HANDBOOK

TO THE MOST EXCELLENT

ORDER OF THE BRITISH EMPIRE

HANDBOOK

TO THE MOST EXCELLENT

ORDER OF THE BRITISH EMPIRE

CONTAINING BIOGRAPHIES, AND A FULL LIST OF PERSONS
APPOINTED TO THE ORDER, SHOWING THEIR
RELATIVE PRECEDENCE

EDITED BY
A. WINTON THORPE

Originally Published as

BURKE'S HANDBOOK
TO THE MOST EXCELLENT
ORDER OF THE BRITISH
EMPIRE

CONTENTS.

ABBREVIATIONS.

A.D.C.	...	Aide-de-Camp.
A.F.C.	...	Air Force Cross.
Adj. ...	...	Adjutant.
Adm.	...	Admiral.
A.M.I.C.E. ...	...	Associate Member of the Institution of Civil Engineers.
A.R.A.	...	Associate of the Royal Academy.
B. ...	...	Baron.
b. ...	...	born.
B.A. ...	...	Bachelor of Arts.
Bart.	...	Baronet.
B.C.L.	...	Bachelor of Civil Law.
B.D. ...	...	,, Divinity.
B.Sc.	...	,, Science.
C.A. ...	...	County Alderman.
C.B. ...	...	Companion of the Order of the Bath.
C.B.E.	...	Commander of the Order of the British Empire.
C.C. ...	...	County Councillor.
C.H. ...	...	Member of the Order of Companions of Honour.
C.I. ...	...	Lady of the Imperial Order of the Crown of India.
C.I.E.	...	Companion of the Order of the Indian Empire.
C.M.G.	...	,, ,, ,, St. Michael and St. George.
C.S.I.	...	,, ,, ,, the Star of India.
C.V.O.	...	Commander of the Royal Victorian Order.
Comm.	...	Commander.
D. ...	...	Duke.
d. ...	...	daughter.
D.B.E.	...	Dame Commander of the Order of the British Empire.
D.C.L.	...	Doctor of Civil Law.
D.D. ...	...	,, Divinity.
D.F.C.	...	Distinguished Flying Cross.
D.L. ...	...	Deputy Lieutenant.
D.P.H.	...	Diploma in Public Health.
D.S.C.	...	Distinguished Service Cross.
D.Sc.	...	Doctor of Science.
D.S.O.	...	Companion of the Distinguished Service Order.
E. ...	...	Earl.
F.B.A.	...	Fellow of the British Academy.
F.R.A.S.	...	,, Royal Astronomical Society.
F.R.C.P.	...	,, ,, College of Physicians.
F.R.C.S.	...	,, ,, ,, Surgeons.
F.R.G.S.	...	,, ,, Geographical Society.
F.R.S.	...	,, ,, Society.
F.S.A.	...	,, Society of Antiquaries.
G.B.E.	...	Knight Grand Cross or Dame Grand Cross of the Order of the British Empire.
G.C.B.	...	Knight Grand Cross of the Order of the Bath.
G.C.I.E.	...	,, ,, Commander of the Order of the Indian Empire.
G.C.M.G.	...	,, ,, Cross of the Order of St. Michael and St. George.
G.C.S.I.	...	,, ,, Commander of the Order of the Star of India.
G.C.V.O.	...	,, ,, Cross of the Royal Victorian Order.
H.E.I.C.S.	...	In the service of the Honourable East India Company.
Hon. ...	...	Honourable.
H.I.H.	...	His or Her Imperial Highness.
H.H. ...	...	,, Highness.
H.R.H.	...	,, Royal Highness.

H.S.H.	...	His or Her Serene Highness.
I.C.S.	...	Indian Civil Service.
I.S.C.	...	,, Staff Corps.
I.S.O.	...	Imperial Service Order.
J.P. ...	...	Justice of the Peace.
K.B.E.	...	Knight Commander of the Order of the British Empire.
K.C. ...	...	King's Counsel
K.C.B.	...	Knight Commander of the Order of the Bath.
K.C.I.E.	...	,, ,, ,, Order of the Indian Empire.
K.C.M.G.	..	,, ,, ,, Order of St. Michael and St. George.
K.C.S.I.	...	,, ,, ,, Order of the Star of India.
K.C.V.O.	...	,, ,, ,, Royal Victorian Order.
K.G. ...	...	,, of the Order of the Garter.
K.G. St. John		,, of Grace of St. John of Jerusalem.
K.J. St. John		,, of Justice of St. John of Jerusalem.
K.P. ...	...	,, of the Order of St. Patrick.
K.T. ...	...	,, ,, the Thistle.
L.G. St. John		Lady of Grace of St. John of Jerusalem.
L.J. St. John		,, Justice of St. John of Jerusalem.
LL.D.	...	Doctor of Laws.
LL.M.	...	Master of Laws.
M. ...	...	Marquis.
m. ...	...	marrried.
M.A. ...	...	Master of Arts.
M.B. ...	...	Bachelor of Medicine.
M.B.E	...	Member of the Order of the British Empire.
M.C. ...	...	Military Cross.
M.Ch.	...	Master of Surgery.
M.D. ...	...	Doctor of Medicine.
M.P. ...	...	Member of Parliament.
Mus. Doc. ...		Doctor of Music.
M.V.O.	...	Member of the Royal Victorian Order.
O.B.E.	...	Officer of the Order of the British Empire.
O.M. ...	...	Order of Merit.
P.C. ...	...	Privy Councillor.
R.A. ...	...	Royal Academician.
R.A. ...	...	,, Artillery.
R.A.F.	...	,, Air Force.
R.A.M.C.	...	,, Army Medical Corps.
R.A.S.C.	...	,, ,, Service Corps.
R.D. ...	...	Naval Reserve Decoration.
R.E. ...	...	Royal Engineers.
R.F.A.	...	,, Field Artillery.
R.G.A.	...	,, Garrison Artillery.
R.H.A.	...	,, Horse Artillery.
R.M.A.	...	,, Marine Artillery.
R.M.L.I.	...	,, ,, Light Infantry.
R.N. ...	...	,, Navy.
R.R.C.	...	,, Red Cross.
s. ...	...	Son.
T.D. ...	...	Territorial Decoration.
V. ...	...	Viscount.
V.A. ...	...	Lady of the Royal Order of Victoria and Albert
V.C. ...	...	Victoria Cross.
V.D. ...	...	Volunteer Decoration.
W.S. ...	...	Writer to the Signet.

PREFACE.

In compiling the Handbook to the Order of the British Empire the object of the Editor has been to extend and give permanency to the scattered records of those who have been admitted to the Order in recognition of " important services to the Empire " in the hour of its greatest need. Of the origin of the Order at " a moment of almost unrelieved gloom," when "the entire British nation was fully mobilised for war," the story is told in the introductory article which follows, where it is shown that " the Order of the British Empire is in the truest sense of the word the British Democracy's own Order of Chivalry."

From the nature of the circumstances in which it was evolved, it was inevitable that this Order should become, almost at a leap, the most numerous of all Orders of Knighthood in this country. But numbers are only relatively large or small, and of the millions of citizens who were mobilised in military and civil capacities, only some 25,000—of whom nearly half were naval and military—were singled out for decoration with the Order of the British Empire.

The historical interest attaching to the Order made it desirable that some permanent record should be provided, and it has been the endeavour of the Editor to supply a memorial worthy of its subject.

In these pages will be found a full list of those who have been admitted to the Order, arranged in order of precedence under their respective classes. Also as many biographical notes as possible are given ; but so many addresses are lacking, even in the official records, and so many others have been changed and are now untraceable, that in many thousands of instances it has been impossible to get in touch with those concerned in order to obtain the necessary particulars.

It was originally intended to publish only one edition of the Handbook, as it was thought that subsequent additions to the Order would not be sufficiently numerous to justify a reprint. But with so many biographical gaps it may be found desirable to re-issue the volume later, and those concerned, whose biographies do not now appear, are invited to communicate with the Editor with a view to the inclusion of particulars concerning them in any further edition.

That this Handbook will be of lasting interest as a memento of the Great War there is little doubt. It is hoped that it will prove also of considerable value as a reference book, covering ground hitherto barely touched in other publications.

The thanks of the Editor are due to the Officials of the Order who have rendered much practical assistance in a difficult undertaking.

February 19, 1921.

THE ORIGIN OF THE ORDER OF THE BRITISH EMPIRE.

"THE Most Excellent Order of the British Empire" was instituted by Letters Patent under the Great Seal on June 4, 1917. The Great War was at its height, and there was no prospect of its early conclusion. It was, indeed, a moment of almost unrelieved gloom and disappointment for the Allies. The strategical offensive of the spring had broken down. The brilliant tactical victory of the British at Arras had led to no result. General Nivelle's big French offensive on the Aisne had failed decisively. Revolutionary Russia was beginning to fade out of the war in disastrous collapse. At Salonica there was deadlock; at Gaza the British advance on Jerusalem had been checked with heavy loss. At home the dreaded figure of starvation seemed to be on the point of appearing, for the intensive submarine campaign was in full swing, and our food-ships were being sunk in increasing numbers all round our shores. The one bright star was the entry of the United States into the war, but her armies had to be raised and equipped, and the day of their effective help was distant. Such were the grave conditions, though realised, perhaps fortunately, by few, when the King declared his intention of instituting a new Order of Knighthood.

And yet from this broad picture of the situation in midsummer, 1917, has been omitted the one great dominant group of facts in the very foreground which made the institution of this Order a necessity. The entire British nation by that time was fully mobilised for war. With the exception of an infinitesimal fragment of the population, all were harnessed to its remorseless wheels. The war had become an intimate part of everyone's life. Its demands were inexorable and insatiable. From the very beginning it had taken the best. It now took the second best, the third best, and the indifferent. All the energies of the State, all the energies of industry, all the energies of individuals were directed towards the carrying on of a devouring and devastating struggle, which some day—but no one knew when—was to end in the victory of the Allies, because on victory the will of the British people was firmly and immovably set. This unconquerable will to victory on the part of the British people is, next to the heroism of the British soldiers and sailors, the proudest memory of the Great War. Firmly founded on the unshakeable conviction that the cause of the Allies was the cause of Right, the British people—again we may ignore the waverers, and the timid, and the base—were resolved to go on to the end, cost what it might, and snatch the ultimate victory even out of the very jaws of starvation and defeat. There was little or no distinction between men and women. The womanhood of the country was marshalled and mobilised as never before, and showed an equal courage and an equal endurance with the men, and that great outstanding fact was not forgotten by those who framed the Statutes of the Order of the British Empire.

Such were the conditions to meet which the new Order was instituted, for in a nation thus mobilised for war service how else could just recognition be made of those who were rendering signal service to their country? "It is ordained"—so runs the Sixth Statute—"that the persons to be admitted to the Civil Division of the said Order shall be such persons, male or female, as may have rendered, or shall hereafter render, important services to our Empire." Important services—that was, and is, the sole qualification. Eighteen months later, on December 27, after the war had been won, a Military Division of the Order was added; but the original object of the Order was the recognition and encouragement of the non-combatant war worker, who was doing his and her best to keep the fighting services working at their utmost capacity and to look after the well-being of the fighting man at home and at the front, in the ranks and in hospital, wherever he might be, and serving in whatever capacity.

It is in this respect, therefore, that the Order of the British Empire differs in the circumstances of its inception and in the scope of its design from any other Order of Chivalry instituted in this country. In most of the earlier Orders there had been a strong element of exclusiveness, though the idea of equality within the Order had sometimes been emphasized. For example, in the Order of the Garter, though possibly in theory the door was open to any knight of stainless chivalry, in practice it was fast shut to all save those of noble birth and the highest social distinction. Indeed, it soon came to be an unwritten, but no less essential, qualification for admission to the Order of the Garter that the candidate should be "a gentleman of blood," which signified "three descents of *noblesse*, that is to say of name and arms, both of his father's side, and of his mother's side." And so it has remained down to our own times; for the admission even of a statesman so eminent, and a commoner so *bene natus*, as Sir Edward Grey (now Viscount Grey of Fallodon), was an event without parallel since the case of Sir Robert Walpole.

As is well known, the circumstances in which Edward III. came to institute the Order of the Garter are very much disputed by historians, though the historian of the Order, Sir N. H. Nicolas, declared confidently enough that there can be no reasonable doubt that "the illustrious Fraternity was intended to supersede the Round Table which Edward had revived, that it had no loftier origin than a Tournament or Hastilude, and that its Name, Badge, and Motto were derived from no nobler source than a fair Dame's misfortune and a chivalrous Monarch's gallantry." Accepting, therefore, the traditional story of the Tournament and Tilting at Windsor, and the slipping of the Countess of Salisbury's garter at the Ball, could there be a more poignant contrast than that between the Courtly Play of Spears, a Royal Gathering, out of which grew the Most Noble Order of the Garter, and the Bloody Tourney of the Nations of the World, known as the Great War—where the combatants were numbered by millions, and the stakes were Thrones, Dominions, Principalities, Powers, and even human Liberty itself—out of which arose the Order of the British Empire?

It would be easy to heighten this contrast still more by tracing the origins of some of the other great historic Orders of Chivalry. The Order of the Golden Fleece, for example, was instituted at Bruges in 1429, by Philip II., Duke of Burgundy, on his marriage with Isabel of Portugal; the recent downfall of the Hapsburghs has presumably brought the Austrian branch of that proud Order to a sudden end, though the Spanish branch still remains. The Motto of the Order of the Annunziata—"F. E. R. T."—still recalls, by the capital letters of the legend "Fortitudo Ejus Rhodum Tenuit," the relief of Rhodes by Amadeus V. of Savoy. Or, if we look to our British Orders, even as late as 1725, when the Order of the Bath, based on the old Knighthood of the Bath, was instituted for the reward of both civil and military merit, membership was limited to thirty-six Knights, and it was not until after Waterloo that the Order was enlarged to three classes "for the purpose of commemorating the auspicious termination of the long and arduous contest in which the nation has been engaged." Even so, the Bath retained much of its old exclusiveness until it was extended again in 1847 by the inclusion of the new ranks of Civil Knight Commanders and Companions. The Order of St. Michael and St. George shows a similar expansion. Originally instituted in 1818 for natives of the Ionian Islands (then under the British Crown) and Malta, and others "holding high and confidential situations in the Mediterranean," the Order was reconstructed in 1868, and again in 1877, when it was declared to be intended for those who held high office in the "Colonial possessions" of Great Britain, and again in 1879, when its ranks were thrown open to those who had rendered "good service to the Crown in relation to the Foreign Affairs of the British Empire."

INTRODUCTION.

In contradistinction to all these, the idea of the Order of the British Empire was conceived on a grand inclusive plan, and was brought into being with five classes, so that from the outset it might be all-embracing and fully comprehensive, and on a scale reasonably commensurate with the magnitude and universality of the services to be recognized. The only other British Order to possess five classes is the Royal Victorian Order, instituted in 1896, which ranks immediately above that of the British Empire, though nearly all Foreign Orders possess the five classes, which have been justified by practical experience. At the head of the Order are the Sovereign and the Grand Master, who is either to be a Prince of the Blood Royal or "such other exalted personage as the Sovereign may appoint." The first to be appointed to the Grand Mastership, with rank as First or Principal Knight Grand Cross, was the Prince of Wales. The five classes are as follows:—

I. Knights Grand Cross and Dames Grand Cross.
II. Knights Commanders and Dames Commanders.
III. Commanders.
IV. Officers.
V. Members.

Each class consists of two sub-divisions, Military and Civil.

Each sub-division consists of Ordinary and Honorary Members, the latter being foreigners on whom the distinction of being received into the Order is conferred.

Persons not being members of, or eligible for appointment to, any of the five classes may be awarded the Medal of the Order, either Military or Civil.

In each case, whether for Membership or for the Medal, the qualification is the same—the rendering of important service to the Empire. In practice, the award of the Medal is limited to cases of courage, self-sacrifice, or great devotion to duty. Among the first list of Medallists, for example, were many munition workers who had shown great courage and presence of mind in extinguishing fires in explosive factories, shipwright divers, electrical fitters and drillers, who had executed important repairs in the Grand Fleet during action, and workers of all ranks who had shown "great devotion to duty." One man was thus rewarded who, though 72 years of age, returned from Australia, at his own expense, to his old firm, put in for two years an average of 54 hours a week, and though he often fainted at his work "refused to go home, stating that he could not rest whilst he thought his country wanted shells." His name was Thomas Harper.

The great innovation of the Order of the British Empire—and of the Companionship of Honour which was instituted about the same time—was the inclusion of women side by side with men. Never before had there been full admission of women to all degrees of any important Order of Knighthood, and the innovation coincided with the acceptance by the British Parliament of the principle of Women's Suffrage. As has been already said, the womanhood of the country had been mobilised for war service, not indeed as completely as its manhood, for in the circumstances of the case that was impossible, but with no trace of compulsion, for whatever services women performed they performed voluntarily. Theirs, however, was a service absolutely indispensable to victory, and it was rendered with cheerfulness, thoroughness, endurance, devotion and efficiency beyond all praise.

The idea of the admission of women to an Order of Knighthood was far older than most people knew, and curiously enough it was the most exclusive of all the ancient Orders of Chivalry which had given them the largest privileges. Soon after the institution of the Order of the Garter we find a sort of quasi-admission of ladies of high rank, who were presented with Robes of the Order of the Garter, and who wore the Badge of the Order on their left arm. Between 1376 and 1494 some sixty ladies received this signal mark of distinction, and they were usually known as "Dames de la Fraternité de St. George." Several monumental effigies survive showing these ladies wearing the Garter, and in one or two cases apparently (e.g. that of Margaret, wife of Sir Robert Harcourt) the adornment was placed on the recumbent figure without the lady having had any strict right to wear it in life. The last entry in the Register of the Order of this gift of the Robes was in connection with Elizabeth, wife of Henry VII.—the Princess Bessy of the old Ballad—and then for some unknown reason the graceful custom was allowed to die out. There was considerable talk of its revival about 1730—not long after the institution of the Order of the Bath—but the idea was not carried out.

At the time of writing, the Order of the British Empire has a total membership in all its various classes of 25,419, the Military members numbering 11,646, and the Civil, 13,773. The Knights and Dames Grand Cross number 94; the Knights and Dames Commanders 537; the Commanders 3,173; the Officers 11,369; and the Members 10,246.

The numbers are large compared with those of any British Order, but they are not so large when one considers what an extensive use was made of the Military sub-divisions to make suitable recognition of the services of large numbers of officers who performed during the war multifarious duties of an indispensable, but in many cases of a non-combatant, character; and above all when one remembers that the whole nation was mobilised for war, and that even the most ordinary industrial occupations took on during the Great War a special war significance. The War overshadowed everything; new values attached to conduct, which became good or bad according as it was helpful or the contrary towards the achievement of victory; public spirit was shown in a thousand different ways as men and women surrendered their own careers and ambitions, and became parts of the Great Machine which existed only for the purpose of keeping our armies and our fleets in the highest state of efficiency. While warfare itself became more pitiless, and the engines of destruction more frightful, the spirit of chivalry spread through all classes, and a nobler idea of the beauty of public service penetrated all ranks alike. Democracy, thus animated, won the war; the Order of the British Empire is in the truest sense of the word the British Democracy's own Order of Chivalry. All classes are blended therein; the old distinctive qualification of being " a gentleman of blood " has gone and left no trace; service is the only test of admission, and the service of women here finds recognition in exactly the same way as the service of men. The newest and latest-born of the British Orders of Chivalry may therefore well be proud of its long list of members, and of the vast unnumbered host of war workers—unrecognised in the way of honorific distinction, but not unappreciated—whose representatives they are.

STATUTES OF THE
MOST EXCELLENT ORDER OF THE BRITISH EMPIRE.

George, R. & J.

GEORGE THE FIFTH, by the Grace of God, of the United Kingdom of Great Britain and Ireland and of the British Dominions beyond the Seas, King, Defender of the Faith, Emperor of India, to all to whom these Presents shall come.

Greeting!

WHEREAS by Letters Patent under the Great Seal of the said United Kingdom of Great Britain and Ireland, bearing date at Westminster the Fourth day of June, 1917, in the Eighth year of Our Reign, We have thought fit and been pleased to institute, erect, constitute, and create, an Order of Knighthood, to be called and known for ever hereafter by the name, style, and designation of "The Most Excellent Order of the British Empire," whereof We, Our heirs and successors for ever shall be Sovereigns:

And whereas by Our aforesaid Letters Patent We did ordain that the said Order should be governed by Statutes and Ordinances and that the Statutes to be observed within the said Order should be established by Us and sealed by the Seal of the Said Order which Statutes so given and in future to be given by Us, Our heirs and successors, to which the said Seal shall be affixed, should be of the same validity and taken and read as if the same and every Article of them had been verbatim recited in the said Letters Patent and passed under the Great Seal of Our said United Kingdom of Great Britain and Ireland:

And whereas in conformity with the said Letters Patent of the fourth day of June, 1917, We did enact and issue certain Statutes and Ordinances to be observed within the said Order bearing the same date wherein a power was reserved to Us, Our heirs and successors of annulling, altering, augmenting, interpreting or dispensing with these Statutes and Regulations or any part thereof by a notification under the Sign Manual of the Sovereign of the Order:

And whereas we deemed it expedient that alterations should be made in the Statutes of the said Order. We therefore in pursuance of the Power vested in Us by the said Letters Patent did make, ordain and establish certain amended Statutes bearing date the twelfth day of April, 1918:

And whereas it is expedient that certain further alterations should be made in the existing Statutes of the said Order:

Now know ye that in pursuance and in exercise of the power vested in Us by the said Letters Patent We have abrogated and annulled and do hereby abrogate and repeal the said Statutes:

And further know all ye to whom these Presents shall come that in substitution thereof We have made, ordained and established, and by these Presents, sealed with the Seal of the said Order, do make, ordain and establish the following Statutes and Ordinances, namely:—

1. It is ordained and enjoined that this Order of Chivalry shall be styled and designated in all Acts, proceedings, and pleadings The Most Excellent Order of the British Empire as in Our said Letters Patent is directed, and by no other designation.

2. It is ordained that the said Order shall consist of the Sovereign and a Grand Master and of five several classes:—I. "Knights Grand Cross" and "Dames Grand Cross." II. "Knights Commanders" and "Dames Commanders." III. "Commanders." IV. "Officers." V. "Members." And it is further ordained that each and every of these five Classes shall likewise contain two

sub-divisions whereof the first shall be styled "Military" and the second "Civil," each of which sub-divisions shall be composed partly of Ordinary and partly of Honorary Members.

3. It is ordained that We, Our heirs and successors, Kings or Queens Regnant of Our said United Kingdom, are and for ever shall be Sovereigns of this Order, to whom doth and shall belong all power of annulling, interpreting, explaining, or augmenting these and every part of these Statutes.

4. We do hereby ordain, direct and appoint that a Prince of the Blood Royal or such other exalted personage as We, Our heirs and successors shall hereafter appoint shall be Grand Master of the said Order, and shall in virtue thereof be the First or Principal Knight Grand Cross of the said Order, to whose custody shall be confided the Great Seal of the Order, which he shall affix to all Statutes, Ordinances, and Instruments according to the regulations touching the issue of every of the said Instruments; and it is further ordained that it shall be his special duty to enforce the due observance of the Statutes and Ordinances of this Order, and that he shall likewise direct the issue of all letters of Summons whenever the Sovereign shall be pleased to command an Investiture of the said Most Excellent Order.

5. It is ordained that all commissioned, warrant and subordinate Officers subject to the Naval Discipline Act or employed under the Order of the Admiralty, and all commissioned and warrant Officers recommended by any Commander-in-Chief in the field or elsewhere, or by the General Officer Commanding, Independent Force, Royal Air Force, or employed under the War Office or Air Ministry, or under the Administrative Headquarters of Dominions or Overseas Forces, or employed under the Ministry of Munitions or the Ministry of National Service on work which, but for the creation of those Departments, would have been performed by the War Office; and all members of the Naval, Army, Dominions, or Overseas Nursing Services, or officials of the Women's Royal Naval Service, Queen Mary's Army Auxiliary Corps, or the Women's Royal Air Force, and such commandants of the Women's Legion or similar organisations as are under contract with or employed by the Admiralty, War Office or Air Ministry shall be eligible for appointment to the Military Division of this Order.

6. It is ordained that the persons to be admitted to the Civil Division of the said Order shall be such persons, male or female, as may have rendered or shall hereafter render important services to our Empire.

7. It is ordained that foreign persons upon whom We may think fit to confer the honour of being received into this Order shall be deemed to be, and described as, Honorary Knights Grand Cross or Honorary Dames Grand Cross, Honorary Knights Commanders or Honorary Dames Commanders, Honorary Commanders, Honorary Officers, and Honorary Members, according to the classes in the Order to which they belong.

8. It is ordained that persons already appointed to this Order who are qualified for the Military Division shall, on the recommendation of the First Lord of the Admiralty, the Secretary of State for War or the Secretary of State for the Royal Air Force as the case may be, be transferred to the Military Division of this Order.

9. It is ordained that when We, Our heirs or successors shall be pleased to nominate and appoint any person to this Order such appointment shall be made by Warrant under Our Royal Sign Manual sealed with the Seal of this Order and countersigned by the Grand Master of the said Order.

10. It is ordained that this Order shall rank next to and immediately after Our Royal Victorian Order, that in all solemn Ceremonies, places and assemblies the Knights Grand Cross of this Order shall have place and precedency next to and immediately after the Knights Grand Cross of the Royal Victorian Order, that the Dames Grand Cross of this Order shall have place and precedency next to and immediately before the wives of Knights Grand Cross of the Most Honourable Order of the Bath, and may on all occasions have, use and enjoy the appellation and style of Dame before their Christian or first names, that the Knights Commanders of this Order shall have place and precedency next to and immediately after the Knights Commanders of the Royal Victorian Order, that the Dames Commanders of this Order shall have place and precedency next to and immediately before the wives of Knights Commanders of the Most Honourable Order of the Bath, and may on all occasions have, use and enjoy the appellation and style of Dame before their Christian or first names, that the men who are Commanders of this Order shall have place and precedency next to and immediately after the Members of the Third Class of the Royal Victorian Order and the women who are Commanders of this Order shall have place and precedency next to and immediately before the Wives of Companions of the Most Honourable Order of the Bath, that the men who

are Officers of this Order shall have place and precedency next to and immediately after the Members of the Fourth Class of the Royal Victorian Order and the women who are Officers of this Order shall have place and precedency next to and immediately before the wives of Members of the Fourth Class of the Royal Victorian Order, that the men who are Members of this Order shall have place and precedency next to and immediately after the Members of the Fifth Class of the Royal Victorian Order and that the women who are Members of this Order shall have place and precedency next to and immediately before the wives of Members of the Fifth Class of the Royal Victorian Order.

11. It is ordained that the Insignia of the Sovereign of this Order shall be of the same material and fashion as are hereinafter appointed for the Knights Grand Cross, save only with those alterations which distinguish Our Royal Dignity.

12. It is ordained that the Grand Master shall wear the Insignia of a Knight Grand Cross, the badge of which for the Grand Master shall be augmented in accordance with the commands of the Sovereign.

13. It is ordained that the Military and Civil Knights and Dames Grand Cross of this Most Excellent Order shall upon all great and solemn occasions wear the badge of the Order, which shall consist of a cross patonce, enamelled pearl, fimbriated or surmounted by a gold medallion with a representation of Britannia seated within a circle gules inscribed with the motto, " For God and the Empire," in letters of gold ensigned with the Imperial Crown or, the whole suspended from a purple riband which in the case of Knights Grand Cross shall be of the breadth of three inches and three-quarters with, for Military Knights Grand Cross, the addition of a vertical red stripe in the centre of the ribbon of the width of about five-sixteenths of an inch, and in the case of Dames Grand Cross shall be of the breadth of two inches and one-quarter with, for Military Dames Grand Cross, a vertical red stripe in the centre of the ribbon of the width of about one-quarter of an inch, passing from the right shoulder to the left side, and they shall wear on the left side of their coats or outer garments an oval Star composed of eight points and charged with a medallion as above.

14. It is ordained that the Military and Civil Knights Commanders shall wear around their necks a riband of the same colour and pattern as that of the Military and Civil Knights Grand Cross of the breadth of one inch and three-quarters, but, in the case of Military Knights Commanders the vertical red stripe is to be of the width of about three-sixteenths of an inch, and pendant therefrom the Badge of the Knights Commanders of the Order, which shall be of similar form and pattern to that appointed for the Knights Grand Cross, but of smaller size, and also that they shall wear on the left side of their coats or outer garments a silver star composed of four equal points and four lesser, charged with a medallion as before, and it is ordained that the Military and Civil Dames Commanders shall wear a badge of similar form and pattern as that appointed for Knights Commanders attached to a riband also similar to that worn by Military and Civil Knights Commanders but tied in a bow and worn on the left shoulder, and that they shall wear a like star.

15. It is ordained that the Military and Civil Commanders shall in the same manner wear the like riband and badge as that appointed for the Military and Civil Knights and Dames Commanders respectively, but that they shall not be entitled to wear the Star.

16. It is ordained that the Military and Civil Officers shall wear a badge of similar form and pattern as that appointed for the Military and Civil Commanders of the Order, but of a smaller size and silver gilt, attached to a riband of the same colour and pattern of the breadth of one inch and a half, but in the case of Military Officers the vertical red stripe is to be of the width of an eighth of an inch, attached to the left breast of their coats or outer garments by men, and tied in a bow on the left shoulder by women.

17. It is ordained that the Military and Civil Members shall wear in like manner the same ribands and badge as that appointed to the Military and Civil Officers of the Order except that the badge shall be in silver.

18. It is ordained that upon the nomination of any person to be a Knight Grand Cross, Dame Grand Cross, Knight Commander, or Dame Commander of this Order, he or she shall be invested with the Insignia of his or her dignity in the Order by Us, Our heirs and successors if he or she be resident at the time in this country, but if he or she be in India by Our Viceroy of India in Our name and on Our behalf, and if he or she be in Canada, Australia, New Zealand, or South Africa by Our Governors General of Canada, Australia, New Zealand, or South Africa respectively

in Our name and on Our behalf; and that on the day of the Investiture the person to be invested shall be introduced into the presence of the Sovereign, the Viceroy of India, or the Governor General of Canada, Australia, New Zealand, or South Africa, as the case may be, by the Officer of the Order or other Officer deputed to be in attendance bearing the proper Insignia of the Order, when the Sovereign, Viceroy, or Governor General having in the case of Knights Grand Cross and Knights Commanders conferred the Honour of Knighthood upon the person so nominated if he have not previously received the said Honour, will then proceed to invest him or her with the Ensigns of the said Order in the following manner :—The Sovereign, Viceroy or Governor General will invest the new Knight Grand Cross, Dame Grand Cross, Knight Commander or Dame Commander with the riband and badge and will deliver or place on his or her left side the star of the said Order appertaining to his or her dignity.

19. It is further ordained that it shall be competent for Us, Our heirs and successors by a Warrant or Warrants under Our Sign Manual countersigned by the Grand Master and sealed with the Seal of this Order to authorise some distinguished person in Our Service or other person to perform in Our name and on Our behalf the Ceremony of investing Knights Grand Cross, Dames Grand Cross, Knights Commanders, or Dames Commanders with the Insignia of their respective dignities or to permit the Ceremony of Investiture to be dispensed with. And We reserve to Ourselves, Our heirs and successors, by Our or their Warrant or Warrants as aforesaid, full power and authority to permit and authorise the person or persons not invested by Us to wear the Insignia and enjoy the privileges appertaining to their respective dignities in as full and ample a manner as if they had been invested by Us, Our heirs and successors.

20. It is ordained that on the promotion of a person to a higher class of this Order the Insignia of the class theretofore worn by him or her shall be returned to the Registrar of the Order for the service of the Order, and that on the resignation or decease of an Official of the Order his Badge of Office shall be restored for the service of the Order.

21. It is ordained that for the greater honour and dignity of the Knights Grand Cross and Dames Grand Cross of this Order it shall and may be lawful for them upon all occasions to bear Supporters to their Arms; and We do by these Presents direct and command Our Garter Principal King of Arms for the time being to grant Supporters to such Knights Grand Cross and Dames Grand Cross of this Order as shall not otherwise be entitled thereto and it shall also be lawful for Knights Grand Cross and Dames Grand Cross of this Order to surround their Armorial Bearings with the circle and motto of the Order and to suspend therefrom a representation of their riband and badge and for Knights Commanders, Dames Commanders, and Commanders of this Order to surround their Armorial Bearings with their circle and motto of the Order and to suspend therefrom a representation of their riband and badge and for the Officers and Members of the Order to suspend a representation of their riband and respective badges from the bottom of the escocheon containing their Armorial Bearings.

22. It is ordained that the Seal of the Order shall have engraved thereon as follows (that is to say) a representation of Britannia surrounded by a circle containing the motto of the Order " For God and the Empire," and that the Statutes of the Order shall be sealed by and with the same.

23. It is ordained that it shall be competent for Us, Our heirs and successors by an Ordinance signed by the Sovereign and sealed with the Seal of the Order to cancel and annul the appointment of any person to this Order, and thereupon his or her name in the Register shall be erased. But that it shall be competent for the Sovereign to restore to the Order any person whose appointment may have been so cancelled and annulled when circumstances render it just and expedient so to do.

24. It is ordained that a Military and Civil Medal of this Order shall be awarded to persons, not being Members of or eligible for appointment to the five classes of Our said Order, whose services to Our Empire would warrant such mark of Our Royal appreciation and that persons subordinate to those who are eligible for the Military Divisions of the various classes of this Order shall be eligible for the said Military Medal.

25. It is ordained that the medal of the Most Excellent Order of the British Empire for men and for women shall consist of a circular medal in silver, having on the obverse a representation of Britannia within the circle and motto of the .Order and on the reverse Our Royal and Imperial Cypher, and shall be worn on the left side suspended by a ring to a purple riband of one inch and one-sixteenth of an inch in width, with the addition in the case of recipients of the Military Medal of the Order of a vertical red stripe in the centre of the riband of about one-sixteenth of an inch.

26. It is ordained that it shall be competent for Us, Our heirs and successors by a Warrant

under Our Royal Sign Manual to cancel and annul the award of any Medal of the Most Excellent Order of the British Empire, and that thereupon the name of the recipient in the Register shall be erased, but it shall be competent for the Sovereign to restore the medal to any person whose name may have been so erased when circumstances render it just and expedient so to do.

27. It is ordained that the twenty-fourth day of May every year shall henceforth be taken and deemed to be the anniversary of the institution of this Order.

28. It is ordained that the following officials shall be appointed to this Order, that is to say, a

Prelate,

King of Arms,

Registrar,

Secretary,

Gentleman Usher of the Purple Rod.

29. It is ordained that the Prelate of this Order shall wear around his neck pendent to a riband similar to that which is assigned to the Knights Commanders an escocheon of gold enamelled on a field purpure the badge within the circle and motto of the Order, the whole surmounted by an Imperial Crown. Moreover, it shall be lawful for the Prelate to surround his Armorial Bearings with the circle and motto of this Order.

30. It is ordained that the King of Arms of this Order shall be nominated by Us, Our heirs and successors, and that he shall sedulously attend the Service of the Order. And further it is ordained that he shall wear around his neck pendent to a purple riband an escocheon of gold enamelled on a field purpure a representation of Britannia impaling the Arms of the Sovereign surrounded with the circle and motto of the Order and surmounted by an Imperial Crown, that he shall carry the Rod of this Order, which shall have on the two greater squares the Arms of the Order impaled with those of the Sovereign, and on the lesser squares the Arms of the Order, the whole surmounted by an Imperial Crown, and that at all Coronations he shall precede the Knights Grand Cross and shall carry and wear a Crown as Our other Kings of Arms are accustomed to do, which badge, rod and crown shall all be of the same materials with those used and borne by Our Garter Principal King of Arms.

31. It is ordained that the Registrar of this Order shall be the person for the time being holding the Office of Registrar and Secretary of the Central Chancery of the Orders of Knighthood, that he shall record all proceedings connected with this Most Excellent Order in a register to be appropriated for that purpose and shall, under the directions of the Grand Master, prepare all Warrants and other Instruments to be passed under the Seal of the Order and engross the same, that he shall summon the Knights Grand Cross to attend the Sovereign at all investitures of this Order, that he shall wear around his neck pendent to a purple riband an escocheon of gold enamelled on a field purpure the cross of the Order surmounted by a representation of a closed book Gules, clasps Or, within the circle and motto of the Order, the whole surmounted by an Imperial Crown.

32. It is ordained that the Secretary of this Order shall be the person holding for the time being the office of Permanent Under Secretary of State for the Home Department or such other member of the staff of the Home Department as may be nominated by Us, that he shall collect and tabulate the names of those persons who are to be submitted to Us for admission to this Order or to be awarded the Medal of this Order, that he shall wear around his neck pendent to a purple riband an escocheon of gold enamelled on a field purpure the badge of the Order with two pens saltirewise between the angles in pearl enamel within the circle and motto of the Order, the whole surmounted by an Imperial Crown.

33. It is ordained that the Gentleman Usher of the Purple Rod of this Most Excellent Order shall be appointed by Us, Our heirs and successors, shall wear around his neck pendent to a purple riband an escocheon of gold enamelled on a field purpure a representation of Britannia surrounded by the circle and motto of the Order and surmounted by an Imperial Crown, and that he shall carry the Purple Rod of the Order, having at the top an escrol thereon the motto of the Order surmounted by a representation of Britannia.

34. It is ordained that all and every of the officials of this Order shall over and above the duties more specially imposed by the foregoing Statutes execute diligently whatever the Sovereign or Grand Master may be pleased to command touching the interests of the said Order, and that the said Offices of Prelate, King of Arms, Registrar, Secretary, and Gentleman Usher shall be holden during good behaviour.

STATUTES.

35. We do hereby command and enjoin that these Statutes shall be of such and that same force, virtue and effect in every respect as if they had been duly made and the said acts, deeds, matters and things had been duly done on the fourth day of June, 1917.

Lastly.—We reserve to Ourself, Our heirs and successors, full power of annulling, altering, abrogating, augmenting, interpreting or dispensing with these Statutes and Regulations or any part thereof by a notification under the Sign Manual of the Sovereign of the Order.

Given at Our Court at *Saint James's*, the twenty-eighth day of March, One thousand nine hundred and nineteen, in the Ninth year of Our Reign.

By His Majesty's Command.

EDWARD SHORTT.

OBITUARY.

Abhayeswari, Debi Rani, O.B.E.
Adams, George Francis, C.B.E.
Adams, Capt. Herbert Algernon, C.B.E., R.N.
Alcock, Capt. Sir John William, K.B.E.
Allardyce, Constance Angel, Lady, O.B.E.
Amherst of Hackney, Mary Rothes Margaret Cecil, Lady, O.B.E.
Anderson, Brig.-Gen. Sir Francis James, K.B.E., C.B.
Andrews, Capt. Henry John, V.C., M.B.E.
Arbuthnot, Elizabeth Fountaine, Mrs. H. L., M.B.E.
Ashe, Anna Katherine, M.B.E.
Atkins, May Clara, Lady Crofton, M.B.E.
Atkinson, Surg.-Lieut. Charles Henry Fairbank, O.B.E., R.N.V.R.
Atkinson, Major Edward William, D.S.O., O.B.E.

Bailey, Capt. James Conner Maxwell, O.B.E.
Baird, Sir Alexander, Bart., G.B.E.
Barge, Henry Lowthian, O.B.E.
Barnett, Capt. Raymond Theodore Frederick, M.B.E.
Barrow, Capt. Geoffrey Selwyn, O.B.E.
Barwell, Horace George, O.B.E.
Beckwith, Capt. William John, O.B.E.
Bedford, Adeline Marie, Duchess of, G.B.E.
Benningfield, Col. John William, O.B.E.
Bennett, Charles Palmer, M.B.E.
Benyon, Dame Edith Isabel, G.B.E.
Bessborough, Countess of, C.B.E.
Biddulph, Lieut.-Col. Michael, O.B.E.
Birch, Capt. William, M.B.E.
Black, Major John, O.B.E.
Boscawen, Edith Sarah, Lady Griffith, O.B.E.
Bottomley, Herbert Holford, C.B.E.
Bradey, George William Cantwell, M.B.E.
Bradley, Capt. William Allen.
Brindley, (Sir) Harry Samuel Bickerton, K.B.E. (died before investiture).
Brock, Wing-Commander Frank Arthur, O.B.E.
Brown, Margaret Alice, M.B.E.
Brown, Lieut.-Col. William George Charteris, C.B.E.
Bucknor, Augusta Margaret, Mrs., M.B.E.

Cameron, Joan Jessie, O.B.E.
Campbell, Major Charles Duncan Miles, M.B.E.
Capel, Arthur Edward, C.B.E.
Challenor, Bromley, M.B.E.
Chaney, Major Henry Edward, O.B.E.
Christie, Lieut.-Col. Henry Robert Stark, O.B.E.
Christie, Lieut.-Col. William Edward Tolfrey, C.M.G., D.S.O., O.B.E.
Clarke, Edward Russell, C.B.E.
Clarke, Lieut.-Col. William James, M.B.E.
Clarke, Capt. William Robert Bruce-, M.B.E.
Clay, Robert, O.B.E.
Coleridge, Lieut. Colin Toss, M.B.E.
Collingwood, Edith Florence, M.B.E.
Collyer, Lieut.-Col. Arthur Allen, O.B.E.
Condon, Major George Henry Edward, O.B.E.
Cook, Sir Edward Tyas, K.B.E.
Cooke, Major Charles John Bowen, C.B.E.
Coote, William Alexander, O.B.E.
Crack, Howard Wilfred, M.B.E.
Crawford, Hubert, M.B.E.
Crawford, Sir Richard Frederick, G.C.M.G., K.B.E.
Crawley, Reginald S., M.B.E.
Crawshay, Florentina Maria, Mrs. W. T., O.B.E.
Cuffey, Edward, O.B.E.
Cumberland, John Mason, O.B.E.
Cuming, George, O.B.E.
Cunliffe, Sir Walter, 1st Baron, G.B.E.
Cuyler, Lieut.-Col. Charles, Bart., O.B.E.

D'aeth, Major Lewis Narborough Hughes, O.B.E.
Dale, Major Alwyn Percy, O.B.E.
Darley, Major William Hastings la Touche, O.B.E.
Davey, Hon. Arthur Jex, C.B.E.
Davies, Capt. Alonzo Ernest, M.B.E.
Dawson, Margaret Damer, O.B.E.
Deakin, Norris Henry, O.B.E.
Deo, Rajah Sudhal, C.B.E.

Dimmock, Lieut.-Col. Henry Piers, O.B.E.
Discombe, George Morton, O.B.E.
Dixon, George Francis, C.B.E., M.V.O.
Douglas, Margaret Elizabeth, Mrs., C.I., M.B.E.
Downie, Capt. Frederick Habler, O.B.E.
Drew, Henrietta Dorothy, M.B.E.
Duddell, William, C.B.E.
Dudley, Rachel, Countess of, M.B.E.
Dyer, Henry, C.B.E.

Eaves, Capt. Wilberforce Vaughan, O.B.E.
Edwards, Lieut.-Col. Francis William Lloyd, O.B.E., K.R.R.C.
Elliott, Capt. William Herron, M.B.E.
Ellis, John William, M.B.E.
Ellis, Major-Gen. Philip Mackay, O.B.E.
Esslemont, Alfred Sherwood, C.B.E.
Evans, Henry, C.B.E.

Fagan, Charles Edward, C.B.E., I.S.O.
Feilden, Major Edward Leyland Cook, O.B.E.
Ferguson, Major A. R., O.B.E.
Ferguson, Capt. Harold Stuart, M.B.E.
Fetherstonhaugh. Florence, Mrs. R. S., M.B.E.
Fisher, Harry Kaye Cecil, M.B.E.
Forbes, Capt. Charles, O.B.E.
Forbes, Capt. Charles Hay, C.B.E., R.N.
Franklin, Major and Qr.-Mr. Charles, O.B.E.
Franklin, George Cooper, M.B.E., F.R.C.S.
Frasher, Hon. Col. John Pilling, C.B.E.
Furner, Willoughby, O.B.E.

Galloway, Agnes Lottie, Mrs., M.B.E.
Garrett, Lieut.-Col. Arthur ffolliott, O.B.E.
Gaussen, Col. John Samuel, C.B.E.
Gibbs, Victoria Florence de Burgh, Mrs. G. A., C.B.E.
Gildea, Sir James, G.B.E., K.C.V.O. C.B.
Gladwell, Charles John, O.B.E.
Godfray, Brig.-Gen. John William, C.B., C.V.O., C.B.E.
Gore, Major Charles Henry, O.B.E.
Gould, Lieut.-Col. van Jay-, C.B.E.
Graham, Robert Paul, O.B.E.
Gray, Herbert Stanley, M.B.E.
Gray, William Acheson, M.B.E.
Greenwood, Lieut.-Commander Charles, O.B.E., R.N.V.R.
Greenwood, Lieut. Harold Cecil, O.B.E., R.N.V.R.
Grieve, James Dyce, M.B.E.

Hall, Capt. Eric Watson, M.B.E.
Hall, Frederick Eardley John Blackburne, C.B.E.
Hamilton, Lieut. Thomas, M.B.E.
Harbottle, Sir John George, Kt. Bach.
Harris, Major John James Fitzgerald, O.B.E.
Harris, Capt. Worsley John, M.B.E.
Harrison, Lieut.-Col. Percy Wordsworth, C.B.E.
Hazel, Lieut.-Col. Albert William, C.B.E.
Hemmant, Edward Vincent, O.B.E.
Hewitt, Rev. Sydney Rangely, O.B.E.
Hibberdine, William, O.B.E.
Hill, Thomas, O.B.E., J.P.
Hodder, Rev. Charles William, M.B.E.
Hodgson, Lieut.-Col. John Edward, O.B.E.
Hope, George Irving, C.B.E.
Hornabrook, Rev. John Oliver, O.B.E.
Hornby, Lieut.-Col. Cecil Geoffrey, O.B.E., M.C.
Horne, Capt. Clement Cooper, C.B.E., R.N.
Houndle, Henry Charles Herman Hawker, C.B.E., I.S.O.
Howard, Capt. Charles Reginald, O.B.E.
Howard, Robert Jared Bliss, O.B.E.
Howson, William Richard, O.B.E.
Hughes, Marjorie, M.B.E.
Hugill, Herbert, M.B.E.
Hugo, Major FitzHerbert, O.B.E., M.C.
Hulse, Edward James, O.B.E.
Hunter, Lieut.-Col. John Muir, C.S.I., O.B.E.
Hutton, Emily Fenton Armitage, Mrs. J. A., O.B.E.

Ireland, Col. Sir Robert Megaw, K.B.E., C.B., C.M.G.
Ivey, Major T. E., O.B.E.

Jefcoate, Capt. Frank, M.B.E.
Jenkins, Lieut.-Comm. Basil Oliver, C.B.E.

OBITUARY.

Jodhpur, Major H. H., Maharaja of, K.B.E.
Johnson, William, C.B.E.
Jones, Alfred Richard, M.B.E.
Jones, Beatrice Isabel, C.B.E., R.R.C.
Jones, Lieut. Kenneth Charles Johnstone, M.B.E., M.C.
Jones, Major Thomas W. H., O.B.E.
Jones, Samuel Nathan, O.B.E.

Keele, John Rushworth, O.B.E.
Keeling, Lieut.-Col. Bertram Francis Eardley, O.B.E., M.C.
Keene, Major Robert Francis Ruck-, O.B.E.
Keene, William, C.B.E., M.V.O.
Kelly, Robert, M.B.E.
Ker, Leighton Buchanan, M.B.E.
Killby, Capt. William Watson, M.B.E.
King, George Kemp, C.B.E., M.V.O.
Kirwan, Lieut. Theodore, M.B.E.
Knowles, T. Capt. Eustace Oliver, O.B.E.

Lane, Col. Clayton Turner, C.I.E., C.B.E.
Laurie, T. Capt. Donald Saunders, O.B.E.
Lawson, Capt. Harold, M.B.E.
Lee, Major-Gen. Henry Herbert, C.B.E.
Leeming, Capt. James Arthur, O.B.E.
Lever, Major Harry Reginald, O.B.E., R.A.S.C.
Lewlas, Lieut.-Col. John Tweedy, C.B.E.
Lima, Sir Bertram Lewis, K.B.E.
Little, Ernest Knightley, C.B.E.
Little, Staff Pay-Master James Scott, O.B.E.
Llewellyn, Lieut.-Col. Arthur, O.B.E.
Lloyd, Francis Zachary, C.B.E.
Long, Violet Beatrice Alice Lambton, Mrs., O.B.E.
Longstaff, Lieut.-Col. Llewellyn Wood, O.B.E.
Lovelady, Thomas, M.B.E.
Lovett, Brig.-Gen. Alfred Crowdy, C.B., C.B.E.
Lowe, Catherine Howard, Mrs., M.B.E.
Lowe, Gerard Horsfall Corbett, O.B.E.
Luckes, Eva Charlotte Ellis, C.B.E.
Lush, Capt. John, C.B.E.
Luson, Capt. Thomas Gerhard Leslie, O.B.E.
Lyster, Cecil Rupert Chaworth, C.B.E.

Macdowell, Sir Alexander, G.B.E.
MacGilvray, Capt. Thomas Clouston Rae, M.B.E.
MacIntyre, 2nd Lieut. Robert William, M.B.E.
MacKay, Colin, M.B.E.
McLaren, Sir John, K.B.E.
McMillan, Thomas, C.B.E.
Mahaffy, Arthur William, O.B.E.
Mahaffy, Rev. John Pentland, G.B.E.
Maine, Jane, Lady.
Maitland, Adam, M.B.E.
Marsh, Col. William, C.B.E.
Marston, Dorothy, M.B.E.
May, Lieut. William Samuel, O.B.E., R.N.
Melville, Witham, M.V.O., M.B.E.
Mercer, Lieut. William, M.B.E.
Miles, Sir C. W., Bart., O.B.E.
Miles, Henry Stephen, M.B.E.
Mitra, Rai Sahili Rajeshwar, O.B.E.
Moffat, John, O.B.E.
Moncrieff, Lieut.-Col. George Hay, C.B.E.
Moran, 2nd Lieut. John, M.B.E.
Morgan, Charles, O.B.E.
Morgan, Capt. G. B., O.B.E.
Morton, Capt. Harold Swithun, O.B.E.
Murray, Capt. Alexander Gordon Wynch, M.B.E.

Napier, Emily Caroline, M.B.E.
Newton, Major Leslie Cuthbert, O.B.E.
Nicholson, Frank, C.B.E.
Nightingale, Thomas Slingsby, C.B.E.
Niven, Major Douglas Scott, O.B.E.
North, Thomas Keppel, O.B.E.

Oran, Lieut.-Col. Harry Kendall, C.B.E.
Owen, Sir Douglas William, K.B.E.
Owen, William Scott, O.B.E.

Palmer, Lieut.-Col. Werner William Thomas Massiah, O.B.E.
Parker, Charles Sandbach, C.B.E.
Paterson, Lieut.-Col. Andrew Melville, C.B.E.
Perris, George Herbert, C.B.E.
Plunket, William Lee, Lord, G.C.M.G. K.C.V.O., K.B.E.
Pollock, Lieut.-Col. Charles Frederick, O.B.E.
Poole, Capt. and Qr.-Mr. Richard William, M.B.E.
Pratt, Capt. Mervyn Palles, O.B.E.

Quicke, Herbert John, M.B.E.

Ranger, Catherine Sarah, Mrs. Marden-, M.B.E., R.R.C.

Ransome, Capt. and Qr.-Mr. Robert Sheffield, O.B.E.
Restler, Sir James William, K.B.E.
Richardson, John, M.B.E.
Riddiford, Capt. Richard Errol Wardell, O.B.E.
Rimington, Comm. Percy William, O.B.E.
Ritson, Sir Arthur, K.B.E., J.P.
Roberts, Lieut.-Col. Frank Wereat, O.B.E.
Roberts, Col. Henry Robert, C.B.E.
Roberts, Herbert Wallace, M.B.E.
Robertson, Sir Frederick Alexander, K.B.E.
Robertson, Major Robert Arthur Harvey, O.B.E.
Rogers, Frederick Charles, M.B.E.
Rogers, Herbert, M.B.E.
Rouquette, Stewart Henry, O.B.E.
Rutherford, Annie, O.B.E.

Schank, Capt. Henry Alexander, O.B.E.
Scicluna, Corinna, Marchesa, O.B.E.
Scowcroft, Thomas, O.B.E.
Shepherd, Col. Charles Herbert, C.B.E.
Sheridan, Matthew Joseph, O.B.E.
Simmonds, Charles, O.B.E., B.Sc.
Smith, Lieut. Allan Bertram, M.B.E.
Smith, Roland Siddons, O.B.E.
Smith, Hon. Mrs. S. L.
Smith, Col. Stewart Boyle, C.B., C.B.E.
Smith, Thomas, O.B.E.
Smith, Lieut. Ronald Tate-, M.B.E.
Snell, John, M.B.E.
Solomon, Maude Elizabeth, Lady, O.B.E.
Spanton, Capt. John Percival, M.B.E.
Sparks, Capt. John Barnes, C.B.E., R.N.
Sparks, Lieut.-Col. Ralph Harold Austin, O.B.E.
Squires, Lieut. Reginald Alfred, O.B.E.
Stammers, Caroline Elinor, Mrs., M.B.E.
Stamp, William Blatspiel, O.B.E.
Steward, George Charles, K.B.E., C.M.G.
Stewart, George Vesey, M.B.E.
Stigand, Major Chauncy Hugh, O.B.E.
Strong, The Rt. Hon. Sir Thomas Vezey, P.C., K.C.V.O., K.B.E.
Stuart, Laura Elizabeth, Mrs., O.B.E.
Stubbs, John, O.B.E.

Taylor, Lieut.-Col. Gerald Oldroyd Cornock, C.B.E.
Temple, Elfrida Stella, M.B.E.
Thomas, Sir Godfrey John Vignoles, Bart., C.B., C.B.E., D.S.O.
Thomas, Capt. John, O.B.E.
Thompson, Sir William Henry, K.B.E.
Thompson, Capt. William Peter, O.B.E.
Thorne, Charles Augustus, M.B.E.
Tibbles, Frank Parry Relf, M.B.E.
Todd, Col. Octavius, C.B.E.
Towesy, Joseph Henry, O.B.E.
Treves, Major Wilfred Warrick, O.B.E.
Trueman, Lieut.-Col. Arthur Philip Hamilton, O.B.E.
Tuson, Capt. and Qr.-Mr. William, M.B.E.

Vaughan, Major Arthur Owen, D.S.O., O.B.E.
Vellacott, James Richard, M.B.E.
Verel, Capt. Raymond, O.B.E.

Wace, Major Stephen Charles, C.B.E.
Walker, Lieut.-Col. Howard Napier, O.B.E., M.C.
Wallis, Col. Charles Thomas, O.B.E.
Walsh, Lieut. Martin Oliver, M.B.E.
Walters, John, M.B.E.
Ward, Com. Charles Bertram, O.B.E., R.N.R.
Ward, Capt. George Augustus Crosbie, O.B.E., R.N.
Ward, Mary Augusta, Mrs. Humphrey, C.B.E.
Webb, Ellen, Lady, M.B.E.
Wells, Norman Septimus, O.B.E.
Weston, Dame Agnes, G.B.E.
White, Com. Hans Thomas Fell, O.B.E., R.N.
White, John William, O.B.E.
White, Lieut.-Col. Sinclair, C.B.E.
Willcock, Lieut.-Col. Stephen, O.B.E.
Wilkinson, Major Henry Frederick, C.B.E.
Williams, Capt. Arthur Albert, M.B.E.
Willoughby, Lieut.-Col. Frederick, O.B.E., V.D., D.L.
Wills, Lieut.-Col. Norman Septimus, O.B.E.
Wilson, Capt. Wilfred Gordon, M.B.E.
Wood, Edith Frances, M.B.E.
Wood, Frances, Mrs. S.H., O.B.E.
Wright, Capt. John Windham, O.B.E.

Yar Muhammad Khan Mian, M.B.E.

Zigomala, Lieut. John Copeland, M.B.E.

BIOGRAPHIES.

The numbers following the names give a cross-reference to the Precedence Lists at the end of the Handbook, where will be found the date of the appointment to the Order and whether the person named belongs to the Military or Civil division. The initial letters used are: G=Knights Grand Cross; D.G.=Dames Grand Cross; K=Knights Commanders: D= Dames Commanders; C=Commanders; O=Officers; M=Members, In cases of compound surnames the entry will be found under the last name at the end of the single names of similar spelling.

ABBEY, Paymaster-Lieut. Douglas Wilson, M.B.E., R.N. (retired).

ABBEY, Lieut.-Col. Walter Bulmer Tait, C.B.E., I.A.

ABBISS, William Frederick, M.B.E.

ABBOT, Mary Joyce, M.B.E., *b.* 5 Aug. 1891; *d.* of Henry Napier Abbot, of Bristol. *Educ.:* Eastbury School, near Watford, Herts. *War Work:* President, Bristol East Division S. and S.F.A. and War Pensions Committee. *Addresses:* 2, Beaufort Road, Clifton, Bristol; The Cottage, Dulverton, Somerset. (M7176)

ABBOTT, Lieut.-Comm. Bernard Edwin, O.B.E., R.N.R.

ABBOTT, Major Charles Reginald, M.B.E., R.A.F., *b.* 11 June, 1884; *s.* of Dr. C. E. Abbott, of Cheltenham. *Educ.:* Weston-super-Mare and Cheltenham. *War Work:* With the Royal Naval Air Service from Sept. 1914; finally in charge of Marine Acceptance Department in R.A.F. *Address:* 2, Auriol Mansions, Barons Court, London, W. 14 *Clubs:* Royal Automobile; Brooklands Automobile Racing Club. (M1320)

ABBOTT, Francis Charles, C.B.E., B.Sc., M.B., M.S.(Lond.), F.R.C.S.. *b.* 28 May, 1867; *s.* of the late Rev. Arthur Robert Abbott Vicar of Gorleston, Suffolk; *m.* Pauline, *d.* of the late Col. Harry Piesley L'Estrange, of Norwich. *Educ.:* Bruce Castle, St. Thomas's Hospital, and Univ. of London. Late Asst.-Surgeon. St. Thomas's Hospital; Consulting Surgeon, Evelina Hospital; Chief Surgeon, National Fund for Greek Wounded, Greco-Turkish War, 1897. *War Work:* Donor of, Commandant and Surgeon-in-Charge, Red Gables Hospital, Bletchingley; Advisory Surgeon, Redhill War Hospital. *Address:* The Hermitage, White Hill, Bletchingley. (C2404)

ABBOTT, George Edward, O.B.E., JP.

ABBOTT, Col. Herbert Edward Stacy, C.B.E., D.S.O., *b.* 6 April, 1855; *s.* of General H. E. S. Abbott, of Bengal Infantry; *m.* Mary, *d.* of Thomas Aveling, of Rochester, Kent. *Educ.:* Elizabeth College, Guernsey; and R.M. Academy, Woolwich. Brevet Colonel, Royal Engineers; Superintending Engineer in Public Works Dept. of India; Officiating Chief Engineer, Punjab, and Secretary to Govt. in Public Works Dept. *War Work:* R.E. Staff of London District, special charge being R.E. Services War Hospitals in London District. *Address:* 80, King's Road, Richmond, Surrey. *Club:* Junior United Service. (C796)

ABBOTT, John Dixon, M.B.E.

ABBOTT, Capt. John Harold, O.B.E., V.D., Delhi Medal; *s.* of William Abbott, of Edinburgh. *Educ.:* Stokes, Mussoorie, India. Hon. Member Viceroy's Council from April, 1913, to June, 1916; Municipal Commissioner, Jhansi; President, Anglo-Indian Empire League; Member of the Cantonment Committee. *War Work:* Chief (Hon.) Recruiting Officer for the Anglo-Indian Community, responsible for the recruitment of several thousand Anglo-Indians and the Domiciled community. Was responsible for the reform and improvement of many Government services in India; obtained increases of pay for the Indian Medical Department, and has removed certain disabilities in the Police, Postal and Telegraph Department, and in the Educational service; recruited over 5000 volunteers in India and Burma, and in the United Provinces alone over 100 women, trained and untrained, offered their services as nurses. *Address:* Jhansi, U.P., India. (O4007)

ABBOTT, Joseph Edward, O.B.E., *b.* 22 March, 1869; *s.* of W. Abbott, District Superintendent, G.N.R. Assistant to Superintendent of the Line, Great Northern Railway. *War Work:* Services rendered in connection with transport. *Address:* Kelso, Holden Road, Woodside Park, N. (O9866)

ABBOTT, Tom Bland, M.B.E., L.S.A.

ABBOTT, Capt. William George, O.B.E., R.A.S.C. (M.T.)

ABDY, Hon. Brig.-Gen. Anthony John, C.B., C.B.E., *b.* 26 April, 1856; *s.* of His Honour J. T. Abdy, County Court Judge, Regius Professor of Civil Laws, Cambridge; *m.* Alice Laura, *d.* of J. Bonham Carter, of Adhurst, Petersfield. *Educ.:* Charterhouse and R.M.A., Woolwich. Secretary Royal Artillery Institution; Commander R.H.A. and R.F.A., S.A., 1908–1912. *War Work:* Brig.-Gen. commanding various Divisional Artilleries in their formation, and Assistant Military Secretary, Southern Command. *Address:* The White Cottage, Woodbridge. *Club:* Naval and Military. (C418)

ABEL, Walter Charles, M.B.E.

ABELL, Major Charles Francis, O.B.E., R.A.F.

ABELL, Major George Henry, O.B.E., R.A.F.

ABELL, Prof. Thomas Bertrand, O.B.E., M.Eng.,

R.C.N.C. ret., *b.* March, 1880; *s.* of Thomas Abell, of Exmouth; *m.* Gertrude S., *d.* of Edwin F. Brook, of Ryde. *Educ.:* West Buckland School, Royal Naval Engineering College (Devonport), Royal Naval College (Greenwich). Naval Architect. Professor of Naval Architecture, University, Liverpool. *War Work.* Temporary Constructor, Admiralty; Assistant Director of Designs, Admiralty, and subsequently Ministry of Shipping, in the Department of Controller-General of Merchant Shipbuilding. *Address:* 10, Greenbank Drive, Liverpool; The University, Liverpool. *Club:* University (Liverpool). (O9867)

ABELL, Sir Westcott Stile, K.B.E., *b.* 16 Jan. 1920; *s.* of Thomas Abell, of Exmouth; *m.* Beatrice Gertrude, *d.* of Joseph Wyld Davenport, of Chester. *Educ.:* West Buckland School, Royal Naval Engineering College, Royal Naval College, Greenwich. Professional Secretary to Director of Naval Construction; Instructor in Naval Architecture, Royal Naval College; Professor of Naval Architecture, University of Liverpool; Chief Ship Surveyor, Lloyd's Register of Shipping from 1914. *War Work:* Assisting President of Board of Trade until Dec. 1916; Technical Adviser to Shipping Controller, 1917; Member of Merchant Shipbuilding Advisory Committee, 1917; Admiralty Shipbuilding Council, 1917; Reconstruction Committee on Shipping and Shipbuilding. *Address:* 11, Wedderburn Road, Hampstead, N.W. 3. *Clubs:* Savile; Royal Societies'; Royal Automobile. (K337)

ABERCONWAY, Laura, Lady, C.B.E.; *d.* of the late Henry Pochin, M.P., of Bodnant, Denbighshire; *m.* Charles Benjamin Bright M'Laren, 1st Baron Aberconway. *War Work:* Equipped and personally superintended a Hospital for Wounded Officers at her own house in Belgrave Square. This Hospital she ran four and a half years during the War, taking cases of severe wounds. Also lent her country house, Filders, Haslemere, for a Hospital for Soldiers under the Aldershot Command. *Address:* 43, Belgrave Square, S.W. 1; Bodnant, Denbighshire; Chateau de la Garoupe, Antibes, France. (C419)

ABERCROMBIE, Col. Charles Murray, C.M.G., C.B.E., Commanding 16th Bn. Lanc. Fusiliers, *b.* 1874; *m.* Dorothy, *d.* of John Riley, of Purley Court, Sedbury. Served in the S.A. War, 1901–2 (Queen's Medal, 5 Clasps); Great War, 1914–18 (mentioned in despatches, C.M.G.). (C1212)

ABERDEIN, Florence Maud, M.B.E., *b.* 6 Sept. 1893; *d.* of Arthur William Aberdein, of Brentford, Middlesex. *Educ.:* St. Mary's College, Isleworth, Middlesex, and St. George's College, London. Civil Servant. *War Work:* Private Secretary to Chairman of Flour Mills Control, Ministry of Food. *Address:* Eversleigh, The Butts, Brentford, Middx. *Club:* Forum. (M7178)

ABLETT, T. Lieut. (T. Capt.) Charles Anthony, O.B.F., R.E.

ABLETT, 1st Eng. Frank, M.B.E.

ABRAHALL, Bennet HOSKYNS-, C.B.E., *b.* 26 Aug.1858; *s.* of T. Bennet Hoskyns-Abrahall, Barrister-at-Law, Commissioner of Bankruptcy, of Goldspink Hall, Newcastle-on-Tyne, and Kernock, Torquay; *m.* Edith Louise, *d.* of the Rev. W. Egerton Tapp, of 85, Elm Park Gardens, S.W. *Educ.:* St. Peter's School, York; Keble Coll., Oxford (Scholar). Entered Civil Service, Grade I., in 1881, as Clerk in Secretary's Office, G.P.O.; Principal Clerk, 1906; appointed Director of the Investigation Branch, 1910. *War Work:* Special work in connection with duties as Director of the Investigation Branch. *Address:* Rubers Law, W. Byfleet. *Club:* Union. (C922)

ABRAHAM, Constance Palgrave, Mrs., M.B.E.

ABRAHAM, Lieut.-Col. James Johnston, C.B.E., D.S.O., R.A.M.C., *b.* 1876; *s.* of William Abraham, J.P., of Coleraine, Co. Derry; *m.* Lilian, *d.* of Dr. Alex Francis, of London. *Educ.:* Trinity College, Dublin, and London Hospital. Surgeon, The Kensington Hospital and London Lock Hospitals. *War Work:* Captain, Serbian Army, 1914–15 (awarded Order of St. Sava, 4th Class); served British Army, 1915–19; was A.D.M.S., Lines of Communications, Egyptian Expeditionary Force, 1917–19; three times mentioned in despatches. *Addresses:* 38, Harley St., W.1; Coleraine, Co. Derry. *Club:* Savage. (C1367)

ABRAHAM, Lieut. John Conrad, M.B.E.

ABRAHAM, Lieut.-Col. John William, O.B.E., D.L. Co. Middlesex, *b.* 3 June, 1875; *s.* of John George Abraham, of Grove Lodge, Muswell Hill, N.; *m.* Mabel Eleanor, *d.* of George Thomas Wilson, of Tollington Park, N. *Educ.:* Totteridge. Licentiate Royal Institute of British Architects: Oct. 1919, appointed Brigade Major to Middlesex Territorial Cadets with rank of Lieut-Col.; Sept. 1920, appointed Assistant Director of

Road Transport, Ministry of Food (Regents Park). *War Work* : Officer Commanding Transport, Eastern Command, Volunteer Ambulance Convoy ; Radiographer to Middlesex V.A.D. and Order of St. John ; organised, equipped, and ran travelling Cinematograph show, which in 4 years entertained over 100,000 men. (O9868)

ABRAHAMS, Dr. Adolphe, O.B.E., B.A., M.D., B.Ch. (Camb.), M.R C.P., M.R.C.S., *b.* 1884 ; *s.* of Isaac Abrahams, of London. *Educ.:* Bedford ; Cambridge Univ.; St. Bartholomew's Hospital ; Vienna. Consulting Physician. Physician to the Royal Chest Hospital ; Assistant Physician to Westminster Hospital and the Hampstead General Hospital. *War Work :* Major R.A.M.C. ; Officer in charge the Medical Division, Connaught Hospital, Aldershot ; District Consulting Physician Aldershot Command. *Addresses :* 24, Park Crescent, Portland Place, W. 1 ; 50, Rodney Court, Maida Vale, W. *Club :* New Oxford and Cambridge. (O6826)

ABRAHAMS, Major Arthur Cecil, C.B.E. *War Work :* Temp. Hon. Major, Special List ; Deputy Director of Stores, Boulogne, and a Special Red Cross Commissioner in France. (C2405)

ABRAHAMS, Joseph Godchaux, M.B.E.

ABRAHAMSON, Sir Martin Arnold, K.B.E., *b.* 12 Sept. 1870 ; *s.* of late Arnold Abrahamson, of Copenhagen ; *m.* Emma, *d.* of late Bernard Hirschsprung, of Copenhagen. *Educ.:* London and Copenhagen. Electrical Engineer ; Managing Director Industrial Trading Co., Ltd., and Tvermoes and Abrahamson, Ltd., Copenhagen. *War Work :* Vice-President and Chairman of British Red Cross Bureau, Copenhagen ; Organisation of Repatriation of British and Allied Prisoners of War from Germany *via* Copenhagen after Armistice. Assisted O'Grady Commission and Lady Marling (Pres. Br. Red Cr., Copenhagen) in work connected with Repatriation of British Nationals from Russia the beginning of this year. *Address :* 6, Krausesvej, Copenhagen. *Clubs :* Royal Danish Automobile ; Royal Danish Yacht ; Overseas ; Patriotic League, London (K338)

ABRAM, Ethel May, Mrs., M.B.E., *b.* 30 Nov. 1869 ; *d.* of Thomas Francis Rider, M.V.O., of London, S.W. ; *m.* George Stewart, *s.* of George Abram, of London, N.W. *Educ.:* Clapham High School ; " St. Clair," Tunbridge Wells. *War Work :* Commandant, St. Luke's Auxiliary Hospital, Reading, 1914–19, which was staffed by members of V.A.D., Berks 34, affiliated to Reading War Hospital. *Address :* 106, London Road, Reading, Berks. *Clubs :* Ladies' County, Reading ; V.A.D. Cavendish Sq., London, W. (M66)

ABRAMSON, Loc. Capt. Albert, O.B.E.

ABSALE, John Hilling, O.B.E., *b.* 15 Oct. 1851 ; *s.* of John Isaac Absale, of London ; *m.* Caroline Ada, *d.* of Francis Wood, of Hornsey Rise. *Educ.:* Privately. Late Principal, Securities Office, Bank of England, E.C. *War Work :* Principal of the Bank of England Staff, " American Securities Committee." *Address :* Hillingwood, Langley Park Road, Sutton, Surrey. (O1037)

ACFIELD, Wilfred Cosens, O.B.E.

ACHESON, Capt. Albert Edward, C.B.E., R.N. *War Work :* Divisional Naval Transport Officer, Manchester. (C2242)

ACHESON, Annie Crawford, C.B.E.: *d.* of John Acheson, J.P., of Portadown, Ireland. *Educ.:* Victoria College, Belfast ; Royal College of Art, South Kensington. Sculptor. *War Work :* Special splint making for military hospitals as head of Plastic Department of Surgical Requisites Association, Mulberry Walk. *Addresses :* 18, Beaufort Mansions, Beaufort St., S.W. 3 ; 6, Wentworth Studios, Manresa Road, Chelsea. (C923)

ACHESON, Capt. and Qr.-Mr. James, M.B.E. R.A.S.C.

ACHESON, Hon. Capt. and Qr.-Mr. Thomas Stuart, O.B.E.

ACHURCH, Lieut. George Philip, M.B.E., R.A.F.

ACKERS, Irene Mary, M.B.E. ; *d.* of the Rev. F. J. Ackers, of Dorchester, formerly Vicar of Frampton, Dorchester. *Educ.:* Cheltenham Ladies' College, and Somerville College, Oxford. *War Work :* V.A.D. (Nursing Service) 3rd Southern General Hospital, Oxford, Aug. 1916, to Jan. 1918 ; Q.M.A.A.C. (attached Headquarters Western and Scottish Commands), Jan. 1918 to Nov. 1919 ; Assistant Adminstrator, Jan. 1918; promoted Unit Administrator, Nov. 1918. *Address :* 21, The Avenue, Clifton, Bristol. (M6589)

ACKLAND, Robert Craig, C.B.E., M.R.C.S., L.R.C.P., L.D.S., *b.* 1865 ; *s.* of Robert Ackland, of Exeter ; *m.* Ruth Kathleen, *d.* of Edmund Macrory, K.C., of London. *Educ.:* Torquay and London. Senior Dental Surgeon to St. Bartholomew's Hospital ; Dental Surgeon, London Fire Brigade Benevolent Society. *War Work :* Medical Officer in charge of the Red Cross Hospitals for Facial Injuries, 78, Brook Street, W. 1., and 24, Norfolk Street, Park Lane. *Addresses :* 54, Brook Street, W. 1 ; The Hill, Winterton, Norfolk. (C2406)

ACKLAND, Vera, Mrs., M.B.E. ; *d.* of John Richard Philpots, of Moorcroft, Parkstone ; *m.* Donald, *s.* of Robert Ackland, of Exeter. *Educ.:* Brussels. *War Work :* Working Member of 2 Needlework Guilds and 2 canteens, 1914 ; whole time ambulance driver for Comforts and Convoys day and night, 1916 ; Commandant No. 1 Red Cross Hospital, Rock House (130 beds), for penetrating chest wounds, 1917 ; presented to their Majesties the King and Queen when they visited Bath in 1917 ; joint organiser in raising £8,000 for Red Cross and local Hospitals ; raised £3,400 for Y.M.C.A. by Flag Days ; organised Christmas Day Entertainments for troops stationed in Bath. *Address :* 11, The Circus, Bath. (M7180)

ACLAND, Col. Alfred Dyke, C.B.E., T.D.,J.P. (T.F., ret.), Croix-de-Guerre, Knight of Justice, Order of St. John of Jerusalem ; *b.* 19 Aug. 1858 ; *s.* of Sir Henry W. Acland, Bart., of Oxford (*see* BURKE'S *Peerage*) , *m.* Beatrice Danvers, *d.* of the late Rt. Hon. W. H. Smith, of Greenlands, Henley-on-Thames. *Educ.:* Charterhouse. *War Work :* Commanded Royal 1st Devon Yeomanry to 15 Dec. 1914 ; No. 3 Base Remount Department, 6 Jan. 1915, to 8 Feb. 1917 ; Assistant Director Labour Fourth Army, B.E.F., 8 Feb. 1917, to 8 Feb. 1918 ; Labour Commandant Australian Corps, 8 Feb. 1918, to 31 Aug. 1918. *Addresses :* Digswell House, Welwyn ; 306, St. James' Court. *Clubs :* Cavalry ; Brooks's ; Athenæum. (C2407)

ACLAND, Lieut.-Col. Hugh Thomas Dyke, C.M.G., C.B.E., *b.* 1874 ; *s.* of the late Hon. John Barton Arundel Acland, and Emily Weddell *d.* of the Rev. H. J. C. Harper, D.D., Bishop of Christchurch, N.Z. ; *m.* Evelyn Mary, *d.* of the late J. L. Ovans, East Sheen. Served in the S.A. War, 1900–1 ; Great War, 1914–17 ; mentioned in despatches ; C.M.G. *Address :* Christchurch, New Zealand. (C1848)

ACLAND, Katharine, M.B.E., *b.* 28 Sept. 1892 ; *d.* of Col. A. D. (*q.v.*) and Hon. Mrs. Acland, of Digswell House, Welwyn. *Educ.:* At Home. *War Work :* Secretary, Herts Branch, British Red Cross Society ; Assistant Commandant and Secretary, No 5 Australian Auxiliary Hospital, Digswell House, Welwyn ; Secretary of Controller of Entertainments, British Empire Leave Club, Cologne (for British Army of Occupation). *Addresses :* Digswell House, Welwyn ; 306, St. James' Court, S.W. 1. *Club :* V.A.D. (M3480)

ACLAND, Leopold George Dyke, O.B.E., M.C., *b.* 1876 ; *s.* of Thomas Dyke Acland, of Christchurch, N.Z. ; *Educ.:* Christ's College, Christchurch, N.Z. Sheep farmer. *War Services :* with New Zealand Expeditionary Force. *Address :* Springbank Farm, Hororata, N.Z. *Clubs :* Junior Carlton ; Christchurch (N.Z.). (O7973)

ACKLOM, Capt. Cecil Ryther, C.B., C.B.E., *b.* 1872 ; *s.* of Robert Evatt Acklom. Entered R.N., 1885 ; became Lieut. 1893 ; retired (1910), and Com. 1912 ; served in punitive Expedition against Sultan of Vitu, 1890 (medal with clasp); appointed Assist. Superintendent of Royal Gun Factory, Woolwich, 1899, and Superintendent of Royal Naval Torpedo Factory, Greenock, 1910 ; a C.B. (Civil) 1914. *Address :* B.T.H. Co.'s Works, Willesden. *Club :* United Service. (C2214d)

ACRAMAN, Capt. Ivor Yorath, M.B.E.

ACRES, Major (T. Lieut.-Col.) Thomas George, O.B.E.

ACTON, Ellen Marion, C.B.E. *War Work :* Assistant Secretary, Incorporated Soldiers' and Sailors' Help Society. *Address :* Ladies' Park Club, 32, Knightsbridge, S.W. (C2408)

ACTON, Frederick, C.B.E., J.P., *b.* 20 Sept. 1845 ; *s.* of James Acton, of the Elms, Nottingham ; *m.* Frances, *d.* of Simeon Woodhouse, of Mapperley, Notts. *Educ.:* Willoughby House, Nottingham. Sheriff of Nottingham, 1879–80 ; High Sheriff of Lincolnshire, 1915–16 ; J.P. for Lincs. and Nottingham ; Deputy Chairman, Lindsey Sessions ; Hon. President National Deposit Friendly Society ; Chairman Nottingham General Hospital for several years. *War Work :* Chairman of Nottingham General Hospital throughout the War, and actively engaged in dealing with some 7000 wounded ; Deputy Chairman to the Duchess of Portland, inaugurating and carrying on Ellerslie Home, Nottingham, for Sailors and Soldiers of Notts., paralysed consequent on war service ; Deputy Chairman of the Lindsey Appeal Tribunal, etc. *Addresses :* The Elms, Nottingham ; Miramar, Seacroft, Lincolnshire. *Clubs :* Notts. and Lincs. County. (C2409)

ACTON, Major William Cawley, O.B.E., R.A.O.C.

ACWORTH, Col. Louis Raymond, C.B.E., R.A.O.C.

ADAIR, Major Alexander Cecil, O.B.E.

ADAIR, Capt. Francis Robert, M.B.E., R.E.

ADAIR, Brig.-Gen. Hugh Robert, C.B.E., R.A. (ret.), *b.* 8 Sept. 1863 ; *s.* of Gen. Sir C. W. Adair, K.C.B., Royal Marines ; *m.* Sibyl, *d.* of T. Cayzer, of Aigburth, Liverpool. *Educ.:* Cheltenham College ; R.M.A., Woolwich. Joined R.A. 25 July, 1892, retired 15 April, 1920. *War Work :* Lient.-Col., Col., and Brig.-Gen., Royal Artillery. *Address :* c/o Cox & Co., 16, Charing Cross, S.W. 1. (C1441)

ADAM, Capt. Herbert Algernon, C.B.E., R.N., *b.* 3 Jan. 1872 ; *s.* of Rev. B. W. Adams, D.D., of Santry, Co. Dublin ; *m.* Elizabeth Banner Clough, *d.* of Capt. S. Y. Somerset-Johnstone. *Educ.:* Privately and H.M.S. " Britannia." *War Work :* In command of H.M.S. Queen for first two years of War, and landed Anzac Brigade at Dardanelles ; one year, Principal British Naval Transport Officer at Salonika with rank of Commander 2nd Class ; remainder of war employed in convoy work in North Atlantic. *Address :* The Chillies, Uckfield, Sussex *Club :* United Service. (C1175)

ADAM, James, C.B.E., K.C., *b.* 6 Jan. 1870 ; *s.* of Lord Adam, late Senator of the College of Justice (Scotland) ; *m.* Edith, *d.* of the late Rt. Hon. George Young, P.C. *Educ.:* Eton and Oxford. Secretary to Scottish Unionist Whip. *War Work :* Central Recruiting Committee, Scotland ; Red Cross ; General Commission National Service, Scotland ; Deputy Director National Service (London). *Club :* New (Edinburgh). (C420)

ADAM, John Hunter, O.B.E.

ADAM, Mary, M.B.E. ; *d.* of John Birnie Adam, of Newcastle-on-Tyne. *Educ.:* Aberdeen and abroad. *War Work :* Hon. Sec. Comforts Committee (Ladies) for the 16th,

18th, and 19th Battalions Northumberland Fusiliers; Worked at Munitions at Armstrongs', Elswick; Canteen Work Y.M.C.A. and Victoria League (Hospital Dressings Depot). *Addresses:* 8, Osborne Terrace, Newcastle-on-Tyne; Luddick, Kenton, Newcastle-on-Tyne. *Club:* Ladies' Athenæum.

(M7181)

ADAM, Robert, O.B.E.

ADAM, Major Ronald Forbes, D.S.O., O.B.E., R.F.A., *b.* 13 Oct. 1885; *s.* of Sir Frank Forbes Adam, Bart., C.B., C.I.E., LL.D., D.L., of Pownall Hall, Cheshire; *m.* Dorothy, *d.* of Frederick Islay Pitman, of Breymead, Berks. *Educ.:* Eton and R.M.A., Woolwich. *War Work:* France and Italy, 1914 to 1918. *Addresses:* Pownall Hall, Wilmoton, Cheshire; Quebec House, Bordon. *Club:* Naval and Military. (O6341)

ADAMI, Col. John George, C.B.E., F.R.S., M.A., M.D. (Camb.), F.R.C.P. (Lond.), F.R.C.S. (Eng.), F.R.S.S. (Edin.), 1898, Canada 1902, M.A., M.D. (*ad eundem*) McGill 1899, LL.D. (New Brunswick) 1900, Toronto (1912), Sc.D. (T.C.D.) 1912, Vice-Chancellor of the Univ. of Liverpool since 1919, *b.* 12 Jan. 1862; *s.* of the late John George Adami, of Manchester and Ashton-upon-Mersey, Cheshire; *m.* Mary Stuart (died 1916), *d.* of James Alexander Cantlie, of Montreal. *Educ.:* Owens College, Manchester; Christ's Coll. (Camb.), (Scholar); Breslau, and Paris (1st class 1st pt. Nat. Sc. Tripos, 1882; 1st cl. 2nd pt. 1884; Darwin Prizeman, 1885). House Physician, Manchester Royal Infirmary, and Demonstrator of Pathology, Univ. of Camb., 1887; John Lucas Walker Student of Pathology, 1890; Fellow, Jesus Coll., 1891; Advisory Pathologist to the Montreal General and Royal Victoria Hospitals; President, Association American Physicians, 1911–12; Canadian Association Prevention Tuberculosis, 1909–12; Montreal City Improvement League. 1909; Montreal Child Welfare Exhibition, 1912; Col. C.A.M.C., Medical Historical Recorder, Canadian Expeditionary Force; member W.O. Committee on Medical History of the War; Strathcona Professor of Pathology and Bacteriology, McGill University, Montreal, 1892–1919; Fothergillian Medallist, Medical Society, London, 1914. *Address:* The University, Liverpool *Clubs:* Savile; University, Exchange and Athenæum, Liverpool. (C1825)

ADAMS, Alexander, O.B.E. (O6124)

ADAMS, Alfred Montague, M B.E.

ADAMS, Arthur Botwell, O.B.E., *b.* 1 Oct. 1886; *s.* of William Adams, of Loughton, Essex; *m.* Margaret, *d.* of H. T. Baugust. *Educ.:* Marlborough, and Emmanuel Coll., Cambridge. H.M. Inspector of Schools. *War Work:* Administrative Officer, Prisoners of War Dept., Home Office. *Address:* Selby Avenue, St. Albans. (O9870)

ADAMS, Lieut.-Col. Sir Arthur Robert, K.B.E., V.D., *b.* 13 Dec. 1861; *e.s.* of Robert Adams, of Sherborne; *m.* Hilda Isabel (died 1907), *d.* of Philip Jones, Assistant Colonial Treasurer, Straits Settlements. *Educ.:* The Abbey and Foster's Schools, Sherborne. English Solicitor, 1884; Straits Settlements Bar, 1898; Johore Bar, 1917; Unofficial Member of the Legislative Council, Straits Settlements, 1907–19; Senior Unofficial, 1915–19; Municipal Commissioner, Penang, 1891, and subsequent years; has on several occasions acted as Solicitor-General of the Colony; Vice-President S.S. Branch of the Royal Asiatic Society; Fellow, Royal Colonial Institute; First President of the Association of Malaya, 1916–19; P.D.D.G.M. Eastern Archipelago (ruled the district 1910–11); Commandant, Penang Volunteers, 1899–1919; mobilised 1914 till the Armistice; Lieut.-Col. Commanding troops Penang, 1915–18; despatches. *Address:* Rockleigh, Swanage, Dorset. *Clubs:* Junior Carlton; Sports'; Penang, Singapore. (K189)

ADAMS, Edgar, M.B.E.

ADAMS, Dr. Edward William, O.B.E., M.D., *b.* 25 Nov. 1873; *s.* of Dr. E. J. Adams, of Sheffield; *m.* Winifred, *d.* of Turton Chatterton, of Sheffield. *Educ.:* Sheffield and London Univs. Medical Officer, Ministry of Health. *War Work:* In connection with war work of National Health Insurance Commission, England. *Address:* Ministry of Health, Whitehall, S.W. 1. (O9871)

ADAMS, T. Lieut. (A. Capt.) Edwin Plimpton, O.B.E., R.E.

ADAMS, Francis William Rhys, M.B.E., *b.* 16 Oct. 1874; *s.* of Henry Adams, of Pembroke. *Educ.:* St. Paul's School, London. Keeper of Photographs, Imperial War Museum. *War Work:* Orderly at Hopital Temporaire, Arc-en-Barrois, Haute Marne, France, 1915–16, Officer in charge Photographic Exhibitions (Propaganda), Dept. of Information, 1917; Officer in charge Photographic Propaganda, Ministry of Information, 1918. *Address:* Imperial War Museum, Crystal Palace, S.E. (M3481)

ADAMS, Col. Gofton Gee, C.B.E. *b.* 1861; Col. (ret.) R.A.M.C. Served in the Great War, 1914–19 (despatches). (C1442)

ADAMS, Harold Cotterell, O.B.E., *b.* 18 Oct. 1874; *s.* of William Adams, of Gloucester; *m.* Clare, *d.* of Charles Rampini, D.L., LL.D., Advocate. *Educ.:* Bath College and Middlesex Hospital. *War Work:* Civil Surgeon, S. African Field Force, 1900; Major, R.A.M.C., second in Command, 212nd Wessex Ambulance, B.E.F. France. *Address:* Mayhurst, Paignton. (O2391)

ADAMS, Capt. Henry George Homer, C.B.E., R.N., *b.* 10 April, 1879; *s.* of the late Rev. C. E. Adams; *m.* Emma

Florence, *d.* of the late James Craig. *Educ.:* Oxford Preparatory School and H.M.S. "Britannia." Present appointment H.M.C.S. "Aurora." *War Work:* Service in the Grand Fleet, H.M.S. "Russell," Aug. 1914, to July, 1915; H.M.S. "Barham," July, 1915, to Oct. 1918; S.N.O., Corfu, 1 Oct. 1918, to Jan. 1919. *Address:* Camrose, Goring-on-Thames. *Club:* Naval and Military. (C2283)

ADAMS, Herbert Windham, M.B.E., B.A., *b.* 9 March, 1879; *s.* of Baldwin Adams, of Melling Hall, Carnforth; *m.* Evelyn, *d.* of C. Bridgewater Williams, of Richmond. *Educ.:* St. Paul's School, and University Coll., Oxford. Assistant to Manager of Alexander's Discount Co., Ltd. *War Work:* R.A.S.C. and later, Staff Lieut. at War Office (Q.M.G. 6). *Address:* 24, Lombard Street, E.C. 3. *Clubs:* Leander; Vincent's Roehampton. (M5022)

ADAMS, Dr. John, M.B.E., *b.* 1859; *s.* of John Adams, of Glasgow; *m.* Jessie, *d.* of James Reid, of Edinburgh. *Educ.:* Banff, privately, and Glasgow University. Physician. *War Work:* Medical Service Emergency Committee (Scotland) and of its Executive; Local Medical Committee (Chairman), British Medical Association, War Work. *Address:* 1, Queen's Crescent, W., Glasgow. (M3482)

ADAMS, Major John Basil Franklin, O.B.E., R.A.M.C.

ADAMS, Capt. John Cadwallader, O.B.E.

ADAMS, Major John Hughes, O.B.E., R.F.A.

ADAMS, 2nd Lieut. John Leonard, M.B.E., D.S.M., R.A.F.

ADAMS, Capt. Josiah Logan, O.B.E., R.E.

ADAMS, Major Kenneth Lemesle, O.B.E., R.E.

ADAMS, Major Lewis Charles, C.B.E., *b.* 1877; Major and Brevet Lieut.-Col. R.A. Served in the Great War, 1914–19 (despatches). (C1443)

ADAMS, Matthew Henry, M.B.E.

ADAMS, Major Paul, O.B.E.

ADAMS, Richard Percival, O.B.E.

ADAMS, Robert Ernest Kennedy, M.B.E.

ADAMS, Capt. and Qr.-Mr. Robert Frank, M.B.E.

ADAMS, Thomas, C.B.E. J.P., Chm. S.-E. Scotland Joint Committee, Min. of Pensions. (C421)

ADAMS, Capt. Thomas Henry, O.B.E., M.A., *b.* 16 July, 1887; *s.* of Henry Charles Skelton Adams, of Walsall; *m.* Matilda Eliza, *d.* of Charles Deakin, of Old Southgate, London. *Educ.:* Bishop Vesey's Grammar School (Warw.), Universities of Birmingham, Munich, and Strasbourg. Senior Assistant Master. *War Work:* Enlisted as Private Aug. 1914 in 15th Service Batt. R.W.R.; Transferred Aug. 1915 to Gas Companies (Special Bde.) Royal Engineers (Sergt.); 2nd Lieut., Lt., Special Bde. R.E., 1916–17; Captain R.E., Intelligence Officer to Directorate of Gas Services and Special Bde., R.E., G.H.Q., France; Mentioned in Despatches, Dec. 1918. *Address:* Alva, Reservoir Road, Old Southgate, N. 14. (O4941)

ADAMS, Thomas Herbert, M.B.E. Schoolmaster. *War Work:* Honorary Secretary, Lowestoft War Savings Committee. *Address:* 74, The Avenue, S. Lowestoft. (M7183)

ADAMS, William, O.B.E.

ADAMS, Lieut.-Col. William Henry, O.B.E., R.A.O.C.

ADAMS, William John, C.B., C.M.G., O.B.E., J.P.

ADAMS, Col. Sir Henry Edward GOOLD-, K.B.E., C.B., C.M.G., R.A., *b.* 16 May, 1860; 5th *s.* of the late R. W. Goold-Adams. *Educ.:* R.M.A., Woolwich. Entered Army, 1879; Capt., 1887; Major, 1897; Col., 1911; served China, 1901 (despatches, medal, C.M.G.); a member of the Ordnance Board, 1910. *Address:* Jamesbrook, Midleton, Co. Cork. *Club:* United Service. (K128)

ADAMSON, Major and Qr.-Mr. George Herbert, M.B.E., R.A.

ADAMSON, John, C.B.E.; formerly a M.L.A., Queensland. (C1990)

ADAMSON, John Stockton, M.B.E., *b.* 1 Nov. 1877; *s.* of the late John Stockton Adamson, of Liverpool; *m.* Margaret Mackie, *d.* of the late Samuel Kirkness, of Liverpool and Kirkness, Orkney. *Educ.:* Sedbergh Grammar School. Cotton Broker. *War Work:* Commandant of West Lancashire T.F.A. and B.R.C.S., V.A.D. No. 27; organised and trained 400 Voluntary Workers as Stretcher Bearers and Hospital Orderlies at 18 Local and Military Hospitals; during the war worked personally more than 6000 hours. *Address:* Silverdale, Victoria Park, Wavertree, Liverpool. (M1323)

ADAMSON, Lieut.-Col. Robert Hay, C.B.E. Lieut.-Col. and Hon. Col. R.G.A ; Great War, 1914–19 (despatches). (C1444)

ADCOCK, Lieut. Frank, M.B.E., R.E.

ADCOCK, Lieut.-Comm. Frank Ezra, O B.E., R.N.V.R.

ADCOCK, Fred, M.B.E.

ADCOCK, Capt. Frederick Harold, M.B.E., R.F.A. (T.F.)

ADDENBROOKE, Lieut.-Col. Joseph Saunders, O.B.E., R.E.

ADDIE, Col. John Heathcote, C.B.E.; Col. New Armies, and Dep. Director of Agriculture; Great War, 1914–19 (despatches). (C1213)

ADDIE, Julia Constance, Mrs., M.B.E.

ADDINGTON, John Gellibrand Hubbard, Lord, O.B.E., of Addington, co. Buckingham, *b.* 7 June, 1883; *s.* of Egerton, 2nd Baron Addington (*see* BURKE'S *Peerage*). *Educ.:* Christ Church Coll., Oxford. Capt. Bucks Batt., Oxford and Bucks

Light Infantry. Served in the Great War. *Address*: Addington, nr. Winslow, Bucks. *Club*: Bachelor's. (O9712)

ADDINGTON, Maud Florence, O.B.E. *b.* 25, Feb. 1863; *d.* of the late Major the Hon. L. A. Addington, of Ratclyffe, Devon (*see* BURKE'S *Peerage*, Sidmouth V.). *Educ.*: At home. *War Work*: Chief of the Lady Staff on M.S. 3 Cas. War Office, under Major H. Stanton, M.V.O., from 14 Sept. 1915, to 30 Aug. 1919. *Club*: Forum. (O9874)

ADDIS, Frederick Henry, O.B.E., V.D., A.M.Inst.C.E , *b.* 24 Feb. 1862; *s.* of the late H. B. Addis; *m.* Elsie *d.* of G. F. Cumberland, of Selby. *Educ.* Dollar Academy and King's Coll., London. Locomotive and Carriage Supt., Bombay, Baroda, and Central India Rly., Metre Gauge Section, India (retired). *War Work*: Engaged in manufacture and supply of armoured trains, munitions, and rolling stock for Mesopotamia and East Africa; mentioned in despatches. *Address*: 21, Wellington Road, Bridlington, Yorks. *Club*: Royal Societies'. (O4008)

ADDISCOTT, William James, M.B.E.

ADDISCOTT, Elizabeth Mary, M.B.E. (M10244a)

ADDISON, Guy Frederick, M.B.E.; *b.* 5 Nov. 1885; *s.* of George Thomas Addison, of Halifax; *m.* Elsie Annie, *d.* of Alfred Duce, of Dudley. *Educ.*: Halifax. Works Manager, A. Harper, Sons and Bean, Ltd., Waddam's Pool Works, Dudley, Worcestershire. *War Work*: Mass Production of Munitions of War (practice shot, Shrapnel shell, high explosive shell and 60 pdr. B.L. guns). (M7185)

ADDISON, Joseph Bartlett, M.B.E.

ADDISON, Capt. Lancelot Mark, M.B.E., A.I.F.

ADDISON, Stanley, M.B.E. (M10266)

ADDISON, Major Sydney Wentworth, O.B.E., R.A.F.

ADDY, Lieut. Ernest, M.B.E., R.N., *b.* 15 May, 1869; *s.* of George Addy, of Shelley, Huddersfield; *m.* Catherine, *d.* of Charles Howard, of Southsea. *War Work*: Served during the war in H.M. Gunnery School "Excellent," Portsmouth, and at the Admiralty in Director of Naval Ordnance's Department. *Address*: 56, Kenilworth Avenue, Wimbledon Park, S.W. 19. (M1325)

ADEANE, Jean Henrietta, O.B.E., *d.* of Henry John Adeane, of Babraham, Cambridge, M.P. for Cambs., and Hon. Maud Adeane, *d.* of 1st Lord Stanley of Alderley. *War Work*: Commandant, Stanley Hospital for Sailors and Soldiers, Holyhead; President, Free Buffet for Soldiers and Sailors, Holyhead; *Addresses*: Plas Llanfawr, Holyhead; Lennox Lodge, London, S.W. (O9875)

ADEY, Lieut.-Col. John Kellerman, O.B.E.

ADKIN, Paymaster-Lieut. Guy Tempest, M.B.E., R.N.R.

ADKIN, Rev. Walter Kenrick Knight, O.B.E., B.A., R.N.

ADKINS, Lieut. George, M.B.E.

ADKINS, Capt. William John, M.B.E., *b.* 17 Dec. 1865; *s.* of Colour-Sergt. James Adkins, of late 28th Regt. of Foot; *m.* Minnie, *d.* of Hovel Hill, of Prickwillow, Ely, Cambs. *Educ.*: Army Schools. Served in S.A. War (Queen's Medal); King George V. Coronation, Long Service and Good Conduct Medals. *War Work*: Embodied with 6th Gloucester Regt., Aug. 1914 (Qr.-Mstr.); France March, 1915, to Aug. 1917; transferred to R.A.F. April, 1918; Demobilised from R.A.F., Jan. 1920: mentioned in despatches, F.M. Haig (Gazette 1 Jan. 1917). *Addresses*: 16, The Paragon, Bath; 42, Shakespeare Cresent, Manor Park, E. (M5904)

ADLER, Capt. Herbert Marcus, M.B.E., M.A., LL.M., *b.* 16 Jan. 1876; *s.* of Marcus N. Adler, M.A., of London. *Educ.*: City of London School, and St. John's Coll. Cambridge. Barrister-at-law. *War Work*: Adjutant M.T. Training Depot, R.A.S.C., Osterley Park. *Address*: 5, Abercorn Place, N.W. 8. (M5025)

AFFLECK, Florence Bessie, M.B.E., *b.* 25 Mar. 1879; *d.* of John Murray Affleck, of High Wycombe. *Educ.*: Ellerker College. *War Work*: Commandant of V.A.D. Bucks. 52; part organiser of Wycombe V.A.D. Hospital, and afterwards responsible for the catering. *Address*: Priory Avenue, High Wycombe. (M70)

AGABEG, Col. Frank Joseph, O.B.E,

AGLEN, Sir Francis Arthur, K.B.E., *b.* 17 Oct. 1869; *s.* of the late Ven. A. S. Aglen; *m.* Senga Marion, *d.* of Prof. Bayley Balfour. *Educ.*: Marlborough. Inspector-General Maritime Customs, China, since 1911; joined the Customs, 1888; Deputy Commissioner, 1896; Commissioner, Tientsin, 1897; Nanking, 1890–1900, 1901–3; Shanghai, 1900–1; Chief Secretary Inspectorate-General, 1903–4; Commissioner, Hankow, 1906; Deputy Inspector-General, 1910; Officiating Inspector-General, 1910–11; Civil rank, 2nd Class, with Imperial Order; Double Dragon, 2nd Division, 2nd Class; Order of the China Ho, First Class. *Address*: Inspectorate-General of Customs, Peking, China. *Club*: Royal Societies'. (K48)

AGLIONBY, Rosa Frances, M.B.E.; *d.* of Rev. Dr. Aglionby, Vicar of Newbold Pacey, Warwick. *War Work*: Under British Red Cross Society. *Address*: Newbold Pacey Vicarage, Warwick. *Club*: Lyceum. (M7186)

AGNEW, Capt. Andrew, M.B.E.

AGNEW, Andrew, C.B.E., *b.* 28 Feb. 1882; *s.* of Andrew Agnew, of Greenock; *m.* Belle, *d.* of James McClymont, of Girvan. *Educ.*: Greenock. Member Legislative Council, Straits Settlements (ret.); Justice of the Peace. *War Work*: Chairman Mesopotamian River Craft Committee, Singapore; Member Straits Settlements Food Control and Shipping Committees; Commandant Singapore Civil Guard. *Address*: St. Helens Court, Great St. Helens, E.C. (C384)

AGNEW, Charles Morland, O.B.E., M.A., *b.* 14 Dec. 1855; *s.* of Sir William Agnew, of Manchester and London (*see* BURKE'S *Peerage*); *m.* Evelyn Mary, *d.* of William Nayler, of Paddington. *Educ.*: Rugby School, and Trinity College, Cambridge. *War Work*: Red Cross Society, missing and wounded department. *Addresses*: Durrants, Croxley Green, Herts.; 9, Cavendish Square, W. *Clubs*: Reform; Farmers'; Lord's. (O1042)

AGNEW, Sir Patrick Dalreagle, K.B.E., Knight of Grace of the Order of St. John, *b.* 26 April, 1868; *s.* of William Henry Agnew, of Victoria, Australia; *m.* Elizabeth Frances Seaton, *d.* of Lt.-Col. C. F. Massy, of Grantstown, Tipperary. *Educ.*: Bedford Grammar School; Balliol College, Oxford. Joined Indian Civil Service in 1889; Assistant Commissioner in Panjab till 1898; Deputy Commissioner, 1898; Divisional Judge, 1910; Officiating Judge, Chief Court, 1913; retired 1914. *War Work*: Hon. Sec. Indian Soldiers Fund, 1914–16; Managing Director and Vice-Chairman Central Prisoners of War Committee, 1916–19. *Address*: 8, Northmoor Road, Oxford. *Club*: East India United Service. (K339)

AGNEW, Capt. Samuel Montagu, O.B.E., R.N., *b.* 22 Feb. 1867; *s.* of Capt. John de Courcy Agnew, R.N. *Club*: Naval and Military. (O1043)

AHERN, Major Michael David, O.B.E., R.A.M.C.

AHERN, Lieut.-Comm. Michael John, O.B.E., R.N.

AHERNE, Major Denis, O.B.E., R.H.A.

AIKMAN, Andrew, M.B.E.

AINLEY, Lieut.-Col. Richard, O.B.E.

AINSCOUGH, Thomas Martland, O.B.E., M.Com., F.R.G.S., *b.* 12 Aug. 1886; *s.* of J. M. Ainscough, J.P., of Lindley Mount, Parbold, Lancs.; *m.* Mabel, 3rd *d.* of Wm. Lincolne, of Ely, Cambs. *Educ.*: Manchester Grammar School and Manchester Univ. His Majesty's Senior Trade Commissioner in India and Ceylon; travelled widely in China and Eastern Tibet; Special Commissioner of the Board of Trade in China, 1914–15; Secretary of the Board of Trade Textiles Comm., 1916–17; Secretary of the Empire Cotton Growing Committee, 1917; proceeded to India to take up appointment as H.M. Senior Trade Commissioner in India and Ceylon, 1918; Expert Assistant attached to the Commission for the Revision of the Persian Tariff, 1920. *Clubs*: Royal Societies'; Bengal, Calcutta. (O80)

AINSLIE, Lieut. Eustace Montagu Lafone, M.B.E. R.A.F.

AINSWORTH, Ina Cameron, Mrs., M.B.E., *b.* 6 Nov. 1876; *d.* of John Scott; *m.* John, *s.* of John Dawson Ainsworth, of Manchester. *War Work*: Continuous services on behalf of the East African Expeditionary Force. *Address*: 18, Maple Avenue, Chorlton-cum-Hardy, Manchester. (M6407)

AINSWORTH, Col. John, C.M.G., C.B.E., D.S.O., *b.* 16 June, 1864; *s.* of John Dawson Ainsworth, of Manchester; *m.* Ina Cameron, *d.* of the late John Scott. *Educ.*: Privately. H.M. Vice-Consul, E.A.P., 1896–1902; Provincial Commissioner E.A.P. 1895–1917; Military Commissioner for Labour East Africa Expeditionary Force, with rank of Colonel, 1917–18; Chief Native Commissioner E.A.P. from 1918; Member of Executive and Legislative Councils, E.A.P. *War Work*: Recruitment of natives for the King's African Rifles and as carriers for the E.A. Expeditionary Force. *Address*: Chorlton-cum-Hardy, Manchester. (C2013)

AINSWORTH, Lieut.-Col. William John, C.B.E., D.S.O., *b.* 1873; *s.* of late Capt. William Ainsworth (formerly 53rd and 106th L.I.), of Spotland, Rochdale, Lancashire, and Trentham House, Twickenham Park, Middlesex. Entered Durham L.I. 1893; Capt. 1001, Major, 1914; Brevet Lieut.-Col. 1917; served in S. Africa, 1899–1900 (despatches); Staff Officer, 1911; D.A.A.G. 1914; A.A.G. 1916; has 4th class Serbian Order of the White Eagle. *Club*: Junior United Service. (C779)

AIREY, Lieut-Col. Harold Morris, C.B.E.; Hon. Lieut.-Col. R.M. *War Services*: with Wireless Telegraphy during Great War. (C2351)

AIREY Major Rowland Montagu, O.B.E., M.C., *b.* 7 Jan. 1884; *s.* of Major Airey, late 24th Regt. *Educ.*: St. Paul's School, and R.M. College, Camberley. *War Work*: D.A.A.M.G. 37th Division July, 1915 to July, 1917; D.A.D.P. War Office, July, Oct. 1917 to Jan. 1920. *Address*: C/o Sir C. R. McGrigor, Bart., & Co., 39, Panton Street, S.W. *Clubs*: Junior United Service; Marlborough. (O4306)

AIRLIE, Mabell Frances Elizabeth, Countess Dowager of, G.B.E., *b.* 10 March, 1866; *d.* of the Earl of Arran, of Castle Gore, Ireland (*see* BURKE'S *Peerage*); *m.* David, Earl of Airlie, late Lt.-Col. 12th Royal Lancers, killed at Diamond Hill, Pretoria, 11 June, 1900 (*see* BURKE'S *Peerage*). Lady of the Bedchamber to Queen Mary; Vice President, Army Nursing Board; President Forfarshire Branch, Scottish Red Cross. *Addresses*: Airlie Castle, Alyth, N.B.; 56, Ashley Gardens, S.W. (D.G.29)

AITCHISON, Agnes Mary, M.B.E.

AITCHISON, George, M.B.E., C.C., *b.* 2 Jan. 1883; *s.* of William Aitchison, of Briery Hill, Hawick, N.B.; *m.* Marjorie, *d.* of C. H. Hough, J.P., of White Craggs, Ambleside. *Educ.*: Malvern College. County Councillor for Westmorland. *War Work*: Late Major R.A.S.C. *Address*: Quarry Garth, Windermere. (M3164)

AITCHISON, Capt. Robert Smith, M.B.E.

AITKEN, Adeline, M.B.E., *b.* 17 April, 1864; *d.* of Charles Loyd Norman, J.P., D.L., of Bromley Common, Kent; *m.* Major John Christie, *s.* of John Christie Aitken, of St. Andrews, Fife. *War Work*: Chairman, Berwickshire Local Central War Savings Committee; Member of Food Control Committee, Berwickshire. *Club*: Queen's (Edinburgh). (M7188)

AITKEN, Major Allan Beacon, O.B.E., M.C.

AITKEN, Andrew, M.B.E., J.P., C.C.; *s.* of the late Andrew Blair Aitken, of Carsehead, Dalry, Ayrshire; *m.* Annie Barclay Hogarth, *d.* of the late John Hogarth, Provost of Ardrossan. *Educ.*: Royal Academy, Irvine, and High School, Glasgow. Woollen Manufacturer. Member of County Council of Ayrshire, and Convener of Northern District Committee of County Council, also member of Northern District Licensing Court from the time of its inception; Chairman of Dalry Gas-Light Coy., Ltd., Dalry, Ayrshire. *War Work*: Member of County Local Tribunal during all the time of its existence. Chairman of Dalry Parish Council from 1895 to 1915 when war work claimed more attention, therefore resigned that office. *Address*: One Ash, Dalry, Ayrshire. *Club*: Scottish Constitutional (Glasgow). (M1328)

AITKEN, Constance Margaret, M.B.E., *b.* 17 Dec. 1890; *d.* of late Andrew Aitken, of Spalding, Lincolnshire. *Educ.*: Privately. Divisional Superintendent, Ministry of Pensions. *War Work*: 4 years in the Ministry of Pensions engaged on duties connected with the award and payment of disability pensions to soldiers invalided in the Great War. *Address*: Royal Hospital, Chelsea, S.W. 3. (M7189)

AITKEN, David Jeffrey, O.B.E.

AITKEN, James Herbert, O.B.E

AITKEN, Jean Reid, M.B.E., *b.* 30 Jan. 1895; *d.* of Alex. Aitken, of Stranraer. *Educ.*: Stranraer High School and Glasgow and West of Scotland College of Domestic Science. Staff Mistress of Cookery in the Training School for Teachers of Domestic Science, Preston. *War Work*: Head and Organising Cook at Hinton St. George Flax Camp, Somerset, in summer of 1918. *Address*: Bowie Cottage, Stranraer. (M3484)

AITKEN, Major John Christie, M.B.E.

AITKEN, John Malcolm, M.B.E., J.P., F.H.A.S., *b.* 24 Feb. 1855; *s.* of the late Mark Aitken, of Oaklands, Crieff, N.B.; *m.* Isobella Wilson, *d.* of the late William Macindoe, M.D., of Lockerbie. *Educ.*: Crieff, and Edinburgh. Estate Agent to Sir Robert W. Buchanan-Jardine, Bart., Castlemilk; is a Member of Dumfriesshire County Council; chairman of the County Public Health Committee, also of Lockerbie District Committee, and of other Public Bodies. *War Work*: acted as first Town Manager of the Townships at H.M. Factory, Gretna, the duties of which office included the setting up of the numerous services connected with the communal life of the Townships; assisted with recruiting, served on the Dumfriesshire Local Tribunal, and was Chairman of the Lockerbie District Food Production Committee. *Address*: Norwood, Lockerbie, N.B. *Clubs*: Dumfries and Galloway County; Scottish Conservative. (M7190)

AITKEN, Robert Young, O.B.E., M.D., F.R.C.S., J.P.; *Educ.*: Glasgow University. Surgeon, Blackburn Royal Infirmary. *War Work*: Medical Officer in charge, Ellerslie Auxiliary Hospital, Blackburn; Operating Surgeon, Queen Mary's Military Hospital, Whalley. *Address*: Oakfield, Blackburn. (O4346)

AITKENHEAD, William, M.B.E.

AITKIN, Major James Alexander Hamilton, O.B.E., M.B., R.A.M C. (T.F.)

AITON, John Arthur, C.B.E., *b.* 1864; *s.* of John Aiton; *m.* 1895, Adriana W. Stoop of Dordrecht, Holland. Mechanical Engineer, and Chm. Derbyshire Munitions Committee; *Address*: Duffield Park, Derby. *Clubs*: St. Stephen's; Derbyshire. (C85)

AKERMAN, Conrad, M.B.E., M.B.

AKERMAN, Lieut. John Camille, C.B.E.

AKERS, Charles Wrightson, M.B.E.

AKERS, Capt. Wilfred Stuart, O.B.E.

AKHURST, Capt. and Qr.-Mr. William Harry, M.B.E.

ALABASTER, Chaloner Grenville, O.B.E., *b.* 24 July, 1880; *s.* of the late Sir Chaloner Alabaster K.C.M.G.; *m.* Mabel Winifred Mary, *d.* of Col. E. P. Mainwaring, of 39th Garwahl Rifles. *Educ.*: Tonbridge. Barrister-at-Law (Inner Temple), 1904; Acting Attorney-General, Hongkong. 1911, 1912; Member of Legislative Council, Hongkong 1911, 1912, 1919; Deputy Censor of Cables, Hongkong, 1914–17. *Address*: Cheung Chow, Hongkong. *Clubs*: Thatched House; Hongkong; Peak. (O981)

ALBAN, Arthur David, O.B.E., *b.* 12 March, 1862; *s.* of the late Major Thomas Clifton Alban, Bombay Staff Corps; *m.* Amelia Anna, *d.* of the late Alexander Fritsch. *Educ.*: Cheltenham College. H.M. Consul-General at Alexandria, Egypt. *War Work*: H.M. Consul in Cairo during the war. (O2130)

ALBANY, Capt. Sidney Charles, M.B.E.

ALBRECHT, Major Vaudrey Adolph, O.B.E., M.C.

ALBRIGHT, George Stacey, C.B.E., M.A., J.P., *b.* 15 June, 1855; *s.* of Arthur Albright, of Mariemont, Edgbaston; *m.* Isabella Margaret, *d.* of Smith Harrison, of Southwoodford, Essex. *Educ.*: Tottenham; Trinity College, Cambridge. County Alderman, Worcestershire. *War Work*: Panel of Munitions Inventions Department, Nitrogen Products Committee; Airships Committee of Board of Invention and Research. *Address*: Bromsberrow Place, Ledbury. *Club*: New University. (C2410)

ALCIDE, Capt. Edward Augustus, M.B.E., *b.* June, 1869, Shipmaster, commanding S.S. "Inkula." *War Work*: Inspector of Civil Police Force, Ruhleten Camp, 1915–18. *Address*: 34, Alexandra Road, Gt. Crosby, Lancs. (M7192)

ALCOCK, Lieut. Charles William, M.B.E.

ALCOCK, Edgar, M.B.E.

ALCOCK, Commander Reginald, C.B.E., F.R.C.S. (Edin. 1910), J.P., *b.* 1868; *s.* of John Alcock, J.P., of Portland House, Burslem; *m.* Elizabeth Colebrooke, *d.* of Rev. James Cowan, of Crawfordjohn. *Educ.*: Victoria Univ., Manchester. Justice of the Peace for the Borough of Stoke-on-Trent (1920); Senior Honorary Surgeon North Staffordshire Infirmary-Hartshill, Stoke-on-Trent. *War Work*: Senior Surgeon, Stoke, on-Trent War Hospital. *Address*: Chatterley House, Hanley, Staffordshire. (C1150)

ALCOCK, Violet May, M.B.E., *b.* 14 May, 1878; *d.* of C. W. Alcock, late Secretary of the Surrey County Cricket Club. *Educ.*: Privately in England and Germany. Formerly Assistant Editor of the "Girl's Realm"; Secretary to the Lyceum Club Bureau; Employed on Royal Commission on the Income Tax, now by Inland Revenue; Contributed to "Daily Mail," "Pall Mall Gazette," "Lady's Realm," etc., etc. *War Work*: Junior Administrative Assistant in the War. Trade Department. *Address*: Hazelwood, Richmond, Surrey. (M1329)

ALCORN, Alexander, O.B.E.

ALDAM, Sarah Julia WARDE-, Mrs., M.B.E., A.R.R.C.; *d.* of Rev. William Warde, of Hooton Pagnell Hall, Yorks.; *m.* William Wright, J.P., D.L. (who assumed the additional surname of Warde by Royal licence, 1878), *s.* of William Aldam, of Frickley Hall. *Educ.*: At home and in Isle of Wight. Landowner and Lady of the Manor of Hooton Pagnell. *War Work*: Equipped her house at Hooton Pagnell as an Auxiliary Military Hospital (100 beds) and was the Commandant and General Administrator from its acceptance in Aug. 1914, until April, 1919; President of Hooton Pagnell District War Savings Association; President of the S. Yorks Branch of the West Riding Women's Agricultural Committee; also inaugurated and managed three War Working Parties at Hooton Pagnell, Clayton, and South Elmsall. *Address*: Hooton Pagnell Hall, Doncaster, Yorks. *Club*: Albemarle. (M1330)

ALDEN, Lieut. Arthur Rhodes, M.B.E., *b.* 22 Dec. 1894; *s.* of Leonard H. Alden, of Eastwyke, Oxford. *Educ.*: King's Grammar School, Warwick, and High School, Oxford. Civil Servant. *War Work*: Inns of Court O.T.C., June, to Dec. 1915; with 1/11 London Regt. in Egypt and Palestine, Jan. 1916 to Oct. 1917; classified unfit, B1, Oct. 1917, and attached Graves Registration Unit, E.E.F.; appointed to command Mobile section, G.R.U., E.E.F., Jan. 1919. *Address*: Eastwyke, Abingdon Rd., Oxford. (M4666)

ALDER, George, M.B.E.

ALDER, Wilfred, O.B.E.

ALDERMAN, Col. Robert, C.I.E., O.B.E., Indian Army Reserve of Officers; served in Mesopotamia, 1917–18 (despatches; C.I.E.). (O6566)

ALDERSON, Lieut. James Richard, O.B.E., R.A.S.C.

ALDERSON, Major William Frederick, O.B.E.

ALDHAM, Lieut. Michael Seymour, O.B.E., R.A.S.C., (M.T.)

ALDINGTON, Lieut.-Col. Charles, C.B.E., *b.* 20 Dec. 1862; *s.* of John Aldington, of Tanworth, Warwickshire; *m.* Rosina, *d.* of Richard Thomas, of Mullion, Cornwall. *Educ.*: Packwood School. Lieut.-Col. R.E. (Engineer and Railway Staff Corps); General Manager of Great Western Railway. *War Work*: Railway Transport arrangements as Superintendent of the Line, Great Western Railway. *Address*: 53, Eastbourne Terrace, Hyde Park, W. *Club*: Constitutional. (C86)

ALDIS, Arthur Cyril Webb, M.B.E.

ALDOM, Major Herbert Raymond Salisbury, M.B.E. (Mil.), *b.* 28 Dec. 1883; *s.* of H. C. Aldom, of Eastbourne. *Educ.*: Privately. Secretary, Warrenpoint Shipbuilding and Engineering Co. Ltd. *War Work*: Sub-Inspector, Westminster Special Constabulary, 1914; Recruiting Staff, St. Pancras, 1916; Chief Registration Officer, 7th R.D.R.A., 1917; Asst. to Colonel in charge of Records, Hounslow, 1918–20. *Clubs*: Sports; Royal Automobile. (M6591)

ALDRIDGE, Allen Garnies, O.B.E., J.P.

ALDRIDGE, Ernest Charles, M.B.E.

ALDRIDGE, Lieut.-Col. Evelyn, O.B.E.

ALDRIDGE, Samuel Kendrick, O.B.E., F.L.A.A., *b.* 13 Jan. 1873; *s.* of Samuel Aldridge, of Birmingham; *m.* Rose, *d.* of Thomas Briant, of Tring, Herts. *Educ.*: Haberdashers' Company's School, London. Examiner in Exchequer and Audit Dept., London 1892–1912. *War Work*: Accountant in Employment Dept., Ministry of Labour, 1912–16; Chief Accountant, Ministry of Food. 1916; Finance member of National Kitchens Committee 1917; Member of Finance Sub-Committee of War Cabinet Committee on Industrial Unrest, 1919-20. *Address*: 17, St. James' Avenue, London, N.W. 2. (O9878)

ALDRIDGE, William Frederick, M.B.E., *b.* 25 Sept. 1872; *s.* of Richard Paul Aldridge, of Melbourne, Australia; *m.* Ethel May, *d.* of Louis Henry Marks, of Maida Vale, London, W. *Educ.*: Various Secondary Schools. *War Work*: Supervising Clerk, War Office. *Address*: Clifton House, Kilburn Square, N.W. 6. *Club*: Paddington Conservative. (M1333)

ALDWORTH, Dorothea Anne Harvey, Mrs., M.B.E., *d.* of the late Richard William Drew, of Bletchingley House, Surrey; *m.* John Richard Oliver Aldworth, British Resident, Negri Sembilan, F.M.S., *s.* of the late Colonel Robert Aldworth, J.P. of Co. Cork. *War Work*: Worked on behalf of British and Allied War Charities in the Federated Malay States. *Addresses*: British Residency, Seremban, Federated Malay States; Claremont, Dorking, Surrey. *Club*: Forum. (M6408)

ALDWORTH, Capt. Thomas Preston, D.S.O., O.B.E.

ALEXANDER, Alfred, M.B.E., *b.* 14 Feb. 1858 ; *s.* of William Alexander, of Aldeburgh, Suffolk ; *m.* Catherine Mary, *d.* of Henry Spindler, of Thorpeness, Suffolk. *Educ.:* Aldeburgh National School. Fisherman and ex-Coxswain of Thorpeness Lifeboat. *War Work :* Coast Watcher (4 years). *Address :* Alexandra House, Thorpeness, nr. Leiston, Suffolk. (M6097)

ALEXANDER, Capt. Arnold, M.B.E. ; 1/4 Border Regt. (T.F.) attd. M.W.S., I. A. (M10213)

ALEXANDER, Major Arthur Charles Bridgeman, O.B.E. *b.* 23 May, 1873 ; *s.* of Arthur Harvey Alexander, late of Hazelwood, Dufftown, Banffshire ; *m.* Amy Louise, *d.* of William Bowland Faulkner, late of Westergate House, Kingston-on-Thames. *Educ.:* Royal Naval Academy, Gosport, Bedford, and R.M.C. Sandhurst. Gazetted Seaforth Highlanders, May, 1893 ; Promoted Captain, Nov. 1899 ; Invalided and retired on pension, 1912. *War Work :* Served with 3rd Bn. Dorsetshire Regt. May, 1915, to Nov. 1915 ; appointed General Staff Officer, Bermuda Command, Nov. 1915, and gazetted Major, Reserve of Officers, Seaforth Highlanders ; replaced on Retired List, June,1919,on return from Bermuda ; received the thanks of the Army Council for " the valuable services rendered during the war." *Club :* Army and Navy. (O6832)

ALEXANDER, Brig.-Gen. Charles Henry, C.B.E., R.A. (retired), *b.* 2 June, 1856 ; *s.* of John Alexander, of Milford, Carlow ; *m.* Isabel Annie, *d.* of the late Sir Campbell Ross, K.C.B. *Educ.:* Uppingham ; R.M.A., Woolwich. Served in Royal Artillery, 1876–1908 ; Colonel, 1908. *War Work :* Rejoined from retired list, in Great War, 10 Oct. 1914 ; formed 21st Divisional Artillery and commanded it with rank of Brig.-Gen. until after the battle of Loos, 1915 ; subsequently commanded 69th Divisional Artillery, No. 6 Reserve Brigade, R.F.A. (T.), and No. 5 C. Reserve Brigade, R.F.A. ; mentioned in despatches for valuable services during the war ; Brig-General, 1918. *Address :* 96, Bouverie Road, Folkestone. *Club :* Royal Automobile. (C797)

ALEXANDER, Donald Clark, M.B.E.

ALEXANDER, Edith Margaret, Mrs., M.B.E.

ALEXANDER, Eleanor Jane, M.B.E., A.R.R.C., Lady of Grace of St. John of Jerusalem ; *d.* of William Alexander, Archbishop of Armagh and Primate of all Ireland. *War Work :* Commandant of Auxiliary Military Hospital and served on County Committees of the Order of St. John and B.R.C.S. *Address :* Hampton Court Palace. (M7197)

ALEXANDER, Frederick, O.B.E., *b.* 1878 ; *s.* of Robert Alexander, of Liverpool. *Educ.:* Cheltenham College. *War Work :* British Red Cross, France and Italy. *Address,* Ogbeare Hall, Holsworthy, Devon. (O1046)

ALEXANDER, George Edward, O.B.E.

ALEXANDER, George Hamilton, M.B.E. Chief Boatswain, R.N.

ALEXANDER, Major (T. Lieut.-Col.) Heber Maitland, D.S.O., M.B.E., *b.* 1 Feb. 1881 ; *s.* of Major C. A. Alexander, of Ugley, Essex ; *m.* 1st Mary Brenda (*d.* 1914), *d.* of late J. H. B· Walch, of Tasmania, 2nd, Violet Lilian (widow of Major H. M. Hogg, 32nd Lancers, Indian Army), *d.* of Lieut.-Col. S. L. Aplin, C.S.I., late Burmah Commission. *Educ.:* Clifton College and R.M.C. Sandhurst. Indian Army. *War Work :* In command of 9th Mule Corps, Indian Army, France, Sept. 1914, to April, 1915, with Lahore Div. ; Gallipoli, April to Nov. 1915, with Australian and New Zealand Army Corps ; present at first landing in Gallipoli and at battle of Suvla Bay (despatches). *Clubs :* Naval and Military ; Junior Naval and Military. (O8427)

ALEXANDER, Capt. James Ulick Francis Canning, O.B.E.

ALEXANDER, James Young, O.B.E., *b.* 1868. *Educ.:* Dumfries Academy. Director of Alexander Cross and Sons, Ltd., Glasgow. *War Work :* Supervisor of Feeding Stuffs for Scotland. *Address :* 19, Hope Street, Glasgow. *Clubs :* Conservative ; S.A.C. (O9880)

ALEXANDER, Col. John Donald, C.B.E., D.S.O.. *b.* 11 April, 1867 ; *s.* of Very Rev. John Alexander, Dean of Ferns ; *m.* Georgina Eleanor, *d.* of Alexander Going, of Altavila. *Educ.:* St. Columba College, and Trinity College, Dublin. Lieutenant in the R.A.M.C. 30 Jan. 1892, and was promoted Captain 3 years later ; took part in the Tirah Campaign 1897–98 (twice mentioned in despatches) ; also in the South African War of 1899–1902 (three times mentioned in despatches) ; was promoted Major in 1906, Lieut.-Colonel in 1914, and Colonel in 1917. *War Work :* Served during the Great War from October, 1914, till the termination of hostilities in France and Flanders (four times mentioned in despatches, D.S.O., C.B.E.) (C1214)

ALEXANDER, John William, *b.* of July, 1861 ; *s.* of R. L. Alexander, of New Southgate ; *m.* Annie, *d.* of Charles Ferry, of Dalston. *Educ.:* Privately. Merchant. *War Work :* Founder of Voluntary War Hospital Supplies Depot, Southend-on-Sea ; Hon. General Secretary, V.A.D. Transport and Hospital Work. *Address :* Arima, Ailsa Road, Westcliff-on-Sea, Essex. (M1798)

ALEXANDER, Juliet, Mrs., M.B.E.

ALEXANDER, Margaret Katharine Hon. Mrs. Walter, M.B.E. (*see* BURKE'S *Peerage,* Verulam E. and Caledon E.) (M10244)

ALEXANDER, Major Kay, M.B.E.

ALEXANDER, Major Robert Donald Thain, O.B.E·, D.S.O. Capt. and Acting Major, London Regt. *War Services :* Mesopotamia, 1915–18 (despatches). (O4188)

ALEXANDER, Rose, Mrs., O.B.E., *b.* 10 Dec. 1883 ; *d.* of Major H. G. Newcome, of Aldershot Manor ; *m.* Brig.-Gen. E. W. Alexander, V.C., C.B., C.M.G., *s.* of Robert Alexander of Liverpool. *Educ.:* Privately. *War Work :* Chairman and Hon. Organiser, Aldershot War Hospital Supply Depot. and Hon. Sec. Ladies Central Committee, Aldershot Command. *Address :* Horswell House, Kingsbridge, S. Devon. *Club :* Ladies' Empire. (O9881)

ALEXANDER, Samuel Grant, M.B.E., L.R.I.B.A., F.F.S., J.P., Architect, *m.* Sara Margarete Heydon, *d.* of Kenneth Mackenzie, of Cape Town, S.A. *Educ.:* Privately and Raining's College. *War Work :* Hon. County Secretary for Inverness-shire Branch British Red Cross Society ; Hon. Sec. Leys Castle Auxiliary Red Cross, Hospital ; Hon. Sec. Q.M.M.G. Surgical Branch, Highland War Hospital Supply Depot. *Address :* Willow Bank, Inverness. *Clubs :* Highland (Inverness) ; Chelsea Arts. (M1334)

ALEXANDER, Stanley Walter, M.B.E.

ALEXANDER, Brig.-Gen. Sir William, K.B.E., C.B., C.M.G., D.S.O., *b.* 4 May, 1874 ; *s.* of Thomas Alexander, of Brentham Park, Stirling ; *m.* Beatrice Evelyn, *d.* of the late John Ritchie, of Bingham, Parramatta. *Educ :* Kelvinside Academy, Glasgow University, and Göttingen. Managing Director of Messrs Charles Tennant & Company, Ltd., Glasgow. *War Work :* France, 1914–16 ; Director of Administration, National Explosives Factories ; Controller of Aircraft Supply and Production, Ministry of Munitions, 1917–18 ; Director-General of Purchases, Ministry of Munitions (Supply), 1918–19 ; Member of Air Council, 1918–19. *Address :* 4, Whitehall Court, S.W. 1. *Clubs :* Junior Army and Navy ; Royal Air Force ; Conservative, Glasgow ; Ranelagh. (K340)

ALEXANDRE, Capt. Philip George, O.B.E. (Mil.), *b* 2 Feb. 1884 ; *s.* of Philip Luce Alexandre, of Jersey, Channel Islands ; *m.* Mary Elizabeth, *d.* of Joseph Gartside, of Smithy Bridge, Rochdale. Lancs. *Educ.:* Leeds High School. Departmental Manager for the Eagle, Star and British Dominions Insurance Co., Ltd. *War Work :* 11th Yorkshire Regt., 1915 ; in France with 10th Batt. Yorkshire Regiment, Somme, Arras, Cambrai, etc., 1916–17 ; Chief British Signalling Instructor to American Expeditionary Forces in France and Germany, 1918–19 ; mentioned in Marshal Haig's 1918 despatches. *Address :* Clareville, Pool, near Leeds. *Club :* Services (Sheffield). · (O4944)

ALFORD, Rev. Canon Josiah George, C.B.E.,M.A.(Camb.), V.D., T.D.; *b.* 1 Jan, 1847 ; *s.* of the late Chas. Richard Alford, D.D., Bishop of Victoria ; *m.* Catherine Mary, *d.* of the late Colonel J. T. Leslie, C.B. *Educ.:* King's College, London ; and Corpus Christi College, Cambridge. Canon Residentiary of Bristol ; Chaplain (1st Class) Territorial Force ; Hon. Chaplain to the Bishop of Bristol. *War Work :* Mobilised 1914–19 ; attached to R.A.M.C. (T) ; Senior Chaplain Bristol and District, 1915 ; and Gloucestershire, Somerset and North Wilts, 1917 ; afterwards of No 2 Area, Southern Command. *Addresses :* 5, Richmond Hill, Clifton, Bristol ; Park Cottage, Cleeve, N. Somerset. *Club :* Life member Royal United Service Institution. (C1445)

ALFORD, Capt. Sydney Ernest, O.B.E., M.C., *b.* 29 March, 1892 ; *s.* of Rev. S. F. Alford, M.A., of Clifton, Bristol. *Educ.:* Dean Close School, Cheltenham. Schoolmaster. *War Work :* Served as Subaltern, Battery Commander, and Adjutant in 14th Army Brigade, R.F.A. in France and Belgium from March, 1915, to April, 1919 ; thrice mentioned in despatches. *Address :* Rose Hill School, Banstead, Surrey ; 6, The Fosseway, Clifton Bristol. (O4945)

ALING, Gerrit, M.B.E. Censor, Cape Town. (M10256*f*)

ALISON, Charles Hugh, M.B.E.

ALKIN, Richard Ley, O.B.E., M.I.E.E., *b.* 23 Aug. 1878 ; *s.* of Richard Alkin, of Hartshill, Atherstone ; *m.* Annie Maude, *d.* of Capt. H. Franklin, of Hounslow. *Educ.:* Leeds University. Chief Representative, English Electric Co., Ltd., China. *Address :* Shanghai, China. (O4946)

ALLAN, Lieut.-Col. Bryce, O.B.E., T.D., J.P., *b.* 2 June, 1874 ; *s.* of Alexander Allan, of Aros House, Tobermory ; *m.* Hilda Mary, *d.* of the late J. H. Allan, of Shrawley Wood House, Worcester. *Educ.:* Fettes Coll., Edinburgh, and St. John's Coll., Oxford. J.P. for Argyllshire ; Farming and Estate Management ; Sea Scout Commissioner for Scotland. *War Work :* Capt. Argyll Mountain Battery, 4th High. Mtd. Bde., R.G.A., 1914 ; Major Commanding, Ross Mountain Battery, July, 1914 ; took part in landing in Gallipoli on 25 April with 29th Division ; went to France in command C Batty. 317th Bde., July, 1916 ; seconded with regular Army and given command of 6th D.A.C., which eventually went to the Rhine Area, Nov. 1919 ; mentioned in despatches, Nov. 1918 ; French Croix de Guerre, Feb. 1919 ; Territorial Decoration, 1919. *Address :* Lindhu, Tobermory, Argyll. *Club :* New (Edinburgh). (O4948)

ALLAN, Evelyn Julia, Mrs., O.B.E. ; *d.* of Fielding Nalder, Barrister-at-Law, of Lincoln's Inn ; *m.* Charles Edward, *s.* of Francis Stallan Allan, of Edinburgh. *Educ.:* Privately. *War Work :* Hon. Secretary and Asst.-County Director and Organiser of British Red Cross work in Borough of Chelsea ; raised 6 Voluntary Aid Detachments (between 800 and 900 members) ; formed, and was Chairman of, Chelsea Red Cross Workrooms and Depot ; assisted Serbian Red Cross Soc. of Gt. Britain. *Address :* Layham House, near Hadleigh, Suffolk. *Club :* Forum. (O82)

ALLAN, George Macdonald, M.B.E., *b.* 22 Dec. 1863 ; *s.* of Capt. George Arthur Allan, late of 1st West India Regt. ;

m. Isabella Menzies, *d.* of John Whigham, of Hawkhurst. *Educ.:* Dublin. Shipping Agent. *War Work:* At the Admiralty and Ministry of Shipping. *Address:* 155, Camden Road, London, N.W. 1. (M77)

ALLAN, Herbert William, O.B.E., M.R.C.S. (Eng.), L.R.C.P. (Lond.), *b.* 11 Feb. 1869; *s.* of the late Thomas Allan, of York; *m.* Clara Louisa, *d.* of Thomas Rodwell, of Monkseaton, Northumberland. *Educ.:* St. Peter's School, York; Caius College, Cambridge; Guy's Hospital, London. M.O.H. City of Wells, Somerset. *War Work:* Medical Officer to Cedars Red Cross Hospital, Wells, 1915–19; Medical Officer in charge troops, Wells, 1915–16. *Address:* Melbourne House, Wells, Somerset. (O9883)

ALLAN, Ida, Mrs., M.B.E.

ALLAN, James, O.B.E.

ALLAN, James Craig, M.B.E., *b.* 14 Oct. 1884; *s.* of Thomas Gibson Allan, of Helensburgh, N.B. *Educ.:* Hermitage Public School, Helensburgh, and Glasgow University. Solicitor. *War Work:* Commissioned to Cameronians, Dec. 1914; Services abroad, 1915; wounded, Oct. 1915; seconded Recruiting Staff, Jan. 1916; transferred to Ministry of National Service as Appeal National Service Representative (Lanarkshire), 1917; discharged, Dec. 1918, with rank of Captain. *Addresses:* Silverwells, Hamilton; Urr Bank, Helensburgh. *Club:* Lanarkshire County. (M1335)

ALLAN, Capt. James Lambertini, M.B.E., M.A. (Oxon.), *b.* 3 Sept. 1893; *s.* of James Manuel Allan, of Glasgow and Burma. *Educ.:* Charterhouse and Univ. Coll., Oxford. On the active list of the Territorial Army with the 1st City of London Brigade, R.F.A. (T.A.). *War Work:* Joined the 2/3rd West Lancs. Brigade, R.F.A. (T.F.) 57th W. Lancs. Division on its formation in July, 1915, and served with this unit until Jan. 1917, going overseas with it in that month; served overseas until June, 1917, when wounded after the Battle of Messines; attached for duty at the War Office, in Dec. 1917, serving there until demobilised in May, 1919; mentioned in the Press for war services. *Address:* 20, Hans Place, London, S.W. 1. *Clubs:* Oxford and Cambridge; Queen's. (M4319)

ALLAN, Jessie Whyte, O.B.E.

ALLAN, Lieut. John Hunter, O.B.E., R.N.R.

ALLAN, Lieut. (acting Capt.) Norman, O.B.E., R.A.S.C.

ALLAN, Thomas Easton, M.B.E.

ALLAN, Rev. Tom, M.B.E. (M10367)

ALLAN, Lieut. William, M.B.E., *n.* 20 July, 1880; *s.* of William Allan, of Airdrie; *m.* Elizabeth Coats, *d.* of John Jackson, of Blantyre. *Educ.:* E.C. Training College and Glasgow University. Teacher. *War Work:* Enlisted Sept. 1914, in Royal Highlanders (Black Watch); to France as C.Q.M.S. with 9th Service Batt. 15th Div., July, 1915; wounded, 1916; with 3rd Reserve Batt. B.W. till June, 1917; Supply Officer, 173rd Bde.; Supply Officer, 9th Corps Troops. *Address:* Baron Hall, Blantyre, N.B. (M4409)

ALLAN, Major William David, O.B.E.

ALLAN, Major and Qr.-Mr. William Murray, O.B.E.

ALLAN, Edith, Lady HAVELOCK-, *d.* of Thomas C. J. Sowerby, of Snow Hall, Darlington; *m.* Sir Henry Spencer Moreton, Bart., *s.* of Lieut.-Gen. Sir Henry Marshman Havelock-Allan, Bart. (*see* BURKE'S *Peerage*), of Blackwell Grange, Darlington. Deputy President Red Cross Society, County Durham; Assistant County Director V.A.D., Co. Durham; Hon. Commandant, 18th Durham V.A.D. Red Cross; District Commissioner, Girl Guides, Darlington, to 1919. *War Work:* Assistant County Director, V.A.D. Durham; Executive Demobilisation Committee, Co. Durham; Hon. Com. 18th Durham Red Cross Detachment, Woodside Hospital, Darlington, Co. Durham; Executive Committee, Lady Anne Lambton's Work Depot, Durham; Deputy President, Red Cross Society, Co. Durham, 1919. *Address:* Blackwell Grange, Darlington. *Clubs:* Bath; Ladies' Automobile. (O9882)

ALLARD, Capt. Philip, O.B.E., R.M.L.I.

ALLARD, Major William, O.B.E., R.E.

ALLARDICE, Capt. William McDiarmid, O.B.E.

ALLARDYCE, Capt. Kenneth James, M.B.E.

ALLAWAY, Henry, O.B.E. (O11784a)

ALLCARD, Capt. Rupert, O.B.E., *b.* 5 July, 1884; *s.* of E. J. Allcard, of Teddington; *m.* Helen Flora, *d.* of F. J. Whitmore, of Surbiton. *Educ.:* Eton and Trinity Coll., Cambridge. Stockbroker. *War Work:* Active Service in France from May, 1915, to April, 1919, in the Royal Engineers, Signal Service, with the 6th Corps, 34th Div. and 51st Div. and as Acting Major in command of 62nd Div. Signal Co., R.E. *Address:* Gandria, Sydney Road, Walton-on-Thames; 7, Drapers Gardens, E.C. *Clubs:* Oxford and Cambridge; City University; Leander. (O2397)

ALLCHIN, Thomas Cuthbert, M.B.E.

ALLCOCK, William Barnes, M.B.E.

ALLDEN, Harry, O.B.E., *b.* 29 Sept. 1861; *s.* of Richard Allden, late of Stapley Farm, Odiham, Hants.; *m.* Ann, *d.* of George Vincent, of Southsea. *Educ.:* Trafalgar House School, Winchester. Engineer. Appointed Examiner of Naval Ordnance at the Admiralty from 1904 to 1915; from 1915 to 1919 Officer in charge of Royal Naval Gun Factory at Westhoughton. *War Work:* Supervised the manufacture of Gun Mechanism at Contractor's works and assisted the Contractors in the details of manufacture; superintended the equipment and organisation of the Royal Naval Gun Factory at Westhoughton, near Bolton, Lancs. *Address:* Laurel Dene, Hambrook, near Emsworth, Hants. (O84)

ALLEN, Capt. Abraham, O.B.E.

ALLEN, Alan Bruce, M.B.E., 10 April, 1866; *s.* of Rev. R. Collyns Allen, Vicar of Whaddon, Bucks.; *m.* Ella, *d.* of — Holladay, of Slough. *Educ.:* Privately. Fur Expert to Debenhams, Ltd., in charge of all Fur sections. *War Work:* Voluntary Fur Expert in charge of all work concerning their examination and manufacture; also assisted D.E.O.S. with various urgent matters such as anti-gas veils, cleaning furs in France, etc. member of the Fur Trade Board, Great Britain. *Club:* Junior Constitutional. (M82)

ALLEN, Arthur Denby, O.B.E.

ALLEN, Capt. Arthur Dunscombe, M.B.E., R.A.F.

ALLEN, Lieut.-Col. Atwell Hayes, C.B.E.

ALLEN, Capt. Charles Edward, M.B.E.

ALLEN, Capt. Charles Henry, O.B.E., M.B., F.R.C.S., R.A.M.C. *Address:* 5, Wellington Circus, Nottingham.

ALLEN, Lieut. Charles William Edward, M.B.E., M.C., R.A.

ALLEN, Clementina Dorothy, O.B.E., *b.* 23 Aug. 1885; *d.* of Clement Allen, of Southfield, Woodchester. *Educ.:* Privately. *War Work:* County Secretary and Assistant County Director, Gloucestershire Branch British Red Cross Society. *Address:* Southfield, Woodchester, Stroud. (O1049)

ALLEN, David Hugonin Satow, M.B.E. In charge of Recreation and Cinemas at Rouen and Etaples. (M10,256g)

ALLEN, Doreen, M.B.E.

ALLEN, Capt. Edmund Drury, O.B.E.

ALLEN, Col. Edward Watts, C.B.E.; *s.* of Frederick Allen, late of Mottingham, Kent; *m.* Edith Jane, *d.* of Charles Denyer Upham, of Eltham. *Educ.:* Eltham. Secretary and General Manager, Civil Service Supply Assoc., Queen Victoria Street, and Bedford Street, London. *War Work:* 1915, Major A.S.C., Adviser to Director of Transport of Supplies; 1916, Lieut.-Col., Adviser visiting France, Egypt, and Salonica to install new accounting systems, after conducting periodical inspections; 1917, Director Food Production, responsible for the Tractor Cultivation Scheme; 1918, Staff Colonel, installing Costings Accounts in Supply and Transport Depots. *Address:* Elmhurst, Shooters Hill, Kent. *Club:* Devonshire. (C2076)

ALLEN, Elsie Clara, M.B.E., *b.* 29 Sept. 1898; *d.* of Samuel Allen of Dulwich. *War Work:* Three years clerical work, Ministry of Labour Employment Dept. *Address:* 51, Worlingham Road, East Dulwich, S.E. 22. (M7199)

ALLEN, Ernest Joshua, C.B.E.; Director of Railway Materials, Ministry of Munitions. (C87)

ALLEN, Ernest King, C.B.E., *b.* 22 Sep. 1864; 4th son late Robin Allen, Secretary of Trinity House; *m.* Florence Mary, *d.* of Peter Gellatly, J.P., D.L., of Essex. *Educ.:* Privately. Barrister-at-Law. Entered the Public Trustee Office 1 Oct. 1907; appointed Assistant Public Trustee 1915; author of "The Law of Corporate Trustees." *War Work:* As second-in-command of the Department which released 70 per cent. of the staff eligible for military service. The general withdrawal of men from civil life was the primary cause of a great increase in the business of the office, and a serious responsibility and strain fell upon the senior officers who were retained at their posts. *Address:* Yew Tree House, Leatherhead, Surrey. (C88)

ALLEN, Ernest Thomas William, M.B.E. Chief Confidential Clerk, H.M. Signal School, Portsmouth. (M16303)

ALLEN, Francis, M.B.E.

ALLEN, Capt. Francis John, O.B.E., M.C., R.A.M.C.

ALLEN, Frank, M.B.E.

ALLEN, Capt. Frederick John, O.B.E.; *s.* of Joseph Allen, of Burnham, Somerset; *m.* Mary Rachel, *d.* of the late Rev. A. R. Cartwright, of Hornblotton, Somerset. *Educ.:* Clifton and Keble Coll., Oxford. Army Tutor. *War Work:* England, Sept. 1914, to July, 1915; Overseas, France, Belgium, and Germany, July, 1915, to May, 1920. *Addresses:* Jellalabad, Tidworth; 90, Pembroke Road, Clifton, Bristol. *Club:* Cavendish. (O4950)

ALLEN, George James, M.B.E., *b.* 29 Mar. 1879; *s.* of James Vince Allen, of St. Pancras, London; *m.* Caroline Mary, *d.* of Herbert Burgess, of Battle, Sussex. *Educ.:* London. Clerk in the Colonial Office, 1895; lent to the Ministry of Munitions of War, Aug. 1915; Deputy Assistant Secretary in that Ministry, Feb. 1919; Regional Finance Officer, Ministry of Health, March, 1920. *War Work:* Mainly in connection with the organisation of Finance and Establishment services in the Explosives Department of the Ministry of Munitions. *Address:* The Firs, Mill Hill, London, N.W. 7; 111, New Street, Birmingham. (M7201)

ALLEN, Lieut. George Roland Gordon, O.B.E., R.N.

ALLEN, Henry Charles, M.B.E. (M10368)

ALLEN, Herbert Warner, C.B.E., Chevalier of the Legion of Honour, *b.* 8 Mar. 1881; *s.* of Capt. G. W. Allen, R.N., of Woodside, Purbrook; *m.* Ethel, *d.* of Warwick Pemberton, Esq., of Warwick. *Educ.:* Charterhouse; University College, Oxford. Journalist. Paris Correspondent of the *Morning Post*, 1908–15. *War Work:* War Correspondent representing the British Press with the French Armies, 1915–16; representing *Morning Post* and other London newspapers with the French Armies, 1916–17; with B.E.F. in Italy and Italian Armies, 1917–18; with the American E.F., 1918–19. *Addresses:* 66, Park Street, Hyde Park; The Little House, Ham Common, Surrey. *Club:* Savage. (C2411)

ALLEN, Engineer Lieut.-Comm. James, O.B.E., R.N.

ALLEN, Capt. Jesse, O.B.E.

ALLEN, John, M.B.E., *b.* 7 June, 1863. Deputy Chief Constable of Leicestershire. *War Work:* Police Administration. *Address:* County Constabulary Office, Leicester.

(M7202)

ALLEN, John, O.B.E., J.P., M.Inst.T., *b.* 1856; *s.* of George Allen, of Unicarval, Comber, Co. Down; *m.* Elizabeth, *d.* of John Sampson, of Brompton, Yeovil. *Educ.:* Cheltenham College. Engineer; Honorary Advisor to the Ministry of Agriculture on Steam Ploughing; Member of First Council Institute of Transport; Governing Director of Oxford Steam Plough Co., Ltd. *War Work:* Chairman of the Oxford shire Munition Board of Management; Honorary Adviser to Food Production Department on Steam Ploughing; Organiser of all the Steam Ploughs in England for War Work Production; Member of the Advisory Committee of the Road Transport Board. *Address:* Unicarval, Comber, Co. Down. *Clubs:* Constitutional; Royal Automobile; Union Club, Belfast; Royal Ulster Yacht.

(O85)

ALLEN, Margaret Louise, Mrs. Douglas, M.B.E., *b.* 27 Aug. 1874; *d.* of Edward and Annette Fry, of Ipswich; *m.* Douglas, *s.* of Edward Ransome Allen, of Stoke Newington. *Educ.:* Ackworth School (Yorks), and the Mount School, York. *War Work:* British Red Cross, Missing and Wounded Enquiry Bureau, Alexandria, Egypt, Oct. 1915, to Feb. 1919. *Address:* Bulkeley, Ramleh, Alexandria, Egypt.

(M7203)

ALLEN, Mary Sophia, O.B.E., *b.* 12 March, 1878; *d.* of Thomas Isaac Allen, of Clifton, Bristol. *Educ.:* Princess Helena College, Ealing. *War Work:* Women Police Service since Sept. 1914; second in command under the late Miss Damer Dawson, O.B.E.; became Commandant of Women Police Service in May, 1920, at death of Commandant Damer Dawson. *Addresses:* Danehill, Lympne, Kent; 6, Eccleston Square S.W. *Clubs:* Forum; Farm and Garden Union.

(O86)

ALLEN, Major Michael Henry Percival, M.B.E., R.A.F.

ALLEN, Oswald Coleman, C.B.E., *b.* 13 Apr. 1887. Late Private Sectetary to Rt. Hon. Sir R. S. Horne, G.B.E., K.C., M.P., as Minister of Labour; Principal Clerk, Ministry of Labour; Barrister-at-Law, Middle Temple. *War Work:* Asst.-Secty. Committee on Munitions of War, Apr.–May, 1915; late Deputy Asst.-Secty. Ministry of Munitions and Secty. Mission Anglaise de l'Armement, Paris, 1918; Officer Crown of Italy; Chevalier Legion of Honour. *Address:* Ministry of Labour, Whitehall, S.W. 1. *Club:* Cercle Interallié, Paris. (C2412)

ALLEN, Percy Ruskin, O.B.E.

ALLEN, Richard William, C.B.E.,J.P.; eldest *s.* of William Henry Allen, D.L., of Bromham House, near Bedford; *m.* Geraldine Agnew, *d.* of William Joseph Fedden, Clifton, Bristol. Managing Director of W. H. Allen, Son & Co., Ltd., Bedford. *Educ.:* Christ's College, Finchley; King's College, London. Served for nine years Bedfordshire County Council (ret. in 1912); J.P. for the County of Bedford. Member of the Institution of Civil Engineers, awarded Telford Premium 1904; Member of the Council of the Institute of Mechanical Engineers; Member of the Institute of Naval Architects; Member of the Institute of Marine Engineers; Member of the Institute of Metals; Member of the Institute of Iron and Steel; Fellow of the Royal Horticultural Society; Fellow of the Royal Aeronautical Society; Governor of the Royal Agricultural Society; Member of the Management Committee of the Engineering and National Employers Federation; Chairman of the Engineering and National Employers Association for Bedfordshire. *War Work:* Responsible to the Admiralty for the construction of main propelling machinery for submarines, mine-sweepers, trawlers, pinnaces and special auxiliary machinery for all classes of warships; responsible to the Air Ministry for the construction of the " Le Rhone " engine; designed, constructed and equipped special works for the speedy production of the "Le Rhone" Engines. The "Le Rhone" engines were used on all the various fronts and expeditions. *Address:* Woodlands, Clapham, near Bedford. *Clubs:* M.C.C.; R.A.C.; Town and Country, Bedford. (C89)

ALLEN, Stella Ada May, O.B.E.

ALLEN, Thomas Frederick, O.B.E., J.P., *b.* 31 Jan. 1874; *s.* of Frederick Allen, of Kensington, London; *m.* Lilian Marie, *d.* of Edwin Daly, of Kensington, London. *Educ.:* St. Peter's, London. Property Owner, Executor of Estates and Valuator. *War Work:* Mayor of Johannesburg, 1917–19; Chairman of Recruiting Campaign, raised large sums of money for all war funds. *Address:* High Court Buildings, Fox Street, Johannesburg. *Clubs:* Rand; Unionist Party; African Aero; President, Overseas. (O2198)

ALLEN, Walter Macarthur, C.B.E., *b* 31 Jan. 1870; *s.* of the late Sir Wigram Allen, K.C.M.G., of Sydney, New South Wales; *m.* Pearl, *d.* of the late Edward Lamb, formerly Minister for Lands, Queensland, of Sydney, N.S.W. *Educ.:* Leys School and Trinity Hall, Cambridge (B.A. 1893). Barrister, Inner Temple, 1896. *War Work:* Assistant Staff Officer Metropolitan Special Constabulary, Oct. 1914; Director of Supplies thereof, 1915–18; Staff Officer to Sir Edward Ward, Bart., G.B.E., K.C.B., K.C.V.O., 1918 (Commandant-in-Chief, M.S.C.). *Address:* Wyndleshore, Datchet, Bucks. *Clubs:* Conservative; Royal Automobile. (C2413)

ALLEN, William George, O.B.E., *b.* 19 July, 1858; *s.* of Robert Allen, of Pembroke Dock; *m.* Marion, *d.* of James Evans, of Pembroke Dock. *Educ.:* National and Dockyard School. Assistant Expense Accounts Officer, Naval Yard, Hong Kong; Deputy in charge Sheerness; Expense Accounts Officer, H.M. Dockyard, Portsmouth. *War Work:* As Expense

Accounts Officer, Portsmouth Dockyard. *Address:* Lawrenny, Stubbington Avenue, Portsmouth.

(O88)

ALLEN, William Henry, O.B.E.

ALLENBY, Capt. Frederick Claude Hynman, C.B.E., J.P., R.N., *b.* 21 Sep. 1864; *s.* of Hynman Allenby, of Felixstowe, Suffolk (*see* BURKE'S *Peerage*); *m.* Edith Mabel, *d.* of T. Munton Jaffray, of Stydd House, Lyndhurst. *Educ.:* Privately, and H.M.S. "Britannia," Dartmouth. *War Work:* Naval Transport Staff. *Address:* Loanend, Berwick-on-Tweed. *Club:* Naval and Military. (C2243)

ALLENBY, Eng.-Comm. John Norfolk, O.B.E., R.N.

ALLEY, Major Herbert Rutton, O.B.E.

ALLEYNE, Major Charles Forster, O.B.E., Royal Army Service Corps, *b.* 8 Oct. 1882. *War Work:* Went to France with the 1st British Expeditionary Force, Aug. 1914; served on the Staff as D.A.Q.M.G., Aug. 1915. *Club:* Army and Navy. (O8730)

ALLEYNE, Stella Margaret, M.B.E. *Educ.:* Francis Holland School, Graham Street; Clifton High School; Lady Margaret Hall, Oxford. Secretary, British Federation of University Women. *War Work:* Accountant-General's Department, Admiralty; Welfare Section, Labour Regulation Department, Ministry of Munitions. *Address:* 16, Cecil Court, Redcliffe Gardens, S.W. *Club:* Sesame. (M7204)

ALLIBONE, Abraham Cory, O.B.E., *b.* 30 June, 1866. Town Clerk of Wakefield and Solicitor to Corporation and Overseers. *Address:* Sandal, Wakefield. *Club:* Wakefield and County. (O9889)

ALLIN, Lieut.-Col. Henry Chester, O.B.E., R.A.S.C.

ALLIN, Samuel John Henry Wallis, C.B.E., F.I.A., *b.* 9 Feb. 1871; *s.* of John Samuel Wallis Allin, of Sidcup, Kent; *m.* Evelyn Aishton, *d.* of Arthur Procter Dunstan, of Lee, Kent. *Educ.:* Blackheath Proprietary School. Secretary Government Actuary's Department. *Address:* Monabeg, Hatherley Road, Sidcup. (C422)

ALLINGHAM, Lieut. Gerald Carlyle, M.B.E., R.E.

ALLINSON, Ephraim, M.B.E., *b.* 17 March, 1873; *s.* of John Allinson, of Ormside, Westmorland; *m.* as his 2nd wife, Elizabeth Alice, *d.* of George K. Allen, of Rochdale. *Educ.:* Warcop and Asby Schools (Westmorland) afterwards privately at Oldham, Lancs. Joined Oldham (Lancs.) Borough Police Force in Jan. 1896, and after 5 years street duty was selected after competitive examination for clerkship in Chief Constable's office; was Clerk in Charge Office, afterwards Detective Clerk, and subsequently appointed Assistant Chief Clerk; in 1903 was selected out of 600 applicants for appointment as 1st Class Sergt. and Asst. Chief Clerk in the County Chief Constable's office, Beverley, East Yorks.; promoted to Acting Inspector, 1910, 1st Class Inspector 1913, Superintendent and Chief Clerk, Jan. 1915. *Address:* Westwood Avenue, Grayburn Lane, Beverley. (M1337)

ALLISON, George Henry, M.B.E.

ALLISON, James, C.B.E., M.A., LL.B., *b.* 27 April, 1865; *s.* of Matthew Allison, of Dundee; *m.* Kate Constable, *d.* of Peter Young, of Dundee. *Educ.:* St. Andrews and Edinburgh Universities (LL.B. (with distinction), 1888). Lecturer on Scots Law, University of St. Andrews, 1899; Examiner under Law Agents (Scotland) Act, 1873; Searcher of Register of Sasines for Burgh of Dundee; Burgh Prosecutor, Newport, Fife. *War Work:* Chairman of Court of Referees for Dundee District of Scotland; Chairman of Local Munitions Tribunal for Dundee District of Scotland. *Addresses:* 61, Reform Street, Dundee; Craiglea, Newport, Fife. *Club:* Scottish Liberal (Edinburgh). (C2414)

ALLISON, John Neve, O.B.E. *War Work:* Worked in France with the Enquiry Department of the British Red Cross Society, 1915–19. *Address:* Bexhill, Sussex. (O9890)

ALLISON, Richard John, C.B.E., F.R.I.B.A., *b.* 8 Jan. 1869; *s.* of Joseph Charles Allison, of Radlett, Herts. *Educ.:* Private Choir School. Chief Architect H.M. Office of Works. *War Work:* Designed various War Hospitals, including the South African Military Hospital, Richmond Park, and Special Hospitals for Officers; also numerous Institutions for the Ministry of Pensions, and large works for other War Time Departments. *Address:* 63, Hornsey Lane, Highgate, N. 6. (C2415)

ALLISON, Thomas, M.B.E.

ALLNATT, Major Alfred Ernest, M.B.E.

ALLNUTT, Arthur Joseph, M.B.E.

ALLUM, Frederick Warner, C.B.E.; Engineer-in-Ch. Mushk Extension Railway. (C1064)

ALLUM, Herbert George, M.B.E.

ALLUM, Horace Benjamin, M.B.E.

ALLWOOD, John Humber, O.B.E.

ALMOND, the Rev. Col. John Macpherson, C.M.G., C.B.E., D.C.L., *b.* 1872; *s.* of James Almond; *m.* 1901, Nellie Estella Beemer. Is Rector of Trinity Church, Montreal, and Hon. Canon of Christchurch Cathedral, Montreal; S. Africa, 1900, as Chap. Canadian Contingent (Queen's medal with three clasps); Great War, 1914–17, as Director of Chaplains Sers. with rank of Hon. Col. (despatches). *Address:* 54, St. Denis Street, Montreal. (C1826)

ALPIN, Lieut.-Col. William George Patrick, O.B.E., I.M.S., *b.* 15 Sept. 1859; *s.* of William Thomas Alpin, Controller, Post Office, India; *m.* Helen May, *d.* of Charles H. Stoddart, Col. Indian Army. *Educ.:* Oscott College, near Birmingham. Civil Surgeon, United Provinces of India; Medical Officer to 39th Central India Horse; Medical Officer,

14th Jat Lancers; Medical Officer, General Hosp., Suakin, 1885; Medical Officer, Ordnance Field Park, Relief of Chitral, 1895. *War Work:* Medical Officer, Hospital Ship, 1914; S.M.O. Dorset Training Area, and O.C. Military Hosp. Brockenhurst, 1915–16; served with British Red Cross in Egypt, 1916–17; M.O. Prince of Wales' Hosp. for Officers, London, 1917–19.   (O11787)

ALSOP, Lieut. Anthony, M.B.E., Temp. Paymaster, R.A.P.D. *Address:* c/o Messrs. Cox & Co., Charing Cross, S.W.1.   (M10298)

ALSOP, James Willcox, O.B.E., B.A. (Lond,,) LL.D. (Liverpool), J.P., *b.* 6 June, 1846; *s.* of Rev. James Alsop, of Birmingham; *m.* Constance, *d.* of Charles Grey Mott, J.P., of Harrow Weald, Middlesex. *Educ.:* Liverpool Institute; Queen's College, Liverpool. Solicitor; Pro-Chancellor of the University of Liverpool; Chairman of the Liverpool Education Committee. *War Work:* Chairman of Liverpool Local Tribunal. *Business Address:* 14, Castle Street, Liverpool; *Residence:* Ulverscroft, Bidston Road, Birkenhead. *Clubs:* Reform, London; University, Exchange, Conservative, Liverpool.   (O90)

ALSTON, Major Charles Henry, M.B.E., T.D., *b.* 28 Feb. 1843; *s.* of James Wm. Alston, of Stockbriggs, Lanarkshire; *m.* Sara Fullerton, *d.* of John Geo. Brown, of Auchlochan, Lanarkshire. *Educ.:* Loretto and abroad. Served for 20 years in the Queen's Own Glasgow Yeomanry; retired in 1891. *War Work:* Employed on Recruiting Duties from Aug. 1914 to Dec. 1918; Asst. Recruiting Officer, Military Representative at Stirling Tribunal, and National Service Representative, Stirling. *Address:* St. Albans, Stirling. *Club:* Stirling County.   (M7207)

ALSTON, Frances Carr Ross, Mrs., M.B.E.

ALSTON, Hilda, Mrs., C.B,E.

ALSTON, Capt. John Stirling, O.B.E., K.R.R.C.

ALSTON, Rowland Alison, M.B.E., *b.* 2 May 1888; *s.* of Rowland Crewe Alston, of Odell, Co. Bedford (see BURKE'S *Landed Gentry*); *m.* Dorothy Mildred, *d.* of Charles Guy Pym of Cæsar's Camp, Bedfordshire. Late Capt. 3rd Bn. Northamptonshire Regt.; formerly Lieut. Coldstream Guards. *Address:* Harrold Hall, Bedfordshire.   (M3241)

ALTON, Surgeon Lieut.-Com. Francis Cooke, O.B.E. (Mil.), M.B., B.S. (Lond.), R.N., *b.* 17 Feb. 1888; *s.* of Sir Francis Alton, K.B.E., C.B., C.M.G. (*q.v.*) *Educ.:* Bedford School and St. Thomas's Hospital. Late Asst. Anæsthetist, West London Hospital; Anæsthetist, National Dental Hospital. *War Work:* Service in Royal Navy. *Address:* 73, St. James' Street. S.W.1. *Club:* Junior Constitutional.   (O9444)

ALTON, Paymaster Rear Admiral Sir Francis Cooke, K.B.E., C.B., C.M.G., *b.* 24 Aug. 1856; *s.* of late Francis Cooke Alton Chief Inspector of Machinery, R.N.; *m.* Pauline (Lina), *d.* of the late Ernest Barclay. *Educ.:* Private School. *War Work:* Secretary to Principal Naval Transport Officer, France, 1914–17. *Address:* 38, St. Leonard's Road, Exeter. *Clubs:* Devon and Exeter.   (K263)

ALVAREZ, Justin Charles William, I.S.O., O.B.E., M.R.A.S., H.B.M.'s Consul-General (ret.), *b.* 13 May, 1859; *s.* of the late William Thomas Alvarez, Professor of Languages, Lecturer on Spanish and Italian Literature, of 170, Oxford Road, Manchester; *m.* Mary, *d.* of the late Hon. George Pangiris Efendy, of Constantinople. Judge of the Court of Appeal, Member of the Orthodox Patriarchal Council, Mayor of Prinkipo. *Educ.:* Privately and at Manchester Grammar School. Student Dragoman, 1877; Consular Assistant, 1880, first at Salonica, then at Constantinople; Vice-Consul, 1885; H.B.M.'s Consul, Benghazy, 1890; Judicial Reform Commissioner in Crete, 1896–7; H.B.M.'s Consul-General at Tripoli, 1904; in charge at Trebizond, 1912–13. *War Work:* At the commencement of the war with Turkey, sole Censor for Turkish correspondence at first and afterwards Senior Censor; resigned 1919; is a Life Fellow of the Imperial Institute, a Member of the Royal Asiatic Society and of the Society of Biblical Archæology. *Address:* Villa Bonici, Prince of Wales Road, Sliema, Malta. *Club:* Union (Malta).   (O1052)

ALWOOD, Lieut.-Col. William Albert, O.B.E., R.A.O.C.

AMBLER, Joseph Edward, M.B.E., *Educ.:* Whitworth Institute, Manchester. Engineer. *War Work:* Munition Area Officer, Lancaster and Carlisle N.W. Area; Asst. Deputy Director, Shipyard Labour. *Address:* Patterdale Hotel, Patterdale, Ullswater.   (M7208)

AMBROSE, Capt. John Goldwell, O.B.E., M.C.; Capt. R.E.; Great War, 1914–19 (despatches).   (O2400)

AMBROSE, Philip Firmor, M.B.E.

AMERY, William Bankes, C.B.E., *b.* 26 Oct. 1882; *s.* of Thomas Arthur Amery, Norwell, Newark, Notts.; *m.* Adelaide Sophia, *d.* of Col. Herbert Burrows Adcock, of Highfield Lane End, Bucks. *Educ.:* Christ's Hospital. Establishment Officer, Ministry of Transport, 6, Whitehall Gardens, S.W. 1. *War Work:* Assistant Secretary of War Trade Dept. *Address:* 5, Egliston Road, Putney, S.W. 15. *Club:* Royal Automobile.   (C2417)

AMES, Major William Rex, O.B.E.

AMEY, Major Fulcher, M.B.E., R.A.

AMOR, Emma, Mrs., M.B.E.

AMOR, Capt. Stanley Long, M.B.E., R.A.F.

AMORY, Alexandra, Lady HEATHCOAT-, O.B.E., *d.* of Admiral Seymour, G.C.B., and Mrs. Seymour, of Barwick House, Norfolk; *m.* Sir Ian Heathcoat-Amory (Bart.), C.B.E. (*see* BURKE'S *Peerage*). *War Work:* Hospital Work: Knights-

---

hayes Court V.A. Hospital from 1915–19; Commandant V.A. Detachment, Devon 78. *Address:* Knightshayes Court, Tiverton, N. Devon.   (O9891)

AMORY, Sir Ian Murray Heathcoat HEATHCOAT-, 2nd Bt., C.B.E., J.P. and D.L. Co. Devon, *b.* 16 April, 1865; *s.* of Sir John Heathcoat Heathcoat Amory, 1st Bart., J.P., D.L. (*see* BURKE'S *Peerage*); *m.* 6 June, 1893, Alexandra Georgina, O.B.E. (*q.v.*), *e. d.* of the late Vice-Adm. Henry George Seymour, C.B. (*see* BURKE'S *Peerage*, Hertford, M.) *Address:* Knightshayes Court and Hensleigh, Tiverton, Devon. *Club:* Brooks's.   (C2)

AMOS, Alfred, M.B.E., C.A., J.P.; *s.* of James Amos, of Boughton Court, Ashford; *m.* Mary Beatrice Ann, *d.* of William Gillow, of Woodnesborough. *Educ.:* Chatham House, Ramsgate. Yeoman and tenant farmer. *War Work:* Practised and preached grubbing hops in order to grow food; Agricultural War Committee; Local Tribunal for enlisting; Chairman London Farmers Club. *Address:* Spring Grove, Wye, Kent. *Clubs:* National Liberal; London Farmers'; Canterbury Farmers'; Chamber of Agriculture.

AMOS, Mary Beatrice, O.B.E.

AMPHLETT, Theodora Mildred, Mrs., O.B.E.

AMPTHILL, Margaret Lygon, Lady, G.B.E., J.P. (1920), *b.* 8 Oct. 1874; *d.* of the 6th Earl Beauchamp (*see* BURKE'S *Peerage*); *m.* Sir Arthur Oliver Villiers Russell, 2nd Baron Ampthill, G.C.I.E., G.C.S.I., G.B.E., M.A., J.P., D.L. (*see* BURKE'S *Peerage*). Received the Order of the Crown of India in 1899; the Kaisir-i-Hind Gold Medal, 1906; lady of the bedchamber to H.M. the Queen, 1911. *Addresses:* Oakley House, Oakley, Bedford.   (DG7)

AMY, Lillian Eva, Mrs., M.B.E., *b.* 31 May., 1875; *d.* of W. L. Payne, K.C., of Colborne, Ontario, Canada; *m.* Lacey, *s.* of Rev. Thomas Amy, of Burlington, Ontario, Canada. *Educ.:* Toronto, Canada (Conservatory of Music). *War Work:* Mess Sister, Massey-Harris Hospital, Dulwich, England; Lady Superintendent, Associated Equipment Co., Walthamstow London, to Aug. 1917; Lady Superintendent, C. A. Vandervell & Co., Acton, W. 3, from Aug. 1917 and still there. *Club:* Marning Music, Toronto, Canada.   (M1342)

ANASTASIE, Joseph, M.B.E., R.A.M.C.

ANCASTER, Eloise Lawrence, Countess of, O.B.E., *b.* 1884; *d.* of William Laurence Breese, of New York; *m.* Gilbert, 2nd Earl of Ancaster (*see* BURKE'S *Peerage*). *War Work:* Vice-President, Bourne and District Red Cross; Chairman, Bourne and District War Pensions Committee; Chairman, Kestwen Women's War Agricultural Committee, Gresby House, Rutland Gate, London. *Addresses:* Grimsthorpe Castle, Bourne, Lincolnshire; Drummond Castle, Crieff, Scotland.   (O9893)

ANDEL, Harry Rudolph, O.B.E.

ANDERSON, Adelaide Mary, C.B.E., *b.* 8 Apr. 1863; *d.* of Alexander Gavin Anderson, late of 1 Fitzjohn's Avenue, London, N.W. *Educ.:* Queen's College, Harley Street; Girton College, Cambridge; and France and Germany. Civil Servant; H.M. Principal Lady Inspector of Factories, Home Office, Whitehall, S.W. 1. *War Work:* On Central Advisory Committee Women's (Industrial) Employment under Ministry of Labour; on Women's Employment Committee under Ministry of Reconstruction; and throughout War in Factory Department, Home Office, especially on Substitution of Women for men in Industry and Welfare Work. *Address:* 14, Coulson Street, Chelsea, S.W. 3. *Clubs:* University Club for Ladies; Albemarle.   (C91)

ANDERSON, Agnes Hilda, Mrs., M.B.E., *b.* 15 June, 1882; *d.* of Robert Orr, late of Kinnaird, Stirlingshire; *m.* James Arthur, *s.* of Robert Anderson, late of Glasgow. *War Work:* Hon. Secretary for "The Maxillo Facial Hospital," Kennington, S.E., and also for Facial Hospital, 78, Brook Street, W. 1, and for Annex of same, 24, Norfolk Street, W. 1. *Address:* 1, Cleveland Terrace, London, W. 2. *Club:* Ladies' Athenæum, Dover, Street, London.   (M7209)

ANDERSON, Sir Alan Garrett, K.B.E., *b.* 9 Mar. 1877; *s.* of the late James George Skelton Anderson J.P., Managing Director of Orient Line, who *d.* 25 Mar. 1907, and Elizabeth Garrett Anderson, M.D., his wife, who *d.* 17 Dec. 1917, *d.* of Newson Garrett of Aldeburgh, Suffolk; *m.* 9 June, 1903, Muriel Ivy, *d.* of G. W Duncan, of Richmond, Surrey. Partner in firm of Anderson, Anderson & Co., and Director of Midland Rly.; Vice-Chancellor of Royal Commission on Wheat, 1916–17; Chairman of Wheat Executive 1917; Controller of the Navy and Member of Board of Admiralty 1917–18 and Vice-Chairman of Food Council; Ministry of Munitions from 1918; Member of Royal Commission on Sugar Supply from 1918; is Commander of the Crown of Italy. *Address:* 19, Craven Hill, Bayswater, W. *Clubs:* Carlton; United; City of London.   (K10)

ANDERSON, Capt. Albert Roland, O.B.E., J.P., *b.* 17 Sept. 1882; *s.* of Charles Anderson, of Streete House, County Westmeath; *m.* Olga, *d.* of Henry Oberschmoukler, of Kerch South Russia. *Educ.:* Farra, Co. Westmeath. J.P., County Westmeath. *War Work:* Commissioned 1915 from Inns of Court O.T.C.; Served 1915–18, R.A.S.C., Salonika; 1918–20 on Staff South Russia and Constantinople; Twice mentioned in despatches; awarded O.B.E. and Russian Order of St. Stanislaus. *Address:* Streete House, Streete, Co. Westmeath. *Clubs:* Thatched House; United R.A.S.C.   (O6430)

ANDERSON, Capt. Alexander, M.B.E., R.G.A.

ANDERSON, Capt. Alexander, O.B.E., A.R.S.M., *b.* 23 Jan. 1879 ; *s.* of John Anderson, of Owensboro, Kentucky, U.S.A. ; *m.* Ida Marguerite, *d.* of Samuel A. Cockburn, of Cabo Gracias, Nicaragua. *Educ. :* Olivers Mount School and Edinburgh University. Chief Mining Engineer of a Dutch Company in Sumatra. *War Work :* Military service in France ; Experimental and inventions work under Munitions Inventions Department, and for the Admiralty in the Anti-Submarine Division and the Dept. of Torpedoes and Mining. *Address :* 27, Inverleith Row, Edinburgh. (O9053)

ANDERSON, Alexander Colin, O.B.E.

ANDERSON, Alexander Richard, C.B.E., F.R.C.S. ; Surg.-Gen. Hospital, Nottingham ; *s.* of Col. R. Anderson, formerly 56th Regt. ; *m.* 1890, Edith. *d.* of C. E. Tuck, J.P., of Blofield, Norfolk. *Address :* 3, East Circus Street, Nottingham. (C1151)

ANDERSON, Capt. Alfred Thomas Duncan, M.B.E., I.A.R.O.

ANDERSON, Amy Douglas Knyveton, Mrs., O.B.E., *b.* 9 Dec. 1867 ; *d.* of Canon Edward Harland, of Colwich, Staffs. ; *m.* Rupert Darnley, O.B.E., *q.v., s.* of Thomas Darnley Anderson, of Waverley Abbey. *War Work :* Commandant, Waverley Abbey Military Hospital, 1914–19. *Address :* Waverley Abbey, Farnham. *Club :* Ladies' Imperial. (O91)

ANDERSON, Annie Maria, Mrs., M.B.E.

ANDERSON, Capt. Arthur, O.B.E., *b.* 14 Nov. 1872 ; *s.* of Robert Anderson, of Strensall Grange, Yorkshire. *Educ. :* St. Martin's Vicarage, York. Secretary for the York Assembly Rooms ; Commandant of the York Motor Ambulance Detachment ; Hon. Sec. to the York Anti-Tuberculosis Campaign Committee ; Hon. Sec. Soldiers and Sailors Help Society for the West Riding of Yorkshire ; Hon. Sec. to the York Branch of the League of Nations Union ; Hon. Sec. to the York Branch of the National Life Boat Institution. *War Work :* Commandant of the North Riding Field Ambulance Detachment ; Commandant of the York Voluntary Aid Detachments ; Commandant of York Military Auxilliary Motor Ambulance Unit ; Mobilising Officer for the Yorkshire Coast Hospitals Scheme ; President of the York Stranded Soldiers' Dormitories ; Founder of the Yorkshire War Hospitals Depot ; Founder of the York Sphagnum Moss Dressings Depots. *Address :* Strensall Grange ; 44, Coney Street, York. *Club :* York Conservative. (O153)

ANDERSON, Engineer Lieut.-Comm. Arthur Robert, O.B.E , R.N.

ANDERSON, Sir Arthur Robert, Knt., C.I.E., C.B.E., A.M.I.C.E., *b.* 28 July, 1860 ; *s.* of the late James Anderson, of Auchendarroch, Argyllshire ; *m.* Gertrude (who died), *d.* of the late J. D. Fraser, J.P., of Tiverton. *Educ. :* Glasgow Academy and Univ. Educated as a Civil Engineer ; Assistant Engineer to the Southern Maharatta Railway, India, 1882 ; Chief Engineer, 1879 ; Agent of the Madras and Southern Maharatta Railway, 1908 ; Member of the Railway Board, Government of India, 1914–19 ; President since 1919. *Address :* Simla, India. *Clubs :* Caledonian ; United Service, Simla ; Club of Western India, Poona. (C82)

ANDERSON, Charles, M.B.E., *b.* 30 Aug. 1859 ; *s.* of Charles Anderson, of West Hartlepool ; *m.* Catherine Duff, *d.* of John Macfarlane, of West Hartlepool. *Educ. :* Fraserburgh Public School and Cambridge University Extension Lectures. *War Work :* Honorary Secretary, West Hartlepool War Savings Committee ; the Borough won the " Tank " Record in 1918, and the National War Bonds Record 1918–19 for which Tank " Egbert " was awarded to the town. *Address :* Willow House, West Hartlepool. (M1343)

ANDERSON, Major Charles Harrison Murray, O.B.E.

ANDERSON, Charles James, M.B.E.

ANDERSON, Charles John, O.B.E., J.P., *b.* 16 March, 1853 ; *s.* of Thomas Anderson, M.D., F.R.S.E., Professor of Chemistry, of Glasgow University ; *m.* Kate, *d.* of John Barclay, of Shetland. *Educ. :* Yverdun House, Blackheath ; Durham School ; Glasgow University. Justice of the Peace, Middlesex. *War Work :* On National Registrar, Chiswick ; Chairman, Derby Recruiting Canvass Committee, Chiswick ; Member, Military Service Acts Committee, Chiswick ; Chairman, Local Relief Committee, Chiswick ; Chairman, War Pensions, Committee, Chiswick ; Joint Chairman, War Savings Committee, Chiswick ; Member, Food Economy Committee, Chiswick ; Member, Air Raid Committee, Chiswick. *Address :* Kelvin Lodge, Spencer Road, Chiswick, W. *Clubs :* Constitutional ; Grange (Guernsey) ; Glasgow University (London) ; Royal Guernsey Golf, L'Ancrene, Guernsey. (O9894)

ANDERSON, Charles Llewellyn, O.B.E. (O12040)

ANDERSON, Charles Thompson, O.B.E. (O12039)

ANDERSON, Daisy Kate, M.B.E.

ANDERSON, Major David Irving, O.B.E., R.A.M.C.

ANDERSON, David Martin, O.B.E., and Knight of the Crown of Italy, *b* 1880 ; *s.* of the late James Anderson, of Glasgow. *Educ. :* Glasgow High School. Mechanical Engineer ; Director Sir William Arrol & Co., Ltd. *War Work :* Deputy Director-General of Guns, and later Controller of Forgings, Castings, and Stampings for Admiralty, Ministry of Munitions, and Air Board ; Designed and supervised the complete installation of the National Ordnance Factory, Nottingham. *Address :* 5, Queen's Terrace, Glasgow. *Clubs :* Devonshire ; Conservative, Glasgow. (C2418)

ANDERSON, Dora, Mrs., O.B.E.

ANDERSON, Lieut.-Col. Edmund Buller, O.B.E., R.A.

ANDERSON, Eleanor Florence, M.B.E.

ANDERSON, Elizabeth, Mrs., O.B.E.

ANDERSON, Eric Harper, O.B.E.

ANDERSON, Eric Oswald, C.B.E., *b.* 24 July, 1870 ; *s.* of the late H. D. Anderson, of Shenley, Herts. ; *m.* Cicely Violet Mary, *w.* of A. D. Stafford, Royal Warwickshire Regt. Member of Legislative Council, Burma, and Chairman, Burma Chamber of Commerce, 1917–19. *Address :* Rangoon, Burma. *Clubs :* Conservative ; Pegu (Burma). (C1596)

ANDERSON, Frances Lightbourne Trimingham, M.B.E. ; *d.* of William Anderson, J.P., of Inistore, Helensburgh. *Educ. :* St. Bride's School and Holloway College. *War Work :* Honorary Secretary, Soldiers' and Sailors' Families Association, Dumbartonshire Branch ; Member of Naval and Military War Pensions Committee for the County of Dumbarton, and Honorary Secretary for the District Committee for the Parishes of Row and Rosemeath. *Address :* Inistore, Helensburgh. *Club :* Kelvin, Glasgow. (M7210)

ANDERSON, Francis, M.B.E.

ANDERSON, Major Francis Edward, O B.E., R.A.S.C.

ANDERSON, Capt. Francis Henry Middleton, O.B.E., R.A.S.C., *b.* 17 Mar. 1881 ; *s.* of George Carpenter Anderson. *Educ. :* Blundells School. Land Agent. *Address :* Park Cottage, Falmer, Lewes, Sussex. *Club :* Royal Automobile. (O4951)

ANDERSON, Lieut.-Col. Frederick Walter Gale, O.B.E.

ANDERSON, George, M.B.E., *b.* Edinburgh, 23 July, 1866. *Educ. :* George Watson's College. Chartered Accountant (Edinburgh) ; Actuary, Preston Savings Bank ; Member of National Savings Committee. *Address :* 3, Bank Parade, Preston. *Club :* Winckley Club, Preston. (M1946)

ANDERSON, George Reinhardt, M.B.E., F.R.C.S., L.R.C.P. (Lond.), *b.* 18 May, 1864 ; *s.* of Henry Bunting Anderson, M.R.C.S., of London and Bournemouth ; *m.* Eleanor Annie, *d.* of Rev. Bamford Burrows, of Poulton-le-Fylde. *Educ. :* New College, Eastbourne, and St. Thomas' Hospital, London. Senior Hon. Medical Officer and Chairman, Medical Board, The General Infirmary, Southport, Medical Referee Workmen's Compensation Act. *War Work :* Medical Officer in charge of Military Annexes, Southport Infirmary, 265 beds ; Temporary Divisional Surgeon, V.A.D., The Grange and Woodlands, St. John's Hospital, 500 beds ; Surgeon in charge Battalion 1915, during training ; Member of the Local Medical War Committee. *Address :* " Lansdowne," 36, Hoghton Street, Southport. Lancs. (M7212)

ANDERSON, Hon. Major George William Strachan, M.B.E. Senior Assistant Censor, Headquarters, Australia. (M10256*h*)

ANDERSON, Gladys, Mrs., M.B.E.

ANDERSON, Helen Agnes, Mrs., M.B.E. (M10368)

ANDERSON, Henry, M.B.E.

ANDERSON, Major H. Graeme, M.B.E., M.D., Ch.B., F.R.C.S., R.A.F., *b.* 1 Aug. 1882 ; *s.* of Nicol Anderson, of Glasgow. *Educ. :* Glasgow Univ. ; King's Coll. ; London Hospital. Consulting Surgeon ; Surgical Consultant to the Royal Air Force ; Surgeon to St. Mark's Hospital : Senior Assistant Surgeon to Belgrave Hospital. *War Work :* Surgeon-Lieutenant R.N. Aug. 1914 ; attached as surgeon to original R.N.A.S. expeditionary force, Antwerp, 1st Battle of Ypres, Dunkirk ; Aviator's Certificate of Royal Aero Club, No. 3758, 26 Oct. 1916 ; transferred to Royal Air Force, April, 1918 ; author of " The Medical and Surgical Aspects of Aviation." *Addresses :* 75, Harley Street, W. 1. *Clubs :* Caledonian ; Royal Air Force ; Royal Aero ; London Flying. (M3352)

ANDERSON, Capt. Hugh A., M.B.E.

ANDERSON, James, C.B.E., *b.* 22 Jan. 1857 ; *s.* of Wellwood Anderson, of Dumfries, Scotland ; *m.* Arabella Williamson, *d.* of William Williamson, of Smyrna. *Educ. :* Dumfries Academy, N.B. Chief Electrician on various Cable Steamers of the Eastern Telegraph ; Electrician at Malta and Divisional Manager in the Levant and Agent in Turkey of the Eastern Telegraph Co ; H.B.M. Consul for Syra and the Grecian Archipelago from 1888 till 1892. *Foreign Decorations :* Commander of Saviour (Greece) : Commander of Medjidieh and Cretan Medal (Turkey). *War Work :* Maintenance of Submarine Cable Communications ; Chairman in Athens of the Patriotic League of Britons Overseas. *Address :* c/o H. S. King & Co., 9 Pall Mall, London. (C2419)

ANDERSON, James Alexander, M.B.E. (M10244*c*)

ANDERSON, Lieut.-Col. James Dalgleish, C.B.E., D.S.O. ; Major Cape Auxiliary Horse Transport, and temporary Lieut.-Col. attached R.A.S.C. ; German S.-W. Africa, 1914–15 (despatches). (C1215)

ANDERSON, Lieut.-Col. James Douglas, O.B.E., R.G.A.

ANDERSON, James Edward, C.B.E., M.I.M.E., *b.* 3 April, 1871 ; *s.* of Rev. Wm. Anderson, Minister of Fettercairn ; *m.* Agnes Meikle, *d.* of Andrew Davidson, of Ayr. *Educ. :* Privately and Montrose Academy and Gordon's College, Aberdeen. Engineer ; Deputy Chief Mechanical Engineer, Midland Railway, Derby. *War Work :* Responsible for all Munitions turned out of the Works (Locomotive) of the Midland Ry. Co. at Derby *Address :* 52, Empress Road, Derby. (C2420)

ANDERSON, Lieut.-Col. John Hubback, C.M.G., C.B.E., M.B., B.S. 1908, M.D. 1910, A.A.M.C., A.D.M.S., Australian Imperial Forces Headquarters, *b.* 20 Aug. 1883 ; *s.* of Dr. J. F. Anderson, of Woodend, Maloa, Victoria ; *m.* Ruby C., 2nd *d.* of H. C. Moffatt, of Goodrich Court, Ross, and Hamptworth Lodge, Hants. *Educ. :* Longford Grammar School, Tasmania ;

Ormond Coll., Univ. of Melbourne. Senior Demonstrator of Anatomy, Univ. of Melbourne, 1909–11; Hon. Out-patient Physician, St. Vincent's Hospital, Melbourne, 1911; in private practice, Benalla, Victoria, 1914; enlisted A.I.F., 1914; served Gallipoli, Egypt, France, in various positions (despatches twice). *Address :* 28, Carlisle Mansions, Carlisle Place, S.W. 1. (C92)

ANDERSON, Major John Samuel, O.B.E.

ANDERSON, Julia Ada, Mrs., M.B.E.

ANDERSON, Louis Dessurne, O.B.E.

ANDERSON, Capt. Louis Goodrich Abbot, M.B.E., *b.* 10 July, 1872 ; *s.* of Major-Gen. E. Abbot Anderson, of Kilkenny, Ireland ; *m.* Beatrice Kathleen, *d.* of James Edward Huggins, of Dublin. *Educ. :* Oxford Military College. Actor, under the name of Louis Goodrich ; served in Ceylon Planters' Rifle Corps in the Boer War, 1900. *War Work :* Enlisted in 28th Batt. London Regt., in Aug. 1914 ; proceeded overseas (France) Dec. 1914 ; Commissioned, 18 April, 1915 ; Adjutant of No. 15 Officer Cadet Batt. from 10 Sept. 1916 to 7 May, 1919 ; mentioned in despatches. *Address :* 10, Palace Mansions, Kensington, W. 14. *Clubs :* Green Room ; Denham Golf. (M5019)

ANDERSON, Dr. Louisa Garrett, C.B.E., M.D., B.S., *b.* 1873 ; *d.* of Jas. George Skelton Anderson and Elizabeth Garrett Anderson, M.D. of London. *Educ. :* St. Leonards ; Bedford College ; London School of Medicine for Women. Surgeon to the Roll of Honour Hospital for Children, Harrow Road, and Consulting Surgeon Elizabeth Garrett Anderson Hospital, Euston Road. *War Work :* Joint Organiser of Women's Hospital Corps and Surgeon to the Auxiliary Hospitals in Claridge's Hotel, Paris, and Chateau Mauricien, Wimereux, 1914–15, and Chief Surgeon to the Military Hospital, Endell St., London, 1915–1919. *Address :* 116, Park St., Grosvenor Square, London. (C3)

ANDERSON, Lydia Elizabeth, Lady, C.B.E.

ANDERSON, Mary Addison, M.B.E., *b.* 2 Oct. 1895 ; *d.* of Mrs. William Anderson, of Leven. *Educ. :* Kirkcaldy High School. *War Work :* Served with Women's Legion, Feb. 1917 to Sept. 1917 ; Gazetted Unit Administrator of Q.M.A.A.C. ; was in Command of Q.M.A.A.C. stationed in Portsmouth Town till June, 1919. *Address :* Leven, Fife. (M6593)

ANDERSON, Mary Gardiner, M.B.E., Q.M.A.A.C., *b.* 14 March, 1895 ; *d.* of Robert S. Anderson, of Peebles, N.B. *Educ. :* High School, Peebles, and Edinburgh School of Domestic Science. *War Work :* Women's Legion, 13 months ; Q.M.A.A.C., 2 years. *Address :* South Bank, Peebles, N.B. (M6594)

ANDERSON, Maurice Fitzgerald, O.B.E.

ANDERSON, Capt. Maxwell Hendry, C.B.E., *b.* 1879 ; *s.* of the Rev. J. H. Anderson ; Bar. Middle Temple, 1909 ; entered R.N. 1893, and is Capt. (ret.) ; was Local Govt. Board Member of Central (Unemployed) Body for London, 1914–19 ; appointed Attorney-Gen. of Gibraltar, 1919. *Clubs :* Gibraltar ; United Service ; National Liberal. (C1176)

ANDERSON, Capt. Neil Gordon, O.B.E., R.A.S.C,

ANDERSON, Major Neville, O.B.E., *b.* 11 Jan. 1881 ; *s.* of the late W. M. Anderson, Esq., of Oxted, Surrey. *Educ. :* Rugby, and Oriel College, Oxford. Barrister-at-Law ; A special Commissioner of Income Tax. *War Work :* 2 Lt. in London Rifle Brigade, Feb. 1915 ; France, Jan. 1916 to March, 1919 ; served on Staff of Headquarters First Army as D.A.A.G., Jan. 1916 to March, 1919 ; Capt., April, 1916 ; Major Feb. 1918 ; three times mentioned in despatches ; M.B.E., 1917 ; O.B.E., 7 Jan. 1919. *Address :* 4, Ralston Street, Chelsea, S.W. *Clubs :* Brooks's ; Bath. (O2401)

ANDERSON, Percival James, M.B.E.

ANDERSON, Lieut. Percy, M.B.E.

ANDERSON, Mrs. Powell, O.B.E. Rendered valuable war services. (O11922)

ANDERSON, Capt. Robert Cairns Amis, O.B.E.

ANDERSON, Major Robert Gray, O.B.E., R.A.V.C.

ANDERSON, Assistant Paymaster Capt. Robert William, M.B.E., *b.* 19 July, 1873 ; *s.* of Mathew William, of Dublin ; Lilian Maud, *d.* of Lawson H. Stockdale, of Preston. *Educ. :* Ripley Hospital, Lancaster. *War Work :* Royal Army Pay Dept. *Address :* Army Pay Office, Woolwich. (M5033)

ANDERSON, Capt. Roy Dunlop, D.S.O., O.B.E.

ANDERSON, Major Rupert Darnley, O.B.E., D.L., J.P., *b.* 29 April, 1859 ; *s.* of Thomas Darnley Anderson, of Waverley Abbey, Farnham, Surrey ; *m.* Amy Douglas Knyveton, O.B.E. (*q.v.*), *d.* of Canon Edward Harland, of Colwich, Staffs. *Educ. :* Eton and Trinity Hall, Cambridge. *Address :* Waverley Abbey, Farnham, Surrey. (O8035)

ANDERSON, Capt. Thomas Andrew Irving, O.B.E., R.A.V.C.

ANDERSON, Thomas George, O.B.E.

ANDERSON, Major Thomas Lynewolde, O.B.E., A.I.F.

ANDERSON, Lieut. Toni Percival, M.B.E., *b.* 29 Dec. 1884 ; *s.* of Robert Anderson, of York. *Educ. :* York Minster Choir School. Portrait painter. *War Work :* Served with R.A.S.C. in France, afterwards was an official artist and did portraits of distinguished general officers, which are now in the Royal Collection and the property of H.M. The King. *Address :* 22, Baker Street, W. (M5034)

ANDERSON, William, O.B.E., *b.* 11 July, 1853 ; *s.* of John Anderson, of Glasgow ; *m.* Ada, *d.* of Thomas Smith, of Ulverston, Lancs. *Educ. :* Partick Academy. Chairman Glasgow Liberal Council ; President Central Division Liberal Association, Glasgow ; Vice-Chairman Scottish Liberal Federation ;

Chairman Wm. Anderson & Co., Ltd., Glasgow ; Chairman R. A. Whytelaw, Son & Co., Ltd., Glasgow ; Director Scottish Ontario and Manitoba Land Co. ; Director North British Canadian Investment Co. *War Work :* Chairman Central Division Advisory Committee, Glasgow ; Member Textile Shipping Commission, Manchester. *Addresses :* 12, Princes Square, Glasgow ; 11, Sherbrooke Avenue, Glasgow. (O1057)

ANDERSON, Major William, O.B.E., M.B., Ch.B., F.R.C.S. (Ed.) ; R.A.M.C., *b.* 16 May, 1886 ; *s.* of George Anderson, J.P., of Nether Aucharnie Forgue, Aberdeenshire ; *m.* Barbara Matthew, *d.* of David Gibson, of Redhill Surrey. *Educ. :* Banff Academy, Aberdeen and Edinburgh Universities. Surgeon. Assistant Surgeon, Aberdeen Royal Infirmary. *War Work :* British Red Cross Hospital, Netley, 1914 ; R.A.M.C., France, Feb. 1915 to Dec. 1918 ; Hospitals in England, Dec. 1918 to May, 1919. *Address :* 10, Albyn Place, Aberdeen. (O4956)

ANDERSON, William Dunlop, O.B.E., M.B., M.R.C.S., J.P., *b.* 10 July, 1858 ; *s.* of Alexander Dunlop Anderson, of Ardsheal, Argyllshire. *Educ. :* Trinity College, Cambridge ; St. George's Hospital, London. Commissioner of Income Tax. *War Work :* Hon. House Surgeon and Radiographer, Cumberland Infirmary, 1914–17 ; Anæsthetist and M.O. in charge X-rays, Fusehill War Hospital, Carlisle, 1917–18. *Address :* Chestnut Hill, Keswick. *Club :* Royal Highland Yacht, Oban. (O11788)

ANDERSON, William James, C.B.E., J.P., *b.* 30 Nov. 1851; *s.* of William Anderson, Chartered Accountant, Glasgow ; *m.* Eleonora, *d.* of Alexander Kay, of Cornhill, Lanarkshire. *Educ. :* Glasgow Academy and Abbey Park. St. Andrews. Chartered Accountant. *War Work :* Honorary Treasurer and Member of Council and Executive Committee of the Scottish Branch of the British Red Cross Society. *Address :* Strathairly, Largo, Fife. *Clubs :* Western, Glasgow ; University, Edinburgh. (C93)

ANDERSON, Capt. William John Skeat, M.B.E., R.F.A.

ANDERSON, William Thomas, C.B.E., *b.* 1872. *Educ. :* Grammar School, Darlington. Member of Institution of Minign and Metallurgy ; Consulting Engineer to Transvaal Mining Companies *War Work :* 1917, Chief Technical Adviser to Mineral Resources Department ; 1918, Controller of Iron Ore Mines of Cumberland and Lancashire ; 1919, Chief Labour Adviser, Ministry of Munitions. *Clubs :* Rand, Johannesburg ; Royal Automobile (London). (C2422)

ANDERSON, Capt. Wilfred Arthur DUNCOMBE-, O.B.E.

ANDERSON, Joan Anderson SCOTT-, M.B.E., *b.* 1856 ; *d.* of Thomas Shaw, of Australia ; *m.* Thomas Scott, *s.* of Thomas Anderson, of Selkirk. *Educ. :* Switzerland. *War Work :* President, Kirkhope Branch of Selkirk Red Cross. *Address :* Ettrick Shaws, Selkirk. (M7213)

ANDERTON, James Edwin, M.B.E., M.R.C.S., L.R.C.P., *b.* 25 March, 1853 ; *s.* of James Anderton, of Ormskirk, Lancashire ; *m.* Hannah, *d.* of William Shaw, of Ashton-under-Lyne. *Educ. :* Sandringham School, Southport. Medical Medical Officer, Hayfield Union ; Medical Officer of Health, New Mills District Council ; Certifying Factory Surgeon. *War Work :* Medical Officer, New Mills V.A.D. Hospital. *Club :* Constitutional (Manchester). (M7214)

ANDREW, Bennett Harvey, M.B.E., M.D., *b.* 1865 ; *s.* of Charles Andrew, of Hemsworth, Yorks. ; *m.* Sarah Edith, *d.* of James Berry, of Bath. *Educ. :* Privately and King's College Hospital. Medical Practitioner. *War Work :* M.O. in charge Thame V.A.D. Hospital. *Address :* Newbury House, Walliscote Road, Weston-super-Mare. (M7215)

ANDREW, Rev. G. Findlay, O.B.E.

ANDREW, Major George Lionel, O.B.E.

ANDREW, Lieut.-Col. Phillip Oywalk, O.B.E.

ANDREW, Capt. Richard Hynman, O.B.E., M.C.

ANDREWES, Lieut. Cyril John, M.B.E., R.A.S.C.

ANDREWES, Major Sir Frederick William, Knt Bach., O.B.E., M.D., F.R.S., R.A.M.C., *b.* 31 March, 1859 ; *s.* of Charles James Andrewes, J.P., of Broad Oak, Reading ; *m.* Phyllis Mary, *d.* of John Hamer, J.P. *Educ. :* Christ Church, Oxford ; St. Bartholomew's Hospital, London. Professor of Pathology, University of London ; Pathologist, St. Bartholomew's Hospital. *War Work :* Pathologist, 1st General London Hospital ; Member of War Office Committee on Tetanus ; Member of War Office Committee on Dysentery ; Tetanus Inspector, London (N. of Thames). *Address :* 1, North Grove, Highgate, N. 6. (O6839)

ANDREWES, Lieut. Robert Lancelot, M.B.E.

ANDREWS, Lieut.-Col. Albion Ernest, O.B.E., *b.* 16 June, 1877 ; *s.* of Albion George Andrews, of Wells, Somerset ; *m.* Blanche Derham, *d.* of Rev. H. Bernard Derham-Marshall, of Norton Canon, Herefordshire. *Educ. :* Weymouth College. At present commanding 1st Batt. The Hampshire Regiment. Served in South Africa, 1902 ; Somaliland, 1903–4 ; France, 1917–18 ; N. Russia, 1918–19 ; Army of the Black Sea, 1920. *Addresses :* Messrs. Cox and Co., 16, Charing Cross, London, S.W. 1 ; Messrs. Harris and Harris, Diocesan Registry, Wells, Somerset. (O9713)

ANDREWS, Annie, Mrs., M.B.E., *b.* 27 July, 1872 ; *d.* of Robert Bell, J.P., Craigie Lea, New Scotland, Transvaal ; *m.* George Samuel Burt, M.I.C.E., *s.* of George Robert Andrews, M.I.C.E., of Bournemouth, England. *Educ. :* Pietermaritzburg, Natal. *War Work :* Governor-General's Fund, since Sept. 1914 ; still serving as committee member ; head of a department in the office. *Address :* Jabula, 77, St. Patrick's Road, Houghton Ridge, Johannesburg. (M2870)

ANDREWS, Arthur William, M.B.E.

ANDREWS, Major Charles Eric, O.B.E.

ANDREWS, Charles Henry, M.B.E.

ANDREWS, Major Cyril Rogers, M.B.E., R.A.F.

ANDREWS, Elizabeth, M.B.E.; *d.* of Rev. W. R. Andrews, of 27, Enys Road, Eastbourne. *War Work :* Secretary to the Eastbourne Belgian and French Refugees Committee. *Address :* 27, Enys Road, Eastbourne. (M7217)

ANDREWS, Capt. Ernest Courtney Harold Norman, M.B.E., R.G.A.

ANDREWS, Capt. Francis Arthur Lavington, C.B.E., R.N., King's Harbour Master since 1912, *b.* 1869. *Address :* H.M. Dockyard, Malta. *Clubs :* United Service ; St. James's. (C423)

ANDREWS, Major Frank Leon, O.B.E., D.C.M., *b.* 17 Nov. 1870 ; *s.* of the late John William, of London ; *m.* Margaret Maria, *d.* of T. B. Bickerton, of Hove, and niece of the late Rear-Admiral Sir Richard Bickerton, Bart. *War Work :* Service in India ; South Africa, Medal and 8 clasps ; King's Medal and 2 clasps ; D.C.M. and 1 clasp ; 2 mentions, 10 Sept. 1901, and 29 July, 1902. *Club :* Junior Army and Navy.

ANDREWS, George, M.B.E.

ANDREWS, Lieut.-Col. George Henry, O.B.E.

ANDREWS, Helen, Mrs., M.B.E., *b.* 13 April, 1863 ; *d.* of Robert Ardill, of Fallowfield, Manchester ; *m.* Thomas James, *s.* of Isaac Andrews, of Comber, Co. Down. *Educ. :* In France and Germany. *War Work :* Controller of Buffet for Sailors and Soldiers, Co. Down Railway, Belfast ; Vice-President, S.S.F.A. ; Vice-Chairman, Local War Pensions Sub-committee, Comber, Co. Down. *Address :* The Square, Comber, Co. Down. *Club :* Lyceum. (M7219)

ANDREWS, Capt. Henry Leonard Herbert, M.B.E.

ANDREWS, Eng.-Comm. Henry Osmond, O.B.E., R.N.

ANDREWS, Horace George, M.B.E.

ANDREWS, Lieut. Joseph Claude, M.B.E., R.A.F.

ANDREWS, Leonard, M.B.E., M.Inst.C.E., *b.* 16 April, 1869 ; *s.* of Henry Andrews, of Little Langford, Salisbury. *Educ. :* Bedford County School. Consulting Engineer, Johnson Matthey, and Co. Ltd., 78, Hatton Garden, E.C. 1. *War Work :* Engineering Superintendent, Metropolitan Munitions Committee *Address :* The Hut, West End Lane, Pinner. *Club :* St. Stephen's. (M3491)

ANDREWS, Lieut. Leslie Frank, M.B.E.

ANDREWS, Major Neale, O.B.E., R.A.S.C.

ANDREWS, Surgeon Capt. Octavius William, C.B.E., M.B., R.N.

ANDREWS, Lieut. Sidney Byron, M.B.E., R.E. (M10299)

ANDREWS, Walter Gower, M.B.E., J.P., *b.* 1866 ; *s.* of Thornton Andrews, M.Inst.C E., J.P., of Cefn Eithen Swansea. *Educ. :* Cheltenham College. *War Work :* Military Representative on the Tribunals for Abergavenny Borough and Abergavenny Rural District. *Address :* Aberbaiden, nr. Abergavenny, Mon. *Club :* Junior Athenæum. (M7220)

ANDREWS, Capt. George Edward GENGE-, O.B.E., M.P., B.S., *b.* 1 Aug. 1888 ; *s.* of George Edward Genge-Andrews, of Rimpton House, Rimpton, Bath. *Educ. :* Guy's Hospital. Medical Assessor, Ministry of Pensions. *War Work :* Civilian Medical Officer i/c Troops, Lewes, Sussex, from Aug. to Dec. 1914 ; Lieut. and Capt. R.A.M.C., 16 Dec. 1914 to 16 Dec. 1916 ; Civilian M.O. i/c 332 Field Ambulance Hospital, May 1917 to Nov. 1918. *Address :* 49, Beaufort Mansions, Beaufort Street, Chelsea, S.W. 3. *Club :* Guy's Hospital. (O4374)

ANGEL, Frederick William, M.B.E.

ANGEL, Capt. Sydney James Hounsell, O.B.E., *b.* 14 Dec. 1872 ; *s.* of Richard Angel, of Bridport, Dorset, *m.* Katharine, *d.* of John Alex Barker, of Upton Manor. *Educ. :* Upton Cross. Merchant Service. *War Work :* Commanded H.M.S. "Australind" ; was taken up by the Admiralty at the outbreak of War ; was conveying troops, horses, guns, ammunition, etc., to ports of France ; sent to Egypt in March, 1915 ; took part in Gallipoli landing on 25 April, 1915 ; carried troops from Egypt to Mudros until July, 1915, then returned to Southampton and was on duty in the Channel until the cessation of hostilities. *Address :* Rozel, Westbourne Grove, Westcliff-on-Sea. *Club :* Maritime. (O3603)

ANGEL, Capt. Walter Douglas, M.B.E.

ANGELL, Capt. Bruce Othniel, M.B.E., R.A.F.

ANGELL, Charles Henry Cooper, O.B.E.

ANGELL, Col. Frederick John, C.B.E., Assistant Director of Ordnance Services, Southern Command, late Col. Royal Irish Fusiliers, *b.* 1861. Served Egyptian Expedition, 1884 ; Bechuanaland Expedition, 1884–85. (C94)

ANGELO, Alfred, O.B.E.

ANGELS, Mary Colquhoun, Mrs. FOX-, M.B.E. (M10369)

ANGIER, Frederick Leigh, O.B.E., M.R.C.S.

ANGUS, John, M.B.E., B.Sc. Glasgow. *War Work :* Assistant Constructor (Temporary) Department of Director of Naval Construction Admiralty. (M7221)

ANGUS, Maj. Robert, O.B.E., R.E.

ANGUS, Major William Brodie Gurney, O.B.E., M.C., M.A., M.D. (Cantab.), F.R.C.S. (Edin.), *b.* 28 June, 1884 ; *s.* of C. J. Angus, of Hampstead. *Educ. :* Oundle School ; Christ's College, Cambridge ; London Hospital. *War Work :* Joined Aug. 1914; served in Gallipoli, Egypt, France ; was Surgical Specialist in Casualty Clearing Stations ; and for a

time Medical Officer in charge 108 Army Brigade, R.F.A. *Address :* 14, North Square, London, N.W. 4. (O4959)

ANNAN, Margaret, M.B.E. *Educ. :* Wycombe Abbey School. Administrative Assistant in the Offices of the War Cabinet. *Address :* Pentlands, Mitcham, Surrey. (M7222)

ANNAND, John Fowler, O.B.E., M.Sc. ; *s.* of Adam Annand, of Keig, Aberdeenshire ; *m.* Mary Anderson, *d.* of Robert Harvey, of Aberdeen. *Educ. :* Aberdeen, Edinburgh, and on the Continent. Divisional Forest Officer, Forestry Commission (Eastern Division, Scotland), was formerly Adviser and Lecturer in Forestry at Armstrong College (University of Durham), and Superintendent of Crown Woods in County Durham. *War Work :* During the War held the position of Divisional Officer in charge at Newcastle-upon-Tyne, of the Board of Trade Timber Supply Department and was responsible for the purchase and manufacture of large quantities of home timber used for war purposes in France and in England. *Address :* 156, Union Street, Aberdeen. (O9897)

ANNE, Major George Charlton, O.B.E., R.A.F., *b.* 11 Feb. 1886 ; *s.* of Ernest Lambert Swinburne Anne, of Burghwallis, Co. York. (*see* BURKE's *Landed Gentry*) ; *m.* Amy Violet, *d.* of late James Montagu, of Malton Park, Yorkshire (*see* BURKE's *Landed Gentry*) ; Capt. King's Own Yorkshire Light Infantry; *Address :* Fieldhead, Thornet, W. Leeds. (O3248)

ANNETT, Henry Edward, M.B.E., M.D.

ANNING, Lieut. William James, M.B.E., R.N.R.

ANSCOMBE, Capt. Richard Stanley, O.B.E.

ANSELL, George Frederic, C.B.E.

ANSON, Major Ernest St. George, O.B.E., *b.* 23 April, 1875 ; *s.* of Lieut.-Col. A. G. Anson, of Royal Marine Artillery (retired) ; *m.* Blanche Evelyn, *d.* of C. C. W. Hoare, of H.M. Civil Service (retired). *Educ. :* Clifton College. Joined East Surrey Regt., 9 Dec. 1896, as 2nd Lieut. ; served throughout with that unit except as below. *War Work :* At outbreak of war, was employed training arafts for the front until Jan. 1915 ; proceeded to the Ypres district, Jan. 1915 ; evacuated to England very severely wounded, 20 Feb. 1915 ; attached General Staff, War Office, M.I.S., 20 Dec. 1915 ; appointed to Imperial General Staff, M.I.S. War Office, 1 March, 1917 to 31 Dec. 1919 ; rejoined East Surrey Regt., 1 Jan. 1920. *Address :* c/o Messrs. Cox and Co., 16, Charing Cross, S.W. 1. (O8731)

ANSON, Major George Frank Wemyss, O.B.E. (O11722)

ANSON, Major George Wilfred, M.B.E., M.C., *b.* 2 June, 1893 ; *s.* of G. E. Anson, of Windy Brow, Kendal ; *m.* Dinah *d.* of A. A. Bourne, of Cheltenham. *Educ. :* Winchester and Trinity College, Oxford. *War Work :* Served with 7th Royal North Lancashire Regt., 1914–17 (France) ; adjutant two years ; Adjutant, No 11 Officer Cadet Batt., 1918–20. *Address :* Copthorn, Downleaze, Sneyd Park, Bristol. *Club :* Cavendish. (M5036)

ANSON, Maud, Mrs., M.B.E.

ANSTEY, Eng.-Comm. Henry Charles, O.B.E., R.N.

ANSTEY, Norman, O.B.E.

ANSTRUTHER, Hon. Dame Eva Isabella Henrietta, D.B.E., *b.* 25 Jan. 1869 ; *e.d.* of the 4th Baron Sudeley (*see* BURKE's *Peerage*) ; *m.* Henry Torrens, 2nd *s.* of the late Sir Robert Anstruther, 5th Bt., M.P., of Balcaskie (*see* BURKE's *Peerage*). *Address :* 25, Curzon St. W. 1. (D8)

ANSTRUTHER, Mildred Harriet, Lady, C.B.E., *b.* 2 June, 1863 ; *d.* of Edward Hussey, of Scotney Castle ; *m.* Sir Ralph William, *s.* of the late Sir Robert Anstruther, Bt., of Balcaskie. *War Work :* Soldiers and Sailors Families Association ; War Pensions ; Red Cross ; Food Control. *Addresses :* Balcaskie, Pittenweem ; 10, Evelyn Mansions, London, S.W. *Clubs :* Queen's, Edinburgh ; New Victorian. (C95)

ANSTRUTHER, Eleonora, Hon. Mrs. James LLOYD-, M.B.E.

ANTHONY, Isaac John, M.B.E.

ANTILL, Lilian Mary, Mrs., C.B.E., *b.* 1879 ; *d.* of John Bassett Christian, of Tudor Elizabeth Bay, Sydney, N.S. Wales ; *m.* late Major E. A. Antill, Royal Aust. Field Artillery. *War Work :* Organiser of War Chest Fund at Sydney. *Address :* Javisfield, Picton, N.S. Wales. (C357)

ANTOINE, Ivy, Madame Andre, M.B.E., *b.* 18 April, 1884 ; *d.* of late Capt. Arthur Gooch, 16th Lancers, of 7, Queen's Gardens, Windsor ; *m.* André Joseph Antoine, *s.* of Monsieur C. E. Antoine, of Paris. *Educ. :* "The Beehive," Windsor. *War Work :* Worked at Bow House, Bow, for the late Lady St. Davids, also a short time at the Missing and Wounded Office, Norfolk House, Pall Mall ; 1915, went to Abbeville to work in The Church of England Soldiers' Rooms, where she stayed till March, 1919. *Address :* 101, Rue Gravel, Levallois, Perret, Seine. (M8227)

ANTROBUS, George Pollock, O.B.E.

APPERLY, David Cooper, M.B.E., *b.* 17 Feb. 1846 ; *s.* of David Apperly, of Stroud, Glos. ; *m.* 1st, Louisa, *d.* of James Mackenzie, of Kilmalcolm, 2ndly, Beatrice, *d.* of Dr. W. Soltau Eccles, of Norwood. *Educ. :* Privately. Hon. Treasurer, and Chairman of Council of Mr. Fegan's Homes Incorporated ; Director and Chairman of several Companies. *War Work :* Established and President of the Langton Green War Hospital Supply Depot (Affiliated to Queen Mary's Needlework Guild, Carpenters Branch). *Club :* Royal Automobile. (M7226)

APPLEBEY, Malcolm Percival, M.B.E.

APPLEBY, Capt. Geoffrey Edmund, M.B.E.

APPLEBY, Lieut.-Col. Kinloch Arthur, O.B.E.

APPLETON, Edith Elizabeth, O.B.E.

APPLETON, Janet, Mrs., M.B.E.; *d.* of the Rev. Canon Parish, Master of Greatham Hospital, Co. Durham; *m.* Rev. Charles Reginald, *s.* of the Rev. T. Appleton, Rector of Ludgershall, Bucks. *War Work:* V.A.D. work 1914–19 at 1st Durham Aux. Hospital, Whinney House, Gateshead, and at St. John's Ambulance Brigade Hospital, Saltwell Towers Gateshead. *Address:* 17, Osborne Terrace, Gateshead, Co. Durham. (M7227)

APPLETON, Mary, Mrs., M.B.E., *b.* 17 Oct. 1858; *d.* of Æneas Joseph Dymott, of London; *m.* Thomas Alfred, Surgeon, *s.* of James Appleton, of London. *Educ.:* Wells, Somerset. Commandant, V.A.D., L. 158. *War Work:* For 5 years Commandant and Organiser of the Red Cross Voluntary work, and Hon. Sec. of the Gifts and Comforts Department at Special Military Surgical Hospital, Shepherd's Bush; also under the Ministry of Pensions; One year at Fulham Military Hospital. *Address:* 34, Stevenage Road, Bishop's Park, Fulham, S.W. 6. (M7228)

APPLETON, William Archibald, C.B.E., *b.* 1859; *s.* of Edward John Appleton, of Lenton; Sec. Lace Makers' Trade Union, 1896–1907; Sec. Gen. Federation of Trade Unions; British Correspondent to International Federation of Trade Unions, and Member of Advisory Committee on National Insurance. *Address:* The Larches, Stevenage, Herts.; Hamilton House, Bidborough Street, W.C. 1. (C1)

APPLETON, Lieut. William Arnold, M.B.E., R.N.V.R.

APPLEYARD, Agnes, Mrs., M.B.E.,; *d.* of Hugh Dickie, B.A., LL.D., of Kilmarnock, Scotland; *m.* Charles W. Appleyard, *s.* of Isaac Appleyard, of Scarborough. *War Work:* On Administrative Committee of Gov.-General's Fund, Johannesburg; did special work in connection with Widows' pensions and the education of the War orphans. *Address:* 126, Houghton Drive Johannesburg. (M6341)

APPLEYARD, Major George Crossley, O.B.E.

APPLEYARD, Lieut. Rollo, O.B.E., R.N.V.R., D.S.O. O.B.E.

APPLIN, Lieut.-Col. Reginald Vincent Kempenfeldt, D.S.O., O.B.E., Commanding 14th (King's) Hussars, *b.* 11 April, 1869; *e.s.* of the late Capt. V. J. Applin, late R.M.T.; *m.* Beatrice Caroline Buchan. *Educ.:* Newton Coll. and Sherborne. Entered British North Borneo Service as a Cadet, 1889; served through Syed and Mat Salleh Rebellions, 1895–97 (medal and clasp); served through South African War, 1899–1901; District Commissioner, Bloemfontein (medal, 4 clasps, despatches twice, D.S.O.); battles Messines and Passchendaele, 1917 (despatches twice, Brevet Lieut.-Col.). *Address:* c/o Cox & Co., 16, Charing Cross, S.W. 1. *Club:* Junior United Service. (O8732)

APSEY, Sir John, K.B.E., *b.* 18 March, 1859; *s.* of the late John Apsey, of Sheerness; *m.* 1st, Esther Elizabeth (died 1917), *d.* of the late Nathaniel Finch, of Sheerness, 2nd, Mabel, *d.* of James Jesse Coles, South Hayling. *Educ.:* Royal Naval Coll., Greenwich. Manager of H.M. Dockyard, Portsmouth, since 1907; Chief Constructor, H.M. Dockyard, Malta, 1902; superintended the building of the following battleships of the Super-Dreadnought type, viz.: "Bellerophon," "St. Vincent," "Neptune," "Orion," "King George V.," "Iron Duke," "Queen Elizabeth," and "Royal Sovereign," these being in each case the leading ship of their class. *Address:* 2, The Parade, H.M. Dockyard, Portsmouth. (K450)

APTHORP, Beatrice Mary, O B E

ARBERY, Major James, M.B.E.

ARBUTHNOT, Constance, Lady, M.B.E.; *d.* of Sir William Milman, 3rd Bart. (*see* BURKE'S *Peerage*); *m.* Sir Alexander John Arbuthnot, K.C.S.I., C.I.E., *s.* of the Right Rev. Alexander Arbuthnot, D.D., Bishop of Killaloe. *Educ.:* Privately. Commandant, 130 Hants B.R.C.S.; Foundation Manager, Newtown School. *War Work:* Correspondent for Local Belgian-Relief Fund (Kingsclere) 1914–19; Correspondent for Newtown for Soldiers' and Sailors' Families Assoc. and for Group of workers under Newbury Hospital Supply Depot, 1915–19; convalescent officers received, 1915–16; Newtown House accepted for Auxiliary Hospital (Class A), and opened 17 Dec. 1916; enlarged to 31 beds, 1918; closed 30 June, 1919; organised Hospital and acted as commandant; mentioned in despatch, 1919. *Address:* Newtown House, Newbury. (M7229)

ARBUTHNOT, Elizabeth Fountaine, M.B.E. *Address:* 26, Cadogan Square, London, S.W.1.

ARBUTHNOT, Evelyn Mary, O B E.

ARBUTHNOT, Capt. Lionel Gough, M.B.E., *b.* 24 Sept. 1870; *s.* of Hugh Gough Arbuthnot. *Educ.:* Harrow and Trinity College, Cambridge. *War Work:* Enlisted Oct. 1914; Commission, April, 1915; proceeded to Gallipoli, Oct. 1915; remained until evacuation; served in Egypt, and proceeded to France, June, 1916; remained there until Aug. 1917, when severely wounded; after recovering, proceeded to Salonika, and was appointed A.D.C. to Gen. Plunkett, Chief of the Military Mission with the Serbian Army. Received the Serbian Order of the White Eagle. *Club:* M.C.C. (M5037)

ARBUTHNOT, Major Malcolm Alexander, O.B.E., *b.* 23 Sept. 1878; *s.* of W. R. Arbuthnot, late of Plawhatch, East Grimstead; *m.* Florence Jessie, *d.* of G. S. Boileau, of Sydney. *Educ.:* Trinity College, Cambridge. Stockbroker. *War Work:* 2nd Batt. Seaforth Highlanders, Western Front, till wounded, and then Staff Capt. and Deputy Assistant Adjutant-General, War Office. *Address:* 69, Courtfield Gardens, S.W. 5. *Club:* Wellington. (O6841)

ARCHDALE, Rev. Mervyn, O.B.E.

ARCHDALE, Capt. Nicholas Edward, C.B.E., R.N.

ARCHER, Major Basil Henry, O.B.E.

ARCHER, Henry George Fuller, O.B.E. (O11936)

ARCHER, Henry William, O.B.E.

ARCHER, Sir John, K.B.E., *b.* 13 June, 1860; *s.* of late John Archer, of Lenzie, Dumbartonshire; *m.* Ella Beatrice, *d.* of J. C. Sharpe, of Longhope, Glos. *Educ.:* Privately. *War Work:* Chairman, Advisory Committee, Customs and Excise, on Wines and Spirits, 1917–19. *Address:* Devonshire Lodge, Richmond, Surrey. *Clubs:* Junior Carlton; Constitutional; Royal Automobile. (K129)

ARCHER, Major John Oliver, O.B.E., R.F.A., S.R. *Address:* R.F.A., Woolwich, S.E.

ARCHER, Major Samuel Frank Alderson, O.B.E., F.A.

ARCHER, Thomas William, M.B.E.

ARCHER, William David, O.B.E., *b.* 4 March, 1860; *s.* of David Archer, of Croydon. *Educ.:* Whitgift School, Croydon. Late Principal Ship Surveyor, Board of Trade. *War Work:* Marine Department, Board of Trade. *Address:* 3, Birdhurst Rise, Croydon. (O9900)

ARCHEY, Capt. Gilbert Edward, O.B.E.

ARCHIBALD, David, M.B.E., *b.* 31 Aug. 1862. Station Master, Waverley Station, Edinburgh. *Address:* 2, West Mayfield, Edinburgh. (M7231)

ARCHIBALD, Major George Grassie, O.B.E.

ARD, Rachel Maud, M.B.E., *b.* 1871; *d.* of Rev. A. J. Ard, M.A., late Vicar of S. Savionia, Tollington Park, London, N. *Educ.:* At home, France and Italy with governesses. *War Work:* Commandant of Rusthale V.A.D. Hospital, Tunbridge Wells. *Address:* Heatherleigh, Hungershall Park, Tunbridge Wells. (M1)

ARDEE, Brig.-Gen. Lord Reginald Le Normand, C.B., C.B.E., *b.* 24 Nov. 1889; *s.* of 13th Earl of Meath; *m.* Aileen May, *d.* of 4th Earl of Dunraven. *Educ.:* Wellington College. Served in the South African War 1900–2 (Queen's Medal three clasps, King's Medal two clasps). *War Work:* Commanding 1st Batt. Grenadier Guards when war began; transferred to command of 1st Batt. Irish Guards, Sept. 1914; wounded Ypres, Nov. 1914; attached Munitions Inventions Department; 1915–16; commanded 4th Guards Brigade, Feb. to April, 1918; gassed, 1918; commandant Etaples Administrative District, June, 1918, to July, 1919. (C1216)

ARDERN, Frederick, M.B.E., *b.* 21 Dec. 1883; *s.* of Thomas Henry Ardern, of Stockport; *m.* Lavinia Mary, *d.* of James Royle, of Stockport. *Educ.:* Stockport and Manchester. Assistant Overseer and Collector of Rates for the parishes and Urban Districts of Handforth and Hazel Grove-cum-Bramhall; Secretary, Hazel Grove and Wilmslow War Pensions Committee (Cheshire); Member, Hazel Grove sub-committee, Cheshire Old Age Pensions Committee. *War Work:* Sub-District Representative, Sailors' and Soldiers' Families Association; Sub-District Representative Incorporated Sailors' and Soldiers' Help Society; Member, local Prince of Wales' Fund Committee; Hon. Sec., Ashton-under-Lyne and Stockport War Pensions District Committee, afterwards known as Hazel Grove and Wilmslow District Committee (Cheshire); Hon. Auditor, Hazel Grove War Savings Association; Special Constable, Cheshire County Constabulary. *Address:* "Withernsea," Queen's Road, Hazel Grove, Cheshire. (M7232)

ARGLES, Agnes, O.B.E., *b.* 21 March, 1866; *d.* of W. H. Wakefield, of Sedgwick, Kendal; *m.* Thomas A., *s.* of F. A. Argles, of Eversley, Milnthorpe. *War Work:* Chairman of Executive and Disablement Committees for Westmorland War Pensions; Commissioner for Westmorland Girl Guides; President of Westmorland Musical Festival. *Address:* Eversley, Milnthorpe, Westmorland. (O9901)

ARGLES, Capt. Guy Arthur Eustace, O.B.E., R.A.S.C.

ARGO, Archibald, M.B.E.

ARIS, Capt. Alexander Frederick, O.B.E., R.A.S.C.

ARKLE, Alderman Arthur Henry, O.B.E., J.P., *b.* 29 Aug. 1858; *s.* of W. B. Arkle, of Oxton, Birkenhead. *Educ.:* Marlborough. Chairman, Birkenhead Education Committee. *War Work:* Chairman, War Pensions Committee; Chairman, Recruiting Advisory Committee; Mayor of Birkenhead, 1914–1915. *Address:* Elmhurst, Oxton, Birkenhead. *Club:* Athenæum (Liverpool). (O9902)

ARKLE, Major John Stanley, O.B.E., M.B. R.A.M.C., *s.* of Thomas Nixon Arkle, of Gosforth, Northumberland; *m.* E. B., *d.* of William Wade, of Gosforth. Hon. Asst. to Ophthalmic Dept., Royal Victoria Infirmary, Newcastle-on-Tyne. *War Work:* Served with R.A.M.C., Sept. 1914 to Nov. 1915; attached to 12th Batt. The Royal Scots, Nov. 1915 to April, 1919; No. 3 Casualty Clearing Station. *Address:* 14, Jesmond Road, Newcastle-on-Tyne. (O2403)

ARKLIE, Edgar Vincent, M.B.E.

ARLAND, Lieut. John Alfred, M.B.E.

ARMAN, Edward William James, O.B.E., *b.* 24 Jan. 1856; *s.* of Orlando Arman, of Hungerford, Berks.; *m.* Kate Elizabeth, *d.* of Joseph Seelie Greenhow, of Chelmsford. *Educ.:* Hungerford Grammar School, and Privately. *War Work:* Member, Portsmouth War Pensions Committee; Member, Portsmouth War Economy Committee; Member, Portsmouth War Savings Committee; President, Portsmouth Post Office War Savings Association; Divisional Food Commissioner, South Midland Division; Hon. Sec. Berkshire County War Memorial. *Address:* 23, Kendrick Road, Reading. (O9903)

ARMBRUSTER, Major Charles Hubert, O.B.E.

ARMBRUSTER, Hubert, M.B.E.

ARMISTEAD, Thomas, M.B.E.

ARMITAGE, Cecil Henry, C.B.E., D.L., *b.* 1877; *s.* of

Frederick Armitage, of Northallerton, Yorks; *m.* Mary Marchent Edwards *d.* of John Edwards, of Taunton. *Educd.:* King William's College. County Red Cross Hon. Sec. an. County Director. *War Work:* County Director, Derbyshire; Red Cross County Hon. Sec.; Hon. Sec. Derbyshire Soldiers' Comforts Assoc. *Address:* Longstone Grange, near Bakewell, Derbyshire. *Club:* Derbyshire County. (C97)

ARMITAGE, Major Charles Leathley, D.S.O., O.B.E., *b.* 1871; *s.* of the late Rev. Arthur Armitage, of Breckenbrough, Cheltenham; *m.* 1901, Esther, who *d.* 1914, *d.* of Richard Armitage. *Educ.:* Winchester. Entered King's Liverpool Regt., 1892, and became Capt. 1900; retired 1907. *War Services:* Served during 1914–15, as Capt. and Brevet Major Worcestershire Regt. (wounded, despatches); is Ch. Constable of Southport. *Club:* Union (Southport). (O6844)

ARMITAGE, Elsie Barbara, M.B.E., *b.* 10 Sept. 1878; *d.* of A. C. Armitage, of Kirroughtree, Newton Stewart. *War Work:* Secretary, British Soldiers' and Sailors' Institute, Boulogne. *Address:* Kirroughtree, Newton Stewart, Scotland. (M3492)

ARMITAGE, Ethel, Mrs., M.B.E.

ARMITAGE, Louisa Mary, O.B.E., *b.* 12 Aug. 1864; *d.* of S. F. Armitage, J.P., of Pell Hall, Little Hulton, Bolton, Lancs. *Educ.:* Mme. Yeatman's School, Neuilly, Paris. *War Work:* From 1912 to 1920 worked amongst the British Soldiers in Miss Sande's Homes, of which there are eight in India. *Address:* Sutton Seale, Macclesfield, Cheshire. (O9804)

ARMITAGE, Capt. Philip Melland, O.B.E., R.F.A. (T.F.).

ARMITAGE, Stanley Holt, O.B.E.

ARMITAGE, T. 2nd Lieut. Walter Cleveland, M.B.E., R.A.S.C.

ARMITAGE, Major William Bryan, O.B.E., late R.A.F., now Capt. 8th Bn. Lancashire Fusiliers (T.F.)

ARMITSTEAD, Henry, M.B.E.

ARMITSTEAD, 2nd Lieut. Thomas, M.B.E.

ARMOUR, George Denholm, O.B.E., *b.* 30 Jan. 1864; *s.* of Robert Armour, of Waterside, Busby, Lanarkshire; *m.* Mary Emma, *d.* of John Robb. *Educ.:* St. Andrews. *War Work:* In Army Remount Service; appointed to command of F. Squadron, Remount Depot, Swaythling, April, 1915, with rank of Major; exchanged to Salonica, June, 1917, to command 42nd Remount Squadron; in Dec. 1917 was promoted to Staff as D.A.D.R. and to command Remount Depot, Salonica, with temporary rank of Lieut.-Col.; awarded Greek Military Medal, 3rd Class. *Address:* Parkside, Corsham, Wilts. *Club:* Savage. (O6431)

ARMOUR, Major John Douglas, O.B.E.

ARMOUR, William Staveley, M.B.E., M.A., Barrister-at-Law, *b.* 28 Dec. 1883; *s.* of the Rev. J. B. Armour, M.A., of Ballymoney Ireland. *Educ.:* Campbell Coll., Belfast; Jesus Coll. Oxford. President Oxford Union, 1907. Indian Education Service; Headmaster, Queen's Coll. School, Benares; Inspector of Schools, Lucknow, etc. *War Work:* On Special Duty, Northern Army Headquarters, India, 1917; Supt. Publicity Bureau, Education Dept. U.P., 1918–19. (M6101)

ARMSTRONG, Arthur Campbell, O.B.E.

ARMSTRONG, Capt. Cyril, M.B.E., R.A.M.C., *b.* 11 May 1893; *s.* of John H. Armstrong, of Sunderland; *m.* Elizabeth Childs, *d.* of the late Stanley Dorling, of Sunderland. *Educ.:* Argyle House School, Sunderland. *War Work:* Served with No. 10, General Hospital; 1/5 Lincolnshire Regt., France, 1914–15; West Africa, May, 1916, to July, 1917; Registrar, Military Hospital, Rochester Row, S.W. 1., Sept. 1917 to May, 1919. *Address:* Raincliffe, Roker, Sunderland. (M5038)

ARMSTRONG, Capt. Francis Harold Courtenay, O.B.E.

ARMSTRONG, Francis Joseph, O.B.E., *b.* 14 Jan. 1865; *s.* of the late Joseph Armstrong, of Ipswich; *m.* Annie May, *d.* of the late Frederick Davies, of London. *Educ.:* Ipswich. Junior Assistant Secretary, in the Scottish Education Department, and Secretary to the Advisory Council of the Department. *War Work:* Increased departmental duties owing to the absence, on military service, of the younger members of the staff, and evening work on munitions. *Address:* 7, Rillbank Terrace, Edinburgh. (O3604)

ARMSTRONG, Lieut.-Col. Francis Logie, O.B.E., *b.* 5 Sept. 1886; *s.* of C. N. Armstrong, of Montreal, Canada; *m.* Marjorie Hilton, *d.* of Lieut.-Col. A. J. Wilkes, K.C., of Brantford, Canada *Educ.:* St. Alban's School, Royal Military College, Kingston. Director of Records, Department of Militia and Defence, Ottawa. *War Work:* D.A.A.G. Canadian Record Office, London; Staff Captain 4th Can. Inf. Brigade, France; General Staff Officer H.Q. 3rd Can. Div. France; Officer-in-Charge Canadian Records, London, Eng.; Director of Records, Militia H.Q. Ottawa. *Address:* Rockcliffe, Ottawa, Canada. *Clubs:* Junior Naval and Military; Royal Ottawa Golf. (O97)

ARMSTRONG, Comm. Francis Philip, O.B.E., R.N.V.R., *b.* 16 Oct. 1871 *s.* of Sir G. C. H. Armstrong, Bart.; *m* Pucheria Margaret, *d.* of George Fox, J.P., D.L., of Elmhurst Hall, Lichfield. *Educ.:* Charterhouse and Magdalen College, Oxford. *War Work:* Aug. 1914, to Feb. 1916, Admiralty; Feb. 1916, to Feb. 1917, in charge of Commission for selection of officers and mechanics for Auxiliary Patrol in Canada and New Zealand; Mar. 1916, to Dec. 1918, Commander Yacht Patrol, Portsmouth, and in Command of Coastal Motor-boat Base at Haslar; Jan. 1919, to Aug. 1919, Assistant Maintenance Captain, Portsmouth. *Address:* Oxleys, Beaulieu, Hants. *Club:* Junior Carlton.

ARMSTRONG, Capt. George Medlicott, O.B.E., R.A.O.C.

ARMSTRONG, Capt. George William, M.B.E., R.F.A.

ARMSTRONG, Lieut.-Col. Godfrey George, O.B.E.

ARMSTRONG, Henry, O.B.E.

ARMSTRONG, Capt. Howard Wolfenden, M.B.E.

ARMSTRONG, Major James Alexander, O.B.E.

ARMSTRONG, Col. John Alexander, C.M.G., C B.E., *b.* 1862; *s.* of late Thomas Armstrong; *m.* 1890, Ida, who *d.* 1904, *d.* of — Spittal. *Educ.:* Toronto Univ. Is a Surg. Dentist, Col. Canadian Forces, and Director of Dental Sers. Overseas Mil. Forces of Canada; was a Member of Public Sch. Board, Ottawa, 1906–17 (elected Chm. 1912). *Address:* 102, James Street, Ottawa. *Clubs:* National Liberal; Sports'; Wellington: Laurentian (Ottawa). (C1827)

ARMSTRONG, John Henry Nicholas, O.B.E.

ARMSTRONG, John Warneford Scobell, C.B.E., *b.* 1 Mar. 1877; *s.* of John Scobell Armstrong, of Nancealverne, near Penzance. *Educ.:* Abroad. Called to the Bar at the Inner Temple on 5 July, 1905, and joined the Western Circuit; author of the "Trade Continuation Schools of Germany," published by the Eighty Club in 1913. *War Work:* Assistant Postal Censor, 1914–15; from 1915 to June, 1919, was in charge of a subsection of the Directorate of Military Intelligence, War Office, and responsible to the Chief Postal Censor for the policy of the Postal Censorship in relation to Commerce and to the Economic Blockade; from June, 1919, to Feb. 1920, served as Temp. Assistant Legal Adviser to the Foreign Office; now serving as Temp. Legal Adviser to the Reparation Claims Department of the Board of Trade. Received, 25 June, 1920, Les Palmes d' Officier d' Academic conferred by the President of the French Republic. *Address:* 5, Montagu Street, Portman Sq., London, W. *Clubs:* St. James'; Eighty; M.C.C. (C2424)

ARMSTRONG, John William, O.B.E.

ARMSTRONG, Nevill Alexander Drummond, O.B.E.

ARMSTRONG, Robert Bayles, M.B.E.

ARMSTRONG, Capt. Samuel Richard, O.B.E., R.A.M.C.

ARMSTRONG, Capt. Sereld John, O.B.E., M.C., R.E., *b.* 25 May, 1894; *s.* of Rear-Admiral J. G. Armstrong. *Educ.:* Cheltenham College and Royal Military Academy, Woolwich. *War Work:* France, Jan. 1915 to Nov. 1918, in 2nd Field Squadron. *Address:* Brompton Barracks, Chatham. *Club:* United Service. (O4963)

ARMSTRONG, 2nd Lieut. Thomas Edward Steele, M.B.E.

ARMSTRONG, Col. Thomas Graves Lowry Herbert, C.B.E., *b.* 1586; Col. and Hon. Brig.-Gen. (ret.); Great War, 1914–19 (despatches). (C1446)

ARMSTRONG, Flight.-Lieut. Tom, M.B.E., R.A.F.; L.R.C.S.

ARMYTAGE, Frederic Fairburn, M.B.E., L.R.C.P. and S. Ed., L.F.P. and S.G., *b.* 18 March, 1861; *s.* of James Armytage, of Hartshead, Yorks. *Educ.:* Edinburgh University. *War Work:* Med. Officer to Clifford Street and Nunthorpe Hall V.A.D. Hospitals, York, and Askham Grange V.A.D. Hospital, near York. *Address:* Acomb, York. (M7235)

ARNEIL, Lieut. London, O.B.E., R.F.A.

ARNISON, Christine Mary, M.B.E.; *d.* of William Prince Trustram, of Cheapside, London; *m.* William Drewett, *s.* of George Arnison, of Allendale, Northumberland. *Educ.:* Blackheath High School, London, S.E. *War Work:* 1st Northern General Hospital, Newcastle. *Address:* 4, Lovaine Place, Newcastle-on-Tyne. (M7236)

ARNOLD, Capt. Alfred Henry, O.B.E., *b.* 4 Aug. 1890. Esquire of Order of St. John of Jerusalem in England; Order of Nile (4th Class); Chevalier, Order King George of Greece; mentioned in despatches. *War Work:* Secretary, H.Q. Collections Committee, B.R.C.S. and Order of St. John, 1914; attached H.Q. Staff, Red Cross Commission, France, 1914–15; Secretary, Malta, Egypt, and Near East Commissions, B.R.C.S. and Order of St. John, 1915–19. *Address:* 2, Sherbrook Gardens, Winchmore Hill, N. 21. (O9906)

ARNOLD, Col. Alfred James, C.B.E., D.S.O., *b.* 1866; *s.* of Alfred Roberts Arnold, of Bournemouth; *m.* H. May, *d.* of the late R. Hardwick, J.P., of Cheshire. *Educ.:* Privately and Corpus Christi College, Cambridge. *War Work:* Commanded 20th Batt. Manchester Regt., also 1st G. B. Royal Welsh Fusiliers. *Address:* Hafod Wen, Harlech. *Clubs:* Arthur's; Cavalry; British Empire. (C798)

ARNOLD, Major Allan Cholmondeley, O.B.E., M.C.

ARNOLD, Hon. Lieut.-Col. Francis Havard, O.B.E., R.A.O.C.

ARNOLD, Capt. George, M.B.E., *b.* 21 Feb. 1862; *s.* of George and Sarah Arnold, of Goole; *m.* Sarah Ellen, *d.* of Jonathan Sales, of Goole. *Educ.:* National School, Goole. Master Mariner in the employ of the Lancashire and Yorkshire Railway Co. *War Work:* Employed in Cross-Channel Transport during the whole of the War. *Address:* 4, Sutton Street, Goole. (M3493)

ARNOLD, Henry George, M.B.E.

ARNOLD, Lieut.-Col. Herbert Tollemache, C.B.E. D.S.O., *b.* 1867; Major, Brevet Lieut.-Col., and Staff-Paymaster Army Pay Depart.; Great War, 1914–18 (despatches), was 2nd class Assist. Accountant, Accounts Depart., 1905–9. (C1217)

ARNOLD, Percy, O.B.E.

ARNOT, John Wilkie, M.B.E. Works Manager and Engineer to the Hereford Filling Factory. (M10304)

ARNOT, Capt. William, O.B.E.

ARNOT, Lieut. William Mills, M.B.E., R.A.F. (T.F.)

ARNOTT, Caroline Sydney, Lady, D.B.E., Lady of Grace of the Order of St. John of Jerusalem, J.P., *b.* 22 March, 1859 ; *d.* of Sir Frederick Williams, 2nd Bart., of Tregullow, Cornwall, and Heanton Court, N. Devon ; *m.* Sir John Arnott, Bart. *s.* of Sir John Arnott, 1st Bart., of Woodlands, Cork (*see* BURKE'S *Peerage*). *War Work :* Vice-President for Dublin City Branch of the Sailors' and Soldiers' Help Society ; President, Dublin Committee of " Farewell " to British Troops, Aug. 1914 ; President and Organiser, Dublin Depot for Food Supplies to the Prisoners of War of the Royal Dublin Fusiliers ; Chairman, National War Savings Committee for Leinster, Munster and Connaught ; Chairman, National Waste Paper Department of Irish Hospital Supply Depot. *Address :* 12, Merrion Square, Dublin. (D9)

ARNOTT, Major Edward Whiston, O.B.E., R.F.A. (T.F. Reserve), *b.* 7 May, 1883 ; *s.* of the late Edward Arnott, J.P., of the Garth, Monmouth ; *m.* Julia, *d.* of the late William Alfred Baker, J.P., of Avishays, Newport. Barrister, Inner Temple ; Assistant Secretary, War Compensation Court. *War Work :* Served with Expeditionary Forces in France and Egypt ; 1914-15 Star. *Address :* 11, Old Court Mansions, Kensington, London, W. 8. *Clubs :* Junior Carlton ; New University. (O6846)

ARNOTT, Florence Evelyn, Mrs., M.B.E.

ARNOTT, Francis William, M.B.E., *b.* 21 Sept. 1888 ; *s.* of Thomas Richard, of Coventry ; *m.* Ellen Annie, *d.* of Arthur Henton, of Leamington Spa. *Educ.:* Bablake and King Henry VIII. Schools, Coventry. Superintendent, Carriage and Erecting Dept., The Daimler Co., Ltd., Coventry. *War Work :* Superintendent, Aeroplane Dept., The Daimler Co., Ltd., Coventry. *Address :* 35, Chester Street, Coventry. (M7237)

ARRIGO, Edgar, M.B.E., *b.* 15 April, 1870 ; *s.* of Oswald Arrigo, of Valetta, Malta ; *m.* Marietta, *d.* of Alfonso Rocco Peralta, of Valetta. *Educ.:* Lyceum, Malta. *War Work :* At the Secretariat, Malta. *Addresses :* 126, Strada San Domenico, Valetta ; Casino Maltese, Valetta. (M6410)

ARSCOTT, Capt. William Herbert, O.B.E.

ARTHUR, Major Harry Robert, O.B.E., R.A.O.C.

ARTHUR, Janet Stevenson Bennet, Lady, M.B.E.

ARTHUR, Capt. John Stanley, O.B.E., B.Sc. (Lond.), A.I.C., R.A.M.C. T.F., *b.* 1887 ; *s.* of John Joseph Arthur, of Dulwich, S.E. ; *m.* Mabel, *d.* of Edmund Burges Horner, of Lincs. *Educ.:* Alleyn's School, Dulwich, S.E. ; London University. Chemist ; Senior Assistant to Lee's Reader of Chemistry, Christ Church, Oxford, 1904–11 ; Science Master, Oxford High School, 1912–16 ; Assistant Chemist to the Empire Motor Fuels Committee, 1920. *War Work :* Officer-in-charge, War Office Experimental Water Station ; introduced the system of Sterilisation of Water by Chlorine Gas, as adopted by the War Office ; designer of Water Purification Plants for War Office, 1916–19, and India Office, 1919–20. *Address :* 2, Halsmere Road, Myatt's Park, S.E. 5. (O8735)

ARTHUR, Rev. John William, O.B.E., M.D., Ch.B., *b.* 23 April, 1881 ; *s.* of John William Arthur, of Glasgow, Scotland. *Educ.:* Glasgow Academy and Glasgow University. Ordained Medical Missionary and Chairman of the Mission Council of the Church of Scotland Mission, Kikuyu, British East Africa. *War Work :* Captain and Officer Commanding the Kikuyu Missions Volunteers (K.M.V.), attached to the Military Labour Bureau (M.L.B.), the German East Africa Expeditionary Force ; served from 16 April, 1917, to 16 Jan. 1918. *Addresses :* 9, Athole Gardens, Glasgow ; Church of Scotland Mission, Kikuyu, Kenya Colony. *Club :* Nairobi. (O9907)

ARTHUR, Major Lionel Francis, D.S.O., O.B.E., 26th Cav. (O11723)

ARTHUR, Olive Juana, Mrs. James, M.B.E.

ARUNDEL, Grace, M.B.E.

ARUNDELL, Lieut.-Col. Hon. George Vere Arundell MONCKTON-, D.S.O., O.B.E., 1st Life Guards, *b.* 24 March, 1882 ; *e.s.* of the 7th Viscount Galway. *Educ.:* Christ Church, Oxford. Served Great War, 1914–17 (despatches, D.S.O.). *Address :* Serlby, Bawtry, Yorks. (O5588)

ASBRIDGE, Harry Hales, M.B.E.

ASCOTT, Major William, O.B.E., D.A.D.V.S. 43rd (Wessex) Div., *b.* 29 May, 1864 ; *s.* of Henry Ascott, J.P., of Bideford ; *m.* Frances Anne, *d.* of William John Keyte, of Westward Ho ! *Educ.:* Devon County School. Veterinary Surgeon. *War Work :* At Mobilisation was a Capt., R.A.V.C., (T.F.), attached to R. N. Devon Yeomanry ; did duty on East Coast until Regt. sent to Gallipoli as Infantry in Sept. 1915 ; then sent to France, seeing service first with the 12th Div. and from Oct. 1916, to March, 1919, with the 56th Div., as D.A.D.V.S. ; thrice mentioned in despatches ; awarded O.B.E. (Mil.), and Order de Reconnaisance (France). *Address :* West Bridge, Bideford, North Devon. (O2404)

ASCOUGH, Matthew Mather, M.B.E.

ASCROFT, Lieut. Robert William, M.B.E.

ASH, Alfred James, O.B.E.

ASH, T. 2nd Lieut. Ernest, O.B.E.

ASH, T. Lieut. Frederick Cecil, M.B.E., M.G.C.

ASH, Major Harold Garton, O.B.E., M.C., *b.* 26 June, 1884 ; *s.* of the late Charles Frederick Ash, of Derwent House, Finchley. *War Work :* Joined from T.F. reserve, Aug. 1914 ; service with 2/17th Batt. London Regt. ; Staff Capt., 180th Infy. Brigade, March, 1915 to Dec. 1917 ; appointed D.A.Q.M.G., Yeomanry Div. (afterwards 4th Cavalry Div.), Dec. 1917, to Dec. 1918 ; and served in France, 1916,

afterwards Salonika, 1917, and Palestine, 1917–18. *Address :* Grassmere, Edgware, Middlesex. (O6131)

ASH, Capt. William Maxwell VACY-, O.B.E.

ASHCROFT, Capt. William, M.B.E.

ASHDOWN, Sir George Henry, K.B.E., I.S.O., Legion of Honour, D S M. American Navy, *b.* 1857 Director of Stores, Admiralty. *Address :* Waratah, Effingham Road, Surbiton. (K341)

ASHER, Augustus Gordon Grant, C.B.E., *b.* 18 Dec. 1861 ; *s.* of John Gordon Asher, Major, Bombay Staff Corps ; *m.* Emme Berry, *d.* of Charles George Barclay, of Dura, Cupar, Fife. *Educ.:* Loretto and Brasenose College, Oxford. County Clerk and Treasurer of Midlothian ; Secretary of Association of County Councils in Scotland ; Clerk of Lieutenancy of Midlothian. *War Work :* Confidential work in connection with the Defence of the East Coast of Scotland ; Hon. Sec. National Relief Fund for Midlothian ; Hon. Sec. Midlothian War Savings Committee. *Address :* 10, Atholl Crescent, Edinburgh. *Clubs :* New Edinburgh ; Wellington. (C424)

ASHFORD, Major and Qr.-Mr. Frederick Henry, O.B.E., R.E.

ASHFORD Capt. John. O.B.E., M.I.Mech.E., *b.* 1870 ; *s.* of Francis E. Ashford, of Birmingham ; *m.* Annie, *d.* of G. Shelvoke, of Handsworth. *Educ.:* Private School and Sir Josiah Mason's Science College, Birmingham. Engineer. Superintendent Central Workshop Division, Public Works Department, Punjab, India. *War Work :* Manufacture of Munitions and other Military requirements. *Address :* Amritsar, Punjab, India. (O2084)

ASHFORD, Mary Adelaide, Mrs., M.B.E.

ASHFORD, William, O.B.E., M.R.C.S., L.R.C.P., *b.* 18 Dec. 1871 ; *s.* of the late William Ashford, of Woodbury, Devon ; *m.* Elise Mary, *d.* of Capt. Charles Irwin, of R. Irish Fusiliers. *Educ.:* Exeter and St. Thomas' Hospital, London. Medical Practitioner. *War Work :* Topsham V.A. Hospital ; Medical Officer, Nov. 1914, to March, 1915 ; O.C. and M.O. March, 1915, to April, 1919 ; Medical Officer to troops at Topsham, and Member of Exeter Medical Board. *Address :* 1, Riversmeet Terrace, Topsham, Devon. (O9909)

ASHHURST, William Henry, C.B.E., *b.* 29 Dec. 1851 ; *s.* of John Henry Ashhurst, of Waterstock (*see* BURKE'S *Landed Gentry*) ; *m.* Catherine Sophia, *d.* of Arthur Henry Clarke Brown, Kingston Blount, Oxon. *Educ.:* Eton and Cambridge. Chairman Oxfordshire County Council ; D.L. and J.P. Oxon. *War Work :* Chairman Ashhurst War Hospital, Littlemore, Oxon. ; Member of the County Recruiting Committee. *Address :* Waterstock, Wheatley S.O., Oxford. *Clubs :* Carlton ; Oxfordshire County. (C2425)

ASHLEY, Anne, M.B.E.,; *d.* of Sir William Ashley, Vice-Principal, University of Birmingham (*see* BURKE'S *Peerage*). *Educ.:* Edgbaston High School for Girls and University of Birmingham. Assistant Organiser, Central Care Committee (under Birmingham Education Committee), 1913–16, Board of Trade, 1916–20. Recorder of Section F (Economic Science and Statistics) of British Association for the Advancement of Science, 1916. *Address :* 40, Mortlake Road, Kew. (M7239)

ASHLEY, Ernest Gilman, M.B.E.

ASHLEY, Lieut.-Col. Frank, C.B.E., Croix de Guerre, *b.* 1870 ; *m.* Cecilia, *d.* of F. C. Walker. *Educ.:* Clifton Coll. British Red Cross Commissioner, Malta. *Address :* Southcroft, Stratford-on-Avon. (C99)

ASHLEY, Martha Nixon Greenwood, Mrs., M.B.E.; *d.* of C. V. F. Greenwood, of Middletown, N.J., U.S.A. ; *m.* Harry Leigh Ashley, *s.* of the late Atherton Edward. *Educ.:* Saint Gabriel's School, Peekskill, New York, U.S.A. *War Work :* Organised Red Cross Work and Surgical Dressings Bureau in Havana, Cuba. *Addresses :* King's Highway Farm, Middletown, New Jersey, U.S.A. ; c/o United Railways of Havana, Havana, Cuba. (M7240)

ASHMOLE, William Hadley, M.B.E., *b.* 5 Aug. 1874 ; *s.* of Elias Ashmole, of Kent. *Educ.:* Swansea. Borough Treasurer of Swansea. *War Work :* Hon. Sec. Local War Savings Committee ; organised War Loan Campaigns ; Treasurer to War Pensions Committee, Prince of Wales' Fund, Mayor's War Comforts Fund, etc. *Address :* Guildhall, Swansea. *Clubs :* Swansea and County. (M7241)

ASHTON, Antonio, O.B.E.

ASHTON, Arthur, M.B.E.

ASHTON, Major Cecil Charles Gough, O.B.E.

ASHTON, George Kerfoot, M.B.E.

ASHTON, Harold, M.B.E.

ASHTON, Helen, Mrs., O.B.E., *b.* 1869 ; *d.* of the Rev. Speer Willis, M.A., R. of St. Matthew's, Manly, N.S. Wales ; *m.* 1898, the Hon. James Ashton, M.L.C. *War Work :* With N.S. Wales Div., Australian Red Cross (Order of Reconnaissance Française). *Address :* Theila, Double Bay, Sydney, N.S. Wales. (O2142)

ASHTON, Capt. John Herbert, M.B.E.

ASHTON, Joseph, O.B.E.

ASHTON, Paymr.-Lieut. Reginald William Alexander, O.B.E., R.N.

ASHTON, Capt. and Qr.-Mr. Robert, M.B.E. R.A.M.C.

ASHWELL, Lieut.-Col. Herbert George, O.B.E., R.A.M.C.

ASHWELL, Lena Margaret, O.B.E., *b.* 1871 ; *d.* of Capt. Chas. Ashwell Botter Pocock, R.N., of the Royal Navy ; *m.* Henry John Forbes. *s.* of Robert Simson. *Educ.:* Church School, Toronto ; Trinity University ; and in Switzerland. Actress ; Proprietor and Manager of Kingsway Theatre.

War Work: Organiser of the movement called "Concerts at the Front," which sent concerts and entertainments to the fighting men during the war, in France, Egypt and Palestine; also to the men of the Adriatic Fleet; entertainments at the rate of 14,000 a year were being given at the time of the Armistice; 600 artistes helped Miss Ashwell in this work, and one hundred thousand pounds was raised. *Address:* 36, Grosvenor Street, W. 1. (O57)

ASHWORTH, Tom, M.B.E., *b.* 18 Oct. 1867; *s.* of the late Thomas Lewis Ashworth, of Heathwood, Bowdon, Cheshire. *Educ.:* Bowdon College. *War Work:* Chairman of the Altrincham District War Pensions Committee; Hon. Sec. National Relief Fund, Altrincham; Hon. National Registration Clerk, Altrincham U.D.C.; Hon. Sec. Altrincham Bowdon Hale and District Committee War Pensions Acts, 1915–18. *Address:* Heathwood, Heald Road, Bowdon, Cheshire. *Club:* Conservative (Altrincham). (M7243)

ASHWORTH, Wilfred Adam, M.B.E.

ASKEW, Percy, M.B.E., *b.* 27 March, 1876. *Educ.:* Hutton Grammar School. *War Work:* Acting Paymaster, Army Pay Dept., Preston; mentioned in despatches, March, 1919. *Address:* 18, Queen's Road, Fulwood, Preston. (M7244)

ASKIN, Thomas Cuming, M.B.E., B.A., M.D. (T.C.D.), J.P., Suffolk, *b.* 11 March, 1864; *s.* of the late Rev. W. B. Askin, M.A., of Dublin. *Educ.:* Royal School, Armagh, and Trinity College, Dublin. Medical Practitioner. *War Work:* Civilian Medical Practitioner in charge of 17 Cyclist Batt., Devonshire Regt., 1916–17, and 28 Cyclist Batt., Essex Regt., 1917–18, at Bawdsey Manor and Hollesley, Suffolk, also other troops. *Address:* Alderton, Woodbridge, Suffolk. (M10261a)

ASKWITH, Ellen, Lady, C.B.E., *d.* of the late Archibald Peel, of Westlea, Herts.; *m.* George Ranken, Lord Askwith, *s.* of the late General Askwith, R.A., 119, St. George's Square, Military Attaché in Spain. *Educ.:* At home. *War Work:* Lady President Y.M.C.A. London Docks; organised and ran 6 Canteens there; organised the Horseferry Road Hostel and Canteen (taken over by the Australians); started first National Kitchen; sat on three Govt. Committees—Women's Unemployment, War Savings, Imperial War Museum. *Addresses:* 5, Cadogan Gardens, London, S.W. 3; Oak Knoll, Sunningdale. (C100)

ASLETT, William Stacey, M.B.E., M.R.C.S., L.R.C.P.

ASPDEN, Hartley, C.B.E., J.P., *b.* 1858. Director for many years of Amalgamated Press, Ltd.; present Director of J. Sears & Co. (Trueform Boot Co.) Ltd.; the Leigh Trust, Ltd. *War Work:* Organising Director of the Beyond Seas Association which includes the Royal Club for Overseas Ladies; the New Zealand Officers' Club and the Canadian Officers' Club. *Address:* West Court, Purley Surrey. *Club:* National Liberal, S.W. (C924)

ASPINALL, Gladys Hester. See Birks, Gladys Helen.

ASPINALL, Lieut.-Col. Hugh Harry Haworth, O.B.E., I.A.

ASTBURY, Sarah, M.B.E.

ASTIN, Arthur, M.B.E.

ASTLE, William, O.B.E., J.P., *b.* 9 Nov. 1869; *s.* of William Astle, of Heaton Norris; *m.* Lillie, *d.* of John Hulme, of Heaton Norris. *Educ.:* Stockport. Managing Editor, "Stockport Advertiser," and "Cheshire Daily Echo"; President, Lancashire, Cheshire and Derbyshire Federation of Weekly Newspapers. *War Work:* Largely in connection with assistance to wives and families of soldiers and sailors serving in the war in following voluntary capacities: Hon. Sec. Stockport Division, Soldiers' and Sailors' Families Association, and Soldiers' and Sailors' Help Society; Hon. Sec. Stockport War Pensions Committee, and Chairman, Cheshire County War Pensions Committee. *Address:* Overdale, Bramhall, Cheshire. (O9911)

ASTON, Major Reginald Godfrey, O.B.E., R.E.

ASTON, Capt. Thomas, M.B.E.

ATCHERLEY, Ethel Mary, M.B.E.

ATCHESON, William, O.B.E.

ATCHLEY, Major Charles Atherton, O.B.E., R.E.

ATHA, Charles Gurney, O.B.E.

ATHERTON, Lieut.-Col. George Bramall, O.B.E.

ATHERTON, T. Major Stanley, O.B.E.

ATHERTON, Lieut. William Thomas Finlay, M.B.E., R.F.A.

ATHOLL, Dame Katherine Marjory, Duchess of, D.B.E., *b.* 6 Nov. 1874; *d.* of Sir James Ramsay, 10th Bt. of Bamff (*see* BURKE'S *Peerage*); *m.* 1899, John George Stewart Murray, K.T., C.B., M.V.O., 8th Duke of Atholl (*see* BURKE'S *Peerage*). (D24)

ATKIN, Lieut. Edward, O.B.E., R.G.A.

ATKIN, Capt. Percy Harland, O.B.E., J.P., *b.* 26 July, 1863; *s.* of the late G. Atkin, of Wharncliffe, Yorkshire. *Educ.:* University and King's Colleges, London. Barrister-at-law, Oxford Circuit; formerly Capt., Lancashire Fusiliers, served in Boer War, 1899–1901; Military Commandant of Hopetown District; J.P., Cape Colony; British Commissioner to St. Louis Exhibition, U.S.A., 1904, and to New Zealand International Exhibition, 1906. *War Work:* Employed in Special Confidential Enquiries at New Scotland Yard, and as Secretary to a Military Service Committee under National Service Ministry. *Address:* Hadlow Park, Hadlow, Kent; 3, Plowden Buildings, Temple, E.C. 4. *Clubs:* Garrick; Constitutional; Cecil. (O3605)

ATKIN, Peter Wilson, O.B.E., M.A., LL.M., J.P., *b.* 4 Feb. 1859; *s.* of George Atkin, J.P., of Rock Ferry, Cheshire; *m.*

Netley Everett, *d.* of William Keyser, of Pensacola, Florida, U.S.A. *Educ.:* Royal Institution, Liverpool; Mill Hill School; Jesus College, Cambridge. Stipendiary Magistrate of Salford. *War Work:* Chairman Salford Tribunal; Chairman of Moorlands Hospital, Kersal. *Address:* 6, Park Lane, Kersal, Manchester. *Clubs:* Liverpool Reform; Brazenose, Manchester; Reform, London; Leander. (O101)

ATKINS, Charles Henry, M.B.E., R.A.S.C.

ATKINS, Gertrude, M.B.E.

ATKINS, Capt. Henry Albert, M.B.E. *b.* 9 April, 1871; *s.* of J. W. Atkins, of Slough, Bucks.; *m.* Frances Hannah, *d.* of William Rigelsford, of Woolston. *Educ.:* British School, Slough. Enlisted in 19th Hussars, 21 Nov. 1888; proceeded with regiment to India, 1891; left India for South Africa, Sept. 1899; took part in Boer War, including the following engagements and operations: Tinta Inyoni, Lombard's Kop, Defence of Ladysmith, Laings Nek, Orange Free State, Belfast, Lydenburg, Western Transvaal; granted Queen's Medal with 4 clasps, King's S.A. Medal with 2 clasps, Medal for Long Service and good conduct; discharged as Squadron Sergeant Major, Nov. 1911; enlisted in Staffs. Yeomanry, 6 Mar. 1912; appointed S.S.M. same date. *War Work:* Mobilised on 4 Aug. 1914; commissioned as Lieut. and Qr.-Mr., 28 April, 1915, proceeded overseas (Egypt), Oct. 1915; Western Desert; 1916; operations on Sinai Peninsula, 1916–17; mentioned in despatches, 6 July, 1917; first and second battles of Gaza, Beersheba, Jerusalem; invalided to England, Feb. 1918; served in Ireland, 1918, until Aug. 1919. *Address:* 33, St. John's Street, Wolverhampton. (M5040)

ATKINS, Mary Clara Crofton, M.B.E.

ATKINS, Major William Ringrose Gelston, O.B.E.

ATKINS, Col. Cyril Randell CROFTON-, C.B.E., *b.* 1867; Col. Notts and Derbyshire Regt., and a T. Brig.-Gen.; Sierra Leone, 1898–9 (medal with clasp); S. Africa, 1899–1902 (despatches, Brevet Major, Queen's medal with four clasps, King's medal with two clasps; Great War, 1914–19 (despatches). (C1533)

ATKINSON, Alice Lilian, O.B.E.; *d.* of the late Wm. Chapman Atkinson. *Educ.:* Ladies' College, Cheltenham, and Newnham College, Cambridge. Classical Mistress, St. George's School, Edinburgh. *War Work:* In Queen Mary's Army Auxiliary Corps: (1) was Senior Area Controller in Western Command, 1917; (2) as Controller, was head of the Corps in Scotland, 1918–20. *Address:* 19, Pentland Terrace, Edinburgh. *Club:* University, W. 1. (O3084)

ATKINSON, Lieut. Arthur, O.B.E., R.E.

ATKINSON, Capt. Arthur George, M.B.E., M.D., *b.* 3 May, 1881; *s.* of J. G. Atkinson. *Educ.:* St. Olave's Grammar School, London and Trinity Coll., Cambridge. Physician and Surgeon. *War Work:* R.A.M.C. (T.F.), Oct. 1914 to April, 1919. *Address:* 27, Sunham Road, Upper Norwood, S.E. 19. (M5041)

ATKINSON, Major Arthur Joseph, M.B.E. Esquire of the Order of St. John of Jerusalem.

ATKINSON, Carleton Richard Buckley, M.B.E.

ATKINSON, Dorothea, Mrs., M.B.E., *b.* 1881; *s.* of Charles F. Hicks, of Silverdale, Lancs.; *m.* John Parkinson, *s.* of Dr. John P. Atkinson, of Saffron Walden. *Educ.:* Manor Mount Girls' Collegiate School, Forest Hill. *War Work:* Local Secretary to the S. & S.F.A. for Saffron Walden; Commandant of Red Cross Hospital, Saffron Walden. *Address:* The Grange, Saffron Walden. (M1360)

ATKINSON, Edward Hale Tindal, C.B.E. Chevalier Legion of Honour, *b.* 19 Sept. 1878; *s.* of Henry Tindal Atkinson, Judge of County Courts. *Educ.:* Harrow; Trinity College, Oxford. Barrister-at-Law. *War Work:* Asst.-Sec. and Sec. War Trade Advisory Committee; Asst.-Sec. Civil Aerial Transport Committee; Lieut. R.N.V.R. (R.N.A.S.); Capt. and Major R.A.F.; Legal Adviser Air Section, Peace Conference, Paris; British Secretary International Air Commission, Paris. *Address:* 4, Essex Court, Temple, E.C. 4. *Clubs:* Royal Automobile; Royal Aero. (C2426)

ATKINSON, Major Edward William, D.S.O., O.B.E.

ATKINSON, Major Felton Clayson, O.B.E., R.A.F.

ATKINSON, George Arthur, M.B.E., *b.* 21 July, 1879; *s.* of W. H. Atkinson, of Liverpool; *m.* Dorothy Amy, *d.* of Frederick Boxer, late R.N., Deal, granddaughter of Admiral Sir Thomas Boxer, K.C.B. *Educ.:* Liverpool. Journalist. *War Work:* General Secretary, British Red Cross Commission, Salonika; Member of the Order of St. Sava, Serbia; mentioned in Salonika despatches. *Address:* Croft, Nower Hill, Pinner, Middlesex. (M7248)

ATKINSON, Georgina Jane, O.B.E., *b.* 1848; *d.* of Rev. Thos. Atkinson, of Kirby Sigston. Allerton Division North Riding, Hon. Sec. to Soldiers' and Sailors' Families Association. *War Work:* Hon. Sec. of the North Riding of Yorkshire Voluntary Workers' Association of Working Parties during the War, which contributed 200,000 articles to the Director-General V.O. (Sir E. Ward) Fund. *Address:* Vine Cottage, Northallerton. (O1063)

ATKINSON, Lieut.-Comm. Harold Gordon, O.B.E., R.A.F.

ATKINSON, Harold Waring, M.B.E., M.A., *b.* 2 July, 1868; *s.* of William Atkinson, M.Inst.C.E., of Erwood, Beckenham, Kent. *Educ.:* Merchant Taylor's School, London, and Trinity College, Cambridge. Assistant Master, Dean Close School, Cheltenham, and Rossall School, Fleetwood; Headmaster, Boys' High School, Pretoria; sometime additional Examiner and Inspector for the University of London;

occasional Examiner to the Civil Service Commissioners. *War Work*: Special Constable, Feb. 1916 to July, 1917; Y.M.C.A., London, May, 1916, to June, 1917; worker, and later, Hon. Librarian, British Prisoners of War Book Scheme (Educational), Jan. 1917, to closing. *Address*: West View, Eastbury Avenue, Northwood, Middlesex. (M3499)

ATKINSON, Capt. Herbert Benjamin, O.B.E. A.E.F.

ATKINSON, Lieut.-Col. John, O.B.E. (O2407)

ATKINSON, John Parkinson, M.B.E., M.A. (Cantab.), M.R.C.S.(Eng.) L.R.C.P. (Lond.), *b.* 5 Feb. 1869; *s.* of the late John Parkinson Atkinson, M.D., J.P., V.D., of Saffron Walden; *m.* Dorothea, *d.* of the late C. E. Hicks, of Silverdale, Lancs. *Educ.*: Privately; Clare College, Cambridge; King's College, London. Surgeon, Saffron Walden Hospital; Medical Officer, Friends' School, Training College and Post Office Saffron Walden, and All Saints' Orphanage, Ashdon. *War Work*: Commandant, Essex 41, B.R.C.S.; Medical Officer in charge, Saffron Walden Hospital, Walden Place Red Cross Hospital. *Address*: The Grange, Saffron Walden. *Club*: Overseas. (M7429)

ATKINSON, Lucy Mary Montagu, M.B.E., *b.* 2 Dec. 1890; *d.* of the late Lieut.-Col. R. H. Atkinson, 14th and 55th Regts. of 2, Lansdowne Grove, Devizes, Wilts. *Educ.*: St. Anne's, Abbotts Bromley, Staffs. *War Work*: Quartermaster, Auxiliary Military Hospital, Devizes, Wilts, from Jan. 1915 to Feb. 1919; Radiographer, Military Hospital, Tidworth, from April, 1919, to present date, still serving. *Addresses*: X-Ray Dept., Military Hospital, Tidworth; 2, Lansdowne Grove, Devizes. (M1361)

ATKINSON, Margaret Winifred, M.B.E., *b.* 17 Jan. 1890; *d.* of Dr. William Atkinson, of Clapham. *Educ.*: Streatham Hill School. *War Work*: 1915 to 1920, Superintendent Women's Legion Cookery Section; Unit Administrator Q.M.A.A.C. *Address*: 2, The Sweep, Clapham Common. S.W. 4. (M96)

ATKINSON, Capt. Thomas John Day, O.B.E., B.A. (T.C.D.), J.P., *b.* 4 March, 1882; *s.* of Thomas J. Atkinson, D.L., of Cavangarden, Co. Donegal; *m.* Cicely H. B., *d.* of H. B. Hawkshaw, Commander, R.N. *Educ.*: Trinity College, Dublin (Mod. B.A., 1903). Barrister-at-law; Joint Secretary Commissioners of Charitable Donations and Bequests for Ireland. *War Work*: Capt., Unatt. List, (T.F.), 1911; Temp. Capt., 5th Service Bn. R. Irish Fusiliers, 1914; Staff Capt., 31st Inf. Brigade, 1915; severely wounded in Action, 16 Aug. 1915 (Gallipoli), invalided home; Staff Capt., G.H.Q. Ireland, 1917–19. *Address*: Carrigrenane, Killiney, Co. Dublin. *Clubs*: University (Dublin); Royal St. George Yacht (Kingstown). (O3085)

ATKINSON, Lieut. William, O.B.E., R.N.R.

ATKINSON, George James MOUNCEY-, O.B.E., M.R.C.S.(Eng.) L.R.C.P. (Lond.), *b.* 12 July, 1876; *s.* of George Mouncey-Atkinson, of London; *m.* Rhoda, *d.* of Major W. McIlsoham, of London. *Educ.*: St. Paul's School and St. Mary's Hospital, London. *War Work*: Attached 1st London General Hospital. *Address*: Bampton, Oxfordshire. (O4348)

ATTENBOROUGH, Lieut. Ernest, M.B.E. R.E. (S.R.).

ATTER, Capt. Harold Frederic, O.B.E., *b* 5 Sept. 1879; *s.* of Frederic Atter, of Peterborough; *m.* Amy Dorothy, *d.* of John Barber, of Leeds. *Educ.*: Kings' School, Peterborough. Solicitor; Member of the firm of Greaves and Atter, Solicitors, Wakefield; Clerk and Solicitor to the West Riding of Yorkshire Rivers Board. *War Work*: Oct. 1914, to Sept. 1917, service with 4th Batt. K.O. Yorks L.I. in England and France; Sept. 1917, to April, 1918, Staff Captain, 138th Infantry Brigade, B.E.F., April, 1918, to March, 1919, Staff Captain. H.Q. First Army, B.E.F. *Address*: Glenthorn, Wakefield. (O2408)

ATTERBURY, William Joseph, M.B.E.

ATTHILL, Major Anthony William Maunsell, M.V.O., O.B.E., *b.* 10 Aug. 1861; *s.* of Henry Maunsell Atthill, of St. Peter Port, Guernsey; *m.* Minnie Maude, *d.* of Michael Redgrave of Witham, Essex. *Educ.*: King Edward VI. School, Norwich and Privately. Chairman, Royal Norfolk Veterans Association since 1898. *War Work*: Served with Royal Army Service Corps from Aug. 1914, to Feb. 1920; took part in Gallipoli expedition and was Officer in charge, Field Supply Depot, Suvla. *Address*: Hillcrest, Bourne Hall Road, Bushey, Herts. *Club*: United R.A.S.C. (O6852)

ATTRILL, 2nd Lieut. Charles, M.B.E., R.A.F.

ATTWELL, Sydney Watson, M.B.E.

ATTWOOD, Edward Lewis, O.B.E., *b.* 7 Oct. 1871. *Educ.*: Royal Naval College, Greenwich. Chief Constructor, Admiralty; Member Royal Corps of Naval Constructors; Member Institution of Naval Architects. *War Work*: Warship Designing Staff at Admiralty, H.M.S. "Repulse," "Renown," and "Hood." *Address*: 35, The Drive, Ilford, Essex. (O1064)

ATTWOOD, Capt. Reginald Guy, O.B.E., R.E.

ATWELL, Capt. William, M.B.E., M.C.

AUBREY, Major Herbert Arthur Reginald, O.B.E., M.C., K.S.L.I.; *s.* of Dr. J. Aubrey, of Cowes; *m.* Marion, *d.* of Tom Houghton, of Southwell. *Educ.*: Epsom College, and R.M.C. Sandhurst. *War Work*: France, Sept. 1914, to Aug. 1915, as Adjutant K.S.L.I.; wounded, Hooge, 1915; Staff Officer, Trinidad, 1916; Brigade Major, 4th Brigade, R.F.C., 1917; Staff Officer, 5 Group R.A.F., 1918; despatches Jan. 1915; Jan. 1918, French Croix de Guerre avec palm. *Address*: c/o Messrs. Cox & Co., 16, Charing Cross, S.W. 1. *Clubs*: Cavendish; R.A.F. (O3252)

AUCHINLECK, Major Claude John Eyre, D.S.O., O.B.E., *b.* 1884; *s.* of the late Col. John Claude Auchinleck, R.A.

Educ.: Wellington Coll. Major, Indian Army; Mesopotamia, 1915–19 (despatches, Croix de Guerre). (O6568)

AUDLAND, William Edward, M.B.E., M.R.C S., L.R.C.P.

AUDUS, Major and Quartermaster Henry Joseph Francis, O.B.E., R.A.M.C., *b.* 31 March, 1860; *s.* of Francis Audus, of London. Went through the Zulu Campaign, 1879 (medal); Egypt, 1882 (medal and bar Tel-el-Kebir); Suakin, 1884 (bar El-Teb and Tamani). *War Work*: France, 1914–1919. *Address*: 38A, Tweedy Road, Bromley, Kent. (O1065)

AUGER, Capt. Albert Raymond, M.B.E.

AUKER, Capt. Lawrence, O.B.E., R.A.F.

AULD, Major Samuel James Manson, O.B.E., M.C.

AULD, Lieut.-Col. William, O.B.E.

AURET, Francis Victoria, M.B.E.

AUSTEN, Major Alfred Reade GODWIN-, O.B.E., M.C.

AUSTEN, Harold Cholmley Mansfield, O.B.E.

AUSTIN, Albert Sydney, M.B.E.

AUSTIN, Capt. Alfred Edward, O.B.E.

AUSTIN, Arthur, M.B.E., R.N.

AUSTIN, Lieut. Bertram Herbert, M.B.E., R.F.A.

AUSTIN, Major Frederick William, O.B.E

AUSTIN, Gertrude Hannah, M.B.E., *b.* 3 June, 1877; *d.* of Joshua Austin, of Tipton. *Educ.*: Tipton. Assistant Secretary, Tipton War Pensions Sub-Committee. *War Work*: Appointed Hon. Sec., S. and S.F.A., in Aug. 1914 and still holds that position, awarded Certificate of Merit; Hon. Sec. to Statutory Committee and continued Hon. Sec. to War Pensions Committee for a short period, subsequently appointed salaried officer; assisted in organising Flag Days for the raising of funds for sending parcels to Prisoners of War, paying Railway Fares to Wives and Dependants to enable them to visit relatives in Hospitals, and Christmas Treats to children of Sailors and Soldiers; voluntary work in connection with National Registration and Food Control. *Address*: Gladstone House, Castle Road, Tipton, Staffs. (M7250)

AUSTIN, Henry Edmund, M.B.E., M.P.

AUSTIN, Lieut.-Col. Sir Herbert, K.B.E., M.I.M.E., M.P., (C.U.) King's Norton, Birmingham, since 1919; *b.* 8 Nov. 1866; *m.* Helen, *d.* of James Dron, merchant. *Educ.*: Rotherham Grammar School; Brampton Coll. Chairman and Managing Director of Austin Motor Co., Ltd., and Chairman Wolseley Sheep Shearing Machine Co., Ltd.; served apprenticeship to Engineering at Langlands Foundry, Melbourne; managed several small works in Melbourne; came over to England in 1890 to control the manufacture of the Wolseley Sheep Shearing Machine; made a director, 1900; was Manager of the Wolseley Tool and Motor Car Co., Ltd., Birmingham, 1900–5; commenced manufacture of motor cars on own account at Longbridge Works, Northfield, Birmingham, 1906. *Address*: Lickey Grange, near Bromsgrove. *Clubs*: Carlton; Junior Carlton; Unionist; Royal Automobile; British Empire; 1900; Conservative (Birmingham). (K11)

AUSTIN, Thomas George, M.B.E.

AUSTIN, Walter, M.B.E., R.N.

AUSTIN, Chief Gunner Walter Alexander, M.B.E., R.N.

AUSTIN, William, O.B.E., *b.* 29 Aug. 1869; *s.* of Nathan Austin, of Southampton; *m.* Margaret, *d.* of Henry Stoneman, of Newport, Mon. *Educ.*: Southampton. Secretary Y.M.C.A. *War Work*: Secretary Y.M.C.A. for 3rd, 4th, and 5th Army Areas in France, 1915–1917; Secretary Y.M.C.A. for Italy and Gibraltar, 1918–1919. *Address*: 149, Clive Road, Canton, rdiff. (O1017)

AUSTIN, William Walter, M.B.E.

AVELINE, William Rebotier, O.B.E., M.Inst.M.E., *b.* 15 Sept. 1867; *s.* of W. Talbot Aveline, F.G.S. of Wrington, Somerset; *m.* Lillian Ethel, *d.* of Henry Whatley, of Clifton, Bristol. *Educ.*: Bath and University College, Bristol. Chief Engineer of the Asiatic Petroleum Co. Ltd., of St. Helen's Court, Great St. Helens, London, E.C. *War Work*: For the Ministry of Munitions in connection with the manufacture of high explosives and for the War Office in connection with the supply of petroleum spirit for the use of the B.E.F. *Address*: Greengates, Carshalton, Surrey. *Club*: R.A.C. (O3607)

AVELING, Lieut. Arthur Francis, C.B.E., R.N.V.R., *b.* 10 Aug. 1893; *s.* of Thomas Luke Aveling, M.I.C.E., J.P., of Rochester. *Educ.*: Harrow. Director of Messrs. Aveling & Porter, Ltd., Rochester. 3rd Secretary H.M.'s Diplomatic Service. *War Work*: Served with 1st Royal Naval Brigade during operations around Antwerp, 5 Oct. 1914; interned in Holland on fall of Antwerp; Sept. 1916, to Feb. 1919, Attaché at H.M. Legation, The Hague; Head of Department dealing with Protection of British Interests and Prisoners of War in Enemy Countries. *Address*: Boley Hill House, Rochester, Kent. *Clubs*: Royal Thames Yacht; Wellington; National Liberal. (C2427)

AVERN, Lieut. James Waters Earnscliffe, O.B.E.

AVERRE, Major William James, O.B.E., A.S.C.

AVERY, Capt. John Edgar, O.B.E.

AWBURN, Harriett, Mrs. (Madam Halle), M.B.E., *b.* 24 April, 1864; *d.* of James Pearson, of High Crook, Northumberland. *Educ.*: Cheshire. *War Work*: Founder of the Earl Roberts' Rest House at Pentonville Road, King's Cross, London, where considerably over a million Sailors and Soldiers were welcomed and fed during the four years of its existence. *Addresses*: 48, Brook Street, London, W.; 3H, Maida Vale Mansions, W. *Club*: Lyceum. (M7254)

AWCOCK, Capt. Charles Henry, O.B.E., R.G.A. and R.A.F.

AWDRY, Olive Muriel, Mrs., M.B.E., *b.* 1884; *d.* of Louis H. Tosswill, of Exeter; *m.* Robert William, *s.* of

Charles Awdry. *War Work*: Hon. Sec., Wilts Women's War Agricultural Committee, and Hon. Sec. Salisbury Plain Garden Produce Association. *Address*: Little Cheverell, Devizes, Wilts. (M7255)

AXFORD, Capt. Sidney Robert, O.B.E. R.A.F.

AXTEN, Capt. Ernest Henry, M.B.E., R.E.

AXTEN, Lieut. Henry James, M.B.E., R. Fus. and R.A.F.

AYDEN, Capt. Arthur John, M.B.E.

AYLING, A. Artificer-Engr. William, M.B.E., R.N.

AYLMER, Capt. Arthur Lintott, O.B.E.

AYLMER, George Mason, M.B.E., *b.* 2 Jan. 1887; *s.* of G. W. Aylmer, of Fincham, Norfolk; *m.* Margaret Anderson, *d.* of C. McLachlan, of Ealing. *Educ.*: St. John's College, Hurstpierpoint. H.M. Inspector of Taxes, 1st Class, No. 2 District, Belfast. *War Work*: Founder and Hon. Sec. Belfast Inland Revenue War Savings Association. *Address*: 36, Bawnmore Road, Belfast. (M7256)

AYLWARD, Major and Qr.-Mr. William, O.B.E., R.A.S.C.

AYLWIN, Major William Edgar, O.B.E., R.A.F., *b.* 6 July, 1882; *m.* Emma Mathilde, *d.* of C. H. Parker, of Chatham. *Educ.*: Sir Joseph Williamson's School, Rochester. Royal Air Force. *War Work*: Service in France, Gallipoli, Egypt, and at War Office and Air Ministry. *Address*: 39, Moyser Road, S.W. 16. *Club*: R.A.F. (O3255)

AYRE, Amos Lowrey, O.B.E.

AYRE, Charles Pascoe, O.B.E.

AYRE, Paymr.-Comm. Leslie Charles Edward, O.B.E., R.N.

AYRES, Henry John, M.B.E.

AYRES, Robert Alfred, M.B.E.

AYRTON, George, M.B.E.

AYTOUN, Lieut.-Col. Andrew, C.M.G., C.B.E., D.S.O., *b.* 2nd July 1860; *m.* Helen Lilias, 4th *d.* of the late Robert Graham, of Fintry. Embarkation Commandant; joined Argyll and Sutherland Highlanders, 1881; Captain, 1890; Major, 1902; served South Africa, 1900–1; in Command of 4th Queensland Imperial Bushmen; retired 1908. (C1448)

AZEVEDO, 2nd Lieut. Alec Eustace, M.B.E., R.A.F.

AZZOPARDI, Francesco, O.B.E.

BABER, Shum Shere Jang Bahadur Rana, General of the Nepalese Army, G.B.E. (Hon. Mil.) cr. 1920; K.C.S.I. (Hon.) cr. 1919; K.C.I.E. (Hon.) cr. 1916; *b.* 27 Jan. 1888; 2nd *s.* of Maharaja Sir Chandra of Nepal, *q.v.*; *m.* 1903 Deva Vakta Lakshmi Devi: 3 *s.*, 2 *d.* Director-General Police Forces, Katmandu, since 1903; was present at the Delhi Coronation Durbar, 1903; visited Europe, 1908; was in charge of shooting arrangements during King George's shoot in Nepal Terai, 1911; attached to the Army Headquarters, India (March, 1915, to Feb. 1919), as Inspector-General of Nepalese Contingents in India during the Great War (despatches, specially; thanks of Commanders-in-Chief in India; K.C.S.I., K.C.I.E., for Meritorious Service; received the 1st Class Order of the Star of Nepal with the title of Supradipta Manyabara, 1918; the thanks of the Nepalese Government and a Sword of Honour); Waziristan Field Force 1917 (despatches; special mention by the Commander-in-Chief in India; the Nepalese Military decoration for bravery); at Army Headquarters, India (June to Sept.) as Inspector-General of Nepalese Contingent during Afghan War, 1919 (despatches, G.B.E.). *Address*: Singha Durbar and Baber Mahal, Katmandu, Nepal, *via* India.

BABONAU, Major Alexander Frederick, O.B.E., M.B., I.M.S.

BACK, Stanley, M.B.E., R.N.

BACKHAUS, Lieut. Frederick, M.B.E.

BACKHOUSE, Edith Frances, M.B.E.

BACKHOUSE, Edwin, M.B.E.

BACKHOUSE, Indiana Richenda, M.B.E., *b.* 10 July, 1886; *d.* of Charles H. Backhouse, of Westbury Court, Westbury-on-Severn. *Educ.*: Wantage, Berks. *War Work*: British Red Cross, V.A.D.; Quartermaster, and latterly Commandant, of the Lydney Red Cross Hospital, Gloucestershire. *Address*: Westbury Court, Westbury-on-Severn, Glos. (M3501)

BACON, Major Charles Raymond Kenrick, O.B.E.

BACON, Constance Alice, Mrs. Nicholas, C.B.E., *b.* 14 May, 1870; *d.* of Alexander Leslie-Melville and the Hon. Mrs. Leslie-Melville, of Branston Hall, Lincoln; *m.* Nicholas Henry, *s.* of Sir H. Bacon, Bart., of Thonock, Gainsborough, and Raveningham Hall, Norwich. Deputy President Norfolk Branch B.R.C.S. from 1912. *Address*: Raveningham Hall, Norwich. *Club*: V.A.D. (C925)

BACON, Lieut. Cyril William, O.B.E., R.A.O.C.

BACON, Eustace Vivian, M.B.E., M.A. (Oxon.), F.Z.S., F.R. Met. Soc., *b* 12 April, 1881; *s.* of the late Rev. H. V. Bacon, late rector of East Tisted, Alton, Hants. *Educ.*: Bilton Grange; Marlborough; Rugby; and Hertford College (Scholar), Oxford. Barrister-at-Law. Statistician, London Metal Exchange. *War Work*: Aug. 1914, to June, 1915, Assistant to Hon. Sec. Committee of Clearing Bankers; June, 1915, to Dec. 1919, Administrative Assistant, Secretary's Department, Ministry of Munitions. *Address*: 3, Sheffield Terrace, Kensington, W. 8. *Clubs*: Roehampton; Royal Corinthian Yacht. (M102)

BACON, Frederick Joseph, C.B.E., F.S.I., *b.* 21 Oct. 1853; *s.* of Frederick Bacon, of Pimlico; *m.* Thérèse Joséphine, *d.* of Edouard Violette, of Camden Town. *Educ.*: St. Peter's Collegiate School, Eaton Square, S.W. Junior Examiner H.M. Office of Works, 1876; Assistant Surveyor of Lands, Admiralty,

1903; Assistant Treasury Valuer, 1906; Treasure Valuer, 1909–1920. *War Work*: Great additional work in consequence of the occupation of lands and premises for the War Emergency. *Address*: Clare Lodge, Park Hill, Clapham, S.W. (C101)

BACON, Lieut. James, M.B.E., R.E. (T.F.).

BACON, Rupert Alfred, O.B.E.

BADCOCK, Lieut.-Col. George Henry, O.B.E.

BADCOCK, Lieut.-Col. Gerald Eliot, C.B.E., D.S.O., R.A.S.C., *b.* 1883; *m.* Dorothy (died 1919), *y.d.* of the late James Watt Gibson-Watt, of Doldowlod, Radnorshire. Served in the Great War, 1914–18 (despatches, D.S.O., Bt. Lieut.-Col.). (C1368)

BADDELEY, Henry, M.B.E., *b.* 19 Sept. 1872; *s.* of Henry Baddeley, of Smallthorne; *m.* Hannah, *d.* of George Hulme, of Leek. *Educ.*: Army Schools. Retired Army Officer, late Lieut., 21st (E. of I.) Lancers. *War Work*: In connection with expeditions on the North-West Frontier, and 3rd Afghan War whilst holding the appointment of Station Staff Officer, Risalpur, N.W.F.P., India. *Address*: Pindi House, High Lane, Burslem, Stoke-on-Trent. (M6502)

BADELEY, Henry John Fanshawe, C.B.E., *b.* 1874; *s.* of Henry Badeley, late of Guy Harlings, Chelmsford, Essex. *Educ.*: Radley; Trinity College, Oxford. Taxing Officer and Principal Clerk Judicial Department, House of Lords. *War Work*: County Director (T.F.A.) of County of London; Voluntary Aid and Auxiliary Hospitals. *Addresses*: 2, Morpeth Terrace, S.W.; Bude, N. Cornwall. *Clubs*: Travellers'; Wellington. (C2428)

BADGER, Capt. James Carol, O.B.E.

BADGER, Major Reginald, O.B.E., 12th Lancers, *b.* 14 March, 1882; *s.* of T. W. Badger, of Red House, Rotherham. *Educ.*: Charterhouse. *Address*: Carlton Park, Market Harborough. *Club*: Cavalry. (O8738)

BADOCK, Sir Walter, K.B.E., C.S.I., *b.* 8 March, 1854; *s.* of the late William Frederick Badock, of The Manor House, Westbury-on-Trym, near Bristol; *m.* Ellen May, *d.* of Charles Britten, of Bowes Park, N. *Educ.*: Privately and London University. Accountant-General at India Office, 1907–19, and Director of Funds, 1909–19. *War Work*: As Accountant-General was in charge, under the Secretary of State in Council of India, of a Department of nearly 200 members which dealt with all receipts and payments of the Government of India in this country, prepared the Home Accounts presented to Parliament and the Home Budget of that Government and had the management of the unprecedentedly large balances which the war operations in all parts of the world and the disturbances of exchange caused to be accumulated here. As Director of Funds superintended the various Family Pension Funds established for the Indian Civil and Military Services and administered pensions to the widows and orphans of Indian officers who fell in the war. As Official Agent to the Administrator-General in India (1909–19) distributed the assets of Estates of all deceased officers and other persons remitted by the Administrator-General to this country. *Club*: East India United Service. (K342)

BADSHAH, Kavas Jamas, O.B.E.

BAGENAL, Major Charles James, O.B.E.

BAGENAL, Philip Henry, O.B.E., *b.* 18 June, 1850; *s.* of Philp Bagenal, of Benekerry, Co. Carlow; *m.* Hariot Jocelyn, *d.* of Walter Hore, late of Rathwade, Co. Carlow. *Educ.*: St. Columba's College, Co. Dublin. B.A. Oxford; Barrister-at-Law, English and Irish Bar; late General Inspector of the Local Govt. Board, Whitehall. *War Work*: During the whole period of the War was employed on extra services by the Local Govt. Board in superintending the care of Belgian Refugees in East and West Riding of Yorkshire and in similar work connected with the establishment of Military Tribunals. *Address*: 11, Spencer Hill, Wimbledon, S.W. 19. (O103)

BAGGALLAY, Patience Gertrude, M.B.E.

BAGGE, 2nd Lieut. Harry James, M.B.E., R.A.F.

BAGNALL, Major Arthur Henry, O.B.E.

BAGNALL, Francis Edward, O.B.E.

BAGNALL, Major Ralph, O.B.E.

BAGNALL, Paymaster-Sub.-Lieut. Reginald Douglas, M.B.E., R.N.V.R.

BAGNALL, Lieut. Richard Dayrell, O.B.E.

BAGOT, Major Christopher George Seymour, M.B.E.

BAGSHAW, William, O.B.E., *b.* 15 Feb. 1874; *s.* of the late H. B. Bagshaw, formerly of Millbrook, Cheshire, and latterly of Oldham; *m.* Bessie, *d.* of the late William Bagshaw, of Oldham. *Educ.*: Oldham High School and privately. Town Clerk of Lincoln. *War Work*: Commanded the 4th V.B. Lincolnshire Regt. from its formation to disbandment; was a special constable in the early part of the War, and a member and the Clerk of the Lincoln Military Service Tribunal. (O9916)

BAGSHAWE, Bernal, C.B.E.

BAGSHAWE, Lieut.-Col. Edward Leonard, C.I.E., D.S.O., O.B.E., *b.* 15 Nov. 1876. *Educ.*: St. Cuthbert's Coll., Ushaw; Dover Coll.; R.I.E. Coll. R.E., Indian Telegraph Dept.; Basra; entered Telegraph Service, 1897; Field Service, 1915. *Club*: East India United Service. (O6569)

BAGSHAWE, Capt. Francis John, M.B.E.

BAGSHAWE, Lieut.-Col. Herbert Vale, C.B.E., D.S.O., R.A.M.C., A.D.M.S., G.H.Q., Cairo, *b.* 31 Aug. 1874; *s.* of William Augustus Edward Bagshawe, M.A. (*see* BURKE'S *Landed Gentry*, BAGSHAWE OF OAKES AND WORMHILL). Served Great War, 1914–18, (D.S.O., despatches, Bt. Lieut.-Col.). *Address*: Cairo, Egypt. (C1369)

BAGWELL, William Henry, M.B.E. Local Government Officer. *War Work :* 2½ years Accountant at Church Army Headquarters in France. *Address :* 40, Old Ford Road, Victoria Park, E. 2. (M7260)

BAIGENT, Major Cyril Victor, O.B.E., M.C., M.B.

BAIGENT, William, M.B.E.

BAIKIE, William Baikie, M.B.E., Provost of Kirkwall, *b.* 12 April, 1853 ; *s.* of Samuel Baikie, of Kirkwall, *m.* 1st Margaret H. D. Isbister, *d.* of James L. Isbister, of Upper Scapa St. Ola, Orkney, 2nd Margaret Murray, *d.* of William Murray, Contractor, of Glasgow. *Educ. :* Grammar School. Managing Director of S. Baikie and Son, Timber Merchants and Importers and Building Contractors. *War Work :* Entered Kirkwall Town Council in Nov. 1897 ; promoted to the Magistracy in 1904 ; acted as one of its representatives on the Orkney Harbours Commissioners, the Orkney County Council and Commissioners of Supply for several years and also one of the Meason's Trustees for the St. Magnus Cathedral and a Trustee of the Balfour Hospital ; in 1913, elected Provost of Kirkwall, and in 1914 had a very considerable amount of personal connection with the work of the British Navy : acted as Chairman of the Local Tribunal, Seaforth Highlanders' fund for their disabled and dependants, Belgian and Serbian Relief Funds, and personally carried out the local collection of King George's Fund ; also acted as Chairman of the Orkney Local Food Control Committee and was one of the active members of the Orkney War Savings Committee which raised nearly half a million of money in the county. *Address :* Palace Road, Kirkwall. *Club :* Kirkwall Unionist (President). (M7261)

BAILEY, Col. Alfred John, C.B.E., T.D., J.P., *b.* 26 July, 1867 ; *s.* of the late Sir William Bailey, of Sale Hall, Cheshire ; *m.* Ethel Ellis, *d.* of James Johnson, of Pendleton. *Educ. :* Manchester Grammar School and Victoria University, Manchester. Governing Director of Sir W. H. Bailey & Co., Ltd., Engineers, Manchester ; Director of Grain Elevator Estates, Ltd., Manchester. *War Work :* Second in command 7th Lancashire Fusiliers on outbreak of War ; commanded 2/7th Lancashire Fusiliers, Oct. 1914, to April, 1915 ; commanded 3rd Line Grouped Units, East Lancashire Division, April, 1915. to Sept. 1917 ; Member of East Lancashire Territorial Association, 1915–19. *Address :* Chaseley, Bowdon, Cheshire. *Clubs :* Royal Automobile ; British Empire ; Constitutional, Manchester. (C1449)

BAILEY, Major Arthur Charles, O.B.E., R.E.

BAILEY, Gunr. Arthur Herbert, M.B.E., R.N.

BAILEY, Arthur Stowaway, O.B.E.

BAILEY, Benjamin Edwin, O.B.E., J.P., *b.* 6 Jan. 1856 ; Freeman of London Felt Makers' Company. *Educ. :* Liverpool College. Registrar of Births and Deaths, Walton District, West Derby, Liverpool. *War Work :* Chairman of Food Control ; Chairman of Houses ; Hon. Sec. War Savings, etc. ; Chairman of Hospitals ; Mayor of Bootle, 1917. *Address :* 49, Merton Road, Bootle, Liverpool. *Club :* Chairman, Bootle Conservative. (O9917)

BAILEY, Clement William, M.B.E.

BAILEY, Cyril, M.B.E., *b.* 13 April, 1871 ; *s.* of Alfred Bailey, of Lincoln's Inn ; *m.* Gemma, *d.* of the late Dr. Mandell Creighton, Bishop of London. *Educ. :* St. Paul's School, Balliol College, Oxford. Fellow of Exeter College, Oxford, 1894 ; Fellow of Balliol College, 1902. *War Work :* Ministry of Munitions, Labour Department. *Addresses :* Balliol College ; the King's Mound, Oxford. *Clubs :* Savile ; Alpine. (M1366)

BAILEY, Duncan, O.B.E., M.I.Mech.E., *b.* 1875 ; *s.* of Duncan Bailey, of Birmingham ; *m.* Jessie Marion Hancox, *d.* of John W. Jeens, of Gloucester. *Educ. :* King Charles I. School, Kidderminster. Managing Director, C. Roberts & Co., Railway Rolling Stock Manufacturers, Wakefield. *War Work :* Member of Wakefield Munitions Committee ; designed, erected, and equipped 18 pound Shrapnel Shell Forging Plant for 30,000 shells per week. *Address :* Chapelthorpe, Wakefield. *Clubs :* R.A.C. ; Wakefield County. (O1069)

BAILEY, Florence Emily, Mrs., M.B.E.

BAILEY, George William, M.B.E.

BAILEY, Gertrude Mary, Mrs., C.B.E., J.P., *d.* of James Buchanan, of Sunderland ; *m.* the late Charles Henry Bailey, Partner in Firm of C. H. Bailey, Newport and Barry ; Director Cardiff Junction Dry Dock and Engineering Co., Ltd., Cardiff ; Director Buchanan Shipping Investment Co., Ltd., Newport, Mon. ; Member of Newport Education Committee ; Director of Royal Gwent Hospital, Newport, Mon. ; President Monmouthshire Training Centre for Midwives ; Court of Governors King Edward VII. Welsh National Memorial ; Court of Governors University College of South Wales and Monmouthshire ; Lady President Newport Borough Centre of The Order of St. John of Jerusalem, Priory for Wales. J.P. for the County Borough of Newport, Mon. *War Work :* Chairman Monmouthshire Prisoners of War Committee ; President of Munition Workers' Creche ; organised Canteens for the Welfare of Munition Workers ; President National Shell Factory Canteen ; Belgian Refugee Committee ; Received Medaille de la Reine Elisabeth. *Address :* Stelvio, Newport, Monmouthshire ; Gliffaes, Brecknockshire. (C425)

BAILEY, Harold James, O.B.E., F.I.C., *b.* 13 Dec. 1879 ; *s.* of Rev. John Bailey (Baptist Minister), of London, Sheffield, etc. ; *m.* Edith, *d.* of Howell Powell, of Pontypridd. *Educ. :* Summerfield School, Wesley College, Sheffield, and University College, Sheffield. Fellow of Institute of Chemistry, Russell Square, W. C. 1. ; Inspector of Alkali, etc., Works (under

Ministry of Health). *War Work :* Technical Adviser to the Acid and Fertiliser Branch of the Explosives Supply Department of the Ministry of Munitions. *Address :* Ingleside, Health Park Avenue, Cardiff. (O9918)

BAILEY, Capt. Herbert John, M.B.E., R.E.

BAILEY, James Rhodes, M.B.E., *b.* 23 Feb. 1886. Assistant Port Master, Great Central Railway, Grimsby Docks, Lincs. *War Work :* Dock administration for the Great Central Railway Co. ; from June, 1917, to Dec. 1918 was in London, Board of Trade, as Chief Intelligence and Statistical Officer in the Department of the Timber Controller. *Address :* 81, Oxford Street, Cleethorpes, Lincs. (M7265)

BAILEY, Lieut.-Col. John Henry, R.E. (ret.), C.B.E. *War Work :* Served as an Assistant Director of Fortifications and Works at the War Office. (C2077)

BAILEY, Margaret Fanny, Mrs., M.B.E.

BAILEY, Col. Percy James, D.S.O., O.B.E., *b.* 1878 ; *e.s.* of the late Sir James Bailey, of Lofts Hall, Saffron Walden, and 58, Rutland Gate, S.W. ; *m.* 1907, Dorothy Jessica, *d.* of Thomas Gibson Bowles (formerly M.P. for King's Lynn), of 25, Lowndes Square, S.W. Entered Lancers 1895, became Capt. 1901, and Major 1908 ; served in S. Africa 1899–1902 as Signalling Officer, present at action of Poplar Grove (severely wounded) ; Great War, 1914 (wounded, prisoner) ; was Adj. and Quartermaster at Cav. Sch. 1905–9 ; appointed a Dep. Director of Remounts with rank of Col. 1919. *Address :* Fosseway House, Stow-on-the-Wold, Gloucestershire. (O6859)

BAILEY, Reginald Threlfall, M.B.E., M.R.C.S. (Eng.) L.R.C.P. (Lond.), *b.* 19 July, 1873 ; *s.* of Col. Francis James Bailey, M.R.C.S. (Eng.), L.R.C.P. (Lond.), L.S.A. (Lond.), of Liverpool. *Educ. :* Liverpool College ; Liverpool University ; Liverpool Royal Infirmary. Medical Superintendent, the Mill Road Infirmary, Liverpool, 901 beds ; late Senior Resident Medical Officer, the Mill Road Infirmary, Liverpool ; House Physician, and House Surgeon, to the Ophthalmological, Laryngological, Aural, and Lock Departments, Liverpool Royal Infirmary ; Member the Liverpool Medical Institution ; Member and Hon. Librarian, the Historic Society of Lancashire and Cheshire. *War Work :* Officer Commanding, the Mill Road Military Hospital, Liverpool ; 12,519 acutely wounded Sailors and Soldiers treated, 3,625 operations from May, 1915, to Aug. 1919 ; Medical Officer in charge of troops, 3rd West Lancashire Brigade, Royal Field Artillery, Liverpool, 1914–16. *Address :* 51, Grove Street, Liverpool. *Club :* Athenæum, (Liverpool). (M10261b)

BAILEY, Robert William Harvey, M.B.E.

BAILEY, Sidney Alfred, M.B.E.

BAILEY, Thomas Henry, M.B.E.

BAILEY, Major William Edward, M.B.E.

BAILLIE, Amelia Martha, Mrs., M.B.E.

BAILLIE, Elizabeth Margaret, M.B.E., *d.* of Major James Rose, Lord Lieutenant of Nairnshire, of Kilravock Castle, Nairnshire ; *m.* Ronald Hugh, O.B.E. (*q.v.*), *s.* of Lieut.-Gen. Duncan Baillie, Royal Horse Guards. of Loch Loy, Nairn (*see* BURKE S *Landed Gentry*). President, Roxburghshire Branch of the Scottish Mothers Union and Member of the Executive Council (Scotland). *War Work :* Secretary and Treasurer, S.S.F.A. Roxburghshire ; Member, War Pensions Committee, Roxburghshire ; Member, Food Control Committee, Roxburghshire. *Address :* Jedbank, Jedburgh, N.B. (M1369)

BAILLIE, Sir Frank, K.B.E., *b.* 19 Aug. 1875 ; *s.* of John Baillie and Marion Wilton ; *m.* Edith Julia, *d.* of the late Aubrey White, C.M.G., Deputy Minister of Lands and Mines for Ontario. President, Canadian Aeroplanes, Ltd., Bankers Bond Co., Ltd., and Burlington Steel Co., Ltd. ; commenced business career as a clerk with the Central Canada Loan and Savings Co., Toronto ; became private secretary to the late Senator G. A. Cox ; Accountant, Central Canada Loan and Savings Co., 1896 ; Secretary, 1898 ; Assistant Manager, 1901 ; General Manager, Metropolitan Bank, Toronto, 1902 ; formed the firm of Baillie, Wood and Croft, members of the Toronto Stock Exchange, 1903 ; organised the Burlington Steel Co., Ltd., Hamilton, 1910 ; the Bankers Bond Co., Ltd., Toronto, 1912 ; and Dominion Steel Foundry Co. Ltd., Hamilton, 1912. *War Work :* 1914, Organised the Canadian Cartridge Co. Ltd., Hamilton, to manufacture Brass Cartridge Cases for the British Government ; Director of Aviation for Canada, Imperial Munitions Board, Dec. 1916 ; organised and became President of Canadian Aeroplanes, Ltd., acting for British Government. *Address :* 146, Crescent Road, Toronto. *Clubs :* Albany ; Lambton Golf and Country ; Mississanga Golf ; National ; Royal Canadian Yacht ; Toronto ; Victoria ; Hamilton Golf, Hamilton. (K49)

BAILLIE, Capt. and Qr.-Mr. George Bertram, M.B.E., R.A.S.C.

BAILLIE, Granville Hugh, M.B.E.

BAILLIE, James Black, O.B.E.

BAILLIE, Lieut. Roderick, M.B.E., R.A., *b.* 5 Aug. 1871 ; *s.* of Alexander Baillie ; *m.* Alice Lilian, *d.* of James Glover. *Educ. :* Banff Academy and Edinburgh University. *War Work :* Military Secretary's Division, War Office. *Address :* c/o Messrs. Cox and Co., 16, Charing Cross, S.W. 1. (M5049)

BAILLIE, Ronald Hugh, O.B.E., J.P., D.L., *b.* 1863 ; *s.* of Lieut.-Gen. Duncan Baillie, Royal Horse Guards. of Loch Loy, Nairn (*see* BURKE'S *Landed Gentry*) ; *m.* Elizabeth Margaret, M.B.E. (*q.v.*), *d.* of Major James Rose, Lord Lieut. of Nairnshire, of Kilravock Castle, Nairn. *Educ. :* Wellington

College. Sheriff Substitute of Roxburghshire. *War Work:* Chairman, War Pensions Committee of Roxburghshire; Member, S.E. of Scotland Joint Disablement Committee; Member, Executive Council Association of War Pension Committees of Scotland; Member, Advisory Council of Scottish Region (War Pensions); Chairman, Roxburghshire Red Cross Committee; Chairman, both Roxburghshire Recruiting Tribunals; Chairman, Roxburghshire Fuel Committee. *Address:* Jedbank, Jedburgh, N.B. *Clubs:* Carlton; New (Edinburgh). (O9919)

BAILLIEN, Major Clive Latham, O.B.E., R.A.F.

BAILY, Major Clifford Allan, O.B.E.

BAILY, Edwin, M.B.E., M.B. C.M., J.P., *b.* 1860; *s.* of John Baily, of Calne; *m.* Anne Eleanor, *d.* of Robert Hope Johnstone, of Annandale. *Educ.:* Privately and Edinburgh University. *War Work:* 1915–19, on the Staff as Hon. Physician to the S. African Ambulance; under the French Government at the Croix Rouge Française, at L'Hôpital Beau Rivage, Cannes, France; in 1919, appointed Hon. Member of the Medical Staff of the British Officers' Convalescent Home, Hotel California, Cannes. *Address:* Cannes, France. (M7268)

BAILY, Harold, M.B.E., *b.* 29 Nov. 1869; *s.* of Walter Baily, of Hampstead. *Educ.* University College School and College. *War Work:* Sub-Commissioner, British Red Cross, Taranto. *Address:* 4, Rosslyn Hill, Hampstead, London, N.W. 3. *Clubs:* National Liberal; Eighty. (M7269)

BAILY, Joseph Macdonald, O.B.E., M.A., *b.* 26 Aug. 1865; *s.* of Rev. Canon Baily, of Ryton, Co. Durham; *m.* Ellen Millicent, *d.* of Rev. T. J. Morris, of Hampton-in-Arden, Warwickshire. *Educ.:* Magdalen College School and Oriel College, Oxford. Barrister-at-law; Chairman, Newcastle-upon-Tyne Court of Referees. *War Work:* Chairman, Newcastle-upon-Tyne Munitions Tribunal. *Address:* 94 Osborne Road, Newcastle-upon-Tyne. *Club:* Northern Counties, (Newcastle-upon-Tyne). (O9920)

BAILY, Robert Edward Hartwell, M.B.E.

BAIN, David, C.B.E., *b.* 1855; *s.* of William Bain, of Reay, Caithness. Controller of Timber Supplies, Ministry of Munitions. *Address:* 2, Downhurst, Parson St., Hendon, N.W. (C103)

BAIN, Herbert Barr, M.B.E.

BAIN, Mary Jane, Mrs., O.B.E., *b.* 11 Aug. 1854; *d.* of Rev. John Taylor, of Southport; *m.* Albert Wellesley Bain, J.P., *s.* of John Marsland Bain, of Belfast. *Educ.:* Stockport. *War Work:* Chairwoman, Harrogate Women's Sewing League, it being the first organisation of its kind, opening on 8 Aug. 1914; the League raised £12,000 and sent out 1,180,472 articles. (O9921)

BAINBRIDGE, Col. William Frank, C.M.G., D.S.O., *b.* 1873; *s.* of Maj.-Gen. F. T. Bainbridge, of Cheltenham; *m.* 1902, Violet Maud, *e. d.* of Capt. Joseph Henderson, of Rylstone, Yorkshire, and Rylstone House, Cheltenham. *Educ.:* Cheltenham Coll. Cameronians (Scottish Rifles), 1894; Capt. I.S.C. (now Indian Army), 1901; Major, 1909: Brevet Lieut.-Col 1913; Lieut.-Col. 1916, and Brevet Col. 1919; served on N.-W. Frontier of India, 1897–8 (medal with clasp); China, 1900; present at relief of Pekin (despatches twice); Great War, 1914–19, as a Gen. Staff Officer (despatches, Order of the Nile, Brevet Col.). *Club:* Junior Army and Navy. (O3083)

BAINES, Major Denis Lynch, O.B.E.

BAINES, Major Edward George Graham Talbot, O.B.E.

BAINES, Florence, Mrs., M.B.E. (M10431)

BAINES, Sir Frank, C.B.E., M.V.O., *b.* 7 Dec. 1878. *Educ.:* Privately. Architect, Surveyor, Civil Engineer; Director of Works; H.M. Office of Works and Public Buildings. *Address:* Hillside, Loughton Essex. (C104)

BAINES, Lieut. George Norman, M.B.E.

BAINES, Hubert, C.B.E., *b.* 29 June, 1874. *Educ.:* Privately. Chief Electrical and Mechanical Engineer, H.M. Office of Works. *War Work:* Factory construction and development of process in connection with production of Munitions of War; Member of Fire Protection Advisory Committee, Ministry of Munitions. *Address:* Bryn Mawr, Church Hill, Loughton. (C2424)

BAINES, John William Owen, M.B.E.; *s.* of Edwin Frederick Baines, of High Wycombe; *m.* Maude Ann, *d.* of Herbert Denwood Harrison, of Ipswich. *Educ.:* Perse Grammar School, Cambridge. *War Work:* Director, Flour and Bread Section, Ministry of Food. *Address:* Aveling, 17, Constitution Hill, Ipswich. *Clubs:* Junior Athenæum; Ipswich and Suffolk. (M1370)

BAINTON, Edward Cecil, M.B.E.

BAIRD, Capt. Alexander Edwin, O.B.E.

BAIRD, Alexander McDonald, M.B.E.

BAIRD, Andrew Henry, O.B.E. (O8739)

BAIRD, Blanche Mary, Mrs., M.B.E., *b.* 3 Aug. 1881; *d.* of the late Alfred Pyne, of Roydon, Ware, Herts.; *m.* Hugh Robert, *s.* of the late Hugh Baird. *Educ.:* Privately. *War Work:* Superintendent of 5, Y.M.C.A. Dock Canteens under Lady Askwith. *Address:* 34, Hartwood Road, Stamford Brook. *Club:* New Century. (M7273)

BAIRD, Constance Kennedy, M.B.E.

BAIRD, Douglas Heriot, C.B.E., *b.* 23 May, 1883; *s.* of Hugh Harper Baird, of Glasgow; *m.* Dorothea Frances, *d.* of Henry Templer Prior, of Esher. *Educ.:* Charterhouse;

London Univ. *War Work:* Contracts for supply of Bacteriological Apparatus to H.M. Allied Armies; started at the request of the Government, Glass Works for the manufacture of Scientific Laboratory Glassware; Manager of H.M. Filling Factory, Walthamstow, for filling poison gas shells, 1915–17; Member of the New Industries Reconstruction Committee, subsection of Dr. Addison's reconstruction committee. *Address:* Halidon, Esher, Surrey. *Club:* Cavendish. (C2430)

BAIRD, Brig.-Gen. Edward William David, C.B.E., J.P., *b.* 1864; 6th *s.* of the late William Baird of Elie (*see* BURKE'S *Landed Gentry*); *m.* Millicent Bessie, 2nd *d.* of Maj.-Gen. Sir Stanley Clarke G.C.V.O. (*see* BURKE'S *Peerage*). *Educ.:* Eton. Formerly Capt. 10th Hussars; served with Imperial Yeomanry S. African War, 1900; Hon. Maj. in the Army, 1901; Lieut.-Col. Commanding (Hon. Col. 1906) Suffolk Hussars I.Y., 1901–6; served Great War 1914–17 (T. Brig.-Gen. since May, 1916); Member of Jockey Club since 1894; won St. Leger with Woolwinder, 1907. *Address:* Forse, Caithness; Kelloe, Berwickshire; *Clubs:* Turf; Cavalry; Naval and Military. (C799)

BAIRD, Malcolm, O.B.E.

BAIRD, Lieut.-Col. Randolph Eustace Wemyss, O.B.E.

BAIRD, Major William Merrilees, O.B.E., T.D., *b.* 7 Feb. 1879; *s.* of the late William Baird, Engineer, of Glasgow; *m.* Eileen Beatrice, *d.* of A. C. Bryson, B.C.S. (retired), of Sidmouth. *Educ.:* Hamilton Crescent School and Royal Technical College, Glasgow. Senior Partner in William Baird and Son, Structural Engineers, Anniesland, Glasgow. *War Work:* Served with Army in France, on the Headquarters Staff of the 51st (Highland) Division and 61st (South Midland) Division, from 1 May, 1915 to 10 Feb. 1919. *Address:* 6, Spring Gardens, North Kelvinside, Glasgow. *Club:* Royal Scottish Automobile (Glasgow). (O4968)

BAIRNSFATHER, Capt. George Edward Beckwith, C.B.E., R.N. (ret.), *b.* 16 Sep. 1855; *s.* of Peter Bairnsfather, D.L., of Dumbarrow, Forfarshire, great-grandson of Patrick Miller, Laird of Dalswinton, Dumfriesshire, who was the first to use steam for the propulsion of boats. He was accompanied on his first voyage by Alexander Nasmyth, Artist, father of the inventor of the Nasmyth Steam Hammer; *m.* Charlotte Emily, *d.* of H. Roberts, of Cambridge. *Educ.:* St. Andrews, N.B. Joined H.M.S. "Britannia," Sept. 1869, ret. Sept. 1905. *War Work:* Divisional Naval Transport Officer at Dover; organised and conducted the Naval Transport Work at that Port from Oct. 1914, to May, 1918, when something close on one million sick and wounded were landed, besides large numbers of troops were despatched and received in addition to much material. *Address:* "Brumana," Farnham. (C426)

BAIRSTOW, Prof. Leonard, C.B.E., F.R.S., F.R.Ae.S. F.Inst.P., *b.* 25 June, 1880; *s.* of Uriah Bairstow, of Halifax, Yorkshire; *m.* Eleanor Mary, *d.* of William Hamer, of Wandsworth Common. *Educ.:* Royal College of Science, South Kensington. Professor of Aerodynamics at the Imperial College of Science and Technology; Expert Adviser in Aerodynamics to the Air Ministry; Member of the Aeronautical Research Committee and of the Advisory Committee on Civil Aviation. *War Work:* Superintendent of the Aerodynamics Department of the National Physical Laboratory, 1914–17; Expert Adviser to the Research Department of the Air Ministry, 1917–19. *Address:* The Imperial College of Science and Technology, South Kensington, S.W. 7. (C9)

BAISS, Llewelyn Arnold, O.B.E., M.R.C.S.

BAKER, Ada Mary, M.B.E.

BAKER, Capt. Alan Hugh Sancroft, O.B.E., R.F.A.

BAKER, Alfred Gabriel, O.B.E., *b.* 26 Oct. 1867; *s.* of Henry Baker, of Canterbury; *m.* Louisa, *d.* of William Blackwell, Oundle, Northants. *Educ.:* Abroad. Superintendent of Training Classes for Disabled Sailors and Soldiers, The Queen's Hospital, Frognal, Sidcup. *War Work:* Hon. Financial Sec. Y.M.C.A., East Kent Division, two years; Organising Superintendent Queen Mary's Workshop, Royal Pavilion, Military Hospital, Brighton. *Addresses:* The Queen's Hospital, Frognal, Sidcup, Kent; 18 St. George's Place, Canterbury. (O108)

BAKER, Eng. Lieut.-Comm. Alfred Henry, O.B.E., R.I.M.

BAKER, Alma, C.B.E.; founded Malayan Aircraft Fund. (C2014)

BAKER, Arthur, C.B.E., *b.* 21 May, 1861; *s.* of George Baker, of Barnet; *m.* Leila, *d.* of H. Pulman. *Educ.:* Robert College, King's Coll. London. Merchant; Chairman, G. and A. Baker, Ltd., and of Edwards and Sons, Near East, Ltd. *War Work:* Serbian Red Cross, Hon. Sec.; Commissioner British Red Cross, Roumania. *Address:* 370, Grande Rue de Péra, Constantinople. *Club:* Club de Constantinople. (C926)

BAKER, Capt. Arthur Frederick, O.B.E., R.A.S.C.

BAKER, Atheling Herbert, M.B.E.

BAKER, Augustus, M.B.E.

BAKER, Cecil, Mrs., C.B.E.; Hon. Sec. British Ambulance Committees. (C5)

BAKER, Capt. Charles Matthew, M.B.E., A.E.F.

BAKER, Conyers, O.B.E., *b.* 30 Jan. 1885; *s.* of Charles Conyers Massy Baker, of Lismacue, Bansha, Co. Tipperary, Ireland (*see* BURKE'S *Landed Gentry*); *m.* Geraldine Susan Dorothea, *d.* of Very Rev. R. J. S. Devenish, Dean of Cashel, of Cashel, Co. Tipperary, Ireland. *Educ.:* Privately. Member of Incorporated Law Society of Ireland ; Provincial Secretary, Burma Y.M.C.A. *War Work :* Y.M.C.A. Work in Burma and Salonica. *Address :* Central Y.M.C.A., Rangoon, Burma.

BAKER, Flight-Lieut. Cyril Bennett, O.B.E., R.A.F.

BAKER, Major C. H., O.B.E., R.E.

BAKER, Edward Charles Stuart, O.B.E.

BAKER, Edwin Emmanuel, M.B.E. ; *s.* of late Major E. Baker, R.H.A., of Woolwich ; *m.* Annie, *d.* of Mary Buckley, of Birr, Ireland. *Educ. :* Privately. For 20 years Superintending Clerk, War Office. *War Work :* Dealing with all questions in connection with the Territorial Force, including decorations and drafts to the seat of War, casualties, etc. *Address :* 32, Leonard Road, Southall. *Clubs :* Conservative (Southall) ; Comrades of Great War. (M7274)

BAKER, Ernest Frederick, M.B.E., S.S.M., R.A.S.C.

BAKER, Francis, M.B.E.

BAKER, Capt. Francis Barrington, M.B.E., M.A. (Cantab.), R. of O., *b.* 1892 ; *s.* of James Barrington Baker, M.D., of Finchley, London. *Educ. :* King's School, Rochester, and Peterhouse, Cambridge. Assistant to Managing Director of Willis, Sindall and Syrett Ltd., 4, Lloyds Av., E.C. 3. *War Work :* 1914-19, York and Lancaster Regt. ; 1915-16, France ; 1916-17, R.E. Record Office, Chatham ; 1917-19, R.E. Record Office (Transportation Branch), Tavistock Sq., W.C. 1 ; 1919, Capt., R. of O. *Addresses :* Grove Lodge, Church End, Finchley, N. 3 ; Peterhouse, Cambridge. (M4291)

BAKER, Capt. Francis Pearson, M.B.E.

BAKER, Lieut.-Col. Frank, O.B.E., T.F.R., *b.* 7 March, 1875 ; *s.* of William Baker, of Wellesbourne, Warwick. *Educ. :* Wellesbourne. Soldier ; Enlisted into the Royal Welsh Fusiliers 9 March, 1893, and served continuously until 27 May, 1920, in Malta, Crete, Egypt, Crete, China, India, France and Flanders. *War Work :* Commissioned 19 Dec. 1914, assisted to raise and train 2 5th Batt., Royal Welsh Fusiliers, was retained on Home Service until June, 1916 for training purposes ; on the Brigade Staff and 2nd in Command of a Batt. ; proceeded to France, 4 June, 1916 ; seconded to Labour Corps, 13 Aug. 1917 ; Commanded 32 Labour Group, Mar. 1919, to May 1920 ; mentioned in despatches, awarded O.B.E. ; mentioned in French despatches ; received the thanks of the Mayor and Commune of Arques and the Sous-Prefect of St. Omer for personal services to the Commune of Arques during hostile aircraft action from June, to Sept. 1918 ; awarded La Médaille de la Reconnaissance Française and Diploma ; received thanks of Chinese Authorities for work with Chinese, especially the 78th C.L.C. which did most excellent work during the war and always in the forward and fighting area. *Address :* 46, York Road, Northampton. *Club :* R.A.C. (O2409)

BAKER, Major Frederick Guy Stirling, O.B.E.

BAKER, Eng.-Lieut.-Comm. Frederick John, O.B.E., R.N.

BAKER, George, O.B.E.

BAKER, George Stephen, O.B.E.

BAKER, Gerald Percival, M.B.E., *b.* 18 March, 1879 ; *s.* of Lawrence James, of Brambridge Park, Eastleigh ; *m.* Rachel, *d.* of Col. F. Howell, of Trewellwell, Solva. *Educ. :* Harrow and Cambridge. Barrister-at-law. *War Work :* No. 2 Motor Ambulance Convoy, France and No. 3 Motor Ambulance Convoy, Italy. *Address :* Llanunwas, Solva, Pembrokeshire. *Clubs :* United Universities ; M.C.C. (M7275)

BAKER, Lieut. Gordon St. George Wildman, O.B.E., R.N.F.

BAKER, Major Harry Cecil, O.B.E.

BAKER, Major Herbert, O.B.E., R.A.S.C.

BAKER, Prof. Herbert Brereton, C.B.E., M.A., D.Sc., F.R.S. ; *s.* of Rev. John Baker, of Blackburn ; *m.* Muriel, *d.* of Harry J. Powell, of Whitefriars. *Educ. :* Manchester Grammar School and Balliol College, Oxford. Professor of Chemistry, Imperial College, S.W. 7. *War Work :* Member of Trench Warfare Committee of the War Office ; Chemical Warfare Committee of the Ministry of Munitions : of the Panel of the Admiralty Board of Invention and Research ; Chemical Adviser to the War Office on Purification of Water for the Army. *Addresses :* Imperial College, S.W. 7 ; Latchmoor House, Gerrards Cross, Bucks. (C4)

BAKER, Horace William, M.B.E.

BAKER, Isabel Noeline, M.B.E., 25 Dec. 1879 ; *d.* of John H. Baker, of Christchurch, New Zealand. *Educ. :* Privately. Hon. Sec. National Association of Landswomen. *War Work :* Organising Secretary for Surrey under the Women's Branch of the Board of Agriculture. *Address :* Monk's Path, Warwick's Bench, Guildford. (M7277)

BAKER, Isabella Winifred, Mrs., M.B.E.

BAKER, James Mitchell, C.B.E., D.S.O., *b.* 1878. S. African War, 1899-1902, mentioned in despatches ; served in Great War, 1914-18 ; German S.W. Africa, Egypt, France and Flanders ; mentioned in despatches. (C1879)

BAKER, Col. Jasper, O.B.E., R.A.O.C.

BAKER, Capt. John, M.B.E., R.A.S.C.

BAKER, John, M.B.E., *b.* 11 May, 1852. An Elective Auditor for the Borough of Hove, Sussex. *War Work :* Hon. Sec. to the Hove Local Central Committee for War Savings since June, 1916. *Address :* 2, Lansdowne Square, Hove, Sussex. (M105)

BAKER, John Edgar, O.B.E.

BAKER, John Frederick William, M.B.E., *b.* 22 April, 1877 ; *s.* of John William Nicholls, of Plymouth, Devon. ;

m. Florence Mary, *d.* of Samuel Sheriff, of Plymouth. *Educ. :* Naval and Military Schools, Devonport. Officer in charge, H.M. Naval Store Depot, Langley, Birmingham. *War Work :* On outbreak of war, was stationed at H.M. Naval Yard, Hong Kong, China, serving in the Naval Store Branch, Admiralty ; recalled to England in April, 1915, and was appointed to take charge of H.M. Naval Store Depot, Langley, near Birmingham. *Address :* 14, Durban Road, Peverell, Plymouth ; 2, Richmond Hill, Langley, Birmingham. (M7279)

BAKER, John William, O.B.E., J.P., *b.* 1868 ; *s.* of John Baker, of Oakwood Grange, Rotherham ; *m.* Ada, *d.* of Henry Bingley, of Rotherham. *Educ. :* Doncaster Grammar School and Sheffield University. President of Rotherham Chamber of Commerce, 1917-21 ; Member of Labour Advisory Committee. *War Work :* Chairman of John Baker & Co., Rotherham, who directed all their resources to Shell making ; Member of Board of Management of the Rotherham National Shell Factory. *Address :* Elm Tree Bank, Rotherham ; Wyke Holme, Bridlington, Yorks. (O110)

BAKER, Major Joseph Samuel, O.B.E.

BAKER, Maggie Ethel, M.B.E.

BAKER, Muriel Carew, M.B.E., *b.* 29 July, 1892 ; Clerical Assistant, British Legation, The Hague. *War Work :* Secretarial work at Foreign Office, Downing Street ; Canteen work, Regent's Park ; Secretarial work at Peace Conference, Paris. *Address :* 24, Lewisham Road, Dartmouth Park, N.W. 5. (M7282)

BAKER, Prof. Percy Montague, M.B.E., B.Sc., A.M.I.M.E., A.M.I.E.E., *b.* 27 Aug. 1872 ; *s.* of John Richard Baker, of Handsworth, Birmingham. *Educ.* Birmingham. Professor of Electrical Engineering, Bombay ; Director of Instructional Factories in the Ministry of Labour. *War Work :* Technical Adviser on the Training of Munition Workers ; concerned with the equipment and running of factories for the training of men and women for the production of munitions *Address :* Livingstone Road, Handsworth, Birmingham. *Clubs :* Royal Societies ; Royal Bombay Yacht ; Bombay Gymkhana. (M105)

BAKER, Capt. Richard Lawrence, O.B.E. (Res. of Officers), *b.* 1877 ; *s.* of Lawrence J. Baker, of Brambridge Park, Eastleigh ; *m.* Katie, *d.* of the late Ambrose Shere Massey. *Educ. :* Eton and Trinity Hall, Cambridge. *Address :* The Cwm, Monmouth. *Club :* Army and Navy. (O1074)

BAKER, Rosa Agnes, Mrs. CLINTON-, M.B.E., *b.* 4 July 1899 ; *d.* of the late William Henderson, of Berkley House, Frome ; *m.* Rear-Admiral Lewis Clinton-Baker, C.B., C.B.E. *q.v.* ; *s.* of the late William Clinton-Baker, of Bayfordbury, Hertford. *War Work :* V.A.D., Frome Detachment, B.R.C.S., 1914-17 ; Superintendent, Frome War Hospital Depot, 1915-18 ; Superintendent Church Army Club ("Charmys"), Marble Arch, London, 1918-19. *Address :* H.M. Dockyard, Chatham (temporary). *Club :* Empress. (M8442)

BAKER, Sir Thomas, K.B.E., J.P., rendered valuable services in connection with the Great War. Late Mayor of Plymouth. (K343)

BAKER, Thomas, O.B.E., M.R.C.S., L.S.A., *b.* 26 March, 1852 ; *s.* of Thomas Brown, of Cosham, Hants ; *m.* Laurie Hannah, *d.* of — Glasspool of Southampton. *Educ. :* Southsea Diocesan Grammar School and Privately. Assistant M.O., St. George's, Hanover Square Union, Infirmary ; District M.O., Havant, Public Vaccinator ; M.O. to Post Office, etc. *War Work :* In charge of Auxiliary Hospital, V.A.D. for duration of the War. *Address :* 25, Western Parade, Southsea, Hants. (O11789)

BAKER, Thomas Edgar, M.B.E.

BAKER, Major Wilfred Bertram, O.B.E., 10th Gurkha Rifles, I.A.. has Order of the Star of Nepal, 3rd Class. (O8433)

BAKER, William Ernest, M.B.E.

BAKER, Vice-Admiral William Henry Baker, O.B.E., R.N., *b.* 7 Dec. 1862 ; *y.s.* of the late Henry John Baker Baker, of Elemore Hall, Co. Durham, J.P. and D.L. for County Durham ; *m.* Harriett Constance, *y.d.* of Henry N. Middleton D.L., J.P. and C.A. Northumberland, late Rifle Brigade, of Lowood, Melrose, N.B. *Educ. :* H.M.S. "Britannia," Dartmouth. Lieut.-Col. and County Commandant, Northumberland Volunteer Force ; went to sea as Naval Cadet, 1878 ; on board H.M.S. "Sultan" in Sea of Marmora during Russo-Turkish War ; assisted in landing troops during the occupation of Cyprus, 1878 ; served in Egyptian Campaign, 1882 (medal and Khedive's Star) ; with expedition against Sultan of Vitu, E. Africa, 1890 (medal and clasp) ; on special commission to Massi-Kissu and Umptali, Mashonaland, 1891 ; Order of the Red Eagle of Prussia, 2nd Class, 1907 ; Rear-Admiral 1913 ; retired, 1913. Vice-Admiral 1918. *Address :* Buston House, Lesbury, Northumberland. *Club :* Naval and Military. (O6861)

BAKER, Rear-Adm. Lewis CLINTON-, C.B., C.B.E., *b.* 16 March, 1866 ; *s.* of William Clinton-Baker, of Bayfordbury, Herts. (see BURKE'S *Landed Gentry*). *m.* Rosa Agnes, *d.* of William Henderson, of Berkley House, Frome. *Educ. :* H.M. Training Ship "Britannia," Dartmouth. *War Work :* Midshipman at Bombardment of Alexandria in H.M.S. "Monarch" ; served in South African War, 1900, as Commander of H.M.S. "Gibraltar" ; in command H.M.S. "Berwick" as S.N.O. in West Indies, Aug. 1914, to March, 1915 ; captured three enemy supply ships ; in command H.M.S. "Hercules" at Jutland ; in command H.M.S. "Benbow," 1916-17 ; promoted to Rear Admiral and appointed in command of 1st Minelaying Squadron, and responsible for the laying of the Northern Mine Barrage, 1917-18. *Clubs :* Army and Navy ; United Service. (C1918)

BAKEWELL, Major George Victor, O.B.E., late R.A.M.C., *b.* 10 Sept. 1887 ; *s.* of George Bakewell, of Longton, Stoke-on-Trent. *Educ.* : Epsom College ; Clare College, Cambridge ; London Hospital. Medical Practitioner. *War Work* : Joined the army as Lieut., R.A.M.C. Sept. 1914 ; demobilised with rank of Major March, 1919 ; saw active service in France and with the Salonica Army from Nov. 1915, to Nov. 1918, when invalided home ; twice mentioned in despatches. *Address* : London End, Beaconsfield, Bucks. (O3016)

BAKEWELL, Robert Turle, O.B.E., M.B., M.R.C.S., L.R.C.P. Anæsthetist to St. John and St. Elisabeth Hospital. (O11890)

BALAAM, Charles John, O.B.E., *b.* 18 July, 1876. Divisional Controller Employment Department, Ministry of Labour. *Address* : 20, Orchard Street, Portman Square, W. 1. (O1075)

BALBI, Major Henry Alexander, M.B.E., Royal Malta Artillery (retired), *b.* 14 Oct. 1867 ; *s.* of the late Raffaele Balbi, LL.D., of Malta Bar and Civil Service ; *m.* the late Eileen Moira, *d.* of the late Fleet Surgeon Brien P. S. Macdermott, M.D., R.N. *Educ.* : The Lyceum, Malta, and Privately. District Superintendent, St. John Ambulance Brigade Overseas, Malta, and late Chairman, St. John Ambulance Association, Malta ; Executive Committee, Baden Powell Boy Scouts, Malta ; Malta Athletic Club ; President, Malta Art Amateur Association, Malta Football Association ; Member, Board of Visitors Civil Prison ; Member of Committee Public Library and of Garrison Library, Malta ; Hon. Sec. Malta Society of Arts, Manufactures and Commerce, for which awarded Gold Medal and appointed Hon. Vice-President ; Gunnery Instructor. 1st Class ; A. Inspector of Warlike Stores ; Commanded the Royal Malta Artillery in Egypt, 1900–5. *War Work* : District Superintendent, St. John Ambulance Brigade Overseas, Malta ; Chairman, St. John Ambulance Association, Malta ; Member " Our Day " Committee, Malta ; " London Gazette," " Malta Government Gazette," and letter of thanks from Governor of Malta for assistance in organising emergency military hospital in 1920, Appointed Esquire, Order of St. John of Jerusalem in England ; Chief Postal Censor, Malta, 3 Aug. 1914, to 15 Sept. 1919. *Addresses* : c/o The London County Westminster and Parr's Bank, Ltd., 52, Threadneedle Street, London, E.C. 2 ; c/o The Anglo-Maltese Bank, Malta. (M6598)

BALDERS, Major Dudley Vere Morley, O.B.E., M.C., *b.* 28 Oct. 1883 ; *s.* of the late Lieut.-Col. Charles Morley Balders, King's Dragoon Guards, of West Barsham, Norfolk ; *m.* Violet Agnes Fairlie, *d.* of the late Lieut.-Col. Arthur Watson, the Suffolk Regt. *Educ.* : Isle of Wight College and Royal Military College, Sandhurst. Appointed 2nd Lieut., Suffolk Regt., 22 April, 1903 ; Lieut., Suffolk Regt., April, 1905 ; Capt., Suffolk Regt., Feb. 1914 ; Major, Suffolk Regt., 22 April, 1918 ; Adjutant, 1st Battalion Suffolk Regt., 30 Dec. 1913 to 23 Oct. 1915 ; served all Regimental soldiering with 1st Batt. Suffolk Regt., England, Malta, Egypt, prior to the war. *War Work* : Adjutant, 1st Suffolk Regt., France and Flanders, 16 Jan. 1915 to 13 May, 1915 ; wounded (remained at duty), 26 April, 1915 ; wounded, evacuated to hospital, 8 May, 1915, 2nd battle of Ypres ; Instructor, Officers' School of Instruction in London University O.T.C., 6 Sept. 1915 to 6 March, 1916 ; Staff Capt., 198th Inf. Brigade, 6 March, 1916 to 22 Sept. 1916 ; D.A.A. and Q.M.G., 2nd Cyclist Div., 23 Sept 1916 to 4 Dec. 1916 ; D.A.A. and Q.M.G., 66th Div., 4 Dec. 1916 to 17 Feb. 1917, England ; D.A.A.G., 66th Div. France and Flanders, 18 Feb. 1917 to 17 Feb. 1919 ; D.A.A.G., British Base, Rotterdam, Holland, 18 Feb. 1919, to 3 Nov. 1919 ; D.A.A.G., G.H.Q., France and Flanders, 30 Nov. 1919, to 22 March, 1920 ; D.A.A. and Q.M.G., East Anglian Div. (T.A.), 16 April, 1920. *Address* : c/o Messrs. Cox and Co., 16, Charing Cross, London. *Club* : United Service. (O4972)

BALDOCK, Henry Augustus, M.B.E.

BALDRY, Walter Burton BURTON-, O.B.E., *Educ.* : King's College, London, and Queen's College, Oxford. Stockbroker. *War Work* : R.N.V.R. Aug. 1914. to Oct. 1914 ; Lieut. Oxford and Bucks. Lt. Infantry, May, 1915 ; Capt., May, 1916 ; Recruiting Staff Officer. June, 1916 ; commanded School of Instruction for Recruiting Officers, 1917 ; Secretary Eastern Region, Ministry of National Service, 1918. *Address* : c/o Authors' Club, Whitehall Court, S.W. 1. *Clubs* : Wellington ; Authors' ; New City. (O1076)

BALDWIN, Arthur George, M.B.E., *b.* 21 March, 1874 ; *s.* of Henry Baldwin, of Rayleigh, Essex, Builder ; *m.* Ethel Daisy, *d.* of William H. Scriven, of Chelmsford, Civil Servant. *Educ.* : Rayleigh Collegiate School. *War Work* : Aerodrome Constructing ; Chairman, Works Committee, Handley Page's Extensions. *Address* : 89, Dollis Road, Church End, Finchley London, N. 3. (M7283)

BALDWIN, Rev. Charles Henry Robert, M.B.E., *b.* 14 May, 1881 ; *s.* of Rev. Francis Baldwin, of Stede Hill, Harrietsham, Kent. ; *m.* Silvia Louise, *d.* of Reginald Emson, of London. *Educ.* : Denstone College and Lincoln Theological College. British Chaplain, Gothenburg ; British Vice-Consul, Gothenburg. *War Work* : Secretary to British Consulate General 1916 and now held ; Secretary for Sweden British Red Cross Society 1915, to end of war ; collected about £10,000 ; carried out survey of Graves of Officers and men of R.N. for Admiralty 1917 ; Hon. Chaplain repatriation camp, British prisoners of war, Ljungbyhed, Sweden, 1919 ; Commissioner for Sweden, Imperial War Graves Committee, 1920. *Address* : British Consulate General, Gothenburg. *Clubs* : Royal Bachelors' (Gothenburg) ; Royal Gothenburg Yacht. (M7284)

BALDWIN, Christine, Mrs. Guy Melfort, M.B.E.,

BALDWIN, Edmund Chaplin, O.B.E., F.C.A., F.C.I.S., F.F.I., *b.* 3 Sept. 1861 ; *s.* of the late William Chaplin Baldwin ; *m.* Dorothy, *d.* of the late W. L. Barraclough, M.A. *Educ.* : Privately. Chartered Accountant, Chartered Secretary, Public Auditor appointed by the Treasury under the Friendly Societies Acts. *War Work* : Hon. Sec. Sussex County Voluntary Organisation for supplying comforts to Sailors and Soldiers during the War (War Office Scheme), under Col. Sir Edward Ward, Bart., G.B.E., *q.v. Address* : 9, Windlesham Avenue, Brighton. *Clubs* : Junior Constitutional, London ; Windlesham Bowling Club, Brighton. (O1077)

BALDWIN, Lieut.-Col. John Eustace Arthur, D.S.O., O.B.E., *b.* 13 April, 1892 ; *s.* of John Herbert Lacey Baldwin, of the Hall, Thornton-le-dale ; *m.* Kathleen Betsy, *d.* of the late Tom W. L. Terry, of Trentholme, York. *Educ.* : Rugby and Sandhurst. *War Work* : Cavalry till 24 Sept. 1914 ; Royal Flying Corps, Royal Air Force, Independent Force in France for various periods from Jan. 1915 till Nov. 1918. Resigned commission in 8th Hussars on appointment to a permanent commission in R.A.F. *Clubs* : Cavalry ; Bath. (O8041)

BALDWIN, Lucy, Mrs. Stanley, C.B.E., *b.* 1870 ; *d.* of Edward Lucas Jenks Ridsdale, of Rottingdean, Sussex ; *m.* Rt. Hon. Stanley Baldwin, P.C., J.P., M.P., Financial Secretary to the Treasury since 1917, *s.* of Alfred Baldwin, M.P., of Wilden, Stourport (*see* BURKE'S *Landed Gentry*) *Educ.* : At home. *War Work* : Donor and Commandant Wilden Red Cross Auxiliary Hospital, 1914–19. *Addresses* : Astley Hall, Stourport, Worcestershire ; 93, Eaton Square S.W. 1. *Club* : Ladies' Imperial. (O1078)

BALDWIN, Sam, M.B.E., M.Sc., A.I.C., *b.* 11 Oct. 1880 ; *s.* of Greenwood Baldwin, of Todmorden, Yorks ; *m.* Amy Elizabeth, *d.* of Charles Joseph Hiley, of Todmorden, Yorks. *Educ.* : Grammar School and Owens College, Manchester. Superintendent and Works Manager, Explosives and Chemical Products, Ltd., Great Oakley, Harwich, Essex. *War Work* : Engaged in the manufacture of all kinds of explosives and chemicals for Home and Allied Governments. *Address* : Sandholm, St. George's Avenue, Dovercourt. (M7285)

BALDWIN, Capt. Walter James, M.B.E., *b.* 13 Dec. 1881 ; *s.* of James Anthony Windum Baldwin, of Chelsea ; *m.* Alizabeth Annie, *d.* of Phillip Edmund Weston, of Highgate. *Educ.* : United Westminster School and Emmanuel School, Wandsworth Common. Buyer and Works Manager to old established and well-known firm of London Manufacturers in the textile trade ; Eleven years' service in Volunteers and T.F. before the war. *War Work* : Mobilised with T.F., 4 Aug. 1914 (rank Sergt.) ; gazetted 11 Oct. 1915 ; In France with 33rd Division from Nov. 1915 to Dec. 1916 (battles of Somme and Ancre) ; proceeded East, May, 1917 ; service on Sinai Desert, Palestine, Syria ; promoted Capt., 11 Oct. 1918. *Address* : Tower House, Southcote Road, Bournemouth. (M3165)

BALE, Capt. Francis Herbert, O.B.E, R.A.S.C.,

BALFE, Kathleen, M.B.E. Catholic Soldiers' Club, Abbeville. (M10257a)

BALFOUR, Brig.-Gen. Sir Alfred Granville, K.B.E., C.B., *b.* 25 March, 1858 ; *s.* of John Balfour, of Balbirnie, Fife (*see* BURKE'S *Landed Gentry*) ; *m.* Frances, *d.* of Sir Benjamin Simpson, K.C.I.E. *Educ.* : Eton. Joined 71st Highland Light Infantry, 1879 ; Commissioner Royal Hospital, Chelsea. *War Work* : Embarkation Commandant, Port No. 1, Southampton, Aug. 1914 to Aug. 1919 ; Officer Legion of Honour ; Distinguished Service Medal, U.S.A. ; Commander Crown of Belgium ; Commander Order St. Maurice and St. Lazarus, Italy ; 3rd Class Rising Sun, Japan ; 3rd Class White Eagle, Serbia. *Address* : 7, Durham Place, Chelsea. *Clubs* : Turf ; Naval and Military ; Wellington ; Pratt's. (K303)

BALFOUR, Capt. Alfred Stevenson, Royal Indian Marine, O.B.E., *b.* 11 Jan. 1870 ; *s.* of Lewis Balfour ; *m.* Millicent, *d.* of Sir James Balfour, Knt., C.V.O., of Edinburgh. *Educ.* : Tonbridge School and H.M.S. " Conway." *War Work* : In charge of mine-sweeping operations and armed patrols, Madras, India. *Address* : 10, Albany Street, Edinburgh. (O4009)

BALFOUR, Bertha Elsie, Mrs., M.B.E. (M10432)

BALFOUR, David, O.B.E.

BALFOUR, Major Edward William Sturgis, D.S.O., O.B.E., M.C., *b.* 1884 ; *s.* of Edward Balfour, of Balbirnie, co. Fife ; *m.* 1914, Ruth, *d.* of the Rt. Hon. Gerald William Balfour, P.C. Entered R.A. 1904, Major Dragoon Guards, 1918 ; served during Great War, 1914–18, mentioned in despatches. (O6863)

BALFOUR, Lieut.-Col. Harry Hyndman, O.B.E., *b.* 31 May, 1873 ; *s.* of the late George W. Balfour, of Edinburgh ; *m.* Bertha Elsie, *d.* of the late Sir Benjamin Greenacre, of Durban, Natal. *Educ.* : Edinburgh and Brussels. Late Medical Officer to Rand Mines, Johannesburg ; served in Boer War, including Siege of Ladysmith (King's and Queen's Medals, 5 bars), late P.M.O., Transvaal. *War Work* : Sept. 1914, Acting Assistant Director of Medical Service in Natal South Africa ; later attached to South African Medical Corps in Europe ; was Divisional Medical Officer in South African Military Hospital ; mentioned in despatches, O.B.E. *Address* : 62, Queen's Road, Richmond, S.W. *Club* : Durban. (O8005)

BALFOUR, Sir Isaac Bayley, K.B.E., M.A., M.D., D.Sc., LL.D., F.R.S., King's Botanist in Scotland, Regius Keeper of Royal Botanic Gardens, Edinburgh ; Professor of Botany. Univ. of Edinburgh since 1888, *b.* 31 March, 1853 ; *s.* of John Hutton Balfour, Professor of Botany, Univ. of Edinburgh, 1845–79 ;

m. Agnes, *d.* of the late Robert Balloch, Glasgow. *Educ.:* Edinburgh Academy ; Universities of Edinburgh, Strasbourg, and Würzburg. Transit of Venus Expedition to Rodriquez, 1874 ; Regius Professor of Botany, Univ. of Glasgow, 1879–84 ; explored Island of Socotra, 1880 ; Sherardian Professor of Botany, Univ. of Oxford, and Fellow of Madgalen Coll., 1884–88. *Address :* Inverleith House, Edinburgh. *Clubs :* Athenæum ; University, Edinburgh.

BALFOUR, Hon. James Moncreiff, O.B.E. *b.* 6 July, 1878 ; *s.* of the Lord Kinross, of Glasclune (*see* BURKE'S *Peerage*) ; *m.* Madeline Maude, *d.* of James Graham-Watson, of Kingston Grange, Liberton, Midlothian. *Educ.:* Cheltenham, and Balliol College, Oxford. Was Writer to the Signet and was Deputy to the Financial Adviser to the Persian Government at Teheran. *War Work :* Capt. Scottish Horse, Aug. 1914, to Aug. 1915 ; Staff Capt. in this country and then attached 3rd Echelon in France, 1915–17 ; Assistant Secretary, National Service, 1917–19. *Addresses :* 23, He iot Row, Edinburgh ; Teheran, Persia. *Clubs :* New (Edinburgh) ; Orleans.
(O6864)

BALFOUR, Jessie Edith, M.B.E. ; *d.* of James Balfour, late of Clapham Common, S.W. *War Work :* Commandant, No. 16, City of London, Red Cross Hospital, Finsbury Square, E.C.
(M7286)

BALFOUR, Capt. and Qr.-Mr. John, M.B.E., A.I.F.
BALFOUR, Major Nigel Harington, O.B.E., R.A.S.
BALFOUR, Robert John, O.B.E.
BALGARNIE, Capt. Wilfred, O.B.E., M.B. (Lond.), F.R.C.S. (Eng.), R.A.M.C., *b.* 24 Sept. 1863 ; *s.* of Robert Balgarnie, of Scarborough. *Educ.:* Privately ; St. Bartholomew's Hospital ; London and Leeds Universities. County Medical Director British Red Cross Society ; Medical Referee Ministry of Pensions and Workmen's Compensation Act. *War Work :* Medical Officer Minley and Tylney Auxiliary Military Hospitals ; Temporary Captain R.A.M.C. *Address :* The Dutch House, Winchfield.
(O1)

BALL, Capt. Alexander Douglas, O.B.E.
BALL, Capt. and Qr.-Mr. Edward, O.B.E.
BALL, Major Eric Percy, O.B.E.
BALL, Francis Livingstone, M.B.E.
BALL, Lieut. Frank Clement, M.B.E.
BALL, Frederick Ernest, M.B.E.
BALL, Capt. George Joseph, O.B.E.
BALL, Capt. Harry Standish, O.B.E., R.E.
BALL, James, M.B.E., *b.* 1874 ; *s.* of Ebenezer Ball, of Derby ; *m.* Bertha Christella, *d.* of Thomas Carnall, of Derby. *Educ.:* Derby Technical College. Publicity Expert ; District Food Officer, Derbyshire. *War Work :* Hon. Food Distribution Officer, Derbyshire ; Executive Officer, Derby and District Food Control Committee ; Hon. Sec., Derby National Kitchens ; assisted in Recruiting and Registration and other war services. *Address :* 202, Kedleston Road, Derby. *Clubs :* Derby Town ; Markeaton Golf.
(M7288)

BALL, Dr. John, O.B.E., D.Sc., Ph.D., M.Inst.C.E., Assoc. R.S.M., F.G.S., F.R.G.S., *b.* 1872 ; *s.* of the late Ebenezer Ball, of Derby ; *m.* Kate, *d.* of the late James Russell Waite, of Darlington. *Educ.:* Royal College of Science and Royal School of Mines, London. Director of Desert Surveys, Egypt ; Author of numerous works on Geology, Geography, and Surveying. *War Work :* Reconnaissance surveys in the Libyan Desert, in conjunction with military patrols, and assistance to the Intelligence Division, General Staff. *Address :* Maison Mandofia, Garden City, Cairo, Egypt. *Clubs :* Royal Societies' ; Turf (Cairo).
(O2131)

BALL, Major John Clement, D.S.O. O.B.E., Major Canadian Artillery ; Great War, 1914–19 (wounded, despatches, Belgian Croix de Guerre).
(O5978)

BALL, Capt. Lionel Percy, O.B.E., R.A.F.
BALL, Capt. Sydney Arthur, M.B.E.
BALL, Capt. Walter Craven, O.B.E., R.E.
BALL, Walter Mills, M.B.E.
BALL, William Theodore, O.B.E.
BALL, William Valentine, O.B.E., M.A. (Cantab.), *b.* 10 Feb. 1874 ; 2nd *s.* of the late Sir Robert Stawell Ball, LL.D., F.R.S., of Cambridge ; *m.* Kathleen Mary, *d.* of the late George Butt, I.C.S. *Educ.:* Tonbridge School ; King's College, Cambridge ; Lincoln's Inn and Middle Temple. Barrister-at-Law ; Assistant Recorder of Leeds ; an Examiner of the Court. *War Work :* R.N.A.S. Anti-Aircraft Corps, 1915–16 ; Military Service (Civil Liabilities) Commissioner for Essex, 1916–19 ; Kensington Red Cross Depot (Metal Shop), 1915–18. *Addresses :* 1, Brick Court, Temple, London, E.C. ; 18, Holland St., Kensington, London, W. *Club :* Athenæum.
(O1079)

BALLANCE, Sir Hamilton Ashley, K.B.E., C.B., *b.* 28 July, 1867 ; *s.* of the late Charles Ballance, of Clapton, Middlesex ; *m.* Ruth, *d.* of the late Rev. G. S. Barrett, D.D., of Norwich. *Educ. :* Mill Hill School, and Univ. Coll., London. Consulting Surgeon ; Surgeon, Norfolk and Norwich Hospital. *War Work :* Consulting Surgeon, British Armies in France. *Address :* All Saints Green, Norwich.
(K268)

BALLANTINE, Alice Liardet, M.B.E. ; *d.* of Thomas Ballantine, of Greenock, Scotland. *Educ.:* Bournemouth. *War Work :* Quartermaster, Crag Head Hospital, Bournemouth ; had the ordering and giving out of all stores, checking all accounts, paying salaries and wages, and seeing to all renovations and repairs, etc. *Addresses :* 13, Landseer Road, Bournemouth, West ; Kilvaree, Douglas Pier, Argyleshire, Scotland.
(M3505)

BALLANTINE, Ethel Cadogan Burton, M.B.E.
BALLANTYNE, Allan Opie, M.B.E.
BALLANTYNE, Andrew, M.B.E.
BALLANTYNE, Major David, O.B.E.
BALLANTYNE, John, O.B.E.
BALLARD, Com. George Norman, C.B.E., R.N., *b.* 1874 ; *s.* of the late G. A. Ballard, M.C.S., of Philiptown, Selkirk. Great War, 1914–19.
(C2241)

BALLARD, Capt. Gilbert Alfred, O.B.E., Assoc. M.Inst. C.E. etc., *b.* 22 Aug. 1887 ; *s.* of W. J. Ballard, of Birmingham ; *m.* Dorothy, *d.* of T. Milner, of York. *Educ.:* Birmingham Technical School of Engineering. Borough Surveyor, Grantham. *War Work :* 5th R.E. Labour Batt. 1915–16, chiefly work in the Ypres Salient ; Headquarters R.E. Staff XIX Army Corps, B.E.F., 2 years, 1917–19. *Address :* Guildhall, Grantham.
(O4974)

BALLARD, Joseph Alfred William, M.B.E., *b.* 1 Aug. 1875 ; *s.* of the late John Suter Ballard, R.N., of Portsmouth ; *m.* Emily Georgina, *d.* of the late John Woodhouse, of Portsmouth. *Educ.:* Abingdon Road Academy, Southsea. Civil Servant ; entered the Civil Service in 1890 and has held appointments in the Board of Trade and the Admiralty. *War Work :* Served at the Admiralty throughout the War and took a leading part in the work of provision, preparation, and supply of Torpedoes, Paravanes, and Anti-Submarine Devices to the British and Allied Fleets. *Address :* 6, Merchiston Road, Catford, S.E. 6.
(M109)

BALLEINE, Rev. Austen Humphrey, O.B.E.
BALLINGER, John, C.B.E., M.A., *b.* 12 May, 1860 ; *s.* of Henry Ballinger, of Whitchurch, Herefordshire ; *m.* Amy Amelia, *d.* of Captain David Boughton, of Cardiff. Librarian of the National Library of Wales. *War Work :* Custody of National Treasures removed to the National Library of Wales from the British Museum, the National Portrait Gallery, Lambeth Palace, and the Guildhall of the City of London. *Address :* Sherborne House, Aberystwyth.
(C2431)

BALLS, Lieut. William Daniel Chamberlain, M.B.E.
BALME, Archibald Hamilton, O.B.E.
BALMER, Hon. Capt. Ruth, O.B.E., M.B., R.A.F.
BALMFORD, Joseph William, M.B.E.
BALLY, Major Edward Downes, O.B.E.
BALSTON, Major Thomas, O.B.E., M.C.
BALTHAZER, Helen, Mrs., M.B.E.
BALY, Edward Charles Cyril, C.B.E., M.Sc., F.I.C., F.R.S., *b.* 9 Feb. 1871 ; *s.* of the late Edward Ely Baly, of London ; *m.* Ellen Agnes, *d.* of Thomas Jago, of London. *Educ.:* Aldenham School and University College, London. Grant Professor of Inorganic Chemistry, University of Liverpool. *War Work :* Deputy Inspector of High Explosives, Liverpool Area. *Address :* 14, Sunnyside, Princes Park, Liverpool. *Club :* University, Liverpool.
(C427)

BAM, Lieut.-Col. Sir Pieter Cauzius Van Blommestein STEWART- Kt., O.B.E., J.P., M.L A. ; *b.* 99 July, 1869 ; *s.* of the late J. A. Bam, M.L.A. ; *m.* Ena Dingwall Tasca *d.* and co-heir of the late Alexander G. J. Stewart of Ards, Co. Donegal (*see* BURKE'S *Landed Gentry*), and assumed by Royal Licence the prefix surname and the additional arms of Stewart on his marriage, 1910. *Educ.:* Cheltenham ; Normal Coll. and South African Coll., Capetown ; Diocesan Coll., Rondebosch ; Cheltenham Coll. Entered Cape Garrison Artillery, 1892 ; retired with rank, 1901 ; served South African War (medal) ; contested Cape Town, 1904 ; Victoria West, 1904 ; Chairman of the General Executive of South African Exhibition, 1907 ; raised, in 1915, and in command of the 3/7th Batt. the London Regt. ; Chief Recruiting Officer City of London Territorials, May–Sept., 1915 ; Founder and first Chairman, and present Vice-President, of the South African National Union ; special medal granted in 1910 by King Edward for services rendered in connection with the coronation of the Union of South Africa ; connected with many Imperial organisations in England and South Africa ; J.P. Co. Donegal. *Addresses :* 61, Addison Road W. 14 ; Ards, Cashelmore, Co. Donegal ; Sea Point, Capetown. *Clubs :* Sports ; Royal Automobile ; City, Cape Town.

BAMBER, Herbert, O.B.E., *b.* 1880 ; *s.* of John Bamber ; *m.* Mary Elizabeth, *d.* of Thos. Bridge, of Preston. *Educ.:* Xaverians, Preston. Controller of Coal Mines. Export Representative for South Wales and Monmouthshire. *War Work :* General Distribution Branch, Coal Controller's Dept,. 1917 ; Coal Controller's Representative for Scotland, 1917–19 ; acted as a British Delegate, Central European Coal Commission, 1919, and Reparation Commission, Coal Sub-Commission, Paris, 1919–20. *Address :* The Crossways, Parkmoor, Herts.
(O9929)

BAMBER, Capt. Wyndham Lerriee, C.B.E. R.N. (ret.) ; Drafting Com. and Assist. Director Mobilization Div., Admiralty during Great War.
(C2232)

BAMFORD, Lieut.-Col. Harry William Morrey, O.B.E., M.C., Croix de Guerre, South African Infantry. Saw Service with Cape Mounted Riflemen (Boer War) ; Transvaal Mounted Rifles (Zulu Rebellion, 1906) ; Natal Police in Northern Zululand ; Natal Light Horse ; 2nd South African Infantry. *War Work :* Served throughout S. African Rebellion, 1914, and G.S.W.A. campaign, 1914–15, as Adjutant Natal Light Horse ; then to Egypt with South African Brigade throughout Sennussi Campaign (wounded at Halazin) ; then to France with South African Brigade till end of the War (wounded at Delville Wood in July, 1916 ; very severely wounded Le Cateau, Oct. 1918) ; Brigade Major 90th Infantry Brigade in 1917 and later commanded 2nd South African Infantry and South African Composite Regiment; mentioned in despatches. *Address:* National Bank of South Africa, Ltd., Circus Place, London Wall, E.C. (O1081)

BAMFORD, Herbert Richard, M.B.E., *b.* 4 June, 1864. Staff Clerk, Board of Trade. *War Work:* Settlement of estates of deceased merchant seamen. *Address:* East Oakley, Basingstoke. (M7293)

BAMFORD, Louisa Orme, Mrs., M.B.E., *b.* 25 Dec. 1863; *d.* of Thomas Orme Farmer, of Ashbourne, J.P.; *m.* Thomas Henry Broughton, *s.* of John Bamford, of Ashbourne. *Educ.:* 2u Stanley Gardens, Notting Hill. *War Work:* Quartermaster, Ashbourne V.A.D. Hospital, 1915–19. *Address:* Ashbourne, Derbyshire. (M1374)

BAMFORD, Lieut.-Col. Percy, O.B.E., T.D.

BAMFORD, Capt. Reginald Mayall, O.B.E., M.R.C.V.S., R.A.V.C., *b.* 16 Nov. 1892; *y. s.* of Herbert Richard Bamford, M.B.E. (*q.v.*), of Oakley, Hants; *m.* May, *d.* of F. H. Roche, of Princes Street, E.C. *War Work:* Attached 12th Infantry Brigade, Aug. 1914 to Aug. 1915; commanded 41st Mobile Veterinary Section till Feb. 1917, and later commanded the Base Veterinary Hospital, Basra, Mesopotamia. *Address:* Oakley, Hants. (O2259)

BAMFORD, Walter Cecil, M.B.E.

BAMPFIELD, Capt. George Charles, O.B.E.

BAMPFIELD, Capt. Lewis Adolphus, M.B.E.

BAMPTON, Lieut. John Augustus Hamilton, M.B.E., I.A.R.O., attd. R.E.

BANBURY, Charlotte Marie Louise, Mrs., O.B.E.

BANCROFT, Blanche, Mrs., M.B.E.

BANCROFT, James, M.B.E.

BANDON, Hon. Georgiana Dorothea Harriet, Countess of, C.B.E., *o.c.* of the 7th Baron Carbery (*see* BURKE'S *Peerage*); *m.* James Francis Bernard, K.P., 4th Earl of Bandon (*see* BURKE'S *Peerage*). *Addresses:* Castle Bernard, Bandon; Coolkelure, Dunmanway, Co. Cork. (C2432)

BANFIELD, Richard, O.B.E.

BANGAY, Surg.-Lieut. James Darrington, O.B.E., R.N., M.B. (O12021)

BANGER, Lieut. and Qr.-Mr. John Henry Adolphus, M.B.E., *b.* 7 Nov. 1884; *s.* of the late Adolphus Banger, Royal Marines. *Educ.:* Walmer. Confidential Clerk to Director of Organisation, War Office. *War Work:* Served in France with Royal Engineers from Aug. 1914–16, and subsequently in the General Staff and Adjutant-General's Departments of the War Office; twice mentioned in despatches, and once mentioned in Secretary of State's Communiqué; awarded Médaille Militaire by French Government. *Address:* 62, Kent Road, Gravesend, Kent. (M3243)

BANGOR, Maxwell Richard Crosbie Ward, 6th Viscount, O.B.E., R.A., *b.* 4 May, 1868; Eldest surviving *s.* of the 5th Viscount and Mary, *d.* of Henry King, Ballylin, King's Co.; *m.* Agnes Elizabeth, 3rd *d.* of the late Dacre Hamilton of Cornacassa, Monaghan. *Educ.:* Harrow, and R.M.A., Woolwich. Entered Army 1887; Capt. 1898; Major, 1906; retired 1912; served Great War, 1914–19; Lieut.-Col. Reserve of Officers (O.B.E.); Member of the Church of Ireland. *Address:* Castle Ward, Downpatrick, Co. Down. *Clubs:* Army and Navy; Royal Yacht Squadron (Cowes); Royal Ulster Yacht. (O2412)

BANISTER, Lieut. Fred, M.B.E., I.A.R.O.

BANISTER, George Henry, C.B.E., M.I.C.E., *b.* 1856; *s.* of William Banister, J.P., of Devonport; *m.* Lydia Eleanor, *d.* of William Davies, of Charlton, Kent. *Educ.:* Woolwich, Whitworth Scholar. Mechanical Engineering Director, Engineering Works, Messrs. Vickers, Limited, Barrow-in-Furness. *War Work:* Manufacture of War material for Navy and Army. *Address:* Monks Croft, Barrow-in-Furness. *Club:* County, Barrow-in-Furness. (C927)

BANISTER, John, O.B.E., *b.* 1874; *s.* of Arthur Banister, F.C.A., London; *m.* Ada, *d.* of John Brown, of Aspenden, Herts. *Educ.:* City of London School. *War Work:* War Trade Intelligence Department; British Food Missions to Vienna and Prague. *Address:* Secretary of Commission for the Distribution of the Rolling Stock of the former Austro-Hungarian Monarchy, The Hofburg, Vienna. (O9930)

BANKART, Alfred Seymour, M.B.E.

BANKS, Lieut. Francis Rodwell, O.B.E., R.N.V.R.

BANKS, Major George Bertram, O.B.E.

BANKS, Isaac, O.B.E., M.D., M.B., *b.* 3 March, 1867; *s.* of Isaac Banks, of Rockspring, Cork; *m.* Florence Adelaide, *d.* of Dr. Evan Jones, of Aberdare. *Educ.:* Cork; Dublin; London. *War Work:* Surgeon-in-Charge, Aberdare and Merthyr Red Cross Hospital; 208 beds. *Address:* 2, Park Lane, Aberdare, S. Wales. (O4349)

BANKS, Capt. James Harvey, O.B.E., R.A.S.C. and R.A.F.

BANKS, Major Thomas Rivers, M.B.E., *b.* 27 Jan. 1883; *s.* of Rivers Banks, of Stockport; *m.* Barbara Elder, *d.* of James Forbes Duthie, of Thurso, Caithness. *Educ.:* Abbey School, Beckenham, Kent, and Manchester Univ. *War Work:* 2/Lieut. Lancashire Fusiliers, April, 1915, to June, 1915; R.A.S.C. (M.T.), June, 1915, to Jan. 1920; with Mediterranean Ex. Force, Oct. 1915, to Dec. 1915; Mesopotamia Ex. Force, Jan. 1916, to April, 1919 (mentioned in despatches); Q.M.G.2, War Office, July, 1919, to Jan. 1920; Acting Deputy Assist. Director of M.T., G.H.Q., Mes. Ex. Force, Oct. 1919, to April, 1920. *Addresses:* Dean Row, Wilmslow, Cheshire; 23, Orange Street, W.C. 2. *Clubs:* Royal Automobile; Reform. (M4261)

BANNATYNE, Lieut. Archibald Brown, O.B.E., R.N.R.

BANNATYNE, Capt. Arthur Gordon, M.B.E., R.A.S.C., *b.* 5 July, 1885; *s.* of late Lieut.-Col. J. M. Bannatyne, of 8th King's Liverpool Regt.; *m.* Frances Nesta, *d.* of late C. M. Holland, of Bryn-y-grog, Wrexham. *Educ.:* Westward Ho, and King's College, Cambridge. (M5053)

BANNATYNE, Lieut.-Col. Gilbert Alexander, O.B.E., M.D., F.R.C.P., R.A.M.C., *b.* 25 April, 1867; *s.* of Lieut.-Col. John Millar Bannatyne, late 8th King's Liverpool Regt.; *m.* Amy Vivian, *d.* of Surgeon-General William Walker, Indian Medical Service. *Educ.:* Glasgow University and Paris. Honorary Consulting Physician, Royal United Hospital and Royal Mineral Water Hospital. *War Work:* Commandant, Bath War Hospital, March, 1916, to June, 1919; twice mentioned for valuable services. *Address:* 21, The Circus, Bath. *Club:* Bath County. (O6869)

BANNATYNE, Victoria Vera, M.B.E., Medaille de la Reine Elisabeth, *b.* 11 Sept. 1887; *d.* of James FitzGerald Bannatyne, of Haldon, Exeter, and Fanningstown, Co. Limerick. *Educ.:* Privately. *War Work:* Secretary to Devon and Cornwall War Refugee Committee and Quartermaster in charge V.A.D. Rest Club, Trouville, France. *Address:* Parke, Bovey Tracey; Fanningstown, Co. Limerick. (M110)

BANNER, Major Allan William, O.B.E., *b.* 18 July, 1878; *s.* of Allan William Banner, of Liverpool; *m.* Charlotte Mary, *d.* of Thomas Dalton, of Glyn Isa, North Wales. *Educ.:* Privately and Liverpool University. Director of Public Companies. *War Work:* O.T.C., Epsom, Sept. 1914; Paymaster, Northern Command, June, 1915; Certified unfit, Dec. 1915; Voluntary Enlishment, Category 4B, May, 1916; 2nd Lieut., Accounts Officer, R.E., Southampton; Lieut., Inspector of Accounts, Richboro', Manston, Eastchurch, and Hawkinge; Capt., Chief Accounts Inspector of I.W. and D.R.E. Branches and Depots; Major, Deputy Managing Director and Chief Accountant National Shipyards, Chepstow, Beachley, and Portbury; South Africa, on special duty for Ministry of Shipping. *Addresses:* 199, Piccadilly, London, W. 1; South Terrace, Littlehampton. *Clubs:* Littlehampton Golf; Southampton Yacht; Royal Automobile. (O9931)

BANNER, Myra, Mrs., M.B.E. (M10244d)

BANNER, Wilfred, M.B.E., *b.* 9 Jan. 1872; *s.* of Rev. George John Banner, M.A. (Oxon.), of Roby, near Liverpool; *m.* Emily Louisa, *d.* of the late Joseph Tiffin, of Montreal, Canada. *Educ.:* Royal Institution, Liverpool; Privately; Zürich University. *War Work:* War Trade Intelligence Department, and now Foreign Office. *Address:* 35, Courtfield Road, London, S.W. 7. *Club:* Royal Automobile. (M7294)

BANNERMAN, Alexander, M.B.E.

BANNERMAN, David Armitage, M.B.E., B.A., an Esquire of the Order of St. John of Jerusalem, *b.* 27 Nov. 1886; *s.* of the ate David Bannerman; *m.* Muriel, *d.* of T. R. Morgan, of Craigieburn, Moffat, N.B. *Educ.:* Wellington College, and Pembroke College, Cambridge. Special Assistant, Dept. of Zoology, British Museum (Nat. Hist.). *War Work:* Served on staff of the Earl of Donoughmore, K.P., and of Sir Arthur Lawley, G.C.S.I., G.C.I.E.; K.C.M.G., at headquarters of British Red Cross Society in France for 28 months, and afterwards at headquarters in London of B.R.C.S. *Address:* 6, Palace Gardens Terrace, Kensington, W. 8. *Club:* British Ornithologists'. (M1376)

BANNERMAN, Lieut. Glenney Franklin, M.B.E., *b.* 9 Dec. 1896; *s.* of William Gunn Bannerman, of Toronto, Co. York. *Educ.:* Tottenham High School; Jarvis Collegiate Institute; Victoria Coll., Univ. of Toronto. Student at Toronto Univ. in Honour Political Science. *War Work:* Enlisted at Toronto May, 1915, with 2nd Univ. Coy.; served in France with P.P.C.L.I., Aug. 1915 to May, 1917; commissioned to South Staffordshire Regt., Dec. 1917; served in France with 1st. Bn. K.S.L.I., Sept. 1918 to Oct. 1918; 1/6th Batt. South Staffs. Regt., Oct. 1918 to Feb. 1919; attached to Brigade Headquarters Repatriation Centre, Winchester, March, 1919, to Aug. 1919. *Address:* 56, Rose Avenue, Toronto; Victoria Coll., Univ. of Toronto. *Club:* O.R.B., Toronto. (M05999)

BANNING, Stephen Thomas, C.B.E. (C2214d)

BANNON, Lieut. John Joseph, M.B.E.

BANTOFT, William, O.B.E., *b.* 17 Nov. 1848 *s.* of William Bantoft, of Ipswich; *m.* Ellen Jane, *d.* of Robert Bond, of Ipswich. *Educ.:* Privately. Town Clerk and Clerk of the Peace for Ipswich. *War Work:* Secretary to Local Tribunal, and Assistant to the successive Mayors in all the various works undertaken by them during the War. *Address:* 8, Westerfield Road, Ipswich. (O9932)

BARBARY, Capt. John Ewart Trounce, M.B.E., R.A. (T.F.)

BARBER, Lieut. Arthur Powell, M.B.E., A.C.A., R.F.A. (T.), *b.* 25 July, 1887; *s.* of James Barber, of Hendon; *m.* Margery Leader, *d.* of C. H. Bellhouse, of Weymouth. *Educ.:* Merchant Taylors School, London. Assistant Controller, Munitions Accounts. *War Work:* Served in H.A.C. and R.F.A.; twice wounded; attached Ministry of Munitions. *Address:* The Cottage, Shenley, Hertfordshire. (M7295)

BARBER, Lieut. Charles Gordon, M.B.E., I.A.R.O.

BARBER, Francis Amy, M.B.E.

BARBER, Capt. George Henry, M.B.E., R.A.V.C.

BARBER, Capt. James, M.B.E. *b.* 18 Sept. 1877; *s.* of John Barber, of Portsmouth, Hants; *m.* May Lightowler, *d.* of William John Villars, of City Road, London. *War Work:* Original Army of Occupation, Egypt, Camel Corps School; served as

Adjutant and Acting Quartermaster, Camel Corps, Canal Zones, from outbreak of War to Dec. 1915 ; appointed Adjutant of Imperial Camel Corps, Egypt, Jan. 1916, and served as such till Aug. 1918 ; in Palestine, Syria ; appointed to Frontier District Administration as O.C. Camel Corps Depot, 1 Aug. 1918. *Address* : O.C. Depot, Camel Corps, Frontier Districts Administration, Khanka, Egypt. *Club* : Turf (Cairo). (M3166)

BARBER, Capt. James William, C.B.E., *b*. 2 Aug. 1884 ; *s*. of the late James Barber, of Cardiff ; *m*. Daisy Florence, *d*. of Frederick Harman, of St. Leonards. Consulting Engineer. *War Work* : Designer of the Government "Cinemotor" used by the Ministry of Information for propaganda and information purposes during the War ; subsequently appointed Director of Cinematography, National War Aims Committee. *Address* : 60, Welbeck Street, Cavendish Square, W. 1. (C2433)

BARBER, Lieut. Louis Walter, M.B.E., M.C.

BARBER, Mabel Emily, O.B.E.

BARBER, Maude Helen, M.B.E. ; *d*. of the late Charles Worthington Barber, of Prestwich, Lancashire. *Educ.* : Privately. *War Work* : Commandant of High Beach Aux. Military Hospital (Voluntary Aid Detachment, Kent, 64), Westgate-on-Sea, from Feb. 1916 to closing of hospital, Feb. 1919. *Address* : St. Bernard's, Westgate-on-Sea. (M7296)

BARBER, Capt. Percy Charles, M.B.E., R.A.F.

BARBER, Capt. and Qr.-Mr. Richard Alexander, O.B.E., R.E.

BARBER, Samuel Henry, M.B.E., *b*. 1876 ; *s*. of Samuel Barber, of Northampton. *Educ.* : Northampton Grammar School. Auctioneer and Estate Agent ; Fellow of the Auctioneers' and Estate Agents' Institute of the United Kingdom ; Director Northampton Conservative Building and Land Society. *War Work* : Commandant Northampton Special Constabulary. *Address* : Rostrevor, Queen's Park Parade, Northampton. (M113)

BARBER, Major and Qr.-Mr. Thomas, O.B.E., T.D., J.P., *b*. 16 Jan. 1863 ; *s*. of John Barber, of Hertford ; *m*. Clara, *d*. of Robert Chaplin, of Hertford. *Educ.* : Hertford Grammar School. *War Work* : Mobilised on outbreak of War ; proceeded to France, Nov. 1914 ; served with Unit 1st Herts T.F. overseas from that date till return of Cadre in April, 1919 ; twice mentioned in despatches. *Address* : 36, Castle Street, Hertford. *Club* : Conservative (Hertford). (O2413)

BARBER, William, O.B.E., M.A., J.P., *b*. 1863 ; *s*. of John Barber, of Tererran, Moniaive ; *m*. Ella Craig, *d*. of Andrew Lusk, of Caigton. *Educ.* : Dumfries Academy ; Glasgow University. Member of Scottish Land Court. *War Work* : Director of Cultivation for Scotland. *Address* : Millburn, Dumfriesshire ; 32, Dick Place, Edinburgh. (O113)

BARBER, William Clarence, M.B.E.

BARBER, William David, O.B.E., I.S.O.

BARBIER, Isabella Eugenie Marie, M.B.E.

BARBOUR, Anna Edwards, O.B.E., *b*. 25 Nov. 1875 ; *d*. of Robert Barbour, of Paterson, New Jersey, U.S.A. ; *m*. Harold Milne Barbour, *s*. of John D. Barbour, of Lisburn, Ireland. *Educ.* : Dobbs Ferry, New York, U.S.A. *War Work* : Presented Government with Motor Ambulances at the beginning of the War ; from 1914 to 1919 Chairman of Dunmurry Work Guild which raised funds to purchase materials for over 80,000 articles, clothing and hospital requisities which were made and sent to all parts of war area ; also assisted in establishing first Red Cross Hospital in Ulster, known as Hilden Convalescent Hospital for soldiers of all the Allied countries. *Addresses* : Strathearne, Dunmurry, Co. Antrim, Ireland ; Ben Ingan, Donaghadee, Co. Down. (O1083)

BARBOUR, Capt. Archibald Robinson, O.B.E.

BARCLAY, Alfred Ernest, O.B.E., M.D.

BARCLAY, Colville Adrian de Rune, C.B., C.B.E., M.V.O., *b*. 17 Sept. 1869 ; *s*. of Sir Colville A. D. Barclay, Bart., of Pierston ; *m*. Sarita Henriqueta, *d*. of Herbert Ward. *Educ.* : Privately. H.M. Envoy Extraordinary and Minister Plenipotentiary to the Court of Sweden. *War Work* : Counsellor and H.M. Minister Plenipotentiary, H.M. Embassy, Washington. *Address* : British Legation, Stockholm. *Clubs* : St. James's ; Travellers'. (C7)

BARCLAY, Lieut.-Col. George, O.B.E., V.D., *b*. 12 Dec. 1865 ; *s*. of Lawrence Barclay, of Dunedin, New Zealand ; *m*. Laura Edith, *d*. of George Chas. Graham, of Milton, N.Z. *Educ.* : Tokomairiro Grammar School, Milton, N.Z. Railway Manager. *War Services* : Served with the New Zealand Engineers in the New Zealand Expeditionary Force in Gallipoli, Egypt, France, Belgium, and England, 1915–19 ; Chevalier of the Order of Danilo ; twice mentioned in despatches ; Knight of Grace of the Order of St. John of Jerusalem. *Address* : Te Kohanga, Hamilton Road, Anderson's Bay, Dunedin, New Zealand. (O7978)

BARCLAY, Hannah Maud, Mrs., M.B.E., *b*. 23 March, 1872 ; *d*. of Edward North Buxton, of Knighten, Buckhurst Hill ; *m*. Francis Hubert, *s*. of Joseph Gurney Barclay, of Leyton. *Educ.* : At home. *War Work* : Commandant of Women's Red Cross Detachment, Norfolk 6 ; Superintended Red Cross Hospital at Colne House, Cromer, during War, from March, 1915, to Feb. 1919. *Address* : The Warren, Cromer, Norfolk. (M7297)

BARCLAY, Henry Gladstone, M.B.E. (M5056)

BARCLAY, Major Robert Leatham, C.B.E. M.A., *b*. 1869 ; *s*. of Robert Barclay, of High Leigh, Hoddesdon, Herts. (see BURKE's *Landed Gentry*) ; *m*. 31 Mar. 1898, Alice Eugenia, *d*. of Horace Smith - Bosanquet of Broxbournebury (see

BURKE'S *Landed Gentry*). Major Yeo., and Assist. to Ch. Inspector of Quarter-Master-Gen.'s Sers. (C1450)

BARCLAY, William Robb, O.B.E., A.M.I.E.E., *b*. 15 Nov. 1875 ; *s*. of James Laing Barclay, of North East Aberdeenshire. *Educ.* : Privately ; Technical School ; University College, Sheffield. Lecturer in Electro-Metallurgy, University of Sheffield, 1911–19 ; Chairman, Sheffield Local Section of the Institute of Metals, 1918–20 ; Joint-examiner in Electro-Metallurgy, City and Guilds of London Institute ; Works Manager, Henry Wiggin & Co., Ltd., Metallurgists, Birmingham, 1919. *War Work* : Undertook, in 1915, for Messrs. Greenwood & Batley, Ltd., of Leeds, the organisation of new sources of supply of copper-nickel alloys for the manufacture of rifle and machine-gun bullets ; joined the staff of the Ministry of Munitions in 1916 ; appointed Assistant Director and Metallurgist to the non-ferrous rolled metal section ; in this capacity was responsible for the technical oversight of supplies of cartridge and bullet metals for small-arms and quick-firing ammunition ; also acted as Technical Director to the Electro-Metallurgical Committee, Ministry of Munitions. *Address* : 65, Beaconsfield Road, Cannon Hill, Birmingham. *Club* : Clef (Birmingham). (O9935)

BARCLAY, Jeanie, Mrs. COATS-, O.B.E.

BARCROFT, Joseph, C.B.E., F.R.S., *b*. 26 July, 1872 ; *s*. of Henry Barcroft, D.L., of The Glen Newry ; *m*. Mary Agnetta, *d*. of Sir Robert S. Ball, F.R.S., of Cambridge (late Lowndean Prof. of Astronomy). *Educ.* : Botham School, York ; The Leys School, Cambridge ; King's College, Cambridge. Fellow of King's College, Cambridge ; Reader in Physiology University of Cambridge ; Member of the Council of the Royal Society. *War Work* : Member of the Chemical Warfare Committee ; Superintendent in Physiology to Ministry of Munitions. *Address* : 13, Grange Road, Cambridge. *Clubs* : Athenæum ; C.U. Cruising. (C428)

BARDSLEY, Robert Vickers, M.B.E.

BARFF, Comm. Arthur Douglas, O.B.E., R.N.

BARHAM, Col. Thomas Foster, O.B.E.

BARING, Eva Hermione, Lady, M.B.E., *b*. 30 June, 1876 ; *d*. of the late A. Mackintosh of Mackintosh, of Moy Hall, Inverness ; *m*. Sir Godfrey, 1st Bart. (see BURKE's *Peerage*), *s*. of Lieut.-Gen. Charles Baring, of 36, Wilton Place, W. *War Work* : Commandant, Northwood House Red Cross Auxiliary Hospital, Cowes, I.W., Dec. 1914, to Feb. 1919. *Address* : Nubia House, Cowes, I.W. *Club* : Ladies' Automobile. (M3566)

BARING, Brig.-Gen. Hon. Everard, C.V.O., C.B.E., *b*. 1865 ; *s*. of Edward Charles Baring (see BURKE's *Peerage*, Revelstoke, B.) ; *m*. Lady Ulrica Duncombe, *d*. of 1st Earl of Feversham (see BURKE's *Peerage*). *Educ.* : Eton, and R.M.C. Formerly Lieut.-Col. 10th Hussars ; Military Sec. to Viceroy of India, 1899–1905 ; served in Soudan, and at Khartoum. *Addresses* : 26, Hyde Park Street, W. ; Slightholme Dale, Kirby Moorside, Yorkshire. *Clubs* : Turf ; Naval and Military. (C1451)

BARING, Harold Herman John, M.B.E., *b*. 4 Mar. 1869 ; *s*. of Thomas Charles Baring of High Beech, Essex (see BURKE's *Landed Gentry*) : *m*. 24 Oct. 1898, Mary Heigh, *d*. of John Augustus Churchill of New York. *Address* : High Beach, Loughton, Essex. (M7298)

BARING, Capt. the Hon. Hugo, O.B.E.

BARING, Major Hon. Maurice, O.B.E., Chevalier Legion of Honour, *b*. 1874 ; *s*. of the 2nd Lord Revelstoke. *Educ.* : Eton ; Cambridge. Diplomatic Service ; 3rd Sec. 1898–1904 ; Author and Journalist. *War Work* : Intelligence Corps, attached R.F.C. 1914 ; R.F.C. Equipment Officer, 1915 ; Staff Captain, 1916 ; Major, 1917 ; Personal Secretary to C.A.S. Sir Hugh Trenchard, Jan.–May, 1918 ; S.O. 2 Royal Air Force, Staff Officer Independent Air Force, May–Oct. 1918. *Address* : Pickwick's Villa, Dulwich Village, S.E. 21. (O1085)

BARING, Major Thomas Esme, O.B.E., *b*. 7 May, 1882 ; *s*. of Francis C. Baring, of Timsbury Manor, Romsey, Hants (see BURKE's *Landed Gentry*) ; *m*. Deirdre Mary Hughes, *d*. of Hughes Martin, J.P., of Tullaghreine, Co. Cork. *Educ.* : Eton. *War Work* : H.Q. Staff, Southern Command, Aug. 1914, to April, 1916 ; H.Q. Staff, Western Command, June, 1916, to Jan. 1917 ; B.E.F., France, April, 1916, to June, 1916 ; Tank Corps, July, 1917, to May 1918 ; General Staff, Western Command, May, 1918, to Oct. 1918 ; General Staff, British Mission, Siberia, Oct. 1918, to July, 1919. *Address* : Rifle Depôt, Winchester. *Clubs* : Arthur's ; M.C.C. (O9040)

BARKAS, Thomas Cooke, O.B.E., M.B., B.S.

BARKER, Lieut. Albert, O.B.E., R.N.V.R.

BARKER, Major Charles Ainslie, O.B.E.

BARKER, Col. Charles William Panton, C.B.E., Solicitor, Sunderland ; Clerk to the Borough Magistrates. *War Work* : Rendered valuable services in Sunderland. (C3131)

BARKER, Christabel Buchanan, M.B.E., *b*. 7 Oct. 1878 ; *d*. of Rev. Johnson Barker, of New College Chapel, Hampstead. *Educ.* : The Clergy Daughters' School, Bristol. House Mistress of Fawcett House, Godolphin School, Salisbury. *War Work* : Divisional Secretary of B.R.C.S. (Salisbury D.S. Wilts Div.). *Address* : Fawcett House, Salisbury (M7299)

BARKER, Major Eric Clement, M.B.E., *b*. 27 Sept. 1883 ; *s*. of Alfred J. F. Barker, of Constantinople and Esher, Surrey. *Educ.* : Rugby and Royal Agricultural College, Cirencester. Land Agent. *War Work* : Joined 4th King's Shropshire Light Infantry in Sept. 1914 ; commissioned Oct. 1914, and after training with regiment in Wales and Isle of Man, proceeded overseas early in 1916 to join British Salonika Force as Officer

Interpreter (French, Modern Greek, German) ; in Sept. 1916, appointed 1st Class Agent, Intelligence Corps, with rank of Captain, and acted in this capacity at H.Q. XII. Corps until Aug. 1917, when appointed to General Staff Intelligence, General H.Q. Salonika, as G.S.O. 3 ; promoted General Staff Officer, 2nd Class, 4 Nov. 1918 ; proceeded to Constantinople, where attached to Gen. Staff Intelligence till demobilisation in July, 1919. *Address :* Stokesay Cottage, Onibury, Shropshire. *Club :* Public Schools. (M4764)

BARKER, Ernest Bernard, M.B.E., R.A.F.

BARKER, Evelyn, Mrs., M.B.E.

BARKER, Capt. Francis Brock, O.B.E., R.E., *b.* 30 March 1893 *s.* of H. Y. Barker, of Selber House, Hough Green, Chester. *Educ. :* Stonyhurst College. *War Work :* Signal Service in Gallipoli and Salonika. *Address :* Selber House, Hough Green, Chester. *Club :* Naval and Military. (O3017)

BARKER, Capt. Frederick Allan, O.B.E., I.M.S., M.B.

BARKER, Lieut.-Col. Frederick George, C.B.E., M.A., J.P., of Stanlake Park, Berks. ((see BURKE'S *Landed Gentry*) formerly Lieut.-Col. Comdg. 3rd Bn. R. Berks Regt., now Lieut.-Col. Special List, *b.* 27 Oct. 1866 ; *m.* Lucille Mary, *d.* of Cartmell Harrison of Bramley, Hants. Great War, 1914–19 (despatches) *Address :* Stanlake Park, Reading. (C1452)

BARKER, Lieut.-Col. Frederick Rowland, M.B.E., M.B. (Lond.), R.A.M.C. (ret.), *b.* 18 Mar. 1853 ; *s.* of Edmund John Barker M.D., of The Mount, Aldershot ; *m.* Esther Clare, *d.* of Felix Morley, M.A., of Cambridge. *Educ. :* Epsom College and St. Thomas's Hospital. Lecturer and Examiner B.R.C.S. Served on the Red Cross National Aid Society, Turco-Servian War, 1876 (5th Mejidieh) ; the Stafford House Committee, Turco-Russian War, 1877–78 (4th Osmanieh) ; in South African War (Queen's Medal, three bars). *War Work :* Hon. Sec., British Red Cross Society, Worthing Branch ; raised four detachments V.A.D., Sussex. *Address :* Lyncourt, Chaucer Road, Worthing. (M7300)

BARKER, Harold Hastings, M.B.E.

BARKER, Nellie, M.B.E.

BARKER, Capt. and Qr.-Mr. Herbert, M.B.E., M.C., 5th K.O. Yorkshire L.I., *b.* 11 Aug. 1871 ; *s.* of John Barker, of Birstall, Leeds ; *m.* Hannah Mary, *d.* of John Barraclough, of Morley, Leeds. *Educ. :* Mirfield Grammar School. Served 1st V.B., K.O.Y.L.I., 1888–90 ; joined Regular Army, 12 Oct. 1891 ; served Channel Islands, Ireland, Mauritius, South Africa, West Africa (Southern Nigeria), and late War in France, Belgium, and Germany, from 13 April, 1915, to 9 Sept. 1919 ; appointed quartermaster 5th K.O.Y.L.I., 4 May, 1912. *War Work :* Served with 2nd K.O.Y.L.I. in South Africa, in charge Machine Guns, and awarded South African Medal with clasps for Belmont, Modder River, Wittebergen, Transvaal, and South Africa, 1901 ; served in Southern Nigeria ; in charge Machine Guns with Lagos Hausas, during the Aro Expedition ; awarded African General Service Medal with clasps, Aro, 1901 and 1902 ; mentioned for gallant conduct ; mentioned in Sir Douglas Haig's Birthday Honours List, 1917 ; awarded M.C. New Year's Honours List, 1919, and M.B.E., Dec. 1919. *Address :* Minden House Cantley Lane, Doncaster. (M6521)

BARKER, Capt. John Percival, M.B.E., *b.* 27 Sept. 1888 ; *s.* of John Barker, of Melbourne, Australia ; *m.* Lucy Hay, *d.* of Dr. G. Affleck Scott, of Ballarat, Australia. *Educ. :* Melbourne Church of England Grammar School. Fruit farmer. *War Work :* Enlisted 2nd Lieut., Aug. 1915 ; Captain, Jan. 1916 to March, 1916 ; Salonika, March, 1916, to March 1919 ; Staff Captain, Dec. 1918 ; Caucasus, March, 1919 to Sept. 1919 ; Anatolia, Oct. 1919 ; Salonika, Nov. 1919,to June, 1920 *Address :* White Rivers Estates, Nelspruit, Transvaal, South Africa. (M4765)

BARKER, Lilian Charlotte, C.B.E., *b.* 21 Feb. 1874 ; *d.* of James Barker, of Sweffling, Suffolk. *Educ. :* Whitelands College, Chelsea. Principal of Cosway St. L.C.C. Women's Institute ; Principal Officer Training Dept. Ministry of Labour ; Executive Officer Central Committee for Women's Training and Employment. *War Work :* 1st Commandant Women's Legion, Cookery Section ; Lady Superintendent Royal Arsenal, Woolwich. *Address :* 99, Hornsey Lane, N. 6. *Club :* Forum. (C6)

BARKER, Capt. Norman Leslie, O.B.E., R.E.

BARKER, Raymond Thomas, M.B.E.

BARKER, Thomas, M.B.E.

BARKER, Tom Battersby, C.B.E.

BARKER, William, M.B.E. *b.* 11 July, 1858 ; *s.* of John Barker, of Darlington ; *m.* Margaret Jane, *d.* of the late Horace St. Paul Armstrong, of Darlington. *Educ. :* Privately. Clerk and Steward, and Clerk to the Visiting Committee of the North Wales Counties Mental Hospital, Denbigh ; Fellow of the Treasurers' and Cashiers' Corporation ; Chairman of Colliery Holdings, Ltd. *War Work :* Chairman of Denbigh Food Control Committee ; Chairman of Food Economy Committee ; Member of County Appeal Committee under the Profiteering Act ; Chairman of the House Committee of the County Council Farm Institute. *Address :* Meadowside, Denbigh. (M7301)

BARKLEY, Thomas Yuille, O.B.E., M.B., Ch.B., *b.* 28 Dec. 1891 ; *s.* of Martin Barkley, of Lenzie, Dumbartonshire ; *m.* Mary Hughena Jean, *d.* of John Cameron, of Oban. *Educ. :* Dunfermline High School. *War Work :* Served in Salonika, France and Russia, from 1915–19 ; Lieut.-Col. in command of 27th Casualty Clearing Station ; thrice mentioned in despatches. *Address :* Woodcroft, Oatlands, near Weybridge, Surrey. (O3018)

BARKSHIRE, Major Charles Robert, O.B.E., R.E.

BARKWORTH, Minnie Mabel, Mrs., M.B.E. ; *d.* of Malcolm McNeile, Capt., R. Navy ; *m.* John Raymond, Capt., R. Engineers. *War Work :* Four years in the Wounded and Missing Dept. (Brit. Red Cross and Order of St. John). *Club :* Ladies' Imperial. (M7303)

BARLING, Edith Madge, M.B.E. ; *d.* of Sir Gilbert Barling, Bart., C.B., C.B.E., F.R.C.S. (see BURKE'S *Peerage*). *War Work :* Nursing Officer, Birmingham Nursing Corps, St. John Ambulance Brigade ; Commandant, V.A.D., Worc. 82 ; served 1914–19 ; Snow Hill Rest Station, 1914 ; Highbury V.A.D. Hospital, 1915 ; Commandant, 4th Auxiliary Hospital, Moseley, 1916–17 ; Commandant, Mayfield Aux. Hospital for Officers, 1918. (M3507)

BARLING, Lieut.-Col. Sir Gilbert, Bart., C.B., C.B.E., M.B., B.S. (Lond.), F.R.C.S., J.P., R.A.M.C.(T.F.), *b.* 30 April, 1855 ; *s.* of the late William Barling, of Newnham-on-Severn, Glos. ; *m.* Katherine Jaffray, 2nd *d.* of Henry Edmunds, of Elmsdale, Edgbaston, Birmingham. *Educ. :* St. Bartholomew's. Vice-Chancellor University of Birmingham and Ingleby Lecturer, Consulting Surgeon, Birmingham General Hospital ; late Dean of the Medical Faculty, University of Birmingham ; late Examiner in Surgery, University of Cambridge. *Address :* Blythe Court, Edgbaston, near Birmingham. (C1986)

BARLOW, Sir Clement Anderson Montague, K.B.E., LL.D., M.A., M.P. (C.), South Salford, since Dec. 1910 ; Barrister-at-Law ; Parliamentary Secretary to the Ministry of Labour since April, 1920 ; partner in firm of Sotheby, Wilkinson and Hodge ; *s.* of the late Dean of Peterborough. *Educ. :* Repton (Head of the School), King's Coll., Cambridge (Classical Exhibitioner, 2nd Class Classical Tripos, 1st Class Law, Senior Whewell Scholarship, Yorke University Prize Essay). Called to the Bar, Lincoln's Inn, 1895 ; Scholarship, Middle Temple ; Studentship, Inns of Court ; has practised mainly in educational and charity cases ; sometime Lecturer, London School of Economics ; Examiner in Law, London Univ. ; L.C.C. (M.R.) East Islington, 1907–10, and Vice-Chairman, Parliamentary Committee ; for three years Sec., Cambridge House Settlements ; contested South London, Jan. 1910. *War Work :* Raised, with local committee, the Salford Brigade of 5 Battalions (about 7000 men), clothing and equipping them on behalf of the War Office, and built a hut camp for them at Conway, 1914–15 ; Chairman of Select Committee on Soldiers' Pensions, and of Int. Dept. Comm. on Tuberculous Soldiers, 1919. *Address :* 107, Jermyn Street, S.W. *Clubs :* Carlton ; Leander ; Rye Golf ; Union (Manchester). (K50)

BARLOW, Henry Arthur, M.B.E., *b.* 6 Jan. 1863 ; *s.* of Henry Barlow, of Newcastle-on-Tyne ; *m.* Irene, *d.* of Edward Simmonds, of Wandsworth. *Educ. :* Private Schools at Newcastle-on-Tyne and Harrogate. Staff Clerk, War Office. *Address :* 51, Montserrat Road, Putney, London, S.W. 15. (M3508)

BARLOW, James, M.B.E., J.P.

BARLOW, James Alan Noel, C.B.E., B.A., J.P., *b.* 1881 ; *s.* of Sir Thomas Barlow, K.C.V.O., M.D., 1st Bart (see BURKE'S *Peerage*) ; *m.* Emma Nora, *d.* of Sir Horace Darwin, K.B.E., F.R.S. (see BURKE'S *Peerage*). *Educ. :* Corpus Christi Coll., Oxford. *War Work :* Deputy Controller, Labour Supply Dept. Ministry of Munitions ; Assist. Secretary, Ministry of Labour. *Address :* The Warren, Chesham Bucks. (C105)

BARLOW, Lucy Marjorie Kathleen Pratt Mrs., O.B.E.

BARLOW, Sydney, M.B.E., A.C.A., *b.* 18 Sept. 1890 ; *s.* of Frank Barlow, of Kersal. Regional Finance Officer, Ministry of Pensions, North Western Regional Headquarters, Manchester. *War Work :* Finance and Accounts Dept., Ministry of National Service, London, S.W. 1. *Address :* 296, Great Clowes Street, Higher Broughton, Manchester. (M7305)

BARLOW, Dr. Thomas William Naylor, O.B.E., M.R.C.S. (Eng.), L.R.C.P. (Lond.), D.P.H. (Camb.), Barrister-at-law, of Lincoln's Inn, *b.* 30 Sept. 1868 ; *s.* of Josiah Barlow, C.E., of Liverpool ; *m.* Pearl Barlow, *d.* of James McCrossin, of Uralla, N.S.W., Australia. *Educ. :* King Edward's Grammar School, Lichfield ; Liverpool University ; Lincoln's Inn. Medical Officer of Health, County Borough of Wallasey ; Vice-President, Incorporated Society of Medical Officers of Health. *War Work :* Civil Medical Officer in charge of Wallasey Town Hall Military Hospital (450 beds). *Address :* 23, North Drive, Wallasey, Cheshire. *Clubs :* Wallasey Golf ; Liverpool Cricket ; Liverpool Medical Institution. (O11790)

BARLOW, Capt. William Tait, M.B.E., R.G.A., *b.* 1888 ; *s.* of Major Wm. Barlow, V.D., of West Hartlepool, Durham ; *m.* Marjorie Dana, *d.* of Dr. Chas. Loomis Dana, M.D., of New York. *Educ. :* North Eastern County School, Barnard Castle, County Durham. Steamship Manager. *War Work :* France, 1915–16, 19th Heavy Battery (R.G.A.) ; New York, 1917–19, Director, British Ministry of Shipping. *Address :* 53. West 53rd Street, New York. (M3509)

BARMBY, Capt. Aiden James Wharton, O.B.E., R.A.F.

BARNABY, Capt. Hazen Ottis, M.B.E., R.F.A. (T.F.), and R.A.F.

BARNABY, Stanley Skoulding, M.B.E., *b.* 23 Sept. 1879 ; *s.* of Wm. Hy. Barnaby, of Great Yarmouth ; *m.* Amy Mary, *d.* of Thomas Collier, of Gt. Yarmouth. *Educ. :* Gt. Yarmouth Grammar School. G.P.O., July, 1895, to Aug. 1895 ; H.M. Customs, Yarmouth, Aug. 1895 to Sept. 1899 ; Ministry of Agriculture and Fisheries since Jan. 1900. *War*

Work : June, 1915, to 31 March, 1920, Transport Department, Admiralty (Ministry of Shipping), Naval Sea Transport Branch, Commissioned Fleet Auxiliary Section. *Address :* 137, Boundaries Road, S.W. 12.   (M7306)

BARNACLE, Arthur Henry, O.B.E., P.L.G., *b.* 3 Nov. 1863. *War Work :* National Kitchens. *Address :* Idalia, Waveley Road, Coventry.   (O9936)

BARNARD, Albert Alfred, O.B.E.

BARNARD, Major Arthur John Chichester, O.B.E.

BARNARD, Cyril Wyndham, M.B.E., *b.* 26 March, 1867 ; *s.* of Sir Herbert Barnard, of 23, Portland Place, W. ; *m.* Emma Flora, *d.* of the late Frederick Goodman Hunt. *Educ. :* Eton. *War Work :* Special Constable. *Address :* 3, Linden Gardens, Tunbridge Wells.   (M7307)

BARNARD, Edmund Broughton, O.B.E., M.A., D.L. ; *s.* of William Barnard, of Sawbridgeworth and Harlow ; *m.* Alice Maud, *d.* of Charles Richardson, of Wimbledon. *Educ. :* Brighton College, and Downing Coll., Cambridge. Chairman, Hertfordshire County Council ; Chairman, Metropolitan Water Board 1908–20 ; Chairman, Lee Conservancy Board. Member, Agricultural Council for England. *War Work :* Chairman, Herts Agricultural Committee ; Chairman, Military Tribunal. *Clubs :* Reform ; National Liberal.   (O9937)

BARNARD, Ernest Augustus William, O.B.E.

BARNARD, John Henry, O.B.E., M.D., M.R.C.S., *b.* 1852 ; *s.* of the late Robert Barnard, of Liverpool and Ffynnon Grouw, N. Wales. *Educ. :* University of Paris and Guy's Hospital. Late Physician to the Siamese Legation, Paris. *War Work :* Medical Examiner of recruits ; whole-time Medical Officer from 31 Oct. 1916, to 31 May, 1920, to Bermondsey Military Hospital, Ladywell Road, Lewisham, S.E. *Address :* 35, Russell Road, Kensington, W. 14.   (O11791)

BARNARD, John Henry Owen, M.B.E., *b.* 23 June, 1874. *Educ. :* Municipal Secondary School, Bolton. Tramways General Manager. *War Work :* Area Secretary, Board of Trade Tramways Committee. *Address :* Parkside, Green Lane, Bolton.   (M7308)

BARNARDISTON, Katherine Weston, Mrs., O.B.E. ; *d.* of E. G. Elwes, of Felixstowe, and widow of late Gen. Sir George Digby Barker, G.C.B., J.P., of Clare Priory, Suffolk (*d.* 1914) ; *m.* Lieut.-Col. Ernald, D.S.O., R.E., *s.* of the late Col. N. Barnardiston, of The Ryes, Sudbury, Suffolk (*d.* 1916) (*see* BURKE'S *Landed Gentry*), and Lady Florence, 5th *d.* of the 4th Earl of Dartmouth (*d.* 1917) (*see* BURKE'S *Peerage*). *War Work :* Worked in Wounded and Missing Inquiry Bureau, British Red Cross and Order of St. John, first in London, and afterwards as head of Cairo Branch, 1915–16 ; head of Record Department, Central Prisoners of War Committee, 1916–17. *Address :* 10, Barton Street, Westminster. *Club :* Ladies' Empire.   (O1088)

BARNARDO, Col. Frederick Adolphus Fleming, C.I.E., C.B.E., B.Sc., M.D., M.R.C.P., F.R.C.S. ; *b.* 4 June 1874 ; *s.* of the late George Charles Ferdinand Barnardo ; *m.* 1910, Violet Kathleen Ann, *d.* of the late Henry Teviot Kerr, of Monteviot, Darjeeling, India. *Educ. :* Edinburgh Univ. (M.A., B.Sc., M.B. 1899) ; F.R.C.S. 1912, M.R.C.P. (Edinburgh) 1913. Col. Indian Med. Ser. ; S. Africa, 1900–2 (Queen's medal with three clasps, King's medal with two clasps) ; Somaliland, 1902–3 (medal with two clasps). *War Services :* Assist. Director of Med. Sers. (Embarkation) Bombay, 1917, and Dist. Surg. St. John Ambulance Brig. (Women's), Bombay, 1918. *Address :* 9, Queen's Road, Bombay. *Clubs :* Junior United Service ; Royal Automobile.   (C2028)

BARNE, Dorothy Kate, Mrs., M.B.E.

BARNE, Major the Rev. George Dunsford, O.B.E.

BARNE, William Bradley Gosset, C.B.E.   (C3175)

BARNES, Annie Ethel, Mrs., O.B.E.

BARNES, Capt. Douglas, M.B.E., A.I.F.

BARNES, Edgar George, O.B.E., M.D. (Lond.), M.R.C.S., L.S.A., J.P., *b.* 14 Dec. 1848 ; *s.* of George Barnes, of Stradbroke, Suffolk ; *m.* Florence Campbell, *d.* of William Ranby Goate, Major 35th Royal Sussex Regt. *Educ. :* Private School and St. George's Hospital, London. Formerly M.O.H., Hartismere Rural and Eye Urban Districts, Suffolk ; President, of Medical Defence Union ; Member of Council, British Medical Association ; President and Hon. Sec., East Anglian Branch, British Medical Association ; President, Norwich Medico-Chirurgical Society. *War Work :* Red Cross County Director for Jersey ; Hon. Sec., Jersey Branch, British Red Cross Society ; Hon. Sec. and Treasurer, Jersey Joint War Committee of B.R.C.S. and S.J.A.A., etc. *Address :* St. Edmunds, Pontac, Jersey, C.I.   (O9938)

BARNES, Edith Helen, Lady, M.B.E. ; *d.* of Rev. Preb. R. H. Barnes, Vicar of Heavitree, Exeter ; *m.* Sir Hugh Shakespear, *s.* of James Barnes, of Indian Civil Service. *Educ. :* High School, Exeter.. *War Work :* V.A.D. W. Byfleet Military Hospital ; Chairman of Committee of West Byfleet Military Hospital ; on committee, West Byfleet Belgian Refugee Home ; head of Packing Department, Prisoner of War Parcels for R.A.F., Surrey House, Marble Arch. *Address :* 29, Camden House Court, Kensington, W. 8.   (M3510)

BARNES, Edwin Clay, C.B.E., J.P., D L., *b.* 6 April, 1864 ; *s.* of Alfred Barnes, of Ashgate Lodge, Chesterfield. *Educ. :* Wellington College and Trinity College, Cambridge. Chairman Derbyshire County Council ; Chairman Chesterfield Royal Hospital. *War Work :* Member of Appeal Tribunal, Derbyshire ; Chairman War Pensions Committee ; Assistant County Director, British Red Cross Society, Derbyshire.

Address : Ashgate Lodge, Chesterfield. *Clubs :* Oxford and Cambridge ; Reform ; Royal Automobile.   (C2344)

BARNES, Major Frank Purcell, D.S.O., O.B.E., A.M.I.A.E., *b.* 2 Nov. 1880 ; *s.* of Rev. Canon J. P. Barnes, of Ballycastle, Co. Antrim ; *m.* the late Florence Alice, *d.* of C. P. Beck. *Educ. :* Bilton Grange ; Tonbridge ; Magdalen Coll., Cambridge. Chief Instructor M.T. (Mechanical Transport) School of Instruction. *War Work :* Commanded 1st Base M.T. Depot, France, from its inception, organising it and taking it out from England ; this Depot supplied all the M.T. Personnel, Vehicles, and Stores for the B.E.F., and for this he held temporary rank of Lieut.-Col. *Addresses :* Ballycastle, Co. Antrim ; Turner's Green Farm, Fleet, Hants.   (O1089)

BARNES, Lieut.-Col. George Edward, C.B.E., R.M.A., *b.* 19 Aug. 1865 ; *s.* of Geo. R. Barnes, M.D., of Ewell, Surrey ; *m.* Florence Annie, *d.* of Capt. E. Barkley, R.N., of Westholme, British Columbia. *Educ. :* Cheltenham College. *War Work :* Instructor of Gunnery, R.M.A., 1915–17 ; Officer commanding Recruits' Depot, 1917–19. *Address :* Crofton, Vancouver Island, British Columbia.   (C1914)

BARNES, Lieut. George Edwin Olaf, O.B.E., R.N.

BARNES, Harold Charles Edward, C.B.E., *b.* 11 May 1871 ; *s.* of William Black-Barnes, of Collingbourne Lodge, Sandown, Isle of Wight : *m.* Anna Katharine, *d.* of Albert Edward Marvin, of The Grove, Carisbrook, Isle of Wight. *Educ. :* Smythe's Naval School, Portsmouth. Govt. Auditor of Kenya Colony and Zanzibar Protectorate. *War Work :* Director of Military Audit (Mil. Precedence, Lieut.-Col.) during the German East African Campaign (despatches). *Address :* Nairobi, Kenya Colony. *Club :* Sports (London).   (C745)

BARNES, Major Harold Douglas, O.B.E., T.D., *b.* 7 May, 1876 ; *s.* of Edmund Barnes, D.L., J.P., of 220, Camden Road, London. *Educ. :* Malvern College. Solicitor ; Clerk to Justices, St. Pancras Div. ; Major, 7th Batt. London Regt. ; D.A.A.G., War Office Staff. *War Work :* Mobilised 5 Aug. 1914 ; proceeded overseas with 7th Batt. London Regt., British Expeditionary Force, 16 Mar. 1915 ; very severely wounded battle of Festubert, in May, 1915 ; attached to Judge Advocate General's Office, Nov. 1916 ; appointed Staff Captain, Feb. 1917 ; mentioned, Mar. 1918 ; O.B.E. (Mil.), Jan. 1919 ; appointed D.A.A.G., Jan. 1919. *Address :* 68, Victoria Street, S.W. 1. *Club :* Public Schools.   (O3088)

BARNES, Helen Elizabeth, M.B.E.

BARNES, Henry, O.B.E., M.D., LL.D., F.R.S.E., J.P., *b.* 20 July, 1842 ; *s.* of Joseph Barnes, of Aikton, Cumberland ; *m.* Emily Mary, *d.* of Thomas Barnes, of Bolton, Lancashire. *Educ. :* St. Bees, Cumberland ; Edinburgh University. Physician Cumberland Infirmary, 1873 to 1904 ; Consulting Physician, 1904 to date ; Senior Ex-President British Medical Association ; Chairman Cumberland War Justices, 1904 to date. *War Work :* Hon. Sec. and Treasurer Cumberland Branch British Red Cross Society, 1907 to 1919. *Address :* 6, Portland Square, Carlisle. *Club :* County, Carlisle.   (O117)

BARNES, James Burden, O.B.E.

BARNES, 2nd Lieut. James Cecil Lawson, M.B.E., H.A.C.

BARNES, James Sidney, O.B.E.

BARNES, John, M.B.E., R.N.

BARNES, John Albert, O.B.E.

BARNES, Katharine Florence, M.B.E.   (M10371)

BARNES, Major Lawrance Edward, O.B.E., R.E.

BARNES, Leonard Stewart, O.B.E., M.R.C.S., L.R.C.P. (Eng.), *b.* 11 July, 1869 ; *s.* of John George Barnes, R.N., of Weymouth, Dorset ; *m.* Emily, *d.* of Charles Harrison Allan. *Educ. :* Weymouth College and St. Bartholomew's Hospital. Surgeon and Physician to Welwyn Hospital ; Medical Officer to 3rd Div. Hitchin R.D. ; Examiner to St. John's Ambulance. Publications : "Martin's First Aid," "Home Nursing." *War Work :* Auxiliary V.A.D. Hospital, St. Paulswalden, 1914–15 ; Private Hospital for Wounded Belgians, Little Berkhampstead, 1914–16 ; Auxiliary V.A.D. Hospital, Kingswalden, 1915–17 ; Auxiliary V.A.D. Hospital, Bragbury, 1915–17 ; Auxiliary V.A.D. Hospital, Knebworth, 1917–18 ; Special Constable, 1914–19. *Addresses :* Whitwell, Welwyn, Herts. ; 16, South Audley Street, London.   (O9939)

BARNES, Mary Elizabeth, Mrs., O.B.E.

BARNES, Minnie Craig, Mrs., M.B.E.

BARNES, Rev. Sidney Reeves, O.B.E., *b.* 1871 ; *s.* of the late Rev. B. T. Barnes, of Wombwell, Yorkshire ; *m.* Ethel Alberta, *d.* of the late Law Liversidge, of Fixby, Huddersfield. *Educ. :* St. Paul's Sch., and Worcester Coll., Oxford. R. of Ashwell, and a Chap. to the Forces (T.F.) ; sometime Capt. 5th Batt. York and Lancaster Regt. (T.D.) ; became Hon. Lieut. in the Army, 1902 ; S. African War, 1899–1902 (medal with five clasps) ; Great War, 1914–19 (despatches, 1914–15 Star). *Address :* Ashwell Rectory, Oakham.   (O2415)

BARNES, Thomas James, O.B.E.

BARNETT, Ada, M.B.E. ; *d.* of Edward Barnett, of Kenton Court, Sunbury-on-Thames. *War Work :* Commandant of Kingswood Park Hospital, Tunbridge Wells. *Address :* 7, Church Road, Tunbridge Wells. *Club :* Services.   (M3511)

BARNETT, Major Albert Edward, M.B.E., R.A.M.C.

BARNETT, Lieut.-Col. Alfred George C.B.E.. *b.* 23 June, 1883 ; *s.* of James Barnett, of Barnes ; *m.* Mabel Lilian Beatrice, *d.* of H. O. Strong, of Redland, Bristol. *Educ. :* Alleyn's School and Birkbeck College. Deputy Director of Contracts and

Labour, H.M. Office of Works. *War Work*: Assistant Director of Forestry, British Armies in France. *Address*: 8, Ranelagh Avenue, Barnes, S.W. 13. (C1219)

BARNETT, Capt. Alfred Henry, M.B.E.

BARNETT, Lieut. Edwin Ernest, M.B.E.

BARNETT, Ezra John, M.B.E.,

BARNETT, Lieut. Geoffrey Arthur, M.B.E.

BARNETT, Henrietta Octavia Weston, Mrs., C.B.E., *b* 4 May, 1851; *d.* of Alexander Rowland, of Champion Hall, Kent; *m.* Samuel Augustus, *s.* of Francis Augustus Barnett. *Educ.*: At home. Hon. Manager of the Hampstead Garden Suburb Trust, Ltd.; Director of the Institute Council; Vice-Chairman of the Governors of the Barnett School; Member of the Trust Committee under the Profiteering Act. *War Work*: Helped to establish the Hampstead Hospital; established 12 tenements for War Widows and their children; was President of the Overseas Hospitality Committee; held office in the H.G.S. War Supply Depot; conducted V.A.D. classes. *Addresses*: 1, South Square, Hampstead Garden Suburb; Aldrington, Hove, Sussex. (C10)

BARNETT, James Rennie, O.B.E., *b.* 6 Sept. 1864; *s.* of James Barnett, of Johnstone, Renfrewshire; *m.* Annie Caird Cowan, *d.* of David A. Finlay, J.P., of Glasgow. *Educ.*: Neilson Educational Institution, Paisley; Technical College, Glasgow; Glasgow School of Art, and Glasgow University. Naval Architect and Yacht Designer; Consulting Naval Architect to the Royal National Lifeboat Institution. *Address*: G. L. Watson & Co., Naval Architects, 53, Bothwell St. Glasgow. *Clubs*: Royal Northern Yacht; Royal Clyde Yacht. (O119)

BARNETT, Margaret Elizabeth, M.B.E.

BARNETT, Samuel Henry Gilmore, M.B.E.

BARNFIELD, Capt. Allen Stewart, O.B.E. R.A.F.

BARNFIELD, Capt. William George, M.B.E.

BARNS, George Delbridge, M.B.E.

BARNS, Stephen Allen, M.B.E.

BARNSLEY, Major George, O.B.E, *b.* 17 June, 1874; *s.* of Henry Barnsley, of Sheffield; *m.* Mabel Kate, *d.* of Frederick Gittus, of Mildenhall, Suffolk. *Educ.*: Wesley Coll., Sheffield, and Moravian School, Neuwied-on-Rhine. Steel, File, and Tool Manufacturer. *War Work*: Officer Commanding Recruiting Area. *Address*: 6, Victoria Road, Broomhall Park, Sheffield. (O1091)

BARNSLEY, T. Warrant Officer John G., M.B.E.; Royal Indian Marine.

BARNWELL, Capt. Frank Sowter, O.B.E., A.F.C., R.A.F.

BARON, Barclay, O.B.E., *b.* 28 Feb. 1884; *s.* of Sir Barclay J. Baron, Kt., of Bristol (d. 1919); *m.* Rachel Caroline, *d.* of the late Abel Smith, M.P., of Woodhall, Hertford. *Educ.*: Clifton College and University College, Oxford. *War Work*: Secretary, Y.M.C.A., Havre Base, 1915–16; Fourth Army, 1917; Second Army, 1917–18. *Address*: 175A, Long Lane, Bermondsey, S.E. *Club*: Cavendish. (O1362)

BARON, Herbert Harry, M.B.E.

BARON, Hilda Madeleine, Mrs., M.B.E.

BARR, Lieut. Charles Nicholson, M.B.E., R.G.A.

BARR, Sir James, Knt. Bach., C.B.E., LL.D. F.R.C.P., F.R.S.E., *b.* 25 Sept. 1849; *s.* of Samuel Barr, J.P., of Claremont, Co Tyrone; *m.* Isabella Maria, *d.* of J. Woolley, of Liverpool. *Educ.*: Londonderry; Glasgow. Consulting Physician, Liverpool Royal Infirmary; Vice-President, B.M.A.; Medical Visitor, Turbrook Asylum; Visiting Physician, Haydock Lodge Asylum; Physician, Stanley Hospital; Northern Hospital, Liverpool. *War Work*: Lieut.-Col. 1st Western General Hospital, R.A.M.C.; County Director for West Lancs. Vol. Aid. Ass. T.F. with control of Fifty Voluntary Aid Hospitals; Chief Transport Officer for the Wounded Soldiers in West Lancashire; County Director, West Lancashire Territorial Force Association. *Addresses*: 72, Rodney St. and Otterspool Bank, Aigburth, Liverpool. *Clubs*: Conservative and Athenæum, Liverpool. (C2435)

BARR, John, C.B.E.

BARR, Lieut. Philip Henry, M.B.E., R.A.F.

BARR, Venie Ainsworth, Mrs., C.B.E.

BARRACLOUGH, Lieut. Jackson Gurth, M.B.E.

BARRACLOUGH, Sir Samuel Henry Egerton, K.B.E., Col. Military Forces; Staff Australian Imperial Forces. (K346)

BARRAS, Lieut. Harold Wilmot, M.B.E.

BARRATT, Major Arthur Walker, M.B.E.

BARRATT, (May) Katharine Mathilde, Mrs. CROSS-, O.B.E.; *d.* of Henry Goldsmith, of Ramsey, Isle of Man; *m.* Major-Gen. William Cross-Barratt, C.B., C.S.I., D.S.O., commanding 9th Secunderabad Division. *War Work*: 1914–18, Soldiers' and Sailors' Families Association; President, Dalhousie Branch, Red Cross Work and Lahore Cantonment; Officers' Family Fund; Station Hospital and Family Hospital and entertainment of Soldiers, British and Indian; 1918–20, Entertainment and Comforts, Troops Bangalore and 9th Div.; Welfare and care of women and children, British troops; Local Officers' Family Fund, and President Organised League of Help, British and Indian Troops; organised and raised subscription for Silver Wedding Fund. (O8244)

BARRATT, Frances, Lady LAYLAND-, C.B.E., a Lady of Grace of the Order of St. John of Jerusalem; *d.* of Thomas Layland, of Stonehouse, Wallasey, Cheshire; *m.* Sir Francis Layland-Barratt, Bart., M.A., LL.B., J.P., D.L., *s.* of Francis Barratt, of St. Austell, Cornwall. *Educ.*: At home. *War Work*: Commandant of the Red House Hospital, a First Line

Hospital for non-commissioned officers and men at Cromer, Norfolk, and Commandant of Lady Layland-Barratt's Hospital for Officers, The Manor House, Torquay, 1914–19. *Address*: The Manor House, Torquay. *Club*: Bath. (C2438)

BARRELL, Major William Henry, O.B.E., T.D., R.G.A. (T.F.), *b.* 25 Feb. 1882; *s.* of William Henry Barrell, of Southsea; *m.* Beatrice Grant, *d.* of Thomas Page, of Southsea. *Educ.*: Portsmouth Grammar School. *War Work*: Coast Defence, England; France, 1915–16; Major Instructor of Gunnery, Siege Artillery School, 1917; Salonika, 1918; Constantinople, 1919; Senior Control Officer, Allied Police Commission, 1919–20. *Address*: Morval, High Street, Portsmouth. (O8676)

BARRETT, Col. Dacre Lennard, C.B.E., R.M.L.I., *b.* 11 Sept. 1858; *s.* of the late Henry Alfred Barrett, Rector of Chedgrave, Vicar of Langley, Norfolk; *m.* Maud Mary, *d.* of the late H. C. Hast, of 31, Russell Road, Kensington. *Educ.*: Marlborough. Entered Royal Marines, 1 Sept. 1876; distinguished Military Law; Fortification; first-class Gunnery Instructor; Army Gymnastics and Physical Training. *War Work*: Served General Staff Royal Marines, R.N. Division. Dunkirk, as Chief Paymaster to both Services; head of Postal Service during operations round Antwerp; as command paymaster for short time, then Brigade Paymaster R.M. Walmer, Shellingstone, Chatham, Blandford, Aldershot, from 7 Sept. 1914, to 18 May, 1919. *Address*: Vigers Hall, Tavistock. *Clubs*: Fly Fishers'; Marlborough; Public Schools. (C1915)

BARRETT, Dr. Edith Helen, C.B.E.

BARRETT, Florence Elizabeth, Lady, C.B.E., M.D., M.S.; *d.* of the late Benjamin Perry, of Avonleigh, Stoke Bishop; *m.* Sir William Fletcher, F.R.S., *s* of. the Rev. W. G. Barrett (*see* BURKE'S *Peerage*). *Addresses*: 31, Devonshire Place, W.; Carrigoona, near Bray, Co. Wicklow. (C8)

BARRETT, Geoffrey Foster, O.B.E.

BARRETT, Hannah Madge, M.B.E., A.C.I.S., *b.* 1879; *d.* of the late John Barrett, of Hungerford, Berks. *Educ.*: Privately. *War Work*: In charge of Nurses' Pay and Contracts Department, Joint War Committee, British Red Cross Society and Order of St. John of Jerusalem. *Address*: 6, Claremont Road, Cricklewood, N.W. 2 (M7313)

BARRETT, Capt. Hugh Scott, O.B.E.

BARRETT, Lieut.-Col. Sir James William, K.B.E., C.B., C.M.G., Order of the Nile (3rd Class), R.A.M.C. and A.A.M.C., *b.* 27 Feb. 1862; *s.* of James Barrett, of South Melbourne; *m.* Marian, *d.* of Charles Rennick, of Melbourne. *Educ.*: Melbourne University and King's College, London. Consulting Surgeon, Victorian Eye and Ear Hospital; Ophthalmologist, Melbourne Hospital; Member of Council and Lecturer on the Physiology of the Special Lenses in the University of Melbourne. *War Work*: Consulting Oculist, Egypt, 1915; A.D.M.S., Australian Force in Egypt, 1918; Consulting Aurist, A.E.F., 1916–18; President, Invaliding and Classification Board, Della District, 1916–18; First Secretary, Australian Red Cross; Member War Work Committee, Y.M.C.A., Egypt. *Address*: 105, Collins Street, Melbourne. Australia. *Club*: Melbourne. (K116)

BARRETT, Kate Eveline, M.B.E.; *d.* of the late J. Platt Barrett, F.E.S. *Educ.*: Aske's (Hatcham). Superintendent (Acting), Accountant-General's Dept., G.P.O. *Address*: Westcroft, South Road, Forest Hill, S.E. 23. (M7314)

BARRETT, Kenneth Delmar, M.B.E.; *s.* of C. R. Barrett, J.P., of Co. Durham; *m.* Dorothy Grace, *d.* of Douglas H. Barry, of Collingham Gardens, S.W. *Educ.*: Rossall. Marine Engineer. *War Work*: Outside Manager Messrs. R. & W. Hawthorn Leslie & Co., Ltd., Engineers and Shipbuilders, Newcastle-on-Tyne. *Address*: Berisal, Graham Park Road, Gosforth, Northumberland (M120)

BARRETT, Mary Beatrice, Mrs. Cowdell, O.B.E. (O11963)

BARRETT, Milan, Mrs., M.B.E.; *d.* of William Laud, of Camberwell; *m.* Leonard, *s.* of Richard Bray Barrett, of Dulwich. *Educ.*: Mary Datchelor School, Camberwell. *War Work*: Hon. Sec., Streatham War Savings Committee; Hon. Sec., Streatham Food Control Sub-Committee; Hon. Sec., Streatham Peace Celebration Committee. (M7315)

BARRETT, Lieut. Richard William, O.B.E., R.N.R.

BARRETT, William James, M.B.E., *b.* 16 Sept. 1857; *s.* of the late J. A. Barrett, of Old Charlton, Kent; *m.* Mary Jane, *d.* of the late W. Curtis, of Poole, Dorset. *Educ.*: Birkbeck Schools, Peckham. Civilian Inspector of Equipment and Stores, Royal Dockyard, Woolwich. *Address*: 29, Little Heath, Charlton, S.E. 7. (M121)

BARRIE, Charles Coupar, C.B.E., J.P., M.P., *b.* 1875; *s.* of Sir Charles Barrie, D.L., of Dundee. *Educ.*: Blanlodge School, N.B. Shipowner and Merchant: M.P. for Elgin Burghs, 1919; M.P. for Banffshire, 1920. *War Work*: Voluntary services to Admiralty Transport Dept. and Ministry of Shipping 1916–20; Member of Supreme Economic Council to Peace Conference 1919; Representative of Minister of Munitions, Paris; Member of Disposals Board; on Advisory Council to Department of Overseas Trade. *Addresses*: Airlie Park, Broughty Ferry, N.B.; 6 Dean's Yard, Westminster, S.W. *Clubs*: Oriental; Royal Automobile; National Liberal. (C429)

BARRIE, David Watson, O.B.E.

BARRINGTON, Sir Charles Burton, Bart., M.B.E., M.A., J.P., D.L., *b.* 1848; succeeded his father, as 5th Bart., 1890 (*see* BURKE'S *Peerage*); *m.* Mary Rose, *d.* of Sir Henry Hickman

Bacon, 10th Bart. of Redgrave, and 11th Bart. of Mildenhall (*see* BURKE'S *Peerage*). *Educ.:* Rugby, and T.C.D. High Sheriff, Co. Limerick, 1879 and Hon. Col. Special Reserve. *Address:* Glenstal, Newport, Limerick. *Clubs:* Union; Kildare Street; Carlton. (M3112)

BARRINGTON, Lieut. Herbert Cecil, M.B.E., *b.* 31 July, 1877; *s.* of Herbert Barrington, of Lynmouth, N. Devon, and Burpham. *Educ.:* Privately. Land Agent. Qualified Associate of the Land Agents' Society; (late) Sub-Agent to Sir A. Hargreaves Brown, Bart., Lady Gerrard, and others. *War Work:* R.A.S.C., H.T., Depot work. *Address:* 80, Piccadilly. *Clubs:* Royal Thames Yacht; Royal Corinthian Yacht. (M5062)

BARRINGTON, Lieut.-Comm. Thomas Barwell, M.B.E., R.N.V.R.

BARRIOS, Dr. Benjamin, C.B.E., *b.* 31 March, 1878; *s.* of the late General Pedro Barrios. *Educ.:* City of Mexico. Member of the Mexican Bar, 1899; of the Spanish Bar, College of Madrid, 1911; of the Bar of Lima, Peru; Member of the Bar of Bolivia, Salvador, Costa Rica; Barrister-at-Law, England, Lincoln's Inn, called 1912; Attaché to the Mexican Legation in London, 1908; Minister Plenipotentiary to Guatemala, 1914; Member of the Council of the International Law Association, London; Member of the Société des Gens de Lettres, Paris; Commander of the Order of Elizabeth, Spain, 1910; Chevalier de la Legion d'Honneur, France, 1916; Commander of the Order of the Redeemer, Greece, 1918; Chevalier do l'ordre de Leopold, Belgium, 1918; Editor of the fortnightly review, " America Latina," London and Paris. *Addresses:* 103, Portman Mansions, W.; 54, Gresham Street, E.C. (C106)

BARRITT, Capt. Wesley, O.B.E.

BARRON, Lieut.-Col. Alexander, M.B.E., *b.* 21 Aug. 1861; *s.* of Robert Barron, of Skene; *m.* Elizabeth, *d.* of Martin Culbert, of 78th Rosshire Buffs. *Educ.:* Aberdeen. Seaforth Highlanders, 1879; Argyllshire Highlanders, 1880; A. and S. Highlanders, 1881; R.A.S.C., 1890; War Office, 1890–99; General Sir Redvers Buller's Advance Supply Depot, South African War, 1899–1902; twice mentioned in despatches. *War Work:* With Mechanical Transport, R.A.S.C. on outbreak of Great War, assisted in despatching companies from Seaforth overseas, and started M.T. Depot at Bulford; was D.A.D.T.M.T. 9, Mobilisation and Embarkation Area, Bulford; assisted in formation and supervised details of preparation and despatch for overseas of some 600 M.T. Companies, and about 2000 H.A.M.T. Sections; mentioned in despatches three times; retired 1920. *Address:* Granton Lodge, 10, Great Western Place, Aberdeen. *Club:* R.A.S.C. (M123)

BARRON, Lieut.-Col. Cyril Alexander, O.B.E., R.A.S.C.

BARRON, Rev. Douglas Gordon, O.B.E., V.D., *b.* 21 Oct. 1854; *s.* of the Rev. Peter Barron, of Unit. Presb. Minister, Dunning, Perthshire; *m.* Louise Eliza, *d.* of Robert Brydon, of The Dene, Seaham, Harbour. *Educ.:* St. Andrews' University. Minister at Dunnottar, Kincardineshire. *War Work:* Local War Pensions Committee, Kincardineshire; Member of Sailors' and Soldiers' Federated Association. *Address:* Dunnottar Manse, Stonehaven, Kincardineshire. (O0942)

BARRON, Lieut.-Col. Frederick Wilmot, O.B.E., R.A.

BARRON, Jonathan, M.B.E., Ex-R.N.R., *b.* 11 Nov. 1861; *s.* of William Barron, of Mevagissey; *m.* Elizabeth, *d.* of Joseph Giles, of St. Austell. *Educ.:* Privately. Cornwall County Fishery Officer; Coastal Surveyor (State Insurance of Fishing Vessels) under the Board of Agriculture and Fisheries. *War Work:* Confidential work under the Admiralty and in conjunction with the Board of Agriculture and Fisheries. *Address:* " The Cuddy," Polkirt, Mevagissey, Cornwall. (M124)

BARRON, Major John Bernard, O.B.E., M.C.

BARRON, Lieut.-Col. Neil MacKechnie, O.B.E., R.A.

BARRON, Major Sidney Norman, O.B.E., M.C., Legion d'Honneur, A.M.I.C.E., P.A.S.I., late R.E.; *s.* of Sidney Barron, of Kingstown, Co. Dublin; *m.* Irene M., *d.* of the late Rev. G. A. Robins, of Eccleston and Southborough. *Educ.:* Aravon School, Bray; Trent College, Derbyshire; Owens College, Manchester. Civil Engineer; B.Sc. (Engineering). *War Work:* Trained and went to France with 82nd Field Co., R.E., 1914–16; Staff Officer to Chief Engineer, 3rd Corps, B.E.F., 1916–19. *Address:* 13, Emperor's Gate, S.W. 7. (O2416)

BARROW, Alfred, O.B.E.

BARROW, Capt. Claude, M.B.E.

BARROW, Ellen Janet, M.B.E.; *d.* of J. B. Barrow. *War Work:* Superintendent of C. of E. Soldiers' Institutes at Killinghall and Catterick Camps. *Club:* Three Arts. (M7316)

BARROW, Lieut.-Col. Harold Percy Waller, C.M.G., D.S.O., O.B.E., *b.* 1876; Lieut.-Col. Roy. Army Med. Corps; S. African War, 1900–2 (Queen's medal with three clasps, King's medal with two clasps); Dep. Assist. Director-Gen. Med. Sers., 1914 (Belgian Order de la Couronne). (O2415)

BARROW, Jess, Mrs. GRAHAM-, M.B.E., *b.* 5 April, 1886; *d.* of Russell Witherington, of Sonning-on-Thames; *m.* Edward Percy, *s.* of Charles John Graham-Barrow, of Camden Town, N. *Educ.:* Western House, The Park, Nottingham. *War Work:* Clerical work in Recruiting Office, Southend-on-Sea, Essex, from 1915–17; serving with Queen Mary's Army Auxiliary Corps, from 1917 to demobilisation, 1920. *Address:* Cathedral School, Shanghai, China. (M5298)

BARROW, Oscar Theodore, C.S.I., C.B.E., *b.* 1854; *s.* of

Jacob Barrow; *m.* 1888, Helen Emma Winefride, *e. d.* of the late Reginald Reynolds, of Clarendon Square, Leamington. *Educ.:* Beaumaris Gram. Sch., and Gloucester Sch. Entered I.C.S. 1875; Accountant-Gen. of Bengal, 1891; of Bombay, 1894; Sec. to Govt. of India in Finance Depart. 1906, and Comptroller and Auditor-Gen. of India, 1906; retired, 1910; Fellow of Bombay Univ. *Address:* Kareol, Weybridge, Surrey. *Clubs:* East India United Service; Hurlingham. (C107)

BARROWCLIFF, Marmaduke, M.B.E.

BARROWS, Comm. Elliot Thomas, C.B.E., *b.* 16 April, 1860; *s.* of William Henry Barrows; *m.* Cora, *d.* of James Fuller. *Educ.:* Public Schools. Ex-Member Board of Managers; Vice-President and President New York Produce Exchange; Ex-Member Common Council; Ex-Police Commissioner; Ex-Member Board of Health, City of Plainfield, New Jersey, U.S.A. *War Work:* Director British Ministry of Shipping, U.S.A., 1918, and Deputy Director-General, 1918 to date. *Address:* 406, Produce Exchange, New York City, U.S.A. *Clubs:* Plainfield Country; New England Society; Sons of the Revolution; The Pilgrims; St. George's Society; Military Order of the Loyal Legion; Veteran Society Seventh Regiment National Guard, State of New York (C2439)

BARROWS, Lucy Adeline, M.B.E., *b.* 19 Nov. 1878; *d.* of Joseph Barrows, of Edgbaston, near Birmingham. *Educ.:* Edgbaston Church of England College for Girls, and private school. *War Work:* Asst. Hon. Sec., War Pensions Committee and Citizens' Society, Birmingham. *Address:* 44, Russell Road, Moseley, near Birmingham. *Club:* Three Counties (Birmingham). (M7318)

BARRY, Major Arthur Cressy, M.B.E.

BARRY, Arthur J., M.B.E.; Assistant Censor, New York. (M10257b)

BARRY, Lieut.-Col. Arthur John, C.B.E., Officer Legion of Honour, Knight of Grace Order of St. John of Jerusalem in England, Croix de Guerre, M.Inst.C.E. R.E. (T.), *b.* 1859; *s.* of Chas. Barry, F.R.I.B.A., of London; *m.* Mabel Maude, *d.* of Col. Ostrehan, I.A. *Educ.:* Uppingham. Consulting Engineer, Bombay Port Trust, Aden Port Trust, Shanghai Nankin Railway, Shanghai Hanchow Ningpo Railway, Canton-Kowloon Railway, British and Chinese Corporation, Ltd., etc. *War Work:* Went to France, under auspices of B.R.C.S., in Sept. 1914, on mission to search for missing and wounded; raised Volunteer Convoy of Motor Ambulances for service on French front, also under the auspices of the B.R.C.S. in conjunction with the late Mr. Richard Norton, founder of a society known as the Anglo-American Volunteer Ambulance Corps; became Officer in General Command of B.R.C.S. Motor Ambulance Convoys, supported by the special fund of the B.R.C.S., known as the " Dennis Bayley " Fund, serving on French front. *Addresses:* 2, Queen Anne's Gate, London, S.W. 1; Twisly, Catsfield, Sussex. *Clubs:* Athenæum; Wellington; St. Stephen's; Sussex County, etc. (C928)

BARRY, David, O.B.E.

BARRY, Lady Grace, M.B.E.

BARRY, Lieut. Jack Leslie, M.B.E., I.A.

BARRY, John Armstrong, M.B.E., *b.* 8 Jan. 1881; *s.* of Arthur Barry, of Dundee. *Educ.:* High School, Dundee, and Edinburgh University. Solicitor; Secretary, Dundee Local War Pensions Committee; Hon. Sec. and Treasurer, Dundee Branch Incorp. Soldiers and Sailors Help Society; Joint Hon. Secretary, Lord Roberts' Memorial Workshops Committee for Central Scottish Area; Lieut. H.M. Cadet Force. *War Work:* Sailors and Soldiers Help Society; War Pensions; Flag Days. *Address:* 7, Fort Street, Magdalen Green, Dundee. (M3514)

BARRY, Capt. John Hewitt, O.B.E., *b.* 13 Sept. 1891; *s.* of the late James Hewitt Barry, of London and Calcutta. *Educ.:* Heidelberg College, Heidelberg, Germany. Shipping. *Club:* Conservative. (O4979)

BARRY, Capt. Louis Charles, M.B.E., R.F.A.

BARRY, Col. Stanley Leonard, C.M.G., C.B.E., D.S.O., M.V.O., J.P., *b.* 31 Dec. 1873; *s.* of Sir Francis Barry, of St. Leonard's Hill, Windsor; *m.* Hannah, *d.* of James Hainsworth, of 34, Phillimore Gardens, W. *Educ.:* Harrow. Late 10th Hussars. *War Work:* France, 1914–15; Asst.-Military Secretary Forces in Great Britain, Horse Guards, 1916–18. *Address:* Spencer House, Wimbledon Common, S.W. 19. *Clubs:* Turf; Marlborough; Boodle's. (C1454)

BARRY, Col. Thomas David Collis, C.B.E. Lieut.-Col. and Hon. Col. R.A.F.; Great War, 1914–19 (despatches). (C852)

BARRY, Thomas Ernest, M.B.E.

BARRY, Major James Robert BURY-, O.B.E.

BARRY, Capt. Kenneth A. WOLFE-, O.B.E.

BARRY, Bernard John WOLFE-, O.B.E., *b.* 20 Jan. 1877; eldest *s.* of late Sir John Wolfe-Barry, K.C.B.; *m.* Gertrude Emily, *d.* of T. E. Allt. *Educ.:* Winchester and New College, Oxford. Called to the Bar and now in business in the City of London as partner in the firm of Linley & Co. *War Work:* Gazetted 2nd Lieut. R.G.A. Jan. 1915; B.E.F. June, 1915; wounded, Dec. 1915; transferred R.F.C. 1916; Lieut.-Col. Royal Air Force, April, 1918; demobilised, 1919. *Address:* 74, Onslow Gardens, London, S.W. 7. *Clubs:* Athenæum; Bath. (O1094)

BARSDORF, Ralph, M.B.E., B.A., *b.* 1869; *s.* of Augustus Barsdorf, of London and South Africa; *m.* Jess Louisa, *d.* of William Spencer, of The Mount, Stansted, Essex. *Educ.:* Clifton College, Bristol and Brasenose College, Oxford. Barrister-at-law. *War Work:* Assistant Secretary, War Refugees

Committee ; Secretary, Belgian Refugee Department, Local Government Board which succeeded the Committee ; Corporal, Inns of Court Reserve Corps, 1915–18. *Address :* The Maltings, Manuden, Essex. (M7320)

BARSTOW, Brig.-Gen. Henry, C.B.E. Major and Brevet Lieut.-Col. Indian Army ; N.W. Frontier of India, 1897–8 (medal with clasp) and 1901–2 (clasp) ; Director of Personal Sers., Headquarters Staff, India. (C2029)

BARSTOW, Capt. Thomas Clement Erskine, O.B.E., I.A.

BARTELS, Olive, O.B.E., M.B.E.

BARTER, Eng.-Comm. Frederick, O.B.E., R.N.

BARTER, John Reginald, O.B.E. (O11948)

BARTER, Richard Henry, O.B.E., *b.* 24 Oct. 1875 ; *s.* of Capt. Henry Barter, of 2nd Queen's Regiment ; *m.* Alice Isabella, *d.* of Captain R. Wade Thompson, of Clonskeagh Castle, Co. Dublin. *Educ. :* Wellington and Queen's College, Cork. Resident Medical Officer, St. Ann's Hill, Co. Cork, Ireland. *War Work :* Medical Officer of Auxiliary Military Hospital, St. Ann's Hill, Co. Cork. *Address :* St. Ann's Hill, Co. Cork, Ireland. *Club :* Cork. (O4350)

BARTH, Hon. Jacob William, C.B.E., *b.* 23 July, 1871 ; *s.* of the late William Wright Barth ; *m.* Ida Russell, *d.* of the late Harry Burmand. *Educ. :* Heidelberg and Oxford. Crown Advocate, East Africa Protectorate, 1902–05 ; Puisne Judge of H.M. High Court of East Africa, 1905–14 ; Attorney-General, East Africa Protectorate, 1914–20 ; Chief Justice, Kenya Colony, 1920. *War Work :* J.A.G., East African Forces ; Legal Adviser to British Expeditionary Force, East Africa. *Address :* Nairobi, Kenya. *Club :* Sports'. (C1144)

BARTHOLOMEW, Col. Allen Gilbert, O.B.E.

BARTHOLOMEW, Lieut.-Col. Arthur Wollaston, C.M.G., C.B.E., D.S.O., *b.* 5 May, 1878 ; *s.* of A. C. Bartholomew, of Park House, Reading ; *m.* Helen May Ethel, *d.* of the late Major-General W. W. Anderson, of Glen Urquhart, Inverness. *Educ. :* Marlborough and Trinity College, Oxford. (C2067)

BARTHOLOMEW, Cadet-Col. Clarence Edward, O.B.E., *b.* 15 Aug. 1879 ; *s.* of Gilbert Bartholomew, of London ; *m.* Dorothy Cottam, *d.* of H. W. Perry, of Melbourne, Australia. *Educ. :* Clifton. A Director of Bryant and May, Ltd. ; Col. Commandant of the London Division, Church Lads' Brigade Cadets ; Colonel Commanding Cadet Battalion Philanthropic Society's Farm School, Redhill ; Treasurer, London Diocesan Council for the Welfare of Lads. *Address :* 6, Kidderpore Gardens, Hampstead, N.W. 3. *Club :* Constitutional.

BARTHOLOMEW, John, O.B.E., M.A., LL.D., F.S.A. (Scot.) J.P. Advocate, *b.* 1870 ; *s.* of Hugh Bartholomew, of Glenorchard ; *m.* 29 Dec. 1920, Phillis Gray *e.d.* of J. Scott Anderson, Advocate, of Gorscodden House, Drumchapel, Dumbartonshire. *Educ. :* Glasgow Academy and Glasgow University. *War Work :* Military Representative, Edinburgh Recruiting Tribunal, Feb. to July, 1916 ; Commissioner, Military Service (Civil Liabilities) Department, July, 1916, to May, 1920. *Address :* Glenorchard, Torrance, near Glasgow. *Clubs :* Royal Societies', London ; University, Edinburgh ; Western, Glasgow. (O1096)

BARTHOLOMEW, William, M.B.E., *b.* 2 March, 1881 ; *s.* of J. Bartholomew, Retired Collector of Inland Revenue, Somerset House. *Educ. :* Bedford. Civil Servant ; served in S. African War ; awarded medal and 2 clasps ; also on special service for the War Office in S. Africa ; served for 5 years in Malta and Egypt in the Army Accounts Dept *War Work :* Contracts Department, War Office. *Address :* 67, Blenheim Gardens, Wallington, Surrey. (M7321)

BARTHOLOMEW, Lieut.-Col. William Barker, O.B.E.

BARTIE, Lieut. Edward William, M.B.E., R.D.C.

BARTLETT, Capt. Charles Alfred, C.B., C.B.E., *b.* 1868 ; *s* of the William Sydney Bartlett ; *m.* 1898, Edith Kate, *d.* of J. R. Ellis, of Hillcrest, Gorleston. Capt. R.N.R. and a Younger Brother of Trinity House ; Great War, 1914–17 (despatches) ; an A.D.C. to H.M. *Address :* 22, Marine Terrace, Waterloo, Liverpool. (C2440)

BARTLETT, Capt. Edmund Burton, O.B.E.

BARTLETT, Capt. Edward George, O.B.E., M.C., K.O.Y.L.I.

BARTLETT, Ellis ASHMEAD-, C.B.E. (C3106a)

BARTLETT, Frederick William, O.B.E.

BARTLETT, Capt. Horace John, O.B.E., R.A.S.C.

BARTLETT, Lieut. John Holderness, O.B.E., R.N.R.

BARTLETT, Major the Rev. Reginald, O.B.E., *b.* 21 March, 1878 ; *s.* of Charles Henry Bartlett, of Bristol ; *m.* Alice Mary, *d.* of Leonard Bennett, of Wotton-under-Edge, Gloucestershire. *Educ. :* Bristol and Western College. Missionary under the London Missionary Society in New Guinea for a number of years ; now District Secretary for the London Missionary Society, for the Midland and Eastern Counties. *War Work :* Chaplain att. 49th Div. West Ridings, from May, 1915 ; later appointed Assistant Principal Chaplain, Headquarters Southern Command, Salisbury ; Demobilised July, 1919. *Address :* London Missionary Society, County Chambers, Birmingham. (O6875)

BARTLETT, Tom, M.B.E., *b.* 7 July, 1864 ; *s.* of Joseph Bartlett, of Clayhidon, Devon ; *m.* Bessie, *d.* of William Bishop, Littlehampton, Sussex. *Educ. :* Parish School, Clayhidon, Devon. Works Foreman. *War Work :* Secret Service. *Address :* Clarence Villa, 72A, High Street, Shoeburyness, Essex. (M7322)

BARTLEY, Lieut.-Col. Bryan Cole, C.B.E. (Mil.), *b.* 23 June, 1875 ; *s.* of late Sir George Bartley, K.C.B., of Shovelstrode Manor, East Grinstead ; *m.* Gertrude Emily, *d.* of late

W. Strickland, of Yorkshire. *Educ. :* Haileybury College and University College, London. Engineer, Managing Director Public Companies in S. Africa, with offices in Johannesburg, Bulawayo, Durban, London, etc. Captain in Railway Pioneer Regiment in Boer War, received Queen's Medal and 4 Clasps. *War Work :* Joined R.N.V.R. in June, 1915, at Admiralty ; went R.N.A.S., France, 1916 ; Assistant Controller Aircraft Production, Aug. 1917, and made commander R.N.V.R. ; Lieut.-Col. R.A.F., 1918. *Address :* 845, Salisbury House, London Wall. *Clubs :* Carlton ; Junior Carlton ; Royal Air Force ; Rand, Johannesburg. (C1886)

BARTLEY, William, M.B.E., B.A., J.P., *b.* 3 Jan. 1885 ; *s.* of Charles Bartley, of Fairview, Enniskillen ; *m.* Leslie Marion, *d.* of Robert Brown, of Woggonora and Kahmoo, Queensland. *Educ. :* St. Columbe Coll., Londonderry ; Educational Inst., Dundalk, and Dublin Univ. Straits Settlements Civil Service. *War Work :* Military Censor ; Director of War Trade, Straits Settlements ; Secretary to the Committee of Food Control, S.S. ; Member of the Advisory Committee to the Shipping Controller ; Captain and O.C. Malay Company Singapore Volunteer Infantry ; Agent for the Food Controller, Singapore ; Secretary to the Commission on Profiteering. *Addresses :* Fairview, Enniskillen ; c/o Hon. Colonial Secretary, Singapore. *Club :* Singapore. (M6413)

BARTOLO, Antonio, M.B.E.

BARTON, Albert Edward, M.B.E. (M10372)

BARTON, Col. Alfred Yarker, C.B.E. ; *b.* 1864 ; Col. in Army ; Great War, 1914–19 (despatches). (C1455)

BARTON, Major Bertram Claude, O.B.E., R.A.S.C. ; *s.* of Rev. H. C. M. Barton, M.A. *Address :* Stubley Old Hall, Littleborough, Lancs. (O6436)

BARTON, Capt. Charles Percival, O.B.E., *b.* 20 Sept. 1880 ; *s.* of Charles T. Barton, of Kidderminster. *Educ. :* Malvern Coll. *War Services :* With the Expeditionary Force in France, 1916–19. *Address :* Park View, Belbroughton, Worcestershire. (O4979)

BARTON, Eleanor, M.B.E., *b.* March, 1860 ; *d.* of Bertram F. Barton, of Straffan House, Co. Kildare, Ireland. *Educ. :* At home. *War Work :* Q.M.N.W. Guild and canteen work ; 3 years Commandant of Clayton Court Red Cross Hospital, East Lyss, Hants. *Address :* Easton, East Lyss. *Clubs :* Ladies' Athenæum ; V.A.D. Ladies'. (M7324)

BARTON, Emma Alice, Mrs., O.B.E., Lady of Grace of the Order of Jerusalem, *b.* 1 May, 1878 ; *d.* of George William Lowther, of Swillington House, Yorkshire ; *s.* of Sir Charles Bingham Lowther, 4th Bart. (*see* BURKE'S *Peerage*) *m.* Henry John Hope, *s.* of John Hope Barton, of Stapleton Park, Yorkshire, and Saxby Hall, Lincolnshire (*see* BURKE'S *Landed Gentry*). *Educ. :* At home. Vice-President Osgoldcross Division (Yorkshire) of the St. John's Ambulance Association. *War Work :* Organised 4 V.A.D. Hospitals in Osgoldcross and worked personally as Commandant and Quartermaster at Stapleton Park. *Addresses :* Stapleton Park, Pontefract, and Saxby Hall, Brigg. (O1097)

BARTON, Ernest Mortlock, O.B.E., *b.* 4 July, 1867 ; *s.* of Thomas Mortlock Barton, of The Mount, Ware, Herts ; *m.* Anna Jane, *d.* of Philip Benns, of Kirby Cane, Bungay, Suffolk. *Educ. :* Ware Grammar School 1875–80 and Merchant Taylors' School, 1880–84. articled 1884 to J. C. Park M.I.C.E. Locomotive Superintendent, North London Railway, Bow, London, E. ; Assistant to Messrs. Joseph Westwood and Co., Constructional Engineers, Millwall, E., 1887–91 ; Assistant Engineer, Chief Engineer's Office, Great Western Railway, Paddington, W., 1891–94 ; entered Director of Works Department, Admiralty 1894 and served in all grades up to the position of Superintending Civil Engineer, which position he still holds. *War Work :* All works in connection with the land defences of Scapa Flow ; seaplane and Kite Balloon Stations in the Orkneys ; Construction of Seaplane Stations and Rigid and Non-Rigid Aerodromes, throughout Scotland for the Admiralty and all works in connection therewith ; Oil Fuel Depots at various sites in Scotland and the Orkneys ; Oil Fuel Pipe Line from Clyde to Forth, (36 miles) and all Jetties, Pumping Stations, etc., in connection with same. *Address :* Trinity House, H.M. Dockyard, Portsmouth. (O6944)

BARTON, Ernest Wilfred Edwards, M.B.E.

BARTON, Capt. George, M.B.E.

BARTON, Gilbert William, M.B.E.

BARTON, Harriet, Mrs. Maurice Charles, M.B.E.

BARTON, Harry, M.B.E.

BARTON, Lilian, Mrs., M.B.E.

BARTON, Rachel Mary, Mrs., M.B.E.

BARTON, Lieut.-Col. Robert John Ferguson, O.B.E., R.A.F.

BARTON, Surg.-Lieut. Samuel Saxton, O.B.E.

BARTON, Sybil Edith, O.B.E., Kaisir-i-Hind Medal, 1915, *b.* 8 June, 1872 ; *d.* of A. M. Smith, of Albert Mervyn (Wales) ; *m.* Percy Alfred, *s.* of Thomas Barton, of Kent. *War Work :* St. John Ambulance Association and Red Cross Society, Hon. Sec. Sept. 1914 to Jan. 1920 ; Hon. Sec. Rupee Fund, 1918 to June, 1920. *Address :* Brunten Road, Bangalore. (O8234)

BARTRAM, Euphemia Walker, Mrs., O.B.E., *b.* 30 April, 1871 ; *d.* of the late Alexander Rhind, of New York, *w.* of the late George, *s.* of R. A. Bartram, J.P., of Sunderland. *War Work :* St. George's Soldiers' Rest, Sunderland, run for five years by voluntary subscriptions from friends amounting to over £3000, visited (on an average) weekly by 1500 soldiers ;

St. George's Y.M.C.A. Hut (£1000) sent out to France. *Address :* Holme Field, Sunderland. (O9945)

BARTRUM, Marian, Mrs., M.B.E., *b.* 26 Dec. 1856 ; *d.* of Rev. R. T. Burton, M.A., of Stott Park, Lake Side, Lancs. ; *m.* the late Rev. Edward Bartrum, D.D., Headmaster of Berkhampstead Grammar School and late rector of Wakes Colne, Essex. *Educ. :* St. Mary's Hall, Kemp Town, Brighton. *War Work :* 1914, Training V.A.D. and knitting and bandage making ; 1915, Bandage Classes and sewing and getting V.A.D.'s into Hospitals ; 1916 till April, still working for France, Serbia and our own Red Cross, 4000 bandages ; V.A.D. Hospital opened 19 June, 1916 till 5 March, 1919. *Address :* Lynwood, Lindale, Grange-over-Sands. (M7325)

BARTRUM, Capt. Vere Ayscott, O.B.E., R.A.V.C.

BARWELL, Henry Edward, M.B.E.

BARWICK, Capt. Frederick Mortimer, O.B.E., R.I.M., Knight of Grace of the Order of St. John of Jerusalem, J.P. Parts of Lindsey, Lincs., *b.* 1857 ; *s.* of late Joseph Barwick, of St. Margaret's, Twickenham ; *m.* Ethel Gordon, *d.* of the late Oriel Walton, of Maperton House, Wincanton, by daughter of Lord Cecil Gordon (*see* BURKE'S *Peerage*, Huntley, M.). *Educ. :* Privately and Somerset College. *War Work :* Served in the Chin Lushai Expedition, 1890, despatches, medal with clasp ; Manipur Expedition, 1891-2, despatches, medal with clasp ; Egypt, Suakin Field Force, 1896, medal with clasp ; Central Africa medal ; Naval Supply Officer, the Humber. *Address :* Scarths Hall, near Grimsby, Lincs. *Club :* Constitutional. (O123)

BASCH, Bertha, M.B.E., *b.* 21 March, 1890 ; *d.* of J. Granger, of Barberton ; *m.* Emanuel, J.P., *s.* of Edward Basch, of Plymouth. *Educ. :* Springfield, near Capetown. Hon. Sec. Ladies' Red Cross Working Party, 1914-20 ; Hon Sec. and Treas. of Women's Auxiliary Comrades of the Great War. *War Work :* Meeting all trains and entertaining soldiers passing through Bulawayo to B.E.A. and S.W.A. and Europe, and providing them with comforts, etc. *Address :* Suburbs, Bulawayo, Rhodesia. (M2927)

BASDEN, Albert Edward, M.B.E.

BASHFORD, Capt. Ernest Francis, O.B.E., R.A.

BASHFORD, Capt. Radcliffe James Lindsay, O.B.E. R.A.O.C.

BASS, Edith, O.B.E., B.A. ; *d.* of the late Thomas Bass, of Grange House, Streatham Hill, and Greenroyd, Teignmouth. *Educ. :* Laleham and Newnham College, Cambridge. Principal Lady Superintendent, Admiralty. *Clubs :* Forum ; Berkeley. (O9946)

BASS, Major and Qr.-Mr. William, O.B.E.

BASSET, Helen, Mrs., M.B.E. ; *d.* of the late Admiral Sir William Dowell, G.C.B. ; *m.* the late Walter, *s.* of the late Charles H. Basset, of Watermouth Castle, N. Devon. *War Work :* Hon. Sec., Soldiers' and Sailors' Fund Association and War Pensions, Bideford District, from Aug. 1914, to Sept. 1919. *Address :* Mallacleave, Bideford, N. Devon. (M7328)

BASSET, Lieut.-Col. William Fortescue, O.B.E., *b.* 7 April, 1879 ; *s.* of Richard Basset, of Bonvilstone, Glamorgan ; *m.* Mary Sturgis, of Givons, Leatherhead. *Educ. :* Marlborough. Served 14 years in Rifle Brigade, adjutant of 2nd Batt. ; 3 years A.D.C. to Lord Kitchener when he was C.-in-C. in India. *War Work :* Staff Captain, D.A.A.G. and A.A.G. at War Office ; transferred to Ministry of National Service as Deputy Director of Recruiting for London and South-Eastern Region. *Address :* The Manor House, Petersham, Surrey. *Clubs :* Naval and Military ; Royal Automobile. (O124)

BASSETT, Arthur Tilney, O.B.E., Chevalier of the Order of Leopold (Belgium) ; *s.* of Henry Tilney Bassett, of Norwich ; *m.* Mary, *d.* of William Barton. *Educ. :* Privately and Trinity College, Dublin. Secretary, Welsh Church Fund. Author of various works. *War Work :* London Defences C.P.O., R.N.V.R. (Anti-Aircraft Corps) ; War Refugees Committee ; Italian Red Cross ; Metropolitan Observation Service. *Club :* National Liberal. (O9947)

BASSETT, Ernest Thomas Walter, M.B.E., *b.* 14 May, 1876 ; *s.* of John Bassett, of Plymouth, Devon ; *m.* Flora Harriett, *d.* of Edward Howlett, of Gt. Yarmouth. *Educ. :* Middlesborough and Durham County. Manager, 1st Class, Ministry of Labour Employment Department ; Secretary to the Portsmouth Local Employment Committee (Ministry of Labour) ; Secretary to Technical Advisory Committees for the training of disabled Sailors and Soldiers ; Secretary to Building Trade Apprenticeship Committee, Portsmouth. *War Work :* Recruiting of skilled and unskilled labour for H.M. Dockyards ; Selection of skilled workers for Shipyards (Australians and Canadians) on arrival in England ; Special Officer detached for Employment under Ministry of Munitions during 1915-16 and part of 1917 and attached the Southern Command selecting skilled workers for transfer from Army to Munition work ; Special Officer attached to Southern Command, 1916-17 for Substitution. *Address :* 38, Worthing Road, Southsea, Hants. (M7327)

BASSETT, Major Francis Marshall, O.B.E., Bedfordshire Regt., *b.* 14 June, 1873 ; *s.* of the late Frederick Bassett, of The Heath, Leighton Buzzard, Bedfordshire ; *m.* Violet Alice, *d.* of Lieut.-Col. R. C. H. Germon, of Barn Hawe, Edenbridge, Kent. *Educ. :* Uppingham. Served in the South African War ; mentioned in Lord Roberts' despatches. *War Work :* Served in the European War in Flanders as a Regimental Officer ; seriously wounded 1st battle of Ypres, Oct. 1914 ; since 1917 various duties at home ; placed on h.p. list on

account of wounds ; granted Croix de Guerre (French). *Address :* The Barracks, Bedford. (O6877)

BASSETT, Lieut.-Col. John Retallack, D.S.O., O.B.E., *b.* 1878 ; Lieut.-Col. (retired) Roy. Berkshire Regt. ; served in S. Africa 1899-1902 (Queen's medal with three clasps, King's medal with two clasps) ; Great War, 1914-18 (despatches). (O6878)

BASSETT, John William Abell, M.B.E., J.P.

BASSETT, Rosa, M.B.E., B.A., *b.* 9 Aug. 1871 ; *d.* of John Bassett, of St. John's, London, S.E. *Educ. :* Roan School, Greenwich ; London School of Economics. Headmistress of the County Secondary School, Streatham. *War Work :* Initiated scheme of selecting educated women and girls for special clerical posts in Government Offices. *Address :* 9, Conyers Road, Streatham, S.W. 16. *Club :* University. (M4)

BASSOM, Arthur Ernest, O.B.E.

BASTARD, Capt. Ernest William, O.B.E.

BASTARD, Lieut.-Col. William Edmund Pollexfen, O.B.E., D.L., J.P., *b.* 12 April, 1864 ; *e.s.* of the late Rev. W. P. Bastard, of Kitley, Devon (*see* BURKE'S *Landed Gentry*) ; *m.* 7 April, 1890, Rosamond Isobel, *e.d.* of Abraham Briggs Foster, of Conwell Hall, Co. Stafford (*see* BURKE'S *Landed Gentry*). *Educ. :* St. John's Coll., Oxford. *War Work :* Officer Commanding Devonshire Fortress, Royal Engineers (T.F.). *Address :* Kitley, Yealmpton, Devon. *Clubs :* Junior Carlton ; Royal Western Yacht (Plymouth). (O6879)

BATCH, Edward, M.B.E., *b.* 17 Jan. 1886 ; *s.* of James Batch, of Chelsea ; *m.* Jessie, *d.* of James Smith, of Hampstead. *Educ. :* Westminster City School. Civil Servant ; Director, Imported Timber Disposal Section, Board of Trade. *War Work :* Assistant Controller, Timber Supplies Dept., Board of Trade ; Secretary, Timber Sub-Committee, Inter-Allied Maritime Council ; Secretary, Timber Allocation Sub-Committee ; War Priorities Committee, War Cabinet ; Member of the Tonnage Priority Committee, Ministry of Shipping. *Address :* 43, Melrose Avenue, Wimbledon Park, S.W. 19. (M1387)

BATCHELDOR, William, M.B.E., R.F.A.

BATCHELOR, Capt. Arthur, O.B.E., *b.* 21 June, 1874 ; *s.* of George Batchelor, of Rochester ; *m.* Margaret, *d.* of William Carnaby, of Dulwich. *Educ. :* Sir Joseph Williamson's Mathematical School, Rochester. Cement Manufacturer. *War Work :* Served with R.A.S.C. from May, 1915, to March, 1919 ; Just over one year in England and the remainder in France ; went overseas with 11 Divisional Supply Column, July, 1916 ; transferred to IV Corps Supply Column, Jan. 1917 ; mentioned in despatches three times. *Address :* Blatchington, Seaford. *Club :* United R.A.S.C. (O4981)

BATCHELOR, Emily, C.B.E., *b.* 17 Jan. 1886 ; *d.* of Frank J. Batchelor, of Northampton. *Educ. :* Church of England College, Birmingham. and Roedean, Brighton. *War Work :* April, 1915, to Aug. 1915, Y.M.C.A. Rugeley ; Oct. 1915, to Aug. 1916, as V.A.D. 1st Southern General Hospital ; Aug. 1916, to Dec. 1916, French Red Cross at Troyes, France ; Aug. 1917, to Dec. 1917, as worker ; Jan. 1918, to March, 1919, as Directoire Women's Emergency Canteens, Gare du Nord, Paris. *Addresses :* 10, Cumberland House, Kensington Road, W. 8 ; Burnside, Shottery, near Stratford-on-Avon. *Club :* Midland Counties, Birmingham. (C2441)

BATCHELOR, Capt. John William, O.B.E.

BATCHELOR, Mary Anne Northway, Mrs., O.B.E.

BATCHELOR, Capt. Ronald George, MB.E., R.N.

BATE, Comm. Francis William, O.B.E., R.N.R., R.D.

BATE, Henry Francis, O.B.E., J.P.

BATE, John Osborn Shepperton, M.B.E. (M10433)

BATE, Mary, Mrs., M.B.E., *b.* 1862 ; *d.* of Rev. Richard Williams, Wesleyan Minister ; *m.* Joseph, *s.* of Rev. Joseph Bate, Wesleyan Minister. *Educ. :* Trinity Hall, Southport, and Dr. Williams', Dolgelly. *War Work :* Worked in Soldiers' and Sailors' Canteen at Chatham and Strood, and Munition Workers' and Soldiers' Canteen at Queen's Ferry, Avonmouth and Bristol. *Address :* The Edge, Congleton.

BATE, Surg.-Capt. Richard Francis, O.B.E., R.N.

BATE, Col. Thomas Elwood Lindsay, C.I.E., C.B.E., *b.* 1852 ; Indian Med. Ser. 1875 ; retired 1910 ; Civil Surg., Gujerat 1880 ; Inspector-Gen. of Prisons, Punjab, 1891, and of Civil Hospitals 1905. (C108)

BATE, William, M.B.E.

BATEMAN, Edward Colston, M.B.E., *b.* 9 Nov. 1870 ; *s.* of Samuel Tyler Bateman, of Bath ; *m.* Louise, *d.* of William Stocks, of Bath. *Educ. :* Park House Academy, Combe Down, Bath. General Manager of H.M. Stationery Office Press, London and Harrow. *War Work :* Organised supplies of large quantities of printed matter of all kinds for use of War Office and of British Expeditionary Forces, and in connection with propaganda work for Dept. of Information ; Member of Hertfordshire Special Constabulary. *Address :* Helesborough, Rickmansworth Road, Watford, Herts. (M7320)

BATEMAN, Capt. Frank Graham, M.B.E.

BATEMAN, Major George Deane, O.B.E., R.A.F.

BATEMAN, Major James Cecil, O.B.E.

BATEMAN, John, M.B.E., J.P.

BATEMAN, Walter Slade, O.B.E. (O12041)

BATES, Charles William, M.B.E., *b.* 11 April, 1882 ; *s.* of Major Bates, of Walton-on-Naze. *Educ. :* Walton-on-Naze. Y.M.C.A. Secretary. *War Work :* Y.M.C.A. work at Dardanelles, Egypt, Salonika, Turkey. *Address :* 13, Russell Square, London, W.C. 1. (M1389)

BATES, Ellen Marie, Mrs., O.B.E. Secretary of St. Dunstan's during practically the whole of its existence. Responsible for the detail work of the whole organisation. (O11891)

BATES, Henry Baker, M.B.E., J.P.

BATES, Herbert, O.B.E.

BATES, Capt. Hubert Tunstall, O.B.E., R.A.M.C.

BATES, Lilian Douglas, Mrs., O.B.E.

BATES, Major Mark, O.B.E., F.R.C.S., B.A., B.M., B.Ch.(Oxon.), *b.* 22 Jan. 1881 ; *s.* of Tom Bates, of Worcester. *Educ.*: Cathedral King's School, Worcester; St. John's College, Oxford ; St. Bartholomew's Hospital, London. Hon. anæsthetist to Worcester General Infirmary ; Medical Referee to Ministry of Pensions. *War Work*: Surgical Specialist No. 15 General Hospital, No. 26 C.C.S. and No. 33 C.C.H. E.E.F. and S.M.O. Haifa Area. *Address*: 33 The Tything, Worcester. (O6038)

BATES, Mary Beatrice, M.B.E. ; *d.* of Ralph Bates, of Stalybridge. *War Work*: Commandant V.A.D., Cheshire 112 B.R.C. Auxiliary Hospital, The Old Hall, Mottram-in-Longdendale, Cheshire. *Address*: Acres Bank, Stalybridge, Cheshire. (M7331)

BATES, Sir Percy Elly, Bart., G.B.E., Officer of the Legion of Honour, *b.* 12 May, 1879 ; *s.* of Edward Percy Bates, of Liverpool ; *m.* Mary Ann Lefroy, *d.* of Very Rev. William Lefroy, D.D., Dean of Norwich. *Educ.*: Winchester. Director of Cunard Steam Ship Co., Ltd. ; Thos. & Jno. Brocklebank, Ltd. ; Anchor Line (Henderson Bros.), Ltd. ; Commonwealth and Dominion Line. Ltd. ; London Joint City and Midland Bank, Ltd. ; London and Kano Trading Co. Ltd. ; partner in Edward Bates & Sons ; Sheriff of Cheshire, 1920. *War Work*: Head of Commercial Branch Transport Dept. of Admiralty, 1916 ; Director of Commercial Services, Ministry of Shipping, 1917–19 ; Member of Shipping Control Committee, 1919. *Address*: Hinderton Hall, Neston, Cheshire. *Clubs*: Oriental ; Windham's ; Fly Fishers' ; Royal Automobile. (G62)

BATES, Paymaster Lieut.-Comm. Reginald Barrington, O.B.E., R.N.

BATES, Sir Richard Dawson, Knt. Bach., O.B.E., J.P., *b.* 23 Nov., 1876 ; *s.* of the late Richard Dawson Bates, solicitor, of Sydenham, Belfast ; *m.* 8 April, 1920, Jessie Muriel, *y. d.* of Sir Charles John Cleland, K.B.E., M.V.O., D.L., of Bonville Maryhill, Glasgow (*q.v.*), Sec. of the Ulster Unionist Council since 1906. *War Services*: Acted as Hon. Sec. of the Ulster Volunteer Force Hospitals, and Hon. Sec. of the Ulster Volunteer Force Patriotic Fund, which raised over £100,000 for the augmenting of War Pensions. *Address*: Furloe, Holywood, co. Down. *Clubs*: Constitutional ; Ulster (Belfast) Royal Ulster Yacht ; Royal North of Ireland Yacht. (O3613)

BATES, Thomas Edward Bowen, O.B.E., J.P., *b.* 13 June, 1860 ; *s.* of Joseph Bates, of Dudley, Staffordshire ; *m.* Maria Jane, *d.* of James Bennington, of Cleveland, Yorks. *Educ.*: Darlington. Alderman of Borough Council ; Chairman, Board of Guardians ; Chairman of Housing Committee, all of Darlington. *War Work*: Chairman, War Pensions Committee since commencement ; during second term of office as Mayor 1917, formed 4th Batt. D.L.I. ; in addition worked as instructor for engineering for munition workers and disabled soldiers and sailors. *Address*: Clissoldhurst, South Terrace, Darlington. (O9953)

BATES, Walter, M.B.E., R.N.

BATES, William, O.B.E., M.Inst.C.E., *b.* 4 June, 1863 ; *s.* of William Bates, M.D., F.R.C.S., of Manchester ; *m.* Alice Mary, *d.* of Robert Hailstone, of Hampstead, London. *Educ.*: Bruce Castle School ; University College, London. Engineer to Rea, Limited, Liverpool. *War Work*: The coaling of H.M. Ships, Transports and Hospital Ships in the Port of Liverpool. *Address*: "Tregenna," Mount Pleasant, Oxton, Cheshire. (O1100)

BATES, William Edward, M.B.E. *Educ.*: Borough Road Training College. Head Master of General Boys' School, Bridport. *War Work*: Hon. Sec., Bridport and District War Savings Committee. *Addrsse*: General Bosy' School, Bridport. (M7332)

BATES, William Richard, O.B.E., *b.* 5 Feb. 1856 ; *s.* of William Tunstall Bates, of Hope Street, Liverpool ; *m.* Margaret, *d.* of Thomas James Critchley, of Ilkley. *Educ.*: Birkdale. Late Chairman, Urban District Council ; Past President, Leeds and West Riding Medico-Chirurgical Society ; Honorary Associate of St. John of Jerusalem. *War Work*: Anæsthetist, 2nd Northern General Hospital (Honorary) ; Medical Officer, Auxiliary Military Hospital, Ilkley ; Chairman, Ilkley Tribunal ; Member of Medical Board, Keighley. *Address*: Fernhill, Ilkley. (O9954)

BATESON, Rev. Joseph Harger, C.B.E., *b.* 5 March, 1865 ; *s.* of Thomas Bateson, J.P., of Kendal ; *m.* Rose, *d.* of Alfred Edmeades, of Winchester. *Educ.*: Friends' School, Kendal ; and Queen's College, Taunton. Secretary, Wesleyan Royal Navy, Army and Air Force Board ; Chaplain, Upper Burmah Field Force, 1886–8, received medal and two clasps ; Hon. Chaplain, Territorial Force, 1913. *War Work*: Hon. Chaplain to the Forces, 1st Class, 1917 ; Principal Chaplain (ranking as Brig.-General), 1918 ; War Member of Interdenominational Advisory Committee on Chaplaincy Services, War Office. *Address*: 30, Marlborough Mansions, Hampstead, London, N.W. 6. (C2078)

BATGER, Janet Mary, Mrs., M.B.E.

BATH, Paymaster-Lieut. Alan George, O.B.E., R.N.

BATH, Capt. Charles Hubert, O.B.E.

BATHER, Muriel Emmeline, Mrs., O.B.E. ; *d.* of Spencer Henry Bickham, J.P., of Underdown, Ledbury, Herefordshire ;

m. Edward William Bather, Lord of the Manor of Meole Brace (*see* BURKE'S *Landed Gentry*). *Educ.*: Highfield, Hendon. *War Work*: Commandant of Cyngfeld Hospital, Shrewsbury. *Address*: Nobold Grange, Salop. *Club*: Shropshire Ladies' County. (O126)

BATHER, Capt. Rowland Henry, O.B.E., R.N.

BATHGATE, Adam, M.B.E.

BATHO, Charles Philip Arthur, M.B.E. (M10434)

BATHO, Capt. George William Hyde, O.B.E., R.G.A.

BATHURST, Frederick Marlay, O.B.E., *b.* 1865 ; *s.* of Frederick Bathurst, Archdeacon of Bedford (deceased) ; *m.* Mary Blanche, *d.* of R. P. Fetherstonhaugh Frampton (deceased), of Moreton, Dorset. *Educ.*: Winchester. *War Work*: British Red Cross, Inquiry Department. *Address*: The Warren, Lydney, Glos. *Club*: Conservative. (O9955)

BATHURST, Katherine Mary Delicia, Lady HERVEY-, O.B.E., *d.* of the late Alexander Dick-Cunyngham, and widow of J. H. Nevill ; *m.* 1919, Capt. Sir Frederick Edward William Hervey-Bathurst, 5th Bart., D.S.O. *Address*: Somborne Park, Stockbridge. (O9956)

BATSON, Capt. Herbert MacKenzie, O.B.E.

BATT, Lieut.-Col. Reginald Cossley, C.B.E., M.V.O., *b.* 29 Oct. 1872 ; *s.* of William Foster, of Cae Kenfy, Abergavenny ; *m.* 1st, 1903, Violet, *y.d.* (*d.* 1910) of Robert Millington Knowles, J.P., D.L., of Colston Bassett Hall, Notts., issue 4 sons ; 2ndly Eileen Augusta, *s.* of Henry William Russell Domvile, of Pentre Cottage, Abergavenny. *Educ.*: Wellington and Sandhurst. Adjutant 4th Royal Fusiliers. 1900–4 ; Adjutant 3rd V.B. Norfolk Regt., 1905–7 ; Commanded 6th Batt. Royal Fusiliers, 1913–17. *War Work*: Commanded 6th Batt. Royal Fusiliers, 1913–17. *Address*: Gresham Hall, Norwich. *Club*: Army and Navy. (C1456)

BATTEN, Beatrix Marguerite Fox, M.B.E., *b.* 4 April, 1886 ; *d.* of T. H. Batten, of Chislehurst. *Educ.*: "Coedbel," Chislehurst ; Girton College, Cambridge. *War Work*: Commandant of Abbey Lodge Hospital, Chislehurst, Oct. 1914, to March, 1919. *Address*: Foxdeane, Chislehurst. (M1301)

BATTEN, Capt. Edward Fetherstonhaugh, M.B.E.

BATTEN, Frederick William, M.B.E., *b.* 11 Jan. 1885 ; *s.* of William Frederick Batten ; *m.* Henrietta, *d.* of Robert Ferris. *Educ.*: Polytechnic Institute, Battersea. Civil Servant. *War Work*: Assisting in Naval Prize matters in the department of the Procurator-General. *Address*: 57, Topsham Road, Upper Tooting. (M3517)

BATTEN, Col. Herbert Cary George, O.B.E., J.P., D.L., *b.* 3 March, 1849 ; *s.* of John Batten, F.S.A., J.P., D.L., of Aldon, Somerset ; *m.* Isabel Frances, *d.* of the late Gen. Sir Robert Bright, G.C.B. *Educ.*: Cheltenham College and Trinity Hall, Cambridge. Barrister-at-law, Inner Temple and Banker ; director, London County Westminster and Parrs Bank ; Hon. Col., 3rd Batt., Dorset Regt. *War Work*: Commanded the Bristol Branch of the National Reserve and was County Commandant of the Bristol Volunteer Regiment. *Addresses*: Abbots Leigh, near Bristol ; Keyford, North Coker, Yeovil. *Club*: New University. (O6881)

BATTEN, John Thomas, M.B.E., R.N.

BATTEN, Winifred Eleanor Sarah Mount, M.B.E., M.M. ; *d.* of Col. John Mount Batten, C.B., of Upcerne, Dorset. *Educ.*: Private and Switzerland. *War Work*: Worked in Canteen at Boulogne, 1915 ; 1916–18, Motor driver British Red Cross Society and Order of St. John of Jerusalem in Fance ; Commandant Etaples Motor Ambulance Convoy, March, 1917, to Nov. 1918 ; Assistant Commandant, W.R.A.F., Air Ministry, Nov. 1918, to Sept. 1919. *Address*: Upcerne Manor, Dorset. (M1393)

BATTERBURY, Lieut. George Henry, M.B.E., I.A.R.O.

BATTERSBY, James Allan, O.B.E., *b.* 27 March, 1871 ; *s.* of Thomas Battersby, of Shrewsbury ; *m.* Loie Allen, *d.* of Lewis Beale, of Biddenden, Kent. *Educ.*: Shrewsbury. Barrister-at-Law (Middle Temple) ; Clerk to the Guardians, to the Assessment Committee, and Superintendent Registrar of the City of Nottingham. *War Work*: Organised Local Representative Committee of "King's Fund" ; Hon. Sec. of War Pensions Committee from its formation to 31 Dec. 1919. *Address*: Elm Bank, Nottingham. *Club*: Nottinghamshire County. (O127)

BATTLE, George Richard, M.B.E., A.M.I.E.E., *b.* 19 Jan. 1878. Admiralty District Electrical Engineer, Newcastle-on-Tyne. *War Work*: Electrical Engineer in charge of the Royal Naval Dockyard and establishments at Invergordon, N.B. *Address*: Commercial Union Buildings, 41–47, Pilgrim Street, Newcastle-on-Tyne. (M3518)

BATTLE, Richard, M.B.E., *b.* May, 1855 ; *s.* of Hugh Battle, of County Mayo, Ireland ; *m.* Emma, *d.* of Thomas Wright, of Aston, Stone, Staffordshire. *Educ.*: Stone Grammar School. Town Clerk of Stafford ; Clerk to Stafford (Higher) Education Committee ; Clerk to Stafford Borough Local Pension Committee. *War Work*: Clerk to the Local Registration Authority for the Borough of Stafford under the National Registration Act, 1915 ; Clerk to the Local Tribunal for Stafford Borough established under the Military Service 1916–18 Acts ; Clerk to the Stafford Borough Local War Pensions Sub-Committee from Oct. 1916, to April, 1918 ; Executive Officer of Stafford Borough Food Control Committee from Sept. 1917, to 30 June, 1920. *Address*: Meyrick Road, Stafford *Club*: County Conservative, Stafford. (M7334)

BATTLE, Lieut. William Sooley, M.B.E., *b.* 8 Aug. 1889 ; *Educ.*: Privately. Partner (senior) in Agence Franciscoley

Antwerp-Belgium, and Soleil Levant Films, Antwerp, Cinematograph Experts and Specialities. *War Work*: Joined and gazetted 60th (London) Divisional Train, 3 Feb. 1915; later 50th (Northumbrian) Divisional M.T. Company; promoted to present permanent rank, Oct. 1915 (T.F.); in France, active service, over 3 years; amongst many other duties was O.T.C. Cinemas, 50th Division, during the whole time this Division ran them. *Addresses*: c o 49, Harley Street, London, W.; Rue des Fortifications 22, Antwerp, Belgium. (M4417)

BATTY, Rev. Basil Staunton, O.B.E., M.A., F.R.A.S., *b.* 12 May, 1873; *s.* of William Edmund Batty, Vicar of Fulham; *m.* Emily Kathleen Foquet, *d.* of the late John Sutton, of Henley Park, Oxon. *Educ.*: St. Paul's School and Selwyn College, Cambridge. Vicar of St. Gabriel's, Warwick Square, S.W.; member of Board of the Church Army and also of the Archbishop's Lambeth Advisory Committee. *War Work*: Chairman of the London Diocesan Committee for the Social and Spiritual care of munition workers; member of Church Army Military Committee; visited French and Italian Fronts on special missions; Decorated by Italian Government for services rendered. *Address*: 4, Warwick Square, S.W. 1. *Club*: Oxford and Cambridge; Leander: New. (O3614)

BATTY, Capt. Edgar Douglas, O.B.E.

BATTY, Edmund, O.B.E., *b.* 28 Sept. 1879; *s.* of Edmund Batty, of York; *m.* Emily, *d.* of David Hodgson, of York. *Educ.*: Alleyn's School, College of God's Gift, Dulwich. *War Work*: Assistant Controller of Scientific Instrument, Glassware, and Potash Production Department of the Ministry of Munitions. *Address*: Sydney Road, Richmond, Surrey. (O9957)

BATTY, Capt. George Henry, M.B.E.

BATTY, James, M.B.E.

BAVIN, Lieut. Arthur Julian Walter, O.B.E., R.A.S.C., *b.* 12 Jan. 1896; *s.* of Major J. T. Bavin, of Berkhamsted; *m.* Joyce, *d.* of E. A. Ebblewhite, J.P., of Middle Temple. *Educ.*: Berkhamsted School. *War Work*: 2 years 4th Divisional Train, France; 2½ years 1st Corps M.T. Column, France; 9 months British Military Mission to Baltic States. *Address*: Buller Barracks, Aldershot. *Clubs*: Services; R.A.S.C.; United R.A.S.C. (O9734)

BAWDEN, Lieut. Cornelius Roberts, M.B.E., R.E.

BAWDEN, Capt. Frederick Henry, O.B.F.

BAXENDALE, Lieut. Basil Francis, O.B.E., R.N.V.R.

BAXENDALE, Gertrude Mary, Mrs. VINCENT-, M.B.E., *o.c.* of the late Richard Birley Baxendale, of Blackmore End, Welwyn, Herts.; *m.* 1883, late Col. Arthur Hare Vincent, J.P. (died 1916), formerly commanding 3rd King's Own Hussars, of Summerhill House, Co. Clare, Ireland, assumed the additional surname of Baxendale on succeeding to the Blackmore End Estate. *War Work*: Lent Blackmore End for use as a Military Hospital from Sept. 1915, till six months after Peace was declared. *Address*: 35, Portman Square, W. 1. (M2963)

BAXENDEN, Capt. Thomas George, O.B.E., R,AF,

BAXTER, Capt. Arthur, O.B.E., R.A.S.C.

BAXTER, Capt. Charles Botterill, O.B.E., R.A.M.C., M.B., F.R.C.S.

BAXTER, Capt. David Charles, O.B.E., R.A.M.C., *b.* 25 May, 1879. *War Work*: O.C. 33 Advanced Depot, Medical Stores. *Addresses*: c/o Holt & Co., 3 Whitehall Place; Base, Medical Stores, Basrah, Mesopotamia. (O4987)

BAXTER, Major David Lionel MacKenzie, O.B.E., R.A.S.C.

BAXTER, Edith, Lady, O.B.E., J.P. for Forfarshire; *d.* of Major-General J. L. Fagan; *m.* Sir George Baxter, Bart., LL.D., *s.* of Rt. Hon. W. E. Baxter, of Kincaldrum, Forfarshire. *War Work*: War Pensions under Ministry of Pensions, and Training of Disabled Men under Ministry of Labour; and Soldiers' and Sailors' Families Association. *Address*: Invereighty, Forfarshire. (O128)

BAXTER, Fane Fleming, O.B.E., *b.* 8 Jan. 1873; *s* .of Herbert Fleming, of Sibdon Castle, Salop.; *m.* Mary Scovill, *d.* of Ambrose Ives Upson, of U.S.A. *Educ.*: Uppingham and Jesus College, Cambridge. Artist. *War Work*: War Refugee Committee. *Address*: 12, Upper Phillimore Gardens, W. 8. *Club*: Arts. (O9958)

BAXTER, Lieut. George, O.B.E., R.E.

BAXTER, Harry Percy, M.B.E.

BAXTER, Capt. Henry George, M.B.E.

BAXTER, Peter McLeod, O.B.E.

BAXTER, Lieut.-Col. Robert Hugh Neville, O.B.E., I.A.R.O.

BAXTER, Stewart, M.B.E.

BAYES, Major John George, O.B.E., R.A.F.

BAYES, Sidney Henry, M.B.E., R.E.

BAYFORD, Robert Frederic, O.B.E., K.C., J.P., *b.* 24 Sept. 1871; *s.* of Robert Augustus Bayford, K.C., of Netley Hill, Botley, Hants; *m.* Catharine Mary, *d.* of Henry Goodenough Hayter, of Sidmouth. *Educ.*: Eton and Trinity Hall, Cambs. *War Work*: Commander, Metropolitan Special Constabulary. *Address*: 20, Cleveland Square, Hyde Park, W. *Clubs*: Oxford and Cambridge; Athenæum. (O9959)

BAYLAY, Brig.-Gen. Frederick, O.B.E.

BAYLAY, Willoughby Lake, O.B.E.

BAYLEY, Col. Arthur George, C.B.E., D.S.O., *b.* 5 July, 1878; *s.* of Kennett Bayley, of Inchicore, Dublin. *Educ.*: Shrewsbury. *War Work*: Brig.-Major 41st Infantry Brigade; G.S.O. 2/56th Division; Chief Instructor Senior Officers School, Aldershot; G.S.O 1/14th Division; Superintendent of Training, Machine Gun Training Centre, Grantham. *Club*: Army and Navy. (C1458)

BAYLEY, Capt. Benjamin Croft, M.B.E., A.M.I.E.E., R.E. (T.), *b.* 2 April, 1889. *Educ.*: Wolverhampton Grammar School. Prior to the war, represented the British Thomson-Houston Company, Ltd., Electrical Engineers and Manufacturers, at their Birmingham Office, now holds the position of Assistant Engineer in the Contract Dept. of the British Thomson-Houston Company, Ltd. Rugby. *War Work*: In Jan. 1915, was given a commission in the North Midland Divisional Royal Engineers (T), and in June, 1915, embarked for France and joined the 1.1st North Midland Field Co., R.E. (T) of the 46th Division, which was then working in the line in front of Kemel, Belgium; remained with this Company until June 1916, during which time the Company maintained and consolidated various parts of the line from Ypres down to the neighbourhood of Doullens; in Oct. 1915, took part in the attack on the Hohenzollern Redoubt; returned to England as a casualty in June, 1916, and was then transferred to Anti-Aircraft Searchlight Experimental work with the London Electrical Engineers, R.E. (T.), where he was Officer-in-Charge of the Experimental Workshops until July, 1919. *Addresses*: British Thomson-Houston Co, Ltd., Contract Dept., Rugby; Duncroft, Hillmorton Paddox, Rugby. (M3244)

BAYLEY, Constance Theodora, M.B.E., R.A.F.

BAYLEY, Lieut.-Col. Edward C., C.I.E., O.B.E.

BAYLEY, Lieut.-Col. Sir Henry Dennis READETT-, K.B.E., D.L., J.P., R.A.M.C. (V.), *b.* 8 Dec. 1878; *s.* of Thomas Bayley, M.P., of Lenton Abbey and Langor Hall, Notts., who was M.P. for the Chesterfield Div. of Derbyshire 1892 to 1906; *m.* Audrey Cecil, *d.* of Sir John Turney, of Gedling House, Notts., 1 son 4 dau. *Educ.*: Tettenhanger College, St. Albans, and Private Tutors. Managing Director Digby Colliery (Nottingham) Co. Ltd.; Director Manners Colliery (Ilkeston) Co. Ltd.; Renishaw Iron Works (Chesterfield); Smith Bros. & Co., Ltd. (Hyson); Humber Coal (Hull) Co., Ltd.; Director Alban Richards & Co., Ltd., 19 St. James', London; South African Carbide and By-Products Co., Ltd., 13 St. Helens Place, London, E.C.; was member of the Notts. C.C. 1904-1908 and High Sheriff E. Yorks. 1920. *War Work*: Interested in the Transport of Wounded; he raised £700,000 worth of ambulances and ambulance equipment, mobile hospitals, including 30 motor hospital boats for Mesopotamia; the Dennis Bayley Fund Ambulances were on all the Allied Fronts; Sir Dennis was mentioned in General French's despatches in Jan. 1915, has the 1914-15 medal, was decorated on the Field with the Croix-de-Guerre, and made Officier of the French Legion of Honour; he is a Knight of Grace of the Order of St. John of Jerusalem in England; he was made a K.B.E. in 1918 for War Services; the family's Orphanage at Beeston and the Creche in Nottingham are well known, and have been in existence nearly 50 years. The Bayley Hospital in Nottingham was full of Belgian wounded in Sept. 1914, and during the War had 1600 cases. *Addresses*: Lenton Abbey, Notts.; and Hunmanby Hall, E. Yorks. *Clubs*: Bath; Reform; R.A.C.; Notts. County; Hull and East Riding; Scarborough. (K130)

BAYLEY, Roland, O.B.E.

BAYLEY, Lieut.-Col. Stuart Farquharson, O.B.E., I.A.

BAYLISS, Edward Swayn, M.B.E., *b.* 16 April, 1864; *s.* of the late Edward Swayn Bayliss, late of Pontypridd; *m.* Sophia Alice, *d.* of the late Lieut. James Dyer, R.N. *Educ.*: Dockyard School, Portsmouth. Contract Officer, Admiralty. *War Work*: Service in Admiralty Contract Dept. *Address*: Friaryhurst, Pollards Hill East, Norbury, S.W. 16. (M1395)

BAYLISS, Gilbert Thomas, M.B.E.

BAYLY, Lieut.-Col. Abingdon Robert, D.S.O., O.B.E., *b.* 7 March, 1871; *s.* of the late General A. A. Bayly, Colonel Commandant Royal Artillery. *Educ.*: Marlborough; Lausanne; R.M.A., Woolwich. Commanding 4th Brigade R.F.A., Ross Barracks, Shorncliffe, Kent. *War Work*: O.C. 118th Batt. 1st Division in retreat from Mons; Staff Officer attached to Interned Branch of British Legation in Switzerland. *Address*: c/o Cox and Co., 16 Charing Cross, London, S.W *Club*: Royal Automobile. (O6882)

BAYNE, Bertha Marguerite, Mrs., M.B.E.; *d.* of John Corlett La Mothe, J.P., of Ramsey, Isle of Man; *m.* John Bayne, M.A., B.Sc. *Educ.*: At home and in Switzerland. Woman Farmer; Lecturer and teacher in Agriculture; Seven years Sub-Warden, Lady Warwick's Agricultural College, Reading and Studley. *War Work*: Organisation of Women's War Work on Land and of Women's War Agricultural Committees; appointed, 1915, Agricultural Adviser to Board of Trade, and in 1916 transferred to Board of Agriculture as Chief Woman Inspector of the Land Army. *Address*: Spring Park, Shirley, Surrey. *Club*: Forum. (M130)

BAYNE, Charles Walter, C.B.E., *b.* 1872; *s.* of William Bicknell Bayne, of Littlehampton; *m.* 1896, Kate Blythman, Gen. Manager, Central Uruguay Railway, and Local Director Standard Life Assurance Co., and of Monte Video Telephone Co. *Address*: Montevideo, Uruguay. *Club*: Uruguay (Montevideo). (C929)

BAYNES, Charlotte Augusta, Mrs., O.B.E.

BAYNES, Lieut.-Col. Douglas Dyneley, O.B.E.

BAYNES, Edward William, O.B.E., *b.* 1 Dec. 1880; *s.* of the late Edward Baynes, of Antigua, West Indies; *m.* Dorothy Margaret, *d.* of the late F. W. Beauchamp, of Colwall, Herefordshire. *Educ.*: Antigua Grammar School and privately. Colonial Service, Leeward Islands, West Indies, 1899-1912; transferred to Home Civil Service, 1912; Second Class Clerk, 1912, First Class Clerk, 1913 in National Health

Insurance Commission now part of Ministry of Health), and Secretary to National Health Insurance Joint Committee, 1919. *War Work*: Assisted in Propaganda Department, 1914–17; Private Secretary to Secretary of Ministry of Shipping, Jan. 1917, to Oct. 1919, and from April, 1920; also Private Secretary to Parliamentary Secretary, Ministry of Shipping, April, 1920. *Address*: The Manor House, Datchet, Windsor. *Club*: Isthmian. (O9969)

BAYNES, Lucy Draffen, M.B.E., *b.* 31 Aug. 1887; *d.* of Joseph Hanbury Baynes, M.B., Ch.B., of Manchester. *Educ.*: Manchester High School for Girls; Lady Margaret Hall, Oxford. *War Work*: Junior Administrative Assistant, War Office. *Address*: 28, College Court, W. 6. (M7336)

BAYNHAM, Lieut.-Comm. Henry, O.B.E., R.N.

BAYNHAM, Comm. Sir Walter de Mouchet, K.B.E., R.D., R.N.R., *b.* 27 July, 1876; *s.* of John Francis Baynham, of Charlton, Dover, Kent; *m.* Edith Jane Chevallier, *d.* of Alfred Chevallier Preston, M.D., of Swaffham Prior, Cambridge. *Educ.*: Private School. Marine Superintendent to Orient Steam Navigation Co., Ltd.; Younger Brother, Trinity House. *War Work*: Navigation Commander and 2nd in command H.M.S. "Otranto" from 8 Aug. 1914, to 23 June, 1917; commanded transport "Ormonde," Nov. 1917, to Nov. 1918. *Address*: "Coronel," Main Road, Sidcup, Kent. (K345)

BAZELEY, Marjorie Letitia, Mrs., M.B.E., *b.* 24 July, 1874; *d.* of the late Col. Henry Dumaresq, R.E., of Bideford, N. Devon; *m.* Henry Russell, *s.* of Henry Montague Bazeley, of Bideford, Devon. *Educ.*: At home. *War Work*: Commandant of Red Cross Auxiliary Hospital at "Commons," Northam, N. Devon, from March, 1915, to Feb. 1919. *Address*: Bracken Brae, Bideford, N. Devon. (M3520)

BAZETT, Capt. Henry Cuthbert, O.B.E. M.C., R.A.M.C.

BAZLEY, Walter Stanley, M.B.E.

BEACH, Col. Thomas Boswall, C.M.G., C.B.E., R.A.M.S, (ret.), *b.* 28 May, 1866; *s.* of the late Rev. W. R. Beach, M.A., late Royal Army Chaplains Dept. *Educ.*: Bloxham School and King's College, London. *War Work*: A.D.M.S. Alexandria, Egypt, for duration of War; mentioned in despatches twice and awarded C.M.G., 1916, and C.B.E., 1919. *Address*: Ailsa House, King's Road, Reading. (C1370)

BEACHAM, Capt. Robert William, O.B.E., M.C.

BEACHCROFT, Betty, Mrs., M.B.E.

BEACHCROFT, Major Philip Maurice, O.B.E., *b.* 3rd March, 1879; *s.* of Philip Edward Beachcroft, of Wingates, Boyne Hill, Maidenhead; *m.* Patience Marguerite, *d.* of Thomas Ward Wilson, of Uploders, Bridport, Dorset. *Educ.*: Uppingham School, and Magdalen College, Oxford. Barrister-at-Law; M.A., Oxon. *War Work*: 1914–15, C.P.O., R.N.A.S.; 1916, Royal Artillery; 1916–17, France; A. Capt. 1917, H.Q. Staff, No. 9 District, Eastern Command, 1918–19; Head of legal discipline at Air Ministry; mentioned in despatches, Jan. 1919; Officer B.E. (Mil. Div.), June, 1919. *Addresses*: 1, Essex Court, Temple, E.C. 4; 48, The Ridgeway, N.W 4. *Clubs*: New University. (O8044)

BEADON, Lieut.-Col. Roger Hammet, C.B.E., *b.* 16 Jan. 1887; *s.* of John Hammet Beadon, J.P., of Blackerton, East Anstey, Devon. *Educ.*: Clifton College. Captain and Brevet-Lieut.-Col. Royal Army Service Corps. *War Work*: Africa, 1914; War Office, 1915–17; Italy, 1917; B.E.F. France, Sept. 1917; G.H.Q. Italy, 1917; D.A.A. & Q.M.G. Supreme War Council, Versailles, 1917–18; Peace Conference, 1919–20, as Representative of Q.M.G.; Asst.-Adjutant and Quartermaster-General Allied Committee of Versailles, 1920. *Club*: Junior United Service. (C1459)

BEAL, Major Richard Edward Bruce, O.B.E., M.C., R.A.S.C.

BEALE, Capt. Alan Oswald Rufus, M.B.E., M.C., *b.* 10 April, 1891; *s.* of Louis Stephen of Tunbridge Wells; *m.* Dorothy Mary, *d.* of John Booker, of Crowborough. *Educ.*: Tonbridge School and Royal Military College. *War Work*: France, 1st Batt. Bedfordshire Regt., June, 1915, to June, 1918; wounded twice; Adjutant and Staff Captain, Italy, Nov. 1917, to April, 1918; Russia (Murmansk), Nov. 1918, to Oct. 1919; placed on Res. of Regular Officers, March, 1920. *Address*: Bettenham, Biddenden, Kent. *Club*: Sports. (M6991)

BEALE, Lieut. Basil Perry, O.B.E., M.C., R.A.S.C.

BEALE, Frances Helen FitzGerald, Mrs., M.B.E., *b.* 5 Feb. 1852; *d.* of John Alex FitzGerald, of Mountmellick, Ireland; *m.* late Frederic FitzGerald Beale. *War Work*: S. and S.F.A. and Local War Pensions Committee. Queens Co.; also acting entirely as Sub-Local, Mountmellick; acted for Prisoners of War, Mountmellick and Maryborough. *Address*: Mountmellick. Queens Co., Ireland. (M7339)

BEALE, Lieut. Geoffrey Scott, M.B.E.,

BEALE, Helen Mary, O.B.E., W.R.N.S.

BEALE, Sir John Field, K.B.E., *b.* 15 Jan. 1874; *s.* of late James Samuel, of Standen, East Grinstead; *m.* Daisy Emma, *d.* of James Aylward Game. *Educ.*: Harrow and Trinity College, Cambridge. Deputy Chairman, Midland Rly. Co.; Director, Guest, Keen & Nettlefolds, Ltd.; Director, Anderson, Green & Co., Ltd. (Managers "Orient" Line). *War Work*: Vice-Chairman of Wheat Commission; Chairman of Wheat Executive; Chairman of Committee of Representatives of Allied Food Council; First Secretary, Ministry of Food; British Representative on Inter-Allied Council of Supply and Relief, Paris. *Addresses*: 49, Porchester Terrace, London, W. 1; and North Bay, Oulton Broad. *Clubs*: Junior Carlton; Norfolk and Suffolk Yacht; Royal Cruising and Tamesis. (K51)

BEALE, Richard Henry, M.B.E., *b.* 9 Jan. 1877; *s.* of Richard John Beale, of Fowey, Cornwall; *m.* Alice, *d.* of Edmund Roberts, of Plymouth. *Educ.*: Fowey Grammar School. Master Mariner. *War Work*: Employed as Master of Steamers on Admiralty work in the French and Norwegian Traders, in the danger zones, during the duration of the War. *Address*: Peverell, Torquay, Devon. (M7340)

BEALE, Lieut. Walter William, O.B.E.

BEALES, Major William Lear, O.B.E.

BEALL, Major Frank William, O.B.E., R.A.S.C., *b.* 19 June, 1884; *s.* of the late W. E. Beall; *m.* Helen Marion, *d.* of Hamilton Hunter, C.M.G. *Educ.*: Bedford School. *War Work*: France, Aug. 1914; Salonika, Dec. 1915–19; Constantinople, June, 1919, to present date; four times mentioned in despatches; Brevet Major; O.B.E. *Address*: c/o Sir C. R. McGrigor, Bart. and Co., 39, Panton Street, S.W. (O6437)

BEALL, Paymaster-Lieut. Norman Hugh, O.B.E., R.N.

BEAMAN, Lieut. Val Ardern Hulme, M.B.E., I.A.R.O. (M6780*a*)

BEAMER, Ernest Edward Boyce, O.B.E.

BEAMISH, Capt. Eric Hamilton, O.B.E.

BEAMISH, Major Francis Teulon, O.B.E., A.M.C.

BEAMISH, Capt. William Robert de la Cour, O.B.E., R.E.

BEAN, Lieut. Arthur, O.B.E., R.N.R.

BEAN, Jane Ann, Mrs., O.B.E.

BEAN, John Harper, C.B.E., *b.* 1885; *s.* of Alderman Sir George Bean, of Oakham Lodge, Dudley. Director of Harper, Sons and Bean, Ltd., of Dudley. *Address*: Tansley Hill House, Dudley. (C109)

BEAN, Lieut. Robert Charles, M.B.E.

BEANES, Warwick Henry, M.B.E.

BEARD, Charles Albert, M.B.E., *b.* 21 Nov. 1855; *s.* of the late Charles Beard, of Woolwich and Hampton-on-Thames; *m.* Supheme Louise, *d.* of the late Alexander Joskey, of Woolwich. *Educ.*: Woolwich. Superintending Clerk, Admiralty. *War Work*: Purchase of timber for Admiralty and Air Ministry (Aeroplane) requirements; represented the Admiralty as a member of the Commission Internationale d'Achat des Bois, Home Grown Timber Committee, Engineering Standards Committee (Timber, etc.); Special Constabulary, T Division, Service Medal; conducted sales of obsolete War ships and enemy War ships. *Address*: Crescent Road, Kingston Hill. *Club*: O.P. (M7341)

BEARD, Ernest Somerville, M.B.E.; *s.* of T. H. Beard, of Truro; *m.* Clara, *d.* of Capt. T. Trethewey, of Newquay. *Educ.*: Hart House, Tregoney, and Truro College, Truro. Wholesale and Retail Shoe Factor. *War Work*: Quartermaster, Hon. Sec. and Transport Officer, R.N. Auxiliary Hospital, Truro, Oct. 1915, to March, 1919. *Address*: Somerville. Truro. (M7)

BEARD, Lieut. John James, M.B.E.

BEARD, Joseph James, C.B.E.

BEARD, Marian Gertrude, O.B.E.

BEARD, Norah, Mrs., M.B.E.

BEARD, Richard Frith, M.B.E.

BEARD, Capt. Samuel Trevor, O.B.E., R.A.M.C., *b.* 1 Feb. 1876; *s.* of the late John H. Beard, of Hendsford, Staffs; *m.* Frances Ada, *d.* of the late Hubert Coombes, of Stratford-on-Avon. *Educ.*: Abergavenny Grammar School. L. & N. W. Rly. Official; Hon. Serving Brother Order of St. John of Jerusalem; Scoutmaster, B.P. Boy Scouts; Corps Supt. St. John Ambulance Brigade; served in S. African War, 1900–1. *War Work*: Mobilised Aug. 1914 as a Quartermaster of the Military Home Hospital Reserve of the St. John Ambulance Brigade; was posted for duty with the R.A.M.C. on Salisbury Plain, in which area he served in several hospitals until May, 1917, when he proceeded to France; carried out the duties of Quartermaster of a Field Ambulance in the 25th Div. for over two years, taking part in the retreats of the Somme, the North, and the Marne, and the final advance. *Address*: 2, Grosvenor Road, Abergavenny, Mon. *Club*: Royal Automobile. (O4989)

BEARD, Lieut. William, M.B.E.

BEARDER, John William, M.B.E., B.A., Ph.D., *b.* 18 April, 1869; *s.* of William Corthan Bearder, of Nottingham; *m.* Ada, *d.* of Archibald Morris, of Belfast. *Educ.*: Nottingham High School. Headmaster, Northallerton Grammar School. *War Work*: Hon. Sec. North Riding Distress Committee (National Relief Fund), which was also responsible for Belgian Refugees in the North Riding; awarded 1920 Médaille du Roi Albert avec rayure. *Address*: Grammar School, Northallerton. (M131)

BEARDMORE, Joseph George, O.B.E., *b.* 17 Jan. 1872; *s.* of Isaac Beardmore, of Parkhead Forge. *Educ.*: Uppingham. *War Work*: Manufacture of Bullet Proof plates for 18-pounder Field Guns and plate details for 18-pounder, 6-in. Howitzer, and 8-in. Howitzer Carriages; also the construction of 8-in. Howitzer Trails. *Address*: Lymington Lodge, Bothwell, Lanarkshire. (O9962)

BEARDSLEY, Eleanor Jemima, M.B.E., *b.* 3 Nov. 1879; *d.* of John Joseph Beardsley, of Nottingham. *Educ.*: Nottingham. Civil Servant; Chief Woman Officer, North-Western Division, Ministry of Labour. *War Work*: Initiation and Organisation of the Military Laundry Scheme, in Sept. 1914, for the Eleventh Division of Kitchener's Army stationed at Belton Park Camp, Grantham; Recruitment of women for the various State Services, Q.M.A.A.C., W.R.N.S., W.R.A.F.,

W.L.A., N.A.C.B. *Address :* 4, Bridge Street, Withington, Manchester. (M7342)

BEARE, Surg.-Lieut. Stanley Samuel, O.B.E., R.N., *b.* 1890 ; *s.* of Samuel Beare, of Torquay ; *m.* Cecil Mary Guise, *d.* of Captain Francis Horner Lyell, of Ruckmans, Oakwood Hill. *Educ. :* Newton Abbot and Middlesex Hospital. Resident Medical Officer to the Middlesex Hospital, W. 1. *War Work :* Surg.-Lieut., R.N., 1914–19 ; H.M.S. "Orvieto," minelayer ; Medical Officer to Auxiliary Patrol, Dover, 1916–19 ; present in Zeebrugge and Ostend attacks, 1918 ; mentioned in Vice-Admiral Sir Roger Keyes's despatches. *Address :* The Middlesex Hospital, W. 1. (O4920)

BEASLEY, Capt. Horace Owen Compton, O.B.E.

BEASLEY, Madeleine, M.B.E.

BEASLEY, Major Myddelton, O.B.E., R.E.

BEATE, Capt. Basil Perry, O.B.E., M.C., R. of O., *b.* 7 Sept. 1895 ; *s.* of Sydney Benjamin Beale, of Sutton, Surrey ; *m.* Helen Ada, *d.* of the late E. V. Carey, of Lyne Capel, Surrey. Enlisted in Inns of Court O.T.C. ; Aug. 1920 ; Commissioned R.A.S.C., Oct. 1914 ; served in France and Belgium, Nov. 1914, to May, 1915 ; granted regular commission, Dec. 1915 ; served with 6th Corps, R.A.S.C., May, 1915, to Sept. 1918 ; Staff Capt. 98th Inf. Brigade H.Q. Oct. 1918, to Jan. 1919 ; mentioned in despatches. *Address :* c/o Mrs. E. V. Carey, Swanston, Whitchurch, Oxon. (O2422)

BEATH, David Leslie, O.B.E., *b.* 3 March, 1873 ; *s.* of David Beath, of Melbourne, Australia ; *m.* Hilda Rosalie Gertrude, *d.* of the late Fredk. Wm. Lawrence, of Bath. *Educ. :* Merchiston and St. Bart.'s Hospital. Hon. Associate Order of St. John of Jerusalem ; Medical Officer, Magdalen Hospital School, Bath ; Medical Officer, Kingswood School, Bath ; Hon. Medical Officer Bath Preventive Mission. *War Work :* Medical Officer in Charge, Newton Park Hospital ; Medical Officer, Kingswood Hospital, Bath ; Medical Officer Bath War Hospital. *Address :* Clan House, Sydney Gardens, Bath.

BEATON, George Howard, O.B.E.

BEATON, Surg.-Lieut. Thomas, O.B.E., M.D., R.N.

BEATSON, Sir George Thomas Beatson, K.C.B., K.B.E., B.A. (Cantab.), D.L., *b.* 26 May, 1848 ; *s.* of the late Surgeon General George Stewart Beatson, C.B., of Campbeltown, Argyllshire. *Educ. :* King William's College, I.O.M. ; Cambridge University ; Edinburgh University. Surgeon. *War Work :* Chairman of the Scottish Branch B.R.C.S. *Address :* 7, Woodside Crescent, Glasgow. *Clubs :* Junior Constitutional ; Western Club (Glasgow) ; Scottish Conservative (Edinburgh). (K52)

BEATSON, Lieut.-Col. Leonard Frank, O.B.E., *b.* 28 Dec. 1865 ; *s.* of Rev. L. B. Beatson, who died 1894 ; *m.* Gladys, *d.* of Lieut.-Col. H. Pipe-Wolferstan, of the Cameronians. *Educ. :* King's School, Canterbury, and R.M.C., Sandhurst. *War Work :* Raised and commanded the 12th Service Batt. the East Surrey Regt. ; Commanded the 29th (Works) Batt. the Middlesex Regt., also Commandant Eastern Command Labour Centre ; served during the War from Sept. 1914, to Sept. 1919. *Address :* Redstone, Brighton Road, Sutton, Surrey. (O3090)

BEATTIE, Lieut.-Col. Alexander Elder, M.C., M.C., *b.* 25 Jan. 1888 ; *s.* of Major Alexander Beattie, of Stirling, Scotland ; *m.* Janet Dunbar, *d.* of Thomas Kirkaldy, of Woodford. *Educ. :* Stirling. Brevet Major in the Queen's Regt. ; at present Staff Officer, West Africa Frontier Force. *War Work :* Active Service on Nigerian-Cameroon Frontier, Aug. 1914 ; Staff Officer, Northern Railway, Jebessi River, and Jaunde Road Columns, Cameroons Expeditionary Force ; severely wounded ; Staff Officer at Colonial Office Dec. 1915, to end of war. *Address :* 69, Gloucester Crescent, Regent's Park, London. *Clubs :* Junior United Service ; Royal Automobile ; Sports. (C2397)

BEATTIE, Capt. Arthur Joseph, M.B.E., M.C., R.A.

BEATTIE, Capt. and Qr.-Mr. Edward Allsop, M.B.E., R.A.M.C.

BEATTIE, Sir James, K.B.E., *b.* April, 1861 ; *y.s.* of Charles Beattie, of Aberdeen ; *m.* Mary, *e.d.* of William Minty, of Aberdeen. Chairman, Messrs. A. & A. Henry & Co. *War Services :* In charge of Jute Supplies, War Office, and Hon. Director of Flax Office, Department of the Surveyor-General of Supply, War Office. *Addresses :* 52, Eaton Square, S.W. ; Canmore, St. Andrews, Fife.

BEATTIE, John Millar, M.B.E.

BEATTIE, Rachel, Lady, M.B.E., J.P. ; *d.* of Thomas Brien, of Lanistown House, Co. Dublin ; *m.* Rt. Hon. Sir Andrew Beattie, P.C., *s.* of John Ladlie Beattie (*see* BURKE'S *Peerage*), of Co. Down. *Educ. :* Ireland. *War Work :* Services in Dublin. *Address :* 46, Fitzwilliam Square, Dublin. (M7343)

BEATTY, Andrew Henry, O.B.E.

BEATTY, Francis Montague Algernon, O.B.E.

BEATTY, Lieut. Herbert James, M.B.E.

BEATTY, Rose Mabel, Mrs., C.B.E., *b.* 1879 ; Comdt.-in-Chief and Founder of Green Cross Corps. (C430)

BEATTY, Lieut.-Col. William Dawson, C.B.E., A.F.C., R.E., and R.A.F. Has Order of Military Merit of Spain.

BEATTY, Major William John, O.B.E., R.A.S.C.

BEAUCHAMP, Agneta Frances, O.B.E.

BEAUCHAMP, Col. Sir Frank, Bart., C.B.E., J.P., *b.* 6 Oct. 1866 ; *s.* of the late W. B. Beauchamp, of Norton Hall, Bath ; *m.* Mabel Constance, *d.* of the late J. N. Bannoir, of New Romney. *Educ. :* Privately. Member of Somerset County Council. *War Work :* Served for 18 months

as O.C.A.S.C. at Fonant, as I.Q.M.G.S. Headquarters Southern Command ; was then sent on a special mission by the War Office to the War Department, Washington, U.S.A., in an advisory capacity and served until the Armistice. *Address :* Woodborough House, Bath. *Clubs :* Carlton ; Ranelagh ; Hurlingham : Bath and County, Bath. (C1460)

BEAUCLERK, Dame Beatrix Francis, Lady Osborne De Vere, G.B.E., Lady of Grace, *b.* 25 March, 1877 ; *d.* of 5th Marquess of Lansdowne. K.G. (*see* BURKE'S *Peerage*) ; *m.* 1st, 6th Marquess of Waterford, K.P. (d. 1911), 2nd, Lord Osborne de Vere Beauclerk, *s.* of 10th Duke of St. Albans (d. 1898) (*see* BURKE'S *Peerage*). *Educ. :* Privately. *War Work :* President and Chairman of Irish War Hospitals Supply Depots ; Chairman of Co. Waterford Local War Pensions Committee ; President of Irish Munition Makers' Canteens ; Hon. Sec. Soldiers' and Sailors' Families Association ; Vice-President Soldiers' and Sailors' Help Society, Co. Waterford. *Addresses :* Curraghmore, Portlaw, Co. Waterford ; 8, Hyde Park Gardens, London. W. (D.G.28)

BEAUFORT, Capt. Victor Alexandre, O.B.E., M.C., *b.* 23 June, 1890 ; *s.* of the late Major Francis Beaufort, of Royal Artillery ; *m.* Enid Margaret, *d.* of the late Charles Robin, of Jersey. *Educ. :* St. Davids, Reigate, and Wellington. Joined 3rd Devon Regt. S.R., 1908 ; passed into Regular Army, 1st Batt. Devon Regt., 1911 ; appointed Adjutant, 4th Devon Regt. (T.F.), 1920. *War Work :* Served with 1st Devon Regt. from commencement of War till seriously wounded on the Aisne, 26 Sept. 1914 ; employed at War Office till Sept. 1915 ; joined R.F.C. Balloon Section, Sept. 15 ; served with No. 1 Kite Balloon Section in France till May, 1916 ; Invalided home ; took 21st Balloon Company to Palestine, May, 1917 ; served there till Armistice ; returned to England and organised the London-Paris Aerial route for Peace Conference. *Address :* Bovey Tracey, Devonshire. *Clubs :* Conservative ; Junior Naval and Military ; Hurlingham ; Wells, (O8046)

BEAUMONT, Major Eugene Guy Euston, O.B.E., R.A.S.C.

BEAUMONT, Lieut.-Col. Godfrey Lancaster, O.B.E., R.M.L.I., *b.* 25 Aug. 1864 ; *s.* of the late James Beaumont, of Rainhill Hall, Lancashire ; *m.* Eily Elizabeth, *d.* of the late George Augustus Dawes, of The Hall, Kenilworth. *Educ. :* Downside College, Woburn Park, and Royal Naval College, Greenwich. Joined Royal Marine Light Infantry, Sept. 1884 ; retired as Major, 1903 ; served at Intelligence Dept., Admiralty ; Adjutant, Royal Malta Militia ; Recruiting Staff Officer, London, Belfast, Bristol. *War Work :* Called up 1914 ; served on board H.M.S. "Euryalus," Western Patrol ; later, in H.M.S. "Swiftsure" and H M.S. "Lord Nelson," throughout Dardanelles Campaign ; present at landing and evacuation of Gallipoli, also bombardment of Smyrna ; made Temp. Brig.-Gen. and Chairman Inter-allied Board of Controls at Athens ; G.S.O. (N.), 1st Class, Rio de Janeiro ; mentioned in despatches ; received thanks of the British Government for political services at Athens ; awarded O.B.E., promoted to substantive Lieut.-Col., and made Commander of the Order of the Redeemer (Greece). (O9516)

BEAUMONT, Major Henry, O.B.E.

BEAUMONT, Major and Qr.-Mr. Henry George, O.B.E., R.A.S.C.

BEAUMONT, Violet Marie-Louise, Lady, O.B.E. ; *d.* of the late F. Wootton Isaacson, M.P., of 18, Upper Grosvenor Street ; *m.* Henry, 9th Lord Beaumont. *Educ. :* Privately. *War Work :* Vice-President British Red Cross ; Commandant V.A.D. 86, Sussex ; Commandant and part donor Officers' Red Cross Hospital, Slindon House, Arundel ; President Soldiers' and Sailors' Families Assocn., West Sussex ; Registrar for Women on the Land (Slindon) ; Representative for Slindon Voluntary Women Workers' (Sir Edward Ward's Scheme). *Addresses :* Slindon House, Arundel ; 49, Eaton Place, S.W. 1. *Club :* Bath. (O1102)

BEAUSIRE, Clara Constance, C.B.E., *b.* 7 Feb. 1871 ; *d.* of Joseph Beausire, of Wethersfield, Noctorum, Birkenhead. *Educ. :* At home and in Germany. *War Work :* Vice-President Birkenhead Division since 1913 ; organised Hospitals, Depots, etc., also Comforts Committees for 4 Military Hospitals in Division of Birkenhead ; Secretary to the Mendell Home for Discharged and Disabled Sailors and Soldiers, 1917–19, and now acting as Secretary to the Manor Hill Hospital, Birkenhead, Cheshire Branch B.R.C.S. for Discharged and Disabled Sailors and Soldiers. *Address :* Wethersfield, Noctorum, Birkenhead. (C2443))

BEAUTEMENT, Lieut. Harold, O.B.E., R.N.R.

BEAVAN, Ernest Charles Edward, M.B.E.

BEAVAN, Francis John, O.B.E.

BEAVER, Edith Maude, M.B.E.

BEAVER, Ida Scott AUDSLEY-, O.B.E.

BEAVER, Major Robert Atwood, O.B.E., R.A.M.C.

BEAVIS, Arthur Beagley, C.B.E. ; *b.* 1867 ; *s.* of James Beavis. Financial Adviser British Salonica Force. (C405)

BEAVIS, Capt. Philip Ernest, O.B.E., R.A.

BEAVON, John, M.B.E., *b.* 26 March, 1858 ; *s.* of James Beavon, of Birmingham ; *m.* Miriam Maud Lilian, *d.* of — Hardcastle, of London. *Educ. :* Wesleyan Schools, Westminster, and Bow. Chief Examiner of Small Arms, Army Inspection Department, Royal Small Arms Factory, Enfield Lock. *War Work :* Supervision of the above department, under the Chief Inspector of Small Arms, War Office, and, later, Ministry of Munitions, and Technical Adviser in all small arm matters. *Address:* 14, Portland Avenue, Stamford Hill, N. 16. (M7345)

BEAZLEY, Capt. Arthur Tetley, M.B.E.

BEAZLEY, Herbert George, M.B.E.

BEBB, Herbert Llewellyn Mountfort, O.B.E.

BEBB, Capt. Roland Harry, O.B.E.

BECHER, Maj.-Gen. (Hon.) Andrew Cracroft, C.B.E., *b.* 26th Aug. 1858 ; *s.* of Gen. Sir Arthur Becher, K.C.B. ; *m.* Elizabeth Dalyell, *d.* of James Raphael Stewart, M.A. *Educ.:* Wellington College and Sandhurst. Norfolk Regiment, 1878–1904 ; commanded 1st Batt. 1900–04 ; retired, 1905 ; commanded 2nd Lothian (Vol.) Brigade, 1906–08 ; commanded Durham L.I. (Terr.) Brigade, 1908–14 ; served in the Afghan War, 1879–80, and South African War, 1899–1900. *War Work:* Aug. 1914, A.A. and Q.M.G. 3rd Army Central Force ; commanded 63rd Division (at home), 1915–16, and Southern Command Depot, 1917–18. *Address:* Northam Lodge, Northam, N. Devon. *Club:* Naval and Military. (C1461)

BECHER, Major Cecil Leycester, M.B.E., 7th Dragoon Guards (ret.), *b.* 11 Aug. 1844 ; *s.* of Sullivan James Becher, of Indian Civil Service ; *m.* Emily Sophia Mary, *d.* of Col. William Grove, of Indian Army. *Educ.:* Sidney College, Bath. 19¾ years as Officer of the 7th Dragoon Guards, and subsequently 12 years in the Army Pay Department ; Egyptian War Medal, 1882 ; Khedivial Star, Bar to Medal, Tel-el-Kebir. *War Work:* Treasurer for Essex of the Sailors' and Soldiers' Families Association, from Nov. 1899, to Sept. 1919, and other local War work associations. *Address:* 40, Creffield Road. Colchester. (M7346)

BECHER, Dame Ethel Hope, G.B.E., R.R.C., *b.* 1867 ; *s.* of Col. A. W. R. Becher, of Hammersley, Penn, Bucks. *Educ.:* Privately. Trained London Hospital, Whitechapel, E. Ward Sister, 1893–99 ; Principal Matron Queen Alexandra's Imperial Military Nursing Service, 1903–10 ; Matron-in-Chief, 1910–19 ; South African War, 1899–1902, R.R.C. ; (two medals) : Sister, Army Nursing Service Reserve. *War Work:* Matron-in-Chief of Queen Alexandra's Imperial Military Nursing Service and its Reserve Headquarters, War Office (bar to R.R.C.) ; Lady of Grace, Order of St. John of Jerusalem. *Address:* 35, Mecklenburgh Square, W.C. 1 . (D16)

BECK, Albert George, M.B.E., *b.* 6 June, 1870. *Educ.:* At private school and at Royal Dockyard School, Portsmouth, till 1889. Entered Portsmouth as Dockyard Engine Fitter Apprentice, 1885–92 ; became Chargeman of Engine Building, 1894 ; appointed Inspector of Engine Fitters, Feb. 1901 ; Promoted Foreman, Engineering Branch, Nov. 1906. *War Work:* Appointed by Admiralty, 8 Aug. 1914, as Senior Assistant to the Engineer Captain on the Staff of Rear-Admiral Laurence E. Power, C.B., C.V.O., for organising, negotiating, and supervising repairs to H.M. Warships and Chartered Vessels carried out by Engineering Firms on the Tyne, and at Sunderland, Middlesbrough, and Blyth during the War. *Address:* 108, Orchard Road, Southsea, Portsmouth. (M7347)

BECK, Conrad, C.B.E., *b.* 1864 ; *s.* of Joseph Beck, of Stoke Newington, N. ; *m.* Annie, *e. d.* of John Collings, of Leighton Buzzard. Chm. and Managing Director of R. and J. Beck, Ltd., and Pres. British Optical Instrument Manufacturers' Asso. ; author of " The Theory of the Microscope," etc. *Address:* 34, Upper Addison Gardens, Kensington, W. (C431)

BECK, Frank Harold, M.B.E.

BECK, Oliver Lawrence, C.B.E., D.S.O.

BECKENHAM, Harry Anstead, M.B.E., *b.* 6 Nov. 1890. Civil Servant, Admiralty, since 1910. *Club:* Tavistock Residential, Tavistock Square, W.C. (M7349)

BECKER, Sir Walter (Frederick), K.B.E., *b.* 9 March, 1855 ; *s.* of Frederick Becker, of Falmouth ; *m.* Delphine Clotilde Thérèse, *d.* of Alphonse de Martelly, of London. *Educ.:* Falmouth Classical and Grammar School. Ex-shipowner ; Member of the Executives of Local Societies : The Turin Society for the Prevention of Cruelty to Animals ; The Society for the Protection of Youthful Offenders, etc. ; The Italo-Britannic League, etc. ; formerly Chairman of Maternity and Rescue Home, Turin, founded and maintained by himself ; Founder of Italian Steamship Lines, Member of Boards of Directors of Italian Steamship Companies ; Consul-General for the King of Siam. *War Work:* Founded and maintained British Military Hospital at Turin ; Rest House and Reading Room for British Sailors and Soldiers ; Free Buffet and Meals at Turin Station, for British Sailors and Soldiers passing through from all parts ; Propaganda Work during the War. *Addresses:* Val Salice, Turin (Italy) ; Villa Delphine, Roquebrune-Cap-Martin (France). *Clubs:* R.A.C. ; Royal Cornwall Yacht ; Union, Genoa and Rome ; Automobile Club of Italy. (K53)

BECKETT, Capt. Charles Stephenson, O.B.E.

BECKETT, Ivy Nina, Mrs., C.B.E.

BECKETT, Rev. Maurice Thomas, O.B.E.

BECKETT, Muriel Helen Florence, Mrs. Rupert, C.B.E., *b.* 3 Jan. 1878 ; *d.* of Lord Berkeley, Charles Sidney Paget (*see* BURKE'S *Peerage*, Anglesey, M.) ; *m.* Hon. Rupert (Evelyn), J.P., D.L., 3rd *s.* of the late William Beckett, O.B.E. *Addresses:* Stone House, Moor Allerton, Leeds ; 34, Grosvenor Square, W. (C432)

BECKETT, William Marrow, M.B.E., Assoc.M.Inst.C.E., Mem. Soc. Eng., *b.* 12 April, 1860 ; *s.* of William Beckett, of Northwich, Cheshire ; *m.* Martha, *d.* of Rev. Jacob Sturton, M.A., R.D., J.P., of Woodborough Rectory, Wilts. *Educ.:* Whitchurch Grammar School, and Victoria University,

Manchester. Consulting Civil Engineer in Manchester, 1900–14 ; now practising as Consulting Engineer at 10, Throgmorton Avenue, London, E.C. ; previous appointments as Resident Engineer on Preston Dock Works, Manchester Ship Canal. and Aire and Calder Navigation. *War Work:* 2½ years Assistant Inspector of Carriages for the War Office in the North-West District ; 2 years Assistant Water Engineer to the Air Ministry. *Addresses:* 42, Hammelton Road, Bromley, Kent ; 10, Throgmorton Avenue, London, E.C. (M7350)

BECKETT, Lieut.-Col. (Acting Brig.-Gen.) William Thomas Clifford, C.B.E., D.S.O., V.D., M.I.C.E., R.E., T.F.R., *b.* 29 Aug. 1862 ; *s.* of Col. W. H. Beckett, of Indian Army ; *m.* Bessie, *d.* of the late Maj.-Gen. C. S. Thomason, R.E., Bengal. *Educ.:* Dover College ; Tonbridge School ; Crystal Palace Engineering School. Civil Engineer ; Agent and Chief Eng. B.N. Ry., 1905 ; Lieut.-Col. B.N. Ry. Volunteers ; held appointments in Egypt later. *War Work:* Commanded S. Div. Special Constab. ; did Censor's work in French, Italian, Spanish, and Portuguese ; under Lord Derby's Scheme was given command of 12th (Pioneer) Batt. Loyal North Lancs. Regt. ; served in France, Salonika, Syria and again in France ; transferred to R.E. and is in Siberia, where he holds the command of the British Ry. Mission. *Addresses:* 111, Iverna Court, Kensington, W. 8 ; Grantown-on-Spey, Scotland. *Club:* Oriental. (C2212b)

BECKWITH, Arthur, O.B.E., A.M.I.C.E., C.C. ; J.P., *b.* 12 June, 1860 ; *s.* of Edward Lonsdale Beckwith, of The Knoll, Eastbourne ; *m.* Edith Annie, *d.* of Dr. Heckstall Smith, of Hove. *Educ.:* Eton. County Councillor ; Director, Neath and Brecon Rly. Co., and Towgood and Beckwith, Ltd. *War Work:* Chairman, Breconshire War Pensions Local Committee. *Address:* Moor Park, Llanbedr, Crickhowell, S. Wales. *Club:* Thatched House. (O9968)

BEDDALL, Herbert Bowman, M.B.E., F.S.I., N.D.A., M.R.A.C., *b.* 28 Dec. 1880 ; *s.* of J. F. Beddall, of London ; *m.* Edith, *d.* of the late Dr. F. S. Watson, of Princes Risborough, Bucks. *Educ.:* Bedford School ; and Royal Agricultural College, Cirencester. Articled to J. R. Eve & Son, Bedford ; District Valuer at Truro ; Valuation Department, Inland Revenue (held appointment since 1910, previously Agent to the late Wm. Coryton, J.P., Pentillie Castle, Cornwall). *War Work:* Acted as Surveyor to the Cornwall Agriculture Executive Committee, and Sub-Commissioner under the Ministry of Agriculture, during the Food Production Campaign, 1917–19. *Address:* Elston, The Avenue, Truro, Cornwall. (M133)

BEDDINGTON, Reginald, O.B.E., *b.* 15 Aug. 1877 ; *s.* of D. L. Beddington, of 4, Sussex Square, W. 2 ; *m.* Sybil Elizabeth, *d.* of D. Q. Henriques, of 17, Sussex Square, W. 2. *Educ.:* Rugby, and Corpus Christi College, Oxford. Barrister-at-law. *War Work:* Commandant, F Division, Metropolitan Special Constabulary, and member of London Ambulance Column. *Address:* 25, Cambridge Square, W. 2. *Club:* Flyfishers : Devonshire. (O9969)

BEDDISON, Francis William, M.B.E.

BEDDOE, James Stuart, M.B.E.

BEDDOES, Major Claude Eagles Willoughby, O.B.E.

BEDDOW, Muriel Grace, M.B.E.

BEDFORD, Col. Herbrand Arthur Russell, 11th Duke of, K.G., K.B.E., Marquess of Tavistock, Earl of Bedford, Baron Russell of Chenies, Baron Russell of Thornhaugh, Baron Howland of Streatham, F.R.S., *b.* 19 Feb. 1858 ; *suc.* his brother, 10th Duke, 1893 ; *m.* Mary du Courroy, *d.* of the late Ven. W. H. Tribe, Archdeacon of Lahore. *Educ.:* Balliol Coll., Oxford. Lord Lieutenant of the County of Middlesex since 1898 ; a Trustee of the British Museum ; Chairman, Bedfordshire County Council ; late Col. 3rd Bn. Bedfordshire Regt. ; formerly A.D.C. to King Edward and King George ; J.P. ; President of the Zoological Society of London since 1899 ; Church of England ; Liberal Unionist ; joined Grenadier Guards, 1879 ; served in Egyptian Campaign, 1882 (medal with clasp and Khedive's Star) ; A.D.C. to Lord Dufferin, Viceroy of India, 1884–88. *Addresses:* Woburn Abbey, Bedfordshire ; 15, Belgrave Square, W. *Club:* Brooks's. (K309)

BEDFORD, Richard William, M.B.E.

BEDINGFELD, Lieut.-Col. Henry Howard, O.B.E. (Mil.), *b.* 7 May, 1859 ; *s.* of Major-Gen. Philip Bedingfeld, of Windsor ; *m.* Helen Wellesbourne, *d.* of William Venour, of Saundersfoot, Pembrokeshire. *Educ.:* Privately, and Royal Military College, Sandhurst. Gazetted 11th Foot from R.M.C., 1879. *War Work:* Served in France, 1915, 9th Batt. Devon Regt. (1st New Army) ; later, in command, 11th (R.) Batt. Devon Regt., afterwards the 44th Training Reserve Batt. ; then in command 2nd Vol. Batt. Hants. Regt. ; 1914–15 Star ; British War Medal ; Victory Medal ; O.B.E., 1919 (Mil.). *Address:* Flemings, Hayling Island. (O6889)

BEDNELL, Alfred, O.B.E., *b.* 1869 ; *s.* of James Bartleet Bednell, of Coventry. *War Work:* Secretary Ministry of Munitions Board of Management, Coventry ; Vice-Chairman, Ministry of Munitions Board of Management, Midland Area ; Director War Savings Department, Coventry. *Address:* Stoke Park, Coventry. (O135)

BEECROFT, Alfred, M.B.E.

BEECROFT, Capt. Arthur Edward, M.B.E., B.A., LL.B., late R.E., *b.* 12 June, 1887 ; *s.* of E. R. Beecroft, J.P., of Tunbridge Wells ; *m.* Beryl Constance, *d.* of Thomas Salt, M.R.C.S., L.R.C.P., of Birmingham. *Educ.:* Tonbridge School ; The Leys School ; Cambridge University. Barrister-at-Law. *War Work:* University and Public School Force, Royal Fusiliers,

Aug. to Sept. 1914; Despatch Rider, R.E., Oct. 1914; 2nd Lieut., R.E. (Signals), 11 Nov. 1914; Gallipoli, Suvla Bay, with 11th Div. (invalided), 6 Aug. 1915; Home Service with Signals (Captain), 1916–1919. *Address:* 3, Essex Court, Temple; Saltley, Beaconsfield, Bucks. (M1401)

BEEDEN, Harry, M.B.E., *b.* 1872; *s.* of Thomas Beeden, of Elston, Notts.; *m.* Emma, *d.* of William Weatherhogg, of Fishtoft, Lincs. *Educ.:* Grantham British School and National School. Clothier. Poor Law Guardian; Borough Councillor; Building Society Director. *War Work:* Secretary, Local Central War Savings Committee; National Service Committee; Food Economy Campaign; Official Correspondent to the Ministry of Food; Congregational Church Soldiers' Social Club. *Address:* 9, St. Catherine's Road, Grantham. (M7352)

BEEDIE, Capt. Robert Mitchell, M.B.E., *b.* 31 March, 1875; *s.* of Rev. R. M. Beedie, of Old Calabar; *m.* Margaret Ann, *d.* of William Beedie, of Whitehill, New-Deer. *Educ.:* Partick Academy and Hamilton Crescent School, Partick. Member of Glasgow and West of Scotland Interviewing Board, Appointments Dept. Ministry of Labour (Honorary). *War Work:* Master Transports, "Hurst," "Hunsdon" and "War Music"; "Hurst" attacked by submarine on surface, action lasted 1¼ hours, and "Hurst" escaped, 18 April, 1917; "Hurst" torpedoed, no lives lost, 3 Oct. 1917; "Hunsdon" torpedoed, 1 life lost, 18 Oct. 1918. *Address:* 54, Airlie Gardens, Hyndland, Glasgow. (M7353)

BEEMAN, C. May, C.B.E. Organising Secretary, Alexandra Day. (C3132)

BEER, Lieut. Arthur James, M.B.E.

BEER, George Stephen, O.B.E.

BEER, Lina, Mrs., O.B.E., *b.* 1871; *d.* of — Stern, of Liverpool; *m.* Walter Beer, of Liverpool. *Educ.:* Liverpool. *War Work:* Commandant, Bradstones Auxiliary Hospital, Liverpool; equipped hospital of 50 beds, and ran it for two years. *Address:* 11, Livingston Drive, Sefton Park, Liverpool. (O9970)

BEESLEY, Major Lewis Henry, M.B.E., *b.* 1882; *s.* of the late Henry Beesley, of The Bank House, Wirksworth, Derbyshire. *Educ.:* Wirksworth Grammar School. *War Work:* Commissioned April, 1915, to Rifle Brigade; Capt. Sept. 1915; went to France, Feb. 1916; invalided home with shell shock, July, 1916; served on Military Intelligence Staff from Nov. 1916, to Sept. 1919; in May, 1918, was gazetted as Major, and appointed British Liaison Officer between British and American Governments for Postal Censorship; went to America in May, 1918, and travelled all over America, Canada, and down to the West Indies to visit American Censorship Stations. (M5069)

BEETON, Capt. Bernard James, M.B.E., R.A.F.

BEETON, Sir Mayson Moss, K.B.E. Rendered services in connection with the Newfoundland Forestry Corps. (K348)

BEETON, Capt. and Qr.-Mr. Thomas Guy, M.B.E.

BEEVER, Lieut. Claude Henry, M.B.E., R.N.

BEEVOR, Susan Heard, Mrs., O.B.E.; *d.* of Dabney Charles, of Boston, U.S.A.; *m.* John Hare, *s.* of Sir Thomas Beevor, Bart., of Hargham, Norfolk. *War Work:* In Oct. 1914, started a small Hospital, 10 beds in Wroxham; in spring of 1915 handed the Hospital over to Wroxham V.A.D. Detachment; at once opened a hospital of 50 beds in her own home. *Address:* Newhouse, Penshurst, Kent. *Club:* Ladies' Empire. (O136)

BEGBEY, Lieut.-Col. Henry, O.B.E., R.A.O.C.

BEGBIE, Col. Frank Warburton, C.B.E., Knight of Grace of the Order of St. John of Jerusalem, M.R.C.S.(Eng.), L.R.C.P. (Lond.), *b.* 13 June, 1864; *s.* of James Warburton Begbie, M.D., LL.D., of Edinburgh; *m.* Catherine Mary, *d.* of Walter Reynolds, J.P., of Hawkswick, St. Albans. *Educ.:* Fettes and St. Bart.'s Hospital. Member of Board of Pensions, Plymouth Area. *War Work:* Commandant Eastbourne, Ripon, Black pool: Training Battalions Liaison Officer to American Medical Units; O.C. No. 6 General Hospital, Rouen: A.D.M.S. Dieppe, Le Tréport, Dunkerque; A.D.M.S. Cornwall, Devon, Somerset, and Gloucester. *Address:* 1, Carlton Hill, Exmouth, Devon. *Club:* Junior Naval and Military. (C1220)

BEGG, Alexander Clarke, O.B.E., M.D., *b.* 21 Feb. 1873; *s.* of the late Alexander Campbell Begg, of Dunedin, N.Z.; *m.* Catherine Willis, *d.* of the late Charles A. Ainslie, of Swinton Park, Peebles, N.B. *Educ.:* Boys' High School, Dundee, and Edinburgh University. Hon. Physician to the Swansea Hospital; Chairman, Swansea Division of the British Medical Association. *War Work:* Medical Officer, Hedd Fan, Parc Wern, and Brynmill Red Cross Hospitals; Chairman, Local Medical War Committee. *Address:* 74, Walter Road, Swansea, S. Wales. (O9971)

BEGG, Donald Glassford, M.B.E., *b.* 24 May, 1870; *s.* of Robert Begg, of Ayr. *War Work:* Hon. Sec.. Committee for the River Plate Contingent. *Address:* 32, Corfton Road, Ealing, W. *Club:* Argentine. (M1402)

BEHRENS, Capt. Edgar Charles, O.B.E., *b.* 13 May, 1885; *s.* of G. Behrens, of Withington, Manchester. *Educ.:* Rugby School. Merchant. *Address:* 5, Queens Road, Ilkley, Yorks. *Club:* Bradford. (O6891)

BEITH, Major Ian Hay, C.B.E., M.C.. *b.* 17 April, 1876; *s.* of John Alexander Beith, of Altnacriag, Oban; *m.* Helen Margaret, *d.* of P. A. Shipes, of Polmont Park, Stirlingshire. *Educ.:* Fettes College, Edinburgh; St. John's College, Cambridge. Author. *War Work:* Served 10th Argyll and Sutherland Highlanders; then Machine Gun Corps. *Address:* 21,

Bruton St., W. *Clubs:* Garrick; Caledonian; Royal Automobile. (C4433)

BELBEN, Frank, O.B.E., M.B., F.R.C.S., *b.* 16 April, 1869; *s.* of Thomas Belben, of Poole, Dorset. *Educ.:* Haileybury; Christ's College, Cambridge; St. Bartholomew's. Surgeon (Consulting); Surgeon to Royal Victoria and West Hants Hospital, Bournemouth; Consulting Surgeon to Milford Cottage Hospital. *War Work:* Hon. Surgeon, Boscombe, Crag Head, and Christ Church Military Hospitals, Bournemouth; St. John Ambulance Brigade, and Grata Quies Auxiliary Hospitals, Bournemouth. *Address:* 25, Knyverton Road, Bournemouth. *Club:* Bournemouth. (O9972)

BELCHAMBER, Lieut. Douglas Foster, M.B.E., M.G.C.

BELCHAMBER, Frederick Augustus, O.B.E.

BELCHEM, Capt. and Qr.-Mr. Owen King, O.B.E., M.C.

BELCHER, The Hon. Charles Frederic, M.B.E., M.A., LL.B., *b.* 11 July, 1876; *s.* of George Frederick Belcher, of Geelong, Australia; *m.* Sara, *d.* of Harman Visger, of London. *Educ.:* Geelong Grammar School and Trinity College (University of Melbourne). Barrister-at-Law, Attorney-General, Nyasaland Protectorate. *War Work:* Translation of wireless interceptions and captured documents in Uganda during 1914–17. Served in Uganda Volunteer Reserve 1914–1916. *Address:* Zomba, Nyasaland. *Club:* Zomba. (M6414)

BELCHER, Edmund Charles, M.B.E.

BELCHER, Major Ernest Albert Crossley, C.B.E., M.A. (Oxon.), *b.* 1872; *s.* of the late Albert Belcher, of Barnet, Herts. *Educ.:* Queen's College, Taunton, and Lincoln College, Oxford. Natal Civil Service, 1901–07; Assistant Master and House Tutor, Clifton, 1908–12; Headmaster, Christ's College, New Zealand, 1912–14. *War Work:* Second-in-Command D.C.L.I., 1915–16; Director Agricultural Section, Navy and Army Canteen Board, 1916–17; Director of Vegetable Supplies, Ministry of Food, 1917–18; Contested (U.) Holland with Boston Division of Lincolnshire, 1918. *Address:* The Mill House, Clewer, Windsor. *Clubs:* Oxford and Cambridge; Junior Army and Navy; Royal Colonial Institute. (C434)

BELCHER, Evelyn, M.B.E., *b.* 1882; *d.* of Francis Wm. Belcher, of Chippenham. *Educ.:* Privately. *War Work:* Quartermaster of Chippenham Red Cross Hospital; responsible for all housekeeping and accounts for 100 beds 3¼ years. *Address:* 12, Marshfield Road, Chippenham. (M137)

BELFIELD, Florence, Lady, C.B.E.; *d.* of late Sir James Rathborne; *m.* Sir Henry Conway, K.C.M.B. (see BURKE'S *Peerage*), *s.* of late John Belfield, J.P., of Primley Hill, S. Devon. *Address:* 4, Roxburgh Mansions, Kensington Court, W.8. *Clubs:* Junior Carlton, Bachelors', and Ranelagh. (C751b)

BELFIELD, Lieut.-Gen. Sir Herbert Eversley, K.C.B., K.C.M.G., K.B.E., D.S.O., *p.s.c.*, *b.* 25 Sept. 1857; *s.* of the late Capt Belfield, J.P., Malmains, Glos.; *m.* 1st, Emily Mary, *e.d.* of the late Rt. Rev. Hibbert Binney, D.D., Bishop of Nova Scotia; 2nd, Evelyn Mary, *d.* of the late Albon Taylor, Elm Grove, Barnes. *Educ.:* Wellington Coll. Director of Prisoners of War 1914–20; served Ashanti, 1895–96, as Chief Staff Officer (despatches, Brevet Lieut.-Col., Star); South Africa, 1899–1902 (despatches twice, C.B., D.S.O.); A.A.G., 1st Army Corps, 1902–3, commanded 4th Infantry Brigade, 1903–7; Commanded 4th Division, 1907–11; Colonel, Duke of Wellington's Regt., 1909; a Governor of Wellington College, and a Commissioner of the Duke of York's Royal Military School; Grand Officer, Ordre de la Couronne (Belgium). *Address:* 15, Thurloe Court, S.W.3. *Club:* Army and Navy. (K297)

BELFIELD, Major Sydney, C.B.E., *b.* 1862; *s.* of the late John Finney Belfield, of Primley Hill, Paignton; *m.* 1902, Annie, *d.* of Charles Mitchell, of Jesmond Towers, Newcastle-on-Tyne. Major and temporary Lieut.-Col. R.A.; S. Africa, 1899–1900 (Queen's medal with clasp); Great War, 1914–19 (despatches). (C1463)

BELL, Capt. and Brevet-Major Aidan Isaac, O.B.E., R.M.L.I., *b.* 15 July, 1885; *s.* of Charles Ernest Bell, of Park House, Durham, and Teresa Mary Bell, nee Salvin, of Burn Hall, Durham; *m.* Eleanor Christina, *d.* of Edward G. Dove, J.P., of Oaklands, Riding Mill-on-Tyne. *Educ.:* Oratory School, Edgbaston, Birmingham. Joined the Royal Marine Light Infantry, 1 Sept. 1904. *War Work:* Served in H.M.S. "Leviathan," H.M.S. "Agincourt," H.M.S. "Shannon" until end of 1916; then appointed Naval Intelligence Officer at Callao, Peru, S. America, until 1 Jan. 1920; awarded rank of Brevet Major, 1 Jan. 1919, for good services during the War. *Clubs:* Junior Naval and Military. (O9414)

BELL, Capt. Adolphus Edmund, C.B.E., *b.* 1850; *s.* of Edmund Frederick Bell, of Kensington, W. An Elder Brother of Trinity House. *Address:* 23, Down Street, Mayfair. W. *Clubs:* Isthmian; Junior Athenæum. (C882)

BELL, Capt. Alec Jeffrey, O.B.E., late Indian Cavalry, *b.* 20 May, 1885; *e.s.* of Charles Jeffrey Bell, of St. Leonards-on-Sea; *m.* 13 Oct. 1920, Christina Hannah, *e.d.* of W. G. Badham, of Four Oaks, Warwickshire. *Educ.:* Malvern. East India Merchant, Calcutta. *War Work:* Assistant Director of Remounts, Baghdad. *Address:* 22, Strand Road, Calcutta. *Clubs:* Bengal; New Oxford and Cambridge; East Sussex. (O6572)

BELL, Andrew, M.B.E., J.P., *b.* 1868; *s.* of Andrew Bell, of Leith; *m.* Rachel, *d.* of James Ballingall, of Leith. *Educ.:* Free Church Normal School, Edinburgh. Gen. Sec., Y.M.C.A., Glasgow. *War Work:* Y.M.C.A. Hut work in Egypt; in Glasgow, organising two Huts and organising and running six hostels for Service men, and one hostel for relatives of wounded. An aggregate of over 544,000 men were accommodated overnight in the former, and 3,869 in the latter; in all these ministered to the physical and social needs of about 2,155,000 Service men. *Address:* Y.M.C.A. Club, 100, Bothwell Street, Glasgow. (M7355)

BELL, Andrew Riddell, O.B.E.

BELL, Major Arthur Hugh. D.S.O., O.B.E., R.E., *b.* 16 April, 1878; *s.* of Edward Bell, of Hampstead, London, N.W.; *m.* Gabrielle, *d.* of the late J. Kennedy, I.C.S. *Educ.:* Charterhouse. Commissioned 2nd Lieut., R.E., 23 March, 1898. *War Work:* Served with a field company in Flanders from July, 1915, to Feb. 1916; subsequently on Indian Frontier, mostly in Waziristan; awarded the O.B.E. for work in India during the War. *Address:* c/o Messrs. Cox & Co., 16, Charing Cross. (O8436)

BELL, Arthur Morton, O.B.E., M.I.Mech.E., J.P., *b.* 1865; *s.* of Richard Morton Bell, of Sandy, Beds.; *m.* Frances Maud, *d.* of Henry Lee, of Dunton. *Educ.:* Private schools. Mechanical Engineer, formerly Loco. Dept., Great Eastern Rly., England, now Carriage and Wagon Supt., Great Indian Peninsula Rly. *War Work:* Design and construction of military troop trains, ambulance cars; pontoon structures for Mesopotamia, etc.; munitions, hospital furniture, etc. *Address:* 7, Khatau Mansions, Bombay. (O4012)

BELL, Charles David Jarrett, M.B.E.

BELL, Lieut.-Col. Charles Francis, C.B.E., D.S.O., *b.* 4 July, 1882; *s.* of late Charles Bell, J.P., of Norley Hall, Norley, Cheshire; *m.* Rita, *d.* of E. J. McCabe, Scranton, Penna., U.S.A. *Educ.:* Greenbank School, Liverpool; and Sedbergh, Yorks. Director of Road Transport, Ministry of Food; awarded C.B.E. (Civil) for special work in connection with the Railway Strike, 1919. *War Work:* Joined R.A.S.C. Sep. 1914, took part in retreat from Antwerp; first battle of Ypres; overseas service, 1914 to 1917; awards, 1914 Star and Bar, Mention in Despatches, D.S.O., British War Medal and Victory Medal; Home Service, 1917 to 1919; A.Q.M.G. War Office Demobilisation Work; awarded O.B.E. (Military). *Address:* 25, Weymouth St., London, W. 1. *Club:* Royal Automobile. (C2444)

BELL, Capt. Charles Hugh, O.B.E., R.A.F.

BELL, Lieut.-Col. Charles Thornhill, O.B.E., Kaisir-i-Hind medal, R.A. (ret.), *b.* 18 Dec. 1862; *s.* of Rev. W. C. Bell, of Indian Ecclesiastical Establishment. *Educ.:* Royal Military Academy, Woolwich. Supt., Indian Ordnance Factories; Gun Carriage Factory, Bombay; Gun and Shell Factory, Cossipore. *War Work:* Supt., Gun Carriage Factory, Jubbulpore; Superintending Engineer, London Area; Inspector Gun Carriages; Technical Adviser, Trench Mortar Inspection. *Address:* 3, Cambridge Place, Bromley, Kent. (O3616)
tary. (O6893)

BELL, Constance Mildred, M.B.E. Responsible for the welfare of Blinded Officers, St. Dunstan's. (M10305)

BELL, Lieut.-Col. Edward, M.B.E., *b.* June, 1868; *s.* of Peter Bell, of Wexford, Ireland; *m.* Elizabeth Alice Edith, *d.* of Henry George Stubbs. *Educ.:* Privately and at Clarke's C.I. School, Dublin. Commandant, Local Forces, Leeward Islands, British West Indies, and Chief Inspector, L.I. Police Force; Member of Executive Council, Leeward Islands, with affix of "Honourable"; thanks of H.M. Government for services in riots at Antigua in 1918, and Police Medal for gallantry in 1914 (wounded). *War Work:* Enlisted and trained contingents to the B.W.I. Regiment; in charge of discipline of Royal Marine Artillery Battery, Antigua. *Address:* Court Lodge, St. John, Antigua. (M1250)

BELL, Enoch, M.B.E., J.P.

BELL, Evelyn Mary, Mrs., O.B.E.

BELL, Florence, Lady, D.B.E.; *d.* of late Sir Joseph Olliffe, M.D.; *m.* as his 2nd wife Sir Thomas Hugh R. Bell, 2nd Bart.; *suc.* his father, 1904 (see BURKE'S *Peerage*). *Addresses:* Rounton Grange and Mount Graer Priory, Northallerton, Yorkshire; 95, Sloane Street, S.W. (D25)

BELL, Francis James, M.B.E., *b.* 15 May, 1866. *Educ.:* Uppingham. Registrar of the Kingston County Court; Clerk to the County Justices (Kingston Division), and Commissioners of Taxes (Kingston and Elmbridge Division). *War Work:* Chief Officer of Kingston, Surbiton, and District Fire Brigade; Member of Home Office Fire Brigades Co-ordination Committee, 1917–18, and of Advisory Committee, 1918–19; Vice-Chairman of the National Fire Brigades Association. *Address:* Chillington, Lovelace Gardens, Surbiton. (M7357)

BELL, Capt. George, O.B.E., Aust. A.M.C.

BELL, Major George Gerald, O.B.E., R.E.

BELL, Gertrude Margaret Lowthian, C.B.E.; *d.* of Sir Thomas Hugh Bell, Bart., by his first marriage (see BURKE'S *Peerage*). *War Work:* Rendered valuable services to B.R.C.S. during Great War, and was Asst. Political Officer to Mesopotamian Exped. Force. (C11)

BELL, Harold Idris, O.B.E., M.A., *b.* 2 Oct. 1879; *s.* of Chas. C. Bell, of Epworth (Lincs.); *m.* Mabel Winifred, *d.* of Ernest Ayling, of Crouch End. *Educ.:* High School, Nottingham; Oriel College, Oxford; Universities of Berlin and Halle. First Class Assistant, Dept. of MSS., British Museum. *War Work:* Editor of Food Supplement to the Daily Review of the Foreign Press, published by the General Staff. *Address:* 8, Birchington Road, Crouch End, N. 8. (O9975)

BELL, Henry McGrady, C.B.E., *b.* 25 Oct. 1880; *s.* of James Wills Bell, of Dundee; *m.* Illa, *d.* of Prof. Adam Schwappach, of Eberswalde. *Educ.:* Dundee High School; Morrison's

Academy, Crieff; and on the Continent. Director, Price & Pierce Ltd., London and New York. *War Work:* Acting-Consul at Helsingfors to 1919; Acting Chargé d'Affaires in the Diplomatic Service, 1920. *Addresses:* 27, Clement's Lane, London E.C. 4; 269, Banbury Road, Oxford. *Club:* St. Stephen's S.W. (C2445)

BELL, Capt. Herbert, O.B.E., R.E. (T.F.)

BELL, Hubert Dowson, O.B.E.

BELL, Capt. James Logan, O.B.E., R.A.S.C.

BELL, Major James MacKintosh, O.B.E.

BELL, Lieut. John Aiton, O.B.E., I.A.R.O.

BELL, Eng.-Comm. John Fawcett, O.B.E., R.N.

BELL, 2nd Lieut. Lee, M.B.E.

BELL, Marcus, O.B.E. (O11949)

BELL, Lieut.-Col. Matthew Gerald Edward, O.B.E. *b.* 24 July 1871; *s.* of Matthew John Bell, of Bourne Park, Kent (see BURKE'S *Landed Gentry*); *m.* Hon. Mary, late Maid of Honour to Queen Alexandra, *d.* of Sir William Hart Dyke, Bart., of Lullingstone Castle (see BURKE'S *Peerage*). *Educ.:* Eton. Late Rifle Brigade. *War Work:* General Staff, Central Force, Eastern Command, and Supreme War Council, Versailles. *Address:* Bourne Park, Canterbury, Kent. *Club:* Marlborough. (O4304)

BELL, Capt. Morris James, O.B.E.

BELL, Lieut. Norman, M.B.E., A.S.C.

BELL, Lieut.-Col. Richard Carmichael, D.S.O., O.B.E., late 38th (K.G.O.) Central India Horse, *b.* 21 June, 1868; *s.* of Rev. Canon J. S. Bell, of St. Patrick's Cathedral, Dublin; *m.* Mildred Charlotte, *d.* of Rev. B. C. Davidson-Houston, of St. Johns, Sydney Parade, Dublin. *Educ.:* Trinity College, Startford-on-Avon. Served in the Tirah Expedition, 1897–8; Seistan Boundary Commission in Persia and S. Afghanistan, 1903–6. *War Work:* Served in France, Dec. 1914 to Oct. 1919; commanded 15th Batt. (1st London Welsh) Royal Welsh Fusiliers, Nov. 1915, to Oct. 1916; Battle of the Somme, July, 1916; attack on and capture of Mametz Wood, Battle of Cambrai, Nov. 1917. *Club:* Junior United Service. (O2435)

BELL, Robert, C.B.E.; in N.-E. Railway Co.'s Service. (C438)

BELL, Capt. Robert Arthur, O.B.E.

BELL, Capt. Rudolph John, O.B.E., M.C., R.A.S.C.

BELL, Sir Thomas, K.B.E., *b.* Sersawa, British India, 1865; *e.s.* of the late Imrie Bell, M.I.C.E.; *m.* Helen, *d.* of Malcolm Macdonald. *Educ.:* King's Coll. School; Royal Naval Engineering Coll., Devonport. Director, John Brown & Co., Ltd. Entered, in 1886, the Engineering and Shipbuilding Works of James and George Thompson, Clydebank, which were subsequently purchased by John Brown & Co., Ltd., of Sheffield and Clydebank; Resident Director in charge since 1909; Deputy Controller of Dockyards and Shipbuilding, Admiralty, May, 1917, to Dec. 1918; a Vice-President of the Institute of Naval Architects; M.I.C.E., and Member of other technical societies; also of General Committee of Lloyd's Register of Shipping. *Address:* Auchentoshan, Dalmuir, Dumbartonshire. *Clubs:* Reform; Royal Automobile; New (Glasgow). (KB)

BELL, Capt. Thomas Carmichael, O.B.E.

BELL, Thomas Norman Jarvis, O.B.E.

BELL, Major Victor Douglas, O.B.E., R.A.F.

BELL, Violet Caroline, M.B.E., V.A.D.

BELL, William Thomas, O.B.E.

BELL, Kathleen Audrey Danvers BAINBRIDGE-, *b.* 1894; *d.* of the Rev. F. C. Bainbridge-Bell. *Educ.:* Queen's College, London. *War Work:* Secretarial work at Ministry of Munitions and Ministry of Food, 1915–19. *Address:* The Vicarage, Catford. *Club:* Halcyon. (M1404)

BELL, Major Clive Vincent MOBERLY-, O.B.E., *b.* 15 Jan. 1885; *s.* of Charles Frederick Moberly-Bell; *m.* Elizabeth Enid, *d.* of A. A. Grenville Malet. *Educ.:* Marlborough. *War Work:* D.A.Q.M.G., Southern Command, Salisbury; D.A.Q.M.G., 10th Corps, B.E.F.; A.Q.M.G., Eastern Command, London. *Club:* Junior Naval and Military.

BELL, Lieut.-Col. Ernest FitzRoy MORRISON-, O.B.E., *b.* 19 April, 1871; *s.* of Sir Charles Morrison-Bell, Bart., of Otterburn Hall, Northumberland; *m.* Maud Evelyn, *d.* of Lieut.-Col. F. Henry, of Elmestree, Tetbury, Glos. *Educ.:* Eton. Late 9th Lancers. *War Work:* Served with 7th Reserve Regt. of Cavalry from Aug. 1914, to April, 1917; commanded 2/1 Royal Wilts Yeomanry, April, 1917, to end of War. *Addresses:* 5, Cambridge Gate, Regents Park, N.W. 1; The Close, Tetbury, Glos. *Clubs:* Carlton, Cavalry, Royal Automobile. (O7492)

BELLAIRS, Major Robert George, O.B.E., I.A.R.O., *b.* 13 Jan. 1876; *s.* of J. G. Bellairs-Stevenson, of Ranikhet, U.P., India; *m.* Kathleen Mary, *d.* of C. T. Ambler, of Monghyr. *Educ.:* Neuenheim College, Heidelberg. Teaplanter; at present Colonization Officer, Kumaon, Ind., Soldiers' Settlements, Kausanie, Almora. *War Work:* Recruited men for 50th Kumaon Rifles; raised 36th Kumaon Labour Corps; served in France, Sept. 1917, to July, 1918; in Mesopotamia, from Oct. 1918, to Jan. 1920, as C.O. of the 73rd and 109th Kumaon Lab. Corps, respectively. *Address:* Kausanie P.O., via Almora, U.P., India. *Club:* Overseas. (O2116)

BELLAMY, Albert, C.B.E., *b.* 1870; *s.* of the late James Bellamy; *m.* 1899, Mary, *d.* of the late John Fisher, of Halifax. Formerly Pres. National Union of Railwaymen. *Address:* 93, Fox Street, Stockport. (C16)

BELLAMY, Major Charles Glynn Hughes, O.B.E.

BELLAMY, Hugh Maurice, O.B.E. (O9714)

BELLANEY, Major David Ernest, M.B.E., *b.* 1872; *s.* of David Bellaney, of Lucan. *Educ.:* Kingsley College. *War Work:* Purchasing Officer on Remount Commission in Canada and United States of America during period of War. *Address:* Esker House, Lucan, Ireland. *Club:* White's. (M139)

BELLASIS, Gwendolen Edith, M.B.E.; *d.* of E. S. Bellasis, late of P.W. Dept., India. *Educ.:* Badminton House; Clifton; and Ladies' College, Cheltenham. *War Work:* Four years in War Trade Dept., for which she received the thanks of the Government and the M.B.E. *Address:* Enmore, Guildford. (M104)

BELLEW, Capt. Edward Henry, M.B.E.

BELLHOUSE, Gerald, C.B.E., B.A., *b.* 13 April, 1867; *s.* of William Bellhouse, of Alderley Edge, Cheshire; *m.* Edith Marion, *d.* of W. R. R. Gemmell, of Alderley Edge. *Educ.:* Fettes College, Edinburgh, and Trinity College, Cambridge. H.M. Deputy Chief Inspector of Factories. *War Work:* Organised arrangements for special overtime and for substitution of female for male labour in munition and other factories (Home Office); Member of Health of Munition Workers Committee (Ministry of Munitions); Chief Commissioner National Service Department; Chairman Civil War Workers Committee (Ministry of Reconstruction); Member of Supplementary Rations Committee (Ministry of Food). *Address:* 6, Eaton Square, London, S.W. 1. *Club:* United University. (C110)

BELLMAN, Harold, M.B.E., F.S.S., *b.* 16 Feb. 1886; *s.* of Charles Henry Bellman, formerly of Penzance, Cornwall; *m.* Kate, *d.* of Edwin Peacock, of Brondesbury Park. *Educ.:* Paddington and Privately. Asst. Sec., the Abbey Road Permanent Building Society. *War Work:* Principal Assistant (Administrative) Establishment Branch of the Secretariat of the Ministry of Munitions of War, 1915–20; Assistant Commander, Headquarters Central Detachment Metropolitan Special Constabulary Reserve. *Address:* Etchingham Park Road. Finchley. *Club:* Eighty. (M1358)

BELLWOOD, Major Cecil Power, O.B.E.

BELLWOOD, Surg.-Lieut. Kenneth Bonson, O.B.E., R.N.

BELT, Capt. Charles Burnley, M.B.E., M.C., D.C.M., R.A.F.

BELTON, Capt. Andrew, O.B.E., R.A.F.

BEMROSE, Capt. William Lloyd, O.B.E., T.F.

BENDALL, James Lucas, O.B.E., *b.* 1857; *s.* of the late Charles Bendall, of Wells, Somerset. *Educ.:* Grammar School, Wells, Somerset. H.M. Civil Service, Board of Trade, from Dec. 1875. *War Work:* Clerk in charge of Accounts at the Board of Trade. *Address:* Sheen Park Gardens, Richmond, Surrey. *Club:* National Liberal. (O9978)

BENDELL, Lieut. Albert, M.B.E., R.N.

BENDER, Capt. William Edward Gustave, M.B.E., I.A.R.O.

BENET, Lieut.-Col. Henry Vere Fane, C.B.E., *b.* 1863; Major (ret.), and T. Lieut.-Col.; served in Russia during Great War; has Legion of Honour. (C436)

BENEY, Major Arthur, O.B.E., *b.* 26 March, 1883; *s.* of W. A. Beney, J.P., of Beckenham; *m.* Evelyn, *d.* of E. Simpson, of Toronto. *Educ.:* Westminster School. Machinery Exporter. *War Work:* D.A.D.T., 5th Army. *Address:* Oakleigh, Shepherd's Hill, Highgate. *Clubs:* Junior Athenæum; M.C.C. (O2426)

BENJAMIN, Florence, Mrs., M.B.E., *b.* 23 Dec. 1867; *d.* of A. L. Lazarus, of Palace Court, W.; *m.* Henry S., *s.* of Solomon Benjamin, of Brunswick House, Clifton Gardens, London, W. *Educ.:* Girton House. *War Work:* Head of a Surgical Bandage Department at the British Red Cross Central Workrooms, Burlington House, Piccadilly, W. *Address:* 15, Pembridge Crescent, London, W. 11. (M1406)

BENN, Sir Arthur Shirley, K.B.E., M.P. (C.), Plymouth, since 1910; *b.* 1858; *e.s.* of the late Rev. J. W. Benn, M.A., Rector of Carrigaline and Douglas, Co. Cork, and Maria Louisa, *d.* of the late Gen. Christopher Hamilton, C.B., and Hon. Mrs. Hamilton, *d.* of the 2nd Lord Castlemaine; *m.* Alys Marie, *d.* of F. A. Lüling, of Springhill, Alabama. *Educ.:* Clifton Coll.; abroad. Student, Inner Temple. Lived for some time in Canada; was British Vice-Consul, Mobile, and Managing Director, Hunter, Benn & Co.; held commission in Canadian Garrison Artillery; returned to England, 1902; contested Battersea, 1909 and 1910; Member, L.C.C., 1907–11; Chairman, Highways Committee, 1901–10. *Address:* Bolton Gardens, S.W. *Clubs:* Carlton; Royal Thames Yacht; Royal Western. (K131)

BENN, Charles Anthony, O.B.E. (O11784)

BENN, Capt. Edward Hugh, M.B.E., R.A.S.C.

BENN, Ernest John Pickstone, C.B.E., *b.* 25 June, 1875; eldest *s.* of Sir John W Benn, Bart.; *m.* Gwendoline Dorothy, *d.* of the late F. M. Andrews, of Edgbaston. *Educ.:* Privately. Managing Director Benn Brothers, Ltd.; Editor "Ways and Means." *War Work:* Assistant Director, training section, Ministry of Munitions, 1916–17; Chairman, Trade Organisation Commissioners, Ministry of Reconstruction, 1917–18; Founder of the Industrial Reconstruction Council and of the Higher Production Council; Treasurer, Industrial League. *Addresses:* Blunt House, Oxted, Surrey; 8, Bouverie St. E.C. 4. *Clubs:* Savile; Union; Reform. (C437)

BENN, Capt. Walter, M.B.E., R.E.

BENNET, Mary Barbara, O.B.E.

BENNETT, Ada Mary, M.B.E.

BENNETT, Agnes, Mrs., M.B.E., Queen Elizabeth's Belgium Medal, *b.* 10 Dec. 1857; *d.* of James Tait, of Ayrshire, Scotland; *m.* William, *s.* of A. Brice Bennett, of Wargrave, Berks. *Educ.:* Mauchline High School, Ayrshire, and Leeds, Yorks. President from 1914–18, and from 1919 to present date, Loyal Women's Guild, Umtali Branch; President Girl Guide Local Association, Umtali; Member Hospital Advisory Board; Member Advisory Committee of Maternity Home. *War Work:* Organised Belgian Fete in 1914 for the relief of Belgian Refugees; from 1914 the Loyal Women's Guild Organised and controlled the bulk of War Relief Work in Umtali, including Comforts for the men at the front and in hospitals, in South-West Africa, East Africa, and at home, particularly to the 2nd Rhodesian; and also raised substantial sums for the British Red Cross Society, the S. A. Red Cross Society, and the Mashonaland Central War Fund for returned disabled Rhodesians. *Address:* Darlington, Umtali, S. Rhodesia. (M6415)

BENNETT, Major Alexander John Munro, O.B.E., T.D.

BENNETT, Alice Mary, M.B.E., Q.M.A.A.C.

BENNETT, Lieut.-Col. Allan Edward Kingston, O.B.E.

BENNETT, 2nd. Lieut. Archie, M.B.E.,

BENNETT, Arthur Henry, O.B.E., LL.B. (Lond.), *b.* 17 Sept. 1862; *s.* of Arthur Bennett, of Leicester; *m.* Gertrude, *d.* of R. P. Swain, of Leicester. *Educ.:* Privately. *War Work:* Executive Officer, Leicester Food Control Committee; Distribution Officer for Leicestershire, under the Ministry of Food. *Address:* 111, Dorset Road, Bexhill-on-Sea. (O3617)

BENNETT, Arthur Russell, M.B.E.

BENNETT, Catherine Elizabeth, O.B.E., W.R.N.S.

BENNETT, Capt. Douglas Raymond, O.B.E., R.E.

BENNETT, Edward, M.B.E., *b.* 16 Sept. 1857; *s.* of the late Rev. Henry Bennett, of The Vicarage, St. Nicholas-at-Wade, Thanet; *m.* Joanna Margaret, *d.* of the late Nicol Macphail of Edinburgh. *Educ.:* Dover College. Appointed to Savings Bank Department, General Post Office, 1875; Principal clerk, 1911; Vice-President of Association of Men of Kent and Kentish Men. *War Work:* Direction of correspondence relating to the Post Office, issues of War Loan, Exchequer Bonds and National War Bonds. *Address:* 14, Cyril Mansions, Battersea Park, S.W. 11. (M9360)

BENNETT, Edward George, O.B.E. (O11950)

BENNETT, Capt. Edward Morden, O.B.E., R.N.

BENNETT, Ernest Lampeer, M.B.E.,

BENNETT, Ernest Reginald, M.B.E., R.N.,

BENNETT, Frank Douglas, O.B.E.

BENNETT, Geoffrey Thomas, O.B.E., Sc.D., F.R.S., *b.* 30 June. 1868. Fellow of Emmanuel College, Cambridge. *War Work:* Ministry of Munitions and Admiralty Compass Department. *Address:* Emmanuel College, Cambridge. *Club:* Royal Societies'. (O140)

BENNETT, George Edward, M.B.E.

BENNETT, George Richard, M.B.E.

BENNETT, George Wilfred, M.B.E.

BENNETT, Capt. Gilbert Hedley, M.B.E.

BENNETT, Isaac Vaughan, M.B.E., *b.* 30 April, 1879; *s.* of the Rev. Henry G. Bennett, of Southport; *m.* Joan, *d.* of Wm. Lovell Bonnett, of Harpenden. *Educ.:* Silcoates School, Wakefield, and privately. Civil Servant in Naval Store Dept. of Admiralty. *War Work:* Principally as Naval Store Officer, H.M. Dockyard, Haulbowline, Queenstown, Ireland; also at Admiralty and at H.M. Dockyard, Portsmouth. *Address:* 4, Dockyard Terrace, Sheerness. (M3526)

BENNETT, Major James, O.B.E., R.A.S.C.

BENNETT, Major James William, O.B.E., V.D.

BENNETT, Joseph, M.B.E.

BENNETT, Josephine Katherine, M.B.E.

BENNETT, Leonora, Mrs., M.B.E.; *d.* of Theo. Thorne Ricketts, of Greystones, Paignton; *m.* Lawrence Henry, M.A., M.B. Oxon., who died 1918, *s.* of Henry Bennett, J.P., of Somersetshire. *Educ.:* Privately. Joined B.R.C. Society, 1910. *War Work:* Joined The Larches V.A. Hospital, Paignton, S. Devon, Aug. 1914; became V.A.D. Quartermaster and remained as such 3½ years at The Larches; joined Barrington Aux. Hosp. for Officers, Paignton, S. Devon, 1918, as V.A. Quartermaster, remained for six months, leaving in Oct. 1918; mentioned in despatches, Oct. 1918. (M7363)

BENNETT, Paymaster-Lieut.-Comm. Martin Gilbert, O.B.E., R.N.

BENNETT, Nina Bessie, M.B.E., *b.* 16 June, 1878; *d.* of Charles Hudson Bennett, of First House, Cooden, Bexhill, and 68, Coleman Street, W.C. *War Work:* Commandant, Cooden V.A.D. Hospital, from 25 Aug. 1914, to 18 Jan. 1919; attached Canadian C.A.M.C. at Cooden and Epsom Camps from Jan. to July, 1919. *Address:* First House, Cooden, Bexhill. *Club:* Lady Golfers. (M7364)

BENNETT, Major Norman Carmichael, O.B.E., M.C.

BENNETT, Peter Frederick Blaker, O.B.E., A.I.A.E., *b.* 16 April, 1880; *s.* of Frederick C. Bennett, of London; *m.* Agnes, *d.* of the late Joseph Palmer, of Birmingham. *Educ.:* King Edward's School, Five Ways, Birmingham. Joint Managing Director, Joseph Lucas, Ltd.; Managing Director, The Lucas Electrical Co., Ltd., and Thomson-Bennett Magnetos, Ltd.; Chairman, The British Ignition Apparatus Association; Chairman, The British Aero Magneto Manufacturers Association. *War Work:* The establishment of a Magneto manufacturing Industry in Gt. Britain, which was previously a German monopoly. *Address:* Ardencote, Four Oaks, Warwickshire. *Club:* Royal Automobile. (O9980)

BENNETT, Reginald Allbon, O.B.E., *b.* 7 Jan. 1878 ; *s.* of Rev. Augustus Frederick Bennett, of St. Leonards-on-Sea ; *m.* Olive Janet. *Educ.:* Privately and in France and Germany. Served under the British North Borneo Government in Borneo, and on resignation spent life in foreign travel in all parts of the world, including exploring and shooting trips in South America, Australia, and Northern Africa. *War Work:* Superintending Aliens Officer (under Home Office) at Liverpool, Sep. 1915, to Aug. 1916 ; in charge of same work for all S. Wales Ports from Aug. 1916, to May, 1919. *Clubs:* Authors' ; Primrose. (O1106)

BENNETT, Major Thomas Edwin, O.B.E., D.S.O., *b.* 1881 ; Major, R.A.S.C. ; Great War 1914–18 (despatches). (O2427)

BENNETT, Lieut. Thomas Parks, M.B.E.

BENNETT, Qr.-Mr. and Capt. Thomas William, O.B E.,

BENNETT, Lieut. Thomas Witchell, O.B.E., *b.* 10 April, 1879 ; *s.* of T. L. Bennett, of Old Sodbury. *Educ.:* Long Ashton School, Bristol. Farmer. *War Work:* Oct. 1914 to March, 1916, in charge of a Remount Depot ; March, 1916, to Feb. 1918, with the 6th Service Batt., King's Own Scottish Borderers in France ; March, 1918, with the 2/2 Scottish Horse in Scotland and Ireland until May, 1919. *Address:* Cross Hands Farm, Chipping Sodbury, Glos. (O4999)

BENNETT, Violet, Mrs., O.B.E. (O11951)

BENNETT, Lieut.-Col. William, D.S.O., O.B.E., M.B. *Educ.:* Edinburgh Univ. (M.B. and C.M. 1898) ; Lieut.-Col. ; three clasps) ; Somaliland, 1903–4 (medal with clasp) R.A.M.C. ; S. African War, 1900–1902 (Queen's medal) ; Great War, 1914–19 (despatches, Croix de Guerre). (C5000)

BENNETT, William Henry, M.B.E.

BENNETT, William Roger, M.B.E., *b.* 27 Jan. 1872 ; *s.* of William Bennett, of Leamington Spa ; *m.* Jeanie Morrison, *d.* of John Hunter, of Edinburgh. *Educ.:* Westminster Wesleyan Training College. *War Work:* Clerk at War Office (Movements Directorate) ; Railway and Shipping arrangements for troop movements, including the movement of New Army Divisions to overseas theatres of war ; United States Army Divisions through United Kingdom to France. *Address:* 36, Crouch Hall Road, Crouch End, London, N. 8. (M1407)

BENNETT, Capt. Ernest Pendarves LEIGH-, M.B.E., R.A.F.

BENNETT, Major John STERNDALE-, O.B.E.

BENNETT, John Wheeler WHEELER-, C.B.E.

BENNETTE, Capt. Bernard John Taylor, O.B.E.

BENNETTS, Paymaster-Comm. Sydney, O.B.E., R.N.

BENOY, William John, M.B.E., R.N.

BENSKIN, Gladys Sheffield, Mrs., C.B.E. ; *d.* of M P. Grace, of 40, Belgrave Square ; *m.* 1st, Major Raymond Hamilton Grace, 13th Hussars ; 2nd, Major Joseph Benskin, O.B.E., D.S.O., R.E., *s.* of Thomas Benskin, of Glenthorne, Harrow Weald. *War Work:* Nursing and Canteen Work ; Secretary to Mesopotamian Relief Fund. *Addresses:* Knole, Frant, Sussex ; and 2, Prince's Gate. (C507)

BENSKIN, Major Joseph, O.B E., R.E., *b.* April, 1883 ; *s.* of T. Benskin, of Watford ; *m.* Gladys Sheffield, *d.* of M. P. Grace, of 40, Belgrave Square. *Educ.:* Harrow. *War Work:* Commanded 89th Field Company, R.E., France and Belgium ; Brigade Major, 178th Infantry Brigade, 39th Division ; D.A.A.G in War Office ; A.A.G. in Eastern Command. *Address:* Knole, Frant, Sussex. *Club:* Army and Navy. (O6897)

BENSON, Bessie, Mrs., M.B.E.

BENSON, Edward Frederic, M.B.E.

BENSON, Col. Frank, C.B.E., *b.* 27 Sept. 1878 ; *s.* of Rev. W. J. Benson, of Farnborough ; *m.* Stephana Rose, *d.* of Rev. J. G. Pooley, late of Stonham Aspal, Suffolk. *Educ.:* Halleybury. General Manager, Canteen and Mess Co-operative Soc., Ltd., 1911. *War Work:* Hon. Gen. Manager, Expeditionary Force Canteens, 1914 ; *War Work:* Hon. Gen. Manager, Expeditionary Force Canteens, 1914 ; Member, Expeditionary Force Canteens Committee, 1915 ; Asst.-Managing Director, Navy and Army Canteen Board, 1917 ; Colonel, Deputy Controller, War Office, 1918 ; served in France and Italy. *Address:* Down Cottage, Wrotham, Kent. *Club:* Union, Trafalgar Sq. (C.438)

BENSON, Major and Qr.-Mr. George Augustus, O.B.E., D.C.M., *b.* 5 Dec. 1861 ; *s*l of Samuel Benson, of Sligo. *Educ.:* National School, Sligo. First Commission, R.A.M.C., June, 1900 ; retired Feb. 1911 ; promoted Major, July, 1917. *War Work:* Officer-in-charge, R.A.M.C. Section, 3rd Echelon, France, 1914–19. *Address:* Ballincar, Sligo. (O5002

BENSON, Lieut. Hugh, O.B.E., R.F.A., S.R.

BENSON, John, M.B.E., *b.* 1 Aug. 1864 ; *s.* of Thomas Benson, of Unthank, Kirkoswald, Cumberland. *Educ.:* Privately. Dairy Proprietor and Expert ; Member of Council of British Dairy Farmers' Association ; Examiner in Dairying to National Agricultural Examination Board ; for 7 years Chief Instructor at British Dairy Institute, and for 5 years Manager and Chief Instructor, Midland Agricultural and Dairy College. *War Work:* Engaged under Ministry of Agriculture on establishment of Co-operative Cheese Factories, and as temporary Inspector of Cheese-making Schools throughout England during latter part of the War. *Address:* Kettering, Dairy, Dalkeith Place, Kettering, Northants. *Club:* Farmers'. (M7367)

BENSON, Capt. John James Charles, M.B.E., R.A.O.C., *b.* 6 July, 1867 ; *s.* of John Edgecombe Benson, of Plymouth ; *m.* Elizabeth Eleanor, *d.* of John S. Toop, of Devon. *Educ.:*

Plymouth Public School ; Normal School, South Kensington ; Royal College of Science. Assistant Inspector of Ordnance Machinery, Royal Army Ordnance Corps. *War Work:* Repairs to armament of Navy in South African waters, from 1914 to date, and maintenance of Land Armament. *Address:* 5, Searle Street, Trafalgar Park, Cape Town, South Africa. (M6602)

BENSON, Philip de Gylpyn, O.B.E.

BENSON, Lieut.-Col. Ralph Hawtrey Rohde, O.B.E., R.A.

BENSON, Capt. Trevor Gaulter, M.B.E., Croce di Guerra, Italy, *b.* 5 March, 1893 ; *s.* of Alfred Benson, of Kingswood, Surrey. *Educ.:* Eton. Director, J. W. Benson, Ltd., 62 & 64, Ludgate Hill, and 25, Old Bond Street, W. *War Work:* Served in France and Italy with R.A.S.C., M.T. ; proceeded overseas, March, 1915, and remained there until the end of the War. *Address:* Kingswood Court, Tadworth, Surrey. (M2307)

BENSON, William John, C.B.E., F.R.G.S. ; *s.* of John Benson, of Leamington ; *m.* Emma, *d.* of the late Charles, Richardson, of Springfield, Magheralin, Ireland. *Educ.:* Privately. Banking and Mining appointments in South Africa and London. *War Work:* Rendered voluntary service to Ministry of Munitions, Whitehall ; Director of Russian Munition Supplies, also a Director of other Sections and acted as Deputy Director-General of "B"Section, Ministry of Munitions ; received the Order (with Star) of St. Stanislas for special services rendered to the Russian Government in the earlier stages of the war. Created O.B.E. 1917 ; C.B.E. 1918. *Address:* 10 Leonard Place, Kensington, London, W. 8. *Club:* Conservative, St. James' Street (C930)

BENSON, Major William John Phillip, O.B.E.

BENT, Col. Arthur Milton, C.M.G., C.B.E., *b.* 17 Nov. 1870 ; *s.* of the late George Bent, Lieut.-Col. King's Own Borderers ; *m.* Lucie St. George, *d.* of — Ormsby, of Blackrock, Dublin. *Educ.:* Wellington and Sandhurst. Served for 29 years in the Royal Munster Fusiliers, attaining rank of Brevet-Colonel. *War Work:* Commanded 2nd Batt. Royal Munster Fusiliers in France, 1914 ; severely wounded ; mentioned in despatches twice ; C.M.G., C.B.E. and Brevet of Colonel. *Club:* Army and Navy. (C1887)

BENTALL, William Charles, O.B.E., F.R.C.S.E., *b.* 13 May, 1875 ; *s.* of Edw. Ch. Bentall, of Lanyon, Ryde, I. of W. ; *m.* Ethel Mary, *d.* of Barlow Pearton, of Reading. *Educ.:* Vickery's Naval Academy, Portsmouth and Edinburgh. Surgeon, Southport Hydropathic Hospital ; late Lecturer Anatomy and Surgery, Neyoor Medical School, S. India. *War Work:* Medical Officer in charge, Southport, St. John Hospital (500 beds) ; Medical Officer in charge, Birkdale Officers' Hospital ; Surgeon, Southport Cottage Hospital. *Address:* Grove House. Southport ; Dwerry House, Mawdesly, Ormskirk. (O4351)

BENTHALL, Major John Lawrence, C.B.E. ; *m.* 1919, Henrietta, *d.* of the late R. Watson Hall, of Lowton St. Mary's, Lancashire. Major, Territorial Force Reserve (T.D.), and a Director of Vickers, Ltd. *Address:* 10, Queen's Gate Gardens, S.W. (C931)

BENTINCK, Lieut.-Col. Baron Walter Guy, C.M.G., C.B.E., D.S.O., late Rifle Brigade, *b.* 1864 ; *s.* of the late Walter Theodore Edward, Baron Bentinck (*see* BURKE'S *Peerage*) ; *m.* Anne Elizabeth, *d.* of the late Col. William Burnett Ramsay, Rifle Brigade, of Banchory Lodge. *Educ.:* Marlborough College and Royal Military College, Sandhurst. Served in Rifle Brigade from 1885–1905 ; S. African War, 1899–1902 ; wounded, despatches, D.S.O., Queen's and King's Medals and 8 clasps ; Resident Magistrate, Transvaal ; Acting Imperial Secretary to H.E. The High Commissioner and Governor, South Africa. *War Work:* G.H.Q., 3rd Echelon, B.E.F. ; Intelligence Directorate, War Office ; and in charge of No. 2, Infantry Record Office, Preston. *Address:* House of Scolty, By Banchory, Kincardineshire, N.B. *Club:* Travellers'. (C2079)

BENTLEY, Capt. R., M.B.E.

BENTLEY, Capt. Walter Owen, M.B.E., R.A.F.

BENTLEY, Lieut.-Col. William Joseph, O.B.E.

BENTLIF, Surgeon Lieut.-Col. Philip Barnett, M.B.E., R.M.I.J., *b.* 1859 ; *s.* of Philip Bentlif, of Salisbury ; *m.* Agnes Houston, *d.* of George Thomson, of Dumfries. *Educ.:* Grammar School, Salisbury and Middlesex Hospital, London. Surgeon, Jersey General Hospital ; Consulting Physician, Jersey Infirmary and Dispensary ; President, St. John's Ambulance Association (Jersey Centre) ; Fellow Royal Society of Medicine. *War Work:* O.C. Medical Co., R.M.I.J. ; Medical Officer, Military Hospital, Jersey, and in charge of troops. *Clubs:* Victoria (Jersey) ; Royal Societies'. (M5074)

BENTLY, Capt. Harold Rothwell, O.B.E., *b.* 22 Dec. 1886 ; *s.* of Rev. H. R. Bentley ; *m.* Lota Mary, *d.* of Dr. H. F. Bailey. *Educ.:* Rugby and R.M.C., Sandhurst. Joined 1st Batt. Cheshire Regt., 1906 ; Adjutant, 4th Cheshire Regt., 1912–14. *War Work:* Brigade Major, 1915–16 ; employed under Air Ministry, 1918–19 ; Adjutant, 2nd Cheshire Regt., May, 1919, to present time. *Club:* Junior United Service. (O8049)

BENTTLER, Lieut.-Col. Edward Gerald Oakley, O.B.E., R.A.F.

BENTWICH, Major Norman de Mattos, O.B.E., M.C.

BENTWICK, Lieut.-Col. Walter Guy, C.B.E.

BENYON, Edith Marion, M.B.E., *b.* 1880 ; *d.* of J. M. Benyon, of Englefield House, near Reading (*see* BURKE'S *Landed Gentry*). *Educ.:* Privately. *War Work:* Assistant Commandant, Englefield Auxiliary Hospital. *Address:* Englefield House, near Reading. (M7368)

BENZIE, Lieut.-Col. Robert Marr, O.B.E.. T.D., *b.* 13 Dec. 1868 ; *s.* of Robert Marr Benzie, of Langside, Glasgow ; *m.* Annie Young, *d.* of Hugh Lamberton, of Surbiton, Pollokshields. *Educ.:* High School and Glasgow University. Chartered Accountant ; R.W.M. of Lodge " Pollok" ; Ex-Visitor of Incorporation of Maltmen and other public offices in the City of Glasgow. *War Work :* Went to France as 2nd in Command of 5th Scottish Rifles on 5 Nov. 1914 ; awarded 1914 Star and Bar ; mentioned in despatches by Lord French, 25 June, 1915 ; promoted Lieut.-Col. 4 Oct. 1915, and placed in command of 2nd Batt. 5th Scottish Rifles ; served with this Batt. in counties Cork, Clare, and Kerry from 4 Jan. 1917, to 11 April, 1918, when appointed Military Member of Travelling Medical Board, Irish Command ; mentioned for valuable services by Lord French, 28 May, 1917 ; awarded O.B.E. (Mil.) 28 May, 1919. *Addresses :* 121, St. Vincent Street, Glasgow ; Chlauchlands, Pollokshields. *Clubs :* Various (Glasgow).

(O6899)

BEOR, Lieut.-Col. Bertram Richard White, O.B.E., R.A.F. Officer of the Order of the Crown of Belgium.

BERESFORD. Charles Frederick Delaval, M.B.E., *b.* 30 Dec. 1879 ; *s.* of Lieut.-Col. G W. Beresford, of Harlington ; *m.* Violet Eva, *d.* of Thomas Beament, of Ottawa. *Educ.:* Abroad. British Vice-Consul at Cherbourg. *Address :* British Vice-Consulate. Cherbourg.

(M1409)

BERESFORD, Dorothy, Mrs., M.B.E.   (M10244e)

BERESFORD, Major Gerald Waddington, O.B.E., R.A.M.C.

BERESFORD, Lieut. Henry Edward, M.B.E., R.E.

BERESFORD, Lieut. John Baldwin, M.B.E.,

BERESFORD, Major John de la Poer, O.B.E.

BERESFORD, Denis Robert PACK-, O.B.E., J.P., D.L., B.A., M.R.I.A., *b.* 23 March, 1864 ; *s.* of Denis W. Pack-Beresford, of Fenagh, Co. Carlow ; *m.* Alice (*d.* 2 June, 1918), *d.* of James A. Lyle, of Glandore, Kilrea. *Educ.:* Rugby ; Christ Church, Oxford. *War Work :* Hon. Sec. and County Director, Co. Dublin British Red Cross Society ; Member of Joint War Committee for Leinster, Munster and Connaught ; Hon. Sec. and Organiser of the National Egg Collection for all Ireland. *Addresses :* Fenagh House, Bagnalstown, Co. Carlow ; and The Tansey, Baily, Co. Dublin. *Clubs :* Kildare St., Dublin ; Royal Irish Auto.

(O2)

BERISFORD, Harold, O.B.E.

BERISFORD, Margaret, Mrs., M.B.E.. *b.* 11 Oct. 1868 ; *d.* of Rev. Joseph Rippon, of Congleton ; *m.* Harry Berisford, J.P., *s.* of Charles Berisford, J.P., of Congleton. *Educ.:* Trinity Hall, Southport. *War Work :* Secretary of War Pensions Sub-Committee ; Quartermaster of Red Cross Detachment.

(M7369)

BERKELEY, Major and Brevet Lieut.-Col. Christopher Robert, C.M.G., D.S.O., O.B.E., *b.* 18 Jan. 1877 ; *s.* of Major H. W. Berkeley, of Fieldgate House, Kenilworth, 2nd son of Robert Berkeley, of Spetchley Park, Worcester ; *m.* Nest, *d.* of Col. J. A. Rradney, C.B., of Talycoed Court, Monmouth. *Educ.:* Oratory School, Edgbaston, and R.M. College, Sandhurst. Served in the South African War, 1899–1902 ; Queen's medal, six clasps, King's medal, two clasps ; D.S.O., twice mentioned in despatches (wounded). *War Work :* European war, 1914–18 ; with 2nd Batt. the Welsh Regt., Aug. 1914, to Feb. 1915 ; Brigade Major, 3rd Infantry Brigade, 1st Division, Feb. 1915, to April, 1916 ; D.A.A. and Q.M.G., 15th Division, April, 1915, to Aug. 1916 ; A.A. and Q.M.G., Temp. Lieut.-Col., Aug. 1916, to Oct. 1918, 15th Division ; A.Q.M.G., G.H.Q., France, Oct. 1918, to Oct. 1919 ; Brevet Lieut.-Col., 1 Jan 1916 ; C.M.G., O.B.E., six times mentioned in despatches (wounded). *Address :* Fieldgate House, Kenilworth. *Club :* Army and Navy.

(O2428)

BERKELEY, Eva Mary FitzHarding Milman Foley, Lady, M.B.E., *b.* 4 March, 1875 ; *d.* of Maj.-Gen. Milman, R.A. ; *m.* Lieut.-Col. Frank Wigram Foley, C.B.E., D.S.O., who commanded a battalion Princess Charlotte of Wales' (Royal Berkshire Regt.). *War Work :* Struan House Aux. Hospital, Reading ; Commandant, Berks. 52 V.A.D., 1914–17 ; Staff Nurse, Branksmere Aux. Hospital, Southsea, 1917.

(M7370)

BERKELEY, John Henry Astley, O.B.E.

BERKELEY, Major Rupert Edric Gifford, O.B.E., I.A.

BERKLEY, Major Ernest James Gibson, M.B.E., F.R.C.S. (Eng.), R.A.M.C. (T.) (retired) ; *s.* of Thomas Berkley, of Alnwick, Northumberland ; *m.* Amelia Julia, *d.* of Capt. Wallace Meyer, 38 M.N.L.I., India. *Educ.:* City of London School ; Charing Cross Hospital. Surgeon. *War Work :* South African Campaign, 1900–1, Capt. R.A.M.C. (Volunteer) ; Hon. Com., and sometime second-in-command, 2nd Batt. S. L. Rifle Volunteers ; Officer-in-charge Southwark Ambulance Emergency Corps ; Officer-in-charge Southwark V.A.D. Hospital ; M.O.-in-charge 64 Depot, T.F. ; Divisional Inspector B.R.C.S. ; M.O. for 1294 B.R.C.S. ; Capt. Southwark Rifle Club ; Lecturer and Examiner, B.R.C.S. *Address :* 70, Camberwell Road. S.E. 5.

(M7371)

BERLANDINA, Major Herbert Hillel, O.B.E., M.C., R.E.

BERNACCHI, Lieut. Louis Charles, O.B.E., R.N.V.R.

BERNARD, Albert Victor, M.B.E., M.D.

BERNARD, Alice Eleanor, M.B.E., M.A. (Dublin).

BERNARD, Col. Sir Edgar Edwin, K.B.E., C.M.G., *b.* 5 Nov. 1866 ; *e.s.* of Col. Count Bernard ; *m.* Beatrice Mary, *d.* of Edward Carrington Wright, J.P. *Educ.:* R.M.C., Sandhurst. Financial Secretary to Government of Soudan ; joined Devon Regt., 1887 ; Capt. Army Service Corps, 1892 ; Brevet Major, 1898 ; Major, 1900 ; Local Lieut.-Col., 1901 ; Lieut.-Col. and Local Col. 1907 ; Brevet Col., 1913 ; served in India, 1887–90 ; Ashanti Expedition, 1895–96 (Star) ; Nile Expedition, 1898, as D.A.A.G. on Staff of General Officer Commanding-in-Chief ; present at battle of Khartoum (despatches, Brevet Major, Egyptian Medal with clasp, medal) ; and Coronations, 1902 and 1911 ; has been employed with Egyptian Army since 1899 ; is a Pasha of Egypt, and has Medjidieh, 2nd Class, and Osmanieh, 3rd Class. *Club :* United Service.

(K250)

BERNARD, Lieut.-Col. John, O.B.E. R.A.S.C.

BERNARD, Lieut. Oliver Percy, O.B.E., M.C., R.E.

BERNARD, Lieut.-Col. William Kingsmill, C.B.E., R.A.S.C.

BERNAU, Lieut.-Col. Henry Ferdinand, O.B.E., M.C.

BERNAYS, Lieut. Geoffrey Charles Arrowsmith, M.B.E., R.E.

BERNAYS, Rev. Stewart Frederick Lewis, O.B.E., M.A., *b.* 3 Oct. 1866 ; *s.* of the Rev. Leopold John Bernay, of Stanmore Rectory ; *m.* Lilian Jane, *d.* of The Rev. John Stephenson, of Boston, Lincs. *Educ.:* Durham and Trinity, Oxford. *War Work :* Chaplain to the Forces. *Address :* The Rectory, Stanmore. *Club :* Flyfishers'.

(O6904)

BERNE, Capt. James Leo, O.B.E., *b.* 11 April, 1885 ; *s.* of late Lieut.-Col. J. C. Berne, of Southsea. *Educ.:* Dulwich College. Served with Sierra Leone Batt. West African Frontier Force, 1907–12 ; Asst.-Dist. Commissioner British Somaliland, 1912 ; District Commissioner, 1914 ; Senior Asst.-Sec. to Government, Tanganyka Territory, 1920 ; served with Franco-Liberian Boundary Commission, 1908 (thanks French Govt.) ; served with Anglo-French Boundary Commission, 1911 ; British Mission to Abyssinia, 1917 ; received 3rd Class Star of Ethiopia. *War Work :* Admiralty War Staff Intelligence Division, 1916 ; Remount Purchase Officer, Egyptian Expeditionary Force, 1917–17 ; Recruiting Officer, King's African Rifles, 1917–18. *Address :* Dar-es-Salaam, Tanganyka Territory, East Africa. *Club :* Junior Army and Navy, S.W.

(O983)

BERNERS, Major John Anstruther, O.B.E.

BERRIDGE, Major Harold, O.B.E.

BERRIDGE, Sir Thomas Henry Devereux, K.B.E., Knt. Bach. 1912, *b.* 6 July, 1857 ; *s.* of Rev. W. Berridge, formerly headmaster of Upholland Grammar School, Lancs., and Vicar of Lowton St. Mary's, Lancs. ; *m.* Agnes (d. 1909), *d.* of Frederick Campion, of Frenches, Redhill. *Educ.:* Upholland Grammar School and privately. Articled to Maskell Peace of Wigan, Solicitor to Mining Assoc. of Great Britain ; admitted solicitor, 1878, member of the firm of Burn and Berridge, Solicitors to the Government of Newfoundland ; M.P. (L.), Warwick and Leamington, 1906–10 ; contested same division, 1903 and 1910. *War Work :* Chairman, Executive Committee Royal Air Force Voluntary Hospitals and other work in connection with various War Departments. *Addresses :* 6, Austin Friars, E.C. ; 11 & 12, Southampton Street, Bloomsbury, W.C. ; 20, Elm Park Gardens, S.W. ; Greenwood, Alkham, near Dover. *Clubs :* Reform ; Royal Automobile ; National Liberal ; Eighty.

(K349)

BERRIMAN, Algernon Edward, O.B.E., M.I.Mech.E., M.I.A.E., F.R.Ae.S., *b.* 1882. Chief Engineer, Daimler Co. *Address :* Beauchamp House, Kenilworth. *Clubs :* R.A.C. ; R.Ae.C.

(O141)

BERROW, Major John, O.B.E., 19th (Q.A.O.R.) Hussars, *b.* 29 April, 1867. *Address :* Garrison Adjutant, Gibraltar.

(O6905)

BERROW, William Lewis, O.B.E., I.S.O., *b.* 1862 ; *s.* of the late John Burrow, of Newport, Salop, and Worcester. *Educ.:* Newport (Salop) Grammar School. Foreign Office since 1881. *Address :* 34, Montrell Road, Streatham Hill, S.W. 2. *Club :* North Surrey Golf.

(O142)

BERRY, Arthur, O.B.E., M.A., *b.* 28 Dec. 1862 ; *s.* of Edward Berry, of London ; *m.* Harriet Mary, *d.* of W. H. F. Johnson, J.P., of Cambridge. *Educ.:* Whitgift School, Croydon ; University Coll. School, London ; University Coll., London ; King's Coll., Cambridge. Fellow and Assistant Tutor of King's Coll., Cambridge ; University Lecturer in Mathematics. *War Work :* Attached to G.H.Q., Mediterranean Expeditionary Force, as 2nd Lieut., 1915–16 ; Consulting Mathematician to Air Dept., Admiralty, and to Technical Department, Air Ministry, 1916–18. *Addresses :* Meadowside, Grantchester Meadows, Cambridge ; King's College, Cambridge.

(O9982)

BERRY, Major Harry Poole, O.B.E., T.D., M.B., R.A.M.C. (T.F.), *b.* 8 May, 1859 ; *s.* of Henry Thomas Berry, of Islington, London ; *m.* Rosina Jessie, *d.* of Alexander Currie, of Lloyds and Blackheath. *Educ.:* Islington Proprietary School and Guy's Hospital. Medical Officer of Health, Borough of Grantham ; School Medical Officer, Borough of Grantham ; Senior Medical Officer, Grantham Hospital. *War Work :* Reg. Med. Officer, 1.4 Batt. Line Regt. ; M.O. in charge Red Cross Hospital, Grantham ; Major and O.C. Linc. R.A.M.C. *Address :* The Priory, Grantham.

(O9983)

BERRY, John Joseph, M.B.E., J.P., *b.* 26 March, 1885; *s.* of John Berry, of Newcastle-upon-Tyne ; *m.* Margaret, *d.* of James Burns, of Newcastle-on-Tyne. *Educ.:* St. Joseph's Home, Pailton, near Rugby and St. Dominic's Church School, Newcastle-on-Tyne. *War Work :* Hon. Sec. of the Elswick and Scotswood Workers War Relief Fund ; Soldiers' Comforts Fund and Allies Hospital Fund ; raised over £176,000 by means of contributions from the workers at Messrs. Sir W. G. Armstrong Whitworth & Co.'s Works at Elswick and Scotswood, Newcastle-on-Tyne ; Member of over 30 War Committees, and Chairman of about 10 War Committees. *Address :* 62, Balmoral Terrace, Heaton, Newcastle-on-Tyne. (M7372)

BERRY, Mary Ann, M.B.E., Q.M.A.A.C.

BERRY, Rev. Seymour Brendon Sterling, O.B.E., M.A. Hon. C.F., *b.* 13 July, 1885 ; *s.* of Right Rev. Lord Bishop of Killaloe, Ireland ; *m.* Marguerite, *d.* of Fred Spafford, of Lancs. *Educ. :* Oswestry Grammar School and Trinity College, Dublin. *War Work :* Chaplain to the Forces. *Address :* c o Clarisford, Killaloe, Co. Clare, Ireland. (O8050)

BERRY, Sir Walter Wheeler, K.B.E., J.P., Development Commissioner ; Representative of Board of Agriculture on the Hop Control Committee, and various other committees ; Member of Agricultural Advisory Council. *Address :* Gushmere Court, Selling, Faversham ; *Club :* National Liberal. (K350)

BERRY, William, O.B.E., B.A., LL.B. (Cantab.), *b.* 9 May, 1864 ; *s.* of John Berry, of Tayfield, Fifeshire (d. Dec. 1877) (*see* BURKE'S *Landed Gentry*) ; *m.* 1906, Wilhelmina (d. 1907), *d.* of the late Allan Barns Graham, of Craigallian, Co.Stirling and Limekilns, Co. Lanark (*see* BURKE'S *Landed Gentry*). *Educ. :* Eton and Trin. Coll., Cambridge. Advocate ; J.P., Fifeshire. *War Work :* Chairman, Fifeshire War Pensions Local Committee ; Chairman, Joint (Disablement) Committee for Central Scotland ; Member of Regional Advisory Council and of Scottish Joint Instituional Committee, Ministry of Pensions ; Member of Scottish General Training Committee, Ministry of Labour ; Chairman, Emergency Committee for Tay District of Fifeshire, and Chief Special Constable ; Member of Military Tribunal, Cupar and St Andrews Districts of Fifeshire, and for the Burghs of Newport and Auchtermuchty. *Club :* New (Edinburgh). (O9984)

BERRY, Lieut. William James, M.B.E., A.R.C.

BERRY, Major Winslow Seymour Sterling, O.B.E., M.B., R.A.M.C., *b.* 8 June, 1880 ; *s.* of T. Sterling Berry, Lord Bishop of Killaloe ; *m.* Louisa Mary Seymour, *d.* of Rev. Canon H. C. Murphy, of Tuam. *Educ. :* Corrig School, Kingstown, and University of Dublin (T.C.D.). Medical Inspector, Local Government Board, Ireland. *War Work :* M.O. in charge, 9th R. Ir. Fus. ; D.A.D.M.S., 10th British Army Corps, B.E.F., and Army of the Rhine. *Address :* Beach House, Bantry. *Club :* Cork (Bantry). (O5005)

BERRYMAN, Lieut.-Col. Henry Arthur, O.B.E., R.A.M.C. (ret.), *b.* 3 Dec. 1865 ; *s.* of J. P. Berryman, of St. Austell, Cornwall ; *m.* Adeline Maude Marjorie, *d.* of Charles Paget. *Educ. :* Newton College. *War Work :* D.A.D.M.S., A.D.M.S., Headquarters, Western Command, Chester. *Club :* Junior United Service. (O6906)

BERRYMAN, Capt. Mark, M.B.E.

BERSEY, Stanley Howard, O.B.E., F.C.A., *b.* 18 July, 1877 ; *s.* of Thomas Bersey, of London. *Educ. :* London. Chartered Accountant ; partner in Sissons, Bersey, Gain, Vincent & Co. *War Work :* Joined Ministry of Munitions, Explosives Finance Department in 1915 ; appointed Section Director in 1917, and Assistant Controller, and subsequently, in 1918, Controller of Explosives Finance and Contracts Department. *Address :* 53, New Broad Street, E.C. *Club :* City Carlton. (O9985)

BERTENSHAW, Benjamin James, M.B.E.

BERTHON, Lieut.-Col. Charles Peter, O.B.E.

BERTHOUD, Edward Henry, O.B.E.

BERTRAM, Edith, Lady, C.B.E., *d.* of Rees Jones, J.P. of Porthkerry, Glamorganshire ; *m.* Sir Anton Bertram, Knt. Bach., Chief Justice of Ceylon, *s.* of Rev. R. A. Bertram. *Educ. :* Privately. Member of Cardiff Board of Guardians for six years ; first lady appointed by the Governor to serve as Poor Law Relief Commissioner in the West Indies. *War Work :* Hon. Sec. of Queen Mary's Needlework Guild from 1915, of Ceylon Branch ; President of Y.W.C.A. in Ceylon, etc., etc. *Addresses:* Porthkerry, Colombo ; Barry Cottage, N. Eliya. (C2015)

BERTRAM, Francis George Lawder, C.B.E., *b.* 12 Aug. 1875 ; only *s.* of the late Francis Godfray Bertram, late of Beaulieu, St. Heliers, Jersey ; *m.* Mabel Catherine, *d.* of W. Peck Smith, of Tilne, Notts. *Educ. :* St. Paul's School (Scholar) and Pembroke College, Oxford (Scholar), M.A. H.M. Inspector of Schools (both of Elementary and Secondary), Board of Education, 1901–15. *War Work :* Ministry of Munitions (Contracts Dept., Secretary Reconstruction Dept., Secretary of various Munitions Council Committees, Secretaria Officer for Ordnance), 1915–19 ; War Office (Personal Assistant to Surveyor-General of Supply), Jan. to June, 1919 ; Air Ministry Principal Civil Aviation Dept., and Secretary to Advisory Committee on Civil Aviation June. 1919). O.B.E. 1918, C.B.E. 1920. *Addresses :* St. Keyne, Shrublands Road, Berkhamsted, and Air Ministry, Kingsway. (C2447)

BERTRAM, Robert, M.B.E.

BERWICK, William Edwin, M.B.E., R.A.F.

BESANT, Frederick William, M.B.E.

BESANT, Lieut.-Comm. Henry Francis, O.B.E., R.N.

BESANT, Capt. Reginald Edgar, O.B.E.

BEST, Alfred, O.B.E., D.C.M., Capt. T. Major, Lancs. Fus. (O6908)

BEST, Charles William, M.B.E.

BEST, Eleanor, M.B.E., W.R.N.S.

BEST, Hon. James William, O.B.E., *b.* 3 May, 1882 ; *s.* of George, 5th Baron Wynford, of Wynford Eagle, Dorset ;

m. Florence Mary Bernarda, *d.* of Sir Elliott Lees, 1st Bart., D.S.O. (d. 1908). *Educ. :* Wellington College and Royal Indian Engineering College, Coopers Hill. India Forest Service. *War Work :* Supply of fodder, grass, forest products, and timber. *Address :* Chikalda, Berar, India. *Club :* Junior Carlton. (O4013)

BEST, Capt. Sigismund Payne, O.B.E.

BEST, Thomas Alexander Vans, C.M.G., C.B.E., *b.* 1870 ; *s.* of the late Alexander Vans Best, F.R.C.P., F.R.C.S. ; *m.* 1904, Lady Helena Leopoldine, *d.* of the late Rear-Adm. the Hon. Victor Alexander Montagu, C.B. (*see* BURKE'S *Peerage*, Sandwich, E.). *Educ. :* Cheltenham, and Magdalen Coll. Oxford. Acting Vice-Consul, Chinde 1902 ; Acting Dep. Commr., Nyasaland, 1903 ; Colonial Sec., Falkland Islands, 1909 ; Colonial Sec., Leeward Islands, 1913 ; Colonial Sec., Trinidad and Tobago, 1919 ; administered Govt., Falkland Islands, 1919–10, and Leeward Islands 1914, 1915, and 1916, *Addresses :* Port of Spain, Trinidad ; 4, Cadogan Mansions, Sloane Square, S.W. *Club :* St. James's. (C385)

BESTE, Comm. Henry Aloysius Bruno DIGBY-, O.B.E. R.I.M.

BESTWICK, William, M.B.E.

BESZANT, Capt. George William, M.B.E., *b.* 1868 ; *s.* of John Beszant, of Axbridge, Somerset ; *m.* Elina Gertruαe, *d.* of George Deacon, of Kingsdown, Bristol. *Educ. :* Axbridge, Somersetshire. Served in the Royal Field Artillery from May, 1888, until May, 1913 ; commissioned Sept. 1914 ; promoted Captain, July, 1916 ; demobilised, Nov. 1919. *War Work :* Posted 12th Northumberland Fusiliers as Quartermaster, Sept. 1914 ; took part in the Battle of Loos, Sept. 1915 ; invalided from France and posted Anti-Aircraft Reserve Brigade, where he formed and commanded a battery until it was finally dissolved. *Address :* 80, Barmouth Road, Wandsworth, S.W. 18. (M5077)

BETHELL, Major Leonard Arthur, O.B.E., 2/10 Gurkha Rifles. I.A. (O11724)

BETHELL, Phyllis Mary Hermione, O.B.E., *b.* 26 April, 1889 ; *d.* of William Bethell and the late Hon. Mrs. Bethell, of Rise Park, Hull. *War Work :* Asst. County Director ; Secretary for 3 Holderness Red Cross Divisions ; also Secretary and Organiser of the Hull and Holderness Gifts of vegetables and fruit for the sailors, run under the Vegetable Produce Committee, London. *Address :* Rise Park, Hull, East Yorkshire. (O9986)

BETHELL, Thyra Talvase, Mrs., M.B.E.

BETHILL, William Edmund, M.B.E.

BETHUNE, Capt. Henry Leonard, C.B.E., R.N. ; *s.* of the late Adm. Charles Ramsay Drinkwater Bethune, C.B., R.N. Great War, 1914–19 (despatches). (C2276)

BETTERIDGE, Lieut. George William, M.B.E., I.A.R.O.

BETTERIDGE, Capt. Harold Leonard, M.B.E., R.A.F.

BETTERTON, Henry Bucknall, C.B.E., M.P., *b.* 1872 ; *s.* of Henry Inman Betterton, J.P., of Woodville, Leicestershire ; *m.* Violet, *d.* of J. S. Gilliat, D.L., M.P., of Chorleywood Cedars. *Educ. :* Rugby and Christ Church, Oxford. M.P. (Rushcliffe, Notts.). *War Work :* Member of Advisory Board, War Trade Intelligence Department ; Liaison Officer with War Office, Admiralty and Ministry of Munitions. *Addresses :* 166, Ashley Gardens, S.W. ; Fedsden, Roydon, Ware. *Clubs :* Carlton ; Wellington ; Notts County. (C2448)

BETTINGTON, Major Egerton Mitford, O.B.E.

BETTINGTON, Maud, Mrs., M.B.E.

BETTS, Comm. Ernest Edward Alexander, C.B.E., R.N.

BETTS, Lieut.-Col. Hyla Hume, C.B.E., R.E.

BETTS, Major Lionel Oxborrow, O.B.E.

BETTY, Lieut.-Col. Hubert Kemmis, D.S.O., O.B.E., *b.* 1872 ; *s.* of the late Col. Joshua Frederic Kemmis Betty, R.A. (*see* BURKE'S *Peerage*, Medlycott, Bt.) ; *m.* 1907, Ethel Antoinette Watts. *Educ. :* Wellington Coll. Great War, 1914–18, as Lieut.-Col. Canadian Forces (despatches). (O6015)

BETTY, Lieut.-Col. William Redmond Prendergast Kemmis, O.B.E.

BEVAN, Edward Morris, M.B.E., *b.* 30 June, 1882 ; *s.* of Benjamin Bevan, of Burry Port ; *m.* Ethel Mary, *d.* of Walter Turner, of Chard. *Educ. :* Borough Road College and London University. Headmaster Twyn School, Caerphilly. *War Work :* Hon. Sec. Caerphilly Local Central Committee for War Savings, 1916–19, and chairman for 1920 ; Member of Local War Pensions and Food Control Committee. *Address :* Brynden, Corbett Crescent, Caerphilly. (M7376)

BEVAN, Edwyn Robert, O.B.E., M.A., *b.* 15 Feb. 1870 ; *s.* of Robert Cooper Lee Bevan, of Trent Park, New Barnet, Herts (*see* BURKE'S *Landed Gentry*) ; *m.* Mary, *d.* of the 3rd Baron Radstock, of Castle Town, Queens Co., Ireland. *Educ. :* Monkton Combe School, Bath and New College, Oxford. Hon. Fellow of New College, Oxford ; author of " The House of Selencus," " The Land of Two Rivers," " German Social Democracy during the War," etc. *War Work :* Department of Information, May, 1915, to April, 1918 ; Foreign Office (Political Intelligence Department), April, 1918, to April, 1919. *Address :* 5, York Terrace, N.W. 1. *Clubs :* Athenæum ; Cavendish. (O9987)

BEVAN, Ernest Alltree, O.B.E.

BEVAN, F. H., M.B.E.

BEVAN, Comm. George Hope, O.B.E., R.N.,

BEVAN, 2nd Lieut. Gilbert John Beckford, M.B.E., I.A.

BEVAN, Jean, Mrs., O.B.E., *b.* 1876 ; *d.* of the late Sir Algernon Coote, Bart., H.M.L., of Ballyfin, Queen's Co., Ireland (*see* BURKE'S *Peerage*) ; *m.* Ivor, *s.* of F. A. Bevan, late of

1, Tilney Street, Mayfair, W, and of 54, Lombard Street, E.C. *Educ.:* Privately and in Brussels. Member of the Special Grants Committee, Ministry of Pensions, 1919 ; Member of the London War Pensions Committee, 1920; Member of the United Services Fund, London District Childrens' Home Committee, 1920. *War Work :* Hon. Sec. of the North Hackney Division, Soldiers' and Sailors' Families Association, 4 Aug. 1914, to present day ; Hon. Sec. and member of the Stoke Newington War Pensions Sub-Committee, 1 July, 1916, to present day ; Hon. Sec. North Hackney Sub-Office, and Member of the Hackney War Pensions Sub-Committee. *Address :* 65, Eccleston Square, S.W. 1. *Club :* Forum.   (O3619)

BEVAN, Hon. Dame Maud Elizabeth. Mrs., D.B.E., J.P., *b.* 1856 ; *d.* of Henry, 1st Viscount Hampden and 23rd Baron Dacre, G.C.B., of Glynde Place, Lewes (*see* BURKE'S *Peerage*) ; *m.* David Augustus, *s.* of Richard Lee Bevan, of Brixworth Hall, Northampton. *Educ.:* Privately. *War Work :* President Herts County Branch, B.R.C.S. ; Commandant of Herts V.A.D. 18, of Royston V.A.D. Hospital (70 beds). *Address :* Burloes, Royston, Herts. *Club :* Sesame.   (D26)

BEVAN, Marmaduke, M.B.E., S.S.-M., R.A.S.C.   (M4420)

BEVERIDGE, Capt. Edmund Walter St. Clair, M.B.E. (M7030*d*)

BEVERIDGE, Rev. John, M.B.E., M.A., B.D.,E.B. ; S.B.A., F.B.E.A., *b.* 29 June, 1857 ; *s.* of Robert Morris Beveridge, of Ayr ; *m.* Alice Alexandra Henderson, *d.* of James Henderson, of Sydney, N.S.W. *Educ.:* Ayr Academy and Glasgow University. Minister of the United Presbyterian Church, Stow, Midlothian, 1882–93 ; English Presbyterian Church, Wolverhampton, 1893–1900 ; United Free Church, Dundee, 1900–13 ; Fossoway, 1913–19 ; Gartmore, Perthshire, 1919. *War Work :* Hon. Commissioner of the Scottish War Savings Committee. *Address :* Manse, Gartmore, Perthshire. (M7377)

BEVERIDGE, Capt. Thomas Blackwood, O.B.E., *b.* June, 1896 ; *s.* of Col. Rev. W. W. Beveridge, T.D., of Port Glasgow. *Educ.:* The Academy, Greenock. *War Work :* Served in the Great War in Gallipoli, Egypt, Palestine ; mentioned in despatches, Jan. 1919. *Address :* Hillside, Port Glasgow, Scotland.   (O2866)

BEVERIDGE, Col. Wilfred William Ogilvy, C.B., C.B.E., D.S.O., *b.* 1864 ; *s.* of James Spowart Beveridge ; *m.* 1889, Mary, *d.* of George Spencer-Walker. Entered R.A.M.C. 1890 ; Col. Army Med. Ser. 1917 ; S. Africa, 1902 (despatches) ; Great War, 1914–19, on Staff (despatches, Russian Order of St. Stanislaus, Legion of Honour) ; some'ime Med. Officer, Roy. Army Clothing Factory ; Med. Officer. London Dist. 1910 ; Professor of Hygiene, Roy. Army Med. Coll., 1912.   (C1221)

BEVERLEY, Capt. Samuel, O.B.E., R.A.

BEVERLY, Elizabeth, M.B.E., *b.* 21 Jan. 1884 ; *d.* of John T. Beverly, of Forest Gate. Matron-Superintendent, Bethnal Green Guardians' Schools at Leytonstone. *Address :* Leytonstone House, Leytonstone.   (M7378)

BEVIS, Major Cecil Bevis, O.B.E.

BEWICK, Ralph Martin, C.B.E.

BEWICKE, Major Calverly, O.B.E., M.C.

BEWLEY, Constance Lillie, Mrs., M.B.E..; *d.* of the late William Henry Bewley, of Rockville, Co. Dublin ; *m.* Walter, *s.* of the late Samuel Bewley, of Sandford Hill, Dublin. *Educ.:* Weston-super-Mare and Westfield College, London. *War Work :* Hon. Sec. of the Dacca Ladies' War Fund (for supplying comforts to the troops in Mesopotamia) from April, 1916, to April, 1918. *Address :* c/o Messrs. H. S. King & Co., Cornhill, London.   (M6108)

BEYNON, Lieut. John, M.B.E., R.A.S.C.

BEYNON, Sir John Wyndham, Bart., C.B.E. Esquire of the Order of St. John of Jerusalem, *b.* 2 Dec. 1864 ; *s.* of Thomas Beynon, J.P., D.L., County of Monmouth, High Sheriff, 1890, of Newport, Mon.(*see* BURKE'S *Peerage*). *Educ.:* Clifton College and Abroad. Largely interested in the Iron, Steel and Coal Industry of South Wales ; Chairman of many of the Colliery Companies of Monmouthshire. *War Work :* J.P. High Sheriff County Monmouth, 1917–18 ; County Director of Red Cross and St. John of Jerusalem ; commanded Mon. R.A.S.C., M.T. (V.) with rank of Major. *Addresses :* The Coldra near Newport, Mon. ; 6, Charles St., Mayfair, W. 1. *Clubs :* Carlton ; Royal Automobile.   (C2450)

BEYNON, Ruth, M.B.E. ; *d.* of Richard and Annie Beynon, of Birkenhead. *Educ.:* Higher Tranmere High School, Birkenhead. London organiser, Y.M.C.A. Womens' Auxiliaries. *War Work :* Secretary, Y.M.C.A. Munitions Auxiliary Committee ; Asst.-Sec. Y.M.C.A. Munitions Department. *Address :* Woodley, Leigh-on-Sea, Essex. (M7379)

BEYNON, Vernon Bryan CROWTHER-, M.B.E., M.A., F.S.A., *b.* 21 Oct. 1865 ; *s.* of the late Rev. S. B. Crowther-Beynon, of Beckenham, Kent ; *m.* Mary, *d.* of the late Rev. Frederick Walter Giffard, of Wootton. Lincs. *Educ.:* Wellington College and Trinity College, Cambridge. Barrister-at-Law. *War Work :* Hon. Sec., Beckenham Belgian Relief Committee ; served in Metropolitan Special Constabulary (and now a member of the Special Constabulary Reserve). *Address :* Westfield, Beckenham, Kent. *Club :* Royal Societies'.   (M7380)

BEYTS, Clement Ayerst, O.B.E.

BEYTS, William George, C.B.E.

BHARUCHA, Capt. Phirozshah Byramji, O.B.E., D.S.O., I.M.S., F.R.C.S.   (O11725)

BHORE, Joseph William, C.B.E., I.C.S.

BHORE, Margaret Wilke, Mrs., M.B.E.

BIBBY, Frank, C.B.E., J.P., D.L., *b.* 4 Jan. 1857 ; *s.* of James Jenkinson Bibby, of Hardwicke Grange, Shrewsbury ; *m.* Edith Mary, *d.* of Maj.-Gen. Sir Stanley Clarke, G.V.C.O., C.M.G. *Educ.:* Eton. Chairman of Bibby Steamship Co. ; Director of Great Western Railway. *War Work :* Chairman of Shropshire and Herefordshire Appeal Tribunals ; provided stabling and accommodation and carried on big Remount Depot for the Director of Remounts during whole of War. *Addresses :* Hardwicke Grange, Shrewsbury ; 39, Hill Street, Mayfair, London. *Clubs :* Turf ; Carlton ; Royal Yacht Squadron ; Jockey.   (C2451)

BICKERSTAFFE-DREW, Right Rev. Monsignor Count Francis Browning Drew, C.B.E., K.H.S., LL.D., *b.* 11 Feb. 1858 ; *s.* of Rev. Henry Lloyd Bickerstaffe, of Boylestone, Co. Derby and of Mona Brougham, *d.* of Rev. P. W. Drew of Heathfield Towers, Co. Cork ; assumed additional name of Drew, 1879. *Educ.:* King Edward VI.'s School, Lichfield ; Oxford and St. Thomas's Seminary, W. Acting-Chaplain to H.M. Forces, 1886–92 ; Chaplain to the Forces, 1892–1919 ; Senior R.C. Chaplain, Plymouth, 1892–99 ; Malta, 6681–1905 ; Salisbury Plain, 1905–19 ; Assistant Principal R.C. Chaplain, 1918–19 ; Private Chamberlain to Pope Leo XIII., 1891–1903 ; to Pius X., 1903 ; Domestic Prelate of His Holiness from 1904 ; Protonotary Apostolic from 1912 ; received Cross " Pro Ecclesia et Pontifice, 1901 ; Knight of the Holy Sepulchre, 1909 ; Member of Special Council of University of Malta, 1899. *War Work :* Proceeded to Front as Chaplain on outbreak of War, Aug. 1914 ; at battles of Mons, Marne, Aisne, Ypres, etc., and in retreat from Mons (Star 2 roses, General Service Medal, Victory Medal and Silver Oak leaf) ; mentioned in both Lord French's despatches, and later in Sec. of State's despatch. *Address :* The Manor House, Winterbourne Gunner, Salisbury. *Club :* Authors'.   (C1465)

BICKERSTETH, John Joseph, O.B.E. *Address :* Cottingham House, Cottingham, Hull.   (O9989)

BICKET, Brig.-Gen. William Neilson, C.B.E. ; Great War, 1914–18, as Brig.-Gen. (despatches).   (C800)

BICKLEY, Nora Magdalen, Mrs., M.B.E., *b.* 21 July, 1880 ; *d.* of Commander E. P. Statham, R.N. ; *m.* Francis Lawrance, *s.* of Francis Bridges Bickley, of British Museum. *War Work :* Women's Emergency Corps (Interpreter) ; Junior Administrative Assistant in the Treasury Solicitor's Department (Law Courts Branch). *Address :* 58, Biddulph Mansions, Elgin Avenue, W. 9.   (M1412)

BICKLEY, Lieut. Reginald Couteney, O.B.E., R.N.

BIDDISCOMBE, George, M.B.E., D.C.M., *b.* 2 March, 1880 ; *s.* of James Biddiscombe, of Greenwich ; *m.* Edith Emily, *d.* of George Bayles, of Clapham Park. Clerk, War Office. *War Work :* Engaged throughout the War on the organisation and administration of all hospitals in the United Kingdom for the treatment of the sick and wounded. *Address :* 29, Chertsey Street, Church Lane, Tooting, S.W 17. (M7381)

BIDDLE, Lois, M.B.E., *b.* 4 Jan. 1894 ; *d.* of Leonard Frederick Biddle, of Liverpool *Educ.:* Central Foundation, Girls' School, London, and Ursuline Convent, Londerzeel, Belgium. *War Work :* Assistant Superintendent of Clerical Staff, of Contraband Committee, Foreign Office ; and Peace Conference, Paris. *Address :* 207, Ebury St., London, S.W. 1. (M147)

BIDDULPH, Capt. Alfred James, O.B.E.,M.C., R.F.A.

BIDDULPH, Eleanor, Lady, O.B.E. ; *d.* of late Samuel Thompson of Muckamore Abbey, Co. Antrim ; *m.* Sir Theophilus George Biddulph, 8th Bart. (*see* BURKE'S *Peerage*). *Address :* Pavilion, Melrose, N.B.   (O9990)

BIDWELL, Eivir Linda, M.B.E.

BIDWELL, Right Rev. Monsignor Manuel John, C.B.E., D.D., Bishop of Miletopolis, Auxiliary to Cardinal Bourne, *b.* 29 June, 1872 ; *s.* of Charles Toll Bidwell, F.R.G.S. *Educ.:* Paris ; King's College, London ; Academia Ecclesiastica, Rome. *Addresses :* St. Mary's Rectory, Cadogan St., S.W. ; San Carlos, St. Jean de Luz, Basses Pyrénées. (C439)

BIDWILL, William Edward, O.B.E.

BIGBY, Dorothy Anne, M.B.E., M.A. (Lond.). *Educ.:* Cheltenham Ladies' College and University College, London. Research and examining work. *Address :* Stonehill's Mansions, Streatham.   (M7383)

BIGG, Capt. William Charles, O.B.E., R.A.S.C.

BIGGE, Edith Lindsay, Lady SELBY-, O.B.E. *b* 16 Oct 1864 ; *d.* of Right Hon. J. R. Davison, M.P., of Underriver House, Sevenoaks ; *m.* Sir Lewis Amherst Selby-Bigge, Bart., K.C.B. (*see* BURKE'S *Peerage*), *s.* of Charles Selby-Bigge, of Linden, Northumberland, and Ightham Mote, Kent. *War Work :* Member of Executive of Young Women's Christian Association collection of funds, organisation of " Flag Days," establishment of Hostels. *Addresses :* 127, Sloane Street, S.W. 1 ; Kingston Manor, Lewes, Sussex.   (O3620)

BIGGE, Lieut.-Col. George Orde, O.B.E., R.E.

BIGGS, Ambrose Joseph, M.B.E..

BIGGS, Arthur Holland, M.B.E.

BIGGS, Lieut.-Col. Charles William, O.B.E., R.E.

BIGGS, Lieut. Jack Pelham Percival Leslie, M.B.E., R.A.F.

BIGGS, Capt. John James Egerton, O.B.E., R.A.M.C. (T.F.).

BIGHAM, Lieut.-Col. Hon. Charles Clive, C.M.G., C.B.E., J.P., D.L., *b.* 18 Aug. 1872 ; *s.* of Viscount Mersey, of 22, Grosvenor Place, S.W. 1 ; *m.* Mary Gertrude, *d.* of late Sir Horace Seymour, K.C.B., Deputy Master, Royal Mint. *Educ.:* Eton ;

Sandhurst R.M.C. Grenadier Guards, Reserve of Officers; H.M. Diplomatic Service; Board of Trade; Secretary to Royal Commissions; Intelligence Dept., War Office. *War Work*: Rejoined Grenadier Guards, 5 Aug. 1914; Brigade Major, Brigade of Guards and General Staff Officer, 2nd Grade, London District, 1914; Provost Marshal, Mediterranean Expeditionary Force and Military Attaché, Egypt, 1915; General Staff Officer, 1st Grade, Egypt, France, 1916; in command of British Military Mission to French War Office, 1916–19 (1914–15 Star, two medals; despatches, 1917; Officer of Legion of Honour, 1918; C.B.E. (Military), Lieut.-Col. and Officer Crown of Italy, 1919). *Address*: 22, Eaton Place, London, S.W. 1. *Clubs*: United Service; Bachelors'. (C1466)

BIGLEY, Francis William Hudson, M.B.E., M.A., B.Ch.

BIGNOLD, William Henry, M.B.E.

BIKANER, Hon. Major-Gen. H. H. Maharaja Raj Rajeshawar Siromani Sri Sir Ganga Singh Bahadur, Maharaja of, G.C.S.I., G.C.I.E., G.C.V.O., G.B.E. (1921), K.C.B., A.D.C. to the King, *b.* 3 Oct. 1880; *s.* of Maharaj Sri Lall Singhji Bahadut. Hon. LL.D., Cambridge and Edinburgh; D.C.L. Oxford; granted Hon. Commission of Major, British Army, 1900, and attached 2nd Bengal Lancers; Lieut.-Col. 1909; Col. 1910; Major-Gen. 1917; was selected as one of the Representatives of India at Imperial War Cabinet and Conference, 1917 and 1919; received Freedom of the Cities of London, Edinburgh, Manchester, and Bristol; is Patron and President of many Institutions and Associations; served with British Army in China, 1901; in command of Bikaner Camel Corps (despatches); served in Great War in France and Egypt (despatches, bronze star); has Grand Cordon of the Order of the Nile; and 1st Class Kaisir-i-Hind medal; and is Donat of the Order of St. John of Jerusalem in England. *Address*: Bikaner, Rajputana India. *Clubs*: Marlborough; Western India Turf; Willingdon Sports, Bombay. (G68)

BILDERBECK, Capt. William John How, O.B.E., A.P.D.

BILLINTON, Lieut.-Col. Lawson, C.B.E., R.E.

BILLS, Eng.-Comm. Walter William, O.B.E., R.N.

BILSLAND, Robert, O.B.E., J.P., *b.* 1 Oct. 1859; *s.* of Robert Bilsland, of Glasgow; *m.* Jeanie, *d.* of James McKean, of Dumbartonshire. *Educ.*: Dumbarton Academy and Glasgow High School. Alderman, West Suffolk County Council; Member of Education and other Committees of above Council; Chairman of West Suffolk War Agricultural Executive Committee; Member of the Mildenhall Rural District Council. *War Work*: Chairman, War Agricultural Executive Committee; represented the Board of Agriculture on the West Suffolk Appeal Tribunal; Member of the Mildenhall Tribunal. *Address*: Brandon House, Lakenheath, Brandon. *Club*: National Liberal. (O1110)

BILTON, Christina Turnbull, M.B.E. (M1414)

BING, Herbert, O.B.E., M.I.Mech.E., *b.* 1870; *s.* of Herbert Bing, of Teynham, Kent. *Educ.*: Faversham. Director: The Clement Stevens Pneumatic Engineering Co. Ltd.; 28, Spencer Street, London, S.W. 1. *War Work*: Managing Director, National Filling Factories, Banbury, 1915, Gainsborough, 1917, and Chittening, 1918. *Address*: 32, Rollscourt Avenue, Herne Hill, S.E. 24. (O148)

BINGHAM, Lieut.-Col. Sir Albert Edward, 2nd Bt., O.B.E., V.D., J.P., *b.* 23 Nov. 1868; *o.s* of Sir John Edward Bingham, 1st Bt. of West Lea, Sheffield, and Maria, *d.* of the late William Fowcett, of Clarke House, Sheffield; *m.* Lucy, *d.* of the late Duncan L. McAllum, of Gosforth. *Educ.*: Blair Lodge. Master Cutler of the Cutlers' Company, Sheffield, Lieut.-Col. West Riding Division, R.E. (T.); Member, West Riding of York Territorial Force Association; Proprietor of Walker and Hall, Sheffield (Silver, Cutlery, and Electro-plate manufacturers). *Address*: Rauby House, near Retford, Notts. *Clubs*: Junior Constitutional; Royal Automobile; The Club, Sheffield. (O6912)

BINGHAM, Lieut. and Qr.-Mr. Charles Frederick, M.B.E.

BINGHAM, Constance Gwendoline, O.B.E., *d.* of the late Robert Bingham. *Educ.*: St. Scholastica's School, Oxford. *War Work*: Secretary, Contraband Committee, Foreign Office, S.W. 1, and Superintendent, Women Staff, Peace Conference, Paris. (O9991)

BINGHAM, Capt. the Hon. Edward Barry Stewart, V.C., O.B.E., R.N, *b.* 26 July, 1881; *s.* of the 5th Baron Clanmorris, of Creg Clare, Co. Galway, and Bangor Castle, Ireland (see BURKE'S *Peerage*); *m.* Vera, *d.* of E. Temple-Patterson, of Culford Gardens, London. *Educ.*: Arnold House, Llanddulas and H.M.S. "Britannia," Dartmouth. Royal Navy (active list). *War Work*: Lieut.-Com. in H.M.S. "Invincible" 1914–15; Commander in H.M.S. Destroyer "Hornet," 1916; Commander of H.M.S. "Nestor," at battle of Jutland, 1916; H.M.S. "Nestor" sunk during battle; prisoner of war in Germany, 1916; interned in Holland, 1918, until Armistice; awarded V.C. for Jutland and St. Stani-laus (2nd class); O.B.E. for services whilst prisoner of war in Germany. *Address*: 57, Bedford Gardens, Campden Hill, London, W. 8. *Clubs*: United Service; Ranelagh. (O9642)

BINGHAM, Major William Henry, C.B.E., I.A.

BINGLE, Capt. William Reginald, M.B.E., A.I.E.

BINGLEY, Mabel Katherine, Lady, O.B.E., *b.* 19 Dec. 1869; *d.* of Col. G. A. Way, C.B., late of Spaynes Hall, Great Yelpham, Essex; *m.* Major-General Sir Alfred Horsford Bingley, K.C.I.E., C.B. (*see* BURKE'S *Peerage*), *s.* of Peregrine Taylor Bingley. *War Work*: Member of Indian Joint War Committee of British Red Cross Society and Order of St. John of Jerusalem; Member of Committee of Delhi-Simla Red Cross Work Party. *Address*: Simla, India. (O4015)

BINGLEY, Major Robert Noel Glanville, O.B.E.

BINNEY, Major Arthur Thomson, O.B.E., R.A.S.C.

BINNEY, Harold William Meares, O.B.E., *b.* 20 Jan. 1878; *s.* of the late William Binney, of London; *m.* Ivy St. Claire, *d.* of the late Edward Harley, of Cardiff. *Educ.*: University College School, London. *War Work*: Sometime Chief Commissariat Officer and Deputy Director, Middlesex Branch, Joint V.A. Organisation, British Red Cross and Order of St. John. *Address*: 14, Manor Mansions, Belsize Grove, Hampstead. (O3621)

BINNIE, Annie Janet, Mrs., M.B.E., *b.* 15 Feb. 1880; *d.* of James Deas, of Manchester; *m.* William Bryce Binnie (Major), *s.* of William Binnie, of Airdrie. *Educ.*: Manchester High School. *War Work*: Feb. 1915, to May, 1918, Record Clerk and Registrar to the Commissioner, British Red Cross and Order of St. John, at Headquarters, Boulogne, France; Jan. 1919, to July, 1919 (inclusive) engaged on the reclassification and compilation of the permanent records of the Commission in France. *Address*: Church House, The Ridgway, Mill Hill, London. (M1415)

BINNIE, Lieut. and Qr.-Mr. James Ballentyne, M.B.E.

BINNS, Arthur, M.B.E.

BINNS, Aubrey Brian, M.B.E.

BINNS, A. Lieut.-Col. Cuthbert Evelyn, O.B.E., R.M., *b.* 26 Nov. 1880; *s.* of Walter Rupen, of Constantinople; *m.* Edith Mildred, *d.* of Charles Edwards, of Constantinople. *Educ.*: American College. *War Work*: Joined Royal Naval Division, March, 1915, and served throughout Dardanelles campaign, transferred to Egypt, May, 1916; thence appointed to Assistant Military Attaché British Legation at Berne; after Armistice attached to Staff of Admiral De Robeck, British High Commissioner at Constantinople; promoted during the war to A. Lieut.-Col.; received Greek Order of Redeemer, French Legion of Honour, Italian Order of St. Maurice and Lazarus. *Club*: Constantinople. (O4332)

BINNS, Douglas Thomson, O.B.E. Temp. Assistant Commercial Attaché, Copenhagen. (O11789c)

BINNS, Capt. Frederick, M.B.E., A.P.D.

BINNS, Joseph, M.B.E.

BINNS, Oswell Barritt, O.B.E.

BINNY, Lieut.-Col. Steuart Murrey, O.B.E., A.P.D.

BINYON, Major Basil, O.B.E. R.A.F.

BIRBECK, Thomas Edson, M.B.E.

BIRCH, Major Alfred Granville, O.B.E., R.A.S.C.

BIRCH, Bertha, Mrs., M.B.E.

BIRCH, Charles, M.B.E.

BIRCH, Lieut.-Comm. Frank, O.B.E., R.N.V.R.

BIRCH, George, M.B.E.

BIRCH, George Ernest, O.B.E., *b.* 19 July, 1877. Chief Clerk to Governor General of Union of South Africa and Secretary, King Edward VII Order of Nurses. *Address*: Government House, Cape Town. (O8345)

BIRCH, George Hubert, M.B.E., *b.* 30 June, 1880; *s.* of A. F. M. Birch, of Mysore Educational Service; *m.* Alice, *d.* of James Lennon, of Cork, Ireland. *Educ.*: Grammar School, Karachi, Sind, India. Bombay Civil Service; held appointments of Assistant to the Commissioner in Sind; Assistant Commissioner of Salt Excise and Opium in Sind; Deputy Controller of prices for Sind; Controller of Rents, Karachi; Collector of Income Tax in Sind. *War Work*: Honorary General Secretary, Y.M.C.A., Karachi; Honorary Secretary, Hospital Nursing Association; Honorary Secretary, Boy Scouts, Sind Local Association; Volunteer, Long Service Medal (1915); Honorary Secretary, Domiciled European and Anglo-Indian Recruitment Committee; Member of following War Committees: Sind Aeroplane and Ambulance Fund; Sind "Our Day" Fund; Sind Recruitment Committee; Karachi Passage Control Committee; War Loan Committee; Karachi Rent Committee (Member and Secretary), Sind Resettlement Committee. *Address*: Karachi, Sind, India. (M4116)

BIRCH, Lieut. George Russell, M.B.E.

BIRCH, Janet Elizabeth, Mrs., M.B.E., *b.* 21 May, 1877; *d.* of Arthur Travis Clay, of Rastrick and Filey, Yorks.; *m.* John Kenneth Beaufoy Birch, Com., R.N., *s.* of John Grant Birch, of Bedfont, Middlesex. *Educ.*: Privately, and University College, London. *War Work*: Commandant, E.R. 34 Yorks, 1914–19 (V.A.D. Hosp. Filey). *Address*: Bourne End, Filey, Yorks. (M3529)

BIRCH, John, M.B.E.

BIRCH, Lieut.-Col. Lewis Henry Peregrine, O.B.E., R.A.

BIRCH, Capt. Montague, O.B.E., *b.* 1893; *s.* of Theodore Birch, of Paris, France. *Educ.*: City of London School. Engineer (Motor and Mechanical). *War Work*: Enlisted in R.A.S.C. Mechanical Transport, 7 Aug. 1914, as despatch rider; Commissioned 24 Oct. 1914, when with No. 1 Ammunition Park; Commanded same unit in 1917, also Commanded for short periods, 5th Aux. Petrol Co., No. 1 Divisional M.T. Co.; now Commanding 789 M.T. Co., India. *Addresses*: 40, Tulse Hill, London; 46 Rue St. Placide, Paris. (O5010)

BIRCH, Lieut. William Kenning, O.B.E.

BIRCH, Major Wyndham Lindsay, D.S.O., M.B.E., Croix de Guerre, *b.* 22 March, 1879; *s.* of Sir Arthur Birch; *m.* Susan, *d.* of the Earl of Hardwicke. *Educ.*: Marlboro. Prime Warden of Fishmongers' Company, 1919–20. *War Work*:

Served as a Private in the London Scottish as a Subaltern in the West Yorkshire Regt.; as an Observer and Pilot in the R.F.C. and R.A.F. in France, Salonica, Palestine, Syria and Somaliland; twice mentioned in despatches. *Address:* 22, Albert Road, Regent's Park. *Clubs:* Pratt's; Arthur's; Bachelors'; R.A.C. (M1417)

BIRCHBY, Henry William Britain, M.B.E., *b.* 15 Feb. 1882; *s.* of Thomas John Birchby, of Portsmouth; *m.* Helen Maude. *Educ.:* Royal Hospital School, Greenwich. Assistant Naval Store Officer, Admiralty. *War Work:* Work in connection with the supply of Naval Stores and maintenance of the R.N. Air Service, and of the Airship Service after the transfer of heavier-than-air machines to the Air Ministry. *Address:* 52, Chestnut Road, Raynes Park, S.W. 19. (M7388)

BIRD, Capt. Douglas Joseph, M.B.E., *b.* 14 April, 1894; *s.* of H. F Bird, of Cambridge; *m.* Evelyn Marjorie, *d.* of C. J. Hobbs, of Chester. *Educ.:* Gresham's School, Holt Norfolk. *War Work:* Served in the 2 5th Batt., The York and Lancaster Regt., at home and in France; also as Chief Instructor, Hawarden Castle Officers' Convalescent Hospital. *Address:* The Bungalow, Downham Market, Norfolk. (M1418)

BIRD, Capt. Edmund Ivan Montford, M.B.E., R.A.F.

BIRD, Henry Linsell, M.B.E., *b.* 5 April, 1879; *s.* of James Bird, of Ilford; *m.* Harriet Emily, *d.* of William Nichols, of Ilford. *Educ.:* Ilford C. of E. School and East Ham Technical College. Works Superintendent to the Ilford Urban District Council. *War Work:* Managed the Ilford Council's Government Contracts for the manufacture of 18-pounder shells, ·303 British Cartridge Dies, Japanese and Russian Cartridge Dies, and Needle Holders; of the total articles supplied (250,000) not one was rejected. *Address:* 41, Quebec Road, Ilford, Essex. (M7389)

BIRD, Herbert Ruben, M.B.E.

BIRD, Major James, O.B.E., R.A.F.

BIRD, Jessie, Mrs., M.B.E.

BIRD, Major Lawrence Wilfred, D.S.O., O.B.E., *b.* 1883; *s.* of Arthur Bird, J.P., of The Grange, Great Bookham; *m.* 1916, Hilda, *d.* of the late Richard Alfred Lett, M.D., of Wakefield. *Educ.:* Harrow, and Trin. Coll., Camb. Major, Roy. Berkshire Regt.; Great War, 1914–18 (despatches twice). (O6914)

BIRD, Mary Cecilia, M.B.E., Q.M.A.A.C.

BIRD, Capt. Richard Martin, M.B.E.

BIRD, Capt. Ronald Trevor Wilberforce, O.B.E. Dorsetshire Regt.

BIRD, Major William Arthur Henry, O.B.E., Sikh Pnrs., I.A. (O11726)

BIRD, Brevet-Col. William John Butterworth, O.B.E., *b.* 27 Nov. 1852. *Educ.:* Clifton College and Royal Military Academy, Woolwich. Royal Artillery and Indian Army. *War Work:* Served in Guernsey throughout the war. (O9993)

BIRDWOOD, Lieut.-Col. George Christopher McDowall, C.B.E.

BIRKET, Major Myles HIGGIN-, O.B.E., J.P., Order of the White Eagle, Serbia, 4th Class, *b.* Nov. 7 1874; *s.* of the late William Higgin-Birket, of Birket Houses, Cartmel Fell, Lancs. *Educ.:* Heversham School, Westmorland; and University College, London. Landed Proprietor; Major, Lancashire Fusiliers (S.R.). *War Work:* Served with 2nd Lancashire Fusiliers, Sept. 20 to Oct. 23, France and Belgium, 1914; attached Foreign Office, London, March to Oct. 1915; attached General Staff G.H.Q. Salonika, Oct. 1915, to Oct. 1918; Camp Commandant G.H.Q. Salonika and G.H.Q. Army of the Black Sea, Constantinople, Nov. 1918, to March, 1920. *Address:* Birket Houses, Windermere. *Club:* Royal Windermere Yacht. (O1028)

BIRKETT, Annie, O.B.E., *b.* 24 Sept. 1872; *d.* of John Birkett, of Kendal. *Educ.:* Privately. Certificated Hospital Nurse; Proprietress of Nursing Home, 7, Mandeville Place, W. *War Work:* Organiser and Commandant, Miss Birkett's Hospital for Officers, 7, Mandeville Place, W.; had over 1300 officers in from overseas, of which only 2 died; Hospital opened Sept. 1914, closed 30 April, 1919. *Address:* River House, Elstead, Surrey. (O9994)

BIRKETT, Matthew Stevenson, O.B.E., *b.* 29 April, 1882; *s.* of John Birkett, of Sydenham; *m.* Janet Frew, *d.* of James B. Allan, J.P., of Motherwell. *Educ.:* London University. Statistical Officer to National Federation of Iron and Steel Manufacturers. *War Work:* Assistant Controller of Statistics, Ministry of Munitions. *Address:* 27, Collingtree Road, Sydenham, S.E. 26. (O3622)

BIRKETT, Tom, M.B.E., F.S.I., *b.* 30 Jan. 1863; *s.* of Joseph Birkett, of Foxton House, Penrith, Cumberland; *m.* Ada Elizabeth, *d.* of Michael Bird, of Ealing. *Educ.:* Sedburgh School and College of Agriculture, Downton. *War Work:* Sub-Commissioner (Cumberland and Westmorland) Board of Agriculture and Fisheries Food Production Department. *Address:* Foxton House, Penrith, Cumberland. (M151)

BIRKIN, Ethel Lilian, O.B.E., *d.* of Sir T. J. Birkin, Bart., of Ruddington Grange, Nottingham. *Educ.:* Privately and Halliwick Manor, London. Sister-in-Charge, Birkin Red Cross Clinic for Discharged Sailors and Soldiers, Nottingham, 1919 (present temporary occupation). *War Work:* Commandant and Matron, Bayley Red Cross Hospital, Nottingham, 1914 to 1919. *Addresses:* B.R.C.C., 16, Upper College St., Nottingham; and Ruddington Grange, Notts. (O3)

BIRKIN, Major Philip Austin, O.B.E.

BIRKMYRE, Sir Archibald, Bt., C.B.E., *b.* 28 June 1875; *s.* of the late Henry Birkmyre of Port Glasgow;¹ *m.* 8 Dec. 1896, Annie, *e₃ d.* of Capt. James Black. Partner in Birkmyre Bros., Jute Manufacturers and Merchants, Calcutta, Bengal. *Address:* 6, Clive Row, Calcutta. (C698)

BIRKS, Lieut. Falconor Moffat, O.B.E., R.A.S.C. (T.F.).

BIRKS, Lieut.-Col. Gerald Walker, O.B.E.

BIRKS, Gladys Helen, M.B.E., *b.* 11 Jan. 1889; *d.* of Lieut.-Col. H. H. Aspinall, O.B.E., of Coonoor, India, late Indian Army; *m.* 15 Dec. 1920, H. L. Birks, Tank Corps. *Educ.:* Privately. *War Work:* V.A.D. Canteen work; Unit Administrator, Q.M.A.A.C., 1917–19. *Address:* Lane End, Headley, Bordon, Hants. (M6596)

BIRLEY, Wing-Comm. James Leatham, C.B.E., *b.* 1884; *s.* of the late Francis Hornby Leatham, of Clarides, Lingfield, Surrey. Squadron-Leader and Acting Wing.-Com. and Med. Officer R.A.F.; European War, 1914–19 (despatches). (C2335)

BIRMINGHAM, Rt. Rev. Henry Russell Wakefield, Bishop of, C.B.E., D.D., *b.* 1 Dec. 1854; *s.* of F. Wakefield, J.P., Broomfield, Co. Wicklow, and Emily, *d.* of Leatham Howard; *g.g.s.* of Gilbert Wakefield, the celebrated scholar; *m.* Frances, *d.* of Henry Dallaway. *Educ.:* Tonbridge School; the Lycée Bonaparte, Paris; Bonn, Germany; Cuddesdon, Oxford. Curate of St. Peter's, Vauxhall, 1877–78; Barnes, 1878–81; Vicar of All Saints', Swanscombe, 1881–83, Lower Sydenham, 1883–88, Sandgate, 1888–94; Lecturer on English Literature, Crystal Palace, 1887–91; Member of the London School Board, 1897–1900; Mayor of St. Marylebone, 1903–4–5; Rector of St. Mary's, Bryanston Square, 1894–1909; Prebendary of St. Paul's, 1908–9; Dean of Norwich 1909–11; Chairman of Central Committee on the Unemployed; Member of the Royal Commission on the Poor Law; President of the Free and Open Church Society; President of the National Council of Public Morals; Vice-President of the British Workers' League. *Address:* Bishop's Croft, Birmingham. *Clubs:* Athenæum; Reform. (C2187)

BIRRELL, Lieut. Edward, M.B.E., R.E.

BIRRELL, Hugh, M.B.E.

BIRSE, Capt. Arthur Herbert, M.B.E.,

BIRT, Lieut.-Col. Arthur Watson, O.B.E.

BIRTLES, John Edward, M.B.E.

BIRTWISTLE, Philip, M.B.E.

BISACRE, Frederick Francis Percival, O.B.E., M.A., B.Sc., *b.* 1885; *s.* of George Bisacre, of Southborough, Kent; *m.* Jean Margaret, *d.* of Walter Wilfrid Blackie, of Glasgow. *Educ.:* Privately and Trinity College, Cambridge. Engineer and Publisher. *War Work:* Engineer-in-Chief's Department, Admiralty, attached for Experiments and Research. *Address:* 1 Florentine Gardens, Hillhead, Glasgow. (O9995)

BISDEE, Lieut.-Col. John Hutton, O.B.E.

BISHOP, Alice Margaret, M.B.E.

BISHOP, Lieut. Arthur Grimwade, M.B.E.

BISHOP, Capt. Charles Alder, O.B.E., R.A.S.C.

BISHOP, Major Charles Arthur, O.B.E., R.M.A., *b.* 22 Feb. 1879; *s.* of the late Capt. E. Bishop, of Bath; *m.* Charlotte Mary, *d.* of the late George Keys Betham, of Indian Forest Service. *Educ.:* Bedford. 2nd Lieut. Royal Marine Artillery, 1 Sept. 1897,; Adjutant, Wicklow Garrison Artillery Militia, 1906–8; Assistant Inspector of Naval Ordnance, Jan. 1912; Assistant to Superintendent, Naval Ordnance Design, June, 1919 (Admiralty). *War Work:* Inspection of Military and Naval Ordnance stores throughout the war. (O9996)

BISHOP, Capt. and Qr.-Mr. John Evitt, M.B.E., R.F.A.; *b.* 13 Aug. 1854; *s.* of Charles Bishop, of London; *m.* Susan Alice, *d.* of J. Sloane, of Cork. *Educ.:* Chichester Cathedral Choristers School. *War Work:* Rejoined Army in Aug. 1914, at 60 years of age; after having served almost continuously in the ranks for 45 years, served for 5 years; mentioned in despatches, "London Gazette," 23 Feb. 1917, for good work, and 1 Jan. 1919, for valuable services. *Address:* 75, Gladstone Road, Edge Hill, Liverpool. (M3245)

BISHOP, Lieut.-Col. Joseph George, O.B.E.

BISHOP, Louise Emma, Mrs., M.B.E.; *d.* of the late Col. William Lamb, Indian Army; *m.* Col. Edward Barry Bishop (late Commandant 3rd Gurkha Rifles), *s.* of Gen. George Williams Bishop. *War Work:* Hon. Sec. S. and S.F.A. and special work for Ministry of Pensions in Jersey. *Address:* Mayfield, Millbrook, Jersey. (M7392)

BISHOP, Capt. Nathaniel, O.B.E.

BISHOP, Pearl Hall, Mrs., O.B.E.

BISHOP, Major Percy, O.B.E., R.A.F., *b.* 26 June, 1888; *s.* of Frank Bishop, of Uxbridge; *m.* Dorothy, *d.* of William Freeman, of London. *Educ.:* Kendrick School, Reading, and Polytechnic School of Engineering, Regent Street, London, W. Assistant-Engineer (Design) at Royal Aircraft Establishment, Farnborough, Hants; subsequently Deputy Chief Inspector of Aeroplanes with the Aeronautical Inspection Department. *War Work:* Engaged on the supervision of the design of War Aeroplanes, experimental work in connection with Aircraft, and controlling the Inspection of War Contracts; mentioned in despatches, 1917. *Address:* Helenslea, Arlow Road, Winchmore Hill. London, W. 21. *Club:* R.A.F. (O8051)

BISHOP, 2nd Lieut. Robert Odell, M.B.E.

BISHOP, Rosa Ethel, Mrs., O.B.E.

BISHOP, Richard Winsor, M.B.E., *b.* 15 Sept. 1861; *s.* of John Corry Bishop, of Sherborne, Dorset; *m.* Edith Mary, *d.* of Francis Gaydon, of Norwood. *Educ.:* King's School, Sherborne. Councillor, City of Norwich. *War Work:* Special Constabulary; Promoter of combined effort by this force in support of War Loan : Tank Week, £50,000 was subscribed by about 600 members—a record for the country ; Member of City of Norwich Tribunal. *Addresses :* Beech Lodge, Norwich ; Coombe Lodge, E. Liss, Hants. (M1421)

BISHOP, Capt. Stanley, M.B.E., R.G.A. (S.R.), *b.* 11 Oct. 1885 ; *s.* of Herbert Bishop. of Ongar, Essex ; *m.* Cicely, *d.* of William Monger, of Faversham, Kent. *Educ. :* Privately. Journalist. *War Work :* 4 years' service with Forces, first R.N.V.R., later commission R.G.A. (S.R.) ; twice mentioned in despatches. *Address :* 100, Fordhook Avenue, W. 5. *Club :* Press. (M5082)

BISHOP, Lieut. Walter George, O.B.E., R.N.

BISHOP, William George, M.B.E.

BISHOP, William Henry, M.B.E., M.B., B.S., *b.* 4 Feb. 1867 ; *s.* of Rev. Henry Halsall Bishop, late Vicar of St. Andrew's, Sunderland. *Educ. :* City of London School and Durham Univ. *War Work :* Medical Officer, 14th Northumberland V.A.D. Hospital, 1915–19. *Address :* Wylam, Northumberland. (M7394)

BISPHAM, Capt. George, O.B.E., M.B.E., I.R.A.O.

BISPHAM, Capt. James Webb, O.B.E.

BISSET, Capt. the Rev. Mordaunt Elrington, M.B.E., *b.* 8 Dec. 1859 ; *s.* of J. F. Elrington Bisset, of Lessendrum, Huntly, N.B. *Educ. :* Cheltenham Coll. and Penbroke Coll., Cambridge. *War Work :* Chaplain at R.M. Chapel, Wellington Barracks, from 1915. *Address :* 8, Chantrey House, Eccleston Street, S.W. *Clubs :* Union ; Royal Automobile. (M5083)

BISSET, Capt. Ormond Douglas, M.B.E., *b.* 5 Feb. 1891 ; *s.* of James Smith Bisset, of Liverpool ; *m.* Gertrude Gwendolen, *d.* of the Rev. Carey Bonner, of London. *Educ. :* High School, Liverpool Institute. Merchant ; Reserve of Officers, Royal Marines. *War Work :* Served in Gallipoli, France, and Transport Dept., Ministry of Shipping. *Address :* Cranley, Cecil Street, Gordon, nr. Sydney, N.S.W. *Clubs :* United Berkeley ; Union (Sydney). (M7395)

BISSET, Eng.-Lieut. William David, M.B.E., R.N.

BISSETT, Capt. James, O.B.E., Can. A.S.C.

BISSETT, John, O.B.E., M.Inst.M.E., *b.* 14 March, 1882 ; *s.* of Rev. George Alexander Bissett, of Houndwood, Berwickshire. *Educ. :* Reston School, Berwickshire ; George Watson's College, Merchiston Castle School and Heriot Watt College, Edinburgh. Director, Messrs. Platt Bros. & Co., Ltd., Oldham. *War Work :* Secretary and Engineering Manager to the Board of Management of the Manchester and District Armaments Output Committee. *Clubs :* Albion, Oldham ; Royal Automobile. (O151)

BISSLAND, Emma, Mrs., M.B.E.

BIVAR, Capt. Roderick BELLI-, M.B.E., R.A.F.

BLACHFORD, Lieut.-Col. James Vincent, C.B.E., R.A.M.C.

BLACK, Alexander, M.B.E.

BLACK, Paymaster-Sub-Lieut. Alfred Stephen, M.B.E., R.N.R,

BLACK, Archibald, O.B.E., J.P. Ex-Provost of Oban. (O11892)

BLACK, Archibald Campbell, O.B.E., M.A., LL.B., *b.* 31 Dec. 1877 ; *s.* of Archibald Campbell Black, of Glasgow ; *m.* Charlotte Wyllie, *d.* of Sir Thomas Mason, of Glasgow. *Educ. :* Albany Academy ; Glasgow University. Advocate. *War Work :* Captain and Adjutant 2/7th Batt. Royal Scots ; attached War Office, April, 1917 ; attached Ministry of National Service, Oct. 1917, to 31 Dec. 1918 ; relinquished Commission with rank of Captain, May, 1919. *Address :* 61, Great King St., Edinburgh. *Clubs :* University and Scottish Conservative ; Caledonian, London. (O152)

BLACK, Charles William, Senior, M.B.E.

BLACK, Dora Winifred, M.B.E.

BLACK, Major George Cumine Strahan, O.B.E.

BLACK, Major Gordon Boyes, M.B.E.

BLACK, Lieut. Graeme Morrison, M.B.E.

BLACK, Herbert Duncan, M.B.E. Rendered patriotic services. (M10306)

BLACK, Lieut. Hutcheson Campbell, O.B.E., R.E.

BLACK, Rev. James, O.B.E., *b.* 8 Nov. 1879 ; *s.* of James Black, LL.D., of Sheriffston, Elgin ; *m.* Roberta Cecilia (who died) *d.* of R. C. Williamson of Edinburgh. *Educ. :* Elgin Academy ; Universities of Aberdeen and Edinburgh. Chaplain, Church of Scotland, Simla, India (formerly Minister of the parish of Balfron, Sterlingshire). *War Work :* Hon. Sec. Order of St. John and British Red Cross Society in India. *Addresses :* The Manse, Simla, India ; Sheriffston, Elgin. *Clubs :* Caledonian (London) ; University (Edinburgh) ; Western (Glasgow) ; U.S. Club (Simla). (O4016)

BLACK, Muriel, Mrs., M.B.E.

BLACK, Major N., O.B.E.

BLACK, Rena Denholm Menzies, M.B.E.

BLACK, William George, C.B.E., LL.D., J.P., *b.* 23 Dec. 1857 , *s.* of George Black, of Glasgow, Solicitor ; *m.* Anna Robertson Black (died 1920), *d.* of Robert Blackie, Publisher, of Blackie & Son, Glasgow. *Educ. :* Glasgow University. A Manager of Glasgow Royal Infirmary and Chairman of its Ophthalmic Committee ; Vice-President of St. Munro's College, Glasgow ; a Director of Glasgow Eye Infirmary ; of Glasgow Deaf and Dumb Institution, and of Association for Relief of Incurables. *War Work :* Chairman of Scottish V.A.D. Committee ; Member of Central Joint V.A.D. Committee, London ; War Executive of Scottish Branch, Red Cross Society ; Member of Advisory Board of the Ministry of Labour as to post-war

Training of Officers (attached to 4th Army Headquarters, Namur) ; Chairman of Selective Committee (Western Lowlands of Scotland) ; Chairman of Officers' Interviewing Board of Ministry of Labour for Glasgow and West of Scotland. *Addresses :* Ardmay, Arrochar, Dumbartonshire ; Ramoyle, Dowanhill Gardens, Glasgow. *Clubs :* Carlton ; Royal Societies' ; 1900 ; University, New Edinburgh ; Royal Scottish Automobile, Glasgow. (C932)

BLACKADDER, David, M.B.E.

BLACKALL, William Walker, M.B.E., R.A.

BLACKBURN, Lieut. Albert Edward, O.B.E., R.N.R.

BLACKBURN, Alfred Charles, M.B.E.

BLACKBURN, Rev. Burdus Redford, M.B.E., *b.* 16 Nov. 1888 ; *s.* of B. R. Blackburn, of Tynemouth. *Educ. :* St. Catharine's Coll., Cambridge. *Address :* The Vicarage, Cleator Moor, Cumberland. (M2978)

BLACKBURN, Lieut.-Col. Charles Bickerton, O.B.E., Aust. A.M.C.

BLACKBURN, Major Lionel Oddy Gaskell, O.B.E., R.A.S.C.

BLACKBURN, Robert, O.B.E., A.M.I.C.E., F.R.Ae.S., *b.* 26 March, 1885 ; *s.* of G. W. Blackburn, of Leeds ; *m.* Jessica, *d.* of Dr. Thompson, of Birmingham. *Educ. :* University of Leeds. Ebgineer ; Managing Director of the Blackburn Aeroplane and Motor Co., Ltd. *War Work :* Responsible for the design, construction, and production of Aircraft ; in particular of Torpedo Aircraft. *Address :* Bowcliffe, Boston Spa, Yorks. *Clubs :* Royal Aero ; West Riding (Leeds). (O9998)

BLACKBURN, Major Thomas, O.B.E., *b.* 27 April, 1882 ; *s.* of the late Francis Blackburn, of Longtown, Cumberland ; *m.* Isabella Johnstone, *d.* of Robt. E. Moffat, J.P., of Canonbie, Dumfriesshire. *Educ. :* Bede College, Durham. Secretary of the Edinburgh and East of Scotland College of Agriculture, 13, George Square, Edinburgh. *War Work :* Joined K.O.S.B. at outbreak of war ; promoted Captain Feb. 1915 ; severely wounded at the Battle of Loos, 25 Sept. 1915, and taken prisoner by the enemy ; right leg amputated ; exchanged to Switzerland May, 1916 ; repatriated to this country, 1917 ; appointed to the War Office (Military Secretary's Dept.) ; promoted Major, Dec. 1918 ; mentioned in despatches, March, 1919 ; invalided from the Service, Jan. 1920, and permitted to retain rank of Major. (O6921)

BLACKBURN, Lieut. Walter James, M.B.E., R.F.A.

BLACKBURN, William Ernest, C.B.E.

BLACKBURNE, Editha Marjorie, Mrs. IRELAND-, M.B.E., *b.* 26 May, 1891 ; *d.* of Henry John Bromilow, of Rainhill, Lancashire ; *m.* John Ireland-Blackburne, *s.* of Col. Ireland-Blackburne, C.B., of Hale Hall, Lancashire. *Educ. :* Privately. *War Work :* Hon. Sec. of the Prisoners of War Department, Liverpool Civic Service League, War Depot. *Address :* Salmon Arm, British Columbia, Canada.

BLACKDEN, Mary Helen Bennett, Mrs., M.B.E.

BLACKDEN, Brig.-Gen. Leonard Shadwell, C.B.E.

BLACKER, George, C.B.E., MD., F.R.C.P., F.R.C.S., *b.* 23 Oct. 1865 ; *s.* of the late General L. Blacker, ; *m.* Shirley Elvina, *d.* of Rev. T. J. Bowen, of Clifton, Bristol. *Educ. :* Cheltenham College ; and University College London. Obstetric Physician University College Hospital ; Lecturer at and Dean of the Medical School. *War Work :* With R.A.M.C., Hospital Ship, M.E.F. and Egypt ; Univ. Lond. O.T.C. ; O. i/c Ext. Military Aux. Univ. Coll. Hospital. *Addresses :* 45, Wimpole Street, W. ; Tarwood House, S. Leigh, Oxon. *Club :* Royal Automobile. (C3073)

BLACKETT, Edward Joseph, O.B.E., M.R.C.S., L.R.C.P., *b.* 1870 ; *s.* of Joseph Byron Blackett, of Green Street, Park Lane, W.1 ; *m.* Rosalie Beatrice Still. *Educ. :* Stonyhurst Coll. and St. George's Hospital. *War Work :* Acted as Medical Officer in charge of the following Hospitals for Officers during the period Aug. 1914, to June. 1919 · H.R.H. Princess Louise's, Kensington Palace ; The Hon. Mrs. Rupert Beckett's, 34, Grosvenor Street, W. 1 ; Bathurst House Hospital, 12, Belgrave Square, S.W. 1 ; Theodore Hospital, Mount Street W. 1 ; Harcourt House, Cavendish Square, W. 1 (Convalescent Hospital). *Address :* 33, South Audley Street, W. 1. *Club :* Public Schools. (O4352)

BLACKETT, Frances Charlotte Isabella, M.B.E., *b.* 19 April, 1870 ; *d.* of John Stephens Blackett, of Inverard, Aberfoyle. *Educ. :* At home and at Oxford. Member of Perthshire Insurance Committee ; Hon. County Sec. Perthshire Red Cross ; Hon. Sec. Perthshire Federation of Nursing Associations. *War Work :* Hon. Sec. Perthshire Branch B.R.C.S. ; Searcher for Missing Enquiry Dept. B.R.C.S. *Address :* Inverard, Aberfoyle, Perthshire, Red Cross Office. Perth. (M154)

BLACKETT, Rear-Admiral Henry, C.B.E., R.N., *b.* 28 Nov. 1867 ; *s.* of late John Charles Blackett, R.N. of Thorpe Lea, Egham (see BURKE'S *Peerage*, Blackett, Bart.) ; *m.* Hon. Pamela Mary Fisher, *d.* of John, 1st Baron Fisher, G.C.B. (see BURKE'S *Peerage*). *Club :* Army and Navy. (C1178)

BLACKETT, Capt. Mortimer Charles, M.B.E.

BLACKETT, Col. William Cuthbert, C.B.E., T.D., LL.D., M.Sc., J.P., D.L., *b.* 18 Nov. 1859 ; *s.* of Dr. Wm. Cuthbert Blackett, M.I.M.E of Durham ; *m.* Anne, *d.* of W. Waddingham, of Durham. *Educ. :* Durham School and Durham University N/C College. President of the Institution of Mining Engineers ; Managing Director Charlaw and Sacriston Collieries Co., Ltd. *War Work :* Commanded 8th Durham Light Infantry ; raised, organised and commanded other battalions ; Military Representative Colliery Recruiting Courts Durham and Northumberland ; served in France in 1918 ;

County Commandant Durham Volunteer Corps. *Address:* Acorn Close, Sacriston, near Durham. *Clubs:* Durham County Club; London Conservative Club. (C1469)

BLACKHURST, Arthur, M.B.E. *War Work:* Army, Medical Dept., War Office. *Address:* 37, Clayton Avenue, Wembley, Middlesex. (M7399)

BLACKLEDGE, Major William Thomas, M.B.E., T.D., M.S., Edin., R.A.M.C. (T.F.), *b.* 1862; *s.* of William Blackledge, of Chorley, Lancashire; *m.* Sarah Elizabeth, *d.* of J. Taylor, J.P., of Coleshill, Flintshire. *Educ.:* Edinburgh Univ. *War Work:* Major 2nd West Lancs. Field Ambulance, Aug. 1914–16; President, Officers' Medical Board, Mersey Defences, 1917–20; President, Army Recruiting Board, 1916–17. *Address:* 2, Somerset Place, Newsham Park, Liverpool. *Club:* Athenæum (Liverpool). (M10261*d*)

BLACKLER, Paymaster-Comm. Leonard, O.B.E., R.N.

BLACKLEY, Lucie Ida, Mrs., O.B.E., *b.* 6 April, 1883; *d.* of Richard Allen, of Cavan; *m.* Travers Robert, *s.* of Travers Robert Blackley, of Dublin. *Educ.:* Cedar House, Slough, Bucks. *War Work:* Organised all the National Schools in Co. Cavan in various war work, knitting, etc.; acted as Hon. Sec. for the entire War Work Committee from Aug. 1914, to closing of this work in 1919. *Address:* Drumbar, Cavan, Ireland. (O9999)

BLACKMAN, Ida Louisa, M.B.E.

BLACKMAN, Major William Stephen, O.B.E., R.M.L.I.

BLACKMORE, Lieut. Alfred Charles, M.B.E., R.A.F.

BLACKMORE, Major Charles Nelson Lindsley, M.B.E.

BLACKMORE, Constance Marie, M.B.E.

BLACKMORE, Capt. Herbert Stuart, O.B.E., R.A.M.C. (O11727)

BLACKSHAW, Major George Neville, O.B.E., R.E.

 BLACKSHAW, James William, M.B.E., *b.* 8 June, 1895; *s.* of Arthur Joseph Blackshaw, of Doncaster. *Educ.:* Doncaster Grammar School. Regional Registrar, Ministry of Pensions, Yorkshire Region H.Q., 7, Boar Lane, Leeds. *War Work:* After discharge from 3rd Batt. K.O.Y.L.I. appointed official in charge Retail Business Licensing Order, East Central Region, Ministry of National Service; subsequently appointed Finance Officer and later Secretary. *Address:* 22, Denison Road, Hexthorpe, Doncaster. (M7401)

BLACKSHAW, John Frank, O.B.E., *b.* 22 May, 1875; *s.* of John Blackshaw, of Marton, Cheshire; *m.* Winifred Mary, *d.* of William Trimmer, of Alton, Hants. *Educ.:* Macclesfield Grammar School and Bangor University, N. Wales. Formerly Assistant Professor West of Scotland Agricultural College, Glasgow; formerly Principal Midland Agricultural and Dairy College, Kingston-on-Soar, Derby; formerly H.M. Inspector Board of Education. *War Work:* Food Production; designed and supervised the carrying out of scheme which resulted in an increased home production of Dairy Produce during and immediately following War. *Address:* The Cottage, Bromsgrove, Worcs.; *Club:* Farmers'. (O11117)

BLACKSTOCK, George, O.B.E.

BLACKSTOCK, Capt. George Gooderham, O.B.E., M.C.

BLACKWELL, Lieut. Cecil Patrick, M.B.E.

BLACKWELL, Major Francis Victor, C.B.E., M.C., *b.* 12 May, 1890; *s.* of John Blackwell, of Shipley, Yorks.; *m.* Elsie Marguerite, *d.* of Benjamin Illingworth, of Bradford. *Educ.:* Belle Vue and Privately. *War Work:* Joined Duke of Wellington's West Riding Regiment, June, 1915; went out to France, 1st Jan. 1916; awarded Military Cross for gallantry battle of the Somme; wounded Oct. 1916; invalided home; promoted Captain and attached Northumbrian Reserve Brigade, June, 1917; sent with British Military Mission to America, Oct. 1917; commanded group of British officers, Camp Dodge, Iowa; attached British War Mission, and afterwards the Canadian Mission in London; was assistant to Director, Victory Loan, 1919. *Address:* 5, St. James's Place, S.W. 1; Underwood, Thames Ditton, Surrey. (C2454)

BLACKWELL, Harry Cooper, M.B.E., *b.* 9 Dec. 1875; *s.* of Henry Blackwell, late Chief Constable of Shrewsbury. *Educ.:* Newport Grammar School, I. of W., and Shrewsbury High Schools. Chief Inspector of the Criminal Investigation Department, Birmingham. *War Work:* Engaged during the war period upon the supervision and registration of aliens, and upon work of a confidential nature for various Government Departments. *Address:* 16, Melton Road, King's Heath, Birmingham. (M1425)

BLACKWELL, Capt. Henry, O.B.E.

BLACKWELL, Hilda, M.B.E.; *d.* of the late Wm. Henry Blackwell, late Rector of Avington, Berks. *Educ.:* Privately. Temporary Health Visitor, County Borough of Brighton, 1902–3; Health Visitor, County Borough of Plymouth, 1903–4; Women Sanitary Inspector, Metropolitan Borough of Southwark, 1904–12. *War Work:* Organiser of Women Patrols under National Union of Women Workers, 1914–15; Temporary Officer, Ministry of Labour Employment Dept., 1915–17; Deputy Principal Officer, Women's Section, National Service Dept., 1917; Private Secretary to Conjoint Secretary, Ministry of National Service, 1917–18; Private Secretary to Secretary, Ministry of National Service, 1918–19. *Address:* 29, Eastern Avenue, Reading, Berks. (M1426)

BLACKWELL, Margaret Brown, Mrs., M.B.E.

BLACKWELL, Thomas Geoffrey, O.B.E., *b.* 28 July, 1884; *s.* of Thomas Francis Blackwell, of Harrow Weald; *m.* Shirley Maud Lawson-Johnston. *Educ.:* Harrow and New College, Oxford. Deputy Chairman, Crosse and Blackwell, Ltd.,

Director Metropolitan Electric Supply Association, Ltd. *War Work:* 1914–16 Admiralty War Staff (Trade Division); 1916–19 Restriction of Enemy Supplies Department, Ministry of Blockade. *Address:* Haresfoot House, Berkhamsted. *Clubs:* Carlton; Union; Burlington Fine Arts; M.C.C.; R. and A. Golf. (O4)

BLACKWOOD, Lieut. Edgar Derwent, M.B.E., R.E.

BLACKWOOD, Capt. Noel Pinkstan O'Reilly, M.B.E., I.R.A.O.

BLADEN, Rev. Albert Percy, O.B.E., A.I.F.

BLADES, Major John, O.B.E., R.E.

BLAGROVE, Col. Henry John, C.B., C.B.E., *b.* 30 June, 1854; *s.* of H. J. Blagrove, of Gloucester Place, Hyde Park, and Cardiff Hall, Jamaica; *m.* Violet, *d.* of Frederick Walton, of Cwm, Aberangell, N. Wales. *Educ.:* Eton and Magdalen College, Oxford. Late 13th Hussars. *War Work:* Afghan War, 1879; Egyptian Campaign, 1882; South African War, 1899; commandant Prisoners of War Camp, Leigh, 1915–17. *Address:* Dowdeswell Court, Gloucestershire. *Clubs:* Army and Navy; Cavalry; New, Cheltenham. (C2081)

BLAIKIE, Lieut. Thomas Hugh Conolly, M.B.E., R.F.A. (T.F.).

BLAIN, Herbert Edwin, C.B.E., M.Inst.T., *b.* 14 May, 1870; *s.* of Arbuthnot Harrisson Blain, of Liverpool and Gt. Grimsby. *Educ.:* Privately. Operating Manager Metropolitan District Railway, London Electric Railway, Central London Railway, City and South London Railway and London General Omnibus Co., Ltd.; Hon. Sec. London "Safety First" Council and British Industrial "Safety First" Association; Hon. Sec. and Member of Council Institute of Transport; Vice-President Industrial League and Council; Member of Technical Committee on London Traffic, etc. *War Work:* Assisted Government in provision of War Motor Transport and Personnel and in the training of motor drivers for the A.S.C. (M.T.), also in the provision of Air Raid Shelter facilities. *Addresses:* 2 & 3, The Sanctuary, Westminster, S.W. 1; Electric Railway House, Westminster Broadway, S.W. 1. *Clubs:* Constitutional and O.P. (C2456)

BLAIR, Capt. Alexander, M.B.E., R.A.O.C.

BLAIR, Atholl, M.B.E.

BLAIR, Comm. David, O.B.E., R.N.R.

BLAIR, Frank Younger, O.B.E.

BLAIR, Capt. John Milligan, M.B.E., *b.* 26 Dec. 1887; *s.* of Sir Robert Blair, LL.D., M.A., B.Sc. (*see* BURKE'S *Peerage*). *Educ.:* Mill Hill School, Middx. The British Union Oil Co. Ltd. *War Work:* Enlisted Aug. 1914; Commissioned Oct. 1914; served N.W.F. India, 1915–16, 1/5th East Surrey Regt.; Mesopotamia, 1917–19, Indian Signal Service; mentioned in despatches and awarded M.B.E. *Address:* 19, Ardwick Road, Hampstead, N.W. 2. (M4846)

BLAIR, Malcolm, M.B.E.

BLAIR, Robert, M.B.E.

BLAIR, Major Reginald Stanley HUNTER-, M.B.E.

BLAKE, Alfred, M.B.E., R.N.

BLAKE, Engineer-Capt. Albert Valentine, C.B.E.; Engineer-Capt. R.N., and Engineer Overseer, Wallsend Slipway Co., and J. S. White & Co. (C2214*c*)

BLAKE, Sir Arthur Ernest, K.B.E., J.P., *b.* 5 Jan. 1869; *s.* of the late Henry Blake, of Chesterfield; *m.* Florence Emily, *d.* of the late John Angrave Howitt, of Nottingham. *Educ.:* St. Mary's House, Chesterfield. Trustee and Hon. Treasurer of the Nottingham Savings Bank. *War Work:* Special Services in connection with War Loans and Savings Banks, Local Services in Parliamentary Recruiting; War Savings; War Aims, Tribunal and Emergency Committees; Special Constabulary, etc. *Address:* West Leake Manor, Notts. *Clubs:* Borough Club, Nottingham; Junior Carlton. (K351)

BLAKE, Capt. Arthur Locke, O.B.E.

BLAKE, Capt. Charles Frederick, O.B.E., R.A.S.C.

BLAKE, Charles Thomas, M.B.E.

BLAKE, Edwin Holmes, C.B.E., F.S.I., M.R.S.I., F.I.S.E., *b.* 1873; *s.* of T. H. Blake, of Reading; *m.* Rosa, *d.* of the late A. W. Parry, A.M.I.C.E., F.S.I., etc., of Reading. *Educ.:* Reading. Secretary of the Auctioneers' and Estate Agents' Institute of the United Kingdom; author of well-known works on Drainage and Sanitary subjects; has contributed a large number of "papers" on Professional subjects to the proceedings of various Professional Institutions such as The Surveyors' Institution, The Auctioneers' and Estate Agents' Institute, etc.; formerly a member of the firm of Parry, Blake and Parry, Civil Engineers and Surveyors, of Westminster. *War Work:* Deputy Chief Live Stock Commission at the Ministry of Food, 1918–20. *Address:* Balham, S.W. (C2457)

BLAKE, Ellen Una, Mrs., M.B.E.

BLAKE, Frank, O.B.E.

BLAKE, Capt. George Shearsley, M.B.E.

BLAKE, Major Harold Henry, O.B.E., R.A.M.C.

BLAKE, Harry, O.B.E., *b.* July, 1855; *s.* of the late Col. E. S. Blake, C.B., Bombay Horse Artillery (now R.H.A.); *m.* Gertrude, *d.* of the late Thomas Bingham. *Educ.:* Privately. Senior Partner of Hogg and Robinson, 34, Leadenhall Street, E.C., Merchants and Shipping Agents to Transport Department, Admiralty; Members of Lloyds. *War Work:* Attending to shipments of Imperial Government Stores and other confidential work connected therewith; his firm have held this post for upwards of 50 years, and he has personally directed this Department for 46 years; his firm are sole Shipping Agents in this capacity for Government Stores (not coal), and have acted since the first and only appointment was made in 1870. *Address:* Craigmyle, Sunningdale, Berks. *Clubs:* Badminton; Royal Automobile. (O1118)

BLAKE, Jack Percy, M.B.E.

BLAKE, Capt. James Thompson, C.B.E.; Capt. R.N., Div. Naval Transport Officer, Folkestone, during Great War, 1914–19 (despatches). (C2244)

BLAKE, Owen Vincent, O.B.E., *b.* 9 Aug. 1864; *s.* of James Blake, of St. Just-in-Roseland, Cornwall; *m.* Emily May, *d.* of Frank Charles Westoby, of London. *Educ.:* Local Schools and privately. Chief Accountant, Foreign Office, London. *War Work:* Financial work in connection with the Foreign Office and Ministry of Blockade. *Address:* 13, Wilton Crescent, Wimbledon (O3624)

BLAKE, Percival, M.B.E.

BLAKE, Percy Francis Ward, M.B.E., *b.* 23 Dec. 1874; *s.* of Horatio Francis Blake, of Ponton Lodge, Sunbury, Middlesex; *m.* Vera Hartley, *d.* of Walter Swain, of Manchester. Master Mariner in the firm of Messrs. John T. Rennie, Son & Co., 4, East India Avenue, London, E.C., subsequently Marine Superintendent for the Harrison-Rennie Line; at present Marine Superintendent for the United States Shipping Board, 8, Grosvenor Gardens, S.W. 1; was 20¼ years in the Royal Naval Reserve, resigned in 1913 with 11½ years seniority as Lieutenant. *War Work:* was appointed Marine Superintendent at Norfolk, Virginia, U.S.A., by the Ministry of Shipping, for the purpose of expediting the dispatch of Convoys from Hampton Roads, also the dispatch of vessels from the Gulf of Mexico ports, and regulating the quantity of bunkers for same, thus ensuring that every vessel carried her maximum of cargo. *Address:* Beechworth, The Green, Wanstead, Essex. (M7405)

BLAKE, Lieut. Wm. Betts, M.B.E., R.A.O.C.

BLAKE, Lieut.-Comm. William Henry, M.B.E., R.N. *War Work:* Attached to H.M.S. "President" for duty in Naval Store Department, Admiralty. (M10244f)

BLAKE, Major William Lascelles Fitzgerald, O.B.E.

BLAKEMORE, Lieut.-Col. Frederick, O.B.E., R.E.

BLAKENEY, Col. William Edward Albemarle, C.B.E.

BLAKER, Sir John George, 1st Bart., O.B.E., Mayor of Brighton, 1895–98, *b.* 1854; *s.* of J. G. Blaker; *m.* Lily, *d.* of Samuel Cowell. *Educ.:* Privately; Sandgate and Brighton. Elected Councillor, 1886; Alderman, 1893. *Address:* The Romans, Stanford Avenue, Brighton. (O1119)

BLAKER, Lieut.-Col. William Frederick, D.S.O. O.B.E. Knight of the Legion of Honour, R.H.A.. and R.F.A.. *b.* 9 April, 1877; *s.* of A. Reichwald, of Beckenham, Kent; *m.* Helen Elisabeth, *d.* of Nathaniel Payne Blaker, of Hurstpierpoint, Sussex. *Educ.:* At home and in France and Germany. *War Work:* Served on the Headquarters Staff of the Indian Cavalry Corps in France from Nov. 1914, to June, 1915; from Feb. 1916 ,to May, 1919, served on the General Headquarters Staff in Mesopotamia; thrice mentioned in despatches. *Address:* Park House, Twineham, Sussex. *Club:* Army and Navy. (O4189)

BLAKEWAY, Evelyn, Mrs. Denys Brook, O.B.E.

BLAKEY, George, O.B.E., J.P., Mayor of Wakefield, *b.* 3 Feb. 1859; *s.* of Joseph Blakey, of Wakefield; *m.* Ada, *d.* of David Grimshaw, of Calverley (Leeds). *Educ.:* Green Coat School, Wakefield. Freeman of London (Feltmakers); Governor of Clayton Hospital, Chairman Housing Committee, Chairman Food Committee, and War Savings Committee, Wakefield; Chairman Disablement and War Pension Committee, 3 years. *War Work:* Chairman of Food, War Pensions, War Savings, and Housing Committees; President War Hospital Fund. *Address:* Pinderfields House, Wakefield. *Club:* County (Wakefield). (O10000)

BLAMEY, Helen Dale, M.B.E., *b.* 30 Oct. 1887; *d.* of James Blamey, of Penryn, Cornwall. *Educ.:* Godolphin School, Salisbury. Late Social Worker, United Girls' Schools' Settlement, 19, Peckham Road, Camberwell, S.E. 5. *War Work:* Late Hon. Sec. Camberwell (A) London War Pensions Committee; Member Camberwell Joint Disablement Sub-Committee; late Hon. Sec. Camberwell (N.) Branch, Soldiers' and Sailors' Help Society; late Hon. Sec. Camberwell and Peckham Division, Soldiers' and Sailors' Families Association. *Address:* Penryn, Cornwall. (M7406)

BLAMEY, Thomas, M.B.E., J.P.

BLAMIRES, Mary, Mrs., M.B.E., *b.* 1 Dec. 1867; *d.* of Thomas Broadbent, of Huddersfield. *Educ.:* Huddersfield Girls' Coll. *War Work:* President of Women's Committee for Soldier's and Sailors; President of Prisoners of War Committee; Member of Belgian Relief Committee. Received, in recognition of late husband's valuable service, the Serbian Order of St. Sava, the Medaille de la Reine Elizabeth. (M1429)

BLANC, William, C.B.E.

BLANCHARD, Edward Cooper, M.B.E., Medal of King Albert of Belgium, *b.* 22 May, 1865; *s.* of Edward Blanchard, late of Boulogne-sur-Mer. *Educ.:* France and Germany. Attached to Continental Department of Office of the Superintendent of the Line, South-Eastern and Chatham Railway, London Bridge Station, S.E. 1. *War Work:* Secretary of Belgian Railways Refugee Sub-Committee, appointed by the Railway Executive Committee to look after Belgian Railwaymen and their families living as refugees in Great Britain and Ireland. (M7407)

BLANCHFLOWER, Comm. Edward Charles, O.B.E., R.N.

BLANCK, Lieut. Sydney Frank, M.B.E., R.A.F., *b.* 1887;

s. of William Blanck, of Acton, W.; *m.* Edith, *d.* of William Howell, of Acton, W. *Educ.:* Westbourne School. Automobile Engineer. *War Work:* Served with British Ambulance Committee, B Convoy, 1914–15; was engineer in charge of workshops of Munition Inventions Dept., Experimental Ground; largely responsible for production of M.I.D. Message Carrying Rocket and other inventions; later was transferred to R.A.F. Experimental Staff on Rockets and Flares. *Addresses:* 126, Chestnut Grove, New Malden, Surrey; 65, Brouncker Rd., Acton, W. (M7408)

BLAND, Albert, M.B.E., 2nd Lieut. Gen. List. (M6959)

BLAND, Lieut. and Qr.-Mr. Frederick Edward, M.B.E., R.I.F.

BLAND, Capt. Maurice George, O.B.E., A.M.I.C.E., A.M.I.E.E., R.E (T.F.)

BLANDFORD, Edward Cornelius, M.B.E., *b.* 10 March, 1860; *s.* of Josiah Blandford, of Sheerness, Kent; *m.* Harriett Jane, *d.* of George Young, of Sheerness. *Educ.:* National School, Sheerness. Foreman of Storehouses and Inspecting Officer, Naval Store Dept., Admiralty. *War Work:* Organisation for Supply of Stores at Naval Bases in England, Ireland, and Scotland, also Foreman of Storehouses at R.N. Store Depot, W. I. Docks, packing and shipment of Stores and subsequently appointed to R.N. Air Service at White City, London, in charge of general supervision in packing, shipment, storing, and erection of fittings for the reception of Aeroplane and Seaplane Spares, Airship Spares, and Motor and Aircraft Engine Spares and Armament and Naval Stores generally in use in the Air Service at home and abroad. *Address:* 70, Seymour Gardens, Ilford, Essex. (M7499)

BLANDFORD, Herbert John George, O.B.E.,

BLANDFORD, Col. Laurence James, C.B.E., T.D., M.D., *b.* 30 July, 1876; *s.* of Col. J. W. Blandford, K.H.P., J.P., of Stockton -on-Tees; *m.* Clara, *d.* of H. Hobson, of Stockton-on-Tees. *Educ.:* Repton, Durham. AD.M.S. South Midland Division T.F.; D.C.M.S. Ministry of Pensions. *Address:* Bleabeck, Worcester. *Club:* Junior Army and Navy. (C1470)

BLANE, Amy Henrietta, Lady, O.B.E.; *d.* of Col. G. F. Leverson, C.B., C.M.G., of Sheldons, Hook, Hants; *m.* Charles Rodney, *s.* of Capt. Rodney Blane, R.N. *War Work:* Y.M.C.A. in France and England. (O11784c)

BLANE, William, C.B.E., *b.* 1864; *s.* of the late Robert Blane, of Galston, Scotland; *m.* 1892, Bertha Annie, *d.* of the late W. H. Roberts, Ch. Surveyor of Inland Revenue, late of Somerset House. *Educ.:* Privately. Mining and Mechanical Engineer; Founder of Blane & Co. (Ltd.), consulting engineers and contractors; has been Advisory Engineer to several Colonial Govts.; author of "Lays of Life and Hope," etc., and many articles on engineering and economics. *War Work:* 1915–17 Senior Technical Asst. in charge of War Office Contracts Branch at Sheffield; 1917–19 Asst. Director of Army Contracts in charge of D.C. 1; Member of Army Contracts Board; War Office Representative on Petroleum Products Committee; Member of Establishment Committee, etc. *Address:* Thruxton, Hants. *Club:* Savage. (C13)

BLANEY. George, M.B.E.

BLANFORD, Harry Richard, O.B.E., *b.* 15 June, 1884; *s.* of William Thomas Blanford, of London. *Educ.:* Dover Coll. and Cooper's Hill. Indian Forest Service in Burma. *War Work:* Timber supply. *Address:* c/o Grindlay & Co., Parliament Street, S.W. *Club:* E.I.U.S. (O9806)

BLANKENBURG, Sir Reginald Andrew, K.B.E., *b.* 25 Dec., 1876; *s.* of the late Charles Andrew Blankenburg; *m.* 10 Jan., 1903, Laura Veryan, *d.* of the late John Truscott, of Fowey, Cornwall. Entered the service of the B.S.A. Co., 1895; Private Sec. to the Administrator of Matabeleland, 1899; Acting Sec. to Administrator of Rhodesia, 1902; transferred to Transvaal Service as Private Sec. to Lieut.-Governor, 1903; Private Sec. to General Botha, 1907; Chief Clerk to Agent-General for the Transvaal, 1907; Chief Clerk in Office of High Commissioner for the Union of S. Africa in London, 1910; Asst.-Sec., 1912; Official Sec., 1918; Acting High Commissioner, 1919. *Address:* 56, Campden Hill Court, W. 8. (K477)

BLANSHARD, Major Ernest Gladstone, O.B.E.

BLANSHARD, Isabella Miller, Mrs., M.B.E.

BLATCH, William Bernard, M.B.E.

BLAXLAND, George Thomas, O.B.E., *b.* 8 Jan. 1871; *s.* of George Blaxland, of Whitstable, Kent; *m.* Daisy Ada, *d.* of Sydney Nicholls, of Whitstable. *Educ.:* Sandwich, Kent Shipmaster, Mercantile Marine. *War Work:* Lieut. Royal Naval Reserve, from outbreak of hostilities to end of 1915, as Second in Command of a seaplane carrier; thence to end of war in command of troop transports. *Address:* Katoomba, 15, Christchurch Road, Melksham. (O10001)

BLAY, Capt. John Augustus, M.B.E.

BLAYLOCK, Lieut.-Col. Harry Woodbarn, C.B.E.,

BLAYLOCK, Robert, M.B.E.

BLECK, Lieut. George Sebastian, M.B.E,

BLEDISLOE, Charles, Lord, K.B.E., J.P., C.C., *b.* 21 Sept. 1867; *s.* of Charles Bathurst, of Lydney Park, Co. Gloucester; *m.* Hon. Bertha Susan Lopes, *d.* of Henry, 1st Lord Ludlow (*see* BURKE'S *Peerage*). *Educ.:* Sherborne; Eton; Univ. Coll., Oxford; Royal Agric. Coll., Cirencester (gold medallist, 1894). Verderer of the Forest of Dean, 1907; M.P. Wilton Division of Wiltshire, 1910–18; M.A., Oxford, 1892; Barrister-at-Law, Inner Temple, 1892; Capt. Royal Monmouthshire R.E. (S.R.); Parliamentary Sec. to Ministry of Food, 1916–17; Chairman of Royal Commission on the Sugar

Supply and Director of Sugar Distribution, 1917–19 ; Silver Medallist, Royal Agricultural Society ; Chairman of the Federation of County Agricultural Committees ; Chairman of the Central Agricultural Advisory Council ; President, Bath and West of England Agricultural Society ; President, British Dairy Farmers' Association ; Deputy President, Central Landowners' Association ; Chairman, Central Chamber of Agriculture ; Chairman of Governors' of Royal Agricultural College ; Chairman of Managing Committee of Rothamsted Experimental Station ; Director, Lloyds Bank. *Addresses :* Lydney Park, Gloucestershire : Teffont Magna, Wilts. *Clubs :* Carlton ; Oxford and Cambridge ; Conservative ; British Empire ; Burlington Fine Arts. (K12)

BLENKARNE, Capt. Harold Morgan, O.B.E., R.A.S.C.

BLENNERHASSET, Nesta Georgie, O.B.E.

BLENNERHASSET, William Lewis, O.B.E. (O117848)

BLENNERHASSETT, Major Arthur, M.B.E., J.P., D.L. (see BURKE'S *Landed Gentry of Ireland*), *b.* 26 June, 1856 ; *s.* of C. I. A. Blennerhassett, of Ballyseedy, Co. Kerry ; *m.* Clare Nesta Richarda, *d.* of the late Desmond John Edmund Fitzgerald, The Knight of Glin, of Glin Castle, Co. Limerick. (see BURKE'S *Landed Gentry of Ireland*). *Educ. :* Harrow. Starter to Turf Club and Irish N.H.S. Committee ; also Inspector of Courses to Turf Club and Irish N.H.S. Committee. *War Work :* Purchasing horses in Australia and the United State of America from 1914 to end of 1918 for the British Government under Remount Department. *Address :* Ballyseedy, Tralee, Co. Kerry, Ireland. *Clubs :* Kildare Street ; and Royal St. George Yacht. (M159)

BLENNERHASSETT, Nesta, Mrs., M.B.E.

BLENKINSOP, John Mathewson, M.B.E. (M10244)

BLEW, Nellie, O.B.E.

BLEWETT, Joseph, M.B.E., *b.* 16 July, 1878 ; *s.* of Joseph Blewett, of St. Day, Cornwall ; *m.* Hilda, *d.* of Capt. F. Peter Webster, of Plymouth. *Educ. :* St. Day Council School ; Redruth Mining School ; Westminster Training Coll. Headmaster, Gunnislake School ; President, Cornwall County Teachers' Association, 1919–20. *War Work :* Hon. Sec. Calstock War Savings Committee ; Member of R.H.S. Panel of Expert Garden Advisers ; Hon. Sec. Calstock War Refugee Committee ; with his wife organised and superintended the only Sanatorium Colony for War Refugees established in England, for which service he received the Medaille du Roi Albert and his wife the Medaille de la Reine Elizabeth from the King of the Belgians. *Address :* Prospect Terrace, Gunnislake, Cornwall. (M7411)

BLEWETT, Martin, M.B.E.

BLEWITT, Ethel Louisa Herries, M.B.E., B.A., Oxon., *b.* 23 April, 1877 ; *d.* of Major-General Charles Blewitt. *Educ. :* Lady Margaret Hall, Oxford. *War Work :* 1 year in twine factory ; 3½ years Welfare Secretary to Colonel-in-charge R.E. Records, Chatham. *Address :* Lechlade, Glos. (M4339)

BLEWITT, Major-Gen. William Edward, C.B., C.M.G. C.B.E., *b.* 24 Sep. 1854 ; *s.* of William Blewitt, of Pinner ; *m.* Harriett Agnes, *d.* of Jame Rigby, of Moss House, West Derby. *Educ. :* Harrow ; R.M. Academy. Lieut. Royal Artillery, 1874 ; Secretary and Member of Ordnance Committee ; Commandant School of Gunnery for Horse and Field Artillery ; Director of Artillery War Office ; G.O. Commanding Southern Coast Defences ; served in South Africa, 1899–1900. *War Work :* G.O. Commanding Portsmouth Garrison, 1914–16. *Club :* Army and Navy. (C2082)

BLIGHT, Major George Elmo, O.B.E., A.I.F.

BLISS, Gertrude Alice, O.B.E., *b.* 1882 ; *d.* of Arthur Bliss. *Educ. :* Streatham Hill High School. *War Work :* Hon. Sec. Streatham Division, County of London Branch British Red Cross Society. *Address :* 43, Gleneldon Road, Streatham, S.W. 16. (O10003)

BLISS, John William, M.B.E., *b.* 21 Aug. 1860 ; *s.* of William Bliss, of Norton, near Daventry ; *m.* Edith Alice, *d.* of John Nicholas, of Daventry. *Educ. :* Daventry Grammar School. General Manager of the Grand Junction Canal Company. *War Work :* In connection with Transport under the Canal Control Committee (Board of Trade). *Addresses :* 21, Surrey Street, Strand, W.C. 2 ; Chesleigh, New Malden, Surrey. (M7413)

BLISS, Capt. Theodore Stephen, M.B.E., R.E. (T.F.).

BLISS, Lieut.-Col. Thomas Gordon Cumming, C.B.E., *b.* 30 Aug. 1869 ; *s.* of Thomas Bliss, of Bengal, India. *Educ. :* St. Charles' College, W. Lieut. and Capt. 1st., 2nd., 3rd. and 4th Batt. Lancashire Fusiliers, 1889 to 1899 ; now serving as Lieut.-Col. and Staff Paymaster in Royal Army Pay Dept. *War Work :* Command Paymaster Base Tsing Tau operations, 1914 ; Staff Paymaster and Regimental Paymaster and Temporary Chief Paymaster York and Preston, 1915–19. *Address :* Strensall, Yorks. (C1471)

BLISS, Capt. William Edward, O.B.E., R.A.S.C., M.T., *b.* 1889 ; *s.* of Francis Alfred Bliss, of Stewkley, Bucks, and Harrow, Middlesex. *Educ. :* Privately. Locomotive Engineer. *War Work :* With Yeomanry from Aug. 1914 to March 1915 ; in France from May 1915 to July, 1919, with various units, including over 2½ years attached Tank Corps ; commissioned from ranks, March, 1915. Mentioned in despatches. *Address :* Hawarden Lodge, Harrow-on-the-Hill, Middlesex. (O5016)

BLOCK, Capt. Bernard Alfred Leopold, O.B.E., *b.* 21 July, 1883. *Educ. :* Privately. *War Work :* Royal Army Pay Department, London, Salonica, Constantinople Dec. 1914, to Oct. 1919 ; mentioned in despatches. (O8677)

BLOCK, Capt. Isidore Jack, O.B.E., M.C., M.B.

BLOCK, Col. Maurice William Palmer, O.B.E.

BLOIS, Lieut.-Col. Eustace William, O.B.E., *b.* 4 Dec. 1877 ; *s.* of the late Lieut.-Col. W. T. Blois. *War Work :* Adjutant, Remount Depot, Swaythling, 1914–16 ; Headquarters Staff, Salonica Force, 1916–18 ; Deputy Assistant Director of Remounts, Eastern and Northern Commands, 1918–19. *Address :* 25, Elvaston Place, London, S.W. *Club :* Naval and Military. (O6923)

BLOMEFIELD, Lieut.-Col. Wilmot, O.B.E., *b.* 26 Nov. 1878 ; *s.* of Sir T. W. P. Blomefield, Bart., C.B., of Windmill House, Lichfield, Staffs. (see BURKE'S *Peerage*) ; *m.* Lella, *d.* of W. A. Hodges, J.P., of The Hill, East Bridgford, Notts. *Educ. :* Repton. Formerly Assistant Traffic Supt., Buenos Aires Western Railway. *War Work :* 2nd Lieut. R.E. (R.O.D.) 1916, Captain (I.W. and D.) 1917, Major 1917, Lieut.-Col. 1918 ; D.A.D. Movements, War Office, 1919 ; Assistant Director of Movements, 1919 ; Chevalier Legion d'Honneur ; mentioned in despatches. *Address :* The Outspan, Gerrard's Cross, Bucks. (O6924)

BLOMFIELD, Joseph, O.B.E., M.D., B.Ch., B.A. (Cantab), *b.* 1 March, 1870 ; *s.* of the late Louis Blumfeld, Branneck, Hampstead ; *m.* Rosamund Sheila, *d.* of Ernest Lehmann, of Queen Street, Mayfair. *Educ. :* University Coll. Schooi, Gonville and Caius Coll. Cambridge, and St. George's Hospital. Senior Anæsthetist to St. George's Hospital ; Lecturer on Anæsthetics, St. George's Hospital Medical School ; Editorial Representative, Anæsthetic Section, Royal Society of Medicine ; Member of Anæsthetics Committee of the British Association. *War Work :* Administration of Anæsthetics at a large number of Officers' Hospitals, including King Edward VII. Hospital for Officers and the Endsleigh Palace Hospital for Officers ; Special Constable 1 year, and member of the Emergency Corps, Royal Society of Medicine. *Address :* 20, Cornwall Terrace, Regent's Park, N.W. *Club :* United University. (O4353)

BLOMFIELD, Lieut.-Comm. Myles Aldington, O.B.E., R.E.

BLOMFIELD, Lieut. and Qr.-Mr. Sydney Thomas, M.B.E.

BLOOD, Geraldine Mary, Hon Mrs., M.B.E. ; *d.* of 14th Baron Inchiquin, of Dromsland Castle, Co. Clare (see BURKE'S *Peerage*) ; *m.* John Blood. *War Work :* Late President of the Co. Clare Branch Soldiers' and Sailors' Families Association ; President of the Co. Clare Prisoners of War Aid Society. *Address :* 11, Abbey Road, St. John's Wood. (M10244h)

BLOOD, Major Joseph FitzGerald, M.B.E., I.M.S. (ret.), *Educ. :* Trinity Coll., Dublin. Hon. Consulting Surg. Birkenhead Boro' Hospital. *War Work :* In charge R.A.M.C. Hospital, Birkenhead. (M10261a)

BLOODWORTH, William Snow, M.B.E., R.N.

BLOOMBURGH, Capt. Joseph Hugh, O.B.E.

BLOOMFIELD, Constance Caldwell, O.B.E., *d.* of Col. Alleyne Fitz-Herbert Fenton Bloomfield, *s.* of Major John Bloomfield of Castle Caldwell, Co. Fermanagh, Ireland. *Educ. :* Privately. Aug. 1914 Founder and Organising Hon. Sec. Temporary Convalescent Homes Advisory Committee (Duke of Sutherland's Scheme ; Dec. 1914 Founder and Hon. Sec. Soldiers' Clubs Association ; July 1916 Founder, Vice-President and Hon. Director Empire Union Club for H.M. British and Overseas Forces. *Addresses :* 11a Lincoln St., Chelsea ; Halfway House, Great Bookham, Surrey. (O156)

BLOOMFIELD, Hilda, Mrs., M.B.E.

BLOOMFIELD, Comm. James, O.B.E., R.N.V.R.

BLOOR, Major Frank Robert, M.B.E., R.A.O.C.

BLORE, Lieut.-Col. Herbert Richard, C.B.E. D.S.O. ; *b.* 1871 ; Lieut.-Col. King 'sRoy. Rifle Corps ; Chitral Relief Force, 1895 (medal with clasp) ; S. Africa, 1899–1902 (despatches thrice, Brevet-Major, Queen's medal with five clasps, King's medal with two clasps) ; Great War, 1914–18 (despatches) (C2083)

BLOSSOM, James, M.B.E., F.C.R.A., F.C.P.A., *b.* 7 June, 1864 ; *s.* of John Blossom, of Sheffield ; *m.* Ellen, *d.* of John Worrall, of Sheffield. *Educ. :* St. Matthias' School and Montgomery Coll., Sheffield. *War Work :* Vice-Chairman, Sheffield Naval and Military War Pensions Committee ; Chairman, Disablement Sub-Committee and Pensions Appeals Sub-Committee ; Member, Enquiry, Finance, Norbury, King's Fund, Civil Liabilities Sub-Committee ; Member, Sheffield War Savings Committees. *Address :* 24, Grange Crescent, Sheffield. (M7414)

BLOUNT, Angela Mary, M.B.E.

BLOUNT, Clara, Mrs. Edward Aston Charles Marie, O.B.E.

BLOUNT, Edith Margaret, M.B.E. ; *d.* of Major Wm. Blount, of Orleton, Hereford. *Educ. :* St. Mary's Priory, Princethorpe, Rugby. *War Work :* From 1914–17 Soldiers' and Sailors' Families Association ; from 1917, War Pensions Committee. *Address :* Cherrymount, Phibsborough, Dublin. *Clubs :* Ladies' ; Army and Navy. (M7416)

BLOUNT, Lieut.-Col. Edward Augustine, C.B.E. ; *m.* 1902, Marcella Caroline Mary, *d.* of F.-M. Sir (Henry) Evelyn Wood, V.C., G.C.B., G.C.M.G., LL.D. (see BURKE'S *Peerage*, Wood, Bt.). Lieut.-Col. R.E. Sers., and an Inspector of Works ; Great War, 1914–19 (O.B.E.). (C1222)

BLOUNT, Edward Charles Aston Marie, O.B.E.

BLOUNT, Mary, M.B.E. ; *d.* of Major Wm. Blount, of Orleton, Herefordshire. *War Work :* Soldiers' and Sailors' Families Association ; Soldiers' and Sailors' Help Society ; War Pensions Committee, Dublin City. *Address :* Cherrymount, North Circular Road, Dublin. (M1433)

BLOW, Henry Charles, M.B.E., R.E.

BLOWEY, Major Henry Francis Tozer, O.B.E., R.A.F.

BLOXAM, Cadet Lieut.-Col. Frank Abel, M.B.E., F.R.B.S., *b.* 3 June, 1867 ; *s.* of Charles Loudon Bloxam, of King's Coll., London, and Royal Military Academy, Woolwich. *Educ.:* King's Coll. School, London, and King's Coll., London. Sec. London Diocesan Council for Welfare of Lads ; London Division Church Lads' Brigade ; London Diocesan Boy Scouts Association ; Seaside Camps for London Working Boys ; Commandant Seaside Camps for London Working Boys ; Hon. Sec. Advisory Council of Brigade Cadets ; Member, Board of Education Juvenile Organisations Committee. *War Work :* Lads' Welfare Work, and Cadet Work. *Addresses :* 213, Albany Street, N.W. 1 ; 55, Chancery Lane, W.C.2. (M7417)

BLOXAM, Henrietta, M.B.E., la Médaille de la Reine Elisabeth, *b.* 8 June, 1857 ; *d.* of Robert W. Bloxam, of Ryde, Isle of Wight. *Educ.:* At home. *War Work :* Director of the Castlebar Hostel for Belgian (middle class) Refugees (opened by the Ealing Branch of the London Society for Woman's Suffrage, of which was Hon. Sec.) from Oct. 1914 to April, 1919, many of the families remaining throughout this period (50 to 70 guests were always in residence) ; Member of the Ealing Central Belgian Relief Committee. *Address :* Haylands, Sutherland Road, West Ealing. (M7418)

BLOYE, George Herbert, O.B.E., *b.* 21 July, 1870 ; *s.* of George Bloye, of Edgbaston, Birmingham. *Educ.:* King Edward VI. School, Birmingham, and Headingley College. Wesleyan Minister, 1894–1910 ; Free Trade Union, Secretary and Lecturer, 1910–1916 ; Lecturer to Garton Foundation, 1913–15. *War Work :* Sec., Headquarters Collections Committee, British Red Cross Society and Order of St. John. *Address :* 81, Ham Road, Worthing, Sussex. (O10005)

BLUMBERG, Capt. Frederick Thomas, O.B.E., R.M., R.A.M.C. (T.F.)

BLUMBERG, Major Henry d'Arnim, O.B.E., T.D., Croix de Guerre, L.R.C.P., L.R.C.S. (Edin.), *b.* 1867 ; *s.* of the late Henry Blumberg, M.D., J.P., of Southport, Lancs. ; *m.* Ella, *d.* of Charles Powell of Southport. *Educ.:* Rossall, and Edinburgh Univ. Physician and Surgeon ; Senior Physician, North of England Children's Sanatorium ; Medical Referee, Southport. *War Work :* Served as M.O. with 7th Batt. King's (L'pool) Regt. ; present at Festubert and Loos, May and Sept. 1915 ; Somme operations with 55th Div. 1916 ; Ypres, 1917, taking part in the Passchendaele advance, July and Sept. 1917 ; Cambrai, Nov. 1917 ; Locon and Givenchy, 1918 ; invalided after Armistice ; twice wounded ; twice mentioned in despatches. *Address :* 37, Church Street, Southport. *Club :* Union (Southport). (O2434)

BLUNDELL, Agnes Mary Frances, M.B.E. ; *d.* of Francis Blundell, of Crosby. *Educ.:* At home. *War Work :* Work Party for Soldiers, Prisoners of War Guild ; management of the Catholic Women's League Hut, Catterick Camp ; installation of Chapel in Scotton Camp. *Address :* Maes Alyn, Mold, North Wales. (M7419)

BLUNDELL, Annie Elizabeth, Mrs., M.B.E.

BLUNDELL, Lieut.-Col. Charles Wilson, O.B.E., *b.* 29 Dec. 1864 ; *s.* of Richard Hemer Blundell, of Birkenhead ; *m.* Annie Kate, *d.* of Lewis John Sydenham, of Plymouth. *Educ.:* Birkenhead. *War Work :* Served with heavy artillery in England and France from Aug. 1914, to Aug. 1919. *Address :* Lexden, Hartley Avenue, Plymouth. (O8748)

BLUNDELL, Harry James, M.B.E.

BLUNDELL, Major Cuthbert Leigh BLUNDELL-HOLLINSHEAD-, O.B.E.

BLUNDELL, Lieut.-Col. Bryan Seymour MOSS-, D.S.O., O.B.E., *b.* 1878 ; *s.* of John Seymour Moss-Blundell ; *m.* Kate Beatrice Home. *Educ.:* Dulwich Coll. and R.M.C. Entered Yorkshire Regt. 1900 ; became Capt. 1906 ; Major 1915 ; S. African War, 1902 (Queen's medal with two clasps) ; Great War, 1914–15, as Brig.-Gen. (despatches) ; is A.A.G. with rank of Lieut.-Col. (O1124)

BLUNDELL, Henry Seymour MOSS-, C.B.E., LL.D., *b.* 6 Dec. 1871 ; *s.* of John Seymour Moss-Blundell, of Tranby Rise, Hessle, E. Yorks. ; *m.* Elizabeth Hilda, *d.* of A. E. Cumberbatch, of Stratton Chase, Bucks. *Educ.:* Rugby School and St. John's College, Cambridge. Barrister-at-Law ; Chief Inspector of Fisheries. *War Work :* Served in Naval Staff, Admiralty. *Address :* Callipers Hall, Chipperfield, Herts. *Club :* Oxford and Cambridge. (C15)

BLUNT, Rev. Arthur Stanley Vaughan, O.B.E., M.A., *b.* 6 Sept. 1870 ; *s.* of the late Richard Frederick Lefèvre Blunt, Bishop of Hull ; *m.* Hilda Violet, *d.* of John Henry Master, J.P., of Petersham, Surrey. *Educ.:* Harrow, and King's College, Cambridge. Chaplain of the British Embassy Church, Paris, 1912. *War Work :* Hon. Chaplain to Forces, Paris Area, 1915–18 ; Senior Chaplain to the Forces, 1918–19 ; Member of the Ambassador's Advisory Committee for Recruiting, Paris ; Hon. Sec., and then Chairman, British Army and Navy Leave Club, Paris. *Address :* British Embassy Church House, 70, Rue Jouffroy, Paris. *Club :* Royal Societies'. (O10006)

BLUNT, Lieut.-Col. Charles Jasper, C.B.E. ; *b.* 1866. Lieut.-Col. R.A.O.C. ; Chitral, 1895 (medal with clasp) ; Great War, 1914–19 (despatches). (C1472)

BLUNT, Lieut.-Col. Conrad Edward Grant, C.B.E., D.S.O., *b.* 21 Feb. 1868 ; *s.* of late Maj.-Gen. Grant Blunt, Governor of St. Helena (*see* BURKE'S *Peerage*) ; *m.* 1900, Aimée, *d.* of Col. Abel Straghan, C.B. Col. Egyptian Army, late R.A.S.C., Director of Supplies, Egyptian Army ; has Order of Osmanieh (3rd Class), Medjidieh (4th Class), and Order of the Nile (2nd Class). (C1371)

BLUNT, Hon. Edward Arthur Henry, O.B.E., I.C.S., *b.* 14 March, 1877 ; *s.* of the late Capt. F. T. Blunt (*see* BURKE'S *Peerage*) ; *m.* Ada, *d.* of the late Paymaster-Commander C. H. Stone, R.N. *Educ.:* Marlborough Coll., and Corpus Christi Coll., Oxford. Census Superintendent, 1910–12 ; Settlement Officer, Basti District, Basti, 1915–18 ; Provincial Director of Civil Supplies, 1918–19 ; Revenue Sec. to Government, U.P., 1919 ; Financial Sec. to Government, U.P., 1920, which post is still held ; Member of Legislative Council, U.P., 1919, and still continues. *War Work :* Recruiting, Basti District, 1918 ; Director of Civil Supplies, 1918–19 ; mentioned in despatches, 1919 (C.-in-C.'s final despatch). *Address :* Dar-ul-Shafa, Lucknow, Oudh ; Waverley Quarters, Naini Tal, U.P. (O8239)

BLUNT, Major Gerald Charles Gordon, D.S.O., O.B.E., R.A.S.C., *b.* 10 June, 1883 ; *s.* of Gerald Henry Blunt, of Springfield Park, Horsham, Sussex. *Educ.:* Sedbergh, and R.M. Coll., Sandhurst. *War Work :* Nov. 1914 to July, 1916, commanded the First Indian Cavalry Supply Column ; Aug. 1916, commanded the 11th Army Corps Ammunition Park Headquarters ; Sept. 1916–20, commanded the Base Mech. Trans. Depot, Northern Lines of Communication, France ; mentioned in despatches four times ; Commander of the Military Order of Avis, conferred by the President of the Portuguese Republic. *Clubs :* United Service ; Royal Automobile. (O5017)

BLUNT, Lieut. Hubert Porter, M.B.E.

BLUNT, Capt. William Frederick, C.B.E., D.S.O., R.N., *b.* 3 Mar. 1870 ; *s.* of F. W. Blunt, of Culcheth Hall, Teddington ; *m.* Laura Mary Grace Katherine, *d.* of Maj.-Gen. H. W. Mawbey, of R.M.A. *Educ.:* Private School. *War Work :* Commanded H.M.S. " Fearless " as Capt. (1st Flotilla at Heligoland, Aug. 1914, despatches, D.S.O.) ; Ditto to Cuxhaven Raid, Dec. 1914 ; Capt. H.M.S. " Jupiter " Red Sea and Suez Canal, 1915–16 ; Capt. H.M.S. " Gloucester " at Jutland, despatches ; Capt. H.M.S. " Berwick " and " Achilles " 1916–18, Atlantic Convoy Service, C.B.E. *Club :* United Service. (C2306)

BLYTH, Alfred Carleton, C.B.E., *b.* 1865 ; *s.* of the late Alfred Blyth, of 38, Westbourne Terrace, Hyde Park, W. ; *m.* 1891, Frances Ellen, *d.* of Richard Everett Rolls. *Educ.:* Univ. Coll. and Sch., London. Civil Engineer, and Managing Director and Ch. Engineer of Hayes and Northolt Filling Factories. *War Work :* Ministry of Munitions. *Address :* San Martin, Buenos Aires. *Clubs :* Royal Automobile; English (Buenos Aires). (C112)

BLYTH, Alice Maud, M.B.E., *d.* of Charles Horatio Day Blyth, of King's Lynn, Norfolk. *War Work :* Statistics, Ministry of Munitions. (M7421)

BLYTH, Charles Edward, M.B.E.

BLYTH, Dora Elizabeth, M.B.E., *b.* 1882 ; *d.* of late Francis C. Blyth, of Belvedere, Kent. *War Work :* Commandant, V.A.D. Auxiliary Hospital. *Address :* Fairfield, Arboretum Road, Edinburgh. *Club :* Ladies' V.A.D. (M7422)

BLYTH, Ethel Jane, Hon. Mrs. Audley, M.B.E., *b.* 16 April, 1881 ; *d.* of the late Right Hon. Sir John Brunner, 1st Bart., D.L., of Silverlands, Chertsey (*see* BURKE'S *Peerage*) ; *m.* Hon. Audley James, 2nd *s.* of 1st Baron Blyth, of Stansted, Essex (*see* BURKE'S *Peerage*). *Educ.:* Roedean School, Brighton. *War Work :* Commandant of the Grange Auxiliary Military Hospital, Chertsey, 1915–19. *Address :* Silverlands, Chertsey. *Club :* Bath.

BLYTH, Lieut.-Col. James, C.B.E., *b.* 27 May, 1869 ; *s.* of late James Blyth, of 7, Hamilton Place. W. ; *m.* Ethel, *d.* of Dr. C. J. Gibb, of Newcastle-on-Tyne. *Educ.:* Eton. *War Work :* Commanded 3rd Batt. Oxford and Bucks Lt. Infantry. *Addresses :* 25, Norfolk St., Park Lane, W. ; and Iver Grove, Iver, Bucks. *Clubs :* Bachelors' ; Wellington. (C1473)

BLYTH, Lieut.-Col. John Dunbar, O.B.E. (ret.), *b.* 13 April, 1889 ; *s.* of the late William Dunbar Blyth, M.A., LL.D., I.C.S., of Bankipore, Bengal, and The Limes, Bayshill Road, Cheltenham ; *m.* Marguerite, *d.* of the late Henry Westlake, of Brimington Hall, Brimington, Derbyshire. *Educ.:* Cheltenham College ; R.M.A., Woolwich. *War Work :* Royal Engineers to 1 April, 1918 ; Royal Air Force to 2 Aug. 1919. *Address :* Glyn Gwy, Rhayader, Radnorshire. (O11952)

BLYTHE, Archibald Lewis, O.B.E.

BLYTHEN, Capt. Stanley, O.B.E.

BOADELLA, Alfred Herbert, M.B.E.

BOAG, Major and Qr.-Mr. Henry, O.B.E.

BOALTH, Victor Hope, C.B.E. Traffic Manager, N.-W. Railway, India. (C1066)

BOAR, William Henry, O.B.E.

BOARD, William John, O.B.E., *b.* 12 May, 1869 ; *s.* of John Board of Weston-super-Mare ; *m.* Ada, *d.* of Henry Parfitt, J.P., of Pontrewydd, Mon. *Educ.:* Private schools. Town Clerk of the City of Nottingham ; formerly Deputy Town Clerk of Cardiff, 1897–1904 ; and Town Clerk and Clerk of the Peace of Rotherham, Yorks., 1904–12. *War Work :* Secretary Nottingham War Relief Committee ; Secretary Belgian Refugee Committee ; Secretary Mayor of Nottingham's Recruiting Committee ; Clerk to Local Tribunal ; Clerk to Emergency Committee ; Joint Hon. Sec. War Pensions Committee ; Member of Notts. Patriotic Committee and War Savings Committee. *Address :* Lucknow Avenue, Mapperley Park, Nottingham. (O1126)

BOASE, Alice Eleanor, Mrs., M.B.E., M.A. ; *d.* of the Most Rev. and Rt. Hon. J. H. Bernard, Provost of Trinity

College, Dublin ; *m.* George Orlebar, *s.* of the late G. W. Boase, of Dundee. *Educ.:* Alexandra School and Coll., Dublin, and Trinity Coll., Dublin. *War Work:* Temp. Clerk in Contraband Dept. and Foreign Claims Office, Foreign Office, 1915–20 ; member of Secretarial Staff to Peace Conference, Paris. *Club:* Lyceum.   (M144)

BOASE, Lieut.-Col. George Orlebar, C.B.E., R.A.; *s.* of the late G. W. Boase, of Dundee ; *m.* Alice Eleanor, M.B.E., M.A. (*q.v.*), *d.* of the Most Rev. and Rt. Hon. J. H. Bernard, Provost of Trinity College Dublin (*see* BURKE'S *Peerage*).
                                                              (C1474)

BOASE, William Norman, C.B.E., J.P., *b.* 17 Oct. 1870 ; *s.* of Wm. L. Boase, of Dundee ; *m.* Mabel Margaret, *d.* of John Leadbetter, of Broughty Ferry. *Educ.:* Fettes College. Linen Manufacturer. *War Work:* Member of the Flax Control Board ; Member of the Empire Flax Growing Committee ; Chairman Scottish Committee of the Flax Control Board ; Chairman Fife Flax Advisory Committee ; Chairman East of Fife Tribunal Advisory Committee, etc., etc. *Address:* The White House, St. Andrews. *Club:* Royal and Ancient ; Caledonian.   (C1100)

BOAZMAN, Capt. Henry, M.B.E.

BOBART, Henry Hodgkinson, M.B.E., F.S.A.A., *b.* 7 Aug. 1864 ; *s.* of Henry Tilleman Bobart, of Leicester ; *m.* Frances Jane Gwynne, *d.* of Rev. Francis Foulkes, of Bawtry, Yorks. Incorporated Accountant ; partner in the firm of Saunders, Bobart & Saunders, Gresham College, Basinghall Street, London, E.C. *War Work:* Chief Transport Officer of the Middlesex Red Cross Ambulance Column (British Red Cross Society), which during the War transferred 11,061 wounded men from Military to Auxiliary Hospitals in the county ; Commandant of the 23rd Middlesex (Men's) V.A.D., which rendered valuable assistance in the transport of wounded and during Air Raids. *Addresses:* Normanhurst, St. Margaret's-on-Thames, Middlesex ; Gresham College, Basinghall Street, London, E.C. *Clubs:* Royal Corinthian Yacht ; City Livery.   (M3531)

BODEN, Annie Sanetta, Mrs., M.B.E.

BODEN, John Smedley, M.B.E. *b.* 17 April, 1871 ; *s.* of Anthony Boden, of South Hampstead ; *m.* Edith, *d.* of Richard Hicks, of Hull. *Educ.:* King's College School, London. Medical Officer. North Finchley Infant Welfare Centre ; Medical Officer, Hornsey School Clinic ; Clinical Assistant, Eye, Ear, Nose and Throat Departments, Gt. Northern Hospital ; Clinical Assistant, Ophthalmic out-patients, Gt. Ormond Street Hospital. *War Work:* Treasurer, Muswell Hill War Supply Depot ; Medical Officer, Alexandra V.A.D. Hospital (attached Edmonton), ; Acting Out-patient Surgeon, Gt. Northern Hospital. *Address:* 2, Methuen Park, Muswell Hill, N. 10. *Club:* Muswell Hill Golf.   (O11792)

BODEN, Oliver, O.B.E.

BODIN, Samuel, M.B.E.

BODY, Lieut.-Col. John, D.S.O., O.B.E. Capt. and T. Lieut.-Col. E. Kent Regt. *War Work:* Mesopotamia, 1915–19 (despatches, D.S.O. with Bar).   (O6578)

BODY, Lieut.-Col. Kenneth Marten, C.M.G., O.B.E., *b.* 1883 ; *s.* of H. M. Body, of Crediton, Devon ; *m.* 1907, Isabel, *d.* of W. Fell Smith, of Deer Park, Honiton, Devon. Major and Brevet Lieut.-Col. R.A.O.C. ; has Order of Crown of Belgium. *Address:* Kidbrook Gardens, Blackheath, S.E.
                                                              (O6926)

BOGGON, Richard Octavius, O.B.E.

BOGGS, Capt. Arthur Beaumont, O.B.E.

BOGIE, Capt. Robert, M.B.E., A. & S.H., *b.* 31 Oct. 1873 ; *s.* of James Stirling Bogie, of Ashton-under-Lyne ; *m.* Elizabeth Robertson, *d.* of David Gillespie, of Culross. *War Work:* With B.E.F. in France until Nov. 1917 ; subsequently employed in Infantry Record Office, Hamilton, and awarded M.B.E. for services rendered there. *Address:* West Heath Cottage, Congleton, Cheshire.   (M4294)

BOGLE, James Cairns, O.B.E., J.P.

BOHAVE, Albert Edward, O.B.E.

BOILEAU, Lieut.-Col. Etienne Ronald Partridge, C.I.E., C.B.E. Lieut.-Col. Indian Army ; Chitral Relief Force, 1895 (medal with clasp) ; N.-W. Frontier of India, 1897–8 (clasps) ; Tibet, 1903–4 (medal) ; Great War, 1914–19 (despatches).   (C3084)

BOLAM, Brevet Lieut.-Col. Robert Alfred, O.B.E., M.D., R.A.M.C. (T.F.).

BOLAND, Henry Patrick, O.B.E.

BOLAND, Capt. Samuel, M.B.E., R.G.A., *b.* 20 May, 1879 ; *s.* of James Boland, of Dublin ; *m.* Elsie Harriet, *d.* of Henry Edwards, of London. *Educ.:* George Heriot's School, Edinburgh. *War Work:* Active Service, France and Belgium ; wounded 14 June, 1916 ; adjutant, No. 2 Siege Artillery Reserve Brigade, Royal Garrison Artillery, 1917–19. *Address:* Crossways Terrace, Acle, Norfolk.   (M5089)

BOLAS, Harold, M.B.E., B.Sc., A.M.I.C.E., A.F.Æ.S., *b.* 24 Aug. 1887 ; *s.* of James Bolas, of Monton, near Manchester. *Educ.:* Victoria University and Owens College. Designer and Chief Engineer, George Parnall & Co., Coliseum Works, Park Row, Bristol. *War Work:* Chief Assistant Technical Adviser, Air Dept., Admiralty, 1914–17 ; Chief Assistant to Head of Designs Branch, Air Ministry, 1917 ; Aircraft Designer, Parnall & Son, Mivart Street, Bristol, 1917–19. *Address:* 7, Windsor Terrace, Clifton, Bristol. *Club:* Royal Aero.   (M7425)

BOLCKOW, Henry William Ferdinand, M.B.E.

BOLDERO, Marjorie Florence, Mrs., M.B.E., *b.* 15 Feb.

1895 ; *d.* of Arthur T. B. Dunn, of Ludgrove, Herts. ; *m.* Harold Esmond Arnison, *s.* of John Boldero, of Frankham, Mark Cross, Sussex. *War Work:* Dec. 1914, Kensington War Depot, to Dec. 1915 ; Dec. 1915, Empire Hospital, Vincent Square, to Aug. 1916 ; Aug. 1916, B.R.C.S., Wounded and Missing Dept., 18, Carlton House Terrace, S.W., to April, 1919. *Address:* 57, Elm Park Gardens, S.W. *Clubs:* Queen's ; Ladies' Empress.   (M7427)

BOLES, Lieut.-Col Dennis Fortescue, C.B.E., M.P., *b.* 1861 ; *s.* of the late Rev. James Thomas Boles, of Ryll Court, Exmouth, and Moyge, Co. Cork ; *m.* 1894, Beatrice Ringrose, *d.* of the late John Lysaght, of Hengrave Hall, Suffolk. Is a J.P. and D.L. for Somerset ; sometime Lieut.-Col. Comdg. a Batt. Devonshire Regt. ; sat as M.P. for W., or Wellington, Div. of Somersetshire (C), July, 1911 to Nov. 1918 ; elected for Taunton Div. of Somerset, Dec. 1918. *Address:* Watts House, Bishops Lydeard, Taunton. *Clubs:* Junior United Service ; Carlton ; Ranelagh ; Royal Automobile ; Arthur's.
                                                              (C1474)

BOLLAND, Arthur Philip, M.B.E.

BOLLARD, Louisa, Mrs., M.B.E.

BOLT, Daniel Roberts, M.B.E., *b.* 1873 ; *s.* of Daniel R. Bolt (Master Mariner), of London ; *m.* Lucy Mabel, *d.* of W. J. Newbegin, of London. *Educ.:* George Green School. Chief Draughtsman, Poplar Borough Council. *War Work:* Hon. Sec., Poplar War Refugees Committee ; voluntary worker for Aldwych Committee for Stepney, Custom House, and North Woolwich districts ; Member 47th V.A.D., Essex. *Address:* 59, Station Road, Leigh-on-Sea, Essex.   (M1433)

BOLT, George, O.B.E., *b.* 10 Feb. 1857 ; *s.* of Robert Bolt, of Belton, Grantham ; *m.* Ida Clare, *d.* of William Henry Lindsey, of Doncaster. *Educ.:* Middlemore House, Grantham. Divisional Superintendent, Northern Division, Great Northern Railway Co., Grantham. *War Work:* In charge of the railway arrangements for working the military traffic at Grantham (Belton Park and Harrowby Camps), Newark, Retford, Bawtry and Doncaster ; also of the traffic to and from the Aerodromes at Wittering, Buckminster, Spittlegate, Harlaxton, Waddington, and Doncaster. *Address:* Dordon Bank, Grantham.
                                                              (O10009)

BOLTER, Henry James, O.B.E.

BOLTON, Arthur Leon, O.B.E.   (O11953)

BOLTON, Charles, C.B.E., M.D., D.Sc., F.R.C.P., F.R.S. *Educ.:* University College, London. Physician to University College Hospital, London. *War Work:* Physician to University College Hospital branch of Millbank Military Hospital. (C3074)

BOLTON, Brevet Lieut.-Col. Charles Arthur, C.B.E., Manchester Regiment, *b.* 3 Jan. 1882 ; *s.* of Charles Watter Bolton, C.S.I. (deceased), Indian Civil Service ; *m.* Ada Violet Emily, *d.* of the late Sir Henry John Jourdain, K.C.M.G. *Educ.:* Marlborough College and New College, Oxford. Officer in H.M. Land Forces ; passed Staff College 1913–14 and held Staff appointments throughout the Great War. *War Work:* B.E.F. France, Aug. to Dec. 1914 ; M.E.F. Gallipoli, Mar. to Sept. 1915 ; B.E.F. France, June to Dec. 1916 ; Salonika E.F. Macedonia, Dec. 1916 to June, 1917 ; E.E.F. Palestine, July, 1917, to Nov. 1918, and until Sept. 1919 ; six times mentioned in despatches, C.B.E ; Commander of the Order of the Redeemer (Greece) and 3rd Class of the Order of the Nile (Egypt). *Address:* c/o Messrs. S. King & Co., 9, Pall Mall, London, S.W. 1. *Club:* United Services.   (C2057)

BOLTON, Lieut.-Col. Edwin, M.B.E., D.L., *s.* of the late J. C. Bolton, of Carbrook, Co. Stirling ; *m.* 12 April, 1888, Elenor Elizabeth, *d.* of Sir John Hatt Noble Barnham, 1st. Bart. of Larbert and Househill, Co. Stirling (*see* BURKE'S *Peerage*). *Address:* Plean, Bannockburn, Co. Stirling.   (M1436)

BOLTON, Capt. Frederick, M.B.E., R.F.A.

BOLTON, Henry Hargreaves, M.B.E., J.P., *b.* 21 June, 1856 ; *s.* of Henry Hargreaves Bolton, of Heightside, New-church in Rossendale, Lancashire ; *m.* Florence Eliza, *d.* of Thomas Allen, The Manor House, Thurmaston, Leicestershire. *Educ.:* Cheltenham College ; Victoria University, Manchester. Acting Partner, Colliery Firm. *War Work:* First Chairman, War Pensions Committee, Rawtenstall ; Member of Military Tribunal, Rawtenstall ; Hon. Lieut.-Col. 3rd Batt. East Lancashire Volunteers ; Treasurer, Belgian Refugees Committee, Rawtenstall ; on numerous committees for treatment and training of discharged and disabled sailors and soldiers. *Address:* Heightside, Newchurch in Rossendale, Lancashire. *Clubs:* Union ; Reform ; Old Rectory (Manchester) ; Farmers' (London).   (M7428)

BOLTON, Engineer-Comm. Richard Edmund Cornforth, D.S.O., O.B.E. Is Engineer-Com.Roy. Indian Marine. *War Work:* Served in E. Africa, 1916–18 (despatches).   (O4414)

BOLTON, Major Samuel James, O.B.E.

BOLTON, Major Wilfrid Nash, O.B.E.

BOLTON, Lieut.-Col. William Kinsey, C.B.E., *b.* 1861 ; *s.* of John Hammersley Bolton ; *m.* 1st, 1881, Jean Morpeth Gullin ; 2nd, 1894, Margaret Ford. *Educ.:* State Schs., Victoria. Lieut.-Col. Australian Forces, Pres. Returned Sailors' and Soldiers' Imperial League, and a Member of Senate, Commonwealth of Australia ; Great War, 1914–15, Comdg. Defended Ports, Victoria, and at Gallipoli. *Address:* Commercial Club, Ballarat, Victoria, Australia.   (C705)

BONALLO, Nina Helen, Mrs., M.B.E., *b.* 11 Oct. 1868 ; *d.* of the late Capt. Sir James Dunbar, 3rd Bart., R.N., of Boath, Nairnshire (*see* BURKE'S *Peerage*) ; *m.* Rev. James Bonallo, B.D., Parish Minister of Auldearn, *s.* of Rev. David Bonallo, Parish Minister of Blackford. *Educ.:* Privately.

Vice-President, Nairnshire Branch of the Scottish Branch of the British Red Cross Society; Hon. Sec., Nairnshire Branch of the Victoria League. *War Work:* Quartermaster of Ivy Bank Auxiliary Hospital, Nairn, from Nov. 1914, to March, 1919. *Address:* The Manse, Auldearn, Nairnshire. (M7429)

BONAR, Major Hew Hunter, O.B.E., R.A.S.C.

BONAVIA, Marie, Mrs. Edgar, M.B.E.

BOND, Comm. Arthur George Hayes, O.B.E., R.N.

BOND, Charles Hubert, C.B.E., M.D., D.Sc. (Edin.), F.R.C.P. (Lond.), *b.* 6 Sep. 1870; *s.* of late Rev. Alfred Bond, T.C.D., of Chipping, Lancs. and Powick, Worcester; *m.* Janet Constance, *d.* of Frederick Robert Laurie, of Worcester. *Educ.:* University, Edinburgh; King's College, London; and Privately. One of H.M. Commissioners of the Board of Control (Lunacy and Mental Deficiency); Emeritus Lecturer in Psychiatry at Middlesex Hospital Medical School; Examiner in Psychl. Med. for Conjoint Board in England and President-Elect of the Medico-Psychol. Association. *War Work:* One of two of the Commissioners of the Board of Control delegated on behalf of the Board to carry into effect, develop and, with the co-operation of Local Authorities, to organise the Asylum War Hospital Scheme, and whose whole-time services were ultimately lent to the War Office for these duties from 1915 to 1920; under this scheme, by the vacation of asylums of their insane patients and by the retention of the staffs and equipment of these institutions, 24 first-rate war hospitals were established in which over 31,000 medical and surgical beds were provided and at which 480,000 soldiers were treated, that is more than one-sixth of the total number of sick and wounded soldiers from all fronts; Medical Adviser to the Home Office Committee for the provision of Internment Camps for Aliens; Acted as Medical Referee at Scotland Yard in doubtful internment cases; Hon. Medical Adviser to the Ministry of Pensions upon the treatment of, and the provision of institutions for, cases of epilepsy in sailors and soldiers. *Addresses:* Commissioner of the Board of Control, Victoria Street, S.W. 1; and Cevenna, Hall Road, Bushey, Herts. *Club:* Union. (C3075)

BOND, Lieut.-Col. Chetwynd Rokeby Alfred, C.B.E. Major and Brevet Lieut.-Col. Indian Army, and Dep. Assist. Director of Movements at War Office; Isazai Expedition, 1892; Dongola Expedition, 1896 (Egyptian medal); N.-W. Frontier of India, 1897–8 (medal with clasp); is Commander of the Military Order of Aviz of Portugal. (C801)

BOND, 2nd Lieut. Cyril Henry Charles, M.B.E., R.A.S.C., C.M.G.

BOND, Maj.-Gen. Sir Francis George, K.B.E., C.B., C.M.G. (late R.E.), *b.* 10 Aug. 1856; *s.* of Rev. Frederick H. Bond, of Marlborough; *m.* Alice Maud, *d.* of W. Vivian, of 15, Bolton Gardens, London, S.W. *Educ.:* Marlborough and Woolwich. Commissioned R.E. 1876; Adjutant R.E. troops, 1883–87; Bengal Sappers and Miners, 1887–91 and 1896–1901; D.A.A.G. (S. Africa) 1901–2; Commandant Q.O. Sappers and Miners 1902–4; A.Q.M.G. Punjab, 1904–6; D.Q.M.G. India, 1906–8; Director-General Military Works, India, 1908–11; Commanded Southern Brigade, India, 1911–13. *War Work:* Assistant Director of Quartering, War Office, 1914–17; Director of Quartering, 1917–19 (in charge of housing, billeting, etc., of all troops in the United Kingdom and formation of hospitals). *Address:* Stowe, Camberley, Surrey. *Club:* United Service. (K298)

BOND, George Leslie, M.B.E., *b.* 18 Feb. 1891. *Educ.:* Luton Modern School. 1914, Secretary's Office, H.M. Customs and Excise. *War Work:* 1915–19, Principal of the Chemical Division, War Trade Department; 1919–20, Secretary of the Standing Committee on Trusts, Profiteering Act. *Address:* Mill Hill, Middlesex. (M7430)

BOND, Lieut.-Col. James Henry Robinson, C.B.E., D.S.O., *b.* 1871. Lieut.-Col. R.A.M.C., S. Africa, 1899–1902; present at relief of Ladysmith (Queen's medal with six clasps, King's medal with two clasps). *War Work:* Mesopotamia, 1915–18 (despatches). (C103)

BOND, James Ryding, M.B.E.

BOND, John, O.B.E.

BOND, John Robert, O.B.E.

BOND, Mildred Mary, O.B.E., R.R.C.; *d.* of Abraham Bond, of Huntstile, Goathurst, Bridgwater, Somerset. *Educ.:* Weston-super-Mare. Matron, Q.A.I.M.N.S. *War Work:* Queen Alexandra Military Hospital, Millbank, London; Wharncliffe War Hospital, Sheffield; successively Principal Matron Calais, 1st Army, and B.E.F., France. *Address:* Cannington, Bridgwater, Somerset. (O5020)

BOND, Nigel de Mundeville, O.B.E., M.A., *b.* 29 Aug. 1877; *s.* of Nathaniel Bond, of Creech Grange, Dorset (*see* BURKE's *Landed Gentry*); *m.* Dorothy, *d.* of Percival Hambro, of Milton Abbey, Dorset. *Educ.:* Eton, and Magdalen Coll., Oxford. Director, Eyre & Spottiswoode, Ltd.; Deputy Manager, Peabody Donation Fund; Secretary, Oxford University Endowment Fund; Member of the Council and Executive Committee of The National Trust. *War Work:* Contraband Dept., Foreign Office. *Address:* Hatfield Peverel, Essex. *Club:* Union. (O10012)

BOND, Lieut.-Col. Reginald Francis George, O.B.E., R.E., *b.* 15 March, 1868; *s.* of F. T. Bond, M.D., of Gloucester; *m.* Alice Estelle Margaret, *d.* of Col. J. Cowan, of Moffat, Dumfriesshire. *Educ.:* Cheltenham College; R.M.A., Woolwich. Asst. Sec. to the Govt. of India; Deputy Director-General, Military Works, Army Headquarters, India. *War Work:* Served in the East throughout the War, including North West Frontier and Army Headquarters, India, and

Mesopotamia; after the Armistice, organisation of Transport Service, Ministry of Food. *Clubs:* United Service; Caledonian, United Service, Edinburgh. (O10013)

BOND, Major William Cotesworth, O.B.E., *b.* 5 Jan. 1869; *s.* of F. W. Bond, J.P., D.L., of Wargrave Manor, Berks.; *m.* Margaret Helen, *d.* of J. S. Taylor. *Educ.:* Rugby; Trinity College, Cambridge. *War Work:* Joined as 2nd Lieut., A.S.C., 7 Nov. 1916; went to France, 17 Nov. 1916; promoted Capt. 1 Nov. 1917; appointed Assistant Controller of Labour, St. Omer, Andring, and Zeneghem, 17 Mar. 1918, and transferred to Labour Corps; promoted Major, 13 Sept. 1918; Asst. Com. Labour, Abancourt, 3 Nov. 1918. *Address:* Shalesbrook, Forest Row, Sussex. (O5021)

BONE, Wing-Commander Reginald John, C.B.E., D.S.O., R.A.F.; *s.* of Frederick Southall Bone, of Kensington. *Educ.:* Eastman's Naval Academy and H.M.S. "Britannia." Sea-going appointments in Royal Navy till 1909; Submarine Service, 1909–1913; Naval Wing, R.F.C. 1913–19; Royal Air Force, 1919–1920. *War Work:* North Sea, 1914 (including Cuxhaven Raid); Dunkirk, 1915; Ægean, 1915; North Russia, 1918. *Address:* H.Q. No. 3, Group R.A.F. Spittlegate, Grantham. *Clubs:* Junior United Service; Royal Aero. (C2369)

BONE, Major Thomas, O.B.E., R. of O., *b.* 29 Dec. 1879; *s.* of John Bone, of South Shields; *m.* Elsie Nora, *d.* of George William Foote, of Guernsey. *Educ.:* South Shields High School; Royal Veterinary Coll., Camden Town. Lieut., Army Veterinary Corps, May, 1906; Capt., May, 1911; Major on retirement, Nov. 1919. *War Work:* V.O. in charge 27th Bde., R.F.A., 5th Div., 4 Aug. to March, 1915; O.C., 15th Mobile Vet. Section, 8th Div., April to July, 1915; Assist. Director Vet. Services, 5th Div., July, 1915, to Jan. 1918; O.C. No. 1 Veterinary Hospital, Jan. 1918; awards, O.B.E., mentions in despatches, three times. *Address:* Glendale, Southern Rhodesia. (O2966)

BONHOTE, Mary Baxter, Mrs., O.B.E.; *d.* of Rev. C. E. Meeres, of Eastry, Kent.; *m.* John Lewis James, *s.* of Col. John Bonhote, of London. Lecturer, Nat. Health Insurance Bill. *War Work:* War Office, 1915–17; Ministry of Food, 1917–20; Sec., Legal Department; Sec., Orders Committee. *Addresses:* 8, Westbourne Street, Eaton Square, S.W. 1. *Club:* Forum. (O11690)

BONNER, Eveleen Caroline, Mrs., M.B.E., Order of Queen Elisabeth of Belgium; *d.* of the late Frank T. Lewis, of Whitehall Court, London; *m.* George Albert Bonner, Master of the Supreme Court. *War Work:* War Relief Committee, Aldwych; National War Savings Committee, Westminster Canteen, St. Peter's, Eaton Square. *Address:* 78, Ashley Gardens, Westminster. *Club:* Sesame. (M7431)

BONNER, John William Arundel, M.B.E.

BONNER, Lieut. Stanley Abbott, O.B.E., R.E.

BONNER, Lieut.-Col. Thomas William, O.B.E., V.D.

BONNETT, Capt. Claude Herbert Dick, O.B.E., R.A.F.

BONNY, William, O.B.E.

BONNYMAN, Major Francis James Cosmos, O.B.E.

BONNYMAN, 2nd Lieut. John Alexander, M.B.E., late R.A.F.; now Lieut. 3rd Northumberland Brigade, R.F.A.

BONOMI, Lieut.-Col. Joseph Ignatius, C.B.E. Lieut.-Col. (ret.) Roy. Lancashire Regt.; Great War, 1914–19 (despatches). (C1477)

BONSALL, Gertrude Elizabeth, Mrs., M.B.E.; *d.* of J. T. Morgan, J.P., D.L., of Nantcaerio, Aberystwyth; *m.* Hugh Edward, *s.* of John George M. Bonsall, of Fronfraith, Aberystwyth. *War Work:* Raised Detachment, 22 Montgomery, B.R.C.S.; Commandant, Auxiliary Red Cross Hospital, Machynlleth; Head of B.R.C.S. working party, Machynlleth. *Club:* Empress. (M7432)

BONSER, William Frederick, M.B.E.

BONSEY, Harold Robert YERBURGH-, O.B.E., Commandant, J. Div. M.S.C.R., *b.* 27 Nov. 1877; *s.* of the late William Bonsey, Archdeacon and Vicar of Lancaster; *m.* Henrietta Mary, *d.* of Henry Holson Finch, of Goffs Hill, Crawley, Sussex. *Educ.:* The Phibberds, Maidenhead; Forest School, Snaresbrook, Essex. Barrister-at-law, Middle Temple. *War Work:* Metropolitan Special Constabulary since Sept. 1914; Assistant Commander, Dec. 1914; Commander, J, or Hackney Division, June, 1916; Commandant, July, 1919; Commissioner, Military Service Civil Liabilities, Hackney, Islington, and Stoke Newington, Oct. 1916, to May, 1920. *Address:* Upton House, Crawley, Sussex. (O10014)

BONUS, Florence, Mrs., O.B.E.; *m.* Ernest Melvill Bonus. *War Work:* Chairman of Hammersmith Belgian Committee, 1914, to May, 1919. *Address:* 11, Stafford Mansions, Buckingham Gate, S.W. 1. (O10015)

BOOBYER, John Edwards, O.B.E.

BOOKER, Cissie, Mrs., M.B.E.

BOOKER, Capt. George Edward Mussey, C.B.E. Capt. and T. Lieut.-Col. Reserve Regt.; Served in the Great War, 1914–19 (despatches). (C1476)

BOOKER, Lieut. Harry, M.B.E., R.A.F.

BOOKER, Joseph, M.B.E., *b.* 9 May, 1871; *s.* of Frederick Booker, of Westcombe Hill, London, S.E.; *m.* Frances Maud, *e. d.* of Jonathan Crapper, of Ulley Hall, Rotherham. *Educ.:* Kensington School, London; Goldsmiths Institute, London. *War Work:* Engineer Inspector, representing Mechanical Warfare Dept.; in charge at Metropolitan Carriage and Wagon Co., Ltd., Oldbury; responsible for final inspection of all Tanks sent into Commission from the Birmingham area. (M7433)

BOON, John Goodisson, O.B.E., L.R.C.P., L.R.C.S. (Irel.), b. 2 Aug. 1870; s. of the late John Boon, of Bullock, Co. Dublin; m. Olive Dunbar, d. of the late Rev. A. Wood, of Sherborne, Dorset. Educ.: Corrig School, Kingstown, Coleraine; R.C.S. Ireland. M.O. i/c Lady Forester Hospital, Broseley; Cert. Factory Surgeon; M.O. and Public Vaccinator, Broseley District, Madeley Union; M.O. Post Office. War Work: M.O. i/c Lady Forester Civil Auxiliary A. Hospital, Broseley, Shropshire, from Sept. 1914 to April, 1919. Address: Whitehall, Broseley, Shropshire. (O11793)

BOORN, George Stanley, M.B.E.

BOOSEY, Madge, M.B.E.

BOOTH, Albert Joseph, M.B.E.

BOOTH, Alfred Watson, O.B.E.

BOOTH, Lieut. Arthur Newton, M.B.E., R.F.A.

BOOTH, Capt. Charles Henry, M.B.E.

BOOTH, Ernest Witton, M.B.E., A.M. Inst. C.E., b. 12 Dec. 1877; s. of the late Josiah Booth, of Morley, near Leeds; m. Emma Kay, d. of the late John Holder, of Liverpool. Educ.: Morley, near Leeds. Barrister-at-Law, practising at Leeds on the North Eastern Circuit; called to the Bar at the Middle Temple on 2 May, 1917; formerly a civil engineer and surveyor in practice in Manchester. Held appointments as Assistant Engineer to the Corporations of Morley (Yorks), Croydon, and Bolton (Lancs); an Associate (formerly professional associate) of the Surveyor's Institution, and an Associate Member of the Institution of Municipal and County Engineers. War Work: Principally in connection with the Board of Trade, Coal Mines Dept., Household Fuel and Lighting Branch; Divisional Officer in charge of this Branch throughout the West Riding of Yorkshire, and formerly associated with the administration of the Metropolitan Coal Order, 1917–18 winter; during 1916 Acting Deputy Borough Engineer and Surveyor to the Metropolitan Borough of Deptford; and in 1917 Acting Engineer and Surveyor to the U.D.C. of Beddington and Wallington; in these appointments was associated with the works of many other Government departments on work of a special war character. Addresses: No. 9, Park Square, Leeds; 3, Hare Court, Temple, E.C. 4; St. Albans, Apperley Lane, Rawdon, near Leeds. (M7435)

BOOTH, Capt. Erskine, O.B.E.

BOOTH, Frederick Knight, M.B.E., b. 17 March, 1857; s. of Frederick Booth, of Harlesden, London; m. Margaret Annie, d. of Joseph Banister, of Harlesden, London. Educ.: Peckham Day School; King's Coll., London. Senior Surveyor, H.M. Customs and Excise. War Work: Import restrictions, detection of contraband and enemy origin goods. Address: 46, Nicoll Road, Harlesden, N.W.; Custom House, Thames Street, E.C. (M7436)

BOOTH, Frederic Lancelot, O.B.E., M.I.M.E., b. 18 Dec. 1874; s. of Robert Lancelot Booth, of Ashington, Northumberland; m. Isabella Mary, d. of John Charlton, of Ashington. Educ.: Sir Wm. Turner's Grammar School, Coatham, Redcar. Mining Engineer; Manager, Ashington Colliery, Northumberland. War Work: Asst. County Director, V.A.D., Northumberland; Administrator, Ashington V.A. Hospital; Chairman, Ashington Local War Pensions Committee, and a member of Northumberland County Local War Pensions Committee; Rep. of Soldiers' and Sailors' Families Assoc., and Soldiers' and Sailors' Help Society; Chairman, Ashington War Savings Local Committee. Address: The Hawthorns, Ashington, Northumberland. (O10017)

BOOTH, Harry, O.B.E., b. 24 Jan. 1865; s. of Isaac Booth, of Manchester; m. Bertha, d. of William Hall, of Dulwich. Educ.: Turton Hall College, near Leeds; and King's College, London. Irish Land Commission, 1882–83; Board of Trade, 1884–1920; now an Electricity Commissioner appointed under the Electricity (Supply) Act, 1919. War Work: Member of various Committees, including Diversion of Shipping Committee; Contraband Committee; Electrical Services Committee and Electric Power Supply Committee. Address: Electricity Commission, Gwydyr House, Whitehall, S.W. 1. Club: St. Stephen's. (O161)

BOOTH, Henry BENNION-, O.B.E.

BOOTH, John, O.B.E., J.P.

BOOTH, Mary, C.B.E., b. 1885; d. of Bramwell Booth, of London, General of Salvation Army. Educ.: At home. Salvation Army Officer, Divisional Commander, Brighton Division. War Work: Salvation Army with B.E.F. Address: 26, London Road, Brighton. (C933)

BOOTH, Mary Booth, C.B.E., O.B.E.

BOOTH, Maud, M.B.E., b. 4 Aug. 1879; d. of George J. Booth, J.P., of Storrs Hall, Arkholme, Carnforth. Educ.: St. Stephen's College, Clewer, Windsor. War Work: Hon. Sec., S. & S.F.A. (S. Lonsdale Division) from 1914; Hon. Sec., Lancaster Local War Pensions Committee, from July, 1916, to Sept. 1919. Address: Storrs Hall, Arkholme, near Carnforth. (M1442)

BOOTH, Major William Henry, O.B.E., D.S.O., b. 1862; s. of Maj.-Gen. William Booth (formerly R.A.), of Rose Duryard, Exeter; m. 1905, Kathleen Isabel, d. of Sir John Charles Holder, 1st Bt. Educ.: Wellington Coll. Entered the Buffs (E. Kent Regt.), 1882; became Capt. 1893; Major, 1901; ret. 1906; served in S. Africa, 1899–1900 as A.D.C. (despatches, medal); was Railway Transport Officer, 1914, and a Dep. Assist. Director of Railway Transport, 1915–18; is a J.P. for Herefordshire. Address: Brynmelyn, Hay, Herefordshire. Clubs: New (Edinburgh); Army and Navy. (O162)

BOOTHBY, Capt. Francis Stewart Evelyn, O.B.E., D.L.

b. 23 April, 1867; s. of the late Col. Basil Charles Boothby, 95th Regiment; m. Hannah Mildred, d. of the late Robert Swan, J.P., of Lincoln. Educ.: Dover College. Lincolnshire Regiment (reti.) War Work: Secretary Lincolnshire Territorial Army Association. Address: Stonefield House, Lincoln. Club: Flyfishers'. (O163)

BOOTHBY, Comm. Frederick Lewis Maitland, C.B.E., R.N., b. 13 Nov. 1881; s. of Alexander Cunningham Boothby, of St. Andrews, Fife; m. Lady May Katherine Leila, d. of 3rd Earl of Limerick. Educ.: H.M.S. "Britannia." Wing Commander, R.N.A.S. and R.A.F. War Work: Commanded Armoured Car Division, R.N.A.S.; commanded Barrow-in-Furness, Howden Airship Station and Experimental Airship Station, Pulham St. Mary. Address: Overwey, Tilford, near Farnham, Surrey. Clubs: Travellers'; Junior Naval and Military; Royal Automobile; Royal Aero, R.A.F. (C2336)

BOOTY, Capt. Lester Browning, O.B.E. War Work: On Staff of Maj.-Gen. Sir F. W. B. Landon, K.C.M.G., C.B., C.I.Q.M.G.S., War Office; received M.B.E. and was also mentioned for valuable services rendered in connection with the War. Club: Constitutional. (O8749)

BORASTON, Lieut.-Col. John Herbert, C.B., O.B.E., M.A., B.C.L., R.F.A., b. 19 Jan. 1885; s. of Sir John Boraston (deceased), of Ringwood, Beckenham; m. Honor Emily Muriel, d. of Charles Fitzroy Doll, J.P., of Hadham Towers, Much Hadham. Educ.: Malvern, and Merton College, Oxford. Barrister-at-Law; Director of South Suburban Gas Co. War Work: European War, France; Private Secretary to Field Marshal Earl Haig, Feb. 1919 to Jan. 1920. Address: 4, Gower Street, Bedford Square. Club: Oxford and Cambridge. (O1018)

BORG, George, M.B.E., LL.D

BORLAND, Lieut.-Col. James Henry George, O.B.E.

BORLAND, Robert Gordon, M.B.E.

BORLAND, William, M.B.E., R.A.F.

BORLASE, Rev. John Jennings Dingle, M.B.E. B.A., LL.D. b. 10 Feb. 1878; s. of J. W. Borlase, of Devon; m. Anne Adeline, d. of F. F. Eld, J.P., of Seighford, Stafford. Educ.: Sidney Sussex Coll., Cambridge; Trinity Coll., Dublin. Senior Chaplain, Madras Ecclesiastical Establishment. War Work: Chaplain, and organiser of War Funds. Address: Bangalore, S. India. (M6110)

BORLEY, John Oliver, O.B.E.

BORRAJO, Edward Joseph William, M.B.E.

BORRETT, Lieut. Jack Tuthill, O.B.E., R.N.

BORRIE, Capt. David Forbes, O.B.E., R.A.M.C.

BORRIE, Walter, O.B.E.

BORRISSOW, Lieut.-Comm. Charles Kirby, O.B.E., R.N.R.

BORROW, John Richard Travers Eales, M.B.E. (M10374)

BORTHWICK, Albert William, O.B.E.

BORTHWICK, Jemina, O.B.E.

BOSANQUET, Theodora, M.B.E., B.Sc., b. 1880; d. of Frederick O. T. Bosanquet, of Uplyme, Devon. Educ.: Ladies' College, Cheltenham; University College, London. War Work: 1917–18, Editorial Staff, War Trade Intelligence Dept.; 1918–20, Assistant, Ministry of Food; 1920, Asst. Sec., Universities Bureau of the British Empire. Addresses: 38, Cheyne Walk, S.W. 3; Uplyme, Devon. Club: International Women's Franchise. (M3532)

BOSANQUET, Lieut. Thomas Albert Edward James, M.B.E., R.N., b. 9 Nov. 1858; s. of T. Bosanquet; m. Cecilia Irwin Truscot, d. of E. Thomson. Educ.: Tottenham Day College. War Work: Officer of Patrol, Pembroke Dock. Address: 81, Bush Street, Pembroke Dock. (M1444)

BOSTOCK, Adelaide Hannah Eliza Annie, Mrs., M.B.E.

BOSTOCK, Major James, O.B.E., K.O.Y.L.I.

BOSTOCK, Major John Edward, O.B.E., R.E.

BOSTOCK, Capt. Thomas Herbert Geoffrey, O.B.E.

BOSUSTOW, Lieut. John Coulson, M.B.E., D.C.L.I.

BOSWELL, Lieut. Albert Edouard, O.B.E., R.N.R.

BOSWELL, Percy George Hamnal, O.B.E., D.Sc., F.G.S.

BOSWORTH, Major John Thomas, M.B.E.

BOSWORTH, Capt. Laurence Owen, O.B.E., M.C.

BOSWORTH, Lieut.-Col. Samuel Medbury, C.B.E., Capt. and Acting Lieut.-Col. Quebec Regt.; Great War, 1915–19 (despatches). (C1828)

BOTHA, Capt. Gerhardis Maritz, M.B.E.

BOTT, Carl Lotherington, GLEN-, O.B.E., B.A., A.M.I.E.E. Staff Engineer, Grade I., Wireless Telegraphy Staff, H.M. Signal School, Portsmouth. (O11893)

BOTT, Henry, O.B.E., V.D., L.R.C.P.

BOTT, Lieut.-Comm. Leslie Charles, O.B.E., R.N.

BOTT, Olive, M.B.E.; d. of Rev. Richard Bott, of Cotehill Vicarage, Carlisle. Educ.: Englethwaite, Armathwaite, Cumberland. C.O. at Alnwick Camp, Col. Broome Giles, C.B., R.A.M.C.; C.O. at R.E. Camp, Col. J. F. Lister, C.M.G., R.E. War Work: Enrolled Women's Legion, Aug. 1915; enrolled Q.M.A.A.C., Nov. 1917; period of service, 4 years and 4 months. Address: Cotehill Vicarage, Carlisle, Cumberland. (M5092)

BOTTAN, Joseph, M.B.E. (M10375)

BOTTERELL, Percy Dunville, C.B.E., O.B.E.

BOTTERILL, Frank Owen, M.B.E.

BOTTOMLEY, Capt. Clarence Fereday, M.B.E.

BOTTOMLEY, Francis Carr, O.B.E., M.D., b. 1869. Educ.: Giggleswick School; Caius College, Cambridge; St. George's Hospital. Physician, Boscombe Hospital; Commandant, St. John Ambulance Brigade, V.A.D., No. 9 Hants

(Men's). *War Work :* Organised, and was in charge of, hospital transport in Bournemouth, which throughout the war was carried out by the V.A.D. in conjunction with owners of voluntary ambulance ; Hon. Meq. Off. and Chairman of Committee of St. John's V.A.D. Hospital, Bournemouth ; Hon. Physician, Boscombe Military Hospital and Wentworth Lodge Convalescent Hospital for Officers. *Address :* 205, Christchurch Road, Boscombe, Bournemouth. (O10021)

BOTTOMLEY, James Henry, M.B.E., M.N.S., *b.* 8 Nov. 1858 ; *s.* of John Bottomley, of Oldham ; *m.* Elizabeth, *d.* of John Scholes, of Oldham. *Educ.:* Werneth Academy. Conservative Agent for Clapham ; Political Secretary to Sir Arthur Du Cros, Bart., M.P., and Harry Green, M.P. ; National Unionist Central Office, Organising Secretary for the Junior Imperial League ; late Conservative Agent for Newton Division of Lancashire ; the Lancaster Division ; and the Doncaster Division of Yorkshire ; for a great many years Lecturer for Conservative Central Office, National Union of Conservative Associations, Tariff Reform League, Primrose League ; had most active political life ; contested Gateshead-on-Tyne as working men's candidate ; Member of St. Helens Town Council. *War Work :* Chief of Station Staff, Oversea Forces Reception Committee ; Lecturer, War Aims ; Lecturer, Thrift Campaign ; Canvasser for Derby Recruiting Scheme. *Address :* 32, Spencer Road, New Wandsworth, S.W. *Club :* Constitutional. (M7439)

BOTTOMLEY, William Cecil, C.M.G., O.B.E., *b.* 19 Mar. 1878 ; *s.* of the late William Bottomley, of Greenfield, Yorks, and Ashton-under-Lyne ; *m.* Alice Thistle, *d.* of Sir Richard Robinson, of Whitby, Yorks. *Educ.:* Tettenhall College, Staffs. ; Owens College, Manchester ; and Trinity College, Cambridge. Asst.-Sec., Colonial Office. *War Work :* In connection with official duties in the Colonial Office. *Address :* 13, Luttrell Avenue, Putney, London, S.W. (O166)

BOUCHER, Elizabeth Staniforth, Mrs., M.B.E., *b.* 31 Dec. 1844 ; *d.* of the late Rev. J. H. Hext, of Kings Teignton Vicarage, Newton Abbot ; *m.* Alfred Richard, *s.* of James George, of Shedfield, Hants. *War Work :* Treasurer and Secretary of Sailors' and Soldiers' Families Association, Cornwall, during the Boer War and till 1915, since then been Treasurer only. *Address :* Treneau, St. Germans, Cornwall. (M7440)

BOUCHER, Comm. Henry Charles Russel, O.B.E., R.N.

BOUFFLER, Marjorie Minnie, M.B.E., *b.* 9 April, 1893 ; *d.* of George John Bouffler, of 39, Oakfield Road, Stroud Green, N. 4. *Educ.:* Higher Grade Council School, and Commercial School. Personal Clerk to Director of Contracts, Royal Commission on Wheat Supplies, Trafalgar House, Waterloo Place, S.W. 1., since 1916. *Address :* 39, Oakfield Road, Stroud Green, N. 4. (M7741)

BOUGHEY, George Mentith, O.B.E.

BOULDING, Reginald Sidney Henry, O.B.E., B.Sc. (Engineering) B.Sc., A.M.I.E.E., A.C.G.I. ; *s.* of the late Sidney Boulding ; *m.* Janet Alice, *d.* of C. Weldhen, of Mount Hawke, Cornwall. *Educ.:* Dulwich College ; Imperial College of Science and Technology. Physicist on Staff of Admiralty, 1916–19 ; Superintendent Engineer to Submarine Signal Company from 1920. *War Work :* Development of Sound Ranging for naval purposes. *Address :* 35, Leander Road, Thornton Heath, Surrey. *Club :* University of London.

BOULNOIS, Fanny Emma, Mrs., M.B.E. ; *d.* of Peter John Margary, of Devonshire ; *m.* H. Percy, *s.* of William Boulnois, of Gestingthorpe. *Educ.:* Privately. *War Work :* Superintendent of Women War Workers' Canteen, Victoria, Westminster. *Address :* 34, Evelyn Mansions, Westminster, S.W.1. *Clubs :* Ladies' Imperial ; Forum. (M1445)

BOULTER, Capt. Edgar Charles, O.B.E., R.A.S.C., *b.* 21 Sept. 1873 ; *s.* of David Boulter, of Ditchingham ; *m.* Florence Emily, *d.* of William J. Thomas, of Rocheford, Essex. *Educ.:* Bungay, Suffolk. *War Work :* Supplies in France, Aug. 1914 to Dec. 1915 ; O.C. Base Muleteer Depot, Training Establishment ; and O.C. Records from formation of Muleteer Corps until Jan. 1919. *Address :* G.H.Q., Irish Command. (O3021)

BOULTON, Lieut.-Col. Harold, C.B.E., M.B., I.M.S. (C3085)

BOULTON, Capt. Sir Harold Edwin, 2nd Bart., C.V.O., C.B.E. (*see* BURKE'S *Peerage*), *b.* 7 Aug. 1859 ; *s.* of Sir Samuel Bagster Boulton, 1st Bart., of Copped Hall, Crookham Hill Kent ; *m.* Adelaide Lucy, 3rd *d.* of Duncan Henry Caithness Reay Davidson, of Tulloch, Ross-shire (*see* BURKE'S *Landed Gentry*). J.P. West Ham ; M.A. Balliol College, Oxford ; Capt. T.F.R. late Capt. 3rd Batt. Cameron Highlanders and City of London Yeomanry ; K.J. of St. John ; Ovate Bard of Wales, and Chairman and Founder of many Charitable Organizations : Chairman of Burt, Boulton and Haywood, Ltd. ; author of " Skye Boat Song," " Glorious Devon," and many other lyrics ; editor " Song of the North," " Song of Four Nations," etc. ; Hon. Sec. Keats-Shelley Memorial Association. *Address :* Copped Hall, Crookham Hill, Kent ; 58 Great Cumberland Place, W. 1. (C442)

BOULTON, Capt. and Qr.-Mr. James Arthur, O.B.E.

BOUNDY, Elsie Maria, M.B.E. ; *d.* of the late George Langworthy Boundy, of Exeter. *Educ.:* Exeter High School. *War Work :* Mayoress of Exeter's Depot, Devon Prisoners of War ; Hospitality to Troops and Comforts Fund. *Address :* 2, Albany Place, Heavitree Road, Exeter. (M7442)

BOURCHIER, Paymaster Lieut.-Comm. John Arthur Fitz-warine, O.B.E., R.N.

BOURDEAUX, Henry Frank, O.B.E.
BOURDEAUX, John, O.B.E.
BOURKE, Sqdn.-Leader John Patrick, O.B.E., R.A.F.
BOURKE, Hon. Terence Theobald, O.B.E., *b.* 2 April, 1865 ; 4th *s.* of the Earl of Mayo, of Palmerstown, Co. Kildare, formerly Viceroy of India (*see* BURKE'S *Peerage*) ; *m.* Eveline Constance (died 1917), *e. d.* of late Colonel T. W. Haines, of Hasketon Manor, Suffolk (*see* BURKE'S *Landed Gentry*). *Educ.:* Eton. His Britannic Majesty's Consul, Bizerta. *War Work :* Representative of Ministry of Shipping at Bizerta during the war ; gave his services free of any remuneration. *Addresses :* H.B.M. Consulate, Bizerta ; Tunisia, North Africa ; Pekes, Hellingly, Sussex. *Clubs :* White's ; Carlton. (O10023)

BOURN, George, M.B.E.

BOURN, George Frederick, M.B.E., *b.* 11 Nov. 1895 ; *s.* of George Edward Collin Bourn, of Boston, Lincs. *Educ.:* St. Martins-in-the-Fields, Charing Cross. *War Work :* Wounded, 16 April, 1915 ; transferred to War Office Recruiting Staff ; Chief Clerk War Office Recruiting Audit Board ; Chief Assistant to Chief of Registration Dept., Ministry of National Service ; transferred to Home Office. *Address :* 90, Rannoch Road, W. 6. (M7443)

BOURN, Thomas William, M.B.E.

BOURNE, Lieut.-Col. and Qr.-Mr. Frank, O.B.E.

BOURNE, Sir (Henry) Roland (Murray), K.B.E., C.M.G., late Capt. 1st The Royal Scots ; Sec. for Defence, Union of South Africa, *b.* 18 June, 1874 ; *s.* of the late Lieut.-Col. Robert Bourne, J.P., D.L., of Cowarne Court, Herefordshire ; *m.* Lucy Dorothea White. *Educ.:* Radley ; New College, Oxford. *Address :* Stone Cottage, Mecklenenk, Pretoria. *Clubs :* Bath ; Pretoria ; Civil Service (Capetown). (K127)

BOURNE, Lily Anne, Mrs., M.B.E. ; *o.d.* of Frederick Clewlow, of Acton, Staffordshire ; *m.* Thomas Holland, 3rd *s.* of the late Alfred Bourne, of Gnosall, Staffs. *Educ.:* Privately. *War Work :* Assisting to supply surgical appliances in connection with V.A.D., 1914–16 ; Joint Women's V.A.D. Headquarters, 1916–19, as :—Sec. to Lady Oliver, D.B.E., R.R.C., *q.v.* June, 1916, to Nov. 1917 ; transferred as Sec. to the Lady Ampthill, G.B.E., C.I., *q.v.* Nov. 1917, to Sept. 1918 ; transferred to Staff appt., General Service (Home Section), Sept. 1918, to Aug. 1919 ; Head of Clerical section, 1917 ; Assist. Sec. to Joint Women's V.A.D. Committee, 1917–19 ; attached to the V.A.D. H.Qrs., Air Raid Column, Jan. 1917 till demobilisation after Armistice. *Address :* Maidensley, Foston, Derby. (M7444)

BOURNE, Lucie Dorothea, Lady, M.B.E., *b.* 8 Aug. 1885 ; *d.* of Alfred H. White, of the Transvaal, S. Africa (*q.v.*) ; *m.* Sir Henry Roland Murray Bourne, K.B.E., *s.* of the late Lieut.-Col. Bourne, of Cowarne Court, Herefordshire. President of the Defence Forces Aid Funds Committee ; Union of S. Africa. *Address :* Stone Cottage, Pretoria, S. Africa. (M1206)

BOURNE, Thomas Johnstone, C.B.E., M.Inst.C.E., *b.* 1864 ; *s.* of the Rev. Samuel Whitbread, Incumbent of Winfarthing, Norfolk ; *m.* Edith Mary Bridges, of Weston-super-Mare. *Educ.:* St. Edmund's Canterbury and King's College School. Engineer Antofagasta Harbour Works and Persian Railway Syndicate. *War Work :* War Office Representative for the recruitment of the Chinese Labour Corps in China. *Address :* Hascombe,Woking. *Club :* Royal Societies' (C934)

BOURNE, Major Thomas Richard Arter, O.B.E., R.A.S.C. (T.F.)

BOURNE, Lieut.-Col. Walter Fitzgerald, O.B.E., I.A. (retired).

BOURNE, Lieut.-Col. Walter Kemp, O.B.E.

BOUSFIELD, Edith Margaret, Mrs., O.B.E. ; *w.* of the late Rev. Stephen Bousfield. Board of Guardians ; Maternity and Child Welfare, Women's Diocesan Council ; and the voluntary public service. *War Work :* Hon. Administrator of a Washing Scheme for two camps at Grantham ; organised a band of 700 women to wash, also a volunteer band of menders ; numbers washed for at one time reached 25,000 men ; garments washed reached nearly half a million. *Address :* 41, Watergate, Grantham, Lincs. (O10024)

BOUTFLOWER, Capt. Edward Cyril, O.B.E., W. Rid. Regt. (O11728)

BOUTFLOWER, Major Geoffrey, O.B.E., R.A.S.C.

BOUVERIE, Major Humphrey PLEYDELL-, M.B.E.

BOVEY, Lieut.-Col Wilfred, O.B.E.

BOVILL, Lieut.-Col. Carlos, O.B.E., R.A. and R.A.F.

BOWATER, Sir Frederick William, K.B.E., *b.* 8 June, 1867 ; *s.* of William Vansittart Bowater, of Bury Hall, Enfield, Middlesex ; *m.* Alice Emily, *d.* of Joseph Sharp, of Bognor, Sussex. *Educ.:* Privately. Paper maker. *War Work :* Director of Paper to the Ministry of Information. *Addresses :* 39, Hyde Park Gate, S.W. 7 ; and " Copley Dene," Walton Heath, Surrey. *Clubs :* Walton Heath Golf ; Chislehurst Golf ; Gullane Golf ; Constitutional. (K451)

BOWATER, Norman James, O.B.E., B.Sc., *b.* 3 May, 1888 ; *s.* of John J. Bowater, of West Bromwich, Staffs ; *m.* Christine Diana Hardwick, *d.* of Walter Henry Cheetham, M.D., of Guiseley, Yorks. *Educ.:* Birmingham University. Consulting Engineer. *War Work :* Granted commission in H.M. Forces, 5 Nov. 1914 ; proceded to France, July, 1915, and served there continuously until demobilised in July, 1919 ; twice mentioned in despatches, and awarded O.B.E. in *Gazette* of 3 June, 1919. *Addresses :* 40, Westminster Gardens, S.W. 1 ; 28 Hogarth Road, S.W. 5. *Clubs :* Junior Army and Navy ; Roehampton. (O5026)

BOWATER, Sarah Fanny, Lady, O.B.E. ; *d.* of John

Westwood, of Birmingham ; *m.* Sir William, *s.* of William Bowater, of Birmingham. Lady of Grace of the Order of St. John of Jerusalem ; Lady Mayoress of Birmingham, 1909–11, 1914–15. *War Work:* President of Lady Mayoress' War Depot and Prisoners of War Fund. *Address:* Fulford Hall, Warwickshire. *Club:* Three Counties. (O168)

BOWDEN, Edgar Alfred, M.B.E., *b.* 4 June, 1876 ; *s.* of Alderman Bowden, J.P., of Exeter ; *m.* Elizabeth, *d.* of Thomas Greenwood, of Norchway Court, Ashchurch. *Educ.:* Hele's School, Exeter ; Shebbear College, N. Devon. *War Work:* O.C. Exeter Division St. John Ambulance Brigade ; transport and hospital work at Exeter Red Cross Hospitals. (M7445)

BOWDEN, Harry James, O.B.E., R.N.R.

BOWDEN, Hon. Major John, O.B.E., M.I.M.E., A.I.E.E., R.E., *b.* 28 Dec. 1873 ; *s.* of Thomas Bowden, J.P., F.C.A., of Newcastle-on-Tyne ; *m.* Constance, *d.* of Robt. J. O. Hudson, of Newcastle-on-Tyne. *Educ.:* Cranleigh, and Durham College. Engineer. *War Work:* Ministry of Munitions ; Engineer of No. 2 Area developed production of War material in Lancashire, Cheshire, Westmorland, Cumberland and N. Wales ; established National Factories ; assisted Engineering manufacturers to change over from Civil to War productions (Civil O.B.E. for services rendered in this capacity) ; as Deputy Assistant Director of Light Railways under D.G.T., B.E.F., France, designed, constructed and organised central works at Berquette and Beaurainville for maintaining and constructing Light Railway locomotives, rolling stock and other material ; as Lieut.-Col. in command of these works, administered the technical and military operations of six R.E. Companies, labour troops and P.O.W. companies, numbering some 2000 men ; remained in France until after Armistice and returned to the Ministry of Munitions to take up an appointment as Deputy Controller under the Disposal Board. *Address:* 23, Roxborough Park, Harrow-on-the-Hill. (O169)

BOWDEN, Capt. Jonathan Scott, O.B.E., R.A.V.C. (T.F.)

BOWDEN, Joseph, M.B.E.

BOWDEN, Capt. Robert Kenrick CORNISH-, O.B.E., R.E.

BOWDLER, Flight-Lieut. Archibald Penrhyn, O.B.E., R.A.F.

BOWEN, Capt. Albert Stephen, O.B.E., R.A.O.C.

BOWEN, Col. Arthur Winniett, C.B.E. (C1224)

BOWEN, T. Capt. Charles Henry Croasdaile, M.B.E.

BOWEN, Ellen, Mrs., M.B.E.

BOWEN, Capt. Frank Hart, M.B.E.

BOWEN, Lieut.-Comm. Gerald Percival, O.B.E., R.N., *b.* 3 Dec. 1889 ; *s.* of the late Percival Bowen, of Stoke St. Milburgh, Salop ; *m.* Irene Beatrice, *d.* of the Rev. Alfred J. Begbie, M.A. Entered H.M.S. "Britannia," Sept. 1904 ; qualified in Navigation, Nov. 1911. *War Work:* Served as Navigating Officer of H.M.S. "Severn," Senior Officer's Ship, Belgian Coast operations, Oct. to Dec. 1914, and successively as Navigating Officer of H.M. Ships "Paris," "Amphitrite," and "Princess Margaret," in 1st Mine-Laying Squadron, 1915–19 ; Croix de Guerre, and mentioned in despatches, 1918. *Address:* Stenton Lodge Auckland Road, Southsea.

BOWEN, Lieut-Col. James Bevan, O.B.E., R.A.F.

BOWEN, Lieut.-Col. John Francis, O.B.E. R. Berks Regt. Officer of the Order of the Crown of Italy. (O6346)

BOWEN, Thomas, M.B.E., J.P.

BOWEN, William Korff, O.B.E., *b.* 1869 ; *s.* of Major-General G. B. Bowen, H.E.I.C.S., Madras Staff Corps ; *m.* Gertrude Isabella, *d.* of Col. David Adamson, H.E.I.C.S., of Airlie Lodge, Fife. Assist. Sec., The Corporation of Trinity House. *War Work:* General Lighthouse Authority : Admiralty Recommendations. *Address:* Cornwalls, Brentwood, Essex. (O3630)

BOWER, Beatrice Lilian Chivers, O.B.E., *b.* 25 Feb. 1871 ; *d.* of E. C. Bower, of Broxholme, Scarborough. *War Work:* Assist. Sec., Camberwell War Refugee Committee, and other war work. *Address:* 14, Upper Cheyne Row, Chelsea, S.W. (O10025)

BOWER, Artificer-Eng. David, M.B.E., R.N.

BOWER, Elias, M.B.E.

BOWER, Capt. Lancelot Tregonwell Syndercombe, O.B.F.

BOWER, Percival, M.B.E.

BOWER, Major Robert Lister, C.M.G., C.B.E., *b.* 1860 ; *s.* of the late Robert Hartly Bower Lister-Kaye, Bt. (*see* BURKE's *Peerage*) ; *m.* 1893, Annette Norah, *d.* of Henry Head, of Thornhill, Bray, Co. Wicklow. *Educ.:* Harrow. Formerly Major, King's Royal Rifle Corps ; Egyptian War, 1882 ; present at battle of Tel-el-Kebir (medal with clasp, bronze star) ; Soudan Expedition, 1884 ; present at battles of El Teb and Tamai (despatches, two clasps) ; Nile Expedition, 1884–5 (despatches twice, clasp) ; Jebu Expedition, 1892 (medal with clasp) ; Great War, 1914–16 in Egypt as D.A.A.G. ; formerly Resident at Ibadan ; is Ch. Constable of N. Riding of Yorkshire ; has King's Police medal. *Address:* The West House, Thirsk, Yorkshire. *Club:* Naval and Military. (C2460)

BOWER, Thomas Stanley, O.B.E., *b.* 1865 ; *s.* of T. R. Bower, of Southport ; *m.* Alice Maud, *d.* of James Cross, of Burslem. *Educ.:* Heversham. Managing Director, T. R. Bower and Sons, Ltd. ; Director, The Overton Steamship Co. Ltd., The Manchester and North Wales Steamship Co. Ltd., The Stanley Steamship Co. Ltd., and The Prince of Wales Hotel Co. Ltd., Southport. *War Work:* Officer Com. Auxiliary Military Hospital, Frodsham (190 Beds) ; Chairman, Frodsham Advisory Committee ; Leader, Frodsham Special Constabulary.

Address: Overton Hall, Frodsham, Cheshire. *Clubs:* Empire, London ; Union, Southport ; Cotton, Liverpool ; Formby Golf. (O1133)

BOWERBANK, Major Frederick Thompson, O.B.E., M.C., M.D.

BOWERS, Frederick Gatus, O.B.E., A.C.A., *b.* 19 Oct. 1882 ; *s.* of Thomas Frederick Bowers, of Westcliff-on-Sea ; *m.* Carrie Isabel, *d.* of Henry J. Smith, of Eltham, Kent. *Educ.:* Bancroft's School ; and London University (London School of Economics). Chartered Accountant, formerly Associate of the Institute of Municipal Treasurers and Accountants, now Accountant-General of the Ministry of Labour. *War Work:* First, Assistant Director of Munitions Finance, later Controller of Explosives Finance and Contracts, Ministry of Munitions. *Address:* 68, Burlington Avenue, Kew Gardens, Surrey. (O170)

BOWERS, Major John, M.B.E., *b.* 17 Dec. 1858 ; *s.* of Isaac Bowers, of Wicken, Cambs. ; *m.* Mary Hope, *d.* of James Campbell Fraser, of Dunmore, Argyllshire. *Educ.:* Privately. South Africa, 1879 ; Zululand, Battle of Ginginhlovo, and relief of Etshowe (medal with clasp) ; Egyptian Expedition, 1882, reconnaissance of Ramleh ; affair at Tel-el-Mahuta ; action at Kassassin, and battle of Tel-el-Kebir (Bronze Star, medal with clasp) ; South African War, 1899–1900, on Staff ; operations in the Orange Free State, Feb. to May, 1900, including operations at Paardeberg (17 to 26 Feb.) ; actions at Poplar Grove, Dreifontein, Vet River (5 and 6 May), and Zand River ; operations in the Transvaal, in May and June, 1900 including actions near Johannesburg and Pretoria ; operations in Transvaal east of Pretoria, July to 29 Nov. 1900, including action at Belfast (26 and 27 Aug.) ; despatches, *London Gazette*, 16 April, 1901 ; Queen's medal with 5 clasps. *War Work:* Main Supply Depot, Northampton, Aug. 1914 to May, 1917 ; War Office, May 1917 to May, 1919 ; 3 times mentioned in despatches. *Address:* Ingleside, Lynton, North Devon. *Club:* Primrose. (M5093)

BOWERS, Lieut.-Col. Maunsell, O.B.E., *b.* 27 Dec. 1852 ; *s.* of Capt. A. M. A. Bowers, of 37th Regiment ; *m.* Catherine Georgiana, *d.* of George Thornhill, of Diddington, Buckden, Hunts. *Educ.:* Harrow and Sandhurst. Served in the 5th Dragoon Guards from 1872–97 ; commanded the Regiment from 1893–97. *War Work:* Recruiting Officer in charge of Biggleswade, Beds Sub-area, 1915–17 ; in charge of Bedford Recruiting Area under Ministry of National Service, 1917–19. *Address:* Beeston Grange, Sandy, Beds. *Club:* Naval and Military. (O6929)

BOWES, Elizabeth, Mrs., O.B.E. ; *d.* of William Standring, Lieut. Loyal N. Lanc. Regt. ; *m.* William Wentworth Bowes, *s.* of John Bowes, of Carlisle. *War Work:* Hon. Sec. for 4½ years, The Lancashire Fusiliers Prisoners of War Regimental Care Committee. *Address:* Rose Cottage, Broughton, Near Preston. (O10026)

BOWHAY, Capt. Alfred Benjamin, O.B.E., R.A.V.C.

BOWHILL, Capt. Thomas, M.B.E., F.R.C.V.S., F.R.P.S., *b.* 21 May, 1850 ; *s.* of the late James Bowhill, of Ayton, Berwickshire. *Educ.:* Merchiston Castle School, Edinburgh. Veterinary Surgeon ; Veterinary Officer, Uganda Protectorate, East Africa. *War Work:* Served with Colonial Forces, 1877–79 ; in Boer War, Veterinary Officer 14th King's Hussars, also Veterinary Embarkation Officer, Cape Town ; served on Australian and Canadian Remount Commissions and R.A.V.C., 1915–18. *Address:* Veterinary Department, Kampula, Uganda. (M5095)

BOWIE, Janet, Mrs., M.B.E.

BOWING, Eng.-Comm. John, O.B.E., R.N.

BOWIS, William John, O.B.E., Ph.D., F.I.C., *b.* 21 Sept. 1881 ; *s.* of Thomas Bowis, of Nottingham ; *m.* Caroline Ellen, *d.* of Frederic Gillman, of Lorca, Spain. *Educ.:* Nottingham ; Wiesbaden ; and Zürich University. Technical Director of Boots' Pure Drug Co. Ltd. *War Work:* Closely associated with the late Lieut.-Col. Harrison, C.M.G., in the evolution and manufacture on a large scale of the Box Respirator used by the Allied Armies. *Address:* The Gables, Bridgford Road, West Bridgford, Notts. *Clubs:* Trent Valley Sailing ; Nottingham Reform. (O10027)

BOWLES, Charles William, M.B.E., *b.* 1879 ; *s.* of William Edward Bowles, of Corsham, Wilts. ; *m.* Kathleen Maud Juliet, *d.* of Charles William Goodson, of Oxford. *Educ.:* Holloway, and King's Coll., London. State Engineer, Public Works Dept., Patiala Government, Punjab, India ; Lieut. in 5th Punjab Light Horse, Commanding Officer, Amballa Troop of Light Horse. *War Work:* With Indian Cavalry Division in France, 1914–15 ; Construction of barracks for Indian Infantry, officers' quarters, and works appertaining thereto. *Address:* Patiala, Punjab, India. *Club:* Royal Automobile (London). (M6112)

BOWLES, Elizabeth, M.B.E.

BOWLES, Capt. Ernest, O.B.E., M.B.E.

BOWLES, Lieut.-Col. Ludlow Tonson, O.B.E.

BOWLEY, Alfred, M.B.E.

BOWLY, Major William Arthur Travell, C.B.E., M.C., *b.* 18 April, 1880 ; *s.* of the late Commander J. E. Bowly, R.N., *m.* Florence Winifred Astley, *d.* of Major L. Astley Cooper, of Bath (*see* BURKE's *Peerage*, Paston-Cooper, Bt.). *Educ.:* Winchester and Oxford. Major and T. Lieut.-Col. Roy. Warwickshire Regt. ; Served in the Great War, 1914–19 (despatches). *Address:* Dullatur, Camberley. (C1478)

BOWMAN, Alfred Thomas, M.B.E.

BOWMAN, Capt. George Edward, O.B.E., M.G.C.

BOWMAN, James Henry, M.B.E.

BOWMAN, James Robert, M.B.E.

BOWMAN, Hugh, M.B.E. (M10245a)

BOWMAN, Major Humphrey Ernest, C.B.E., M.A., b. 1879 ; s. of late John Frederick Bowman, of 25, Young Street, Kensington, and Galiamor, Ansaig, Inverness-shire ; m. Frances Guinevere, d. of Col. A. H. Armytage (late R.H.A.), of 17, Cambridge Square, Hyde Park. *Educ.:* Eton, and New Coll., Oxford (B.A. 1902; M.A. 1905). Egyptian Ministry of Education since 1903 ; seconded for service with Sudan Government, 1911–13 ; Director of Egyptian Education Office in U.K., 1913–14 ; Director of Education for Mesopotamia, 1918–20. *War Work:* Served with Royal Fusiliers, Sept. 1914, to May, 1916 ; B.E.F., Nov. 1915, to May, 1916 ; Staff Captain, H.Q. Northern Command, 1916–18 ; India, 1918 ; Mesopotamia Expeditionary Force, 1918–20 ; Captain, Jan. 1915 ; Major, Oct. 1918. *Addresses :* 25, Young Street, Kensington, W. 8 ; Ministry of Education, Cairo, Egypt. *Club:* New University. (C2372)

BOWMAN, Richard Oxley, M.B.E., M.D.

BOWMAN, Thomas Anderson, O.B.E.

BOWMAN, William Turnbull, O.B.E., b. 12 May, 1874 ; s. of Robert Bowman, of Amble, Northumberland ; m. Jessie, d. of Alfred Knowles, of Manchester. *Educ.:* "Burns" Private School, Warkworth ; Rutherford College, Newcastleon-Tyne. General Superintendent Housing Schemes for H.M. Office of Works. *War Work:* Was in charge of the Government Housing Scheme, Well Hall, Woolwich, in 1915, for Arsenal Workers, erected 1300 permanent houses in 10 months ; afterwards District Superintendent with Central Stores Department Ministry of Munitions, Jan. 1916, to June, 1920. *Address :* 26, Butler Avenue, Harrow-on-the-Hill. (O172)

BOWN, Major Herbert, O.B.E., B.Sc. (Lond.), b. 4 Nov. 1887 ; s. of Herbert John Bown, of Irlams-o'-th'-Height, Lancashire ; m. Margherita, d. of Michele Costanzo, of Naples. *Educ.:* Manchester University. *War Work:* Service in Egypt, Mesopotamia, India, Persia ; Brigade Major, Wellington, India ; D.A.A.G. Bushire Field Force, Persia ; D.A.A.G. 8th Lucknow Division, India. *Address :* Lincoln's Inn, London. (O9053)

BOWN, Chief Artificer-Eng. Joseph, M.B.E., R.N.

BOWNAS, Francis Osborne, O.B.E.

BOWNASS, Capt. William Everett, O.B.E., M.C., b. 17 May, 1881 ; s. of John Titterington Bownass, of Windermere. *Educ.:* The College, Colwyn Bay. Accountant to Group of Tea Estates belonging to The Bombay Burmah Trading Corporation, Ltd., in Southern India. *War Work:* Oct. 1914, proceeded to England ; obtained commission in Dec. in R.F.A., 5A Reserve Brigade, Athlone, till end of Feb. 1915, then sent to France and posted to "Z" Battery, R.H.A., 8th Div.; served with "Z" and "O" Batteries till Nov. 1915, when appointed Adjutant of 5th Brigade, R.H.A., in which capacity served till Jan. 1917; then posted to 33rd Division, R.A., as Staff Capt. *Address :* The Bombay Burmah Trading Corpn., Ltd., Mudis Group Office, Mudis P.O., S. India. *Clubs :* Quilon ; Malabar (Calicut). (O5030)

BOWRA, Lieut. Edward Valentine, O.B.E., R.E., b. 23 Oct. 1896 ; s. of C. A. V. Bowra, of Peking, China, and The Bower House, Ightham, Kent. *Educ.:* Cheltenham College, and R.M.A., Woolwich. Royal Engineers. *War Work:* B.E.F., France, 1915–18 ; R.E. Signal Service. *Address :* The Bower House, Ightham, Kent. (O5031)

BOWRING, Sir Charles Calvert, K.B.E., C.M.G., b. 20 Nov. 1872 ; s. of the late John Charles Bowring, J.P., of Forest Farm, Windsor Forest ; m. Ethel Dorothy (C.B.E., 1918), d. of the late G. K. Watts, of Indian P.W.D. *Educ.:* Clifton College. Chief Secretary to the Government of the Kenya Colony and Protectorate. *War Work:* President of the Governor's War Council, 1915–17 ; Acting Governor and Commander-in-Chief, 1917–19. *Address :* Nairobi, Kenya Colony. *Clubs :* Union ; Sports. (K317)

BOWRING, Lieut.-Col. Edward Langley, O.B.E., D.S.O., b. 1882 ; . of the late Sir (Charles) Clement Bowring ; m. 1915, Laura Fraser, d. of the late W. Fraser Biscoe. Entered Worcestershire Regt. 1901 ; became Capt. 1908 ; Major 1915 ; S. African War, 1901–2 (Queen's medal with five clasps) ; Great War, 1914–17 on Staff with rank of Lieut.-Col. (despatches). (O6932)

BOWRING, Ethel Dorothy, Lady, C.B.E., d. of late G. K. Watts, Comm. Public Works, E. Africa ; m. Sir Charles Calvert, K.B.E., C.M.G. (*see* BURKE'S *Peerage*), s. of late John Charles Bowring, J.P., of Forest Farm, Bucks (*see* BURKE'S *Landed Gentry*). *Address :* Nairobi, Kenya Colony. (C386)

BOWRING, Lieut. William, M.B.E., R.A.F.

BOWRON, Lieut. Henry, O.B.E., R.A.S.C.

BOWYER, Lieut. Arthur William, O.B.E.

BOWYER, John Charles, O.B.E.

BOX, Harold Arthur, M.B.E., b. 31 May, 1875 ; s. of the late Rev. Wesley Coke Box, Rector of Polebrooke, Northamptonshire. *Educ.:* Oundle and Durham University (Scholar). At first engaged in teaching, subsequently took up Political and Social Work ; Member of Islington Borough Council, 1906–09. *War Work:* Second-in-charge Motor Ambulance Department British Red Cross Society and Order of St. John of Jerusalem from Sept. 1914, to Dec. 1919. *Address :* 187, Wymering Mansions, Maida Vale, W. 9. *Club:* Public Schools. (M164)

BOXALL, George, M.B.E.

BOYANTON, Ernest, M.B.E., b. 10 Dec. 1879. Shipping Agent. *War Work:* Ministry of Shipping, Temporary Assistant. *Address* 28, Kingscliffe Gardens, Wimbledon, S.W. 19. (M7452)

BOYCE, Adam, M.B.E.

BOYCE, Lieut.-Col. Clement James, O.B.E.

BOYCE, Lieut. Ernest Thomas, O.B.E., R.N.V.R.

BOYCE, Godfrey Hale, O.B.E., b. 26 Sept. 1865 ; s. of Matthias Boyce, of London ; m. Gladys Willicombe, d. of John Nicholas Mason, of London. *Educ.:* Sherborne. Solicitor. *War Work:* Hon. Solicitor to Soldiers' and Sailors Families Association. *Address :* 6, Rosslyn Mansions, London, N.W. 6. *Club:* Devonshire. (O1134)

BOYCE, James Stuart, M.B.E., b. 28 Aug. 1878 ; s. of William Newenham Boyce, of Wandsworth ; m. Florence Louise, d. of — Price, of Ross. *Educ.:* Privately. Director and Ceylon departmental Manager to Wholesale Tea Merchants. *War Work:* Assistant Director Tea Supplies, Ministry of Food ; Sec. Tea Advisory Committee ; Chairman Tea Balloting Sub-Committee ; Sergeant in City of London Police Reserve ; Freeman City of London. *Address :* 27, Leppoc Road, Clapham Park, London, S.W. 4. (M7453)

BOYCOTT, Ethel Aline, M.B.E., b. 1870 : d. of Rev. Edmund Boycott, of North Cove, Suffolk. *War Work:* July to Dec. 1915, Voluntary Hospital, Frinton-on-Sea ; Dec. 1915 to July, 1916, in charge of B.R.C.S. Hostel, at Le Touquet ; from July, 1916, to July, 1919, Commandant in Charge of B.R.C.S. Headquarters in France ; mentioned in despatches, 1918. *Address :* Bungay, Suffolk. *Club:* New Victorian. (M7454)

BOYCOTT, Lota, Mrs., M.B.E., b. 13 Oct. 1865 ; d. of the late Edward Griffith Brewer, of Strawberry Hill ; m. Arthur Norman, s. of Richard Boycott, of Rugeley. *Educ.:* Privately. *War Work:* Commandant V.A.D. Hertford 38 (Bricket House, Red Cross Hospital, St. Albans, 1914–19). *Address :* Hill End, St. Albans. *Club:* V.A.D. Ladies' Club, Cavendish Square, W. 1. (M165)

BOYD, Anne Jamieson, M.B.E.

BOYD, Major Arthur, O.B.E., R.A.S.C., b. 22 May, 1882 ; s. of Rev. Wilam Boyd, of 66, Oxford Terrace, London ; m. Dora, d. of R. S. Mason, of Eynsford, Kent. *Educ.:* St. Pauls. General Secretary, Navy and Army Canteen Board. *War Work:* Rejoined Aug. 1914 ; served in France, mentioned in despatches. *Address :* 23, Southwick Street, W. 2. *Club:* Conservative. (O173)

BOYD, Rev. Arthur Hamilton, O.B.E., M.C., T.D., b. 1869 ; s. of Sir John Boyd, of Maxpoffle, Roxburghshire ; m. Penelope Elizabeth, d. of John George Blencowe, of Bineham, Sussex. *Educ.:* Edinburgh Academy and Edinburgh Theol. Coll. Clerk in Holy Orders. *War Work:* 1914 ; apptd. A.C.F., 4th Class, posted Div. Troops, 3rd Cav. Div., B.E.F., France ; 1915, aptd. Senior Chaplain, 3rd Class, 3rd Cav. Div. ; 1916, aptd. D.A.C.G., 2nd Class, Cav. Corps ; mentioned in despatches, 17 Feb. 1915 ; awarded M.C., 18 Feb. 1915 ; mentioned, 22 June, 1915 ; mentioned, 30 Dec. 1918 ; awarded O.B.E. (Mil.) 1 Jan. 1919. *Address :* Slaughan Rectory, Hayward's Heath, Sussex. *Club:* Junior Army and Navy. (O2439)

BOYD, Major Arthur Octavian, O.B.E., R.F.A., b. 29 Sept. 1881 ; s. of James Boyd, of 4; Moray Place, Edinburgh ; m. Margaret Amy, d. of Rev. A. Bramwell. *Educ.:* Rugby and R.M.A. Woolwich. *Address :* 10, Wilbraham Place, Sloane Street, S.W. 1. *Clubs :* Naval and Military ; Royal and Ancient Golf. (O6633)

BOYD, Capt. Clive Kingsley, O.B.E., T.F., b. 4 Sept. 1885 ; s. of Rev. William Boyd, M.A. ; m. Gladys Rolls, d. of J. Rolls Hoare. Member of London Stock Exchange. *War Work:* Active service abroad from Feb. 1915, to April, 1920 ; with No 48 Divisional M.T. Company throughout. *Address :* Cloonmore, Cuckfield, Sussex. *Club:* Conservative. (O6347)

BOYD, Elizabeth Frances, M.B.E., d. of the Rev. W. L. G. Boyd, of Skelmorlie. *Educ.:* Saint Andrews and abroad (France and Italy). Artist (Painter). *War Work:* War Office. *Address :* 38, Harrington Gardens, S.W. 7. *Clubs :* New Century ; Franchise : Lyceum (Paris). (M166)

BOYD, Gladys Margaret, M.B.E.

BOYD, Harry Robert, C.B.E., b. 13 Feb. 1876 ; s. of late Robert Boyd, of 63, Nevern Square, S.W. *Educ.:* Haileybury and St. Paul's. Engaged in business in Shanghai 1899–1911 (China Medal 1900) ; attached Ministry of Finance, Peking, 1914 (Order of the Excellent Crop) ; Assistant Private Secretary to the Under-Secretary of State, Home Office, 1915–17 (O.B.E.) ; Deputy Assistant Secretary, Ministry of National Service, 1917 ; Assistant Secretary, 1918 (C.B.E.) ; attached War Cabinet (Rehabilitation of Trade Section), 1919 ; Assistant Private Secretary to Secretary of State for the Home Department (Right Hon. E. Shortt, K.C., M.P.) 1919–20. *Clubs :* Conservative : Albemarle ; Travellers'. (C2462)

BOYD, Hugh, M.B.E.

BOYD, Lieut.-Col. John Henry, O.B.E., R.E.

BOYD, Lieut.-Comm. John Mossom, O.B.E.

BOYD, Katherine Faraday, M.B.E.

BOYD, Col. Mossom Archibald, C.B.E. ; Col. in Army ; Great War, 1914–19 (despatches). (C1479)

BOYD, Sqdn.-Leader Owen Tudor, O.B.E., M.C., A.F.C., R.A.F.

BOYD, William, C.B.E., b. 5 April, 1876 ; s. of Robert Findlay Boyd, of Moulmein, British Burmah ; m. Helen, d. of William Bow, J.P., of Glasgow. Shipbroker. *War Work:* Lord Northcliffe's Mission to U.S.A.: thereafter Deputy Director-General, British Ministry of Shipping, New York,

U.S.A. *Addresses:* The Sheiling, Dongan Hills, Richmond County, New York, U.S.A.; 24, State Street, New York City. *Clubs:* India House; Bowling Green; Richmond County. (C935)

BOYD, Alexander William KEOWN-, C.B.E., *b.* 19 June, 1884; *s.* of William Keown-Boyd, of Highgate; *m.* the late Joan Mary, *d.* of Maximilian D. D. Dalison, of Hamptons, Kent. *Educ.:* Merchant Taylors' School and St. John's College, Oxford. Sudan Civil Service, now Oriental Secretary to the High Commissioner for Egypt. *War Work:* Service on the staff of the Governor-General of the Sudan and Sirdar of the Egyptian Army, and later with the High Commissioner for Egypt; twice mentioned in despatches in connection with operations in the Sudan and the Hedjaz. *Address:* The Residency, Cairo. *Club:* Royal Societies'. (C2461)

BOYDELL, Thomas, M.B.E.

BOYER, Albert Edward, M.B.E., M.R.C.V.S.

BOYER, Paymaster-Capt. George Christopher Aubin, C.B.E., *b.* 1862; *s.* of George Boyer, of Beaumont, Jersey; *m.* 1894, Gertrude Elizabeth, *d.* of James Allen, of Battenhurst, Ticehurst. *Educ.:* St. James' Collegiate Sch., Jersey. Accountant Officer R.N.; Paymaster-Capt. Royal Fleet Reserve, Devonport; a Com. of Order of Crown of Italy, and a Chevalier of Legion of Honour; Soudan, 1884–5 (medal); China, 1900 (medal); Dongola Expedition, 1896 (medal); Great War, 1916–18, as Naval Base Agent, Boulogne. *Address:* Windsor Villa, Saltash. (C879)

BOYES, Charles Edward, C.B.E., *b.* 1866; *s.* of Major James F. Boyes. Dep. Resident Commr. in Basutoland; assisted recruiting during Great War. (C2016)

BOYLAND, Sydney Edward, O.B.E.

BOYLE, Sir Alexander George, K.C.M.G., C.B.E., *b.* 1872; *m.* 1898, Sibyl Blanche, *d.* of the late Rev. J. T. Hodgson, of Charterhouse. Appointed Private Sec. to Senior Puisne Judge, Straits Settlements, 1893; Assist. Treasurer, Uganda, 1895; Dep. Treasurer, 1900; Collector, 1902; Assist. Sec., 1902; Sub-Commr., E. Province 1905; acted as Sec. to H.M. Commr. Uganda Protectorate 1906–8; as Ch. Accountant, 1899–1900; as First Assist. Accountant, 1900; Sec. to Govt., 1901–2; as Sub-Commr., E. Province, 1903–4; was Dep. Commr., Uganda Protectorate, 1907; acting Ch. Sec. and Gov. there, 1909–10; Colonial Sec., S. Nigeria, 1910–13; since when he has been a Lieut.-Gov. of Nigeria Protectorate; acted as Gov. thereof, 1911. *Address:* Lagos, S. Nigeria; 24, Montpelier Crescent, Brighton. *Clubs:* Sports'; Bath. (C2017)

BOYLE, Sqdn.-Leader Archibald Robert, O.B.E., M.C., R.A.F.

BOYLE, Capt. Cecil Hefferon, M.B.E.

BOYLE, Comm. Harry Lumsden, C.B.E.

BOYLE, Capt. Henry Edmund Gaskin, O.B.E., M.R.C.S., L.R.C.P., R.A.M.C. (T.F.), *b.* 2 April, 1875; *s.* of Henry Eudolphus Boyle, of Barbados, W. I.; *m.* Mildred Ethel, *d.* of John Wildy. *Educ.:* Harrison College, Barbados; St. Bartholomew's Hospital. Anæsthetist; Anæsthetist and Lecturer on Anæsthetics to St. Bartholomew's Hospital; Anæsthetist to St. Andrew's Hosptial, Dollis Hill. *War Work:* Anæsthetist to the following: St. Bartholomew's Hospital, 1st London General Hospital, and St. Andrew's Hospital, Dollis Hill; and the following hospitals for officers: Queen Alexandra's Hospital for Officers at Highgate, The Duchess of Rutland's, The Countess of Carnarvon's, Lady Evelyn Mason's, Miss Birkett's, Sir John Ellerman's. *Address:* 16, Upper Wimpole Street, W. 1. *Clubs:* West Indian; R.A.C. (O8751)

BOYLE, Irene Florinda Maud, M.B.E., *b.* 1895; *d.* of Edward Louis Dalrymple Boyle (*see* BURKE'S *Peerage,* Glasgow, E.), of 40, Cranley Gds., S.W. 7. *War Work:* Clerk in Foreign Office and to British Delegation, Peace Conference, Paris. *Address:* British Legation, Prague, Czecho-Slovakia. (M7459)

BOYLE, Eng.-Comm. James Charles, O.B.E., R.N.

BOYLE, Wing Comm. Hon. John David, C.B.E., D.S.O., Royal Air Force, *b.* 8 July, 1884; *s.* of 7th Earl of Glasgow; *m.* Ethel, *d.* of Sir Henry Hodges, of Melbourne, Victoria. *Educ.:* Winchester. Officer in H.M. Air Force; Air Staff appointment. *War Work:* Served in France and Italy since outbreak of war. *Clubs:* Travellers'; Junior U.S. (C1888)

BOYLE, Lieut. John Valentine, M.B.E., A.I.F.

BOYLE, Louise Judith, Lady, M.B.E., *b.* 13 April, 1873; *d.* of Reuben David Sassoon, M.V.O., of London and Hove (*see* BURKE'S *Peerage*; *m.* Sir Charles Cavendish Spencer Boyle, K.C.M.G. (who died Sept. 1916), *s.* of Capt. Cavendish Spencer Boyle (*see* BURKE'S *Peerage,* Cork, E.). *War Work:* Lent (jointly with husband till his death), from outbreak until close of war, No 6 Third Avenue, Hove, Sussex, for a Red Cross Auxiliary Military Hospital; carried on at this hospital the work of tracing the Missing and Wounded for British Red Cross Society and Order of St. John. *Address:* Lathkil, 5, Hayne Road, Beckenham. (M7460)

BOYLE, Lieut.-Col. Michael, O.B.E., R.A.M.C., *b.* 1865; *s.* of the late Michael Boyle, of Dundalk; *m.* Mary Theresa, *d.* of the late Alfred J. Le Mesurier, Guernsey. *Educ.:* St. Mary's Coll., Dundalk; Queen's Coll., Cork. *War Work:* O.C. No. 3 C.C.S., France; O.C. 28 C.C.S., Salonika. *Address:* Les Terres, Guernsey. *Club:* Grange, Guernsey. (O3022)

BOYLE, Percy, M.B.E., *b.* 21 June, 1869; *s.* of Neil Boyle, of Enniscorthy, Co. Wexford; *m.* Elizabeth Ann, *d.* of Lamble Hodge, of Manchester. *Educ.:* Dublin. Traffic Agent, G.W.Rly.; Lloyd's Agent; Sub-Commissioner of Pilo-

tage; Vice-Consul for Belgium. *War Work:* Traffic Manager, Channel Islands Service; Sub-Commissioner of Pilotage; Shell-stamper under Ministry of Munitions; Special Constable, etc. *Address:* 1, Grosvenor Road, Weymouth. *Club:* Carlyle. (M7461)

BOYLE, Capt. Walter, O.B.E., R.E. (T.F.).

BOYNE, Margaret Selina, Viscountess, C.B.E., *b.* 11 Aug. 1883; *d.* of Earl of Harewood, of Harewood House, Leeds; *m.* Gustavus William, Viscount Boyne, *s.* of 8th Viscount Boyne, of Brancepeth Castle, Durham. *War Work:* Director Brancepeth Castle Auxiliary Hospital with 126 beds; chairman Durham Women's War Agricultural Committee; County President British Red Cross Society; Lady of Grace St. John of Jerusalem. *Address:* Brancepeth Castle, Durham; Burwarton Hall, Bridgnorth, Shropshire; Belgrave House, Belgrave Square, London. *Club:* Forum. (C2463)

BOYS, Sir Francis Theodore, K.B.E., Principal Director of Meat Supplies, *b.* 12 Feb. 1870; *s.* of Henry Scott Boys, Indian Civil Service, and Ethel Rigand *d.* of Capt. Henry Strong; *m.* Christina Josephine de Snaldt, New Zealand. *Educ.:* Harrow. Seven years on sheep station in N. Zealand; sixteen years in business; eight years managing N.Z. Refrigerating Company, London; two years Principal Director of Meat Supplies, Ministry of Food. *Address:* 84, Iverna Court, W. 8. *Clubs:* Royal Automobile; Christchurch (New Zealand). (K202)

BOYS, Capt. Henry Cecil, M.B.E.

BOYS, Henry Ward, C.B.E.

BOYS, Capt. Herbert Augustus, O.B.E., *b.* 19 June, 1882; *s.* of Rev. W. J. Boys, Vicar of Fordingbridge, Hants. *Educ.:* St. John's School, Leatherhead. Manager of Cotton Factory, Wasta, Egypt. *War Work:* R.A.S.C. in France. *Addresses:* Wasta, Egypt; Fairhaven, Milford-on-Sea. *Club:* United Empire. (O5033)

BOYS, Walter Guy Robert, O.B.E., *b.* 12 Oct. 1890; *s.* of Walter Boys, of London; *m.* Marian Pamela, *d.* of the late Harry Wilding McIsack. *Educ.:* Alleyn's School, Dulwich. Deputy Director of Meat Supplies, Ministry of Food. *Address:* Palace Chambers, S.W. 1. *Club:* National Liberal. (O10030)

BOYTON, Robert Alexander Stewart, O.B.E.

BRABAZON, Lieut.-Col. Hon. Claud Maitland Patrick, O.B.E., Irish Guards (retired), *b.* 16 July, 1874; *s.* of 12th Earl of Meath (*see* BURKE'S *Peerage*); *m.* Kathleen, *d.* of Arthur Maitland, J.P., of Shudy Camps Park, Cambridgeshire. *Educ.:* Wellington College; Trinity Hall, Cambridge. *War Work:* Served in R.F.C., R.N.A.S., and R.A.F., during whole of War; seconded from Irish Guards. *Address:* Old Lodge, Titchfield, Hants. *Clubs:* Travellers'; Royal Cruising; Stansted Working Men's. (O8054)

BRABY, Wallace, M.B.E., *b.* 1864; *s.* of Alfred Braby, of London; *m.* Annie Amelia, *d.* of John Henderson, of Hexham. *Educ.:* University School, Hastings. Hon. Sec. of Edith Cavell Homes of Rest for Nurses; and Secretary of Companies. *War Work:* Associated with Australian and New Zealand War Contingent Associations; Edith Cavell Homes of Rest for Nurses; R.N.A.S. Comforts Fund. *Addresses:* 25, Victoria Street, S.W. 1; 191, Park Road, Kingston-on-Thames. *Club:* Overseas. (M7462)

BRACKENBORO, Lieut. Henry Edwin, M.B.E., R.A.F.

BRACKENBURY, Florence Adelia, Mrs., M.B.E.

BRACKENBURY, Hereward Irenius, C.B.E., *b.* 1871; *s.* of General Charles Brackenbury, R.A.; *m.* Winifred, *d.* of the late Sir Benjamin Browne, D.C.L., J.P., of Westacres, Newcastle-on-Tyne. *Educ.:* Dover College. Managing Director Messrs. C. A. Parsons, Heaton Works, Newcastle-on-Tyne; late General Manager Sir W. G. Armstrong, Whitworth & Co., of Elswick Works, Newcastle-on-Tyne. *War Work:* Superintended the manufacture of 13,000 guns, 11,785 carriages, 102 tanks, torpedo tubes, etc. *Address:* Seaton Burn House, Dudley, R.S.O., Northumberland. *Clubs:* Bath; Northern Counties, Newcastle. (C113)

BRADBURN, Albert Edward, M.B.E., *b.* 2 May, 1866; *s.* of William Bradburn, of Pendleton, Manchester; *m.* Annie, *d.* of Frederick William Burt, of Withington, Manchester. *Educ.:* Brindle Heath School, Pendleton, Manchester. City Surveyor's Secretary, Town Hall, Manchester. *War Work:* Secretary of Cold Storage Dept., of the Ministry of Food, at Headquarters, Westminster, from its inception; services were loaned to the Ministry by the Manchester Corporation. *Addresses:* 8, Glebe Place, Chelsea, S.W. 3 (temporary); City Surveyor's Office, Town Hall, Manchester (business). (M7463)

BRADBURY, Capt. Arthur Lyle, O.B.E.

BRADBURY, Capt. George Richardson, M.B.E.

BRADBURY, William Embry, M.B.E., *b.* 19 April, 1859; *s.* of Thos. Wm. Bradbury, of Marylebone. Railway Official. *War Work:* Preparation and carrying out of the scheme for Mobilisation of the Army. *Address:* "Lynwood," Marlboro' Hill, Harrow, Middlesex. (M169)

BRADBURY, Major William Percy, O.B.E., *b.* 15 Feb. 1889; *s.* of William Embry Bradbury (*q.v.*), M.B.E., of Harrow, Middx.; *m.* Winifred May, *d.* of Frederick James, of Twickenham. *Educ.:* London. Deputy Chief Staff Clerk, Supt. of the Line's Dept., L. & N.W. Rly., Euston. *War Work:* Enlisted Jan. 1915 in Royal Engineers; sent to France same month; commissioned as a Lieut. R.E., July, 1915; promoted Capt., Dec. 1915; made a Staff Officer (Deputy Assistant Director), Nov. 1916; promoted Major, Jan. 1917; employed from Jan. 1915, to Aug. 1919 at G.H.Q., France, organising Inland Water Transport arrangements for the Army, under the Director of Inland Water Transport; during the latter part of the war acted as Assistant Director of Inland Water Transport at General Headquarters; twice mentioned in despatches. (O1136)

BRADBY, Matthew Samuel, M.B.E., R.N.

BRADDELL, Lieut.-Col. Monckton O'Dell, C.B.E., M.B., R.A.M.C.

BRADDEN, Elliot, M.B.E.

BRADFIELD, Major Ernest William Charles, O.B.E., M.B., F.R.C.S.E., I.M.S.

BRADFIELD, William Walter, C.B.E., b. 1879; s. of William Bradfield. Director and Manager Marconi Co.. *Address:* 1, St. James's Place, S.W.1. (C448)

BRADFORD, Beryl Angelica Selby, Mrs., M.B.E.; d. of Capt. J. B. Taylor, of 76th Regt.; m. Capt. Sydney Sheridan Bradford, 24th Regt. (who died). *Educ.:* Privately. *War Work:* Organiser for Women Patrols, 6 months; for 2 years Lady Superintendent, Command Pay Office, London; then Lady Controller Women Staff, Air Ministry, until Jan. 1920. *Address:* 11, Bryanston Street, London, W. 1. (M7464)

BRADFORD, Lieut. James, M.B.E.

BRADFORD, Sir John Rose, K.C.M.G., C.B., C.B.E., M.D., D.Sc., Hon. M.D. (Christiania), F.R.C.P., F.R.S., Hon. Major-Gen. A.M.S., b. 7 May, 1863; m. Mary, d. of the late Thomas Ffoulkes Roberts, J.P. *Educ.:* Univ. Coll. School, Coll., and Hospital. Late Member of the Senate, Univ. of London; Senior Physician to the Univ. Coll. Hospital; Holme Lecturer on Clinical Medicine to the Univ. Coll. Hospital Medical School; Sec. of the Royal Society, 1908–15; Senior Medical. Adviser to the Colonial Office; Consulting Physician, B.E.F.; formerly George Henry Lewes Student and Grocer Research Scholar; served Great War, 1914–19 (despatches, C.B., C.B.E.). *Addresses:* 8, Manchester Square, W.; Bryn, near Dinas Mawddwy R.S.O., Merionethshire. *Clubs:* Athenæum; Arts. (C1225)

BRADFORD, Mary, Lady, O.B.E.; d. of Thomas Foulkes Roberts, J.P., of Llanidloes, North Wales; m. Sir John Rose, K.C.M.G., C.B., C.B.E., F.R.S., s. of A. R. Bradford (*see* BURKE'S *Peerage*). *Educ.:* Private school. *War Work:* Letter-writer for the wounded in 13 Stationary, and 24 and 26 General Hospitals, B.E.F.; mentioned in despatches, June, 1916; O.B.E., Jan. 1919. *Addresses:* 8, Manchester Square, W.; Bryn, nr. Dinas Mawddwy, R.S.O., Merionethshire. (O3631)

BRADFORD, William, O.B.E., J.P., b. 17 April, 1868; s. of Richard and Mary Bradford, of North Tawton, Devonshire; m. Sarah Ann Maud, d. of Edward Davis, of Dudley. *Educ.:* Elementary School. Glassmaker; General Financial Secretary to National Flint Glassmakers' Society, since 1906; Town Councillor for Dudley, 10 years; Justice of Peace for Dudley 3 years. *War Work:* Dudley Recruiting Committee; Tribunal; Pensions Committee; Chairman War Savings Committee at Dudley; National Advisory Committee, London; Food Control Committee; Local Advisory Committee; Dudley Food Control Committee; Member of the Committee of Unemployment Act; Member of Executive Council, Joint Industrial Council, London; Member of Housing Town Planning Committee, and several other important committees in London and Dudley. *Address:* 35, Wellington Road, Dudley, Worcs. (O1137)

BRADLEY, Lieut.-Col. Charles Raymond Strathearn, O.B.E., I.A. and R.A.F.

BRADLEY, Henry Edward Manning, M.B.E.

BRADLEY, Capt. James Lennox, O.B.E., R.A.S.C.

BRADLEY, Capt. John Stanley Travers, C.B.E., M.G.C.

BRADLEY, Lesley Ripley, M.B.E. *War Work:* Did valuable work in connection with the Imperial War Museum. (M10307)

BRADLEY, Rose Marian, O.B.E. General Secretary, Women's Legion. (O11894)

BRADLEY, Thomas John, C.B.E., b. 1857. Entered Exchequer and Audit Depart. 1875, and retired as Principal Clerk, 1917. (C114)

BRADLY, Henry George, C.B.E.

BRADSHAW, Frances Evelyn, M.B.E., W.R.N.S.

BRADSHAW, Fleet-Surg. Frank, O.B.E., R.N., b. 7 April, 1866; s. of the late Francis Burgess Bradshaw, of Thurles, Co. Tipperary; m. Mary Frances, d. of the late Rev. Adderley Willcocks Campbell, Tullycorbet, Co. Monaghan. *Educ.:* Royal University of Ireland. Fleet-Surgeon, R.N. (ret.); Deputy Commissioner of Medical Services, Ministry of Pensions. *War Work:* President Army Recruiting Board, Great Scotland Yard; Deputy Commissioner of Medical Services; Ministry of National Services; Deputy Commissioner of Medical Services Ministry of Pensions. *Address:* 13, Palliser Road, West Kensington. W. 14. *Club:* Junior Constitutional. (O1138)

BRADSHAW, Granville Eastwood, O.B.E.

BRADSHAW, Laura Katherine, M.B.E.

BRADSHAW, Capt. Stanley Goodwin, M.B.E., b. 10 Aug. 1889; s. of Bradshaw Charles Goodwin, of Blackheath, Kent. *Educ.:* Lancing. Solicitor. *War Work:* Private in the Inns of Court O.T.C., 1913–14; granted a commission in the 8th Service Battalion of the East Lancashire Regiment in Sept. 1914 and attained the rank of Captain in Jan. 1915; saw service in Belgium and France, 1915–16; appointed a Military Representative for the County of London Appeal

Tribunal under the Military Service Acts. *Address:* 2, Vanbrugh Park, Blackheath, S.E. 3. (M1452)

BRADSHAW, William Graham, C.B.E., b. 1 Sept. 1861; s. of Richard Bradshaw, of 10, Stanhope Street, Hyde Park; m. Dora Sophia, d. of Edward Studd, of Tedworth House, Hants.; and 2, Hyde Park Gardens. *Educ.:* Harrow, and Trinity College, Cambridge. Dep. Chairman London Joint City and Midland Bank since 1891; Chairman Commercial Gas Company. *War Work:* American Dollar Securities Committee. *Address:* Down Park, Crawley Down, Sussex. (C2465)

BRADWELL, William Howard, O.B.E., b. 29 May, 1867; s. of John Howard Bradwell, of Nottingham; m. Carrie, d. of Benjamin North, of Nottingham. *Educ.:* Nottingham High School and Shrewsbury. Past President of the Auctioneers' and Estate Agents' Institute; Past President of the Midland Counties' Tenant-Right Valuers' Association; Member of Council of Central Tenant-Right Valuers' Association. *War Work:* Member of Central Advisory Committee of Cattle Control; Member of the Central Livestock Fund, Chairman of Auctioneers' Pool Committee, under the Cattle Control. *Address:* 7, Cavendish Crescent South, The Park; Nottingham. (O10031)

BRADY, Rev. Canon Henry Westby, O.B.E., M.A.. b. 19 Dec. 1884; s. of Capt. George Westropp Brady, of Bray, Co. Wicklow, and Raheens, Co. Clare. *Educ.:* Privately; St. John's, London; University College, Durham. 1907, Curate Parish Church, Plymouth; 1911, Assistant Seamen's Chaplain, Ports of the River Plate; 1915, Senior Seamen's Chaplain, East Coast, S. America; Chaplain to Anglican Bishop in Argentina and East Coast, S. America; 1918, Canon of St. John's Cathedral, Buenos Aires. *War Work:* As Senior Seamen's Chaplain came in close touch with British ships and shipping during the period of the war; visited coast Ports, arranged for entertainment and welfare ashore and thousands of British Seamen; kept in close touch with the British Legation and the Squadron on the Coast. *Address:* Avenida Leandro Alems 693, Buenos Aires, Rep. Argentina. *Club:* Hurlingham, Buenos Aires. (O10032)

BRADY, Lieut. John Joseph Hugh, O.B.E., R.N.R.

BRADY, Capt. Ralph Hollinshed, M.B.E. (The Cheshire Regt.), b. 1867; s. of William Hollinshed Brady, of Stockport; m. Beatrice, d. of Frederick Beech, of Broughton, Lancs. *Educ.:* Stockport Grammar School; Manchester Grammar School. Land Agent and Auctioneer; Fellow of Surveyors' Institute; Vice-President of The Auctioneers' and Estate Agents' Institute. *War Work:* Appointed by the Ministry of Food (Live Stock Section) Chairman of South Lancashire and Salford Market for the Control and Distribution of Live Stock; Military Representative of Appeal Tribunal for the County of Chester; Secretary of War Agricultural Committee. *Address:* The Bungalow, Wilmslow, Cheshire. *Club:* Egerton, Stockport. (M7466)

BRADY, Lieut. Sydney Edward Joseph, M.B.E.

BRAGG, Sir William Henry, K.B.E., D.Sc., F.R.S., b. 2 July, 1862; s. of Robert John Bragg, of Stoneraise Place, Wigton, Cumberland; m. Gwendoline, d. of Sir Charles Todd, K.C.M.G., F.R.S., F.R.A.S., of The Observatory, Adelaide, South Australia. *Educ.:* King William's College, Isle of Man; Trinity. Elder Professor of Mathematics and Physics, University of Adelaide, 1886–1909; Cavendish Professor of Physics, University of Leeds, 1909–15; Quain Professor of Physics, University of London, 1915; Honorary Fellow of Trinity College, Cambridge; Nobel Laureate for Physics, 1915. *War Work:* Resident Director of the Admiralty Experimental Station at Aberdour. 1916, and Parkeston,1917; Scientific Adviser to the Director of the Anti-Submarine Division, 1918. *Address:* 32, Ladbroke Square, W. 11; *Clubs:* United University; Albemarle. (K352)

BRAGG, William Lawrence, O.B.E., b. 31 Mar. 1890; s. of Sir William Bragg, K.B.E. *Educ:* Trinity College. Prof. of Physics, Manchester University. *War Work:* Technical Adviser on Sound Ranging to the Map Section, General Headquarters, France. *Address:* 49, Heaton Road, Withington, Manchester. (O109)

BRAGGINS, Edith Annie, M.B.E., b. 20 Oct. 1878; d. of Ezra Braggins, of Hermon, Russell Park, Bedford. *Educ.:* Bedford High School for Girls; La Prinlamère, Vevey, Switzerland. *War Work:* Temporary Clerk, Ministry of Shipping, from Feb. 1916. *Address:* 39, Kensington Gardens Square, London, W. 2. (M7467)

BRAID, Major Arthur Reade, O.B.E.

BRAIN, Capt. Hugh Gerner, O.B.E.

BRAIN, Edwin LEWTON-, M.B.E.

BRAITHWAITE, Lieut Col. Francis Powell, C.B.E., D.S.O., M.C., R.E.; m. 1st Oct. 1920, Victoria Alexandrina, Lady Plunket, widow of the 5th Baron Plunket, and d. of the 1st Marquess of Dufferin (*see* BURKE'S *Peerage*). Served in the Great War. 1914–19 (despatches twice. Croix de Guerre). (C1226)

BRAITHWAITE, Capt. Stanley Nesham, M.B.E., b. 6 April, 1878; s. of Joseph Braithwaite, of Wood Green; m. Beatrice, d. of William Aubery, of Southampton. *Educ.:* Margate and Southgate Colleges. *War Work:* In command of Transports "Teviot" and "Cardiganshire," R.M.S.P. "Pardo," "Araguaya," "Desna," "Danube," "Amazon"; mentioned in despatches; present at the Landing at Gallipoli. *Address:* Ashurst, 64, Westwood Road, Southampton. (M7468)

BRAKE, Ethol Primrose, Mrs., M.B.E.

BRAKES, Harry, M.B.E.

BRAMAH, David, C.B.E., M.I.M.E., *b.* 17 June, 1875; *s.* of John Bramah, of Manchester; *m.* Emilia, *d.* of Charles Henry Hobday, of Birmingham and Anglesey, and niece of General Sir Owen Thomas (*see* BURKE'S *Peerage*). Formerly Chief Engineer White Star Line, and latterly General Secretary Marine Engineers' Association; Joint Secretary National Maritime Board (Engineer Officers' Panel); member of Standard Uniform Committee convened by Board of Trade; Member of Committee of National War Savings (Mercantile Section); Recommended introduction of Commissioned Rank R.N.R. for Engineer Officers M.M.; Assisted the Authorities in securing the services of officers for special duty in connection with Fleet Auxiliaries, particularly in staffing No. 12 Special Squadron. *Addresses:* London Bridge House, S.E. 1; Alexandra Road, Leyton. (C2466)

BRAMALL, Ernest Edward Peel, O.B.E., *b.* 5 Jan. 1865; *s.* of the late Edward Charles Bramall; *m.* Constance Eva, *d.* of the late Joseph Haselden. *Educ.:* Lichfield Grammar School. Member of Benisouef (Egypt) Municipality from its commencement to date. *War Work:* Egyptian Expeditionary Force (Labour Directorate); Recruiting Officer (Lieut.), 28 May, 1917, to 29 Aug. 1917; Officer-in-charge Military Labour Bureau Alexandria; Major, 30 Aug. 1917, to 30 April, 1918; Officer-in-charge Labour Area, Alexandria Base, 1 May, 1918, to 7 Feb. 1919; L.G. 7 June, 1918; mentioned in despatches; L.G. 14 June, 1918. *Addresses:* Pickforde, Ticehurst, Sussex; Benisouef, Middle Egypt. *Club:* Turf, Cairo. (O1140)

BRAMALL, Major Harold Egerton, O.B.E., *b.* 13 Sept. 1883; *s.* of W. E. Bramall, of Manchester. *War Work:* With Lancashire Fusiliers, Egypt, 1914; Gallipoli, 1915; Rifle Brigade, Palestine, 1917; Devonshire Regiment, Palestine, 1918–19. *Address:* Holmsdale, Kersal, Manchester. (O6144)

BRAMHALL, Major Charles, O.B.E., R.A.M.C.

BRAMLEY, Lieut. Percy Brooke, O.B.E., I.A.R.O.

BRAMMALL, Major Leslie Hinchcliffe, O.B.E.

BRAMWELL, Hugh, O.B.E., J.P., *b.* 1 Jan. 1861; *s.* of John Byrom Bramwell, of Tynemouth, Northumberland; *m.* Margaret Jane, *d.* of Peter Lang, of Edinburgh. *Educ.:* Cheltenham College, Edinburgh University, and Newcastle College of Science. Mining Engineer, Director of Great Western Colliery Co., Ltd.: Director of Mon. and S. Wales Employers' Mutual Indemnity Society; Chairman of the Treforest Electrical Consumers Co., Ltd. *War Work:* Member of the Glamorgan Colliery Recruiting Court and Member of the Standing Committee on Mining of Privy Council Committee for Scientific and Industrial Research; Member of the Coal Controllers' Advisory Board. *Address:* Pontyquesta, Pontychen, Glam. *Clubs:* Cardiff and County; Public Schools; Albemarle. (O176)

BRAMWELL, Percy, M.B.E., *b.* 6 June, 1865. *Educ.:* Privately. *War Work:* R.N.A.S. Seaplane Inspection (C.P.O.), then Aeronautical Inspection Dept. Ministry of Munitions. *Address:* 5, Woodland Villas, Datchet Common, Bucks. (M1456)

BRANCH, Albert Ernest, O.B.E.

BRANCH, Charles Churchill, O.B.E., F.R.G.S., *b.* 8 May, 1866; *s.* of Charles Branch, of 67, Chester Square, S.W.; *m.* Mary Bernadette, *d.* of R.N. Rawstron, of Weymouth. *Educ.:* Eton; New Coll., Oxford. Barrister-at-law; Member of Council of the Boy Scouts' Association. *War Work:* Commissioner in charge of Imperial Headquarters Boy Scouts' Association; in control of Coast Guard and other public services rendered by the Boy Scouts during the war. *Address:* 67, Chester Square, S.W.1. *Clubs:* Windham; New University. (O10033)

BRANCH, Irene, Mrs., M.B.E.

BRAND, Flight-Lieut. Sir Christopher Joseph Quintin, K.B.E., D.S.O., M.C., D.F.C., R.A.F., *b.* 25 May, 1893; *s.* of E. C. J. Brand, late C.I.D. Johannesburg; *m.* Marie, *d.* of Patrick William Vaughan, of King's Town, Ireland. *Educ.:* Marist Brothers' Colleges, Johannesburg and Uitenhage. Flying. *War Work:* German S.W. Africa, 1914–15; R.F.C. and R.A.F. 1916 to date; commanded 151 Squadron, 1918; 112 Squadron Feb. 1918; 44 Squadron 1919; K.B.E. awarded for Pioneer flight London to Cape Town in company with Col. Sir H. A. Van Ryneveld, K.B.E., D.S.O., M.C., Feb. 4 Brooklands, Mar. 20 Cape Town, 1920. *Club:* R.A.F. (K449)

BRAND, Edward Murray, O.B.E.

BRAND, Lieut. Erie Bergo, M.B.E., R.A.S.C.

BRAND, Ethert, M.B.E., *b.* 1872; *s.* of George Brand, of Richmond, Surrey; *m.* Mary Ann, *d.* of John Colley, of Stretton Baskerville. *Educ.:* Dulwich Coll. London and North-Western Railway. *War Work:* Railway Transport; Ministry of Munitions; Coal Control. *Address:* Dhoon, Marion Road, Mill Hill, N.W. 7. (M7470)

BRAND, Henry, M.B.E.

BRAND, Lieut.-Col. Robert Harvey, O.B.E., R.A.F.

BRAND, Lieut. Stanley Hunt, M.B.E., R.A.S.C.

BRANDER, Capt. James Maudsley O.B.E., R.A.S.C.

BRANDER, William Browne, C.B.E., *b.* 1880; *s.* of William John Brander, of Edinburgh; *m.* 1909, Matilda Baird Thompson. *Educ.:* George Watson's Coll.; Edinburgh Univ. (Hon. M.A.); Balliol Coll., Oxford. Entered I.C.S. 1903; has been Dep.-Commr. Tavoy since 1914. *Address:* Tavoy, Burma. *Club:* East India United Service. (C694)

BRANDER, Archibald Alexander DUNBAR-, O.B.E., I.F.S., F.Z.S., F.R.G.S., *b.* 23 April, 1877; *s.* of the late Capt. James Brander Dunbar-Brander, of Scots Greys and of Pitgaveny, Elgin, N.B.; *m.* Frances Emily, widow of George

Rowell, F.R.C.S. *Educ.:* Marlborough Coll., Coopers Hill. Conservator of Forests, Imperial Forest Service, India. *War Work:* Supplying Forest Produce to the Army Department, chiefly baled Hay, of which some 40,000 tons was supplied. *Address:* Nagput, Central Provinces, India. *Club:* Savile. (O2085)

BRANDON, Major Percy de Bathe, O.B.E.

BRANDON, Comm. Vivian Ronald, C.B.E., *b.* 1882; *s.* of G. S. Brandon, of Oakbrook, Ravenscourt Park, W.; *m.* 1915, Joan Elizabeth Maud, *d.* of Capt. H. V. Simpson, R.N., of Highbrook Cottage, Ardingley. Com. R.N., and Mine Clearance Officer in Norwegian Waters; sentenced at Leipzig, Dec. 1910, to 4 years' imprisonment in a fortress (pardoned May, 1913). *Club:* Junior United Service. (C1146)

BRANFORD, Harold, O.B.E.

BRANSON, Major Frederick Henry Ewart, O.B.E., Royal Army Ordnance Corps, *b.* 18 May, 1878; *s.* of the late James H. A. Branson, 2, Essex Court, Temple; *m.* Helen Mary, *d.* of the late Harold Brown, of 2, Bond Court, E.C. *Educ.:* Bedford; Trin. Coll. Cambridge. *Club:* United University. (O6934)

BRANSON, William Philip Sutcliffe, C.B.E., M.D., F.R.C.P. (sometime Col. (Temp.), A.M.S.), *b.* 1874; *s.* of James H. A. Branson. *Educ.:* Bedford; Trinity College, Cambridge; St. Bartholomew's Hospital. Consulting Physician; Physician to Royal Free Hospital, London; Medical Officer, Sun Life Assurance Society, London. *War Work:* Physician, No. 1 Red Cross (Duchess of Westminster) Hospital, B.E.F., 1914–18; Physician, 48th C.C.S., B.E.F., 1918–19; Consulting Physician, 5th Army, B.E.F., 1919. *Professional Address:* 41, Devonshire Place, London, W. 1; *Private Address:* 9, York House, York St., London, W. 1. *Club:* United University. (C1227)

BRASH, Capt. Ernest Livett, M.B.E., A.P.D.

BRASS, Thomas Francis, O.B.E., J.P.

BRASSEY, Maude Helena, Hon. Mrs. Albert, O.B.E., *b.* 27 April, 1850; *d.* of John Charles Robert, 4th Lord Clanmorris (*see* BURKE'S *Peerage*); *m.* Albert (died Jan. 1918), *s.* of Thomas Brassey, of Heythrop, Chipping Norton. Oxfordshire (*see* BURKE'S *Landed Gentry*). *War Work:* Commandant, V.A.D. Hospital, Chipping Norton, Oxfordshire; Vice-President Soldiers' and Sailors' Families Association; on Committee Red Cross Society, Oxon. *Address:* 29, Berkeley Square, W. 1. (O3633)

BRATBY, Samuel Henry, M.B.E., *b.* 3 Nov. 1878; *s.* of William Bratby, J.P., of Manchester; *m.* Muriel Hope, *d.* of Walter Atkinson, of Timperley. *Educ.:* Sherborne. Member of the Manchester Stock Exchange. *War Work:* A. Capt. R.A.S.C. (T.F.); served in Mesopotamia, 1916–18. *Address:* Boyton, Hale, Cheshire. *Clubs:* Public Schools; Manchester Constitutional; Manchester Tennis and Racquets. (M2980)

BRATHBY, Lieut. George Henry, M.B.E., R.G.A. (T.F.)

BRAY, Rev. Albert Edward, O.B.E., Temp. Chaplain, 4th Class.

BRAY, Denneys de Saumerez, C.B.E. (C1957)

BRAY, Major Eustace Arthur, O.B.E., M.C.

BRAY, Comm. John Evelyn, O.B.E., R.N.

BRAY, Paul Dudley, O.B.E.

BRAYBROOKE, Capt. Henry George, O.B.E., R.A.O.C.

BRAYBROOKE, Henry Mellor, M.B.E., M.A. (Cantab.), *b.* 11 Feb. 1869; *s.* of the late P. W. Braybrooke, F.R.G.S., of Studley, Tunbridge Wells; *m.* Olive Rowena, *d.* of the late E. W. Waller, of Ardtona, Dundrum, Co. Dublin. *Educ.:* Wellington Coll.; Pembroke Coll., Cambridge. *War Work:* Commandant, Oakfield Red Cross Hospital, Hawkhurst, Kent (1914–18), Kent V.A.D., 156. *Address:* Tates, Hawkhurst, Kent. *Club:* Wellington. (M7472)

BRAYBROOKS, Gladys Marian, Mrs., M.B.E.

BRAYDEN, William John Henry, O.B.E.

BREACH, William Hall, O.B.E., M.Inst. T., *b.* Oct. 1860; *s.* of John Robert Breach, of Leeds; *m.* Jane Annie, *d.* of Joseph Broadhead, of Leeds. *Educ.:* Privately. Traffic Manager, Aire and Calder Navigation, Leeds. *War Work:* In connection with the Canal Control, Northern Sub-Committee; and of the Aire and Calder Navigation. *Address:* Ashville, Wheatley Road, Ilkley. (O10036)

BREADMORE, Major Reginald George, O.B.E., R.A.S.C.

BREAKEY, Lieut.-Col. Arthur John, O.B.E., R.A.

BREARS, Lieut. Tom, M.B.E., R.A.O.C.

BREBNER, Capt. Innes Wares, M.B.E.

BRECHIN, Rev. Edwin James, O.B.E., M.A., B.D., *b.* 10 Feb. 1874; *s.* of James Brodie Brechin, of Dundee; *m.* Theodora Mary, *d.* of Rev. W. Smith, of Unst, Shetland. *Educ.:* Dundee High School; St. Andrews Univ. Minister of the Scots Kirk, Paris; Minister of St. James's Church of Scotland, Dulwich, London; now Parish Minister of Avoch, Ross-shire; member of the Avoch Parish Council; of the Black Isle District Committee; of the Rosemarkie and Avoch School Committee. *War Work:* General Superintendent for France of the Scottish Churches' Huts. *Address:* The Manse, Avoch, Ross-shire. (O3634)

BREHM, Mary Chisholm, Mrs., O.B.E.

BREMNER, Eng.-Comm. Archibald Gordon, O.B.E., R.N.

BREMNER, Capt. David, M.B.E.

BREMNER, David Alexander, O.B.E., M.I.M.E., M.I.E.E., M.I.M.M.

BREMNER, Major James Morrison Gardiner, O.B.E., M.B., R.A.M.C. (T.F.).

BREMRIDGE, Major Richard Harding, ' O.B.E., M.A., M.B., B.Ch., B.Sc., R.A.M.C., *b.* 30 Oct. 1870 ; *s.* of Richard Bremridge, of 17, Bloomsbury Sq., W.C. 1 ; *m.* Kathleen, *d.* of James William Britton, Clerk to the Wood Green Council. *Educ.:* Magdalen Coll., Oxford ; St. Bartholomew's Hospital, London. Deputy Commissioner of Medical Services, Ministry of Pensions ; late Deputy County M.O.H., School Medical Officer and County Oculist, Wilts County Council ; late Medical Officer to the Kolar Gold Fields, Southern India ; late M.O. to the Ministry of Justice, Bangkok, Siam. *War Work:* Command Sanitary Officer Southern Command from March, 1917, to April, 1920. Had charge of all matters relating to the health of the troops occupying the camps in the 13 counties, comprising the Southern Command, including the camps and aerodromes of the R.A.F. *Address:* Ministry of Pensions, Northern Region, 14, Clayton Street West, Newcastle-on-Tyne.   (O6936)

BRENAN, Capt. Frederick Rudolf Esmonde Dowes, O.B.E.

BRENNAN, Vincent Talbot, M.B.E.

BRENNAN, Capt. William, O.B.E., R.A.M.C., *b.* 13 Dec. 1871 ; *s.* of Peter Brennan, of Ireland ; *m.* Eliza, *d.* of Henry Crocker, of London. *Educ.:* Mungret Coll., Limerick. Quartermaster. *War Work:* Quartermaster in Casualty Clearing Stations and Field Ambulance in France, 1914–19. *Address:* c/o Messrs. Holt & Co., 3, Whitehall Place, S.W.   (O5036)

BRENT, Margaret, Mrs., M.B.E.

BRERETON, Charles Cecil Trelawny, M.B.E., *b.* 14 Dec. 1889 ; *s.* of the Rev. Cecil Brereton, of Hardham Rectory, Pulborough. *Educ.:* Horsham. District Traffic Superintendent, Indian State Railways, Public Works Department. *War Work:* Throughout the war was in charge of Rawalpindi Frontier District of the North-Western Railway, India ; carried out the Concentration of the Waziristan Field Force Operations, 1917, and numerous other minor Frontier Expeditions. *Club:* R.A.C.   (M4119)

BRERETON, Rev. Eric Hugh, O.B.E., *b.* 17 Nov. 1889 ; *s.* of Capt. W. E. Brereton, late R.A., of Ascot. *Educ.:* Glengorse, Eastbourne, and Univ. Coll., Durham. Senior Chaplain, St. Mary's Cathedral, Edinburgh. *War Work:* T. Chaplain to the Forces (4th Class), 1915 ; promoted 3rd Class, 1918, as S.C.F. 26th Division ; twice mentioned in despatches ; served with B.E.F. and British Salonica Force, 1915–19. *Address:* 7, Cornwall Street, Edinburgh.   (O6440)

BRERETON, Major and Brevet Lieut.-Col. Frederick Sadlier, C.B.E., M.R.C.S., L.R.C.P., J.P., *b.* 5 Aug. 1872 ; *s.* of Franc. S. Brereton, of London ; *m.* Ethel Mary, *d.* of W. J. Lamb, of Southport. *Educ.:* Cranleigh, and Guy's Hospital. Qualified medical man but does not practise ; author of sundry books for boys, and of " The Great War and the R.A.M.C." *War Work:* Secretary Medical History of the War ; organiser of Army Medical War Museum. *Address:* Felden Lodge, Boxmoor, Herts. *Clubs:* Junior United Service ; Authors' ; R.A.C.   (C1480)

BRERETON, Katherine Blanche, M.B.E., R.R.C., *b.* 11 Feb. 1861 ; *d.* of Capt. S. H. Brereton, M.A., of Briningham House, Norfolk. Sister at Guy's Hospital, 1892–1900, Sister in Imperial Yeomanry Hospitals in Delfontein and Pretoria, and Matron of Elandsfontein during the South African War ; member of the Government Concentration Camps Commission to inquire into the condition of Boer Women and Children in South Africa ; Churchwarden, Guardian, and District Councillor ; on the District Housing and other Sub-Committees ; member of the Public Health Committee, County Council ; member of the County National Health Committee. *War Work:* Member of the District Food Control and Profiteering Committees and Military Tribunal ; Parish Representative of Pension Committee ; Sailors' and Soldiers' Association ; and District War Agricultural Committee. *Address:* Briningham House, Melton Constable, Norfolk.   (M7474)

BRERETON, Victor le Gay, O.B.E.   (O11954)

BRESSEY, Lieut.-Col. Charles Herbert, O.B.E., F.S.I., R.E., Chevalier de la Légion d'Honneur, *b.* 3 Jan. 1874 ; *s.* of John T. Bressey, of Wanstead, Essex ; *m.* Lily Margaret Francis, *d.* of Francis Charles Hill, of Wanstead, Essex. *Educ.:* Rouen ; Bremen ; Forest School, Walthamstow. Divisional Engineer, London, Roads Department. Ministry of Transport. *War Work:* Assistant Director of Roads, France ; British Member, Inter-Allied Road Commission, Rhine Province. *Address:* Leicester Road, Wanstead, Essex ; 7, Whitehall Gardens, S.W. 1.   (O2443)

BRETON, Eng.-Comm. Colin Guy, O.B.E., R.N.

BRETON, Norton, M.B.E.

BRETT, Lieut. George Henry, O.B.E., R.N.V.R.

BRETT, Capt. John Vaughan, M.B.E.

BRETT, Lieut.-Col. Hon. Maurice Vyner Baliol, M.V.O., O.B.E., Chevalier of the Legion of Honour, 1906, Officer, 1917, *b.* 24 April, 1882 ; 2nd *s.* of 2nd Viscount Esher ; *m.* Florence Zena Dare. *Educ.:* Eton ; R.M.C. Sandhurst (Sword of Honour, 1902). Entered Coldstream Guards, 1902 ; Capt., 1910 ; 6th Batt. Black Watch, 1911 ; A.D.C. to F.M. Sir John French, 1904–12 ; served in the Great War (France), 1914–19 (despatches four times) ; Sec. to the Garton Foundation ; Librarian to London Museum. *Addresses:* Chilston, Winkfield, Berks ; Roman Camp, Callander, N.B. *Clubs:* Marlborough ; Royal Automobile.   (O1142)

BRETT, Hon. Oliver (Sylvain Baliol), M.B.E., *b.* 23 March, 1881 ; *e.s.* of the 2nd Viscount Esher ; *m.* Antoinette, *d.* of August Hecksher, New York. *Educ.:* Eton. Contested Huntingdon (L.), Jan. and Dec. 1910 ; Assist. Private Sec. (unpaid) to Secretary of State for India (Viscount Morley), 1905–10 ; entered 16th Batt. Co. of London Regt. (Queen's Westminster Rifles), 1914 ; attached to the War Office, 1915–19. *Address:* Chester House, Upper Belgrave Street, S.W. 1. *Clubs:* Marlborough ; Cavendish ; Ranelagh ; Royal Automobile.   (M712)

BRETT, The Rev. William, O.B.E.

BREWER, Surg.-Lieut.-Comm. Charles Samuel, O.B.E., R.N.V.R.

BREWER, Ella Nora Dorothy, M.B.E. *War Work:* Did valuable work in connection with the Imperial War Museum.   (M10380)

BREWER, Lieut. Frederick Henry, O.B.E., R.N.R.

BREWER, Cadet Lieut.-Col. Frederic William, O.B.E., M.A., *b.* 30 Oct. 1867 ; *s.* of Thomas Brewer, of Preston, Lancs. ; *m.* Violette Eliza, *d.* of Rev. W. D. Daniel. M.A., of Wymondham, Norfolk. *Educ.:* Preston Grammar School ; St. Catharine's Coll., Cambridge. Headmaster of Dame Allan's School, Newcastle-on-Tyne ; Officer Commanding 1st Cadet Battalion, Northumberland Fusiliers ; also Officer Commanding Allan's School Cadet Unit. *War Work:* Recruiting and training Territorials, Volunteers and Cadets. *Address:* Dame Allan's School House, Newcastle-on-Tyne.   (O10038)

BREWER, Griffith, O.B.E.

BREWIN, Lieut. George Grahame, M.B.E., I.A.R.O.

BREWIN, Lieut. Harry, O.B.E., R.F.A.

BREWIN, Capt. Thomas James, O.B.E.

BREWIS, Major Andrew Seymour, O.B.E., M.C., M.D.

BREWIS, Arthur William, *b.* 8 Feb. 1884 ; *s.* of the late Edward Brewis. Member of the London Stock Exchange. *War Work:* Executive Officer of Lewisham Food Control ; Hon. Financial Sec., Lewisham Victory War Loan Assoc. ; Hon. Treasurer, Fairlawn Auxiliary Hospital ; *Address:* Eildon Ravensbourne Park, Catford, S.E. 6. *Club:* Conservative (Catford).   (M7475)

BREWIS, Charles Richard Wynn, C.B.E.   (C3186)

BREWIS, Major Roddison Douglas, O.B.E.

BREWIS, Lieut. Thomas Stamp, M.B.E.

BREWITT, 2nd Lieut. Charles Patrick, M.B.E.

BREWSTER, William Thomas, M.B.E., R.A.O.C.

BRICE, Capt. Albert Victor, O.B.E., R.E.

BRICE, Lieut. and Qr.-Mr. Ernest Gottlieb Isdeal, M.B.E., R.A.M.C.

BRICE, Mary Helen Thorpe, M.B.E., *d.* of the late John Brice, jun., of Northampton. Ministry of Labour Employment Exchange. *Address:* 14, Daylesford Avenue, Putney, S.W. 15.   (M1461)

BRICKENDEN, Charles, M.B.E., *b.* 23 July, 1864 ; *s.* of John Brickenden, of Sheerness ; *m.* Edith Jane, *d.* of Edward R. Marsh, of Sheerness. Cartographer. *War Work:* Naval Intelligence at Admiralty. *Address:* 108, Friern Road, East Dulwich, S.E. 22.   (M1462)

BRICKWELL, Alfred James, C.B.E., F.S.I., *b.* 16 Feb, 1870 ; *s.* of the late J. Brickwell, of Hertford ; *m.* Ida Muriel, *d.* of the late Rev. G. Rogers, of London. *Educ.:* Hertford. Surveyor to the Great Northern Railway Company. *War Work:* Director of Cold Storage from Feb. 1918, to date, controlling the Cold Storage of the British Isles and arranging for additional constructon and financing thereof. *Address:* New Barnet, Herts.   (C2467)

BRIDCUT, Lieut.-Col. Sidney Haines, O.B.E., F.R.G.S., A.M.I.E.E., *b.* 16 May, 1886 ; *s.* of the late Alfred Bridcut, of Birmingham; *m.* Clarice May, *d.* of John Meachem, of Moseley, Worcestershire. *Educ.:* Privately ; Mason's Coll., Birmingham. Director of Electrical and Mechanical Services, Mesopotamia. *War Work:* Indian Defence from 1914–16. Commissioned Jan. 1917, and posted to R.E. Unit in Mesopotamia ; Thrice mentioned in despatches ; awarded O.B.E. in Victory Honours List. *Address:* Stratford-on-Avon, Warwickshire. *Club:* Junior Army and Navy.   (O6581)

BRIDGE, Arthur George, M.B.E.   (M10245b)

BRIDGE, Joseph James Rabnett, C.B.E., M.A., H.M. Inspector of Schools, *b.* 8 June, 1875 ; *s.* of Joseph Bridge, of Shrewsbury ; *m.* Kathleen Mary, *d.* of the late Thomas O'Shaughnessey, of Bruff, Co. Limerick. *Educ.:* Shrewsbury School and Gonville & Caius College, Cambridge (Powis Medal for Latin verse, and 1st Class Classical Tripos). 1897–1900, Prof. of Classics, Stonyhurst College ; 1900, Senior Classical Master, St. Edmund's College, Ware ; 1901–2, Prof. of English Literature, University of Calcutta ; 1902, Junior Inspector, Board of Education ; 1904, H.M. Inspector, Board of Education ; 1911, Report on Secondary Education in Ceylon. *War Work:* 1914, Tyneside Irish Brigade Committee ; 1915, lent to War Office ; 1915–19 Secretary, War Office Dependants' Assessment Appeals Committee, *Addresses:* Board of Education, Whitehall ; 47, Front St., Tynemouth, Northumberland.   (C2468)

BRIDGE, Josiah, M.B.E., F.S.A.A., *b.* 31 March, 1865 ; *s.* of George Bridge, of Manchester ; *m.* Mary Roseline, *d.* of Thomas Mason, of Oldham. *Educ.:* Warrington, Manchester and Oldham. Borough Accountant to the South Shields Corporation. *War Work:* Hon. Treasurer of Local War Pensions Committee.   (M7476)

BRIDGEMAN, Sqdn.-Leader Percival Cunningham Allen, O.B.E., R.A.F.

BRIDGER, Donald Keith, M.B.E., *b.* 4 May, 1880; *s.* of the late Archibald Bridger; *m.* Mabel Ireland, *d.* of John William Green, of Southampton; *Educ.:* Cavendish Coll., Southampton. Chief Inspector and Deputy Chief Constable, Great Yarmouth Borough Police. *War Work:* Emergency work in connection with possible hostile landing; Police work during air raids and bombardments, and confidential work with regard to espionage. *Address:* 16, Priory Gardens, Yarmouth. (M7477)

BRIDGER, Stanley Alexander, M.B.E., *b.* 3 Nov. 1870; *s.* of W. S. Bridger, of Havant; *m.* Beatrice Minnie, *d.* of G. Waldren, of Portsmouth. *Educ.:* Mile End House Academy, Portsmouth. Foreman of the Yard, H.M. Dockyard. *War Work:* Arming of merchant vessels, repair of vessels torpedoed near Gibraltar; repair and upkeep of H.M. vessels of all classes. *Address:* 26, Tower Buildings, Yarmouth. *Club:* Overseas. (M1463)

BRIDGES, Capt. Arthur Brodie Hamilton, O.B.E., R.A.M.C.

BRIDGES, Lieut.-Col. Edward James, O.B.E., F.R.I.B.A., *b.* 20 Jan. 1861; *s.* of Edward Curson Bridges, of King's Lynn, Norfolk; *m.* Leah, *d.* of Edward Sweetman, of Ryde, I. of W. *Educ.:* Privately, King's Lynn. Superintending Inspector of Works, Southern Command, Salisbury. *War Work:* Employed in erection of hutting at Salisbury Plain and elsewhere, and in designing buildings, etc., for special War requirements; also in the adaptation of public and private buildings at various places for use as Military Hospitals and winter billets for troops, etc. *Address:* 33, Fowler's Road, Salisbury. (O6938)

BRIDGES, Lieut. Frederick Thomas, M.B.E., R.E.

BRIDGES, Col. James Whiteside, C.B.E. Col. Canadian Army Med. Corps; Great War, 1915–19 (despatches). (C1829)

BRIDGLAND, Richard John, M.B.E.

BRIDGWATER, Major Havard Noel, O.B.E., D.S.O., T.D., Major, Norfolk Regt. Served in the Great War, 1914–19 (despatches) (O6146)

BRIEN, Owen, M.B.E.

BRIERCLIFFE, Major Rupert, O.B.E., M.B., Ch. B. B.Sc. (Public Health) D.P.H., R.A.M.C., (T.F.), *b.* 27 Jan. 1889; *s.* of Thomas H. Briercliffe, of Wheatfield, Bolton. *Educ.:* Victoria Univ., Manchester. *War Work:* Sanitary Officer, 1st East Lancs. Div. (T.F.), Egypt and Gallipoli; Officer i'c District Laboratory, Cairo; O.C. Military Laboratory, Suez; O.C. 30th Sanitary Section; Medical Inspector of Water Supplies, Palestine, L. of C.; P.M.O. Haifa; D.A.D.M.S., O.E.T.A. (South); mentioned in a despatch from General Sir E. H. H. Allenby, G.C.M.G., K.C.B., dated 23 Oct. 1918, for gallant and distinguished services in the field; Director of Health, Palestine. *Address:* Government House, Jerusalem. (O2869)

BRIERLEY, Clement Hall, M.B.E., *b.* 4 June, 1869; *s.* of Samuel Brierley, of Rochdale, Lancashire; *m.* Irene Jessie, *d.* James Love, of Calcutta, India. *Educ.:* Rochdale Grammar School. Superintendent of Prisons (Bombay Jail Department). *Address:* Superintendent, Deccan Convict Gang, Visapur (Ahmednagar District), India. (M2764)

BRIERLEY, Edgar, O.B.E., *b.* 1858; *s.* of James Brierley, of West Hill, Rochdale, *m.* Catharine, *d.* of J. Henry Lancashire, of Rochdale. *Educ.:* Rugby School and University College, Oxford. Stipendiary Magistrate for the City of Manchester. *War Work:* Chairman, Manchester Local Tribunal, 1915–18. (O178)

BRIERLEY, Eustace Carlile, O.B.E. (O5039)

BRIERLEY, Major Norman Howorth, O.B.E., late R.E., *b.* 9 Feb. 1879; *s.* of Abraham Brierley, of Rochdale, Lancashire; *m.* Rachel Mary, *d.* of the late Charles Crofton Black, of Cranham, Essex. *Educ.:* Sedbergh. Mechanical Engineer; Assistant Locomotive Running Superintendent, Buenos Aires, Great Southern Railway. *War Work:* Commissioned 4 Jan. 1915; Captain 12th Batt. Essex Regt.; transferred to Royal Engineers, Nov. 1915; railway work in Salonica; has Order of Serbian White Eagle, 5th Class. Asst. Director Railway Traffic, Sofia, Bulgaria, and subsequently Military Manager of Anatolian Railway. *Address:* Ferro Carril del Sud, Buenos Aires, Argentina. (O6441)

BRIERLY, Major James Leslie, O.B.E.

BRIGGS, Capt. Albert, O.B.E., *b.* 31 Jan. 1887; *s.* of George Briggs, of Blackpool, Lancs.; *m.* Kathleen Annie, *d.* of William Hamilton, of Whitefield, Lancs. *Educ.:* Privately. Solicitor. Sec. of Tyne Iron Shipbuilding Co., Ltd. *War Work:* Royal Engineers; Special Headquarter duties; mentioned for services, 1916; Acting Sec. Dept. of Controller-General of Merchant Shipbuilding. *Address:* Willington Quay-on-Tyne. (O10040)

BRIGGS, Major Arthur Edwin, O.B.E., *b.* 13 Dec. 1889; *s.* of W. E. Briggs, of Kibworth, Leicestershire; *m.* Alison Mary, *d.* of the late W. Hearth, of Leicester. *Educ.:* Wyggeson School, Leicester. Boot Manufacturer. *War Work:* Served overseas four years with the R.A.S.C. *Addresses:* 16, York Street, Leicester; Spinney Close, Kibworth Harcourt, Leicestershire. (O2444)

BRIGGS, Paymaster-Lieut. Charles, O.B.E., R.N.R.

BRIGGS, Col. Edward Featherstone, D.S.O., O.B.E.; *s.* of the late William Briggs, of Clifton, Bristol; *m.* 1918, Violet, *d.* of Ernest Long, of York. Entered R.N. 1905; became Engineer-Lieut. 1908; Squadron-Com. (Roy. Naval Air Ser.), 1914; Wing-Com. 19—; Group-Com. R.A.F. 1918, with rank of Col.; served during Great War, 1914–18 (wounded, taken prisoner, Legion of Honour, Croix de Guerre). (O8057)

BRIGGS, Eloir Baron, M.B.E.

BRIGGS, Col. George Ewbank, O.B.E.

BRIGGS, Prof. Henry, O.B.E., D.Sc., A.R.S.M., *b.* 4 Nov. 1883; *s.* of John Edwin Briggs, of Stott Park, Lakeside; *m.* Myfanwy, *d.* of John Heilyn Williams, of Llanllechid. *Educ.:* Bradford; Imperial Coll., London. Professor of Mining, Heriot Watt Coll., Edinburgh; Univ. Lecturer in Mining, Edinburgh Univ. *War Work:* Technical Adviser, Medical Supplies Committee, War Office; Superintendent, Physical Test Station, Edinburgh. Developed new methods of testing physical fitness. *Address:* Allermuir, Liberton, Midlothian. (O10041)

BRIGGS, Eng.-Comm. Henry Smalley, O.B.E., R.N.

BRIGGS, Major Henry Stackpoole, O.B.E., R.E.

BRIGGS, James, C.B.E.

BRIGGS, Margaret Ellen, Mrs., M.B.E. *War Work:* Founder and President of the Chiddingfold War Hospital Supply Depot. *Address:* Waterfield, Chiddingfold, Surrey. (M7480)

BRIGGS, Mary Alice, Mrs., M.B.E., *b.* 17 June, 1864; *d.* of Richard Stanton, of Lancaster; *m.* William, *s.* of Robert Briggs, of Lancaster. *Educ.:* Privately. Vice-President Lancaster Girl Guides; Vice-President Lancaster I.C.A.A.; Governor of Lancaster Girls' Grammar School; Chairman Lancaster Women Citizens' Association; Member of Education Committee; Member of Local War Pensions Committee. *War Work:* Mayoress of Lancaster, Nov. 1913 to Nov. 1919; Chairman Women Munition Workers Clearing Hostel under Ministry of Munitions; Chairman the King's Own R.L.R. Care Committee for Prisoners of War; Chairman Y.W.C.A. Club for Women Munition Workers; Chairman Comforts Fund for local Territorials; Member of local Belgian Relief Committee; Food Economy Committee, War Pensions, Women's War Employment, and Red Cross Committees. *Address:* The Vale, Lancaster. (M7481)

BRIGGS, Capt. Waldo Raven, O.B.E.

BRIGGS, Major Warwick Wellington, O.B.E., R.A.S.C.

BRIGGS, William, O.B.E., J.P., C.C., *b.* 22 Nov. 1858; *s.* of Robert Briggs, of Lancaster; *m.* Mary Alice, *d.* of Richard Stanton, of Lancaster. *Educ.:* Friends' School, Lancaster. J.P. County of Lancaster; J.P. Borough of Lancaster; Member of Lancaster Town Council; Member of Lancashire County Council; Commissioner of the Port of Lancaster. *War Work:* Mayor of Lancaster from Nov. 1913 to Nov. 1919. President of The King's Own R.L.R. Prisoners of War Care Committee; Chairman of the following committees: War Pensions, Prince of Wales' Relief Fund, Belgian Refugees Committees, Recruiting, National Service, Food Control, Food Economy, War Savings, Billeting (Munition Workers), Coal Control, Charities Collection, Advisory Committee Women's War Employment and Employment Exchanges. *Address:* The Vale, Lancaster. *Club:* County (Lancaster). (O10042)

BRIGGS, William Albert, O.B.E.

BRIGGS, Helen, Mrs. CURRER-, M.B.E.; *m.* the late Arthur Currer, *s.* of Henry Currer-Briggs, of Leeds. City Council Representative of Leeds Girls' High School; Co-opted member Local Pensions Committee Leeds City Council; Chairman of Leeds Poor Children's Holiday Camp Association; Vice-President Leeds Maternity Hospital; Member of Executive Yorkshire Ladies' Council of Education (Incorporated). *War Work:* From Oct. 1914 to Feb. 1916 Hon. Treas. Leeds Belgian Refugee Committee; Gift (£2000) of Operating Theatre 2nd Northern General Hospital Beckett's Park, Leeds; Donor and Administrator of Broad Leys Officers' Convalescent Hospital, 2½ years' Windermere. *Address:* The Garth, Moor Allerton, Leeds. *Club:* Albemarle. (M7479)

BRIGHT, Alfred, M.B.E.

BRIGHT, Alfred Ernest, C.B.E., *b.* 1869; *s.* of C. E, Bright, C.M.G., and the Hon. Mrs. Bright (*see* BURKE'S *Peerage*, Canterbury, V.), of Manor House, Elstree, Herts; *m.* 1st Edith, *d.* of the late J. Tully (who died 1902), 2nd Ruby, *d.* of L. Lloyd. *Educ.:* Melbourne Grammar School, and Eton. Merchant. *Address:* St. Leonards, South Yarra, Melbourne, Victoria. *Club:* Melbourne (Melbourne, Victoria). (C706)

BRIGHT, Lieut. Harold Norman, M.B.E., Yorkshire Regt.; *b.* 2 March, 1894; *s.* of the late John Meaburn Bright, M.D., of Forest Hill. *Educ.:* Epsom Coll. Serving with 1st Batt. (A.P.W.O.) Yorkshire Regt. *War Work:* From Sept. 1914, to Feb. 1915, with 16th Middlesex Regt. (Public Schools Batt.); apptd. 2nd Lieut. 8th Batt. Yorkshire Regt., serving with it at home from Feb. 1915, to Oct. 1915; to France, joining 2nd Battn. Yorkshire Regt. Oct. 1915, serving continuously; April, 1917, present at battles of Somme and Arras, being wounded at Henin, while commanding a company; April, 1915, apptd. Adjutant 52nd West Yorkshire Regt., May, 1918; accompanied battalion to Cologne, March, 1919; became Acting Staff Capt. 3rd Northern Brigade on disbandment of battalion, from April to June, 1919; apptd. to Regular Commission Nov. 1915; promoted Lieut. Oct. 1916. *Address:* c/o Messrs. Holt & Co., 3, Whitehall Place, London, S.W. 1. (M5104)

BRIGHT, Brig.-Gen. Reginald Arthur, C.B., C.B.E. *b.* 1870; *s.* of the late Gen. Sir Robert Onesiphorus Bright, G.C.B., Col. R.A. S. Africa, 1899–1902 (despatches, Queen's medal with four clasps, King's medal with two clasps); Mesopotamia, 1914–18 (despatches). (C3086)

BRIGHTEN, Major Claude William, O.B.E.

BRIGHTEN, Edgcumbe Rendle, O.B.E.

BRIGHTMAN, Capt. Charles John, O.B.E., R.A.S.C.

BRIGHTMAN, Edith Marian, Mrs., M.B.E., *b.* 8 Oct. 1869; *d.* of E. J. Bass, of Chilham; *m.* Frank, *s.* of E. W. Brightman, of Sheerness. *War Work:* Commandant, "Fairfield" V.A.D. Hospital, Kent V.A.D. 146; Hon. Sec. Local War Pensions Sub-Committee, Broadstairs. *Address:* 1, Victoria Gardens, Broadstairs. (M173)

BRIGHTMAN, Lieut.-Col. Eustace Webster, O.B.E., R.A.S.C.

BRIGHTMAN, Major Frank, O.B.E., M.R.C.S.

BRIGHTMAN, Lieut. John Henry, O.B.E.

BRIGHTMAN, Thomas, M.B.E.

BRIMS, Lieut.-Col. Charles William, C.B.E., M.C., T.D., *b.* 1 Nov. 1877; *s.* of David N. Brims, of Newcastle-on-Tyne; *m.* Vera, *d.* of W. S. Vaughan, M. Inst. C.E., J.P., of Gosforth, Northumberland. *Educ.:* Newcastle and abroad. Civil Engineering Contractor; Chairman and Managing Director of Brims & Co., Ltd., Civil Engineering Contractors, of Newcastle and Westminster. *War Work:* Mobilised 5 Aug. 1914, as Capt. in 4th Northumbrian Brigade, R.F.A., T.F.; went to France with 50th Division, April, 1915; promoted Major, 1916; commanded Field Batteries until wounded near Arras in 1917; promoted Brevet Lieut.-Col. and sent to Admiralty and Ministry of Shipping as Director of Extensions to private shipyards and docks; remained there until after Armistice. *Addresses:* Ringstead, Weybridge, Surrey; 50, Buckingham Palace Road, S.W. 1; Pandon Buildings, Newcastle-on-Tyne. *Clubs:* St. Stephen's; Union, Newcastle. (C2470)

BRINDLEY, Louis Kirwan, M.B.E.

BRINDLEY, William, M.B.E., *b.* 8 Nov. 1872; *s.* of William Brindley, of Stoke-on-Trent; *m.* Ada Beatrice, *d.* of William Beebee, of Ettingshall, Wolverhampton. *Educ.:* Eudowed Middle School, Newcastle-under-Lyme. Divisional Officer, Board of Trade (Coal Mines Dept.). *War Work:* Divisional officer in charge of the Midland Division (Counties Staffs., Worcester, Warwick, Shropshire, Hereford), comprising 140 Local Authorities for the Administration of Household Fuel and Lighting Orders, 1918–19. *Address:* Derby House, Bilston, Staffs. (M7484)

BRINGAN, Surg.-Lieut.-Comm. James Campbell, O.B.E., M.B., R.N.

BRINKMAN, Major Rowland, O.B.E.

BRINNAND, John Thomas, M.B.E.

BRINSMEAD, Lieut.-Col. Horace Clowes, O.B.E., M.C., A.I.F. and R.A.F.

BRINSON, Major Harold Neilson, D.S.O., O.B.E.

BRISCOE, Ada Ellen, Mrs., M.B.E.

BRISCOE, Capt. Edward James, O.B.E., R.A.F.

BRISCOE, William Richard Brunskill, C.B.E., M.A., *b.* 14 Jan. 1855; *s.* of Rev. John George Briscoe, of Outwell Rectory, Norfolk; *m.* Janet, *d.* of Rev. Charles Soames, J.P., of Mildenhall Rectory, Marlborough. *Educ.:* Christ's Hospital and Trinity College, Cambridge. Barrister-at-Law, sometime Crown Prosecutor for Egypt. *War Work:* Assistant in the Intelligence Branch of the Department of H.M. Procurator-General. *Addresses:* 10, Porchester Square, W. 2; 1, King's Bench Walk, Temple, E.C., 4. (C2471)

BRISLEY, Maud Isabel, Mrs., M.B.E., *d.* of John Mudon, of Bristol, Gloucestershire; *m.* Alfred Stephen, *s.* of Stephen Brisley, of Birchington, Kent. *Educ.:* Kensington High School. Hon. Divisional Sec. Borough of Wandsworth Branch British Red Cross Society; Member of Wandsworth "B" Local War Pensions Sub-Committee. *War Work:* Organised working parties, weekly teas, and entertainments for wounded men. *Address:* Ivydene, Lower Park Fields, Putney, S.W. 15. (M7486)

BRISSENDEN, Lieut. Edwin Mayhew, M.B.E.

BRISTED, Major Richard Bower, O.B.E., R.E.

BRISTER, Capt. Joseph Fane, O.B.E., Manchester Regt., *b.* 9 Aug. 1887; *s.* of Joseph Charles, of Alnwick, Northumberland, and Manchester; *m.* Florence, *d.* of Edmund Withers, of Hertfordshire. *Educ.:* Hulme Grammar School, Manchester; St. Mary's Coll., Dublin; St. Bede's Coll., Manchester. Staff Capt. 97th Infantry Brigade. *War Work:* Served with Manchester Regt. from Sept. 1914; fought with 66th Div. through the German attack on 5th Army in 1918; served with 25th Inf. Div.; 33rd Ind. Div.; 32nd Infy. (Staff Capt. 97th Infy. Bde.; 32nd Div.); Brigade Bombing Officer 198th Infy. Bde.; mentioned in despatches and awarded the O.B.E. (Mil.). *Address:* China, Japan, and South America Trading Co., Ltd., Kobe. *Club:* Kobe (Japan). (O5044)

BRISTOW, Capt. Frank Anstie, O.B.E., L.I.

BRITT, Gwendoline Mary, M.B.E.

BRITTAIN, Lieut. Arthur William, M.B.E., R.A.F.

BRITTAIN, Ernest George, M.B.E., *b.* 5 May, 1882; *s.* of the late Beniah Brittain, of Willingale, Essex. *War Work:* Expert on the manufacture of the British anti-gas mask. *Address:* Fritton, Brighton Road, Coulsdon, Surrey. (M7487)

BRITTAIN, Sir Harry K.B.E., LL.D., M.P., *b.* 24 Dec. 1873: *s.* of W. H. Brittain, J.P., of Storth Oaks, near Sheffield; *m.* Alida Luisa, *d.* of Sir Robert Harvey, of Dundridge, S. Devon. *Educ.:* Repton; Oxford (Honours in Law). First Member of Parliament for Acton. Officer of the Crown of Belgium. *War Work:* Work carried out in U.S.A. and other work for Government during the War. *Address:* 2, Cowley St., Westminster Abbey. *Clubs:* Carlton; Bath; Constitutional; Pilgrims'; American. (K132)

BRITTAN, Col. Reginald, D.S.O., O.B.E., *b.* 1865; *s.* of Rev. Charles Brittan, of Darley Abbey, Derbyshire; *m.* Alice,*d.*of W.Gisborne, of Allestree, Derbyshire. *Educ.:* Clifton;

Malvern; Sandhurst. Commissioner, Boy Scouts, Bristol. *War Work:* Commanded 14th and 53rd Batts. Sherwood Foresters. *Address:* Failand Hill, Failand, Somerset. *Club:* Sports. (O6644)

BRITTEN, Charles Douglas, M.B.E., A.C.A.; *s.* of C. H. Britten, of Moseley, Birmingham; *m.* Ida Mildred, *d.* of S. Gillatt, of Leeds. *Educ.:* King Edward's Grammar School, Birmingham, and Queen's Coll., Taunton. Chartered Accountant. *War Work:* Member of the Examining Staff of the Costings Investigation Division of the Admiralty from April, 1915; appointed to Head Office Staff as Superintending Accountant, July, 1916, and still holds that appointment. *Address:* 55, Collingwood Avenue, Muswell Hill, N. 10. (M7488)

BRITTEN, Reginald Wellesley, M.B.E., *b.* 8 Jan. 1880; *s.* of the late Lieut.-Col. John Britten, of 106, Cambridge Gardens, W.; *m.* Kathleen Lucy, *d.* of the late Stanley Chapman, solicitor, of 27, Kensington Park Gardens, W., and Bedford Row. *Educ.:* Univ. Coll., School. Member of London Stock Exchange; Freeman of City of London; Member of Livery of Clothworkers Company. *War Work:* Head of Leather Division, War Trade Department; and Sec. to that Committee. *Address:* Little Meadow Farm, Pebworth, Stratford-on-Avon. (M7489)

BRITTEN Capt. Wallace Ernest, O.B.E., R.E.

BRITTEN, Major William Albert, O.B.E., A.P.D.

BRITTO, Valentine, M.B.E., *b.* 11 Dec. 1886; *s.* of Victor Britto, of Karachi, Sind, India. *Educ.:* St. Patrick's High School, Karachi, Sind, India. Clerk-in-charge, Indo-European Telegraph Dept., Bander Abbas, Persian Gulf. *War Work:* Assisted Anglo-Persian Oil Co. during their occupation of Kishin Island during a German attack; worked in the Indo-European Telegraph. *Address:* 21, Cromwell Road, South Kensington, W. 7. *Society:* The Northbrook Society. (M7071)

BRITTON, Ellen Alice, M.B.E.

BRITTON, Lieut. and Qr.-Mr. Walter Peaston, M.B.E.

BROAD, Capt. Archibald du Bourg, M.B.E., I.F.

BROAD, Lieut. Arthur Nowell, M.B.E.

BROAD, Lieut. Frederick Laurence, M.B.E., R.F.A., *b.* 13 May, 1880; *s.* of H. J. Broad, of 38, Teddington Park Road, Teddington, Middlesex; *m.* Rebecca, *d.* of the late Thomas Cone, of Wolstanton, Staffs. *Educ.:* Various Schools. Depot Manager, Central Stores Department, Ministry of Munitions. *War Work:* In connection with Central Stores Department, Ministry of Munitions, Depot 1208, Walton, Liverpool. *Address:* Winkleville, Lancot's Lane, Sutton Oak, St. Helens, Lancs. (M3539)

BROAD, Capt. Gordon Leslie, O.B.E., M.C., A.R.I.B.A., F.S.I., *b.* 29 April, 1885; *s.* of Jas. W. Broad, of Lewes; *m.* Ethel Margaret Forrest, *d.* of Jas. F. Mill, of Chittagong. *Educ.:* Lewes Grammar School. District Architect and Surveyor H.M. Office of Works. *War Work:* Served with 42nd Division Signal Co., R.E., Egypt and Gallipoli, 1914–15; Assistant Director of Army Signals, G.H.Q., Home Forces, 1917; Commandant Egyptian Army School of Signalling, Khartoum, 1918. *Club:* Junior Army and Navy. (O1143)

BROAD, Major Robert Norman Dymoke, O.B.E., I.A.R.O.

BROADBENT, Benjamin, C.B.E., M.A., J.P., *b.* 7 May, 1850; *s.* of John Broadbent, of Longwood Edge; *m.* Louisa A., *d.* of William Keighley, of Huddersfield. *Educ.:* Huddersfield College; King's College, London; Queen's College, Oxford. Freeman of Huddersfield; Mayor of Huddersfield, 1904–5 and 1905–6; Chairman, Health Committee and Alderman; Deputy Chairman, National Association for the Prevention of Infant Mortality. *Address:* Gatesgarth, Lindley, Huddersfield. *Clubs:* Cavendish; Overseas; Huddersfield. (C115)

BROADBENT, Lieut. John Stuart, M.B.E., R.A.S.C., (M.T.).

BROADBENT, Margaret Emily, M.B.E., *d.* of the late Charles Broadbent, of The Hollies, Latchford, Cheshire. *Educ.:* Queen's School, Chester; Liverpool Univ. Commandant Cheshire (32) V.A.D. *War Work:* Officer in charge Raddon Court Red Cross Hospital (76 beds), Latchford, Warrington, from Oct. 1914, till the closing of hospital, May, 1919. (M7491)

BROADLEY, Capt. Phillip John, O.B.E.

BROADMEAD, Edith, Mrs., O.B.E., *b.* 1862; *d.* of George Birch, of Petrograd; *m.* Rev. Philip Palfrey, *s.* of T. P. Broadmead, of Enmore Castle (*see* BURKE'S *Landed Gentry*). *Address:* Olands Hall, Somerset. (O3636)

BROADWAY, Lieut. Eric Evans, M.B.E., K.O.S.B., *b.* 22 Dec. 1896; *s.* of Alexander Boradway; *m.* Gwendolen Mostyn, *d.* of the late Major C. M. F. Watkins, R.E. *Educ.:* Merchiston Castle School, Edinburgh; R.M.C. Sandhurst. *Address:* Heath End House, Farnham, Surrey. (M5105)

BROADWOOD, Anna Maria Hennen, M.B.E.; *d.* of the late Thomas Capel Broadwood, of Lyne, Sussex. *War Work:* Voluntary services for British soldiers in Italian war zone at Gradisca and Arzignano, 1917–18. *Address:* 7, Piazza Independenza, Rome. (M7492)

BROADWOOD, Capt. Francis, O.B.E., J.P., *b.* 25 Dec. 1856; *s.* of Thomas Broadwood, late of Holmbush, Crawley, Sussex; *m.* Mary Sylvestre Charlotte, *d.* of Maximilian H. Dalison, of Hamptons, Tonbridge, Kent. *Educ.:* Harrow and Sandhurst. Retired Captain of South Staffordshire Regiment. *War Work:* National Service, Recruiting, etc. *Address:* Hever Court, Singlewell, Gravesend, Kent. *Club:* Naval and Military. (O1144)

BROATCH, Surg.-Capt. George Thomas, C.B.E., M.B., R.N.

BROCK, Major Charles Henry, O.B.E., I.A.R.O.

BROCK, Lieut. Donald Carey, O.B.E., R.N., *b.* 5 July, 1891; *s.* of the late Rev. H. W. Brock; *m.* Jocelyn Florence, *d.* of Admiral John Denison, D.S.O., of Rusholme, Alverstoke, Hants. *Educ.:* Elizabeth Coll., Guernsey. Naval Cadet, 1904; Midshipman, 1909; Sub-Lieutenant, 1912; Lieutenant, 1914. *War Work:* Lieutenant in H.M.S. "Triumph" at Naval Operations, Dardanelles, and Bombardment of Smyrna, 1915. On board that vessel when torpedoed and sunk by German submarine, May, 1915; Flag-Lieutenant on Staffs of Vice-Admiral Commanding at Gibraltar, 1915–16, and Vice-Admiral Commanding East Coast of England, 1916–18. *Club:* United Service. (O9270)

BROCK, Edith Balfour, M.B.E.

BROCK, Wing-Comm. Frank Arthur, O.B.E., R.N.

BROCK, George Sandison, M.B.E., M.D., F.R.C.P.E., F.R.S.E., Cavaliere of the Order of the Crown of Italy, *b.* 12 April, 1858; *s.* of George Brock, of Braehead, Orkney, and Greenland, Caithness; *m.* 1st, Marianne, *d.* of David Scott; 2nd, Lily Maria, *d.* of John Butler. *Educ.:* Royal High School, Edinburgh; and Univ., Edinburgh. Senior Headquarters Medical Inspector, and Deputy Commissioner of Medical Services; Ministry of Pensions; Late Asst. to Prof. of Pathology, Edinburgh University; District Surgeon Rustenburg, Transvaal; Physician to the British Embassy, Rome. *War Work:* Propaganda work in Italy, 1914–15; Chief Medical Officer, Villa Trento Hospital, near Gorizia, 1915–17; Medical Officer, Brook War Hospital, 1918; Dep. Com. of Med. Services, Ministry of National Service, 1918–19. *Address:* 6, Corso d'Italia, Rome, Italy. *Clubs:* Royal Societies'; Authors'. (M3540)

BROCK, Major William, O.B.E., *b.* 22 Sept. 1873; *s.* of William Brock, of Exeter; *m.* Annie Bradley, *d.* of Charles E. Rowe, of Exeter. *Educ.:* Exeter. Furnishing Warehouseman. *War Work:* Commissioned, Oct. 1914, Devonshire Regt.; proceeded overseas, Gallipoli, May, 1915; served Gallipoli, Egypt, Salonica, demobilised, March, 1919. *Address:* Naucherrow, Spicer Road, Exeter. (O6442)

BROCK, Capt. William Stewart Ranulf, M.B.E., (T.F. Res.).

BROCKBANK, Lieut. Charles Joseph, M.B.E., R.A.F.

BROCKBANK, Edward Mansfield, M.B.E., M.D., F.R.C.P.

BROCKBANK, Col. John Grahame, C.B.E., D.S.O., *b,* 20 Nov. 1883; *s.* of John Ben Brockbank, B.A., of Chappels, St. Bees, Cumberland; *m.* Eirene Marguerite, *d.* of Lionel G. Robinson, of Old Buckenham Hall, Norfolk. *Educ.:* Cranleigh, King's Coll. (London). Mechanical Engineer. *War Work:* Commissioned (Special Reserve), Aug. 1914, A.S.C.; transferred Machine Gun Corps, 1916; transferred Tank Corps. Jan. 1917; appointed Chief Engineer of the Corps, 1918. *Address:* 29, Sussex Place, Regent's Park, N.W. 1. *Clubs:* Badminton; Royal Automobile. (C2047)

BROCKHOLES, William Joseph FITZHERBERT-, C.B.E., D.L., J.P., County Alderman (*see* BURKE'S *Landed Gentry*), *b.* 29 May, 1851; *s.* of Francis Fitzherbert, of Swynnerton Park, Stone, Staffs.; *m.* 1st in 1876, Mary Ida (died 1883), *d.* of the late Robert Berkeley, of Spetchley Park, Worcestershire; 2nd in 1885, Blanche Winifred Mary, *d.* of the late Major-Gen. the Hon. Sir Henry Hugh Clifford, V.C., K.C.M.G., C.B. (*see* BURKE'S *Peerage*, Clifford, B.). *Educ.:* St Mary's College, Oscott. *War Work:* Chairman, Lancashire War Agricultural Executive Committee; Member of the Agricultural Policy Sub-Committee of the Reconstruction Committee; Chairman of the Garstang Tribunal. *Address:* Claughton Hall, Garstang, Lancashire. *Clubs:* Junior Carlton; Wellington. (C160)

BROCKINGTON, William Allport, O.B.E., M.A., King Albert Medal with bar (Belgium), *b.* 18 June, 1871; *s.* of Thomas Alfred, of Birmingham; *m.* Jessie, *d.* of Alexander MacGeoch, of Birmingham. *Educ.:* King Edward's School and Mason University College, Birmingham. Director of Education for Leicestershire; Divisional Director of Industrial Training (Ministry of Labour), for East Midlands Area. *War Work:* County Secretary for National Relief and War Refugees Committees; Organiser of Training for Ministry of Munitions; Major commanding 2nd V.B. Leicestershire Regt.; Chairman, Leicestershire War Pensions Committee. *Address:* Birstall, Leicester. *Club:* County, Leicester. (O5)

BROCKLEBANK, Agnes Sylvia, O.B.E. Chairman of the Central Council, Forage Dept., Civil Supplies, Women's Legion. (O11895)

BROCKLEBANK, Capt. Henry Cyril Royds, C.B.E., R.N.

BROCKLEBANK, Stanley Hartree, M.B.E.

BROCKLEBANK, Thomas Haslehurst, O.B.E.

BROCKLEHURST, Herbert Cecil, M.B.E.

BROCKLESBY, Isabel, Mrs., M.B.E.

BROCKS, Capt. Arthur William, M.B.E.

BRODERICK, Lieut. Richard, O.B.E., R.N.

BRODIE, Arthur William, M.B.E.

BRODIE of BRODIE, Caroline Violet Mary, Mrs., O.B.E., *b.* 11 Sept. 1878; *d.* of Lieut.-Col. Montagu Hope; *m.* 28 Apr. 1904, Ian Ashley Moreton Brodie of Brodie (*see*

BURKE'S *Landed Gentry*). *War Work:* Scottish Branch, B.R.C.S. *Address:* Brodie Castle, Forres.

BRODIE, Capt. Harry Campbell, M.B.E., *b.* 22 June, 1875; *s.* of William John Brodie, of Edinburgh; *m.* Pamela Elizabeth, *d.* of Francis Kirkwell, of Dundee. *Educ.:* Wyggeston Grammar School, Leicester. Capt. and Quartermaster, Leicestershire Regt. *War Work:* British Expd. Force, France, Oct. 1914 to Nov. 1915; Mesopotamian Expd. Force, Nov. 1915 to Nov. 1916; twice mentioned in despatches; Staff Capt., War Office, Aug. 1918, to Aug. 1920. (M5107)

BRODIE, Marial, M.B.E.; *d.* of John Brodie, of Tirydail. Hon. Sec. of Y.W.C.A.; Local worker. *War Work:* Formed Nursing Brigade of St. John Ambulance Association; organised and acted as Commandant at Military Aux. Hospital, Stebonheath, Llanelly. *Address:* Cheriton, Old Road, Llanelly. (M5542)

BRODIE, Rhoda, M.B.E.,; *d.* of Robert Brodie, M.A., of 20, St. Peter's Road, Croydon. *Educ.:* Croydon High School for Girls. Sec. to Croydon Mothers and Infants Welfare Association. *War Work:* Hon. Sec. of Croydon Association of Voluntary Organisations; Leader of Croydon Women Patrols (voluntary and paid); Hon. Sec. Hospitality Committee of Croydon War Refugees Committee; Clerk in Croydon Branch of Sun Life Assurance Association. *Address:* 20, St. Peter's Road, Croydon. (M1468)

BRODIE, Major Richard, M.B.E.,, R.A.M.C.

BRODIGAN, Mary Christina, M.B.E., *b.* 2 Feb. 1875; *d.* of Colonel Brodigan, of Piltown House, Drogheda. Hon. Superintendent of H.R.H. Princess Marie Louise Club for Working Girls, Bermondsey. *War Work:* Org. Sec. Bishop of Southwark's Council for Munition Areas; Warden of Joan of Arc Hostel, Plumstead, Woolwich, for 700 munition workers. *Address:* Piltown House, Drogheda. *Club:* Lyceum. (M7405)

BRODRIBB, Noel Kenrice Stevens, O.B.E. (O11955)

BRODRICK, Thomas Noel, O.B.E., I.S.O., *b.* 25 Dec. 1855; *s.* of the late Thomas Brodrick, of Invercargill, New Zealand; *m.* Helen, *d.* of the late Justin John Aylmer, of Akaroa, New Zealand. *Educ.:* Privately. Under Secretary of Lands and Surveyor-General for Dominion of New Zealand. *War Work:* In connection with settling discharged soldiers upon the land. *Address:* 22, Talavera Terrace, Wellington, New Zealand. (O8318)

BRODRICK, William John Henry, O.B.E.

BROKE, Marie Frances Lisette WILLOUGHBY DE-, O.B.E.

BROMEHEAD, Capt. Francis Edward ORANGE-, O.B.E., R.E., *b.* 9 May, 1893; *s.* of Col. J. E. Orange-Bromehead, of Newbold, near Chesterfield. *Educ.:* Cheltenham Coll. *War Work:* Serving abroad. *Address:* c/o Messrs. Cox & Co., 16, Charing Cross, London, S.W. 1. (O3054)

BROMET, Geoffrey Rhodes, O.B.E. (O3269)

BROMHEAD, Lieut.-Col. Alfred Claude, C.B.E., *b.* 25 July, 1876; *s.* of Sidney S. Bromhead, of Bristol; *m.* Gertrude Carmela, *d.* of Charles W. Comer, of Fitzhead, Somerset. *Educ.:* Dulwich and Paris. Managing Director of the Gaumont Co., Ltd. *War Work:* Rejoined 24th London Regt. in Sept. 1914; appointed Adjutant, 1915; seconded for special duty and sent to Russia, Jan. 1916; saw service with Russian Armies from Riga to Caucasus, including Rumania; decorated twice by Czar; returned Russia with Special Mission to Russian Armies in the Field, 1917, and in 1918 sent to Italy at head of Special Mission to Italian Armies in the Field. *Address:* 37, Ladbroke Grove, Holland Park, W. 11. *Club:* Royal Societies'. (C116)

BROMHEAD, Ethel, M.B.E.,; *d.* of Lieut.-Col. E. R. Bromhead, of Canterbury. *War Work:* Hon. Sec. S. & S.F.A. from 4 Aug. 1914, Assistant Hon. Sec. to War Pensions Committee, June, 1916, and afterwards Hon. Sec., and finally Sec. to the same until February, 1919. *Address:* St. Dunstan's House, Canterbury. *Club:* Sesame. (M7496)

BROMILOW, Major Bernard Heatherington, M.B.E., S.A.S.C.

BROMILOW, Brig.-Gen. Walter, C.B.E., *b.* 11 Aug. 1865; *s.* of the late H. G. Bromilow, J.P., of Southport and St. Helens, Lancs.; *m.* Adelaide Lucy, *d.* of the late W. Price, M.I.C.E. *Educ.:* Private School. *War Work:* Commanded Staffordshire Infantry Brigade, T.F.; 118th Infantry Brigade; 8th Training Reserve Brigade; No, XI District and Infantry Records, Dublin. *Club:* Army and Navy Club. (C1481)

BROMWICH, Frederick Dudman, M.B.E., *b.* 12 Nov. 1872; *s.* of Charles Frederick Bromwich, of Derby; *m.* Katie Neville, *d.* of Charles Morton, of London. *Educ.:* Privately. *War Work:* Organising Entertainments, etc., for the wounded. (M9747)

BROMWICH, Eng.-Capt. George Herbert, D.S.O., O.B.E., R.N. General Manager, Garden Island, New South Wales. *Address:* Garden Island, Sydney, N.S.W. (O11916)

BROOK, Arthur, M.B.E.

BROOK, Capt. Leonard Thornicraft, M.B.E.

BROOK, Mabel Frances, Mrs., M.B.E.; *d.* of the late William Brook, of Healey House, Huddersfield; *m.* Charles, *s.* of the late Edward Brook, of Hoddom Castle, Dumfriesshire. *War Work:* Commandant of Kinmount Red Cross Auxiliary Hospital, Annan, N.B.; Commandant of Glen Stuart Red Cross Auxiliary Hospital, Cummertrees, N.B., March, 1915 to Nov. 1918. *Address:* Kinmount, Annan. (M7499)

BROOK, Capt. (Brevet Lieut.-Col.) Reginald James, C.B.E., D.S.O., Royal Canadian Regt., *b.* 16 Sept. 1885; *s.* of

Arthur and Ruth Brook, of Weybridge, Surrey ; *m.* Eleanor, *d.* of Henry Darlington, of Wigan. *Educ. :* Uppingham. A.A. & Q.M.G., H.Q., M.D. 2 Toronto, Canada. *War Work :* 1914–18, France with Canadian Expeditionary Force (D.A.A.G.) ; 1918–19, Siberia with Canadian Siberian Exped. Force (A.A. & Q.M.G. and G.S.O.). *Address :* A.A. & Q.M.G., M.D. 2, Toronto, Canada.   (C2213a)

BROOK, Major Reginald Vernon Charlesworth, O.B.E., R.A.F.

BROOK, Major Thomas Fleetwood, O.B.E., I.A.

BROOKE, Dorothy, Mrs., M.B.E., *b.* 4 Oct. 1887 ; *d.* of Dr. Horace Lamb, LL.D., D.Sc., F.R.S., of Trinity Coll., Cambridge ; *m.* John Reeve, C.B., *s.* of John Reeve Brooke, of Lincoln's Inn Fields. *Educ. :* Newnham Coll., Cambridge. Studied at British School of Archæology in Athens ; 1912–13, held Chair of Archæology at Bryn Mawr Coll., U.S.A. ; 1913–14, Travelling Fellowship, Newnham Coll., Cambridge. *War Work :* 1915–16, Shift Forewoman, Perivale Inspection Factory, under Woolwich Arsenal ; 1916–18, Administrative Official in Directorate of Recruiting, both under the War Office and National Service Departments ; 1919, Sec. to the London Committee of the Supreme Economical Council ; 1920, Sec. to the Official Committee for Relief in Europe (Treasury). *Address :* 1, Mitre Court Buildings, Temple, E.C.   (M467)

BROOKE, Grace Milicent, M.B.E. ; *d.* of the late Ven. Archdeacon J. Ingham Brooke, of Halifax, Yorkshire. *War Work :* Hon. Sec. of Soldiers' and Sailors' Families Assoc., and London War Pensions Committee, Hammersmith A. Division, from Sept. 1914 to March, 1919. *Club :* Ladies' Athenæum.   (M7300)

BROOKE, Col. Harry Morris Mitchelson, C.B.E.   (C3087)

BROOKE, Capt. Sir Harry Vesey, K.B.E., J.P., D.L., *b.* 1845 ; *s.* of Sir Arthur Brooke, Bart., M.P. (*see* BURKE'S *Peerage*), of Colebrooke, Co. Fermanagh ; *m.* Patricia, *d.* of G. Moir-Byres, J.P., of Tonley, Aberdeenshire (*see* BURKE'S *Landed Gentry*). *Educ. :* Sandhurst. Served for 15¼ years with 92nd Gordon Highlanders. *War Work :* Chairman of Aberdeen District Emergency Committee, District Committee, Gordon Highlanders Prisoners of War Committee, London and Aberdeen, and Soldiers' and Sailors' Help and Families Associations ; Administrator of comforts for 1st and 2nd Batts. Gordon Highlanders during the War. *Address :* Fairley, Countesswells, Aberdeenshire. *Clubs :* Naval and Military ; Royal Northern, Aberdeen.   (K336)

BROOKE, Col. Hugh Fenwick, C.B., C.M.G., C.B.E.

BROOKE, John Walter, O.B.E., J.P., M.I.Mech.E., *b.* 10 June, 1849 ; *s.* of John Brooke, of London ; *m.* Jane Anne, *d.* of John Hogg, of London. *Educ. :* Charterhouse and privately. Alderman, Borough of Lowestoft ; Chairman J. W. Brooke & Co., Engineers, Lowestoft ; Member Institute Mech. Engineers. *War Work :* Recruiting, Chairman Emergency Committee ; Chairman Local Tribunal, and other Committees ; three consecutive years Mayor of Lowestoft, 1915–17. *Club :* Royal Automobile.   (O10046)

BROOKE, Capt. Joshua Rupert Ingham, M.B.E., R.G.A. (T.F.).

BROOKE, Margery Jean, Lady, M.B.E., *b.* 25 April, 1886 ; *d.* of Alexander Geddes, of Blairmore, Aberdeenshire ; *m.* Sir Robert Weston, *s.* of the late Sir John Arthur Brooke, Bart., of Fenay Hall, Huddersfield, and Fearn Lodge, Ross-shire (*see* BURKE'S *Peerage*). *War Work :* Vice-President, Ardgay Branch Red Cross ; War Pensions Committee (Local and Sub). *Address :* Midfearn Cottage, Ardgay, Ross-shire.   (M7501)

BROOKE, Brevet Col. Ronald George, C.B.E., D.S.O. ; *s.* of Sir Victor Brooke, Bart., of Colebrooke (*see* BURKE'S *Peerage*) ; *m.* Haller, *d.* of Orville Horwitz, of Baltimore, Maryland, U.S.A. *Educ. :* Marlborough ; Royal Military College ; Staff College. 7th Hussars and 11th Hussars, retired ; Chitral Relief Force, 1895 (medal with clasp) ; Tirah Expeditionary Force, 1897 (two clasps) ; A.D.C. to Gen. Gatacre during Atbara and Khartoum Campaigns, 1898 (medal with two clasps, Khedive's Medal, D.S.O.) ; South Africa, 1899–1902 (despatches three times, Brevet-Major, Queen's Medal, seven clasps, King's Medal, two clasps) ; Somaliland, 1903 (despatches twice, medal with two clasps, Humane Society Silver Medal, Brevet Lieut.-Col.) ; Great War 1914–19, mentioned for valuable services in connection with the War, Feb. 1917, (Brevet Col. June, 1917, C.B.E. July, 1918). *Address :* Brooke House, Valescure, St. Raphael, France. *Club :* Cavalry.   (C1482)

BROOKE, Edward Geoffrey DE CAPELL-, C.B.E., *b.* 1880. *Educ. :* Radley ; Merton College, Oxford. *War Work :* Prov. Sec. in Chief of Imperial General Staff. *Club :* Travellers'.   (C2472)

BROOKES, Albert Edward, O.B.E., M.Inst.T., M.I.M. & C.E., *b.* 10 Jan. 1870 ; *s.* of Edw. D. C. Brookes, of Manchester and Southport ; *m.* Amy I., *d.* of the late Robt. Wm. White, of Manchester. *Educ. :* Liverpool Institute and Macclesfield Grammar School. County Surveyor, Engineer and Architect, Durham County Council. *War Work :* Acted as Resident Chief Engineer to the Road Board in the Southern and Western Commands in connection with the construction of roads and other engineering works in camps, aerodromes, etc., for the War Office, Admiralty, Ministry of Munitions, Air Ministry, etc. *Address :* Shire Hall, Durham. *Club :* Golfers'.   (O10047)

BROOKES, Arthur Stuart, M.B.E.

BROOKES, Florence, Hon. Mrs. M. Jones, C.B.E. ; *e. d.* of the late Frederick Freeman Thomas, M.P., of Ratton, Co.

Sussex (*see* BURKE'S *Peerage*, Willingdon, B.) ; *m.* 29 April 1899, Hon. Marshall James Brookes, M.A., Brasenose Coll., Oxford, J.P. Lancashire and Cheshire, 2nd *s.* of the 1st Baron Crawshaw. *Address :* Portal, Tarporley, Cheshire.   (C444)

BROOKS, Alice, M.B.E.

BROOKS, Sir Arthur David, G.B.E., J.P., *b.* 6 March, 1864 ; *s.* of Arthur Brooks, of Birmingham ; *m.* Florence Ethel, *d.* of Frederick Howe, of Norwich. *Educ. :* King Edward's School, Birmingham. Solicitor. *War Work :* Lord Mayor of Birmingham, 1917–19 ; Chairman of Food Control Committee ; Chairman of Military Tribunal ; Chairman Fuel and Lighting Committee ; Chairman War Savings. *Address :* Woodcote, Harborne, Birmingham. *Clubs :* Union Club ; Conservative Club, Birmingham ; Municipal and Counties Club, London.   (G31)

BROOKS, Charles John Wood, M.B.E.

BROOKS, Charlotte Elizabeth, Lady, M.B.E., *b* 17 Feb. 1878 ; *d.* of the late Rev. W. A. Bathurst ; *m.* Sir James Henry Brooks, K.C.B., J.P. (*see* BURKE'S *Peerage*), *s.* of James Henry Brooks, of Seychelles (*see* BURKE'S *Landed Gentry*). *Educ. :* Cedar House, Salt Hill, Slough. *War Work :* Voluntary clerical work at Professional Classes War Relief Council, National War Savings, and Admiralty, from March, 1915, to Sept. 1919. *Address :* 11, Cedar House, Marloes Road, Kensington, W. 8.   (M7504)

BROOKS, 2nd Lieut. Ernest, M.B.E.

BROOKS, Florence Ethel, Lady, C.B.E., *b.* 23 July, 1884 ; *d.* of Frederick Howe, of Norwich ; *m.* Arthur David, *s.* of Arthur Brooks, of Birmingham. *Educ. :* Birmingham and Brussels. *War Work :* Lady Mayoress of Birmingham, Jan 1917 to Nov. 1919. *Address :* Woodcote, Harborne, Birmingham. *Club :* Three Counties Club, Birmingham.   (C2473)

BROOKS, George Harold, M.B.E.

BROOKS, 2nd Lieut. George Thomas Adams, M.B.E., R.D.C.

BROOKS, Gladys Muriel, M.B.E., *b.* 9 Dec. 1886 ; *d.* of Herbert Edmund Brooks, J.P., C.A., of Stifford Lodge, Grays, Essex. *Educ. :* Bieberich a/Rhein, Germany, and Roedean School, nr. Brighton. *War Work :* Helped collect and make hospital equipment and clothing ; learned motor-driving to release a man ; Feb. 1915, to Aug. 1915, was with Lady Wimborne's unit for work in Serbia ; decorated with the Serbian Cross of Charity ; Oct. 1915, joined Rosherville V.A.D. Hospital, Kent, for nursing duties ; appointed Commandant, March. 1916, and Assist. Commandant Rosherville and Ingress Abbey V.A.D. Hospital in June, 1917. *Address :* Stifford Lodge, nr. Grays, Essex.   (M7503)

BROOKS, Lieut. Henry Arthur, M.B.E.

BROOKS, Capt. John Chadwick, M.B.E., R.A.O.C.

BROOKS, Lieut. John Rowe, M.B.E.

BROOME, Capt. Lewis John, M.B.E.

BROOME, Capt. Louis Egerton, M.B.E.

BROOME, Comm. Thomas Charles, O.B.E., R.D., R.N.R.

BROOMFIELD, Dorothy, Mrs., M.B.E.

BROOMFIELD, Frederick Harry, M.B.E.

BROOMHALL, Capt. Harold George, M.B.E., *b.* 26 May, 1880 ; *s.* of Edward Barron Broomhall, of Bromley, Kent ; *m.* Dorothy Mary Josephine, *d.* of Walter Grimes, of Altrincham, Cheshire, and Amersham, Bucks. *Educ. :* Privately. *War Work :* Joined R.A.S.C., O.T.C., Aldershot, Dec. 1915 ; commissioned 2nd Lieut. Feb. 1916 ; Acting Lieut., May, 1917 ; Lieut. Aug. 1917 ; Acting Capt. Aug. 1918 ; mentioned March 1918 ; M.B.E., June, 1919 ; engaged in supply work ; Military Member, Port Labour and Transit Committee, King's Lynn, 1919. *Address :* Finchers, Amersham, Bucks. *Club :* United R.A.S.C.   (M6604)

BROSNAN, Rev. John Brodie, M.B.E., R.A.Ch.D.

BROSTER, Major Lennox Ross, O.B.E., M.A., M.D. (Oxon.), R.A.M.C., *b.* 1889 ; *s.* of Charles John Broster, of Cape Colony ; *m.* Edith Mary Victoria, *d.* of D. C. J. Thomas, of Southampton. *Educ. :* Trinity Coll., Oxford. Surgeon, D.A.D.M.S. *War Work :* 14th Division, Feb. 1915, to Dec. 1916 ; Tank Corps, 1916–19 ; D.A.D.M.S. *Address :* 3, Winn Road, Southampton.   (O5046)

BROTHERS, Lieut.-Col. Orlando Frank, O.B.E., M.C., *b.* 1878 ; *s.* of F. W. Brothers, of Blackburn, Lancs. ; *m.* Janet Bell, *a.* of J. McClelland, of Edinburgh. *Educ. :* Hutton, Lancs. Secretary, Transvaal Police, 1900–1906 ; Editor, "The Old Countryman," Vancouver. Boer War, 1899–1902 : Lieut. *War Work :* Canadian Exped. Forces, British Columbia Regiment, Aug. 1914–19 and General Staff. *Clubs :* Junior Naval and Military ; Press (London) ; Tedesco County, Mass., U.S.A.   (O1147)

BROUGH, Major and Bt. Lieut.-Col. Alan, C.M.G., C.B.E., D.S.O., R.E., *b.* 20 March, 1876 ; *s.* of Col. W. R. C. Brough, late Royal Artillery. *Educ. :* Cheltenham College. Royal Engineers. *War Work :* Served with 7th Division from 27 Dec. 1914, to 1 Sept. 1915 ; from 1 Sept. 1915, to 10 July, 1917, with Guards Division ; from 10 July, 1917, to 2 Sept. 1918, transportation in France ; from 2 Sept. 1918, to 2 Jan. 1919, transportation Mesopotamia ; from 2 Jan. 1919, to 17 Nov. 1919, transportation Trans-Caucasus ; from 17 Nov. 1919, to 6 Aug. 1920, South Russia. Temp. Brig.-Gen. *Clubs :* United Service Club ; Pall Mall.   (C2070)

BROUGH, Lieut. Frederick Arthur, M.B.E., R.A.F. (T.F.).

BROUGHAM, Diana Isabel, Hon. Mrs., O.B.E., *b.* 1884 ; *d.* of the late Lord Alington, of Crichel, Wimborne (*see* BURKE'S *Peerage*) ; *m.* Henry, *e. s.* of Lord Brougham and Vaux, of

Brougham, Penrith (*see* BURKE'S *Peerage*). *War Work :* Headquarters, V.A.D. Department, British Red Cross Society and Order of St. John. *Address :* 10, Oxford Square, Hyde Park. *Clubs ;* Ladies' Automobile ; V.A.D. (O3637)

BROUGHAM, Capt. James Henry Chamberlain, M.B.E.

BROUGHTON, Lieut. Cecil Howard, M.B.E., R.E. (M5111)

BROUGHTON, Lieut.-Col. Geoffrey Delves, O.B.E., Welch Regt., *b.* 10 May 1880 ; *s.* of Lieut.-Col Delves Broughton, E. Yorks Regt. (*see* BURKE'S *Peerage*) ; *m.* 1 Sept. 1913, Violet Carnegie, *d.* of H. Anstey and *w.* of Talbot Dean-Pitt, G.S O. (2nd grade). (O8575)

BROUGHTON, Gladys Mary, O.B.E., *b.* 30 Oct. 1883 ; *d.* of William Barnard Broughton, Captain, Dorset Regiment. *Educ. :* High School, Bedford ; University College, London ; School of Economics, London. Inspectress of schools, Central Provinces, India. *War Work :* Welfare Work, Ministry of Munitions. *Address :* 50, Morpeth Mansions, London, S.W. 1. (O8)

BROUSSON, Robert Percy, O.B.E.

BROWETT, Leonard, O.B.E.

BROWN, Hon. Lieut.-Col. Adam, O.B.E., M.B., Ch.B., R.A.M.C., *b.* 21 Dec. 1886 ; *s.* of Richard Cragg Brown, of Seaton, Cumberland. *Educ. :* Workington, Cumberland. *War Work :* Senior Medical Officer, Camel Transport Corps, E.E.F. ; Surgeon to P. of W. Hospitals, Egyptian Hospitals, E.E.F. ; D.A.D.M.S., Egyptian Hospitals, E.E.F. ; O.C. No. 3 Egyptian Stationary Hospital, E.E.F. *Addresses :* Galecroft, Seaton, Cumberland ; Beechwood, Workington, Cumberland. (O6148)

BROWN, Agnes Elizabeth, M.B.E., *b.* 16 Sept. 1876; *d* of Pereira Brown, of Glentworth Hall, Lincs. *Educ. :* Hamilton House, Tunbridge Wells. Councillor, Scarborough Town Council. *War Work :* Sec. and Treas., Mayoress of Scarborough's Prisoners of War Committee ; Sec. and Treas., Mayoress of Scarborough's Branch Working Party, under D.G.V.O. ; also on Committee of Mayoress' Central Committee for War Comforts. *Address :* 6, Cromwell Terrace, Scarborough. (M7506)

BROWN, Capt. Albert James Studd, O.B.E.

BROWN, Albert Thomas, M.B.E. (M1472)

·BROWN, Major and Qr.-Mr. Alexander, M.B.E., M.C., D.C.M.

BROWN, Capt. Alfred Claude, M.B.E. R.A.S.C. (T.F.), *b.* 1885 ; *s.* of Alfred E. Brown, late of Clacton-on-Sea, now of Blythwood, Biggin Hill, Westerham, Kent ; *m.* Nellie, *d.* of M. Greevy, of Birmingham. *Educ. :* Stationers' Co. School, Hornsey, London, N. Inspector of Films for Bengal. *War Work :* Commissioned Oct. 1914 ; N.M.D. Train Leicester ; served during Irish Rebellion, 1916 ; served in Mesopotamia, March, 1917 to Oct. 1919 ; O.C., R.A.S.C., Kirkuk, during Fraser Force operations, 1919. *Address :* The Cottage, Theatre Road, Calcutta. (M7023)

BROWN, Lieut. Alfred Thomas, M.B.E.

BROWN, Lieut. Algernon Gordon, O.B.E., R.F.A.

BROWN, Alice, O.B.E.

BROWN, Alice Elizabeth, Mrs., O.B.E.

BROWN, Lieut. Alwin, O.B.E., R.A.O.C.

BROWN, Annie Kathleen, M.B.E.

BROWN, Archibald, O.B.E., *b.* 4 Nov, 1867 ; *s.* of Archibald Brown, of Westland, New Cumnock, Ayrshire : *m.* Ada Catherine, *d.* of John Steele, of " Mayfield," West Kirby. *Educ. :* New Cumnock Parish School. Brassfounder and Coppersmith. *War Work :* Organising and Commanding the Liverpool Special Constabulary during the War. *Address :* 24, Huntley Road, Liverpool. (O181)

BROWN, Archibald Hall, M.B.E.

BROWN, Arthur Cecil, O.B.E., *b.* 29 Feb. 1876. Agent, Bank of Bengal, Dacca, India. *Address :* Hessle, East Yorkshire ; 53, New Broad Street, E.C. (O4020)

BROWN, Lieut.-Col. Arthur Edmund, O.B.E.

BROWN, Capt. Arthur George, M.B.E., I.M.S.

BROWN, Capt. Arthur Richard Dupuis, M.B.E.

BROWN, Col. Arthur Rudston, O.B.E.,

BROWN, Capt. Arthur Walter, M.B.E.

BROWN, Sir Arthur Whitten, K.B.E., late R.F.A. ; *s.* of A. G. Brown, of Manchester ; *m.* Marguerite Kathleen, *d.* of Major D. H. Kennedy, of Ealing. Decorated for first crossing the Atlantic in an aeroplane, 4.28 p.m. to 8.40 a.m., 14–15 June, 1919. (K353)

BROWN, Lieut. Bertram John, M.B.E., late 6th V. Batt. (P.W.O.) West Yorkshire Regt., *b.* 2 June, 1880 ; *s.* of George Brown, of Smethwick, South Staffs. ; *m.* Gertrude, *d.* of Charles Owen, of Birmingham. *Educ. :* Central Higher Grade School, Smethwick, South Staffs. Manager of the Hippodrome, Leeds, formerly of the Hippodrome, Brighton. *War Work :* Organiser of Vaudeville entertainments by members of the theatrical and music hall profession for the Northern Command hospitals and Mansion House concerts at York. *Address :* 27, Avenue Crescent, Roundhay, Leeds. *Club :* Carlton (Brighton). (M7507)

BROWN, Lieut. Cecil Norman, M.B.E.

BROWN, Capt. Cecil Thomas, M.B.E., R.M.A.

BROWN, Lieut. Charles Frederick, M.B.E., R.N.V.R., *b.* 1895 ; *s.* of F. B. Brown, O.B.E., A.M.I.C.E. *Educ. :* Dulwich College and Christ Church Oxford. *Club :* Primrose. (M175)

BROWN, Major Charles John, O.B.E.

BROWN, Lieut.-Col. Claude, O.B.E., A.D.C.

BROWN, Cuthbert, M.B.E.

BROWN, Daniel MacLaren, O.B.E. (O12042)

BROWN, David, M.B.E.

BROWN, Surg. Sub-Lieut. Donald Eadie, M.B.E., R.N.V.R.

BROWN, Dorothy Ann, Mrs, M.B.E. ; *d.* of the late Edmund Ellery Bowden ; *m.* Frederick John Brown. *War Work :* Commandant of Southwood V.A.D. Hospital, Bickley, Kent, from Oct. 1914, until Feb. 1919. *Address :* St. Cuthbert's, Berkhamsted, Herts. (M7508)

BROWN, Dorothy Ierne, Mrs., O.B.E., *b.* 12 April, 1889 ; *d.* of the late Sir Evelyn Freeth, of Estate Duty Office, Somerset House ; *m.* Stuart Kelson Brown. *Educ. :* Royal Holloway Coll., Surrey. *War Work :* With Mr. Lloyd George in Treasury and Ministry of Munitions ; with Mr. Montagu in Ministry of Munitions, Reconstruction Committee and India Office. *Address :* 5, Holly Place, Hampstead, N.W. 3. (O10436)

BROWN, Lieut. Douglas Archibald Guillan, M.B.E.

BROWN, Comm. Duncan Tatton, O.B.E. R.N.

BROWN, Edward John, M.B.E., F.I.P.S., *b.* 28 March, 1877 ; *s.* of Daniel Alfred Brown, of Eton ; *m.* Margaret, *d.* of John Hogan, of Coniston, Lancs. *Educ. :* St. Mark's Coll., Chelsea. Confidential shorthand writer to the Secretary of State for War since 1907, and previously in the Director of Works Department, Admiralty. *War Work :* Time entirely devoted to official work in personal attendance on successive Secretaries of State with the sole exception of a short period at 10, Downing Street, on the appointment of Mr. Lloyd George to be Prime Minister. *Address :* 53, Pepys Road, Wimbledon, S.W. 19 (M7509)

BROWN, Edward Walter, O.B.E.

BROWN, Capt. Edwin, M.B.E.

BROWN, Emily May, M.B.E., *b.* 9 May, 1891 ; *d.* of Col. Thos. W. Brown, V.D., of Manchester. *Educ. :* Edmundsbury ; Eastbourne ; La Prairie, Vevey, Switzerland. *War Work :* Quartermaster, East Lancs., 98 B.R.C.S., at Woodlawn Auxiliary Military Hospital, West Didsbury, 1914–19. *Address :* 84, Palatine Road, West Didsbury, Manchester. (M7510)

BROWN, Capt. Ernest Addison, M.B.E.

BROWN, Lieut.-Col. Ernest Rudolf, C.B E. Lieut.-Col. Canadian Army Med. Corps ; Great War 1915–19 (despatches). (C1880)

BROWN, Capt. Everard Kenneth, M.B.E., *b.* 19 Aug. 1879 ; *s.* of Rev. John Brown, D.D., of Hampstead, formerly of Bedford. *Educ. :* Bedford. Solicitor ; partner in the firm of Kenneth Brown, Baker, Baker, of Lennox House, Norfolk Street, Strand, W.C.2 ; First Prizeman (Clements Inn and Daniel Reardon Prizes), Law Society's Honours Examination, Nov. 1902. *War Work :* Intelligence Officer, General Staff, Northern Command. *Addresses :* Lennox House, Norfolk Street, Strand, W.C. 2 ; 10, Upper Park Road, Hampstead, N.W. 3. *Club :* Devonshire. (M1477)

BROWN, Florence Fannie, Mrs., M.B.E. ; *d.* of Elliott Robert Odams, of Ives, Huntingdonshire ; *m.* William, *s.* of John Brown, of Manchester. *Educ. :* Cambridge. *War Work :* Vice-President B.R.C. Society, Heaton Chapel Division, East Lancs. ; Searcher, Wounded and Missing, Jan. 1915–19 ; Canadian Visitor, 1915–19 ; on various War Work Committees. *Addresses :* The Laurels, Heaton Mersey, Manchester ; Netherlaw, Kirkcudbright. (M177)

BROWN, Capt. Francis Giles, O.B.E., R.A.F.

BROWN, Major Francis Robert, O.B.E., M.B., Ch.B., F.R.C.S., R.A.M.C., *b.* 29 Sept. 1889 ; *s.* of John Brown, of Hundalee, Jedburgh ; *m.* Hannah, *d.* of George Pearson, of Heath, Leighton Buzzard. *Educ. :* Edinburgh Univ. *War Work :* Edinburgh War Hospital, Bangour ; Surgical Specialist, 28th Gen. Hosp., Brit. Salonika Force ; Surgical Specialist, 27th C.C.S., Brit. Salonika Force, and at Batoum, Army of Black Sea ; mentioned in Gen. Milne's despatch of March, 1919. Russian Order of St. Stanislaus, 2nd Class. *Address :* Muir House, Stow, Midlothian. (O8679)

BROWN, Frank James, C.B.E., M.A., B.Sc. (Lond.), *b.* 5 Feb. 1865 ; *s.* of William Brown, of Skelton, York ; *m.* Lucy, *d.* of Richard Shaw, of Brompton, Yorkshire. *Educ. :* Privately. Assist.-Sec., General Post Office ; Member of British Peace Delegation, in capacity of expert adviser on telegraph matters ; Member of Imperial Communications Committee ; Member of Imperial Wireless Telegraphy Committee. *War Work :* Various official work in connection with maintenance of telegraph communication with the Empire and Foreign Countries. *Addresses :* Secretary's Office, General Post Office, E.C. 1 ; Romney Close, North End, Hampstead, N.W. 3. (C2476)

BROWN, Capt. Frank Leader, O.B.E., R.E.

BROWN, Lieut. Frederick, M.B.E., R.F.A.

BROWN, Major Frederick Alexander William, O.B.E., R.A.O.C.

BROWN, Frederick Benjamin, O.B.E.

BROWN, Frederick Lenox Harman, O.B.E., M.B., C.M. (Edin.), *b.* 1863 ; *s.* of Major Fredk. John Harman Brown, of Cheltenham ; *m.* Dora Annie, *d.* of Vickers Jones, of Coventry. *Educ. ;* Privately ; Edinburgh Univ. *War Work :* Hon. Surgeon, Coventry and Warwickshire Hospital ; Hon. Surgeon, Courtbauld's Hospital. *Address :* St. Oswald, Highweek, Newton Abbot. *Club :* Conservative. (O4354)

BROWN, Major Geoffrey Manwaring, O.B.E., *b.* 15 Jan. 1891 ; *s.* of Frederick William Brown, of Southport, Lancs. ; *m.* Mabel Frances, *d.* of Thomas Bentley-Turner, of Colchester. *Educ. :* Haileybury ; King's Coll., Cambridge. D.A.Q.M.G., at G.H.Q. France. *War Work :* 1914, Adjutant 10th Batt.

Suffolk Regt.; 1915, Captain; 1918 Major. *Clubs*: R.A.C.; Cambridge University Cruising. (O5048)

BROWN, Capt. Geoffrey William, M.B.E.

BROWN, George, M.B.E., *b.* 9 March, 1872; *e.s.* of William Brown, of Dunkinty, Elgin; *m.* Anne, *d.* of David Bruce, of Stirling. *Educ.*: Inverness Coll.; Edinburgh Univ. A member of the Faculty of Advocates; Sec. Scottish Unionist Association. *War Work*: Joint Hon. Sec. East of Scotland Kitchener Recruiting Committee, War Aims Committee, and City of Edinburgh Red Cross Committee, 1914–19. *Address*: 62, Northumberland Street, Edinburgh. *Clubs*: University; Scottish Conservative, Edinburgh. (M7512)

BROWN, Major George Conway, O.B.E., R.E.

BROWN, George Drake, M.B.E., M.A.

BROWN, Sir George McLaren, K.B.E., *b.* 29 Jan. 1865; *s.* of Adam Brown, of Hamilton, Ont., Canada; *m.* Eleanor Grahame, *d.* of John Crerar, K.C., of Hamilton, Ont., Canada. *Educ.*: Shrewsbury, England; Hamilton Grammar School, Ont.; Upper Canada Coll., Toronto, Ont. European General Manager, Canadian Pacific Railway; entered service of the Canadian Pacific Railway, 1887; General Traffic Manager and Executive Representative for B.C., 1892; General Superintendent, hotels, dining and shipping cars, 1902. *War Work*: Lieut.-Col. British Army, Feb. 1917; Col. April, 1918; Assistant Director of Movements, 1917–18; Assistant Director General of Movements and Railways, 1918–19; special duty France, 1918. *Address*: 61, Cadogan Square, London, S.W. 1. *Clubs*: Royal Thames Yacht; Caledonian; Royal Automobile; Constitutional; Ranelagh; City Carlton; St. James' Club (Montreal). (K196)

BROWN, Major George S., O.B.E.

BROWN, Lieut. and Qr.-Mr. George Thomas, M.B.E.

BROWN, 2nd Lieut. George Wauchop Stewart, M.B.E.

BROWN, Capt. Gilbert Alexander Murray, O.B.E., R.E. (T.F.)

BROWN, Major Harold Blumfield, O.B.E., R.G.A. (T.), *b.* 21 Jan. 1882; *s.* of W. B. Brown, J.P., of Ealing, Middlesex; *m.* Gladys, *d.* of C. E. Mieville, of London. *Educ.*: St. Edward's, Oxford. *War Work*: An old Volunteer; went to France in March, 1915, in command of a T.F. heavy battery; later commanded a T.F. Reserve Brigade, R.G.A., at home, until given a Staff appointment. *Address*: Horsemoor Green, Langley, Bucks. *Club*: Junior Army and Navy. (O8756)

BROWN, Major Harry Egerton, O.B.E.

BROWN, Harry Percy, M.B.E.

BROWN, Helen Grace Rae, M.B.E.

BROWN, Major Henry, O.B.E., R.E. (T.F.).

BROWN, Major Henry Harwood, M.B.E.

BROWN, Sir Herbert, K.B.E., *b.* 4 March, 1869; *s.* of Charles Brown, of Westfield, Bonchurch, Isle of Wight; *m.* Anna Flora, *d.* of John Frith, of Oaklands, Croydon. *Educ.*: Privately. Has received the Legion of Honour and the Order of Leopold. *War Work*: Founder of the British Farmers' Red Cross Fund, which raised just over £1,053 000 for the British Red Cross Society; assisted in founding the Baltic and Corn Exchange Hospital; organised an appeal for the Y.M.C.A., which resulted in subscriptions amounting to £500,000; after the Armistice assisted in relief work in the devastated areas of France; directed an appeal for funds for the Officers' Association. *Address*: Coombe Lodge, Addington Hill, Croydon. (K354)

BROWN, Rev. Hugh, O.B.E.

BROWN, Dr. Herbert Henry, O.B.E., M.D.(Lond.), F.R.C.S. *b.* 1862; *s.* of David Brown, of London. *Educ.*: Harrow and London Univ. Surgeon to the East Suffolk Hospital. *War Work*: Surgeon in charge of Broadwater Hospital, Ipswich; Maryland Convalescent Hospital, Sproughton, Ipswich; in charge of wounded at East Suffolk Hospital. *Address*: 3, Museum Street, Ipswich. (O10054)

BROWN, James, C.B.E., J.P., M.P., *b.* 16 Dec. 1862; *s.* of James Brown, of Newton-on-Ayr; *m.* Catherine Macgregor, *d.* of Matthew Steele, of Kilbarchan, Renfrewshire. *Educ.*: Annbank Public School. Gen. Sec. Ayrshire Miners' Union; Gen. Sec. National Union of Scottish Mine Workers. *War Work*: Member of Ayr County Tribunal; of Ayr County Food Committee. *Address*: 56, Annbank by Ayr. (C118)

BROWN, James, M.B.E.

BROWN, James, M.B.E.

BROWN, Lieut.-Col. James Carleton, O.B.E., R.E., *b.* 3 Oct. 1888; *s.* of David Wark Brown, of St. Stephen, N.B., Canada. *Educ.*: Univ. of New Brunswick, Canada. Civil Engineer; Member Engineering Institute of Canada. *War Work*: Lieut. Canadian Infantry, Mar. 1915 to Nov. 1915; transferred to Royal Engineers, Nov. 1915; promoted Captain, Mar. 1916; Acting Major, June, 1918; Acting Lieut.-Col. Oct. 1918; twice mentioned in despatches; second in command 119th Rly. Co., R.E., in France, May, 1916, to Aug. 1916; O.C. 273rd Rly. Co., R.E., British Salonica Force, Sept. 1916, to Oct. 1918; Railway Construction Engr. No. 1, British Salonica Force, Oct. 1918, to March, 1919; Railway Adviser to British Military Mission, S. Russia, Aug. to Oct. 1919; Chief Engineer, Anatolian Railways, Military Operating and Control Staff, from Oct. 1919 to present; General rly. construction and heavy bridge work. *Addresses*: Cox & Co., 16, Charing Cross, London, S.W. 1; c/o Director of Railways, A.B.S., Constantinople, Turkey. (O8680)

BROWN, James Hardy, O.B.E. (O6584)

BROWN, Major James Parry, O.B.E., *b.* 3 Feb. 1880; *s.* of the late Alderman W. H. Brown, J.P., of Newport, Mon.;

m. Hetty, *d.* of the late E. Hartley, J.P., of Newport, Mon. *Educ.*: Newport Collegiate School. Accountant. *War Work*: R.A.S.C. Base Supply Depot, Avonmouth; R.A.S.C., Main Supply Depot, Northampton; O.C., R.A.S.C., Kholmogorskaya, North Russia; O.C., Base Supply Depot, Bakharitza, North Russia. *Address*: Brynheulog, Llanthewy Road, Newport, Mon. (O9681)

BROWN, Janet Gilmour, O.B.E.; *d.* of W. R. Gilmour Brown, of Sutton. Personal clerk to the Prime Minister (Rt. Hon. D. Lloyd George). *Address*: Rochford, Sutton, Surrey. (O10055)

BROWN, Capt. John, M.B.E., M.C., R.A.F.

BROWN, Capt. John, M.B.E.

BROWN, T. Lieut.-Col. John Bayley Fairfax, O.B.E., R.E., *b.* 13 March, 1887; *s.* of B. Fairfax Brown, of Norwood, Taunton; *m.* Dorothy, *d.* of W. T. Tucker, of Loughborough. *Educ.*: Berkhampsted, and Sheffield Univ. Executive Engineer, 3rd Project Division, Public Works Department, Imperial Delhi. *War Work*: Mesopotamia, Deputy Asst. Director of Works (E. & M.), 1917–19; Asst. Director, 1919–20. *Address*: Raisina, Delhi. (O6585)

BROWN, Paymaster-Lieut.-Comm. John Edward Ambrose, C.B.E., R.N.

BROWN, Major John Falconer, O.B.E., M.D.

BROWN, Major John Herald Balfour, O.B.E., M.C., A.M.C., A.I.F.

BROWN, Eng.-Comm. John Steven, M.B.E., R.N.

BROWN, Jonathan Boswell, O.B.E., *b.* 1 Jan. 1871; *s.* of John Brown, of Erith, Kent; *m.* Amy, *d.* of James Schofield, of Erith, Kent. *Educ.*: Privately. Director, Wolsey, Ltd., Leicester. *War Work*: Assistant Director of Wool Textile Production; responsible for all hosiery and underwear required by Army, Navy and other services, British and Allied Governments. Officer of the Order of Leopold II. of Belgium. *Address*: Desford, Leicestershire. *Clubs*: National Liberal; Leicestershire. (O182)

BROWN, Capt. Joseph Hector, M.B.E., I.F.

BROWN, Joseph Pearce, C.B.E., J.P.

BROWN, Capt. Laurence, M.B.E.

BROWN, Capt. Margaret, Mrs., M.B.E.

BROWN, Margaret Bennett, M.B.E.; *d.* of the late Matthew Brown, J.P. for County of Cumberland, of Longtown, Cumberland. *War Work*: Commandant and organiser of Murrell Hill Military Auxiliary Hospital, Carlisle, for four years (Primary Hospital), March, 1915, to April, 1919. *Address*: East View, Carlisle. (M1481)

BROWN, Marian, Lady, M.B.E., *b.* 26 Feb. 1852; *d.* of Rev. Edwin Meyrick, M.A., of Allington Vicarage, Wilts.; *m.* Sir R. Hanbury Brown, K.C.M.G. (*see* BURKE'S *Peerage*). *War Work*: Commandant, V.A.D. Sussex 30 East Lodge Hospital, Crawley Down. *Address*: Newlands, Crawley Down, Sussex. (M7514)

BROWN, Minnie, M.B.E., *b.* 23 June, 1872; *d.* of J. Webster-Brown, of Liverpool and Southport. *Educ.*: Dagfield, Birkdale, and privately. *War Work*: Commandant of the St. John V.A.D. Hospitals, Southport; Acting Matron of the Military Hospital, 30, Queen's Road, Southport. *Address*: 23, Talbot Street, Southport. (M3545)

BROWN, Monica Harcourt, M.B.E., Q.M.A.A.C.

BROWN, Lieut.-Col. Montagu Wilhelm, O.B.E.

BROWN, Nicol Paton, C.B.E., *b.* 9 May, 1853; *s.* of Thomas White Brown, of Glasgow; *m.* Maria Crowley, *d.* of George Crowley Ashby, of Isleworth, Middlesex. *Educ.*: Glasgow Academy; Glasgow University. Muslin Manufacturer; Chairman of John Brown & Son, Ltd., Glasgow; Director of The Albion Motor Car Co., Ltd. Glasgow; Director of Glasgow Chamber of Commerce. *War Work*: Member of Council of War Executive, Scottish Branch British Red Cross Society; Vice-Chairman on Finance Committee; Chairman of Scottish National Red Cross Hospital, Bellahouston. *Address*: 22, Belhaven Terrace, Glasgow, W. *Clubs*: Western Glasgow; Reform; R.A.C.; Pall Mall; R.S.A.C.; Prestwick Golf.(C2479)

BROWN, Patrick Campbell Cowley, M.B.E. Assistant Censor, Straits Settlements. (M10257c)

BROWN, Capt. Percy George, C.B.E., *b.* 1874; *s.* of the late Capt. Robert Brown, 53rd Regt.; *m.* 1914, Mary, *d.* of S. N. Hutchins, J.P., of Ardnagasgel, co. Cork. Com. and Acting Capt. R.N.; employed in Drifters, Nore Area (Croix de Guerre) and on Blockade Duties (Chevalier Legion of Honour) during Great War. (C2215)

BROWN, Lieut.-Col. Percy Gordon, O.B.E., A.M.C.

BROWN, Phyllis Warden, M.B.E., B.A., *b.* 8 June, 1895; *d.* of Charles Andrews Brown, of Bedford. *Educ.*: High School, and Victoria Univ., Manchester. *War Work*: V.A.D. in England and France, 1914–17; 1915 Star; Q.M.A.A.C. Administration in France, 1917–19; awarded M.B.E., June, 1919, as Unit Administrator Queen Victoria Camp, Andrincq, Calais. *Address*: 44, Shakespeare Road, Bedford. *Club*: V.A.D. Ladies'. (M4430)

BROWN, Reginald, M.B.E.

BROWN, Eng.-Lieut.-Comm. Richard Charles, O.B.E., R.N.

BROWN, Robert Burns, M.B.E.

BROWN, Capt. Robert Campbell, O.B.E.

BROWN, Robert Cunyngham, C.B.E., Officer of Christ (Portugal), Order of St. Sava (Serbia), M.D., etc., *b.* 1867; *s.* of Rev. Robert Brown, of Paisley, and Mary Cheyne Hoseason, *d.* of James Hoseason, J.P., of Aywick, Shetland; *m.* Arabella Halyburton, *d.* of Dr. J. J. Johnstone, of Brampton, Cumberland. *Educ.*: Privately and Universities of Glasgow, Durham,

and Frankfurt. Deputy Director-General, Medical Services, Ministry of Pensions. *War Work :* Administrator, Spring-burn-Woodside Central Hospital, Glasgow ; Registrar, 37th General Hospital, Macedonia (attached Royal Serbian Army) ; Officer-in-Charge Medical Divisions 60th and 52rd General Hospitals, Salonika ; Visiting Physician, Mental Cases, Salonika Command ; Dept. Commissioner, Ministry of National Service. *Address :* Rossmore, Chislehurst Common. *Club :* Royal Societies'.
(C2480)

BROWN, Robert Cyril, M.B.E.

BROWN, Lieut. Robert William, M.B.E.

BROWN, Sheila Macpherson, M.B.E., *b.* 18 Feb. 1891 ; *d.* of Major Gideon Brown, of Galashiels, N.B. *Educ. :* Harrogate, and abroad. *War Work :* Served in Women's Legion (Cookery Section) from June, 1916, to Sept. 1917, at Summerdown Camp, Eastbourne ; Q.M.A.A.S.C. as Unit Administrator at Mansfield Park Camp, near Uckfield, Sussex, from Sept. 1917 to Dec. 1919. *Address :* Thorniedean, Galashiels, Scotland.
(M6605)

BROWN, Simon Stubbs, O.B.E., J.P., C.A., *b.* 13 Nov. 1841 ; *s.* of Zephaniah Brown, of Ratley ; *m.* Mary Helen, *d.* of Joseph Owen, of Warrington. *Educ. :* Privately. Late cotton spinner and manufacturer. *War Work :* Chairman of the Lord Derby War Hospital, Warrington. *Address :* Easton Lodge, 2 Regent Road, Birkdale, Lancashire. *Club :* Wigan.
(O10057)

BROWN, Capt. Stanley, M.B.E., R.A.M.C.

BROWN, Theophilus Edward, M.B.E.

BROWN, Lieut. Thomas, M.B.E.

BROWN, Tom, O.B.E., *b.* 10 Sept. 1858 ; *s.* of the late Thomas Brown, of Babington, near Bath ; *m.* Catherine Laura, *d.* of William Charles Govier, of Taunton. *Educ. :* Stratton-on-the-Fosse, near Bath. Deputy Chief Constable of Somerset. *War Work :* In charge of the Somerset Police Force during the War, in consequence of the Chief Constable being on Active Service.
(O10058)

BROWN, Lieut. Vernon, M.B.E.

BROWN, Violet McConochie, Mrs., M.B.E.

BROWN, Capt. Walter Ritchie, M.B.E.

BROWN, Wilfred Gordon, O.B.E.

BROWN, William, C.B.E., J.P., *b.* 11 Aug. 1850 ; *s.* of Andrew Brown, J.P., of Renfrew ; *m.* Jeanie, *d.* of John McDougal, M.D., of Old Kilpatrick. *Educ. :* Renfrew and Paisley Grammar Schools, and Glasgow University. Engineer and Shipbuilder ; Chairman of Messrs. Wm. Simons. & Co., Ltd., Renfrew, Scotland ; Representative of the Burgh of Renfrew on the Clyde Navigation Trust ; late Deacon of the Incorporation of Hammermen, Glasgow. *War Work :* Fully employed with the construction, including the machinery of a large number of twin screw minesweepers, convoy sloops, paddle hospital steamers for Mesopotamia, Oil Tankers, etc., etc. *Address :* 7, Whittinghame Gardens, Glasgow, W. *Club :* New Club, Glasgow.
(C445)

BROWN, Capt. and Qr.-Mr. William, M.B.E.

BROWN, Capt. William, O.B.E., R.A.M.C. (T.F.), M.D.

BROWN, William Henry George, M.B.E.

BROWN, Paymaster Lieut.-Comm. William John Archer, O.B.E., R.N.

BROWN, Rev. William Joseph, O.B.E., *b.* 29 Feb. 1880. *Educ. :* Mount St. Mary's Coll., Chesterfield. *War Work :* R.C. Chaplain, P. W. Camp (Officers), Dyffryn Aled, 1914–15 ; R.C. Chaplain, 38th (Welsh) Division, 1915–19. *Address :* 31. Farm Street, London, W. 1.
(O5050)

BROWN, William Robert, M.B.E.

BROWN, Mary Louisa Hester, Mrs. CLERKE-, M.B.E., *b.* 1857 ; *d.* of John Samuel Bowles, of Milton Hill, Berks. ; *m.* Henry (deceased), *s.* of Arthur Clerke-Brown, of Kingston Blount, Oxon. *Educ. :* At home. *War Work :* Lady Commandant, Swyncombe Red Cross Hospital, Henley-on-Thames, Oxon., for four years. *Address :* Kingston Blount, Oxon. *Club :* Ladies' Imperial.
(M1482)

BROWN, Rear-Adm. Frederick Dundas GILPIN-, C.B.E. Rear-Adm. (ret.), and Capt. Sup., Pembroke Dockyard. *Address :* The Dockyard, Pembroke.
(C2310)

BROWN, Capt. Alfred Ernest HOLMES-, O.B.E., R.G.A., S.R.

BROWN, Cicely LEADLEY-, M.B.E.

BROWN, Capt. and Qr.-Mr. Richard Charles STAPLES-, M.B.E., M.C.

BROWN, Capt. Vere WARD-, O.B.E., M.C., R.A.F.

BROWNE, Col. Abraham Walker, C.B.E. Brevet Col. R.A.M.C. (ret.) ; Great War, 1914–19 (despatches).
(C1483)

BROWNE, Hon. Sir Albert, K.B.E., C.M.G., I.S.O., *b.* 1860 ; *s.* of J. C. Browne, of Bury St. Edmunds ; *m.* 1899, Mabel, *d.* of Dr. U. Lawrence, of Cape Colony. Entered Colonial Office 1877, and became a Clerk in Colonial Sec.'s Office, Cyprus, 1880 ; Assist. Accountant to High Commr., S. Africa, 1891 ; Auditor, Basutoland, 1892 ; Assist. Imperial Sec., S. Africa, 1896 and 1899 ; Financial Adviser, Orange River Colony, 1900 ; Colonial Treasurer thereof 1901 ; retired 1907 ; sometime a Member of Executive, Legislative and Inter-Colonial Councils of Orange River Colony ; was a Member of Board of Inquiry into Postal and Telegraph Administration, Bechuanaland 1892, of National Convention for Union of S. Africa, 1909–10, and of Public Service Re-organisation Commn. 1910–11. *Address :* Government Offices, Bloemfontein, O. R. Colony, South Africa.
(K478)

BROWNE, Capt. Arthur Ernest Bankhead, O.B.E.

BROWNE, Col. Lord Arthur Howe, K.B.E., F.L.S., *b.* 1867 ; *s.* of 5th Marquess of Sligo (*see* BURKE'S *Peerage*) ; Col. Reserve of Officers. *m.* 1919, Lilian Whiteside, widow of Major A. F. Mann, and daughter of Charles Chapman. Served Royal Munster Fusiliers, 1889–1901 ; Punjab Frontier (1897–8, medal and clasp) ; South Africa, 1901–2 (medal with 5 clasps) ; retired 1909 ; General Staff, War Office, 1914–19 ; K.B.E., Brevet Lieut.-Col., Col., Legion of Honour, Grand Officer Order of Christ of Portugal. *Address :* 97, Coleherne Court, S.W. 5. *Club :* Naval and Military.
(K305)

BROWNE, Cecil Pownall, O.B.E.

BROWNE, Lieut. Charles James, M.B.E., K.R.R.C., *b.* 4 Oct. 1882 ; 2nd *s.* of Frederick G. Dillon Browne ; *m.* Dorothy Mary, *d.* of George Chuter. *Educ. :* Privately. Stock Exchange. *War Work :* Gazetted 11th K.R.R.C., March, 1917 ; gassed third Battle of Ypres ; invalided home and attached by W.O. for Special Duty to Commission Internationale de Ravitaillement. *Address :* c/o Messrs. Cox & Co., 38, Lombard Street, E.C. *Club :* Pollards Hill Golf (Norbury, Surrey).
(M4321)

BROWNE, Major Claude Melville, O.B.E., M.C. 3rd Battn. Gordon Highlanders. *Address :* c/o Holt & Co., 3, Whitehall Place, S.W.1.
(O11877)

BROWNE, Capt. Cyril Edward, O.B.E., M.C., R.A.S.C.

BROWNE, Lieut.-Col. Denis Robert Howe, O.B.E., I.A.R.O.

BROWNE, Dorothy Mary, M.B.E.

BROWNE, Douglas, M.B.E.

BROWNE, Major Edward Denis, O.B.E.

BROWNE, Major Francis John, O.B.E.

BROWNE, George Herbert, M.B.E.

BROWNE, Major George Willis, O.B.E.

BROWNE, Gerald Macleay, O.B.E.

BROWNE, Comm. Harold Ernest, O.B.E., R.N.

BROWNE, Henry William Langley, O.B.E., M.D., F.R.C.S.E., LL.D., J.P. County of Stafford, *b.* 26 Nov. 1848 ; *s.* of Benjamin Stocks Browne, of West Bromwich. Consulting Surgeon to West Bromwich and District Hospital. *War Work :* Member of Central Medical War Committee (London) ; Hon. Surgeon, Churchfields Auxiliary Hospital, West Bromwich. *Address :* Moor House, West Bromwich, Staffs. *Club :* Royal Societies'.
(O10060)

BROWNE, Isabel Mary Peyronnel, Lady, O.B.E.

BROWNE, John Coggis, O.B.E.

BROWNE, Mildred Frances, M.B.E.

BROWNE, Lieut.-Col. Philip Henry, C.B.E. Lieut.-Col. in the Army and Assist. Director Inland Water Transport in Mesopotamia during Great War.
(C1422)

BROWNE, Surg.-Comm. Robley Henry John, O.B.E., R.N.

BROWNE, Brig.-Gen. Sherwood Dighton, C.B., C.B.E., *b.* 1862 ; *s.* of the late Gen. Sir Samuel Browne, V.C., of The Wood, Ryde, Isle of Wight ; *m.* Hilda, *d.* of J. P. Law, J.P., of Hallfield, Wetherby. *Educ. :* Wellington Coll. Entered R.A. 1882 ; became Capt. 1890 ; Major, 1899 ; Lieut.-Col. 1906 ; Col. 1911 ; Hon. Brig.-Gen. (ret.), 1919 ; served in Matabeleland Campaign, 1893 ; with Tirah Expedition, 1897–8 (despatches, medal with two clasps) ; during Great War, 1914–17, on Staff (despatches). *Club :* Army and Navy.
(C1229)

BROWNE, Dame Sidney Jane, G.B.E., R.R.C., *b.* 5 Jan. 1850 ; *d.* of Dr. Benjamin Stocks Browne, of Bishop Auckland and West Bromwich. *Educ. :* Privately. Sister in the Army Nursing Service from 1883 ; served at Netley, Woolwich, Aldershot, Curragh Camp, Malta, and in the following campaigns : Egypt, 1884 ; Soudan Campaign, Suakin, 1885 ; Boer War, 1889–1902. First Matron-in-Chief, (War Office) Queen Alexandra Imperial Military Nursing Service, 1902 ; First Matron-in-Chief, Territorial Force Nursing Service (War Office 1908) ; served in the Great War 1914–19 ; mentioned in despatches several times. *Address :* 2, Lyndale, Childs Hill, London, N.W. 2. *Clubs :* Halcyon, St. Andrew's House.
(DG22)

BROWNE, Lieut.-Col. Tom Bousquet, O.B.E., M.I.Mech.E., M.I A.E., M.S.A.E., *b.* 15 July, 1873 ; *s.* of the late Thomas Brooks Browne. *Educ. :* King's Coll., London. Automobile Engineer. President of the Institution of Automobile Engineers, 1913–14. *War Work :* Mechanical Transport, R.A.S.C., Aug. 1914, to April, 1920 ; 3 years of above with B.E.F., France (mentioned in despatches) ; in charge of Heavy M.T. Repair Shops. *Address :* 32, Onslow Square, London, S.W. 7. *Club :* Royal Automobile.
(O6249)

BROWNE, Tomys Reginald, M.B.E., V.D.

BROWNE, Lieut.-Col. William Walker, O.B.E., R.A.M.C.
(O11775)

BROWNE, Major Granville St. John ORDE-, O.B.E.

BROWNFIELD, Lieut.-Col. Harry Munyard, O.B.E., V.D., R.A.M.C. (retired), Hon. Associate Order of St. John of Jerusalem, *b.* 28 Aug. 1861 ; *s.* of S. Brownfield, K.J.V., J.P., of London. *Educ. :* Greenwich Proprietary School and Guy's Hospital. Medical Officer of Health, Petersfield ; Surgeon, Hants. Constabulary ; Medical Referee, Admiralty ; Medical Officer, L. & S.W. Railway Co. ; Medical Officer, Post Office ; Lecturer and Examiner, St. John's Ambulance and Red Cross Society ; Medical Officer Bedales School. *War Work :* Senior Medical Officer in charge of Coldhayes Auxiliary Hospital, East Div. ; Heath Lodge Auxiliary Hospital, Petersfield ; Clayton Court Auxiliary Hospital, East Div. *Address :* The Old College, Petersfield.
(O10061)

BROWNFIELD, Surg.-Lieut. Owen Deane, O.B.E., R.N.

BROWNING, Adeline Elizabeth, Mrs., C.B.E. Rendered service in connection with reception and treatment of returned soldiers and sailors during Great War. (C730)

BROWNING, Albert Charles, M.B.E., late R.A., *b.* 10 Nov. 1868 ; *s.* of Rowland William Browning, of Woolwich, S.E. 18 ; *m.* Edith Blanche, *d.* of Robert Wilkinson, of Calstock, Cornwall. *Educ.:* St. John's National (Higher) School, Devonport, Devonshire. *War Work:* B.E.F., France, Aug. 1914, to Dec. 1915, taking part in the retirement from Mons ; Ministry of Munitions Headquarters, London, in Department of Munitions Design as Clerk in charge of a Branch. *Address:* 116, Kinveachy Gardens, Charlton, S.E. 7. (M7525)

BROWNING, Elizabeth Anne, M.B.E. (M10376)

BROWNING, Lieut.-Col. Frederick Henry, C.B.E. Lieut.-Col. Special List ; Great War, 1914–19 (despatches, Order of Crown of Italy). (C802)

BROWNING, Harry, O.B.E.

BROWNING, Lieut. Herbert, M.B.E., B.A. (Cantab.), (T.F.) *b.* 11 Aug. 1894 ; *s.* of Henry Browning, of Aylesford, Kent. *Educ.:* Latymer Upper School, London, W., and Selwyn Coll., Cambridge. *Address:* The Friars, Aylesford, Kent. (M4770)

BROWNING, Jeffrey, C.B.E., I.S.O.

BROWNING, Capt. Langley, O.B.E., M.C. (F.), *b.* 28 July, 1891 ; *s.* of Lieut.-Col. W. B. Browning, C.I.E., I.M.S. of Cregg House, Fermoy, co. Cork ; *m.* Violet Muriel, *d.* of Allan Cairnes, of The Glen, Drogheda. *Educ.:* Tyttenhanger Lodge, St. Albans, Herts., and Tonbridge School. *War Work:* Campaign, Aug. 1914, to Armistice ; twice wounded ; twice mentioned ; 3 decorations ; Regtl. and Staff Employment, 4th, Guards, 16th and 23rd Divisions, France, Belgium, and Italy. *Address:* c/o Cox and Co., 16, Charing Cross, S.W. 1. (O6350)

BROWNING, Mary Louisa, Mrs., M.B.E., *b.* 4 Oct. 1872 ; *d.* of Rev. Alfred Forbes Sealy, M.A. (Camb.), Director of Education, Cochin, South India ; *m.* George Elliot, *s.* of Arrott Browning, M.I.C.E., Consulting Engineer, Westminster, of Coaley. *Educ.:* Girls' High School, Croydon. Acted as Confidential Secretary and Stenographer to her husband in connection with drawing up detailed reports and correspondence connected with the development of the Cochin Harbour into a great Imperial Harbour and the Radial Railways to connect the same with the rest of India. *War Work:* Started War Relief Fund in Trichur, S. India, to gather in monthly subscriptions, divided amongst War Charities ; boxes of " comforts " sent to War Organisations every month. *Address:* Trichur, S. India ; Sherbrook, Budleigh Salterton, Devon. (M2697)

BROWNING, Col. George DANSEY-, C.B.E., A.M.C.

BROWNLIE, James Thomas. C.B.E., *b.* 23 June, 1865 ; *s.* of Thomas Brownlie, of Dalserth, Scotland : *m.* Ellen Ritche, *d.* of Capt. James Anderson, of Saltcoats, Scotland. *Educ.:* Wason's Academy, Paisley. Chairman of Executive Council of Amalgamated Society of Engineers. *War Work:* Member of National Advisory Committee on War Output ; Central Munitions Supply Committee ; Member of Mission appointed by the Director-General of Recruiting for Munitions work on the output of Munitions in France, Dec. 1915, and other Government Committees. *Address:* 98, Arodene Road, Brixton Hill, S.W. 2. (C14)

BROWNLOW, Col. Charles William, C.M.G., C.B.E., D.S.O., *b.* 1862 ; Col. R.G.A. (ret.) ; Zhob Valley Expedition, 1890 ; Burma Expedition, 1891–2 (medal with clasp) ; N.W. Frontier of India, 1897–8 (medal with clasp) ; Tirah Expedition, 1897–8 (clasp) ; Great War, 1914–18 (despatches). (C1484)

BROWNLOW, Capt. (Royal Australian Navy) Frederick Hugh, O.B.E., V.D., R.A.N., *b.* 8 Aug. 1859 ; *s.* of Edward Brownlow, Coldstream Guards, of Bovingdon, Herts ; *m.* Ellen, *d.* of William Gillespie, of Double Bay, N.S. Wales. *Educ.:* Queen Elizabeth's Grammar School, Southwark. District Naval Officer, New South Wales. *War Work:* Egypt, Soudan, 1885, Advance of Tamai, Medal and Khedive's Star, 1914–19 ; Home Service, Sydney, N.S. Wales ; in charge of R. Australian Auxiliary Services, N.S. Wales Intelligence Officer, etc. *Address:* Mufloma, Ocean Avenue, Double Bay, Sydney, N.S. Wales. *Club:* Royal Sydney Yacht. (O2144)

BROWNRIGG, The Rev. Earnest Graham, O.B.E., M.A.

BROWNSWORD, Walter, M.B.E.

BRUCE, Alexander, M.B.E.

BRUCE Lieut.-Col. Alexander, O.B.E.

BRUCE, Lieut.-Col. Arthur Carlyon, O.B.E., A.P.D. (ret.), *b.* 27 April, 1853 ; *Educ.:* At Private Schools. Served in the Army, 60th Rifles and Army Pay Department, April, 1878, to Dec. 1919 ; War Office Staff, Sept. 1897 to Dec. 1919. *War Work:* Financial Secretary's Department, War Office, 1914–19. *Address:* 246, Ivydale Road, Waverley Park, S.E. 15. *Club:* Junior Army and Navy. (O4805)

BRUCE, Bertha Marguerita, M.B.E.; *d.* of the late Major W. T. Bruce, of Leserragh. *Educ.:* Privately. *War Work:* Welfare Supt., Ministry of Munitions, Birmingham ; Instructress, War Hospital Supply Depot, Dublin. *Address:* Leserragh, Borrisokane, Co. Tipperary. (M181)

BRUCE, Major Charles Edward, C.I.E., O.B.E., I.A., *b.* 28 March, 1876 ; *s.* of R. S. Bruce, C.I.E. of Quetta, Teddington ; *m.* Doris, *d.* of J. Wilding, of Preston. *Educ.:* Wellington and Sandhurst. Indian Army Supernumerary List ; in Political employ under Government of India ; commission, 20th Lancs. Fusiliers, 1896 ; 24th Baluchistan Infy., 1897 ;

served in China, 1900 (medal) ; appointed Political Dept., 1901 ; North-West Frontier Gumatti, 1902 ; served Tank, Bannu, Hazara, Peshawar, Sibi, Zhob, and Loralai ; European War : on special duty as Political Officer, Mari Punitive Force, despatches ; Military O.B.E. ; Afghan War (despatches, C.I.E.). *Address:* Coldingham Lodge, Winchfield, Hants. *Club:* East India United Service, St. James' Square. (O4298)

BRUCE, Charles Matthewes, O.B.E.

BRUCE, Brig.-Gen. Clarence Dalrymple, C.B.E. Major W. Riding Regt. (ret.) ; T. Brig.-Gen. ; Great War, 1914–19 (despatches). (M1485)

BRUCE, Lady Constance Veronica, M.B.E., *b.* 24 Feb. 1880 ; *d.* of the late Victor Alexander, 9th Earl of Elgin and Kincardine (*see* BURKE'S *Peerage*). *Educ.:* Privately. President, County Nursing Association, Fife ; Vice-President. West Fife District, Scottish Branch, British Red Cross Society ; President, Women's Rural Institute, Limekilns and Charlestown ; Vice-President, Culross and Torryburn District Nursing Association. *War Work:* Red Cross Organisation ; Nursing in Military Hospitals. *Address:* Broomhall, Dunfermline. *Club:* United Societies. (M7528)

BRUCE, Edward Walrond de Wells, O.B.E., *b.* 22 March, 1863 ; *s.* of William Downing Bruce, late Judge, F.R.A.S., Knight of the Order of St. John of Jerusalem ; *m.* Amy Cecilia, *d.* of John Timms, B.A., late of Mountside, Victoria, Australia. *Educ.:* Mr. Foster's, Stubbington, Hants, and H.M.S. " Britannia." Late R.N. and retired Commander, P. & O. Company ; Member of Harrow Urban District Council; Poor Law Guardian. *War Work:* In command of Naval Hospital Ship " Plassy," 4 Aug. 1914, to May, 1918, hence to end of War in command of the same ship (turned into a troopship), bringing American Troops over from New York to Glasgow and Liverpool. *Address:* Garlet, Harrow-on-the-Hill. (O1153)

BRUCE, Elizabeth, Mrs., M.B.E., *d.* of Thomas Healey, of Clapham, S.W. ; *m.* Herbert Bruce, M.A., F.R.Hist.S.; *s.* of A. Bruce, of Batley, Yorkshire. *Educ.:* Royal College of Science. *War Work:* War Trade Intelligence Department, 1916–19 (Translator ; Assistant Establishment Officer). *Address:* 57, Cardiff Road, Llandaff, South Wales. (M1485)

BRUCE, Ellen Maud, Lady, O.B.E., *b.* 10 Oct. 1848 ; *d.* of Percy Ricardo, D.L., J.P., of Bramley Park, Surrey ; *m.* Sir Hervey J. Ll. Bruce, Bart., *s.* of the late Rt. Hon. Sir H. Hervey Bruce, Bart., P.C., of Downhill, Londonderry. *War Work:* Commandant and Treasurer V.A.D. Hospital, West Bridgford, Nottingham ; Hospital opened on 25 Jan. 1915, with 20 beds ; closed 31 March, 1919, with 150 beds. *Addresses:* Clifton Hall, Nottingham ; Downhill, Londonderry, Ireland. (O186)

BRUCE, Evelyn Susan, M.B.E.; *d.* of the late Major W. T. Bruce, of Leserragh. *Educ.:* Privately. *War Work:* St. John Ambulance and Red Cross Society ; Hon. Sec., Soldiers' and Sailors' Help Society. *Address:* Leserragh, Borrisokane, Co. Tipperary. (M7529)

BRUCE, Finetta Madeline Julia, the Hon. Mrs. Charles Granville, M.B.E.

BRUCE, George, M.B.E., *b.* 30 May, 1860 ; *s.* of Robert Bruce, of Longside, Aberdeenshire ; *m.* May Mary, *d.* of George May, of Mintlaw, Aberdeenshire and has issue Capt. George Robert Bruce, O.B.E., *q.v. Educ.:* Public Schools, Aberdeenshire. Chief Constable and Procurator Fiscal of Dunfermline ; Author of several well-known articles on Criminal Investigation, Prevention of Crime, Juvenile Offenders, etc. ; for more than a quarter of a century an active member of the Executive and Staff Committees of the S.P.C.C. in Scotland ; gave evidence before several Government Departmental Committees ; acted on various Committees in the interests of Service Men, P. of W., etc. ; performed important Imperial Duties and War Services during and since the Great War, for which he received the thanks of the Home Secretary, the Secretary for Scotland, Admiralty, War Office, etc. ; the recipient of a special letter of thanks from the U.S. Government for services rendered to the U.S. Fleet ; present at the surrender of the German Fleet, 20 Nov. 1918. *Address:* Glenugie, Dunfermline. (M7530)

BRUCE, Capt. George Robert, O.B.E., R.A.M.C. (S.R.), *b.* 19 July, 1884 ; *s.* of George Bruce, of 3, Transy Place, Dunfermline ; *m.* Gertrude Ethel Ratledge, of Southport. *Educ:* Dunfermline High School, St. Andrews and Edinburgh Univs. Medical Officer of Health and School Medical Officer to the Borough of Jarrow-on-Tyne. *War Work:* Specialist Sanitary Officer, Wylye Valley, Salisbury Plain ; Specialist Sanitary Officer, Malta Command. *Address:* 22, Bede Burn Road, Jarrow. (O6950)

BRUCE, Lieut. (T. Capt.) Ian Robert, M.B.E., *b.* 22 June, 1890 ; *s.* of Eric Stuart Bruce, of Airth, Sunningdale. *Educ.:* Beaumont Coll. Staff Captain, 84th Infantry Brigade, Army of the Black Sea. *War Work:* Enlisted in Honourable Artillery Co. Aug. 1914, and proceeded to France with 1st Batt. in Sept. 1914, and served in France and Belgium until April, 1915 ; entered R.M.C., Sandhurst, May, 1915, and gazetted as 2nd Lieut. in Q.O. Cameron Highlanders, Sept. 1915 ; joined 1st Batt. in France in Oct. 1915, and served in Salonica from Oct. 1916, to end of war ; mentioned in despatches by General Milne on two occasions. *Address:* Airth, Sunningdale. (M4771)

BRUCE, Major James Comyn Lewis Knight, O.B.E.

BRUCE, Lieut.-Col. John, O B E

BRUCE, Capt. John, O.B.E., R.A.M.C. (T.F.).

BRUCE, John Charles, O.B.E., *b.* 1880. Manager, Publicity Business throughout Scotland and North of England.

War Work: Acted as Organiser to the Scottish War Savings Committee; organised the Food Economy Campaign in Scotland and conducted the "Tank" "War Weapons Week" and other War Bond Campaigns in Scotland. *Address*: 38 West Savile Terrace, Edinburgh. (O10063)

BRUCE, Marion, Mrs., O.B.E.

BRUCE, Mary Elizabeth, Lady, O.B.E., R.R.C.; *d.* of John Lisson Steele, of Reigate; *m.* Maj.-Gen. Sir David Bruce, K.C.B. (Mil.), C.B. (Civil), F.R.C.S. (*see* BURKE'S *Peerage*), *s.* of David Bruce, of Stirling. Received the R.R.C. for work in Ladysmith during the siege, other than nursing work. *War Work*: During the Great War, work in connection with War Office Committees on Tetanus and Trench Fever; Member of Committee of R.A.M.C. Comforts and Prisoners of War Fund. *Addresses*: Artillery Mansions, Victoria Street; Lister Institute, Chelsea Gardens, S.W. 1. *Club*: Forum. (O10064)

BRUCE, Maye Emily, M.B.E., *b.* 1879; *d.* of Samuel Bruce, of Norton Hall. *Educ.*: At home. *War Work*: Red Cross Work, Commandant of Hospital for 60 beds. *Addresses*: Norton Hall, Campden, Gloucestershire; 23, Cromwell Road, London, S.W. 7. (M182)

BRUCE, Robert Arthur, O.B.E., *b.* 15 April, 1869; *s.* of Robert Bruce, of Bristol.; *m* Alice, *d.* of Edward Vaughan, of Barton Grange, near Taunton. *Educ.*: Clifton Coll., Bristol. Civil and Mechanical Engineer. 1896–1901, Asst. Engineer, Brennan Torpedo Works, Chatham, assisting inventor, Louis Brennan, C.B., in design of torpedo and its installation; 1902–4, Asst. Works Manager, Joshua Buckton & Co., Leeds; 1904–7, Director and Works Manager, Joshua Buckton & Co., Leeds; 1907–10, Asst. Engineer to Louis Brennan, C.B., assisting in development of Brennan Gyrostatic Mono-rail system of transport; 1910–12, Engineer, Hick, Hargreaves & Co., Bolton; 1912–13, Engineer and Manager, British and Colonial Aeroplane Co., Bristol; 1914, Consulting Engineer (Aircraft) to Greek Government. *War Work*: 1914–15, Lieut., R.N.V.R., Royal Naval Air Service; 1915, Manager, Westland Aircraft Works, Yeovil (Branch of Petters, Ltd.); 1916, Manager, Westland Aircraft Works and Director Petters, Ltd.; 1918, Joint Managing Director, Petters, Ltd., Yeovil, and Manager, Westland Aircraft Works. *Address*: The Knoll, Yeovil. *Club*: Constitutional. (O10065)

BRUCE, Robert Randal, M.B.E., J.P., *b.* 17 July, 1868; *s.* of George R. Bruce, of St. Helena; *m.* May, *d.* of Fredk. J. Broadway, of St. Helena. *Educ.*: Head School, St. Helena. Colonial Treasurer; Harbour Master; Shipping Master. *War Work*: Special services rendered as Reporting Officer in connection with Shipping, and duties performed while in charge of Guard Boat, etc. *Address*: The Castle, St. Helena. (M1254)

BRUCE, Capt. Wilfred Montagu, C.B.E., R.N.R., *b.* 26 Oct. 1874; 4th *s.* of the Rev. Lloyd Stewart Bruce, M.A., Canon of York, Rector of Stokesley, Northallerton, and Chaplain to the Archbishop of York; *g.s.* of Sir James Robertson Bruce, 2nd Bt. (*see* BURKE'S *Peerage*); *m.* 25 Nov. 1913, Dorothy Florence, *d.* of Sir Jesse Boot, Bt. (*see* BURKE'S *Peerage*). Awarded Polar Medal, 1913, for the Scott Expedition. (C881)

BRUCE, Violet Dorothy Evelyn, Hon. Mrs. G. J. G., M.B.E.

BRUCE, Lieut.-Col. William, O.B.E., M.B., N.Z.A.M.D., *b.* 12 July, 1887; *s.* of James Bruce, W.S., of Edinburgh; *m.* Martha Louisa, *d.* of Arthur Reed, of Sunderland. *Educ.*: Stubbington; Edinburgh Academy; and Edinburgh Univ. A.D.M.S. Otago Military District, New Zealand. *War Work*: N.Z.E.F. 1915–19. Now Capt. R.A.M.C. *Address*: R.A.M.C. Records. *Club*: British Empire. (O3241)

BRUCE, William Joseph, O.B.E.

BRUCE, William Joseph Willett, O.B.E.

BRUCE, William Robert, O.B.E. (O11931)

BRUCE, Sqdn.-Leader William Robert, O.B.E.

BRUCE, Charles BRUDENELL-, M.B.E., *b.* 6 March, 1885; *s.* of Lord Robert Brudenell-Bruce, of Hayling Island, Hants (*see* BURKE'S *Peerage*); *m.* Else, *d.* of Capt. C. Drechsel, of Danish Navy. *Educ.*: Harrow. Honorary Attaché, British Legation, Copenhagen, 1908–10; *War Work*: War Trade Department, 1915; Acting Second Secretary, British Legation, Christiania, 1916–19; Assistant Commissioner and Secretary-General, Slesvig Plebiscite Commission, 1919–20. *Club*: St. James's. (M1484)

BRUEN, Capt. William, M.B.E., M.C., *b.* 17 April, 1876; *s.* of John Bruen, of Royal Irish Constabulary, Collooney, Co. Sligo; *m.* Agnes, *d.* of Jeremiah Mulvey, of Castlebar, Ireland. *Educ.*: Camphill, Collooney, and Christian Brothers', Castlebar. *War Work*: Served with the Connaught Rangers (2nd Batt.) with the first Army; took part at Mons, the Retreat, the Marne, the Aisne, also 1st Battle of Calais; slightly wounded Sept. 1914, dangerously Oct. 1914; promoted 2nd Lieut. for "Service in the Field," 1914; mentioned in despatches Oct. 1914; awarded the French Medaille Militaire, also the military Cross, appointed Assistant Embarkation Staff Officer at North Wall, Dublin, 1915, and was twice mentioned for valuable services and awarded the O.B.E. for duties in the same capacity. *Club*: Yacht and Boat (Clontarf, Co. Dublin). (O8737)

BRUFFA, John, M.B.E. Chief Press Censor and Censorship Establishment Officer, Malta. (M10257*d*)

BRUGGY, Lieut.-Col. Stephen, D.S.O., C.M.G.R. Lieut.-Col. Australian Commonwealth Forces; S. African War, 1901–2 (Queen's medal with four clasps); Great War, 1914–18 (despatches, 4th class Serbian Order of the White Eagle). (O3232)

BRUMELL, Mary, Mrs., M.B.E., *b.* 1 Aug. 1865; *d.* of George Browne Collins, of St. Columb, Cornwall; *m.* Francis,

s. of Francis Brumell, of Morpeth, Northumberland. *Educ.*: Privately. *War Work*: Treasurer and Quartermaster of No. 6 V.A.D. Hospital, Morpeth, Northumberland. *Address*: Fulbeck, Morpeth. (M3546)

BRUMWELL, Rev. Donald Stanley, O.B.E., A.I.F.

BRUNE, Cecely Alice PRIDEAUX-, M.B.E., *d.* of Sir Philip Grey Egerton, Bart., of Oulton Park, Tarporley (*see* BURKE'S *Peerage*); *m.* Denys Edward, *s.* of Col. C. Prideaux-Brune, of Prideaux Place, Cornwall (*see* BURKE'S *Landed Gentry*). *War Work*: V.A.D. (nursing member) Portal Auxiliary Hospital Cheshire, and Coltesbrooke War Hospital, 1914–15; Commandant V.A.D. 140 London; Commandant in charge Nielka Auxiliary Hospital, Streatham Common. (M7532)

BRUNO, Capt. Hugh Alan BRUNO-, M.B.E., Hampshire Regt., *b.* 4 Sept. 1897; *s.* of Lieut.-Col. H. W. B. Bruno, of The Moorings, Chandlers Ford, Hants. *Educ.*: King Edward VI. Grammar School, Southampton. *War Work*: Commissioned to the Hampshire Regt. March, 1915; served throughout war in Balkans with 10th Batt. the Hampshire Regt. *Address*: The Moorings, Chandlers Ford, Hants. (M4772)

BRUNSHILL, Catherine Lavinia, Mrs., C.B.E., *b.* 15 Aug. 1891; *d.* of Robert Bennett, of Eastbourne; *m.* Major George Stephen, M.C., of the King's Shropshire Light Infantry, *s.* of the late Major Arthur Stephen Brunskill, Major of "The King's Own," and West India Regt. *Educ.*: Zion House Convent, Bayswater, and Elstree. *War Work*: Private Secretary to General Sir Nevil Macready, G.C.M.G., K.C.B., Adjutant-General to the Forces, War Office; Private Secretary to Chief Commissioner of Metropolitan Police, New Scotland Yard. *Address*: 135, Sloane Street, London, S.W. 1. (C963)

BRUNSKILL, Lieut.-Col. John Handfield, D.S.O., O.B.E.

BRUNTON, Guy, O.B.E., F.R.A.I., *b.* 18 July, 1878; *s.* of Spencer Brunton, of 84, Brook Street, W.; *m.* Winifred Mabel, *d.* of Charles Newberry, of Orange Free State. *Educ.*: Privately, and University Coll., London. Archæologist, attached to British School of Archæology in Egypt. *War Work*: 2 years Pay-Sergeant, British Red Cross Hospital, Netley; 4 months Artists' Rifles; 2 years Labour Corps (France). *Address*: 2, Regent's Court, Park Road, London, N.W. 1. (O5054)

BRUNTON, John Dixon, O.B.E., B.Met., F.C.S., *b.* 1872; *s.* of W. N. Brunton, of Edinburgh; *m.* Helen Edwards, *d.* of James Banks, J.P., of Pittcadie. *Educ.*: Edinburgh Institution and Sheffield Univ. *War Work*: Invented aerial bomb proof netting; produced stream line wires for aeroplanes; first manufacture of submarine indicator nets; sat on many Technical Panels, *re* aircraft material. *Address*: Inveresk Lodge, Midlothian. *Clubs*: R.A.C.; R.S.A.C. (Glasgow). (O10067)

BRUNTON, John Norman, O.B.E.

BRUNTON, Robert Godfree, M.B.E.

BRUNYATE, Bertha Maud Vipond, Lady, M.B.E.; *d.* of Andrew Davies, J.P.; *m.* Sir William Brunyate, *s.* of the Rev. W. Brunyate. *War Work*: V.A.D. Cairo (Australian Gen. Hosp. No. 2, etc.,) and Red Cross Librarian, Cairo. *Address*: Boxford, Suffolk. (M7533)

BRUTY, Capt. William Glynes, M.B.E.

BRYAN, Lieut. Godfrey Middleton Eric, M.B.E., R.A.S.C.

BRYAN, John Lockton, M.B.E.

BRYAN, Lieut. Thomas Edward, M.B.E.

BRYANS, Capt. Maurice, O.B.E., R.A.S.C.

BRYANT, Lieut.-Col. Alfred Rolfe, O.B.E., T.D., *b.* 19 Feb. 1881; *s.* of Edward Bryant, of Harold Wood Hall, Essex; *m.* Marta Maria, *d.* of Frederic Krebs, of Copenhagen. *Educ.*: Forest School, Essex. *War Work*: Commandant of Gt. Yarmouth, Jan. to June, 1915; Commanding 4th Reserve Batt. Essex Regt. until disbanded, 1919. (O3098)

BRYANT, Charles William, C.B.E. Managing Director of Brotherhoods (Ltd.). *Address*: Westwood House, Peterborough. (C12)

BRYANT, Sir Francis Morgan, C B.E., M.V.O. (4th Class), I.S.O., *b.* 13 March, 1859; *s.* of the late Thomas Bryant, of Lowestoft; *m.* May, *d.* of H. W. Edmunds, of Edgbaston. Secretary of the King's Private Secretary's Office and Assistant Keeper of the King's Archives since 1913 and Registrar of the Royal Victorian Order since 1916; served on the Staff of Royal Commission for Philadelphia International Exhibition, 1875–6; Paris Universal Exhibition, 1877–8; Melbourne International Exhibition, 1879–81; Secretary to the Comptroller and Treasurer, Marlborough House, 1881–1901; and Chief Clerk to King Edward VII. (when Prince of Wales), 1893–1901; Asst.-Sec. to His Majesty's Privy Purse, 1901–10; Asst.-Sec. and in charge of the King's Private Secretary's Office, 1910–12. *Address*: 17, Lower Grosvenor Place, S.W. 1. (C119)

BRYANT, Frederick, O.B.E.

BRYANT, Lieut.-Col. Frederick Carkeet, C.M.G., C.B.E., D.S.O., *b.* 10 Dec. 1879; *s.* of the late Theodore Henry Bryant, of Juniper Hill, Mickleham; *m.* Rosamund, *d.* of Philip Beresford Beresford-Hope, of Bedgebury Park, Goudhurst. *Educ.*: Harrow and Royal Military Academy. Royal Field Artillery. *War Work*: Commanded Allied Forces in Togoland, 1914; served in France, 1915–17; wounded, 1917; Home Service, 1918; Officier du Legion d'honneur, 1914; Bt. Lieut.-Col., Jan. 1918. *Address*: 2, Cumberland Mansions, Bryanston Square, W. 1. *Clubs*: Army and Navy; Bath. (C1486)

BRYANT, Major George Herbert, O.B.E.

BRYANT, Herbert William, M.B.E.

BRYANT, Mary Louisa, M.B.E., *d.* of Rev. W. F. Bryant,

Vicar of St. Mary's, Tyndall's Park, Clifton, Bristol. *Educ.*: Eastbourne and abroad. Com. B.R.C.S., 126, Somerset; Sec. and Treasurer Bristol Church Day Schools, Women's Branch. *War Work*: Nurse, etc., at Faye House Hospital, Leigh Woods, Bristol; Commandant, Ashton Court Officers' Hospital, Long Ashton, Somerset, from opening till the close in Aug. 1919. *Address*: 4, The Paragon, Clifton. *Club*: Clifton Ladies'.   (M7534)

BRYANT, Capt. Robert Francis, O.B.E., R.A.S.

BRYANT, Robert William, M.B.E.

BRYANT, Major Thomas Hedley, M.B.E., *b.* 10 July, 1865; *War Work*: Hon. Sec. Local Committee of the East Suffolk War Relief Fund; Hon. Sec. Local Committee, East Suffolk Pensions Committee; County Adjutant Suffolk Volunteer Regt. *Address*: Martletwye, Beach Road East, Felixstowe, Suffolk.   (M5118)

BRYANT, Capt. Walter Edward George, M.B.E., R.A.F.

BRYANT, William Henry, M.B.E.   (M10247)

BRYCE, Capt. Francis, O.B.E., K.R.R.C.

BRYCE, James McKie, C.B.E.

BRYDON, James Herbert, C.B.E., *b.* 19 March, 1881; *s.* of James Lockhart Brydon, of Bramhall Park, Cheadle Hulme, Cheshire. *Educ.*: Rossall and Pembroke, Cambridge. Solicitor. *War Work*: Hon. County Secretary and Treasurer B.R.C.S. (Cheshire Branch), Nov. 1914, to Aug. 1917; Hon. County Director for Red Cross and St. John (Cheshire), Aug. 1917, to date. *Addresses*: Bramhall Park, Cheadle Hulme, Cheshire; 56A Mosley St., Manchester. *Clubs*: Constitutional, Manchester, and Public Schools, London.

BRYDONE, James Marr, O.B.E., M.B.

BRYETT, Henry, O.B.E., *b.* 12 Sept. 1873; *s.* of Henry Bryett, of Southchurch, Essex; *m.* Edith Mary, *d.* of Ralph Hooper, of Hornchurch, Essex. *Educ.*: Culham. Board of Education. *War Work*: Organised War Savings in Durham County with 60 Committees and 1800 Associations; Hon. Sec. to Durham County Committee for War Savings and Food Economy. *Address*: 24, Newlands Avenue, West Hartlepool.   (O10069)

BRYNING, Emma Jane, M.B.E.

BRYSON, Lieut.-Charles, M.B.E.

BRYSON, Frederick Francis Smith, M.B.E., M.A., B.Sc., *b.* 9 May, 1884; *s.* of William Bryson, of Kilsyth, Stirlingshire. *Educ.*: Edinburgh and Glasgow Universities. *War Work*: Sub-Section Director, Scientific and Technical Branch, Optical Munitions and Glassware Supply Department, Ministry of Munitions. *Address*: 12, Oppidans Road, London, N.W. 3.   (M185)

BUBB, Charles Henry, O.B.E., L.R.C.P., M.R.C.S., L.D.S. (Eng.). *Educ.*: Wycliffe Coll. and Guy's Hospital. *War Work*: Hon. Dental Surgeon, King George Military Hospital, 1915–19, in connection with the treatment of jaw and facial injuries. *Addresses*: 1, Burlington Gardens, W.; Justacot, Chorley Wood.   (O11794)

BUCHAN, Lieut. Andrew, M.B.E. R.A.

BUCHAN, Lieut.-Col. Charles Forbes, C.B.E. Lieut.-Col. T.F. Reserve; sometime Dep. Assist. Director to Under Sec. of State for War; Great War, 1914–19 (despatches).   (C1487)

BUCHAN, Eng.-Lieut. John Robertson, O.B.E., R.N.

BUCHAN, Capt. Robert, M.B.E., R.N.R.

BUCHAN, William, M.B.E., *b.* 28 July, 1874; *s.* of Edward Buchan, of Peterhead; *m.* Helen, *d.* of McBoyle, of Banffshire. *Educ.*: Public School, Peterhead. Chief Barrack Master, H.M. Naval Hutments, Invergordon. *War Work*: Supervision of all billeting, etc., arrangements for men employed at H.M. Dockyard, Invergordon. *Address*: H.M. Hutments, Invergordon.   (M7535)

BUCHANAN, Andrew, M.B.E., J.P. (County of London), *b.* 12 Oct. 1870; *s.* of Andrew Buchanan, of Murrayfield, Edinburgh; *m.* Henrietta Frances, *d.* of Capt. J. H. Smith, Indian Army. *Educ.*: Royal High School and Daniel Stewart's Coll., Edinburgh. Labour Adviser, Ministry of Food; Fellow of Royal Colonial Institute; Trade Union Founder and Branch President; Lecturer on Industrialism, Economics, and Trade Unionism; Borough Councillor of Paddington for 10 years. *War Work*: Labour Adviser, Ministry of Food; Lecturer for Central Patriotic Committee; Lecturer for Y.M.C.A. to Military Camps. *Address*: 84, Hotham Road, Putney, S.W. 15.   (M7536)

BUCHANAN, Archibald Samuel, M.B.E., *b.* 25 Dec. 1873. Superintendent of Police, Wiltshire Constabulary. *War Work*: In charge of the Amesbury Police Division of Wiltshire (which includes Salisbury Plain) Military District. *Address*: Police Station, Amesbury.   (M7537)

BUCHANAN, Lieut.-Col. Arthur Louis Hamilton, O.B.E.

BUCHANAN, Comm. Frederic Gray, O.B.E., R.N., *b.* 21 Sept. 1887; *s.* of M. R. Gray Buchanan, of Ettrickdale, Bute; *m.* Hilary Joyce, *d.* of M. R. Morrow, of Halifax. *Educ.*: Summer Fields, near Oxford. *War Work*: Lieut.-Commander H.M.S. "Newcastle," 1914–16; H.M.S. "Devonshire," 1916–19; Atlantic Convoy service. *Address*: Ettrickdale, Port Bannatyne, Bute.   (O9066)

BUCHANAN, Lieut.-Col. Henry Meredith, O.B.E., M.B.

BUCHANAN, James Courtney, C.B.E., *b.* 19 Sept. 1877; *s.* of Theodore James Buchanan, of Herne, Kent; *m.* Frances Marjory, *d.* of George Forbes Bassett, M.A. (Oxon.), of Bassett Mount, Bassett, near Southampton. *Educ.*: Christ's Hospital, London (Grecian); Univ. of London; Mitchell Scholarship for Classics and English Literature. Barrister-at-Law of Lincoln's

Inn; late Secretary and House Governor of Metropolitan Hospital, London; appointed Secretary of the Cancer Hospital, London, 14 March, 1920; Officer in charge of Military Section (302 beds) of Metropolitan Hospital, London (1914–19). *Address*: The Lodge, 28, Willoughby Road, Hampstead, London, N.W. 3.   (C2482)

BUCHANAN, Capt. James Frederick, M.B.E.

BUCHANAN, Jane, O.B.E., *b.* 17 Aug. 1871; *d.* of Alexander Buchanan, of Mount Buchanan, Dungiven, Londonderry. Lady Superintendent, Post Office Savings Bank. *War Work*: Official work greatly augmented by the various War Loans, etc.; President of the Savings Bank Branch of Queen Mary's Needlework Guild. *Address*: 9, Exchange Mansions, Golders Green Road, N.W. 4. *Club*: Forum.   (O188)

BUCHANAN, Joseph Andrew William, C.B.E., *b.* 19 April, 1865; *s.* of Joseph Buchanan, of Cookstown, Co. Tyrone, Ireland; *m.* Caroline Hannah, *d.* of Henry Hanning, of Calcutta. *Educ.*: Privately. Comptroller of Accounts H.M. Office of Works. *Address*: 12, Mount Ephraim, Tunbridge Wells. (C2483)

BUCHANAN, Margaret, Mrs., M.B.E.

BUCHANAN, Lieut.-Col. Michael Rowland Gray, O.B.E.

BUCHANAN, Rhoda Agnes, Mrs., M.B.E.

BUCHANAN, Robert John, O.B.E., *b.* 1 March, 1871. Deputy Chief Constable, Wiltshire Constabulary. *War Work*: In charge of the Wiltshire Constabulary during the absence on Service of Lieut.-Col. Hoel Llewellyn, D.S.O., Chief Constable of Wiltshire. *Address*: Central Police Station, Devizes.   (O10070)

BUCHANNAN, Lieut. George Herbert, O.B.E.

BUCK, Edward Horace, M.B.E., *b.* 1 Dec. 1852; *m.* Tamzon Eliza, *d.* of George Parker, of Portsmouth. *Educ.*: City of London School. Outfitter; formerly Master Tailor, R.M.L.I., Gosport. *War Work*: Had charge of National Registration from Aug. 1915, to April, 1919, which was an honorary position. *Address*: 40, High Street, Dartford.   (M7538)

BUCK, Edward John, C.B.E. Hon. Sec. of "Our Day" in India.   (C699)

BUCK, Frank Steele, M.B.E., *b.* 20 Feb. 1878; *s.* of William Richard Buck, of West Ham House, West Ham, Essex; *m.* Margaret Helen Hearne, *d.* of Thomas Bond, F.R.C.S., of Westminster. *Educ.*: Merchant Taylors' School, London. *War Work*: Explosives Department, Ministry of Munitions. *Addresses*: Bembridge, Avenue Road, St. Albans; 22, Austin Friars, London, E.C.; Stock Exchange, E.C.   (M1488)

BUCK, Henry, O.B.E.   (O51195)

BUCK, Margaret, Mrs., M.B.E.

BUCK, Phillip, O.B.E., J.P. Rendered valuable war services in Tottenham.   (O11896)

BUCKINGHAM, Sir Henry Cecil, Kt., C.B.E.; *s.* of Joseph Hicks Buckingham, of Truro, and Lancaster Gate, and Lucy Webster, *d.* of Benjamin Halliwell, of Leeds; *m.* Madeleine, *d.* of William Bull, of Hove, Sussex. *Educ.*: Harrow; France. Joined the firm of J. H. Buckingham & Co., Ltd., 1886; Governing Director since 1899; Chairman, Commissioners of Taxes, Holborn Division; Arbitrator, City of London Court of Arbitration; Sheriff of London, 1910–11; Master Skinners' Company, 1918–19; Member of City of London Advisory Committee, 1916; Member Military Service Committee, Ministry of National Service; Chairman, Board of Trade Section, 1918. *Addresses*: 15, Hans Place, S.W. 1; Seale Lodge, Farnham; Ropemaker Street, E.C. *Clubs*: Junior Carlton; Sports; Ranelagh; M.C.C.   (C2484)

BUCKINGHAM, James Frank, O.B.E., *b.* 1886; *s.* of the late Sir James Buckingham, of Assam, India. *Educ.*: Kelly Coll., Tavistock, Devon. Engineer; partner in firm of J. F. Buckingham, Engineer, Spon Street, Coventry. *War Work*: Inventor and manufacturer of the Buckingham Incendiary Bullet used for the destruction of Zeppelins, Kite Balloons, and Aeroplanes. The firm manufactured large quantities for the British Government and Allies, over 26,000,000 being supplied during the war. *Address*: Dunstan House, Elmdon, near Birmingham.   (O10071)

BUCKINGHAMSHIRE, Sir Sidney Carr Hobart-Hampden-Mercer-Henderson, 7th Earl of, Bt., O.B.E., J.P., D.L., Baron Hobart. Lord-in-Waiting, 1895 (assumed by Royal License in 1903, the additional name of Mercer-Henderson), *b.* 14 March, 1860; *m.* Georgiana, *d.* of Hon. H. Duncan Mercer-Henderson, *d.* of 1st Earl of Camperdown (see BURKE's *Peerage*). *Educ.*: Trinity Coll., Cambridge. *Addresses*: Hampden House, Great Missenden. Bucks.; Fordell, Inverkeithing, Fife. *Club*: Brooks's.   (O6953)

BUCKLAND, Alfred Virgoe, O.B.E.

BUCKLAND, Isabel Maud, Mrs., M.B.E., *b.* 1880; *d.* of Edwin Peters, of 29, Grimston Gardens, Folkestone; *m.* Harry, *s.* of John Carey Buckland, of Goldwell, Great Chart, Kent. *Educ.*: Cheltenham Ladies' Coll. Commandant V.A.D. K/48 (since 1912); Hon. Sec. Ashford Branch N.C.W.; Hon. Sec. E. Kent, for Soldiers' and Sailors' Help Society; Ashford District Commissioner for Girl Guides. *War Work*: Commandant K/48 and officer-in-charge Ashford V.A.D. Hospitals and Woodchurch Hospital (Hendon Place), 1914–19; officer-in-charge Swanton House Pensions' Hospital. *Address*: Chilmington House, Great Chart, near Ashford, Kent. *Clubs*: New Century; V.A.D.   (M7539)

BUCKLAND, Major Lionel, O.B.E., *b.* 10 Dec. 1870; *s.* of Stephen Vine Buckland, of Geelong, Victoria, Australia.

Educ.: Rugby School; Melbourne Univ. Qualified Solicitor; Journalist. *War Work*: Lieut.-Commander, Hood Batt. Royal Naval Division, Sept. 1914, Dardanelles; transferred to R.A.S.C. as Major, March, 1916; served as Deputy Inspector Camel Transport Corps, Egypt, Western Front, Palestine, and Syria, till March, 1919. *Address*: Bulkeley, Alexandria, Egypt. *Clubs*: Union; Alexandria; Athenæum; Melbourne. (O6150)

BUCKLAND, Capt. and Qr.-Mr. Philip Percival, M.B.E.

BUCKLAND, Rawlin George Samuel, M.B.E., *b.* 6 Sept 1853; *s.* of the Rev. Samuel Buckland, M.A., of Great Torrington, North Devon; *m.* Lucy Beatrice, *d.* of Charles Richard Jones, M.D., of Great Torrington. *Educ.*: Privately. Superintendent (retired) Foreign Service, Eastern Extension Australasian and China Telegraph Co. *War Work*: Commandant V.A.D. 108 Devon (Hospital of 100 beds); Military Representative and National Service Representative, Torrington Borough Tribunal; Lance-corporal V.T.C.; Pte. Devon Motor Volunteer Corps; Special Constable; Press Censor for Local Papers. *Address*: 26 South Street, Torrington. (M7547)

BUCKLE, Lieut.-Col. Cuthbert, C.B.E., *b.* 19 March, 1885. *s.* of Henry Rogers Buckle, of Gravesend; *m.* Edith Marion, *d.* of John Kennedy Barlow, of Gravesend. *Educ.*: University of London; City and Guilds of London Institute. Assessor and Surveyor to the Insurance Offices and to Lloyds' Underwriters; Managing Director of Ellis & Buckle, Ltd. *War Work*: Lieut.-Col. R.A.; Anti-Aircraft Defence Comm., London Air Defences. *Addresses*: 9, Walbrook, E.C.; St. Aubin, Cross Lane, Gravesend. (C1488)

BUCKLE, Ethel Agnes, Mrs., M.B.E.

BUCKLER, Georgina Grenfell, Mrs., C.B.E. In Enquiry Depart. for wounded and missing, Red Cross Soc. (C247)

BUCKLETON, Alice Australia Gertrude, O.B.E.

BUCKLEY, Arthur Burton, O.B.E., *b.* 15 Aug. 1877; *s.* of Arthur Burton Buckley, of Genoa, Italy; *m.* Sturata Frances, *d.* of Franz Weyermann, of Hager Hof, Honnef, Germany. *Educ.*: St. Paul's School, and City and Guilds of London Institute. Egyptian Irrigation Service. *War Work*: In Mesopotamia with Sir John Hewett, G.S.C.I., C.I.E., investigating military expenditure. *Clubs*: Turf (Cairo); Royal Thames Yacht. (O10072)

BUCKLEY, Major Edward Duncombe Henry, O.B.E., R.A., *b.* 2 Aug. 1860; *s.* of Alfred Buckley, of New Hall, Salisbury; *m.* Ellen Cecilia, *d.* of Col. F. Pridham, O.S.D. *Educ.*: Eton and R.M.A. *War Work*: Serving in Coast Defence, etc. *Address*: New Hall, Salisbury. *Club*: Travellers'. (O6954.

BUCKLEY, Major Edward John, O.B.E.

BUCKLEY, Lieut.-Col. George Alexander McLean, C.B.E., D.S.O., F.R.G.S., *b.* Oct. 1866; *s.* of the late George Buckley, of Christ Church, New Zealand; *m.* Mabel Gertrude, *d.* of Francis Robert Warren. *Educ.*: Christ's College, New Zealand; Cheltenham College. Retired from Army. *War Work*: Commanded a battalion in France, 1915–17. Cadet Battalion at Oxford 1918–19. *Address*: Bunt's End, Leigh, Surrey. *Clubs*: Bath; Royal Societies'; Royal Thames Yacht. (C1489)

BUCKLEY, James William, O.B.E., *b.* 26 Jan. 1850; *s.* of James Buckley, of Quick Edge, Mossley; *m.* Ann Maria, *d.* of William Ward, of Manchester. *Educ.*: Balliol Coll., Oxford. *War Work*: Deputy Military Representative and National Service Representative appearing before Manchester Tribunal. *Addresses*: Westwood, Altrincham; Moor Crag, Windermere. *Clubs*: Clarendon (Manchester); Royal Windermere Yacht. (O10073)

BUCKLEY, Joan Brunner, M.B.E.

BUCKLEY, Capt. Peter Burton, O.B.E., M.C., R.E.

BUCKLEY, Wilfred, C.B.E., *b.* 13 June, 1873; *s.* of Henry Buckley, of Birmingham; *m* Bertha T. *d.* of Herbert L. Terrell, of New York, U.S.A. *Educ.*: Giggleswick School. *War Work*: Director of Milk Supplies, Ministry of Food, 1917–20; Technical Advisor to Food Controller; Member War Agricultural Executive Committee, Hampshire; Committee on the Production and Distribution of Milk; Poultry Advisory Committee. *Address*: Moundsmere Manor, Basingstoke. *Clubs*: Royal Automobile; Hampshire (Winchester). (C2175)

BUCKLEY, William, C.B.E., J.P., C.C.; *s.* of Joseph Buckley, of Higher Broughton, Manchester; *m.* Kate Lewtas, *d.* of John Carter, of Fleetwood, Lancs. *Educ.*: Privately. J.P. County Borough of Salford and County of Flint; Member Flint County Council, Education, and Insurance Committees; Chairman Meadowslea (Flintshire) Tuberculosis Hospital; Vice-Chairman Llangwyfan Sanatorium Committee, Denbighshire; Governor and Member of Council King Edward Memorial Association for Prevention of Tuberculosis; *War Work*: Chairman N. Wales Munition Committee (covering five counties); Chairman Leeswood Auxiliary Red Cross Hospital, Mold; assisted in recruiting in County of Flint. *Address*: Hafod, Mold, N.Wales; *Club*: Clarendon; Manchester. (C448)

BUCKLEY, Dr. Winifred Finnimore, O.B.E., M.R.C.S., L.R.C.P., *b.* 18 Oct. 1883; *d.* of Robert Burton Buckley, C.S.I. *Educ.*: Kensington High School, Newnham Coll., Cambridge, and Royal Free Hospital. Physician and Surgeon, Temporary Assistant Physician and Registrar Roll of Honour Hospital for Children, Harrow Road; Demonstrator of Anatomy, London School of Medicine for Women, 8, Hunter Street, W.C. *War Work*: Assistant Surgeon and later Surgeon at the Military Hospital, Endell Street, from May, 1915, to Nov. 1919.

Addresses: Roll of Honour Hospital for Children, 688, Harrow Road; 44, Clanricarde Gardens, London, W. 2. (O11795)

BUCKMAN, James, M.B.E.

BUCKMASTER, Dorothy Mary, Mrs., M.B.E., *b.* 26 July, 1885; *d.* of William John Dyer, of 1, Sydney Place, Onslow Square, S.W. 7; *m.* Martin Arnold, *s.* of John Charles Buckmaster, of Hampton Wick. *Educ.*: Kensington and Clapham High Schools and Royal College of Art. *War Work*: 3 years as officer in War Trade Intelligence Dept.; 6 months in Disposal Board. *Address*: 17, Coleherne Mansions, West Bolton Gardens, London, S.W. 5. *Club*: Halcyon. (M7542)

BUCKMASTER, Harry Cuthbert, O.B.E.

BUCKMASTER, Major Henry Stephen Guy, O.B.E.

BUCKMASTER, William, O.B.E.

BUCKNALL, Nathalie, Mrs., M.B.E., *b.* 21 July, 1895; *d.* of Councillor of State Ivan de Fedenko, of Petrograd; *m.* Lieut.-Comm. George, R.N.V.R., *s.* of Charles Herbert Bucknall, of London. *Educ.*: St. Anne's Coll., Petrograd. *War Work*: July, 1914, to Sept. 1915, Czarevitch Alexei's Hospital, Petrograd; 1915–17, Hospital Trains of T.I.H. Grand Duchess Tatiana and Grand Duchess Marie, as voluntary sister of the Kaufman Sisterhood (awarded Gold Medal of St. Anne for these services); 1919 (voluntary), Sister-in-Charge of the aid-post of British Mil. Mission, Ekaterinodar, S. Russia, while her husband was Naval Liaison Officer there (May to Aug.). *Address*: 3, Kensington Hall Gardens, W. 14. (M7543)

BUCKNALL, Capt. Roger, O.B.E.

BUCKNALL, Capt. William Beverley, O.B.E.

BUCKNELL, Norman Charles, O.B.E. (O11958)

BUCKNER, Albert Walter, M.B.E., L.A.M.T.P.I., *b.* 13 Jan. 1876; *s.* of Thomas William Buckner, of Stoke Row, Oxon; *m.* Ellen Mercy, *d.* of Edwin Hatton, of Reading. *Educ.*: Reading Blue Coat School. Clerk to Tilbury Urban District Council and as such responsible for all negotiations on Tilbury Extended Housing Scheme for erection of 1520 workmen's dwellings and construction of important reinforced concrete roads and flood prevention works, whole scheme, costing upwards of two million pounds, having been definitely sanctioned and contracts placed. *War Work*: Executive Food Officer for Tilbury (including Docks); Local Fuel Overseer for Tilbury; Hon. Sec. Tilbury War Pensions Committee, Air Raid Emergency Committee, Local Coal Distribution Committee; Hon. Auditor, Tilbury Supplementary Aid Fund for Discharged Soldiers and Sailors; Clerk to Tilbury War Housing Committee in carrying out erection of 150 workmen's dwellings for transport workers during war. *Addresses*: Clontarf, Dell Road, Grays; Council Offices, Tilbury. (M7544)

BUCKNER, Frederick Percival, M.B.E.

BUCKNER, Lieut. Johnstone Stanley, M.B.E., R.N.

BUCKNILL, Lieut. Thomas Alfred Townsend, O.B.E.

BUDD, Sir Cecil Lindsay, K.B.E., Officer of the Legion of Honour, *b.* 29 Sept. 1865; *s.* of Edward Budd, of Vale Lodge, Leatherhead; *m.* Muriel Edmee, *d.* of Wilfrid A. Bevan, of Combe Court. *Educ.*: Winchester College. Chairman of the London Metal Exchange. *War Work*: Various Committees of the Board of Trade, Ministry of Munitions, and Ministry of Reconstruction; Departmental Controller in Ministry of Munitions. *Addresses*: The Briars, Reigate; 37, St. James's Place, S.W. *Clubs*: Reform; Gresham; M.C.C. (K203)

BUDD, Capt. and Qr.-Mr. Charles, M.B.E., R.A.V.C.

BUDD, Henry George, M.B.E., *b.* 28 Aug. 1873; *s.* of James Budd, of Croydon, Surrey; *m.* Priscilla Penuel, *d.* of F. M. MacDermott, of Henfield, Sussex. *Educ.*: High School, Hungerford. Bank Official. Served in Boer War, 1900, and awarded the Freedom of the City of London. *War Work*: As a member of the London Scottish, appointed Drill Instructor in Sept. 1914, Paymaster-Sergeant in 1915; organised, and appointed Secretary of the London Scottish War Savings Association in 1917. (M7545)

BUDDEN, Henry Ebenezer, C.B.E. Organiser of Overseas Australian Comforts Fund during Great War. (C358)

BUDDLE, Surg.-Lieut. Comdr. Roger, O.B.E., R.N., M.B.

BUDGE, Henry, M.B.E., R.N.

BUDGE, John, M.B.E. (Merchant Service), *b.* 6 April, 1868; *s.* of William Budge, of Kirkhill, Wick; *m.* Georgina, *d.* of William Hendry, of Forse, Caithness. *Educ.*: Landward School, Wick, Caithness. Superintending Engineer and Ship Surveyor. *War Work*: Engaged in Merchant Service during war, carrying war material to France, and also in Russia (from Riga to Petrograd); took home ship with disabled engines from Sweden to West Hartlepool (voluntarily). *Address*: 338, Easter Road, Leith, Scotland. (M7546)

BUDGE, Lieut. James William, M.B.E.

BUDGEN, Capt. William Douglas, O.B.E., R.A.F.

BUDGETT, Georgiana Essie, Mrs., O.B.E.

BUELL, Lieut.-Col. William Senkler, C.B.E. Lieut.-Col. Canadian Forces; Great War, 1915–19 (despatches). (C1831)

BUFFHAM, Major Lewis William, O.B.E.

BUGDEN, Sara Amy, M.B.E., *b.* 15 June, 1855; *d.* of George Bugden, of Berwick St. John, Wilts. *Educ.*: Privately. Certified Mistress (Board of Education). *War Work*: At the outbreak of war was Hon. Divisional Secretary of the Hackney and Stoke Newington Red Cross Division, County of London Branch; Initiated and organised many Red Cross activities in this Division—help to needy Service men on Sick Furlough; establishment of the first Auxiliary Hospital in Hackney and organisation of Air Raid Relief Units. *Address*: 4, Alcester Crescent, Upper Clapton, E. 5. (M7547)

BUGLER, 2nd Lieut. William Thomas Hansford, M.B.E., R.A.S.C.

BUHAGIAR, Peter, M.B.E.

BUIST, Florence May, Mrs., M.B.E., *b.* 11 Jan. 1875; *d.* of Rev. J. C. Whitley, late Bishop of Chhota Nagpur; *m.* Arthur William Buist. *War Work:* Red Cross Depot, Rawalpindi; also visiting soldiers in Hospital and supplying them with comforts. *Addresses:* c/o Alliance Bank of Simla, Ltd., Rawalpindi, India; c/o H. S. King & Co., 9, Pall Mall, London. (M6114)

BUIST, William Huntley, O.B.E., J.P., *b.* 1876; *s.* of Thos. P. Buist, of Dundee; *m.* Jane, *d.* of J. Scivwright, of Cleveland, U.S.A. *Educ.:* High School and Harris Academy, Dundee. *War Work:* 1st Chairman Dundee War Savings Association; Building Convener, Scotland, for Y.M.C.A.; Member of Dundee Food Control Committee; Chairman Advisory Committee Furnishing Trades, etc. *Addresses:* 15, Albany Terrace, Dundee; Whitegates, Balmerino, Fife. *Clubs:* Scottish Liberal; Glasgow Liberal. (O1159)

BULKLEY, Mildred Emily, M.B.E.

BULL, Annie, Mrs., M.B.E., *b.* 15 Dec. 1871; *d.* of Robert Cartmel Fairrie, of Castlerigg, Cumberland; *m.* Lieut.-Col. George Henry, I.M.S., *s.* of Joshua Bull, M.D. *War Work:* Nursing at The Chalet, Hoylake, Cheshire, Sept. 1915, to Jan. 1916; served as Quartermaster Jan. 1916, to Nov. 1919, at the Princess Christian Military Hospital, Englefield Green, Surrey. (M8044)

BULL, Edward BAGNALL-, C.B.E.

BULL, Esther, Mrs., M.B.E.

BULL, Lieut.-Col. Frederick Julius, O.B.E., T.D., Middlesex Regt., *b.* 12 Dec. 1871. *War Work:* Attached G.H.Q. Med. Exped. Force, 1915–16; attached G.H.Q. British Exped. Force, 1916–19; twice mentioned in despatches. *Addresses:* 2, Western Lawns, Hove, Sussex. *Clubs:* Constitutional; Fellow Royal Colonial Institute. (O2448)

BULL, George, C.B.E. Chairman of the Central Council, Forage Dept., Civil Supplies, Board of Trade. (C3133)

BULL, George Frederick, O.B.E.

BULL, George Lucien, C.B.E.

BULL, Maude Ellen, M.B.E.; *d.* of Henry Graves Bull, M.D., J.P., of Harley House, Hereford. Associate of Oxford University Extension Delegacy; Hon. Local Sec. Oxford University Extension (Hereford Centre); Member of L.E.A. for Hereford City, and of Training College Sub-Com. of Hereford County L.E.A.; Hon. Sub-Librarian Hereford Cathedral Library; Hon. Sec. Ladies' Com. N.S.P.C.C. (Hereford and County Branch). *War Work:* Hon. Treas. and Sec. Soldiers' and Sailors' Families Association; Distributor and Member of War Pensions Local Committee for Herefordshire. *Address:* Harley House, Hereford. (M7548)

BULL, Thomas Tollemache Jackson, O.B.E.

BULL, Paymaster-Comm. Wilfrid James, O.B.E., R.N.

BULL, William, M.B.E., R.A.O.C.

BULL, Col. William Henry, O.B.E., F.R.C.S., F.D.

BULLEID, Prof. Charles Henry, O.B.E., M.A., A.M.I.C.E., M.Inst. Met., *b.* 10 Jan. 1883; *s.* of Samuel John Bulleid, of Hatherleigh, Devonshire; *m.* Dorothy, *d.* of S. Neville Cox, of Derby. *Educ.:* Exeter School and Trinity College, Cambridge. Professor of Engineering, University College, Nottingham. *War Work:* General Manager, Nottingham National Shell Factory; Chief Engineer, Admiralty Mining School, Portsmouth. *Address:* 7, Ebers Road, Nottingham. (O1160)

BULLEN, Daisy May, M.B.E., *b.* 9 Aug. 1883; *d.* of Frederick William Bullen, of Holloway. *Educ.:* Camden School for Girls. *War Work:* Sec. Aeronautical Inspection Department War Savings Association. (M7549)

BULLEN, Frederick John, O.B.E. (O11784h)

BULLEN, Gertrude, M.B.E., V.A.D.

BULLEN, Major Thomas, O.B.E., R.A.F.

BULLEN, Capt. William Henry Chambers, O.B.E.

BULLER, Dame Audrey Charlotte Georgina, D.B.E.; R.R.C. *War Work:* Performed valuable work as Administrator, War Hospitals, Exeter, throughout the War. (D61)

BULLER, Capt. Francis Elliot, O.B.E., M.C., R.E.; *b.* 5 Dec. 1888; *s.* of the Rev. S. R. A. Buller, M.A., of Weybridge. *Educ.:* Wellington Coll., and R.M.A. *Address:* c/o Messrs. Cox & Co., Bombay. *Club:* Army and Navy. (O8420)

BULLER, Brig.-Gen. the hon. Sir Henry YARDE-, K.B.E., C.B., D.S.O., M.V.O., brother of the late 2nd Baron Churston, of Lupton, Devonshire; *b.* 2 Nov. 1862; *m.* Adelaide, *d.* of the late Col. Meeking, of Richings Park, Bucks. *Educ.:* Radley Coll. Entered Rifle Brigade 1884; served with Waziristan Expedition, 1894–95; Sudan Expedition 1898, including Battle of Khartum; Crete 1898–99; South African War 1898–1902, including operations on Tugela Heights, Relief of Ladysmith and Laing's Nek; Mil. Attaché at N. European Courts, 1906–11; First Assist. to British Mil. Delegate to Peace Conference at The Hague, 1907; Military Attaché at Paris, Madrid, and Lisbon, 1912–15; Chief of British Mission at French Army Headquarters 1914–17 during Great War; Military Attaché Norway and Sweden 1917–18; Comm. of the Orders of Leopold of Belgium, Dannebrog of Denmark, St. Olav of Norway, Epée of Sweden and Legion of Honour of France; retired 1919. *Address:* Essex Lodge, Windsor. *Clubs:* Travellers'; Naval & Military. (K322)

BULLER, Lieut.-Col. Walter Thomas More, C.B.E. Capt. and Brevet Major, R.A.S.C.; Great War, 1914–19, as Lieut.-Col. (despatches). (C1124)

BULLER, Ralph Buller HUGHES-, C.I.E., C.B.E.,

b. 28 Feb. 1871; *s.* of the late General Sir William Hughes, K.C.B., of Dunley, Bovey Tracey; *m.* Elizabeth, *d.* of the late Very Rev. Norman Macleod, D.D., Dean of the Thistle, of the Barony Church, Glasgow. *Educ.* Marlborough; Balliol Coll., Oxon. Indian Civil Service (retired). joined the Indian Civil Service in 1892, and held various posts including: Settlement Officer; Political Officer; Assistant Secretary to the Government of India, Foreign Dept.; Special Duty, Delhi Durbar: General and Judicial Secretary to Government of Eastern Bengal and Assam; Inspector-General of Police, Eastern Bengal and Assam and Bengal. *War Work:* Inspector-General of Police, Bengal, India, 1914–16; Ministry of Munitions, 1916; Special duty New Scotland Yard, 1916–17; Director of National Service, South Western Region, 1917–18. *Address:* Woodhayes, Whimple, Devon. *Club:* Brooks's. (C2487)

BULLER, Hon. Lilah Constance Cavendish, Lady MANNINGHAM-, O.B.E., *b.* 20 March, 1884, only surviving *d.* of 3rd Baron Chesham (*see* BURKE'S *Peerage*), *m.* Sir Merwyn Edward, 3rd Bt., *s.* of the late Maj.-Gen. Edward Manningham Manningham-Buller and Lady Anne Coke, 2nd *d.* of the 2nd Earl of Leicester. *War Work:* Northamptonshire Red Cross Hospital Supply Depot. *Address:* Brownhill, Spratton, Northampton. (O10078)

BULLIVANT, Lieut. Hugh Edward, M.B.E., R.F.A. (S.R.).

BULLOCH, Marion Maria, O.B.E.,; *d.* of the late Geo. Bulloch, of Kinloch, Dunkeld, Perthshire. *War Work:* County Director, Perthshire V.A.D. *Address:* Kinloch, Dunkeld. *Club:* Ladies' Army and Navy. (O1162)

BULLOCK, Amy Isabel, Lady, O.B.E.; *d.* of James Thomson, D.L., of Middlesex; *m.* Sir George Mackworth Bullock, *s.* of Thomas Henry Bullock, Deputy Commissioner of Berar; one *d.*, Evelyn. *War Work:* With Soldiers' and Sailors' Families Association in England for six months; Bermuda, three years' work for Red Cross; a year and a half at Belgravia "Splint" Depot, London. *Address:* 3, Carlton Hill, N.W. 8. *Club:* Empress. (O984)

BULLOCK, Lieut.-Comm. Charles Arthur, O.B.E., R.N.R., R.D.

BULLOCK, Capt. Christopher Llewellyn, O.B.E., R.A.F.

BULLOCK, Lieut. Frank Henry William, M.B.E., A.M.I.M.E., R.A.S.C., *b.* 1885; *s.* of Capt. W. Bullock, of South Farnboro', Hants. *Educ.:* Privately. *War Work:* Served with army from 12 Nov. 1914, to end of War; in France 1915–17; in Palestine 1917–18; took part in raids on Es Salt and Amam; also in last advance to Damascus. *Address:* 30, York Road, South Farnboro', Hants. (M3169)

BULLOCK, Capt. Harold Malcolm, M.B.E.

BULLOCK, Lieut. Herbert Charles Stuart, M.B.E., R.A.F.

BULLOCK, Lieut. Herbert Poe Story, O.B.E., I.A.

BULLOCK, James Arthur Edward, M.B.E., *b.* 2 Nov. 1871; *d.* of the Rev. Walter Trevelyan Bullock, of Faulkbourn Hall, Essex (*see* BURKE'S *Landed Gentry*); *m.* Helen, *d.* of John Wilks of Stanbridgeford, Bedfordshire. *Educ.:* Rottingdean and Reading. Chief Clerk, Colonial Secretary's Office, Hongkong. *War Work:* Served in Hongkong Defence Force. *Address:* Colonial Secretary's Office, Hongkong. *Club:* Hongkong: Thatched House. (M6420)

BULLOCK, Lieut. John Walter, M.B.E., R.E.

BULLOCK, John William, M.B.E., *b.* 17 May, 1865; *s.* of Thomas Bullock, J.P., of Killynick House, Belturbet, Ireland; *m.* Emma, *d.* of Henry Mitchell, of Westminster. *Educ.:* Farra School, Westmeath, Ireland. Civil Servant, Exchequer and Audit Department. *War Work:* Secretariat Irish Convention; Assisted on public audit of War Accounts. *Address:* Emo, York Road, Cheam, Surrey. *Club:* Whitefriars. (M3547)

BULLOCK, Margaret Annie, M.B.E.

BULLOCK, Ralph, C.B.E., *b.* 1 June, 1868; *s.* of Wm. Hy. Bullock, of South Tottenham. *Educ.:* Privately; Eastern Produce Merchant. *War Work:* Comm. of N. Division Special Constabulary, 1915–20. *Address:* 172, High Road, South Tottenham, N. 15. *Club:* Royal Automobile. (C2488)

BULLOUGH, Frank, M.B.E.

BULLWINKLE, Leonard Albert, O.B.E.

BULMAN, Major George Purvis, O.B.E., R.A.F.

BULMAN, Capt. John James, O.B.E., M.C., R.E.

BULMAN, Mary Helen, Mrs., M.B.E., *b.* 1849; *d.* of Dr. Wm. Roderick, of Oswestry, Salop; *m.* the late Andrew, *s.* of Andrew Bulman, of Kelso. *Educ.:* Cheltenham. *War Work:* Member of Roxburghshire War Pensions Committee; Member of Committee Sailors' and Soldiers' Families Association; Member of Committee, Roxburghshire Sewing Guild. *Address:* Pringle Bank, Kelso, Scotland. (M7551)

BULMER, Francis Bertram, M.B.E.

BULMER, S.S.M. Newlove, M.B.E., R.A.S.C.

BULPITT, Walter Henry, O.B.E.

BULTEEL, Cecil Edward, O.B.E. (O11729)

BULTEEL, Lieut. Walter Beresford, M.B.E.

BUMPUS, Alf'ed Adolphus, M.B.E., J.P. Leicestershire, *b.* 13 Aug. 1851; *s.* of Thomas Bumpus, of Stratford-on-Avon; *m.* Clara E., *d.* of Edward Stevenson, of Loughborough. *War Work:* Chairman of Tribunal, etc. *Address:* Heathfield, London Road, Leicester. (M188)

BUMSTEAD, Richard Edward, M.B.E., J.P., *b.* 1883; *s.* of William Edward Bumstead, of Ashford, Kent; *m.* Kate Maytum, *d.* of William Frederick Cackett, of Canterbury,

Kent. *Educ.*: National School, Ashford, Kent. Railway Engine Driver. *War Work*: Appeal Tribunal, Kent; Soldiers' War Pensions Committee; Food Control Committee; War Savings Committee; Prince of Wales' Fund. *Address*: 264, New Town, Ashford, Kent. (M189)

BUNBURY, Comm. Charles Thomas Alexander, O.B.E., R.N.

BUNBURY, Hon. Thomas Leopold McCLINTOCK-, M.B.E.

BUNCE, Thomas Lockwood, M.B.E., M.I.Mech.E. *b.*, 6 March, 1881; *s.* of John Edwardes Bunce, of Halifax; *m.* Isabel Mary, *d.* of William Colley, of Liverpool. *Educ.*: Halifax Higher Grade School Technical College; West Ham College; Liverpool University. *War Work*: Introduction of female labour in Machine Tool Factories; equipment of shell, projectile and gun factories; Admiralty and shipyard extensions; Ministry of Munitions, London, 1915–20. *Address*: 33, Princes Avenue, Liverpool. (M680)

BUNCE, Lieut. William Leslie, O.B.E.

BUNCH, William Henry, M.B.E.

BUND, John William WILLIS-, C.B.E., D.L., J.P., *b.* 8 Aug. 1843 *s.* of John Walpole Willis, of Wick Episcopi, Worcester; *m.* 1st, Harrietta Penelope, *d.* of Richard Temple, The Nash, Kempsey; 2nd, Mary Elizabeth, *d.* of Col. R. Thackeray, C.B., R.E. *Educ.*: Eton, Caius College, Cambridge. Chairman of Quarter Sessions, Worcestershire and Cardiganshire; Chairman, Worcestershire County Council Standing Joint Committee; Education Committee, Worcestershire; Licensing Committee, Worcestershire and Cardiganshire; Chairman, Severn Fishing Board. *War Work*: Chairman, County Appeal Tribunal, Worcestershire; Chairman, Naval and Military War Pensions Committee and County War Relief Committee. *Address*: Wick Episcopi, Worcester. *Clubs*: Oxford and Cambridge; Constitutional. (C334)

BUNDOCK, Lieut. and Qr.-Mr. Charles, M.B.E.

BUNDOCK, Capt. Charles Slade, O.B.E.

BUNNEY, Michael, M.B.E., F.R.I.B.A., *b.* 3 Feb. 1873; *s.* of John Wharlton Bunney, of Venice; *m.* Edith Adelaide, *d.* of John Hewetson, of Ravenstonedale. *Educ.*: Fettes Coll., Edinburgh. Deputy Chief Architect, Ministry of Health. *War Work*: Assistant Director, Trench Warfare Supply Department, Ministry of Munitions, 1916–18; Resident Engineer, Administrator of Works and Buildings Department, Air Ministry. *Addresses*: Windhill, Meadway, N.W. 4; 33, Henrietta Street, Covent Garden. (M1495)

BUNNING, George Harold STUART-, O.B.E., J.P., *b.* 25 Dec. 1870; *s.* of Edward Bunning, of Cosby, Leicester; *m.* Emily Agnes, *d.* of Ralph George Lucas, of Malton, Yorks. Vice-Chairman, National Civil Service Whitby Council; Secretary, Sub-Postmasters' Federation; Labour Representative International Labour Bureau (League of Nations). *Addresses*: Parliament Mansions, Victoria St., S.W. 1; Portland Lodge, Streatham, S.W. (O60)

BUNKER, Nellie, M.B.E.

BUNT, Richard Charles, M.B.E., R.N.

BUNTING, Lieut. Sheldon Arthur Stewart, M.B.E.

BUNTON, Samuel, M.B.E., J.P.

BURALL, Henry Charles, M.B.E., *b.* 1854; *s.* of Thomas Burall, of Devoran, Cornwall *m.* 1st, Louie, *d.* of Edward Darlow, of Ramsey, Hunts; 2nd, Maud, *d.* of Joseph Reynolds, of Wimblington, Cambs. Councillor to the Borough of Wisbech; Hon. Sec. Wisbech Monumental Memorial Committee; Member of the National Savings Assembly. *War Work*: Hon. Sec. Wisbech Local Savings Committee from 1916. *Address*: Pengreep, Wisbech, Cambs. (M7553)

BURBIDGE, Sir Richard Woodman, Bart., C.B.E., *b.* 7 Dec. 1872 *s.* of the late Sir Richard Burbidge, 1stBart., of Littleton Park, Shepperton; *m.* Catherine Jemima, *d.* of H. J. Grant, of Sodbury House, Clacton. *Educ.*: Privately. Managing Director Harrods (London), Ltd.; Managing Director Harrods (Buenos Aires), Ltd.; Chairman, Dickins & Jones; Director, Swan & Edgars; Managing Director, South American Stores (Gath & Chaves), Ltd.; Hon. Treas. Tariff Commission. *War Work*: Member of Stores Purchases Advisory Committee; Member of Ministry of Munitions Staff, Investigation Committee. *Addresses*: 51, Hans Mansions, Chelsea, S.W. 3; Cisswood Cottage, Mannings Heath, Horsham. *Clubs*: Devonshire; Aldwych; R.A.C. (C937)

BURCH, Major Frederick, O.B.E.

BURCH, Lieut.-Col. William Edward Scarth, C.B.E., *b.* 1863; *s.* John Burch Burch, of Sheffield; *m.* Florence, *d.* of J. Hebblethwaite, of Richmond, Surrey. *Educ.*: Privately and at Poulton House, Hampton-on-Thames. *War Work*: Officer-in-Charge of Records, Royal Flying Corps, from 3 June, 1912, to 25 Feb. 1918; Staff Officer, Class I., Air Ministry, 25 Feb. 1918, to 1 Nov. 1918; Inspector of Q.M.G. Services, Midland Area, R.A.F., from 1 Nov. 1918, to 1 July, 1919. *Address*: 41, Emperor's Gate, South Kensington, London, S.W. 7. (C2344;

BURCHALL, Major Percival Russell, O.B.E., R.A.F.

BURCHARDT, Christiana Mary, O.B.E., *b.* 26 Jan. 1856 *d.* of Otto Burchardt, of Liverpool. *War Work*: County Secretary for Oxfordshire Branch of British Red Cross Society. *Address*: 160, Banbury Road, Oxford. *Club*: Empress. (O3642)

BURCHATT, Ernest Edward, M.B.E.

BURCHELL, Capt. James Melvill, O.B.E.

BURCHER, Frederick Edward, M.B.E.

BURDEKIN, ex-2nd Lieut. Cyril Blake, M.B.E., *b.* 14 Oct. 1887; *s.* of Edward Blake Burdekin, of Nelson, New Zealand;

m. Ada Constance Dorothy. *d.* of John Hamblet Gill, of 21, Woburn Square, London, W.C. 1. *Educ.*: Wellington Coll., New Zealand. *War Work*: Assistant to Asst.-Adjutant General, New Zealand Expeditionary Force. *Addresses*: 21, Woburn Square, London, W.C. 1; N.Z. High Commissioner's Office, Strand, W.C., (M6743)

BURDEKIN, Lizzie, Mrs., M.B.E.

BURDEN, Capt. Albert Edmund Charles, O.B.E., *b.* 5 Dec. 1877. On staff London County Council, 1895–1908; Chief Accountant United Motor Cab Co., Ltd., and General Motor Cab Co., Ltd., 1908–12. *War Work*: Stores manager, British Red Cross and Order of St. John, Malta, Egypt, and Near East Commission, April, 1915, to April, 1920. *Club*: Turf (Cairo). (O10081)

BURDEN, Walter Patrick, M.B.E., R.N.

BURDER, Walter Chapman, M.B.E., Assoc. M.I.C.E., J.P., *b.* 7 Feb. 1848; *s.* of Rev. Alfred Burder, of Oakley, Essex; *m.* Elizabeth J., *d.* of Rev. F. Gifford Nash, of Clavering. *Educ.*: Bishops Stortford and King's Coll., London. Mechanical Engineer, Director of Messenger & Co., Ltd., Loughborough. *War Work*: Commandant, British Red Cross, Leicester, 24; Chairman, Loughborough and District Hospital. *Address*: Field House, Loughborough. (M1497)

BURDETT, Henry Stanton, M.B.E., R.A.F.

BURDITT, George Frederick, C.R.E.

BURDON, Major Edward Griffiths George, O.B.E.

BURDON, Col. Rowland, C.B.E., M.P.; *b.* 1857; *s.* of the late Rev. John Burdon, of Castle Eden, Durham; *m.* 1887, Mary, *d.* of the late Wyndham Slade, of Montys Court, Taunton. Lieut.-Col. Durham L.I. (V.D.), and a J.P. and D.L. for Durham (Sheriff, 1907); unsuccessfully contested S.E. Div. of Durham, 1910; has sat as M.P. for Sedgefield Div. (Co.U.) thereof since Dec. 1918. *Address*: Castle Eden, Durham. (C1490)

BURDON, Lieut. Walter Boyd Chandlers, O.B.E., R.F.A.

BURGE, Capt. Cyril Gordon, O.B.E., R.A.F.

BURGES, Capt. (Pasha and Major-Gen. in Egypt), Frank, O.B.E.; *s.* of Rev. Frank Burges, B.D., of Winterbourne Rectory, Gloucestershire; *m.* Marion Anderson, *d.* of John Cochran. *Educ.*: Winchester, Magdalen Coll., Oxford, and R. M. C. Sandhurst. Joined Gloucestershire Regt. 21 Sept. 1889; seconded Egyptian Army, Jan. 1898, and served in Nile Campaign; present at Battle of Omdurman, 2 Sept. 1898 (mentioned in despatches, British Medal, and Sudan Medal and clasp); Commanded Friendly Arabs, Kordofan Field Force, 1899 (mentioned in despatches, clasp to medal); joined Sudan Civil Administration, March, 1899, at Suakin; commanded Force capturing Oswald Dijna (4th Class Order Medjidieh); transferred to Berber Province, 1901 to 1908; joined the Legal Dept. 1909; Police Magistrate, Khartum, in charge of Criminal Courts, Khartum Prov. (4th Class Osmanieh); made a Pasha, 1917 (2nd Class Order of the Nile). Retired Sept. 1919. *War Work*: Served on the Canal Zone, 1915, as Assist. Provost Marshal, Canal Defences. *Address*: Farncombe House, Broadway, Glos. *Clubs*: Army and Navy; M.C.C. (O9983)

BURGES, Frederick Augustus l'Estrange, M.B.E., M.R.C.S. (Eng.), L.R.C.P. (Lond.), *b.* 1870; *s.* of the late Rev. R. B. Burges, of St. Paul's Vicarage, Birmingham; *m.* Mary Annie, *d.* of Rev. A. L. Wilkinson, of Bromsgrove. *Educ.*: King Edward's High School, Birmingham. Medical Officer to the Post Office, Birmingham; Public Vaccinator, Birmingham District. *War Work*: Hon. Sec. Birmingham Medical War Committee. *Address*: 62, Hockley Hill, Birmingham. *Club*: Garrick (Birmingham). (M7557)

BURGES, Col. William Edward Parry, O.B.E., D.L. M.A., LL.M., *b.* 25 Dec. 1856; *s.* of Edward Burges, of The Ridge, Chipping Sodbury, Glos.; *m.* Ellen, *d.* of William Parry, of Eaton Bishop. *Educ.*: Clifton College, Eton; King's College, London; Trinity College, Cambridge. *War Work*: Chief Recruiting Officer, Bristol; subsequently Commanded 12 (S) Bn. Glostershire Regt.; Commandant Young Officers' School, Pembroke; Chief Military Representative and Appeal Representative, Bristol. *Address*: The Ridge, Chipping Sodbury. *Club*: Junior United Service. (O1163)

BURGESS, Ann, Mrs., M.B.E.

BURGESS, Arthur Edward, M.B.E., *b.* 8 July, 1873; *s.* of Frederick Burgess, of St. Osyth, Essex; *m.* Ethel Mary, *d.* of James Glasscock, of Ilford, Essex. Superintendent of Horticultural Instruction, Surrey County Council; held similar positions in Essex and Hertfordshire. *War Work*: Organising Secretary of the Surrey Horticultural Sub-Committee. This Committee was responsible for a great increase in the number of allotment plots, and rendered assistance to small cultivators generally, thus increasing the home supply of food during the critical days of the war. *Address*: Wolferton, Burton Road, Kingston-on-Thames; County Education Office, Kingston-on-Thames. (M7558)

BURGESS, Arthur William, M.B.E.

BURGESS, Charles Hayward, M.B.E.

BURGESS, Lieut.-Col. Charles Roscoe, C.B.E., D.S.O. Lieut.-Col. S. African Forces; Great War, 1914–19. (C1880)

BURGESS, Elspeth, Mrs., M.B.E.; *d.* of Thomas Robinson, Esq., of Leek; *m.* Arthur Henry Burgess, Surgeon, of Manchester. *War Work*: Organised the 1st Red Cross Hospital in Manchester, and had charge of it for the duration of the War; sat on many committees, and helped generally. *Address*: Milberton Lodge, Victoria Park, Manchester. (M103)

BURGESS, Frederick James, O.B.E.

BURGESS, Paymaster-Sub-Lieut. Herbert Smith, O.B.E., R.N.R.

BURGESS, Major John Frederick, O.B.E., Can.A.M.C.

BURGESS, Kenneth Paul, O.B.E., A.I.N.A., b. 11 July, 1879 ; s. of Joseph Burgess, of Oxford ; m. Helena Mary, d. of Edward S. Lambert, of Red Hill. Assistant-Director of Technical Services, Ministry of Shipping. War Work : Arrangement and supervision of the fitting of ships as transports, for the conveyance of troops ; Hospital ships, and Naval Auxiliaries. Address : "Kennelle," Edgar Road, Sanderstead.
(O193)

BURGESS, Lieut. Robert Ashfield, M.B.E., R.H.A.

BURGESS, William Frederick Richardson, O.B.E. M.D. (Lond.), b. 31 July, 1849 ; s. of the late Frederick Josiah Burgess. Educ. : Privately and Guy's Hospital. Now retired from practice. War Work : Civil Medical Officer, Preston Barracks, Brighton ; Civil Medical Officer, Grove Hospital, Tooting, S.W. Address : 23, High Road, Streatham, S.W. 16. Club : Junior Constitutional. (O11796)

BURGOYNE, Lieut. Clarence, M.B.E.

BURGOYNE, Capt. Sydney Thomas, M.V.O., O.B.E.

BURKE, Capt. Allan Frederick, M.B.E.

BURKE, Lieut.-Col. Bernard Bruce, C.B.E., D.S.O., R.A.M.C., b. 7 Jan. 1876 ; s. of James Marlow Burke, of Westend, Mallow, Ireland ; m. Anna, d. of late Sir Adam Scott Reid, K.C.B., of New Kelso, Strathcarron. Educ. : High School, Dublin and Royal College of Surgeons, Ireland. War Work : France, 3rd Division, 34th Division, 30th Division, 11th Division, 1914–19. Address : c/o Holt & Co., 3, Whitehall Place, S.W. Club : Junior Army and Navy. (C1230)

BURKE, Major Denis Joseph Gerard, O.B.E., D.C.L.I.

BURKE, Capt. Edmund Albert, O.B.E.

BURKE, Paymaster-Lieut. Fred, O.B.E., R.N.R.

BURKE, Hubert Francis Daubeny, O.B.E.

BURKE, Lieut.-Col. Hugh St. George Melville Addison, M.B.E., b. 15 June, 1884 ; s. of Charles Carrington Burke. Educ. : Harrow. War Work : Caterpillar Tractors. Address : Red House, Levington, Ipswich. Club : R. A. C. (M5125)

BURKE, May, Mrs., O.B.E.

BURKE, Vincent Patrick, M.B.E.' M.A., B.Sc., LL.D., b. 3 Aug. 1878 ; s. of Patrick Burke, of St. Jacques, N.F. ; m. Margaret Elizabeth, d. of Capt. Wm. Mulcahy, of St. John's, N.F. Educ. : St. Bonaventure's Coll., St. John's, and afterwards Columbia Univ., New York. Principal High School, Torbay, on leaving college ; Superintendent Education, Catholic Schools, 1899–1920 ; Deputy Minister of Education, N.F., 1920 ; President Council of Higher Education, 1918, (re-elected 1919). War Work : Hon. Sec. Patriotic Association of Newfoundland, 1914 to present date ; Member of following Committees during the war : Finance Committee, Recruiting Committee, Officer's Selection Committee, Forestry Companies Committee, Trustee Patriotic Fund and Hon. Sec. Standing Committee on Military Organisation, which committee acted in lieu of Militia Department until Aug. 1917, and under its direction the Royal N.F. Regiment was recruited, enlisted, and despatched on active service. Address : Allandale Road, St. John's, Newfoundland. Clubs : City ; Ballyhally Golf ; County. (M1242)

BURKITT, Francis Holy, O.B.E.

BURLACE, Capt. Leslie Binmore, O.B.E., B.Sc., A.M.Inst.C.E., b. 5 June, 1891 ; s. of J. B. Burlace, of Ealing. Educ. : St. Paul's School ; and Univ. Coll., London. Civil Engineer. War Work : In ranks 1st Batt. "U.P.S." (Royal Fusiliers), Sept. 1914 ; commissioned R.A.S.C., Dec. 1914 ; served in France, Dec. 1914 to March, 1919. Address : 38, Corfton Road, Ealing, W. 5. Club : New Oxford and Cambridge. (O5058)

BURLAND, Lieut. Leonard, O.B.E.

BURLEIGH, Cecil Charles, O.B.E. Address : Hayes Cottage, Hayes Road, Bromley, Kent. (O10083)

BURLEIGH, John Laurence, M.B.E.

BURLEY, Alison, M.B.E.

BURLING, George Alfred, M.B.E.

BURLS, Herbert Thomas, M.B.E., F.G.S., M. Inst. Ing. Civiles de France, b. 1860 ; s. of Edward William. Educ. : Continent ; Royal School of Mines. Consulting Engineer to several Petroleum Companies. War Work : Geologist Petroleum Production Department Ministry of Munitions. Address : 24, Gloucester Street, Warwick Square. Club : St. Stephen's. (M7559)

BURLTON, Capt. Launcelot Henry Beaumont, O.B.E., M.C., R.A.S.C.

BURMAN, Thomas, M.B.E.

BURMESTER, Major Zante Gower, O.B.E., 31st Lancers I.A. (O11730)

BURN, Major Alexander Henderson, O.B.E., I.A.

BURN, Col. Charles Rosdew, O.B.E.

BURN, Capt. Eric Francis, O.B.E.

BURN, Ethel Louise, Hon. Mrs. Rosdew, O.B.E., Lady of Grace St. John of Jerusalem ; d. of The Lord Leith of Fyvie (see BURKE'S Peerage) ; m. Col. Charles Rosdew, A.D.C. to the King, O.B.E., M.P., s. of Gen. Robert Burn, R.A., of Jessfield. War Work : Went to France, Sept. 1914 with Red Cross Units for special work ; gave up own house, Stoodley Knowle, Torquay, as a First Line Hospital for Officers ; Matron and Commandant Hospital Oct. 1914, to July, 1918 ; went to France as Commandant of Church Army Huts for the 4th Army Infantry School. Addresses : 10, Hill Street, Berkeley Square, W. 1 ; Lea Farm, Surrey. Club : Ladies' Empire. (O196)

BURN, Sir Joseph, K.B.E., F.I.A., F.S.I., Vice-President Institute of Actuaries, b. 6 March, 1871 ; s. of James Burn,

m. Emily Harriet, d. of Richard Smith. Actuary of Prudential Association Co. ; Director of British Italian Corporation ; Member of Central War Saving Committee. War Work : War Savings Movement from time of Montagu Committee ; Statistical work in connection with German casualties ; Member of Royal Commission on Decimal Coinage. Address : Rydal Mount, Potters Bar, Middlesex. (K355)

BURN, Muriel Lyell, O.B.E., b. 12 Nov. 1892 ; d. of Robert George Laing Burn, of Edinburgh. War Work : Assistant Historian to the Official Historian of the Quartermaster-General's Department, and Services with the British Armies in France and Flanders. Address : 48, Waterlow Road, Highgate, N. 19. (M7560)

BURN, Capt. Reginald William, O.B.E R.A.S.C.

BURN, Major Robert Nathaniel, O.B.E., B.E.

BURN, Lieut.-Col. William George, O.B.E., V.D., B.Sc., late R.E., b. 1879 ; s. of William Burn, of Glasgow ; m. Norah Gertrude, d. of W. H. Bell, of York. Educ. : Hutcheson's School and Glasgow Univ. Engineer ; East Indian Railway. War Work : Capt. Indian Army Reserve and Adjutant East Indian Railway Volunteer Rifles, June, 1915, to Aug. 1916 ; Mesopotamia, Aug. 1916, to April, 1920 ; Lieut.-Col. R.E. Assistant Director Inland Water Transport ; twice mentioned in despatches. Addresses : 9, Spring Gardens, Kelvinside, Glasgow ; East Indian Railway, Clive Street, Calcutta. (O6589)

BURNAND, Lieut.-Col. Montague Berthon, O.B.E.

BURNAND, Major Richard Frank, O.B.E.

BURNE, Major Lindsay Elliott Lumley, C.B.E., I.A.
(C245b)

BURNE, Louisa Joan, Mrs., M.B.E., d. of the late Rev. J. B. Burne, of Wasing Rectory, Berks ; m. Richard, s. of the late Richard Higgins, of Leybourne Wood, Kent. Educ. : Privately. War Work : Commandant, Dressing Station, Olympia, Aug, 1914, to Dec. 1914 ; Commandant, V.A.D. Hostels, 3rd London Gen. Hosp., Wandsworth, Aug. 1915, to Aug. 1916 ; Commandant, Kensington Hostel, Sept. 1916 ; Commandant, Central V.A.D. Hostel, May, 1917 to June, 1919. Address : 21, Stanley Crescent, W. 11. Clubs : Lyceum ; V.A.D. Ladies'. (M1499)

BURNE, Lieut.-Col. Newdigate Addington Knightley, O.B.E.

BURNE, Lieut.-Col. (Hon. Brig.-Gen.) Rainald Owen, C.B.E., b. 3 Jan.1871 ; s. of Newdigate Burne, Barrister-at-Law, Albury, Surrey, and Hon. Mrs. Burne, d. of 2nd Viscount Sidmouth ; m. Sybil Mary, d. of David H. Owen, late Senior Registrar, H.M. Court of Probate, Somerset House. Educ. : Bedford Grammar School and abroad. Assistant-Director of Supplies and Transport, Headquarters, Northern Command. War Work : D.A.Q.M.G., 3rd Cavalry Division, France and Belgium ; A.A. and Q.M.G., 23rd Division, France and Belgium ; Commandant (Temp. Brig.-Gen.), Mechanical Transport Recepton and Training Area ; R.A.S.C., Lee, Kent. Club : United Service. (C1492)

BURNET, Sarah Elizabeth, O.B.E., b. 4 Jan. 1886 ; e. d. of John E. H. Burnet, of Bradford. Entered the Labour Exchange Department of the Board of Trade in 1910 ; Assistant Divisional Officer for the London Division ; and Secretary of the London Advisory Committee on Juvenile Employment from 1912 to 1915. Since 1915, in Employment Dept., Ministry of Labour, concerned with the arrangements for recruiting women for the Women's War Services and with the activities of the Women's Section of the Employment Dept. generally. Addresses : Queen Anne's Chambers, Westminster ; 5, St. Andrew's Road, Golders Green, N.W. 4.
(O1164)

BURNET, William Hodgson, M.B.E., L.R.I.B.A., b. 11 March, 1873 ; s. of the late John Burnet, Advocate, of Edinburgh ; m. Janet Agnes, d. of Alexander Taylor Machattie, of London, Ont. Educ. : St. Paul's School, and St. Andrew's and Oxford Univs. Civil Servant. Assistant Architect in His Majesty's Office of Works. War Work : Acted as Architect in charge of the London Anti-Aircraft Defences ; sergeant in the F Division, Special Constabulary (Long Service Medal). Address : 2, Salisbury Tower, Windsor Castle. Club : Savage.
(M1500)

BURNETT, Alexander, M.B.E., b. 13 April, 1883 ; s. of Alexander Burnett, of Stenhousemuir, Stirlingshire ; m. Ethel Maud Norman, d. of Alfred Pearson, of Newcastle. Educ. : Larbert and also Glasgow Training College. School Teacher of Handwork. War Work : Invented Trench Periscope, which was tested and accepted by War Office, Woolwich Arsenal, etc. ; taught pupils to make same ; made and sent over 6000 to troops on all Fronts free of cost—all material collected ; also designed artificial limbs and supplied same to hospitals ; sent several other inventions to War Office and Admiralty for development, Services were given without reward from the beginning to the end of War. (M7561)

BURNETT, Major Alexander Edwin, O.B.E.

BURNETT, Dame Annie Maud, D.B.E., J.P. ; d. of Jacob Burnett, J.P., of Tynemouth. Educ. : Tynemouth, and Vevey, Switzerland. Town Councillor of Tynemouth. Address : 10, Priors Terrace, Tynemouth. (D10)

BURNETT, Lieut.-Col. Charles Stuart, C.B.E., D.S.O., b. 1882 ; s. of John Alexander Burnett (see BURKE'S Peerage, Sempill, B.) ; m. 1914, Sybil Bell. T. Lieut.-Col. R.A.F. ; S. Africa, 1900–1, with Derbyshire Imperial Yeo. (medal with three clasps) ; N. Nigeria, 1904–5 (despatches, medal with three clasps) ; Great War, 1914–18 (despatches, 3rd class Order of the Nile). (C1889)

BURNETT, Sir (Edward) Napier, K.B.E., J.P., M.D. (Glas.), F.R.C.S., F.R.C.P. (Edin.). Knight of Grace of the Order of St. John of Jerusalem. b. 12 July, 1872 ; y. s. of James Burnett, of Fraserburgh ; m. 1903. Educ.: Glasgow Univ. ; Edinburgh ; Dublin. Consulting Surgeon. Chairman Economical Committee, Army Medical Dept., War Office ; Assistant-Surgeon, Hospital for Women, Newcastle. Address : 4, Windsor Crescent, Newcastle. Clubs : British Empire ; Liberal, Newcastle. (K204).

BURNETT, Ernest Joseph, M.B.E., M.B., C.M., M.R.C.P. (Edin.), b. 21 Feb. 1865 ; s. of Wm. Bridgeford Tather Burnett, Cambuslang, Scotland ; m. Emily Maud Margaret d. of John Brownless, of Whorlton Grange, Barnard Castle. Educ.: Private School, East Wemyss, Scotland. Consultant, Saltburn Brine Baths ; Medical Officer, Post Office, N.E. Ry., Saltburn, War Pensions Hostel, Saltburn, and Northern Convalescent Home, Saltburn ; Ex-President, North of England Branch, B.M.A. War Work : Commandant and Medical Officer, Saltburn Auxiliary Hospital, and part-time Saltburn Auxiliary Hospital ; Member of original Committee, N. Riding B. Red Cross Society. Received Board of Trade Long Service Medal as Captain of the Local Life Saving Rocket Brigade. Address : The Red House, Saltburn, Yorkshire. (M7562)

BURNETT, Ethel, O.B.E d. of Sir T. Burnett, Bart., of Leys, of Crathes Castle, Crathes, Kincardineshire, N.B. (see BURKE'S Peerage). Educ.: Privately. President, Kincardineshire Branch, British Red Cross Society. War Work : Acting-President of Kincardineshire Branch, B.R.C.S. from 1915 to 1918 ; afterwards President ; engaged in hospital work. Address : Crathes Castle, Crathes, N.B. Club : Ladies' Army and Navy. (O197)

BURNETT, Ethel Mary, C.B.E., d. of — Burnett. Rendered services during Great War to New Zealand War Contingent Assoc. in London. (C1991)

BURNETT, James, O.B.E.

BURNETT, James Taylor, M.B.E.

BURNETT, Lieut.-Col. John Chaplyn, D.S.O., O.B.E., b. 1863 ; s. of the late Charles Mountford Burnett, M.D. Entered R.A. 1884 ; became Capt. 1893 ; Major, 1902 ; retired 1909 ; now T. Lieut.-Col.; served in S. Africa, 1900-2 (despatches) ; Great War, 1914-18. (O6963)

BURNETT, Lieut.-Col. Leslie Trew, O.B.E.

BURNETT, Mary, M.B.E.

BURNETT, Dame Maud, O.B.E.

BURNETT, Lieut. Thomas Leslie Forbes, M.B.E., R.A.F.

BURNEY, Brig.-Gen. Herbert Henry, C.B., C.B.E., b. 1858 ; s. of the late Rev. Edward Burney, V. of Thornham, Maidstone ; m. 1858, Diana Geraldine, e. d. of Maj.-Gen. John Talbot Coke, of Trusley, Derbyshire. Entered 39th Regt. 1878 ; became Capt. Gordon Highlanders, 1886 ; Major, 1895 ; Brevet Lieut.-Col. 1898 ; Lieut.-Col. and Brevet Col. 1904 ; Col. 1908 ; retired as Hon. Brig.-Gen. 1913 ; served with Egyptian Expedition, 1882-84 ; present at battle of Tel-el-Kebir (medal with clasp, bronze star, 5th class Medjidieh) ; Soudan 1884 ; present at battles of Teb and Tamai (two clasps) ; with Chitral Relief Force, 1895 ; present at storming of Malakand Pass (wounded, medal with clasp), on N.W. Frontier of India, 1897-98 (despatches, two clasps, Brevet Lieut.-Col.) ; S. Africa ; 1899-1902, as A.A.G. (despatches) ; during Great War, 1914-18, on Staff ; was a Professor at Roy. Mil. Coll., Canada, 1899-1900 ; A.A.G., E. Command, 1908-10 ; Brig.-Gen. Comdg. 9th Inf. Brig. 1910-13. (C149)

BURNEY, Capt. Sydney Bernard, C.B.E. Is Assist. Director-Gen. of Voluntary Organisations. (C123)

BURNHAM, John Charles, C.S.I., C.B.E., B.Sc., F.I.C., b. 9 Dec. 1866 ; s. of Charles Burnham, of Camberwell, London ; m. Lilian, d. of Charles Sinclair Cox, of Southend, Bromley, Kent. Educ. Victoria University, Manchester. War Department Chemist, Chemical Dept., Woolwich, 1888-94 ; served on Special Committee on Explosives, 1888-91 ; Chemist-in-Charge, Experimental Cordite Factory, Kirkee, India, 1894-99 ; Manager, Government of India Cordite Factory, Aruvankadu, India, 1899-1915. War Work : Specially recalled from India on loan from the Government of India in Oct. 1915, to take charge of H.M. Factory, Gretna, which was then about to be erected for the manufacture of propellent explosive (Cordite) on an enormously larger scale than had ever before been attempted ; Director of Board of Management, and Superintendent of H.M. Factory, Gretna, 1915-20. Address : Sarkbank, Gretna, Dumfriesshire. (C2490)

BURNIE, William Beckit, O.B.E., D.Sc., b. 1875. Address : 87, Stanford Avenue, Brighton. (O1166)

BURNS, Donald George, M.B.E.

BURNS, Lieut. Edward James, M.B.E., R.A.

BURNS, Hon. Emily Dunbar, O.B.E.; d. of 3rd Baron Inverclyde, of Castle Wemyss (see BURKE'S Peerage). Educ.: At home and in Brussels. War Work : Nursing Member of V.A.D., Dumbarton 28 ; Nursed in Woodlands Auxiliary Hospital from Jan. 1915, and in Gartshore Auxiliary Hospital, also worked at Headquarters B.R.C.S. Joint Women's V.A.D. Dept., Devonshire House, London ; Secretary of the Rosneath Peninsula War Work Parties under the D.G.V.O. ; Secretary of Woodlands Auxiliary Hospital, Kilcreggan. Addresses : Castle Wemyss, Wemyss Bay ; 10, Berkeley Square, London. Clubs : Kelvin (Glasgow) ; Ladies' V.A.D. (O3643)

BURNS, Helen Jaqueline, Mrs., M.B.E.. b. 26 Oct. 1875 d. of Capt. John Hope, R.N., of St. Mary's Isle, Kirkcudbright ;

m. Alan, s. of John William Burns, of Kilmahew, Cardross War Work : Young Women's Christian Association Red Cross Society (Commandant, 24th Dumbartonshire V.A.D.) ; S. & S.F.A. Local War Pensions Committee. Address : Cumbernauld House, Cumbernauld. Club : Kelvin, Glasgow. (M197)

BURNS, Surg.-Lieut.-Comm. Henry, O.B.E., R.N., M.B.

BURNS, Norah Dalrymple, M.B.E.

BURNS, Lieut. Patrick John, M.B.E.

BURNSIDE, Ethel Margaret, O.B.E., b. 19 Dec. 1877 ; d. of the late Rev. Canon Burnside, of Hertingfordbury, near Hertford. Educ.: At home. Inspector under the Ministry of Health, Maternity and Child Welfare Branch ; formerly Inspector of Midwives Herts County Council, 1906-19 ; County Superintendent and Secretary, Herts County Nursing Association, 1909-19. War Work : Hon. Sec. and Assistant County Director, Hertfordshire Branch, British Red Cross Society, from Aug. 1914, to Dec. 1919. Address : 74, Barons Court Road, W. 14. (O198)

BURNSIDE, Robert Henery, M.B.E.

BURNYEAT, John, M.B.E.

BURRAGE, Cyril Charles Webb, O.B.E.

BURRAGE, Lieut. David Alexander, M.B.E.

BURRAGE, Lieut. Henry James, M.B.E., R.M.

BURRELL, Lieut.-Col. Charles William Wilberforce, O.B.E.

BURRELL, Frederic William White, O.B.E.

BURRELL, Lieut.-Col. Sir Merrik Raymond, Bart., C.B.E., J.P., b. 14 May, 1877 ; s. of the late Sir Charles Raymond Burrell, Bart. (see BURKE'S Peerage) ; m. Coralie Archdale Mervyn, d. of John Porter-Porter, of Belle Isle, Co. Fermanagh. Educ.: Eton. High Sheriff for Sussex, 1919. War Work : Inspector of Remounts. Address : Knepp Castle, Horsham, Sussex. Clubs : Cavalry ; Boodle's. (C1494)

BURRIDGE, Major Arthur, O.B.E., b. 1 Jan. 1872 ; s. of Alfred Burridge, late of Herne Hill, London ; m. Daisy, d. of David Banks, of Bloemfontein, Orange River Colony, South Africa. Educ.: Grays College, Essex. War Work : Sub-Div. Inspector Special Constabulary (Metropolitan), 1914-15 ; 1915-20, O.C. Group 1 Co. of Lond. R.A.S.C., M.T. (V.) ; Evacuation of London Military Hospitals, attached to Metropolitan Police throughout Air Raid period ; Transport Officer, Ministry of Food. The whole of the above work was voluntary. Addresses : 6, Copley Park, Streatham Common, S.W. 16 ; 9, Brackley Street, Golden Lane, E.C. 1. (O10086)

BURRIDGE, John Harold, M.B.E., M.R.C.S. (Eng.), L.R.C.P. (London), b. 13 Oct. 1876 ; s. of Alfred Burridge, of London ; m. Maud Frances, d. of Nathaniel Campbell, of Belfast. Educ.: King's Coll. School, King's Coll., and King's Coll. Hospital, London. Hon. Medical Officer, Paddington Green Hospital and Children's Convalescent Home, Slough ; Asst. School Medical Officer for S. Bucks. War Work : Organised and commanded Slough V.A.D. Hospital 1914-19 ; was Commandant and Medical Officer in sole charge (56 beds) ; The hospital was visited by T.M. The King and Queen, in July, 1915. Address : 18, MacKenzie Street, Slough, Bucks. (M1502)

BURROUGH, Hedley Gravett, M.B.E., b. 11 July, 1876 ; s. of Thomas and Maria Burrough, of Broad Chalk, near Salisbury m. Caroline Rosina, d. of Bruce Hersee Potter, of Eastbourne. Educ.: Cleveland House School, Salisbury. Organising Secretary of Y.M.C.A. War Work : In charge of Y.M.C.A. Centres in Kent, Surrey, and Sussex. Address : 26, Duchess Road. Clifton, Bristol. (M198)

BURROW, Leopold Arthur, M.B.E.

BURROWES, Henry Ambrose, M.B.E., M.D., (Lond.), J.P., b. 21 Aug. 1864 ; s. of Rev. Henry Burrowes, of St. Mary's, Waterloo, near Liverpool ; m. Norah Eleanor, d. of Dr. W. P. Brabazon. Educ.: Merchant Taylors' School, St. Crosby, and Liverpool Univ. War Work : Officer in charge and Medical Officer, V.A.D. Hospital, Lymm, Cheshire. Address : Lemain, W. Looe, Cornwall. (M7576)

BURROWES, Major Louis Arundell, O.B.E., R.A.F.

BURROWES, Thomas Fraser, C.B.E. ; m. Lena, d. of Hugh Sproston. Controller of Customs, and Receiver of Enemy Estates, Nigeria. (E388)

BURROWS, Adam Clarke, O.B.E., L.R.C.P., L.R.C.S., F.R.C.S., R.A.M.C., (T.F.)

BURROWS, T. Warrant Officer Alexander, M.B.E., Royal Indian Marine.

BURROWS, Capt. Amos, M.B.E., R.F.A., b. 15th March, 1878 ; s. of the late Amos Burrows ; m. Caroline, d. of John Fox, of Walsall. Educ.: All Saints', West Bromwich. War Work : France from Aug. 1914 till Nov. 1917 ; Italy, Nov. 1917 till Feb. 1919. Address : Bridge Inn, Park Brook, Walsall. (M4725)

BURROWS, Anna Louisa, M.B.E. (Médaille de la Reine Elizabeth), b. 4 Aug. 1861 ; d. of John Edward Bovill, of Sondes Place, near Dorking ; m. Leonard Hedley, Bishop of Sheffield (see BURKE'S Peerage), s. of Leonard Francis Burrows of Rugby School. Educ.: At home and in France. Member of Sheffield Education Committee. War Work : Chairman, Sheffield Prisoners of War Help Committee ; Chairman of Committee of Norfolk Base (Receiving House for Belgian Refugees) ; President of Y.M.C.A. Munition Workers Canteen ; Visitor in all Military Hospitals in S. Yorkshire (Sheffield Dioceses). Address : Bishopsholme, near Sheffield. Club : Church Imperial Ladies'. (M7568)

BURROWS, Col. Edmund Augustine, C.M.G., C.B.E.,

J.P., *b.* 19 March, 1855 ; *s.* of Rev. Canon Burrows, of Rochester Cathedral ; *m.* Mary Claudine, *d.* of the late William Coode, Trevarna, St. Austell, Cornwall. *Educ.:* Wellington College. Lieut.-Col. R.H. and R.F. Artillery. *War Work :* In command of the Training Brigade of Royal Field Artillery, at Newcastle-on-Tyne, 1914–18. *Address :* Manor House, Long Crendon, Thame, Oxon. (C1495)

BURROWS, Col. Harold, C.B.E., A.M.S. (T.F.R.), F.R.C.S., *b.* 1875 ; *s.* of the late Surg.-Major E. P. Burrows ; *m.* Lucy Mary Elizabeth, *d.* of the late H. Wheeler. *Educ.:* Marlborough and St. Bartholomew's Hospital Consulting Surgeon. *War Work :* Consulting Surgeon, First Army, and Army of the Rhine. *Address :* 1, The Cams, Grove Road, Southsea. *Club :* Royal Albert Yacht. (C1231)

BURROWS, Capt. James Douglas, M.B.E., *b.* 9 March, 1885 ; *s.* of the late Frederick James, of the East Surrey Regt., Kingston ; *m.* Edith, *d.* of William Murray, late Garrison Staff of the Army. *Educ.:* Duke of York's Royal Military School. Attached to the War Office Staff, Jan. 1916 ; appointed Staff Captain at W.O., Aug. 1918 ; retired on account of wound received in action and appointed Captain of Invalids at the Royal Hospital, Chelsea, Feb. 1919. *War Work :* Commissioned Royal West Kent Regiment as a 2nd Lieut., Sept. 1914 ; proceeded to France in Nov. 1914 (very severely wounded) ; joined War Office Staff ; promoted Captain in the Essex Regt. and eventually appointed Staff Captain in the Adjutant-General's Department. *Addresses :* 10, Kendall Road, Beckenham, Kent ; Royal Hospital, Chelsea. *Club :* Junior Army and Navy. (M5127)

BURROWS, John Thomas Ladbrooke, M.B.E., R.N.

BURROWS, Kate Ellen, M.B.E., V.A.D.

BURROWS, Thomas Enos, M.B.E.

BURRUP, John Arthur Evans, O.B.E., I.S.O.

BURSTALL, Capt. Edgar Bryan, O.B.E., *b.* 28 May, 1881 ; *s.* of Edgar Burstall, of Barnes, Surrey ; *m.* Marguerite, *d.* of M. Louis Delzons, Chevalier de la Légion d'Honneur, Barrister-at-Law. Directeur politique du "Journal des Debats" of Paris. *Educ.:* Marlborough. *War Work :* R.A.S.C., M.T., Mar., 1915, to July, 1919. (O5062)

BURSTALL, Henry Robert John, M.B.E., M.Inst.C.E., *b.* 12 Jan. 1863 ; *s.* of Henry Abraham Burstall, of London ; *m.* Alice Maud, *d.* of J. W. McLellan, J.P., of Rochester. *Educ.:* Private Schools and Univ. Coll., London. Consulting Engineer to a number of companies. *War Work :* War Office, March, 1915 ; Govt. Superintending Engineer, M. of M., S.E. London, June, 1915 ; Chief Engineer, Contracts Section, Dept. of Explosives Supply, M. of M., from July, 1915, and also Section Director till Aug. 1919 ; under D.G.F. till Jan. 1920. *Addresses :* 14, Old Queen Street, S.W. ; 50, Finchley Road, Westcliff-on-Sea. (M3552)

BURSTON, Lieut.-Col. Samuel Roy, C.B.E., D.S.O., *b.* 1888 ; *s.* of Brig.-Gen. James Burston, V.D. (Gen. Officer Comdg. an Inf. Brig. in Gallipoli), of Melbourne, Australia ; *m.* 1913, Helen Elizabeth, *d.* of the late William Culross, Barrister, of Adelaide. *Educ.:* Melbourne Gram. Sch. and Univ. (M.B., B.S. Melbourne 1910). Lieut.-Col. Australian Army Med. Corps, Assist. Physician to Adelaide Hospital, and Hon. Anæsthetist to Adelaide Children's Hospital ; served during Great War, 1915–18, in Gallipoli, Egypt, and France (despatches). *Address :* Adelaide, S. Australia. *Clubs :* Adelaide ; Naval and Military (Adelaide). (C2193)

BURT, Alexander, junior, M.B.E.

BURT, Comm. Arthur Stanley, O.B.E., R.N.

BURT, Bryce Chudleigh, M.B.E., B.Sc., *b.* 29 April, 1881 ; *s.* of the late Isaac Burt, of Churcham, Gloucester ; *m.* Beatrice Maud, *d.* of the late A. Seary, of Bristol. *Educ.:* Merchant Venturers, Bristol, and Univ. Coll., London. Deputy Director Agriculture, United Provinces, India (Indian Agricultural Service). *War Work :* In India (Wheat and fodder supplies). *Address :* Cawnpore, U.P., India. *Clubs :* Cawnpore ; Naini Tal ; University of London. (M4121)

BURT, Frank Playfair, M.B.E.

BURT, Sir Henry Parsall, K.C.I.E., C.B.E., Knight of Grace of the Order of St. John of Jerusalem, V.D., A.M.I.C.E. *b.* 15 April, 1857 ; *s.* of Henry Potter Burt, of Littlecot, Streatham Common ; *m.* Blanche, *d.* of John Curtis Harrop, of Liverpool. *Educ.:* Clifton College and Royal Engineering College, Cooper's Hill. Manager of North-Western Railway of India, 1907 ; Member of Legislative Council of Punjab, 1908 ; Member of Legislative Council of Gov.-Gen. of India, 1914 ; Director of Indian Railway Companies, India Office, 1915 ; Chairman of several Indian Railway Companies since 1919. *War Work :* Representative throughout the War of the Secretary of State for India, on the Priority Committee of the Ministry of Munitions, and was largely responsible for the control and supply from this country and America of India's requirements, especially in the matter of railway plant and material. *Addresses :* Woodfield, Lytton Grove, Putney Hill, S.W. 15 ; 237, Gresham House, Old Broad Street, E.C. *Clubs :* East India United Service ; Bengal, Calcutta ; Royal Victoria Yacht : Ryde, I. of W. (C450)

BURT, James, M.B.E.

BURT, Jean, M.B.E.

BURT, John, M.B.E., J.P.

BURT, Capt. John Wotherspoon, O.B.E., R.A.F.

BURT, Lieut. Reginald Edward, M.B.E.

BURT, Capt. Reginald Stevens, O.B.E.

BURT, Capt. Walter Leslie, M.B.E., R.A.F.

BURTA, Capt. William, O.B.E. (O199)

BURTENSHAW, Major Arthur, O.B.E., M.C., R.A.S.C., *b.* 25 Aug. 1881 ; *s.* of Major J. Burtenshaw, R.M.L.I. (ret.) ; *m.* Grace, *d.* of C. Brooker, of Strood. *Educ.:* Portsmouth Grammar School ; Mathematical School, Rochester. *War Work :* Joined R.A.S.C. Nov. 1914, proceeding to France same day ; Requisitioning and Supply Officer, 19th Inf. Bde., Jan. to Aug. 1915 ; attached D.D.S.T., 1st Army, Sept. 1915 to March, 1916 ; Senior Supply Officer, 16th (Irish) Division, April, 1916, to April, 1917 ; Senior Supply Officer, 51st (Highland) Division, April, 1917 to Nov. 1917 ; Senior Supply Officer, 58th Div. (London), Nov. 1917 to March, 1919 ; 2nd in charge No. 6 Base Supply Depot, Calais, March to Dec. 1919 ; O.C. same Jan. to July, 1920 ; received Military Cross, May. 1916 ; promoted Capt., March 1915 ; Major, Oct. 1916 ; mentioned in despatches, June, 1917 and Dec. 1918. (O2454)

BURTON, David Fowler, M.B.E., J.P., Co. Alderman, *b.* 7 Oct. 1857 ; *s.* of David Burton, of Cherry Burton. *Educ.:* Rugby School. Barrister-at-law, Middle Temple. *War Work :* 5 years and 4 months, Assistant Paymaster in West Riding (Yorks.) Territorial Association (Separation Department). *Address :* Cherry Burton Hall, Beverley, East Yorks. *Club :* Yorkshire (York). (M7571)

BURTON, Donald, M.B.E., M.Sc., A.I.C., *b.* 29 July, 1892 ; *s.* of Arthur Angell Burton, of Morley, Yorks. *Educ.:* Bradford Grammar School and Univ. of Leeds. Leather Chemist, Co-operative Wholesale Society's Research Department, Manchester. *War Work :* Assistant to Deputy Inspector of High Explosives, University of Leeds ; received a letter from the Minister of Munitions expressing appreciation of the course of action taken at the Explosion at the Low Moor Munitions Company in Aug. 1916, which secured the safety of the magazine and resulted in the preservation of the stock of explosives at the adjacent Picric Acid Factory of Messrs. Breaks & Son, which might otherwise have been lost to the country ; seriously injured at the explosion at Copley in Dec., 1917, while endeavouring to turn on the drenchers after fire had broken out. *Address :* Holmesfield, Morley, Yorks. (M7572)

BURTON, Major Edmund Gerald, O.B.E., R.A.S.C.

BURTON, Frances Westbrook, M.B.E., *d.* of Col. Gerard S. Burton, of The Norfolk Regt. *War Work :* Hon. Sec., Norfolk Regt. Prisoners of War Help Organisation, also Hon. Sec. for 2 years of Norfolk Women's Agricultural Committee and Hon. Sec. for East Norfolk Soldiers' and Sailors' Families Association. *Address :* 129, Newmarket Road, Norwich. (M2553)

BURTON, Rev. Canon Harry Darwin, O.B.E.

BURTON, Rev. Harold John Chandos, M.B.E., M.A., *b.* 12 May, 1878 ; *s.* of Prebendary J. R. Burton, of Bilterely, Ludlow : *m.* Constance Mary, *d.* of Rev. D. Vawdrey, of Arcley Kings. *Educ.:* Trinity Coll., Glenalmond, and Magdalene Coll., Cambridge. Vicar of Stoke S. Milburgh with the Heath, Salop. *War Work :* T.C.F., May, 1917, to April, 1919 ; attached 28th Manchesters, May. to Nov. 1917 ; Brigade Chaplain, 222nd mixed brigade, Nov. 1917, to Jan. 1919 ; attached 25th R.D.B. Jan. 1919, to April, 1919. *Address :* The Vicarage, Stoke S. Milburgh, Ludlow, Salop. (M5129)

BURTON, Henrietta, O.B.E.

BURTON, Lieut.-Col. Henry Walter, O.B.E., R.N.

BURTON, Major Herbert Edgar, O.B.E., R.E.

BURTON, Kenneth, M.B.E.

BURTON, Major Percy Collingwood, M.B.E.

BURTON, Major R.B.S., O.B.E.

BURTON, Major Sydney Collard, O.B.E.

BURTON, Walter William John, M.B.E., Palmes en argent Ordre de la Couronne (Belgium), *b.* 1 Aug. 1880 ; *s.* of John Burton, of Westminster ; *m.* Florence Amelia, *d.* of Frank Moth, of London. *Educ.:* City of Westminster School. Clerk to Chief Inspector, Aliens Branch, Home Office. *War Work :* Regulations governing landing and embarkation of passengers in United Kingdom ; Clerk in charge of clerical staff, Aliens Branch, Home Office. *Address :* 61, Wyndham Road, Kingston-on-Thames. (M7575)

BURTON, Capt. William Arthur, O.B.E.

BURTON, William John, O.B.E.

BURTON, William Parker, O.B.E., J.P., M.F.H., *b.* 29 Oct. 1864 ; *s.* of Henry May Burton, of Ipswich ; *m.* Emily, *d.* of William Chandler, of Ipswich. *Educ.:* Ipswich School. Joint Master of Essex and Suffolk Foxhounds ; Joint Vice-President of Yacht Racing Association ; sailed Shamrock IV. for Sir Thomas Lipton in the America Cup Race ; J.P. for Ipswich Borough. *War Work :* In the spring of 1915 became Honorary Director Pit-prop section, Board of Trade ; transferred services, in winter of 1916, to the Ministry of Food at its inception—now one of the very few original members still serving ; Chairman of the Flour Mills Control Committee, responsible for the manufacture and distribution of flour in the United Kingdom ; Member of the Royal Commission on Wheat Supplies. *Address :* The Cottage, Burstall, Ipswich. *Club :* Royal Thames Yacht. (O200)

BURTT, William Edmund, M.B.E. (M10245)

BURY, Ernest, O.B.E.

BURY, Francis George, C.B.E. Hon. Treasurer, King George and Queen Mary's Club for Oversea Forces. *Address :* 8, Cheniston Gardens, W. 8. (C387)

BURY. Lieut. George Wyman, M.B.E., R.N.V.R.

BURY, John Edwin, M.B.E.

BURY, Lindsay Edward, C.B.E., *b.* 11 June, 1882 ; *s.* of Francis George Bury, C.B.E., of 8, Cheniston Gardens,

Kensington ; *m.* Frances, *d.* of Capt. H. J. Beckwith, of Milli-chope Park, Craven Arms. *Educ.:* Eton and Trinity, Cambridge. Irrigation Department, Public Works Ministry, Egypt. *War Work :* Major, R.E., Suez Canal Defences, 1915–16 ; Colonel, Deputy Director, I.W.T., R.E., Egypt, 1917–18. *Address :* Public Works, Ministry, Egypt. *Clubs :* Turf and Sporting, Cairo ; New University.   (C1372)

BURY, Capt. Raymond, M.B.E.,

BUSBY, Thomas Dalrymple, O.B.E.   (O11958)

BUSBY, Thomas Frederick, M.B.E.

BUSH, Flying Officer Albert Edward, M.B.E., R.A.F., *b.* 8 Oct. 1882 ; *s.* of William Gardner Bush, of Coventry ; *m.* Helen Elizabeth, *d.* of John Ingram, of Coventry. *Educ.:* St. Peter's School and Technical Institute, Coventry. Engineer, Daimler Co., Ltd., Coventry. *War Work :* Design of Transport Vehicles, Aeronautical Engines and Aeroplanes ; Deputy Chief Engineer, Daimler Co., Ltd. ; served on various committees of British Engineering Standards Association for Aircraft Materials ; appointed Engineer in charge of BK2 Engine. *Address :* 4, Avondale Road, Coventry.   (M7575)

BUSH, Helen Ethel, Mrs., M.B.E., *b.* 31 Jan. 1877 ; *d.* of John V. S. Pope, late D.P.I., Burma ; *m.* Col. Harry S. Bush, C.B., C.M.G. ; *s.* of J. Bush, of Hanworth House, Middlesex. *Educ.:* Princess Helena Coll., Ealing, and Brussels. *War Work :* Lady Smith-Dorrien's Hospital Bag Fund and Soldiers' and Sailors' Families Assoc. *Address :* Red Barracks, Woolwich. *Club :* Kenmar.   (M3554)

BUSH, Bt. Col. James Paul, C.M.G., C.B.E., T.D. Ch.M., D.L., *b.* 30 June, 1857 ; *s.* of Lieut.-Col. Robert Bush, of Clifton, Bristol ; *m.* Laura Annie, *d.* of the late John Robertson, of Colac, Victoria, Australia. *Educ.:* Clifton College ; Bristol Medical School ; University College Hospital, London. Consulting Surgeon, Bristol Royal Infirmary, Almondsbury Memorial Hospital and Pontypool Hospital ; Chief Surgeon Bristol Police Force ; Lecturer on Operative Surgery, University of Bristol ; Ex-President, Bath and Bristol Br.B.M.A., and Ex-President Bristol Medico-Chirurgical Society ; Member of Council, Epsom College ; Member of Council, International Surgical Society. *War Work :* Senior-Surgeon, Princess Christian Hospital, Natal Field Force ; P.M.O. H.M. Hospital Ship "Lismore Castle," Boer War, 1899–1900 (medal and clasps and mentioned in despatches) ; Officer Commanding 2nd Southern General Hospital, T.F. and 56 General Hospital, France ; A.D.M.S., No. 2 Area (Bristol), Southern Command (mentioned in despatches, medals and clasps). *Address :* Clifton Park, Bristol. *Clubs :* Constitutional ; Clifton.   (C1232)

BUSH, Capt. James Tobin, C.B.E., *b.* 1874 ; *s.* of James Charles Tobin Bush, of Bromley, Kent ; *m.* 1904, Antonia Harriet Lander, *d.* of John Richard Leonard Cridland, of Copenhagen and Exeter. Capt. R.N. ; in Controller's Depart. Admiralty 1910–12 ; Great War, 1914–19, with Ocean Escort (despatches).   (C1180)

BUSH, Margery, Mrs., O.B.E., *b.* 5 July, 1885 ; *d.* of Edward Scott, M.D., of Stoke Bishop, near Bristol ; *m.* Robert Edwin Bush, *s.* of Robert Bush, of Clifton, Bristol. *Educ.:* Godolphin School, Salisbury. *War Work :* With husband, turned residence into a hundred-bed hospital, Aug. 1914 ; equipped, administered, and paid all costs of running it. *Address :* Bishop's Knoll, Stoke Bishop, near Bristol. (O201)

BUSHE, Surg.-Comm. Charles Kendal, M.B.E., M.D., R.A., R.N.

BUSHBY, Maud Alice, M.B.E., *b.* 1874 ; *d.* of H. J. Bushby, of Wormley Bury, Herts. *War Work :* Secretarial and Staff work for the B.R.C.S. *Address :* 2, Egerton Gardens, S.W. *Clubs :* Forum ; V.A.D. Ladies'.   (M3555)

BUSHELL, Major Christopher Wyndowe, O.B.E., R.N.

BUSHELL, Lieut.-Col. Edward Harry, O.B.E.

BUSHELL, John James, M.B.E., *b.* 25 Jan. 1872 ; *s.* of James Bushell, of Athlone, Ireland ; *m.* Mary Rosalie Beatrice, *d.* of Robert T. D. Popham, of Bermuda. *Educ.:* Manchester (England) High School and private tutors. Member, Board of Trade, Bermuda (Dept. of Govt.) ; Member, Devonshire Parish Vestry, Bermuda ; Secretary, Bermuda Chamber of Commerce ; Managing Editor, "Bermuda Colonist and Daily News " ; author, "All about Bermuda," and other local handbooks and booklets ; correspondent, "Sun " and "New York Herald," etc ; Member, Empire Air League. *Address :* "Palm Vale," Devonshire, Bermuda.   (M6421)

BUSHELL, Sybil Dorothy, M.B.E., *d.* of the late Rev. William Done Bushell, of Harrow School. *Educ.:* Wycombe Abbey. *War Work :* 1915–16 nursed under the Croix Rouge in France, Hôpital Auxiliare, 222 ; 1917–19, worked as Higher Grade Clerk in Commission Internationale de Ravitaillement. *Address :* The Hermitage, Harrow.   (M7576)

BUSHROD, Frank, O.B.E.

BUSS, Major H. A., O.B.E., D.S.C., R.A.F.

BUSSELL, Major Albert Cecil, O.B.E.

BUSSELL, Percy Dale, O.B.E.

BUSTARD, Major Frank, O.B.E., King's Own Royal Lancaster Regt., (T.F.) R., *b.* 20 Feb. 1886 ; *s.* of John Bustard, of Halewood, Liverpool ; *m.* Norah, *d.* of Thomas Hamilton, of Liverpool. *Educ.:* Liverpool Institute. Shipping. Principal of the Passenger Conference Depts. of the White Star, Dominion and American Lines. *War Work :* Military Landing Officer, Mudros ; Asst. Embarkation Staff Officer, Suez ; successively Embarkation Staff Officer, Beirut, Tripoli, Alexandretta, and Mersina : Opening these ports during General Allenby's advance through Palestine and Syria ; mentioned in despatches

4 times. *Address :* May Bank, 58, Victoria Road, Gt. Crosby, Liverpool.   (O2870)

BUSTARD, George, M.B.E.

BUSTEED, Lieut.-Col. Henry Richard, O.B.E., A.F.C., R.A.F.

BUTCHER, Lieut. Alfred William, M.B.E.

BUTCHER, Lieut. Charlie Robert, M.B.E., I.A.R.O.

BUTCHER, Doris Ruth, M.B.E., *b.* 22 Sept. 1896 ; *d.* of Henry Charles Butcher, of London. *Educ.:* Whitelands College School, and City of London College. Secretary. *War Work :* Worked at V.A.D. Headquarters, London, from 1915 to 1918 (staff quartermaster) ; member of London V.A. Detachment, 128. *Address :* 92, Baron's Court Road, W. *Club :* Portsmouth.   (M7577)

BUTCHER, George Henry, M.B.E., *b.* 7 Feb. 1875 ; *s.* of Joseph Butcher, of Berkeley. *Educ :* Cirencester. Managing Director, J. Fryer, Ltd., Hereford ; Managing Director, Newport (Mon.) Motor Co., Ltd. ; Director, Hereford Transport Co., Ltd. *War Work :* Agricultural tractors and transport tractor representative County of Hereford, Food Production Dept.   (M1504)

BUTCHER, Henry James, M.B.E.

BUTCHER, Marjorie Alma, M.B.E., *b.* 24 Dec. 1889 ; *d.* of Henry Charles Butcher, of London. *Educ.:* Onslow Hall School, S. Kensington ; S.W.P. Day College, Chelsea. Private Secretary. *War Work :* Member of V.A.D. London 128 ; worked at V.A.D. Headquarters, London, from 1915–17 ; worked at W.R.N.S. Headquarters, from 1917–19 (Assistant Principal W.R.N.S.). *Address :* 92, Baron's Court Road, W. 14. *Club :* Portsmouth.   (M3556)

BUTCHER, Samuel Foster, O.B.E.

BUTCHER, Sidney Herbert, M.B.E., Chevalier de l'Ordre de la Couronne de Belgique, *b.* 19 July, 1873 ; *s.* of Charles Richard Butcher, of Islington ; *m.* Ada Snell, *d.* of Henry Jackson, of Flamstead End, Cheshunt, Herts. *Educ.:* Cloudesley Grammar School and Burstead House Academy, Billericay, Essex. Master of United Institutions, 38, Parish Street, and 28, Tanner Street, Bermondsey, S.E. 1. *War Work :* The reception of the first War Refugees from Belgium and distribution of same ; The reception, cleansing and feeding of 20,500 Belgian Soldiers in 1915–16, and the establishment of the fourth Belgian Military Hospital and the Belgian Military Bureau, all Belgian troops entering the country passing through the institution. The hospital was visited by Princess Clementine, who invested over 2000 soldiers with medals won on the field of battle, Sir Francis Lloyd, representing the War Office, in attendance, and by H.R.H. Princess Christian and many other notables.   (M1508)

BUTCHER, Capt. Trevor Aveling, O.B.E., R.A.M.C.

BUTCHER, Paymaster-Lieut. Victor George, O.B.E., R.N.R.

BUTE, Augusta Mary Monica, Marchioness of, D.B.E., *d.* of Sir Henry Bellingham, Bart., Castle Bellingham, Co. Louth, and Lady Constance Bellingham, *d.* of the 2nd Earl of Gainsborough ; *m.* John, 4th Marquis of Bute. *War Work :* Donor, with Lord Bute, and Administratrix of Mount Stuart R.N. Hospital, of 110 beds ; entertained 40 Belgian refugees for 2 years ; worked in the 3rd Western General Hospital and Prince of Wales's Hospital for Limbless Sailors and Soldiers, Cardiff ; President, Bute Branch of the British Red Cross Society. *Addresses :* Mount Stuart, Rothesay ; Dumfries House, Ayrshire ; Cardiff Castle, Cardiff.   (D27)

BUTLER, Albert, O.B.E., *b.* 16 Jan. 1862 ; *s.* of George Butler, of Gillingham, Dorset ; *m.* Mary Emily, *d.* of Thomas Catling, late Editor of "Lloyd's" newspaper. *Educ.:* Grammar School, Gillingham, Dorset. Principal Clerk, Royal Ordnance Factories, Woolwich Arsenal. *War Work :* In charge of the manufacturing accounts of the Royal Ordnance Factories and responsible for the correct calculations of the earnings of the employees, some 80,000 men, women and boys. *Address :* Fiona, 23 Vanburgh Hill, Blackheath, S.E. 3.   (O1170)

BUTLER, Major Arnold Charles Paul, O.B.E., K.R.R.C.

BUTLER, Arthur Francis, O.B.E., *b.* 18 June, 1876 ; *s.* of the late Spencer Perceval Butler, of Lincoln's Inn ; *m.* Sibella Akers, *d.* of Edward Norman, of Chelsfield. *Educ.:* Haileybury College ; Pembroke College ; Cambridge. H.M. Inspector, Board of Education. *War Work :* Ministry of Munitions, Labour Supply Department. *Address :* Chelsfield House, Chelsfield. *Club :* United University.   (O203)

BUTLER, Major Charles Walter, O.B.E.

BUTLER, Daphne Kendall, M.B.E.,

BUTLER, Capt. Eustace Norman, M.B.E., R.A.M.C. (T.F.)

BUTLER, Lieut. Fernand Charles, M.B.E., R.A.F.

BUTLER, Sub-Lieut. Francis John, M.B.E., R.N.

BUTLER, Major Frank Norman, O.B.E., R.E.

BUTLER, Capt. Frederick William, O.B.E., R.A.S.C.

BUTLER, Sir (George) Geoffrey (Gilbert), K.B.E., M.A., *b.* 15 Aug. 1887 ; *s.* of Spencer Butler, of Lincoln's Inn ; *m.* Elizabeth Levering, *d.* of J. Levering Jones, of Philadelphia, U.S.A. *Educ.:* Clifton ; Trinity College, Cambridge. Fellow, Librarian and Lecturer in International Law and Diplomacy, Corpus Christi College, Cambridge ; Secretary, Cambridge University Board of Research Studies. *War Work :* Foreign Office ; Balfour Mission to U.S.A. ; Director British Bureau of Information, U.S.A. *Address :* Corpus Christi College, Cambridge. *Clubs :* Carlton ; United University ; Cambridge County.   (K205)

BUTLER, Capt. George Guy, M.B.E., R.A.M.C.

BUTLER, Harold, M.B.E.

BUTLER, Harold Branson, M.B.E., F.R.C.S. (Eng.), b. 13 Oct. 1875 ; s. of Thomas Mapleson Butler, of Guildford ; m. Hilda Bethune, d. of John Denham Smith, late of Hare-stock House, Winchester. *Educ.* : St. Paul's School ; St. Bartholomew's Hospital. Surgeon ; Surgeon to the Royal Surrey County Hospital. *War Work* : Surgeon to Military Annexe of Royal Surrey County Hospital, Clandon Park Military Hospital, and Guildford War Hospital. *Address* : Belmont House, Guildford. *Club* : Royal Societies'. (M7580)

BUTLER, Harold George, O.B.E., b. 21 April, 1877 ; s. of Alexander Butler, of West Wycombe, Bucks. ; m. Eva Beatrix, d. of Alfred Rutt, of 68, Cannon Street, E.C. *Educ.* : Royal Grammar School, High Wycombe. Superintending Inspector of Taxes, Somerset House. *War Work* : Chairman of Black List Committee, under Minister of Blockade ; Assistant Secretary, War Trade Department. *Address* : 16, Woodland Gardens, Muswell Hill, N. 10. (O1171)

BUTLER, Capt. Henry Basil Bacon, M.B.E., b. 1 Feb. 1892 ; s. of Prof. W. R. Butler, M.I.C.E., of King's College, Windsor, and Nova Scotia, Canada. *Educ.* : Shirley House School, Blackheath ; Cheltenham College ; Royal Military College, Kingston, Canada. *War Work* : Served in France and Flanders with various units between Aug. 1914 and Feb. 1919. *Address* : c/o Sir C. R. McGrigor, Bart., & Co., 39 Panton Street, Haymarket. (O2458)

BUTLER, Col. Henry Hugh, C.B.E., b. 1863 ; s. of Lieut.-Gen. — Butler. *Educ.* : Wellington Coll. Col. R.A. (ret.) ; Great War, 1914–19. (C1496)

BUTLER, Henry John, M.B.E., b. July, 1874 ; s. of John Butler, of Ealing. *Educ.* : Privately. Chief Supt. Wimbledon Fire Brigade. *War Work* : Fire protection of Munition Works, Camp, Hospitals ; special precautions during Air Raids. *Address* : 10, Queen's Road, Wimbledon, S.W. 19. *Club* : Kings' (Wimbledon). (M7581)

BUTLER, Herbert George, M.B.E.

BUTLER, Major James Bayley, M.B.E., R.A.M.C. b. 8 April, 1884 ; s. of Col. J. W. S. Butler of Madras Staff Corps ; m. Katherine Mary, d. of Theophilus McWeeney, of Dublin. *Educ.* : Clongowes Wood and Royal Univ. of Ireland. Professor of Botany, Univ. Coll., Dublin., National Univ. of Ireland. *War Work* : Attached H.Q. 48th Division, B.E.F., France ; Commandant Dublin Area Anti-gas School and later Commandant G.H.Q. Ireland Science Schools. *Address* : 81, Ranelagh Road, Dublin. (M5131)

BUTLER, Capt. James Dickson, M.B.E.

BUTLER, James Ramsay Montagu, M.V.O., O.B.E., b. 20 July, 1889 ; s. of the Rev. H. M. Butler, D.D., Master of Trinity College, Cambridge. *Educ.* : Harrow ; Trinity Coll., Cambridge. Fellow of Trinity Coll., Cambridge. *War Work* : Served Gallipoli, Egypt, War Office and France in Great War. *Address* : Trinity College, Cambridge. (O5065)

BUTLER, John Ingham, M.B.E.

BUTLER, John Lawrence, M.B.E., A.M.I.C., A.M.I.M.E.

BUTLER, Leonard Frederick George, M.B.E., b. 29 March, 1888 ; s. of Walter David Butler, of Paulton, Bristol ; m. Clara Elizabeth, d. of Ernest Jeffs, of Bristol. *Educ.* : Sexey's School, Bruton. Designer for Messrs. Brazil Straker, Engineers, Bristol. *War Work* : Experimental work on new designs for Aircraft Engines. *Address* : 22, Walsingham Road, St. Andrew's Park, Bristol. (M7584)

BUTLER, Lily Isabella, C.B.E..

BUTLER, Mildred Mary, Mrs., O.B.E. *War Work* : Donor and Commandant of Heywood Hospital, Cobham, Surrey. (O10089)

BUTLER, Montagu Sherard Dawes, C.B., C.I.E., C.V.O., C.B.E., b. 19 May, 1873 ; s. of late S. P. Butler, Barrister-at-law, of Lincoln's Inn ; m. Ann, d. of Dr. George Smith, C.I.E., Edinburgh. *Educ.* : Haileybury Coll., and Pembroke Coll. Cambridge. Indian Civil Service. *War Work* : Recruiting and other war work in the Attock district, Punjab, India. *Address* : c/o Messrs. H. S. King & Co., 9, Pall Mall, London. *Club* : Bath. (C2373)

BUTLER, Nina, M.B.E., d. of Sir Thomas Butler, K.C.V.O., Secretary to Lord Great Chamberlain Deputy Black Rod, House of Lords (*see* BURKE'S *Peerage*). *War Work* : British Red Cross Enquiry Department for Wounded and Missing, 1915–19. *Address* : Royal Court, Palace of Westminster, S.W. 1. (M3558)

BUTLER, Lieut. Richard Jefferson, M.B.E., K.O.Y.L.I.

BUTLER, Sir Richard Pierce, Bart., O.B.E., J.P., D.L., b. 28 Sept. 1872 ; s. of the late Sir Thomas Pierce Butler, Bart., of Ballin Temple, Co. Carlow, Ireland ; m. Alice Dudley, d. of The Very Rev. The Hon. J. W. Leigh, D.D. *Educ.* : Harrow. Served in S. African War with Mounted Infantry, Queen's Medal and 5 clasps. *War Work* : Served in the Great War as Recruiting Officer, Sept. 1914 to Feb. 1915, then Remount Dept. in France till Nov. 1917, then took first Remount Sqdn. to Italy ; in Sept. 1918 appointed D.D.R. (temp. Lieut.-Col.) to Desert Mounted Corps in Syria ; twice mentioned in despatches. *Addresses* : 63, Pont Street, S.W. 1 ; Ballin Temple, Tullow, Co. Carlow, Ireland. *Clubs* : Wellington and Kildare Street (Dublin). (O2970)

BUTLER, Rev. Richard Urban, O.B.E.

BUTLER, Samuel Flowers, O.B.E.

BUTLER, Sir Cyril KENDALL-, K.B.E., J.P. (*see* BURKE'S *Landed Gentry*), b. 28 July, 1864 ; eldest son of SpencerPerceval Butler, of Lincoln's Inn, and of Mary, only child of the Rev. Nicholas Kendall ; m. Louisa Mary, only child of Joseph

Beaumont Pease, of Darlington. *Educ.* : Harrow. J.P., County of London, and J.P. Co. Berks. ; High Sheriff, Berks., 1906. *War Work* : Divisional Food Commissioner (Ministry of Food), for S.M. Division, 1917–19 ; Chief of the British Section of the Inter-Allied Mission for Food and Relief to Central Europe, 1919–20. *Address* : Bourton House, Shrivenham. *Clubs* : Travellers ; Bath ; Windham ; Hurlingham ; R.A.C. (K356)

BUTTENSHAW, George Eskholme, M.B.E., A.M.Inst. M.E., b. 5 April, 1870. *Educ.* : Rotherham Grammar School, Sheffield Univ. Coll. Engineer ; Director of Frank Pearn & Co., Manchester. *War Work* : Section Engineer, Ministry of Munitions. *Address* : Lynbrook, Chorlton-cum-Hardy, Manchester. (M3559)

BUTTER, Major Charles Adrian James, O.B.E., R.A.F.

BUTTER, Capt. Francis Sam, O.B.E., R.A.S.C.

BUTTERS, Capt. Adams, O.B.E.

BUTTERS, 2nd Lieut. James Waugh, M.B.E.

BUTTERS, John Henry, M.B.E. (M10377)

BUTTERWORTH, Capt. Arthur Bernard, O.B.E., R.A.S.C.

BUTTERWORTH, Lieut.-Col. Jabez, O.B.E., b. 15 June, 1878 ; s. of William Butterworth, of Luddenden ; m. Ann Olga, d. of George Marsden, of Harrogate. *Educ.* : Privately. Solicitor ; Commissioner for Oaths ; Clerk to District Insurance Committee. *War Work* : Army Pay Department, 1914–19. *Address* : 27, St. George's Road, Harrogate. (O1172)

BUTTERWORTH, Reginald, C.B.E.

BUTTON, Howard, C.B.E., b. 20 March, 1875 ; s. of John J. Button, of Fern Bank, Olton, Warwickshire ; m. Beatrice Maud, d. of the late Willoughby F. Smith, of Woodville. *Educ.* : Foundation Scholar of King Edward VI. Grammar School, Birmingham. *War Work* : Served as A.B. for 2½ years in R.N.A.A.C. ; Director of Internal Audits (D.I.A.), Ministry of Munitions of War ; Controller of Munitions Accounts (C.M.A.), Ministry of Munitions of War. *Addresses* : 86, East Sheen Avenue, S.W. 14 ; 61–62, Lincoln's Inn Fields, W.C. 2. *Club* : R.A.C. (C2491)

BUTTON, Surg.-Lieut.-Comdr. Philip Norman, O.B.E., R.N.

BUTTON, Thomas Frederick, M.B.E.

BUXTON, Alfred Mellor, O.B.E., b. 7 May, 1879 ; s. of Alfred Buxton, of Wilmslow ; m. Ethel Marion, d. of G. E. Mawby, of Northampton. *Educ.* : Rossall. Manufacturer. *War Work* : B.R.C.S. Cheshire Branch ; Manager of Food and Stores Department for the County *Address* : Remenham, Wilmslow ,Cheshire. *Club* : Constitutional (Manchester). (O10091)

BUXTON, Lieut. Claude Henry, M.B.E., R.A.O.C.

BUXTON, Edward, M.B.E.

BUXTON, Frances Mary, O.B.E., b. 10 Oct. 1879 ; d. of the late Francis William and Hon. Mrs. Buxton, O.B.E., of 42, Grosvenor Gardens. *War Work* : Four years at Red Cross Wounded and Missing Dept., 18, Carlton House Terrace. *Address* : 43, Hans Place, S.W. 1. (O3646)

BUXTON, Laura, Mrs., M.B.E. ; d. of John Gurney, of Sprowston Hall, Norwich ; m. Edward Gurney, s. of Samuel Gurney Buxton, of Catton Hall, Norwich. *War Work* : Commandant (and owner) of Catton Hall, V.A.D. Hospital, 1915–19. *Address* : Catton Hall, Norwich. *Club* : New Century. (M3561)

BUXTON, Lucy Ethel, Mrs., O.B.E., b. 1867 ; d. of the late Sir Joseph Pease, Bart., of Hutton Hall, Guisborough, Yorks. (*see* BURKE'S *Peerage*) ; m. Gerald, s. of E. N. Buxton, of Knighton, Essex. *Educ.* : Privately. Vice-Chairman, Essex Branch, B.R.C.S. ; Lady President, League of Mercy ; Deputy Chairman, Essex County Nursing Association ; Member of Essex War Pensions Committees. *War Work* : Commandant, Essex 58 and Theydon Towers Hospital, Essex Branch, B.R.C.S. ; Training Centre at Birch Hall Farm, for Land Army ; Pensions Committees. *Address* : Birch Hall, Theydon Bois, Essex. *Clubs* : Ladies' Automobile ; Bath. (O1123)

BUXTON, Mary Aline, Mrs., M.B.E., b. 23 May, 1896 ; d. of Lieut.-Col. F. E. Bradshaw, D.S.O., of 29, Draycott Place, S.W. ; m. Clarence Edward Victor, s. of Sir T. F. Victor Buxton, 5th Bart., of Warlies, Waltham Abbey. *War Work* : Central Prisoners of War Committee. (M7586)

BUXTON, Mary G., The Hon. Mrs. Francis, O.B.E.

BUXTON, Capt. Vincent, O.B.E., b. 25 April, 1893 ; s. of William Henry Buxton, of Bryn Coed, St. Asaph. *Educ.* : France, Germany, and Royal Military Coll., Sandhurst. Flight-Lieut., R.A.F., late the Leicestershire Regt. *War Work* : Served with the 2nd Leicestershire Regt. in France, 1914 and 1915 (Indian Corps) ; attached to the 2nd East Yorkshire Regt. in France, 1915 (28th Div.) ; served with the 2nd Leicestershire Regt. in Mesopotamia, 1916 and 1917 ; attached to 30 Squadron, R.F.C. in 1917 in Mesopotamia ; appointed to Air Staff in Oct. 1917 ; served as S.O. 3 and S.O. 2 (Air) until 1920 ; transferred to R.A.F. in 1919 ; mentioned in despatches by General Sir Stanley Maude, K.C.B., C.M.G., D.S.O., 2 Nov. 1917 ; wounded at battle of Neuve Chapelle, March, 1915 ; Loos, Sept. 1915 and while bombing Arab tribes on the River Euphrates in Feb. 1919. *Address* : Bryn Coed, St. Asaph, N. Wales. *Club* : R.A.F., R.A.C. (O8063)

BUXTON, Violet, Mrs., O.B.E., d. of the late Rev. Dr. T. W. Jex-Blake, of The Deanery, Wells, Somerset ; m. Alfred Fowell, s. of Thomas Fowell, of Easneye, Ware. *War Work* : Lady Almoner of the Manor (County of London) War Hospital, Epsom. *Address* : Fairhill, Tonbridge. *Club* : Albemarle. (O10092)

BYAM, Lieut.-Col. William, O.B.E., R.A.M.C., b. 19 Aug., 1882 ; s. of Maj.-Gen. W. Byam, C.E., of Southampton ; m. Doris Mabert, d. of Edward Stiven, M.D., of Harrow-on-the-Hill. Educ. : Wellington Coll., Berks, and St. George's Hosp., London. Assistant Director of Pathology, London District. War Work : Member of the War Office Trench Fever Investigation Committee ; and in charge of the War Office Trench Fever Investigation Wards, etc. Address : 9, Harley Street, London, W. 1. (O6971)

BYAS, Hugh Fulton, M.B.E.

BYATT, Ernest Henry, M.B.E.

BYGRAVE, Leonard Charles, M.B.E. (M5981)

BYGRAVE, William Thomas, O.B.E., b. 24 Oct. 1865 ; s. of the late Henry Bygrave, of Norwich ; m. Matilda, d. of the late Daniel John Mahon, of St. Marylebone. Educ. : St. Giles and St. Peter Mancroft Schools, Norwich. Director and Secretary of Eastman & Son (Dyers and Cleaners), Ltd., Acton Vale ; Member of Council, Chairman of Finance Committee, and Vice-Chairman of House Committee, Acton Hospital. Vice-President of Acton Philanthropic Society. War Work : Vice-Chairman Acton Local War Pensions Committee ; Chairman Special Disablement King's Fund and Special Appeals Sub-Committees from formation until end of 1919. Address : 11, Cumberland Road, Acton, W. 3. Clubs : Past Masters' ; Priory Constitutional (Acton). (O10093)

BYLES, Emma Mary, M.B.E., b. 25 July, 1865 ; d. of Pierre Beuzeville Byles, of Henley-on-Thames. Educ. : Bradford Girls' Grammar School. Trained Nurse. For 17 years Matron of Lambeth Infirmary, retired Nov. 1918 ; trained Addenbrooke's Hospital, Cambridge. War Work : Organised, and worked shorthanded, accommodation for 300 extra patients to relieve other Institutions which were used for Military Hospitals. A large number of nurses from her training school (Lambeth) volunteered for war work and many received honours. Address : Resthaven, St. Leonard's Road, Horsham. (M3863)

BYNE, Lieut.-Col. Roland Martin, O.B.E., R.M.L.I. (ret.), b. 19 April, 1864. (O1175)

BYRDE, Edwin Augustus, O.B.E. Engineer-in-Chief, Railway Construction, Mesopotamia. (O17189f)

BYRNE, Lieut.-Col. Gerald Bertram Eustace, O.B.E., late Rifle Brigade, b. 10 Nov. 1873 ; s. of Maj.-Gen. T. E. Byrne, of Tekels Castle, Camberley ; m. Aileen Myrtle, d. of Robert Sanderson Whitaker, of Villa Sofia, Palermo. Educ. : Woburn School, Weybridge, and Beaumont College, Old Windsor. War Work : 5th Batt. Rifle Brigade, 1914–18 ; France, 1918–19. Club : Army and Navy. (O5066)

BYRNE, Brig.-Gen. Sir Joseph Aloysius, K.B.E., C.B., b. 2 Oct. 1874 ; s. of the late J. Byrne, D.L., F.R.C.S.I., of Londonderry ; m. 21 July, 1908, Marjorie, d. of the late Allan F. Joseph, of Ghezira, Cairo. Late Royal Inniskilling Fusiliers ; joined 1893 ; Major, 1914 ; Brevet Lieut.-Col. 1915 ; Hon. Brig.-Gen., (ret.) 1916 ; was A.A.G. War Office, 1915–16 ; D.A.G. Irish Command, 1916, and Inspector-General Royal Irish Constabulary, 1916–20 ; served in S. African War 1899–1902 (two medals, seven clasps, wounded). (K133)

BYRNE, Kathleen, Mrs., M.B.E.

BYRNE, Louisa Mary, Mrs., M.B.E. ; d. of the late Andrew Derham, J.P., of Co. Dublin. Educ. : Rathfarnham Abbey, Co. Dublin. War Work : Services on Committee of Tyneside Irish Brigade. Address : 26, Eldon Place, Newcastle-on-Tyne. (M7587)

BYRNE, Capt. and Qr.-Mr. Richard, O.B.E.

BYRNE, Violet Julia, O.B.E. War Work : V.A.D. Headquarters Staff, 1915–20 ; Hon. Sec. Joint Women's V.A.D. Selection Board, 1916–20 ; Commandant V.A.D. London 284, 1917–20 ; appointed Lady of Grace of St. John of Jerusalem, Nov. 1917. Address : 65, Cadogan Place, S.W. 1. Clubs : Ladies' Automobile ; V.A.D. Ladies'. (O10094)

BYROM, Charles Reginald, O.B.E., b. 7 Nov. 1878 ; s. of the late Rev. John Wolsey Unwin, of Overton Rectory, Ellesmere, Salop (took name of Byrom by Deed Poll, 31 Dec., 1907) ; m. Blanche, youngest daughter of the late Nicholas Martindale, of Liverpool. Educ. : Shrewsbury School. Assistant Superintendent of the Line, L. & N.W. Railway. War Work : General Transport of Troops and War Material in this country. Address : 65, Hampstead Way. N.W. 4. (O1176)

BYROM, Thomas Emmett, C.B.E., b. 12 Feb. 1871 ; s. of John Byrom, of Stockport. Educ. : Stockport. War Work : In 1915, engaged at Glasgow for several months in active recruiting campaign, raising men for Voluntary Army ; from 1917 onwards, work in Home Counties raising money for War Bond Campaigns (Tank, and War Weapons Weeks, etc.). Address : 101, Ladbroke Grove, London, W. 11. Clubs : Royal Automobile ; National Liberal. (C249)

BYRON, Fanny Lucy, Lady, D.B.E. ; 4th d. of the late Thomas Radnall, of St. Margarets, Twickenham, and w. of George Frederick William, 9th Baron Byron (see BURKE'S Peerage). Address : Byron Cottage, Hampstead Heath, N.W. (D3)

BYRON, Margaret Dorothy, O.B.E.

BYRSON, T. Warrant Officer John, M.B.E. Royal Indian Marine.

BYTHELL, Capt. William James Storey, O.B.E., R.A.M.C. (T.F.), b. 14 March, 1872 ; s. of John Kenworthy Bythell, of Manchester ; m. Theodora, d. of R. H. Prestwich, of Tarporley, Cheshire. Educ. : Camb. Univ. Radiologist to Salford Royal Hospital, and Manchester Children's Hospital. War Work : In England and France ; Hon. Med. Officer to East

Lancs. Homes for Disabled Sailors and Soldiers. Address : The Grange, Chelford, Cheshire. (O10095)

BYTHELL, Col. William John, C.B.E. Col. R.E. (ret.); Great War, 1914–19 (despatches). (C1497)

CABLE, Lieut.-Col. James Frederick, O.B.E.

CABLE, Norah Evelyn, M.B.E., Q.M.A.A.C.

CABLE, William John, O.B.E., A.C.I.S., b. 8 July, 1872 ; s. of William Cable, of Ipswich ; m. Mary, d. of Charles Hemberger, of Hendon. Secretary to the Society of Friends of Foreigners in Distress, 1903 ; Hon. Sec. to the Russian Benevolent Fund, 1910 ; Secretary to the Central Council of Foreign Benevolent Societies, 1914. War Work : Organisation of Central Council of United Alien Relief Societies, and carrying out special work on behalf of the British Authorities. Address : 7, Fox Lane, Palmer's Green, N. 13. (O204)

CABROL, Right Rev. Fernand, O.B.E., b. 11 Dec. 1855 ; s. of Louis-Pascal Cabrol. Abbot of Farnborough, Hants. War Work : Kept an ambulance in his own house during all the time of the War ; about 2000 soldiers (Belgian and British) were nursed at this ambulance. Address : The Abbey, Farnborough, Hants. (O10096)

CABUCHE, Major Henry Leon, O.B.E., T.D., F.S.A., F.I.B.D., b. 9 Aug. 1876 ; s. of Leon Cabuche, of London ; m. Mabel Louise, d. of Frederick Garon, of Essex. Educ. : Paris ; Privately ; University College, London. Architect and Surveyor. War Work : Mobilised 3 Aug. 1914 ; went to France, 3 Nov. 1914 (1914 Star with bar), as Company Commander in 13th County of London Batt. ; 1915, appointed to Staff of 60th Division, as Chief Instructor in Bombing ; 1916, transferred to W.O. Staff and loaned to Ministry of Munitions as Superintendant of Factory Construction ; 1917, appointed Assistant Controller, Dept. of Engineering ; 1918, appointed Assistant Director of Training of Disabled Soldiers to Ministry of Pensions. Address : 4, Rusholme Road, Putney, S.W. 15. (O117)

CADBURY, Elizabeth Mary, Mrs., O.B.E., M.A., b. 1858 ; d. of John Taylor, of London ; m. George, s. of John Cadbury, of Birmingham. Educ. : Privately and abroad. City Councillor, Birmingham ; Chairman of Birmingham School Medical Service ; Past President of National Council of Women. War Work : Chairman of Belgian Refugees Committee ; Chairman of Serbian Refugees Committee ; Vice-President, Worcestershire Red Cross. Addresses : The Manor House, Northfield ; 1, Druids Point, Malvern. Clubs : Ladies' Empire ; Lyceum ; Forum. (O205)

CADBURY, Laurence John, O.B.E.

CADDINGTON, Major Thomas George Augustus, O.B.E., R.H.A.

CADELL, Fairley Charlotte, Mrs., M.B.E., b. 22 June, 1870 ; d. of Alex. Blair, Sheriff of the Lothians ; m. Hew Francis, s. of Col. T. Cadell, V.C., C.B., of Cockenzie House, Prestonpans, N.B. War Work : President of West Edinburgh Division, Soldiers' and Sailors' Families Assoc. ; Member of the Edinburgh War Pensions Local Committee. Address : 7, Rothesay Place, Edinburgh ; Cockenzie House, Prestonpans, N.B. Club : Ladies' Caledonian (Edinburgh). (M7588)

CADELL, Lieut.-Col. Harry Ernest, C.B.E., b. 1867 ; s. of the late Lieut.-Gen. Alexander Tod Cadell, R.A. Lieut.-Col. R.A. ; Great War, 1914–19 (despatches). (C1498)

CADGE, Capt. Christopher Rawlinson, O.B.E.

CADGE, Lieut.-Col. William Hotson, O.B.E., I.M.S., b. 11 Aug. 1853 ; s. of Christopher Goulder Cadge, of Carlton Colville, Lowestoft ; m. Flora, d. of James Bowless Summers, of Haverfordwest. Educ. : Norwich Grammar School ; St. George's Hospital, London. War Work : Organised and in Medical charge of Ipswich Military Hospital from April, 1915, to June, 1917 ; President of Medical Board, Colchester Military Hospital from July, 1917, to April, 1918 ; from latter date to Dec. 1918, President of Medical Board, Ipswich Military Hospital. Address : Helmingham House, Kirkley Cliff Road, Lowestoft. Clubs : East India United Service ; Norfolk and Suffolk Yacht. (O4355)

CADIZ, Major Charles James Roche Galway, O.B.E.

CADMAN, The Rev. Cecil Frank MILES-, O.B.E.

CADOGAN, Gerald Oakley Cadogan, Earl, C.B.E., b. 28 May, 1869 ; s. of the 6th Earl (see BURKE'S Peerage) ; m. 7 June, 1911, Lilian Eleanor Marie, o. d. of George Stewart Coxon, of Craigleith, Cheltenham. Hereditary Trustee of the British Museum ; Hon. Lieut.-Col. late Suffolk Volunteer Regt. ; formerly Lieut. 1st Life Guards, and Capt. 3rd Batt. Suffolk Regt. ; A.D.C. to the Lords Lieutenant of Ireland, 1895–1905 ; served in South Africa. Addresses : Culford Hall, Bury St. Edmunds ; Chelsea House, Cadogan Place, S.W. 1. (C2085)

CADOUX, Capt. Bernard Temple, M.B.E.

CAFFYN, Margaret Louise, M.B.E., b. 2 July, 1885 ; d. of Alfred Caffyn, of The Chantry, Warbleton, Sussex. War Work : Leader of a Y.M.C.A. Patriotic Club for Soldiers and Girls. (M7589)

CAHILL, R.Q.M.S. Albert, M.B.E., R.A.S.C.

CAHILL, Lieut. John, M.B.E., R.N.

CAHILL, Capt. John Walter Frederick, M.B.E., A.S.C.

CAILLARD, Elizabeth Francis, Lady, O.B.E., Lady of Grace of the Order of St. John of Jerusalem ; d. of Capt. John Hanham (see BURKE'S Peerage, Hanham, Bart.) ; m. 16 June 1881, Sir Vincent Henry Penalver, Knt. Bach., D.L. (see BURKE'S Peerage), s. of the late Camille Felix Désvié Caillard,

County Court Judge, of Wingfield House, near Trowbridge, Wilts. *Addresses:* Wingfield House, near Trowbridge, Wilts.; 42, Half Moon Street, Piccadilly, W. (O2061)

CAIN, Sarah, Mrs., M.B.E., Kaisir-i-Hind bar; *b.* 1855, *d.* of Charles Davies, of Melbourne; *m.* John, *s.* of Henry Cain, of Bedford. *Educ.:* Melbourne, Australia. Missionary. *War Work:* Getting socks, caps, comforters, etc., knitted (about 800 pairs of socks), part of the wool provided by Ladies' Depot, Madras, part brought from lace profits; subscribing Rs. 1383, from proceeds chiefly of Lace Industry, from which profits Miss Wallen also subscribed Rs. 800. *Address:* Dummagudem, S. India. (M6116)

CAINE, Elizabeth, Mrs., M.B.E.; *d.* of the late William Mackenzie, of The Scottish Land Court, Edinburgh; *m.* Nathaniel, *s.* of Nathaniel Caine, of Spital, Cheshire. *Educ.:* Inverness Academy and Cheltenham College. Councillor, Lower Bebington Urban District; Chairman of the Maternity and Child Welfare Committee. *War Work:* Y.M.C.A. Canteen Work; Hon. Secretary, Bebington District War Pensions Committee. *Address:* New Ferry Park, New Ferry, Birkenhead. (M7590)

CAINE, Gordon Ralph Hall, C.B.E. Deputy Controller of Paper. (C3134)

CAINE, Sir Hall, K.B.E., J.P., Officer of Order of Leopold, *b.* 14 May, 1853, *s.* of John Caine, of Isle of Man; *m.* Mary, *d.* of William Chandler, of Walthamstow. *Educ.:* Isle of Man and Liverpool. Author. *War Work:* Propaganda (chiefly in U.S.A.); devoted the whole period of the War to it to the exclusion of all professional work. *Address:* Greeba Castle, Isle of Man. (K134)

CAINE, Lieut. Martin Surney, M.B.E.

CAINES, Clement Guy, M.B.E.

CAIRD, Sir Andrew, K.B.E., *b.* 14 Oct. 1870; *s.* of Andrew Caird, of Montrose; *m.* Anne, *d.* of William Davidson, of Montrose. Journalist and Newspaper Manager. *War Work:* Was Administrator, New York Headquarters, of the British War Mission to the United States of America, 1917-18. *Address:* Glenmard, Arthur Road, Wimbledon Park, S.W. 10. (K54)

CAIRD, Francis Pratt, M.B.E.

CAIRNS, Lieut. David, M.B.E., R.A.F.

CAIRNS, The Rev. David Smith, O.B.E., D.D.

CAIRNS, James, O.B.E., M.A., M.B., Ch.B., D.P.H., *b.* 12 July, 1885; *s.* of Bailie James Cairns of Glasgow. *Educ.:* Allan Glen's School, and Univ. of Glasgow. Principal Medical and Health Officer, Great Indian Peninsula Railway. *War Work:* Sanitary Officer, Deolali, India; Specialist in Prevention of Disease, 34th (The Welsh) General Hospital; D.A.D.M.S. (Sanitary), the 8th (Lucknow) Division. *Address:* Beryl House, Wodehouse Road, Bombay; 12, Holyrood Crescent, Glasgow. *Club:* Royal Bombay Yacht. (O8446)

CAIRNS, Rev. and Hon. Major John, M.B.E., V.D., J.P., 3rd Batt. R. West Kent Regt., *b.* 18 March, 1865; *s.* of James Cairns of Mountpleasant, Berwickshire; *m.* Christina, *d.* of Alexander Jack, of Avoch, Ross-shire, Scotland. *Educ.:* Edinburgh Univ. and United Presbyterian College. Assistant Principal Chaplain, Royal Army Chaplains' Department. *War Work:* Staff Officer, Eastern Command; served on H.M.S. "Aquitania," and Ambulance troopship "Braemar Castle." *Address:* Glencairn, Little Heath, Charlton, S.E. 7. *Club:* National Liberal. (O6973)

CAIRNS, John, M.B.E., J.P.

CAIRNS, William Murray, C.B.E., M.D., C.M.; *s.* of W. S. Cairns, of Hyldagarth, Heswall, Cheshire; *m.* Eleanor Stephenson, *d.* of the Rev. James Anderson, of Polmont, Stirlingshire. *Educ.:* Edinburgh Univ. *War Work:* Medical Officer in Charge Princes Road and Myrtle Street St. John Auxiliary Hospitals, Liverpool; Corps Surgeon St. John Ambulance Brigade; Lecturer and Examiner St. John Ambulance Association. *Address:* 67, Catharine Street, Liverpool. (C2493)

CAITHNESS, Norman Macleod Buchan, 18th Earl of, C.B.E.; Baron Birriedale, Bt., D.L., County of Aberdeen, *b.* 4 April, 1862; *s.* of 16th Earl, and Janet, *d.* of Roderick M'Leod, M.D.; succeeded his brother, 1914; *m.* Lilian, 2nd *d.* of Higford Higford, 23, Eaton Place, S.W. *Educ.:* Uppingham; Trinity Hall, Cambridge. Changed his surname from Sinclair to Buchan, 1911. Captain in 3/5th Batt. Gordon Highlanders. *Address:* Auchmacoy House, Ellon, Aberdeenshire. *Club:* Caledonian. (C1499)

CALDER, Lieut. George, O.B.E., R.A.O.C.

CALDER, James Charles, C.B.E., *b.* Dec. 1869; *s.* of Jas. Calder, of Ardargie, Forgandenny Perthshire; *m.* Mildred Louise, *d.* of Col. Richard Manners, of Royal Scots. *Educ.:* St. Benedicts, Fort Augustus. *War Work:* Controller, Timber Supplies Department, Board of Trade. *Address:* 32, Park Lane; Ledlanet, Milnathort, Scotland. *Clubs:* St. James's; Devonshire; British Empire. London; County, Perth. (C2494)

CALDER, Reginald Colin, O.B.E., *b.* 6 March, 1888; *s.* of the late William J. W. Calder; *m.* Catherine Lily, *d.* of Henry Self, of London. *Educ.:* St. Peter's, London Docks; East London Technical Coll.; King's Coll., London. Second Division Clerk—Admiralty, 19 Oct. 1908, to 16 Jan. 1912; Board of Trade, 17 Jan. 1912, to 12 Jan. 1913; National Health Insurance Commission (England), Jan. 1913, to July, 1917; on loan to the Ministry of Information July, 1917; Establishment Officer in that Ministry April, 1918, to Dec. 1918; on loan to Foreign Office Jan. 1919; appointed First Class Establishment and Accounts Officer in the Foreign Office,

Aug. 1919. *Address:* 47, Langdale Road, Thornton Heath, Surrey. (O3649)

CALDER, William Beale, M.B.E., *b.* 22 June, 1875; *s.* of David Calder, of Pietermaritzburg; *m.* Ethel, *d.* of James Barnes, of Pietermaritzburg. *Educ.:* Pietermaritzburg College. Solicitor. *War Work:* Chairman, Executive Committee, Governor-General's Fund, Durban; Chairman, Sportsmen's Contribution to Governor-General's Fund. *Address:* 543, Currie Road, Durban. *Clubs:* Durban; Durban Royal Yacht; Durban Golf. (M1207)

CALDICOTT, Capt. Charles Holt, M.B.E., R.A.M.C. (T.F.), *b.* 26 Feb. 1871; *s.* of Oswald Holt Caldicott, of Four Oaks, Warwickshire; *m.* Elizabeth Lora, *d.* of Lieut.-General A. Phelps, of Woodbourne Grange, Edgbaston. *Educ.:* King Edward's School, Birmingham. *War Work:* Served with South-Eastern Mounted Brigade Field Ambulance in Gallipoli and Egypt; afterwards in charge of Medical Division, Lewisham Military Hospital. *Address:* Grantbourne, Chatham, Surrey. (M5135)

CALDWELL, Col. Arthur Lewis, O.B.E., R.A.S.C.

CALDWELL, Major Bruce McGregor, M.B.E.

CALDWELL, David, M.B.E.

CALDWELL, Francis, C.B.E., M.V.O.

CALDWELL, Mary Louisa, O.B.E.

CALDWELL, Lieut.-Col. Michael Alexander, O.B.E.

CALDWELL Major Thomas Richey, O.B.E.

CALDWELL, T. Capt. William James, M.B.E.

CALE, Capt. William Frederick, M.B.E.

CALL, Capt. Hamilton, O.B.E., *b.* 8 Sept. 1868; *s.* of the late Stanford Call, of London; *m.* Ada Maria Walsgraves, *d.* of John Angus Hewat, *Educ.:* Privately. Commander, P. & O.S.N. Co.'s Service (ret. 1919). *War Work:* Commanding Royal Naval Hospital Ship "Soudan" (No. 1), Aug. 1914, to April, 1919; attached to Grand Fleet, North Sea, Aug. 1914, to Feb. 1915; attached to Eastern Mediterranean Squadron and served off Gallipoli Peninsula throughout Dardanelles Campaign, Jan. 1916; returned home waters and re-joined Grand Fleet in North Sea, serving with same ship till April, 1919, when "Soudan" was paid off as R.N.H. Ship, re-conditioned and returned to P. & O.S.N. Co. *Addresses:* The Cottage, North Gate, Regent's Park, London; Cornerways, Hillhead, nr. Fareham, Hampshire. *Club:* Golfers'. (O10097)

CALLADINE, Ernest Thompson, O.B.E., *b.* 12 Jan. 1875; *s.* of William Calladine, of Hucknall, Notts.; *m.* Stella *d.* of John Holroyd, of Hucknall, Notts. *Educ.:* Nottingham High School. Manager of the London Joint City and Midland Bank, Hastings. *War Work:* Hon. Sec. Hastings and St. Leonards War Refugees' Committee, 1914-19. *Address:* 18, Priory Avenue, Hastings. (O10098)

CALLAGHAN, John Martin, M.B.E.

CALLAGHAN, Capt. Joseph Aloysius, O.B.E.

CALLAN, Joseph, C.B.E.

CALLANDER, Major Cuthbert BURN-, O.B.E., *b.* 5 Feb. 1886; *s.* of Edward Burn-Callander, late of Preston Hall, Midlothian. *Educ.:* Rugby. Professional Associate of the Surveyors Institution. *War Work:* Served with Montgomeryshire Yeomanry from beginning of War until March, 1916, when was appointed A.D.C. to G.O.C. 56th London Division; Feb. 1917, appointed to Physical and Bayonet Training Staff; Jan. 1918 appointed Superintendent Physical and Bayonet Training; twice mentioned in dispatches. *Address:* Barford, Warwick. *Clubs:* New Oxford and Cambridge. (O5061)

CALLARD, Cuthbert Richard, O.B.E., *b.* 27 Dec. 1874; *s.* of Thomas Black Callard, of Chesham Bois, Bucks.; *m.* Katharine Miriam, *d.* of Charles Atkins Faraday. *Educ.:* Privately. Solicitor. *War Work:* Hon. Sec. to Special Hospitals for Officers (Lord Knutsford's Committee). *Addresses:* Glengariff, Pinner, Middlesex; 3, St. James' Street, London, S.W. 1. *Club:* Devonshire. (O10099)

CALLENDAR, Hugh Longbourne, C.B.E., F.R.S.C.

CALLENDER, Edward Henry William, O.B.E.

CALLENDER, Lieut.-Col. Eustace Maude, C.B.E., T.D., M.D., L.R.C.P., M.R.C.S., R.A.M.C. (T.), *b.* 31 Oct. 1864; *s.* of Samuel Pope Callender of Manchester; *m.* Adelaide Frances Jane, *d.* of John Beeching Stephens, of Maidstone. *Educ.:* Rugby and St. Mary's Hospital, London. Physician, Medical Aid Society for Necessitous Gentlewomen; Medical Officer, St. Agatha's Home; late House Surgeon, House Physician, Resident Obstetric Officer, and Assistant Anæsthetist, St. Mary's Hospital. *War Work:* Commanded 2nd London Genl. Hospital; mobilised 4 Aug. 1914 and continued in command till April, 1917, on which date proceeded to France in command of No. 53 General Hospital, and served with it until April, 1919; disembodied 15 April, 1919; three times mentioned in despatches. *Address:* 73, Sussex Gardens, Hyde Park, W. 2. *Clubs:* St. Albans Medical; Mid-Surrey Golf. (C1233)

CALLEY, Major-Gen. Thomas Charles Pleydell, C.B., C.B.E., M.V.O., J.P., D.L., *b.* 28 Jan. 1856; *s.* of Henry Calley, J.P., D.L., of Burderop Park, Wilts.; *m.* Emily, *d.* of T. P. Chappell, of Weir Bank, Teddington. *Educ.:* Harrow and Christchurch, Oxford. Commanded 1st Life Guards, 1902-6; London Mounted Brigade, 1908-12; M.P. for North Wilts, 1910. *War Work:* Commanded 60th Division, Oct. 1914, to Dec. 1915; Staff Officer for Volunteers, Southern Command, 1916-19. *Address:* Burderop Park, Swindon. *Clubs:* Naval and Military; Guards'. (C1500)

CALLWELL, Lieut.-Comm. Eberhard William Ernest, O.B.E., R.N.

CALNAN, Denis, C.B.E., I.C.S., *b.* 14 May, 1865 ; *s.* of Joseph Calnan, of Bandon, Co. Cork ; *m.* Florence, *d.* of Norman Reid, of Behar, India. *Educ.:* St. Stanislaus' Coll., Fullamore ; Queens' Coll., Cambridge. Commissioner of Bundelkhand, United Provinces. *War Work:* Was mentioned by the Commander-in-Chief in a despatch reviewing the part played by India in the prosecution of the war. *Address:* Jhansi, United Provinces, India. *Club:* East India United Service. (C1958)

CALTHROP, Col. Christopher William CARR-, C.B.E., J.P., I.M.S. (ret.), *b.* 28 July, 1844 ; *s.* of William Charles Calthrop, of Crowland, Lincolnshire ; *m.* Alice Evett, *d.* of Charles James Hartley, of Edgbaston, Birmingham. *Educ.:* Merchant Taylor's School ; Charing Cross Hospital. Has held many professional appointments in connection with University of Lahore, Punjaub, India ; Afghan War of 1878–80 ; P.M.O. Malakand Brigade, Swat Valley Campaign, 1895–96 ; P.M.O. Indian Contingent, Sudan Field Force, 1896–97 ; P.M.O. Assam Brigade, I.G.C.H., Assam, 1899–1904. *Address:* 9, Grange Road, Ealing, W. 5. (C2497)

CALTHROP, Hugh Victor Ekeward, M.B.E.

CALVERLEY, Major Edmond Leveson, O.B.E.

CALVERLEY, Louisa Mary, Mrs., O.B.E. *b.* 19 April, 1870 ; *d.* of Sir Brydges Henniker, Bart., of Newton Hall, Dunmow, Essex ; *m.* Horace Walter, *s.* of Edmund Calverley, Esq. of Oulton Hall, Leeds. *Educ.:* At home. Vice-President and Commandant, Harlow Division, Essex Branch of British Red Cross Society ; Lady of Grace of the Order of St. John of Jerusalem. *War Work:* Had a hospital of sixty beds for men in Harlow, and one of twenty beds for convalescents, in her own house for four years of the War. *Address:* Down Hall, Harlow, Essex. *Club:* Ladies' Automobile. (O1182)

CALVERT, Harry, M.B.E.

CALVERT, Harry Thornton, M.B.E., D.Sc., Ph.D., F.I.C., *b.* 3 May, 1878 ; *s.* of Manoah B. Calvert, of Armley, Leeds ; *m.* Annie, *d.* of John H. Tetley, of Ilkley. *Educ.:* Leeds and Leipsic Universities. Demonstrator of Chemistry, Yorkshire Coll., Leeds ; Industrial Chemist ; Chief Chemist and Deputy Chief Inspector (West Riding of Yorkshire Rivers Board) ; Chemical Inspector (Ministry of Health). *War Work:* Technical Chemist on Lord Moulton's Headquarters Staff (Explosives Supply Department, Ministry of Munitions of War). *Address:* Watergate, Burbage Road, Dulwich, S.E. 24. *Club:* Chemical Industry. (M7593)

CALVERT, Lieut.-Col. James, C.B.E., M.D. Lieut.-Col. R.A.M.C. ; Great War, 1914–19 (despatches). (C1501)

CALVERT, Rupert Harry, M.B.E.

CALVERT, Tom, M.B.E.

CALVEY, Capt. Charles Bernard, M.B.E., R.A.S.C., *b.* 14 June, 1867 ; *s.* of Bryan Calvey, of Dublin ; *m.* Anne Louisa, *d.* of William Marshman, of Catford, S.E. *Educ.:* Privately. *War Work:* Home Base Supply Depot, Newhaven ; Mechanical Transport Training Depot, Osterley Park. *Address:* Fairlight, Bath Road, Hounslow, Middlesex. (M5136)

CALWELL, William, O.B.E., *b.* June, 26 1859 ; *s.* of Robert Calwell, of Annadale, Co. Down ; *m.* Helen Agnes, *d.* of the late Lieut.-Col. Robert Anderson, H.L.I. of Richmond, Yorkshire. *Educ.:* Royal Academical Institution, Belfast ; Queen's Coll. and Univ. of Belfast. Visiting Physician to Royal Victoria Hospital, Belfast ; visiting Physician to U.V.F. Hospitals, Belfast ; M.O., in charge U.V.F. Craigavon Hospital for Neurasthenia ; Consulting Physician to various Hospitals. *War Work:* Visiting Physician to the U.V.F. Hospitals in Belfast ; Medical Officer in charge of U.V.F. Craigavon Neurasthenic Hospital ; Physician to Soldiers in Royal Victoria Hospital, Belfast. *Address:* 6, College Gardens, Belfast. (O10101)

CAMBRAY, Philip George, O.B.E., *b.* 1879 ; *s.* of G. R. Cambray, of Oxford ; *m.* Helen Frances Omash, of Brockley. *War Work:* Commander, X Division, Metropolitan S.C. ; T.F. Res. (Gen. List) ; Staff Lieut., War Office ; Private Secretary to Sir Auckland Geddes, 1917–19. (O209)

CAMBRIDGE, Lieut. Arthur Edward, M.B.E., R.A.F.

CAMBRIDGE, Hilda Margaret, Mrs. PICKARD-, M.B.E., *b.* 19 June, 1873 ; *d.* of John Mortimer Hunt, of 4, Airlie Gardens, W., and Bellevue, Holmwood ; *m.* Arthur Wallace (Fellow of Balliol College, Oxford), *s.* of Rev. O. Pickard-Cambridge, F.R.S., of Bloxworth, Dorset. *War Work:* British Red Cross Society (Wounded and Missing Department), Oxford. *Address:* St. Catharine's, Headington Hill, Oxford. (M7595)

CAMBURN, Caleb, M.B.E., *b.* 4 Aug. 1857 ; *s.* of the late George A. Camburn, of Folkestone. *Educ.:* Folkestone, Peckham and Westminster Training College. Headmaster of Schools at Great Malvern, Bradford, Yorks and now of Council School, Hungerford, Berks. *War Work:* Hon. Sec. of Local Central Savings Committee, Hungerford ; Member of the Food Control Committee ; Chairman of Economy Committee ; Propaganda work in the District. *Address:* Hungerford, Berks. (M7596)

CAMDEN, Joan Marion, Marchioness, C.B.E., *d.* of Lord Henry Nevill, of Eridge Castle, Sussex (*see* BURKE'S *Peerage*) *m.* John Charles Pratt, 4th Marquess Camden (*see* BURKE'S *Peerage*). *War Work:* President, Kent V.A.D.'s ; President, Kent County War Fund which she started and raised a Fund of over £17,000 to assist the V.A.D. Hospitals in the County ; President, Kent Branch Sailors' and Soldiers' Families Association, and President, Kent County Nursing Association. *Address:* Bayham Abbey, Lamberhurst, Kent. (C2498)

CAMERON, Major Alexander, O.B.E., M.B, I.M.S.. (O11732)

CAMERON, Capt. Alexander Duncan, M.B.E., *b.* 2 Aug. 1897 ; *s.* of Alexander Cameron, of Glasgow. *Educ.:* Glasgow Academy. *War Work:* Served in Army from 2 Sept. 1914 commissioned on that date ; France and Flanders, 8th Scottish Rifles ; later Signal Services. *Addresses:* 185, Buchanan Street, Glasgow ; Empire House, 175, Piccadilly, W. 1. *Club:* Services. (M5137)

CAMERON, Allan, M.B.E., *b.* 4 June, 1861 ; *s.* of William Cameron, of Bannockburn, Stirlingshire ; *m.* Mary Stewart *d.* of William Stewart, of Hamilton, Lanarkshire. *Educ.:* Larkhall Academy. Goods and Mineral Superintendent, The Caledonian Railway, Scotland. *War Work:* Superintending the transit of War Material, Troops, etc., during the Great War. *Address:* St. Elmo, Cameron Street, Motherwell, Scotland. (M7597)

CAMERON, Annie Buchanan, O.B.E., R.R.C., *b.* 8 Aug. 1869 ; *d.* of John Cameron, of Fort William, Inverness-shire. A. Matron, Queen Alexandra's Imperial Military Nursing Service ; served in South African War, and continuously since. *Address:* The Military Hospital, Curragh Camp, Ireland. (O4287)

CAMERON, Major Cecil Aylmer, C.B.E., D.S.O. Major Intelligence Corps, and a Gen. Staff Officer at War Office ; served during Great War, 1914–17 (despatches, Legion of Honour, Order of Leopold of Belgium). (C2212c)

CAMERON, Capt. and Qr.-Mr. Cecil Stevenson, O.B.E., M.C.

CAMERON, Charlotte, Mrs., M.B.E., F.R.G.S. ; *d.* of Capt. Jacob Wales-Almy, R.N. ; *m.* Major Donald Duncan Cameron, of Edinburgh (*who died*). *Educ.:* Brighton and France. Represented " Lady's Pictorial," Delhi, Imperial Durbar. *War Work:* Lecturing on the German Colonies ; Propaganda work at her own expense for all War Charities, firstly in England and then for two years throughout America, Alaska and the Yukon ; worked at Free Buffet at Victoria Station, also Red Cross Work at Bournemouth ; Fellow of the Botanical Society ; Fellow of the Royal Geographical Society ; Member of the Society of Authors ; Fellow of the Society of Women Journalists. *Club:* Writers'. (M7598)

CAMERON, Clarence St. Clair, M.B.E.

CAMERON, Cyril Claude, M.B.E.

CAMERON, Capt. Cyril St. Clair, C.B.E. ; *s.* of the late Col. Aylmer S. Cameron, V.C., C.B. ; *m.* 1909, Isabel Edith, *d.* of Peter Hordern, sometime Director of Public Instruction, Burma. Capt. R.N. ; served in Great War, 1914–19 with Anti-Submarine Serv. (despatches). (C2295)

CAMERON, Major Donald Cunninghame, O.B.E., R.A.S.C.

CAMERON, Major Donald Hay, O.B.E., R.A.F.,

CAMERON, Donald Phillips, M.B.E., R.A.F.

CAMERON, Sir Hector Clare, Kt.. C.B.E., M.B., C.M., M.B., LL.D.. Emeritus Professor of Clinical Surgery in the Univ. of Glasgow, *b.* 30 Sept. 1843 ; *s.* of Donald Cameron, Plantation Zeelugt, Demerara, sugar planter ; *m.* Frances (*d.* 1879), *d.* of William Hamilton Macdonald. *Educ.:* St. Andrews, Edinburgh, and Glasgow Univ. Formerly President of the Faculty of Physicians and Surgeons of Glasgow, and Representative of the Faculty at the General Medical Council. *Address:* 18, Woodside Crescent, Glasgow. (C451)

CAMERON, James, M.B.E.

CAMERON, John, M.B.E.

CAMERON, Lieut. John, O.B.E., R.E.

CAMERON, Norman Restell, M.B.E.

CAMERON, Capt. and Qr.-Mr. Thomas Duncan, M.B.E., R.A.M.C. (T.F.).

CAMERON, Lieut. William Macpherson, M.B.E.

CAMERON, William Scott, M.B.E., L.L.R.

CAMFIELD, Capt. and Qr.-Mr. Charles Nathaniel, M.B.E., R.A.S.C.

CAMP, Edwin James, M.B.E., *b.* 11 Oct. 1884 ; *s.* of James Camp, of Leigh-on-Sea ; *m.* Maude, *d.* of the late Alfred James Indge, of Forest Gate. *War Work:* Transport Department of Admiralty and Ministry of Shipping from October 1914. *Address:* 14, Park Road, Hampton Hill, Middlesex. (M7600)

CAMP, Capt. Ernest Walter, O.B.E., *b.* 5 Aug. 1883 ; *s.* of William Camp, of Witham, Essex ; *m.* May, *d.* of S. S. Bloxham, of Blackheath. *Educ.:* Mann's, Witham, Essex. *War Work:* Enlisted Aug. 1914, H.A.C. ; Commissioned March, 1917 ; transferred to 182 Labour Co. same year ; given command of 113th Labour Co. Jan. 1918 ; transferred to command 53rd P.O.W Co. Nov. 1918 ; mentioned in despatches, 1918. (O2461)

CAMP, Henry John, M.B.E.

CAMPAGNAC, Charles Haswell, M.B.E., *b.* 14 Jan. 1886 ; *s.* of A. G. Campagnac, of Lucknow and Burma ; *m.* Gladys, *d.* of C. H. Kirkham, of Myindaik, Southern Shan States, Burma. *Educ.:* Taunton School, Taunton, Somersetshire. Barrister-at-Law of the Middle Temple ; Municipal Commissioner, Rangoon Municipality, elected by the European and Anglo-Indian Community. *War Work:* Recruited for the Burma Contingent, Volunteer Mobile Battery, and Anglo-Indian Forces ; Member of the Burma Fighting Men's Dependants' Fund, and the Recruits and Comforts Fund, Committees ; Hon. Sec. and founder of the Kut Prisoners' Fund Committee. *Address:* 6, Barr Street, Rangoon. (M7075)

CAMPBELL, Alexander, C.B.E., J.P.

CAMPBELL, Alexander, O.B.E.

CAMPBELL, Angela Mary Alice, Lady, M.B.E., *b.* 1863; 2nd *d.* of the 4th Earl of Harrowby (*see* BURKE'S *Peerage*); *m.* 1890, Colin Frederick, *s.* of George William Campbell. *Addresses:* 17, Lowndes Square, S.W. 1; Everlands, Sevenoaks. (M3564)

CAMPBELL, Annie, M.B.E., *b.* 17 March, 1845; *d.* of Dr. Campbell, of Tarbert, Loch Tyne. *Educated:* Privately. *War Work:* Collecting and working for soldiers. *Address:* Kumard, Kiru, Argyllshire. (M1512)

CAMPBELL, Archibald, O.B.E.

CAMPBELL, Archibald Charles, O.B.E., *b.* 4 March, 1868; *s.* of Lieut.-Col. Colin Campbell, of 46th Regt.; *m.* Emma Olive, *d.* of — Ogilvie, of Yulgillar, N.S.W. *Educ.:* Wellington College. President of British Chamber of Commerce for Italy. *War Work:* Munitions. *Clubs:* Isthmian; Union (Geneva). (O3650)

CAMPBELL, Lieut. Archibald Sydney, O.B.E.

CAMPBELL, Archibald Young Gipps, C.I.E., C.B.E., *s.* of the late Archibald Samuels Campbell of Auchimbreck; *m.* 15 Dec. 1910, Frances Irene, 4th *d.* of George Edward Savill Young (*see* BURKE'S *Peerage*, Young, of North Dean); Late Sec. to British Red Cross Commissioner for France; Founder Central Prisoners of War Organisation. (C3107*a*)

CAMPBELL, Major Arthur Colin Clyde, O.B.E., *b.* 16 Aug. 1875; *s.* of William Campbell, of Uppingham and Stoke Dry, Rutland; *m.* Gladys Annie, *d.* of David Theophilus, of Port Elizabeth. *Educ.:* Uppngham. *War Work:* Royal Army Service Corps. *Address:* Greencroft, St. Albans. *Clubs:* Verulam Golf; United R.A.S.C.; R.A.C. (O2263)

CAMPBELL, Hon. Capt. Arthur Lang, M.B.E., Senior Assistant Censor, Second Military District, New South Wales, Australia. (M10257*e*)

CAMPBELL, Lieut.-Col. Charles, O.B.E., I.A.

CAMPBELL, Lieut.-Col. Charles Ferguson, O.B.E., C.I.E., *b.* 1863; *s.* of J. Scarlett Campbell; *m.* 1908, Emily Gertrude Lilian, *d.* of R. D. Steuart Muirhead, and *w.* of Lieut.-Col. A. Gould, 2nd Dragoon Guards. Entered The Buffs (E. Kent Regt.), 1882; became Capt. Indian Army, 1893; Major, 1901; Lieut.-Col. (ret.), 1908; served on N.W. Frontier of India, 1897–98; operations in Kurram Valley (medal with two clasps) and with Tirah Expedition; operations against Khani Khel Chamkani (clasp); was an Extra Equerry to Prince of Wales, 1906–10, and to King George V. 1910–12; acted as A.D.C. to Prince of Wales during tour in India, 1905–6; appointed one of H.M.'s Hon. Corps. of Gentlemen-at-Arms, 1912; Lieut.-Col. Gen. Reserve. *Addresses:* Salcey Lawn, Northampton; 10, Cambridge Square, W. *Club:* Naval and Military. (O8064)

CAMPBELL, Charles Ivor Rae, O.B.E., R.C.N.C., M.I.N.A., *b.* 12 April. 1878; *s.* of J. A. D. Campbell, of Science and Art Dept., S. Kensington; *m.* Edith Muriel, *d.* of T. Trenerry, of Clapham Park. *Educ.:* R.N. Eng. Coll., Keyham, and R.N.C. Greenwich. Naval Constructor; Superintendent of Airship Design and Construction, at Royal Airship Works, Bedford. *War Work:* Sent by Admiralty to United States as Overseer of submarines built by Bethlehem Steel Corp., Dec. 1914; returned Oct. 1915 and was placed in charge of newly formed Airship Design Section at Admiralty; remained on this work until 1920 and was appointed as above on transfer of Airship Work to Air Ministry. *Address:* Royal Airship Works, Cardington, nr. Bedford. (O10103)

CAMPBELL, Charles Stewart, C.B.E., I.C.S., *b.* 14 March, 1875; 3rd *s.* of Frederick Campbell, C.B., V.D., J.P., and *n.* of Sir John William Campbell, 1st Bart., C.B., of Ardnamurchan (*see* BURKE'S *Peerage*). *Address:* c/o Messrs. King, King & Co., Bombay. (C1067)

CAMPBELL, Lieut.-Col. Charles Vincent, O.B.E.

CAMPBELL, Clementina Henrietta, Mrs., M.B.E.

CAMPBELL, Colin, O.B.E.

CAMPBELL, Lieut.-Col. David Bishop, M.B.E.

CAMPBELL, Comm. Donald, O.B.E., R.N.

CAMPBELL, Donald, M.B.E.

CAMPBELL, Lieut. and Qr.-Mr. Donald George, M.B.E., S.L.I.

CAMPBELL, Douglas Robert, M.B.E.

CAMPBELL, Col. Duncan, O.B.E., J.P., D.L., *b.* 11 Sept. 1842; *s.* of James Archibald Campbell, J.P., D.L., of Inverneill, Ardrishaig, Argyll (*see* BURKE'S *Landed Gentry*); *m.* Isabel (who died 1911), *d.* of J. A. Tobin, of Eastham House, Cheshire. *Educ.:* St. Andrews, Fife. Chairman, Territorial Force Association for Argyll; Member County Council for Argyll. *War Work:* Chairman War Pensions Committee for Argyll; Hon. Sec. for Argyll Soldiers' and Sailors' Families Association. *Address:* Inverneill, Ardrishaig, Argyll. *Club:* Junior Carlton. (O10105)

CAMPBELL, Capt. Duncan, O.B.E., R.A.V.C.

CAMPBELL, Emily, Mrs. Muirhead, O.B.E.

CAMPBELL, Ethel Margaret, M.B.E.

CAMPBELL, Florence Ishbel, O.B.E., *b.* 11 July, 1877; *d.* of the late George William Campbell, of 22, Queen's Gate Gardens, S.W. *Educ.:* At Home. *War Work:* Organising Secretary Y.W.C.A. Munition Workers' Welfare Committee. *Address:* Woodview, Eastbourne. (O212)

CAMPBELL, Capt. Francis Ernest Archer, O.B.E.

CAMPBELL, Lieut. Frederick Harold, M.B.E., *b.* 16 Dec. 1879. *War Work:* Served in 60th Rifles throughout the War; proceeded to France with B.E.F. on 13th Aug. 1914; Commissioned for Service in the Field; twice wounded; invalided from the Army, Dec. 1919, as result of injuries received

on Service. *Address:* 15, Haward Road, Gunnersbury, W. 4. (M1513)

CAMPBELL, Col. George Polding, C.B.E. R.E.; N.W. Frontier of India 1897–8 (medal with clasp); Great War, 1914–19 (despatches). (C2031)

CAMPBELL, Georgina Jane, Mrs., M.B.E., *b.* 25 Oct. 1848; *d.* of Lionel Oliver, J.P., of Heacham, Norfolk; *m.* Rev. William Fraser, late Vicar of Kintbury, Berks., *s.* of Capt. W. C. J. Campbell, J.P., of Snettisham, Norfolk. *Educ.:* Privately. *War Work:* Commandant of Cliff House, V.A.D. Hospital, Hunstanton, Norfolk, from Feb. 1915. (M7604)

CAMPBELL, Gerald FitzGerald, C.B.E., B.A., Chevalier Légion d'Honneur, *b.* 26 April, 1862; *s.* of Col. Sir Edward FitzGerald Campbell, Bart., 60th Rifles. *Educ.:* Fettes College, Edinburgh; Clare College, Cambridge. Editorial Staff of "The Times." *War Work:* War Correspondent of "The Times" with the French Armies, 1914–18. *Address:* Albany Chambers, York St., Westminster. *Clubs:* M.C.C.; R.A.C. (C2500)

CAMPBELL, Geraldine Georgina, M.B.E.

CAMPBELL, Gilbert, M.B.E.

CAMPBELL, Gordon Charles Henry, O.B.E.

CAMPBELL, Sir Gordon Huntley, K.B.E., Chairman Collections Committee British Red Cross Society and Order of St. John. (K357)

CAMPBELL, Capt. Harold James, M.B.E., R.F.A.

CAMPBELL, Harry, C.B.E., M.B.E.

CAMPBELL, Henry Kenyon, M.B.E., *b.* 1873; *s.* of John Campbell, of Maryport; *m.* Mary, *d.* of Edward Hope, of Liverpool. *Educ.:* Privately. Chairman Carlisle Education Committee. *War Work:* Secretary, and subsequently General Manager, East Cumberland National Shell Factory, Carlisle. *Address:* 22, Warwick Square, Carlisle. (M1514)

CAMPBELL, Henry Samuel, M.B.E., *b.* 23 Sept. 1862; *s.* of the late Donald Campbell, of Tottenham; *m.* Florence Eliza, *d.* of W. D. Chidson, of Liverpool. *Educ.:* Privately. Collector H.M. Customs and Excise, Weymouth. *War Work:* Detection of enemy cargo and general Departmental War work in the Customs Service in Liverpool. *Address:* 15, Belvidere, Weymouth. (M7606)

CAMPBELL, Lieut.-Col. Hugh, D.S.O., O.B.E., Roy. Fus. (City of London Regt. (T.)). Served in Great War, 1914–19 (mentioned in despatches). (O8065)

CAMPBELL, Capt. Ian Percy Fitzgerald, O.B.E.

CAMPBELL, Ina, Mrs., M.B.E., *b.* 26 Jan. 1870; *d.* of J. W. Valentine, of Whiteabbey, Co. Antrim; *m.* Lloyd, *d.* of John Campbell, of Rathfern, Whiteabbey. *War Work:* Controller of free Rest House, for wounded soldiers and sailors, Belfast. *Address:* Glen House, Whiteabbey, Co. Antrim. (M7607)

CAMPBELL, Isabel Edwards, Mrs., M.B.E. (M10435)

CAMPBELL, James Alexander West, O.B.E., *b.* 6 June, 1866; *s.* of James Campbell, of Callander, N.B.; *m.* Jessie Frances, *d.* of James Parris Hind, of Brockley. *Educ.:* Roan School, Greenwich. Accountant, War Office. *War Work:* War Office. *Address:* St. Bede's, Sefton Road, Addiscombe. (O10107)

CAMPBELL, Comm. James Douglas, O.B.E., R.N.

CAMPBELL, John, O.B.E., I.C.S.

CAMPBELL, John, M.B.E.

CAMPBELL, Lieut. John, M.B.E., R.E.

CAMPBELL, Surg.-Comm. John Alexander Langdorf, O.B.E., R.N.

CAMPBELL, John Archibald, M.B.E., *b.* 12 Dec. 1862; *s.* of the late John Campbell, of Aberdeen and Woolwich Arsenal. *Educ.:* Woolwich. War Department Overseer of Shipping, Woolwich Dockyard. *War Work:* Special services rendered in various Engineering matters, under the Directorate of the Superintending Engineer and Constructor of Shipping (War Office). *Address:* 30, Beechhill Road, Eltham, S.E. 9. (M7609)

CAMPBELL, John Arthur, O.B.E., *b.* 7 Dec. 1877; *s.* of William Gamble, of North Runcton, King's Lynn; *m.* Mary Alicia, *d.* of Richard Worger, of London. *Educ.:* East Anglian School, Bury St. Edmund's. Theatre and Cinema Proprietor, at Grantham and Peterboro'; Proprietor, Theatre Royal, Grantham; Managing Director, The Picture House, Grantham; Lessee, Theatre Royal, Peterboro'. *War Work:* Services to the Troops at Grantham; Organiser of the Military Entertainments; Chairman, Grantham and District Belton Park Hospital Committee Comforts Fund. *Address:* Welby Gardens, Grantham. *Clubs:* Eccentric; The Road. (O10168)

CAMPBELL, Capt. John Cameron, O.B.E.

CAMPBELL, Lieut.-Col. John Hay, C.B.E., D.S.O., R.A.M.C., *b.* 31 Dec. 1871; *s.* of the late Maj.-Gen. T. Hay Campbell, R.A.; *m.* Clara Edith, *d.* of James Hedley, Esq., of Richmond, Yorks. *Educ.:* Tinton House School; St. Mary's Hospital. *Address:* c/o Messrs. Holt & Co., 3, Whitehall Place, S.W. (C1234)

CAMPBELL, John Honeyford, M.B.E. (M10379)

CAMPBELL, Major John MacKnight, O.B.E., M.C., R.A.M.C. (S.R.).

CAMPBELL, John Macmaster, C.B.E., J.P., *b.* 21 Feb. 1859; *s.* of George Campbell, of Inverness; *m.* Jane Christie, *d.* of Alexander Armstrong, of Arnprior, Stirlingshire. *Educ.:* Old Academy, Inverness. Sheriff Substitute of Kintyre, Argyllshire. *War Work:* Army Recruiting in Lanarkshire under Military Authorities; Convener, Campbeltown Branch, British Red Cross Society; Convener, Campbeltown and

Kintyre War Savings Committee ; Commissioner for Argyll-shire for Civil Liabilities Commission ; President, Union Jack Club, Campbeltown, for entertainment of Service men ; member, and for a period Chairman, Appeal Tribunal under Military Service Acts for Argyllshire. *Address :* Norwood, Campbeltown. *Clubs :* Campbeltown ; Liberal Glasgow. (C938)

CAMPBELL, John Maurice Hardman, O.B.E., M.B., B.Ch., *b.* 1891 ; *s.* of John Edward Campbell, F.R.S., of 14, Rawlinson Road, Oxford. *Educ. :* Winchester and New College Oxford ; Medical Registrar and Poulton Research Fellow at Guy's Hospital, London. *War Work :* Capt. R.A.M.C. (S.R.), Mesopotamia and N. Persia. *Address :* 8, Spa Mansions, Bermondsey, S.E. 1. (O6592)

CAMPBELL, John St. Clair, O.B.E.

CAMPBELL, Lieut.-Col. Joseph Alexander, O.B.E.

CAMPBELL, Capt. Lewis Gordon, O.B.E.

CAMPBELL, Lieut. Malcolm, M.B.E., R.A.F.

CAMPBELL, Lieut. Malcolm, M.B.E.

CAMPBELL, Capt. Malcolm Hay Alexander, O.B.E., I.A.

CAMPBELL, Nicol, M.B.E.

CAMPBELL, Olga Margaret, M.B.E. Quartermaster, Endell Street Military Hospital. (M10257f)

CAMPBELL, Lieut.-Col. Hon. Ralph Alexander, C.B.E., *b.* 18 Feb. 1877 ; 3rd *s.* of Hugh Frederick Vaughan, 4th Earl Cawdor (see BURKE'S *Peerage*) ; *m.* 1st, 1 Dec. 1906, Marjorie Theophila, *d.* of the late Sir John Arthur Fowler, 2nd Bart., *d.* 30 Nov. 1911 ; *m.* 2nd, 14 Jan. 1914, Marjorie Edith, *e. d.* of Horace George Devas, of Hartfield, Kent (see BURKE'S *Landed Gentry*). (C1502)

CAMPBELL, Robert Garrett, C.B.E., *b.* 25 Sept. 1858 ; *s.* of John Campbell, of Mossley, Belfast ; *m.* Alicia Anna, *d.* of Henry S. Ferguson, M.D., of Belfast. *Educ. :* Wellington College. *War Work :* Representative of the Irish Flax Spinners on the Flax Control Board, and Chairman of the Irish sub-committee of the Flax Control Board. *Address :* Coolgreany, Fortwilliam Park, Belfast. *Clubs :* Ulster ; Royal Automobile. (C1101)

CAMPBELL, Brevet Lieut.-Col. Robert Morris, C.B.E. *s.* of Rev. Edward Fitzhardinge Campbell, M.A., R.D., of Killyman Rectory, Moy, Co. Tyrone ; *m.* Louise Eleanor, *d.* of Alexander J. Henry, Esq., of Rathescar, Co. Louth. *Educ. :* Corrig School and Dungannon Royal School. Army Service Corps. *War Work :* War Office ; Salonica, D.A.Q.M.G. ; Italy, A.Q.M.G. *Address :* Killyman Rectory, Moy, Co. Tyrone. (C1398)

CAMPBELL, Capt. Roy Niel Boyd, O.B.E.

CAMPBELL, Lieut. Thomas, O.B.E.

CAMPBELL, Vera, M.B.E., *b.* 24 March, 1897 ; *d.* of Archibald Campbell, of Harrow-on-Hill. *Educ. :* Thame, Oxon. and Kensington College. *War Work :* Secretary and Assistant in Ministry of Information. *Address :* 21, Berners St., W. 1. (M3565)

CAMPBELL, Comm. Victor Lindsey Arbuthnot, D.S.O., O.B.E., *b.* 1875 ; *s.* of Capt. Hugh Campbell, R.N. ; *m.* 1903, Lilian, *d.* of Lieut.-Gen. Sir Henry Hamilton Settle, K.C.B., D.S.O. Retired as Lieut. R.N. ; reinstated as Comm. 1917 ; promoted Comm. for service with British Antarctic Expedition, 1910–13 ; served in Great War, 1914–19, Comdg. Drake Batt. R.N. Div. at Antwerp and in Gallipoli ; Comdg. H.M.S. "Milne" with Dover Patrol, H.M.S. "Warwick" at Zeebrugge and Ostend, and with N. Russia Expeditionary Force (despatches thrice, D.S.O. with bar, Croix de Guerre). *Address :* 34, Sloane Court West, Chelsea, S.W. (O4905)

CAMPBELL, William, M.B.E. (M10436)

CAMPBELL, Lieut. William Little, O.B.E.

CAMPBELL, Brig.-Gen. William Maclaren, M.V.O., O.B.E.

CAMPBELL, William Robert, M.B.E., *b.* 14 Oct. 1895 ; *s.* of Colin Campbell, of Newcastle-on-Tyne. *Educ. :* Rutherford College, Newcastle-on-Tyne, England. Chief Accountant, Canadian Press, Ltd., Toronto, Canada. *War Work :* Served with H.M. Forces from Sept. 1914, to Feb. 1918 ; promoted Sergeant ; wounded at 2nd Battle of Ypres, April, 1915 ; served on Headquarter's Recruiting Staff at York and Newcastle-on-Tyne from Nov. 1915, to Oct. 1917 ; Assist. Sec. Northern Region, Ministry of National Services from Nov. 1917, to Nov. 1918. *Addresses :* 7, Warrington Road, Newcastle-on-Tyne, and 2012, Queen St. East, Toronto, Canada. (M1515)

CAMPBELL, Archibald Hamilton James DOUGLAS-, O.B.E.

CAMPBELL, Mary Vereker HAMILTON-, O.B.E., *b.* 2 May, 1867 ; *d.* of the late Col. C. V. Hamilton-Campbell, of Nether-place, Mauchline, Ayrshire. *Educ. :* Privately. Vice-President S. & S. F.A., Ayr Division ; Vice-Chairman, Ayr Burgh Local War Pensions Committee. *War Work :* Joint Convener of Ayrshire County Association, under Director-General of Voluntary Organisations ; also acted as Hon. Sec. S. & S. F.A. (Ayr Division), from outbreak of War in Aug. 1914, for two months. *Address :* Auchincar, Ayr. *Clubs :* Queen's, Edinburgh. (O1184)

CAMPBELL, Lieut.-Col. Henry MONTGOMERY-, O.B.E.

CAMPBELL, Capt. William Henry McNeile VERSCHOYLE-, O.B.E., M.C., B.A.R.

CAMPDEN, Arthur Edward Joseph Noel, Viscount, O.B.E., T.D., Major the Gloucestershire Regt. (T.F.), J.P. Co. Rutland ; *b.* 30 June, 1884 ; *e.s.* of the 3rd Earl of Gainsborough ; *m.* Alice Mary, *e. d.* of Edward Eyre, 1, Belgrave Place, S.W. 1. *Educ. :* Downside ; Exeter Coll., Oxford.

Attaché to the British Legations at Christiania and Stockholm, 1908–12, and to the British Embassy at Washington, U.S.A., 1913–14, when he resigned ; accompanied Dr. Charles Harriss' Musical Festival throughout the British Empire, 1911 ; served Great War, 1915 ; D.A.M.S. Forces in Great Britain ; Horse Guards, 1917–19 ; mentioned for valuable services during the War ; organised, with Dr. Harriss, Imperial Concert of 10,000 voices in Hyde Park on Empire Day, 1919. *Address :* Exton Park, Oakham, Rutland. *Clubs :* White's ; Turf ; M.C.C. (O6976)

CAMPEY, Capt. Thomas Epton, M.B.E.

CAMPION, Charles Austin Bunworth, O.B.E.

CAMPION, Edwin William, O.B.E.

CAMPION, Mary Gertrude, O.B.E.

CAMPOS, Lieut.-Comm. Victor Ribeiro d'Almeida, O.B.E., R.N.R.

CANDLER, Edmund, C.B.E.

CANDLER, Henry, M.B.E., *b.* 15 Aug. 1864 ; *s.* of John Candler M.R.C.S., of Harleston, Norfolk. *Educ. :* Heversham. Clerk in the War Office (retired). *War Work :* On permanent staff of War Office. *Address :* Broad Eaves, Ashtead, Surrey. *Club :* Alpine. (M216)

CANDY, Capt. Algernon Henry Chester, C.B.E. ; *s.* of William Marshall Candy, of 183, Ashley Gardens, S.W. ; *m.* 1914, Isabel, *d.* of Henry Abraham, of Southampton. Capt. R.N. ; was Assist. Director of Torpedoes, 1917–19. (C2216)

CANDY, Major Cairns, O.B.E.

CANDY, Comm. Geoffrey Charles, O.B.E., R.N.

CANDY, Comm. John, O.B.E., R.N.

CANE, Arthur Beresford, C.B.E.

CANE, Arthur Skedling, D.S.O., O.B.E.

CANE, Lucy Mary, Mrs., C.B.E. ; *d.* of William Dermod O'Brien, of Cahermoyle, Ardagh, Co. Limerick (see BURKE'S *Peerage*, Michiquin, B.) ; *m.* 24 Jan. 1894, Arthur Beresford Cane, barrister-at-law, of 66, Elm Park Gardens, S.W. (C1172)

CANHAM, Lieut. Ernest Reginald, O.B.E., R.E.

CANNAN, Capt. Astley Cuthbert, M.B.E.

CANNAN, Eng.-Lieut.-Comm. George William, O.B.E., R.N.

CANNELL, Daniel George, M.B.E., *b.* 19 Aug. 1867 ; *s.* of James Cannell, of Chelsea ; *m.* Dorothy, *d.* of Dr. Arthur Thomas Lloyd Jones, of Wellington, Salop. *Educ. :* Westminster City School. Appointed Second Division Clerk in the Office of Works, Nov. 1885 ; transferred to Royal Hospital, Chelsea, Oct. 1890 ; appointed Staff Clerk Jan. 1904 ; transferred to Ministry of Pensions, Feb. 1917 ; became Principal Clerk, June, 1918. *War Work :* Work in connection with the award of pensions to soldiers disabled during the war. *Address :* 52, Sackville Gardens, Hove, Sussex. (M7611)

CANNELL, Lieut. Harry Hardman, O.B.E., *b.* 29, Oct. 1863 ; *s.* of Fleetwood James Cannell, of Wednesbury, Staffordshire ; *m.* Alice, *d.* of Absalom Evans, of Wolverhampton, Staffs. ; *Educ. :* Royal Orphanage, Wolverhampton. Sec. The Junior Imperial League ; acted as Chief Agent to the Conservative party at Walsall, North Monmouth, Shoreditch, Wednesbury (15 years), South Hackney and Peckham (8 years). *War Work :* Hon. Sec. Peckham Recruiting Committee ; enlisted for General Service under Derby Scheme, Dec. 1915 ; Hon. Sec. Oversea Forces Reception Committee which dealt with over one Million Oversea Troops ; attached as Hon. Lieut., Headquarters, Overseas Military Forces of Canada. *Address :* 1, Sanctuary Buildings, Great Smith Street, S.W. 1. (O10111)

CANNING, Joseph Herbert, O.B.E., F.C.S., *b.* 1875 ; *s.* of the late Thomas Canning, A.M.I.C.E., J.P., of Newport. Mon. ; *m.* Frances Edith, *d.* of the late Alonzo Townsend, of Newport, Mon. *Educ. :* Prior Park Coll., Bath. Engineer and Manager, Newport, Mon. Gas Company ; Member of Council, Institution of Gas Engineers, 1917–20 ; President, Wales and Monmouthshire Institution of Gas Engineers and Managers, 1910 ; Fellow of the Chemical Society. *War Work :* Supervising Engineer for Wales and Monmouthshire for the Gas Section of the Department of Explosives Supply of the Ministry of Munitions ; Member of Lord Moulton's Committee of Gas Engineers ; Divisional (Gas and Coke) Officer, Wales (Southern) Division, for the Board of Trade Coal Mines Department ; also furnished technical advice on gas coals to that Dept. *Address :* Crindau, Newport, Mon. *Club :* Constitutional (Newport). (O10112)

CANNING, Lionel Edgar, O.B.E.

CANNON, Percival Charles, O.B.E.

CANNON, Capt. William Butler, O.B.E., R.A.S.C.

CANNONS, Edwin Galton, O.B.E., *b.* 21 Feb. 1862 ; *s.* of Henry Edwin Cannons of Andover, Hants. *Educ. :* London. Master, Merchant Service, 32 years with Atlantic Transport Co., 27 years in Command, North Atlantic Service. *War Work :* Mediterranean Expeditionary Force, transporting troops, etc., Gallipoli, Salonika, Mesopotamia, and India. *Address :* 43. Walter Road, Swansea, Glam. (O1187)

CANNY, Lieut.-Col. James Clare Macnamara, C.B.E., D.S.O. *b.* 1877 ; *s.* of the late John Macnamara Canny. *Educ.* Uppingham, and Hertford Coll., Oxford. Entered Roy. Munster Fusiliers, 1899 ; became Capt. Army Ser. Corps, 1908 ; Major, 1914 ; Brevet Lieut.-Col. 1915 ; S. Africa, 1900 (despatches) ; Great War, 1914–18 (despatches, Brevet Lieut.-Col.) ; was an Assist. Director of Transportation, 1918–19. *Club :* Isthmian. (C1423)

CANSDALE, Capt. Cyril, O.B.E.

CANT, Lieut. John, M.B.E., R.N.V.R.

CANT, William Edmund, M.B.E., M.D., F.R.C.S., Knight

of Grace, Order of St. John of Jerusalem. *War Work:* Surgeon Auxillary Hospitals, Woodhouse, Gt. Horkesley, Colchester and Gostwycke, Colchester. *Address:* The Mill House, Lexden, Colchester. (M7612)

CANTLEY, John Cargill, M.B.E., *b.* 28 June, 1872; *s.* of the late James Rankine Cantley, of Edinburgh; *m.* Margaret Young, *d.* of the late John Aitken, of Edinburgh. *Educ.:* Church of Scotland Normal School, Edinburgh, and Edinburgh University. Solicitor, Town Clerk, etc. *War Work:* Hon. Sec. St. Andrews National Relief Fund and War Savings Committee; Clerk, Local Military Tribunal; Clerk and Executive Officer, Food Control Committee; Local Fuel Overseer; Hon. Treas. St. Andrews Branch of Queen Mary's Needlework Guild, Belgian Refugees Fund, Red Cross Special Efforts, Serbian Relief Fund and many others; Organised a very large number of Flag Days and other special efforts on behalf of War Charities and was greatly helped by his wife, who, in addition to other war service, acted as Hon. Sec. for over 4 years in connection with a large Canteen for Soldiers and Sailors. *Address:* Woodlands, St. Andrews. (M7613)

CANTLIE, Col. Sir James, K.B.E., M.B. (Aberdeen), LL.D. (Aberdeen), F.R.C.S. (Eng.), R.A.M.C. (T.), *b.* 17 Jan. 1851; *s.* of Wm. Cantlie, of Dufftown, Banffshire; *m.* Mabel Barclay, *d.* of Robert Barclay Brown, of Barnes. *Educ.:* Milner Institution, Fochabers; Aberdeen University; Charing Cross Hospital, London. Surgeon, Seamen's Hospital, London; Lecturer, London School of Tropical Medicine. *War Work:* Hon. Col. R.A.M.C. (T.); Council British Red Cross Society; Principal of College of Ambulance. *Addresses:* 23, Harley St., London; The Kennels, Cottered, Buntingford, Herts. (K55)

CANTLIE, Mabel Barclay, Lady, O.B.E., *d.* of Robert Barclay Brown, of Lindores, Putney; *m.* 7 June, 1884, Sir James, K.B.E., LL.D., M.A., M.B., C.M., F.R.C.S., D.P.H., Hon. Col. R.A.M.C. (T.), *s.* of William Cantlie, of Kirthmore, Banffshire. *Addresses:* 23, Harley Street, W. 1; The Kennels, Cottered, Buntingford, Herts. (O3653)

CAPE, Thomas, M.B.E., J.P., *b.* 5 Oct. 1868; *s.* of Wm. and Catherine Cape, of Crag Head, Durham. *Educ.:* Broughton Endowed School. Miners' Agent. *War Work:* Member of Cumberland County Appeal Tribunal; Workmen's Assessor at the Colliery Recruiting Committee; Member of County Pensions Committee. *Address:* 91, Harrington Road, Workington, Cumberland. (M8)

CAPITO, Charles Erik, O.B.E.

CAPLETON, Ernest Carlile, M.B.E.

CAPON, Capt. Herbert William Thomas, M.B.E.

CAPON, Lieut. Selwyn Norman, M.B.E., R.N.R.

CAPPER, Lieut.-Comm. Henry Douglas, O.B.E., R.N.

CAPRON, Athol John, O.B.E., M.Inst.C.E., M.I.Mech.E., *b.* 3 Jan. 1859; *s.* of the late Rev. G. H. Capron, of Southwick Hall, Oundle, Northants; *m.* Catherine, *d.* of William Dickinson, of Warham Road, Croydon. *Educ.:* Wellington; King's College, London. Managing Director of Davy Bros., Ltd., Engineers, Park Iron Works, Sheffield; Vice-Chairman of Newton, Chambers & Co., Ltd., Thorncliffe, Sheffield; President of the Sheffield and District Engineering Trades Employers Association. *War Work:* Provided machinery for the production of war materials, including hydraulic presses for the manufacture of guns, shells, explosives and Admiralty requirements; also rolling mills for the manufacture of steel and shipbuilding material. *Clubs:* Constitutional, London; The Club, Sheffield. (O214)

CAPSTICK, Major Hugh Patrick, M.B.E., M.C. Agent. *Club:* Birch Lane, Longsight, Manchester. (M7012)

CAPSTICK, Dr. John Walton, O.B.E., D.Sc. (Manch.), M.A. (Camb.), *b.* 31 Aug. 1858; *s.* of Thomas Capstick, of Lancaster. *Educ.:* Manchester and Cambridge Universities. Fellow of Trinity Coll., Cambridge. *War Work:* In 1915 served with the French Army in the Vosges as Ambulance Driver; During 1916, 1917 and most of 1918 was Inspector of shells, guns and mines for the Admiralty; for a few months at the end of the war, was Superintendent of the Admiralty Physical Laboratory. *Address:* Trinity Coll., Cambridge. (O10113)

CARBERY, Lieut.-Col. Edward Oliver Bamford, O.B.E., M.B., R.A.F.

CARBERRY, Lieut.-Col. Anderson Robert Dillon, C.B.E., F.R.C.S. Lieut.-Col. New Zealand Med. Corps; served in Great War, 1915-9 (despatches). (C1849)

CARBONELL, Edith Frances, M.B.E.; *d.* of the late John Carbonell, of Fairleigh, Reigate. *War Work:* Head of Addressograph Department, Central Prisoners of War Committee, Thurloe Place. *Address:* Cranford Lodge, Reigate, Surrey. (M1516)

CARBUTT, Francis, C.B.E., *b.* 30 April, 1863; *s.* of George Henry Carbutt; *m.* E. Pauline, *d.* of Charles H. Runge. *Educ.:* Privately. *War Work:* Under the Joint Committee of the British Red Cross and the Order of St. John of Jerusalem in England. *Addresses:* 19, Hyde Park Gardens, London; Shovelstrode Manor, East Grinstead, Sussex. (C2504)

CARD, Ernest, M.B.E.

CARDEN, Major Edward David, O.B.E., R.E.

CARDEN, Rev. John, C.B.E., M.C.; *b.* 1882. *Educ.:* Dulwich Coll.; is in Holy Orders of the Church of Rome, and a Chap. to the Forces; served in Great War, 1916-19 as Assist. Principal Chap. 1st Army (despatches). *Address:* 3, Prospect Row, Old Brompton, Kent. (C1235)

CARDEN, Capt. John Valentine, M.B.E.

CARDEN, Mary Gertrude, Mrs., O.B.E., *d.* of Henry Blaine, M.L.A., of Grahamstown, South Africa; *m.* Maj.-Gen. George, *s.* of Thomas Carden, of Worcester. *Educ.:* Privately. *War Work:* Hon. Sec. and Organiser, Women Patrols, National Council of Women. *Address:* Lulworth Court Road, Eltham, Kent. *Club:* Forum. (O215)

CARDEW, Evelyn Roberta, Lady, C.B.E., *e. d.* of the late E. J. Firth; *m.* 2 Nov. 1886, Sir Alexander Gordon, K.C.S.I., M.A., I.C.S., *s.* of Rev. J. W. Cardew, M.A., Vicar of West Knoyle, Wilts, and Margaret, 2nd *d.* of the late Michael Francis Gordon of Abergeldie Castle, Aberdeenshire. *Addresses:* The Albany, Madras; St. Margarets, Ootacamund, India. (C1068)

CARDEW, Major Francis Gordon, O.B.E.

CARDEW, Col. George Arthur, O.B.E., V.D., M.R.C.S., *b.* 18 June, 1856. *Educ.:* Queen's Coll., Birmingham; University College Hospital, London. Surgeon. *War Work:* Medical Officer, St. John V.A.D. Hospital, Cheltenham. *Address:* 5, Fauconberg Villas, Cheltenham. (O10114)

CARDEW, Col. George Hereward, C.B.E., D.S.O., *b.* 3 Jan. 1861; *s.* of Rev. Geo. Cardew, of St. Minver, Liss. *Educ.:* Haileybury. *War Work:* A.A. & Q.M.G., 1st Mounted Division, Central Force, 1914-16; Group Commander, Labour Corps, B.E.F., France, 1917-18; assisted as a voluntary worker, War Pensions Committee, Portsmouth, 1919. *Club:* Army and Navy. (C1504)

CARDONA, Lewis BORG-, M.B.E., *b.* 3 June, 1883; *s.* of the late Alexander Borg-Cardona E.T.C., of Malta; *m.* Josephine, *d.* of the late John Calleja Schembri, Notary Public, of Malta. *Educ.:* St. Ignatius College, St. Julians, Malta. Joined the Malta Civil Service in Feb. 1901; served in the Secretariat, the Post Office Department and the Audit Office. *War Work:* Sec. to the Supplies and Prices Board; sec. to the Wheat Board from the date of the constitution of the two Boards in July, 1916, and Dec. 1916, respectively, to June, 1916, the date of their disbandment; in May, 1917 appointed Head Clerk in the newly instituted Food and Commerce Control Office, a position held until the suppression of the Office in March, 1919; since 1 April, 1919, Chief Executive Officer and Sec. to the Control Board; in charge of the operations of the Profiteering Act (Control of Prices) since its inception in Aug. 1917; in May, 1918 refused permission to accept a Commission as Lieutenant R.N.V.R., the Civil Authorities' view being that services in Food Control Work were indispensable. *Address:* 68, Windsor Terrace, Sliema, Malta. (M6422)

CARDWELL, Major Charles Alexander, O.B.E., *b.* 25 1876; *s.* of Thomas Holme Cardwell, of Newnton House, Tetburg, Glos.; *m.* Catherine, Elizabeth, *d.* of Colonel Arthur Leycester Wynter, late of K.O.S.B. *Educ:* Harrow. 2nd Oxfordshire Light Infantry, 1897-1906; 3rd Oxfordshire Light Infantry (Militia), 1906-8; Oxfordshire and Bucks Light Inf. Special Reserve of Officers, 1908, to date. *War Work:* D.A.A.G. (O6451)

CARDWELL, Capt. William Arthur, O.B.E., M.B.

CARDY, William Edward Jesse, M.B.E.

CARELESS, Beatrice, Ann, M.B.E.

CAREW, Lieut.-Col. Frank John, O.B.E.

CAREY, Albert John, M.B.E., R.A.S.C.

CAREY, Alfred David, O.B.E., R.A.F.

CAREY, Arthur William Joseph Greenwood Macleod, M.B.E.

CAREY, Lieut. Basil Ernest, O.B.E., R.N.V.R.

CAREY, Major-Gen. Carteret Walter, C.B.E., M.V.O., *b.* 1853; *s.* of the Rev. Carteret Priaulx Carey; *m.* 1890, Florence Margaret, O.B.E. (*q.v.*), *d.* of W. Ravenhill Stock, of Clevedon, Somerset. Entered Highland L.I. 1873; became Capt. 1882; Major, 1890; Lieut.-Col. 1900; Brevet Col. 1904; Col. 1906; retired 1910; served with Egyptian Expedition 1882; at battle of Tel-el-Kebir (despatches, medal with clasp, bronze star, 4th class Medjidieh); on N.-W. Frontier of India, 1897-8; at capture of Tanga Pass (despatches, medal with clasp); was Comdg. No. 9 Dist. (E. Coast) 1906-10; appointed Gov. of Mil. Knights of Windsor, 1913 (with rank of Maj.-Gen.); acted as Gov. and Constable of Windsor Castle during War 1914-18; received Coronation medals, 1902 and 1911. *Address:* Governor's Tower, Windsor Castle. *Club:* Army and Navy. (C2086)

CAREY, Capt. Geoffrey Newman, M.B.E. Chevalier Star of Roumania with swords, Manchester Regt., *b.* 30 May, 1894; *s.* of Edward Delves Carey. *Educ.:* Privately; Birkbeck College; Brussels; Sandhurst. *War Work:* Enlisted as Private 5 Aug. 1914; joined B.E.F. France, 26 Aug. 1914; gazetted 2nd Battn. Manchester Regt. 6 April, 1916; severely wounded, Battle of the Somme, 1 July, 1916; appointed Executive Shipping and Transport Officer for (*a*) Russian Government Committee, (*b*) Munitions Account, Roumanian Government Committee, (*c*) American Expeditionary Forces, on the staff of the Commission Internationale de Ravitaillement, sub-section, Foreign Office, from Sept. 1916, to Oct. 1918; joined Salonica Army 22 Dec. 1918; appointed to Military Operating and Control Staff of the Chemin de Fer Ottoman d'Anatolie, Constantinople, as Chef du Service Commercial, Chef du Personnel, and Directeur de Ravitaillement, 5 Jan. 1919. *Club:* Isthmian. (M7619)

CAREY, Hattie Maud, M.B.E., Q.M.A.A.C.

CAREY, Joseph James Seymour, M.B.E.

CAREY, Major Leslie Clement, O.B.E.

CAREY, Lieut.-Col. Lewis Adolphus De Vic, O.B.E.

CAREY, Hon. Lucius Plantagenet, O.B.E. (O8763)

CAREY, Surg.-Lieut. **Richard Stocker**, O.B.E., R.N.

CAREY, Capt. **Robert Edward**, M.B.E.

CAREY, Major **Rowland Dobree**, O.B.E., R.A.F.,

CAREY, Capt. **Walter**, C.B.E. ; Capt. R.N. Rendered services at Roy. Naval Depot, Crystal Palace, during Great War. (C1162)

CAREY, Major **William Havilland**, O.B.E.

CAREY, Florence Margaret, Mrs. CARTERET-, O.B.E., *d.* of W. Ravenhill Stock, of Clevedon, Somerset, *m.* Maj.-Gen. Carteret Walter, C.B.E., M.V.O. (*q.v.*), *s.* of the Rev. Carteret Priaulx Carey. *Address :* Governor's Tower, Windsor Castle. (O11897)

CARGILL, Alexander, O.B.E., J.P. for the County of the City of Edinburgh, *b.* 7 Jan. 1851 ; *s.* of James Cargill, M.A., of Aberdeen and Edinburgh ; *m.* Jane, *d.* of David Russell, of Linlithgow. *Educ. :* Privately and Edinburgh University. Manager of Edinburgh Savings Bank, with which institution he has had over 56 years' service. *War Work :* Member of Mr. McKenna's (Chancellor of the Exchequer) Committee on War Loans for small investors (Mr. E. S. Montague, Chairman) ; and original member of Scottish War Savings Committee, Edinburgh, and Convener of the Committee's Publicity and Advertising Schemes ; also Sergeant in the Edinburgh Special Constables from the first. *Address :* 18, Wester Coats Gardens, Edinburgh. *Club :* Scottish Conservative. (O1188)

CARGILL, John Henry, M.B.E., *b.* 20 July 1880 ; *s.* of Dr. Jasper Cargill, of St. Andrew, Jamaica ; *m.* Gwendolen Isabel, *s.* of Samuel Halton Morris, of Bluecastle Est. Westmoreland, Jamaica. *Educ. :* Kingston Church of England Grammar School, Kingston, Jamaica. Solicitor. *War Work :* Raised and commanded the St. Andrew Cos. Jamaica Reserve Regiment from Oct. 1914–19 ; Hon. Sec. The Jamaica Aeroplane Fund Committee. *Address :* Kingston, Jamaica, B.W.I. *Clubs :* West India, London ; Liguanea, Jamaica ; Overseas. (M2932)

CARL, Frederick, O.B.E.

CARLE, James, M.B.E., *b.* 3 Jan. 1871 ; *s.* of Alexander Carle, of New Pitsligo, Aberdeenshire ; *Educ :* Aberdeen University. Advocate and Notary Public ; Member, Aberdeen Educational Trust Juvenile Auxiliary Board of Trade ; Sec. for various Companies, and Sec. Road Transport Section Ministry of Food, Aberdeen area. *War Work :* Legal Military Representative, Ministry of Food ; Distribution Officer for margarine and Sec. Road Transport Board, Aberdeen. *Address :* 217, Union Street, Aberdeen. (M7621)

CARLESS, Col. A., C.B.E., M.B., M.C.R.S. ; T. Col. Army Med. Staff : served in Great War, 1914–19 (despatches). (C1505)

CARLESS, Lieut. William Edward, M.B.E.

CARLETON, Lieut.-Col. the Hon. Dudley Massey Pigott, O.B.E., J.P. *b.* 26 Feb. 1876 ; *s.* of The Baroness Dorchester and the late Capt. Francis Paynton Pigott (16th Lancers), of Greywell Hill ; *m.* Hon. Kathleen Winchfield, Hants., *d.* of William 6th Lord de Blaquiere (died 1920), of Brockworth Manor, Glos., and 3, The Circus, Bath. *Educ. :* Wellington College ; R.M.C. Sandhurst (*see* BURKE'S *Peerage*). Joined 9th Lancers 1896 ; retired 1904 ; J.P. for Hants. ; County Councillor for Hants for six years, previously Director of S. F. Edge, Ltd., previously Managing Director of R Hoe and Co., Printing Press Engineers, retired ; rejoined Army, Aug. 1914 ; served in France, Egypt, Macedonia, 2nd in Command Derbyshire Yeomanry, July, 1917 appointed Military Secretary to General Sir George Milne, Commanding British Salonika Force. *Addresses :* 21, Upper Berkeley Street, London, W. 1 ; Hamlet Lodge, Cowes, I. of Wight. *Clubs :* Carlton, Cavalry, Royal Automobile, Hurlingham. (O6452)

CARLETON, Col. Montgomery Launcelot, C.B.E., *b.* 1861 ; *s.* of the late Gen. Henry Alexander Carleton, C.B. ; *m.* 1908, Marguerite Helen, *d.* of Sir Lionel Edward Darell, 5th Bt. Col. and Hon. Brig.-Gen. (ret.) ; served in Great War, 1914–19 (despatches). (C1506)

CARLILE, Charles, M.B.E., Head Master, Boys' National School, Brixham. *War Work :* Hon. Sec. to Local Comm. for War Savings, Brixham, since its inception. *Address :* New Road, Brixham, Devon. (M7622)

CARLILE, Sir (Edward) Hildred, Bart., C.B.E., T.D., J.P., D.L. (*see* BURKE'S *Peerage*), *b.* 10 July, 1852 ; *s.* of Edward Carlile, of Richmond Hill, Surrey ; *m.* Isabella, 3rd *d.* of C. Hanbury, of Little Berkhampstead, Herts. *Educ. :* Privately. J.P. and D.L., Herts. ; J.P., West Riding of Yorkshire ; formerly Captain 2nd W. Yorks. Yeomanry ; Lieut.-Col. 2nd V.B. West Riding Regt., 1898–1910 ; Hon. Col. of the Battalion (now 5th Batt. W. Riding Regt.), since 1906 ; T.D. ; M.P. (Unionist), Mid-Herts., 1906–19 ; Member, House of Laity, Canterbury Province. *War Work :* Red Cross ; Chairman, Board of Trade Committee on Work of National Importance, 1916–19. *Address :* Ponsbourne Park, near Hertford, Herts. *Club :* Carlton. (C2505)

CARLILE, William Walter, C.B.E., O.B.E., J.P., D.L., *b.* 15 June, 1862 ; *s.* of James William Carlile, of Ponsbourne Park, Hertford ; *m.* Blanche Anne, *d.* of Rev. E. Cadogan, of Wicken, Northants. *Educ. :* Harrow ; Clare College, Cambs. M.P. for North Bucks., 1895–1906. *War Work :* 1914 Star and General Service Medal for work connected with "missing," and "Graves Registration" with Fabian Ware's unit in Flanders and France ; afterwards Military Representative for Recruiting at home. *Address :* Gayhurst, Newport Pagnell, Bucks. *Clubs :* Carlton ; Junior Carlton ; Windham ; Bath ; R.A.C. (O217)

CARLISLE, Rev. John Charles, C.B.E. Vice-President of the Baptist Union. *War Work :* Lectured in Canada and America during the War. (C3135)

CARLISLE, Lieut. and Qr.-Mr. William, M.B.E.

CARLTON, Arthur Roscoe, C.B.E., J.P.; *s.* of Alfred Roscoe, of Brighton, Sussex. High Sheriff of the City of Worcester, 1913–15 ; Mayor, 1916–19 ; Deputy-Mayor, 1919–20 ; served for six years on Devonport County Council, and six years Devonport Board of Guardians. *War Work :* Raised over £20,000 for War Funds and Charities at Bath, Barry, Worcester, Gainsborough, etc. ; organised the formation of the Worcester Volunteer Transport Corps, of which he is Commanding Officer ; founded the British-American Fellowship ; and originated the scheme of hospitality to U.S.A. soldiers in connection with the Fellowship ; originated the "Homes" for Disabled Sailors and Soldiers in the City of Worcester—now being built ; was Sub-Commissioner of National Service under Mr. Neville Chamberlain ; Chairman of the Land Cultivation, Recruiting, Worcester War Relief, and many other committees. *Address :* Colehurst, Worcester. (C2506)

CARLTON, Lieut.-Comm. George Frederick, O.B.E., R.N.R.

CARLTON, Thomas, O.B.E.

CARLYLE, Lieut.-Col. Thomas, O.B.E.

CARMICHAEL, Andrew, M.B.E., *b.* 1857 ; *s.* of Andrew Carmichael, of Greenock ; *m.* Isabel Somerville, *d.* of George Allan, of Greenock. *Educ. :* Greenock Academy and Merchiston Castle. *War Work :* Chief Inspector, Special Constabulary ; services in connection with Recruiting, National Service, and War Saving Certificates. *Address :* 41, Union Street, Greenock. (M7623)

CARMICHAEL, Evelyn George Massey, O.B.E., *b.* 1871 ; *s.* of Lieut.-Col. George Lynedoch Carmichael, K.L.H., 95 Regt., Chief Constable of Worcestershire ; *m.* Dorothea Helen Mary Elizabeth Sutherland, *d.* of Sir James Colquhoun, Bart., of Luss, Lord Lieutenant of Dumbartonshire (*see* BURKE'S *Peerage*). *Educ. :* Harrow, Oriel Coll., Oxford. Chairman, Walsall Court of Referees. *War Work :* Chairman, Coventry, Worcestershire, and Herefordshire Munition Tribunals ; Military Representative (Colliery Courts) Shropshire, Herefordshire, Radnorshire. *Addresses :* 10, King's Bench Walk, Temple, London, E.C. ; Meretown House, Newport, Shropshire. *Clubs :* Bath ; Marylebone ; I Zingari ; Free Forester Cricket. (O10116)

CARMICHAEL, Gertrude, Mrs., O.B.E.

CARMICHAEL, Sir James, K.B.E., *b.* 1858 ; *s.* of the late Robert Carmichael, of Meiklour, Perthshire ; *m.* 1884, Annie, *d.* of James Reid, of Ruthven, Forfarshire. *Educ. :* Privately. A J.P. for London ; Past Pres. Institute of Builders and London Master Builders' Asso., a Member of Standing Council thereof ; Member Govt. Surplus Property Disposal Board ; Chm. of Munitions Works Board, Ministry of Munitions, 1917–19 ; since when he has been Director-Gen. of Housing in England and Wales. *Address :* Redclyffe, Ullathorne Road, Streatham Park, S.W.16. *Club :* Reform. (K206)

CARMICHAEL, Major James Charles Gordon, O.B.E., M.B., Ch.B., D.P.H., *b.* 27 Aug. 1878 ; *s.* of the late Col. J. C. G. Carmichael, I.M.S. ; *m.* Hilda Sade, *d.* of Lieut.-Col. J. Armstrong, I.M.S. (ret.). *Educ. :* United Service College, and Edinburgh University. R.A.M.C. (regular). O.C. 166 Combined Field Ambulance E.E.F., Egypt. *War Work :* O.C. Forrest Hospital Malta ; O.C. St. Andrews General Hospital Malta, 1914, to 1917 ; O.C. 29, Casualty Clearing Station, France ; O.C. 29 Casualty Clearing Station, Germany, 1917–19. *Address :* c/o Messrs. Holt and Co., 3 Whitehall Place, London, S.W. 1. (O5076)

CARMICHAEL, Capt. James Duncan, O.B.E., R.E., *b.* 28 May, 1890 ; *s.* of J. D. Carmichael, of South Shields ; *m.* Nora, *d.* of W. G. Merriman, of Harton, Co. Durham. *Educ. :* Westoe High School. Ironfoundry, Works Manager. *War Work :* Served with the R.E. in France over 4 years. *Address :* Belgrave Gardens, Harton, nr. South Shields. *Clubs :* Masonic and Borough, South Shields. (O5077)

CARMICHAEL, Brevet Lieut.-Col. James Forrest Halketh, C.M.G., C.B.E., late R.E., *b.* 8 July, 1868 ; *s.* of Charles Paget Carmichael, C.S.I. ; *m.* Winifred Mary, *d.* of Rev. John M. Webster, M.A. Served in Burmah, 1893, and in Tirah, 1897–8 (medal, two clasps) ; has Legion of Honour. *War Work :* 1915–17, Asst. Controller Raw Materials, Ministry of Munitions ; 1917–18, Chairman of Alloy Steel Committee ; 1919, Chief Engineer to Crown Agents. *Address :* Artillery Mansions, Victoria St., S.W. 1. *Club :* United Service. (C125)

CARMICHAEL, Montgomery, O.B.E., *b.* 17 May, 1857 ; *s.* of John Carmichael, of Corosal ; *m.* Maud, *d.* of John William Parker, publisher, West Strand. *Educ. :* Brewood Grammar School ; Bonn. H.M. Consul at Leghorn ; H.M. Consul-General to the Republic of San Marino. *War Work :* On duty at Leghorn throughout the war. *Address :* British Consulate, Leghorn. (O10117)

CARMICHAEL, Winifred Mary, Mrs., M.B.E., *b.* 24 Sept., 1885 ; *d.* of the Rev. John Mackeesor Webster, M.A. ; *m.* Lieut.-Col. James Forrest Halkett Carmichael, C.M.G., C.B.E., R.E. ; *s.* of Charles Paget Carmichael, C.S.I. *War Work :* Was president, jointly with Dame Mary Hon. Lady Monro, of The Hon. Lady Monro War Hospital Supply Depot, which was started in Sept. 1914, by Mrs. Carmichael in her own house for the purpose of supplying the needs of the 3rd London

General Hospital; and later formed a unit representing Old Westminster and Pimlico in the Director-General's voluntary organisation scheme for the supply of Military Hospitals. *Address :* 5, Artillery Mansions. (M7624)

CARMODY, Capt. Ernest Patrick, M.B.E., M.R.C.S., L.R.C.P. (Lond.), *b.* 27 March, 1883; *s.* of Prof. P. Carmody, F.I.C., F.C.S., of Lostwithiel, Cornwall. *Educ. :* Queen's Royal Coll., Trinidad; St. Bart.'s Hospital. Physician and Surgeon at Tilehurst, Reading; Neurologist to the Ministry of Pensions; for Berkshire; Chairman of Officers' Boards; Member of the Reading Pathological Society. *War Work :* Civil Surgeon, Reading War Hospital; Capt. R.A.M.C. and R.A.F.M.S.; M.O. to 14th Hants Regt. in France; Sen. Med. Off. for Reading in the R.A.F., while Capt. R.A.F.M.S., and in charge of No. 1 School of Aeronautics. *Address :* Tilehurst, Reading. (M5935)

CARNAC, Wilfred, M.B.E. (M10345)

CARNAC, Lilian Muriel RIVETT-, Mrs., M.B.E.

CARNEGIE, Arthur Alexander, O.B.E.

CARNEGIE, Col. David, C.B.E., F.R.S.E., M.Inst.C.E., etc., *b.* 1868; *s.* of David Carnegie, of Aberdeen; *m.* Frances Ellen, *d.* of Thomas Howard Lloyd, of Leicester. *Educ. :* Gordon's College, Aberdeen, and Royal College of Science, London. Civil and Ordnance Engineer; Hon. Consulting Technical Ordnance Adviser, Canadian Govt.; Oversea Member, Labour Committee, Canadian Govt.; author, "Liquid Steel" and "Can Church and Industry Unite," etc. *War Work :* Member and Ordnance Adviser, Shell Committee, Canada, 1915; and subsequently Member and Ordnance Adviser of Imperial Munitions Board, Canada, 1915–19; Chairman of Commission (Canadian Govt.) to inquire into the feasibility of refining zinc and copper in Canada, 1915; Chairman, Inventions Committee, Canada; Chairman, Committee Changes in Munitions Design. *Address :* Woodlands, Beckenham Hill, Kent. *Club :* British Empire. (C2507)

CARNEGIE, Francis, O.B.E., M.I.C.E., M.I.M.E., *b.* 9 Feb. 1874; *s.* of David Carnegie, of Aberdeen, N.B.; *m.* Theodora, *d.* of Rev. E. W. Matthews, of Bembridge, I. of W. *Educ. :* St. Clement's School, Aberdeen; East London Technical Coll. Appointed to Managerial Staff, Ordnance Factories, as Shop Manager, 1904; as Manager, 1908; as Assist. Superintendent, 1916. *War Work :* Munitions, the manufacture of rifles, bayonets, scabbards, machine-guns, cavalry swords, and bayonets, etc. (O10119)

CARNEGIE, William, M.B.E., M.Inst.C.E., M.I.Mech.E., *b.* 23 May, 1872; *s.* of David Carnegie, of Aberdeen; *m.* Mary Wallace, *d.* of John Brodie, of Woolwich. *Educ. :* Aberdeen and London. Manager, Grimesthorpe Steel Works, Cammell, Laird & Co., Ltd., Sheffield. *War Work :* Manager, Shell Dept., Cammell, Laird & Co. *Address :* Firshill House, Pitsmoor, Sheffield. (M217)

CARNEGIE, Edward Hugo Wakefield FULLERTON-, O.B.E., *b.* 5 Aug. 1870; *s.* of Major-Gen. George Fullerton-Carnegie, I.A.; *m.* Emilie Prange, of Concordia Estancia, Uruguay. *Educ. :* Privately; Dresden and Paris. *War Work :* Department of Information, Foreign Office (temporary clerk in the Political Intelligence Department); Peace Conference in Paris. *Address :* Aytonhill, Newburgh, Fife, N.B. *Club :* St. James. (O10118)

CARNEGIE, Agnes, Mrs. LINDSAY-, M.B.E.

CARNEGY, Violet, Mrs., M.B.E., *b.* 1897; *d.* H. W. Henderson, of 9, Princes Gardens, S.W.; *m.* Capt. Uchtred Elliott Carnegy D.S.O., M.C., *s.* of Major F. E. Carnegy and Mrs. Carnegy of Lour (*see* BURKE's *Landed Gentry*). *War Work :* Lady President of H.M. Factory, Watford, Herts. *Address :* Lour, Forfar, N.B. (M3710)

CARNLEY, Mary, Mrs., M.B.E., R.A.F.

CARO, Lieut. Phillip, M.B.E.

CAROLIN, Major George Tevers, O.B.E.

CARPENTER, Capt. Alexander Scott Jarvis, O.B.E., *b.* 5 Feb. 1878; *s.* of Stephen Carpenter, of Sutton, Surrey; *m.* Eliza, *d.* of William Ramsey, of Sunderland. *Educ. :* Sutton, Surrey. Master Mariner. *War Work :* Command of Transports carrying ammunition etc., from Canada to France and Salonica; in action with submarine, navigating a transport in danger zone single-handed. *Address :* 17, Mount Road West, Sunderland, Durham. (O10120)

CARPENTER, Charles Claude, C.B.E., D.Sc., Knight of Grace of St. John of Jerusalem, M.Inst.C.E., F.C.S., *b.* 1858; *s.* of William Richard Carpenter, R.N., of Woolwich; *m.* Amy Florence, *d.* of Richard Phillips, of Kensington. *War Work :* Consulted by, and carried out work for, Ministry of Munitions. *Address :* 157, Victoria Street, Westminster. *Clubs :* Arts; St. Stephen's. (C2508)

CARPENTER, Charles Howard, O.B.E., *b.* 7 June, 1878; *s.* of John Howard Carpenter, of Kingstown, Ireland, and Teddington, Middlesex; *m.* Beatrice Violet Wynn Isdell, of Hampton Hill, Middlesex. *Educ. :* Christ's Hospital. Barrister-at-Law. Secretary of Chartered Institute of Secretaries of Joint Stock Companies, etc. *War Work :* Lieut. in Royal Naval Volunteer Reserve, attached to Director of Intelligence at Malta; assisted Director-General of Voluntary Organisations working for the fighting forces and the hospitals for wounded; special constable in City of London Police Reserve. *Addresses :* Cornwall Lodge, Hampton Hill, Middlesex; London Wall, E.C.; 4, King's Bench Walk, Temple, E.C. (O1189)

CARPENTER, Capt. Geoffrey Douglas Hale, M.B.E.

CARPENTER, Shipwright-Lieut. George, M.B.E., R.N.

CARPENTER, Capt. Henry, O.B.E., M.C., R.A.S.C.

CARPENTER, Ethel, Mrs. BOYD-, M.B.E., *b.* 2 Jan. 1873; *d.* of Sir Francis Ley, Bart., of Epperstone Manor, Notts, and Lealholm. Yorks (*see* BURKE's *Peerage*); *m.* Henry John, *s.* of the Rt. Rev. William Boyd-Carpenter, K.C.V.O., Bishop of Ripon (died 1918). *Educ. :* Cheltenham Ladies' Coll. *War Work :* Red Cross, Cairo, Egypt. *Address :* Riversea, Kingswear, S. Devon. *Club :* Ladies' Army and Navy. (M7626)

CARR, Alexander, O.B.E.

CARR, Sqdn.-Leader Alfred George Horsley, O.B.E., R.A.F.

CARR, Capt. Charles, O.B.E., *b.* 17 May, 1880; *s.* of Robert Charles Carr, of Aldershot; *jm.* Emmeline Marie Louise, *d.* of — Noverraz, of Cheltenham. *Educ. :* Army Schools and privately. Capt. R.G.A. *War Work :* With the Aden Field Force from July, 1915, till April, 1916; conducted Turkish Prisoners of War from India to Egypt; Instructor in Gunnery at Bombay, India; appointed Fire Commander to the Bombay Defences. *Address :* 7, Beach Road, Southsea. (O8447)

CARR, Lieut.-Col. Charles Cattley, O.B.E. O6980)

CARR, Lieut. Christopher George, O.B.E., R.N.R.

CARR, David Leslie, M.B.E.

CARR, Lieut. David Whiston, M.B.E.

CARR, Col. Edward Elliott, C.B., C.B.E., *b.* 31 May, 1854; *s.* of J. K. Carr; *m.* Rosa E., *d.* of Rev. A. Hall, M.A. *Educ. :* Privately. Col., late commanding 2nd R. Scots Fusiliers; District Inspector in Musketry, N.E. District; Commanding Regimental, afterwards No. 2, District Scotland, 1903–08. *War Work :* 1914, A.A. & Q.M.G., Lowland Division; 1914–15, Inspector, Lines of Communications, Home; 1915–16, Commanded No. 16 Base Depôt, France; 1916–18, Commanded Reinforcements, France; despatches, by Sec. of State for War, Feb. 1917; by Field Marshal Sir D. Haig, Dec. 1917. *Address :* Overmead, Ludlow, Salop. *Clubs :* Army and Navy; Bath. (C1507)

CARR, Edward Hallett, C.B.E., *b.* 28 June, 1892; *s.* of Francis Parker Carr, of 105, Crouch Hill, London, N. *Educ. :* Merchant Taylor's School, London; Trinity College, Cambridge. *War Work :* Foreign Office, June, 1916, to Jan. 1919; Peace Conference, Jan. 1919, to Jan. 1920; at present Temp. Sec. at the British Embassy, Paris, attached to Ambassadors' Conference. *Addresses :* British Embassy, Paris; 105, Crouch Hill, London, N. (C2509)

CARR, Francis Howard, C.B.E., F.I.C., *b.* 13 March, 1874; *s.* of Henry Carr, of Croydon; *m.* Hilda Mary Sykes, of London. *Educ. :* Whitgift Grammar School, Croydon. *War Work :* Supply of Box Respirators, essential drugs, saccharin, etc.; research work in connection with Chemical Warfare. *Address :* The White House, Petersfield, Hants. (C2510)

CARR, Capt. Francis Tullius Fay, O.B.E.

CARR, George Alexander, M.B.E., *b.* 28 April, 1883; *s.* of Joseph Carr, of Heworth; *m.* Eleanor Giles, *d.* of Robert Redhead, of Wallsend. Asst. Traffic Superintendent of Newcastle-on-Tyne Corporation Tramways. *War Work :* Hon. Sec. Board of Trade Tramways Committee (Northern Area). *Address :* 8, Lilac Road, Wallsend. (M7629)

CARR, Capt. Gerald Mossman, M.B.E.

CARR, Major John, M.B.E.

CARR, John Walter, C.B.E., M.D. (Lond.), F.R.C.P. (Lond.), F.R.C.S. (Eng.), *b.* 8 June, 1862; *s.* of John Carr, J.P., of 40, Bloomsbury Square; *m.* Jessie, *d.* of Walter Griffith, of Streatham Hill. *Educ. :* University College School, College, and Hospital. Senior Physician to the Royal Free Hospital; Consulting Physician to the Victoria Hospital for Children, Chelsea; Lecturer on Medicine to the London School of Medicine for Women; Examiner in Medicine to the Royal College of Physicians. *War Work :* Senior Physician to the Military Wing for Officers, Royal Free Hospital, London. *Address :* 19, Cavendish Place, London, W. 1. (C3076)

CARR, John William, M.B.E., R.A.S.C.

CARR, Lieut.-Col. Laurence, O.B.E., D.S.O., *b.* 1888; Capt. and Brevet Major, Gordon Highlanders, and a Gen. Staff Officer with rank of Lieut.-Col.; served in Great War, 1914–18 (despatches). (O2466)

CARR, Capt. Leslie Wilden, M.B.E., R.A.F.

CARR, Mary, O.B.E., *d.* of William Carr, D.L., of Ditchingham Hall, Norfolk. *War Work :* Commandant Detachment 116, Norfolk; ran a Red Cross Hospital of 35 beds at Hedenham Hall from April, 1915, to Dec. 1918. *Address :* Hedenham, Norfolk. *Clubs :* Sesame; Norfolk, Norwich. (O10121)

CARR, Reginald Childers Culling, O.B.E., *b.* 3 Aug. 1864; *s.* of the late Francis Culling Carr-Gomm, of the Chase, Farnham Royal; *m.* Enid Agnes Herbert, *d.* of General Kenney-Herbert, of Madras Cavalry. *Educ. :* Charterhouse and Trinity College, Oxford. Indian Civil Service (Madras), retired. Barrister-at-Law, Inner Temple. *War Work :* Ministry of Food; Director of Enforcement. *Address :* 5, FitzJames' Avenue, W. 14. *Club :* East India United Service. (O1191)

CARR, William, M.B.E., J.P.

CARR, William Theodore, O.B.E., M.P.

CARR, Major Henry Barchard Fenwick BAKER-, O.B.E.

CARRICK, Bt. Lieut.-Col. Charles Ernest Alfred French Somerset Butler, 7th Earl of, Baron Butler (U.K.) of Mt. Juliet and Kilkenny, Viscount Ikerrin, O.B.E., formerly Comptroller of the Lord Lieutenant's Household, Ireland; *o. s.* of the 6th Earl of Carrick, and Kathleen Emily, *d.* of Lieut. Col. Ross; *b.*

15 Nov. 1873 (*see* BURKE'S *Peerage*) ; *m.* Ellen Rosamund Mary, *d.* of the late Lieut.-Col. Lindsay. *Educ.:* Repton ; R.M.C., Sandhurst. Late Lieut. King's Own (Yorkshire Light Infantry). *Address:* Elmfield, Tonbridge, Kent. *Clubs:* Cavendish ; Royal Automobile ; Kildare Street, Dublin. (O218)

CARRICK, Margaret, M.B.E.

CARRINGTON, John William Richard, M.B.E.

CARRINGTON, Capt. Noel Lewis, M.B.E.

CARRINGTON, Major Sidney John Ness, M.B.E., R.E.

CARRINGTON, Capt. William, O.B.E., K.O.Y.L.I.

CARROLL, Henee Materon, Lady, O.B.E. ; *m.* Hon. Sir James Carroll, K.C.M.G., of Wellington, N.Z. (*see* BURKE'S *Peerage*). *Address:* Wellington, New Zealand.   (O934)

CARROLL, Capt. Patrick Alphonsus, O.B.E., R.A.O.C.

CARROLL, Thomas William, M.B.E., *b.* 24 May, 1872 ; *s.* of Michael Carroll, of Pembroke Dock, Pembrokeshire ; *m.* Mary, *d.* of Henry Hitchings, of Pembroke. *Educ.:* Royal Dockyard Schools, Pembroke Dock. Senior Foreman of the Yard, H.M. Dockyard, Portsmouth. *War Work:* Supervising construction of battleships ; repair of warships damaged in action, and general maintenance of ships of the Grand Fleet. *Address:* 108, Oriel Road, N.E. Portsmouth.   (M218)

CARROLL, Capt. William, O.B.E.

CARRUTHERS, Engineer-Capt. David John, C.B.E., R.N. Employed in Engineer-in-Chief's Dept.   (C2217)

CARRUTHERS, Capt. Francis. O.B.E., *b.* 14 Feb. 1892 ; *s.* of Lieut.-Col. F. J. C. Carruthers, of Dixons, Lockerbie, Scotland. *Educ.:* Warriston Moffat, and Malvern Coll. *War Work:* Adjutant, 7th Batt. The East Yorkshire Regt., Sept. 1914 to July, 1916 ; Staff Capt. 50th Infantry Brigade, April, 1917 to April, 1918 ; D.A.Q.M.G. 37th British Division, April, 1918 to March, 1919 ; D.A.Q.M.G. British Army of the Rhine, March, 1919 to Oct. 1919 ; D.A.Q.M.G. British Military Mission South Russia, Nov. 1919 to Feb. 1920. *Address:* c/o Messrs. Cox & Co., 16, Charing Cross, S.W. 1. *Club:* Cocoa Tree.   (O5080)

CARRUTHERS, Major John Harvey de Wuderhold, O.B.E., M.C.

CARRUTHERS, Lieut.-Col. Robert Jardine, O.B.E., D.S.C., R.E., *b.* 27 Sept. 1884 ; *s.* of Joseph Carruthers, of Eslemont, Moffat, N.B. ; *m.* Georgina Rose, *d.* of Sir Robert Liddell, D.L., of Banoge House, Donacloney, Co. Down (*see* BURKE'S *Peerage*). *Educ.:* Elizabeth Coll., Guernsey. Insurance Manager. *War Work:* Minesweeping, East Coast and Dover Patrol, until Nov. 1917 ; awarded D.S.C. Jan. 1916 ; Lieut.-Col. in Command of Marine Companies, Richborough ; responsible for Train Ferries and Cross-Channel Barge Service, Nov. 1917 to March, 1919 ; Croix de Guerre (French). *Address:* Hooper's Farm, Eden Bridge, Kent. *Club:* Caledonian.   (O6982)

CARSE, Lieut. John R., M.B.E.

CARSON, Charles William Charteris, O.B.E.

CARSON, Lieut.-Col. David Simpson, O.B.E.

CARSON, Paymaster-Lieut.-Comm. John Findlay, O.B.E., R.N.V.R.

CARSON, Col. Charles John LLOYD-, C.B.E., *b.* 16 Oct. 1866 ; *s.* of the late John Lloyd-Carson, of Egryn Abbey, Merionethshire ; *m.* Elizabeth Furnival, *d.* of the late Robt. Wilson Oak Lodge, Bitterne, and Sandbach, Cheshire. *Educ.:* King William's College. Commanded 3rd Batt. East Lancashire Regt. ; South African War, 1899–1902 ; European War, 1914–18. *Address:* Stratton Lodge, Leamington, Warwickshire.   (C1669)

CARSTAIRS, Lieut.-Col. Albert Joseph Henry, O.B.E., R.I.R. (ret.), *b.* 3 Oct. 1862 ; *s.* of the late Joseph S. Carstairs, of Bengal Civil Service. *Educ.:* Clifton College. *War Work:* With 6th (Service) Batt. R. Irish Rifles, Aug. 1914 ; Railway Transport Officer, Central Force, Oct. 1914 to March, 1915 ; in France, Train Conducting Officer, March, 1915, to April, 1917 ; in charge of 1st Class Section, G.H.Q., 3rd Echelon, April, 1917, to May, 1919. *Address:* Bowerwood House, Fordingbridge, Hants.   (O5081)

CARSTAIRS, William Ramage, O.B.E.

CARSWELL, Capt. James Ernest Ingham, M.B.E.

CART-DE-LAFONTAINE, Lieut.-Col. Henry Philip, O.B.E., A.R.I.B.A., Officier d'Académie (France), *b.* 30 March, 1884 ; *s.* of Henry T. Cart-de-Lafontaine, of Albert Court, London, S.W. *Educ.:* Privately and abroad ; studied at Ecole des Beaux Arts, Paris. Hon. Sec.-General, Exhibition of British Architecture, Paris, 1914 ; Member of Council of Architectural Assocn. of London, 1911–13 ; Member of Council of Entente Cordiale Society. *War Work:* Mediterranean Expeditionary Force, 1914 ; British Expeditionary Force, 1915 ; Instructor No. 7 O.C.B., Ireland, 1916 ; Instructor in Aerial Topography, No. 2 R.F.C., Cadet Wing, 1917 ; Deputy Asst. Director of Graves Registration, G.H.Q., France, 1918 ; Asst. Inspector, and Inspector of Works, Imperial War Graves Commission, France, 1918–20. *Address:* 33, de Vere Gardens, W. 8. *Club:* Junior Army and Navy.   (O10794)

CARTER, Albert Thomas, C.B.E., D.C.L., *b.* 1861 ; *s.* of the late T. A. Carter, F.R.C.P., of Shottery Hall, Stratford-on-Avon. *Educ.:* Leamington, and at Queen's Coll., Oxford (B.A. 1883 ; M.A. 1888). Bar. Inner Temple 1886 ; Student of Ch. Ch., Oxford, 1895 ; was Reader in Law Inns of Court, 1898–1910. Author of "A History of English Legal Institutions," etc. *Addresses:* Shottery Hall, Stratford-on-Avon ; Christ Church, Oxford. *Clubs:* Oxford and Cambridge ; Savage.   (C18)

CARTER, Capt. Alfred William., D.S.O., M.B.E., R.A.F.

CARTER, Capt. Charles Frederick Beall, M.B.E., R.A.S.C.

CARTER, Lieut.-Col. Charles Herbert Philip, C.B., C.M.G., C.B.E., *b.* 1864 ; *s.* of the late Capt. Willoughby Harcourt Carter, formerly Roy. Fusiliers (City of London Regt.), of Annag Keen, co. Galway ; *m.* 1899, Kathleen Maud, *d.* of James Hartley. *Educ.:* Cheltenham Coll. Entered Black Watch (Roy. Highlanders), 1888 ; became Capt. Roy. Scots (Lothian Regt.), 1897 ; Brevet Major, 1897 ; Brevet Lieut.-Col. 1900 ; Brevet Col. 1906 ; Major, 1908 ; Lieut.-Col. The Cameronians (Scottish Rifles), 1911 ; Col. 1913 ; retired 1913 ; served with Benin Expedition, 1897 (despatches, medal with clasp, Brevet Major) ; Niger Coast Protectorate in command of Force in operations against Kwo Ibibio, 1899 (despatches) ; Benin Territories, 1899 (despatches, medal with clasp ; Ashanti, at relief of Kumasi, 1900 ; in command of S. Nigerian Force (severely wounded, medal with clasp) ; was Comdt. 3rd (Niger) Batt. W. African Frontier Force (Lieut.-Col.), 1900 ; was in command of Gold Coast Regt. (W. African Frontier Force), 1906–9 ; and a Brig. Comm. 1916–17. *Club:* Naval and Military.   (C1508)

CARTER, Charles Maurice, M.B.E.

CARTER, Edward Clark, O.B.E., *b.* 9 June, 1878 ; *s.* of Clark Carter, of Andover, Massachusetts ; *m.* Alice Olin, *d.* of Dr. William H. Draper, of New York. *Educ.:* Phillips-Andover Academy, and Harvard University. Secretary, Harvard University Y.M.C.A. ; National Secretary, Y.M.C.A. of India and Ceylon ; Student Secretary, International Committee, Y.M.C.A. ; Asst.-Sec. English Y.M.C.A. ; Chief Secretary, American Expeditionary Forces, Y.M.C.A. *War Work:* War Secretary, Indian National Y.M.C.A. ; responsible for early administration work in India, for Indian troops in France, and British and Indian troops in India, Mesopotamia and East Africa, from Aug. 1914, to Sept. 1916 ; Oct. 1916 to May, 1917, Asst. Sec., English National Y.M.C.A., with especial reference to recruiting and training ; June, 1917, to Sept. 1919, Chief Secretary American Expeditionary Forces, Y.M.C.A. *Addresses:* 347, Madison Avenue, New York ; 31, Bartlet Street, Andover, Massachusetts. *Club:* Harvard, New York.   (O78)

CARTER, Edward Henry, O.B.E.

CARTER, Major Edward Philip, C.B.E.

CARTER, Lieut.-Col. Ernest Augustus Frederick, C.B.E., Lieut.-Col. and Brevet Col. King's Own Roy. Lancaster Regt. ; served in Great War 1914–19 (despatches).   (C1509)

CARTER, Lieut.-Col. Ernest Pasley, O.B.E. R.A.

CARTER, Capt. Ernest Walker Augustus, O.B.E. R.N.

CARTER, Eustace George, O.B.E., M.R.C.S. (Eng.), L.R.C.P. (Eng.), *b.* 20 July, 1861 ; *s.* of Joseph Barton Carter, of Chapel Allerton, Leeds ; *m.* Josephine Mary, *d.* of Joseph Richardson, of Springfield, Lisburn, Co. Antrim. *Educ.:* Leeds Grammar School. *War Work:* Medical Officer in charge of Gledhow Hall and Roundhay Auxiliary Hospitals, Leeds. *Addresses:* Ivy House, Chapel Allerton, Leeds ; 18. Harrogate Road, Chapel Allerton, Leeds. *Club:* Leeds.   (O10122)

CARTER, Flora Mactavish, Mrs., O.B.E., *b.* 1 April, 1872 ; *d.* of Sir Alexander Ogston, K.C.V.O., of Glendavan, Dinnet, Aberdeenshire ; *m.* George Christopher Carter. *Educ.:* Cheltenham Ladies' College. Late Principal, Dunfermline Physical Training College. *War Work:* Hon. Sec., City of Aberdeen War Work Association ; served as V.A.D. Nurse in Southall Military Hospital, and with First British Eastern Auxiliary Hospital, Belgrade. *Address:* 252, Union Street, Aberdeen. *Club:* Halcyon.   (O1192)

CARTER, Francis Tavor, M.B.E.

CARTER, Sir Frank Willington, Knt. Bach., C.I.E., C.B.E., Director of Turner, Morrison & Co., Ltd., Calcutta, *b.* 16 Jan. 1865 ; *s.* of Rev. W. A. Carter, Fellow and Bursar of Eton Coll. ; *m.* Mary, widow of Comdr. Charles Collins, *e.d.* of Rev. Dacres Olivier. *Educ.:* Cheltenham Coll. Went to India 1891 ; Member of the Legislative Council of Bengal, Jan. 1917 ; Sheriff of Calcutta. *Address:* 6, Lyons Range, Calcutta. *Clubs:* Oriental ; Royal Automobile ; Bengal, Calcutta.   (C687)

CARTER, Capt. Frederick George, O.B.E.

CARTER, Frederick James, M.B.E., R.N.

CARTER, George, M.B.E., *b.* 14 May, 1883 : *s.* of George Carter, of Coventry ; *m.* Kathleen Blanche, *d.* of Thomas James Burney, of Strood. *Educ.:* Bablake School, Coventry ; and Birmingham Univ. Civil Servant (Admiralty) ; served as Assistant Naval Store Officer at Devonport, Portsmouth, Portland, Sydney (N.S.W.), and Admiralty, from 1902–14. *War Work:* At the outbreak of war was appointed to assist the Naval Store Officer, Grand Fleet, and served in various Depot and Store Ships until 1918. *Addresses:* H.M. Dockyard, Chatham ; Cotehele, Maidstone Road. Rochester.   (M1519)

CARTER, Major George James, O.B.E.

CARTER, Sir George (John), K.B.E., M.I.C.E., M.I.N.A., M.I.M.E., J.P., *b.* 1860 ; *s.* of George Dean Carter ; *m.* Edith Harriet, *d.* of the late J. S. Vaux, Sunderland. Managing Director of Cammell, Laird & Co., Ltd., Birkenhead ; Director of Coventry Ordnance Works, Ltd., President of the Shipbuilding Employers' Federation ; was Chairman of the Merchant Shipbuilding Advisory Committee to the Controller of Shipping ; and later a Member of the Shipbuilding Council ; Member of the Council of the Institute of Naval Architects ; Federation of British Industries ; Member of Committee Lloyd's Register ; Member of the Mersey Docks and Harbour Board ; Deputy Chairman, Liverpool Munitions Committee. *War*

Work : Chairman of the Merchant Shipbuilding Advisory Committee ; President of the Shipbuilding Employers' Federation throughout war period ; responsible for the building of a large number of warships and standard type merchant vessels. *Addresses :* Brackenwood, Hr. Bebington, Cheshire ; Dinbren Hall, Llangollen, N. Wales. *Clubs :* Constitutional ; Royal Societies' ; Royal Automobile. (K14)

CARTER, George Wallace, C.B.E., *b.* 1870 ; *s.* of Jonathan Carter, of Banbury ; *m.* Margaret Mary, *d.* of Alfred Pickard, of Leeds. *Educ. :* Privately. *War Work :* Joint Hon. Sec., Parliamentary Recruiting ; Parliamentary War Savings, and National War Aims Committees. *Address :* Fairholme, Pollards Hill West, Norbury, S.W. 16. *Club :* National Liberal. (C452

CARTER, Major Gerald Francis, O.B.E.

CARTER, Major Gerald Vernon, O.B.E., *b.* 25 May, 1883 ; *s.* of the late Rev. Vernon Robert Carter, of Stone Park, Wimborne, Dorset ; *m.* Cicely Joan, *d.* of the Rev. Charles Lewis Kennaway, (*see* BURKE'S *Peerage,* Kennaway, Bart.). *Educ. :* Eton. Commissioned in 16th Lancers ; resigned, 1904 ; joined Dorset Yeomanry as 2nd Lieut. Oct. 1909 ; Egypt, April, 1915 ; Suvla Bay, Aug. 1915 ; A.D.C. to Lieut.-Gen. Sir W. R. Marshall, G.C.M.G., K.C.B., K.C.S.I. Sept. 1915 ; mentioned in despatches, Aug. 1917, and June, 1918 ; Chevalier Legion l'Honneur. *Address :* Waterston Manor, Dorchester, Dorset. (O2265)

CARTER, R.S.M. Henry Lower, M.B.E., N.Z.F.A., *b.* 10 Aug. 1891 ; *s.* of Francis S. Carter, of Lewisham, London. *Educ. :* Derby. Accountant to Messrs. Thomas Cook & Son, Tourists' Agents. *War Work :* With N.Z. Field Artillery in Egypt, Suez Canal, Alexandria, Gallipoli, and Northern France. *Address :* c/o Messrs. T. Cook and Sons, Ludgate Circus, London, E.C. (M4663)

CARTER, Herbert Parkinson, O.B.E.

CARTER, Hester Marion, Mrs., C.B.E., *b.* 1867 ; *d.* of the late James Rose, of Inverness ; *m.* 1904, the Most Rev. William Marlborough Carter, Archbishop of Capetown. *Address :* Bishopscourt, Claremont, Cape of Good Hope. (C376)

CARTER, John Gordon, O.B.E. (O12043)

CARTER, Major John Leslie Graydon, O.B.E., R.A.S.C.

CARTER, Major John Reginald, O.B.E., R.E.

CARTER, Maud Eleanor, Mrs., M.B.E.

CARTER, Rei Alfred Deakin, O.B.E., J.P., M.P., *b.* 3 Dec. 1856 ; *s.* of Joseph Janney Carter, of Manchester ; *m.* Annie (died, 1894), *d.* of William Henry Woodworth, of Southport. *Educ. :* Stanley House, Blackpool ; Owens Coll. and Victoria Univ., Manchester. Director, Manchester Palace Theatre, and Empire Theatre. Preston. *War Work :* Chairman, Lord Derby's Recruiting Campaign, Stretford, Lancs. ; Chairman, Advisory Committee (4 years), Manchester ; Chairman, Brook House Auxiliary Military Hospital, Manchester ; Commander, No. 2 Co., Manchester Special Police (5 years). *Address :* Rushford, Rushford Park, Levenshulme, Manchester. *Clubs :* Constitutional and Arts, Manchester ; Union, London. (O10123)

CARTER, Major Silas Bernard Foley, O.B.E., R.A.F.

CARTER, Stanley Bronislaw, O.B.E., Member Institute of Transport, *b.* 19 July, 1882 ; *s.* of William Henry Carter, of London and Shanghai ; *m.* Dulcie Isabel, *d.* of J. E. Melhuish, of London. *Educ. :* Fettes. District Superintendent, London and North-Western Railway, Northern District, Liverpool. *War Work :* Entrainment of Canadian and American Armies at Liverpool. *Addresses :* Clifton, Helsby, Cheshire ; Lime Street Station, Liverpool. (O10124)

CARTER, Thomas, M.B.E.

CARTER, Qr.-Mr. and Capt. Thomas Benjamin, M.B.E.

CARTER, Comm. Thomas Gilbert, O.B.E., R.N.

CARTER, Major Thomas Moravian, O.B.E., R.A.M.C. (T.F.)

CARTER, Wilfred George, M.B.E., A.M.I.M.E., M.I.A.E., A.F.R.A.S., *b.* 9 March, 1889 ; *s.* of George Alfred Carter, of Bedford ; *m.* Hilda, *d.* of John Frederick Back, of Johannesburg, S.A. *Educ. :* Bedford. Engineer. *War Work :* Chief of Drawing Office, the Sopwith Aviation and Engineering Co., Ltd., Kingston-on-Thames, Designers and Constructors of Airplanes and Seaplanes. *Address :* Denehurst, Kingston-on-Thames. (M7633)

CARTER, William, M.B.E.

CARTER, William Allan, O.B.E., M.I.C.E., J.P., *b.* 27 Nov. 1847 ; *s.* of Frederick Hayne Carter, C.A., of Edinburgh ; *m.* Jane Agnes Mortmer, *d.* of Thomas Blaikie Park, of Haddington. *Educ. :* Edinburgh Academy, Edinburgh. Civil Engineer. *War Work :* Member of Edinburgh Recruiting Tribunal ; Member of Munition Board of Eastern District, Scotland. *Address :* Stamford Hall, Gullane, East Lothian. *Clubs :* Northern, Edinburgh ; Royal Automobile. (O219)

CARTER, Hon. Sir William Morris, Knt. Bach., C.B.E., B.A., B.Ch., Chief Justice, Uganda Protectorate, since 1912, *b.* 9 Dec. 1873 ; *s.* of the late Sidney James Carter, of Canterbury. *Educ. :* King's School, Canterbury ; Brasenose Coll., Oxford. Certificate of Honour, Bar Examination, and Prize of Council of Legal Education in Constitutional Law and Legal History ; called to Bar, Lincoln's Inn, 1899 ; Registrar and Principal Registrar of Documents, East Africa Protectorate, 1902 ; Magistrate, Mombasa, 1902 ; Judge of H.M. High Court of Uganda, and H.B.M. Court of Appeal for Eastern Africa, 1903 ; acted as Principal Judge, Uganda, on several occasions ; T. Capt. Uganda Volunteer Reserve, 1914 ; T. Lieut.-Col.,

1916 ; A.D.T. and Contracts, Uganda, 1916 (despatches) ; Chairman, Supplies Board, Uganda, 1914–17 ; in charge of Local Shortages Section, Ministry of Food, London, 1917–18. *Address :* Entebbe, Uganda. *Clubs :* Royal Societies' ; M.C.C. (C389)

CARTER, Capt. William Tom, O.B.E. ; *s.* of the late Tom Carter, of Warwick. *Educ. :* Warwick. Fellow Library Association ; Private Secretary. *War Work :* Enlisted 7th R. Warwick Regt., 1914 ; commissioned S. Staffs. Regt., 1915 ; Capt. and Adjutant, 1916 ; Acting Staff Capt., 2nd T.R. Brigade, 1916–18 ; Garrison Adjutant, Cannock Chase Res. Centre, 1918–19 ; Staff Capt., 1919 ; assisted in organisation of original Army Education Scheme ; lectured considerably ; Law work as Judge Advocate, including case of Capt. von Müller, of the "Emden." *Address :* c/o Larkholm, Rugeley, Staffs. (O6981)

CARTER, Lieut.-Col. Ian Malcolm BONHAM-, O.B.E., R.A.F.

CARTMAIL, Daisy Olive, M.B.E.

CARTMELL, Annie, Lady, M.B.E. ; *d.* of Thomas Dewell Scott, of London ; *m.* 1880, Sir Harry, Knt. Bach., J.P., *s.* of James Cartmell, of Manchester. *Address :* 9, Victoria Road. St. Annes-on-Sea, Lancashire. (M7634)

CARTWRIGHT, Comm. Charles Chesters, O.B.E.

CARTWRIGHT, Capt. Edward Rogers, O.B.E., R.E.

CARTWRIGHT, Capt. Francis Lennox, C.B.E., D.S.O., *b.* 1874 ; *s.* of the late Rt. Hon. Sir Richard John Cartwright, P.C., G.C.M.G., of King Street, Kingston, Ontario ; *m.* 1901, Ada Marion Carlos, *d.* of Augustus F. Perkins, of Oakdene, Holmwood, Surrey. Hon. Capt. in the Army ; Capt. Canadian Cav. ; sometime Inspector of Canadian N.-W. Mounted Police ; served in S. Africa, 1900–1901, as Capt. Strathcona's Horse (despatches). *Address :* Fort Osborne Barracks, Winnipeg, Manitoba, Canada. (C2313b)

CARTWRIGHT, Mary, M.B.E.

CARTWRIGHT, Major Richard Bernard, O.B.E., A.P.D.

CARTY, Major Samuel Wilfrid, O.B.E., M.C., R.A.S.C.

CARUANA, Most Rev. Dom. Sir Maurus, K.B.E., O.S.B., *b.* 16 Nov. 1867 ; *s.* of Henry Caruana, of Malta. *Educ. :* Malta, and St. Benedict's Abbey, Fort Augustus, Scotland. Took vows as Benedictine, 1885 ; Ordained Priest, 1891. Bishop of Malta and Titular Archbishop of Rhodes, since 1915 ; Archbishop of Malta. *Address :* Archbishop's Palace, Valetta, Malta. (K122)

CARVELL, John Maclean, M.B.E., M.R.C.S. (Eng.), L.S.A., (Lond.), *b.* 20 Aug. 1856 ; *s.* of John Carvell, of Southam, Warwickshire ; *m.* Euphemia Sarah, *d.* of Benjamin Avery, of London. *Educ. :* Brewers' School ; London Hospital. Assistant Commissioner, St. John Ambulance Brigade. *War Work :* Ambulance Organisation and Training, No. 1 district, Order of St. John ; duty with ambulances during air raids. *Address :* 31, Avonmore Road, West Kensington. W. 14. (M7635)

CARVER, Albert Wing, M.B.E., *b.* 25 May, 1866 ; *s.* of the late George Carver ; *m.* Florence, *d.* of the late George Walker, of Wakefield. Clerk to Guardians of Cannock Union ; Clerk to Cannock Rural District Council, etc. *War Work :* Hon. Sec. Cannock and District Recruiting Committee, 1914–15 ; Hon. Clerk Cannock Rural National Registration Authority 1915–18 ; Hon. Sec. Bushbury and Penkridge War Pensions Local Committees, 1916 ; Clerk Cannock Rural Local Tribunal, 1916–18. *Address :* Rydersford, Cannock, Staffs. (M221)

CARVER, Helena Philae Olive Virginia, Mrs., M.B.E., *b.* 8 Sept. 1893 ; *d.* of General Rt. Hon. Sir John Maxwell G.C.B., K.C.M.G., of London ; *m.* Clifford, *s.* of Amos Carver, of New York. *War Work :* War Pensions Officer, York. *Address :* Locust Valley, Long Island, New York. (M7636)

CARVER, Mary Glendinning, M.B.E., *b.* 1872 ; *d.* of Henry Clifton Carver, of Wilmslow, Cheshire. *Educ. :* Private schools in England and Germany. *War Work :* Secretary and Translator, Intelligence Dept., Admiralty. *Address :* 52, Lower Sloane Street, London, S.W. (M1521)

CARVER, Olive McLaren, M.B.E., *Educ. :* St. Leonard's School, St. Andrew's. *War Work :* Commandant, V.A.D. Cheshire 84 ; Joint Officer in Charge Auxiliary Military Hospital, Kilrie, Knutsford. *Address :* Oakhurst, Knutsford. (M7637)

CARVER, Sydney Ralph Pitts, C.B.E.

CARY, Arthur Deering Lucius, O.B.E., *b.* 14 Dec. 1856 ; *s.* of Henry George Cary, County Inspector, R.I. Constabulary ; *m.* 1st, Edith Lucy, *d.* of Capt. C. G. Weller, Elder Brother of Trinity House ; 2nd, Caroline Eleanor, *d.* of Rev. Stephen Radcliff, of Armagh. *Educ. :* Drogheda Grammar School. Librarian, Royal United Service Institution, Whitehall, London. *War Work :* Librarian of the Parliamentary and Reference Section of the War Office Library. *Address :* 55, Thurleigh Road, London, S.W. 12. (O10125)

CARY, Paymaster Henry John, M.B.E., R.N.R.

CARY, Major the Hon. Lucius Plantagenet, O.B.E. (*see* FALKLAND, Master of).

CARY, Reginald Ormsby, O.B.E., *b.* 8 Jan. 1875 ; *s.* of Col. Francis Walter Cary, of East Yorkshire Regt. ; *m.* Lille Benbow Bowen. *Educ. :* Harrison's College, Barbados ; Diocesan College, Cape Town. Managing Director of the Sopwith Aviation and Engineering Co., Ltd., Kingston-on-Thames. *Addresses :* Pompet House, Sunbury-on-Thames ; 8, Hay Hill, W. *Clubs :* Royal Aero ; Royal Automobile. (O1194)

CARY, Lieut. Rupert Tristram Oliver, M.B.E.

CASE, Capt. and Qr.-Mr. Arthur Joseph, O.B.E.,

b. 29 Nov. 1870 ; *s.* of Benjamin Case, of March, Cambridgeshire. *Educ.* : March. *War Work* : Served on Western Front from Sept. 1915 till end of war ; wounded May, 1918 ; mentioned in despatches, June, 1916, and July, 1919. *Address* : 12, Nene Parade, March, Cambridgeshire.   (O5085)

CASE, Thomas Henry Towler, O.B.E., *b.* 13 April, 1864, *s.* of Thomas Henry Case, of Norwich ; *m.* Evelyn, *d.* of William Henry White, of Barnet. *Educ.* : Norwich Grammar School ; Queen's Coll., Oxford. Barrister-at-Law. *War Work* : Assisted in departments of H.M. Procurator-General and Treasury Solicitor. *Address* : Abbotsford, Lyonsdown Avenue, New Barnet, Herts. *Club* : Union.   (O3654)

CASH, Ernest William, M.B.E., M.I.Mech.E., *b.* 18 Aug. 1875 ; *s.* of Edwin Cash, of Cambridge ; *m.* Elizabeth, *d.* of Isaac Draper, of Shorwell, Isle of Wight. *Educ.* : Aukland School, Cambridge ; East London Technical Coll. Works Manager, Skefko Ball Bearing Co., Luton ; Member of Executive Council of Engineering Employers' Federation, Bedfordshire Branch ; previously with the British Thomson-Houston Co., Rugby, and on Mining work in South Africa. *War Work* : Associated with Messrs. Dick, Kerr & Co., in equipping and organising Hackney Marshes National Projectile Factory, London, for the production of 6-inch shells ; afterwards Works Manager of the National Cartridge and Box Repair Factory, Newport, Mon. *Address* : Lancaster House, Kingsley Road, Limbury, Beds.   (M7638)

CASH, C.S.M. Samuel, M.B.E., R.E.

CASH, Rev. William Wilson, O.B.E.   (O6153)

CASHIN, John, O.B.E., F.R.C.S., L.R.C.P., Surgeon R.N. (Retired List), *b.* 29 June, 1854 ; *s.* of Michael Cashin, of Shanraham, Clogheen, Co. Tipperary, Ireland ; *m.* Alice Maud, *d.* of Thomas Were Fox, of Hoe House, Plymouth, Devon. *Educ.* : The Abbey School, Mount Melleray, Cappoquin, Ireland ; Queen's Coll., Cork ; Royal Coll. of Surgeons, Ireland. Formerly Resident Surgeon, Jervis Street Hospital, Dublin, and Demonstrator of Anatomy, Ledwich School of Medicine, Dublin. *War Work* : Medical Officer in charge of 3rd Royal Berkshire Regiment, 3rd Leinster Regiment, 3rd Dorset Regiment, and 2nd Sussex Regiment. *Address* : St. Aubyn's, Osborne Road, Southsea, Hants.   (O4356)

CASHIN, Hon. Sir Michael Patrick, K.B.E., Minister of Finance and Customs of Newfoundland since 1909 ; Member, Colonial House of Assembly for Ferryland District ; *b.* 29 Sept. 1864 ; *s.* of Richard Cashin ; *m.* Gertrude C., *d.* of Capt. P. Mullowney, of Witless Bay. *Educ.* : Bonaventure's Coll., St. Johns, N.F. Trained for mercantile career at St. John's ; engaged in business of fishery merchant at Cape Broyle, 1885, on attaining his majority ; has continued same since ; entered political life in Colonial General Election, 1893 ; joined Liberal Party, 1895 ; led Independent Party in Assembly, 1905–08, when joined with Sir Edward Morris ; represented Colony before Imperial Royal Commission on West India trade at Jamaica, Jan. 1910 ; Acting Prime Minister ; Acting Minister of Militia ; Acting Minister of Shipping, 1918 ; as Minister of Finance raised the first successful Victory Loan in the Colony in 1917–18. *Addresses* : Sea View, Cape Broyle ; 38, Queen's Road, St. Johns.   (K188)

CASOLANI, Henry, M.B.E.

CASS, Gertrude Margaret Carew, O.B.E. ; *d.* of the late Frederick Charles Cass, of Monken Hadley, Herts., and 9 Heene Terrace, Worthing. Homes of Holy Redeemer, Duxhurst, near Reigate. *War Work* : Matron, Morant War Hospital, Brockenhurst, Oct. 1915, to Sept. 1916 ; then Donor, Commandant, and Matron of the Cass Hospital for Officers, Worthing, 1916–19. *Addresses* : 9, Heene Terrace, Worthing ; Duxhurst, Reigate. *Clubs* : Albemarle ; Ladies' Imperial.   (10126)

CASSEL, Capt. Louis, O.B.E.

CASSELS, Lieut.-Col. George Hamilton, C.M.G., O.B.E., Lieut.-Col. 2nd Central Ontario Regt. ; served in Great War, 1915–19 (despatches).   (O3214)

CASSELS, Lieut. Hamilton, M.B.E., R.A.F.

CASSELS, Lieut. James Houston, M.B.E.

CASSELS, John Bordase, M.B.E.

CASSELS, Walter Seton, O.B.E., I.C.S.

CASSERA, Major Anthony Aloysius, O.B.E., R.E., *b.* 11 March, 1893 ; *s.* of Anthony Cassera, of Handsworth, Birmingham. *Educ.* : St. Philip's Grammar School, Edgbaston. Deputy Assistant Director of Engineering Stores. *War Work* : Served in R. Warwickshire Regt., 1914–17 ; Royal Engineers, 1917–19. *Address* : Hall Road, Handsworth, Birmingham.   (O5086)

CASSIDI, Francis Richard, M.B.E., M.D., *b.* 1858 ; *s.* of Francis Peter Cassidi, of Glenbrook, Magherafelt ; *m.* Marion Elizabeth, *d.* of John Duncanson, M.D., of Alloa, N.B. *Educ.* : Rugby, and Trinity College, Dublin. *War Work* : Director of Transport, First Line Hospitals, Derbyshire. *Address* : Glenbrook, Magherafelt. Co. Londonderry.   (M222)

CASSON, Emily Marjorie, M.B.E. ; *d.* of George Robert Casson, of Apsley House, Queen's Road, Richmond. *Educ.* : St. Martin's Coll., Cliftonville, Margate. *War Work* : For first year of war, V.A.D. work in Richmond Red Cross Hospital ; afterwards temp. Clerk in War Trade Statistical Dept. ; then 8 months at Paris Peace Conference.   (M7639)

CASSON, Gertrude Hamilton, Mrs., M.B.E. ; *d.* of Capt. A. Hamilton Russell, of Heath House, Petersfield ; *m.* Herbert Alexander Casson, of Tyn-y-coed, Arthog, Dolgelly, Merionethshire, N. Wales ; *s.* of Rev. George Casson of Olde Court, Torquay. *War Work* : Red Cross Depot, Ambala,

India ; Member of Committee for Monro Soldiers' Canteens. *Address* : Tyn-y-Coed, Arthog, Merionethshire, N. Wales. *Club* : Ladies' Imperial.   (M6119)

CASSY, Capt. Alexander William, O.B.E., R.A.F.

CASTELL, Rose Catherine Clanmorris, Mrs., M.B.E.

CASTELLAN, Major Victor Edward, M.B.E., R.F.A. (T.F.)

CASTINGS, 2nd Lieut. Walter Rumley, M.B.E., R.A.F.

CASTLE, Gordon Harwood, O.B.E.   (O11959)

CASTLE, Hubert William, M.B.E., *b.* 10 March, 1878 ; *s.* of Thomas Smith Castle, of London ; *m.* Lizzie May, *d.* of George Henry Hunt, of London. *War Work* : Asst.-Commander Metropolitan Special Constabulary, 1914–19. *Address* : 20, Muswell Avenue, N. 10. *Clubs* : R.A.C. ; Junior Constitutional.   (M7640)

CASTLE, Capt. Ivor, M.B.E.

CASTLE, Major Leonard James, O.B.E., M.C., *b.* 21 Aug. 1887.   (O6453)

CASTLE, Montague Wilson, M.B.E.

CATCHPOLE, Alfred Edward, M.B.E.

CATERALL, John, M.B.E.

CATHCART, Lieut.-Col. Charles Walker, C.B.E., M.B., *b.* 1853 ; *s.* of the late James Cathcart. *Educ.* : Edinburgh Univ. (M.B. and C.M. 1878). F.R.C.S. (England, 1879 ; Edinburgh, 1880). Consulting Surg. Roy. Infirmary, Edinburgh ; Lieut.-Col. R.A.M.C. (T.F.), 2nd Scottish Gen. Hospital, Edinburgh War Hospital, Edenhall Hostel for Limbless Sailors and Soldiers during Great War, 1914–19. *Address* : 3, Tipperlinn Road, Edinburgh.   (C804)

CATHCART, Major George Elliot, O.B.E., R.A.M.C.

CATHERALL, Lieut. John Eric, M.B.E., R.AF.

CATHERY, Edmund, C.B.E.

CATHLES, Albert, O.B.E., C.A., *b.* 13 May, 1882 ; *s.* of John Cathles, of St. Margaret's, Elie, Fife ; *m.* Ada Rockcliff, *d.* of Thomas Baker, of Coatbridge. *Educ.* : George Watson's College, Edinburgh. *War Work* : Ministry of Munitions ; Assistan Director (Factory Accounts) ; Deputy Director of Factory Accounting ; Assistant Controller of Factory Audit and Costs. *Address* : c/o Price, Waterhouse & Co., 3, Frederick's Place, Old Jewry, E.C. 2.   (O1195)

CATLEUGH, Lieut. John Harwood, M.B.E., R.A.F.

CATLEY, Clare, M.B.E., *b.* 21 Dec. 1883 ; *s.* of J. W. H. Catley, of Scarborough ; *m.* Florence Mary, *d.* of Aquila Ladd Mitchell, of Boston, Lincoln. *Educ.* : St. Martin's Grammar School, Scarborough. Accountant. *War Work* : Section Director of Dept. Factory Audit and Costs ; Sec. of Canteen Finance Committee, Ministry of Munitions of War. *Addresses* : Colwyn, Castle Road, Scarborough ; 24, Westborough, Scarborough.   (M1522)

CATMUR, Benjamin, O.B.E., *b.* 30 May, 1861 ; *s.* of Thomas Catmur, L.C.C., of Whitechapel and Bow ; *m.* Celia, *d.* of Jabez Druitt, of Manor Park and Bow. *Educ.* : Whitechapel Foundation School. Clerk to the Guardians, Hamlet of Mile End Old Town ; Superintendent Registrar of Births, Deaths, and Marriages, District of Mile End Old Town. *War Work* : As Clerk to the Guardians responsible for the whole of the maintenance, staffing, and upkeep of the Mile End Military Hospital ; Hon. Sec. Wounded Soldiers' Entertainment Fund, Mile End Military Hospital ; Member of the 5th City of London (National Guard) Volunteer Regiment, Jan. 1915, to date of Armistice. *Addresses* : Guardians' Offices, Bancroft Road, Mile End, E. 1 ; 4, Wallwood Road, Leytonstone, E. 11.   (O10127)

CATON, Richard, C.B.E., M.D., LL.D., F.R.C.P., J.P., *s.* of Richard Caton, of Heysham ; *m.* the late Annie, *d.* of William Ivory, of St. Roque, Edinburgh. *Educ.* : Scarborough Grammar School ; University of Edinburgh ; Emeritus Professor, University of Liverpool ; Ex-Lord Mayor of Liverpool ; President, Liverpool Royal Infirmary. *War Work* : Chairman of West Lancashire Nursing Service Committee. *Address* : 7, Sunnyside, Prince's Park, Liverpool. *Clubs* : Athenæum, Liverpool ; University, Liverpool.   (C2513)

CATOR, Maud, Mrs., O.B.E., *b.* 5 July, 1866 ; *d.* of Henry John Adeane, of Babraham Hall, Cambridge, and of Lady Elizabeth Yorke, eldest *d.* of Philip, 4th Earl of Hardwicke ; *m.* John, *s.* of Albemarle Caton, of Woodbastwick Hall, Norfolk. *War Work* : Commandant, V.A. Detachment, Norfolk 54 ; organised, equipped, and carried out hospital in own home, 1914–18 ; nursed 1220 soldiers. *Addresses* : Woodbastwick, Norwich ; 52, Pont St., London, S.W. 1.   (O221)

CATOR, Lieut.-Col. Robert, O.B.E., R.M.L.I.

CATTANACH, Jean Lorimer M.B.E., of Peter Lorimer Cattanach, Advocate, of Edinburgh. *Educ.* : Privately ; Edinburgh Univ. ; Paris. *War Work* : British Red Cross, Paris, 1914 ; Assist. Sec. Record and Casualty Office, B.E.F., 1914–15 ; Commandant, V.A.D. (W. Lancs., 86) ; Lady Superintendent, King's Lancashire Military Convalescent Hospital, 1915–18. *Address* : 13, Pembridge Crescent, W.   (M7642)

CATTELL, Major Arthur Shelton Goodricke, O.B.E.

CATTO, Lieut. Andrew Yule, O.B.E., R.N.

CATTO, Thomas Sivewright, C.B.E. In Ministry of Shipping.   (C126)

CAULFEILD, Brig.-Gen. Francis William John, C.B.E., *b.* 1859 ; *s.* of Col. Robert Caulfeild, of Camolin, Wexford, Ireland ; *m.* Alice, *d.* of J. H. Finnemor, of Ballyward Manor, Kilbride, Co. Wicklow. *War Work* : Commanded 65th Infantry Brigade in England, 1914–15 ; served in France as Area Commandant, 1916–18. *Address* : Innishannon, Co. Cork.   (C765)

CAULFEILD, Capt. James Montgomerie, C.B.E., R.N. (ret.), b. 22 Feb., 1855; s. of William Montgomerie Stewart Caulfeild, Lieut.-Col. late Royal Dublin Fusiliers, of Weston Park, Dublin (see BURKE'S *Peerage*, Charlemont, V.); m. 6 Feb., 1889, Kathleen Ruth, d. of the late Lieut.-Col. H. A. Crofton (see BURKE'S *Peerage*, Crofton, Bt.). (C2267)

CAUNTER, Brig.-Gen. James Eales, C.B., C.B.E., b. 1859; s. of the late J. E. Caunter (15th Bengal Native Inf.), of Wave, Ashburton, Devon; m. 1879, Kate, d. of H. Haworth. Entered 69th Regt. 1878; became Capt. 1887; Major, Lancashire Fusiliers, 1898; Lieut.-Col. 1903; Brevet Col. 1906; Col. 1911; and Hon. Brig.-Gen. 1918; ret. 1918; served in S. Africa, 1899–1900, as D.A.A.G., 6th Div.; present at relief of Kimberley, and at actions of Paardeberg, Poplar Grove, and Dreifontein (despatches, Queen's medal with three clasps); was D.A.A.G., Bermuda, 1889–94; Professor of Mil. History and Tactics at R.M.C. 1900–2; Gen. Staff Officer there, 1902–6; S. Midland Div. 1908–11; A.A.G., War Office, 1911–13; Brig.-Gen. in charge of Administration 1913–19. *Address*: Trevora, Torquay. (C453)

CAUSTON, Major Edward Postle Gwyn, O.B.E.
CAUSTON, Ida Jessie, Mrs., M.B.E., b. 14 Dec. 1876;
CAUSTON, Lieut.-Col. Joseph, O.B.E., R.M.E. d. of W. F. Paul, O.B.E., J.P., of Orwell Lodge, Ipswich; m. Joseph, s. of the late Joseph Causton, of Bickley, Kent. *Educ.*: High School, Ipswich; Dresden, and Paris. Commandant of V.A. Detachment, Middlesex; Member of Hendon Rural District Council, and Hendon Board of Guardians. *War Work*: Organised Pinner, V.A.D. Hospital, Feb. 1915, and was Commandant and Officer in Charge of the Hospital all the time it was open, from Feb. 1915, to Feb. 1919. *Address*: Gippeswyck, Pinner, Middlesex. (M1523)

CAUTLEY, Major Harry Llewellyn, O.B.E.
CAUVIN, Major William Stephen, O.B.E.
CAVAGE, Capt. Ronald James, M.B.E.
CAVAN, Samuel Edward, M.B.E.
CAVANAGH, Capt. Henry James, O.B.E., L.D.S., R.C.S., b. 4 April, 1885; s. of John Cavanagh, of Dublin; m. Louise, d. of Daniel Cronin, of Cork. *Educ.*: St. Thomas', Ireland. Dental Surgeon. *War Work*: Served in the R.A.S.C. in Gallipoli, Egypt, and France, Aug. 1914, to April, 1919. *Address*: The Boundary, West Ealing, W. *Clubs*: Services; United R.A.S.C. (O5087)

CAVE, Beatrice Julia, Mrs., O.B.E., b. 20 Sept. 1863; d. of Sir Frederick Martin Williams, Bart., of Tregullow, Scorrier, Cornwall, and Heanton Punchardon, Barnstaple; m. Charles Henry, s. of Sir Charles D. Cave, Bart., of Sidbury Manor, Sidmouth, and Cleve Hill, Downend, Gloucestershire. *War Work*: Vice-President, Lawford's Gate Division, Gloucestershire Branch of the British Red Cross Society; Commandant of Cleve Hill V.A. Hospital, Downend, Gloucestershire, 1914–19. *Address*: Sidbury Manor, Sidmouth. (O1196)

CAVE, Capt. George Ellis, C.B.E. Capt. R.N. Served in Great War, 1914–19, as Div. Naval Transport Officer, Avonmouth (despatches). (C2245)

CAVE, Hugo Charles, M.B.E.

CAVE, Col. Sir Thomas Sturmy, K.C.B., C.B.E., V.D., T.D., T.F. (ret.), b. 23 Sept. 1846; s. of William Cave, of Yatley, Hants.; m. Beatrice Maria, d. of Edward Carlile, of Richmond, Surrey. *Educ.*: Queenswood College. Hon. Col., 4th Hampshires; served in Volunteers and Territorials from 1863; Ensign, 1865; Lieut., 1867; Captain, 1870; Major, 1877; Lieut.-Col., 1886; Col., 1888; commanded battalion, 1888–1906; concurrently A.D.A.F. (Vols.), 1904–06; commanded South Midland Infantry Brigade, 1906–10; commanded Composite Brigade, T.F., at Coronation of King George V. and Queen Mary, 1911. *War Work*: Chairman of War Emergency Committee of National Council of Y.M.C.A., 1914–19. *Address*: Kilworth, Woking. *Clubs*: Constitutional; National. (C454)

CAVE, Wilhelmina Mary Henrietta, Mrs. Charles, O.B.E., b. 1872; d. of Major Francis E. Kerr, late of The Rifle Brigade; m. Charles John Philip Cave, J.P., s. of the late Laurence Trent Cave, of Ditcham Park, Petersfield. *Educ.*: Convent of Sacred Heart, Roehampton. *War Work*: Vice-President, Petersfield Division, Hants Branch, B.R.C.S.; Chairman of two hospital committees; Belgian Refugees (Médaille de la Reine Elizabeth). *Address*: Ditcham Park, Petersfield, Hants. *Club*: Ladies' Athenæum. (O10128)

CAVE, Beatrice Mabel CAVE-BROWNE-, M.B.E.; d. of Sir Thomas Cave-Browne-Cave, C.B., of Burnage, Streatham Common (see BURKE'S *Peerage*). *Educ.*: Girton. *War Work*: Aeronautical research for the Admiralty, Air Department, Air Ministry, and Aircraft Production Department. *Address*: Burnage, Streatham Common, S.W. 16. (M7643)

CAVE, Wing Comm. Thomas Reginald CAVE-BROWNE-, C.B.E., R.A.F., F.R.Ae.S., A.M.I.N.A., A.M.I.M.E., b. 11 Jan. 1885; s. of Sir Thomas Cave-Browne-Cave, Kt., D.L., late of War Office (see BURKE'S *Peerage*); m. Marjorie Gwynne, d. of Albert Wright, of Idle, Yorkshire. *Educ.*: Dulwich Coll., and Royal Navy (Engineering). Deputy Director of Research (Airships), Air Ministry. *War Work*: R.N.A.S., and R.A.F.; design and construction of British non-rigid airships, and later in charge of airship experiments. *Address*: 43, Tierney Road, Streatham Hill, S.W. 2. *Clubs*: R.A.F.; Junior Army and Navy. (C853)

CAVENDISH, Elizabeth Janet, Hon. Mrs. William Edwin, O.B.E.; d. of Thomas Baillie, of New South Wales; m. Brig.-Gen. William Edwin Cavendish, s. of William, 2nd Baron Chesham. *War Work*: Equipped and organised, and was

Commandant of, V.A.D. Hospital, "Whitehall," Sawtry, Huntingdonshire, 1915–18. *Address*: The Farm House, Holkham, Norfolk. (O1197)

CAVILL, Lieut. Herbert John, O.B.E., R.N.R.

CAW, William Strathie, O.B.E., J.P., b. 4 Dec. 1862; s. of William Caw, of Edinburgh; m. Mary, d. of James B. Veitch, of Carlops, Peeblesshire. Treasurer and Clerk of the Royal Infirmary of Edinburgh. *War Work*: Acted as Superintendent of the Royal Infirmary of Edinburgh, in addition to duties as Treasurer and Clerk, from Aug. 1915, to Feb. 1919. *Address*: 19, Queen's Crescent, Edinburgh. *Club*: Scottish Conservative, Edinburgh. (O10129)

CAWOOD, Charles John, M.B.E., J.P. Commissioner, Ministry of Agriculture and Fisheries. *Address*: 47, Esplanade, Scarborough. (M1525)

CAY, Albert, M.B.E., J.P., b. 2 Sept. 1846; s. of Robert Dundas Cay, of Shepperton, Edinburgh; m. Annie, d. of Sir John Jaffray, Bart., of Skilts, Redditch. *Educ.*: Edinburgh Academy, and Edinburgh Univ. Lay Canon of Coventry Cathedral. *War Work*: Hon. Treasurer, Soldiers' and Sailors' Families Assn. for County of Warwick; Hon. Treasurer, Statutory Committee for the County of Warwick; Hon. Treasurer, War Pensions Committee for the County of Warwick; Hon. Treasurer, Munition Workers' Mission, Diocese of Worcester. *Address*: Woodside, Kenilworth, Warwickshire. *Clubs*: Union; R.A.C.; Union, Birmingham. (M7644)

CAYLEY, Dora, M.B.E.

CAZENOVE, Major Percy, O.B.E.

CECIL, Alicia Margaret, Hon. Mrs. Evelyn, C.B.E., d. of Lord Amherst of Hackney; m. Rt. Hon. Evelyn Cecil, M.P., s. of Lieut.-Col. Lord Eustace Cecil, s. of the 2nd Marquess of Salisbury. Lady of Justice of the Order of St. John of Jerusalem; Freedom of the Gardeners' Company and of the City of London; on Committee of Management, Chelsea Physic Garden; Vice-Chairman of the Council of the Society for the Oversea Settlement of British Women. *War Work*: Member of the Joint Collections Committee, St. John and Red Cross; worked in St. John Hospital until Food Production Dept. was formed in 1917, when she became Hon. Asst.-Director of Horticulture. *Address*: 2, Cadogan Square, S.W. 1. *Club*: Ladies' Empire. (C2398)

CHADWICK, Capt. Alan Wentworth, O.B.E., b. 19 March, 1890; s. of Rev. J. H. Chadwick. *Educ.*: St. Edward's, and Queen's Coll., Oxford. *War Work*: 2nd Lieut. Hampshire Regt. (11th Batt. Pioneers), 29 Aug. 1914; served in France, Dec. 1915, to Aug. 1916; and May, 1917, to June, 1919; twice wounded, June, 1916, and June, 1917. *Club*: Isthmian. (O5089)

CHADWICK, Edith Caroline, M.B.E.; d. of Samuel Joseph Chadwick, of Dewsbury. *Educ.*: Privately, and Göttingen. Member of Dewsbury Education Committee, 1914–19; Hon. Sec. Dewsbury Day Nursery, 1913–19; President of Dewsbury Day Nursery, 1919; Hon. Sec. Dewsbury and District Nursing Association, 1918–19. *War Work*: Member, and formerly Vice-Chairman, of Dewsbury War Pensions Committee; Member of Belgian Refugees' Committee; Member of Dewsbury Patriotic Committee; Hon. Sec. of Ladies' Visiting Committee (for visiting wives and families of Sailors and Soldiers, and for distributing weekly grants from Patriotic Committee's Funds). *Address*: Boyne Hill, Chapelthorpe, near Wakefield. (M7646)

CHADWICK, Harry Bernard Clarke, M.B.E.

CHADWICK, Thomas, M.B.E.

CHAFF, Thomas Waycott, M.B.E., M.R.C.S., L.R.C.P.

CHAFFEY, Col. Ralph Anderson, C.B.E., V.D., J.P., b. 1856; s. of the late Major E. Chaffey, of Keinton Mandeville, Somerset; m. Agnes Rosa, d. of the late Dr. Webster (Army Medical), of Balruddery, Otago, N.Z. *Educ.*: Sherborne. Sheep Farmer. *War Work*: Commanding Canterbury Military District, June, 1914, to Nov. 1919. *Address*: Keinton Combe, Waiau, N.Z. *Club*: Christchurch. (C722)

CHAINEY, Capt. George Barrett, O.B.E., R.A.F.

CHALDECOTT, Harold Richards, O.B.E.

CHALKER, Alfred Caulke, M.B.E., b. 25 Sept. 1865; s. of Horace Chalker, of Norwich; m. Edith Anna, d. of Harold Bridger, of Chichester. *Educ.*: Walberton. Stationmaster, Crystal Palace Low Level, L. B. and S. C. Railway. *War Work*: 750,000 seamen, and 500,000 soldiers passed through his station on demobilization. *Address*: Stationmaster, Crystal Palace Low Level, L. B. and S. C. (M7647)

CHALKLEY, Alfred Philip, M.B.E.

CHALKLEY, Major Francis Henry, M.B.E.

CHALLICE, R.S.M. Sydney, M.B.E., b. 12 Jan. 1883; s. of William Challice, of Exwick, Exeter, Devonshire; m. Alice, d. of John Salvin, of Richmond, Yorkshire. *Educ.*: Exwick, Exeter, Devonshire. *War Work*: Western Front, France, Aug. 1914, to June, 1919; mentioned in Sir Douglas Haig's despatches, 14 Dec. 1917, for gallantry and devotion to duty; awarded the Meritorious Service Medal, 1914 Star, British War Medal, Victory Medal, Long Service and Good Conduct Medal. *Address*: The Barracks, Richmond, Yorkshire. (M4444)

CHALLINOR, William Robert, M.B.E., b. 26 Oct. 1872; s. of Alfred Challinor, M.R.C.V.S., of Bolton-le-Moors, Lancashire; m. Elizabeth Openshaw, d. of James Addison, of Gorsefield, Lytham, Lancs. *Educ.*: Bolton Church Institute and Bolton Grammar School. Partner in firm of Langston, Goode & Challinor; Member of the Manchester Stock Exchange; Director of the Star Paper Mill Co. (1920), Ltd., Feniscowles, near Blackburn, Lancs.; Chairman of Directors, Rendevous

Café, Wigan, Lancs. *War Work:* In 1914, joined the Wigan County Borough Police Special Constabulary; acted as intermediary for the Soldiers' and Sailors' Families Association, Wigan Branch, between that centre and the various Army Pay Offices in the area, in all matters affecting Army pay, separation allowances, etc; undertook alien inquiries, and owing to having had private wireless telegraphy station, prior to 1914, continuously served for duty in this connection in various areas; Special Inspector, Wigan County Borough Police, and awarded Special Constabulary Medal. *Club:* Lytham Yacht.   (M228)

CHALLIS, Major Oswald, O.B.E., late R.A.M.C., *b.* 1872. *Educ.:* St. George's. South African War, 1899–1901; severely wounded at Battle of Rhenoster Kop, 29 Nov. 1900; mentioned in despatches, "London Gazette," 7 May, and 10 Sept. 1901; Queen's Medal with 3 clasps; relinquished Commission, May, 1905. *War Work* Employed at War Office (Army Medical Dept.), July, 1915 to June, 1920; promoted to Major, 6 Sept. 1917; mentioned for services, March, 1918. *Address:* 23, Dorset Square, N.W. *Club:* R.A.C.   (O6986)

CHALLONER, Bromley, M.B.E.

CHALMERS, Jessie Elder, Mrs., O.B.E.

CHALMERS, Kenneth Edlmann, O.B.E., *b.* 15 Sept. 1873; *s.* of the late Frederick Chalmers, of Farrants, Bickley, Kent; *m.* Agnes, *d.* of the Rev. Canon Theobald, of Lasham, Alton, Hants. *Edu.:* Eton and Balliol, Barrister; Member of Kent C.C. *War Work:* Hon. Sec. of S. & S.F.A., and afterwards Chairman of Bromley (Kent) War Pensions Committee; Vice-Chairman of Kent Disablement W. P. Committee; Vice-Chairman of Kent County Fund (V.A.D.); Special Constable. *Addresses:* Blackbrook, Bickley, Kent; 8, Fig Tree Court, Temple, E.C. *Clubs:* Reform; Union; Wellington. (O3655)

CHALMERS, Margaret, M.B.E.

CHALMERS, Robert, O.B.E., B.Sc., A.M.I.C.E., late Lieut.-Col. R.M., *b.* 18 June, 1883; *s.* of Robert Chalmers, of Dundee; *m.* Margaret Colville, *d.* of — Duff, of Glasgow. *Educ.:* Dundee High School, and St. Andrews. *War Work:* On Engineering Staff of Messrs. Easton, Gibb & Son, Ltd., Contractors at H.M. Dockyard, Rosyth, till Feb. 1918; March to Aug. 1918, Special Mission to Ægean Ports for the Admiralty Aug. 1918, to Feb. 1919, Tank Factory at Chateauroux. *Addresses:* 79, Stretton Road, Croydon, Surrey; Messrs. S. Pearson and Son (Contracting Dept.), Ltd., 10, Victoria Street, S.W. 1.   (O10131)

CHALMERS, Major Robert Arthur, O.B.E., A.F.C. R.A.F.

CHALMERS, Major William, O.B.E., R.A.O.C.

CHAMBERLAIN, Alfred John, M.B.E., *b.* 2 Nov. 1868; *s.* of Alfred Chamberlain, of West Hampstead, London; *m.* Florence Elizabeth, *d.* of John Oates, of South Hampstead, London. *Educ.:* Privately. Entered Accounting Department, Railway Clearing House, 1883. *War Work:* Lent to Admiralty (Transport Department) by Railway Clearing House, Jan. 1916, for duration of war; transferred to Ministry of Shipping on its formation in 1917; appointed Assistant to Financial Representative, British Ministry of Shipping, New York, May, 1918. *Addresses:* 269, West Seventy-Second Street, New York; 9, Granville Road, St. Albans, Herts.
(M7648)

CHAMBERLAIN, Fernley John, C.B.E., *b.* 19 July, 1879; *s.* of William Henry Chamberlain, of Plymouth; *m.* Gertrude, *d.* of John Holloway, of Stoke-on-Trent. *Educ.:* Plymouth Public and Science and Art Schools. Associate National Secretary of Young Men's Christian Association. *Addresses:* 26, Bedford Place, W.C. 1; 16, Russell Square, W.C. 1.
(C127)

CHAMBERLAIN, Helen, Mrs., *b.* 21 Oct. 1880; *d.* of Edward Jackson, of Tynemouth; *m.* Arthur Chamberlain, *s.* of Arthur Chamberlain, of Moor-Green Hall, Birmingham. *Educ.:* St. Leonard's School; St. Andrew's, N.B. *War Work:* Assistant County Director, S.J.A.B. and Brit. Red Cross Society. *Address:* 6, Cheyne Walk, Chelsea, S.W. (O1199)

CHAMBERLAIN, William, O.B.E., *b.* 3 April, 1849; *s.* of William Chamberlain, of Ruddington, Notts.; *m.* Elizabeth (died 1920), *d.* of James Taylor, of Duffield. *Educ.:* Privately. Royal Colonial Institute, London, appointed Clerk 1874; Chief Clerk 1889; Assist. Sec. 1916; *War Work:* Organised the arrangements for the transport of overseas Wounded Soldiers that were entertained by the R.C.I. and the various City Companies, etc., under the direction of the Council of the Institute, who were responsible for their transport to and from the various hospitals. *Address:* 33, Kempshott Road, Streatham Common, S.W. 16.   (O8881)

CHAMBERLIN, Lieut.-Comm. Trevor Ronald, O.B.E., R.N.

CHAMBERS, Evelyn Marion, M.B.E., *b.* 26 Jan. 1895; *d.* of James Chambers, M.D., of The Priory, Roehampton. *Educ.:* Putney High School, and Lady Margaret Hall, Oxford. *War Work:* Assistant Head Clerk, Offices of the War Cabinet) *Address:* The Priory, Roehampton, S.W. 15.   (M7649)

CHAMBERS, Major F., O.B.E.

CHAMBERS, Francis George, M.B.E.

CHAMBERS, Rev. Frank Hanson, O.B.E.

CHAMBERS, Frank William, O.B.E.

CHAMBERS, Major Frederick Foster, O.B.E., R.A.F.

CHAMBERS, Capt. George Kirby, M.B.E., R.G.A.

CHAMBERS, Lieut.-Col. George Lawson, C.B.E., *b.* 29 March, 1852; *s.* of George Chambers, of Preston, Lancashire; *m.* Gertrude Grace, *d.* of Edward Liddell, of Leith. *Educ.:*

Tettenhall College. Late Member of Legislative Council, Madras; Chairman of Chamber of Commerce, Madras; Commandant, Madras Artillery Volunteers; President, Anglo-Indian Association; Founder of Victoria Technical Institute. *War Work:* Official Consignor (Dyes Dept.), Board of Trade; Officer Commanding 4th Batt. (National Guard), City of London Rifle Vols.; Special Constable, Herts. *Address:* 24, Heath Drive, Hampstead, N.W. 3. *Clubs:* Oriental; Royal and Ancient Golf; St. Andrews; Royal Dornoch Golf.
(C2514)

CHAMBERS, Major Harold Tullis, O.B.E., *b.* 21 Feb. 1891, *s.* of G. C. Chambers, of Wallasey. *Educ.:* Gresham's School, Holt, Norfolk, and King's Coll., Cambridge. Associate of the Chartered Accountants. *War Work:* R.A.S.C., Aug. 1914 to Feb. 1920; with 10th (Irish) Division, Gallipoli, Serbia, 1915; Macedonia 1916; G.H.Q., Salonica, 1916–19; G.H.Q. Constantinople, 1919–20; D.A.D.S.T., G.H.Q. Army of the Black Sea. *Address:* 124, Manor Road, Wallasey, Cheshire. *Club:* R.A.S.C.   (O3025)

CHAMBERS, Harry, M.B.E.. *b.* 1 Feb. 1882; *s.* of Henry Chambers, of Walmer. Staff Clerk, Ministry of Agriculture and Fisheries. *War Work:* Lent to Ministry of Food; Private Secretary to Director-General of Food Production; head of Seeds Branch, Food Production. *Address:* 7, Adelaide Road, Brockley, S.E. 1.   (M230)

CHAMBERS, Helen, C.B.E., M.D., B.S.

CHAMBERS, Henry, M.B.E.

CHAMBERS, James Thomas, C.B.E., *b.* 23 July, 1867. *Educ.:* Boys' Free School, St. Neots, Hunts. Treasurer, National Sailors' and Firemens' Union; Member, National Maritime Board; Trustee, Special Fund for Seamen, Nat. Insurance Act, 1918; Member, Central Committee Minesweepers' Co-operative Trawling Society; Treasurer, Merchant Seamens' War Memorial Society. *War Work:* Specially amongst men of the Mercantile Marine. *Address:* 7, Brougham Road, Acton, W. 3. *Club:* National Liberal. (C2515)

CHAMBERS, Capt. Robert Alexander, O.B.E., I.M.G.

CHAMBERS, Lieut. Sydney Arthur, O.B.E., R.E.

CHAMBERS, Sir Theodore Gervase, K.B.E., *b.* 31 Jan. 1871; *s.* of Charles Harcourt Chambers, Barrister-at-Law, of 2, Chesham Place, S.W.; *m.* Georgina Maria Sandeman. *Educ.:* Tonbridge; St. Paul's; Royal School of Mines. Surveyor. *War Work:* Hon. Sec., Professional Classes Relief Association; Sec. and Controller, National War Savings Committee. *Address:* 8, North Street, Westminster, S.W. 1. *Clubs:* Union; Royal Automobile.   (K135)

CHAMBRE, Capt. John, M.B.E., M.D., R.A.F.

CHAMIER, John Adrian, O.B.E.

CHAMIER, Lieut.-Col. William, C.B.E., V.D.

CHAMIER, Lieut.-Col. William St. George, O.B.E.

CHAMPION, John Alfred Cuthbert, O.B.E.

CHAMPION, Mary Ann, Mrs., M.B.E.

CHAMPION, Major Samuel Stewart, O.B.E., J.P.

CHAMPION DE CRESPIGNY, Lieut.-Col. George Harrison, C.B.E., J.P., *b.* 9 July, 1863; *o. s.* of the late Col. C. B. Champion de Crespigny, of Folkestone, Kent (*see* BURKE'S *Peerage*); *m.* 1890, Gwendoline Blanch, *y. d.* of the late W. C. Clarke-Thornhill, of Rushton Hall, Northants, and Fixby, Yorkshire. *Educ.:* Felstead. Late Lieut. 48th Northamptonshire Regt.; Lieut.-Col. Commanding 3rd Batt. (Special Reserve) Northamptonshire Regt. 1914–1918; afterwards attached Head-Quarter Staff till Armistice. *Address:* 21, York Terrace, York Gate, N.W.1. *Club:* Junior United Service.   (C1510)

CHAMPNESS, Edward Leslie, M.B.E., M.Sc., *b.* 10 Oct. 1891; *s.* of the late Edward Coulter Champness, of London; *m.* Rowena Sanderson, *d.* of the late J. B. Duckworth, J.P., of The Heys, Eastham, Cheshire. *Educ.:* Barnard Castle, and Durham Univ. Naval Architect. *War Work:* Assistant Naval Constructor, Royal Corps of Naval Constructors; on Staff of Director of Naval Construction, Admiralty. *Address:* The Walled Cottage, Dynas Powis, Glamorganshire. (M7652)

CHAMPNEYS, Edith, Mrs., M.B.E., *b.* 14 Aug. 1863; *d.* of Francis Harris, of 24, Cavendish Square, London, S.W.; *m.* the Rev. Francis Weldon Champneys, Rector of Frant, and Canon of Chichester. *Educ.:* Privately, and Queen's Coll. *War Work:* Quartermaster, and from 1916, Commandant, Shernfold Park Hospital, Frant, Sussex. *Address:* The Rectory, Frant, Sussex.   (M7653)

CHANCE, Sir Arthur, Knt. Bach. C.B.E., F.R.C.S.I., F.R.C.P.I.(Hon.), F.R.C.S.(Edin.)(Hon.), *b.* 15 June, 1859; *s.* of Albert Chance and Elizabeth Fleming; *m.* 1st, Martha (d. 1891), *d.* of the late Daniel Rooney, Belfast; 2nd, Eileen, *d.* of the late William Murphy, Dartry. *Educ.:* Univ. Coll., Dublin. Member of Council Royal College of Surgeons, Ireland; Senior Surgeon, Mater Misericordiæ Hospital; Consulting Surgeon, Orthopædic Hospital of Ireland; Consulting Surgeon, Doctor Steevens Hospital; Consulting Surgeon, Dental Hospital of Ireland; Consulting Surgeon, St. Michael's Hospital; Col. A.M.S.; Inspector, Special Military Surgical Hospitals; Irish Command; Member General Medical Council; Medical Visitor in Lunacy under the High Court of Chancery, in Ireland; President, Royal College of Surgeons in Ireland, 1904–6; Surgeon to Jervis Street Hospital, 1884–86; Examiner in Surgery, R.C.S.I., 1893–95, 1896–99; Surgeon in Ordinary to the Lord Lieutenant of Ireland, 1892–95 and 1906–15; Member of Senate of National Univ. of Ireland, 1914. *Address:* 90, Merrion Square, Dublin.   (C1511)

CHANCE, Lieut.-Col. Ernest Washington, O.B.E., T.D.,

LL.B., F.R.G.S., b. 28 Oct. 1880; s. of William Chance, of Leigh. Educ.: Privately; King's Coll., Univ. of London; and Gray's Inn. Barrister-at-Law; served in South Africa, 1901–2, Medal and 3 clasps; assistant Controller of Non-Ferrous Raw Materials, Ministry of Munitions; Member of Raw Materials Committee; Senior Staff Officer, Ministry of Transport, 1920. War Work: Served Aug. 1914, to June, 1919, in Army; raised 35th Divisional Ammunition Column, Royal Field Artillery; raised 13th Batt. Bedfordshire Regt. Address: 1, Essex Court, Temple, E.C. (O6987)

CHANCE, Sir Frederick (William), K.B.E., J.P., D.L., b. 26 Dec. 1852; s. of Edward Chance, J.P., D.L., of Malvern; m. 1st in 1884, Mary, d. of George Berkley Seton-Karr, I.C.S.; d. (1905); 2ndly in 1908, Josephine, youngest d. of Sir Wilfrid Lawson, 2nd Bart. Educ.: Harrow; Caius College, Cambridge. Chairman, Ferguson Bros., Ltd., Carlisle; Director of Bank of Liverpool and Martins; Director, Cockermouth, Keswick and Penrith Railway; formerly M.P. for Carlisle, 1905–10. War Work: Chairman, Local Advisory Committee of Central Liquor Control Board; Hon. Col., Cumberland Volunteer Border Regiment, 1st Batt. Addresses: Morton, Carlisle; Lancrigg, Grasmere. Club: Brooks. (K358)

CHANCE, Major Maurice, O.B.E., b. 28 Oct. 1882; s. of William Chance, of Leigh, Essex. Educ.: Bancroft, and King's Coll. War Work: Officer Commanding London Areas from Brentford to Tilbury Docks, 13th Batt. Bedfordshire Regt., for Transport Work; supervised detachments loading and discharging over million tons of Ammunition; War Stores Food Supplies, under Port and Transit Executive Committee; Commanding Battalion at Croydon until disbandment of unit, Aug. 1919. Address: Fairdene, Dorking. Club: National Liberal. (O6988)

CHANDLER, Alfred, C.B.E., b. 11 Nov. 1853; s. of James Henry Chandler, of Liverpool; m. Catherine, d. of Robert Williams, of Liverpool. Educ.: Liverpool Institute. late General Manager and Secretary, Mersey Docks and Harbour Board, Liverpool. War Work: Administration of the Port of Liverpool, the work of which, during the War, largely exceeded that of any other Port in the United Kingdom. Address: Broadlands, Alexandra Drive, Liverpool. (C455)

CHANDLER, Major Arthur Frederick Neale, O.B.E. R.A.O.C.

CHANDLER, Major Cecil John Golding, O.B.E., R.A.O.C.

CHANDLER, Capt. Charles Kingsley, M.B.E., R.A.F.

CHANDLER, F., O.B.E.

CHANDLER, 2nd Lieut. Frederick Joseph, M.B.E., R.G.A. (T.F.)

CHANDLER, Capt. Hugh Elphinstone, M.B.E.

CHANDLER, Capt. John Marsden, M.B.E.

CHANDLER, T. Warrant Officer S., M.B.E. Royal Indian Marine.

CHANDLER, William George, M.B.E., b. 25 Sept. 1860; s. of the late William Chandler, of Bath; m. Mabel, d. of the late George Baker, of Eastbourne. Educ.: Bath Grammar School. House Furnisher and China Merchant. War Work: Hon. Sec. Darlington War Savings Committee; Deputy Group Leader for Special Constables; Member of the Food Control Committee, etc. Address: 107, Bondgate, Darlington. (M7654)

CHANNER, Frederick Francis Ralph, O.B.E., b. 20 June, 1875; s. of Rev. E. C. Channer, of Durdham Park, Bristol; m. Edith Janie, d. of the late Gen. G. W. Channer, V.C., C.B. Educ.: St. Paul's School, London. Conservator of Forests; Imperial Forest Service of India, 1896. War Work: Special supply of forest hay for the overseas forces in Mesopotamia and Palestine. Address: c/o Lloyd's Bank, Ltd., Market Harborough, England. (O8241)

CHANTER, Francis William, M.B.E., J.P.

CHANTER, Frederick, M.B.E.

CHANTLER, John Dale, M.B.E., s. of John Dale Chantler, of Manchester; m. Ann, d. of Robert Ainscow, of Manchester. Educ.: Privately. J.P., City of Manchester, 1905; Councillor, City of Manchester, from 1907 to date. War Work: Leader Special Constables, Manchester. Address: 274, Dickenson Road, Rusholme, Manchester. (M7657)

CHANTREY, Guy Mortimer, M.B.E.

CHAPLIN, Constance Helena, M.B.E.

CHAPLIN, Frank, M.B.E., b. 1870; s. of Cecil Chaplin. Educ.: Harrow. Banker. Address: 21, Great Cumberland Place. (M1527)

CHAPLIN, Lieut. Henry Slater, O.B.E., R.A.O.C.

CHAPLIN, Margaret Seton, Lady, C.B.E.; d. of the late William Seton Smith; m. 8 Aug, 1895, Sir Francis Drummond Percy, K.C.M.G., s. of Major Percy Chaplin, 60th Rifles, of Chavenage, Tetbury, Glos. Address: Government House, Salisbury, Rhodesia. (C732)

CHAPLIN, Lieut.-Col. Reginald Spencer, O.B.E.

CHAPMAN, Brig.-Gen. Archibald John, C.B., C.M.G. C.B.E., b. 1862; s. of John E. Chapman, of Monkstown, co. Dublin; m. 1895, Annie Evelyn, 2nd d. of George Orr Wilson, formerly of Dunardagh, Blackrock, co. Dublin. Educ.: Privately. Entered Roy. Dublin Fusiliers, 1884; became Capt. 1892; Major, 1901; Brevet Lieut.-Col. 1901; Lieut.-Col. 1906; Brevet Col. 1907; Col. 1910; Commanded 1st R.D.F., 1906–10; Commanded Staffs. Inf. Bde., T.F., 1911–12; Gen. Staff Officer, N. Command, 1912–14; served in S. Africa, 1898–1902 (wounded, despatches three times, Queen's medal

with six clasps, King's medal with two clasps, Brevet Lieut.-Col.); during Great War 1914–18 as Brig.-Comm. (despatches twice, Comm. Legion of Honour); appointed Inspector of Inf. 1915, with rank of Brig.-Gen. Address: Condover House, Shrewsbury. Clubs: Army and Navy; Sports'. (C1984)

CHAPMAN, Major Charles Leonard, O.B.E., R.M.L.I.

CHAPMAN, Edmund Alensby, M.B.E., b. 17 July, 1875; s. of Edmund Chapman, of Ely; m. Amy, d. of Peter Low, of Dalston, N. London. Educ.: St. Mark's, Gillingham; H.M. Dockyard School, Chatham. Foreman of Boilermakers, H.M. Dockyard, Devonport. War Work: Engaged during the war in supervising repairs to Boilers of H.M. Ships. Address: 1, Amhurst Road, Plymouth. (M7658)

CHAPMAN, Edward Henry, M.B.E., b. 14 Sept. 1880; s. of T. T. Chapman, of Gravesend, Kent. Educ.: Clarence Coll., Gravesend, and King's Coll., London. Superintendent, H.M. Stationery Office, Manchester. Addresses: The Hydro, Bowdon, Cheshire; 11, The Grove, Gravesend, Kent. Club: Gravesend Sailing. (M7659)

CHAPMAN, Major Edward Henry, O.B.E.

CHAPMAN, Edward Stuart, O.B.E., b. 23 Oct. 1858; s. of John Chapman, of Gloucester; m. Susan Ella, d. of William Davies. Educ.: Commercial Travellers' School; City of London School. Deputy Accountant and Comptroller-General, Inland Revenue. War Work: Revenue Work. Address: 7, Rodenhurst Road, Clapham, S.W. (O10132)

CHAPMAN, Florence, M.B.E.

CHAPMAN, George Alfred, M.B.E., b. 29 April, 1878; s. of George Chapman, of Folkestone, Kent; m. Nora Vera Rose, d. of William Henry McDermott, of Catonpore, India. Educ.: Lawrence Memorial Asylum, Murree, India. Stationmaster, North-Western Railway, India. Served in the 11th P.A.O. Hussars, Aug. 1893 to Sept. 1902. War Work: Transportation of Troops; also Concentration for Marrie and Afghanistan Field Forces. Address: Lytton Road, Quetta, Baluchistan. (M6122)

CHAPMAN, Major George James, O.B.E., R.E.

CHAPMAN, George Russell, M.B.E.

CHAPMAN, Major Guy Patterson, O.B.E.

CHAPMAN, Major Harry Ernest, O.B.E.; Border Regt.; b. 19 Feb. 1870; s. of Harry Stephenson Chapman, C.E.; m. Catherine Harriette Jessie, d. of the late Arthur Fremlin. Educ.: Royal Naval School. War Work: Deputy Chief Constable of Kent till Nov. 1915; British Adriatic Mission with Serbs, 1916; France, 1916. Address: Sheals Court, Maidstone, Kent. (O10133)

CHAPMAN, Capt. James Austin, O.B.E.

CHAPMAN, James Gardiner, M.B.E.

CHAPMAN, James Henry, M.B.E., b. 8 Feb. 1871; s. of J. S. Chapman, of London; m. Louisa, d. of J. Burke of London. Educ.: High School, Stratford, Essex. Engineer Manager (outside), Messrs. Vickers, Limited, Barrow-in-Furness. War Work: Charge of erection gun mounting machinery and director firing gear, from 1913 to present date. Club: National Sporting. (M7661)

CHAPMAN, John Barnett, O.B.E., b. 25 Aug. 1865; s. of John Chapman, of Hull; m. Annie Louisa, d. of Robert Bailey, of Hull. Educ.: Hull Elementary School, and privately. Town Clerk, and Clerk of the Peace, Burton-upon-Trent. War Work: Secretary to the Burton-upon-Trent Recruiting Committee; Clerk to the Local (Military) Tribunal; sec. to the National Service Committee; Executive Officer to the Local Food Control Committee, and Sec. to the Belgian Refugee Committee; for services rendered in the last-mentioned capacity awarded by H.M. the King of the Belgians the Médaille du Roi Albert avec rayure. Addresses: Ashleigh, Stapenhill, Burton-upon-Trent; Town Hall, Burton-upon-Trent. (O10134)

CHAPMAN, Capt. and Qr.-Mr. John Damian, O.B.E., R.A.M.C. (T.F.)

CHAPMAN, Major Joseph Thomas, O.B.E.

CHAPMAN, Leonard, O.B.E. (O5091)

CHAPMAN, Marie Langslow, M.B.E.

CHAPMAN, Maud Jewell, Mrs., M.B.E., M.A.; d. of John Robertson Reep, Solicitor; m. Stanley Salter Chapman, F.C.A. Educ.: Girton Coll. Cambridge. War Work: Administrative, Ministry of Shipping. Address: The Women's Institute, 92, Victoria Street, S.W. 1. (M7662)

CHAPMAN, Oswald Cotton, O.B.E., b. 7 Sept. 1885; s. of Dr. C. W. Chapman, 121, Harley Street, W. Educ.: Westminster School, and Christ Church, Oxford. Civil Servant. War Work: Sec. Freight and Transport Section, Commission Internationale de Ravitaillement; British Sec. Raw Materials Section, Supreme Economic Council, Paris; after Armistice, in charge of Paris Office of Ministry of Munitions Address: Highwood Coombe, Mill Hill, N.W. (O10135)

CHAPMAN, Paul Morgan, M.B.E., M.D., F.R.C.P. (Lond.), b. 18 Oct. 1852; s. of Evershed Chapman, of Homerton, London; m. Alice Elizabeth, d. of Rev. John Lewis, of Cascob Rectory, Radnorshire. Educ.: Shrewsbury, Univ. Coll., London. Consulting Physician, and Physician in Charge of Venereal Clinic to Herefordshire General Hospital; Medical Referee for Herefordshire and Radnorshire. War Work: Senior Physician Herefordshire General Hospital; Physician in charge of Beechwood V.A.D. Red Cross Hospital, Hereford; Consulting Physician to Sarnesfield V.A.D. Red Cross Hospital, near Hereford, throughout the war. Addresses: Beechwood,

Hereford; 1, St. John Street, Hereford. *Club*: Herefordshire County. (M10261*h*)

CHAPMAN, Richard Herbert, O.B.E., Solicitor and Commissioner for Oaths. *War Work*: Hon. Local Organiser, Enquiry Department for Wounded and Missing, East Lancashire Branch of the British Red Cross Society. *Addresses*: 33, Cheltenham Road, Chorlton-cum-Hardy; 56A, Mosley Street, Manchester. (O10136)

CHAPMAN, Sir Sydney John, K.C.B., C.B.E., *b.* 20 April, 1871; *s.* of the late David Chapman, of Wells, Norfolk; *m.* Mabel Gwendoline, *d.* of T. H. Mordey, J.P., of Newport, Mon. *Educ.*: Manchester Grammar School; Owens Coll.; Trinity Coll., Cambridge. Joint Permanent Sec. Board of Trade; sometime Professor and Dean of Faculty of Commerce in University of Manchester. *War Work*: Board of Trade. *Address*: 3, Oak Hill Park, Hampstead, London, N.W. 3. *Clubs*: New University; Authors'. (C19)

CHAPMAN, Lieut.-Col. T. H., O.B.E., V.D.

CHAPMAN, Walter, O.B.E., M.B.

CHAPPÉ, Penelope Louise, Mrs., C.B.E., *b.* 1869; *d.* of F. W. McEwan, of Durban, Natal; *m.* Paul Laffette Chappé. Pres. Durham Women's Patriotic League and Natal Centre, S. Africa Red Cross Soc.; Hon. Sec. and Treasurer S. African Soldiers' and Sailors' Graves Committee (Durban Branch). *Address*: Brightside, Mitchell Park, Durban, Natal. (C2000)

CHAPPELL, Ernest, C.B.E.

CHARLES, Ernest Bruce, C.B.E., K.C., *b.* 15 June, 1871; *s.* of Rt. Hon. Sir Arthur Charles, of The Woodlands, Sevenoaks (*see* BURKE'S *Peerage*). *Educ.*: Clifton, and New Coll., Oxford. One of His Majesty's Counsel; Recorder of Bournemouth; Commissary General of the Diocese of Canterbury; Chancellor of Hereford; Chancellor of Wakefield. *War Work*: Director of Wounded and Missing Department, British Red Cross in France; Hon. Legal Adviser to British Red Cross in France; Civil Member of the Claims Commission in France. *Address*: The Woodlands, Sevenoaks. *Club*: Savile. (C940)

CHARLES, Esther, M.B.E.

CHARLES, Gertrude Mary, Mrs., M.B.E.

CHARLES, Capt. Sir James Thomas Walter, K.B.E., C.B., R.D., R.N.R., Commanding the Cunard R.M.S. " Aquitania," *b.* 2 Aug. 1865; 2nd *s.* of the late James Charles; *m.* Eleanor Mary, *e.d.* of the Rev. T. Macfarlane, of Clyrd Vicarage, Radnorshire. *Educ.*: Privately. Went to sea in Mercantile Marine, 1880; Sub-Lieut., Royal Naval Reserve, 1891; Lieut. 1895; Commander, 1907; Capt. 1914; Member Departmental Committee on Boats and Davits, 1912–13; Nautical Adviser to the British Delegation, International Conference on Safety of Life at Sea, 1913–14. *Address*: Harestock Close, Winchester. (K359)

CHARLES, Major Richard, O.B.E., F.R.C.S.I.

CHARLESON, Bruno Arthur, O.B.E., *b.* 27 May, 1878; *s.* of Charles Jonas, of Portland (Oregon), U.S.A.; *m.* Contessina Sonia, *d.* of Conte Lenassi, of Gorizia, Italy. *Educ.*: Geneva College. *War Work*: Bureau de secours, Prisoners of War, British Legation, Berne. (O10138)

CHARLESWORTH, Lieut. and Qr.-Mr. Arthur, M.B.E., A.M.C.

CHARLESWORTH, Lieut. William, M.B.E.

CHARLESWORTH, William Herbert Rudolph, M.B.E.

CHARLEY, Lieut.-Col. Harold Richard, C.B.E., Royal Irish Rifles, *b.* 4 April, 1875; *s.* of William Charley, D.L., of Seymour Hill, Dunmurry, Co. Antrim. *Educ.*: Cheltenham. *War Work*: (With B.R.C.) Officer in charge, Technical Instruction for British Interned in Switzerland, 1917–18; Assistant Commissioner, then Commissioner, B.R.C. in Switzerland, 1918–19; Manager, B.R.C., Berlin, March–Aug., 1919. *Address*: Seymour Hill, Dunmurry, Co. Antrim. *Club*: Junior Army and Navy; Royal Automobile (C2516)

CHARLEY, Capt. Leslie William, O.B.E.

CHARLIER, Paymaster-Sub-Lieut. Leonard Clayton, M.B.E., R.N.V.R.

CHARLTON, Capt. Charles Joseph, M.B.E.

CHARLTON, Rowland Hugh, O.B.E.

CHARNAND, Frederick Christian, M.B.E.

CHARNOCK, Lieut. Richard, O.B.E., M.C.

CHARRINGTON, Elinor Mary, Mrs., O.B.E.; *d.* of late Rt. Hon. Sir Richard Baggalay, P.C., Lord Justice of Appeal, of Mapletreuse, Edenbridge, Kent, and 55, Queen's Gate, S.W.; *m.* Major Hugh Spencer Charrington, of Burys Court, Leigh, Surrey. Vice-President, Staffordshire Branch of British Red Cross Society since 1911, and Hon. Commdt., Red Cross Auxiliary Hospital, Burton-on-Trent. *War Work*: 1914–19, President and organiser, Burton War Hospital Supply Depôt. *Address*: Dove Cliff, Burton-on-Trent. *Clubs*: New Century; Ladies' Imperial. (O1205)

CHARRINGTON, John Douglas, O.B.E.

CHARTERIS, Rev. William Cramb, O.B.E., M.C., *b.* 4 July, 1869; *s.* of Ex-Councillor W. B. Charteris, of Castle Douglas, N.B.; *m.* Jeanie Dick, *d.* of the late James Jack, of Glasgow. *Educ.*: The Academy, Castle-Douglas, and privately. Baptist Minister, Ayr. *War Work*: Served as Army Scripture Reader during S. African War in 1900; commissioned as Army Chaplain (Temporary), 8 Dec. 1914, 4th Class; 6 Jan. 1917, promoted 3rd Class; 8 Nov. 1917, promoted 2nd Class; demobilised, 8 April, 1919, with hon. rank of Lieut.-Col. *Address*: Benvue, 11, Ailsa Place, Ayr. (O5094)

CHASE, Alfred James, O.B.E.

CHASE, Alice Eleanor, M.B.E., *b.* 24 Feb. 1892; *d.* of Major L. H. Chase, M.Inst.C.E., of Melbourne, Australia, and Chertsey ,Surrey. *Educ.*: Girton Coll., Cambridge (Med. and Mod. Languages, Tripos, 1914). Officer in charge of Translation and Foreign Press Intelligence Section, Air Ministry. *War Work*: War Office (Military Translation Bureau), Aug. 1915, to Oct. 1916; Board of Trade (Russian Government Committee), Oct. 1916, to April, 1917; Air Ministry (as above), April, 1917, to present time. *Addresses*: 14, Ashburn Gardens, S.W. 7; Pondside, Chertsey. (M7665)

CHASE, Louisa Maud, M.B.E., Q.M.A.A.C.

CHASSAR, Major William Charles, O.B.E.

CHATAWAY, Louiso, Mrs., M.B.E., *d.* of the late Wm. Edgar, of London and Paris; *m.* Norman. *s.* of Rev. James Chataway, late of Rotherwick Rectory, Hampshire. *Educ.*: Privately. *War Work*: Obtaining funds for Red Cross, etc. *Address*: The Residency, Umtali, Southern Rhodesia. (M6434)

CHATER, Eng.-Comm. Francis Arthur, O.B.E., R.N.

CHATFIELD, Frederick, M.B.E., J.P., D.L., *b.* 27 Nov. 1861; *s.* of the late Charles Henry Chatfield, of Surbiton; *m.* Winifred Marian, *d.* of the late Frank E. Lott, J.P., of Burton-on-Trent. *Educ.*: Charterhouse. Alderman, Borough of Appleby. *War Work*: Hon. Sec. and Treas., Appleby District, County of Westmorland, War Pensions. *Address*: Garbridge, Appleby, Westmorland. (M7666)

CHATTERLEY, Lieut.-Col. Frank Martin, O.B.E., T.D., *b.* 6 Aug. 1868; *s.* of John Bishop Chatterley, of Solihull, Warwickshire; *m.* Edith Winifred, *d.* of A. P. Pridmore, of Coventry. *Educ.*: Privately. Director of John B. Chatterley and Sons, Ltd. *War Work*: Mobilised with the 6th Royal Warwickshire Regt., and proceeded to France with the 48th Division; Commanded the 5th Res. Batt. R. Warwickshire Regt., until 22 April, 1919. *Address*: Craycombe, Solihull, Warwickshire. *Club*: Clef, Birmingham. (O6998)

CHATTERTON, Alice Gertrude, Lady, M.B.E., ; *d.* of W. H. Wilson, of Madras; *m.* Sir Alfred (cr. Knt. 1919) (*see* BURKE'S *Peerage*), *s.* of J. H. Chatterton, of Honor Oak. *Educ.*: Bedford High School. *Address*: Yews, Longfield, Kent. (M6124)

CHATTERTON, Elizabeth Eva, Mrs., M.B.E., *b.* 17 March, 1875; *d.* of Francis Albert Waller, J.P., of Shannon Grove, Banagher; *m.* Abraham Chatterton, J.P., *s.* of the late Abraham Thomas Chatterton. *War Work*: Member Co. Wicklow War Pensions Local Committee; Hon. Treasurer, Rathdowne and Bray Sub-Committee. *Address*: Kilgarron, Enniskerry, Co. Wicklow. (M7667)

CHATTERTON, Col. Frank Beauchamp Macaulay, C.M.G., C.B.E., *b.* 28 July, 1873; *s.* of Col. Frank William Chatterton, C.I.E., J.P., of Central Lodge, Upper Norwood; *m.* Annie, *d.* of the late W. M. Marshall, F.R.G.S. *Educ.*: Monkton Combe School, Sandhurst. Formerly served with Prince of Wales Vols., S. Lancs. Regt., 1894–96; Royal Army Service Corps, 1896–1920; promoted Col., July, 1920. *War Work*: Commanding 18th Divisional Train, 1914–15; Assistant Director of Supplies, 1915–17; Assistant Dir. Supplies and Transport, 1917–19 (War Department Liaison Officer with Ministry of Food); at present employed as Dep. Dir. Supplies and Transport, Egyptian Expeditionary Force. *Address*: c/o Sir Charles McGrigor, Bart., & Co., 39, Panton Street, S.W. *Club*: United Service. (C1512)

CHATTERTON, Julia, Mrs., M.B.E., *d.* of Ralph Cook-Watson, of Harrogate; *m.* Frederick, *s.* of George Joseph Chatterton, of Derby. Composer and Lyric Writer. *War Work*: Member of the Cairo V.A.D. No. 2; promoted to-Section Leader, V.A.D., in 1916; Red Cross Kitchen Organisation for Cairo and district; Superintendence of Red Cross work at Boulac Dakrour Convalescent Depot; Musical Direction of the " Cards " Concert Party in Egypt; mentioned in Gen. Sir Archibald Murray's despatches, 1917, and awarded 1914–15 Star. *Address*: 6, Halley House, Vauxhall Bridge Road, S.W. 1. *Club*: Writers'. (M3569)

CHAUNCEY, Alice Louise, M.B.E., W.R.A.F.

CHAUVEL, Major James Allan, O.B.E., A.I.F.

CHAVASSE, Francis Hannah, Lady, M.B.E., *d.* of the late Arthur Ryland, of The Linthurst Hill, Bromsgrove, Worcestershire; *m.* Jan. 1885, Sir Thomas Frederick Chavasse, M.D., F.R.C.S., J.P., who died 17 Feb., 1913. (M7668)

CHAVE, Capt. Sir Benjamin, K.B.E., R.N.R., *b.* 1870; *s.* of late Benjamin Chave, of London; *m.* Rachel Agnes, *d.* of late Rev. Thomas Morgan, M.A., of Dilwyn, Herefordshire. *Educ.*: King Edward VI. Grammar School, Southampton. Master Mariner; Union Castle Mail S.S. Co., Ltd., 3, Fenchurch Street, E.C. 3. *War Work*: Commander, Royal Naval Reserve; served in H.M.S. " Armadale Castle "; Naval Transport Officer in charge at Ludentzbucht, G.S.W. Africa, during Gen. Botha's successful campaign; mentioned in despatches; Commanding Transport " Alnwick Castle " when torpedoed, March, 1917. (K360)

CHAYTOR, Lieut.-Col. D'Arcy, C.M.G., C.B.E., New Zealand Mounted Rifles, *b.* 1873; 3rd *s.* of John Clervaux Chaytor, and Emma, *d.* of the late Edward Fearon, of Nelson, New Zealand; *m.* 1908, Avis Anne, *d.* of Commander Arthur Robert Atherton Edwin, R.N. (ret.). *Educ*: Clare Coll., Cambridge. Served in South Africa, 1899–1901 (medal with four clasps), and in the Great War (despatches). Has Order of the Nile 3rd Class. (O1396)

CHAYTOR, Herbert Stanley, O.B.E., *b.* 20 Jan. 1867;

s. of William Chaytor, of Dublin ; *m.* Edith Constance, *d.* of Capt. J. M. Daly (77th Regt.), of Castledaly, Co. Westmeath. *Educ.:* Royal School, Armagh. Sec. Royal Irish Automobile Club. *War Work:* Irish Automobile Club, Ambulance Service ; Wounded Soldiers' Reception Committee ; Wounded Soldiers' Summer and Winter Clubs ; Repatriated Prisoners Reception Committee ; Central Employment Bureau Discharged Sailors and Soldiers (Mechanics). *Address:* 17, Morehampton Road, Dublin. (O10141)

CHAZAL, Dora Stewart, M.B.E. (M2716)

CHEALES, Lieut.-Col. Ralph Darby, O.B.E., *b.* 29 May. 1869 ; *s.* of Rev. Alan Cheales, of Hagworthingham, Lincs. *Educ.:* Harrow ; Trinity Coll., Cambridge. Indian Frontier, 1895 ; South African War ; European War. *Club:* Junior Naval and Military. (O5095)

CHEATLE, Lieut.-Col. Arthur Henry, C.B.E. Major and Hon. Lieut.-Col. R.A.F.; served in Great War, 1914–19 (despatches, O.B.E.). (C2345)

CHEERS, Capt. Joseph McGregor, M.B.E., I.A.R.O.

CHEESEMAN, 2nd Lieut. Bernard, M.B.E., R.A.F.

CHEESWRIGHT, Lieut. Frederick Grahame, M.B.E.

CHEETHAM, Anastasia, Lady C.B.E., Lady of Grace of the Order of St. John of Jerusalem ; *d.* of M. Muravieff, Russian Ambassador in Rome ; *m.* 1907, Sir Milne Cheetham, K.C.M.G., H.M.'s Envoy Extraordinary and Minster Plenipotentiary in Persia. *Address:* The British Agency, Rome. (C456)

CHEETHAM, Eva Christine, Mrs., O.B.E.

CHEETHAM, Rev. Robert Darbyshire, O.B.E., *b.* 3 Dec. 1850 ; *s.* of John Hurst Cheetham, of Manchester ; *m.* Ameila Jane, *d.* of John Gill, of Cheltenham. *Educ.:* Tettenhall Coll. ; Lichfield Theological Coll. Chairman, Stoke-upon-Trent Board of Guardians, 1908–17 ; Chairman, since 1913 of Staffordshire Vagrancy Committee ; Sec. Staffordshire Missionary Studentships Fund ; Sec. Hanley Rural Deanery. *War Work:* Stoke War Hospital came under Stoke-upon-Trent Board of Guardians ; Member of Committee, War Hospital ; Committee Soldiers' and Sailors' Fund, Hanley ; Chairman of 10 Ward (for War Work) in Hanley. *Address:* Northwood Vicarage, Hanley, Staffordshire. (O10142)

CHELLEW, Major Thomas John, O.B.E., R.G.A.

CHELMSFORD, Frances Charlotte Guest, Lady, G.B.E., C.I. ; *e. d.* of Ivor, 1st Baron Wimborne (*see* BURKE'S *Peerage*) ; *m.* Sir Frederick John Napier Thesiger, G.B.E., P.C., G.C.S.I., G.C.M.G., G.C.I.E., 3rd Baron Chelmsford (*see* BURKE'S *Peerage*). *Address:* 18, Queen's Gate Place, S.W. (G5)

CHELMSFORD, Frederick John Napier Thesiger, Lord, G.B.E., P.C., G.C.S.I., G.C.M.G., G.C.I.E., *b.* 12 Aug., 1868 ; *s.* of the 2nd Baron Chelmsford (*see* BURKE'S *Peerage*) ; *m.* 27 July, 1894, Hon. Frances Charlotte Guest, *e. d.* of Ivor, 1st Baron Wimborne (*see* BURKE'S *Peerage*). M.A. Magdalen Coll., Oxford ; Fellow of All Souls College, 1892–9 ; Hon. Fellow of Magdalen Coll. 1917 ; Barrister-at-Law ; Captain, 4th Batt. Dorsetshire Regiment ; Member of London School Board, 1900–4, and of London County Council, 1904–5 ; Alderman L.C.C. 1913 ; Governor of Queensland, 1905–9, and of N.S. Wales, 1909–13 ; Viceroy of India from 1916 ; Knt. of Justice of the Order of St. John of Jerusalem, was Chancellor of the Order of St. Michael and St. George, 1914–16 ; ex-officio Grand Master of the Star of India and of the Indian Empire from 1916. (G14)

CHENERY, George, M.B.E., R.A.O.C.

CHERITON, Capt. William George Lloyd, O.B.E.

CHERRY, Edward Hazlehurst, M.B.E.

CHERRY, Flight-Lieut. Ernest William Fraser, O.B.E., R.A.F.

CHESHIRE, Capt. Archibald Sidney, M.B.E., R.A.F.

CHESHIRE, Frederic Brandon, M.B.E.

CHESHIRE, Prof. Frederic John, C.B.E., A.R.C.S., *b.* 8 June, 1860 ; *s.* of George Cheshire, of Leeds ; *m.* Mary, *d.* of George Richardson, of Leeds. *Educ.:* Birkbeck College ; Royal School of Mines. Director and a Professor of the Optical Engineering Dept., Imperial College of Science and Technology, South Kensington. *War Work:* Organised with A. S. Esslemont, and Scientific and Technical Director of, the Optical Munition Dept. of the Ministry of Munitions ; also a Deputy Director-General of the Ministry of Munitions. *Address:* Imperial College, South Kensington, London. *Club:* Savile. (C1C9)

CHESHIRE, Herbert Henry, M.B.E.

CHESNAYE, Major Christian Purefoy, C.B.E., *b.* 1869 ; *m.* 1903, Katharine, *d.* of Dr. A. Woddill, of Los Angeles, California. Hon. Major in the Army, and Magistrate and Dist. Commr., N. Rhodesia ; Matabele War, 1895–6, German E. Africa as Political Officer. *Address:* Livingstone, N. Rhodesia. (C733)

CHESNEY, Capt. Dennis, O.B.E., Worcs. Regt., *b.* 1 May, 1892 ; *s.* of E. S. Chesney, of Holmleigh, Alderley Edge, Cheshire. *Educ.:* Marlborough and Sandhurst. *War Work:* Served with the Worcestershire Regt., and on the Staff at home. *Address:* Holmleigh, Alderley Edge, Cheshire. *Club:* Junior Army and Navy. (O6995)

CHESTER, Jack Granado, M.B.E.

CHESTER, Major Stephen Charles Robert, M.B.E., R.A.O.C. (M10215)

CHESTERMAN, Capt. Clement Clapton, O.B.E., R.A.M.C.

CHESTERTON, Capt. Hugh, M.B.E.

CHESTERTON, Sidney James, M.B.E., Cavaliere della Corona d'Italia, *b.* 11 Aug. 1878 ; *s.* of Sidney Rawlins Chesterton, of Kensington. *Educ.:* St. Paul's School. *War Work:* Served in France, Italy and Germany. *Address:* 31, Pembroke Road, Kensington. *Club:* R.A.S.C. (M9)

CHETTLE, Major Henry Francis, O.B.E., R.A.S.C., (ret.), *b.* 23 Dec. 1882 ; *s.* of Henry Chettle, of Hornsey, London, N. ; *m.* the late Margaret, *d.* of William John Morris, of Muswell Hill, London, N. *Educ.:* City of London School and Corpus Christi College, Oxford. Barrister-at-Law, 1908 ; Second Class Clerk, Charity Commission, 1911 ; First Class Clerk, Imperial War Graves Commission, 1919. *War Work:* Lieut., R.A.S.C., Sept. 1914 ; Capt., R.A.S.C., Aug. 1915 ; Staff Capt., D.G.R.E., War Office, Aug. 1916 ; Major, Nov. 1918. *Address:* 12, Treborough House, Great Woodstock Street, W. 1. *Club:* United University. (O1208)

CHETTLE, Mrs. Lisbeth, O.B.E.

CHETWODE, Capt. George Knightley, C.B., C.B.E., R.N., *b.* 10 Dec., 1877 ; *s.* of Sir George Chetwode, 6th Bt., and *b.* of the present baronet ; *m.* 4 Feb., 1908, Alice Clara, *y. d.* of the late Major Vaughan Hanning Vaughan-Lee, of Dillington, Somersetshire (*see* BURKE'S *Landed Gentry*). Served in China, 1900 (medal), and in the Great War ; has Russian Order of St. Stanislaus, 2nd Class with swords ; Legion of Honour ; Hellenes Medal of Military Merit. (C885)

CHETWYND, Capt. Arthur Henry Talbot, O.B.E., M.C.

CHEVENS, Capt. Herbert Glyn, O.B.E.

CHEYNE, Charles, M.B.E., *b.* 10 Sept. 1867 ; *s.* of Charles Cheyne, of Foveran, Aberdeenshire ; *m.* Margaret Spence, *d.* of Benjamin Mundell, of Douglas, Lanarkshire. *Educ.:* Fyvie Public School, Aberdeenshire. Inspector of Police. *War Work:* Services rendered to Military Authorities, and assistance to Belgian Refugees located in town and district. *Address:* 109, Quarry Street, Hamilton, N.B. (M7671)

CHICHESTER, Major the Hon. Arthur Claud Spencer, O.B.E., D.S.O., *b.* 12 Sept., 1880 ; *e. s.* of the 3rd Baron Templemore (*see* BURKE'S *Peerage*) ; *m.* 10 Jan. 1911, Hon. Clare Meriel Wingfield, 2nd *d.* of the 7th Viscount Powerscourt (*see* BURKE'S *Peerage*). *Educ.:* Harrow and Royal Military College, Sandhurst. Major, Irish Guards ; late Capt. Royal Fusiliers ; Deputy Lieut. co. Wexford ; served in the South African War, 1902 (medal with four clasps) ; Tibet Mission, 1904 ; action of Gysautse and march to Lhasa (medal with clasp) ; Great War, 1914–18 (despatches 3 times, Croix de Guerre of Italy). *Address:* 26, Norfolk Crescent W. *Clubs:* Guards' ; Travellers'. (O6354)

CHICHESTER, Dehra, Mrs. Robert Peel Dawson Spencer, O.B.E.

CHICHESTER, Comm. Ivor Francis, O.B.E., R.N.

CHICHESTER, Jocelyn Brudenell Pelham, 6th Earl of, Bt., Baron Pelham of Stanmer, O.B.E., D.L., J.P., Sussex ; Public Works Loan Commissioner ; Bt. Lieut.-Col. 5th Batt. Royal Sussex Regt., *b.* 21 May, 1871 ; *e.s.* of the 5th Earl of Chichester (*see* BURKE'S *Peerage*), and Hon. Alice Carr Glyn, *d.* of the 1st Baron Wolverton (*see* BURKE'S *Peerage*) ; *m.* Ruth, *e.d.* of F. W. Buxton. *Address:* Stanmer, Lewes, Sussex. *Clubs:* Brooks's ; Bath ; Beefsteak. (O229)

CHICHESTER, Shane Randolph, O.B.E., *s.* of Capt. the Hon. F. A. J. and Lady Emily Chichester (*see* BURKE'S *Peerage*) ; *m.* Madeline Herschel, *d.* of Henry A. Whately, of Laurel Lodge, Dancer's Hill, Barnet. *Educ.:* Wellington Coll. and Pembroke Coll., Cambridge. Civil Engineer ; Public Works Dept. (Irrigation), Egypt, 1905–10. *War Work:* Royal Naval Division, Aug 1914 ; later in Ministry of Munitions ; 1914 Star. *Add ess:* Coombe House, Chieveley Newbury, Berks. *Club:* Wellington. (O10143)

CHICHESTER, Lieut.-Col. Walter Raleigh, O.B.E.

CHIDGEY, Hon. Lieut.-Col. Hugh Thomas Arthur, M.B.E., M.S.A., *b.* 16 Nov. 1860. Chief Surveyor for National Housing, Ministry of Health. *War Work:* Mayor of Metropolitan Borough of Stepney (3 years), 1914–17 ; raised the 3/6th County of London (Stepney) Bn. Volunteers ; Commander of Metropolitan Special Constabulary, 1915–18 ; served on Military Service Tribunal Recruiting Committee and War Savings Committee, etc. *Addresses:* 18, Adam Street, Strand, W.C. 2 ; Highclere, High Road, Buckhurst Hill, Essex. (M3571)

CHIDSON, Lieut. Lowthian Hume, M.B.E.

CHIDSON, Lieut. Montagu Reaney, M.B.E., R.A.

CHIESMAN, Harry, M.B.E., *b.* 31 Jan. 1861 ; *s.* of Walter Chiesman, of Leeds ; *m.* Florence Catherine, *d.* of Delamark Waterhouse, of London. *Educ.:* Stationer's School. *War Work:* Recruiting ; Derby Scheme ; National Service ; Tribunal ; Mayor of Lewisham, 1919–20. *Address:* Mayfield, Ravensbourne Park, Catford. (M233)

CHIGNELL, Capt. Robert, O.B.E., R.A.S.C., *b.* 8 May, 1882 ; *s.* of the late B. J. Chignell, of Romsey, Hants ; *m.* Amy, *d.* of the late W. Bosworthick, of Stoke, Devonshire. *Educ.:* Handel Coll., Southampton ; Royal College of Music, London. *War Work:* Served with R.A.S.C. ; Adjutant, 35th Divisional Train during war ; now commanding 297th Company, R.A.S.C., I. & T., Rhine Army of Occupation. *Addresses:* Commanding 297th Company, R.A.S.C., Cologne, Germany ; 23, Edwardes Square, Kensington, W. 8. *Clubs:* Savage, London ; Rhine Army Officers', Cologne. (O2472)

CHILCOTT, Gregory Hall, M.B.E.

CHILCOTT, Capt. Ronald Evered, C.B.E. Capt. R.N. ; served in Great War, 1914–19 (despatches,). (C1916)

CHILD, Capt. Armando Dumas, O.B.E., M.B., C.H.B., D.P.H., R.A.M.C. (S.R.), *b.* 17 July, 1887 ; *s.* of A. Dumas

Child, of Valparaiso. *Educ.:* King's School, Chester; Seven Oaks School. *War Work:* 1914, 15th C.C.S., Lahore Division, B.E.F.; Sanitary Officer, Camiers, 1916–17; Specialist Sanitary Officer, Etaples administrative district, 1917–19. *Addresses:* 51, York Street, Buckingham Gate, S.W. 1; Traders Cottage, Rye, Sussex; 12, Great Ormond Street, W.C. 1. (O2473)

CHILD, Lieut.-Col. Arthur James, O.B.E., M.C., B.Sc., A.I.C., *b.* 19 April, 1888. *Educ.:* Marlborough. (O8068)

CHILD, Capt. Cyril Holland, M.B.E.

CHILD, Capt. Gerald Alfred, O.B.E., M.R.C.S., L.R.C.P., R.A.M.C. (T.F.), *b.* 8 Feb. 1871; *s.* of the late Rev. Alfred Child, of Upper Clatford, Hants; *m.* Louie Child, *d.* of the late Richard Hughes, of Ealing. *Educ.:* St. Edward's, Oxford; Marlborough Coll.; Oxford Univ.; St. Thomas's Hospital. *War Work:* In charge of Hampshire Automobile Club Ambulance Work, mostly removing wounded from hospital ships in Southampton Docks. The H.A.C. Ambulance conveyed 211,400 mostly serious cases, and travelled 605,800 miles; Surgeon-in-charge of Westcliffe War Hospital, 1914-18; Co-designer with Major Leslie of the "Leslie and Child Ambulance" which has been adopted by the War Office. *Address:* Gate House, Hythe, near Southampton. (O8764)

CHILDERS, Mary Alden, Mrs., Erskine, M.B.E.

CHILDS, Lieut. Edmund, M.B.E., R.G.A., *b.* 23 Jan. 1884; *s.* of Edmund Childs of Gosport, Hants; *m.* Christina Mary, *d.* of the late William Fennell, of Gosport. *Educ.:* Garrison School, Fort Rowner, Gosport. *War Work:* German East Africa, Oct. 1914, to March, 1915; Mesopotamia, March, 1915, to Armistice. *Addresses:* 29, Astley Avenue, Dover; No. 31, Fire Command, R.G.A., Bere Island, Bantry, Co. Cork. (M2983)

CHILDS, Emma Catherine, Mrs., M.B.E., B.Sc., *b.* 9 Feb. 1869; *d.* of the late Alfred Whiting Pollard, of Reading, Berks; *m.* William Macbride, *s.* of the late Rev. William Linington Childs, M.A., formerly Vicar of St. George's, Portsea. *Educ.:* The Mount School, York; Somerville Coll., Oxford. *War Work:* Commandant V.A.D., Berks 50; in Command of V.A.D. Nurses detailed for duty at the station on the arrival of convoys for the War Hospitals in Reading, May, 1915, to Oct. 1916; Commandant of Sutherlands Auxiliary Hospital, Reading, Nov. 1916, to Feb. 1919. *Address:* Principal's Lodge, Reading. (M7673)

CHILDS, James, M.B.E., *b.* 23 Dec. 1867; *s.* of John Childs, of Greenock; *m.* Isabella, *d.* of Peter Copeland, of Walker-on-Tyne. *Educ.:* Newcastle-on-Tyne. Assistant Iron Manager at C. S. Swan and Hunter's, Shipbuilders, Walls-end-on-Tyne. *War Work:* Engaged on the building of Submarines, Standard, and Oil Vessels. *Address:* Brandle-how, Grange Villas, Wallsend-on-Tyne. (M1531)

CHILL, Hon. Capt. Edwin Albert, O.B.E., M.D., C.M., F.R.G.S., *b.* 5 Mar. 1861; *s.* of Arthur Wellington Chill, Advocate, of Burma, Further India; *m.* Evelyn Maude, *d.* of W. H. Colman, of London. *Educ.:* King's College School, London; Edinburgh University. Surgeon, Ealing School Clinic; Medical Referee of several Life Assurance Cos.; Lecturer and Examiner, St. John Ambulance Association. *War, Work:* Chief Commandant, Central Middlesex (V.A.D.); Assistant County Director, Middlesex; Capt.ain, R.A.M.C. (V.), attached to the County of London R.A.S.C., M.T. (V.); Officer in command, Auxiliary Military Hospital, Southall; Medical Examiner, Recruits for Territorial Force. *Club:* Edinburgh University. (O1204)

CHILSTON, Aretas Akers-Douglas, 1st Viscount, of Boughton Malherbe, Baron Douglas, P.C., G.B.E., D.L. (*see* BURKE'S *Peerage*); *b.* 21 Oct. 1851; *o.s.* of Aretas Akers, Malling Abbey, Kent; *m.* Adeline, *e.d.* of H. Austen Smith, Hayes Court, Kent. *Educ.:* Univ. Coll., Oxford. Barrister, Inner Temple; late Capt. E. Kent Yeomanry Cavalry; M.P.(C.) for St. Augustine's Division of Kent, 1880–1911; Whip to Conservative Party, 1883–95; Patronage Sec. to Treasury, 1885–86, 1889–92, and for a short time, 1895; First Commissioner of Works, with seat in Cabinet, 1895–1909; Secretary of State, Home Department, 1902–06. *Addresses:* Chilston Park, Maidstone; 34 Lower Belgrave Street. (G48)

CHILTON, Ruth Helen Jane, M.B.E. (M01245f)

CHILTON, Elizabeth, Mrs., M.B.E.

CHILVER, Capt. Jas. Thomas, O.B.E.

CHINERY, Elizabeth, Mrs., M.B.E., Lady of Grace of the Order of St John of Jerusalem in England, *b.* 24 Aug. 1853; *d.* of Miles Ponsonby Knubley, of Plumbland Rectory, Cumberland; *m.* Edward Fluder, *s.* of Edward Chinery, of Long Melford, Suffolk. *Educ.:* Harrow. Commandant, V.A.D., 70 Hants.; Lady Superintendent, St. John Ambulance Brigade (Lymington Nursing Division); President and P.G. of the Loyal Elizabeth Chinery Lodge of Oddfellows. *War Work:* Commandant of Home Mead Auxiliary Hospital and Annexes, Lymington. *Address:* Lymington, Hants. (M235)

CHING, Horace Edwin, M.B.E., *b.* 16 Oct. 1874; *s.* of Samuel Ching, of Cardiff; *m.* Daisy Alice Hurd, *d.* of Rev. A. F. Barley. *Educ.:* Cardiff. Deputy Manager in Egypt for Messrs. Cory Brothers & Co., Ltd., Colliery and Coal Depot Owners. *War Work:* Lighterage Control Executive Committee, Port Said, for which mentioned in Gen. Allenby's despatches. *Address:* Port Said, Egypt. (M7674)

CHIPMAN, Leontine, O.B.E., *b.* 11 Feb. 1864; *d.* of Col. L. de V. Chipman, of Kenville, Nova Scotia. *Educ.:* Halifax, Nova Scotia; Bradford, U.S.A.; London. Guardian and Rural District Councillor for the Alnwick district of North-

umberland. *War Work:* 1914, Royal Victoria Infirmary, Newcastle-on-Tyne; Auxiliary Hospitals at Howick, Northumberland, and at Weymouth; 1915–16, year at 37 and 37A formation at Dieppe, under the French Red Cross; 1916–19, organiser and head of Soldiers' Rest, Alnwick, Northumberland. *Club:* V.A.D. (O10145)

CHIPPENDALE, Martha, M.B.E., *b.* 14 March, 1867; *d.* of John Chippendale, of Yeadon, Yorks. *Educ.:* Public School. Salvation Army Officer. *War Work:* Assist. Sec. of Naval and Military League War Work of the Salvation Army. *Address:* 42, George Lane, Lewisham, S.E. 13. (M1532)

CHIRNSIDE, Capt. John Percy, C.M.G., O.B.E., *b.* 1865; *s.* of the late Andrew Chirnside, of Haprick, Berwickshire; *m.* Ethel Mary, *d.* of G. O. Ross-Fenner. *Educ.:* Geelong Gram. Sch., Victoria; was a M.L.A. for Victoria, 1894–1904, and a Sup. in Remount Ser. 1917–19; Great War (despatches twice). *Address:* The Manor, Werribee, Victoria, Australia. (O6997)

CHIRNSIDE, Capt. Robert Gordon, O.B.E., A.I.F.

CHISHOLM, Capt. Percy, M.B.E.

CHISHOLM, Robert, C.B.E. Sup. of William Beardmore and Co.'s, Ltd., Ordnance Factories. (C457)

CHITTENDEN, Doris Mary, M.B.E. *War Work:* Sec. in connection with Board of Trade, Coal Mines Department, Household Fuel and Lighting Branch. (M7675)

CHIVERS, George Tanner, O.B.E., *b.* 19 June, 1864; *s.* of Eli Chivers, of Landport, Portsmouth; *m.* Rose Jane, *d.* of James Butchers, of Northend, Portsmouth. *Educ.:* Portsmouth Royal Dockyard School. Headmaster of Portsmouth Royal Dockyard School; formerly Headmaster of Royal Dockyard Schools at Devonport and Pembroke Dock, and Assistant Master at Royal Naval Engineering College, Keyham. *War Work:* Education and training of apprentices and boys employed in Portsmouth Dockyard. *Address:* Zealandia, East End, Havant, Hants. *Club:* Havant. (O3656)

CHOLMELEY, Francis Robert, O.B.E.

CHOLMONDELEY, Lord George Hugo, O.B.E., M.C., *b.* 17 Oct. 1887; *s.* of Marquess of Cholmondeley (*see* BURKE'S *Peerage*). *Educ.:* Eton. Stock Exchange, E.C. *War Work:* Notts R.H.A., England, Aug. 1914, to April, 1915; Egypt, April, 1915, to Feb. 1917; G.H.Q., E.E.F., Egypt and Palestine, April, 1917, to March, 1919. *Clubs:* Turf; R.A.C. (O6156)

CHOLMONDELEY, Hon. Brig.-Gen. Hugh Cecil, C.B., C.B.E. (Mil.), D.L., J.P., *b.* 1 Dec. 1852; *s.* of the Hon. Thomas Grenville Cholmondeley, of Abbots Moss, Northwich, Cheshire; *m.* Mary Stewart, *d.* of Payne Townshend, of Derry, Ross Carbery, Co. Cork. *Educ.:* Rugby. Vice-Chairman, Shropshire T.F.A.; County Council; Chairman, Local War Pensions Committee, Salop. *War Work:* Commanded Prisoners of War Camp, Lancaster, Handforth, Shrewsbury; commanded 3rd Batt. London Rifle Brigade; commanded 173rd Inf. Brigade; County Commandant, Shropshire Volunteer Regt.; Staff Officer for Volunteer Services, Western Command. *Address:* Edstaston, Wem, Salop. *Club:* Army and Navy; Bath. (C1513)

CHOLMONDELEY, Winifred Ida, Marchioness of, O.B.E., *b.* 24 April, 1862; *d.* of late Col. Sir Nigel Kingscote, of Kingscote; *m.* George Henry Hugh, 4th Marquess of Cholmondeley (*see* BURKE'S *Peerage*). *War Work:* Vice-President of Broxton Division, Cheshire Branch, B.R.C.S.; now President of Cheshire Branch, B.R.C.S.; donor of Higgensfield Auxiliary Hospital, B.R.C.S. *Address:* Cholmondeley Castle, Malpas, Cheshire. (O10146)

CHOMLEY, Mary Elizabeth, O.B.E., *b.* 1871; *d.* of His Honour Judge Chomley, of Victoria, Australia. *Educ.:* Privately. Hon. Sec., Victoria League (of Victoria), 1908–14; Hon. Sec., Arts and Crafts Society of Victoria, and connected with committees of numerous philanthropic and Art Societies in Australia. *War Work:* Assisted at the Belgian War Refugees Camp, Earl's Court; was Superintendent of the House Staff at Princess Christian's Hospital for Officers for a few months; and in 1916 organised the Prisoners of War branch of the Australian Red Cross, and supervised it until its close in 1919; was appointed the same year, by H.M. Government, to accompany a delegation of women to Australia to inquire as to openings there for women from the United Kingdom. *Club:* Alexandra, Melbourne. (O1919)

CHORLTON, Alan Ernest Scopic, C.B.E.

CHOWN, Major Stanley Gordon, O.B.E., C.A.M.C.

CHOYCE, Col. Charles Coley, C.M.G., O.B.E., M.D., B.Sc., F.R.C.S., *b.* 1875; *s.* of Henry Charles Choyce, of Auckland, New Zealand; *m.* Gwendolen Alice, *d.* of F. C. Dobbing, J.P., of Chislehurst, Kent. *Educ.:* New Zealand and Edinburgh University. Director of Surgical Unit, University College Hospital Medical School; Surgeon, University College Hospital; Surgeon, Great Northern Central Hospital; Consulting Surgeon, Seamen's Hospital, Greenwich. *War Work:* Col., Army Medical Service; Officer in charge, Surgical Division, 19th General Hospital; Consulting Surgeon, Egyptian Expeditionary Force. *Address:* University College Hospital Medical School. (C780)

CHRIMES, Capt. Frank, C.B.E.

CHRISTIAN, Capt. Charles, M.B.E., R.E.

CHRISTIAN, Edward Hompesch, O.B.E., *b.* 2 April, 1859; *s.* of Major Hugh Henry Christian, of Bilton Lodge, Edinburgh, N.B.; *m.* Olive Susan, *d.* of Henry Luff, M.D., of Seaton. *Educ.:* Glasgow Academy; Glen Park, Greenock. *War Work:* Station Guide at Victoria Station, from Nov. 1915, controlling the billeting of troops, and directing soldiers to their destinations at night, and generally looking after travelling troops. *Addresses:* West Huntington Hall, York; 2, Wilton Street, Grosvenor Place, S.W. *Club:* R.A.C. (O10147)

CHRISTIAN, Louis de Bylandt, O.B.E., M.B., C.M., *b.* 20 Jan. 1862; *s.* of Major Hugh Henry Christian, of Bilton Lodge, Duddingston, Edinburgh; *m.* Emmeline, *d.* of James R. A. Douglas, of Hounslow. *Educ.:* Univ. of Edinburgh; Royal High School, Edinburgh. Surgeon, Hounslow Hospital; Surgeon, Metropolitan Police; Certifying Surgeon (Factory Act). *War Work:* Commandant Auxiliary Military Hospital, Percy House, Isleworth. *Address:* Stanley House, Hounslow. (O10148)

CHRISTIAN, H.R.H. Princess, G.B.E., C.I.

CHRISTIE, Amie, M.B.E.; *d.* of Peter Christie, of Tayport, Fife. *Educ.:* St. Andrews and Edinburgh. Missionary in Kalua, Bengal, with U.F. Church of Scotland. *War Work:* Commandant of 1/10th R. Scots Hut, N. Berwick, and Scottish Churches Hut, Rouen, France. *Address:* Riverlea, Blairgowrie, Perthshire. (M7676)

CHRISTIE, Capt. Fred, M.B.E., R.A.F.

CHRISTIE, 2nd Lieut. Harold, M.B.E.

CHRISTIE, Lieut.-Col. James, O.B.E.

CHRISTIE, James Roberton, O.B.E., LL.B., K.C., *b.* 1866; *s.* of John Gilkison Christie, of Glasgow. *Educ.:* Glasgow and Albany Academies; Hutcheson's Grammar School; Glasgow and Edinburgh Univs. Advocate (Scottish Bar, 1891); Clerk of Justiciary for Scotland, 1917. *War Work:* Assisted with Y.M.C.A. Rest Huts for Sailors and Soldiers in Edinburgh; lectured on behalf of War Charities; superintended a Department of Intelligence Work under Forth Garrison in the Scottish Command area; was one of the founders of, and took an active part in, the work of the Edinburgh Hospitality League. *Address:* 2, Doune Terrace, Edinburgh. *Clubs:* Cavendish; University and Conservative (Edinburgh); Glasgow Conservative. (O10149)

CHRISTIE, John Cubie, O.B.E.

CHRISTIE, Capt. and Qr.-Mr. Joseph James, O.B.E.

CHRISTIE, Col. Joseph MacNaughtan, C.B.E., M.D., C.M. (Glasg.), F.R.C.S. (Edin.), F.R.F.P.S. (Glasg.), N.Z. Army Medical Department, *b.* 5 May, 1871; *s.* of John Christie, of Glasgow; *m.* Vita Alice Mary, *d.* of Reginald Bayley, of Otemai, New Plymouth, N.Z. *Educ.:* Glasgow High School and Univ., Dublin and Berlin. *War Work:* Surgical Specialist, H.M. N.Z. Hospital Ship "Maheno" (2nd Charter); Consulting Surgeon to the Forces in New Zealand. *Address:* c/o Dr. W. W. Christie, 12, Rosslyn Terrace, Kelvinside, Glasgow. (C1850)

CHRISTIE, Capt. Lionel Ronald, O.B.E.

CHRISTISON, Lieut. Fred Hamilton, M.B.E.

CHRISTISON, Lieut. McCulloch, M.B.E.

CHRISTMAS, Jessie, Mrs., O.B.E., W.R.A.F.

CHRISTOPHERS, Major Samuel Richard, C.I.E., O.B.E., I.M.S. *Address:* Central Research Institute, Kasauli, India. (O2266)

CHRISTOPHERSON, Alice Catherine, Mrs., M.B.E., *b.* 1 June, 1867; *d.* of George F. Howe, of Bruxelles and Paris; *m.* Nelson, *s.* of William Butler Christopherson, of Blackheath. *Educ.:* Convent des "Dames Urseline," Warre-Notre-Dame, Bruxelles. *War Work:* Commandant V.A.D. Hospital, Gardenhurst, Bexley, Kent, 1914–19. *Address:* Newlands, Bexley, Kent. (M7677)

CHRISTOPHERSON, Douglas, C.B.E., *b.* 1868; *s.* of the late Derman Christopherson, of Blackheath, S.E.; *m.* 1910, Alma, *d.* of the late W. Griffiths, of Cardiff. *Educ.:* Bedford. Served during Matabeleland Rebellion and S. African War; Vice-Chm. Johannesburg Local Committee Gov.-Gen.'s Fund; Chm. Disabled Soldiers' Board, Johannesburg. *Address:* Johannesburg, Transvaal. (C378)

CHRISTOPHERSON, John Brian, C.B.E., M.A., M.D. (Cantab.), F.R.C.S. (Eng.), F.R.C.P. (Lond.), *b.* 1870; *s.* of Canon B. Christopherson, Rector of Falmouth; *m.* Joyce Eleanor, *d.* of J. A. Ormerod, M.D., Consulting Physician to St. Bartholomew's Hospital. *Educ.:* Clifton Coll.; Caius Coll.; St. Bartholomew's Hospital; Vienna. Examiner in Tropical Diseases, Royal College of Physicians (London); late Director of the Sudan Medical Department. *War Work:* Surgeon at the Bury Hospital (Red Cross), Vrynatschka Banja, Serbia, 1915; Member of the Commission on Medical Establishments (France), appointed by War Office, 1917. *Address:* 29, Devonshire Place, W. 1. (C2365)

CHRISTOPHERSON, Lieut. Kenneth, M.B.E., *b.* 3 Feb. 1865; *s.* of Derman Christopherson, of Blackheath. *Educ.:* Uppingham. *War Work:* Staff Capt. Home Counties Reserve Brigade from Oct. 1916, to April, 1919. *Address:* Flat 1, 246, Gloucester Terrace, Hyde Park, W. 2. (M5156)

CHUBB, Capt. Harry Emory, O.B.E., R.A.S.C.

CHUBB, William Lindsay, M.B.E., M.D. Medical Officer, Menley and Farnborough Court Auxiliary Hospitals, Farnborough, Hants. (M10257g)

CHUNE, Helen Gertrude, M.B.E.; *d.* of H. C. Chune, M.R.C.S., of Much Wenlock. *War Work:* Quartermaster, Red Cross Hospital (100 beds), Highland Moors, Llandrindod Wells. *Address:* Kelmscot, Llandrindod Wells. (M1533)

CHURCH, Arthur Frederick, C.B.E. Ch. Engineer Uganda Railway. (C2018)

CHURCH, Charlotte Mary Viola, M.B.E.; *d.* of the late Rev. A. J. Church. *Educ.:* Privately. *War Work:* Foreign Trade Dept. of the Foreign Office. *Club:* Ladies' Athenæum. (M7678)

CHURCH, Major Eric James, O.B.E., Can. A.S.C.

CHURCH, Col. George Ross Marryat, C.M.G., C.B.E., late R.A., *b.* 16 Mar. 1868; *s.* of Gen. Thomas Ross Church, C.I.E.; *m.* Emily, *d.* of Henry Whymper, C.I.E. *Educ.:* Trent College, Nottingham. *War Work:* General Staff, General Headquarters, France, to May, 1918; commanding Army Troops, Independent Air Force, June, 1918, to Armistice; Despatches, "London Gazette," seven times; Officer, Legion d'Honneur; Officer Ordre de Leopold; Croix de Guerre, Belge. *Address:* Elmfield House, Bickington, Barnstaple. (C1236)

CHURCH, Major Thomas Henry, M.B.E.

CHURCH, Capt. William Drummond, C.B.E. Capt R.N.; served in Great War, 1914–19, with Ocean Escort (despatches). (C1181)

CHURCH, Mabel Ellen, Mrs. KING-, M.B.E., *d.* of the late John Robert Malcolm, of Tellera Mulla, S. Wynaad, S. India; *m.* Lionel James Church. *War Work:* Hon. Sec. Ladies' Depot, Madras War Fund, Tellicherry, Malabar, S. India; working and despatching units to France, Mesopotamia, and Madras Hospital Ships. (M7115)

CHURCHILL, Col. Arthur Gillespie, C.B., C.B.E., *b.* 17 Aug. 1860; *s.* of Charles Churchill, J.P., of Weybridge Park; *m.* Katherine Mary, *d.* of Gen. Sir William Payn, K.C.B. *Educ.:* Eton and Royal Military College. Joined 12th Lancers, 1880; Military Attaché, Tokyo and Korea, 1898–1903; Colonel, 1902; Gen. Staff Officer, 1st Grade, Scottish Command, 1904–08; retired, 1909. *War Work:* Called up on 30 July, 1914, to organise the Cable Censorship; Chief Cable Censor until Jan. 1918, when invalided by Medical Board, owing to injuries received in a street accident; awarded C.B., C.B.E., Legion of Honour (Officer), for services during the War. *Address:* Graylands, Horsell, Surrey. *Clubs:* Army and Navy; M.C.C. (C458)

CHURCHILL, Henry, O.B.E., *b.* 26 Nov. 1890; *s.* of the Rev. W. H. Churchill, of Stone House, Broadstairs. *Educ.:* Eton. *War Work:* Prince of Wales Fund; Postal Censorship; Foreign Office. *Address:* 5, Lower Grosvenor Place, S.W. 1. *Club:* St. James. (O230)

CHURCHILL, Lieut.-Col. Herbert Forbes, O.B.E.

CHURCHILL, Laura, Mrs., M.B.E., *d.* of Edward Raffe, of Essex; *m.* Henry William Reynolds, *s.* of William Henry Churchill, Warminster. *Educ.:* Croydon. Commandant, 98th East Lancs. B.R.C.S.; Hon. Treasurer of Women's Liberal Association for Didsbury. *War Work:* Commandant of Woodlawn Hospital, West Didsbury, continuously for 4½ years. *Address:* Westwood, Didsbury, Manchester. (M3573)

CHURCHILL, Augusta, Lady Edward SPENCER-, O.B.E., *d.* of the late Major George Drought Warburton, R.A., M.P., and the late Lady Northwick (see BURKE'S *Peerage*); *m.* Lord Edward Spencer Churchill, *s.* of Duke of Marlborough (see BURKE'S *Peerage*). *Educ.:* Privately. Deputy President, Red Cross, Berkshire; on the Executive Committee and Hon. Sec. for Windsor, Eton, and Clewer Branch R.S.P.C. Children; President, Chairman, Windsor Branch R.S.P.C. Animals. *War Work:* Commandant, Windsor Detachment Red Cross; Commandant of own Hospital for Convalescent Officers; Organiser, President, and Secretary of Windsor War Hospital Supply Depot; worker for 3 years at Church Army Canteen for munition makers at Hayes. *Addresses:* Queensmead, Windsor; 28, Grosvenor Street, London, W. 1. *Clubs:* Alexandra; Ladies' Automobile. (O10151)

CHURCHILL, Clementine Ogilvy, Mrs. Winston L. SPENCER-, C.B.E.; *d.* of the late Sir Henry Montague Hozier, K.C.B. (see BURKE'S *Peerage*, Newlands, B.) and Lady Henrietta Blanche, his wife, *d.* of the 7th Earl of Airlie (see BURKE'S *Peerage*); *m.* 12 Sept. 1908, Rt. Hon. Winston Leonard, P.C., M.P., *e.* *s.* of Lord Randolph Churchill (see BURKE'S *Peerage*, Marlborough, D.). (C130)

CHURCHWARD, George Charles, M.B.E.

CHURCHWARD, George Jackson, C.B.E. Ch. Mechanical Engineer Great Western Railway; J.P. for Wilts. *Address:* Newburn House, Swindon, Wilts. (C459)

CHURCHWARD, Rev. Marcus Wellesley, C.B.E., M.A., *b.* 11 Nov. 1860; *s.* of Benjamin Hannaford Churchward, of Devonshire; *m.* Mary Ella, *d.* of Joseph Woodall. *Educ.:* King's School, Rochester; St. John's, Cambridge. C.F. retired; Asst. Sec. S.P.G. *War Work:* Asst. Chaplain-General, London. *Address:* 38, The Chase, Clapham, S.W. 4. *Club:* Church Imperial. (C2087)

CHURSTON, John Reginald Lopes, Lieut.-Col. Lord, M.V.O., O.B.E., Scots Guards (see BURKE'S *Peerage*), *b.* 9 Nov. 1873; *s.* of 2nd Lord Churston, of Co. Devon; *m.* Jessie, *d.* of Alfred Smither. A.D.C. to the Viceroy of India, 1902–3, and to H.R.H. Duke of Connaught, 1904–6; served in S. A. War, 1900–1 (medal with 4 clasps). *War Work:* D.A.Q.M.G., London District, I.Q.M.G.S., London District. *Address:* 25, Knightsbridge, S.W.; Lupton House, Brixham, Devonshire. *Clubs:* Turf; Guards'. (O7000)

CHURTON, Ethel Blanche, Mrs., O.B.E.

CHUTE, Rev. Anthony William, O.B.E., M.A., *b.* 17 Dec. 1884; *s.* of Chaloner William Chute, of The Vyne, Basingstoke. *Educ.:* Winchester; Magdalen Coll., Oxford. Vicar of St Oswald's, West Hartlepool, 1919. *War Work:* Chaplain to the Forces, attached to 23rd Division, in France, Belgium, and Italy, 1916–19. *Address:* St. Oswalds, West Hartlepool. (O6355)

CHUTE, Lieut.-Col. Mervyn Lyde, O.B.E., A.M.I.M.E.,

F.Z.S., b. 11 Feb. 1881 ; s. of Rev. Edward Russell Chute, o Moulton, Norfolk ; m. Frances Josephine, d. of Rev. Canon Armour, D.D. *Educ.*: St. Paul's School, London. Mechanical Engineer, with appointments in S. Africa, West Indies, and at home. *War Work*: First commissioned as 2nd Lieut., R.A.S.C.; transferred in 1917 to Royal Engineers ; appointed to Staff of Director-General of Transportation ; final rank, Lieut.-Col. *Address*: Furgarth, Kirknewton, Northumberland. *Club*: Cavendish. (O1211)

CHUTER, Arthur George, M.B.E., b. 1 May, 1877 ; s. of the late John William Chuter, of Andover, Hants ; m. Hilda, d. of Charles Holdcroft, of Acton. *Educ.*: Grammar School, Andover. Sec., British Sections at (a) Golden Fleece Exhibition, Bruges, 1907 ; (b) Exhibition of Seventeenth Century Flemish Art, Brussels, 1910 ; (c) International Miniature Exhibition, Brussels, 1912 ; Assist. Sec. Committee of Trustees of National Gallery on Export of Works of Art ; Accountant, Exhibitions Branch, Board of Trade, 1913 ; Chief Staff Officer, Exhibitions Division Dept. of Overseas Trade, 1920. *War Work*: Accountant and Establishment Officer, Commission Internationale de Ravitaillement. *Address*: 22, Highview Road, Ealing, W. 13. *Club*: Junior Constitutional. (M1535)

CIPRIANI, Albert Henry, M.B.E.

CIRCUITT, Capt. George Francis Langdale, M.B.E., R.A.S.C.

CLANWILLIAM, Muriel, Countess of, M.B.E.: d. of Russell Stephenson, and w. of Hon. Oliver Howard (see BURKE'S *Peerage*, Carlisle, E.) ; m. 27 April, 1909, Arthur Vesey Meade, M.C., 5th Earl of Clanwilliam (see BURKE'S *Peerage*). (M7679)

CLAPCOTT, Charles Blackstone, O.B.E., b. 9 July, 1867 ; s. of Major Charles Clapcott, 32nd Light Infantry ; m. Sylvie, d. of E. d'Avigdor. *Educ.*: Privately, and Jesus Coll., Cambridge. Judge, Native Court of Appeal, Cairo, Egypt. *Address*: Cairo, Egypt. (O10153)

CLAPHAM, 2nd Lieut. Athol England, M.B.E., R.A.S.C.

CLAPHAM, Major Douglas, D.S.O., O.B.E. *Club*: United Service. (O1212)

CLAPHAM, John Harold, C.B.E., Litt.D., b. 13 Sept. 1873 ; s. of John Clapham, of Prestwich, Manchester ; m. Mary Margaret, d. of W. E. Green, of Ross, Hereford. *Educ.*: Leys School ; King's College, Cambridge. Fellow of King's College, 1898–1904, and since 1908 ; Professor of Economics, Universtiy of Leeds, 1902–8 ; Dean of King's College, 1908–13 ; Tutor, 1913 ; Lecturer in Economic History in the University. *War Work*: Special Inquiry Work for the Board of Trade, 1916 ; Deputy Director, War Inquiries, 1917 ; Representative of Board of Trade on Priorities Committee, War Cabinet, 1918 ; Member of Post War Priorities Committee, 1919. *Addresses*: King's College ; Storey's End, Cambridge. *Club*: Alpine. (C460)

CLAPP, Rev. Charles Herbert, M.B.E.

CLAPPERTON, Gladys Laura, Mrs., M.B.E.

CLAPSHAW, Major and Qr.-Mr. Aquila, O.B.E., R.A.M.C.

CLARE, Lieut. Harold Ernest, O.B.E., R.N.R.

CLARE, Capt. Samuel, M.B.E., R.F.A.

CLARE, Major Herbert John NEWTON-, O.B.E.

CLARE, Capt. Walter Shackfield NEWTON-, M.B.E., R.A.F.

CLAREMONT, Adel Dorothy, Mrs., M.B.E.

CLARENCE, Capt. Arthur Arderne, O.B.E.

CLARET, Capt. Frank Henry, O.B.E.

CLARIDGE, Capt. John Watson Lawson, M.B.E., I.A.

CLARK, Adrian, O.B.E., late Lieut.-Col. R.A.F. *Address*: 3, Temple Gardens, Temple, E.C. (O8069)

CLARK, Alfred Percy Stanley, M.B.E., b. 4 June 1889 ; s. of Alfred Clark, of London ; m. Kathleen Grace, d. of — Cheale, of Lewes, Sussex. *Educ.*: Grocers' Company's School. Manager, The Anglo-Egyptian Bank, Ltd., Jerusalem. *War Work*: Banking for E.E.F., and Occupied Enemy Territory Administration (South). *Address*: c,o Anglo-Egyptian Bank, Ltd., Jerusalem. (M7682)

CLARK, Alice Fanny, Mrs., M.B.E. *War Work*: Sailors' and Soldiers' Families Association ; Royal Patriotic Corporation ; Hull Patriotic Fund ; War Pensions Committee, Hull. *Address*: 29, Coltman St., Hull. (M7681)

CLARK, Col. D'Arcy Melville, O.B.E., M.B.E.

CLARK, Donald George, O.B.E.

CLARK, Edward Mellish, O.B.E., M.A. (Cantab.), b. 25 Sept. 1874 ; s. of John Willis Clark, of Scroope House, Cambridge ; m. Lilian Mary Hart, d. of Sir A. J. C. Milman, K.C.B., of Speaker's Court, Westminster, Clerk of the House of Commons (see BURKE'S *Peerage*). *Educ.*: Harrow, and Trinity Coll., Cambridge. Local Director of Barclays Bank, Limited, Cambridge ; Chairman of New Theatre, Cambridge, Limited. *War Work*: Chairman, Cambridgeshire Local War Pensions Committee ; Hon. Treasurer, Borough of Cambridge, War Pensions Committee ; Hon. Treasurer, Cambs. and Isle of Ely Branch of the Soldiers' and Sailors' Families Association. *Address*: Binnbrook, Cambridge. *Clubs*: United Univs. ; Cambridge County ; University Pitt ; University A.D.C. (O10154)

CLARK, Elizabeth Mary, Mrs., M.B.E., b. 30 June, 1860 ; d. of Sir William Lenox-Conyngham of Spring Hill, Co. Derry (see BURKE'S *Peerage*) ; m. Col. James Jackson Clark, H.M.L. for Co. Derry, s. of James Johnston Clark, of Largantogher, Co. Derry. *Educ.*: Privately. *War Work*: Red Cross and other War charities. *Address*: Largantogher, Maghera, Co. Derry, Ireland. (M7683)

CLARK, Sir Ernest, Kt. Bach., C.B.E., b. 13 April, 1864 ; s. of Samuel Henry Clark ; m. Mary, d. of John Thomas Cox Winkfield, J.P., Barrister-at-Law, Middle Temple ; Assist.-Sec., Board of Inland Revenue ; Secretary of Royal Commission on Income Tax. *Address*: 16, Clareville Grove, S. Kensington. *Club*: Junior Athenæum. (C461)

CLARK, Eng.-Lieut. Ewbank, M.B.E., R.N.

CLARK, Capt. Frederick Ourry, O.B.E.

CLARK, Major George, O.B.E., R.A., b. 3 Aug. 1857 ; s. of the late George Clark. *Educ.*: Waltham Abbey Commercial School. Adjutant, R.A. Regimental District Staff, 1897–1902 ; Superintending Officer, A.G.C. War Office, 1902–1916 ; Staff Officer to G.O.C., Woolwich, 1916–19. *Address*: 19, Sherard Gardens, Eltham. (O231)

CLARK, George Henry, M.B.E., b. 1 Aug. 1852 ; s. of John Clark, Builder, of Stepney, London ; m. Laura Andane, d. of Charles Robinson, of Plymouth. *Educ.*: Privately. Chief Clerk, Plymouth Garrison. *War Work*: Served 50 years with R. Dublin Fusiliers and as Civil Clerk, Corps of Military Staff Clerks ; awarded Long Service and Meritorious Service Medals ; Chief Clerk, Plymouth Garrison, during the whole of the war ; heavy work necessitating attendance at all times, Offices being open day and night ; received the personal thanks of all of the officers including the Generals Commanding ; Received thanks of Secretary of State (War Office List). *Address*: 16, Alton Road Plymouth. *Club*: Freemasons', Plymouth. (M7684)

CLARK, Lieut. Gordon Lilico, O.B.E., R.N.R.

CLARK, Gowan Cresswell Strange, C.M.G., O.B.E., b. 1856 ; s. of the late Gowan Clark, of Shrewsbury ; m. 1885, Caroline Ann, d. of James Kemsley. Sometime Ch. Traffic Manager of Cape Govt. Railways ; Assist. Gen. Manager, S. African Railways. *Address*: South African Railway Offices, Johannesburg, Transvaal. (O956)

CLARK, Harry, M.B.E.

CLARK, Capt. Henry Fox Atkinson, M.V.O., O.B.E., R.A.F.

CLARK, Capt. Henry William Alfred, C.B.E., R.D. Com. and Acting Capt. R.N.R.; served in the Great War, 1914–19, as Commodore of Convoys (despatches). (C1182)

CLARK, Herbert Ernest, M.B.E.

CLARK, Major Herbert James, O.B.E., b. 13 May, 1866 ; s. of the late Rev. William Clark, C.M.S. ; m. Mary Elizabeth Howard, d. of the late Rev. T. Howard Gill, of Paris, and Tonbridge, Kent. *Educ.*: Privately. Indian Railways. *War Work*: Commissioned in R.A.S.C., Oct. 1914 ; served in France, Belgium, and Germany ; twice mentioned in despatches was with Indian and British Cavalry for greater part of war ; latterly in command of the Army Patrol Installation, Reisholz, Army of the Rhine. *Address*: 58, Upperton Road, Eastbourne.

CLARK, Lieut. Horace Gordon, M.B.E.

CLARK, Capt. Hubert Charles, M.B.E., R.A.S.C. (O5099)

CLARK, Capt. Hugh Bryan, O.B.E., M.C., b. 5 June, 1887 ; s. of Francis J. Clark, J.P., of Street, Somerset ; m. Lilian Genevieve Brooking, d. of George Brooking, of Iquique, Chile. *Educ.*: Bootham School, York, and Leighton Park School, Reading. Director of C. and J. Clark, Ltd., Street, Somerset ; Director of Mid-Somerset Electric Lighting Co. *War Work*: Nov. 1914, to Feb. 1915, with French Red Cross in France ; 1915, April to July, with British Red Cross in Belgium and France ; Aug. 1915, to Jan, 1919, with British Armies in France. *Address*: Butleigh, near Glastonbury, Somerset. (O5100)

CLARK, Hugh Cook, M.B.E., M.I.M.E., b. 3 June, 1874 ; s. of Robert Neilson Clark, of Montrose, Scotland ; m. Helen, d. of — Spalding, of Montrose. *Educ.*: Academy, Montrose. Engineer (Mechanical) ; Head Engineer ; His Majesty's Mint, Calcutta. *War Work*: Supervising Coinage operations for India and the Colonies ; also erection of machinery and production of copper-driving bands for shells and gauges for the Ordnance Department. *Address*: His Majesty's Mint, 47, Strand, Calcutta. (M6126)

CLARK, J. A. M.B.E., M.B., M.S., Egyptian Army. (M10349)

CLARK, Capt. James Jeffery, O.B.E.

CLARK, James John, O.B.E., M.B.E., J.P., b. 1870 ; s. of the Rev. James Clark, of Palmerston ; m. Joy, d. of — Mowatt, of Aberdeen. *Educ.*: Palmerston High School. Mayor, Dunedin, 1915–19 ; Member, City Council since 1908 ; Dunedin Drainage Board, Domain Board, and Prices Investigation Tribunal. *War Work*: President, Otago Patriotic Assocn. ; Chairman, Soldiers' Welfare Committee ; Member, N.Z. War Funds Council ; Member, Governor-General's Advisory Board of Hospital Ships. *Address*: Union Street, Dunedin, N.Z. *Club*: Otago (Dunedin). (C1992)

CLARK, Lieut. John Martin, M.B.E.

CLARK, Col. Sir John Maurice, Bt., M.B.E., V.D., D.L., J.P., b. 7 March, 1859 ; s. of the late Sir Thomas Clark, Bart., of Edinburgh (see BURKE'S *Peerage*) ; m. Helen Marden, d. of the late Rev. Henry M. Douglas, of Kirkcaldy. *Educ.*: Edinburgh Academy ; Edinburgh Univ. Publisher (Senior Partner of T. & T. Clark, Publishers, Edinburgh) ; Chairman of the Scottish Life Assurance Company, Limited ; Extraordinary Director of the British Linen Bank ; Deputy Lieutenant for the County of Midlothian. *War Work*: Vice-Chairman, Midlothian County Association Territorial Army ; Military Representative (and later National Service

Representative) for the County of Midlothian. *Address*: 17, Rothesay Terrace, Edinburgh. *Club*: University, Edinburgh. (M236)

CLARK, Joseph Sains, M.B.E.

CLARK, Major Lionel Melville, O.B.E., b. 29 April, 1878; s. of William Trested Clark, of Rivermead, Rickmansworth, Herts. *Educ.*: Highgate School. Solicitor. *War Work*: Joined the supply branch of the R.A.S.C. at Reading in May, 1915 as a Lieut.; subsequently saw service in Gallipoli, Egypt, and Palestine; rose to rank of Major, and on demobilisation in June, 1919, was a Deputy Assistant Director of Supplies. *Address*: 95, Gresham Street, E.C. *Club*: Devonshire. (O2874)

CLARK, Major Louis Spencer, M.B.E.

CLARK, Lydia, M.B.E.

CLARK, Lieut. Martin Harry, M.B.E., b. 12 July, 1882; s. of the late Harry Clark, of Croydon. *Educ.*: Whitgift Grammar School, Croydon. *War Work*: 1st Batt. County of London Volunteer Regiment, Feb. 1915; O.T.C., Grove Park, Dec. 1915; 2nd Lieut. Jan. 1916; Lieut. July, 1917; Overseas, France, Jan. 1916, to Jan. 1919; posted to 62nd Siege Battery Ammunition Column, April, 1916; A.S.C. Personnel of 62nd Siege Battery, transferred to 96th Siege Battery, June, 1916; remained with this battery until Armistice; mentioned in despatches (Sir Douglas Haig's), Nov. 1918. *Address*: Craigside, Heathhurst Road, Sanderstead, Surrey. (M4445)

CLARK, Owen Aly, M.B.E., J.P.

CLARK, Col. Robert, O.B.E., V.D.

CLARK, Lieut.-Col. Robert Leaver, D.S.O., O.B.E., b. 1862; m. 1914, Dorothy, d. of J. E. Moulton, of King's Heath, Worcs. Entered Army Ordnance Dept. 1896; became a Ch. Inspector of Ordnance Machinery with rank of Hon. Major, 1907; Hon. Lieut.-Col. 1915; S. Africa, 1900 (despatches twice); holds Serbian Order of White Eagle. (O2875)

CLARK, Lieut.-Comm. Roland Arbuthnot, O.B.E., R.N.

CLARK, Lieut.-Col. William Henry Dennis, O.B.E.

CLARK, Lieut. William Morrison, M.B.E.

CLARKE, Andrew Campbell, M.B.E., M.D., Ch.B.

CLARKE, Antoinette, Mrs., M.B.E.

CLARKE, Vice-Adm. Arthur Calvert, C.M.G., C.B.E., D.S.O., b. 1848; s. of the late William Gray Clarke; m. 1895, Margaret MacGregor, d. of J. L. Adams, of U.S.A. Entered R.N. 1861; became Lieut. 1872; Com. 1883; Capt. 1891; Rear-Adm. 1904 (retired 1903); Vice-Adm. 1908; served during Abyssinian Campaign 1868 (medal); China 1900 (medal); is an Officer of Legion of Honour; T. Capt. Roy. Naval Reserve. *Club*: United Service. (C1917)

CLARKE, Arthur Ernest, M.B.E., M.D., b. 2 Aug. 1873. *Address*: The Old House, Rickmansworth. (M7687)

CLARKE, Major Arthur John, O.B.E., M.C., D.C.M.

CLARKE, Capt. Sir Arthur Wellesley, K.B.E., J.P., Lieut.-Comm., R.N.R. (ret.), b. 7 Jan. 1857; s of John Joseph Clarke, of Cork; m. Rosina Margaret, d. of David Hopkins, H.B.M. Consul. *Educ.*: Cork. Elder Brother of Trinity House; J.P., County of London; Member, Port of London Authority (Chairman of River Committee, P.L.A.); Chairman, Marine Society (the "Warspite"); Deputy-Chairman, Seamen's Hospital, Greenwich (the "Dreadnought"); Deputy-Chairman, King George's Fund for Sailors; Member of Committee, Sailor's Home and Red Ensign Club; of Royal Alfred Aged Seamen's Institution: C.B.E. (Mil.) 1919; K.B.E. (Civil) 1920. *Address*: 5, Hamston House, Kensington Court Place, W. 8; Trinity House, E.C. 3. (C888)

CLARKE, Charles Agacy, C.B.E., I.C.S.

CLARKE, Col. Charles Childs, M.V.O., O.B.E., b. 1861; s. of the late Rev. Charles Childs Clarke (formerly V. of Thorverton); m. 1916, Shiela Mary, o. d. of the late Andrew D. Tolmie, of Aldersier, Stirling. Entered R.M. 1879; became Capt. 1889; Major, 1897 (h.p. 1902); Hon. Lieut.-Col. 1908; Brevet Col. 1918; served with Egyptian Expedition, 1882 (medal, bronze star); commanded R.M. detachment during T.R.H. the Duke and Duchess of Cornwall and York's Colonial Tour of 1901; appointed a Barrack Master, 1903; Paymaster at Roy. Marine Depot, 1914. *Club*: United Service. (O9523)

CLARKE, Capt. Charles Hugh, O.B.E.

CLARKE, Dora Gunning Elwin, M.B.E.; d. of Major-General William Calcott Clarke, Madras Staff Corps. *Educ.*: Privately. *War Work*: Commandant, Romney Marsh V.A.D. Hospital, Littlestone-on-Sea, Kent. *Address*: Casa D'Este, Bordighera. Italy. *Clubs*: New Victorian; V.A.D. (M7688)

CLARKE, Douglas Allen, M.B.E.

CLARKE, Edith, Mrs., M.B.E., b. 27 Oct. 1844; d. of the late Edward Nicolls, R.N.; m. Charles Clarke, I.P.S. *Educ.*: Privately. Pioneer of Domestic teaching; for 45 years Principal of the National Training School of Cookery, *Address*: 6, Kensington Mansions, Trebovir Road, Earl's Court, S.W. 5. (M239)

CLARKE, Ernest Herbert, M.B.E., R.A.M.C. (T.F.)

CLARKE, Ethel May, M.B.E., b. 7 May, 1873; d. of Henry Thoburn Clarke. *Educ.*: Privately. *War Work*: Joined Women's Legion, July, 1915, and was sent to Summerdown Convalescent Camp in Aug. 1915; was promoted Superintendent eleven months later, and posted to Dunstable; 7 months later was transferred to Netheravon Cavalry School; joined the W.A.A.C. in 1917 when it was formed from the nucleus of W.L., and remained in that Corps when it became

known as Q.M.A.A.C., in the capacity of Unit Administrator; demobilised, Feb. 1920. *Address*: c/o Mrs. Wood, Harefield Mills, Middlesex. *Club*: Women's United Services. (M6615)

CLARKE, Francis William, M.B.E., M.A., b. 26 May, 1879; s. of the late John Frank Clarke, of St. Andrews, Worcester Park. *Educ.*: Harrow. University Lecturer; formerly Professor of English Literature, Deccan College, Poona, India. *War Work*: Temp. second class clerk, Colonial Office, Dec. 1915, to Dec. 1918. (M1540)

CLARKE, Lieut. Frederick, M.B.E., R.A.

CLARKE, Geoffrey Rothe, O.B.E., J.P., I.C.S., b. 4 July, 1871; s. of George Richard Clarke; m. Hilda Geraldine, d. of Lieut.-Col. C. Seymour. *Educ.*: Trinity College, Dublin. Director-General Posts and Telegraphs, India. *War Work*: Ministry of Munitions, Dept. of Inspection; sent on special duty to U.S.A. and Canada in connection with output of munitions. *Address*: Simla, India. *Clubs*: East India United Service; Bengal. (O233)

CLARKE, Lieut. George Edgar, O.B.E., R.N.V.R.

CLARKE, George Whitlock, M.B.E.

CLARKE, Capt. and Brevet-Major Gerald, O.B.E., b. 1 April, 1883; s. of A. H. Clarke, of Bulcote, Nottingham; m. Marjorie Agnes, d. of Col. J. O. Hodgson (R.A. ret.), of Andover. *Educ.*: Charterhouse. Territorial Army, Staff *War Work*: Served in the Great War, France, 1915–19. *Address*: The Cedars, Duffield, Derby. *Club*: Services. (O5102)

CLARKE, Harold Thomas, O.B.E.

CLARKE, Helen Blanche, Mrs., M.B.E., b. 1873; d. of Walter Scott Copeland, of Dalbeattie, N.B.; m. William Edward, s. of William Clarke, of York. *Educ.*: Addlestone, Surrey. *War Work*: Quartermaster 3 years, and Commandant 2 years, of V.A.D. Hospital, Strood, Kent. *Address*: Strood, Kent. (M7690)

CLARKE, Lieut. Henry, M.B.E.

CLARKE, Henry Charles, M.B.E. Clerk, Railway Clearing House; Head of a Financial Section, Ministry of Shipping. (M10309)

CLARKE, Rear-Adm. Henry James Langford, C.B.E., R.N. Served in Great War, 1914–19, as Senior Naval Officer and Port Convoy Officer, Dakar (despatches). (C1183)

CLARKE, Lieut.-Col. Herman, C.B.E. T. Major and Acting Lieut.-Col. R.E.; served in Great War, 1914–19 (despatches). (C1514)

CLARKE, Lieut. Hugh Franklin, M.B.E., R.G.A.

CLARKE, Lieut. James Alexander, O.B.E.

CLARKE, Lieut. James Bryce, O.B.E.

CLARKE, Lieut. James Richard Plomer, O.B.E., R.N.V.R.

CLARKE, Lieut. James Thomas Morton, O.B.E., M.B.E., R.A.S.C.

CLARKE, John Courtenay, C.B.E., R.N.R.

CLARKE, Col. John Thomas, C.B.E., Can. A.M.C.

CLARKE, Capt. Joseph, M.B.E., R.E., (T.F.)

CLARKE, Capt. Joseph Edward, O.B.E., Royal Sussex Regt., b. 8 July, 1875. *War Work*: Served in France from May, 1915, to Feb. 1919. *Address*: 2nd Batt., Royal Sussex Regt., Jamaica. (O5103)

CLARKE, Joseph Percival, C.B.E., M.Inst.C.E., b. 15 Oct. 1862; s. of Thomas Charles Clarke, M.Inst.C.E.; m. Elizabeth, d. of Edward Glover, of Buenos Aires. *Educ.*: Marlborough. Civil Engineer; constructed many railways in S. America; 1902–06, Gen. Manager, Leopoldina Rly., Brazil; 1907–14, Gen. Manager, Buenos Aires Gt. Southern Rly.; at present director of Buenos Aires Gt. Southern Rly., Entre Rios Rlys. Cordoba Central, and other Rlys. *War Work*: 1915–17, assisted Ministry Munitions Priority Dept.; 1917 to Armistice, was Deputy-Director, Inland Waterways and Docks, War Office. *Address*: 20, Rosary Gardens, S.W. 7. *Clubs*: Argentine; Ranelagh: Stoke Poges. (C462)

CLARKE, Leslie Ebenezer, M.B.E.

CLARKE, Comm. Maurice Harvey, O.B.E., R.N.R.

CLARKE, Lieut. (T. Lieut.-Col.) Orme Bigland, C.B.E., B.A., b. 1880; s. of Frederick, M.A., heir presumptive to the Rev. Sir Charles Clarke, of Dunham, Bt. (*see* BURKE'S *Peerage*); m. 19 June, 1905, Elfrida, e. d. of Alfred Roosevelt, of New York. *Educ.*: Magdalen Coll., Oxford. Barrister-at-law of the Inner Temple. *War Work*: Valuable services in relation to the legal Administration of occupied territory. *Club*: Oxford and Cambridge. (C3107b)

CLARKE, Percival Herbert, M.B.E.

CLARKE, Percy Daniel, M.B.E., b. 5 Aug. 1892; s. of Robert Henry Arundel Clarke, of The Lawn, Kingsholm, Gloucester; m. Violet Bessie, d. of William James Barrett, of Gloucester. *Educ.*: Gloucester. Executive Officer Food Control Committees, and Deputy Registrar of Marriages. *War Work*: Food Control; also associated with work of Local Tribunal, War Pensions, and Dependants' Separation Allowances. *Address*: 7. Howard Street, Gloucester. (M7692)

CLARKE, Reuben Arthur, M.B.E.

CLARKE, Major Richard Charles, O.B.E., M.C.

CLARKE, Major Richard Christopher, O.B.E., M.B., M.R.C.P., (Lond.), b. 15 June, 1885; s. of John Henry Clarke, of Clifton, Bristol; m. Mabel Kate, d. of F. R. Hall, of Oxford. *Educ.*: Clifton College, University of Bristol; Middlesex Hospital. Hon. Physician to Bristol Royal Infirmary; Hon. Physician to Cossham Memorial Hospital, Bristol. *War Work*: R.A.M.C. (T.F.), France, March, 1915, to Jan. 1919; mentioned in despatches ; attached 4th Gloucestershire Regt., and 19th Casualty Clearing Station. *Address :* 29, Victoria Square, Clifton, Bristol. *Club :* Clifton. (O5104)

CLARKE, **Thomas Henry**, M.B.E., *b.* 15 June, 1883 ; *s.* of Thomas Clarke, of Woolwich ; *m.* Catherine Elizabeth, *d.* of Farquhar Beaton Gollan, of Woolwich. *Educ. :* Woolwich High School and King's College, London University. Civil Servant, War Office. *War Work :* Contracts Dept., War Office, and Ministry of Munitions ; Secretary, Sir Albert Stanley's Mechanical Transport Contracts Committee. *Address :* 118, Dunvegan Road, Eltham, S.E. 9. (M240)

CLAY, **Col. Thomas Henry Matthews**, C.M.G., C.B.E., D.S.O., M.B., *b.* 1869 ; *s.* of the late Staff Surg. Thomas Matthews Clarke, M.B., Army Med. Depart. ; *m.* 1905, Susan Morrell, *d.* of Philip E. Chapin, of Washington, District of Columbia, U.S.A. *Educ. :* Trinity Coll., Dublin (B.A. and M.B.). Entered Army Med. Depart. 1897 ; became Capt. Roy Army Med. Corps, 1900 ; Major, 1909 ; Lieut.-Col. 1915 ; and Col. Army Med. Ser. 1918 ; served at Candia, 1898 (wounded, despatches twice) ; Med. Adviser to H.R.H. Prince George of Greece, 1901–3 ; appointed Physician and Surg. to Roy. Hospital, Kilmainham, 1912 ; Knight of Order of Saviour of Greece. *Clubs :* Army and Navy ; Royal Automobile. (C805)

CLARKE, **Lieut. Thomas Walter**, M.B.E.

CLARKE, **Walter Leonard**, M.B.E.

CLARKE, **Lieut. William Francis**, O.B.E., R.N.V.R.

CLARKE, **Lieut.-Col. William Gay**, C.B.E., R.E., *b.* 16 July, 1869 ; *s.* of John Clarke, of Chieveley ; *m.* Norah Helen, *d.* of Dr. William Bodkin, of Chelmsford. *Educ. :* King's College, London. *War Work :* Acting Director of Inland Waterways and Docks. *Club :* Thatched House. (C2088)

CLARKE, **Lieut.-Col. William James**, O.B.E.

CLARKE, **Lieut.-Col. William James**, M.B.E., R.A.

CLARKE, **William John**, C.B.E., *b.* 13 March, 1857 ; *s.* of John Clarke, of Haddenham, Bucks., and Plymouth ; *m.* Annie Georgina, *d.* of Joseph Godfrey, of Plymouth, and has issue, three sons. *Educ. :* Clewer House School, Windsor. Thirty-seven years in the Admiralty Service ; entered by competitive examination in 1882, and retired in 1919 ; from 1882–94, served at Devonport, Portsmouth, Gosport and Bermuda ; in 1894, appointed Superintending Civil Engineer of H.M. naval establishments at Malta, and afterwards served in a similar capacity at Chatham, the Admiralty (Whitehall), and Devonport, until 1912 ; in that year appointed Assistant-Director of Works at the Admiralty, and later Deputy-Director of Works, and consequently served at the Admiralty during the whole of the War ; Fellow of the Royal Colonial Institute, and late M.Inst.C.E. *Address :* Wayside, Brockenhurst, Hants. *Club :* Royal Societies'. (C2518)

CLARKE, **Leslie CHATFEILD-**, M.B.E., M.I.M.E. M.J.I.E., *b.* 1865 ; *s.* of the late Thomas Chatfeild-Clarke, J.P., F.R.I.B.A., of Westbourne Terrace, Hyde Park, W., and Wootton, Isle of Wight ; *m.* Grace Brown Moore, *d.* of William Moore, of Belfast. *Educ. :* Rev. C. Young's School, Brighton ; Rev. T. R. Stebbing's School, Turbridge Wells. Vice-Chairman of the Isle of Wight Rural District Council ; Guardian, Isle of Wight Union. *War Work :* Assistant Commandant and Superintendent, Northwood Red Cross Auxiliary Hospital, Cowes, I. of W., 1914–18. (M7691)

CLARKE, **Hope Elizabeth HOPE-**, O.B.E. Founder and Organiser of the Silver Thimble Fund. (O11898)

CLARKE, **Col. John de Winton LARDNER-**, C.B.E., R.A. (Retired), *b.* 19 May, 1858 ; *s.* of the late Major John Lardner-Clarke, R.A. ; *m.* Mary Elizabeth Augusta, *d.* of late Henry Askew Robinson, M.R.C.S., widow of late Alan E. Chambré, of Halhead Hall, Cumberland. *Educ. :* Privately. *War Work :* Military Intelligence Department, War Office, from Aug. 1914, to Aug. 1919. *Address :* Parkholme, Warblington, Havant, Hants. *Clubs :* Army and Navy ; Royal Dorset Yacht ; Royal Albert Yacht. (C2134)

CLARKE, **Major Mervyn Hanbury LOWTHER-**, O.B.E.

CLARKE, **Capt. James Thomas MORTON-**, O.B.E., *b.* 31 Aug. 1880. Served in the South African Campaign, Staff Captain, War Office (Quartermaster General's Dept.). *Clubs :* R.A.C. ; United R.A.S.C. (O7494)

CLARKE, **Capt. Geoffrey SOMERS-**, O.B.E., R.A.F.

CLARKE, **Lieut.-Col. Charles Camden WISEMAN-**, O.B.E.

CLARKSON, **Elkanah**, M.B.E.

CLARKSON, **Francis George**, M.B.E.

CLARKSON, **Eng.-Rear-Adm. Sir William**, K.B.E., C.M.G., A.D.C., R.A.N., *b.* 26 March, 1859 (*see* BURKE's *Peerage*) ; *s.* of James Nicholson Clarkson, of Whitby, Yorks. ; *m.* Louisa Clarissa, *d.* of James C. Hawker, of Adelaide, South Australia. *Educ. :* Privately. 3rd Naval Member of the Naval Board of Administration ; Director of Transports ; Controller of Shipping, Australia. *War Work :* The organisation and direction of transport for conveying Australian troops to Europe ; the Organisation and Control of Merchant Shipping. *Address :* Mombah, 12, Como Avenue, South Yarra, Victoria, Australia. *Club :* The Australian, Melbourne. (K117)

CLAUGHTON, **Harold**, M.B.E.

CLAUSEN, **Lieut. Hugh**, O.B.E., R.N.V.R.

CLAUSON, **Albert Charles**, C.B.E., K.C., *b.* 14 Jan. 1870 ; *s.* of Charles Clauson, and of Julia Burton, daughter of Rev. John Wall Buckley (*see* BURKE's *Peerage*, Wrenbury, B.) ; *m.* Kate, *d.* of James Thomas Hopwood, of Lincoln's Inn (*see*

Southborough, Baron). *Educ. :* Merchant Taylors' School, and St. John's College, Oxford. Bencher (1914) of Lincoln's Inn; Past-Master of Merchant Taylors' Company. *War Work :* Legal Member (unpaid) of the Staff of the Controller of the Navy, at the Admiralty, 1917–18 ; attached to Lord Southborough's Indian Reforms Commission, 1918–19. *Addresses :* 13, Old Square, Lincoln's Inn, W.C. 2 ; Hawkshead House, Hatfield, Herts. *Clubs :* Athenæum ; United University; Albemarle. (C2519)

CLAUSON, **Capt. Gerald Leslie Makins**, O.B.E.

CLAVELL, **Lieut. Richard Charles**, O.B.E., R.N.

CLAY, **Capt. Ernest**, M.B.E., *b.* 19 Dec. 1874 ; *s.* of Philip Clay, of Nottingham ; *m.* Emma Rose, *d.* of Thomas Brown, of Dublin. *Educ. :* St. John's College, Gibraltar, and Army. Adjutant, 6th Batt. London Regt. *War Work :* South Africa, 1899–1902 ; France, as R.S.M., March–June, 1915 ; Adjutant, 6th Batt. London Regt., Oct. 15, to present date. *Address :* 41, Mountfold Road, Stamford Hill. (M5161)

CLAY, **Major Ernest Charles**, C.B.E., *b.* 2 Dec. 1872; *s.* of Charles John Clay, of Holly Bush Hall, Staffs. ; *m.* Dorothy Mary, *d.* of John L. Press, of Reymerstone Hall, Norfolk, and Clifton, Bristol. *Educ. :* Marlborough and New College, Oxford. Called to the Bar, Lincoln's Inn, 1899. *War Work :* Temp. Major and D.A.A.G., Headquarters Staff, War Office. *Address :* Little Court, Banstead, Surrey. *Club :* Royal Automobile. (C1515)

CLAY, **Capt. Frank Septimus**, O.B.E., R.A.V.C.

CLAY, **Frederick Septimus**, M.B.E.

CLAY, **Col. Henry**, C.B.E. ; Col. (retired) ; Dep. Director of Recruiting, E. Command. (C806)

CLAY, **Major and Qr.-Mr. Henry**, C.B.E.

CLAY, **Col. John**, C.B.E., M.B., M.R.C.S., R.A.M.C. ; served in the Great War, 1914–19 (despatches). (C1237)

CLAY, **Joseph Miles**, O.B.E., I.C.S., *b.* 6 Sept. 1881 ; *s.* of the late Arthur Lloyd Clay, I.C.S. ; *m.* Edith Marguerite Florence, *d.* of Edwin T. Hall, of Dulwich, S E. *Educ. :* Winchester ; New College, Oxford. Deputy Commissioner of the Garhwal District, U.P., India. *Address :* c/o Messrs. Grindlay and Co., Parliament Street, S.W. (O2064)

CLAY, **Laura Beatrice**, M.B.E., *b.* 1892 ; *d.* of Laurence Clay, of Kingskerswell, Devon. *Educ. :* Manchester High School. Late Controller, Northern Command, Q.M.A.A.C. *War Work :* Four years' service with the Women's Legion and the Q.M.A.A.C. ; now on relief work in Poland. *Address :* South Hill, Kingskerswell, Devon. (M3254)

CLAY, **Mignon Elvira, Mrs.**, M.B.E., *d.* of Louis Andre, of Paris ; *m.* Joseph, *s.* of James Henry Clay, of Giggleswick. *Educ. :* France, and Dresden Conservatorium of Music. *War Work :* Sec. and Vice-Chairwoman Leeds City Association ; D.G.V.O., Clothing and Hospital Needs Committee. *Address :* Riddings, Long Preston Yorks. (M7694)

CLAY, **Robert**, O.B.E., J.P.

CLAY, **Major William Henry Christy**, O.B.E.

CLAYE, **Fred Wainwright**, M.B.E., R.A.S.C.

CLAYTON, **Rev. Albert Charles**, O.B.E. Board for Tamil Christian Literature, Madras. *War Work :* Edited " War News " for the Publicity Board of the Government of Madras. *Address :* Ingleby, Kodaikanal, South India. (O9810)

CLAYTON, **Charles Henry James**, M.B.E.

CLAYTON, **Major Emilius**, O.B.E., R.F.A., *b.* 19 June, 1884 ; *s.* of Col. Emilius Clayton, late R.A., of Charlcombe Manor, Bath ; *m.* Irene Dorothy Constance, *d.* of the late Col. Thomas Edmund Strong, I.A., of Claremont, Exeter. *Educ. :* Bradfield ; Royal Military Academy, Woolwich. *War Work :* Served with the British Army in Flanders, the Balkans, and South Russia, during the European War. *Address :* Charlcombe Manor, Bath. *Club :* Sports. (O7002)

CLAYTON, **George Christopher**, C.B.E., J.P.

CLAYTON, **Brig.-Gen. Sir Gilbert Falkingham**, K.B.E., C.B., C.M.G., F.R.G.S., Lieut.-Col. R. of O., R.A., *b.* 6 July, 1875 ; *s.* of Lieut.-Col. W. L. N. Clayton, Sandown ; *m.* Enid Caroline, 2nd *d.* of Frank Napier Thorowgood, 24, Elm Park, Gardens, S.W. *Educ. :* Isle of White Coll. ; R.M.A., Woolwich. Entered Army, 1895 ; Capt. 1901 ; employed by Egyptian Govt., 1900–10 ; Sudan Govt. since 1910 ; served Nile Expedition, 1898 (despatches, Egyptian Medal, 2 clasps, medal) ; Director of Intelligence in Egypt, 1914–17 ; Chief Political Officer, Egyptian Expeditionary Force, 1917 ; European War, 1914–19 (K.B.E., C.B., C.M.G., despatches six times) ; Officer, Legion of Honour : 4th Class Osmanieh ; 3rd Class Medjidieh ; Officer, St. Maurice and Lazarus and St. Stanislaus : Grand Commander, Order of King George I. of Greece. *Address :* War Office, Cairo. *Club :* United Service. (K274)

CLAYTON, **Harry**, M.B.E., *b.* 15 April, 1888. *Educ. :* Dover College. *War Work :* Assistant Controller, Munitions Accounts Department, Ministry of Munitions. *Address :* Wayside, Cheam, Surrey. *Clubs :* Cocoa Tree ; Road. (M3575)

CLAYTON, **James**, M.B.E., M.I.M.E., *b.* 17 Nov. 1872 ; *s.* of Jabez Clayton, of Bollington, Stockport, Cheshire ; *m.* Mary Gertrude, *d.* of Samuel Collins, of Derryork, Dungiven, Co. Derry, Ireland. *Educ. :* Gorton Schools, and Municipal School of Technology, Manchester. Locomotive Engineer ; Personal Assistant to Chief Mechanical Engineer, South-Eastern and Chatham Railway ; Member of Council of Institution of Locomotive Engineers. *War Work :* Planning and equipment of Overseas Railway Workshops ; charge of Indenting and inspection of all Railway Material, the supply of which was undertaken by the Chief Mechanical Engineers Dept., S.E. and C. Ry., Ashford, for all theatres of war ;

designs of Anti-Aircraft Gun Carriage for Sir Percy Scott, R.N. *Addresses :* Langton, 36, Albert Road, Ashford, Kent ; Chief Mechanical Engineer's Dept., S.E. and C. Ry. (M7695)

CLAYTON, Lieut. Norman Willis, M.B.E. M.C.

CLAYTON, Thomas, M.B.E., J.P.

CLAYTON, William Ellis, O.B.E.

CLEARY, Right Rev. Henry William, O.B.E., R.C.

CLEAVER, Lieut.-Col. Frederick Holden, C.B.E., D.S.O., *b.* 1875 ; Lieut.-Col. R.A.F. ; served in the Great War, 1914–19 (despatches). (C854)

CLEAVER, Harris Pengest, O.B.E.

CLEEVE, Major Charles Edward, O.B.E., *b.* 31 May, 1891 ; *s.* of Frederick Cleeve, D.L., of Limerick ; *m.* Josephine Eugenie, *d.* of Alfred Talbot, of Westcliffe-on-Sea. *Educ. :* St. Edward's School, Oxford ; Christ's Coll., Cambridge. Merchant. *War Work :* Joined R.A.S.C., Mechanical Transport Branch, in April, 1915 ; served with 52 M.T. Coy., Aldershot, till April, 1916 ; went to France with No 1 Water Tank M.T. Coy. as Adjutant ; took over Command of Coy. in Feb. 1917 ; twice mentioned in despatches ; relinquished commission, April, 1919. *Address :* Calgarth, St. Margaret's Road, Hoylake. (O5107)

CLEEVE, Lieut.-Col. Herbert, C.B.E., R.A.S.C., (R. of O.), *b.* 15 Sept. 1870 ; *s.* of C. K. Cleeve ; *m.* Clara F., *d.* of John F. Holt, of U.S.A. *Educ. :* Wellington College. Joined 1st Batt. South Wales Borderers, 1892, from 4th Batt. Queen's Own Royal West Kent Regt. ; transferred to A.S.C., 1896 ; served South African War, 1899–1901 (despatches, twice) ; Queen's medal, seven clasps. *War Work :* European War, 1914–19 (despatches, twice), cr. C.B.E. (Military), 1919. *Club :* Naval and Military. (C1518)

CLEGG, Alfred, M.B.E., J.P., *b.* 23 June, 1872 ; *s.* of Albert Clegg, of New Hey, Lancs. ; *m.* Frances, *d.* of Samuel Binns, of Oldham, Lancs. Head Master of Crompton East Crompton School ; Chairman, Crompton Urban District Council. *War Work :* Chairman of the Military Service Tribunal, War Pensions Committee, Food Control Committee, and War Savings Committee. *Addresses :* 31, College Road, Oldham ; East Crompton, Shaw, Lancs. (M1542)

CLEGG, Bella (Rebecca), Mrs., M.B.E. *b.* 28 Nov. 1848 ; *d.* of Joseph Sills, of Orsett, Essex ; *m.* the late Harry Clegg, J.P., D.L., A.C.C.. Plas Llanfair, Anglesey. *s.* of Kay Clegg, Solicitor, of Oldham, Lancs. Chairman of District Nursing Association ; Vice-Chairman, Bryn Menai Nursing Home ; on Committee, North Wales Nursing Association ; Board of Governors, Carnarvonshire and Anglesey Infirmary. *War Work :* Commandant of Bodlendch Auxiliary Hospital, Menai Bridge, 1915–19. *Address :* Bryn Llwyd, Menai Bridge, Anglesey. *Clubs :* Ladies' Imperial : Empress. (M1543)

CLEGG, Elizabeth, Mrs., M.B.E. *War Work :* Joint Hon. Sec., Central Advisory Committee (Care Committee), Royal Dublin Fusiliers, Dublin. *Address :* 11, Kenilworth Road, Dublin. (M3576)

CLEGG, Ethel Theodora, M.B.E., *b.* 12 March, 1891 ; *d.* of Leonard Johnson Clegg, of Sheffield. *Educ. :* The Grange, Buxton ; Vevey, Switzerland. *War Work :* Joined Women's Legion, Military Cooking Section, Aug. 1916 ; worked at Folkestone Rest Camps until transferred to Headquarters Chatham Garrison, Feb. 1918 ; promoted Deputy Controller, Eastern Command, Feb. 1918 ; transferred to Q.M.A.A.C. Headquarters Staff, Eastern Command, London, 1919 ; demobilised Nov. 1919. *Address :* West Hey, Whiteley Wood, Sheffield. (M1544)

CLEGG, Fanny, M.B.E. *War Work :* From Aug. 1914, to Jan. 1919, engaged in voluntary work amongst the wives and dependants of Soldiers and Sailors, first through the Soldiers' and Sailors' Families Assn.. and later the War Pensions Committee. *Address :* Walmsley House, Rochdale. (M7697)

CLEGG, Herbert Edmund, M.B.E., R.A.S.C.

CLEGG, Comm. John Harry Kay, O.B.E., M.B.E.

CLEGG, Margaret Penelope, M.B.E., *b.* 7 Nov. 1846 ; *d.* of Walter Clegg, M.R.C.S. (Eng.), L.S.A., of Boston, Lincolnshire. *Educ. :* Privately. *War Work :* 4½ years Commandant of the Red Cross Auxiliary Hospital, Holden House, Boston, Lincs. ; Officer-in-charge of Surgical Clinic for Discharged Sailors and Soldiers, under the Ministry of Pensions, East Midlands Centre. *Address :* Portarlington, Carlton Road, Boston, Lincs. (M243)

CLEGG, Capt. Robert Edward, M.B.E., S.A.S.C.

CLEGG, Capt. Sydney James, O.B.E., R.A.M.C. (T.F.)

CLEGG, Lieut. Thomas Harry, M.B.E., M.C.

CLEGG, Sir William Edwin, Kt. Bach., C.B.E., J.P. for the West Riding of Yorkshire and City of Sheffield, LL.D. (*honoris causa*), Sheffield University, *b.* 21 April, 1852 ; *s.* of William Johnson Clegg, of Cliffe Tower, Sheffield. *Educ. :* Sheffield and Gainford, near Darlington. Ex-Lord Mayor of Sheffield, 1898–99 ; Alderman of the City ; Member of the Sheffield Town Trust : Chairman of the Sheffield Education Committee ; Corporation Tramways Committee ; Sheffield Licensing Committee ; Member of the Council of the Sheffield University ; Chairman of the Applied Science Committee of the Sheffield University ; Member and Treasurer of the Derwent Valley Water Board. *War Work :* Propaganda work in connection with recruiting ; Chairman of the Sheffield Military Tribunal ; Chairman of the Sheffield District Munitions Court, under the Munitions of War Acts ; Chairman of the Court of Referees for the Yorkshire and East Midlands Division. under the Ministry of Labour (Employment Department). *Clubs :* National Liberal ; Sheffield ; Sheffield Reform. (C463)

CLELAND. Sir Charles, K.B.E., M.V.O., D.L., J.P., *b.* 15 April, 1867 ; *s.* of Charles Cleland, of Bonville, Maryhill ; *m.* Jessie Houston, *d.* of William Burrell, of Elmbank, Bowling. *Educ. :* Glasgow Academy, and privately. Chairman, Glasgow Education Authority ; Income Tax Commissioner for City of Glasgow ; Chairman, Glasgow Unionist Association. *War Work :* Chairman, Glasgow Local War Pensions Committee ; Chairman, South West of Scotland Joint (Disablement) Committee. *Address :* Bonville, Maryhill, Glasgow. *Clubs* Conservative ; Scottish Constitutional, Glasgow. (K16)

CLELAND, John Storkwyn, M.B.E. (M10337)

CLEMENS, Major Lionel Alfred, O.B.E., M.C.

CLEMENT, Sir Thomas, K.B.E., Chairman of the Cheese and Butter Department, Ministry of Food. (K207)

CLEMENTI, Marie Penelope Rose, Mrs., M.B.E. ; *d.* of Vice-Admiral C. J. Eyres, R.N., D.S.O., of Denmark House, Rochester ; *m.* Cecil, *s.* of the late Colonel Montagu Clementi. *War Work :* President of British Guiana War Relief Needlework Guild (affiliated to Queen Mary's Needlework Guild). *Address :* Denmark House, Rochester. (M6427)

CLEMENTS, Dora, Mrs., O.B.E., Q.M.A.A.C.

CLEMENTS, Wing Com., Edward Cecil, O.B.E., R.A.F., M.S. Ophthalmic Surgeon, Lincoln County Hospital. *War Work :* Major, R.A.M.C. (T.F.) ; Squadron Leader, R.A.F. Med. Service. *Address :* 3, Lindum Road, Lincoln. (O9620)

CLEMENTS, Fred, M.B.E.

CLEMENTS, Lieut. and Qr.-Mr. Frederick James, M.B.E., R.E.

CLEMENTS, Major Thomas, O.B.E. *b.* 23 Aug. 1868 ; *s.* of the late Frank Clements, of Ingham, Norfolk ; *m.* Fanny Bartley, *d.* of the late Samuel Weller, of East Grinstead. *Educ. :* Privately. Served continuously in the Durham Light Infantry since May, 1887. *War Work :* Served on the Staff Headquarters, Second Army, France, and also with the Italian Expeditionary Force from Jan. 1917, to April, 1919 ; mentioned in despatches, London Gazette, 1st Jan. 1919 ; awarded Croce di Guerra (Italian), Dec. 1918. *Address :* c/o Messrs. Holt and Co., 3, Whitehall Place, S.W. (O2911)

CLEMENTS, Lieut. and Quartermaster William Joseph, M.B.E., *b.* 8 Dec. 1887 ; *m.* Jessie Hatherll, *d.* of the late John Handy, of Cardiff. *Educ. :* Grocers' Company School. Insurance Official ; served in Grenadier Guards. *War Work :* Joined and helped to form 10th Batt. Royal Fusiliers (Stock Exchange Batt.) in 1914, with rank of R.Q.M. Sergt. ; proceeded with them to France in 1915, and remained with them until May, 1917, with the exception of a few months in 1916, when temporarily attached to the 13th Batt. The Rifle Brigade, as Quartermaster ; promoted to Lieut. and Quartermaster to 13th Batt. The Rifle Brigade in May 1917, and remained with that Brigade until demobilisation May, 1919. *Address :* 15, Lupus Street, S.W. 1. (M4449)

CLEMISHAW, 2nd. Lieut. John, M.B.E., R.E.

CLEMSON, Flight-Lieut. Alfred William, O.B.E., D.S.C.

CLERICI, Major Charles John Emile, C.I.E., O.B.E., R.E., *b.* 1877 ; *s.* of Ernest Clerici, of Milan, Italy ; *m.* Constance Jessie *d.* of Yates Brooks, of Victoria, Australia. Assistant Director-General, Posts and Telegraphs of India. *War Work :* Served in Mesopotamia, 1914–20 ; Director of Postal Services, 'Iraz and Persian Lines of Communication ; mentioned in despatches. *Address :* Colpelly, Abbott Street, Sandringham, Pretoria, Australia. (O2267)

CLERK, Sir Dugald, K.B.E., D.Sc., LL.D., F.R.S., J.P. *b.* 31 March, 1854 (*see* BURKE's *Peerage*) ; *s.* of the late Donald Clerk, of Glasgow ; *m.* Margaret, *d.* of the late Alex. Hannay, of Westburn, Helensburgh, N.B. *Educ. :* Anderson's College, Glasgow ; Yorkshire College of Science, Leeds. Civil Engineer ; inventor and investigator in internal combustion engines since 1876 ; member of the University Grants Committee. *War Work :* Chairman, Royal Society, Engineering Section Committee for War, 1914–19 ; member of the Advisory Committee for Aeronautics ; Chairman, Internal Combustion Engine Sub-Com. of that body ; member, Air Inventions Committee ; member of Panel Board of Invention and Research ; director of Engineering Research, Admiralty Engineering Laboratory, 1916–19. *Addresses :* Lukyns, Ewhurst, Surrey ; 57–58, Lincoln's Inn Fields, W.C. 2. *Clubs :* Athenæum ; Reform ; Royal Automobile ; Royal Clyde Yacht. (K15)

CLERK, Lieut.-Col. Robert Mildmay, O.B.E. Hon. Sec., Somerset Branch of the Soldiers' and Sailors' Families Association. (O11899)

CLERKE, Major Augustus Basil Holt, C.B.E., *b.* 1871 ; *s.* of Col. Shadwell H. Clerke, formerly Roy. Scots ; *m.* Mabel, *d.* of J. Seymour Salaman. *Educ. :* Cheltenham ; R.M.A. Major R.A. (ret.) ; Managing Director of Hadfields (Limited), of Sheffield ; appointed Assist. Inspector of Steel, 1889 ; Ch. Inspector, Ordnance Coll. 1905 ; Inspector, Roy. Arsenal, Woolwich 1918. *Club :* United Service. (C131)

CLEVELAND, Major Arthur John, O.B.E., R.A.M.C.

CLEVELAND, Sir Charles Raitt, K.C.I.E., K.B.E., Director of Central Intelligence, India, since 1910 ; *b.* 1866 ; *m.* Mary Kathleen, *d.* of Col. W. T. Hogg. *Educ. :* Christ's Coll., Finchley ; Balliol Coll., Oxford. Entered Indian Civil Service, 1885 ; Assistant Commissioner, C.P., 1887 ; Settlement Officer, 1891 ; Commissioner of Excise, 1894 ; Deputy Commissioner, 1897 ; Inspector-General Police, C.P., India, 1900 ; D.C.I., 1910 ; King's Police Medal, 1909. *Address :* Simla and Calcutta, India. *Clubs :* East India United Service ; United Service, Simla ; Bengal, Calcutta. (K46)

CLIBBON, Percy Gordon, M.B.E., R.N.

CLIFF, Capt. Arthur, O.B.E.

CLIFF, Edith Maud, O.B.E.

CLIFFORD, Elizabeth Lydia Rosabelle, Lady, C.B.E.; *d.* of the late Edward Bonham, Consul at Calais, and *w.* of Henry Philip Ducarel de la Pasture (*see* BURKE'S *Peerage,* Foreign Titles); *m.* 24 Sept. 1910, Sir Hugh Charles, K.C.M.G., *s.* of Sir Henry Hugh Clifford, V.C., K.C.M.G., C.B., and *g. s.* of the 7th Baron Clifford of Chudleigh (*see* BURKE'S *Peerage*).   (C390)

CLIFFORD, Lieut.-Col. Ernest Stanley, D.S.O., O.B.E., *b.* 1873; *s.* of Samuel Le Poer Trench Clifford, a judge of Punjab. Joined Punjab Light Horse, 1896; served in S. Africa, 1900, with Lumsden's Horse; as Lieut. W. Australian Mounted Inf.; in charge of W. Australian Scouts; present at action of Moore Vlej; capture of Bettah Commando (despatches); Major and T. Lieut.-Col. Canadian Forces; Assist. Provost Marshal.   (O7902)

CLIFFORD, Col. Ernest Thomas, C.B.E., C.B.E., V.D., R.E. (T.F.); served in the Great War, 1914–19 (despatches).
                                         (C1516)

CLIFFORD, Brig.-Gen. Walter Rees, C.B.E. Col. and Hon. Brig.-Gen. (retired); served in the Great War, 1914–19 (despatches).   (C1517)

CLIFFORD, Major William Henry, O.B.E.

CLIFT, Agnes, Mrs., M.B.E.

CLIFT, Surg.-Comm. Hugh, O.B.E., R.N.

CLIFT, James Augustus, C.B.E., K.C., *b.* 1857; *s.* of Theodore Clift, merchant, of St. John's, Newfoundland. Bar, Newfoundland 1884, and K.C. 1904; Vice-Chm. of Standing Committee of Patriotic Assoc., and a Member of Pensions Board and Mil. Board; elected to Newfoundland Parliament 1889. *Address:* St. John's, Newfoundland.   (C383)

CLIFT, Lieut. George Neilson, M.B.E., R.A.F.

CLIFT, John George Neilson, M.B.E.   (M3365)

CLIFT, Mildred, M.B.E.

CLIFTON, Major Arthur John, O.B.E., Durham L.I., *b.* 27 Jan. 1887; *s.* of the late James Clifton, of Cheltenham, Glos. *Educ.:* Privately. Inspector of Armoured Motor Batteries in India. *War Work:* Pioneer of the armoured car in India; played a leading part in organising armoured motor batteries for use in India and on the north-west frontier of India; Commanded A.M. Batts. on all operations on the N.W.F. between 1915 and 1919; author of first official manual on A.M. Tactics; mentioned in despatches six times; awarded O.B.E., Croix de Guerre with palm (French), and Brevet Majority. *Addresses:* Hazle Dean, Cheltenham; c/o Army Headquarters, Simla, India. *Clubs:* R.A.C.; various Indian.
                                      (O2366)

CLIFTON, Rev. Edward James, O.B.E.

CLIFTON, Capt. Ernest Hamilton, O.B.E.

CLINCH, Sidney Herbert, M.B.E.

CLINCKETT, Robert James, M.B.E., *b.* 30 May, 1846; *s.* of Robert Clinckett, of Barbados W.I. *Educ.:* Privately. Official Assignee. *War Work:* Treasurer for British, French and Belgium Red Cross Societies; Local Controller of Clearing Office under Peace Treaty Order, 1919. *Address:* Strathclyde, Bridgetown, Barbados, W.I.   (M2933)

CLINE, Major John George, O.B.E., Can. M.G.C.

CLINKARD, Lieut. Charles Ernest, M.B.E.

CLIPPERTON, Ella Elizabeth, Mrs. Charles Bell Child, O.B.E.

CLITHEROW, Col. John Bourchier STRACEY-, C.B.E.

CLIVE, Major Harry, O.B.E., T.D., *b.* 7 May, 1880; *s.* of Col. R. C. Clive, V.D., D.L., of Gravenhunger Hall, Woore, Crewe; *m.* Dorothy, *d.* of Joseph Clive, of Combe Flory, Somerset. *Educ.:* Newcastle; Staffordshire. Porcelain Manufacturer; Merchant (Raw Materials). *War Work:* Mobilised 5th N. Staffs Regt., Aug. 1914; overseas, 46th Division, Feb. 1915; Staff Capt. North Midland Brigade; D.A.Q.M.G. Headquarters Northern Command, York. *Address:* Ela's Gorse, Willoughbridge, Market Drayton, Salop. (O7004)

CLOETE, Col. Evelyn Rivers Henry Josias, C.B.E. Col. R.A. (ret.); Soudan, 1885 (medal with clasps, bronze star); served in the Great War, 1914–19 (despatches).   (C807)

CLOGSTOUN, Capt. Herbert Cunningham, C.I.E., O.B.E., *b.* 1857; *s.* of Major Herbert Mackworth Clogstoun, V.C.; *m.* 1885, Emily Ursula Anne, who died 1897, *d.* of Maj.-Gen. A. Hoseason, Madras Army. *Educ.:* Wellington Coll. Was in Bengal Police, 1882–87; Special Assist. to Bengal Govt. 1887–91; employed under Foreign Depart. of Govt. of India in Rajputana and Central India, 1891–1906; has been Tutor to Maharajah Holkar of Indo, and Police Assist., Rajputana; retired 1912; is T. Capt. in the Army.   (O5109)

CLOGSTOUN, Capt. Herbert Prinsep Somers, O.B.E., R.A.F.

CLONBROCK, Augusta Caroline, Baroness, O.B.E., *b* 1839; *d.* of the late Edward, 2nd Baron Crofton; *m.* the late Luke Gerald, 4th Baron Clonbrock (*see* BURKE'S *Peerage*). President of G.F.S., and of Mothers' Union, Dioceses Killaloe, Clonfert, etc.; President, Ladies Committee Mount Bellew Workhouse, and of Co. Galway Assn. for Promotion of Temperance; started, and for many years President, Clonbrock and Castlegar Poultry Society. *War Work:* President, Co. Galway War Fund Association. *Address:* Clonbrock, Ahascragh, Ireland.   (O10156)

CLOSE, Col. Sir Charles (Frederick), K.B.E., C.M.G., F.R.S., *b.* 10 Aug. 1865; *s.* of Maj.-Gen. F. Close, R.A., of Shanklin; *m.* Gladys Violet, *d.* of Theodore Percival,

of Shanklin. *Educ.:* Jersey and Royal Military Academy. Commissioned in R.E., 1884; on Survey of India, 1889–94; in charge Niger-Cameroon Boundary Survey, 1895; British Commissioner, Nyasa-Tanganyika Boundary Commission, 1898: S. African War, 1900; Chief Instructor in Surveying, Chatham, 1902–05; Head of Geographical Section, General Staff, 1905–1911; Director General, Ordnance Survey, 1911; Halley Lecturer, Oxford, 1914; Boundary Commissioner under Representation of the People Bill, 1917. *War Work:* During the war the Ordnance Survey was the main source of supply for the millions of trench and other maps required by the British Armies on the Western Front. *Addresses:* Ordnance Survey, Southampton; Coytbury, St. Giles's Hill, Winchester. *Club:* Army and Navy.   (K56)

CLOSE, Ella, O.B.E.

CLOSE, Lieut.-Col. Francis Morton, O.B.E., B.E.

CLOSE, Harold Arden, C.I.E., C.B.E., *b.* 13 Dec. 1863; *s.* of Gen. H. P. Close, Bombay Staff Corps; *m.* Edith Mary, *d.* of W. A. Robinson. *Educ.:* Cheltenham. Appointed to Indian Police in 1884; Inspector-General, North West Frontier Province, 1909–20. *War Work:* Served on Indian North-West Frontier throughout the War; received King's Police Medal in 1917. *Address:* Peshawar, Branksome Park, Bournemouth. *Club:* E.I.U.S.   (C1070)

CLOSE, Rev. Richard Bevill Middleton, O.B.E., M.A., R.A.

CLOTHIER, Lieut. Frederick Nelson, M.B.E., R.N.V.R.

CLOUGH, Frederic Horton, C.B.E.

CLOUGH, Major Henry Kenny, O.B.E., *b.* 19 Dec. 1876; *s.* of the late Rev. John Clough, M.A., Rector of Wilford, Nottinghamshire; *m.* Mabel Grace, *d.* of the late Rev. C. A. Hodgson, B.A., Rector of Barton-in-Fabis, Nottinghamshire. *Educ.:* Repton. Commissioned in Regular Army, and appointed to The King's Own Regiment, 4 May, 1898. *War Work:* Adjutant, 3rd Battalion The Kings' Own Regt.; 2nd in Command 2nd Battalion The King's Own Regt.; in Command 2nd Battalion The King's Own Regt.; with British Expeditionary Force, France; wounded May, 1915; Deputy Assistant, Adjutant-General at Headquarters, Northern Command, March 1916, to Feb. 1920. *Address:* c/o Messrs. Cox & Co., 16, Charing Cross, London, S.W. 1. *Club:* Cocoa Tree. (O7006)

CLOUGH, William, M.B.E.

CLOUSTON, Lieut. Noel Stewart, O.B.E., R.E.

CLOUSTON, Thomas Harold, O.B.E., *b.* 1875; *s.* of Sir Thomas S. Clouston, of Edinburgh (*see* BURKE'S *Peerage*); *m.* Ada Mary Stuart, *d.* of Major-Gen. A. A. Bruce, of Edinburgh. *Educ.:* Merchiston School, and Roy. School of Mines, Lond. Mining Engineer. *War Work:* Section Director of Trench Warfare Dept., and later of Dept. of Engineering. *Address:* Langskaill, Church Road, Wimbledon, S.W. *Clubs:* Union; R.A.C.: Royal Wimbledon Golf.
                                    (O10157)

CLOUT, Capt. Charles William, M.B.E.

CLOUX, Frank Louis Whitmarsh, M.B.E., A.R.I.B.A., *b.* 27 Aug. 1885; *s.* of P. F. L. Cloux, of Folkestone; *m.* Hilda, *d.* of T. B. Woodfall, of Dulwich. *Educ.:* Harvey Grammar School, Folkestone. Assistant Architect in H.M. Office of Works. *War Work:* Engaged upon design and erection of buildings, etc., used for war purposes. *Address:* Gables, East Dulwich Grove, S.E. 24.   (M7701)

CLOVER, Major Edgar, O.B.E., R.A.S.C.

CLOVER, Capt. Frederick William, M.B.E.

CLOVER, Margaret Dorothy, Mrs., M.B.E.

CLOW, Lieut.-Col. William, C.B.E.

CLOWER, William, O.B.E.

CLOWES, Edith Emily, Mrs., M.B.E.; *d.* of George, Warren, of Woolton, Liverpool; *m.* Peter Legh Clowes, of Burton Court. *War Work:* Acting Hon. Sec. County Branch B.R.C., 1915–16; County Agricultural and Horticultural organisation and Committee work for food production; District Hon. Sec. Soldiers' and Sailors' Families Association. *Address:* Burton Court, Eardisland, Herefordshire. (M244)

CLOWES, Ethel Robin, O.B.E.

CLOWES, Mary Knight, O.B.E.

CLOWES, Nina Maud Dacre, Mrs., O.B.E.; *d.* of E. Sparshall Willett, M.D., J.P., of Wyke House, Isleworth; *m.* William Archibald Clowes. *War Work:* Hon. Organising Sec. Surbiton War Hospital Supply Depot; Hon. Superintendent Surbiton Y.M.C.A. Hut. *Address:* Berwyn, Ditton Hill, Surbiton.   (O10159)

CLUBB, Leonard, O.B.E.

CLUCAS, Capt. Alfred Henry, M.B.E.

CLUETT, Alfred William Ayers, M.B.E.

CLUMECK, Marie, M.B.E., *b.* 6 Sept. 1886; *d.* of Abraham Frankel, of Singapore; *m.* Victor, *s.* of Nathaniel Clumeck, of Egypt. *Educ.:* French Convent, and Raffles Girls' School, Singapore. *War Work:* British Red Cross, and Star and Gartar. *Address:* Waringa Hill, 2, Paterson Road, Singapore.
                                      (M1257)

CLUTTERBUCK, Major Lewis St. John Rawlinson, O.B.E., R.A., *b.* 30 June, 1884; *s.* of Col. L. A. Clutterbuck. *Educ.:* Bath College; R.M.A., Woolwich, Inspector, Inspection Dept., Woolwich Arsenal; Military Interallied Commission of Control in Germany. *Address:* c/o Messrs. Cox & Co. 16, Charing Cross, S.W. 1.   (O3659)

CLUTTERBUCK, Millie Gertrude, M.B.E.

CLUTTERBUCK, Peter Henry, C.I.E., C.B.E., *b.* 1868; *s.* of the late Alexander Clutterbuck (*see* BURKE'S *Peerage,* Barrow, Bt.); *m.* 1896, Rose Winifred, *d.* of Alfred Barrow

Wilson Marriott. Formerly Dist. Sup. of Police, Central Provinces, India. Entered Indian Forest Service, 1899; became Dep. Conservator, 1897; Conservator, 1913; has been Ch. Conservator of United Provinces since 1915; has Kaisir-i-Hind Medal. *Address :* Naini Tal, United Provinces, India. (C2375)

CLUTTERBUCK, Sydney Ernest, M.B.E.

CLUVER, Paul Dietrich, O.B.E.

CLYDESDALE, Alexander M'Alister, M.B.E. (M10378)

COALES, Capt. Herbert Wallis, O.B.E., M.C., R.E.

COAST, Ernest Frederick, M.B.E.

COATES, Major Christopher George, O.B.E., *b.* 1883; *s.* of Joseph Coates, of Hampstead. Chartered Accountant. *Addresses :* 26, Willoughby Road, Hampstead, London, N.W.; 18, Rue Chauveau-Lagarde, Paris. (O2972)

COATES, David Wilson, C.B.E., *b.* 1886; *s.* of Fletcher Coates, of Broadwater, Beckenham; *m.* 1913, Mabel, *d.* of the late Thomas Goodley, of Knapwell, Cambridgeshire. *Educ.:* St. John's Coll., Camb. (B.A. and LL.B. 1907, M.A. 1911). A partner in firm of Elles, Salaman, Coates & Co., chartered accountants; appointed Chief Accountant, Coal Mines Depart., Board of Trade 1917, and Financial Sec. 1919. *Address :* Hughenden, Cator Road, Sydenham, S.E. *Club :* St. Stephen's. (C464)

COATES, Capt. Edward Clive, O.B.E.

COATES, Ernest, M.B.E.

COATES, Lieut.-Comm. Joseph Edward, O.B.E., R.N.V.R.,

COATES, Lieut. Joseph Michael Smith, O.B.E., M.G.C.

COATES, Lavinia, O.B.E.

COATES, R. H., M.B.E.

COATES, Capt. and Qr.-Mr. Thomas, O.B.E.

COATES, Lieut.-Col. Thomas Seymour, O.B.E.

COATES, Col. William, C.B., C.B.E., V.D., D.L., County Palatine, Lancashire. Chairman, East Lancashire Branch, B.R.C.S. *War Work :* A.D.M.S., Western Command; Chairman, East Lancashire Branch, B.R.C.S.; and of Totally Disabled Sailors' and Soldiers' Homes. *Addresses :* Ingleside, Whalley Range, Manchester; 17, Market Street, Manchester. (C2522)

COATS, Marie Jeanne, Lady, O.B.E., Lady of Grace St. John of Jerusalem, *b.* 20 March, 1860; *d.* of Charles Henri Oldam, Member of Council General of Basse Alsace; *m.* James, *s.* of the late Sir Peter Coats, of Auchendrane, Scotland (*see* BURKE'S *Peerage*). *War Work :* Equipped 30 Hill Street, Berkeley Square, as a Hospital for 22 to 25 Officers, and maintained it for 3 years. *Address :* 7, Place Malesherbes, Paris, France. (O10161)

COBB, Major Charles, O.B.E.

COBB, Sir Cyril Stephen, K.B.E., M.V.O., M.A., B.C.L. M.P. (Coalition) West Fulham, since 1918; Chairman of the London County Council, 1913–14; Barrister-at-Law; *b.* 1861. *Address :* 5, Cornwall Terrace, N.W. (K136)

COBB, Col. Henry Frederick, C.B.E., F.S.I., *b.* 11 March, 1881; *s.* of Herbert Mansfield Cobb, C.B.E., of Mockbeggar, near Rochester; *m.* Annie Margaret; *d.* of Edwin Walter Wix, of 1, Old Court Mansions, Kensington. *Educ.:* Rugby. Fellow of Surveyors' Institution; Fellow of Auctioneers' Institute. *War Work :* Chief Valuer and Compensation Officer to Directorate of Lands of War Office, Ministry of Munitions, Air Force, Disposal Board; Member of various committees. *Addresses :* 5, Rutland House, Kensington, W. 8; 61 & 62, Lincoln's Inn Fields, W.C. *Clubs :* Windham; Roehampton. (C2089)

COBB, Lieut. Henry Percy, M.B.E., R.A.S.C.

COBB, Henry Venn, C.S.I., C.I.E., C.B.E., M.A., LL.B., *b.* 24 Aug. 1864; *s.* of the late Rev. Clement F Cobb, M.A., late of Teston, near Maidstone, Kent. *Educ.:* King's School, Canterbury; Trinity College, Cambridge. Indian Civil Service; British Resident in Mysore; and Chief Commissioner of Coorg, India. *War Work :* In Kashmir, Mysore, Bangalore and Coorg; received medal from the Govt. of India for Voluntary War Work in India, 1914–19; also medal from the Commander-in-Chief in India, for recruiting work during the war; also Medaille de la reconnaissance Française from the French Govt. for work in aid of la Croix rouge Française; worked also as a volunteer for three months in the Ministry of Munitions. *Address :* 1, St. James's Street, London, S.W. 1. *Clubs :* East India U.S.; Bath. (C1959)

COBB, Herbert Mansfield, C.B.E. Hon. Adviser to War Office and Ministry of Munitions, on Land Questions. (C465)

COBB, Prof. John William, C.B.E., *b.* 6 Feb. 1873; *s.* of James Cobb, of Leeds; *m.* Alice, *d.* of John Eadie, of Paisley. *Educ.:* Modern School, Leeds; Yorkshire College, Leeds. Livesey Professor of Coal Gas and Fuel Industries in the University of Leeds. *War Work :* Deputy Inspector, High Explosives (Leeds Area); chemical control of Benzene and Toluene production from gas works, Yorks. and Lincolnshire; Adviser on Furnaces to Dept. of Glassware Production, Ministry of Munitions. *Address :* University, Leeds. (C942)

COBB, Robert Bennett, M.B.E.

COBB, Monica Mary GEIKIE-, M.B.E., B.A. (Lond.), *b.* 8 March, 1891; *d.* of Rev. Dr. Geikie-Cobb, of St. Ethelburga's Church, Bishopsgate. *Educ.:* Queen's Coll., Harley Street; Univ. Coll. University of London. *War Work :* Joint Sec. Professional Classes War Relief Council for relieving distress occasioned by the war amongst the professional classes. *Addresses :* 40, Cathcart Road, S.W. 10; Rishangles, Eye, Suffolk. (M7704)

COBBOLD, Alfred Townshend, O.B.E., *b.* 4 Nov. 1852;

s. of Rowland Townshend Cobbold, of Dedham, Essex; *m.* Alice Bessie, *d.* of Robert Lindley Nunn, of Ipswich. *Educ.:* Felsted. Solicitor. Clerk of the Peace for East Suffolk and for West Suffolk; Clerk of the East and West Suffolk County Councils; Clerk to the Lieutenancy for Suffolk (Honorary). *War Work :* Sec. East and West Suffolk Appeal Tribunals; Hon. Sec. East Suffolk War Relief Committee; Member of West Suffolk War Relief Committee; Special Constable, East Suffolk; Hon. Treas. Bramford War Savings Committee. *Address :* Bramford House, nr. Ipswich. *Clubs :* County, Ipswich; West Suffolk County, Bury St. Edmunds. (O10162)

COBBOLD, Herbert St. George, C.B.E.

COBDEN, Alfred Sydney, M.B.E.

COBDEN, Major George Gough, O.B.E.

COBURN, Marmaduke Robert, O.B.E.

COCHRAN, Alexander, C.B.E., M.I.N.A., *b.* 1879. *Educ.:* Shrewsbury Sch.; Chairman and Managing Director Burn & Co. (Limited), of Calcutta; Chairman Indian Iron and Steel Co. (Limited) of Calcutta, and other companies. *Address :* Calcutta. *Clubs :* Oriental; Royal Dorset Yacht; Bengal (Calcutta). (C1960)

COCHRAN, Dora Alexandrina, M.B.E., V.A.D.

COCHRANE, Andrew, O.B.E.

COCHRANE, Blair Onslow, O.B.E.

COCHRANE, Edith Rose, M.B.E.; *d.* of Henry Cochrane, of The Longlands, Middlesbro'. *Educ.:* Ladies Coll., Bath. Treas. War Savings Association. *War Work :* Naval and Military War Pensions; War Savings; Work on Land; Voluntary Workers' Organisation. *Address :* The Hawthorns, Loftus in Cleveland, Yorkshire. (M7706)

COCHRANE, Ethel, M.B.E.; *d.* of Henry Cochrane, of The Longlands, Middlesbro'. *Educ.:* Ladies' Coll., Bath. Sec. War Savings Association. *War Work :* Naval and Military War Pensions; War Savings; Work on Land; Voluntary Workers' Organisation. *Address :* The Hawthorns, Loftus in Cleveland, Yorkshire. (M7707)

COCHRANE, Ethel Isabel Virginia, Mrs., M.B.E.

COCHRANE of CULTS, Gertrude Julia Georgina, Lady, O.B.E., *d.* of 6th Earl of Glasgow (*see* BURKE'S *Peerage*); *m.* Thomas Horatio Arthur Ernest, 1st Baron Cochrane, *s.* of the 11th Earl of Dundonald (*see* BURKE'S *Peerage*). *Address :* Crawford Priory, Cupar, Fife. (O10163)

COCHRANE, Hon. Katherine Elizabeth, M.B.E.

COCHRANE, Major (acting Lieut.-Col.) Robert Cecil, C.B.E., F.R.C.V.S., R.A.V.C., *b.* 11 May, 1871; *s.* of John Cochrane, M.A., T.C.D., J.P., of Combermore, Lifford, Co. Donegal, Ireland; *m.* Lily Holmes, *d.* of Oliver Tennant, of Bethlehem, O.R.C., South Africa. *Educ.:* Privately. Royal Army Veterinary Corps. Served throughout South African War, Oct. 1899 to 1902; mentioned in despatches; served throughout the Great War in France, Italy, and at home. *Address :* Ardavon, Westcombe Park Road, Blackheath. *Club :* Junior Army and Navy. (C2090)

COCHRANE, Lieut.-Col. Thomas Henry, M.V.O., C.B.E., *b.* 1867; *e. s.* of the late Rev. Thomas Cochrane; *m.* 1909, Jeanie, *d.* of the late William Wilkin Lumb, of Meadow House, Whitehaven. Entered R.E. 1888; became Capt. 1898; Major, 1906; Lieut.-Col. 1914; was an Inspector of Iron Structures at Headquarters, 1905–9. *Club :* Royal Automobile. (O7009)

COCHRANE, Capt. William Percy, O.B.E.

COCK, Edward, M.B.E.

COCK, James Wearne, M.B.E.

COCKBURN, Capt. Clarence Beaufort, O.B.E. (Mil), *b.* 14 Jan. 1892; *s.* of Lestock W. Cockburn, M.D., of Hamilton, Ontario, Canada. *Educ.:* Trinity College School, Port Hope, Canada; and R.M.C., Kingston, Ontario, Canada. *War Work :* Served in France and Belgium from Aug. 1914, to Sept. 1919. *Address :* c/o Sir C. R. McGrigor, Bart., & Co., Panton Street, Haymarket. *Club :* Northern Counties. (O2475)

COCKBURN, Major David, O.B.E., *b.* 29 July, 1860; *s.* of William Hamilton Cockburn, of Hamilton. *Educ.:* St. John's Grammar School, Hamilton, and Glasgow University. Solicitor, and Joint County Clerk of Dumbartonshire. *War Work :* Secretary, Dumbartonshire Territorial Force Association; Executive Officer, Food Control Committee for County of Dumbarton; Acting County Adjutant, Dumbartonshire Volunteers; Joint Hon. Treasurer, Local War Pensions Committee for County of Dumbarton; Joint Hon. Sec., County of Dumbarton Civil Relief Fund; Member of Committee of Dumbartonshire Branch, British Red Cross Society; Burgh of Dumbarton War Relief Committee; County of Dumbarton Fund for Relief of Disabled and Wounded Soldiers; Dumbarton and Alexandria Local Employment Committee; Soldiers' and Sailors' Families Association. *Address :* Netherton, Dumbarton. *Club :* Conservative, Glasgow. (O1222)

COCKBURN, Dorothy, M.B.E.

COCKBURN, Major Ernest Radcliffe, O.B.E., *b.* 17 Sept. 1875; *s.* of the late Robert Adolphus Cockburn, of Fetcham Lodge, Leatherhead, Surrey; *m.* Jean Henderson, *d.* of George Rodger, of Selkirk. *Educ.:* Harrow. Joined 3rd Wiltshire Regt., 1894; 2nd Batt. Duke of Edinburgh's Wiltshire Regt., 1897; served South African War, 1899–1902 (Queen's medal, 5 clasps, King's medal, 2 clasps); promoted Capt., Manchester Regt., for distinguished service in the Field, 1901; retired, and appointed Secretary Ayrshire Territorial Force Association, 1912; promoted Major and "mentioned." 1917; appointed Chief Constable of the County of Ayr, 1919. *War Work :* Secretary, Ayrshire Territorial Force Association, administering 1st, 2nd and 3rd Ayrshire Yeomanry; 1st and 2nd Ayrshire R.H.A.; 1st, 2nd and 3rd First Lowland Brigade, R.F.A.; 1st, 2nd and 3rd Fourth Batt. Royal Scots Fusiliers; 1st, 2nd and 3rd Fifth Batt. Royal Scots Fusiliers; 11th and 12th Batt. Royal Scots Fusiliers. *Address :* Headquarters, County Constabulary, Ayr. *Club :* Army and Navy. (O1223)

COCKBURN, Brig.-Gen. George, C.B.E., D.S.O. (late Rifle Brigade), *b.* 9 Jan. 1856; *s.* of Admiral J. H. Cockburn; *m.* Alice Lindsay, *d.* of Hazell Rodwell, of Ipswich. *Educ. :* Eton. Served in Rifle Brigade, 1876–1905. *War Work :* A.A. & Q.M.G., 1st London Territorial Division; Commanded 43rd Light Infantry Brigade (New Army); Commanded Reserve Brigade (18th), Ripon Camp; and Tay Defences. *Club :* Naval and Military. (C1519)

COCKBURN, George Bertram, O.B.E.
COCKBURN, Major George Ernest, O.B.E.
COCKBURN, James Lowrie, M.B.E.
COCKBURN, John Alexander, M.B.E.
COCKBURN, John Henry, O.B.E.; *s.* of Charles Cockburn; *m.* Louisa Annie, *d.* of Anthony Berriman, of Percy House, Pocklington. Solicitor (Honours); Sec. of South Yorkshire Coal Trade Association; author of the following works; *Law of Coal and other Minerals, Law of Private Railway Sidings and Traffic, Law of Checkweighing. War Work :* Sec. of South Yorkshire District Coal Supplies Committee. *Address :* Rotherham, Yorkshire. *Clubs :* Constitutional (London); Rotherham. (O10165)
COCKBURN, Major Ronald, O.B.E. R.A.F.
COCKBURN, Major Walter George, O.B.E., R.A.O.C.
COCKE, Major Thomas Dudley, O.B.E.
COCKELL, Major Norman Alexander Lindsey, O.B.E., *b.* 21 June, 1865; *s.* of William James, of Simla, India. *Educ. :* Dulwich and Oxford. President Association of Master Lightermen and Bargeowners (Port of London). *War Work :* Enlisted as private in Royal Fusiliers (regulars) on 6 Sept. 1914; severely wounded in June, 1916, at Givenchy (France); Hon. Consultant to Ministry of Shipping, 1917–20. *Addresses :* 56, Rodney Court, W. 9; Old Trinity House, E.C. (O10166)
COCKELL, Lieut.-Col. Anthony Stuart BUCKLAND-, O.B.E., M.C.
COCKERAM, William Henry, C.B.E.
COCKERELL, Douglas Bennett, M.B.E.
COCKERELL, Florence Elizabeth, Mrs., M.B.E.
COCKERELL, Lieut.-Col. Frederick Peyps, O.B.E., M.C.
COCKERELL, Major Henry, O.B.E., R.A.F.
COCKERELL, John Pepys, O.B.E.
COCKERELL, Capt. Leslie Maurice, O.B.E., M.I.M.E., *b.* 2 Nov. 1872; *s.* of Sydney John, of Beckenham; *m.* Gladys Marguerite, *d.* of J. H. Stretton, of London. *Educ. :* Privately. Mining Engineer; travelled in U.S.A., New Zealand, Mexico, Alaska, Canada, Brazil, Guianas, Italy, Spain, Uruguay. *War Work :* Special work War Office, 2 years; and subsequently Controller of Department for Development of Mineral Resources, Ministry of Munitions. *Address :* 10, FitzGeorge Avenue, London, W. *Club :* Isthmian. (O10168)
COCKING, Albert, M.B.E., *b.* 18 July, 1893; *s.* of Elwyn James Cocking, of Nottingham. *War Work :* Church Army Commissioner for Egyptian Expeditionary Force (Egypt and Palestine). *Address :* 140, Kirkewhite St., Nottingham. (M13)
COCKINGTON, Arthur John, O.B.E., *b.* 25 March, 1865; *s.* of John Cockington, of Highbury. *Educ. :* The Central Foundation School, Cowper Street. Assist. Sec. General Medical Council. *War Work :* Acting Registrar, General Medical Council, 1914–19, during absence of Registrar on war service. *Address :* 44, Hallam Street, W. 1. (O10169)
COCKS, Albert Edward, O.B.E.
COCKS, Edward Charles, M.B.E.
COCKS, Capt. Robert, M.B.E., A.I.F.
COCKS, William, C.B.E., *b.* 1860; *s.* of W. H. Cocks, of Swansea; *m.* 1915, Ella Mary, *d.* of George Webb, of Brighton. *Educ. :* Privately. An Engineer and Shipbuilder, and Managing Director of Channel Dry Docks Co. of Cardiff. *Address :* Gwithian, Rogermoor Road, Penarth, Glamorganshire. *Club :* Royal Automobile. (C466)
COCKSHOTT, John James, O.B.E., *b.* 1847; *s.* of Hargreaves Cockshott, of Preston, Lancashire; *m.* Jane, *d.* of George Kent, of Walton-le-Dale, Lancashire. *Educ. :* Kirkham Grammar School. Solicitor. *War Work :* Chairman of St. John Primary Hospital for Wounded Soldiers at Southport, being the largest Voluntary Hospital for Wounded Soldiers in Great Britain. *Address :* 31, Queen's Road, Southport. (O10170)
CODD, Arthur William, O.B.E., B.A., *b.* 8 May, 1863; *s.* of the late John Codd, of Ventnor, I. of Wight; *m.* Florence, *d.* of William Whitley, late of Woodstock. *Educ. :* Privately, and London Univ. Chief Cartographer, Hydrographic Department, Admiralty, S.W. *Address :* 48, Westbere Road, N.W. 2. (O3663)
CODDINGTON, Lieut.-Col. Herbert Adolphe, D.S.O., O.B.E.
CODLING, William Richard, C.B.E., M.V.O., *b.* 5 April, 1879; *Educ. :* Enfield Grammar School; King's College, London. Civil Servant. Controller of H.M. Stationery Office, King's Printer of Acts of Parliament; Holder, by Letters Patent issued under the Great Seal, of Copyright in all Government publications. *War Work :* Served successively in H.M. Stationery Office during the War in the following capacities : Superintendent of Demands; Superintendent of Publications and Distribution; Accountant; Deputy Controller; was responsible for the printing of all the Books, Forms,

Coupons, and Cards used in the rationing of food in the United Kingdom; paid three visits of inspection to the Western Front during the War in connection with the Army Printing and Stationery Services. *Address :* H.M. Stationery Office, Westminster, London, S.W. 1. *Club :* Union. (C467)
CODRINGTON, Adela Harriet, Lady, C.B.E.,; *d.* of Melville Portal, of Laverstoke, Hants, and Lady Charlotte, daughter of Gilbert, 2nd Earl of Minto; *m.* Lieut.-Gen. Sir Alfred Edward Codrington, K.C.V.O., C.B. Member of Rutland County Education Committee; President of Mothers' Union, Army Division; Chairman of V.A.D. Selection Board. *War Work :* Chairman of London Women Patrols Committee. *Address :* 110, Eaton Square, S.W. 1; Preston Hall, Uppingham. (C2525)
CODRINGTON, Major Geoffrey Ronald, D.S.O O.B.E., *b.* 13 May, 1888; *s.* of Sir Alfred Edward Codrington, K.C.V.O., C.B. (*see* BURKE'S *Peerage*). Major in Leicestershire Yeomanry; was Staff Capt. and D.A.Q.M.G. in the Great War; has Order of St. Maurice and St. Lazarus of Italy. (O5116)
COE, Capt. Charles George, M.B.E., R.A.F
COFFEY, Frank William, M.B.E.
COGGAN, Robert Denby, O.B.E.
COGGAN, William, O.B.E.
COGHLAN, Capt. Daniel, O.B.E., A.I.S.A., Medaille d'Honneur (Senior Div.), *b.* Feb. 1881; *s.* of Daniel Coghlan, of Skibbereen, Ireland. *Educ. :* Privately. Confidential Sec. (Harrods' Stores). *War Work :* Joined as a private; Commissioned in France; promoted to Capt.; mentioned in despatches; thanked by 2nd Army Commander for excellent work performed by his company (126th Armed Labour Coy.); awarded Medaille d'Honneur avec glaives en vermeil by President of France. *Addresses :* 5, Cadogan Street, London, S.W.; Skibbereen, Ireland. (O5117)
COGHLAN, Lieut. Edward Maurice Ernest, M.B.E., R.E.
COGHLAN, 2nd Lieut. George Edmond, M.B.E., R.E.
COGHLAN, Capt. Gerald Spencer, M.B.E., M.C.
COHEN, Hannah Floretta, O.B.E.,; *d.* of Sir Benjamin L. Cohen, Bart., of 30 Hyde Park Gardens, W., and Shoreham, Kent (*see* BURKE'S *Peerage*). *Educ. :* Rocdean, and Newnham. *War Work :* Hon. Treas. West Kent Women's War Agricultural Committee; Temp. First Division Clerk, H.M. Treasury. *Addresses :* 18, Albert Court, S.W.; Shoreham, Kent. *Club :* Ladies' Univ. (O10171)
COHEN, Sir Herbert Benjamin, Bart., O.B.E., M.A., *b.* 26 April, 1874; *s.* of Sir Benjamin Louis Cohen, Bart. (*see* BURKE'S *Peerage*); *m.* Hannah Mildred (Nina), *d.* of Henry Behrens, of 34, Gloucester Square, W. *Educ. :* Clifton Coll.; King's Coll., Cambridge. Barrister-at-law; Governor, St. Bartholomew's Hospital. *War Work :* Served as Major in 4th Batt. Royal West Kent Regt., 1900–20; Embarkation Staff Officer, 1916–19. *Addresses :* 6, King's Bench Walk, Temple, E.C. 4; Sandy Hatch, Hythe, Kent. *Club :* Junior Carlton. (O7013)
COHEN, Marjorie Emmeline, M.B.E., *b.* 1892; *d.* of Benjamin A. Cohen, K.C., of Champions, Limpsfield, Surrey. *Educ. :* The Manor House, Limpsfield. *War Work :* Nursing and Quartermaster's duties at Charing Cross Convalescent Home, and Furzedown Auxiliary Hospital, Limpsfield. *Address :* Champions, Limpsfield, Surrey. (M7711)
COHEN, Philip, O.B.E., *b.* 20 Sept. 1870; *s.* of J. Cohen, of Edgbaston, Birmingham; *m.* Ruby, *d.* of Edward Lee, C.C.D.L., of London. *Educ. :* King Edward VI. High School, Birmingham. Solicitor. Consul of Republic of Honduras; Supt. City Division (Birmingham) St. John Ambulance Brigade. *War Work :* District Director, 1st Southern General Hospital Command Area; Enquiry Department for Missing Wounded and Prisoners of War, British Red Cross and Order of St. John. *Addresses :* 232, Hagley Road, Edgbaston, Birmingham; 7, Waterloo Street, Birmingham. (O10172)
COHEN, Sir Robert WALEY-, K.B.E., *b.* Sept. 1877; *s.* of Nathaniel Louis Cohen, of Courtlanos, East Grinstead, and 11, Hyde Park Terrace, W.; *m.* Alice Violet, *d.* of H. E. Beddington, of Heatherside, Newmarket, and 15, Hyde Park Sq., W. *Educ. :* Clifton and Emmanuel College, Cambridge. Director, Shell Transport and Trading Co., Ltd.; Managing Director, Anglo-Saxon Petroleum Co., Ltd. *War Work :* Petroleum Adviser to the War Office. *Address :* Caen Wood Towers, Highgate, N. 6. *Clubs :* Reform; Royal Automobile; Oxford and Cambridge; Musical. (K361)
COKAYNE, Capt. Thomas M.B.E.
COKE, Major Basil Elmsley, O.B.E., R.E.
COKE, Capt. John Gilbert de Odingsells, C.B.E., R.N.
COKE, Mabel, Lady, M.B.E., *y. d.* of Thomas William, 2nd Earl of Leicester, K.G., J.P., D.L. (*see* BURKE'S *Peerage*). (M7713)
COKE, Phyllis Hermione, Hon. Mrs. Arthur George, M.B.E.
COKER, Major Lewis Aubrey, O.B.E., R.F.A., *b.* 30 Aug. 1883; *s.* of Col. L. E. Coker, of Bicester House, Oxfordshire; *m.* Margaret Rosalys, *d.* of W. Mirrlees, of Mt. Blow, Cambs. *Educ. :* Clifton Coll. *War Work :* Served in France, Belgium, and Macedonia, and Russia; Mons Star; Croix de Guerre avec palmes; St. Stanislaus of Russia, 2nd Class; three times mentioned in despatches. *Clubs :* United Service; R.A.C. (O6793)
COLAM, Capt. Rosslyn Leigh, M.B.E.
COLBECK, Capt. Charles Edward Beeby, O.B.E., R.N.
COLBECK, Major Edmund Harry, O.B.E., M.D.

COLBECK, Hon. Flight-Lieut. Paul, M.B.E., R.A.F., *b.* 1878 ; *s.* of the late Edward John Colbeck, of Alexandria, Egypt ; *m.* Grace Marie, *d.* of J. Falshaw Hobson, of Durham. *Educ.:* Sedbergh School. Formerly Electrical Engineer ; Manager of branch for Hubert Davies & Co., Johannesburg, from 1904–15. *War Work :* Rejoined 2/6th Batt. Northumberland Fusiliers as temp. Capt., May, 1915 ; transferred to 2/7th Batt. Northumberland Fusiliers as temp. Major, Aug. 1915 ; transferred to R.F.C., now Royal Air Force, Oct., 1917 ; joined Egyptian Expeditionary Force, Jan. 1917 to date. *Address :* R.A.F. Aircraft Depot, Egypt, Aboukir, Egypt. *Club :* New, Johannesburg, S. Africa. (M5944)

COLBORNE, Christina Johanna Petronella, Mrs., M.B.E., *b.* 1869 ; *d.* of Louis Auguste Desvages, of Dordrecht, South Africa ; *m.* E. W. P. Colborne. *Educ.:* South Africa. *War Work :* Hon. Sec. Bloemfontein Branch, Victoria League ; Provincial War Relief Executive ; Red Cross Committee ; Hon. Treas. Women's Auxiliary Comrades of the War. *Address :* Bloemfontein, Orange Free State, South Africa. (M2875)

COLBOURNE, Robert Bertram, M.B.E.

COLBOURNE, Walter Sydney, O.B.E., R.N.R.

COLBY, Henry James, M.B.E., R.F.A.

COLCHESTER, Annie Frances Julia, Mrs., M.B.E., *b.* 19 Aug. 1872 ; *d.* of Fleet Paymaster H. T. Nettleton, R.N., M.R.C.S.E. ; *m.* Maurice Herbert, *s.* of Henry Sparrowe, Colchester, of Ipswich. *Educ.:* St. Margaret's House, Twickenham ; Bedford Coll., York Place, London. *War Work :* Hon. Sec. Croydon Local War Savings Committee ; Member of National Kitchens, Food Control, and Profiteering Committees (Croydon). *Address :* Beechcroft, 2, Park Hill Road, Croydon. (M7715)

COLCLOUGH, Paymaster-Capt. Beauchamp Urquhart, C.B.E. ; Paymaster-Com. and Acting Paymaster-Capt. R.N. ; served inthe Great War, 1914–19 (despatches). (C1919)

COLCLOUGH, Capt. William Caesar Sarsfield, M.B.E.,

COLDSTREAM, Major John Clayton, O.B.E., I.A.

COLDWELL, Major Reginald Charles, O.B.E.

COLE, Albert Percy, M.B.E. (M10245g)

COLE, Annie Violet, Mrs., M.B.E. ; *d.* of Col. E. Shaw, I.A. ; *m.* Col. Edward Hearle Cole, C.B., C.M.G. *War Work :* Organised a Prisoner of War Depot in own house, for four years. *Addresses :* Dumfries House, Cheltenham ; and Coleyana, Okara, N.W. Railway, Punjab. (M7716)

COLE, Comm. Archibald Charles, O.B.E.. R.N.

COLE, Major Aubrey du Plat Thorold, O.B.E., M.C., *b.* 3 June, 1877 ; *s.* of Canon E. P. Cole, of Bristol. *Educ.:* Cheltenham and Sandhurst. *War Work :* Served in East Africa till May, 1915 ; then Adjutant 1st Lovat's Scouts, with whom served on Gallipoli Peninsula, including evacuation ; Staff Capt., Alexandria, and D.A.Q.M.G. at G.H.Q., German East Africa, 1916–18. *Addresses :* 23, Great George Street, Bristol ; Abbotsham Court, Bideford. *Clubs :* Naval and Military ; Bath ; Sports ; Royal Automobile. (O2308)

COLE, Charles Henry, M.B.E.

COLE, Lieut. Claude Willoughby, M.B.E.

COLE, Lieut.-Col. Cole Edward Cooper, O.B.E., Can. A.M.C.

COLE, Capt. David Henry, M.B.E., R.A.S.C.

COLE, Edward George, M.B.E., J.P.

COLE, Francis Joseph, M.B.E., F.S.I., *b.* 24 Aug. 1876. Surveyor. Appointed to the Civil Engineer in Chief's Dept., Admiralty, 1901 ; served at Home Dockyards and Naval Stations abroad, and, during the war, at the Admiralty. *Address :* 16, Hitherfield Road, Streatham, S.W. 16. (M7717)

COLE, Major Fritz William, M.B.E.

COLE, Major Harold Linter, O.B.E., R.E.

COLE, Lieut. Harold Ralph C., M.B.E.,

COLE, Harold William, C.B.E.

COLE, Col. Henry Walter George, C.S.I., O.B.E., I.A., *b.* 8 March, 1866 ; *s.* of late Lieut.-Col. H. H. Cole, R.E. ; *m,* Mai Kathleen, *d.* of Col. W. Shapter Hunt, H.L.I. *Educ.:* Wellington and Sandhurst. Lieut. 5th Fusiliers, 1885 ; 2nd K.E.O. Gurkhas, 1888 ; Hazara, 1888 ; Lushai, 1888–89 ; Chinlushai, 1889–91 ; N.E. Frontier, 1891 ; Despatches twice, and thanks of Government of India ; Assam Commission, 1891–20 ; Supdt. Lushai Hills, 1905–10 ; Political Agent, Manipur, 1914–17 ; Director Temporary Works, Delhi, 1912–13 ; Director, Exhibitions Division Dept. Overseas Trade. *War Work :* Labour Corps, and Labour Commandant 22nd and 2nd Corps, 1917–19 ; Despatches twice, and O.B.E. *Address :* Keynsham Manor, Saltford, Somerset. *Clubs :* United Service ; United Sports. (O5119)

COLE, Col. Herbert Covington, C.B.E., Chief Valuer and Compensation Officer, Land Directorate, War Office. (C468)

COLE, James Edward, M.B.E., *b.* 8 Nov. 1875 ; *s.* of James Cole, of Aylesford, Kent ; *m.* Constance Lavinia, *d.* of Walter Larkin, of Brenchley, Kent. *Educ.:* Aylesford. Marine Surveyor. *War Work :* Technical Assistant under Machinery Construction Department, Ministry of Shipping. *Addresses :* 223, Boxley Road, Maidstone, Kent ; Via Alla Nunziata 18, Genoa. (M7718)

COLE, Lieut.-Col. John Albert, O.B.E.

COLE, Laura Edith, O.B.E., *b.* 29 Aug. 1869 ; *d.* of Robert C. Cole, of London. Matron, Graylingwell Mental Hospital. (O10173)

**COLE, Lilian Seymour, Mrs., O.B.E., *m.* Alfred Clayton Cole. *War Work :* Commandant of Red Cross Auxiliary Hospital in own Home, West Woodhay House, Berkshire.

Addresses : 64, Portland Place, W. ; West Woodhay, nr. Newbury. (O10174)

COLE, Lieut. Lowry Arthur Casamaijor, M.B.E.

COLE, Robert Clifford, M.B.E., *b.* 13 Feb. 1892 ; *s.* of Robert Cole, of Staplehurst, Kent ; *m.* Maisie Isbeth, *d.* of — Fuller, of Wheatley Hill, Durham. *Educ :.* Sir A. Judd's Commercial School, Tonbridge ; King's Coll., London. H.M. Office of Works, Head of section hands and Accommodation Division. *War Work :* Providing accommodation for Government Staffs in London ; Assist. to Sec. of War Cabinet Committee on Accommodation ; 2nd Lieut. Royal Marine Artillery. *Address :* Wilsley, 134, Headstone Road, Harrow-on-the-Hill. *Club :* Bloomsbury House, Cartwright Gardens, W.C. (M7719)

COLE, Robert Frank, M.B.E., I.A.

COLE, Seymour, M.B.E., C.C., J.P., House and Estate Agent, *b.* 6 Feb. 1860 ; *s.* of Wadham Cole, of Devon and Wolverhampton ; *m.* Deborah Morgan, *d.* of J. Dymmock, Builder, of Redland, Bristol. *War Work :* Was Hon. Sec. and Officer-in-charge of the Red Cross Hospital, Sussex Lodge, Newmarket ; also interested in public affairs, as Chairman of the Urban District Council and a Member of the West Suffolk County Council ; the Food Committee and Coal Control. *Addresses :* 5–8, Station Road, and Rutland Cottage, Newmarket. *Clubs :* Junior Conservative ; Subscription Rooms (Newmarket). (M7720)

COLE, Stanton Wilding, O.B.E., *b.* 1880 ; *s.* of R. Wilding Cole, of Hillside, Puttenham, Surrey ; *m.* Florence Annie, *d.* of Dr. Chetwood. *Educ.:* King's School, Canterbury. Engineer ; Managing Director of Messrs. Burney and Blackburne, Ltd., 38, Conduit Street, London, W. 1. *War Work :* Manufacture of Stokes Guns ; majority of experimental work on Stokes Gun Mountings and Trench Warfare, Bombs, Fuses, etc. *Address :* The Elms, Tongham, Surrey. (O10175)

COLE, Sybil, Mrs., M.B.E.

COLE, 2nd Lieut. William, M.B.E., R.A.F.

COLE, William George, O.B.E.

COLEFAX, Sir (Henry) Arthur, K.B.E., K.C., *b.* 1866 ; *s.* of the late J. S. Colefax, of Bradford ; *m.* Sibyl, *d.* of the late W. S. Halsey, Indian Civil Service. *Educ.:* Bradford ; Merton College, Oxford ; Strassburg University. Solicitor-General, Palatine of Durham ; King's Counsel ; formerly M.P., S.W. Manchester. *War Work :* Controller of Optical Munitions ; Glassware and Polish Production, under Ministry of Munitions ; work for Admiralty. *Address :* Argyll House, Chelsea, S.W. 3. *Clubs :* Athenæum ; Garrick ; United University. (K362)

COLEGRAVE, Elizabeth Violet, Mrs., M.B.E., Lady of Grace of the Order of St. John. *War Work :* Lady Supt. of H.R.H. Princess Christian's Hospital at Norwood. *Addresses :* Bracebridge, Norwood ; Denmark Terrace, Brighton. *Club :* Ladies' Athenæum. (M3579)

COLEGRAVE, Capt. William Henry, O.B.E., R.D., R.N.R.

COLEING, Charles Thomas, O.B.E., J.P., *b.* 7 Jan. 1861. *s.* of Charles Coleing, of Hampstead Road. *Educ.:* Univ. Coll. School, London. Draper. *War Work :* Chairman, War Savings Committee, St. Pancras ; Chairman of Advisory Committee to Military Representative, St. Pancras ; Member of various Employment Committees, London ; Member of Central Profiteering Committee, County of London ; Chairman of L.C.C. Consultative Committee on Vocational Education for the Distributive Trades. *Address :* 135, Hampstead Road, N.W. *Club :* Junior Constitutional. (O10176)

COLEMAN, Capt. Amos Hubert, O.B.E., M.B., R,A.M.C.

COLEMAN, Arthur Charles, M.B.E., *b.* 2 June, 1874 ; *s.* of the Rev. E. O. Coleman, of London ; *m.* Dora Isabel, *d.* of Charles Hope Harris, of Adelaide, S. Australia. *Educ.:* Kingswood School, Lansdown, Bath. Engineer. *War Work :* Assistant Inspector of Munitions ; subsequently transferred to U.S.A., and promoted Deputy Inspector and Inspector-in-charge, Pittsburgh district. *Address :* Grange House, Grange, South Australia. (M1553)

COLEMAN, Col. George Henry, O.B.E., V.D.

COLEMAN, Capt. Patrick Eugene, O.B.E.

COLEMAN, Lieut. Patrick Peter, O.B.E., R.N.

COLEMAN, Capt. Reginald Ernest, O.B.E.

COLEMAN, Lieut.-Col. Thomas Everit, O.B.E.

COLEMAN, William Francis, M.B.E., R.N.

COLMORE, Capt. Reginald Blayney, O.B.E , R.N.

COLERIDGE, Ellen Gertrude, Mrs., O.B.E., *d.* of the late Frederick Swabey, of 69, Pont Street ; *m.* Rennell Coleridge, *s.* of William Rennell Coleridge, of Salston, Ottery St. Mary. *Educ.:* (See BURKE'S *Peerage*). *War Work :* Assistant County Director, Devonshire Voluntary Aid Organisation, etc. *Addresses :* Salston, Ottery St. Mary ; 69, Pont Street, S.W. (O01177)

COLERIDGE, Frances May, M.B.E. ; *d.* of Charles C. C. Coleridge, of Plymouth. *Educ.:* Privately. *War Work :* 3½ years in British Legation, Copenhagen, as stenographer, etc., during the war ; work was of extremely confidential nature ; archivist to Commission Internationale Slesvig during taking of plebiscite under Treaty of Versailles. *Addresses :* 5, Park Road, Wisbech ; 11, Porchester Terrace, Hyde Park. (M3580)

COLERIDGE, Col. Hugh Fortescue, C.B.E., D.S.O., *b.* 11 Jan. 1859 ; *s.* of Frederick John Coleridge, of Cadbury, Devon ; *m.* Kathleen Grace Fane, *d.* of Admiral J. H. Bainbridge. *Educ.:* R.M.C., Sandhurst. *Address :* Langstone, Moortown, Tavistock. *Club :* Naval and Military. (C1520)

COLERIDGE, Major Percy Lovel, O.B.E., I.A.

COLES, Lieut. Harry Victor, M.B.E.. Can. M.G.C.

COLES, Major Lawrence Walter, O.B.E.

COLES, Richard James, C.B.E., *b.* 17 Nov. 1862; *s.* of John Thomas Coles, of Bedfont, Middlesex; *m.* Dorothy Jane, *d.* of Walter Henry Dredge, of Kingston, Surrey. *Educ.:* Cranford Hall School, Middlesex. Civil Servant; Financial Assistant Secretary, Ministry of Pensions. *War Work :* Devised system for payment of Army Pensions weekly when war commenced; appointed Supt. of Army Pension Issue Office early in 1915; appointed Asst. Director-General of Finance, Ministry of Pensions, in April, 1917; appointed Acting Director-General of Finance, in Sept. 1918; and Financial Asst. Sec., in May, 1920. *Addresses :* Cromwell House, Millbank (Ministry of Pensions); 32, Lingfield Avenue, Kingston, Surrey. (C943)

COLES, Walter George, O.B.E.

COLES, Capt. John Monck CAMPION-, M.B.E.

COLEY, Phillip, O.B.E. J.P.

COLEY, Major William, M.B.E., *b.* 13 April, 1858; *s.* of Abram Coley. *Educ.:* Army Schools. Quartermaster in Royal Artillery and Depôt, Argyll and Sutherland Highlanders. *War Work :* Carried out the duties of a quartermaster from first week of the War to the finish. Received special promotion, M.B.E., and thanks of the Government for work performed during the war. *Address :* Belsize, London Road, Leigh-on-Sea. (M255)

COLLARD, Lieut.-Col. and Staff Paymaster Alexander Arthur Lysons, C.B.E., R.A.P.D.; *b.* 10 June, 1871; *s.* of Rev. Canon J. M. Collard, of Salisbury; *m.* Kathleen Louisa, *d.* of William C. Turner, Indian Civil Service. *Educ.:* Woodcote House; Windlesham; Clifton College. *War Work :* Employed at War Office, Aug. 1914, to March, 1917; Regimental Paymaster, No. 2, Preston Army Pay Office, March, 1917, to Sept. 1919. (C1521)

COLLARD, Major Alfred Stephen, C.B.E., J.P., *b.* 1865; *s.* of James A. Collard, of Liverpool; *m.* Florence, *d.* of James Haigh, of Ledsham, Cheshire. Served with the Soudan Expedition, Relief of Gordon, 1885. *War Work :* Commanding Officer, British Red Cross, Stretcher-bearers and Orderlies, in France and Belgium, 1914–19; mentioned twice in despatches. *Addresses :* Ledsham Hall, Cheshire; 169, Gt. Portland St., W. *Club :* Junior Carlton. (C469)

COLLARD, Col. Arthur William, C.B.E.

COLLARD, Cecil Wharton, M.B.E.

COLLAS, Major Francis Jervoise, O.B.E., M.C.

COLLEDGE, Major Francis William, M.B.E.

COLLER, Frederick Ernest Watts, O.B.E., *b.* 27 March, 1876; *s.* of the late Rev. W. E. Coller, of Manchester; *m.* Norah Beatrice, *d.* of the late James Annandale, of Shotley Bridge, Durham. *Educ.:* Privately. Shipyard Manager and a Local Director at Sir W. G. Armstrong, Whitworth & Co. Ltd.'s. Naval Yard, Newcastle-on-Tyne; Member of the Central Board of the Ship-building Employers' Federation; Member of the Institution of Naval Architects; Member of the N.E.C. Institution of Engineers and Shipbuilders. *War Work :* Construction and repairs of vessels for the Royal Navy. *Address :* Dipton Foot, Riding Mill, Northumberland. (O10)

COLLES, Paymaster-Lieut. Ernest Dudley Gordon, O.B.E., R.N.

COLLET, Lieut. Arthur William, M.B.E.

COLLET, Lieut. Richard Awdrey White, M.B.E., R.A.F.

COLLETT, Charles Benjamin, O.B.E., M.I.Mech.E., *b.* 10 Sept. 1871; *s.* of William Collett, of London; *m.* Ethelwyn May, *d.* of Rev. Henry Simon, of London. *Educ.:* Merchant Taylors' School and London University. Deputy Chief Mechanical Engineer, Great Western Railway. *War Work :* Railway work and assistance in the manufacture of Ordnance and Munitions for the Admiralty, War Office, and Ministry of Munitions. *Address :* 5, Church Place Swindon, Wilts. (O1229)

COLLETT, Lieut.-Comm. John Alsager, O.B.E., R.N.

COLLEY, Capt. Thomas Bellasyse, M.B.E.

COLLEY, Lieut.-Col. William Harold, O.B.E., *b.* 31 July, 1888; *s.* of William Colley, of Tollerton, York. *Educ.:* St. Peter's, York; Emmanuel Coll., Cambridge. Master, Uppingham School, Rutland. *War Work :* Served in France and Belgium with 2nd Bn. A.P.W.O. Yorks Regt.; Capt., Jan. 1915; Acting Major, Nov. 1916; Temp. Lieut.-Col., Commanding 16th Manchester Regt., April, 1918, to June, 1919; wounded, Ypres; mentioned in despatches, June 1918, and June, 1919; awarded the Belgium Croix de Guerre, Chevalier de l'Ordre de Leopold; 1914 Star. *Addresses :* The Beeches, Tollerton, York; Uppingham School, Rutland. (O12044)

COLLIE, James, O.B.E.

COLLIER, Major Edwin Arthur, O.B.E., R.E.

COLLIER, 2nd Lieut. Frank Norton Proctor, M.B.E.

COLLIER, Hon. John, O.B.E., *b.* 1850; *s.* of the 1st Lord Monkswell (*see* BURKE'S *Peerage*); *m.* Ethel Gladys, *d.* of Rt. Hon. Professor Huxley. *Educ.:* Eton. Artist. *War Work :* Temp. Clerk in the Parliamentary Department of the Foreign Office. *Address :* 69, Eton Avenue, London, N.W. 3. *Clubs :* Athenæum; Arts. (O11695)

COLLIER, Joseph Veasy, M.B.E.

COLLIER, Major Mortimer Calmady, O.B.E., T.D., R.A.S.C. (T.F.), *b.* 14 Dec. 1874; *s.* of Lieut.-Col. M. J. Collier, of Foxhams, Horrabridge, Devon. *Educ.:* Eton. Military Member, Devon County Territorial Association, 1908–19. *War Work :* Commanded Devon and Cornwall Brigade Coy., R.A.S.C., at outbreak of war; subsequently Senior Supply

Officer, 29th Division, taking part in landing, Gallipoli Peninsula, 25 April, 1915; commanded 29th Divisional Train (acting Lieut.-Col.); Officer Commanding Royal Army Service Corps at Fovant, Wareham, Weymouth, and Queenstown, from July, 1916, to March, 1920. *Address :* Foxhams, Horrabridge, Devon. *Club :* Royal Western Yacht, Plymouth. (O7017)

COLLIER, Lieut.-Col. Richard Hamilton, D.S.O., O.B.E.; Lieut.-Col. R.A.F. (Special Reserve); served in the Great War, 1917–18 (despatches). (O8071)

COLLIER, Willoughby, M.B.E.

COLLINGS, F. J., O.B.E. (O9056*g*)

COLLINGS, Major T. J., O.B.E., Can. A.M.C.

COLLINGWOOD, Alfred Henry, O.B.E., Town Clerk and Clerk of the Peace for the City of Carlisle; Solicitor. *War Work :* Acted as Clerk to the Carlisle Local Tribunal; Hon. Sec. of the Carlisle Local War Pensions Committee; Executive Officer, Carlisle Local Food Control Committee. *Address :* Cote Cottage, Skinburness, Cumberland. (O10180)

COLLINGWOOD, Capt. Bertram James, O.B.E., R.A.M.C.

COLLINGWOOD, Sir William, K.B.E., M.Inst.C.E., J.P., *b.* 18 Aug. 1855 (*see* BURKE'S *Peerage*); *s.* of the late George Collingwood, Hon. E.I.C., of Stratford St. Mary, Suffolk; *m.* Maria Elizabeth, *d.* of Rev. G. T. Lermit, LL D., of St. Florence, Tenby. *Educ.:* Dedham Grammar School. Civil Engineer; Managing Director, The Vulcan Foundry, Ltd. *War Work :* Chairman of the Manchester and District Armament Output Committee, 1915–18. *Address :* Dedham Grove, near Colchester. *Clubs :* St. Stephen's; Constitutional; Argentine. (K18)

COLLINS, Lieut.-Comm. Abraham Bennett, M.B.E.

COLLINS, Alice Godiva Thorold, M.B.E., *b.* 10 July, 1869; *d.* of the late Rev. J. A. Welsh Collins, Chaplain H.M. Forces, Vicar of Newton St. Cyres, Devon. Assist. Commandant Devon 50 V.A.D. *War Work :* Exeter War Hospitals, Section III., 1 Nov. 1914; The Beacon V.A. Hospital, Sidmouth, Jan. to Feb. 1915; Quartermaster Exeter War Hospital, Section IV., March, 1915, to Nov. 1916; Quartermaster V.A. Hospital, Peak House, Sidmouth, Nov. 1916, to Feb. 1919; Commissariat Officer Exeter War Hospital, Headquarters, Feb. 1919, to Jan. 1920. *Address :* Winslade Cottage, Sidmouth, Devon. (M7722)

COLLINS, Major Arthur Francis St. Clair, O.B.E., M.C., R.A.S.C.

COLLINS, Lieut. Arthur Rutherford Dundas, O.B.E., R.N.R.

COLLINS, Lieut.-Comm. Charles Edward, O.B.E., R.N.

COLLINS, Major Charles Howell Groset, O.B.E., D.C.L.I.

COLLINS, Christabel, M.B.E., *b.* 23 March, 1895; *d.* of Edward Treacher Collins, F.R.C.S., of 17, Queen Anne Street, Cavendish Square, London, W. 1. *Educ.:* Queen's Coll., Harley Street, London. *War Work :* Joint Women's V.A.D. Department, British Red Cross Society and Order of St. John, Oct. 1915, to March, 1920; Auxiliary Hospital Section and V.A.D. Scholarship Scheme; given rank of Assist. Staff Commandant, 27 Oct 1919; Member of detachment London 146; mentioned in despatches, 14 Aug. 1918; awarded M.B.E., 1 Jan. 1920. *Addresses :* 17, Queen Anne Street, Cavendish Square, London, W. 1; Yewgate, Remenham Hill, Henley-on-Thames. (M7723)

COLLINS, Rev. Edward Hyacynth, O.B.E., *b.* 7 July, 1876; *s.* of John Collins, of Youghal. *Educ.:* St. Thomas Coll., Newbridge; St. Mary's, Tallaght Roman Univ. Prior of the Black Abbey, Kilkenny. *War Work :* Chaplain to the Forces, 4th Class, Salonica, Egypt, East Africa, France; Assist. Principal Chaplain, Northern Command, 3rd Class; mentioned in despatches, East Africa and France. *Address :* Black Abbey, Kilkenny. (O7019)

COLLINS, Edward Redvers Kerington, M.B.E.

COLLINS, Elizabeth Ann, Mrs., O.B.E. (O11961)

COLLINS, Ellen Evelyn, M.B.E., *b.* 1892; *d.* of Marcus Evelyn Collins. *Educ.:* Bedford High School. *War Work :* Head of the Collecting Box Department, County of London Branch of the British Red Cross Society and Order of St. John of Jerusalem. *Address :* The Chestnuts, Wooburn, Bucks. *Club :* Ladies' V.A.D. (M3581)

COLLINS, Lady Evelyn Anne, O.B.E., *b.* 7 Feb., 1882; *d.* of James Henry Robert, 7th Duke of Roxburghe (*see* BURKE'S *Peerage*); *m.* 23 Nov., 1907, Major William Fellowes Collins, Royal Scots Greys, of Kirkman Bank, Knaresborough, Yorks. (*see* BURKE'S *Landed Gentry*). *Address :* Knaresborough House, Knaresborough. (O10181)

COLLINS, Emily Ida, M.B.E. (M10380)

COLLINS, Frank Moore, O.B.E., *b.* 1872; *s.* of George Collins, of Lyme Regis; *m.* Isabella, *d.* of Frederick Caldcleugh, of Durham. *Educ.:* Bishop Barrington School, Bishop Auckland. Accountant, International Labour Office. *War Work :* Chairman, Sheerness Urban District Council; Superintendent Relief Work British and Foreign Sailors' Society; Member of Red Cross Committee for relief of repatriated civilians. *Addresses :* 24, Sackville Gardens, Ilford, Essex; La Chatelaine, Geneva. (O10182)

COLLINS, Lieut. Frederick, O.B.E., M.C.

COLLINS, George Alfred, M.B.E., *b.* 10 Nov. 1862; *s.* of George Collins, of Shirehampton; *m.* Mary Ann, *d.* of George Lait, of Avonmouth. *Educ.:* Shirehampton National School, and Bristol Trade and Mining School. Traffic Manager of the Bristol Corporation Docks, Avonmouth; Vice-Chairman,

Shirehampton Parish Church Council. *War Work:* Import and Export traffic at Avonmouth Docks; Chairman, War Savings Committee. *Address:* The Green, Shirehampton
(M1558)

COLLINS, George William, M.B.E.

COLLINS, Gladys Mary, M.B.E., W.A.A.C.

COLLINS, Capt. Godfrey Ferdinando Stratford, O.B.E.

COLLINS, Lieut.-Col. Sir Godfrey Pattison, K.B.E., C.M.G., *b.* 26 June, 1875; *s.* of the late Alexander Glen Collins, of Aunet Lodge, Skilmorlie, N.B.; *m.* 26 April, 1900, Margaret Jane Faith, *d.* of J. C. A. Henderson, late Lieut.-Col. R.A.S.C., formerly a Midshipman, R.N. M.P. for Greenock since 1910; was Member of War Office Supplies Committee, 1912–13; Parliamentary Private Sec. to the Rt. Hon. J. E. B. Seely, M.P., 1910–14, and to the Rt. Hon. J. W. Gulland, M.P., 1915; Inspector of Q.M.G.'s Services, 1915–16; Junior Lord of the Treasury, 1919–20; served in the Great War in Egypt, Gallipoli and Mesopotamia. *Address:* 40, Rutland Gate, S.W. *Clubs:* Reform; Ranelagh; Western (Glasgow).
(K253)

COLLINS, Capt. Harold Edmund, O.B.E.

COLLINS, Capt. Hugh Michael, O.B.E., I.M.S.

COLLINS, John Howarth, M.B.E.

COLLINS, Katharine Wilson, Mrs., M.B.E.; *d.* of John McNeill, J.P., of 1, Great Western Terrace, Glasgow; *m.* Charles Millington, *s.* of Edward Collins, J.P., of Kelvindale. *War Work:* President of Maryhill Division Soldiers' and Sailors' Families Association; Member of War Pensions Local Committee. *Addresses:* Kelvindale, Maryhill, Glasgow; Rowardennan Lodge, Rowardennan, Loch Lomond. (M7725)

COLLINS, Lesbia, M.B.E.

COLLINS, Lionel Dennis, M.B.E., R.N., *b.* 17 Aug. 1849; *s.* of the late Frederick Collins; *m.* Sarah Ann, *d.* of the late Richard Warren. *Educ.:* North Summercoates, Lincolnshire. *War Work:* Under the Board of Agriculture and Fisheries. *Address:* 10, Grove Road, Fareham, Hants.
(M257)

COLLINS, Major Lionel Peter, D.S.O., O.B.E., 1/4th Gurkha Rifles. (O11733)

COLLINS, Lieut.-Col. Michael Abdy, O.B.E., M.D. M.R.C.S., R.A.M.C.

COLLINS, Percy John, O.B.E., *b.* 3 March, 1871; *s.* of the late Rev. J. W. Collins of Lawrence-on-Sea, Thanet, Kent. *Educ.:* South Eastern Coll., Ramsgate. Master Mariner. *War Work:* Commander of Troop Transport. *Addresses:* c/o The Aberdeen Line, George Thompson & Co., Ltd., 7, Billiter Square, London, E.C. *Club:* Junior Constitutional.
(O10184)

COLLINS, Sibyl Ida, Mrs. Abdy, M.B.E.

COLLINS, Timothy, M.B.E., R.E.

COLLINS, Major and Qr.-Mr. William Henry, M.B.E.

COLLINS, Lieut. William Joseph, M.B.E.

COLLINSON, Alfred Howe, C.B.E., M.I.C.E., *b.* 1866; Controller of Inspection of Munitions, Ministry of Munitions; has Order of Double Dragon of China. *Addresses:* 1, Down Street, Mayfair, W. 1; Westfield Lodge, Hayling Island, Hants. *Club:* Junior Athenæum. (C21)

COLLINSON, Arthur, O.B.E.

COLLINSON, Beatrice Annie, M.B.E., A.R.R.C., Hon. Serving Sister of St. John of Jerusalem, *b.* 13 Dec. 1875; *d.* of Thomas Collinson, of Kendal. *Educ.:* Kendal Friends' School. Member of State Insurance Committee for Westmorland; Hon. Sec. Women's Liberal Association, S. Westmorland; Member of sub-committee, War Pensions, and many other committees of public interest; also the Lady Superintendent, since 1908, of the Kendal Nursing Division of the St. John Ambulance; Commandant of the V.A.D., Westmorland 2, since Oct. 1911. *War Work:* Four and a quarter years of continuous service as head of the Auxiliary Military Hospital, Stramongate, Kendal, 130 beds. *Address:* 19, Highfield, Kendal, Westmorland. (M258)

COLLIS, Frederick, M.B.E.

COLLISHAW, Major Raymond, D.S.O., D.S.C., D.F.C.; Major, R.A.F. Served in the Great War, 1914–18 (despatches). (O11892)

COLLISSON, Capt. Percival Lorimer, O.B.E.

COLLS, Herbert Ailby, M.B.E., *b.* 1 July, 1876; *s.* of Thomas Arthur Colls, I.S.O., Tufnell Park; *m.* Florence Alice, *d.* of Thomas Oldham Williams, of Highgate. *Educ.:* King's Coll., Strand. War Risks Insurance Office, Board of Trade. *War Work:* Government War Risks Insurance, Marine and Aircraft. *Address:* 3, Kingsdown Avenue, South Croydon.
(M7728)

COLLYMORE, Frederick Appleton, M.B.E.

COLMAN, Edith Margaret, O.B.E.

COLMAN, Capt. Joseph Leonard, M.B.E.

COLMORE, Major Reginald Blayney Bulteel, O.B.E., R.A.F.

COLONA, Gilbert Edmond Chalmers, M.B.E.

COLQUHOUN, Lieut. Arthur Hugh, O.B.E., R.A.O.C.

COLQUHOUN, Lieut. Edgar Edmund, M.B.E., R.A.F.

COLQUHOUN, Emily Margaret, M.B.E.; *d.* of Andrew Colquhoun, of Stirling. *Educ.:* Stirling. *War Work:* Hon. Assist. Sec. Argyll and Sutherland Prisoners of War Fund and Stirlingshire Work Depôt; also Hon. Sec. Soldiers' Mending Bureau. *Address:* 8, Royal Gardens, Stirling. (M7729)

COLQUHOUN, Lieut. James Clifton, M.B.E.

COLQUHOUN, Lieut. Victor Alexander, O.B.E., R.F.A. (T.F.)

COLSON, Charles Henry, O.B.E., Commander Order of Redeemer, Greece, M.Inst.C.E., *b.* 24 April, 1864; *s.* of Charles Colson, C.B.; *m.* Isabel Maude, *d.* of Capt. Neville, R.N. *Educ.:* Privately. Deputy Civil Engineer-in-Chief, Admiralty. *War Work:* Admiralty; British Naval Mission to Greece. *Address:* 9, Thornton Avenue, Streatham Hill. (O3665)

COLT, Thomas Archer, O.B.E., L.R.C.P., M.R.C.S., *b.* 29 Dec. 1851; *s.* of Sir Thomas Colt, Bart., of Torquay (*see* BURKE's *Peerage*); *m.* Annie M., *d.* of William Kennett. *Educ.:* Shrewsbury School; Univ. Coll. Hospital, London. *War Work:* Commandant, Brankesmere Red Cross Hospital, Portsmouth, 1915–18. (O10187)

COLTMAN, Capt. Edward Sinnott, O.B.E., R.A.S.C., *b.* 30 April, 1892; *s.* of Joseph Coltman, F.C.I.S. *War Work:* Trooper, City of London Yeomanry (Rough Riders), Aug. 1914, to April, 1915; served as 2nd Lieut. with 3rd, 12th, 14th, and 16th Batts. The Prince of Wales's Own (West Yorkshire Regt.), April, 1915, to Nov. 1916; transferred as Lieut. to R.A.S.C., Nov. 1916 to Sept. 1917; M.T. at Grove Park, Sept. 1917, to March, 1918; Taranto, Italy (Mediterranean L. of C.), Mar. 1918, to March, 1920; Staff Capt. S. & T. Directorate G.H.Q., Italy, April, 1920, to present day; War Office Q.M.G.S. *Address:* The Laurels, Grove Park, Kent. *Club:* United Sports. (O2973)

COLTMAN, Grace, Mrs., M.B.E.

COLTMAN, Walter William, M.B.E., J.P.

COLVILE, Major Charles Rowe, O.B.E., *b.* 29 July, 1870; *s.* of Lieut.-Col. C. F. Colville, of 16, Harrington Gardens, S.W.; *m.* Norah, *d.* of John Henry Bovill, of Buckland, Betchworth, Surrey. *Educ.:* Marlborough Coll. *War Work:* Major, 6th Batt. K.R.R.C.; Staff appointments in France; and attached Royal Fusiliers. *Address:* Ivyhouse Farm, E. Malling, Kent. *Club:* Cavendish. (O5124)

COLVILLE, Lieut.-Col. Charles Eliezer, O.B.E., V.D., J.P. for Perthshire, *b.* 22 Nov. 1859; *s.* of Charles David Colville, of Ayton; *m.* Caroline Sophia, *d.* of Foster Gray, of Edinburgh. *Educ.:* George Watson's Coll., and Edinburgh Univ. Solicitor; Town Clerk, Crieff. *War Work:* Mobilised with 6th Black Watch on 4 Aug. 1914; raised and commanded 3 6th Black Watch; Commanded 4th Res. Batt. Royal Scots Fusiliers from April, 1916, until demobilisation in May, 1919; mentioned, 1917. *Address:* Eversley, Crieff, Perthshire. *Club:* Scottish Conservative. (O7021)

COLVILLE, Capt. Cyril Prichard, O.B.E.

COLVILLE, Hon. George Charles, M.B.E., *b.* 22 Feb. 1867; *s.* of 1st Viscount Colville, of Culross; *m.* Cynthia, *d.* of 1st Marquess of Crewe (*see* BURKE's *Peerage*). *Educ.:* Winchester, and Trinity Coll., Cambridge. Barrister-at-Law. *War Work:* Military Service Tribunal Advisory Committee. *Clubs:* Carlton; Turf; Royal Yacht Squadron. (M1562)

COLVIN, Clement Preston, O.B.E., *b.* 12 July, 1879; *s.* of Clement Sueyd Colvin, C.S.I., of London; *m.* Dorothea Mary, *d.* of George Mair, of Sydney, N.S.W. *Educ.:* Dulwich Coll. Deputy Traffic Manager on the Burma Railway Co., Rangoon, Burma. *War Work:* Chief Recruiting Officer for Technical Labour in the Province of Burma, for service with the Indian Military and Naval forces overseas. *Address:* c/o The Burma Railway Co., Rangoon, Burma. *Club:* Devonshire. (O9811)

COLVIN, Lieut.-Col. Forrester Farnell, C.B.E., J.P., *b.* 22 Jan. 1860; *s.* of Beale Blackwell Colvin, of Monkhams, Waltham Abbey, Essex, and Pishiobury, Herts; *m.* Isabella Katharine, *d.* of Lord Rathdonnell, of Lisnavagh, Rathvilly, Co. Carlow (*see* BURKE's *Peerage*). *Educ.:* Cheam and Marlborough. 9th Lancers, 1880–1903. *War Work:* Served with 9th Lancers, S. Africa, 1899–1901; commanded column under General H. Plumer, 1901–2; Divisional Staff Officer to Colonel C. P. Crewe, Cape Colony, 1902; twice mentioned in despatches; Brevet Lieut.-Col. 1900; appointed to command 2nd Dragoons, 1903; commanded 7th Res. Regt. of Cavalry, Aug. 1914, to Feb. 1917; commanded 6th Res. Regt. of Cavalry, Feb. 1917, to 31 May, 1918; mentioned in W.O. Gazette, 24 Feb. 1917; Horse Adviser, 2nd Corps B.E.F. Nov. 1918, to April, 1919. *Address:* Shermanbury Grange, Henfield, Sussex. *Clubs:* Naval and Military; Cavalry. (C1523)

COLVIN, Lady Gwendoline Audrey Adeline Brudenell, C.B.E., *b.* 3 Aug. 1869; *d.* of 2nd Earl of Stradbroke; *m.* Richard Beale, *s.* of Beale Blackwell Colvin, of Monkhams, Essex. *War Work:* Chairman, Executive Committee, Essex Branch, British Red Cross Society; Asst. Commandant, Essex, 16, Voluntary Aid Detachment. *Address:* Monkhams, Waltham Abbey, Essex. (C944)

COLVIN, Capt. Ragmar Musgrave, C.B.E.,; was Assist. Director Plans Div. during Great War. (C2234)

COLWILL, Lieut.-Comm. George Henry, O.B.E., R.N.

COLYER, Claude Gray, O.B.E., M.R.C.S., L.R.C.P., L.D.S. *b.* 20 April, 1889; *s.* of Horace O. Colyer, of Ryde, I. of W.; *m.* Gladys May, *d.* of Robert King, of Port Elizabeth, S.A. *Educ.:* Charing Cross; Univ. Coll.; Royal Dental Hospitals. *War Work:* Dental Surgeon to the No. 4 C.C.S., B.E.F., Nov. 1914, to May, 1915; No. 54 C.C.S., May, 1915, to May, 1918; Advisory Dental Surgeon, First Army, B.E.F., May, 1918, to Feb. 1919. *Address:* Burnham, Claygate, Surrey. (O5125)

COLYER, Sir James Frank, K.B.E., L.R.C.P., F.R.C.S., L.D.S.R.C.S. (Eng.), Dental Surgeon and Lecturer on Dental Surgery to Charing Cross Hospital; Surgeon to the Royal Dental Hospital, London. *Address:* 11, Queen Anne Street, Cavendish Square, W. 1. (K444)

COMBE, Capt. Harvey Alexander Brabazon, M.B.E.

COMBE, Major James Scarth, O.B.E.

COMBE, Col. Lionel, C.B.E., *b.* 1861 ; *s.* of the late Maj.-Gen. James John Combe, Indian Army ; *m.* 1893, Katherine Louise, *d.* of William Shipp. Formerly Roy. Dublin Fusiliers ; served in the Great War, 1914–19 (despatches).   (C808)

COMBE, Nigel Victor, M.B.E., J.P., *b.* 12 Jan. 1873 ; *s.* of the late Matthew Combe, M.D., Deputy Surgeon-General, R.A. ; *m.* Margaret Hornby, *d.* of the late Ven. Archdeacon Walker, of Chichester. *Educ.:* Charterhouse, and Trinity Coll., Cambridge. *War Work:* Hon. Sec. Allowances Sub-Committee of the West Sussex War Pensions Committee ; Hon. Sec. West Sussex Soldiers' and Sailors' Families Association. *Address:* Hollist, Midhurst, Sussex. *Club:* Oxford and Cambridge.   (M7731)

COMBEN, Robert Stone, C.B.E., *b.* 5 April, 1868 ; *s.* of R. S. Comben, of Woodford Bridge, Essex ; *m.* late Charlotte Alice, *d.* of late John Hawkins, of Dorchester. *Educ.:* Holy Trinity School, Weymouth. *War Work:* Mayor of the Borough of Weymouth and Melcombe-Regis, 1915–18 ; Chairman of Military Tribunal, Food Control Committee, Local Fuel Committee, etc. ; was successful, with the aid of fellow-townspeople, in raising considerable sums for War Charities, Local Hospitals, etc., during the period of office. *Address:* 11, Rodwell Avenue, Weymouth, Dorset.   (C2527)

COMBER, Charles Thomas Thornton, O.B.E., M.D., M.R.C.S., L.R.C.P., *b.* 29 Jan. 1864 ; *s.* of Rev. Charles Thomas Comber, of Oswaldkirk, Yorks. *Educ.:* Mercers' School, and St. Bartholomew's Hospital. Late Surgeon-Capt., Warrens Mounted Infantry, S. Africa ; Vice-President National Medical Union ; Chairman Lewisham Medical War Committee ; O.C. of R.A.M.C. units, 2nd Brigade ; London Div., National Reserve. *War Work:* Four years Surgeon to the Lewisham Military Hospital ; also 3 years in charge of the Electrical and Massage Special Department of the same hospital. *Address:* 27, Rushey Green, Catford, S.E. 6.   (O11798)

COMBER, Lieut.-Comm. Thomas Geoffrey, O.B.E., R.N.

COMBES, Lieut. Percy Matthew, M.B.E., R.G.A. (S.R.)

COMBRIDGE, Cornelius, O.B.E., J.P., *b.* 1856 ; *s.* of Daniel Thomas Combridge, of Hove, Sussex ; *m.* Annie, *d.* of Mark Barker, of Bristnall Hall, Worc. *Educ.:* Brighton Grammar School. Member of Birmingham City Council. *War Work:* Chairman of Executive, Birmingham War Savings Committees. *Address:* 7, Westfield Road, Edgbaston. *Club:* Conservative, Birmingham.   (O3666)

COMER, George Richard, M.B.E., Inter. B.Sc., *b.* 3 Jan. 1878 ; *s.* of T. H. Comer, of Boston ; *m.* Emma Martha Margaret, *d.* of the late Charles Atkinson, of Fishtoft, Lincs.. *Educ.:* St. Mark's Coll., Chelsea, S.W. Headmaster, Tower Road School, Skirbeck ; Worshipful Master (1920) of Franklin Lodge of Free Masons, No. 838, Boston ; Member Skirbeck Parish Council. *War Work:* Hon. Sec. Boston and District War Savings Committee ; Hon Sec. Skirbeck War Savings Association ; Hon. Sec. Skirbeck Emergency Defence Committee, and Special Constables. *Address:* 7, San Francisco Terrace, Boston, Lincs.   (M7732)

COMERFORD, Matthew, M.B.E.

COMINS, Capt. Francis Aloysius, O.B.E., A.I.F.

COMPLIN, Major Edward Charles, O.B.E.

COMPTON, Hon. Paymaster Lieut.-Commander Charles Leonard, M.B.E., R.N.R., *b.* 3 May, 1866 ; *s.* of the late Charles Compton, of H.M. Dockyard, Woolwich ; *m.* Anne Ferguson, *d.* of late James Wilson, of Old Charlton, Kent. *Educ.:* Privately. Senior Staff Officer ; General Register and Record Office of Shipping and Seamen, London. *War Work:* During the War period was in charge (under the Registrar-General of Shipping and Seamen) of the Royal Naval Reserve Department of the General Register and Record Office of Shipping and Seamen, London. *Addresses:* General Register and Record Office of Shipping and Seamen, Tower Hill, London, E. 1 ; Royal United Service Ins'itution, Whitehall, London, S.W. ; Bouverie Place, Folkestone.   (M260)

COMPTON, Major Clifton William McGrath, O.B.E.

COMPTON, Lord Douglas James Cecil, C.B.E., 9th Lancers (retired), *b.* 15 Nov. 1865 ; *s.* of 4th Marquess of Northampton of Castle Ashby, Northampton (*see* BURKE'S *Peerage*) ; *m.* Dollie, *d.* of M. Woolf. *Educ.:* Eton. Col., commanded 9th Lancers 1902–11, served with his regiment throughout the Boer War, 1899–1902. *War Work:* Commanded a Depôt on Line of Communication, 1915–19. *Address:* Delmonden Manor, Hawkhurst, Kent. *Club:* Turf.   (C470)

COMPTON, Edna Katherine, Mrs., M.B.E.

COMPTON, Capt. Edward Bathurst, O.B.E., R.N.

COMPTON, Henry, M.B.E., J.P., Major (retired) Essex Vol. Artillery, Eastern Div. R.A., *b.* 22 May, 1853 ; *s.* of John Compton, of Dorset ; *m.* Mary Temperley, *d.* of W. L. Darke, of Plaistow, Essex. *Educ.:* Privately. *War Work:* Hon. Sec. Kingston Soldiers' and Sailors' Families Association ; and War Pensions Sub-Committee, 1914–19 ; Chairman, Kingston Surbiton and Fistrict Red Cross Hospital, 1915–19. *Address:* 50, Kensington Palace Mansions, W. 1. *Clubs:* Royal Thames Yacht ; Constitutional.   (M7734)

COMPTON, Major John, M.B.E., T.D., Officier d'Academie, *b.* 1 Dec 1864 ; *s.* of Charles Compton, of Royal Dockyard, Woolwich ; *m.* Kate Mary, *d.* of William Pye, of Old Charlton, Kent. *Educ.:* Privately. Postmaster, Folkestone. *War Work:* Employed on Postal Work at Folkestone during the Great War. *Address:* 9, Millfield, Folkestone.   (M3584)

COMYNS, Algernon Charles, O.B.E., *b.* 17 Nov. 1867 ;

s. of the late Charles William Comyns, Principal Clerk, Admiralty ; *m.* Elizabeth Annie, *d.* of John Washington Whinyates, of Liverpool, and U.S.A. *Educ.:* City of London School. Superintending Clerk, Accountant General's Dept., Admiralty. *Address:* 7, Stafford Mansions, Albert Bridge Road. S.W. 11. *Club:* Eccentric.   (O10188)

CONACHER, Hon. Major Charles Leonard, O.B.E., *b.* 17 May, 1873 ; *s.* of the late John Conacher, of 69. Westbourne Terrace, Hyde Park, W. ; *m.* Violet Mary, *d.* of Henry Merrett, of Bishop's Cleeve, Glos. *Educ.:* Oswestry Grammar School (Old Foundation). 1896–1910, General Manager, Isle of Wight Central Rly. ; 1910–14, Traffic Manager, Cambrian Railways. *War Work:* Commissioned in Oct. 1914, as a Railway Transport Officer on War Office Headquarters Staff ; transferred to Ministry of Munitions upon first formation in June, 1915, and still so engaged on executive work ; decorated for War Services in Jan. 1919 (first list), and awarded two special mentions. *Address:* Heathfield, New Barnet, Herts.   (O247)

CONCANON, Col. Henry, O.B.E., T.D., J.P., *b.* 1861 ; *s.* of Christopher Concanon, of Walton-on-the-Hill ; *m.* Isobel, *d.* of Joseph Ion Wharton, of Soulby. *Educ.:* Privately. Joint Manager and Liverpool Director, White Star, Dominion. and American Lines ; Chairman, Liverpool Steamship Owners' Association ; Member of Mersey Docks and Harbour Board. *War Work:* Transportation overseas of troops, munitions, and foodstuffs ; on various committees, Red Cross, Recruiting, Labour, etc. ; formerly commanded 7th Batt. The King's (Liverpool Regiment). *Addresses:* 30, James Street, Liverpool ; Beechside, Allerton, Liverpool. *Clubs:* Exchange, Liverpool ; Junior Constitutional, London.   (O1230)

CONCHIE, Jean, Mrs., M.B.E.

CONDER, Walter Tasman, M.B.E.   (M10380)

CONEY, Lieut. Cecil Frederick, M.B.E.

CONGDON, Lieut. William Sydney Philip, O.B.E., R.N.R.

CONGREVE, Eirene, Mrs., M.B.E.   (M10245h)

CONIBEAR James Handford M.B.E.

CONINGHAM, Major Alfred Evelyn, O.B.E., M.C., R.E.

CONINGHAM, Geraldine Emily, Mrs. M.B.E.

CONYNGHAM, Elsie Margaret, Lady, O.B.E.   (O2053)

CONN, Robert, M.B.E.

CONNAL, Lieut.-Col. Kenneth Hugh Munro, O.B.E., T.D., J.P., *b.* 28 Feb. 1870 ; *s.* of William Connal, of Solsgirth, Dollar ; *m.* Kitty MacTudoe, *d.* of A. Cochran, of Glasgow. *Educ.:* Cheltenham. Vice-Chairman, City of Glasgow T.F. Association ; served 1½ years in the South African Campaign. *War Work:* Three years 'active service in Egypt, Gallipoli and France ; invalided home from France Oct. 1917 ; Divisional Road Transport Officer, West of Scotland Division, 1918, till Road Transport Board dissolved in 1919. *Address:* Monktonhead, Monkton, Ayrshire. *Clubs:* Cavalry, London ; Western, Glasgow.   (O10189)

CONNAL, Sophia Lucy Mackworth, Mrs., M.B.E., B.Sc.

CONNAN, Capt. John Cranmer, O.B.E., R.A.O.C.

CONNELL, Jessie Murdoch, Mrs., M.B.E., *b.* 10 Jan. 1882 ; *d.* of Sir Henry Robson, of Aubrey Lodge, Kennington, London ; *m.* Alexander, *s.* of John Connell of Appin, N.B. *Educ.:* Privately. *War Work:* Commandant St. John V.A.D. Hospital, Myrtle Street, Liverpool. *Address:* 4, Alexandra Drive, Sefton Park, Liverpool.   (M262)

CONNELL, John, M.B.E., M.C., R.A.S.C.

CONNELL, Sir Robert Lowden, K.B.E., *b.* 1867 ; *s.* of Thomas Connell, of Moresby, Cumberland (*see* BURKE'S *Peerage*) ; *m.* Sarah, *d.* of John Webster, of Bootle. *Educ.:* Privately. Shipowner and Underwriter ; Senior partner, Lowden, Connell & Co., Liverpool. *War Work:* Chairman War Stores Committee, 1917 ; Deputy Controller Army Salvage, 1917–19 ; Member of the Disposal Board Surplus Government Stores, 1919–20. *Address:* Glencaple, Blundellsands, Liverpool. *Clubs:* Reform ; Royal Automobile ; Argentine ; Liverpool Reform.   (K137)

CONNER, Lieut.-Col. Daniel Goodwin, O.B.E., R.A.F.

CONNER, James, M.B.E., M.I.M.E.. M.I.E.E.

CONNERY Capt. William Lawrence, M.B.E. Manchester Regt., *b.* 25 Nov. 1875 ; *s.* of Lieut.-Col. M. H. Connery, M.C., of Willow Bank, Ashton-under-Lyne ; *m.* Lily Gertrude, *d.* of J. J. Carroll, of Dundalk. *Educ.:* Salford Catholic Grammar School. *War Work:* South African War, 1899–1902 ; mentioned twice in despatches by Lord Roberts and Lord Kitchener ; Great War, 1914, with 2nd Batt. Manchester Regt. ; mentioned in Lord French's despatches, Feb. 1915. *Address:* Willow Bank, Ashton-under-Lyne.   (M6620)

CONNETT, Capt. William, M.B.E., *b.* 15 March, 1860 ; *s.* of William Connett, of Appledore ; *m.* Louisa, *d.* of John Chesterfield, of Portreath. *Educ.:* Appledore. Master Mariner. *War Work:* Colliery Transport, S.S. "Treleigh" ; valuable services rendered during the war. *Address:* Hill View, Portreath, Redruth, Cornwall.   (M1564)

CONNICHIE, Henry Joseph Bexfield, M.B.E.

CONNOLLY, Capt. Hugh Francis, M.B.E.

CONNOLLY, Matthew, M.B.E.

CONNOLLY, Thomas Francis, M.B.E., M.Sc., Fellow of Optical Society, *b.* 1878 ; *s.* of John Connolly of Monaghan, Ireland : *m.* Emma Adèle, *d.* of A. Richez. *Educ.:* St. Francis Xaviers Coll. ; Liverpool Univ. ; Royal Coll. of Science, S. Kensington. Civil Servant (Technical Science). *War*

Work: Optical Munitions. *Address:* 45, Dryburgh Road, Putney, S.W. 15. (M7737)
CONNOLLY, William Frederick, M.B.E.
CONNOLLY, William Patrick Joseph, C.B.E., I.S.O., Principal Clerk, Chief Sec.'s Office, Dublin Castle. *Address:* 63, Merrion Road, Dublin. (C945)
CONNOR, Anthony John, M.B.E.
CONNOR, William James, M.B.E.
CONNORS, Eng.-Lieut.-Comm. Ernest John, O.B.E., R.N.
CONROY, Lieut.-Col. Charles O'Neil, O.B.E., K.C., *b.* 24 Jan. 1871; *s.* of James Gervais Conroy, K.C., of Dublin; *m.* Mary Agnes, *d.* of George Weathers, M.R.C.S., of London. *Educ.:* St. Bede's College, Manchester; Univ. College and School, London; Wren and Gurney, London. General Counsel and Treasurer, Reid Newfoundland Co., St. John's, Newfoundland; Lieut.-Col. commanding Catholic Cadet Corps of Newfoundland. *War Work:* Executive Member, Standing Committee of Newfoundland Patriotic Association, which raised and equipped Royal Newfoundland Regiment. *Address:* "Raheen," Bonaventure Avenue, St. John's, Newfoundland. *Clubs:* City; Knights of Columbus. (O974)
CONSTABLE, Andrew Henderson Briggs, C.B.E., K.C., *b.* March, 1865; *s.* of William Briggs Constable, of Benarty, Fife; *m.* Elizabeth, *d.* of James Simpson, of Mawcarse, Kincross. *Educ.:* Dollar Academy; University of Edinburgh. Dean of the Faculty of Advocates. *War Work:* Supervisor of Military Representatives, and afterwards Representative of the Scottish Office to Tribunals, under Military Service Acts, in Scotland. *Address:* 23, Royal Circus, Edinburgh. *Clubs:* University, Edinburgh; Wellington, London. (C2528)
CONSTABLE, Arthur Douglas, O.B.E.
CONSTABLE, Capt. Clifford Edward, O.B.E., M.C., *b.* 20 Aug. 1876; *s.* of Marmaduke Constable, of Millbrook, Southampton; *m.* Sarah Snow, *d.* of Daniel Kimball, of Boston, U.S.A. *Educ.:* Eastman's; R.N. Academy; "Britannia." Holds Life Saving Certificate; served in the Boer War with B.S.A. Mounted Police. *War Work:* Joined 2nd King Edward's Horse as trooper in Aug. 1914; through N.C.O. ranks to commission in Regt.; finally Capt and Adjutant; left Regt. May, 1917, and joined Welsh Division (38th Div.), and served with them till end of Sept. 1918; Camp Commandant of Headquarters Lines of Communication until demobilisation in May, 1919; twice mentioned in despatches. (O5126)
CONSTABLE, Eng.-Comm. James Sandford, O.B.E., R.N.
CONSTABLE, Eng.-Lieut.-Comm. William Charles O.B.E.
CONSTABLE, Alice Amelia BROWN-, M.B.E., Q.M.A.A.C.
CONSTANTINE, Arthur Heaton, M.B.E., *b.* 21 Jan. 1885; *s.* of Arthur Constantine, of Bolton, Lancs.; *m.* Mary, *d.* of Frank Cornell, of Birmingham. *Educ.:* Nottingham High School and Univ. Coll. Engineer. *War Work:* Served with the forces, Aug. 1914, to Jan. 1916; afterwards assistant works manager to National Ordnance Factory, Nottingham. *Address:* 55, Coney Green Drive, Longbridge, Birmingham. (M7739)
CONSTANTINE, William Windley, M.B.E., A.M.I.Mech.E., M.I.A.E., *b.* 18 Sept. 1886; *s.* of the late Arthur Constantine, Solicitor, of Blackburn. *Educ.:* Nottingham High School and Univ. Coll. Chief Designer (Engine Dept.), Crossley Bros., Ltd., Erwood Park Works, Manchester. *War Work:* Served in H.M. Forces from Sept. 1914, to June, 1916 (5th King's Royal Rifles and Machine Gun Corps); transferred to Ministry of Munitions, June, 1916, and became Chief Technical Assistant to Director of Munitions, Mechanical Transport; later transferred to Mech. Warfare Dept. (Tanks), and was appointed Section Director, Engine Design; voluntary member of Advisory Committee (Engines) to Disposal Board. *Address:* 42, Peel Moat Road, Heaton Moor, Stockport. (M7740)
CONSTERDINE, Rudolph, M.B.E., *b.* 15 July, 1887; *s.* of Rev. J. Consterdine, M.A., Rector of Edgware, Middlesex. *Educ.:* St. Lawrence Coll., Ramsgate; Univ. Coll. Reading. *War Work:* Served with the Y.M.C.A. (British) at Bedford, Dieppe (Sec.), and Third Army Area (Sec.); Y.M.C.A. (Chinese) Third Army Area (Sec.) Headquarters for France (Assist. Sec.); Holds the Order of Wen-Hu (5th Class). *Addresses:* Y.M.C.A., Cairo, Egypt; Edgware Rectory, Middlesex. (M1565)
CONWAY, Agnes Ethel, M.B.E.
CONYERS, Ada Blanche, Mrs., M.B.E.
CONYERS, Evelyn Augustus, C.B.E., R.R.C. Matron-in Chief, Australian Army Nursing Service. (C1142)
CONYNGHAM, Elsie Margaret, Lady LENOX-, O.B.E., *d.* of Surgeon-Maj.-Gen. Sir (Alexander) Frederick Bradshaw, K.C.B.; *m.* 15 Nov. 1890, Col. Sir Gerald Ponsonby, 5th *s.* of the late Sir William Fitzwilliam Lenox-Conyngham, K.C.B., of Springhill, Co. Londonderry. (O2053)
CONYNGHAM, Eva, Mrs. LENOX-, O.B.E., *b.* 10 Sept. 1879; *d.* of Edmund Sanders Darley, of Fern Hill, Co. Dublin; *m.* the late Hubert Maxwell, Lieut.-Col., D.S.O., *s.* of Col. Sir William Lenox-Conyngham, of Springhill, Co. Derry (*see* BURKE's *Landed Gentry of Ireland*). *War Work:* Hon. Sec. Wounded Soldiers' Club, Dublin. *Address:* Fern Hill, Sandy Ford, Co. Dublin. (O10190)
CONYNHAM, Lieut.-Col. William Arbuthnot LENOX-, O.B.E., T.F., Res.
COODE, Montgomery Penrose, O.B.E., *b.* 20 May, 1853;

s. of Gen. John Penrose Coode, of Madras Army. *Educ.:* Haileybury Coll. and R.I.E. Coll., Coopers Hill. Late Indian Public Works Department; Superintending Engineer in Burma; retired in 1907; late M.Inst.C.E.; Fellow Royal Colonial Institute. *War Work:* Hon. Treas. and Sec. Devonport War Hospital Supply Depôt. *Address:* 13, Penlee Gardens, Devonport. *Clubs:* E.I.U.S.; Royal Western Yacht Club, Plymouth. (O10191)
COOK, Albert Ruskin, O.B.E., M.D. (Lond.), B.A. (Camb.), B.Sc. (Lond.), Chevalier de L'Ordre de Léopold *b.* 2 March, 1870; *s.* of William Henry Cook, of Hampstead, N.W.; *m.* Katharine, *d.* of J. Timpson. *Educ.:* St. Paul's School; Trinity Coll., Cambridge; St. Bart.'s Hospital (Science Exhibitioner, St. Paul's School; Major Scholar, Trinity Coll., Camb.; Shuter Scholar, Bart.'s). 1st Class Nat. Science Tripos, Part I., 1st Class, Part II.; S.M.O., Mengo Hospital; C.M.S., Kampala, 1897; President Uganda Branch of B.M.A. *War Work:* Officer in charge Mengo Base Hospital, Uganda, 1914–17; on the Staff of Bermondsey Military Hospital, 1918; late Capt. Uganda Medical Service; medal with 2 clasps for Uganda Nubian Rebellion, 1897–98. *Addresses:* P.O. Box 125, Kampala, Uganda; C.M.S., Salisbury Square, London, E.C. (O985)
COOK, Albert Sydney, M.B.E., *b.* 22 March, 1894; *s.* of F. Alford Cook, of Burgess Hill, Sussex. *Educ.:* S. London School. *War Work:* Served in France with London Regt.; later joined Military Secretary's Branch and served on H.Q. Staff of 5th, and then 4th, Army until the cessation of hostilities, when recalled to join a new branch at War Office. *Address:* 20, Barry Road, Dulwich. (M7741)
COOK, Major Alexander, O.B.E., Aust. A.M.C.
COOK, Lieut. Alexander James, O.B.E., R.N.R.
COOK, Capt. Charles Lever, M.B.E.
COOK, Fred Compigne, M.B.E.
COOK, Grace Muriel Mrs., O.B.E.
COOK, Lieut.-Col. Herbert George Graham, C.B.E., M.D., F.R.C.S., R.A.M.C., *b.* 1864; *s.* of Thomas William Cook, of London; *m.* Mabel Mary, Norton. *Educ.:* Charterhouse; St. Bartholomew's Hospital. Surgeon, King Edward VII. Hospital, Cardiff; Medical Officer, H.M. Prison, Cardiff. *War Work:* Surgeon-in-Charge, Glamorgan and Monmouthshire Hospital; attached to French Xth Army, at Berck Plage, Pas-de-Calais, 1914–15; Lieut.-Col., Commanding Welsh Hospital, Netley, April, 1916–19. *Address:* 22, Newport Road, Cardiff. (C2091)
COOK, Col. James, O.B.E., T.F. Res.
COOK, James, M.B.E.
COOK, Katharine, Mrs., M.B.E., *d.* of John Timpson, of Northampton; *m.* Albert Ruskin, *s.* of Dr. W. H. Cook, of Hampstead. *Educ.:* Guy's Hospital. Superintendent of Maternity Training School, Kampala, Uganda; for 21 years Matron, Mengo Hospital, Kampala, 1897–1918. Medal and clasp, Uganda, 1897–98. *War Work:* March, 1918, Matron, Base Hospital, Mengo; 1914–17 Superintendent, Kampala Branch, Red Cross Society. *Addresses:* P.O. Box 125, Kampala, Uganda; c/o C.M.S., Salisbury Square, London, E.C. (M1257)
COOK, Lieut.-Col. Leonard Barnaby, O.B.E.
COOK, Col. Percival Robert, C.B.E., N.Z.A.M.D., *b.* 6 Dec. 1867; *s.* of Edmund Cook, of Dunedin, N.Z.; *m.* Lilian Maud, *d.* of James C. Wilkin, of Christchurch. Surgeon to Masterton Hospital. *War Work:* Officer Commanding troops on New Zealand Hospital Ship "Marama," from Dec. 1915, to May, 1918; A.D.M.S. Wellington Military District, June, 1918, to Feb. 1919. *Club:* Masterton. (C1851)
COOK, Percy Frederick, M.B.E., Q.M.S., R.A.M.C.
COOK, Richard Frederic, M.B.E.
COOK, Capt. Robert Ewing, O.B.E., R.A.F.
COOK, Major Sidney George, O.B.E.
COOK, Thomas, O.B.E.
COOK, Capt. Victor Chandler, O.B.E., R.A.S.C.
COOK, Major William Ernest, O.B.E., R.N.
COOK, William Frederick, M.B.E.
COOK, Capt. William Littlejohn, O.B.E., Gordon Highlanders, *b.* 21 July, 1883; *s.* of George Milne Cook, D.L., of Beaconhill, Murtle, Aberdeenshire; *m.* Xenia, *d.* of Oscar Steveni, of Petrograd. *Educ.:* Merchiston Castle. *War Work:* Served in France with unit, 1915; attached Admiralty for special service in Russia, 1916–17; Norway, 1917–18; Egypt, 1918. *Address:* Anderson Drive, Aberdeen. *Club:* Royal Northern, Aberdeen. (O8771)
COOK, William Wallace, O.B.E. *Address:* Worcoppice House, White Hill, Caterham, Surrey. (O10193)
COOKE, Air-Commodore Bertram Hewett Hunter, C.M.G., C.B.E., D.S.O., *b.* 1874; *s.* of John Edward Cooke, formerly R.N.; *m.* 1903, Mary Henrietta, *d.* of the late T. H. Cardwell, of Newnton, Tetbury, Gloucestershire. Lieut.-Col. Rifle Brig. (Prince Consort's Own), and attached to R.A.F. with rank of Air-Commodore; Nile Expedition, 1898 (medal, Egyptian medal with clasp); S. African War, 1900–1902, on special service (wounded, Queen's medal with five clasps); served in the Great War, 1914–18, on Staff (severely wounded, despatches four times, Brevet Lieut.-Col., Russian Order of St. Stanislaus with swords, Croix de Guerre). (C1800)
COOKE, Major Cedric Franklin, O.B.E., R.A.S.C., *b.* 12 Aug. 1882; *s.* of Henry Cooke, late of Thong, Gravesend, Kent; *m.* Mabel Dorothy, *d.* of Hamilton Stein, of Mauritius. *Educ.:* King's School, Rochester. *War Work:* Raised 18th Divisional Train, 1914; D.A.Q.M.G. 13th Division, 1915;

Staff Captain, War Office, 1916 ; and D.A.D.T. Eastern Command, 1916–19. *Address :* R.A.S.C., Mauritius. *Club :* Junior Naval and Military. (O8772)

COOKE, Clara Mabel, Mrs., M.B.E., *b.* 9 May, 1870 ; *d.* of Richard Rudyard, of Scalby Hall, near Scarborough ; *m.* Major Thomas Percy, *s.* of J. A. Cooke. *Educ. :* Scarborough and Dresden. *War Work :* Commandant, Olton Auxiliary Hospital for 5 years. *Address :* Eskdale, Kineton Road, Olton, Warwickshire. (M7745)

COOKE, Lieut.-Col. Claude Edward Arthur, C.B.E.

COOKE, Cuthbert Cresswell, M.B.E.

COOKE, Edward Henry William, M.B.E.

COOKE, Sir (Edward) Marriott, K.B.E.. M.B. (Lond.), M.R.C.S. (Eng.), A.K.C., *b.* 4 Feb. 1852 ; *s.* of Henry Edward Cooke, of Harrow-on-the-Hill ; *m.* Mary Anne Henrietta Cecil, *d.* of Sir George Brooke-Pechell, 5th Bart., of Alton House, Alton, Hants. *Educ. :* Cholmeley's School, Highgate ; King's College Hospital, London. Commissioner of the Board of Control since 1914 ; Chairman of that Board, 1916–18 ; Commissioner in Lunacy, 1898–1914 ; formerly Medical Officer and Superintendent Worcester County and City Lunatic Asylum, and previously Medical Superintendent of the Wilts. County Asylum. *War Work :* Was largely concerned with the initiation and development of a scheme for the establishment of some 24 well equipped War Hospitals, formed by the conversion of County and Borough Lunatic Asylums in England and Wales, whereby over 31,000 beds were provided, which during the five years they were available afforded treatment for nearly 500,000 sick and wounded soldiers. *Addresses :* 43, Coleherne Court, South Kensington, S.W. 5 ; 66, Victoria Street, S.W. 1. *Club :* Conservative. (K138)

COOKE, Frank Alexander, M.B.E., D.C.M.

COOKE, Frank James, M.B.E.

COOKE, Henry Moore Annesley, O.B.E.

COOKE, Herbert Sutton, O.B.E.

COOKE, Howard Francis Vernon, M.B.E., B.A., *b.* 9 Feb. 1867 ; *s.* of Rev. R. H. Cooke, B.D., of Healaugh, Yorkshire ; *m.* Ethel Margaret, *d.* of W. H. Cobb, of Southwoods Hall, Thirsk. *Educ. :* Malvern Coll., and Emmanuel Coll., Cambridge. Electrical Engineer. *War Work :* Ministry of Munitions, Salvage Dept. ; Sergt. Metropolitan Special Constabulary ; awarded 1914 Star and Long Service Medal. *Address :* 36, Cleveland Road, Ealing. *Club :* New University. (M7749)

COOKE, Brevet-Major Ion Alexander Scott, O.B.E., F.R. Colonial Inst., *b.* 12 Oct. 1888 ; *s.* of the Rev. Edward Alexander Cooke, M.A., Vicar of St. Paul, Brentford. *Educ. :* St. John's, Leatherhead. 2nd Lieut. 4th Connaught Rangers, 1907 ; Lieut., 1910 ; Capt., 1915 ; Brevet-Major, 1918 ; Private Sec. to Sir Lawrence Wallace, K.B.E., C.M.G., Administrator of N. Rhodesia, May, 1912, to Aug. 1913 ; Private Sec. to Lieut.-Col. H. W. Kempster, C.M.G., Commissioner of Land Settlement for Rhodesia, in Australia, New Zealand, and Canada, Oct. 1913, to Aug. 1914. *War Work :* Served in 2nd Batt. Connaught Rangers, Sept. to Nov. 1914 ; Battles, Aisne and 1st Battle of Ypres ; Egypt and Palestine, April, 1915, to Nov. 1918 ; despatches, "London Gazette," June, 1916, and 1917 ; Brevet-Major, New Years' Honours, 1918 ; O.B.E. New Year's Honours, 1919 ; 1914 Star and Rosette. *Address :* Devon Estates, Malacca. *Clubs :* Junior United Service, Charles Street, S.W. ; Malacca Club, Malacca, S. Settlements. (O3287)

COOKE, James Henry, M.B.E., M.B., R.A.M.C.

COOKE, John Galwey, O.B.E., M.B., B.Ch., *b.* 1859 ; *s.* of the Rev. Ambrose Cooke, of Killinane, Co. Tipperary. *Educ. :* Trinity Coll., Dublin. Hon. Consulting Surgeon, County Infirmary, Londonderry ; late Surgeon to County Infirmary, Londonderry. *War Work :* Surgeon-in-charge, County Infirmary, Londonderry (Auxiliary Naval and Military Hospital) ; Acting Hon. Surgeon to Officers of Buncrana Naval Base. *Address :* 67, Clarendon Street, Londonderry. *Club :* Northern Counties, Londonderry. (O10194)

COOKE, Joseph, O.B.E.

COOKE, Margery Randal, Mrs., O.B.E.

COOKE, Martin Alfred, O.B.E., T.D., M.R.C.S., L.R.C.P., L.S.A., R.A.M.C. (T.F.), *b.* 1872 ; *s.* of Alfred Square Cooke, of Stroud, Glos. ; *m.* May, *d.* of Thomas W. Elvy, of Stroud. *Educ. :* Wycliffe Coll., Stonehouse ; Weymouth Coll. ; St. Barts. Hospital. *War Work :* Lieut.-Col. R.A.M.C. (T.F.) ; L.M. Bde. Field Ambulance ; O.C. Tooting Grove Military Hospital, S.W. *Address :* 12, Central Hill, Upper Norwood, S.E. 19. (O7027)

COOKE, Capt. Philip Andrew, O.B.E., M.C.

COOKE, Lieut.-Col. Robert Joseph, O.B.E.

COOKE, Thomas Fothergill, O.B.E.

COOKE, Capt. William Edward Hinchley, O.B.E.

COOKE, William Herrick, M.B.E., *b.* 1881 ; *s.* of William Cooke, of Leicester ; *m.* Elizabeth, *d.* of John Clarke, of Market Basworth. *Educ. :* Leicester. Master, Poor Law Institution. *War Work :* Recruited 200 able-bodied men from the Casual Wards ; afterwards turned the whole of the Poor Law Institution into Hospital for the sick. *Address :* Poor Law Institution, Worksop, Notts. (M7750)

COOKE, William John, M.B.E.

COOKE, Philip Tatton DAVIES-, O.B.E., J.P., D.L, *b.* 15 May, 1863 ; *s.* of P. B. Davies-Cooke, of Gugraney, Mold, N. Wales (*see* BURKE'S *Peerage*) ; *m.* Doris, *d.* of R. C. Donaldson Hudson, of Cheswardine, Market Drayton. *Educ. :* Eton and Cambridge. J.P. *War Work :* Chairman Flintshire War Agricultural Committee ; Member of County Advisory Com-

mittee ; Major, Volunteers. *Address :* Gugraney, Mold, North Wales. *Clubs :* Carlton ; Travellers'. (O10197)

COOKE, Sir Clement KINLOCH-, Kt., K.B.E., B.A., LL.M., M.P. (U.), Devonport, since 1910 ; *o.s.* of the late Robert Whall Cooke, of Sunnyside, Brighton ; *m.* Florence, *y.d.* of the late Rev. J. L. Errington ; assumed additional surname of Kinloch. *Educ. :* Brighton Coll. ; St. John's Coll., Cambs. ; Mathematical Tripos ; Law Tripos ; Barr. 1883 ; Oxford Circuit ; H.M. Counsel for Mint in Berkshire ; legal adviser to House of Lords Sweating Commission, 1886–88 ; Private Sec. to Earl of Dunraven (Under-Secretary of State for Colonies) ; Examiner under Civil Service Commission for H.M.'s Factory Inspectorships ; Edited " English Illustrated Magazine," " Observer," " Pall Mall Gazette " ; Founder and Editor, " Empire Review " ; Hon. Sec. to Allied Colonial Univ. Conference held at Burlington House, 1903 ; Member L.C.C., 1907–10 ; of Educational Authority for County of London ; of London (Central) Unemployed Body ; of County of London Territorial Force Association ; Governor of Imperial College of Science and Technology ; Chairman, Central Emigration Board ; and of S.W. Advisory Committee, London Secondary School for Girls ; Member of Conjoint Committee for Promotion of Commercial Education ; Fellow of the Royal Colonial Institute ; Ruling Councillor of the Iddesleigh Habitation of the S.W. London United Habitation of the Primrose League. *Addresses :* 3, Mount Street, Grosvenor Square, W. 1 ; 2, Garden Court, Temple, E.C. *Clubs :* Athenæum ; Carlton ; St. Stephen's ; United ; Beefsteak ; M.C.C. ; Royal South-Western Yacht. (K208)

COOKSEY, Lieut. Frank Reginald, M.B.E.

COOKSEY, Henry James, M.B.E., *b.* 24 Sept. 1875 ; *s.* of Philip Henry Cooksey, of Camberwell ; *m.* Maud Watt. *Educ. :* Privately. Superintending Clerk, War Office. *War Work :* Clerk-in-Charge, Territorial Officers' section, Military Secretary's Department, War Office ; served in the N.W. Frontier, 1897–8 Campaigns, India. *Address :* Undermount, Sydenham Hill Road, Sydenham, S.E. (M267)

COOKSON, Christopher, M.B.E., Egyptian State Telegraphs. (M10350)

COOKSON, Kenneth, O.B.E.

COOKSON, Percy Charles, M.B.E., J.P., *b.* 6 July, 1827 ; *s.* of the Rev. Osmond Cookson, of Adelaide, South Africa ; *m.* Adelaide Elizabeth, *d.* of late Georges De La Montaigne, of Paris. *Educ. :* Denstone Coll., Leeds Grammar School, and Privately. Civil Servant ; Magistrate ; Native Commissioner and Justice of Peace for Northern Rhodesia. *War Work :* Forwarding supplies for Fife Garrison on Rhodesian Northern Border ; supplying Military Porters for' Rhodesian and Nyasaland Field Forces operating in German East Africa and Portuguese East Africa. *Address :* Fort Jameson, East Luangwa District, Northern Rhodesia. *Club :* United Service (Livingstone). (M6429)

COOKSON, Lieut.-Col. Philip Blencowe, C.M.G., O.B.E., J.P., *b.* 30 Oct. 1871 ; *s.* of John Blencowe Cookson, of Meldon Park, Morpeth ; *m.* Gwendoline, *d.* of Henry Arthur Brassey, of Preston Hall, Kent (*see* BURKE'S *Peerage*). *Educ. :* Eton. 1st Life Guards, April, 1894–1911 ; served on N.W. Frontier of India, 1897–98 ; S. African War, 1899–1900. *War Work :* European War, 1914–18, Lieut.-Col. Northumberland Hussars. *Address :* Meldon Park, Morpeth, Northumberland. *Clubs :* Turf ; White's. (O7028)

COOKSON, Thomas Hatton, M.B.E., *b.* 17 Sept., 1878 ; *s.* of Henry Cookson, of West Derby, Liverpool ; *m.* Winifred Susan, *d.* of Richard Preston Bishop, of Starcross, Devon. *Educ. :* Shrewsbury School. Merchant. *War Work :* In charge of the Liverpool Office of the Oils and Fats Branch, Ministry of Food. *Address :* Rose Lea, Willaston, near Birkenhead. *Club :* Old Hall, Liverpool (M7751)

COOMBE, Arthur Henry, M.B.E., *b.* 10 Oct. 1865 ; *s.* of William Coombe, of Torrington, North Devon ; *m.* Kate, *d.* of Richard Starling, of Clapham. *Educ. :* Shebbear College, North Devon. *War Work :* Duties connected with the post of Registrar to the Accountant-General of the Navy, in whose department, during the war period, the number of communications received in the Registry averaged two and a quarter millions per annum. *Address :* 42, Tierney Road, Streatham Hill, S.W. (M268)

COOMBES, George Noble, M.B.E.

COOMBES, Sydney Cooper, M.B.E., *b.* 1 Sept. 1871 ; *s.* of Walter James Coombes, of Ryde, Isle of Wight ; *m.* Edith Alathea, *d.* of George Brewster, of Marston, Staffs. *Educ. :* Privately. Hon. Magistrate, Rangoon, from 1907–10 ; President, Rangoon Trades Association ; Hon. Treas. Viceroy's Reception Committee, Rangoon ; Judge, Burma Arts and Crafts Exhibition ; Delhi-Durbar Medal for Public Service, Rangoon, 1911. *War Work :* Naval Supply Officer, Colombo Ceylon, from Jan. 1917, to July, 1919. *Club :* Overseas. (M7752)

COOMBES, Lieut. and Qr.-Mr. William James, M.B.E., R.A.

COOMBS, Edward Alfred, M.B.E., F.S.A.A., *b.* 10 Jan. 1866 ; *s.* of the late Alfred Coombs, of Beckenham, Kent. Treasurer of the Royal Borough of Kensington ; Fellow of the Society of Incorporated Accountants and Auditors ; Fellow and Past President of the Institute of Municipal Treasurers and Accountants (Incorporated). *War Work :* Member of the Advisory Committee on Accounts and Audit of the National War Savings Committee ; Hon. Treas. of the Kensington Central Committee for War Savings ; Hon. Treas. of Kensington Food Control Committee and Kensington National

Kitchens. *Addresses:* The Town Hall, Kensington, W. 8; Longside. Beckenham, Kent. (M1568)

COOMBS, Capt. Frederick Middleton, O.B.E., R.A.V.C.

COOMBS, 2nd Lieut. Percy, M.B.E., R.A.F.

COOMBS, Lieut.-Comm. Thomas Edward, O.B.E., R.N.R., *b.* 1884; *s.* of John Coombs, of Somersetshire; *m.* Kathleen, *d.* of Rev. H. A. S. Pitt, of Devonshire. *Educ.:* Wells Grammar School. Master Mariner, R.N.S.R. *War Work:* Second in Command H.M. Auxiliary Cruiser "Patia," 1915–19; in Command H.M.T.G. "Gossamer," till April, 1919, employed in minesweeping; in command H.M.S. "Gainsborough," April to Nov. 1919, employed in sweeping mines off the Belgian coast. *Address:* 32, Khartoum Road, Highfield, Southampton.
(O9664)

COOMBS, William Walter, M.B.E., *b.* 24 Oct. 1866; *s.* of the late Hillary Coombs, of Crewkerne, Somerset; *m.* Emma, *d.* of James Jarman, of Ipswich. *Educ.:* Crewkerne Grammar School and London University. Civil Servant (Board of Trade). *War Work:* Work in connection with Trading with the enemy. (M269)

COONEY, Capt. Ralph Carson, O.B.E.

COOPE, Amy Monica, M.B.E.

COOPE, Capt. Raymond Henry, O.B.E., Mercantile Marine, *b.* 21 May, 1856; *s.* of the late John Coope; *m.* Alice Maud, *d.* of the late William Speechley. *Educ.:* School ship "Conway." In the service of the B.I.S.N.C.-L. 44 years, 36 years of which were in command of ships on the Indian coast. *War Work:* In command of the "Elephanta" when war broke out on 10 Aug. 1914, ship taken by Indian Govt. as troop transport; served whole war to date of Armistice; carried some 50,000 men without accident; mentioned despatches 3 times; present first actions, Mesopotamia, and last at Hodeida against Turks. *Address:* 510, Lytham Road, Blackpool, Lancashire. (O1231)

COOPER, Alice, O.B.E.

COOPER, Allan Ernest, M.B.E., *b.* 1874; *s.* of John Cooper, of Lapworth; *m.* Elizabeth Ann, *d.* of Philip Blight, of Ilfracombe. *Educ.:* King Edward's School, Aston. *War Work:* Production of Side Arms. *Address:* 22, Holly Road, Edgbaston Birmingham. *Club:* R.A.C. (M1569)

COOPER, Capt. Ansell Edgar, M.B.E., R.A.O.C.

COOPER, Paymaster-Lieut.-Comm. Archibald Frederick, O.B.E., R.N.

COOPER, Bertram George, M.B.E.

COOPER, Major Bryan Ricco, M.B.E.

COOPER, 2nd Lieut. Cecil Aubrey, M.B.E., R.E.

COOPER, Capt. Charles Herbert, M.B.E., I.A.R.O.

COOPER, Col. Charles James, C.B.E., T.D.

COOPER, Lieut.-Comm. Charles Purcell, O.B.E., R.D., R.N.R.

COOPER, Charlotte Leonora, Lady, O.B.E.; *d.* of Thomas Crambton, of Grove Park, Middlesex; *m.* 7 Sept. 1876, Sir Edward Ernest Cooper, 1st Bt. of Berrydown Court (*see* BURKE'S *Peerage*). *Address:* Berrydown Court, Overton, Hants. (O3668)

COOPER, Daniel George Arthur, O.B.E., S.M., J.P., *b.* 1 July, 1861; *s.* of George Sisson Cooper, of Wellington. *Educ.:* Privately; Wellington Coll. 1889–1914, Registrar Supreme Court and Court of Appeal, and Sheriff, Wellington District; Feb. 1914, Stipendiary Magistrate, Wellington. *War Work:* Nov. 1914, to Nov. 1918, Chairman, 1st Wellington Military Service Board; 25 Aug. 1915, Chairman, War Pensions Board for New Zealand. *Address:* Wellington. Wellington. (O8223)

COOPER, Edward Stroud, M.B.E.. *b.* 17 Sept. 1881; *s.* of Thomas Cooper, of Bishops Waltham; *m.* Martha Cecilia Florence, *d.* of the late John Gregg Corbitt, of Belfast. *Educ.:* Queen's Park Coll., Harrow Road, W. *War Work:* Assistant to Sec. Railway Executive Committee, Board of Trade; volunteered for Army in 1915 and rejected. *Address:* 75, Wrottesley Road, Harlesden, N.W. 10. (M7754)

COOPER, Eleanor Valentine, M.B.E., *b.* 14 Feb. 1874; *d.* of Edward Llewelyn Cooper, of Coventry and West Worthing. *Educ.:* Kensington and Bedford. Joined Red Cross Society in 1911; appointed Quartermaster of Sussex 78 in 1913 (Feb.) *War Work:* Quartermaster of "Cecils" Red Cross Hospital, Worthing, Dec. 1914, to March, 1919. *Addresses:* Seaholme, Heene Road, W. Worthing; 3, Heath Gardens, Petersfield, Hants. (M1570)

COOPER, Elizabeth, O.B.E., *b.* 20 Sept. 1861; *d.* of James Cooper, of Southampton. *Educ.:* Shirley, Southampton. Member of Council of the Royal National Mission to Deep Sea Fishermen. *War Work:* Hon. Superintendent of work among Minesweepers at Fishermen's Institute of the Royal National Mission to Deep Sea Fishermen, Milford Haven; also Hon. Sec. and Treasurer of Milford Haven and South Wales Minesweepers' Comforts Supply Association. *Address:* Caerleon, Wokingham, Berks. (O249)

COOPER, Ernest Napier, O.B.E.

COOPER, Ethel Beatrice, O.B.E.; *d.* of John Wilson Cooper, of Wincanton, Somerset (late a Principal of War Office, Whitehall, London). *Educ.:* Clapham High School. *War Work:* Organiser and Hon. Sec. Clapham War Relief Fund; also on the Executive Committee, Wandsworth Division, British Red Cross Society. *Address:* 43, The Chase, Clapham Common. London, S.W. (O10199)

COOPER, Ethel Mary, M.B.E.

COOPER, Lieut.-Col. Eustace Nugent Fitzgeorge de Radcliffe, O.B.E., M.C., R.F.A.

COOPER, Lieut. and Quartermaster Francis John, M.B.E., *b.* 19 Jan. 1879; *s.* of John Cooper, of Chipping Norton. *Educ.:* Burford Grammar School. Nurseryman. *War Work:* Enlisted, Sept. 1914, in Oxf. and Bucks Lt. Infy., became Quartermaster of 6th (Serv.) Batt.; on disbandment of that battalion, in Feb. 1918, became Quartermaster of the 20th Batt. M.G. Corps; service in France, July 1915, to April, 1919. *Address:* The Hollies, Chipping Norton. (M4454)

COOPER, Major Frederick Ernest, O.B.E., R.A.F.

COOPER, Major Geoffrey Beauchamp Astley, O.B.E., I.A.

COOPER, Capt. George Alexander Conacher, O.B.E., R.E.

COOPER, Harold Merriman, O.B.E., M.B., *b.* 25 Feb. 1873; *s.* of Horace Cooper, M.R.C.S., J.P., of Marlborough, Wilts.; *m.* Amy Wentworth, *d.* of Wentworth Tyndale, M.B., of Hampton, Middlesex. *Educ.:*. Marlborough Coll.; St. George's Hospital; London Univ. Surgeon to St. Mary's Cottage Hospital, Hampton; Poor Law Medical Officer; Public Vaccinator; District Medical Officer, Metropolitan Water Board. *War Work:* Medical Officer County of Middlesex Red Cross Hospital, Hanworth Park; Medical Officer, St. Mary's Cottage Hospital (Military Hospital), Hampton; Hon Sec. Local Medical War Committee, South Middlesex; Medical Officer, Whitehall Red Cross Hospital, Hampton Court. (O10200)

COOPER, Capt., Harold Octavius, O.B.E., R.F.A., *b.* 3 Aug. 1887; *s.* of J. E. Cooper, of Knodishall, Suffolk; *m.* Yvonne Suzanne, *d.* of Arthur Cornet-Auquier, of Chalon-sur-Saone, France. *Educ.:* Dean Close School, Cheltenham, and Corpus Christi Coll., Cambridge. Assistant Master, Dulwich College. *War Work:* Commissioned to the R.F.A. in June, 1915; Posted to C. Battery, 47th Bde., R.F.A., in France, Sept. 1915; appointed Reconnaissance Officer, R.A., to 14th Div., 1916, XIX Corps, 1917, and 4th Army, 1918. *Address:* 6, Hillcrest Road, Upper Sydenham, S.E. (O5123)

COOPER, Harry, M.B.E., I.A.

COOPER, Col. Harry, (ret.), C.M.G. C.B.E., J.P., D.L., *b.* 14 April, 1847; *s.* of late Henry Cooper, of Shooter's Hill, Kent; *m.* Emily Charlotte Ernestine, *d.* of late Capt. Henry Caldwell, C.B., R. N.. *Educ.:* Brentwood Gr. School . Royal Military College, Sandhurst. Late 47th Foot, and Staff; com. Essex Inf. Brig. 1905–11; Vice-Chairman, Essex Terr. Force Assoc., 1908–14; and commanded No. 3 Dist. 1915–17; Fenian Raids, Canada, 1866; Ashanti, 1873–74; Burma, 1886; Sudan, 1896; S. Africa, 1899–1902; France, 1914; Vice-Consul, Bosnia, 1877–8; Asia Minor, 1879–80; A.D.C. to Viceroy, India, 1884–8; A.D.C. to the Sovereign, 1898–1904. *Address:* Pakenham Lodge, Bury St. Edmund's, Suffolk. *Club:* United Service, London. (C1525)

COOPER, Major Harry, O.B.E., R.A.O.C.

COOPER, Harry Gordon, M.B.E., M.B., B.C. (Cantab.), M.A., M.R.C.S., L.R.C.P., *b.* 5 Jan. 1871; *s.* of Percy Byssche Cooper, of Manchester; *m.* Edith Warde, *d.* of Peter Johnson, of Manchester. *Educ.:* Manchester Grammar School; Emmanuel Coll., Cambridge; Victoria University. Physician and Surgeon. *War Work:* Hon. Surgeon, St. John Ambulance Brigade; Assistant County Director, Red Cross, Cheshire; Hon. Surgeon, Stamford Hospital, Dunham Massey, John Leigh Hospital, Temporary Red Cross Hospital and R.A.O.D., Altrincham. *Address:* Foye, 43, Manchester Road, Altrincham. (M1571)

COOPER, Major Henry, M.B.E.

COOPER, Henry Harold, M.B.E.

COOPER, Major Henry Sloane, O.B.E.. M.C.

COOPER, Lieut. Herbert Millburn, M.B.E., *b.* 12 April, 1885; *s.* of Joseph Cooper, of London; *m.* Jennie Frances, *d.* of William Downey, of London. *Educ.:* Privately and St. Paul's. Electrical and Mechanical Eng. *War Work:* Assistant Inspector (2 years), District Inspector (2 years) of Shell, Ontario District, under Imperial Ministry of Munitions. *Address:* 2335, Yonge Street, Toronto, Ont., Canada. (M272)

COOPER, Howard Samuel, M.B.E.

COOPER, James, M.B.E.

COOPER, James Alexander, C.B.E., J.P. Temporary Principal Clerk Finance Dept., War Office. (C471)

COOPER, Col. James Charles, C.B.E., *b.* 29 Feb. 1864: *s.* of James Cooper, of Caversham, Reading; *m.* Mary Campbell Simpson, *d.* of Hon. T. W. Hislop, of Wellington, New Zealand. *Educ.:* Brighton Coll. Insurance Manager for N.Z.; the Liverpool and London and Globe Insurance Company, Limited; twenty-five years Artillery Officer. *War Work:* Mobilized Aug. 1914, as Coast Defence Commander, and served in C.D.C. till 1920; Red Cross Work for three years, Lyttelton and Christchurch, New Zealand. *Address:* 86, Browns Road, St. Albans, Christchurch. New Zealand. *Clubs:* Canterbury (Christchurch); Wellesley (Wellington); Otago (Dunedin). (C1852)

COOPER, Major James Percy Carre, O.B.E.

COOPER, John, M.B.E.

COOPER, Juanita Carlota, Mrs., M.B.E.

COOPER, Major Lyall Newcomen, C.B.E., D.S.O. Major, R.E.; served in the Great War, 1914–18 (despatches). (C781)

COOPER, Marion Helen, M.B.E., *b.* 1874; *d.* of Rev. Canon J. H. Cooper, Vicar of Cuckfield, Sussex. *War Work:* Commandant of Red Cross Hospital, Cuckfield. *Address:* Tentercroft, Cuckfield Sussex. (M7758)

COOPER, Mary, Lady, C.B.E.; *d.* of George Smith, of Chicago, Illinois; *m.* Sir George (Bart.), *s.* of Alexander

Cooper, of Elgin N.B. (*see* BURKE'S *Peerage*). *Educ.*: Lake Forest, U.S.A., and England. *War Work*: Commandant and Donor of Hospital at Hursley Park, Winchester, from 1914–19; also maintained Belgian refugees during same period. *Addresses*: 26, Gros- venor Square, London; Hursley Park, Winchester; The College, Elgin, N.B. (C2529)

COOPER, Philip Ward, O.B.E., *b.* 8 March, 1877; *s.* ou Horace Cooper, M.R.C.S., L.R.C.P., J.P. County of Wilts.; *m.* Katharine, *d.* of Charles Rolls Foster, of Armaside, Hampton Hill. *Educ.*: Marlborough. Provincial Commissioner, Uganda Protectorate. *Address*: Fort Portal, Toro, Uganda. *Club*: Sports. (O8382)

COOPER, Major Raymond Willoughby, O.B.E., R.E.

COOPER, Lieut. Richard Tennant, M.B.E., R.E.

COOPER, Lieut.-Col. Robert Higham, C.B.E. Major and Acting Lieut.-Col. R.A.M.C.; served in the Great War, 1914–19 (despatches). (C1238)

COOPER, Robert Llewellyn Wilson, M.B.E., *b.* 21 March, 1874; *s.* of Robert Cooper, of Luton; *m.* Edith Harriet, *d.* of James Taylor, of Aberdeen. *Educ.*: Cowper Street Foundation School, City of London. Customs and Excise Department of Civil Service. *War Work*: Head of Section in Ministry of Shipping. *Address*: 79, The Avenue, Muswell Hill, London. (M3588)

COOPER, Major Robert William, O.B.E., M.C.

COOPER, Rose Ellen, The Hon. Mrs., O.B.E.

COOPER, Major Samuel Edward, M.B.E., R.E.

COOPER, Capt. Thomas, M.B.E.

COOPER, Thomas Mackay, O.B.E,. M.A., LL.B.,; *s.* of John Cooper, C.E., of Edinburgh. *Educ.*: George Watson's Coll., and Edinburgh Univ. Advocate of the Scottish Bar. *War Work*: Secretarial Assistant, War Trade Department; Liaison Officer with Ministry of Munitions, and War Priorities Committee of the War Cabinet. *Address*: 28, India Street, Edinburgh. *Club*: Northern, Edinburgh. (O10202)

COOPER, Major Vivian Bolton Douglas, M.B.E., R.E.

COOPER, Wilbraham Villiers, O.B.E.

COOPER, Capt. Walter Jackson, M.B.E., R.A.F.

COOPER, Rev. William Henry Hewlett, M.B.E.

COOPER, Lieut.-Col. William Linford Edward, O.B.E.

COOPER, Willie, O.B.E. (O11785b)

COOPER, Lieut.-Col. William Naunton Roger GILBERT-, O.B.E.

COOPER, Lieut.-Col. William Weldon HERRING-, D.S.O., O.B.E., *b.* 1873; *s.* of the late Harman Herring-Cooper, of Shrule Castle, Carlow. Entered Army Service Corps, 1901) became Capt. 1906; Major, 1914; Brevet Lieut.-Col. 1918; is an A.Q.M.G.; served in S. Africa, 1902 (despatches). (C2059)

COOTE, Comm. Bernard Trotter, O.B.E., R.N., *b.* 9 April, 1880; *s.* of Sir Algernon Coote, Bart., of Ballyfin (*see* BURKE'S *Peerage*); *m.* Grace Harriet, *d.* of the late Very Rev. John Joseph Robinson, D.D., Dean of Belfast (*see* BURKE'S *Peerage*—Avebury B). *Educ.*: Royal Navy; entered H.M.S. "Britannia," 1893 Industrial Welfare Society, 51, Palace Street, S.W. 1. *War Work*: In charge of the physical and recreational training of the Royal Navy. *Address*: Clifton House, Cart Bridge, Surrey. (O9077)

COOTE, Major John Methuen, O.B.E.

COPE, Capt. Alan Lachlan Silverwood, M.B.E., *b.* 19 Feb. 1891; *s.* of William Silverwood Cope, of 24, Collingham Gardens, S.W.; *m.* Elizabeth Masters, *d.* of Dr. Carl Stone, of Chicago, Ill., U.S.A. *Educ.*: Rugby; Univ. Coll., Oxford. *War Work*: Served with 1st Batt. The Buffs (E. Kent Regt.) in France, 1914; Acting Brigade Major, Dover Infantry Brigade, 1915–16; Adjutant, 1st Garrison Batt. The Buffs, 1916–17; Ministry of National Service, 1917–18; Co-ordination of Demobilisation Section, War Cabinet, 1919. *Address*: 24, Collingham Gardens, S.W. *Clubs*: Cavendish; Leander. (M5626)

COPE, Geoffrey Silverwood, M.B.E., *b.* 15 Feb. 1889; *s.* of William Silverwood Cope, of 24, Collingham Gardens, S W. 5. *Educ.*: St. Andrew's School, Eastbourne; Rugby; New College, Oxon. *War Work*: Joint Societies, British Red Cross and Order of St. John; Sec. Equipment Committee, The King George Hospital, S.E. 1, Nov. 1914 to June, 1915; Transport Officer, The King George Hospital, June, 1915, to Sept. 1916; Sec. The King George Hospital, Sept. 1916, to Oct. 1919. *Address*: 24, Collingham Gardens, S.W. 5. (M1572)

COPE, Surg.-Comm. Lidbroke Frank, O.B.E., R.N.

COPE, Lieut. Noel Harwood, M.B.E.

COPE, Major Thomas Francis, O.B.E.

COPELAND, Capt. David Patrick, O.B.E.

COPELAND, Capt. John Hugh, M.B.E., I.A.R.O. (M6780e)

COPEMAN, Edward Arden, M.B.E.

COPLAUS, Meyer, O.B.E. (O6356)

COPLESTON, Ada Emily, M.B.E., Q.M.A.A.C., *b.* 30 March, 1885; *d.* of William Francis, of Harlow, Essex; *m.* William Horace, *s.* of William Copleston, of Cambridge. *Educ.*: Pitman's Metropolitan School, Southampton Row, W.C. *War Work*: Served in France with Queen Mary's Army Auxiliary Corps; was first attached to the 4th Army Infantry School at Flexicourt, near Amiens; later to the Royal Army Ordnance Corps, in Calais. *Address*: c/o Mrs. Gower, Market Deeping, nr. Peterborough. (M4485)

COPLESTON, Comm. Reginald Gay, O.B.E., R.N

COPLESTONE, Frederick, C.B.E., J.P. Editor of the "Cheshire Chronicle." (C3186)

COPLEY, Brig.-Gen. Sir Alington BEWICKE-, K.B.E., C.B., J.P., D.L., *b.* 8 April, 1855 (*see* BURKE'S *Peerage*); *s.* of R. C. Bewicke Bewicke, of Coulby Manor, Cleveland; *m.* Selina Frances, *d.* of Sir Charles Watson, Bart., of Fulmer, Bucks (*see* BURKE'S *Peerage*). *Educ.*: Rugby; Merton College, Oxford; Sandhurst. 60th Rifles, 1877; A.D.C., India, 1880; D.A.A.G., West Indies, 1890; D.A.A.G., Ireland, 1892; Military Sec. Bengal, 1896; General Staff, Northern Command, 1908; Commanding 17th Infantry Brigade, 1910; Commanding West Riding Volunteers, 1914; Nile Expedition, 1884–5; N.W. Frontier, Chitral, 1895; Kurram 1897; Samana, 1897; Tirah, 1898; S. Africa, 1899. *Address*: Sprotborough Hall, Doncaster. *Clubs*: Carlton; Naval and Military; Yorkshire. (K299)

COPPINGER, Major Francis Romney, O.B.E., B.A., M.B., R.A.M.C., *b.* 10 May, 1883; *s.* of Valentine J. Coppinger, Barrister-at-Law, Dublin. *Educ.*: Dublin University. In charge of the Vaccine Department, Royal Army Medical College, Grosvenor Road, London, S.W. *War Work*: Field ambulance, and specialist in the prevention of disease, Aden Field Force, 1914–16; D.A.D.M.S. (Sanitary), Burma Division, 1916–18. *Address*: Royal Army Medical College, Grosvenor Road, London, S.W. 1. (O8454)

COPPINGER, Capt. Robert Henry, C.B.E., *b.* 1877; *s.* of the late Valentine John Coppinger, Barrister-at-law; *m.* 1909, Georgiana Katherine Grace, *d.* of the late G. Bousfield Long, of Chipping House, Wotton-under-Edge. Capt. R.N.; served in the Great War, 1914–19, with Dover Patrol and Ocean Escort (despatches). (C1184)

COPPOCK, Harry Stowe, O.B.E., B.Sc., Assoc. M.Inst. C.E., *b.* 13 Jan. 1880; *s.* of John George Coppock, of Cardiff; *m.* Ivy Jessie, *d.* of John Edgar, of Melbourne, Australia. *Educ.*: University College, Cardiff. Manager of the Gun Department at the Elswick Works of Sir W. G. Armstrong, Whitworth & Co., Ltd., Newcastle-on-Tyne. *War Work*: As manager of the Gun Department at the Elswick Works, was responsible for the manufacture of guns of all calibres, including the 18-inch long-range naval guns and the 18-inch long-range howitzers for land service; the output of guns from Messrs. Armstrong-Whitworth during the war period was approximately one-third of the national output. *Address*: c/o Edgar, 4 Bellevue Terrace, Edinburgh. (O251)

COPUS, Clarence George, M.B.E.

CORADINE, Sarah Ann, Mrs., M.B.E.

CORAH, John Reginald, M.B.E.

CORBET, Katharine, Hon. Mrs., M.B.E., Lady of Grace, St. John of Jerusalem, *b.* 1861; *d.* of 23rd Baron de Clifford (*see* BURKE'S *Peerage*; *m.* Reginald Corbet, J.P., *s.* of H. R. Corbet, of Adderly, Market Drayton. *War Work*: Commandant, Adderly Military Auxiliary Hospital, Shropshire; Organiser Y.M.C.A. Camp Work; Y.M.C.A. Member for Midland Division, National Auxiliary Committee Y.M.C.A. *Address*: Adderly, Market Drayton. *Clubs*: Ladies' Automobile; Forum. (M1574)

CORBET, Lieut. Francis Wellington, O.B.E.

CORBET, Rosamond, Mrs. Bertram D'Avenant, O.B.E., R.A.M.C.

CORBETT, Major Daniel Maurice, O.B.E., B.A., M.B., B.Ch., B.A.O., L.M., R.A.M.C., *b.* 17 Aug. 1882; *s.* of Daniel Corbett, F.R.C.S.I., of Dublin; *m.* Eleanor Louise, *d.* of Charles Samuel Hawkes, of Beckenham and Rio de Janeiro. *Educ.*: Trinity College, Dublin. *War Work*: Served in France and Belgium, Macedonia and Serbia. *Address*: c/o Holt and Co., 3, Whitehall Place, S.W. *Club*: Junior United Service. (O5133)

CORBETT, Major Edward Richard Trevor, M.B.E., J.P. (Salop), *b.* 8 Aug. 1872; *s.* of Edward Corbett, of Longnor, Salop; *m.* Marie, *d.* of Major W. E. Stuart, late 15th Hussars. *Educ.*: Eton and Trinity College, Cambridge. Chairman, Atcham Rural District Council. *War Work*: District Recruiting Officer, and subsequently Secretary, West Midland Region, under Ministry of National Service. *Address*: Longnor Hall, Shrewsbury. *Club*: Junior Army and Navy. (M276)

CORBETT, Comm. Godfrey Edwin, C.B.E.; *s.* of the late Capt. Frank Corbett, 33rd Regt., of Presteigne, Radnorshire. Com. (ret.) R.N.; Great War, 1914–18, on Blockade Patrol and with Ocean Escort (despatches). (C1185)

CORBETT, Lieut.-Col. Robert Lorimer, C.B.E., R.A.O.C.

CORBETT, Sybel, C.B.E.

CORBISHLEY, Mary Cecilia, O.B.E., R.R.C.

CORBY, Capt. Hugh George, M.B.E., R.A.F.

CORBYN, A.Lieut. Frederick James Harold,O.B.E.,R.N.R.

CORDEAUX, Edith, Mrs., M.B.E.

CORDEAUX, Col. Edward Kyme, C.B.E., Croix de Guerre (Belge), late Lincolnshire Regt., *b.* 7 Dec. 1866; *s.* of John Cordeaux, F.R.G.S., J.P., of Great Coates House, near Grimsby; *m.* Hilda (M.B.E.), *d.* of Sir Henry Bennett, D.L., J.P., of Grimsby. *Educ.*: Oakham School; Dresden. J.P. for Lincolnshire (parts of Lindsey) since 1899; S. African War, 1900–01 (Queen's medal and four clasps, despatches); European War, 1914–19; mentioned in despatches. *Address*: Brackenborough Lawn, Louth, Lincolnshire. *Club*: United Service. (C1239)

CORDEAUX, Hilda Eliza Agar, Mrs., M.B.E., *b.* 27 Oct. 1870; *d.* of Sir Henry Bennett, D.L., J.P., of Westlands, Grimsby; *m.* Col. Edward Kyme Cordeaux, C.B.E., *s.* of John Cordeaux, J.P., of Great Coates, Lincs. *Educ.*: Berlin; Lausanne. *War Work*: Commandant, Auxiliary Red Cross Hospital, Louth, Lincolnshire. *Address*: Brackenborough Lawn, Louth, Lincolnshire. (M277)

CORDEAUX, Capt. Melville Charles Dymoke, M.B.E.,M.C., b. 21 Aug. 1882 ; s. of the late Edward Cordeaux, I.C.S. *Educ.*: Privately. Served in the R.G.A. Militia, and R.F.A. (S.R.), from March, 1904, to July, 1911. *War Work*: Served in the R.G.A. (T.F.) from Aug. 1914, until disembodied, Sept. 1919 ; severely wounded at the Battle of Arras, 27 April, 1917.
(M5179)

CORDEAUX, Lieut.-Col. William Wilfred, O.B.E., J.P., b. 20 Nov. 1860 : s. of John Cordeaux, of Great Coates, Co. Lincoln ; m. Edith, d. of Capt. T. Hilton, late 19th Foot, of Sole Street, Faversham. *Educ.*: Bute House, Petersham, and St. John's Coll. Cantab. *War Work*: Cavalry Record Office, Canterbury. *Address*: Hopebourne, Harbledown, Canterbury.
(O8775)

CORDER, Lieut.-Col. Arthur Annerley, C.M.G., O.B.E. Served in the Great War, 1914–18, as Lieut.-Col. Army Ordnance Depart. (despatches). *Address*: Geendoon, Havant, Hants.
(O2877)

CORDINGLEY, Major John Walter, O.B.E., R.A.F.

CORDNER, Lieut. Edward James O'Cimidi, O.B.E., R.A.S.C. (T.F.)

CORFIELD, Lieut.-Col. Frederick Alleyne, D.S.O., O.B.E., b. 1884 ; s. of the late Frederick Channer Corfield, of Ormonde Fields, Derbyshire (*see* BURKE'S *Peerage*, Alleyne, Bt.) ; m. 1907, Mary Graham, d. of the late T. Bowater Vernon, of Hanbury, Wellington, Surrey. Major, R.A.S.C., and an A.A. and Q.M.G. with rank of Lieut.-Col. ; served in the Great War, 1914–18 (despatches). *Address*: Chatwall, Cardington, Salop.
(O5135)

CORFIELD, Mary Hay, Hon. Mrs., O.B.E., b. 14 Feb. 1871 ; d. of John, 1st Lord Inverclyde, of Castle Wemyss (*see* BURKE'S *Peerage*) ; m. Claud Evelyn Lacy, s. of the Rev. Frederick Corfield, Vicar of Shirley. President of the Mothers' Union in the Diocese of Bath and Wells ; Divisional Commissioner of Girl Guides in the County of Somerset ; a member of the Diocesan Conference of the Diocese of Bath and Wells an elected Represen.ative of the National Assembly of the Church of England. *War Work*: President of the Taunton War Hospital, Supply Depot ; President of the Central Club for young people, started during the war. *Address*: The Vicarage, Taunton.
(O10204)

CORIN, Major Herbert John, O.B.E., R.A.F., L.D.S., R.C.S.

CORK, Major Reginald Philip, O.B.E., b. 18 March, 1884 ; s. of Alfred Philip Cork, of Sloane Court, S.W. *Educ.*: Trent and Eastbourne. Member of the London Stock Exchange Served with the 22nd Batt. London Regt. (The Queens), and the Machine Gun Corps. *Club*: Junior Army and Navy.
(O5136)

CORKE, Edward Stanton, M.B.E.
(M10438)

CORKERY, Lieut.-Col. Martin Percy, O.B.E., R.A.M.C.

CORKHILL, Percy Fullerton, C.B.E., b. 21 Nov. 1873 ; s. of Thomas Corkhill, of Kirkmichael. *Educ.*: Liverpool. Solicitor ; Secretary to the Lord Mayor of Liverpool ; Hon. Tres., Association of Local War Pensions Committees. *War Work*: Honorary Organiser of Roll of Honour Fund, Lord Mayor's Million Shilling Fund ; Lord Mayor's Silver Badge Fund ; Hon. Sec., "Lusitania" Fund ; Joint Hon. Sec., Soldiers' and Sailors' Help Society. *Address*: 18, Rufford Road, Liverpool.
(C2530)

CORKING, Qr.-Mr. and Capt. James William, O.B.E., R.A.M.C. (T.F.)

CORKRAN, Florence Caroline Seymour, C.B.E., b. 6 May, 1851 ; d. of Sir Charles Lennox Peel, K.C.B. ; m. Charles Seymour, late Col., Grenadier Guards, s. of Charles Corkran, Long Ditton, Surrey. Lady of Justice of the Order of St. John of Jerusalem ; Order of the League of Mercy. *War Work*: Officers' Families Fund with Marchioness of Lansdowne, both in the South African War and the Great War. *Address*: 39, Lowndes Square, S.W.
(C2531)

CORKRAN, Helena Muriel Seymour, M.B.E. ; d. of Col. Charles Seymour Corkran, of 39, Lowndes Square, London. *War Work*: Queen Mary's Needlework Guild (voluntary), Head Officer, St. James' Palace, Aug. 1914–19. *Address*: 39, Lowndes Square, W.
(M7761)

CORKRAN, Sybil Florence, M.B.E. ; d. of Col. Seymour Corkran, late Grenadier Guards. *War Work*: Officers' Families' Fund, from Sept. 1914, to Feb. 1919. *Address*: 39, Lowndes Square, S.W.
(M3589)

CORLESS, Richard, O.B.E., M.A., b. 10 Oct. 1884 ; s. of James Corless, of Goosnargh, nr. Preston, Lancs. ; m. Etheline, d. of Samuel Oaten, of Tunbridge Wells. *Educ.*: Preston Grammar School, and Sidney Sussex Coll., Cambridge. Superintendent of Instruments, Meteorological Office. *War Work*: Arrangements for the supply of Meteorological Instruments to Navy, Army and Royal Air Force. *Address*: 21, Wimborne Gardens, West Ealing, W. 13.
(O3670)

CORLETT, Arthur Ready, O.B.E., b. 8 Sept. 1873 ; s. of the late Rev. John Corlett, of St. John's, Isle of Man ; m. Eleanor Jane, d. of William Christian, of Douglas, Isle of Man. *Educ.*: King William's College, Castletown, Isle of Man. Third Officer, Manchester Fire Brigade, July, 1898 ; Second Officer, April, 1904 ; Chief Officer, Nov. 1916. *War Work*: As Chief Officer, Manchester Fire Brigade, attended fires in premises engaged in the production of munitions of war, especially, high explosives. *Address*: Headquarters, Fire Dept., London Road, Manchester.
(O10205)

CORLETTE, Major Hubert Christian, O.B.E., F.R.I.B.A., R.B.C., b. 27 June, 1869 ; s. of late Rev. Canon James Christian

Corlette, D.D. (Oxon.), of Ashfield, Sydney, N.S.W., Australia m. Florence Gwynedd, d. of Arthur V. Davies-Berrington, of Pant-y-Goitre, Monmouthshire. *Educ.*: Sydney Grammar School ; Sydney Univ. ; Univ. Coll., London ; Royal Academy of Arts, (School of Architecture), London ; Seade School of Fine Art. *War Work*: Major, 1st King Edward's Horse, The King's Oversea Dominions Regiment (Special Reserve Cavalry) on outbreak of War ; attached R.F.A., 1915–16 ; employed on Staff Duty, 1916–18 ; attached to Ministry of Agriculture, 1918–20, under War Office orders, as Head of Labour Section for recruiting and demobilisation duty. *Addresses*: 28, Palace Gardens Terrace, W. 8 ; 2, New Square, Lincoln's Inn, W.C. *Club*: Arts.
(O10206)

CORMACK, George, M.B.E., b. 6 Jan. 1852 ; s. of Donald Cormack, of Wick ; m. Jane Johnston, d. of Alexander Blackhall, of Fraserburgh. *Educ.*: Public School, Fraserburgh. 35 years' service as Fishery Officer, under the Fishery Board for Scotland (now retired). *War Work*: For the services rendered as a Fishery Officer, under the Fishery Board for Scotland, and as Fish Executive Officer, under the Ministry of Food ; these duties were carried on during the war to the entire satisfaction of the above Departments, and also the satisfaction of the traders and members of the community of Fraserburgh Fishery District.
(M7762)

CORMACK, Brig.-Gen. John Dewar, C.M.G., C.B.E., b. 1870 ; s. of the late Alexander Cormack, of Dumbarton ; m. 1902, Fanny, d. of the late John Lister, of Leeds. *Educ.*: Glasgow Univ. (B.Sc. double 1st class Honours, 1892) ; D.Sc. Brussels ; M.I.C.E., M.I.M.E., M.I.E.E. Is an Hon. Brig.-Gen., Regius Professor of Civil Engineering and Mechanics, Glasgow Univ., and a Chevalier of Legion of Honour ; sometime Professor of Mechanical Engineering, Univ. Coll., London ; appointed Chief Contracts Officer, Mil. Aeronautics at War Office, 1915 ; Assist. Director, Aircraft Equipment, 1916, and Director there of Supply and Production (Air Board), 1917 ; was Chief Representative Air Board and Chief Representative Aero Supply Dept., Ministry of Munitions in U.S.A., 1917–18 ; author of various scientific and literary papers. *Addresses*: 11, Park Terrace, Glasgow ; 37, Hyde Park Gate, S.W.
(C1125)

CORNABE, Comm. William Eckford, O.B.E., R.N.

CORNELL, Frederick Carruthers, O.B.E.

CORNER, Kate Agnes, M.B.E.

CORNER, Sylvia, M.B.E.

CORNER, Capt. William, O.B.E., b. 25 Nov. 1893 ; s. of William Corner, of Inverness. *Educ.*: Inverness Royal Academy, and Modern Univ. Medical practitioner. *War Work*: R.A.M.C. ; now attached to the new Civil Hospital, Bagdad, Mesopotamia. *Address*: Brookside, Drummond Road, Inverness.
(O6600)

CORNETT, Major Alexander Don, O.B.E.

CORNEY, Lieut. and Qr.-Mr. Albert, M.B.E.

CORNISH, William Delhi, O.B.E., J.P.

CORNS, Eng.-Lieut. Frederick Samson, M.B.E., R.N.R., b. 13 Dec. 1857 ; s. of W. L. Corns, of Newton Heath, Nr. Manchester ; m. Alice Milocent Ursula, d. of P. W. Smyth, of South Norwood, London, S.E. *Educ.*: Privately. Engineer (retired). *War Work*: Serving on board the Cable ship, "John Pender," as Chief Engineer while maintaining, laying, and repairing submarine cables, etc. *Address*: 36, Connaught Avenue, Plymouth. *Club*: Plymouth.
(M7763)

CORNWALL, Lieut.-Col. James Handyside Marshall, C.B.E. D.S.O., M.C., R.F.A., b. 27 May, 1887 ; s. of James Cornwall, 24 Drumsheugh Gardens, Edinburgh. *Educ.*: Edinburgh Academy ; Cargilfield ; Rugby ; Woolwich. *War Work*: Served in France and Belgium, Aug. 1914, to Jan. 1918 ; employed in Military Intelligence, War Office, Jan. 1918, to April, 1919. *Clubs*: United Service ; Royal Automobile ; Phyllis Court.
(C2094)

CORNWALL, Lily Elizabeth Frances, M.B.E. (M10246a)

CORNWALLIS, Hon. Col. Fiennes Stanley Wykeham, C.B.E., T.D., J.P., D.L., b. 17 May, 1864 ; s. of the late Major Fiennes Cornwallis, of Chacombe, near Banbury ; m. 1886, Mabel, d. of the late Capt, O. P. Leigh, of Belmont, Cheshire. *Educ.*: Eton. Chairman, Kent County Council ; Chairman, Kent War Agricultural Executive Committee ; Prov. G.M. Kent Freemasons ; Trustee, R.A.S.E. and Past President ; formerly M.P. for Maidstone. *War Work*: Major, Hon. Col., 2/1st West Kent Yeomanry ; War Agricultural Executive Committee. *Address*: Linton Park Maidstone. *Club*: Carlton.
(C472)

CORNWALLIS, Lieut.-Col. Kinahan, C.B.E., D.S.O., Major and T. Lieut.-Col. Special List ; served in the Great War, 1914–19 (despatches, Order of the Nile).
(O1273)

CORNWALLIS, Lieut. Oswald Wykeham, O.B.E., R.N.

CORRALL, Capt. George Edward, O.B.E.

CORRIE, Donald Welldon, M.B.E., B.A. (Cantab), b. 29 Aug. 1886 ; s. of Edward Knowles Corrie, of 4, Chislehurst Road, Richmond, Surrey ; m. Vera Maude, d. of William Brown, J.P., of Challoners, Rottingdean, Sussex. *Educ.*: Eton Coll. (Foundation Scholar), 1901–5 ; King's Coll., Camb. (Scholar), 1905–10. Chancellor's English Verse Medallist, 1907 ; called to Bar (Inner Temple), 1911 ; appointed Junior Examiner, Board of Education, 1914. *War Work*: Lent to Ministry of Munitions, July, 1915, to June 1920 ; Private Sec. to Director of Munition Contracts, 1915 ; Sec. to Canadian Branch (R.I.M.B.), 1916–18 ; Statistical Branch, D.M.R.S., 1918–20 ; War Office (Factories Branch) June to Nov. 1920. *Address*: Cromden Lodge, Reigate, Surrey. *Clubs*: M.C.C. ; Eton Ramblers ; Butterflies ; Cryptics.
(M1576)

CORRIE, Lieut. William Edward, M.B.E.

CORRIE, William Malcolm, O.B.E., *b.* 3 April, 1851 ; *s.* of John Malcolm Corrie, of Itchen Abbas, Hants ; *m.* Margaret Louisa, *d.* of Macgregor Laird, of Birkenhead. *Educ.:* Winchester. *War Work :* Organised and directed throughout the war a hospital (bénévole) for wounded officers at Biarritz, offered and financed by Mr. J. Kennedy Tod, of New York ; helped to organise and maintain throughout the war a Corps of Brancardiers and Ambulances for the convoys of wounded, receiving thanks of the French Government and the Medaille de la reconnaissance Française ; helped to organise and maintain a club for wounded soldiers, and agency for tracing missing wounded and dead. *Addresses :* Kelwood, St. John's, Woking ; Gurutzea, St. Jean de Luz, B.P., France. *Club :* British, Biarritz, B.P.   (O10207)

CORRIGAN, Major Albert Arthur, M.B.E.

CORRIGAN, John, M.B.E.,

CORRY, Alice Maude, Mrs., M.B.E,

CORSCADEN, Fannie Evelyn, Mrs., M.B.E., *d.* of Bartholomew McCorkell, of Richmond, Londonderry ; *m.* Robert Corscaden. Vice-President Londonderry Women's Unionist Association ; Member of Executive Committee, Ulster Women's Unionist Council. *War Work :* Committee of Sailors' Rest, Londonderry (British and Foreign Sailors' Society) ; presented a house to render premises large enough to deal with torpedoed crews and thousands of other sailors ; supported and worked for Red Cross, Regimental Comforts, etc. ; gave a room in her house for packing and collection in connection with Red Cross Stores. *Address :* Richmond, Londonderry. *Club :* Ladies' Army and Navy.   (M7764)

CORSI, Anthony Joseph, M.B.E.

CORSI, Manual Gregory, M.B.E.

CORT, Capt. William Percy, M.B.E., Special Reserve R.F.C., and Unemployed List R.A.F., *b.* 7 July, 1890 ; *s.* of William Smith Cort, J.P., of Market Harborough ; *m.* Edith Emma, *d.* of Joseph Stapleford, of Leicester. *Educ.:* Privately, and Edward VII Grammar School. *War Work :* One of the original six night-flying pilots of the Royal Flying Corps ; commanded first night-flying detachment, R.F.C., in East London ; after active overseas service returned to command the first R.A.F. School of Wireless Telephony, Penshurst, Kent. *Addresses :* 52, Howitt Road, Belsize Park, N.W. 3 ; Sibbertoft, Northants. *Club :* R.F.C.   (M3371)

CORY, Major Evan James Trevor, O.B.E., R.A.M.C.(T.F.)

CORY, Mabel Emily Hartridge, Mrs., M.B.E.

COSENS, Peter Hunter, M.B.E., *b.* 25 May, 1865 ; *s.* of Rev. A. T. Cosens, Broughton, Peeblesshire. *Educ.:* Royal High School, and Univ. of Edinburgh. Writer to the Signet. *War Work :* Hon. Sec. Scottish Freshwater Fisheries Commission. *Address :* 17, Hope Terrace, Edinburgh. *Club :* Conservative, Edinburgh.   (M7765)

COSGRAVE, Capt. Frederick John, M.B.E., *b.* 3 Dec. 1870 ; *s.* of Frederick Michael Cosgrave, of Co. Kildare, Ireland ; *m.* Ellen Agnes, *d.* of Thomas Strudwick, of Arundel, Sussex. *Educ.:* Claremont Academy. Joined 4th Dragoon Guards, 1889 ; served in India, 1894–1904 ; took part in the Relief of Chitral, 1895 (medal and clasp) ; Tirah Campaign, 1897 (medal and clasp) ; N.-W. Frontier of India, 1897–98 (Medal and clasp). *War Work :* During Great War, served with 2nd Mounted Division in Egypt, Gallipoli (Suvla Bay Landing, Aug. 1915) ; Senussi Campaign, 1915–16 ; and Turkish Invasion of Egypt, Feb. 1915. *Address :* Shabani, Rhodesia.   (M5180)

COSGRIFF, Eugene, M.B.E.

COSGROVE, James, O.B.E., *b.* 21 Aug. 1879 ; *s.* of late James Cosgrove, of Aberdeen ; *m.* Elizabeth, *d.* of William Ritchie, of Aberdeen. *Educ.:* Aberdeen. Chief Engineer, P. & O. Steam Navigation Co. *War Work :* Transport of troops, during the whole period of the War. *Address :* 110, De Vere Gardens, Cranbrook Park, Ilford.   (O1236)

COSGROVE, Capt. and Qr.-Mr. Thomas Patrick, M.B.E.

COSSEY, Capt. Harry John Moore, O.B.E., R.A.S.C.

COSSGROVE, Capt. David Cecil Wallace, M.B.E.

COSTELLO, Lieut. George Arthur, M.B.E., R.E.

COSTELLO, Frederick, O.B.E.

COSTER, Gaius William, M.B.E.

COSTIGAN, Charles Samuel, M.B.E., *b.* 12 June, 1870 ; *s.* of the late Charles Costigan, of Liverpool ; *m.* Eleanor Clementina, *d.* of the late Thomas Daniels, T.C., of Liverpool and Southport. *Educ.:* Liverpool College. Fellow of the Auctioneers' Institute ; Sec. of the Sefton Hall Co., Ltd., Liverpool ; Auctioneer, Appraiser and Fire Loss Assessor. *War Work :* Commandant of the West Lancashire T.F.A. Voluntary Aid Detachment No. 25 ; O.C. of the Liverpool Ambulance Co. ; supplied the V.A.D. Orderlies at 6 Hospitals in Liverpool. *Addresses :* 97, Park Road, and 1, Upper Park Street, Liverpool, S. ; Merllyn, Hartington Road, Sefton Park, Liverpool.   (M7767)

COSWAY, Leopold Harold Baskerville, O.B.E. (O8075)

COTTELL, Amy Joan, M.B.E., *b.* 13 Nov. 1887 ; *d.* of Mark Cottell, of St. Breward, Bodmin. *Educ.:* Privately, and Goldsmiths' Coll., New Cross. *War Work :* British War Mission on Lord Northcliffe's personal staff. *Address :* 63, Taunton Road, Lee, Kent.   (M1578)

COTTELL, Lieut.-Col. and Bt. Col. Reginald James Cope, C.B.E., Knight of Grace of Order of St. John of Jerusalem, late R.A.M.C., *b.* 13 Oct. 1858 ; *s.* of late Major J. W. Cottell, H.E.I.C.S. ; *m.* Edith Clementina, *d.* of James Ruthven, of Hull. Physician and Surgeon to the Royal Hospital, Chelsea ; Officer-in-Charge, The King George Hospital, London ; South African War. 1899–1902 (Queen's

medal, three clasps, and King's medal, two clasps). *War Work :* Medical Officer in charge of Recruiting, Stratford, London, 1914–15, and from May, 1915, to Sept. 1919, Officer-in-charge of the King George Hospital, Stamford Street, London. *Address :* 7, Phillimore Terrace, Kensington, W. 8.   (C1526)

COTTER, Joseph, O.B.E.

COTTERELL, Mabel, O.B.E., *d.* of George Cotterell, of York. *Educ.:* York High School, and privately. Organising Sec. to Women's National Committee to secure State Purchase and Control of the Liquor Trade. *War Work :* Opened Girls' Patriotic Clubs at Ipswich, Chatham, Hull, for Y.W.C.A., 1915 ; Lady Superintendent Welfare Department, H.M. Factory, Gretna, N.B., 1916–19. *Addresses :* Parliament Mansions, Victoria Street, S.W. 1 ; 64, Belsize Lane, N.W. 3.   (O1237)

COTTERELL, Thomas Sturge, M.B.E., J.P., *b.* 10 March, 1865 ; *s.* of Frederick Fowler Cotterell, of Clevedon, Somerset. *Educ.:* Sidcot School, Somerset ; Olivers Mount, Scarborough. Justice of the Peace for Bath since 1902 ; City Councillor, Bath, for 14 years. *War Work :* Senior Superintendent of H.M. Magazines during the war for Ministry of Munitions. *Address :* High Cleare, Bath, Somerset.   (M1579)

COTTLE, Adela, Mrs., C.B.E.,

COTTLE, Clifford John, M.B.E. ; *s.* of John Cottle, of Bristol ; *m.* Sarah, *d.* of George Chittenden, of Snodland, Kent. *Educ. :* Council School, Bristol. Church Army Evangelist. *War Work :* Friends of the Wounded Department, Church Army ; organised outings and personal care of lonely men ; 27,000 taken for drives, concerts, garden parties, the whole cost of which was borne by the Church Army. *Address :* 187, Marylebone Road, London, N.W. 1.   (M3590)

COTTLE, Flying Officer Jack, M.B.E., D.F.C.

COTTLE, Lieut. and Qr.-Mr. Joseph, M.B.E., R.A.M.C., *b.* 23 Feb. 1886 ; *s.* of Joseph Cottle, of Bristol ; *m.* Ethel May, *d.* of William Rogers, of Bath. *Educ. :* Russell Town, Bristol. Joined H.M. Forces Feb. 1902, and served in the ranks until June, 1917, when promoted in the field to a commission as Lieut. and Qr.-Mr. ; proceeded on Active Service March, 1915, and served overseas until Aug. 1919, during which time was with Field Ambulance doing front-line work ; served in France, Belgium, and Italy ; appointed O.C. 2/1st N.M. Field Ambulance (Cadre), May, 1919. *Address :* 3, Congleton Road, St. George, Bristol. *Clubs :* Regimental ; Broad Plain Social, Bristol.   (M4726)

COTTLE, Capt. Peter James, O.B.E., M.C., R.E.

COTTON, Alonzo, M.B.E., *b.* 6 Oct. 1862 ; *s.* of Thomas Nathaniel Cotton, of Bristol ; *m.* Sarah Ann, *d.* of John Hares, of Bristol. Supt. of Transport, St. John Ambulance Brigade, City of Bristol Corps. *War Work :* Commandant V.A.D., S.J.A.B., Bristol 5 ; disembarking and embarking wounded from H.M. Hospital Ships at Avonmouth Dock ; Bristol Special Constabulary. *Address :* 100, Barton Hill Road, Bristol. *Club :* R.A.O.B., Bristol.   (M3591)

COTTON, Annie, Mrs., M.B.E. ; *d.* of the late Venble. Alfred Pott, Archdeacon of Berks. *War Work :* Lent private house as hospital, 1915–18 ; Commandant of the Red Cross V.A.D. Convalescent Home, 1918–10.   (M7768)

COTTON, Archibald James, M.B.E.

COTTON, Col. Arthur Stedman, C.M.G., C.B.E., D.S.O., A.M., R.F.A., *b.* 18 Aug. 1873 ; *s.* of the late Major J. W. M. Cotton, J.P., late of 21st Hussars, and 9th Foot ; *m.* Rose, *d.* of the late Robert Bousfield, D.L. of County of Kent. *Educ.:* Merchant Taylors' and R.M.A., Woolwich. *War Work :* Served from Aug. 1914 to the Armistice on the Western Front and occupation of Germany ; British Military Mission to S. Russia, 1919–20 ; 3 times wounded, 9 times mentioned in despatches ; awarded Bt. Lieut.-Col., 1916 ; Bt. Col., 1919 ; C.M.G., 1919 ; C.B.E., 1920 ; D.S.O., 1915 ; and A.M. (Gazette 16 July, 1920) ; Foreign decorations : St. Vladimir (Russia), 3rd Class ; St. Maurice and St. Lazarus (Italy) Officer ; Croix de guerre avec palmes (France) ; Croix de guerre (Belgium). *Address :* Perron Lodge, Branksome, Bournemouth. *Club :* Army and Navy. (C3126)

COTTON, Charles, O.B.E., F.R.C.P., M.R.C.S. (Eng.), Knight of Grace of St. John of Jerusalem, *b.* 7 Feb. 1856 ; *s.* of Hugh Powell Cotton, of Seaway, Cockington, Torquay ; *m.* Adelaide, *d.* of the late Major-Gen. Robert Thomas Leigh, Bengal Staff Corps, of Ilfracombe, Devon. *Educ.:* Western Grammar School ; King's Coll., London ; St. George's Hospital. Commissioner Commanding No. 8 District (Kent, Surrey, and Sussex) St. John Ambulance Brigade ; Hon. Librarian, Christ Church Cathedral, Canterbury. *War Work :* Assist. County Director (formerly County Director) Kent V.A.D. Organisation. *Address :* Briarfield, Ethelbert Road, Canterbury. (O10208)

COTTON, George Frederick, M.V.O., M.B.E.

COTTON, Harry, M.B.E., B.Sc., F.R.Met.S., *b.* 17 June, 1889 ; *s.* of J. T. Cotton, of Hanley, Staffs. ; *m.* Lilian, *d.* of G. R. Hall, of Hanley, Staffs. *Educ.:* Victoria Univ. of Manchester. Senior Lecturer in Electrical Engineering, Univ. Coll., Nottingham. *War Work :* Observer in Meteorological Section, R.E. *Address :* Waverley House, Waverley Street, Nottingham.   (M4557)

COTTON, James Temple, M.B.E., *b.* 12 Nov. 1879 ; *s.* of George Frederick Cotton, of Clapham ; *m.* Laura Beatrice, *d.* of W. G. Dunnett, of Ipswich. *Educ.:* Stationers' Company's School, and Birkbeck Coll. Held appointments in various Government Depts., including Board of Trade, Scottish Education Office, Estate Duty Office, Inland Revenue, Office of Works, Admiralty, and Air Ministry. *War Work:* Trade Division, Admiralty. Civil assistant to Assist. Chief of Naval Staff; and Secretary's Department of Admiralty. *Addresses:* Ellerslie, Westcott, Dorking; Air Ministry, Kingsway, W.C. 2. (M1581)

COTTON, Capt. Maurice John, O.B.E.

COTTON, Major Percy Vernon, O.B.E.

COTTON, Major Vere Egerton, O.B.E., R.G.A. (T.), *b.* 5 May, 1888; *s.* of the late Charles C. Cotton. *Educ.:* Repton; Magdalene Coll., Cambridge. *Address:* 2, Blackburne Terrace, Hope Street, Liverpool. (O2974)

COTTON, Major William Ernest Leslie, O.B.E., M.C., Croix de Guerre, *b.* 31 July, 1888; *s.* of Ernest E. Cotton, J.P., of Bromsgrove, Worcestershire; *m.* Doris May, *d.* of William Rowe, of Worcester. *Educ.:* Bromsgrove School. Engineer; director of Easton, Lloyd & Co., Ltd., Birmingham. *War Work:* Mobilized 5 Aug. 1914; commanding a company in the 8th Bn. the Worcestershire Regt., T.F.; France, March, 1915; Brigade Transport Officer; Staff Capt. 144 Inf. Brigade, 1916–17; D.A.Q.M.G., H.Q., Fourth Army, 1917–19; now 2nd in Command, 8th Bn. Worcestershire Regt. *Address:* 43, Britannia Sq., Worcester. (O2480)

COTTON, Olive Harriet STAPLETON-, Mrs., O.B.E., *b.* 1883; *d.* of the late Col. Sir Edward Cotton-Jodrell, K.C.B., of Reaseheath Hall, Nantwich; *m.* Richard Greville Arthur Wellington, *s.* of Col. Hon. R. Stapleton-Cotton, of Llwynon, Anglesey (*see* BURKE'S *Peerage*). *War Work:* Vice-President, Cheshire B.R.C.S. till 1915; Hon. Commandant V.A.D. Cheshire No. 4; organised V.A.D. Hospital, Nantwich, Nov. 1914; In Portsmouth was from outbreak of war member of S. & S. F. A., and subsequently of War Pensions Committee; Member of N.S.P.C.C. and Royal Portsmouth Hospital Committee of Management, representing War Pensions Committee; Chairman of Royal Naval Crèche for War Orphans; Member of Portsmouth Navy League Education Committee. *Address:* Lennox Road, Portsmouth. (O10017)

COTTON, Capt. Richard Greville Arthur Wellington STAPLETON-, C.B.E., M.V.O., R.N., *b.* 7 Nov. 1873; *s.* of Richard Southwall George Stapleton-Cotton, heir-presumptive to the Viscounty of Combermere (*see* BURKE'S *Peerage*); *m.* 9 Aug. 1910, Olive Harriet, O.B.E., *y. d.* of Lieut.-Col. Sir Edward T. D. Cotton-Jodrell, K.C.B. Served in the Great War; has Order of the Crown of Italy. (C2282)

COTTRELL, Comm. William Henry, C.M.G., O.B.E.; *s.* of the late Major W. F. Cottrell; *m.* 1889, Louisa Celestina Baglietto. Com., Roy. Naval Vol. Reserve; served at Dardanelles, 1915 (despatches). (O3476)

COTTS, Sir William Dingwall Mitchell, K.B.E., J.P., *b.* 15 July, 1871; *s.* of William Cotts, of Sanquhar, Dumfriesshire, N.B.; *m.* Agnes Nivison, *d.* of Robert Sloane, of Sanquhar, Dumfriesshire, N.B. *Educ.:* Privately, and at Wallace Hall Academy, Dumfriesshire. Colonial Merchant; Shipowner and Colliery Proprietor. *War Work:* Services in connection with Recruiting. *Addresses:* 24, Hans Place, S.W.; 8, St. Helen's Place, E.C. *Clubs:* City, Cape-town; London—New City; National Liberal; Automobile; Thatched House; Royal Societies'. (K313)

COUBROUGH, Anthony Cathcart, C.B.E., M.A., B.Sc. M.I.E.E., M.I.M.E., *b.* 1877; *s.* of Anthony Sykes Coubrough, J.P., of Blanefield, Stirlingshire. *Educ.:* Albany Acad., and Univ. of Glasgow. Engineer; Gen. Manager for India of Mather and Platt (Limited), engineers, of Manchester, London and Calcutta; Controller, Munitions Board, 1917–19. *Club:* Bengal (Calcutta). (C1071)

COUCHMAN, Sir Francis Dundas, K.B.E., M.Inst.C.E, *b.* 15 Feb. 1864; *s.* of the late Thomas Barnes Couchman, of Henley-in-Arden, Warwickshire; *m.* Isabella McLean (Daisy), *d.* of the late Lieut.-Col. Donat Edward McMahon. Entered State Railways, India, 1886; was Consulting Engineer for Railways, Calcutta, 1899–1900; Under-Sec. to Government of India, Railway Branch, 1901–5; Sec. and Consulting Engineer for Railways, Burma, 1906–8; Chief Engineer Burma Railways, 1909–12; Agent and General Manager, 1912–15; Member of the Railway Board from April, 1915, to Nov., 1920. *Address:* Instow, N. Devon. *Club:* East India United Service. (K328)

COULCHER, Mary Caroline, C.B.E., *b.* 1852; *d.* of Rev. George Coulcher. *Educ.:* Lymington House School, Clapham Park. Vice-President, British Red Cross Society for Ipswich; late Lady District Supt. St. John Ambulance Brigade, and a Lady of Grace of the Order of St. John of Jerusalem in England; has Coronation Medal, 1911, and Service Medal (2 bars). *War Work:* Commandant, V.A.D., Suffolk 22; Commandant, Gippeswyk Hall Military Isolation Hospital, Ipswich, and Broadwater Auxilliary Hospital, Ipswich; East Suffolk War Relief Committee Executive. *Address:* Beechholme, Ipswich. *Club:* V.A.D. Ladies'. (C2533)

COULON, Major Frederick Coulon, O.B.E., M.G.C.

COULSON, Lieut.-Col. Basil John Blenkinsopp, C.B.E., K.O.S.B.

COULSON, Edith Mabel, M.B.E.; *d.* of the late Corry Coulson, of Newtownbutler, Co. Fermanagh. *Educ.:* Dublin and Germany. Asst. Private Sec. to H.E. The Lord Lieutenant of Ireland. *War Work:* Department of Recruiting for Ireland, 1915–16; Assist. Private Sec. to H.E. The Lord Lieutenant. *Address:* Vice-Regal Lodge, Dublin. (M7770)

COULSON, Bt. Lieut.-Col. Frank Morris, C.B.E., *b.* 10 July, 1880; *s.* of Morris Coulson, of High Holborn; *m.* Beatrice Mary, *d.* of Arthur William Anderson, of Prince's St.,

Hanover Sq., W. *Educ.:* Privately. Interested in the work of the Dutch painters of the seventeenth century; South Africa, 1901–02; Queen's medal and 5 clasps. *War Work:* Acting paymaster, 1914, Warwick; Capt. and Paymaster, May, 1917, Warwick; Major and Staff Paymaster, Oct. 1917, Lichfield and War Office; Bt. Lieut.-Col. Jan. 1919, War Office. *Address:* 34, Telford Avenue, S.W. 2. *Club:* The Officers' Association. (C2096)

COULSON, Lieut. Horace Wilkinson, M.B.E., R.E. (T.F.).

COULSON, Capt. Thomas, O.B.E.

COULSON, William Ernest, M.B.E., A.I.C.S., *b.* 18 May, 1865; *s.* of George Coulson, of Cherry Burton; *m.* Mary Elizabeth, *d.* of Henry Creaser, of Dunnington, York. *Educ.:* Dyson's Boarding School, Beverley. Previously Member of the Cottingham Urban District Council for ten years, including Chairman. *War Work:* 1st Representative Ministry of Shipping, Malta Dockyard; Chairman of the Food Control Committee, and Allotment Committee; Member of the Tribunal; Chairman, Urban District Council; Member of the Charities Act Committee. *Clubs:* Hull Constitutional; Pacific; Hull Exchange; Hornsea. (M7771)

COULTER, Lieut. Percival Arthur, M.B.E.

COUNAHAN, Michael Tyrell, M.B.E., *s.* of Gerald Counahan, of C. Louth; *m.* Theresa, *d.* of James Cantwell, of Dublin and Co. Tipperary. Collector of Customs and Excise, Cork, Ireland. *War Work:* Examination of papers of ships brought into Queenstown, etc., by Admiralty, under Retaliation Prize Traders, which led to the confiscation of enemy property of about £250,000; controlled work of Alien Officers; put in force orders respecting illegal shipment of oil; as Head Receiver of Wrecks took charge of and disposed of perhaps the largest number of Droits in the U.K.; acted generally in co-operation with the Navy as regards ships, routes and notification of enemy submarines. *Address:* 6, Wellesley Terrace, Wellington Road, Cork. (M7772)

COUPER, Chief Carpenter John, M.B.E., R.N.

COUPER, John Charles, O.B.E., *b.* 1867; *s.* of Charles Tennant Couper, of Woodstone Row, Dumbartonshire; *m.* Elsie Winifred, *d.* of Benjamin Hall Blyth, C.E., of Edinburgh. *Educ.:* Winchester, Edinburgh University. Writer to His Majesty's Signet; Pursebearer to His Majesty's Lord High Commissioner to the General Assembly of the Church of Scotland. *War Work:* Chief Military Representative, City of Edinburgh Tribunals, and thereafter Chief National Service Representative for Edinburgh Area, including counties of West Lothian, Peebles, etc., 1915–18. *Address:* 17, Palmerston Place, Edinburgh; Kaimend, North Berwick. *Clubs:* New Edinburgh; Hon. Co. of Edinburgh Golfers. (O1239).

COUPER, Col. John Duncan Campbell, C.B.E.; Col. R.E.; served in the Great War, 1914–19 (despatches). (C1240)

COUPER, Major Peter, O.B.E.

COURAGE, Comm. Archibald Vesey, O.B.E., R.N.

COURAGE, Francis Zoe, Mrs., M.B.E.

COURATIN, Paul Evelyn, M.B.E.

COURSE, Sarah Denton, Mrs., M.B.E.

COURT, Charles Edward, O.B.E., *b.* 1869; *s.* of the late John Court, of Kendal; *m.* Mary J., *d.* of E. R. Martindale, of Crake Trees, near Kendal. 1916–19, Chairman of the Ulverston Urban District Council. *War Work:* Chairman of the following Committees: War Savings, Food Control, Red Cross, and Y.M.C.A. Hut Week; Member of the Tribunal. *Address:* Elm Lodge, Ulverston, Lancs. (O10210)

COURT, Eleanor Rosina, M.B.E.

COURT, Lieut. Henry Darlington Harold, M.B.E., R.E.

COURT, Lilian, M.B.E.

COURT, Lilian Ethel, M.B.E.

COURT, Capt. Sidney Herbert, O.B.E.. R.E.

COURT, William Albert, M.B.E., *b.* 2 June, 1877. Surveyor of Stores, H.M. Dockyard, Chatham. *War Work:* Admiralty Constructive Repair Overseer, Glasgow; in this capacity was responsible for the oversight of the docking and refitting of all H.M. vessels sent to the upper reaches of the Clyde for repair during the war. (M7775)

COURTNEY, Wing-Comm. Christopher Lloyd, C.B.E., D.S.O.; Wing-Comm. R.A.F.; served in the Great War, 1914–18 (despatches). (C855)

COURTNEY, Col. Edward Arthur Waldegrave, C.M.G., C.B.E., *b.* 1868; *e. s.* of the late Maj.-Gen. Edward Henry Courtney, C.V.O., R.E., Governor of Mil. Knights of Windsor; *m.* 1894, Hilda Maria, *y.d.* of the late T. E. Chapman, of Silksworth Hall, Co. Durham. Entered Lancashire Fusiliers, 1889; became Capt. Army Service Corps, 1896; Major, 1903; Lieut.-Col. 1912; Col. 1917; served during S. African War, 1899–1901; present at actions of Paardeberg, Driefontein, and Poplar Grove, and at relief of Kimberley (Queen's medal with six clasps). *War Services:* 1914–18, as Dep. Director and then as Director of Requisition Services (despatches, Order of Leopold of Belgium, Legion of Honour, Croix de Guerre); Dep. Assist. Director of Supplies and Transport, E. Command, 1906–10; is Assist. Director of Supplies and Transport, N. Command. *Clubs:* York; United Service. (C473)

COURTNEY, Wing-Comm. Ivon Terence, C.B.E.; Wing-Comm. R.A.F.; served in the Great War, 1914–19 (despatches). (C2337)

COURTNEY, Janet Elizabeth, Mrs. William Leonard, O.B.E.

COURTNEY, Capt. Reginald Aloysius, M.B.E., R.A.F.

COURTNEY, Reginald Sydney, O.B.E.

COUSENS, 2nd Lieut. Arthur Bertie, M.B.E., R.A.S.C.

COUSINS, Lieut.-Col. Arthur George, C.B.E., *b.* 1880; *s.* of Harry Cousins, of Braunton, Devon; *m.* Kate, *d.* of Robert Riches. *Educ.:* City of London School. Director of Public Companies, including, Ferguson Bros. (Port Glasgow), Ltd.; Murdoch and Murray, Ltd. (Port Glasgow); Fearnley Bros. (1920), Ltd.; Gwynnes Engineering Co., Ltd.; Hartlepools Paper Mill Co., Ltd.; Investment Registry, Ltd. (Managing Director). *War Work:* Served European War, 1914–18; mentioned in despatches. *Addresses:* The White House, Nether Street, Finchley, N.; Bix Manor Farm, near Henley-on-Thames. *Clubs:* Junior Carlton; R.A.C.   (C1527)

COUSINS, Capt. Robert William, O.B.E., R.A.S.C.

COUTTS, Capt. Colin, M.B.E.

COUTTS, Major Frederick, M.B.E., T.D., *b.* 3 May, 1870; *s.* of John Coutts, of Invergowrie; *m.* Elizabeth, *d.* of James Robertson, of Fallows. *Educ.:* West End Academy, Dundee. General Manager and Engineer, Paisley Districts Tramways; on staff of technical advisers to Transport Board. *War Work:* Served in the Army, 1914–16; Hon. Sec. to Board of Trade (Trams Dept.) for Scotland, 1917–19. *Address:* Knightswood, Elderslie, Renfrewshire.   (M7776)

COUTTS, Lieut.-Col. Malcolm, O.B.E., R.A.S.C.

COUTURIER, The Rt. Rev. Felix Bishop, O.B.E., M.C., D.D., *b.* 29 March, 1876; *s.* of Antony Couturier, of Lyons. *Educ.:* France; St. Charles' Coll., Bayswater. Member of the English Province of the Dominican Order (Blackfriars); consecrated Bishop of Myriophytos, April, 1919; appointed Visitor Apostolic to Egypt, April, 1919. *War Work:* Gazetted Chaplain to the Forces, Jan. 1915; served in Egypt from June, 1915, to March, 1919, and held the appointment of Assistant to the Principal Chaplain of the Egyptian Expeditionary Force; awarded the Military Cross, and mentioned thrice in despatches by General Sir Archibald Murray; twice mentioned in despatches by F. M. Lord Allenby. *Address:* St. Dominic's Priory, Southampton Road, N.W., 5.   (O2878)

COUZENS, Arthur Wilson, M.B.E.

COVENTRY Fulwar Cecil Ashton, O.B.E.

COVENTRY, Mary Jane, M.B.E., *b.* 1860; *d.* of George Andrew Coventry, of Shanwell, Kinross-shire, N.B. *War Work:* Convenor of County Auxiliary Red Cross Hospital; Vice-President, B.R.C.S.S.B., Kinross-shire.   (M7778)

COWAN, Capt. Alexander Henry, M.B.E., T.F. Res.

COWAN, David John, O.B.E., M.C., *b.* 25 May, 1896; *s.* of E. W. Cowan, M.I.C.E., M.I.E.E., F.R.E.S., of London; *m.* Katharine Mary, *d.* of Rev. B. J. Snell, M.A., B.Sc., of London. *Educ.:* Magdalen Coll. School, Oxford; St. Bartholomew's Hospital. Balkan Representative of The North British Rubber Co., Ltd., Edinburgh. *War Work:* Served in France as a private in R.A.M.C., Aug. to Nov. 1914; Lieut., 5th Conn. Rangers, Ireland, Nov. 1914, to Sept. 1915; Lieut., 5th Conn. Rangers, British Salonica Force, Sept. 1915, to Aug. 1919; attached to British Military Mission, Sofia, Dec. 1918, to Aug. 1919; promoted Acting Capt., March, 1919; demobilised, Aug. 1919. *Addresses:* c/o Messrs. Cox & Co., F Branch, 16, Charing Cross, S.W. 1; Piazza dell' Unita 6, Trieste, Italy.   (O4488d)

COWAN, Edith Ducksey, O.B.E.   (O11962)

COWAN, Eric Tennant, O.B.E., *b.* 17 Jan. 1891. *War Work:* Aug. 1914, to present date served in France with 17th Batt. Lancashire Fusiliers. *Address:* Edendarroch, Oxton, Cheshire.   (O2452)

COWAN, Col. Harry James, O.B.E.

COWAN, Major and Qr.-Mr. Herbert Gladstone, M.B.E., D.C.M.

COWAN, Howard Denys Russell, M.B.E., *b.* 23 Oct. 1883; *s.* of Rev. R. D. Russell Cowan, of Bushley, Tewkesbury; *m.* Gertrude, *d.* of F. F. Perssé, of Roxborough, Co. Galway. *Educ.:* Merchant Taylors' School, and Abroad. Vice-Consul at Havana, Cuba, 1911–20.   (M280)

COWAN, John, M.B.E., M.I.M.E., *b.* 13 Feb. 1873; *s.* of John Cowan, of Irvine; *m.* Margaret Dickie, *d.* of John Macmillan, of Irvine. *Educ.:* Irvine Academy. Mechanical Engineer; Chief Inspector of Boilers, Bengal Government. *War Work:* In charge of Priority Certificates for all imports into Bengal from 1917. *Addresses:* 13, Alexandra Court, Calcutta; 4, Government Place West, Calcutta.   (M4128)

COWAN, Major John, O.B.E., R.E. (T.F.)

COWAN, Col. John Marshall, C.B.E., M.D. T. Col. Army Med. Ser.; served in the Great War 1914–19 (despatches).   (C1374)

COWAN, Lieut. Percy John, M.B.E.

COWAN, Lieut. Peter Hood, O.B.E.

COWAN, Capt. Robert Cecil, O.B.E.

COWAN, William, M.B.E.

COWARD, Capt. Noel Anthony, O.B.E., R.A.M.C., M.D.

COWARD, Randulph Lewis, O.B.E., *b.* 17 May, 1860; *s.* of the late James Coward; *m.* Amy Florence, *d.* of Joseph Longbottom, of Leeds. *Educ.:* Chapel Royal, St. James's. Financial Dept. of the War Office. *Address:* 14, St. George's Square, S.W. 1.   (O10211)

COWCHER, William Brainsford, O.B.E.

COWDROY, Charlotte Jane Howarth, M.B.E., *b.* 5 Jan. 1864; *d.* of S. H. Cowdroy, of the Manchester Cowdroys. Principal of Crouch End High School and Coll., London, N. 8; teacher, lecturer, author of various articles on Education. *War Work:* Originator, Organiser, and Hon. Treas. of Hornsey Prisoner of War Fund. *Address:* Elm House, London, N. 8.   (M7779)

COWELL, Edward Hudson, O.B.E.

COWELL, Marie, O.B.E. Hon. Sec., North Riding of Yorkshire Branch of Soldiers' and Sailors' Families Association.   (O11900)

COWEN, Jane, O.B.E.

COWIE, Lieut.-Col. Henry Edward Colvin, C.B.E., D.S.O.; *b.* 1872; *s.* of the late Henry George Cowie, of Tiverton, Devon; *m.* 1903, Mary Theodora, *e. d.* of the Rev. Daniel Thomas, Rector of Hamerton, Hunts. *Educ.:* Shrewsbury, and at R.M.A. Entered R.E. 1893; became Capt. 1904; Major, 1913; China, 1900–1902 (despatches, medal with clasp); served in the Great War, 1914–19, with rank of Lieut.-Col.   (C1241)

COWIN, Norris Tynwald, M.B.E.

COWLEY, Alexander Percy, M.B.E.

COWLEY, Capt. Ernest, M.B.E.

COWLEY, Capt. James Arthur, M.B.E., *b.* 22 Aug. 1870; *s.* of James Cowley, of Northwich; *m.* Katharine Marion, *d.* of David Davies, of Carmarthen. *Educ.:* Sir John Deane's School, Northwich. Clerk to Urban District Council of Northwich (appointed in 1896); Hon. Sec. Victoria Infirmary, Northwich; for 25 years a member of the Executive Council of the Urban District Councils Association, of which he was formerly Chairman; 20 years a member of Law and Parliamentary Committee; Member of Lancashire and Cheshire Industrial Council for Local Authorities (Non-Trading Departments). *War Work:* One of the two founders of the Northwich Volunteer Training Corps; appointed 2nd Lieut. and Treas. of the 8th Bn. Cheshire Regt.; then appointed Transport Officer of the Bn., subsequently given rank of Capt. and Command of No. 2 Company of the Cheshire R.A.S.C.; M.T. (V.); Hon. Sec. of the following: Sailors' and Soldiers' Families Association, Sailors' and Soldiers' Help Society, Prince of Wales' Fund, Northwich District War Fund, Northwich War Pensions Committee, Northwich Fuel and Lighting Committee, National Service Committee, Mid Cheshire Orthopædic Clinic for Discharged Sailors and Soldiers; and Member of Cheshire War Pensions Committee, Cheshire Joint Committee for Sailors' and Soldiers' Families Association, and Soldiers' and Sailors' Help Society, Northwich and District Prisoners of War Committee, Northwich Patriotic Committee, Part Time Committee, National Kitchens Committee, Food Control Committee, Recruiting Committee for Women's Land Army; Hon. Adviser, Queen Mary's Hospital Supply Guild; Clerk to Military Service Tribunal, and National Registration Authority; first recruiting agent after outbreak of War, and afterwards voluntary worker on Recruiting Committee; inaugurated the Allotments Holders' Association for the District. *Address:* Lyndhurst, Hartford, Cheshire.   (M7780)

COWLEY, Col. James William, O.B.E.

COWLEY, Marie, Lady, O.B.E.   (O11964)

COWLEY, Norah Louisa, M.B.E.

COWLEY, Lieut.-Col. Robert Mansfield, O.B.E., V.D., East Indian Railway Volunteers, *b.* 9 Sept. 1864; *s.* of Capt. Patrick Cowley, of Dublin; *m.* Monica, *d.* of Joseph Robinson, of Elvetham. *Educ.:* The Coll., Southampton; King's Coll., London. General Traffic Manager, East Indian Railway. *War Work:* Railway Transport, India. *Address:* Hillsdown, Ocklynge Avenue, Eastbourne.   (O4030)

COWLING, Eleanor, Mrs., M.B.E.

COWLING, Capt. John, O.B.E.

COWPER, Major Lionel Ilfred, O.B.E., *b.* 19 Dec. 1881 *s.* of John Cowper, and *g.s.* of Frederick Cowper, of Carleton Hall, Penrith, Cumberland (*see* Burke's *Landed Gentry*); *m.* Edith Margaret Jane, *d.* of Charles Lister, J.P., D.L., of Agden Hall, Lymm, Cheshire. *Educ.:* Cheltenham and Sandhurst. Commission in The King's Own (Royal Lancaster Regt.), 8 Jan. 1901. *Club:* Naval and Military.   (O7037)

COWPER, Mary Bourne, Mrs., M.B.E., *Educ.:* London and Hanover. *War Work:* Hon. Organiser and Sec. of Leighton Buzzard War Hospital Supply Depot. *Address:* The Manor House, Leighton Buzzard.   (M7781)

COWPER, Muriel, O.B.E.

COWTAN, Arthur Barnard, O.B.E.

COX, Lieut. Aedan, O.B.E.

COX, Lieut. Alexander, M.B.E.

COX, Alfred, O.B.E., M.B., B.S. (Univ. Durham), *b.* 1866; *s.* of Thomas Cox, of Darlington; *m.* Florence Amelia, *d.* of Thomas Cheesman, of Newcastle-on-Tyne. *Educ.:* Albert Road School, Darlington, and University of Durham. Medical Secretary, British Medical Association. *War Work:* Member, Duke of Devonshire's Committee for providing medical attendance for dependants of sailors and soldiers; Joint Secretary, Central Medical War Committee for providing doctors for services, with due regard to civilian needs. *Addresses:* Cotfield, Fairdene Road, Coulsdon, Surrey; 429, Strand, W.C. 2. *Club:* National Liberal.   (O1240)

COX, Observer Officer Albert John, M.B.E., R.A.F.

COX, Arthur William Franklin, M.B.E.

COX, Belle, Lady, O.B.E.

COX, Bernard Henry, O.B.E.

COX, Charles Edwin, M.B.E.

COX, Constance Louise, Mrs., M.B.E.

COX, Major Edward Geoffrey Hippisley, C.B.E., *b.* 29 Aug 1884; *s.* of Edward Hippisley Cox; *m.* Ethel Milsted, *d.* of Mountague Edye. Major, Queen's Westminster Rifles; served during European War, 1914–19; Staff-Capt., 1915; Deputy Asst. Quartermaster-General, 1916; Deputy Asst. Adjutant-General, 1917; Asst. Adjutant-General, London

District, (temp. Lieut.-Col. in Army), 1918; despatches; Bt. Major in Army, *Address :* 3A, Dean's Yard, Westminster, S.W. *Clubs :* Carlton ; St. Stephen's. (C1528)

COX, Capt. Edward Orme, M.B.E., I.A.E.O.

COX, Sir Edward Owen, G.B.E. Chairman Overseas Shipping Committee, Australia. (G66)

COX, Major Edwin Charles, C.B.E. Major, Engineer and Railway Staff Corps, and Sup. of the Line S.E. and Chatham Railway ; has Order of Leopold of Belgium. (C134)

COX, Ethel Sophie, Mrs., M.B.E.

COX, Evelin Florence Conran, Mrs., M.B.E.

COX, Frederick Nutter, O.B.E.

COX, Capt. and Qr.-Mr. George, M.B.E.

COX, George Henry, M.B.E.

COX, Gerald, O.B.E., *b.* 22 Sept. 1883 ; *s.* of Joseph Goodenough Cox, of Falmouth ; *m.* Isabel Scott, *d.* of William Scott, of London. *Educ. :* Kelly Coll., Tavistock. Late Managing Director, Cox & Co., Engineers and Shipbuilders. *War Work :* Shipbuilding ; Ship Repairing ; Ship Salving. *Address :* 6, Western Terrace, Falmouth, Cornwall. (O10216)

COX, Sqdn.-Leader Henry Ashley, O.B.E., R.A.F.

COX, Lieut. Herbert Spencer, O.B.E., R.N.R.

COX, Lieut. Horace Beresford, O.B.E., R.G.A. (T.F.)

COX, Capt. Humphrey John Hamilton, *b.* 26 March, 1889 ; *s.* of Howard W. Cox. *Educ. :* Gresham's School, Holt, Norfolk. *War Work :* Served with the 2nd Batt. Devon Regt. in France, Nov. to Dec. 1914 ; attd. 2nd Batt. Dorsets, Mesopotamia, April, 1915, to March, 1916 ; Assistant to officer in command M.G.C. Record Office, Nov. 1916, to date. *Address :* c/o H. W. Cox, 23, The Embankment, Bedford. (O4272)

COX, Irene Winifred, O.B.E.

COX, James Henry, M.B.E.

COX, John Hugh, C.I.E., C.B.E.

COX, Joseph Peter, M.B.E.

COX, Major Joshua John, O.B.E., M.D., F.R.C.S., R.A.M.C. (T.F. Res.)

COX, Capt. Keith Trenchard, M.B.E.

COX, Oswald, O.B.E.

COX, Lieut.-Col. Percy Alexander, O.B.E.

COX, Percy Walter, M.B.E., *b.* 13 Sept. 1888 ; *y.s.* of William Cox, of Maidstone ; *m.* Beatrice Constance, *d.* of E. A. Gardner, of Maidstone. *Educ. :* Maidstone Grammar School. Tenant Farmer ; Chief Executive Officer and Sec. to the Kent County Agricultural Executive Committee ; previously some time Hon. Sec. Kent Farmers' Union, and Editor of the Farmers' Union Journal. *War Work :* In connection with present appointment, and previously as Labour Officer to the above-mentioned Committee ; also sometime member of the Agricultural Advisory Committee, Ministry of Food. *Address :* Coombe Farm, Maidstone. *Club :* Farmers', London. (M7784)

COX, Ralph Bouverie, M.B.E.

COX, Stephen, M.B.E.

COX, Sybil Mary, Mrs., O.B.E., *b.* 1865 ; *d.* of T. M. Wegnelin ; *m.* Reginald Henry, *s.* of Frederick Cox, of Cox's Bank. *War Work :* Manager of Messrs. Cox & Co.'s Casualty Enquiry Office, at Harrington House, from Oct. 1914, till the office was closed in Feb. 1919. *Addresses :* 4, Cavendish Square, W. ; Manor Cottage, Old Windsor. (O10217)

COX, Lieut. Sydney, M.B.E., *b.* 8 March, 1881 ; *s.* of the late Horace Cox, of Downe House, Duke's Drive, Eastbourne ; *m.* Florence May, *d.* of the late J. Tranter, of Bromsgrove. *Educ. :* Harrow. *War Work :* Went out in charge of the " Wessex," the first Red Cross Launch to be despatched to Mesopotamia, in Oct. 1915 ; during the first six months of 1916, while attached to No. 3 Hospital at Basra, the " Wessex " carried over 12,000 sick and wounded men ; Commissioned, Jan. 1918. *Addresses :* Oakfields, Carter's Hill, Arborfield, near Reading ; The Bungalow, Grand Lake, Newfoundland. (M3593)

COX, Thomas, C.B.E., J.P. Member of National War Aims Committee. (C474)

COX, Veronica Mary Machell, M.B.E.

COX, Col. Arthur Francis HAMILTON-, C.B.E., *b.* 6 April, 1861 ; *s.* of Charles John Cox, J.P., of London ; *m.* Susan Josephine, *d.* of J. van der Riet, of Simonstown, S. Africa. *Educ. :* Privately. Appointed Lieut., Royal Inniskilling Fusiliers, Feb. 1886 ; transferred to Royal Army Pay Dept., June, 1895. *War Work :* Command Paymaster, S. Africa ; Command Paymaster, Northern District ; Command Paymaster, Southern District. *Address :* Command Pay Office, Salisbury. (C1601)

COX, Lieut.-Col. Ernest William HART-, O.B.E.

COX, George HART-, M.B.E.

COX, Major Reginald WOODRUFF-, O.B.E., T.D., *b.* 16 Aug. 1883 ; *s.* of Edward William Cox, of London. *Educ. :* St. George's School, Windsor Castle. Merchant and Shipper. *War Work :* Proceeded to France with Regt. (Queen Victoria's Rifles), 4 Nov. 1914, and served continuously till Dec. 1919 ; held rank of Temp. Lieut.-Col. from Oct. 1917, to Jan. 1920 ; mentioned thrice in despatches, and awarded Order of Wen-Hu of China. *Address :* 56, Davies Street, Berkeley Square, W. (O5143)

COXHEAD, Lieut.-Col. Thomas Langhorne, D.S.O., O.B.E., late R.G.A., Military Knight of Windsor, *b.* 8 Oct. 1864 ; *s.* of Henry George Coxhead, formerly of Hardwicke House, Ham Common, Surrey ; *m.* Eliza Loet, *d.* of Rev. D. Winter Morris, of St. Ishmaels, Milford Haven. *Educ. :* Bute House, Petersham. Brigade-Major, China Field Force, 1900-1 ;

D.A.A.G., R.A., 1900-02. *War Work :* On Coast Defences, Portsmouth Garrison, 1914-15 ; Commanding R.G.A. Depot, Brockhurst, 1915-19. *Address :* 15, Castle Yard, Windsor Castle. (O7039)

COXON, Major Alfred Walter, O.B.E., *b.* 11 July, 1872 ; *s.* of Alfred Coxon, of London ; *m.* Muriel, *d.* of the Rev. T. W. M. Lund, of Liverpool. *Educ. :* Marlborough Coll. and Trinity Coll., Cambridge. *War Work :* Army Paymaster in France and North Russia. (O6774)

COXWELL, Charles Blake, O.B.E.

COY, Capt. Frederick, O.B.E.

COYLE, James, M.B.E.

COYNE, Lieut. Denis, M.B.E., R.F.A.

COYNE, Capt. Russell, M.B.E.

CRABB, Mary Maud, Mrs., O.B.E., *b.* 7 May, 1864 ; *d.* of Alan Bruce Charles Bellamy ; *m.* the late Richard William, *s.* of William Crabb, R.N. *War Work :* With Lady Lugard's Belgian Hospital, 1914 ; French Red Cross Crépy en Valois, 1915-16 ; travelling and organising Sec., War Dept., Y.W.C.A. 1917-20. *Address :* 19, Westcliff Terrace Mansions, Pegwell Bay, Ramsgate. (O10219)

CRABB, Lieut. William Charles Pascoe, O.B.E., D.S.C., R.N.

CRABBE, Lieut. Sidney Charles, M.B.E., *b.* 12 July, 1886 ; *s.* of John Crabbe, of London ; *m.* Ivy Hildegarde, *d.* of John Glynn-Barnes, Kensington. *Educ. :* Christ's Hospital. *War Work :* R.A.S.C., M.T., April, 1916 to Jan. 1920 (France). *Address :* 10, Norland Square, Holland Park, London, W. 11. (M6524)

CRABBIE, Capt. John Edward, O.B.E., *b.* 11 April, 1879 *s.* of George Crabbie, of Blairhoyle ; *m.* Cecilia Cochrane, *d.* of the late Patrick Turnbull, C.A. *Educ. :* Edinburgh Academy, and Oxford Univ. Advocate. *War Work :* Joined 6th Black Watch in Oct. 1914, as 2nd Lieut. ; promoted Capt., Jan. 1915 ; sent to work as Military Representative for the Counties of the Lothians and Peebles, and the cities of Edinburgh and Leith, in March, 1916. *Address :* 5, Ainslie Place, Edinburgh. *Clubs :* Vincent's, Oxford ; Caledonian United Service, Edinburgh ; Public Schools, London. (O7040)

CRABTREE, Major Ernest Granville, O.B.E., R.A.M.C.

CRACKNELL, Nora Frances Elizabeth, M.B.E.

CRADDOCK, Frances Henrietta, Lady, C.B.E. ; *y. d.* of the late Gen. H. R. Browne, C.B. ; *m.* 1888, Sir Reginald Henry, K.C.S.I., I.C.S., *s.* of the late Surgeon-Major William Craddock, 1st Gurkha Rifles. (C1962)

CRAFT, Capt. and Qr.-Mr. Samuel Louis, M.B.E.

CRAFTER, Richard Andrew, O.B.E.

CRAGG, Rev. Roland Herbert, O.B.E. (O11878)

CRAGG, Capt. and Qr.-Mr. William Joseph, O.B.E.

CRAIG, Alexander, C.B.E., J.P.

CRAIG, Alexander Meldrum, M.B.E., Can. A.S.C.

CRAIG, Alexander Robertson, M.B.E., *b.* 2 Oct. 1881 ; *s.* of the late William John Craig, of Liverpool. Chief Archivist, The Residency, Cairo, with local rank of Third Sec., in H.M. Diplomatic Service. *Address :* The Residency, Cairo, Egypt. (M2820)

CRAIG, Capt. Archibald Maxwell, R.M.L.I.

CRAIG, Capt. Colin McKean, O.B.E., M.D., R.A.M.C.

CRAIG, Emily Mary, Lady TUDOR-, C.B.E. ; 2nd *d.* of Rev. James Lukin, of Felbrigg Lodge, Romsey, Hants ; *m.* 26 Oct., 1898, Major Sir Algernon Tudor, 2nd *s.* of the late Rev. Allen Tudor-Craig, M.A., Oxford. Incumbent of Marbœuf Church, Paris (*see* BURKE'S *Family Records*). (C2535)

CRAIG, Eustace Neville, O.B.E.

CRAIG, Lieut. Graham, M.B.E.

CRAIG, Capt. Hugh Morton, O.B.E.

CRAIG, James Douglas, O.B.E.

CRAIG, John, C.B.E. Managing Director, David Colville and Sons, Ltd. (C476)

CRAIG, John, M.B.E., M.B., Ch.B., *b.* Feb. 1876. *Educ. :* Glasgow Univ. *War Work :* Active service in the field, Feb. 1916, to Nov. 1917 ; mentioned in despatches (Battle of Somme) ; Medical Officer in charge Grange Street Military Hospital, Manchester, 1918-19. (M10262b)

CRAIG, Capt. John Gibson, O.B.E., R.A.M.C.

CRAIG, Juliet Sisley, Mrs., M.B.E.

CRAIG, Lieut.-Col. Maurice, C.B.E., M.D., F.R.C.S., R.A.M.C., *b.* 29 March, 1866 ; *s.* of William Simson Craig, M.D., F.R.C.P., of Bedford ; *m.* Edith de Saumarez, *d.* of A. Kentish Brock, of The Hermitage, Guernsey. *Educ. :* Bedford Grammar School ; Gonville and Caius College, Cambridge ; Guy's Hospital, London. Physician (Consulting) ; Physician for, and Lecturer in, Psychological Medicine, Guy's Hospital ; Consulting Physician (Psychological Medicine), Ministry of Health ; Consulting Physician (Neurological), Ministry of Pensions. *War Work :* Lieut.-Col., R.A.M.C. ; Asst. Physician to Neurologist, Headquarters, War Office ; Consulting Neurologist Physician, Headquarters, Medical Board, War Office ; Consulting visiting Physician to Lord Knutsford Special Hospital for Officers. *Addresses :* 87, Harley Street, W. ; Salona, East Preston, Sussex. *Club :* Oxford and Cambridge. (C1529)

CRAIG, Lieut.-Col. Newman Lombard, C.B.E., D.S.O. ; *b.* 1884 ; Capt. R.A.S.C. ; Q.M.G. with rank of Lieut.-Col. ; served during the Great War, 1914-18 (despatches). (C5147)

CRAIG, Lieut.-Col. Robert Annesley, C.M.G., C.B.E., *b.* 1869 ; *s.* of R. S. Craig, of Belfast ; *m.* 1904, Helen Mary Stewart, *d.* of the Very Rev. Graham Craig, of Clonmacnois.

Lieut.-Col. R.A., and Sup. of Research, Roy. Arsenal, Woolwich. *Club:* United Service. (C1530)

CRAIG, Robert James, M.B.E.

CRAIG, Capt. Thomas, O.B.E., R.A.V.C. (T.)

CRAIG, Walter Elder, M.B.E., *b.* 15 March, 1881 ; *s.* of Walter T. Craig, of Wick. *Educ.:* Wick. *War Work:* Raised funds by means of Flag Days, etc., in aid of Belgian Relief Fund, Serbian Relief Fund, etc. ; rendered sympathetic service on behalf of relatives of soldiers and sailors of the town and district. *Addresses:* Miller Street, Wick ; 96, High Street, Wick, Caithness. (M7788)

CRAIG, William, O.B.E., *b.* 27 Feb., 1849 ; *s.* of John Craig, of Dumbarton ; *m.* Margaret Anne, *d.* of William Babtie, of Dumbarton. *Educ.:* Dumbarton Academy, and Glasgow Univ. County Clerk ; Clerk of the Peace ; Clerk to Lieutenancy of Dumbartonshire. *War Work:* Clerk, Local Tribunals for County of Dumbarton ; Hon. Sec. to the following : War Pensions Committee for County, County Fund for Relief of Disabled and Wounded Sailors and Soldiers connected with the county, County of Dumbarton Civil Relief Fund, Food Control Committee. *Address:* Inverleven, Dumbarton. *Clubs:* Conservative ; Automobile, Glasgow. (O1244)

CRAIG, William Brownfield, O.B.E., *b.* 1867 ; *s.* of W. J. Craig, of Sandown, I.W. *War Work:* Assistant County Director, British Red Cross Society. *Address:* Torrhill, Ivybridge, S. Devon. (O257)

CRAIG, William James Robert, M.B.E., R.E.

CRAIG, Major Sir John Algernon Tudor TUDOR-, K.B.E. F.S.A., *b.* 3 Jan. 1873 ; *s.* of Rev. Allen Tudor-Craig, M.A., Incumbent of Marbœuf Church, Paris ; *m.* Emily Mary (C.B.E.), *d.* of Rev. James Lukin, of Felbrigg Lodge, Romsey. Major, late 4th Bn. Royal Irish Rifles, 1902 ; Sec. Inc. Sailors' and Soldiers' Help Society, since 1903, and of Veterans Relief Fund, since 1908 ; Gold Staff Officer in Westminster Abbey, and Staff Officer to Colonial Coronation Contingent, 1911 ; D.A.A.G., 1914-20 ; Director, Admiralty Convalescent Homes, 1914-20 ; Acting Assistant Provost Marshal, London District, 1915-20 ; Comptroller, Lord Roberts' Memorial Fund and Workshops, since 1915 ; Member, London War Pensions Committee, since 1916 ; Esquire of the Order of St. John of Jerusalem, 1914 ; C.B.E. 1918 ; Chevalier of the Order of the Crown of Belgium, 1920. *Addresses:* Craigston, Bisley, Surrey ; 2, Cresswell Gardens, S.W. 5. *Club:* St. James's. (K209)

CRAIGIE, Muriel, M.B.E., Q.M.A.A.C.

CRAIK, Major George Thomas, O.B.E., R.A.O.C.

CRAILSHAM, Major Harry Rollo, O.B.E.

CRAMOND, John McGregor, O.B.E.

CRAMP, Annie Elizabeth, Mrs., M.B.E., *b.* 23 Jan. 1875 ; *d.* of Henry Welton, of Coventry ; *m.* the late Charles Frederick, *s.* of Charles Frederick Cramp, of Coleshill. *Educ.:* Coventry High School. *War Work:* Commandant, V.A.D. Warwick 70. *Address:* High Street, Coventry. (M7789)

CRAMPTON, Capt. Denis Burke, C.B.E., M.V.O., D.S.O., R.N. ; *b.* 1873 ; *s.* of the late John Burke Crampton ; *m.* 1904, Evangeline Beatrice, *d.* of Col. E. Dickinson, R.E. Entered R.N. 1886 ; became Lieut. 1894 ; Comm. 1904 ; Capt. 1911 ; Brass River Expedition 1895 (medal with clasp), bombardment of Zanzibar, 1896. *War Services:* 1914-19, present at operation against the " Königsberg " (despatches, Legion of Honour) ; has 2nd class Russian Order of St Stanislaus (with plaque) ; 4th class of Order of Redeemer of Greece, and of Order of the Dannebrog of Denmark ; is a Comm. of Order of Crown of Italy. *Clubs:* Junior United Service ; Royal Yacht Squadron. (C2286)

CRAMPTON, Lieut.-Col. Philip John Ribton, C.B.E. Lieut.-Col and Brevet Col. R.A. (ret.) ; served in the Great War, 1914-19 (despatches). (C1531)

CRAN, Lieut.-Col. George, M.B.E., V.D., M.D., J.P., 7th Gordons, *b.* 1852 ; *s.* of Alex Cran, F.R.C.S.E. ; *m.* Annie Emslie, *d.* of Al. Emslie Smith, of Summerhill, Aberdeen. *Educ.:* Tarland, and Aberdeen Univ. Med. Officer to Banchory, Durris Strachan, and Biore Parish Councils. *War Work:* Med. Officer to Durris Hospital. *Address:* Walbrook, Banchory. (M7790)

CRAN, Lieut.-Col. James, O.B.E.

CRAN, Capt. Peter McLellan, O.B.E., R.E.

CRANE, Capt. Bertie Frederick, M.B.E., R.A.F.

CRANE, Lieut.-Col. Charles Paston, D.S.O., O.B.E., B.A., *b.* 1857 ; *s.* of the Rev. William Crane, Residentiary Canon of Manchester ; *m.* Mary Alice Caroline, *d.* of late Col. Henry Mills Skrene, J.P., D.L. (see BURKE's *Peerage,* Temple, E.). *Educ.:* Exeter Coll, Oxford. Entered R.I.C. as Cadet 1879 ; was Private Secretary to Insp.-Gen. R.I.C. 1895-1897 ; Resident Magistrate in Ireland since 1897 ; S. Africa, 1900-1901, as Capt. and Adj. 12th Batt. Imperial Yeomanry ; Great War as Major and Lieut.-Col. Comdg. a battalion of Infantry (mentioned in despatches). *Address:* Killarney, co. Kerry. *Club:* Wellington. (O259)

CRANE, Major Francis Leopold, O.B.E., A.I.F.

CRANE, Capt. James Henry, M.B.E., R.A.M.C. (T.)

CRANE, Capt. Lucius Fairchild, O.B.E.

CRANE, Major Robert Eugene, O.B.E., F.R.G.S., *b.* 8 Jan. 1879 ; *s.* of Robert Newton Crane, of 4, Temple Gardens, E.C. ; *m.* Aline, *d.* of F. C. Van Duzer, of 43, Stanhope Gdns., S.W. *Educ.:* Charterhouse. *War Work:* France and Belgium, Sept. to Nov. 1914 ; Adjutant, 11th Bn. Loyal North Lancashire Regt., 1914-16 ; Brigade Major, Portland Garrison, 1916-18 ; D.A.A.G., War Office, 1918-19. *Address:* Santa

Barbara, California, U.S.A. *Club:* Junior United Service. (O7043)

CRANFIELD, Major Guy William, M.B.E., R.A.F.

CRANFIELD, Mary, O.B.E.

CRANFORD, Lieut.-Col. Robert Langley, C.B.E., *b.* 18 May, 1867 ; *s.* of Robert Cranford, of Dartmouth, Devon ; *m.* late Ethel Constance, *d.* of C. H. Stanley, of Liverpool. *Educ.:* Preparatory School, Dartmouth and Blundell's School, Tiverton. R.A. Veterinary Corps. *War Work:* A.D.V.S., London District ; A.D.V.S., Southern Army, H.D. ; D.D.V.S., L. of C., Northern (France) ; D.D.V.S., 5th Army ; A.D.V.S., X. Corps, Bonn. *Address:* 1, Friars Terrace, York. (C1242)

CRANFORD, Capt. Stanley Charles Russell, O.B.E., *b.* 21 April, 1880 ; *s.* of late Charles Frederick Crawford, of Streatham Common ; *m.* Sybil Dorothy, *d.* of Edward S. Elvey, of Streatham Common. *Educ.:* Streatham Coll. ; King's Coll., London. Barrister-at-law of Inner Temple. Deputy Judge Advocate General, Mesopotamia Expeditionary Force. *War Work:* Capt. 5th E. Surrey Regt. ; served N.W. Frontier (India) ; Mesopotamia Exped. Force. ; N. Persian Force, 1914 to date. *Addresses:* 3, Temple Gardens, Temple, E.C. ; 29, Lewin Road, Streatham Common, S.W. ; Gen. H.Q., Bagdad. (O4201)

CRANG, James, M.B.E.

CRANKSHAW, Major Eric Norman Spencer, M.B.E.

CRANMER, Capt. Alexander Thomas, M.B.E., R.A.F.

CRANMER, Lieut. William Ernest, M.B.E., R.A.F.

CRANSTON, Brig.-Gen. Sir Robert, K.C.V.O., Knt. Bach., C.B., C.B.E., V.D., T.D., LL.D., F.R.S.A., J.P., D.L., *b.* 2 June, 1843 ; *e. s.* of Robert Cranston, J.P., D.L., of Edinburgh and Elizabeth, his wife, *d.* of the late James Dagleish, of Edinburgh ; *m.* 1 July, 1868, Elizabeth, *e. d.* of James Simmel Gilbert of Edinburgh. Fellow of the Educational Institute of Scotland ; late Member of School Board ; formerly Treasurer of City of Edinburgh ; Lord Provost and Lord Lieutenant, 1903-6 ; late Colonel in Territorial Force ; formerly Commanding Lothian Brigade, and Col.-Comd. Queen's Rifle Vol. Brigade ; raised and commanded 15th and 18th Batts. Royal Scots ; Comdg. 77th Training Reserve Batt. in 1917 ; Chairman of Cranston's Hotels, and Officer of Legion of Honour ; Knt. Comm. of St. Olaf of Norway. *Address:* Corehouse, 19, Merchiston Avenue, Edinburgh. *Clubs:* Junior Constitutional ; Conservative (Edinburgh) (C477)

CRANSTON, 2nd Lieut. Thomas, M.B.E., R.E.

CRAPNELL, Stanley Richard, M.B.E. ; *s.* of Richard Gilbert Crapnell, of Portsmouth ; *m.* Emma Elizabeth, *d.* of John Barnes, of Portsmouth. *Educ.:* Privately. *War Work:* Hon. Sec. Prisoners of War Fund for Duke of Wellington's (West Riding) Regt. (M7791)

CRAPPER, Capt. Harold Sugden, M.B.E.

CRASKE, Mabel Annetta, M.B.E. (M10246b)

CRASKE, Mary, M.B.E., *b.* 6 Oct. 1852 ; *d.* of Wm. Giles Craske, of Lowestoft. *Educ.:* Privately. *War Work:* Registration Work, Aug. 1915 ; Volunteer Clerk in Recruiting Office, Sept. 1915 to Sept. 1917 ; Volunteer Clerk in Food Control Office, Sept. 1917 to March, 1920 ; Helped in Canteen for Sailors and Soldiers, Dec. 1916 to March, 1919. *Address:* 4, Cleveland Road, Lowestoft, South. (M7792)

CRASTER, Capt. Albert Kenneth Graves, O.B.E.

CRASTER, Barbara Marion, M.B.E., W.R.N.S.

CRASTER, Lieut.-Col. Edmund Henry Bertram, C.B.E., *b.* 1869 ; *s.* of the late Edmund Craster, of Beadnell Tower, Chathill, Northumberland ; *m.* 1902, his cousin, Margaret Eleanor Mary, *d.* of Col. William Robert Craster. Lieut.-Col. R.G.A. ; served in the Great War, 1914 (despatches). (C1532)

CRASTER, Major George, D.S.O., O.B.E. (O11734)

CRASTER, Lieut.-Col. John Evelyn Edmund, O.B.E., R.E.

CRAUFURD, Emily Maud, Mrs. HOUISON-, O.B.E. ; *d.* of Major-Gen. Fairfax Hassard, C.B., Royal Engineers ; *m.* William Reginald, *s.* of John Reginald Houison-Craufurd, of Craufurdland, Kilmarnock, and Braehead, Cramond Brig, Edinburgh (see BURKE's *Landed Gentry*). *War Work:* Vice President Kilmarnock Division Red Cross Society ; Chairman Dick Auxiliary Hospital, Kilmarnock ; President, Maternity and Child Welfare Centre, Kilmarnock ; Work Party, Fenwick by Kilmarnock. *Address:* Craufurdland Castle, Kilmarnock. (O10221)

CRAUFURD, Brig.-Gen. John Archibald HOUISON-, C.M.G., C.B.E., *b.* 1862 ; *s.* of the late Lieut.-Col. John Reginald Houison-Craufurd, of Craufurd, Kilmarnock, and Braehead, Midlothian ; *m.* 1903, Eleanor Louisa, *d.* of the late F. F. Dalrymple-Hay, of Dunlop (see BURKE's *Peerage*). Lieut.-Col. Indian Army (ret.), and Hon. Brig.-Gen R.A.F. (retired) ; Burma 1886-9 (medal with clasp), China 1900-1 as D.A.Q.M.G. (despatches, medal), Somaliland 1903 (medal with clasp). Served in the Great War as A.Q.M.G. Scottish Command, 1916-18 (despatches) ; was D.A.A.G. India 1899-1903. *Addresses:* Dunlop House, Dunlop, Ayrshire ; Borland, Kilmarnock. *Clubs:* East India United Service ; New (Edinburgh). (C866)

CRAVEN, Commissary and Capt. Albert, O.B.E.

CRAVEN, Lieut.-Comm. Charles Worthington, O.B.E., R.N.

CRAVEN, Edward Joseph Eclipsis, M.B.E.

CRAVEN, Henry, O.B.E., *b.* 11 Nov. 1866 ; *s.* of Charles Alfred Craven, of Dewsbury (Yorks), Engineer ; *m.* Mary Amy, *d.* of William Waud, of Baslow, Derbyshire. *Educ.:* Merchant

Taylors' School. Solicitor ; Town Clerk and Clerk of the Peace, Sunderland, Co. Durham. *War Work :* Recruiting, Derby Canvass ; work in connection with the raising of 160th (Wearside) R.F.A., and 20th (Service Battalion) D.L.I. ; work in connection with a local Military Hospital, and raising £30,000 therefor ; work in connection with Mayor's Local Relief Fund, the Prince of Wales' Fund, the Mayoress's Serbian Fund, and the King's Fund ; Hon. Sec. War Savings ; work in connection with Tank and Guns Week ; Hon. Sec. Food Control Committee ; Hon. work in connection with Air Raid Claims, Fuel Control, and War Allotments ; Hon. Sec. to Local War Pensions Committee. *Address :* 5, West Lawn, Sunderland. *Club :* Sunderland.   (O10222)

CRAVEN, Lieut.-Col. John, O.B.E.

CRAVEN, Capt. the Hon. Rupert Cecil, O.B.E.

CRAVEN, William George Robert Craven, Earl of, O.B.E.   (O8789)

CRAWFORD, Alexander, M.B.E.

CRAWFORD, Andrew, C.B.E., *b.* 7 Sept. 1871 ; *s.* of John Crawford, of Raillies, Largs, N.B. ; *m.* Ursula Ritchie, *d.* of John Orr, of Largs, N.B. *Educ. :* Largs Public School ; Glasgow High School. Steamship Owner and Broker. *War Work :* Assistant Accountant-General, Ministry of Shipping (Voluntary). *Address :* "Underbank House," Largs, N.B. *Clubs :* Conservative ; Scottish Automobile, Glasgow ; Junior Constitutional, London.   (C946)

CRAWFORD, Capt. Andrew, M.B.E., R.A.M.C.

CRAWFORD, Barbara Grace Rutherfurd, M.B.E., M.B., Ch.B. (Glasg.) ; *d.* of the late Rev. J Rutherfurd, B.D., of Renfrew ; *m.* George Robert, *s.* of George Crawford, of Rothbury, Northumberland. *Educ. :* Brighton High School, and Glasgow Univ. Medical Officer, H.M. Factory, Queen's Ferry, Chester. *War Work :* Medical Officer, Military Auxiliary Hospital, Southampton, 1914–15 ; and Leicester, 1915–17 ; Chief Medical Officer, H.M. Factory, Queen's Ferry, Chester, 1917–20. *Address :* Mancot Royal, by Chester.   (M1596)

CRAWFORD, Capt. Charles Wispingto Glover, C.B.E., R.N. Div. Naval Transport Officer ; served in the Great War, 1914–19 (despatches).   (C2246)

CRAWFORD, Daniel, M.B.E., J.P., 18 Aug. 1868 ; *s.* of Daniel Crawford, of Potterells Farm, Hatfield ; *m.* Janie Jessie McEwan, *d.* of James Melville, of Crummock, Beith, N.B. *Educ. :* St. Albans. Vice-Chairman, District Council ; Member County Agricultural Committee ; Chairman, County Branch National Farmers' Union. *War Work :* Chairman, Farm Produce for Herts ; Board of Agriculture Representative at County Appeal Tribunal ; Member of War Agricultural Executive Committee, detailed to arrange Prisoner of War Camps in Herts for Agriculture ; Member of Civil Supplies Forage Committee for Herts. *Address :* Birchwood, Hatfield.   (M7794)

CRAWFORD, Frederick Leslie, O.B.E.

CRAWFORD, Gertrude Alice, Mrs., M.B.E.

CRAWFORD, Harriette Sophia, Mrs., M.B.E.

CRAWFORD, Lieut. James, M.B.E.

CRAWFORD, Lieut.-Col. James Muir, O.B.E., M.B., Edinburgh, I.M.S., *b.* 5 Aug. 1866 ; *s.* of James Alexander Crawford, of the Bengal Civil Service ; *m.* Winifred Edith, *d.* of Frederick Joseph Wernick, of Lingia, Darjeeling. *Educ. :* Edinburgh University ; Bonn University ; St. George's Hospital. Served on the N.E. Frontier of India ; Chin-Lushai, 1892–3 ; N.W. Frontier of India, Malakand and Buner, 1897–8 ; China, Boxer Rebellion, 1900. *War Work :* Commanded "Y," Indian General Hospital at Brighton, 1914–15 ; and at Suez, 1916 ; commanded Lady Chelmsford War Hospital at Benares, 1916–19. *Address :* c/o Messrs. Grindlay & Co., 54, Parliament Street, S.W. 1. *Club :* Oriental.   (O2065)

CRAWFORD, Lieut. James Robert, O.B.E., R.N.V.R.

CRAWFORD, Major John Martin Maynard, O.B.E., R.A.M.C.

CRAWFORD, Capt. Stanley Charles Russell, O.B.E.

CRAWFORD, Thomas, M.B.E.

CRAWFORD, Col. Robert Gordon SHARMAN-, C.B.E.

CRAWLEY, Cecil Gordon, C.B.E., *b.* 1862 ; *s.* of John S. Crawley, of Stockwood, Luton ; *m.* Violet Chadwick. *Educ. :* Eton, and at Magdalene Coll., Cambridge ; is Director-Gen. Mechanical Depart., Public Works Min., Egypt. *Address :* Zamalek, Ghezirch, Cairo. *Clubs :* Windham ; Arthur's. (C354)

CRAWLEY, Cecil, Mrs., M.B.E.   (M1598)

CRAWLEY, Major Charles, O.B.E.

CRAWLEY, Gertrude, M.B.E. ; *d.* of John Crawley, of Whaplode Manor, Holbeach, S. Lincs. *Educ. :* Merton Coll. Croydon W. ; Madeley House, Richmond ; Inst. de Mlle. Tavernier, Boulogne-sur-Mer. Member of Lincs. Art Society ; Vice-President of Holbeach and District Red Cross Dst., No. 9, S. Lincs. (Hdqrs., Grantham) ; Hon. Sec. Prisoners of War Fund, etc. *War Work :* New Red Cross District ; General Red Cross Work in the various branches required. *Club :* V.A.D. Ladies'.   (M7796)

CRAWLEY, James, M.B.E.

CRAWLEY, Lieut.-Col. Richard Parry, D.S.O., O.B.E., M.V.O., *b.* 1876 ; *o. s.* of the late Rev. William Parry Crawley, Vicar of Walberton, Sussex ; *m.* 1904, Alice Vida Mary, *d.* of the Rev. David Crawford Cochrane, Master of Etwall Hospital, Derby. *Educ. :* At Winchester. Entered S. Wales Borderers 1897, became Capt. Army Ser. Corps, 1903, Major, 1914 ; Brevet Lieut.-Col. 1918 ; S. Africa, 1899–1902 (wounded,

despatches) ; served in the Great War, 1914–18 (Brevet Lieut.-Col. ; appointed Assist. Director, Supplies and Transport, Headquarters of Administration Services, 1918.   (O6795)

CRAWLEY, Violet Elizabeth, Mrs., M.B.E., V.A.D.

CRAWSHAY, 2nd Lieut. de Barri, O.B.E., Kent Royal Army Service Corps M.T. (V.), *b.* 2 June, 1857 ; *s.* of the late Francis Crawshay, of Treforest, Glamorganshire, and Bradbourne, Hall, Sevenoaks, Kent ; *m.* Rose Mary, *d.* of Rev. Walter Young, of Pettigo, Co. Donegal, Ireland. *Educ. :* Privately. *War Work :* Red Cross Transport of 10 hospitals in Sevenoaks (Kent) Area ; recruit ditto, during 1914–15 ; supervisor of Telegraph wires, Motor Patrol Guard, 1914–15 ; O.C. section 38 of Kent R.A.S.C. M.T. (V.): *Address :* Rosefield, Sevenoaks, Kent. *Clubs :* Royal Automobile ; Kent Automobile ; Brooklands Automobile Racing.   (O10223)

CREAGH, Lieut.-Col. Edward Cottingham, O.B.E., I.A.

CREAGH, Elizabeth Pymer, Mrs., O.B.E., R.R.C.

CREASE, Comm. Thomas Evans, C.B., C.B.E., *b.* 1875 ; *m.* Louise, *d.* of the late John Johnson, of Thetford, Norfolk. Entered R.N. 1888, and became Lieut. 1895, and Comm. 1905 ; retired 1910 ; was Naval Assist. to Controller of the Navy, 1917–19, with rank of Capt. ; has Orders of Rising Sun of Japan and of St. Maurice and St. Lazarus, and Legion of Honour. *Address :* Riverholm, Datchet.   (C883)

CREE, Capt. Harold Frederick, M.B.E., *b.* 12 May, 1887 ; *s.* of Joseph Collins Cree. *Educ. :* Tonbridge School. *War Work :* Served with 3rd Battn. The Buffs from March, 1915. to June, 1915, and with 2nd Battn. The Buffs from June, 1915 to Aug. 1919. *Clubs :* Junior Naval and Military ; Tientein, Peking.   (M4776)

CREE, Isabella Warden, M.B.E., *b.* 13 June, 1883 ; *d.* of Thomas Scott Cree, LL.D., of Glasgow. *Educ. :* Cheltenham. *War Work :* Hon. Sec., Aug. 1914, to Dec. 1918, Headquarters Clothing Committee and Stores and Despatch Committee of Scottish Branch, British Red Cross Society. *Address :* 18, Beaumont Gate, Glasgow. *Clubs :* Lady Artists', Glasgow ; Halcyon.   (M1599)

CREE, Laura Alexander Bell, Mrs., O.B.E. (20 Feb. 1918), *b.* 6 April, 1877 ; *d.* of Alexander T. Bell, M.D., of Baltimore, Maryland, U.S.A. ; *m.* Charles Deacon, *s.* of Robert Scott Cree, of Glasgow. *Educ. :* Baltimore, U.S.A. *War Work :* For the Scottish Branch, B.R.C. Society, voluntary full time worker from Aug. 1914, to April, 1919, at St. Andrews Halls, Glasgow ; Convener, Headquarters Organising Clothing Committee for Scotland ; Convener, "Stores and Despatch Committee for Scotland," Member, War Executive Committeee for Scotland ; Medal of "Elizabeth" (Belgium), conferred December, 1919, etc. *Address :* Gartferry, Ayr, Scotland. *Clubs :* Kelvin ; Literary, Glasgow.   (O261)

CREE, Thomas Deacon, O.B.E., *b.* 26 Feb. 1871 ; *s.* of Robert Scott ; *m.* Beatrice Mary, *d.* of Capt. H. V. Cowley. *Educ. :* Scotland. Merchant. *War Work :* Political Officer with I.E.F. "D" ; attached to Staff of 6th (Poona) Division ; twice mentioned in despatches. *Address :* Baghdad. (O10224)

CREEGAN, Edward Patrick, M.B.E., *b.* 9 Aug. 1859 ; *s.* of Hugh Creegan, of Dundalk, Ireland ; *m.* Christiana, *d.* of William Wells, of Tilton, Leicester. Many years Chief Superintendent of map drawing Dept., at Ordnance Survey Office, Southampton.   (M285)

CREMETTI, Major Eugene, O.B.E.

CRERAR, Major Robert, O.B.E.

CRESSWELL, Adelaide Elizabeth, Lady, O.B.E. ; *d.* of Justice Stow, a Judge of the Supreme Court of S. Australia ; *m.* 1888, Rear-Adm. Sir William Rooke, K.C.M.G , K.B.E., R.N. (ret.), *s.* of Edmund Cresswell of Gibraltar.   (O920)

CRESSWELL, Gwladys Catherine, M.B.E. ; *d.* of the late Pearson R. Cresswell, C.B., F.R.C.S., of Dowlais, Glamorgan. *War Work :* One of the Commandants (for the Merthyr Division) and Sec. at the Aberdare and Merthyr Red Cross Hospital from Oct. 1915, to April, 1919. *Address :* The Mount, Merthyr Tydfil.   (M7797)

CRESSWELL, Capt. Herbert Pinkney, M.B.E.

CRESSWELL, John Edwards, C.B.E., M.B., *b.* 12 March, 1864 ; *s.* of late Edmund Cresswell, of Gibraltar ; *m.* Catherine Burleigh, *d.* of Mathew Towgood, of Ceylon. *Educ. :* Bruce Castle School and Cavendish College, Cambridge. Egyptian Public Health. *War Work :* P.M.O., Government Hospital. *Address :* Government Hospital, Suez.   (C2536)

CRESSWELL, Rear-Adml. Sir William Rooke, K.C.M.G., K.B.E., R.N., Australian Service ; First Naval Member of R.A.N. Board of Administration ; *b.* 20 July, 1852 ; 3rd *s.* of the late Edmund Cresswell, Deputy P.M.G. for Gibraltar, and Post Office Surveyor for Mediterranean, and of Mary Margaret Ward, *d.* of Rev. W. Fraser, Rector of N. Waltham, Hants. ; *m.* Adelaide Elizabeth, O.B.E., and *d.* of the late Mr. Justice Stow, Judge of Supreme Court of S. Australia. *Educ. :* Aitken's School, Gibraltar ; Eastman's R.N. Academy, Southsea ; "Britannia." Joined Navy, 1866 ; H.M.S. "Phœbe," 1867 ; Sub-Lieut. 1871 ; specially promoted, boat action, Larost River, 1873 ; H.M.S. "London," Suppression of Slave Trade, 1875–78 ; received thanks of Foreign Minister for service there ; retired after being invalided, 1878 ; took service under S.A. Govt., 1885 ; Commander, 1891 ; Post-Capt., 1894 ; Rear-Admiral, 1911 ; Decorated for Imperial and Colonial services 1897 ; China Medal, 1900. Now farming. *Address :* Navy Office, Melbourne. *Clubs :* Queensland, Brisbane ; Melbourne, Melbourne.   (K255)

CRESWELL, Major Francis Samuel, O.B.E., R.F.C.

CRESWICK, Capt. James Paul, O.B.E., *b.* 25 Sept. 1866; *s.* of James Creswick, of Molesey, Surrey; *m.* Maude, *d.* of George Morris, of Keynsham, Somerset. *Educ.:* South Lambeth Grammar School. County Transport Officer, Kent Voluntary Aid Detachment; o/c Group 3, Kent R.A.S.C., M.T.(V.); Area Transport Officer, Ministry of Food. *Address:* Addiscombe Court, Wilbury Rd., Hove. *Clubs:* Authors'; Whitefriars; London Scottish Rifles' Lodge. (O10225)

CREWDSON, Lieut., T. Capt. Bernard Francis, C.B.E., Irish Guards, *b.* 9 July, 1887; *s.* of F. W. Crewdson, Gilling Grove, Kendal. *Educ.:* Uppingham; King's College, Cambridge. Chief of British Relief Mission to Poland, 1919. *War Work:* Border Regiment, in Gallipoli and France, 1915–17; Irish Guards, France, 1917–18; -Ministry of Munitions, Labour Supply Dept., 1916. *Address:* Karolinengasse 5, Vienna. *Clubs:* United University; American; Guards'; A.D.C.; Warsaw Rowing. (C2537)

CREWE, Capt. and Qr.-Mr. Frank, O.B.E.

CREWE, Helen Agnes Josephine, Lady, O.B.E.; *d.* of Hon. Joseph Orpen, M.L.C., Surveyor-General of Rhodesia; *m.* 11 July, 1887, Sir Charles Preston, K.C.M.G., C.B. *s.* of Frederick Crewe (*see* BURKE'S *Peerage*, Crewe, M.). *Address:* East London, Cape Colony. (O2200)

CRIBBES, George, O.B.E.

CRICHTON, Brevet-Major George Keeble, M.B.E., M.C., *b.* 5 Oct. 1888; *s.* of Walter Crichton, of Belgrave, Rutherglen, Lanarkshire; *m.* Catherine Bryce Fairley, *d.* of Thomas Topping, of Edinburgh. *War Work:* Recalled from Territorial Force Reserve on 5 Aug. 1914, and posted to the Lowland Divisional Train, R.A.S.C. (T.); appointed Adjutant, Lowland Divisional Train, 6 Oct. 1914; appointed Senior Supply Officer, 10th Division, and promoted T.-Major, R.A.S.C., 1 Jan. 1916; appointed Deputy Assist.-Adj. and Quartermaster-Gen., G.H.Q., Egyptian Expeditionary Force, 29 Dec. 1917; appointed Assist.-Adj.-Gen. (O.E.T.A.), G.H.Q., E.E.F., and promoted T. Lieut.-Col. 16 Sept. 1918; appointed Assist. Administrator (Class X), O.E.T.A. (Palestine), and Lieut.-Col. 17 Nov. 1918; disembodied to Territorial Force, 12 Sept. 1920; awarded Military Cross, Jan. 1917; Brevet-Major, June 1918; mentioned in despatches, O.B.E., Jan. 1919. Order of the Nile, Jan. 1920; *Addresses:* 24, Queen Street, Glasgow; 16, Crown Terrace, Dowanhill, Glasgow. *Clubs:* Conservative, Glasgow; R.A.C., London. (O2879)

CRICHTON, Capt. Henry Lumsden, M.B.E., R.A.F.

CRICHTON, Lady Jane Emma, C.B.E. C.I.; *o. d.* of Thomas George, P.C., G.C.S.I., 1st Earl Northbrook; *m.* 29 Jan., 1890, Col. the Hon. Sir Henry George Lewis Crichton, K.C.B., 3rd *s.* of John 3rd Earl Erne, K.P. (C2538)

CRIGHTON, Jean, Mrs. Cullen, O.B.E. (O8349)

CRIGHTON, John, O.B.E.

CRICHTON, Eng.-Capt. Peter Thomson, C.B.E., *b.* 1863; *s.* of John Crichton, Engineer R.N., of Southsea; *m.* 1888, Alice Maud, *d.* of George Perfect, of Portsmouth, Eng. Capt. R.N. (ret.); Consulting Engineer; served in the Great War 1914–19, on Staff. *Address:* 41, Chapel Walks, South Castle Street, Liverpool. (C2308)

CRIDLAND, Frank, C.B.E. (C3187)

CRIPPS, Lieut.-Comm. Arthur Edward William, O.B.E., R.N.R.

CRIPPS, Lieut. George Wilfitt, M.B.E.

CRIPPS, Gerald Faulkner, M.B.E.

CRIPPS, Major Henry Rivers, M.B.E.

CRIPPS, Major the Hon. Leonard Harrison, C.B.E.; *b.* 21 April, 1887; 3rd *s.* of Sir Charles Alfred Cripps, 1st Baron Parmoor (*see* BURKE'S *Peerage*); *m.* 5 April, 1913, Miriam Barbara, *d.* of Sir Mathew Ingle Joyce, Justice of the High Court. (C135)

CRIPPS, Lucy Davis, M.B.E., M.B., Ch.B.

CRISFORD, George Northcote, C.B.E., B.A. (Cantab), *b.* 19 Feb. 1880; *s.* of George Stephen Crisford, F.I.A., of Kingshill House, Swindon; *m.* Effie Mary, *d.* of the late William Saul, M.D., of Boscombe. *Educ.:* Merchant Taylors' School and Emmanuel College, Cambridge. Colonial Civil Service; District Commissioner, East Africa (retired 1916); Jan. 1919, General Manager, Mac Fisheries, Ltd., 33, St. James' Square, S.W. 1; Director, Mac Fisheries, Ltd., Charles Saunders, Ltd.. Mac Line Drifters & Trawlers Co., Ltd., Sprigens, Ltd., The Premier Fishmeal Co., Ltd. *War Work:* Captain, East Africa Forces, D.A.A.G.; War Office; Director of National Service, Northern Region; Inspector of Regions, Ministry of National Service. *Address:* 2, Titchfield Road, Regents Park, N.W. 1. *Clubs:* Royal Societies'; Sports. (C947)

CRISP, Annette Ina, M.B.E., W.R.N.S.

CRISP, Eng.-Capt. Arthur Samuel, C.B.E. Eng.-Capt. R.N.; served in the Great War. 1914–19 (despatches). (C1920)

CRISP, Cadet Lieut.-Col. Charles Doland, O.B.E.

CRISP, Helena Jane, M.B.E., V.A.D.

CRISP, John, O.B.E.

CRISPIN, Edward Smyth, C.B.E. (C3182)

CRISWELL, Major Walter, O.B.E., A.M.I.C.E. Civil Engineer. *War Work:* 5½ years' service in Royal Engineers in Gallipoli, France, North Russia. (O6796)

CRITCHINSON, William Thomas, M.B.E.

CRITCHLEY, Herbert Lawson, O.B.E., *b.* 1877; *s.* of James Critchley, of Bury, Lancashire; *m.* Edith, *d.* of Seth Holding, of Adlington, Lancs. *Educ.:* Bury Grammar School. Works Manager, Locomotive Works, Sir W. G. Armstrong Whitworth's, Newcastle-on-Tyne. *War Work:* Director of

Technical and Efficiency Dept. for National Shell and Projectile Factories, Ministry of Munitions, 1915–17; Assist. Controller, Dept. of Engineering, Ministry of Munitions, 1917–19. *Address:* Dinglesyde, Queen's Road, Monkseaton, Northumberland. (O10228)

CRITCHLEY, William Edwin, M.B.E., R.A.F.

CRITCHLOW, Major John, O.B.E., R.E.

CRITIEN, Attilio, M.B.E., M.D., M.A.

CROAD, Hector, O.B.E.

CROAL, George Crammond, O.B.E.

CROCKER, Lieut.-Col. Arthur Albert, O.B.E., *b.* 20 Oct. 1872; *s.* of Arthur William Crocker, of 3, Second Avenue, Hove; *m.* Dorothy Seymour, *d.* of Lieut.-Col. William Howard, of East Lodge, Bexhill-on-Sea. *Educ.:* Golden Parsonage, Hemel Hempstead, and Harrow. *War Work:* Served with 3rd Battn. Essex Regt., Harwich, on mobilisation; 2nd in command of 11th Service Battn. Essex Regt. B.E.F.; promoted to command 3rd Battn. Essex Regt., June, 1917 Battn. stationed at Harwich, Rugeley and Kinsale. *Club:* Junior United Service. (O7049)

CROCKER, Lieut. Gordon George, M.B.E., B.A. Cantab, *b.* 14 June, 1893; *s.* of George Henry Crocker, of South Molton, Devon. *Educ.:* Cheltenham and Clare College, Cambridge. Private Secretary to the Financial Adviser to the Persian Government, 1920. *War Services:* Inniskillings (6th Dragoons) Special Reserve, attached to the General Staff for Intelligence Work. *Address:* Thorne, Enford, Taunton. *Club:* Oxford and Cambridge. (M289)

CROCKETT, Capt. Leonard Marshall, O.B.E.

CROCKETT, William Gordon, M.B.E., *b.* 18 Dec. 1880 *s.* of the late Alexander Irvine Crockett, of Finchley. *Educ.:* Kentish Town High School. First Class Clerk, Stores Department, India Office. *War Work:* Work in connection with the purchase and supply of stores (Ordnance, Clothing, etc.) to the Indian Army. *Address:* 10, Bowrons Avenue, Alperton, Middlesex (M290)

CROFT, Charles Rowland, M.B.E.

CROFT, Ernest Samuel, O.B.E., *b.* 7 May, 1867; *s.* of Christopher F. Croft, of London; *m.* Helen Louise, *d.* of Thomas Whiting, of London. *Educ.:* North London Collegiate School, and King's College, London. Assistant Accountant-General of the Navy. *Address:* Red Lodge, The Park, Hampstead, N.W. 3. (O263)

CROFT, Lieut. George Henry Belton, M.B.E.

CROFT, Geraldine May, O.B.E., V.A.D.

CROFT, Capt. Tom, O.B.E.

CROFTON, Augusta Maude, Mrs., M.B.E.; *d.* of Gen. Sir Henry Lefroy, C.B., K.C.M.G.; *m.* the late Capt. Duke Crofton, R.N., *s.* of Gen. R. H. Crofton. *War Work:* Soldiers' and Sailors' Families Association Sec., Co. Leitrim. *Address:* Lakefield, Mohill, Co. Leitrim. (M7799)

CROFTON, Lieut. Richard Llewellyn, M.B.E., R.A.F.

CROKER, Alice Georgiana, O.B.E., *b.* 12 March, 1845; *d.* of the late Capt. Crocker, late 17th Lancers, and Lady Georgina Croker, of Ballynagarde, Limerick. *Educ.:* Privately. Sec. Royal Irish Association for Employment and Training of Women from 1886–1903; Sec. Irish Training School of Domestic Economy, Dept. of Agriculture and Technical Instruction for Ireland, 1903–10. *War Work:* Hon. Treas. Dublin Committee Royal Dublin Fusiliers Prisoners of War, 1914–19. *Address:* 4, St. Mary's Road, South, Dublin. (O10229)

CROKER, Major Crofton, O.B.E.

CROLL, Col. G. D., C.B.E. Lieut.-Col. and T. Col. Australian Army Med. Corps; served in the Great War, 1915–19 (despatches) (C1395)

CROMAR, George Scott, M.B.E.

CROMBIE, Lieut. Colin Ross, M.B.E., *b.* 1877; *s.* of John L. Crombie, M.D., of North Berwick. *Educ.:* Abbey School, North Berwick. *War Work:* Enlisted in the R.A.S.C., Nov. 1914; went overseas to France in April, 1915; drove a lorry for 9 months; commissioned in R.A.S.C., Nov. 1915; was put in charge of Hydraulic Tyre Press with 3rd Army; created record for Solid Tyre fitting in France, having put on 100 Solid Tyres to 588 vehicles in one week, during the push in Nov.–Dec. 1915; stayed with 3rd Army in charge of "J" Mobile Tyre Press until demobilised in April, 1920. *Clubs:* Scottish Conservative, Edinburgh; R.A.S.C., London. (M4460)

CROMBIE, Henry, M.B.E.

CROME, Lieut. Harry, M.B.E.

CROMPTON, Capt. Charles, O.B.E., A.M.I.E.E., R.E. (T.), *b.* 1864; *s.* of Robert Crompton, of Liverpool; *m.* Mary Rebecca, *d.* of John Curphey, of Liverpool *Educ.:* The Grange School, Bootle, Liverpool, and Liverpool Univ. (Engineering Section). Assistant Superintending Engineer, Post Office Engineering Department, Scotland (East) District, G.P.O., Edinburgh. *War Service:* Adviser to General Officer Commanding-in-Chief, Scottish Command, on communications (Telegraph and Telephone); also in charge of all War Emergency communications for Admiralty, War Office, Air Ministry, Ministries of Munitions, Food, Timber, Wool, etc., in the East and North of Scotland, and Islands of Orkney, Shetland and Western Hebrides. *Address:* 27, St. Clair Terrace, Edinburgh. (O10230)

CROMPTON, Claud, O.B.E., *b.* 1876; *s.* of Col. Crompton, C.B., R.E.; *m.* Jeanetta, *d.* of Sir Thomas Gordon, K.C.B., K.C.I.E., C.S.I. *Educ.:* Harrow and Trinity College, Cambridge. *War Work:* Inspector of Small Arms Ammunition, and Consulting Engineer for Electric Power Station, and Heating and Lighting Plant, at the Government M. T. Depot, Slough. *Address:* 61, Vanbrugh Park, Blackheath, S.E. 3. *Club:* Royal Automobile. (O264)

CROMPTON, Capt. James, O.B.E., I.A.

CROMPTON, Rev. James, O.B.E., M.A., *b.* 19 July, 1886; *s.* of Henry D. Crompton, of Edgbaston. *Educ.:* West House, Edgbaston; Sedbergh; Caius Coll., Cambridge. Late Capt. 10th Jats I.A., now in Holy Orders. *War Work:* France, 1914–15; N.W.F. India, 1916–17; Mesopotamia, 1918; Salonica, 1918–19; South Russia, 1919; Anatolia, 1919; retired, Nov. 1919. *Address:* c/o Thos. Cook and Son, London. *Club:* Junior Naval and Military. (O8683)

CROMPTON, Robert, C.B.E., *b.* 1869; *s.* of Robert Crompton, of Bolton; *m.* Rosaline, *d.* of Charles Allen, of Warrington. *Educ.:* Blue Coat School, Warrington. Solicitor, M.L.C., Fiji, a Member of Roy. Colonial Institute, and Vice-Pres. British Empire Producers Asso.; sometime Solicitor, Supreme Court, England. *Address:* Tamavua House, Suva, Fiji. (C734)

CROMWELL, Oliver Underwood, M.B.E., *b.* 29 Nov. 1877; *s.* of Joshua Cromwell, of Bradford; *m.* Annie, *d.* of Edwin Ogden Ratcliffe, of Bingley. *Educ.:* Borough West School, and Technical Coll., Bradford. Superintendent of Police. *War Work:* Organising special constables; alien and military enquiry work; executive officer, Ministry of Food; fuel overseer; Sec. Profiteering Tribunal; Organising Sec. Trade pools for Food distribution; organised local transport for distributing food and coal during National Railway Strike, 1919. *Address:* St. Ives, Armthorpe Lane, Doncaster. (M7800)

CROOK, Major and Qr.-Mr. Arthur, O.B.E.

CROOK, Shipwright-Lieut. George Henry Holland, M.B.E., R.N.

CROOK, John Rowland, O.B.E.

CROOK, William Montgomery, O.B.E., B.A., F.R.G.S., *b.* 1860; *s.* of the late Rev. W. Crook, D.D., of Galway. *Educ.:* Methodist College, Belfast; Drogheda Grammar School; Trinity College, Dublin. Head Classical Master, Wesley College, Dublin; Assistant Editor, "Methodist Times"; Editor, "Echo"; Sec. Eighty Club; Sec. Home Counties Liberal Federation. *War Work:* Hon. Organiser, Church Collections for Red Cross Society, 1914–18, which raised about £300,000 for Red Cross. *Addresses:* 5, Spencer Mansions, Queen's Club Gardens, West Kensington, W. 14; 42, Parliament Street, S.W. 1. *Clubs:* Devonshire; National Liberal; Eighty. (O1248)

CROOKE, Jane Duttie, Mrs., M.B.E.

CROOKE, Victor, M.B.E., *b.* 18 Oct. 1866; *s.* of William Hugh Crooke, of Preston; *m.* Alice, *d.* of Edward Walker, of Wolverhampton. *Educ.:* Wolverhampton. Clerk and Solicitor; Deputy Town Clerk of Walsall, and Executive Officer for the Borough of Walsall Food Control Committee. *War Work:* National Registration; National Service in London and Walsall; Food Control work for Walsall; Allotment extension; acted as Hon. Sec. for Mayor's After-War Fund, and also in similar capacity to Walsall War Memorial Fund. *Address:* Woodstock, Borneo Street, Walsall. (M3596)

CROOKHAM, Rev. William Thomas Rupert, C.B.E. Was Rector of Haddenham, Camb. 1893–1905, since when he has been Vicar of Wisbech. *War Services:* 1914–19, as 1st class Chaplain to Forces (despatches). *Address:* The Vicarage, Wisbech. (C1534)

CROOKS, Capt. David Robert, M.B.E., A.I.F.

CROOKS, Capt. Lindsay, M.B.E., R.A.F.

CROOKSTON, John Gray, C.B.E., *b.* 12 Sept. 1864; *s.* of Thomas Crookston, of Glasgow; *m.* Ella, *d.* of Vladimir Déline, of Petrograd. *Educ.:* Odessa and Glasgow. Engineer and Naval Architect; Vice-President of the Russian Shipbuilding Co., and of the Chantiers Navals de Nicolaieff; Managing Director of the Salamander Steel Works of Riga. *War Work:* Controller of the British Ministry of Information (Russian Section); Builder of the Russian Black Sea Fleet; Manufacture of Munitions of War, etc. *Address:* Galernaya 63, Petrograd; and Cotham House, Weybridge, Surrey. *Clubs:* Mining and Metallurgical; Petrograd Yacht Club; British Club of Petrograd. (C948)

CROPPER, Ann Ellen, Mrs., M.B.E.

CROPPER, Edward, O.B.E.

CROPPER, Marjorie Constance, Mrs., M.B.E., *b.* 24 March, 1888; *d.* of Josceline Fitzroy Bagot, Bart., of Levens (*see* BURKE'S *Peerage*); *m.* James Winstanley, *s.* of Charles James Cropper, of Ellergreen, Kendal. *War Work:* County Sec. to S. and S.F.A. at beginning of war; subsequently District Sec. to Statutory Committee and N. and M. War Pensions Committee till the end of the war; member of Executive, Finance, and Disablement Committees for County; organised Club for soldiers' wives. *Address:* Summer How, Kendal.

CROSBIE, Flight-Lieut. Dudley Stuart Kay, O.B.E., R.A.F.

CROSBIE, Sir John Chalker, K.B.E., *b.* 11 Sept. 1876; *s.* of George Graham Crosbie, of Dumfries, Scotland; *m.* Mitchie A., *d.* of Josiah Manuel, of Exploits, Nfld. *Educ.:* Methodist Coll., St. John's, Newfoundland. Managing Owner of Crosbie and Company; elected to Newfoundland Legislature for District of Bay de Verde 1908; re-elected 1909–13; Member, Executive Council, 1909; Acting Prime Minister, 1918; re-elected to Legislature for Port de Grave, 1919. *War Work:* Chairman of Tonnage Committee of the Executive Council,

1917; Minister of Shipping, 1917–19. *Address:* Devon Place, Kingsbridge Road, St. John's, Newfoundland. *Clubs:* City; St. Andrews; Old Colony; Ballyhaly Golf; Curling. (K312)

CROSBIE, Maxwell Arthur, O.B.E., *b.* 20 July, 1881; *s.* of Maxwell Crosbie, of Southampton and London; *m.* Margaret, *d.* of John Shaw, of Boston (Lincs.) *War Work:* In connection with erection and running of plant for manufacture of Chemical Filling for Box (Anti-gas) Respirators, at Messrs. Boots Pure Drug Co.'s Works at Nottingham. *Address:* 11, Leonard Avenue, Nottingham. (O3675)

CROSBIE, Capt. William Maxwell, M.B.E., R.E.

CROSBY, Ada, M.B.E.

CROSBY, Josiah, C.I.E., O.B.E., *b.* 25 May, 1880; *s.* of J. P. Crosby, of Southport; *Educ.:* Royal Grammar School, Newcastle-on-Tyne, and Gonville and Caius Coll., Cambridge. H.B.M. Consul, Saigon, Cochin-China; at present officiating as H.B.M. Consul-General at Batavia, Java. *War Work:* In performance of duties as a member of His Majesty's Consular Service in Siam. *Address:* H.B.M. Consulate-General, Batavia, Java. *Clubs:* British (Bangkok); Batavia Cricket; Royal (Bangkok); Sports (Siam). (O267)

CROSBY, Capt. Reginald Douglas, O.B.E., M.C.

CROSHER, William Samuel, M.B.E.

CROSLAND, Clarence Field, M.B.E.

CROSS, Arthur, M.B.E.

CROSS, Capt. Arthur Gordon, M.B.E., M.C.

CROSS, Bertram Charles, M.B.E.

CROSS, Lieut. Cecil Woodrow, O.B.E., R.N.V.R.

CROSS, Capt. Charles Garsed, M.B.E.

CROSS, Lieut.-Comm. Charles Henry Dennis, O.B.E., R.N.R.

CROSS, Edward Alfred, M.B.E.

CROSS, Ernest, M.B.E.

CROSS, Grenville Burgess, M.B.E.

CROSS, Lieut. James, O.B.E., R.N.R.

CROSS, Minnie Eleanor Elizabeth, M.B.E., *b.* 14 June, 1869; *d.* of Charles Thomas Cross, of Acton and City of London. *Educ.:* Miss Frances Mary Buss's School and H. and C. Coll. Responsible Mistress of Tollington Park L.C.C. Women's Institute. *War Work:* Asst. Lady Supt. of Royal Arsenal, Woolwich; and Supt. of the Juvenile Unemployment Educational Centre, Woolwich, after the Armistice and until Aug. 1919. (M1600)

CROSS, Richard Basil, O.B.E., *b.* 18 March, 1881; *s.* of late Thomas Cross, of Beckenham, Kent; *m.* Janet Helen, *d.* of Peter Hurst. *Educ.:* Dulwich and Corpus Christi College, Oxford. (Scholar, C.C.C.; 1st Class Classical Moderations, 2nd Class Litt. Hum.); Civil Servant, Assistant Secretary, Ministry of Health; formerly Private Secretary to successive Presidents of the Local Government Board. *Address:* Ravensbourne, Epsom, Surrey. *Club:* R.A.C. (O268)

CROSS, Robert, M.B.E.

CROSS, Robert William Ryder, M.B.E.

CROSSE, Rev. Arthur John William, C.B.E., T.D., B.A., *s.* of the late Archdeacon A. B. Crosse. Res. Canon of Norwich Cathedral; *m.* Mary Charlotte, *d.* of the late William Sisson, of Wrexham. *Educ.:* Dedham Grammar School; London University; Leeds Clergy School. Vicar of Rye, Sussex, 1888; Vicar of S. Cyprian's, Durban, S. Africa, 1902; Vicar of S. James, Barrow, 1906; Vicar of S. Cuthbert's, Carlisle, 1910; Vicar of Stow Bardolph and Rector of Wimbotsham, 1919; Territorial Chaplain to the Forces since 1890; now 1st Class. *War Work:* Chaplain in 1914 to the 11th Border Regt. (the Lonsdales); Chaplain to 97th Brigade, 1915; Senior Chaplain to 32nd Division at the Front, from Nov. 1915, to April, 1919; 3 times mentioned in despatches. *Address:* Stow Vicarage, Downham, Norfolk. (C766)

CROSSE, Lieut. James Frederick, M.B.E.

CROSSINGHAM, Agatha Gwendoline Rees, M.B.E.

CROSSKEY, Lieut.-Col. Cecil, O.B.E., V.D., R.A.S.C. (T.F.)

CROSSKILL, Lieut.-Col. Reginald Charles Osborne, O.B.E., Cadet Norfolk Artillery, *b.* 17 Feb. 1888; *s.* of C. R. Crosskill, of Norwich. *Educ.:* King Edward VI. Grammar School; King Edward VI. Commercial School (Norwich and Wymondham). Officer Commanding Cadet Norfolk Artillery (affiliated to 1st East Anglian Brigade, R.F.A.); President and Chairman, 1st V.B. Norfolk Regt. Veterans' Association; President, Cadet Norfolk Artillery Old Comrades' Association; Hon. Sec. Norfolk Miniature Rifle Association; Hon. Sec. Norfolk Branch Ex-Officers National Union. *War Service:* Mercantile Marine; Volunteer and Cadet Forces training and organising; awarded British War Medal, and British Mercantile Marine War Medal. *Addresses:* Highbury Lodge, Thorpe Road, Norwich; Royal Field Artillery Barracks, All Saints' Green, Norwich. (O10231)

CROSSLEY, Professor Arthur William, C.M.G., C.B.E., D.Sc., LL.D., F.R.S.; *s.* of the late Richard Crossley, of Accrington; *m.* 1901, Muriel, *d.* of the late R. Lamb, of Liverpool. Professor of Chemistry, Pharmaceutical Soc.; Professor of Chemistry in King's Coll., Univ. of London; Foreign Sec. Chemical Soc.; Officer of Legion of Honour; sometime Lieut.-Col. R.E. *Address:* King's College, Strand, W.C. 2. (C2097)

CROSSLEY, Audrey, Mrs., M.B.E.; *d.* of Alfred Thomson, of Belfast; *m.* Basil Charles, *s.* of Arthur C. Crossley, of Belfast. *Educ.:* Brussels and Hamburg. *War Work:* Qualified Red Cross nurse, Theydon Towers, Essex, Sept. 1915, to Dec. 1916; Section Head, Ministry of Pensions,

London, Feb. 1917, to April, 1918 ; joined British War Mission in New York, May, 1918 ; appointed superintendent Cabling Dept., June, 1918. *Address :* 28, Gledhow Gardens, S.W. 5. (M3598)

CROSSLEY, Major Eric, O.B.E.

CROSSLEY, Capt. George Henry, M.B.E., *b.* 1895 ; *s.* of Henry Leonard Crossley, Tapton Croft, Sheffield ; *m.* Jessie, *d.* of B. Howkins, of Bromham, Bedford. *Educ. :* Wesley Coll. Sheffield. *Address :* Beachcroft, Baslow, Derbyshire. (M5198)

CROSSMAN, Francis Ward, O.B.E., M.B.

CROSSMAN, Major Robert Francis, O.B.E.

CROSTHWAITE, Capt. Arthur Tonley, O.B.E., R.A.S.C.

CROSTHWAITE, Major Charles Gilbert, O.B.E., *b.* 3 June, 1878 ; *s.* of Sir Robert Crosthwaite, K.C.S.I. ; *m.* Joan, *d.* of Major-Gen. A. C. Becher, C.B.E. *Educ. :* Shrewsbury School and Sandhurst. Political Department, Government of India. *Address :* c/o Messrs. Thos. Cook and Son, Ludgate Circus. (O8245)

CROSTHWAITE, Lieut.-Col. Henry Robert, C.I.E., C.B.E., *b.* 1876 ; *s.* of the late Sir Charles Crosthwaite, K.C.S.I. ; *m.* 1896, Ada Elizabeth Berry. *Educ. :* Clifton ; Oxford Univ. Entered I.C.S. 1897 ; Assist. Commr. Central Provinces 1902 ; Registrar Co-operative Credit Socs. 1911 ; also Dep. Commr. 1915 ; Sec. Central Provinces War Board ; T. Lieut.-Col. Indian Army Reserve of Officers. *Address :* Jubbulpore, Central Provinces, India. *Club :* Savile. (C2377)

CROSTHWAITE, Capt. William Henry, O.B.E.

CROTHERS, Capt. Wallace Guy Murdock, M.B.E., R.A.F.

CROTTY, Capt. Trevor, M.B.E.

CROUCH, Paymaster Lieut.-Comm. Charles Henry Anson, O.B.E., R.N.

CROUCHER, Lieut. Edward William, M.B.E., R.N.

CROUCHER, Wilfred Gladstone, M.B.E., *b.* 4 Dec. 1883 ; *s.* of the late Rev. Charles Croucher, of Victoria, British Columbia ; *m.* Mary Kate, *d.* of George Bennett, of Staple Hill, Bristol. *Educ. :* The Merchant Venturers Technical Coll., Bristol. *War Work :* Hon. Sec. Bridgwater Local Committee for War Savings ; Joint Hon. Sec. Parliamentary Recruiting Committee ; Joint Hon. Sec. War Aims Committee ; Hon. Sec. Peace Celebrations and War Memorial Committee ; Member of Bridgwater Food Control Committee. *Address :* The Cottage, Wembdon, Bridgwater, Somerset. (M7809)

CROW, Ada Maud, M.B.E., *b.* 20 Oct. 1885 ; *d.* of William Crow, of Boreham, Essex. *War Work :* Canteen and Relief Work at the Missions to Seamen's Station, Stornoway, Isle of Lewis, N.B. *Address :* St. Margarets, Ferndale Road, Woking. (M7810)

CROW, Alwyn Douglas, O.B.E., *s.* of John Kent Crow, D.Sc., F.I.C., of Blackheath. *Educ. :* Westminster School, and Queens' College, Cambridge. Director of Ballistic Research, Woolwich Arsenal ; Associate Member of the Ordnance Committee, etc. *War Work :* Temp. commission, East Surrey Regt., 20 Oct. 1914 ; promoted to temp. Capt., 11 Nov. 1915 ; served in France, 1916 ; wounded at Delville Wood, Sept. 1916 ; appointed to Research Dept., Woolwich, March, 1917, and served there for the rest of the war ; mentioned in despatches, 1918. *Address :* 20, West Park, Eltham, Kent. *Club :* Devonshire. (O1249)

CROW, John, M.B.E.

CROWDEN, Capt. and Qr.-Mr. Henry Clarence, M.B.E.

CROWDY, Edith Frances, C.B.E., Serving Sister of the Order of St. John of Jerusalem ; *d.* of James Crowdy. *Educ. :* Privately. Divisional Secretary for Paddington British Red Cross Society, 1912. *War Work :* Senior Staff Commandant, V.A.D., H.Q. ; Deputy Director, Women's Royal Naval Service, 1917–19. *Club :* Portsmouth. (C921)

CROWDY, Isabel, O.B.E., A.R.C.M., *d.* of James Crowdy *Educ. :* Privately ; Royal College of Music. General Secretary of the Society for the Oversea Settlement of British Women. *War Work :* V.A.D. Quartermaster ; Commandant and Area Commandant in France, from 1914–18 ; Assistant Director, Inspection and Training of Women's Royal Naval Service, 1918–19. *Clubs :* Portsmouth Blue Triangle ; V.A.D. (O1251)

CROWDY, Mary, O.B.E., also Serving Sister of the Order of St. John of Jerusalem ; *d.* of James Crowdy. *Educ. :* Privately. *War Work :* Assistant-Principal Commandant V.A.D.s in France ; V.A.D. work from Jan. 1913, till present date ; V.A.D. work in France, 19 Oct. 1914, to 17 July, 1919. *Address :* 100, Beaufort St., Chelsea. *Club :* Portsmouth ; V.A.D. Ladies'. (C478)

CROWDY, Dame Rachel Eleanor, D.B.E., R.R.C., *b.* 3 March, 1884 ; *d.* of the late James Crowdy, M.A., of 8, Orsett Terrace, Hyde Park. *Educ. :* Hyde Park New College, London. 1912–14, Lecturer and Demonstrator, National Health Soc. ; Health Member of the Secretariat of the League of Nations ; Member of Voluntary Aid Advisory Committee ; Joint Women's V.A.D. Committee ; International Committee of Girl Guides ; Associate of Social Students Union. *War Work :* Served with B.E.F., from 1914–19, as Principal Commandant of V.A.D.s, France and Belgium ; Awards, 1916, despatches ; 1916, Royal Red Cross (2nd Class) ; 1917, Royal Red Cross (1st Class) ; 1917, Lady of Grace, Order of St. John of Jerusalem ; 1919, Dame of the British Empire ; Mons Star. *Address :* 100, Beaufort Street, Chelsea. *Club :* Portsmouth. (D33)

CROWE, Lieut. George Gordon, M.B.E., Mons Star, *b.*

29 March, 1891 ; *s.* of George Cranmer Crowe, of Southsea ; *m.* Rene Flora, *d.* of Albert W. Partridge, of Lewisham. *Educ. :* Sir Joseph Williamson's Mathematical School, Rochester, Kent. Assurance Clerk. *War Service :* Nov. 1914, to Nov. 1915, served with the British Red Cross Society in France (Anglo-Belge Hospital, Calais) ; Dec. 1915, to March, 1916, Salonika ; April, 1916, to Nov. 1918, Mesopotamia (promoted Lieut.) ; Nov. 1918, to March, 1919, Persia, Lieut. in charge Red Cross Depot for distribution of stores to Hospitals and Ambulances. *Address :* 7, Beaufort Gardens, Lewisham, S.E. 13. *Club :* Ibis. (M1607)

CROWE, Major Henry Aubrey, O.B.E., R.A.V.C.

CROWE, Lieut. Joseph John, O.B.E., R.E.

CROWE, William, M.B.E. (M10246c)

CROWFOOT, John Winter, O.B.E.

CROWLEY, Cuthbert, O.B.E., *b.* 1883 ; *s.* of the Rev. H. E. Crowley, of Albury Rectory, Surrey ; *m.* Jeanie Margaret, *d.* of John Currey, formerly of 30, Great George Street, Westminster. *Educ. :* Portsmouth Grammar School and Downton Agricultural Coll. Previous to 1914, farming in Western Canada. *War Work :* Served in France and Flanders in 5th Batt. Canadian Infantry ; discharged disabled in 1916 ; subsequently acted under the British Red Cross Society as Director of Kitchener House Club for disabled Sailors and Soldiers from 1917 to 1920. *Address :* Ridgway, Fordwich Lane, Canterbury, Kent. (O8676)

CROWTHER, Ethel Annie, O.B.E. (O11964)

CROWTHER, Lieut. Harold Oakes, M.B.E., I.A.R.O.

CROWTHER, Lawrence, O.B.E., *b.* 5 June, 1880 ; *s.* of Joe Crowther, of Golcar, nr. Huddersfield ; *m.* Clara, *d.* of Thomas Wood, of Golcar, nr. Huddersfield. *Educ. :* Huddersfield. Stock Broker. *War Work :* Hon. Sec. Huddersfield War Savings Committee ; Member of Advisory, Yorks (West Riding) Committee ; Chairman, Golcar Committee ; Treas., Belgian Refugees Committee ; Member of Food Control, War Pensions, and War Distress, Committees ; Hon. Sec. War Memorial Committee. *Address :* Ridgmont, Huddersfield. *Clubs :* Huddersfield Liberal ; Huddersfield Golf ; Elland Golf. (O10233)

CROWTHER, Major Walter, M.B.E.

CROWTHER, William, O.B.E., J.P., *b.* 30 April, 1845 ; *s.* of John Crowther, of Golcar ; *m.* Eliza Anne, *d.* of Law Heppenstall of Golcar. *Educ. :* Huddersfield Coll. Woollen Cloth Manufacturer. President of the Huddersfield and District Manufacturers' Association ; Chairman of W. and E. Crowther, Ltd., Globe Worsted Co., Ltd., etc. *War Work :* Acted on the following Committees : Wool Control Board, Wool Council, Dilution of Labour in the Woollen Trade, Allocation of Contracts for Military Cloths. *Address :* Field House, Slaithwaite. *Club :* Huddersfield. (O2677)

CROWTHER, Comm. William Reginald Denys, O.B.E., R.N.

CROXFORD, Charles Henry, O.B.E.

CROXTON, Edith Miriam, Mrs., M.B.E.

CROYDON, Capt. George, O.B.E., R.G.A.

CROYSDILL, Clifford William, C.B.E., *b.* 26 June, 1874 ; *s.* of the late Thomas Henry Croysdill, of London. *Educ. :* Privately. Assistant-Director of Navy Victualling. *War Work :* Served throughout the War as Superintendent of the Royal Victoria Yard, Deptford, S.E., the principal Admiralty Victualling Establishment. *Address :* Superintendent's House, Royal Victoria Yard, Deptford, S.E. *Club :* Union (Malta) ; Sports'. (C2539)

CROZIER, William, O.B.E., *b.* 3 Sept. 1875 ; *s.* of John Crozier, of Glassford, Lanarkshire ; *m.* Margaret Wilson, *d.* of James Young, of Rutherglen. *Educ. :* Glassford and Glengowan Public Schools. Assistant Superintendent of the Line, Caledonian Railway. *War Work :* Transport arrangements in connection with mobilisation in 1914, and in connection with general movements of troops and war material during the period of the War. *Address :* Braehead, Kirkhill, Lanarkshire. (O10236)

CRUDDAS, Hamilton Maxwell, O.B.E.

CRUDDAS, William John, O.B.E.

CRUICKSHANK, Alexander Jaffray, O.B.E.

CRUICKSHANK, Alexander Thomas, O.B.E.

CRUICKSHANK, George, M.B.E., *b.* 15 Jan. 1880 ; *s.* of John Cruickshank, Solicitor, of Elgin ; *m.* Margaret Henry, *d.* of James Henry Powrie, Perth. *Educ. :* Elgin Academy, and Glasgow Univ. Solicitor, Clerk and Treasurer to Haddington County Council and Western District Committee of the County Council. *War Work :* In connection with County Council, including War Pensions, National Registration, and Tribunal, etc. *Address :* Clarenceville, Haddington. *Club :* Conservative (Edinburgh). (M7812)

CRUICKSHANK, James, M.B.E., *b.* 2 June, 1865 ; *s.* of Alexander Cruickshank, of Barnes, S.E. ; *m.* 1st Elizabeth Antonia, *d.* of Alfred Hallamore, of Bromley, Kent ; 2ndly, Alice Jane, *d.* of the late Percy Swan Golds, of Goring, Sussex. *Educ. :* Leeds Middle Class School and King's Coll., London. Civil Servant, Air Ministry (late of War Office). *War Work :* At War Office and Ministry of Munitions (Aircraft Production Dept. on loan). *Address :* Amberley, Bridle Road, Purley, Surrey. (M7813)

CRUICKSHANK, James Bell, M.B.E., M.B.. C.M'

CRUICKSHANK, Lieut.-Col. Jasper Wallace, O.B.E., R.A.F.

CRUICKSHANK, Major Percy Hamilton, O.B.E., R.A.

CRUICKSHANK, Capt. Robert Scott, O.B.E., R.A.S.C.

CRUICKSHANK, William, M.B.E.

CRUICKSHANK, Rev. William Walker, O.B.E., M.A., B.D., *b.* 8 Oct. 1880 ; *s.* of James Smith Cruickshank, of Logie, Newton ; *m.* Mary Walker, *d.* of James Durno, of Uppermill. *Educ.:* Aberdeen Univ. *War Work:* Chaplain to the Forces, Nov. 1915, to Nov. 1919, attached 15th (Scottish) Division, 39th General Hosp., 17th C.C.S., 36th C.C.S. *Address:* 74, Gough Road, Edgbaston, Birmingham. (O5156)

CRUISE, Lieut. Albert John, M.B.E.

CRUM, Sir Walter Erskine, Knt. Bach., O.B.E., *b.* 2 Sept. 1874 ; *s.* of the late Walter Ewing Crum, of Thornliebank, Renfrew ; *m.* Violet Mary, *d.* of the late C. H. B. Forbes. President, Bengal Chamber of Commerce, 1919–20 ; Member Indian Imperial Legislative Council, 1919–20 ; Major, Calcutta Light Horse, 1913–20. *Address:* Ashton Grange, nr. Chester. *Club:* Union. (O2077)

CRUMP, Charles, O.B.E.

CRUMP, Major Edward Harold, O.B.E., R.E.

CRUMP, Lieut.-Col. Eldon Annesley, O.B.E.

CRUMP, Percy Charles, O.B.E., F.I.A., *b.* March, 1879 ; *s.* of Edwin Henry Crump, of Finsbury Park ; *m.* Ada Minnie, *d.* of Walter George Diggon, of E. Finchley. *Educ.:* Stroud Green Grammar School and Lady Owen's, Islington. Controller, Investments Department, Prudential Assurance Co., Ltd. *War Work:* Assistant to Sir George E. May, Manager of American Dollar Securities Committee, National Debt Office, 1916–19. *Address:* Claverley, Bramber Road, North Finchley. (O10239)

CRUTCHFIELD, Henry, O.B.E.

CRUTCHLEY, Capt. Ernest Tristram, O.B.E., R.E. (T.).

CUBITT, Hon. Helen Laura, C.B.E., *b.* Nov. 1855 ; eldest *d.* of George, 1st Lord Ashcombe. *War Work:* Care of Convalescent Officers under Red Cross. *Address:* Lyncourt, Torquay. (C2540)

CUBBON, Capt. Richard, M.B.E.

CUCKOW, Capt. Philip Edwin, O.B.E.

CUDDEFORD, Arthur Charles, M.B.E., *b.* 25 Feb. 1875. *Educ.:* Privately. Assistant Sec. British Red Cross Society. *War Work:* As Assistant Sec. British Red Cross Society, was engaged in administration work on behalf of the sick and wounded soldiers and sailors. *Address:* 40, Clifford Gardens, Willesden, N.W. 10. (M7814)

CUDLIP, Eng.-Capt. Edwin William, O.B.E., R.N.

CUDLIP, Ethel Annie Lina PENDER-, M.B.E. ; *d.* of the late Rev. Pender-Cudlip and Annie Thomas, of Sparkwell, Devon. Singer. *War Work:* Superintendent of the Women's Ration Packing Factory at the Supply Reserve Depot, Deptford, S.E. *Address:* 45, Norfolk Square, W. *Club:* New Century. (M1609)

CUDMORE, Lieut. and Qr.-Mr. Frederick William, M.B.E., R.A.M.C.

CUFF, Anna Holland, Mrs., O.B.E.

CUFF, Ethel, Mrs., M.B.E.

CUFF, Herbert Edmond, O.B.E., M.D. (Lond.), F.R.C.S. (Eng.), *b.* 27 Jan. 1864 ; *s.* of John Cuff, of Binderton, Sussex ; *m.* Nancy, *d.* of Dr. Philip Nunn, of Bournemouth. *Educ.:* Proprietary School, Blackheath, Kent. Principal Medical Officer to the Metropolitan Asylums Board, London. *War Work:* Resident Head of the Belgian Refugee Camp at the Alexandra Palace. *Addresses:* Woodside, Bookham, Surrey ; Metropolitan Asylums Board, Victoria Embankment, E.C. (O270)

CUFF, Stanley Geikie, M.B.E., *b.* 18 April, 1879 ; *s.* of Reverend William Cuff, of Shoreditch Tabernacle, London ; *m.* Mabel Lucy, *d.* of the late Reuben Message, of Norwood. *Educ.:* Bishop's Stortford Coll. *War Work:* Special Constabulary, Aug. 1914, to Feb. 1917 ; H.M. Forces, March, 1917, to Feb. 1918 ; Assistant Director of Tea Supplies, Ministry of Food, March, 1918, to May, 1919. *Addresses:* 7 Cardigan Mansions, Richmond Hill, Surrey ; 134, Fenchurch Street, London, E.C. *Club:* Old Stortfordians. (M7815)

CULBARD, Amelia Jane Chisholm, M.B.E., *b.* 1860 ; *d.* of William Culbard, J.P., of Oldmills, Elgin. *Educ.:* Elgin. *War Work:* District Head of Soldiers' and Sailors' Help Society ; Commandant Red Cross and organiser of Sphagnum moss and war dressing work parties. *Address:* Oldmills, Elgin (M1610)

CULL, Paymaster-Lieut-Comm. Malcolm Giffard Stebbing, O.B.E., R.N.

CULLEN of Ashbourne, Brien Ibrican, Lord, K.B.E. (*see* BURKE'S *Peerage*), *b.* 12 July, 1864 ; *s.* of George Edward Cokayne, of Roehampton ; *m.* Grace Margaret, *d.* of Rev. Hon. John Marsham. *Educ.:* Charterhouse. Deputy Governor and Governor of Bank of England, from April, 1915, to March, 1920, and served on several Government Committees. *Address:* Exeter House, Roehampton, S.W. 15. *Club:* Junior Carlton. (K17)

CULLEN, Jean Crickton, Mrs., O.B.E.

CULLEN, Capt. William John, M.B.E.

CULLEY, James, M.B.E., J.P., C.C., *b.* 15 Sept. 1878 ; *s.* of James Culley, of Kintbury, Berks. ; *m.* Lillian Annie, *d.* of James Hubbard, of Birmingham. *Educ.:* Public Elementary School. J.P. County Middlesex ; Member of the M.C.C. ; Member of Southall-Norwood Urban District Council. *War Work:* Chairman, Local Tribunal ; Chairman, Southall-Norwood U.D.C. 1915–17, also of National Service Committee ; Member of Middlesex War Pensions Committee, and Secretary of Southall and Hayes Sub-Local War Pensions Committee ;

Vice-Chairman, Middlesex Committee on Industrial Training, and a member of Advisory Committee on Munition Workers and Advisory Resettlement Committee, Ministry of Labour. (M7816)

CULLEY, Mrs. Zella Evelyn LEATHER-, O.B.E., *b.* 20 Oct. 1875 ; *d.* of John E. A. Dick Lander, of Huntleywood, Berwickshire ; *m.* the late Arthur George, late Coldstream Guards, *s.* of Arthur Hugo Leather-Culley, of Fowberry Tower, Northumberland. Member of Alnwick Board of Guardians since 1912 ; Vice-President, British Red Cross Society, Northumberland Branch, since 1909. *War Work:* Commandant Northumberland V.A.D. 4, Auxiliary Hospitals, Alnwick, and Command Depot Dressing Station, Alnwick ; Alnwick Red Cross Work Rooms. *Address:* The Green Gate, Alnwick, Northumberland. *Club:* Forum. (O3678)

CULLING, James William Henry, C.B.E., *b.* 25 Oct. 1870. Deputy-Director of Victualling, Admiralty. *War Work:* In connection with the Supply Services of the Fleet. (C2541)

CULLIS, Mary Aeldrin, M.B.E., *b.* 25 Oct. 1883 ; *d.* of Thomas Henry, of London. *Educ.:* Streatham Hill High School and Somerville Coll., Oxford. *War Work:* One year ambulance driving in Salonica ; one year ambulance driving, attached to French Army, Amiens, France ; two years running a Soldiers' Club in Amiens and later Abbeville, France ; one year in charge of a Y.M.C.A. Bookshop in Abbeville, France. *Address:* Alliston, Boscombe Manor, Bournemouth. *Club:* Ladies' University. (M7817)

CULLIS, Prof. Winifred Clara, O.B.E., D.Sc., *b.* 2 June, 1875 ; *d.* of Frederick John Cullis, of Kempsford House, Gloucester. *Educ.:* King Edward VI. High School for Girls, Birmingham, and Newnham. Professor of Physiology in the University of London attached to the London (Royal Free Hospital) School of Medicine for Women ; Member of the Industrial Fatigue Research Board, of the Girton College Council, and of the National Council for Combating Venereal Diseases. *War Work:* Propaganda work for the National War Savings movement, and for the National Council for combating Venereal Diseases, and from Dec. 1917 to May, 1918, filled the duties of the Chair of Physiology in the University of Toronto, Canada, and lectured widely in Eastern Canada. *Address:* 47, Belsize Avenue, Hampstead, N.W. 3. *Clubs:* Lyceum ; University Club for Ladies ; University of London. (O10243)

CULLUM, Henry John, M.B.E.

CULPIN, George Francis, O.B.E., *b.* 18 Nov. 1861 ; *s.* of the late Millice Culpin, of Stevenage ; *m.* Florence Sarah, *d.* of the late George Wright, of Stevenage. *Educ.:* Stevenage Grammar School and private boarding school, Rothbury College, Stroud Green, N. Acting Chief Examiner, War Office. *War Work:* Chief Examiner in the Directorate of Lands, which took over Lands and Buildings for war emergency purposes for the War Office, Ministry of Munitions, and Air Ministry, either under agreement or Defence of Realm powers, and dealt with compensation therefor. *Address:* Valence Manor, Clavering, Essex. *Club:* Farmers'. (O10244)

CULROSS, James, M.B.E., M.A., M.B., C.M., *b.* 20 Feb. 1864 ; *s.* of the late Rev. James Culross, M.A., D.D., of Bristol ; *m.* Helen Drummond, *d.* of James Grant, of Philadelphia. *Educ.:* City of London School ; Glasgow Academy ; Glasgow Univ. Medical Officer, Newton Abbot Hospital. *War Work:* Assistant Medical Officer to Newton Abbot V.A. Hospital ; afterwards O.C. Palmes en Or de l'Ordre de la Couronne conferred by King of the Belgians, Jan. 1920. *Address:* Roseneath, Newton Abbot, S. Devon. (M3599)

CULSHAW, Frank, M.B.E.

CULVER, Albert Leopold, M.B.E.

CULVER, Edith Bruce, Mrs., O.B.E., *b.* 15 Mar. 1869 ; *d.* of Joseph Chambers Mortlock ; *m.* William Robert Richard, *s.* of William Thomas Culver. *Educ.:* Privately. Headquarters Staff, Commandant, Kent Voluntary Aid Detachments ; Hon. Sec., Railwaywomen's Convalescent Home, Lavenham, Suffolk. *War Work:* Organising Secretary, Gravesend Division, Kent V.A.D.s ; Commandant, Rosherville V.A.D. Hospital, 1 year ; Chatham Area, Transport Officer, 2 years ; Kent Headquarters Staff, Commandant, 3 years. *Address:* Broomfield Hall, Swanley, Kent. *Club:* V.A.D. Ladies'. (O1254)

CUMBERBATCH, Hugh Carlton, O.B.E.

CUMBERLAND, Major Hugh Carlton, O.B.E., M.C.

CUMBERLAND, Capt. Thomas Daily, O.B.E., R.A.M.C., M.B.

CUMBERLEGE, Col. Archibald Farrington, O.B.E., R.E., *b.* 2 Sept. 1870 ; *s.* of the late Lieut. A. F. Cumberlege, R.E. ; *m.* Beatrice, *d.* of the late Colonel W. Warner, of the Madras Cavalry. *Educ.:* Blundell's School. China Campaign, 1900–01. *War Work:* Mesopotamia 1915. (O8456)

CUMBERLEGE, Major Barry Stephenson, O.B.E., B.A., *b.* 5 June, 1891 ; *s.* of Charles Farrington Cumberlege, of 1, Freeland Road, Ealing, W. 5 ; *m.* Louella Louisa, *d.* of James Gillis, of Matapedia, Quebec, Canada. *Educ.:* Durham School : Emmanuel Coll., Cambridge. *War Work:* Mechanical Transport, R.A.S.C. ; served overseas from Oct. 1914, to Feb. 1919 (mentioned in despatches). (O5159)

CUMBERLEGE, Major Cleland Bulstrode, D.S.O., O.B.E., *b.* 1875. Entered Army 1902, became Capt. Bedfordshire Regt. 1910 ; Major, 1915 ; S. Africa, 1900–1902, with Imperial Yeo. (Queen's medal with three clasps, King's medal with two clasps) ; served in the Great War, 1914–15 (despatches). (O7055)

CUMBERLEGE, Comm. Marcius Victor, O.B.E., R.E.

CUMING, Ethel Maud, Mrs., M.B.E., b. 15 Oct. 1864; d. of the late Col. Herbert Locock, C.B., R.E., of Frensham Grove, Farnham; m. Edward William Dirom, s. of the late Col. E. W. Cuming, 79th Q.O. Cameron Highlanders, of Crover, Co. Cavan, Ireland. Educ.: Privately, and Les Ruches, Fontainebleau. War Work: Commandant, B.R.C.S., V.A D London 100; Divisional Quartermaster and Asst. Hon. Sec. and Acting Divisional Sec., Kensington Division, B.R.C.S. Address: 20, Pembroke Road, Kensington, W. 8.

CUMING, Lieut.-Col. Robert John, D.S.O., O.B.E., b. 1872; Major and Brevet Lieut.-Col. Indian Army; China, 1900 (medal); Mesopotamia. 1914–18 (despatches). (O6602)

CUMING, Adm. Robert Stevenson Dalton, C.B.E., D.S.O., J.P., D.L., R.N., b. 10 Sept. 1852; s. of Col. Cumming, of Coulton, Cheltenham; m. Henrietta Florence, d. of Sir James Gibson Craig, Bart., of Riccarton, Midlothian (see BURKE'S Peerage). Educ.: Privately. War Work: Captain R.N.R. Yachts "Aries" and "Atalanta," North Sea, Irish Seas, and Mediterranean; Commodore in Charge of Larne Naval Base. Address: Eastbury Manor, Nr. Worcester. Clubs: United Service: Worcester County. (C2218)

CUMMING, Major Adam Bennett, O.B.E.

CUMMING, Alexander, O.B.E.

CUMMING, Alexander Charles, O.B.E., D.Sc.

CUMMING, Andrew Lawrence, M.B.E.

CUMMING, Lieut.-Col. Arthur Willie, O.B.E.

CUMMING, Beatrice, Mrs., O.B.E.

CUMMING, George, O.B.E., J.P.

CUMMING, Capt. Howard, O.B.E., R.A.F.

CUMMING, Ida Georgina, M.B.E.

CUMMING, Janet Barun, M.B.E., d. of John Cumming, of Kathlea, Dufftown. Educ.: Mortlach Public School and Privately. Gen. Sec., Scottish Y.W.C.A., 45, Melville Street, Edinburgh. War Work: Organising Secretary, Scottish Y.W.C.A. Clubs, Canteens, Hostels, Rest Homes, etc., for Munition and other war workers. (M297)

CUMMING, John Fleetwood, O.B.E., J.P., D.L., b. 5 Aug. 1863; s. of Lewis Cumming, of Cardow, Morayshire; m. Isabel, d. of Arthur Field, of London. Educ.: Aberdeen Univ. War Work: Military Representative and National Service Representative on Recruiting, Morayshire; Member of Executive Committee, Increased Food Production; Member of Food Control for County, then Chairman; Member of County Territorial Association, Morayshire. Addresses: The Dowans, Aberlour, Banffshire; East Cliff, Lossiemouth. Clubs: Conservative; Caledonian. (O3679)

CUMMING, Marjorie Stevenson, Mrs., O.B.E.

CUMMING, Capt. Percy, M.B.E.

CUMMING, Phoebe Eleanor, Mrs., M.B.E. (M10246e)

CUMMINGS, David Charles, C.B.E., b. 16 Dec. 1861; s. of George David Cummings, of Greenwich, S.E. Educ.: Roans School, Greenwich. Apprentice to Shipbuilding Trade, 1876; joined Trade Union, 1880; District Delegate for Yorkshire, 1895; Member of Leeds School Board, 1898; General Secretary of Union (Boilermakers and Ironshipbuilders) 1900; J.P. for Newcastle-on-Tyne, 1907; Member of Parliamentary Committee, Trade Union Congress, 1902–8; Chairman and President, 1905–6; joined Board of Trade, 1908; transferred to Chief Industrial Commissioner, as Assistant Industrial Commissioner, 1911; transferred to Ministry of Labour, 1916; Member of Industrial Court, 1919. War Work: Settling Trade and Labour disputes; Volunteer, 17th Division. Clubs: Catford Cricket and Lawn Tennis; Bellingham Bowling Club; Lewisham Volunteers'. (C479)

CUMMINGS, Hon. Emanuel Henry, M.B.E., J.P., M.L.C., b. 27 March, 1863; s. of Henry Benjamin Cummings, Merchant, of Freetown, Sierra Leone; m. Alice Maude, d. of William Ray Taylor, Merchant and Govt. Contractor, Ashantee Expedition, 1874. Educ.: Wesleyan Boys' High School, Freetown, and Queen's Coll., Taunton. Merchant, Member of the Legislative Council of Sierra Leone, 1913–17, re-appointed for another 5 years; Charity Commissioner since 1896; Justice of the Peace, 1902; Visiting Justice of the Gaol, 1902; Member of the Board of Education. During the war was Mayor of Freetown for 3 successive years; as Mayor interested himself in Red Cross Work and forwarding War Charities. Addresses: 18, Earl Street, Effnah House, Freetown, Sierra Leone, W.C. Africa. (M1260)

CUMMINGS, John Thomas, M.B.E.

CUMMINS, Hon. Paymaster-Capt. Henry Ashley Travers, C.B.E., O.B.E., R.N.

CUMMINS, Herbert Ashley Cunard, O.B.E.

CUNINGHAME, Helen Ethel, Mrs., M.B.E., d. of James McDouall, of Logan, Wigtonshire; m. Richard John, s. of Capt. John William Herbert Cuninghame. War Work: Assistant County Director, Deputy President Wigtonshire Branch, British Red Cross Society. Address: Hensol, Mossdale, Kirkcudbrightshire. Club: Ladies' Caledonian (Edinburgh). (M7824)

CUNINGHAME, Margaret Georgiana, M.B.E., b. 12 July, 1876; d. of Col. Cuningham, of 11th Hussars. War W)rk: Hon. Sec. and Superintendent to the Ayrshire Surgical Work Depot in Ayr, from 1915–19. Address: Belmont, Ayr, Scotland. (M298)

CUNLIFFE, Hon. Cecilie Victoria, Lady, O.B.E., b. 18 Feb. 1865; d. of Col. Hon. William Edward Sackville West, s. of George Earl De la Warr; m. late Sir Robert Alfred Cunliffe, 5th Baronet, of Acton Park, Wrexham. War Work: President

of Girls' Friendly Society which did work among munition workers in factories, providing hostels and rest homes in various parts of England. Address: River, Tillington, Petworth. Club: Ladies' Imperial. (C2542)

CUNLIFFE, Major Ernest Nicholson, O.B.E., M.D., R.A.M.C. (T.).

CUNLIFFE, Capt. Norman, M.B.E.

CUNLIFFE, Walter, O.B.E.

CUNLIFFE, William, O.B.E., J.P., b. 9 Nov. 1844; s. of Walter Cunliffe, of Rochdale. Educ.: Privately. Corn Miller. War Work: Chairman of Rochdale War Tribunal. Address: Dean Bank, Rochdale. Club: Rochdale and District Reform. (O274)

CUNNINGHAM, Group-Capt. Alexander Duncan, C.B.E. Wing-Com. and Acting Group-Capt. R.A.F.; served in the Great War, 1914–19 (despatches). (C2332)

CUNNINGHAM, Sub.-Lieut. Andrew, M.B.E., R.N.V.R.

CUNNINGHAM, Lieut.-Col. Aylmer Basil, C.B.E., D.S.O., b. 1879; Major and Brevet Lieut.-Col. R.E.; served in the Great War, 1915–18 (despatches, Croix de Guerre, Brevet Lieut.-Col.). (C782)

CUNNINGHAM, Barbara Martin, O.B.E., M.B., Ch.B.

CUNNINGHAM, Rev. Canon Bertram Keir, O.B.E. M.A., b. 26 March, 1871; s. of the late George Miller Cunningham, of Leithenhopes, Peebleshire (see BURKE'S Landed Gentry). Educ.: Marlborough and Trinity Coll., Cambridge. Principal of Westcott House, Cambridge; Chaplain to the King; Hon. Canon of Winchester Cathedral; Examining Chaplain to the Bishop of Exeter; Chairman of the India Chaplaincies Board (C. of E.). War Work: Principal Chaplain to the Chaplains' School of Instruction in France, Jan. 1917, to April, 1919. Addresses: Westcott House, Cambridge; Leithen, Innerleithen, Scotland. Club: Oxford and Cambridge. (O5160)

CUNNINGHAM, Lieut. Charlie Allen Chichester, O.B.E.-R.N.R.

CUNNINGHAM, Edith Usher, M.B.E.; d. of Col. John Usher Cunningham, of Birkenhead. Educ.: Privately. War Work: Organiser and head of Red Cross Work Depot, Birkenhead, Aug. 1914, to July, 1919; Hon. Treas. Cheshire Regt., Prisoners of War Fund, Birkenhead; Member of Committee, Work for Women's Association, Birkenhead. Club: Forum. M1612)

CUNNINGHAM, Lieut.-Col. Frederick George, O.B.E.

CUNNINGHAM, Brig.-Gen. George Glencairn, C.B., C.B.E., D.S.O., b. 24 July, 1862; s. of Major William Cunningham, of Indian Army; m. Dorothy Louisa, d. of R. Yeo, of Drayton House, Ealing. Educ.: Wellington and R.M.C. Sandhurst. Joined the Army, 22 Oct. 1881; commanded a Brigade, South African War. War Work: Commanded Special Reserve Brigade, Plymouth Garrison, 5 Aug. 1914, to 30 Nov. 1916; served on Base Commander's Staff at Dieppe and Boulogne, 14 Aug. 1917, to 2 March, 1918; and as Base Commandant at Brest, 3 March, 1918, to 23 Oct. 1918. Address: Boyne House, Cannongate Road, Hythe, Kent. Club: Junior United Service. (C1536)

CUNNINGHAM, Gordon, M.B.E.

CUNNINGHAM, John, O.B.E.

CUNNINGHAM, Major John Francis, O.B.E., F.R.C.S., R.A.M.C., b. 25 Sept. 1875; s. of the late J. K. Cunningham, Sec Tor, Axminster; m. Phyllis Lovell, d. of the late L. B. Clarence, Judge of the Supreme Court Ceylon, of Coaxden, Axminster. Educ.: Sherborne; St. Thomas's Hospital Surgeon, Central London Ophthalmic Hospital; Ophthalmologist, Bethlem Royal Hospital. War Work: Served as Major, R.A.M.C.; Ophthalmic Surgeon attached to B.E.F., France. Address: 27, Weymouth Street, London, W. 1. (O5161)

CUNNINGHAM, Lallie, C.B.E., d. of Josias Cunningham, Glencairn, Belfast. Educ.: Privately and Edinburgh. War Work: Docks Free Buffet for Sailors and Soldiers; worked at other Free Buffets; Sailors' Fund and parcels for overseas; Quartermaster, St. John's Ambulance Ass., V.A.D. Address: Glencairn, Belfast. (C2543)

CUNNINGHAM, Mary Elizabeth, C.B.E.; d. of Josias Cunningham, of Glencairn, Belfast. Educ.: Privately; Belfast; London and Edinburgh. Manager under School Board. War Work: Controller, Free Buffet for S. & S., Gt. Nor. Rly.; Assistant S. & S. Service Club; President, "Torpedoed Crews" and Welcome Home Fund; Commandant of St. John Amb. Ass., V.A.D.; Demonstrator of St. John Amb. Ass.; Hospital Trains Buffet, run by V.A.D.; and helped in many other ways; inquiry for missing and wounded; Comrade of the Gt. War (Women's Section). Address: Glencairn, Belfast. (C2544)

CUNNINGHAM, Lieut.-Col. Percy Henry, O.B.E., I.A.

CUNNINGHAME, James Fraser, M.B.E., J.P., b. 1870; s. of William Cunninghame, of Leith. Educ.: Edinburgh Institution. Assistant Sec. Scottish Employment Council and Deputy Controller, Retail Business Licensing Section (Ministry of Labour). War Work: Honorary Sec., Derby Recruiting Scheme and National Service Scheme for Burgh of Leith; Chairman of Leith War Pensions Bureau; Member of Military Recruiting Advisory Committee for Burgh of Leith. Clubs: Scottish Conservative (Edinburgh); Scottish Constitutional (Glasgow); Unionist (Leith). (M3600)

CUNNINGTON, Capt. Frederick Joseph, O.B.E., Member of the Order St. John of Jerusalem, b. 1 Oct. 1870; s. of Joseph Cunnington, of Ingham Lodge, South Mimms, Herts.;

m. Mary Henrietta, *d.* of Dr. Edward Williams M'Call, of Highgate. *Educ.:* Owen's School, Islington. *War Work:* In Sept. 1914, raised, organised, and equipped the Middlesex Volunteer Transport Corps, which was re-named, in 1918, The Eastern Command Volunteer Ambulance Corps; resigned the Command in 1917, on appointment as Detraining Officer, Eastern Command, attached to A.D.S.T., E. Command, 50, Pall Mall. *Address:* 26, Cranley Gardens, Muswell Hill, N. 10.
(O275)

CUNNINGTON, Lily Maria, Mrs., M.B.E.

CUNYNGHAM, Lieut -Col. Sir William Stewart DICK- of Prestonfield, Bt., C.B.E., *b.* 20 Feb. 1871; *s.* of the late Sir Robert Keith Alexander Dick-Cunnyngham, Bt., of Prestonfield; *m.* Evelyn, *d.* of Arthur Fraser, of 58, Gloucester Terrace, Hyde Park, W. *Educ.:* Harrow and R.M.C., Sandhurst. 2nd Lieut., 1892, 42nd Royal Highlanders; A.D.C. to G.O.C.-in-C., Scotland, 1897; served in S. African War (despatches); P.S to Chief of the General Staff, War Office, 1905. *War Work:* commanded 10th Bn. Black Watch in France and Balkans, 1915–17 (despatches twice); commandant, G.H.Q., Reinforcement Camp, Italy, 1918 (C.B.E. and Croix di guerra); War Office, Dept. of Q.M.G., 1919–20; retired April, 1920. *Address:* Prestonfield, Edinburgh. *Clubs:* Army and Navy; New (Edinburgh). (C1405)

CUNYNGHAME, Lieut.-Col. Sir Percy Francis, 10th Bt. O.B.E., J.P., R. of O., late Middlesex Regt., *b.* 21 Feb. 1867; *s.* of Sir Francis George Thurlow Cunynghame, 9th Bt.; *m.* Maud Albinia Margaret, *d.* of Major John Handcock Solywn-Payne, of Badgeworth, Glos. Formerly Resident and Officer Administering Govt. of British Protectorate of Sarawak; J.P. for County of Gloucester. *War Work:* 9th Batt. Royal Fusiliers; A.P.M., 40th Division; Adjutant. 41st I.B.D., France, with rank of Captain, and as Commandant, Italy, with rank of Lieut.-Col. *Address:* 20, Cheyne Gardens, S.W. 3. *Club:* Junior United Service. (O2975)

CURLETT, Kathleen Lottie, O.B.E., W.R.A.F. (O9640)

CURLING, Major Joseph, O.B.E., R.F.A.

CURNOW, Benjamin Henry, M.B.E., *b.* 3 Dec. 1871; *s.* of Henry Curnow, of Southfields, Wandsworth; *m.* Wilhelmina Harriet, *d.* of John McManus, of Dublin. Controller of Furniture Section of H.M. Board of Public Works, Ireland. *War Work:* Officially equipped National Shell and Cartridge Factories, Canteens, War Hospitals, Convalescent Hospitals, Ministry of Munitions Offices, Ministry of Pensions Offices, Recruiting Councils, etc. *Address:* 8, Church Avenue, Upper Rathmines, Co. Dublin. *Club:* Miltown Golf. (M3601)

CURR, Thomas, O.B.E.

CURRALL, Henrietta Frances, Mrs., M.B.E.

CURRAN, Lieut.-Col. Theophilus John, O.B.E.

CURRAN, Lieut.-Col. William John Patrick ADYE-, O.B.E., *b.* 24 March, 1877; *s.* of Lieut.-Col. F. G. Adye-Curran, of Esker House, Upper Rathmines, Dublin. Lieut.-Col., R.A.M.C., Specialist in Operative Surgery. *War Work:* Surgery and Command of an Ambulance Train and several hospitals. *Address:* c/o Holt & Co. (O2394)

CURRE, Col. William Edward Carne, C.B.E., J.P., D.L., C.C., *b.* 26 June, 1855; *s.* of Edward Mathew Curre, of Itton, Monmouthshire; *m.* Augusta, *d.* of Crawshay Bailey, of Maindiff Court, Monmouthshire. *Educ.:* Harrow and Oxford. *War Work:* Served lines Communication, M.E.F., 1915; invalided; Chairman, Mon. War Pensions Committee; Chairman, Mon. War Agricultural Executive Committee; on Executive Welsh National Fund. (C2545)

CURREY, Muriel Innes, O.B.E., W.R.N.S.

CURRIE, Gertrude Barclay, Mrs., M.B.E.; *d.* of W. A. Peterkin. *War Work:* Hon. Superintendent, H.R.H. Princess Louise Mine Sweepers' Hut, Granton. *Addresses:* Larkfield, Wardie Road, Edinburgh; Inverawe, Argyllshire. *Club:* Ladies' Caledonian (Edinburgh). (M3602)

CURRIE, Isabel, Mrs., O.B.E.

CURRIE, Sir James, K.B.E., C.M.G., J.P., Controller, Training Department, Ministry of Labour; Director, Training Munition Workers, Labour Supply Dept., Ministry of Munitions, 1916–18; J.P., Wiltshire; *b.* 31 May, 1868; *s.* of the late Rev. James Currie, LL.D., of Edinburgh; *m.* Hilda Beatrice, *o.d.* of the late Sir Thomas Hanbury, K.C.V.O., la Mortola, Ventimiglia, Italy. *Educ.:* Fettes Coll., Edinburgh; Edinburgh and Oxford Univs. Member of Governor-General's Council for the Soudan, 1911–14; Principal of the Gordon Coll., Khartoum, and Director of Education in the Soudan, 1900–14; 2nd Class Medjidieh, 3rd Class Osmanieh. *War Service:* 1916–18, Director Training Munition Workers Labour Supply Dept., Ministry of Munitions; 1918, Controller, Department, Industrial Training, Ministry of Labour. *Addresses:* 4, Prince's Gardens, S.W.; Upham House, Aldbourne, Wilts. *Club:* Reform, Brooks's. (K363)

CURRIE, Lorna May, Mrs., O.B.E. (O11965)

CURRIE, Marguerita Copeland, M.B.E.

CURRIE, Major Philip John Reginald, O.B.E., M.C., K.R.R.C., *b.* 2 March, 1889; *s.* of the late William Reginald Currie, Rushden House, Northamptonshire. *Educ.:* Malvern and Sandhurst. *War Work:* Expeditionary Force, Aug. 1914; Adjutant 2nd K.R.R.C., B.E.F.; G.S.O. III., XV. Corps, B.E.F.; Brigade Major, 25th Infantry Brigade, B.E.F.; Brigade Major, 3rd Australian Training Brigade; G.S.O. II., Supreme War Council Versailles; mentioned in despatches 3 times. *Address:* Hambledon House, Child-Okeford, Blandford, Dorset. *Clubs:* Naval and Military; Bath. (O4306)

CURRIE, Richard, M.B.E.

CURRIE, Lieut. Thomas Dickson, M.B.E.

CURRINGTON, Capt. Stanley, M.B.E. (R.A.F.), *b.* 2 Nov. 1892; *s.* of J. T. Currington, of London. *Educ.:* Penrith House School; Christ's Coll., Cambridge. *War Service:* Commissioned Duke of Wellington's (West Rid. Regt.), 29 June, 1915; served Overseas with 10th Ser. Bn. D. of W. West Rid. Regt. (wounded, Oct. 1916); attached H.Q. No 2 Section, Tyne Garrison, from April, 1917, to July, 1918; appointed Adj. and Administrative Officer to P.M.O. H.Q. Midland Area, R.A.F., 10 July, 1918 and later to H.Q. Northern Area, R.A.F. *Address:* c/o Messrs. Cox & Co., 110, St. Martin's Lane, W.C. (M5953)

CURRY, Lieut. Charles Townley, M.B.E,

CURRY, Capt. Edward, M.B.E., R.F.A.

CURRY, James William, O.B.E.

CURRY, Brig.-Gen. Montagu Creighton, C.B., C.B.E., D.S.O., *b.* 1856; *s.* of Col. R. M. Curry; *m.* 1897, Amy Mary, *d.* of the late Henry Moulton-Barrett. Entered 11th Regt. 1877, became Capt. Devonshire Regt. 1885, and Major 1897 (transferred to Lincolnshire Regt. 1901); Lieut.-Col. 1902. Brevet Col. 1905, Col. 1907 (retired 1913), and Hon. Brig.-Gen 1917; served with Tirah Expedition, 1897–98 (medal with two clasps); in S. Africa, 1899–1901, as Station Comdt.; subsequently in command of Imperial L.I. with rank of Lieut.-Col. (despatches); was Assist.-Inspector of Warlike Stores, 1890–94 in command of 4th Dist., W. Command, 1909–13; appointed to command a Brig. 1914; Staff Capt. 1917. *Address:* Torwood, Torquay. *Club:* Junior United Service. (C1535)

CURRY, Major Philip Arthur, O.B.E., *b.* 5 Sept. 1889; *s.* of Philip E. Curry, of Southampton; *m.* Anita Godwin, *d.* of R. J. Godwin, of Larchmont, New York. *Educ.:* Blundell's School. Manager, White Star Line, Montreal. *War Work:* Oxford and Bucks L.I., Dec. 1914, to May, 1916; Embarkation Staff Officer, May, 1916, to Jan. 1917; Director of Embarkation, British Ministry of Shipping, New York, Feb. 1917, to Dec. 1919. *Address:* 386, Sherbrooke Street, Montreal, P.Q., Canada. *Clubs:* Trojans (Southampton); Canada and St. James's (Montreal). (O3681)

CURRY, William Fortescue, O.B.E., J.P., *b.* 3 Jan. 1864; *s.* of Thomas Parsons Curry, of Falmouth, Cornwall. *Educ.:* Falmouth Grammar School. Manager of the African Boating Co., Ltd.; Member of Durban Harbour Advisory Board. *War Work:* Admiralty and Military, landing and shipping men and material. *Address:* Point, Durban, Natal. *Club:* Durban. (O10250)

CURSITER, Capt. Stanley. O.B.E., R.S.W., *b.* 1887; *s.* of John Scott Cursiter, of Kirkwall; *m.* Phyllis Eda, *d.* of David Hourston, of Greenfield, Orkney. *Educ.:* Kirkwall School. Artist. President of the Society of Scottish Artists; Member of the Royal Scottish Society of Painters in Water Colour. *War Work:* Trained with Inns of Court O.T.C.; Commissioned to 7th Scottish Rifles, and served with the Cameronians (1st Scottish Rifles); attached to 4th Field Survey Coy. R.E. in charge of reproduction and distribution of maps with 2nd Army, 4th Army, and Army of Occupation, Cologne. *Address:* 28, Queen Street, Edinburgh. *Clubs:* Scottish Arts (Edin.); Cap and Gown (Edin.). (O5162)

CURSLEY, Capt. Samuel, M.B.E., J.P., *b.* 18 June, 1867. Lace Manufacturer. *War Work:* Recruiting. *Address:* Berberry, Derby Road, Long Eaton. *Club:* County (Derby). (M3260)

CURSONS, George, M.B.E., J.P., Order of the Belgian Crown, *b.* 1872; *s.* of William Henry Cursons, of Park St., Grosvenor Square, W.; *m.* Clara, *d.* of Charles Preddy, of Norwood. *Educ.:* Privately. J.P., Middlesex, 1907, and J.P., Kent, 1914; Director and Trustee of Public Companies, including the Cairn Line of Steamships, Golden Valley Estates of South Africa, Sir J. L. Huleth and Sons (S. Africa), Sunderland Tramway Co., Murdoch and Murray, Ferguson & Co.; Chairman The Royal Nations! Lifeboat Institution, and National Institute for the Blind, Herne Bay Branch. *War Work:* Chairman, Herne Bay Urban District Council for 1915–18; Chairman of the Prince of Wales' Committee, Recruiting Committee, Local Tribunal, Food Control Committee, War Savings Committee, War Relief Committee, Belgian Relief Committee, Prisoners of War Committee, Troops Entertainment Committee, Canadian Relief Committee, and Navy and Army Veterans' Association; Member of the Pensions Committee and National Council Y.M.C.A.; on the Board of Management, London Temperance Hospital. *Address:* Ranelagh, Herne Bay, Kent.

CURTIS, Agnes, Mrs., O.B.E.

CURTIS, Amy, M.B.E., Q.M.A.A.C.

CURTIS, Annie, Mrs., M.B.E., Q.M.A.A.C.

CURTIS, Capt. Cecil Montagu Drury, C.B.E.

CURTIS, Frederick, O.B.E., F.R.C.S. (Eng.), L.R.C.P. (Lond.), F.R.G.S., M.B.O.U., *b.* 9 Feb. 1873; *s.* of the late Albert Curtis, M.R.C.S. (Eng.), L.R.C.P. (Lond.) of Staines. *m.* Edith Margaret, *d.* of the late Frederic Green, M.A. (Lond.), of Inner Temple, London. *Educ.:* Bootham School, York; Guy's Hospital. Surgeon, Medical Officer, Reigate and Redhill Hospital, etc. *War Work:* Medical Officer in charge of Redhill War Hospital; Medical Officer, Merstham Red Cross Hospital; Surgeon, Red Gables War Hospital, Bletchingley; Controlling Surgeon, Redhill Curative Post and Dorking Curative Post. *Address:* Alton House, Redhill, Surrey. *Club:* British Ornithological.

CURTIS, Capt. John Dorrien Constable, M.BE., M.C., R.A.F.

CURTIS, John William, M.B.E.

CURTIS, Rev. Levi, M.B.E., A.M., D.D., *b.* 22 Feb. 1858; *s.* of Apollos and Harriet Curtis, of Newfoundland; *m.* Lillie Cordelia, *d.* of George Mason Black, of New Brunswick. *Educ.:* Methodist Coll., St. John's, and Mount Allison Univ., Sackville, N.B., Canada. Superintendent of Education; Editor, "Monthly Greeting," etc. *War Work:* Member of Patriotic Association, Recruiting Committee, and Civil Re-establishment Committee; raised through Methodist Schools $4546.36 for the Cot Fund; travelled hundreds of miles and delivered numerous addresses in recruiting men for the Army and Navy, etc. (M1243)

CURTIS, Sir (Richard) James, K.B.E., *b.* 1868; *s.* of late William Curtis, of Rotton Park, Birmingham; *m.* Edith, *d.* of George Rowe, of Edmonton. *Educ.:* North Devon and Birmingham. Solicitor and Clerk to the Birmingham Board of Guardians and Assessment Committee. *War Work:* Food Commissioner, Midland Division; at request of Lord Rhondda initiated the first local rationing scheme; was Deputy Commissioner, National Service, in 1917; Honorary Organiser for provision of Military Hospitals, 1915–17; Chairman, Birmingham Discharged Soldiers' Committee, 1915–19; Member of Local Government Reconstruction Committee; Member of Ministry of Health, Consultative Council on Local Government; Honorary Clerk to, and member of, Birmingham Military Tribunal, which dealt with one hundred thousand appeals. *Addresses:* St. Mary's Road, Harborne, Birmingham; Ashton-under-Hill, Gloucestershire. *Club:* Union, Birmingham. (K210)

CURTIS, Capt. Walter John Brice, O.B.E., R.A.F.

CURTIS, William, M.B.E., (M10312)

CURTIS, Capt. and Qr.-Mr. William Arthur, M.B.E., R.A.S.C.

CURWEN, Elizabeth Gordon, Mrs., M.B.E., *b.* 1863; *d.* of Gen. Sir William Cameron, K.C.B., K.C.M.G., of Nea House, Christchurch, Hants (*see* BURKE'S *Peerage*); *m.* Chaloner F. H., *s.* of Eldred Curwen, of Withdeane Court, Brighton. *War Work:* Donor of Auxiliary Hospital, Class A, for 4 years, March, 1815, to March, 1919, and Commandant of same for same period. *Address:* Brooke Lodge, Weedon, Northants. *Club:* Ladies' Park. (M7829)

CURWEN, Capt. John Spedding, O.B.E., 3rd Loyal North Lancs Regt., *b.* 27 June, 1891; *s.* of J. F. Curwen, F.S.A., J.P., of Heversham, Westmorland. *Educ.:* Sedbergh, Yorks. *War Work:* France, 1915 (1st Loyal N. Lancs Regt.); N. Russia, 1919 (British Relief Force); awarded the Russian Order of St. Anne, 3rd Class, with Cross Swords and Bow; mentioned in despatches for Allied Services with the Archangel Force, N. Russia. *Address:* Heversham, Westmorland. (O9687)

CURZON, Edith Bassett, Mrs., C.B.E., *b.* 13 June, 1861; *d.* of Charles H. Basset, of Watermouth Castle, Ilfracombe; *m.* Ernest Charles Penn, *s.* of Col. the Hon. Ernest George Curzon (*see* BURKE'S *Peerage*). *Educ.:* privately. *War Work:* Received wounded Belgian soldiers, 1914; English soldiers in house as Convalescents, same year, until 1916; after that received Convalescent Officers in Castle and Annexe, 1916–19. *Address:* Watermouth Castle, Ilfracombe, N. Devon. (C480)

CUSENS, George Charles, M.B.E., *b.* 23 April, 1887; *s.* of Thomas Cusens, of Portsmouth, London and Cambridge; *m.* Lily, *d.* of John Samuel Sowden, of Devonport and Portsmouth. *Educ.:* Organised School of Science, Portsmouth. Civil Servant *War Work:* Took a leading part in the provision, production, and supply of Mines and Anti-Submarine Appliances generally, to the Naval Service and Allies. *Address:* 42, Craven Gardens, Wimbledon, S.W. 19. (M300)

CUST, Adm. Sir Herbert Edward PUREY-, K.B.E., C.B., R.N., *b.* 26 Feb. 1857; *s.* of the late Very Rev. Arthur Perceval Purey-Cust. Dean of York; *m.* Alice Ella, *d.* of of the late G. S. Hepburn, of Smeaton, Australia. *Educ.:* Temple Grove, East Sheen. *War Work:* Commodore, R.N.R. in charge of Auxiliary Patrol, Orkneys. *Address:* Hollyside, West Hill, Highgate, N. 6. *Club:* United Service. (K260)

CUTBUSH, Mabel Jane, O.B.E.

CUTFORTH, John Ashlin, M.B.E. (M10246g)

CUTHBERT, Alexander, M.B.E.

CUTHBERT, Helena Eliza, Mrs., M.B.E.

CUTHBERT, Kathleen Alice, Mrs. James Harold, O.B.E.

CUTHBERTSON, Clive, O.B.E., F.R.S., *b.* 29 Nov. 1863 *s.* of William Gilmour Cuthbertson; *m.* Mildred Maude Mary, *d.* of Major Charles Hesketh Aldersey Gower. *Educ.:* Trinity College, Glenalmond; University College, Oxford. Indian Civil Service, 1884; Under-Secretary, Government of Bengal, Financial and Municipal Dept., 1888–90; retired, owing to ill-health, 1896; Assistant Private Secretary to the Marquess of Salisbury, 1899–1902. *War Work:* Staff Sergeant, Instructor of Musketry, 1914–15; Temporary Clerk, Foreign Office, 1915–19. *Address and Club:* East India United Service, 16 St. James' Square. S.W. (O277)

CUTHBERTSON, John, M.B.E., F.R.S.E., F.E.I.S., *b.* 15 Aug. 1859; *s.* of David Cuthbertson; *m.* Lilias Ann, *d.* of Capt. John Bowman, of Tain. *Educ.:* Glasgow University. Secretary and Treasurer, The West of Scotland Agricultural College. *War Work:* Member of County Pension Committee; Member of Food Production Committee; Member of Red Cross Committee; Chairman, Local Pension Committee. *Address:*

6, Charles Street, Kilmarnock. *Clubs:* Kilmarnock; Barassie Golf. (M301)

CUTHBERTSON, Major John Ernest Moncrieff, O.B.E., *b.* 27 May, 1887; *s.* of the late Robert Moncrieff Cuthbertson, of Uitenhage, S. Africa; *m.* Gladys Muriel Lucy, *d.* of Herbert Melville Guest, J.P., of Klerksdorp, S. Africa. *Educ.:* St. Andrews Coll., Grahamstown, South Africa. Journalist *War Work:* German West Africa with South African Forces, 1914–15; in British Salonica Forces as O.C., No. 4 Advanced Horse Transport Depot, and No. 3 Base Horse Transport Depot, 1915–19; O.C. R.A.S.C. Chester District, Western Command, 1919–20. *Address:* Box 1, Klerksdorp, Transvaal, South Africa. *Club:* City (Chester). (O6458)

CUTHBERTSON, William Darling, M.B.E., *b.* 3 Feb. 1863; *s.* of Robert Cuthbertson, of Edinburgh and Glasgow; *m.* Jessie, *d.* of Samuel Hanning, of Manchester. *Educ.:* Glasgow. Archivist of British Embassy, Paris. *Addresses:* British Embassy, Paris; Villa "La Fougeraie," Le Vésinet (Seine et Oise), France. (M1613)

CUTLER, Ernest Edward, M.B.E.

CUTLER, Major Roy Victor, M.B.E., M.C., *b.* 1 Nov. 1892; *s.* of Charles F. Cutler, of Elsternwick, Melbourne; *m.* Evelyn, *d.* of Charles H. Westropp, of Melford Place, Long Melford. *Educ.:* Melbourne University. Architect and Engineer (Military). *War Work:* Left Australia with 1st Division, attached to 2nd Field Co., Engineers; was at the landing and evacuation of Gallipoli; most of the battles in France; and Commandant of the Brightlingsea Engineer's Training Depot, 20 Feb. 1917, to 26 Nov. 1917. *Address:* 88, Were St., Brighton Beach. *Club:* Naval and Military, Melbourne. (M30)

CUTTING, Lieut.-Col. Frank, O.B.E., R.E.

CUTTRISS, Charles Arthur, M.B.E.

DABELL, Capt. and Quartermaster William Bates, M.B.E., M.C., *b.* 5 May, 1873. With 2nd Batt. Grenadier Guards (Q.-M.-Sergt.) in South Africa, 1900–2. *War Work:* Joined 1st Batt. Welsh Guards on formation, 26 Feb. 1915; with battalion on Western Front, 17 Aug. 1915, till 12 March, 1919. (M6525)

DACOMB, Major Leonard Sydney, O.B.E., J.P., B.S.A. Police, *b.* 15 Aug. 1871; *s.* of Charles Dacomb, of Durban, Natal; *m.* Agnes Jane, *d.* of Alfred Marks, of England. *Educ.:* High School, Durban, Natal. Joined British South Africa Police, Nov. 1896, still serving. Mashonaland Rebellion, 1896–97; Boer War, 1899–1902. *War Work:* Rhodesia, 1914–19. *Address:* Salisbury, Rhodesia. (O8006)

DA COSTA, Attamont, M.B.E.

DADSON, Mary Alice Portlock, M.B.E.; *d.* of Capt. Portlock Dadson, J.P., late R.M.L.I., R.B.G. *Educ.:* Privately. *War Work:* Assisted in organising Gifford House Auxiliary Hospital, Roehampton, S.W. 15, in Aug. 1914; Quartermaster, V.A.D., London, 96, St. John Ambulance Brigade; appointed Acting Commandant, 29 April, 1918, and Assist. Commandant, 27 Aug. 1918. *Address:* c/o Edward Stenning, 64, Cannon Street, E.C. 4. (M7830)

DADSON, Major Reginald Thornton, O.B.E., F.S.I., *b.* 17 March, 1881; *s.* of James Thornton Dadson, of Finchley; *m.* Christian Colquhoun, *d.* of James Mill, of Nairn. *Educ.:* Harrow. Surveyor. *Addresses:* 2, John Street, Bedford Row, W.C. 1; Taplow. *Clubs:* Junior Army and Navy; Public Schools. (O5165)

DADSON, Sophie Portlock, O.B.E.; *d.* of Capt. W. Portlock Dadson, J.P., late R.M.L.I., R.B.C. *Educ.:* At home. Lady Superintendent, St. John Ambulance Brigade, Commandant, London, 96. *War Work:* Organised and Administered Gifford House Auxiliary Hospital, Roehampton, S.W., 1914–19. *Address:* c/o E. Stenning, 64, Cannon Street, E.C. (O10252)

DAFFERN, Thomas Wells, O.B.E., F.C.A., F.S.A.A., *b.* 16 Nov. 1883; *s.* of Thomas Mason Daffern, of Coventry. Director, Hertford Street Motor Co., Ltd.; M.A.G. Engine Co., Ltd.; Mohawk Cycle Co., Ltd. *War Work:* Deputy Controller, Aircraft Production Accounts, Ministry of Munitions of War. *Addresses:* Broadwater, Coventry; 5, Church Row, Fulham, S.W. 6. *Clubs:* Isthmian; Coventry and County (Coventry). (O10253)

DAGGER, Richard, O.B.E., M.D., L.R.C.P. L.R.C.S.

DAGLISH, Edith, Mrs., O.B.E. (O11966)

DAGLISH, Gladys, M.B.E., *b.* 5 Sept. 1889; *d.* of J. Daglish, J.P., of Tynemouth, Northumberland. *Educ.:* St. Leonard's School, St. Andrews, Fife. *War Work:* Joined Q.M.A.A.C., July, 1917; went to France, Aug. 1917, as a gardener (Forewoman) to British Cemetery, Etaples; became an Administrator, March, 1918; was in France till March, 1919. *Address:* Wynbury, Leyburn, Yorkshire. (M4462)

DAGLISH, James, M.B.E.

DAGNALL, Capt. William John, O.B.E.

DAILLEY, Lieut. Wilfred Gordon Beale, O.B.E., R.A.O.C.

DAIN, John Henry, O.B.E., *b.* 1874; *s.* of William Dain, of Lincoln; *m.* Amy, *d.* of Ben Green, of Hyde. *Educ.:* Winterton Grammar School. Chief Constable of the City of Norwich. *War Work:* War Office, Intelligence. *Address:* Guildhall, Norwich. (O10254)

DAINTON, Major Sydney Herbert George, O.B.E.

DAINTON, Major William Charles ANNABLE-, M.B.E. (Mil.), *b.* 29 April, 1884; *s.* of William Charles Annable-Dainton, of Bath ; *m.* Alda Marie, *d.* of William Taylor, of Burton-on-Trent. *Educ.:* Bath Forum School ; St. John's Coll. Planter and Accountant ; now Chief Accountant to the British Central Africa Co., Ltd., Nyasaland. *War Work:* Gallipoli, Egypt, Sinai, Syria, Palestine, and France with the 5th Lancashire Fusiliers ; Assistant D.A.P.M., Marseilles ; D.A.P.M., Rouen ; A.P.M., Syren Force, Murmansk, N. Russia. *Addresses:* 2, Scalpcliffe Road, Burton-on-Trent ; Blantyre, Nyasaland. *Club:* Junior Army and Navy. (M6990)

DAINTREE, Capt. John Dodson, C.B.E., *b.* 1864 ; *s.* o John Osborne Daintree, of Lolworth, Cambridgeshire ; *m.* 1893, Mary Francis, *d.* of Rear-Adm. Edward Kelly. Capt. R.N.: Senior Inspector, Life-Saving Apparatus, Board of Trade. *Address:* 48, Pembridge Villas, W. (C892)

DAKIN, Frances George, M.B.E.

DAKIN, Flight-Lieut. Humphrey Burns, M.B.E., R.A.F.

DAKIN, Margaret Evelyn HARRISON-, M.B.E., *b.* 25 March, 1882 ; *d.* of J Harrison-Dakin, of Brittany Lodge, Edwardes Sq., Kensington. *Educ.:* Private Governesses and Caldecote Towers, Bushey. *War Work:* Battersea Branches of the Soldiers' and Sailors' Families Assn., and Soldiers' and Sailors' Help Society, from Jan. 1915, till the formation of the War Pension Committee ; then Hon. Sec. of the Battersea Sub-Committee of the L.W.P. Committee until the end of July, 1919. *Address:* Brittany Lodge, Edwardes Sq., Kensington. (M7832)

DAKYNS, Winifred,' Mrs., C.B.E., *b.* 16 Sept. 1875 ; *d.* of the late John Pattinson, of Newcastle-on-Tyne ; *m.* Henry Graham, *s.* of the late Henry Graham Dakyns, of Higher Coombe, Haslemere. *Educ.:* Gateshead High School for Girls and Newnham College, Cambridge. *War Work:* Aug. 1914, to Nov. 1917, at Headquarters of the V.A.D. Department, B.R.C.S., and Order of St. John ; Nov. 1917, to Dec. 1919, Assistant Director Women's Royal Naval Service. *Address:* 7, Thurloe Court, Chelsea, S.W. 3. *Club:* University for Ladies. (C1173)

DALDY, Major Alexander William, O.B.E., I.A.

DALE, Albert Ernest, M.B.E., *b.* 6 Nov. 1892 ; *s.* of Robert David Dale, of Aylsham, Norfolk ; *m.* Sylvia Sarah Minnie, *d.* of A. Woodcock, of Petworth, Sussex. *Educ.:* Wesleyan School, and King Edward VI. Grammar School, Retford. Notts. Civil Servant. *War Work:* Recruiting for the technical branches of the Army and for the Royal Air Force. *Address:* 29, Acris Street, Wandsworth Common, S.W. 18. (M7824)

DALE, Charles Ernest, C.M.G., C.B.E., *b.* 26 Feb., 1867 ; *s.* of the late James George Dale ; *m.* 1892, Matilda Ada, *d.* of the late Edmund Parr. *Educ.:* Greenwich ; King's Coll., London. Appointed Assist. Director of Customs, S. Nigeria, 1895 ; Acting Director-Gen. of Customs and Postmaster-Gen. 1896 ; Treasurer, 1898 ; Acting Sec. to Administration, 1900 ; also Acting Collector of Customs, 1900, again Acting Sec. to Administration, 1903, and Financial Commr. on Amalgamation of S. Nigeria and Lagos, 1906 ; on special duty in connection with transfer of Niger Co.'s Territory to Colonial Office, 1899, and as Treasurer to Lagos Govt. 1904 ; elected an M.E.C. and M.L.C. 1905 ; acted as Colonial Sec., and Dep. Gov. of the Colony, 1908 ; retired, 1914 ; is a Fellow of Soc. of Accountants and Auditors (Incorporated Accountants), and of Roy. Statistical Soc. *War Work:* Passport Office, Foreign Office, Jan. 1915 ; Colonial Audit Department, Aug. 1915 ; Deputy Asst.-Director, War Office, Feb. 1917, to end of the War. *Address:* 72, The Ridgeway, Golders Green, N.W. *Club:* Sports'. (C2546)

DALE, Cicely Susan, M.B.E., *b.* 1863 ; *d.* of Rev. Lawford W. T. Dale, late of Vicarage, Chiswick, Middlesex. *Educ.:* At home. Commandant of V.A.D. Kent 36. T.F. Hythe, Kent. *War Work:* For 4½ years Military Commandant and Registrar of the Bevan V.A.D. Hospital, Sandgate, Kent (300 beds, 12,109 patients treated). Worked the whole of the time without holiday, week-day or Sunday. (M7835)

DALE, Major Claude Henry, O.B.E., *b.* 13 May, 1882 ; *s.* of the late Hylton W. Dale, of London ; *m.* Gwendolen Monica, *d.* of the late Brisco-Ray, of London. *Educ.:* King's College School, London ; Bedford Grammar School ; Royal Military Coll., Sandhurst. Gazetted 2nd Lieut. in Royal Welch Fusiliers in 1900 ; retired in 1907 ; joined 4th Extra (S.R.) Batt. Royal Warwickshire Regt. *War Work:* Called up for service with 4th Extra (S.R.) Batt. Royal Warwickshire Regt. on 1 Aug. 1914 ; sent to France in Nov. 1914 ; given Staff appointment Jan. 1915 ; invalided to England at end of Oct. 1915 ; found permanently unfit for further service abroad ; held various Staff appointments at home until Nov. 1919. *Address:* Hawkenbury Hall, Staplehurst, Kent. *Club:* Naval and Military. (O7060)

DALE, Henry Hallett, C.B.E., M.D., F.R.S., *b.* 1875 ; *s.* of the late Charles James Dale ; *m.* 1894, Ellen, *d.* of F. W. Hallett, of Highgate, N. *Educ.:* The Leys Sch., and Trinity Coll., Camb. (M.A. 1903, M.D. 1909). Member of Scientific Staff Med. Research Committee. *Address:* Mount Vernon House, Holly Hill, Hampstead, N.W. (C949)

DALE, Major John, O.B.E., M.D., B.Sc., *b.* 2 May, 1885 ; *s.* of James Francis Dale, of Coleshill, Warwickshire ; *m.* Wynifred Mary, *d.* of — Evans, of Sydney, N.S.W. *Educ.:* Birmingham. Late Assistant Medical Officer of Health for Birmingham ; now Assistant Commissioner of Public Health, Western Australia (1920). *War Work:* Sanitary Officer, 48th Division (1915) ; then D.A.D.M.S. (Sanitation), 2nd

Army, B.E.F. *Addresses:* Public Health Dept., Perth, W.A. ; 14, Dean Street, Cottesloe, Perth, W.A. (O5166)

DALE, Mary Frances, M.B.E. *b.* 2 July, 1881 ; *d.* of Bruno George Dale, of London. *Educ.:* Convent of Notre Dame, London, N. Music mistress at the boarding school of the "Sainte Famille." *War Work:* Services to sick and wounded soldiers at the Pensionnat de la Sainte Famille, Esplanade Noyon, Amiens, the school being occupied by the British troops from 1914 till Dec. 1919. (M7833)

DALE, Rev. Percy John, O.B.E., M.A.. *b.* 23 May, 1876 *s.* of Henry John Dale, of Leckhampton, Glos. ; *m.* Dorothy, *d.* of Rev. C. J. S. Churchill, of Shrewsbury. *Educ.:* Magdalen Coll., Oxford. Rector of West Dean with East Grinstead, and Sec. and Treasurer of the Salisbury Diocesan Board of Finance. *War Work:* Hon. Sec. of the Church of England Board for the Welfare of the Imperial Forces within the Diocese of Salisbury. *Address:* Dean Rectory, Salisbury. (O10255)

DALE, Major and Qr.-Mr. William Henry, O.B.E., M.C., R.E.

DALE, Capt. William John, M.B.E.

DALE, Capt. Wilfred John, O.B.E., R.A.V.C.

DALE, Henry Angley LEWIS-, M.B.E., M.I.C.E., A.M.I.Mech.E., *b.* 26 Aug. 1876 ; *s.* of Henry Lewis-Dale, of Altona, Crewe ; *m.* Minnie Elizabeth, *d.* of Arthur Lewis-Dale, of Morwell, Colwyn Bay. *Educ.:* Nantwich and Acton Grammar School ; Owen's Coll., Manchester (Ashbury Exhibitioner in Civil Engineering). Entered Admiralty Service as Civil Engineer, 1901 ; served in Royal Dockyards, Chatham, Pembroke Dock, and Malta ; 1919, Superintending Civil Engineer on the Staff of Air Officer Commanding Coastal Area, Royal Air Force. *War Work:* Works construction, Admiralty and Royal Air Force ; also acted as Hon. Warden Navy House, Chatham, by appointment of the Bishop of Rochester ; Chairman of House Committee and Building Committee ; Hon. Architect of large extension scheme carried out during the war, and opened by H.R.H. the Duke of Connaught. (During his Wardenship upwards of 250,000 men of H.M. Navy enjoyed the hospitality of the Home) ; Member of the Council of the Institution of Professional Civil Servants ; Member of Air Ministry Departmental Whitley Council ; Committee Gibraltar Diocesan Assn. *Address:* Coastal Area Head Quarters, R.A.F., Tavistock Place, W.C. (M7836)

DALGLEISH, Capt. William Brown, O.B.E.

DALGLEISH, Wing-Commander James William OGILVY-, O.B.E., R.A.F., *b.* 20 March, 1888 ; *s.* of James Ogilvy-Dalgleish, late Captain, 29th Foot, of Glebelands, Wokingham, Berks. ; *m.* Guinevere. *d.* of Myles Kennedy, of Stone Cross, Ulverston. *Educ.:* Harrow and Royal Navy. *War Work:* Served throughout the War with Royal Naval Air Service and Royal Air Force. Now on retired list through ill health contracted on active service. *Club:* United Service. (O1260)

DALLAS, Col. Alexander Egerton, C.M.G., O.B.E., *b.* 1869 ; *m.* 1894, Frederica Katherine, *d.* of the late Capt. William Montagu Leeds (*see* BURKE'S *Peerage*, Leeds, Bart.). Lieut.-Col. Indian Army ; served in Burma 1889–92 (medal with clasp), and during Great War, 1914–17 as Col. on Staff (despatches). (O847)

DALLINGER, Percy Gough, O.B.E., *b.* 8 Oct. 1867 ; *s.* of late Rev. W. H. Dallinger, D.Sc., D.C.L., LL.D., F.R.S. *Educ.:* At Wesley College, Sheffield, and Trinity College, Dublin. Civil Servant. *Address:* 17, Unwin Mansions, Queen's Club Gardens, West Kensington. (O280)

DALLY, Thomas, C.B.E., *b.* 17 Oct. 1860 ; *s.* of James Dally, of Llansbigdig, Pembrokeshire ; *m.* Edith, *d.* of William Trindall, of Pembroke Dock. *Educ.:* National School ; Royal Dockyard School ; Royal Naval College, Greenwich. Chief Constructor and Superintendent of Naval Construction, Admiralty. *War Work:* Refit and repair of warships at Malta ; Design Work on warships, Admiralty ; Supervision of all warships building by contract. *Address:* Pinedale, 56, Parkwood Road, Boscombe, Bournemouth. (C481)

DALMAHOY, Emily Marion, M.B.E.

DALMAHOY, Lilias Edith Jean, M.B.E.

DALRYMPLE, James, C.B.E.

DALRYMPLE, Col. Joseph, C.M.G., O.B.E. Lieut.-Col. and Acting Col. R.A.M.C. ; served in the Great War, 1914–18 (O1261)

DALRYMPLE, Lady Marjorie Louise, O.B.E., *b.* 23 Feb. 1888 ; *d.* of 11th Earl of Stair, of Oxenfoord Castle, Dalkeith, Scotland (*see* BURKE'S *Peerage*). *Educ.:* At home. Made Lady of Grace of Order of St. John of Jerusalem, Dec. 1917. *War Work:* Making Provisional Limbs in London for last 2 years of War ; previously in France for 2½ years. *Addresses:* Lochninch, Castle Kennedy, Wigtonshire ; Oxenfoord Castle, Dalkeith, Scotland. *Clubs:* Bath ; Victoria. (O10256)

DALRYMPLE, Thomas, M.B.E., *b.* 1865 ; *s.* of Thomas Dalrymple, of Kirkintilloch ; *m.* the late Carrie Thompson, *d.* of William Thompson, of Woolwich. *Educ.:* Kirkintilloch. *War Work:* Since Sept. 1914 devoted himself exclusively to carrying on the Soldiers' Social Institute at Bridge of Allan. (M7838)

DALRYMPLE, William, M.B.E.

DALSTON, Capt. Norman Howard Maxwell, M.B.E., New Zealand Expeditionary Force, *b.* 15 March, 1862 ; *s.* of William Maxwell Dalston, of Christchurch ; *m.* Marguerite Maxwell, *d.* of Charles Edward Mason, of Norwood. *Educ.:* Privately. Chartered Accountant, New Zealand ; General Manager New Zealand Midland Railway. *War Work:*

Aug. 1914, to June, 1915, Hon. Organising Sec., New Zealand War Contingent Association ; June, 1915, to July, 1920, Quartermaster, and subsequently O.C., No 2 New Zealand General Hospital, Walton-on-Thames. *Address :* c/o National Bank of New Zealand, 17, Moorgate Street, E.C. 1. *Club :* Constitutional. (M1617)

DALTON, Lieut. Ernest Albert Llewellyn, M.B.E.

DALTON, James Henry Chesshyre Dalton, M.B.E., M.D., J.P., *b.* 15 April, 1861 ; *s.* of Henry Dalton, of Manchester ; *m.* Alice Tenison, *d.* of Rev. T. Mosse, of Dover. *Educ.:* Marlborough Coll. ; Trinity Coll., Cambridge. Alderman, Cambridge Town Council ; Councillor, Cambridgeshire County Council ; Chairman of the Public Health Committees of the County and Borough Councils ; Member of the Cambridge Board of Guardians and the Cambridgeshire Insurance Committee. *War Work :* Member of Cambridge Borough War Pensions Committee, and Chairman of the Disabled Soldiers' Sub Committee. *Address :* The Plot, Adams Road, Cambridge. *Club :* Constitutional. (M7840)

DALTON, Michael, O.B.E., *b.* 26 Jan. 1875 ; *s.* of Patrick Dalton, of Ballylanders, Co. Limerick ; *m.* Evelyn, *d.* of Gundry Stephens, of Bristol. *Educ.:* Privately. Asst. Controller, Central Stores Dept., Ministry of Munitions. *Address :* 27, Gt. Elms Road, Bromley, Kent. (O10257)

DALTON, William, M.B.E., *b.* 24 Feb. 1855 ; *s.* of Rev. W. B. Dalton, of Little Burstead, Essex ; *m.* Katharine Beaton, *d.* of John Hammond, of Newmarket. *Educ.:* Felstead. Member, Essex County Council ; Sec. Brentwood Cottage Hospital. *War Work :* Essex County War Pensions Committee ; Chairman of Brentwood War Pensions Committee ; Sec. Brentwood War Hospital Supply Depot ; Member of District Local Tribunal ; Member of District Food Control Committee. *Address :* Hutton Burses, Brentwood, Essex. *Clubs :* Portland ; Devonshire. (M7841)

DALTRY, Major Henry James, O.B.E.

DALWOOD, Lieut.-Col. John HALL-, C.B.E.

DALY, Agnes, M.B.E.

DALY, Amy, Mrs., M.B.E. ; *d.* of the late Rev. C. W. Pritchard, of Withington Rectory, Herefordshire ; *m.* James Thomas, *s.* of Michael Daly, of County Galway. *War Work :* In 1912 was made Commandant of Warwick N 44 V.A.D., and organised lectures and practical training for the Detachment ; on 29 Jan. 1914, to 15 March, 1919, Commandant of " The Warren " Auxiliary Hospital, Leamington Spa, which commenced with 44 beds and afterwards increased to 60 beds by the building of outside wards. *Address :* Raford, Kenilworth Road, Leamington Spa, Warwickshire. (M1618)

DALY, Major Charles Calthrop de Burgh, O.B.E., R.A.M.C. (Ret.), *b.* 23 April, 1861 ; *s.* of Ulick James Daly, of Dublin ; *m.* Emily Lucy, *d.* of Christopher French, of Cloonyquinn, Co. Roscommon. *Educ.:* Christ's Hospital. Medical Superintendent, Special Surgical Hospital, Blackrock, Co. Dublin. *War Work :* As Civil Practitioner, Nov. 1914, to April, 1915 ; Lieut. April, 1915 ; Capt. April, 1915 ; Acting Major, 1918 ; retired Major, March, 1920 ; in charge of special Malarial Hospital and Limbless Hospital ; Med. Sup. Ministry of Pensions ; Special Surgical Hospital, Dublin, from March, 1920, to present date. *Address :* Priory Lodge, Blackrock, Co. Dublin. *Club :* Dublin Univ. (O8782)

DALY, Hon. Florence Maria, M.B.E.

DALY, Lieut. Oscar Bedford, M.B.E.

DALYELL, Elsie Jean, O.B.E., M.B., Ch.M.; *d.* of J. M. Dalyell, of Sydney, Australia. *Educ.:* Sydney High School ; Univ. of Sydney, Australia. Medical Practitioner ; Beit Memorial Research Fellow. *War Work :* Bacteriologist, 6th Reserve Hospital, Serbia, 1915 ; for Hôpital Auxiliare 301, France, 1916 ; and for R.A.M.C. in Malta, Macedonia, and Constantinople, 1916–19. *Address :* Lister Institute of Preventive Medicine, London. (O6459)

DALZELL, Reginald Alexander, C.B.E., *b.* 28 Aug. 1865 ; of Nicol Alexander Dalzell, M.A., of Edinburgh (Conservator of Woods and Forests) ; *m.* Katherine Ann, *d.* of James Livingston, of Edinburgh. *Educ.:* Dulwich. Traffic Supt. (Telephones), London ; Provincial Supt., West of England ; Chief Inspector, Telegraph and Telephone Traffic. *Address :* 1, Cleveland Road, Ealing, W. (C2549)

DALZIEL, Norman Pearson, O.B.E.

DAMANT, Lieut.-Comm. Guybon Chesney Castell, O.B.E., R.N.

DANA, Robert Washington, O.B.E., *b.* 16 June, 1868 ; *s.* of William P. W. Dana, of Boston, U.S.A. ; *m.* Anna, *d.* of William Kane, of New York. *Educ.:* Clifton Coll., and Pembroke Coll., Cambridge. Civil Engineer ; Secretary of the Institution of Naval Architects ; and Editor of the Transactions, I.N.A. *War Work :* At Ministry of Munitions assisted in organising the Artillery Supply Branch under Sir Charles Ellis, G.B.E., from July, 1915, to June, 1917 ; then at Admiralty under the Director of Naval Construction, June, 1917, to Jan. 1919. *Address :* 15, Cranley Place, S.W. 7 ; 5, Adelphi Terrace, W.C. 2. *Clubs :* Athenæum ; New University. (O281)

DANCE, Charles William, O.B.E., *b.* 23 Dec. 1849; *s.* of Thomas Dance, of Lowestoft ; *m.* Sara, *d.* of Jeremiah Warford, of Pakefield. *Educ.:* Lowestoft and Aldeburgh-on-Sea. Fishery Adviser and Valuer to the Admiralty ; Board of Trade, Expert Surveyor and Valuer, under Fisheries Act, 1891. *War Work :* Adviser to the Admiralty in connection with Assessment of Compensation for losses of Fishing Vessels ; and Special Service duties throughout the War.

Address : Shipcote, Lowestoft, North. *Club :* National Maritime. (O10259)

DANCE, Lieut. Frank, M.B.E., R.A.F.

DANCE, Samuel Richard, M.B.E., A.M.Inst.I., *b.* 10 Nov. 1869. Fish Traffic Superintendent, G.E.R., Grimsby Docks. *War Work :* Technical Adviser on Fish Transport, Ministry of Food. (M7842)

DAND, Lieut. James Huddart, M.B.E., R.A.F.

DANE, Frederick Hopper, M.B.E., *b.* 13 Nov. 1871 ; *s.* of Richard Henry, of Canterbury. *Educ.:* St. Philip's. Member, Essex County Council, and Ilford Urban District Council (Chairman, 1912–13) ; Overseer, Parish of Ilford. *War Work :* Chairman, Finance Committee, Ilford War Pensions and Civil Liabilities Committees ; Member, Ilford Tribunal (Military Service Act). *Addresses :* 20, De Vere Gardens, Ilford, Essex ; 1A, St. Helen's Place, E.C. (M7843)

DANE, James Whiteside, M.B.E., D.L., Co. Fermanagh, *b.* 22 June, 1856 ; *s.* of William Auchinleck Dane, of Killyreagh, Co. Fermanagh. *Educ.:* Portora ; Enniskillen Royal School. Clerk of the Crown and Peace, Co. Kildare. *War Work :* Originated and started the Co. Kildare Committee to send warm clothing and comforts to the Royal Dublin Fusiliers ; started the Royal Dublin Fusiliers Central Advisory Committee, and co-ordinated therein the above to three other Committees which had been promoted with same object, thus avoiding overlapping, and acted as Hon. Sec. of both, later sharing the office of latter with Mrs. Clegg ; assisted in Recruiting Campaign in Co. Fermanagh, under auspices of the County Council, when County Council of Kildare, had failed to do anything about Recruiting ; at its request organised a Recruiting Campaign in Co. Kildare and was thanked therefor by the Lord Lieutenant of Ireland. *Address :* Garryard, Johnston, Straffan, Co. Kildare. *Clubs :* Hibernian ; United Service, Dublin ; Royal Automobile of Ireland ; Fermanagh County ; Enniskillen. (M7844)

DANE, John Stevenson, M.B.E.

DANGER, Frank Charles, C.B.E. *War Work :* Rendered valuable services to the Ministry of Shipping. (C3137)

DANIEL, Lieut.-Col. Charles James, C.B.E., D.S.O., *b.* 3 Nov. 1861 ; *s.* of late Rev. R. Daniel, B.D., Vicar of Osbaldwick, near York ; *m.* Agnes Margaret, *d.* of late Admiral T. Saumarez, C.B., of Jersey. *Educ.:* St. Peter's School, York, and Sandhurst. Late Loyal N. Lancs. Regt. *War Work :* In charge No. 1 Record Office, Preston. *Address :* Hillside, Fulwood, Preston. *Club :* Army and Navy. (C1117)

DANIEL, Lieut.-Col. Edward Yorke, C.B.E., R.M., *b.* 2 July, 1865 ; *s.* of Rev. Robert Daniel, B.D., of York ; *m.* Agnes Elizabeth, *d.* of Paymaster-in-Chief A. Turner. *Educ.:* York. *War Work :* Secretary, Historical Section, Committee of Imperial Defence. *Clubs :* United Service ; Royal Automobile. (C136).

DANIEL, Major Walter, O.B.E., R.E.

DANIELL, Col. Frederick Francis Williamson, C.B.E. Col. and T. Brig.-Gen. ; served in the Great War, 1914–19 (despatches). (C1537)

DANIELL, Capt. Humphrey Averell, O.B.E.

DANIELL, Major John Acheson Staines, D.S.O., O.B.E., *b.* 1882 ; *s.* of the late Col. William S. Daniel ; *m.* 1916, Ellen Mary, *d.* of S. Taylor, of Ponchen End, Boxmoor. Entered King's Own Yorkshire L.I. 1901, and became Major, Indian Army, 1916 ; served in the Great War, 1914–15 (despatches). (O8558)

DANIELL, Major John Clarmont, O.B.E., *b.* 8 March, 1869 ; *s.* of the late Col. James le Geyt Daniell, 22, Wilton Crescent, London, S.W. ; *m.* Julie Linda, *d.* of Lindo St. Myers, of 10, Culross Street, Park Lane. *Educ.:* Harrow. *War Work :* Staff Capt., 162 Infy. Bde., Aug. 1914, to July, 1915 ; Bde. Major, 3/1 S. Midland Division, 1915 to 1916 ; Military Inspector Canteen Board, Feb. 1917 ; service in France and Italy, Nov. 1917, to March, 1918 ; D.A.Q.M.G., H.Q., Eastern Command, 1918, to Oct. 1919. *Club :* White's. (O8783)

DANIELL, Col. Thomas Edward St. Clare, O.B.E., M.C.

DANIELS, Major Arthur Marston, O.B.E., I.A.

DANIELS, Lieut. Ernest Stuart, O.B.E., R.N.R.

DANIELS, Major Henry Douglas, O.B.E.

DANIELS, Major Lindsay Sydney, O.B.E., R.E.

DANIELS, Margaret Frances, M.B.E.

DANIELS, Sir Percy, K.B.E., *b.* 15 Aug. 1875 ; *s.* of Edward Daniels, of London ; *m.* Florence Grace, *d.* of John Robert Pakeman, C.B.E. *Educ.:* Mill Hill School. *War Work :* Chief of Leather Mission to U.S.A., from 1917 to Aug. 1919. *Address :* 41, South Street, Mayfair, W. 1. *Clubs :* City of London ; Junior Carlton. (K211)

DANN, John Charles, M.B.E.,

DANN, Capt. William Squire, M.B.E.

DANNATT, Elsie Mary, M.B.E., W.R.N.S.

DANNATT, Frank Cedrio, O.B.E.

DANSEY, Lieut.-Col. Edward Mashiter, O.B.E.

DANSON, Major Thomas, M.B.E., R.A.O.C.,

DARBY, T. Lieut.-Col. Alexander Whyte, O.B.E., *b.* 5 Sept. 1883 ; *s.* of G. M. N. Darby, of India ; *m.* Margaret Binnie, *d.* of Thomas Binnie Ralston, V.D., J.P., of Bothwell, Scotland. *Educ.:* Dollar Academy and Glasgow University. Mining Engineer. *War Work :* Home Service, 3rd Hundred Thousand, Oct. 1914, to Aug. 1915 ; Active Service, France, Aug. 1915, to Nov. 1915 ; Balkans, Nov. 1915, to June, 1919 ; Guzetted, Sept. 1914 ; Lieut. 11th Service Batt. The Cameronians (Scottish Rifles) ; Capt. and Adjt., Nov. 1914 ; Major, 1917 ; Lieut.-Col., 1919 ; Com. Itia Base and L. of C. ; three times mentioned in despatches. *Address :* 104, Raeburn Place, Edinburgh. *Clubs :* Scottish Liberal, Edinburgh ; R.S. Automobile, Glasgow. (O6460)

DARBY, Capt. George, O.B.E., M.C. (O11879)

DARBY, Capt. John Edward, M.B.E.

DARBY, Margaret, M.B.E.

DARBY, Major Maurice Ormonde, O.B.E., R.A.F.

D'ARCY, Lieut. George Graham, M.B.E.

D'ARCY, William James Buchanan, M.B.E., *b.* 18 March, 1844 ; *s.* of William Arthur, of Regent's Park, London. *War Work :* Joined the Special Police, Aug. 1914 ; disbanded, Nov. 1919 ; did over 2100 duties. *Clubs :* Unionist, Southchurch ; Masonic, Southend. (M7848)

DARGIE, Albert, M.B.E.

DARKER, Charlotte Tarry, M.B.E.

DARLEY, Major Henry Read, D.S.O., O.B.E., *b.* 13 June, 1865 ; *s.* of T. F. Darley, Esq., of Leeson Park, Dublin ; *m.* Marjorie, *d.* of H. Champion, of 83, Onslow Gardens, S.W. *Educ. :* Clifton ; Trinity Coll., Cambridge ; Sandhurst. Barrister-at-law ; late Capt., 4th Dragoon Guards ; Sec. Cavalry Club. *War Work :* Assist. Military Sec., Eastern Command ; A.D.C. to G.O.C., 11th Division, B.E.F., France ; Staff Capt. Remounts, Eastern Command. *Address :* Fircroft, Stoke Poges, Bucks. *Club :* Cavalry. (O7064)

DARLEY, Major and Qr.-Mr. Thomas Henry, O.B.E. A.I.F.

DARLING, John Ford, C.B.E., *b.* 1864 ; *s.* of John Darling, of St. Martin's, Perthshire ; *m.* Margaret Catherine (died 1907), *d.* of Thomas Munro, of Perth. *Educ. :* St. Martin's School and privately. Was General Manager, London Joint Stock Bank, Ltd. ; subsequently a Managing Director, and now a Director, London Joint City and Midland Bank ; member of Colonial Economic Development Committee. *War Work :* In the summer of 1918 paid two visits to Spain for the purpose of negotiating a loan for the British Government through the Rio Tinto Co., which was successfully accomplished. *Address :* Hollycombe, Englefield Green, Surrey. *Clubs :* Carlton ; Conservative ; Royal Automobile. (C950)

DARLOW, Ellen Frances, Mrs., M.B.E., *b.* 23 May, 1867 ; *m.* Thomas Herbert, *s.* of Thomas Darlow, of Ramsey, Hunts. *Educ. :* Westlands, Birkdale ; Bonn, Klostermanns Höhere Töchterschule. Member of Ruislip-Nortnwood Urban District Council. *War Work :* Quartermaster, Northwood V.A. Hospital, from Nov. 1914, to June, 1915 ; after that Commandant, until close of Hospital, Jan. 1919. *Address :* Beauleigh, Northwood, Middlesex. (M305)

DARNELL, Edward, O.B.E.

DARNELL, George, O.B.E.

DARNELL, Capt. Thomas Noah, M.B.E.

DARNLEY, Florence Rose, Countess of, D.B.E. ; *d.* of John Stephen Morphy, of Kerry and Beechworth, Australia ; *m.* Ivo Francis Walter, Earl of Darnley. *Educ. :* Australia. President of Gravesend Girl Guides ; Chatham Brownies ; Y.W.C.A. Hut, Gravesend ; St. Bartholomew's Linen League, Rochester ; Nurse's Association of Cobham and Shorne ; Cobham Hall Arts and Crafts. *War Work :* Hospital in own home, Cobham Hall, from Oct. 1914, to Dec. 1918 ; helped with V.A.D. Hospitals ; President of three Y.W.C.A. Huts ; organised concerts each winter for patients of surrounding and own hospital ; organised Flag days. *Address :* Cobham Hall, Kent. *Club :* Ladies' Empire. (D42)

DARRACH, William Elliot, M.B.E.

DARROCH, Rev. John, O.B.E.

DARTMOUTH, Mary, Countess of, C.B.E., *d.* of Thomas William, 2nd Earl of Leicester ; *m.* 1879, William, 6th Earl of Dartmouth (*see* BURKE'S *Peerage*). *Addresses :* Patshull House, Wolverhampton ; Woodsome Hall, near Huddersfield ; 37, Charles Street, Berkeley Square, W.

DARTNELL, Lieut.-Col. George Bruce, O.B.E., R.A.S.C.

DARWIN, Major George Henry, M.B.E., M.D., B.Sc. (Vic), F.R.C.P. (Edin.), *b.* 29 June, 1852 ; *s.* of Dr. Henry Darwin, of Masbro', Yorkshire ; *m.* Amelia Elizabeth, Lady of Grace, Order of St. John, *d.* of John Bradshaw, of Withington, Manchester. *Educ. :* Rotherham Grammar School, Manchester University, London, Edinburgh and St. Andrews. M.O. Lancashire and Yorkshire Railway ; for over 40 years interested himself in Ambulance work, as Judge, Examiner and Lecturer ; devoted much time to service in the Volunteers, Territorials and National Rese rve; was awarded the Volunteer Officers' Decoration, also King George's Coronation Medal, for assisting in the formation and organisation of the National Reserve Force, a regiment of which he raised, to a strength of 685, at Southport, and Commanded for over two years ; also assisted in the formation of the Medical Staff Corps, Manchester ; formed a battalion of Engineers at Manchester (not taken over by Government). *War Work :* During the war, was the first Medical Officer called up in Manchester for recruiting, etc., and afterwards was attached to the 2nd Western General Hospital ; was M.O. in charge of the Princess Street Military Hospital, and assisted at the New Bridge and Refuge Hospitals ; 5 years attended at H.Q., 6th Manchester Regiment ; undertook the Examination of railwaymen for R.T.O., France, examined a number of Candidates for Commissions, and in addition attended committees at St. John's Gate, London ; an application by him for re-Commission for Active Service was not accepted on the grounds of age. *Addresses :* Wentworth, Lethbridge Road, Southport ; 97, Railway, 79, Corporation Street, Manchester. *Club :* Southport Conservative. (M10262d)

DARWIN, Sir Horace, K.B.E., F.R.S., M.A., J.P., Assoc.-M.Inst.C.E., *b.* 13 May, 1851 ; *s.* of Charles Robert Darwin, of Down, Kent ; *m.* Hon. Emma Cecilia Farrer, *d.* of Thomas Henry, 1st Lord Farrer, of Abinger Hall. *Educ. :* Trinity College, Cambridge (M.A. 1877). Chairman of the Cambridge and Paul Instrument Co., Ltd. ; Director of the Cambridge Gas Co. ; Member of the Royal Commission on Oxford and Cambridge Universities ; Mayor of Cambridge, 1896–7. *War Work :* Chairman of the Air Inventions Committee, 1918–19 ; Member of the Advising Committee for Aeronautics, 1909–20 ; Member of the Munitions Inventions Department Panel. *Address :* The Orchard, Cambridge. *Club :* Athenæum.

DASHPER, Alice Hester, Mrs., O.B.E., *b.* April, 1869 ; *m.* Charles F., *s.* of Capt. W. Dashper, of Dartmouth. *War Work :* Hon. Sec. Women's Emergency Corps, South-ampton, dealing first with distress amongst women and girls ; opened charity workrooms ; cheap meals for workers ; organised War Hospital Supply Depot in 1915 ; Hon. Sec. for Southampton Baby Week in 1917. Organised and now Hon. Director of " Hostel for Mothers and Babies," Highfield, Southampton. *Address :* Southerns, Bassett, Southampton. (O10264)

DASHWOOD, Arthur Paul, O.B.E., *b.* 17 July, 1882 ; *s.* of Sir George Dashwood, Bart., and Lady Mary Dashwood (*see* BURKE'S *Peerage*) ; *m.* Edmée Elizabeth Monica, *d.* of Henry de la Pasture. *Educ. :* Rugby. Civil Engineer. *War Work :* Richborough ; and Water Transport on East Coast Africa. *Addresses :* Johore Bahru ; The Warren, Abingdon. *Club :* Isthmian. (O6745)

DASHWOOD, Cyril Russell, O.B.E.

DASHWOOD, Col. Edmund William, C.B.E., *b.* 9 Sept. 1858 ; *s.* of the Rev. S. V. Dashwood (*see* BURKE'S *Peerage*, Dashwood of Oxfordshire) ; *m.* 23 Jan. 1908, Geva, *d.* of the late Comdr. H. J. Stanley, R.N., of Cavers-Carre, Melbourne. *Club :* Naval and Military. (C1538)

DASHWOOD, Gova Vereker, Mrs., M.B.E.

DASHWOOD, Capt. Sidney Lewes, M.B.E., R.E. (T.) and R.A.F., *b.* 25 Nov. 1882 ; *s.* of Robert Lewes Dashwood, of The Mount, Yarmouth, I. of W. *Educ. :* Radley Coll. ; Christ Church, Oxford. *War Work :* R.F.C. on Western Front. *Address :* Ellangowan, Grouville, Jersey. *Club :* Constitutional. (M1623)

DAUBENEY, Brig.-Gen. Edward Kaye, C.B.E., D.S.O., *b.* 23 May, 1858 ; *s.* of Thomas Daubeney, of Eastington, Cirencester ; *m.* Eileen Gertrude, *d.* of Sir Peter FitzGerald, Bart., 19th Knight of Kerry, of Valencia, Ireland. *Educ. :* Wellington. La*t*e of South Staffordshire Regiment ; served in the Sekukuni and Zulu Campaigns, 1878–9 (Ulundi) ; Nile Expedition, 1884–5 ; Egyptian Frontier, 1885–6 (Ginnis). *War Work :* Commanded Gloster and Worcester Brigade, T.F., 1914 ; 182nd (Warwick) Inf. Brigade, 1915 ; Highland T.F. Res. Brigade, 1916–18. *Address :* Eastington, Cirencester. *Club :* Army and Navy. (C810)

DAUBENY, Mabel Agnes, M.B.E., *d.* of General Daubeny, C.B. *War Work :* District Head and Hon. Sec. of Soldiers' and Sailors' Help Society (Bristol branch) ; Hon. Sec. Men's branch, Bristol War Pensions. *Address :* 12, Christchurch Road, Clifton, Bristol. (M1625)

DAUBENY, Col. Reginald Ernest, C.B.E., *b.* 9 Nov. 1877 ; *s.* of E. Donajowski, of Heathside, Finchley Road, N.W. 2 (changed name by Deed Poll, dated 18 Feb. 1918), *m.* Louie, the late *d.* of H. J. Bletcher, of Castlethorpe Hall, Brigg. *Educ. :* Univ. Coll. School, London, and Royal Mil. College, Sandhurst. 2nd Lieut. the King's Own Regt., 1896 ; Lieut., 1898 ; Capt., 1900 ; Major, Royal Army Pay Depot, 1916 ; Brevet Lieut.-Col., 3 June, 1917 ; Lieut.-Col., 15 Feb. 1920 ; Temp. Col. and Chief Paymaster, May, 1917, to June, 1920. *War Work :* Organised Army Pay Office, Terr. Force, London District ; assisted in reconstitution of Army Pay Office, Dublin, destroyed in Sinn Fein Rebellion, 1916 ; inaugurated and organised Labour Corps Pay Office at Nottingham, which comprised eventually 7,500 clerks and 750,000 accounts. *Clubs :* Army and Navy ; Junior Carlton. (C1126)

DAUBUZ, Major Claude, O.B.E., M.C., R.A.F.

DAUKES, Capt. Sidney Herbert, O.B.E., M.B., B.A., D.P.H., D.T.M. and H., R.A.M.C., *b.* 20 April, 1879 ; *s.* of Rev. F. Whitfield Daukes, M.A., of Beckenham ; *m.* Emma Maria, *d.* of William Kempsell, of Reigate. *Educ. :* Lancing College ; Caius College, Cambridge ; London Hospital. Doctor of Medicine ; Curator, Wellcome Research Bureau ; late senior School Medical Officer, Norfolk. *War Work :* Specialist Sanitary Officer with B.E.F., France ; Commandant. School of Army Sanitation, Leeds ; Lecturer, R.A.M.C. School of Hygiene, Blackpool. *Address :* 27, Cator Road, Sydenham. (O8785)

DAUNCEY, Lieut.-Col. Thursby Henry Ernest, O.B.E.

DAUNTESEY, Lieut.-Col. William Bathurst, C.B., C.B.E. (assumed by Royal Licence, Oct. 1912, the surname and arms of Dauntesey), *b.* 18 Oct. 1864 ; *s.* of Rev. Robert Harkness, of St. Giles, Dorset ; *m.* Evelyn, *d.* of Capt. William Dauntesey (*see* BURKE'S *Landed Gentry*), of Agecraft Hall, Lancashire. *Educ. :* Wellington College. Royal Marine Artillery, 1882–1912. *War Work :* Commanded 9th Royal Cheshire Regt., and 14th K.O.Y.L.I. (France), 1912–1918. *Address :* Lovells Court, Marnhull, Dorset. *Clubs :* Naval and Military ; Royal Automobile. (C2098)

DAVENPORT, Lieut. Charles Malcolm, O.B.E., R.F.A., S.R.

DAVENPORT, Capt. Colin, O.B.E., R.A.V.C. (O11735)

DAVENPORT, Daniel, M.B.E.

DAVENPORT, Flora Gladys, M.B.E., *b.* 6 Oct. 1881 ; *d.* of John Davies Davenport, of 17, Kensington Park Gardens, and Lincoln's Inn. *Educ.*: At home. Commandant V.A.D. London, 4. *War Work*: Commandant-in-Charge of War Refugees' Dispensary at 265, Strand, W.C.; of B.R.C.S. Recreation Hut and Canteen, No 7 Convalescent Camp, Boulogne and Commandant at Kensington Red Cross (Weir) Hospital, Balham. *Address*: 17, Kensington Park Gardens, W. 11. *Club*: Portsmouth Blue Triangle. (M7852)

DAVENPORT, Lieut. Hugh Richard BROMLEY-, O.B.E.

DAVENPORT, Muriel, Mrs. BROMLEY-, C.B.E., *b.* 1879 ; *d.* of late John Head, of Alington House, Ipswich ; *m.* Hugh Richard, *s.* of W. Bromley Davenport, of Capesthorse, Chelford, Cheshire. *War Work*: Vice-President and Founder, Hove War Hospital Supply Depot ; Hon. Sec. Invalid Comforts Fund for Prisoners of War. *Address*: 6, Medine Terrace, Hove. (C482)

DAVENPORT, Col. William BROMLEY-, C.M.G., C.B.E., D.S.O., T.D., J.P., *b.* 1863 ; *s.* of the late Col. William Bromley-Davenport. M.P. for W. Warwickshire (*see* BURKE'S *Landed Gentry*). *Educ.*: Eton ; Balliol Coll., Oxford. Hon. Col. Staffordshire Yeo.; Lieut.-Col. in the Army; Lieut.-Col. Territorial Force Reserve (formerly Lieut.-Col. Staffordshire Yeo.; Chairman of Cheshire Territorial Forces Assoc. ; sometime Parliamentary Private Sec. to Sec. of State for Home Depart. (Rt. Hon. Sir Matthew White Ridley, Bart., M.P.); appointed Financial Sec. to the War Office 1903, and Finance Member of Army Council, 1904 ; served in S. Africa, 1900, as Lieut.-Col. 4th Batt. Imperial Yeo. (despatches); Great War, 1916-19, Comdg. a Brig. and as an Assist. Director of Labour and Comdt. of a Labour Army in France (Order of Crown of Italy) ; M.P. for Cheshire, Macclesfield Div. (C), 1886-1906. *Addresses*: Capesthorne Hall, Chelford, Cheshire ; Wootton Hall, Ashbourne. (C1228)

DAVEY, Annie, Mrs., O.B.E.

DAVEY, Benjamin Alfred, M.B.E.

DAVEY, Comm. Charles Henry, O.B.E.

DAVEY, Grace Emilie, O.B.E., *b.* 23 Jan. 1878 ; *d.* of Theophilus Davey, of Ronford. Civil Servant. *War Work*: Superintendent of Women Staff (with rank of Section Director), Headquarters, Ministry of Munitions, 1915-18 ; Chief woman officer, Ministry of Munitions, 1918-20. *Address*: Western Road, Romford. (O10267)

DAVEY, Harold William, O.B.E.

DAVEY, Herbert John, M.B.E., *b.* 31 Oct. 1875 ; *s.* of George Samuel Davey ; *m.* Ann Ruth, *d.* of James Howell, of London. *Educ.*: Kennington Oval Boys' School ; Birkbeck College. Inspecting and Testing Engineer ; Chief Inspector to David Kirkaldy & Son, of London, 1900-14 ; Senior partner, Davey and Bell, 11, Arundel Street, Strand, W.C., 1914 to date. *War Work*: Consultant on mechanical tests of materials for Gun Ammunition to the Technical Directorate of Inspection of Gun Ammunition, Royal Arsenal, Woolwich, 1915-18 ; Inspector of Mercury Fulminate and Detonators for Naval, Land, and Air Services, 1915-18 ; Technical Inspector of Tubes, Primers, and Percussion Caps, 1915-18. *Addresses*: 11, Arundel Street, Strand, W.C. 2 ; 25, Danecroft Road, Herne Hill, S.E. 24. (M7854)

DAVEY, Shipwright-Lieut. John Henry, M.B.E.

DAVEY, Major William Hamilton, O.B.E., M.A., B.L.; *s.* of Robert Davey, of Greenholme, Carrickfergus, Co. Antrim ; *m.* Ruby Irene, *d.* of W. S. Mollan, of Marlborough Park, Belfast. *Educ.*: Royal Academical Institution ; Queen's University ; Belfast ; and King's Inns, Dublin. Barrister-at-law, North-East Circuit, Ireland. *War Work*: Combatant Officer, 24th Northumberland Fusiliers (Tyneside Irish Brigade), France and Flanders, 1916-18 ; lent to Irish Recruiting Council Aug. to Nov. 1918 ; British Troops in France and Flanders, 1919-20. *Address*: 48 Bawnmore Road, Belfast, Ireland. (O10269)

DAVID, Maud Anne, O.B.E., *b.* 1872 ; *d.* of the late Edward David, of The Hendre, Llandaff. *War Work*: S.S.F.A. ; S. African War, Great War. *Address*: The Hendre, Llandaff, S. Wales. (O3683)

DAVID, Morgan Edwin, M.B.E., J.P.

DAVIDS, Capt. Maurice, O.B.E.

DAVIDSON, Albert, C.B.E. Managing Director of Hattersley and Davidson (Limited), of Sheffield. *Address*: Sheffield.

DAVIDSON, Capt. Alec Stuart, M.B.E. (late R.E.), *b.* 10 June, 1891 ; *s.* of Harold Davidson, of Teddington, Middlesex ; *m.* Kathleen Muriel, *d.* of C. W. Cresswell Hine, of Dorking. *Educ.*: Oundle School, Northants. Engineer. *War Work*: H.M. Army, Sept. 1914, to Feb. 1919. *Address*: Moleway, Dorking, Surrey. (M5207)

DAVIDSON, Major Arthur Madgwick, O.B.E., Aust. A.M.C.

DAVIDSON, Capt. Colin Keppel, O.B.E., R.A.

DAVIDSON, Lieut.-Col. Edward Humphrey, C.B.E., M.C.

DAVIDSON, Elizabeth, Mrs., M.B.E.

DAVIDSON, Ellen Beatrice, Mrs., O.B.E. (O11758)

DAVIDSON, Ethel Sarah, C.B.E., R.R.C. ; *d.* of — Davidson ; matron, Australian Army Nursing Staff ; served in the Great War. 1915-19. (C1840)

DAVIDSON, Frances Joan, Mrs., O.B.E., *b.* 29 May, 1894 ; *d.* of Right Hon. Sir W. H. Dickinson (*see* BURKE'S

Peerage) ; *m.* John Colin Campbell, *s.* of Sir James Mackenzie Davidson (*see* BURKE'S *Peerage*). *War Work*: Member of Central Prisoners of War Committee. *Address*: 10, Barton Street, Westminster. (O10270)

DAVIDSON, George, O.B.E.

DAVIDSON, George Frederick, O.B.E.

DAVIDSON, Capt. Hugh Stevenson, O.B.E., R.A.M.C., M.B., F.R.C.S.

DAVIDSON, Col. James, C.B.E., J.P., D.L., late 8th Hussars, *b.* 15 Sept. 1853 ; *s.* of the late William Davidson ; *m.* Margaret, *d.* of Col. Edward Ring Berry, of Hyde Park Gate. *Educ.*: Privately, and Aberdeen University. *War Work*: Chairman, Kincardineshire War Pensions Committee ; Chairman, Joint Disablements Committee for Northern Area of Scotland ; Chairman, City of Aberdeen War Pensions Committee ; Vice-Chairman, and from 23 Aug. 1918, Chairman, Kincardineshire Territorial Force Assoc. ; Member, Joint Institutional Committee for Scotland ; Member, Representative Joint Disablement Committee for Scotland ; Member, Local Advisory Committee, Ministry of Labour ; Secretary, Kincardineshire Branch, S. & S. F. Assoc. ; Military Member, Local Emergency Committee, Kincardine ; County Commissioner, Boy Scouts (the Scouts watched the whole coast of Kincardineshire). *Address*: Balnagask, Aberdeen. *Clubs*: Arthurs' ; Royal Automobile. (C2551)

DAVIDSON, Capt. James MacFarlane, O.B.E.

DAVIDSON, James Stewart, O.B.E., J.P. ; *s.* of Rev. G. S. Davidson, of Kinfauns Parish Church, Perthshire ; *m.* Agnes F., *d.* of Rev. P. McLaren, of Fraserburgh Parish Church, Aberdeenshire. *Educ.*: Royal High School and, University, Edinburgh. *War Work*: Hon. Sec. and Treasr. County of Aberdeen War Work Association. *Address*: Cairnlee, Bieldside, Aberdeenshire. *Club*: Scottish Conservative, Edinburgh. (O282)

DAVIDSON, Lieut.-Col. John, O.B.E., R.E. (S.R.).

DAVIDSON, Major John, O.B.E., I.A.R.O.

DAVIDSON, John Hay, M.B.E.

DAVIDSON, Dame Margaret Agnes, Lady, D.B.E., *b.* 21 April, 1871 ; *d.* of General the Hon. Sir Percy Fielding (*see* BURKE'S *Peerage*) ; *m.* Walter Edward, K.C.M.G., Governor of the State of New South Wales, Australia (*see* BURKE'S *Peerage*) ; *s.* of James Davidson, of Killyleagh, Co. Down, Ireland. *Address*: Government House, Sydney, N.S.W., Australia. (D23)

DAVIDSON, Marion, Mrs., M.B.E.

DAVIDSON, Capt. Norman Granville Walshe, O.B.E. F.R.C.S., R.A.M.C.

DAVIDSON, Robert Gibson, O.B.E., M.B., Ch.B., *b.* 2 Oct. 1880 ; *s.* of the late Alexander Duncan Davidson, of Cullen, Banffshire, and London. *Educ.*: Aberdeen. *War Work*: Anæsthetist to Hospital for treating injuries to the jaw, at Norbury, Croydon, 1915-19. *Address*: Thornton Heath, Surrey. *Club*: Royal Societies'. (O11800)

DAVIDSON, Col. Stuart, C.B.E., *b.* 1859 ; Formerly Col. R.E., and Chief Technical Examiner for Works, War Office ; retired 1919. (C138)

DAVIDSON, Williamina Saida, O.B.E., Hon. Serving Sister of the Order of St. John of Jerusalem since 1912, *b.* 15 Nov. 1856 ; *d.* of Patrick Davidson, of Inchmarlo, Kincardineshire, N.B. Hon. Lady Superintendent for 25 years of the Glasgow Soldiers' Home ; and of the Barry Camp Soldiers' Home. *War Work*: In 1914 in 48 hours secured sufficient money and in 3 months built a spacious temporary Soldiers' Home, which has paid its own way and had an average attendance of soldiers during war time of over 1000 per night ; the new permanent Soldiers' Home into which the temporary one has now been transferred, costing about £16,000, was opened, free of debt, on 26 May, 1920, by His Grace the Lord High Commissioner, the Duke of Atholl, K.T., C.B., D.S.O., M.V.O., T.D., and on 9 July, 1920, was visited by Their Majesties the King and Queen and Princess Mary. *Address*: Royal Soldiers' Home, Colinton, Midlothian. (O10272)

DAVIE, James Gordon, M.B.E., *b.* 14 July, 1883 ; *s.* of John Davie, of Airlie, Kirriemuir, N.B. ; *m.* Janet Gow, *d.* of William Lyon, of Airlie. *Educ.*: Airlie Public School ; Webster's Seminary, Kirriemuir. Banker, with National Bank of Scotland, Ltd., London. *War Work*: Chief Cashier to Butter and Cheese Import Committee of Ministry of Food. *Address*: 122, Christchurch Road, Streatham Hill, S.W. 2. *Clubs*: Dulwich Bowling ; Scottish Banks Rifle. (M7855)

DAVIES, Agnes, M.B.E.

DAVIES, Capt. Alewyn Thomas, M.B.E., A.S.C.

DAVIES, Alfred Maurice, O.B.E. (O11785d)

DAVIES, Alfred Thomas, C.B.E., M.P., *b.* 17 July, 1881 ; *s.* of John Thomas Davies of Llanarthney ; *m.* Joanna Elizabeth, *d.* of John Lewis, of Llanelly. *Educ.*: London Polytechnic and abroad. Chairman, Charles Hatton & Co., Ltd. ; Director, Glynbeady Tin Plate Works ; South Wales Fuel Co., Ltd. ; Old Silkstone Collieries, Ltd. ; a governor of Middlesex Hospital and of Bart.'s Hospital. *War Work*: Hon. Sec., Welsh Prisoners of War Fund ; Hon. Sec., All Welsh Service in Westminster Abbey ; Assistant, Ministry of Munitions, Priority Branch. *Addresses*: The Eagles, West Hill, Highgate ; Gore Farm, East Dean, near Eastbourne, Sussex. *Clubs*: Junior Carlton ; Constitutional ; 1900 ; Royal Automobile, etc. (C2552)

DAVIES, Sir Alfred Thomas, K.B.E., C.B., J.P., D.L., *b.* 11 March, 1861 ; *s.* of Wm. Davies, of Liverpool ; *m.* 1st, Margaret Esther (d. 1892), *d.* of Thomas Christian Nicholas, of

Liverpool; 2nd, Mary, *d.* of Charles Colton, of Liverpool and Birkdale, Lancs. *Educ.*: Waterloo High School and Univ. Coll. of Wales, Aberystwyth. Solicitor (admitted 1883); Notary Public (adm. 1887); Cursitor of the County Palatine of Lancaster since 1895; Permanent Secretary to the Welsh Department of the Board of Education since 1907; Member of the Imperial Education Conferences of 1907 and 1911; of the Departmental Committee on the National School of Medicine for Wales, 1914; and of the Ancient Monuments Board for Wales; Librarian of the Priory for Wales of the Order of St. John of Jerusalem; Governor of the University College of Wales, Aberystwyth. *War Work*: Founder and Hon. Director of the British Prisoners of War Book Scheme (Educational). *Addresses*: Jesmond, Blackheath Park, S.E. 3; Yewtree Cottage, Medmenham, Marlow, Bucks. *Club*: Reform. (K57)

DAVIES, Alphonso William James, M.B.E.

DAVIES, Capt. Andrew William, O.B.E., R.N.

DAVIES, Major Arthur, C.B.E. Hon. Major and Hon. Sup. St. John's and British Red Cross Combined War Gift Depot. (C1963)

DAVIES, Arthur Vernon, O.B.E., M.B., Ch.B., Knight of Grace of the Order of St. John of Jerusalem in England, *b.* 10 June, 1872; *s.* of Edwin Edgar Davies, of Bridgend, Glamorgan; *m.* Annie Maude, *d.* of J. Brooke Unwin, M.D., of Dunchurch. *Educ.*: Privately, and Owens' Coll., Manchester. M.O.H., Crompton; Certifying Factory Surgeon, Crompton. *War Work*: Assist. Com. for Lancs St. John Ambulance Brigade; Assist. County Director, B.R.C.S., representing the S.J.A.B. on the East Lancs County Committee, and all the St. John V.A.D. Hospitals in East Lancs. *Address*: Glenarm House, Shaw, Lancs. (O10273)

DAVIES, Ashton, M.B.E.

DAVIES, Lieut. Bertram Harold, O.B.E., R.N.R.

DAVIES, Lieut. Charles Beverley, M.B.E.

DAVIES, Major Charles Frederick Fellows, O.B.E.

DAVIES, Charles Llewelyn, C.B.E., *b.* 29 June, 1860; *s.* of Rev. John Llewelyn Davies. *Educ.*: Marlborough; Trinity College, Cambridge. Clerk in Local Government Board, 1884; transferred to Treasury, 1888; Assistant Paymaster-General since 1910. *Address*: 10, Lupus Street, Pimlico, London. S.W. 1. (C139)

DAVIES, Lieut.-Col. Charles Robert, O.B.E.

DAVIES, Clara Maud, Mrs., M.B.E., *b.* Oct. 1866; *d.* of Henry Moore, of Sampford Peverell, Devon; *m.* Lieut.-Col. Henry Davies, C.M.G., *d.* of Henry Davies, of Cheltenham; *Educ.*: Cheltenham Ladies' College, and Brussels. *War Work*: Interpreter for Belgians at Folkestone and Deal, placed 400 in private houses; organised Church Hall, Dover, for soldiers and wives to meet; organised entire Red Cross Depot for stores for Admiralty Pier, and all surgical work for Military Hospitals; Com. and Supt. Red Cross and St. John; organised and ran Hostel for V.A.Ds and W.L., Dover. *Addresses*: 10, de Vere Gardens: 37, Salisbury Road, Dover. (M7857)

DAVIES, Rev. David, M.B.E., *b.* 25 June, 1886; *s.* of David Davies, of Morlach, Cross Inn S.O., Cardigs. *Educ.*: St. David's Coll. School, and St. David's Coll., Lampeter. Clerk in Holy Orders. *War Work*: Chaplain to the Forces with 114 Brigade, 38th Division, on the Western Front. *Address*: Moeloch, Cross Inn S.O., Cardiganshire, S. Wales. (O6461)

DAVIES, David Gordon, M.B.E.

DAVIES, Lieut. David Owen, M.B.E.

DAVIES, David Thomas, O.B.E., F.S.I., *b.* 14 Oct. 1868; *s.* of M. Davies, of Llanfyllin, of Montgomeryshire, N. Wales. *Educ.*: Oswestry High School. Land Surveyor and Valuer; Superintending Valuer for Wales (Inland Revenue Dept.). *War Work*: Commissioner for South Wales for Food Production under Ministry of Agriculture and Fisheries; Land Valuer and Adviser to the Admiralty in requisitions under Defence of Realm Regulations. *Address*: Willsden, Rhiwbina, Cardiff. *Club*: Cardiff and County. (O10274)

DAVIES, Edward Futcher, O.B.E.

DAVIES, Major Edward Owen, O.B.E.

DAVIES, Edwin Harold, O.B.E.

DAVIES, Emily Geraldine, Mrs., M.B.E.; *d.* of Edward Harte, of Wells, Somerset; *m.* Evan Coleman Davies, *s.* of Evan James Davies, of Monmouth. *Educ.*: Home. *War Work*: Was Commandant of The Cedars Hospital, Wells, Somerset, from 1915–19; had over 1000 patients during the time (the hospital was worked entirely by voluntary workers). *Address*: Wells, Somersetshire. (M7858)

DAVIES, Ernest, C.B.E.

DAVIES, Ernest Herbert, O.B.E.

DAVIES, Lieut. Ernest James, O.B.E.

DAVIES, Evan Edward, O.B.E., *b.* 20 June, 1879. Solicitor; Clerk to the Maesteg Urban District Council, and Solicitor to the Joint Burial Board, 1912; Member of the Glamorgan County Council for Maesteg Division, 1906; Alderman, 1912; Member of Local Group of Managers and Chairman of Maesteg Secondary School Governors; Executive Officer Local Food Control Committee; Solicitor to Maesteg District of South Wales Miners' Federation. *Address*: Brynhanlog, 38, Victoria Avenue, Porthcawl. (O10277)

DAVIES, Capt. Fred, M.B.E.

DAVIES, Frederick Charles, O.B.E.

DAVIES, George, M.B.E., J.P.

DAVIES, Capt. George Frederick, M.B.E.

DAVIES, Col. George Freshfield, C.B., C.M.G., C.B.E.,

b. 1872; Entered Lincolnshire Regt. 1892, and became Lieut.-Col. 1915, and Brevet Col. 1917; served in the S. African War 1899–1902, present at relief of Ladysmith (despatches, Queen's medal with four clasps, King's medal with two clasps), and in the Great War, 1914–19, in Palestine, as Dep. Director of Supplies and Transport, with rank of Col. (despatches). (C1375)

DAVIES, Gwilym Meirion, M.B.E., *b.* 17 June, 1882; *s.* of William Thomas Davies, of Shrewsbury; *m.* Elizabeth Rigg, *d.* of Alan Mackune, of Anglesey. *Educ.*: Shrewsbury. Solicitor; Labour Advisor to Metropolitan-Vickers Electrical Co., Ltd. *War Work*: Manchester War Relief Committee; Organising Secretary, N.W. Area of Ministry of Munitions. *Address*: 15, Higher Downs, Bowden, Cheshire. (M312)

DAVIES, Lieut. Harry Cornwall, O.B.E., R.E.

DAVIES, Capt. Henry, O.B.E., *b.* Oct. 1860. *Educ.*: Normal Coll.; Bangor; Univ. Coll., Cardiff. Director of Mining Instruction, Glamorgan County Council; Member of Cardiff City Council. *War Work*: Returned from Germany two days before War declared; enlisted as private soldier with three sons on mobilisation day; did strenuous recruiting work; proceeded to France as Capt. in R.W.F.; wounded on Somme in 1916; subsequently attached to Royal Engineers as District Officer Roads and Transport; appointed Education Officer; mentioned in despatches. *Address*: County Hall, Cardiff. (O10279)

DAVIES, Henry Ivor, M.B.E., *b.* 1 May, 1872; *s.* of Joseph Davies. *Educ.*: Westminster City School; King's College, London. Appointed to the War Office, Oct. 1890; transferred to Ministry of Pensions, Feb. 1917; promoted First Class Clerk, June, 1917; Deputy Principal Clerk, Oct. 1919. *Address*: 44, Blenheim Gardens, N.W. 2. (M7861)

DAVIES, Horace Victor, M.B.E. Censor, Sierra Leone. (M10257h)

DAVIES, Hugh Christopher, M.B.E.

DAVIES, Isabel Warwick, Mrs., M.B.E., *b.* 2 Jan. 1883; *d.* of Maj.-Gen. D. K. Evans, 6th Royal Warwickshire Regt.; *m.* Maj.-Gen. H. R. Davies, C.B., *s.* of Lieut.-Gen. H. F. Davies, of Elmley Castle, Worcs. *Educ.*: Dorchester. *War Work*: Joint Sec. of Prisoners of War Fund for Oxfordshire and Buckinghamshire Regiments; Sec. of 2nd (Oxford and Bucks) Light Infantry Comforts Fund. *Address*: Godmanstone Manor, Dorchester, Dorset. (M7862)

DAVIES, Ivor, M.B.E. Lloyd's Agent at Algiers. *War Work*: Sec. Military Exemption Committee for Algeria; salvage and repairs to torpedoed steamers. *Address*: 1, rue Colbert, Algiers. (M1632)

DAVIES, James, O.B.E. (O11957)

DAVIES, James David, O.B.E., *b.* 4 Jan. 1857; *s.* of Edward Davies, of The Court, Merthyr Tydvil, Glam.; *m.* Eleanor Mary, *d.* of Frederick Cobb, of Frensham, Surrey. *Educ.*: Christ's Coll., Brecon. Surgeon, Royal Isle of Wight County Hospital. *War Work*: Hazelwood Red Cross Hospital, Ryde; M.O. in Command Troops, Ryde District. *Address*: Belmont, Ryde, I.W. *Clubs*: Army and Navy; Royal Victoria Yacht. (O10289)

DAVIES, Capt. John, O.B.E., R.A.O.C.

DAVIES, John Cecil, C.B.E., J.P., Legion of Honour, *b.* 23 Sept. 1864; *s.* of Thos. Davies, of Swansea; *m.* Emma Jane, *d.* of John Edmunds, of Coed-y-Paen, Monmouthshire. *Educ.*: Normal College, Swansea. Managing Director of Baldwins, Ltd., etc.; Member of the Council of the University College of Swansea; Member of Llanelly Board of Guardians and Gowerton Council. *War Work*: One of the founders of the Swansea National Shell Factory; Member of the Executive Committee appointed by the Ministry of Munitions to control shell factories; represented Ministry in allocation of steel supplies. *Address*: The Mount, Gowerton, Glam. *Clubs*: Swansea and Counties; Bristol Channel Yacht. (C2553)

DAVIES, Major John Francis, O.B.E., I.A.

DAVIES, Major John Hallmark, O.B.E., R.A.F.

DAVIES, John Howell, M.B.E.

DAVIES, John Robert, C.B.E., M.A., *b.* 1856; eldest *s.* of the late Richard Davies, of Treborth, Bangor, Lord-Lieut. of Anglesey. J.P., Anglesey and Carnarvonshire; D.L., Anglesey. *Address*: Ceris, Bangor, N.Wales. (C2554)

DAVIES, Lieut. John Trevor, M.B.E., I.A.

DAVIES, Paymaster-Sub.-Lieut. John Wilfred, M.B.E. R.N.V.R.

DAVIES, Sir Joseph, K.B.E., J.P., M.P., *b.* 11 Dec. 1866; *s.* of Thomas Seth Davies, of St. Issells, Pembroke; *m.* Blanche, *d.* of John Heron Wilson, of Cardiff. *Educ.*: Bristol Grammar School. Chairman, A.G.W.I. Petroleum Corporation, Ltd.; Status Investment Trust, Ltd.; Director, Cambrian Railways; Anglo-Baltic and Mediterranean Bank, etc.; M.P., Crewe Division; J.P., County of Glamorgan. *War Work*: Representative for Wales on Cabinet Committee for Prevention of Unemployment and Distress, 1914–16; Secretary, Prime Minister's Secretariat, 1917–19; visited U.S.A., 1917, on Government Mission. *Address*: 29, Chester Terrace, Regent's Park. N.W. 1. *Clubs*: Bath; Reform. (K58)

DAVIES, Capt. Joseph Edward, O.B.E., R.A.S.C.

DAVIES, Julia, M.B.E.

DAVIES, Capt. Leofric Pearson, O.B.E.

DAVIES, Capt. Llewellyn Wynne, O.B.E., M.D., Ch.B., *b.* 18 April, 1875; *s.* of Rev. D. Davies, of Llansilin Vicarage, Oswestry. *Educ.*: Oswestry Grammar School, Shropshire; Edinburgh Univ.; King's Coll., London; Berlin. Member of the West African Medical Service since 1911; Senior House

Surgeon and Physician, East Suffolk and Ipswich Hospital, 3 years; House Physician and Acting Medical Superintendent, Hospital for Sick Children, Great Ormond Street, London; Clinical Assistant, Ear, Nose and Throat Hosp., Golden Square, London; House Physician and House Surgeon, Dreadnought Hospital, Greenwich. *War Work:* Medical Officer, Northern Column Cameroon Expeditionary Force, W. Africa, Nov. 1914, to May, 1916; acting Assistant Surgeon, Dreadnought Hospital, Greenwich, June, 1916, to Sept. 1916; Medical Officer and Surgical Specialist, No 42 Indian General Hosp., Mesopotamia, March, 1917, to July, 1917; Sanitary Officer and Civil Surgeon, Kurna, Mesopotamia, July, 1917, to Jan. 1918; Officer Commanding No. 57 C.S. Hospital, Mesopotamia, Jan. 1918, to Feb. 1919; Surgical Specialist, No. 57 C.S. Hospital, Mesopotamia; mentioned in despatches, Aug. 1918; Medical Officer Special Battalion at Rawal Pindi, India, March to May, 1919; S.M.O. Kohat-Kurram Force (Afghanistan Campaign), May to July, 1919. *Address:* c̸o Lloyds Bank, Ltd., Penzance, Cornwall.   (O4203)

DAVIES, Louisa, Mrs. Russell, M.B.E.,

DAVIES, Magdalen Augusta Lavinia, Lady, C.B.E.   (C3106a)

DAVIES, Mildred Lucy, Mrs., M.B.E.

DAVIES, Morgan, M.B.E. *b.* 1 May, 1868; *s.* of B. A. David Davies, of Wernddu, Pontardawr; *m.* Elizabeth, *d.* of Jenkin Bevan Morgan, of Alltwen. *Educ.:* Elementary School; Trehanor Grammar School; Pontardawr Collegiate School. Solicitor. *War Work:* Chairman of Pontardawr Rural District Council in 1914; Chairman, Pontardawr Military Tribunal; Chairman of the Local War Distress Fund Committee; Chairman, Belgian Refugee Committee; Member of the Local Military Committee; acted as Hon. Sec. under Lord Derby Scheme; acted as Executive Officer to the Pontardawr Food Control Committee from 1 Jan. 1918, to 31 March, 1919; now Member of the Pontardawr District Council and Board of Guardians; Local Representative on the University College of Swansea.   (M7864)

DAVIES, Owen, M.B.E.

DAVIES, Major Reginald Laidlaw, O.B.E., M.B., F.R.C.S., R.A.M.C. Chevalier, Legion of Honour.

DAVIES, Richard, C.B.E., J.P., *b.* 15 July, 1853; *s.* of David Davies, of Crockerbtown, Cardiff, Glam.; *m.* Mary, *d.* of James Barnes, of Kensington. *Educ.:* Privately. Member of the London Stock Exchange; one of H M. Lieutenants for the City of London; J.P. for the County of Middlesex; Member of the Territorial Force Association for the City of London; a Trustee of the Crystal Palace; Vice-Chairman of the Sir John Cass Foundation; Member of the Corporation of London. *War Work:* Chairman of the City of London Branch of the British Red Cross Society; Member of the City of London Military Tribunal; Chairman (during the War) of the City of London Branch of the National Lifeboat Society. *Addresses:* 10–11, Austin Friars, E.C.; Inglewood, 21 Highbury Quadrant, N.   (C2555)

DAVIES, Capt. Richard Llewellyn, M.B.E., R.A.S.C.

DAVIES, Robert Yarnell, M.B.E..

DAVIES, Lieut. Sellick, M.B.E., R.A.S.C.

DAVIES, Sophia Katherine, M.B.E.

DAVIES, Thomas, O.B.E.

DAVIES, Thomas, M.B.E., J.P., *b.* 10 April, 1874; *s.* of Henry Davies, of Cilwaunyddfawr; *m.* Frances Mary, *d.* of Edward Davies, J.P., of Creig Evan. *Educ.:* Capel Evan Council School. Farmer. *War Work:* Chairman of Newcastle-Emlyn Rural Tribunal; Member of Carmarthenshire War Agric. Committee; Member of Rural Food Control Committee; Member of the Carmarthenshire Women's War Agricultural Committee; Chairman of Newcastle Emlyn District Agric. Committee; Member of the Live Stock Control Committee; Chairman and Organiser of West Carmarthenshire Prisoners of War Committee; Promoter of Soldiers' Ploughing School. *Address:* Cilwaunyddfawr, Newcastle Emlyn, South Wales.   (M1634)

DAVIES, Capt. Thomas Edward, M.B.E.

DAVIES, Thomas Evan, O.B.E., Chevalier Legion d' Honneur, *b.* 16 Nov. 1873; *s.* of late David Evan Davies, of Dowlais; *m.* Margaret Elizabeth, *d.* of late Rev. William Johnson Bain, of Aberdeen. *Educ.:* Cardiff. Civil Engineer. *War Work:* Liaison Officer in charge of machinery supplies to Allies; Director of Crane Section, Ministry of Munitions; in charge of various hutment contracts for War Office, and submarine defences for Admiralty. *Address:* The General Electric Co., Witton, Birmingham. *Clubs:* Central and Engineers, Rio de Janeiro.   (O1269)

DAVIES, Major Walford, O.B.E., R.A.F.

DAVIES, Walter, M.B.E., J.P. for the County of Middlesex, *b.* 24 Oct. 1857; *s.* of Chas. William Davies, of London. *War Work:* Hon. Sec., Ealing National Emergency Fund (Prince of Wales' Fund); Military Representative; National Service Representative; Hon. Sec. and Treasurer, Ealing War Hospitals Workshop. *Address:* Downhurst, Ealing, W. 5. *Club:* Constitutional.   (M314)

DAVIES, William, M.B.E.

DAVIES, Major William Henry Saxon, O.B.E.

DAVIES, William John Abbott, O.B.E.

DAVIES, William Lloyd, M.B.E.

DAVIES, Lieut. William Thomas, M.B.E., *b.* 25 Oct. 1874; *s.* of Michael Davies, of Bridgend, Glamorganshire; *m.* Florence Eleanor, *d.* of William John Leat, of Tondu, Glam. *Educ.:* Bridgend Board and Grammar Schools and Cardiff Higher

Grade. Manager; Ministry of Labour. *War Work:* Joined as Private 10th Batt. Rifle Brigade, 10 Sept. 1914; promoted Sergt 12 Sept.; went to France, July, 1915; granted commission, Aug. 1915; returned to England, Sept. 1915, and posted to 10th Batt. Welsh Regt.; transferred to 3rd Garr. Batt. Royal Welsh Fusiliers; proceeded to Egypt, July, 1916, on Prisoner of War work. *Club:* Masonic.   (M4674)

DAVIES, Dorothy Mortlock, Mrs. KEVILL-, M.B.E.; *d.* of Ernest Lacon, of Ormesby Hall, Norfolk; *m.* Capt. W. A. S. H. Kevill-Davies, 7th Hussars, of Croft Castle, Herefordshire. *War Work:* Hon. Sec. Women's War Agricultural Committee and Horticultural Committee; Hon. Sec. of County Federation of Women Institutes. *Address:* The Highwood, Leominster, Herefordshire.   (M1631)

DAVIES, Ethel, Mrs. PRICE-, O.B.E., *b.* 19 May, 1872; *d.* of C. E. Charlesworth, J.P., of Conyngham Hall, Knaresborough; *m.* Lieut.-Col. Stafford D. Price-Davies. Vice-President, Montgomeryshire British Red Cross Society. *War Work:* Started a hospital, Broadway House, Churchstoke, Montgomeryshire, which continued until the end of the War. *Address:* Marrington Hall, Chirbury, Salop. *Clubs:* Ladies' Imperial, London; Shropshire Ladies' County, Shrewsbury.   (O1267)

DAVIES, Capt. Edward Owen WATKIN-, O.B.E.

DAVIES, Rev. William WYNN-, O.B.E., B.A. (1st) (Lond.). *Educ.:* Grammar School, Beaumaris; University College of Wales, Aberystwyth. Minister of Capel Mawr, Rhos; Chairman of Managers of Rhos Council Schools; Member of Governing Body of Ruabon County School. *War Work:* Chairman of War Savings and Rhos Food Production Committees; Vice-Chairman of East Denbigh War Aims Committee; and varied and valuable administrative and platform work. *Address:* Rhos, Wrexham, N. Wales.   (O10281)

DAVIS, Albert Alfred, M.B.E.

DAVIS, Lieut. Alexander Horace, O.B.E., M.C., R.G.A., *b.* 2 Feb. 1886; *s.* of Charles Davis, of Cumbrae, Wharf Road, Bournemouth; *m.* Olive May, *d.* of Francis Dungey, of Plymouth. *Educ.:* Westbourne British School, Bournemouth. *War Work:* Embarked for France with 2nd Siege Battery, R.G.A., Sept. 1914; commissioned for service in the field, Sept. 1915; served with 102 Siege Bty. in France, from May, 1916, to Mar. 1917; appointed Staff Capt.. VI. Corps, H.A., Mar. 1917; appointed Staff Capt., IX. Corps, R.A., July, 1919.   (O2487)

DAVIS, Anna Gronow, Mrs., M.B.E.

DAVIS, Capt. Bernard Langridge, O.B.E., R.A.M.C. (T.).

DAVIS, Capt. Bryant Fitzwilliam Richard, O.B.E.

DAVIS, Lieut.-Col. Cecil, O.B.E., (T.).

DAVIS, Charles, M.B.E.

DAVIS, Lieut.-Col. Charles Herbert, C.B.E., D.S.O.

DAVIS, Lieut.-Col. Charles Thomas, O.B.E.

DAVIS, Adm. Edward Henry Meggs, C.M.G., O.B.E., *b.* 1846; *s.* of the late Capt. John E. Davis; *m.* 1895, Ethel Mary, *d.* of the late F. C. Lambe, of Flushing, Cornwall. Entered R.N. 1860; Lieut. 1870; Com. 1878; Capt. 1887; Rear-Adm. 1901; Vice-Adm. (ret.), 1905; Adm. 1908; served at bombardment of Kagosima, Japan, 1863; at capture of Simonoseki Forts, Japan, 1864; during Kaffir War, 1877–78; with Naval Brig. (specially promited), and during Zulu War, 1879 (medal with three clasps); hoisted British flag on 13 islands of the Gilbert group, W Pacific, 1892; J.P. for Sussex. *Address:* Rathedmond, Bexhill-on-Sea. *Club:* Naval and Military.   (O10283)

DAVIS, Capt. Eugene Charles Henry, M.B.E.

DAVIS, Florence Mary, Mrs., O.B.E., *b.* 16 Oct. 1863; *m.* Arthur Walker Davis. Trained nurse, 1885–90, King's College Hospital, London; Charge-nurse, J. J. Hospital, Bombay, 1891–96; Sister, R. Sussex County Hospital, 1896–99; Matron, Hove Sanatorium, 1899–1904. *War Work:* From Sept. 1914, to Oct. 1918, as Sister, R. Sussex County Hospital; Matron, with the first B.R.C.S. unit at Boulogne; Sister-in-Charge, Mrs. Hanbury Tracey's Hospital, Woodcote; Matron, V.A.D. Hospital, Porchester Terrace, London, W.; and Interviewing Matron, etc., Devonshire House, and 83, Pall Mall, W. *Address:* Highdown, Rhodes Minnis, Elham, Canterbury.   (O3687)

DAVIS, Major Francis Robert Edward, O.B.E., R.A.F.

DAVIS, Capt. Frank Gordon, M.B.E., R.A.S.C.

DAVIS, Georgina Jessie Chisholm, Mrs., M.B.E.,

DAVIS, Gershom Willoughby Cecil, M.B.E., A.C.A., *b.* 28 July, 1880; *s.* of the late Alfred Davis, of Willow Grange-Keston, Kent; *m.* Hilda Margaret, *d.* of the late Judge Vickers, of Kingston, Jamaica, B.W.I. Chartered Accountant of the firm of Linnett, Davis & Co., 42, Poultry, E.C. *War Work:* In Accounts Dept., Ministry of Munitions; appointed Assistant Controller of Munitions Accounts on 31 May, 1919; later a member of Accounts Liquidation Committee, and other Sub-Committees for winding up affairs of Accounts Dept., Ministry of Munitions. *Addresses:* 42. Poultry, E.C.; 2, Moscow Court, Bayswater, W.   (M7870)

DAVIS, Harry Lewer, O.B.E.

DAVIS, Henry William Carless, O.B.E.

DAVIS, John, M.B.E., R.G.A.

DAVIS, Comm. John Cecil, O.B.E., R.N.

DAVIS, John Samuel Champion, C.B.E., V.D., M.A., J.P., D.L., *b.* 21 Feb. 1859; *s.* of Rev. S. Davis, of Burrington, N. Devon; *m.* Minna Sophia, *d.* of William Butt, of Axmouth, Devon. *Educ.:* Rossall and Balliol College. Indian Civil Service, 1880–1906; D.L. and J P. for Devon; Member of

Devon County Council; Member of Devon Territorial Force Association; Deputy Chairman, Exeter Diocesan Board of Finance; County Director, British Red Cross Society. *War Work:* Control of Red Cross and V.A.D. work in Devon. *Address:* Kingford, Burrington, N. Devon. *Clubs:* New University; Devon and Exeter. (C142)

DAVIS, Capt. Kenneth Randall, O.B.E., Royal Warwick shire Regt. (T.), *b.* 1867; *s.* of J. Davis, of Bournemouth; *m.* Jane, *d.* of W. Dolamore, of Bournemouth. *Educ.:* Privately. *Address:* Broadmeadow, Solihill, Warwickshire. *Clubs:* R.A.C.; Union, Birmingham. (O3688)

DAVIS, Lilian Bertha, M.B.E., *b.* 25 Dec. 1896; *d.* of Francis J. M. Davis, of Bath. *Educ.:* Alexandra School, Dublin. Appointed Woman Clerk, Savings Bank Dept., General Post Office, Jan. 1916. *War Work:* Loaned to War Trade Department as administrative assistant, 1916–19. (M7871)

DAVIS, Capt. Leslie Stalman, O.B.E., R.A.S.C.

DAVIS, Mary Elizabeth Mrs., O.B.E.

DAVIS, Owen, M.B.E.

DAVIS, Paymaster Lieut.-Comm. Reginald Unwin, O.B.E., R.N.

DAVIS, Capt. Robert, M.B.E., R.E.

DAVIS, Capt. Sidney Alfred, D.S.O., O.B.E. Lieut.-Gen. List and Acting Capt.; served in the Great War, 1914–16 (despatches) (O7070)

DAVIS, Lieut. Spencer, M.B.E.

DAVIS, Lieut. Sidney George, O.B.E., LL.B. (Lond.) *b.* 15 Dec. 1883; *s.* of Walter James Davis, of Wandsworth Common. *Educ.:* King's and University Colleges, London. Solicitor. *War Work:* Attached Staff D.R. 7(b), War Office, London; transferred to Ministry of National Service; served at London Headquarters as Personal Assistant to Con troller of Registration and Director of National Service, London and South Eastern Region; Joint Secretary, Registration Advisory Board; gave evidence for M.N.S.to Civil War Workers Committee (Ministry of Reconstruction); Joint Representative on Committee of Manning (Ministry of Shipping). *Addresses:* 19, Park Road, Wandsworth Common, S.W.; Donington House, Norfolk Street, Strand, W.C. 2. *Club:* Royal Societies'. (O271)

DAVIS, Sydney Carlile, M.B.E., *b.* 1878; *s.* of Orlando Davis, J.P., of Plymouth; *m.* Saidie, *d.* of the late Thomas Pickering Pick, F.R.C.S., of London. *Educ.:* Plymouth Coll. Solicitor and Notary Public, Vice-Consul for Sweden; Hon. Solicitor, National Chamber of Trade; Hon. Sec. Plymouth Incorporated Mercantile Association. *War Work:* Clerk to the Plymouth Panel of the Devon County Appeal Tribunal, under the Military Service Act; Road Transport Officer for Plymouth Area of S.W. Division of Ministry of Food; organiser of Road Transport Services for Plymouth and Cornwall during Railway Strike, 1919. *Address:* Plymouth. (M7872)

DAVIS, Thomas Ruddock, O.B.E., F.I.S., F.I.D., *b.* 7 Dec. 1884; *s.* of Thomas Dewar Davis, of Newcastle-on-Tyne and Streatham; *m.* Keturah, *d.* of George Crowter, of West Norwood. *Educ.:* Lancaster Coll. One of the first members of the Incorporated Institute of Shipbrokers; Director of W.R. Smith and Sons (London), Ltd.; Director of Cornborough Shipping Line, Ltd.; Fellow of Institute of Directors. *War Work:* Joined the firm of Ross T. Smyth & Co., appointed to buy all the grain for the Allies under Asquith Government; negotiated all the chartering of tonnage for carrying grain purchases; subsequently technical shipping assistant to the Royal Commission on Wheat Supplies; finally managing the Commission's City Chartering Bureau. *Addresses:* Bonheur, Braxted Park, Streatham; Exchange Chambers, St Mary Axe, E.C.3. (O10285)

DAVIS, Capt. Valfred Emanuel, M.B.E.

DAVIS, Lieut. William, O.B.E., I.A.R.O.

DAVIS, Lieut.-Col. William Northcote, O.B.E., V.D., J.P.

DAVIS, Comm. William Thomas, M.B.E., R.N.V.R.

DAVIS, Evelyn Mary, Mrs. BRAMWELL-, O.B.E.; *d.* of Albert R. Till, of Crookham House, nr. Newbury, Berks; *m.* the late Percy Bramwell-Davis, Capt. Highland Light Infantry, *s.* of Richard Bramwell-Davis, K.C. *War Work:* Sec. Berkshire War Pensions Local Committee. *Address:* c o A. S. B. Tull. Esq., Crookham House, nr. Newbury, Berks. *Club:* Ladies' Empress. (O10254)

DAVISON, Major Charles Gray, O.B.E.

DAVISON, Daniel, O.B.E.

DAVISON, Capt. Duncan Athol, O.B.E., Royal Irish Fusiliers, *b.* 20 Aug. 1887; *s.* of Duncan Davison, of Sedgefield House, Sedgefield, Durham. *Educ.:* Bedford and Sandhurst. Gazetted 2nd Lieut. R. Irish Fusiliers, 9 Oct. 1907; Lieut., 12 Dec. 1909; Capt., 27 Oct. 1914; appointed Assistant Instructor, School of Musketry, Hythe 1 Jan. 1914; Assist. Instructor, School of Musketry, Hythe (temp.) 20 Dec. 1915; Assist. Instructor, Machine-gun Corps, British Armies in France, 18 Oct. 1916; Commandant, School of Musketry, Ireland (T. Major), 1 June, 1917; Chief Instructor, School of Musketry, Ireland (T. Major), 13 July, 1918; Adjutant, 2nd R. Irish Fusiliers, 11 Aug. 1919; served with 1st Bn. R. Irish Fusiliers in France and Flanders, 18 Dec. 1914, to 1 May, 1915; wounded, 2nd Battle of Ypres, 25 April, 1915. *Clubs:* Naval and Military; Junior United Service. (O8788)

DAVISON, Edward Anderson, M.B.E.

DAVISON, 2nd Lieut. James Edwin, M.B.E., R.E.

DAVISON, John William, M.B.E., M.I.Mech.E., *b.* 6 May,

1864; *s.* of James Davison, of Low Fell, Co. Durham; *m.* Mary Dorethea, *d.* of William Clemson Cowgill, of Old Colwyn. *Educ.:* Ravensworth Academy, Co. Durham; Dr. Ehrlich's Private School, Newcastle-on-Tyne. Sub-Commissioner, Glam. County St. John Ambulance Brigade, Priory for Wales; Chief Mech. and Constructional Engineer to the Great Western Colliery Co., Ltd., Pontypridd; Member of the Council of the South Wales Institute of Engineers. *War Work:* Organised Flag Days and collected Funds towards War Hospitals; supervised the conveying of the wounded from station to hospitals, and charge of orderlies at the hospital; Commandant of V.A.D.; 1st Lieut., 6th Vol. Batt. Glamorgan Volunteers; charge of sentries and guards on night duty, Cardiff Docks, 1917–18; Instructor in trench work, obstacles, and bombing to the battalion. *Address:* Rhondda House, Pontypridd. (M7874)

DAVISON, Minnie Gibson, Mrs., O.B.E., *b.* 11 Dec. 1870; *d.* of Robert Henry Brooks, of North Shields; *m.* Thomas, *s.* of Charles Davison, of Cornsay, Durham. *Educ.:* Cleminson's Private Seminary, Bishop Auckland. *War Work:* Col. of New castle Women's Volunteer Reserve; raised the above corps, which was the first of its kind in the country, to train women to replace men called up for war service; organised and carried on sailors' and soldiers' canteen and free rest rooms at Central Station, Newcastle; supplied comforts for soldiers at home and abroad; catered and provided for refugees passing through the Port of Newcastle. (O10287)

DAVISON, William Henderson, O.B.E., M.B., D.P.H., Barrister-at-Law, *b.* 26 Feb. 1880; *s.* of Henderson Davison, of Larne, Co. Antrim; *m.* Gladys, *d.* of late Hill Norris, M.D., J.P., of Aston. *Educ.:* Royal School, Dungannon, and Edin burgh University. Assistant Medical Officer of Health, City of Birmingham. *War Work:* Major, R.A.M.C. (T.F.); D.A.D.M.S. Sanitation, Third Army, H.Q., B.E.F.; Com mandant, Fourth Army School of Sanitation, Peronne; Divisional Sanitary Officer, 61st South Midland Division, B.E.F. *Address:* 11, Vernon Road, Edgbaston, Birmingham. (O2488)

DAVISON, Sir William Henry, K.B.E., J.P., D.L., M.P.; *s.* of Richard Davison, of Beechfield, Ballymena, Co. Antrim; *m.* Beatrice Mary, *d.* of Sir Owen Roberts, D.L., J.P. D.C.L., of Henley Park, Guildford, Surrey, and Plas Dinas, Carnarvon. *Educ.:* Shrewsbury and Oxford (M.A. Honours, Jurisprudence). Barrister-at-Law; M.P. for South Kensing ton; Alderman of the Royal Borough of Kensington; Mayor of that borough from 1913–19, inclusive; D.L. and J.P. for County of London; Fellow of Society of Antiquaries and Vice-President, Royal Society of Arts. *War Work:* Raised men for two territorial battalions and one service battalion of the New Army (the 22nd Batt. Royal Fusiliers, Kensington); in connection with the latter, undertook the personal responsibility of housing, clothing, and equipping the men and selecting the officers who trained the battalion for active service in a camp which he erected at Horsham; for this he received the thanks of the Army Council; Hon. Commandant, Kensington Volunteer Battalion; Chairman, Kensington Military Service Tribunal; Chairman of Kensington Division, British Red Cross Society; President, Kensington War Hospital Supply Depots. *Address:* 14, Kensington Park Gardens, W. 11. *Clubs:* Athenæum; Carlton; Oxford and Cambridge. (K59)

DAVOREN, Carmen, M.B.E.

DAVSON, Lieut.-Col. Ivan Buchanan, O.B.E.

DAVY, Lieut. Cyril, M.B.E.

DAVY, Major Frederick, O.B.E.

DAVY, Col. Sir Henry, K.B.E., C.B., M.D. D.Sc.

DAVY, Sir Henry, K.B.E., C.B., M.D., D.Sc., F.R.C.P., Col. R.A.M.C. (T.), T. Col. A.M.S., *b.* 18 Jan.1855; *s.* of Henry Davy, of Ottery St. Mary, Devon; *m.* 1st, 6 Jan. 1885 Beatrice Mary, *d.* of W. J. Tucker, of Chard, Somerset, *d.* 9 Dec. 1905, 2ndly, 10 Jan. 1920, Mary, *d.* of the late Samuel Octavius Gray of Swaines, Rudgwick, Sussex, and widow of John Mor timer, M.D., of Southernhay, Exeter. President of British Med. Association, 1907–8; Physician to Roy. Devon and Exeter Hospital since 1881; Consulting Physician, S. Command, 1915. *Address:* Southernhay House, Exeter. *Clubs:* Garrick, Devon, and Exeter. (K286)

DAVY, Capt. Gerald Henry, O.B.E., M.D., *b.* 1883. *Educ.:* Hymers Coll.; Gonville and Caius Coll., Cambridge; the London Hospital. *War Work:* Temp. Commission, R.A.M.C., May, 1915; Gallipoli, Aug. to Dec. 1915; Meso potamia, Feb. 1916, to Oct. 1918. *Address:* 301, Beverley Road, Hull. (O4204)

DAVY, Lila, C.B.E., *b.* 1873; *d.* of the late George Baynton Davy, of Owthorpe, Notts., and Spean Lodge, Spean Bridge, Scotland. *War Work:* 1914–15, Quartermaster, Brae Locha ber V.A.D., County of Inverness; Chairman, Local Ways and Means Committee, Brae Lochaber; 1915–17, served in France with V.A.D., 128, London; 1917–20, served in France in Queen Mary's Army Auxiliary Corps, acting as Chief Controller overseas, from Sept. 1918. Despatches four times. *Address:* Spean Lodge, Spean Bridge, Scotland. (C1243)

DAVY, Francis Herbert Mountjoy Nelson HUMPHREY-, O.B.E., *b.* 9 April, 1880; *s.* of Alfred Humphrey-Davy, M.D., M.Ch., of The Red House, Bournemouth West; *g.g.gs.* of Frances Herbert, Viscountess Nelson, and descended paternally from the 10th Earl of Ross, and maternally from the 4th Earl of Moray. *Educ.:* London Univ.; University Tutorial Coll., London. Founder of the All-British Industrial Movement by forming the Union Jack Industries League, becoming Hon. Sec.

1905, and Vice-Chairman, 1911; Sub-Editor, London News Agency, 1908–14; joined "The Times" Staff, 1914; a Private Secretary to Viscount Northcliffe since 1915. *War Work:* Work in connection with the British War Mission to the United States, 1917. *Addresses:* "The Times," Printing House Square, E.C. 4; The Red House, Bournemouth West. (O3689)

DAVYS, Maud Lilian, O.B.E., *b.* 1 Nov. 1887; *d.* of the late Lieut.-Col. T. C. H. Spencer, of Beechview, Blackheath; *m.* Lieut.-Col. Gerard Irvine Davys, *s.* of Cochran Davys, of Sligo. *Educ.:* London, Paris, and Weimar. First Assistant, Military Food Laboratory, Kasauli, India; prior to War, Assistant, Brigade Laboratory, Jubbulpore; Assistant, Quetta Malaria Investigation (all of which has been entirely voluntary and unpaid). *War Work:* Assistant, Cholera Investigation, Kampti; Voluntary War Work in London; Clerk, No. 2 Ambulance Train; Assistant, Brigade Laboratory, Jullundur; First Assistant, Bacteriological Laboratory, Bombay; First Assistant, Brigade Laboratory, Ambala; First Assistant, Military Food Laboratory, Kasauli. *Address:* Kasauli, Simla Hills, India. (O4031)

DAW, Major Thomas, M.B.E.

DAWES, Elizabeth Lilian, Mrs., M.B.E., *b.* 30 March, 1878; *d.* of J. R. Roberts, of Cwm-y-Glo, Carnarvon; *m.* Joseph Harold Cowburn, *s.* of the late Joseph Dawes, of Cheadle, Cheshire. *Educ.:* Home and Colonial Coll; Gray's Inn, London. *War Work:* Acting Quartermaster, Detention Hospital, Addison Villas, Northampton, 3 months; Nurse, General Hospital, Northampton, 2 months; Acting Commandant, Wothorp Stampford R.F.A. Hospital, 2 months; Quartermaster, Abington Av. Aux. Mil. Hospital, Northants, 3 years. *Address:* 1, Park Avenue, Northampton. (M7875)

DAWES, Helen Frances, M.B.E.

DAWES, 2nd Lieut. Henry, M.B.E., R.A.F.

DAWES, Major Henry Halford, O.B.E.

DAWES, Hugh Campbell Frederick, D.S.O., O.B.E.

DAWES, Jesse Cooper, O.B.E., *b.* 21 Oct. 1878; *s.* of James C. Dawes, of Wolverhampton; *m.* Alice Gertrude, *d.* of Joseph Clarke, of York. Public Cleansing and Salvage Inspector, Engineering Department, Ministry of Health. *War Work:* Assistant Director and Chief Technical Adviser to the National Salvage Department. *Addresses:* Ministry of Health; Radnor Avenue, Harrow. (O10288)

DAWKINS, Charles William, C.B.E., *b.* 22 July, 1870. *War Work:* Controller of Contracts, Ministry of Information; Member Advisory Committee, Agricl.Machinery Dept., Ministry of Munitions. *Clubs:* British Empire; National Liberal. (C951)

DAWKINS, Capt. Ernest Walton, M.B.E., *b.* 24 Dec. 1876; *s.* of Charles Dawkins, of Southampton; *m.* Katherine, *d.* of Patrick King, of Tralee. *War Work:* Charge of a Wing of an Army Pay Office. *Address:* Fairmead, The Mount, Shrewsbury. (M6625)

DAWKINS, Horace Christian, M.B.E., *b.* 1867; *s.* of Clinton George Dawkins, of the Foreign Office (*see* BURKE'S *Landed Gentry,* Dawkins of Over Norton); *m.* Marjorie Vesey, *d.* of Sir Vesey Holt, K.B.E. *Educ.:* Eton; Balliol. Clerk Assistant, House of Commons. *War Work:* Commander, "G" Division, Metropolitan Special Constabulary, 1914–18. *Address:* 9, Onslow Square, S.W. *Club:* Travellers'. (M316)

DAWKINS, William Paxton, M.B.E., Clerk in the Civil Service. *War Work:* Temporary Clerk at the Foreign Office from Sept. 1914; accompanied Viscount Milner on a Special Mission to Russia, 1917; accompanied Mr. Balfour (Secretary of State for Foreign Affairs) to America, 1917; attached to Staff of the Earl of Reading, High Commissioner and Special Ambassador to United States, 1918–19, and subsequently (in 1919) to Staff of Viscount Grey of Fallodon, Special Ambassador to United States; Confidential Clerk to Sir Auckland Geddes, H.M. Ambassador at Washington, 1920. *Address:* British Embassy, Washington, D.C., U.S.A. (M7876)

DAWNAY, Lieut.-Col. Alan Geoffrey Charles, C.B.E., D.S.O., *b.* 24 March, 1888; *s.* of Lewis Payn Downay, 2nd *s.* of the 7th Viscount Downe (*see* BURKE'S *Peerage*); *m.* 3 Aug. 1914, Elizabeth Sofia, *d.* of George Bulteel, of Brook Lodge, Ascot, Capt. and Brevet Major, Coldstream Guards' G.S.O. (2nd grade) 1916, and 1st grade from 1916. Served in the Great War (despatches six times, Brevet); has Order of the Nile, Silver Medal for Military Valour of Italy; Legion of Honour. *Address:* c/o Messrs. Cox & Co., 16, Charing Cross, S.W. 1. (C1376)

DAWNAY, Sybil Mary, O.B.E., *b.* 7 April, 1876; *d.* of Hon. William Frederick Dawnay, of Brampton House, Northampton. *Educ.:* Privately. *War Work:* Hon. Sec., and in charge of Stores Dept., for Northamptonshire County Association for the Administration of Voluntary Work, under Sir Edward Ward; also Stores Dept. of Northamptonshire Red Cross Committee, 1915–19. *Address:* Brampton House, Northampton. (O1273)

DAWSON, Agnes, M.B.E., B.Sc. (Econ.), *b.* 22 Sept. 1876; *d.* of William Dawson, M.I.C.E., of Leyton, Essex. *Educ.:* Privately; London and Munich Univ. Statistician, E.M. 7 and M.S.(M.) Sections, Ministry of Munitions, 1916–18. Chief Statistician, Appointments Department, Ministry of Labour, since Sept. 1918. *Addresses:* 113, Wallwood Road, Leytonstone, Essex; London School of Economics, Clare Market, Kingsway. (M7877)

DAWSON, Agnes Elizabeth, Mrs., M.B.E.

DAWSON, Dame Aimee Evelyn, Lady, G.B.E., *d.* of the late Gordon Pirie, of Chateau de Barenne, France (*see* BURKE'S *Landed Gentry*), and *w.* of Herbert Oakley; *m.* 15 Dec. 1903,

Sir Douglas Frederick Rawdon, G.C.V.O., C.B., C.M.G.; *s.* of Thomas Vesey Dawson, 2nd *s.* of the 2nd Lord Cremorne, and brother of the 3rd Lord Cremorne and 1st Earl of Dartrey (*see* BURKE'S *Peerage*). *Addresses:* Remenham Place, Henley-on-Thames; Stable Yard, St. James's Palace, S.W. 1. (DG9)

DAWSON, Lieut. Albert Edward, O.B.E., R.N.V.R.

DAWSON, Capt. Alexander John, M.B.E., R.A.F.

DAWSON, Col. Algernon Cecil, C.B.E., J.P., D.L. for Norfolk, *b.* 3 May, 1849; *s.* of Rev. J. Dawson, of Rollesby Hall, Norwich; *m.* Helen Louise, *d.* of Maj.-Gen. C. Daniell, C.B. *Educ.:* Abroad. Captain, 3rd D.G.; Major, Norfolk Artillery; Lieut.-Col. and Hon. Col., 1st V.B. Norfolk Regt.; *War Work:* Supervising Officer, Vulnerable Points, No. 1 District, Eastern Command; Col., Royal Defence Corps. *Address:* Manor House, Catton, Norwich. *Clubs:* Naval and Military; Norfolk. (C811)

DAWSON, Anne, M.B.E.

DAWSON, Arthur James, O.B.E.

DAWSON, Arthur Robert, M.B.E., I.S.O., R.N.R., *b.* 13 May, 1861; *s.* of Rev. William James Dawson, of Southampton; *m.* Mary Alice, *d.* of Rev. Edward Dodds. *Educ.:* New Kingswood Coll., Lansdown, Bath. Collector of Customs and Excise, Cardiff; Registrar of Shipping; Receiver of Wrecks, etc. *War Work:* Entrusted with important duties relating to the control of shipping and the import and export trade. *Address:* 8, Victoria Road, Penarth, Cardiff. (M1639)

DAWSON, Cecily, M.B.E., *b.* 1878; *d.* of John Walker Dawson, of London. *Educ.:* Grey Coat Hospital, S.W., and Paris. *War Work:* Registrar, Ministry National Service. *Address:* Innisfree, Downs Court Road, Purley. *Club:* Fabian Society. (M7880)

DAWSON, Errington, O.B.E., *b.* 17 Sept. 1850; *m.* Leonora, *d.* of Francis Churchill Cannell, of Lisbon. A Managing Director of Garland Laidley & Co., Ltd., Lisbon, Oporto and Vigo. *Address:* Garland, Laidley & Co., Ltd., Lisbon, Portugal. (O10289)

DAWSON, Capt. Frank Donald, O.B.E.

DAWSON, Frederick William, M.B.E.

DAWSON, George William, M.B.E.

DAWSON, Hannah, M.B.E.

DAWSON, Paymaster-Capt. Henry, C.B.E., R.N. *War Work:* employed at Naval Base, Great Yarmouth. (C2296)

DAWSON, Lieut. Herbert Milner, M.B.E.

DAWSON, Capt. John Kenneth Bonsfield, O.B.E.

DAWSON, Keith Cyril Darlington, M.B.E. (M10216)

DAWSON, Minnie Ethel, Lady, O.B.E., *y. d.* of Sir Alfred Fernandez Yarrow, 1st Bt. (*see* BURKE'S *Peerage*); *m.* 18 Dec. 1900, Sir Bertrand Edward Dawson, G.C.V.O., K.C.M.G., C.B., 1st Baron Dawson of Penn (*see* BURKE'S *Peerage*). (O1275)

DAWSON, Sidney Stanley, O.B.E., J.P., F.C.A., *b.* 1868. *Educ.:* Blue Coat Hospital, Liverpool. Mayor of Wallasey (Cheshire), 1915–16; Professor of Accountancy (Birmingham University), 1907–10. *War Work:* Chairman, Wallasey War Pensions Committee; Chairman, Wallasey War Savings Committee; Member of Cheshire County Appeal Tribunal (under Military Service Acts). *Addresses:* 51, North John Street, and Prince's Park, Liverpool. *Clubs:* Constitutional, London; Conservative, Liverpool. (O10290)

DAWSON, Major Thomas Henry, C.M.G., C.B.E. Major New Zealand Inf. (C1853)

DAWSON, William, O.B.E.

DAWSON, Lieut. William, M.B.E., R.A.F.

DAWSON, Major William Bell, M.B.E.

DAWSON, Lieut.-Col. William Richard, O.B.E., M.D., F.R.C.P.I., R.A.M.C., *b.* 11 Sept. 1864; *s.* of the late Very Rev. Abraham Dawson, Dean of Dromore, Ireland; *m.* Florence A. E., *d.* of the late Robert W. Shekleton, Q.C., of Dublin. *Educ.:* Royal School, Dungannon, and T.C.D. H.M. Inspector of Lunatic Asylums, Ireland; Consulting Neurologist to the Ministry of Pensions; co-Editor, "Journal of Mental Science." *War Work:* Specialist in Nerve Diseases (including Mental Disease) to the troops in Ireland, with commission in R.A.M.C., first as Major, promoted Lieut.-Col., 1917, from 15 Sept. 1915, to 3 March, 1920; President, Special Medical Board, for 2 years; also worked for St. John Ambulance Brigade, etc. *Address:* 7, Ailesbury Road Dublin. *Clubs:* University, Dublin; Swiss Alpine. (O7071)

DAWTRY, W. F., M.B.E.

DAY, Albert Cecil, C.B.E., *b.* 9 Nov. 1884; *s.* of C. F. Day, of Eastington, Glostershire; *m.* Clara Katharine, *d.* of the late W. Fisher, of Lydney, Glostershire. *Educ.:* Northleach Grammar School and privately. Official Sec. to the Governor-General and Commander-in-Chief of New Zealand. *Address:* Secretary's Lodge, Government House, Wellington, New Zealand. *Club:* Wellington. (C1993)

DAY, Albert Sinclair, M.B.E., *b.* 13 Nov. 1873; *s.* of B. N. Day, of Calcutta; *m.* Maria Meta Charlotte, *d.* of E. Nyss, of Calcutta. *Educ.:* Reid Christian College, Lucknow. Sec. to Chief Justices Sir Louis Kershaw, Sir Arthur Strachey, Sir John Stanley, Kt., K.C.I.E., C.B.E., Sir Henry Richards, Kt., K.B.E., and Sir Grimwood Mears, Kt. *War Work:* Chief Clerk, and later Hon. Sec. U.P. Special War Fund, the activities of which may be measured by its War Charities amounting to over 33⅓ lakhs of rupees; also connected with Lady Richard's Red Cross and St. John's Ambulance Association, U.P., and the Prisoners' Bread Fund. *Address:* 11 Strachey Road, Allahabad, U.P. (M7083)

DAY, Rev. Arthur, O.B.E.

DAY, Major Benjamin, O.B.E., R.E.

DAY, Ven. Charles Victor Parkerson, C.B.E., T.D., M.A., late Archdeacon of Mackay, b. 1864 ; s. of Theodore H. C. Day, M.A., of Limpenhoe Rectory, Norfolk ; m. Helen Constance, d. of Mark Lambert, of Whitley Hall, Northumberland. Educ.: Oundle, Durham, and Cuddesdon College, Oxon. Commissary to the Bishop of North Queensland ; Vicar of Glastonbury, Somerset ; formerly Vicar of Wotkey, Somerset ; Principal of Abbey School, Beckenham, Kent ; late Canon and Subdean of Townsville Cathedral, Queensland ; late Vicar of Christ Church, Milton, Brisbane ; domestic Chaplain to the Bishop of Brisbane ; Archdeacon of Mackay, N. Queensland ; Rector of Southwood and Limpenhoe, Norfolk. Served as Chaplain in S. A. War, Queen's and King's Medals with five clasps. Also served in Great War 1914-19. Mentioned in despatches. Address : The Abbey House, Glastonbury, Somerset. Club : Royal Colonial Institute. (C1104)

DAY, Capt. Christian Richard John, O.B.E., R.A.S.C.

DAY, Major Edmund, O.B.E.

DAY Edward Philip, M.B.E., b. 27 Oct. 1881 ; s. of Ernest Clement Day, of Beaconsfield Terrace, Peterborough. Educ.: St. Peter's Peterborough. Headmaster, All Saints' School, Bingham, Nottingham. War Work : In connection with War Savings Movement and Victory Loan Campaign in South Notts. : Local Sec. for Lord Derby's Recruiting Scheme. Addresses : Bingham, Nottingham, and Beaconsfield Terrace, Peterborough. (M7881)

DAY, Rev. Edward Rouviere, C.M.G., b. 1867 ; s. of the late Robert Day, J.P., F.S.A., of Myrtle Hill House, Cork ; m. 1893, Lydia Constance Mary Bremner. Educ.: Cork Gram. Sch., and Trin. Coll., Dublin (B.A. 1891, M.A. 1896). Chap. to the Forces (1st Class), with rank of Col. ; served in the S. African War, 1900-2 ; present at relief of Ladysmith (despatches twice, Queen's medal with six clasps, King's medal with two clasps, promoted) ; and in the Great War, 1914-18 (despatches five times) ; appointed Principal Chap. Egyptian Expeditionary Force, 1918, with rank of Brig.-Gen. Address : Ivy Cottage, Whittington, Lichfield. (C1377)

DAY, Ernest Cockburn, M.B.E.

DAY, Florence, M.B.E., R.A.F.

DAY, Frederick Thomas, M.B.E.

DAY, George, M.B.E., F.R.C.S.E., b. 1 Nov. 1872 ; Thomas Day, of Norwich ; m. Isabella Blackwood, d. of the late John Muckersie, of Kirkcaldy, N.B. Educ.: Privately. Physician and Surgeon. War Work : Medical Officer in Trench Warfare Depot, Hanley, Staffs. (afterwards H.M. Cylinder Depot), where poison gas of various kinds was evacuated ; also work on Recruiting Boards. Address : Lichfield House, Hanley, Staffs. (M6733)

DAY, George, M.B.E.

DAY, Lieut. George Albert John, M.B.E., R.G.A.

DAY, Gertrude Margaret, M.B.E., b. 20 Dec. 1875 ; d. of Colonel Francis J. Day, Royal Engineers. Educ.: Private Schools. War Work : Board of Trade, Juvenile Advisory Committee, Deptford ; Agricultural Organiser (under the Selborne Scheme), 1916-17 ; Board of Agriculture Travelling Inspector, and originator of " Test of Efficiency trials for Women Workers " ; in 1918 was appointed Chief Organiser of Markets for Small Holders under the Horticultural Section of the Board. Address : 66, Oxford Gardens, London, W. 10. Club : Albemarle. (M11641)

DAY, James John, O.B.E., M.R.C.S., L.R.C.P., D.P.H., b. 1873 ; s. of the late James John Day ; m. 1903, Mabel Grace, d. of William John Gordon. Served in the S. African War as Civil Surg. ; and in the Great War attached R.A.M.C. ; Med. Officer Niger Coast Protectorate, 1899-1900, and Assist. Med. Officer Metropolitan Asylums Board, 1901-3. Address : Mayfield, Sandwich, Kent. (C4357)

DAY, Maud FitzGerald, M.B.E., b. 1871 ; d. of Robert John FitzGerald Day, J.P., late of Beaufort, Co. Kerry, Ireland. Educ.: Privately. War Work : Assistant Hon. Sec. South Staffordshire Regt. Prisoners of War Fund. (M7884)

DAY, Lieut.-Col. Robert William, D.S.O., O.B.E.

DAY, Lieut.-Comm. Roderick Wilson, O.B.E., R.N.R.

DAY, Victor Grace, O.B.E.

DAY, Lieut. William, M.B.E.

DAY, Capt. William Leigh Maule, O.B.E., M.D. (Oxon.), R.A.M.C., b. 1877 ; s. of William White Day, M.D., of Edmonton ; m. Gertrude Kate, d. of Surgeon-General Manners Smith, F.R.C.S., I.M.S. Educ.: Charterhouse ; Exeter Coll., Oxford ; Guy's Hospital. Surgeon, Essex County Hospital. War Work : Surgical Specialist, Military Hospital, Curragh. Address : 4, Lexden Road, Colchester. (O8790)

DAY, William Thomas, M.B.E., b. 26 Sept. 1861 ; s. of the late John Day, of Birmingham ; m. Millicent Florence Beatrice, d. of Nathaniel Dauncey Griffin, of Bristol. Educ.: Bradford Villa School, Edgbaston, Birmingham. Director of E. G. Wrigley & Co., Ltd. War Work : Small Tool Department, Ministry of Munitions. Address : The Lodge, Stanley Avenue, Alperton, Wembley, Middlesex. Club : Royal Automobile. (M7886)

DAYAL, Seth Prabh, M.B.E.

DAYNES, Qr.-Mr. and Lieut. William Herbert, O.B.E.

DEACON, Clara, M.B.E. ; d. of Capt. T. Hooper Deacon of Swindon, Wiltshire. War Work : Commandant of B.R.C Hospital, The Baths, Swindon, Aug. 1914, till June, 1915 Linen Sister at Q.M.C.A. Hospital, Roehampton House, Roehampton Lane, from Aug. 1915, till Jan. 1916, then Assistant Matron there till 1 Jan. 1917 ; 8 Jan. appointed Matron at the

Prince of Wales' Hospital, Cardiff, and Commandant in May of that year, which position she still holds. (M7887)

DEACON, Edgar Reginald, O.B.E.

DEACON Henry Wade, C.B.E., b. 18 Oct. 1852 ; s. of Henry Deacon, of Widnes. Educ.: King's College, London. J.P. for County of Lancaster ; Chairman, Finance Committee County Council, etc. War Work : Chairman, Lancashire War Pensions Committee, and work in connection with hospitals. Address : 8, Ullet Road, Liverpool. Clubs : Reform ; National Liberal. (C2556)

DEACON, Capt. Martin, O.B.E., R.E.

DEACON, Mary Ariel Stewart, Mrs., M.B.E., M.B., B.S., b. 1871 ; d. of James Stewart, of Cheltenham ; m. Major Thomas Deacon. Educ.: Public Day School, Cheltenham ; London School of Medicine for Women. (M1642)

DEAKEN, Margaret, Mrs., M.B.E.

DEAKIN, Major Charles, O.B.E.

DEAKIN, Capt. Ralph, O.B.E.

DEAKIN, Vera, O.B.E.

DEAN, Major Arthur Cecil Hamilton, D.S.O., O.B.E., b. 1878 ; s. of Charles Percy Dean ; m. 1901, Elizabeth Rybot. Major R.G.A. and Chief Instructor, R.M.A ; served in the Great War, 1914-17 (despatches). (O7073)

DEAN, Capt. Basil, M.B.E.

DEAN, Edward George, M.B.E.

DEAN, Frederic William Charles, M.B.E.

DEAN, Capt. George Edward, M.B.E., I.A.R.O.

DEAN, Lieut. George Edward Morgan, M.B.E.

DEAN, Ida Florence, Mrs., M.B.E.

DEAN, Seth Ellis, M.B.E.

DEAN, Capt. Walter Thomas, M.B.E., R.G.A.

DEANE, Augusta, O.B.E.

DEANE, Charles Chatterton, O.B.E., M.D., J.P., b. 1867) s. of Alexander Sharp Deane, of Newlawn, Co. Dublin, and Monkstown, Co. Dublin ; m. Adelaide Elizabeth, d. of Henry A. Stocker, of Co. Cork. Educ.: Privately, and Trinity Coll., Dublin. Medical Officer, Loughgall ; Life Member of the St. John Ambulance Association ; Justice of the Peace, Co. Armagh. War Work : Armagh County Director of the Royal British Red Cross and St. John Ambulance Association throughout the period of the Great War. Club : Armagh County. (O10293)

DEANE, Phyllis Lucy, Mrs. James, M.B.E.

DEANE, Lieut.-Col. Richard Woodforde, C.B.E. ; formerly Lieut.-Col. and Brevet Col. (ret.) ; served in the Great War, 1914-19, on Staff (despatches). (C1539;

DEANE, Major Robert, O.B.E., M.B.E.

DEARDEN, Clarence Reginald, O.B.E., b. 23 July, 1872 ; s. of Jonathan Dearden, of Sheffield ; m. Edith Ellen, d. of George Booker, of Sheffield. Educ.: Royal Grammar School, Sheffield ; Sheffield School of Medicine ; London Hospital. War Work : Medical Officer in charge Orthopædic Hospital, Penarth, Glamorgan. Address : Glenburn, St. Brannock's Road, Ilfracombe. Club : Ilfracombe. (O10294)

DEARING, Lieut. Sidney Arthur, M.B.E., R.E.

DEARNLEY, Qr.-Mr. and Capt. Walter Nathan, O.B.E.

DEAS, Acting Major Percy, O.B.E., b. 18 April, 1899 ; s. of Adam Deas, J.P., N.P., of Duns. Educ.: Rossall and Edinburgh Univ. Solicitor, partner with Adam Deas, in firm of A. and P. Deas, Solicitors, Duns. War Work : Organised purchase and issue of supplies for South Scottish Brigade ; A.D.C. to Duke of Montrose, March, 1915 ; embarked for Salonica ; transferred to 10th Irish Div., and proceeded to Servian and Bulgarian Frontier, Dec. 1915 ; O.C. 840 Park Co., 10th Div. Train, Aug. 1916 ; transferred to Egyptian Camel Transport Corps, Palestine ; proceeded to Tripoli, June 1918 ; mentioned in despatches Nov. 1918. Address : Briery Bank, Duns, Scotland. (O6165;

DEASE, Lieut.-Col. Conley Edward, O.B.E.

DEASE, Mabel Mary Frances, Mrs., O.B.E., b. 2 Oct. 1873 ; d. of Ambrose More-O'Ferrall, V.L., J.P., Balyna, Co. Kildare (see BURKE's Landed Gentry of Ireland) ; m. Edmund James, s. of Edmund Dease, of Rath, Ballybrettas, Queen's Co. Educ.: Privately. War Work : 1st Commandant, V.A.D., 776, St. John's Ambulance Assoc.; organised Nenagh War Hospital Supply Depot : from 1916-19, Chief Lady Superintendent, Inspection Dept. and Central Store Dept., Ministry of Munitions. Address : Rath, Ballybrettas, Ireland. Clubs : Empress ; Alexander (Dublin) ; Automobile, Dawson St. (Dublin). (O14)

DEASE, Mary O'Kelly, M.B.E. (M10246g)

DE BARCAYE, Capt. Hugo Seeman, M.B.E.

DE BATHE, Lieut.-Col. Maximilian John, O.B.E., s. of the late Gen. Sir H. P. de Bathe, Bart., K.C.B., of Knightstown, Co. Meath ; Wood End, Chichester ; and de Bathe Barton, North Tawton (see BURKE's Peerage). Educ.: Harrow. Recreations : Big Game shooting ; racing, principally in Belgium, where he has won many races and has a training stable at Stockel. War Work : Joined 3rd Gloucester Regt., April, 1885, proceeded India with 18th Hussars, Nov. 1889 ; appointed 8th Hussars, April, 1893 ; proceeded S. Africa, Oct. 1899 ; attached Imperial Light Horse (was present in Ladysmith during the siege) ; retired, 1901 ; appointed Major and second-in-command 7th Wilts, Nov. 1914 ; proceeded with battalion to France, Sept. 1915 ; proceeded, Nov. 1915, with battalion to Salonica ; continuously in front line trenches till end of 1917 ; proceeded Ypres Salient, Jan. 1918 ; promoted Lieut.-Col. commanding 28th L. Group with advancing army up to the Armistice ; mentioned five times in despatches for services in front line ; retired, Dec. 1919. *Address :* 74, South Audley Street, Mayfair. *Club :* Cavalry. (O5179)

DE BAVAY, Capt. Auguste John Charles, O.B.E., *b.* 19 Feb. 1890 ; *s.* of A. J. F. De Bavay, O.B.E., of Kew, Melbourne, Australia ; *m.* Vera, *d.* of Ernest A. Tolley, of Adelaide. *Educ. :* St. Francis Xavier Coll., Kew, Melbourne. Bacteriologist. *War Work :* Joined R.A.S.C. (M.T.), Aug. 1915 ; served in France, March, 1916, until April, 1919. *Address :* 125, Wattle Street, Fularton, Adelaide. *Club :* Naval and Military, Adelaide. (O11968)

DE BAVAY, Auguste Joseph Francois, O.B.E., Pro Eclesia and Pontifici, Chevalier Ordre de Leopold, Officier de la Couronne, Belgium, *b.* 9 June, 1856 ; *s.* of Xavier de Bavay, of Vilvorde-Bruxelles, Belgium ; *m.* Anne, *d.* of — Hinzlé, of Melbourne. *Educ. :* Namur and Jambloux (Belgium). Consulting Chemist, Defence Department, and private companies ; Director, Amalgamated Zinc De Bavay Co., Ltd., and Electrolytic Zinc Co. of Australasia, etc. *War Work :* At the request of Minister for Defence, evolving process and designing plant and manufacture of Calcium Acetate for Acetone and Cordite ; Inventor of De Bavay's process for the recovery of Zinc Blende. *Address :* Glencara, Studley Park Road, Kew, Melbourne. *Club :* Athenæum (Melbourne). (O11970)

DE BEAUFORT, Arnaud Jan, O.B.E. (O11784)

DEBENHAM, Amy, O.B.E., *b.* 11 Feb. 1867 ; *d.* of Frank Gissing Debenham, of Cheshunt Park. *Educ. :* At home. Hon. Sec. (East Enfield) Enfield War Pensions ; Hon. Sec. (Cheshunt) Herts War Pensions. *War Work :* Soldiers' and Sailors' Families Association, and Soldiers' and Sailors' Help Society, throughout war until War Pensions Act ; then working for War Pensions, and still continuing, in capacities described above. *Address :* Cheshunt Park, Herts. (O10295)

DEBENHAM, Major Frank, O.B.E., B.A., B.Sc., *b.* 26 Dec. 1883 ; *s.* of the late Rev. J. W. Debenham, of Sydney, Australia ; *m.* Dorothy, *d.* of the late John T. Lempriere, of Melbourne, Australia. *Educ. :* The King's School, N.S.W. ; The Univ., Sydney, N.S.W. ; and Cambridge Univ. Royal Geographical Society's Lecturer in Cartography and Surveying, at Cambridge Univ. ; Fellow of Gonville and Caius Coll., Cambridge. *War Work :* Commission in 7th Batt. Oxford and Bucks Light Infantry ; temp. Major in July, 1915 ; wounded, Aug. 1916, in Macedonia ; further service in England, training of troops. *Address :* Caius College, Cambridge. (O7075)

DEBENHAM, Walter Charles, M.B.E.

DE BLAQUIÈRE, Lucienne, Lady, O.B.E., *d.* of George Desbarats, of Montreal, Canada, and *widow* of the late Baron de Blaquiere (*see* BURKE'S *Peerage*). *War Work :* Vice-President, British Red Cross Society, from 1910 ; Commandant, No. 1, Red Cross Hospital, Lansdown Place, West Bath, 1914–17 ; organised and raised equipment and funds for Officers Convalescent Home, 28, 29 and 30, Marlborough Buildings, 1914 ; organised Red Cross Comforts for Soldiers, 1916. *Address :* 3, The Circus, Bath. *Club :* Ladies' Empire. (O1121)

DE BOISE, Frank, M.B.E. (M1158)

DE BURY and DE BOCARME, Lieut.-Col. Henry Robert Visart, Count, C.B.E., *b.* 11 June, 1872 ; *m.* 7 May, 1898, Agnes Mary, *d.* of the late Charles Robertson, and widow of Charles Paul Derrick, of Singapore. Lieut.-Col. Canadian Ordnance Corps and A.D.C. to the Lieut.-Governor of Manitoba ; Assist. Director of Ordnance Services, 1917 ; late Capt. Royal Artillery, formerly Garrison Adjutant, St. Lucia, 1902–5 ; Professor Royal Military Coll., Canada, 1905–10 ; obtained a Royal Licence, 19 Nov. 1910, authorising him and the heirs male of his body in succession to bear and use the title of Count in this country (*see* BURKE'S *Peerage*). *Addresses :* Bury, Hainault. Belgium ; St. John's, New Brunswick. (C772)

DE CASTRO, Edith, Mrs., M.B.E.

DE CHAIR, Major George Herbert Blackett, O.B.E., M.C., Royal Sussex Regt., *b.* 1891 ; *s.* of the late Richard Blackett De Chair and Mrs. Richard De Chair, of Emsworth, Sussex ; *m.* Mary Janet, *d.* of the late Henry J. Pearson, of Bramcote, Notts. *Educ. :* Norwich and Sandhurst. *War Work :* France, with B.E.F. *Address :* Gen. Staff, Aldershot Command. (O5181)

DE CHAYAL, Dora Stewert, Mrs., M.B.E.

DE CORDOVA, Judith, Mrs., M.B.E.

DE DOMBASLE, Lieut.-Col. Guy Cyril St. Pourgin, O.B.E.

DEEDES, Lieut. John Gordon, M.B.E. R.E., (T.).

DEEDES, Ralph Bouverie, O.B.E., M.C. (O11776)

DEEDES, Rose Elinor, Mrs., M.B.E.

DEEKS, Stephen John, O.B.E. (O11785e)

DE FALBE, Lieut.-Col. Christian Frederick George William, O.B.E. T.F. Res.

DE FELICE, Capt. Rodolfo, M.B.E.

DEFRIES, Wolf, M.B.E. (M10246h)

DE FONSEKA, Edmund Clarke, M.B.E.

DE FRANCIA, Capt. Jeane, O.B.E., R.A.F.

DE FREITAS, Anthony, O.B.E.

DE FREITAS, Dora Florence, Mrs., M.B.E.

DE FREITAS, Capt. Julian Mignon, O.B.E., B.A., LL.B., *b.* 26 July, 1889 ; *s.* of Domingo S. De Freitas, of Grenada, B. West Indies. *Educ. :* St. Augustine's Coll., Ramsgate ; Haileybury Coll. ; Clare Coll., Cambridge ; Inner Temple. Law Student ; passed Bar Trial ; proposed : Cocoa Planter, West Indies. *War Work :* Inns of Court O.T.C., Nov. 1914 ; 2nd Lieut. 11th Batt. Gloucester Regt., Jan. 1915 ; Mesopo-

tamia, 1916–18 ; Persia, July, 1918, to Nov. 1918 ; Caucasus (Baku), Nov. 1918, to Aug. 1919 ; Constantinople, Allied Police, Sept. 1919 ; wounded before taking of Kut, 1917. *Club :* West India. (O8685)

DE GLANVILLE, Oscar, O.B.E.

DE GRAY, Lieut.-Comm. Nigel, O.B.E., R.N.V.R.

DE GRUCHY, Amy Douglas, M.B.E. ; *d.* of Capt. Thomas de Gruchy, of St. Martin's, Jersey. *Educ. :* Elson House High School, Leytonstone. Civil Servant ; First Class Clerk, Post Office Savings Bank. *War Work :* Lent to the War Office and employed in administering the estates of deceased soldiers and supervising temporary staff. *Address :* 24, Sheen Gate Mansions, East Sheen, S.W. 14. (M8290)

DE GRUCHY, Frederick de Quetteville, O.B.E.

DE GRUCHY, William Geary, O.B.E., *b.* 26 May, 1883 ; *s.* of Thomas De Gruchy, of St. Heliers, Gersey, Channel Islands; *m.* Doris Ida, *d.* of William Palmby, of Kensington. *Educ. :* Mercer's School. Joint Manager in New Zealand Commonwealth and Dominion Line, Ltd. (Cunard Line, Australasian Service). *War Work :* Hon. Sec. Shipowners Provision Pool. *Address :* Oriental Bay, Wellington, N.Z. *Clubs :* Wellington N.Z. ; Wellesley (Wellington, N.Z.). (O10544)

D'EGVILLE, Sir Howard, K.B.E. *Educ. :* St. Cath. College Cambridge. Barrister-at-Law (Middle Temple) ; Organiser and Secretary of Empire Parliamentary Association (United Kingdom Branch) ; editor of " Journal of the Parliaments of the Empire," and of publications of Empire Parliamentary Association ; was member of War Cabinet secretariat, 1917–19 ; Commissioner, Military Service (Civil Liabilities) Committee, 1916 ; organised visit of representatives of Dominion Parliaments to Coronation of King George V., 1911 ; and visit of Lords and Commons Delegation to Canada, Australia, New Zealand and South Africa, 1916 ; and War Visit of Representatives of Dominion Parliaments to United Kingdom, 1916 ; author of " Imperial Defence and Closer Union," " The Invasion of England " ; " War Legislation of the Empire." *Address :* Lamb Building, Temple, E.C. 4. (K452)

DE HAVILLAND, Capt. Geoffrey, O.B.E., A.F.C.

DE HOGHTON, Major Daniel, M.B.E.

DE HOGHTON, Col. Sir James, Bart, C.B.E., J.P., D.L., *b.* 2 Feb. 1851 ; *s.* of Henry Bold Hoghton. of Hoghton Tower, Lancashire ; *m.* the late Aimée Jean, *d.* of John Fraser Grove, of Ferne, Wilts. *Educ. :* Cheltenham ; Sandhurst. *War Work :* County Commandant, Lancashire Volunteer Corps. *Club :* Army and Navy. (C1541)

DEIGHTON, Albert, M.B.E.

DE JERSEY, Lieut.-Col. William Grant, C.B.E. ; Lieut.-Col. and Brevet Col., R.A. (ret.) ; served in the Great War, 1914–19 (despatches). (C1542)

DE KNOOP, Evelyn Elizabeth, Mrs., M.B.E., *b.* 22 June, 1879 ; *d.* of Charles John Fletcher, of Dale Park, Sussex. *War Work :* Commandant, Auxiliary Military Hospital at Calveley Hall. *Addresses :* Singewick House, Buckingham ; 39, Bryanston Square, London, W. (M8726)

DE KOCK, Lieut.-Col. Gervase Meyer, D.S.O., O.B.E. ; Lieut.-Col. S. African Forces. *War Services :* German S.-W. Africa, 1914–15, Commanding a Commando (despatches). (O2384)

DE LA BERE, Lieut.-Col. Hugh Pleydell, O.B.E., Royal Scots Fusiliers, *b.* 21 June, 1867 ; *s.* of the late Henry De la Bère, C.B., late Accountant-General of the Army, of Kinnersely Castle, Hereford ; *m.* Wyllie, *d.* of John Tawse, of Edinburgh, N.B. *Educ. :* Dulwich and Sandhurst. Joined Royal Scots Fusiliers, 1886 ; Capt., 1895 ; Major, 1905 ; Lieut.-Col., 1915. *War Work :* Served with 1st Batt. Royal Scots Fusiliers in Flanders and France, 1915, in temporary command ; appointed Inspector of Guns and Rifles, Ishapore, India, 1915. *Club :* Junior Army and Navy. (O8462)

DE LA BOURDONNAIS, H.H. Prince Charles Mahe de Chenal, O.B.E. (O7441)

DELACOMBE, Lieut.-Col. Harry, O.B.E.

DE LA COUR, Major George, O.B.E., R.A.

DE LA COUR, —, M.B.E. Superintendent of the School of Cookery, Atholl Crescent, Edinburgh. (M10310)

DELANTE, Major Frederic Joseph, O.B.E.

DELANY, Thomas William, O.B.E.

DELANY, Major William, O.B.E.

DE LA POER, The Hon. Mrs. Mary Olivia, O.B.E., Lady of Grace of St. John of Jerusalem in England ; *d.* of William, 1st Baron Emly, of Tervoe, Co. Limerick, *m.* Edmond, 1st Count de la Poer (*see* BURKE'S *Peerage*) ; *s.* of John William Power, of Gurteen. *War Work :* Lady Div. Superintendent of Clonmel Nursing Division of St. John's Ambulance Brigade, Clonmel Hospital Supply Depot. *Address :* Glen Poer, Kilshelan, Co. Waterford. (O3872)

D'ELBOUX, Louis, O.B.E.

DE L'HOPITAL, Winefride Mary, Mrs., O.B.E., W.R.N.S.

DE LISLE, Rev. Hirzel Frederick, M.B.E., M.A., *b.* 4 Dec. 1868 ; *s.* of the Rev. H. C. de Lisle ; *m.* Dorothy Pell, *d.* of Richard Pell Edmonds, of Ripplemead Dohn, Cape Province. *Educ. :* Brentwood, Essex, and Lincoln Coll., Oxford. Rector, St. Mark's, Cape Town ; Chaplain to the Forces, S.A. Rebellion, S.W.A., Nyasaland and E. Africa. *Address :* 70, Roeland Street, Cape Town. (M4989)

DELIUS, Comm. Daniel Edwin St. Martin, O.B.E.

DELMEGE, James Anthony, O.B.E. (Mil. Div.), *b.* 4 March, 1887 ; *s.* of Deputy Inspector-General A. G. Delmege, R.N. *Educ. :* Oundle. Asst. Medical Officer of Health, Smethwick, Staffs. *War Work :* R.A.M.C., 1914–18 ; Specialist

Sanitary Officer to 22nd Division, British Salonica Force. *Address:* Holly Lane Hospital, Smethwick. (O3029)

DELPRAT, Guillaume Daniel, C.B.E. *War Service:* In connection with steel supplies. (C359)

DE MAINE, Capt. Lionel Thomas, M.B.E.

DE MEL, Vidanelage Henry Lawson, C.B.E., *b.* 1877; *s.* of Vidanelage Jacob De Mel, of Villa De Mel, Horton Place, Cinnamon Gardens, Colombo; *m.* 1900, Caroline Elsie, *d.* of the late S. H. Jayewickrema Mudaliyar, of Kurunegala, Ceylon. *Educ.:* Roy. Coll., Colombo. Proctor of Supreme Court, Ceylon, and Notary Public; head of the firm of H. L. De Mel and Co., produce and plumbago merchants and estate agents, of 3, Queen Street, Fort Colombo; a J.P. for Ceylon; Town Commr. for Colombo, Commr. Local Loans and Development Fund; a Member of Ceylon Med. Advisory Board; Ceylon Railway Advisory Board; of Consultative Committee on Roads; Pres. of Plumbago Merchants' Union; Vice-Chairman Ceylon Low Country Products Assoc.; a Member of Board of Agriculture; Pres. Ceylon Young Men's Christian Assoc.; Vice-Pres. Sinhalese Young Men's Assoc.; and Founder of De Mel Free Library; has been a Member of Municipal Council for Colombo, Slave Island Ward since 1908; rendered services to Ceylon Govt. during the Great War. *Addresses:* Elsmere, Horton Place, Cinnamon Gardens, Colombo; Kande, Walauwa, Kadugannawa, Ceylon. *Club:* Orient (Colombo). (C391)

DEMETRIADI, Sir Stephen, K.B.E., *b.* 6 March, 1880; *s.* of the late C. E. Demetriadi, of Prestwich, Lancashire; *m.* Gulielma Norah Mabel, *d.* of R. G. Bates, formerly of Calcutta. *Educ.:* Marlborough. In the firm of Ralli Brothers, East India Merchants, 25, Finsbury Circus, E.C. *War Work:* With the Naval and Military War Pensions, etc., Statutory Committee, 1916–17; Asst. Sec., Special Grants Committee, Ministry of Pensions, 1917–18; Director of Awards of Pensions to Demobilised men, Ministry of Pensions, 1919. *Address:* 89, Cadogan Gardens, S.W. *Clubs:* Bath, Oriental; Bengal, Turf, Calcutta. (K364)

DE MOLE, Lancelot Eldin, C.B.E., *b.* 13 March, 1880; *s.* of Wm. F. de Mole, of Adelaide, S. Australia; *m.* Josephine, *d.* of G. F. Walter, of Bendigo, Victoria, Australia, and Bristol, England. *Educ.:* Berwick Grammar School, and Church of England Grammar School, Melbourne, Victoria. Invented (1912) a type of Tank which was highly commended by the Royal Commission on Awards to Inventors, and who stated that they considered the invention very brilliant, but unfortunately unappreciated because in advance of its time. *Address:* 79, Jeffcott Street, N. Adelaide, S. Australia. (C2813)

DE MONTMORENCY, Geoffrey Fitzhervey, C.I.E., C.B.E., I.C.S., *b.* 23 Aug. 1876; *s.* of the Venble. Archdeacon of Ossony, of Castle Morres, Ireland. *Educ.:* Malvern Coll., Pembroke Coll., Cambridge. Deputy Sec. to the Government of India. *War Work:* Recruiting and War Loans in the Punjab. *Addresses:* Delhi, India; Castle Morres, Knocktopher. Ireland. *Club:* Travellers'. (C2378)

DE MONTMORENCY, Hervey Angus, O.B.E., *b.* 27 Sept. 1888; *s.* of Hervey Lodge de Montmorency; *m.* Eleanor Katharine, *d.* of Rev. E. R. J. Nicolls. *Educ.:* Winchester and Brasenose College, Oxford. Second Class Clerk, National Health Insurance Commission (England), 1912; Principal Clerk, Ministry of Health, 1919. *War Work:* Work at Transport Department, Admiralty and Ministry of Shipping. *Address:* 24, Well Walk, Hampstead, N.W. 3. (O287)

DE MONTMORENCY, Hervey Guy, Francis Edward, O.B.E. (O5183)

DEMPSEY, Lieut. Cornelius Thomas, M.B.E.

DEMPSTER, William Thomas, M.B.E. *Educ.:* King's College Hospital, London. *War Work:* Founder, Organiser, Commandant, and sole Hon. Surgeon, South Croydon Relief Hospital, 1914–19, affiliated to Horton (County of London War Hospital, Epsom). *Address:* 94, Brighton Road, S. Croydon. (M7888)

DEMUTH, Lieut. Richard Harold, O.B.E., R.N.V.R.

DENBY, Clara Sophia, Lady, O.B.E., *b.* 26 Sept. 1856; *d.* of Jeremiah Slater, of Stanningley; *m.* Sir Ellis *s.* of John Denby, of Shipley. *Educ.:* Fulneck and Wil ow Hall, Halifax. *War Work:* Queen Mary's Needlework Guild, and many other things for the help of the Soldiers and Sailors in Shipley and at the Front. *Address:* Chapel House, nr. Skipton. (O10298)

DENDY, Edward Evershed, C.B.E., *b.* 17 Sept. 1861; *s.* of the Rev. John Dendy, B.A.; *m.* Edith, *d.* of Herbert New, of Evesham. *Educ.:* Manchester Grammar School. Metal Manufacturer; Managing Director of Williams, Foster & Co., Ltd., and Pascoe Grenfell and Sons, Ltd. *War Work:* Chairman of Semi-Manufactured Non-ferrous Metals, Ministry of Munitions. *Address:* Miramar, Langland Bay, Mumbles, Glam. (C144)

DENDY, Frederick Walter, O.B.E., D.C.L., *b.* 9 Dec. 1849; *s.* of Frederick Dendy, of Gorleston, Suffolk; *m.* 1st, Jessie, *d.* of John Percy Baumgartner, of Gorleston; 2nd, Honor Elizabeth, *d.* of Walter Lamplugh Brooksbank, of Lamplugh Hall, Cumberland. District Registrar of the High Court, and Registrar of the County Court at Newcastle-upon-Tyne. *War Work:* Deputy-Chairman under the Lord Mayor of the Newcastle Panel of the Northumberland Appeal Tribunal; Chairman of the Tyne and Blyth Maritime Board. *Addresses:* Eldon House, Jesmond, Newcastle-upon-Tyne; High Mousen, Belford, Northumberland. (O288)

DENDY, John, O.B.E.

DENHAM, Arthur Christopher, O.B.E., J.P., *b.* 1873; *s.* of Thomas Nathaniel Denham of Birmingham. Barrister-

at-Law; Director of various Companies: Member of L.C.C., 1918–19. *War Work:* Military Representative, Stepney, 1915–16; Assistant Controller, Priority Dept., Ministry of Munitions, 1916–18. *Address:* 30, Audley House, Margaret St., W. 1. *Club:* National Liberal. (O1280)

DENHAM, Godfrey Charles, C.I.E., C.B.E., *b.* 1883; *s.* of Charles Denham; Sup. of Police, Bengal; officiated as Dep. Director of Central Intelligence. (C1073)

DENHAM, Lieut.-Col. Harold Alfred, O.B.E.

DENHOLM, John Maxwell, M.B.E.

DENHOLM, Walter Windebank, M.B.E.

DENING, Lieut. Maberley Ester, M.B.E.

DENISON, Lieut. Amos Allan, M.B.E., M.C., R.A.F.

DENISON, Brig.-Gen. Henry, C.B., C.B.E., T.D., J.P., D.L., *b.* 10 March, 1847; *s.* of Stephen Charles Denison, Deputy Judge Advocate General; *m.* Edith Kate, *d.* of Pierce Taylor, of West Agwell, Devon. *Educ.:* Rugby and Royal Military Academy, Woolwich. Entered R.E., 1867; retired as Major and Hon. Lieut.-Col., 1887; Sherwood Rangers Yeomanry, 1887–1910; commanded regiment, 1904–10; C.B. (Civil), 1909. *War Work:* Commanded, 2/1 Scottish Horse Brigade and Lincolnshire Coast Defences, 1915–16; Recruiting, Kensington, South London and Woolwich Areas, 1916–18. *Address:* 41, Evelyn Gardens. *Club:* Naval and Military. (C1544)

DENLEY, Clara Sophia, Lady, O.B.E.

DENMAN, Gertrude, Lady, C.B.E., J.P., *b.* 7 Nov. 1884; *d.* of Viscount Cowdray; *m.* 1903, Thomas, 3rd Baron Denman, P.C., G.C.M.G. (*see* BURKE'S *Peerage*). Chairman, National Federation of Women's Institutes. *War Work:* 1914, Organised with Mrs. Quirk, Lady Sclater, Mr. E. F. Benson and Sir T. Pile, Bart., "Smokes for Soldiers and Sailors"; 1915, formed Women's Section of National Poultry Society; 1916, was appointed Chairman of sub-committee of Agricultural Organisation Society, which was responsible for formation of Women's Institutes in 1917; Board of Agriculture took over this work and appointed Lady Denman Assistant Director of the Women's Branch of the Bd. of Agric.; by Jan. 1919, Women's Institutes had been formed in 774 villages in England and Wales, and by Jan. 1920, 1500 had been formed. *Addresses:* 43, Upper Grosvenor Street, W.; Balcombe Place, Sussex. *Clubs:* Bath; Forum. (C2557)

DENNE, Mark Thomas, O.B.E.

DENNETT, Sydney, M.B.E.

DENNING, Arthur du Pre, O.B.E.

DENNIS, Sir Alfred Hull, K.B.E., C.B., *b.* 31 July 1858; *s.* of the late John Dennis, of Wonston, Crowborough; *m.* 7 Jan. 1905, Dorothy Caroline, *e.d.* of Sir Henry Sutton, formerly Judge of High Court. Barrister-at-Law, Inner Temple, 1885; Assist. Solicitor to Treasury from 1901. *Address:* 10, Eaton Mansions, Eaton Squre, S.W. *Club:* Reform.

DENNIS, Anna Emily, M.B.E., *b.* Dec. 1855; *d.* of Meade Caufield Dennis, of Fort Granite, Co. Wicklow. Hon. Sec. Soldiers' and Sailors' Families Association, West Wicklow; Hon. Sec. and Treas. Local War Pensions Sub-Committee, Baltinglass No. 1 District, Co. Wicklow. *War Work:* Worked as voluntary worker for Soldiers' and Sailors' Families Association, Statutory Committee, and Local War Pensions Committee, as Hon. Sec. and Treas. since 1914, and is still working for them. *Address:* Eadstown Lodge, Stratford-on-Slaney, Co. Wickow, Ireland. (M7891)

DENNIS, Lieut.-Col. Bertram Ramsey, O.B.E., M.B.

DENNIS, Lieut.-Col. Charles Edgar, O.B.E., Aust. A.M.C.

DENNIS, Horace Arthur, M.B.E.

DENNIS, Sir Raymond Herbert, K.B.E., Joint Managing Director of Dennis Bros., Ltd., Guildford. *War Work:* In connection with the supply of motor lorries and fire engines. *Address:* Guildford. (K365)

DENNIS, Rendall Hamilton, M.B.E.

DENNISS, George Hamson, C.B.E., *b.* 1854; *s.* of Hamson George Denniss, of London; *m.* Jeanne Madeleine Pauline Dubouchet. *Educ.:* University College and School. Barrister-at-Law; Assistant Solicitor for the Customs and Excise. *War Work:* Legal work. *Address:* 2, Gliddon Road, West Kensington. (C2558)

DENNISTON, Adam Fairrie, M.B.E.

DENNISTON, Comm. Alastair Guthrie, O.B.E., R.N.V.R., *b.* 1 Dec. 1881; *s.* of James Denniston; *m.* Dorothy Mary, *d.* of Arthur Gilliat, of Leeds. *Educ.:* Bowdon College, Cheshire; Bonn; Paris. Civil Servant. *War Work:* Naval Intelligence Division. *Address:* 48, Royal Avenue, Chelsea, S.W. 3. (O290)

DENNISTON, Major John Dewar, O.B.E.

DENNISTON, Mary Grace, Mrs., M.B.E., *b.* 14 Sept. 1896; *d.* of J. J. Morgan, of 134, Holland Road, Kensington; *m.* John Dewar Denniston, O.B.E., *s.* of James Lawson Denniston, I.C.S. *Educ.:* Norland Place School, London. *War Work:* 3½ years secretarial work at Ministry of Munitions. *Address:* 5, Polstead Road, Oxford. (M7892)

DENNISTOUN, Robert Maxwell, Hon. Mr. Justice, C.B.E., B.A., K.C., *b.* 24 Dec. 1864; *s.* of James Frederick Dennistoun, K.C., of Castleknock, Peterborough, Ont.; *m.* Mildred, *d.* of Rev. J. W. R. Beck, M.A., Canon of St. Alban's Cathedral, Rector of Peterborough, Ont. *Educ.:* Queen's University, Kingston. K.C. Bencher, Law Society of Upper Canada; Bencher, Law Society of Manitoba; Governor of Trinity College School; Judge of the Court of Appeal for Manitoba. *War Work:* Colonel, Canadian Expeditionary

Force ; commanded 53rd Batt. Can. Infantry ; Deputy Judge Advocate General on H.Q. Staff ; European War, 1914–19 ; Publications : " Notes on Military Law " ; " Notes on District Courts Martial." *Address* : 166, Roslyn Road, Winnipeg. *Clubs* : Manitoba ; St. Charles' Country. Winnipeg.   (C145)

DENNY, Barbara Mary, Mrs. C.B.E.

DENNY, Henry Samuel, C.B.E., *b.* 13 March, 1872 ; *s.* of Thomas Denny, of Kent ; *m.* Edith Mary, *d.* of George Mare, of London. *Educ.* : High School, Sydney ; School of Mines, Ballarat, Victoria, (in the University of Melbourne). Consulting Metallurgical, Chemical, and Mining Engineer ; Member, Inst. Mining and Metallurgy ; Member, Inst. Petroleum Technologists ; Member American Inst. Mining and Metallurgical Engineers ; Member, South African Inst. of Engineers ; Managing Director, Denny Chemical Engineers Co., Ltd. ; Consulting Engineer to various private interests. *War Work* : Redesign, construction, and organisation of H.M. Factory, Penrhyndeudraeth, N. Wales ; Litherland, near Liverpool ; Langwith, Notts. ; Head of Technical Commission, nominated by Lord Moulton, to assist Gen. Plumer in the occupied area of the Rhine, after the Armistice. *Addresses* : 810–811, Salisbury House, London, E.C. (Phone : London Wall, 140) ; 2, Rotherwick Court, Golder's Green, N.W. (*Phone* : Finchley, 2469.) *Clubs* : Mining and Metallurgical ; Chemical Industries.   (C483)

DENNY, Capt. Maurice Edward, C.B.E., *b.* 11 Feb. 1886 ; *s.* of Sir Archibald Denny, Bart., LL.D., of Dumbarton ; *m.* Marjorie, *d.* of William Lysaght, C.B.E., of Castleford, Chepstow. *Educ.* : Tonbridge and abroad. Deputy Chairman of Messrs. William Denny and Brothers, Ltd., Shipbuilders and Engineers, Dumbarton. *War Work* : Army (Acting Major, M.G.C.), and at Admiralty. *Address* : Ardenvohr, Cardross, Dumbartonshire. *Clubs* : Windham ; New (Glasgow).   (C494)

DENNY, Norah Madeline, M.B.E., *b.* 16 June, 1892 ; *d.* of Frederick A. Denny, of 73, Grosvenor Street, W., and Horwood House, Winslow, Bucks. *Educ.* : Privately. *War Work* : Wounded and Missing Enquiries Dept., British Red Cross Society, 18, Carlton House Terrace, S.W. *Addresses* : 73, Grosvenor Street, W. ; Horwood House, Winslow, Bucks.   (M1647)

DENNY, Rosalind Mary, M.B.E., *b.* 4 Sept. 1894 ; *d.* of F. A. Denny, of 73, Grosvenor Street, W., and Horwood House, Winslow, Bucks. *Educ.* : Privately. *War Work* : Wounded and Missing Dept., British Red Cross Society, 18, Carlton House Terrace. *Addresses* : 73, Grosvenor Street, W. 1 ; Horwood House, Winslow, Bucks.   (M3610)

DENNY, Major William Alfred Charles, O.B.E., *b.* 20 April, 1871 ; *s.* of late Lieut. A. Denny, R.N. (*see* BURKE'S *Peerage*—Denny, Bart., of Tralee), of Tralee, Co. Kerry ; *m.* Lucy Florence, *d.* of the late Major-Gen. H. Coningham. *Educ.* : Windsor, and Staff Coll., Camberley. Reserve of Officers Army Service Corps ; late Leinster Regiment ; South African War, thrice mentioned in despatches, promoted Brevet-Major, Medal, 6 clasps, D.A.A.G., South China, 1902–3 ; Director-General, Military Intelligence Canadian Headquarters Staff ; raised and Commanded Canadian Corps of Guides, 1903–6 ; organised Canteen Services for two Divisions Kitchener's Army at Salisbury, 1914 ; Deputy Controller Welfare Supervision Dept., Woolwich Arsenal, 1916, and Controller Catering Dept. ; and Managing Director Improved Public House Co., Ltd. *Address* : c/o Sir C. McGrigor, Bart., & Co., 39, Panton Street, Haymarket, S.W. *Clubs* : Royal Automobile ; Aldwych ; Royal Golf (Eltham).   (O7078)

DENNY, Major William Bernard Valentine, M.B.E., *b.* 8 Nov. 1878 ; *s.* of William Henry Denny, of Kennington. *War Work* : Territorial Officer with 1st London Div. ; Requisition Officer to 28th Division in France and Salonica ; Commanded 18th (Indian) Divisional Train in Mesopotamia. *Address* : 142, Hailsham Avenue, Streatham, London, S.W. *Club* : R.A.S.C.   (M4269)

DENNYS, Major Guy Tulloch, O.B.E., *b.* 14 May, 1884 ; *s.* of Lieut.-Col. C. J. Dennys, of Indian Army ; *m.* Melita Mary, *d.* of Sir George Hart, K.B.E., C.I.E., I. G. of Forests, India (*q.v.*). *Educ.* : Eastbourne Coll. Major, 31st Punjabis, Indian Army. *Address* : 2, Warwick Mansions, 117, Warwick Road, Earlscourt, London.   (O6607)

DENNYS, Lieut.-Col. Sir Hector Travers, K.B.E., C.I.E., Indian Army (ret.), *b.* 9 March, 1864 ; *s.* of Gen. Julius Bentall Dennys, of Bengal Staff Corps ; *m.* Lucy Maud Massy, *d.* of Lieut.-Gen. George Wheeler, of Bengal Staff Corps. *Educ.* : Cheltenham Coll. and Sandhurst. Joined Manchester Regt. in 1885 ; Indian Army in 1887 ; Punjab Police in Nov. 1889 ; Inspector-Gen. of Police from April 1914 to March, 1919. *Address* : c/o Barclays Bank, Ltd., Sidmouth, S. Devon. *Club* : East India United Service.   (K246)

DENNYS, Lucy Maud Massy, Lady, M.B.E., *b.* 31 Jan. 1864 ; *d.* of Lieut.-Gen. George Wheeler, of the Bengal Staff Corps ; *m.* Hector Travers, *s.* of Gen. Julius Dennys, of the Bengal Staff Corps. *Educ.* : Privately. *War Work* : Did valuable service at Lahore throughout the Great War. *Address* : c/o Barclay's Bank, Ltd., Sidmouth, S. Devon. (M54)

DENSHAM, Sir Harry Percival, K.B.E. Chairman, United Tanners' Federation. *Address* : Cuerdon Hall, Thelwall. (K443a)

DENT, Major Arthur, O.B.E., M.C., *b.* 5 June, 1870 ; *s.* of Rev. R. F. Dent, M.A. (Cantab.), Vicar of Coverdale, Wensleydale, Yorkshire. *Educ.* : St. Edmund's School, Canterbury. Insurance Manager ; Fellow of Chartered Insurance Institute. Joined Territorial Army Service Corps in 1908 ; promoted Capt. and Officer in charge Supplies, Durham

Light Infantry Brigade, 1913 ; embarked for France, April, 1915, with 50th (Northumbrian) Division ; Divisional Senior Supply Officer with rank of Major, 1917 ; was with this famous division 1915–18 ; twice mentioned in despatches. *Address* : 145, Pilgrim Street, Newcastle-on-Tyne. *Club* : Royal Automobile.   (O5184)

DENT, Edith Vere, Mrs., O.B.E., *b.* 25 Sept. 1863 ; *d.* of Francis Hanbury Annesley, of The Manor House, Clifford Chambers, Stratford-on-Avon.; *m.* Robert Wilkinson, *s.* of Thomas Wilkinson John Dent, of Flass, Crosby Ravensworth. *War Work* : Raised 3 Voluntary Aid Detachments ; President, Westmorland Branch of the British Red Cross Society. The Westmorland Hut at Netley built, and beds maintained, by this branch, also a hospital at Appleby, and about £16,000 and much needlework, sent to the Central Fund. *Address* : Flass, Crosby Ravensworth, Shap, Westmorland.   (O10301)

DENT, Major Herbert Crowley, M.B.E., Army Medical Staff (ret.), *b.* 17 July, 1860 ; *s.* of William Yerbury Dent, of War Dept., Woolwich Arsenal ; *m.* May Burton, *d.* of late Rev. William Park, of Rampside (Lancs.). *Educ.* : King's Coll. School ; King's Coll. ; and King's Coll. Hospital, London. Hon. M.O. Cromer Hospital ; Hon. M.O. Norfolk and Norwich Convalescent Home, Cromer ; Cromer Commissioner, District Councillor, etc. *War Work* : Hon. Medical Recruiting Officer, North Norfolk ; Hon. M.O. in charge Auxiliary Military Hospitals (Cromer Area), 1914–19 ; Member of Committee of Prince of Wales' Fund, Canadian Fund, Prisoner of War Fund, Food Control, Coal Control, etc. *Address* : 2, Cliff Avenue, Cromer.   (M7893)

DENT, Hubert Augustus, M.B.E.

DENT, Lancelot Wilkinson, O.B.E., *b.* 19 Oct. 1868 ; *s.* of Rev. Charles Dent, M.A., of 104, Gloucester Terrace, W., and The Cottage, Sunningdale ; *m.* Beatrice Holdsworth (A.R.R.C.), *d.* of Rt. Hon. Sir Joseph Dimsdale, Bart., P.C., K.C.V.O., of 29, Sussex Square, W. (*see* BURKE's *Peerage*). *Educ.* : Eton, and Trinity Hall, Cambridge. Member of the Lieutenancy of the City of London. *War Work* : Founder and Head of the Ambulance Column, attached to the London District ; in charge of the transport of all the sick and wounded who came to the London District from Aug. 1914, to Oct. 1917. *Address* : 83, Westbourne Terrace, W. *Clubs* : Oxford and Cambridge ; Ranelagh ; Bengal (Calcutta). (O2141)

DENT, Richard Court, Chevalier, O.B.E., J.P., *b.* 21 July, 1860 ; *s.* of Major Richard Dent, of London (late 16th Beds.) ; *m.* Agnes, *d.* of Capt. W. C. Jackson, of East London, S.A. *Educ.* : Adelaide House, Jersey, and Brecon, S. Wales. Mercantile. *War Work* : Work done in connection with Imperial purchase of S.A. Wools, etc., as Chairman of Advisory Board, East London. *Address* : East London, Cape Province. South Africa.   (O8350)

DENTON, Capt. Harold Bentley, O.B.E., R.A.F.

DE PARAVICINI, Major Percy Chandos Farquhar, O.B.E.

DE PAULA, Lieut.-Col. Frederic Rudolf Mackley, O.B.E.

DE PENCIER, Right Rev. Bishop Adam Urias, O.B.E., R.A.F.

DE PLEDGE, Cecil Fenwick, O.B.E., J.P., Co. Durham, *b.* 9 Jan. 1858 ; *s.* of the Rev. Joseph Price de Pledge, J.P., of Satley Vic., Co. Durham ; *m.* Winifred, *d.* of George Mathew, of Sunderland. *Educ.* : Richmond and Reading. Deputy Provincial Grand Master of Durham. *War Work* : Commandant, Sunderland Special Constables ; Chairman, Sunderland Emergency Committee. *Address* : 11, The Elms, Sunderland.   (O11145)

DE POIX, Major Ralph Claude Busick Tyrel, O.B.E., B.A., *b.* 29th May, 1890 ; *s.* of Edmond Tyrel de Poix, Broome Place, Norfolk. *Educ.* : Oratory School, Edgbaston, and Christ Church, Oxford. Barrister-at-Law (Inner Temple). *War Work* : Served in 4th Batt. (T.) Norfolk Regt. in the Dardanelles, and in France with the R.A.F. as a flying officer, and subsequently as Staff Capt. to H.Q. Middle East R.A.F., and Staff Officer to 10th and 9th Brigades R.A.F. in France. *Address* : 23, Phillimore Gardens, W. 8. *Clubs* : Oxford and Cambridge ; Cavendish.   (O8083)

DE PUTRON, Adele Mary, O.B.E., *b.* 4 July, 1887 ; *d.* of the Rev. Godfrey Pierre de Putron, of Bertozerie, Guernsey. *Educ.* : Cheltenham. *War Work* : Deputy Controller, Q.M.A.A.C. Rouen and G.H.Q., France, 1917–20 ; mentioned in despatches ; Scoutmaster, Boy Scouts' Association, 1914–17. *Addresses* : Bertozerie, Guernsey ; 102, Abbey Road Mansions, St. John's Wood, N.W. *Club* : New Century.   (O5186)

DE RHE PHILIPE, Mary Catherine, Mrs., M.B.E.

DE ROBECK, Major John Henry Edward, M.B.E.

DERRICK, Col. George Alexander, C.B.E., V.D., *b.* 1860 ; *s.* of George Derrick, of Southampton ; *m.* 1905, Julia Anna, *d.* of Jacob Hutkin, of Poltava, Russia. Public Accountant. and Lieut.-Col. Comdg. Singapore Vol. Corps (ret. as Col. 1919) ; J.P. for Singapore. *Address* : Mount Elizabeth House, Singapore. *Clubs* : Singapore, and Sports' (London).   (G735)

DE ROTHSCHILD, Major Lionel Nathan, O.B.E., M.P.

DE ROTHSCHILD, Marie, Mrs. Leopold, C.B.E., *b.* 31 March, 1862 ; *d.* of Achilles Perugia ; *m.* the late Leopold de Rothschild, C.V.O., Baron of the Austrian Empire, one of His Majesty's Lieutenants for the City of London. *War Work* : President, Middlesex Red Cross Society ; on the Executive Committee of the Officers' Families Fund. *Addresses* : 5, Hamilton Place, W. 1 ; Gunnersbury Park, Acton ; Ascott, Wing, Leighton Buzzard. *Clubs* : Ladies' Automobile ; Bath.   (C2919)

DE ROUGEMONT, Frank Alexander, O.B.E., *b.* 11 Sept. 1881; *s.* of the late Commander Frank Rougemont, R.N., of 52, Lancaster Gate, W.; *m.* Gladys Mary, *d.* of the late Thomas Bulteel, J.P., of Radford, near Plymouth. *Educ.:* Kelly Coll., Tavistock, and Continent. Banker. 3rd Class Medjidieh 1911. *War Work:* Sub-Commissioner, British Red Cross and Order of St. John for Port Said and district, 1915–19; twice mentioned in despatches; O.B.E. 1918; Hon. Associate, Order of St. John of Jerusalem, 1918. *Addresses:* Port Said, Egypt; c/o Baring Brothers & Co., London. *Clubs:* Royal Cruising; M.C.C.; Union (Port Said). (O1825)

DE ROUGEMONT, Muriel Evelyn, Mrs., O.B.E.; *d.* of Evelyn Heseltine, of Great Warley, Essex *m.* Brig.-Gen. C. H. (Roger) de Rougemont, C.B., C.M.G., D.S.O., M.V.O., late Royal Artillery, and has issue, two sons. *War Work:* Commandant, Coombe Lodge Auxiliary Military Hospital, from Nov. 1914, to May, 1919; also nursed at Middlesex Hospital, Clacton-on-Sea, Oct. 1914; and Commandant, Brentwood Temporary Red Cross Hospital, Aug. 1914. *Address:* Great Warley, Essex. *Clubs:* V.A.D.; Forum. (O291)

DERRY, Major Arthur, D.S.O., O.B.E., *b.* 1874; *s.* of the late William Derry, of Houndiscombe, Plymouth; *m.* 1902, Collette Caroline, *d.* of the Rev. William Oxland, R.N., Vicar of Alston, Cumberland. *Educ.:* Wellington Coll. Joined Welsh Regt. 1895; became Capt. 1902; Major, 1914; served in S. Africa, 1899–1902, in command of Welsh Co. of 6th Regt. of Mounted Inf. (despatches twice, Queen's medal with five clasps, King's medal with two clasps); was a D.A.A. and Q.M.G. 1912–15; on Staff, 1915–19 (despatches); has Order of St. Maurice and St. Lazarus of Italy. *Club:* United Service. (O5793)

DE ST. CROIX, Capt. Leslie Lawson, M.B.E., *b.* 8 Aug. 1885; *s.* of Philip Charles de Ste. Croix, of Jersey. *Educ.:* Privately. *War Work:* Artists' Rifles; 3rd Batt. Royal Militia, Island of Jersey; Royal Army Service Corps; Staff of Quartermaster-General to the Forces. *Address:* 5, Hastings Terrace, Jersey. *Clubs:* Conservative; United R.A.S.C.; Royal Colonial Institute; Victoria (Jersey); Royal Jersey Golf. (M5220)

DE SALIS, Major Herbert Joseph Norman, O.B.E., R.E., S.R.

DE SARIGNY, Major Rene, O.B.E., R.A.F.

DE SAROJINI, Mrs., M.B.E. (M4133)

DE SAUMAREZ, Jane Anne, Lady, O.B.E.; *e. d.* of Capt. Charles Acton Vere Broke, R.E.; *m.* 10 Oct. 1882, Sir James St. Vincent Saumarez, 4th Baron de Saumarez, of Saumarez, Guernsey (*see* BURKE'S *Peerage*). (O1184)

DE SAUSMAREZ, Anne Elizabeth, Lady, G.B.E., Medaille de la Reine Elizabeth; *d.* of Rev. F. W. Mann, of Castel, Guernsey; *m.* Sir Havilland Walter (*see* BURKE'S *Peerage*), *s.* of Rev. Havilland de Sausmarez, of Guernsey. President and Hon. Sec. of British Women's Work Association for our Sailors and Soldiers and their families, which was formed to enable British Women in China to do such work. The headquarters of the Association were in Shanghai whilst there were 23 other centres of work scattered throughout China and one at Vladivostock. The Association was a branch of Queen Mary's Needlework Guild, and sent donations of clothing and hospital requirements to the number of 1,230,760 articles wherever directed by Her Majesty. *Address:* Sausmarez Manor, St. Martins, Guernsey. (G32)

DESBOROUGH, Capt. Arthur Peregrine Henry, C.B.E., late R.A., *b.* 10 Sept. 1868; *s.* of late Maj.-Gen. John Desborough, C.B., R.A.; *m.* Alice Henrietta Rosalie, *d.* of Maj.-Gen. E. L. Bland, R.E. *Educ.:* R.M. Academy, Woolwich. Entered R.A., 23 July, 1887; appointed H.M. Inspector of Explosives, Home Office, July, 1899; appointed Superintendent, R.N. Cordite Factory, Holton Heath, 1915; services lent to U.S. Govt. for an inquiry into accidents in American Coal Mines, in 1908; services lent to Canadian Govt. to advise on the regulation of the Explosives Industry, 1910. *Clubs:* Army and Navy. (C2560)

DESBOROUGH, Walter, M.B.E.

DES CLAYES, T. Major Camille, O.B.E., *b.* 12 Feb. 1887; *s.* of C. L. Des Clayes. *Educ.:* Bedford Modern School. Merchant, Alexandria, Egypt. *War Work:* 2nd Lieut., Dec. 1915; Capt., May, 1916; Major (and Deputy Inspector, Camel Transport Corps, attd. Anzac Mtd. Div.), Feb. 1917; served with Egyptian Camel Transport Corps, attd. E.E.F.; throughout war; mentioned in despatches, Dec. 1916; June, 1918; Jan. 1919; Order of Nile, 4th Class, Jan. 1919. *Address:* Union Club, Alexandria, Egypt. *Clubs:* Junior Athenæum; Turf (Cairo); Union (Alexandria, Egypt). (O2884)

DE SEGUNDO, Charles Sempill, O.B.E. V.D., M.B., B.S.

DES FORGES, Charles Lee, M.B.E., *b.* 20 July, 1879; *s.* of Walter H. des Forges, of Nottingham; *m.* Alice Mary, *d* of late George Stretton, of Nottingham. *Educ.:* Privately. Solicitor; Town Clerk and Clerk of the Peace; County Borough of Rotherham. *War Work:* Clerk to Military Tribunal; Hon. Sec. War Pensions Committee; Hon. Sec. Mayor's Recruiting Committee. *Address:* Grove House, Rotherham. *Clubs:* Rotherham; Royal Automobile. (M1727)

DESMOND, Lieut. Arthur Edward, M.B.E., R.E. (T.).

DE SOISSONS, Louis Emmanuel Jean Guy de Savoie, Carignan, O.B.E. (O6360)

DE SOISSONS, Pierre Amedee de Savoie, Barignan, O.B.E. (O5187)

DE SOUSA, Capt. Pascal John, O.B.E., I.M.S. (O11736)

DE SOYSE, Mary Margaret, Mrs., M.B.E.

DESPARD, Beatrice Lorne, Mrs., O.B.E., *d.* of Thomas Jarvis, of Mount Jarvis, Antigua; *m.* 1st, Major R. W. Dennistown, N. Staffs. Regt.; 2ndly, Capt. Herbert John, C.B.E.(*q.v.*), *s.* of Richard Carden Despard, of Queen's Co. *War Work:* Vice-President, Lanarkshire Executive Committee, Scottish Branch, Brit. Red Cross Society; President tor Hamilton S.B., B.R.C.S. and V.A.D.; Commandant, V.A.D., Lanark 36; Commandant, Caldergrove Auxiliary Hospital, Hallside; Convener, Lanarkshire Clothing Branch, S.B., B.R.C.S.; also War Work Parties, under Sir Edward Ward. *Club:* Kelvin, Glasgow. (O1282)

DESPARD, Capt. Herbert John, C.B.E., D.L., Royal Scots Fus. and 1st W.I. Regt. *b.* 7 Feb. 1860; *s.* of Richard Carden Despard, of Queen's Co.; *m.* Beatrice Lorne, O.B.E., *d* of Thomas Jarvis, of Mount Jarvis, Antigua, W.I. *Educ.:* King's College; Sandhurst. Chief Constable, Lanarkshire. *War Work:* Hon. Sec. S. & S. Families Association, Lanarkshire Branch. *Addresses:* Balgreen, Hamilton, N.B. *Club:* Naval and Military. (C2561)

DES VOEUX, Hylda Henrietta, Lady, C.B.E., *b.* 22 Feb. 1879; *d.* of the late Sir Victor Brooke, 3rd Bart., of Colebrooke, Brookeboro', Co. Fermanagh; *m.* Sir Frederick des Voeux, 7th Bart. *Educ.:* France. Hon. Controller, Overseas Club and Patriotic League, General Buildings, Aldwych, London, W.C. 2. *War Work:* Chairman, Overseas Club, Soldiers' and Sailors' Fund. *Address:* 50, Gillingham St., Eccleston Square, London, S.W. 1. *Clubs:* Overseas; English-Speaking Union. (C657)

DES VOEUX, Lieut.-Col. Henry, O.B.E.

DES VOEX, Violet Samana, M.B.E.

DE TRAFFORD, Capt. Rudolf Edgar Framin, O.B.E.

DE TURCKHEIM, Alfred Frederic, O.B.E., *b.* 19 June, 1863; *s.* of late Baron de Turckheim, of Alsace, France. *Educ.:* Versailles and Zurich. Engineer. *War Work:* Transport. *Address:* Sydney House, Bedford Park. *Club:* Royal Societies'. (O11508)

DE TUYLL, Lieut. Frank, M.B.E.

DEVAS, Rev. Francis Charles, O.B.E. (O5188)

DEVAS, Rev. Philip Dominic, O.B.E., O.F.M., *b.* 16 March, 1888; *s.* of Charles Stanton Devas. *Educ.:* Beaumont Coll.; Stonyhurst, and in Franciscan Order *War Work:* Chaplain, Jan, 1915, to April, 1919; garrison duty in England, Jan. 1915; 1/1st South Midland Field Ambulance, May, 1915; transfer ed to 1/6th Gloucestershire Regt., May, 1916; transferred as S.C.F. (P.C.'s Dept.) to 57th Div., March, 1917; appointed to 1st Royal Munster Fusiliers, May, 1918. *Address:* The Friary, Woodford Green, Essex. (O5189)

DEVENISH, Bertha, Mrs., O.B.E., *b.* 26 April, 1862; *d.* of the late G. P. Bidder, Q.C., of Ravensbury Park, Mitcham, Surrey; *m.* Henry Weston, *s.* of Henry Devenish, of The Lawn, Whitchurch, Hants. *Educ.:* Privately. *War Work:* On 7 Aug. 1914, originated and personally established a Women's League of Service for Mitcham, in order to collect together and organise all work that Mitcham Women might wish to do for the War. It was joined by about 500 women, who worked under it in many war activities till April, 1919. Organised a "Queen's Workroom" for Mitcham; started the first War Savings Association in Surrey. Was Hon. Sec. to the Mitcham War Savings Committee since March, 1916; member of the Surrey War Distress Committee, Surrey War Agricultural Committee, Surrey War Savings Committee, Women's Advisory Committee to the National War Savings Committee, Lord Mayor's Committee for organising the War Loan Campaign and Food Campaign, 1917; Registrar for Women in Agriculture. *Address:* Mount House, Parkstone, Dorset. *Club:* Sesame. (O16302)

DEVEREUX, Augustine, M.B.E.

DEVEREUX, Ethel Mary, Mrs., M.B.E.

DE VILLE, Flight-Lieut. Edward Alexander de Lossy, O.B.E., R.A.F.

DEVINE, Capt. Henry, O.B.E., M.D., R.A.M.C.

DEVINE, Major James, O.B.E., R.E.

DEVINE, Major James Arthur, D.S.O., O.B.E., *b.* 1869; *s.* of the late Capt. Thomas Devine, Dep. Surveyor-Gen., Ontario; *m.* 1916, Mary Hilda, *d.* of the late Henry Miles, of Liverpool. *Educ.:* Trin. Coll. Dublin (M.A. and M.D. 1897). Physician. Major, Canadian Army Med. Staff; Professor of Manitoba Medical College; Member of Council of Manitoba Univ.; Professor of Clinical Med.; sometime Major, Canadian Permanent Forces; appointed Major, R.A.M.C. 1915; served in the S. African War, 1900–2 with Canadian Mounted Rifles (despatches). *Address:* Fort Garry Court, Winnipeg, Manitoba. (O7081)

DEVINE, John, O.B.E.

DEVLIN, Capt. Joseph, O.B.E.

DEVONSHIRE, Sir James Lyne, K.B.E., *b.* 4 Oct. 1863; *s.* of late Thomas Harris Devonshire, of 1, Frederick's Place, E.C., and Mill Gap, Eastbourne; *m.* Wilhelmina Walker, *d.* of Charles Sidey, of Kensington. Member and Hon. Treas. of Inst. of Elect. Eng., and a Member of the Inst. of Transport. Member of Electric Power Supply Committee, appointed by Board of Trade; Member of Committee appointed by Board of Trade to consider position of Electrical Trades after the War; Member of Consultative Council on National Health Assurance (Approved Societies' Section); Chairman, National Trade Advisory Committee of disabled Sailors and Soldiers (Electricity, Power and Light); during the war Member of Middlesex Appeal Tribunal, Military Service Acts; Chairman of

Tramways (Board of Trade) Committee. *Address:* 48, Queen's Gate, S.W. *Clubs:* St. Stephen's; Ranelagh; Royal St. George's Golf; Royal Wimbledon Golf.   (K366)

DEVONSHIRE, Marie Vulliamy, M.B.E.

DEW, Lieut. Reginald Francis, M.B.E., R.E. (T.).

DEW, Capt. William James, M.B.E., R.A.F.

DEWAR, Capt. Alfred Charles, O.B.E., R.N.

DEWAR, Capt. Kenneth Gilbert Balmain, C.B.E.; *m.* 1914, Gertrude Mary, *d.* of the late Frederick Stapleton-Bretherton, J.P., of The Hall, Rainhill, Lancashire (*see* BURKE'S *Peerage*, Petre, Bt.). Capt. Q.W.; served at Peace Conference, 1919.   (C2352)

DEWAR, Major Michael Bruce Urquhart, O.B.E., R.E. (T.).

DE WARDT, John Isaac, O.B.E.

DE WATTEVILLE, Major Herman Gaston, C.B.E.; Major and Brevet Lieut.-Col., R.A.; served in the Great War, 1914–19 (despatches).   (C1543)

DE WET, Lieut. Nicholas Johannes, M.B.E.

DE WET, Comm. Thomas Oloff, C.B.E.; Com. R.N., and Div. Naval Transport Officer, Vancouver; served in the Great War, 1914–19 (despatches).   (C2247)

DEWHURST, Counsell, O.B.E., J.P.

DEWHURST, John Henry, M.B.E., M.D., M.R.C.S.

DEWHURST, Major Norman, O.B.E., *b.* 25 Nov. 1877; *s.* of late T. H. Dewhurst, of Skipton, Yorks. *Educ.:* Sedbergh. Solicitor. *War Work:* Commanding 50th Divisional (formerly Northumbrian Division) Supply Column, France, 1915–17; No. 7 Divisional Motor Transport Co., Italian Ex. Force, 1918–19. *Address:* 12, Market Place, Bishop Auckland, Co. Durham. *Clubs:* Golfers; Whitehall Court.   (O2902)

DEWING, Lieut.-Col. Robert Henry, O.B.E., late Indian Army, *b.* 6 Aug. 1863; *s.* of the late E. M. Dewing, of Carbrooke Hall, Norfolk; *m.* Norah Emma, *d.* of the late Rev. H. Hunter, of Wath. *Educ.:* Brighton College; Sandhurst. *War Work:* Raised and trained 13th Batt. East Yorkshire Regt.; also commanded it in Egypt and France; later commanded a Reserve Batt. in England, 1917–19. *Address:* Grove House, Sible Hedingham, Essex. *Clubs:* E. I. United Service; M.C.C.; I.Z.; Alpine; Sports.   (O3109)

DEWING, Lieut.-Col. Sidney Herbert, O.B.E.

DE WITT, Capt. Ferdinand, O.B.E., R.A. (T.).

DE WOLF, Capt. Francis George, O.B.E., M.C.

DE WOLFF, Capt. (acting Major) Charles Esmond. C.B.E., LL.B., *b.* 25 Nov. 1893; *s.* of C. Louis De Wolff, of Purley, Surrey; *m.* Ada Marjorie, *d.* of Henry R. Arnold, of-Hatch End, Middlesex. *Educ.:* Portsmouth Grammar School; King's College, London; London University. Regular Army. *War Work:* Served in Dardanelles, Macedonia, and South Russia; O.B.E., 1919; C.B.E., 1920; 4 times mentioned in despatches; Russian Order of Vladimir, 4th Class. *Address:* Mansion Hotel, Richmond, Surrey.   (C2360d)

DE WOOLFSON, Major Albert Henry Frederick, O.B.E., R.E.

DEWRANCE, Sir John, K.B.E., *b.* 13 March, 1858; *s.* of John Dewrance, of Tilford, Farnham, Surrey; *m.* Isabella, *d.* of Frances Trevithick, of Penzance. *Educ.:* St. John's Wood Preparatory; Charterhouse; and King's College, London. Member of the Institution of Civil Engineers; Member of Council of the Institute of Mechanical Engineers and the Institute of Metals; Member of the Institute of Naval Architects; Member of the Iron and Steel Inst., and many other learned societies; President of the Engineering and the National Employers' Federation. *War Work:* Member of Advisory Committee of the Treasury; Ministry of Munitions Ministry of Labour; Department of Oversens Trade. *Address:* Cranmore Place, Chislehurst, Kent. *Clubs:* Junior Carlton; St. Stephens; Gresham; Royal Automobile.   (K367)

DEXTER, Edward, O.B.E.

DEXTER, Thomas, M.B.E.

DEXTER, Thomas Edward, O.B.E., *b.* 22 April, 1857; *s.* of Thomas Philip Dexter, of Southborough, Kent; *m.* Alice Maud, *d.* of Thomas James Stafford, of London. *Educ.:* Highbury College, London. Civil Service Clerk, Dublin Castle, 1876; Education Dept., Whitehall, 1877–83; Secretary's Dept., Admiralty, 1883–89; Officer in charge of Expense Accounts, Sheerness Dockyard, 1893–1901; Devonport Dockyard, 1901–1918; Admiralty representative on Plymouth Insurance Committee, 1912–18. *War Work:* Discharge of official duties under war conditions from 4 Aug. 1914, to retirement, on 8 Oct. 1918, at the completion of 42 years' service; general assistance, under the Insurance Act, to men of Navy and Army, invalided for tuberculosis; receiving official letters of thanks from Board of Admiralty, and National Health Insurance Commission (England) on retirement. *Address:* 9, Ravenlea Road, Folkestone. *Club:* Radnor, Folkestone.   (O1284)

DEY, Alexander, M.B.E., M.B., C.M. (Aberdn.), *b.* 5 Aug. 1854; *s.* of Alexander Dey, of Milltown, Tomintoul Banffshire; *m.* Eva Mary, *d.* of Thomas Nash Ward, of Hempnall House, Norfolk. *Educ.:* Aberdeen University. Medical Officer of Health, Rural District of Glendale; Medical Officer and Public Vaccinator, Wooler, Chatton, Districts; Surgeon, Glendale Dispensary; Surgeon to Constabulary; Certif. Factory Surgeon, Glendale, Northumberland. *War Work:* Medical Officer, 12th Northumberland V.A.D. Hospital, Fowberry Hetton, and 13th Northumberland V.A.D. Hospital, Etal Manor, Cornhill-on-Tweed.   (M7897)

DEZEST, Frank, M.B.E.

D'HARTY, William Cornelius, M.B.E., 3rd Class Star of Ethiopia for services rendered to the Government of Abyssinia. Civil Servant (His Majesty's Office of Works). *War Work:* Resident Architect at Aintree, Liverpool, for the Construction of Filling and Amatol Factories, A.O.D. Stores, Shell Stores, etc. *Address:* Saltleigh, Hampton Road, Strawberry Hill. (M7899)

DHAT, H.H. Raja Sir Udalji Rao Puat of, K.B.E. (K44)

DIACK, Sir Alexander Henderson, K.C.I.E., C.V.O., C.B.E., *b.* 13 Feb. 1862; *s.* of the late John Diack, of Aberdeen; *m.* Mylsie, *d.* of the late Robert Alfred Molley. *Educ.:* Aberdeen University and King's College, Cambridge. India Civil Service, 1881–1916; retired after serving 6 years as Financial Commissioner of the Punjab, having previously been 4 years Chief Secretary to the Punjab Govt. *War Work:* in the Ministry of Munitions, Aug. 1916, to April, 1917; and thence onward in connection with the administration of artificial limbs and appliances, in the Ministry of Pensions. *Address:* Lane End, Putney Heath Lane, London, S.W. 15.   (C2562)

DIAMOND, Sir William Henry, K.B.E., *b.* 23 Sept 1865; *s.* of Thomas Diamond, of Cardiff. Engineer and Ship Repairer. Director of local companies, etc. *War Work:* President of the Dry Dock Owners and Ship Repairers' Association for the Bristol Channel, during the whole of the War period. *Address:* Deane House, Newport Road, Cardiff. *Club:* Devonshire.   (K368)

DIBBEN, Lieut.-Comm. Arthur Douglas Harry, O.B.E., R.N.

DIBBEN, Major Cecil Reginald, O.B.E.

DICHMONT, Katherine, Mrs., O.B.E., *b.* 30 Oct. 1863; *d.* of Alexander Maclean, of Largs, Ayr, Scotland; *m.* Archibald, *s.* of George Dichmont, of Oswaldtwistle, Lancs. Prior to marriage was mistress of a Girls' High School in Accrington, Lancashire, for nearly two years. *War Work:* President of the Fairhaven Working Party, which forwarded comforts to South-West Africa, to East Africa, the Hospital Ship "Ebain," the Belgian Refugees, and overseas contingents, and entertained Australian and New Zealand wounded passing through, and was responsible for all delicacies and flowers to the Alexandra Hospital. *Address:* Fairhaven, Green Point, Cape Town, S. Africa.   (O2201)

DICK, Col. Sir Arthur Robert, K.B.E., C.B., C.V.O.

DICK, Gladys Helen, M.B.E., *d.* of A:chd. W. Dick, of 48, Lilybank Gardens, Glasgow. *Educ.:* Privately. Sec. Girls' Auxiliary United Free Church of Scotland. *War Work:* Welfare Supervisor, Aisne Factory, Renfrew, one of the munition factories managed by Babcock and Wilcox, Ltd., Renfrew. *Address:* 48, Lilybank Gardens, Glasgow. (M3612)

DICK, Helen Maybel Kathleen, Mrs., O.B.E., *b.* 22 Aug. 1874; *d.* of S. W. Wyllys-Pomeroy, of Boston, Mass., U.S.A.; *m.* Major Thomas Aitken Dick, R.F.A., *s.* of T. Dick, of Edinburgh, Imperial Chinese Maritime Customs. *Educ.:* Privately. *War Work:* Commandant, V.A.D. L/72 British Red Cross Society, from Jan. 1914, to July, 1919; Joint Commandant, Chelsea V.A.D. Hospital, 13, Grosvenor Crescent, March, 1915, to April, 1919. *Address:* Rushford Warren, Christchurch, Hants. *Clubs:* Bath; Hurlingham; V.A.D.; Solent Yacht.   (O10305)

DICK, Henry Charles, M.B.E.

DICK, James Scott, M.B.E., B.Sc., A.I.C., *b.* 3 Nov. 1889; *s.* of William Dick, of Kirkcaldy, Fifeshire; *m.* Marion Edith, *d.* of William Narborough, of Woolwich. *Educ.:* Kirkcaldy High School and St. Andrews Univ. Research Chemist at Research Department, Royal Arsenal, Woolwich. *Address:* 6, Blendon Terrace, Plumstead, London, S.E. 18. (M7901)

DICK, Margaret Mary Douglas, O.B.E.

DICK, Marion Edith, Mrs., M.B.E., B.Sc. (Lond.); *d.* of late William Narborough, of Woolwich; *m.* James Scott, *s.* of William Dick. *Educ.:* Blackheath High School, and Royal Holloway Coll., London Univ. Lecturer in Science. *War Work:* Chemist, Research Dept., Woolwich Arsenal. *Address:* 6, Blendon Terrace, Plumstead S.E. 18. (M7902)

DICK, Octavius Petty, M.B.E.

DICKENS, Henry Charles, O.B.E., *b.* 7 Oct. 1878; *s.* of Henry Fielding Dickens, K.C., of 8, Mulberry Walk, S.W.; *m.* Fanny, *d.* of H. Rungo, of 25, Berkeley Square. *Educ.:* Beaumont College, and Trinity Hall, Cambridge. Barrister-at-Law. *War Work:* Civil Liabilities Commissioner. *Address:* 52, Chepstow Villas, W. 11; 4, Essex Court, Temple.   (O292)

DICKENS, Lieut. William Samuel, M.B.E., I.A.R.O.

DICKENS, Capt. Willie Hyde, O.B.E.

DICKER, Capt. Arthur Seymour Hamilton, M.B.E.

DICKER, Lieut. Gilbert Charles Hamilton, M.B.E.

DICKERSON, Major Frederick Thomas, O.B.E.

DICKEY, Archibald Alexander George, M.B.E., M.D., J.P., *b.* 20 Sept. 1861; *s.* of Rev. J. P. Dickey, of Carnone, Raphow, Co. Donegal, Ireland; *m.* Marion, *d.* of late John Yeates, of Botcherly Hall, Carlisle. *Educ.:* Queen's Coll. Belfast. *War Work:* Officer-in-Charge and Medical Officer, Colne Auxiliary Military Hospital. *Address:* Overdale Hall, Whitefield, Manchester.   (M1650)

DICKIE, James, M.B.E.

DICKIE, Robert Charles, O.B.E.

DICKIE, Major William Stewart, O.B.E., R.A.M.C., F.R.C.S.

DICKINS, Sidney John Oldacres, M.B.E., M.D. Brux., M.R.C.S. (Eng.), L.R.C.P. (Lond.), *b.* 24 Aug. 1869; *s.* of Charles Dickins, of Monken Hadley, Middlesex; *m.* Cicely

Margaret, *d.* of William Whitchurch Taunton, of Worcester. *Educ.*: Totteridge Park School; St. Bart.'s Hospital; Univ. Brux. Medical Officer and Public Vaccinator, Horsham Union, and of Cuckfield Union; Medical Officer, St. Joseph's Orphanage, West Grinstead. *War Work*: Commandant and Medical Officer of Sussex V. V.A.D. from 1912-15; at his own expense, fitted up a machine shop, with 15 machines, and commenced making fuse bodies, fuse caps, and finally fuse hammers for high explosive shells, until the end of the war. *Address*: Cowfold, Sussex. (M16)

DICKINSON, Emily Frances, Mrs., M.B.E., *b.* 1874; *d.* of Thomas Francis Sewell, of Colne-Engaine, Essex; *m.* Henry Basham, *s.* of Joseph Dickinson, of Wavertree, Liverpool. *Educ.*: Privately, and Endsleigh House, London. *War Work*: Commandant, Essex County Hospital, Colchester; Vice-President, British Red Cross Society, Lexden and Winstree Div., Colchester. *Club*: V.A.D. Ladies'. (M1652)

DICKINSON, Frances Joan, M.B.E.

DICKINSON, Major Francis Sidney, O.B.E., Aust. A.S.C.

DICKINSON, Capt. and Qr.-Mr. George Joseph, O.B.E.

DICKINSON, Capt. James, O.B.E.

DICKINSON, Major and Qr.-Mr. Joseph Espin, O.B.E.

DICKINSON, Major Richard Frederick O'Toole, O.B.E., M.B., B.A.O., M.Sc., R.A.M.C.; *s.* of Richard Randall Dickinson; *m.* Ita Mary Pauline, *d.* of Hugh Macken, of Dublin. *Educ.*: Blackrock Coll., and the Univ. Coll., Dublin, Medical School. Deputy Assistant Director of Hygiene, 5th Division, Ireland. *War Work*: Medical Officer of a unit in the 6th Division in 1914-15; afterwards, Specialist Sanitary Officer, Trouville Base, and Deputy Assistant Director of Med. Services (Sanitation), 1st British Army in the Field, and later held the same appointment at G.H.Q. British Rhine Army. *Address*: Bayview, Sandy Cove, Co. Dublin. (O8191)

DICKINSON, William, M.B.E.

DICKINSON, William Henry, O.B.E., M.B.

DICKINSON, Capt. William Henry, O.B.E., R.A.S.C.

DICKINSON, Right Hon. Sir Willoughby Hyett, P.C., K.B.E., J.P., D.L., *b.* 9 April, 1859; *s.* of Sebastian Stewart Dickinson, of Brown's Hill, Stroud, Glos.; *m.* Minnie Elizabeth, *d.* of Sir Richard Meade, K.C.I.E. *Educ.*: Eton and Cambridge (Trinity College). Barrister-at-Law; formerly M.P. for North St. Pancras, 1906–1918. *War Work*: Chairman of the War Office Appeals Committee (Soldiers' Dependants); Member of the London Central Relief Committee (Prince of Wales' Fund); Member of War Refugees Committee. *Address*: 4, Egerton Gardens, S.W. 3. *Clubs*: Reform; National Liberal. (K61)

DICKINSON, Capt. William Michael Kington, O.B.E., R.A.M.C.

DICKS, Capt. Eustace James Carey, M.B.E., M.D., B.S. (Lond.), R.A.M.C.(V.), *b.* 3 June, 1883; *s.* of F. R. Dicks, of Cheltenham; *m.* Ethel, *d.* of J. How, of Cheltenham. *Educ.*: Epsom Coll., and St. Mary's Hospital, London. Medical Officer, Framlingham College. *War Work*: Medical Officer, Easton Park Red Cross Hospital. *Address*: The Limes, Framlingham, Suffolk. (M7903)

DICKS, Capt. Henry Leage, C.B.E., R.N., *b.* 1870; *s.* of the late Henry Dicks, of Haslecourt, Woking. *War Work*: Served as Senior Naval Officer, Extended Defence Officer, and Capt. of Auxiliary Patrols, Cromarty. (C2235)

DICKSON, Beatrice Beaupré, Mrs., M.B.E.

DICKSON, Lieut.-Col. Ernest, C.M.G., C.B.E.; Lieut.-Col. R.A.S.C.; served in Mesopotamia, 1915-18 (despatches). (C1105)

DICKSON, Lieut. Eric James, M.B.E., I.A.R.O. (M10217)

DICKSON, Prof. Henry Newton, C.B.E., M.A., D.Sc., *b.* 24 June, 1866; *s.* of William Dickson, of Edinburgh; *m.* Margaret Stephenson, of Duns, N.B. *Educ.*: Edinburgh University. An Assistant Editor of the "Encyclopædia Britannica." *War Work*: Head of Geographical Section of the Naval Intelligence Department, Admiralty. *Address*: 125, High Holborn, London, W.C. 1. *Club*: Royal Societies'. (C485)

DICKSON, Isabel Anne, O.B.E., *b.* 12 Dec. 1872; *d.* of John Farquhar Dickson, of Panbride House, Carnoustie. *Educ.*: St. Leonard's School, St. Andrew's; Girton College, Cambridge. Acting Principal, Women's College within the University of Sydney, New South Wales; Acting Principal, Bedford College, University of London; H.M. Inspector of Schools; Acting Assistant Secretary, Board of Education. *War Work*: Lent to Board of Agriculture and Fisheries. *Addresses*: Deuchar, Forfarshire; 17, Pelham Crescent, S.W. 7. *Club*: Lyceum. (O1285)

DICKSON, Major James, O.B.E., R.A.F.

DICKSON, Lorna, Mrs., M.B.E.

DICKSON, Norman, O.B.E.

DICKSON, Major Robert Milne, O.B.E., M.D., R.A.M.C., *b.* 13 Dec. 1880; *s.* of William Dickson, of Newport, Fife; *m.* Katherine Wilson, *d.* of William Cunningham, of Dundee. *Educ.*: St. Andrew's Univ. Ophthalmic Specialist, Aldershot Command. *War Work*: Medical Officer, King's Dragoon Guards; Commandant, Bath War Hospital. *Address*: Youngsdale, Newport, Fife. (O7087)

DICKSON, Robinson Simpson, O.B.E., M.D., *b.* 30 Oct 1868; *s.* of Joseph Dickson, M.D., of Whitehaven, Cumberland; *m.* Marguerite Victoria, *d.* of William George Rice, J.P., Bowes Park, N. 22. *Educ.*: Ghyll Bank Coll., Whitehaven, and Glasgow Univ. Police Surgeon, Wood Green, N. 22; Surgeon Passmore Edwards Hospital, Wood Green; Surgeon Linen and Woollen Drapers Institution. *War Work*: Surgeon to

Roseneath Auxiliary Military Hospital, Winchmore Hill, N., for 5 years, and Med. Off. to Auxiliary Military Hospital, Palmers Green, N. 3, for 2½ years; Surgeon to Wood Green and Southgate Clinic for Disabled Soldiers. *Address*: 129, Palmerston Road, Bowes Park, N. 22. (O10308)

DICKSON, Major William, O.B.E. R.A.O.C.

DIGBY, Emily, M.B.E., *d.* of the late Sir Kenelm Digby, G.C.B., of King's Ford, Colchester (*see* BURKE'S *Peerage*). *War Work*: Joint Hon. Sec. Colchester War Pensions Local Committee. *Address*: King's Ford, Colchester. (M7904)

DIGBY, Lady Lilian Mary Harriet Diana, M.B.E., A.R.R.C., *b.* 10 Feb. 1872; *d.* of Henry George, 2nd Earl of Ravensworth, of Ravensworth Castle, Gateshead; *m.* Hon. Gerald Fitzmaurice, Capt. R.N., *s.* of the 9th Baron Digby. of Minterne, Dorset (*see* BURKE'S *Peerage*). *War Work*: 3 years and 9 months' service in Holnest Auxiliary Military Hospital (Primary Class), as Commandant and Nurse. *Address*: Lewcombe Manor, Dorchester. *Club*: V.A.D. (M327)

DIGGINS, Capt. Arthur, O.B.E., T.D., *b.* 10 Nov. 1867; *s.* of John Diggins, of Totnes, Devon; *m.* Eva, *d.* of J. T. A. Crofton, J.P., of Dublin. Civil Servant. *Address*: The Homestead, Richmond, Surrey. (O1287)

DIGGINS, William Samuel, M.B.E.

DIGGLE, Capt. Frank Holt, O.B.E. M.B., F.R.C.S., R.A.M.C.

DIGNAM, Edmund Grattan, O.B.E.

DIKE, Capt. and Qr.-Mr. Edward Henry, O.B.E.

DILBY, Arthur George, M.B.E.

DILKE, Beaumont Albany FETHERSTON-, M.B.E.,M.A., M.B. (Cantab.) *b.* 14 Nov. 1875; *s.* of the late Theodore Henry Percival Dilke, of The India Office, S.W.; *m.* Phoebe Stella *d* of Rev. W. Riland Bedford, M.A., of Sutton Coldfield, Warwicks. *Educ.*: St. John's Coll., Cambridge, and St. George's Hospital, London. Physician; Medical Officer in the West African Medical Service in Nigeria. *War Work*: Acted as Assistant Surgeon to the Colonial Hospital at Gibraltar during the War. *Address*: Maxstoke Castle, Coleshill, Warwickshire. *Club*: Union. (M6439)

DILKS, Alice Irene, M.B.E., *b.* 23 May, 1887; *d.* of Arthur Dilks, M.A. (Oxon) of Sanderstead, Surrey. *Educ.*: Ladies' Coll., Eastbourne, and Newnham Coll., Cambridge. Secretary and Treasurer to the Bureau of Municipal Research, Dayton, Ohio, U.S.A., 1912-16. *War Work*: Administrative Assistant, Ministry of Munitions, 1916-20. *Address*: 118, Mayfield Road, Sanderstead, Surrey. (M7907)

DILL, John Frederick Gordon, O.B.E., M.D.

DILL, Major Thomas Melville, O.B.E., R.G.A.

DILLON, Surgeon-Major Luke Gerald, O.B.E., F.S.A.,J.P., Co. Durham, *b.* 24 April, 1862; *s.* of Charles Blake Dillon, of Springlawn, Co. Roscommon; *m.* Elizabeth Mary, *d.* of the late Hon. Hubert Dormer. *Educ.*: Queen's Univ., Galway (*See* BURKE'S *Peerage*, Dillon Viscount Dillon, descendants of Thomas, 4th son of Theobald, 1st V. Dillon). *War Work*: Medical Officer in charge of Seaham Hall Auxiliary Military Hospital, Seaham Infirmary, and all troops stationed at Seaham during the war, including the 4th D.L.I. for 3½ years. *Address*: Hawthorn Tower, Seaham, Co. of Durham. (O11802)

DILLON, Malcolm, M.B.E., J.P., *b.* 1859; *s.* of Anthony Dillon, J.P., of Wrexham; *m.* Clara Elizabeth, *d.* of Walter W. U. Palmer, of Southacre, Norfolk. *Educ.*: Mercers' School. Chief Agent to the Marquis of Londonderry. *War Work*: Member of Recruiting and War Savings Committees; County Sec. Soldiers' and Sailors' Families Association; Chairman, Seaham Tribunal; Hon. Sec. and Treas. Seaham Hall War Hospital; Deputy Chairman, Durham County Sailors' Fund; Sec. Seaham Division Soldiers' Help Society; Member of Durham County War Pensions Committee; Chairman of Emergency Committee. *Address*: Dene House, Seaham Harbour. (M7908)

DILLON, Richards Henry, C.B.E.

DILLON, Lieut. Robert, M.B.E.

DILLON, Stella Margaret, M.B.E., *b.* 26 Dec. 1889; *d.* of Col. the Hon. R. V. Dillon. *War Work*: Nursing in Bedfordshire Hospitals; Member of No. 4, Bedford V.A.D., 1918-19; Quartermaster of same detachment working at Kempston Military Hospital, Bedford. *Address*: Biddenham Manor, Bedfordshire. (M7909)

DILLON, Thomas Cantrell, O.B.E., M.D.

DILWORTH, Lieut. Charles, M.B.E.

DIMMER, Lieut.-Col. John Francis, O.B.E.

DIMMOCK, Capt. Henry Lionel Ffortington, O.B.E., *b.* 2 Feb. 1885; *s.* of Lieut.-Col. H. P. Dimmock, O.B.E.,; *m.* Beatrice Mary, *d.* of the late Ernest Kent, formerly of Hanley Castle, Worcestershire. *Educ.*: Clifton and Royal Military Academy. Captain in 9th Brigade, Royal Garrison Artillery. *War Work*: Embarked with 7th Division, Sept. 1914; commanded 146th Heavy Battery, R.G.A., Dec. 1917; Senior Instructor, 1st Army Artillery School, Nov. 1919; commanded 290th Siege Battery, R.G.A., Nov. 1918. *Address*: Stagsdene, Stonehill, Bordon, Hants. (O2487)

DIMMOCK, Lieut.-Col. Henry Peers, O.B.E.

DIMOCK, Capt. John Francis Douglas, O.B.E.

DIMSDALE, Beatrice, Eliza Bower, Lady, *b.* Aug. 1853; *d.* of Robert Hunt Holdsworth; *m.* the late Right Hon. Sir Joseph C. Dimsdale, Bart., K.C.V.O. *War Work*: Civil Administrator of Fishmongers' Hall Hospital from Oct. 1914, to Feb. 1919. (O1290)

DINGLE, Henry James, M.B.E., *b.* 14 Nov. 1865; *s.* of Henry James Dingle, of Dean, near Salisbury; *m.* Mary Ann, *d.* of Henry Lewis, of Boyle, Ireland. *Educ.:* Romsey. *War Work:* Superintending Clerk, No. 2, Infantry Records, Exeter. *Address:* 15, West Street, Trowbridge, Wilts.   (M4296)

DINGLI, Capt. Adrian, O.B.E., R.M.A.

DINSDALE, Lieut. Thomas Errington Coutts, M.B.E.

DINWIDDIE, Capt. Melville, O.B.E., D.S.O., M.C.; Capt. Gordon Highlanders; served in the Great War 1914–17 (despatches).   (O5194)

DINWIDDIE, Agnes Letitia BLOUNT-, M.B.E. Supervisor, Judge Advocate-General's Office, War Office.   (M10310)

DISNEY, Rev. Anthony Edward Denny, M.B.E., *b.* 1859; *s.* of the late Rev. William Henry Disney, Rector of Winwick, Northamptonshire; *m.* Katharine Gertrude, *d.* of the late Rev. Henry Lacon Watson, J.P., Rector of Sharnford, and Hon. Canon of Peterborough. *Educ.:* Privately, and Lichfield Theological Coll. Rector of Stoney Stanton since 1885, holding many public offices in Diocese of Peterborough and County of Leicester. *War Work:* Chairman of the Hinckley Local Tribunal; Chairman of the Hinckley and District Joint Food Control Committee; Chairman of the Hinckley Rural Fuel and Light (Coal Control) Committee; Member of the Hinckley District War Agricultural Committee (Men's); Chairman of the Hinckley District War Agricultural Committee (Women's); Vice-Chairman of the Hinckley District Sub-Committee, Naval and Military Pensions; Member of the Joint Food Distribution Committee for County of Leicester; District Representative of Q.M.A.A.C. *Address:* The Rectory, Stoney Stanton, near Hinckley, Leicestershire. *Club:* County (Leicester).   (M1654)

DISRAELI, Marion Grace, Mrs., O.B.E., *b.* 1875; *d.* of the late Edward Silva, of Testcombe, Hants; *m.* Coningsby Disraeli, D.L., T.D., C.A., J.P., nephew and heir of the late Earl of Beaconsfield. *War Work:* Red Cross Organisation; War Pensions work; Vice-President, Buckinghamshire Soldiers' and Sailors' Families Association. *Address:* Hughenden Manor, Bucks.   (O3690)

DITCHFIELD, Richard Thomas, M.B.E., *b.* April, 1855. *War Work:* Filled the position as responsible head in connection with National Service, Chorley Parliamentary Division; was responsible for the preparation and presentation of the cases coming before six tribunals; rendered valuable service at the Recruiting Office, and was Hon. Sec. for the Derby Scheme for the Borough of Chorley. *Address:* Windsor Road, Chorley.   (M7910)

DITTMAN, Capt. (acting Lieut.-Col.) William Ewart, O.B.E., *b.* Oct. 1880; *s.* of Wm. T. Dittman, J.P. *Educ.:* Portsmouth Grammar School. *War Work:* As Lieut.-Col. commanding 2nd A.A. Mobile Brigade, 1917; A.A. Defences, Redhill, 1918; A.A. Defences, Dover, 1919. *Address:* 24, Saint Ronan's Road, Southsea.   (O3111)

DIVE, Horace, M.B.E.   (M1655)

DIVER, Paymaster Lieut. James Michael, M.B.E., R.N.R.

DIVES, Evelyn Scott, Mrs., O.B.E. Hon. Sec., Hove War Hospital Supply Depot.   (O11789*g*)

DIX, Arthur Harold, O.B.E., *b.* 6 Aug. 1876. *Addresses:* 7, Mincing Lane, London, E.C.; Forest Dene, Worth, Sussex.   (O10130)

DIX, Edith Amy, Mrs., M.B.E.

DIX, Lieut. Henry Philip, O.B.E., M.C., R.N.V.R.

DIX, Major Robert Malam, O.B.E., R.A.S.C.

DIX, Selina, M.B.E., M.I.H., Medallist Dom. Sci., *b.* 15 March, 1859; *d.* of the late Edward Dix, of Beeston, Notts. *Educ.:* Beeston; Lincoln Training Coll.; Nottingham Univ. Coll. Head Teacher, Wheatley St. Girls' School, and Principal, Wheatley St. Women's Institute, Coventry. *War Work:* Vice-Chairman, Coventry Women's Advisory Committee for War Employment; Chairman, Sub-Committee Recreation for War Workers; Member of Housing Sub-Committee, War Workers; Red Cross Committee; Food Economy Campaign Committee; Chairman, Care of Maternity Committee; Lecturer, Food Economy Campaign; Chairman and Co-foundress, Dunsmoor Nursery and Maternity Home; assisted in raising very large sums of money for war charities; Treasurer, Wheatley St. War Savings' Association. *Address:* 4, Fairfax Street, Coventry.   (M1656)

DIXEY, Evelyn Hilda, M.B.E., *b.* 24 Aug. 1891; *d.* of H. E. Dixey, D.L., J.P., of Malvern, Worcs. *Educ.:* Malvern and Brussels. *War Work:* Quartermaster of Red Cross Hospital, Malvern, from Oct. 1914, to May, 1919; three separate buildings, 100 patients in all. *Address:* Woodgate, Malvern, Worcestershire.   (M1657)

DIXON, Comm. Alan, O.B.E., R.N.

DIXON, Arthur Lewis, C.B.E., B.A., *b.* 30 Jan. 1888; *s.* of Rev. Seth Dixon, Wesleyan Minister; *m.* Marie Price. *Educ.:* Kingswood School, Bath; Sidney Sussex College, Cambridge. Assistant Secretary, Home Office. *Address:* Dudbrooke House, Eardley Road, Sevenoaks. *Club:* National.   (C146)

DIXON, Lieut. Arthur Tollemache, O.B.E., D.C.L.I.

DIXON, Lieut.-Col. Charles Egerton, O.B.E.

DIXON, Qr.-Mr. and Major Charles Joseph, O.B.E.

DIXON, Charles William, M.B.E., *b.* 29 April, 1888; *s.* of late John W. Dixon, of Manchester. *Educ.:* Clifton; Balliol College, Oxford. 2nd Class Clerk, Colonial Office, 1911; Private Secretary to the Permanent Under Secretary of State, 1917; Principal, 1920. *Address:* Colonial Office, S.W. 1.   (M328)

DIXON, Edgar Geoffrey, O.B.E., A.C.A., *b.* 11 May, 1880; *s.* of William Dixon, of Liverpool; *m.* Beatrice Edith, *d.* of Col. J. Binning, C.I.E., of Calcutta. *Educ.:* Rossall. Chartered Accountant; Director, Turner, Morrison & Co., Ltd., 6, Lyons Range, Calcutta. *Address:* Post Box No. 68, Calcutta. *Clubs:* Oriental (London); Bengal; Saturday; Tollygunge; Jodhpur; Barrackpore, all of Calcutta.   (O8286)

DIXON, Edgar George, O.B.E.

DIXON, Edward, O.B.E.

DIXON, Major Edward Travers, O.B.E., R.A.

DIXON, Elizabeth Amy, Mrs., M.B.E.

DIXON, Major Frederick Frank, O.B.E.

DIXON, George Finley, M.B.E.

DIXON, Capt. George Seymour, M.B.E., *b.* 28 July, 1895; *s.* of Mrs. K. Deighton Dixon, of Newcastle-on-Tyne. *Educ.:* Sherborne School; Wye Agricultural Coll., Kent. Civil Service. *War Work:* Enlisted Aug. 1914; Commissioned 28 Oct. 1914; Adjutant, 2/4th Buffs (E.K.R.), June, 1915, to Sept. 1917; Assist. Brigade Major, 86th Brigade, 29th Division, Oct. 1917, to Jan. 1918; wounded, Battle of Lys, 11 April, 1918; Adjutant, 1st Royal Guernsey Light Infantry, July, 1918, to Jan. 1919; General Staff Officer, 3rd Grade, at G.H.Q., B.E.F., France, Jan. 1919, to May, 1919; G.S.O., 3rd Grade, G.H.Q., British troops in France and Flanders, May to Oct. 1919; Staff Capt., G.H.Q., British troops in France and Flanders, Oct. to Dec. 1919. *Address:* The Inglenook, Ashtead, Surrey. *Club:* New Oxford and Cambridge. (O5197)

DIXON, Gertrude Caroline, C.B.E.

DIXON, Col. Graham Patrick, C.B.E., Aust. A.M.C.

DIXON, Harold Bailey, C.B.E., F.R.S., Ph. D., M.A.

DIXON, Capt. Herbert, O.B.E., M.P.

DIXON, Jennie, Mrs., M.B.E., B.A. (Lond.); *d.* of M. Earlam, of Davenham, Northwich; *m.* John Frank, *s* of J. J Dixon, of Northwich. *Educ.:* Northwich High School, and Univ. Coll., Aberystwyth. *War Work:* Quartermaster, and afterwards Commandant and Officer in charge of the Dowery Auxiliary Military Hospital, Nantwich, Cheshire. *Address:* 8, Dysart Buildings, Nantwich, Cheshire.   (M7912)

DIXON, Kate Alice, Mrs., M.B.E., *b.* June, 1874; *d.* of John Robinson, of Esher; *m.* Charles Harvey, *s.* of Henry Dixon, of Watlington. *War Work:* Sec. and Guarantor to the Uppingham Auxiliary Hospital; Sec. to the Herb Section and Horticultural Section Women's Legion, Rutland Branch. *Address:* Gunthorpe, Oakham. *Club:* Ladies' Athenæum.   (M7913)

DIXON, Comm. Kennet, C.B.E., R.N. *War Work:* Employed in Office of Admiral Comdg. Coastguard and Reserves and as Port Mine Sweeping and Mine Clearance Officer. (C2219)

DIXON, Rev. Leonard Alexander, O.B.E., *b.* 2 July, 1889; *s.* of the Rev. Canon Dixon, of Toronto, Canada. *Educ.:* St. Alban's School, Toronto; Univ. of Toronto; and Wycliffe Coll., Toronto. Sec. Foreign Department, International Committee Y.M.C.A. *War Work:* Gen. Sec. Y.M.C.A. with Mesopotamian Expeditionary Force, 1915–19. *Address:* 5, Russell Street, Calcutta, India.   (O1292)

DIXON, Capt. Robert Garside, O.B.E., M.B., Ch.B., *b.* 1881; *s.* of George Edward Dixon, of East Chevin, Otley; *m.* Gertrude, *d.* of James Storey, of Ben Rhydding. *Educ.:* Leeds Univ. Hon. Surgeon, Bingley Cottage Hospital; Medical Referee under Pensions Ministry. *War Work:* 2nd West Riding Field Ambulance, Aug. 1914, to Jan. 1915; Surgical Specialist (acting Major), 58th (West Riding) Casualty Clearing Station, France, Jan. 1915, to Feb. 1919. *Address:* Old School House, Bingley, Yorks.   (O5198)

DIXON, Major Sydney Wentworth, O.B.E., *b.* 6 March, 1868; *s.* of William Hepworth Dixon. Late Capt. 3rd Batt. The Manchester Regt. (Militia); joined R.A.S.C. Horse Transport, Aug. 27, 1914.   (O8796)

DIXON, William Chester, O.B.E.   (O5199)

DIXON, Surg.-Lieut. Walter Ernest, O.B.E., M.D., R.N.

DIXON, Walter Reginald, M.B.E.

DIXON, William Vibart, O.B.E., *b.* 25 Dec. 1850; *s.* of Rev. John Dixon, M.A. Camb., Vicar of Hoe, etc. Suffolk; *m.* Muriel, *d.* of Richard Ernest Langhorne, of Woolley Moor House, near Wakefield. *Educ.:* Aldeburgh Grammar School. Deputy Clerk of Peace and County Council of West Riding of Yorks.; Solicitor, West Riding Asylums Board. *War Work:* Hon. Sec. of various bodies, including W. Riding Appeal Tribunal, E. Central Division; W. Riding War Agricultural and Executive Committees; W. Riding War Pensions Committee; W. Riding Distress Committee etc.; Chairman of Thorner Sailors' and Soldiers' Fund. *Address:* Westfield House, Thorner, near Leeds. *Club:* Wakefield and County.   (O296)

DOBB, Capt. Harry Raymond, O.B.E., *b.* 19 Dec. 1890; *s.* of Harry Dobb, of Shiplake, Oxfordshire. *Educ.:* Tonbridge School, and Pembroke Coll., Cambridge. *War Work:* Served in France, 1914–15; Salonica, 1915–16; England, 1916–19; North Russia, 1918–19. *Address:* Martlets, Shiplake, Oxfordshire. *Clubs:* Leander; Isthmian; Officers', Aldershot.   (O9716)

DOBBIN, Roy Samuel, O.B.E., M.D., B.Ch., B.A.O., B.A., *b.* 5 May, 1872; *s.* of Samuel Dobbin, of Dublin, Ireland. *Educ.:* Trinity Coll., Dublin. Professor of Midwifery and Gynæcology, Government School of Medicine, Cairo, Egypt. *War Work:* Surgical Specialist, British Expeditionary Force, France; served also with the armies of the Black Sea. *Address:* Khedivial Buildings, rue Emad et Dine, Cairo. *Club:* Turf (Cairo).   (O5200)

DOBBIN, Lieut.-Col. William James Knowles, C.B.E. Lieut.-Col. Rifle Brig. (T.F.); served in the Great War, 1914–19 (despatches). (C1378)

DOBBIN, Major William Wood, M.B.E., A.M.F., *b.* 11 April, 1859; *s.* of George Dobbin, of Armagh, late R.E.; *m.* Kate Shaw, *d.* of Henry McLaughlin, of Osborne Park, Belfast. *Educ.:* Royal Academical Institution, Belfast. Adjutant, Victorian Mounted Rifles; Commanded 3rd Victorians, South African War (King and Queen's Medals, 7 Bars); Governor, Irish Prison Service, 1903; Borstal, 1902. *War Work:* Commandant local St. John Ambulance Brigade, 1914; County Director, Joint Red Cross and St. John Organisations; 500 Ex-Borstal young men joined the colours. (M7915)

DOBBINGS, William, M.B.E., *b.* 1859; *s.* of William Dobbings, of Leeds, Yorks; *m.* Elizabeth, *d.* of Matthew Waugh, of Bradford, Yorks. *Educ.:* Kippax (Yorks.) Collegiate School. Foreman, Royal Arsenal Thames Shipbuilding Co., etc. *War Work:* Manufacture of Ordnance; Dilution Officer, Ministry of Munitions; Investigation Officer, Ministry of Munitions and Ministry of Labour. *Address:* 238, Plumstead Common Road, London, S.E. 18. (M7916)

DOBBS, Col. Charles Fairlie, C.B.E., D.S.O.; *b.* 1872. Major and Brevet Lieut.-Col. Indian Army; served in Aden, 1903–4, and in the Great War, 1914–18. (C3089)

DOBBS, Col. Conway Richard, O.B.E., R.E.

DOBBS, Col. George Cadell, O.B.E., Indian Army (retired), *b.* 3 July, 1849; *s.* of Major-Gen. R. S. Dobbs, Madras Staff Corps; *m.* Sophy de Moleyns, *d.* of Rev. William Prior Moore, M.A. *Educ.:* Privately. Commissary-General, Bengal and Bombay. *War Work:* Hon. Sec. to Executive Committee, Soldiers' and Sailors' Help Society, Irish Branch. *Address:* Winton Lodge, Monkstown, Co. Dublin. (O3691)

DOBIE, Herbert, M.B.E., M.D. (Edin.), M.R.C.S., L.R.C.P., *b.* 6 June, 1865; *s.* of Dr. W. M. Dobie, of Chester; *m.* Margaret Ann, *d.* of James McIsaac, of Parkend, Saltcoats. *Educ.:* Marlborough; Edinburgh Univ.; London, Vienna, and Dresden. *War Work:* Medical Officer in charge of Eaton Hall Auxiliary Military Hospital, near Chester; afterwards in charge of Oakfields Auxiliary Military Hospital, Upton, Chester. *Address:* Northdene, Chester. (M7917)

DOBLE, Capt. William Alfred, M.B.E., A.P.C., E.A.F.

DOBRÉE, Alfred, C.B.E.; *b.* 1864; *s.* of the Rev. Canon Osmond Dobrée, of Colwich, Staffordshire. Consulting Engineer; Member of Royal Institution, Royal Asiatic Soc., and Royal United Service Institution, Hon. Member R.A. Institution, Member Ordnance Committee, Min. of Munitions, and a Fellow of Physical Soc. *Address:* 11, Palace Street, Buckingham Gate, S.W.1. *Club:* Savile. (C487)

DOBSON, Major Andrew Edward Augustus, O.B.E., M.A.; *b.* 1 Jan. 1885; *s.* of Col. A. F. Dobson, late I.M.S.; *m.* Deborah Clare, *d.* of the Rev. T. Sarsfield Hall, late Vicar of Doddington, Kent. *Educ.:* Heidelberg and Warwick. Obtained a commission as 2nd Lieut. in the Royal Garrison Artillery from the Royal Military Academy, 29 July, 1904; promoted Lieut., 29 July, 1907; passed as Instructor Signalling, Aldershot, 1908; German Interpreter, 1908; passed Advanced Class (*P.A.C.*), 1912; appointed Assist. Inspector, Inspection Department, Woolwich Arsenal, 27 March, 1913. *War Work:* Was retained during the whole of the war in the Inspection Department, when the department was taken over by the Ministry of Munitions from the War Office; promoted Capt., 30 Oct. 1914; appointed Inspector, 14 April, 1916; promoted Major, 31 Oct. 1918; for valuable services rendered in connection with the war, promoted Brevet Major, 3 June, 1917; mentioned in despatches, 24 Feb. 1917. *Address:* 123, Coleraine Road, Blackheath, S.E., 3. (O7092)

DOBSON, Bernard Henry, C.B.E., I.C.S., *b.* 1 Jan. 1881; *s.* of Austin Dobson, of 75, Eaton Rise, Ealing, W.; *m.* Margaret Eleanor, *d.* of the late Col. M. T. Sale, C.M.G., R.E. *Educ.:* Clifton College; Emmanuel College, Cambridge. Assistant Commissioner, Punjab; Settlement Officer, Chenab Colony, 1911–15; Deputy Commissioner, Lyallpur, 1919. *War Work:* War Office, 1915–16; Assistant Director, Commission Internationale de Ravitaillement, 1916–19; Member of Lord Milner's sub-committee of the War Cabinet on Russian Supplies, 1917–18. *Clubs:* Athenæum; Bath; United Service; Simla. (C2565)

DOBSON, Capt. Geoffrey William, O.B.E., R.A.F.

DOBSON, 2nd Lieut. George Herbert, M.B.E. (M10218)

DOBSON, Capt. Maurice Rowland, O.B.E., M.B., R.A.M.C.

DOBSON, Capt. William, M.B.E.

DOBSON, Lieut. William Frederick, M.B.E., R.E.

DOCKER, Capt. Cyril Talbot, M.B.E.

DOCKERY, Owen, M.B.E., H.S.B., Divisional Superintendent, St. John Ambulance, *b.* 1859; *s.* of T. Dockery, of Dublin; *m.* Mary, *d.* of John Quinn, of Co. Tyrone. *War Work:* District Head, Soldiers' and Sailors' Help Society, and Soldiers' and Sailors' Families Association; Member of Local War Pension Committee; rendered first aid to a large number (over 300) torpedoed crews who arrived in Galway Bay during the war; also to His Majesty's Forces during the Rebellion in 1916. (M7918)

DOCKRELL, Capt. George Shannon, O.B.E.

DOD, Capt. Francis Sandford, O.B.E., F.A.I., F.C.I.A., *b.* 27 July, 1888; *e. s.* of Francis Augustus Dod, J.P., F.A.I., of Stoke Newington; *m.* Bertha Ivy, *d.* of Lieut.-Col. J. J. Fox,

O.B.E., of Streatham. *Educ.:* Merchant Taylors' School. Surveyor, Assessor, and Auctioneer; Freeman of the City of London; Liveryman of the Farriers' Company. *War Work:* 2nd Lieut. A.S.C., Oct. 1915; Lieut., Feb. 1916; Capt., May, 1918; served in Malta as Purchasing and Compensation Officer, Nov. 1916 to, June, 1917; Staff Capt. (Q.M.G. Dept.), War Office, July, 1917, to Feb. 1919. *Addresses:* Rosslyn, Manor Road, N. 16; 11, Grocers' Hall Court, London, E.C. 2. *Clubs:* Sports; Royal Army Service Corps. (O7094)

DODD, John William, O.B.E.

DODD, Peter, M.B.E.

DODDS, Lieut. Archibald Forbes, O.B.E., R.A.O.C.

DODDS, Helen, Lady, C.B.E.; 2nd *d.* of Capt. E. Picton Baumgarten, late 10th Hussars; *m.* 19 June, 1889, Sir James Miller, K.C.B. (*see* BURKE'S *Peerage*), 2nd *s.* of the Rev. James Dodds, D.D., Minister of Corstophine, Midlothian. (C488)

DODDS, Major Jackson, O.B.E., R.A.O.C.

DODDS, Lionel, O.B.E., B.A., M.D., *b* 1881; *s.* of Thomas Dodds, of Buenos Aires; *m.* Helena, *d.* of Robert Rodman, of Glasgow. *Educ.:* National Coll.; Univ. of Buenos Aires. Medical Doctor; Assist. Oculist to the Univ. Hospital; Chief Oculist to the Alvear Hospital. *War Work:* Revised the eyesight of all the volunteers from the Argentine Republic; tested them for glasses, and put them in condition for service. *Address:* Maipu 794, Buenos Aires. *Club:* Strangers'. (O10313)

DODDS, Mary Janet, O.B.E., *b.* 8 Nov. 1869; *d.* of Rev. James Dodds, D.D., of Corstorphine Parish Church. *Educ.:* Park School, Glasgow; Ladies' Coll., Edinburgh; School of Medicine for Women, Edinburgh. Medical Missionary, and Deaconess, Church of Scotland, Poona, India. *War Work:* Scottish Churches' Huts, Dreghorn, Colinton. *Club:* Caledonian, Edinburgh. (O10314)

DODDS, Lieut. Theodore Edwin, M.B.E., R.F.A.

DODDS, Thomas Liddell, O.B.E., J.P., *b.* 5 Feb. 1846; *s.* of William Dodds, of Newcastle; *m.* Jane Widdofield, *d.* of Stephen Raseby, of Durham. *Educ.:* Hexham. Ex-Mayor of Birkenhead; Chairman of Licensing Bench. *War Work:* Chairman of Tribunal; Sub-Commissioner for Birkenhead and District. *Address:* 8, Charlesville, Birkenhead. (O1293)

DODGSON, Capt. Arthur Douglas, O.B.E., *b.* 22 Aug. 1884; *s.* of William Henley Dodgson, of Keston; *m.* Juliet Henrietta, *d.* of F. Hugh Capron, of Northgate, Regent's Park. *Educ.:* Winchester, and Christ Church, Oxford. Stock Broker. *War Work:* R.A.S.C., Newhaven, Egypt, Palestine, Syria; Officer in charge Supplies, Jaffa, Sarona, Beirut, and Tripoli. *Address:* 13, Kent Terrace, Regent's Park, N.W. 1. (O6169)

DODGSON, Campbell, C.B.E., *b.* 13 Aug. 1867; *s.* of William Oliver Dodgson, of Manor House, Sevenoaks; *m.* Frances Catharine, *d.* of Rev. W. A. Spooner, DD., Warden of New College, Oxford. *Educ.:* Winchester and New College, Oxford. Keeper of Prints and Drawings, British Museum, 1912. *War Work:* Assistance given to the propaganda work conducted at Wellington House, and afterwards by the Ministry of Information. *Address:* 22, Montagu Square, W. 1. *Clubs:* Athenæum; Burlington Fine Arts. (C489)

DODINGTON, Lieut.-Col. Roger MARRIOTT-, O.B.E., T.D., D.L., J.P. (*see* BURKE'S *Landed Gentry*), *b.* 30 July, 1866; *s.* of Thomas Marriott-Dodington, of Horsington; *m.* Mary Emeline Bertha, *d.* of Gen. Couper, I.S.C., of Combe, Dulverton. *Educ.:* Eton and Cambridge. *War Work:* Commanded West Somerset Yeomanry till autumn of 1916; then went to France on Staff of 1st Corps; mentioned in despatches, and O.B.E. for services. *Address:* Horsington House, Templecombe, Somerset. *Clubs:* Cavalry; Oxford and Cambridge. (O5541)

DODWORTH, Capt. Benjamin, O.B.E., T.F. Res.

DODSWORTH, Robinson Irving, O.B.E

DODSWORTH, Sir Matthew Blayney SMITH-, Bart., O.B.E., J.P., *b.* 26 Oct. 1856; *s.* of the late Sir Matthew Dodsworth, Bart., of Newland Park (*see* BURKE'S *Peerage*); *m.* Agnes Eliza, *d.* of John Crowder. *Educ.:* Richmond (Yorks.), and Oxford (Univ. Coll.). *War Work:* As Member of the National Council of Y.M.C.A. and Chairman of the Yorkshire Union Council of Y.M.C.A., engaged in work among the troops. *Address:* Thornton Watlass Hall, Bedale, Yorks. (O1294)

DODWELL, Charles Money, M.B.E., *b.* 20 Jan. 1892; *s.* of Edward Dodwell. *Educ.:* City of London School. Deputy Accounts Officer, Admiralty. *War Work:* Advisory work on Navy Separation Allowances. *Address:* Foxley Hall, Purley, Surrey. (M1659)

DOERY, George Henry, O.B.E.

DOGGRELL, Capt. Enos, M.B.E., *b.* 8 May, 1875; *s.* of Enos Doggrell, of Motcombe, Dorset. *Educ.:* Shaftesbury. *War Work:* Adjutant and Armament Major, R.G.A., South Gibraltar. *Address:* Ivy Cottage, Semley, Shaftesbury, Dorest. (M5225)

DOHERTY, Arthur Edward, M.B.E.

DOHERTY, Francis Cecil, M.B.E., B.A., *b.* 10 Nov. 1892; *s.* of William Pemble Doherty; *m.* Marjorie Banks, *d.* of George Sargent, of Chelmsford. *Educ.:* Westminster School, and Christ Church, Oxford. Assist. Master, Radley Coll., Berks *War Work:* Lieut., 5th Batt. Essex Regt. (T.F.). *Address:* East Cottage, Radley, Abingdon, Berks. (M5226)

DOIDGE, Major Herbert Frederick, O.B.E., R.A.S.C.

DOIDGE, Major R. C., O.B.E.

DOIG, Annie Emilia, M.B.E.; *d.* of James Scott Elliot, of Blackwood, Dumfriesshire; *m.* late Capt. Doig, Scottish Borderers. Y.M.C.A. *War Work:* France, 1914–16; "All Welcome Hut," Victoria, 1916–19. (M329)

DOIG, Claude Prendergast, O.B.E. (O7096)

DOIG, David, M.B.E., J.P.

DOLAND, Lieut.-Col. George Frederick, O.B.E., *b.* 1 May, 1872 ; *s.* of George Richard Doland, of Balham, London, S.W. ; *m.* Minnie Mary, *d.* of George Richardson, of Balham, London, S.W. *Educ.*: Privately. Member of Wandsworth Borough Council 10 years. *War Work*: Founder and Officer Commanding County of London Royal Army Service Corps, Motor Transport (Volunteers). *Address*: Taainga, Clarence Road, Clapham Park, S.W. 4. (O7097)

DOLLOND, Alfred Walter, M.B.E., *b.* 28 June, 1861 ; *s.* of the late William Dollond ; *m.* Louisa, *d.* of David Beadle, of Ightham, Kent. *Educ.*: Sir Anthony Browne's School, Brentwood. Clerk in War Office. *War Work*: Record of prisoners of war captured by the enemy. *Address*: Westcroft, Salisbury Road, Carshalton, Surrey. (M9720)

DOLMAGE, Capt. Francis Alfred Emilio, M.B.E.

DOLPHIN, John Byron, O.B.E., Chevalier de l'Ordre de Leopold, *b.* 19 April, 1877 ; *s.* of the late Rev. John Maximilian Dolphin, formerly of Long-Eaton Vicarage, Derbyshire (Hon. Canon of Southwell) ; *m.* Bertha Alice Lucy, *d.* of Thomas Furnival, of Bishopstone, Sussex. *Educ.*: Oundle School, Northants. H.M. Vice-Consul at Liége, Belgium, from 1907–14 inclusive. *War Work*: Assist. Representative, afterwards Representative, of Ministry of Munitions, at National Projectile Factory, Birtley, Co. Durham, 1915–19. *Address*: 3, Avenue du Hetre, Sclessin, Liége, Belgium. (O10515)

DOLTON, Capt. Herbert Edward, O.B.E.

DOMINY, Lieut.-Comm. Reginald Hugh, C.B.E., R.N.R.

DOMVILLE, Edward James, O.B.E., J.P., M.R.C.S. (Eng.), L.R.C.P. (Lond.), *b.* 14 Sept. 1848 ; *s.* of Rev. D. E. Domville, Chaplain, R.N. ; *m.* Lucy, *d.* of William Danby, of Elmfield, Exeter. *Educ.*: Royal Naval School, New Cross. Mayor of Exeter, 1893–94 ; Justice of the Peace, City and County of Exeter ; Consulting Surgeon, Royal Devon and Exeter Hospital. *War Work*: House Surgeon to Royal Devon and Exeter Hospital. *Address*: Shutes, Symondsbury, Bridport, Dorset. (O10316)

DON, Sir William, K.B.E., J.P., D.L., *b.* 1861 ; *s.* of James Don, of Dundee ; *m.* Martha Nicoll, *d.* of J. H. Lindsay, of Dundee. *Educ.*: Dundee High School. Deputy Lieutenant of the County of the City of Dundee ; Ex-Lord Provost of the City of Dundee. *War Work*: Chairman of Recruiting Committee ; National Service Committee ; Local War Pensions Committee ; Local Tribunal, etc. *Address*: Ardarroch, Dundee. *Club*: Eastern, Dundee. (K62)

DONALD, Cecile, Mrs., M.B.E., *b.* 1872 ; *d.* of Rev. George Woodberry Spooner, M.A., of Inglesham Vicarage, Gloucestershire Lieut.-Col. 1/4th Border Regt. ; *m.* William Nanson, *s.* of John Donald, of Carlisle. *Educ.*: Ascham Coll., Oxford ; Florence, Italy. Mayoress of Carlisle, 1917–18. *War Work*: Commandant of Chadwick Auxuliary Military Hospital from 1915–18. *Address*: Inglesham, The Scaur, Carlisle. (M1661)

DONALD, Major-Gen. Colin George, C.B., C.B.E. *War Work*: Did valuable work in connection with the Imperial War Museum. (C139)

DONALD David Angus M.B.E. (M10247)

DONALD, Duncan, O.B.E., *b.* 30 June, 1864 ; *s.* of A. J. S. Donald ; *m.* Isabelle Anne, *d.* of W. W. Robertson. *Educ.*: Bishop Cotton School, Simla. Indian Police, retired ; now serving as Superintendent Central Jail, Lahore. *War Work*: Served in the Burma War (medal and clasp) ; subsequently earned the King's Police Medal ; mentioned and thanked by H.E. The Commander-in-Chief for war work during 1915–17. (O8287)

DONALD, Ethel Maud, M.B.E.

DONALD, George GRAY-, O.B.E., R.E.

DONALD, Capt. George Reid, M.B.E.

DONALD Capt. Robert, M.B.E., R.A.F.

DONALD, Robert, M.B.E., *b.* 7 May, 1879 ; *s.* of Robert Donald, of Banchory. *Educ.*: Central Public Higher Grade School, Banchory. General Merchant, Town Councillor ; Sec. to the St. Ternan Lodge of Oddfellows. *War Work*: Sec. and Treas. of the Banchory War Savings Association ; also of the Upper Deeside District Local Central War Savings Committee. *Address*: Woodside, Arbeadie, Banchory, Kincardine, Scotland. (M7921)

DONALD, William, M.B.E.

DONALD, Capt. William Hamish, O.B.E.

DONALDSON, Ada Maud, Mrs., M.B.E.

DONALDSON, Major Arthur William Hunter, O.B.E., M.B., B.Ch. (Oxon.), M.R.C.S., L.R.C.P., R.A.M.C., *b.* 12 Oct. 1885 ; *s.* of Daniel Donaldson, of Vancouver, B.C., Canada. *Educ.*: Hertford Coll., Oxford ; St. Thomas' Hospital, London. Medical Officer, Somaliland Protectorate. *War Work*: Attached Cambridge Hospital, Aldershot, Jan. to July, 1915 ; Surgical Specialist, 18th Casualty Clearing Station, France, till April, 1919. *Addresses*: St. Thomas' Hospital, S.E. 1 ; c/o Medical Dept., Berbera, British Somaliland. (O5026)

DONALDSON, Lieut. Ernest, O.B.E., R.N.R.

DONALDSON, George Lester, M.B.E.

DONALDSON, Norman Patrick, C.B.E.

DONALDSON, Qr.-Mr. and Capt. Robert Inglis, O.B.E.

DONCASTER, Robert, O.B.E., J.P.

DONKIN, Major Herbert Julyan, M.B.E., R.E.

DONNAN, Frederick George, C.B.E., M.A., Ph.D., D.Sc., F.I.C., F.R.S., *b.* 6 Sept. 1870 ; *s.* of William Donnan, of Holywood, Co. Down, Ireland. *Educ.*: Universities of Belfast ; Berlin ; and London. Professor of General Chemistry University College, University of London ; A Vice-President of the Chemical Society of London, and of the Faraday Society. *War Work*: Member of the Munitions Inventions Panel, and of the Nitrogen Products Committee of the Munitions Inventions Department ; Member of the Chemical Warfare Committee, Ministry of Munitions of War ; rendered assistance to the Department of Explosives Supply, the Admiralty Hydrogen Committee, and the Air Ministry. *Address*: 23, Woburn Square, London, W.C. 1. *Clubs*: Savile ; University, Liverpool ; Royal North of Ireland Yacht. (C2568).

DONNELLY, Major John William, O.B.E., A.I.F.

DONNER, Anna Maria, Lady, D.B.E., *d.* of W. A. Cunnham, of Manchester ; *m.* Sir Edward Donner, 1st Bart., *s.* of Edward Sedgfield Donner, of Scarborough. *War Work*: Vice-President, Fallowfield and Burnage Division, British Red Cross Society ; Organiser of Fairview Auxiliary Hospital, Fallowfield ; President, Manchester War Hospital Supply Depot. *Address*: Oak Mount, Fallowfield, Manchester. (D28)

DONOHUE, Col. William Edward, C.B.E., M. Inst. C.E., R.A.S.C., *b.* May, 1861 ; *s.* of Timothy Donohue, of Clonakilty, Co. Cork ; *m.* Frances Martha, *d.* of John Everett, of London. *Educ.*: Privately and Royal College of Science, London. Chairman of Motorists Association, Egypt ; Director, Egyptian Transport Company, Alexandria. *War Service*: Chief Inspector of Mechanical Transport and Officer in charge of Home Base Depots, for supply of Equipment and Mechanical Transport Stores, Aug. 1914–16 ; Inspector of Mechanical Transport Services, Eastern theatres of operations, Egypt, Salonika, East Africa, Mesopotamia, Persia, Palestine, 1916–19. *Address*: 25, Harrington Gardens, South Kensington, London. *Clubs*: Royal Automobile (London) ; Union (Alexandria, Egypt). (C490).

DONOHUE, Lieut. William James, O.B.E., R.N.

DONOVAN, Capt. Thomas Christopher, O.B.E., M.C., R.G.A., *b.* 24 Dec. 1881 ; *s.* of Thomas Donovan, of Dublin ; *m.* Bridget Mary, *d.* of Thomas Moran, of Dublin. *Educ.*: Donnybrook National School. Enlisted at Dublin into the Royal Garrison Artillery, 5 Oct. 1899 ; rank of Master Gunner at outbreak of war ; served in Malta, Ceylon, Hongkong, Singapore and Sierra Leone. *War Service*: Ministry of Munitions, 18 Nov. 1915, to April, 1916 ; 127th Siege Battery, Salonica, July, 1916, to Jan. 1917 ; Ammunition Duties, R.A.O.C., Salonica, Jan. 1917 to Feb. 1919 ; in charge of Ammunition Services, Denniken's force, South Russia, March, 1919, to Dec. 1919 ; awarded O.B.E. for this service and given the order of Saint Anne, Class II., by Russian authorities ; granted M.C. for saving an ammunition depot on fire, caused by air raid ; mentioned in despatches. (O9740)

DOOLAN, Edmond, M.B.E., R.F.A.

DOOLEY, Lieut. John, M.B.E., R.N.

DOOLEY, Lieut. Raymond, M.B.E.

DOONER, Lieut.-Col. William Dundas, C.M.G., O.B.E. ; *b.* 1876 ; *o. surv. s.* of William Toker Dooner, of Ditton Place nr. Maidstone. Entered Roy. Irish Fusiliers 1895 ; Major, Brevet Lieut.-Col. R.A.O.C. ; S. African War, 1899–1900, with Roy. Irish Fusiliers (severely wounded, Queen's medal with two clasps). *Address*: 4, Rosary Gardens, S.W.7. *Club*: Army and Navy. (O7008)

DOONER, Col. William Toke, M.B.E., J.P. Hon. Sec., Chatham Military Division of Soldiers' and Sailors' Families Association. (M10312)

DOOR, Reginald Edmund, M.B.E.

DOPPING-HEPENSTAL, Major Lambert John, O.B.E., D.L., J.P., R.E. (ret.), *b.* 3 Aug. 1859 ; (*see* BURKE'S *Landed Gentry*) ; *s.* of the late Col. R. A. Dopping-Hepenstal, D.L., J.P., of Derrycassan, Granard ; *m.* Amy Maude, *d.* of Major C. R. W. Tottenham, D.L., J.P., of Woodstock, Co. Wicklow, and Plas Berwyn, N. Wales. *Educ.*: Harrow and Woolwich. *War Work*: Volunteered for service 4 Aug. 1914, and served through out the Great War until Nov. 1919 ; awarded Egyptian War Medal and Star, 1882. *Address*: Derrycassan, Granard, Co. Longford ; 73, Harcourt Street, Dublin. *Club*: Kildare Street, Dublin. (O8797

DORAN, David John, M.B.E., *b.* 1860 ; *s.* of W. J. Doran, of Ireland ; *m.* Eliza Ann, *d.* of John Kelly, Freeman of City of London, and Freemason. *Educ.*: Aberystwyth Grammar School. Principal Clerk, Chief Goods Manager's Office, Great Western Railway, Paddington. *War Work*: Had to deal with the conveyance of all descriptions of explosives, inflammable liquids, dangerous chemicals, gases, etc., for the Great Western Railway, and in association with other Railway Companies ; also the problems arising in connection therewith ; Member of Railway Companies Joint Standing Committee on Explosives ; holds Long Service Medal and King's Medal for service in Metropolitan Special Constabulary. (M7923)

DORAN, Lieut.-Col. John Crampton Morton, C.B.E., D.S.O. ; *b.* 1880 ; *s.* of the late Rev. J. Wilberforce Doran, of Souldern, Oxon ; *m.* Hester Maude, *d.* of Edward Field, of Blackdown Hill, Leamington. *Educ.*: St. Edward's School, Summertown, Oxford. Entered Army Service Corps, 1902 ; Major, 1914 ; Brevet Lieut.-Col. 1918 ; served during S. African War, 1901–1902 (medal with five clasps); in Somaliland ; 1908–10 (medal with clasp) ; Great War, 1914–15, on Staff (despatches twice) ; appointed Dep. Assist. Director of Supplies, War Office, 1915, and an Assist. Director, 1917. *Address*: Charlbury, Oxon. (C1545)

DORMAN, Sir Arthur John, K.B.E., J.P., N.R., Yorks ; *b.* 8 Aug., 1848 ; *s.* of late Charles Dorman, of Ashford, Kent ; *m.*

18 Sept., 1873, Clara Share, *d.* of late George Lockwood, of Stockton-on-Tees. Chairman of Messrs. Dorman, Long & Co., of Middlesbrough. *Address:* Grey Towers, Nunthorpe, Yorks. *Clubs:* St. Stephen's and Junior Athenæum. (K63)

DORMAN, Capt. Bedford Lockwood, O.B.E., *b.* 1879; *s.* of Sir Arthur J. Dorman, K.B.E., of Grey Towers, Nunthorpe; *m.* Constance Phelps, *d.* of A. S. Hay, of Sacombe Park, Ware. *Educ.:* Rugby and Trinity College, Cambridge. Barrister-at-Law. *War Service:* Temp. Lieut., A.O.D., Dec. 1914; Staff Captain, Directorate of Artillery. War Office, 1916. *Address:* Enterpen Hall, Hutton Rudly. *Club:* Conservative. (O1297)

DORMER, Alfred James, M.B.E., *b.* 30 March, 1866; *s.* of Richard Dormer, of Reading; *m.* Edith, *d.* of James Malham, of Reading. *Educ.:* St. Mary's School, Reading. *War Work:* Welfare of Soldiers in Reading. *Address:* 68, Elgar Road, Reading. (M7924)

DORMER, Capt. Charles Joseph Thaddeus, Lord, C.B.E., R.N., J.P., D.L., Gent. Usher, (*see* BURKE'S *Peerage*), *b.* 24 Feb. 1864; *s.* of the late Hon. Sir James C. Dormer, K.C.B., *m.* Caroline May, *d.* of Col. Sir Spencer Cavendish Clifford, Bart., of Westfield, Ryde, Isle of Wight. *Educ.:* Oscott Coll. J.P. and D.L. for Warwickshire; Gentleman Usher to H.M. the King. *War Service:* Admiralty War Staff; Chairman of a Committee, War Trade Department. *Address:* Grove Park, Warwick. *Club:* Naval and Military. (C147)

DORRELL, William John, M.B.E.

DORRIEN, Olive Crofton, Lady SMITH-, D.B.E.; *o. d.* of Col. John Schneider, of Oak Lee, Furness Abbey; *m.* 3 Sept., 1902, Gen. Sir Horace Lockwood, G.C.B., G.C.M.G., D.S.O. (*see* BURKE'S *Peerage*), 5th *s.* of Col. Robert Algernon Smith-Dorrien, of Haresfoot, Herts (*see* BURKE'S *Landed Gentry*). (D19)

DORRINGTON, Lieut. Frederick James, M.B.E., R.A.O.C.

DOTT, George, M.B.E., J.P., *b.* 26 July, 1855; *s.* of William Dott, of Moffat; *m.* Georgina, *d.* of William Law, of Midlothian. *Educ.:* Newington Public School, Edinburgh. Member of Glasgow Town Council; ex-Chairman of Glasgow Parish Council; Chairman of Old Age Pensions Sub-Committee, District 7, Glasgow. *War Work:* Member of Glasgow Local Committee, War Pensions Acts, 1915-19; Chairman of Central and Kelvingrove Division, 64, Berkeley Street. *Addresses:* 42, Elderslie Street, Glasgow; Brookville, North Mount Vernon, Tollcross. (M7925)

DOTTRIDGE, Edwin Thomas, C.B.E., Chevalier of the Order of the Crown of Italy, *b.* 1876; *s.* of Alfred James; *m.* Mabel Florence, *d.* of the late Walter Hudson, of Hastings, and widow of the late Clement Tulloch of the Hong Kong and Shangai Banking Corporation. *Educ.:* Privately. Director of Messrs. J. Travers & Sons, Ltd. *War Work:* 1916, Visited Italy (Rome, Piacenza, Palma, Turin, Ancona, Bari, Naples, Messina, Catania, Syracuse) for the purpose of making a report to the President of the Board of Trade; 1917, visited Rome for the purpose of investigating and making a report to the Foreign Office on certain trade matters; 1917-19, organised and carried out a scheme for the solution of a semi-political difficulty in connection with food supplies. *Address:* 47, St. George's Court, Gloucester Road, Kensington. *Club:* Junior Constitutional. (C2569)

DOUBLEDAY, Capt, Charles Edward, O.B.E., *b.* 21 June, 1871. *Educ.:* Simon Langton School, Canterbury. Principal Clerk, Paymaster-General's Office, S.W. 1. *War Work:* Served in the Civil Service Rifles from mobilisation, 4 Aug. 1914, to 11 Oct. 1918; Hon. Sec. of the Civil Service Rifles Regimental Aid Fund and Prisoners of War Committee; O.B.E. awarded for services in the Paymaster-General's Dept. subsequent to Oct. 1918. *Address:* Paymaster-General's Office, Whitehall, S.W. (O10317)

DOUGALL, John, M.B.E.,

DOUGAN, James Lockhart, C.B.E., M.A., *b.* 1 Jan. 1874; *s.* of John Dougan, of Belfast; *m.* Margaret, *d.* of John Morton, of Glasgow, *Educ.:* Oxford University. City Librarian, Oxford, to 1919. *War Work:* Hon. Sec., War Emergency Fund, Oxford; Hon. Sec., National Service Committee, Oxford; Director of Missing and Wounded Department for the Mediterranean Area (British Red Cross); Hon. Executive Officer, Food Control Committee, Oxford; Assistant Divisional Commissioner, South Midland Division Ministry of Food, Member of Inter-allied Commission of Relief for Southern Europe; Representative in Vienna of Vienna Emergency Relief Fund. *Address:* 20, Beech Croft Road, Oxford. (C2570)

DOUGHERTY, Aileen Margaret, M.B.E.

DOUGHTY, Beatrice Mary Constance, M.B.E., *b.* 19 July, 1861; *d.* of Rear Admiral Frederic Proby Doughty, of Woodbridge, Suffolk. *Educ.:* Privately in England; 2 years in Paris and Frankfurt-am-Main; studied painting 2 years in Monsieur Blanc Garin's studio, Brussels; 1 year Lady Pupil at Guy's Hospital (certificate). Co-opted member of Lowestoft Education Committee, and Chairman of School Management; Hon. Sec. Waifs and Strays Society, Lowestoft Home. *War Work:* President of Welcome Club for men of H.M. Forces and local girls, 1915-19; took part of school nurse's work when she was called up on Territorial Scheme; Night Nurse and Kitchen Assist. as required at Gunton Cottage Hospital for several months, 1915-19. *Address:* 1, High Street, Lowestoft. (M7926)

DOUGHTY, Frederick George, M.B.E., R.N.
DOUGLAS, Alfred, O.B.E., *b.* 9 Oct. 1872; *s.* of John

Douglas, of The Mains, Kirkoswald, Cumberland; *m.* Isobel Muriel Mary, *d.* of Lieut.-Col. W. H. D. Clark, of Hadley Wood. *Educ.:* Privately. Assistant Accountant-General of the Navy. *Address:* 64, Bedford Avenue, High Barnet. (O1298)

DOUGLAS, Allie Vibert, M.B.E.
DOUGLAS, Annie Jane, M.B.E.
DOUGLAS, Col. Archibald Philip, C.M.G., C.B.E. (C3091)
DOUGLAS, Capt. Archibald Sholto George, O.B.E.

DOUGLAS, George, M.B.E., F.R.P.S., *b.* 13 July, 1884; *s.* of Thomas Douglas, of Edinburgh; *m.* Thomasina Jane Clapperton, *d.* of John Douglas, of Peebles, Scotland. *Educ.:* Sciennes Public School, and Heriot Watt College, Edinburgh. Photographer; Superintendent, Photo-Process Office, Survey of Egypt, Giza (Mudiria), Egypt. *War Work:* Reproduction of maps, etc., for the Armies on the Gallipoli, Sinia, Palestine, and Arabian Fronts; Aerial Photographic Survey, X-ray work at the Giza Red Cross Hospital, Egypt. *Address:* Survey of Egypt, Giza (Mudiria), Egypt. *Club:* Gezira Sporting (Cairo). (M1144)

DOUGLAS, Capt. George Robert Poynter, O.B.E., M.C., *b.* 7 July, 1881; *s.* of the late T. Kennedy Douglas, M.B., C.M., of Scone, Perth; *m.* Jessie Ewan, *d.* of Col. Ewan Campbell, T.D., of Kingussie. *Educ.:* Perth Academy; Edinburgh University. *War Work:* 2 years with Highland Cyclist Batt.; 2½ years attached 8th Cheshires in Mesopotamia; 7 months M.L.O. to British Military Mission to South Russia. *Address:* Mount Place, Scone, Perth. (O9741)

DOUGLAS, Gwendoline Ethel, Mrs. Sholto, M.B.E.
DOUGLAS, Helen Mary Isabel, Mrs., O.B.E.
DOUGLAS, Paymaster-Lieut.-Comm. James, O.B.E., R.N.V.R. (S.A.)
DOUGLAS, Lieut. John Turner, M.B.E.
DOUGLAS, Capt. Robert Douglas Argyll, M.B.E., S.A.M.C., M.D.

DOUGLAS, Robert James, O.B.E., J.P., *b.* 19 April, 1865; *s.* of John Douglas, of Gordon St., Forres; *m.* Jeannie Henderson, *d.* of Alex. Baillie Gordon, of Helensburgh. *Educ.:* Forres Academy. Provost of Forres, 1908-20; Member of Morayshire Territorial Force Association and Morayshire County Council. *War Work:* Chairman, Military Tribunal, Food Control, Coal Control, and of Area Road Transport Committee for Northern Division of Scotland; Member of Red Cross Committee and of V.A.D. Hospital, Forres. *Address:* Ormidale, Forres. (O10318)

DOUGLAS, Lieut.-Col. Robert Vaughan, C.B.E., R.A., *b.* 29 June, 1881; *s.* of the late C. P. Douglas, of Chester; *m.* Gladys Mary, *d.* of Col. John Lewes, of Llanlear, Cardiganshire. *Educ.:* Cheltenham and Royal Military Academy. *Address:* c/o Messrs. Cox & Co., 16, Charing Cross, S.W. 1. *Club:* Army and Navy. (C2099)

DOUGLAS, Lieut. the Hon. Ronald John Sholto, O.B.E.
DOUGLAS, Samuel Henry, O.B.E., I.S.O., 26 July, 1858. *Address:* 119, Westminster Road, Handsworth, Birmingham. (O10319)

DOUGLAS, Comm. Sholto Grant, C.B.E., *b.* 1867; *s.* of the late Adm. Sholto Douglas, C.B.; *m.* 1896, Elizabeth, *d.* of the late J. W. Foran, of St. John, Newfoundland. R.N. (ret.); Div. Naval Transport Officer; served in the Egyptian Campaign, 1882 (medal, bronze star); Great War, 1914-19 (despatches); has King Edward VII. Coronation medal. *Address:* Sheet, Petersfield, Hants. (C2248)

DOUGLASS, Rev. Frederick Wingfield, O.B.E., M.C., M.A., Hon. C.F., *b.* 22 June, 1866; *s.* of J. H. Douglass, of Market Harborough. *Educ.:* Oakham; Christ Church, Oxford; Cuddesdon College. *War Service:* I.A.R.O., 2nd Lieut.; Acting Captain, 64 Bengal Labour Co.; France, 1917-18; T.C.F., 4th Class; B.E.F., 1918-19. *Address:* Oxford Mission, Calcutta, India. (O2498)

DOUGLASS, James Douglas Thessiger, M.B.E. (M6781a)

DOUGLASS, Major James Henry, O.B.E., M.D., D.P.H. R.A.M.C., *b.* 1877; *s.* of W. Douglass, of Stella, Penzance, Cornwall, late Engineer-in-Chief, Irish Lights; *m.* Constance, *d.* of Robert Arthur Holmes, late of Peterfield, Nenagh, Tipperary, Ireland. *Educ.:* Shrewsbury and Trinity Coll., Dublin. Entered service in Jan. 1904. Civil Surgeon, South African War, 1902, Queen's Medal, 3 clasps. *War Work:* From mobilisation to April, 1915, Company Officer, 14th Co. R.A.M.C., Dublin; May, 1915, to July, 1916, S.M.O., West African Command, Sierra Leone; Aug. to Nov. 1916, Dublin District; Dec. 1916, to April, 1919, France and Belgium; May, 1919, to Dec. 1919, Eastern Siberia. *Address:* Stella, Penzance, Cornwall. (O5207).

DOUGLASS, James Robertson, M.B.E., M.Inst.C.E., Hon. Lieut. 2nd Vol. Batt. The Black Watch, Royal Highlanders, *b.* 31 Aug. 1869; *s.* of Alexander Forbes Douglass, of The Mains, Haddo House, Aberdeenshire; *m.* Grace Hunter, *d.* of John Menzies Baillie, of Culter Allers, Lanarkshire. *Educ.:* Cargilfield, Edinburgh; Fettes College, Edinburgh; Edinburgh Univ. Assist. Harbour Engineer, Dundee Harbour Trust. *War Work:* Engaged in War Work in connection with the Ministry of Shipping, the War Office, and the Admiralty. *Address:* Greybank, Magdalen Yard Road, Dundee. (M7927)

DOUIE Lieut.-Col. Lawrence Adam, C.B.E. (C1138)

DOULTON, Alice Duneau, M.B.E., *d.* of Frederic Doulton, of Dulwich, S.E. *Educ.:* Privately. *War Work:* Aug. 1914, to Jan. 1920, Hon. Sec. Soldiers' and Sailors' Families Association; Hon. Sec. War Pensions Committee, Camberwell. *Address:* 22, Underhill Road, East Dulwich, S.E. 22. (M7928)

DOUTHWAITE, Capt. and Qr.-Mr. William Bernard, O.B.E.

DOVE, Edward James, O.B.E. Ministry of Food. (O11901)

DOVE, Lieut. John Scott, O.B.E., R.N.

DOVE, Margaret Anne, Mrs., M.B.E.

DOVE, Capt. Percy William, O.B.E., R.A.M.C., M.B.

DOVER, Alice Eliza, Mrs., M.B.E., *b.* 11 Feb. 1866; *d.* of Richard Wright, of London; *m.* Horace Walter, *s.* of John William Dover, of Princes Risborough, Bucks. *Educ.:* Southwell, Nottingham. *War Work:* Superintendent Northamptonshire Regimental Prisoners of War Depot; Member of Lady Buller's Hospital Supply Depot; member of Northampton Naval and Military War Pension Committee; Member of House Committee, Lady Margaret Spencer's Home of Rest for Convalescent Soldiers. *Address:* Holyrood, St. James, Northampton. *Clubs:* Ladies' (Northampton); Kingsthorpe Golf. (M7930)

DOW, James William, M.B.E., M.I.M.E.; *s.* of William Dow, of Branxton, Dysart, Fife; *m.* Mary, M.B.E. *q.v.*, *d.* of George Penty, of Thorntree Hill, Grimston, York. *Educ.:* Privately. Assist. Manager of the Carriage and Wagon Dept., North-Eastern Railway, at York. *War Work:* Special War Work in connection with the making of munitions. *Addresses:* Thorntree Hill, Grimston, York; 15, St. Olave's Road, York. *Club:* York City. (M1666)

DOW, Mary, Mrs., M.B.E.; *d.* of George Penty, of Thorntree Hill, Grimston, York; *m.* James William, M.B.E.*q.v.*, *s.* of William Dow, of Branxton, Dysart, Fife. *Educ.:* Dunnington, and Longley Coll., Easingwold. *War Work:* Voluntary clerical work in connection with recruiting; 5 years' voluntary service with the Y.M.C.A., serving in their canteens, organising concerts, etc., for the troops. *Addresses:* Thorntree Hill, Grimston, York; 15 St. Olave's Road, York. (M7931)

DOWBIGGIN, Annie, M.B.E., R.R.C.; *d.* of the late Richard Dowbiggin. Matron, Hospital, Edmonton, N. 18; Member of the following: General Nursing Council; Council, Royal British Nurses Association; Matrons Council of Great Britain and Ireland; Executive Committee and Vice-President, National Union of Trained Nurses. *War Work:* Matron, Special Military Surgical Hospital, Edmonton, N. 18. *Club:* Lyceum. (M3616)

DOWDELL, Staff Qr.-Mr. Sergt. George James, M.B.E., *b.* 21 Nov. 1882; *s.* of the late Edwin Dowdell, of Semley, Wilts.; *m.* Mabel Bond, *d.* of the late William John Baker, of Taunton, Somerset. *Educ.:* Semley School. Royal Army Pay Corps. *War Work:* Nursing Staff Accounts; Supt. Clerk, Clearing House and R.A.S.C. Accounts, Malta. *Address:* Army Pay Office, Perth, Scotland. (M5230)

DOWDING, Dorothy Carwithen, O.B.E.; *e.d* of the Rev. W. Berkeley Dowding (late Senior Chaplain to the Forces). *Educ.:* Royal School, Lansdowne, Bath. *War Work:* Nursed in hospital in London and the Isle of Wight, 1914–16; in January, 1917, was appointed personal assistant to Sir Bertram Cubitt, K.C.B., the Assist. Sec. of the War Office; in Jan. 1919, became a private secretary to Sir Reginald Brade, G.C.B., the Secretary of the War Office, and to his successor, Sir Herbert Creedy, K.C.B., C.V.O., in Jan. 1920. *Club:* New Victorian. (O10320)

DOWELL, Brig.-Gen. George William, C.M.G., C.B.E.

DOWER, Edward Maxwell, M.B.E.

DOWER, Mary, Mrs. GOUGH-, O.B.E., *b.* 7 Dec. 1863; *d.* of William Berresford-Gough, of Ballykerogue, Co. Waterford; *m.* John, *s.* of Capt. Augustin Dower, of Abbeyside. *Educ.:* The Convent, Stradbally. Hon. Sec. Dungarvan Local War Pensions Committee. *War Work:* Valuable work on the Co. Waterford War Pensions Committee; Hon. Sec. Dungarvan War Pensions Local Committee; mentioned to the Secretary of State for War for general Red Cross work; Hon. Recruiter, Q.M.A.A.C. *Address:* The Terrace, Dungarvan, Co. Waterford. (O10321)

DOWIE, Lieut.-Col. Lawrence Adam, C.B.E.

DOWLER, Edwin Harold, M.B.E.

DOWLING, Eng.-Comm. Horace Edward, O.B.E., R.N.

DOWLING, Lieut.-Col. Thomas, O.B.E., T.D., Croix de Guerre (Belgium), *b.* 24 Jan. 1867; *s.* of John Dowling, of Bishop Auckland; *m.* Constance Mary, *d.* of Sir Edward Fraser, D.C.L., J.P., of Nottingham. *Educ.:* Bishop Auckland. Solicitor. *War Service:* Served as Senior Supply Officer to the 50th (Northumbrian) Division and 3rd Division in France and Belgium; commanded, 63rd (Northumbrian) Divisional Train and the 41st Divisional Train in France, Belgium, Italy and Army of Occupation, Cologne; mentioned in despatches three times. *Address:* York House, Bishop Auckland. *Club:* R.A.S.C. (O2499)

DOWN, Lieut.-Comm. Sir Charles Edward, K.B.E., R.N.R., *b.* 13 July, 1857; *s.* of Rev. Chas. J. Down, of Ilfracombe, N. Devon; *m.* Gertrude Louisa, *d.* of Very Rev. Dean May, of Demerara. *Educ.:* Marlborough and Switzerland. Marine Superintendent of Royal Mail Steam Packet Co. *War Work:* Command of various steamers until June, 1917; work employed in reconditioning of company's steamers after their employment as merchant cruisers, hospital ships, transports, etc. *Addresses:* R.M.S.P. Co., 18, Moorgate St., E.C.; 52, Hardy Road, Blackheath, S.E. (K369)

DOWN, Major Halkett Walton Money, O.B.E., *b.* 18 June, 1868; *s.* of Edward Augustus Down, of Sussex Towers, Southsea, Hants; *m.* Hilda Catherine, *d.* of George Burnand, of Marnhull, Dorset. *Educ.:* All Saints' Coll., Bloxham, Oxon.

Commission in the 1st Bn. Prince of Wales' (North Staffordshire) Regt., 13 Sept. 1893; transferred to Royal Army Pay Dept., 13 Dec. 1902. *War Work:* Field Cashier to Headquarters, 7th Division, under General Sir Thomas Capper, 1 Sept. 1914; Headquarters IV. Corps, under General Sir Henry Rawlinson; landed at Ostend, 6 Oct. 1914, for relief of Antwerp; was present at 1st Battle of Ypres, and Neuve Chapelle; appointed Command Paymaster, Jamaica, B.W.I., 29 Sept. 1916; specially mentioned in despatches, 16 March, 1918, and 3 July, 1919. (O7100)

DOWN, Major John Egbert, O.B.E.

DOWN, Percy Bissett, M.B.E., M.I.Mech.E., *b.* June, 1876; *s.* of G. B. Down, of Muswell Hill. *Educ.:* Stamford Hill Collegiate School, Stamford Hill. *War Work:* Inspection Dept., Royal Arsenal, Woolwich. *Address:* 100, Duke's Avenue, Muswell Hill, N. 10. (M334)

DOWN, Thomas Beadle, M.B.E.

DOWNES, Doris Mary, Mrs., O.B.E.

DOWNES, Sarah Elizabeth, O.B.E. (O11069)

DOWNES, Thomas, O.B.E.

DOWNEY, Thomas, O.B.E.

DOWNIE, Major Fairbairn, C.B.E., A.M.I.Mar.E., *b.* 19 July, 1880; 7th *s.* of Robert Downie of Dalmally (N.B.), and Newcastle-upon-Tyne. *Educ.:* School of Science and Art, Newcastle-upon-Tyne, and privately. Associate Member of Institute of Marine Engineers; travelled extensively throughout Europe, the Near and Far East and American Continent. *War Work:* Serving as Lieut., London Scottish Regt., T.F., on outbreak of war; went to France, Sept. 1914; promoted Captain, Oct. 1914; invalided home, suffering from shell concussion and sprained shoulder, Nov. 1914; entered Ministry of Munitions, July, 1915, and sent to Ireland where he organised and equipped six National (Shell, Fuse and Cartridge) factories, besides starting 60 private firms on munition manufacture; was Director and Superintendent Engineer; resigned position in Ireland, 4 Feb. 1918; received letters of appreciation of services from the Minister, G.O.C.-in-C. H.M. Forces, Ireland, etc.; entered War Office, 1 March, 1918, during which time French and Belgian factories were visited and reported upon; received special letters from M. of M. and G.O.C.-in-C., The Forces, Ireland, for services rendered in connection with Rebellion, Easter week, Dublin, 1916; mentioned in despatches "London Gazette," 25 Jan. 1917; promoted to Brevet rank of Major (King's Birthday Honours List), June 1917; promoted substantive rank of Major, seniority 20 June, 1917, "London Gazette," 15 March, 1918. *Club:* National Liberal. (C2571)

DOWNIE, Thomas Steel, O.B.E.

DOWNING, Lieut.-Col. Henry John, D.S.O., O.B.E., *b.* 20 Jan. 1862; *s.* of Samuel Downing, LL.D., Professor, Civil Engineering, T.C.D., of Monkstown, Co. Dublin.; *m.* Emily Harriett, *d.* of Capt. Arthur French Lloyd, of 52nd Oxfordshire Light Infantry. *Educ.:* Rugby, and Trinity Coll., Dublin. Gazetted to the Royal Irish Regiment, 1882; Capt., 1889; Adjutant, 1898; Major, 1901; Commanding 1st Batt. the Royal Irish Regiment, 1908–12. *War Work:* Commanded 8th (Service) Batt. Royal Inniskilling Fusiliers, Oct. 1914, to June, 1916; 10th (Training) Batt. East Lancashire Regt., June, 1916, to Jan. 1918; 3rd Vol. Batt. Devon Regt., Oct. 1918, to Jan. 1920. *Address:* Velwell House, nr. Totnes, S. Devon. (O7101)

DOWNING, Pansy, M.B.E., *b.* 1886; *d.* of Major David Fitzgerald Downing, of Royal Artillery. *Educ.:* Cheltenham Ladies' College. *War Work:* Temporary clerk in Military Intelligence Dept., War Office, from 1916–19. *Club:* Halcyon. (M7934)

DOWNING, Robert Edward, M.B.E.

DOWNS, James, O.B.E., J.P., *b.* 2 June, 1856; *s.* of James Downs, of Hull and Bridlington; *m.* Ethel Ester, *d.* of the late William Wilson, of Hull. *Educ.:* Privately and at High School of Glasgow. Chairman, Rose, Downs and Thompson, Ltd., Hull, London and Shanghai; Chairman, Barnsley Canister and Engineering Co., Ltd.; President, Hull Cricket Club; President, Hull Literary and Philosophical Society; Member of Council of Hull Chamber of Commerce; Justice of the Peace for the City and County of Kingston-upon-Hull. *War Work:* Largely engaged in the manufacture of munitions of War; Chief Special Constable, Commander of a Force of 5000 men. *Address:* Dunedin, The Park, Hull. *Clubs:* National Liberal; 1917, London; Scottish Liberal (Edinburgh); Hull and East Riding (Hull). (O297)

DOWNS, John Henry, M.B.E.

DOWSING, Herbert Leopold, M.B.E., M.R.C.S. (Eng.), L.R.C.P. (Lond.), *b.* 29 Aug. 1860; *s.* of William Dowsing, of Hull; *m.* Mary Elizabeth, *d.* of Edmund Johnson Tomalin, of Hull. *Educ.:* Salway House, Leyton; The Leys School, Cambridge; St. Bartholomew's Hospital, London. Late Surgeon, Hull and Sculcoates Dispensary. *War Work:* Hon. Assist. Physician, St. John's V.A.D. Hospital, Hull. *Address:* 275, Beverley Road, Hull. (M7935)

DOWSON, Ernest Macleod, C.B.E., *b.* 19 Nov. 1876; *s.* of Ernest Dowson, late of Indian Telegraph Dept.; *m.* Hilda, *d.* of Rev. S. Pascoe, of Newquay, Cornwall. *Educ.:* Isle of Wight College and City and Guilds Engineering College. Surveyor-General of Egypt, 1909–19; Under Secretary of State for Finance, Egypt, 1919. *War Work:* The Survey of Egypt; was charged with the map work required for the Near Eastern theatres of war (Gallipoli, Egypt, Palestine), and supplied officers for the field parties; initiated use of air photography for map work in Gallipoli, which was gradually developed throughout these theatres. *Address :* Gezira, Cairo, Egypt. (C353)

DOWSON, Kenneth, O.B.E.

DOWSON, Major Oscar Follett, O.B.E., R.A.S.C. (T.F.).

DOYLE, Capt. James Bernard Harvey, O.B.E.

DRACOPOLI, Capt. Ignatius Nicholas, M.B.E., R.A.F.

DRAGE, Elinor Katharine, M.B.E.

DRAISEY, John William James, M.B.E., R.N.

DRAKE, Annie, Mrs., M.B.E.

DRAKE, Bernard Harpur, C.B.E.

DRAKE, Ellen Mary, M.B.E., *b.* 10 Oct. 1874 ; *d.* of William H. Warner, of Percy Lodge, East Sheen ; *m.* Courtenay H. Drake, F.R.C.S. *War Work :* Relief work for Belgium Refugees, 1914 ; joint head of bandage department, Streatham War Supply Depot, organised by Mrs. James, M.B.E., and Mrs. Grimwade, M.B.E. ; voluntary worker King George Hospital, 1915, under Lady Wynne ; Organiser and Hon. Treas. of needlework and handicrafts for wounded soldiers at Tooting Military Hospital, Church Lane, S.W., since 1916. *Address :* 1, Leigham Avenue, Streatham, S.W. (M7938)

DRAKE, Lieut.-Col. Francis Richard, C.B.E., R.A.F. Served in the Great War, 1914–19 (despatches). (C856)

DRAKE, Frank, M.B.E., *b.* 7 Aug. 1873. Sanitary Department, Durban Corporation. *War Work :* In charge of British Red Cross motor boats, East Africa. *Address :* Chamberlain Buildings, Durban, Natal. (M1669)

DRAKE, Col. Henry Dowrish, C.B.E., R.M.A., *b.* 8 Dec. 1859 ; *m.* Jessie Heatley, *d.* of Surgeon-Gen. Alfred Crocker. Entered R.M. Artillery, 1877. Served in Australia and Western Pacific, 1881–5 ; Asst. to Prof. of Fortifications, R.N. College, Greenwich, 1885–7 ; Staff College, Camberley, 1888–9 ; D.A.A.G. and D.A.A.G. for Instruction Southern District, 1890–95 ; medal of the Royal Humane Society for saving life, 1892 ; particular Service Squadron, Mediterranean and Channel Fleets, 1896–97 ; Naval Intelligence Department, Admiralty, 1897–99 ; Professor of Fortifications, R.N. Coll., Greenwich, 1899–1904 ; D.A.Q.M.G., Major of General Staff ; Directorate of Military Operations, War Office, 1904–6 ; Directing Staff, Staff College, Deolali and Quetta, India, 1906–12 ; G.S.O., 1st Grade, retired 1912 ; serving in special appointment, War Office, since 1914. *Address :* 41, Oakley Street, Chelsea. S.W. 3. *Club :* United Service ; Savile. (C491)

DRAKE, James Ernest, O.B.E.

DRAKE, Lieut.-Comm. James Woodard, O.B.E., R.N.R.

DRAKE, John, M.B.E.

DRAKE, John Collard Bernard, O.B.E., *b.* 7 March, 1884 ; *s.* of the late Felix Drake, of East Coker, Somerset. *Educ. :* Blundell's ; Balliol Coll., Oxford. Indian Civil Service : Deputy Secretary to the Government of India, Department of Industries. *War Work :* 1917–18, Provincial Hon. Sec. Joint War Committee (St. John Ambulance Association), and " Our Day " organisation, in Bihar and Orissa, India. *Addresses :* East Coker, Yeovil, Somerset ; c/o Messrs. King, Hamilton & Co., Calcutta. *Clubs :* East India United Services, London ; United Services, Simla. (O4034)

DRAKE, Major John Hughes, O.B.E.

DRAKE, Lieut. Tom, M.B.E., *b.* 17 May, 1885 ; *s.* of Dennys Drake, of Orpington, Kent. *Educ. :* Uppingham. *War Work :* Served 1 year France, Sept. 1914, London Scottish, as private ; Commissioned 3/1st Herts Yeomanry, Sept. 1915, to March, 1917 ; seconded Machine Gun Corps, Cavalry, March, 1917, until demobilisation, Jan. 1919. *Address :* 64, Parliament Hill, Hampstead Heath, London, N.W. (M1670)

DRAKE, Capt. William Barnard, O.B.E., 1st Bn. S. Wales Borderers, *b.* 1871 ; *s.* of the late Sir W. H. Drake, K.C.B., of War Office, London ; *m.* Katherine Alice. *d.* of C. J. Lacy, of Basingbourne House, Fleet, Hants. *Educ. :* Sherborne. *War Work :* Served in Egypt, 1915–16 ; Embarkation Staff, Mesopotamia, 1916–18 ; Embarkation Staff, Hull, Tilbury, Devonport, 1919. *Address :* Cotmaton House, Sidmouth, S. Devon. (O6009)

DRAKE, William Henry Milverton, O.B.E., *b.* 27 Jan. 1885 ; *s.* of Edward Drake, of Exeter ; *m.* Ethel Kate, *d.* of William Betts, of Oxford. *Educ. :* Exeter College School. Assist. National Sec. Y.M.C.A. Headquarters, W.C. 1 ; in Y.M.C.A. work for 17 years ; held General Secretaryships at Devonport and Oxford. *War Work :* Secretary-in-Charge of the Department of Personnel for Y.M.C.A. war work with the troops at home and overseas. *Address :* Sutties Hotel, Bedford Place, W.C. 1. (O3694)

DRAKE, Kathleen TYRWHITT-, M.B.E., *b.* 27 Dec. 1874 ; *d.* of the late William T. Tyrwhitt-Drake, Boro'gate, St. Albans, sometime Vicar of Gt. Gaddesden, Herts. *War Work :* District Chairman, St. Albans Division, Herts Local War Pensions Committee. *Address :* Boro'gate, St. Albans. (M7939)

DRAKEFORD, William Dusantoy, M.B.E., *b.* 21 Jan. 1868 ; *s.* of the late Rev. David James Drakeford, M.A., of Elm Grove, Sydenham ; *m.* Catherine May, *d.* of the late Col. Henry Dixon, Indian Army, of Sydenham. *Educ. :* Westminster School, 1882–84, and Clare Coll., Cambridge. B.A. 1889, M.A. 1893. Clerk, War Office. *War Work :* War Office, Military Secretary's Department. *Address :* 4, Girdlers Road, West Kensington, W. 14. (M7940)

DRAPER, Capt. Charles Frederick, O.B.E.

DRAPER, Christopher Robert Burroughes, M.B.E., J.P. N. Rhodesia, Magistrate and District Commr., N. Rhodesia, *b.* 9 June. 1878 ; *s.* of the Rev. W. H. Draper, M.A. (Oxon), Middleton Rectory, Bicester. *Educ. :* Stubbington House,

Fareham, and H.M.S. " Worcester." *War Work :* Organisation and supply of transport and food for Military Porters engaged German East African campaign. *Address :* Livingstone, N. Rhodesia. (M1263)

DRAPER, Lieut.-Comm. Philip Nelson, O.B.E., R.N.R.

DRAPER, Thomas Percy, C.B.E., K.C. ; *b.* 1864. Called to the Bar, Inner Temple, 1891 ; K.C. 1910 ; Chairman, W. Australian Red Cross. *Address :* Perth, W. Australia. (C707)

DRAPES, Thomas Lambert, M.B.E., B.A., M.B., B.C. (Cantab), M.R.C.S., L.R.C.P., *b.* 4 Aug. 1878 ; *s.* of Thomas Drapes, M.B., of Enniscorthy, Co. Wexford, Ireland. *Educ. :* Epsom Coll. ; Sidney Sussex Coll., Cambridge : St. Mary's Hospital, W. M.O.H. Chepstow Urban and Rural District Councils, and Chepstow Port Sanitary Authority. *War Work :* M.O. Red Cross Hospital Portskewett, Mon. *Address :* St. Maur, Chepstow, Mon. *Club :* Junior Constitutional. (M7941)

DRAY, Evelyn Muriel, M.B.E.

DRAYSON, Col. Alfred Percy, O.B.E., T.D., D.L. (Surrey) *b.* 5 Aug. 1877 ; *e. s.* of Alfred W. Drayson, of Ditton Grange, Ditton Hill, Surrey ; *m.* Dorothy Frances, *d.* of Francis G Johns, of Glenthorne, Enfield. *Educ. :* Highgate School. Director of Alfred W. Drayson & Sons., Ltd. *War Work :* Commanded 6th East Surrey Reg., 1913–20 ; (India, Oct. 1914–19) ; Served with Aden Field Force, 1917–18 ; Commanded Rawalpindi, May to Oct. 1916 ; Commanded Agra, 1918 ; Mention Despatches twice ; awarded Croix de Guerre. *Address :* Trohork, Langley Avenue, Surbiton, Surrey. *Club :* Junior Army and Navy. (O2367)

DRAYSON, Capt. and Qr.-Mr. Thomas, O.B.E., R.A.

DRAYTON, Gertrude, O.B.E.

DREAPER, William Porter, O.B.E., F.I.C., *b.* 1868 ; *s.* of John Shaw Dreaper, of London ; *m.* Florence Barbara, *d.* of George Jecks, of Barnet. *Educ. :* Privately, and City and Guilds Coll. Finsbury. Consulting Chemical Engineer ; Hon. Consulting Chemist to Silk Association ; Editor of " Text Books of Chemical Research and Engineering," Author of " Notes on Chemical Research," " Chemistry and Physics of Dyeing," etc. *War Work :* Superintendent of H.M. Factories at Sutton Oak, St. Helen's, and Ellesmere Port, Cheshire. *Address :* 27, Willow Road, Hampstead Heath, N.W. 3, London. (O10325)

DREDGE, Lieut. Austin Edward Makinson, M.B.E., R.A.S.C., *b.* 8 July, 1882 ; *s.* of the Rev. N. Dredge, M.A., of Pettaugh, Suffolk. *Educ. :* Clairville House School, Ross-on-Wye. *War Work :* Mobilised 4 Aug. 1914 ; Gallipoli, July, 1915 ; Egyptian Expeditionary Force, Dec. 1915 ; Mesopotamian Exp. Force, June, 1916 ; remaining with that force until 15 Nov. 1919. *Addresses :* Windervie, Ufford, Suffolk ; Whittington Barracks, Lichfield. *Club :* R.A.S.C. (M4864)

DREW, Brig.-Gen. Bertie Clephane Hawley, C.M.G., C.B.E., R.A.F. ; *b.* 1880. Served in China, 1900 (medal) ; N.-W. Frontier of India, 1901–2 and 1903–4 (medal) ; Great War, 1914–18 (despatches, promoted). (C1892)

DREW, Florence Grace, Mrs., M.B.E.

DREW, Major Francis Grenville, O.B.E., R.E.

DREW, James William, M.B.E.

DREW, Lieut.-Col. John Summers, O.B.E.

DREW, Lorna Auchterlonie, M.B.E.

DREW, Lieut.-Comm. Thomas Bernard, O.B.E., R.N.

DREW, Lieut.-Col. Tom Maxwell, O.B.E., *b.* 28 Feb. 1869 ; *s.* of Henry Drew, of Peamore Cottage, near Exeter ; *m.* Cecilia Margaret, *d.* of Brabazon Campbell, of The Northgate, Warwick. *Educ. :* Malvern and Leamington Colleges. Served in the Leicestershire Regt. for 31 years, from 1888 to 1919. *War Work :* Served in Gallipoli and France ; Commanded the 17th Recruiting Area and the Depot of the Leicestershire Regt., from July, 1916, to March, 1919. *Address :* East Ridgeway, Northaw, Hertfordshire. *Club :* Naval and Military. (O7103)

DREW, Rev. Monsignor Francis BICKERSTAFFE-, C.B.E., B.D. : see Bickerstaffe.

DREYER, Capt. Frederic Charles, C.B. (Mil. and Civ.), C.B.E. (Mil.), R.N., *b.* 8 Jan. 1878 ; *s.* of John L. E. Dreyer, M.A., Ph.D., of 14, Staverton Road, Oxford ; *m.* Una Maria, *d.* of the late Rev. J. T. Hallett, Vicar of Bishops Tachbrook, Warwickshire ; 3 sons, 2 daughters. *Educ. :* Royal School Armagh and H.M.S. " Britannia," Director of Gunnery, Division Naval Staff Admiralty, since April, 1920 ; Commodore and Chief of Staff to Admiral of the Fleet, The Right Hon. Viscount Jellicoe, of Scapa, G.C.B., O.M., G.C.V.O., during his Mission to India and the Dominions, Feb. 1919, to Feb. 1920. *War Work :* Capt. H.M. Battleship " Orion," Grand Fleet, Aug. 1914, to Oct. 1915 ; Capt., H.M. Battleship " Iron Duke,' Fleet Flagship of Admiral Sir John Jellicoe, G.C.B., O.M., G.C.V.O., Commander in Chief, Grand Fleet, Oct. 1915, to Nov. 1916 ; (Battle of Jutland—Despatches, Military C.B.). Assistant Director, Anti-Submarine Division, Naval Staff Admiralty, Dec. 1916, to March, 1917 ; Director of Naval Ordnance, March, 1917, to June, 1918 ; Director of Naval Artillery and Torpedo, Naval Staff Admiralty, June, 1918, to Feb. 1919. Has Orders of St. Stanislaus, 2nd Class, with Star ; St. Anne, 2nd Class ; and Rising Sun, 3rd Class, American Navy Distinguished Service Medal ; is Officer of Legion of Honour. *Address :* 35, Bury Road, Alverstoke. *Clubs :* United Service, Naval, Portsmouth. (C890)

DREYER, Lieut.-Col. George S., C.B.E., R.A.F. Served in the Great War, 1914–19 (despatches). (C2346)

DREYER, Lieut.-Col. Georges, C.B.E., O.B.E., R.A.M.C., B.S.,

DRIBERG, James Douglas, O.B.E., M.C., F.R.C.S., *b.* 30 July, 1890 ; *s.* of the late J. J. S. Driberg, I.C.S., of Crowborough, Sussex. *Educ.:* Lancing Coll., and London Hospital. Surgical Registrar to, and assist. to, Surgical Unit, London Hospital. *War Work:* M.O. 6th Buffs ; Surgical Specialist, 35 General Hospital, Calais. *Address:* 46, Queen Anne Street, London, W. 1. *Club:* R.A.C. (O5211)

DRINKWATER, Katharine Rosebery, Mrs., O.B.E., J.P., M.B., B.S., B.Sc., D.P.H., *b.* 11 Nov. 1872 ; *d.* of Henry Mason Jay, M.D., of Chippenham, Wilts. ; *m.* Harry Drinkwater, J.P., M.D., F.R.S. (Edin.), *s.* of the late James Drinkwater, of Liverpool. *Educ.:* Bath High School ; Bedford College, London ; London School of Medicine for Women ; Royal Free Hospital, London. General Medical Practitioner ; Assist. School Medical Officer to the Wrexham Education Committee. *War Work:* 1916–17, Medical Officer in charge of Staff and Departments and Military Families Hospital, Malta (R.A.M.C.) ; 1914, with Mrs. Berners, organised Roseneath Military Auxiliary Hospital, Wrexham. *Address:* Lister House, Wrexham, N. Wales. (O1300)

DRINKWATER, Sidney William, M.B.E.

DRISCOLL, Eng.-Lieut. Robert, O.B.E., R.N.

DRIVER, Lieut. George Osborne Hitchin, M.B.E., Can. A.S.C.

DROGHEDA, Kathleen, Countess of, C.B.E. ; *d.* of Charles M. Pelham Burn ; *m.* 1909, Henry Charles Ponsonby Moore, 10th Earl of Drogheda (*see* BURKE'S *Peerage*). (C953)

DROWER, Gertrude Louise, M.B.E.

DROWER, John Edmund, C.B.E., *b.* 1853 ; *s.* of George Marwood Drower, of Axminster ; *m.* Bessie Florence, *d.* of Edwin Chivers, of Tavistock. *Educ.:* Privately. Fellow of the Royal Astronomical Society and of the Surveyor's Institution. *War Work:* Assistant Director of Army Contracts, having Charge of Works ; Held the post until the end of the war, when he organised the Department of Building Material Supplies for the Ministry of Munitions, and became its first Director. *Addresses:* 49, Mount Ephraim Road, Streatham, S.W. 16 ; 28, Victoria Street, S.W. 1. *Club:* St. Stephen's. (C954)

DRUDGE, Capt. Ernest O., M.B.E., R.A.F.

DRUITT, Hilda, M.B.E., R.A.S.C.

DRUITT, Reginald Ernest, O.B.E., *b.* 1882 ; *s.* of Theodore Druitt, of London ; *m.* Ivy Millicent, *d.* of Walter Scott-Smith, of London. *Educ.:* Coopers' Company's Grammar School. *War Work:* Greek Ships Committee (Foreign Office) Inter-Allied Chartering Executive. *Address:* Southwood, Plough Lane, Purley, Surrey. (O1301)

DRUM, Col. L., C.B.E. Canadian Forces ; served in the Great War, 1915–19 (despatches). (C1349)

DRUMMOND, Charles James, M.B.E., J.P., Officier d'Academie, France, *b.* 30 July, 1848 ; *s.* of Charles Drummond, of Ipswich ; *m.* Helena Catherine, *d.* of Humphrey Deen, of Chislehurst. *Educ.:* Queen Elizabeth's School, Ipswich. Ex-Chief Labour Correspondent, Board of Trade ; Local Labour Correspondent, Ministry of Labour ; Vice-Chairman, Tin Box and Paper Box Trade Boards ; a Chairman of Scottish Board, Coal Mines (Minimum Wage) Act, 1912 ; Member of Chairmen's Panel, Arbitration and Conciliation Act. *War Work:* Prince of Wales' Committee ; City of London Local Tribunal ; Civil Liabilities Committee ; Local Food Control Committee, City of London ; Appeal Tribunal, Profiteering Act, 1919, City of London ; Ministry of National Service, Sub-Commissioner for Trade Exemptions. *Address:* Northfield, 21, Dalmore Road, Dulwich, S.E. 21. *Club:* Constitutional. (M1673)

DRUMMOND, Capt. Cyril Alexander Fraser, O.B.E. R.A.

DRUMMOND, David, C.B.E., M.D.

DRUMMOND, Capt. and Qr.-Mr. John Raymond, M.B.E., Aust. A.M.C.

DRUMMOND, Mary Jane, M.B.E., *b.* 28 Aug. 1869 ; *d.* of Walter Scott Drummond, of Charlton, Kent. *Educ.:* Roan School, Greenwich, S.E. 10. Divisional Sec. Greenwich and Woolwich Division, County of London Branch, of the British Red Cross Society. *War Work:* Aug. 1914, to July, 1915, assisting in training recruits for V.A.D.'s ; July, 1915, to May, 1917, part time V.A.D. in Southwood Red Cross Hospital, Eltham, part time assisting Div. Sec. Headquarters, Charlton House, Charlton ; May, 1917, to present time Divisional Sec. ; also helped collect funds for Belgian Homes in Charlton from Sept. 1914, to Sept. 1918. *Address:* 42, Wellington Road, Old Charlton, Kent. (M7945)

DRUMMOND, Capt. Robert, O.B.E., J.P., *b.* 1856 ; *s.* of John Drummond, of Trinity, Edinburgh. *Educ.:* Edinburgh. Civil Engineer and Road Surveyor. *War Work:* Chairman of Local Tribunal, Paisley ; Member of Joint Roads Committee, London ; Chairman of Investigation Sub-Committee for Scotland. *Address:* Fairfield, Paisley. *Clubs:* Paisley ; Art (Glasgow) ; R.A.C. (London). (O1302)

DRUMMOND, Lieut.-Col. Francis Dudley, WILLIAMS- C.B.E., J.P., D.L., *b.* 27 June, 1863 ; *s.* of Sir James Drummond, of Hawthornden and Edwinsford ; *m.* Marguerite Violet Maud, *d.* of Sir Andrew Agnew, Bart., of Locknaw. *Educ.:* Eton and Trinity College, Cambridge. Chairman, Court of Quarter Sessions for County of Carmarthen and of County Petty Sessions ; Chairman, Carmarthenshire Territorial Force Association ; Alderman, County Council ; Fellow Surveyors Institute ; Member of Government Reconstruction Committee on Forestry and Member of Council, Bath and

West Society. *War Work:* Served on County Appeal Tribunal and War Agr. Committee. Raised County V.T.C. Battalion ; Commissioner for Wales (Agr.) National Service ; Appointed Live Stock Commissioner for 7 South Wales Counties, under Ministry of Food ; Vive-Chairman, consultation committee for Wales under Forestry Commission ; served on various agricultural Forestry and Grouse Disease Commissions and taken active part in public life and developments of south and west Wales. *Address:* Hafodneddyn, Llandilo. *Club:* Travellers. (C955)

DRURY, Amy Gertrude, Lady, C.B.E., *b.* 2 June, 1863 ; *d.* of John Middleton of 3, Porchester Gate, W. 2 ; *m.* the late Admiral Sir Charles Carter Drury, G.C.B., G.C.V.O., K.C.S.I., *s.* of Le Baron Drury, of Rothsey, New Brunswick. *Educ.:* At home. Hon. General Secretary ot the Royal Naval Friendly Union of Sailors' Wives ; Division Commissioner of Girl Guides for S.W. Kent ; Member of the Ashford District Board of Education ; President Tenterden Women's Institute ; Member Joint Parliamentary Advisory Committee. *War Work:* Relief and assistance of wives and families of naval men who were wounded or killed. Chairman of Ladies' Advisory Committee of the Navy League Overseas Relief Fund. *Address:* Homewood, Tenterden, Kent. (C2573)

DRURY, Comm. Edward Dumerque, O.B.E., R.N.R.

DRURY, Edward Herbert Merivale, M.B.E.

DRURY, Geoffrey Herbert, O.B.E.

DRURY, Lieut.-Col. Richard Frederick, C.B.E. Hon. Lieut.-Col. in the Army. (C857)

DRURY, Capt. Thomas, O.B.E. (Mil.), *b.* 20 Feb. 1878 ; *s.* of the Rev. W. F. Drury, late Vicar of Holy Trinity, Burton-on-Trent, and Hornby, Bedale, Yorkshire. *Educ.:* St. John's School, Leatherhead, and University of London. Schoolmaster. *War Work:* Gazetted to 11th Batt. Duke of Wellington's Regt., 24 July, 1915 ; posted to 12th (Lab.) Batt. Duke of Wellington's Regt., March, 1916 ; promoted Capt. and appointed Adjutant 12th (Lab.) Batt. Duke of Wellington's Regt., 20 July, 1916 ; transferred to Labour Corps, 13 April, 1917 ; Adjutant, 40th and 27th Labour Groups, 13 April, 1917, to 22 Nov. 1919. *Address:* 22, Bisham Gardens, Highgate, London, N. 6. (O5212)

DRURY, Lieut.-Col. William Price, C.B.E., R.M.L.I. (ret.), *b.* 8 Nov. 1861 ; *s.* of the late William Drury, Paymaster-in-chief, R.N. ; *m.* Marguerite Florence Shirley, *d.* of the late Rev. Pender H. Cudlip, Vicar of Sparkwell, S. Devon. *Educ.:* Brentwood School, Essex, and Plymouth College. Author and Dramatist (" The Flag Lieutenant " and other plays) ; Member of the Naval Intelligence Department, 1900–1 ; Was Chief Organiser of Lord Robert's National Service League before the War. *War Work:* Rejoined Royal Marines at Chatham on outbreak of War, having been invalided out of the Service in 1903 ; Commanded Anti-Aircraft Battery, Portsmouth Harbour, 1914–15 ; Served as Intelligence Officer at Plymouth (*a*) on staff of Garrison Commander, (*b*) on Staff of Naval Commander-in-Chief, 1915–17 ; Regimental duty during remainder of war ; Was awarded O.B.E. primarily for active service in Crete, Sept. 1898. *Address:* St. Germans, Cornwall. *Club:* Garrick. (C1921)

DRYSDALE, Charles Vickery, O.B.E., D.Sc.

DRYSDALE, Duncan, M.B.E.

DRYSDALE, Major John Douglas, O.B.E.

DRYSDALE, Capt. John Syme, M.B.E.

DUARTE, Edgar Thurston, M.B.E., S.M., R.F.A.

DUBERLY, Ida Mary Villiers, Mrs., O.B.E., *b.* Dec. 1856 ; *d.* of Richard Farrer, of Michelstown, Co. Cork ; *m.* Arthur Grey, *s.* of James Duberly, of Gaynes, Huntingdonshire. *War Work:* Hon. Sec. to the Bedfordshire branch of the Soldiers' and Sailors' Families Association, and Beds. Soldiers' and Sailors' Help Society ; Commandant of the Cardington V.A.D., No. 32 ; Member of the Bedfordshire War Pensions Committee. (O10327)

DUBERLY, Capt. Montagu Richard William, O.B.E.

DU BERN, Jules Emile, O.B.E.

DUBOIS, Frederick, M.B.E.

DU BOISE, Ferdinand de Ricquebourg, M.B.E.

DU BREUL, Major Frederick Alexander, O.B.E.

DU BUISSON, Major Henry, O.B.E., Lincolnshire Regt. (ret.), *b.* 9 Nov. 1857 ; *s.* of the late James Du Buisson, of Wandsworth Common, Surrey ; *m.* Ismé, *d.* of Alexander Hamilton, W.S., of Edinburgh. *Educ.:* Marlborough Coll., and Sandhurst. *War Work:* Assist. Cable Censor, Aug. 1914, to Oct. 1914 ; second in command, Depot Lincoln, and subsequently in command, Oct. 1914, to Nov. 1918. *Address:* St. Wilfreds, nr. Ryde, Isle of Wight. *Club:* Junior United Service. (O3639)

DU CANE, Major Charles George, O.B.E.

DU CAUR, Arthur George, M.B.E. (M10245)

DUCK, Surg.-Lieut. William Agar Scholefield, O.B.E., R.N.

DUCKETT, Lieut. William Knight, M.B.E., R.E. (T.F.)

DUCKWORTH, Lieut. Francis Robinson Gladstone, M.B.E.

DUCKWORTH, Robert, M.B.E.

DU CROZ, Grace Jessie, Mrs., O.B.E.

DUDDING, Bernard Phineas, M.B.E., A.R.C.Sc., *b.* 16 Dec. 1885 ; *s.* of Phineas John Dudding, of Gillingham, Kent ; *m.* Lilian, *d.* of William Petchey, of Dover. *Educ.:* Wesleyan Higher Grade School, Gillingham, Kent ; Royal College of Science, London. Assistant at National Physical Laboratory, Teddington, 1911–18 ; Senior Assistant on the Staff of the

Research Laboratories of the General Electric Company, England. *War Work:* Development of measuring appliances used in the production and examination of screw gauges for Munitions of all kinds. *Address:* The Nook, Hampton Road, Teddington, Middlesex. (M339)

DUDDING, Major Thomas Scarborough, O.B.E., R.A.M.C.

DUDDY, Philip Menross, M.B.E., *b.* 7 Feb. 1872 ; *s.* of Joseph Duddy, late Chief Inspector, City Police ; *m.* Mary, *d.* of George Hilder, of Rolvenden, Kent. *Educ.:* Weymouth Coll. Senior Staff Clerk, Secretary's Office, H.M. Customs and Excise. *War Work:* Principal of the Registry of the Secretary's Office Customs and Excise ; the Secretary's Office maintained a continuous service night and day throughout the war. *Addresses:* 4, Park Villas, Loughton, Essex ; Secretary's Office, Custom House, Lower Thames Street, London, E.C. 3. (M7947)

DUDFIELD, Capt. Reginald Samuel Orme, O.B.E., R.A.M.C. (T.F.)

DUDGEON, Arthur Frederick, O.B.E., B.A.

DUDGEON, Florence Margaret, M.B.E.

DUDGEON, Gerald Cecil, C.B.E. ; *b.* 1867 ; *s.* of the late Robert Ellis Dudgeon, M.D., of 53, Montagu Square, W. ; *m.* 1907, Isabel Annie, *d.* of the late R. Ballard, of Palumpur, Kangra Valley, Punjab, and widow of Percy Fitzgerald Campbell (*see* BURKE'S *Peerage*, Campbell, Bt.). *Educ.:* St. Marylebone and All Souls' Grammar School (King's Coll., Prizeman). Sup., and subsequently Gen. Inspector of Agriculture, British W. Africa and Protectorate, 1905–10 ; Director-Gen. Depart. of Agriculture, Egypt, 1910–12 ; Consulting Agriculturist, Ministry of Agriculture, with rank of Director-Gen. 1912–18 ; sometime on Staff of Indian Museum, Calcutta ; Fellow of Entomological Society ; has 2nd class of Order of the Nile ; author of " The Agricultural and Forest Products of British West Africa," and of various articles on Agricultural, Economic, and Natural History subjects. *Address:* 1, Zetland House, Cheniston Gardens, W. *Club:* Royal Societies'. (C702)

DUDGEON, Prof. Leonard Stanley, C.M.G. C.B.E., F.R.C.P., London ; *b.* Oct. 1876 ; *s.* of John Hepburn Dudgeon of Haddington, N.B.: *m.* Norah Edith, *d.* of Richard Hugh Orpen, of Ardtully, Kenmare, Co. Kerry. *Educ.:* St. Thomas's Hospital. Professor of Pathology, Univ. of London ; Bacteriologist-in-Chief, St. Thomas's Hospital ; Examiner in Pathology, Royal Army Medical College. *War Work:* Col. A.M.S. Consulting Bacteriologist, H.M. Forces ; Eastern Mediterranean, 1915–19 ; Member of War Office Committee of Infectious Diseases ; Gallipoli and Egypt, 1915 ; Thrice mentioned in Despatches ; Order of St. Sara, Serbia, 1917, 3rd Class. *Address:* 6, Stanhope Street, Hyde Park, W. 2. *Club:* Union. (C1409)

DUDGEON, Margaret, Mrs. Robert Francis, O.B.E.

DUDLEY, Capt. Cyril Raymond, M.B.E.

DUDLEY, Lieut. Edward Joseph Scott, M.B.E.

DUDLEY, George James, O.B.E., M.R.C.S., L.R.C.P., *b.* 8 Sept. 1867 ; *s.* of the late Samuel Dudley, of Dudley ; *m.* Sarah Jane, *d.* of the late Luke Jewkes, J.P., of Dudley. *Educ.:* Dudley Grammar School, and Queen's Coll., Birmingham. Medical Practitioner ; Hon. Surgeon, Stourbridge Dispensary ; Surgeon to Post Office. *War Work:* Medical Officer to Wordsley Military Hospital, 1915–17 ; Medical Officer, Studley Court Red Cross Hospital, 1914–19 ; Commandant, Studley Court Red Cross Hospital, 1915–17 ; Examiner of Recruits ; lecturer to St. John Ambulance Association and Red Cross Society. *Address:* 13, High Street, Stourbridge. (O10328)

DUDLEY, Capt. Harold Ward, O.B.E., R.E.

DUDLEY, Surg.-Lieut.-Comm. Sheldon Francis, O.B.E., R.N.

DUDLEY, Sophie, Mrs., M.B.E.

DUDLEY, William Edward, O.B.E., J.P.

DUFF, Col. Charles de Vertus, C.B.E. Capt. and T. Col. 2nd Reserve Batt., S. African Forces ; served in the Great War, 1915–19 (despatches). (C1366)

DUFF, Sir Hector Livingstone, K.B.E., C.M.G. ; *b.* 1872 ; *s.* of the late J. P. Duff, of Edderton House, Edderton. Appointed Asst. Resident Nyasaland, 1897 ; Resident 1907 ; Acting Deputy Governor, 1911 ; Chief Secretary to the Government and Senior Member Executive and Legislative Councils, 1914 ; Acting Governor and Commander-in-Chief, 1918–19. *War Work:* Served with Nyasaland Field Force, 1914–18 ; twice mentioned in despatches ; 1914–15 Star ; General Service War Medal ; Victory Medal ; African General Service Medal and clasp. Appointed Chief Political Officer to General Northey's Forces, 1916 ; administered Military Government of occupied enemy territory in East Africa, 1916–18. *Address:* The Old Residency, Zomba, Nyasaland. *Club:* Junior Carlton.

DUFF, Mildred Mabel Gordon, Mrs., O.B.E.

DUFF, Thomas Duff Gordon, C.B.E., J.P., D.L., *b.* 11 Aug. 1848 ; *s.* of Major Lachlan D. Gordon Duff, of Drummuir and Park, Banffshire ; *m.* 1st, 1875, Pauline Emma, *d.* of late Sir Chas. Tennant, Bart., 2nd, 1893, Mildred Mabel, O.B.E., *d.* of late E. C. Walker, of Chester. *Educ.:* Harrow and Trinity College, Oxford. Vice-Lieutenant, Banffshire ; Chairman Standing Joint Committee, Banffshire. *War Work:* Chairman Terr. Force Assoc. till 1919, and of Agricult. Executive Committee. *Address:* Drummuir, Keith. *Clubs:* New Edinburgh ; Royal Automobile, London. (C2574)

DUFF, Edith Florence, Lady GRANT-, C.B.E., Lady of Grace of the Order of St. John of Jerusalem, *b.* 12 Jan. 1877 ; *d.* of Sir George Bonham, Bart., of Knowle, Cranleigh (*see*

BURKE'S *Peerage*) ; *m.* Sir Evelyn Mountstuart, K.C.M.G., *s.* of the late Rt. Hon. Sir Mountstuart Grant-Duff, *War Work:* Founder and Organiser of the British Section, Bureau de Secours aux Prisonniers de Guerre, Berne, Switzerland, known as the Berne Bread Bureau, 1915 ; founder and organiser of the British Legation Red Cross Organisation in Switzerland, 1914. *Address:* Earl Soham Grange, Framlingham, Suffolk. (C492)

DUFF, Victoria Adelaide Alexandrina GRANT-, M.B.E.

DUFFERIN AND AVA, Harriot Georgiana, Marchioness of, D.B.E., *d.* of Archibald Rowan Hamilton, of Killyleagh Castle, co. Down ; *m.* 23 Oct. 1862, Frederick Temple, 1st Marquis of Dufferin and Ava (*see* BURKE'S *Peerage*). *Address:* Clandeboye, co. Down. (D2)

DUFFES, Hilda Ethel Paterson, M.B.E.; M.A., *d.* of the late George Macpherson Duffes, of 10, Carlton Street, Edinburgh ; and Forres, Morayshire. *Educ.:* Edinburgh Ladies' Coll., and Edinburgh Univ. *War Work:* Was engaged in war work in the Ministry of Shipping, in connection with the control of transfers of vessels and the Inter-Allied Ship-Purchasing Committee. *Addresses:* 11, Denning Road, Hampstead ; 10, Carlton Street, Edinburgh. (M7949)

DUFFETT, Lieut.-Comm. Edward, O.B.E., R.N.

DUFFIELD, Major Edgar Willoughby, O.B.E.

DUFFIELD, Walter Dowsett, O.B.E., *b.* 15 Feb. 1874 ; *s.* of John Duffield, of York. *Educ.:* Thirsk High School. Assist. Director, Ministry of Transport. *War Work:* Assist. Director, Statistical Branch, Admiralty. *Address:* Greenvale Road, S.E. 9. *Club:* Junior Constitutional. (O1033a)

DUFFIN, Lieut.-Col. Earle Calder, O.B.E.

DUFFUS, Major Chester Stairs, O.B.E., M.C., *b.* 1 March, 1891 ; *s.* of W. Stairs Duffus, of Halifax, Nova Scotia ; *m.* Evelyn Ursula, *d.* of Major G. D. Giles, of Brora, Sutherlandshire. *Educ.:* Oundle. Company Director. *War Work:* R.A.F., 2¼ years in France. *Address:* Corner House, Brentwood, Essex. *Club:* R.A.F. (O3298)

DUFFY, Capt. Michael Louis, O.B.E., R.E.

DUFFY, Major Thomas Augustine, O.B.E.

DUFORT, Cyril John NESBITT-, O.B.E., *b.* 28 April, 1892 ; *s.* of the late J. C. Dufort, of London. *Educ.:* Cheltenham Coll., and London Univ. Engineer. *War Work:* Served with 230th Siege Battery, R.G.A., France, and later, Staff Capt., War Office, Whitehall, S.W. *Address:* 12, Thurloe Place, S.W. 7. *Club:* Royal Automobile. (O7510)

DU FRAYER, Major Alfred Henry, O.B.E.,

DUFTON, Dorothy, M.B.E.

DUGDALE, Ethel Innes, Mrs., O.B.E., A.R.R.C.

DUGDALE, Hilda, M.B.E., *d.* of the late Adam Dugdale, D.L., of Griffin Lodge, Blackburn, Lancashire ; and Gilmonby Hall, Bowes, Darlington. *War Work:* Hon. Sec. Blackburn Prisoners of War Committee. *Address:* Griffin Lodge, Blackburn. *Clubs:* Forum ; Ladies' Imperial. (M7590)

DUGDALE, Maud Violet, Mrs., O.B.E., *d.* of G. Woodroffe late Royal Horse Guards ; *m.* James Lionel, *s.* of John Dugdale, of Crathorne. *War Work:* Com. Red Cross Auxiliary Hospital ; Local War Pensions Committee, etc., etc. *Address:* Crathorne Hall, Yarm-on-Tees, Yorks. *Club:* Bath. (O1305)

DUGGAN, Eva, M.B.E., *b.* 1891 ; *d.* of Dr. M. Duggan, of Altrincham. *Educ.:* Roedean, Brighton, and Paris. *War Work:* Sec. to President of The Ordnance Committee, Woolwich. *Address:* Clevedon, Altrincham. (M3617)

DUGGAN, Paymaster-Lieut.-Comm. Eyre Sturdy, O.B.E., R.N.

DUGGAN, George Chester, O.B.E., M.A., Chevalier of the Orders of Leopold II. and of the Legion of Honour, *b.* 5 Feb. 1885 *s.* of George Duggan, of Provincial Bank House, Dublin, and Ferney, Greystones, Co. Wicklow ; *m.* Elsie Gore, *d.* of Rev. R. Blair, of the Rectory, Ballinamallard. *Educ.:* The High School, Dublin, and Trinity College, Dublin. Clerk, Class I., Transport Dept. Admiralty, 1908–10 and Chief Secretary's Office, Dublin, 1910–14 ; Superintending Clerk Transport Dept. Admiralty, and Ministry of Shipping, 1915–19 ; Superintending Clerk, Chief Secretary's Office, 1919–20 ; Principal Clerk, Chief Secretary's Office, 1920. *War Work:* Directorate of Military Sea Transport, Admiralty, and Ministry of Shipping. *Address:* Mount Anville Lodge, Dundrum, Co. Dublin. (O302)

DUGGAN, Capt. and Qr.-Mr. Harry Van Norman, M.B.E.

DUGGAN, Lieut.-Col. and Qr.-Mr. Martin Joseph, O.B.E.

DUGGAN, Rev. Mother Mary, M.B.E., Medaille de la Reine Elizabeth, *b.* 21 Nov. 1856 ; *d.* of Matthew Duggan, of Kilkenny. *Educ.:* Convent of the Faithful Virgin, Norwood and Bernardine Abbey of Soleilmont, Belgium ; Lady Superior of the Sisters of Charity at Holly Mount, Tottington, near Bury, Lancs. *War Work:* Sheltered over 440 Belgian Refugees from 1914 to 1919 ; provided Auxiliary Military Hospital where over 1200 sick and wounded soldiers were nursed from Oct. 1914, to Jan. 1919. *Address:* Holly Mount, Tottington. (M7951)

DUGGAN, Motherwell, M.B.E., M.R.C.S., L.R.C.P.

DUGGLEBY, Constance Mary, Mrs., M.B.E.; *d.* of the late Frederick William Huddleston, of Lincoln and Plumstead ; *m.* the late Septimus, *s.* of the late Stephen Waldby Duggleby, of Cottam, Yorks. *War Work:* Confidential Sec. to the Officer Commanding the Military Hospital, Lewisham, from its opening in May, 1915, to its closing in May, 1919. *Address:* Lewisham, London, S.E. (M7955)

DUGON, Lieut. Arnold Louis, M.B.E., R.M.L.I.

DUGUID, Lieut. David Robertson, M.B.E., R.A.O.C. (M10300)

DUKAULT, Capt. Joseph Rene Jacques, O.B.E., Can., A.V.C.

DUKE, Major Basil Lawrence, D.S.O., O.B.E., R.F.A. b. 1882 ; Educ.: Wellington. War Work : France and Belgium, Nov. 1914, to Armistice. (O4282)

DUKE, Capt. Edward, O.B.E., b. 22 May, 1882 ; s. of Sir Henry Edward Lord Justice Duke ; m. Odette, d. of Edmond Roger, of Paris. Educ.: Dulwich and Neuchatel. Barrister-at-Law ; Sec. to the President of the Probate Admiralty and Divorce Division. War Work : Employed in Intelligence Dept., War Office, from Aug. 1914, to Nov. 1914) ; after that A.P.M. of 24th Division, France and Flanders, 1916 to Armistice ; Intelligence, War Office, receiving thanks of American, French, and Belgian Governments. Addresses : 37, Alleyn Park, S.E. 21 ; 5, Essex Court, Temple, E.C. 4. Club : Roehampton. (O8799)

DUKE, Capt. Herbert Lyndhurst, O.B.E.

DUKE, Reginald Franklin Hare, C.B.E. Commercial Secretary, 1st Grade, H.M. Diplomatic Service. (C3106c)

DUKE, Richard Hare, O.B.E.

DUKES, Cuthbert, O.B.E., M.D., D.P.H., b. 24 July, 1890 ; s. of the Rev. E. J. Dukes, of Friern Barnet ; m. Ethel, L.R.C.P., L.R.C.S., d. of the Rev. J. Popplewell, of Bolton, Educ.: Caterham School ; Univ. Coll., London ; Edinburgh. Univ. Bacteriologist ; Fellow of the Royal Society of Medicine. War Work : Late Major, R.A.M.C. ; Medical Specialist to No. 3 Casualty Clearing Station. Address : 18, Gordon Square, W.C. 1. (O5213)

DUKES, Sir Paul, K.B.E. ; b. 10 Feb., 1889 ; s. of the Rev. E. J. Dukes, B.A., of Bridgwater. Educ.: Caterham. School, and Conservatoire of St. Petersburg. Assistant to Mr. Albert Coates at the Imperial Marinsky Opera House, Petrograd, 1913-15. War Work : Member of the Anglo-Russian Commission, Petrograd, and representative of the Commission at the Foreign Office, London, 1915-18 ; Chief of British Intelligence Service in Russia, 1918-19. Address : 18, Gordon Square, W.C.1. Club : Royal Societies'. (K443d)

DULANTY, John Whelan, C.B.E. Assist. Sec. Establishment Depart. Ministry of Munitions. (C493)

DULEY, Capt. Cyril C., M.B.E.

DULMAGE, Lieut.-Col. Anson, O.B.E.

DUMBELL, James Burns, O.B.E., J.P., A.M.I.Mech.E., b. 7 Sept. 1869 ; s. of James Stone Dumbell, of Wolverhampton ; m. Minnie, d. of the late Dr. Robert Lamb, of London. Educ.: Wolverhampton Grammar School. Managing Director of Motor Manufacturing Co. War Work : Founder and organiser of local fund for providing food parcels for 1000 Wolverhampton men imprisoned in Germany, and caring for the welfare and comfort of all soldiers from the district. Address : The Lowlands, Tettenhall, Staffs. (O10332)

DUMBLE, Lieut.-Col. Wilfred Chatterton, C.B.E., O.B.E., R.E.

DUN, Major George, O.B.E., K.C.S.B. (T.F.)

DUNALLEY, Mary Frances, Lady, M.B.E., d. of the late Major-Gen. R. Ouslow Farmer, R.A., of Apsley Guise, Bedfordshire ; m. Henry O'Callaghan Prittie, 4th Baron Dunalley, D.L., J.P., Representative Peer for Ireland. War Work : President of Co. Tipperary Red Cross Society ; Prisoners of War Fund ; Nenagh Branch Soldiers' and Sailors' Families Association ; Soldiers' and Sailors' Help Society, North Riding, Co. Tipperary ; Member of St. John Ambulance Brigade, and Local War Hospital Supply Depot ; Chairman, North Riding, Co. Tipperary, War Pensions Committee. Address : Kilboy, Nenagh, Co. Tipperary. (M7954)

DUNBAR, Paymaster-Capt. Charles Augustus Roger Flood, C.B.E., R.N. (ret.). (C889)

DUNBAR, Frank Hay, M.B.E.

DUNBAR, Capt. Henry John, O.B.E., M.D., F.R.C.S., b. 17 July, 1880 ; s. of the Rev. John W. Dunbar, M.A., of Edinburgh. Educ.: Watson's Coll., Edinburgh ; Edinburgh Univ. Medical Practitioner. War Work : T. Major, R.A.M.C. (T.F.) ; served with 2nd Welsh Field Ambulance in Dardanelles, Egypt, and Palestine. Address : 47, Cathedral Road, Cardiff. (O6172)

DUNBAR, Major Leslie, O.B.E., R.A.M.C., M.B.

DUNBAR, Major Robert Murray, O.B.E., M.C., S.A.S.C.

DUNBAR, Capt. and Qr.-Mr. William Robert, M.B.E., R.A.S.C.

DUNCALFE, Lucy Harding, Mrs., O.B.E., d. of Thomas Fenn, late of Stonebrook House, Ludlow, Salop. War Work : Vice-President of British Red Cross Society for Wolverhampton ; Head of Red Cross organisations for the borough, and sent many thousands pounds to " Our Day " fund ; opened large workrooms and Hospital Supply Depot in the town. Address : Stockwell End House, Tettenhall, Staffs. (O10333)

DUNCAN, Paymaster Sub.-Lieut. Alec James, M.B.E., R.N.R.

DUNCAN, Lieut. Charles, M.B.E., R.F.A.

DUNCAN, Capt. David Blaikie, O.B.E., 1st Sco. Rifles, b. 27 June, 1878. Educ.: James Gillespies Merchant Co., Edinburgh. War Work : Served in France and Flanders from 15 Aug. 1914, to 24 Aug. 1919. Address : H.Qrs. (British Section) Inter-Allied Commission of Control, A.C.O., 85, Berlin ; 13 Garrioch Quadrant, Kelvinside North, Glasgow. (O5216)

DUNCAN, Elsie Eppielow, M.B.E.

DUNCAN, George, M.B.E., b. 23 Aug. 1866 ; s. of Calder Duncan, of Aberdeen ; m. Margaret Ann, d. of James Cameron, of Aberdeen. Educ.: Ruthrieston Public School, and Ramage's

Academy. Engineer ; Chief Engineer in ocean-going vessels ; Superintendent of the Aberdeen Floating Docks. War Work : As Superintendent of the Floating Docks, was responsible for the docking of over 2000 vessels for the Admiralty. Address : 4, Milburn Street, Aberdeen. (M7055)

DUNCAN, Capt. George, C.B.E. Com. and Acting Capt. R.N. (C891)

DUNCAN, George Douglass, M.B.E.

DUNCAN, Surg.-Comm. George Ernest, O.B.E.. R.N.

DUNCAN, George Forest, M.B.E. ; s. of William Duncan, of New Deer, Aberdeenshire ; m. Charlotte Gordon, d. of Robert Campbell, of Farr, Sutherlandshire. Educ.: Free Church Training Coll., Glasgow. Teacher. War Work : Inspector-in-Charge of Special Constables, Rutherglen and District, for 3½ years. Address : 13, Jedburgh Avenue, Rutherglen.(M7957)

DUNCAN, Capt. George Wilson, M.B.E., M.C.

DUNCAN, Rev. George Simpson, O.B.E., B.D., b. 8 Mar. 1884 ; s. of Alexander Duncan, of Forfar. Educ.: Forfar Academy ; Edinburgh Univ. ; St. Andrews Univ. ; Trinity Coll., Cambridge. Professor of Biblical Criticism, Univ. of St. Andrews. War Work : Chaplain to the Forces ; attached to General Headquarters, British Armies in France, 1915-19 ; twice mentioned in despatches. Address : St. Mary's Coll., St. Andrews. (O2501)

DUNCAN, George Leopold, M.B.E.

DUNCAN, Lieut. Godfrey Alexander, M.B.E.

DUNCAN Henry Clare, O.B.E. (O9760)

DUNCAN, Houston, O.B.E.

DUNCAN, James, O.B.E.

DUNCAN, Rev. James, O.B.E., M.A., S.C.F. (hon). b. 1882 ; s. of W. A. Duncan, of Deeside, Scotland. Educ.: Hatfield Coll., Durham Univ. Clerk-in-Holy Orders ; Rector of Willington. War Work : R.A.C. Dept., 1914-19 ; 16th K.R.R.C. (C.L.B.) Batt., 1914-17 ; Senior Chaplain, 58th (London) Division, 1917-19 ; Author of " With the C.L.B. Battalion in France " (Skeffington, 1916). Address : The Rectory, Willington, Co. Durham. (O1306)

DUNCAN, Major James Matthews, O.B.E., T.D., M.A., M.D., b. 17 June, 1874 ; s. of Charles Duncan, of Deebank, Aberdeenshire ; m. Muriel, d. of G. S. Stephenson, M.D., of Manor House, Grimsby. Educ.: Grammar School, Aberdeen ; Aberdeen Univ ; West London Hospital. Medical Referee, Ministry of Pensions ; Naval Surgeon ; Certifying Factory Surgeon ; Hon. Physician, Ascot Cottage Hospital. War Work : M.O., 5th Bn. Lincs Regt. ; O.C. Ambulance Train, France ; O.C. 46 Stationary Hospital, France. Address : Murtle, Sunninghill, Berks. (O5217)

DUNCAN, Leland Lewis, M.V.O., O.B.E., F.S.A., b. 24 Aug. 1862 ; s. of Leland Crosthwait Duncan, of H.M. Customs. Educ.: Lewisham Grammar School. Clerk, War Office. since 1882. War Work : In charge of Army Printing and Stationery Services at the War Office. Address : Rosslair, Lingards Road, Lewisham. (O303).

DUNCAN, Margaret Elmslie, M.B.E. (M10247c)

DUNCAN, Peter Milne, O.B.E. (O12044)u

DUNCAN, Robert, M.B.E.

DUNCAN, Capt. Thomas, M.B.E.

DUNCAN, Capt. William, O.B.E., R.A.M.C. (T.F.)

DUNCAN, Capt. William Lindsay, M.B.E.

DUNCOMBE, Lieut.-Col. Charles William Ernest, C.B.E., J.P., for N.R. Yorks., b 15 March, 1862 ; e. s. of Cecil Duncombe, of the Grange, Nawton, Yorks., and uncle of the present Earl of Feversham (see BURKE'S Peerage) ; m. 1st, 8 Feb. 1890, Lilian Bertha, step-d. of Archibald Stuart Wortley (died 14 Feb. 1904), 2nd, 26 July, 1910, Frances Adelaide. e. d. of the late Rev. H. M. Villiers (see BURKE'S Peerage, Clarendon, E.) and w. of Arthur Francis Walrond (see BURKE'S Landed Gentry). Address : 11, Montagu Square, W. Clubs : Carlton ; White's. (C148)

DUNCOMBE, Emily Katharine Louisa, M.B.E. Commandant, Horticultural Section, Women's Legion, Rutland. (M10313)

DUNDAS, Major Allan Charlesworth, O.B.E.

DUNDAS, Betty, Mrs., M.B.E., Q.M.A.A.C.

DUNDAS, Lieut.-Col. Patrick Henry, C.B.E., D.S.O., b. 1871 ; s. of Donald William Dundas. Entered Indian Army 1894 ; became Capt. 1901, Major, 1910 ; Brevet Lieut.-Col. 1917 ; Lieut.-Col. 1919 ; served on N.-W. Frontier of India, 1897-98 (medal with clasp) ; in China, 1900 (medal) ; Great War, 1914-17 (despatches) ; Staff-Capt., India, 1907-8 ; Brig.-Major, 1909-11 ; appointed an A.Q.M.G. 1916. (O6612)

DUNDERDALE, Robert Harold Webster, M.B.E., M.R.C.P. L.R.C.P.

DUNDERDALE, Wilfred Albert, M.B.E., Lieut. R.N.V.R. (M10365)

DUNELL, Lieut. Alan Gordon, M.B.E., R.A.S.C.

DUNELL, Marion, Mrs., M.B.E.

DUNFEE, Col. Vickers, V.D., J.P., b. 30 April, 1861 ; Educ.: King's College and School. Commandant City of London Police Reserve ; Deputy Alderman, Ward of Vintry, War Work : Gallipoli, Egypt, France. Address : Guildhall, E.C. Club : Royal Automobile Club. (C1546)

DUNHAM, Walter, M.B.E., R.A.S.C.

DUNK, Harry William, M.B.E. Address : Percy Road, Bexley Heath. (M1680)

DUNKIN, William Henry, M.B.E.

DUNKLEY, Lieut. George William, O.B.E., R.M.A.

DUNKLEY, Capt. Stanley Fitz-Roy, O.B.E., b. 16 Aug. 1889 ; s. of Joseph E. Dunkley, of Northampton and Montreal ; m.

Doris Evelyn, *y. d.* of William James Webb, Managing Director, London Public Company. *Educ.:* St. Mark's Coll., London. Technical Clerk, The Gas Light and Coke Company, Westminster. *War Work:* Mobilised Aug. 1914 with R.N.V.R., in which he had five years previous service ; Secretary to G.O. Commanding 63rd (R.N.) Division Reserves until 1916 ; Staff Capt. with H.Q. 63rd (R.N.) Division, Oct. 1916, to Feb. 1920. *Address:* 25, Bishops Mansions, Putney Bridge, S.W. 6. *Club:* Vesta Rowing. (O9787)

DUNLEATH, Nora Louisa Fanny, O.B.E.

DUNLEY, James, M.B.E.

DUNLOP, Major Charles, D.S.O., O.B.E. Major in the Army ; served in the Great War, 1915–19. (O1307)

DUNLOP, Elizabeth Dorothea, M.B.E.

DUNLOP, Frederick George, O.B.E.

DUNLOP, Lieut. and Quartermaster Robert, M.B.E., Reserve of Officers Union Defence Force, *b.* 22 Feb. 1874 ; *s.* of William Dunlop, of Greenock, Scotland ; *m.* Marion, *d.* of William Gray, of Edinburgh. *Educ.:* Moray House and Heriot Watt College, Edinburgh. Registered Public Accountant ; Commissioner for Oaths ; Secretary, Chamber of Commerce and Public Comparies. *War Work:* Organising Secretary and Treasurer (Natal) Governor General's Fund ; Hon. Sec., Disabled Soldier's Board ; Hon. Sec., Returned Soldier's Committee, Maritzburg. *Address:* 280, Prince Alfred Street, Pietermaritzburg. (M1212)

DUNLOP, Sir Thomas, Bart., G.B.E., LL.D., J.P., D.L., *b.* 2 Aug. 1855 ; *s.* of Thomas Dunlop, of Glasgow ; *m.* 1st, Dorothy Euphemia, 2nd, Margaret, both *ds.* of Peter Mitchell, of Longniddry, E. Lothian, *Educ.:* Glasgow Academy. Shipowner and Flour Importer. *War Work:* Lord Provost of Glasgow, 1914–17 during which period did a considerable amount of recruiting and raised large sums of money for war purposes and relief funds. *Address:* 6, Park Terrace, Glasgow. *Clubs:* Conservative, Art and New Clubs, Glasgow ; Conservative, Edinburgh. (G23)

DUNLOP, Capt. William, O.B.E., R.A.M.C., S.R.

DUNLOP, Lieut.-Col. William Bruce, D.S.O., O.B.E. (O11737)

DUNLOP, Capt. William George, O.B.E., M.C., *b.* 9 June, 1892 ; *s.* of William Dunlop, of Haysmuir, Ayr. *Educ.:* St. Ninians, Moffat ; Fettes Coll., Edinburgh. Chartered Accountant. *War Work:* Capt. Ayrshire Royal Horse Artillery (T.F.) ; served on Staff of A. and N.Z. Mtd. Div., and of XXth Army Corps ; mentioned in despatches, March, 1917, Oct. 1918, March, 1919. *Address:* Haysmuir, Ayr, Scotland. *Club:* Junior, Glasgow. (O6173)

DUNLOP, William Louis Martial, O.B.E.

DUNLOP, Mary Janet MURRAY-, M.B.E. ; *d.* of A. C. S., Murray-Dunlop, of Corsock and Edinbarnet, Scotland. *War Work:* Commandant of Auxiliary Hospital, Class B., Glendarroch, Kirkcowan, Wigtownshire, Jan. 1915–Jan. 1919 ; the Hospital ran for 16 months on voluntary contributions. *Address:* Corvisel, Newton Stewart, Wigtownshire. (M7963)

DUNN, Alfred Cuthbert, C.B.E. (C3188)

DUNN, Capt. Arthur Edward, C.B.E., R.D., R.N.R. Served in the Great War, 1914–19 (despatches). (C2291)

DUNN, Ellen S., Mrs., M.B.E.

DUNN, Frederick William, O.B.E., B.A., B.Sc., A.R.C.Sc., *b.* 11 Dec. 1869 ; *s.* of the late William Henry Dunn, of Bristol and Parkstone, Dorset ; *m.* Helen Elizabeth Dunn, *d.* of David Durham, of Stonehaven. *Educ.:* Merchant Venturers Technical Coll. Bristol ; Royal Coll. of Science for Ireland ; Glasgow Univ. ; London Univ. Science Research Scholar of Exhibition of 1851 ; Barrister at Law ; Examiner, H.M. Patent Office. *War Work:* attached to the Higher Clerical Staff of the Ordnance Factories, Royal Arsenal, Woolwich, from 17 Aug. 1914, to 16 March, 1919. *Address:* 8, Westmount Road, Eltham, S.E. 9. (O10337)

DUNN, George Owen William, O.B.E., *b.* 25 Oct. 1854 ; *s.* of Major W. J. Dunn, of Royal Marine Light Inf. ; *m.* Charlotte, *d.* of Daniel de Castro, of East Sheen. *Educ.:* Royal Indian Engineering Coll., Coopers Hill. Late Chief Engineer, Bombay Public Works Department, and Chairman Bombay City Improvement Trust, 1904–9 ; Member of the Bombay Legislative Council, 1905–9 ; President of the Bombay Municipal Corporation, 1908–9. *War Work:* Metropolitan Special Constabulary, D division, Constable, Sergeant, and Inspector, 1914–16 ; First Division Clerk, India Office, 1916–19. *Address:* 60, Bickenhall Mansions, W. 1. *Clubs:* East India United Service, Byculla, Bombay. (O10338)

DUNN, Harold Stuart, M.B.E., R.N.

DUNN, James D., O.B.E., ; *s.* of the late James Dunn, of Glasgow ; *m.* Florence Kerr, *d.* of John Ward, of Dumbarton. *Educ.:* Glasgow Academy, and Fettes Coll., Edinburgh, Ship Broker. *War Work:* Ministry of Shipping. *Addresses:* 33, Kingsborough Gardens, Glasgow ; 31, St. Vincent Place, Glasgow. *Clubs:* New, Glasgow ; Caledonian, London. (O3695)

DUNN, James Stormont, C.B.E. Reuter's Agent in S. Africa. (C2001)

DUNN, Marion Prudence, M.B.E.

DUNN, Patrick Smith, C.B.E.

DUNN, Capt. Robert Charles, O.B.E.

DUNN, Lieut. Robert Ewart, O.B.E., R.N.R.

DUNN, Major Wilfred James, O.B.E., R.A.M.C.

DUNNE, James, M.B.E.

DUNNE, Laura Catharine, Mrs., M.B.E., *b.* 18 Dec. 1885 ; *d.* of Admiral W. H. Henderson ; *m.* James Stuart, Major,

D.S.O., F.R.C.S.I., R.A.M.C., *s.* of William Dunne, of Edenderry, King's Co., Ireland. *Educ.:* Privately and at Wycombe Abbey School. *War Work:* Professional Classes War Relief Council, Oct. 1914, to June, 1915 ; Intelligence Division, Admiralty, June, 1915, to Jan. 1920. *Address:* 3, Onslow Houses, London, S.W. 7. (M8709)

DUNNE, Walter Clement Goddard, M.B.E.

DUNNE, Col. William, C.B., C.B.E., J.P., R.A.S.C. (ret.), *b.* 5 March, 1855 ; *s.* of Jeremiah Dunne, J.P., of Aghavoe, Ballacolla, Queen's County ; *m.* Mary Agnes, *d.* of James Higgins, of Valentia Island, co. Kerry. *Educ.:* St. Patrick's College, Carlow. *War Work:* Served as O.C., A.S.C., at the Curragh from 9 Aug. 1914 to 19 May, 1916, and as District Barrack Officer, Scottish Command, from 1 Dec. 1916, to 8 March, 1920. *Address:* Jonestown, Edenderry, King's County. *Club:* Hiberian United Service, Dublin. (C1547)

DUNNETT, Rev. George Victor, O.B.E., B.D., *b.* 9 Dec. 1878 ; *s.* of Rev. Wm. Dunnett, M.A., V.D., of Kilmarnock ; *m.* Jane, *d.* of Rev. R. G. Forrest, D.D., of Edinburgh. *Educ.:* Kilmarnock Academy ; Edinburgh Univ. Parish Minister, Cockburnspath ; subsequently Grange Parish, Edinburgh. *War Work:* Chaplain to the Forces, 1915–19, in M.E.F. and B.E.F. ; twice mentioned in despatches. *Address:* Grange Parish Church, Edinburgh. (O1308)

DUNNETT, Rev. William Alexander, O.B.E.

DUNNING, Lieut. Thomas William John, O.B.E., R.N.R.

DUNRAVEN AND MOUNTEARL, Windham Thomas Wyndham-Quin, Earl of, K.P., P.C., C.M.G., O.B.E., *b.* 12 Feb. 1841 ; *m.* 1869, Florence Elizabeth, *d.* of Lord Charles Lennox Kerr, *s.* of the 6th Marquess of Lothian (see BURKE'S *Peerage*). *Addresses:* Dunraven Castle, Southerdown, Glamorgan ; Adare Manor, co. Limerick ; Kenry House, Putney Vale, S.W. ; 22, Norfolk St., Hyde Park, W. *Clubs:* Athenæum, Turf, Marlborough, Beefsteak, and Royal Yacht Squadron. (O4425)

DUNSCOMBE, Lieut.-Col. Nicholas Blake, O.B.E.

DUNSHEATH, Capt. Percy, O.B.E.

DUNSTAN, Capt. and Qr.-Mr. Albert Edward, O.B.E., R.A.S.C.

DUNSTAN, Malcolm James Rowley, O.B.E., M.A., F.R.S.E., I.C., *b.* 19 Aug. 1863 ; *s.* of John Dunstan, of Chester Castle ; *m.* Edith Rose Walton, of Ipswich. *Educ.:* Bedford Grammar School ; S. Paul's ; Merton College, Oxford (Postmaster). Principal, South Eastern Agric. College, Wye. *War Work:* District Commissioner (Board of Agriculture) Kent, Surrey and Sussex. *Address:* Wye, Kent. *Club:* R.A.C., London. (O304)

DUNSTERVILLE, Col. Arthur Bruce, C.M.G., O.B.E.

DUNSTERVILLE, Capt. Arthur Geoffrey, O.B.E.

DUNVILLE, Lieut.-Col. John, C.B.E., O.B.E., R.A.F.

DUNWOODIE, Lallah Bessie, C.B.E., R.R.C. Lady Sup. Queen Alexandra's Military Service Nursing, India. (C2032)

DUNWOODY, Robert Browne, O.B.E.

DUPE, Mabel Alethea, Mrs., M.B.E.

DUPRÉ, Frederick Harold, M.B.E., F.C.S.

DUPRÉ, Percy Vivian, M.B.E.

DUQUEMIN, Eveline Mary, Mrs., O.B.E., *b.* Dec. 1878 ; *d.* of James Haydon Gill, of Bath ; *m.* Francis William, *s.* of the late James Duquemin, M.I.C.E., of Guernsey. *Educ.:* Whitelands Coll. Chelsea. *War Work:* Served on Committee of Governor-General's Fund, South Africa (Johannesburg Branch), since inception ; Vice-Chairman of same for 2 years ; Hon. Sec. of Witwatersrand Disabled Soldiers Board ; and member of same ; Member of Govt. Advisory Board for Returned Soldiers for Johannesburg. *Address:* Box 4846, Johannesburg. *Clubs:* Country, Johannesburg ; Transvaal Automobile. (O8351)

DURANT, Percy, O.B.E.

DURANT, William James, M.B.E.

DURBRIDGE, Lieut. William, M.B.E., R.F.A. (T.F.)

DURELL, Col. Arthur James Vavasor, C.B., C.B.E.

DURELL, Rev. Canon John Carlyon Vavasor, C.B.E., B.D., *b.* 1 June, 1870 ; *s.* of Rev. J. V. Durell, late Rector of Fulbourn ; *m.* Ellen Maud, *d.* of H. Wood Payne, of Bombay. *Educ.:* Wellington and Clare College, Cambridge. Rector of Rotherhithe ; Chaplain Rotherhithe and Bermondsey Hospital ; Rural Dean of Bermondsey ; Surrogate for Diocese of Southwark ; Examining Chaplain to the Bishop of Southwark ; Hon. Canon of Southwark. *War Work:* Chief Commissioner of the Church Army in France, Belgium and Germany. (C2577)

DURELL, Margaret, M.B.E.

DURHAM, Francis Hermia, C.B.E., *b.* 1873 ; *d.* of the late Arthur E. Durham. Chief Woman Inspector, Central Offices, Employment Depart., Ministry of Labour. *Addresses:* 151, Colcherne Court, S.W. 5 ; Lea Cottage, Otterton, S. Devon. (C149)

DURHAM, Lieut.-Col. Frank Rogers, C.B.E., M.C., R.E.

DURHAM, John Hope, M.B.E., *b.* 9 Aug. 1886 ; *s.* of Capt. William Thomas Durham, of Upper Teddington, Middlesex ; *m.* Eliza, *d.* of the late Robert Roscoe Felix Davey, of St. Withburga's, East Dereham, Norfolk, and Brompton Square, London, S.W. *Educ.:* Privately. Examiner of Letters, Italian and Spanish (Trade) Branches, H.M. Postal Censorship, 1915 Sec. British Vice-Consulate, Venice, 1919 ; Chief Clerk to

Controller of Railways for the Inter-Allied Plebiscite Commission for Upper Silesia, 1920. *War Work :* Confidential Sec. to G.S.O. attached to the Military Intelligence Service for the British Armies in France, 1915–19. *Address :* Palazzo Vendramin Calergi, Venice, Italy. (M7967)

DURHAM, James Alexander ROBERTSON-, O.B.E.

DURIE, Robert DEWAR-, O.B.E., M.C.

DURLER, Nora Kathleen, Mrs., O.B.E.

DURLEY, Richard John, M.B.E., M.Inst.C.E., *b.* 1868; *Educ. :* Bedford Modern School; Univ. Coll. London. Engineer; Sec. Canadian Engineering Standards Association. *War Work :* Officer i/c Gauges and Standards, Department of Inspection, Imperial Ministry of Munitions (Canada). *Address :* 654, Rideau St., Ottawa. *Clubs :* Univ., Montreal; Rideau, Ottawa. (M347)

DURNFORD, Philip Barton, O.B.E.

DURNFORD, Sir Walter, G.B.E., V.D., LL.D., J.P., *b.* 1847; *s.* of Richard Durnford, Bishop of Chichester. *Educ.* Eton and King's College, Cambridge. Provost of Eton College; Senior Fellow of Eton College; J.P. for Cambridgeshire and Cambridge Borough. *War Work :* Chairman of War Board for recommending members of Cambridge University for Commissions. *Address :* The Lodge, King's College, Cambridge. *Clubs :* United University; M.C.C.; Leander. (G40).

DURRAN, William, M.B.E.

DURRANT, Sir Arthur Isaac, C.B.E.

DURRANT, Rt. Rev. Henry Bickersteth, C.B.E., M.A., D.D. *Educ. :* Highgate School; Pembroke Coll., Camb.; Fellow, Allahabad Univ. 1906. Served in the Great War in Mesopotamia, 1915–19 (despatches); appointed Bishop of Lahore, 1913. *Address :* Bishopsbourne, Lahore. (C1143)

DURRANT, Walter Charles, M.B.E.

DUTHIE, Lieut.-Col. Arthur Murray, O.B.E., D.S.O. *b.* 12 June, 1881; *s.* of John Firminger Duthie, Director of Botanical Survey, Northern India; *m.* 1917, Yseult, *d.* of the late Edmond de la Poer, of Gurteen le Poer, Kilsheelan, Ireland. *Educ. :* Marlborough; R.M.A. Woolwich. Entered the Army, 1899; served in the S. African War, 1902 (Queen's medal, two clasps); Great War, in France, 1914–18 (despatches five times; Legion of Honour); Baluchistan Force, Afghanistan War, 1919. *Club :* Army and Navy. (O2504)

DUTHIE, Barbara Elder, M.B.E., T.F.N.S.

DUTHIE, David Hutcheon, O.B.E.

DUTHIE, David Whamand, O.B.E.

DUTHIE, Sir John, K.B.E., J.P.

DUTT, Mrs., M.B.E.

DUTTON, Beatrice Aimee, Mrs., M.B.E.

DUTTON Mildred, M.B.E., *b.* 27 Sept. 1884; *d.* of James Dutton, of Carlton Road, Bolton. *Educ. :* Conamur, Sandgate, Kent, and at home. *War Work :* Deputy Hon. Sec. of Bolton War Pensions Committee from Dec. 1916, to March, 1919, and member of the Committee from Oct. 1917, to June, 1919. *Address :* Cranford, Carlton Road, Bolton, Lancs. (M7968)

DUTTON, Peter Irving, M.B.E., *n.* 4 April, 1880; *s.* of Peter Dutton, of Lancaster; *m.* Hilda Mary, *d.* of the late Benjamin Cork Huntly, M.A., of Hutton Grammar School, Preston. *Educ. :* Royal Grammar School, Lancaster. Clerk and Steward, Lancashire County Asylum, Winwick, Warrington. *War Work :* Clerk and Steward, The Lord Derby War Hospital Winwick, Warrington (3300 beds) from March, 1915. *Address :* Hollins Lane, Winwick, Warrington. *Clubs :* The Warrington, Warrington. (M7969)

DUTTON, Major Ralph Matthew Legge, O.B.E., M.C., R.A., *b.* 21 Sept. 1882; *s.* of the Revd. William Ewart Dutton, of Lothersdale, Yorks. *Educ. :* King's School Canterbury; Royal Military Academy, Woolwich. *War Work :* In East Africa, 1914–17; Persia (Bushin Field Force), 1918–19; North-West Frontier of India (Waziristan), 1919–20. *Address :* c/o Cox & Co., 16, Charing Cross, S.W. 1. (O9054a)

DUVAL, Ethel, Mrs., O.B.E.

DUVAL, Rev. Stephen Peachey, O.B.E., D.D., *b.* 12 Nov. 1870; *s.* of Stephen Smith Duval, of The Hollies, St. Albans Road, Highgate Road, N.W. 5.; *m.* Maud, *d.* of Thomas Norman, of Weston Park, Bath. *Educ. :* Sir Roger Chomeley's School, Highgate; Brasenose Coll., Oxford. Rector of Colne, Lancs.; Surrogate in the Diocese of Manchester. *War Work :* Hon. Treas., Colne Division, Soldiers' and Sailors' Families Association, 1914–16; District Head and Hon. Sec. Colne District, Incorporated Soldiers' and Sailors' Help Society from 1915; Member of Colne Local War Pensions Committee, and Chairman of Separation Allowances Sub-Committee from 1916; Member of Lord Roberts' Memorial Workshops, Burnley and District Committee. *Address :* The Rectory, Colne, Lancs. *Club :* Old Rectory, Manchester. (O11341)

DWANE, Ernest Henry, M.B.E.

DWANE, Lieut.-Col. Herbert Milton, O.B.E.

DWYER, Lieut.-Col. Ernest, C.B.E., M.C., R.A.S.C. Served in the Great War, 1914–19 (despatches). (C1437)

DYAS, Capt. Richard Seymour Vivian, O.B.E.

DYAS, William George, M.B.E.

DYASTON, Ernest Clement, M.B.E.

DYBALL, William Moore, O.B.E.

DYER, Capt. Albert John, M.B.E., I.A.R.O.

DYER, Alfred Thomas, M.B.E.

DYER, Edward Jerome, O.B.E., M.B.E.

DYER, Major James Frederick, O.B.E., R.A.F.

DYER, John Luther, M.B.E,

DYER, Robert Broomfield, M.B.E,. J.P. (Wigtownshire),

b. 21 March, 1863; *s.* of William Dyer, of Dalkeith, Midlothian. *Educ. :* Sheuchan School, and Stranraer Academy. Provost of Stranraer, Scotland; Member of Stranraer Town Council; and Parish Council; Chairman County Joint Hospital Committee; Vice-Chairman County Poor House Board; Chairman of the Association of Parish Councils of Scotland; Member of the Joint Sanatorium Board for Dumfries and Galloway; Provincial Grand Secretary of Free Masonry in Galloway; *War Work :* Chairman of Stranraer Burgh Advisory Committee; Chairman of the Rhins War Pensions Committee; Chairman of Wigtownshire War Pensions Committee; Member of Soldiers' and Sailors' Disablement and Employment Committee for Wigtownshire; Member of the Territorial Force Association of the County. *Address :* Albion House, Stranraer, Scotland. (M7973)

DYER, Terence Armiston Stewart, M.B.E., *b.* 2 Nov. 1874, *s.* of the Revd. Frederick T. Stewart Dyer, of St. John's, Bournemouth. *Educ. :* Falmouth Grammar School, and Crystal Palace School of Engineering Consulting and Inspecting Engineer. *War Work :* Representative in the United States of America of Messrs Rendel, Palmer and Tritton, Consulting Engineers to the War Office and Ministry of Munitions, and had charge of the construction of all Locomotives ordered in the United States by the War Office for service in France, Greece, Egypt, Mesopotamia, etc. *Address :* 28, Rue du Meridien, Brussels, Belgium. (M3621)

DYKE, Arthur James, C.B.E., *b.* 1872; *s.* of Thomas Dyke. Assist. Sec. Board of Customs and Excise, 1910–19; Sec. 1919. *Address :* Custom House, Lower Thames Street, E.C. (C150)

DYKE, David Nicholas, O.B.E., A.R.I.B.A., *b* 24 June, 1881; *s.* of Edward Dyke, of Bournemouth; *m.* Christina Jessie, *d.* of Walter William Wright, of Southgate. *Educ. :* Collett House School, Bournemouth. Architect; Architect and Surveyor, H.M. Office of Works. *War Work :* Design and erection of Hospital Buildings for the wounded at British Red Cross Hospitals; Design and erection of Canteen and Welfare Buildings in Controlled Munition Factories; Purchase and acquisition of many hundreds of properties to enable the Government to accommodate War Staffs. *Addresses :* H.M. Office of Works, Westminster, S.W.; Velindre, Finchley Park, North Finchley. (O16342)

DYKE, Lieut.-Col. John Samuel, O.B.E., M.V.O., *b.* 14 Aug. 1859; *s.* of Samuel Dyke, of Warwick; *m.* 1st 1894, Anna Elizabeth (*d.* 1907), *d.* of Burrhold Bergner, of Fulda, Germany, 2ndly Harriett, *d.* of William Walker, of Whitehall, Chingford, Essex, and *widow* of Lieut.-Col. William Wellington Lake, late R.A.M.C. *Educ. :* Warwick. Formerly of The Queen's Regiment; Adjutant and Qr. Mr. and afterwards Commandant, Duke of York's Royal Military School; Served in Burmese Exped., 1886–9 (Medal and two clasps); South African War, 1900–2 (twice mentioned in despatches, Queen's Medal and two clasps, King's Medal and two clasps). *War Work :* employed as Commandant Duke of York's Royal Military School during the Great War. *Address :* 20, Kingsnorth Gardens, Folkestone. *Club :* Junior Army and Navy. (O7109)

DYKES, Ellen, Mrs., O.B.E., C.C. Warwickshire County Council. *War Work :* Hon. Sec. Leamington Spa Division of Soldiers' and Sailors' Families Association since 1914; and Sec. of Leamington War Pensions Sub-Committee, July, 1916, to May, 1920. *Address :* 12, Milverton Crescent, Leamington Spa. (O10343)

DYKES, Kathleen Ellison, M.B.E., *b.* 15 Sept. 1894; *d.* of Sir Thomas Oliver, of Ayr, N.B.; *m.* Kingsley, *s.* of Alfred Herbert Dykes, of Shortlands, Kent. *War Work :* Hon. Sec. Ladies' Committee. Tyneside Scottish Brigade (N.F.); V.A.D. at Northumberland War Hospital, Newcastle-on-Tyne; No. 9 Red Cross Hospital, Calais; and No. 1 Red Cross Hospital, Le Touquet. *Address :* Ottinge Court Farm, Elham, nr. Canterbury. (M7974)

DYKES, Capt. Kingsley, O.B.E., M.C.

DYMOCK, Lieut.-Col. Arthur, O.B.E.. R.A.O.C.

DYMOND, Charles Joseph, O.B.E., J.P., *b.* 21 Aug. 1857; *s.* of Joseph John Dymond, of Exeter; *m.* Margaret Harris, *d.* of John Bennett Alexander, of Newcastle-on-Tyne. *Educ. :* Oliver's Mount School, Scarboro'. *War Work :* Y.M.C.A. work in home camps; Northumberland County Medal for British Red Cross and St. John Ambulance Association for convoy of wounded and air raid work. *Address :* 1, Windsor Terrace, Newcastle-on-Tyne. (O10344)

DYMOND, Edmund Robert, O.B.E., Assoc. M.Inst.C.E., J.P., *b.* 1865; *s.* of W. P. Dymond, of Penmorva, Falmouth; *m.* Dorothy Emma, *d.* of the late Rev. Preb. Harris D.D. *Educ. :* Clifton Coll.; Bristol Univ. Coll.; Crompton's, Chelmsford. *War Work :* Mayor of Hereford, Nov. 1916–Nov. 1919; Chairman of Nat. Service Committee, War Savings Committee, Women's Welfare Committee, Billeting (Civilian) Committee, Labour Employment Committee; Member of Fuel, Food, and Red Cross Committees. *Address :* Hampton Grange, Hereford. *Club :* Hereford County. (O10345)

DYMOND, Mary Evelyn, O.B.E., *b.* 9 Aug. 1865; *d.* of George Dymond, of Edgbaston. *Educ. :* Privately. *War Work :* Hon. Manager, Church of England Soldiers' Institute, Swanage, 1915–19. (O10346)

DYSON, Lieut.-Col. Harry Hugo Bernard, D.S.O., O.B.E., *b.* 1 June, 1869; *s.* of William Henry Dyson; *m.* Nora, *d.* of Alfred Leighton Whittell, of Woodside, Llandaff. *Educ. :* R.M.C., Sandhurst. Entered Royal Scots, 1889; Capt., 1897;

Major, 1907; Lieut.-Col., 1917; D.A.A.G., Poona, 1903–7; appointed G.S.O., 1915. *War Work:* European War, 1914–19; despatches, 1915, 1917, 1918, and 1919; awarded D.S.O. and O.B.E. *Address:* The Bays, Burnham, Bucks. *Club:* Army and Navy. (O5221)

DYSON, John Richard Haigh, M.B.E., L.R.C.P. and L.R.C.S. (Ed.), L.R.F.P., and S. (Glasgow), *b.* 19 Jan. 1865; *s.* of Alexander Dyson, of Honley, nr. Huddersfield; *m.* Edith, *d.* of Thomas Grant, of Huddersfield. *Educ.:* Huddersfield Coll. and Univ. Coll. Hospital, London. *War Work:* Medical Officer, Honley Auxiliary Hospital, nr. Huddersfield. *Address:* Prospect House, Honley, nr. Huddersfield. (M7579)

DYSON, Major William, O.B.E., M.D., R.A.M.C. (T.), *b.* 19 May, 1872; *s.* of John Dyson, of Manchester; *m.* Margaret Mabel, *d.* of William Speirs, of Cleator. *Educ.:* Rossall, Victoria University, Vienna. Physician; Dermatologist, Manchester Royal Infirmary; Physician, Manchester and Salford Hospital for Skin Diseases; Lecturer in Dermatology, Victoria University of Manchester. *War Work:* (1) R.M.O. to 1/8th Lancashire Fusiliers, Egypt and Gallipoli; (2) Dermatologist to the Forces in Alexandria, Egypt; (3) Officer i'c Med. Division, 78th General Hospital, Egypt and Palestine; Mentioned in Despatches (Sir Edmund Allenby's) for services rendered between March and September, 1918. *Addresses:* Birch Polygon, Rusholme, Manchester; 96, Mosley Street, Manchester. *Club:* Clarendon. (O2859)

EACHUS, Lieut. Thomas, O.B.E., R.N.V.R.

EADIE, Harold George, M.B.E., *b.* 7 Oct. 1874; *s.* of G. W. Eadie, of Montreal, Canada; *m.* Marjorie Sanborn, *d.* of Hon. James K. Ward, of Montreal, Canada. *Educ.:* The Grange, Eastbourne, and Uppingham. *War Work:* Sec. to the Ministry of Munitions at Birmingham, 1916–18, and Superintendent of Offices, 1918–19. *Address:* Rokeby, Cheltenham. *Club:* Golfers'. (M350)

EADIE, Robert, M.B.E. (M10440)

EADY, Lieut.-Col. Frederick William Edward, O.B.E., R.M.L.I., *b.* 3 Jan. 1864; *s.* of Edward Eady, youngest son of William Eady, of Campsbourne; *m.* Maud Evelyn, *d.* of late Edward Loraine, of Loraine House, Wallington. *Educ.:* Sherborne. Lieut. R.M.L.I., 1 Sept. 1883; Retired, 7 Sept. 1905. *War Work:* Recruiting Staff Officer; Royal Navy and Royal Marines, Scotlan.. *Address:* Bay Cottage, Fyfield, Weyhill, Hants. (O4426)

EADY, Comm. George Griffin, O.B.E., R.N.V.R.

EAGAR, Edward Herbert, M.B.E., *b.* 9 Oct. 1864; *s.* of the late Charles Henry Eagar, Civil Engineer. *Educ.:* City Middle Class School, Cowper Street, E.C.; King's College, London, Civil Service Dept. Senior Examiner; Paymaster General's Office, Whitehall, S.W.1. *War Work:* Head of Pensions Section for Widows, Children and other Relatives of Army Officers. *Address:* St. Denis, Normandy Avenue, High Barnet, Herts. (M351)

EAGAR, Margery, Mrs., M.B.E., W.R.N.S.

EAGER, Joseph Henry, M.B.E.

EAGER, Major Richard, O.B.E., M.D., M.P.C., R.A.M.C. (T.), *b.* 14 June, 1881; *s.* of the late Dr. Wilson Eager, of Woodbridge, Suffolk; *m.* Marion Jane, *d.* of C. H. Tremlett, of The Quarries, Exeter. *Educ.:* Aldenham School, Elstree, Herts, and Aberdeen Univ. Physician, Deputy Medical Superintendent, the Devon Mental Hospital, Exminster; Neurologist, "Out Patient Clinic," the Palace Hospital, Exeter. Divisional Prize Medico-Psychological Association 1914, Bronze Medal and Prize 1919. *War Work:* O.C. 2/1st Wessex Field Ambulance, 1914; Resident Medical Officer Neurological section, the Royal Victoria Hospital, Netley, 1916; Medical Officer in charge of the Mental Division (1000 beds), the Lord Derby War Hospital, Warrington, June, 1916, to Oct. 1918; attached Special Neurological Hospital and School of Instruction, Maghull, nr. Liverpool; Resident Medical Officer, the Ashhurst War Hospital for Functional Nervous Disorders, nr. Oxford, Oct. 1918, to Feb. 1919. *Address:* The Devon Mental Hospital, Exminster. (O8801)

EAGLES, Joseph William, M.B.E., *b.* 15 Feb. 1865; *s.* of Joseph Eagles, of Wigan, Lancs; *m.* Elizabeth, *d.* of Thomas Bryan, of Peterboro'. *Educ.:* Sheffield. Engineer and Manager, Coalville Urban District Council Gas Dept., nr. Leicester. *War Work:* Hon. Sec. Coalville and District War Savings Assoc. since commencement; Vice-Chairman, Profiteering Committee; Member of the Food Control Committee; Member of the Local Fuel Committee; Special Constable. *Address:* Whitwick, nr. Leicester (M7977)

EAGLETON, Comm. Henry Arthur, O.B.E., R.N.R., R.D.

EALES, Sydney York, M.B.E.

EALES, Capt. William John, O.B.E., has Croix de Guerre of Italy. (O2977)

EAMES, Florence Mabel, M.B.E.

EAMES, Col. William L'Estrange, C.B., O.B.E.

EARCHWAN, Archibald, O.B.E. (O5991)

EARL, Major Austin, C.B.E., O.B.E., R.G.A.

EARL, Edward Franklyn, M.B.E. Accountant to the Ministry of Shipping since its formation. (M10314)

EARL, Frederick, O.B.E.

EARLE, Major Augustus Thornhill, O.B.E., *b.* 5 Feb. 1872; *s.* of Augustus John Earle, of Liverpool and County Wexford. *Educ.:* Liverpool Institute. *War Work:* Mobilized Aug. 1914, as Capt. 4th (S.R.) Bn. King's Regt; Proceeded

to France, 29 Sept., and posted to 1st Bn. King's Regt.; served in that unit on the Aisne and the whole of the First Battle of Ypres; Served subsequently, Gallipoli and Egypt, 1915–16, and France, 1916–19. *Address:* Bank of Liverpool; 160, Argburth Road, Liverpool. *Club:* Conservative, Liverpool. (O5222)

EARLE, Betty, Mrs., M.B.E., *b.* 27 Feb. 1863; *d.* of Fife Scott, of Newcastle-on-Tyne; *m.* Cecil Arthur, *s.* of Arthur Earle, of Childwall Lodge, Wavertree. *War Work:* Camberley Military Hospital, Sept. 1914, to March, 1920. *Address:* Earles Court, Camberley, Surrey. (M7979)

EARLE, Gerald Frederick, C.B.E.

EARLE, William Francis, O.B.E., *b.* 17 Jan. 1857; *s.* of the late George Earle, of High Rhones, Sheriff Hutton, York; *m.* Jean Graham, *s.* of John Gibson, of Standerton, Transvaal. *Educ.:* Huddersfield Coll., Yorkshire. *War Work:* Chairman, Advisory Wool Committee under Imperial Government Purchase Scheme; Fellow, Royal Colonial Institute, London. *Address:* Lynden, Bellevue Road, Durban. *Club:* Durban, Durban, Natal. (O8352)

EARP, Charles Anthony, C.B.E. (C3189)

EARP, Hon. George Frederick, C.B.E. (C3190)

EARP, Major Lewis Thomas Jerome, O.B.E., R.A.O.C.

EARWAKER, Capt. Ralph Parsons, O.B.E., R.A.S.C.

EASBY, Nora, O.B.E., R.R.C. Q.A.I.M.N.S.R.

EASON, John Charles Malcolm, O.B.E., *b.* 22 June, 1880; *s.* of Charles Eason, J.P., of Dalkey, Co. Dublin. *Educ.:* Trinity Coll., Dublin. *War Work:* Joint Hon. Sec. National Savings Committee for Leinster, Munster, Connaught. *Address:* 4, Alma Road, Monkstown, Co. Dublin. (O10437)

EASON, Paymaster-Lieut.-Comm. Victor Cecil Gould, O.B.E., D.S.C., R.N.

EAST, Alfred Ernest, M.B.E.

EAST, Capt. Arthur William, M.B.E.

EAST, Percy Harry, M.B.E.

EAST, Major George Frederick Lancelot CLAYTON-, O.B.E.

EASTCOTT, Henry John, M.B.E.

EASTEN, Stephen, O.B.E., J.P., *b.* 26 Feb. 1867; Building Contractor; President of the National Federation of Building Trade employers of Great Britain and Ireland; City Councillor and Chairman of the Estates and Property Committee. *War Work:* Chairman of the Local Tribunal. *Address:* Esperance, Akenside Terrace, Jesmond, Newcastle-on-Tyne *Club:* Junior Constitutional. (O309)

EASTGATE, Capt. and Qr.-Mr. Henry, M.B.E.

EASTHAM, William Pelham, O.B.E., *b.* 16 June, 1854; *s.* of William Eastham, of Maidstone, Kent; *m.* Margaret, *d.* of George Stevens, of Ramsgate. *Educ.:* Grammar School, Gt. Yarmouth. Capt. of Trinity House Steam Vessels until 1904, then Marine Supt.; Retired since 1918. *War Work:* Admiralty work under Trinity House jurisdiction. *Address:* Richmond House, Hardingstone, Northampton. (O3697)

EASTICK, Capt. and Qr.-Mr. Alfred, M.B.E.

EASTICK, Charles Esau, M.B.E., F.C.S.

EASTMAN, Capt. Edward George, O.B.E., *b.* 1885; *s.* of late Edward John Eastman of Alcombe, Sydenham; *m.* Emily, *d.* of George Henry West, of Newent, Glos. *Educ.:* Dulwich College. Civil Servant. *War work:* Capt. 25th Middlesex Regt., Service in Siberia; With battalion when mined in "Tynddrews," off Cape of Good Hope, 1917. *Address:* C/o London County and Westminster Bank, Orpington. *Club:* Hong Kong. (O4291)

EASTON, Col. George, C.B.E., T.D., D.L.

EASTON, Major Philip George, C.B.E., D.S.O., *b.* 15 Dec. 1878; *s.* of late John Easton, M.D., of 19, Norfolk Crescent, Hyde Park, W.; *m.* Winifred, *d.* of Philip Witham, of Whitmoor House. *Educ.:* Lancing College, St. Mary's Hospital. Deputy Assistant Director General Army Medical Service. *War Work:* No. 3 Field Ambulance; D.A.D.M.S., 1st Corps; D.A.D.M.S.. Base and L. of C., Salonika; D.A.D.G., War Office. *Address:* Whitmoor House, Sutton Park, Nr. Guildford. *Club:* Junior Army and Navy. (C1548)

EASTWOOD, Dorothy Sybil Montagu, Mrs., M.B.E., W.R.N.S.

EASTWOOD, Lieut.-Col. Frederick Norman, O.B.E., M.C., *b.* 1877; *s.* of the late Frederick Eastwood, J.P., of Huddersfield; *m.* Edith Mary, *d.* of the late Charles Beaumont Waller, M.D., of Sydenham, S.E. *Educ.:* Loretto School; Elizabeth Coll., Guernsey; Pembroke Coll., Oxford. *War Work:* Joined 2/22 London Regt., 1914; raised and commanded 3/22 London Regt., 1915; served with 2/22 London Regt. in France, 1916; in Salonika, 1917; with E.E.F., 1917–18; with E.E.F. as Base Commandant, Alexandretta, Syria, 1918–19; mentioned in despatches,. *Address:* c/o Barclays Bank, Sydenham, London. (O6174)

EASTWOOD, Mabel, M.B.E.

EASTWOOD, Capt. and Qr.-Mr. Samuel Cosby, M.B.E.

EASTWOOD, William Hastings, O.B.E.; *s.* of William Eastwood, of Liverpool; *m.* 1st, Jeannie, *d.* of the late James Welsh, 2nd, Marion Brokenshar, *d.* of Charles E. L. Gregson, of Waterloo, Lancs. *Educ.:* Liverpool Institute. Member of Waterloo-with-Seaforth Urban District Council, and of Education Committee. *War Work:* Served as Chairman of the following Committees—Local War Pensions Committee (Waterloo-with-Seaforth), Waterloo Recruiting Committee (Derby Scheme), Military Advisory Committee, National War Campaign; Member of Roll of Honour Committee; also served in the V.T.C. and the Volunteer Force throughout the war. *Address:* Rosemarkie, Victoria Road, Waterloo, Lancashire. *Club:* Liverpool Reform. (O10348)

EATEN, Sybil Frances, O.B.E.

EATHERLEY, Capt. William, O.B.E., B.A. (Cantab.), *b.* 29 Dec. 1877; *s.* of Nathan Hunt Eatherly. *Educ.:* Merchant Taylors, and Queen's College, Cambridge. *War Work:* 289 Siege Battery, R.G.A.; Artillery liaison officer, 6th Squadron, R.F.C.; Staff Capt., Heavy Artillery in Italy. *Address:* 54, Grosvenor Street, W. *Club:* Almack's. (O2978)

EATON, Capt. B. J., O.B.E.

EATON, Capt. Henry Rayner, O.B.E.

EATON, Lieut.-Col. William Arnold, O.B.E., The Buffs, *b.* 7 April, 1870; *s.* of Rev. Canon J. R. T. Eaton. *Educ.:* Marlborough and Sandhurst. *Address:* Sondes House, Bekesbourne, Canterbury. *Club:* Naval and Military. (O3114)

EBBEN, Lieut.-Col. Henry Stuart, O.B.E., R.A.F., *b.* 9 Dec. 1884; *s.* of Rev. H. Ebben, of Bournemouth; *m.* Grace Henriette Spaner, of East London, So. Africa. *Educ.:* Salisbury School. Member of the Stock Exchange. *War Work,* R.F.C., and R.A.F.; Director of Manning at the Air Ministry and subsequently Officer i/c R.A.F. Records. *Addresses:* 10, Throgmorton Avenue, London, E.C.2: 32, Harrington Gardens, London, S.W.7. (O310)

EBDEN, Agnes Murray, Mrs., C.B.E.; *d.* of Col. Murray Mackenzie, R.H.A.; *m.* Charles John Ebden. Deputy President, B.R.C.S. and Order of St. John of Jerusalem, Hastings and St. Leonards; Lady of Grace of Order of St. John of Jerusalem in England; Order of Mercy. *Addresses:* Baldslow Place, Baldslow, Sussex; Newton House, Alvanfort, Lanarkshire. (C151)

EBDEN, Elizabeth, Mrs., M.B.E.

EBERLE, Alderman James Fuller, O.B.E., *b.* 1854; *s.* of the Rev. J. A. Eberle. *Educ.:* Clifton Coll., and Dr. C. T. Hudson's, of Manilla Hall. Alderman of Bristol, and Chairman of the Museum and Art Gallery, where over 50,000 wounded soldiers were entertained by citizens during the winter months. *War Work:* A member of the Bristol Recruiting Committee upon the outbreak of the war, becoming Chairman of this Committee (after the death of Sir Herbert Ashman Bart., and Sir Joseph Weston Stevens). *Address:* 110, Pembroke Road, Clifton, Bristol. *Clubs:* Royal Automobile; Constitutional, Bristol. (O10349)

EBORALL, Edith, M.B.E.; *d.* of Cornelius Willes Eborall, of London. *Educ.:* Privately. *War Work:* Hon. Sec. and Treas. Church of England Soldiers' Club, Woodward Hall, Folkestone, from Aug. 1914, to June, 1919. *Address:* Birnam Lodge, Manor Road, Folkestone. (M7981)

EBORALL, Herbert, M.B.E., *b.* 14 March, 1881; *s.* of Alfred Eborall, of Hastings, Sussex; *m.* Ivy Ivory, of Moss Bury, Herts. *Educ.:* King's College, London. Civil Service; Admiralty since 1898. *War Work:* In A.G.'s Department of the Admiralty. (M352)

EBRAHIM, Sir Fazulbhoy, C.B.E.

ECCLESTON, 2nd Lieut. Henry Charles, M.B.E., R.E.

ECHLIN, Lieut. Joseph Edward O'Brien, O.B.E., R.E. (T.).

ECKERSLEY, Frank, O.B.E., M.I.M.E., F.S.I., *b.* 12 March, 1873; *s.* of James Eckersley, of Atherton, Lancashire; *m.* Frances, *d.* of John Burgess, of Alderley Edge. *Educ.:* Privately, and Owens College (now Manchester Univ.). Mining Engineer to the Duchy of Lancaster. *War Work:* Inspector on behalf of the Controller of Coal Mines, and Technical Adviser to the Lancashire, Cheshire, and North Wales Pitwood Committee. *Address:* Abbotsford, Kenilworth Avenue, Harrogate. (O10350)

ECKFORD, 2nd Lieut. Francis George, M.B.E., R.A.F.

ECKFORD, Reg. Henderson, M.B.E.

ECROYD, Capt. Frederick Thomas, M.B.E., A.M.I.C.E.

EDDEN, Major Reginald Percival Sidney, O.B.E.

EDDISON, Albert, C.B.E. Gen. Manager of Kynoch (Limited). (C494)

EDDY, Charles, M.B.E., R.N.

EDDY, Edward George, M.B.E., *b.* 22 June, 1878; *Educ.:* Kidderminster Grammar School. Managing Director; Member of Freemasons Lodge, "Hope and Charity," No 377. *War Work:* Hon. Financial Sec. of the Kidderminster Local Central Committee for War Savings, and Joint Sec. Food Campaigns. *Address:* Berkswell, Kidderminster. (M1685)

EDE, Henry William, M.B.E., *b.* 5 April, 1875; *s.* of William Edward Ede, of Kilburn, London; *m.* Florence, *d.* of Rev. Hugh Doig, of Saddleworth. Assistant Irish Traffic Manager, London and North-Western Railway. *War Work:* Transport Work, Port of Dublin; Chairman of Cross-Channel Traffic Regulation Committee, Dublin, 1917–19; special services in connection with survivors of torpedoed ships, etc. *Address:* 31, Oaklands Park, Ballsbridge, Co. Dublin. (M7982)

EDE, Stuart Strickland Moore, M.B.E.

EDEN, Charles Hamilton, O.B.E., *b.* 2 April, 1855; *s.* of the Rev. John Patrick Eden, of Sedgefield, Co. Durham; *m.* Caroline Sophia, *d.* of the Rev. C. H. Ford, of Bishopton, Co. Durham. *Educ.:* Haileybury. Vice-Chairman and Managing Director of Messrs. Vivian & Sons, Ltd., Swansea, smelters and manufacturers of copper, lead, zinc, and brass, etc. *War Work:* Munitions supplies in shell bands and copper, brass, and zinc materials, to Admiralty and War Office. *Address:* Glyndermen, Black Pill, S.O., Glamorgan. (O10351)

EDEN, Capt. Geoffrey Morton, M.B.E., *b.* 1891; *s.* of the Hon. George Eden, of 6, Cromwell Place, S.W.; *m.* Dorothy

Ida, *d.* of Prebendary F. Clyde Harvey, of Hailsham, Sussex. *Educ.:* Eton. Engineer. *War Work:* With 1/6th Batt. East Surrey Regt., and later with the R.A.S.C., M.T. *Address:* 6, Cromwell Place, S.W. *Club:* Royal Automobile. (M5018)

EDEN, Mary Frances Dove, Mrs., M.B.E.

EDEN, Morton Frederick, M.B.E., *b.* 16 June, 1865; *s.* of Charles Calvert Eden, of H.M. Diplomatic Service; *m.* Maria Theresa, *d.* of—MacMahon, of New South Wales. *Educ.:* Clifton Coll., and abroad. *War Work:* Military Mission in Albania. *Address:* Glen Eden, Jenolan Caves, N.S.W. (M3623)

EDEN, Sybil Frances, Lady, O.B.E. (O10352)

EDGAR, Alice, M.B.E.

EDGAR, Caroline Elizabeth Grattan, Mrs., M.B.E.

EDGAR, Ethel, Lady, C.B.E.; *d.* of John Pindar, of Montreal, Canada; *m.* Sir Edward Mackay Edgar, 1st Bart. of Chalfont Park, Bucks. (see BURKE'S *Peerage*). *War Work:* Member of Ladies' Auxiliary Committee (Munitions Section) Y.M.C.A. *Addresses:* Merton Hall, Watton, Norfolk; 17, Grosvenor Square, W. 1. (C152)

EDGAR, James Winterbottom, M.B.E., *b.* 8 July, 1872; *y. s.* of Robert Edgar, of Greenheys, Manchester. *Educ.:* Choriton High School, and Manchester Commercial School. *War Work:* Registration; Hon. Investigator and Subsistence Officer (National Service); Hon. Sec. Flag Days; Hon. Inspector (Food Control); Hon. Sec. County Borough of Salford War Savings Committee; secretarial work Lancashire, Fusiliers Prisoners of War Fund (raised £425); and Hon. Organiser Lancashire Fusiliers "Penny" Fund, also for Lancs prisoners of war. *Address:* Downham Villa, Sale, Cheshire. *Club:* Old Rectory, Manchester. (M7984)

EDGAR, Jonathan Cyril, M.B.E. Chief Clerk to a Section of the Surplus Stores and Salvage, War Office. (M10315)

EDGAR, Major Peter Maxwell, O.B.E.

EDGCUMBE, John Aubrey Pearce, C.B.E., *b.* 21 Sept. 1886; *s.* of Sir Robert Edgcumbe, of Reperry Manor (see BURKE'S *Landed Gentry*); *m.* Hilda Eva, *d.* of Victor Pettit. *Educ.:* Winchester, Magdalene Col., Cambridge. Board of Trade, May 1910 to Feb. 1912; National Health Insurance Commission (England), Feb. 1912 to Dec. 1916; War Trade Statistical Dept., Dec. 1913 to Feb. 1919 (Director, April 1918), Paris Conference, Feb. to June, 1919; Dept. of Overseas Trade, June, 1919, to date. *Address:* Dept. of Overseas Trade, 35, Old Queen Street, S.W. (C2581)

EDGE, Lieut. Arthur Broughton, M.B.E., R.A.

EDGE, George, O.B.E., *b.* 8 Oct. 1854. Chief Superintendent and Deputy Chief Constable, Shropshire County Police. *Address:* 39, Belle Vue Road, Shrewsbury. (O10353)

EDGE, Major Percy Granville, O.B.E., R.A.F.

EDGECOMBE, Ethel, Mrs., M.B.E.; *d.* of Thomas Goffey, of Blundellsands, Lancs; *m.* Henry Herbert, *s.* of George Edgecombe, of Blundellsands, Lancs. *Educ.:* Privately; Cheltenham Coll. *War Work:* Soldiers' and Sailors' Club, Liverpool, March, 1915, to June, 1919. *Address:* Park Corner, Blundellsands, Lancashire. (M1687)

EDGINGTON, Major Herbert, O.B.E., R.A.S.C.

EDGINGTON, Capt. Walter, O.B.E., *b.* 3 Feb. 1877; *s.* of late Rev. Charles N. Edgington, of Boxford, Berks. *Educ.:* Rugby and New College, Oxford. Land Agent; Partner in the firm of Messrs. H. J. Wigram & Co., Retford, Notts. *War Work:* Gazetted 2nd Leiut. in R.A.S.C., 23 Oct. 1914; Served with B.E.F. in France, Belgium, and Germany from Nov. 1914, to July, 1920; 3 years with Guards division, acting as Senior Supply Officer on arrival at Cologne in Dec. 1918. *Address:* 30, Carolgate, Retford. *Club:* R.A.C. (O5226)

EDGINTON, Major Clyde, C.B.E.

EDGELL, Comm. John Augustine, O.B.E., R.N.

EDIS, Col. Sir Robert William, K.B.E., C.B., V.D., J.P., D.L., *b.* 13 June, 1839; *s.* of the late Robert Edis, of Huntingdon; *m.* 10 July, 1862, Elsie (who died 22 Dec., 1897), *d.* of the late James Anton, of Westminster, S.W. Hon. Col., late Col. Commandant 28 Bn. (Artists) the London Regt.; was A.D.C. to Earl of Albemarle under Geneva Convention in Franco-German War; Architect of many important works, including Constitutional and Junior Constitutional Clubs, and additions to the Royal Residences at Sandringham; Author, amongst other works, of *Decoration and Furniture of Town Houses*. *Address:* The Old Hall, Ormesby St. Margaret, Norfolk. *Clubs:* Junior Constitutional; Norfolk. (K307)

EDKINS, Capt. Beresford Harry Huey, M.B.E.

EDMEADES, Alfred, C.B.E., D.L.

EDMED, Frank George, O.B.E., B.Sc., F.I.C., A.R.C.Sc., *b.* 19 Nov. 1876; *s.* of Frank Tomlin Edmed, of Brighton. *Educ.:* Brighton Grammar School, and Royal Coll. of Science, London. Superintending Chemist, Admiralty Inspection Dept., Holton Heath. *War Work:* Deputy Head Chemist; Directorate of Chemical Inspection; Ministry of Munitions. *Address:* Coleraine, Penn Hill Avenue, Parkstone, Dorset. (O1311)

EDMISTON, Iris Dorothy, M.B.E.; *d.* of Walter Edmiston, of London. *War Work:* Personal and Private Sec. to the Rt. Hon. Lord Pirrie (Chairman of Harland & Wolff, Ltd.), Controller-General of Merchant Shipbuilding. *Address:* 26, Thurleigh Road, S.W. 12. (M7985)

EDMOND, John, O.B.E., J.P., *b.* 12 April, 1845; *s.* of the late William Edmond of Ballochruin, Killearn; *m.* Jane, *d.* of the late Robert Binnie, of Avonbank. *Educ.:* Balfron Public School. County Councillor, Governor, West of Scotland Agri. College; Governor of Royal (Dick) Veterinary College,

War Work : Chairman of Stirling County Tribunal. *Address :* Gallamuir, Bannockburn. (O211)

EDMOND, Lieut. Robert, O.B.E. R.N.V.R.

EDMONDS, Paymaster-Lieut.-Comm. Archibald Charles Mackay, O.B.E., R.N.

EDMONDS, Squadron Leader Charles Humphrey Kingsman, D.S.O., O.B.E., R.A.F., *b.* 20 April, 1891 ; *s.* of Charles Edmonds, of Lymington ; *m.* Lorna Karim Chadwick, *d.* of Colonel George Osborn, of Lavington. One *s. b.* 5 Oct. 1920. *Educ. :* St. Andrew's Southborough ; Osborne College ; Dartmouth College. Late Officer in Royal Navy, now in Royal Air Force. *War Work :* Served in Balkan War, 1912–13 ; Served in Great War, 1914–19. Flying over the North Sea, Belgian and German Coasts ; in the Dardanelles Campaign ; in Egypt, Red Sea, and Aden ; Adriatic (anti-submarine warfare) ; Twice on the Admiralty War Staff. *Club :* United Service Club. (O3301)

EDMONDS, Major Courtenay Harold Wish, O.B.E., R.E.

EDMONDS, John Francis, M.B.E.

EDMONDS, William Stanley, O.B.E.

EDMONDSON, Lieut.-Col. James Heslam, C.B.E. Lieut.-Col. and Quartermaster R.A.S.C. (retired) ; Great War, 1914–19 (mentioned in despatches). (C1549)

EDMUNDS, Elizabeth, Mrs., M.B.E. *War Work :* French Red Cross, 1914–16 ; Lady Welfare Superintendent to H.M. Factory, Pembrey, South Wales, from 1917 to Feb. 1919. *Club :* New Century. (M3625)

EDMUNDS, Flavell, M.B.E., M.R.C.S.E., L.R.C.P. (Lond.), *b.* 20 Dec. 1870 ; *s.* of Wilfred Edmunds, F.R.H.S., of Chesterfield ; *m.* Marjorie, *d.* of Roderick A. Fowler, of Brussels. *Educ. :* Chesterfield Grammar School, and London Hospital, Hon. Surgeon to the Chesterfield Royal Hospital. *War Work :* Medical Officer in charge of Auxiliary Hospital, Ashgate, Chesterfield ; M.O. to Red Cross Society, Chesterfield District. *Address :* Avenue House, Chesterfield. (M7986)

EDMUNDS, John Parry, M.B.E., *b.* 31 July, 1863 ; *s.* of Ephraim Edmunds, of Llandaff ; *m.* Mary, *d.* of William Treseder, of Cardiff. *Educ. :* Llandaff Cathedral School. Shipowner ; Managing Director of Edmunds and Radley, Ltd., Cardiff ; director of other companies. *War Work :* Inspector, Special Police for County of Glamorganshire. *Address :* White Lodge, Whitchurch. Glamorgan. *Clubs :* Whitchurch, Radyr, and Llandrindod Wells Golf. (M3626)

EDMUNDS, Leslie Wynn, M.B.E., M.A., *b.* 29 Dec. 1872 ; *s.* of H. W. Edmunds, of Birmingham ; *m.* Laura, *d.* of R. Smythe, of Killiney. *Educ. :* Radley and Queen's College, Oxford. Senior Inspector, Congested District Bd., Galway. *War Work :* T. Lieut.-Comm. R.N.V.R., from 1915–19. *Address :* C.D.B., Galway. *Club :* Leander and Royal Cruising Club. (O312)

EDMUNDS, Wilfred Hawksley, O.B.E., J.P., *b.* 29 April, 1868 ; *s.* of Wilfred Edmunds, of Chesterfield ; *m.* Florence, *d.* of Joseph Clayton, of Chesterfield. *Educ. :* Chesterfield Grammar School. Mayor of Chesterfield 1919–21 ; Alderman of Chesterfield Town Council, and of Derbyshire County Council ; Chairman of Derbyshire Asylums Committee ; Chairman of Derbyshire Public Health and Maternity and Child Welfare Committees. *War Work :* Chairman of Chesterfield Borough Food Control, and Chesterfield District Area Food Control Committees ; Member of Chesterfield Recruiting Tribunal ; Chesterfield Soldiers' Parcels Committee, and other War Emergency Committees. *Address :* Scarsdale House, Chesterfield. (O10354)

EDSER, Major Edmund, O.B.E., R.A.M.C.

EDWARDES, Lieut.-Col. Alexander Coburn, C.B.E.

EDWARDES, Charles Whitfield, M.B.E., *b.* 1884 ; *s.* of Robert Edwardes, of Clifton, Bristol. *Educ. :* Merchant Venturers Technical Coll., Bristol. Admiralty Overseer. *War Work :* Principal Admiralty Electrical Repair Overseer Tyne District, for H.M. Fleet and Ships. *Address :* 41, Coquet Terrace, Newcastle-on-Tyne. (M7984)

EDWARDES, David John William, O.B.E., *b.* 20 April, 1864 ; *s.* of Capt. Browne Edwardes, of Rhyd-y-gorse, Carmarthen. *Educ. :* Stubbington House, Fareham, Hants. *War Work :* Deputy Coast Watcher, R.N., from 1915–18. *Address :* St. Regulus, Shirley Warren, Southampton. *Clubs :* Royal Southern Yacht and Cocoa Tree. (O313)

EDWARDS, Maj.-Gen. Sir Alfred Hamilton MacKenzie, K.B.E., C.B., M.V.O., *b.* 22 Sept., 1862 ; *y.s.* of the late William Edwards, formerly Bengal C.S., of Craigton, co. Ross ; *m.* 24 Sept., 1892, Kate. O.B.E. (*q.v.*), *d.* of the late John Henderson, of Middlethird, co. Berwick, and has had issue, an only son, William Hardinge Colvin, Lieut. 1st Bn. Black Watch, *b.* 30 July, 1893, killed in action 9 May, 1915. Comdt.-Gen. Rhodesian forces from 1912 ; late 5th Dragoon Guards ; formerly 1st Dragoon Guards ; served with Hazara Expedition, 1888 (despatches, medal with clasp) ; in S. African War 1899–1902, defence of Ladysmith (wounded, despatches, Queen's medal with four clasps, King's medal with two clasps, Brev.-Lt.-Col., C.B.) ; comdt. Transvaal Vols. 1903-5 ; Mil. Sec. to Viceroy of India 1905 ; A.A.G. Northern Command, India. 1906 ; ret. 1907 ; Chief Constable Metropolitan Police 1907–12. *Address :* Salisbury, Rhodesia, S. Africa. *Club :* United Service, London. (K480)

EDWARDS, Arthur Joseph, M.B.E.

EDWARDS, Bogdan Edward Jastrzebski, M.B.E., M.B., C.M., *b.* 1860. *Educ. :* Edinburgh. School Medical Officer ;

Medical Officer of Health ; Poor Law Medical Officer. *War Work :* Commandant of Boothroyde and Longroyde Hospitals. (M7989)

EDWARDS, Charles James, O.B.E., *b.* 5 Nov. 1865 ; *s.* of Charles Edwards, of London ; *m.* Lucy Heath, *d.* of Benjamin Pearce, of Bournemouth. *Educ. :* Private Schools. Superintending Clerk ; Accountant General's Department, Admiralty. *War Work :* Finance Branch ; Ministry of Shipping. *Address :* Brookfield, Chiswick Lane, Chiswick W.4. (O314)

EDWARDS, Capt. Charles Joseph, M.B.E.

EDWARDS, Charles Lewis, C.B.E.

EDWARDS, Lieut.-Comm. Charles Peter, O.B.E., R.N.V.R.

EDWARDS, Edith Constance, Mrs., M.B.E., *d.* of Maurice Newton, *m.* Reuben Edwards. *Educ. :* Privately. *War Work :* War Hospital Supply Depot ; Organizer of Flag Days ; Commandant of Red Cross Detachment. *Address :* 22, New Cavendish Street, Portland Place. W. (M355)

EDWARDS, Elizabeth Alice, M.B.E.

EDWARDS, Emma Dorothy, Mrs., M.B.E., *d.* of William Durning Holt, of Liverpool ; *m.* the late Stanley Edwards. *War Work :* 2 years Soldiers' and Sailors' Families Association ; 2 years Commandant of Crofton Auxiliary Hospital, Aigburth, Liverpool. *Address :* 17, Ullet Road, Liverpool. (M7991)

EDWARDS, Ernest Arthur, M.B.E.

EDWARDS, George, C.B.E. Auditor and Controller, Imperial Munitions Board, Canada. (C153)

EDWARDS, George, O.B.E.

EDWARDS, George Henry, O.B.E., *b.* 1865 ; *s.* of late John Edwards of Haywards Heath, Sussex ; *m.* Alice, *d.* of William Henry Blatch, J.P., of Basingstoke. *Educ. :* City of London School. In the Civil Service ; Secretary to the Aliens Department, and Assistant Secretary, Metropolitan Police Office, New Scotland Yard ; a member of various Departmental and other Committees ; *War Work :* Private Secretary to the Commissioner of Police of the Metropolis. *Address :* 15, Kidderpore Avenue, Hampstead, and New Scotland Yard. *Clubs :* National ; Artists'. (O315)

EDWARDS, Gladys Maude, M.B.E., *b.* 1895 ; *d.* of H. A. Edwards, of Hampstead, N.W. *Educ. :* Neuville Coll., East Finchley. *War Work :* Secretary to Sir John Beale, K.B.E. *Address :* 17, Park Drive, Hampstead, London. (M3627)

EDWARDS, Capt. Graham Richard Leicester, C.B.E., R.N. Great War, 1914–19 with Dover Patrol (mentioned in despatches). (C2358)

EDWARDS, Major Harry Melville, O.B.E.

EDWARDS, Col. Henry John, C.B., C.B.E., M.A., *b.* 8 Sept. 1869 ; *s.* of Major Henry Charles Edwards, V.D., of Woodbridge, Suffolk ; *m.* Margaret Ethel, *d.* of Rev. Arthur Ashton, B.D., Rector of Uggeshall, Wangford, Suffolk. *Educ. :* Woodbridge ; Bath College ; Trinity College, Cambridge. Fellow (late Tutor), and Classical Lecturer, Peterhouse, Cambridge ; late Commanding Cambridge University, O.T.C. *War Work :* Secretary, Eoard of Military Studies, University of Cambridge ; Commanding Cambridge University O.T.C. ; Commandant, Cambridge University School of Instruction, 1914–16 ; Commanding No. 2 Officer Cadet Battalion, and O.C. Troops, Cambridge, 1916–18 ; War Office Representative, University of Cambridge, 1918–19. *Address :* Peterhouse, Cambridge. *Club :* United University. (C1550)

EDWARDS, Hester Mary, Mrs., M.B.E., *b.* 1876 ; *d.* of John Greenwood, of Todmorden, Yorks. ; *m.* Edward, *s.* of Arthur Edwards, of Manchester. *Educ. :* Centre Vale, Yorks. *War Work :* Women's Legion and Q.M.A.A.C. *Address :* 14, Royal Hospital Road, Chelsea, S.W.3. *Club :* Women's United Services. (M356)

EDWARDS, Ina Leonora, M.B.E., *b.* 23 July, 1897 ; *d.* of John J. H. Edwards, late of Craigton, Ross-shire, N.B. *Educ. :* Abbot's Hill, Hemel Hempstead. *War Work :* V.A.D., B.R.C.S., 1916–17 ; Military Auxiliary Red Cross Hospital, Goring, Oxon., from Oct. 1917, to Oct. 1919 ; Q.M.A.A.C., serving as Company Commander A. Compy., Connaught Club, London ; retired Deputy Admin. (M6630)

EDWARDS, Ivor, M.B.E.

EDWARDS, James Herbert, O.B.E.

EDWARDS, Jean, Mrs., O.B.E.

EDWARDS, John, C.B.E., O.B.E.

EDWARDS, Capt. John Augustus, O.B.E., R.A.V.C.

EDWARDS, John Vaughan, O.B.E.

EDWARDS, Joseph, M.B.E.

EDWARDS, Kate, Lady, O.B.E., *d.* of late John Henderson, of Middlethird, co. Berwick ; *m.* 1892 Maj.-Gen. Sir Alfred Hamilton Mackenzie Edwards, K.B.E. (*q.v.*). (O2220)

EDWARDS, Major Lionel Charles, O.B.E., R.A., *b.* 14 Sept. 1882 ; *s.* of Lionel Edwards, of Ashburnham House, Bedford. *Educ. :* Bedford School, and Royal Military Academy, Woolwich. *War Work :* In France, Adjutant, West Riding Heavy Battery (T.F.) ; Commanded 144th Heavy Battery, R.G.A. ; employed at War Office 1917 to end of war. *Address :* c/o Messrs. Cox & Co., 16, Charing Cross, London. (O7114)

EDWARDS, Mabel Constance, M.B.E., J.P., *d.* of Robinson John Park, of Liverpool ; *m.* William Henry, *s.* of Henry Edwards, of Winchester. *Educ. :* Ladies' Coll., Cheltenham. Justice of the Peace for the County of Lancaster. *War Work :* For Soldiers' and Sailors' Families Association and Ministry of Pensions in Liverpool and Formby ; Member

174

of Committee of Lancashire Territorial Nursing Association for providing comforts to hospitals. *Address:* The White Cottage, Freshfield, Lancs. (O7993)

EDWARDS, Eng.-Lieut.-Comm. Macleod Gamul Arthur, O.B.E., R.N.

EDWARDS, Mary, Mrs., O.B.E., W.R.A.F.

EDWARDS, Rev. Nathaniel Walter Allen, O.B.E., M.C. *b.* 9 May, 1877; *s.* of Rev. N. W. Edwards, of Westcott, Budleigh. Salterton, Devon. *Educ.:* S. John's School, Leatherhead, and S. John's College, Cambridge. Clerk in Holy Orders. Vicar of S. John the Evangelist, Walworth, S.E. *War Work:* Chaplain to the Forces, 4th Class. *Addresses:* S. John's Vicarage, Larcom Street, Walworth, S.E.17. and Westcott, Budleigh Salterton, Devon. (O5229)

EDWARDS, Percy, O.B.E., M.R.C.S., L.R.C.P., *b.* 21 Sept. 1863; *s.* of James Latchford Edwards, of Rochester; *m.* Eleanor Blanche, *d.* of Henry Smith, of Dartmouth. *Educ.:* Mill Hill, School, and Univ. Coll. Hospital, London. Hon. Sec. Liverpool Division, British Medical Association; Hon. Medical Officer, Liverpool Seamen's Orphanage. *War Work:* Member, Medical Advisory Board, Ministry of National Service; Hon. Sec. Liverpool Medical War Committee; Chairman of Recruiting and Pensions Boards. *Address:* 1, Newsham Drive, Liverpool. *Club:* Athenæum, Liverpool. (O10358)

EDWARDS, Major Reginald Owen, O.B.E., R.E.

EDWARDS, Richard, M.B.E., *b.* 29 Sept. 1877; *s.* of Richard Edwards, of Litherland, Lancs; *m.* Gwladys Jane Marie, *d.* of Howel Thomas, of Local Government Board, and FitzGeorge Avenue, Kensington. *Educ.:* Waterloo. Sec. Ipswich District, Alliance Assurance Co. *War Work:* Hon. Sec. Suffolk Prisoners of War Help Committee. *Address:* South Lodge, Parkside Avenue, Ipswich. *Club:* Ipswich and Suffolk. (M3628)

EDWARDS, Lieut.-Col. Robert Richards, C.B.E.; Major and Brevet Lieut.-Col. S. African Permanent Staff. (C1881)

EDWARDS, Roger Bellis, M.B.E., M.B.

EDWARDS, Capt. T. H., O.B.E. R.A.O.C.

EDWARDS, Capt. Walter Bernard, O.B.E.. M.C.

EDWARDS, Lieut. William, M.B.E., *b.* 11 Dec. 1882; *s.* of Sergt.-Major J. Edwards, of the Royal Artillery; *m.* Lillian, *d.* of John Coppleston, of Barnes. *Educ.:* Ancona Road School, Plumstead; Woolwich Polytechnic. Enlisted, 3 May, 1900; S. Africa War, 1900–1902; India, Jan. 1904, to Nov. 1911; S. Africa, 1911–14; France 1915–16. *War Work:* Promoted from R.Q.M.S. to R.S.M., 1915; commissioned for services in the Field, March, 1916; Garrison Adjutant, Larkhill, 1917–18; Staff Capt., No 3 Area, S. Command, Dec. 1918, to April, 1920; mentioned in despatches, Feb., 1920. *Address:* Cavalry Barracks, Hounslow, Middlesex. (M3262)

EDWARDS, Lieut.-Col. William Bickerton, C.B.E., *b.* 1870; *s.* of the late Rev. Bickerton Edwards, Vicar of Bettws-yn-Rhos; *m.* Elizabeth, *d.* of William Daniel, J.P., of Pen-y-bont, Crynant, Neath. *Educ.:* Glasgow Univ. (M.B. and C.M. 1894). In charge of Plague Operations, Villore, S. India, 1898–9; Lieut.-Col. R.A.M.C. commdg. a Field Ambulance with British Expeditionary Force, 1916–17; is a Knight of Grace of Order of St. John of Jerusalem in England, and Commr. Medical Services, Welsh Region, Ministry of Pensions. *Address:* Tyn-y-Craig, Crynant, Neath. (C1551)

EDWARDS, William Buckland, M.B.E., B.Sc., F.I.C., *b.* 17 April, 1871; *m.* Grace Marion, *d.* of Thomas Arthur Stephens, of Brondesbury, N.W. *Educ.:* Mill Hill School, and Central Technical Coll. Principal Assist. Chemist in Directorate of Chemical Inspection, Woolwich. *Address:* 1, Vanbrugh Park Road, Blackheath, S.E. 3. (M7996)

EDWARDS, William Ernest, M.B.E., *b.* 18 May, 1866; *s.* of Charles William Edwards, of Watford, Herts; *m.* Elizabeth, *d.* of Richard Bannard, of Brackley, Northants. *Educ.:* St. Mary's School, Watford. Chief Clerk, Goods Dept., L. and N.W. Rly., Northampton. Supt. of Headquarters Division, St. John Ambulance Brigade, Northampton. *War Work:* Food Controller for Auxiliary Military Hospitals of Northamptonshire; Transport Officer for unloading ambulance trains and transport of wounded. (M7997)

EDWARDS, 2nd Lieut. William Manning, M.B.E.

EDWARDS, William Rea, O.B.E.

EDWARDS, William Robert, O.B.E.

EDWARDS, Annie DOULTON-, M.B.E.

EDWARDS, Thomas Ramsay KING-, M.B.E., M.D., *b.* 31 Aug. 1874; *s.* of William King-Edwards, J.P., D.L., of Dartans House, Tyrone; *m.* A. Blanche, *d.* of Canon Stack, of Derry Cathedral, of Moville, Ireland. *Educ.:* Trinity Coll., Dublin. Medical Officer, Thame Union; M.D. Ewelm Alms Houses; Assistant Inspector Schools, Oxford Co. *War Work:* Commandant M.O. of V.A.D., Oxford, and Medical Officer and Commandant, Swyncombe Red Cross Hospital. *Address:* The Old House, Watlington, Oxon. (M7995)

EDWARDS, Hugh Copner WYNNE-, O.B.E.

EDYE, Ernest Henry Huish, M.B.E., M.A., J.P., I.C.S., *b.* 2 June, 1884; *s.* of Ernest Edye, of Syon House, East Budleigh, S. Devon; *m.* Alice Dorothy, *d.* of J. N. Stuart, Broomhill, Harrow. *Educ.:* Stubbington; Harrow; and Balliol Coll., Oxford. Superintendent Census operations, United Provinces, India. *War Work:* In charge of various districts in United Provinces, India; Recruiting; temporarily commissioned in Indian Army Reserve of Officers. *Address:* United Provinces, India. (M4130)

EGAN, George, O.B.E.

EGAN, Hulda, Mrs., O.B.E. (O10441)

EGAN, Kate, M.B.E.

EGAN, Col. Michael Henry, C.M.G., C.B.E., *p.a.c.,* R.A.O.C., *b.* 7 May, 1865; *s.* of Capt. Edward Egan, of Royal Artillery; *m.* Ina, adopted *d.* of C. Fane. *Educ.:* Marlborough House, Hove; Royal Academy, Gosport; R.M. College, Sandhurst. A.D.O.S. Malta. *War Work:* With R.A.O.C. France and England; Chief Inspector, R.A.C.D.; Original Anti-Gas War Office Committee; Commanded the Royal Army Ordnance Corps, Woolwich. *Address:* The Castille, Malta. *Club:* Army and Navy. (C1552)

EGAN, Lieut. and Qr.-Mr. William, M.B.E.

EGERTON, Ada Maud, Lady, O.B.E., *b.* 10 Feb. 1861; *d.* of the late Canon Nash, of Tolpuddle, Dorset; *m.* Sir Walter Egerton, K.C.M.G., of Mayfield, Sussex (*see* BURKE's *Peerage*). *War Work:* Organised branch of Queen Mary's Needlework Guild in British Guiana. *Address:* Fir Toll, Mayfield, Sussex. (O989)

EGERTON, Christian Mary, M.B.E., *b.* 17 June, 1876; *d.* of Admiral the Hon. Francis Egerton. *War Work:* Enquiry Office for Missing and Wounded. *Address:* St. George's Hill, Byfleet. (M1692)

EGERTON, Dorothy Charlotte, O.B.E., *b.* 6 Oct. 1874; *d.* of Admiral the Hon. Francis Egerton, of St. George's Hill, Byfleet. *War Work:* Commandant, Blytheswood Auxiliary Hospital, Byfleet, Surrey. *Address:* St. George's Hill, Byfleet. (O10360)

EGERTON, Mabelle Annie, Lady, C.B.E., *b.* 1865; *d.* of 1st Earl Brassey, of Normanhurst, Sussex (*see* BURKE's *Peerage*); *m.* Charles A., *s.* of Edward C. Egerton, of Mountfield Court. Member of Central Midwives Board. *War Work:* Rouen Station Coffee-shop, 1914–19; mentioned in C.-in-C.'s despatches, 1917. *Address:* 32, Ashley Gardens, S.W. 1. (C407)

EGERTON, Capt. Philip, C.B.E., R.N. (Emergency List), *b.* 3 May, 1866; *s.* of late Philip Henry Egerton, Indian Civil Service (*see* BURKE's *Peerage*, Gray-Egerton, Bart). (C2268)

EGFORD, George Henry, M.B.E., D.S.C., R.N.

EGGAR, James, C.B.E.

EGGAR, Mildred Fanny, M.B.E., *b.* 1875; *d.* of the late Edward Aldous; *m.* Frederick Henry, *s.* of Sir Henry Cooper Eggar, M.V.O. National Indian. Association, Calcutta; Soldiers' Furlough Home, Calcutta. *Addresses:* Alipore Park, Calcutta; The Cedars, Strawberry Hill, Middlesex. *Club:* New Empress. (M4137)

EGGAR, Capt. Thomas Macdonald, O.B.E., R.A.F.

EGGINTON, Col. John, O.B.E., T.D.

EGGLESHAW, Frank Herbert, M.B.E.

EGLINTON AND WINTON, Janet Lucretia, Dowager Countess of, D.B.E., LL.D., *d.* of Boyd Alex. Cuninghame, R.N., *s.* of John Cuninghame, of Craigends, co. Renfrew; *m.* George Arnulph, 15th Earl of Eglinton and Winton, *s.* of the 13th Earl of Eglinton (*see* BURKE's *Peerage*). *War Work:* President Ayrshire Red Cross and Member of Scottish War Executive Red Cross; President of County of Sailors' and Soldiers' Families Assoc.; Naval and Military Pensions. *Address:* Skelmorlie Castle, Ayrshire, Scotland. (D457)

EGLEN, A. Paymaster-Lieut. Arthur Harold, O.B.E., R.N.R.

EHRENFEST, Muriel Alice Adela, M.B.E.

EHRMANN, Major Albert, O.B.E., T.D., R.A.M.C. (T.F.), *b.* 13 June, 1864; *s.* of Ferdinand Ehrmann, of Melbourne, Australia. *Educ.:* Scotch Coll., Melbourne; Univ. of Melbourne, and Univ. Coll. Hospital, London. Lecturer and Examiner First Aid, Nursing and Health, London County Council; Lecturer, Examiner, Hon. Life Member, St. John Ambulance Association; Hon. Divisional Surgeon Hospital Saturday Fund. *War Work:* Medical Officer various Depots and Units; on the Staff of D.D.M.S., London District; Registrar of 2nd London General Hospital, T.F. *Address:* 255, Camden Road, N. (O7115)

EICHHOLZ, Alfred, C.B.E., M.A., M.D., *b.* 26 Nov. 1869; *s.* of Adolphus Eichholz, of Manchester; *m.* Ruth, *d.* of Dr. Hermann Adler, Chief Rabbi. *Educ.:* Manchester Grammar School; Emmanuel College, Cambridge; S. Bartholomew's, London. Chief Medical Inspector, Board of Education, Whitehall S.W. *Addresses:* Board of Education, Whitehall, S.W.; 47, Addison Gardens, W.14. (C956)

ELAND, Ruth Adelaide, M.B.E., *b.* 22 Nov. 1893; *d.* of Rev. Charles Tucker Eland, of Burston Rectory, Diss, Norfolk. *Educ.:* Abbotsford, Broadstairs; Mounthurst, Oak Hill Park, Hampstead. *War Work:* Finance Department, War Office. (M8000)

ELBORNE, Sydney Lipscomb, M.B.E., M.A., F.G.S., A.I.C., *b.* 6 July, 1890; *s.* of William Elborne, M.A., of Peterborough. *Educ.:* Trinity Coll., Cambridge. Called to the Bar by the Inner Temple, Jan. 1919. *War Work:* 1915, Temp. Assist. Chemist to War Department and Ministry of Munitions; 1916, appointed Assist. Inspector (technical) in the Directorate of Inspection of High Explosives, Inspection Department, Royal Arsenal, Woolwich (resigned May, 1919). *Addresses:* 6, Crown Office Row, Temple, London, E.C. 4; Wootton House, Peterborough. (M1693)

ELBOURNE, Edward Tregaskiss, M.B.E.

ELCOMBE, Minnie Eliza, Mrs., M.B.E.

ELDER, Andrew, M.B.E., R.N.R.

ELDER, David, O.B.E., J.P. for the County of the City of Glasgow, *b.* 16 Oct. 1867; *s.* of Robert Elder, of Perth; *m.* Elizabeth Sorley, *d.* of the late Rev. Walter Buchan, of the

United Presbyterian Church, Boveedy, Kilrea, Co. Londonderry. *Educ.:* Private Schools; Hutcheson's Grammar School; Glasgow Univ. Assistant City Assessor, Glasgow. *War Work:* Acted as Assist. Sec. of the Glasgow Corporation Belgian Refugee Committee. *Addresses:* City Chambers, Glasgow; Castlewood, Cathcart, Glasgow. (O10361)

ELDERTON, William Palin, C.B.E., *b.* 26 June, 1877; *s.* of the late William A. Elderton; *m.* Enid Muriel, *d.* of George Podmore, of Grange over Sands. *Educ.:* Merchant Taylors' School. Actuary to the Star Assurance Society, 1912–13; Actuary and Manager to the Equitable Life Assurance Society since 1913. *War Work:* Statistical Adviser to Ministry of Shipping, 1916–20. *Addresses:* 24, Mount Ephraim Road, S.W.16; Quill Hall Cottage, Amersham Common, Bucks. *Club:* City of London. (C2586)

ELDRED, Capt. Arthur George, C.B.E.

ELDRED, Paymaster-Capt. Edward Henry, C.B.E., R.N. Great War, 1914–19 (mentioned in despatches). (C1922

ELDRED, Edwin Charles, O.B.E., *b.* 11 July, 1867; *s.* of the late Edgar Eldred, of The Gables, Petersfield. *War Work:* Controller of Staff, War Trade Department, for four years, 1915–19. At present the Collector, H.M. Customs and Excise, Swansea. *Addresses:* Strathfield, Brighton Road, Purley, Surrey, and Custom House, Swansea. (O318)

ELDRED, Elizabeth Francis, M.B.E., Q.M.A.A.C.

ELDRIDGE, Capt. Ernest James Morritt, O.B.E., *b.* 25 July, 1896; *s.* of Cecil J. E. Eldridge, of Mossley Hill, Liverpool. *Educ.:* Liverpool Institute. Medical Student. *War Work:* Served in France and Belgium with the 1/6th (Rifle) Batt. The King's (Liverpool) Regt.; wounded at Hill 60, April, 1915; afterwards served at home and in Ireland; appointed to the Staff as Railway Transport Officer, Holyhead, March, 1918; when on board s.s. "Rathmore," which had collided with a Government trawler, took command of some 700 troops, and was responsible for their orderly transfer to destroyers. *Address:* 15, Cassville Road, Mossley Hill, Liverpool. *Club:* Students' Union, Liverpool Univ. (O8802)

ELDRIDGE, Capt. George Bernard, C.B.E., R.N.

ELDRIDGE, William John, M.B.E.

ELEY, Major Henry Gerard, M.B.E., R.E.

ELFORD, Archibald Sefton, O.B.E. M.A., *b.* 5 June, 1878; *s.* of Edwin Elford, of Tregear, Exeter, Devon; *m.* Sybil Audrey, *d.* of Richard Edward West, of Firth Dene, Reigate, Surrey. *Educ.:* Magdalen College School, Oxford, and St. John's College, Oxford. Assistant Secretary, Essex Education Committee; Inspector of Schools, L.C.C.; Director of Education, Wolverhampton; Deputy Chairman, Australasian Steamship Owners' Federation, Melbourne, Australia. *War Work:* Ministry of Shipping, St. James' Park, London; Military Sea Transport Department; Accompanied Special War Mission to the United States of America, in 1918; Assisted in formation of Public School Battalions. *Address:* Australasian Steamship Owners' Federation, 509, Collins Street, Melbourne. *Club:* Union Society, Oxford. (O3700)

ELGEE, Capt. Ernest Alfred, O.B.E.

ELGEE, Lieut.-Col. Samuel Charles, O.B.E.,R.A.M.C., L.M.

ELGOOD, Cornelia Bonte Sheldon, Mrs., O.B.E., M.B. (Lond.), Medaille de la Reconnaissance Francaise, *b.* 19 July, 1874; *d.* of the late Professor Sheldon Amos; *m.* Percival George (Lieut.-Col. R. of O., C.M.G.), *s.* of the late G. J. Elgood, J.P. *Educ.:* London Univ. Senior Lady Medical Officer, Ministry of Education, Egypt. *War Work:* Voluntary Work, Cairo, Egypt; *Address:* Villa Beata, Heliopolis, Egypt. *Club:* Sesame. (O10362)

ELGOOD, Frank Minshull, O.B.E., F.R.I.B.A., *b.* 5 Mar. 1865; *s.* of George I. Elgood, of Hampstead; *m.* Frances Isabel Lloyd, *d.* of Charles John Allen, of Bedford Row. *Educ.:* King's College, London. Architect; Housing Commissioner under Ministry of Health. *War Work:* Various local Committees; Church Army Commissioner for Recreation Huts in France; Vice-Chairman Naval and Military Committee; Church Army, etc. *Addresses:* The Close, Northwood; 98, Wimpole Street, W.1. *Club:* Arts. (O1316)

ELGOOD, Lieut. Leonard Alsager, O.B.E., M.C.

ELIOT, Anne Huyshe, Mrs., M.B.E.

ELIOT, Lieut.-Col. Christian Edward Cornwallis, O.B.E.

ELIOT, Capt. John Alfred Roy, M.B.E., A.P.D.

ELIOT, Kate Marianne, M.B.E., M.A., *b.* 11 Aug. 1890; *d.* of Henry John Eliot, of Charmouth, Dorset. *Educ.:* Southlands School, Exmouth; Westfield Coll.; Univ. of London. Lecturer in History, St. Margaret's Coll., Ripon, Yorks. *War Work:* Clerical work at Custom House, E.C., and at Admiralty, 1917–19. *Address:* St. Margaret's Coll., Ripon, Yorks. (M8001)

ELIOT, Lieut.-Comm. Montague Charles, O.B.E.

ELIOT, Major and Brevet Lieut.-Col. Nevill, C.B.E., R.A., *d.* 25 Oct. 1880; *s.* of the late Sir John Eliot, K.C.I.E., of Bonporteau, Cavalaire, Var, France; *m.* Margaret Winifred, *d.* of Admiral C. L. Oxley, of The Hall, Ripon. *Educ.:* Malvern and Royal Military Academy. Gazetted 2nd Lieut., R.G.A., 1899, promoted Capt. 1906, Major 1914, Brevet Lieut. Col. 1918. *War Work:* Posted to Inspection Department, Royal Arsenal, 1915; transferred to Ministry of Munitions (Dept. of Munitions Design) 1916; War Office (Directorate of Artillery), 1919. *Club:* Army and Navy. (C2103)

ELIOT, Capt. Ralph, C.B.E., R.N. Great War, 1914–19 (mentioned in despatches). (C2269)

ELIOTT, Comm. Gerald Otho Rooskie, O.B.E., D.S.C., R.N.R.

ELKAN, Lieut.-Col. Clarence John, D.S.O., O.B.E., R. of O., *b.* 15 May, 1877; *s.* of John Elkan, M.V.O., of 40, Hanover Gate Mansions, Regent's Park; *m.* 3 March, 1915, Gladys, *d.* of William Dagnall, of Cape Town. *Educ.:* City of London School. *War Work:* With 1st Royal Irish Fusiliers (Fourth Division), from 5 August, 1914, until appointed on Staff, July, 1915; A.Q.M.G., General Head Quarters and Head Quarters Lines of Communication. *Address:* 25, Windsor Court, Moscow Road, Bayswater, W. *Clubs:* Army and Navy; Junior United Service. (O5233)

ELKIN, Charlotte Emily, M.B.E. Q.M.A.A.C.

ELKINGTON, Capt. James Llewllyn Meredith, O.B.E.

ELKINGTON, William, M.B.E.

ELKINS, Walter Henry, O.B.E.

ELKINS, Major Walter Henry, O.B.E., I.A.R.O.

ELLERTON, Flight-Lieut. Alban Spenser, O.B.E., R.A.F.

ELLERY, Major Cecil Langdon, O.B.E.

ELLERY, Kathleen Frances Elizabeth, Mrs., M.B.E.

ELLES, Col. Arthur Warre, O.B.E., *b.* 16 June, 1864; *s.* of the late Lieut. Gen. Sir William Kidston Elles, K.C.B.; *m.* Janet, *d.* of Rev. John Gilberd Pearse, of Exeter. *Educ.:* Westward Ho (United Service Preparatory College); Heidelberg; Clifton College; Sandhurst. Served in K.O. Yorkshire L.I.; Adjutant 1st Batt. 1890–93; Commanded 2nd Batt. 1906–10; A.D.C. India, 1893–96; D.A.A.G., S. Africa, 1899–1902; At Staff College, 1898–99; Naval War College, 1910; Now District Commissioner Boy Scouts, Gosport. *War Work:* General Staff, 1914–16; Recruiting Staff, 1916–17; and National Service 1918. *Address:* 4, Anglesey Crescent, Alverstoke, Hants. *Club:* Naval and Military. (O1317)

ELLES, Edmund Hardie, O.B.E., *b.* 12 Sept. 1867; *s.* of Jamieson Elles, of Wimbledon, Surrey; *m.* Ina Katharine Hilda, *d.* of W. B. Skene, of Pitlour and Hallyards, Fife. *Educ.:* Winchester, and New Coll., Oxford. *War Work:* Textile adviser to War Trade Intelligence Department. *Address:* 79, Onslow Square, S.W. *Club:* United University. (O10363)

ELLES, Gertrude Lilian, M.B.E., D.Sc., *b.* Oct. 1872; *d.* of Jamieson Elles of Ridgway Place, Wimbledon. *Educ.:* Wimbledon, and Newnham Coll., Cambridge. Fellow and Lecturer, Newnham Coll., Cambridge. *War Work:* Commandant Red Cross Hospital, Wordsworth Grove, Cambridge. *Address:* Newnham Coll., Cambridge. (M8002)

ELLICOCK, Samuel, O.B.E. School Inspector (Board of Education). *War Work:* Hon. Secretary of Leicester and Leicestershire War Savings Committees. (O1318)

ELLINGTON, Air Vice-Marshal Sir Edward Leonard, K.C.B., C.M.G., C.B.E., R.A.F., *b.* 30 Dec. 1877; *s.* of E. B. Ellington. *Educ.:* Clifton and R.M.A. Woolwich. Director General of Supply and Research, Air Ministry; Member of the Air Council. *War Work:* 49th Battery, R.F.A., 3rd Div. Aug. 1914; B.M., 8th Inf. Bde.; B.E.F., Aug. to Sept. 1914; D.A.Q.M.G., G.H.Q., B.E.F., Oct. 1914 to Feb. 1915; A.A. and Q.M.G., 2nd Cav. Div., March 1915 to July, 1915; G.S.O.1., 2nd Army H.Q., July, 1915 to Feb. 1916; G.S.O.1., M.O.1., W.O., Feb. 1916, to Dec. 1916; Brig.-Gen. G.S., 8th Corps, B.E.F., Jan. 1917, to Nov. 1917; D.D.G.M.A., W.O., Nov. 1917, to Jan. 1918; D.G.M.A., W.O., Jan. 1918, to April, 1918; C.G.E., Air Ministry, May, 1918, to Feb. 1919. *Address:* Cox & Co., 108–111, St. Martin's Lane, W.C.2. *Club:* United Service. (C1894)

ELLIOT, Alexander Macbeth, O.B.E., M.D.

ELLIOT, Bessie Clarke, Mrs., M.B.E.

ELLIOT, Frederick Barnard, C.B.E., *b.* 1877; *s.* of Col. G. A. Elliot, of the Royal Irish Regt.; *m.* Ermyngarde, *d.* of Edmond de la Poer, of Gurteen le Poer, Co. Waterford. H.M. Lieutenant for the County and City of Waterford. *Educ.:* Eton and Trinity College, Oxford. *War Work:* Obtained a Commission in the 5th (Service) Batt., Royal Berkshire Regiment, Sept. 1914; Served in France and Flanders, 1915; Severely wounded, Nov. 1915; Appointed Freight Manager to the Wheat Commission, 1916; Director of Shipping, Ministry of Food, 1917; Director of Freights International Food Council, 1918; Chevalier of the Legion of Honour; Officer of the Orders of the Crown of Italy, and Leopold II., of Belgium. *Address:* 3 Sloane Court, S.W.3. *Club:* Union. (C2587)

ELLIOT, Frederick Mitchell, O.B.E.

ELLIOT, George, O.B.E.

ELLIOT, Col. Gilbert Sutherland McDowell, C.B.E., R.E.

ELLIOT, Lieut.-Col. Henry Charles Schomberg, O.B.E., C.A.M.C.

ELLIOT, Sir James Duncan, K.B.E., M. Inst. C.E., *b.* 18 June, 1862; *s.* of Rev. Henry Lettsom Elliot, of Gosfield Vicarage, Halstead, Essex, and grandson of Sir Henry Miers Elliot, K.C.B., and The Rev. John Wall Buckley; *m.* Dora Marguerite Jeannette, *d.* of James McIntosh. *Educ.:* Felstead and Portsmouth Dockyard, and Royal Naval College, Greenwich. Assistant under Sir A. M. Rendel, K.C.I.E., 1887; Assistant to John Carruthers, 1900; Partner with John Carruthers, 1903, Consulting Engineers, New Zealand Gov., etc. (Carruthers and Elliot), and Consulting Engineer to New Zealand Gov., etc., on own account, 1918. *War Work:* Committee on Production, May, 1917 to Nov. 1918; Interim Court of Arbitration, Nov. 1918, to Nov. 1919; Industrial Court, Nov. 1919. *Address:* 22, Vineyard Hill, Wimbledon, S.W.19. *Clubs:* St. Stephen's and Fly Fishers'. (K453)

ELLIOTT, Lieut.-Col. Alfred Charles, C.B.E., *b.* 20 Sept. 1870 ; *s.* of the late Sir Charles Elliott, K.C.S.I., C.I.E., of Fernwood, Wimbledon Park, S.W. (*see* BURKE'S *Peerage*) ; *m.* Maud, *d.* of the late Thomas Beeching, J.P., of The Manor House, Tunbridge Wells. *Educ.:* Elstree, Harrow, and Sandhurst. Indian Army and in Civil Employ in the Punjab Commission ; now Commissioner, Ambala Division, Punjab. *War Work:* Raised between 13,000 and 14,000 recruits as Deputy Commissioner, Gurgaon District, Punjab ; raised money for the 1st and 2nd War Loans, and "Our Day ;" twice mentioned in despatches of the Commander-in-Chief in India for Red Cross work. *Addresses:* Fernwood, Wimbledon Park, S.W. ; Paget House, Ambala Courts. *Club:* E.I.N.S.
(C691)

ELLIOTT, Arthur Campbell, M.B.E., M.B., C.M.

ELLIOTT, Sir Bignell George, K.B.E., F.R.G.S.

ELLIOTT, Blanche Beatrice, M.B.E. ; youngest *d.* of Joseph Elliott, Chalet Pontac, Jersey, late Inspector of Schools, Central Provinces, India. *Educ.:* Jersey. Journalist. *War Work:* Worked at Ministry of National Service since its inception ; acted as private Sec. to F. H. McLeod, C.B., Chairman of Reserved Occupations Committee, and Commissioner for Trade Exemptions. *Address:* Le Chalet Pontac, Jersey. *Club:* Writers'. (M1694)

ELLIOTT, Charles Edward, M.B.E.

ELLIOTT, Charles John, M.B.E.

ELLIOTT, Claude Aurelius, O.B.E.

ELLIOTT, Comm. Frank, O.B.E., R.N., *b.* 10 Oct. 1885 ; *s.* of Frank Elliott, of Totland Bay, I. of W. ; *m.* Edith Lily, *d.* of Gen. Sir William Nicholls, K.C.B., R.M., of 79, Warwick Road, London, S.W. 5 (*see* BURKE'S *Peerage*). *Educ.:* Bedford Grammar School. Joined " Britannia " in 1900 ; served in Mediterranean and China as Midshipman ; Mediterranean as Sub.-Lieut. ; with Lord Charles Beresford in " King Edward VII." as Lieut. ; qualified in gunnery in 1908 ; served as Gunnery Officer of " Prince George " and " Commonwealth " ; joined Turkish Naval Mission under Admiral Sir Arthur Limpus in 1912 ; sent home to take over Turkish Dreadnoughts " Reshadyeh " and " Sultan Osman 1st," 1914 ; served 8 months of the war in ex-Turkish ship " Agincourt " ; served remainder of war (and Jutland) in " Benbow," Admiral Sturdee's Flagship ; promoted to Commander, June, 1918. *Address:* c/o Sir W. Nicholls, K.C.B., R.M., 79, Warwick Road, London, S.W. 5. (O9333)

ELLIOTT, Major George Frederick, M.B.E.

ELLIOTT, Col. Gilbert Sutherland McDowell, C.B.E., R.E., *b.* 1863. Served in S. Africa, 1899–1900 (twice mentioned in despatches, Brevet Lieut.-Col., Queen's medal with four clasps) ; Kano-Sokoto Campaign, 1903 (medal and clasp) ; Great War, 1914–19, in N. Russia (mentioned in despatches). (C1440)

ELLIOTT, Capt. James Boyne, O.B.E., R.A.F.

ELLIOTT, Lieut. and Qr.-Mr. James Henry, M.B.E.

ELLIOTT, John, O.B.E., M.D., B.S., B.Sc. (London), F.R.C.S., F.R.C.P., J.P., *b.* 29 Sept. 1861 ; *s.* of John Elliott, of Whitchurch, Salop ; *m.* Margaret, *d.* of William Weaver, of Stanney Grange, nr. Chester. *Educ.:* Queen's College, Taunton ; Owen's College ; S. Bartholomew's Hospital. Hon. Physician, Chester Royal Infirmary. *War Work:* Hon. Consulting Physician to Eaton Hall Hospital for Officers, and to the Military Hospitals at Kimnel Park, Park Hall, and Prees Heath Camps ; Consulting Physician, Chester War Hospital. *Address:* 24, Nicholas St., Chester. *Clubs:* Royal Automobile ; University of London. (O4358)

ELLIOTT, Mabel Beatrice, M.B.E., *b.* 28 May, 1885 ; *d.* of the late Edwin Downton Elliott, of London. *Educ.:* London and Abroad. *War Work:* Censor in charge of women's staff of Postal Censorship, 1914–19. *Addresses:* 1, Elm Grove, Cricklewood, N.W. 2 ; 195, Victoria Street, S.W.1. (M359)

ELLIOTT, Paymaster-Lieut. Maurice Herbert, M.B.E., R.N.

ELLIOTT, Capt. Myles Layman Farr, M.B.E.

ELLIOTT, Major Stanley, O.B.E., B.Sc. (Lond.) F.I.C., *b.* 1889 ; *e. s.* of Frank Elliott, of London ; *m.* 7 Sept., 1920, Fanny Cecilia, *y. d.* of the late C. C. Claremont of Southsea, and Mrs. Claremont, of the Park, Hampstead. *Educ.:* Enfield Grammar School, and King's Coll., London. Analyst to the Royal Army Medical Coll. *Address:* Royal Army Medical Coll., S.W. 1. *Club:* Chemical Industry. (O7117)

ELLIOTT, Lieut.-Comm. Stephen Percy, O.B.E., R.N.R.

ELLIOTT, T. Warrant Officer George P., M.B.E. Royal Indian Marine.

ELLIOTT, Col. Thomas Renton, C.B.E., D.S.O., M.A., M.D., F.R.S., *b.* 1877 ; *s.* of A. W. Elliott, of Springfield House, Willington, Co. Durham ; *m.* Martha, *d.* of the late A. K. McCosh, of Cairnhill, Airdrie, Lanarkshire. *Educ.:* Durham Sch., and Trin. Coll., Camb. Consulting Physician, A.M.S. ; Physician to Univ. Coll. Hospital ; on Staff of Medical Research Committee ; served in Great War, 1914–18 (mentioned in despatches). *Address:* 8, Cheyne Walk, Chelsea, S.W. 1. (C1245)

ELLIOTT, Major (Brevet Lieut.-Col.) William, C.B.E., D.S.O., R.A.S.C., *b.* 14 March, 1879 ; *s.* of William Elliott, late of Tortington Manor, Nr. Arundel, Sussex. *Educ.:* Cranleigh. Deputy Food Controller Upper Silesia, late Deputy Director of Supplies Transport E.E. Force. *War Work:* On the S.T. directorate staff of the M.E.F., and the E.E.F. 1915, to 1920 ; Gallipoli, Senussi, Sinai and Palestine

operations. *Addresses:* C/o Sir C. McGrigor, Bart. and Co., Ltd., 39, Panton Street, S.W. *Club:* R.A.S.C. (C1379)

ELLIOTT, William, M.B.E.

ELLIS, Amy Amelia, Mrs., M.B.E., *b.* 23 Nov. 1874 ; *d.* of Thomas Jeffs, of Grimsby ; *m.* Thomas Wokes, *s.* of Joseph Ellis, of Hull. *Educ.:* Grimsby. *War Work:* Local Secretary for B.R.C.S. until 1916, and Commandant of Women's V.A.D., Lincs. 36 ; Commandant and Matron of S. Aidan's Red Cross Hospital from Oct. 1914, until March, 1919, when Hospital was closed. *Address:* 121, Grimsby Road, New Cleethorpes, Grimsby. (M361)

ELLIS, Albert Edward, M.B.E. ; *s.* of Thomas Ellis, of Manchester ; *m.* Laura Louise, *d.* of George Plucknett, of Queen Camel. *War Work:* Commandant V.A.D. 33, East Lancs. B.R.C.S. ; Officer in Charge, unloading Ambulance Trains, Mayfield Station, Manchester. *Address:* 16, Egerton Terrace, Ardwick, Manchester. (M8007)

ELLIS, Capt. Arthur Evelyn Paul, M.B.E.

ELLIS, Major Arthur William Mickle, O.B.E., Can. A.M.C.

ELLIS, Col. Charles Conyngham, C.B., C.B.E., *b.* 1852 ; *s.* of the late Col. Francis Ellis. Entered R.E. 1872 ; Capt. 1884 ; Major, 1891 ; Brevet Col. 1903 ; Col. 1903 ; ret. 1909 ; served with Chitral Relief Force, 1895 (mentioned in despatches, medal with clasp) ; was Chief Engineer, India, 1904–7. *Address:* Sunningdale, Ascot. *Club:* Army and Navy. (C1553)

ELLIS, Sir Charles Edward, G.B.E., K.C.B., J.P., *b.* 12 Sept. 1852 ; *s.* of John Devonshire Ellis, J.P. of Worksop, Notts. ; *m.* Inez Blanche Faviell, of Down Place, Guildford. *Educ.:* Lancing and Trinity College, Cambridge. Barrister Inner Temple ; Managing Director, John Brown & Co., Ltd. ; Director, Great Eastern Railway ; Vice-President and Hon. Treasurer of Institution of Naval Architects. *War Work:* Joined Ministry of Munitions, July, 1915 ; Director-General of Ordnance Supply, 1916–17 ; Member of Council of Ministry, 1917–18 ; Continental Representative of Ministry in Paris, 1918 ; Commander of the Legion of Honour ; 1st Class ; Order of St. Anne (Russia) ; Grand Officer of Order of Crown of Italy ; Commander of Order of the Crown of Belgium. *Addresses:* Rampton Manor, Notts. ; 26, Hans Place, S.W.1. *Clubs:* Reform ; Oxford and Cambridge ; St. Stephen's. (G41)

ELLIS, Charles Leonard, M.B.E.

ELLIS, Major Edward George, O.B.E.

ELLIS, Lieut. Frederick Rowland, M.B.E., M.G.C.

ELLIS, Brevet Major George William, O.B.E., B.Sc. (Lond.) A.I.C., *b.* 1882 ; *s.* of Rev. W. Ellis, of London ; *m.* Mary Taylor, *d.* of John Fraser, B.A., of London. *Educ.:* Wisbech Grammar School, and London University. Scientist ; For some time Research Chemist and Demonstrator at the Physiological Laboratory, London University, S.W., and at St. George's Hospital Medical School ; Author of various scientific publications. *War Work:* O.C. 27th Sanitary Section, 2nd London Sanitary Company, R.A.M.C. (T.F.) ; Deputy Inspector of Q.M.G. services G.H.Q., France ; Deputy Assistant Controller of Salvage G.H.Q. France ; Inventor of the " Ellis Field Fat Extracting Plants," and of other salvage devices used in France. *Address:* 8, Gloucester Road, S.W.7. (O2508)

ELLIS, George Stanley, M.B.E.

ELLIS, Surg.-Lieut. Gordon Ernest Dormer, O.B.E., R.N.

ELLIS, Lieut. Harry Charles, M.B.E., R.A.S.C.

ELLIS, Capt. Hector Charles, O.B.E.

ELLIS, Henrietta Christobel, C.B.E., *b.* 15 Jan. 1886 ; *d.* of William Charles Ellis, M.A., Rector of Bothal, Morpeth (*see* BURKE'S *Peerage*, Howard de Walden, B.). *Address:* The Rectory, Bothal, Morpeth. (C1554)

ELLIS, Col. Herbert Charles, C.B.E., R.A.F., *b.* 24 Feb. 1874 *s.* of the late Col. C. H. Fairface Ellis, R.A. ; *m.* Monica Helen, *d.* of the late Lieut.-Col. H. G. Fincham, A.O.D. *Educ.:* Stonyhurst College, and R.M.C., Sandhurst. Joined Royal Berkshire Regt., 10 Oct. 1894 ; Transferred Army Pay Department, 18 Jan. 1901 ; Transferred Royal Air Force, 1 April, 1918. *War Work:* Served in France and Belgium with 5th Cav. Brigade, and 2nd Cav. Division, 12 Aug. 1914 to 15 Feb. 1915 and at Base till 16 Aug. 1915. *Address:* Glasslyn, Brentwood, Essex. *Clubs:* Army and Navy ; Royal Air Force. (C858)

ELLIS, Inez Blanche, Lady, O.B.E., *d.* of William Frederick Faviell, of Down Place, Guildford ; *m.* Sir Charles Edward, G.B.E., K.C.B., B.A., J.P. (*see* BURKE'S *Peerage*), *s.* of late John Devonshire Ellis, J.P., of Worksop. *Addresses:* Rampton Manor, Retford, Notts. ; 26, Hans Place, S.W. (O10367)

ELLIS, Major (retired) James Logan, O.B.E., Late 4th Batt. P.W.O. West Yorkshire Regt., *b.* 23 March, 1872 ; *s.* of the late James Walter Ellis, of Cranstonhill, Stirling, N.B. ; *m.* Marianne Gertrude, *d.* of late Drummond Bond Wingrove, of Langley House, Totton, Hants., and widow of the late Major H. G. Crofton of Inchinappa, Ashford, Co. Wicklow (*see* BURKE'S *Peerage*). *Educ.:* Privately. *War Work:* Recruiting Staff Officer, 65, Area Pontefract and Assistant Director of Recruiting Ministry of National Service n charge of south-west Yorkshire area. *Addresses:* Inchinappa, Ashford, Co. Wicklow ; Alum Court, Alumhurst Road, Bournemouth. *Clubs:* Kildare Street, Dublin ; Royal St. George Yacht Club ; New Club, Cheltenham. (O3115)

ELLIS, James Valentine, O.B.E., *b.* 19 Oct. 1874 ; *s.* of Joseph Ellis, of Skiddaw Lodge, Keswick ; *m.* Victorine, *d.* of Adolph Vogne, of Guémené-sur-Scorff, Brittany, France. *Educ.:* Liverpool Institute. Commercial and General Manager of the Workington Branch of the United Steel Co., Ltd. *War Work :* Organising supply of Shell Steel, etc. *Address :* Calva House, Workington. *Club :* Constitutional. (O1319)

ELLIS, John Henry, O.B.E., *b.* 6 March, 1855 ; *s.* of the late Charles Ellis, of Rodmell Place, Sussex ; *m.* Emily Cowley, *d.* of the late Joseph Smith, of Cirencester. *Educ. :* Privately ; Honorary Consulting Town Clerk and Clerk of the Peace, Plymouth ; Chairman of the Plymouth and Stonehouse Gas Light and Coke, Co. *War Work :* Clerk to Local Tribunal of Plymouth ; Honorary and voluntary services to Military and other Departments of Government. *Address :* Heathfield, Canford Cliffs, Bournemouth. *Clubs :* Royal Western Yacht Club of England, Plymouth ; Junior Constitutional. (O321)

ELLIS, Kate Hannah, Mrs., O.B.E.

ELLIS, Minnie, M.B.E.

ELLIS, Lieut. Norman Nuttall, M.B.E., A.P.C.

ELLIS, Qr.-Mr. and Major Philip, O.B.E., R.E.

ELLIS, Lieut. Reuben, M.B.E., *b.* 13 Sept. 1880 ; *s.* of John Dennis Ellis, of Holt, Norfolk. *Educ. :* Gresham Grammar School, Holt, Norfolk. *War Services :* 1914, 1st Eastern Rifles, South African Rebellion ; 1916, 4th South African Horse, B.E.A. and G.E.A. ; 1917, 19 King's African Rifles, Mounted Infantry, G.E.A. and P.E.A. ; now serving with K.A.R.M.I. in Turkanaland. *Address :* King's African Rifles, Mounted Infantry, Nairobi, B.E.A. (M4244)

ELLIS, Major Richard Stanley, O.B.E., M.C., R.F.A., *b.* 31 July, 1884 ; *s.* of R. Henry Ellis, of Eastbourne ; *m.* Margaret Sneyd, *d.* of Lieut.-Col. J. R. Colvin. *Educ. :* Wellington Coll. *Address :* c/o Messrs Barclays Bank, Ltd., 54, Lombard Street, E.C. *Club :* Junior United Service. (O7118)

ELLIS, Lieut. Samuel Howard, M.B.E., R.A.F.

ELLIS, Shipwright Lieut.-Comm. Thomas, O.B.E., R.N.

ELLIS, Thomas Peter, O.B.E., I.C.S.

ELLIS, Lieut.-Col. Sir William (Henry), G.B.E., D. Eng., J.P., R.E. (T.) ; *s.* of John Devonshire Ellis, of Thurnscoe Hall, Rotherham ; *m.* Lucy Runington, *d.* of Francis Tetley, of Leeds. *Educ. :* Uppingham and Leeds University. Master Cutler of Sheffield, 1914–17 ; Doctor of Engineering Sheffield University ; Justice of the Peace for Sheffield ; Member of the University Council, Infirmary Board, Savings Bank Town Trustees, Church Burgesses of all Sheffield ; Managing Director of John Brown & Co., Ltd ; Sheffield and Clydebank and other public Companies ; Member of the Overseas Committee Board of Trade ; Member of the Council of Civil Engineers ; Vice President of the Iron & Steel Institute ; Member of the Executive Board of the National Physical Laboratory ; Member of the Cambridge University Appointments Board. *War Work :* Chairman of the Sub-committee of the War Trade Committee ; Deputy Chairman of the Disposals Board. *Address :* Weetwood, Eccesall, Sheffield. *Clubs :* Carlton and Alpine. (G24)

ELLIS, Lieut.-Col. Charles Henry Brabazon, HEATON-, C.B.E., J.P., D.L., Bedfordshire Regt. (retired), *b.* 11 May, 1864 ; *s.* of Edward Heaton-Ellis of Wyddiall Hall, Buntingford, Herts. ; *m.* Marion, *d.* of Herbert McCartny of Summerhill, Tamworth, N.S. Wales. *Educ. :* Harrow and Trinity College, Cambridge. Justice of the Peace and Deputy Lieut. for County of Herts. *War Work :* Att. to Admiralty during war for special service on west coast of Scotland and Islands. *Address :* Wyddiall Hall, Buntingford, Herts. *Club :* United Service. (C1610)

ELLIS, Rear-Adm. Sir Edward Henry Fitzhardinge HEATON-, K.B.E., C.B., M.V.O.

ELLIS, Gertrude, Lady HEATON-, O.B.E., *b.* 26 Aug. 1871 ; *d.* of Arthur Holme Sumner ; *m.* Rear-Admiral Sir Edward Heaton-Ellis, K.B.E., C.B., M.V.O. *War Work :* Sec. to Paris Local Pensions Committee. *Address :* 56, Boulevard Raspail, Paris (VI). (O10366)

ELLISON, Anne, Mrs., M.B.E.

ELLISON, Capt. Craufurd Tait, O.B.E., K.R.R.C., *b.* 12 Oct. 1888 ; *s.* of the Rev. John Henry Joshua Ellison, M.V.O., of 92, Palace Gardens Terrace, Kensington ; *m.* Marjorie, *d.* of Lieut.-Col. Richard Damer Wynyard, of Cornwall Lodge, Dorchester. *Educ. :* Rottingdean School ; Eton ; and the R.M.C., Sandhurst. *War Work :* France, Aug. to Sept. 1914 ; severely wounded, 14 Sept. 1914 ; Staff employ at home subsequently. *Address :* c/o Messrs. Cox & Co., 16, Charing Cross. *Clubs :* Royal Automobile ; M.C.C. (O9055b)

ELLISON, Frank, M.B.E.

ELLISON, Mabel, Mrs., M.B.E.

ELLISON, Major William Reynolds, M.B.E.

ELLISON, Capt. William Richard, M.B.E., R.A.

ELLISSEN, Lieut.-Col. Herbert, C.B.E., R.A.S.C.

ELLSON, George, O.B.E., *b.* 2 June, 1875 ; *s.* of Charles Ellson, of Ripley, Derbyshire ; *m.* Frances Mabel, *d.* of Septimus Ryott, of Newbury, Berks. *Educ. :* Ripley Coll., Derbyshire. Resident Engineer, South Eastern and Chatham Railway. *War Work :* Railway service, South Eastern and Chatham Railway. *Address :* Cortina, Plough Lane, Purley, Surrey. (O10368)

ELLWOOD, Arthur Addison, O.B.E.

ELMES, Cecil Henry, C.B.E., M.B.E.

ELMORE, 2nd Lieut. Percy, M.B.E., R.A.S.C.

ELMSALL, William de Cardonnel, M.B.E.

ELMSLIE, Christiana Deanes, C.B.E., R.R.C., Matron Queen Alexandra's Imperial Military Nursing Service Reserve. (C1555)

ELMSLIE, Engr. Lieut.-Comm. Edmund Cooch Stewart, M.B.E., R.N.R., *b.* Nov. 1862 ; *s.* of John Stewart Elmslie, of London ; *m.* Mary Amy, *d.* of Evan Butler, of Cheltenham. *Educ. :* Haberdashers' (Aske's) School, London ; Real Gymnasium ; Chalmers' Technical Coll. ; Göteborg, Sweden. Joined Eastern Tel. Co. as 3rd Engr., C.S. " Amber," Jan. 1889 ; promoted Chief Engr., Jan. 1897 ; retired as Senior Chief Engr., 30 March, 1920 ; appointed Asst. Eng., R N.R., 1887 ; Engineer, 1890 ; placed on retired list as Engr. Lieut.-Comm., 1917. *War Work :* As Chief Engr. of Eastern Tel. Co.'s C.S. " Electra," on various Cable Repairs between England and Gibraltar from Aug. 1914, to Nov. 1915, and in various parts of the Mediterranean Sea, and Adriatic Sea from Nov. 1915, to Oct. 1918. *Address :* 1, Eastbourne Villas, College Road, Cheltenham. *Club :* The Exiles, Twickenham. (M8011)

ELMSLIE, Major Reginald Cheyne, O.B.E., R.A.M.C. (T.), F.R.C.S.

ELPHINSTONE, Sir (George) Keith (Buller), K.B.E., *b.* 1865 ; *s.* of Hon. Edward Buller Elphinstone, of Inveresk Lodge, Musselburgh, N.B. : *m.* Katharine Amy, *d.* of Col. A. J. Wake, R.A. (ret.). *Educ. :* Charterhouse. Managing Director of Messrs. Elliott Brothers (London), Ltd., Engineers. *War Work :* Design and Manufacture of Fire Control Apparatus for H.M. Navy. *Address :* The Old Mill Cottage, Wargrave, Berks. *Club :* Windham. (K370)

ELSDON, Francis William, M.B.E., *b.* 6 Oct. 1869 ; *s.* of Charles Elsdon, of London ; *m.* Annis Emma, *d.* of Francis Latham, of Woolwich. *Educ. :* Scotch Schools ; Woolwich. Foreman ; Chief Inspector of Armaments Department, Royal Arsenal, Woolwich. *War Work :* Responsible for the compilation, in the Chief Inspector of Armaments' Department, Royal Arsenal, Woolwich, of historical Records of all guns and howitzers issued to His Majesty's Army, Navy, and Air Services. *Address :* 18, Old Mill Road, Plumstead Common, S.E. 18. (M1697)

ELSMERE, Maude Alice, O.B.E.

ELSNER, Lieut.-Col. Otto William Alexander, C.B.E., D.S.O., R.A.M.C., *b.* 4 June, 1871 ; *s.* of Frederick W. Elsner, of Stillorgan, Co. Dublin, Ireland ; *m.* Agnes Josephine, *d.* of John Lamb, of Grahamstown, Cape Colony, S.A. *Educ. :* Grammar School, Galway and R.C.S. (Ire.). *War Work :* Embarked 1914, with 6th Cavalry Field Ambulance with 3rd Cav. Div. (Oct. 1914 to March, 1915) ; Joined 9th (Scottish) Div., April, 1915 as O.C. 27th Field Ambulance till April, 1917 ; A.D.M.S. 9th (Scottish) Div., May, 1917 to Occupation of Rhine Bridge heads, 1918–19 ; In all engagements of 3rd Cav. Div. and 9th Scottish Div. ; Awarded D.S.O., 1917, Croix de Guerre (Belg.) 1918, C.B.E., June, 1919 ; Mentioned in Despatches five times. *Address :* c/o Holt & Co., 3, Whitehall Place, London, S.W.1. (C1246)

ELSTOB, Paymaster Lieut.-Comm. Eric Bramley, O.B.E., R.N.

ELSWORTHY, Capt. Alexander Lockhart, M.B.E.

ELTHAM, R.Q.M.S. James Frederick, M.B.E., R.E. (M67816)

ELTON, Henry Brown, O.B.E., B.A., M.B., B.C. (Cant.), M.R.C.S., L.R.C.P. (Lond), *b.* 1882 ; *s.* of the late Charles Tierney Elton, of Southwell, Taunton, Som. ; *m.* Mary Constance, *d.* of J. Percy Maule, of Huntingdon. *Educ. :* Sherborne and Caius College, Cambridge. *War Work :* Capt. R.A.M.C., 1915–16, France and Salonica ; M.O. Llandovery and Dolygarreg Auxiliary Red Cross Hospitals 1917–18. *Address :* Glenview, Llandovery, S. Wales. (O4357)

ELTON, Lieut.-Col. Herbert Averill, O.B.E., R.E. *Address :* 37, Kidbrook Park Road, Blackheath. (O7120)

ELTON, Mabel Therese, M.B.E.

ELOVEDER, Viscountess, C.B.E.

ELVEDEN, Gwendolen, Viscountess, C.B.E., *d.* of 4th Earl of Onslow (*see* BURKE'S *Peerage*) ; *m.* Rupert Edward Cecil Lee, C.B., C.M.G., Viscount Elveden, *e. s.* of Sir Edward Cecil Guinness, K.P., G.C.V.O., F.R.S., LL.D., 1st Earl of Iveagh. *Addresses :* Pyrford Court, near Woking ; 11, St. James' Square, S.W. 1. (C2588)

ELVY, Thomas Elvy, O.B.E.

ELWES, Mrs. Aline, O.B.E.

ELWES, Capt. Francis Guy Robert, O.B.E.

ELWES, Henry Geoffrey, M.B.E.

ELWES, Capt. William Burton, O.B.E., R.E.

ELWOOD, Elisha, O.B.E.

ELWORTHY, Ernest George, M.B.E.

ELWORTHY, Capt. Robert Richard, O.B.E., M.D., R.A.M.C.

ELWORTHY, Capt. William Rowe, O.B.E., A.C.A., T.F. Reserve, General List, *b.* 12 March, 1881 ; *s.* of Isaac George Elworthy, of Gippeswyk, Cambridge ; *m* Lizbeth Farrant, *d.* of John Kettle Driver. of Astwood, Cambridge. Chartered Accountant, holding numerous public appointments ; appointed by the Treasury as Public Auditor under the Friendly Societies Acts and Industrial and Provident Societies Acts. *War Work :* Acting Sec. Cambs. and Isle of Ely Territorial Force Association, 5 Aug. 1914, to Oct. 5, 1919 ; mentioned in " London Gazette " by Sec. of State for War for valuable services rendered in connection with the War. *Address :* Homelands, Hills Road, Cambridge. (O7121)

EMBELTON, Major David Moore, O.B.E., Aust. A.M.C.

EMBERTON, John, C.B.E., J.P.

EMBLETON, Rev. Hugh John, O.B.E., R.N., M.A.

EMBLING, Rev. Hugh John, O.B.E., R.N., M.A.

EMERSON, Lieut. George Michael, O.B.E.

EMERSON, Katherine, Mrs. George Henry, O.B.E..

b. February, 1864 ; *d.* of Edward Meahger, Esq., of St. John's, N.F. ; *m.* George Henry, *s.* of Lewis Wilkins Emerson, of St. John's, N.F. *Educ.:* Mount St. Vincent Academy, Halifax, Nova Scotia. *War Work:* Treasurer, Women's Patriotic Association of Newfoundland from Sept. 1914 to the end of the War. *Addresses:* Rennies Mill Road, and Virginia Water, St. John's, Newfoundland.   (O975)

EMERSON, Lieut. Thomas William, M.B.E., T.F. Res.

EMERY, Lieut. Herbert Denham, O.B.E., R.N.V.R.

EMERY, Horace Milton, M.B.E.

EMETT, Frederick William, O.B.E., F.R.G.S., *b.* 30 Aug. 1865 ; *s.* of William Henry Emett, of South Kensington ; *m.* Charlotte Agnes, *d.* of Capt. W. Pearce, of London. *Educ.:* Kensington Grammar School ; Director Intelligence Bureau of Reuters. *War Work:* Ministry of Information. *Address:* 9, Cumberland Road, Kew. *Club:* Devonshire.   (O134)

EMLER, Frederick William, M.B.E., *b.* 4 Feb. 1868 ; *s.* of William Emler, of London ; *m.* Sarah Ansley, *d.* of Thomas Hobbs, of Westminster. *Educ.:* Public Elementary School. Senior Staff Officer, Board of Trade. *War Work:* Control of Accounts dealing with War Risks Insurance of Ships, Cargoes, Seamen's effects, and many other war accounts of a confidential nature ; Bronze Medal of Royal Humane Society. *Address:* 24, Gonvile Road, Thornton Heath, Surrey.   (M8014)

EMLEY, Capt. Maurice Woodman, O.B.E., R.E. (T.).

EMMET, Major Ernest Arnold, O.B.E.

EMMETT, George Ernest, M.B.E.

EMMETT, Lieut.-Col. Joseph James Cheere, O.B.E.

EMMOTT, Alfred, Lord, P.C., G.C.M.G., G.B.E. (*see* BURKE'S *Peerage*), *b.* 8 May, 1858, *s.* of Thomas Emmott, of Brookfield, Oldham and Anchorsholme, Poulton-le-Fylde ; *m.* Mary Gertrude, *d.* of John William Lees, of Waterhead, Lancs. *Educ.:* Grove House School and London University. B.A. (Lond.), J.P. Lancashire and Oldham ; Mayor of Oldham, 1891–92 ; M.P. for Oldham, 1899–1911 ; Deputy Speaker of the House of Commons and Chairman of Ways and Means, 1906–11 ; Parliamentary Under Sec. for the Colonies, 1911–14 ; *War Work:* First Com. of Works, Aug. 1914 to May 1915 ; Director War Trade Department, Jan. 1915 to March, 1919. *Address:* 30, Ennismore Gardens, S.W. *Clubs:* Reform ; Brooks's ; Hurlingham.   (G4)

EMPSON, Agnes Dyke, Mrs., O.B.E., *b.* 28 Feb. 1861 ; *d.* of John Barton Arundel Acland, of Holnicote, Mt. Peel, N.Z. ; *m.* Walter, *s.* of Rev. Arthur John Empson, of Eydon Rectory, Northants. *War Work:* Work done in England from 1915 to 1919 in connection with New Zealand War Contingent Association, and New Zealand Red Cross. *Address:* Mt. Peel, Rangitata, New Zealand.   (O2182)

EMRA, Major Frederic Harcourt, O.R.E., M.E.I.C., *b.* 13 June, 1881 ; *s.* of the Rev. William Henry Atkinson Emra, M.A., of Chippenham, Wiltshire ; *m.* Margaret Gordon, *d.* of Francis Henry Chrysler, K.C., of Ottawa. *Educ.:* Eaton House School, Aldeburgh, and Bromsgrove. With Mr. C. H. Keefer, C.E., of Ottawa, and various engineering appointments, chiefly on railway exploratory, location, construction and maintenance work, on Grand Trunk Pacific and Canadian Pacific Railways of Canada, and South Eastern and Chatham and Dover Railway ; at present in private practice in firm of F. H. Emra and Partners, Civil and Mechanical Engineers, of Ottawa. *War Work:* 1915, Assistant District Engineer, South Eastern and Chatham and Dover Railway ; July, 1915, commission in 1st Canadian Pioneers ; severely wounded, Courcellette, Oct. 1916 ; returned to France Jan. 1917, as an engineering officer with 2nd Canadian Railway Troops ; invalided to England, Sept. 1917, in consequence of mustard gas burns on old wound, and seconded to Admiralty, Oct. 1917, as advisory civil engineer in new department of Auxiliary Shipbuilding : 1918, Resident Engineer, London and South Eastern District, and in charge of engineering and technical administration at headquarters for all residencies ; 1919 till resignation in 1920, acting as Director of Shipyard Extensions, and responsible for all financial commitments of Public Funds, and general executive as well as technical work, in connection with extensions to private shipyards, docks, engine and boiler works, and all kindred industries, occasioned by the war ; 1919–20, Director of Shipyard Extensions. *Addresses:* Hope Chambers, Ottawa ; 25, McLeod Street, Ottawa ; c/o London Joint City and Midland Bank, Gloucester Road, London, S.W. *Clubs:* Engineering Institute of Canada, Montreal ; Engineers', Toronto ; Rock and Fell Climbing, Kendal ; Minto Skating, Ottawa.   (O10379)

ENGELBACH, Lieut.-Comm. Charles Richard Fox, O.B.E., R.N.V.R., *b.* 20 May, 1876 ; *s.* of Lewis William Engelbach, C.B., of Richmond, Surrey ; *m.* Florence Ada, *d.* of Albert Neumegen, of London. *Educ.:* Sandringham House School, Southport. *War Work:* Asst. Examination Officer Hull, Aug. 1914 to Aug. 1915 ; Manager Gun Mounting Dept., Coventry Ordnance Works, Aug. 1915 to March, 1919. *Address:* 13, Edwardes Square, Kensington, W. 8. *Clubs:* Royal Automobile ; United Sports ; Drapers' Hall, Coventry.   (O10371)

ENGLAND, Alfred Colborne, O.B.E.

ENGLAND, Harry, M.B.E.

ENGLAND, Major Philip Remington, O.B.E., R.A.S.C.

ENGLAND, Major Richard Travell, O.B.E.

ENGLAND, Walter W., O.B.E.

ENGLEFIELD, Lieut. William, M.B.E.

ENGLEHEART, Lieut.-Col. Evelyn Linzee, C.B.E.

ENGLEHEART, Matilda Mary (Maye), Mrs., M.B.E. ;

d. of Augustus Walter Arnold, Deputy-Lieut., County of Middlesex, J.P., of Sussex Place, Hyde Park, and Gifford's Hall, Stoke-by-Nayland ; *m.* Henry L. D., *e. s.* of Sir Gardner Engleheart, K.C.B., of 28, Curzon Street, Mayfair. *Educ.:* Privately. *War Work:* President, Sec., and Treas. Boxford and Hadleigh Division, Soldiers' and Sailors' Families Association, and Naval and Military War Pensions. *Address:* The Priory, Stoke-by-Nayland, Suffolk.   (M8616)

ENGLISH, Col. Charles Ernest, O.B.E.

ENGLISH, Major William, O.B.E., R.A.S.C.

ENNESS, Mrs. Minnie, O.B.E.

ENNIS, Rev. Alexander Dallas Lecky, O.B.E., *b.* 9 July, 1870 ; *s.* of the late John Ennis, of Enniscorthy ; *m.* Florence Mary, *d.* of the late Rev. C. Ellington McKay, M.A., of Dublin. *Educ.:* Trinity Coll., Dublin (Master of Arts), Chaplain to H.M. Forces, 2nd Class. *War Work:* Chaplain to the Brigade of Guards at the Guards' Chapel, Wellington Barracks, S.W., 1914–15 ; Senior Chaplain, Shorncliffe Camp, 1915–16 ; Senior Chaplain, Cannock Chase Reserve Centre, 1916–19. *Address:* 2, Secretary's Lane, Gibraltar. *Club:* Junior United Service.   (O7126)

ENNIS, Lawrence, O.B.E. ; *s.* of Arthur Ennis, of West Calder, Scotland ; *m.* Margaret, *d.* of Peter Phillips, of U.S.A. *Educ.:* Scotland and America. General Manager, Dorman, Long & Company Ltd., Steel and Iron Manufacturers, Middlesbrough. *Address:* Genessee Lodge, Linthorpe, Middlesbrough. *Clubs:* Cleveland, Middlesbrough ; American, London. (O1322)

ENRIGHT, Paymaster Lieut.-Comm. William George Ewart, O.B.E., R.N.

ENSOR, Major Frederick Charles Curme, O.B.E., R.A.O.C.

ENTHOVEN, Augusta Gabrielle Eden, Mrs., M.B.E., *b.* 1869 ; *d.* of Rt. Hon. W. G. Romaine, C.B., The Priory, Old Windsor, Berks ; *m.* the late Major C. H. Enthoven, R.E. Writer. *War Work:* On War Refugees Committee. 20 Aug. 1914, to 24 Dec. 1916 ; Central Prisoners of War, Manager of the whole of the Records Department till close of office, from 27 Dec. 1916. *Address:* 97, Cadogan Gardens, S.W. 3.   (M8017)

ENTWISTLE, Joseph, M.B.E., *b.* 28 Aug. 1876 ; *s.* of Frederick Entwistle, of Middleton, Lancs. ; *m.* Nora, *d.* of George Buckley, of Knottend, Preesall, Lancs. *Educ.:* Queen Elizabeth's Grammar School, Middleton. Town Clerk, Morecambe. *War Work:* Hon. Sec. Soldiers' and Sailors' Families Association, Soldiers' and Sailors' Help Society (Bacup Branches) ; Clerk to Local Tribunal, Bacup ; Hon. Sec. Local War Pensions Committee, Bacup. *Address:* 125, York Terrace, Lancaster Road, Morecambe.   (O8018)

ERBY, Lieut. Henry William, M.B.E., R.A.O.C.

ERLEBACH, Capt. Cyril Woodland, O.B.E.

ERRINGTON, Capt. John Perrin, O.B.E., T.F. Reserve, *b.* 7 Sept. 1881 ; *s.* of John Errington, of Kirkandrews-on Eden, Carlisle. *Educ.:* Carlisle Grammar School ; Old Coll., Windermere. Deputy Registrar, Carlisle County Court ; Deputy District Registrar, High Court of Justice, Carlisle. *War Work:* Service in India. *Address:* Kirkandrews-on-Eden, Carlisle   (O8464)

ERSKINE, Col. Henry Adeane, C.B., C.M.G., C.B.E., D.L., *b.* 1 March, 1857 ; *s.* of late Rev. Thomas Erskine, Rector of Alderley, Cheshire (*see* BURKE'S *Peerage*, Erskine, B.) ; *m.* Florence Eliza Palmer, *d.* of Ven. Frank Robert Chapman, Archdeacon of Sudbury and Canon of Ely. Hon. Col. of Northumberland T. and S. Column, A.S.C., late comdg. (V.D.) Col. and Deputy Director of Supplies, 1917 ; has Order of Leopold of Belgium. *Address:* Milton Lodge, Gillingham, Dorset.   (C1247)

ERSKINE, James Francis, C.B., C.M.G., M.V.O., O.B.E., J.P., D.L., *b.* 14 June, 1862 ; *s.* of Sir Henry David Erskine, K.C.V.O., of Cardross, Port of Monteith, Perthshire (*see* BURKE'S *Peerage*. Buchan, E.) ; *m.* Margaret Beatrix, *d.* of late Henry Lambton, of Redfield, Winslow. Brig.-Gen. (ret.) late Scots Guards ; served in Soudan, S. Africa, and in Great War. *Address:* Ledeamerock, Dunblane, Perthshire. *Club:* Guards'.

ERSKINE, Walter Hugh, M.B.E., *b.* 27 April, 1870 ; *s.* of Sir David Erskine, K.C.V.O., of Cardross, Port of Monteith, Perthshire. *Educ.:* Charterhouse. Asst. Sergeant-at-Arms, House of Commons. *War Work:* Asst.-Commander, Metropolitan Special Constabulary, 1914–19. *Address:* House of Commons, S.W. 1. *Club:* Wellington. (M8019)

ERWIN, Lieut. Harry, O.B.E., R.A.O.C.

ESHELBY, Frederick George, M.B.E.

ESPELEY, Lieut. Arthur James, O.B.E.

ESPLEN, James Johnstone, O.B.E., *b.* 2 Nov. 1875 ; *s.* of William Esplen, of Liverpool ; *m.* Winifred, *d.* of John Wallace Taylor, J.P., of Sunderland *Educ.:* Privately and Liverpool University. Consultant Naval Architect. *War Work:* Shipbuilding programme, U.S.A. and Canada (as Chief Technical Advisor to Sir Joseph Maclay, P.C.) ; Later appointed Technical Director, British Ministry of Shipping, U.S.A., in charge of repairs and fitting out of British Ships for carriage of American Troops. *Clubs:* R.A.C. ; Engineers' (New York).   (O3704)

ESPLEN, Sir John, K.B.E., A.Inst.N.A., *b.* 13 May, 1863 ; *s.* of the late William Esplen, of Blundellsands ; *m.* 26 Jan., 1898, Laura Louise, *d.* of the late John Dickenson, of Sunderland. Senior partner in the firm of Messrs. Esplen Sons, and Swainston, Ltd., Naval Archicets ; Director of Overseas Ship Purchase, Ministry of Shipping. *Addresses:* Heron Bridge, Eaton Road, Chester ; Esplanade, Waterloo, Liverpool. *Club:* Junior Conservative, Liverpool.   (K141)

ESPLIN, Annie, M.B.E.
ESSLEMONT, Dora Longhair, Mrs., O.B.E., Q.M.A.A.C.
ESSLEMONT, George Gale, M.B.E.
ESTILL, Harriet, M.B.E.
ESTILL, John Henry, O.B.E., *b.* 10 Aug. 1870 ; *s.* of William Estill, of Scalby, Scarboro', Yorks. ; *m.* Alice Mary, *d.* of William Henwood, of Hull. *Educ. :* Hackness ; Privately ; Hull Technical School. Commercial Manager, Port of London Authority. *War Work :* Organising Sec., Lord Mayor of London's Appeal, 1918, British Red Cross and Order of St. John ; raised £816,000. *Address :* 109, Leadenhall Street, London, E.C. *Club :* Gresham. (O10373)
ETCHES, Major Charles Edward, O.B.E., *b.* 1872 ; *s.* of late Edward Etches, of Derby. *Educ. :* Uppingham and Sandhurst. Res. of Officers ; Assistant Sec. National Rifle Association. *War Work :* General Staff, Eastern Command ; Comm. Eastern Command School of Musketry ; Chief Inst., The School of Musketry. *Address :* Bisley Camp, Brookwood, Surrey. *Club :* Naval and Military. (O3119)
ETESON, Col. Harold Carleton Wetherall, C.B.E., R.A., *b.* 24 Aug. 1863 ; *s.* of Major General F. Eteson, of Dover ; *m.* Marian Elisabeth, *d.* of Jonas ap Jones, of Canada. *Educ. :* Privately. Entered Royal Military Academy, 1880 ; Commissioned Lieut. Royal Artillery, 1882 ; Retired Lieut. Col. and granted rank of Col., 1919 ; 2nd Class Assist. Insp. Warlike Stores, 1893 ; Inspector of Warlike Stores (Gibraltar), 1893 ; Officer in charge Danger Buildings, R. Laboratory, Woolwich, 1897 ; Assist. Supt. R. Lab., Woolwich, 1899. *War Work :* O.C., North Section Royal Artillery, Gibraltar, 1914 ; O.C. Thames Section, Thames and Medway Garrison, 1915–19. *Address :* C/o Cox & Co., 16 Charing Cross, London, S.W.1. (C1556)
ETHELSTON, Ruth Frances, Mrs., M.B.E.
ETHEREDGE, Charles Douglas, M.B.E. *War Work :* Rendered valuable services to the Small Craft Dept., Ministry of Shipping. (M10316)
ETHERIDGE, Arthur Thomas, M.B.E.
ETHERIDGE, Lieut.-Col. Cecil de Courcy, C.B.E., D.S.O. *b.* 1859 ; *s.* of the late Maj.-Gen. Alfred Thomas Etheridge, C.S.I., of 47 Selborne Road, Hove, Sussex. *Educ. :* Privately and R.M.C. Entered 6th Regt. 1878 ; Capt. Roy. Warwickshire Regt. 1886 ; Major 1896 ; retired 1898 ; was Lieut.-Col., Manchester Regt., 1914–15, and Lieut.-Col., Durham L.I., 1915–16 ; subsequently Lieut.-Col. E. Yorkshire Regt. ; is Lieut.-Col. Reserve of Officers, and Sec. City of Edinburgh Territorial Force Assoc. ; served in Afghan War, 1878–80 (medal), with Nile Expedition, 1898 ; present at battle of Khartoum (medal, Egyptian medal with clasp, 4th class, Order of Osmanieh) ; and in S. Africa, 1900–1902 (mentioned in despatches, Queen's medal with three clasps, King's medal with two clasps). (C1540)
ETHERIDGE, Herbert, M.B.E., *b.* 10 June, 1884 ; *s.* of Richard Etheridge, of Hanwell ; *m.* Alice Emma. *d.* of Henry William Hall, of Barnet. *Educ. :* St. John's School, Penge. Acting Deputy Accounts Officer, Accountant-General's Department, Admiralty. *War Work :* Served at Admiralty during the war. *Address :* 76, Milton Road, Hanwell, W. 7. (M8021)
ETHERTON, George Hammond, O.B.E.
EUNSON, Milicent, Mrs., M.B.E., *b.* 4 June, 1873 ; *d.* of Rev. Canon Sanders, of Rothley Vicarage, Leicester ; *m.* George, *s.* of John Eunson, of Northampton. *Educ. :* Clergy Daughters' School, Bristol. *War Work :* Voluntary worker. War Pensions Committee (Borough), Northampton. *Address :* Abington Hill, Northampton. (M8022)
EUSTACE, Lieut. Albert Victor, M.B.E., *b.* 10 Aug. 1883 ; *s.* of Robert Eustace, of Blandford, Dorset ; *m.* Florence Daisy, *d.* of the late Frederick John Head, of Bournemouth. *Educ. :* Milldown School, Blandford, Dorset. Commercial traveller. *War Work :* Rejected on medical grounds, but ultimately accepted in the 13th Batt. Royal Berkshire Regt., Aug. 1916 ; proceeded overseas, Sept. 1916 ; commissioned, April, 1917, to 160 Lab. Co. (4th Devon Lab. Co.), which he commanded Dec. 1918 to Feb. 1919 ; relinquished his commission owing to ill health contracted on active service, June, 1920. *Addresses :* c/o Mrs. Stenlake, 29, Blackall Road, Exeter ; Strathyre, Edgehill Road, Bournemouth. (M4474)
EUSTACE, Major-Gen. Alexander Henry, C.B., C.B.E., D.S.O., *b.* 1863 ; *s.* of Col. J. T. Eustace, formerly 60th Rifles ; *m.* 1904. Evelyn Mary, *d.* of the late Samuel Stonestreet, of Cape Town. Entered E. Surrey Regt., 1885 ; became Capt., Indian Army, 1896 ; Major, 1903 ; Lieut.-Col. 1907 ; Col. 1911, and Maj.-Gen. 1917 ; served with Hazara Expedition, 1888 (medal with clasp) ; and 1891, as Intelligence Field Officer ; and in Somaliland, 1903–4 (mentioned in despatches) ; comdg. Kohat Brigade, N. Army, India. *Club :* East India United Service. (C2033)
EUSTACE, Marjory Edith, Mrs. ROBERTSON-, C.B.E. *d.* of Major Thomas Leith, of Petmathen, Oyne, Aberdeenshire (see BURKE'S *Peerage.* Carnwath) ; *m.* 1906, Major Charles Legge Eustace Robertson-Eustace, D.S.O., who d. Organiser and Administrator, First Rest Club for Nursing Sisters in France during Great War. (C957)
EVANS, Abel Joseph, M.B.E., J.P.,
EVANS, Agnes Louisa, Mrs., M.B.E., *b.* 1867 ; *d.* of Deputy Surg.-Gen. St. John Stanley, of The Court, Wrexham ; *m.* Arthur Ernest Evans, M.B.E., J.P., D.L. (*q.v.*), *s.* of Edward Evans, J.P., D.L., of Bronwylfa, near Wrexham. *Educ. :* Privately. Woman's Sub-Committee, Ministry of Labour ; President Mothers' Union ; Chairman Queen Victoria Nursing

Association ; Chairman Girl Guides, L. A. Committee Waifs and Strays, Boy Scouts, Children's Welfare C.C. ; Member Welsh Church Council. *War Work :* Commandant Roseneath Red Cross Hospital, Wrexham. *Address :* Vrondeg Hall, Bronwylfa, near Wrexham. *Club :* V.A.D. (M3632)
EVANS, Comm. Alfred Englefield, O.B.E., R.N.
EVANS, Annie Elethea, M.B.E. (M10382)
EVANS, Major Arthur, O.B.E., M.C., R.E.
EVANS, Capt. Arthur Ernest, M.B.E., J.P., D.L. Co. Denbigh, ex-High Sheriff (1914–15), R.A.S.C., M.T. (V.), *b.* 28 April, 1866 ; *s.* of the late Edward Evans, J.P., D.L., of Bronwylfa, near Wrexham ; *m.* Agnes Louisa, M.B.E. (*q.v.*), *d.* of Deputy Surgeon St. John Stanley, A.M.S., of The Court, Wrexham. *Educ. :* Leamington and privately. Chairman, Local Employment Committee ; President Miners' Disablement Association ; Commissioner, Boy Scouts ; Chairman County Licensing Committee ; Chairman Appointments Committee ; represents North Wales, Royal Agricultural Council ; Director, International Horse Show, Olympia. *War Work :* Remount Purchasing Officer, North Wales, and Depot Superintendent ; Chief Military Representative, 23rd Area. *Address :* Vrondeg Hall, Bronwylfa, near Wrexham, N. Wales. (M1700)
EVANS, Arthur Henry, O.B.E., M.S., F.R.C.S., R.A.M.C., *b.* 6 Jan. 1872 ; *s.* of the late Samuel Evans, of Neath, Glamorgan ; *m.* Dorothy Evans, *d.* of Lawrance Briant, of Forest Green. Surgeon, Imperial Yeomanry Field Hospital S. Africa, 1900 ; mentioned in despatches ; Surgeon and Lecturer on Surgery, Westminster Hospital, since 1902 ; Surgeon, 4th London General Hospital, 1914–18 ; Freemasons War Hospital, 1916–19 ; Alford House, Park Lane War Hospital for Officers, 1914-18 ; London Temperance Hospital since 1913 ; Royal Chest Hospital since 1910 ; Consulting Surgeon, Bethlem Royal Hospital since 1910. *Address :* 28, Devonshire Place, W. 1. (O7128)
EVANS, Major Arthur Kelly, O.B.E., M.C., R.M.L.I.
EVANS, Major Audrey Thomas, O.B.E., R.A.F.
EVANS, Lieut. Bernard Scott, M.B.E., M.C.
EVANS, Capt. Cecil Hugh Silvester, O.B.E.
EVANS, Christopher Douglas, O.B.E.
EVANS, Claude Victor, M.B.E.
EVANS, Corris William, O.B.E., *b.* 8 May, 1886 ; *s.* of late William Evans, C.B., of 14, Meadway, N.W. 4. *Educ. :* Highgate School and St. John's College, Oxford. Solicitor ; In Department of Treasury Solicitor. *War Work :* 2nd Lieut., Bedfordshire Regt. ; Lieut., March, 1917 ; Served 1914–18 ; Wounded, June, 1916, subsequently seconded for service to Ministry of Shipping, March, 1917 to April, 1919. *Address :* 28, South Eaton Place, S.W.1. *Club :* Devonshire. (O324)
EVANS, Major David Howard, O.B.E., *b.* 25 Feb. 1880 ; *s.* of the late Thomas Evans, Esq., Stoneyhurst, Kent ; *m.* Violet Isabella, *d.* of the late Major J. C. Grant, 2nd (Queen's) R.W. Surrey Regt., of Rathconrath House, Mullingar, Co. Westmeath, Ireland. *Educ. :* Harrow. *War Work :* Served South African War with 20th Mounted Infantry, 1901 ; 1914–15 2nd Reserve Cavalry ; 1916, attached Cavalry Corps Headquarters ; 1917, A.P.M., 40th Division ; 1918–19, A.P.M., Taranto Base, Italy. *Clubs :* Army and Navy ; Cavalry. (O2979)
EVANS, Edith Mary, M.B.E.
EVANS, Rev. Edward, M.B.E.
EVANS, Edward Victor, O.B.E., F.I.C., F.C.S., *b.* 12 Dec. 1882 ; *s.* of J. Edward Evans, of Sydney, Australia ; *m.* Annie, *d.* of T. D. Leng. *Educ. :* King's Coll., London. Chief Chemist and Products Manager, South Metropolitan Gas Co., London. *War Work :* Connected with the manufacture of explosive bases and poison gas. *Address :* 206, Lewisham High Road, London. *Club :* Savage. (O10376)
EVANS, Edwin, M.B.E.
EVANS, Ethel Frances, Mrs., O.B.E., *b.* 25 Aug. 1885 ; *d.* of James Cotesworth Hill, of Gloucester ; *m.* Edward Blackwall, *s.* of Rev. Ed. Evans, of Blackwall, Kirk Ireton, Derbyshire. *War Work :* Commandant of Gloucester Red Cross Hospital, 1914–19. *Address :* Old House, Wotton, Gloucester. *Club :* V.A.D. (O10377)
EVANS, Evan, M.B.E., R.N.
EVANS, Evan Laming, C.B.E., M.A., M.D., B.C. (Cantab.), F.R.C.S., *b.* 3 Sept. 1871 ; *s.* of late Worthington Evans, of 47, York Terrace, Regents Park ; *m.* Vivien, *d.* of Hugh Lloyd Roberts, C.B., of Middle Temple. *Educ. :* Eastbourne College, Trinity College, Cambridge ; St. Bartholomew's Hospital, E.C. Surgeon to the Royal National Orthopædic Hospital ; Surgeon (for Orthopædic cases), to the West End Hospital for Nervous Diseases ; Surgeon, Royal Surgical Aid Society ; Surgeon, Special Military Surgical Hospital, Shepherds Bush ; Consulting Surgeon, National Industrial Home for Crippled Boys ; President of the subsection of Orthopædic Surgery, Royal Society of Medicine. *War Work :* Orthopædic Surgery under the War Office, and British Red Cross Society at numerous Hospitals. *Address :* 50, Seymour Street, Portman Square, W.1. *Clubs :* United University ; Mid-Surrey ; Royal Cinque Ports ; Huntercombe Golf. (C2589)
EVANS, 2nd Lieut. Evan Reginald, M.B.E., R.F.A.
EVANS, Major Fisher Henry Freke, D.S.O., O.B.E., J.P., D.L. Co. Donegal, *b.* 21 April, 1868 ; *s.* of Capt. Richard Fisher Evans ; *m.* Marie Louise Evans, *d.* of Major Arthur Kyle Haslett, R.E. Rossall and Peterhouse, Cambridge (B.A. 1890). High Sheriff, Co. Donegal, 1911. *War Work :* Served with Loyal North Lancashire Regiment, 1914–17 ; Chairman, Eastern Division Road Transport Board, Road

Transport Department of the Ministry of Food. *Addresses :* Carnagarve, Moville, Co. Donegal ; 2, Brookside, Cambridge. *Club :* Junior United Service. (O10378)

EVANS, Frank Hedley, M.B.E.

EVANS, Capt. Frederic, M.B.E., R.A.M.C. (T.F.), F.I.H., M.R.I.P.H., M.R.San.I., F.R.Hist.S., *b.* 18 Aug. 1888 ; *s.* of Thomas Christopher Evans, of Ty Cynwyd, Llangynwyd, Glam. *Educ. :* Maesteg Higher Grade School ; Carmarthen Coll. ; St. Catharine's Coll., Cambridge. *War Work :* England, 8 Feb. 1915 to 4 Dec. 1915 ; B.E.F., France, 4 Dec. 1915, to 23 April, 1918 ; North Russia Forces, 16 June, 1918, to 23 Sept. 1919 ; British Army of Rhine, Nov. 1919 ; D.A.D. Hygiene, Chatham Medical Dist., Dec. 1919, to Oct. 1920 ; has Crosses of Order of St. Stanislaus and St. Anne of Russia (with swords) : mentioned in despatches, "London Gazette," Jan. 1919. *Address :* Ty Cynwyd, Llangynwyd, Bridgend, Glam. (M5005)

EVANS, Frederick George, O.B.E.

EVANS, Capt. Frederick James, C.B.E., R.N., *b.* 1867 ; *s.* of Capt. Frederick John Evans. Served in Great War as Div. Naval Transport Officer, Middlesbrough (mentioned in despatches). (C2249)

EVANS, Sir Frederick, K.C.M.G., K.C.V.O., C.B.E., *b.* 6 May, 1847 ; *s.* of William Frederick Evans, of Admiralty ; *m.* Ellenwood Katharine Carr, *d.* of William Wood Heath, of Antigua, British West Indies. *Educ. :* Privately. Colonial Civil Service ; Colonial Secretary of Southern Nigeria, Gold Coast, Leeward Islands, Jamaica and Gibraltar. *War Work :* Organisation and Control of Food and Supplies and general service at Gibraltar as Colonial Secretary. *Address :* Bywood, Branksome Park, Bournemouth. (C392)

EVANS, Flight-Lieut. Geoffrey Fanington, O.B.E., R.A.F.

EVANS, Col. George Henry, C.I.E., C.B.E., V.D., *b.* 28 Nov. 1863. *Address :* Kalaw, South Shan States, Burma. (C2034)

EVANS, Capt. George Windham Wright, M.B.E.

EVANS, Lieut.-Col. Granville Pennefather, C.B.E.

EVANS, Gladys Richardson, M.B.E., *b.* 19 July, 1881 ; *d.* of Richardson Evans. *Educ. :* St. Hilda's Hall, Oxford. Borough Councillor (Wimbledon). *War Work :* Hon. Sec. Wimbledon and Merton Belgian Refugees Committee (Medal of Queen Elizabeth of Belgium) ; Hon. Sec. Women Patrols Sub-Committee of the Women's Local Government Association for Wimbledon. *Address :* The Keir, Wimbledon Common, London, S.W. 19. *Club :* Univ. for Ladies, 4, George Street, London, W. (M8027)

EVANS, Capt. Griffith Charles, O.B.E.

EVANS, Harold Butler Wyn, M.B.E (M10247e)

EVANS, Lieut. Harold Ernest, O.B.E., R.N.

EVANS, Harry Loft, M.B.E., M.R.C.S. (Eng.), L.R.C.P. (Lond.), *b.* 1876 ; *s.* of T. M. Evans, Surgeon, of Hull ; *m.* Esme Lucy, *d.* of J. Stuhlman, of The Grange, Hessle. *Educ. :* Epsom Coll., and St. Thomas's Hospital. Late resident surgeon, Hull and Sculcoates Dispensary ; Hon. Anæsthetist (late senior casualty surgeon) Hull Royal Infirmary, and John Symons Home for Incurables ; late Sec. to East Yorkshire Division, and East Yorkshire and N. Lincs. Branch of British Medical Association. *War Work :* Hon. Anæsthetist to St. John's V.A.D. Hospital ; Sec. of Hull Medical War Committee. *Address :* 101, Princes Avenue, Hull. (M8028)

EVANS, Major Henry John Archibald, M.B.E., R.F.A.

EVANS, Capt. Henry Morton Glyn, C.B.E., J.P., *b.* 20 Aug. 1874 ; *s.* of David Evans, of Langennech Park, Carmarthenshire ; *m.* Hilda Dalrymple, *d.* of W. H. Delano, C.E., of 13, Barkston Gardens, South Kensington ; *Educ. :* Llandovery. High Sheriff, Carmarthenshire, 1914–15. *War Work :* Recruiting 41st Area ; Ministry National Service,· Welsh Region. *Addresses :* Plasissa and Llangennech Park. *Clubs :* Constitutional ; Royal Automobile. (O1323)

EVANS, Major Herbert, C.B.E., J.P., *b.* Feb. 1868 ; *s.* of John Evans, of Burton-on-Trent ; *m.* Jennie, *d.* of Robert Mitchell, of Peterhead. *Educ. :* Regent Street Polytechnic, London. Director-General of Local Administration, Ministry of Pensions. *War Work :* Combatant Officer, Middlesex Regt., Aug. 1914 to Feb. 1917 ; Principal Private Sec. and Chief Inspector to Minister of Pensions. *Address :* St. Albans Avenue, Bedford Park, W. *Clubs :* Carlyle ; Primrose ; Eccentric. (C2593)

EVANS, Herbert, M.B.E.

EVANS, Herbert Walter Lloyd, O.B.E., *b.* 22 Aug. 1877 ; *s.* of John Lloyd Evans, of Dartford, Kent ; *m.* Susan Georgina *d.* of Thomas Thatcher, of West Peckham, Kent. *Educ. :* City of London School. Assistant Superintendent, Royal Mint. *War Work :* Special work in connection with munitions. *Address :* 11, Dunvegan Gardens, Eltham, S.E. 9. (O1324)

EVANS, Lieut.-Col. John, O.B.E.

EVANS, Capt. John Edward, M.B.E.

EVANS, John Owain, C.B.E.

EVANS, Paymaster-Lieut. Joseph Owen, M.B.E., R.N.R.

EVANS, John Thomas, M.B.E., *b.* 15 May, 1861 ; *s.* of John Evans, of Haverfordwest ; *m.* Frances Bell, *d.* of Richard Dawkins, of Pembroke Dock. *Educ. :* National School, Pembroke Dock, and H.M. Dockyard School, Pembroke Dock. Acting Foreman of H.M. Dockyard ; Treas. of Pembrokeshire Permanent Building Soc. *War Work :* Fitting out and repairing warships· and Special Service vessels for destruction of submarines ; rendering assistance to vessels damaged by submarine attacks, and salvage work of same when necessary. *Address :* 101, Gwyther Street, Pembroke Dock. (M8030)

EVANS, Maude Ellefred, M.B.E.

EVANS, Richard, O.B.E.

EVANS, Lieut. Richard Endell, M.B.E., R.E. (T.).

EVANS, Lieut. Richard Samuel, O.B.E., R.N.R.

EVANS, Capt. Samuel Earnest, M.B.E.

EVANS, Sidney, M.B.E.

EVANS, Thomas, C.B.E., J.P.

EVANS, Thomas Henry Royston, O.B.E., J.P.

EVANS, Victor Hallen, M.B.E. (M10383)

EVANS, Walter David, M.B.E., *b.* 19 Dec. 1863 ; *s.* of David Evans, of London ; *m.* Rosa Mary, *d.* of W. Jolliffe, of Southampton. Previously Examiner of Naval Ordnance Work ; Foreman of Factory at R.N.O. Depot, Invergordon, and R.N.O. Depot, Portsmouth. *War Work :* Duties in connection with guns on board ships of H.M. Fleet and Auxiliaries, etc., also on board new ships under construction. (M8031)

EVANS, William James, C.B.E.

EVANS, William James, M.B.E.

EVANS, Capt. William John, M.B.E., R.A.O.C.

EVANS, Major William Martin, O.B.E., M.C., R.E.

EVANS, Major William Owen, M.B.E., J.P. for County of Glamorgan, R.A.M.C. (T.F.) (ret.), *b.* 8 July, 1869 ; *s.* of Rev. John Evans, of Trebanos House, Pontardawe, Glamorgan ; *m.* Gwladys Mary, *d.* of Dr. Griffith Griffiths, J.P., of Pontardawe. *Educ. :* Trebanos Grammar School ; Llandovery Coll. ; Glasgow Univ. ; Univ. Coll., London. Dist. Med. Officer, No. 1 Dist., Pontardawe Union ; Med. Officer Pontardawe Guardians Institution and Infirmary ; Med. Officer to G.P.O. and Board of Education. *War Work :* Member and Deputy President Swansea Med. Board ; Major, 2nd in command, Welsh Border Mounted Brigade Field Ambulance ; late in command 2nd line Welsh Border Mounted Brigade Field Ambulance ; invalided Mar. 1915 ; Med. Officer in charge Glanrhyd and Pontardawe Auxilliary Hospital, St. John Ambulance ; Hon. Serving Brother St. John of Jerusalem in England. (M8033)

EVANS, Major and Qr.-Mr. William Richard, O.B.E., R.E.

EVANS, Capt. William Sandford, O.B.E.

EVANS, Major William Stanley, O.B.E., R.A.S.C.

EVANS, Lieut.-Col. Charles Harford BOWLE-, C.M.G., C.B.E., I.M.S., *b.* 19 Oct. 1867 ; *s.* of the late John Bowle-Evans, of Byletts, Pembridge, Herefordshire, J.P., D.L. ; *m.* Ellen, *d.* of Major Gen. W. T. Stevenson, C.B. *Educ. :* Cheltenham Coll. ; Emman. College, Cambridge ; St. Bartholomew's Hospital, London. *War Work :* In Command Lucknow Casualty Clearing Station : France, 1914–16 ; Despatches, 3 June, 1915, C.M.G. ; India, Commanding Dhra Dun War Hospital, 1916–18, Despatches ; Persia, A.D.M.S., Bushire Force, T. Col., 1918–19, Despatches.

EVANS, William Augustus BULKELEY-, O.B.E., M.A., *b.* 20 March, 1869 ; *s.* of Col. W. B. Evans ; *m.* Adelaide Kathleen, *d.* of Charles Dufresne, of Montreal. *Educ. :* Wellington and Oxford. Barrister-at-law ; Sec. and Standing Counsel to Headmasters' Conference ; Co-Editor of "Public Schools Year Book" ; representative in Great Britain for McGill Univ., Montreal ; member of Council of Royal Colonial Institute. *War Work :* Hon. Sec. and Treas. of Public Schools Hospitals at Rouen and Netley (collected £36,000) ; member of Central Collections Committee of British Red Cross Society (received O.B.E. for services) ; Chairman of Central Council of Overseas Club for 3 years ; Director of Exports and Imports Branch of Food Ministry from Jan. 1917 to Armistice (foreign decorations) ; Inspector of Legal Section of Special Constabulary (H.Q. C.D.) from Aug. 1914 to disbandment in 1919 (long service medal). *Addresses :* 12, King's Bench Walk, Temple, E.C. ; Cleveland, Maidenhead. *Clubs :* Savile ; St. James'. (O10379)

EVANS, Capt. George LEE-, O.B.E.

EVANS, Annie, Mrs. LLOYD-, O.B.E., *b.* 25 April, 1844 ; *d.* of the late Thomas Pierce, of Berriew, Montgomeryshire ; *m.* John Lloyd, J.P. for Warwickshire, ex-Mayor of Warwick, *s.* of the late John Evans, solicitor, of London. *Educ. :* at Berriew School. Poor-law Guardian ; President of Warwick Sisterhood ; Member of County Maternity, Child Welfare, Mental Deficiency, and National Insurance Committees ; Governor of Warwick King's Schools. *War Work :* As Mayoress of Warwick organised working parties to supply troops with clothing and comforts on active service ; member of War Pensions and Warwickshire Women's Land Army Committees. *Address :* High Street, Warwick. (O10374)

EVANS, Gweneth Kate MOY-, M.B.E.

EVATT, Capt. James Wrigley, M.B.E., 1st Lancashire Fusiliers, *b.* 4 Feb. 1891 ; *s.* of Rev. R. B. Evatt, formerly of Mt. Louise, Smithborough, Co. Monaghan, Ireland ; *m.* Helen Alice, *d.* of Rev. Charles Chaytor, of Worcester. *Educ. :* The Old Coll., Windermere ; Rugby School ; Royal Mil. Coll., Sandhurst. *War Work :* Attached Trench Warfare Dept., Ministry of Munitions, 1915 ; Adjutant, H.Q. Bomb School, Clapham, 1915 and 1917 ; Attached Munitions Design Dept., Ministry of Munitions, 1917 ; Adjutant and Experimental Officer, Trench Warfare Dept., Ministry of Munitions, 1918 ; France, Aug. 1914 ; wounded on the Aisne ; mentioned in Sir J. D. P. French's despatches, May, 1915 ; gassed at Ypres, May, 1915 ; mentioned in despatches by Sec. of State for War, 1919. *Address :* Unstead Cottage, Shalford, Surrey. *Club :* Junior United Service. (M5251

EVE, Col. Arthur Stewart, C.B.E., D.Sc., M.A., b. 1862 ; s. of the late J. R. Eve ; m. 1905, Elizabeth Agnes Brooks, of Montreal. *Educ.* : Berkhamsted Sch., and Pembroke Coll., Camb., and McGill Univ. Assist. Master, Marlborough Coll., 1887–1903 ; Lecturer and Professor, McGill Univ., 1903–15 ; and Resident Director of Research, Admiralty Experimental Station, Parkestone Quay and Harwich, 1917–19 ; has been Macdonald Professor of Physics, McGill Univ. since 1912 ; Col. Canadian Forces, and a F.R.S. *Address* : 490, Mountain Avenue, Montreal. (C496)

EVE, Capt. George Thomas, O.B.E., M.C., R.E.

EVE, Sir Herbert Trustram, K.B.E.

EVE, William Charles Pittuck, M.B.E., b. 21 Aug. 1888. *Educ.* : Privately. Surveyor, H.M Office of Works. *War Work* : Section Director, Construction Branch, Gun Ammunition Filling Dept., Ministry of Munitions. *Address* : 88, Broom Road, Teddington. (M8034)

EVELYN, Gwendolen O.B.E., b. 10 May, 1886 ; d. of Francis Lyndor Evelyn, of Kinsham Court, Presteign. *Educ.* : Cheltenham Ladies College. *War Work* : Commandant of Corton Hospital, Presteign. *Address* : Corton, Presteign. *Clubs* : V.A.D. (O1326)

EVENS, Elizabeth Mary, Mrs., M.B.E., b. Oct. 1860 ; d. of William Dean Wathen, of Fishguard, Pem. ; m. Arthur Tudor, s. of James Evens, of Little Sneyd, Stoke Bishop, Bristol. *Educ.* : Privately. *War Work* : Commandant of Foye House Red Cross Hospital, Leigh Woods, Bristol, during the whole time it was open, May, 1915, to May, 1919. *Address* : c/o Mrs. Davey, Holyrood, Falmouth, Cornwall. *Club* : V.A.D. Ladies'. (M1705)

EVEREST, Edward Percy, M.B.E.

EVEREST, Major William Charles Robert, O.B.E., R.A.O.C.

EVERETT, Basil Preston, O.B.E.

EVERETT, Lieut. Charles Falconer Guy, M.B.E.

EVERETT, Sub-Lieut. Douglas Henry, M.B.E., R.N.

EVERETT, Lionel Decimus Longcroft, O.B.E., b. 17 June, 1877 ; s. of Arthur Joseph Everett, of Berry Pomeroy Vicarage, Devon. *Educ.* : Newton Coll., Devon. Joined Wilts Constabulary, Aug. 1895 ; appointed Supt. Wilts. Constabulary, Oct. 1905 ; Chief Constable, Preston, Lancs., May, 1908 ; Asst. Chief Constable of Liverpool, March, 1912. *War Work* : Police work generally, and direction of Criminal Investigation and Alien Registration. *Club* : Athenæum (Liverpool). (O10380)

EVERETT, Major Ralph Marven, M.B.E.

EVERETT, Capt. (T. Major) Raymond Charles, O.B.E., 2nd King Edward's Horse, b. 15 Jan. 1879 ; s. of Frederic Everett, of Swaffham, Norfolk ; m. Gladys Mary, d. of Thomas Moore, of Great Yarmouth. *War Work* : Served in the Boer War 1899 to 1902 ; Zulu Campaign, 1906. Great War from 29 Aug. 1914 ; Staff Capt., 3rd Echelon, B.S.F., 5 Sept. 1916 to 7 Dec. 1918 ; mentioned in despatches, 30 Jan. 1919 ; Deputy Asst. Director Graves Registration, Army of the Black Sea, 9 Feb. 1919. *Address* : 19, St. George's Road, Worthing. *Club* : Constitutional. (O8687)

EVERETT, Lieut. Raymond Walter, M.B.E., R.A.F.

EVERETT, Capt. Reginald Marsh, O.B.E., R.A.F.

EVERETT, Lieut. Roland Tylor, M.B.E.

EVERIDGE, John, O.B.E., b. 10 Nov. 1884 ; s. of J. W. Everidge, of Surbiton, Surrey ; m. Kathleen Isobel, d. of Henry James Robertson, J.P., of East Molesey, Surrey. *Educ.* : King's College School. Assistant Surgeon, King's College Hospital, London ; Hon. Consulting Surgeon, St. John's Hospital, Twickenham ; Hon. Consulting Surgeon, Surbiton Hospital. *War Work* : Service in R.A.M.C. (T.), Aug. 1914, to March, 1919, with rank of Capt. (acting Major), i/c of Surgical Division, 54th General Hospital, B.E.F. France, etc. Mentioned in despatches. *Address* : 6, Upper Wimpole Street, W.1. (O5241)

EVERITT, Robert Gordon, O.B.E.

EVERITT, Major Stuart Oswald, O.B.E., R.A.F.

EVERSON, Lieut. Thurston Hicks, M.B.E., R.A.S.C.

EWART, David, O.B.E., M.D., F.R.C.S., b. 6 July, 1865 ; s. of Robert Ewart, of Dumfries-shire, Scotland. *Educ.* : Privately and at the Universities of Edinburgh and New Zealand. Honorary Surgeon Royal West Sussex Hospital, and Consulting Medical Officer, Graylingwell Hospital. *War Work* : Surgical specialist, Royal West Sussex Hospital and Graylingwell War Hospital. *Address* : 31, North Street, Chichester. (O4360)

EWART, Lieut.-Col. Ernest Andrew, O.B.E., b. 20 Jan. 1878 ; s. of Major John Knox Ewart, R.A. *Educ.* : Aberdeen and Banff Grammar Schools. *War Work* : Served France 1914–17, in R.F.A., from then to Armistice in R.F.C. and R.A.F ; During last year of war made trips to Home and delivered lectures to aircraft workers and in various other ways tried to stimulate aircraft production. *Address* : 10, Pembroke Studios, Pembroke Gardens, W.8. *Club* : Savage. (O1327)

EWART, Evelyn, Mrs., M.B.E.

EWART, Surg.-Lieut. Francis, O.B.E., M.B., R.N.

EWART, Major Gerald Valentine, C.B.E.

EWART, William Herbert Lee, C.B.E., b. 6 Sept. 1881 ; s. of the late William Lee Ewart, of Northbrook, Godalming ; m. Katherine Carsandra, d. of late Commander Sebastian Gassiot, R.N. *Educ.* : Eton and Trinity College, Cambridge. *Address* : Radipole House, Weymouth, Dorset. *Clubs* : Travellers' ; Royal Dorset Yacht Club. (C2594)

EWEN, Lieut. David, M.B.E., b. 10 May, 1891 ; s. of James Ewen, of Ballechin, Ballinluig ; m. Beatrice Mabel, d. of John Avery, of Skegness. *Educ.* : Ballinluig School. Stationer. *War Work* : Served with Fife and Forfar Yeomanry in Gallipoli, Egypt, and Palestine. *Address* : 19, Lumley Road, Skegness, Lincs. (M4675)

EWEN, Lieut. David Alexander, M.B.E.

EWEN, Elias, M.B.E.

EWEN, John Taylor, O.B.E., B.Sc., M.I.Mech.E., F.R.S.E., H.M.I.S., J.P., b. 9 Sept. 1863 ; s. of James Ewen, Woodmerchant, Millbank House, Forfar ; m. Isabella Jane, d. of Rev. John Ross of Balloch, Alyth, Perthshire. *Educ.* : Forfar Academy ; University College, Dundee ; Edinburgh University. H.M. Inspector of Schools in Scotland. *War Work* : Secretary of the Board of Management of the Munitions Committee for north-east Scotland District.; Chairman of Aberdeen Branch of Scottish Veterans' Garden City Association, and Member of Central Executive. *Address* : Clairmont, 54, Albert Drive, Pollokshields, Glasgow. (O3706)

EWING, Elizabeth Annie, M.B.E., b. 26 April, 1868 ; d. of Rev. Thomas John Ewing, of Kenninghall, Norfolk. *Educ.* : East Anglian Girls' Coll., Bishop's Stortford, and Salcombe House, Loughton, Essex. Missionary of Baptist Mission since 1889 ; Principal of the James Memorial Bible Institute. *War Work* : Since Nov. 1911 member of the St. John's Overseas Brigade, A Division, for Women ; Superintendent of the Indian Nursing Division of the St. John Ambulance Brigade Overseas, and lecturer for the St. John Association. *Address* : James Memorial Bible Institute, 45, Lower Circular Road, Calcutta, India. (M2798)

EWING, Isabella Mercer, O.B.E. ; d. of Robert Ewing, of Fintalich, Muthill, Perthshire. *Educ.* : Private Schools. Formerly Controller Q.M.A.A.C. ; at present employed as Women's Training Officer, Ministry of Labour, Scottish Division. *War Work* : Canteen Work (Voluntary) in Edinburgh, 1915 ; joined Queen Mary's Army Auxiliary Corps, 1917 ; gazetted Unit Administrator, Sept. 1917 ; promoted Deputy Controller Western Command, Feb. 1918, and Controller Western Command Dec. 1918 ; twice mentioned. *Address* : 1, Eyre Crescent, Edinburgh. (O7130)

EWING, Peter Dewar, C.B.E. ; sometime Gen. Manager, Ailsa Shipbuilding Co., Troon. *Address* : Troon, Ayrshire. (C155)

EXHAM, Major Harold, O.B.E., I.A.

EXHAM, Col. Simeon Hardy, C.B., C.B.E., b. 1850 ; s. of the late Thomas Exham, of Monkstown, Co. Cork ; m. 1873, Emily, d. of the late Rev. Godfrey Clarke Charles William Smith, Vicar of Aghabullogue, Co. Cork. Entered R.E., 1871 ; and ret. as Lieut.-Col. (with rank of Col. in the Army) 1901 ; re-joined, 1914 ; served during Afghan War, 1878–9 ; present at capture of Ali Musjid (medal with clasp). *Address* : Walton House, Walton, Suffolk. (C812)

EYKYN, Surg.-Lieut. Frederick Bentley, O.B.E., R.N.

EYLES, Sir Alfred, K.C.B., K.B.E., J.P., b. 8 Dec. 1856 ; s. of Thomas Eyles of Wilts ; m. 1st (died 1914), Emmeline, d. of William Lewis Kemp, of Plumstead, Kent, 2nd, Catherine Crampton, d. of J. R. S. Hayward, M.D., of Maldon, Essex. Entered Admiralty, 1876 ; Superintending Clerk 1897 ; Assistant Accountant General 1903 ; Deputy Accountant General, 1904 ; and Accountant General of the Navy, 1906 ; Retired, 30 Nov. 1918 ; Grand Cordon of the Order of the Sacred Treasure of Japan. *War Work* : Served at the Admiralty throughout the war. *Address* : Brambletye, The Ridgeway, Woking, Surrey. (K212)

EYLES, Herbert Charles, M.B.E., b. 25 Sept. 1869 ; m. Jane Ursula Howard. First Class Clerk. H.M. Office of Woods, Forests, and Land Revenues. *War Work* : Supervision of work connected with supply and conversion of timber from Crown Forests. *Address* : Harringay, Granville Road, Sidcup. (M8035)

EYRE, Edmond, O.B.E.

EYRE, Gervas Malcolm, O.B.E., J.P., b. 17 May, 1862 ; s. of Col. Henry Eyre, C.B., of Rampton, Notts. ; m. Julia Philadelphia, d. of Digby Cayley, of Brompton, Yorks. *Educ.* : Eton. *War Work* : County Sec., East Riding Yorks. Branch of British Red Cross. *Address* : Bishop Burton, Beverley. *Club* : Boodle's. (O10382)

EYRE, Capt. John Benedict, M.B.E., Cavalier of the Order of the Crown of Italy. (M4730)

EYRE, John, O.B.E.

EYRE, Julia Philadelphia, Mrs., M.B.E.

EYRE, Capt. Richard Philip Hastings, M.B.E., R.A.S.C.

EYRES, Lieut. Charles Lionel, M.B.E., R.E.

EYRES, Edmund, M.B.E.

EZECHIEL, Lieut.-Col. James, O.B.E.

EZRA, Alfred, O.B.E.

EZRA, Capt. Ellice, M.B.E., I.A.R.O.

FABER, Lieut. George Valdemar, O.B.E. M.C., R.E. (T.F.). (O12061)

FABER, Oscar, O.B.E., D.Sc.

FACER, Hedley Humphrey, M.B.E.

FACEY, Edith Mary, Mrs., M.B.E.

FACEY, Lilian Maud, Mrs., M.B.E.

FACHE, George Cox, O.B.E.

FAGAN, Capt. Charles Horace John, O.B.E., R.A.M.C. (T.F.), b. Oct. 1877; s. of Charles Edward Fagan, C.B.E., I.S.O., of British Museum (Natural History); m. Dorothy Enid, d. of Sir Hercules Read, LL.D., President Society of Antiquaries, of British Museum. Educ: St. Paul's School, London; Caius Coll., Cambridge; St. George's Hospital. Medical Officer, Prison Service. War Work: Registrar, 3rd London General Hospital; later Officer Commanding 3rd London General Hospital. Address: 5, Heathfield Gardens, Wandsworth Common, S.W. 18.   (O7132)

FAGAN, Lieut. Charles Walter, M.B.E.

FAGAN, Rhoda Kathleen, Mrs., M.B.E., b. 10 March, 1886; d. of John Heppell, of Newcastle-upon-Tyne; m. David Patrick, s. of the late Frederick Fagan, of Sheffield. Educ.: Dame Allan's School, Newcastle-on-Tyne. War Work: General comforts and entertainments work in connection with the Northumberland War Hospital, and the Soldiers' Aid Fund, Bangalore, India. Address: 4, Harewood Grove, Darlington.   (M6140)

FAGE, James Alfred, M.B.E.

FAGGE, Mabel Muriel Hilton, O.B.E.; d. of Charles Hilton Fagge, M.D., F.R.C.P., 72, Grosvenor Street. War Work: Registrar to Queen Mary's Convalescent Auxiliary Hospital, Roehampton House; Organiser, Administrator, and Registrar to the Central Registry, Limbless Sailors and Soldiers, controlling the distribution of all amputation cases due to the War to the various fitting centres for artificial limbs in the U.K. Address: 72, Grosvenor Street, W.   (O10383)

FAICKNEY, Robert, M.B.E.

FAIL, Lieut.-Col. Frederick, O.B.E.

FAILES, Rev. Bernard James, O.B.E., R.N., M.A.

FAIR, Blanche Alicia, O.B.E.

FAIR, Robert Wilson, M.B.E.

FAIRBAIRN, Capt. Bernard William Murray, O.B.E., R.N., b. 18 April, 1880; s. of Rev. W. M. Fairbairn, o1 The Great House, Timberscombe, Somerset; m. Alice Mary, d. of the late William Phillipps. Educ: H.M.S. "Britannia." Address: Hughenden, Crown Hill, S. Devon.   (O9387)

FAIRBAIRN, Major David Alexander, O.B.E.

FAIRBAIRN, Elizabeth Brown, M.B.E., Q.M.A.A.C.

FAIRBAIRN, Ethel Fulton, M.B.E.

FAIRBAIRN, Frederick William, M.B.E.

FAIRBAIRN, Capt. James Ross, O.B.E., Service Batt. The Durham Light Infantry, b. 22 June, 1869; s. of the late James Fairbairn, late Bandmaster, 1st Lanc. Fusiliers; m. Helen Eliza, d. of the late John Fairbairn, of Coldstream. Educ.: Twickenham Grammar School, and privately. Served for 30 years in Royal Artillery, including a period of 2 years in 1st Lanc. Fusiliers. War Work: Acting Staff Capt. 1st Training Res. Bde., 1915–19; Asst. Officer to Officer in Command No. 1 Inf. Records, York, 1919 to date. Address: c/o Messrs. Holt & Co., 3, Whitehall Place, London, S.W.   (O7134)

FAIRBAIRN, John, O.B.E., Esquire of the Order of St. John of Jerusalem in England, b. 14 Jan. 1863; s. of J. A. Fairbairn, of Legerwood, Claremont, Cape Province; m. Winifred, d. of A. Difford, of Cape Town. Educ.: South African Coll. Clerk assistant to the Senate of the Union of South Africa; Sec. S.A. National Art Gallery, etc. War Work: Hon. Sec. Red Cross South Africa, now Vice-Chairman South African Red Cross Society (Cape Province); Member of Council St. John's Ambulance Society, of Returned Soldiers' Vocational Training Board, etc. Address: Hyvotmill, Wynberg, Cape. Club: Civil Service.   (O8353)

FAIRBAIRNS, Mary Elizabeth, M.B.E., Q.M.A.A.C.

FAIRBANK, Amy Helena Margaret, M.B.E. (see Morgan, Amy Helena Margaret).

FAIRBANK, Capt. Harold Arthur Thomas, O.B.E., D.S.O., M.B., M.S., F.R.C.S., R.A.M.C., b. 1876; s. of the late T. Fairbank, M.D., of Windsor; m. 1909, Kathleen, d. of the late A. G. Ogilvie. Educ.: Epsom Coll., London. Surg. to In-Patients, Hospital for Sick Children; served in the Great War, 1914–18 (despatches).   (O6466)

FAIRBANK, John Gerald Atkinson, O.B.E., M.B., M.R.C.S., L.R.C.P., L.D.S., R.C.S., Temp. Sub-Lieut. R.N. b. 12 March, 1882; s. of the late John Harrison Atkinson. Dental Surgeon to the Hospital for Facial Injuries, 1916; Royal Naval Hospital, Stonehouse, 1916–17; H.M.S. "Bacchante," as Surgeon, 1917; H.M.S. "Pembroke," as Inspecting Medical Officer (Dental), 1917–19. Address: 15, George Street, Hanover Square; 58, Digby Mans., W. Clubs: University (London); Cruising; Royal Southampton Yacht.   (O9463)

FAIRBANK, William, C.V.O., O.B.E., C.C., J.P., b. 6 July, 1850; s. of Thomas Fairbank, of Highbury and Wensleydale, Yorks; m. Caroline Florence, d. of John Woodcock, of The Elms, Wigan and Woodcode House, Lancs. Surgeon to His Majesty's Household at Windsor Castle; late Mayor of Windsor, now Deputy Mayor; Hon. Consulting Surgeon to King Edward VII. Hospital; J.P. for Berks and New Windsor; Consulting Surgeon to the Royal Ventnor Hospital; Knight of Grace of the Order of St. John of Jerusalem. Queen Victoria Jubilee Medal with bar, Edward VII. and George V. Coronation Medals. War Work: Training nurses and ambulance men for the front. Club: Cavendish. (O1330)

FAIRBROTHER, 2nd Lieut. Hugh Kingsley, M.B.E., R.A.F.

FAIRBROTHER, Thomas, M.B.E.

FAIRBROTHER, Capt. William George, M.B.E.

FAIRE, Arthur William, C.B.E., D.L., J.P., b. 21 Sept. 1854; s. of Watkin Lewis Faire, of Leicester. Educ.: Stoneygate School. Member and County Director, Leicestershire Territorial Association; Chairman Melton Conservative Associa tion; Hon. Treasurer and Life Governor, Vaughan College; Past President Leicester Chamber of Commerce; Member of Executive Association British Chamber of Commerce; Knight of Grace, Order of St. John of Jerusalem. War Work: Assistant Commissioner St. John Ambulance; County Director, Transport of Wounded to 5th Northern General Hospital; in charge of Leicestershire Auxiliary Hospitals and Rest Rooms; Enquiries, Missing and Wounded. Address: Elmcote, Knighton, Leicester. Clubs: R.A.C.; British Empire. (C2596)

FAIREY, Charles Richard, M.B.E., b. 5 May, 1887; s. of Richard Fairey, of St. Neots, Hunts.; m. Joan, d of John Markey, of Simla, India. Educ.: Merchant Taylors' School, Chairman and Managing Director of the Fairey Aviation Co., Ltd., Hayes, Middlesex; Aeronautical Engineer, engaged in flying since 1910. War Work: Designer of Seaplanes; produced the following types, all of which were used on Government service: "The Campania," "Hamble Baby," Types IIIA., IIIB., IIIC., F2, N9; The Campania, Hamble Baby and IIIc types were in general production. Addresses: Grove Cottage, Iver, Bucks; 175, Piccadilly. Clubs: Royal Aero; Royal London Yacht. (M8040)

FAIRFAX, James Oswald, C.B.E. Chairman N.S. Wales Div., Australian Branch of British Red Cross Society. (C415)

FAIRFIELD, Josephine Letitia Denny, C.B.E., M.D. Served in the Great War, 1914–19, with W.R.A.F. (despatches). (C2349)

FAIRHOLME, Capt. Edward George, O.B.E., R.A.V.O.(T.), b. 1873; s. of late Capt. Charles Fairholme, R.N.; m. Eleanor, d. of W. Laurence Chew, J.P., of Hankelow Court, Cheshire. Educ.: Privately and Chatham House, Ramsgate. Chief Secretary, Royal Society for the Prevention of Cruelty to Animals; founded R.S.P.C.A. Fund for Sick and Wounded Horses, (authorised by Army Council) which collected £250,000 for War horses and mules. War Work: Deputy-Assistant Director of Veterinary Service, B.E.F. Address: 15, Neville Street, Onslow Gardens, S.W. 7; 105, Jermyn Street, S.W. 1. Club: Savile. (O329)

FAIRHOLME, Marie Antoinette Marthe, Mrs., M.B.E., d. of Emile Gouin of Paris; m. Frederick Charles, s. of late Capt. Charles Fairholme, R.N. War Work: Commandant of V.A.D. Derby 38, and of Red Cross Hospital, Hathersage, Derbyshire. Addresses: Churchdale Hall, Bakewell, Derbyshire; Fort Charles, Salcombe, S. Devon. Club: V.A.D. Ladies'. (M372)

FAIRHURST, Archibald, O.B.E.

FAIRLEY, Lucy Rosalind, M.B.E.

FAIRLEY, Major Niel Hamilton, O.B.E., Aust. A.M.C.

FAIRLEY, William, M.B.E.

FAIRLIE, Jessie Mary, Mrs., M.B.E., d. of Thomas Downes, of Glasgow; m. James, s. of Henry C. Fairlie, of Glasgow. War Work: Convener of Ladies Committee for packing parcels for East Stirlingshire Prisoners of War Fund from June, 1915, until Nov. 1918. Address: Watling Lodge, Falkirk, Stirlingshire. (M8043)

FAIRWEATHER, Amelia, Mrs., M.B.E.

FAIRWEATHER, Francis Harold, O.B.E., M.D., C.M., b. 1871; s. of William Fairweather of Heaton Lodge, Huddersfield; m. Maud, d. of James Vincent Bell, F.R.C.S., of Rochester. Educ.: Shrewsbury School and Edinburgh University. Late Senior Surgeon, now Consulting Surgeon St. Bartholomew's Hospital, Rochester. War Work: Surgeon (Military Wards) at Fort Pitt Military Hospital, Chatham and St. Bartholomew's Hospital, Rochester. Address: Warrennes, Hockley, Essex (O4361)

FAITHFUL, Major George Ferdinand Hay, O.B.E., I.A., R.A.F.

FALCONER, Lieut.-Col. Alexander Robertson, C.B.E. New Zealand Med. Corps; served in S. Africa, 1902 (Queen's medal with two clasps); and in the Great War, 1915–19 (despatches). (C1854)

FALCONER, Capt. Arthur Wellesley, C.B.E., D.S.O., M.D., M.R.C.P. (Lond.), R.A.M.C. (T.F.), b. 1880; s. of the late Robert Falconer, solicitor, of Stonehaven; Educ.: Aberdeen Univ. Served in the Great War, 1914–18 (despatches). Address: 18, Bon Accord Square, Aberdeen. (C1410)

FALCONER, James, M.B.E.

FALCONER, Bey, John, O.B.E., b. 12 Sept. 1861; s. of John Falconer, of Glasgow; m. Jessie, d. of John Clark Forrest, of Auchinraith. Educ.: Glasgow. Capt. of Port Suez, Egypt. War Work: Sub-Commissioner, British Red Cross, for Suez and Red Sea. Address: Port House, Suez. Clubs: Turf, Cairo; Royal Scottish Automobile. (O10385)

FALGAR, Capt. Richard Joseph, M.B.E., I.A.R.O.

FALK, Oswald Toynbee, C.B.E. b. 1879; s. of H. John Falk, of West Kirby; m. Guendolen, d. of the late Capt. Gerald Stracey. Educ.: Rugby and Balliol College, Oxford. Director National Mutual Life Assurance Society. War Work, Temporarily attached to the Treasury during the war and one of the British Financial Delegates at the Peace Conference, Paris, 1919. Address: Pixham End, Dorking. Clubs: Union and City University. (C2597)

FALKLAND, MASTER OF (Lucius Plantagenet Cary), O.B.E., b. 23 Sept. 1880; s. of Byron Plantagenet Cary, 12th Viscount Falkland (see BURKE'S Peerage); m. 6 April, 1904, Ella Louise, e. d. of E. W. Catford. Capt. and Brevet Major Reserve of Officers, Gren. Guards; with King's African

Rifles, 1903–5; Dep. Gov. Wandsworth Prison, 1910–14; served in S. African War, 1900–2; Great War, 1914–18; Chevalier Legion of Honour. *Address:* 17, Roland Gardens, S.W. (O8763)

FALKNER, Lieut.-Col. Henry George, O.B.E., R.A.M.C. (T.F.), *b.* Sept. 1870; *s.* of Henry Falkner, of Co. Dublin, Ireland; *m.* Mabel, *d.* of — van Troostwyk, of Holland. *Educ.:* Dover Coll. M.O.H. Lynton; Admiralty Agent and Surgeon Lynmouth; Surgeon Lynton Hospital. *War Work:* A.D.M.S., 63rd, 71st and 66th Divisions; also Officer-in-Charge Maudsley Neurological Hospital, Denmark Hill, London. *Address:* Castle Hill House, Lynton, N. Devon. (O7135)

FALKUS, Richard Uriah, I.S.O., M.B.E., *b.* 1849; *s.* of Richard John Falkus; *m.* Margaret, *d.* of the late John Richards, of Lelant, Cornwall. Formerly Staff Clerk at Admiralty. *War Work:* Retired after 40 years' service, in 1910; volunteered at beginning of war for service anywhere and in any capacity; served over 4 years at Admiralty; for the first two years as Dept. Expense Accounts Officer in Acct.-General's Dept.; subsequently, as Head of Central Registry in Secretary's Dept. *Address:* Carn Brea, Shalford, Guildford. (M8045)

FALLE, Lieut.-Comm. Harold de Carteret, O.B.E., A.M.I.E.E., R.N.V.R., *b.* 5 Nov. 1884; *s.* of the Very Rev. Samuel Falle, M.A., Dean of Jersey; *m.* Frances Mabel, M.D., *d.* of George Huxley, *Educ.:* Cheltenham Coll.; Victoria Univ., Manchester. Electrical Engineer. *War Work:* Commissioned as Lieut. R.N.V.R., 27 Sept. 1914, and appointed to H.M.S. "Emperor of India" for special electrical duties with the Grand Fleet; appointed to the Staff of Rear Admiral Sir W. C. M. Nicholson, K.C.B., 1st Battle Squadron, 1917–19. *Address:* 18, York House, York Street, W. 1. (O9334)

FALLON, Thomas Joseph, M.B.E. *Educ.:* Belvedere Coll. (S.J.), Dublin. Assist. Sec., Irish Public Health Council. *War Work:* Hon. Sec. Belgian Refugees Committee, Ireland; Sec. Petrol Control Committee, Ireland. *Address:* 121, North Circular Road, Dublin. (M8046)

FALLS, Rev. George Oliver, C.B.E. T. Chaplain to Canadian Forces during the Great War, 1915–19 (despatches). (C1350)

FALLS, Lieut.-Col. Horace Edward, C.B.E.

FANE, Lieut. Frederick Navaire, O.B.E.

FANE, Samuel Maddams, M.B.E.

FANNER, Henry Robert, M.B.E.

FANSHAWE, Capt. Basil Hew, C.B.E. R.N. *War Service:* 1914–19, Admiralty Ports Officer, Scapa (despatches). (C2278)

FANSHAWE, Major (A. Lieut.-Col.) Lionel Arthur, D.S.O., O.B.E., R.A., *b.* 7 March, 1874; *s.* of Sir Arthur Fanshawe, K.C.I.E., C.S.I., C.V.O., of 14, Draycott Place, London (*see* BURKE'S *Peerage*); *m.* Eva, *d.* of the late Lieut.-Col. Sholto-Pemberton, R.A. *Educ.:* Dulwich Coll.; Pembroke Coll., Oxford. *War Work:* Served on the Indian N.W. Frontier and in Mesopotamia. *Address:* c/o H. S. King & Co., 9, Pall Mall. *Club:* Junior Naval and Military. (O6616)

FARADAY, Major William, M.B.E., *b.* 3 March, 1861; *s.* of Robert Faraday, of Long Preston, Yorks.; *m.* Jane Henderson, *d.* of George Gibson, of Edinburgh. *Educ.:* National School and Continuation Classes. *War Work:* General A.S.C. duties, Malta and France; Commanded 12 Field Bakeries, Havre, 1915; afterwards, duty with No. 1 Reserve M.T. Depot Grove Park and Lee, S.E. *Address:* 141, Comiston Rd., Edinburgh. (M377)

FARDELL, Flora Emily, O.B.E., *d.* of late Sir George Fardell, M.P., of 2, South Eaton Place, S.W. 1. *Educ.:* at home. Vice-President Ladies' Grand Council, Primrose League; Manager Moberly School. *War Work:* Hon. Sec. Education Committee, Officers' Families Fund 1914–20. (O3707)

FARDON, John Henry, M.B.E., M.R.C.S. (Eng.), L.R.C.P. (Lond.). *Educ.:* Bristol Univ. Hon. Surgeon Birkenhead Borough Hospital. *War Work:* Surgeon Borough Hospital, Birkenhead; Medical Officer in Charge of the Temple Road and Bidston Avenue Military Hospitals. *Address:* 11, Charlesville Birkenhead. *Club:* Constitutional, Birkenhead. (M10262f)

FARGUS, Major Nigel, D.S.O., O.B.E., *b.* 2, July, 1881 *s.* of Henry Robert Fargus, of Milton House, Strawberry Hill; *m.* Charlotte Mary, *d.* of the late Wilfred Trimmer. *Educ.:* Rugby, Sandhurst. 1st Bn. The Royal Scots, General Staff, D.A.A.G.; Temp. Lt.-Col. Cmdg. 11th Royal Scots. *War Work:* Served with the B.E.F., France, Flanders and Germany. Wounded. *Address:* Ollerton Lodge, nr. Knutsford. *Club:* Caledonian, London. (O5243)

FARIS, Major John George, O.B.E., I.A.

FARISH, Eng.-Comm. James Risk, O.B.E., R.N.R.

FARLEY, Edwin Wood Thorp, M.B.E., J.P.

FARLEY, Major Reuben Llewelyn, O.B.E., R.A.F.

FARMER, Capt. Frank, M.B.E., A.P.D.

FARMER, Lieut. Frank Morley, M.B.E., R.A.S.C.

FARMER, George Albert, M.B.E. (M10384)

FARMER, Col. George Devey, C.B.E. Canadian Army Med. Corps. (C840)

FARMER, Henry Edward, M.B.E., F.R.I.B.A., M.T.P.I.; *s.* of Edward Farmer, of Rockford, Salop.; *m.* Florence, *d.* of I. I. Gittings, of Goscote. *Educ.:* Privately. *War Work:* Chief Architect to the Ministry of Shipping; designed and supervised Working Class Dwellings, Men's Hostels, Boys'

Riveting Schools, etc., in connection with existing shipyards, and laid out, designed and supervised, the new Chepstow. *Address:* Rushall Hall, Walsall. *Club:* Primrose. (M3635)

FARMER, Capt. Horace Edwin, O.B.E.

FARMER, Robert Crosbie, O.B.E., D.Sc., Ph.D.

FARMER, Samuel William, O.B.E., J.P.

FARMER, William Henry, M.B.E., Chief Superintendent of Police; Chief Clerk of the Worcestershire Constabulary; awarded the King's Coronation Medal in 1911 for meritorious Service. *War Work:* Duties] under D.O.R.A., Emergency Orders and Regulations; extra duties and responsibilities during the absence of the Chief Constable (1914–19) from the County on Service during the Great War; mentioned in 1918 for services rendered to Department at War Office during war. *Address:* Station House, Castle Street, Worcester. (M8047)

FARMERY, John, M.B.E., *b.* 11 Oct. 1872. Chief Officer of Fire Brigade, Ilford. *War Work:* Served on Home Office Fire Brigades Committee for fire defence of Metropolis; Fire extinguishing operations at various factories engaged on Munitions of War; also at fires caused by, and during enemy air raids on London and district; dealt with enemy "Gotha" aeroplane brought down in flames in London area during the last raid, Whit-Sunday and Monday, 1918. *Address:* Central Fire Station, Ley Street, Ilford, Essex. (M8048)

FARNDALE, Joseph, O.B.E., *b.* 6 April, 1864; *s.* of Thomas Farndale, of Wakefield; *m.* Emma, *d.* of William Selby, of Wakefield. *Educ.:* Field House Academy, Aberford. Chief Constable of Bradford; formerly Chief Constable of Margate and York. (O10386)

FARNELL, Beatrice Isabel, M.B.E.

FARNELL, Henry Dawson, O.B.E., J.P., F.R.C.S.

FARNHAM, Samuel, M.B.E., R.E.

FARNLEY, Arthur Hambleton, M.B.E., R.N.

FARNSWORTH, Alfred William, O.B.E.

FARNSWORTH, Frank Smedley, M.B.E.

FARQUAHAR, Lieut.-Col. FitzRoy, O.B.E.

FARQUHAR, Rev. Henry, M.B.E., B.D.

FARQUHARSON, Lieut.-Col. A. S. L., C.B.E. Major and Brevet Lieut.-Col. Oxford Univ. Officers' Training Corps. (C1557)

FARQUHARSON, Alexander, M.B.E., M.A.

FARQUHARSON, Major Christopher William, O.B.E.

FARQUHARSON, Com. John Philips, D.S.O., O.B.E., *b.* 1884; *s.* of Capt. A. J. Farquharson, R.N., of Stowell Park, Wilts; *m.* 1919, Phyllis Ruth, *e. d.* of Major Francis Edward Prescott, of Bockleton Court, Tenbury. Served in the Great War, 1914–19 (despatches, Croix de Guerre). (O3490)

FARR, Muriel Edith, O.B.E.; *g.d.* of the late Archdeacon Farr, L.L.D., Cambridge, and Adelaide, South Australia. Member of Literary Staff of South Australian "Register," and contributor to South Australian and Inter-state papers and periodicals. *War Work:* Joint founder (with Mrs. Carew Reynell) of League of Loyal Women of Australia; Joint Sec. for one year, and now President of Executive Committee and Council; Hon. Sec. Women's "Yes" Committee, 2nd Conscription Referendum; Member Executive Committee Anzac Hospitality Fund; State War Council's Soldiers' Hostel; Soldiers' combined Recommendations Committee, South Australian Comforts Fund Vice-President South Australian Branch Australian League of Nations Union. *Address:* 29, Jeffcott Street, North Adelaide, S. Australia. *Club:* Queen's, Adelaide. (O2149)

FARR, William Edward, C.B.E., J.P., *b.* October, 1872; *s.* of Albert Hart Farr, of Weston, Herts; *m.* Hilda Lomas, *d.* of James Walker, of Leeds and Harrogate. *Educ.:* Privately. Solicitor; Alderman of Leeds City Council; J.P. for City of Leeds; Member of Council of Leeds University; Chairman Leeds Higher Education Committee; Joint Hon. Sec. Leeds Luncheon Club; Hon. Sec. Leeds Liberal Federation. *War Work:* Chairman Leeds Parliamentary Recruiting Committee; Chairman Leeds Advisory Committee; National Service Representative at Leeds Appeal Tribunal; Chairman Leeds Employment Committee. *Address:* 1, Central Bank Chambers, Leeds. *Clubs:* Leeds Liberal; National Liberal. (C2598)

FARR, Capt. Arthur James Melancthon SAVILLE-, O.B.E., R.A.S.C.

FARRA, Robert Edward, M.B.E.

FARRADAY, Major William, M.B.E.

FARRAN, Rev. George Erle, M.B.E., D.D., *b.* 1868; *s.* of F. Farran, of Berkhampstead. *Educ.:* Rugby; Oriel Coll., Oxon. Vicar of Kingsbury, N.W. *War Work:* Commandant City of London Red Cross Soc.; Sec. and Registrar of No. 8 Red Cross (Baltic and Corn Exchange) Hospital, Paris Plage, and Boulogne, 1915–19. *Address:* Kingsbury Vicarage, N.W. 9. *Club:* Oxford and Cambridge. (M3636)

FARRAN, Major George Lambert, D.S.O., O.B.E.

FARRAN, Helen Isabel, M.B.E., *b.* 20 Oct. 1879; *d.* of George H. Farran, of Georgeville, Rathgar, Dublin. *Educ.:* Dulwich High School; Guernsey Ladies' Coll. *War Work:* Hon. Worker and member of the Soldiers' and Sailors' Families Association, 1914–17; Hon. worker and member, Local War Pensions Committee (City of Dublin), 1917–20. *Address:* Georgeville., 16, Highfield Road, Rathgar, Dublin. (M8051)

FARRANCE, Lieut. Harry, M.B.E.

FARRANT, Mary Josephine, Mrs., M.B.E.; *d.* of Rev. J. L. Kitchin, of Heavitree, Exeter; *m.* the late Mark, *s.* of Samuel Farrant, J.P., of Amberd, Taunton. *Educ.:* Privately, and Cheltenham. Asst. Probation Officer, Home Office; Asst. Sec. Women's Farm Settlement in South Africa; Certificated by Examination of Sanitary Inspector's Examination Board. *War Work :* Senior Lady Superintendent, Command Pay Office of London. *Address :* 66, Portland Court, London, W. 1. (M8052)

FARRAR, Major John William, O.B.E., Aust. A.M.C.

FARRELL, Rev. Bernard, O.B.E.

FARRELL, Major Gilbert Valentine, O.B.E., I.A., *b.* 30 Sept. 1884 ; *s.* of T. F. Farrell, of Hull ; *m.* Dorothy, *d.* of Sir John Sherburn, of Brantingham Thorpe, Brough, East Yorks (*see* BURKE'S *Peerage*). *Educ. :* The Oratory, Birmingham and Sandhurst. *Addresses :* Brantingham Thorpe, Brough, East Yorks ; c/o Henry S. King & Co., 9, Pall Mall, London, S.W. 1. *Clubs :* Junior United Service. (O7136)

FARRELL, Henry William, M.B.E.

FARRELL, Lieut. James Robert, M.B.E.

FARRELL, Margaret Georgina Mary, M.B.E., W.R.N.S.

FARRELL, Capt. Robert, O.B.E.

FARREN, Hugh Richard, O.B.E.. J.P.

FARREN, Capt. William Scott, M.B.E.

FARRER, Hon. Cecil Claude, O.B.E., B.A., *b.* 8 May, 1893 ; *s.* of Lord Farrer, of Abinger ; *m.* Evelyn Hilda *d.* of E. T. Crook, of Woodlands Hall, Bridgnorth. *Educ. :* Eton and New College, Oxford. 1st class market officer in Department of Overseas Trade. *War Work :* Secretary Allied Rationing and Statistical Committee, Ministry of Blockade. *Address :* 100, Palace Gardens Terrace, Kensington, W. 8. *Club :* Oxford and Cambridge Musical. (O69)

FARRER, Major Edward Richard Blackburne, O.B.E., M.C., Chevalier, Legion of Honour, *b.* 21 May 1892 ; *s.* of Canon H. W. Farrer, of Salisbury ; *m.* Cynthia Betty, *d.* of J. W. Stanton, of Chepstow. *Educ.* Sandroyd, Sherborne College and Corpus Christi, Cambridge. Transport Manager, Mac Fisheries, Ltd., 33 St. James Square. *War Work :* Joined R.A.S.C. 1 Sept. 1914. Served in France with 3rd Cav. Division from 31 Sept. 1914–Aug. 1916. D.A.D.S., 3rd Army from Aug. 1916 till 20 Oct. 1919. Five mentions in despatches. *Address :* 16, Emperor's Gate, London S.W. 7. (O1114)

FARRER, Julia Frances, M.B.E., A.R.R.C., *b.* 19 Sept. 1860 ; *d.* of Frederick Willis Farrer, of 66, Lincoln's Inn Fields. *Educ. :* Privately. Trained nurse attached to 46 V.A.D., London. *War Work :* Served 13 months with French troops in France and Tenedos ; 2¼ years nursing garrison in Mudros (Doughty Wylie Unit) ; 16 months Red Cross nursing, London and Bowood ; 5 months with Church Army Canteens, France and Flanders. *Address :* 10, Colosseum Terrace, N.W. 1. (M8054)

FARROW, Arthur Edward, M.B.E. *Address :* 19, Rossall Road, Ansdell, Lyntham. (M8055)

FARROW, Capt. Frederick Denny, O.B.E., R.E.

FARROW, William, M.B.E., *b.* 19 March, 1867 ; *s.* of Thomas Bucknall Farrow, of York ; *m.* Fanny, *d.* of William Brooke, of Huddersfield. *Educ. :* Priory St. School, York. *War Work :* Hon. Sec. Disablements Committee. Sale and Ashton-on-Mersey War Pensions ; also Y.M.C.A., Piccadilly, Manchester ; and Enemy Aliens Relief Work. *Addresses :* 80, Chapel Road, Sale, Cheshire ; 1, Temple Street, Manchester. (M8056)

FARTHING, Capt. William Walter, O.B.E. R.A.F.

FARWELL, George Douglas, M.B.E., A.M.I.C.E., A.M.I.M.E.. *b.* 24 Dec. 1877 ; *s.* of Frederick George Farwell, of Totnes, Devon. ; *m.* Eleanor Grace, *d.* of Everard Jones, of Gwynfryn, Cardiganshire. *Educ. :* Weymouth. *War Work :* Ministry of Munitions, Section Director, Gun Ammunition Dept., 1915–18 ; Section Director, Dept. of Engineering, 1918–20. *Address :* 12, Cyril Mansions, S.W. *Club :* Royal Automobile. (M8057)

FASEY, William, M.B.E.

FASS, Herbert Ernest, O.B.E.

FASSON, Major Thomas William, O.B.E.

FATHERS, Alice Mary, M.B.E.

FATHERS, Henry, C.B.E., I.S.O., *b.* 25 Nov. 1860 ; *s.* of Joseph Fathers, of Middlesex ; *m.* Alice Jane, *d.* of A. J. Jordan, of Walmer. *Educ. :* Adelphi School and Kailey's College, London. Appointed Clerk at Admiralty 1 April 1879 ; and employed in the Naval Ordnance Department. In 1891 was transferred to the Naval Ordnance Store Department then formed to deal with the provision and supply of guns and ordnance stores for the Navy : appointed Asst. Superintendent of Ordnance Stores on 17 April 1909 and Deputy Director of Armament supply on 24 March, 1917. *Address :* Trewinian, 24, Burnt Ash Hill, Lee. (C2599)

FARRELL, Comm. Douglas, M.V.O.. O.B.E.

FAULKNER, Alfred Edward, C.B.E., *b.* 3 July, 1882 ; *m.* Florence Edith Nicoll. *Educ. :* St. Albans School and King's College, London. Transport Department Admiralty, 1901–1917 ; Civil Assistant Director of Transports, Admiralty, 10 April, 1920. *War Work :* Transport Department Admiralty, from 1901 to March, 1917 ; Deputy Director of Military Sea Transport Ministry of Shipping, 1 Mar. 1917 to 27 Sep. 1919 ; Director of Military Sea Transport, Ministry of Shipping, 28 Sept. 1919 to 31 Jan. 1920 ; Acting Director of Transports and Shipping, Ministry of Shipping, 1 Feb. 1920. *Address :* 26, Clarence Road, St. Albans. (C2600)

FAULKNER, Lieut. Henry Robert, M.B.E.

FAULKNER, Roger, O.B.E., *b.* 17 April, 1859 ; *s.* of John Faulkner, of Pavenham, Beds. ; *m.* Mary Frances, *d.* of John Coulson, of Derby. *Educ. :* Bedford. Deputy Chief Constable of Derbyshire. *War Work :* Was solely in charge of the County Constabulary, Derbyshire, from 17 April, 1916, to 31 May, 1918, when a new Chief Constable was appointed. (O10387)

FAULKNER, Sydney Neal, O.B.E.

FAUNTHORPE, Lieut.-Col. John Champion, C.B.E., M.C.

FAURE, Pieter Jacobus van Breda, O.B.E.

FAVA, Albert Bernard, O.B.E. For important services in connection with the Naval Intelligence Division during the War. (O11902)

FAVELL, Millicent, M.B.E. *War Work :* Secretary to War Trade Committee. *Address :* 119, Gleneldon Road, Streatham, S.W. 16. (M8058)

FAVIELL, Com. Douglas, M.V.O., O.B.E., *b.* 1884 ; *s.* of Frederick Henry Faviell, of Highstanding, near Barnstaple ; *m.* 1910, Mary Sanderson, *d.* of Professor John Hunter. Entered R.N. 1899 ; became Lieut. 1906, Lieut.-Comdr. 1914, and Comdr. 1917 ; served in the Great War, 1914–19 ; present at battle of Jutland (despatches, promoted) ; has 3rd Class of Japanese Order of the Sacred Treasure. (O9538)

FAVIELL, Mary Sanderson, Mrs. Douglas, M.B.E., Q.M.A.A.C.

FAWCETT, Capt. Edward George Duncan, O.B.E., R.A.O.C.

FAWCETT, Edward Pinder, C.B.E., *b.* 3 Mar. 1874 ; *s.* of John Edward Fawcett, of Sheffield ; *m.* Alice Elizabeth May, *d.* of W. H. Clifford, of Wexford. *Educ. :* Leys School and Caius College, Cambridge. Indian Civil Service. *War Work :* Recruiting and raising War Loan. (C696)

FAWCETT, Frederick, O.B.E.

FAWCETT, Percy William, O.B.E.

FAWCETT, Walter, M.B.E.

FAWCUS, Lieut.-Col. Alfred, O.B.E.

FAWCUS, Arthur Francis, O.B.E. *War Work :* Attached to the Fleet Coaling Section of the Naval Stores Department at the Admiralty. *Address :* Littleworth Close, Esher, Surrey. (O10390)

FAWCUS, Lieut.-Col. James Scott, O.B.E.

FAWDRY, Capt. Thomas, M.B.E., R.A.F.

FAWKES, Surg.-Lieut. Marmaduke, O.B.E., R N., M.B.

FAWSITT, Lieut. Hubert Harcourt Morland, M.B.E.

FAWSSETT, Frank, M.B.E., M.B., B.S. (Lond.), *b.* 31 Dec. 1864 ; *s.* of Rev. Robert Fawssett, one time Rector of Salmonby, Lincs. ; *m.* Margaret Louisa, *d.* of Augustus Springett, J.P., of Hawkhurst, Kent. *Educ. :* Bedford School ; Privately ; St. Thomas' Hospital. Chief Surgeon East Sussex Constabulary ; Medical Visitor Private Licensed Houses for Lunatics in East Sussex ; Consulting Physician, Victoria Hospital, Lewes. *War Work :* Medical Officer V.A.D. Hospital, St. Annes, Lewis ; Medical Officer V.A.D. Hospital, East Chiltington, nr. Lewes ; Civil Medical Practitioner-in-Charge Troops, Lewes. *Address :* 83, High Street, Lewes, Sussex. *Club :* Lewes and County. (M8059)

FAYRER, Lieut.-Col. Sir Joseph, 2nd Bt., C.B.E., M.A., (Cantab,) M.D. C.M., (St. Andrews), F.R.C.S.E., L.R.C.P., L.R.C.S., L.F.P.S., L.M. Edin. and Glasgow ; Knight of Grace of the Order of St. John of Jerusalem, *b.* 8 Mar. 1859 ; *s.* of Surgeon-Gen. Sir Joseph Fayrer, 1st Bt., of London ; *m.* Ella, *d.* of Col. William Augustin John Mayhew. *Educ. :* Rugby ; Trin. Coll. Camb. ; St. George's Hospl., Edinburgh. *War Work :* Organised and commanded 2nd Scottish General Hospital. *Address :* Meadow Walk, Edinburgh. *Club :* The New, Edinburgh. (C813)

FEAR, Thomas Richard, M.B.E., late R.S.M. Duke of Yorks' Royal Military School, *b.* 22 May, 1861 ; *s.* of Frank Smith, of Weston-super-Mare ; *m.* Mary Ann, *d.* of James Hockett, of New Barnet. *Educ. :* Penparke School, Aberystwyth. *War Work :* At the outbreak of the war organised 20 centres in the County of Cardiganshire with a view to obtaining men trained for H.M. Forces, and was successful in obtaining over 500 before the Derby Scheme came into force ; raised by public subscription over £2000 for various war organisations, £1559 of which was expended in a personally conducted fund, called the "Comforts for Fighters' Fund," which enabled him to send to men serving overseas 6239 parcels, each containing a letter written by him ; 4052 letters were received and acknowledged, all of which have been deposited in the National Library of Wales. *Address :* Highbury, Dinas Terrace, Aberystwyth. (M8660)

FEARENSIDE, Major Edmund, O.B.E.. D.S.O., *b.* 1881 ; *s.* of the late Thomas Charles Fearenside, of Burton, Westmorland. *Educ. :* Queen's Coll., Oxford. Schoolmaster ; Major and Acting Lieut.-Col. comdg. a Battn. Manchester Regt. ; served during the Great War, 1914–17 (wounded, despatches). (O7138)

FEARFIELD, Marjorie Pollard, Mrs., M.B.E., *b.* 20 June, 1892 ; *d.* of William Stafford, of Nottingham ; *m.* Cecil John Fearfield. *War Work :* Assist. Transport Officer, British Red Cross Society, Nottingham. *Addresses :* Nottingham ; Craig Ohn, Simla, India. (M8061)

FEAST, Edith Mary, Mrs., M.B.E.

FEATHERSTONE, John Thomas, M.B.E.

FEDARB, Frederick J., O.B.E

FEDDEN, Alfred Hulbert Roy, M.B.E.

FEDDEN, Katharine Waldo Douglas, Mrs., C.B.E., *b.* 1873 ; *d.* of Henry Livingstone Douglas, of New York ; *m.* 1st, 1894, Francis Kinloch Hunter ; 2nd 1907, Romilly Fedden. Chairman of Belgravia War Hospital Supply Depot, 1915–19.

Address: 69, Beaufort Mansions, Chelsea, S.W. 3. *Club:* Sesame. (C958)

FEGAN, Col. Magrath Fogarty, C.B.E., R.A.

FEHR, Frank, C.B.E., *b.* 2 July, 1874 ; *s.* of Henry Fehr, of London ; *m.* Jane, *d.* of Thomas Poulter, J.P., of London. *Educ :* Privately. Senior partner Thornett and Fehr, 27, Leadenhall St. and Chairman and Director various Colonial Companies ; Underwriter at Lloyds. *War Work :* Holland, 1915, restricting exports to Germany ; Ministry of Food, 1917–19, being Asst. Director. Oilseeds Supply ; sent to Paris Conference, Holland, Belgium, United States and Egypt to negotiate for the Ministry of Food. *Address :* Hatton House, Chislehurst and Marwood, Lympne. *Clubs:* St. Stephen's and Constitutional. (C2601)

FEILDEN, Lieut.-Col. Randle Montague, C.B.E., *b.* 17 July, 1871 ; *s.* of late Sir W. L. Feilden, Bart., of Lancashire (*see* BURKE'S *Peerage*). *Educ.:* Charterhouse : R.M.C. Late of Oxfordshire and Buckinghamshire Light Infantry ; is a Pasha in the Egyptian Army and Civil Secretary of the Sind Government. *War Services:* Employed in the Sind throughout the War. *Clubs:* Army and Navy ; Pall Mall ; Royal Automobile ; Junior Constitutional. (C704)

FEILDER, W. M. *See* Taylor, W. M., Mrs.

FEILDING, Hon. Francis Henry Everard Joseph, O.B.E., B.A., LL.B.,, *b.* 6 March, 1867 ; 2nd *s.* of Rudolf William Basil, 8th Earl of Denbigh (*see* BURKE'S *Peerage*) ; *m.* 27 Nov. 1919, Stanislawa, *d.* of Eustachiusz Tomczyk, of Warsaw. Barrister-at-law ; Lieut. R.N.V.R., 1914, late R.N. ; served in Egypt, 1882 ; has 4th Class Order of the Nile and of El Nahda of Hedjaz. *Address :* 5, John Street, W. *Clubs:* Savile ; Royal Automobile ; Beefsteak ; Bath. (O4427)

FEILING, Ethel Bessie, Mrs., M.B.E.

FEILING, Gladys Maud, Mrs., O.B.E., *b.* 22 May, 1879 ; *d.* of late Col. Compton Norman, Royal Welsh Fusiliers. *Educ.:* Rippingale, Eastbourne and Freiburg. Late Deputy Controller Q.M.A.A.C. *War Work :* Clerical Work in Recruiting Office, Liverpool Area ; Joined Q.M.A.A.C. in Nov. 1917 ; Served in France from Dec. 1917 till Feb. 1919 ; served in Cologne, from Feb. 1919 till Sept. 1920, under Provost Marshal. *Address :* West Harting Cottage, Petersfield. (O5246)

FEILING, Capt. Keith Graham, O.B.E.

FELKIN, Capt. Samuel Denys, M.B.E., R.A.F.

FELL, Aubrey Llewellyn Coventry, C.B.E., *b.* 8 July, 1869 *s.* of the late Samuel Grayson Fell, of Ickham Hall, Canterbury ; *m.* Isabel Leckie Ewing, *d.* of the late Thomas Mantel Fielding, of Ingfield Manor, Billingshurst, Sussex. *Educ.:* Christ's College, Finchley, and Hanover Square School of Engineering. General Manager, London County Council Tramways since 1903 to date. *War Work :* Member Metropolitan Munitions Committee Tramways (Board of Trade) Committee ; Home Office Committee on employment of disabled soldiers and many other Committees and Conferences relating to War Service and transport. *Address :* Ryestead Common, Chiddingfold. *Club:* Sports'. (C2602)

FELL, Frederick Chandos Courtenay, O.B.E.

FELL, Lieut.-Col. Louis Frederick Rudston, D.S.O., O.B.E. Capt. and T. Major, R.A.F. ; Depot Comdr. with rank of Lieut.-Col. ; served in the Great War, 1914–19 (despatches). (O3306)

FELL, Marion Isobel, Mrs., M.B.E., *b.* 2 March, 1877 ; *d.* of Robert Wallace ; *m.* Matthew Henry Gregson, *s.* of John Fell, J.P., D.L., of Flan How, Ulverston, Lancs. *War Work :* Commandant, Fair' View Auxiliary Hospital, Ulverston. *Address :* Flan How, Ulverston, Lancs. (M3638)

FELL, Major James Pemberton, O.B.E.

FELL, Brig.-Gen. Robert Black, C.B., C.B.E., *b.* 5 Nov. 1859 ; *s.* of John Fell, J.P., D.L., of Flan How, Ulverston. *Educ.:* Windermere Coll. Served in Zulu War of 1879 ; Anglo-Boer War of 1901–2 ; Commanded 2nd Batt. Scottish Rifles, 1903–7 ; Scottish Rifle Brigade (T.F.), 1908–12 ; Ceylon Volunteer Forces, 1913, to Sept. 1914 ; 102nd (Service) Infantry Brigade, 1914, to May, 1915 ; 51st (Service) Infantry Brigade, June, 1915, to July, 1916 ; 16th Terr. Reserve Brigade, Nov. 1916, to March, 1917 ; Ceylon Defence Force, April, 1917, to June, 1919. *Club:* Junior United Service. (C1558)

FELL, William, O.B.E.

FELLOWES, Rt. Hon. Sir Ailwyn Edward, K.C.V.O., K.B.E., *b.* 10 Nov. 1855 ; *s.* of Edward Fellowes, 1st Baron De Ramsey, of Ramsey ; *m.* Agatha Eleanor Augusta, *d.* of 2nd Baron Hylton, of Ammerdown (*see* BURKE'S *Peerage*). *Educ.:* Eton, Cambridge. *Address :* Honingham, Norwich. *Clubs:* Carlton ; Boodle's. (K1)

FELLOWES, Alfred Ernest, M.B.E.

FELLOWES, Major Charles Grincill, O.B.E., R.A.

FELLOWS, Evelyn Emma, O.B.E. ; *d.* of George Fellows, late of Beeston Fields, Nottingham. *War Work :* Hon. Sec. 1915–19, Nottingham War Hospital Supply Depot. *Address :* Strancliffe, Barrow-on-Soar, Loughborough. (O10392)

FELLOWS, George, O.B.E., J.P.

FELLOWS, Gertrude Elizabeth, M.B.E.

FELLS, John Manger, C.B.E., *b.* 1858 ; *s.* of William Fells, of Deal, Kent ; *m.* late Henrietta Emily, *d.* of William Julian, of Chelsea. *Educ.:* Deal College and privately. Incorporated Accountant. (Member of Council of Incorporated Soc. of Accountants and Auditors). *War Work :* As private Secretary to Mr. Andrew Weir (Lord Inverforth) assisted in the organisation of the department of the Surveyor General of Supply at the War Office ; Member of several War Office Committees, including the Cost Accounting Committee ; Work in connection

with the Red Cross for which awarded Honorary Life Membership of the British Red Cross Society. *Addresses :* 128, Goldhurst Terrace, Hampstead, N.W. 6 ; 7 Union Court, Old Bond St. E.C. *Club:* National Liberal. (C2603)

FELTON, Charles, M.B.E., R.N.

FELTON, Edgar Hall, M.B.E., M.R.C.S., L.R.C.P.

FELTON, John Robinson, O.B.E.

FELTON, Muriel Harriet, Mrs., O.B.E.

FENDER, Thomas, O.B.E.

FENDICK, Eng.-Comm. Walter Robert, O.B.E., R.N.

FENELON, Martin Joseph, M.B.E., *b.* 1860 ; *s.* of Thomas Fenelon, of Seskin, Bagenalstown, Co. Carlow, Ireland ; *m.* May, *d.* of the late Alderman Michael MacDonnell, Limerick. *Educ.:* The French Coll., Blackrock, Co. Dublin. Permanent Civil Service, War Office ; detached for duty at the Headquarters Scottish Command. *War Work :* Audit of Army Accounts and financial advice. *Address :* 4, Morningside Park, Edinburgh. (M8066)

FENN, Lieut. Ernest Edward, O.B.E., R.E.

FENN, Sydney Albert, M.B.E., R.A.O.C., *b.* 23 April 1881 ; *s.* of Edward Fenn, of Norwich ; *m.* Elizabeth Louise, *d.* of Silas Wingrove, of Salisbury. *Educ.* Elementary School, Nelson St., Norwich. 1st Class Warrant Officer. *War Work :* France, (Havre and Nantes), August, 1914 to 31 Jan. 1915 ; joined 7th Div. at Sailley-sur-la-Lys, 1 Feb. 1915 to 22 Nov. 1917 ; Italy, 22 Nov. 1917 to 31 March, 1919 ; awarded Meritorious Service Medal after Somme operations, 1916 and the M.B.E. after operations between the Piave and the Tagliamento. *Address :* Brentleigh, Wain-a-Long Rd., Salisbury. (M4731)

FENNELLY, Capt. Philip, M.B.E.

FENNER, Major Ralph Lennox, O.B.E.

FENNER, Major Sidney, O.B.E., M.C.

FENNING, Lieut. Robert William, M.B.E., R.E. (T.F.).

FENTON, Capt. Alexander, M.B.E.

FENTON, Capt. Cecil, M.B.E.

FENTON, Edith, M.B.E.

FENTON, Capt. Henry Walter, M.B.E.

FENTON, Capt. John, M.B.E.

FENTON, Charles Ernest, M.B.E., *b.* 6 Nov. 1870 ; *s.* of Charles C. Fenton, of Bromsgrove ; *m.* Ellen Vinnie, *d.* of Philip Levens, of Bromsgrove. *Educ.:* Bromsgrove and Birmingham. Staff Officer, Post Office Stores Dept. *War Work ·* With Telegraphic and Telephonic apparatus for the various branches of War service ; organisation of the work undertaken in the factories attached to the Post Office Stores Department. *Address :* Connisville, Powys Lane, Palmers Green, N. 13. (M383)

FENTON, Major Samuel Greame, O.B.E., *b.* 29 May, 1886 ; *s.* of Francis Gregory Fenton, of Paris ; *m.* Dorothy Margaret, *d.* of David Sturrock, of Dundee. *Educ.:* St. Paul's. Engineer. *War Work :* O. i/c Workshops. No. 6 M.A.C ; O.C., 9th Div. A.S.P. ; O.C. D.G.T. (M.T.) Workshops, G.H.Q. *Address :* 78, Rue Michel Ange, Auteuil, Paris, 16me. *Club:* Royal Automobile. (O5249)

FENTON, William Walter, O.B.E., B.A., M.D. (Dublin), *b.* 8 Jan. 1860 ; *s.* of Richard Fenton, of Grange Park, Tullow, Co. Carlow, Ireland ; *m.* Florence E., *d.* of Col. Charles J. Hill, J.P., of Coventry, Warwickshire. *Educ.:* Bective Coll., Dublin ; Trinity Coll., Dublin. Surgeon Wincanton and East Somerset Hospital ; Medical Officer Wincanton Union District and Infirmary ; Medical Officer Wincanton Isolation Hospital and Sanatorium. *War Work :* Medical Officer to Wincanton Red Cross Hospital. *Address :* Ash House, Wincanton. (O10396)

FENWICK, Major David Eardley, O.B.E., M.C., M.D.

FENWICK, Capt., Brevet Major, Lieut. Col. Edwin Hurry, C.B.E., F.R.C.S., R.A.M.C., *b.* 1856 ; *s.* of Samuel Fenwick ; *m.* Annie, *d.* of John Fenwick, Elder Brother of the Trinity House. *Educ.:* Privately and abroad (Leipzic, Berlin). Consulting Surgeon to the London Hospital ; President, International Society of Urology ; late Lecturer on Clinical Surgery. *War Work :* Officer in charge Military wards London Hospital ; Officer Commanding, Military Hospital, Bethnal Green. *Address :* 53, Bedford Gardens, Kensington. (C1559)

FENWICK, Major Ernest Guy, M.B.E., J.P., C.C. Rutland ; *s.* of Chas. R. Fenwick ; *m.* Elsie Robarts. *Educ.:* Eton. *War Work :* British Remount Commission in Canada and Argentine Republic, 1914–19. *Address :* North Luffenham Hall, Stamford. *Clubs:* Turf ; White's. (M1709)

FENWICK, Major George Ernest Oswald, O.B.E., M.C., F.R.C.S.

FENWICK, Harriet Francis, M.B.E.

FENWICK, Capt. Henry Clennell, O.B.E., R.N.R., R.D.

FENWICK, Paymaster-Comm. Maurice George Fenwick Bissett, O.B.E., R.N.

FERARD, Arthur George, C.B.E., M.A., Oxon., *b.* 6 May, 1853 ; *s.* of Charles Cotton Ferard, of Ascot Place, Winkfield, Berks ; *m.* Sarah Margaret, *d.* of William M. Miller, of Halifax, Nova Scotia and 55, Lancaster Gate, London, W. *Educ.:* On the continent, Brighton Coll., and University Coll. Oxford. Assistant Secretary, Post Office Dept. ; entered by open competition Grade I ; General administration ; Special missions to the continent, *e.g.,* British delegation to Universal Postal Union Congress, 1906 ; Ghent Exhibition, etc. ; Committees of Keats–Shelley Association and Memorial, Rome ; Handel Society etc. ; Borough Councillor, Marylebone, 1919 ; Board of Queen Charlotte's Hospital ; Chairman of Victoria Hospital for Children, Chelsea, 1920. *War Work*: Deputy Chief Censor of telegrams on breaking out of war in 1914; Organiser and hon. secretary, 1914–1919 of Post Office Relief Fund for the dependants of Post Office servants who joined the colours to the number of 85,000; Special Hospital and Convalescent Homes for wounded P.O. servants; feeding of 1000 prisoners, care of widows and orphans, many thousands in number. *Address*: 38, Montagu Square, London, W. 1. *Club*: Oxford and Cambridge. (C2604)

FERARD, John Edward, C.B.E., *b.* 22 Jan. 1889; *s.* of Charles Cotton Ferard, of Winkfield, Berks; *m.* Kathleen Marion, *d.* of E. A. Dennys, of India Public Works Dept. *Educ.*: Eton; Magdalen College, Oxford. Secretary, Judicial and Public Dept, India Office. *War Work*: At the India Office. *Address*: 21, Sumner Place, S. Kensington, S.W. *Club*: Oxford and Cambridge. (C156)

FERGUSON, Alfred Cornwall, O.B.E., M.D.

FERGUSON, Lieut.-Col. Alpin, M.B.E.

FERGUSON, Amy, Mrs., M.B.E.; *d.* of Percy Rockliff, of London; *m.* Edward, *s.* of Edward Ferguson, of Penicuik. *Educ.*: Leyton County School. *War Work*: Sec. to Chairman, and Sec. Royal Commission on the Sugar Supply. *Address*: 132, Station Road, Wood Green, N. 22. (M1710)

FERGUSON, Anna Wise, Mrs., M.B.E.; *d.* of Josias Cunningham, of Glencairn, Belfast; *m.* John, *s.* of James Ferguson, of Silversprings, Templepatrick. *Educ.*: Belfast, and Drumsheugh Gds., Edinburgh. *War Work*: Joint Sec. Shipwrecked Crews' Fund; Sec. Welcome Home Fund; Assist. Belfast Dock Free Buffet; Great Northern Railway Free Buffet, Belfast; Sec. Reception of the Wounded Buffets, Belfast. *Address*: Silversprings, Templepatrick, Co. Antrim. (M8067)

FERGUSON, Eng.-Comm. Anthony, O.B.E.

FERGUSON, Lieut.-Col. Arthur George, C.B.E., *b.* 22 June 1862; *s.* of Lt.-Col. G. A. Ferguson, of Pitfour Mintlaw, Aberdeenshire; *m.* Janet Norah, *d.* of Sir Alexander Baird, of Urie. *Educ.*: Eton. Served in the Rifle Brigade, 1883 to 1904; H.M. Inspector of Constabulary for Scotland, 1904 to date. *War Work*: Commanded Training Battn. of the Rifle Brigade from 1914 to 1918. *Address*: 6, Belgrave Crescent, Edinburgh. (C2605)

FERGUSON, Charles Henry, M.B.E., M.B., Ch.B., *b.* 23 Jan. 1877; *s.* of Hugh Ferguson, of Warrington, Lancs; *m.* Ada Mary, *d.* of Robert Muir, of London and Glasgow. *Educ.*: Warrington Grammar School, and Liverpool Univ. *War Work*: Held Commission in R.A.M.C. and served in France, Dec. 1915, to Nov. 1916; Medical Officer in Charge, Tootal Road Military Hospital, 2nd Western General Hospital, Manchester, 1917–18. *Address*: 2, Park Road, Pendleton, Manchester. (M10262f)

FERGUSON, Major Donald, O.B.E.

FERGUSON, Rev. Fergus, O.B.E., M.A., B.D., *b.* 12 Nov. 1876; *s.* of Fergus Ferguson, of Glasgow; *m.* Eliza Goodfellow, *d.* of John B. Fleming, of Glasgow. *Educ.*: Glasgow High School, and Glasgow Univ. Minister of North United Free Church, Perth, Scotland. *War Work*: Territorial Chaplain; on active service May, 1916, to Aug. 1919, with Salonica Expeditionary Force, and as Senior Presbyterian Chaplain to Mesopotamian Force. *Address*: Denehurst, Bridgend, Perth, Scotland. (O6467)

FERGUSON, Fergus James, C.B.E., *b.* 27 Nov. 1878; *s.* of George Ferguson, of Greenock. *Educ.*: Privately. After brief period of press-work joined the staff of Reuter's Ltd., which he has represented in Persia, Egypt, Morocco and Balkan countries. *War Work*: Acted as official correspondent at headquarters of Salonica Army on behalf of Reuter's and Press Association; subsequently attached General Allenby's force in Palestine and Syria. *Address*: Club de Constantinople, Constantinople. (C2606)

FERGUSON, Frances Madeleine, Mrs., M.B.E.

FERGUSON, Gilbert, Mrs., M.B.E.

FERGUSON, Major James, O.B.E., R.F.A.

FERGUSON, James Strathearn, M.B.E., M.I.M.E., *b.* 1869; *s.* of John Ferguson, of Airdrie, N.B.; *m.* Agnes Smith, *d.* of Alex Dunlop, of Galston, Ayrshire. *Educ.*: Glasgow, Technical Coll. Senior Partner, Ferguson and Palmer, Railway and Contracting Engineers, 9, Victoria Street, Westminster, S.W. 1. *War Work*: Sectional Director, Railway Material Department; had charge of the supply of all Broad Gauge rolling stock required by our Armies. *Addresses*: Rutford House, Rutford Road, Streatham, S.W. 16; 9, Victoria Street, Westminster, S.W. 1. *Club*: Royal Automobile. (M8067)

FERGUSON, Sir John, K.B.E., *b.* 19 May, 1870; *s.* of George Ferguson, of Rosslyn, Aberdeenshire; *m.* Adelaide, elder daughter of Col. Telfer-Smollett, of Bonhill and Cameron, Dumbartonshire. *Educ.*: Aberdeen. Joint General Manager of Lloyds' Bank and Member of Council of Institutes of Banks in England. *War Work*: Chairman of the following War Office Committees; Contractors Accounts (1917); Overtime (1918); Overstaffing Enquiry, (1918); also Establishment, (1918–20) and Russian Accounts Committees, Ministry of Munitions (1920); Financial Adviser on Housing to Ministry of Health, 1920. *Addresses*: 21, Hans Place, London S.W. 1; Norsted Manor, Chelsfield, Kent. *Clubs*: Ranelagh; Carlton; Royal Automobile; City of London; New, Edinburgh; Pilgrims, Canada; Henley Stewards'. (K142)

FERGUSON, 2nd Lieut. John, M.B.E., R.E.

FERGUSON, John Alexander, O.B.E., M.A., Edin. B.A. Oxon: I.C.S., *b.* 2 Feb. 1880; *s.* of John Ferguson, of 5, Wemyss Place, Edinburgh; *m.* Noel, *d.* of V. E. de Bros, M.I.C.E., of P.W.D. India. *Educ.*: Edinburgh and Oxford.

Registrar, High Court, Lahore. *War Work*: Captain, 5th Punjab Light Horse, Indian Defence Force; Secretary, Punjab, Second Indian War Loan. *Address*: 8, Racecourse Rd., Lahore. *Club*: Punjab, Lahore. (O4038)

FERGUSON, 2nd Lieut. John Herbert, M.B.E., R.A.F.

FERGUSON, Louis, O.B.E.

FERGUSON, May Glendening, Mrs., M.B.E.

FERGUSON, Capt. Montgomery Dubois, O.B.E., B.A., M.D., B.Ch., D.P.H., R.A.M.C., *b.* 29 Nov. 1881; *s.* of Montgomery Ferguson, of Dublin; *m.* Alberta, *d.* of Joseph Sheffield, J.P., O.B.E., of Harrogate. *Educ.*: Aldenham School, Herts. Assistant Physician, York County Hospital. *War Work*: France, Feb. 1915–April, 1919; Specialist Sanitary Officer, Boulogne Base, May, 1916 to April 1919; Gazetted Lieut., 7 Dec. 1914; Capt., 7 Dec. 1915; Mentioned in Despatches, May 1918; Cavalier of the Order of Aviz (Portuguese), 1919. (O5251)

FERGUSON, Engineer-Capt. Samuel Pringle, C.B.E. R.N., *b.* 1870; *s.* of Samuel Ferguson. Served in the Great War, 1914–19. (C1923)

FERGUSON, Major Spencer Charles, M.B.E., J.P. *b.* 13 Aug. 1868; *s.* of the late Chancellor Richard S. Ferguson, J.P., F.S.A., of Carisle; *m.* Caroline Agnes, *d.* of the late Col. T. A. Irwin, of Justice Town, Cumberland. *Educ.*: Shrewsbury, and Christ's Coll., Cambridge. J.P. for the County Borough of Carlisle, and County of Cumberland. *War Work*: Embarkation Staff Officer, and Deputy Assistant Adjutant-General for Embarkation, Southampton. *Address*: Holmwood, Brockenhurst, Hants. *Clubs*: Army and Navy; Pall Mall; County, Carlisle. (O7141)

FERGUSON, Major Wallace, O.B.E.

FERGUSON, William Francis, M.B.E. (M10385)

FERGUSON, Lady Helen Hermione MUNRO-: *see* Novar, Helen Hermione, Viscountess, G.B.E.

FERGUSSON, Capt. John Caldwell, M.B.E., M.C., R.A.M.C., *b.* 21 Dec. 1890; *s.* of James H. Fergusson, F.R.C.S.I., of Londonderry; *m.* Agnes Margaret, *d.* of James Wells, of Sackville Street, Dublin. *Educ.*: Foyle Coll., Londonderry; Univ. Coll., London; Royal Coll. of Surgeons, Dublin. *War Work*: No. 10 General Hospital, France; Medical Officer-in-Charge, 9 North Stafford Regt. Military Hospital, Cork. *Qddress*: White House, Brotton, Yorks. (M5259)

FERGUSSON, Margaret Heriot, M.B.E., *b.* 20 Jan. 1893; *d.* of Thomas Fergusson, of Hampstead. *Educ.*: Privately and abroad. Late Deputy Principal, W.R.N.S. *War Work*: Cook in V.A.D. Hospital, and afterwards started and ran Canteen for the Headquarter Staff of Women's Royal Naval Service. *Address*: Dinmurchie, 26 Belsize Crescent, N.W. 3. (R8072)

FERGUSSON, Robert Loftus, M.B.E., *b.* 1877; *s.* of F. J. Fergusson, of Calcutta. *Educ.*: Haileybury and Heidelberg Colleges. Officer of North Eastern Railway. *War Work*: Ministry of Munitions, in charge of Motor Transport Section; during 1919–20 filled position of Director Munitions Inland Transport. *Address*: Westwood House, Beverley. (M1711)

FERMOR, Lewis Leigh, O.B.E., D.Sc.

FERNIE, James, M.B.E. (M10442)

FERNIE, Capt. Ralph, O.B.E., R.A.F.

FERNIE, Major William James, O.B.E., R.A.F.

FERNLEY, Alderman James, O.B.E., J.P.; *s.* of James Fernley, of Heaton Norris. *Educ.*: Commercial School, Stockport. Cotton Yarn Merchant. *War Work*: Active worker in connection with Soldiers' and Sailors' Families Association; Chairman of Local War Pensions Committee from inception. *Address*: Elmstead, Mile End, Stockport. (O10397)

FERNS, Walter, M.B.E.

FERRAR, Major and Brevet Lieut.-Col. Henry Minchin, C.B.E., *b.* 25 March, 1863; *s.* of A. M. Ferrar, D.L. of Belfast, Ireland; *m.* Laura, *d.* of John Hargreaves, of Maiden Erlegh, Berks. *Educ.*: Royal Military Academy. Late Royal Artillery, now Inspector of Remounts for Royal Artillery. *War Work*: Remount work. *Address*: Hook House, Hook, Hants. *Club*: Army and Navy. (C1560)

FERRAR, Major Michael Lloyd, O.B.E.

FERRIER, Capt. Charles Gordon, O.B.E.

FERRIER, Thomas Archibald, C.B.E., *b.* 1877; *s.* of the late T. H. Ferrier, W.S., of Edinburgh. Officer-in-Charge of Mathematical Instrument Office, Survey of India, Calcutta. *Address*: Calcutta. (C1074)

FERRIS, Lieut. Pierce, M.B.E., R.N.

FERRY, Capt. Cuthbert Edmund Caulfield, O.B.E., R.A.M.C. (T.F.).

FERRY, Major Edward Stanton Henry, O.B.E., I.A.

FETHERSTONE, Lieut. Henry Barry, M.B.E., M.C., R.F.A.

FETHERSTONHUGH, Florence, M.B.E.

FETHERSTONHAUGH, Margaret, Mrs., O.B.E; *d.* of Major-Gen. T. G. A. Oakes, C.B.; *m.* Col. J. D. Fetherstonhaugh, D.L., *s.* of R. S. Fetherstonhaugh, of Rockview, Killucan. Ireland. *Educ.*: Privately. *War Work*: Hon. Sec. Soldiers' and Sailors' Help Society for Ireland; Member Red Cross Council for Ireland; collected £2000 and sent and endowed 2 Motor Ambulances from Co. Westmeath; worked as a V.A.D. at Waverley Abbey Red Cross Hospital; twice mentioned by the War Office. *Address*: Rockview, Killucan, Ireland. (O10398)

FETHERSTONHAUGH, Victoria Emma Shaw, Mrs., M.B.E.

FETHERSTONHAUGH, Lieut.-Col. William Albany, C.B.E., D.S.O., *b.* 1876 ; *s.* of the late William Albany Fetherstonhaugh, of Beechhurst, Farnham Royal; *m.* 1915, Adela Mary, *d.* of Claud Thornton Cayley (*see* BURKE'S *Peerage*, Cayley, Bt.) *Educ.* : Privately and R.M.C. Major and Brevet Lieut.-Col. Indian Army ; was A.D.C. to Gen. Officer Comdg. Quetta Div. 1908–12 ; Tirah Expedition, 1897–8 (medal with two clasps) ; Great War, 1914–18, on Staff (despatches, Legion of Honour, Brevet Lieut.-Col.). *Address :* Cavalry Club. (C3093)

FETHERSTONHAUGH, Lieut.-Col. William Samuel, C.B.E. Canadian Forestry Corps, attached R.A.F. (C773)

FEUERHEERD, Marietta Robertine, M.B.E. ; *d.* of H. L. Feuerheerd, of Miramar, Oporto, Portugal, and Anita, his wife, *a. d.* of Hon. A de Landeville, of Joinville. *Educ.* : England and France. *War Work :* Organiser and Manager of the Soldiers' and Sailors' Rest Room and Free Buffet at Euston Station, the first of its kind, started at the request of Lord Kitchener, with the financial aid of Miss Margaret Boulton ; the Buffet was open from 4 Feb. 1915, to 5 July, 1919, serving on an average 100,000 men monthly. *Address :* Miramar, Oporto, Portugal. (M8073)

FFINCH, Capt. Matthew Benjamin Dipnall, C.B.E., D.L., J.P., *b.* 18 Dec. 1866 ; *s.* of Matthew S. Ffinch, of The Old House, Deptford, Kent ; *m.* Crystal, *d.* of Sir Claude Ch. de Crespigny, Bart., of Champion Lodge, Maldon, Essex (*see* BURKE'S *Peerage*). *Educ.* : Haileybury ; R.M.C. Sandhurst. Gazetted to Prince of Wales' N. Stafford Regt., 30 Jan. 1886 ; late Asst. Chief Constable of Essex. *Address :* Langford Meads, Maldon, Essex. *Clubs :* Naval and Military ; M.C.C. ; Shikar. (C15)

FFISKE, William Henry, O.B.E., *b.* 8 April, 1879 ; *s.* of Henry ffiske, of Brundall, Norfolk ; *m.* Jane Ewing, *d.* of Alexander B. Dansken, of Glasgow. *Educ.* : Norwich and Bury St. Edmunds Grammar Schools. Managing Director, Boulton and Paul, Ltd., Norwich and London ; On Council of Norwich Chamber of Commerce ; Member of Local Labour Advisory Committee, Assessor on Court of Referees, etc. *Clubs :* Junior Carlton ; Royal Aero. (O1334)

FFOOKS, Capt. William Archdall, O.B.E.

FFORDE, Comm. Thomas Roderick, O.B.E., R.N.

FFOULKES, Katharine Mary, Mrs. M.B.E., *b.* 25 May, 1878 ; *d.* of Sir George Baker Wilbraham, Bart., of Rode Hall, Cheshire (*see* BURKE'S *Peerage*) ; *m.* the Rev. Piers John Benedict, *s.* of Judge Wynne Ffoulkes, of Chester. *Educ.* : Privately. *War Work :* Acted for 6 months as Commandant of Congleton Red Cross Hospital, Cheshire (25 beds) ; Commandant of Rode Hall Red Cross Hospital, Cheshire (55 beds) for two years ; raised the V.A.D. detachment to run the hospital. *Address :* Rode Rectory, Scholar Green, Cheshire. (M8074)

FFRENCH, Alfred E., M.B.E.

FIASCHI, Lieut.-Col. Piers, O.B.E., Ausr. A.M.C.

FIDLER, George Thomas, M.B.E., *b.* 18 Jan. 1883 ; *s.* of Thomas Fidler, of Ardfert, Co. Kerry ; *m.* Emily Caroline, *d.* of Thomas Copley, of Timogue, Queen's Co. *Educ.* : Cork Grammar School. Civil Servant ; Sec. Departmental Committee on the Irish Flax-growing Industry, 1910–11. *War Work :* Deputy Head of Branch of Military Sea Transport Department, Ministry of Shipping, responsible for transport of Military Personnel, Stores, and Equipment across English Channel, and in Mediterranean. *Address :* Ikotobo, Clontarf, Dublin. (M3640)

FIDOE, Alfred Joseph, M.B.E., *b.* 16 Jan. 1876 ; *s.* of Alfred Fidoe, of Dudley. *Educ.* : Prospect House Academy, Stourbridge, Worcs. Clerk and Steward, Oxford County and City Mental Hospital, Littlemore, nr. Oxford. *War Work :* Mental Hospital converted into a War Hospital, April, 1918 ; acted as Sec. and Steward of the Hospital. *Address :* Littlemore, nr. Oxford. (M8075)

FIDOE, Katharine Mary, M.B.E.

FIELD, Capt. Christopher Senior, O.B.E.

FIELD, Capt. David, M.B.E.

FIELD, Capt. Edward Elgar, O.B.E., D.C.L.I. (T.F.), and R.E.

FIELD, Edward Hubert, M.B.E., M.C., *b.* 28 Oct. 1884 ; *s.* of Edward Field, of Leamington, Warwickshire ; *m.* Catherine Lilian, *d.* of T. W. Sorby. *War Work :* Joined 4th S. Midland Howitzer Bdge., R.A., Sept. 1914 ; proceeded to France, March, 1915 ; twice mentioned in despatches. *Address :* Borve, Woldingham, Surrey. (M4478)

FIELD, Lieut. Eric Athelstane, M.B.E.

FIELD, Herbert Stanley, O.B.E.

FIELD, John William, M.B.E., *b.* 2 Feb. 1878 ; *s.* of Edwin Field, of Ealing W. ; *m.* Edith Anne, *d.* of Edward J. B. Downing, of Westminster. *Educ.* : Aylesbury Grammar and City of Westminster Schools. Civil Servant ; Staff Officer in Foreign Office. *Address :* 93, Coldershaw Road, West Ealing, W. 13. (M8076)

FIELD, Joseph Henry, O.B.E., LL.B. (London), *b.* 1865 ; Town Clerk and Clerk of the Peace, Huddersfield. *War Work :* Clerk to Huddersfield Local Tribunal ; Clerk to Separation Allowances Committee ; Joint Secretary, Huddersfield Recruiting Committee ; Secretary Huddersfield War Relief Committee ; Legal Adviser to Huddersfield Food and Coal and Fuel Control Committees. *Address :* Town Hall, Huddersfield. (O1336)

FIELD, Mabel Clara Hawkes, M.B.E., *b.* 26 Oct. 1875 ; *d.* of Capt. G. Lainson Field, of Talton House, Nr. Stratford-on-Avon. *Educ.* : Privately ; Malvern. *War Work :* Commandant of V.A.D., Warwick 4 ; worked as Assistant Commandant at the Town Hall Hospital, Stratford-on-Avon, from Oct. 1914, to March, 1915 ; and from May, 1915 to March, 1919, was in charge of V.A. Hospital, Whytegates, Stratford-on-Avon. *Addresses :* Talton House, Stratford-on-Avon ; Milton Keynes Rectory, Newport Pagnell. (M3641)

FIELD, Mathilde, Mrs., M.B.E.

FIELD, Michael Birt, M.B.E.

FIELD, Capt. Raymond Ernest, O.B.E.

FIELD, Rev. Major William, O.B.E., Hon. S.C.F., *b.* 1874 ; *s.* of William Field, of Norwich ; *m.* Constance Ethel, *d.* of William Philip Creak, of Great Yarmouth. *Educ.* : Crescent Range College, Manchester, and London University. Minister of Religion. *War Work :* Served in Egypt, Italy, France, Belgium and with Army of Occupation in Germany, in all, four years ; three times mentioned in despatches ; Awarded O.B.E. and Croix de Guerre (Belgium) ; made an Hon. Senior Chaplain to H.M. Forces. *Address :* The Manse, Cleckheaton, Yorks. *Club :* Masonic. (O5254)

FIELD, Lieut. William Samuel, O.B.E., R.A.O.C.

FIELD, Lieut.-Col. William Vincent, O.B.E., R.A.M.C.

FIELDEN, Dora, Mrs., O.B.E. ; *d.* of Thomas Henry Ismay, of Dawpool, Thurstaston ; *m.* Joshua Fielden, *s.* of Joshua Fielden, of Nutfield Priory, Redhill. *War Work :* Commandant of V.A.D. Hospital from 1914–18. *Address :* Kineton House, Kineton, Warwickshire. (O333)

FIELDEN, Mysie, Mrs., M.B.E.

FIELDER, Charles James, M.B.E.

FIELDER, Charles Lavington, M.B.E.

FIELDER, Sub.-Lieut. Stanley, O.B.E., R.N.R.

FIELDHOUSE, Arthur, M.B.E., C.S.M.

FIELDHOUSE, William John, C.B.E., *b.* 1858 ; *s.* of Thomas Fieldhouse, of Newport, Salop. ; *m.* 1882, Lucy, *d.* of Abraham Wood. *Educ.* : Newport Grammar Sch. Head of the firm of Geo. H. Hughes (Limited), of St. Stephen's Wheel Works, Birmingham ; a Director of Brampton Brothers (Limited) ; J.P. for Warwickshire. *Address :* Ansty Manor, Wootton Wawen, Warwickshire. *Club :* Royal Thames Yacht. (C158)

FIELDING, Sir Charles Wm., K.B.E.

FIELDING, Frederick, M.B.E., *b.* 19 Nov. 1863 ; *s.* of John Osborn Fielding, of Graveley Manor, Cambs. *Educ.* : Croydon. *War Work :* Hon. Sec. Buckden Centre British Red Cross Society, and Buckden Centre Huntingdonshire Volunteer Regt. *Address :* York House, Buckden, Huntingdon. (M8078)

FIELDING, Henry, M.B.E.

FIELDING, Thomas Henry, M.B.E.

FIELDING, Capt. Walter Harrison, M.B.E., *b.* 9 Aug. 1889 ; *s.* of the late Thomas Edward Fielding, of Southport, Lancs. ; *m.* Marjorie Octavia Adair, *d.* of F. G. Adair Roberts, of Oakhill Lodge, Hampstead, N.W. *War Work :* Enlisted in 28th London Regt. (Artists Rifles), 1914 ; commissioned as 2nd Lieut. R.E. 1915 ; promoted Capt. 1916 ; served in Gallipoli, Sinai and on Suez Canal ; Engineer-in-Charge of R.A.F. buildings at Aboukir, Egypt, 1917–19 ; mentioned in despatches. *Address :* Briarside Cottage, Letchworth. (M3380)

FIENNES, Florence Agnes, Lady TWISLETON-WYKEHAM-, O.B.E. ; *d.* of John Rathfeldar, of Wynberg, Cape Colony, and widow of Arthur Woodward Fletcher ; *m.* Hon. Sir Eustace Edward Twisleton-Wykeham-Fiennes, Bart. (*see* BURKE'S *Peerage*). *Addresses :* Government House, Victoria Mohé, Seychelles ; Studland House, Studland Bay, Dorset ; 86, Eaton Terrace, S.W. (O1337)

FIENNES, Gerard Yorke TWISLETON-WYKEHAM-, C.B.E., Order of Leopold I., Belgium, *b.* 18 July, 1864 ; *s.* of Rev. Hon. Wingfield Twisleton-Wykeham-Fiennes, of Colne House, Rickmansworth ; *m.* Gwendolen, *d.* of Francis Gisborne, of Holme Hall, Bakewell. *Educ.* : Winchester, New Coll., Oxford. Journalist. *War Work :* Naval Correspondent of "Observer," all through ; General Editor, National War Aims Committee, Oct. 1917 to Armistice. *Address :* Colne House, Rickmansworth. *Club :* Savile. (C2607)

FIFE, William, O.B.E., J.P., *b.* 11 Jan. 1857 ; *s.* of William Fife, of Fairlie. Naval Architect ; Member of the Institute of Naval Architects. *War Work :* Department of Aeronautical Supplies. *Address :* The Place, Fairlie, Ayrshire. *Clubs :* Royal Thames Yacht ; Conservative, Glasgow ; Royal Automobile. (O3712)

FIGG, Capt. and Qr.-Mr. Charles Arthur, O.B.E., R.A.M.C.

FIGGINS, Eng.-Capt. John William, O.B.E., R.N.

FIGGIS, Howard Bradley, M.B.E., *b.* 20 Jan. 1868 ; *s.* of Samuel Figgis, J.P., of Montagu Grove, Hampstead, N.W. ; *m.* Edith Annie, *d.* of Sir Corbet Woodall, D.S.C., of Walden Chislehurst (*see* BURKE'S *Peerage*). *Educ.* : Uppingham. Rubber and General Produce Broker. *War Work :* Member of City of London Advisory Recruiting Committee. *Address :* Heathlands, Hampstead Heath, N.W. *Club :* Reform. (M1715)

FIGGIS, Ruby Norah, M.B.E., V.A.D.

FILER, Samuel, O.B.E.

FILDES, Surg.-Lieut.-Comm. Paul G., O.B.E., R.N.V.R.

FILGATE, Lieut.-Col. Arthur Robert Patten MACARTNEY-, C.B.E.

FILL, Major Samuel John Vincent, O.B.E., R.A.F.

FILLION, Rev Joseph, M.B.E.

FILMER, Lieut. Walter George Harry, M.B.E.

FINCH, Daisy Amelia, M.B.E. ; *d.* of Marshall Finch, of

Tunbridge Wells. *Educ.:* St. James' School, Tunbridge Wells. Telephonist, G.P.O. *War Work:* Three years at General Headquarters, Home Forces, one year at the War Cabinet, Whitehall Gardens. *Address:* 82, Albert Road, Alexandra Park, N. 22. (M8080)

FINCH, Lieut. George Ingle, M.B.E.

FINCH, Lieut.-Col. Hamilton Walter Edward, D.S.O., Middlesex Regt., *b.* 1868. Served in the Great War, 1914–17 (despatches). (C1561)

FINCH, Josiah Robert, O.B.E. (O12047)

FINCH, Lionel Hugh Knightley, O.B.E. (O4488c)

FINCH, Madeline Constance, M.B.E. Secretariat, Ministry of Munitions. (M10317)

FINCH, Marie Isabel, M.B.E. (M1716)

FINCH, Lieut.-Comm. Sidney, O.B.E., R.N.R. (ret.), *b.* 1868 ; *s.* of Robert Finch, of Blackheath, S.E. ; *m.* Florence May, *d.* of Lance Smith, of N.S.W. *Educ.:* H.M.S. "Worcester." Master Mercantile Marine. *War Work:* In command of troopships, and of Hospital ship "Kalyan," Archangel, 1918–19. (O10400)

FINCH, Major William Robert Edward Heneage, O.B.E.

FINCHAM, Capt. John William George, O.B.E.. A.C.F.

FINCKEN, Major Vernon Shaw Taylor, O.B.E.

FINDLAY, Elizabeth Susan, M.B.E.

FINDLAY, Ellen Kent, Mrs., M.B.E.

FINDLAY, Surg.-Lieut. George William Marshall, O.B.E.. M.B., R.N.

FINDLAY, Lieut.-Col. Harold, C.B.E., E. Kent Regt. ; served in the Great War, 1914–19 (despatches). (C1562)

FINDLAY, James, O.B.E.

FINDLAY, James Arthur, M.B.E., J.P., *b.* 16 May, 1883 ; *s.* of Robert Downie Findlay, of Woodside House, Beith ; *m.* Annie Gertrude, *d.* of Theodore Walker, F.R.G.S., of Glenn Hall, Leicestershire. *Educ.:* Ardvreck ; Fettes Coll. ; Geneva Univ. Chairman, Beith Parish Council ; Hon. Sec., Ayrshire Branch, British Red Cross Society ; Member, Glasgow Stock Exchange. *War Work:* Hon. Sec. Ayrshire Branch, British Red Cross Society ; Official organiser for Ayrshire Red Cross Week, 1917–18 ; Chairman, War Savings Association, Beith Branch ; Chairman, War Pensions Committee, Beith ; Member of Lord Eglinton's County Fund to relieve distress caused by the war. *Address:* Woodside House, Beith, Ayrshire. *Clubs:* Royal Thames Yacht ; New, Glasgow. (M3644)

FINDLAY, Jean Elmslie Henderson, C.B.E.

FINDLAY, Sir John Ritchie, K.B.E., D.L., J.P., *b.* 1866 ; (*see* BURKE'S *Peerage*) ; *s.* of J. R. Findlay, of Aberlour ; *m.* Harriet Jane, *d.* of Sir Jonathan E. Backhouse, of the Rookery, Middleton Tyas (*see* BURKE'S *Peerage*). *Educ.:* Harrow ; Balliol, Oxford. Proprietor of "The Scotsman." *War Work:* Chairman of Scottish National Housing Company ; member Scottish Advisory Committee, and of the Prince of Wales' Fund. *Addresses:* 3, Rothesay Terrace, Edinburgh ; Aberlour, Banffshire. *Clubs:* Brooks's ; New, Edinburgh. (K20)

FINDLAY, Lieut.-Col. Richard John, O.B.E., R.A.O.C.

FINDLAY, Lieut.-Col. William Henri de La Tour d'Auvergne, D.S.O., O.B.E., *b.* 1864 ; *s.* of the late Col. Alexander Findlay, of Nairn ; *m.* 1st, 1894, Isabella Maria, who d. youngest *d.* of the Rev. Canon Hodgson, of Horsham, Sussex ; 2nd, 1917, Josephine May, *d.* of Thomas Vaughan Anthony, of 14, Daleham Gardens, Hampstead, N.W. Lieut.-Col. Canadian Army Ser. Corps ; served in the S. African War with Roy. Sussex Regt. ; Great War, 1914–19 (despatches, Croix de Guerre). *Address:* Sunny Hills, Port Williams, Nova Scotia, Canada. (O5994)

FINDLEY, Capt. Harold Bruce, O.B.E. Can. A.D.C.

FINK, Kenneth De Quincey, M.B.E.

FINLAY, Lieut.-Col. Frank Dalzell, O.B.E., P.S.C., *b.* 1868 ; *s.* of Frank D. Finlay, of Belfast. Tirah Expedition N.W. Frontier, India, 1897. *War Work:* Commanded Wiltshire Regt. ; General Staff. *Clubs:* United Service ; Garrick ; M.C.C. (O1339)

FINLAY, Paymaster-Rear-Adm. George, C.B.E., R.N. Accountant Officer, Depot Ship, Queenstown. (C2270)

FINLAY, Capt. George, O.B.E., Aust. A.M.C., A.I.F.

FINLAY, Lieut. Harry William, M.B.E.

FINLAY, Lieut. John, M.B.E., I.A.R.O.

FINLAY, May, M.B.E.

FINLAY, Hon. Sir William, K.B.E., K.C., Officer Legion d'Honneur ; Officer Order of St. Maurice and St. Lazarus (Italy), *b.* 15 Oct. 1875 ; *s.* of Robert Bannatyne, 1st Viscount Finlay, of Nairn, ; *m.* Beatrice Marion, *d.* of Edward Kirkpatrick Hall, of Kevin, Nairn, N.B. *Educ.:* Eton ; Trinity College, Cambridge (President of Union). Junior Counsel to the Inland Revenue, 1905–14 ; King's Counsel, 1914. *War Work:* Assisted in Procurator-General's Department (Intelligence), 1915 ; Chairman of Contraband Committee, Foreign Office, 1916 ; Vice-Chairman of Allied Blockade Committee, 1917–19 ; Temporary Legal Adviser, Foreign Office, 1918–19. *Addresses:* 31, Phillimore Gardens, W. 8 ; Fairway, Great Bedwyn, Wilts. *Club:* United University. (K454)

FINLAY, Sergt. William George, M.B.E., *b.* 25 Nov. 1864 ; *s.* of the late George Finlay, of Newcastle-on-Tyne ; *m.* Annie, *d.* of Frederick Coppin, of Newcastle-on-Tyne. Received an Army Education, and awarded a First Class Certificate of Education, Civil Service Examination, by the Horse Guards, War Office, 26 March, 1890. One of the Founders of the Northumberland Veterans' Association, Newcastle-on-Tyne, for Veterans of the Army and Navy ; Hon.

Sec. of the Society from its first inception on 18 Oct. 1908, till retirement during the present year (1920) ; laboured for upwards of 20 years in the work of social reform, etc., amongst the Veteran Sailors and Soldiers of Newcastle-on-Tyne, and District (received the thanks of the late Field Marshal Lord Roberts, V.C.). *War Work:* Recruiting for Kitchener's Army during the early stages of the War, and instrumental in the formation for the duties of Home Defence, of the National Reserve of the County (Northumberland). *Address:* 39, Seventh Avenue, Heaton, Newcastle-on-Tyne. (M8081)

FINLAYSON, David John, O.B.E.

FINLAYSON, Capt. Duncan, O.B.E., J.P., *b.* 23 Dec. 1863 ; *s.* of Roderick Finlayson, of New Kelso, Strathcarron ; *m.* Katherine Wylie. *Educ.:* Lochcarron Public School. Chief Constable of Ross and Cromarty. *War Work:* County Director of Red Cross Society ; Convener of County Recruiting Committee under Voluntary System ; Member of County Territorial Force Association. *Address:* Marsûle, Craig Road, Dingwall. (O1340)

FINLAYSON, Major William Thomas, O.B.E., R.A.M.C.

FINLINSON, Ethel Mary, Mrs., M.B.E., *b.* 4 June, 1877 ; *d.* of the late John M. Roberts ; *m.* Capt. Alfred Louis Finlinson, South Staffordshire Regt. *War Work:* V.A.D. No 2, B.R.C. Hospital, France, 1915–16 ; Private Sec. to the Controller of Gun Ammunition Filling Dept., Ministry of Munitions, 1917–19. *Address:* Whittington Barracks, Lichfield, Staffs. (M8082)

FINN, Major Charles Napier, O.B.E., Aust. A.M.C.

FINNEY, Capt. Wilfred Josiah, O.B.E., Can. F.A.

FINNIMORE, Benjamin Kingston, M.B.E.

FINNIS, Com. George Home, C.B.E., R.N. Served in the Great War, 1914–19 (despatches). (C2353)

FINNIS, Comm. George Home, C.B.E., O.B.E., R.N.

FINNIS, Col. Henry, C.S.I., C.B.E., late R.E., *b.* 9 Feb. 1853 ; *s.* of Steriker Finnis, D.L., J.P. of Dover ; *m.* Mary, *d.* of John Leahy, M.D., late of Indian Medical Service. *Educ.:* Wellington ; R.M.A., Woolwich. Served in India as an R.E. officer, 1876–1910 ; Afghan War, 1878–80 ; retired, Feb. 1910. *War Work:* Re-employed Oct. 1914 as C.R.E. 36th (Ulster) Division, and C.R.E. Cannock Chase, till Mar. 1919. *Address:* The Cottage, Hillingdon, Uxbridge. (C814)

FINNIS, Herbert, M.B.E.

FINNIS, Capt. Herbert Cobb, O.B.E., I.A.

FIRMIN, 2nd Lieut. Cyril Alfred, M.B.E., R.A.F.

FIRMIN, Major Norman Haynes, O.B.E., Tyne Electrical Engineers, R.E., *b.* 4 July, 1883 ; *s.* of Arthur Firmin, of London ; *m.* Lucy Isabel, *d.* of the late William Short, of Newcastle-on-Tyne. *Educ.:* King's Coll. School. Personal Assistant to Manager of Newcastle-upon-Tyne Electric Supply Co., Ltd. ; Sec. of County of Durham Electric Power Supply Co., and County of Durham Electrical Power Distribution Co., Ltd. *War Work:* Embodied in Special Service Section of Tyne Electrical Engineers, July, 1914 ; commanded No. 9 (Tyne) Mobile Searchlight Co., March 1916 to Oct. 1917 ; seconded for duty at Admiralty as Sec. to Director of Experiments and Research, March 1918 ; appointed Assistant-Director of Experiments and Research (for Administration), Oct. 1918. *Address:* Cotfield, Hexham-on-Tyne. (O10401)

FIRMINGER, Eveleen Sarah, Mrs., M.B.E., *b.* 18 Dec. 1871 ; *d.* of the Rev. P. E. Miles, of Calcutta ; *m.* the Ven. Walter Kelly, Archdeacon of Calcutta, *s.* of the Rev. T. A. C. Firminger. *Address:* St. John's House, Calcutta. (M6142)

FIRMISTONE, Emily Florence, O.B.E., *b.* 1856 ; *d* of the late Rev. Edward Firmstone, of Winchester. *Educ.:* Privately. Town Councillor ; Woman Guardian ; Prison Visitor. *War Work:* Organiser of Westgate Club and Canteen for soldiers, 1914–19, Winchester. *Address:* Pyotts' Cottage, Winchester. (O10402)

FIRTH, Lieut. Bernard, O.B.E., R.N.R.

FIRTH, Clare Jane, Mrs., M.B.E., R.R.C., *b.* 14 Oct. 1868 ; *d.* of late S. A. Turner, of Egham, Surrey ; *m.* Joseph, *s.* of John Firth, of Dudley Hill, Bradford, Yorks. *Educ.:* Egham. Matron of Withington Poor Law Institution (3000 beds). *War Work:* Matron-in-charge, Nell Lane Military Hospital, West Didsbury, Manchester, 1916–19. *Address:* Nell Lane Hospital, West Didsbury. *Club:* Withington Golf. (M392)

FIRTH, John William, M.B.E.

FIRTH, Col. Sir Robert Hammill, K.B.E., C.B., *b.* 1 Dec. 1857 (*see* BURKE'S *Peerage*) ; *s.* of John Firth, H.E.I.C.S. ; *m.* Mary, *d.* of William Knight, of Appledore, Devon. *Educ.:* Privately ; Univ. Coll., London. Entered A.M.S., Aug. 1883 ; Lieut.-Col. 1903 ; Col. 1912 ; retired, 1919 ; formerly Professor Mil. Hyg. Royal Army Med. Coll., London. Hazara Expedition, 1888 ; Tirah Expedition, 1897–8 ; served in France, 1915–19 ; mentioned in despatches three times. *Address:* 4, Canfield House, Hampstead, N.W. 3. *Club:* Junior United Service. (K269)

FISH, Capt. Colin, O.B.E., R.E.

FISH, Capt. George Drummond, M.B.E.

FISH, Major Phillip Henry, O.B.E., R.A.S.C.

FISH, Walter George, C.B.E., *b.* 3 June, 1874 ; *s.* of George Fish, late of Herne Hill, London ; *m.* Nellie, *d.* of D. T. Oakley. *Educ.:* Westminster City School. Director of Associated Newspapers, Ltd. *War Work:* Honorary Director of Publicity to Coal Control Department during critical period of the war. *Address:* 10, Herne Hill, London, S.E.24. *Club:* Devonshire. (C959)

FISHER, Amy Anderson, Mrs., M.B.E.

FISHER, Cecil James, O.B.E. (O6618)

FISHER, Charles Browning, C.B.E., *b.* 1863. *Educ.:*

Winchester. Land Agent; a Director of Northamptonshire Union Bank (Limited); and Agricultural Adviser to Ministry of Food. *Address:* Clipston House, Market Harborough. *Club:* Junior Carlton.   (C960)

FISHER, Major Charles Stanley, O.B.E.

FISHER, Major and Brevet Lieut.-Col. Charles Taylor, O.B.E., R.A.O.C., *b.* 1 Jan. 1877; *s.* of Rev. W. F. Fisher, of Wooton, I. of Wight; *m.* Violet Isabella, *d.* of William Wheeler, of Chatburn. *Educ.:* Privately. Regular Army. *War Work:* C.O.O. Sierra Leone, Feb. 1914 to May, 1915; C.O.O. Southampton Clothing Area, June, 1915 to Dec. 1915; A.D.O.S. East Africa, Jan. 1916 to March, 1918; D.D.O.S. North Russia Expeditionary Force (Archangel), June, 1918 to Sept. 1919. *Address:* c/o Sir C. R. McGrigor, Bart., & Co., 39, Panton Street, Haymarket, London, S.W.   (O2313)

FISHER, Lieut. Claude Frederick Urquhart. M.B.E., T.F. Res., *b.* 4 June, 1891; *s.* of C. Urquhart Fisher, L.C.C., of Hyde Park, W. *Educ.:* Westminster School. Asst. District Commissioner, the Boy Scouts' Association, Lowestoft. *War Work:* Served with 2/1 E.A. (Essex) R.G.A., Heavy Battery, Aug. 1914, to Feb. 1919. *Address:* 16, High Street, Lowestoft.   (M5263)

FISHER, Lieut. Douglas Blake, O.B.E., R.N.

FISHER, Edward Lamley, M.B.E.

FISHER, Ellinor Jane, Mrs., M.B.E., *b.* 23 May, 1868; *d.* of J. H. Whitaker (Cotton Manufacturers), of Burnley, Lancashire; *m.* John Henry (Timber Merchant), of Hull. *Educ.:* Privately. Lady Supt., Kingston Division St. John Ambulance Brigade, Hull; Lady Supt. Hull Society Prevention of Cruelty to Children. *War Work:* Assistant Prince of Wales' Fund (6 months); Belgian Refugee Work (decoration, Queen Elisabeth Medal); V.A.D. Nurse, 7 months, Naval Hospital, Hull; Canteen Work, Hull; for two years Head Steward St. John V.A.D. Hospital, Hull. *Address:* Willerby Hall, Willerby, near Hull.   (M8055)

FISHER, Ethel Sophia, M.B.E.; *d.* of John Bowden, of Manchester; *m.* Edwin Robert, *s.* of Robert Fisher, of Ystalyfera. *Educ.:* Bowdon, Cheshire. *War Work:* President of the Ammanford Branch of the Soldiers' and Sailors' Families Association, and Member of the War Pensions Committee. *Address:* Wansbeck, Ammanford, South Wales.   (M8086)

FISHER, Frederick Furryan, O.B.E., *b.* 3 Oct. 1878; *s.* of Frederick William Fisher, of Ravenscroft, Penge; *m.* Blanche, *d.* of George Nicoll, of Epping. *Educ.:* Privately, and King's Coll., London. Asst. Director of Contracts, Admiralty. *War Work:* Dealing with contracts for warships, auxiliary vessels, and aircraft for H.M. Navy. *Address:* Cranford, Hadley Wood, Middlesex.   (O10403)

FISHER, Frederick Ludolph, M.B.E., A.M.I.E.E., *b.* 2 Sept. 1876; *s.* of Charles Fisher, of Hampton-on-Thames, Middlesex; *m.* Hetty McEwan, *d.* of William Jackson, of Lenzie, Scotland. *Educ.:* City of London School. *War Work:* Chief Electrical Engineer of the Cable Ship " Amber," engaged in repairing the submarine cables between England and the Mediterranean throughout the war. *Address:* c/o Eastern Telegraph Company, Electra House, Finsbury Pavement, London, E.C. 2.   (M8087)

FISHER, Capt. George Wilfred, O.B.E.

FISHER, Honoria Mary, M.B.E.

FISHER, Major Hubert Frank, O.B.E., R.A.F.

FISHER, Hubert William Warwick, M.B.E., *b.* 25 Dec. 1890; *s.* of John and Mary Fisher, of Enfield Lock; Civil Servant. *War Work:* Registrar, War Trade Dept.; and Sec. to the Transhipment and Re-export Committees, War Trade Dept. *Address:* Orwell, Albury Ride, Cheshunt. (M8088)

FISHER, Janet Aitken, Mrs., M.B.E.

FISHER, John Campbell, O.B.E., *b.* 6 June, 1880; *s.* of the Rev. Canon Robert Fisher, of the Rectory, Stokesley, Yorks.; *m.* Agnes Beatrice, *d.* of John Douglas Close, of Nottingham. *Educ.:* Oakham and Sidney Sussex College, Cambridge. Clerk, Colonial Audit branch, Exchequer and Audit dept., 1902; asst. auditor, Lagos, 1903; N. Nigeria, 1905; local auditor, 1909; examnr., 1910; 1st div. clk. (2nd cls.), central office, 1910; auditor, Malta, 1913; senior clerk, central office, 1919. *War Work:* In Malta; Member of Supplies and Prices Board, Wheat Board, and Control Board; Head of Food Control Office. *Address:* 20, Manor Road, Beckenham, Kent. *Club:* Beckenham.   (O991)

FISHER, Josephine Hilda, Mrs., M.B.E., *b.* 1874; *d.* of Joseph Williamson, of Scarborough; *m.* Herbert, *s.* of John Fisher, of London. *Educ.:* " Westlands," Scarborough. *War Work:* Joined the V.A.D. in 1913; Four years Commandant at Balgowan Hospital, where over 5000 patients were treated. *Address:* " Cawood," Tudor Road, Beckenham, Kent.   (M19)

FISHER, Katharine, M.B.E.; *d.* of John Fisher, of Boston Spa. *Educ.:* Privately. *War Work:* Hospital work at Zagazig and Fayoum, Egypt; Industrial Relief work at Armenian Camp, Port Said; Relief work, Jerusalem and Damascus, Orphanage, Soup kitchens, Laundry, and Repair shop for Army clothing. *Address:* Oak Bank, Whitehaven, Cumberland.   (M8089)

FISHER, Major Otto Sarony, O.B.E., M.R.C.V.S., R.A.V.C., *d.* 27 Dec. 1877; *s.* of S. W. Fisher, of Scarborough. *Educ.:* Scarborough; Private School. M.R.C.V.S. *Address:* c/o Messrs. Holt & Co., 3, Whitehall Place, London. (O5257)

FISHER, Samuel Joseph, M.B.E., *b.* 28 Jan. 1860; *s.* of Samuel Fisher, of Cheltenham; *m.* Elizabeth Annie, *d.* of John Anthony Carr, of East Murton, Co. Durham. *Educ.:*

British School, Cheltenham; Boro' Road Coll., London. Schoolmaster. *War Work:* Hon. Sec. Local Central War Savings Committee, Burton-on-Trent.   (M8090)

FISHER, Comm. Sir Thomas, K.B.E., R.N., *b.* 1883; *s.* of Thomas Fisher, of Birmingham; *m.* Aimée, *d.* of Walter Loveridge, of Codsall. *Educ.:* H.M.S. " Britannia." Retired from Royal Navy, 1910, with rank of Commander; General Manager, Canadian Pacific Ocean Services. *War Work:* served afloat in Reserve Fleet as Flag-Com.; at the Admiralty, and at Washington in the United States, as representative of the Ministry of Shipping. *Addresses:* 103, Sloane Street; 8, Waterloo Place, S.W. *Clubs:* United Service; St. James.   (K371)

FISHER, Major Walter Harington, O.B.E., M.B., R.A.M.C. (T.), *b.* 19 Sept. 1876; *s.* of J. E. Fisher, of Higham-on-the-Hill, Leicestershire. *Educ.:* Cambridge and London Hospital. *War Work:* Mediterranean Expeditionary Force and Egyptian Expeditionary Force, April, 1915, to June 1920. *Address:* Pembroke House, Cleethorpes, Lincs. *Club:* Royal Societies'.   (O6181)

FISHER, Paymaster-Lieut. William Newton, O.B.E., R.N.R.

FISK, Elsie Beatrice, M.B.E.

FISKEN, Alice Maude, M.B.E.

FISKEN, Lily Edith, M.B.E.

FISON, Edmund Towers, O.B.E., *b.* 13 Nov. 1869; *s.* of Cornell Henry Fison, of Ford Place, Thetford, Norfolk; *m.* Gertrude Mary, *d.* of F. W. King, of Rushford Lodge, Thetford, Norfolk. *Educ.:* Repton and Corpus Christi College, Cambridge. Surgeon to Salisbury Infirmary; M.O. i/c Troops Salisbury; M.O.H. and School Medical Officer, Salisbury. *War Work:* Surgeon to Salisbury Infirmary; Medical Officer to Troops, Salisbury. *Address:* 2, St. John Street, Salisbury.   (O4363)

FITCH, Sir Cecil Edwin, K.B.E., M.A., LL.B., *b.* 13 Oct. 1870; *s.* of Edwin Fitch, of Frognal Priory, N.W.; *m.* Lillian, *d.* of Col. Alexander Gordon, of Hamilton, Ohio. *Educ.:* Privately, and Jesus College, Cambridge. Barrister-at-law, 1895; Unionist Candidate, E. Norfolk, Jan. 1910, and mid-Gloucester, Dec. 1910. *War Work:* Raised some 3000 recruits; Examiner for Lord Bryce's Commission on Belgian Atrocities; Enlisted, Jan. 1915; Commissioned Lieut., March, 1915; Capt., May, 1915 (Gloucester Regt.); Major, Nov. 1915, (Worcester Regt.), Lieut.-Col., R.W.F., April, 1917; Mentioned in Despatches. *Addresses:* Gordon Dene, Princes Road, Wimbledon Park, S.W.19; St. Anslem, Walmer, Kent. *Clubs:* Carlton; Oxford and Cambridge; Ranelagh.   (K372)

FITCH, Rev. Edward Arnold, O.B.E., C.F., *b.* 23 Feb. 1880; *s.* of Rev. E. H. Fitch, of Burgh-by-Sands, Cumberland; *m.* Dorothy Ingram, *d.* of Rev. Dr. Shaw, of Thame Grammar School, Oxon. *Educ.:* Denstane College; Bradford Technical College; Edinburgh Theological College. Curate, St. James, Leith, 1905–10; Chaplain to Forces, 1910; Stations—Woolwich, Curragh, Harrismith, Pretoria, Bloemfontein, Wareham. *War Work:* C.F., 15th Inf. Brigade, B.E.F.; C.F. 41st Division, B.E.F.; D.A.C.G., XIXth Corps, B.E.F.; A.C.G., Havre Area, B.E.F. *Address:* " The Homestead," Wareham, Dorset.   (O1024)

FITCH, Paymaster-Lieut. Henry Maldon, O.B.E., R.N.

FITCH, Major Vernon Frederick, O.B.E., T.D., R.F.A. (T.), *b.* 20 May, 1880; *s.* of Herbert Fitch, of Kensington. *Educ.:* St. Paul's, London. Director of Herbert Fitch & Co., Ltd., Printers, London. *War Work:* Raised and trained 2/3rd and 3/3rd London Brigade, R.F.A. (T.); trained first 1500 R.F.A. Derby Recruits; served with the B.E.F. as Battery Commander in the 56th (London) and 36th (Ulster) Division. *Club:* Royal Automobile.   (O7147)

FITCHETT, Capt. and Qr.-Mr. William Graham Lawson, M.B.E., R.A.M.C.

FITT, Adelaide, Mrs., M.B.E., *b.* 20 June, 1854; *d.* of Joseph Fogerty, of Henry Street, Limerick; *m.* Charles H., *s.* of Edward Fitt, of Corbally, Limerick. *Educ.:* Privately. *War Work:* Member of Local War Pensions Committee, Limerick, since 1914. *Address:* Maryville, Corbally, Limerick, Co. Limerick, Ireland.   (M8091)

FITTALL, Robert John, O.B.E., *b.* 1870; *s.* of the late John Edward Fittall, of Derby; *m.* Florence Emma, *d.* of the late John Fearn, of Derby. Solicitor and Town Clerk of Plymouth; Registration Officer and Deputy Clerk of the Peace. *War Work:* Clerk to Local Tribunal; Executive Officer Food Control Committee, and Area Organising Officer for Cornwall and a district of Devon. *Addresses:* 6, Osborne Villas, Devonport; Bickleigh, Devon. *Club:* The Royal Western Yacht (Plymouth).   (O10404)

FITTON, John Herbert, O.B.E. For work in connection with the Wool Textile Dept.   (O11903)

FITZGERALD, Lieut.-Col. Arthur, O.B.E., I.A.

FITZGERALD, Edward, C.B.E.; Deputy-Chairman, Canadian Committee, Hudson's Bay Company, *b.* 9 Nov. 1874; *s.* of Charles Lionel John, of Ottawa; *m.* Kate, *d.* of John Bulmer, of Montreal, Quebec. *Educ.:* Model School, Ottawa, Canada. *War Work:* Imperial Munitions Board (Canada). *Address:* 807, Electric Ry. Chambers, Winnipeg, Manitoba, Canada. *Club:* Manitoba.   (C159)

FITZGERALD, Edward Henry, O.B.E., *b.* 1857; *s.* of John B. FitzGerald; *m.* Jessie, *d.* of Wm. Kirtland. *War Work:* Special Committee, Tea Brokers' Association, London. *Address:* c/o Stenning, Inskipp & Co., 14, Mincing Lane, E.C.   (O10405)

FITZGERALD, Francis John, C.B.E., J.P., M.A., LL.B., *b.* 4 July, 1864; *s.* of the Hon. Nicholas FitzGerald, of Melbourne, Australia; *m* Hon. Mina Susanna Georgina, *d.* of William Henry John, 11th Baron North, of Wroxton Abbey, Banbury. *Educ.:* Oscott and Trinity College, Dublin. Barrister-at-Law, Middle Temple; Recorder of Newbury. *War Work:* 1914, served in France with hospital unit attached to the Expeditionary Force; 1914 Medal; 1916–19, Chairman of the Oxfordshire Appeal Tribunal. *Addresses:* Wroxton, Banbury; 3, Pump Court, Temple, E.C.4. *Clubs:* Carlton; Marlborough. (C961)

FITZGERALD, Frank, M.B.E., R.A.S.C.

FITZGERALD, Lieut.-Col. Gordon William, O.B.E., R.A.M.C. (T.F.)

FITZGERALD, Henry Frederick, M.B.E.

FITZ-GERALD, Rev. Henry Purefoy, M.B.E., F.L.S., M.A., *b.* 27 May, 1867; *s.* of Lieut.-Col. R. Purefoy FitzGerald of Preston, Candover, Hants.; *m.* Lilian Mary, *d.* of W. Langton, of Gatcombe House, I. of W. *Educ.:* Clifton Coll.; Keble Coll., Oxford. Senior Science Master, Wellington Coll., 1893–1908. *War Work:* Commandant, Lidwells Auxiliary Military Hospital, Goudhurst, Kent; Member of Tribunal; Food Control; Coal Control; War Agricultural Committee's representative; Chairman, Cranbrook War Agricultural Sub-Committee; Head Special Constable, Goudhurst. *Address:* Lidwells, Goudhurst, Kent. *Clubs:* New; Oxford and Cambridge. (M8092)

FITZGERALD, The Rev. James Charles, O.B.E.

FITZGERALD, Capt. John Sidney North, M.B.E., M.C.

FITZGERALD, John Thomas, M.B.E. (M10386)

FITZGERALD, Marion, Mrs., C.B.E., *b.* 1860; *d.* of Mahony Harte, of Batterfield House, Co. Kerry; *m.* Robert John, *s.* of Sir Peter FitzGerald, Bart., Knight of Kerry, of Valencia Island, Ireland. *War Work:* President, Co. Kerry Soldiers' and Sailors' Families Association; Chairman, Co. Kerry War Pensions Committee; Commandant, Kerry 4 V.A.D.; President and Hon. Sec., Red Cross Working Association. *Address:* 10, Milner Street, Cadogan Square, S.W. (C2609)

FITZGERALD, 2nd Lieut. Maurice Bolton, M.B.E., R.A.U.

FITZGERALD, Capt. Maurice Edward William, O.B.E., R.E.

FITZGERALD, Major Thomas Patrick, O.B.E., *b.* 16 Aug. 1853; *s.* of the late Rev. T. M. FitzGerald; *m.* Sarah, *d.* of William Waite, of Glenavy, Co. Antrim. *Educ.:* Kingswood School, Bath. *War Work:* Senior Assistant Officer, R.G.A. Record Office, Dover. *Address:* 3, Belgrave Road, Monkstown, Co. Dublin. (O8806)

FITZGERALD, William, O.B.E.; *s.* of William Sanderson FitzGerald, of Dunedin, New Zealand; *m.* Kathleen May, *d.* of William Woodville Shelmerding, of Dunedin N.Z. and Manchester. *Educ.:* Oamaru (N.Z.) Grammar School, Otago (N.Z.) University; Edinburgh Univ. Medical Practitioner; Assistant Director (Medical Intelligence Branch) Medical Services Division, Ministry of Pensions; formerly Surgeon-Capt. New Zealand Volunteer Medical Staff Corps; Medals in Anatomy and Practice of Medicine at Royal College of Surgeons, Edinburgh. *War Work:* Examiner of Recruits (under War Office) Manchester and Liverpool; member of Liverpool No. 1 Medical Board; Deputy Commissioner of Medical Services (Ministry of National Service); in charge of Liverpool Recruiting Medical Boards. *Address:* c/o High Commissioner for New Zealand, N.Z. Government Offices, Strand, London. (O11785g)

FITZGERALD, Lieut.-Col. William Coulson, O.B.E.

FITZHERBERT, Lieut.-Col. Norman, C.M.G., D.S.O., New Zealand Exp. Force, *b.* 29 March, 1863; 4th *s.* of Sir Henry FitzHerbert, 3rd Bt. (*see* BURKE'S *Peerage*); *m.* 22 April, 1898, Esther Beresford, 2nd *d.* of the late Henry Sproule, of Ennis, Co. Clare, and widow of Neville Sinclair, M.D. Served in the S. African War and in the Great War. *Address:* Aberfeldie, Wanganui, New Zealand. (C2197)

FITZJOHN, Lieut.-Col. Geoffrey Nigel, O.B.E.

FITZMAURICE, Henry, M.B.E.

FITZMAURICE, Lieut.-Col. Robert, O.B.E., D.S.O., R.F.A., *b.* 1866; served in the Great War, 1914–17 (despatches). (C2106)

FITZPATRICK, Alice Harriet, M.B.E., *b.* 5 June, 1876. *War Work:* Sec. of Bowood V.A.D. Hospital, Sept. 1916 to June, 1919. *Address:* Little Cacketts, Brasted, Kent. (M8093)

FITZPATRICK, Col. Ernest Richard, C.B.E., D.S.O., *b.* 1878. Major and Brevet Lieut.-Col. N. Lancashire Regt., a Dep. Director of Personal Services at the War Office, with rank of Col.; served in the S. African War, 1899–1902 (Queen's medal with four clasps, King's medal with two clasps); Great War, 1914–18 (despatches, Brevet-Lieut.-Col.) (C1564)

FITZPATRICK, Gerald Coleman, O.B.E. (O12046)

FITZPATRICK, Lieut.-Col. Herbert Lindsay, C.B.E. On Special List; Red Cross Commr., Salonica (Order of White Eagle); Knight of Grace of Order of St. John of Jerusalem in England. (C161)

FITZPATRICK, James Alexander Ossory, C.I.E., C.B.E., LL.B. (C1075)

FITZPATRICK, Matthew Joseph McKEAN-, M.B.E., M.I.E.S.S., *b.* 9 July, 1868; *s.* of Peter McKean, of Glasgow; *m.* Kyle, *d.* of John Kyle, of Glasgow. *Educ.:* St. Margaret's R.C. School, Kinning Park, Glasgow. Consulting Engineer (Marine), late Senior Engineer, Marine Dept., Nigeria. *War*

Work: Appointed Staff Engineer (Nigerian Marine Contingent), Cameroon Expedition; Principally engaged on Salvage of vessels wrecked by enemy to form barrage of Duala River; Vice-President of the Priority Committee, appointed by the Governor-General of Nigeria, to control the requisitions of Government and merchant demands for material to be used in the Colony during the war. *Address:* Rosegarth, Bearsden, Glasgow. *Club:* Corona. (M1264)

FITZROY, Muriel, Hon. Mrs. C.B.E., *b.* 8 Aug. 1869; *d.* of late Col. Hon. Archibald Douglas Pennant; *m.* Capt. Hon. Edward Algernon FitzRoy, M.P., *s.* of late Charles, 4th Baron Southampton (*see* BURKE'S *Peerage*). *War Work:* Commandant in charge of General Service V.A.D.'s in Military Hospital's at home and abroad; Staff Commandant H.Q. Staff of British Red Cross Society and the Order of St. John. *Address:* Fox Hill, West Haddon, Rugby. *Clubs:* Ladies' Imperial; Ladies' V.A.D. (C497)

FITZSIMON, Lieut. Samuel Ernest Sydney, M.B.E.

FITZWATER, Wilfred George, M.B.E., S.S.M., R.A.S.C.

FITZWILLIAM, Maud Frederica Elizabeth, Countess, O.B.E., *d.* 9 July, 1877; *d.* of Lawrence Dundas, 1st Marquess of Zetland, of Aske, Co. York; *m.* William Charles De Meuron 7th Earl Fitzwilliam (*see* BURKE'S *Peerage*). *War Work:* Y.M.C.A. Munition Workers Canteens; Earl Fitzwilliam's Wentworth Hunt and Stud. *Addresses:* (see Fitzwilliam, Earl). (O10406)

FITZWILLIAM, Sir William Charles de Meuron Wentworth-Fitzwilliam, Earl, K.C.V.O., C.B.E., D.S.O.; *b.* 1872, *s.* of William, Viscount Milton, *e. s.* of William Thomas Spencer, 6th Earl Fitzwilliam; *m.* 1896 Lady Maud Dundas, D.B.E. (*q.v.*), *d.* of the Marquis of Zetland (*see* BURKE'S *Peerage*). *Addresses:* Wentworth Woodhouse, Rotherham, Yorks.; 4, Grosvenor Square, W. 1; Coollattin, Shillelagh, Co. Wicklow. (C1565)

FLACK, Lieut. (Capt.) Hugh Linley, M.B.E., R.A.S.C. (S.R.), *b.* 28 April, 1891; *s.* of the late D. L. Flack, of Airedale, Worthing, Sussex; *m.* Neste. Margaret, *d.* of W. J. Jones, of The Grange, Highbury New Park, London, N. 5. *War Work:* Served with 3rd Batt. Buffs.; transferred to R.A.S.C.; served in France and Mesopotamia. *Address:* c/o Airedale, Worthing. (O6620)

FLACK, Hon. Lieut.-Col. Martin William, C.B.E., M.B., R.A.F. Served in the Great War, 1914–19 (despatches). (C859)

FLANAGAN, Mary, M.B.E. (M10248a)

FLANNERY, Capt. Harold Fortescue, M.B.E., B.A., A.M.I.C.E., *b.* 13 Dec. 1883. *s.* of Sir James Fortescue Flannery, Bart., of Wethersfield Manor (*see* BURKE'S *Peerage*); *m.* Maud Ethel, *d.* of St. George Boswell, of Quebec. *Educ.:* Trinity Hall, Cambridge. Director of Flannery, Baggallay and Johnson, Ltd. *War Work:* Regimental Duty, 1914–15; Proof Officer, Canada, 1915–17; Headquarter Staff, Ministry of Munitions, 1917–19. *Address:* 11, Chester Place, Hyde Park. *Club:* Union. (M395)

FLAVELL, Thomas, M.B.E.

FLEET, Rear-Adm. Ernest James, C.B.E. Retired Capt. R.N.R.; served in E. Sudan, 1884–5; Vitu Expedition, 1890; Great War, 1914–19 (despatches). (C1924)

FLEET, Vice-Adm. Henry Louis, C.B.E., J.P., R.N., *b.* 1 May, 1850; *s.* of John George Fleet; *m.* Alice Mary, *d.* of William Frank Elliot. *Educ.:* St. Paul's. County Director of Berkshire Branch, B.R.C.S., from 1913 to present date. *Address:* The Camber, Coley Avenue, Reading. *Club:* United Service. (C498)

FLEISCHL, Major Walter, O.B.E., R.A.O.C.

FLEMING, Arthur Percy Morris, C.B.E., M.Sc. (Tech.), M.I.E.E., *b.* 16 Jan. 1881; *s.* of Frank Fleming, of Marvel, Isle of Wight; *m.* Rose Mary, *d.* of the late William Ash, of Newport, Isle of Wight. *Educ.:* Portland House Academy, Newport (I. of W.), and City and Guilds College. Manager of Research and Education Dept., Metropolitan Vickers' Electrical Co., Ltd., Manchester; Special Lecturer at College of Technology, Manchester; Past Chairman, Institution of Electrical Engineers (North Western Centre); Author of Engineering as a Profession; Principles of Apprentice Training; Insulation and Electrical Windings; Industrial Research in the U.S.A., etc. *War Work:* Organised at the request of the Admiralty, and was Vice-Chairman of, the Lancashire Anti-Submarine Committee; organised a centre at the Royal Naval Depot, Crystal Palace, London, for the selection and training of anti-submarine staff. *Address:* West Gables, Hale Road, Hale, Cheshire. *Club:* Engineers'. (C2610)

FLEMING, Lieut.-Col. Baldwyn Henry Francis, O.B.E., *b.* 12 Jan. 1880; *s.* of Baldwyn Fleming, of Westaway, Godalming, Surrey; *m.* Frances Isabel, *d.* of Frank Verrall, of The Manor House, Lewes. *Educ.:* Beaumont College, Old Windsor. Officer H.M. Land Forces Commission, Aug. 1900. *War Work:* Military Service; Latterly Officer, i/c Machine Gun Corps Records. *Address:* Westaway, Godalming, Surrey. *Club:* Junior United Service. (O4327)

FLEMING, Edith May, M.B.E., *b.* 28 Oct. 1895; *d.* of Henry Jones Fleming, of Westcliff-on-Sea. *Educ.:* Holmwood Coll., Westcliff-on-Sea. *War Work:* Temp. Clerk, War Office, since Aug. 1916. *Address:* 52, Elderton Road, Westcliff-on-Sea. (M8094),

FLEMING, Frederick Alexander, M.B.E., *b.* 7 Sept. 1873; *s.* of Peter Fleming, of Newport, Fife. *Educ.:* Dundee High School. Engineer; General Manager of The Grimsby Ice Co., Ltd., Fish Docks, Grimsby. *War Work:* Manager of The National Shell Factory, Grimsby. *Address:* 4, Mill Road, Cleethorpes, Lincs. (M8095)

FLEMING, Frederic John, M.B.E.

FLEMING, Capt. Geoffrey Balmanno, M.B.E., M.D., R.A.M.C. (T.F.), *b.* 20 Feb. 1882 ; *s.* of William James Fleming M.D., of Glasgow. *Educ.:* Haileybury Coll., and King's Coll., Cambridge. Dispensary Physician, Royal Hospital for Sick Children, Glasgow. *War Work:* Mediterranean Expeditionary Force, 1915 ; East African Expeditionary Force, 1916–19 ; Acting Major, 1917–19. *Address:* 13, Lynedoch Crescent, Glasgow. *Club:* Western (Glasgow). (M3043)

FLEMING, Major Henry Slane, O.B.E.

FLEMING, James Finlayson, O.B.E., M.B., Ch.B., *b.* 2 April, 1875 ; *s.* of Rev. Andrew Gibb Fleming, of Paisley. *Educ.:* Paisley Grammar School, Glasgow University. Medical Practitioner. *War Work:* Medical officer in charge Dunfermline Auxiliary Military Hospital. *Address:* Dunsloy, Dunfermline, Fife. (O4364)

FLEMING, Rev. James William, O.B.E., M.A., B.D., D.D., *b.* 28 Aug. 1855 ; *s.* of John Fleming, of Ballindalloch, N.B. ; *m.* Elizabeth Ann, *d.* of Rev. Hugh McDiarmid, D.D., of Callander, N.B. *Educ.:* Aberdeen and Edinburgh Universities. Minister of the Scots Church, Buenos Ayres. *War Work:* Member of various Committees in the Argentine Republic. *Address:* Calle Peru 352, Buenos Ayres. *Club:* The Strangers' (Buenos Ayres). (O10409)

FLEMING, Capt. John Arnold, O.B.E., J.P., *b.* 20 Nov. 1871 ; *s.* of Sir James Fleming, of Rutherglen ; *m.* Wilhelmina Reid, *d.* of Wm. Brand, of Glasgow. *Educ.:* Albany Academy and Edinburgh Univ. Hon. Sec. of Scottish Pottery Manufacturers Society ; Representative for Scotland on National Council of Pottery ; President, St. Rollox Liberal Association. *War Work:* Chemist on refractory materials for Munitions, being a Fellow of Royal Society, Edinburgh ; also mediator on Labour in Potteries in Scotland. *Address:* Locksby, Helensburgh, Dumbartonshire. *Clubs:* New ; Liberal (Glasgow). (O10407)

FLEMING, Brevet Lieut.-Col. John Gibson, C.B.E., D.S.O., R.E., *b.* 9 Jan. 1880 ; *s.* of William James Fleming of Glasgow ; *m.* Blanche Mabel, *d.* of — Déglon, of Barberton. *Educ.:* Haileybury ; Royal Military Academy, Woolwich. *War Work:* Military service ; France and Flanders. *Clubs:* United Service ; R.A.C. (C1249)

FLEMING, Lieut.-Col. John Grant, O.B.E., V.D., J.P., *b.* 14 Feb. 1859 ; *s.* of John Fleming, of Marionburgh, Ballindalloch ; *m.* Lillias Joan, *d.* of W. Cullard, of Oldmills, Elgin. *Educ.:* Edinburgh University. Solicitor and Bank Agent ; Clerk of Lieutenancy for Banffshire. *War Work:* Representative of War Office at Tribunals ; Lieut.-Col. Commanding 4th Vol. Batt., Gordon Highlanders. *Address:* Reidharm House, Keith. *Club:* Conservative, Edinburgh. (O1342)

FLEMING, Lieut.-Col. John Kenneth Sprot, O.B.E., I.M.S.

FLEMING, John Lancelot, O.B.E., *b.* 1883 ; *s.* of Thomas Fleming, of Ambleside ; *m.* Elizabeth J., *d.* of Joseph Pimbley, of Altcar. *Educ.:* St. George's, Liverpool. Diocesan Sec., Church of England Temperance Society ; Police Court Mission and St. George's Home for Boys. *War Work:* Business Manager of over ninety C.E.T.S. Recreation Rooms, etc., in Kent ; Officer of Special Constabulary, and on Special Service. *Addresses:* 41, Hoole Road, Hoole, Chester ; 39, Lower Bridge Street, Chester. (O10408)

FLEMING, The Rev. Michael Joseph, M.B.E.

FLEMING, Sarah Kate, Mrs., O.B.E. ; *d.* of Marshall Kirkland Hindmarsh, of Perthshire ; *m.* Robert, *s.* of John Fleming, of Perthshire. *Educ.:* St. Andrews and Germany. *War Work:* Converted her home into a hospital for officers and ran it entirely at her own expense. *Addresses:* 27, Grosvenor Square, London, W ; Joyce Grove, Nettlebed, Oxon. (O10410)

FLEMING, Major William Ernest, O.B.E., M.C.

FLESHER, James Arthur, O.B.E.

FLETCHER, Wing-Com. Albert, C.M.G., C.B.E., M.C., R.A.F., *b.* 1881. (C499)

FLETCHER, Lieut.-Col. Alexander Kempson, O.B.E.

FLETCHER, Arthur George Murchison, C.B.E., *b.* 27 Sept. 1878 ; *s.* of Dr. G. Fletcher, of Highgate ; *m.* Violet Dorothy, *d.* of Col. Rogers-Harrison, of Cheltenham. *Educ.:* Cheltenham, and Trinity Coll., Oxford. Civil Servant ; Acting Colonial Secretary, Hong-Kong. *War Work:* Chairman, Shipping Control Committee, and Vital Requirements Committee, Hong-Kong. *Address:* 132, The Peak, Hong Kong. *Club:* Royal Societies'. (C2019)

FLETCHER, Basil, M.B.E.

FLETCHER, Capt. Cecil John, O.B.E., A.I.F.

FLETCHER, Clarence George Eugene, C.B.E., *b.* 19 Sept. 1875 ; *s.* of George Fletcher, of Kingston-on-Thames ; *m.* Nellie, *d.* of Robert Molyneux, of Toot'ng, Surrey. *Educ.:* St. Mark's College and Privately. Barrister-at-Law ; Town Clerk of Islington ; Clerk to the Assessment Committee ; formerly Town Clerk of Bethnal Green ; Editor of Mackenzie and Lushington's Registration Manual (3rd edition), and author of Fletcher's Registration of Electors, 1908 ; President of London Town Clerks' Association, 1918. *Address:* 100, Highbury, New Park, N.S. (C2611)

FLETCHER, Surg.-Lieut. Comm. Edward Ernest, O.B.E., R.N.V.R., L.D.S.

FLETCHER, Paymaster-Sub-Lieut. Evelyn Norman Robert, M.B.E., R.N.

FLETCHER, Fanny, M.B.E.

FLETCHER, Frank Purser, O.B.E.

FLETCHER, Frederick John, M.B.E.

FLETCHER, Henry Francis, O.B.E., *b.* 20 Sept. 1866 ; *s.* of Henry Fletcher, of Higham (Notts.) ; *m.* Clara, *d.* of Alexander Scott. *Educ.:* City of London School. President, British Chamber of Commerce, 1917–18 ; founded Canadian Section of that Chamber, 1906 ; Joint Managing Director, Pitt & Scott, Ltd. *War Work:* Vice-Chairman, Paris Colony Committee formed on outbreak of War ; Member of Executive British Army and Navy Leave Club, Paris ; Member Advisory Committee to Recruiting Officer in Paris. *Addresses:* 10, Rue de la Source, Paris ; 25, Cannon Street, London. *Clubs:* New City, London ; Imperial (Paris). (O10411)

FLETCHER, Lieut.-Col. Henry Rivers, O.B.E.

FLETCHER, Lieut. John William, M.B.E.

FLETCHER, Nora Kathleen, O.B.E., R.R.C. ; *d.* of late J. W. Fletcher, M.A. Oxon. J. P., of Sydney, Australia. *Educ.:* At home. Member A.T.N. Assoc. ; College of Nursing London. *War Work:* Principal Matron British Red Cross and Order of St. John of Jerusalem, for France and Belgium, Oct. 1914 to May 1919. Decorations : C.B.E., R.R.C., 1914 Star, (British War Medal, Victory Medal ; Order of St. John of Jerusalem ; Order of Elizabeth of Belgium ; Order of Gratitude in gilt, France, and mentioned in Despatches, June, 1915. *Address:* c/o Commercial Banking Co. of Sydney, 18, Birchin Lane, E.C. ; Eamont, Greenwich, Sydney, Australia. (C2612)

FLETCHER, Stanley Hewitt, O.B.E.

FLETCHER, Violet Eastwood, M.B.E., *b.* 30 April, 1878 ; *d.* of the late John James Fletcher, Civil Engineer and Surveyor, of Botolph House, Eastcheap, E.C. *T.:* Training Coll., Stockwell. Certificated Teacher in London Education Service. Joined Camberwell Division B.R.C.S., when formed, in Feb. 1911. *War Work:* Divisional Matron, Camberwell Division, B.R.C.S., Feb. 1914 ; Commandant, Hanover Park, V.A.D. Hospital, Rye Lane, S.E. 15, Jan. 1916 to April, 1919 ; General Divisional Work. *Address:* 26, Crofton Park Road, Brockley, S.E. 4. (M8097)

FLETCHER, Col. Walter Blunt, O.B.E., *b.* 22 Mar. 1853 ; *s.* of James Fletcher, of Hampton Court ; *m.* Emily Gertrude Whitworth of Noctorian, Bidston, Cheshire. *Educ.:* Cheltenham. Various appointments on the Staff. Was in Field Artillery and served in Horse Artillery and Garrison Artillery ; Chief Staff Officer, Transvaal District, South Africa. *War Work:* Secretary, Wilts County Association. *Address:* Kingston Cottage, Bradford-on-Avon, Wilts. *Club:* Junior United Service. (O335)

FLETCHER, Sir Walter Morley, K.B.E., M.D.

FLETCHER, William Frederick Ashby, O.B.E.

FLETT, John Smith, O.B.E., D.Sc., LL.D., F.R.S., *b.* 1869 ; *s.* of James Ferguson Flett, of Kirkwall, *m.* Mary Jane, *d.* of David Meason. *Educ.:* Edinburgh University. Director, H. M. Geological Survey. *War Work:* Consulting geologist to Naval, Military and Civil departments in Scotland. *Address:* 28, Jermyn St., S.W. 1. (O1344)

FLEW, Major Edwin Howard, O.B.E., A.P.C.

FLICK, Lieut.-Col. Charles Leonard, C.M.G., C.B.E., J.P., *b.* 20 Dec. 1870 ; *s.* of Richard Flick, The Holt, Woodbridge, Suffolk ; *m.* Marie Louise, *d.* of Joseph Milward, of West Bromwich. *Educ.:* Felstead School, Essex. *War Work:* Commanded 31st Canadian Cavalry at outbreak of War, proceeded to England with 1st Canadian Contingent ; attached to 12th Royal Fusiliers, 1 March, 1915 ; commanded 7th Essex in Gallipoli ; commanded 6th Devons in Mesopotamia ; G.O.C. Euphrates, June, July, and Aug. 1918 ; commanded No. 2 Special Battalion in India and on N. W. Frontier during April, May, June, and July, 1919 ; commanded 6th Devons in England from Aug. 1919, to March, 1920. *Address:* c/o Military District No. 11, Victoria, B.C. (C1114)

FLINN, Major William Henry, O.B.E.

FLINT, Lieut. Alfred William, M.B.E.

FLINT, Frederick Theodore, M.B.E.

FLINT, Capt. and Qr.-Mr. George William, O.B.E.

FLINT, Samuel, O.B.E., J.P.

FLINT, Major Samuel Kirk, O.B.E.

FLINT, Violet Amy, Mrs., M.B.E.

FLOERSHEIM, Cecil Louis Ferdinand, C.B.E., *b.* 23 Jan. 1871 ; *s.* of Louis FerdinandFloersheim, of 12, Cadogan Square, W. ; *m.* Maud Beatrice Sleath, *d.* of James W. Skelton. *Educ.:* Eton ; Christ Church, Oxford. Barrister-at-Law. *War Work:* Royal Patriotic Fund Corporation 1914–16 ; Statutory Committee, 1916–17 ; Ministry of Pensions, 1917–19 ; *Addresses:* 29, Kensington Court Mansions, W. ; Pennyhill Park, Bagshot. *Club:* Oxford and Cambridge. (C2613)

FLOOD, Capt. Charles Bertram, O.B.E.

FLOOD, Lieut. Otto Barnes Patrick, O.B.E., R.N.R.

FLOOK, Capt. Walter Bryan, O.B.E., R.A.S.C.

FLOWER, John Walter, M.B.E.

FLOWER, Leila Beatrice, Mrs., O.B.E.

FLOWER, Major Stanley Smyth, O.B.E.

FLOWERS, Capt. Cyril, O.B.E., R.F.A. (T.F.).

FLOWERS, Capt. Stephen, O.B.E., M.C., R.E. (T.F.)

FLUDDER, Capt. George, M.B.E., R.E.

FLUDYER, Augusta Frances, Lady, M.B.E. ; 3rd *d.* of the late Sir Edward Borough, 2nd Bt. (*see* BURKE'S *Peerage*) ; *m.* 9 Sept. 1876, Sir Arthur John Fludyer, 5th Bt., J.P., D.L. and C.C. for Rutland. *Address:* Ayrton Hall, Uppingham, Rutland. (M1722)

FLYNN, The Rev. William Joseph, O.B.E., M.B.E.

BIOGRAPHIES.

FOÀ, Ferdinand Eugene, O.B.E.

FOAKES, Commander Edward Lindsay ASHLEY-, O.B.E., R.N. (ret.), *b.* 6 April, 1865; *s.* of W. H. Foakes, of Brighton; *m.* Idonea Maria. *d.* of Hon. H. F. F. A. Barrington, of Portland, Cape Colony. *Educ.:* Privately. Nautical Adviser General Post Office. *War Work:* Naval Assistant Director of Postal Services. *Address:* 55, Nassau Road, Barnes, S.W. 13. *Club:* Roehampton Club. (O100)

FOGARTY, Major Joseph Patrick, O.B.E., M.C., Aust. A.M.C., A.I.F.

FOGG, Capt. Herbert George, O.B.E., M.C., R.A.S.C., *b.* 7 Feb. 1879; *s.* of George Thomas Fogg, of Manchester; *m.* Cecily Ellen, *d,* of the late Albert Chamberlain, of London. *Educ.:* Military Schools. Officer-in-Charge Barracks, Hong Kong. *War Work:* With B.E.F., France, from Aug. 1914; M.E.F., Dardanelles; Egyptian Expeditionary Force. *Address:* R.A.S.C., Hong Kong, China. (O7155)

FOGGO, Watson, M.B.E.

FOLEY, Col. Frank Wigram, C.B.E., D.S.O., *b.* 1865; *s.* of Capt. E. Foley, R.N.; *m.* The Baroness Berkeley (*see* BURKE'S *Peerage*). *Educ.:* Tonbridge. *War Work:* Raised and commanded in France 5th Battn. Royal Berkshire Regt.; Severely wounded in France. *Address:* Southcote Lodge, Camberley. *Clubs:* United Service Club; M.C.C.; Free Foresters. (C1566)

FOLEY, Major Gerald, O.B.E., B.A., R.E., *b.* 1 Ap. 1886; *s.* of Ven. Archdeacon Foley, B.D., of Tralee. *Educ.:* Tipperary Grammar School and Trinity College, Dublin. District Inspector, Royal Irish Constabulary. *War Work:* Royal Irish Regiment; served in Salonica, Palestine and France. *Address:* R.I.C., Naas, Co. Kildare. (O5260)

FOLEY, Mary Gladys Corinne, O.B.E. R.R.C., M.M., Q.A.I.M.N.S.

FOLEY, Major Peter Trant, O.B.E., M.B.E.

FOLEY, Capt. Walter Barham, O.B.E., R.A.M.C. (S.R.), M.B.

FOLKER, Herbert Henry, O.B.E., M.R.C.S. (Eng.), L.R.C.P. (Lond.), *b.* 16 July, 1864; *s.* of William H. Folker, of Shelton, Stoke-on-Trent; *m.* Eliza Georgina, *d.* of Taylor Ashworth, of Shelton. *Educ.:* Epsom Coll.; Charing Cross Hospital. Consulting Ophthalmic Surgeon, North Staffs Infirmary and Eye Hospital; late Ophthalmic Surgeon, Blind Asylum, Stoke-on-Trent; late Certifying Factory Surgeon, Hanley, Staffs; late Ophthalmic Referee, County Court No. 26. *War Work:* County Director B.R.C., Staffs; .Capt. R.A.M.C., April, 1915, to Oct. 1917; Northern Command Headquarters, York; Deputy Commissioner of Medical Services, Nov. 1917 to date, Ministry of Pensions. (O10415)

FOLKER, Horace SHEPHERD-, C.B.E., F.A.I., *b.* 17 June, 1859; *s.* of the late Alfred Hanley Folker, of Guildford; *m.* Margaret (who died), *d.* of the late George Osborne Barratt, of London. *Educ.:* Brighton Grammar School. *War Work:* Hon. Director of the Uniforms and Equipment Dept. of the Joint War Committee, British Red Cross Society and Order of St. John; Member of the Joint War Council; also served on committees of the B.R.C.S. Finance and Compassionate Fund, 1914–19; Fire Survey Force for Prevention of Fires in Red Cross Hospitals. *Address:* Westfield, Cheam Road, Sutton, Surrey. (C162)

FOLLAND, Henry Phillip, M.B.E.

FOLLETT, Lieut.-Col. Henry Spencer, C.B.E., J.P., *b.* 27 July, 1866; *s.* of Sir Charles Follett, C.B.; *m.* Dorothy Margaret, *d.* of W. N. Champion, of Riddlesworth Hall, Norfolk. *Educ.:* Wellington and R.M.C. Sandhurst. *War Work:* Commanded 17th Divisional Train, England and France 1914–16; Commanded Officers Command Depot, Eastbourne, 1916–19. *Address:* Rockbeare House, S. Devon. *Clubs:* Boodle's; Cavalry. (C1567)

FOLLETT, Robert Charles, M.B.E., *b.* 5 May 1872; *s.* of Edward Way Follett, of Bighton Manor, Alresford, Hants; *m.* Florence, *d.* of late Walter Carr, of Batley, Yorkshire. *Educ.:* Ockham Grammar School, Kingsley, Hants. H.M. Inspector under the Aliens Act. *War Work:* Adjutant to the City of Hull Special Constabulary Force, numbering 3,000 Officers and Men; For work in connection with Belgian War Refugees, received from H.M. the King of the Belgians the Golden Palms of the Order of the Crown. *Address:* Mead House, Anlaby Park, Nr. Hull. *Club:* Constitutional, Hull. (M398)

FOLLOWS, Major John Henry, C.B.E., *b.* 9 Sept. 1869; *s.* of Amos Follows, of Sandiacre, Derbyshire; *m.* Amy *d.* of Edward Farnsworth, of Riddings, Derbyshire. *Educ.:* Risley Grammar School. General Superintendent of the Midland Railway, England. *War Work:* Directed transport of troops and war traffic generally over the whole area covered by the Midland Railway System; accompanied Government Commission to Italy as Railway Representative in 1917. *Address:* The Poplars, Spondon, Nr. Derby. (C163)

FOOKS, Amy Harriet, M.B.E.; *d.* of John Fooks, of Cottesmore, Brentwood. *Educ.:* Brighton High School. *War Work:* General Service (V.A.D.) and Labour Superintendent at Colchester Military Hospital from 1916–1919. *Address:* Cottesmore, Brentwood. (M8100)

FOOKS, Philip Edward Broadley, M.B.E., R.G.A. (T.F.), *b.* 9 May, 1884; *s.* of Edward J. Fooks, of Langton House, Langton Green, Kent; *m.* Mary Beatrice, *d.* of Major R. H. Graham, of Longley Hall, Huddersfield. *Educ.:* St. Augustine's, Ramsgate; New Coll., Oxford. Solicitor. *War Work:* Anti-aircraft defences and G.S.O., II., H.Q. London Air De-

fence Area, Horse Guards. *Address:* St. Maddens, Chislehurst; 60, Carey Street, Lincoln's Inn. *Club:* Oxford and Cambridge. (M1724)

FOORD, Walter James, M.B.E., *b.* 7 June,1874; *s.* of Q.M.S. Foord, 9th Lancers; *m.* Plevna Mary, *d.* of Q.M.S. Harrison, R.M.L.I. *Educ.:* Royal Hibernian Military School. Government Clerk. *War Work:* Chief Clerk, Registry, Headquarters, Southern Command, Salisbury. *Address:* Thirlmere, 22, Carlton Road, Bournemouth. (M8101)

FOOT, Rear-Adm. Cunningham Robert de Clare, C.B.E., R.N. (ret.), *b.* 1864; *s.* of the Rev. Cunningham Noel Foot, formerly R. of Dogmersfield, Hants.; *m.* Mary, *d.* of Rear-Adm. John Ingles. *War Work:* 1914–19 with Ocean Escort (despatches). *Address:* Upper Restoration House, Maidstone Road, Rochester. *Club:* United Service. (C1186)

FOOT, George Edgar, O.B.E.

FOOT, Phyllis Margaret, Mrs., M.B.E., *b.* 1888; *m.* Robert William, O.B.E., M.C. *Educ.:* Hyde Park New Coll., and France. *War Work:* Administrative Assistant and Staff Officer, Gun Ammunition Dept., Ministry of Munitions, 1915–19. *Address:* 14A, Chester House, Eccleston Place, S.W. 1. *Club:* Roehampton. (M1725)

FOOT, Capt. Robert William, O.B.E., M.C., R.F.A.

FOOTMAN, Harold, O.B.E.

FOOTNER, Capt. Bertram Maughan, M.B.E., R.A.M.C. (T.F.)

FORAN, Major Robert, O.B.E., A.P.C.

FORBER, Edward Rodolph, C.B.E. Secretary Military Service (Civil Liabilities) Committee. (C164)

FORBES, Alexander, C.B.E., *b.* 30 May, 1860; *s.* of Charles and Elizabeth Forbes, Belmont, Meigle, Perthshire; *m.* Elizabeth McGlashan Low; *d.* of Capt. Peter Low, of Dundee. *Educ.:* Meigle Public School, Perthshire. Manager, Standard Oil Co. of New York at Rangoon; Hon. Magistrate, Rangoon, since, 1906; Member of the Municipal Committee of Rangoon since 1903. *Addresses:* Strathmore, Boundary Road, Rangoon; Craigatin House, Pitlochry, Perthshire. (C2380)

FORBES, Major Alister Esme Buchan, O.B.E.

FORBES, Arthur Charles, O.B.E., F.H.A.S., M.R.I.A., *b.* 1866; *s.* of John Malcolm Forbes, of Farnham Royal, Bucks. *Educ.:* Beaconsfield School; Edinburgh University. Forestry Officer; Assistant Commissioner, Forestry Commission. *War Work:* Assistant Controller, Timber Supplies (Ireland). *Address:* Avondale, Rathdrum, Co. Wicklow. (O3715)

FORBES, Brig.-Gen. Sir Arthur Wm., K.B.E., C.B., *b.* 17 Sept. 1858 (*see* BURKE'S *Peerage*); *s.* of the late Francis Charles Forbes, I.C.S.; *m.* 1892, Marion Harriet, *d.* of Gen. Sir Horace Searle Anderson, K.C.B., late Indian Army. Embarkation Officer, Devonport, 1916–18, and at Liverpool 1918. *Address:* 11, Linton Road, Oxford. *Club:* Junior United Service. (K278)

FORBES, Barbara Donald, Mrs., M.B.E.; *d.* of John Jackson, of Shawhill and Solway Bank, Dumfriesshire; *m.* James Forbes, M.V.O., formerly commissioner to Queen Victoria and afterwards to Hugh Morrison, of Islay. *War Work:* Red Cross, Islay, County of Argyll. *Address:* Eallabus, Bridgend, Islay. (M8102)

FORBES, Major Hon. Bertram Aloysius, O.B.E.

FORBES, Duncan, M.B.E., M.D., B.Sc., D.P.H., *b.* 7 Dec. 1873; *s.* of Duncan Forbes, Engineer, of Perth; *m.* Kathleen Penfold, *d.* of Edwin Penfold Hall, of Brighton. *Educ.:* Perth Academy and Edinburgh Univ. Medical Officer of Health for Brighton. *War Work:* Fever cases from camps mid-Sussex, attended at Brighton Fever Hospital, particularly cerebrospinal fever; assistance to Military Authorities in sanitary matters in connection with hospitals, including Indian Hospital in Brighton; opinions given to Brighton tribunal and military authorities as to doubtful tuberculosis cases. *Address:* Town Hall, Brighton; 4, Goldsmid Road, Brighton. (M1726)

FORBES, Eliza Mary, M.B.E., *b.* 1856; *d.* of Alexander Clerk Forbes, J.P., of Whitchurch, Oxon. *Educ.:* Privately. *War Work:* Commandant of Devon 58; in charge of Red Cross Hospital, Chudleigh, from Oct. 1914 to Feb. 1919. *Address:* Swanston House, Chudleigh, Devon. *Club:* V.A.D. (M3645)

FORBES, Lieut. Gordon Harold Norman, O.B.E.

FORBES, James, M.B.E.

FORBES, Lieut. and Qr.-Mr. James George Annand, M.B.E., R.A.M.C., *b.* 4 June, 1885; *s.* of George Forbes, of Glasgow; *m.* Henda Catherine, *d.* of Duncan Cameron, of Edinburgh. *Educ.:* Oldmeldrum, Aberdeenshire. Controller of Stores, Ministry of Pensions Hospital, Orpington, Kent. S.A. Campaign, 5 clasps, Queen's Medal. *War Work:* Served in France with 4th Stationary Hospital, Aug. 1914 to Nov. 1916; Sanitary Inspector at Poperinghe, Belgium, April, 1917; with 4th London Field Ambulance, proceeded to N. Russia, Nov 1918 to Nov. 1919. *Address:* Ministry of Pensions Hospital, Orpington. (M6996)

FORBES, Wing-Comm. James Louis, O.B.E., R.A.F.

FORBES, Mary Constance, M.B.E.; *d.* of Captain T. Arthur Forbes, R.N., of West Coates, Berwick-on-Tweed. *Educ.:* At Home. *War Work:* Hon. Sec. Red Cross Clothing Committee, Edinburgh; also canteen work. *Address:* 11, Darnaway St., Edinburgh. *Club:* Ladies' Army and Navy. (M399)

FORBES, Paymaster-Sub-Lieut. Robert, M.B.E., R.N.V.R.

FORBES, Col. Ronald Foster, D.S.O., O.B.E., *b.* 1881;

O

s. of the late Lieut.-Col. John Foster Forbes, of Rothiemay Castle, Banffshire; *m.* 1911, Joan Roseta (who obtained a divorce 1917), *d.* of Herbert James Torr, of Morton Hall, Lincolnshire. *Educ.:* Privately. Major, Highland L.I.; Comdt. of a Sch. of Instruction, with rank of Col.; served in the S. African War, 1899–1901 (Queen's medal with three clasps); Great War, 1914–18, as Lieut.-Col. Comdg. a Batt. (despatches); was A.D.C. to Govr. of N.S. Wales, 1913. *Clubs:* Naval and Military; Caledonian. (O5264)

FORBES, William, M.B.E., J.P.

FORBES, Comm. William Stronach Foster, O.B.E., R.N.

FORBES, Major William Wood, O.B.E., L.R.C.P., L.R.C.S. Ed., L.R.F.P. & S. Glas.; *s.* of the late Fleet-Surgeon Charles Forbes, M.D., R.N. *Educ.:* Edinburgh Univ. *War Work:* R.A.M.C, Gallipoli, Mesopotamia, and Egypt; mentioned in Lord Allenby's despatches; 1914–15 Star. (O2893)

FORBES, Capt. Bertram Francis Alex GORDON-, O.B.E., R.A.O.C.

FORD, Allen Edward, O.B.E.

FORD, Arthur Clow, M.B.E., B.A., L.C.P., *b.* 23 Jan. 1882; *s.* of George Ford, of Portobello, N.B.; *m.* Cecilia Jessie, *d.* of William Kinvig, of Portobello, N.B. *Educ.:* George Watson's Coll., Edinburgh; Universities of London and Lausanne. Sec. at the Central Offices of the Univ. of London. *War Work:* Chairman of the School for British Civilian Prisoners of War interned in Ruhleben Camp, Spandau, Germany from 1914–18. *Address:* La Rosiaz, Court Road, Upper Caterham, Surrey. (M8105)

FORD, Hon. Cadet Col. Commandant Everard Allen, O.B.E., *b.* 29 June, 1845; *s.* of Rev. Joseph Ford, of Hampstead; *m.* Rachel, *d.* of Rev. Sir St. Vincent Hammick, Bart., of Milton Abbot, Devon (*see* BURKE'S *Peerage*). *Educ.:* Edinburgh Academy. *War Work:* Col. Comdt. London Diocesan Church Lads' Brigade and Commissioner for Diocesan Boy Scout Association. *Address:* 2, Eldon Road, Hampstead. *Club:* Junior Carlton. (O3716)

FORD, Major George Newton, O.B.E., *b.* 24 Sept. 1874; *s.* of Ernest Ford, of Edinburgh; *m.* Adelaide Dickinson, *d.* of John Ten Broeck Hillhouse, of New York. *Educ.:* St. Paul's School, London. District Superintendent L. & N.W. Rly.; Traffic Superintendent N.L.R.; Sec. N. & S.-W. U. Rly. Joint Committee. *War Work:* Served in France; Capt. and Major, London Scottish; Brigade Major East Lancashire (R.) Brigade, and Yorkshire Coast Defences. *Address:* 69, Oxford Gardens, London, W. *Club:* The Bath. (O7158)

FORD, Capt. Harry Gilbert, O.B.E., R.A.F.

FORD, Lieut. Harry Spry, M.B.E., R.A.S.C.

FORD, John, M.B.E.

FORD, Major John Theodore, O.B.E., 3rd Batt. Hampshire Regt. (ret.), *b.* 31 Aug. 1881; *s.* of Arthur Vernon Ford, M.R.C.S., of Portsmouth, Hampshire; *m.* Ethel Mary St. Clair, *d.* of the late Surgeon-General James Davis, A.M. Staff. *Educ.:* Portsmouth Grammar School. Assistant Treas. and Comptroller, Shanghai Municipal Council, China. *War Work:* Gallipoli Expedition; afterwards specially employed; date of first commission, Sept. 1902; retired Jan. 1920. *Address:* c/o Municipal Council, Shanghai, China. *Club:* Junior Naval and Military. (O7159)

FORD, Norman Thomas, O.B.E.

FORD, Comm. Reginald Bertram, O.B.E., R.N.R.

FORD, Brevet Lieut.-Col. Richard Vernon Tredinnick, C.B.E., R.M.A., *b.* 18 Feb. 1878; *s.* of the late Arthur Vernon Ford, M.R.C.S., of Sea View, Isle of Wight. Adjutant, Royal Marine Artillery, 1904–9; Brigade Major, Royal Marine Artillery, 1912–17; D.A.A.G., Royal Marines, 1918 to date. *War Work:* Brigade Major, Royal Artillery on outbreak of war, afterwards commanded R.M.A. Heavy Siege Train and Heavy Group of Heavy Siege Guns on the coast of Belgium; recalled in July 1918 to take up appointment of D.A.A.G., Royal Marines at the Admiralty. *Club:* Junior Army and Navy. (C2309)

FORD, Major Stanley William, O.B.E.

FORD, Lieut. Thomas, M.B.E., R.E.

FORD, Thomas Benjamin, M.B.E., *b.* 3 Nov. 1886; *s.* of Joseph John Ford, of Islington, London, N. *Educ.:* France; Privately; Northern Polytechnic Institute, London, N. Confidential Shorthand Writer; Clerk and Archivist to His Majesty's Secretary of State for Foreign Affairs. *Addresses:* 84, Normandy Avenue, Barnet, Herts; Foreign Office, Downing Street, London, S.W. 1. (M8106)

FORD, William George, M.B.E., A.M.Inst.T., *b.* 23 Jan. 1879; *s.* of William Ford, of West Dean, Sussex; *m.* Winnie Ethel, *d.* of T. H. Inkson, of Norwich. *Educ.:* Privately. Assistant Divisional Road Transport Officer, Ministry of Food. *War Work:* Road Transport Board, Board of Trade; subsequently Ministry of Food. *Address:* 59, Lensfield Road, Cambridge. (M8107)

FORD, Lieut. ST. CLAIR-, M.B.E.

FORDHAM, Edward Wilfrid, O.B.E., B.A., LL.B., *b.* 30 Nov. 1874; *s.* of John Hampden Fordham, of 9, Phillimore Gardens, W. 2, and Melbourn Bury, Royston, Herts; *m.* Sybil Harriet, *d.* of Charles Langdon-Davies, of London. *Educ.:* St. Paul's School; and Trinity Coll., Cambridge. Chief Clerk, Solicitor's Department, Ministry of Labour. *War Work:* Legal Assistant, Ministry of Munitions; Special Constable. *Address:* Mill Vale, Bromley, Kent. *Club:* Royal Automobile. (O10147)

FORDHAM, Major John Guerney, O.B.E.

FORDHAM, Lieut. Percy John Richmond, M.B.E.

FORDYCE, John Gordon, C.B.E. Chief Engineer, s.s. " Grantully Castle." (C3107c)

FOREMAN, Major Cornelius William, O.B.E., Res. of Officers, *b.* 17 Dec. 1881; *s.* of Charles Foreman, of Salisbury; *m.* Ethel Mary, *d.* of Philip Henry Palmer, of St. Leonards. *Educ.:* Privately. Land Agent. Served in the Imp. Yeomanry, South African War, 1900–2. *War Work:* Res. of Officers, posted to R.A.S.C. on being called up in 1914; Transport Officer, Northern Lines Communication, March, 1915, to Aug. 1916; 55th Div. Train, Aug. 1916 to Nov. 1916; Adjt. 65th Div. Train, Curragh, Dec. 1916 to March, 1918; O.C. R.A.S.C. Fermoy, S.D., March, 1918, to Dec. 1919. *Address:* Springfield, Fermoy. (O7160)

FOREMAN, Sir Henry, O.B.E. M.P. for Hammersmith since 1918; Mayor of Hammersmith since 1913; Col. of Hammersmith Cadet Corps, and raised Heavy Battery and Ammunition Column in Great War. *Address:* 4, York Mansions, Earls Court, S.W. 5. (O336)

FORESHEW, Ernest, M.B.E.

FORMAN, Rev. Adam, C.B.E., *b.* 1876; *s.* of John Turnbull Forman, of Liverpool; *m.* Flora Gordon, *d.* of James Smith, of Liverpool. *Educ.:* Loretto and Pembroke College, Cambridge. *War Work:* Hon. Secy., Joint Sphagnum Moss Committee for Scotland for supplying dressings to Military Hospitals and H.M. Forces. *Address:* Craigielands, Beattock, Scotland. (C962)

FORMAN, Bernard Gilpin, M.B.E., M.B., B.S., Ch.B., *b.* 26 July, 1874; *s.* of John Forman, of Churchill House, Edinburgh; *m.* Fanny Evelyn, *d.* of Vincent Charles Stuart Wortley Corbett, of Chilton Moor House, Fencehouses, Co. Durham. *Educ.:* Merchiston Castle School, Edinburgh, and Edinburgh Univ. Medical Officer of Health, Scalby Urban District Council; Hon. Life Member British Red Cross Society. *War Work:* Commandant and Medical Officer, Cober Hill Hospital, Cloughton, Scarborough. *Address:* The Beeches, Cloughton, Scarborough. (M8108)

FORMBY, Capt. Hugh Carlton, O.B.E.

FORMBY, Lieut.-Col. John, O.B.E.

FORREST, Alfred Wightman, M.B.E., M.B., C.M.

FORREST, Lieut. David, O.B.E.

FORREST, Lieut.-Col. James, C.M.G., O.B.E., *b.* 1859; *s.* of the late James Forrest, J.P., of Thornhill, Stillorgan, Co. Dublin. *Educ.:* Rugby, and Trinity Coll., Dublin. *War Work:* Served Nile Expedition, 1898 (despatches, Egyptian Medal, 2 clasps, medal); S. Africa, 1899–1902 (Queen's medal, 3 clasps; King's medal, 2 clasps); European War, 1914–19; twice mentioned in despatches. *Address:* Lymehurst, Blackrock, Co. Dublin. *Club:* Naval and Military. (O6366)

FORREST, John William, O.B.E., *b.* 13 March, 1867, *s.* of John Forrest, of Blackburn; *m.* Alice Dugdale, *d.* of William Carr, of Blackburn. *Educ.:* Blackburn Grammar School. Town Councillor; Chairman Blackburn Education Committee; Chairman Corporation Finance Committee; Chairman Blackburn Conservative Association; Member Central Executive Cotton Spinners' and Manufacturers' Association. *War Work:* Recruiting; War Savings; organised War Pensions Committee, Blackburn; Chairman until July, 1919. *Address:* Meins Road, Blackburn. *Clubs:* Union and Conservative; Blackburn. (O10418)

FORREST, Major Robert, M.B.E., *b.* 4 Oct. 1875; *s.* of George Forrest, of Edinburgh and Woolwich; *m.* Amy, *d.* of the late W. J. Thompson, of Plymouth and London. *Educ.:* Privately, and King's Coll., London. Civil Servant. *War Work:* Capt. 5th Batt. The Bedfordshire Regt.; on Special Service, 30 July, 1914; Active Service, Suvla Bay (Gallipoli), Egypt, Sinai; 2 years Adjutant, 5th (R.) Batt. Bedfordshire Regt., a training battalion for officers and men; special mention for work done in this battalion and decoration awarded. *Address:* Ampthill, Beds. (M3265)

FORREST, Thomas Walker Ainsworth, M.B.E., J.P.

FORREST, William Robinson Lidderdale, M.B.E., M.I.C.E.

FORRESTER, Elizabeth, Mrs., M.B.E.

FORRESTER, James, O.B.E., J.P.

FORRESTER, Miriam, M.B.E.

FORRESTER, Lieut.-Comm. William Thomson, O.B.E., R.N.R.

FORSDICK, Major Edward Thomas, O.B.E.

FORSDICK, Major and Qr.-Mr. William Henry, O.B.E.

FORSDIKE, George Frederick, O.B.E., J.P., *b.* 1872; *s.* of John Forsdike, of Llanelly Car.; *m.* Edith, *d.* of John Thomas, of Pontypridd. *Educ.:* Bridgwater; Cardiff College. Solicitor until 1919; Stockbroker, June, 1919; Lord Mayor of Cardiff 1919–20. *War Work:* Chairman Cardiff Military Tribunal; Member Executive Committee, Priority for Wales (Order of St. John); Ambulance Driver under St. John Ambulance; Inspector Cardiff Special Police; served in French Army 1917–18; Rouge Croix Française at Verdun. *Address:* Cathedral Road, Cardiff. *Clubs:* National Liberal; R.A.C.; County, Cardiff. (O1348)

FORSDYKE, Lieut. Albert Victor Wells, M.B.E., R.A.S.C.

FORSTER, Andrew, M.B.E., M.I.M.E.

FORSTER, Aquila, M.B.E.

FORSTER, Arnold John, M.B.E.

FORSTER, Major Charles Matthew, O.B.E., R.E. (T.F.).

FORSTER, Lieut.-Col. David, D.S.O., B.A., *b.* 1878; *s.* of Lieut.-Col. W. D. Forster; *m.* 1903, Isabel Frances, *d.* of Lieut.-Gen. H. A. Brownlow. Major and Brevet Lieut.-Col., R.E.; a Gen. Staff Officer, with rank of Lieut.-Col.; served in the S. African War, 1899–1900 (Queen's medal with two clasps); Great War, 1914–17 (wounded, despatches, Brevet Lieut.-Col.) (C1987)

FORSTER, Douglas Wakefield, M.B.E., *b.* 20 Dec. 1874; *s.* of Matthew Forster, of Jesmond Park, Newcastle-on-Tyne, late of Bishop Middleham Hall, Co. Durham; *m.* Nora Scott, *d.* of Ashley Leggatt, M.D., of 2, Walton Place, Chelsea. *Educ.:* Sedbergh School. *War Work:* Chairman of Pensions Committee; Vice-Chairman of Food Control Committee; Member of Tribunal; Hon. Sec. War Savings Committee. *Address:* The Cottage, Bishop Middleham, Ferryhill, Co. Durham. (M8113)

FOSTER, Major Edward Seymour, M.B.E.

FORSTER, Major Frederick Norman, M.B.E., R.E.

FORSTER, 2nd Lieut. George Henry, M.B.E., R.E.

FORSTER, John, O.B.E., J.P., *b.* 23 Dec. 1853; *s.* of Samuel Forster; *m.* Esther, *d.* of William Twist, of St. Helens. *Educ.:* Farnworth Grammar School. Engineer and Glass Manufacturer. *War Work:* Manufacture of Shells and Glass Containers; Chairman of Local Tribunal; Member of various War Committees. *Address:* Cowley Hill, St. Helens, Lancashire. *Clubs:* National Liberal; British Empire. (O10420)

FORSTER, John James, O.B.E.

FORSTER, Lieut.-Comm. John Vernon, O.B.E., R.N.R.

FORSTER, Matthew, M.B.E., J.P., *b.* 30 Aug. 1847; *s.* of Matthew Forster, of Sunderland; *m.* Mary, *d.* of William Hogdson, of London. *Educ.:* Privately. Chairman, Forster Bishops Middleham Brewery Co., Ltd.; Director of the Newcastle Breweries Co., Ltd.; Local Director of the Lord Roberts Memorial Workshops, Newcastle-on-Tyne. *War Work:* Hon. Sec. Soldiers' and Sailors' Help Society for the Co. of Durham; Hon. Treas. and Sec. for the Earl of Durham's County of Durham Fund for the Northern Branch of the L.R.M. Workshops. *Address:* Greenhill, Jesmond Park, Newcastle-on-Tyne. *Clubs:* Northern Counties (Newcastle); County (Durham). (M8114)

FORSTER, William, M.B.E.

FORSYTHE, Capt. Gordon Harris, M.B.E., F.A.

FORT, George Seymour, C.B.E., *b.* 1858; *s.* of the late Rev. Richard Fort. *Educ.:* Uppingham Sch., and Oxford Univ. (B.A., 1884). Sometime Capt. King Edward's Horse; was Private Sec. to High Commr. of New Guinea, 1885; to Govt. of Victoria, 1887–89; to Govt. of S. Africa, 1891. *War Work:* Hon. Sec. S. African Hospital and Comforts Fund. (C720)

FORTESCUE, 2nd. Lieut. Albert Edward Muspratt, M.B.E., R.A.F.

FORTESCUE, Prof. Cecil Lewis, O.B.E., M.A., *b.* 15 Jan. 1881; *s.* of Lewis Fortescue, of Barnack, Northamptonshire; *m.* Mary Dorothea, *d.* of R. T. Wright, of Trumpington, Cambridge. *Educ.:* Oundle and Christ's College, Cambridge. Professor of Physics; Royal Naval College, Greenwich. *War Work:* Attached to H.M. Signal School, Portsmouth for experimental work. *Address:* Royal Naval College, Greenwich, S.E. 10. (O338)

FORTESCUE, Emily, Countess, C.B.E., *b.* 1859; *d.* of William Richard 2nd Lord Harlech; *m.* Hugh, 4th Earl Fortescue, K.C.B. (*see* BURKE's *Peerage*). *War Work:* President, Devon Branch Red Cross. *Address:* Castle Hill, South Molton, Devon. (C2614)

FORTESCUE, Col. H., C.B.E.

FORTESCUE, Marjorie Ellinor, Hon. Mrs. Denzil, O.B.E., *b.* 30 December, 1893; *d.* of Colonel Charles Trotter, C.B., and Hon. Mrs. Trotter, O.B.E., of Barton Hartshorne Manor, Buckingham; *m.* Hon. Denzil George Fortescue, M.C., *s.* of Hugh 4th Earl Fortescue, K.C.B. (*see* BURKE's *Peerage*). *War Work:* Stores Department, H.Q. British Red Cross Society, 83, Pall Mall, 1914–19. *Address:* 10 South Eaton Place, London, S.W.1. (O11501)

FORTINGTON, Edna Winifred, Mrs., M.B.E.

FORTINGTON, Harold Augustus, O.B.E.

FORTYE, Grace, M.B.E.,

FORWOOD, Major Harry, O.B.E., D.C.M., M.G. Corps, *b.* 5 March, 1890; *s.* of H. Forwood, of Ramsgate; *m.* Helen Edith, *d.* of — Horn, of Minster, Thanet. *Educ.:* Christ Church Boys' School, Ramsgate. *War Work:* Served as Machine-gun Sergt. in the 1st Batt. of the Buffs.; proceeded to France, Sept. 1914 with the 6th Division; twice wounded, Oct. 1914 and Sept. 1915; commissioned, 1916; Asst. Instr. at M.G.T.C., Grantham; to Armistice; Instructor of Machine Gunnery to Gen. Denikin's Army, March to June, 1920. *Address:* 22, Avenue Road, Grantham. (O9743)

FORWOOD, Sir William Bower, K.B.E., D.L., J.P., *b.* 21 Jan. 1840; *s.* of Thomas B. Forwood, J.P., of Thornton Manor, Cheshire; *m.* Elizabeth Constance, *d.* of General Hughes Fleming, D.L., of Rydal Hall, Westmorland. Director of the Cunard Steamship Co.; Director of the Bank of Liverpool. *Address:* Bromborough Hall, Cheshire. *Club:* Constitutional. (K67)

FOSBERY, Major Widenham Francis Widenham, C.M.G., O.B.E., R.D.C., *b.* 1869; third *s.* of the late Capt. Widenham Francis Fosbery, formerly of Mosstown, co. Westmeath; *m.* 1898, Alice Martha, younger *d.* of the late Surg.-Gen. J. Lamprey, Army Med. Staff. *Educ.:* Privately. Appointed Consular Agent, Niger Coast Protectorate, 1893; Dist. Commr., 1896; Resident, Benin City, 1898; Acting Div. Commr., Niger Coast Protectorate, 1900; Div. Commr., 1902; Senior Div. Commr., S. Nigeria Protectorate, 1903; Acting High Commr., 1903; Acting Sec. to Administration, 1904; Dept. High Commr.

1905; Provincial Commr., M.E.C., M.L.C., and Acting Gov., S. Nigeria, 1906; Dep. Gov. and Acting Colonial Sec., 1906; Consul for German Protectorate of the Cameroons, 1909; Political Officer with Central Div. Expedition, 1896 (severely wounded); with Benin Expedition, 1899 (medal with clasp); with Ishan Expedition, 1901 (medal with clasp); with Asaba Hinterland Expedition, 1902 (clasp); with Igarra Expedition, 1903 (clasp). *Address:* Thurloe House, Cromwell Place, S.W. (O7164)

FOSSATI, Mary Mussely, M.B.E., *b.* 16 May, 1888; *d.* of John Fossati, of Manchester. *Educ.:* Courtrai (Belgium), and Convent Higher Grade School, Bury (Lancashire). *War Work:* As a result of collections made, and the generous help of the Ladies of the Red Cross and the authorities of the town of Courtrai, clothing and food was supplied by her to hundreds of British prisoners passing through Courtrai. (M8118)

FOSSEY, Frederick Walter, M.B.E.

FOSTER, Capt. and Qr.-Mr. Albert Percy, O.B.E.

FOSTER, Lieut.-Col. Alfred James, C.M.G., C.B.E.

FOSTER, Lieut.-Col. Arthur Bruce, C.B.E.

FOSTER, Major Arthur Norman, O.B.E., F.R.C.V.S., R.A.V.C., T.F., *b.* 15 Jan. 1882; *s.* of Philip Foster, of Red House, Clifton, Derbyshire; *m.* Mary Dorothy, *d.* of Ernest Norvill, of 32, Lancaster Road, W. Norwood, S.E. *Educ.:* Queen Elizabeth's Grammar School, and Rossall. Vet. Officer, Uganda; Graduated, M.R.C.V.S. (Lond.), 1903; Fellowship, 1909; 1903–6, General Practice; 1907–9, Vet. Inspector. Sheffield Corporation; 1909–12, V.O. Sierra Leone and Gambia; 1913, General Practice; 1914, V.O. Uganda, seconded for the Service, and took up appointment, June, 1920; Gazetted Lieut. R.A.V.C., March, 1909; Capt., Sept. 1914. *War Work:* Mobilised with W.R.D.R.E., Aug. 1914; transferred to Command Doncaster Vet. Hospital, Nov. 1914, and converted establishment from a Civil to a Military basis, under Lieut.-Col. A. W. Mason, O.B.E., R.A.V.C., F.R.C.V.S. (Croix de Guerre); Establishment complete by Dec. 1914; formed 1/1st West Riding Mobile Vet. Section, and proceeded to Western Front as O/C that unit, April, 1915; appointed D.A.D.V.S. of 49th (W.R.) Division with rank of Major, July, 1917; appointed to command 47th Mobile Vet. Section, May, 1919; appointed D.A.D.V.S.Forward Districts in France and Flanders. *Addresses:* Veterinary Officer, Mbale, Uganda; Red House, Clifton, Derbyshire. *Clubs:* Constitutional; New; Oxford and Cambridge. (O5267)

FOSTER, Capt. Charles La Trobe, O.B.E., R.A.S.C.

FOSTER, Cicely Penrose, M.B.E. (Mil.), *b.* 26 April, 1885; *d.* of Col. L. C. Foster, V.D., D.L., J.P., of Trevills, Liskeard, Cornwall. *War Work:* Quartermistress and Acting Commandant, V.A.D. Cornwall 56, till Jan. 1916; went to France in Jan. 1916 as V.A.D. attached to the Army Ordnance Department at Calais and Le Havre for inspection of P.H. Gas Helmets from Jan. 1916 to July, 1917; transferred to Q.M.A.A.C., attached Royal Army Ordnance Corps as Technical Administrator; Superintended the work of the French Female Labour in the R.A.O.C. Receipts Depot at Valdelièvre, Calais, till Aug. 1919; transferred to the Accounts Branch of the R.A.O.C. at Vendroux, Calais, and worked there as Technical Unit Administrator till the Q.M.A.A.C. was demobilised, 31 Dec. 1919; returned to Vendroux as a civilian attached R.A.O.C. and continued work in the Accounts Branch R.A.O.C. Vendroux till Mar. 1920. (M4483)

FOSTER, Capt. Dennis, O.B.E.

FOSTER, Capt. Edward, O.B.E., R.A.S.C., *b.* 26 Oct. 1881; *s.* of Henry Foster J.P., of Ludlow; *m.* Kathleen, *d.* of C. J. Exley, of Arleston, Willington. *War Work:* O.C. 332 Co. R.A.S.C.; went overseas with the 38th (Welsh) Division; mentioned in despatches, Nov. 1917 and Nov. 1918. (O5268)

FOSTER, Evelyn Mary, Mrs., O.B.E., *b.* 10 Oct. 1881; *d.* of Bernard E. Cammell, of The Gate House, Merrow; *m.* Wilfrid Lionel (Major, late R.H.A.), *s.* of Henry Foster, of Malvern. *War Work:* Royal Artillery Prisoners of War Fund. *Address:* Henwood Manor, Tettenhall, Staffs. (O10421)

FOSTER, Capt. Francis Kenelm, O.B.E., *b.* 10 May, 1877; *s.* of T. Nelson Foster, of Cheltenham; *m.* Maude Emilie Probyn, *d.* of Maj.-Gen. G. Swinley, C.B. (late R.A.), of Cheltenham. *Educ.:* Cheltenham. Seed Crusher. *War Work:* Served with 48th (S. Mid.) Division (T.F.), 1914–18. *Address:* Allt Dinas, Cheltenham. *Clubs:* New Club, Cheltenham; Gloucester Club, Gloucester. (O6367)

FOSTER, Frank, O.B.E.

FOSTER, Major Frank Broome, O.B.E., *b.* 27 July 1878; *s.* of C. W. Foster, of Exmouth, Devon. *Educ.:* Rugby. Stockbroker. *War Work:* Supplies, Nantes, Rouen, 1914–15; 28th Div. and 33rd Div. 1915–17; S.S.O. 49th 1917–19; Despatches three times. *Addresses:* 24, Market St., Mayfair; Stock Exchange. *Clubs:* Isthmian Club R.A.C. (O3269)

FOSTER, Henry Knollys, M.B.E., *b.* 30 Oct. 1873; *s.* of Rev. H. Foster, of 5, The College, Malvern; *m.* Ellen Geraldine *d.* of Canon Pelly, of Great Malvern and Hollington, Sussex. *Educ.:* Malvern and Trinity College, Oxford. Land Agent. *War Work:* Chief Executive Officer of the Herefordshire War Agriculture Executive Committee; Lieut. in Herefordshire V.T.C. *Address:* Wargrave House, Hereford. *Club:* United Sports; I Zingari; Free Foresters. (M405)

FOSTER, Col. Henry Nedham, C.M.G., C.B.E., *b.* 1878. Major and Brevet Lieut.-Col. and T. Col., R.A.S.C.; served in S. Africa, 1900–2 (despatches, Queen's medal with five clasps, King's medal with two clasps). (C1570)

FOSTER, James, O.B.E.

FOSTER, James Evelyn, M.B.E., *b.* 19 July, 1898 ; *s.* of Percival R. Foster, of Misterton, Teignmouth, Devonshire. *Educ.:* Exeter School, Exeter. Electrical Engineering, Rees Roturbo Co., Ltd., Wolverhampton. *War Work:* Served 4 years as Officer in charge Workshops in the Mechanical Transport, R.A.S.C. ; joined as private in Aug. 1916 ; commissioned Dec. 1916 ; demobilised in Jan. 1920 ; served in France, Belgium, and Germany. *Addresses:* c/o Messrs Usher, Ltd., Engineers, Old Court House St., Calcutta ; Misterton, Teignmouth, Devonshire. (M1728)

FOSTER, Lieut.-Col. John George, O.B.E., R.A.M.C., *b.* 30 May, 1872 ; *s.* of the late Rev. Robert Foster, one time Chaplain, Royal Hibernian Military School. *Educ.:* High School and Trinity Coll., Dublin. *War Work:* Served in Mesopotamia, 1914 to end of campaign ; mentioned three times in despatches ; promoted Brevet Lieut.-Col. *Address:* c/o Holt & Co., 3, Whitehall Place, S.W. (O6622)

FOSTER, Major John Vere, O.B.E.

FOSTER, Major Kennedy, O.B.E., R.A.M.C.

FOSTER, Marion Ferguson, M.B.E., *b.* 26 May, 1881 ; *d.* of James Yates Foster, of Whitefriars, Penwortham, Preston, Lancs. *Educ.:* Ladies' Coll., Cheltenham. *War Work:* Aug. 1914, Canteen work ; Sept. to Dec. 1914, Hospital Depot Work and Belgian Refugees ; Jan. 1915 to May, 1919, Head Clerk Auxiliary Military Hospital, Moor Park, Preston (250 beds). *Address:* Whitefriars, Penwortham, Preston. (M8119)

FOSTER, Lady Mary Louise Elizabeth, Dowager Duchess of Hamilton, O.B.E. ; *d.* of 7th Duke of Manchester ; *m.* 1st, 1873, William Alexander, 12th Duke of Hamilton, who died 1898 ; 2ndly, Robert Carnaby Foster. *Address:* Easton Park, Suffolk. (O337)

FOSTER, Col. Michael George, O.B.E., M.D., F.S.A., F.R.C.P., *b.* 13 Dec. 1864 ; *s.* of Sir Michael Foster, K.C.B. F.R.S. of Great Shelford, Cambs. ; *m.* 1st Charlotte, *d.* of Gen. R. Shipley, C.B. of Twyford, Hants ; 2nd, Margaret Manning widow of Hon. W. E. Russell, Governor of Commonwealth, Massachusetts, U.S.A. *Educ.:* Trinity College, Cambridge ; Univ. Coll. Hosp. London ; B.A. 1884 ; M.A. 1888. *War Work:* Consulting Physician British Troops in France and Flanders. *Address:* Benington, Harrogate, Yorks ; Villar San Giovanni, San Remo, Italy. *Clubs:* Athenæum ; Cambridge County. (O5271)

FOSTER, Sir Norris Tildesley C.B.E., *b.* 1855 ; *s.* of the late Frederick Foster, of Barton-under-Needwood ; *m.* Eliza, *d.* of Elijah Barnett, of Edgbaston. *Educ.:* King Edward's School, Birmingham, and at Oxford Univ., M.A. Called to Bar at the Inner Temple, 1891 ; Joined Midland Circuit ; was member of Warwickshire County Appeal Tribunal ; also Chairman for Ministry of Labour at Court of Referees ; Vice-President, University Graduates Club ; Member of General Purposes, Finance, and Administration Committee of the War Pensions and Citizens Committee ; Founder and Chairman of Birmingham Streets Collection Committee ; at present Hon. Treasurer of War Pensions Committee ; has taken a leading part in the Unionist Parliamentary work. *Address:* Southfield, Priory Road, Edgbaston, Birmingham. (C2615)

FOSTER, Major Phipps Bentley, O.B.E., *b.* 7 Aug. 1883 ; *s.* of Leonard Foster, of Kirklington Hall, Southwell ; *m.* Madeline Vernon, *d.* of R. L. Crankshaw, of Dunkwy, Gweedore, Co. Donegal. *Educ.:* Uppingham ; Oxford. *War Work:* Raised three R.F.A. Batteries ; France, 1916 ; Voluntary work, Board of Agriculture, 1918–19. *Address:* Woodbury Park, Sandy, Beds. *Club:* Marlborough ; Bath. (O10422)

FOSTER, Reginald, O.B.E.

FOSTER, Robert John, O.B.E., *b.* Jan. 20 1864 ; *s.* of John Foster, of Selby, Yorks ; *m.* Ellen Gertrude, *d.* of John Gorrell, of Lancaster. *Educ.:* Sheffield College. Director of Flax Cultivation, Ltd. *War Work:* Flax Commissioner for Eastern Area (England), under Ministry of Agriculture and Fisheries. *Address:* Westbrook House, Peterborough. (O3718)

FOSTER, Thomas Burdall, M.B.E.

FOSTER, Major Wilfrid Lionel, C.B.E., D.S.O., *b.* 2 Dec. 1874 ; *s.* of Henry Foster, of Malvern College ; *m.* Evelyn Mary *d.* of Bernard E. Cammell, of Merrow. *Educ.:* Malvern and R.M.A. Woolwich. *War Work:* organised the Royal Artillery Prisoners of War Fund. *Address:* Henwood Manor, Tettenhall, Staffs. *Clubs:* Army and Navy. (C963)

FOSTER, Lieut. William, M.B.E., R.E.

FOSTER, William Melville, M.B.E., M.A., B.C.L., F.R.G.S., *b.* 31 Oct. 1871 ; *s.* of John Edwin Foster, M.R.C.S., L.R.C.P., of Mayfield, Huddersfield ; *m.* Mary Anson, *d.* of Matthew George Farrer, of Kemerton, Gloucestershire. *Educ.:* Dover College ; Christ Church, Oxford ; Geneva. Barrister-at-Law (Inner Temple) ; late Private Secretary to H.E. the Governor of Jamaica. *War Work:* Private Secretary, Director of Munitions Contracts, War Office ; later Head of Section, Ministry of Munitions. *Address:* 14, Iverna Court, Kensington. *Clubs:* The Royal Colonial Institute ; Royal Geographical Society ; Oxford and Cambridge ; Ranelagh and Roehampton. (M406)

FOSTER, Col. Sir William Yorke, Bart., C.B.E., late R.A., *b.* 1 April, 1860 ; *s.* of the late Sir William Foster Bt., of Norwich ; *m* Aileen Ethel, *d.* of Col. Augustus Berkeley Portman. *Educ.:* Eton. Royal Horse and Royal Field Artillery from 1880 to 1910 ; Staff Capt. and D.A.A.G. R.A. May, 1892 to May 1897. *War Work:* Asst. Adjt.-General, Southern Command, 1914–17. Records Staff, 1917–19. *Clubs:* Naval and Military ; The Norfolk, Norwich. (C165)

FOUCAR, Alexander Ferdinand Emile, O.B.E., M.B.E.

FOULERTON, Brevet-Major Alexander Grant Russell, O.B.E., F.R.C.S., R.A.M.C. (T.F.), *b.* 22 April, 1863 ; *s.* of Alexander Foulerton, Capt. H.M. Indian Navy. *Educ.:* Kensington School. County Medical Officer, East Sussex ; Chairman, Board of Studies in Hygiene, Univ. of London ; Lecturer on Hygiene at the London School of Medicine for Women, and in the Hygiene Department of Univ. Coll., London ; formerly director of the Cancer Research Laboratories at the Middlesex Hospital. *War Work:* D.A.D.M.S. (Sanitation) B.E.F., France (1914–15 Star) ; O.C. Hygiene Department, Royal Army Medical Coll. *Addresses:* Wealdside, Lewes ; Morpeth Terrace, Victoria Street, S.W. 1. *Club:* Royal Automobile. (O7165)

FOUNTAIN, Annie Christine, C.B.E. ; *d.* of late Joseph Fountain, of Birthwaite Hall, Darton. Colliery Proprietor. *War Work:* Recruiting, Hospital and Red Cross. *Address:* Birthwaite Hall, Darton, nr. Barnsley. (C964)

FOURIE, Louis, M.B.E.

FOWELE, Edward Turner, M.B.E.

FOWLDS, Hon. George, C.B.E., *b.* 1860 ; *s.* of the late Matthew Fowlds, of Fenwick, Scotland ; *m.* 1884, M. A., *d.* of John Fulton, of Chiphall, Fenwick, Ayrshire. *Educ.:* Waterside Sch., Ayrshire ; Andersonian Coll., Glasgow. Was Minister of the Crown, New Zealand, 1906–11, holding Portfolios of Education, Customs, Public Health, Defence, Justice, and Public Hospitals ; Dep. Chm. Auckland Univ. Coll. Council, and a Trustee Jubilee Institute for the Blind. (C723)

FOWLE, Edward, M.B.E.

FOWLE, Helène, Mrs., M.B.E. ; *d.* of Baron de Caters, of Antwerp, Belgium ; *m.* Col. John Fowle ; *s.* of Edmund Fowle, of Newton Abbot. *War Work:* Belgian refugees. *Address:* 9, Hume Street, Dublin. (M408)

FOWLE, Col. Sir Henry Walter Hamilton, K.B.E., *b.* 1871, *s.* of late T. E. Fowle, D.L., of Chute Lodge, Hants, and Durrington Manor, Wilts. Commissioner of Enemy Subjects in S. Africa, 1915, and Custodian of Enemy Property, 1916–19 (*see* BURKE'S *Peerage*)

FOWLE, Col. Thomas Ernle, C.B.E., A.A., and Q.M.G., S. Africa ; served with the Chitral Relief Force, 1895 (medal with clasp) ; in S. Africa, 1902 (despatches, Queen's medal with two clasps) (C815)

FOWLE, William, M.B.E., V.D

FOWLER, Col. Charles Edward Percy, O.B.E., F.R.C.S., A.M.S., *b.* 1866 ; *s.* of Charles Edward Fowler, of Milverton Court, Somerset ; *m.* Mary Dorothy Hopper, *d.* of William Whytehead Boulton, J.P., of Beverley, E. Yorks. *Educ.:* Clifton ; St. Mary's Hospital. Asst. Prof. of Hygiene, R.A.M. College, London, 1903–7 ; Mil. Representative Malarial Commission Mauritius, 1907 ; M.O.H., Gibraltar, 1908–12 ; Commandant, Army School of Sanitation, Aldershot, 1913–14 ; retired 1914. *War Work:* A.D.M.S., Aldershot Command ; Member Army Sanitary Committee, 1914–16 ; mentioned in despatches Brevet Lt.-Col. Aug. 1917 ; A.D.M.S., E.E.F., Mil. Malarial Commission of Egypt, (O.B.E., Mar. 1918) ; A.D.M.S., Delta District ; A.D.M.S., 54th Division (mentioned in Despatches, E.E.F., May 1919) ; gazetted to reserve as Colonel A.M.S. *Address:* Ash Green, Surrey. *Club:* Conservative. (O1025)

FOWLER, Capt. Charles Henry, M.B.E., *b.* 4 Jan. 1885 ; *s.* of the late R. H. Fowler. *Educ.:* Dulwich Coll. ; Trinity Coll., Cambridge. Managing Director, Messrs. John Fowler & Co., Leeds, Ltd., Agricultural Engineers. *War Work:* Chief Ordnance Engineer (Manchester District), Dept. of Gun Manufacture, Ministry of Munitions, 1915–17 ; Director of Field and Siege Artillery Production, Dept. of Gun Manufacture, Ministry of Munitions, 1918–19. *Address:* Moor House, Moortown, Leeds, Yorkshire. *Club:* Windham ; Royal Automobile. (M1732)

FOWLER, Charles Roy, M.B.E.

FOWLER, Ethel Ada, Mrs., M.B.E.

FOWLER, Eveline Georgina, M.B.E., ; *d.* of Ernest William Fowler, of Gunton Old Hall, Suffolk. *Educ.:* At home. *War Work:* Hon. Matron of the Gunton Cottage Hospital for Sailors and Minesweepers from 1915–19. *Address:* Gunton Old Hall, nr. Lowestoft, Suffolk. (M409)

FOWLER, Lieut.-Col. George Curran Orr, O.B.E., R.A.V.C., *b.* 15 Dec. 1859 ; *s.* of L. Hamilton Fowler, of Dhufield Greenock, N.B., and Rangoon ; *m.* Louisa, *d.* of James Mann, of Levanne, Gouroch, N.B. *Educ.:* Privately, and Neuwiedam-Rhein. *War Work:* 5th Div. H.Q. France ; A.D.V.S. 65th Division ; D.A.D.V.S. Irish Command. *Address:* Messrs. Holt & Co., Ltd., 3, Whitehall Place, S.W. *Club:* R.C.Y.C. (O7166)

FOWLER, George Herbert, C.B.E., B.A., Ph.D., F.L.S., *b.* 1861 ; *s.* of Rev. John Fowler, of Lincoln. *Educ.:* Eton, Oxford ; Leipzig. *War Work:* Hydrographic and Intelligence Departments, Admiralty 1914–19. *Address:* The Old House, Aspley Guise, Bedfordshire. *Club:* Arts. (C166)

FOWLER, Gertrude Irene, M.B.E.

FOWLER, Temp. Lieut.-Col. Sir Henry, K.B.E., *b.* 29 July, 1870 ; *s.* of Henry Fowler, of Evesham ; *m.* Emmie Needham, *d.* of Philip Smith, of Horwich, Lancs. *Educ.:* Evesham and Mason Science College, Birmingham. Chief Mechanical Engineer, Midland Railway ; President Institution of Automobile Engineers ; Hon. Secretary, Association of Railway Locomotive Engineers. *War Work:* Director of Production, Ministry of Munitions ; Superintendent of Royal Aircraft Factory ; Assistant Director-General of Aircraft

Production, 1917–18 ; Ministry of Munitions Representative on Aircraft Mission to the United States of America and Canada, 1918 ; Chairman of the Light Alloys Sub-Committee ; Chairman of Aircraft Committee of British Engineering Standards Association, 1918 ; Chairman of Conference to form the International Aircraft Standards Commission, 1918 ; Chairman of the first Inter-Allied Conference on the Standardisation of Aircraft Components ; Deputy-member of Munitions Council, 1918–19. *Address :* Derwent House, Milford, Derby. *Club :* Royal Automobile ; R.A.F. (K68)

FOWLER, Lionel John Porter, O.B.E., *b.* 24 Feb. 1892 ; *s.* of John Porter Fowler, of Tredegar ; *m.* Kathleen Grace, *d.* of Henry Jeffcoat, of Lymington. *Educ. :* Privately. *War Work :* Production Engineer, The Sopwith Aviation and Engineering Co., Ltd., Kingston-on-Thames. *Address :* Woodvale, Petersham, Surrey. (O10425)

FOWLER, Margaret Mary Maitland, Mrs. O.B.E. ; *d.* of Rev. John George Trotter, Canon of Birmingham ; *m.* George Herbert Fowler, 8th Sherwood Foresters (killed in France, Oct. 1915)., *s.* of George Fowler, of Basford Hall, Nottingham. *Educ. :* Grassendale ; Southbourne-on-Sea, Hants ; Paris. *War Work :* Commandant (Warwick 68 B.R.C.S.) Weddington Hospital, Nuneaton, Warwickshire ; Vice-President, B.R.C.S. for Atherstone Division. *Address :* 43, Binswood Avenue, Leamington Spa. *Clubs :* Lyceum ; V.A.D. (O3719)

FOWLER, May, Mrs. Francis John, O.B.E.

FOWLER, Capt. Ralph Howard, O.B.E.

FOWLER, Col. Robert, O.B.E., Aust. A.M.C.

FOWLER, Robert Copp, O.B.E., F.S.A., *b.* 5 Nov. 1867 ; *s.* of the Rev. Newell Vicat Fowler, late vicar of Ulting, Essex ; *m.* Mary Dorothea, *d.* of John Goodacre, late of Ashby Parva and Ullesthorpe, Leicestershire. *Educ. :* Winchester College, and New College, Oxford. Assistant Keeper of the Public Records. *War Work :* Casualties Branch, War Office. *Address :* Wayside, West End Lane, Pinner. *Club :* United University. (O1352)

FOWLIE, Mary, Mrs., M.B.E.

FOX, Arthur Wingate, M.B.E. (M10248)

FOX, Major Charles Horace, M.B.E., R.E.

FOX, David Henry, O.B.E., *b.* 7 May, 1863 ; *s.* of James Fox, of Shepherdswell ; *m.* Susan, *d.* of John Benefield, of Waltham, Kent. *Educ. :* Shepherdswell Elementary School. Chief Constable of Dover ; Captain of the Fire Brigade. *War Work :* Special work in connection with the issue of 40,000 Permit Books to the civilian population of Dover, Dover being considered a special Military Area ; duty in connection with air raids of which there were 113 calls and 18 actual raids, also two bombardments and 4 fires caused by bombs dropped from enemy aircraft. (O10426)

FOX, Capt. Edward Thornton, O.B.E., J.P. (Southern Rhodesia), British South Africa Police, *b.* 29 May, 1881 ; *s.* of Edward Robert Fox, of Leicester ; *m.* Helen Edith, *d.* of William Alexander Brunton, C.I.E., of London. *Educ. :* Privately ; Wyggeston Grammar School, Leicester ; Real Gymnasium I. Hanover. Sec. Department of Defence, Southern Rhodesia ; 1st Vol. Batt. Leicestershire Regt. 1898–1906 ; Lieut. ; joined British South Africa Police, April 1906 ; transferred to Southern Rhodesia Civil Service, April 1909 ; retransferred to B.S.A.P. June 1913, and appointed Lieut. and Asst. Controller on the Staff of the Commandant-General, Rhodesia Forces ; Capt. 1st July, 1918 ; appointed Sec. Department of Defence, Southern Rhodesia, Feb. 1920 ; was Sec. to the Public Committee to enquire into the system of Defence for Southern Rhodesia, 1916. *War Work :* On Active Service with B.S.A. Police, Southern Rhodesia, from Aug. 1914 to June, 1919, as Asst. Controller Rhodesian Defence Force (Administrative Services, Supplies, etc.), and Controller, Pay and Accounts Branch, Rhodesian Defence Force. *Address :* Salisbury, S. Rhodesia. (O8010)

FOX, Capt. Frank, O.B.E., R.A.

FOX, Capt. Harold Arthur, O.B.E., R.A.S.C.

FOX, James Bartholomew, M.B.E., S.M., R.G.A.

FOX, Lieut.-Col. and Qr.-Mr. James Joseph, O.B.E.

FOX, Major John, O.B.E., R.A.S.C.

FOX, John Jacob, O.B.E.

FOX, Joseph Vincent, O.B.E., M.B., C.M.

FOX, Marshall Nathaniel, M.B.E., *b.* 1872 ; *s.* of the late Nathaniel Fox, J.P., of Falmouth ; *m.* Annie Elizabeth, *d.* of the late L. H. Leslie, of North Shields. Six years Joint Sec. of Friends' Foreign Mission Association, London ; since 1909 a Missionary in Mount Lebanon, Syria, leaving in Oct. 1914. *War Work :* March, 1916, to March, 1918, Controller of Industries at the Armenian Refugee Camp, Port Said, and Hon. Govt. Inspector, from then until March, 1920, General Sec. (hon.) of the Syria and Palestine Relief Fund, founded by Bishop MacInnes, and being the united effort of 12 British Missionary Societies ; expenditure in Palestine over £120,000, in Syria over £35,000. *Addresses :* c/o F.F.M.A., 15 Devonshire Street, Bishopsgate, E.C. ; 15, Penwerris Terrace, Falmouth. (M8124)

FOX, Major Robert Michael Douglas, O.B.E., L.I.

FOX, Tom, O.B.E.

FOX, Lieut. Thomas Laurence, O.B.E., *b.* 21 Sept, 1893; *s.* of Thomas Barter Fox, of Melbourne, Australia. *Educ. :* Scotch Coll., Melbourne, and Melbourne Univ. *War Work :* Served in Egypt, France, Salonica, South Russia, Constantinople, Army of Black Sea, with 1st Division, Australian T.F. ; awarded Russian Order of St. Anne, 2nd Class. *Club :* United R.A.S.C., London. (O7944)

FOX, Violet Beatrice, M.B.E.

FOX, Lieut. Walter, O.B.E., R.E., T.F.

FOX, Walter St. John, O.B.E., Esquire of the Order of St. John of Jerusalem, *b.* 28 Feb. 1855 ; *s.* of Thomas Samuel Fox, of Farnborough, Kent. *Educ. :* Tonbridge. *War Work :* Commandant of the Headquarters Central Detachment of the Metropolitan Special Constabulary. *Clubs :* Union ; Constitutional ; M.C.C. (O10428)

FOX, Capt. William Harris, M.B.E., *b.* 17 March, 1878 ; *s.* of Joseph William Fox, of Barrie, Ontario, Canada ; *m.* Emily Gilberetta, *d.* of Gilbert H. York, of Coburg, Ontario. *Educ. :* Univ. of Toronto. Electrical Engineer. *War Work :* Quartermaster, Ontario Military Hospital, Orpington, Kent ; this hospital was built and operated by the Government of Ontario, and was the largest Canadian Hospital in England, having 2100 beds and a staff of 300. (M1733)

FOX, Eng.-Comm. William Henry, O.B.E., R.N.R.

FOX, Eleanor Birch, the Hon. Mrs. WILSON-, C.B.E., *b.* 18 March, 1871 ; *d.* of the 1st Baron Basing (*see* BURKE'S *Peerage*), of Hoddington, Hants. ; *m.* Henry Wilson-Fox, M.P. for Tamworth Division of Warwickshire. *War Work :* Chairman of South African Comforts Committee ; Member of South African Hospital and Comforts Fund, and of London War Pensions Committee ; Chairman of Hackney War Pensions Sub-Committee. *Address :* 20, Lowndes Square, S.W. 1. (C379)

FOXALL, Arthur Squire, M.B.E.

FOYSTER, Arthur Henry, M.B.E., M.I.E.E., *b.* 13 Dec. 1869 ; *s.* of the late Rev. G. A. Foyster, of Guise House, Aspley Guise. *Educ. :* Haileybury. *War Work :* Assist. Inspector of Small Arms Ammunition. (M1735)

FOYSTER, Constance Helena, M.B.E., *b.* 17 Feb. 1878 ; *d.* of the Rev. Henry Brereton Foyster, Rector of St. Clement's, Hastings, and Prebendary of Chichester. *Educ. :* Privately. *War Work :* Commandant of Old Hastings House, British Red Cross Hospital, Hastings, from May, 1915, to April, 1920. *Address :* The Vicarage, Colemans' Hatch, Sussex. *Club :* V.A.D. Ladies'. (M8126)

FOZARD, Capt. Harry Edwin, M.B.E., R.A.F., *b.* 8 Dec. 1883 ; *s.* of Edwin Charles Fozard, of London ; *m.* Florence Chiswell, *d.* of William Myles Chadwick, of Sheffield. *Educ. :* Privately, and Royal Indian Engineering Coll. Engineer (Mech.) ; Assoc. Member of Institute of Mech. Engineers. *War Work :* Inspector of Aeroplanes ; Officer in charge, Northern Area, A.I.D. *Address :* 7, Dartmouth Road, Chorlton-cum-Hardy. *Club :* Constitutional, Manchester. (M3648)

FRAMPTON, Capt. Henry Frank, O.B.E.

FRAMPTON, Capt. Napier Paul, M.B.E., A.R.S.M., R.A.S.C., *b.* 28 Nov. 1871 : *s.* of the late Walter Frampton, of Adelaide, South Australia ; *m.* Ada Lilian, *d.* of the late Edward Lovell Dwyer, Commander R.N., of Launceston, Tasmania, and grandniece of the late Admiral Sir Sidney Smith. *Educ. :* Saint Peter's Coll., Adelaide, and Royal School of Mines, South Kensington. Engaged in Mining in Australia. *War Work :* Enlisted 5 Jan. 1915 ; Sergt.-Major in France, with 10th Div. ; on Supply Ships at Anzac, Suvla Bay, at Supply Depots at Tel-el-Kebir, Romani, and railhead depots across Sinai Peninsula ; obtained Commission, Jan. 1917, and joined 54th Div. as Brigade Supply Officer, and later Requisitioning Officer with XXI. Corps troops ; June, 1918, made Capt. and Supply Officer, XXI. Corps troops ; in charge of Corps Depot at Ras-el-ain during General Allenby's advance in Sept. 1918 ; went into hospital with malaria, Nov. 1918, in Beirut. *Address :* 32, Disraeli Road, Ealing, W. 5. (M3174)

FRANCE, Reginald, M.B.E.

FRANCE, William Ernest, M.B.E., *b.* 6 Dec. 1880 ; *s.* of James France, of Old Trafford ; *m.* Catherine Moncrieff, *d.* of David Ames, of Croydon. *Educ. :* Bishops Stortford Coll. Bank Manager ; Manager, Manchester and Liverpool District Bank, Knutsford and Northwich ; now Sub-Manager, Manchester and Liverpool District Bank, Southport. *War Work :* Hon. Sec. Knutsford War Savings Committee. *Addresses :* Park Cottage, Knutsford ; Delamere Road, Ainsdale, near Southport. (M8127)

FRANCES, Edith, Mrs., M.B.E. Organiser, Soldiers' Rest and Refreshment Camp, Beira. (M10258a)

FRANCEYS, Amy Constance, Mrs., M.B.E., *b.* 13 Feb. 1878 ; *d.* of Alderman Joseph Heap, of Blackpool ; *m.* Lionel Hope Franceys, *d.* of Edw. B. Franceys, of Southport. *Educ. :* Northlands High School, Blackpool. *War Work :* Soldiers' and Sailors' Families Association ; Local War Pensions Committee ; Voluntary Aid Association ; Prisoners of War Committee. *Address :* Hopetoun, Read's Avenue, Blackpool, Lancs. (M8128)

FRANCIS, Ada Emily, M.B.E., Q.M.A.A.C.

FRANCIS, Alfred George, O.B.E., B.A. (Cantab.), M.B., B.S. (Lond.), F.R.C.S. (Eng.), *b.* 25 Nov. 1862 ; *s.* of Charles Wordley Francis, of Southchurch, Essex ; *m.* Frederica Jane, *d.* of the Rev. Walter Marcon, Rector of Edgefield, Norfolk. *Educ. :* Univ. Coll. School ; Univ. Coll., London ; King's Coll., Cambridge ; St. Bartholomew's Hospital, London. Late Surgeon, Hull Royal Infirmary. *War Work :* Chairman, Recruiting and Pension Boards, East Central Region. *Address :* 101, Beverley Road, Hull, E. Yorkshire. (O10429)

FRANCIS, Lieut. Arnold Eardley, M.B.E., *b.* 21 Jan. 1881 ; *s.* of F. W. Francis, J.P., of Leamington Spa. *Educ. :* Leamington Coll. *War Work :* Served in R.A.S.C. *Address :* Garthside, Rugby Road, Leamington Spa. (M4486

FRANCIS, Lieut.-Col. Charles John, C.B.E., R.E. Served in the Great War, 1914–19 (despatches). (C1571)

FRANCIS, Major Frederick Howard, D.S.O., O.B.E. Australian Army Ser. Corps ; served during the Great War, 1914–16 (despatches). (O8616)

FRANCIS, George Chaplin, M.B.E.

FRANCIS, Guy, M.B.E.

FRANCIS, Harvey, O.B.E., M.D.

FRANCIS, Herbert William Sidney, O.B.E.

FRANCIS, John Horace, O.B.E.

FRANCIS, Joseph, O.B.E., J.P., b. 1859. For many years associated with the public work of Southend-on-Sea ; elected Mayor in 1900 and again the first Mayor of the County Borough in 1913 and continued in office throughout the war ; founded the National Benefit Assurance Company Limited in 1890 ; Chairman or Director of several Marine Insurance and other Companies ; Chairman of the City of London Maternity Hospital for many years ; Member of the Board of the Orphan Working School ; Past Master of the Worshipful Company of Gardeners. War Work : Was Chairman of the War Tribunal, Treasurer of the War Pensions Committee, and Chairman of many other Committees formed in connection with the War ; Member of the Committee of Queen Mary's Royal Naval Hospital ; Honorary Commandant of the National Guard, (later the 4th Volunteer Battalion of the Essex Regiment), of which he was gazetted Lieut.-Colonel ; President of the League of Mercy for south-east Essex. Officer of the Order of the Crown of Belgium. Addresses : Bude, Southend-on-Sea ; National House, Newgate Street, E.C.1. Club : Royal Societies'. (O341)

FRANCIS, Katharine Lilian, Mrs., M.B.E. ; d. of Rev. C. Peach, of Evenlode Rectory, Worcestershire. Educ. : Brighton. War Work : Hon. Sec. Red Cross Committee, Chepstow, since 1911 ; Commandant, Chepstow Red Cross Hospital, V.A.D. Mon. 6, 1918. Address : St. Tewdric, Chepstow. Club : Sesame. (M8130)

FRANCIS, Percy Alexander, M.B.E.

FRANCIS, Percy James, O.B.E.

FRANCIS, Surg.-Lieut. Thomas Evan, O.B.E., M.D., D.P.H., R.N.

FRANCIS, Elizabeth Lydia, Mrs. BULT-, M.B.E., b. 11 June, 1854. War Work : Five years at the Euston Y.M.C.A. Hut, 3½ years of that time Superintendent of above ; donor of the Royal Naval Hut, Harwich, and part donor of the Naval Hut, Rosyth. Addresses : 21, Taviton Street, London, W.C.1 ; The Fern House, Little Marlow, Bucks. (M1736)

FRANEY, George Ernest, O.B.E.

FRANK, Peter, O.B.E.

FRANKAU, Col. Claude Howard Stanley, C.B.E., D.S.O., M.B., F.R.C.S. Capt. and Brevet Major and Acting Col. Served during the Great War, 1914–18 (despatches). (C1250)

FRANKISH, Lieut. John Raven, M.B.E., R.A.F.

FRANKLAND, Percy Faraday, C.B.E., J.P., F.R.S., Ph.D., LL.D., Sc.D., Officer of the Order of St. Maurice and St. Lazarus, b. 1858 ; s. of Sir Edward Frankland, K.C.B. m. Grace Coleridge, d. of Joseph Toynbee, F.R.S. Educ. : University College School ; Royal School of Mines ; Würzburg University. Emeritus Professor of Chemistry and late Dean of the Faculty of Science in the University of Birmingham ; Past-President of the Chemical Society and of the Institute of Chemistry of Great Britain and Ireland ; Past Vice-President of the Royal Society. War Work : Deputy Inspector of High Explosives (Birmingham Area) ; Member of Panel, Board of Invention and Research (Admiralty) ; Examiner of Coal Tar for the High Explosives Committee of the Ministry of Munitions ; Member of the Anti-Gas Committee and of the Chemical Warfare Committee of the Ministry of Munitions ; Member of the Executive War Committee of the Royal Society ; Chairman of the Chemical Section of the Royal Society War Committee ; Chairman of the Reserved Occupations Committee of the Royal Society. Address : House of Letterawe, Loch Awe, Argyllshire N.B. (C2616)

FRANKLIN, Arthur Sumpter, M.B.E., b. 22 Jan. 1872 ; s. of William Alfred Franklin, of Portsmouth, Hants ; m. Rose Fanny, d. of Alfred George Curtiss, of Portsmouth, Hants. Educ. : St. Saviour's School, Paddington. Assistant Manager, National Cartridge and Box Repair Factory, Dagenham Dock, Essex. Address : Howgate, Donnington Road, Willesden, N.W. 10. (M8131)

FRANKLIN, Major Edward, O.B.E., R.A.O.C. (T.F.)

FRANKLIN, Capt. Frederick Joseph, O.B.E., b. 10 Feb. 1878 ; s. of Jos. Norris Franklin, J.P. for Devonshire, of Huxham, Exeter. Educ. : Blundell's, Tiverton. Served with the Royal 1st Devon Yeomanry Cavalry in Boer War (King's and Queen's Medals, with clasps) ; Commissioned to A.S.C. in 1901, becoming transport officer to Gen. French's flying columns in Cape Colony ; resigned commission after Boer War ; later accompanied Gen. Piet Cronje and Gen. Ben Viljoen to America ; returned to Natal and served in Bambatas Rebellion, Natal, 1908 ; served with Canadian Forces in World's War, 1915–16 (recruiting branch) ; secured commission, R.A.S.C. ; proceeded with B.E.F. to North Russia as O.C. Remounts to Syren Force ; had charge of transportation of troops by sledge from Soroha to Archangel, with rank of Major ; mentioned in despatches. Addresses : Riverside, Grantham, Lincs ; Hubbard Woods, Ill., U.S.A. Clubs : Royal Army Service Corps ; Adventurers', U.S.A. ; Scarboro', U.S.A. ; Exeter and County National, U.S.A. (O9717)

FRANKLIN, Major George Denne, O.B.E., I.M.S., M.B.

FRANKLIN, Leonard Benjamin, O.B.E., J.P., b. 15 Nov. 1862 ; s. of Ellis A. Franklin, of 35, Porchester Terrace, W. ; m. Laura Agnes, d. of William Laderburg, of 2, Inverness Terrace, W. Educ. : King's College, London ; Athenée Royale, Bruxelles. War Work : appointed Local Government representative at Folkestone and charged with direction of the Belgian Refugee work there ; later on assisted in Housing Schemes of Local Government Board. Addresses : 32, Hyde Park Gardens, N.2., London ; The Grange, Goudhurst, Kent. Clubs : Reform ; National Liberal ; Eighty. (O342)

FRANKLIN, Lilian Annie Margueretta, M.B.E.

FRANKLIN, Mabel, M.B.E.

FRANKLIN, Olga Heather, M.B.E., W.R.N.S.

FRANKLIN, Richard, O.B.E., b. 1876. Educ. : Colchester Grammar School, and King's Coll., London. Engineer. War Work : Was engaged from Sept. 1914, until the Armistice on work of a special character for the Admiralty, as whole-time Director of Davey, Paxman & Co., Ltd., London and Colchester. Address : Gidea Park, Essex. Club : British Empire. (O10433)

FRANKLIN, Robert Francis, O.B.E., b. 30 August, 1863 ; s. of late Henry Franklin, of Cottenham, Cambridge ; m. Edith Rosa, d. of late Myles Gilbert, of Needham Market, Suffolk. Educ. : Privately and at King's College, London. Clerk, Admiralty 1879–92 ; Assistant Secretary, Chatham Dockyard, 1892–1900 ; Assistant Cashier, Sheerness Dockyard 1900–1 ; Secretary to Admiral Superintendent, Devonport Dockyard, 1901 ; still serving. War Work : Secretary to Admiral Superintendent, Devonport Dockyard. Address : 2, The Terrace, H.M. Dockyard, Devonport. Club : Royal South Western Yacht, Plymouth. (O343)

FRANKLIN, Col. Will Hodgson, C.B.E., D.S.O., R. of O., b. 1873 ; s. of William Franklin, of Liverpool ; m. Sarah, d. of Hon. George Knowling, of St. John's, Newfoundland. Educ. : Liverpool Institute. His Majesty's Trade Commissioner in East Africa. War Work : Served in Royal Newfoundland Regt., Capt. 1914 ; Major, 1915 ; attached to Suffolk Regt., Lieut.-Col., 1916 ; attached to and commanded Batt. Royal Warwickshire Regt. ; severely wounded, Somme, July, 1916 ; Col., R. of O., 1919 ; (D.S.O., twice mentioned in despatches) ; Chief Instructor, Torquay Area, 1918. Address : P.O. Box 220, Nairobi, Kenya Colony. Clubs : City St. John's (Newfoundland) ; British Empire. (C2204)

FRANKLING, Albert Edward, M.B.E.

FRANKLING, Herbert George, C.B.E M.R.C.S., b. 1876 ; s. of the late George Frankling. Hon. Surg., Harrogate Infirmary ; m. 1906, Florence, who died 1917, d. of the late Joseph Ashmall. Address : 10, York Road, Harrogate. (C1152)

FRANKS, Paymaster-Lieut. Maurice Cardinall, O.B.E., R.N.R.

FRANKS, Capt. Rudolph Keane, M.B.E., b. 7 June, 1879 ; s. of Edward Franks, late of India Office, and grandson of George Cattermole, R.A. Educ. : St. Peter's Coll., Westminster. War Work : Joined Queen's Own Oxfordshire Hussars (Yeomanry) as trooper in Aug. 1914 ; proceeded to France with that regt. in Sept. of the same year ; took commission in 2/1st North Somerset Yeomanry, 1915 ; appointed Musketry Instructor to the regiment, 1916, after having gained 1st Class Instructor's Certificate at Bisley ; promoted Capt. and Adjutant, 1917. Address : Drayton St. Leonard, Oxon. (M5270)

FRASER, Major Angus George, M.B.E.

FRASER, Lieut.-Comm. Bruce Austin, O.B.E., R.N.

FRASER, Catherine, M.B.E., M.B., Ch.B.

FRASER, Lieut.-Col. Cecil, C.M.G., O.B.E., M.C., R.A.F. Served in the Great War, 1914–19 (despatches). (O3305)

FRASER, Constance Lady, C.B.E. ; d. of Col. Edwin Maude ; m. Nov. 1888, Sir Stuart Mitford Fraser, K.C.S.I., C.I.E., I.C.S., s. of the late J. Denholm Fraser, J.P. (C1965)

FRASER, Capt. Clive Stewart, M.B.E. Chief Censor, Straits Settlements. (M10258b)

FRASER, Lieut. David, M.B.E., S.A.S.S.

FRASER, Capt. David Hammand, O.B.E., M.C., M.A., M.D., B. Ch. (Camb.), b. 25 Dec. 1878 ; s. of Roderick Fraser, of 331, Norwood Road, S.E. ; m. Annie Isabel, d. of Dr. McMullen, of Parliament Hill, N.W.3. Educ. : Privately ; Gonville and Caius College, Cambridge ; London Hospital, E. Anæsthetist, Hampstead General and Great Northern Hospital : Medical Referee, Ministry of Pensions, Hampstead Division ; Lecturer, General Midwives Board. War Work : Captain R.A.M.C. and R.A.F. Medical Service ; attached 15th Field Ambulance, 28th Brigade R.F.A., 1st Army H.Q., 2nd Wing R.A.F., 65 Wing R.A.F. and M.O.i/c Special Air Force Wards, 14 General Hospital Wimereux. Address : 28, Belsize Avenue, N.W.3. (O2238)

FRASER, Sir Drummond, K.B.E., b. 1867 ; s. of late W. Murray Fraser, of London and Manchester. Joint Managing-Director of Manchester and Liverpool Banking Co. ; rendered valuable services in connection with War Savings Movement. Address : Earlscliffe, Altrincham, Cheshire.

FRASER, Evelyn Margaret, M.B E., d. of Hon. Lord Fraser, Senator of the College of Justice. War Work : Edinburgh War Dressings (Sphagnum Moss). Address : 31, Chester St. Edinburgh. Clubs : Queen's, Edinburgh ; Park, London. (M407)

FRASER, Florence, Mrs., b. 9 June, 1851 ; d. of Edward H. Finch Hatton, of Long Stratton, Cambridgeshire ; m. Hugh, s. of John Fraser, of Achnagairn, Inverness-shire. Educ. : At home. War Work : Commandant of Marsandra

Red Cross Hospital, Weymouth, Dorset. *Address :* Wittenham, Rodwell, Weymouth, Dorset. (O3720)

FRASER, Lieut.-Col. Forbes, C.B.E., Capt. and Acting Lieut.-Col. R.A.M.C. Served in the Great War, 1914–19 (despatches). (C1252)

FRASER, Capt. Francis William Ian Victor, O.B.E., M.C., R.A.F.

FRASER, Lieut. George Alexander, M.B.E., M.A., *b.* 9 June, 1877 ; *s.* of Wm. Stuart Fraser, W.S., of 42, Melville Street, Edinburgh ; *m.* Mary Elizabeth, *d.* of William Ramsbotham, of Manchester. *Educ. :* Edinburgh Academy and Edinburgh Univ. (M.A.). Chartered Accountant ; partner of the firm of R. and E. Scott, C.A., 64, Queen Street, Edinburgh. *War Work :* Trooper, Lothians and Border Horse, Sept. 1914, to March, 1915 ; gazetted, 2nd Lieut., 8th K.O.S.B., March, 1915 ; Lieut., Nov. 1915 ; wounded on the Somme, Aug. 1916 ; attached Adjutant-General's Branch, War Office, from May, 1917, to Feb. 1919. *Address :* Carcraig, Davidson's Mains, Midlothian. *Clubs :* Univ., Edinburgh ; Caledonian, London. (M5272)

FRASER, Capt. George Gerald Rae, M.B.E., R.A.F.

FRASER, Lieut.-Col. George William Frederick, O.B.E., R.A.F.

FRASER, Capt. Gordon Colquhoun, C.B.E., R.N. *War Work :* Rendered service as Capt. in charge of Defensive Mining. (C1163)

FRASER, Gordon Lushington, M.B.E.

FRASER, Henry Paterson, M.B.E.

FRASER, Hugh, O.B.E.

FRASER, Hugh, M.B.E.

FRASER, Irene Gladys, Mrs., C.B.E. General Superintendent of the St. Dunstan's Establishments in London and Provinces. (C3141)

FRASER, James, M.B.E.

FRASER, Comm. James Gordon, O.B.E., R.N.

FRASER, Major James Wilson, C.M.G., O.B.E., J.P., *b.* 31 May, 1862 ; *s.* of the late Capt. John Fraser, of Balnain, Inverness-shire ; *m.* Edith Knowles, *d.* of the late Andrew Knowles, of Swinton Old Hall, Lancashire. *Educ. :* The Coll., Inverness, and Royal Military Coll., Sandhurst. Major (ret.), 1st Batt. The Cheshire Regt. *War Work :* Served continuously in France from Nov 1914, till April, 1919, first with the 4th Batt. Seaforth Highlanders, and subsequently on the Staff (D.A.Q.M.G.) ; twice mentioned in despatches. *Address :* Leckmelm, by Garve, Ross-shire. (O5275)

FRASER, Jessie, Mrs., O.B.E.

FRASER, John Hugh Ronald, O.B.E., B.A., I.C.S., *b.* 15 March, 1878. *Educ. :* Haileybury, and Pembroke Coll., Cambridge. Serving under Political Department of Government of India. *Address :* c/o India Office, Whitehall. (O8254)

FRASER, Lieut. John James, M.B.E., R.A.S.C.

FRASER, Katherine Roy, M.B.E., *b.* 1870 ; *d.* of Gilbert Paterson ; *m.* James William Fraser. *War Work :* Nine months with Y.M.C.A. Huts in Le Havre ; afterwards in charge of Y.M.C.A. Hut on Flotta, Scapa Flow. *Address :* Merton Cottage, Liberton, Midlothian. (M1740)

FRASER, Laura Vivienne, Mrs., M.B.E. ; *d.* of Herman Crichton Bell, of Queenstown ; *m.* John Blackburne Fraser, Civil Commissioner and Magistrate, Riversdale, Cape ; *s.* of the late Lieut.-Gen. G. H. J. A. Fraser. *Educ. :* Perth, Scotland. *War Work :* Soldiers' Hut, De Aar Station, South Africa ; Gifts and Comforts Organisation Committee. *Address :* Riversdale, c/o Magistrate, Cape Province, S. Africa. (M1216)

FRASER, Malcolm, O.B.E., *b.* 25 May, 1873 ; *s.* of John Fraser, of Drummond, Inverness, Scotland ; *m.* Caroline, *d.* of Capt. James Watson, of Napier, New Zealand. *Educ. :* Rainings' School, Inverness, Scotland. New Zealand Government Statistician. *War Work :* Responsible for administration of N.Z. "Military Service Act, 1916," so far as it applied to civil registration ; originated and conducted system of balloting for conscripts thereunder. *Address :* Rawhiti Terrace, Kelburn, Wellington, N.Z. (O8330)

FRASER, Norman Graham, M.B.E., A.F.C., R.A.F.

FRASER, Capt. Percy Louis Alexander, M.B.E., J.P., *b.* 26 Oct. 1867 ; *s.* of Lionel Mordaunt Fraser, of Inverness-shire, Scotland ; *m.* Christina Isabel, *d.* of Valentine Plummer, of United States of America. *Educ. :* St. Mary's Coll., Trinidad. Superintendent of H.M. Prisons, Trinidad and Tobago. *War Work :* Trinidad Light Horse ; was Commandant of Prisoners of War Camp, Trinidad, Aug. 1914, to Feb. 1920. Commissioned officer in local forces mobilised for defence of Colony ; supervised mounting of guns on two islands for defence of Trinidad ; received thanks of Governor for services rendered during war. *Address :* H.M. Prisons, Port of Spain, Trinidad, B.W.I. *Club :* St. Clair (Port of Spain). (M1266)

FRASER, Lieut.-Col. Pierce Butler, O.B.E., D.S.O., *b.* 1881. *s.* of George John Fraser. Major R.A.S.C. and an A.Q.M.G., with rank of Lieut.-Col. ; served in the Great War, 1914–17 (despatches). (O8584)

FRASER, Robert, M.B.E.

FRASER, Sarah Louise, M.B.E., M.D., B.S. (Lond.), *b.* 28 Jan. 1874 ; *d.* of Hugh Innes Fraser, of Inverness, N.B. *Educ. :* Bedford Coll., London ; Royal Free Hospital School of Medicine for Women, London. Hon. Consulting Physician, Maternity Hospital, York ; Hon. Medical Officer for Diseases of Women and Children, York Dispensary. *War Work :* Hon. Medical Officer, Clifford Street V.A.D. Hospital, York, from May, 1915, to July, 1916 ; Hon. Medical Officer, Nunthorpe Hall V.A.D. Hospital, York, from July, 1916, to April, 1919. *Address :* 124, The Mount, York. (M8135)

FRASER, Lieut.-Col. Thomas, C.B.E., D.S.O., M.B., R.A.M.C., and Assist.-Director of Med. Ser. Served in the Great War, 1914–18 (despatches). (C1251)

FRASER, Thomas Houston, M.B.E.

FRASER, Capt. Thomas Lockhead, O.B.E., R.A.M.S.

FRASER, William, C.B.E., *b.* 1889 ; Managing Director, Phumperston Oil Co. (Limited), 135, Buchanan Street, Glasgow. (C500)

FRASER, William Stuart, O.B.E.

FRAZER, Major George Warren, O.B.E., R.A.S.C.

FRAZER, Lieut. Thomas, O.B.E.

FRAZER, Wilson Ray, O.B.E., *b.* 1873 ; *s.* of Joseph Frazer, of London ; *m.* Grace Haldane, *d.* of Charles H. Robbs, M.D., of Grantham. *Educ. :* Dulwich Coll. ; Oxford. Principal in Ministry of Health. *War Work :* Sec. of the Military Service (Civil Liabilities) Department during the demobilisation ; and inaugurated the scheme for giving financial assistance to ex-service men to restart them in civil life. *Address :* 6, College Gardens, Dulwich, S.E. (O10434)

FREDERICK, Sir Charles Edward St. John, Bart, O.B.E., *b.* 11 Sept., 1876 ; *s.* of Sir Charles Edward Frederick, 7th Bt. ; *m.* 1911, Ada Louisa, *d.* of Cæsar Czarnikow, of Effingham Hill, Surrey, and widow of Lieut.-Col. George Seymour Charles Jackenson, D.S.O. (*see* BURKE'S *Peerage*). (O5277)

FREDERICK, Capt. George Charles, C.B.E., R.N., (retired), *b.* 1855 ; *s.* of George Septemus Frederick ; *m.* Nellie, *d.* of George Peter Martin, C.B., R.N., of Highlands, Emsworth, Hants. *Educ. :* Eastman's and H.M.S. "Britannia." Entered Royal Navy, 1869 ; promoted Commander R.N. December 1893 and Captain (retired) 1908 ; Employed at Admiralty as Assistant Hydrographer 1892–1900 ; and as Naval Adviser Harbour Department, Board of Trade 1900–10. *War Work :* On War Staff at the Admiralty, serving under the Trade Division, first as Admiralty representative on the Liverpool and London War Risks Association Committee and subsequently in addition as Shipping Intelligence Officer until May, 1919. *Address :* Lou Souliou, Boulouris-sur-Mer, St. Raphael, Var, France. *Club :* United Service. (C167)

FREEBORN, 2nd Lieut. Leonard, M.B.E., R.A.F.

FREEGARD, Capt. Charles Gordon, M.B.E.

FREEL, Lieut.-Col. and Qr.-Mr. Joseph, O.B.E., D.L.I.

FREEMAN, Alice, Mrs., O.B.E., Medaille de la Reine Elizabeth, *b.* 26 Jan. 1860 ; *d.* of Marcus Goodbody, of Inchmore, Clara, King's Co., Ireland ; *m.* Richard Birt, *s.* of John Freeman. *War Work :* Organiser and Manager of Free Buffet, Kingsbridge Station, Dublin. *Address :* 13, Ailesbury Road, Dublin. (O10435)

FREEMAN, Arthur David, O.B.E.

FREEMAN, Eng.-Comm. Benson Fletcher, O.B.E., R.N.

FREEMAN, Capt. George Herbert, M.B.E., R.G.A. (S.R.), *b.* 3 Oct. 1880 ; *s.* of George Deane Freeman, of Woodlane, Falmouth ; *m.* Patricia Tegfryn, *d.* of William Tegfryn Pryce, of Cardiff. *Educ. :* St. Paul's. Solicitor. *War Work :* Joined Artists Rifles, Nov. 1915 ; gazetted 2nd Lieut., R.G.A. (S.R.), Aug. 1916 ; Lieut., Feb. 1917 ; A. Capt. and Adjutant 75th Brigade R.G.A., March, 1918 ; proceeded to Salonica, Jan. 1917, and returned to England, Jan. 1919 ; demobilised, March, 1919 ; twice mentioned in despatches. *Addresses :* Cavendish House, London Road, St. Albans ; 23, Bedford Row, W.C. *Club :* Camera ; Law Society. (M4785)

FREEMAN, John Joseph, C.B.E., J.P., *b.* 8 April, 1851. *War Work :* Red Cross and other work. *Address :* Shepperton-on-Thames. (C2617)

FREEMAN, Major Max, O.B.E., R.A.F.

FREEMAN, Lieut. Percy Tom, M.B.E., R.E. (T.F.).

FREEMAN, Philip Anthony Mallows, M.B.E.

FREEMAN, Sir Philip Horace, K.B.E., M.A., *b.* 27 May, 1878 ; *e. s.* of late George Broke Freeman, Barrister-at-law ; *m.* Phyllis Mary, *d.* of late Edward Scott. *Educ. :* Marlborough and Trinity College, Cambridge. Admitted Solicitor, 1904 ; Member of the firm of Peacock and Goddard of Gray's Inn. *War Work :* Honorary Sec. of the Business Committee of the Officers' Families Fund 1914–19. *Address :* 5 Cadogan Court, S.W.3. (K373)

FREEMAN, Robert, O.B.E.

FREEMAN, Lieut. Sidney Charles, O.B.E., R.N.V.R.

FREEMAN, Sidney Thomas, M.B.E. (M15971)

FREEMAN, Sterry Baines, C.B.E., M.I.C.E., M.I.N.A., *b.* 1875 ; *s.* of Captain T. W. Freeman, of Great Crosby ; *m.* Edith Gertrude, *d.* of Peter Ashcroft, of Great Crosby. *Educ. :* Merchant Taylors' School, Great Grosby, and Gymnasie, Luneburg, Hanover. Superintendent Engineer, Alfred Holt and Co. ; Member of British Marine Engineering, Design and Construction Committee and of British Engineering Standards Committee. *War Work :* Supervising the engineering staff and material of the fleets of the Ocean S.S. Co. and China Mutual S.S. Co., carrying troops and munitions throughout the War ; Chairman Liverpool Superintendent Engineers' Committee 1916–17 ; Representative of the Director of Experiments and Research upon Engineer-in-Chief's Committee at the Admiralty. *Addresses :* India Buildings, Liverpool ; Palm Grove, Oxton Cheshire. (C2618)

FREEMAN, Lieut.-Col. Arthur Peere WILLIAMS-, D.S.O., O.B.E., *b.* 1877 ; *s.* of the Rev. Henry Peere Williams-Freeman, Rector of Turner's Puddle, Dorset ; *m.* 1908, Hilda Gwladys, *d.* of Lieut.-Col. Robert Erasmus Saunders, of Alton Pancras, Dorset. Major and Acting Lieut.-Col. Duke of Cornwall's L.I. ; served with the Tirah Expedition, 1897–98 (two clasps) ; Great War, 1914–19 (despatches thrice). (O5936)

FREEMANTLE, 2nd Lieut. Robert McGorman, M.B.E., R.A.F.

FREER, Capt. Harry Branston, O.B.E., R.A.S.C.

FREER, Maude Alice, M.B.E.

FREESTONE, Capt. Sidney, M.B.E., M.C., Essex Regt., b. 16 Oct. 1870. *Educ.:* Board School, Sawston, Cambridgeshire. *War Work:* Served in the South African Campaign, 1901 and 1902, and the Great War, Aug. 1914, to Nov. 1918, France and Belgium; thrice mentioned in despatches. (M6526)

FREETH, Dorothy Irene, O.B.E.

FREETH, Capt. Francis Arthur, O.B.E., M.Sc., Cheshire Regiment (T.F.), b. 2 Jan. 1884; s. of Edward Henry Freeth, of Liverpool; m. Ethel Elizabeth, d. of G. N. Warbrick, of Silecroft. *Educ.:* University of Liverpool. Chief Chemist, Messrs. Brunner, Mond and Co. Ltd.; Fellow of the Institute of Chemistry; Fellow of the Institute of Physics; Fellow of the Physical Society of London; Member of the Institute of Metals, the Faraday Society and the Dutch and American Chemical Societies. *War Work:* Mobilised August, 1914, served in France, Feb.–March, 1915; assisted in the manufacture of explosives at Messrs. Brunner, Mond and Co. Ltd. from April, 1915 till the Armistice. *Address:* Heysmere, Sandiway, Cheshire. *Club:* Chemical Industry. (O1355)

FREITAS, Hubert St. Clair, M.B.E.

FREITIGRATH, Capt. Otto Tennent Eastman, O.B.E., R.A.S.C.

FREIR, Walter Leo, C.B.E.

FREKE, Ambrose Eyre HUSSEY-, M.B.E.

FREMANTLE, Barberina Rogers, Hon. Lady, C.B.E., b. 5 Feb. 1843; d. of Robert McIntosh Isaacs, of Sydney, New South Wales; m. Hon. Sir Edmund Robert Fremantle, Adm., G.C.B. C.M.G., s. of Thomas Francis, 1st Lord Cottesloe. *War Work:* Emergency Committee of Navy League; Hospital Work; Several War Committees. *Address:* 44, Lower Sloane Street, London, S.W.1. (C2620)

FREMANTLE, Lieut.-Col. Francis Edward, O.B.E.

FREMANTLE, Major John Morton, M.B.E.

FREMANTLE, Vera Evelyn Selina, Mrs., M.B.E.; d. of Henry Marsh, C.I.E., of Springmount, Queen's Co., Ireland; m. Selwyn Howe Fremantle, C.S.I., C.I.E., I.C.S., s. of Admiral the Hon. Sir E. R. Fremantle, of 44, Lower Sloane Street, London (see BURKE'S *Peerage*). *War Work:* Hon. Sec. Red Cross, Allahabad. *Address:* Commissioner's House, Meerut, U.P., India. (M2698)

FRENCH, Hon. Essex Eleonora, O.B.E., d. of Viscount French (see BURKE'S *Peerage*). (O347)

FRENCH, Henry Leon, C.B., O.B.E., b. 30 Dec. 1883; s. of Frederick E. French, J.P., of Southsea, Portsmouth; m. Clare, d. of the late Charles Grimes, F.R.G.S., of Southsea. *Educ.:* Privately. Entered Civil Service by open competition and appointed to Board of Agriculture, 1901; promoted to First Division, 1909; Assistant Secretary of the Ministry of Agriculture and Fisheries, 1920. *War Work:* Secretary of Lord Milner's Committee on Home Production of Food, 1915; Joint Secretary of Lord Selborne's Committee on Agricultural Policy, 1916–17; Private Sec. to Sir Arthur (now Lord) Lee, Director General of Food Production, 1917; General Sec. of the Food Production Department, 1917–19. *Address:* 91, Upper Tulse Hill, S.W.2. (O348)

FRENCH, Lieut.-Col. Herbert, C.B.E., M.D., F.R.C.P., R.A.M.C. Served in the Great War, 1914–19 (despatches). (C1573)

FRENCH, Herbert Edward, M.B.E., b. 27 April, 1867; s. of Thomas John Blencoe French, of Maldon, Essex; m. Lily, d. of Capt. George Beckett, of Thorne, near Doncaster. *Educ.:* Hull Adelaide Wesleyan, and Trinity House Navigation Schools. Master Mariner; Younger Brother, Hull Trinity House. *War Work:* Master of the S.S.'s "Zero" and "Kovno," of the Ellerman's Wilson Line of Hull, during the whole period of the war, trading between different ports in the United Kingdom and France, to Archangel and Norway. *Address:* Maribo, 193, North Boulevard, Hull, E. Yorks. (M8139)

FRENCH, Hilda Dillwyn, M.B.E.

FRENCH, James Frederick, M.B.E., b. 21 Nov. 1884; s. of Frederick French, of Newcastle, Staffordshire; m. Gertrude, d. of Alfred Barber, of Brondesbury. *Educ.:* Haberdashers' Company School (Aske's, Hatcham, London, S.E.). Staff Officer, H.M. Foreign Office. *War Work:* Acting Staff Officer, Ministry of Blockade, and Foreign Office. *Address:* 25, Torbay Road, Brondesbury, N.W. 6. (M8140)

FRENCH, Sir John Russell, M.B.E., b. 5 March, 1847; s. of Major John French, of Bengal Light Infantry; m. Margaret Anne, d. of William Lilly Hawkins, of Christchurch, New Zealand. *Educ.:* The King's School, Parramatta, Sydney. General Manager of Bank of New South Wales, Sydney. *War Work:* Hon. Treas. and Financial Adviser to various large Patriotic Funds. *Address:* Vange, Fairfax Road, Belle Vue Hill, Sydney, N.S.W. *Clubs:* Union (Sydney); Christchurch (New Zealand). (K186)

FRENCH, Capt. John William, M.B.E., b. 8 Feb. 1873; s. of John French, of London; m. Evangeline Mary, d. of Percy Gower, of Cape Town and Rhodesia. Civil Service, Imperial and South African. *War Work:* German South-West African Campaign. *Address:* Sunnyside, Pretoria. (M2880)

FRENCH, Lewis, C.I.E., C.B.E., J.P., b. October, 1873; s. of David French, of Eltham, Kent; m. Margaret Ruth Gilliam, d. of Sir Charles Lewis Tupper, K.C.I.E., C.S.I., of East Molesey, Surrey. *Educ.:* Merchant Taylors' School

and St. John's Coll., Oxford. Indian Civil Service; Secretary to Government of the Punjab. *War Work:* Sec. for Military affairs to the Punjab Goverment; Sec. to the Provincial Recruiting Board. *Address:* U.S. Club, Simla. *Club:* East India United Services. (C1966)

FRENCH, Lieut. Louis Emanuel, M.B.E.

FRENCH, Reginald Thomas George, O.B.E.

FRENCH, William Henry, M.B.E., b. 31 July, 1874; s. of William Duncan French, of Kendal. *Educ.:* Kendal Green School. Engineer; partner, Burkitt and French, 76, Victoria Street, Manchester, Engineers; partner, Collins and Company, Cheetham Hill, Manchester, Engineers. *War Work:* Munitions Area Dilution Officer, in charge of Manchester, Bolton, Bury, and Ashton Districts, acting for the Badges and Protected Occupation Section of the Ministry of Munitions. *Address:* 39, Campbell Road, Longsight, Manchester. *Club:* Engineers', Manchester. (M8142)

FRERE, Frank Horace, O.B.E., A.K.C., M.Inst.C.E., b. 12 July, 1869; s. of Horace Frere, of Lauriston Road, Wimbledon Common, S.W. (see BURKE'S *Landed Gentry*, under John Frere, of Roydon Hall); m. Alice Mary, d. of James McInnes, Kincaid, Milton of Campsie, and widow of Patrick Graham, of Skelmorlie. *Educ.:* Haileybury Coll.; Engineering Department, King's Coll., London. Associate of King's Coll., 1888; Member of the Institution of Civil Engineers, 1905; now Western Divisional Engineer, Midland Railway, Derby. *War Work:* Responsible for the layout and construction of siding accommodation, workmen's platforms, etc., provided for the Government on the Western Division (Derby to Bristol, Avonmouth, and Bath) of the Midland Railway, comprising some 30 different works in all. *Address:* Coombe Crest, Belper Road, Derby. (O10437)

FRERE, Letitia Helen, M.B.E.

FREW, Capt. Harry, M.B.E.

FREWEN, Edward James, M.B.E.

FREWEN, Violet Helen, M.B.E.; d of the late Col. Edward Frewen, C.B., of Brickwall, Northiam, Sussex. *War Work:* Commandant, Red Cross Auxiliary Hospital, Northiam, Sussex, for 3¼ years; registrar for Northiam for Women's Land Army. *Address:* Brickwall, Northiam, Sussex. *Club:* Forum. (M8144)

FREYBERG, Comm. Geoffrey Herbert, O.B.E., R.N.

FRICKER, Guy Carey, O.B.E., b. 1860; s. of Henry Robinson Tricker; m. Lena, Maud Marian, d. of John Symonds Bockett. *Educ.:* Privately. Founder and Managing Director of Fricker's Metal Co., Ltd., Luton, Beds. *War Work:* Inventing, for disposal of Government during war, a successful process for highly refining metallic zinc as required for making cartridge brass, etc. *Address:* The Limes, Milton Road, Harpenden, Herts. (O1356)

FRIEDLANDER, Grace Christian, Mrs., M.B.E.

FRIEND, Dorothy, M.B.E.

FRIEND, Maj.-Gen. the Right Hon. Sir Lovick Bransby, P.C., C.B., K.B.E., R.E., b. 25 April, 1856; s. of the late Frederick Friend. Appointed Lieut. 1873; Capt. 1885; Major, 1893; Lieut.-Col. 1900; Brevet Col. 1904; Col. 1906; Maj.-Gen. 1916; was Instructor in Fortification, R.M.C., 1883–4; Sec. R.E. Committee, 1884–9; Director of Works, Egypt, 1900–4; Assist. Director of Fortifications, Headquarters, 1906–8; Brig.-Gen. comdg. Coast Defences, Scottish Command, 1908–12; Maj.-Gen. in charge of Administration, Ireland; G.O.C. Ireland, 1913–16; served with the Nile Expedition, 1898; has 3rd Class Osmanieh and 3rd Class Medjidieh, Commander, Order of Leopold, Belgium Legion of Honour, and has Croix de Guerre. *Clubs:* Naval and Military; United Service. (K193)

FRISBY, Elizabeth Rowley, M.B.E.; d. of late Joseph Frisby, of Leicester. *Educ.:* Girls' Wyggeston School, Leicester. *War Work:* In Aug. 1914, organised the Leicester members of the Women's Social and Political Union and started a clothing depôt for distribution of garments among the needy families of soldiers; in Nov. 1914, joined the Women Patrols, London, and performed duty at Waterloo, Euston and Liverpool Street Stations; in 1915 was actively engaged on work for the W.S.P.U. to gain Government recognition for Women Munition Workers; in Jan. 1916, in conjunction with her mother and two sisters, gave and equipped a Y.M.C.A. hut which was erected in the camp of the 11th Loyal North Lancs. Batt. at Seaford, Sussex; with her youngest sister took entire charge and management of hut, and accompanied the Batt. upon its removal to Luton, and afterwards to Parkeston, Harwich, and to Margate; in April, 1918, organised and ran, on behalf of the Y.M.C.A., the small canteens attached to recruiting offices in various parts of London under the National Service Ministry; on completion of the above work, ran two Y.M.C.A. huts in the Shepherd's Bush District, until April, 1919. *Addresses:* The Cedars, Stoneygate, Leicester; Queen's Club Gardens, London, W. *Clubs:* International Women's Franchise; Leicestershire Golf; Seacroft Golf. (M414)

FRITH, Lieut.-Col. Cyril Halsted, C.B.E. Major and Brevet Lieut.-Col. Oxfordshire and Bucks. L.I.; served in the Great War, 1914–19 (despatches). (C1574)

FRITH, Comm. William Willoughby Cole, O.B.E.

FRIZELLE, Frances Emily, Mrs., M.B.E.

FROGGATT, Capt. Charles Edward, O.B.E., R.N.R., R.D.

FROGLEY, Major Walter James, O.B.E., b. May, 1874; s. of William Frogley, of Challow, Faringdon; m. Kathleen Georgina, d. of the late Rev. D. A. Doudney. *Educ.:* King

BIOGRAPHIES. Fullerton

Alfred's School, Wantage. *War Work :* Served in Horse Transport in Alexandria, Serbia, Salonica, and Constantinople ; commanded 29th Reserve Park from June, 1915, to March, 1919. *Address :* Seend, Melksham, Wiltshire. *Club :* Services. (O8689)

FROOD, Bertha Helen, Mrs., O.B.E.

FROOD, Mary Sophia, M.B.E.

FROOD, Major Thomas Martin, O.B.E., R.A.M.C.

FROST, Ann Lucy, Mrs., M.B.E. ; *d.* of the late Sir Thomas Gibbons Frost, of Chester ; *m.* Francis Aylmer, *s.* of Francis Aylmer Frost, of Reddish, Stockport. *Educ. :* Belstead School, Ipswich. *War Work :* Quartermaster, Raddon Court (B.R.C.S.) Hospital, Warrington, Aug. 1914, to March, 1915 ; Commandant, Thelwall Heys (B.R.C.S.) Hospital, Cheshire, March 1915 to Feb. 1919. *Address :* Grappenhall Hall, near Warrington. (M8145)

FROST, Major Augustine Thomas, O.B.E., R.A.M.C., M.B.

FROST, E. J. Allan, O.B.E.

FROST, Brig.-Gen. Frank Dutton, C.B.E. Capt. and Brevet Major, Indian Army ; T. Brig.-Gen. Supply and Transport Corps. *War Work :* Mesopotamia, 1914–19 (despatches). (C1424)

FROST, Lieut.-Col. Geoffrey Meadows, O.B.E.

FROST, Capt. George Hewitt, O.B.E., I.A.R.O.

FROST, Mark Edwin Pescott, O.B.E., I.S.O.

FROST, Capt. Oliver Harry, M.B.E., M.C., R.A.F.

FROST, Percy, M.B.E., *b.* 20 Dec. 1858 ; *s.* of John Dixon Frost, of Hull ; *m.* Violet Lyle, *d.* of John Richardson, of Adelaide, South Australia. *Educ. :* Marlborough. H.B.M.'s Vice-Consul, Perugia, Italy. *War Work :* Head of English Propaganda in the Province of Umbria, Italy. *Address :* British Vice-Consulate, Perugia, Italy. (M8146)

FROST, Major Robert Henry, M.B.E., R.A.S.C.

FROST, Capt. Sydney George, M.B.E.

FROST, Lieut. Wilfred John Thomas, M.B.E.

FROST, Capt. William Arthur, O.B.E., M.B., B.Ch. R.U.I., R.A.M.C., *b.* 30 March, 1886 ; *s.* of Edmond Frost, M.D., J.P., of Newmarket-on-Fergus, Co. Clare, Ireland ; *m.* Josephine Marion, *d.* of Col. John Stirling Stirling, R.A., of Gargunnock, Stirlingshire, Scotland. *Educ. :* Catholic Univ., Dublin. *War Work :* Served in India during entire period of the war ; was Senior Medical Officer, Hyderabad, Sind, 'rom Feb. 1915, to June, 1919. *Address :* Beech Lawn, Newmarket-on-Fergus, Co. Clare, Ireland. (O8471)

FROSTICK, James Arthur, C.B.E.

FROUD, William Percy, M.B.E., *b.* 13 April, 1859 ; *s.* of late William Froud, of Brighton ; *m.* Mary Ann *d.* of late Joseph Fenner, of Brighton. *Educ. :* Clarendon House School, Brighton. Joint Superintendent, Joint South-Western and Brighton Committee, Portsmouth. *War Work :* Railway Transport. *Address :* Terminus House, Town Station, Portsmouth, Hants. (M415)

FROUDE, Comm. Ashley Anthony, C.M.G., O.B.E., J.P., R.N.V.R., *b.* 28 June, 1863 ; *s.* of James Anthony Froude, of Salcombe, Devon ; *m.* Ethel Aubrey, *d.* of Capt. A. P. Hallifax, of Halwell House, Kingsbridge. *Educ. :* Westminster ; Oriel Coll., Oxford. *War Work :* Hydrophone Service, in Anti-Submarine Division. *Address :* Collapit Creek, Kingsbridge, S. Devon. *Clubs :* New Univ. ; Royal Western Yacht. (O9276)

FROUDE, Major Charles William, M.B.E., R.G.A., *b.* 9 Feb. 1881 ; *s.* of Charles Froude, late R.H.A. ; *m.* Mary, *d.* of Samuel Howard. *Educ. :* Elementary Schools. *Address :* 39, Wrottesley Road, London, S.E. 18. (M5274)

FROWD, Eng.-Capt. Wm. Smeeton, C.B.E.

FRY, Capt. Alfred Andrew, M.B.E., R.A.F.

FRY, Alfred Joseph, M.B.E., *b.* 1 Nov. 1876 ; *s.* of George Fry, of London ; *m.* Florence Annie, *d.* of William Francis Wright, of London. *Educ. :* St. Thomas' Charterhouse, London. *War Work :* Deputation to Mesopotamia in erecting X-Ray apparatus, 1915 ; Electrician to the X-Ray Institute and Orthopædic Hospital, Lady Chelmsford War Hospitals at Mussoorie and Dehra Dun. *Address :* X-Ray Institute, Dehra Dun, U.P., India. (M6146)

FRY, Beatrice, Mrs., O.B.E.

FRY, Dorothy Margaret, M.B.E.

FRY, Capt. Douglas Gaskoin, M.B.E.

FRY, Ellen Margaret, Lady, O.B.E., *d.* of the late Sir John Goldie Taubman, of The Nunnery, Isle of Man ; *m.* Major-Gen. Sir William Fry, K.C.V.O., C.B., Lieut.-Govr., Isle of Man (*see* BURKE's *Peerage*). *War Work :* Training of wounded soldiers, in hospitals, in handicraft. *Address :* Government House, Isle of Man. (O10438)

FRY, Frederick William, M.B.E.

FRY, George Samuel, C.B.E., *b.* 18 Aug. 1853 ; *s.* of Robert William Fry, of Stamford Hill, Middlesex ; *m.* Artemisia Julia, *d.* of William Cleversley, of Camberwell. *Educ. :* St. Ann's School, Tottenham ; Commercial College, Stoke Newington. Formerly Accountant-General to the Board of Trade. *War Work :* Member of Committee for Licensing Export of Coal, 1916–19. *Address :* 15, Walsingham Road, Hove, Sussex. *Club :* Royal Colonial Institute. (C168)

FRY, Lieut.-Col. John James, M.B.E.

FRY, Theodore Wilfrid, O.B.E.

FRY, Lieut. and Qr.-Mr. Walter, M.B.E.

FRY, Major Walter, Arnold Le Roy, O.B.E.

FRYE, Major Colin Charlwood, O.B.E., R.A.M.C. (T.F.)

FRYER, Lieut.-Col. Cecil Robert, O.B.E., *b.* 11 Jan. 1864 ; *s.* of the late Col. F. D. Fryer, J.P., D.L., of Moulton Paddocks, Newmarket ; *m.* Margaret Fanny, *d.* of the late Very Rev. P. F. Eliot, D.D., K.C.V.O., Dean of Windsor. *Educ. :* Cheltenham. Served in the Suffolk Regt. from Nov. 1885, to Jan. 1914 ; Hazara Expedition, 1888 (medal with clasp) ; South Africa, 1902 (Queen's Medal with 2 clasps) ; served in the Humber Garrison, Northern Command, in the rank of Major, D.A.A. and Q.M.G., from Aug. 1914, to July, 1917, and in rank of Lieut.-Col., A.A. and Q.M.G., from July, 1917, to April, 1918 ; attached to the Staff, Northern Command, from April. 1918, to Dec. 1918 ; commanded Dispersal Unit at Ripon from Dec. 1918, to April, 1919 ; twice mentioned in the "London Gazette" for "valuable services rendered during the war." *Club :* Army and Navy. (O7171)

FRYER, Frances Mary, Mrs., M.B.E., *b.* 2 March, 1874 ; *d.* of Alfred Cooke, of Derby ; *m.* Arthur Tomlinson, *s.* of Joseph Fryer, of Derby. Member of Derby Borough War Pensions Committee, and Children's Welfare Sub-Committee ; Hon. Sec. Disabled Soldiers' Land Settlement Committee ; Hon. Sec. Derbyshire Golf Club, House Committee ; Joint Hon. Sec. Sherwood Foresters Prisoners of War Regimental Care Committee, Oct. 1915, to April, 1920 ; Hon. Sec. and Treas. Soldiers' and Sailors' Families Association, Derby Borough Division. *Address :* 34, Renals Street, Derby. (M8148)

FRYER, George Ernest, O.B.E., M.R.C.S.

FRYER, Lieut. Sydney Ernest, M.B.E.

FRYER, Walter John, C.B.E., *b.* 28 March, 1871 ; *s.* of Frederick George Henry Fryer, of Norfolk ; *m.* Margaret, *d.* of George Nyren, of Brighton. *Educ. :* Brixton Grammar School. Consulting Engineer. *War Work :* Member of Board of Control with Lord Rothermere and Manager (without pay) of the Royal Army Factories at Pimlico, etc. ; was Controller of the Section responsible for the reclothing of the Demobilised Armies. *Address :* Kalyis House, Maidenhead, Berks. *Club :* Constitutional. (C965)

FRYER, Walter John, C.B.E. Hon. Manager, Royal Army Clothing Department Factories. (C965)

FUGE, Capt. William Valentine Greatraks, M.B.E., R.G.A.

FUHRMAN, Major Osmond Charles William, O.B.E., A.I.F.

FULCHER, Lieut. Ernest William Popplewell, M.B.E.

FULCHER, Lieut.-Col. George Arthur, O.B.E., R.A., *b.* 25 Nov. 1869 ; *s.* of James Fulcher, of Litcham, Norfolk. *Educ. :* Military School, Woolwich. Deputy Assistant-Director of Artillery. *War Work :* Artillery Department, War Office. *Address :* 66, Hayes Road, Bromley, Kent. (O352)

FULFORD, Catherine, M.B.E.

FULFORD, Edward Oliver Heywood, M.B.E.

FULFORD, Major Henry Edward, O.B.E., R.A.S.C.

FULLAGAR, Leo Alfred, M.B.E., *b.* 3 April, 1883 ; *s.* of the Rev. H. S. Fullagar, of Hunworth Rectory, Norfolk. *Educ. :* Framlingham Coll. ; Caius Coll., Cambridge. Chief Engineer to the British Cyanides Co., Ltd., Oldbury, Worcs, and Allied Companies ; constructed H.M. Potash Factory, Oldbury. *Address :* Parkhurst, Harborne, Birmingham. (M1746)

FULLER, Capt. Charles, M.B.E, R.E.

FULLER, Elfrida Mary, Lady, M.B.E. ; *e. d.* of William Henry Iremonger, D.L., of Wherwell Priory, Hants. ; *m.* 17 Jan. 1911, Sir Francis Charles Bernard Dudley, K.B.E., C.M.G. (*see* BURKE's *Peerage*), *s.* of the late Capt. Charles F. Fuller, 15th Royal Lancers. (M6442)

FULLER, Sir Francis Charles, K.B.E., C.M.G., *b.* 22 Nov. 1866 ; *s.* of Capt. Charles Fuller, of Florence ; *m.* Elfrida Mary, *d.* of William Iremonger, of Wherwell Priory, Hants. *Educ. :* Saint Charles' Coll., Cardinal Manning's School. Colonial Civil Service. Fiji, 1884 ; Resident Commr. Roturah, 1889 ; District Commr. Lagos, 1892 ; Resident of Ibadan, 1897 ; Col. Treas. Lagos, 1901 ; Asst. Sec. to Govt. Malta, 1902 ; Chief Commr. Ashanti, 1905. *Clubs :* Travellers' ; Garrick ; Royal Automobile. (K318)

FULLER, Shipwright Lieut. James, M.B.E., R.N.

FULLER, Mabel Frances, M.B.E., *b.* 18 Oct. 1888. *War Work :* Sec. to Director of Stores and Transports, British Red Cross Society and Order of St. John. (M8150)

FULLER, Mabel, Mrs. Robert Fleetwood, O.B.E.

FULLER, Mary Francis, Mrs., M.B.E. ; *d.* of James Samuel Drury, M.D., F.R.C.S., of 13, Radnor Place ; *widow of* the late Herbert Henry Fuller, Mayor of Paddington. *War Work :* Worked during whole period of war for the Ladies' Emergency Committee, Navy League, as Hon. Sec. *Address :* 31, Palace Court, W. 2. *Club :* Albemarle. (M8151)

FULLER, Flight-Lieut. Norman Berwick, M.B.E., R.A.F., *b.* 5 Nov. 1893 ; *s.* of the late Herbert H. Fuller, of 31, Palace Court, Bayswater, W. *Educ. :* Harrow ; Christ Church, Oxford. Seconded from the R.A.F. to the Civil Administration in Mesopotamia ; Assist. to Civil Commissioner, Bagdad. *War Work :* 2nd Lieut., K.R.R.C., Aug. 1914, to Dec. 1915 (France 1915) ; transferred to R.F.C., Dec. 1915 (France, 1916–17) ; Capt., 1917 ; to Mesopotamia, 1918 ; Commanding R.A.F. Detachment in N. Persia with Gen. Dunsterville's Expedition to Baku, 1918 ; mentioned in despatches. *Address :* 31, Palace Court, W. 2. *Clubs :* Cavendish ; R.A.F. (M5973)

FULLER, Walter Everard, M.B.E.

FULLERTON, Alexander Moffitt, O.B.E., *b.* 14 Oct. 1865 ; *s.* of the Rev. Alexander Fullerton, of Dalkey, Co. Dublin ; *m.* May, *d.* of Samuel McComas, J.P., of Dalkey, Co. Dublin. *Educ. :* The Coll., Lurgan, and Wesley Coll.

Dublin. Deputy Chief Clerk, General Valuation and Boundary Survey of Ireland. *War Work :* Vice-Chairman, Soldiers' Central Club, Dublin ; Hon. Treas. Army Women's Hostel, Dublin ; Corps Officer, St. John Ambulance Brigade. *Addresses :* 1, Alexandra Terrace, Dalkey, Co. Dublin ; 6, Ely Place, Dublin. (O10440)

FULLERTON, Capt. James Glen Anderson, M.B.E., *b.* 20 July, 1873 ; *s.* of James Fullerton, of Johnshaven ; *m.* Amelia Cowper, *d.* of David Valentine, of Montrose. *Educ. :* Johnshaven Public Schools, and Montrose Academy. Shipmaster. *War Work :* Transport. *Address :* 25, Bents Road, Montrose. *Clubs :* Overseas ; Burns, Montrose. (M1747)

FULLERTON, James, C.B.E.

FULLJAMES, Edith Marianne, M.B.E., *b.* 1 Nov. 1867 ; *d.* of M. G. Totterdell, of Portsmouth ; *m.* Gilbert, *s.* of John Fulljames, of Portsmouth. *Educ. :* Southsea. *War Work :* Commandant of Oatlands, Kingston Crescent, Portsmouth, V.A.D. Auxiliary Hospital, equipped and staffed by members of Detachment, Hants 66 ; acted as Officer in Charge of this Hospital from 1914–19. *Address :* St. Briavel, Queen's Grove, Southsea. (M8152)

FULTON, 2nd Lieut. Angus Robertson, M.B.E., R.A.F.

FULTON, Lieut.-Col. David, C.M.G., C.B.E. Australian Light Horse Regt ; served in the Great War, 1915–19 (despatches). (C792)

FULTON, David Bowie, O.B.E.

FULTON, Hamilton, O.B.E., 28 July, 1880 ; *s.* of Hamilton Fulton, of Milford, Salisbury ; *m.* Gwendoline Tremaine, *d.* of Ernest Godfree, late of Wykeham Lodge, Hersham, and 39, Porchester Terrace, W. *Educ. :* Marlborough and in France. Director and General Manager of Martinsyde, Ltd., Woking, Aeroplane Designers and Aeronautical and General Engineers ; Director and General Manager, Accumulators of Woking, Ltd. ; Management Committee of Society of British Aircraft Constructors (S.B.A.C.) ; Executive Committee of London and District Association of the Engineering and National Employers' Federation, etc. *War Work :* Ministry of Munitions Committee on Aircraft Production ; Director and General Manager of Martinsyde, Ltd. *Addresses :* Carlton House, Regent Street, S.W. ; Byways, Berkhamstead. *Clubs :* Junior Carlton ; City of London. (O3221)

FULTON, Capt. John Sidney, O.B.E., M.C., *b.* 11 June, 1890 ; *s.* of the late James Fulton, of 11, Mayfield Terrace, Edinburgh ; *m.* Edith Jeannette, *d.* of Capt. H. M. J. McCance, late of the Royal Scots. *Educ. :* Merchiston Castle, Edinburgh ; R.M.C., Sandhurst. *Address :* 13, Craven Terrace, Lancaster Gate, W. 2. (O5278)

FULTON, Paymaster Sub.-Lieut. Robert Arthur, M.B.E., R.N.V.R.

FURBER, Edward Price, C.B.E., M.R.C.S. (Eng.), L.R.C.P. (Lond.), *b.* 1864 ; *s.* of Charles Furber ; *m.* Olive, *d.* of George Mann, of Hamilton Terrace. *Educ. :* Charterhouse ; St. Bartholomew's Hospital. *War Work :* Medical Officer to the McCaul Naval and Military and Mackinnon Hospitals ; Obstetric Physician to Lady Howard de Walden's Maternity Hospital for Officers' wives. *Address :* 25, Welbeck Street, Cavendish Square. (C3079)

FURBER, Major Montague, O.B.E.

FURLER, Capt. and Qr.-Mr. Herbert John, M.B.E., R.A.M.C. (T.F.)

FURLEY, John Talfourd, O.B.E., *b.* 31 March, 1878 ; *s.* of the late Henry Furley, Rector of Kingsnorth, Kent. *Educ. :* Tonbridge School. Secretary for Native Affairs, Gold Coast Colony ; Member of Executive and Legislative Councils, Gold Coast Colony. *War Work :* Political Services in Togoland, W. Africa. *Club :* Junior Constitutional. (O993)

FURLONG, Lieut. Dennis Walter, O.B.E., M.C., R. Berks Regt., *b.* July, 1897 ; *s.* of Walter Furlong, of the War Office. *Educ. :* Emmanuel School, Wandsworth Common. *War Work :* France, 1916–19 ; Germany and Russia on General Lord Rawlinson's Staff, 1919. *Club :* Junior Naval and Military. (O5280)

FURLONG, Rev. Hubert, O.B.E.

FURLONG, Margaret Helen, M.B.E.

FURLONG, Capt. (A. Major) Sydney Verner, O.B.E., M.D., R.A.M.C., *b.* 1891 ; *s.* of Wm. V. Furlong, M.D., of 16, Pembroke Road, Dublin. *Educ. :* St. Columba's Coll., and Trinity Coll., Dublin. *War Office :* Officer Commanding 300th Nigerian Field Ambulance, East African E.F., and Administrative Medical Officer, Dodoma Area, Jan. 1919. *Address :* 16, Pembroke Road, Dublin. (O674)

FURNER, Duncan Campbell, M.B.E., *b.* 4 July, 1861 ; *s.* of William Campbell Furner, of Brighton, *g.s.* of Judge William Furner, D.S.O. J.P. for Sussex, great-grand-nephew of Sir Thomas Francis Freemantle, G.C.B. (Vice-Admiral of the Blue), a participator in the glories of Copenhagen and Trafalgar, and through him a cousin of Lord Cottesloe and Earl Middleton (*see* BURKE'S *Peerage*) ; *m.* Mary Elizabeth Eleanor, *d.* of Michael O'Reilly, M.D., of Windmill Place, Bishop's Stortford, Herts. *Educ. :* Cranleigh. *War Work :* Joined Hove Special Constabulary, Aug. 1914 ; appointed Superintendent in 1916 ; Member of the Special Committee, Prince of Wales' Fund, and Hove War Memorial Committee. *Address :* 11, Palmeira Avenue, Hove, Sussex. *Clubs :* Hove ; Brighton and Hove Golf. (M8153)

FURNISS, 2nd Lieut. John Hunt, M.B.E., R.A.F.

FURNIVAL, Capt. John Megarry, M.B.E., R.A.F.

FURSE, Jean Adelaide, Lady, O.B.E. ; *d.* of Henry Evans-

Gordon, of Prestons, Ightham, Kent ; *m.* 1899 Lieut.-Gen. Sir William Thomas Furse, K.C.B. (*see* BURKE'S *Peerage*). (O10,442)

FURSE, Dame Katharine, D.B.E., *b.* 1875 ; *d.* of John Addington Symonds, of Bristol, *m.* Charles Wellington Furse. *Educ. :* At home. Director of Companies. *War Work :* 1914–17, as a V.A.D. (Commandant-in-Chief of V.A.D.s, 1915–17) ; 1917–19, Director Women's Royal Naval Service. *Address :* 112, Beaufort Street, Chelsea. (DG4)

FYFE, Lieut. Robert George, M.B.E., R.A.F.

FYFE, Thomas Alexander, C.B.E., *b.* 5 June, 1852 ; *Educ. :* Perth ; Edinburgh University. Sheriff Substitute of Lanarkshire (appointed in 1895, and still in office). *War Work :* Chairman of Munitions Tribunals in Scotland, 1915–20 ; Chairman of Labour Unrest Commission—Scotland Division—1917 ; on the Board of Trade and Labour Ministry Panel of Arbiters under Munitions of War Acts, and Conciliation Act, 1896. *Addresses :* County Buildings, Glasgow ; 1, Kingsborough Gardens, Glasgow, W. (C169)

FYNN, Ethel May, Mrs., M.B.E.

FYSON, Alfred, M.B.E.

GABAIN, Adele Mary, M.B.E., *b.* 20 Nov. 1886 ; *d.* of Victor Henrotin, of Chicago, U.S.A. ; *m.* George Gabain, *s.* of Henry Gabain, of Caterham Valley, Surrey. *Educ. :* France and Switzerland. *War Work :* First lady worker in Y.M.C.A., France, Nov. 1914 ; Lady Superintendent, Havre, until May, 1919. *Address :* 3, Boulevard de Strasbourg, Le Havre, France. (M3092)

GABB, Capt. Samuel Alwyne, O.B.E., M.C., Worcestershire Regiment, *b.* 28 May, 1886 ; *s.* of James Percy Alwyne Gabb, M.D., of Guildford, Surrey ; *m.* 11 Nov. 1920, Edith Nora Florence, *o.d.* of A. Seymour, of Guildford. *Educ. :* Epsom College. *War Work :* Served in France and Belgium from 14 Aug. 1914, to 10 March, 1919 ; Adj. Worc. Regt., Aug. 1914 to June, 1915 ; Staff Service, July, 1915, to March, 1919. *Addresses :* Poyle Mount, Guildford, Surrey ; Portobello Barracks, Dublin. (O2519)

GABE, Howell Woodwell, O.B.E., F.R.C.S. (Edin.), *b.* 6 Sept. 1884 ; *s.* of Dr. J. B. Gabe, of Petrepoeth House Morriston. *Educ. :* Llandovery College, Wales ; Middlesex Hospital. Consulting Surgeon ; Hon. Surgeon, Swansea General and Eye Hospital ; Consulting Surgeon (Southern portion), Western Command. *War Work :* A. Major, R.A.M.C. ; Surgical Specialist ; Casualty Clearing Station, B.E.F., France. *Address :* 3, Brunswick Place, St. Helen's Road, Swansea. (O5281)

GABITES, Lieut.-Col. George Edward, C.B.E., New Zealand Med. Corps ; S. Africa, 1901–2 (Queen's medal with four clasps) ; Great War, 1915–19 (mentioned in despatches). (C1855)

GABRIEL, Lieut.-Col. Edmund Vivian, C.S.I., C.M.G., C.V.O., C.B.E., *b.* 28 March, 1875 ; *s.* of the late Edmund Gabriel, of Babbacombe Glen, Devon. *Educ. :* Emmanuel Coll., Cambridge. Indian Civil Service. *War Work :* Special duty, Government of India (1914) ; War Office, M.O. Branch (1915) ; British Military Mission with Italian Armies in the Field (1915–17) ; General Staff Intelligence Officer with the British Ægean Squadron (1917–18) ; Financial Adviser, Occupied Enemy Territory, E.E.F., and Assistant Administrator, Palestine (1918–20) ; has Order of St. Maurice and St. Lazarus of Italy. *Address :* Gubbio, Umbria, Italy. *Club :* Marlborough. (C1380)

GADBAN, Capt. Victor John, O.B.E., *b.* 12 April, 1880 ; *s.* of Paul Gadban, of 7, Upper Brook Street, W. ; *m.* Ellen Mary, *d.* of Rev. Henry Gretton, of Otley, Suffolk. *Educ. :* Winchester, New College, Oxon. Solicitor. *War Work :* Active Service, France and Flanders. *Address :* Alton, Hants. (O5822)

GADD, Helen, Mrs., M.B.E., *b.* 31 Aug. 1862 ; *d.* of the late William Bingham, of Hampstead, N.W. ; *m.* Lieut.-Col. William Laurence Gadd, R.G.A., *s.* of the late William Gadd, of Manchester. *Educ. :* North London Collegiate School for Girls. Commandant, V.A.D. Kent 92. *War Work :* Commandant, Yacht Club V.A.D. Hospital, Gravesend, Kent 92, 1914–19. *Address :* 7, Landsowne Square, Rosherville Kent. (M1749)

GADDUM, Arthur Graham, M.B.E. *War Work :* Organising the Boy Scout movement in Greece. *Address :* Bowdon, Cheshire. (M8154)

GADSBY, Capt. Philip, O.B.E., A.O.D., and R.A.F.

GAGNON, Lieut.-Col. Joseph Thomas Emile, O.B.E.

GAHAN, The Rev. Horace Stirling Townsend, M.B.E.

GAHAN, Patrick John, M.B.E.

GAIGER, Grace Elizabeth, M.B.E.

GAIR, Capt. Charles John Dickenson, O.B.E., F.C.S., *b.* 22 March, 1883 ; *s.* of Rev. John Gair, of Durham ; *m.* Emily Jane, *d.* of George Garlett, of London. *Educ. :* Elmfield Coll., York, and City and Guilds Technical Institute, Finsbury. Works Chemist to the South Metropolitan Gas Co., London ; Capt. R.A.M.C. (T.F.) 1st London Sanitary Co. *War Work :* Gazetted Lieut., R.A.M.C. (T.) Dec. 1914 ; Chemical Investigation of Poison Gas, Analytical work on Foods, etc., at Royal Army Medical Coll., Millbank ; April, 1915, went to France, present, Battle of Festubert ; invalided, 1915 ; Salisbury Plain, 1916 ; Officer in charge of Sanitary Services at Headquarters, Eastern Command, 1917–18 ; went to Holland, Nov. 1918, on Repatriation Commission work. *Address :*

39, Cranston Road, Forest Hill, London, S.E. 23. *Club*: Territorial Officers'. (O7173)

GAIR, Christina Ellen, Mrs., M.B.E., *d.* of A. Duncan Fraser, M.D., D.P.H., J.P., of Stratheric, Falkirk. *War Work*: Commandant and Administrator of Wallside Auxiliary Hospital, Falkirk, from Nov. 1914, to Jan. 1919. *Addresses*: Kilmalieu, Ardgour, Argyllshire; The Kilns, Falkirk, Stirlingshire. *Club*: Ladies' Caledonian (Edinburgh). (M8156)

GAIR, Lieut.-Col. Sinclair, O.B.E.

GAIRNS, James Mather, C.B.E.; *b.* 5 April, 1880, *s.* of the late John Gairns, of Kirklawhill, Skirling, Peeblesshire, Scotland; *m.* Mary Gray, *d.* of Robert Gray Murray, of Spittal, Biggar, Lanarkshire. *Educ.*: Dollar Academy. Audit and Accounts Officer on the Bengal and North-Western and Tirhut State Railways, India, from 1902–16; joined transport Dept. of the Admiralty in Dec. 1916; went to New York in April, 1918, as Representative in the United States and Canada of the Accountant-General Ministry of Shipping. *Club*: Caledonian. (C2622)

GAISFORD, Gertrude Emma Frances, M.B.E., *d.* of Charles Green Gaisford, of Devizes, Wiltshire. *War Work*: 3½ years as Matron and Commandant of St. Mary's Red Cross Hospital, Worthing. *Address*: Cranmere, Victoria Road, Worthing. (M8157)

GAISFORD, Harriet Helen, Mrs., M.B.E.

GAIT, Christian Maud, Lady, C.B.E.; *d.* of Col. Stephen, I.M.S.; *m.* Sir Edward Albert, K.C.S.I., C.I.E., I.C.S., Lieut. Governor of Bihar and Orissa from 1915 (*see* BURKE'S *Peerage*), *s.* of late John James Gait. *Address*: Ranchi, India. (C2381)

GAITSKELL, Capt. and Brevet Major Henry Walter, O.B.E., R.G.A., *b.* 1 Dec. 1884; *s.* of Col. W. J. Gaitskell, R.M.A.; *m.* Eileen Constance, *d.* of the late Col. Irving S. Allfrey, Somerset L.I. *Educ.*: Cheltenham Coll., and R.M.A., Woolwich. Served during the war in the Proof and Experimental Establishment, Research Department, Royal Arsenal, Woolwich. (O8809)

GALBRAITH, Major James Ponsonby, O.B.E., R.E.

GALBRAITH, Marion, Mrs., M.B.E.,

GALBRAITH, Samuel, O.B.E.

GALE, Major Arthur John, O.B.E., J.P., C.C., *b.* 2 March, 1881; *m.* Maude Ellen, *d.* of Richard Edward George, of London. Director of Private Companies; Middlesex County Councillor; Chairman, Friern Barnet U.D.C. *War Work*: Transporting wounded from terminus stations to temporary hospitals; conveying German prisoners to encampments; Air Raid duty; training of low category men for home defence, etc. *Address*: San Jacopino, Oakleigh Park, N. 20. *Clubs*: Road; Eccentric. (O10443)

GALE, Ernest John Albert, M.B.E., R.E.

GALE, Frederick Robert, M.B.E., *b.* 1877; *s.* of Robert Gale, of Kensington and Hastings; *m.* Emily Frances, *d.* of the Rev. Frederick Tapply, of Lyminge, Kent. *Educ.*: St. Mary's Coll., Harlow. Editorial Staff of "The Statist," 1895–1910; Member, Inst. of Journalists, 1004; L.R.B. (T.F.), 1895–1910. *War Work*: Rejoined London Rifle Brigade, Nov. 1914; O.-R.-Sergt., 3rd L.R.B., May, 1915, to Aug. 1916; commissioned to A.O.D., afterwards R.A.O.C., Aug. 1916; Staff of D.A.G., 3rd Echelon, B.E.F., Nov. 1917; G.H.Q., British troops in France and Flanders, April to Sept. 1919; retired as Capt. *Address*: c/o London County Westminster and Parr's Bank, Ltd., Kensington High St. W. 8. (M3124)

GALE, Capt. Henry Arthur, M.B.E., R.E.

GALE, Rev. James Randolph Courtenay, O.B.E., M.A., Royal Army Chaplains Dept. (T.), 2nd Class, *b.* 1857; *s.* of Dr. James Gale, of Buckfast Abbey, Devon, and Hampstead; *m.* Mary Simpson, *d.* of Edwin Jago, Paymaster-in-Chief, R.N. *Educ.*: Privately, and St. John's, Cambridge. Vicar of Christ Church, Sutton, 1888; University Extension Lecturer, Cambridge (Staff), 1905–18, and London, 1904–18. *War Work*: Hon. Sec. Sutton and District Territorial and Recruiting Committee, Military Representative; Chairman, Sutton War Hospital Supply Depot; Hon. Sec. Sutton War Pensions Local Committee; Local Representative, Soldiers' and Sailors' Help Society; Hon. Sec. Soldiers' and Sailors' Families Association, Sutton Division. *Address*: Christ Church Vicarage, Sutton, Surrey. (O10444)

GALES, Major John Russell, M.B.E.

GALILEE, Mary Edith, M.B.E., *b.* 1866; *d.* of James Robert Galilee, of Leytonstone. *Educ.*: City of London. Y.W.C.A. Sec. *War Work*: Girl Guide Organisation; organising and carrying on large canteen and hut for Women Munition workers at Hayes, Middlesex. *Address*: Y.W.C.A. Hut, Hayes, Middlesex. (M419)

GALL, Christian McDowall, M.B.E., *b.* 11 Jan. 1890; *d.* of Alexander Gall, of Alloa, N.B. *Educ.*: Edinburgh Ladies' College. *War Work*: Private Sec. to Member of Munitions Council. *Address*: 12, Barlow Road, Alloa. (M420)

GALL, Robert Laing Bruce, C.B.E.

GALLAGHER, John, O.B.E., *b.* 27 July, 1884; *s.* of Michael Gallagher, of Methil, N.B.; *m.* Isabella Smith, *d.* of Alexander McRuvie, of Leven, N.B. *Educ.*: Buckhaven, N.B. Officer of Customs and Excise. *War Work*: Hon. Sec. to Edenderry War Pensions Committee, Belgian Relief Committee, and Soldiers' Parcel Fund; Member of the Joint War Pensions Committee for Leinster and Connaught, the King's County War Pensions, the Leinster Regiment Prisoners of War and other committees; initiated training schemes for disabled soldiers. *Address*: Windsor Terrace, Edenderry, King's County. (O10445)

GALLAND, Alfred Jules Louis, O.B.E.

GALLIE, Sydney, M.B.E., R.E.

GALLIER, William Henry, C.B.E.

GALLON, Lieut. Thomas Heaton, M.B.E.

GALLAWAY, James Henry, M.B.E., Knight of the Royal Orders of St. Stanislaus of Russia and Isabel la Catolica of Spain, *b.* 3 June, 1875; *s.* of George Galloway, of Gooderstone; *m.* Mary (died May, 1919), *d.* of Isaac Galloway, of Oxburgh. *Educ.*: St. Margaret's and Technical Schools, King's Lynn; and privately in London. Superintendent of Police, and Deputy Chief Constable of the Isle of Wight since 1906; formerly second-in-command of Cambridge Police. *Address*: Kingsfield, Newport, Isle of Wight. (M3654)

GALLOWAY, Major Alexander Rudolf, O.B.E., M.A., M.B., C.M., *b.* 9 July, 1864; *s.* of James Galloway, of Inverurie and Calcutta; *m.* Mary Helene, *d.* of George Curry, of Newcastle-on-Tyne. *Educ.*: Aberdeen Univ. and London. Ophth. Surgeon, Eye Institution and Royal Blind Asylum, Aberdeen; Ophth. Surgeon, Aberdeen Education Authority; Ophth. Surgeon, County of Aberdeen Educ. Authority; Ophth. Surgeon, Ministry of Pensions Medical Board, Aberdeen; Lecturer on Ophthalmology, Aberdeen Univ. *War Work*: Ophthalmic Surgeon, 1st Scottish General Hospital, R.A.M.C. (T.); Ophth. Surgeon to Recruiting Medical Boards and Ministry of National Service, Aberdeen. *Address*: 250, Union Street, Aberdeen. (O1044)

GALLOWAY, Sir James, K.B.E., C.B., *b.* 10 Oct. 1862; *s.* of James Galloway, of Inverurie, Aberdeenshire, and Calcutta; *m.* Jessie Hermina, *d.* of Robert Orr Sawers, of Dunbar, East Lothian, and Calcutta. *Educ.*: Chanonry School, Aberdeen; University of Aberdeen. Physician; Senior Physician, Charing Cross Hospital; Consulting Physician, Metropolitan Asylums Board. *War Work*: Major R.A.M.C. (T.F.), att. 4th London General Hospital; Col. (A.M.G.) Consulting Physician, 1st and 2nd Armies, B.E.F. (Despatches); Chief Commissioner for Medical Services; Ministry of National Mobile Service. *Address*: 54, Harley Street, London, W.1. (K69)

GALLOWAY, Major James Muir, O.B.E. R.F.A. (T.).

GALLOWAY, Kathleen Frances Elaine, M.B.E., *b.* 5 May, 1898; *d.* of Lewis Stanley Galloway, of Birkdale. *Educ.*: Leatherhead Court, Surrey. *War Work*: Voluntary assistant to the Sec. Wives' and Dependants' Branch, Local War Pensions Committee, Southport. *Address*: 14, Lulworth Road, Birkdale, Lancashire. (M8159)

GALLOWAY, Mary Helene, M.B.E., *b.* 10 Nov. 1871; *d.* of George Curry, of Newcastle-on-Tyne; *m.* Alexander Rudolf, *s.* of James Galloway, of Calcutta. *War Work*: Hospital Visitor, Joint Disablement Committee for the Northern Area of Scotland, Ministry of Pensions. (M8160)

GALTON, Mary Louisa, Mrs. WHELER-, M.B.E., *b.* 30 Dec. 1863; *d.* of James Dugdale, of Wroxall Abbey (*see* BURKE'S *Landed Gentry*); *m.* Edward Wheler (who by Royal Licence, on 11 Jan. 1913, was authorised to use the additional surname and arms of Galton) (*see* BURKE'S *Landed Gentry*), *s.* of Edward Wheler, of Leamington. Commandant, V.A. Detachment, Warwick 36. *War Work*: Commandant, Guy's Cliffe Hospital, Warwick, 21 May, 1915, to 19 Dec. 1918. *Address*: Claverdon Leys, Warwick. *Club*: Ladies' Army and Navy. (M1751)

GALTREY, Capt. Sidney, O.B.E.

GALVIN, Capt. Alfred, M.B.E., I.A.R.O.

GALWEY, Major William Richards, O.B.E., M.B., R.A.M.C.

GAMAGE, Lieut. Cecil Murdoch, M.B.E., R.E., (T.).

GAMBELL, Comm. Thomas Francis, C.B.E.

GAMBLE, Major Charles William, O.B.E., R.A.F.

GAMBLE, Major Henry, O.B.E., R.A.V.C., *b.* 15 Jan. 1877; *s.* of John Gamble, of Shouldham Thorpe, Norfolk; *m.* Dorothy Constance, *d.* of Thomas Carlton, of Hampstead. *Educ.*: Cranleigh School, and Royal Veterinary College, London, N.W. Fellow of the R.C.V.S.; Officer du Mérite Agricole. *War Work*: Commanded No. 5 Mobile Veterinary Section, 5th Division, from Aug. to Oct. 1914; appointed A.D.V.S., 1st Cavalry Division, from Oct. 1914, to Aug. 1916; commanded No. 1 Veterinary Hospital at La Chapelle-aux-Pots from Aug. 1916, to June, 1917; appointed A.D.V.S., XIII. Corps, with temporary rank of Lieut.-Col., from June, 1917, to April, 1919. *Address*: Instow, Barnstaple, North Devon. *Club*: Junior Naval and Military. (O5283)

GAMBLE, John Dunn, M.B.E., *b.* 11 April, 1876; *s.* of Rev. J. W. Gamble, of the Manse, Lisburn, Ireland; *m.* Jane Isabelle, *d.* of Joseph Adams, of Rakane House, Cootehill. *Educ.*: At Lisburn. Organising Sec. for Ireland, British and Foreign Sailors' Society Committees; North of Ireland Central Association Sea Cadets Corps, Belfast; Sea Scouts Committees, Dublin and Londonderry. *War Work*: Amongst the Sailors, Buncrana, Lough Swilly, and Derry; opening Sailors' Rest and organising relief work on behalf of thousands of torpedoed sailors. *Addresses*: Lisnagarvey, Lisburn Co. Antrim; Gt. James Street, Londonderry; 18, Dock Street, Belfast. (M431)

GAMBLE, Mercier, M.B.E., M.D., Ch.B., *b.* 1876; *s.* of Samuel Gamble, of Manchester and Sheffield; *m.* Constance M., *d.* of Laban Spencer, of Manchester. *Educ.*: Leys School, Cambridge; and Manchester Univ. Medical Officer, Withington Institution and Hospitals, and Dr. Rhodes' Memorial

Home, West Didsbury, Manchester. *War Work:* Temp. Hon. Lieut.-Col. R.A.M.C.; Registrar, Nell Lane Military Hospital, West Didsbury, Manchester, the Central Hospital having 3484 beds. *Address:* 9 Broadway, Withington, Manchester. (M10262g)

GAMBLE, William Michael Hudson Julius, M.B.E.

GAME, Capt. Henry, O.B.E.

GAME, Winifred, M.B.E., L.R.A.M., A.R.C.M., *b.* 13 Oct. 1885; *d.* of James Aylward Game, of The Mount, Great Missenden, Bucks. *Educ.:* Roedean School, near Brighton. *War Work:* Commandant, V.A.D. Herts 50, Ken Cottage; and Ewen Hall V.A.D. Hospitals, Barnet. *Address:* Merton Lodge, Byng Road, Barnet. (M1753)

GAMLEN, Robert Loraine, O.B.E.

GAMMON, Edith Olive, M.B.E. (M10248d)

GAMMON, Capt. Frank Leonard, O.B.E.

GAMMON, Capt. John Charles, O.B.E.

GAMMON, John Thomas, M.B.E., R.C.N.

GAMON, Major Humphrey Percival, O.B.E.

GANDELL, William Raleigh Kerr, O.B.E., *b.* 5 Aug. 1870; *s.* of the late Rev. Robert Gandell, of Oxford; *m.* Millicent Anne, *d.* of the late Joseph Warter. *Educ.:* Uppingham. Retired Civil Servant. *War Work:* Director of the British Industries Fair, organised by the Board of Trade. *Address:* 18, Hornton Court, London, W. 8. *Clubs:* Windham; Roehampton. (O355)

GANDER, Bernard Vincent, M.B.E., B.Sc., *b.* 23 Jan. 1894; *s.* of the late James Gander, of London, late Managing Director Ganders' Ltd., Indiarubber and Leather Merchants; *m.* Dorothy Maude, *d.* of A. J. Field, of London. *Educ.:* Central Foundation School, London; Univ. Coll. (Univ. of Lond.); and Sheffield Univ. Demonstrator and Assist. Lecturer in Metallurgy, Sheffield Univ., 1917–19; Chemistry and Science Master, Sutton Valence School, Kent, since 1919. *War Work:* Lieut. 11th Essex. and later the Army Cyclist Corps, 1914–19; saw active service in France, 1915; present at Loos, Ypres, and the Somme; invalided, 1916, and whilst unfit in England assisted in the Technical Training of Unfit and disabled officers in Sheffield Univ. For that purpose loaned to the Ministry of Labour. *Addresses:* Sutton Valence School, Kent; 76, Romford Road, London. (M3655)

GANDY, Lieut.-Comm. Eric Worsley, O.B.E., Officer Legion d'honneur, B.A. (Cantab), M.R.C.S., L.R.C.P., *b.* 6 July, 1879; *s.* of the late William Gandy, of South Street, Park Lane, London, W.; *m.* Margaret, *d.* of John Kenyon, of Rawtenstall, Lancashire. *Educ.:* Privately; Westminster and Emmanuel College, Cambridge. Teacher of anæsthetics, and anæsthetist to Westminster Hospital, Royal Ear Hospital, Chelsea Hospital for Women, and Norwood Cottage Hospital. *War Work:* Carrying 4½ years' despatches to Fleets and Embassies in Paris, Athens, Rome, and other places in Mediterranean. *Addresses:* 2, Cambridge Street, Hyde Park, W. *Club:* United Sports. (O356)

GANDY, Comm. Gerard Knipe, O.B.E., R.D., R.N.R., *b.* 7 Jan. 1859; *s.* of Gerard Gandy, of Kendal, Westmorland; *m.* Favell Lee, *d.* of Rev. Horace Meyer, M.A., of Clifton, Bristol. *Educ.:* H.M.S. "Worcester." Commander in the Union Castle Mail Steamship Company, Ltd., 314, Fenchurch Street, London, E.C. Now in command of H.M. Hospital Ship "Carisbrook Castle," H.M. Transports "Briton," "Saxon," and "Balmoral Castle," in which were carried over 70,000 troops. *Address:* Rodney, Brockenhurst, Hants. *Club:* Southampton Yacht, Solent. (O1360)

GANDY, Henry Garnett, C.B.E., M.A., D.L., *b.* 28 Aug. 1860; *s.* of Capt. Henry Gandy, J.P., D.L., of Skirsgill Park, Penrith, Cumb. *Educ.:* Eton, and Trinity Coll., Cambridge. *War Work:* T.F.A. County Director; Vol. Aid Detachments and Auxiliary Hospitals of Cumberland and Westmorland. *Address:* Skirsgill Park, Penrith, Cumberland. *Club:* New University. (C2625)

GANDY, Major Henry George, D.S.O., O.B.E., R.E., *b.* 27 Nov. 1879; *s.* of the late Capt. Charles Gandy, King's Dragoon Guards, and Mrs. Dorothy Jane Gandy, of Wester Hall, Humshaugh, Northumberland. *Educ.:* Sedbergh School, Yorkshire. *War Work:* 2nd Corp Signals, Aug. 1914 to April 1915; Brigade Major, School of Military Engineering, Chatham, from 1 Jan. 1916, to 10 Oct. 1918. *Address:* Wester Hall, Humshaugh, Northumberland. *Club:* Junior Naval and Military. (O1361)

GANE, Percy James, M.B.E.

GANGE, Lieut. Comm. Ambrose Day, O.B.E., R.N.R. (ret.), *b.* 6 Nov. 1871; *s.* of William Henry Gange, of Bickenhall, Taunton, Somerset; *m.* Henrietta, *d.* of James Henry Bruce, of Scotland. *Educ.:* Independent Coll. (now Taunton School), Taunton. Master of Cable Steamer "Faraday." *War Work:* Repairing and laying Submarine Telegraph Cables; laying Murmansk Archangel Cable. *Addresses:* 50, Elmfield Road, Upper Tooting, S.W. 17; Imperial Merchant Service Guild, Liverpool. (O10449)

GANN, Edmond Thomas, O.B.E., *b.* 3 Oct. 1860; *s.* of Thomas Gann, of Whitstable; *m.* Ellen Grace, *d.* of the late E. H. Curling, of Whitstable. *Educ.:* Commercial (now Wraight's) School, Faversham. Sec. Army Sanitary Committee, Army Medical Advisory Board, and Consultants' Council; Civil Assist. to Director-General Army Medical Service; appointed Principal Clerk, Pensions Ministry, Jan. 1919. *Address:* Tankerton, Whitstable. (O10450)

GANN, Ernest Harry, M.B.E., B.A., late Capt. and Qr.-Mr. R.A.M.C., *b.* 8 Oct. 1891. *War Work:* Served with the R.A.M.C. in Egypt and Palestine. *Address:* 5, Vicarage Road, Sunbury, Middlesex. (M4677)

GANSON, Robert Dowell, O.B.E., J.P. for Orkney and Zetland, *b.* 25 Sept. 1855; *s.* of Hay Ganson, of Scatsta, Delting, Shetland; *m.* Mary Gillespie Wallace, *d.* of James Wallace, of Hall Quarter, Stirlingshire. *Educ.:* Moorfield Parish School, Delting, and Anderson Institute, Lerwick. Ex-convener of County of Zetland; Provost of the Burgh of Lerwick; Vice-Chairman of the Education Authority of Shetland; Honorary Sheriff-substitute of Zetland. *War Work:* Member of the Appeal Tribunal for Caithness, Orkney, and Zetland; Chairman of War Pensions Committee of the County of Zetland; Chairman of the Appointing Committee for Food Control, etc., in the County. *Address:* Brentham House, Lerwick. *Club:* Zetland, Lerwick. (O1362)

GANT, Wilfred Robert Pinfold, M.B.E., *b.* 18 Jan. 1872; *s.* of Robert Boddy Gant, of Woolwich; *m.* Florence Elizabeth, *d.* of Alfred Stone, of Plumstead. *Educ.:* Privately. Civil Service. *War Work:* Accountant-General's Departmental Admiralty. *Address:* 26, Greenholm Road, Eltham. (M8163)

GANTEAUME, Patrick Padroy Joseph, M.B.E., J.P., *b.* 1875; *s.* of Henry Ganteaume, of Torquay; *m.* Elizabeth Cochrane, *d.* of John Goodeir Robertson, of Edinburgh. *Educ.:* Edinburgh. Senior Surgeon, Frere Hospital, East London, Cape Province. *War Work:* Surgeon No. 1 General Hospital, Wynberg, Cape Colony; Mayor of East London, 1917 and 1918; Chairman Governor-General's Fund, 1917 and 1918; Chairman Recruiting Committee, 1917–18. *Address:* Inch-Marls, East London, C.P. *Clubs:* East London; East London Sporting. (M2882)

GARCIA, Henry John Edward, O.B.E.

GARD, Albert, M.B.E.

GARD, William Garrard Snowdon, M.B.E., LL.B. (Lond.), *b.* 11 Jan. 1848; *s.* of William Snowdon Gard, of Hampstead; *m.* Mary Ann Harriet, *d.* of Walter Frederick Ball, of Hampstead. *Educ.:* Univ. Coll. School and Univ. Coll., London. Solicitor; Commandant, Red Cross V.A.D. 49 London; Chairman, Hampstead Red Cross Divisional Committee; Member of St. Pancras Red Cross Divisional Committee; Member of Executive Committee of County of London Branch, B.R.C.S.; Member of Hampstead Distress Committee, and representative of Hampstead on M.A.B. and C.U.B.L. *War Work:* Raised R.C. V.A.D.'S 49 and 322; organised and directed Air Raid Ambulance work in North St. Pancras Chairman, Rosslyn Lodge A. Military Hospital Committee, and since, of Hampstead R.C. Clinics Committee; private in Hampstead Volunteers. *Addresses:* 10 Hampstead Hill Gardens, Hampstead, N.W. 3; 2, Gresham Buildings, Basinghall Street, E.C. *Club:* Royal Colonial Institute. (M8164)

GARDE, Engineer-Capt. Robert Boles, C.B.E., R.N., *b.* 1863; *s.* of H. W. Garde, M.B.; *m.* 1899, Amy Ethel, *d.* of T. M. Richards, of Plymouth. Admiralty Engineer Overseer at J. S. White and Co.'s, of Cowes, and at Doxford's, of Sunderland. (C2221)

GARDINER, Alice Marie, Mrs., M.B.E., *d.* of the late John Godden, of Bartley, New Forest; *m.* Henry Gardiner, musician. Secretary to o/c Met. Obs. Service, 1916–19; Intelligence Officer, Women Police Service. *War Work:* Joined the Women Police Service in May, 1915, and was seconded to Commander Paget, C.B.E., of Admiralty Intelligence, May, 1916, who organised and commanded the Metropolitan Observation Service, consisting of some 1200 officers and men; the only woman in M.O.S. (M3656)

GARDINER, Lieut. Edward Cecil, M.B.E., *b.* 7 Nov. 1884; *s.* of the late T. J. Gardiner, of Cheltenham; *m.* Dorothy Frances Elizabeth, *d.* of the late Capt. Horace Rochfort, R.N., of Cheltenham. *Educ.:* Cheltenham Coll., and R.M.C., Sandhurst. Late Planter. *War Work:* 2nd Batt. Devon Regt., and later served as Topographical Officer to Gen. Lord Rawlinson, at Headquarters 4th Army. *Address:* Isca House, Exmouth. *Club:* Junior Army and Navy. (M4488)

GARDINER, Frederick Henry, M.B.E.

GARDINER, Major Herbert William, O.B.E. (O11777)

GARDINER, Robert Fulton, M.B.E., *b.* 2 May, 1861; *s.* of Thomas Gardiner, of Coupar-Angus; *m.* Agnes, *d.* of Alexander King, of Kilmarnock. Organising Sec. Temperance Committee, Church of Scotland, since 1898; Member of many public committees for the promotion of Temperance and Social Reform. *War Work:* Business Manager for Church of Scotland Committee on Territorial work from 1914, and Business Manager of the Scottish Churches Huts, in France and Germany, 1916–19. *Address:* 3, Dixon Road, Crosshill, Glasgow. (M8167)

GARDINER, Stanley James, M.B.E., R.A.F.

GARDINER, William Rattray, M.B.E., *b.* 9 June, 1858. *Educ.:* Perth Academy, N.B. *War Work:* War Emergency and Finance Committees of Y.M.C.A. National Council; Hon. Treas. S. Eastern Divisional Union of Y.M.C.A.'s. *Address:* Mount Edgecombe, Redhill, Surrey. *Club:* National Liberal; British-Russia. (M8168)

GARDNER, Annie Elizabeth, O.B.E., *b.* 3 Aug. 1874; *d.* of Walter Silvester Gardner, of Cookham, Berks. *Educ.:* Queen's Coll., Harley Street. Civil Servant; Chief Woman Officer, London and South-Eastern Division, Employment Dept., Ministry of Labour. *War Work:* Recruitment of Women for all branches of War Work—Munitions, Land, Women's Services, etc. *Address:* 13, Arundel Gardens, W. 11. *Clubs:* Halcyon; Forum. (O357)

GARDNER, Arthur Edward, M.B.E.

GARDNER, Lieut.-Col. Charles James Hookham, C.B.E.

Major and T. Lieut.-Col. Yorkshire Regt. ; Great War, 1914–19 (mentioned in despatches). (C1575)

GARDNER, Dorothy, M.B.E., *b.* 24 Oct. 1878 ; *d.* of Herbert Wilson Gardner, of Armitage, Rugeley. *Educ. :* Privately and Paris. *War Work :* Y.M.C.A. worker at Rouen, Abancourt, and Dieppe, from April, 1915 to May, 1919. *Address :* Armitage, Rugeley, Staffs. (M3657)

GARDNER, Major FitzRoy, C.B.E.

GARDNER, Capt. Frederick William, C.B.E., D.C.M., R.A.O.C.

GARDNER, Lieut.-Comm. George Frederick, O.B.E., R.N.R., *b.* 23 Nov. 1869 ; *s.* of Thomas Gardner, of Wimbledon, Surrey ; *m.* Kate, *d.* of Ernest Riley, of London. *Educ. :* Malden Coll. Master Mariner. *War Work :* In command of H.M.S. Ships " Carisbrook Castle " and " Braemar Castle," and of base hospital ship at Murmansk during the winter of 1918 and at the evacuation of Archangel. *Address :* c/o The Union Castle Mail S.S. Co., London, E.C. 3. (O10451)

GARDNER, Major George Herbert, O.B.E.

GARDNER, Henry Willoughby, M.B.E., M.D., F.R.C.P., *b.* 1861 ; *s.* of Henry Gardner, of Liverpool ; *m.* Mary Louisa, *d.* of the late Rev. E. F. Rambant, of Blackrock, Dublin. *Educ. :* Charterhouse, and St. Bartholomew's Hospital. Senior Physician the Royal Salop Infirmary ; Consulting Physician Baschurch Surgical Home, Lady Forester Hospitals, Broseley and Much Wenlock. *War Work :* Consulting Physician Barrington War Hospital ; Physician to Quarry Place Auxiliary A. Hospital, Shrewsbury ; and the Royal Salop Infirmary ; Medical Officer to the Baschurch Surgical Home. *Address :* Shrewsbury. *Club :* London University. (M8166)

GARDNER, Jessie, Mrs., M.B.E. ; *d.* of Walter Wylie and Jane Younger of Alloa, N.B. ; *m.* the Rev. Robert, *s.* of Robert Gardner, of New Kilpatrick. *Educ. :* Westray House, Alloa, N.B. *War Work :* Hon. Sec. of Bo'ness Red Cross Committee from 1915 ; President of Bo'ness Red Cross Work Party ; Member of Prince of Wales' Relief Fund Committee ; Organiser of Ladies' Voluntary Work Party at Bo'ness for the making of Cartridge and Igniter Bags for the Royal Navy, August, 1915–March, 1917. *Address :* The Manse, Bo'ness, Linlithgowshire, N.B. (M8169)

GARDNER, John, O.B.E.

GARDNER, Lieut. John Campbell, O.B.E., M.A. (Cantab), B.Sc. (Dunelm), A.M.Inst.C.E., M.Inst.M.E., Wh.Ex. Carnegie Research Scholar, Iron and Steel Institute, *b.* 1 April, 1878 ; *s.* of the late Thomas Gardner, of Middlesbrough. *Educ. :* Middlesbrough High School ; Armstrong College, Durham Univ. ; Trinity College, Cambridge. General Manager of Works, Ferranti, Ltd., Hollinwood, Lancs. *War Work :* Enlisted as Sapper in the R.N.D.E. in Oct. 1914 ; commissioned, Jan. 1915 ; served through Gallipoli Campaign ; mentioned in despatches for work at Helles Evacuation ; Deputy Representative, subsequently Representative, Ministry of Munitions, N.P.F., Birtley, Co. Durham ; Asst. Supt., National Ordnance Factories, Leeds ; Supt. N.O.F., Hunslet, Leeds. *Address :* 47, Victoria Road, Broomhall Park, Sheffield. (O3723)

GARDNER, Capt. John Cyril, O.B.E., R.A.S.C.

GARDNER, Joseph William, O.B.E.

GARDNER, Nora Hilton, M.B.E., *b.* 15 Dec. 1872 ; *d.* of Rev. Hilton Gardner, of Stanley, Lancashire. *Educ. :* Privately. *War Work :* Quartermaster, Hoole Bank Red Cross Hospital, Chester, 1914–17 ; V.A.D. General Service Superintendent, Chester War Hospital, 1917–19. *Address :* Upton Heath, Chester. *Clubs :* V.A.D. Ladies', Cavendish Square (M424)

GARDNER, Capt. Reginald Lowood, M.B.E.

GARDNER, Major T. Cyril, O.B.E. ; *m.* Bridget Chilton *d.* of Herbert E. Friend. *War Work :* In Malta and France. *Club :* North Rhodesia. (O2522)

GARDNER, Thomas Edward, O.B.E.

GARDNER, William Reid, M.B.E., *b.* 12 Sept. 1873 ; *s.* of John Smith Gardner, of Alreoch, Milngavie ; *m.* Margaret Weatherstone, *d.* of William Weatherstone Wilson, of Manchester. *Educ. :* Strathblane Public School, and Allan Glen's School, Glasgow. Solicitor ; Treasurer to the Burgh of Milngavie ; Agent of the Royal Bank of Scotland, Milngavie ; Sec. to the Local War Pensions Committee, Milngavie ; Fuel Overseer to the Burgh of Milngavie ; Sec. and Treas. Milngavie Angling Club ; Treas. Milngavie Bearsden Cricket and Tennis Clubs. *War Work :* Sec. & Treas. to the Committee of Local War Pensions, New Kilpatrick Division, Dumbartonshire ; Treas. to the Soldiers' and Sailors' Families Association. *Address :* Carbeth, Milngavie. (M8170)

GARDOM, Edward Theodore, O.B.E.

GARFORD, Marian, M.B.E., *b.* 29 Jan. 1866 ; *d.* of the late John Garford. *Educ. :* Privately. *War Work :* Clerk in Promotions Branch of Military Secretary to Kitchener's Armies, War Office. *Club :* Ladies' Imperial. (M8171)

GARFORTH, Comm. Francis Edmund Musgrave, C.B.E., R.N.

GARFORTH, Hylda Maria Madeleine, Hon. Mrs., M.B.E., *b.* Oct. 1856 ; *d.* of the 8th Baron Middleton, of Birdsall House, Yorkshire (*See* BURKE's *Peerage*) ; *m.* William Henry, *s.* of William Garforth, of Wiganthorpe, Yorkshire. *Educ. :* Uppingham and Cambridge. *War Work :* Commandant of Lady Sykes Aux. Mil. Hospital, Eddlethorpe, Yorkshire ; later, Brompton Aux. Mil. Hospital, Yorkshire. *Address :* Malton, Yorkshire. (M.3658)

GARLAKE, Dorothy Eleanor, Mrs., M.B.E.

GARLAND, Arthur Edward, M.B.E., F.I.C., BSc.,

A.R.C.S., *b.* 28 April, 1880 ; *s.* of Arthur Edward Garland. *Educ. :* Alleyn's School, Dulwich ; Univ. Coll., London ; Royal Coll. of Science, London. Research Chemist, Imperial Institute ; Assistant Chemist, Directorate of Chemical Inspection, Woolwich Arsenal. *Address :* Newhill Villa, Shrewsbury Lane, Woolwich Arsenal. (M8172)

GARLAND, Charles Tuller, O.B.E., *b.* 16 Nov. 1874 ; *s.* of James A. Garland, of New York ; *m.* the late Margaret W., *d.* of the late Francis Williams. *Educ. :* Columbia Univ., New York. *War Work :* Lieut. 2nd Life Guards ; invalided out of Army Nov. 1916 ; afterwards provided and kept up the Garland Home, 4, Norfolk Street, Park Lane, W. *Clubs :* St. James'; Orleans; Bath. (O10455)

GARLAND, Herbert, M.B.E.

GARLAND, Hilda Margaret, M.B.E., *d.* of W. G. de F. Garland, of Farrs, East Molesey. *War Work :* In charge of Treatment and Training Section of London War Pensions Committee, Central Office. *Address :* Farrs, East Molesey, Surrey. (M8173)

GARLAND, John William, O.B.E., J.P.

GARLICK, Edith, M.B.E.

GARLICK, Richard, M.B.E.

GARNER, Arthur, M.B.E.

GARNER, Col. Cathcart, C.B.E., M.B. ; formerly Col. R.A.M.C. ; Great War, 1914–19 (mentioned in despatches). (C783)

GARNER, Harry, M.B.E., C.C., *b.* 18 July, 1865 ; *s.* of William Garner, of Barwell ; *m.* Laura, *d.* of Thomas Argyle, of Hinckley. Boot Manufacturer ; Past High Chief Ranger of the Ancient Order of Foresters ; County Councillor ; Parish Councillor ; Chairman of Council School Managers. *War Work :* Chairman of Hinckley Rural Advisory Committee, Ministry of National Service ; Chairman of Belgian Refugees Local Committee ; rendered services in connection with Recruiting, and the War Loan. *Address :* Overdale, Barwell, near Hinckley. (M8174)

GARNER, Joseph Richardson, O.B.E.

GARNER, Lizzie, Mrs., M.B.E., *b.* 30 Dec. 1853 ; *d.* of William Radford, of Newark-on-Trent ; *m.* Thomas Willcox, *s.* of James Garner, of Ancaster. *Educ. :* Privately. Member of Board of Guardians, Newark ; Member of Notts. Executive B.R.C.S. Committee ; Member of Charity Organisation Society Committee, and St. Barnabas' Home for Waifs and Strays, and S.P.C. Children. *War Work :* Commandant of Red Cross Hospital from Oct. 1914 to March 1919. *Address :* The Old Hall, Newark-on-Trent. (M3659)

GARNER, Walter Wesley, C.B.E. (C3191)

GARNETT, Caroline Sugden, Mrs. Stewart, M.B.E., *b.* 8 Nov. 1854 ; *d.* of Elkanah Armitage, of The Rookery, Manchester ; *m.* Stewart, *s.* of Henry Garnett, of Wyreside, Lancaster. *War Work :* Commandant of 54 East Lancs. Detach., and worked a Hospital, B.R.C., Pendleton Division, " Fairhope " Hospital, 4½ years. (M425)

GARNETT, Frank Walls, C.B.E., J.P., *b.* 1867 ; *s.* of the late William Garnett, of Bowness, Westmorland ; *m.* 1895, Susannah, *d.* of Joseph Goddard, of The Priory, Hampstead, N.W. President, Roy. Coll. of Veterinary Surgeons, 1914–19. *Address :* Dalegarth. Windermere. (C170)

GARNETT, Helen Maude Dorothy, M.B.E.

GARNETT, James Clerk Maxwell, C.B.E., M.A., Barrister-at-law, *b.* 13 Oct. 1880 ; *s.* of Dr. William Garnett, of the Chestnuts, Hampstead Heath, and Sea View, Isle of Wight ; *m.* Margaret Lucy, *d.* of Professor E. B. Poulton, F.R.S., of Oxford. *Educ. :* S. Paul's School ; Trinity College, Cambridge. General Sec. of the League of Nations Union ; formerly Principal, College of Technology, Manchester ; and Dean of the Faculty of Technology in the Victoria University of Manchester. *War Work :* Directed the war-time activities of the College. These included, firstly, the supply of highly trained men to the technical and other branches of the Navy, Army, and Air Force, and, secondly, the invention or design, and—until the increasing demand made large scale production necessary—the actual manufacture of many implements and materials (mechanical, electrical, metallurgical, chemical, and textile), that helped to win the War. The Manchester District Armament Output Committee, and the Lancashire Anti-Submarine Committee, had their headquarters in the College, and owed to it some of the remarkable success that attended their activities. An account of the war work of the College was prepared at the request of the War Office, and has recently been published by the College Press. *Address :* 1, Foley Avenue, Hampstead, N.W. 3. *Clubs :* Athenæum; Leander. (C966)

GARNIER, Capt. Alan Parry, M.B.E., M.C., Northumberland Fusiliers, *b.* 9 Aug. 1886 ; *s.* of the late Comm. Keppel Garnier, R.N.; *m.* Hilda de Burgh, *d.* of the late de Burgh d'Arcy. *Educ. :* Uppingham ; R.M. Coll., Sandhurst. Gazetted to Northumberland Fusiliers, Jan. 1906 ; Capt., Aug. 1914 ; Major, Dec. 1915 ; Brigade Major, Oct. 1916. Employed with West African Frontier Force, Aug. 1910, to May, 1914 ; G.S.O., 3rd Grade, at G.H.Q., Egyptian Exped. Force, 1915 ; G.S.O. War Office, 1919. *Address :* 42, Montpelier Square, London, S.W. *Club :* Junior Naval and Military. (M3268)

GARNIER, Capt. Charles Newdigate, O.B.E.

GARNIER, Rev. Thomas Vernon, O.B.E., M.A., *b.* 18 July, 1875 ; *s.* of Rev. Canon Thomas Parry Garnier and Hon. Mrs. Garnier, of Cranworth, Norfolk. *Educ. :* Winchester ; Trinity College, Oxford. Vicar of Tring, Herts. *War Work :* C.F., Dec. 22, 1915 ; 6th Essex Garrison Batt.,

Mudros ; 24 C.C.S., Egypt ; 66th Inf. Brigade, 12th Cheshire Regt., Macedonia ; S.C.F., 22nd Div., April, 1918. *Address :* The Vicarage, Tring. (O3040)

GARNSEY, Sir Gilbert Francis, K.B.E., *b.* 21 March, 1883 ; *m.* Miriam Howles, B.Sc. *Educ. :* Wellington, Somerset. Partner in the firm of Price Waterhouse, & Co., Chartered Accountants, London, United States, Canada, Mexico, South America, Egypt, France, Holland, etc. *War Work :* Engaged on Government inquiries ; served on Departmental Committees ; joined, in an honorary capacity, the Finance Department of the Ministry of Munitions, 1916 ; Deputy Director Munitions Accounts, 1917 : Director Internal Audits, 1917 ; Controller Munitions Accounts, 1918 ; Chairman Finance Committee, and Finance Member of the Munitions Council, 1918 ; Member of Demobilisation Board, 1918 ; and afterwards Member of Munitions Council in charge of Liquidation of Contracts, 1919 ; Member of Advisory Council, and Chairman of Finance Committee, of Ministry of Health in connection with Government Housing Scheme, 1919 ; Member of Committee of Inquiry appointed by Minister of Health into affairs of Metropolitan Water Board, 1920. *Addresses :* 3, Frederick's Place, Old Jewry, E.C.2. ; Spencer Lodge, Greenaway Gardens, Hampstead, N.W.3. *Telegraphic Address :* Accountants Stock, London. *Telephone :* City 4694 and Hampstead 1371. *Clubs :* Union ; Gresham ; Royal Automobile ; Ranelagh.

GARRARD, Alice Mary, Mrs., M.B.E. (M10446)

GARRATT, Major Clarence Herbert Garratt, O.B.E., Royal Army Pay Department, *b.* 29 May, 1870 ; *s.* of the late John Oswald Garratt, of Peterborough ; *m.* Elise Caroline, *d.* of William Barker, of Smyrna. *Educ. :* Bedford Grammar School, and Royal Military Coll. *War Work :* France, Aug. 1914, to June, 1916 ; North Russia, May, 1919 to Oct. 1919. *Address :* Seaside Cottage, Herne Bay. (O9689)

GARRATT, Dorothy Agnes, M.B.E. For work in connection with the Imperial War Museum. (M10318)

GARRATT, George Campbell, O.B.E., M.D., *b.* 1869. Physician and Anæsthetist, Royal West Sussex Hospital. *War Work :* Physician, Graylingwell War Hospital, Chichester. *Address :* Chichester. (O11803)

GARRATT, Herbert, M.B.E. Town Clerk, Todmorden. *War Work :* Hon. Sec. Local War Pensions Committee ; Hon. Sec. of Local Committee for the Prevention and Relief of Distress ; Executive Officer Local Food Control Committee. (M8175)

GARRATT, Lieut.-Col. Lawrence Challoner, O.B.E.

GARRAWAY, Major Frank Harold, O.B.E., M.C., *b.* 23 March, 1888 ; *s.* of John Archibald Garraway, deceased ; *m.* Winifred, *d.* of H. Wordley, of Dorney, Bucks. *Educ. :* Privately. *War Work :* 1914–19, A.D.C. to Gen. Sir William Fry, Kt. Bach., C.B., C.V.O. ; A.P.M., 58th Division, England ; Staff Capt., 173rd Inf. Bde., France ; D.A.O.M.G., 50th Division, France ; twice mentioned in despatches. *Address :* Barge Cottage, Taplow, Bucks. (O5284)

GARRAWAY, T. Warrant Officer Leonard, M.B.E., Royal Indian Marine. (M3112a)

GARRETT, Col. Arthur Newson Bruff, C.B.E., T.D. J.P., *b.* 24 July, 1868 ; *s.* of Major N. D. Garrett, R.A., of Aldeburgh, Suffolk ; *m.* Elise Grant, *d.* of Kenneth Mackenzie, of Borlum-Beg, Inverness-shire. *Educ. :* Portsmouth Grammar School. Director, Coalport China Company ; J.P. (1909), Shropshire. *War Work :* Commanded 4th King's Shropshire L.I., 1914–18 ; G.S.O., Straits Settlements, 1916–17 ; Comd. 2/1 Royal N. Devon Hussars, 1918–19 ; Comd. 2nd Cyclist Brigade, Athlone, 1919. *Address :* The Cottage, Coalport, Shropshire. (C1756)

GARRETT, Charles Scott, M.B.E., D.Sc.

GARRETT, Edith, Mrs., M.B.E.

GARRETT, Lieut.-Col. Frank, C.B.E., T.D., A.M.I.C.E., A.M.I. Mech. E., J.P., *b.* 9 Dec. 1869 ; *s.* of Frank Garrett, of Aldringham House, nr. Leiston, Suffolk ; *m.* Evelyn Rosa, *d.* of Henry Brooks, of Hersham Lodge, Walton-on-Thames. *Educ. :* Rugby. County Councillor for East Suffolk ; J.P. for Suffolk ; Chairman, Leiston U.D.C. ; Director Agricultural and General Engineers, Ltd. ; Chairman and Managing Director, Richard Garrett & Sons, Ltd. *War Work :* Comd. 4th Suffolk Regt. in France, 1914–15. *Address :* Aldringham House, nr. Leiston, Suffolk. *Club :* St. Stephen's. (C171)

GARRETT, Lieut.-Col. Frederick Charles, O.B.E.

GARRETT, James Charles, M.B.E.

GARRETT, Lieut.-Col. John Raymond, O.B.E., R.M.L.I., *b.* 7 June, 1869 ; *s.* of W. R. Garrett, late of co. Carlow. *Educ. :* Clifton Coll. *War Work :* Divisional Paymaster, Royal Marine Division, Plymouth. *Address :* Royal Marine Barracks, Plymouth. (O9540)

GARRETT, Capt. Peter Bruff, C.B.E., R.N. *b.* 14 July, 1866 ; *s.* of Major N. D. Garrett, R.A., of Aldeburgh, Suffolk ; *m.* Alice Maude Mary, *d.* of the late Jone Stone, Weybridge, Surrey. *Educ. :* Mr. Foster's, Stubbington ; H.M.S. "Britannia," Dartmouth. Naval Officer, retired 1911, and was called up Aug., 1914, serving throughout the war, to Sept., 1919 ; Joined H.M.S. "Britannia," July, 1879, served in different ranks of Naval Cadet, Midshipman, Sub-Lieut., and Lieut., finally retiring with the rank of Comdr., as above. *War Work :* From August, 1914 to May, 1915, Naval Transport Staff at Newhaven, Sussex ; June, 1915 to Jan. 1918, served as Divisional Naval Transport Officer and Senior Naval Officer at Newhaven, Sussex, employed embarking stores, ammunition, etc., for the B.E.F., France and elsewhere. Feb. 1918 to Sept. 1919, employed as Divisional Naval Transport Officer

at Portsmouth, embarking the heavy gear, *i.e.* locomotives, tanks, railway wagons, ambulance coaches, etc., and being in charge of all merchant vessels entering Portsmouth harbour, and responsible for their upkeep. *Address :* Glen Isla, Oatlands Park, Surrey. (C2250)

GARRETT, Major Thomas Richard Henty, O.B.E., R.A.F.

GARROD, Heathcote William, C.B.E.

GARROW, Alexander, M.B.E., *b.* 14 June, 1846 ; *s.* of Robert Garrow, of Alteymsh, Dallas, Morayshire ; *m.* Janet, *d.* of Donald Grant, of Torchaster, Dallas. *Educ. :* Dallas Public School. Retired Supervisor of Inland Revenue. *War Work :* Voluntary Registration, Recruiting Tribunals, and Local War Pensions Committee. *Address :* 18, Hay Street, Elgin. (M8177)

GARROW, Robert George, C.B.E., R.E.

GARRY, Francis Nicholas Arbuthnot, O.B.E., M.A., *b.* 1 Feb. 1861 ; *s.* of the late Canon Nicholas T. Garry, of Taplow Rectory, Bucks ; *m.* Anne Georgina, *d.* of Swinton S. Melville, of Starmead, Wokingham. *Educ. :* Aldin House, Slough ; Eton ; Christ Church, Oxford. Member of Reading School Board, 1892–1897 ; Chairman of ditto, 1896–97 ; Member of Berks. Education Committee, 1912–19. *War Work :* Sub-Divisional Officer, Berks Police Special Reserve, Wokingham Sub-Division, Sept. 1914, until May, 1916 ; Temp. 1st Division Clerk in the Foreign Office, 1917–20. *Address :* 28, Kensington Mansions, S.W.5. *Clubs :* United University ; Berkshire, Reading. (O10458)

GARRY, Thomas Gerald, M.B.E., M.D., Mch., M.A.O., R.U.I. *Educ. :* Galway and Dublin. Hon. Physician, Anglo-American Hospital, Cairo ; Consulting British Physician, Pistany, Czecho-Slovakia. *War Work :* Hon. Sec. St. John Ambulance Association (Egyptian Centre) ; Lecturer and Examiner to the British Red Cross and Order of St. John ; Member of the Executive Committee B.R.C. and Order of St. John (Cairo branch) ; T. Major R.A.M.C., attached to Citadel Hospital, Cairo. *Address :* 12, Shani Elwi, Cairo. *Club :* Turf, Cairo. (M8178)

GARSIA, Lieut.-Col. Herbert George Anderson, C.B.E., D.S.O., *b.* 5 Feb. 1871 ; *s.* of Lieut.-Col. Michael Clare Garsia, C.B. ; *m.* Myra Mary, *d.* of Sir George Fottrell, K.C.B., of Dublin. Financial Sec., Egyptian Army. *Club :* United Service. (C2364)

GARSIDE, Cecil, M.B.E., M.C., R.A.S.C.

GARSIDE, Constance Elizabeth, M.B.E.

GARSON, Capt. Herbert Leslie, O.B.E., M.C., R.A.M.C.

GARSTIN, Lieut. Richard Hart, O.B.E., R.M.

GARSTIN, Sir William Edmund, G.C.M.G., G.B.E., Grand Cordon Medjidieh and Grand Cordon Osmanieh ; British Government Director, Suez Canal Co., since 1907 ; engaged on Red Cross Work in England during the war ; *b.* 29 Jan. 1849 ; 2nd *s.* of the late Charles Garstin ; *m.* Mary Isabella, *d.* of the late Charles Augustus North, 56, York Terrace, N.W. *Educ. :* Cheltenham Coll. ; King's Coll., London. Entered Indian Public Works Dept., 1872 ; sent to Egypt, 1885, and retired from India, 1892 ; Inspector-General of Irrigation, Egypt, 1892 ; Under-Secretary of State for Public Works in Egypt, 1904–8. *Address :* 17, Welbeck House, Wigmore Street, W. *Clubs :* Turf ; Travellers' ; Brooks's. (G32)

GARTON, Albert, M.B.E.

GARTON, Sir Richard Charles, G.B.E., Kt. Bach., *b.* 8 Oct. 1857 ; *s.* of William Garton, of Southampton ; *m.* Ellen, *d.* of Andrew Durrant, of Chelmsford. *Educ. :* Owen's College, Manchester ; Marburg University. Fellow Institute of Chemistry ; Head of the firm of Messrs. Gorton, Sons & Co., Battersea ; High Sheriff of Surrey, 1913. *Address :* Lythe Hill, Haslemere. *Clubs :* Carlton ; Conservative ; Royal Thames Yacht Club. (G25)

GARTON, Lieut.-Col. and Qr.-Mr. William George Alfred, O.B.E.

GARTON, Major Willoughby Lewis, M.B.E., R.A.S.C.

GARTSIDE, Vincent, M.B.E., M.I.Mech.E., *b.* 6 April, 1877. Mechanical Engineer (Machine Tools) ; Director of John Holroyd & Co., Ltd., Milnrow, nr. Rochdale. *War Work :* Designer of Special Machine Tools for Manufacture of Rifles, Shells, etc., and for two years at Ministry of Munitions, Whitehall ; first in charge of Russian section of Machine Tool Dept., and after in charge of Dept. controlling transfer of idle and second-hand Machine Tools on to War Work. *Addresses :* 20, Manor Road, Richmond, Surrey ; 34, Victoria Street, S.W. 1. *Club :* Royal Automobile. (M10248e)

GARVAGH, Florence, Lady, M.B.E., Order of Mercy ; *d.* of Baron de Bretton, of Denmark. *War Work :* Red Cross Working Centre ; Packing and despatching of parcels to Prisoners of War ; organised concerts and entertainments for the Wounded. *Address :* 1, Orme Square, W.2. (M1761)

GARVAN, Claire Frances, O.B.E. (O11972)

GARVEY, Lieut.-Comm. John William Frederick, O.B.E., M.A., D.L. Co Mayo, R.N.V.R., *b.* 1856 ; *s.* of John C. Garvey, D.L., of Murrisk Abbey, Westport, Ireland ; *m.* Harrie Taylor, M.B.E., for six years Master North Mayo Hounds. *Educ. :* Trinity Coll., Dublin. *War Work :* Controller of Recruiting Co. Mayo, and also, as Lieut.-Comm. R.N.V.R., in charge of Civilian Coast Watchers ; now Chairman Co. Mayo War Pensions Committee. *Address :* Downhill, Ballina, Co. Mayo. *Clubs :* Univ. ; Friendly Brothers, Dublin. (O359)

GARVEY, Harrie, Mrs., M.B.E.

GARVICE, Major Chudleigh, D.S.O., O.B.E., *b.* 1875 ; *s.* of Charles Garvice, of Bradworthy, N. Devon ; *m.* Isabel, *d.* of

Andrew Orriston, of Tasmania. *Educ.*: Tiverton. Major-General Reserve of Officers, and Commandant of Police, Alexandria, Egypt. *War Work*: Served in Egypt on Western Front as G.S.O. 2, Western Field Force; also as Military Control Officer, Alexandria, till end of the War. *Address*: Commandant's House, Alexandria, Egypt. *Club*: Naval and Military. (O4118)

GARWOOD, Edmund John, M.B.E., *b.* 6 July, 1874; *s.* of the late Edmund James Garwood, of Bushey Hill Road, Camberwell; *m.* Etheline, *d.* of the late John Robinson, of Gosport. *Educ.*: Sir Walter St. John's School, Battersea. Clerk in the War Office. *War Work*: Mobilization Directorate, War Office, on outbreak of war; served with H.M. Forces, from 11 March, 1915, to Jan. 1919, as 1st class Staff Sergeant-Major, R.A.S.C., in Mediterranean and Mesopotamian E. Forces; Mobilisation Directorate on return from service. *Address*: 43, Hillcrest Road, Walthamstow, Essex. (M8181)

GARWOOD, Eng.-Comm. Hugh Sydney, O.B.E., R.N.

GASCOIGNE, Laura Gwendolen, Mrs. Douglas TRENCH-, C.B.E.; *d.* of the late Capt. Sir Douglas Galton, K.C.B.; *m.* 1892, Frederic Richard Thomas Trench-Gascoigne, D.S.O. (*see* BURKE'S *Peerage*, Ashtown, B.). Comdt. Lotherton Hall Auxiliary Hospital, Aberford; Lady of Grace of Order of St. John of Jerusalem in England. *Addresses*: Himbleton Manor, Droitwich; Craignish Castle, Ardfern, Argyllshire; Lotherton Hall, Aberford, Leeds. *Club*: Sesame. (C173)

GASELEE, Stephen, C.B.E., M.A., F.S.A., *b.* 9 Nov. 1882; *s.* of Henry Gaselee, of 75, Linden Gardens, Bayswater, W. 2; *m.* May Evelyn, *d.* of E. Wyndham Hulme, of Clare, Sevenoaks. *Educ.*: Eton and Cambridge. Fellow of Magdalene College, Cambridge, since 1909; Librarian of the College, 1909–1919; Librarian of the Foreign Office, 1920. *War Work*: Temporary Clerk in Foreign Office, 1916–1919; Liaison Officer with Ministry of Information, 1918–1919. *Address*: 24, Ashburn Place, S.W. 7. *Clubs*: Athenæum; Carlton; United University Club. (C174)

GASK, Eleanor, M.B.E.; *d.* of Henry Gask. *War Work*: St. Bartholomew's Women's Guild. *Address*: 7, Harley House, Regent's Park, N.W.1. (M3661)

GASKELL, Arthur, O.B.E. (O9541)

GASKELL, Catherine Julia, M.B.E., *b.* 1879; *s.* of Walter Holbrook Gaskell, F.R.S., The Uplands, Gt. Shelford, Cambs. *Educ.*: Roedean School, Brighton; Newnham Coll. *War Work*: Commandant 1st Borough Red Cross Hospital, Cambridge, Nov. 1914, to March, 1915, and St. Chads V.A.D. Hospital, Cambridge, May, 1915, to May, 1919. *Address*: 26, Barton Road, Cambridge. *Club*: V.A.D. Ladies'. (M3662)

GASKELL, Helen Mary, Mrs., C.B.E., *b.* 1855; *d.* of Rev. Canon Melville, of Worcester Cathedral; *m.* Capt. Henry Brooks, *s.* of Henry Lomas Gaskell, of Kiddington Hall, Oxfordshire. *War Work*: Inaugurated by Mrs. Gaskell, Sept. 1914 the "War Library" to supply the Sick and Wounded of the British Army and Navy in all the War areas with literature. The War Library was taken over by the British Red Cross and Order of St. John in Sept. 1915; Mrs. Gaskell and Dr. Hagberg Wright of the London Library appointed Co-managers; Six million books supplied during the war. *Addresses*: Kiddington Hall, Oxon; 14, Lower Seymour Street, London, W. 1. *Club*: Sesame. (C25)

GASKELL, Holbrook, O.B.E.

GASKELL, Col. Joseph, C.B.E., J.P., D.L., *b.* 1849; *s.* of William John George Clare Gaskell, of Greenhill, Penarth, Glamorganshire; *m.* 1874, Emily Mary, *d.* of Richard Hill of Camden House, Cardiff. *Educ.*: Privately. Lieut.-Col. and Hon. Col. R.F.A. (T.F.) (V.D.); Vice-Chm. and Acting Chm. of Territorial Force Assoc. for Glamorgan; Chm. of William Hancock and Co. (Limited). *Addresses*: Cumberland Lodge, Llandaff; The White House, Llanwit Major. *Club*: National. (C175)

GASKILL, Jackson, O.B.E., *b.* 12 July, 1864; *s.* of Jackson Gaskill, of Brighton; *m.* Amy, *d.* of John Hiskett, of Frome, Somerset. Principal Clerk of the Estate Duty Office, Somerset House. *War Work*: Responsible for the collection of an important branch of the Revenue; as the War proceeded and the staff were gradually withdrawn for military duties, acute difficulties were experienced in carrying on with the reduced staff; undertook, in consequence, much strenuous work in order that the flow of Revenue might not be seriously diminished. *Address*: 29, Killieser Avenue, Streatham Hill, London, S.W. (O10459)

GASKIN, John, M.B.E.

GASPARRO, Francis Christopher, M.B.E., R.N.

GATACRE, Hon. Beatrix Wickens, Lady, O.B.E., *b.* 21 Jan. 1868; *d.* of the late Rt. Hon. Lord Davey, Lord of Appeal; *m.* the late Major-Gen. Sir William Forbes Gatacre, K.C.B., D.S.O., *s.* of Edward Lloyd Gatacre, J.P., of Gatacre Hall, Shropshire. *War Work*: From July, 1915 to Jan. 1916, worked for Messrs. Vickers, Ltd., at Erith, as lathe-hand in the shell-turning shop; from Jan. 1916, to Oct. 1918, was Hon. Treas. to the Crowborough V.A.D. Hospital; and in March, 1917, became Commandant also (V.A.D Sussex, 46); from Oct. 1918, to March, 1919, was Principal Commandant of V.A.D.s in Italy; from May to Nov. 1919, served as Commandant of the ex-V.A.D.s working for the British Empire Leave Club in Cologne. *Address*: c/o Col. the Hon. H. S. Davey, C.M.G., Norton Bavant Manor, Warminster. (O10460)

GATEHOUSE, Major Hugh, O.B.E.

GATES, Lieut.-Col. Edward Alfred, O.B.E., M.D., R.A.M.C., *b.* 16 April, 1874; *s.* of the late Philip Chasemore,

K.C., Inner Temple; *m.* Mary, *d.* of the late Major-Gen. Charles Fowler, R.E. *Educ.*: Westminster School, and St. Thomas Hospital. *War Work*: M.O. 25th R. Fusiliers, East Africa; Consulting Physician, Forward Area, B.E.F., Italy. *Address*: 5, Burwood Place, W.2. *Club*: Athenæum. (O6370)

GATES, Capt. Thomas Frank, C.B.E.

GATES, Capt. William Henry, M.B.E.

GATLIFF, Capt. Geoffrey Gatliff, M.B.E., R.E.

GATTIE, Capt. Brian Berkeley, M.B.E., *b.* 18 July, 1893; *s.* of A. E. B. Gattie, of London; *m.* Madeleine Marie, *d.* of W. S. Giffin, of Birmingham. *Educ.*: Alleyn's School, Dulwich. Interested in the Timber Trade. *War Work*: Active Service, Jan. 1915 to Jan. 1919. *Address*: 55, Mount Ararat Road, Richmond, Surrey. (M4786)

GATTIE, Major Vernon Rodney Montagu, C.B.E., M.A. (Oxon.), *b.* 29 May, 1885; *s.* of Walter Montagu Gattie. *Educ.*: Tonbridge School and Worcester College, Oxford. Barrister-at-law. *War Work*: Member of the British Military Mission to the Peace Conference, 1919; Member of the Committee of Enquiry into Breaches of the Laws of War, 1919–20. *Address*: 5, Paper Buildings, Temple, E.C. 4. *Clubs*: Carlton; Garrick. (C2107)

GATTY, Lina Mary, Mrs. SCOTT-, O.B.E., C.C., *b.* 24 Feb. 1873; *d.* of Sir William Hart Dyke, Bart., of Lullingstone Castle, Kent; *m.* Alexander John, *s.* of the late Sir Alfred Scott-Gatty, Garter King of Arms, of Welwyn, Herts. County Councillor. *War Work*: Head of Centre of Huntingdon Red Cross Hospital; Organiser of Voluntary War Working Parties; Sec. of County Soldiers' and Sailors' Families Association; Chairman of War Pensions Committee. *Address*: Castle Hill, Huntingdon. *Club*: Empress. (O1367)

GAULT, Lieut.-Col. Andrew Hamilton, D.S.O., O.B.E., *b.* 1882; *s.* of the late R. F. Gault, of Montreal; *Educ.*: McGill Univ. Consul-Gen. for Sweden in Canada, 1911–13; Major and T. Lieut.-Col. Canadian Inf.; A.D.C. on Personal Staff; Pres. of Gault Bros. Co. (Limited), of Montreal; served during S. African War, 1902 (Queen's medal with three clasps); Great War, 1915–19 (mentioned in despatches, 3rd class Order of St. Anne). *Address*: 595, Sherbrooke Street, Montreal. *Clubs*: Mount Royal; St. James's (Montreal). (O5998)

GAULT, Rev. James Archibald, O.B.E., A.I.F.

GAULT, Lieut. William James, M.B.E., Can. F.A.

GAUNT, Capt. Arthur, O.B.E.

GAUNT, Lieut.-Col. Cecil Robert, D.S.O., O.B.E., *b.* 1836; *s.* of His Honour the late Judge Gaunt, of Melbourne; *m.* 1904, Maud, *d.* of the late Maj.-Gen. C. I. Moorsom. Major (ret.) 4th Dragoon Guards; Lieut. Col. R. of O.; served on N.-W. Frontier of India, 1897–98 (mentioned in despatches, medal with two clasps); S. Africa, 1899–1902 (Queen's medal with four clasps, King's medal with two clasps); Mesopotamia, 1915–17 (mentioned in despatches). (O8473)

GAUNT, Percy Reginald, C.B.E., *b.* 6 Nov. 1875; *s.* of John W. Gaunt, of Summerfield, Bramley, nr. Leeds; *m.* Ethel Mary, *d.* of Abimelech Hainsworth, of Farsley, Leeds. *Educ.*: Leeds Boys' Modern School; Leeds University. Mill Manager and a Director of Reuben Gaunt & Sons, Ltd., Farsley, nr. Leeds; Freeman of the City of London; President of the Leeds University Textile Association; District-Commissioner for the Farsley District (West Riding of Yorkshire), B.P. Boy Scouts' Association; President of Woodhall Hills Golf Club, Calverley; President of Liberal Club, Farsley. *War Work*: Honorary Assistant-Director of Wool Textile Production, War Department, Bradford, during the war. Reponsible for arranging supplies of materials (cloths, serges, etc.) required by the Admiralty and Royal Marine Divisions, Post Office, Customs, Prisons, India Office, Crown Agents for the Colonies, Egyptian Services, South African Services, and any other Government Services (other than the Army); also for the British Railways, Police Forces, Tramways, Asylums, Corporations, Schools. *Address*: Elmwood, Calverley, nr. Leeds. *Clubs*: National Liberal; Union, Bradford; New Leeds & County Liberal. (C2627)

GAUNT, Walter Henry, O.B.E., *b.* 13 Jan. 1874; William Gaunt, of Bradford; *m.* Kate, *d.* of Alfred Brooks Kearsley, of Manchester. *Educ.*: Manchester Grammar School. Goods distribution and traffic adviser (Messrs. J. Lyons & Co., Ltd.); member of Land Agents' Society and the Institute of Transport. *War Work*: Erection of munition factories and housing; Superintendent of distribution, Coal Mines Dept., (Board of Trade): Chief special constable of Letchworth, Hertfordshire. *Address*: Ladybarn, Letchworth, Herts. (O1368)

GAUNTLETT, Major Eric Gerald, C.B.E., D.S.O., M.B., B.S., F.R.C.S., L.R.C.P., R.A.M.C. (T.), *b.* 1 Nov. 1885, *s.* of T. Lee Gauntlett, of Putney, S.W.; *m.* Hilda Margaret, *d.* of James Gerrard, of Edinburgh. *Educ.*: King's College School; King's College Hospital. Assistant Surgeon, Paddington Green Children's Hospital; Senior Surgical Registrar and Tutor, King's College Hospital; Clinical Assistant Great Northern Central Hospital; Fellow Royal Society of Medicine; Member; Harverian Society late Sambrooke Surgical Registrar House Surgeon and House Physician, King's College Hospital; House Surgeon, Royal Free Hospital; Resident Medical Officer, City of London Lying-in Hospital. *War Work*: Major (T. Lieut.-Col.) R.A.M.C. (T.F.), late Consulting Surgeon to the Salonica Forces; Service in Malta, Gallipoli, Egypt, Salonica (1914–19); Mentioned in Despatches three times. *Address*: Shanghai, China. *Club*: Royal Automobile. (C1411)

GAUNTLETT, Mager Frederic, C.I.E., C.B.E., b. 12 Oct. 1873 ; s. of Charles Augustus Gauntlett, of London ; m. Sophie Gertrude, d. of William James Weller, of London. Educ.: Dulwich Coll., and Emmanuel Coll., Cambridge. Indian Civil Service ; Comptroller and Auditor-General in India. War Work : Assistant Director, Contracts and Purchases Department, Admiralty ; Assistant Director Priority Section, Admiralty ; Sec. Shipyard Labour Department. Address : Arthington, Barton Road, Torquay. Club : East India United Service. (C176)

GAUSSEN, Marguerite, Mrs., M.B.E. ; d. of the late Judge Kelly, of Newtown, Co. Galway, Ireland ; m. the late Capt. David, s. of David Gaussen, of Duncote, Northants. War Work : Worked in Canteens in France. Address : Newtown, Co. Galway, Ireland. Club : Empress. (M3663)

GAVIN, Lieut.-Col. Frederick James, O.B.E.

GAVIN, William, C.B.E., M.A., b. 31 May, 1886 ; s. of the late James Merricks Gavin ; m. Lilian M. T. Forteath, d. of the late W. E. Hilliard and step-d. of Lieut.-Col. F. W. H. Forteath, of Newton, Morayshire, N.B. Educ.: Uppingham and Trinity College, Cambridge. Gold Medal for Research, Royal Agricultural Society, 1912 ; Scientific adviser to Lord Rayleigh's Dairies, 1910 ; Manager, Duke of Marlborough's Farms, 1913. War Work : Late Lieut. R.N.V.R. ; Sec. and Deputy-Director, Army Cattle Committee, 1917 ; Director of Flax Production, 1918 ; Director of Land Reclamation, Ministry of Agriculture, 1919. Address : Coombe House, Coombe, Oxfordshire. Club : United University. (C2628)

GAY, Charlotte Evelyn, O.B.E., b. 22 Feb. 1867 ; d. of Rev. Alf. Henry Gay, Weston House, Albury, Guildford. War Work : Collecting and arranging for parcels being despatched to Prisoners of War in connection with the Church Army. Addresses : The Church Army Headquarters, 55, Bryanston Street, W.1 ; Weston House, Albury, Guildford. (O10461)

GAYE, Major Arthur Stretton, O.B.E., R.A.S.C.

GAYE, Rev. Prebendary Herbert Charles, O.B.E., b. 12 March, 1858 ; s. of Rev. C. H. Gaye, R.D., of St. Matthews, Ipswich ; m. Frederica Louisa, d. of Rev. F. Rudston-Read, of Withyham Rectory, Sussex. Educ.: Ipswich ; Felsted ; Lincoln Theol. College. Vicar of Crewkerne, Somerset, 1897–1907 ; Prebendary of Wells Cathedral, 1905. War Work : Chaplain to 20th Divisional Artillery, 1914–16 ; Senior Chaplain to 20th Div. 1916 ; Senior Chaplain, Dieppe Area, 1916–19 ; Mentioned in despatches, Nov. 1918. Address : Havencliff. Seaton, Devon. Club : Junior Constitutional. (O2823)

GAYER, Mary Hazell, Mrs., O.B.E.

GAYTON, Joseph, M.B.E.

GEAKE, Capt. William Henry Gregory, M.B.E., A.M., b. 23 Feb. 1880 ; s. of John Venning Geake, of Reading, Berks ; m. Sybella Isabella, d. of Montgomery Marsh, of Gibraltar. Educ.: Sydney Grammar School. Consulting Engineer, Australian Defence Dept. ; O.C. Australian Research Section. War Work : Enlisted with 13th Batt., A.I.F., 1916, transferred to Munitions Inventions Dept., 1917 ; Inventor of Geake Gun, also message-carrying rocket and infantry flare used during 1917–18 operations ; Wounded, Claremont, 1917 ; Awarded Albert Medal in connection with rescue work at munitions explosion; Address : Mt. Errington, Sydney. Clubs : Imperial Service. Royal Sydney Yacht, Sydney. (M428)

GEAR, Elizabeth Anne, Mrs., M.B.E. ; d. of Alexander Hughes, of Fettercairn, N.B. War Work : Joint Organiser, Hon. Sec., and Treas. of Pinner War Hospital Supply Depot. Address : Varnham, Pinner, Middlesex. (M8185)

GEARD, Reginald Cheniston, O.B.E. (O11930)

GEARING, Ernest Handley, M.B.E., R.N.

GEARY, Arthur Bernard, O.B.E.

GEARY, Major George Reginald, O.B.E.

GEARY, Henry Valentine, M.B.E.

GEDDES, Capt. Alexander Ebenezer McLean, O.B.E., R.E.

GEDDES, Rt. Hon. Sir Eric Campbell, P.C., G.C.B., G.B.E., LL.D., M.P. (see BURKE'S Peerage) ; s. of Auckland Geddes ; m. Ada Gwendolen, d. of the Rev. A. Stokes. Educ.: Merchiston ; Oxford Military Coll. Minister of Transport. War Work : In Sept. 1914 raised, equipped, and housed the 17th Northumberland Fusiliers ; Deputy Director-General Munitions Supply, 1915–16 ; Director-General Military Railways, and Insp.-General of Transportation, 1916–17 ; Hon. Major-Gen., 1917 ; additional member Board of Admiralty, Navy Controller, 1917 ; Temp. Hon-Vice-Admiral, 1917 ; First Lord of the Admiralty, 1917–19 ; Minister without Portfolio, Jan. to Aug. 1919 ; first Minister of Transport, Aug. 1919 ; Knight, 1916 ; K.C.B. (Mil.) 1917 ; P. C. and G.B.E., 1917 ; G.C.B. (Civil), 1919 ; despatches twice ; Grand Officer of Legion of Honour ; Comm. Order of Leopold of Belgium ; Croix de Guerre Belge ; LL.D. (Sheffield) ; M.P. Cambridge Borough since 1917. Address : 12A, Manchester Square, London, W.1. Clubs : Windham ; Marlborough. (G9)

GEDDES, George, M.B.E., J.P.

GEDDES, Lieut.-Col. George Hessing, C.B., C.B.E., b. 1864 ; s. of Col. John Geddes, formerly 44th and 76th Regts. of 4, Suffolk Square, Cheltenham ; m. 1905, Vera Harriet, d. of Maj.-Gen. Charles Alexander Cuningham, Indian Army. Educ.: Cheltenham. Entered R.A., 1884 ; Capt. 1893 ; Major, 1900 ; Lieut.-Col. 1910 ; retired, 1919 ; served in S. Africa, 1902 (Queen's medal with three clasps) ; Great War. 1914–16 (twice mentioned in despatches, Legion of Honour) ; Instructor in Gunnery, R.H.A., and R.F.A., 1904–8. Club : Naval and Military. (C1578)

GEDDES, Lieut.-Col. Rex Wilshire, O.B.E.

GEDDES, Capt. William John, O.B.E., b. 19 Jan. 1882. Cartographers' Manager. War Work : Served in R.F.A. and afterwards att. to 5th Field Survey Battn., R.E., as O.C. Map Printing Company. Mentioned in despatches. Address : 92, Ebury Street, London, S.W. 1. (O5287)

GEDDES, Capt. William Louis, O.B.E.

GEDGE, Capt. Denny Victor, M.B.E. ; s. of James Gedge, of London. Sec. Bedfordshire Territorial Force Association. Address : 48, De Parys Avenue, Bedford. (M5281)

GEDGE, John Henry Barnes, M.B.E.

GEDYE, Lieut.-Col. Nicholas George, O.B.E., B.Sc. Officer of the Crown of Belgium, b. 23 May, 1874 ; s. of the late Joseph Gedye, of Weston-super-Mare : m. Vera Gladys Emeline, d. of the late John Templeton, of Radclive, Bucks. Educ.: Bristol Grammar School, and Birmingham Univ. Civil Engineer : M.Inst.C.E. ; Chief Engineer, Tyne Improvement Commission, 1910–15 ; Chief Civil Engineer for Docks, Harbours, and Inland Waterways, Ministry of Transport, Oct. 1919. War Work : Superintending Engineer, Ministry of Munitions, 1915–17 ; Major R.E., April 3, 1917 ; served on staff of Director-General of Transportation, B.E.F., 1917–18 ; Lieut.-Col. R.E., Oct. 1918 ; seconded for service under Civil Engineer-in-Chief, Admiralty, Nov. 1918, to Oct. 1919, as Assistant, and later acting Director of Special Construction and in charge of Reconstruction work in Belgian Ports ; mentioned in despatches, 1918. Addresses : 5, Victoria Street, Westminster, S.W. 1 ; Ministry of Transport, 6, Whitehall Gardens, S.W. 1. Club : St. Stephen's, Westminster, S.W. 1. (O9650)

GEE, Alan, O.B.E.

GEE, Frederick Whitfield, M.B.E.

GEE, Lieut. George Augustine, M.B.E., M.C., R.G.A. (M4489)

GEER, Lieut. Ernest Walter, M.B.E., R.A.F.

GEIPEL, Lieut. Kenneth Shute, O.B.E., R.E.

GELDART, Professor William Martin, C.B.E., M.A., B.C.L., b. 7 June, 1870 ; s. of the late Rev. E. M. Geldart, of Croydon ; m. Emily, d. of the late Ferdinand Falk, of Croydon. Educ.: Whitgift Grammar School ; St. Paul's School ; Balliol College, Oxford. Barrister-at-Law, Lincoln's Inn ; Fellow of St. John's College, Oxford, 1892–99 ; Fellow and Lecturer Trinity College, Oxford, 1901–9 ; All Souls Reader in English Law, Oxford, 1906–09 ; Vinerian Professor of English Law and Fellow of All Souls College, Oxford, since 1909. War Work : Ministry of Munitions, 1915 ; Department of the Treasury Solicitor, 1915–1919. Addresses : All Souls' College ; 10, Chadlington Road, Oxford. (C26)

GELL, Henry Willingham, O.B.E., M.D., b. 15 Oct. 1856 ; s. of John Philip Gell, of Kirk Langley, Derbyshire ; m. Edith Georgiana, d. of Richard Bradshaw, of Stanhope Street, Hyde Park, W. Educ.: Balliol Coll., Oxford. Treas. Royal Berkshire Hospital ; Chairman, Newbury Hospital ; Co-opted Member, Mental Deficiency Committee, Berks C.C. ; Director, Commercial Gas Company, London. War Work : Hon. Member of the Staff of Reading War Hospital. Address : Woolhampton Court, Berks. Clubs : New University ; Berkshire County. (O11804)

GELL, Hon. Brig.-Gen. Harry Anthony CHANDOS-POLE-, C.B.E., J.P., D.L., b. 19 Nov. 1872 ; s. of Henry Chandos-Pole-Gell, of Hopton Hall, Derbyshire ; m. Ada, d. of Thomas Henry Ismay, of Dawpool, Cheshire. Educ.: Eton. War Work : Served with Coldstream Guards South Africa, and Great War ; Hon. Brig.-Gen. in Army ; Hon. Col. 4th North Midland (Howitzer) Bde., R.F.A. ; late Major, Derbyshire Yeomanry ; County Commandants Derbyshire Volunteer Corps ; Chairman Derbyshire War Agricultural Committee. Address : Heverswood, Brasted, Kent. Clubs : Guards' ; Boodle's. (C128)

GEMMEL, Brevet-Col. Archibald Burns, C.B.E., b. 1862 ; s. of James Gemmel, M.D., of Dunoon, Argyllshire ; m. Margaret Miller Alice ; d. of William Cooper Thomson, M.D., of Glasgow. Educ.: Greenock Academy ; Glasgow University. General Practitioner. War Work : O.C. 1st Western General Hospital ; 57th General Hospital, B.E.F. Address : 114, Prince's Rd., Liverpool. Club : Racquet, Liverpool. (C1579)

GEMMEL, Col. Archibald Burns, C.B.E., Lieut.-Col. and Brevet Col. R.A.M.C. ; Great War, 1914–19 (mentioned in despatches). (C1579)

GEMMELL, Alice Caroline Anne, M.B.E. ; d. of Andrew Gemmell, of Haddington. Educ.: Cheltenham Coll. War Work : Sec. V.A.D. Committee, B.R.C.S., Edinburgh. Commandant Edinburgh 24 V.A.D. Address : 3, Deanpark Crescent, Edinburgh. Club : Queen's, Edinburgh. (M8189)

GEMMELL, Lieut.-Col. William Alexander Stewart, D.S.O., O.B.E., b. 1874 ; Major, R.A. ; ret. 1911 ; rejoined, 1914, and ret. as Lieut.-Col. 1919 ; served in S. Africa, 1899–1902 (Queen's medal with three clasps, King's medal with two clasps) ; Great War, 1914–19 (mentioned in despatches). (O7179)

GEMMILL, Jane, Mrs., M.B.E., b. 17 July, 1855 ; d. of John Ferguson, of Glasgow ; m. William, s. of Peter Gemmill, of Glasgow. Educ.: Privately. Hon. Sec. British Women's Temperance Association, Scotland (Vice-President, Glasgow District). War Work : Convener of two Belgian Homes House Committees ; Hon. Sec. to two canteens in Munition Works ; Member of Committee of B.W.T.A. Soldiers' Club ; Chairman, Partick War Savings Association ; President, Partick Infant Welfare Visitors. Address : 45, Westbourne Gardens, Glasgow. (M1763)

GENDERS, Reginald, M.B.E., B.Met.A.I.C., *b.* 14 July, 1891; *s.* of William Genders, of Sheffield; *m.* Elsie Doris, *d.* of Edwin Stoakes, of Sheffield. *Educ.:* Sheffield Univ. Research Metallurgist, Royal Arsenal, Woolwich. *War Work:* Investigating work in connection with war materials. *Address:* 84, Wellington Road, Charlton, London, S.E. 7.   (M8190)

GENDLE, Major Albert Edgar, O.B.E., R.A.F.

GENN, Capt. Otto Herman HAWKE-, C.B.E. Capt. R.N.; Served in the Great War, 1914-19 with Ocean Escort (mentioned in despatches).   (C2312)

GENOWER, Reginald, M.B.E.

GENT, William Henry, M.B.E.

GENTLE, Robert, M.B.E., *b.* 30 Oct. 1853; *s.* of Andrew Gentle, Arngask. *Educ.:* Arngask Parish School, and Edinburgh Univ. Late Accountant, Scottish Education Department, Edinburgh. *War Work:* Services rendered in the Department owing to the long continuance of the war. *Address:* 2, Windsor Street, Edinburgh.   (M3664)

GENTRY, Capt. Frederick Charles, M.B.E.

GENTRY, George, O.B.E.

GEOGHEGAN, Ethel Constance, M.B.E.; *d.* of the late Lieut.-Col. A. O. Geoghegan, R.A.M.C., of Dublin. *Educ.:* Blackheath High School; St. Anne's Coll., Lancashire; and Rouen. *War Work:* Private Sec., Ministry of Munitions, 1915-19; Voluntary Canteen Work, Royal Arsenal, Woolwich, for which obtained long service badge. *Address:* 92, St. John's Park, Blackheath, London.   (M1764)

GEOGHEGAN, William, M.B.E., *b.* 1867; *s.* of Charles Geoghegan, F.R.I.A.I., of Dublin; *m.* Adela Maud, *d.* of Thomas F. Gell, of Seedley, Lancashire. *Educ.:* Dublin. *War Work:* Assistant Controller St. John Ambulance Assn.; Joint Red Cross County Director, City of Dublin; recruiting Military Home Hospital Reserve; Red Cross Organisation and Administration from August, 1914, to 1920. *Addresses:* St. Michael's, Eglinton Road, Donnybrook, Co. Dublin; 19, Kildare Street, Dublin.   (M430)

GEORGE, Capt. Charles Dennis Victor, O.B.E., R.E.

GEORGE, Capt. FitzRoy, O.B.E.

GEORGE, Capt. John, O.B.E.

GEORGE, Dame Margaret Lloyd, G.B.E.; *d.* of Richard Owen, of Criccieth, Carnarvon; *m.* Right Hon. David Lloyd George, P.C., LL.D.; *s.* of the late William George of Bulford, Co. Pembroke, and of Liverpool, and Elizabeth his wife, *d.* of late Rev. David Lloyd, of Carnarvon. *Addresses:* Brynawton, Criccieth, Co. Carnarvon; The Firs, Fairmile, Esher, Surrey; 10, Downing Street, S.W.   (DG33)

GEORGE, Capt. Richard Westropp, M.B.E., R.E.

GEORGE, Samuel, M.B.E.

GEORGE, Capt. Wilfred Harold, O.B.E., R,E.

GEORGE, William, O.B.E.

GEORGE, William Frank, M.B.E., *b.* 2 Nov. 1881. Schoolmaster. *War Work:* Hon. Sec. Aldershot Central War Savings Committee, 1917; organised Food Economy Campaign and Demonstrations; Member of Local Advisory Committees, 1917-18; Patriotic Fund and Welcome Home Committee; Special Constable. *Address:* 11, St. Michael's Road, Aldershot.   (M2193)

GEORGE, William Henry Harrison, M.B.E.

GEORGE, Capt. Willy Oswald, M.B.E.

GEORGE, Arthur Hereford WYKEHAM-, M.B.E.

GEORGES, Edith Alexa, Mrs., M.B.E.; *d.* of the late George Milne, of Westwood, Aberdeen; *m.* the late Capt. Theodore Georges, *s.* of Col. Clayton Georges. *Educ.:* Privately. *War Work:* Organiser, Commandant, and Administrator of Hospital for Officers, Pembroke Lodge; also Commandant of V.A.D., London 248. *Club:* Ladies' Athenæum.   (M8194)

GERARD, Lieut. Charles Edward, M.B.E.

GERARD, Harold, M.B.E.

GERHARDI, T. Lieut. (T. Capt.,) William Alexander, O.B.E. Gen. List.   (O12062)

GERMAN, Major Sir James, K.B.E., J.P. (late the Welsh Regiment), *b.* 3 April, 1875; *s.* of the late John German, of London; *m.* Gwladys Rose, *d.* of Thomas J. Eynon, of Penarth. *Educ.:* Exeter. Chairman of James German, Ltd., Stockbrokers, and a director of several Shipping Companies; President of the Cardiff Battalion of the Boys' Brigade. *War Work:* Raised the Welsh tunnelling companies of the Royal Engineers; secured large numbers of volunteers for the colours; raised many thousands of pounds for charity, and also for sending recruiting bands to various towns. *Address:* Duffryn Efrwd, Nantgarw, nr. Cardiff. *Clubs:* National Liberal; Glamorgan County.   (K374)

GERRARD, Capt. Thomas Maitland, M.B.E., R.A.F.

GERVERS, Dorothy, Mrs. Charles T., O.B.E.

GETHIN, Major Randolph George, M.B.E.

GETHING, Charlotte, Mrs. BALTHASAR-, M.B.E., *b.* 14 Nov. 1865; *d.* of William Monds, of Hythe, Kent; *m.* William John Balthasar-Gething. *Educ.:* Privately. 1st Class Army Schoolmistress; retired after twenty-nine years' service in Army Schools. *War Work:* Lady Superintendent, Army Pay Office, Woking; Deputy Administrator, W.R.A.F.; l/c W.R.A.F.'s Central Pay Office, R.A.F., Woking; Lady Superintendent l/c *ex* W.R.A.F.'s Civil Subordinate Female Clerks, Central Pay Office, R.A.F., Woking. *Address:* Rawdon, Church Crookham, Fleet, Hants.   (M3460)

GIBAND, Agnes Mary, Mrs., M.B.E.

GIBB, Sir Alexander, G.B.E., C.B. (Mil.), D.S.M. (American), Member of Société des Ingénieure Civils de France, retired with rank of Brig. Gen. 1919; *b.* 12 Feb. 1872; *s.* of the late Alexander Easton Gibb, late of Beamsley Hall, Skipton, Yorks.; *m.* Norah Isabel, *y. d.* of the late Fleet-Surgeon Lowry John Monteith, R.N. *Educ.:* Rugby; University College, London. Director-General of Civil Engineering, Ministry of Transport: Late Managing Director of Easton Gibb & Son, Ltd., contractors for the construction of H.M. Dockyard, Rosyth, and other large Engineering Works; Chairman of Technical Committee on London Traffic; Chairman of Light Railways Investigation Committee. Com. of the Order of the Crown of Belgium; Fellow of the University College, London; M.I.C.E., M.I.M.E.; Member Inst. of Transport; A.I.N.A., F.R.S. (Edin.), *War Work:* Chief Engineer, Ports Construction to British Armies in France and Belgium, 1916-18; Deputy-Director of Docks (O), B.E.F., France from March, 1917 to Jan. 1918; British Representative (Technical) Commission Militaire des Ports Belges; British Representative (Technical) Commission Technique des Ports Belges; Civil Engineer-in-Chief, Admiralty, 1918-19; Member of Committee appointed to deal with the question of the use of French, Belgian, and Italian Ports for demobilisation purposes. Member of Naval Committee appointed to deal with financial and economic questions arising in connection with the Naval terms of Peace between Great Britain and the Allies, and the Central Powers. *Addresses:* Woodrow High House, Amersham, Bucks.; Gruinard House, by Aultbea, Ross-shire, Scotland. *Clubs:* Reform; Ranelagh; Caledonian; New, Edinburgh.   (G49)

GIBB, Allan, M.B.E., *b.* 13 April, 1890; *s.* of Joseph Gibb, of Millport, Scotland; *m.* Helen Anne, *d.* of Thomas Harris, of Exeter. Civil Servant. *War Work:* Contracts Dept., Ministry of Munitions. *Address:* The Holt, St. James Road, Sutton.   (M431)

GIBB, Major Andrew Dewar, M.B.E.

GIBB, Elizabeth, M.B.E., Adjutant (Salvation Army), *b.* 18 May, 1885; *d.* of Alexander Gibb, of Peterhead, Scotland. *War Work:* From June, 1915, to June, 1919, engaged in Hospital Visitation (in the interests of the British wounded); also had oversight of various huts and hostels in connection with the Salvation Army. *Address:* 108C, Stokes Croft, Bristol.   (M8195)

GIBB, Brig.-Gen. Evan, C.M.G., C.B.E. D.S.O., *b.* 12 March, 1877; *s.* of the late William Gibb, of Craigton, Fintry, Scotland *m.* Beatrice Ramsay, *d.* of Major-Gen. H. J. Hallowes, of 94, Piccadilly. *Educ.:* Rossal and R.M.C., Sandhurst. *War Work:* Served with British Expeditionary Force in France. *Address:* Inwoodbarn, by Tongham, Surrey. *Club:* Royal Automobile.   (C1253)

GIBB, Maurice Sylvester, C.B.E., J.P. Managing Director. *Addresses:* 1, The Grove, West Hartlepool; Central Marine Engine Works, West Hartlepool.   (C2629)

GIBB, Lieut.-Col. Ronald Charles, C.B.E., R.A.S.C.

GIBB, William Doig, O.B.E., M.I.C.E., *b.* 11 April, 1866; *s.* of John Smith Gibb, of Edinburgh; *m.* Mary, *d.* of William Hardie, of Newcastle on Tyne. *Educ.:* George Watson's College, Edinburgh. *War Work:* Technical Adviser to the Department of Explosives Supplies, Ministry of Munitions. *Address:* 166, E. Dulwich Grove, London, S.E. 22.   (O362)

GIBB, Capt. William Morrison, O.B.E.

GIBB, William Thomas, O.B.E., J.P.

GIBB, Aubrey Patrick HUGHES-, O.B.E., 17 March 1885; *s.* of Francis Hughes Gibb, of The Manor House, Tarrant Gunville; *m.* Sibyl Frances, *d.* of the Rev. G. Edmundson Litt. D., Vicar of St. Saviour's, Upper Chelsea. *Educ.:* Wellington; Trinity College, Cambridge. Private Sec. to Viscount Astor (Parliamentary Sec. Ministry of Health), Assistant General Inspector, Ministry of Health. *War Work:* Private Sec. to Food Controller, 1917-18, to Parliamentary Sec Ministry of Food, 1918, and to Ministry of Health, 1919. *Address:* 2, Tedworth Square, Chelsea, S.W. 3. *Club:* Ranelagh.   (O443)

GIBBARD, Col. Thomas Wykes, C.B., C.B.E., M.B. M.R.C.S. *Educ.:* King's Coll., London, and Durham Univ. Lieut.-Col. and Brevet Col. R.A.M.C.; S. Africa, 1902 (Queen's medal with four clasps); Great War, 1914-18.   (C1254)

GIBBINS, Gwendolen Mary Gladys, Mrs., M.B.E., *d.* of Henry M. Madge, M.D., of Upper Wimpole Street; *m.* Herbert Bowly, M.D., *s.* of Frederick Gibbins, of Neath, S. Wales *Educ.:* Baker's St. High School. *War Work:* Commandant Shoreham V.A.D. Hospital, Kent. *Address:* 24, Allen House, Allen Street, Kensington.   (M8935)

GIBBON, Major Edward, O.B.E., M.B., R.A.M.C.

GIBBON, Rev. Henry Hensman, O.B.E.

GIBBON, Ioan Gwilym, C.B.E., B.A., *b.* 1874; *s.* of David Gibbon, of Treherbert, Glamorgan. *Educ.:* Oswestry High School and London Univ. Assist. Sec. Min. of Health *Address:* Ministry of Health, Whitehall, S.W.   (C177)

GIBBON, Major Thomas Holroyd, O.B.E., B.A., M.D., B.Ch., B.A.O., R.A.M.C., *b.* 29 March, 1879; *s.* of Brigade Surgeon-Major E. A. Gibbon, of Sleedagh, Wexford; *m.* Elizabeth Mary, *d.* of Harry Joseph Cooper. *Educ.:* Haileybury Coll., and Trinity Coll., Dublin. *War Work:* France and Italy. *Address:* c/o Messrs. Holt & Co., 3, Whitehall Place.   (O6371)

GIBBONS, Major Gerald Francis Petvin, O.B.E., M.B., B.Sc. (Lond.), M.R.C.S., L.R.C.P., Royal Army Medical Corps (Special Reserve), *b.* 9 June, 1892; *s.* of Henry Gibbons, M.D., J.P., of Desborough; *m.* Donalda, *d.* of W. S. Cameron, M.R.C.S., of

Hampton Hill. *Educ.*: Market Harborough Grammar School; Epsom College; St. Bartholomew's Hospital. Medical Referee, Ministry of Pensions: Late Senior House Physician, St. Bartholomew's Hospital. *War Work*: Att. 27th Field Ambulance (9th Division) Oct. 1914 to Oct. 1915; Att. No. 2, C.C.S., Oct. 1915 to Feb. 1917; Att. H.Q. 2nd Army, Feb. 1917 to to Aug. 1917; Deputy Assistant-Director of Medical Services 37th Division, Aug. 1917 to Feb. 1919; With B.E.F., France, May, 1915 to Feb. 1919; Mentioned in despatches, Midsummer 1918, and Peace Gazette. *Address*: St. Anthony's Hill, Desborough, nr. Market Harborough. (O5290)

GIBBONS, Hope, M.B.E.,

GIBBONS, Lieut. (Acting Major) Oliver Thomas Brice, O.B.E., Machine Gun Corps, *b.* 11 Aug. 1896; *s.* of the late Oliver Thomas Gibbons, of Leytonstone; *m.* Peggie, *d.* of — Redmond, of Ireland. (O5291)

GIBBONS, Lieut. Robert Reginald, O.B.E.

GIBBONS, Lieut.-Col Sir Walter, K.B.E., *b.* 14 May, 1871; *s.* of John Gibbons, of Wolverhampton; *m.* Nellie Isabella, *d.* of the late George Adney Payne, of St. Malo, Herne Bay; Remarried, 1 July, 1913, Doris Blanche, *d.* of Charles Lee, J.P., of Cavendish Court. *Educ.*: Privately. Road Transport Adviser to the Ministry of Food; Hon. Treas. Automobile Association and Motor Union; Commanding Officer, Royal Army Service Corps, County of Middlesex. *War Work*: Instrumental in raising the necessary funds and presenting to the French, Belgium, and English Governments upwards of 300 Ambulances; Received the thanks of the President of the French Republic for Ambulances presented. Presented a number to the British Red Cross Society, to the War Office and the Territorial Force Association of the County of Middlesex; gave a Hospital at Stonebridge Park to the British Red Cross Society and presented them with a cheque for one thousand guineas towards the upkeep of same; instituted a Red Cross column consisting of 20 Ambulances and maintained them for dealing with the wounded at the various London Hospitals. *Address*: 1, Hanover Terrace, Regent's Park, N.W. 1. (K375)

GIBBONS, William Michael, O.B.E.

GIBBS, Capt. Brandreth, O.B.E.

GIBBS, Capt. Gerard Yardley, M.B.E., R.A.S.C., *b.* 8 May, 1887; *s.* of Kenneth Yardley, of Hatterscroft, Sawbridgeworth; *m.* Carol, *d.* of H. Herbert Francis, of Loughton. *Educ.*: Bradfield Coll. *War Work*: Served in Gallipoli and Mesopotamia; three times mentioned in despatches; organised Arab (Native) Labour, North of Bagdad. *Address*: 2, Luxborough House, Northumberland Street, W. (M4273)

GIBBS, Henry, O.B.E., *b.* 6 Nov. 1865; *s.* of the late Isaac Gibbs, of Somersetshire; *m.* Emma Girdlestone-Brown (dec.), *d.* of the late James Girdlestone-Brown, of Terrington, Norfolk. *Educ.*: King's College, London. Wool Merchant; Director of Kreglinger & Fernau, Ltd., Sydney, Melbourne, Brisbane, Freemantle, Australia, and Christchurch, N.Z. *War Work*: Officer in Charge of Colonial Wool Stocks in the U.K. (voluntary). *Address*: Terrington Grange, Northwood, Middlesex. *Club*: Royal Automobile. (O3725)

GIBBS, Hon. Mildred Dorothea, O.B.E., *b.* 2 May, 1876; *d.* of Lord Aldenham, of Aldenham and Clifton Hampden (*see* BURKE'S *Peerage*). *Educ.*: Privately. *War Work*: Commandant of V.A.D. 116 London; Administrator, Hostel for Invalid Belgian Refugees; in charge of Posting Department for V.A.D. Members of County of London. *Addresses*: 37, Portland Place, W.; Clifton Hampden, Abingdon. *Clubs*: Ladies' Empire; V.A.D. (O10465)

GIBBS, Sir Philip Armand Hamilton, K.B.E., *b.* 1877; *s.* of Henry James Gibbs, of Board of Education, Whitehall; *m.* Agnes, *d.* of the Rev. W. J. Rowland. *Educ.*: Privately; Author of many novels, historical works, and the following books on the European War: "The Soul of the War"; "The Battles of the Somme"; "From Bapaume to Passchendaele"; "Open Warfare and the way to Victory"; "The Realities of War." *War Work*: War Correspondent with the British Armies on the Western Front, 1914–19. *Address*: 114, Stamford Hill, London, N. (K376)

GIBBS, Lieut. Stanley, O.B.E., R.N.V.R.

GIBLETT, Major Robert Harold, O.B.E., A.M.I.A.E., Com. Portuguese Military Order of Avis, of Milton, Oxford. *b.* 22 Jan. 1889; *s.* of Thomas Giblett. *Educ.*: Privately; Mechanical Engineer; Automobile and I.C. Engine Designer; has written extensively on Engineering, Motor, and general subjects. "*Design and Productive Efficiency,*" 1912; "*The Recognition of Contemporary Demand,*" 1913. Numerous other articles and sketches. *War Work*: Sept, 1914, 2nd Lieut., Royal Engineers; Nov. 1914, Lieut., Inspector of Mechanical Transport, engaged on supervision of Mobile Workshop Construction; Aug. 1915, as Capt. R.A.S.C., assisted in reorganisation of Base Mech. Transport Depot in France; Jan. 1917, Major, Chief Stores Officer, Base M.T. Depot, Northern Lines of Com., France; Nov. 1917, 2nd in Command, 4th Heavy Repair Shop, Rouen; was President of Committee for interviewing and selecting skilled tradesmen; Member of M.T. Accessory Standardisation Committee; Assisted Portuguese in organisation of Mech. Transport Depot for their forces, for which made Com. of Portuguese Military Order of Avis; †twice mentioned in despatches. *Address*: Bryngwyn, Milton-on-Wychwood, Oxon; 7–15, Rosebery Avenue, E.C.1. *Club*: Royal Automobile. (O5292)

GIBSON, Alfred Edgar, O.B.E., C.A., *b.* 1886; *s.* of

Robert Gibson, of Edinburgh; *m.* Katharine, *d.* of the late James Oliver, of Edinburgh. *Educ.*: Daniel Stewart's Coll., Edinburgh, and Edinburgh Univ. Accountant, William Beardmore & Co., Ltd., Parkhead, Glasgow. *War Work*: Section Director, Department of Factory Audits and Costs, Ministry of Munitions. *Address*: c/o William Beardmore & Co., Ltd., Parkhead, Glasgow. (O10466)

GIBSON, Agnes, Mrs., M.B.E.

GIBSON, Capt. Alan Keith, O.B.E., M.C.

GIBSON, Lieut.-Col. Arthur Clare Vernon, O.B.E., R.A.O.C.

GIBSON, Capt. Charles Mends, O.B.E., R.N.

GIBSON, Prof. Charles Stanley, O.B.E., M.A., B.Sc., M.Sc., F.I.C., *b.* 8 Feb. 1884; *s.* of Joshua Gibson, Esq., of Manchester. *Educ.*: Grammar School, Manchester, Corpus Christi College, Oxford. Professor of Chemistry; Guy's Hospital. *War Work*: Honorary Adviser to the Chemical Warfare Department, Ministry of Munitions. *Addresses*: Guy's Hospital, London; 15, Birch Lane, Longsight, Manchester, England. *Clubs*: Royal Societies'; Turf (Cairo). (O3726)

GIBSON, Edward, M.B.E.

GIBSON, Finlay Albert, O.B.E.

GIBSON, Lieut. Francis Edmund, M.B.E., R.F.A.

GIBSON, Comm. Frederick John Butler, O.B.E., R.N.

GIBSON, Lieut. George E., M.B.E.

GIBSON, George McLean, O.B.E., A.M.Inst.C.E., M.I.Mech.E., *b.* 6 March, 1877; *s.* of William Gibson, of Withington, Manchester; *m.* Sarah Ellen *d.* of the late Samuel Midgley, of Kingston-upon-Hull. *Educ.*: Privately. Deputy Housing Commissioner, Region B (Yorkshire), under the Ministry of Health; late Chief Assistant Engineer, Blyth Harbour Commissioners, Blyth, Northumberland; Assistant Engineer, North-Eastern Railway Docks Department. *War Work*: Assistant Superintendent, Building Works Dept., Royal Arsenal, Woolwich; for 4½ years in charge of a Division, being responsible for Civil Engineering, Factory Construction, and also for the Construction of Temporary Houses and Hostels for Munition Workers. *Addresses*: Quebec House, Quebec Street, Leeds; Merlewood, King's Road, Harrogate. (O10468)

GIBSON, Grace, Mrs., M.B.E.; *d.* of William Gott, of Glasgow; *m.* James, *s.* of Robert Gibson, of Greenlaw, Berwickshire. *Educ.*: Glasgow. *War Work*: Hon. Stores Manager, Stores and Despatch Committee, Scottish Branch of the Red Cross Society, Headquarters, Glasgow. *Address*: 28, Park Gardens North, Broomhill, Glasgow. (M1766)

GIBSON, Sir Herbert, K.B.E., *b.* 8 July, 1863; *s.* of the late Thomas Gibson, of 1, Eglinton Crescent, Edinburgh; *m.* Madeleine Jessie, *d.* of the late Rev. W. J. Savell, M.A., L.L.M., of Wallington, Surrey. Landowner and live stock breeder in the Argentine Republic. *War Work*: Commissioner for Church Army Huts with the II. and V. Armies, B.E.F., France, and subsequently Wheat Commissioner for H.M.G. in the Argentine and Uruguayan Republics and head of Inter-Allied Commission for the purchase of cereals in those countries, 1917–19. *Address*: Compton Hurst, Eastbourne. *Clubs*: St. James'; Jockey (Buenos Aires). (K213)

GIBSON, Herbert Mends, O.B.E., *b.* 1868; *s.* of Charles George Gibson, of Plymouth; *m.* Adèle Buckingham, *d.* of Joseph J. Andrews, of Plymouth. *Educ.*: Plymouth Grammar School. Chief Superintendent, Manchester Ship Canal. *War Work*: Chairman, Transport Committee, East Lancashire Branch British Red Cross Society. *Address*: Greyfriars, Hale, Cheshire. *Clubs*: Clarendon; Constitutional, Manchester; R.A.C., London. (O1370)

GIBSON, Hope, C.B.E., *b.* 23 May, 1859; *s.* of the late Thomas Gibson, of 1, Eglinton Crescent, Edinburgh; *m.* Agnes Russell, *d.* of the late John Waddell, of The Inch, Bathgate. Argentine landowner and stock breeder; Senior partner in the house of Gibson Brothers, Buenos Aires. Produce Brokers and Merchants. *War Work*: Chairman, British Chamber of Commerce in the Argentine Republic, 1913–18; President of the Inter-Allied Committee representing six Allied Chambers of Commerce in Buenos Aires during the War. *Addresses*: Estancia "Los Inglesitos," Prov. of Buenos Aires; 1833, Rodriguez Peña, City of Buenos Aires. *Clubs*: Jockey, and Strangers, Buenos Aires, Argentine. (C967)

GIBSON, Comm. Isham Worsley, O.B.E., M.V.O.

GIBSON, James Albert, M.B.E., M.D., D.P.H., *b.* 16 Sept. 1865; *s.* of James Gibson, of Edinburgh; *m.* Lilian Mary, A.R.R.C., *d.* of the Rev. H. Colson. *Educ.*: Edinburgh Univ. Medical Officer of Health. *War Work*: Specialist Sanitary Officer (with rank of Capt.) for Section 1, Portsmouth Garrison, Aug. 1914, to March, 1919; Hon. Medical Officer in Charge; Secty. Red Cross Hospital, Gatcombe House, I. of W., 1914–17; County Medical Director for I. of W. British Red Cross Society, 1914 to present time. *Address*: Castle View, Carisbrooke, I. of W. (M8197)

GIBSON, Lieut. James Baily, M.B.E., R.A.S.C.

GIBSON, Jane, M.B.E., Q.M.A.A.C.

GIBSON, Jane Margaret Frances, M.B.E., Controller, Southern Command, Q.M.A.A.C.; *d.* of the late Jasper Gibson. *Educ.*: Harrogate. *War Work*: 1914–15, took charge, under Lady Milman, of the needlework rooms at the Primrose League (Red Cross), in Victoria Street, S.W.; in 1915, joined the Women's Legion and served as Superintendant at Dartford Military Hospital; 1917, appointed Area Controller, Q.M.A.A.C., Eastern Command; 1919, appointed Controller, Q.M.A.A.C., Southern Command. *Address*: 30a, Trebovir Road, S.W. 5. (M433)

GIBSON, John Constant, C.B.E. For voluntary services in the Contract Dept., Admiralty, from 1917 to 1919. In charge of contract work for auxiliary vessels. (C3142)

GIBSON, Capt. John George, M.B.E., T.D., b. 6 Novr 1879; s. of Major J. G. Gibson, of Edinburgh; m. Elino. Ewen, d. of Edmund Risoliere Burrell, of Blackheath, S.E. 3. Educ.: Haileybury Coll. Senior Partner in Begbies, Ross & Gibson. War Work: Served in France from Sept. 1914 with 1st Batt. Hon. Artillery Company (Infantry). Address: 6, St. Germans Place, Blackheath, S.E. 3. (M4300)

GIBSON, Lieut. John Montgomery, M.B.E.

GIBSON, John Watson, O.B.E.

GIBSON, Joseph Hamilton, O.B.E., M.Eng. (L'pool), M.I.C.E., b. 2 Feb. 1869; s. of Capt. Joseph Gibson, of Liverpool; m. Margaret. Educ.: Liverpool Institute, Civil Engineer, London and Liverpool; Past-President, Liverpool Engineering Society; Member of Council, Inst. of Naval Architects. War Work: Member of the following Committees:—Board of Invention and Research, British Marine Engineering Design and Construction, British Engineering Standards, etc. Addresses: 7, St. James' Road, Wallasey; 32, Victoria St., Westminster; 34 Castle St., Liverpool. Clubs: St. Stephen's (London); University (Liverpool). (O363)

GIBSON, Lawrence, M.B.E.

GIBSON, Myra MacIndoe, Mrs., C.B.E., b. 26 May, 1884; d. of W. M. Dunlop, M.D., late Medical Superintendent of St. Pancras Infirmary, London; m. Edward Hotham, s. of Edward Graeme, of Chislehurst. Educ.: Private Tuition; Frances Mary Buss Schools, London. Temporary Honorary General Manager, League of Remembrance (1914–19), 1, Marlborough Gate, W. 2. War Work: 1914–15, Honorary Sister-in-Charge of Christchurch Auxiliary Hospital, Chislehurst; 1916–20, Honorary General Manager, The Central Depot (H.R.H. Princess Beatrice's), 2, Cavendish, Sq., W. 1. Addresses: 37, Rutland Court, S.W. Clubs: Halcyon; Phyllis Court; Harewood Downs; League of Remembrance (1914–19). (C502)

GIBSON, Major Norman Maxwell, O.B.E., Aust. A.M.C.

GIBSON, Lieut.-Col. Orland Kingsley, O.B.E., b. 1878; s. of W. C. Gibson, of Ottawa, Ontario, Canada; m. Mona, d. of S. Whalen, of Renfrew, Ontario, Canada. Educ.: Ottawa Collegiate Institute, Toronto Unkversity, Royal College of Dental Surgeons of Ontario. Dental Surgeon. War Work: Deputy-Director of the Canadian Army Dental Services, Overseas Militia Forces of Canada. Addresses: 102, Bank Street, Ottawa, Canada House; 9, Thornton Avenue, Ottawa, Canada. Club: Laurentian (Ottawa). (O7909)

GIBSON, Major Richard Edward, O.B.E., R.A.M.C. retired), b. 8 July, 1891; s. of Henry Francis Gibson, of Ashley, Ashbourne, Derbyshire; m. Daphne Margaret, d. of the late Venerable R. C. Fletcher, Archdeacon of Blackburn, and Rector of Chorley. Educ.: Elizabeth College, Guernsey, C.I.; Edinburgh University; London Hospital. Medical Practitioner. War Work: With B.E.F., France, Aug. 1914 to March, 1919; No. 8 General Hospital; Queen Mary's Convalescent Hospital for Officers, Nice; 92nd Field Ambulance; 161st Brigade, R.F.A.; Medical Officer to General Sir Hubert Gough, K.C.B., K.C.V.O., G.O.C. Fifth Army; Deputy Assistant Director of Medical Services Cavalry Corps; Mentioned in Despatches, Jan. 1918, and June, 1918; Awarded O.B.E., June, 1918. Address: Senlis, Les Gravées, Guernsey, Channel Isles. Club: Grange, Guernsey. (O1371)

GIBSON, Robert, C.B.E.

GIBSON Lieut.-Col. Robert John Harvey, C.B.E. Lieut.-Col. Liverpool Regt. (T.). (C816)

GIBSON, Thomas George, M.B.E.

GIBSON, Capt. Thorey Carbutt, O.B.E., Spec. Res. Irish Guards, b. 11 Aug. 1883; s. of the late Arthur Buxton Cummings Gibson, of Newborough Hall, Fourstones-on-Tyne; m. Elizabeth, d. of Maurice Wetzlar, of London. Educ.: Charterhouse, and New Coll., Oxford. British Sec.-General, Austrian Section, Reparations Commission. War Work: Military Censorship, War Office; served in Irish Guards; Assistant Military Attaché, British Legation, Berne; Special Mission to Germany, 1918–19; attached British Delegation, Peace Conference. Address: 11, Douro Place, London, W. 8. Club: Bath. (O8812)

GIBSON, Capt. W., M.B.E.

GIBSON, William, C.B.E.

GIBSON, William Alfred, O.B.E. (O11973)

GIBSON, William Charles Ernest, M.B.E., b. 14 Jan. 1868; s. of the late Rev. H. A. Gibson, of Linslade Vicarage, Leighton Buzzard; m. Alice Laura, d. of Edward Salzmann. Educ.: Privately. For 20 years in business in the East (now retired). War Work: Commdr. Metropolitan Special Constabulary, T. Division, Aug. 1914 to March, 1919. Address: Mayfield, Somerset Road, Wimbledon Common, S.W. Sports? (M435)

GIBSON, William Howieson, O.B.E., D.Sc. (Lond.), b. 20 Feb. 1885; s. of John Howieson Gibson, of Edinburgh; m. Janet, d. of Walter Simpson, of Aberdeen. Educ.: Mathematical School, Rochester; Univ. Coll. School; and Univ. Coll., London. Chief Chemist, York Street Flax Spinning Co., Ltd., Belfast. War Work: Research Work on High Explosives, T.N.T., Tetryl, Guncotton, etc., at Research Dept., Woolwich Arsenal; Directive and Consultative Work as Principal Assistant to Sir Robert Robertson, K.B.E., F.R.S. Address: Shane's Cottage, Ward Avenue, Bangor, Co. Down. Clubs: Chemical Industry; Univ. of London. (O10469)

GIBSON, William John, O.B.E.

GIBSON, William Walker, O.B.E., R.A.F.

GICK, William John, C.B.E., O.B.E.

GIDDY, Lilian Napier, Mrs., M.B.E.

GIELGUD, Capt. Lewis Evelyn, M.B.E.

GIFFARD, Lieut.-Col. Jack, O.B.E.

GIFFARD, Mary Constance, Mrs., O.B.E.; d. of Richard Holt Briscoe, of Caynton, Shropshire; m. Walter Thomas Courtenay, d. of Walter Peter Giffard, of Chillington, Staffs (see BURKE'S Landed Gentry). War Work: Vice-President of Wolverhampton (Reval) Branch of B.R.C.S.; Hostess of Belgian Refugees, of Shell Shock Cases, and of Australian Officers. Address: Chillington Hall, Staffordshire. (O10471)

GIFFARD, Thomas Arthur Walter, M.B.E., B.A., b. 2 Aug. 1882; s. of Walter T. C. Giffard, J.P., D.L., of Chillington, Staffs; m. Angela Erskine, d. of Sir William Trollope, Bart., of 5, Montagu Square, W. Educ.: Harrow and Christ Church, Oxford. Formerly a Member of the Stock Exchange; now at the Board of Trade. War Work: General Staff, Military Intelligence Dept., War Office. Addresses: 16, Alexander Square, S.W. 3; Chillington Hall, Wolverhampton. Club: Wellington. (M436)

GIFFARD, Major Walter Longueville, O.B.E.

GIFFIN, Major William Herbert Dore, O.B.E., R.A.S.C. (T.).

GIFFORD, Emma, Mrs., M.B.E., b. 1861; d. of Ernest Rossiter, of Taunton; m. James William, s. of James Benjamin Gifford, of Chard. Educ.: Dover, and Bedford Coll., London. Commandant V.A.D. Somerset 52, from Aug. 1911; School Manager; Warden of Women's S. Somerset Unionist League; Hon. Sec. Chard Nursing Assocn. Received freedom of Borough of Chard 1920. Author of "Table of Natural Sines." War Work: Chard Belgian Refugees' Committee until Dec. 1915; Commandant of V.A.D. Hospital from Dec. 1915, to May, 1919. Address: Oaklands, Chard, Somerset. (M8200)

GIFFORD, Major Herbert Llewellyn, O.B.E., Royal Irish Rifles, b. 10 Oct. 1873; s. of the late Major-Gen. H. H. F. Gifford, 13th Hussars; m. Mary Eileen Barrett, d. of Mrs. Stokes, of Hove. Educ.: Bedford. War Work: Proceeded to France with 2nd Batt. Royal Irish Rifles, B.E.F., in Aug. 1914; took part in Operations at Mons and subsequent retreat, Le Cateau, the Marne, the Aisne, Ypres, and Armentières; severely wounded; G.S.O., 3rd Grade, General Staff, War Office; Brigade Major, 60th Infantry Brigade; D.A.A.G. 67th Division. Club: Junior United Service. (O8813)

GILBERT, Lieut.-Comm. Archibald, O.B.E., R.N.

GILBERT, Col. Arthur Robert, C.B.E., D.S.O., b. 1863; s. of the late Rev. Clement Gilbert, of Strumpshaw Hall, Norfolk; m. 1903, Edith Muriel, d. of Herbert Cook, of Thwaite, Norwich. Educ.: Cheltenham Coll. Entered Roy. Sussex Regt., 1882; Capt. 1892; Brevet Major, 1900; Major, 1902; Lieut.-Col. 1907; Col. 1911; served with Soudan Expedition, 1885; with Hazara Expedition, 1888 (medal with clasp); with Tirah Expedition, 1897–98; in S. Africa, 1900–2 (mentioned in despatches, Queen's medal with four clasps, King's medal); commanded a Territorial Force Brig., 1912–17. Club: Junior Army and Navy. (C1580)

GILBERT, George Julian, M.B.E., b. 11 June, 1877; s. of Myles Gilbert, of Needham Market, Suffolk. Educ.: Theobold's Endowed School, Needham Market. Civil Servant. War Work: On the staff of the Government Committee on the Prevention and Relief of Distress, and the Military Service (Civil Liabilities) Department. Address: Sundridge Mansion Hotel, Bromley, Kent. (M437)

GILBERT, James Ainsworth, O.B.E., b. 23 Dec. 1879; s. of Richard James Gilbert, of Wickham Lodge, Wickham Bishops, Essex; m. Agatha Mary, d. of Browlow Rudinge Martin, M.B., of Killeshandra, Co. Cavan. Educ.: City of London School. Bank of Bengal, India. War Work: Hon. Sec. Bengal War Fund; received thanks of French, Russian, Serbian, and Japanese Governments; Mentioned, Commander-in-Chief's (India) Despatches, 25 June, 1919. Addresses: Agra, U.P., India; Briarkot, East Withering, Sussex, England. Club: United Service. (O4041)

GILBERT, Violet Adeline, M.B.E., d. of Jeremiah Gilbert, of Leamington. Educ.: Privately. War Work: Personal Clerk to Minister of Agriculture. Address: 1, Mount View Road, London, N. 4. (M438)

GILBERT, Grace Catherine Rose, Mrs. DAVIES-, C.B.E., b. 10 Dec. 1861; d. of George Massey Dawson, of Ballinacourte, Co. Tipperary, and widow of Carew Davies-Gilbert. War Work: Deputy President of the Eastbourne Division, Sussex, of the British Red Cross Society. Address: The Manor House, Eastbourne. (C968)

GILBERTSON, Mary Campbell Bisset, Mrs., M.B.E., d. of John Ferguson, of Glasgow; m. John, s. of Robert B. Gilbertson, of Lerwick. Trained at Glasgow Royal Infirmary, and afterwards Sister there; Member of Coll. of Nursing, Glasgow Centre. War Work: Matron, Gilbert Bain Memorial Hospital, Lerwick, Shetland, which was chiefly given over for Naval and Military patients. Address: 168, Cumlodden Drive, Glasgow, N.W. (M8261)

GILBURD, William Robert, M.B.E.

GILBY, Lieut. Frank, M.B.E., R.N., b. 19 Sept. 1866; s. of Thomas Gilby, of Great Brickhill, Bucks; m. Ada, d. of George Gilby, of Great Brickhill, Bucks. Educ.: National School, Warwick; British School, Cirencester, Gloucestershire. Naval Torpedo Officer. War Work: Aug. 1914 to Nov. 1915, assisting in construction of H.M. Ships ; Nov. 1915, Torpedo duties with Grand Fleet, Destroyer Flotillas, North Sea, till June, 1918 ; June, 1918, till end of war, Construction duties. *Address* : Commanding Officer, Hornsea Island ; c/o H.M.S. "Vernon," Portsmouth. (M1769)

GILCHRIST, Archibald, O.B.E., J.P., *b.* 1877 ; *s.* of James Gilchrist, J.P., D.L., of Bellcairn, Dumbartonshire ; *m.* Euphemia, *d.* of William Mitchell, Shipbuilder, of West Hartlepool. *Educ.* : Albany Academy ; Andersonian College ; Royal Technical College. Engineer and Shipbuilder ; Director of Swan, Hunter and Wigham Richardson, Ltd., Barclay, Curle & Co. Ltd., the British Hydraulic Foundry Co., Ltd., and other industrial concerns. *War Work* : Building of various types of warships, aeroplanes, seaplanes, etc. *Address* : Highfield, Kelvinside, Glasgow. *Clubs* : Constitutional ; British Empire. (O367)

GILCHRIST, Archibald John, O.B.E., M.C., M.B., M.R.C.S., L.R.C.P., *b.* 21 Oct. 1884 ; *s.* of the late John Gilchrist. *Educ.* : Harbord Street, C.I. ; University of Toronto ; London Hospital. *War Work* : Lieut. R.A.M.C. (S.R.), 1914, att. 1st Worcesters ; promoted Capt. 1915 ; 10th General Hospital, Rouen, 1916–19 ; A. Major, 1918 ; Officer in charge Surgical Division, 10th Gen. Hospital, 1917–19. *Address* : 455, Palmerston Bend, Toronto, Canada. (O5294)

GILCHRIST, Elizabeth MacFarlane, M.B.E., Q.M.A.A.C.

GILCHRIST, George Prowse, M.B.E.

GILCHRIST, Lieut. Henry Thomas, M.B.E., *b.* 3 June, 1897 ; *s.* of H. Gilchrist, of Rathsallagh, Colbinstown, Co. Wicklow. *Educ.* : St. Columba's Coll., Rathfarnham, and The High School, Dublin. *Addresses* : Rathsallagh, Colbinstown, Co. Wicklow, Ireland ; c/o O.C., R.A.S.C., Delta Area, Old Army H.Q., Rue Kasr-el-Nil, Cairo. (M4735)

GILCHRIST, John MacAnslan, O.B.E.

GILCHRIST, Capt. Norman Stephen, O.B.E., R.A.F.

GILES, Arthur, M.B.E.

GILES, Major Arthur Herbert Wainwright, O.B.E.

GILES, Major Godfrey Douglas, O.B.E., R.F.A. (T.).

GILES, Lieut.-Col. Godfrey Hill, C.B.E.

GILES, Lieut. Harry Herbert, M.B.E., R.A.F.

GILES, Capt. (A. Major) Hylton Lloyd, O.B.E., *b.* 18 June, 1880 ; *s.* of Hammond Giles, of Norwich ; *m.* Phyllis Naomi, *d.* of Dr. John Herbert Stacy, of Norwich. *Educ.* : Blundells School, Devon. Manager of the Norwich Branch of the Alliance Assurance Co., Ltd. *War Work* : Mobilised 4 August, 1914 ; demobilised June, 1919 ; 2 years in France on G.H.Q. Staff, 3rd Echelon, B.E.F. *Address* : Blundells, Mile End Road, Norwich. *Club* : Norfolk and Norwich. (O5295)

GILES, John Dudgeon, O.B.E., M.D., Ch.B. (Edin)., *b.* 28 Jan. 1880 ; *s.* of the late Rev. Alexander Giles, M.A. (Aberdeen), of Ashkirk, Selkirkshire ; *m.* Annie, *d.* of Charles Edward Wright, of London. *Educ.* : George Watson's College, Edinburgh ; University of Edinburgh ; King's College, London ; and Middlesex Hospital, London. Medical Superintendent of Salford Union Infirmary, Pendleton, Manchester. *War Work* : Medical Officer-in-Charge of Hope Auxiliary Military Hospital Pendleton, Manchester, from 1915–19. *Addresses* : Sunnyside, Lancaster Road, Pendleton. Manchester ; Hope Hospital, Stott Lane, Pendleton, Manchester. (O4366)

GILES, Robert, M.B.E.

GILES, Robert Edgar, M.B.E., *b.* 2 Feb. 1889 ; *s.* of William Giles, of Battersea ; *m.* Helen Hibble, *d.* of James Gates, of Portchester, Hants. *Educ.* : Strand School. *War Work* : Sec. to the Admiralty Sub-Committee, and Principal of the Admiralty Division, War Trade Department. *Address* : 53, Manchuria Road, Clapham Common, S.W. 11. (M1770)

GILFILLAN, Samuel James, O.B.E., M.B.

GILHESPY, Paymaster-Lieut.-Comm. John William Edward, O.B.E., R.N.

GILL, Daisy Lee Heywood, Mrs., M.B.E.

GILL, Major Ernest William, O.B.E., R.E.

GILL, Frank, O.B.E.

GILL, Lieut.-Comm. Henry Dale, O.B.E., R.N.

GILL, Col. James Geoffrey, C.B.E., D.S.O., L.R.C.P.I., L.M., L.R.C.S.I., R.A.M.C. ; served in S. Africa, 1899–1902 (Queen's medal with four clasps, King's medal with two clasps) ; during Great War, 1914–17 (mentioned in despatches). (C3094)

GILL, Major James Herbert Wainwright, O.B.E., R.E.

GILL, Capt. John Galbraith, D.S.O., O.B.E., M.C.

GILL, Lilias Ida, M.B.E., W.A.A.C.

GILL, Wing.-Com. Napier John, C.B.E., M.C., R.A.F., *b.* 5 April, 1890 ; *s.* of Robert T. Gill, of Airleywight House, Bankfoot, Perthshire ; *m.* Daisy, *d.* of Henry Cotton, of London. *Educ.* : Summerfields, nr. Oxford ; Rugby ; Woolwich. *Address* : 1, Chester Place, Hyde Park, London, W. (C860)

GILL, Capt. Walter Brudenell, O.B.E., R.E.

GILL, William Briggs, O.B.E.

GILL, Joseph WITHERS-, O.B.E., *b.* 7 Dec. 1864 ; *s.* of John Withers Gill, of Thetford Manor, Norfolk ; *m.* Gertrude Bethune, *d.* of Horatio Bethune Leggatt, of Brownwich, Hants. *Educ.* : London and Cambridge. Nigerian Political Service (ret.). *War Work* : Section Director, Ministry of Munitions. *Addresses* : 33 Stanhope Gardens, S.W. 7. (O10474)

GILLAM, Capt. Vernon, M.B.E., R.F.A., *b.* 21 Jan. 1884 ; *m.* Cecilia Ethel Mary, *d.* of John Haines, of Brighton. *Educ.* : Privately. O.C. Artillery Ranges, Salisbury Plain. *War Work* :

Served with 7th Division, B.E.F., in Belgium, during 1st Battle of Ypres ; was commissioned for service in the field, in Jan. 1915 ; appointed Assist. Instructor Gunnery at Shoeburyness ; Assist. Commandant, R.A. Practice Camp, for training of new armies (Artillery), until Nov. 1917. (M5288)

GILLAM, Major Vincent Andrew, O.B.E., York and Lancaster Regt., *b.* 21 Jan. 1884 ; *s.* of the late Frank Andrew Gillam, of 18, West Cromwell Road, South Kensington ; *m.* Ida Dorothy, *d.* of Sir Kenneth Kemp, Bart. (*see* BURKE'S *Peerage*), of Mergate Hall and Gissing Hall, Norfolk. *Educ.* : Wellington Coll., and Royal Military Coll., Sandhurst. *War Work* : Served with B.E.F., France, 1914 ; Deputy Assist. Adjutant-General, Headquarters, Eastern Command, 1916–17 ; War Office, 1917–20. *Club* : Army and Navy. (O7185)

GILLANDERS, Francis Geraldine, Mrs. MACKENZIE-, M.B.E., *b.* 26 Aug. 1878 ; *d.* of George Francis Gillanders, J.P., D.L., of Highfield (*see* BURKE'S *Landed Gentry*) ; *m.* Capt. Edward Baskerville (who assumed by Royal Licence, on his marriage, the additional name of Gillanders), *s.* of William Dalziel Mackenzie, J.P., D.L., of Fawley Court, Bucks, and Farr, Inverness (*see* BURKE'S *Landed Gentry*). Vice-President, Ross and Cromarty Branch Red Cross. *War Work* : President and Convener, Highfield War Hospital Supply Depot ; President and Convener, Highfield Comforts Fund ; President and Chairman, Mrs. Mackenzie-Gillanders' Prisoners of War Fund ; District Representative and Member of Women's Agricultural County Committee ; organised Fetes, Sales, Flower and Flag Days, etc. *Address* : Highfield House, Muir of Ord ; Corriechallie Lodge, Muir of Ord. (M8204)

GILLER, George Samuel, M.B.E.

GILLESPIE, Eng.-Comm. Andrew, O.B.E., R.N.R.

GILLESPIE, Sub.-Lieut. Gerald James, M.B.E., R.N.V.R.

GILLESPIE, Major Harold Evelyn, O.B.E., R.M.L.I.

GILLESPIE, James, M.B.E.

GILLESPIE, James Macgregor, O.B.E.

GILLESPIE, Margaret, Mrs., M.B.E.

GILLESPIE, Lieut.-Col. Rollo St. John, C.I.E., O.B.E.

GILLESPIE, Sara, Mrs., M.B.E.

GILLESPIE, Lieut. William Ernest, M.B.E., R.A.S.C.

GILLESPIE, William James, M.B.E., J.P., *b.* Sept. 24, 1870 ; *s.* of Matthew Gillespie, of Glentriplock ; *m.* Jessie, *d.* of — Anderson Ferguson. Farmer ; J.P. for County of Wigtown ; Chairman, Mochrum Parish Council, and Mochrum School Management Committee ; President of Portwilliam Dairy Farmers' Association, and Farmers' Union ; Member of District Committee of County. *War Work* : Deputy Head Coast Watcher, E. Bay of Luce. *Address* : South Barsalloch, Portwilliam, Wigtownshire. (M3667)

GILLETT, Capt. Bernard George, O.B.E., I.A.R.O.

GILLETT, Edwin, O.B.E.

GILLETT, Henry William, M.B.E.

GILLETT, John Cornelius, M.B.E., *b.* 14 Jan. 1852 ; *s.* of Cornelius Gillett, of Walthamstow ; *m.* Matilda, *d.* of George Gollop, of Poole, Dorset. *Educ.* : City of London School. Silk Manufacturer (ret.). *War Work* : Member of the Local War Pensions Committee, and Chairman of its Disablement Sub-Committee ; Chairman of the Committee for Juvenile Employment under Ministry of Labour ; Hon. Sec. of the local branch of the Soldiers' and Sailors' Help Society ; Member of Comm ttee of Local Soldiers' and Sailors' Families Association, and of the Essex Council for Industrial Training. *Address* : 2, Prospect Hill, Walthamstow, E. 17. (M8207)

GILLETT, Thomas, M.B.E., M.I.M.E., M.I.A.E., *b.* 29 Dec. 1886 ; *s.* of John Gillett, of Peel, Lancashire ; *m.* Helen, *d.* of Thomas McLaren, of Cupar, Fife. *Educ.* : Holy Trinity, Guildford. Managing Director, Gillett, Stephen & Co., Ltd., Bookham. *War Work* : Manufacture of Aero Engines and Spares. (M1773)

GILLIARD, Capt. and Qr.-Mr. William Thomas, M.B.E.

GILLIES, Major Austin Bain, O.B.E., Can. F.A.

GILLIES, Major Harold Delf, C.B.E., F.R.C.S., R.A.M.C.

GILLIES, Capt. James, C.B.E.

GILLIES, Capt. James Adam Kirkwood, O.B.E., R.D.C.

GILLIES, Lieut. John, O.B.E., R.N.V.R.

GILLIGAN, Lieut.-Col. Geoffrey Goyer, D.S.O., O.B.E., Major and Acting Lieut.-Col. Argyll and Sutherland Highlanders, attached Notts. and Derbyshire Regt. ; S. Africa, 1900–1 (Queen's medal with three clasps) ; Somaliland, 1908–10 (medal with clasp) ; Great War, 1914–18 (menticned in despatches). (O5297)

GILLING, Lieut.-Col. Henry Thomas, O.B.E., T.D., R.F.A. (T.).

GILLINGHAM, James Searle, M.B.E.

GILLMAN, Arthur William, O.B.E., *b.* 1862. Bank Manager. *War Work* : Hon. Treas., London War Pensions Committee, Wandsworth C. ; and Streatham Ambulance Fund. *Address* : 16, Tooting Bec Gardens, Streatham, S.W. 16. (O10476)

GILLMAN, Capt. Herbert, O.B.E., R.G.A.

GILLON, Dorothy Gladys, M.B.E., *d.* of the late Henry Gillon, I.C.S. *Educ.* : Privately. Editress. *War Work* : On the personal staff of Lord Northcliffe at the headquarters of the British War Mission, New York, U.S.A. ; canteen work at the Little Theatre, Y.M.C.A., Adelphi, London, W.C. 2. *Addresses* : 4, Madeira Park, Tunbridge Wells, Kent ; The Fleetway House, Farringdon Street, E.C. 4. (M1774)

GILLON, Nina, Mrs. Stair Andrew Gillon, O.B.E.

GILLOTT, Mary Aloysia, M.B.E. b. 21 June, 1878; d. of Thomas Gillott, of Eastwood, Nottingham. Educ.: Ursuline Convent, Upton, Essex. War Work: Commandant of Eastwood V.A.D. Hospital from May, 1915, to March, 1919. Address: Uplands, Eastwood, Nottingham. (M8208)

GILMORE, Alice Maud, O.B.E. (O11741)

GILMORE, Fred Peter, M.B.E.

GILMORE, Major Thomas Edward, O.B.E., R.A.F.

GILMOUR, David, C.B.E.

GILMOUR, David, O.B.E.

GILMOUR, James, M.B.E.

GILMOUR, John, O.B.E., J.P. Provost of Inverary for many years. (O11904)

GILMOUR, Robert, O.B.E.

GILMOUR, Robert, M.B.E.

GILMOUR, Robert Scott, M.B.E.

GILPIN, Brig.-Gen. Frederic Charles Almon, C.B., C.B.E., b. 1860; s. of Lieut.-Col. B. T. Gilpin; m. Georgiana, d. of the Rev. Canon Stephenson, of Weymouth. Educ.: Wellington College; Sandhurst. Served in the S. African War, 1899–1900; Despatches, 17 June, 1902; Brevet. Lieut.-Col.; and the European War, 1914–18; Despatches, 1914. Address: Cavendish, Suffolk. (C1581)

GILPIN, Major and Qr.-Mr. George, O.B.E.

GILPIN, William John, M.B.E., L.R.C.P., M.R.C.S.

GILROY, Lieut. Henry Errington, O.B.E., R.N.R.

GILROY, James Boyd, M.B.E.

GILROY, John, O.B.E.

GILRUTH, Jeannie, Mrs., O.B.E.

GIMBERT, Lieut. William Bertie, O.B.E., R.F.A.

GIMINGHAM, Capt. Conrad Theodore, O.B.E., R.E.

GIMSON, Margaret, M.B.E. War Work: Charge of Registration Department of the Leicester War Pensions Committee for the whole period of the war. Addresses: 4, Belmont Villas, New Walk, Leicester; Rockyfield, Ulverscroft, near Leicester. (M1777)

GINGOLD, Lieut. Frederick Maurice, M.B.E., A.P.D.

GIOVANETTI, Constantine William, C.B.E., M.L.A., b. 13 Aug. 1867; s. of Gottardo Giovanetti, of Victoria, Australia; m. Marion Frances Elizabeth, d. of Eli Hellier, of Victoria, Australia. Educ.: Strangways High School, Victoria, Australia. War Work: Mayor of Pretoria, 1915–20, and as such was Chairman, Recruiting Committee, Governor-General's Fund; Member of Central Executive of Governor-General's Fund; Chairman, Returned Soldiers' Committee; Chairman and Treasurer, Roberts Heights Hospital Entertainment Committee; Chairman, Disabled Soldiers' Board; Member of Hospital Commission re Treatment of Soldiers from East Africa. Address: Melbourne, 908, Church Street, Arcadia, Pretoria. Clubs: Pretoria Unionist; Pretoria County. (C3210)

GIRARD, Mrs. Marie, O.B.E.

GIRDLESTONE, Emily, Mrs., M.B.E.

GIRDWOOD, Alexander Forsyth, M.B.E.

GIRLING, Marjorie, M.B.E., b. 21 Feb. 1894; d. of Frank E. Girling, of Suffolk. Educ.: North London Collegiate School for Girls. War Work: April, 1916, to Feb. 1920; temp. clerk at War Office; previous to that, helped at the Local Red Cross Depot; in Sept. 1918, mentioned in Civil Service Honours List. Address: West Marden, Emsworth, Hants. (M3669)

GITTINGS, Gwendoline, Mrs., M.B.E.

GITTINGS, Lieut. Thomas Albert, O.B.E., R.F.A.

GITTINS, Henry, C.B.E.

GIVEN, Ernest Cranston, C.B.E., M.Inst.C.E., M.I.Mech.E., M.Inst.N.A., b. 11 Nov. 1870; s. of late John Given; m. Winifred Mary, d. of Ronald Currie, M.D., J.P., of Skelmorlie. Educ.: Harrow and Liverpool Univ. Consulting Engineer; General Manager, Slough Trading Co., Ltd. War Work: Hon. Organiser Liverpool Munitions of War Committee, No. 2 National Filling Factory, No. 2 National Amatol, 1915; Director of Airship Production, Admiralty, 1917–19; Director-General of Factories, Ministry of Munitions, 1919–20. Address: Clewer Hill Lodge, Windsor. Clubs: Union; Royal Automobile. (C3106a)

GIVEN, John Cecil Mackmurdo, M.B.E., M.D.

GJERS, Annie Gatenby, Mrs., O.B.E.

GLACKAN, Sydney Hugh, M.B.E.

GLADSTONE, Lieut. Albert Charles, M.B.E.

GLADSTONE, Herbert John, Viscount, P.C., G.C.B., G.C.M.G., G.B.E. (see BURKE'S Peerage), b. 7 Jan. 1854; s. of the late Rt. Hon. William Ewart Gladstone, four times Prime Minister, of Hawarden; m. Dorothy Mary, d. of Rt. Hon. Sir Richard Paget (see BURKE'S Peerage), of Cranmore Hall, Shepton Mallet. Educ.: Eton; University College, Oxford; 3rd Class Classics, 1874; 1st Class. History School, 1876; History Lecturer, Keble College, 1877–80. Contested Middlesex County, 1880; Private Secretary to Mr. Gladstone, 1880–81; a Lord of the Treasury, 1881–85; Finance Sec., War Office, 1886; Under-Sec. Home Office, 1892–94; First Commissioner of Works, 1894–95; Chief Whip to the Liberal Party, 1899–1906; Secretary of State for Home Affairs, 1905–10; M.P. (L), Leeds, W., 1880–1909; First Governor-Genl., South Africa, 1909–14; President, National Physical Recreation Society. War Work: Chairman, War Refugees Committee, 1914–18; Chairman, South African Hospital and Comforts Fund, and Ambulance Hospital, Cannes. Address: 4, Cleveland Square, St. James', London, S.W. 1; Dane End, Ware, Herts. Clubs: Reform; National Liberal; Bath.

GLADSTONE, Maud Ernestine, Hon. Mrs., C.B.E., L.G. St. John, b. 1865; d. of the late Lord Rendel, of Hatchlands, Surrey; m. Henry Neville, s. of the late Rt. Hon. W. E. Gladstone, of Hawarden Castle, four times Prime Minister. War Work: Vice-President, British Red Cross Society, Chester City Division; Chairman of the Committee of Hoole House and Hoole Bank Auxiliary Military Hospital, Chester; Officer in-Charge, Parkgate (Chester) Auxiliary Military Hospital; and associated with numerous War Work Committees. Addresses: Hawarden Castle, Flintshire; Burton Manor, Chester; 78, Eaton Square, London, S.W. (C969)

GLADWELL, 2nd Lieut. Athelstan Louis, M.B.E.

GLADWELL, Ethel Dorothy, Mrs., M.B.E., b. 23 Feb. 1895; d. of John Mitchell Brown, I.S.O., of Ramelton, Co. Donegal, and London; m. Ernest Arney, s. of Henry William Gladwell, of Cheapside, E.C. Educ.: Aske's Haberdashers' School for Girls, Hatcham; and Camberwell School of Art. Member of the Irish Literary Society. War Work: Joined the Staff of the Ministry of Information in April, 1917; assist. in Articles Section, and Superintendent of Typing Section, until March, 1919. Address: 22, Chiswick High Road, W. 4. (M3670)

GLADWYN, Sidney Charles, M.B.E., A.M.Inst.C.E., M.I.S.Inst., b. 8 Sept. 1885; s. of William Charles Gladwyn, of Woolwich; m. Constance Evaline, d. of Joseph Beaumont, of Sheffield. Educ.: Woolwich Polytechnic and Sheffield Univ. Assistant Engineer and Chief Draughtsman to Samuel Osborn and Co., Ltd., Sheffield; Consulting Engineer, London. War Work: Chief Designer and Chief Draughtsman, Royal Laboratory, Woolwich Arsenal; in charge of Design of Ammunition. Addresses: 63, Quentin Road, Blackheath, S.E. 13; Royal Laboratory Dept., Ordnance Factories, Woolwich. (M8214)

GLANELY, Ada Mary, Lady, C.B.E.; d. of the late Thomas Williams, of Pergam, Cardiff; m. 14 Sept., 1897, Sir William James Tatem, 1st Baron Glanely (see BURKE'S Peerage). War Work: Services at Caerphilly. Addresses: The Court, St. Fagan's Cardiff; Lackham, Lacock, Wiltshire; Exning House, Exning, Newmarket. (C3144)

GLANFIELD, Olive, M.B.E.

GLANUSK, Editha Elma, Lady, C.B.E.; o. d. of Warden Sergison (see BURKE'S Landed Gentry), of Cuckfield Park, Sussex; m. Joseph, Henry Russell, 2nd Lord Glanusk, of Crickhowell (see BURKE'S Peerage). War Work: President, Breconshire Red Cross, Penoyre Hospital. Address: Glanusk Park, Crickhowell, S. Wales. (C2632)

GLANUSK, Joseph Henry Russell, 2nd Lord, C.B., C.B.E., D.S.O., J.P. (see BURKE'S Peerage), b. 26 Oct. 1864; s. of 1st Lord Glanusk, of Glanusk Park, Crickhowell; m. Editha Elma, d. of Major Warden Sergison (see BURKE'S Landed Gentry), of Cuckfield Park, Sussex. Educ.: Eton; Sandhurst. Major, Grenadier Guards (retired 1903). War Work: Commanded Breconshire Territorials in Aden and India, 1914–16; commanded London Command Depot, Shoreham, 1916–18. Addresses: Glanusk Park, Crickhowell, Breconshire. Clubs: Guards'; Carlton. (C1582)

GLANVILLE, Lieut. Ernest Alfred, M.B.E.

GLANVILLE, William Henry, O.B.E., b. 1859; s. of Charles Glanville, of Abingdon; m. Lilian Blanche, d. of George Ferguson, of East Molesey. Educ.: Abingdon Grammar School. Director of Sampang (Java) Rubber Plantations; Director of National Electric Theatres, Ltd. War Work: Munitions Area Inspector for Wales and South West England. Address: Hurstfield, East Molesey. Club: Junior Constitutional. (O10480)

GLASBY, Capt. Walter George, O.B.E., R.G.A.

GLASER, Herbert, O.B.E.

GLASIER, Major Frank Bedford, C.M.G., C.B.E., R.E., b. 1872; s. of J. S. Bedford Glasier, of Hunstanton. General Manager and Chief Engineer, Sierra Leone Government Railway, 1899–1901; Lagos (Slate) Railway, 1901–12. War Work: Assisted at Board of Trade, Oct. 1914, O.A.O.R.T., Movements Directorate, War Office, 1915 to Oct. 1919. Address: Hunstanton, Norfolk. Club: Sports'. (C1462)

GLASON, Capt. John Apollonius, M.B.E., b. 18 April, 1893; s. of Samuel Glason, of Littlehampton; m. Dorothy Mary, d. of Charles East, of Farley Hill, Reading. Educ.: St. Bernardine's Coll., Buckingham, and Univ. Coll., Reading. Schoolmaster. War Work: Enlisted 28th Batt. London Regt. (Artists Rifles), Dec. 1915; 2nd Lieut. 4th Lanc. Fus., Sept. 1916; Lieut., March, 1918; promoted Capt., Dec. 1918; service overseas in France and Flanders, Dec. 1916 to June, 1919. Address: 78, Queen's Road, Reading. (M4490)

GLASS, Alexander, O.B.E.

GLASS, Henry Matier, O.B.E.

GLAYSHER, Henry Charles, M.B.E., b. 12 June, 1872; s. of the late James Glaysher, of London, formerly Chief Engineer, Imperial Ottoman Mint, and Imperial Arsenal, Constantinople; m. Jessie, d. of Daniel White, of Highgate. Educ.: Camden High School, and King's Coll., London. War Work: Chief Examiner, War Office. Address: 18, Leyborne Park, Kew Gardens, Surrey. (M8215)

GLAYZER, Edward John, M.B.E.

GLAZE, Charles William Livock, O.B.E.

GLAZEBROOK, Capt. Edward John, M.B.E., D.C.M. (M10220)

GLAZEBROOK, Monica, M.B.E., Hon. Serving Sister of Order of St. John of Jerusalem, b. 1887; d. of Sir Richard

Glazebrook, K.C.B., of Cambridge (*see* BURKE'S *Peerage*). *Educ.*: Privately. Private Secretary. *War Work*: Private Sec. to Principal Commandant of V.A.D.'s, Boulogne Base, B.E.F., from Jan. 1915 to July, 1919; previously Sec. to War Emergencies Relief Committee, and Soldiers' and Sailors' Families Association, in Teddington, Middlesex, Aug. 1914 to Dec. 1914. *Address*: Coton End, Grange Road, Cambridge. *Club*: Blue Triangle.   (M1779)

GLEDHILL, John, O.B.E.

GLEESON, Lieut.-Col. Andrew Fitzwilliam, O.B.E., *b.* 27 Jan. 1860. *War Work*: Quartermaster-General's Department, War Office. *Address*: Moyallon, Fairlawn Park, Chiswick, W. 4.   (O7189)

GLEESON, Edward John, O.B.E., Superintendent of Police, Baluchistan, *b.* 14 May, 1867. *War Work*: Awarded the O.B.E. for successful fights with Pathan raiders during the Afghan War, 1919.   (O9819)

GLEGG, Comm. Robert, M.B.E., *b.* 22 May, 1855; *s.* of Robert Glegg, of Aberdeen; *m.* Mary Farquhar, *d.* of William Hobrow, of Colchester and Aberdeen. *Educ.*: Aberdeen. Mercantile Marine, Commanding s.s. "Atholl." *War Work*: Served as Commander in Naval Transport Service from Sept. 1914 till Jan. 1919; his steamer, the "Lovat," was sunk by "Emden" in Bay of Bengal, Sept. 1914; took over command of s.s. "Atholl" in Feb. 1915, and continued to command her until the end of the war.   (M3672)

GLEGHORN, Thomas Richard, O.B.E.

GLEICHEN, Lady Helena, O.B.E., Lady of Grace St. John of Jerusalem, Italian Bronze Medal for Valour, *b.* 1 Feb. 1873; *d.* of Admiral Prince Victor of Hohenlohe, and Lady Laura Seymour (*see* BURKE'S *Peerage*). *Educ.*: Privately; Westminster; Calderon; Rollshoven; Arthur Lemon (Art). Artist. *War Work*: Ambulance work, France, 1915; X-Ray work, France, 1915; Joint Commandant, X-Ray section, Italy, 1915–17; American Comité des Terres devastées de la France, Soissons, 1919. *Address*: St. James' Palace, London; Neuadd, Crickhowell, S. Wales. *Club*: Sesame. (O10484)

GLEN, Elizabeth Hope, O.B.E., *b.* 18 Aug. 1892; *d.* of the Rev. J. P. Glen, of Ardrishaig. *Educ.*: Newnham Coll., Cambridge (Economics Tripos of the Univ. of Cambridge). Assistant Technical Adviser to the Special Grants Committee, Ministry of Pensions. *War Work*: Sec. to the City of Norwich War Pensions Committee, and Hon. Sec. to Norwich Soldiers' and Sailors' Families Association, 1916–19. *Address*: The Manse, Ardrishaig, Argyll, Scotland.   (O10485)

GLEN, James Hutchinson, M.B.E.

GLEN, James Morrison, M.B.E.

GLENARTHUR, Janet Stevenson Bennett, Lady, O.B.E., *d.* of the late Alexander Bennett McGrigor, LL.D. (*see* BURKE'S *Landed Gentry*), of Cairnoch, Stirlingshire; *m.* Matthew, 1st Lord Glenarthur, of Carlung (*see* BURKE'S *Peerage*), *s.* of the late James Arthur, of Carlung and Barshaw. *Educ.*: Privately. *War Work*: Vice-President of Ayrshire Branch, British Red Cross Society; Member of War Executive Scottish Branch British Red Cross Society; Commandant Troon Red Cross Auxiliary Hospital; Commandant of V.A.D. Ayr 20; President of Troon and District Depot for war work parties; Convener of Troon and District War Pensions Committee; Member of Executive Committees of Carrick House Auxiliary Hospital, and Ayr and Kilmarnock Red Cross Hospital. *Address*: Fullarton, Troon, Ayrshire. *Club*: Kelvin, Glasgow.   (C99)

GLENCROSS, Lieut. Julian, M.B.E.

GLENDINNING, Henry, C.B.E. Director of Brunner, Mond & Co. Ltd. *Address*: Winnington House, Northwich, Cheshire.   (C180)

GLENDINNING, Capt. William Purvis, M.B.E.

GLENNIE, Comm. Hugh Gardiner, O.B.E., R.N.

GLENNIE, Maud, M.B.E.

GLENNIE, Patrick Gordon, M.B.E.

GLENNY, William James, O.B.E., *b.* 14 Nov. 1873; *s.* of T. Armstrong Glenny, of Ryde, I. of W.; *m.* Jessie Reid, *d.* of J. McLeish, of Blairgowrie, Perthshire. *Educ.*: Wilson's Grammar School, Camberwell; B.A. (Lond.). Fellow Royal Statistical Society; Translator to Board of Trade, 1906–14; Senior Staff Clerk, Board of Trade, 1914–18; Director of Division, Dept. of Overseas Trade, 1918. *War Work*: Assistant Sec., Dominions Royal Commission, Work at Board of Trade and Dept. of Overseas Trade (Foreign Office and Board of Trade). *Addresses*: Dept. of Overseas Trade, S.W. 1; 61, Kingsmead Road, S.W. 2. *Club*: Royal Societies'.   (O270)

GLENTON, Arthur Hastings Septimus, O.B.E., *b.* 10 Aug. 1879; *s.* on the late Henry Robert Glenton, of Newcastle-on-Tyne; *m.* Grace Hilda, *d.* of the late William Wright, of Manchester. *Educ.*: Science and Art School, Newcastle-on-Tyne. Chartered Accountant. *War Work*: Divisional Accountant at the Coal Mines Control in charge of Scotland and South Wales and Monmouthshire Divisions for a period of two years, April, 1917, to Mar. 1919. *Address*: Alma Villa, Moorside, Fenham, Newcastle-on-Tyne. *Club*: Northern Conservative and Unionist, Newcastle-on-Tyne.   (O11785*h*)

GLEW, Frederick Harrison, M.B.E., Member Royal Institution, Röntgen, Optical, Pharmaceutical Societies, etc., *b.* 28 April, 1858; *s.* of Richard Harrison Glew, of Wakefield;

m. Anne, *d.* of Henry Lownds, of Clifton-on-Trent. *Educ.*: Wakefield Grammar School. Radiologist and Chemist. *War Work*: Radium expert to the Ministry of Munitions throughout the war period, in charge Radium Stores; Research Work on Luminous Compounds and Gun Sights for night firing, etc. *Address*: 156, Clapham Road, London, S.W. 9.   (M1782)

GLOSSOP, Charles Henry, M.B.E., J.P., *b.* 10 July, 1856; *s.* of Gilderoy Glossop, of Bakewell; *m.* Robina Grigor, *d.* of George Taylor, of Hassop. Bank Manager (ret.). *War Work*: Hon. Treas. Derbyshire Branch, British Red Cross Society. *Address*: Parkwood, Bakewell.   (M8217)

GLOVER, Capt. Edward Norman, O.B.E., R.A.M.C.

GLOVER, Inez Marguerite, M.B.E. For work in connection with Queen Alexandra's Hospital.   (M10319)

GLOVER, James Alison, O.B.E., M.D., D.P.H., *b.* 21 Feb. 1876; *s.* of James Grey Glover, of Highbury; *m.* Katharine, *d.* of Charles P. Merriam, of London. *Educ.*: St. Paul's; St. John's Coll., Cambridge; Guy's Hospital. Medical Officer, Ministry of Health. *War Work*: Sanitary Officer, Malta. M.O. attd. 6th Batt. West Riding Regiment, B.E.F.; worked research, cerebro-spinal fever. *Addresses*: Ministry of Health, S. W. 1; 23, Rosslyn Hill, N.W. 3.   (O7190)

GLOVER, Kathleen, Mrs., O.B.E.

GLOVER, Thomas, C.B.E.

GLUCKSTEIN, Francesca, Mrs., M.B.E.

GLUCKSTEIN, Joseph, O.B.E.

GLUCKSTEIN, Major Montague, O.B.E., R.E., *b.* 13 Oct. 1886; *s.* of Isidore Gluckstein, of 24, Lyndhurst Road, Hampstead; *m.* Hannah, *d.* of Coleman Joseph, of London. *Educ.*: City of London School. Director of Lyons & Co., Ltd. *Address*: 56, Palace Court, Bayswater.   (O7191)

GLYN, Margot Elinor, O.B.E. Member since 1916 and Commandant of the Women's Legion Canteen at Woolwich under the Ministry of Munitions from Nov. 1916-17.

 (O11905)

GLYN, Augusta CARR-, O.B.E.; *d.* of Capt. Carr-Glyn, of Wood Leaze, Wimborne. *Educ.*: Privately. Commandant, V.A.D. Dorset 6. *War Work*: Commandant of Beaucroft Red Cross Hospital, Wimborne, Dorset, for 4 years. *Address*: Wood Leaze, Wimborne. *Club*: Ladies' V.A.D.

 (O10488)

GLYNN, Lieut.-Col. Thomas George Powell, C.M.G., O.B.E., *b.* 13 July, 1863; *s.* of the late Lieut.-Col. T. G. H. Glynn; *m.* Beatrice Emily, *d.* of the late Ernest Peplow Ford. *Educ.*: Privately. Adj. King's Regiment, 1887–91; Adj. London Rifle Brigade, 1892–97; Staff during S. African War; Commanded 1st King's Regt., 1907–12. *War Work*: Commanded Infantry Base Depôt, 1914–18; O.C. Reinforcements, 1918. *Address*: 23, Chester Square, S.W. 1. *Club*: Naval and Military.   (O1375)

GOAD, Capt. David, O.B.E., R.A.F.

GOAD, Edwin Henry, M.B.E., *b.* Oct. 1865; *s.* of Edwin Curtis Goad, of Hackbridge; *m.* Gertrude Sophia, *d.* of Sir George Lampson, Bart., of Albert Gate. *Educ.*: Eton. Merchant. *War Work*: Chief of No 1 Section, Borough of Reigate Special Police, for the first 3 years of the war, after which appointed Chief of the whole force. *Address*: Holly Court Merton Lane, Highgate, W. *Club*: City of London.

 (M8218)

GOAD, Frederick Lockhart, M.B.E.

GOAD, Capt. Harold Elsdale, O.B.E., Cavalier of the Order of the Crown of Italy.   (O3041)

GOADBY, Sir Kenneth Weldon, K.B.E., Medical Referee for Industrial Poisoning, County of London, since 1913; Lecturer on Bacteriology, National Dental Hospital, since 1904; late Lecturer on Oral Hygiene, London School of Tropical Medicine, *b.* 7 March, 1873; *s.* of Rev. J.J. Goadby, *m.* Constance Eva, *d.* of G. Olding. *Educ.*: Grammar School, Henley-on-Thames; University Extension College, Reading; Guy's Hospital. Studied Bacteriology and Bacteriological Research, Guy's Hospital, 1899–1902; investigated Operation of Phosphorus Rules for Match Factories for H.M.'s Home Office; investigated Causes and Pathology of Lead Poisoning (Departmental Committee Home Office; since engaged in Bacteriological and Pathological Research, Investigation of Lead Poisoning in Industrial Processes, and Pathology and Bacteriology of Disease of the Mouth and Upper Air Passages, and Rheumatoid Arthritis; Erasmus Wilson Lecturer R.C. Surgeons, 1907, and Hunterian Professor in 1911; Hon. Bacteriological Specialist for Vaccine Therapy, Royal Herbert Hospital, Woolwich (during War); Member of War Office Committee for the Study of Tetanus. *Address*: 83, Harley Street, W. *Club*: Royal Automobile.

 (K71)

GOALEN, James Thomas, O.B.E., J.P., *b.* 31 Jan. 1878; *s.* of James Goalen, of Leith; *m.* Jane Groundwater, *d.* of Peter Duncan, of Belmont, Eskbank. *Educ.*: Daniel Stewart's College. Member of the Leith Town Council; Magistrate of Leith; Convener of the Leith Corporation Tramways; Vice-Chairman Leith National Health Insurance Committee; Member Edinburgh and Leith Gas Commissioners. *War Work*: Chairman, Leith War Savings Committee; Member of Prince of Wales' National Relief Fund; Chairman, Food Economy Committee of Leith. *Addresses*: 141, Constitution Street, Leith; Allerly, Russell Place, Trinity.   (O371)

GOATE, Lieut. Ernest Edward, M.B.E., R.E.

GOBBITT, Paymaster Sub-Lieut. Reginald Harry Sutton, M.B.E., R.N.R.

GOBEY, Francis Edward, O.B.E.

GOBLE, Annie Harriet, Mrs., M.B.E.

GOBLE, Stanley James, O.B.E. (O3316)

GOBLE, R.S.M. William Richard, M.B.E., *b.* 3 June, 1876 ; *s.* of Charles George Goble, of Brighton ; *m.* Annie May, *d.* of Ernest McCulloch, of Dublin. *Educ.:* Brighton, York Place Secondary School. *War Work:* Taken Prisoner of War at Le Cateau in Aug. 1914, sent to Sennelager bei Paderborn, Germany, and there organised, under the German authorities, a Prisoner of War Camp of over 4000 British troops ; maintained and administered discipline under extremely adverse circumstances. *Address:* 49, Hartington Road, Brighton.
(M43669)

GODDARD, Alexander, C.B.E., *b.* 17 Oct. 1867 ; *s.* of Joseph Goddard, J.P., of The Manor House, Newton Harcourt, Leicester ; *m.* Ellen Henrietta, *d.* of Edward Stonhewer Illingworth, J.P., of Borough Court, Hants. *Educ.:* Haileybury College, and Royal Agricultural College, Cirencester. Secty. to Rt. Hon. Robert Hanbury, M.P., President Board of Agriculture, 1901–2, and to Rt. Hon. Earl of Onslow, President Board of Agriculture 1902–5 ; Secty. The Surveyors' Institution, 1905 to present. Appointed Member of Agricultural Committee for England 1920. *War Work:* Hon. Secy., Agricultural Consultative Committee ; Hon. Sec., Agricultural Reconstruction Committee ; Hon. Sec., Professional Classes' War Relief Council ; Secty. Royal Commission on Agriculture ; Hon. Sec. National Agricultural Council ; Hon. Sec., Village Clubs Association. *Address:* 2, Cleveland Square, W. 2. *Club:* National. (C503)

GODDARD, Major Charles Ernest, O.B.E., M.D., T.D., A.K.C., M.R.C.S., L.R.C.P., R.A.M.C. (T.), *b.* 31 Oct. 1859 ; *s.* of the late Lieut.-Col. T. Goddard ; *m.* Eleanor Lucy, *d.* of Samuel Skelton, of Wembley Orchard. *Educ.:* Privately ; King's College, London ; King's College Hospital. Medical Officer of Health, Wembley ; County Councillor, Middlesex C.C. ; Hon. Assoc. Order St. John ; Lecturer, Examiner and Life Member, St. John Amb. Assoc. ; Hon. Surg. St. John Amb. Brigade ; Divisional Surgeon Metropolitan Police ; Fellow Society Medical Officers' of Health ; Fellow Royal Institute Public Health ; Fellow (*honoris causa*) Royal Sanitary Institute ; Assoc. King's College, London, 1883 ; Todd Medal and Prize, 1880 ; Tanner prize, 1881 ; Certificate of Honour, Surgery (Lister), 1880 ; late R.M.O., N. London Hospital for Consumption, Hampstead, 1884. *War Work:* Commanding Officer 2nd London Sanitary Company, R.A.M.C. (T.F) ; attached 1st Cavalry Division, Ypres, 1914–15 ; mentioned in Despatches, 1915 ; President and Senior Chairman, Chelsea, Holborn and City of London Medical Boards, 1916–18 ; Deputy Commissioner of Medical Services, Ministry of National Service, 1917–19 ; served Pension Ministry, 1918–19 ; holds decorations, O.B.E., Hon. Assoc. of St. John of Jerusalem, Territorial Long Service Decoration. Medals, Queen Victoria Diamond Jubilee, Edward VII. Coronation, 1914–15 Star, General Service and Allies. *Address:* Harrowdene House, Wembley, Middlesex. *Club:* St. Stephen's. (O1377)

GODDARD, Lieut. Eric Norman, O.B.E., M.C., I.A.

GODDARD, 2nd Lieut. Ernest, M.B.E.

GODDARD, Ernest Hope, C.B.E., *b.* March 3, 1879 ; *s.* of the late Arthur Goddard of Herne Hill. *Educ.:* Privately and City of London School. Assistant Editor of the " Illustrated London News " since 1909 and of the " Sketch" since 1905 ; Acting Editor of both papers 1916–18. *War Work:* Did much work for the Ministry of Information ; afterwards for the News Department, Foreign Office ; was an officer in H.Q.C.D., Metropolitan Special Constabulary (Medal ; Mention). Now in M.S.C. Reserve. *Address:* 23, Holmdene Avenue, Herne Hill, S.E. 24. *Clubs:* Arts ; Savage. (C970)

GODDARD, Lieut.-Col. Francis Ambrose D'Oyly, O.B.E., Roy. Mun. Fus., R.O. *Address:* 45, Warwick Road, S.W. (O2527)

GODDARD, Lieut. Norris, O.B.E., R.N.V.R.

GODDARD, Major Richard Ernest, O.B.E., R.A.F.

GODDARD, Capt. Thomas Neilson, M.B.E.

GODDEN, Guy Langham, O.B.E., R.A.F.

GODDEN, Eng.-Lieut.-Comm. James William Mineard, O.B.E.

GODDING, Col. (Temp. Lieut.-Col.) James, O.B.E., T.D., M.R.C.S., L.R.C.P., R.A.M.C. (T.), *b.* 1862. Barrister-at-Law ; Medical Officer, Port of London Authority. *War Work:* O.C. 1/17 Batt. London Regt., Aug. 1914 to Oct. 1915 ; O.C. 53rd Div. Inf. Base Depot, Egypt, Dec. 1915 to July, 1917 ; O.C. 17th General Hospital, Egypt, July, 1917 to May, 1920. *Address:* Southdene, The Avenue, Wanstead, Essex, E.11.
(O2896)

GODDING, James William Sleigh, M.B.E., J.P.

GODFERY, Capt. Masters van Someren, O.B.E., R.G.A., *b.* 7 Dec. 1887 ; *s.* of Col. M. J. Godfery, A.S.C. (late) ; *m.* Marjorie Coplestone, *d.* of F. Coplestone, C.B.E., J.P., of Chester (*q.v.*). *Educ.:* United Services Coll., Westward Ho ! and Royal Military Academy, Woolwich. *Address:* c/o Messrs. Cox & Co. (R.A. Dept.), 16, Charing Cross, S.W. (O8815)

GODFRAY Lieut.-Col. John Charles Lerrier, O.B.E., M.C.

GODFRAY, Capt. Mowatt, M.B.E.

GODFREY, Albert Hamilton, M.B.E., J.P., (Surrey) *b.* 6 Oct. 1864 ; *s.* of Albert Henry Godfrey, J.P. (Gloucester), Lt.-Col., late 73rd Regt., Indian Mutiny, of Linden House, College Lawn, Cheltenham ; *m.* Florena Margaret Bowring. *d.* of the late Major-Gen. Edward Melville Lawford. *Educ.:* Leamington and Angers (France). *War Work:* Chairman of the following : Woking Urban District Council, 1914–20. Local Tribunal (Military Service Acts) ; Soldiers' and Sailors' Families Association ; Naval and Military War Pensions Committee ; Chertsey Division Parliamentary Recruiting Committee ; Surrey Road Transport Committee ; Lighting and Fuel Control ; Member Food Control Committee ; Special Constable. *Addresses:* The Dell, Woking, Surrey ; Brooke House, Ash-in-Canterbury. *Club:* Union. (M444)

GODFREY, Lieut. Alfred Philip, M.B.E.

GODFREY, Nora, Mrs., M.B.E.

GODFREY, Capt. Stanley Charles, M.B.E., M.C.

GODINHO, Capt. Paul Xavier, M.B.E., I.M.S.

GODLEY, Lieut.-Col. Alfred Davis, O.B.E.

GODLEY, Major Francis William Crewe, O.B.E., R.A.S.C., *b.* 25 Jan. 1893 ; *s.* of Major H. C. Godley, D.S.O., of 48th Regt. ; *m.* Kathleen May, *d.* of Edward Jenner-Davis, J.P., of Stonehouse, Gloucestershire. *Educ.:* Cheltenham ; R.M.C., Sandhurst. *War Work:* Service in R.A.S.C. 1914–18. *Address:* Christchurch Lodge, Cheltenham. *Club:* R.A.S.C. (O5299)

GODLEY, Lieut.-Col. Godfrey Archibald, C.B.E. S. African Forces ; rendered services in connection with raising of Native Labour Corps in S. Africa during Great War.
(C2002))

GODLEY, Lieut.-Col. Richard Shearman, *b.* 24 Sept. 1876 ; *s.* of Lieut.-Col. William Alexander Godley, of 56th Essex Regt. ; *m.* Muriel Margaret Dorothea, *d.* of Lieut.-Col. A. W. Matterson, of Rosedale, Pietermaritzburg, Natal. *Educ.:* United Services Coll., Westward Ho ! Devon. Deputy-Commissioner, South African Police ; Justice of the Peace, Natal. *War Work:* Served through Matabele Rebellion, 1896 ; Mashonaland Rebellion, 1897 ; S. African War, 1900–2 ; General Service within the Union of S. Africa, 1914–18. *Address:* South African Police Headquarters, Pietermaritzburg, Natal. *Club:* Isthmian, 105, Piccadilly, W. 1. (O8355)

GODMAN, Dame Alice Mary, D.B.E., *b.* 1868 ; *d.* of the late Major Percy Chaplin, J.P., 60th Rifles, Royal Gloucestershire Hussars ; *m.* Frederick Du Cane, D.C.L., F.R.S., who died. County Commissioner of Sussex Girl Guides ; President, Horsham and Worthing Unionist and Coal. Assoc. ; Member of Central Advisory Committee. *War Work:* Vice-President British Red Cross Society, Horsham Division ; Member of British Red Cross Hospital (Netley) Sub-Committee ; Organising Red Cross work and War Savings. *Addresses:* South Lodge, Horsham ; 45, Pont Street, S.W.1. (D11)

GODMAN, Lieut.-Col. Edward Shirley, O.B.E.

GODSELL, Cornelius, M.B.E,

GODSELL, Capt. James Stanley Peel, M.B.E.

GODWIN, Capt. George, O.B.E., *b.* 18 Aug. 1874 ; *s.* of Walter Godwin, of Upham, Hants ; *m.* Lois, *d.* of John Edwards, of Reigate. *Educ.:* St. Peter's School, Bournemouth. Unionist Agent, Guildford Division of Surrey. *War Work:* Sergt. "H " Coy., C.I.V., South Africa, 1899–1900 (Queen's Medal with 4 clasps) ; 9th and 14th Batts. The Queen's, Royal West Surrey Regt., 1915–17 ; Salonica Force, 1916–19 ; Labour Corps (O.C. 95th Coy.), 1917–19 ; twice mentioned in despatches of C.-in-C., British Salonica Force. *Addresses:* Guildford, Surrey ; Puttenham, Guildford, Surrey. (O6472)

GODWIN, George Batley, M.B.E., S.A.I.E., *b.* 24 Sept. 1879 ; *s.* of the late Harold Frederick Godwin, of London ; *m.* Evelyn Alexandra, *d.* of the late William Owen, of the South African Railways and Cape Volunteer Medical Staff Corps. *Educ.:* King's Coll. School, London, and Clifton Coll. Late Assistant General Manager of the Koffyfontein Mines, Ltd., Koffyfontein, Orange Free State ; now Chief Engineer of the New Jagersfontein Mining and Exploration Co., Jagersfontein, Orange Free State. *War Work:* Union Defence Force during Free State Rebellion ; 5th Mounted Brigade throughout G.S.W. African Campaign ; Chief Draughtsman in the London headquarters of the Dept. of Explosives Supply, 1915–16 ; Manager of the Cordite Factory, H.M. Factory, Gretna, 1916 to Oct. 1919 ; sailed for England immediately G.S.W.A. campaign was culminated, and within a few days was granted commission in Field Artillery, but before being gazetted was enrolled in the Dept. Explosive Supply, for Ministry of Munitions service. *Addresses:* P.O. Box 134, Jagersfontein, Orange Free State, South Africa. (M3221)

GODWIN, Herbert James, O.B.E., M.B., B.S., F.R.C.S. M.R.C.S., L.R.C.P., *b.* 1873 ; *s.* of the late Dr. Godwin, of Twyford, Winchester ; *m.* Florence Marion, *d.* of the late Capt. G. Appleby, (Scottish Rifles) of Durham. *Educ.:* St. Bartholomew's Hospital, London. Senior Hon. Surgeon, Royal Hampshire County Hospital, Winchester ; Consulting Surgeon to Basingstoke, Andover, Fleet, and Odiham Cottage Hospitals ; served through the South African War as Civil Surgeon, 2 Medals, 5 Clasps. *War Work:* Surgical Specialist to Military Hospital, Hursley Park, nr. Winchester ; Surgeon to Lady Cooper's Hospital for Officers, Hursley Park ; Surgeon to Lady Portal's Red Cross Hospital, Laverstoke, Whitchurch,

Hants ; Surgeon to Red Cross Section, Royal Hampshire County Hospital ; Surgeon to Basingstoke Red Cross Hospital ; Surgeon to Mrs. Johnson's Red Cross Hospital, Stockbridge, Hants. *Address :* The Friary, Winchester, Hants. *Club :* Hampshire County. (O4367)

GOFF, Emily Gertrude, Mrs., M.B.E,

GOFF, Capt. Hugh Stuart Trevor, O.B.E., *b.* 21 Aug. 1885 ; *s.* of the late Lt.-Col. Trevor Goff, of Everton Grange, Lymington, Hants. *Educ. :* Private School. *War Work :* Enlisted R.A.S.C. Aug. 21st 1914 ; landed France, Sept. 4th, 1914 ; served continuously overseas till end of War ; thrice mentioned in despatches. *Address :* 22, Nevern Square, Earls Court, S.W.5. (O5300)

GOFFIN, Col. (Hon.) Sydney Frederick Herbert, O.B.E., B.A., LL.B., (Cambridge), *b.* 16 Sept. 1878 ; *s.* of Robert Hemlington Goffin, of Wakes Colne, Essex, and Westminster : *m.* Alice Elizabeth, *d.* of the late John Henry Fricker, of Liverpool. *Educ. :* Westminster City School ; Jesus College, Cambridge. 1st Division Civil Servant, War Office. *War Work :* Assistant Auditor Western Command 1914–17 ; Assistant Financial Adviser B.E.F. France, and Financial Adviser, Rhine Army. *Address :* War Office, S.W.1. *Club :* United University, Pall Mall, S.W. (O2528)

GOGGIN, Capt. John, M.B.E., R.A.P.D., *b.* 24 April, 1872 ; *s.* of James Goggin, B.A., of Ballinasloe, Ireland ; *m.* Margaret. *d.* of Joseph Phillips, of Middlewich. *Educ. :* Breakey's Academy, Ballinasloe, and Privately. *Address :* 49, Effingham Road, Lee, S.E., 12. (M5291)

GOING, Fanny Augusta, Mrs., M.B.E.

GOLD, Lieut.-Col. Ernest, D.S.O., O.B.E., R.E., *b.* 1881 ; *s.* of John Gold, of Lapworth, Warwickshire ; *m.* 1907, Catherine, *d.* of the late John Harlow, of Edinburgh. Great War, 1914–18, Major and acting Lieut.-Col. (Meteorological Section) (despatches) ; appointed Assist. Director of Forecasting, Meteorological Office, 1919. (O2520)

GOLD, Gerald Gilbey, O.B.E.

GOLD, Lieut.-Col. Harcourt Gilbey, O.B.E., R.A.F.

GOLD, Maud Mary, Mrs. Guy, M.B.E., *b.* 1879 ; *d.* of the late Rt. Hon. Sir John Brunner, Bart., of Silverlands, Chertsey (*see* BURKE's *Peerage*) ; *m.* Major Guy G. Gold, *s.* of Sir Charles Gold, of Stansted, Essex (*see* BURKE's *Peerage*). Vice-President, Essex Branch B.R.C.S. *War Work :* Commandant, V.A.D. Hospital, Braintree. *Address :* Abbots Hall, Shalford, Braintree. (M1785)

GOLDFINCH, Sir Arthur Horne, K.B.E. Director of Raw Materials, War Office ; *b.* 10 May, 1866. *Educ. :* Privately. Entered the service of Duncan, Fox & Co., General Merchants, Valparaiso, 1881 ; became a partner of that firm (Liverpool, London, Chile and Peru), 1903 ; retired from business 1913 ; Liberal Candidate for Colchester, 1914–1918. *Address :* 8, Rosecroft Avenue, Hampstead, N.W. 3. *Clubs :* Devonshire ; National Liberal ; Royal Automobile. (K72)

GOLDIE, Major Kenneth Oswald, O.B.E.

GOLDIE, Valentine Francis Taubman, O.B.E.

GOLDIE, Surg.-Lieut. Walton Leigh Mackinnon, C.B.E., F.R.C.S., R.N.

GOLDING, Lieut. George Francis, M.B.E., R.A.F.

GOLDING, Capt. Thomas, C.B.E.

GOLDINGHAM, Isobel Frances, M.B.E., *d.* of John Dalrymple Goldingham, Indian Civil Service (late). *Educ. :* Privately. *War Work :* Assisted in forming the Women Police Service which trained, equipped, and controlled over one thousand Policewomen serving under the Ministry of Munitions in Explosives and National Filling Factories. *Address :* 2, Lyndale, Child's Hill. *Club :* Forum. (M1786)

GOLDINGHAM, Major Robert Elphinstone Dalrymple, O.B.E., R.E., *b.* 2 Sept. 1874 ; *s.* of the late John Dalrymple Goldingham, late I.C.S. of Norfolk. *Educ. :* Cheltenham College and R.M.A. Woolwich. *War Work :* Served in France with B.E.F. May, 1916 to April, 1919. *Club :* United Service. (O5301)

GOLDMAN, Major Charles Sidney, M.B.E., R.G.A. (T.).

GOLDMAN, 2nd Lieut. Julius Israel, M.B.E., R.A.S.C.

GOLDNEY, Alice Frances Holbrow, Lady, O.B.E., *d.* of Major F. C. N. Goldney, of the Indian Army ; *m.* the late Hon. Sir John Tankerville, Kt., 3rd *s.* of Sir Gabriel Goldney, Bart., of Corsham (*see* BURKE's *Peerage*). *Educ. :* Beresford House, Ealing. *War Work :* Commandant of Corsham V.A.D. Hospital, from June, 1915, to August, 1919. *Addresses :* Monks Park, Corsham, Wilts. ; Hanover Court, Hanover Square, W. (O10491)

GOLDNEY, Major Henry Wetherall, O.B.E., M.C., R.G.A., *b.* 12 July, 1885 ; *s.* of Col. W. H. Goldney ; *m.* Barbara, *d.* of Col. W. St. John Richardson. *Educ. :* Portsmouth Grammar School. *War Work :* Served in France and Belgium with heavy battery from Aug. 1914 to May 1915, and from July 1915 to May 1918 ; Staff Appointment (Brigade Major) in France and Belgium from May 1918 to after Armistice ; wounded twice, mentioned in despatches 4 times. *Address :* c/o Messrs. Cox & Co., Charing Cross, S.W. 1. (O5302)

GOLDSMID, Cyril Julian, O.B.E., *b.* 14 Oct. 1890 ; *s.* of Sidney H. Goldsmid, of 35, Chesham Place, London ; *m.* Anna Emily, *d.* of Major MacGillycuddy, of Flesk Castle, Killarney. *Educ. :* Eton and Univ. Coll., Oxford. Barrister-at-Law ; Lieut. 9th (Q.R.) Lancers (Special Reserve). *War Work :* France, 1914–17 ; Italy, 1917–18. *Address :* 16, Hill Street, Knightsbridge, S.W. 7. *Clubs :* Carlton ; Cavendish. (O6374)

GOLDSMID, Lionel Frederic, O.B.E., *b.* 22 Aug. 1880 ; *s.* of Frederic Lestock Goldsmid, of Indian Police, Bombay

Presidency ; *m.* Alison Margarette, *d.* of W. H. Dodd, of Melbourne, Australia. *Educ. :* Cheam School ; Bradfield College, Berks ; Magdalen College, Oxford. Civil Servant ; Higher Division Clerk, Admiralty 1904 ; Superintending Clerk, Admiralty, 1908 ; Assistant Accountant-General, Ministry of Shipping, 1917. *War Work :* Transport Department Admiralty ; Ministry of Shipping. *Addresses :* Transport Department, Admiralty ; 138, Trinity Road, Wandsworth Common, S.W.17. (O373)

GOLDSMITH, Edward, O.B.E., *b.* 24 Nov. 1868 ; *s.* of Adolphus Goldsmith, of London ; *m.* Georgina, *d.* of Arthur Kennedy, of Cultra, Ireland. *Educ. :* St. Leonards. *War Work :* Commander, C. Division, Metropolitan Special Constabulary. *Addresses :* 10 Connaught Square ; Cavenham Park, Suffolk. *Club :* Marlborough. (O3729)

GOLDSMITH, Major Frank, O.B.E.

GOLDSMITH, Lieut. Frank, M.B.E., M.M., R.G.A.

GOLDSMITH, Lieut.-Col. George Mills, C.B.E., R.A.M.C.

GOLDSMITH, Wing-Comm. Norman, O.B.E., R.A.F.

GOLDSMITH, Col. Perry Gladstone, C.B.E., Can. A.M.C.

GOLDSWORTHY, Frederick James, M.B.E.

GOLDSWORTHY, Lieut. John Arthur, O.B.E., R.N.R.

GOLIGHER, Brig.-Gen. Hugh Garvin, C.B.E.

GOLIGHTLY, Col. Robert Edmund, C.B.E., D.S.O., *b.* 1856 ; *s.* of Rev. Canon Golightly, of Shipton Moyne ; *m.* Agnes Francis, *d.* of T. McDowell Aikin. *Educ. :* Eton and Sandhurst. Secretary Council of County Territorial Associations. *War Work :* Section Commander, 1914–15 ; Defence Commander No. 1 Lines of Communication, 1916–17 ; Assist. Director Territorial and Volunteer Forces, 1918–20. *Address :* The Pines, Amberley, Stroud, Gloucester. (C504)

GOLLA, Capt. Frederick Lucien, O.B.E., M.B., R.A.M.C. (T.).

GOLLAN, Sir Henry Cowper, Knt. Bach., C.B.E., M.A., K.C. ; *b.* Coquinibo, Chile, 8 Jan., 1868 ; *s.* of the late Sir Alexander Gollan, K.C.M.G. ; *m.* 1908, *s.* of James Nelson Morris, of St. Louis, U.S.A. *Educ. :* Charterhouse, Edinburgh Univ. Called to the Bar 1891. Northern Circuit ; became Private Secretary to Sir Frederick Lugard, G.C.M.G., 1899 ; went to Northern Nigeria with him and became first Attorney-General, Chief Justice of Northern Nigeria, 1901 ; transferred to Bermuda as Chief Justice and President of the Legislative Council, 1904 ; Attorney-General of Trinidad, 1911–18 ; Attorney-General of Ceylon since 1919. *Address :* Colombo, Ceylon. *Club :* Empire. (C393)

GOLLANCE, Ernest Marcus, M.B.E., *b.* 21 Aug. 1885 ; *s.* of the Rev. Prof. H. Gollancz, M.A., D.Lit., of London ; *m.* Dorothy, *d.* of Walter B. Styer, LL.B., Solicitor, of London. *Educ. :* Univ. Coll. School, London, and Privately. Solicitor. *War Work :* Head of Division and Chairman of Committees, War Trade Department. *Address :* 1, St. Cuthbert's Road, Shoot-up Hill, London, N.W. *Club :* Royal Automobile. (M8224)

GOLLIN, Alfred, C.B.E.

GOLLIN, George, O.B.E.

GOLLIN, Walter Josephson, M.B.E.

GOMERSALL, Edward, O.B.E.

GOMES, Bernard Francis, M.B.E.

GONET, Adolphe Joseph Louis, M.B.E.

GONNER, Edward Carter Kersey, C.B.E., Litt.D., *b.* 5 Mar. 1862 ; *s.* of Peter Kersey Gonner, of South Hampstead ; *m.* Nannie Ledlie, *d.* of James Crawford Ledlie, of Cork. *Educ. :* Merchant Taylors' School ; Lincoln College, Oxford. Professor of Economic Science, University of Liverpool ; Economic Adviser, Ministry of Food. *War Work :* Chairman of War Savings Committee, County of Chester (1917) ; Director of Statistics, Ministry of Food (1917–19) ; one of the Chairmen in the Committee on Production and Interim Court of Arbitration (1918–19). *Address :* The Gables, Willaston, nr. Birkenhead. *Club :* University, Liverpool. (C505)

GONSALVES, Major George, O.B.E., R.A.S.C., M.Inst. C.E., *b.* 11 Mar. 1872 ; *s.* of John Gonsalves, of Trinidad, British West Indies. *Educ. :* University College School and University College, London. Consulting Civil Engineer. *War Work :* Commissioned a Lieut. in the R.A.S.C. 1914 ; attached to B.E.F., France from Oct. 1914 till demobilised in May, 1919 ; for the last two years of the war commanded No. 3 Advanced Supply Depot, France ; mentioned in despatches, 1 Jan. 1919 and decorated O.B.E.(Mil.), 2 Jan. 1919. *Address :* Harewood House, Freelands Road, Bromley, Kent. *Clubs :* Junior Army and Navy ; Sundridge Park Golf. (O2530)

GOOCH, Eva Conway Everard, Mrs., M.B.E., *b.* 25 Dec. 1880 ; *d.* of Richard Everard Jones, of Fassfern, Invernesshire ; *m.* Edward Sinclair, *s.* of the late John Verot Gooch, of Cooper's Hill, Bracknell. *War Work :* Organised Lochiel Auxiliary Red Cross Hospital, Banavie ; Commandant, Detachment, Inverness 42 ; Sec. Berkshire Yeomanry Prisoners of War Association. *Address :* Torcastle, Banavie, Inverness-shire. *Club :* Forum. (M8226)

GOOCH, Henry Martyn, M.B.E., *b.* 1874 ; *s.* of the Rev. W. Fuller Gooch, of West Norwood, S.E. *Educ. :* Central Hill Coll., Upper Norwood, and Stanley House School, Cliftonville. General Sec. The World's Evangelical Alliance (British Organisation), Incorporated. *War Work :* Organiser of the Queen's Hall, W., and the Mansion House United War Prayer Meetings ; services as public lecturer and writer in the interests of war aims and issues. *Addresses :* Lansdowne, 67, Chestnut Road, Norwood, S.E. 27 ; 19, Russell Square, W.C. 1. (M8229)

GOOCH, Lieut. Herbert, M.B.E. (M448)

GOOCH, Ivy, M.B.E.

GOOD, Lieut.-Com. Henry John Graham, O.B.E., R.N. (retired).

GOOD, John, O.B.E.

GOOD, Minnie Agnes, Mrs., O.B.E.

GOOD, Thomas, O.B.E.

GOOD, Lieut.-Col. Thomas Saxty, O.B.E., R.A.M.C.

GOODALL, Amy Sophia, M.B.E.

GOODALL, Clarence Noel, O.B.E.

GOODALL, Edward Basil Herbert, M.B.E.

GOODALL, Lieut.-Col. Edward Wilberforce, O.B.E., M.D., R.A.M.C. (T.).

GOODALL, Lieut.-Col. Edwin, C.B.E., M.D., F.R.C.P., R.A.M.C.

GOODALL, Lieut. Francis Harrison, M.B.E., R.E.

GOODALL, Capt. James Roberts, O.B.E., Can. A.M.C.

GOODALL, Stanley Vernon, M.B.E.

GOODBODY, Lydia Maria, Mrs., M.B.E., b. 15 Nov. 1857; d. of the late Thomas White Fisher, of Dublin; m. Marcus, s. of the late Marcus Goodbody, of Obelisk Park, Blackrock. Educ.: Privately. War Work: Member of the Executive Committee, Royal Dublin Fusilier Bureau; Chairman of the Dependants Aid Committee, Royal Dublin Fusiliers; Organiser and Manageress of the Irish War Hospital Supply Sub-Depot, Blackrock, Co. Dublin; Hon. Commandant of Blackrock (No. 50) Detachment B.R.C.S. Address: Talbot Lodge, Blackrock, Co. Dublin. (M8228)

GOODCHILD, Alwyn Valerie, Mrs., M.B.E., V.D.

GOODCHILD, Major Thomas Phillip, O.B.E.

GOODDEN, Caroline, Mrs., M.B.E., b. 20 Sept. 1848; d. of the Rt. Hon. Sir Bernhard Samuelson, Bart., P.C., F.R.S. (see BURKE'S Peerage); m. John Robert Phelips, s. of John Goodden of Compton House, Sherborne, and Ann his wife d. of Rev. Robert Phelips, Vicar of Yeovil (see BURKE'S Landed Gentry, Phelips of Montacute). War Work: Local President, Soldiers' and Sailors' Families Association; Commandant of Auxiliary Hospital for 20 N.C.O.'s and private soldiers in own house for 4 years. Address: Compton House, Sherborne, Dorset. Club: Ladies' Imperial. (M8230)

GOODDEN, Major Robert Blunde, O.B.E.

GOODE, Henry Abel, C.B.E.

GOODE, Richard Allmond Jeffrey, C.B.E., b. 1873; s. of the late Rev. Thomas Allmond Goode, a Missionary with the Soc. for Propagation of the Gospel, Newfoundland; m. 1904, Agnes, d. of Thomas Codrington, M.I.C.E., of Twickenham Park, S.W. Educ.: Fettes Coll., Edinburgh. Appointed Magistrate and Govt. Sec., N.-E. Rhodesia, 1900; Judge of Administrator's Court and Govt. Sec., N.-W. Rhodesia, 1908; Govt. Sec., N. Rhodesia, 1911. Address: Livingstone, N. Rhodesia. Clubs: United Services (Rhodesia); West Indian. (C394)

GOODE, Capt. Thomas Charles, M.B.E., b. 26 Jan. 1881; s. of Valantine Charles Goode, of Leicester; m. Mary Agnes Grace, d. of Edward Dobinson, of Sheffield. Educ.: St. Mary's School, Richmond, Yorks. Commission Agent. War Work: Served on N.-W. Frontier, India, with 19th Yorkshire Regt.; Commissioned into 13th P.A. Somerset Light Infantry; served as Adjutant to No. 3 C.B.I. Depot, India; Adjutant to No. 1, Reserve Battalion (India); Adjutant and latterly as Commandant to Furlough Recreation Camp, Wellington, India. Addresses: Brampton Villa, 114, Burton Road, Withington, Manchester; 27, Dickenson Street, Manchester. (M6509)

GOODE, Sir William Athelstane Meredith, K.B.E., b. 10 June, 1875; s. of Rev. T. A. Goode; m. Cecilia, d. of Dr. C. A. Sippi, London, Ontario. Educ.: Foyle College, Ireland. President of the Austrian section of the Reparation Commission, British Director of Relief Missions and Member of the Supreme Economic Council, Paris, 1919; Liaison Officer of the Ministry of Food with the United States and Canadian Food Administration since 1917; Director of the Cable Department, Ministry of Food; Hon. Sec. and Organiser of the National Committee for Relief in Belgium; Member of the Newfoundland and West Indian Military Contingent Committees. Served as Purser in British Merchant Marine; in 4th United States Cavalry, 1894; Assistant Night City Editor "New York Recorder," 1895; City Editor, "New York Mercury"; with the Associated Press of America, 1896–1904, representing them on Admiral Sampson's flagship throughout the Spanish American War, and in England for six years as Special Correspondent; News and Managing Editor, "Standard," 1904–10; Joint News Editor, "Daily Mail," 1911; Commander of the Order of the Crown of Belgium; Commander of the Order of Queen Isabella the Catholic; Hon. British Committee, Panama-Pacific Exposition, 1914. Addresses: Vienna; 49, Westbourne Gardens, W. 2. Clubs: West Indian; Pilgrims; Savage; Press: Royal Ulster Yacht (Belfast); British Schools and Universities (New York). (K73)

GOODENOUGH, Henrietta Margaret, Hon. Lady, O.B.E., b. 22 Feb. 1874; e. d. of 4th Lord Sheffield, of Alderley Park, Chelford (see BURKE'S Peerage); m. Sir William Edmund, K.C.B., M.V.O., s. of the late James Goodenough, Commodore. Educ.: At home. War Work: War Pensions Committee, Portsmouth. Addresses: Parsons Pightle, Coulsdon, Surrey; Admiralty House, Simonstown, S.A. (O3733)

GOODERHAM, 2nd Lieut. George Frederick Robert M.B.E., R.F.A.

GOODERIDGE, Capt. Robert Aubrey, O.B.E., R.A.V.C.

GOODEVE, Capt. Thomas Edward, O.B.E., R.E.

GOODFELLOW, Thomas Ashton, C.B.E., b. 16 Sept. 1865; s. of the late Thomas Goodfellow, of Hyde, Cheshire; m. Eleanor Winifred, d. of W. J. Robertson, of Manchester. Educ.: The Owens College, Manchester. Doctor of Medicine; Member of Consultative Council on Medical and Allied Services to the Ministry of Health. War Work: Medical Officer in charge Lawnhurst Red Cross Hospital, Didsbury and the Didsbury Lodge Auxiliary Military Hospital; Chairman Manchester Medical War Committee; Assistant County Director, British Red Cross Society, East Lancs. Branch; Deputy Chairman of Committee, "John Leigh" Memorial Hospital, Woodbourne, Brooklands, Cheshire. Address: 60, Palatine Road, West Didsbury, Manchester. Club: Brasenose, Manchester. (C2635)

GOODHART, Lieut.-Comm. Leander McCORMICK-, O.B.E., R.N.V.R.

GOODIER, Lieut.-Comm. Robert Simes HULME-, O.B.E., R.N.R.

GOODISON, Mary, Mrs., M.B.E.

GOODLAND, Joshua, M.B.E., b. 17 July, 1873; s. of Gillmore Goodland, of Exmouth, S. Devon; m. Florence Annie, d. of Dr. William Holdsworth, of Thames Ditton. Educ.: Coombe Down, Bath and Trinity Hall, Cambridge. Barrister-at-Law. War Work: Legal Adviser to the Priority Department of the Ministry of Munitions. Addresses: 144, Ashley Gardens, S.W. 1.; 1 Paper Buildings, Inner Temple. Club: Bath. (M451)

GOODMAN, Coleman, O.B.E.

GOODMAN, Cyril, C.B.E., M.A., M.R.C.S., L.R.C.P., M.B., B.C., b. 1870; s. of Henry Goodman, J.P., of St. Ives, Hunts.; m. 1902, Sue, d. of the Hon. Cassius M. Clay, of Auvergne, Paris, and Kentucky, U.S.A. Educ.: St. John's Coll., Camb. Assist. Director-Gen., Depart. of Public Health, Egypt. Address: Gezira, Cairo, Egypt. Club: New University. (C703)

GOODRICH, Walter Francis, M.B.E.

GOODSIR, Gertrude Esperance, Mrs., O.B.E.

GOODWIN, Capt. and Qr.-Mr. Arthur, M.B.E., R.A.S.C.

GOODWIN, Aubrey, O.B.E., M.D., B.S. (Lond.), F.R.C.S. (Edin.), M.R.C.S., L.R.C.P. (Lond.), b. 4 Sept. 1889; s. of the late Professor Alfred Goodwin, M.A., of London; m. Elsa Mary, d. of the late John Rudhall, of Brighton. Educ.: Univ. Coll. School College, Medical School and Hospital, London. Gynæcologist and Obstetric Surgeon; Obstetric Tutor to Westminster Hospital. War Work: T. Capt. R.A.M.C. from Oct. 1914 to March, 1919; Staff Officer to Director of Medical Services, Malta, from Nov. 1916 to Jan. 1919, with the local rank of Major. Addresses: 37, Cavendish Mansions, West Hampstead, London, N.W. 6; 72, Wimpole Street, W. Club: Union, Malta. (O7179)

GOODWIN, Charles Arthur, M.B.E.

GOODWIN, Ernest, O.B.E., M.A. (Cantab.) late T. Capt. Special List, b. 17 July, 1877; s. of Felix Goodwin, of 26, Wake Green Road, Moseley, Birmingham; m. Mary, d. of the late James Cook, of Ardrossan, Ayrshire. Educ.: King Edward's School, Birmingham; Emmanuel College, Cambridge. War Work: Adviser on Explosives, Trench Warfare Supply Department; Advisory Member, Trench Warfare (Research) Dept.; Officer of the Gun Ammunition Filling Dept. (S. section), all of the Ministry of Munitions. Address: 15, Stafford Terrace, Kensington, W. 8. Club: New University. (O376)

GOODWIN, Frederick Rice, C.B.E., b. 17 April, 1877; s. of Frederick Charles Goodwin, of London; m. Annie Louise, d. of Henry Harold Rogers, of London. Educ.: Peckham Grammar School. County Councillor for County of Middlesex; President Cinematograph Association of Great Britain and Ireland. War Work: The King's Fund for the disabled (Propaganda Committee); the Training of Disabled men for Ministry of Labour and Ministry of Pensions and other work for the Disabled. Address: Fort Haven, Shoreham-by-Sea, Sussex. Clubs: Royal Automobile: Road. (C2636)

GOODWIN, Capt and Qr.-Mr. George, O.B.E., R.E.

GOODWIN, Capt John Henry, M.B.E., Mercantile Marine, b. 8 June, 1850; s. of Edward Jonathan Goodwin, Master Mariner, of Liverpool; m. Emily Caroline, d. of James Williamson, of Kirkcudbright. Educ.: Privately. President of the Mercantile Marine Service Association, Tower Building, Water Street, Liverpool. War Work: At sea in the Mercantile Marine, 1914–19; National Maritime Board. Address: 18, St. Catherine's Road, Bootle, Liverpool. Club: Mercantile Marine Service Association, Tower Building, Liverpool. (M8233)

GOODWIN, John Thomas, M.B.E., b. 3 May, 1877; s. of Thomas Goodwin, of Butterley, Derbyshire; m. Margaret Ann, d. of Atkinson, of Pentrich. Educ.: Privately; Ripley Coll.; and Ockbrook Moravian School. General Manager and Engineer of Iron Foundries of Messrs. The Sheepbridge Coal and Iron Co., Chesterfield; Capt. of Derbyshire Motor Transport, A.S.C. (V.), Chesterfield; Divisional Superintendent of Sheepbridge and District Ambulance Brigade. War Work: Undertook the manufacture of large practice shot for Admiralty, received their congratulations upon the splendid success made; further increased output with equal success, afterwards made all sizes of practice shot for Admiralty; lso made Cast Iron Shells for Ministry of Munitions, and carried out many experiments for them; also made Aerial Bombs, Stokes' Shells, Depth Charge Throwers, Trench Howitzer Bombs, making in all over 10,000 tons of cast iron munitions ; further, made over 10,000 tons of General Engineering casting of all descriptions for the requirements of Ministry of Munitions and Admiralty. *Address :* The Red House, Old Whittington, Chesterfield.

(M1788)

GOODWIN, Minnie, Mrs., M.B.E.

GOODWIN, Walter, M.B.E.

GOODWYN, Lieut.-Col. Julius Henry, O.B.E.

GOODYEAR, Charles Ernest, O.B.E., A.R.C.Sc., Wh. Sch., R.C.N.C., Member of the Royal Corps of Naval Constructors, *b.* 25 March, 1874 ; *s.* of William Henry Goodyear, of Devonport ; *m.* Mabel, *d.* of James Beesley, of Manchester and London. *Educ.:* Stoke Public School, Devonport ; Dockyard School, Devonport ; Royal College of Science, London ; and Royal Naval Coll., Greenwich. Assist. Constructor, Admiralty ; Constructor H.M. Dockyard, Portsmouth ; Senior Constructor, Admiralty ; Chief Constructor, H.M. Dockyard, Gibraltar ; for many years Examiner to the Board of Education, in the subject of Naval Architecture. *War Work :* Service for Admiralty at Portsmouth Dockyard, and various private ship-building firms, in connection with expediting the completion of latest war vessels ; also, the fitting out of merchant vessels for various kinds of war service. *Address :* Admiralty Quarters, Rosia, Gibraltar. (O10495)

GOODYEAR, Clarie Helen, M.B.E.

GOODYEAR, Lieut. Geoffrey, M.B.E., M.G.C.

GOODYEAR, Mabel, M.B.E.

GOODYEAR, Percy, M.B.E.

GOODYER, Thomas Boyce, O.B.E., A.I.E.E., M.Inst.T., *b.* 1865 ; *s.* of Richard Boyce, of Wisbech, Cambs. ; *m.* Jessie Mary, *d.* of Albert Taylor, of Birmingham. *Educ.:* Royal High School, Edinburgh. Traffic Manager, Birmingham Tramways ; General Traffic Superintendent, British Electric Traction Co., Ltd. ; Tramways Manager, Croydon Corporation Tramways ; Hon. Sec. Metropolitan Municipal Tramways Council ; Member of Executive Council, Municipal Tramways Association ; Past President, Municipal Tramways Association ; Member of Council Tramways and Light Railways Association. *War Work :* Hon. Sec. Tramways (Board of Trade) Committee (Metropolitan and East Coast Area) ; served on numerous committees in connection with Tramways Transport during the war. *Address :* Tramways Offices, Thornton Heath, Surrey. *Club :* Constitutional. (O10496)

GOOLD, Eng.-Comm. Hubert, O.B.E., R.N.

GOOLDEN, Lieut.-Comm. Archibald Campbell, O.B.E., R.N.

GOOLDEN, Capt. Walter Herbert Lewis, O.B.E.

GORDON, Alexander Stewart, O.B.E., M.D. (Edin.), D.P.H., *b.* 1 Aug. 1880 ; *s.* of Henry Gordon, of Bloomfield, Bathgate ; *m.* Marguerite Evelyn, *d.* of Allan Fulton Brotchie, of Costa, Orkney. *Educ.:* Bathgate Academy ; George Heriot's School, Edinburgh ; Univ. of Edinburgh ; Royal Coll. of Physicians and Surgeons, Edinburgh. Fellow Obstetrical Society, Edinburgh ; Member of Harveian Society, Edinburgh ; M.O.H. Inverkeithing ; Assist. M.O.H., Port of St. Davids School, and Medical Inspector ; Parish M.O., late House Surgeon, Royal Infirmary, Edinburgh ; M.O. Red Cross Society ; M.O. troops (R.G.A., and R.E.) Inner Forth Defences ; Medical Referee various Life Assurance Companies ; M.O. Post Office, Inverkeithing and North Queensferry. *War Work :* Admiralty Surgeon, H.M. Dockyard, Rosyth, H.M. Coastguard, and Boom Defence, North Queensferry, H.M. W.T. Station, Rosyth ; Assist. Medical Transport Officer, Rosyth ; organised medical department at Rosyth where, during the war, 10,000 men were employed ; Admiralty M.O.H. for whole Rosyth area and H.M. Ordnance Depot, Crombie ; Casualty Surgeon, all dockyard contractors ; M.O. Holloway Brothers, Housing Contractors, Rosyth ; M.O. National Reserve (Royal Highlanders) ; M.O. Inverkeithing Emergency Ambulance Corps. *Address :* Rosebery House, Inverkeithing, Fife. *Club :* Dunfermline Golf. (O10497)

GORDON, Lieut.-Col. Annesley de Renzy, D.S.O., O.B.E., R.A.V.C. (O6188)

GORDON, Major Archibald Alexander, C.B.E., M.V.O., J.P., Attaché à la Maison Militaire de S.M. le Roi des Belges, *b.* Sept. 1867 ; *s.* of the late Dr. William Eagleson Gordon, of Bridge-of-Allan, Stirlingshire ; *m.* Maude, *d.* of the late Major General E. Davidson-Smith, of the 95th Regiment. *Educ.:* Edinburgh Collegiate School ; Edinburgh University and abroad. C.A. of Edinburgh (1889) ; late Major 9th (Highlanders) The Royal Scots ; Member of the King's Body Guard for Scotland (Royal Company of Archers) ; from 1906–1920, Private Secretary to the Duke of Wellington, K.G., G.C.V.O. *War Work :* Served with Staff of Royal Naval Division during Siege of Antwerp ; and after same as Attaché to the Military Household of H.M. the King of the Belgians and as Belgian King's Messenger (1914–18), the former of which appointments he still retains ; Hon. Organiser and Hon. Secretary of the Belgian Relief Fund ; received several War awards and cited in Belgian and French despatches. *Address :* Monksbarn, Maugersbury, Stow-on-the-Wold, Gloucestershire. *Club :* Constitutional, London. (C27)

GORDON, Capt. and Qr.-Mr. Arthur Douglas, M.B.E.

GORDON, Capt. Cedric Foskett, O.B.E., M.C., R.A.F.

GORDON, Sir Charles Blair, G.B.E., *b.* 22 Nov. 1868 ; *s.* of the late John Gordon and Jane Roy ; *m.* Edith Annie Brooks, Seaforth, Ontario. *Educ.:* Montreal High School. Representative of Minister of Munitions and Director-General of War Supplies for Great Britain at Washington, U.S.A.,

since 1917 ; President Dominion Textile Co., Ltd., 112, St. James Street, Montreal ; Vice-President Bank of Montreal ; President Penmans, Ltd. ; President Hillcrest Collieries, Ltd. : President Dominion Glass Co. ; Vice-President Montreal Cotton Co. ; Vice-President, C. Meredith Co. ; Director, Royal Trust Co. ; Director, Ritz-Carlton Hotel ; Director, Provincial Paper Co. ; Chairman, Metropolitan Parks Commission ; Governor, McGill University ; Vice-Chairman of the Imperial Munition Board, Ottawa, 1916. *Address :* British War Mission, Munsey Building, Washington, U.S.A. *Clubs :* Mount Royal (Montreal) ; Hunt, Senneville Golf (Canada) ; Montreal Jockey ; Royal St. Lawrence Yacht ; Royal Montreal Polo (Montreal). (G33)

GORDON, Flight-Lieut. David, O.B.E., R.A.F.

GORDON, Dora Helen, Mrs., O.B.E.

GORDON, Douglas George Hamilton, O.B.E., J.P., *b.* 7 Aug. 1852 ; *s.* of the late Hon. Rev. Douglas H. Gordon, and the late Lady Ellen Gordon, of The Close, Salisbury (*see* BURKE'S *Peerage*) ; *m.* Edith Anne, *d.* of — Bullock, of Faulkbourne Hall, Essex. *Educ.:* Eton. Sec., Air League of the British Empire. *War Work :* Chairman of Committee "D" of the Appeal Tribunal for the County of London and the City of London. *Address :* 46, Dover Street, London, W.1. *Club :* Arts. (O10499)

GORDON, Major Edward Ian Drumearn, O.B.E.

GORDON, Major Edward Montgomery, O.B.E., Can. A.S.C.

GORDON, Frank Lindsay, M.B.E.

GORDON, Frank Sinclair, M.B.E., R.N.

GORDON, George, M.B.E.

GORDON, Capt. George, O.B.E., *b.* 7 Sept. 1886 ; *m.* Hilda, *d.* of the Hon. C. H. Pearson (*see* BURKE'S *Peerage*). *Educ.:* Cheltenham Coll., and R.M.C. Sandhurst. Ministry of Pensions. *War Work :* Adjutant, 8th (Res.) Batt. Argyll and Sutherland Highlanders, and 16th Batt. Argyll and Sutherland Highlanders, Nov. 1914, to Dec. 1916 ; Navy and Army Canteen Board, Dec. 1916, to July, 1917 ; War Office, July, 1917, to Nov. 1917 ; Ministry of National Service, Nov. 1917, to April, 1919. *Address :* Quarry Wood Hall, Marlow, Bucks. *Club :* Junior United Service. (O7199)

GORDON, George Henry, M.B.E.

GORDON, George Robert, O.B.E., M.D., B.Ch., *s.* of Joseph Gordon, of Ireland ; *m.* Alice Maud, *d.* of George Gordon, of London. *Educ.:* Dublin and Belfast. Medicine and Surgery. *War Work :* M.O. in charge of Hartly College Red Cross Hospital. *Address :* "Ashfield," College Road, Whalley Range, Manchester. (O10500)

GORDON, Gladys, Mrs., M.B.E.

GORDON, Grace, M.B.E.

GORDON, Capt. Grahame Masey, O.B.E., M.C., R.E.

GORDON, Major Harry Francis Adam, O.B.E., York and Lancaster Regt., and R.A.F., *b.* 8 April, 1887 ; *s.* of the late Major-Gen. A. H. A. Gordon, of York and Lancaster Regt. ; *m.* Elsie Kathleen, *d.* of F. G. M. Kennedy, J.P., of Shelbourne, Limerick. *Educ.:* Bedford and R.M.C. Sandhurst. *War Work :* Active service, France and Mesopotamia. (O8104)

GORDON, Lieut.-Col. Henry Erskine, O.B.E., J.P., D.L., Lanarkshire Yeomanry (retired), *b.* 1849 ; *s.* of the late John Gordon, of Aikenhead, Cathcart N.B. ; *m.* Bertha Agnes, *d.* of the late Major John Finlay, of Castle Toward, Argyllshire. *Educ.:* Private School ; Trinity College, Cambridge. Director Caledonian Railway Co., Cathcart Railway ; Chairman Lanarkshire and Ayrshire Railway ; Director Union Bank of Scotland ; Director Coltness Iron Co. ; Alquife Mines and Railway Co. ; Warwickshire Coal Co. ; Local Chairman, Norwich Union Insurance Society. *War Work :* Chairman of Renfrewshire Tribunal ; Aikenhead Auxiliary Hospital. *Address :* Aikenhead House, Cathcart. *Club :* Western and Automobile, Glasgow ; New, Edinburgh ; New University, London. (O278)

GORDON, Henry Sharpe, O.B.E., J.P., *s.* of Henry Gordon, of Dumfries, N.B. ; *m.* John Ann, *d.* of Hugh Gilmour, of London. *Educ.:* Dumfries Academy ; Merchiston Castle, Edinburgh. Solicitor and Banker (ret.). *War Work :* Hon. Sec. Dumfriesshire Local War Pensions Committee ; Military Representative for Dumfriesshire. *Address :* Glenae, Amisfield, N.B. *Clubs :* Dumfries and Galloway County ; Scottish Conservative, Edinburgh ; Royal Automobile, London. (O10501)

GORDON, Isidore Heyam, M.B.E.

GORDON, James, C.B.E.

GORDON, James Edward, O.B.E., M.R.C.S. L.R.C.P., *b.* 1872 ; *s.* of Jas. H. Gordon, M.D., of Salisbury ; *m.* Blanche Violet, *d.* of the late Campbell MacGill, F.R.G.S. V.D., of Stratford-sub-Castle, Salisbury. *Educ.:* Weymouth College ; Glasgow University and St. Bartholomew's Hospital. Medical Superintendent, Isolation Hospital, Salisbury ; Hon. Physician to Salisbury Infirmary. *War Work :* Chiefly at above Hospitals, for treatment of infectious diseases amongst troops in the Salisbury Plain District. (O4368)

GORDON, James Scott, O.B.E. B.Sc., *b.* 10 Dec. 1867 ; *s.* of Robert Gordon, of Stragollen, Strabane, Co. Tyrone ; *m.* Martha Jane ; *d.* of Alexander Moore, of Mile Cross, Co. Down. *Educ.:* Edinburgh University. First Principal of Cheshire Agricultural and Horticultural College, Holmes Chapel ; Deputy Assistant Secretary and Chief Agricultural Inspector to the Department of Agriculture for Ireland. *War Work :* Food Production under Dept. of Agriculture, Ireland. *Addresses :* Stragollen, Strabane, Co. Tyrone, Ireland ; Abbey View, Montestown, Co Dublin. (O1380)

GORDON, James Tennant, O.B.E.

GORDON, Major James William, O.B.E., R.A.F.

GORDON, Capt. John de la Hay, M.C., Indian Army, *m.* 5 Oct. 1920, at Aden, Esmé Violet, *d.* of Cecil Bevan. (O2275)

GORDON, Lewis, C.B.E. Dep. Controller Small Arms Munition, Ministry of Munitions; has Legion of Honour. (C181)

GORDON, Lisa Mary, M.B.E., Q.M.A.A.C.

GORDON, Lieut.-Col. (Hon.) Mervyn Henry, C.M.G., C.B.E., M.D. (Oxon.) *b.* 22 June 1872; *s.* of Rev. Prebendary H. D. Gordon, M.A., Rector of Harting, Sussex; *m.* Mildred Olive, *d.* of Sir William Power, K.C.B., F.R.S. *Educ.:* Marlborough and Oxford. Bacteriologist to St. Bartholomew's Hospital; Member of Army Pathology Advisory Committee. *War Work:* Consulting Bacteriologist to the War Office for Cerebro-spinal fever. *Address:* St. Bartholomew's Hospital, E.C. 1. (C1584)

GORDON, Lieut.-Col. Philip James, O.B.E., I.A.

GORDON, Robert, O.B.E., *b.* 27 June, 1866; Clerk for Manning duties, Mobilisation Dept., Admiralty. *Address:* 73, Sydenham Road North, Croydon. (O2315)

GORDON, Major Stewart, M.B.E.

GORDON, Capt. Thomas Grove, M.B.E., R.A.F.

GORDON, Paymaster-Lieut.-Comm. Walter Hamilton, O.B.E., R.D., R.N.R.

GORDON, William, O.B.E., LL.D.

GORDON, Col. William Eagleson, V.C., A.D.C. to the King; 1913; *b.* 4 May 1866; appointed the Gordon Highlanders, 1888; served with Chitral Relief Expedition 1895, including the storming of Malakand Pass (medal with clasp); with Tirah Expeditionary Force, 1897–98 (clasp); and as Adjutant 1st Batt. Gordon Highlanders throughout the South African campaign, 1899–1902 (dangerously wounded at Magersfontein; despatches, V.C.). Lieut.-Col. 1907; Brevet-Col. 1913; served European War, 1914; Officer Commanding No. 1 District, 1916–20; half-pay, 1920. *Club:* Naval and Military.

GORDON, William James, O.B.E.

GORDON, Capt. William Lennox, O.B.E.

GORDON, Col. Gwynnedd CONWAY-, C.B.E., R.A.S.C., *b.* 1868; *s.* of the late Col. Lewis Conway-Gordon, C.I.E.; *m.* 1894, Gwyneth, *d.* of Sir Arthur William Mackworth 6th Bt. (*see* BURKE'S *Peerage*). Great War, 1914–19 (despatches). (C1524)

GORDON, John Cornwall DUFF-, M.B.E., *b.* 17 Aug. 1869; *s.* of Cosmo Duff-Gordon, and *g.* *s.* of Sir William Duff-Gordon, 2nd Bt. (*see* BURKE'S *Peerage*). *War Work:* Voluntary worker, Catholic Women's League. *Address:* 61, Warwick Street, S.W. (M10258c)

GORDON, Lieut.-Comm. Hugh HAMILTON-, O.B.E.

GORDON, Ellinor Maud, Mrs. MORE-, M.B.E., *b.* 22 May, 1862; *d.* of Œneas Macbean, Writer to H.M. Signet, Edinburgh; *m.* Harry, *s.* of George More-Gordon, Charleton, Montrose. *War Work:* Commandant of No. 1 and No. 2 V.A.D. Red Cross Hospitals, Montrose, Scotland, from Jan. 1915, to April, 1919. *Address:* 4, Panmure Terrace, Montrose, Scotland. (M8235)

GORDON, Edward PIRIE-, M.B.E., J.P., *b.* 1853; *s.* of Patrick Pirie-Gordon, of Buthlaw, Aberdeenshire; *m.* Louisa, *d.* of Rev. W. Handley, M.A., Rector of Winthorpe, Notts. *Educ.:* Harrow. *War Work:* Hon. Sec. Breconshire War Distress Fund; Member, Breconshire Local War Pensions Committee; Hon. Treas. Breconshire Soldiers' and Sailors' Families Association, and Soldiers' and Sailors' Help Society; Chairman of Crickhowell District Tribunal, War Savings Association, Food Control, Welcome Home Committees; Hon. Treas. Crickhowell War Pensions Committee, and War Memorial Cottage Hospital, etc. *Addresses:* Gwernvale, Crickhowell, Breconshire; Buthlaw, Aberdeenshire. (M8234)

GORDON, Lieut.-Col. Walter Gordon WOLRICE-, O.B.E., *b.* 29 Jan. 1861; *s.* of Henry Wolrice-Gordon, of Hallhead and Esslemont. *Educ.:* Eton. Soudan, 1884 (wounded); Nile Expedition, 1884–85; South African War, 42nd Royal Highlanders, 1899–1902; 19th Royal Fusiliers, 1915–18. *Address:* Esslemont, Aberdeenshire. *Clubs:* Naval and Military: Cavendish; Travellers'; New (Edinburgh). (O5948)

GORE, Major Charles Henry, O.B.E.

GORE, Col. St. John Corbet, C.B., C.B.E., *b.* 10 Dec. 1859. *Educ.:* Winchester. Late Commanding 5th Dragoon Guards (retired); Brigade Commander 2nd South Midland Mounted Brigade 1908–11; Military Secretary, to General Sir Archibald Hunter, Aldershot Training Centre, since 1914; Gazetted to 5th Dragoon Guards, 22 Jan. 1879; served with the Heavy Camel Regt. in Soudan in 1884 (medal and star); to India in 1893 with 5th Dragoon Guards; served as Military Secretary to both Sir Baker Russell and Sir George Luck in Bengal 1879–99; commanded cavalry at battle of Elands Laagte, Oct. 1899; siege of Ladysmith (despatches thrice, Queen's Medal, 4 Clasps, King's Medal, 2 Clasps, C.B.). Clerk of the Cheque and Adjutant, His Majesty Body Guard. *Address:* 5, Hans Place, S.W. *Club:* Naval and Military. (C182)

GORE, Capt. Aubrey Edmond PERY-KNOX-, O.B.E., K.O.Y.L.I., *b.* 27 Oct. 1883; *s.* of the late Edmond Pery-Knox-Gore, of Coolcronan, Ballina, Co. Mayo; *m.* Monica, *d.* of Capt. J. S. Bridges, of Woodcote, Fleet, Hants., and Lady Grace Bridges (*see* BURKE'S *Peerage*). *Educ.:* Malvern. *Address:* Coolcronan, Ballina, Co. Mayo. (O7569)

GORE, Lieut.-Col. William Arthur Gore SAUNDERS-KNOX-, O.B.E., R.A.

GORELL, Col. Ronald Gorell Barnes, Lord, C.B.E., M.C., B.A., *b.* 16 April 1884; *s.* his brother as 3rd Baron, 1917. *Educ.:* Winchester; Balliol Coll., Oxford. Called to the Bar, Inner Temple, 1909; on the editorial staff of "The Times"; formerly Capt. Rifle Brigade; Temp. Col. and Dep. Div. of Staff Duties, War Office, 1917; Dep. Dir. for Education in Army, 1918 (mentioned in despatches). *Address:* 1, John St., Adelphi, W.C. *Club:* Garrick.

GORGES, Brig.-Gen. Edmund Howard, C.B., C.B.E., D.S.O., *b.* 1868; *s.* of the late Capt. R. A. Gorges, R.M.A.; *m.* 1900, Sylvia Rosalie, *d.* of the late Lieut.-Col. Henry Fitz-John Townshend, J.P., of Castletownshend, co. Cork. *Educ.:* R.M.C., Sandhurst. Entered Manchester Regt. 1887; Capt. 1896; Major, 1901; Brevet Lieut.-Col. 1906; Brevet Col. 1913; Lieut.-Col. W. African Regt. 1912; Comdt. thereof, 1913; and Col. 1917; served in Uganda, 1897–99 (medal with two clasps); in S. Africa, 1900 (Queen's medal with two clasps); in command of Turkana Punitive Expedition, 1901 (despatches), in Somaliland, 1904; Comdg. Camel Corps and Mounted Inf. with Nandi Field Force, 1905–6; in command of 1st Batn. King's African Rifles (despatches, medal with clasp); and in Cameroons, 1914–16, Comdg. British Contingent (despatches, Legion of Honour); commanded troops in E. Africa and Zanzibar, 1907; appointed a Brig. Com. 1916, with rank of Brig.-Gen. (C1587)

GORMAN, Capt. James Thomas, M.B.E.

GORMAN, William, M.B.E.

GORMAN, Major GORMAN-, M.B.E.

GORRIE, Capt. Henry James, O.B.E., R.A.M.C. (T.).

GORRINGE, Emmeline Mary Vallance, Mrs., M.B.E., *d.* of John Bradford, R.N.; *m.* William Hugh, J.P., *s.* of Hugh Gorringe, J.P., of Kingston-by-Sea and Southwick, Sussex. *Educ.:* Privately. *War Work:* Superintendent of Canteen and Hostel, National Projectile Factory, feeding 6000 daily, and Soldiers' Club, Shoreham-by-Sea; and of Soldiers' and Sailors Families Assoc. *Address:* Oving, Chichester, Sussex. *Clubs:* Ladies' Army and Navy; Forum. (M1794)

GORTON, Lieut.-Col. Sandford George, M.B.E., R.N.R., *b.* 9 Oct. 1883; *s.* of Sandford Thomas Gorton, of London; *m.* Haldane Mary, *d.* of Rev. R. E. Hutchison, of N.S.W., Australia. *Educ.:* Leatherhead; H.M.S. "Worcester." Commanding Officer of Admiralty Cable Ship. *War Work:* Submarine Cable operations for Engineering Dept. of General Post Office at home and in Russia; Lent to Admiralty for duty in Anti-Submarine Division with rank of Lt.-Comdr., R.N.R. *Address:* 79, Hervey Road, Blackheath, S.E. *Club:* Junior Army and Navy. (M459)

GORVIN, John Henry, C.B.E., *b.* 1 Sept. 1886; *s.* of John Hall Gorvin, of Bideford, Devon; *m.* Winifred, *d.* of Rev. James Seldon, of Newport, Mon. *Educ.:* King's College, London. General Secretary, International Committee for Relief Credits, Paris. *War Work:* Freight Manager to Royal Commission on Wheat Supplies; Director of Requirements to Allied Food Council; British Secretary to Allied Scientific Food Commission. Officer of the Order of the Crown of Belgium. *Address:* 3, Rue Francois I., Paris. *Club:* Reform. (C2638)

GOSCHEN, George Joachim, Viscount, of Hawkhurst, C.B.E., *b.* 1866; eldest *s.* of 1st Viscount Goschen and Lucy, *d.* of John Dailley (*see* BURKE'S *Peerage*); *m.* Lady Evelyn Gathorne-Hardy, 5th *d.* of 1st Earl of Cranbrook (*see* BURKE'S *Peerage*). *Educ.:* Rugby; Balliol Coll., Oxford. Joint Parliamentary Secretary, Board of Agriculture, since 1918; late 2nd Vol. Batt. East Kent Regt.; was Private Secretary to Governor of New South Wales, and (unpaid) to his father at the Admiralty; M.P. (C.) E. Grinstead, Sussex, 1895–1906; A.D.C. to Lord Roberts, Commander-in-Chief.; Lieut.-Col. 2/5th Buffs. East Kent Regt. *Addresses:* Seacox Heath, Hawkhurst; 25, Rutland Gate, S.W. 7. *Club:* Carlton. (C183)

GOSCHEN, Sir William Henry Neville, K.B.E., D.L. (Essex). *b.* 30 Oct. 1865; *s.* of Henry Goschen, of Heathfield, Addington, Surrey; *m.* Christian, *d.* of Col. J. A. Grant, C.B., C.S.I., of Househill, Nairn. *Educ.:* Eton. Partner, Goschens and Cunliffe; Director, Nat. Prov. and U. Bank of England; Chartered Bank of India, A. and Ch.; British Trade Corp.; Prime Warden of Goldsmiths' Co., 1919–20; Chairman London Clearing Bankers' Committee, and of Central Assoc. of Bankers, 1918. *War Work:* Hon. Recruiting Officer, Military Representative, Epping Sub-Area; Member Committee Financial Facilities for Trade; Currency and Foreign Exchange Committee, Gold Production Committee, Chairman Treasury Committee on Housing Finance. *Address:* Durrington House, Harlow, Essex. *Clubs:* Carlton; Wellington. (K377)

GOSFORD, Louisa Montague, Countess of, D.B.E., *d.* of the 7th Duke of Manchester; *m.* Sir Archibald Brabazon Sparrow Acheson, K.P., 4th Earl of Gosford. Is a Lady of Grace of the Order of St. John of Jerusalem; Lady of the Bedchamber to H.M. Queen Alexandra. *Addresses:* Gosford Castle, Market Hill; Redhill, Co. Armagh; 24, Hyde Park Gardens, W. (D46)

GOSLING, Francis Godwin, O.B.E., *b.* 13 April, 1873; *s.* of the late Chas. Gray Gosling, of Bermuda; *m.* Alice Emily, *d.* of Joseph L. Trimingham, of Bermuda. *Educ.:* Salter's Grammar School, Bermuda. Assistant Colonial Sec.; Clerk Executive Council, Registrar of Patents, Designs, and Trade Marks; Chairman, Board of Pilot Commissioners, Board of

Fisheries, and Governors of the General Hospital. *War Work :* Administrative work as Acting Colonial Sec. and Asst. Colonial Sec.; Recruiting, and raising of War funds. *Address :* Hamilton, Bermuda Islands. *Club :* Royal Bermuda Yacht. (O8385)

GOSLING, Lieut.-Col. Graham, Ø.B.E.

GOSLING, Hon. Lieut. William, M.B.E., *b.* 19 Dec. 1875; *s.* of Jacob Gosling, of Great Yarmouth. Schoolmaster; Headmaster, Cobholm Boys' Council School, Great Yarmouth. *War Work :* War Savings Sec.; Lieut., 2nd Batt. Norfolk Volunteers. *Address :* 112, Southtown, Great Yarmouth. (M8237)

GOSLING, Major William Richard, O.B.E.

GOSS, Surg.-Lieut. Leslie Stewart, O.B.E.

GOSS, Lilian May, M.B.E.; *d.* of Col. A. J. Y. Goss, of Little Sneed, Stoke Bishop, Bristol. *Educ :* Cheltenham Ladies' Coll. *War Work :* Visited the British Hospitals, and for 2½ years had charge of a branch of the Bristol Inquiry Bureau at the Southmead Section, 2nd Southern General Hospital, Bristol. (M8238)

GOSSAGE, Alfred Milne, C.B.E., M.D., F.R.C.P., *b.* 13 Mar. 1864; *s.* of William Herbert Gossage, of Melbourne, Australia; *m.* Bertha Pillans, *d.* of Pillans Stevenson, of Montreal, Canada. *Educ. :* Clifton College, Magdalen College, Oxford. Senior Medical Assessor, Ministry of Pensions; late Senior Physician, Westminster Hospital and East London Hospital for children; Examiner in Medicine, Universities of Oxford and Durham and Conjoint Board, London. *War Work :* Major, R.A.M.C., (T.); Ministry of Pensions. *Addresses :* 118, Gloucester Place, Portman Square, W. 1; Houndesfield, Chalfont St. Giles. *Club :* Savile. (C2639)

GOSSAGE, Major Charles Ingram, O.B.E., A.O.C.

GOSSE, Hope Wilkes, M.B.E., M.R.C.S., L.R.C.P.

GOSTLING, Thomas Preston, O.B.E., M.R.C.S., L.R.C.P., L.S.A., *b.* 22 Sept. 1858; *s.* of T. P. Gostling, of Diss; *m.* Margaret, *d.* of Ray McCall, of Worthing. *Educ :* Paul and Cadge, Norwich; Univ. Coll. Hospital, London. Consulting Surgeon, Worcester General Infirmary. *War Work :* Surgeon to, and member of, Committee of Battenhall V.A.D. Hospital, Worcester; Surgeon in charge of Soldiers, Worcester General Infirmary. *Address :* Sunnyside, Winchester Road, Worthing. (O11805)

GOTT, Violet Alice, Mrs., O.B.E., *b.* 1868; *d.* of General Waddington, J.P., of Pangbourne, Berks; *m.* Colonel George Arthur Gott, J.P., *s.* of William Gott, of Armley House, Leeds. *War Work :* Commandant of Alton Red Cross Auxiliary Hospital; Vice-President British Red Cross Society, Alton Division, Hants Branch. *Address :* Willhall, Alton, Hants. (O1384)

GOTT, Capt. Walter, O.B.E., of Lithgows, Ltd., Ship-, builders, Port Glasgow, *b.* 17 Oct. 1880; *s.* of E. Gott, of Bradford; *m.* Kitty, *d.* of J. Harland, of Bradford. *Educ :* Bradford Grammar School. *War Work :* Royal Engineers (Inland Waterways and Docks); and Statistical Officer to Controller-General of Merchant Shipbuilding (Ministry of Shipping). *Address :* 38, Campbell Street, Greenock. (O10503)

GOTTO, Capt. Robert Porter Corry, O.B.E., *b.* 20 Jan. 1881; *s.* of A. C. Gotto, C.E., B.Sc., of Belfast; *m.* Olive, *d.* of R. B. Walkington, J.P., of Belfast. *Educ. :* Uppingham. Managing Director, James P. Corry & Co., Ltd., Timber Importers, Belfast. *War Work :* Army Service Corps, Egypt, Sinai, Palestine, Syria. *Address :* The Laurels, Adelaide Park, Belfast. *Club :* Ulster Reform. (O6189)

GOTTS, John Benjamin, O.B.E.

GOUDGE, J. A., C.B.E. For work in connection with the welfare of ex-officers. (C3145)

GOUDGE, Joseph Ernest, O.B.E., I.C.S., *b.* 22 April, 1869; *s.* of Joseph Goudge, of Swindon, Wilts.; *m.* Phyllis Ethel, *d.* of John Hooke, of Croydon. *Educ. :* Queen's Coll., Taunton and Pembroke Coll., Oxford. Indian Civil Service, United Provinces. *War Work :* Recruiting work in Oudh. *Address :* c/o Messrs. Grindlay & Co., 54, Parliament Street, S.W. *Club :* The East India United Service, S.W. (O2061)

GOUDIE, Peter Augustus, O.B.E., *b.* 20 May, 1879; *s.* of William Payne Goudie, of Derby. Editor, "Continental Daily Mail," Paris. *Address :* 34, Rue des Vignes, Passy, Paris. (O10505)

GOUGH, Lieut.-Col. Alan Percy George, C.M.G., C.B.E., D.S.O., J.P., D.L., *b.* 1863; *s.* of the late Gen. Sir John Bloomfield Gough, G.C.B., of Knockeevan, Clonmel, co. Tipperary; *m.* 1895, Mary Georgina Lloyd, *d.* of the late Francis William Lloyd Edwards (*see* BURKE'S *Peerage*, Ashtown, B.). *Educ. :* Wellington Coll. Entered Roy. Welsh Fusiliers, 1882; Capt. 1892; Major, 1900; retired, 1902; served with Burma Expedition 1885-87 (despatches twice, medal with clasp); in S. Africa, 1899-1902 (despatches twice, Queen's medal with five clasps, King's medal with two clasps); during Great War, 1914-16 (despatches); formerly Major and Hon. Lieut.-Col. Denbighshire Imperial Yeo.; Hon. Lieut.-Col. Reserve of Officers. *Address :* Gelliwig, Pwllheli, N. Wales. *Club :* Naval and Military. (C1588)

GOUGH, Arthur Edward, O.B.E.

GOUGH, Major Arthur Trevor, O.B.E., M.C., R.F.A.

GOUGH, Lieut. Herbert John, M.B.E., B.Sc., *b.* 26 April, 1890; *s.* of Henry James Gough, of Ealing; *m.* Sybil, *d.* of Richard Messer Holmes, of Coggeshall. *Educ. :* Univ. Coll. School. Research Engineer; Assistant in Engineering Department, National Physical Laboratory. *War Work :* Four years on active service with the Royal Engineers (Signal Service) in France; mentioned in despatches, Nov. 1917, in

connection with battle of Arras, and subsequent advance; awarded M.B.E. (Military Division) for maintaining forward telephone communications, Aug. to Sept. 1918. *Address :* 8, Christchurch Avenue, Teddington, Middlesex. (M3126)

GOUGH, Joseph Salmon, O.B.E., J.P.

GOUGH, Kathleen Mona, M.B.E., *b.* 1886; *d.* of Col. Hon. G. H. Gough, C.B. (*see* BURKE'S *Peerage*). *Address :* 13 Grosvenor Place, S.W. 1. (M8240)

GOUGH, Capt. and Qr.-Mr. Robert Thomas, M.B.E., R.E.

GOUK, William, M.B.E.

GOULD, Lieut.-Col. Sir Alfred Pearce, K.C.V.O., C.B.E., M.S., F.R.C.S., *b.* 1852: *s.* of Rev. George Gould, of Norwich; *m.* Florence, *d.* of late Rt. Hon. Lord Justice Lush. *Educ. :* Amersham Hall School, University College and Medical School. Consulting Surgeon, Middlesex Hospital; late Vice-Chancellor, University of London. *War Work :* Surgeon-in-Charge and later Officer Commanding, Third London General Hospital, Aug. 1914 to Aug. 1920; Member and Chairman of Health Committee of Advisory Committee; of the Statutory Pensions Committee; Medical Member of Officers' Appeal Board under Ministry of Pensions; Medical Member of Officers' Appeal Tribunal under the Lord Chancellor; Chairman of Executive Committee of the War Emergency Fund. *Addresses :* 10, Queen Anne Street, W. 1; Ashe, Ashburton. *Clubs :* Athenæum; University of London. (C1589)

GOULD, Claude William Shepard, M.B.E.

GOULD, Harold Miller, M.B.E., *b.* 15 May, 1889; *s.* of George Gould, of Ipswich; *m.* Robina Williamson, *d.* of George Melvin, of Edinburgh. *Educ. :* Ipswich Middle School. *War Work :* Y.M.C.A. work, England, 1914; France, 1915-19. *Address :* 1, Brunswick Square, Gloucester. (M1796)

GOULD, William Edward Thomas, M.B.E.

GOULD, Lieut. Willis, O.B.E.

GOULD, Capt. Edward Sabine BARING-, O.B.E.; R.A.S.C.

GOULDEN, Capt. Charles Bernard, O.B.E., R.A.M.C.

GOULDING, Major and Qr.-Mr. Edward Sainsbury, O.B.E., T.D., *b.* 11 Sept. 1875; *s.* of E. K. Goulding, of Liverpool. Fellow of the Society of Incorporated Accountants. *War Work :* Serving as quartermaster of the 6th (Rifle) Battn. The King's Liverpool Regt. on outbreak of war; assisted to mobilise the battalion, went to France with it in Feb., 1915, and served abroad with the battalion until demobilisation; twice mentioned in despatches; has been for many years Secretary of the Lancashire Rifle Association, and interested in the promotion of Rifle Shooting. *Addresses :* 4, Wellesley Road, Princes Park, Liverpool. *Club :* Conservative, Liverpool. (O2533)

GOULDING, Harry Wilson, O.B.E., *b.* 25 Feb. 1858: *s.* of Thomas Alfred Goulding, of Cam, Glos.; *m.* Mary, *d.* of George Hadley, of Cam, Glos. *Educ. :* Brownes Green Collegiate School, and Wolverhampton Grammar School. Consulting Engineer, late Chief Engineer, Soho Foundry, Birmingham; Messrs. Palmer's, Ltd., and Woolwich Arsenal, R.C.D.; work embraced Mechanical, Electrical, and Constructional Engineering and Building Construction. *War Work :* Special Investigator, Ministry of Munitions of War; Chief Dilution Officer, and Chairman of the Enlistment Complaints Committee, South Western Division. *Address :* 28, Lyndon Road, Olton, Warwickshire. (O10508)

GOUT, Lieut. Evelyn Rudolf Albert John, M.B.E.

GOVER, Capt. William Cyril, O.B.E., R.G.A.

GOVINDARAJULU, Rose, M.B.E. (M6149)

GOW, Major Peter Graham, M.B.E.

GOW, Capt. Reginald Ronald, O.B.E.

GOWAN, Major Francis Edward, O.B.E.; *s.* of F. E. Gowan, of Kinsale, Co. Cork; *m.* Ora, *d.* of Rev. John Magill, of Carnlough, Co. Antrim. *Educ. :* King's Coll., London. *War Work :* Served on the Staff of the Financial Adviser to the Commander-in-Chief, British Expeditionary Force, France, 1915-19, with rank of Major; mentioned in despatches. *Addresses :* War Office; and Woodlands, Constable Close, Golders Green, London, N.W. 4. (O10509)

GOWAN, George D'Olier, M.B.E.

GOWANS, Capt. James Dakers, O.B.E.

GOWANS, Thomas, O.B.E.

GOWARD, Major Raymond Spencer, M.B.E.

GOWER, Lieut. John Forbes, M.B.E., R.A.S.C.

GOWER, Lieut. and Qr.-Mr. John Richard, M.B.E.

GOWER, Sir Robert Vaughan, Kt. Bach., O.B.E., F.R.G.S., J.P., C.C., *b.* Nov. 1880; *e. s.* of the late Alderman Joshua Robert Gower, J.P., of Boughton House, Tunbridge Wells; *m.* Dorothy Susan Eleanor, *o. d.* of the late Herbert McClellon Wills, D.L., J.P., of Exeter, Co. Devon, and 1st cousin of the 1st Baron Lee of Fareham. *Educ. :* Privately. Law Society Honours and Final, 1903; Alderman, Borough Royal of Tunbridge Wells, since 1913; Deputy Mayor, 1910-11-12-13; Mayor, 1917-18-19; County Councillor for Kent since 1910; J.P. for Tunbridge Wells; appointed Military Representative, Kent Tribunal, 1915-17; Commissioner (L.G.B., unpaid) for promoting co-operation amongst traders to secure carrying on of businesses of men called to colours; Fellow of Society of Genealogists; President of Society of Prevention and Relief of Cancer; Member of General Council of National Canine Defence League, and of the Vermin Repression Society; Member of Law Society; Liveryman, Needlemakers' Society; Chairman, Tunbridge Wells Conservative and Unionist Association. *Address :* Boughton Colemars, Matfield, Kent. *Clubs :* Carlton; Junior Carlton; United; Kent County. (O3738)

GOWER, Capt. Cecil Octavius Gresham LEVESON-, M.B.E.

GOWER, Col. Charles Cameron LEVESON-, C.M.G., O.B.E., b. 30 June, 1866; s. of the late Capt. H. B. B. Leveson-Gower, of Bill Hill, Berks (see BURKE'S Peerage); m. Beatrice, d. of H. F. Makins, of 180, Queen's Gate, S.W. Educ.: Cheltenham Coll. Late Indian Cavalry, and Royal Field Artillery. War Work: Commanded Brigade, R.F.A., in France, 1915–16; Inspector of Guns, 1917–19. Address: 13, Cottesmore Gardens, Kensington. Club: Cavalry. (O7387)

GOWING, Major Reginald Mack, O.B.E., Aust. A.M.C.

GOWING, Warden, O.B.E.

GRACE, George William, O.B.E., b. 1880; s. of James Grace, of Sunderland; m. Gertrude, d. of R. T. Boothroyd, of West Hartlepool. Director of Connell and Grace, and The Quayside Shipping Co., Ltd., and The Side Shipping Co., Ltd., Newcastle. War Work: Some time in the Royal Engineers (Inland Waterways and Docks Dept.); transferred 1917 to the Ministry of Shipping, where, under Sir Ernest W. Glover, was responsible for the management of the large fleet of Scandinavian vessels requisitioned by the British Government during the War. Address: Proctor House, Newcastle-on-Tyne; Leasyde, Gosforth, Newcastle-on-Tyne. (O10510)

GRACE, Lieut. Theodore Phillip, M.B.E.

GRACE, Gladys Sheffield, Mrs. Raymond Sheffield HAMILTON-, C.B.E.

GRACEY, Edmund, M.B.E.

GRACEY, Hugh Kirkwood, C.B.E., J.P., I.C.S., b. 23 Nov. 1868; s. of David Gracey, of Banbridge; m. Mabel Alice (M.B.E.), d. of George Frederick Berrill. Educ.: City of London School and St. Catharine's College, Cambridge. Commissioner of the Kumaon Division, United Provinces, India; was also settlement officer of Cawnpore, and has been district officer of many districts; is ex-officio political agent to H.H. The Raja of Tehri (Garhwal). War Work: Was in administrative charge of all branches of war work, including the organization of recruiting and war loans, in the Gorakhpur division, U.P.; was also a member of the provincial war committee; mentioned, for valuable war services, in the Gazettes of India, dated 3 June, 1918, and 29 July, 1919. Address: Hatton Hall, Naini Tal, U.P., India. (C1967)

GRACEY, Mabel Alice, Mrs., M.B.E.

GRACIAS, Hyginus Dominie, M.B.E. (M6150)

GRACIE, Sir Alexander, K.B.E., M.V.O., b. 14 Nov. 1860; m. Catherine Fullerton, d. of Walter Rutherford of Glasgow. Chairman and Managing Director, Messrs. Cammel Laird & Co., Ltd. Address: Montgomerie Crescent, Glasgow. Club: Junior Carlton. (K74)

GRACIE, Lieut. Duncan McAuley, M.B.E., R.N.V.R.

GRACIE, Major Farquhar, O.B.E., R.A.M.C. (T.).

GRACIE, Robert Spencer, O.B.E.

GRACIE, William McAuley, M.B.E., A.M.Inst.T., b. 14 Sept. 1887; s. of Duncan Gracie, of H.M. Customs, Moville; m. Olga Mary, d. of William Kaye, of Doncaster. Educ.: Privately. Chief Clerk, Chief Goods Manager's Office, Great Central Railway. War Work: Transport arrangements in connection with Government traffic. Address: Fernlea, Harrow-on-the-Hill. (M8243)

GRADDON, Ernest Edgar, O.B.E.

GRAEME, Patrick Neal Sutherland, C.B.E., J.P., Deputy Judge Advocate, Civil Branch of Judge Advocate-General's Office. (C3142)

GRAFF, Francis Stephen, O.B.E., b. 28 Feb. 1868; s. of Stephen J. Graff, C.B., of 45, Amherst Road, Ealing. Educ.: Privately. Sec. of the Agricultural Organisation Society. War Work: Agricultural organisation; served on committees at Ministry of Agriculture and Ministry of Food. Address: 50, Courtfield Gardens, West Ealing. Club: National Liberal. (O10512)

GRAFTON, Alexander, O.B.E.

GRAHAM, Lieut. Allan James, C.B.E., B.A., b. 16 May, 1883; s. of John Graham, of Mohrcroft, Aigburth Drive, Liverpool; m. Norah Russell, d. of William Delafield. Educ.: Marlborough and Trinity Coll., Oxford. War Work: Lieut. Liverpool Scottish, and later Commercial Adviser to the British Legation, Copenhagen. Address: 158, Fenchurch Street. Club: Prince's. (C2640)

GRAHAM, Arthur John Wood, O.B.E.

GRAHAM, Major Charles Frederick Oliver, O.B.E., R.M.L.I.

GRAHAM, Lieut.-Col. Charles Percy, C.B.E., D.S.O.

GRAHAM, Capt. Charles Ronald, O.B.E.

GRAHAM, Major Charles Townley, O.B.E., I.A.

GRAHAM, Rev. Christopher, O.B.E., M.A., R.N.

GRAHAM, Christopher Colborne, M.B.E.

GRAHAM, Lieut. Cuthbert, M.B.E., R.E.

GRAHAM, Major David James, O.B.E., M.D., F.R.C.P., R.A.M.C. (T.).

GRAHAM, Capt. David Livingstone, O.B.E., M.B.

GRAHAM, David Morgan, M.B.E., J.P.

GRAHAM, Duncan, O.B.E.

GRAHAM, Gilbert Maxwell Adair, C.B.E., b. 19 June, 1883; s. of James Graham, D.L., of Carfin and Stonebyres, Lanarkshire; m. Phyllis Elinor, d. of F. de Mierre Turner, of Oporto. Educ.: Eton, and New College, Oxford. War Work: Served on the Quartermaster-General's Staff at the War Office. Address: Quinta da Povoa, Oporto, Portugal. Clubs: Union; Bath; New (Edinburgh). (C1590)

GRAHAM, Major Harold John, O.B.E.

GRAHAM, Helen, M.B.E.

GRAHAM, James, C.B.E., b. 26 Nov. 1870; s. of James Graham, of Stirling, N.B.; m. Louisa Edith, d. of Robert Rule, of Glasgow and Crieff. Educ.: Charterhouse and Glasgow University. War Work: Commercial Assistant in Ministry of Shipping, April, 1917, to Feb. 1919. Addresses: Hollingden-Woldingham, Surrey; 7, East India Avenue, E.C. Clubs: Thatched House; Public Schools. (C2641)

GRAHAM, Capt. and Qr.-Mr. James, M.B.E., D.C.M.

GRAHAM, James, M.B.E., B.A., R.U.I., b. June, 1861; s. of James Graham, of Carnlea, Ballymena, Co. Antrim, Ireland Educ.: The Model School, Ballymena; Private tuition; Correspondence Coll., Burlington House, Cambridge. Surveyor, H.M. Customs and Excise, Long Room, Custom House, London. War Work: During the War was Surveyor in charge of the Special Export Branch, established for the initial departmental control of merchandise, etc., allowed to be entered at the Custom House, London, for exportation to foreign destinations under the Law and Regulations relating to Trading with the Enemy. Address: 11, Thornby Road, Lower Clapton, N.E. (M6639)

GRAHAM, Capt. James Wells, O.B.E.

GRAHAM, Jannet, M.B.E.

GRAHAM, Capt. John Irvine, C.B.E., R.N., b. 17 July, 1862; s. of Colonel J. H. Graham; m. Hazel Dorothy, d. of General Sir Thomas Graham, K.C.B. Educ.: Elizabeth College, Guernsey, and Royal Navy. Captain R.N. (retired), and now Inspector-General of Customs, Waterguard. Address: 48, Evelyn Gardens, S.W. 7. Club: Army and Navy. (C2642)

GRAHAM, Major John St. John, O.B.E.

GRAHAM, Joseph, O.B.E.

GRAHAM, Lieut.-Col. Joseph William, O.B.E., R.E.

GRAHAM, Mary Bremner, O.B.E.

GRAHAM, Mary Louise, Marchioness of, O.B.E., b. 1 Nov. 1884; d. of 12th Duke of Hamilton (see BURKE'S Peerage); m. James, Marquess of Graham, s. of 5th Duke of Montrose, of Buchanan Castle (see BURKE'S Peerage). War Work: Vice-President Red Cross, Plomesgate Division, Suffolk, and Arran Division, Bute; worked 1 year 10 months as V.A.D. in Easton Park Red Cross Hospital, Suffolk; 5½ months as probationer in Scottish National Red Cross Hospital; 1 year 11 months as Commandant Arran Auxiliary Red Cross Hospital, Isle of Arran. Address: Brodick Castle, Isle of Arran. (O382)

GRAHAM, Maurice, C.B.E. For valuable services to the Ministry of Shipping in the capacity of Construction Engineer. (C3147)

GRAHAM, Lieut.-Col. Robert Balfour, M.B.E., V.D., F.R.C.S., D.P.H., J.P., b. 25 Aug. 1859; s. of the late Rev. M. H. N. Graham, Minister of Parish of Maxton; m. Ella, d. of Henry T. Balfour, of Clock House, E. Barnet. Educ.: Welfield Academy Kelso Grammar School; Edinburgh Univ.; and Medical School. M.O.H. Leven; County Director Fife Red Cross; Member, War Pensions Committee and Soldiers' and Sailors' Help Society, etc. War Work: Lieut.-Col. R.A.M.C.; County Director Red Cross, 1913–14; 1915–16, Senior Medical Officer, Command Depot for wounded men; 1916–17, President Headquarters and Special Recruiting Medical Boards; 1917–18, Officer Commanding Hospital for Officers. Address: Levenbank, Leven, Fife. Club: Scottish Conservative (Edin.). (M8246)

GRAHAM, Lieut.-Col. Robert Blackall, C.B.E., b. 1874; s. of Col. R. B. Graham. Educ.: Wellington Coll, and R.M.C. N.-W. Frontier of India 1897–98 (medal with clasp); S. Africa, 1899–1900 (Queen's medal with clasp); Great War, 1914–19 (mentioned in despatches). Address: Malvern Lodge, Cheltenham. (C1458)

GRAHAM, 2nd Lieut. Robert Clark, M.B.E., R.A.F.

GRAHAM, Lieut. Ronald, M.B.E.

GRAHAM, Sophia Augusta, M.B.E.; d. of Rev. Malise Reginald Graham, of Arthuret, Longtown, Cumberland. Educ.: Privately. President of Northern Ladies' Hockey Association; Diocesan Head of G.F.S. Sick Department; Member of Cumberland Nursing Association Executive Committee; Sec. of Longtown and District Nursing Association; Member of Committee (Executive) of Cumberland Branch of the British Red Cross Society; Chairman of Executive Committee of Association for Rescue and Preventative Work, Carlisle; Governor of Cumberland Infirmary; Member of Longtown War Pensions Sub-Committee; Commandant Cumberland V.A.D. 18 (Longtown); a Manager of the Arthuret and Kirkandrews-upon-Esk Council Schools. War Work: Commandant of Claremont, Scaurbank and Glingerbank Hospitals, Longtown, Cumberland; Member of the Cumberland and Westmorland Red Cross Working Party Committee; Member of the Cumberland War Agricultural Committee. Address: Arthuret, Longtown, Cumberland. Clubs: V.A.D. Ladies', London; North London Rifle; Ladies', Carlisle. (M3676)

GRAHAM, Sydney, C.B.E.

GRAHAM, Eng.-Comm. Thomas Alexander, O.B.E., R.N.R.

GRAHAM, Thomas Harkness, O.B.E., b. 5 Sept. 1880; s. of John Graham, of Lochmaben; m. Ruth, d. of Harry Kennedy, of Bootle. Educ.: University of Liverpool. Librarian, Royal College of Physicians of Edinburgh; Registrar of the Branch Medical Council for Scotland. War Work: Secretary of the Scottish Medical Service Emergency Committee;

Secretary of the Central Professional Committee for Scotland, under the Military Service (Medical Practitioners' Regulations) Act ; Secretary of the Advisory Medical Board for Scotland, Ministry of National Service. *Address* : 8, Keith Terrace, Blackhall, Midlothian. *Club* : Scottish Arts, Edinburgh.
(O1385)

GRAHAM, Capt. Vivien Horace, O.B.E., Can. A.S.C.

GRAHAM, Capt. Walter, M.B.E., C.A.F.

GRAHAM, William, M.B.E., *b.* 14 Dec. 1894 ; *s.* of A. Graham, of Bradford ; *m.* Bessie, *d.* of G. Warnock, of Strathaven, N.B. *Educ.* : Bradford and London. Official of Board of Trade. *War Work* : Sec. of Trade and Licensing Committee, and Dyes Dept. Board of Trade ; represented the U.K. at various International Conferences on dyes, particularly regarding the supply of dyes by Germany as reparation under the Peace Treaty. *Addresses* : Downs Court Road, Purley ; Board of Trade, Great George Street, S.W. 1. (M8249)

GRAHAM, Eng.-Comm. William Air, O.B.E., R.N.R., R.A.M.C.

GRAHAM, Capt. William Thomson, O.B.E., R.A.M.C., *b.* 1885 ; *s.* of J. T. Graham, M.D., M.R.C.S., of Perth. *Educ.* : Perth Academy ; Edinburgh Univ. *War Work* : Served with Mesopotamia and Egyptian Expeditionary Forces, 1914–19. *Address* : c/o Messrs. Holt & Co., 3, Whitehall Place, London, S.W. 1. (O6190)

GRAHAM, Winifred Maud, Mrs. Ogilvie, M.B.E., *b.* 23 Sept. 1893; *d.* of Rev. Canon J. B. Harford, of Ripon Cathedral; *m.* Capt. Ogilvie Blair Graham, D.S.O., *s.* of O. B. Graham, of Larchfield, Lisburn. *Educ.* : Malvern ; Oxford. *War Work* : Headquarters, Q.M.A.A.C., France. *Addresses* : Larchfield, Lisburn, Co. Down, Ireland ; c/o 4th Batt. Rifle Brigade, Quetta, Baluchistan. (M4505)

GRAHAM, Capt. Hamilton Maurice HOWGRAVE-, O.B.E.

GRAINGER, Edwin Charles, M.B.E., M.C., *b.* 24 July, 1879 ; *s.* of Edwin Grainger, of Chilworth, Surrey ; *m.* Fannie, *d.* of John Hale. *Educ.* : Secondary Schools. *War Work* : Served with the Queen's W. Surreys, from Aug. 1914, to April, 1918, in France and Belgium ; 11th R. Sussex Regt., Sept. 1918, to Aug. 1920, in N. Russia. *Address* : c/o Messrs. Cox & Co. (M6997)

GRANARD, Beatrice, Countess of, O.B.E., *d.* of Ogden Mills, of Haatsbury, Duchess County, U.S.A. ; *m.* Right Hon. Bernard Arthur William Patrick Hastings Forbes, 8th Earl of Granard, K.P., G.C.V.O. *Addresses* : Forbes House, Halkin Street, S.W. ; Castle Forbes, Newtown Forbes, Co. Longford ; 73, Rue de Varenne, Paris. (O10516)

GRANDIN, Capt. Ernest, M.B.E.

GRANGE, Major Charles D'Oyly, O.B.E., F.R.C.S., R.A.M.C., *b.* 29 Aug. 1887 ; *s.* of W. D'Oyly Grange, M.D., of Harrogate ; *m.* Dorothea, *d.* of the late C. J. Forster, of Gateshead-on-Tyne, *Educ.* : Harrogate Coll. ; Univ. of Leeds ; St. Bartholomew's Hospital. Assistant Surgeon, Harrogate Infirmary. *War Work* : Officer in Charge Surgical Division, Northumberland War Hospital, Newcastle-on-Tyne, May, 1915, to June, 1919. *Address* : 104, Station Parade, Harrogate. (O8818)

GRANT, Agnes Jane, Mrs., M.B.E. ; *d.* of Robert Ross, of Cape Town, S. Africa ; *m.* Alexander Fraser Grant, *s.* of Duncan Grant, of Edinburgh. *Educ.* : Private School, Cape Town. *War Work* : Organising and managing a canteen for sailors and soldiers at Simon's Bay, South Africa. *Address* : Bosky Dell, Simonstown, S. Africa. *Clubs* : Services, London ; Alexandra, Cape Town. (M8250)

GRANT, Alexander, O.B.E., *b.* 1869 ; *s.* of Alexander Grant, of Edinburgh ; *m.* Margaret St. Clair, *d.* of John Dunnett, of Bower, Caithness. *Educ.* : Edinburgh. On the staff of the " Glasgow Herald," 1892–1918 ; Parliamentary Staff, 1899–1918 ; Council of the Newspaper Press Fund 1907–19. *War Work* : Appointed Superintendent of Publicity, Ministry of Pensions, April, 1918 ; Organiser of the King's Fund for Disabled Officers and Men, Nov. 1918, to June, 1920. *Address* : 11, Salford Road, Streatham Hill, S.W. 2. *Club* : London Press. (O10517)

GRANT of DRUMINNOR, Alexander Philip Fullerton, M.B.E., *b.* 29 May, 1887 ; *s.* of Philip Alexander Holland (latterly Grant). *Educ.* : Eton and Cambridge. Agriculturalist ; Inspector of small live stock. Ministry of Agriculture. *War Work* : Ministry of Munitions (Military Personnel), 1915–20. *Address* : Druminnor, Rhynie, Aberdeenshire. *Clubs* : New Univ. ; Farmers'. (M3677)

GRANT, Major Andrew, M.B.E., M.B., R.A.M.C.

GRANT, Lieut.-Col. Sir Arthur, Bt., C.B.E., D.S.O., J.P., D.L., Gordon Highlanders, late 12th Lancers, retired 1909, *b.* 14 Sept. 1879 ; second *s.* of 9th Bart. and Mary, *d.* of Capt. H. Sholto-Douglas, late 42nd Highlanders ; *m.* Evelyn, 7th *d.* of the late Collingwood L. Wood, of Freeland, Perthshire. Entered Army 1899, served South Africa 1899–1902 (despatches, Queen's medal, 5 clasps, King's medal, 2 clasps, D.S.O.) ; Great War, 1914–15 (wounded). *Address* : House of Monymusk, Aberdeen. *Clubs* : Carlton ; Naval and Military ; Royal Automobile ; Royal Northern (Aberdeen). (C2113)

GRANT, Eng.-Capt. Arthur Robert, C.B.E., R.N.

GRANT, Lieut. Arthur Syme, O.B.E., R.N.V.R.

GRANT, Capt. Charles Cameron, M.B.E.

GRANT, Capt. Donald Ernest, M.B.E.

GRANT, Duncan Walter, C.B.E.

GRANT, Emma Egerton, Mrs., M.B.E ; *m.* Charles E.

GRANT, D.L. *War Work* : Hon. Sec. Naval and Military War Pensions Committee ; Vice President Scottish Branch British Red Cross Society. *Address* : Monkcastle, Kilwinning, Ayrshire. (M8251)

GRANT, Ethel Ogilvie, M.B.E.

GRANT, Major James Forgan, O.B.E., R.A.M.C., *b.* 23 Nov. 1882. *Educ.* : Marischal Coll., Aberdeen. Commissioned, July, 1907. *War Work* : Convoy duty, 1914–15 ; India, 1915–16 ; Mesopotamia, 1917–18 ; Kurdistan, 1919. *Address* : c/o Messrs. Holt & Co., 3, Whitehall Place, London. *Club* : Caledonia. (O9762)

GRANT, Sec. Lieut. Leslie Iam, M.B.E., M.M., R.E.

GRANT, Lilian, Mrs., O.B.E.

GRANT, Capt. Malcolm Kenneth, O.B.E., R.N.

GRANT, Neil Forbes, C.B.E., *b.* 1 Aug. 1882 ; *s.* of James Grant, of Forres, Scotland. *Educ.* Milne's Institution, Fochabers ; Edinburgh University ; Oxford University (Scholar of Brasenose College). Journalist ; Foreign Editor of the " Morning Post " since 1918. *War Work* : Attached Foreign Office and subsequently Ministry of Information, acting as Editor of Cables and Wireless Section. *Address* : 12, Merton Hill Road, Wimbledon, S.W. *Club* : United University. (C971)

GRANT, Norman, M.B.E.

GRANT, Capt. Robert Charles, O.B.E.

GRANT, Col. Ronald Charles, D.S.O., O.B.E., *b.* 1864 ; *s.* of Lieut.-Col. James Murray Grant, of East London, Cape Colony ; *m.* 1898, Mina, *d.* of the Rev. James Stewart, M.D., D.D., of Lovedale, S. Africa. Basutoland, 1880–81 (medal with clasp) ; S. Africa, 1899–1900 (despatches, Queen's medal with four clasps, King's medal with two clasps) ; Lieut.-Col. and temporary Col. Union of S. Africa, Permanent Force. (O2399)

GRANT, Col. Samuel Charles Norton, C.B., C.M.G., C.B.E., *b.* 1854 ; *s.* of the late George Grant, R.N. ; *m.* 1882, Ina, *d.* of the late Maj.-Gen. J. C. Blackwood De Butts, R.E. Entered R.E. 1874 ; Capt. 1885 ; Major, 1894 ; Lieut.-Col. 1901 ; Brevet Col. 1904 ; and Col. 1908 ; retired, 1911 ; served in S. Africa, 1900 (despatches) ; employed under Colonial Office in Cyprus, 1878–79 and 1880–86 ; in W. Africa, 1895–96 ; and under Foreign Office with Anglo-Portuguese Boundary Commn. 1892–93 ; with Venezuela Boundary Arbitration Commn. 1899 ; and on Indian Topographical Survey Commn. 1905 ; was D.A.A.G at Head Quarters, 1897–99 ; Director-Gen. of Ordnance Survey Board of Agriculture and Fisheries, 1908–11. *Address* : The White Cottage, Norton, near Yarmouth, Isle of Wight. (C508)

GRANT, Selwyn Seafield, O.B.E., M.I.E.E., *b.* 16 Sep. 1877 ; *s.* of the late Lieut.-Gen. Douglas Grant, of Indian Army ; *m.* Mary, *d.* of the late John Spencer Curwen. *Educ.* : St. Paul's School. Director of J. Curwen and Sons, Ltd ; Contracts Manager, J. G. White & Co., Ltd. *War Work* : Superintending Engineer, London and S.E. England, Ministry of Munitions. *Address* : 31, Glenloch Road, N.W. 3. *Club* : St. Stephen's. (O387)

GRANT, Capt. Stuart Colquhoun, O.B.E., T.D., Herts. Yeomanry, *b.* 7 Feb. 1873 ; *s.* of Col. G. Colquhoun Grant, Chief Commissioner, Karachi, Sind, India ; *m.* Grace Lilian, *d.* of F. G. Potter, of New York. *Educ.* : Charterhouse. Member London Stock Exchange, 1896 ; now Secretary Guards' Club ; served in the South African War (Queen's Medal). *War Work* : A.D.C. to G.O.C. E. Mounted Brigade, Aug. 1914 ; A.D.C. to G.O.C., 29th and 13th Divisions, Gallipoli, June, 1915 ; A.D.C. to G.O.C., 40th Division, France, June, 1916 ; Camp Commandant, I. Corps, Sept. 1916 till end of War ; twice mentioned in despatches ; Territorial Decoration ; two mentions ; Queen's Medal, S.A. War ; 1915 Star ; Overseas Medal ; Victory Medal ; George V. Coronation Medal. *Address* : 7, Kent Terrace, Regent's Park, N.W. *Clubs* : Boodle's ; Junior United Service, etc. (O2536)

GRANT, William, O.B.E.

GRANT, Lieut. William, M.B.E., R.N.V.R.

GRANT, William Charles, M.B.E.

GRANT, Major William Francis Newby, O.B.E.

GRANT, Lieut.-Col. William Griffith, O.B.E., F.R.G.S.

GRANT, Sir James DUNDAS-, K.B.E., *b.* 13 June, 1854 ; *s.* of James Dundas-Grant, of Edinburgh ; *m.* Helen, *d.* of Edward Frith, of London. *Educ.* : Edinburgh Academy ; Dunkirk Coll. (France) ; Universities of Edinburgh and Würzburg (Germany) ; various London Medical Schools. Aurist and Laryngologist ; Consulting Aurist to Ministry of Pensions ; Surgeon (Throat and Ear), Brompton Hospital for Consumption and West End Hospital for Nerve Diseases ; Teacher University of London ; Consulting Surgeon, Central London Throat and Ear Hospital, Royal Academy of Music, Royal Society of Musicians, Scottish Hospital ; Manager, Royal Institution. *War Work* : President, Special Aural Board and Director of Clinics (Ministry of Pensions) ; Visiting Aural Surgeon to King George Hospital, Endsleigh Palace Hospital, Lord Knutsford Special Hospitals, Freemasons' Hospital, New Zealand Hospital, Anglo-Russian Hospital, etc. *Address* : 148, Harley Street, W. 1. *Clubs* : Athenæum ; British Empire ; Royal Automobile. (K455)

GRANT, Capt. George Bertram MACPHERSON-, M.B.E., J.P., D.L., F.R.G.S., *b.* 26 Jan. 1868 ; *s.* of Sir George Macpherson Grant, 3rd Bart. of Ballindalloch and Invereshie (see BURKE's *Peerage*) ; *m.* Dorothy Eleanor, *d.* of J. D. Kellic MacCallum, of Quinton Rising, Northampton. *Educ.* : Eton. Formerly Engineer, in Argentine Republic and

BIOGRAPHIES.

Gray

Sudan. *War Work:* Joined 4th Cameron Highlanders, Aug. 1914, and was transferred to Naval Ordnance Inspection, under Chief Inspector of Naval Ordnance. *Address:* Craigo House, Montrose. *Club:* Bath. (M6948)

GRANTHAM, Jane Marian, Mrs., M.B.E.

GRANVILLE, Agatha, M.B.E.; *d.* of the late James Granville. *War Work:* Red Cross Hospital Assistant at Orwa-el-Wosha Hospital (No 19 Gen. Hos.), Alexandria, 1916–17; Lady Superintendent Alexandria Ladies' Red Cross Workroom, 1918–20. *Address:* c/o Dr. A. Granville, C.M.G., C.B.E., Carlton, Alexandria, Egypt. (M8253)

GRANVILLE, Alexander, C.M.G., C.B.E., M.R.C.S., L.R.C.P., *b.* 6 Mar. 1874; *s.* of James Granville. President, Quarantine Board of Egypt. *War Work:* Commissioner, British Red Cross and Order of St. John, for Egypt, Palestine and Syria. *Address:* Carlton, Alexandria, Egypt. *Club:* Athenæum. (C2644)

GRANVILLE, Major (T. Lieut.-Col.) Court, O.B.E., 3rd (S.R.) Bn. The Devonshire Regt., *b.* 6 May, 1872; *s.* of the late Sub-Dean Roger Granville, M.A., of Pilton House, Exeter; *m.* Mabel Beatrice, *d.* of the late Col. Dumaresq, R.E., of Bideford, N. Devon. *Educ.:* Sherborne School, and United Services College, Westward Ho. *War Work:* 1914, France and Belgium, with 1st Battn. The Devonshire Regt.; 1916 to end of war, with E.E.F. in command of The Garrison Battn., Royal Warwick Regt, then transferred to Garrison Battn., The Devonshire Regt.; Commandant at Ismailia, Ramleh (Palestine), Jerusalem, and Haifa areas. *Address:* The Cottage, Birchanger, Bishops Stortford, Essex. (O2899)

GRANVILLE, Capt. Dennis, M.V.O., O.B.E., *b.* 14 April, 1863; *s.* of the late G. H. Granville, of Wellesbourne, Warwick; *m.* Beatrice Margaret, *d.* of Sir George Walter, Bart., of Woodcote, Warwick. *Educ.:* Haileybury. Served in the Royal Warwickshire Regiment, 1883–1898; Chief Constable of Dorset since April, 1898. *Address:* Somerleigh Gate, Dorchester. *Clubs:* Naval and Military; Royal Dorset Yacht. (O1386)

GRAPES Major John, O.B.E.

GRASETT, Edward Douglas, O.B.E., *b.* 20 July, 1876; *s.* of Edward Grasett, of Bracknell, Berks; *m.* Caroline, *d.* of J. J. Jackson, of Manchester. *Educ.:* Lancing College, Sussex. Traffic Superintendent, North Staffordshire Railway, Stoke-on-Trent. *Address:* 15, The Villas, Stoke-on-Trent. (O1387)

GRASETT, Capt. Geoffrey William, O.B.E., R.A.S.C.

GRASSICK, Major Frederick, O.B.E.

GRATINCK, Doris Hilda, Mrs., M.B.E

GRATTAN, Caroline Elizabeth, M.B.E.

GRATTAN, Col. Henry William, C.B.E., D.S.O., R.A.M.C. Dep. Director of Hygiene at War Office; Great War, 1914–19 (despatches). (C1257)

GRATTAN, Brig.-Gen. O'Donnel Colley, C.B.E., D.S.O., *b.* 1855; *s.* of the late Henry Colley Grattan; *m.* 1877, Helen Randal, *d.* of the late Maj.-Gen. Henry Luke Le Poer Trench (*see* BURKE'S *Peerage*, Clancarty, E.). *Educ.:* Privately, and at R.M.C. Sandhurst. Entered 8th Regt. 1876; Capt. The King's (Liverpool Regt.), 1882; Major, 1892; Lieut.-Col. 1900; Brevet. Col. 1904 (retired 1905); Hon. Brig.-Gen. 1919; Afghan War, 1878–80 (medal with clasp); S. Africa, 1899–1900; present during siege of Ladysmith (despatches, medal with clasp); Brig. Com. 1st W. Riding Brig. Territorial Force, 1909–13; appointed to command an Inf. Brig. 1914. *Club:* United Service. (C2114)

GRAVE, Capt. Frederick, M.B.E., R.A.F.

GRAVES, Lieut.-Comm. Cornelius Blackwell, O.B.E., R.N.R.

GRAVES, Frances Marjorie, M.B.E., *b.* 17 Sept. 1884; *d.* of William S. Graves, of Newells, Horsham, Sussex. *Educ.:* Privately, and Chateau de Dieudonne, Bornel, France. *War Work:* Foreign Office. *Address:* 3, Stone Buildings, Lincoln's Inn, W.C. 2. *Club:* Le Lycéum, 8 rue de Penthlèvre, Paris. (M1800)

GRAVES, Margrett Massy, Mrs., M.B.E.; *d.* of Major-Gen. R. A. Napper, of Belleville, New Ross, Co. Wexford; *m.* Anthony Elly, *s.* of A. E. Graves, of Rosbercon Castle, New Ross. *War Work:* Ran Soldiers' Buffet at Rosslare, and also Waterford, during the war, and had egg collection for wounded soldiers. (M8254)

GRAVES, Reginald Coupland, M.B.E.

GRAVES, Robert Ernest, C.B.E., *b.* 22 Dec. 1866; *s.* of James Palmer Graves, J.P., of Waterford, Ireland; *m.* Marion, *d.* of John Burt, of Ventnor, Isle of Wight. *Educ.:* Portora Royal School, Enniskillen. H.M. Inspector of Factories, Home Office, 1890; H.M. Superintending Inspector, 1908; H.M. Chief Inspector, 1920. *War Work:* Director of Substitution in the National Service Department; Deputy Commissioner for Trade Exemptions, Ministry of National Service; Deputy Chairman of Reserved Occupations Committee since its formation in Oct. 1915. *Address:* Cowley Cottage, Cowley, Uxbridge. *Club:* Royal Automobile. (C184)

GRAVES, The Rev. Robert Vernon Ottley, O.B.E.

GRAVES, Robert Windham, C.M.G., O.B.E., *b.* 6 July, 1858; *s.* of late Dr. Charles Graves, Bishop of Limerick, 1866–99; *m.* Bessie Catherine, *d.* of John R. Thomson, of Constantinople. *Educ.:* Marlborough. Temporarily Financial Adviser to British High Commissioner, Constantinople, 1919–20; formerly H.B.M. Consul-General in Crete and Salonica: British Delegate on Macedonian Financial Commission, 1907–09; Adviser to Turkish Ministry of Finance, 1909–13,

and Ministry of Interior, 1914. *War Work:* Accompanied Mediterranean Expeditionary Force to Dardanelles, April, 1915; temporary Staff Captain, July, 1915; with G.H.Q., Mediterranean Expeditionary Force and Egyptian Expeditionary Force, during 1915–18; General Staff Officer, 3rd Grade, Aug. 1918; mentioned in despatches; Chevalier of the Legion of Honour; Officer of the Greek Order of the Redeemer; temporary Lieut.-Colonel, November, 1918, and Deputy Chief Political Officer, Egyptian Expeditionary Force. *Address:* 30, Rue Cabristan, Pera, Constantinople. *Clubs:* Athenæum; St. James': Albemarle. (O2900)

GRAVESON, Major Henry, O.B.E.

GRAVETT, Lieut. George William, M.B.E., M.D., R.A.M.C., I.A.R.O.

GRAY, Ada Leila, Mrs., M.B.E., *b.* 24 Aug. 1875; *d.* of Henry Wilson, of 3, Stanhope Street, Hyde Park, W.; *m.* Charles Harold, *s.* of John Gray, of Melbourne, Australia. *Educ.:* Privately. *War Work:* Four years Lady Superintendent, Army Pay Department, York, 1916–20. *Address:* c/o National Bank, Gloucester Gardens, Hyde Park, W. (M8255)

GRAY, Major Alexander Charles Edward, O.B.E., M.D., *b.* 1864; *s.* of Alexander Gray, of Edinburgh; *m.* Mabel, *d.* of Charles Hastings, of Silsden, Yorks. *Educ.:* Edinburgh Collegiate School, and Edinburgh Univ. Physician. Member Special Neurological Board, Ministry of Pensions. *War Work:* Officer in Charge Medical Division, and Cerebrospinal Fever Wards, Fulham Military Hospital. *Addresses:* 2, Stanhope Gardens, S.W. 7; Little Mead, Holtye, Cowden, Kent. *Club:* Savile. (O1203)

GRAY, Major Alexander Mungo, O.B.E., T.D., T.F. Reserve, *b.* 17 Oct. 1886; *s.* of Robert Gray, O.B.E., of Glasgow; *m.* Frances Sagar, *d.* of Joseph Mullineaux Dewhurst, J.P., of Birkdale. *Educ.:* The Glasgow Academy; The Leys School, Cambridge. Cotton Manufacturer, Messrs. Carrington and Dewhurst, Ltd., Grove Mills, Eccleston, near Chorley, Lancashire. *War Work:* France, Captain, 5th Bn. The Cameronians (Scottish Rifles), T.F., Nov. 1914); invalided, May, 1915; returned to France, May, 1916; assistant to Colonel W. Bromley Davenport, C.M.G., C.B.E., D.S.O., T.D., Labour Commandant, Second Army H.Q.; twice mentioned in despatches. *Address:* 29, Westcliffe Road, Birkdale, Lancashire. *Clubs:* Royal Automobile; Royal Yacht, Hunter's Quay. (O2538)

GRAY, Alice, M.B.E., *d.* of Alexander Gray, M.B., C.M., of Bradford, Yorks. *Educ.:* Girls' Perse School, Cambridge. Managing Director Sefton Gate Nursing Home, Ltd., Llandudno; Administrator of Plas Tudno Hospital for Pensioners. *War Work:* Organiser and Administrator of Plas Tudno Auxiliary Hospital (donor of 50 beds) in 1914, enlarged to 186 beds, 1915; the hospital closed May, 1919, after having 2600 men through it: reopened June, 1919, Pensioners Hospital, 27 beds. *Address:* Sefton Gate, Llandudno. (M3679)

GRAY, Andrew, M.B.E.

GRAY, Lieut.-Col. Archibald Montagu Henry, C.B.E. Major and temporary Lieut.-Col. R.A.M.C.; Great War, 1914–19 (despatches). (C1258)

GRAY, Major Arthur Claypon Horner, O.B.E., R.A.M.C.

GRAY, Charles Harold, M.B.E.

GRAY, Donald Nixon, M.B.E., R.N.

GRAY, Edith Mary Spencer, Mrs., O.B.E., *b.* 19 May, 1866; *d.* of James Leonard Wilson, of Wimbledon; *m.* the Rev. Ernest Awdry, R.D., *s.* of the Rev. Joseph Henry Gray, of Keynsham. *Educ.:* St. Helens, Clifton, Bristol. *War Work:* From 1914–17, Nursing at Plumton House Hospital, Bury St. Edmunds; from 1918–19, Commandant in charge of Personal Department, Suffolk Branch of British Red Cross Society, Bury St. Edmunds. *Address:* Lydgate Rectory, Newmarket. (O10519)

GRAY, Capt. Elliott Cecil George, M.B.E., R.A.S.C.

GRAY, Ethel, C.B.E., R.R.C.; Matron Australian Army Nursing Staff; Great War, 1915–19 (despatches). (C1841)

GRAY, Capt. Frank James, O.B.E., R.A.F.

GRAY, Lieut. George, M.B.E.

GRAY, Major George Douglas, O.B.E., M.D., R.A.M.C.

GRAY, Col. Sir Henry McIlree Williamson, K.B.E., C.B., C.M.G., M.B., C.M., F.R.C.S. (Edinburgh), J.P., *b.* 1870; *s.* of A. R. Gray, of Aberdeen; *m.* Katharine Anne, *d.* of Dr. Rattray, of Aberdeen. *Educ.:* Merchiston Castle School, Edinburgh; Aberdeen University; and in London and abroad. Surgeon, Royal Infirmary, Aberdeen; Consultant Surgeon, Royal Hospital for Sick Children, Aberdeen; J.P. for Aberdeen; served in the South African War, 1899–1901. *War Work:* European War, 1914–19, Consultant Surgeon, B.E.F., France; Consultant in Special Military Surgery, Home Service. *Address:* 34, Albyn Place, Aberdeen. *Club:* Royal Northern, Aberdeen; Caledonian. (K291)

GRAY, Lieut. Herbert Chester, M.B.E., R.F.A.

GRAY, Major Hubert Wilfred, O.B.E.

GRAY, James Carter, O.B.E.

GRAY, Lieut.-Col. John, O.B.E., T.D., R.A.M.C. (T.), *b.* 20 Mar. 1869; *s.* of Alexander Gray, of Inverurie, Aberdeenshire; *m.* Nora, *d.* of William Robinson, M.D., F.R.C.S. (Eng.), of Sunderland. *Educ.:* Grammar School, Aberdeen; Aberdeen University. M.O.H., Stanhope U.D.; Surgeon to Police; Medical Superintendent to the Durham County Sanatorium for Men, at Stanhope. *War Work:* Serving in 6th D.L.I. at the outbreak of hostilities; promoted to Major in Nov.

1914 ; transferred to R.A.M.C. in March, 1915, with rank of Major, in command of 2/3 Northumbrian Field Ambulance ; promoted to Lieut.-Col. in July, 1915 ; served at home in Newcastle, Retford, and Aldershot till Aug. 1916 ; sent out with unit to British Salonica Force, where served till April, 1919 ; on unit being demobilised returned to England, being demobilished in May, 1919 ; mentioned twice in despatches ; received O.B.E. (Military Division) in spring of 1918, and T.D. *Address :* Ury House, Stanhope, Co. Durham.   (O3042)

GRAY, **John,** O.B.E., M.A., B.Sc., J.P., I.C.S., *b.* 26 Feb. 1882 ; *s.* of John Gray, of Arduthie Road, Stonehaven ; *m.* Evelyn Mary, *d.* of William Rhodes James, of Canowie, Coonoor, Nilgiris, India. *Educ :* Gordon's Coll. ; Aberdeen Univ. ; Trinity Coll., Cambridge. Deputy Sec. to Government of Madras, Reforms Department. *War Work :* Assistant Director, and Director of Civil Supplies, Madras. *Clubs :* Madras, Madras ; Ootacamund, Nilgiris.   (O9820)

GRAY, **Lieut.Joseph Alexander,** O.B.E., R.E.

GRAY, **Julie Hunter, Mrs.,** M.B.E. ; *d.* of the late Prof. William Dittmar, LL.D., F.R.S., of Glasgow ; *m.* James Hunter, K.C., *s.* of the late William Gray, of Edinburgh. *Educ :* Glasgow. *War Work :* Organised and ran the canteen of the St. Marylebone War Hospital Supply Depot for 4½ years ; the very considerable profits derived therefrom were spent upon materials for the wounded. *Address :* 17, Chantry House, Eccleston Street, London, S.W. 1. *Club :* Bath.   (M8256)

GRAY, **Percy,** M.B.E., *b.* 6 Sept. 1855 ; *s.* of Thomas Gray, of Orlebar, Old Charlton, Kent ; *m.* Minnie, *d.* of J. B. Sandbach, of Cheadle, Cheshire. *Educ :* Wellington Coll. Indian Civil Service from 1876–1905 ; Registrar, High Court of Judicature for North-Western Provinces ; Magistrate and Collector of various Districts in the United Provinces ; ending as Commissioner of a Division ; obtained Honours in Sanskrit. *War Work :* Instrumental in raising the Bude Volunteer Training Corps in Dec. 1914 ; commanded the Corps from April, 1915, to Feb. 1917, with rank of 2nd Lieut. ; was for 2 years (1917–18) employed by the Admiralty in London in recruiting labour for the Army from the shipyards of Great Britain (not Ireland). *Address :* Orlebar, Bude, North Cornwall. *Club :* Public Schools.   (M1802)

GRAY, **Major Reginald Wentworth,** O.B.E., Leinster Regt., *b.* 24 Feb. 1879 ; *s.* of Sir Reginald Gray, K.C., late Attorney-General of Bermuda (now retired) ; *m.* Edith Frances, *d.* of George Curgenven, late of Westcliffe-on-Sea, Essex. *Educ :* Saltus Grammar School ; Hamilton, Bermuda. *War Work :* France, Dec. 1914 to March, 1915, Training Staff, Etaples ; July–Oct. 1915, with 2nd Battn. ; Nov.–Dec. 1915, 2nd in Command 6th Battn., in Salonica ; Jan.–April, 1915, 2nd in Command 13th Cheshire Regt. on the Somme ; wounded, 5 Sept. 1916 ; right leg amputated, 9 Sept. 1916 ; in Command M.G.C. Section, Rouen, Feb. 1918–May, 1919, with rank of Lieut.-Col. ; mentioned in despatches, Nov. 1918 ; awarded O.B.E., Jan. 1919 ; Commanded Records G.H.Q. France, May–Dec. 1919 ; now employed 2nd in Command, No. 1 Record Office, Hanwell. *Address :* 59, Abingdon Villas, W. 8.   (O5313)

GRAY, **Robert,** M.B.E., LL.B., S.S.C., *b.* 18 May, 1876 ; *s.* of Rev. Robert Gray, of Edinburgh ; *m.* Mary Eliza, *d.* of William Henry Johnson, of Edinburgh. *Educ :* George Watson's Coll., and Edinburgh Univ. *War Work :* Executive Officer, Midlothian Food Control Committee. *Addresses :* 45, George Square, Edinburgh ; 45, Frederick Street, Edinburgh.   (M1803)

GRAY, **Robert,** O.B.E., *b.* July, 1853 ; *s.* of Capt. Alexander Gray, of Irvine and Port Glasgow ; *m.* Jane Ann, *d.* of Joseph Russell, of Port, Glasgow. *Educ :* Greenock Academy. *War Work :* Was chiefly to do with committees, and on an enquiry into the workings and expenses of the Forage Dept., after the Forage Dept. was demobilised ; was Chairman of the Central Council (Civil Supplies) Forage Dept. for Scotland ; and member of Central Council, London. *Addresses :* 94, Hope Street, Glasgow ; Craigrownie, Cove, Dumbartonshire. *Club :* Liberal, Glasgow.   (O391)

GRAY, **Robert,** M.B.E.

GRAY, **Brevet Major Ronald Birdseye,** O.B.E., *b.* 24 March, 1892 ; *s.* of James Gray, of Henley-on-Thames. *Educ :* Taunton. Chartered Accountant ; Partner, firm of G. N. Read, Son, Cocke, and Watson. *War Work :* Assistant Controller, Accounts Dept., Ministry of Munitions ; joined Queen's Westminster Rifles ; transferred Army Pay Dept., Salisbury, Jan. 1915 ; gazetted to R.A.S.C., July, 1915, and transferred to Ministry of Munitions, Oct. 1916. *Address :* 6, River Terrace, Henley. *Club :* Royal Automobile.   (O10521)

GRAY, **Capt. Valentine Edgar,** M.B.E.

GRAY, **Lieut.-Comm. William,** O.B.E., R.N.

GRAY, **William,** M.B.E.

GRAY, **William David,** O.B.E.

GRAY, **Robert Whytlaw WHYTLAW-,** O.B.E., Ph.D.

GRAYNDLER, Edward, O.B.E.

GRAYSON, **Lieut.-Col. Sir Henry Mulleneux,** K.B.E., M.P. (see BURKE'S *Peerage*), *b.* 26 June, 1865 ; *s.* of Henry Holdrege Grayson, J.P., of Liverpool ; *m.* Dora Beatrice, *d.* of Frederick William Henry Harrington, of Liverpool. *Educ :* Winchester College. Member of Parliament for Birkenhead West ; High Sheriff of Anglesey, 1917–18 ; Director of Ship Repairs (Hon.), Admiralty, 1917 ; Chairman of H. and C. Grayson, Ltd., Liverpool ; Director of several Shipping and Shipbuilding Companies ; Commander of the Order of the

Crown of Italy, 1918 ; Officer of the Legion of Honour, 1919 ; Commander of the Order of Leopold II., 1920 ; C.B.E., 1920 ; K.B.E., 1920. *Addresses :* 100, Lancaster Gate, Hyde Park, London, W. 2 ; Ravens Point, Holyhead. *Clubs :* Carlton ; Union ; Conservative, Liverpool.   (K456)

GRAYSON, **Rev. Joseph Watson,** M.B.E., Temp. Chaplain 4th Class.

GREAME, **Sir Philip LLOYD-,** K.B.E., M.C., M.P., *b.* 1 May, 1884 ; *s.* of Colonel Y. G. Lloyd-Greame, of Sewerby, Bridlington (see BURKE'S *Peerage*) ; *m.* May Constance, *d.* of Rev. Ingram Boynton of Barmeston, Yorks. *Educ :* Winchester ; University College, Oxford. Called to the Bar, 1908 ; Conjoint Secretary to Ministry of National Service, 1917–18. *War Work :* Major in the Army, 1914 to 1917 ; Chairman of Permanent Labour Committee of War Cabinet ; War Priorities Committee, 1918 ; Member of Select Committee on National Expenditure ; Select Committee on High Prices and Profits. *Address :* 8, Wetherby Place, South Kensington. S.W. 7. *Clubs :* Carlton ; Oxford and Cambridge.   (K378)

GREATHEAD, **Alice Charlotte, Mrs.,** M.B.E., *b.* 1866 ; *d.* of Dr. Spackman, of Harpenden ; *m.* the late Daniel Charles Robinson, *s.* of — Greathead, of Grahamstown, S. Africa. *Educ :* Dulwich High School ; S. Omer, France. *War Work :* Hon. Sec. for the Red Cross Working Parties of Harpenden ; collected during the last four years of the war an average of over £100 a month, and converted the same, by means of organising working parties, etc., into hospital garments, bandages, etc. *Address :* 6, Carlton Bank, Harpenden. (M8258)

GREATOREX, **Ronald Henry,** M.B.E. Censor, Johannesburg.   (M10258d)

GREAVES, **Constance Mary, Mrs.,** M.B.E., *b.* 26 Jan. 1862 ; *d.* of James Dugdale, of Wroxall Abbey, Warwick ; *m.* Richard Methuen, *s.* of John W. Greaves, of Bericote, Leamington. *War Work :* Organised and equipped Auxiliary Military Hospital in own house, and ran it for over 3 years as Commandant and Matron, 50 beds. *Address :* Wern, Portmadoc. *Club :* Ladies' Athenæum.   (M471)

GREAVES, **Capt. Francis Ley Augustus,** O.B.E., R.A.M.C. (T.).

GREAVES, **Isabel,** M.B.E.

GREAVES, **John Ernest,** C.B.E., J.P., D.L. *b.* 1847; *s.* of John Whitehead Greaves, of Plas Weunydd, Festiniog; *m.* Marianne, *d.* of Edward Rigby, M.D., of Berkeley Square, London. *Educ :* Edinburgh and Oxford. Lord Lieutenant County of Carnarvon ; Chairman Quarter Session, Carnarvonshire ; J.P., D.L., Merionethshire ; Alderman County Council, Carnarvonshire ; President Carnarvonshire Territorial Association. *War Work :* Chairman Carnarvonshire County Tribunal. *Addresses :* Bron Eifion, Criccieth : Glangwna, Carnarvon. *Clubs :* Reform ; Royal Automobile.   (C509)

GREAVES, **Richard Henry,** M.B.E.

GREAVES, **Stanley Haldane Linford,** M.B.E., *b.* 17 June, 1885 ; *s.* of Haldane Greaves, of Hampstead ; *m.* Ada, *d.* of William Bailey, of Purley, Surrey. *Educ :* Banister Court School, Southampton. Chartered Accountant. *War Work :* With Ministry of Munitions from Nov. 1916, to Aug. 1919. *Address :* Winterbourne, Dixon's Green, Dudley.   (M3681)

GREAVES, **Lieut. and Qr.-Mr. Walter,** M.B.E., R.A.M.C.

GREEK, **Elizabeth Constance Vittoria,** M.B.E.

GREEK, **T. Warrant Officer Albert Victor,** M.B.E Royal Indian Marine.

GREEN, **Alexander John,** M.B.E.

GREEN, **Alfred John,** M.B.E.

GREEN, **Alice,** M.B.E.

GREEN, **Capt. Arthur James,** M.B.E., J.P., *b.* 23 Oct. 1856 ; *s.* of the late Benjamin Green, of Grahamstown, S. Africa ; *m.* Frances Emmeline, *s.* of Benjamin Green, of Grahamstown, S. Africa. *Educ :* Bedford ; South Africa (Cape Province). Merchant ; Ex-Mayor of Kimberley ; Chairman, Kimberley Hospital Board ; Director, Building Society ; retired Capt., Kimberley Regt. (Volunteers). *War Work :* Chairman, Governor-General's Fund, and Member, Central Executive ; Member, Recruiting Committee ; Member, Advisory Board ; District Grand Master, Central Division, E.C. (Masonic). *Address :* Box 92, Kimberley, S.A. *Club :* Kimberley.   (M2887)

GREEN, **Arthur Stanley,** M.B.E., M.B., B.S.

GREEN, **Capt. Douglas Harold,** O.B.E., M.C., R.E.

GREEN, **Rev. Earnest William,** O.B.E., M.A., Chaplain to the Forces (3rd Class).

GREEN, **Edward William,** O.B.E., M.I.M.E., M.I.Mech.E., M.I.C.E., M.I.N.A., *b.* 7 Jan. 1873 ; *s.* of Sir Frederick Green, K.B.E., of Hainault Lodge, Essex ; *m.* Janet Pattison Kerr, *d.* of Robert Assheton Napier, of Sauchfield, Glasgow. *Educ :* Harrow, and Vevey, Switzerland. Marine Engineer and Ship Repairer. *War Work :* Fitting out and repairing ships for Admiralty, War Office, and other Government Departments. *Address :* The Priory, Theydon Bois, Essex. *Clubs :* Junior Carlton ; City of London ; R.A.C.   (O392)

GREEN, **Edwin Collier,** O.B.E., M.R.C.S., L.R.C.P., *b.* 30 Sept. 1858 ; *s.* of Samuel G. Green, of Streatham ; *m.* Constance Pamela, *d.* of William Grafton Curgenven, of Derby. Hon. Ophthalmic Surgeon, Derbyshire Royal Infirmary ; Derbyshire Hospital for Sick Children, and Burton-on-Trent General Infirmary. *War Work :* Assistant County Director, South Derbyshire Branch, and Hon. Sec. Derby Borough Division, British Red Cross Society ; Head of War Hospital Supply Depot, Derby. *Address :* 27, Friar Gate, Derby.   (O10522)

GREEN, Elizabeth Selino, Mrs., M.B.E.

GREEN, Ethel Mary, Mrs. Lycett, O.B.E., Lady of Grace of the Order of St. John of Jerusalem ; *d.* of the late Arthur Wilson, of Tranby Croft, Hull (*see* BURKE'S *Landed Gentry*) ; *m.* Edward Lycett Green, *s.* of Sir Edward Green, Bt., of Wakefield (*see* BURKE'S *Peerage*). *War Work* : Vice-President (York District No. 5) St. John Ambulance Association since Aug. 1914 ; Commandant of Nunthorpe V.A.D. Hospital from Oct. 1915 until April, 1919. *Addresses* : Ashfield, York, and Ken Hill, King's Lynn. (O1026)

GREEN, Major Francis Arthur, O.B.E.

GREEN, Sir Frederick, K.B.E., J.P., Knighted 1912 (*see* BURKE'S *Peerage*), *b.* 1845 ; *s.* of Frederick Green, of Princes Gardens, Kensington ; *m.* Alice, *d.* of Sir Daniel Cooper, Bt. *Educ.* : Harrow. Shipowner ; J.P. (Essex) ; High Sheriff 1918 ; Director, G.E. Railway Co., and Suez Canal Co. *War Work* : Military Representative. *Address* : Oaklawn, Wimbledon Park, Surrey. *Clubs* : City of London ; Travellers' (Paris). (K214)

GREEN, Capt. Frederick Michael, O.B.E., *b.* 11 March, 1882 ; *s.* of Michael A. Green, of 26, Upper Hamilton Terrace, N.W. 8. *Educ.* : St. Paul's School, Kensington ; City and Guild's Technical Coll. Chief Engineer, Armstrong, Whitworth Aeroplane Co. *War Work* : Engineer in charge of design at Royal Aircraft Establishment, Farnborough, from 1910 to end of 1917 ; responsible for design of various engines and aeroplanes used in war ; 1917 to end of war Aeronautical Engineer, Messrs. Siddeley Dean Motor Co. *Address* : 26, Upper Hamilton Terrace, N.W. 8. *Clubs* : Royal Automobile ; Royal Aero ; Drapers', Coventry. (O10523)

GREEN, George James, M.B.E., R.N.

GREEN, Lieut. Gerald Gilbert, M.B.E.

GREEN, Henry Martyn, M.B.E., *b.* 3 March, 1874 ; *s.* of William Edwin Green, of Bristol ; *m.* Annie Elizabeth, *d.* of William Eyles, of Wick, nr. Bath. *War Work* : Ministry of Munitions, Central Stores Department. *Address* : Box 582, Bulawayo, Rhodesia. (M8261)

GREEN, Capt. Henry William, M.B.E.

GREEN, Hettie Mary, Mrs., M.B.E., *b.* 20 Feb. 1870 ; *d.* of F. R. Radford, J.P., of Cedar Lodge, The Park, Nottingham ; *m.* John Alfred Henderson, who died 27 April, 1919. *War Work* : Hon. Secretary, General Service Section, Notts. Voluntary Aid Detachments ; Commandant, Notts. 40 V.A.D. *Address* : 37, Newcastle Drive, The Park, Nottingham. (M473)

GREEN, Lieut.-Col. James Alexander, O.B.E., M.C., C.R.A., *b.* 26 May, 1879 ; *s.* of the late James England Green ; *m.* Gertrude Catharine, *d.* of the late Alderman Alfred Taylor, of the Red House, Bath. *Educ.* : George Watson's College Edinburgh. Principal Clerk, Treasury, Pretoria (retired medically unfit, 31 March, 1920). Served in South African War, 1899–1902 (Queen's Medal and 5 clasps). *War Work* : Served with the Transvaal Scottish Regiment (the Atholl Highlanders) from Aug. 1914 to Oct. 1916, in South African Rebellion, in G. S. W. A., and Europe ; also in Europe as Officer i/c South African Records from Oct. 1916 to end of war. *Address* : East Lassintullich Lodge, Kinloch Rannoch, Perthshire. (O393)

GREEN, Major John, O.B.E.

GREEN, Capt. John Alfred Henderson, C.B.E.

GREEN, Sir John Little, Knt. Bach., O.B.E., *b.* 6 Sept. 1862. Director of Rural Industries, Ministry of Agriculture ; projected and carried on the Village Industries movement, giving much evidence on this and other rural topics to Government Committees ; has travelled extensively in search of information of an agricultural and rural character ; a strong believer in the policy of occupying ownership ; worked in a voluntary capacity for the Government in connection with the War from its outbreak to its conclusion, receiving the thanks of the Army Council, the Food Production Department, and the Ministry of Agriculture. *Address* : 2, Belmont Park, Lee, S.E. 13. *Clubs* : Constitutional ; Farmers'. (O1393)

GREEN, Capt. Joseph, M.B.E., M.D., D.P.H., R.A.M.C. (T.).

GREEN, Leslie Benton, M.B.E.

GREEN, Lieut. Lionel Havercroft, M.B.E.

GREEN, Margaret, Mrs., O.B.E.

GREEN, Mary Anne, Mrs., O.B.E.

GREEN, Capt. Robert, M.B.E., M.B., R.A.M.C.

GREEN, Col. Sebert Francis St. David's, C.B.E., M.D., M.R.C.S., L.R.C.P. (London), A.M.S., *b.* 16 Mar. 1868 ; *s.* of the Rev. A. J. M. Green, M.A., of Glencoe, Clevedon, Somersetshire ; *m.* Evelyn Caroline Marion, *d.* of Major Gorges Hely, J.P., D.L., of Foulk's Court, Johnstown, Co. Kilkenny, Ireland. *Educ.* : Christ's Hospital ; St Bartholomew's Hospital ; and Durham University. A.D.M.S. of the 5th Division, Headquarters, Curragh Camp, Co. Kildare, Ireland. *War Work* : Proceeded from India to France in October, 1914, with the Rawal Pindi British General Hospital ; appointed to command that unit in March, 1915, and took it to Mesopotamia in December, 1915 ; appointed A.D.M.S. of Amara, July, 1916, and A.D.M.S. of the Base, M.E.F., in May, 1917 ; appointed O.C. the Prince of Wales' Hospital for Officers at Marylebone in Sept. 1918. *Address* : Bretforton, Moorend Park Road, Cheltenham. *Club* : Services. (C1106)

GREEN, Capt. and Qr.-Mr. Thomas, O.B.E.

GREEN, Thomas Ernest, C.B.E.

GREEN, Major Thomas George, M.B.E., V.D., *b.* 18 Feb. 1865 ; *s.* of Thomas George Green, of Hull, Yorkshire ; *m.* Elizabeth, *d.* of Charles Pearce, of St. John's Wood. *Educ.* :

Government High School, Lahore, Punjab, India. Letterpress and Lithographic Printer ; Superintendent of Government Printing, Central Provinces, Nagpur, India. *War Work* : Capt. Nagpur Volunteer Rifle Corps ; promoted Major on the breaking out of the war ; took over duties of Adjutant in addition to Civil duties ; reorganised the Nagpur Rifles from a Volunteer Corps into the 2nd Nagpur Rifles of the Indian Defence Force ; commanded the Corps from April, 1917, till July, 1918 ; organised and sent three contingents for service in German South Africa. (M2725)

GREEN, Lieut. and Qr.-Mr. William, M.B.E., R.E.

GREEN, Lieut. and Qr.-Mr. William Holmes, M.B.E.

GREEN, William Isaac, M.B.E.

GREEN, Major William Robert, O.B.E., R.A.O.C.

GREEN, Frederick William EDRIDGE-, C.B.E., M.D., F.R.C.S., *b.* 14 Dec. 1863 ; *Educ.* : St. Bartholomew's Hospital ; Durham University. *s.* of St. John's College, Cambridge. Oculist London Pensions Boards. *War Work* : Late Chairman Ophthalmic Board ; Central London Medical Boards, National Service. *Address* : 99, Walm Lane, London, N.W. 2. *Clubs* : Savage ; Wigwam. (C2646)

GREEN, Surg.-Capt. Henry William GORDON-, O.B.E., R.N.

GREEN, Helen Mowbray, Mrs. VINCENT-, O.B.E. ; *d.* of Stanley Kemp-Welch ; *m.* Dr. Vincent Green, of Wimbledon. *War Work* : Founder and Hon. Organiser of the Wimbledon War Workers' Depot, and five Sub-Depots, a voluntary organisation for the manufacture of surgical requisities and comforts for the wounded. *Address* : Greyroofs, Wimbledon Hill. (O10524)

GREENACRE, Walter, O.B.E.

GREENALL, Cyril Edward, O.B.E., J.P., *b.* 9 May, 1866 ; *s.* of Rev. Canon Greenall, of Grappenhall, Cheshire ; *m.* Susannah, *d.* of Sir Gilbert Greenall, Bart., of Walton Hall, Cheshire (*see* BURKE'S *Peerage*). *Educ.* : Malvern. *War Work* : Hon. Director and Chairman of the Kesteven (Lincs) War Agricultural Committee. *Address* : The Manor, Carlton Scroop, Grantham. *Club* : Wyndham. (O10526)

GREENALL, Fred, M.B.E.

GREENALL, Capt. James Macintosh, C.B.E., R.A.S.C.

GREENAWAY, Lieut.-Col. Thomas Joseph, M.B.E. ; *s.* of Thomas Sunday Greenaway, of London ; *m.* Hannah, *d.* of Hartley Duerden, of Nelson, Lancs. Salvation Army Officer. *War Work* : Served on Executive Committees of War Refugees, Soldiers' and Sailors' Families Assn., War Savings, Soldiers' Recreations, Prince of Wales' Fund, etc., at Cardiff ; had charge of all hostels and huts in many of the Base Areas of France, and developed the same kind of buildings in First Army Areas ; also hostels for relatives visiting graves in France and Flanders ; Officer in Charge of Disposals of S.A. huts, etc., with the B.E.F. *Address* : 101, Queen Victoria Street, London. (M8263)

GREENE, John Arch, C.B.E.

GREENE, Paymaster-Lieut. John Wilmer, O.B.E., R.N.R.

GREENE, Kathleen, O.B.E.

GREENE, Major Wilfred Arthur, O.B.E., M.C.

GREENE, William Henry Clayton, C.B.E., M.B. F.R.C.S.

GREENE, Major William Howe, O.B.E., F.R.I.B.A., F.R.A.I.C., *b.* 30 June, 1865 ; *s.* of John Howe Greene, of Liverpool. *Educ.* : Privately, and Liverpool Institute. Articled to Edmund Kirby, F.R.I.B.A., Liverpool, Architect ; engaged in rebuilding large portion of St. John's Newfoundland, after the Great Fire of 1892. *War Work* : Aug. 1914, to Jan. 1916, Musketry Instructor and Chairman of Musketry Committee, Newfoundland Regt., at St. John's, N.F. ; Jan. 1916, to July, 1919, Capt. and Musketry Officer to Royal Newfoundland Regiment in Ayr (Scotland), and Winchester (England) ; mentioned in despatches. *Address* : c/o Bank of Montreal, St. John's, Newfoundland. *Clubs* : Bally Haley County, St. John's, N.F. ; Royal Colonial Institute. (O8027)

GREENFIELD, Edith Mary, M.B.E.

GREENHALGH, Frederick William, M.B.E.

GREENHAM, George Frederick, M.B.E.

GREENHILL, Major Frederick William, O.B.E.

GREENHOUGH, Capt. Arthur Basil Wickham, M.B.E., M.C., R.A.F.

GREENING, Capt. Thomas, M.B.E., R.A.F.

GREENLAND, Dora Mrs., M.B.E.

GREENLAND, William John Steward, M.B.E.

GREENLEES, Capt. Alexander McPhee, O.B.E., M.C.

GREENLEES, Janet Campbell, M.B.E., *b.* 28 March, 1886 ; *d.* of Matthew Greenlees. *Educ.* : St. Leonard's School, St. Andrews, Fife. *War Work* : Administrative Orderly, Endell Street Military Hospital, London ; Welfare Department. No 1 Filling Factory, Leeds ; Q.M.A.A.C. *Address* : Langdale, Dowanhill, Glasgow. *Club* : Kelvin, Glasgow. (M5303)

GREENLESS, Lieut. Robert Wallace, M.B.E., R.G.A. (T.).

GREENLY, Lieut.-Col. John Henry Maitland, C.B.E., B.A., Herefordshire Regt. (T.), *b.* 25 July, 1885 ; *s.* of Edward Howorth Greenly, of Titley Court, Titley, Herefordshire ; *m.* Joan Isabel, *d.* of Owen R. Dunell, of Findon Place, Findon, Sussex. *Educ.* : Charterhouse and Trinity, Oxford. Civil Engineer. *War Work* : Captain 1914 ; Major, 1916, Lieut.-Col., 1917 ; Staff work as Staff Captain and Brigade Major, 1915–16 ; served in the Ministry of Munitions as

Assistant Controller of Inspection of Munitions, 1917–1920. *Address:* Fernacres Cottage, Fulmer, Bucks. *Clubs:* New University; Royal Automobile. (C1591)

GREENSLADE, Capt. Cyrus, O.B.E., Devonshire Regt., *b.* 13 May, 1892 ; *s.* of William Francis Greenslade, of Torquay ; *m.* Edith Margaret, *d.* of James Johnson, of Bath. *Educ.:* Blundell's. *Address:* The Cot, St. Mary Church, Torquay. (O9735)

GREENSLADE, Louisa Grace, Mrs., M.B.E.

GREENSTREET, Lieut.-Col. Reginald Hawkins, C.I.E, O.B.E.

GREENUP, William, M.B.E., *b.* 14 Dec. 1888 ; *s.* of John William Greenup, of Whalley Range, Manchester ; *m.* Dorothy Edna, *d.* of Charles Booth Clegg, of Coulsdon, Surrey. *Educ.:* The Hulme Grammar School, Manchester. Entered the Civil Service in 1908, and appointed to the Admiralty in 1909. *War Work:* Navy shipbuilding contracts. *Address:* Chorlton, Old Lodge Lane, Purley, Surrey. *Club:* Civil Service Rifles. (M8267)

GREENWAY, Bessie, M.B.E., *b.* 1865 ; *d.* of the late John David Greenway. *Educ.:* Privately. *War Work:* Commandant, Wesleyan Hall V.A.D. Kent 80 Hospital, Farnborough, Kent. *Address:* Ardoch, Farnborough, Kent. *Club:* New Century. (M8267)

GREENWELL, Major Sir Bernard Eyre, Bart., M.B.E., *b.* 29 May, 1874 ; *s.* of late Sir Walpole Greenwell, Bart., of Marden Park, Surrey (*see* BURKE'S *Peerage*) ; *m.* Anna, *d.* of Admiral Sir Leopold McClintock, K.C.B. (*see* BURKE'S *Peerage*). *Educ.:* Harrow, and Trinity Coll., Cambridge. *War Work:* Assistant Inspector, Woolwich Arsenal. *Address:* Marden Park, Surrey. *Club:* Carlton. (M5204)

GREENWELL, Lieut.-Col. Charles Okey, O.B.E

GREENWELL, His Honour Judge Francis John, C.B.E., D.L., J.P., *b.* 20 Oct. 1852 ; *s.* of Francis Greenwell, of Durham ; *m.* Constance Frances Sybil, *d.* of His Honour Judge Bradshaw, of Newcastle-on-Tyne. *Educ.:* Durham School ; Balliol College, Oxford. Judge of County Courts, Circuit No 1 (Northumberland, Newcastle-on-Tyne, etc.) from 1895. Chairman of Quarter Sessions, County of Durham. *War Work:* Appeal Tribunal (Military Service Acts) for County of Durham, Deputy Chairman. *Address:* Greenwell Ford, Lanchester, Durham. *Club:* Durham County. (C511)

GREENWELL, Capt. Percy, O.B.E., R.A.S.C., *b.* 20 Oct. 1885. *Educ.:* Royal Grammar School, Newcastle-on-Tyne. *War Service:* Gazetted Feb. 1915 ; served with Expedy. Force in France and Italy ; was Officer Commanding the first troop train of the Italian Expeditionary Force (1917) ; appointed to the Order of the British Empire (3 June, 1918) for "distinguished service in connection with military operations" ; mentioned in despatches by General Plumer. *Address:* 13, Oxford Drive, Waterloo, Liverpool. (O2248)

GREENWOOD, Alfred Craven, O.B.E., J.P., *b.* 26 Aug. 1863 ; *s.* of the late Charles Greenwood ; *m.* Julia Wickham *d.* of C. J. Leigh, of Richmond, Virginia, U.S.A. and New York. *Educ.:* Merchant Taylors' School. Colonial Treasurer of Gibraltar and Chairman of the Sanitary Commission. *War Work:* Control of Food, Feeding Stuffs, Fuel, Water and General Stores for supply of Civil and Floating Population, H.M. Fleet Auxiliaries, Merchant Shipping, Allied and Neutral Men-of-war ; Introduction of Paper Currency. *Address:* The Haven, Gibraltar. *Club:* Junior Carlton. (O2223)

GREENWOOD, Capt. Charles Stainforth, M.B.E.

GREENWOOD, Edwin Climson, O.B.E., M.R.C.S., L.R.C.P., *b.* 1861 ; *s.* of Charles Greenwood, of Ewell, Surrey ; *m.* Marie McIver, *d.* of Capt. William Gill, of New Brighton. *Educ.:* Guy's Hospital. Medical Superintendent, Hospital of St. John's and St. Elizabeth ; Div. Surgeon, Metropolitan Police ; Asst. Commander, Metropolitan Police Reserve. *War Work:* M.O. in Charge, Acheson Hospital for Officers ; Anæsthetist at Hospital St. John's and St. Elizabeth, 1915–18 ; Assistant Commander, Special Constabulary. *Addresses:* Hanover House, St. John's Wood ; Cookham. *Club:* R.A.C. (O11806)

GREENWOOD, Fred, M.B.E., J.P. ; *s.* of Robert Greenwood, of Colne, Lancs ; *m.* Mary, *d.* of James Stansfield, of Haverholt, Colne. *Educ.:* Westminster Training Coll. Schoolmaster. *War Work:* Treas. of District Recruiting Committee ; Hon. Sec. of the Local National War Savings, National Service, and Economy Committees. *Address:* The Crescent, Park Avenue, Nelson. *Club:* Liberal. (M8269)

GREENWOOD, George David, O.B.E., *b.* 9 Nov. 1881 ; *s.* of George David Greenwood, of Canonbury, London ; *m.* Maud Eliza, *d.* of Gane Clark, of Forest Gate and South Africa. *Educ.:* City of London School. Charterhouse. Assistant Accountant-General, Ministry of Shipping. *War Work:* Standard Shipbuilding, and commercial questions affecting Ministry of Shipping. *Address:* Glenesk, Wimbledon Park Road, S.W. 19. (O10528)

GREENWOOD, Josémée Marguerite, M.B.E.

GREENWOOD, Major Jonathan William, C.B.E. Major S. African Forces ; German S.-W. Africa, 1914–15 (despatches), (C752)

GREENWOOD, Margery, Lady, C.B.E., *b.* 1886 ; *d.* of Walter Spencer, of Fownhope Court, Herefordshire ; *m.* Rt. Hon. Sir Hamar Greenwood, Bart. K.C., M.P. (*see* BURKE'S *Peerage*). *War Work:* One of the founders of the Women's Section of the Comrades of the Great War, and first Chairman

of its Headquarters Committee. *Address:* 2, Wetherby Gardens, London S.W. 5. (C2647)

GREENWOOD, Robert Morrell, C.B.E. M.A., LL.M., *b.* 21 Jan. 1868 ; *s.* of John Broadley Greenwood, of Morton Bingley, Yorks ; *m.* Margaret Emma, *d.* of Rev. C. E. Leir, of Ditcheat Rectory, Somerset. *Educ.:* Privately and at Trinity College, Cambridge. Chief Clerk in Treasury, Solicitors' Department. *Address:* 67, Cambridge Terrace, W. 2. *Club:* Oxford and Cambridge. (C512)

GREENWOOD, Capt. T., M.B.E.

GREENWOOD, William, M.B.E., *b.* 1862 ; *s.* of Joseph Greenwood, of Dent, Yorkshire ; *m.* Lily, *d.* of Richard Johnson, of Manchester. *Educ.:* Grammar School, Dent, nr. Sedbergh. Divisional Commander in the Salvation Army. *War Work:* Sec. for the Salvation Army, visiting camps throughout the United Kingdom, railway stations, and piers ; looking after stranded soldiers and helping them through London, providing accommodation for them in S.A. hostels. *Addresses:* 101, Queen Victoria Street, London ; Hotel de Nantes, 46 and 48, Rue St. Severn, Rouen, France. (M1813)

GREENWOOD, William Frederick, C.B.E.

GREER, Mary, Mrs., O.B.E. ; *d.* of the late Gen. G. de la Poer Beresford, of 203, Knightsbridge, London ; *m.* Joseph Henry, Capt. late H.L.I., *s.* of the late Gen. Harpur Greer, The Grange, Co. Tyrone. *Educ.:* Privately. *War Work:* Commandant Officers' Hospital, 17 months ; Head of Irish Red Cross Workrooms, Dublin ; on the Committee of Irish Joint War Committee and the Joint Red Cross of St. John of Jerusalem. *Address:* Curragh Grange, The Curragh, Co. Kildare. (O3736)

GREER, Lieut. Alured Ussher, O.B.E.

GREER, Capt. William Niven, O.B.E., M.B., R.A.M.C. (O9057e)

GREET, Capt. Cecil Ansley, O.B.E.

GREG, Major John Ronald, C.B.E., *b.* 1866 ; *s.* of Albert Greg, of Escowbeck, Caton ; *m.* Esther, *d.* of the late John Fell, D.L., of Flan How, Ulverston. *Educ.:* Rugby, and privately. Justice of the Peace for Lancashire ; Member of the Warwickshire Territorial Force Association ; o/c South Midland (Warwick) R.G.A., 1908–1915. *Address:* 5, Sussex Square, Hyde Park, London, W. 2. *Clubs:* Conservative ; Ranelagh. (C513)

GREG, Capt. Arthur Hyde, O.B.E., M.B., F.R.C.S., R.A.M.C.

GREG, Lieut.-Col. Robert Alexander, C.B.E.

GREGG, Capt. James, O.B.E., R.A.V.C.

GREGORY, Col. Alfred, O.B.E., F.S.I., *b.* 15 June, 1855 ; *s.* of Alfred Gregory. Assistant Director of Fortifications and Works ; Chief Inspector of Works, War Office (ret.). *War Work:* France, 1914–15. *Address:* Walden House, Bellinge Road, Herne Bay, Kent. *Club:* Constitutional. (O1396)

GREGORY, Alfred John, O.B.E., M.D., B.S., J.P., *b.* 30 Aug. 1859 ; *s.* of George Johnstone Gregory, of Studleigh Park, Melbourne, Australia ; *m.* Jennie Hamilton, *d.* of George Talbot James, of Streatham, London. *Educ.:* City of London School, and France and Germany. Permanent head of the Department of Public Health and Local Government, Colony of the Cape of Good Hope (retired). *War Work:* Pathologist and Bacteriologist to the Richmond Park War Hospitals. *Clubs:* Civil Service, Cape Town ; Royal Automobile, London. (O10529)

GREGORY, Alfred Thomas, M.B.E., J.P., *b.* 23 Nov. 1852 ; *s.* of Thomas Gregory, of Bath, Somerset ; *m.* Ada, *d.* of James Barnes, J.P., of Tiverton, Devon. Mayor of Tiverton 1911–18. *War Work:* Chairman of Tribunal, Food Control Committee, Recruiting Committee, War Savings Committee, Soldiers' Hospitality Committee, Refugees' Committee. *Address:* Hillside, Tiverton, Devon. (M8271)

GREGORY, Arthur Lamden, M.B.E.

GREGORY, Capt. Arthur Leslie, M.B.E., M.C., R.A.F.

GREGORY, Basil Francis, M.B.E.

GREGORY, Charles William, M.B.E., *b.* 1892. Civil Servant ; Chief Storekeeper P.W.D. Kenya Colony ; Food Controller, E.A. and Uganda Protectorates. *War Work:* Boer War, 1899–1902 ; Capt., Supply and Transport, 1914. *Address:* Mombasa. *Club:* English (Mombasa). (M6445)

GREGORY, Capt. Ernest Foster, C.B.E., R.N. Great War, 1914–19, as Port Convoy Officer, Gibraltar (despatches). (C2287)

GREGORY, Ethel Amy, M.B.E., *b.* 5 Jan. 1894 ; *d.* of Peter Gregory, of East Ilsley, Berks. *Educ.:* Queen Anne's School, Caversham. *War Work:* Shorthand-typist in Military Intelligence Department, War Office, from 1915. *Address:* 2, Caledonia Place, S.W. 1. (M8273)

GREGORY, Frances Violet, M.B.E.

GREGORY, Com. George, C.B.E., D.S.O., *b.* 1872 ; *s.* of John S. Gregory, of Sandhurst ; *m.* 1904, Margaret Amy, *d.* of Graham Ross, of 29, Huntley Gardens, Glasgow. Com. R.N. ; an Elder Brother of Trinity House ; Great War, 1914–19, as Naval Transport Officer (despatches, Order of the Nile). *Address:* Clifton Down House, Clifton, Bristol. *Club:* Junior Army and Navy. (C2251)

GREGORY, Harry William George, M.B.E

GREGORY, Capt. Hugh Manley, O.B.E., R.A.S.C. (T.).

GREGORY, John, O.B.E., *b.* 7 Dec. 1877 ; *s.* of John Gregory, of Oughtibridge, Yorkshire. (O10530)

GREGORY, John, M.B.E., M.I.M.E., *b.* 28 May, 1871 ; *s.* of Thomas Gregory, of Eccles. *Educ.:* Central School, Manchester. Vice-President, Institution of Mining Engineers,

1915–19 ; President, N. Staffordshire Institute of Mining Engineers, 1914–18 ; President, North Staffordshire Colliery Owners' Association, 1918–20 ; Director of Sneyd Collieries, Ltd., Burslem ; Managing Director, Sneyd Bycars Co., Ltd., Burslem. *War Work :* Charging of shells. *Address :* Melrose, Ellesmere Park, Eccles, Manchester. (M1816)

GREGORY, Eng.-Lieut.-Comm. Leslie, O.B.E., R.N.

GREGORY, Winifred, Mrs. GORDON-, M.B.E. ; *d.* of the late Dr. J. R. Wallace, of Calcutta, and widow of the late Cyril Thornton Jensen, *s.* of Carl Godfrey Jensen, of Calcutta ; *m.* Hubert Clarence Gordon-Gregory, of Calcutta. *Educ. :* Loretto Convent, Calcutta, and privately in England. *War Work :* 3½ years at the War Office (Jan. 1917 to Aug. 1920), clerical work and interviewing officers and ladies who had received war decorations ; sole charge since June, 1918, of the section which makes arrangements for attendances at Investitures. *Address :* 78, Thurlow Park Road, Dulwich, S.E. (M8639)

GREGSON, Alvero Church, M.B.E.

GREGSON, George Woolley, M.B.E.

GREGSON, Major Lancelot Mare, O.B.E.

GREGSON, Thomas, M.B.E.

GREHAN, Major Francis, O.B.E.

GREIG, Major Albert David, O.B.E., M.C., R.A., *b.* 16 Feb. 1882 ; *s.* of Albert David Greig, Accountant and Comptroller-General of Customs, London ; *m.* Mabel Frances, *d.* of Paymaster-in-Chief Henry Vaughan Forrest, R.N. *Educ. :* Dulwich Coll., and St. John's Coll., Oxford. *War Work :* Aug. 1914, to May, 1915, Adjutant, Northumbrian (North Riding) and Durham R.G.A., Heavy Batteries ; May, 1915, to July, 1916, with No 108 Heavy Battery (Ypres) ; July, 1916, to Aug. 1917, Staff Capt., R.A. 5th Army, on the Somme ; Aug. 1917, to March, 1919, D.A.A. and Q.M.G. 5th Army, Passchendaele. *Addresses :* Brigade-Major, Rangoon Brigade, Rangoon, Burma ; c/o Messrs. Cox & Co., London. (O5317)

GREIG, Lieut. Alexander, M.B.E.

GREIG, Lieut.-Comm. Alexander Collie, O.B.E., R.D., R.N.R.

GREIG, Comm. Donald, O.B.E., R.N.

GREIG, Lieut. Donald McNeil, O.B.E.

GREIG, John, C.B.E., ; *s.* of John Greig, of Leith. *Educ. :* George Watson's College, Edinburgh. Partner of firm of Easton, Greig and Co., Steam Shipowners, 30, George Square, Glasgow. *War Work :* Gave voluntary services to Ministry of Shipping, 1917–19 ; acted as Commercial Adviser to Director of Military Sea Transport in 1917 ; thereafter as Deputy Director of the Ship Management with supervision of the overseas tramp tonnage under requisition by the Government. *Address :* Brentham Park, Stirling, N.B. *Clubs :* New, Glasgow ; Junior Constitutional. (C2648)

GREIG, John Isdale, M.B.E., M.A., B.Sc., M.B., Ch.B., *b.* 6 Nov. 1882 ; *s.* of John C. Greig, of Glasgow ; *m.* Jeanie Peden, *d.* of the late Robert Rose, of Bridge of Allan. *Educ. :* Glasgow High School, and Glasgow Univ. Medical Practitioner. *War Work :* R.A.M.C., East African Expeditionary Force. *Address :* 23, Townsend Place, Kirkcaldy. (M4959)

GREIG, Capt. Kenneth Clunie, O.B.E., R.A.O.C.

GREIG, Margaret Eunice, Mrs., M.B.E. ; *d.* of Sir Thomas Storey (*see* BURKE'S *Peerage*), of Westfield, Lancaster, and Plas Nantyr, Chirk ; *m.* James Lewis, *s.* of George Greig, of Eccles. *War Work :* Organiser of work party and of hospital egg collection at Eccles, Kelso ; donor and superintendent of Officers' Convalescent Hospital, Eccles, Kelso. *Address :* Eccles, Kelso. *Club :* Queen's, Edinburgh. (M8276)

GREIG, Phyllis Evelyn, Mrs., M.B.E., *b.* 5 Jan. 1898 ; *d.* of John M. Jackson, Barrister-at-Law, of Lucknow, U.P., India ; *m.* Major John Percival Sellon, R.E., *s.* of late Col. P. H. Greig, R.A., of Winchester. *Educ. :* Lausanne and London. Peace Conference, Paris (Commission on International Labour Legislation), secretarial staff. *War Work :* In connection with the Civilian Internment Camps Committee, Home Office, and the French Aviation Commission in London. *Address :* c/o Lloyds Bank, Ltd., 40, Rosslyn Hill, N.W. 3. (M8277)

GREIG, Major William Best, O.B.E.

GRENSIDE, Thomas Reed, O.B.E.

GRENVILLE, Lieut. the Hon. Harry Nugent MORGAN-, O.B.E.

GRESLEY, Major Herbert Nigel, C.B.E., M.Inst.C.E., M.I.M.E., M.Inst.E.E., Railway Staff Corps, R.E., *b.* 19 June, 1876 ; *s.* of the late Rev. Nigel Gresley, of Netherseal, Leicestershire (*see* BURKE'S *Peerage*). Locomotive Engineer, Great Northern Railway, Doncaster. *War Work :* Organisation of Manufacture of War Munitions in Railway Works at Doncaster. *Address :* Avenue House, Doncaster. (C2649)

GRESSON, Lieut.-Col. Robert Holmes Arbuthnot, O.B.E., *b.* 26 June, 1872 ; *s.* of Major W. H. Gresson, of Fernleigh, Cheltenham ; *m.* Theodora Violet, *d.* of Sir Archdale Earle, K.C.S.I., K.C.I.E. (*see* BURKE'S *Peerage*), late Commissioner of Assam. *Educ. :* Fettes. Head of Firm of Jardine, Skinner & Co., Calcutta ; Sheriff of Calcutta ; Governor, Mayo Hospital ; Committee, General Hospital, and Soldiers' Club, Calcutta ; steward, Royal Calcutta Turf Club ; President, Tillygrange Club ; President, Bank of Bengal. *War Work :* Hon. Treas. Red Cross, Nuneaton ; went to France as Lieut. to an advanced Remount Squadron in Nov. 1914 ; subsequently Adjutant, then Superintendent, of a Squadron in England, finally Assistant Director of Remounts in Egypt and Palestine three times mentioned in despatches.

Clubs : Isthmian ; Caledonian ; Conservative ; Sandown ; Kempton ; Newmarket ; Cheltenham ; Southdown, Lewes. (O7207)

GRETTON, Col. John, C.B.E., V.D., J.P., M.P., *b.* 1867 ; *s.* of the late John Gretton, of Burton-on-Trent ; *m.* Maud Helen, *d.* of 4th Baron Ventry (*see* BURKE'S *Peerage*), of Burnham, Co. Kerry. *Educ. :* Harrow. Chairman, Bass, Ratcliff and Gretton, Ltd., Burton-on-Trent. *War Work :* Commanded 1/6 North Stafford Regt., Oct. 1914, to May, 1915 ; 3rd North Midland Division, Sept. 1915, to April, 1916 ; Chairman, Rutland War Agricultural Committee ; Chairman, Rutland Pensions Committee ; Member of various Government War Committees. *Addresses :* Stapleford Park, Melton Mowbray ; 66, Ennismore Gardens, S.W. 7. *Clubs :* Carlton ; Marlborough ; Beefsteak ; R.Y.S. (C1593)

GRETTON, Capt. Richard Henry, M.B.E.

GREVILLE, Charles Beresford Fulke, Lord, O.B.E., J.P., D.L., late 7th Hussars, *b.* 3 March, 1871 ; *s.* of 2nd Baron Greville (died 1909) (*see* BURKE'S *Peerage*) and Lady Beatrice Violet Graham, *d.* of 4th Duke of Montrose (*see* BURKE'S *Peerage*) ; *m.* 1909, *d.* of late J. W. Peace, of Leybourne Grange, Kent, and widow of Henry Kerr, of New York, U.S.A. A.D.C. to Lord Lieutenant of Ireland, 1892–93 ; A.D.C. to Governor of Bombay, 1900–4 ; Military Secretary to Governor-General of Australia, 1904. *Address :* 27, Belgrave Square, S.W. 1. *Clubs :* Turf ; Carlton ; Bachelors'. (O5319)

GREVILLE, Mabel, Hon. Mrs. Alwyne, O.B.E., *s.* of the late Ernald Smith, of Selsdon Park, Croydon ; *m.* Alwyne Henry Fulke, M.V.O., D.L., 2nd *s.* of 4th Earl of Warwick (*see* BURKE'S *Peerage*). *War Work :* Organiser British Red Cross Society, County of Essex Depot. *Address :* 6, Aldford Street, Park Lane. *Club :* Ladies' Automobile. (O397)

GREY, Charles William, M.B.E.

GREY, John Temperley, O.B.E., M.R.C.S., L.R.C.S.

GREY, Mabel Laura, Countess, C.B.E. ; *o. d.* of 2nd Earl of Selborne, K.G. of Blackmoor, Hants (*see* BURKE'S *Peerage*) *m.* Charles, 4th Earl Grey (*see* BURKE'S *Peerage*). *War Work :* County President, B.R.C.S., Northumberland Branch ; Commandant 1st Northumberland V.A.D. Hospital, 1914–15 ; Member Selection Board V.A.D. Headquarters, 1915–19. *Addresses :* Howick, Lesbury, Northumberland ; 9, Chester Terrace, Regent's Park. *Clubs :* Forum : V.A.D. Ladies'. (C973)

GREY, Mary Lizette, M.B.E. ; *d.* of the late George Grey, J.P., of Milfield, Northumberland. *Educ. :* Privately and in France. *War Work :* Organiser and Commandant of Etal Manor V.A.D. Hospital for four years. *Address :* Milfield, Wooler, Northumberland. (M1817)

GREY, Capt. Percy, M.B.E., I.A.

GREY, Lieut.-Col. Sir Raleigh, K.B.E., C.M.G., C.V.O., M.L.C. Rhodeias, *b.* 24 March, 1860 (*see* BURKE'S *Peerage*) ; *m.* 1901, Mary Isobel, *d.* of C. H. Cadogan, of Brinkburn Priory, Northumberland, and widow of A. H. Browne of Callaly Castle, Northumberland. *Educ. :* Durham ; Brasenose Coll., Oxford. Entered Army 1881 ; Capt. 1885 ; served in the Zulu War, 1888 ; formerly Lieut.-Col. Commanding Bechuanaland Border Police : Matabele War, 1893 (medal) ; accompanied Dr. Jameson into the Transvaal, 1896 ; served South Africa, 1899–1900 (Brevet Major, despatches twice, Queen's Medal, 4 clasps, King's Medal) ; retired 1904. *Address :* Salisbury, Southern Rhodesia ; Loebottle Hall, Whittingham, Northumberland. *Clubs :* Naval and Military ; Windham ; Cavalry. (K319)

GREY, Lady Sybil, O.B.E., *b.* 1882 ; 2nd *d.* of 4th Earl Grey (*see* BURKE'S *Peerage*). (O1398)

GREY, Thomas, O.B.E., J.P.

GREY, Comm. Grenville GRENVILLE-, O.B.E., R.N.V.R.

GRIBBON, Lieut.-Col. Walter Harold, C.M.G., C.B.E., The King's Own Royal Lancaster Regt., has Order of the Star of Roumania with Swords, and Legon of Honour. (C1594)

GRICE, 2nd Lieut. Geoffrey, M.B.E.

GRIDLEY, Sir Arnold Babb, K.B.E. ; *b.* 16 July, 1878 ; *s.* of Edward Gridley, of Cheltenham ; *m.* Mabel, *d.* of Oliver Hudson, of Fakenham, Norfolk. *Educ. :* Bristol Grammar School ; Downs School, Clifton. Assistant Manager, Newcastle Electric Supply Co. and Manager, Cleveland and Durham Electric Supply Co. *War Work :* Controller of Electric Power for Ministry of Munitions. *Address :* Clevelands, Saltburn-by-the-Sea. *Clubs :* Devonshire ; Royal Automobile.

GRIER, Francis, M.B.E.

GRIERSON, Capt. and Quartermaster, Ernest Moore, O.B.E., R.A.M.C. (T.F.), *b.* Aug. 1890. *War Work :* Served with 50th Division throughout the War. (O5320)

GRIERSON, George Arthur, O.B.E., M.B.

GRIERSON, Lieut.-Col., William Wylie, C.B.E., Engineer and Railway Staff Corps, R.E. (T.) ; *s.* of James Grierson, of Kensington. *Educ. :* Rugby. Member of Council of Institute of Civil Engineers ; Chief Engineer Great Western Rly. Co. *War Work :* Attached to War Office, Railway Home Defence. *Addresses :* 38, Hyde Park Gate ; Southcroft, Seaford. *Club :* Junior Carlton. (C185)

GRIERSON, Capt. Philip Francis HAMILTON-, M.B.E., *b.* 15 April, 1883 ; *s.* of Sir P. J. Hamilton-Grierson, LL.D. (*see* BURKE'S *Peerage*). *Educ. :* Edinburgh Academy ; Trinity Coll., Oxford. Advocate ; District Judge, Sudan Civil Service. *War Work :* Served Aug. 1914, to March, 1919, 1/5th R. Scots. Fusiliers, Lieut. ; Staff Capt. ; twice mentioned in despatches ; served Gallipoli, Egypt, Sinai, and Palestine,

Addresses: 7, Palmerston Place, Edinburgh; El Obeid, Sudan. *Club:* University, Edinburgh. (M3180)

GRIEVE, Catherine Ramsay Laburn, Mrs., M.B.E.

GRIEVE, George Butler, O.B.E., *b.* 27 Oct. 1879; *s.* of Thomas Grieve, of Greenock. *Educ.:* Greenock Academy and Holmscroft Public School. Accountant. *War Work:* Hon. Sec. and Treas. of the Greenock Central War Savings Committee; Sec. of the Food Economy Campaign, and organiser of the Publicity Campaign for all the War Loans; various other work. *Clubs:* Royal West of Scotland Amateur Boat; Imperial Union. (O10534)

GRIEVE, Major Richard Albany, O.B.E.,

GRIFFIN, Capt. Arthur Cecil, O.B.E., B.A. *b.* 30 March, 1888; *s.* of Horace William Griffin, of Wallasey, Cheshire; *m.* Beryl Kathleen Ditton, *d.* of John Ditton Flynn, C.I.E., of Bombay. Commissioned in Royal Engineers, 1910; India, as Assistant Engineer, Indian State Railways, 1911–14; recalled home on outbreak of War and appointed Adjutant of Musketry, R.E.; 1916, Mesopotamia, appointed to Railway Directorate; 1917, Deputy Assistant Director of Railways at G.H.Q.; 1918, promoted T. Major; 1919, War Office; twice mentioned in despatches. *Club:* Junior Army and Navy. (O4209)

GRIFFIN, Capt. and Qr.-Mr. Arthur James, M.B.E., R.F.A.

GRIFFIN, Lieut.-Col. Atholl Edwin, C.B.E., D.S.O., *b.* 1877; *s.* of Caleb Nelson Griffin, of Wingham, Ontario; *m.* 1905, Jessie Anne, *d.* of John Murray. *Educ.:* Public Sch., Canada, and at Pennsylvania Coll., Philadelphia. A Civil Engineer, Constructor of Railroads; Lieut.-Col. Canadian Railway Troops; Great War, 1914–19 (despatches). *Address:* Vancouver, Canada. *Club:* Vancouver. (C1555)

GRIFFIN, Capt. Edward Christian, O.B.E.

GRIFFIN, Eugene Patrick, M.B.E.

GRIFFIN, James Henry, M.B.E., *b.* 28 Feb. 1869; *s.* of John Tricket Griffin, of Sandown, I.W.; *m.* Eleanor Amy, *d.* of Alfred Janaway, of Winchester. *Educ.:* St. John's School, Gosport, Hants. Deputy Chief Constable of Hants. (M1819)

GRIFFIN, John, O.B.E., *b.* 3 Dec. 1882; *s.* of Henry Charles Griffin, of Wick St. Lawrence, Somerset; *m.* Muriel, *d.* of Adolphus Taylor, of Worle, Somerset. *Educ.:* Privately. Civil Servant; on Supplementary Establishment, Stores Department, General Post Office; Staff Clerk, War Office; Assistant Controller, Ministry of Munitions. *War Work:* Purchased supplies of clothing, furs, helmets, jerkins, and other miscellaneous textile and leather stores; organised various trades to manufacture special items required for war, and to increase output to meet abnormal demands; organised salvage schemes to recover supplies to supplement raw material required for manufacture of cloth, blankets, leather, paper, cordite, and cellulose. *Address:* 25, Nightingale Lane, Hornsey, London, N. 8. (O10535)

GRIFFIN, William Sashford, O.B.E.

GRIFFITH, Alison Lockhart, Mrs., M.B.E., *b.* 17 Dec. 1876; *d.* of William Long, of Grahamstown; *m.* Charles, *s.* of Charles D. Griffith, C.M.G., of Grahamstown. *Educ.:* Wesleyan High School, Grahamstown. Worked in connection with the Governor-General's Fund for Returned Soldiers; Red Cross, etc. *Address:* Ermelo, Transvaal, South Africa. (M2888)

GRIFFITH, Paymaster-Lieut. Charles Harry, O.B.E., R.N.

GRIFFITH, Lieut.-Col. Edward Hugh, C.B.E., *b.* 2 Sept. 1858; *s.* of the late J. T. Griffith, of 3, Prince's Gate, S.W.; *m.* Marguerite Gwendoline, *d.* of the late Lieut.-Col. Ward Simpson, Royal Irish Regt. *Educ.:* Harrow and Sandhurst. Retired after 25 years service in The Leicestershire Regt.; Afghan, Burmah, South Africa, and Great War. *War Work:* Deputy Assist. Adj.-Gen., G.H.Q. Home Forces, 1914–15; Dept. Assist. Adj.-Gen., Eastern Command, 1916–17; Assist. Adj.-Gen. Training Division Royal Flying Corps, 1917; 1st Class, Staff-Officer, Royal Air Force, 1918–19. *Addresses:* Barton House, Wroxham, Norfolk; Rings Hill, Wouldham, Kent. *Club:* Naval and Military. (2338)

GRIFFITH, Rev. Ellis Hughes, M.B.E.

GRIFFITH, Francis Charles, O.B.E., J.P., *b.* 9 Nov. 1878; *s.* of the late F. R. Griffith, Civil Engineer, P.W.D. India, and of Clevedon, Somerset; *m.* Ivy Morna, *d.* of George Jacob, I.C.S. (retired). *Educ.:* Blundell's. Indian Police; Commissioner of Police, Bombay City. *War Work:* Was in charge throughout the war of the Criminal Investigation Department of the Bombay City Police which was very closely concerned with most of the special duties arising out of the War. *Address:* Head Police Office, Bombay, India. (O8256)

GRIFFITH, Lieut. George Devonald, M.B.E.

GRIFFITH, George Herbert, O.B.E., 3rd Class Order of the Nile, 4th Class Mejidiels, *b.* 14 May, 1877; *s.* of the late Rev. J. W. Griffith, B.A., Pentraeth, Anglesey; *m.* Mary St. Lo, *d.* of the late Capt. W. St. Lo Malet, 8th Hussars. *Educ.:* Oswestry School. Goods Manager, Egyptian State Rlys., Cairo; formerly on the L.N.W. Rly., England. *War Work:* Traffic Superintendent, Egyptian State Rlys, Alexandria; was in charge of railways at Port of Alexandria during the War. *Clubs:* Turf, Cairo; Union, Alexandria. (O1027)

GRIFFITH, Capt. Griffith, M.B.E.

GRIFFITH, Capt. Gronwy Robert, O.B.E., R.W. Fus.

GRIFFITH, Capt. Llewelyn Wyn, O.B.E.

GRIFFITH, Louisa, M.B.E., *b.* 21 April, 1863; *d.* of William Griffith, of Co. Down, Ireland. *Educ.:* Model School, Sligo. *War Work:* Matron, Hackney Infirmary, which had a floor in the City of London Infirmary for two years; Soldiers were treated in this Infirmary for four months. (M1821)

GRIFFITH, Walter Spencer Anderson, C.B.E., M.D., F.R.C.S., F.R.C.P. *b.* 1854; *s.* of the late Rev. John Griffith, LL.D., sometime Head Master of Brighton College; *m.* Isabelle Fairweather, *d.* of William Jackson Kennedy, of Lisaghmore, Kirkcaldy. *Educ.:* Brighton College; Downing College, Cambridge; St. Bartholomew's Hospital. Consulting Obstetric Physician, St. Bartholomew's Hospital. *War Work:* Chairman St. Marylebone War Hospital Supply Depot; Consulting Physician (Army Sisters and Nurses); Queen Alexandra's Military Hospital, Millbank. *Address:* 96, Harley Street, W. *Club:* New University. (C2650)

GRIFFITH, Sir William Brandford, C.B.E., *b.* 9 Feb. 1858; *s.* of the late Sir William Brandford Griffith, K.C.M.G., of Windsor, Barbados, late Governor of the Gold Coast; *m.* Eveline Florence Elizabeth, *d.* of Penrose Nevins, of Settle. *Educ.:* Jersey; Harrison College, Barbados; University College, London. Barrister-at-Law; late Chief Justice of the Gold Coast; has administered the Government of Lagos and held dormant commission to act as Governor of the Gold Coast; President of Special Court for trial of human leopard cases in Sierra Leone, 1912. *War Work:* Special Constable "D" Division, 1914–20; Volunteer, Inns of Court Reserve, 1914–19; Assisted Air Board, 1917; and transferred to Ministry of Pensions, 1917; Legal Adviser to Ministry of Pensions 1918. *Addresses:* 2, Essex Court, Temple, E.C.4; 90 Newman Street, W. 1. *Club:* Constitutional. (C2651)

GRIFFITHS, Arthur, O.B.E., *b.* 22 May, 1875; *s.* of John Griffiths, of Hartland, N. Devon. Accountant, Sec. and Superintendent of East Suffolk and Ipswich Hospital, Ipswich; Director of Felixstowe Gas Co. *War Work:* Acted as Officer in Charge of E. Suffolk and Ipswich Hospital of 300 beds; was responsible for the official work in connection with five other Hospitals; carried out all the work of transfers, furloughs, etc., for those hospitals; made the arrangements for the reception of all convoys of wounded to Ipswich; examined and reported on several buildings for the Government as to their suitability for hospitals; purchased all fittings and equipment for the additional accommodation provided for the wounded and all supplies and provisions for military patients here during the war. *Address:* East Suffolk and Ipswich Hospital, Ipswich. (O10537)

GRIFFITHS, Arthur, O.B.E., *b.* 11 March, 1875. Borough Treas., Camberwell. *War Work:* Hon. Executive Officer, Food Control Committee, H.R.H. Prince of Wales National Relief Committee, Local Central Committee, War Savings; Hon. Accounting Officer, 33rd (Camberwell) Divisional Artillery. *Address:* Town Hall, Camberwell; 70, Burbage Road, Herne Hill, S.E.24. (O10538)

GRIFFITHS, Lieut.-Col. Charles, O.B.E., 16th Cavalry, Indian Army, *b.* 19 Oct. 1862; *s.* of Col. Leonard Griffiths, R.A., of Sandhurst; *m.* Winifred, *g.-d.* of Sir Alfred Hickman (*see* BURKE'S *Peerage*), of Wightwick, Staffordshire. *Educ.:* Honiton and Sandhurst. *War Work:* Deputy Assistant Director of Remounts, Western Command. *Address:* Bryn-y-Mor, Penysarn, Anglesey. *Club:* Junior Army and Navy. (O7209)

GRIFFITHS, Charles Bedlington, O.B.E.

GRIFFITHS, Lieut.-Col. Cyril Tracy, C.M.G., O.B.E., *b.* 1873; *s.* of the late Charles Cecil Griffiths, of Sydney, N.S. Wales; *m.* Eugénie, *d.* of R. T. Kirby, of Sydney, N.S. Wales. *Educ.:* privately. Farmer and grazier; Lieut.-Col. Australian Forces; served in S. Africa, 1901–2 (Queen's medal with three clasps, King's medal with two clasps); during Great War, 1916–18, as an A.A.G. (despatches). *Address:* Sydney, N.S. Wales. (O7956)

GRIFFITHS, Lieut. David John, M.B.E.

GRIFFITHS, David Llewellyn, O.B.E., *b.* 20 May, 1880; *s.* of James Griffiths, of Penarth, South Wales; *m.* Winifred Rose, *d.* of the late George Gwinnell, of Cheltenham. *Educ.:* Monmouth Grammar School. Solicitor and Clerk to Council, Aldershot; Hon. Solicitor and Treas. Aldershot War Pensions Committee; Clerk Aldershot Old Age Pensions Committee. *War Work:* Hon. Sec. and Treas. Soldiers' and Sailors' Families Association at Aberdare and Aldershot; Hon. Sec. and Organiser Aberdare and Aldershot Patriotic Funds; Hon. Sec. and Tresa. Aldershot War Pensions Committee; Hon. Sec. Belgian Refugees Fund, Aberdare; Executive Officer, Aldershot Food Control Committee. *Address:* St. Catherines, Aldershot. *Club:* Camberley Heath Golf. (O10540)

GRIFFITHS, George Edward, M.B.E.

GRIFFITHS, Griffith Nathan, M.B.E., *b.* 11 April, 1856; *s.* of John Griffiths, of Mydrim, Carmarthen; *m.* Ellen Ann, *d.* of Eli Billingham, of Gloucestershire. *Educ.:* National School. Railway Inspector; Member of the Llanelly Borough Council. *War Work:* Military and National Service Representative for the Llanelly District during the war. *Address:* 11, Copper Works Road, Llanelly. (M8279)

GRIFFITHS, Helen Maud, Mrs., M.B.E.

GRIFFITHS, Herbert Richard, O.B.E., 7 Nov. 1864; *s.* of Richard Griffiths, of Bristol; *m.* Olive Minnie, *d.* of A. W. Harrison, of Bristol. *Educ.:* Bristol Grammar School.

Divisional Superintendent (Operations) Great Western Railway. *War Work :* Worked in connection with the Railways. *Address :* 19, Henleaze Gardens, Durdham Downs, Bristol. *Club :* Bristol Liberal.

GRIFFITHS, Ida Mildred Mary, M.B.E., *b.* 6 Dec. 1882 ; *d.* of the late Vincent Griffiths, C.B., of Twickenham. *Educ. :* Privately. Organiser to the Women's Branch National Unionist Assocn. ; Member of the Middlesex War Pensions Committee, and Local War Pensions Committee. *War Work :* Entire care of Soldiers' and Sailors' Families and Dependants from 1914 ; District Head Soldiers' and Sailors' Families Assocn., and District Head Soldiers' and Sailors' Help Society. *Address :* 4, Syon Row, Twickenham. *Club :* Forum.
(M8280)

GRIFFITHS, Marion, Mrs., M.B.E. ; *d.* of Edwin Colman, of W. Didsbury ; *m.* Thomas Percy, *s.* of Thomas Griffiths, of Didsbury. *War Work :* Devoted Service on behalf of the Patients of the Nell Lane Military Hospital, W. Didsbury, Manchester. *Address :* Westover, W. Didsbury, Manchester.
(M8281)

GRIFFITHS, Major Noël Marshall, O.B.E., *b.* 27 Dec. 1875 ; *s.* of Vincent Griffiths, C.B., of Yelverton Lodge, Twickenham ; *m.* Kathleen Charlotte, *d.* of Ernest Edye, of Syon, East Budleigh, Devon. *Educ. :* Winchester. Chartered Accountant ; District Auditor under Ministry of Health. *War Work :* Commissioned R.A.S.C., May, 1915 ; with 31st Divisional Train in France, March. 1916 to Aug. 1917 ; transferred to War Office, Deputy Assistant Director of Quartering. *Address :* 5, Wallands Crescent, Lewes. *Club :* Sports.
(O7210)

GRIFFITHS, Sarah, Mrs., M.B.E.

GRIFFITHS, Sarah Gilbert, Mrs., O.B.E.

GRIFFITHS, Brig.-Gen. Thomas, C.M.G., C.B.E., D.S.O. Col. and T. Brig.-Gen. Australian Imperial Forces ; Great War, 1914–19, at Administrative Headquarters (despatches).
(C844)

GRIFFITHS, Thomas Henry, O.B.E., *b.* 13 Nov. 1872 ; *s.* of Thomas James Griffiths, of 30, Hill Avenue, Worcester ; *m.* Annie Alexandra, *d.* of William Emus Smith, of Worcester. *Educ. :* St. John's School, Worcester. Assistant to the City Engineer, Worcester, until the outbreak of war ; resigned office to devote time to War Pensions work. *War Work :* Hon. Sec. Soldiers' and Sailors' Families Assocn. for City of Worcester, since South African War in 1900 ; Hon. Sec. fo City of Worcester Soldiers' and Sailors' Families Relief Committee since Aug. 1914 ; Sec. to City of Worcester War Pensions Committee. *Address :* Kingscliffe, 15, Battenhall Road, Worcester.
(O10452)

GRIFFITHS, Rev. Trevor, O.B.E., *b.* 28 Feb. 1871 ; *s.* of the Rev. F. W. Griffiths, Vicar of Coalpit-Heath, Bristol ; *m.* Emily Louisa, *s.* of H. E. Bennett, J.P., of Sparkford Hall. *Educ. :* Hereford Cathedral School ; Worcester Coll. Oxford (M.A.) ; Lichfield Theolog. Coll. Rector of Sparkford, 1899. *War Work :* Temp. C.F. 1916 ; served in France with 41st C.C.S. 2½ years ; also with British Interned in Switzerland ; mentioned in Army Routine Orders (5th Army), Feb. 1918, for "Act of Courage." *Address :* Sparkford Rectory, Somerset.

GRIFFITHS, Walter James, M.B.E., *b.* 1857. Assistant Manager and Chief Draughtsman, Royal Carriage Dept., Woolwich Arsenal. *Address :* 228, Burrage Road, S.E.18.
(M8283)

GRIFFITHS, Q.M.S. William Crynant, M.B.E., R.E.

GRIFFITHS, Lieut.-Col. Charles du Plat RICHARDSON-, D.S.O., O.B.E., *b.* 1855 ; *s.* of the late Lieut.-Col. T. Richardson-Griffiths, of Armagh ; *m.* 1894, Florence F., *d.* of H. Schwale, of Lymm, Cheshire. *Educ. :* Merchiston. Entered 13th Regt. 1875 ; Capt. Bedfordshire Regt. 1885 ; Major Gloucester Regt. 1896 ; Hon. Lieut. Col. 1917 ; ret. 1903 ; Afghan War, 1879–80 (medal) ; S. Africa, 1900–2, present at relief of Kimberley and battles of Paardeberg and Driefontein (mentioned in despatches) ; served in Great War, 1914–19.
(O7631)

GRIGGS, Capt. Alfred George, M.B.E., R.A.F.

GRIGOR, Lieut.-Col. William Ernest, O.B.E.

GRIGSON, Lieut. Thomas Reginald, O.B.E., R.E.

GRIMBLY, James Thomas, M.B.E., *b.* 5 June, 1874 ; *s.* of Thomas Philip Grimbly, of Hackney, N.E. ; *m.* Eliza Jane, *d.* of Francis Carter, of Owlesbury, Hants. Civil Servant. *War Work :* Supervising Clerk in War Office ; engaged in recruiting work during first period of war ; afterwards in Military Secretary's Dept., War Office. *Address :* Cooma, 17, Bockhampton Road, Kingston-on-Thames.
(M482)

GRIMBLY, Richard Henry, O.B.E., M.R.C.S.

GRIME, Joseph Crookes, M.B.E., F.I.S.A., J.P., *b.* 21 Sept. 1874 ; *s.* of Joseph Grime, J.P., of Manchester ; *m.* Florence Mary, *d.* of John Hall, of Enniskillen. *Educ. :* Manchester Technical School. Deputy Chairman Manchester Watch Committee ; Chairman Discharged Prisoners Aid Society ; Chairman Borstal Committee, H.M. Prison, Manchester ; Board of Managers, Ancoats Hospital, Babies Hospital ; Governor Fylde Reformatory and Holmes Chapel Reformatory ; Member of Manchester City Council for nine years. *War Work :* Commander Special Police ; Member of Manchester Tribunal, Red Cross Society, St. John's Ambulance, etc. *Addresses :* 36, Peter Street, Manchester ; Sandhurst, South Shore, Blackpool. *Clubs :* Arts ; St. Anns Old Links ; Aldwych, etc.
(M8284)

GRIMES, John, M.B.E., *b.* 10 Nov. 1859 ; *s.* of Wm. Howlett Grimes, of Bubbenhall, Warwickshire ; *m.* Mary Alice, *d.* of John Alfred Baker, of Kenilworth. *Educ. :* Privately, and Kenilworth and All Saints' School, Bloxham. *War Work :* Hon. Treas. of St. Pierre Auxiliary Red Cross Hospital for Privates, and Clyne House Auxiliary Red Cross Hospital for Officers, Cardiff ; also for Glamorgan Branch, B.R.C.S., Eastern Division, Cardiff.
(M3685)

GRIMMOND, Margaret Isabella, Mrs., M.B.E.

GRIMSDALE, Blanche Emma, Mrs., M.B.E., *b.* 2 Aug. 1856 ; *d.* of Edgar Webster, of Chester ; *m.* Arthur Robins, *s.* of Daniel Grimsdale, Uxbridge. *Educ. :* Chester. *War Work :* Gerrards Cross War Hospital Supply Depot, in connection with 2, Cavendish Square, April, 1915, to Dec. 1918. *Address :* Ravenscroft, Gerrards Cross.
(M8285)

GRIMSDALE, William, M.B.E.

GRIMSDALL, Lieut. Henry, M.B.E., *b.* 21 Sept. 1855 ; *s.* of Thomas Newberry Grimsdall, of Kensington ; *m.* Ellen Matilda, *d.* of William Deane, of Albion Grove, Barnsbury, N. *Educ. :* St. Thomas Charterhouse School. High Bailiff, Shoreditch County Court of Middlesex. *War Work :* Joined Special Constabulary as Sub-Inspector Aug. 1914, a V.A.D. Company 1915, which subsequently became part of Middlesex R.A.M.C. (V) Eastern Command, Volunteer Ambulance Convoy. This Corps did all the work of Transfer of Wounded solders for four Base and eighty Auxiliary Hospitals ; promoted from private to Adjutant and was actually on duty for five years and a half. *Address :* 22, The Avenue, Hornsey, N. ; *Club :* Hornsey Constitutional.
(M483)

GRIMSDICK, Capt. John Dennin, O.B.E.

GRIMSEY, John Robert, M.B.E., J.P.

GRIMSHAW, Wilfred, O.B.E.

GRIMSHAW, Capt. William Edwin, O.B.E., R.A.

GRIMSLEY, Ellen Maud, M.B.E., *b.* 1885. *Educ. :* Wyggeston Girls' School, Leicester. Secretarial work. *War Work :* Secretary to the County Director for Leicestershire ; and Commandant of Leicester, V.A.D. Reserve. *Address :* 13, Evington Street, Leicester.
(M484)

GRIMSTON, Lieut.-Col. Lionel Augustus, C.I.E., O.B.E.

GRIMWADE, Isabella Emily, Mrs., M.B.E.

GRIMWADE, Surg.-Lt.-Comm. Sidney Wilfred, O.B.E., M.B., R.N.

GRIMWOOD, Lieut.-Col. James, D.S.O., O.B.E., *b.* 1872 ; *s.* of the late G. A. Grimwood, of Shern Hall, Walthamstow ; *m.* 1917, Amy Mander, *d.* of G. Mander Allender, and widow of Lieut. C. E. Fenwick, R.N. *Educ. :* Forest School, Walthamstow ; Marburg Univ. Germany ; R.M.C. Head of the firm of Grimwood, Roberts and Co. (Incorporated Accountants), of Coleman Street, E.C. ; Lieut.-Col. S. Wales Borderers ; Great War, 1914–17 (despatches) ; appointed Adviser on Cost Accounts to Financial Sec. to War Office, 1917. *Address :* The Old Ferry House, Wraysbury, Bucks. *Clubs :* City Carlton ; Bath.
(O3738)

GRINDLEY, Major Hugh Henry, O.B.E., R.F.A. (T.F.)

GRINLING, Major William James, C.B.E., (retired) Engineer and Railway Staff Corps, *b.* 7 Aug 1855 ; *s.* of William Grinling, of Crouch End ; *m.* Eleanor Alice, *d.* of R. C. Sutton, of Nottingham. *Educ. :* Privately. Chief Traffic Manager of the Great Northern Railway up to August, 1919 ; Director East Lincolnshire Railway. *War Work :* In addition to special railway work during the war, served on a number of Committees connected with Railway Executive Committee and Ministry of Munitions. *Address :* Carisbrooke, Coolhurst Road, Crouch End, N.8.
(C2652)

GRINSELL, Capt. George Herbert, O.B.E., R.F.A. (T.).

GRINSELL, Lieut.-Col. Jack, O.B.E., S.A.M.C.

GRINSHED, Major Harold, O.B.E.

GRIPPER, Lieut.-Col. Basil Jasper, O.B.E., V.D., J.P., *b.* 24 July, 1861 ; *s.* of Jasper Gripper, of Hertford ; *m.* Georgina Agnes, *d.* of N. Tarral, M.D., of Havre, France. *Educ. :* Chatham House, Ramsgate. Secretary Territorial Force Association, Herts. *Address :* Hartham House, Hertford.
(O1401)

GRISS, Lieut.-Col. John Ellis, O.B.E., R.N.

GRIST, Capt. William Alfred, M.B.E.

GRITTON, John, M.B.E.

GROGAN, Brig.-Gen. Edward George, C.B., C.B.E., J.P., *s.* of George Grogan, J.P., Carabineers and 7th Royal Fusiliers, of Seafield, Co. Dublin ; *m.* Ida Georgina Mary, *d.* of F. R. Forman, of Craig-Park, Midlothian. *Educ. :* Cheltenham College. Served in the 42nd Royal Highlanders (The Black Watch) in expedition to Coomassie 1873–74 (wounded at battle of Amoaful, medal and clasp) ; South African Campaign, in Command of the 1st Bn. The Black Watch (despatches, medal with 4 clasps, C.B.) ; Colonel Commanding Black Watch Brigade, Territorial Force ; retired 1907 ; appointed to command a Brigade with temporary rank of Brigadier-General, 16 Nov. 1914. *Address :* Torrevagh, St. Andrews. *Clubs :* United Services ; Royal and Ancient Golf.
(C2653)

GROGAN, Commander Edward Harry, O.B.E., R.N., *b.* Nov. 1876 ; *s.* of Brigadier General E. G. Grogan, C.B., C.B.E., of Torrevagh, St. Andrews ; *m.* Elizabeth Beckett, *d.* of T. Clayhills-Henderson, of Invergowrie, Forfarshire. *Educ. :* Stubbington and "Britannia." Egyptian Government Director Ports and Lights Administration, holds rank of Bey ; Gambria, 1894 ; East Coast 1895, wounded ; China 1900. *War Work :* Naval Transport Service and Ministry of Shipping.

1914–1919. *Address:* Port House, Arsenal, Alexandria, Egypt. *Club:* United Service. (O907)

GRONOW, Albert George, C.B.E.

GROOM, Major Edmond Arthur Hudson, O.B.E., *b.* 14 Feb. 1876 ; *s.* of E. C. Groom, of Ashwicken Hall, Norfolk ; *m.* Jennie, *d.* of W. R. Taylor, of South Cave, E. Yorkshire. *Educ.:* Haileybury. *War Work:* 10 months in England with 10th Norfolk Regt. and 1st (R.) Garrison Bn. Suffolk Regt.: France with 11th Royal Berks Labour Bn., Oct. 1916 to Sept. 1917 ; Commanded 36th Labour Co., Sept. 1917 to Jan. 1919 ; when Co. disbanded. All service in France in forward area ; after armistice commanded 319 P.O.W. Co. *Address:* Heacham, King's Lynn, Norfolk. (O2545)

GROOM, Professor Percy, M.B.E., M.A., D.Sc., F.L.S., *b.* 12 Sept. 1865 ; *s.* of F. R. Groom, J.P., of Hereford ; *m.* Mary, *d.* of George Harrop, of Horbury (Yorks). *Educ.:* Universities of Birmingham, Bonn, Cambridge. Professor of Technology of Woods and Fibres, Imperial College, South Kensington ; Consultant on Timber Research to the Department of Scientific and Industrial Research. *War Work:* The Technical Expert on Timber to the Air Ministry ; Voluntary work for various Government Departments (Foreign Office, Home Office, Board of Trade, War Office and Admiralty). *Addresses:* North Park, Gerrards Cross, Bucks ; Imperial College, South Kensington. *Club:* Savile. (M487)

GROOM, Susannah, M.B.E., *b.* 4 Sept. 1863 ; *d.* of the late William Groom, of Boston. *Educ.:* Ingelow House, High School, Boston. Principal of small Private School. *War Work:* from Aug. 1914 to Oct. 1914 was preparing hospitals ; Dec. 1914 was put in charge of Allan House Auxiliary Hospital and worked it as Commandant until it was closed, June, 1919. *Address:* 18, Carlton Road, Boston, Lincolnshire. (M486)

GROOME, Capt. Auckland William Wollaston, M.B.E., *b.* 6 March, 1885 ; *s.* of W. Wollaston Groome, M.D., of Suffolk House, Surbiton ; *m.* Margaret Grace, *d.* of W. H. Cleburne, of Summerstown, C. Cork. *Educ.:* Charterhouse. *Address:* Charlton Hill, Wroxeter, Shrewsbury. *Club:* Royal Air Force.

GROOME, Lieut. Frederick Thompson, O.B.E., R.N.R.

GROOME, Capt. Walter, M.B.E., R.A.M.C.

GROSE, Fred, M.B.E., J.P., *b.* 1858 ; *s.* of Joseph Grose, of St. Austell ; *m.* Gertrude, *d.* of Wm. Matthews, L.C.C., of Anerley, S.E. *Educ.:* Privately. Hon. Inspector Army Contracts. *Address:* Chesham Park, Anerley, S.E. (M1824)

GROSE, Woodman Cole, M.B.E., *b.* 23 Feb. 1859 ; *s.* of John Grose, of Appledore, St. Ives, Cornwall ; *m.* Clara, *d.* of Robert Loosemore. *Educ.:* Wadham House, Liskeard ; Devon County School. Civil Servant. *War Work:* Worked as Staff Clerk in the Finance Department of the War Office. *Address:* 159, Gleneldon Road, Streatham, S.W.16. (M3687)

GROSER, Phyllis, M.B.E. For work in connection with Queen Alexanrda's Hospital. (M10320)

GROSVENOR, Caroline Susan Theodora, Hon. Mrs. Norman Grosvenor, C.B.E., *b.* 15 June, 1858 ; *d.* of Rt. Hon. James Stuart Wortley ; *m.* the late Hon. Norman Grosvenor, *s.* of Lord Ebury (*see* BURKE'S *Peerage*). Chairman Women's Farm and Garden Union ; Vice-Chairman Society for Oversea Settlement of British Women. *War Work:* Helped to start Women's National Land Service Corps (first organised body of women to work on the land). *Address:* 30, Upper Grosvenor Street, W. *Club:* Ladies' Empire. (C2399)

GROSVENOR, Lady Mabel Florence Mary, M.B.E., younger *d.* of 4th Earl of Erne ; *m.* Lord Hugh William Grosvencr, 1st Life Guards (killed in action, Oct. 1914), *s.* of 1st Duke of Westminster. *Address:* 9, Southwick Crescent, W. (M3698)

GROSVENOR, Rosamund Argharad, Lady Henry, C.B.E., *d.* of the late Edward Lloyd, of Castella, Glamorgan ; *m.* 1st Edward Seymour Greaves, of Glen Etive, Argyll, and Watchbury, Warwickshire ; 2ndly, Lord Henry Grosvenor (died 1914), 3rd *s.* of 1st Duke of Westminster (*see* BURKE'S *Peerage*). *Address:* Quenby Hall, Leicestershire. (C186)

GROUNDS, Thomas Collier, M.B.E., *b.* 8 Nov. 1864 ; *s.* of Frederick William Grounds, of Wisbech ; *m.* Kate Annette, *d.* of Miles John Dobson, of Greenwich. *Educ.:* Chapel Royal, St. James's. Partner, Hogg and Robinson, Admiralty Shipping Agents ; Organist, St. Olave's, Hart Street, Mark Lane, E.C. *War Work:* In connection with position as Shipping Agents for British Admiralty, and special work for the French and Italian Governments. *Address:* 2, Devon Mansions, Lewisham, S.E. (M1825)

GROVE, Brig.-Gen. Edward Aickin William Stewart, C.B., C.B.E., (late the Queen's Own, Royal West Kent Regt., J.P., Surrey, *b.* 4 April, 1852 ; *s.* of Capt. Edward Grove, of Dolgnog-Machynlleth ; *m.* Georgina Annie, *d.* of Rev. G. Atkinson, of Kettlethorpe, Lincs. *Educ.:* Bedford School. Lieut. 2nd Royal Cheshire Militia, 1872 ; Lieut. 97th Regiment, 1873 ; Captain, The Queen's Own (Royal West Kent Regt.), 1881 ; Brevet Major, 1882 ; Major, 1886 ; Lieut.-Col., 1896 · Brevet-Col., 1900 ; served in the Transvaal Campaign 1881 ; Egyptian Expedition 1882 ; present at the battles of Kassassin and Tel-el-Kebir ; and was Assistant Provost Marshal to 2nd Division (medal with clasp, bronze star, and Brevet of Major) ; with Soudan Exhibition 1884–85, as D.A.A. and Q.M.G. (clasp) and in South Africa 1899–1901, in command of the 2nd Bn. The Queen's Own (Royal West Kent Regt.) and afterwards of Krugersdorp sub-district, (despatches twice, C.B., medal with four clasps) ; Graduated at Staff College 1883 ;

was D.A.A. and Q.M.G., Canada, 1885–87 and D.A.A.G. E. District 1887–88, ; C.S.O., Scottish District 1902–5 ; Brig.-General Commanding 8th Brigade, 3rd Division 1905–9 ; retired 1909. *War Work:* Inspector Lines of Communication, 1914 ; Commanding Halton Park Camp ; raised seven Foreign Service Garrison Bns. ; Commanding No. 7 District 1916–18. *Addresses:* 135, Whitehall Court, S.W. 1 ; Oakhill Court, Bucknell, Salop. *Clubs:* Junior United Service ; Flyfishers' ; R.A.C. (C1595)

GROVE, Frank, O.B.E.

GROVES, Charles Nixon, C.B.E., M.A., M.D., Bch. ; Oxford, *b.* 16 Feb. 1871 ; *s.* of Charles Groves, of Sherwood ; *m.* Frances, *d.* of Dr. F. M. Millar, J.P., of London. *Educ.:* Bradfield ; Oxford ; The London Hospital. *War Work:* Medical Officer in charge of the Darell Hospital for Officers, London ; twice mentioned in lists of Secretary of State for War. *Address:* 72, Bishops Road, W. 2. (C2654)

GROVES, Herbert Austen, C.B.E., LL.B. (Lond.), *b.* 1880 ; *s.* of the late Rev. W. H. Groves. Solicitor and Parliamentary Agent ; Home Office (Prisoners of War Branch), 1915–17 ; and member of Committee on Proposals for Employment of Prisoners of War 1916–17 ; Admiralty 1917–19 ; and Assistant Secretary (Board) 1919. *Clubs:* St. Stephen's ; Royal Automobile. (C974)

GROVES, Mary, Mrs., M.B.E.

GRUBB, Charles John Edward, M.B.E.

GRUBB, Major John James, O.B.E., *b.* 11 Feb. 1859 ; *s.* of the late Sergt-Major John Grubb, of the School of Musketry, Hythe, Kent ; *m.* Lily Kate, widow of Joseph Leigh, of Streatham. *Educ.:* Cheriton, Kent. Joined 2nd Bn. 2nd Queen's Regt., 1877 ; served at Army Headquarters, India, 1890–93 ; commissioned Quartermaster, 1st Batt. The Queen's W. Surrey Regt. Feb. 1893 ; employed at War Office, Oct. 1903 ; retired July, 1906. Continuing in employment at War Office ; appointed Deputy-Assistant Director, Nov. 1917. *War Services:* N.-W. Frontier of India, 1897–98 ; Malakand Operations in Bajour and in the Mammed Country (Medal with Clasp) ; Tirah, 1897–98, Capture of the Sampagha and Arkunga Passes ; reconnaissance of the Saran Sar and action of Nov. 1897 ; Operation against the Khuni Khel Chamkains ; Operations in the Bazar Valley, 1897 (Clasp) ; The Great War, 1914–18 ; employed on Staff at War Office ; brought to notice of Secretary of State for valuable work ; promoted Major June, 1916. (O7215)i

GRUMBAR, Julian Charles, M.B.E., Chevalier Ordre de Leopold, *b.* 19 June, 1880 ; *s.* of Alphonse Grumbar, of Sarreguemines, France ; *m.* Elizabeth Frances, *d.* of the late Harris Lebus. Member Committee Société Française de Bienfaisance. *War Work:* Member of Executive War Refugees Committee ; Hon. Attaché Belgian Consulate ; 2nd Lieut., Buffs. *Addresses:* 58, Kensington Court, W. ; Bolebroke Cooden, Sussex. *Clubs:* City Carlton. (M1826)

GRUNDY, Allan Wilson, M.B.E.

GRUNDY, Emily Susan, Mrs., M.B.E., *b.* 17 April, 1871 ; *d.* of Walter Baily, of Hampstead, N.W. ; *m.* Edmund Fordham, *s.* of Edmund Herbert Grundy, of Bury, Lancs., and Royston, Herts. *Educ.:* North London Collegiate School. *War Work:* Work in connection with the meeting and accommodation of British Refugees from Germany, Austria, Russia, and Belgium ; and also Hon. Sec. of a Hostel for Belgian Refugees. *Address:* 14, Thurlow Road, Hampstead, N.W. (M8291)

GRUNDY, Lily, M.B.E.

GRUNDY, Robert Taylor, O.B.E., 3rd Class Order of, the Nile, *b.* 19 Nov. 1866 ; *s.* of Frank Grundy, of Bury, Lancs, and Sherbrooke, P.Q., Canada. *Educ.:* Christ College, Brecon, South Wales. Deputy Traffic Manager of the Egyptian State Railways. *War Work:* Railway Officer in Charge at Suez in 1914, arranging despatch by rail of the Indian Army as they arrived ; afterwards stationed at Ismailia, up to 1917, in charge of movement of all troops in the Suez Canal zone, between Port Said, Ismailia, Suez, etc. *Address:* Gezira House, Cairo. *Clubs:* Turf, and Gezira Sporting, Cairo ; Union and Sporting, Alexandria. (O11819)

GRUNDY, Samuel Percy, O.B.E., *b.* 20 Sept. 1880 ; *s.* of Albert Walker Grundy, of Oak Lodge, Prestwich, Manchester *m.* Sarah Eleanor, *d.* of Henry Russell Greg, of Lode Hill, Styal. *Educ.:* Shrewsbury 1894–9 ; Balliol, 1899–1902. Gen. Secretary, Manchester City League of Help till 1919 ; Hon. Secretary, Manchester Committee for National Savings ; Hon. Secretary, National Council of Social Service. *War Work:* Hon. Secretary and Voluntary Workers Sub-Committee, Manchester Committee, National Relief Fund ; Hon. Secretary, Manchester War Savings Committee. *Address:* West Wood House, Bagley Wood, Oxford. *Club:* Cavendish. (O1403)

GRUNER, Lieut. Harold Eric, M.B.E., R.N.V.R.

GRYLLS, Charles John Tench Bedford, C.B.E.

GRYLLS, Lieut.-Col Glynn, O.B.E., R.A.

GUAN, Lee Choon, M.B.E.

GUAYS, Lieut.-Col. Francis Lewis, O.B.E., *b.* 1880 ; *s.* of V. Guays, of East Grinstead ; *m.* Madeleine Lucy, *d.* of J. O. Fison, J.P., of Stutton Hall. *Educ.:* King's College, London. Contractor, Farmer, and Planter. *War Work:* Despatch rider, Transport and Labour Directorate, Mesopotamia and Persia. *Address:* 31, Queensborough Terrace, W. 2. (O4210)

GUBBINS, Helen Hartopp, Mrs., M.B.E., *b.* 1870 ; *d.* of Walter Barnard Byles, of 3, Prince's Gardens, London ; *m.* Joseph Hartopp, D.L., *s.* of Thomas Wise Gubbins, of Dunkathal,

Co. Cork. *Educ.:* Privately. *War Work:* Organised and worked in conjunction with her sister-in-law, Miss Maud Gubbins, the Needlework Department for the Co. Cork Red Cross Depot at 11, King Street, Cork, from May, 1915, to March, 1919. *Address:* Lota Park, Glanmire, Co. Cork. *Club:* Victoria. (M3689)

GUBBINS, Capt. Martin Nepean Traill, O.B.E., M.C., R.A., *b.* 16 April, 1891; *s.* of F. C. Gubbins, of Nonington, near Dover; *m.* Joan Audrey, *d.* of J. Proctor Humphris, of Kingston Hill. *Educ.:* Cheltenham Coll. and Royal Military Academy, Woolwich. Assistant Military Secretary to His Excellency The Governor and C.-in-C., Malta. *War Work:* Proceeded to France Aug. 1914; Staff Capt. R.A. 2nd Army Corps, 1916 to Dec. 1916; Staff Capt. R.A. 9th Corps, Jan. 1918, to July, 1918; Staff Officer to Inspector-General of Artillery. *Address:* The Palace, Malta. *Clubs:* Army and Navy; Union, Malta. (O7216)

GUBBINS, Matilda Ida, Mrs., M.B.E.

GUBBINS, Lieut.-Col. Stamer, D.S.O., O.B.E., *b.* 1882; *s.* of Evans Hartopp Gubbins, of Milltown, Co. Limerick. *Educ.:* Church of England Grammar School, Melbourne. Entered Roy. Fusiliers (City of London Regt.), 1902; Capt. 1912; Major, 1914; served during S. African War, 1901–02, as Lieut. Victorian Mounted Rifles (Queen's medal with five clasps); during Great War, 1914–17, as Lieut.-Col. Comdg. a Batn. of his Regt., and as D.A.A.G. (despatches) (O6129)

GUDE, Capt. Gerald, O.B.E., R.A.F.

GUERIN, Major and Qr.-Mr. Charles Joseph, O.B.E., R.A.S.C.

GUEST, Capt. the Right Hon. Frederick Edward, P.C., C.B.E., D.S.O., M.P., *b.* 14 June, 1875; *s.* of 1st Baron Wimborne, of Wimborne, Dorset (*see* BURKE'S *Peerage*); *m.* Amy, *d.* of Henry Phipps, of New York. *Educ.:* Winchester. *War Work:* Capt. 1st Lifeguards; White Nile, 1900 (despatches); South Africa, 1901–2; A.D.C. to F.M. Sir John French, 1914–16 (despatches); East Africa, 1916–17 (despatches twice), D.S.O. *Address:* Templeton, Priory Lane, Roehampton. *Club:* Turf (C1259)

GUEST, Capt. the Hon. Lionel George William, O.B.E.

GUGGISBERG, Decima Moore, Mrs. H. (Decima Moore), C.B.E., Medaille de Reconnaissance; *d.* of Edward Henry Moore, of Brighton; *m.* Brig.-Gen. Frederick Gordon, C.M.G., D.S.O, Legion d'Honneur, Governor and C.I.C. Gold Coast Colony, *e. s.* of the late Frederick Guggisberg, of Toronto. *Educ.:* Boswell House College, Brighton. *War Work:* Constant and consequentive work from Aug. 1914 to May, 1920; originator and a founder of the Women's Emergency Corps on 9 Aug. 1914; the first organisation of women to replace men. from which sprang the Women's Volunteer Reserve. the Women's Legion, the National Food Fund, and the Women's Emergency Canteen, working in Paris, Compiegne, Chauny, etc.; founder and organiser of the West African Chop Box Fund; Directrice de la Cantine at Depot des Eclopes at Conty, Compiegne, Corneuve, Rambervelles, Vosges; Nurse at Hospital Militaire 103, Amiens, France; Member of Committee British Women's Hospital; one of the founders and hon. secretaries, British Army and Navy Leave Club, Paris; founder of Leave Club Emergency Unit; originator, founder and hon. director-general of British Empire Leave Club, Cologne, Germany. *Address:* Government House, Accra, Gold Coast Colony. *Club:* Ladies' Army and Navy. (C514)

GUILD, James Bennett, M.B.E.

GUILFORD, Rev. Canon Edward, O.B.E., Kaisir-i-Hind Medal, with Bar, *b.* 25 Nov. 1853; *s.* of Henry Guilford, of Portsea, Hants; *m.* Elizabeth Rose, *d.* of George Augustus Grimwood, of Suffolk. *Educ.:* Brighton; C.M.S. Coll., Islington, London. Missionary to the Sikhs of the Punjab, Church Missionary Society; President of Municipal Committee, Tarn Tàran; Member of Amritsar District Board; Chairman of Punjabi New Testament Revision Committee. *War Work:* Capt. Indian Army Reserve Officers, 1918; Recruiting, Propaganda, Supplying Literature and Comforts for the English and Indian Troops on Active Service; Chaplain to the 71st Punjabi Christian Regiment. *Address:* Tarn Tàran, Amritsar District, Punjab. (O8257)

GUILFORD, Hannah, M.B.E.

GUILFOYLE, Sqdn.-Leader, William James Yule, O.B.E., M.C., R.A.F.

GUILLEMARD, Bernard James, O.B.E., M.D.

GUINNESS, Lieut.-Col. Earnest Whitmore Newton, O.B.E.

GUINNESS, Florence, Mrs., M.B.E.

GUINNESS, M.B.E., Kenelm Edward Lee, M.B.E.

GUINNESS, Capt. Owen Charles, O.B.E., 2nd Bn. Worcestershire Regt., *b.* 14 Sept. 1894; *s.* of Col. C. D. Guinness, of Clermont Park, Dundalk. *Educ.:* Uppingham. *War Work:* B.E.F., France from Aug. 1914 to Oct. 1919. *Address:* Clemont Park, Dundalk. *Club:* Naval and Military. (O5321)

GUISE, Major Anselm Verner Lee, O.B.E.

GUISE, Harry Rivett Cecil, O.B.E.

GULL, Q.M.S. Alfred Henry, M.B.E., R.E.

GULL, Sir William Cameron, Bt., O.B.E., J.P., C.C. (*see* BURKE'S *Peerage*), *b.* 6 Jan. 1860; *s.* of William Wittrey Gull, of Brook Street, Grosvenor Square. *Educ.:* Eton and Christ Church, Oxford. Alderman, Berks C.C.; Chairman Public Health Committee and of the Berks and Bucks Joint Sanatorium. *War Work:* Bradfield Local Tribunal; later appointed Military

Representative for the Borough of Reading; Bradfield Local Food Control Committee; Berkshire Pensions Committee. *Address:* Frilsham House, Yattendon, Newbury, Berks. *Clubs:* Athenæum; R.A.C. (O1405)

GULLETT, Capt. Sydney Wolton, O.B.E., A.I.F.

GULSTON, Agneta Annie Justina Stepney, M.B.E.; *d.* of George Stepney Gulston, of Derwydd, Llandebie. *Educ.:* Privately. *War Work:* Hon. County Sec., Carmarthenshire Branch B.R.C.S.; Commandant Llandilo Women's V.A.D., Carmarthen 8 B.R.C.S. *Address:* Derwydd, Llandebie, Carmarthenshire. *Clubs:* Ladies' Park; Carmarthen and County Ladies'. (M3690)

GUMBLEY, Major Douglas William Mew, O.B.E.

GUMMER, Capt. Philip Edward, M.B.E., R.E.

GUNDILL. William Edward, O.B.E., *s.* of W. N. Gundill, of Dewsbury. *Educ.:* Batley Grammar School. General Manager, Henry Cullingworth and Sons, Wool and Rag Auctioneers, Dewsbury. *War Work:* Assisted to organise Army Clothing Depot, Dewsbury, 1916; organised and managed Government scheme for return of tailors' cuttings (khaki, etc.), and issue of same for re-manufacture, 1916–18; Officer i/c Salvage Inspectorate (War Office), 1918–19 (unpaid); Expert Adviser (Textiles) to Disposals Board, 1919–20; superintended disposal of surplus army woollen rags, 1919. (O402)

GUNN, Alexander, M.B.E.

GUNN, Donald Benjamin, M.B.E., R.A.F.

GUNN, Edith Milner, M.B.E.

GUNN, Frank Lindsay, C.B.E. (C3195)

GUNN, George, M.B.E., M.D., F.R.C.S.E., *b.* 1879; *s.* of George Gunn, of Melbourne, Australia; *m. d.* of U. A. Ritson, D.L. of Durham. *Educ.:* Melbourne, Australia, and Edinburgh Univ. Local Physician, Royal Liverpool Children's Hospital, Heswall. *War Work:* Medical Officer Parkgate Military Hospital, and Neston Red Cross Hospital. *Address:* Neston. Cheshire. (M8295)

GUNN, James, M.B.E., *b.* 18 Feb. 1869; *s.* of John Gunn, of Golspie, Sutherland; *m.* Ellen, *d.* of the Rev. G. Wallace Home, of Bangalore. *Educ.:* Glasgow Academy. Superintending Clerk. *War Work:* India Frontier, 1897–98; War of 1914–19, employed with General Headquarters, 3rd Echelon, B.E.F. France; mentioned in despatches; M.S.M.; Indian Medal, 1895, one clasp; 1914–15 Star; British War Medal; Victory Medal; L. S. and G. C. Medal; Territorial Efficiency Medal. *Address:* 14, Eton Place, Hillhead, Glasgow, W. (M4476)

GUNN, Capt. and Qr.-Mr. James Robert, O.B.E., A.I.F.

GUNN, Capt. John, M.B.E.

GUNN, Col. John Alexander, C.B., O.B.E.

GUNNELL, Capt. Dudley, O.B.E.

GUNNION, Thomas, M.B.E.,

GUNSON, Alice Maud, Mrs., M.B.E.

GUNSON, James Henry, C.B.E., *b.* 1877; *s.* of William Gunson, of Aside, Lancashire; *m.* 1905, Jessie, O.B.E., *d.* of James Wiseman. Mayor of Auckland. *Address:* Auckland, New Zealand. (C1914)

GUNSON, Jessie, Mrs., O.B.E.; *d.* of James Wiseman; *m.* James Henry, *s.* of William Gunson, of Aside, Lancashire. *Address:* Auckland, New Zealand. (O939)

GUNTER, Lieut.-Col. Clarence Preston, O.B.E., R.E.

GUNTER, Eustace Edward, O.B.E., M.I.E.E., F.R.G.S., *b.* 30 Sept. 1873; *s.* of Lieut.-Col. Edward Gunter, *p.s.c.*, late of Clifton, Bristol; *m.* Harriett Lawrence, *d.* of the late John Little, M.D., of Singapore. *Educ.:* Dover College; King's College School; City and Guilds Engineering College. Appointed Assistant Superintendent, Indian Telegraph Dept. in August, 1893; transferred to Indo-European Telegraph Department and appointed Director, Persian Gulf Section; ex-officio in political charge and J.P. for Makran Coast; in charge telegraph in November, 1912; communications between India and Mesopotamia during War; raised Telegraph Company of Sind Volunteer Rifles; Captain in 23rd Sind Rifles, Indian Defence Force. *Address:* Woodlands, Bonus Road, Karachi, India. *Clubs:* Sind, Karachi; East India United Service. (O2069)

GUNTHER, Lieut. Frederick Albert, M.B.E.

GUNTON, Ernest, M.B.E.

GUNTON, George, M.B.E.

GUNTON, Major Herbert Charles, M.B.E. R.E.

GURDON, Ada, Mrs., O.B.E.

GURLEY, Major John Herbert, O.B.E. R.A.M.C.

GURLING, Albert Edwin, M.B.E. (M10248h)

GURLING, James, M.B.E., *b.* 11 April, 1889; *s.* of John Gurling, of London; *m.* Eliza, *d.* of George Bartlett, of London. *Educ.:* Elementary. *War Work:* Inspection of Aeronautical Material. (M1831)

GURNEY, Catherine, O.B.E., *b.* 19 June, 1848; *s.* of Joseph Gurney, of Tyndale Lodge, Wimbledon. *Educ.:* Privately. Founder (1883), till 1917, Hon. Secretary, from 1917 President, of International Christian Police Association; Founder and Hon. Secretary of Police Convalescent Homes, Hove, Sussex and Harrogate, Yorks; Founder and Hon. Sec. of Provincial Police Orphanages at Redhill, Surrey and Harrogate, Yorks. *War Work:* Equipped and carried on Auxiliary Military Hospitals at Hove, Sussex and Harrogate, Yorks, from November, 1914 to January, 1919. *Addresses:* 1a Adelphi Terrace, London W.C. 2; Woodlands, Redhill, Surrey; St. Andrews, Harrogate. *Club:* The New Alliance. (O3789)

GURNEY, Cecily Jane, M.B.E., *b.* 1884; *d.* of J. H. Gurney, J.P., F.Z.S., etc., of Keswick Hall, Norwich (*see*

BURKE'S *Landed Gentry*). *Educ.:* Privately. *War Work:* 3¼ years nursing and administrating Auxiliary Hospital of 36 beds under the British Red Cross Society. *Address:* Keswick Hall, Norwich. *Club:* Ladies' Park. (M8278)

GURNEY, Lieut. John Cedric, O.B.E.

GURNEY, Mabel Annie, Mrs., M.B.E.

GURNEY, Sarah Gamzu, Mrs., M.B.E., *b.* 1879; *d.* of Walter Garstang, of Blackburn; *m.* Robert, *s.* of John Gurney, of Norwich. *Educ.:* Somerville Coll., Oxford Late Commandant. *War Work:* Commandant, V.A.D. Hospital at Stalham; Vice-President, Tunstead and Happing Division of B.R.C.S. *Address:* Ingham Old Hall, Stalham, Norfolk. *Club:* Forum. (M3691)

GURTEEN, Horace, M.B.E., *b.* 1880; *s.* of Jabez Gurteen, J.P., of Sturmere, Essex; *m.* Margaret Annie, *d.* of the late Rev. James Calvert Fowler, of Nottingham. *Educ.:* Bedford. Manufacturer. *War Work:* British Red Cross Ambulance Convoy. *Address:* Eastcotts, Kedington, Suffolk. (M8299)

GUSH, Comm. Alfred William, C.B.E. R.N.

GUSH, Eng.-Comm. Arthur Sydney, R.N.

GUTHRIE, Capt. Alan, M.B.E., *b.* June, 1881; *s.* of James Guthrie, of Northallerton. *Educ.:* North Eastern County School, Barnard Castle, and Yorkshire Coll., Leeds. Leather Expert to Madras Government, 1911. *War Work:* Two years in Mesopotamia with Madras Artillery Volunteers and as Embarkation Officer, June, 1915, to July, 1917; Deputy Controller Hides, Madras June, 1917, to July, 1919. *Address:* Department of Industries, Madras. (M6152)

GUTHRIE, Brenda, M.B.E.

GUTHRIE, Capt. Sir Connop, K.B.E., Grenadier Guards (S.R.), *b.* 1882: *m.* Ella, *d.* of the late Sir Malcolm McEacharn, of Galloway House, Wigtownshire. Special Representative of British Ministry of Shipping in U.S.A., 1916–19; Member of the United States Government Shipping Control Committee, 1918; served in the Great War, 1914–15 (wounded); Chevalier Legion d'Honneur; Commendatore, Crown of Italy; Distinguished Service Medal (U.S.A.). *Address:* 36, Charles St., Berkeley Square, W.1. *Clubs:* Guards'; Pratt's; Ranelagh. (K76)

GUTHRIE, Lieut.-Col. Robert Lindsay, O.B.E.

GUTHRIE, Lieut.-Col. Robert Lyall, O.B.E., M.A., M.D., Barrister-at-Law, R.A.M.C. (T.); *s.* of James Guthrie, of Hope Park, Broughty Ferry, Scotland. *Educ.:* Edinburgh Univ. Coroner for the Eastern District of the County of London. Medical Officer, Law Union and Rock Insurance Co.; Member of Council London and Counties Med. Protection Society, and Assurance Medical Society; late Deputy-Coroner N.E. London. *War Work:* Served in France as M.O. 7th London R.F.A., 1915; Registrar and subsequently Officer in Charge Fulham Military Hospital, Brevet-Major, 1917; Officer in Charge and Commandant Belmont Prisoners of War Hospital, 1917–19. *Addresses:* 39, Carlyle Square, S.W.; 180, Fleet Street, E.C. *Club:* St. Stephen's. (O7218)

GUTHRIE, William Alexander, M.B.E.

GUTSCHE, Col. Clemens, C.B.E. Col. S. African Forces; German S.-W. Africa, 1914–15 (despatches). (C753)

GUTTERIDGE, Lieut. Leonard, M.B.E., I.A.R.O.

GUY, Capt. Edward Martin, O.B.E.

GUY, Capt. Percy Claude, M.B.E.

GWATKIN, Capt. Archibald James, O.B.E.

GWATKIN, Capt. Reginald Dugleby Stapleton, M.B.E., *b.* Oct. 1883; *s.* of the late Alexander George Stapleton, of Ceylon; *m.* Kathleen Maude, *d.* of Fred Paddock, F.G.S., of Cookhouse, Cape Colony. South African Permanent Artillery. *War Services:* South African War; Great War; campaigns in German S.-W. Africa; Palestine; Mesopotamia (Dunster force); Caucasus (acting C.R.A. Baku). *Address:* Roberts Heights, Pretoria. (M4276)

GWYER, Capt. Percy Edward, M.B.E., R.M.A.

GWYN, Mrs. MOORE–, O.B.E., *b.* 6 May, 1851; *d.* of William Jephson; *m.* Joseph Edward, who assumed the additional surname of Gwyn, *s.* of Joseph Moore. *War Work.* Had charge of 3 Hospitals, Red Cross and Pensions in Neath; Vice-President of S. and S. Families Association, Pen-Committee and Vice-President of the Red Cross in Glamorgan. sions *Address:* Dyffryn, Neath, S. Wales. (O1408)

GWYNNE, Clement Wansbrough, O.B.E., B.A., J.P., I.C.S., *b.* 3 July, 1883; *s.* of C. T. Gwynne, of Leek, Staffordshire; *m.* Kathleen Hawker, *d.* of Dr. E. O. Kingdon, of Holsworthy, Devonshire. *Educ.:* Newcastle, and St. John's Coll., Oxford. Member of the Indian Civil Service; Deputy Secretary to the Government of India, Home Department. *War Work:* Commission in the I.A.R.O., T. Major; Assist. Sec. Army Department, Government of India; Sec. Indian Soldiers' Board; Hon. Sec. Imperial Indian Relief Fund. *Address:* The Park, Simla. *Club:* United Service (Simla). (O9025)

GWYNNE, Major Frederick William Davies, O.B.E.

GWYNNE, Rt. Rev. Bishop Llewellyn Henry, C.M.G., C.B.E., D.D., *b.* 1863; *s.* of Richard Gwynne, formerly of Kilvey, near Swansea. *Educ.:* Swansea Grammar School; St. John's Hall, Highbury. Was Curate of St. Andrew's, Nottingham, 1889–92; V. of Emmanuel, Nottingham, 1892–99; appointed Archdeacon of Sudan and Suffragan Bishop in Khartum, 1908; Great War, 1914–19; Deputy-Chaplain General (mentioned in despatches). *Address:* The Clergy House, Khartum. *Clubs:* Westminster; National. (C1260)

GWYNNE, Neville G., C.B.E., M.A., Cambridge, *b.* 2 Aug. 1868; *s.* of the late James E. A. Gwynne, of Folkington Manor,

Sussex; *m.* Isabel Violet, *d.* of the late Admiral Charles Wake (*see* BURKE'S *Peerage*, Wake, Bt.) *Educ.:* Lancing College; Pembroke College, Cambridge. President of London and District Engineering Employers; Chairman of the British Engineers' Association; Chairman Engine Section of Society British Aircraft Constructors; Managing Director of Gwynnes Engineering Co., Ltd.; Chairman of Hammersmith Branch, London. *War Work:* War Pensions Committee; President Hammersmith Branch of Federation of Demobilised Soldiers and Sailors. *Clubs:* Carlton; Oxford and Cambridge; Bachelors'. (C2656)

GWYTHER, Louise Banks, Mrs., M.B.E.

GYE, Irene Alice, M.B.E., W.R.N.S.

GYLES, John William, M.B.E.

GYNGELL, Major and Qr.-Mr. George Henry, O.B.E. *War Work:* Served during the period of the Great War with the 3rd Batt. Dorset Regt. at Weymouth; assisted in the formation of two Garrison Battalions for service overseas, and in the establishment of a Depot of the A. I. F. at Weymouth. *Address:* Charminster, Dorchester. (O7219)

HACK, Rev. Robert, M.B.E., M.A., S.C.F., *b.* 21 April, 1868; *s.* of George Robert, of Melton Mowbray; *m.* Bertha, *d.* of Henry Davies, J.P., of Carus Lodge, Lancaster. *Educ.:* Melton Mowbray and Univ. Coll., Durham. Vicar of St. Paul's, Slough; formerly missionary of Church Missionary Society in India; Hon. Chaplain, Government of India. *War Work:* Chaplain to Forces, 1915–16, B.E.F., France; C.F. at G.H.Q. St. Omer, and later of the 19th Infantry Brigade, 2nd Division; 1916–19, Exped. Force, British East Africa, and C.F. at Maktau, Dar-es-Salaam, Nairobi, and Nakuru; 1919, S.C.F. Shorncliffe Command; 1920, S.C.F. Warley, Essex. *Address:* St. Paul's Vicarage, Slough, Bucks. (M4960)

HACKER, Lieut. Douglas Walter Stewart, M.B.E., R.G.A. (S.R.)

HACKER, 2nd Lieut. William Henry, M.B.E., R.E.

HACKETT, John, M.B.E., *b.* 5 Aug. 1872; *s.* of William Hackett, of Kensington; *m.* Edith Constance Louisa, *d.* of George Moore, of Wareham, Dorset, and Fulham. *Educ.:* Birkbeck Coll., London. Chemist. *War Work:* In charge of accounts for Medical, Surgical, X-Ray, Electro-Medical, Dental, Pathological, and Bacteriological Supplies for the Army in the Army Medical Department (A.M.D. 3) of the War Office since 22 Feb. 1915; Editor of the official "Priced List of Medical Stores." *Address:* 168, Holland Road, Kensington, W. (M8301)

HACKETT, Major and Qr.-Mr. Patrick, O.B.E.

HACKETT, Col., Robert Isaac Dalby, C.B.E., M.A., M.D., *b.* 31 March, 1857; *s.* of Thomas Hackett, J.P., of Castle Armstrong, King's Co.; *m.* Evelyn Mary Wynne, *d.* of Evan Jones, of Chester. *Educ.:* Chesterfield School; Birr and Queen's University, Ireland. Retired officer of Army Medical Service. *War Work:* Senior Medical Officer, Dorset Training Area and of Portland Defences and official visitor of Auxiliary Hospitals. *Address:* Ocala, Cheltenham. *Club:* The New, Cheltenham. (C1597)

HACKETT, William Jennens, M.B.E., F.S.I., F.A.I., F.L.A.A., *b.* 16 June, 1877; *s.* of William Hackett, of St. George's, Shifnal, Salop; *m.* Florence Margaret, *d.* of Robert Adams Hall, of Newcastle-on-Tyne. *Educ.:* Privately, U.S.A., and Rutherford Coll., Newcastle-on-Tyne. Chartered Surveyor and Valuer; Articled to James Scott, F.S.I., of Newcastle-on-Tyne, and in 1910 joined the staff of the Valuation Department of the Board of Inland Revenue. *War Work:* Hon. Sec. of Newcastle-on-Tyne Local Central Organising Committee for War Savings, from 1916–19; assisted to form and control about 370 War Savings Associations with approximate membership of 50,000, and apart from continuous routine work largely organised and carried through: War Loan Campaign in 1917; Autumn Campaigns in 1916 and 1917; Tank Week, Business Men's Week, and War Weapons Week in 1918. During this period raised upwards of £45,000,000 for war purposes from Newcastle's population of approximately 272,000. Was for some time a member of the Food Committee, and in June, 1917, had the honour of being presented to their Majesties the King and Queen. *Addresses:* 25, Coquet Terrace, Newcastle-on-Tyne; 32, West Street, Gateshead. *Clubs:* Valuers'; Pen and Palette; City of Newcastle Golf; Chartered Surveyors' (M1833)

HACKING, Major Arthur, O.B.E.

HACKING, Capt. Douglas Hewitt, O.B.E., M.P., *b.* 4 Aug. 1884; *s.* of J. Hacking, J.P., C.C. of Clayton-le-Moors; *m.* Margery Allen, *d.* of H. H. Bolton, J.P., of Newchurch-in-Rossendale. *Educ.:* Giggleswick and Manchester University. Member of Parliament for Chorley Division of Lancashire; Chairman Rishton Urban District Council; Vice-Chairman Accrington Unionist Association. *War Work:* Commission East Lancashire Regiment and Mechanical Transport, attached to Heavy Artillery; joined up Aug. 1914, 2 years in France. *Address:* 20, Arthur Road, Wimbledon, S.W. 19. *Clubs:* Constitutional; St. Stephen's; Wimbledon Royal. (O2546)

HADCOCK, Lieut.-Col. Sir (Albert) George, K.B.E., F.R.S., late R.A., late Lieut.-Col. Commanding 1st Northumbrian Brigade, R.F.A. (T.F.), *b.* 1861; *m.* d. of Lieut.-Gen. J. W. Rideout, I.S.C. Director of Sir W. G. Armstrong Whitworth & Co., Ltd.; Director of Thames Ammunition Works; Associate Member of Institute of Naval Architects. *Address:* Elswick Works, Newcastle-on-Tyne. (K144)

HADDAD, Capt. Gabriel, O.B.E.

HADDEN, Frederick Weston, M.B.E.

HADDO, George Gordon, Earl of, O.B.E., J.P. D.L., L.C.C., *b.* 20 Jan. 1879 ; *e.s.* of John Campbell, 1st Marquis of Aberdeen and Temair ; *m.* Mary Florence, *d.* of the late Joseph Clixby, of Owmby Cliff, Lincs. *Educ. :* Cargilfield, Edinburgh ; Harrow ; St. Andrews Univ. ; Balliol Coll., Oxford. Represented Peckham on L.C.C. since 1910 ; one of the representatives of the L.C.C. on the Metropolitan Water Board since 1913, and on the body of Trustees for the Crystal Palace since 1914. *War Work :* Member of War Emergency Committee of National Council of Y.M.C.A.'s ; Supervisor and Treasurer for war centres of the Y.M.C.A. in London and the Home Counties ; Vice-Chairman of Ellon District War Emergency Committee, Aberdeenshire. *Addresses :* 16, Cambridge Square, W. 2 ; Haddo House, Aberdeen. *Clubs :* Brooks's ; National Liberal ; New (Edinburgh) ; Royal Northern (Aberdeen). (O10546)

HADDON, Lieut.-Col. Andrew, O.B.E., V.D.

HADDON, Lieut. Reginald Cutler, O.B.E., R.A.S.C.

HADFIELD, Charles Frederick, M.B.E., M.A., M.D. (Cantab), M.R.C.S., L.R.C.P., *b.* 17 June, 1875 ; *s.* of the late Geo. H. Hadfield, J.P., of Ross, Herefordshire ; *m.* W. F. E., *d.* of the late Alexander W. MacDougall, of Blackheath. *Educ. :* The Leys School, Cambridge ; Trinity Coll., Cambridge ; St. Bartholomew's Hospital. Anæsthetist ; Senior Anæsthetist, Prince of Wales' General Hospital ; Assist. Anæsthetist, St. Bartholomew's Hospital, E.C. *War Work :* Anæsthetist, City of London Military Hospital, 1915–19. *Addresses :* 42, Devonshire Street, Portland Place, W. 1 ; The Old Rectory, Leaden Roding, Dunmow, Essex. (M10262*h*)

HADFIELD, Ernest, O.B.E.

HADFIELD, Francis Belt, Lady, C.B.E., *d.* of Col. S. M. Wickersham, of Alleghany, Pennsylvania ; *m.* Sir Robert A. Hadfield, 1st Bart., F.R.S., J.P. (*see* BURKE'S *Peerage*). *Address :* 22, Carlton House Terrace, S.W. 1. (C188)

HADFIELD, John White, M.B.E.

HADLEY, Arthur Edward, C.B.E., 5 Dec. 1870 ; *s.* of Edward Alfred Hadley, M.A., of London. *Educ. :* Charterhouse. Managing Director of The Victoria Falls and Transvaal Power Company, Ltd. *War Work :* Deputy Director-General, Inspection Department, Ministry of Munitions. *Address :* 66, Palace Court, Hyde Park, London. *Club :* Ranelagh. (C189)

HADLEY, Frederick Augustus, M.B.E. (M10387)

HADLEY, Joanna Margaret, Mrs., M.B.E., *b.* 3 July, 1861 ; *d.* of Henry T. Wells, R.A., of London, and *wi.* of Ernest Charrington ; *m.* Wilfred James Hadley, M.D., F.R.C.P. *War Work :* Organiser, Commandant, and Sec. of The Kitto Relief Hospital, Reigate (Auxiliary Military Hospital, Class " A "), for 4¼ years. *Addresses :* Parkside, Reigate, Surrey ; 33, Queen Anne Street, London, W. 1. (M8303)

HADKINSON, Frederick, M.B.E. (M10192)

HADKINSON, Capt. Percival, O.B.E.

HADNUTT, William, M.B.E.

HADOW, Sir (William) Henry, C.B.E., *b.* 27 Dec. 1859 ; *s.* of Rev. W. E. Hadow, Vicar of South Cerney, Cirencester. *Educ. :* Malvern and Worcester College, Oxford. Fellow, Tutor and Dean of Worcester College, 1888–1909 ; Principal of Armstrong College, Newcastle-upon-Tyne, 1909–19 ; Vice-Chancellor of Sheffield University, 1919. *War Work :* Director of Education (for Y.M.C.A.) on Lines of Communication in France, 1918 ; Assistant Director of Staff duties (Education) at the War Office, 1918–19. *Address :* The Grange, Ecclesall, Sheffield. *Clubs :* Athenæum ; Oxford and Cambridge. (C2657)

HADRILL, Capt. Henry Clement, O.B.E., R.A.S.C.

HAFFIELD, Walter Milford Paget, M.B.E., *b.* 5 Sept. 1880 ; *s.* of Cooper Haffield, B.A., of Eden Park, Kingstown. *Educ. :* Privately. *War Work :* Voluntary work in connection with the St. John Ambulance Brigade at the unloading of Hospital Ships, etc. ; in charge of Wounded Soldiers' Reception Committees work at Kingstown from Feb. 1915, to Dec. 1919. *Address :* Summer-Hill House, Kingstown, Co. Dublin. (M8304)

HAGAN, Rev. Edward James, O.B.E.

HAGGARD, Godfrey Digby Napier, O.B.E.

HAGGARD, Sir Henry Rider, Knt. Bach., K.B.E., J.P., *b.* 22 June, 1856 ; *s.* of William M. Rider Haggard, of Bradenham Hall, Norfolk ; *m.* Mariana Louisa, *o.c.* of Major Margitson (19th Regt.), of Ditchingham House, Norfolk. *Educ. :* Privately. Sec. to Sir Henry Bulwer, Governor of Natal, 1875 ; on the Staff of Sir Theophilus Shepstone, special commissioner to the Transvaal, 1877 ; with late Gen. Brooke, R.E., formally hoisted the British flag over the South African Republic at Pretoria, on the Queen's Birthday, 1877 ; Sec. to Secocoeni Commission ; Master High Court of the Transvaal, 1878 ; Barrrister, Lincoln's Inn, 1884 ; Chairman of Committee, Society of Authors, 1896–98 ; journeyed through England investigating condition of agriculture and of rural population, 1901 and 1902 ; British Government Special Commissioner to ¡eport on Salvation Army Settlements, U.S.A., etc., 1905 ; Chairman Reclamation and Unemployed Labour Committee of the Royal Commission on Coast Erosion and Afforestation, 1906–11 ; Nominated Hon. Life Fellow of R. Colonial Institute, and presented with illuminated address of thanks, by Council of the R.C. Institute, in recognition of " conspicuous services to the British Empire," 1916 ; elected a Vice-President R. Colonial Institute, 1917 ; Member, Empire Settlement Committee, 1917. *War Work :* Served on Dominions Royal Commissions,

1912–1917 and Empire Settlement Committee ; Hon. Representative Royal Colonial Institute to consult with Governments of the Dominions as to the After-War Settlement of Ex-Service Men, 1916 ; has travelled round the world on Empire Service, etc. *Addresses :* Ditchingham House, Norfolk ; North Lodge, St. Leonards-on-Sea. *Clubs :* Athenæum ; National ; Cecil ; Pilgrims'. (K215)

HAGGARD, Lilias Margitson Rider, M.B.E., *b.* 9 Dec. 1892 ; *d.* of Sir Rider Haggard, of Ditchingham, Norfolk (*q.v.*). *Educ. :* St. Felix School, Southwold. *War Work :* Joined Voluntary Aid Detachment, Norfolk 116, early in 1915, and worked in the Hedenham Auxiliary Hospital, Norfolk, Exmouth Hospital, Devonshire, and Morden Grange Hospital, Wimbledon, until 1918 ; also worked for some months for the Royal Automobile Club as Voluntary Driver. *Address :* Ditchingham House, Norfolk. *Club :* Albemarle ; V.A.D. (M8305)

HAGGART, Capt. James Dewar, O.B.E., J.P., *b.* 22 March, 1875 ; *s.* of Peter Haggart, Woollen Manufacturer, of Aberfeldy, Perthshire ; *m.* Millicent Frances, *d.* of George Bourne, of Oakdene, Edgbaston, Birmingham. *Educ. :* Morrison Academy. Crieff. Woollen Manufacturer ; Provost of Aberfeldy ; Chief Magistrate of the Burgh ; Chairman, local School Committees ; Chairman of Horticultural Society, etc. *War Work :* Gave up his house, Eilean Riabhach, as an Auxiliary Hospital for 4¼ years ; encouraged all local efforts in connection with Red Cross Fund, Prince of Wales' Fund, The Queen Mary Needlework Guild, Prisoner of War Fund ; Chairman of Aberfeldy Burgh Tribunal and Local Food Control ; Member of County War Pensions and Disablement Committee ; raised a local company of volunteers. *Address :* Eilean, Riabhach, Aberfeldy. *Clubs :* R.A.C.; Conservative (Edinburgh) ; Royal Scottish Automobile (Glasgow).

HAGGITT. Major Edward Dashwood, O.B.E.

HAGUE, S., M.B.E.

HAHN, Lieut. and Qr.-Mr. Adolph, M.B.E., R.E.

HAHN, Carl Hugo Linsingen, M.B.E.

HAIG, Lieut.-Col. David Price, O.B.E.

HAIG, Capt. John Alicius, O.B.E., B.A., and Legion of Honour, *b.* 1857 ; *s.* of John Haig, of Cameron Bridge, Co. Fife ; *m.* Jessie Marion, widow of Sir Edmund Waller, 5th Bart. (*see* BURKE'S *Peerage*). *Educ. :* Clifton Coll.; Trinity Coll., Cambridge (B.A.). *War Work :* Transport Officer, 1st Dorset Regt., Somme, 1916 ; Transport Officer, Mhow Cav. Bde., 1916–18 ; A.D.C. to Lieut.-Gen. Sir Chas. Kavanagh, K.C.B., Commanding Cav. Corps, 1918–19 ; Staff Capt. Namur No. 4 Area, 1919. *Address :* Lawfield, Ladybank, Fife. (O5325)

HAIG, Mary Lilian, M.B.E., *d.* of William James Haig, of Dollarfield, Dollar. *War Work :* Vice-President, British Red Cross Society (Scottish Branch) ; A.C.D. for Clackmannan and Kinross, Co. Branch. *Address :* Dollarfield, Dollar. (M8306)

HAIG, Lieut.-Col. Thomas Wolseley, C.S.I., C.M.G., C.B.E., *b.* 1865 ; *s.* of the late Major Robert Wolseley Haig, R.A., F.R.S. ; *m.* 1892, Beatrice, *d.* of Michael Lloyd Ferrar, I.C.S. *Educ. :* Wellington Coll., and R.M.C., Sandhurst. Entered Seaforth Highlanders 1884 ; Capt. I.S.C. (now Indian Army), 1895 ; Major, 1902 ; Lieut.-Col. 1910 ; served with Burma Expedition, 1887–89 ; Staff Officer Bhamo Command (medal with clasp) ; joined Berar Commn. 1892, and was successively Assist. Commr., Inspector-Gen. of Police, Jails, Stamps, Registration, and Excise, and Civil and Sessions Judge ; entered Political Depart. 1901 ; First Assist. Resident at Hyderabad, 1902 ; Assist. Sec. to Govt. of India in Foreign Depart. 1907 ; was Political Agent in Alwar, 1907–8 ; Officiating Political A.D.C. to Sec. of State for India, 1909–10 ; Consul at Kerman, 1910–12 ; Consul-Gen. for Khorassan, 1912–16, since when at Isfahan. *Address :* British Consulate-General, Ispahan, Persia. *Clubs :* Constitutional ; Caledonian United Service. (C2656)

HAIGH, Bernard Parker, M.B.E., D.Sc., *Educ. :* University of Glasgow. Assistant Professor, R.N. College, Greenwich. *War Work :* Consulting Engineer, Admiralty. *Address :* R.N. College, Greenwich. (M496)

HAIGH, Ernest Varley, C.B.E., *b.* 20 May, 1883 ; *s.* of Sam Haigh, of Slaithwaite, Yorkshire. *Educ. :* Huddersfield College. Works Manager in Messrs. J. and P. Coats, Ltd., at home and in Russia and Mexico ; Member of the Institute of Mechanical Engineers. *War Work :* Controller, Trench Warfare Supply Dept. and of Department of Engineering, Ministry of Munitions. *Address :* Services Club, 19, Stratford Place, W. 1. *Clubs :* Royal Thames Yacht ; Royal Corinthian Yacht ; Services. (C190)

HAIGH, George William, M.B.E., *b.* 17 June, 1869 ; *s.* of the late William Haigh, of Huddersfield ; *m.* Georgina Alice, *d.* of the late William James Smith. *Educ. :* Moldgreen Board School, and Huddersfield Technical Coll. Hon. Serving Brother to the Order of St. John of Jerusalem in England ; Corps Superintendent, Huddersfield Corps of the St. John Ambulance Brigade ; Commandant, 27th and 172nd Voluntary Aid Detachment, York ; Hon. Sec. Huddersfield and Holmfirth District Fire Brigades' Friendly Society. *War Work :* As Hon. Supt. of Transport to the Huddersfield War Hospital (9th General), arranged all transport and personally superintended Special and Serious Cases to and from the Hospital, and to the other Commands and Institutions ; procured voluntary transport and superintended all convoys of wounded soldiers to Huddersfield ; and as Commandant of the 27th and 172nd Voluntary Aid Detachment, York, prepared and mobilised for the R.A.M.C.

over 200; formed Ladies' V.A.D. Company for Honley Auxiliary Hospital; arranged transport by motor, etc., of over 78,000 wounded soldiers and patients; assisted with ambulance in transport of wounded soldiers to Halifax St. Luke's Hospital; assisted in the organisation of Treats and Motor Trips to the wounded soldiers at the War Hospital and its auxiliaries. *Address:* 14, Victoria Street, Moldgreen, Huddersfield. (M8307)

HAIL, Lieut. Frederick William, O.B.E., R.N.R.

HAILES, Brevet-Lieut Col. David Augustus, O.B.E., R.M.L.I. (ret.), *b.* 30 Dec. 1863; *s.* of the late Major-Gen. J. C. Hailes, Royal (Bombay) Artillery; *m.* Amy Alice Powell. *Educ.:* Privately; Marlborough. *War Work:* Recruiting Staff Officer, Royal Navy and Royal Marines, Manchester District. *Address:* 210, Upper Chorlton Road, Manchester, S.W. (O4432)

HAILEY, Hammett Reginald Clode, C.I.E., C.B.E., I.C.S.

HAINES, Augustus John Thomas, O.B.E.

HAINES, Acting Lieut. Ernest, M.B.E.

HAINES, Capt. Henry Ronald, O.B.E., R.M.L.I., *b.* 31 July, 1886; *s.* of Charles Haines, of the Manor House, Locking, Somerset; *m.* Phœbe Olivia, *d.* of Col. H. T. S. Yates, R.A., of Weymouth. *Educ.:* Elizabeth Coll., Guernsey. *War Work:* Served in Grand Fleet throughout the war. *Club:* Junior Naval and Military. (O9240)

HAINES, Samuel James, M.B.E., A.M.

HAINES, William Joseph, C.B.E.

HAINS, Charles Brazier, M.B.E.

HAINS, John James, M.B.E.

HAINWORTH, Edward Marrack, M.B.E., M.D., B.S., B.Sc. (Lond.), F.R.C.S., *b.* 14 March, 1870; *s.* of Henry Hainworth, of Blackheath, Kent.; *m.* Charlotte Elizabeth, *d.* of W. P. Burkinshaw, of Hessle, E. York. *Educ.:* Roan School, Greenwich, and St. Thomas's Hospital. Sen. Surgeon, Hull Royal Infirmary; Sen. Surgeon, Victoria Children's Hospital, Hull. *War Work:* St. John's V.A.D. Hospital, Hull; and Brooklands Officers' Hospital, Hull. *Addresses:* 14, Albion Street, Hull; Wolfreton House, Kirk Ella, near Hull. (M8509)

HAIR, John Hugh, M.B.E., J.P., D.L. (County of Moray), *b.* 17 Nov. 1859; *s.* of John Hair, of Hampstead, London; *m.* Lizzie Forsyth, *d.* of James Johnston, of Newmill, Elgin. *Educ.:* Univ. Coll. School, London. Formerly Joint Managing Director, Glenlossie-Glenlivet Distillery Co., Ltd., Elgin; Member of County Council for Morayshire. *War Work:* County Director, Morayshire Branch, British Red Cross Society; Member of County Military Advisory Committee. *Address:* Skerry Cliff, Lossiemouth, Morayshire. (M8310)

HAKE, Major Henry Engelbert, O.B.E., T.D., *b.* 23 Aug. 1868; *s.* of Henry Hake, late Vicar of Chilvers Coton, nr. Nuneaton. *Educ.:* Leamington College. *War Work:* Mobilised, 5 Aug. 1914; Proceeded to France, March, 1915; Various appointments in France; Adjutant of Army Railheads from Nov. 1917, to 1919. (O5326)

HAKING, Lieut.-Gen. Sir Richard Cyril Byrne, G.B.E., K.C.B., K.C.M.G., late Hants. Regt., *b.* 24 Jan. 1862; *s.* of late Rev. Richard Haking; *m.* Rachel Violette, *d.* of late Sir Henry James Burford Burford-Hancock, C.M.G., Chief Justice of Gibraltar. Commdg. 5th Inf. Brig., Aldershot Command, from 1911; served with Burmese Expd., 1885–7; S. Africa, 1899–1900; in Great War (despatches); has Order of St. Vladimir of Russia (4th Class with swords); Legion of Honour, Croix de Guerre of France and Belgium; Military Order of Avis of Portugal, and Sacred Treasure of Japan; is Grand Officer, Order of the Crown of Italy and of Belgium; appointed High Commissioner for Danzig, Jan. 1921. *Address:* Aldershot. *Clubs:* Army and Navy; United Service; Arthur's. (G67)

HALAHAN, Col. John Crosby, C.B.E., A.F.C., R.A.F. Served in Great War, 1914–19 (mentioned in despatches). (C861)

HALAHAN, Surg.-Comm. Thomas Dufour, O.B.E., R.N., M.B., F.R.C.S., B.A.

HALCROW, Marjorie, Mrs., M.B.E., R.A.F.

HALDANE, Henry Chicheley, O.B.E., *b.* 10 May, 1872; *s.* of James Haldane, of Edinburgh; *m.* Norah, *d.* of William Bowden, of Hope, Derbyshire. *Educ.:* Charterhouse and B.N.C., Oxford. *War Work:* Enlisted West Kent Yeomanry, Sept. 1914; received Commission in Lothians and Border Horse, Nov. 1914; served in Flanders and France from Sept. 1915, to Feb. 1918; mentioned in despatches. *Address:* Pavings, King's Langley, Herts. *Club:* Oxford and Cambridge. (O858)

HALE, Felix, M.B.E., *b.* 15 April, 1855; *s.* of John Hale, of Chippenham, Wiltshire; *m.* Hannah, *d.* of Thomas Rees, of Neath, South Wales. *Educ.:* St. Paul's School, Chippenham. Locomotive Foreman (Great Western Railway). *War Work:* Arrangement of Engine Power in connection with running of ambulance trains, movement of troops, and ammunition trains. *Address:* 9, Ormsby Street, Reading. (M8311)

HALE, Lancelot Hugh Dowman, M.B.E.

HALE, Muriel Alice Mary, M.B.E., *d.* of George C. Hale, of Knowsley, Prescot. *War Work:* V.A.D. in Liverpool Merchants Mobile Hospital at Etaples; Lady Superintendent at Amatol Munition Factory, Aintree; Commandant and Matron of Women Munition Workers' Hospital at Knowsley Hall. *Address:* Knowsley, Prescot, Lancs. *Club:* Ladies' Park. (M8312)

HALE, Lieut. Reginald, M.B.E., *b.* 1888. *Educ.:* Owen's

School, Islington. *War Work:* Service with the Red Cross Commission in Mesopotamia and Persia as Director of Finance and Personnel. (M8513)

HALE, Lieut. Sylvester Gresham, M.B.E.

HALE, Major Thomas, O.B.E.

HALE, Col. Thomas Wyatt, C.B., C.M.G., C.B.E., *b.* 1864; *m.* 18—, Annette Hannah, *d.* of the late Daniel Bailey, of Moorock, Ballycumber, King's Co. Entered Wiltshire Regt. 1885; Lieut.-Col. Army Ordnance Depart. 1905; Col. 1913; Benin Expedition, 1897 (medal with clasp); with Nile Expedition, 1898 (despatches, 4th Class Medjidie, Egyptian Medal); Great War, 1914–18 (despatches twice); was a Director of Ordnance Sers. 1918–19, with rank of Brig.-Gen. (C1399)

HALE, Lieut. Walter Churchill, O.B.E., M.C., R.F.A. (T.).

HALE, William Stather, O.B.E.

HALE, Thomas Edward SHERWOOD-, M.B.E., J.P. Gloucestershire (*see* BURKE'S *Landed Gentry*), *b.* 28 Feb. 1861; *s.* of the late Thomas Henry Sherwood-Hale, Royal Scots Fusiliers, and Ann, *d.* of R. B. Hale, of Alderley, Glos.; *m.* Mary Sophia, *d.* of Fredk. Addington Goodenough. *Educ.:* Dulwich Coll. *War Work:* Canteen management in Gloucestershire and Wilts.; also on staff of Filling Factory, Quedgeley, Glos. *Address:* Alderley, near Wotton-under-Edge, Glos. (M1834)

HALER, Percy James, M.B.E., B.Sc. (Vict. and Leeds), A.M.I.Mech.E., A.I.E.E., *b.* 20 Aug. 1876; *s.* of William Henry Haler, of Ilkley (late of the Board of Education, Whitehall); *m.* Edith, *d.* of Arthur Redshaw, of Leeds. *Educ.:* Leeds Central High School, and Leeds Univ. Principal, Leyton Technical Institute, and Supervisor of Evening Studies, Leyton. *War Work:* Superintendent of the Engineering Department, Hackney Technical Institute. London County Council, June, 1915, to Dec. 1918, producing limit and position gauges for the Ministry of Munitions. *Address:* 17, Mornington Road, Chingford, E. 4. (M8314)

HALES, Rev. James Tooke, O.B.E. C.F., *b.* 7 Sept. 1863; *s.* of the late Rev. George Hales, of Barningham, York. *Educ.:* Eton, and Lichfield Theol. Coll. Chaplain H.M. Forces since 1900. Principal Chaplain Mesopotamian Exped. Force, 1920. *War Work:* Served in France with 3rd Division, Aug. 1914; remained with wounded on the retreat from Mons, and was taken into Germany and allowed to remain in men's camp at Sennelager, until Feb. 1915; subsequently at Shoreham and Curragh Camps. *Address:* G.H.Q. Baghdad. (O7224)

HALES, Lieut. Walter Percy, M.B.E., I.A.R.O.

HALES, Capt. Willie, M.B.E., *b.* 1874. Served for 24 years in the Royal Artillery. *War Work:* Assist. Inspector of Shells, Inspection Department, Royal Arsenal, Woolwich. *Address:* 5, Chancelot Road, Abbey Wood, S.E. 2. (M1835)

HALFORD, Capt. Ernest Samuel, O.B.E., R.A.F.

HALFORD, Lieut.-Col. Michael Francis, O.B.E., Y. & L. Regt. (retired).

HALL, Lieut.-Col. Alexander Nelson, O.B.E., J.P., D.L., *b.* 25 July, 1865; *s.* of A. W. Hall, of Barton Abbey, Oxon (*see* BURKE'S *Landed Gentry*); *m.* Susan, *d.* of Col. G. C. Porter, of Fairford Park, Glos. *Educ.:* Charterhouse and Oriel Coll., Oxford. Chairman and Managing Director of Hall's Oxford Brewery, Ltd. *War Work:* Commanded 2/1st Queen's Own Oxfordshire Hussars. *Address:* Burton Abbey, Steeple Aston, Oxon. *Club:* Carlton. (O2226)

HALL, Major Alfred Kingsley, O.B.E., R.A.F.

HALL, Alice Mary, M.B.E., *b.* 1863; *d.* of Benjamin Hall. *Educ.:* High School, Battersea. Matron of The Dreadnought Hospital. *War Work:* Superintending the Nursing of the Royal Navy and Merchant Seamen during the war at the Dreadnought Hospital, Greenwich. *Address:* Dreadnought Hospital, Greenwich. (M1837)

HALL, Aline Margaret, M.B.E. For work in connection with the Imperial War Museum. (M10321)

HALL, Annie, Mrs., O.B.E., *b.* 1867; *d.* of S. I. Hubble, of Barnes; *m.* Benjamin James, *s.* of Rev. R. Hall, B.A., of Leamington. *Educ.:* Wyggeston School, Leicester. *War Work:* Converted own private house into a hospital at the commencement of the War, and acted as Commandant during the whole period of the War. *Address:* Fieldend, Eastcote, Middx. *Club:* Lyceum. (O1411)

HALL, Anthony, M.B.E.

HALL, Lieut. Archibald Holte, O.B.E., R.N.V.R.

HALL, Eng.-Comm. Arthur Colin, O.B.E., R.N.

HALL, Arthur Henry, C.B.E., *b.* 17 Aug. 1876; *s.* of H. S. Hall, of Clifton; *m.* Maud Henrietta, *d.* of Lieut.-Col. Webster, of Blackheath. *Educ.:* Clifton; Trinity Hall, Cambridge. 1st Class Mech. Sciences Tripos; Engineer, M.I.C.E., M.I.M.E.; at present Controller Disposal Board, in charge of factory stores, miscellaneous stores and aircraft disposals. *War Work:* 1914–17, Woolwich Arsenal, Asst. Supt. Mechanical Engineering Dept.; In charge of lay-out and equipment of new factories; 1917, Director of Mine Production, Admiralty; In charge of production of all weapons, torpedoes, mines, paravanes, hydrophones, depth charges, etc., used in the submarine warfare. *Address:* 1, Eliot Vale, Blackheath. *Club:* Authors'. (C191)

HALL, Audrey Elizabeth Kathleen, M.B.E. (M10249a)

HALL, Major Bertram Arthur Montagu, O.B.E., R.A., *b.* 7 Dec. 1879; *s.* of late Col. Montague Hall, Royal Munster Fusiliers, Fairlight, Ryde, I.W.; *m.* Iris Mary, *d.* of F. Cory Yeo, J.P., of Holme Park, Sonning-on-Thames, Berkshire. *Educ.:* I. W. College; Royal Military Academy, Woolwich. Regular Army.

War Work: Served with No. 7 Mountain Battery, Dec. 1914 to Dec. 1915, with the B.E.F. France, and the same Battery from Dec. 1915 till Sept. 1916 with Salonica Expeditionary Force; invalided to England; rejoined B.E.F. France, April, 1917; commanded various batteries until Feb. 1918; appointed Commandant 2nd Army Artillery School, Feb. 1918 to Feb. 1919; Despatches, Dec. 1918 and June, 1919; Belgian Croix de Guerre, O.B.E. *Address:* The Old Abbey, Exeter. *Club:* Junior Naval and Military. (O5327)

HALL, Lieut. Bertram James Leslie, M.B.E., R.E., (T.).

HALL, Lieut. Charles Frank, O.B.E. (O11743)

HALL, Charles John Ernest, O.B.E., J.P.; *s.* of Charles John Hall, of Manchester and Windermere; *m.* Maud Constance Swire, of Ashton. *Educ.:* Privately. Chairman, Disley Council. *War Work:* Red Cross Transport in Cheshire (Assistant County Director (Transport) B.R.C.S., Cheshire Branch). *Address:* Disley, Cheshire. *Clubs:* Brasenose; Royal Clyde Yacht; Royal Windermere Yacht. (O1412)

HALL, Charles Leavers, M.B.E.

HALL, Lieut.-Comm. Charles Stuart, O.B.E., R.D.

HALL, Major and Qr.-Mr. Douglas, O.B.E.

HALL, Lieut. and Qr.-Mr. Edgar, M.B.E.

HALL, Elizabeth Ellen, Mrs., M.B.E.; *d.* of the late Charles Florance Young, of 22, Cranley Gardens, S.W.; *m.* Charles Henry Edward, *s.* of the late Capt. H. E. Hall, of Knockbrack Athenry, Co. Galway. *Educ.:* Privately. *War Work:* Commandant, V.A.D. Kent 102. *Address:* Birchley, Biddenden, Kent. *Clubs:* Sesame and Bath. (M8315)

HALL, Ernest Frederick, M.B.E.

HALL, Lieut. Ernest Virtue, M.B.E.

HALL, Evelyn Alice, Mrs., M.B.E.

HALL, Lieut.-Col. Sir Frederick, K.B.E., D.S.O., M.P., Lieut.-Col. R.F.A., *b.* 7 Oct. 1864; *s.* of Herbert Hall; *m.* 1892 Annie Ellen, *d.* of Dr. Henry Hall. *Educ.:* Privately. Member of Lloyds and Baltic; contested Dulwich L.C.C. 1907–1910, and Parliament, 1910; served in Great War. *Address:* Grafham Grange, Bramley, Surrey. *Clubs:* Carlton; Junior Carlton; Constitutional; St. Stephen's. (K77)

HALL, Frederick Joseph, M.B.E.

HALL, Frederick Walter, O.B.E., *b.* 1874; *s.* of Rev. T. O. Hall, late of Stretton Rectory, Oakham; *m.* Phyllis, *d.* of H. H. Baghall, of Avishays, Chard, Somerset. *Educ.:* Oundle. Land Agent for the Marquis of Zetland and the Duke of Northumberland. *War Work:* Member of North Riding, Yorkshire War Agricultural Committee and latterly Chairman. *Address:* Olliver, Richmond, Yorkshire. *Club:* Windham. (O1413)

HALL, Frederick Holland, M.B.E.

HALL, George, M.B.E., *b.* 3 Dec. 1851; *s.* of Major George Hall, of Poona, Bombay Presidency; *m.* Henrietta Elizabeth, *d.* of Henry Faulconer, of Poona. *Educ.:* Doveton Coll., India. Deputy Supt. Survey of India (retired); Member of the Municipal Council, Bangalore; Hon. Treas. Friend-in-Need Society; Director, Bank of Bangalore; Member, Mythic Society. *War Work:* Visited the hospitals and supplied papers and books; placed car at the disposal of the authorities for the convalescents; Member of the Red Cross Society. (M6156)

HALL, Lieut.-Col. George Clifford Miller, C.M.G., D.S.O., *b.* 26 Jan, 1872; *s.* of Capt. W. H. Hall, R.N., ; *m.* Annie Elizabeth Mary, *d.* of FitzRoy Kelly, of Lincoln's Inn. *Educ.:* Repton and Royal Military Academy, Woolwich. Was in Royal Engineers; now Lieut.-Col., Reserve of Officers. *War Work:* Assistant Director of Railway Transport, Egyptian Expeditionary Force. *Address:* 23, Cranley Gardens, London, S.W. 7. *Clubs:* Army and Navy; Garrick. (C2058)

HALL, Capt. George Frederick, M.B.E., *b.* 18 April, 1898; *s.* of G. A. Hall, of Olgra House, Moore Road, Mapperley, Nottingham. *Educ.:* Nottingham High School, and Nottingham Univ. Coll. *War Work:* Served with the East Yorkshire Regt. overseas, with 8th and 11th Battalions, May, 1917, to June, 1919. *Address:* Olgra House, Moore Road, Mapperley, Nottingham. *Club:* Nottingham and Notts United Services. (M1839)

HALL, Major George Leslie, O.B.E., R.E.

HALL, George Thomas, M.B.E.

HALL, Lieut.-Col. George Thompson, C.M.G., C.B.E.

HALL, Comm. Hamilton John Burnett, O.B.E., R.N.

HALL, Capt. Harold Stanley George, M.B.E., Aust. I.F.

HALL, Harry Francis, M.B.E.

HALL, Capt. Harry Reginald Holland, M.B.E.

HALL, Henry, M.B.E., *b.* 13 July, 1873; *s.* of the late Edward Hall. *Educ.:* City of Westminster School. Senior Staff Clerk in Ministry of Health. *War Work:* Intelligence Department of the Local Government Board, which department collected information with regard to distress due to the war, and later supervised the work of Local and Appeal Tribunals, under the Military Service Acts; also served as a Special Constable. *Address:* 48, Ringford Road, West Hill, Wandsworth, S.W. 18. (M1840)

HALL, Ven. Henry Armstrong, O.B.E., B.D., *b.* 2 June, 1853; *s.* of the late George Hall, late 52nd Light Inf.; *m.* Catherine Gertrude, *d.* of John Ross Hutchinson, H.E.I.C.S. *Educ.:* Christ's Hospital; Abroad. Chaplain to the King; Archdeacon of Richmond; Rector of Methley. *War Work:* Dept. Asst. Chaplain Gen. (A/Asst. C.G.), Northern Command; Organiser and Director of Schools of Instruction for Army Chaplains; In conjunction with Bishop of Ripon formed Diocesan Board and erected Churches and Recreation Huts for the Troops at Ripon, Catterick, and elsewhere; Brought to notice of Sec. of State for War, London Gazette, Feb. 1917. *Address:* Methley Rectory, Leeds. *Club:* Leeds. (C1598)

HALL, Lieut. Henry Leonard, M.B.E., R.A.F.

HALL, Major Herbert Gordon Lewis, O.B.E., R.A.S.C., *b.* 10 July, 1886; *s.* of Brig.-Gen. Lewis Hall, C.B.; *m.* Narayanee, *d.* of Capt. Judge, 2nd K.E.O. Gurkhas. *Educ.:* Magdalen Coll. School, Oxford, and Sandhurst. (O1414)

HALL, Paymaster-Capt. Hugh Seymour, C.B.E., R.N.; *s.* of the late Rev. G. Rome Hall, of Birtley, Northumberland. *Educ.:* Shaftesbury Grammar School. Paymaster-Com, and Acting Paymaster-Capt. R.N.; Paymaster of Contingencies, Admiralty. *Address:* Westmorland House, Wark-on-Tyne, Northumberland. (C895)

HALL, James, M.B.E.

HALL, Rev. James Thomas, O.B.E., B.D., *b.* 22 July, 1886; *s.* of Isaac Hall, of Co. Cavan, Ireland; *m.* Agnes Mary Frances, *d.* of the Rev. T. Burns, D.D., of Edinburgh. *Educ.:* Edinburgh Univ. Minister of the Parish Church of Tillicoultry, Clackmannanshire, Scotland. *War Work:* Chaplain to the 8th Casualty Clearing Station, B.E.F., from Dec. 1915, to Oct. 1916; Chaplain to 2nd King's Own Scottish Borderers from Oct. 1916, to March, 1919, with interim work as Acting Senior Chaplain (non. C. of E.) to Fifth Division. *Address:* The Manse, Tillicoultry. Clackmannanshire. (O5328)

HALL, Jane, Mrs., O.B.E.

HALL, John, M.B.E., J.P.

HALL, Col. John, O.B.E., V.D., D.L.; *s.* of James Hall, of The Lodge, Castleton, Derbyshire; *m.* Olive, *d.* of Andrew Fernie, of Stratton St. Margaret, Wilts. *Educ.:* The Collegiate School, Sheffield. Solicitor; Clerk to County Justices, Petty Sessional Division of Bury. *War Work:* Commanded 2/5th, 3/5th Lancashire Fusiliers, 1914–16; served in France; Commandant of Prisoner of War Camps, Frith Hill, Blandford, and Ripon, 1916 to conclusion of war. *Address:* Gorsey Brow, Chesham, Bury. (O8823)

HALL, Rev. John, O.B.E., *b.* 22 Oct. 1863; *m.* Isabella Stuart, *d.* of John Stuart, R.I.C., of Galway. *Educ.:* Edinburgh Univ., and New Coll., Edinburgh. Minister of United Free Church of Scotland. *War Work:* Convener of Home Mission Committee of United Free Church of Scotland; Joint Convener of Scottish Churches' Huts. *Address:* 2, Greenhill Terrace, Edinburgh. (O10550)

HALL, John Frederick, O.B.E., I.C.S.

HALL, John Herbert, O.B.E., *b.* 18 Sept. 1861; *s.* of John Hall, of Bolton; *m.* Margaret, *d.* of Jethro Scowcroft, of Moorfield, Bolton. *Educ.:* Rugby. Solicitor and Notary; Clerk to the Justices, County Borough of Bolton. *War Work:* Military Representative, and afterwards National Service Representative. *Address:* South Bank, Heaton, near Bolton. *Club:* Reform, Bolton. (O10551)

HALL, Capt. John John, M.B.E.

HALL, Col. Sir John Richard, Bart., C.B.E., Major 3rd Res. Batt. Irish Guards, late Coldstream Guards, *b.* 14 Nov. 1865; *s.* of late Lieut.-Gen. Julian Hamilton Hall, 5th *s.* of 5th Bart. (*see* BURKE'S *Peerage*); *m.* Sophia, *d.* of H. Duncan, and widow of Capt. S. A. Olliver, D.S.O. *Address:* 21, Dorset Square, N.W. 1. *Clubs:* Turf; Beefsteak; St. James's; Guards'. (C1599)

HALL, Major Leonard Joseph, O.B.E., R.E.

HALL, Martin Julian, O.B.E.

HALL, Mary Eleanor, Mrs., M.B.E., *b.* 9 April, 1876; *d.* of Thomas Blakey, of Bowthorpe Hall, Selby, Yorks; *m.* James William Hall. *Educ.:* Howden National School; gained Teacher's Certificate at Belle Vue, Bradford. Cookery Instructress, 1905–9; gained 1st Class Cookery Diploma at Leeds Training School. *War Work:* Commandant of the Castle Auxiliary Hospital, Cockermouth, 1917–19; trained the V.A.D.s in cookery one year before opening hospital, so that all cooking, bread-making, etc., was done by the V.A.D.'s on the hospital premises, the hospital being carried on by voluntary workers only. *Address:* Evening Hill, Cockermouth. (M8319)

HALL, Matthew, M.B.E.

HALL, Capt. Norman McLeod, O.B.E., R.E.

HALL, Oscar Standring, O.B.E., J.P., M.I.Mech.E., *b.* 1862; *s.* of Samuel Standring Hall, of Bury; *m.* Eleanor Burrows, *d.* of Dr. James Kerr, of Crawshawbooth. *Educ.:* Bury Grammar School; Germany; Manchester Technical School; Owens Coll. Vice-Chairman, Bury Insurance Committee; Chairman of the Medical Benefit Sub-Committee of the Bury Insurance Committee since the inception of the Insurance Act in 1912; ex-President of the Bury and District Chamber of Commerce. *War Work:* Director of two large Engineering Works, actively engaged in many directions for war supplies; visited Paris, Spa, and Wiesbaden on behalf of the Government in connection with the Armistice Commission and Peace Conference. *Address:* Tenterden, Bury, Lancashire. *Clubs:* Reform, Manchester; Manchester Literary. (O10552)

HALL, Lieut. Percival Stanhope, O.B.E., R.A.S.C.

HALL, Rev. Richard, O.B.E.

HALL, Lieut.-Col. Robert, O.B.E., R.A.F.

HALL, Robert Mills, O.B.E., M.B., C.M., *b.* 12 Sept. 1872; *s.* of Robert Hall, of South Shields; *m.* Alice Eleanor, *d.* of James Clark, of South Shields. *Educ.:* Edinburgh Univ. Surgeon.

War Work : Organised, and became Principal Medical Officer, Enfield Military Hospital. *Address :* The Crossways, Village Road, Enfield. *Club :* Royal Automobile. (O10554)

HALL, Rosina Marion, M.B.E., b. 25 Nov. 1894 ; d. of Herbert William Hall, of Tiverton, Devon. *Educ. :* Mary Datchelor Girls' School. Stenographer. *War Work :* Confidential Sec. to Col. J. G. Adamson, C.M.G., Officer in charge London Infantry Records, for over five years. *Address :* 42, Tressillian Road, Brockley, S.E. 4. (M4341)

HALL, Lieut. Samuel Howard, O.B.E., R.N.V.R.

HALL, Capt. Sidney Lewis, O.B.E., R.E.

HALL, Thomas, M.B.E.

HALL, Thomas Andrew, C.B.E., B.A., M.I.C.E., b. 1867 s. of William Hall, of High Street, Portadown, co. Armagh. *Educ. :* Univ. of Ireland. Govt. Engineer for Newfoundland since 1906 ; was Sec. to Tonnage Committee, Min. of Shipping, and Board of Coal Control for Newfoundland during Great War. *Address :* St. John's, Newfoundland. (C2008)

HALL, Capt. Vincent Claud, O.B.E., R.E., S.R.

HALL, Walter, O.B.E.

HALL, William Carby, O.B.E., F.R.I.B.A., b. 21 April, 1864 ; s. of John Hall, of Leeds ; m. Helena, d. of Daniel Womersley, of Leeds. *Educ. :* St. Martin's Grammar School, Scarborough, and privately. Member of the Council, Royal Institute British Architects ; President of the Leeds and Yorkshire Architectural Society ; Member of the Council of the National Housing and Town Planning Association ; Member of the Concrete Institute, and Member of the Town Planning Institute ; Past Provincial Grand Director of Ceremonies for the province of West Yorkshire. *War Work :* Deputy Commissioner under the Ministry of Food, North, Eastern Division (Yorkshire), from Aug. 1917, to Nov. 1919 ; since then Commissioner ; Chief Superintendent in the Leeds Police, Special Reserve, from Nov. 1941 to the disbanding of the Reserve in 1919. *Addresses :* Church House, Roundhay, near Leeds ; Prudential Buildings, Park Row, Leeds. *Club :* Leeds and County Conservative. (O10556)

HALL, Lieut.-Col. William Henry, O.B.E.

HALL, Capt. William Wellington, O.B.E., R.A.F.

HALLAM, Ernest Robert Francis, M.B.E.

HALLAND, Capt. Gordon Herbert Ramsay, O.B.E., b. 13 April, 1888 ; e. s. of the Rev. J. T. Halland, M.A., Rector of Blyburgh, Kirton-in-Lindsey, Lincolnshire ; m. Helen Claudine Blanche, d. of Major-Gen. John McNeill Walter, C.B., C.S.I., D.S.O., late Devonshire Regt., of Rosedale, Napier Gardens, Hythe, Kent. Entered Indian Police, 1908 ; District Superintendent of Police, Punjab, since 1913 ; on special duty in H.M. the King's Camp at Delhi Durbar, 1911. *War Work :* Entered Indian Army Reserve of Officers, June, 1915 ; served with General Staff, Intelligence, Army Headquarters, India, till Oct. 1919 ; Capt. June, 1919 ; T. Major and G.S.O. 2 from Nov. 1918 to Oct. 1919 ; mentioned in despatches. *Address :* c/o Messrs. Grindlay & Co., 54, Parliament Street, London. S.W. *Club :* East India United Service. (O2368)

HALLE, Elinor, C.B.E., b. 1856 ; d. of the late Sir Charles Hallé. Sculptor. *War Work :* Invented *papier mache* appliances, splints, boots, etc., for maimed and injured limbs. *Address :* 26, Yeoman's Row, Brompton Road, London, S.W. (C515)

HALLE, Madame, M.B.E.

HALLETT, Frederic Greville, O.B.E., b. 25 May, 1860 ; s. of James Alfred Hallett, of Merton Lodge, Putney ; m. Margaret Elizabeth, d. of James R. Lane, F.R.C.S., surgeon to St. Mary's Hospital, Paddington. *Educ. :* Westminster ; Switzerland. Sec. to the Examining Board of the Royal Colleges of Physicians and of Surgeons ; Sec. of the Imperial Cancer Research Fund ; Director of Examinations, Royal College of Surgeons of England ; late Commissioner of B.P. Scouts for Hammersmith District. *War Work :* Honorary Sec. of the Committee of Reference, a Statutory Committee under the Military Service Acts dealing with the staffing of civilian hospitals, the calling up of Members of the Staffs, various other matters affecting the Hospitals in the London Area, Boards of Medical Assessors, Tribunal of Appeal. *Addresses :* 8–11, Queen Square, Bloomsbury, W.C. 1 ; Point Close, Long Wittenham, Abingdon, Berks. *Club :* Constitutional. (O1416)

HALLETT, Lieut.-Comm. Henry Philip, M.B.E., D.S.C. (M6780g)

HALLETT, Capt. Theodore John, C.B.E., R.N. Served in Great War, 1914–19 (mentioned in despatches). (C234)

HALLETT, Norton Joseph HUGHES-, O.B.E., b. 8 Aug. 1854 ; s. of Rev. James Hughes-Hallett, of Higham, Canterbury, and Little Dunmow, Essex ; m. Alice Louisa, d. of the late Rev. Canon John Denton, of Ashby-de-la-Zouch. *Educ. :* Haileybury. Clerk of Peace and County Council of Derbyshire. *War Work :* In 1914 organised and became Hon. Sec. and Treas. of Derbyshire County War Relief Fund, whereby a sum of nearly £100,000 was raised ; Hon. Sec. and Treas. to County War Pensions Committee ; Sec. to County Belgian Refugees Committee and County Appeal Tribunal. *Address :* The Knoll, Derby. *Club :* Derbyshire County. (O10557)

HALLIDAY, Lieut. Charles William, M.B.E., R.E.

HALLIDAY, William Jamieson, M.B.E., J.P., b. 14 June, 1849 ; s. of the late Ninian Halliday, of Yett Johnstone ; m. 1st, Many Ann Fisher Scott Robson widow of the late Michael Robson, Master Mariner ; 2nd, Margaret Thomson Watson,

d. of the late Thomas Watson, of Dumfries. *Educ. :* Gretna Parish School, and Annan Academy. Vice-Chairman (Acting Chairman), National Health Insurance Committee for the County of Dumfries. *War Work :* Recruiting Campaign, War Savings, Appeal Tribunal (under Military Service Acts) for the Sheriffdom of Dumfries and Galloway ; Naval and Military Pensions Committee, Chairman, Lockerbie District ; Lieut. 3rd Volunteer Batt., King's Own Scottish Borderers. *Address :* Esthwaite, Lochmaben, Dumfriesshire. (M8322)

HALLIFAX, Charles Joseph, C.B.E., b. 1867. *Educ. :* Blundell's School, Tiverton, and Balliol Coll., Oxford. Entered I.C.S. 1887 ; Commr. of a Div. ; a Member of Council of Lieut.-Gov. of Punjab. (C688)

HALLIFAX, Edwin Richard, O.B.E.

HALLIFAX, Percy, M.B.E.

HALLIGAN, Major Joseph Thomas, O.B.E.

HALLIWELL, David, M.B.E., A.Inst.T., b. 20 Jan. 1875 ; s. of William Halliwell, of Upholland ; m. Mary, d. of Henry Duncan, of Burnley. *Educ. :* Upholland ; privately ; Manchester Univ. Assist. to Supt. of the Line, Lancashire and Yorkshire Railway. *War Work :* Organisation of transport, original Expeditionary Force to France ; transport facilities for Lathom Park Remount Depot ; general facilities in connection with movement of men and munitions during the war ; Associate Member of the Institute of Transport. *Address :* Hardy Grove, Worsley. *Clubs :* Worsley and Ellesmere Recreation and Golf. (M8324)

HALLIWELL, John, M.B.E., b. 1867 ; s. of John Halliwell, J.P., of Bury, Lancs ; m. Jeanie, d. of John Thompson, of Bannockburn. *Educ. :* Owens Coll., Manchester. *War Work :* S.M.O. Winchcombe V.A.D. Hospitals, and Cleeve Hill Red Cross Hospital. *Address :* Bayshill Road, Cheltenham ; Braddon's Hill House, Torquay. (M8325)

HALLIWELL, Major William Arthur, O.B.E., b. 16 Dec. 1885 ; s. of the late Thomas Halliwell, of Eccles, Lancs. ; m. Blanche, d. of Joseph Wharton Pollitt, of Colwyn Bay, N. Wales. Cotton Merchant. *War Work :* Served for 5 years in Egypt, Gallipoli, Sinai, Palestine, and Syria. *Address :* St. Heliers, Bramhall, Cheshire. *Club :* Reform (Manchester). (O6194)

HALLORAN, John William, M.B.E., b. 8 Oct. 1866 ; s. of William Archer Halloran, of Walsall, Staffordshire ; m. Margaret Annie, d. of Capt. David Brown (Mercantile Marine), of Liverpool. *Educ. :* Queen Mary's Grammar School, Walsall, Staffordshire. Town Clerk of Chatham ; Solicitor and Clerk to Rochester and Chatham Joint Sewerage Board. *War Work :* Arranged and prepared a scheme for carrying out the provisions of the National Registration Acts, 1915, for Chatham ; organised, in conjunction with the Mayor, numerous meetings in support of voluntary recruiting, also under the Derby Scheme, prior to the Military Service Acts; organised meetings and collections and other means for raising money for the Prince of Wales' Fund ; acted as Clerk to the Military Service Tribunals ; assisted in raising funds for Kentish Prisoners of War ; work in connection with raising the Special Police. *Address :* Normacot, Maidstone Road, Chatham. *Club :* Municipal ; County. (M499)

HALLORAN, Capt. William James, M.B.E., b. 11 Feb. 1865 ; s. of Cornelius Halloram, of Port Louis, S.A. ; m. Agnes Amelia, d. of Patrick Ball, of Dover. *War Work :* South Africa, 1899–1900 ; served in Royal Fusiliers, Sept. 1914, to Oct. 1915 ; and in 1st Garr. Batt. Cheshire Regt. from Oct. 1915, to Nov. 1919, at Gibraltar. (M5318)

HALLSWORTH, Lieut. Harry Mainwaring, O.B.E., R.E.

HALSE, Edyth Mary, Mrs., M.B.E., d. of the late John Henry Smalpage, of East Sheen ; m. Stanley Clarence, s. of the late Richard Clarence, of Inverness Terrace, London. *Educ. :* Privately. *War Work :* Waltham Abbey Hospital ; Lady Lawrence's Canteen, Enfield Lock ; Y.M.C.A. Cantonment, Enfield Lock (Hon. Superintendent) ; Vice-President N. and N.W. Area of London Y.M.C.A. *Address :* 23, Richmond Mansions, S.W. 5. *Club :* Ladies' Army and Navy. (M1844)

HALSEY, Capt. Arthur, C.B.E., R.N., b. 1869 ; s. of the Rt. Hon. Thomas Frederick Halsey, P.C. ; m. Blanche Helen Kerr, d. of the late Adm. Mark Robert Pechell (see BURKE'S *Peerage*, Brooke Pechell, Bart.). (C896)

HALSEY, George, M.B.E., b. 1872 ; s. of George Halsey, of London ; m. Gladys Winifred, D.Sc. (Lond.), d. of Henry Matthews Martyn, of Exeter. *Educ. :* Privately. Senior Assistant, Department of the Comptroller of the London County Council. *War Work :* Assistant Director of Finance, Ministry o. Food. *Address :* St. Clair, Effingham Road, Surbiton. (M8326)

HALSEY, Sir Laurence Edward, K.B.E., Principal Accountant Prince of Wales' National Relief Fund. *Address :* 64, Elm Park Gardens, S.W. 10. (K216)

HALSEY, Walter Johnston, O.B.E., J.P., D.L., b. 1 June, 1868 ; s. of Rt. Hon. Sir Thomas Fredk. Halsey, Bt., of Gaddesden Place (see BURKE'S *Peerage*) ; m. Agnes Marian, d. of W. Macalpine Leny, of Dalswinton, Dumfries (see BURKE'S *Landed Gentry*). *Educ. :* Eton, and Magdalen College, Oxford. Served in Great War as Lieut.-Col. 4th Batt. Bedfordshire Regt., and in Mesopotamia as Staff Capt. and D.A.A.G. (mentioned in despatches). *Addresses :* Westfield, Hatfield ; 32, St. James' Place. *Clubs :* Carlton ; United University. (O2965)

HALY, Herbert John, M.B.E.

HAM, Edwin George, M.B.E.   (M10388)

HAMBELTON, Lieut.-Comm. Alexander Elvin Sherwin, C.B.E.

HAMBLETON, Lieut. Herbert Adolph, O.B.E.. R.F.A.

HAMBLY, George Francis, O.B.E.

HAMBRO, Sir Charles Eric, K.B.E., *b.* 30 Sept. 1872; *s.* of Sir Everard A. Hambro; *m.* Sybil Emily, *d.* of Martin R. Smith, of Warren House, Hayes. *Educ.:* Eton; Trinity Coll., Cambridge. Partner in C. J. Hambro & Son; a Director of Royal Exchange Assurance Co.; and Director of the Great Eastern Railway Co. *Address:* Pickhurst Mead, Hayes, Kent.   (K252)

HAMBRO, Lieut.-Col. Harold Everard, C.B.E., *b.* 1876; *s.* of Sir Everard Alexander Hambro; *m.* Katharine Alethea, *d.* of William Charles Scott (*see* BURKE'S *Peerage*, Sheffield, B.). Formerly Capt. R.A.; served in Great War, 1914-19, as Major and Brevet Lieut.-Col. Remount Ser. (despatches). *Address:* Coldham Hall, Bury St. Edmunds.   (C1600)

HAMER, Dorothy, M.B.E.

HAMERSLEY, Lieut.-Col. John Henry, O.B.E., Order of St. Anne, 3rd class, Russia, late Cheshire Regt., *b.* 20 April, 1842; *s.* of Hugh Hamersley, of Pyton, Oxon.; *m.* Lucy, *d.* of Rev J. Clutterbuck, of Long Wittenham, Berks. *Educ.:* Privately and Sandhurst. Chief Constable of Cheshire. *War Work:* Sec. and Treas. to Cheshire Regt. Prisoners of War Aid Association. *Address:* Lindenwood, Budleigh Salterton, Devon   *Club:* Junior Constitutional.   (O10558)

HAMILL, Capt. John Molyneux O.B.E., R.A.M.C.

HAMILTON, Albert Edwin, M.B.E.

HAMILTON, Capt. Albert, O.B.E., R.A.S.C.

HAMILTON, Lieut.-Col. Alexander George, O.B.E., T.D., M.B., Ch.B., R.A.M.C. (T.), *b.* 14 Dec. 1875; *s.* of A. Hamilton, of Deganwy, North Wales; *m.* Edith Laura, *d.* of Henry Deacon, of Cardiff. *Educ.:* Edinburgh University. Surgeon: Hon. Assistant Surgeon, Chester Royal Infirmary; Hon. Surgeon, Chester Benevolent Institution; Medical Referee, Ministry of Pensions. *War Work:* Officer Commanding 1/1 Welsh Border Mtd. Brigade Field Ambulance, 1914-17; 231st Field Ambulance, 74th (Yeo.) Division, 1917-19. *Address:* 4, Stanley Place, Chester.   (O5331)

HAMILTON, Andrew, C.B.E., *b.* 26 April, 1862; *s.* of William Hamilton, J.P., of Pollokshields, Glasgow; *m.* Mary Alexandra, *d.* of Lewis Mackay, of Lyttle Park, East Killbride. *Educ.:* Privately; Andersonian University, Glasgow; Naval Architect. *War Work:* Honorary Assistant Director of Merchant Ship production. *Address:* 9, Denman Drive, Newsham Park, Liverpool. *Club:* Reform, Liverpool.   (C2660)

HAMILTON, Claude Aubrey Douglas, M.B.E. (M10353)

HAMILTON, Major Claude Melville Bruce, O.B.E. Late Notts and Derby Reg.

HAMILTON, Charles Gipps, O.B.E.

HAMILTON, Emily Moore, M.B.E., W.R.A.F.

HAMILTON, Ethel Mary, M.B.E.

HAMILTON, Capt. Frank Tracey, M.B.E., R.E., (T.).

HAMILTON, Lieut.-Col. Frederick Arthur, O.B.E., (I.A.)

HAMILTON, Lieut. James, O.B.E., R.N.V.R.

HAMILTON, Lieut. James Jack, O.B.E., R.N.R.

HAMILTON, Jane Ethel, M.B.E.; *d.* of Rev. John Sinclair Hamilton, M.A., of Dublin. *Educ.:* Victoria Coll., Belfast, and Lausanne. Women's Training Officer for Scotland, Ministry of Labour. *War Work:* Lady Supt. G.N. Staff, War Office, and Ministry of Munitions; Welfare Officer for Scotland and Ireland, Ministry of Munitions. *Addresses:* 5, Crown Gardens, Glasgow; and Moorfield, Cullybackey, Ireland.   (M1845)

HAMILTON, John Baillie, C.B.E.

HAMILTON, Kate Gibson, Mrs., O.B.E.; *d.* of the late Andrew Middlemass, of Edinburgh; widow of Lieut.-Col. Arthur Percival Hamilton, M.C., The Queen's Regt., *s.* of the late Maj. P. Hamilton, R.H.A. *Educ.:* Edinburgh. *War Work:* Searching for Missing (Red Cross); opened the Hamilton Hospital, 73, Harrington Gardens, for Officers; and when the War Office closed it at termination of war, reopened it for Ministry of Pensions, finally closing in May, 1920. *Addresses:* 19, Bolton Gardens, S.W.; Foxhill, Charles Hill, Farnham, Surrey.   (O10559)

HAMILTON, Margaret Gordon, Mrs. Hans, M.B.E., *b.* 3 July, 1854; *d.* of John Bond Cabbell, of Cromer Hall, Norfolk, and Aldwick, Sussex; *m.* Henry Best Hans, Col. and Ex-Judge, *s.* of Ven. George Hans Hamilton, D.D., Archdeacon of Northumberland and Canon of Durham. *War Work:* Canteens, and on many War Committees; Chairman of the Y.W.C.A. Canteen for Army Pay Clerks at Blackheath. *Address:* 5, Cranley Gardens, S.W. 7. *Club:* Alexandra.   (M3695)

HAMILTON, Mary Duchess of, O.B.E.: *see* Foster, Lady Mary Louise.

HAMILTON, Major Norman Chivas, O.B.E., D.S.C., R.A.S.C.

HAMILTON, Capt. Patrick Swinglehurst, M.B.E.

HAMILTON, Capt. Ronald James, O.B.E.

HAMILTON, Capt. William Lockhart, O.B.E., Aust.A.S.C.

HAMILTON, Lieut. William Vickery, M.B.E., S.A.S.C.

HAMILTON, Georgina Julia, Mrs. FINDLAY-, M.B.E., *b.* 1865; *d.* of Charles Vereker Hamilton-Campbell, of Netherplace; *m.* George Douglas, *s.* of Thomas Dunlop Findlay, of Easterhill. *Educ.:* Leamington and London. (*See* BURKE'S *Landed Gentry*). *War Work:* President of Surgical Work Party and President of Sphagum Work Party, Kilmarnock;

Member of Joint Political War Funds Association; Head of Land Army of South Ayrshire; Vice-President of Red Cross of Ayrshire; President of House Committee Dick. Institute, Red Cross Hospital (150 beds); originated the War Gardens in Scotland, starting 87 in Hurlford, a mining village, in 1915. *Address:* Carnell, Hurtford, Ayrshire. *Clubs:* Empress; Kelvin, Glasgow.   (M388)

HAMILTON, John STIRLING-, M.B.E., M.A., M.B., B.C. (Cantab.), M.R.C.S., L.R.C.P., *b.* 2 Dec. 1873; *s.* of the late Gen. Sir William Stirling-Hamilton, Bart., C.B., R.A. *Educ.:* Privately; Jesus Coll., Cambridge; and St. Bartholomew's Hospital, London. Late House Physician at St. Bartholomew's Hospital. *War Work:* Carrying on Opposition Practice from 1914-20; M.O. in charge Huskard's Auxiliary Military Hospital, 1914-19; Hyde Auxiliary Military Hospital, 1914-18; The Court, Ingatestone, Convalescent Hospital, 1915; M.O. in charge troops billeted in village at various times and two Anti-Aircraft Gun Stations, at Ingatestone and Stock, 1917-20. *Address:* Brandiston House, Ingatestone, Essex.   (M10263)

HAMILTON, Henry Killermann WEDDERBURN-, O.B.E.

HAMLETT, Capt. Harry Williams, O.B.E., R.F.A., (T.F.)

HAMLIN, Lieut.-Col. Richard James, O.B.E., R.A.O.C.

HAMLYN, Henrietta, Mrs. Hamlyn, M.B.E.

HAMLYN, Capt. Ralph Ashton, O.B.E., R.A.S.C.

HAMLYN, Mary Sylvia CALMADY-, M.B.E., J.P., *b.* 1881; *d.* of the late Vincent Waldo Calmady-Hamlyn, J.P., M.A. (Balliol Coll., Oxford), Barrister-at-law, Capt. R.N.D. Yeomanry Cavalry. *Educ.:* Wycombe Abbey. Appointed Member, Devon Agricultural Wages Board, Devon Agricultural Executive, and Devon Profiteering Appeals Tribunal; Governor, Seale Hayne Agricultural College, and Okehampton Secondary Schools; Chairman, Devon Women's Institutes' Executive. *War Work:* Travelling Inspector, Board of Agriculture and Fisheries; Member, Devon County Military Appeals Tribunal; Chairman, Great Bidlake Women's Farm Committee. *Address:* Bidlake Vean, Bridestowe, Devon. *Club:* Forum.   (M8330)

HAMMICK, Lucy Mabel, M.B.E.; *d.* of Sir Murray Hammick, K.C.S.I., C.I.E. (*see* BURKE'S *Peerage*). *War Work:* Queen Mary's Needlework Guild, St. James' Palace. *Address:* 23, Brunswick Gardens, Kensington.   (M8331)

HAMMOND, Lieut. Bert Ernest, O.B.E., R.N.V.R.

HAMMOND, Brig.-Gen. Dayrell Talbot, C.B., C.B.E., J.P., *b.* 24 Dec. 1856; *s.* of J. H. Hammond, J.P., of Preston, Lancs.; *m.* Emma Adelaide Sobieski, *d.* of William Ince Anderton, J.P., D L., of Euxton Hall, Chorley, Lancs. *Educ.:* Rossall; Cheltenham College. *War Work:* Lieut.-Col.-Commdg. 4th Batt. Connaught Rangers; A.A.Q.M.G., 16th (Irish) Division; Brig.-Gen. Commdg. 25th (Irish), Reserve Infantry Brigade; Military Adviser, Irish Recruiting Council. *Address:* Corballis, Dunoany, Co. Meath. *Clubs:* Cocoa Tree; Stephen's Green; Dublin.   (C977)

HAMMOND, Edith, M.B.E.   (M10249b)

HAMMOND, Egbert Laurie Lucas, C.B.E., *b.* 1873; *s.* of the late Rev. Canon Joseph Hammond; *m.* Effie Townsend, *d.* of the Rev. George Townsend Warner. *Educ.:* Newton Abbot Coll., and Keble Coll., Oxford. In Indian Civil Service; Controller of Munitions, Bihar and Orissa. *Addresses:* Patna, Bihar and Orissa, India. *Club:* United Service.   (C1968)

HAMMOND, Emily Mary, Mrs., M.B.E.; *d.* of John Evans, of Essex; *m.* Charles Thomas, *s.* of George Hammond, of Lamberhurst, Kent. *Educ.:* Privately. *War Work:* 4½ years' service with Q.M.G. 3 Staff, War Office, Whitehall, S.W. 1. *Address:* 31, Gleneagle Road, Streatham, S.W. 16.

HAMMOND, Ernest Walter, M.B.E.

HAMMOND, Lieut.-Col. Frederick Dawson, C.B.E., D.S.O., *b.* 1881; *s.* of the late Col. Frederick Hammond, C.B., I.S.C. Entered R.E. 1900; Capt. 1910; Major, 1916; Brevet Lieut.-Col. 1917; served during S. African War, 1901-2 (Queen's medal with five clasps); Great War, 1914-17 (despatches, Legion of Honour).   (C1602)

HAMMOND, Major John Henry, O.B.E., Aust. A.P.C.

HAMMOND, Stephen Thomas, M.B.E., R.N.

HAMMOND, William Cecil, O.B.E.

HAMMOND, Major William Charles Thomas, O.B.E., R.N.

HAMMOND, Capt. William Stanley, O.B.E., R.A.F.

HAMNETT, Paymaster-Lieut. Bernard, O.B.E, R.N.

HAMPDEN, Sir Thomas Rudolph, C.B.E.

HAMPSHIRE, Frederick, M.B.E., *b.* 20 April, 1866; *s.* of John Hampshire, of Horbury; *m.* Martha, *d.* of Thomas Addy, of Doncaster. *Educ.:* St. Peter's School, Horbury. Member of the Horbury Urban District Council for eleven years, having held the position of Chairman of the Council, and Chairman of the Public Health Committee; at present Chairman of the Housing and Town Planning Committee; President of Ambulance Association; Life Member of the Horbury Common Lands Trust; Member of the West Riding Provincial Industrial Council. *War Work:* Chairman Military Service Tribunal, Local War Pensions Committee, Local War Relief Committee, War Savings Committee, and Food Economy Campaign; Member of Food Control Committee, and Local Fuel and Lighting Committee. *Address:* Hill Crest, Horbury, near Wakefield. *Clubs:* Masonic, Mirfield; Conservative, Horbury.   (M8333)

HAMPTON, Lieut. and Qr.-Mr. Charles Sweet, M.B.E., M.C.

HAMPTON, Clement Edward, M.B.E.

HAMPTON, Lieut. and Qr.-Mr. Thomas, M.B.E., D.C.M. *War Work:* Served in the Black Watch for 22¼ years previous to the Great War; in possession of Queen's South African Medal with 4 clasps, also Long Service and Good Conduct Medal; re-enlisted Sept. 1914, and proceeded overseas with the 9th Batt. Black Watch; awarded D.C.M., 1916; promoted Lieut. and Quartermaster in the 19th Royal Scots in April, 1916, subsequently serving with the 11th and 8th Batt. Royal Lancashire Regt., 1st Batt. The Essex Regt., and the Mission for the Repatriation of Russian Prisoners of War; served continuously overseas from July, 1915, to Nov. 1919. (M4497)

HANAFY, John Zaky, O.B.E., M.R.C.S., L.R.C.P.

HANBURY, Arthur Marcus, O.B.E., *b.* 1875; *s.* of Capel Hanbury; *m.* Norah Diana, *d.* of F. W. Maude, of New Romney, Kent. *Educ.:* Eastbourne Coll. *War Work:* Ministry of Munitions, Labour Supply Dept.; Section Director, Dilution of Labour. *Address:* 47, Oakley Street, Chelsea. *Club:* Savile. (O10561)

HANBURY, Effield Dorothy Cecil, Mrs., O.B.E., *b.* 29 May, 1889; *d.* of J. F. Symons-Jenne, Esq., of Watlington Park, Oxon.; *m.* Cecil, *s.* of Sir Thomas Hanbury, K.C.V.O., of La Mortola, Italy. *War Work:* Dorset Branch, B.R.C.S. *Addresses:* Kingston Maurward, Dorchester, Dorset; La Mortola, Ventimiglia, Italy. (O1419)

HANBURY, Major Everard Ernest, O.B.E., J.P., *b.* 1862; *s.* of Capt. Gurney Hanbury, of Holmwood Lodge, Ascot; *m.* Lilian, *d.* of the late C. T. Murdoch, D.L., J.P., M.P., of Buckhurst, Wokingham. *Educ.:* Eton and Sandhurst. Served with the Scots Guards, 1881 to 1902; Egyptian War, 1882; South African War, 1900. *War Work:* British Expeditionary Force, 1914–15; Home Service, 1915–19. *Address:* Watership House, Sydmonton, Newbury. *Clubs:* Guards'; Bachelors'. (O7235)

HANBURY, Major Geoffrey Hyde Barday, O.B.E., R.A.S.C.

HANBURY, Rev. Guy Somerset, O.B.E., M.A., Hon. C.F., *b.* 19 Feb. 1887; *s.* of Edgar Hanbury, of Eastrop Grange, Highworth, Wilts. *Educ.:* Winchester; Christ Church, Oxford; Bishop's Hostel, Farnham. Assistant Curate, St. George's, Portsea, Portsmouth, 1913–17; Vice-Principal, St. Francis Coll., Mundah, Queensland, and Mission Chaplain, Diocese of Brisbane, 1920. *War Work:* Member of Portsmouth Volunteer Ambulance Corps, 1916–17; Temp. C. F., 1917–19; attached successively to 7th Corps, Heavy Artillery, Rest Camp, 65th Brigade R.G.A., 72nd Bde. R.G.A., 79th Bde. R.G.A., and 2/1 D.L.I., all in B.E.F., in France and Belgium. *Address:* St. Francis Coll., Mundah, Queensland, Australia. (O5335)

HANBURY, John James, O.B.E., M.I.M.E., J.P. Middlesex, *b.* 1 Feb. 1846; *s.* of George John Hanbury, of Hastings; *m.* Henrietta, *d.* of Richard Wood, of Sowerby Bridge, Yorkshire. *Educ.:* Owens. *War Work:* Member of Committee for National Relief; Chairman of the Recruiting Committee for the Harrow Division (under Lord Derby's Scheme), and afterwards Chairman of the Advisory Recruiting Committee for Willesden until its disbandment. *Address:* Edgeley, York Road, Exeter *Club:* Constitutional. (O10562)

HANBURY, Lieut. Nigel, M.B.E., *b.* 5 Aug. 1879; *s.* of George Hanbury, of Hitcham House, Burnham, Bucks; *m.* Evelyn Marion, *d.* of Herbert Arbuthnot, of 76, Westbourne Terrace, London. *Educ.:* Eton. Merchant. *War Work:* Served with the Coldstream Guards, Staff, 18th Division, in France, from Sept. 1916, till Jan. 1918. *Clubs:* Carlton; Guards'. (M4498)

HANBURY, Noel, C.B.E., *b.* 1881; *s.* of Sampson Hanbury, of Bishopstowe, Torquay (*see* BURKE's *Landed Gentry*); *m.* E. M. Lillie, *d.* of William Ferrand, of St. Ives, Yorks. *Educ.* Eton. County Director of Hampshire. *War Work:* Aug. 1914 to Oct. 1918, Hon. Administrator of Winchester Auxiliary Hospitals; Oct. 1918, County Director V.A.O., Hants. *Address:* St. Cross Grange, Winchester. (C2662)

HANCOCK, Aline Marie, Mrs., M.B.E.

HANCOCK, Annie Maria, O.B.E. (O11977)

HANCOCK, Capt. Charles Frederick, O.B.E.

HANCOCK, Lieut. Frank, M.B.E.

HANCOCK, Frederick, M.B.E., B.A., *b.* 13 Dec. 1883; *s.* of William Hancock, of London. *Educ.:* Wellington and Clare Coll., Cambridge. Chartered Accountant. *War Work:* Five years in Rouen, organising entertainments and games for the reinforcement camps, under the Rouen Recreation Committee. *Address:* Clophill House, Clophill, Beds. (M1847)

HANCOCK, George Charles, C.B.E., M.R.C.S., L.R.C.P., D.P.H. Medical Supervisor of Army Contracts at Home. (C3148)

HANCOCK, Capt. (Act. Major) Thomas Watson, O.B.E., F.R.C.S., M.R.C.S., L.R.C.P., R.A.M.C. (T.), *b.* 1890; *s.* of J. A. Hancock, of Norwich; *m.* Rosella Isabel *d.* of the late T. Walker, of Wolverhampton. *Educ.:* Bracondale School, Norwich; London Hospital. Surgeon; late Resident Surgical Officer and House Surgeon, Norfolk and Norwich Hospital. *War Work:* Surgical Specialist, 47th Casualty Clearing Station, B.E.F.; mentioned in despatches, 1918–19. *Address:* 40, St. Giles St., Norwich. *Clubs:* London Hospital Sports Union; British Medical Association; Norfolk Motor. (O2551)

HANCOCK, William Hern, M.B.E., *b.* 13 Aug. 1880; *s.* of Henry Sydney Hancock, of Sydney Place, St. Austell, Cornwall; *m.* Irene Eugénie, *d.* of Thomas Heath, of Southfield, Kingskerswell. *Educ.:* Hart House School, Burnham,

Somerset. *War Work:* Acting Staff Clerk, Intelligence; Division, Admiralty, 1914–15; Assistant Sec. to Chief of Staff, 1916–17; Staff Clerk in charge of Operations Division, 1917; Sec. to Deputy First Sea Lord, 1918. *Address:* 29, Ellerton Road, Wandsworth Common, S.W. 18. (M8337)

HANCOCK, Capt. (A. Major) William Venning Glanvill, O.B.E., R.G.A. (T.), *b.* 27 April, 1892; *s.* of William G. Hancock, of St. Ives, Cornwall. *Educ.:* Kelly College, Tavistock. Accountant, Barclays Bank, Ltd. *War Work:* Mobilised in Cornwall R.G.A. (T.F.), Aug. 1914; Service on A.A. in France, 1916–19, commanding "D" Anti-Aircraft Battery and subsequently Central A. A. Group, L. of C.; Service in Germany with " R." A.A.Bty., 1919. Twice mentioned in despatches. *Address:* St. Ives, Cornwall. *Club:* Junior Army and Navy. (O5336)

HANCOCK, Alice Maud Nancy, Lady BURFORD-, M.B.E. (*see* BURKE's *Peerage*); *d.* of Rev. G. R. Nankivell, of Crediton, N. Devon, widow of Sir Henry James Burford-Hancock. *War Work:* Commandant London 40 Searcher after the Missing and Wounded; engaged on Air Raid action. *Address:* 10, Penywern Road, S.W. 5. (M8335)

HANCOX, Cecil John, M.B.E.

HAND, John Pierce, M.B.E., *b.* 2 March, 1883; *s.* of John Hand, of St. Johns, Newfoundland; *m.* Helen, *d.* of George F. Scott, of Ashville, N.C., U.S.A. *Educ.:* St. Patricks Hall, St. Johns, Newfoundland. President, Bermuda Chamber of Commerce, 1916–17–18–20; Chairman, Bermuda Government Board of Trade: Member Government Trade Development Board. *War Work:* Organiser "600 Club," Bermuda, to assist dependents and returned soldiers; Member various Bermuda Government Commissions; sent to Ottawa, Washington, and New York. *Address:* Hamilton, Bermuda. *Club:* Royal Bermuda Yacht. (M1270)

HANDASYDE, George Harris, O.B.E.

HANDFORD, John James William, O.B.E.

HANDFORD, Margaret Emma, Mrs., M.B.E., *b.* 13 July, 1868; *s.* of John Davis Peard, of Croydon; *m.* the Rev. William Boycott, Vicar of St. Peter's, Barnsley; *s.* of William Handford, of Lucknow, India. *Educ.:* Woodford House, Croydon. *War Work:* Soldiers' and Sailors' Families Association Representative, Barnsley; Soldiers' and Sailors' Help Society Friend, Barnsley; Local War Pensions Committee, Barnsley; War League of Help Committee, Barnsley. *Address:* St. Peter's Vicarage, Barnsley, York. (M8339)

HANDLEY, Capt. Arthur, O.B.E., R.A.S.C., *b.* 1 Aug. 1892; *s.* of Arthur Handley, of Warminster. *Educ.:* Privately, and King's Coll., London Univ. Export Merchant. *War Work:* Joined R.N. Armoured Car Div., Nov. 1914, which was disbanded in Aug. 1915; transferred to the R.N.A.S., but owing to a crash, resigned in Nov. 1915, and was granted a commission in the R.A.S.C. (M.T.), Jan. 1916; was on the Somme, April to Sept. 1916, and served in Palestine and Syria, 1917–19; twice mentioned in despatches. *Address:* Corbie Steps, Harehills Lane, Leeds. *Clubs:* Leeds; R.A.S.C. (O6195)

HANDLEY, Kirk, M.B.E.

HANDMAN, Capt. Adolph Herbert, M.B.E., R.A.F.

HANDOVER, Harry George, O.B.E., J.P.

HANDS, Aletta Catherine, Lady, O.B.E.; *s.* of Philippus Albertue Myburgh, of Elsenburg, Mulders Vlei, Cape Colony; *m.* Sir Harry Hands, K.B.E., *s.* of Josiah Hands, of Kings Norton, Birmingham. *Educ.:* Good Hope Seminary, Cape Town. *War Work:* Mayoress of Cape Town, 1915–18; President of Troops' Refreshment Committee; Member of Executive Committee of Gifts and Comforts Organisation, and various other Committees for War work. *Address:* Talana, Claremont, Cape Town. (O2202)

HANDS, Sir Harry, K.B.E., *b.* Sept. 1860; *s.* of Josiah Hands, of King's Norton, Birmingham; *m.* Aletta Catharine, *d.* of Philip A. Ryburgh, M.L.A., of Etseuburg, Mulders Vlei, Cape Colony. Major of Cape Town, 1912–13; Greater Cape Town, 1915–18; Commander Order of Leopold of Belgium. *Address:* Talana, Claremont, Cape Colony, S. Africa. *Clubs:* City; D.A.C. (Cape Town). (K315)

HANDS, William Joseph, C.B.E., *b.* 10 July, 1865; *s.* of Joseph Hands, of Moulsoe, Bucks. H.M. Divisional Inspector of Schools (East Central Division) Board of Education. *War Work:* Assistant Director, Dilution of Labour Branch, Ministry of Munitions; Deputy Director-Gen. National Labour Supply, Ministry of National Service; Controller, Ministry of National Service: Sec. of Ministry of National Service and Reconstruction; Controller of Profiteering Act Department, Board of Trade. *Address:* 130, Kedleston Road, Derby. (C2663)

HANDY, Lieut. William, M.B.E., R.E.

HANDYSIDE, Surg. Rear-Adm. Sir Patrick Brodie, K.B.E., C.B., R.N. (ret.), *b.* March, 1860; *s.* of John Brodie Handyside; *m.* Lilly Chester, *d.* of Lieut.-Col. F. H. Blenkinsop, I.M.S. *Educ.:* Edinburgh. *War Work:* Royal Naval Hospitals, Plymouth and Chatham. *Address:* Edgehill, Gallane, N.B. *Clubs:* Junior United Services, London; Caledonian United Services, Edinburgh. (K259)

HANKEY, Basil Howard Alers, C.B.E., *b.* 1868; *s.* of E. A. Hankey, of Notton House, Lacock; *m.* Maud Wyndham *d.* of Col. Goodden, of Compton House, Sherborne. *Educ.:* Sherborne. County Director of Red Cross for Wilts. *War Work:* *Address:* Stanton Manor, Chippenham, Wilts. *Clubs:* Windham. (C516)

HANKEY, Major George Frederick Barnard, O.B.E.

HANKEY, Lieut.-Col. John Cyril Giffard Alers, C.B.E., M.V.O., b. 1873. Formerly Lieut.-Col. R.A.; Extra Equerry to Princess Christian. (C1603)

HANKEY, Major William Hubert Alers, O.B.E.

HANKINS, Albert Edward, M.B.E., b. 21 June, 1871; s. of the late George Hankins; m. Mary Ann, d. of the late Thomas Henry Usher. Clerk, War Office. Address: 10, Albert Road, Hounslow. (M1848)

HANKINS, Ivy Winifred, M.B.E.

HANKINSON, Charles James, M.B.E., J.P.; s. of Thomas James, of Bournemouth; m. Violet Downs, d. of William Downs, C.E. Educ.: Mill Hill School and privately. Author, Lecturer, and Journalist. War Work: Qualified as Munitions Engineer, 1915; head of a Supply Section, Ministry of Munitions, 1916–18; first Superintendent Archives Registry, Ministry of Munitions, 1919–20; Lecturer for Belgian Refugees Fund; Lecturer for War Office; Lecturer for Y.M.C.A. throughout the War. Address: 1, Park Hill, Ealing, W. 5. Clubs: Whitefriars; After Dinner. (M8341)

HANKINSON, George, M.B.E., b. 24 Feb. 1862; s. of Thomas and Aley Hankinson, of Scarborough; m. Mary Lettice, d. of Collingwood Smailes, of Scarborough. Educ.: Privately. Member of Society of Incorporated Accountants and Auditors; Clerk to Bridlington Guardians, Rural District Council, Harbour Commissioners; Superintendent Registrar; Registrar of Borough Debentures, etc. War Work: Hon. Sec. East Riding of Yorkshire County Relief Committee (Prince of Wales' Fund), Canadian Rent Fund Committee, Rural District Tribunal, Bridlington District Food Control Committee, Local Fuel Overseer, etc. Addresses: Long Lane, and Ashbourne, Marton Road, Bridlington. (M502)

HANMAN, William Thomas, C.B.E.

HANNA, Major Arthur Leonard, M.B.E.

HANNA, Ellen Victoria, Mrs., M.B.E., b. 24 May, 1876; d. of the late Wm. Ridgway Jackson, of Belfast; m. Henry, s. of John Hanna, of Belfast. Educ.: Friends' School, York. War Work: Soldiers' Canteen Buffet, and Soldiers' Central Club, Dublin, from Sept. 1914 to present date. Address: 83, Pembroke Road, Dublin. (M8342)

HANNA, Capt. William Gemmill Chalmers, O.B.E., C.A., b. 27 March, 1879; s. of Thomas Chalmers Hanna, of Littlelaught, Ayrshire; m. Alice Maud, d. of James Russell Middleton, I.C.S. Educ.: Loretto School. Sec. Edinburgh Canadian Mortgage Co., Ltd. War Work: Lieut., Scottish Horse Yeomanry, 1914–15; Lieut., 4th Seaforth Highlanders; Staff Capt., G.H.Q.; France, 1915–19; mentioned in despatches (twice). Club: University, Edinburgh. (O5337)

HANNAFORD, Claude, M.B.E.

HANNAFORD, Sarah Ann Pike, M.B.E.

HANNAH, John Miller, O.B.E., J.P.

HANNAN, George James Bryce, M.B.E., b. 20 Jan. 1882; s. of William Campbell Hannan, of Edinburgh. Educ.: Public School, Dublin, and Polytechnic, London. Inspection Department, Royal Arsenal, 1896–1914. War Work: Joined British War Mission in U.S.A., Dec. 1914; Bethlehem, Pa., 1915; Pittsburgh, Pa., 1915–17; Chief Clerk Combined British and American Government Aeronautical Inspection Departments, Buffalo, N.Y., 1917–18; New York, 1918–19. Address: Hawthorndene, Balcaskie Road, Eltham, London. Clubs: Overseas, Aldwych. (M8344)

HANNAY, Major Charles Graham, O.B.E., b. 1867; s. of H. E. S. Hannay, R.I.N., J.P., of Dibrugarh, Assam; m. Lucy, d. of James Ramsden, of Meltham, Yorks. Educ.: Eastbourne and privately. Tea planter, Assam. War Work: Remount purchasing officer, 1914; R.A.S.C., S.S.O. 22nd Division, B.E.F. and Salonica E.F.; Officer in charge, 661 Co. R.A.S.C. No. 1 R.H.T. Depot, Park Royal. Address: Gordon Lodge, Eastbourne. Clubs: Golfers'; United R.A.S.C. (O7238)

HANNAY, Major George Daniel, M.B.E. R.A.F.

HANNAY, Jane Ewing, Mrs., O.B.E.

HANNAY, Major Donald RAINSFORD-, O.B.E., R.A.F.

HANNEN, Lancelot, C.B.E., B.A., b. 10 Dec. 1866; s. of Benjamin Hannen; m. Delia Mary, d. of T. Ramsey Dennis, Paymaster-in-Chief, R.N. Educ.: Radley; Trinity Hall, Cambridge. War Work: Head Partner of the Firm of Christie, Manson and Woods, who conducted four Great Red Cross Sales of works of art during the War; a Trustee of British Empire Leave Club at Cologne; owner-driver on the London Ambulance Column. Address: 11A, Portland Place, W. 1. Clubs: United University; Ranelagh; Royal Automobile; Leander. (C978)

HANNEN, Capt. Nicholas James, O.B.E. R.A.S.C.

HANNEY, Capt. Michael John, M.B.E., A.P.D.

HANNING, Charles Horatio, M.B.E., R.N.

HANNON, Marion Coulson, M.B.E.

HANNYNGTON, Mary, Mrs. John Arthur, O.B.E.

HANRAHAN, William George Augustin, M.B.E.

HANSCOMB, Henry Charles, M.B.E., b. 15 Oct. 1874; s. of the late William Robert Hanscomb, of Battersea; m. Annie Caroline, d. of the late Spencer Bannister, of Fletching. Educ.: Battersea. Appointed ex-soldier clerk, War Office, Oct. 1908; South Africa 1899–1902, with 1st Batt. The Border Regiment (Queen's Medal, 5 clasps; King's Medal, 2 clasps). War Work: Clerical duties at the War Office; served in the Wandsworth V.T.C. Address: 57, Kelmscott Road, Wandsworth Common, S.W. 11. (M8345)

HANSCOMBE, Lieut. Stanley William, M.B.E., b. 17 May, 1894; s. of Wm. Hanscombe, of Cambridge. Educ.: Privately, The County School, Cambridge. Incorporated Accountant.

War Work: Enlisted in 69th (East Anglian) Divisional Cyclist Company; subsequently transferred to O.T.C., Grove Park, S.E., and commissioned to the R.A.S.C. (Mechanical Transport) on 15 January, 1917; promoted to Lieut. 15 July, 1918. Addresses: Kenilworth, Pretoria Road, Cambridge; 4, Capel Villas, Capel Road, East Barnet, Herts. (M4501)

HANSEN, Alina, M.B.E.

HANSEN, Sven Wohlford, M.B.E.

HANSFORD, Capt. Albert Urbane, M.B.E., R.A.F.

HANSFORD, Ernest William Harry, M.B.E.

HANSON, Clarence Oldham, M.B.E., b. 21 Feb. 1871; m. Elizabeth Margaret Sinclair Shepherd. Educ.: Winchester; Cooper's Hill. Assistant Conservator of Forests, Indian Forest Department, 1893 (retired 1904); Instructor, School of Forestry, Forest of Dean, under Office of Works, 1904; Assistant Deputy Surveyor Dean Forest, 1914; Divisional Officer, Forestry Commission, 1920. War Work: Lent to the Timber Supply Dept., April, 1916, to Nov. 1917, and was in charge of their operations in Devon and Cornwall. Addresses: 3, Malvern Place, Cheltenham; 8, The Close, Exeter. (M504)

HANSON, Lieut. Herbert James, O.B.E., R.N.V.R.

HANSON, Lieut.-Col. John Richard, O.B.E.

HANSON, Lieut.-Col. Paul Rennard, O.B.E., b. 22 Oct., 1882; s. of George F. Hanson, of Montreal; m. Mary Edith, d. of William H. Irwin, of Montreal. Educ.: Ontario Public School. Sales Manager, Dunlop Tyre and Rubber Goods Company, Ltd., Canada, Montreal Division. War Work: Enlisted September, 1914, Royal Montreal Regiment, 14th Battalion; wounded 23 April, 1915; mentioned in despatches, June 1916. Address: 702, Grosvenor Avenue, Montreal, Quebec. Clubs: Montreal; St. George's; Country. (O1425)

HANSON, Surgeon-Commander Reginald John Edward, O.B.E., M.A. (Cantab.), F.R.C.S., R.N.V.R., b. 16 August, 1870; s. of the Rev. H. Hanson, of London; m. Blanche Southwood, d. of Charles Lee Lewes, of London. Educ.: Haileybury; Trinity College, Cambridge; St. Mary's Hospital. Ophthalmic Surgeon, attached to London Division, Royal Naval Volunteer Reserve. War Work: In Hospital carriers "Plassy" and "Asturias," 1914–15; R.N. Hospital, Haslar, 1915–19 (ophthalmic surgeon); organised ophthalmic cliniques in Grand Fleet, 1914; inventor of improvements to periscopes, gun-sighting telescopes and theodolites adopted in the Royal Navy. Addresses: 20, Kensington Park Gardens, London, W. 11; Hayling Island, Hants. Clubs: Oxford and Cambridge; Cruising Association; Union Society, Cambridge. (O1426)

HANSON, Rev. Robert Edward Vernon, O.B.E., M.A., Deputy Chaplain-in-Chief, Royal Air Force, b. 29 March, 1866; s. of Joseph Hanson, of Clapham Common; m. Margaret, d. of Thomas Fox Simpson, of Tunbridge Wells. Educ.: King's College, London, and Emmanuel Coll., Cambridge. War Work: Senior Chaplain, 6th Division, B.E.F., France; Senior Chaplain, Winchester and District; Deputy Chaplain-in-Chief, Royal Air Force. Address: 62, Park Lane, Wallington, Surrey. Club: Royal Air Force. (O7239)

HANTON, 2nd Lieut. Peter Kydd, M.B.E., R.E.

HAPPELL, David, M.B.E.

HARBEN, Guy Philip, O.B.E.

HARBINSON, T. Major William Dawson, O.B.E., R.A.O.C.

HARBORD, Frank William, C.B.E., F.I.C., A.R.S.M., F.C.S., Chevalier Legion d'Honneur, b. Dec. 1860; s. of J. Massingham Harbord, of Norwich; m. Marian, d. of Vernon Smith. Educ.: Privately and Royal School of Mines. Consulting Metallurgist; Member of Council Iron and Steel Institute; Member of Council, Institution of Mining and Metallurgy; Civil Member, Ordnance Committee Royal Arsenal. War Work: Acted as Consulting Metallurgist at the Ministry of Munitions. Addresses: 16, Victoria Street, S.W. 1; Englewick, Englefield Green, Surrey. Clubs: St. Stephen's; Mining and Metallurgical. (C29)

HARBORD, Capt. Richard Arthur, O.B.E., Mercantile Marine, b. 13 March, 1859; s. of Wm. Harbord, M.R.C.S. (Eng.), L.S.A. (Lond.), of Wainfleet, Lincs.; m. Rose Helen, d. of James Chamberlain, of Hull. Educ.: Magdalen College School, Wainfleet. War Work: In command of H.M. transport "Lepanto." Address: 45, Melrose Street, Hull. Club: International Shipmasters', Bombay. (O10564)

HARBOTTLE, Lieut. Denis Leslie, M.B.E., R.A.S.C., b. 20 April, 1894; s. of John George Harbottle, of Newcastle-on-Tyne. Educ.: Monkton Combe School. War Work: Served in Canadian Expeditionary Force and afterwards commissioned in R.A.S.C. Address: 12, Victoria Terrace, Low Fell, Durham. (M4877)

HARBURN, Ellen Frances, M.B.E.

HARCHER, Ernest Edwin, M.B.E., R.A.S.C.

HARCOURT, Eveline Alice Marian, M.B.E.

HARCOURT, Henry, C.B.E., I.C.S., b. 20 Sept. 1873; s. of R. F. Harcourt, M.A., of Woodford, Essex; m. Elsie Mary, d. of John Knight, of Woodford. Educ.: Merchant Taylors', London, and Pembroke Coll., Oxford. Deputy Commissioner, Gundaspur, Punjab. Called to the Bar (Middle Temple) 1920. War Work: Recruiting and War Loans in Rohtak, D.I., Punjab. Addresses: Gundaspur, Punjab; Upper Norwood, S.E. 19. (C1076)

HARCOURT, Mary Ethel, Viscountess, M.B.E., J.P.; Lady of Grace of the Order of St. John of Jerusalem, d. of Walter Hayes Burns, of New York, U.S.A., m. Lewis, 1st Viscount Harcourt, s. of Rt. Hon. Sir William Harcourt, Nuneham

Park, Oxford. *War Work :* Joint Founder and Hon. Secretary American Women's War Relief Fund ; Hon. Secty. and Acting Commandant American Women's Hospital for Officers, Lancaster Gate ; Commandant Nuneham Park, Auxiliary Hospital for Officers. *Addresses :* 69, Brook Street, W. 1. ; Nuneham Park, Oxford. *Clubs :* Bath ; American Women's.   (DG17)

HARDEN, Lieut.-Col. Henry Spencer SCOTT-, O.B.E. ; has Croix de Guerre of Italy.   (O2255)

HARDIE, Anne, M.B.E. M.A., ; *d.* of John Hardie, J.P., of Elgin, N.B. *Educ. :* Elgin Academy ; Aberdeen Univ. ; France and Germany. Principal, Mahbubia Girls' School, Hyderabad, Deccan, India. *War Work :* Supt. of Press Section in Mobilisation Directorate, War Office ; Sec. of Women War Workers' Resettlement Committee. *Address :* Saifabad, Hyderabad, Deccan, India. *Club :* Secunderabad.   (M8350)

HARDIE, James March, M.B.E.   (M10390)

HARDIE, John, M.B.E.

HARDIE, Major John Leslie, D.S.O., O.B.E.

HARDIE, Muriel, M.B.E., W.R.N.S.

HARDIE, Surg.-Comm. Robert, O.B.E.. M.D., R.N.

HARDIMAN, John Percy, C.B.E., I.C.S., *b.* 24 May, 1874 ; *s.* of G. J. Hardiman, of Kidderminster ; *m.* Gertrude Emma, *d.* of Percival Smith, of Hampstead. *Educ. :* Malvern, and Oriel College, Oxford. Indian Civil Service ; Commissioner, Tenasserim Division, Moulmein, Burma. *War Work :* Controller of Munitions, Burma ; Liquidator of Hostile Firms, Burma ; Custodian of Enemy Property, Burma ; President, Exemption Tribunal, Rangoon Brigade Area. President, Selection Committee, Rangoon Brigade Area. *Address :* 13, Compayne Gardens, N.W. 6. *Club :* Pegu, Rangoon, Burma.   (C1077)

HARDING, Alfred Burcham, M.B.E.

HARDING, Alfred John, O.B.E., *b.* 24 Sept. 1878 ; *s.* of John Goulding Harding, of Tetbury, Gloucestershire. *Educ. :* Christ's College, Brecon ; St. John's College, Cambridge. Assistant Secretary Colonial Office.   (O406)

HARDING, Lieut. Arthur George, O.B.E.. R.A.O.C.

HARDING, Major Cecil Redfern, O.B.E., *b.* 24 Jan. 1874 ; *s.* of William S. Harding, of Harborne, Staffs. *Educ. :* Rugby. *War Work :* Commissioned in Reserve Batt. Irish Guards, Aug. 1914 ; joined 1st Battn. Irish Guards Sept. 1914 in France ; severely wounded at Ypres, Nov. 1914 ; appointed Staff Capt., H.Q. Staff, London District, 1916 ; Deputy Assistant Adjt.-Gen., London District, 1917-19. *Address :* Albany, Piccadilly, W. 1. *Clubs :* Guards' ; Arthur's ; St. James's ; Beefsteak.   (O7240)

HARDING, Major Edward Hadley, O.B.E.

HARDING, Egerton Stephen Somers, O.B.E., M.A., *b.* 30 Aug. 1886 ; *s.* of Francis E. Harding, of Old Springs, Market Drayton ; *m.* Elizabeth Muriel Scott, *d.* of Gen. Sir James Browne, K.C.B., K.C.S.I., R.E. *Educ. :* Oratory School, and King's College, Cambridge. *War Work :* Founded and directed the " Catholic Club, B.E.F." (huts and chapels for soldiers in France and Germany). *Address :* Old Springs, Market Drayton.   (O1427)

HARDING, Ethel Emma, Mrs., M.B.E., *b.* 5 Dec. 1869 ; *d.* of J. E. King, of Chatham ; *m.* Arthur James, *s.* of L. J. Harding, of Chatham. *Educ. :* Chatham. *War Work :* Lady Superintendent, Army Pay Offices, Chatham.   (M8351)

HARDING, John Rudge, O.B.E., *b.* 5 Dec. 1861 ; *s.* of Thomas Harding, of Elvetham, Hants. *Educ. :* Privately. An actor for thirty years before the War, under the Management of Sir John Hare, Mr. and Mrs. Kendal, Mr. Cyril Maude, Mr. Fred Terry, Miss Ellen Terry, etc. ; played many parts in London, including Rev. James Bartlett, in " Cousin Kate," at the Haymarket Theatre ; Spencer Pringle, in ' The Brass Bottle," at the Vaudeville ; Mr. Coote, in " Kipps " ; The Prince of Wales, in " The Scarlet Pimpernel," etc. *War Work :* Served with British Red Cross Society from Aug. 1914, first as Secretary in Auxiliary Home Hospitals Department, and afterwards as Secretary to " Star and Garter " Committee, which appointment is still held. *Address :* 34, Elm Park Mansions, Park Walk, S.W. 10. *Club :* Green Room.   (O3742)

HARDING, Col. John Stafford Goldie, M.B.E., J.P. Devon, Devonshire Regt. (ret.), *b.* 1856 ; *s.* of Capt. Thomas Goldie Harding, of Hallsannery, Bideford, Devon ; *m.* Louisa Francis William, *d.* of Col. Francis Farrant, of Buckland House, Dover. *Educ. :* Clifton. *War Work :* Chief Recruiting Officer for the County of Devon from 4 Aug. 1914, to Sept. 1918. *Address :* 2, The Terrace, Instow, North Devon.   (M1852)

HARDING, Capt. Kenneth O'Brien, O.B.E., I.A.

HARDING, Margaret, Mrs., M.B.E.

HARDING, Col. Philip Edward, O.B.E., M.C.

HARDING, Lieut.-Col. Richard Spalding, O.B.E.

HARDING, Capt. Robert Arthur Cotton, M.B.E. ; *s.* of A. R. Harding ; *m.* Muriel Annie Fredericka, *d.* of H. H. Hextall. *Educ. :* Eton ; Oxford. *War Work :* R.F.A. (T.F.) in India and Mesopotamia. *Address :* 51, Coleherne Court, London. *Club :* Bath.   (M4277)

HARDING, Lieut.-Col. William, C.B.E., M.D., R.A.M.C.

HARDING, William Percy, O.B.E.

HARDING, Lieut. Wyndham John Dorney, M.B.E.,

HARDISTY, Arthur Hobson, O.B.E., *b.* 1872 ; *s.* of William Hobson Hardisty, of Fartown, Huddersfield ; *m.* Henrietta, *d.* of the late Jabez Smith, of Eccles. *Educ. :* Mellor's Acad., and Technical Coll., Huddersfield. Engineer ; Hon. Sec. and Gen. Manager National Shell Factory, Hudders-

field, during Great War ; a musical composer ; author of numerous works on industrial questions. *Address :* The Hollies, Halifax Old Road, Huddersfield.   (O3743)

HARDISTY, Major William Frederick James, O.B.E., D.L., *b.* 13 July, 1858 ; *s.* of Rev. W. Hardisty, of Eton College ; *m.* Margaret Elaine, *d.* of A. T. H. Evans, of Manchester. *Educ. :* Eton. 29th (Worcestershire) Regt., 11th May, 1878 ; retired, July, 1906. *War Work :* Secretary, Territorial Force Association, Warwickshire. *Address :* Sydney Lodge, Leamington.   (O1428)

HARDMAN, Frances Mary Holford, Mrs., O.B.E. ; *d.* of late General Sir Thomas W. McMahon, Bart., C.B. ; *m.* late John Wreford Julian Hardman, Capt., Royal Dragoons, *s.* of Frederick Hardman. *Educ. :* Privately. Commandant, 2nd Dorset V.A.D. *War Work :* Commandant, The Castle Hospital, Serborne, 1914-19. *Address :* The Lattice House, Sherborne, Dorset.   (O1429)

HARDMAN, James, M.B.E.

HARDMAN, Capt. and Qr.-Mr. Walter, M.B.E.

HARDWICK, Lieut. Frank, M.B.E., R.E.

HARDWICK, Capt. Noel de Courcy, O.B.E., I.A.R.O.

HARDWICKE, Ellen, Countess of, C.B.E., *b.* 1881 ; *s.* of late James Russell, of New Zealand ; *m.* Charles Alexander, 8th Earl of Hardwicke. *War Work :* New Zealand Red Cross ; New Zealand War Contingent Association ; Belgian Refugee Work ; Norfolk House, Overseas Club ; New Zealand Officers' Club. *Address :* 13, Queensberry Place, London.   (C724)

HARDY, Capt. Charles Talbot, C.B.E., R.N.

HARDY, Major Confred Napier Mitchell, O.B.E., A.P.D.

HARDY, Dorothy Clara, M.B.E., *b.* 15 Feb. 1882 ; *d.* of Thomas Bush Hardy, R.B.A., of London. *Educ. :* Privately. *War Work :* In charge of women Munition Volunteer Records at the Ministry of Munitions.   (M8352)

HARDY, Major Frank Buckland, O.B.E., *b.* 6 Nov. 1868 ; *s.* of late General Campbell Hardy, of Dover ; *m.* Ethel, *d.* of Angus Macgregor, of Kerry, Malvern. *Educ. :* Tonbridge. Late Lieut. South African Constabulary, and Resident Justice of the Peace, Lydenbury District, Transvaal. *War Work :* In Royal Army Service Corps, 1914-19, France, Palestine, Germany. *Address :* 105, Jermyn Street, S.W.   (O5343)

HARDY, Frank Philip, M.B.E.

HARDY, Gladys Rivers, O.B.E., *d.* of the late W. M. Hardy, of Tasmania. *Educ. :* Tasmania. *War Work :* Commandant, The Garland Home, Norfolk Street, Park Lane, W. 1. *Address :* 36, Thayer Street, Manchester Square, W. 1.   (O10566)

HARDY, Henry Harrison, M.B.E.

HARDY, Major Henry Stewart, M.B.E., M.C.

HARDY, Capt. Hermann Alfred, O.B.E., Can. A.S.C.

HARDY, Ismay Gertrude, Mrs., M.B.E.

HARDY, Major John Lawton, O.B.E., E.A.F.

HARDY, Margaret Jane, M.B.E.

HARDY, Capt. Victor, M.B.E.

HARDY, Capt. Walter, O.B.E., R.G.A.

HARDY, William Eversley, M.B.E., M.I.E.E., *b.* 1876 ; *s.* of Major W. E. Hardy, late R.A., *m.* Gertrude Maye, *d.* of Laurence John Birthby. *Educ. :* United Services College, Westward Ho ; Currie Engineering School, Folkstone. General Manager and Engineer, Bath Electric Tramways, Ltd. *War Work :* Technical Representative Coal Mines Dept., Area 13. Hon. Sec., Advisory Committee, Area 3, Tramways (Board of Trade) Committee. *Address :* York Villa, Kensington, Bath.   (M8356)

HARDY, Margaret Joy COZENS-, M.B.E., *b.* 30 June, 1893 ; *d.* of Sydney Cozens-Hardy, of Glavenside, Letheringsett, Norfolk (*see* BURKE'S *Landed Gentry*). *Educ. :* Grassendall, Southbourne, Hants. *War Work :* Probationer, London Hospital ; Nurse at Cambridge Military Hospital, Aldershot ; Pensions Office, Norwich, 1917-19. *Address :* Glavenside, Letheringsett, Norfolk.   (M8354)

HARE, Dorothy Christian, C.B.E., M.D., W.R.N.S.

HARE, Major and Brevet Lieut.-Col. Charles Tristram Melville, C.B.E., *b.* 9 Feb. 1870 ; *s.* of Charles E. Hare, of Lee-on-Solent ; *m.* Marie Gertrude, *d.* of Volker van Waverveen, of The Klarenbeek, Holland (G.). *Educ. :* Stamford and Sandhurst. *Address :* 34, Sloane Court, S.W. 3. *Club :* United Service.   (C1604)

HARE, Francis Edward, M.B.E., *b.* 10 Nov. 1873 ; *s.* of Thomas Hare, of West Bay, Bridport, Dorset ; *m.* Rose Mary, *d.* of Thomas Hopkinson, of Ashover, Derbyshire. *Educ. :* Wellingore Hall College, and Lincoln Grammar School. Estate Manager. *War Work :* Commandant, V.A.D. Warwick 17 ; Organising Divisional Sec., Coleshill Division, Warwickshire Branch, British Red Cross Society ; Commandant, St. Gerard's Auxiliary Hospital, 1915-19 ; Member of Headquarters Council, Warwickshire Branch, B.R.C.S. ; Recruiting Officer, Home Hospitals Reserve, R.A.M.C. *Address :* Cross Heath, Coleshill, Birmingham.   (M8357)

HARE, George Frederick, M.B.E., *b.* 7 Feb. 1884. *Educ. :* Laughton's School, Boston, and P. T. Centre, Boston. Headmaster of Spalding Goodfellow's School. Commissioned Lay Reader, Lincoln Diocese ; formerly a member of the Spalding Urban Council. *War Work :* Hon. Sec., Spalding and District War Savings Committee ; Sec. Spalding District War Agricultural Committee ; Member Spalding Urban Food Control Committee, and Spalding Profiteering Tribunals. *Address :* Goodfellow's, Spalding.   (M8358)

HARE, Major Richard George Powel, O.B.E., R.A.O.C.,

b. 8 October, 1882; *s.* of Lieut.-Col. Robert Powel Hare, R.H.A., of Bath, *s.* of late Commander Richard Hare, R.N.; *m.* Ruby Geraldine, *d.* of John Warry, of Clifton, Bristol. *Educ.:* Dulwich. *War Work:* D.A.D.O.S., 6th Division, B.E.F., and Midland Division, British Army of the Rhine. *Address:* 47, Wymering Mansions, Elgin Avenue, London, W. (O2554)

HARE, Samuel, O.B.E., J.P., *b.* 1862; *s.* of John Hare, of Crook, Co. Durham; *m.* Mary Elizabeth, *d.* of Edward Williams, of Brymbo, N. Wales. *Educ.:* Gainford Academy, nr. Darlington. Mining and Civil Engineer. *War Work:* Producing Benzol, Toluol, etc., for war purposes. *Address:* Howlish Hall, Bishop Auckland. *Club:* Royal Automobile. (O407)

HARE, William Henry, M.B.E., *b.* 25 March, 1872; *s.* of the late William Henry Hare, of Louth; *m.* Edith, *d.* of the late Felix Goodwin, of Upper Hall, Louth. *Educ.:* Elstow School, Bedford. *War Work:* Establishment Officer, National Savings Committee, Salisbury Square, E.C. 4; formerly Staff Clerk, Board of Education. *Address:* 62, Barrington Road, Crouch End, N. 8. (M3697)

HAREWOOD, Rev. Ernest James, O.B.E.

HARFORD, Winifred Maud B., M.B.E., Q.M.A.A.C.

HARGOOD, Harry, O.B.E., J.P. D.L., *b.* 12 March, 1842; *s.* of Admiral W. Hargood, J.P., D.L., of Worthing; *m.* Elizabeth Mary, *d.* of the Rev. George Croke Rowden, D.C.L., of Oak Lawn, Weybridge, Surrey. *Educ.:* Rottingdean. Member R. National Life Boat Institution Committee; President of Worthing Branch, R.N.L.B. *War Work:* Chairman of Graylingwell War Hospital, Chichester, and Worthing Advisory Committee. *Address:* North Lodge, Worthing. *Club:* Worthing County. (O10567)

HARGRAVE, Paymaster-Lieut. John Eustace, O.B.E., R.N.

HARGRAVE, Mary Montague, Mrs., O.B.E.; *d.* of Major Thomas Spring; *m.* Abraham Addison, *s.* of A. A. Hargrave. *War Work:* Organiser, Soldiers' and Sailors' Club; Organiser and District Controller, National Egg-Collection; Member Co. Kerry Local War Pensions Committee; worker, British Red Cross; Interviewer, Repatriated Prisoners of War; on committee Soldiers' and Sailors' Family Association; S. Friend and Acting Co-Secretary Soldiers' Help Society, supplied local men prisoners of war with tobacco etc., at Limbury. (O105687)

HARGRAVE, Capt. William Bowen, O.B.E., R.A.F., *b.* 20 April, 1894; *s.* of Col. H. J. Hargrave, of Upton Lodge, Acle, Norfolk; *m.* Ethel May, *d.* of W. F. Batsford, of Essex. *War Work:* At commencement of War with Suffolk Regt.; transference to R.F.C., Sept. 1914; served overseas and at home with that corps. *Address:* C.F.S. Upavon, Wilts; Lipton Lodge, Acle, Norfolk. *Club:* R.A.F. (O8111)

HARGREAVES, Lieut. Gordon John Cooper, O.B.E.

HARGREAVES, Paymaster-Capt. Herbert James, C.B.E. Paymaster-Com. and Acting Paymaster-Capt. R.N.; Great War, 1914–19 (mentioned in despatches). (C2279)

HARGREAVES, John Henry, C.B.E., J.P.

HARGREAVES, Lieut. Laurence Appleyard, O.B.E., R.A.S.C. (T.).

HARINGTON, Wanda Grace, M.B.E., *d.* of the late Herbert S. Harington, of Kelston, Simla, India, and granddaughter of the late Col. T. L. Harington, 5th Bengal Cavalry. *Educ.:* Privately. *War Work:* Secretarial work at War Office from Jan. 1916, to Nov. 1920; worked at Queen Mary's Needlework Guild, Mulberry Walk, Chelsea. *Address:* Forum Club, 6, Grosvenor Place, Hyde Park Corner, S.W. 1. (M8359)

HARGROVES, Capt. and Qr.-Mr. William Robert, M.B.E., R.A.S.C.

HARISON, U., M.B.E.

HARKER, Edward, O.B.E.

HARKER, John Allen, O.B.E., F.R.S., *b.* 23 Jan. 1870; *s.* of the late Rev. John Harker, of Stockport; *m.* Ada Laura Maud, *d.* of Thomas Richardson, C.C., J.P., of Alston. *Educ.:* Stockport Grammar School; Univ. of Manchester, and Tübingen. Chief Assistant at National Physical Laboratory, Teddington. *War Work:* Acted as organiser of the work of the Nitrogen Products Committee, and Director of the Research in the Ministry of Munitions; visited Norway, Sweden, France, and America on work of the Ministry; was torpedoed on Cunarder "Andania." *Addresses:* Clarghyll Hall, Alston; 7, Houghton Place, N.W. 1. *Club:* National Liberal. (O408)

HARKER, Rev. Thomas Alphonsus, O.B.E.

HARKER, Surg.-Lieut.-Comm. William Edmund, O.B.E., M.D., R.N.V.R.

HARKNESS, Edith Geraldine, M.B.E. Hon. Sec. of the Hastings and Battle Division of the Soldiers' and Sailors' Families Association. (M10322)

HARLE, Charles, M.B.E. (M10354)

HARLEY, David, O.B.E.

HARLEY, Lieut. Ernest William James, M.B.E., R.A.O.C.

HARLOCK, Emily, Mrs., M.B.E., *b.* 2 Nov. 1864; *d.* of Alfred Robinson, of Lymm, Cheshire; *m.* Edward Baker, J.P., *s.* of John Harlock, J.P., of Banbury. *Educ.:* Privately. *War Work:* Hon. Sec. for 4 War Savings Associations; Hon. Sec. District Nursing Association; Member of the Cheshire County Insurance Committee. *Address:* Newton House, Middlewich, Cheshire. (M8560)

HARLOCK, Wilfred, M.B.E., J.P.

HARLOW, Frederick James, M.B.E., B.Sc., A.R.C.Sc., D.I.C., F.Inst.P., *b.* 13 Sept. 1886; *s.* of James Thomas Harlow,

of Preston, Canterbury; *m.* Isabel Elsie, *d.* of J. F. Pettman, of St. Nicholas, Thanet. *Educ.:* Simon Langton School, Canterbury; and Roya. College of Science, London. Head of Department of Mathematics and Physics, Sir John Cass Technical Institute, London. *War Work:* X-ray and Electro-medical Physicist, Army Medical Department, War Office; Secretary, War Office X-Ray Committee; Secretary, War Office Electro-medical Committee. *Addresses:* St. Nicholas, Castlebar Park Road, Ealing, W. 5.; Sir John Cass Technical Institute, Jewry Street, E.C. 3. (M8362)

HARLOW, Lieut.-Col. George Henry, O.B.E., R.A.S.C.

HARMAN, Lieut. Edmund, M.B.E.

HARMAN, Rowland George, M.B.E.

HARMER, Ronald Frederick, M.B.E., *b.* 22 March, 1892; *s.* of William Scotford Harmer, of Cirencester, Glos.; *m.* Alison Scott, *d.* of Walter Charles Harmer, of London. *Educ.:* Cirencester Grammar School; New College School, Oxford; formerly a member of the Editorial staff of the "Morning Post." Secretary and Manager, Review of the Foreign Press, Ltd., Greycoat Buildings, 99–101, Horseferry Road, Westminster, S.W. *War Work:* Enlisted in the London Scottish, Aug. 1914; Commission 1/5th Gordon Highlanders, April, 1915; served in France, July to Dec. 1915; attached Military Intelligence Dept. War Office, 1916–19; promoted Capt. 1917. *Address:* River Court, Cirencester, Gloucestershire. (M5334)

HARMER, Sir Sidney Frederic, K.B.E., Sc.D., F.R.S., *b.* 9 March, 1862; *s.* of Frederic William Harmer, J.P., Hon. M.A. (Cantab.), F.G.S., of Oakland House, Cringleford, Norwich; *m.* Laura Russell, *d.* of Arthur Pearse Howell, of Bengal Civil Service, formerly Fellow of St. John's College, Oxford. *Educ.:* University College, London; King's College, Cambridge. Fellow of King's College, Cambridge, 1886–1914; Lecturer, 1886–1908; Assistant-Tutor, 1890–1908; Superintendent of the University Museum of Zoology, 1892–1908; Keeper of Zoology, British Museum (Natural History), 1909–20; Director of the Natural History Departments of the British Museum since 1919. *War Work:* Officially concerned in assisting the Trustees of the British Museum to advise various Government Departments on scientific questions referred to them in connexion with the War. Among these were the whales and whaling industry of South Georgia, the South Shetland Islands and other Southern localities. Enormous quantities of oil were obtained from these sources, and these were of vital importance, not only in the manufacture of explosives, but in providing material which must otherwise have been taken from the food-supply of the country. *Addresses:* British Museum (Natural History), Cromwell Road S.W. 7; 30, Courtfield Gardens, S.W. 5. *Club:* Savile. (K380)

HARNDEN, Alfred Charles, M.B.E.

HARNESS, Lieut. Robert John, M.B.E., R.N.

HARNETT, Capt. Edward St. Clair, M.B.E., R.A.F.

HARNETT, Leslie Bennett, M.B.E., *b.* 15 June, 1868; *s.* of Jeremiah Harnett, of Hamilton, Bermuda; *m.* Ina Clifton, *d.* of George Vallis, of Sutton, Somersetshire. *Educ.:* Baltimore, U.S.A. *War Work:* Executive Officer and Secretary, Supply Control Board, Bermuda. *Address:* Glynhir, Pembroke, Bermuda. *Clubs:* Royal Bermuda Yacht; Hamilton Dinghy, Hamilton (Bermuda). (M2945)

HARNETT, William Augustus, M.B.E., *b.* 15 Jan. 1873; *s.* of the late William Harnett, of Herne Bay, Kent.; *m.* Annie Grace, *d.* of the late George Jones, of Hill Farm, Downham, Norfolk. *Educ.:* Herne Bay. Civil Servant at the Admiralty. *Address:* Crayholme, Knoll Road, Sidcup, Kent. (M8364)

HARNETT, William Falkiner, C.B.E., *b.* 1869; *s.* of Falkiner Minchin Harnett, of Shannon Lawn, Glin, co. Limerick; *m.* Mary Isabella, *d.* of Dr. F. P. Philips, of Exeter. *Educ.:* Grammar School, Drogheda. Entered I.C.S. 1893; Locomotive and Carriage Supt., Bengal State Railway, 1911; Lieut.-Col. Comdg. 12th E. Bengal Railway Batn., Indian Defence Force (V.D.). *Addresses:* Indian State Railways, Bengal; 12, Victoria Terrace, Exeter. *Club:* Bengal United Service. (C1078)

HAROLD, Joseph, M.B.E., D.C.M., R.A.S.C.

HAROLD, May, Mrs., M.B.E. (M7099)

HARPER, Capt. Arthur David, O.B.E., F.L.G.A., *b.* 2 June, 1875; *s.* of Thomas Harper, of Wolverhampton; *m.* Susan Harper, *d.* of Thomas Reynolds, of Liverpool. *Educ.:* Windsor Higher Grade School, Liverpool. Late Principal Assistant of the Town Clerk's Department, Liverpool City Council; recently appointed Clerk and Superintendent Liverpool Markets and Abattoir. *War Work:* Joint Secretary Parliamentary Recruiting Committee; subsequently Commissioned and attached to Liverpool Area; appointed Area Registration Officer; and Headquarters Staff Officer; appointed to Secretariat North-Western Region, under Ministry of National Service, and transferred to Chester as Assistant Director for Cheshire. (O1432)

HARPER, Charles Henry, O.B.E.

HARPER, Edward Thomas, M.B.E.

HARPER, Francis Henry, M.B.E., *b.* 2 March, 1877; *s.* of the late Francis Hill Harper, of New Malden, Surrey; *m.* Ida Louise, *d.* of William Larkin, of Putney. Acting Staff Officer, Colonial Office. *War Work:* Military Department of the Colonial Office. *Address:* 93, Oakhill Road, Putney, S.W. 15. (M8366)

HARPER, George, O.B.E.

HARPER, John Bradford, O.B.E.

HARPER, Lieut.-Col. John Robinson, C.B.E., R.A.M.C. Served in the Great War, 1914–19 (mentioned in despatches). (C1261)

HARPER, Capt. John Stanley, M.B.E., R.E.

HARPER, Major Reginald Tristram, O.B.E., R.A.V.C.

HARPER, Sydney, M.B.E.

HARPHAM, Major Harold D., O.B.E.

HARPUR, Lieut. John Latimer, M.B.E., R.A.S.C.

HARPUR, Major William Lewis, O.B.E., R.E.

HARRAP, George Edward, M.B.E.

HARREL, Right Hon. Sir David, G.B.E., K.C.B., K.C.V.O., I.S.O.

HARREL, Com. William Vesey, C.B., C.B.E., M.V.O., *b.* 1866; *s.* of the Rt. Hon. Sir David Harrel, P.C., K.C.B., K.C.V.O., I.S.O., of Shankill, co. Dublin (*see* BURKE'S *Peerage*), Roy. Irish Constabulary, 1886–98; Inspector of Prisons in Ireland, 1898–1902; Assist. Commr. of Dublin Metropolitan Police, 1902–14; Com. R.N.V.R.; Knight of Grace of the Order of St. John of Jerusalem in England. *Clubs:* Kildare Street: Royal St. George Yacht. (C1164)

HARRIDENCE, Lieut. Robert Treslove, M.B.E. (M10223)

HARRIES, 2nd Lieut. Ernest Bertram, M.B.E.

HARRIES, Major George Samuel, M.B.E.

HARRIES, Herbert Frederick, O.B.E.

HARRIES, Owen, M.B.E., *b.* 26 April, 1864; *s.* of Peter Harries, of Fishguard; *m.* Alice Annie, *d.* of James Henry Clements, of Charlotte Town, P. E. Island. *Educ.:* Long Ashton School, Somersetshire. Assistant Manager, The Cunard Steam Ship Co., Ltd., Southampton. *War Work:* Represented the Cunard Steam Ship Co., Ltd., in connection with steamers engaged in transport service during whole period of the war. *Addresses:* Maritime Chambers, Southampton: and The Green House, Compton, Winchester. *Club:* Royal Southampton Yacht. (M8368)

HARRIES, Thomas Henry, M.B.E.

HARRINGTON, Lieut. Athur George, O.B.E., R.N.

HARRINGTON, Ernest John, O.B.E., *b.* 4 June, 1864; *s.* of George Harrington, of London; *m.* Augusta Elkington, *d.* of Tate Mansford, of London. Deputy Accountant-General, General Post Office. *Address:* 21, Hampstead Lane, N. 6. (O10569)

HARRINGTON, Capt. George, M.B.E., R.M., (ret.), *b.* 7 Aug. 1876; *s.* of George Harrington, of London; *m.* Alice Maude, *d.* of George Franks, of Portsmouth. *Educ.:* Crouch End, Board School, London. Joined H.M. Service in the Royal Marine Artillery, May, 1893; served for 21 years; discharged to Pension, May, 1914, with the rank of Quartermaster-Sergeant. Granted a Temporary Commission as Lieut. and Qr.-Mr., Royal Marines, May, 1915 for service with the Land Defences, Scapa Flow; promoted Captain and Qr.-Mr. Aug. 1918. *Addresses:* 23, Somerset Road, Brentford, Middlesex; 41, Douglas Road, Lenton Sands, Nottingham. (M3469)

HARRINGTON, Henry Augustus, M.B.E., *b.* 10 July, 1864; *s.* of the late John William Harrington. *Educ.:* Army Schools, Local Director of Ports, Alexandria, Egypt. *War Work:* Canteen work, and general interest in the moral welfare of the troops (British) quartered in Alexandria during the War. *Addresses:* The Overseas Club, General Buildings, Aldwych, London, W.C.; Post Office, Alexandria, Egypt. (M8370)

HARRINGTON, Henry William, M.B.E.

HARRINGTON, Lieut. John, M.B.E., Aust. A.O.C.

HARRIS, Andrew, M.B.E., F.R.C.S., L.R.C.P.

HARRIS, Capt. Archibald John, O.B.E. R.E.

HARRIS, Sir Arthur Ambrose Hall. K.B.E., J.P., *b.* 15 October, 1854; *s.* of Henry Vinton Harris, of Stoke, Devonshire, England; *m.* Sarah Morris, *d.* of William B. Lambe, B.C.L., of Montreal, Canada. *Educ.:* Devonport; Stoke Grammar School. Served in various official capacities in Grand Trunk Railway, 1884 to 1902, when he joined the Canadian Pacific. *War Work:* Director-General British Ministry of Shipping (Canada) August, 1914, to March, 1920. *Clubs:* St. James's, Montreal; Rideau, Ottawa. (K78)

HARRIS, Sir Austin Edward, K.B.E., *b.* 1870; *s.* of Frederick William Harris, J.P., D.L.; *m.* Cara Veronica, *d.* of George Maxwell Batten, I.C.S. *Educ.:* Harrow. Director of Lloyds Bank. *War Work:* Assistant Surveyor-General of Supply; Chairman of the Board of Contracts, W.O. *Address:* 10, Catherine Street, Buckingham Gate. *Clubs:* Arthurs'; Garrick; Ranelagh. (K381)

HARRIS, Charles, M.B.E.

HARRIS, Sir Charles, G.B.E., K.C.B., *b.* 2 March, 1864; *s.* of late John Harris, of Ivybridge, Devon; *m.* Lisbeth, *d.* of late Ferdinand Schiller, of Calcutta. *Educ.:* Bradford Grammar School; Balliol, Oxford (Scholar). First in open competition for Home Civil Service, 1886; entered War Office, 1887; Assistant Financial Secretary, 1908; Joint Secretary, 1920. *War Work:* Permanent Head of Finance, Department of the War Office throughout the War. *Addresses:* War Office, Whitehall; Lofftuss, The Drive, Wimbledon. (G51)

HARRIS, Charles Hubert, M.B.E.

HARRIS, Lieut.-Col. Charles Sydney, O.B.E., *b.* 25 May, 1871; *s.* of the late John Harris, of Hawkmoor, Bovey Tracy, Devon. *Educ.:* Bedford Grammar School; Sandhurst. Gazetted 2nd Lieut. 2nd K.O. Yorkshire L.I. July, 1891; promoted Capt. 1899; transferred to Army Pay Department, Sept. 1903; retired with rank of Lieut.-Col., Jan. 1920. *War*

Work: Command Paymaster, Ceylon, 1914–18; Regimental Paymaster. No. 2 Army Pay Office, Shrewsbury, 1918–19; Medals: Tirah Campaign, Medal and 2 clasps, 1897–98; South African War, Queen's Medal and 3 clasps, King's Medal and 2 clasps. *Address:* Osborne House, Stoke, Devonport. (O7243)

HARRIS, Lieut. Claude Pickering, M.B.E., I.A.

HARRIS, Capt. Edgar David, M.B.E.

HARRIS, Major Edward Ross, O.B.E.

HARRIS, Elizabeth Frances, Mrs., M.B.E., *b.* 1870; *d.* of the late Alderman Crawford, of Sligo; *m.* John Nugent, *s.* of Henry Bradshaw Harris, of Co. Clare, Ireland. Chief Organiser of the National Federation of Womens' Institutes, Iddesleigh House, Caxton Street, Westminster, S.W. 1. *War Work:* Head of the Women's Institutes Section of the Ministry of Agriculture (Women's Branch). *Address:* 42, Dalebury Road, Wandsworth Common, London, S.W. 17. *Club:* Forum.

HARRIS, Major Emanuel Vincent, O.B.E., R.E.

HARRIS, Ernest Alfred, C.B.E.

HARRIS, Ethel, M.B.E.

HARRIS, Faith Frances, Mrs., M.B.E., *b.* 29 July, 1888; *d.* of C. J. Bowen Cooke, C.B.E., of Chester Place, Crewe; *m.* Dudley Raymond, *s.* of Arthur B. Harris, M.D., J.P., of Falmouth. *Educ.:* The Laurels, Rugby. *War Work:* Private Secretary to Deputation from Board of Trade visiting America for purchase of railway material for British Railways; afterwards in charge of allocation of material from various ports to the different Railway Companies. *Address:* 2, Bank Place, Falmouth. (M8373)

HARRIS, Francis George, M.B.E., R.A.S.C.

HARRIS, Francis William Robert, M.B.E.

HARRIS, George Arthur, O.B.E. (O7245)

HARRIS, Hon. Capt. George Hardy, M.B.E., *b.* 9 Feb. 1853; *s.* of George William Harris, of Nether Priors, Halstead, Essex. *Educ.:* Rugby. Solicitor. *War Work:* County War Pensions Committee; County Adjutant, Volunteer Battalions, Devonshire Regiment. *Addresses:* 25, Southernhay, Exeter; Woodway, Teignmouth. *Clubs:* Devon and Exeter; Royal Automobile. (M8375)

HARRIS, Lieut.-Comm. George Henry, O.B.E., R.N.R., *b.* 7 March, 1854; *s.* of William Stanley Harris, of Lymington; *m.* Bertha Josephine, *d.* of Miles Berkeley, of Sibbertoft. *Educ.:* H.M.S. "Conway." Master Mariner; Younger Brother Trinity House. *War Work:* Commander H.M. Hospital Ship "Oxfordshire," Aug. 1914 to May 1918, serving in North Sea, English Channel, Mediterranean, Persian Gulf, East and South Africa; commanded S.S. "Lancashire," July 1918, carrying American troops from Boston, U.S.A. *Address:* 3, Quadrille Court, Lymington, Hants. *Club:* Primrose. (O1435)

HARRIS, George Montagu, O.B.E., *b.* 1868; *s.* of Rev. G. C. Harris, of Torquay, Prebendary of Exeter; *m.* Violet Estelle, *d.* of Lieut.-Col. E. Martineau. *Educ.:* Winchester; New College, Oxford. Barrister-at-Law; Secretary to County Councils Association, 1902–1919; now in Ministry of Health. *War Work:* Assistant Hon. Secretary Surrey War Distress Committee; Temporary Clerk of Peace and County Council, East Sussex; Clerk to E. Sussex Appeal Tribunal; Hon. Secretary, E. Sussex War Agriculture Committee, War Pensions Committee, War Distress Committee, etc.; Lieut. 6th Royal Sussex Volunteer Regt. *Club:* Reform. (O1436)

HARRIS, Helen, Mrs., M.B.E.; *d.* of Joseph Offenbach, of New York City, U.S.A.; *m.* Lionel W., *s.* of Alderman Lewis Harris, of Dublin. *War Work:* Recruiting; Organising; attached Ministry of Food Dec. 1916 to Feb. 1919. *Address:* 4, Upper Grosvenor Street, W.1. *Club:* American Women's Club, 41, Hereford Street. (M3699)

HARRIS, Henry Arthur, M.B.E.

HARRIS, Henry Lewis, M.B.E., *b.* 9 Feb. 1860; *s.* of the late Lewis P. Harris, F.R.G.S. *Educ.:* Dartford Grammar School, Kent. Schoolmaster. *War Work:* Organising subscriptions in aid of Red Cross, and other War Funds in the district. *Address:* Serowe, Bechuanaland Protectorate, S. Africa. *Club:* Overseas; Mountain, South Africa. (M2946)

HARRIS, Sir Henry Percy, K.B.E., J.P., M.P., D.L., *b.* 2 Sept. 1856; *s.* of Sir George David Harris, of 32, Inverness Terrace, W. (*see* BURKE'S *Peerage*); *m.* Ethel Alice Chivers, *d.* of Edward Chivers Bower, of Broxholme, Scarborough. *Educ.:* Eton, and Christ Church, Oxford. Barrister-at-law; M.P.; Chairman London County Council, 1907–8. *War Work:* Chairman London War Pensions Committee. *Addresses:* 98, Gloucester Terrace, London, W.; Cherry Croft, Forest Row, Sussex. *Clubs:* Carlton; Oxford and Cambridge. (K22)

HARRIS, Lieut.-Col. Herbert Sextus, O.B.E.

HARRIS, The Reverend John Charles, M.B.E.

HARRIS, Capt. John Richard, O.B.E., R.A.M.C., S.R.

HARRIS, Joseph Orlando, D.S.O. Sub-Lieut. R.N.V.R.; Great War, 1914–19 (mentioned in despatches). (C125)

HARRIS, Leonard David John, M.B.E.

HARRIS, Lieut. Leopold Jonas, O.B.E., R.E.

HARRIS, Lillie Crawford, Mrs., M.B.E.

HARRIS, Marjorie Maxwell, M.B.E.

HARRIS, Mary Gertrude, M.B.E.

HARRIS, Eng.-Comm. Percy George, O.B.E., R.N.

HARRIS, Major Samuel Wallace, M.B.E.

HARRIS, Major Thomas Guy Marriott, O.B.E.

HARRIS, Major Walter Reginald, O.B.E., T.D., *b.* 4 July, 1865 ; *s.* of Henry Harris, of Guildford ; *m.* Ellen Florke, *d.* of James Lee Jones, of Guildford. *Educ.:* Guildford. Secretary to the County Club, Guildford. *War Work :* Joined 2nd Volunteer Batt. The Queen's R.W.S. Regt. Dec. 1887 ; Commission May, 1904, Lieut. and Qr.-Mr. ; Promoted Capt. April, 1906 ; Major Feb. 1911 ; Mobilised Aug. 1914 ; fitted out numerous drafts for overseas ; appointed, with Assist. Adjt., by G.O.C. 225 Brigade, to organise new Batts. for 25th Division. 34th Middlesex Regt., 13th Border Regt., 13th East Surrey Regt. ; served during the war at Chatham, Maidstone, Canterbury, Guildford, Tunbridge Wells, Seaford, and Lowestoft ; demobilised and relinquished commission on account of ill health July, 1919. *Address :* Amesbury, Stoke Road, Guildford. (O7246)

HARRIS, William, M.B.E., R.N.

HARRIS, William Blandford, M.B.E., *b.* 8. Dec. 1872; *s.* of William Harris, of Upwell, Wisbech ; *m.* Bertha, *d.* of George Trueman, of Ventnor. *Educ.:* Wisbech Grammar School. Civil Servant. *War Work :* Secretary's Office of the General Post Office. *Addresses :* Secretary's Office, G.P.O., E.C. ; 27, Valley Road, S.W.16. (M1855)

HARRIS, William Rowland, M.B.E.

HARRIS, William Thomas Harper, M.B.E.

HARRISON, Sir Cecil Reeves, K.B.E., *b.* 1856 ; *s.* of James William Harrison, of St. Martin's Lane, W.C. 2 ; *m.* Caroline Clara, *d.* of Dr. Benjamin Winstone, of Russell Square, London. *Educ.:* Univ. Coll., London. Director, Harrison & Sons, Ltd., Printers in Ordinary to H.M. The King. *War Work :* Official printing for Army and Navy, and various Government Departments. *Addresses :* Woodcote, Chislehurst, Kent ; Hillside, Charmouth, Dorset. *Clubs :* Union ; Royal Automobile. (K145)

HARRISON, Charles Henry, O.B.E., M.C.

HARRISON, Col. Cholmeley Edward Carl Branfill, C.M.G., C.B.E., *b.* 1857 ; *s.* of the Rev. J. Branfill Harrison ; *m.* Mary Evelyn, *d.* of John Bazley-White (*see* BURKE'S *Peerage*, Rothes, E). Formerly Comdg. 1st Batn. Roy. W. Kent Regt.; Boer War, 1881 ; Egyptian Expedition, 1882 (medal, bronze star) ; S. Africa, 1900 (despatches, Queen's medal with two clasps) ; Great War, 1915–18 (despatches). *Address :* 15, Cromwell Road, Hove, Sussex. *Club :* Army and Navy. (C1262)

HARRISON, Major Christopher Heathfield, O.B.E. (O11779)

HARRISON, Major Cuthbert Alfred Lakin, O.B.E., R.A.F.

HARRISON, Elsie Lydia, M.B.E., *b.* 1882 ; *d.* of Frederick Stone Harrison, of London. *War Work :* Deputy Controller Women's Staff, M.I. 5 W. O. *Address :* 2, Howitt Road, Belsize Park, N.W.3. (M8381)

HARRISON, Emily Margaret, Mrs. O.B.E. ; *d.* of Robert Brown Watson, of Sudworth, New Brighton ; *m.* Frederic James, *s.* of James Harrison, of Dornden, Tunbridge Wells ; Wallasey, Cheshire ; Hare Appletree, near Lancaster. *War Work :* President, Soldiers' and Sailors' Families Association (Potteries, South Division) ; President, War Hospital Supply Depot, Shelton ; President and Chairman, Stoke War Hospital Committee ; Member Executive Committee North Staffs Regt. Prisoners of War Association ; Member Staffs County Women's War Agricultural Committee. *Addresses :* Maer Hall, Staffs ; Hare Appletree, near Lancaster ; 227, St. James' Court, S.W. 1. (O410)

HARRISON, Evelyn, M.B.E.

HARRISON, Florence Ada, Mrs., O.B.E.

HARRISON, Major Francis Edward, O.B.E., R.E.

HARRISON, Major Frank, O.B.E., M.C.

HARRISON, Capt. Frank, O.B.E.

HARRISON, Freda, M.B.E., *b.* 2 Nov. 1899 ; *d.* of Joseph Harrison, of Wrexham. *War Work :* Divisional Assistant for North Wales Division, Ministry of Food. *Address :* 10, Bryn Acton, Chester Road, Wrexham. (M8383)

HARRISON, Frederick, M.B.E.

HARRISON, Lieut.-Comm. Geoffrey Brancker, O.B.E., R.N.

HARRISON, George, M.B.E., D.C.M., R.A.S.C.

HARRISON, George Alfred, O.B.E.

HARRISON, Gwynedd Helen Lightfoot, M.B.E.

HARRISON, Harry, M.B.E.

HARRISON, Lieut. Henry, O.B.E., M.C.

HARRISON, Capt. Henry Coromandel Watsford, O.B.E., Aust. A.S.C.

HARRISON, Hilda Mary, M.B.E., *d.* of Frederick Stone Harrison, of Highgate. *Educ.:* Privately, High School. *War Work :* Head of Dept. dealing with disposal of Surplus Plant, Waste Products, Scrap Metals, Clothing, etc., from Explosive Factories under Ministry of Munitions. *Club :* Women's International Franchise. (M8385)

HARRISON, Capt. James, M.B.E.,

HARRISON, John Atkinson, O.B.E., M.B., C.M.

HARRISON, John, C.B.E., LL.D., D.L., *b.* 17 Aug. 1847 ; *s.* of Sir George Harrison, M.P., of Edinburgh ; *m.* Helen Georginia, *d.* of George Roberts, of Selkirk. *Educ.:* High School, Edinburgh. Chairman Edinburgh Public Library and Savings Bank. *War Work :* Chairman City of Edinburgh Tribunal and Finance Committee of Local Red Cross Society. *Address :* 3, Napier Road, Edinburgh. *Club :* Northern, Edinburgh. (C192)

HARRISON, Capt. John Stubbs, O.B.E., R.F.A. (T.),

b. 27 July, 1883 ; *s.* of Alfred James Harrison, M.D., Clifton, Bristol. *Educ.:* Clifton. Solicitor. *War Work :* Commissioned as 2nd Lieut. in S.M. Brigade R.F.A. (T.F.) Oct, 1914 ; A.D.C. to C. R. A. 61st Division, April, 1915, to Dec. 1915 ; Staff Capt. 69th Division, Jan. 1916 ; Staff Capt. G. H. Q. Great Britain (Anti-Aircraft), 1918. *Address :* 24, Orchard Street, Bristol. *Clubs :* Royal Automobile ; Clifton. (O7245)

HARRISON, Lieut. Joseph Lawrence, M.B.E., R.A.O.C.

HARRISON, Kate, M.B.E.

HARRISON, Capt. Leonard Charles, M.B.E., R.E.

HARRISON, Lieut.-Col. and Brev.-Col. Louis Kenneth, C.B.E., B.A., M.B., R.A.M.C. (T.), *b.* 19 Dec. 1871 ; *s.* of John E. Harrison, of Buxton ; *m.* Edith, *d.* of the late Septimus March, of Aberystwyth. *Educ.:* Repton ; Caius College, Cambridge ; St. Bartholomew's Hospital. Member of the Leicestershire and Rutland Territorial Association ; President, Leicester Medical Society 1920–1921. *War Work :* Officer Commanding and Administrator of the 5th Northern General Hospital which, with its sections and auxiliaries, contained 5,200 beds and admitted 75,000 patients. *Address :* Springfield, Springfield Road, Leicester. (C1605)

HARRISON, Muriel Evelyn, M.B.E.

HARRISON, Rosamond Mary, O.B.E. ; *d.* of Frederic James Harrison, of Maer Hall, Staffs ; Hare Appletree, Lancashire ; Wallasey, Cheshire. *War Work :* Organising Hon. Sec. North Staffordshire Regiment Prisoners of War Association (1800 men). *Addresses :* Maer Hall, Newcastle, Staffs ; 180, St. James' Court, Buckingham Gate, S.W.1. (O10572)

HARRISON, Stanley, O.B.E. (O11786*b*)

HARRISON, Sydney Thomas Walker, M.B.E.

HARRISON, Lieut. Thomas, O.B.E., R.N.R.

HARRISON, Tom Curtis, M.B.E. (M10392)

HARRISON, Major Walter Lewis, O.B.E., F.R.C.V.S. R.A.V.C. (T.).

HARRISON, William, O.B.E.

HARRISON, Lieut.-Col. William Edward, O.B.E., M.I.M.E., J.P. (Staffs), C.C., *b.* 14 August, 1875 ; *s.* of Captain William Bealey Harrison of Aldershawe, Lichfield ; *m.* Edith *d.* of Herbert W. Gardiner, of Armitage, Rugeley, Staffs. *Educ.:* Eton ; Oriel College, Oxford. Member of Staffordshire County Council, Tutbury Rural Council and Board of Guardians ; Vice-President British Friesian Cattle Society ; Chairman of Cannock Chase Coal Owners Association. *War Work :* C.R.E. 46th (North Midland Division) from mobilisation to Oct. 21 1914 ; C.R.E. 59th (North Midland Division) April, 1915 to March, 1916 ; Acting Commanding, Engineers' Training Centre, Deganwy, March, 1916 to June, 1916 ; Second in Command, Deganwy, June, 1916 to March, 1918 ; Command of Special Brigade Depot R.E. (Devonport) March, 1918 to January, 1919 ; mentioned in despatches 24 Feb. 1917, for War Services. *Address :* Wychnor Park, Burton-on-Trent. *Clubs :* Windham ; Royal Automobile. (O1439)

HARRISON, Capt. William John, M.B.E., M.A., R.G.A. (S.R.), *b.* 17 June, 1884 ; *s.* of R. Limmer Harrison, South Benfleet, Essex ; *m.* Ethel Marianne, *d.* of E. W. Harvey Piper, of Clapham, S.W. *Educ.:* Dulwich Coll., and Clare Coll., Cambridge. Fellow, Assistant Tutor and Lecturer of Clare College, Cambridge ; University Lecturer in Mathematics. *War Work :* Assistant Proof and Experimental Officer, Research Dept., Woolwich Arsenal. *Address :* Elmstead, Great Shelford, Cambs. (M1856)

HARRISON, Surg.-Comm. William Rhodes, O.B.E., R.N.

HARRISSON, Sydney Thirlwall, C.M.G., O.B.E., *b.* 1865 ; *s.* of Henry Loud Harrisson. *Educ.:* Blackheath. Appointed Assist. Accountant, Public Works Depart. Gold Coast, 1894 ; Ch. Accountant, 1897 ; Assist. Accountant, W. African Frontier Force, 1898 ; Ch. Accountant, 1899 ; Treasurer, N. Nigeria, 1900 ; Comptroller of Customs, Barbados. *Address :* Bridgetown, Barbados. *Clubs :* Sports ; Bridgetown (Barbados). (O8388)

HARRISSON, William Walter, M.B.E.

HARROLD, John Blake, M.B.E.

HARROP, William, O.B.E.

HARROWBY, Mabel Danvers, Countess of, D.B.E., *b.* 26 Feb. 1867 ; *d.* of late Rt. Hon. W. H. Smith M.P., and Emily, 1st Viscountess Hambleden ; *m.* John Herbert Dudley, 5th Earl of Harrowby. Chairman Executive Committee, Staffordshire County Nursing Association ; Vice-President Mothers' Union. *War Work :* Organised Country and London Hospitality for Overseas' Officers. *Addresses :* Sandon Hall, Stafford ; Norton House, Campden, Gloucestershire ; 10, Upper Belgrave St., London, S.W. 1. (D43)

HARRY, 2nd Lieut. Herbert Edward, M.B.E.

HARRY, Richard John, M.B.E.

HARRY, William, C.B.E.

HARSLEY, Martha, Mrs., M.B.E., *b.* 2 Nov. 1860 ; *d.* of the late Robert Ellerby, of Marfleet, Hull ; widow of John (died 1919), *s.* of Robert Harsley, of Hull. *Educ.:* Hull. *War Work :* Member of Committee of Soldiers' and Sailors' Family Association, Soldiers' and Sailors' Help Society, and Hull War Pensions Committee ; Investigator (voluntary) Hull Great War Trust. *Address :* 18, Elm Avenue, Garden Village, Holderness Road, Hull. (M8391)

HARSTON, John Edwin, O.B.E., *b.* 18 May, 1857 ; *s.* of John Harston, of Littleborough, Lancashire ; *m.* Bessie Annie Northey, *d.* of Thomas Plucknett, of Plymouth. *Educ.:* Privately. H.M. Inspector of Factories. *War Work :* Commissioner in the National Service Department for the Midland

Division ; and as Acting Superintending Inspector of Factories (Midland Division). *Address* : Elmwood, Olton, Warwickshire.
(O1440)

HARSTONE, Lieut.-Col. John Brunton, D.S.O., O.B.E., *b.* 1879 ; *s.* of Robert Brunton Harstone. T. Lieut.-Col. Canadian Forces ; served in the Great War, 1914–18 (mentioned in despatches). (O1441)

HART, Charles James, M.B.E.

HART, Col. Charles Joseph, C.B., C.B.E., V.D., T.D., J.P., D.L., *b.* 15 Aug. 1851 ; *s.* of Charles Hart, late of Harborne Hall, Staffordshire. *Educ.* : Haileybury. Honorary Colonel, 5th Bn. Royal Warwickshire Regt. ; Member of Warwickshire Territorial Force Association ; Chairman of Hart, Son, Peard, and Co., Ltd. War Work : Commandant Birmingham National Reserve 1909–1914 ; Chief Recruiting Officer, Curzon Hall, Birmingham 1914–1916 ; Commanding Troops, Birmingham, 1915–1917 ; Competent Military Authority for Arms and Ammunition, Birmingham, 1915–1917 ; President of Quartering Committee, 1917–1920. *Address* : Southbank, Warwick New Road, Leamington. (C1606)

HART, Cyril Herbert, M.B.E.

HART, Ernest Sidney Walter, M.B.E., *b.* 11 July, 1870 ; *s.* of Sidney George Hart, of Chislehurst, Kent ; *m.* Ella Mary, *d.* of Charles Prime, M.I.C.E., P.W.D., of Ceylon. *Educ.* : Privately. Clerk of the Peace and Clerk of the County Council of Middlesex ; Clerk to the Middlesex Lieutenancy and Advisory Committee ; Registration Officer and Acting Returning Officer for the Parliamentary County of Middlesex. *War Work* : Joint Sec. of the Middlesex Military Appeal Tribunal, and in connection therewith the investigation of the subject of the enlistment in the Army of unfit men. Valuable evidence on this subject was given before the Select Committee of the House of Commons in July, 1917. As a result of the Committee's Report, Civilian Medical Boards superseded Military Boards. *Address* : Guildhall, Westminster. *Club* : St. Stephen's. (M1859)

HART, Sir George Sankey, K.B.E., C.I.E., *b.* 14 April 1866 ; *s.* of David Hart, of Blackheath, London, S.E. ; *m.* Georgina Mary, *d.* of Thornton Temple. *Educ.* : St. Paul's School, and Cooper's Hill. Indian Forest Service ; Assistant and Deputy Conservator Forests, Punjab, 1887–1906 ; Conservator Central Provinces, 1906–8 ; Conservator Bengal, 1908–10 ; Chief Conservator Central Provinces, 1910–13 ; Inspector-General of Forests to the Government of India. 1913. *War Work* : Duties as Inspector-General of Forests, *Address* : c/o Mercantile Bank of India, 15, Gracechurch Street, London, E.C. (K329)

HART, Capt. Gilbert, O.B.E., M.C., R.E.

HART, Henry, M.B.E.

HART, Lieut.-Col. Henry Travers, C.B.E., R.A., *b.* 6 May, 1873 ; *s.* of Colonel E. C. Hart (late R.E.), of Bournemouth ; *m.* Phyllis Hope, *d.* of Colonel H. M. Matthews (late Queen's), of Fareham. *Educ.* : Sedbergh. Regular Army. *War Work* : Commanding 13 Siege Battery, France 1915 ; Chief Instructor Bexhill Siege School, 1915–1916 ; C.R.A., South Africa, 1916–1919. *Address* : c/o Messrs Cox and Co. 16, Charing Cross, S.W. (C2117)

HART, James, M.B.E., *b.* 14 May, 1855 ; *s.* of James Hart, of Hackney, London ; *m.* Annetta Emily, *d.* of George Welby, of Plumstead, Kent ; *Educ.* : Tudor House School, Hackney, and School of Pharmacy. Entered R.N. Medical Service as Dispenser in 1878 ; served at Haslar, Chatham, Yarmouth, Malta, Haulbowline, and Plymouth R.N. Hospitals. *War Work* : Superintending Pharmacist R.N. Hospital, Plymouth, in charge of medical stores for the Devonport Division of the Fleet and establishments attached. *Address* : 38, Glenhouse Road, Eltham Park, S.E.9. (M8394)

HART, James MacGregor, O.B.E., *b.* 20 April, 1878 ; *s.* of Thomas Hart. of Glasgow ; *m.* Isabel Gilbert, *d.* of R. W. Cameron, of Greenock. *Educ.* : Glasgow ; Glasgow Univ. Chartered Accountant. *War Work* : Hon. Treas. Scottish National Council, Y.M.C.A., and Glasgow Y.M.C.A. *Addresses* : 17, Broomhill Terrace, Partick, Glasgow ; 142, St. Vincent Street, Glasgow. (O10574)

HART, Jane Elizabeth, Mrs., M.B.E.

HART, Major Kenneth Eugene, O.B.E. M.C.

HART, Maurice Roberts Wilson, M.B.E.

HART, Philip Theodore, O.B.E., *b.* 3 Dec. 1868 ; *s.* of Alderman Henry Hart, J.P., of Canterbury ; *m.* Hannah, *d.* of Maurice Levene, of London. *Educ.* : Dover Coll. *War Work* : Hon. Sec. Parliamentary Recruiting Committee ; Chairman Local Military Advisory Committee, Military National Service Committee, and Dover Branch Red Cross Society. *Address* : 68, Bouverie Road, W. Folkestone. *Clubs* : Royal Cinque Ports Yacht, Dover ; Hythe Golf. (O10575)

HART, Surrey Rutherford, M.B.E., *b.* 26 June, 1856. Late Principal Clerk, General Post Office. *Address* : 34, Bernard Gardens, Wimbledon, S.W. (M8395)

HART, Thomas Wheeler, C.B.E., M.B., Ch.B., *b.* 13 May, 1875 ; *s.* of Rev. Dudley Hart, of Stretford ; *m.* Edith, *d.* of — Heywood, of Manchester. *Educ.* : Manchester Grammar School, and Manchester University. *War Work* : County Director, East Lancashire Branch British Red Cross Society. *Address* : Avenham House, Edge Lane, Stretford, nr. Manchester. (C30)

HART, Eng.-Capt. William, O.B.E., R.N.

HART, William Edward, O.B.E.

HART, Capt. William Whiddon, M.B.E., R.A.F.

HART, Major James Milleville RAVEN-, O.B E.

HARTCUP, Major William Richard Monyns, O.B.E., *b.* 22 Nov. 1882 ; *s.* of H. J. Hartcup, of Upland Hall, Bungay, Suffolk ; *m.* Marjorie Ellison, *d.* of J. E. Woods, of Swarland Hall, Northumberland. *Educ.* : Shrewsbury. Army 1901 to 1919 ; Chief Constable, Isle of Ely, Aug. 1919. *War Work* : Adjutant, 5th Durham L.I. ; Brigade Major, 189 Infantry Brigade and 194 Infantry Brigade ; attached H.Q. Irish Command, Dublin ; D.A.A. and Q.M.G. Headquarters, Ripon Reserve centre. *Address* : St. Edmunds, Newmarket. *Club* : Army and Navy. (O8127)

HARTINGTON, Edward William Spencer Cavendish, Marquess of, M.B.E., J.P. for Derbyshire, Mayor of Buxton, 1920–21, *b.* 6 May, 1898 ; *s.* of the 9th Duke of Devonshire, of Chatsworth ; *m.* Mary Alice, *d.* of the 4th Marquess of Salisbury, of Hatfield (*see* BURKE'S *Peerage*). *Educ.* : Eton ; Cambridge. *War Work* : Derbyshire Yeomanry, 1914 ; served in Egypt and Gallipoli ; attached Intelligence Dept. War Office ; British Mission, French War Office, 1916–18 ; served on British Delegation, Peace Conference, 1918–19. *Addresses* : 2, Upper Belgrave Street, S.W. ; Chatsworth, Bakewell. *Clubs* : Brooks's ; Turf. (M5330)

HARTLAND, Lilian Mary, Mrs., M.B.E., *b.* 18 July, 1880 ; *d.* of Thomas W. Windeatt, of Totnes ; *m.* Thomas, *s.* of Thomas Hartland, of Bromesberrow Court, Glos. *Educ.* : Privately ; Weimar, Germany. *War Work* : Quartermaster and Asst.-Comdt. Totnes V.A. Hospital, Dec. 1914, to March, 1919. *Address* : N.P. Bank House, Totnes. (M1861)

HARTLEY, Major Alan Pickup, O.B.E., R.A.F., *b.* 4 Nov. 1887 ; *s.* of J. P. Hartley, of Cheadle-Hulme, Cheshire. *Educ.* : King's School, Grantham. Cotton Manufacturer, *War Work* : Sep. 1914, Pte. 6th Manchester ; Nov. 1914. Bombing Officer, 6th Cheshire Regt. ; transferred to R.F.C. June, 1916 ; Pilot ; specialised in Aerial Armament ; commenced and ran the " Wing of Practical Armament," Uxbridge . *Addresses* : Hill Top Avenue, Cheadle Hulme ; Palatine Bank Bldgs. Manchester. *Club* : R.A.F. (O8114)

HARTLEY, Albert, M.B.E.

HARTLEY, Major Arthur Clifford, O.B.E., R.A.F.

HARTLEY, Major Harold, C.B.E., M.C.

HARTLEY, Harry, O.B.E.

HARTLEY, Major Harry, C.B.E., R.E. Technical Wool Officer, War Office. (C1263)

HARTLEY, Capt. James Norman Jackson, O.B.E., M.B., Edin., F.R.C.S., (Edin. and England), T.C., *b.* 2 July, 1889 ; *s.* of James Henry Hartley, of Keighley. *Educ.* : Edinburgh University. Assistant to the Professor of Clinical Surgery and Surgical Clinical Tutor, Edinburgh University. *War Work* : Surgeon to the Surgical Observation Hut, Etaples ; Surgeon Specialist, H.M.T.S. " Egypt " ; and various General Hospitals. *Address* : c/o Mrs. Christie, 20, Royal Crescent, Edinburgh. (O5354)

HARTLEY, Richard Frederick, O.B.E.

HARTLEY, Capt. Richard Warburton, M.B.E., R.A.S.C. (T.F.),

HARTLING, Edward Hadley, O.B.E. (O2380)

HARTNELL, Walter George, M.B.E.

HARTREE, William, O.B.E., M.A., 8, April, 1870 ; *s.* of late John Penn Hartree ; *m.* Eva, *d.* of Dr. Edwin Rayner, of Stockport. *Educ.* : Tonbridge ; Trinity College, Cambridge. *War Work* : Anti-aircraft Section of the Munitions Inventions Department. *Address* : Newton Road, Cambridge (O1444)

HARTSHORN, Major Arthur Hastings, O.B.E., R.E. (T).

HARTSHORN, Hon. Major Stuart, C.B.E., *b.* 30 June, 1867 ; *s.* of James Hartshorn, of Nottingham ; *m.* Ida Clara' *d.* of William Evans, J.P., of Knighton, Leicester. *Educ.* : Chigwell School. Retired Lace Manufacturer. *War Work* : Hon. Sec. Nottingham Recruiting Committee and Nottingham Notts' Voluntary Workers Association ; District Recruiting Officer, No 6 District, Lichfield, for Counties Lincoln, Leicester, Nottingham, Derby, Rutland, Stafford, Wolverhampton ; Sec. Yorkshire and East Midland region and Northern Region, Ministry of National Service. *Address* : Knighton, Magdale Road, Nottingham. *Clubs* : Nottingham Borough ; Nottingham County. (C979)

HARTSHORN, Vernon, O.B.E., J.P.,M.P. (Lab.), Ogmore Division of Glamorganshire since Dec., 1918 ; served on the Coal Trade Organization Committee ; and also on the Coal Controller's Advisory Committee. *Address* : Maesteg, Bridgend, Glam. (O412)

HARTY, Capt. William, O.B.E.

HARVEY, Anita Maria, Mrs., M.B.E., *b.* 24 Jan. 1875 ; *d.* of Philip Symons, of Bodmin, Cornwall ; *m.* Charles Henry, *s.* of Isaac Harvey, of London. *Educ.* : Northfield Seminary, Northfield, Mass., U.S.A. Missionary of the Baptist Missionary Society, London. *War Work* : Two years at St. John Ambulance Nursing Sisters' Convalescent Home for wounded British troops, Calcutta ; engaged in massage and doctors' rooms ; four years at Sambhu Nath Pundit Hospital, Calcutta, training candidates for Military Hospitals ; during four years gave " First Aid " and " Home Nursing " lectures to qualify people for war work. *Address* : c/o Baptist Missionary Society, 19, Furnival Street, Holborn, London, E.C. 4. (M4147)

HARVEY, Arthur Kenneth, O.B.E. (O2381)

HARVEY, 2nd Lieut. Austin Mozart, M.B.E.

HARVEY, Major Bertram Lionel, O.B.E., I.A.R.O.

HARVEY, Lieut.-Comm. Cecil Russell Hains, O.B.E. R.N.

HARVEY, Christina, Mrs., M.B.E.
HARVEY, Col. David, C.M.G., C.B.E., M.D., M.B., Ch.B., *b.* 1871. *Educ.:* Glasgow Univ. Lieut.-Col. R.A.M.C.; Dep. Director of Pathology at War Office, with rank of Col.; served in S. Africa, 1900–2 (Queen's medal with three clasps, King's medal with two clasps). (C1607)
HARVEY, Rev. Edward Douglas Lennox, O.B.E., M.A., J.P., *b.* 26 Dec. 1858; *s.* of W. J. Harvey, of Carnousie, Banffshire. *Educ.:* Harrow; Trin. Coll., Cambridge. *War Work:* Recruiting; Appeal Tribunal, West Sussex; Chairman Local War Pensions Committee. *Address:* Beedingwood, Horsham, Sussex. *Clubs:* Conservative; Automobile. (O10576)
HARVEY, Major Edward John Morewood, M.B.E.
HARVEY, Edward Murray, O.B.E. (O11786c)
HARVEY, Comm. Edwin William, M.B.E., R.N.R.
HARVEY, Emma Jessie, Mrs., O.B.E., *b.* 26 Sept. 1867; *d.* of Philip Rawson, J.P., D.L., of Woodhurst, Crawley, Sussex. *War Work:* Raised funds to equip and maintain hut of 20 beds at B.R.C. Hospital, Netley, for four years; Commandant V.A.D. Sussex/70, and other Red Cross work; Head of War Hospital Supply Depot, Horsham; organised Hut Week Campaign for Y.M.C.A. in Horsham and district; work in connection with Women's Land Army. *Address:* Beedingwood, Horsham, Sussex. *Clubs:* Albemarle. (O10577)
HARVEY, Sir Ernest Maes, K.B.E., *b.* 1 Jan. 1872; *s.* of Julius Harvey, of Ipswich; *m.* Blanche, *d.* of Edward Pogson, of St. Kitts. *Educ.:* Ipswich. Banker; Director British Columbia Electric Rly. Co. *War Work:* Treasury Representative Archangel, 1918–19; Financial Adviser to British Representative, Inter-Allied Rhineland Committee, 1919; Financial Adviser, Austrian Section, Reparation Committee, Vienna, 1920. *Addresses:* Inveresk, Watford; Hill House, Aldeburgh, Suffolk. *Clubs:* Union; Tuesday. (K382)
HARVEY, Sir Ernest Musgrave, K.B.E., *b.* 27 July, 1867; *s.* of Rev. Preb. C. M. Harvey, late of Hillingdon, Middlesex; *m.* Sophia, *d.* of Capt. Catesby Paget, late of Aspley Guise, Woburn. *Educ.:* Marlborough. Chief Cashier, Bank of England; Chevalier, Legion d'Honneur; Chevalier, Order of Leopold of Belgium. *Address:* 29, Cranley Gardens, S.W. 7. (K457)
HARVEY, Ethel, Mrs., M.B.E.
HARVEY, Lieut.-Col., Francis George, C.B.E., D.S.O. Lieut.Col. S. African Forces; A.Q.M.G.; served in Great War (German S.-W. Africa, 1914–15 (despatches, Legion of Honour). (C754)
HARVEY, Major Frank Barrington, O.B.E., R. of O.
HARVEY, Sir George Samuel Abercromby, K.B.E., C.M.G., *b.* 21 Oct. 1854; *s.* of William James Harvey, J.P., of Carnousie, Turriff, N.B.; *m.* Elizabeth Diana Lily, *d.* of the late Colonel John Craigie-Halkett, of Cramond, Midlothian. *Educ.:* Trinity College, Glenalmond. Late The Black Watch, Royal Highlanders, then Egyptian Government Service. *War Work:* Provost-Marshal Cairo and Upper Egypt, 1916–17. *Address:* 10, West Eaton Place, London, S.W. 1. (K185)
HARVEY, Lieut.-Comm. James Robertson, O.B.E., R.N.
HARVEY, Capt. John, C.B.E., R.N.
HARVEY, Capt. Joseph Massey, O.B.E.
HARVEY, Joshua Harold, O.B.E., M.R.C.S., L.R.C.P., *b.* 22 Nov. 1867; *s.* of Joshua Harvey, of Broadmoor, Pembrokeshire; *m.* Emily Jane, *d.* of George Harries, of Trevaccoon, Pembrokeshire. *Educ.:* Privately and Guy's Hospital. *War Work:* Civil Medical Practitioner in charge of 3rd Dorsetshire Regt. and other troops stationed at Wyke Regis near Weymouth. *Address:* The Willows, Wyke Regis, Dorset. (O4371)
HARVEY, Capt. Nicholas Charles, M.B.E.
HARVEY, Lieut. Percy Edgar, O.B.E., R.E,
HARVEY, Lieut. Ralph Oswald, O.B.E.
HARVEY, Major Robert Bald, O.B.E., A.S.C.
HARVEY, Capt. Robert Bleeck Leech, O.B.E., *b.* 19 Aug. 1887; *s.* of Charles O. Harvey, of Bristol. *Educ.:* Clifton College, and R.M.C. Sandhurst. Appointed 2nd Lieut. Royal Berkshire Regt. 1906; seconded for service with the Colonial Office, 1911. *War Work:* Served with 4th King's African Rifles in the East African Campaign; Intelligence Officer, Uganda, 1914; Adjutant 1/4 King's African Rifles, 1916; T. Major, 2nd in command 2/4 King's African Rifles, 1916; commanding 5/4 King's African Rifles, 1917; T. Lieut.-Col. 1918; served in Somaliland Operations, 1919–20; twice mentioned in despatches. *Address:* 4, Worcester Crescent, Clifton, Bristol. *Club:* Army and Navy. (O6749)
HARVEY, Tom Horace, O.B.E. For services rendered to the Ministry of Food. (O11906)
HARVEY, Lieut. William, M.B.E., R.A.S.C.
HARVEY, William, M.B.E., *b.* 10 Sept. 1862; Harness, Trunk and Bag Manufacturer. *War Work:* Chief Inspector of Special Constabulary, Stockport; Organised Traders' Co. of Special Constables, acting under Chief Constable. *Address:* Russell Place, 102, Prince's Street, Stockport. (M516)
HARVEY, Winifred Beatrice, M.B.E., *b.* 11 Aug. 1888; *d.* of Colonel H. J. Harvey, of Newlands, Guernsey; *Educ.:* Ladies' College, Guernsey. *War Work:* Secretarial Work for the Guernsey Branch of the Soldiers' and Sailors' Families Association; Member of the Guernsey Local War Pensions Committee. *Address:* Newlands, Guernsey. (M8396)
HARVIE, Charles Frederick, O.B.E.
HARWARD, Mabel, Mrs., M.B.E., *b.* 1 Sept. 1875; *d.* of Benjamin Scarf, of Cliffe Hill, Bradford; *m.* the Rev.

Reginald Cuthbert, *s.* of the Rev. Edwin C. Harward, Vicar of Middleton-by-Wirksworth. *Educ.:* Isleworth and Lausanne. *War Work:* British Soldiers' Institute, Boulogne-sur-Mer. *Address:* 7, Boulevard Daunow. Boulogne-sur-Mer. (M8397)
HARWARD, Rev. Reginald Cuthbert, M.B.E., M.A., *b.* 30 Nov. 1871; *s.* of Edwin Cuthbert Harward, of Middleton Vicarage, Wirksworth, Derby.; *m.* Mabel, *d.* of Benjamin Scarf, of Bradford, Yorks. *Educ.:* Denstone Coll.; Chichester Theol. Coll.; Durham University. Resident English Chaplain (since 1912), Holy Trinity Church, Boulogne-sur-Mer, France. *War Work:* British Soldiers' and Sailors' Institute, Boulogne Base. *Address:* 7, Boulevard Daunow. Boulogne-sur-Mer. (M8398)
HARWARD, Capt. Robert Blake, O.B.E.
HARWOOD, Capt. Alfred, M.B.E.
HARWOOD, George, M.B.E.
HARWOOD, Gertrude, Mrs., M.B.E.
HARWOOD, Lieut.-Comm. Henry Harwood, O.B.E., R.N.
HARWOOD, James Henry, M.B.E.
HARWOOD, John Edward, O.B.E., *b.* 3 March, 1870; *s.* of John Harwood, of Manchester; *m.* Sophia Marion, *d.* of Rev. E. D. Hall, M.A., of Coln S. Denys, Glos. Mayor of Shoreditch, 1909–10. *War Work:* Member of Profiteering Appeal Tribunal; representative at the Electricity Conference, Act, 1919; Shoreditch Borough Councillor; Military Tribunal, Shoreditch; Right-half Co. Comm. City of London Police Reserve, 1914; to 1918. *Address:* 32, Brondesbury Park, N.W. 6. *Club:* Junior Constitutional. (O10580)
HARWOOD, Margaret, M.B.E.
HARWOOD, Ralph Endersby, C.B.E., F.S.S., *b.* 28 March, 1883; *s.* of Charles Harwood, of Shefford; *m.* Kitty, *d.* of William Rule Endersby, of Old Warden, Bedfordshire. *Educ.:* Modern School, Bedford. Assistant Sec., H.M. Treasury: Telegraphist, G.P.O., 1898; Second Division Clerk, at India Office and Royal Hospital, Chelsea (1901–03); Estate Duty Office (1903–11); Accountant-General's Dept., Inland Revenue, 1911–12; N. H. Insurance Committee, 1912; Staff Clerk, 1912; Assistant Accountant, 1912–13; Clerk, Class I., 1913, at N. H. I. C. *War Work:* Assisted Rt. Hon. Sir John Anderson, K.C.B., in the control of the British drug supply till April 1915; then seconded to War Trade Dept. in connection with the blockade of Germany; Appointed Controller of the War Trade, Statistical Dept. on its formation in 1916; Chairman of Inter-Allied Rationing and Statistical Committee, 1917–18; Appointed Principal, Finance Dept., Air Ministry, 1918; Principal Establishment Officer and Assistant Sec. of H.M. Treasury, 1919. *Addresses:* Homefield, Warlingham; Treasury, S.W. 1. (C193)
HASELER, William Rabone, O.B.E., *b.* 1860; *s.* of W. H. Haseler, of Birmingham; *m.* Florence, *d.* of William Ryland, of Birmingham. *Educ.:* Privately. Manufacturer; Commissioner of Income Tax; Guardian of Birmingham Assay Office; Governor of Handsworth Grammar School. *War Work:* Commander of the "C" Division of Special Constabulary of Birmingham. *Address:* 43, Handsworth Wood Road, Birmingham. (O10581)
HASKINS, Arthur, M.B.E.
HASKINS, Edith Mabel, M.B.E.; *d.* of Joseph Haskins, of Warmley Tower, Warmley, Glos. *Educ.:* Clifton High School. *War Work:* Gazetted Assistant Administrator Q.M.A.A.C., Oct. 1917; attached to General Headquarter Staff (Ireland) from Nov. 1917 to June, 1919, as Assistant Controller Q.M.A.A.C. Ireland, dealing with general administration of Q.M.A.A.C. camps, Ireland. *Address:* 28, Caversham Road, London, N.W. 5. (M6643)
HASLAM, Francis Meadows, M.B.E.
HASLAM, Capt. Thomas Wilfred, O.B.E.
HASLAM, Lieut. William Heywood, O.B.E., R.N.V.R.
HASLEHUST, Harold Maitland, M.B.E., I.A.
HASSALL, Lieut.-Col. Owen, O.B.E.
HASSELL, Charles Joseph, O.B.E., *b.* 20 Aug. 1857; *s.* of Joseph Hassell, A.K.C. (Lond.), Professor of Education; *m.* Hannah Elizabeth, *d.* of Joseph Barrett, of London. *Educ.:* Islington Proprietary School and King's College, London. Collector of H.M. Customs and Excise, London Port. *War Work:* In charge of the Outdoor Department of Customs in London, which had many special and important duties imposed upon it by legislation and Orders in Council consequent upon the war. *Address:* Tregarthen, Windsor Road, Finchley. (O10582)
HASTHORPE, Alice, M.B.E.
HASTIE, Peter, M.B.E.
HASTIE, Major Stuart Henderson, O.B.E., M.C.
HASTINGS, Albert, M.B.E.
HASTINGS, Lieut.-Comm. Edward George Godolphin, O.B.E., R.N.
HASTINGS, Frank, C.B.E.
HASTINGS, Eng.-Comm. James Frederick Arthur, O.B.E., R.N.
HASTINGS, William, O.B.E.
HASWELL, John Watson, M.B.E.
HASWELL, Robert, M.B.E. Secretary, William Doxford & Sons, Ltd., Shipbuilders, Sunderland. *Address:* 27, Thornhill Gardens, Sunderland. *Club:* County Constitutional. (M522)
HASZARD, Lieut. Gerald Fenwick, O.B.E., D.S.C. R.M.

245

HASZARD, Lieut. Henry Vivian Moore, O.B.E., R.N.V.R.

HATCH, Sir Ernest Frederick George, Bart., K.B.E., *b.* 12 April, 1859; *s.* of the late John William Hatch and Matilda Augusta, his wife, *o. d.* of Hugh Snell, of Callington, Cornwall, Barrister-at-law; *m.* 12 Oct. 1900, Lady Constance Blanche Godolphin Osborne *y.d.* of the 9th Duke of Leeds (*see* BURKE'S *Peerage*). M.P. for the Gorton Division of S.E. Lancashire, 1895-1906; Chairman and Treasurer of University College Hospital and has been Chairman of various Departmental Committees (Home Office, Board of Trade, Local Government Board and Insurance Commissioners); and on the panel of Chairmen of Court of Arbitration; is Commander of the Order of the Crown of Belgium, and Member of the Order of St. John of Jerusalem. *Address:* 20, Portland Place, W. (K334)

HATCH, Ethel Francis, M.B.E., Q.M.A.A.C.

HATCH, Frederick Henry, Ph.D., O.B.E., M.Inst.C.E., Past President Inst. Mining and Metallurgy, *b.* 1864. *Educ.:* Univ. Coll., London, and Bonn Univ. Mining Engineer: S. Africa, Spain, Canada, United States, India, Abyssinia, Natal, Zululand, Urals; reported on the gold resources of India for the Indian Government in 1900-1, and the mineral resources of Natal and Zululand for the Natal Government; at present member of the Governing Body of the Imperial Mineral Resources Bureau, and Director of the Mineral Resources Development Department of the Board of Trade. *War Work:* Member of the Home Iron Ore Supply Committee of the Iron and Steel Department of the Ministry of Munitions; Member of Commission to examine the condition of the Iron and Steel Works in the occupied areas of Germany, in Belgium, and in France; member of the Departmental Committee appointed by the Board of Trade to enquire into the economic position of the Iron Ferrous Mining Industry; Author of "The Iron and Steel Industry of the U.K. under War Conditions." *Clubs:* Athenæum; Bath. (O10583)

HATCH, Lieut. William Ashton, M.B.E., R.E.

HATFIELD, Ada Sophia Lucy, O.B.E.; *d.* of James Berriman Tippetts, of Highbury and St. Leonards; *m.* George Frederick Hatfield, *s.* of Charles William Hatfield, of Doncaster. *Educ.:* Privately. *War Work:* Hon. Sec. to the Y.M.C.A. 1915-20, for the National Women's Auxiliary; Hon. Auditor of Ladies' Alpine Club; a Governor of the Green Cross Club; *Address:* 11, Bedford Square, London, W.C. 1. *Clubs:* Albemarle; Forum; Ladies' Alpine. (O414)

HATHERLEY, Cyril George, O.B.E.

HATTERSLEY, John, O.B.E.

HATTON, George, C.B.E., J.P.

HATTON, James Thomas, M.B.E.

HAUGHTON, Major Henry Wilfred, D.S.O., O.B.E.

HAUGHTON, Francis George, M.B.E., *b.* 14 June, 1863; *s.* of Henry Charles Haughton, of London; *m.* Kate, *d.* of Samuel Edward Sturman, of London. *Educ.:* Stoke Newington; City of London Coll. Surveyor of Customs and Excise, Kirkwall; Registrar of Shipping; Receiver of Wrecks; Registrar of Royal Naval Reserve; Superintendent of Mercantile Marine, and Agent for Admiralty Prize Court, for Orkney Islands. *War Work:* Mobilised the R.N. Reserve in Orkney in Aug. 1914; dealt with custody of prize ships and cargoes, and derelict torpedoed vessels, and flotsam from these and other wrecks; also all general Customs duties in relation to the duty-free stores supplied to the large fleets of His Majesty in Orkney waters. *Address:* St. Bernards, Bulstrode Road, Hounslow. (M8404)

HAUGHTON, Marjorie Wilhelmina, O.B.E., *b.* 19 Sept. 1893; *d.* of Benjamin Haughton, J.P., of Cork. *Educ.:* Polam Hall School, Darlington. *War Work:* Hon. Sec. Soldiers' and Sailors' Free Buffet at Cork Station of Gt. Southern and Western Railway; Hon. Lady Sec. Soldiers' and Sailors' Hostel, Y.M.C.A., Cork. *Address:* Wellington Road, Cork. (O10585)

HAULTAIN, Capt. William Francis Theodore, O.B.E., M.C., B.A., M.B., B.Ch. (Cantab), late R.A.M.C. (S.R.), *b.* 14 Jan. 1893; *s.* of F. W. N. Haultain, M.D., of 12, Charlotte Square, Edinburgh; *m.* Winifred, *d.* of Major J. D. Outram, of Edinburgh. *Educ.:* Edinburgh Academy; Cambridge and Edinburgh Universities. *War Work:* Capt. R.A.M.C. (S.R.), B.E.F. and E.E.F. *Address:* 5, Queen's Terrace, Aberdeen. (O6197)

HAUSWELL, Francis, M.B.E. (M10249d)

HAUXWELL, Samuel, O.B.E.

HAVES, Paymaster-Lieut.-Comm. Robert, O.B.E., R.N.

HAVES, Paymaster Thomas, O.B.E., R.N.

HAVILAND, Capt. Reginald Henry, M.B.E.; *s.* of the late Rev. A. C. Haviland, of Lilley, Herts. *Educ.:* Wellington. *War Work:* Oct. 1914, obtained Commission, in 4th Batt. Durham Light Infantry; attached to Staff of Tyne Garrison, July, 1915, to July, 1916; with Army Canteen Committee, now Navy and Army Canteen Board, from July, 1916, to date. *Addresses:* St. Michael's Manor, St. Albans; 10, Hanover Square, London, W. *Club:* Bath. (M5332)

HAVILAND, Capt. Wilfred Pollen, M.B.E., Argyll and Sutherland Highlanders (T.F.), *b.* 14 April, 1881; *s.* of the late Rev. Arthur Haviland, of Lilley, Herts.; *m.* Beryl Marion, *d.* of the late Lieut.-Col. Sir Edward Durand, Bart., C.B. *Educ.:* Charterhouse and Kings' Coll., Cambridge. Stock Exchange. *War Work:* With 1/8th Argyll and Sutherland Highlanders (Princess Louise's), served in France, 1915-18; General Staff from Aug. 1917, to March, 1919; twice mentioned

in despatches. *Address:* Whitlars, King's Langley, Herts. *Club:* Isthmian. (M5333)

HAVOCK, Donald St. John, M.B.E.

HAWES, Albert Henry, O.B.E. (O11744)

HAWES, Charles Henry, M.B.E., *b.* 10 Dec. 1876; *s.* of Philip James Hawes, of Market Drayton, Shropshire; *m.* Nellie Louisa, *d.* of Thomas Moore, of Havant, Hants. *Educ.:* Longparish, Hants. Clerk, War Office. *War Work:* Clerical work at War Office in connection with Transportation of Troops and Stores. *Address:* 9, Fairfield Terrace, Havant, Hants. (M3701)

HAWES, George William Spencer, O.B.E.

HAWK, William, C.B.E., J.P., *b.* 1851; *s.* of William Hawk, of Kernock, Cornwall; *m.* Florence, *d.* of John Clemence of Howton, Cornwall. Chairman of Cornwall County Council and War Agricultural Committee. *Address:* Kernock, St. Mellion, Cornwall. (C194)

HAWKE, Dora Annie, Mrs., M.B.E.

HAWKE, Edward Drummond Hay, O.B.E., L.R.C.P. (Lond.), M.R.C.S., *b.* 7 June, 1867; *s.* of Edward Henry Hawke, of Tolgulla, Scarrier, Cornwall; *m.* Dora Annie, *d.* of Charles Park, of Hampstead. *Educ.:* Merchant Taylors' School; Charing Cross Hospital. *War Work:* M.O. of Shortlands V.A.D. Hospital, and of Shortlands Depot, R.A.S.C. (M.T.) *Address:* 9, Tolgulla, Shortlands, Kent. (O4372)

HAWKE, Leah Lucy, Mrs., M.B.E.

HAWKE, William, C.B.E., J.P.

HAWKER, Brig.-Gen. Claude Julian, C.M.G., C.B.E., *b.* 1867. Lieut.-Col. Coldstream Guards; Nile Expedition, 1899; served in Great War in Mesopotamia, 1915-18 (mentioned in despatches). (C1107)

HAWKER, Francis Feodor Wynne, M.B.E., *b.* 14 April, 1857; *s.* of James Hawker, of Plymouth; *m.* Ada St. John Melliar, *d.* of Rev. C. F. Garratt, of Bickleigh. *Educ.:* Winchester Coll. Wine Merchant. *War Work:* Y.M.C.A.; Treas. of Plymouth War Hospital Supply Depot; collection and forwarding of clothing to Ruhleben Camp; visiting Hospitals; entertaining wounded. *Address:* Hele House, Batsleigh, Roborough, S. Devon. *Club:* Royal Western Yacht; British Empire. (M1867)

HAWKER, Frank, M.B.E., *b.* 9 March, 1868; *s.* of Thomas Hawker, of Birmingham; *m.* Nora Jane, *d.* of James Rollason, of Moseley, Birmingham. *Educ.:* Gower Street Schools, and Privately. Manufacturer; founder of Frank Hawker Carpathian Silver Co., Ltd.; Director and Chairman of Hawkers, Ltd., and The British Needle Co. Ltd.; member of the Birmingham City Council, since 1911 an Overseer for Handsworth. *War Work:* Rendered valuable services to the Ministry of Munitions for the production of Fuse parts, especially Safety Shutters, which prevented our shells exploding in our guns or near our men. *Address:* Milenda House, Devonshire Road, Handsworth Wood, Birmingham. *Club:* Midland Conservative. (M1866)

HAWKES, Lieut. Comley, M.B.E., M.C., R.A.O.C.

HAWKES, Lieut.-Col. Frank Roxburgh, O.B.E., I.A.R.O.

HAWKES, Harry George, M.B.E.

HAWKES, Major John Alfred, O.B.E.

HAWKES, Violet, M.B.E.

HAWKESWORTH, Paymaster-Lieut. Richard Arthur, O.B.E., R.N.

HAWKINS, Lieut. Albert Gordon Jones, M.B.E.

HAWKINS, Albert Victor, M.B.E., *b.* 16 Oct. 1871; *s.* of Alexander Hawkins, of London; *m.* Barbara Walker, *d.* of William Dodds, of London. *Educ.:* Privately. Superintendent, Criminal Investigation Department, New Scotland Yard, S.W. *War Work:* Special Police (C.I.D.) work. *Address:* 18, Ravenscourt Park, W. 6. (M523)

HAWKINS, Beatrice Helen, M.B.E., *b.* 22 Nov. 1887; *d.* of Isaac Thomas Hawkins, A.M.I.C.E., formerly Col. Civil Service, and Mrs. Mary Hope Hawkins, and sister of Lieut. Lionel Hope Hawkins, 1st King's Dragoon Guards, the well-known polo player, who was killed in action, Oct. 1914. *Educ.:* The Abbey Coll., Stroud; Madame Yateman's, Neuilly, Paris. *War Work:* Winter 1914-15 worked in connection with the Soldiers' and Sailors' Families Association; in Autumn 1915 worked in motor repair works, gaining certificate for running repairs, etc.; also worked for Belgian Food Relief, driving van to Covent Garden, collecting and distributing food, etc.; worked at Woolwich Arsenal, and was one of the first ladies to obtain a certificate as an examiner of shell filling; afterwards entered the War Office in Military Secretary's Dept. *Address:* 5, Emperor's Gate, S.W. 7. *Clubs:* Ladies' Army and Navy; Hurlingham. (M8407)

HAWKINS, Florence Beatrice, Mrs., M.B.E.

HAWKINS, Capt. Harold John Charlton, O.B.E., R.A.S.C.

HAWKINS, Capt. George, O.B.E., R.A.S.C., *b.* 19 Aug. 1893; *s.* of G. P. Hawkins, of Cambridge. *Educ.:* Perse and Christ's College, Cambridge. *War Service:* Served at the front in France from Jan. 1915 to 11 Nov. 1918 continuously; Enlisted Aug. 1914; Served with 28th, 33rd, and 3rd Infantry Divisions; Latterly S.S.O. 3rd Division. *Address:* Brunswick Walk, Cambridge. (O5358)

HAWKINS, Major Henry, O.B.E.

HAWKINS, Lieut.-Col. Herbert Pennell, C.B.E., R.A.M.C. (T.), *b.* 30 June, 1859; *s.* of Rev. Robert Hawkins, Vicar of Lamberhurst; *m.* Hester Vera, *d.* of Fleetwood Rynd, of

Mount Armstrong. *Educ.*: Eton and Oxford. Physician (retired). *War Work*: O.C. 5th London General Hospital. *Address*: Lackenhurst, Shipley, Sussex. *Club*: New Univ.
(C1608)

HAWKINS, John Alfred, M.B.E.

HAWKINS, Capt. John Frederick, O.B.E., R.A.F.

HAWKINS, Sarah Annie Moss, M.B.E. Clerk in Civil Service. *War Work*: Work in connection with War Savings Certificates. *Addresses*: 5, Argyle Road, Woodside Park, N.; Money Order Dept., G.P.O.
(M8409)

HAWKINS, Thomas Shirley, M.B.E.

HAWKS, Lieut.-Col. George Augustus, O.B.E., I.A.

HAWKSFORD, Capt. Francis Henry, O.B.E.. R.A.F.

HAWKSWORTH, Capt. John Ledlie Inglish, O.B.E.

HAWKSWORTH, William, O.B.E.

HAWLEY, Arthur, O.B.E., M.B., M.R.C.S., L.R.C.P.

HAWORTH, Col. Frederic, O.B.E., T.D., V.D., J.P., D.L., *b.* 8 May, 1857; *s.* of Richard Haworth, J.P., of Didsbury. Lancashire; *m.* Mary Simmons, *d.* of Robert Hodgkinson, of Cheadle, Cheshire. *Educ.*: Privately. Cadet Colonel Commandant for Cumberland and Westmorland; Hon. Col. 7th Batt. Lancs. Fus.; Member of Westmorland Territorial Force Association. *War Work*: Raised and trained Westmorland Section of the 11th Batt. (Lonsdale) Border Regt. County Commandant, Cumberland and Westmorland Volunteer Regt. *Address*: Ashley Green, Loughrigg, Ambleside. *Clubs*: Arts; Royal Windermere Yacht. (O7256)

HAWS, Capt. Albert Henry, O.B.E., *b.* 29 March, 1871; *s.* of Charles Henry Haws, of Witcham; *m.* Alice M., *d.* of Charles Strowlger, of Colchester. *Educ.*: Sutton. *War Work*: Enlisted in 1st King's Dragoon Guards, 1914; Commissioned Lieut.-Qr.-Mr. in the Scottish Horse Yeomanry, Sept. 1914; gazetted Capt. Sept. 1917; served in the Dardanelles, under Lord Tullibardine, C.B., D.S.O., M.V.O., Oct. 1915, to Dec. 1915; posted to 2nd Brigade, Scottish Horse Yeo., East Coasts, Nov. 1916; posted to 1st King's Dragoon Guards, and proceeded to France, June, 1917; India, 1917–19, mentioned in Gen. Monro's despatches for distinguished services during the operations; medals, 1914 Star, British War, 3rd Afghan 1919, Allied, and Long Service. *Address*: Kingsleigh, Nutfield Road, Thornton Heath, Surrey. *Club*: Primrose. (O11744)

HAWSON, Millar Wright, M.B.E.

HAWTREY, Capt. Wilfred Robert John, O.B.E., *b.* 22 Feb. 1875; *s.* of Rev. H. C. Hawtrey, of Nursling; *m.* Mary Dixon, *d.* of W. M. Chinnery, of Hatchford. *Educ.*: Royal Naval School, and Weymouth. *War Work*: Helped to form 9th D.A.C., March, 1915; Commanded 51st B.A.C., April, 1915, to May, 1915, and "D" Bty., 51st Bde., and "B" Bty., 53 Bde., France; Loos, Ypres, Armentières, Somme, wounded 1916; Mobilisation, W.D. Staff. May, 1917, to May, 1919; Secretary, King's Fund, Ministry of Pensions. *Address*: Bray Rise, Bray, Berks. *Club*: R.A.C. (O1588)

HAY, Algernon Richard Francis, O.B.E.

HAY, Althea Maud, M.B.E.; *d.* of David Hay, M.I.C.E., of 6, Abbey Road Mansions N.W., and Little Hill, Melton, Suffolk. *Educ.*: St. Winifred's, Eastbourne, and Lady Margaret Hall, Oxford. *War Work*: Four years in the Intelligence Department, Ministry of Shipping; previously teaching in boy's school to relieve a master for Active Service. *Address*: 6, Abbey Road Mansions, N.W. *Club*: Ladies' Univ.
(M1871)

HAY, Major Arthur Kennet, D.S.O., O.B.E., *b.* 1884; Major R.A.; Gen. Staff Officer; served in the Great War, 1914–18 (mentioned in despatches). (O2988)

HAY, Charlotte Maud, M.B.E., Q.M.A.A.C.

HAY, David Allan, *b.* 1878; *s.* of James Hay, of Paisley; *m.* Frances Margaret, *d.* of Thomas Walker, of North Berwick. *Educ.*: Paisley Grammar School; Glasgow University. Chartered Accountant. *War Work*: Hon. Sec., and Hon. Treas., of Soldiers' and Sailors' Families Association, Glasgow Branch. *Address*: Lorraine Gardens, Downhill, Glasgow, W. *Club*: Glasgow Conservative. (O3745)

HAY, Lieut.-Col. George Lennox, C.B.E., D.S.O., *b.* 1873. Capt. and Brevet Lieut.-Col. Army Ordnance Depart.; served in Great War, 1914–18 (mentioned in despatches). (C784)

HAY, Henrietta Louisa, M.B.E.; *d.* of the late Sir Robert Hay, Bart., of Haystoun. *War Work*: Organising of Canteens for women war workers for Young Women's Christian Association. *Addresses*: 24, Thurloe Square, London, S.W.; The Lees, Innerleithen, Scotland. (M525)

HAY, James, O.B.E. (O11979)

HAY, Capt. James George, D.S.O., O.B.E., *b.* 1878; sometime an A.A. and Q.M.G.; S. Africa, 1899–1900 (Queen's medal with three clasps); served in the Great War, 1914–18 (mentioned in despatches). (O2558)

HAY, James Lawrence, O.B.E.

HAY, Kenneth Robert, O.B.E., M.A., M.B., M.R.C.S., L.R.C.P., *b.* 1873; *s.* of the late Alexander S. Hay, of Sacombe Park, Ware, Herts; *m.* Rachel, *d.* of Ernest Beek, of Gt. Amwell, Ware, Herts. *Educ.*: Sherborne and Cambridge. *War Work*: Hon. Medical Officer, Officers' Hospitals at 24, Park Street, W., and 53, Cadogan Square, S.W.; Resident Civilian Medical Officer at 1st London General Hospital, Camberwell, June, 1916, to Dec. 1918. *Address*: 47, Hill Street, Berkeley Square, W. 1. *Club*: Oxford and Cambridge.
(O11809)

HAY, Capt. Peter Stewart, O.B.E.

HAY, Comm. The Hon. Sereld Mordaunt Alan, O.B.E., *b.* 25 Nov. 1877; *s.* of Major-Gen. Charles Gore Hay, 19th Earl of Erroll, K.T., C.B., T.D. (*see* BURKE'S *Peerage*), of Aberdeenshire, Scotland; *m.* Violet, *d.* of Col. Duncan Spiller, of 23, Vale Avenue, S.W. *Educ.*: Privately; H.M.S. "Britannia." Under-Sec. Imperial Institute, South Kensington; Orange Farmer, owning two orange farms, Penhurst and Riverside, at Selborne on the Sunday's River, South Africa. *War Work*: Assist. Naval Transport Officer, under Capt. R. C. Lambert, D.S.O., R.N., during German South-West African Campaign, 1914–15; Staff Officer to the R.N.V.R., South African Division, 1914–19; Author of the "History of the R.N.V.R., South African Division," which has been accepted by Gen. Smuts as the official History of the Corps. *Clubs*: Junior Naval and Military. (O9668)

HAY, Capt. Sydney Hartley, M.B.E.

HAY, 2nd Lieut. William Ross, M.B.E., R.E.

HAY, Mary Elizabeth DALRYMPLE-, O.B.E.; *d.* of the late Admiral the Rt. Hon. Sir J. C. Dalrymple-Hay, Bart., G.C.B. *War Work*: Navy League; in charge of the N.L. Naval Units. *Address*: 9, Vincent Square Mansions, S.W. 1. *Clubs*: Bath; Mid-Surrey Golf. (O10589)

HAY, Eveline Anstey, Mrs. DRUMMOND-, M.B.E., *b.* 20 Jan. 1874; *d.* of the late Rev. E. T. Bennett, of Castle Roe, Coleraine; *m.* Francis Edward, M.V.O., H.M. Consul-General at Lyons; *s.* of the late Sir Francis R. Drummond-Hay. *War Work*: Head of Clothing Department of Belgian War Refugees Committee, Folkestone; organiser of seven Depots in connection with Queen Mary's Needlework Guild, in Brazil; Deputy Commandant Kenry House Hospital for Officers, Kingston Hill; received from the King of the Belgians the Medaille de la Reine Elizabeth. *Address*: British Consulate-General, Lyons, France. (M8411)

HAYCOCK, Herbert Clement, O.B.E., *b.* 27 March, 1874; *s.* of W. T. Haycock, of London; *m.* Marguerite Lucy, *d.* of Robert Finch, of Dulwich. *Educ.*: Archbishop Tenison's School. Chairman and Managing Director of Haycock, Cadle and Graham, Ltd., of Camberwell. *War Work*: Voluntary Administrative Officer, Road Transport Board, Board of Trade. *Address*: The Nook, Gipsy Hill, Upper Norwood. S.E. 19. *Club*: National Liberal. (O10590)

HAYCRAFT, George Tolman, O.B.E.

HAYDEN, Lieut.-Col. Frederick Arthur, D.S.O., O.B.E., *b.* 1861; *s.* of the late Rev. Charles Frederick Hayden, Vicar of West Hendred, Berks; *m.* Henrietta Grace Lambeart, *d.* of the late Col. Anthony Stewart, I.S.C. *Educ.*: Winchester. Entered 33rd Regt. 1881; Capt. Duke of Wellington's (W. Riding Regt.), 1888; Major, 1898; Lieut.-Col. 1908; ret. 1912; served in S. Africa, 1900–2 (despatches); served in Great War as Lieut.-Col. Comdg. a Batt. Duke of Wellington's (W. Riding Regt.), 1914–16. *Address*: 52, Warwick Road, Earl's Court, S.W.5. (O7257)

HAYES, Agnes, M.B.E.

HAYES, Annie Rosina, Mrs., M.B.E.

HAYES, Arthur William, M.B.E., *b.* 16 Dec. 1873; *s.* of William Hayes, of Blidworth, Notts.; *m.* Elizabeth Eleanor, *d.* of Thomas Glass, of Wingate, Durham. *Educ.*: Hucknall. *War Work*: Directed the whole of the Y.M.C.A. activities in the County of Kent; also for a time the sleeping of soldiers in London; Twice complimented by His Majesty. *Address*: Deneholme, Elm Avenue, Nottingham. (M526)

HAYES, Capt. and Qr.-Mr. Denis, M.B.E.

HAYES, Lieut.-Col. Edwin Charles, C.B.E., *b.* 1868. Lieut.-Col. R.A.M.C.; China, 1900 (medal); Great War, 1914–19 (mentioned in despatches). (C1264)

HAYES, Lieut. Ernest George, M.B.E.

HAYES, Capt. Francis Bernard, O.B.E., R.A.V.C.

HAYES, Fredric James, M.B.E., *b.* 1867; *s.* of Louis Milroy Hayes, of Manchester; *m.* Lucy Violet, *d.* of Samuel Horton, of Liverpool. *Educ.*: Privately. Merchant. *War Work*: Chairman Y.M.C.A. War Emergency Committee, Lancashire Division. *Addresses*: Rochester Terrace, Buxton; Victoria Street, Manchester. *Clubs*: Clarendon (Manchester); Old Rectory (Manchester). (M527)

HAYES, Capt. and Qr.-Mr. George Frederick Lacey, M.B.E.

HAYES, George Patrick, O.B.E.

HAYES, Surg.-Capt. George Sullivan Clifford, O.B.E.

HAYES, James Waldegrave, M.B.E.

HAYES, John Joseph, M.B.E.

HAYES, Lillian May McCaully, Mrs., M.B.E.

HAYES, Robert, O.B.E. (O3509)

HAYES, Major Robert Cholerton, O.B.E., R.F.A.

HAYFORD, Joseph Ephraim Casely, M.B.E.

HAYLEY, Major Sydney Thomas, D.S.O., O.B.E.

HAYLOCK, Ernest Edwin, O.B.E.

HAYMAN, Albert Melville, O.B.E. Organiser, Accounts Branch, Mesopotamian Railways. (O11789h)

HAYNE, Frederick William, O.B.E.

HAYNE, Louis Brightwell, M.B.E., M.A., M.D. (Cantab), *b.* 19 July, 1869; *s.* of Henry Hayne, of Tunbridge Wells; *m.* Margaret Lillias, *d.* of Murdock Shaw Morison. *Educ*: Tonbridge School; Gonville and Caius Coll., Camb.; St. George's Hospital, London. Physician Harrogate Infirmary. *War Work*: Medical Officer in Charge, Grove House Auxiliary Hospital, Harrogate. *Address*: Sheen House, Harrogate.
(M8414)

HAYNES, Eng.-Lieut.-Comm. Frederick Gambier, O.B.E., R.D., R.N.R.

HAYNES, George, M.B.E.

HAYNES, Capt. George William, M.B.E.

HAYNES, Lieut.-Col. (T. Brig.-Gen.,) Kenneth Edward, C.M.G. C.B.E., R.A., b. 2 Aug. 1871; s. of Lieut.-Col. E. C. Haynes, of Bridge, Kent; m. Katharine Mary Elizabeth, d. of Rev. Canon J. H. Carr, of Adisham, Kent. *Educ.:* Malvern; Royal Military Academy. Regular Army. *War Work:* Superintendent of Experiments; Member of Ordnance Committee. *Address:* c/o Messrs. Cox & Co., 16, Charing Cross, S.W. 1. *Club:* Army and Navy. (C1609)

HAYSE, Thomas William James, M.B.E.

HAYTER, Major Gordon Willis, O.B.E., M.I.A.E., b. 14 Jan. 1888; s. of John Short Hayter, of Wimborne. *Educ.:* Christ's Hospital. Engineer. *War Work:* R.A.S.C. from Oct. 1914, to date; 2 years Italy as Inspector of Mech. Transport. *Address:* 57, Chancery Lane, W.C. *Club:* Royal Automobile. (O6378)

HAYTER, Capt. John, M.B.E., R.G.A.

HAYTER, William George, C.B.E.

HAYTER, Sir William Goodenough, K.B.E., b. 1869; s. of Henry Goodenough Hayter; m. Alethea, d. of the Rev. J. H. Slessor; Rector of Headborne Worthy, Hants; Barr.-at-Law, Lincoln's Inn, 1895; Civil Judge in the Soudan, 1903; Asst. Legal Adviser in Egypt, 1904; Khedival Counsellor 1913; Sultan's Counsellor, 1915; Chairman, Cotton Control in Egypt; acted as Judicial Adviser in 1904–6, and as Financial Adviser in 1919; has Orders of the Nile and Medjidie 2nd Class. *Address:* Lamalek, Gezira, Cairo. *Clubs:* Turf, Gezira. Sidmouth. (K466)

HAYTHORNE, Winifred Scott, O.B.E. (M.), b. 11 June, 1891; d. of the late T. J. S. Haythorne, M.D., of Liverpool. *Educ.:* Belvedere School, Girls' Public Day School Trust, Liverpool; Somerville College, Oxford; London School of Economics. Since May, 1920, General and Organising Sec. to the Women's Political and Industrial League, 92, Victoria St. S.W.1. *War Work:* Assistant Administrator, W.A.A.C., 1917; Q.M.A.A.C. Controller, London District, 1918; Q.M.A.A.C. Deputy Chief Controller Overseas, 1918; Mentioned in despatches, 16 March, 1919. *Club:* Forum. (O3128)

HAYWARD, Annie, M.B.E.

HAYWARD, Curling, M.B.E.

HAYWARD, Ernest Addison Stanley, O.B.E.

HAYWARD, Lieut.-Col. Edwyn Walton, C.B.E. Commr. Australian Red Cross Society. (C416)

HAYWARD, John Robert Baxter, M.B.E. Civil Service, War Office, 1898–1902; Earl Marshal's Staff, King Edward VII. Coronation (medal). *War Work:* Sec. of Union Jack Club; specially mentioned for services by Sec. of State for War, 1918; Hon. Sec. and Manager Westminster Club, 1915–19. *Address:* 91A, Waterloo Road, London, S.E. 1. (M8416)

HAYWARD, Major Percy Christopher Gallimore, M.B.E.

HAYWARD, Capt. William, M.B.E., R.A.F.

HAYWARD, William, M.B.E.

HAYWARD, Margaret Frances CURTIS-, M.B.E., b. 23 Oct. 1848; s. of John Curtis-Hayward, of Quedgeley House, Gloucester. *Educ.:* Cheltenham Ladies' Coll. *War Work:* Hon. Sec. Soldiers' and Sailors' Families Association, Gloucestershire; Hon. Sec. Quedgeley District Nursing Association; Member of Local War Pensions Committee. *Address:* Quedgeley House, Gloucestershire. (M8417)

HAYWOOD, Lieut. and Qr.-Mr. Harry, M.B.E.

HAYWOOD, Lieut. Norman Alphonso, M.B.E.

HAZARD, Major Cecil James, O.B.E., M.C., b. 24 Nov. 1883; s. of James Dare Hazard, of Sandown, I. of Wight. *Educ.:* Wimborne Grammar School, Dorset. Until Aug. 1914, topographical surveyor to the Administration of Northern Rhodesia, C. Africa. *War Work:* Enlisted as a private in Aug. 1914; Lieut. Hampshire Regt., Sept. 1914; Capt. Oct. 1914; Major May, 1916; wounded and prisoner, March, 1918; on release in Nov. 1918 was promoted Lieut.-Col. and appointed O.C. Troops in Denmark and Base Commandant, Copenhagen, in charge of Repatriation of Prisoners of War. *Addresses:* Redcliff, Sandown, I. of Wight, England; Finca Seamay, Alta Verapaz, Guatemala, C. America. (O8829)

HAZEL, Alfred Ernest William, C.B.E., M.A., B.C.L., LL.D., b. 1869; s. of the late John Hazel, builder and contractor, of West Bromwich; m. Ethel Annie, d. of the Rev. W. G. Percival, of Holloway, N.; *Educ.:* West Bromwich Wesleyan School; King Edward's School, Birmingham; Jesus Coll., Oxford. Called to the Bar, Lincoln's Inn, 1898; Fellow, Dean, and Bursar of Jesus Coll.; Lecturer on Law at Queen's and Pembroke Colls., Oxford; Reader of Constitutional Law and Legal History to Inns of Court; Senior Proctor, Oxford Univ., 1910–11; M.P. for W. Bromwich (L), 1906–10; appointed first Recorder of Burton-on-Trent, Nov. 1912. *Addresses:* Jesus College, Oxford; Oxenford House, West Bromwich; 3, Temple Gardens, E.C.; 77, Colmore Row, Birmingham. *Clubs:* Reform; National Liberal. (C195)

HAZLEHURST, George, O.B.E.

HAZLERIGG, Grey, O.B.E.

HAZELTON, Major George, O.B.E., R.A.F.

HEAD, Arthur, M.B.E. (M10448)

HEAD, Lieut. Geoffrey, O.B.E.

HEAD, Herbert Harry, M.B.E., b. 12 March, 1887; s. of Harry Head, of Faversham; m. Florence Lilian Alice, d. of — Gowers. *Educ.:* Faversham District National Schools; Henry Wreight's School, Faversham; Faversham

Teachers' Training Centre. Assistant Master under Board of Education; Fellow of Institute of Specialist and Commercial Teachers; Executive Staff of Clark's Coll.; Manager Staff Training Dept., Harrods, Ltd., S.W. 1. *War Work:* Accounts Dept. of Ministry of Munitions, Assistant Director; Sec. in the Finance Dept.; Private Sec. to the Assistant Financial Sec.; Travelling Audit Staff of Ministry of Munitions. *Address:* 31. Tollenhall Road, Palmers' Green, N. 13. *Club:* National Liberal. (M3704)

HEADLAM, Capt. Cuthbert Morley, D.S.O., O.B.E., b. 27 April, 1876; s. of late Francis John Headlam, formerly Stipendiary Police Magistrate, Manchester; m. Georgina Beatrice, d. of late George Baden Crawley. *Educ.:* King's School, Canterbury; Magdalen College, Oxford. Barrister-at-Law, Clerk of Public Bills and Clerk of the Journals, House of Lords. *War Work:* Went to France with the Bedfordshire Yeomanry, in June, 1915, and remained until the end of the war; was A.D.C. to the Earl of Cavan while that officer was in command of the 50th Division and Guards Division; Subsequently served as General Staff Officer, 3rd Grade, with Second Army; as G.S.O. 2 with VIII. Corps, and as G.S.O. 1 with rank of Lieut.-Col. at G.H.Q., B.E.F. *Address:* 4, Montagu Place, W. 1. *Clubs:* Travellers'; Beefsteak; Pratt's. (O5360)

HEADLAM, Sir John Emerson Wharton, K.B.E., C.B., D.S.O., D.L., Co. Durham. b. 16 April, 1864; s. of Morley Headlam, J.P., of Gilmonby Hall, Yorkshire, and of Whorlton Grange, Durham; m. Mary Charlotte, d. of Perceval Wilkinson, J.P., of Mount Oswald, Co. Durham. *Educ.:* King's College School; Royal Military Academy. Entered Royal Artillery, 1883; served in South African War, 1900–02 (Brevet Lieut.-Col., D.S.O.); Director of Staff Duties and Military Training in India, 1908–13. *War Work:* Commanded Divisional Artillery, 5th Division, Aug. 1914 to Feb. 1915; Artillery Second Army to Dec. 1915; Major-Gen. R.A. at G.H.Q., 1916; Liaison Officer, Ministry of Munitions; accompanied Lord Milner's Mission to Russia, 1917; in charge of Artillery Mission to U.S.A., 1918; promoted Major-Gen. for Distinguished Service in the Field; Commander of the Legion of Honour, Order of St. Anne of Russia, 1st Class with Swords, American D.S.M. *Address:* Cruck Meole House, Hanwood, W. Shrewsbury. *Clubs:* Army and Navy; Cavalry; Shropshire. (K254)

HEADLAND, Robert Vincent, O.B.E., b. 6 April, 1876; s. of the late Robert Headland, late Assistant Controller, Central Telegraph Office; m. Zoe Antoinette, d. of Alfred Phillips, of Brookdene, Bournemouth. *Educ.:* Privately. Principal Staff Officer, Finance Dept., Board of Trade. *War Work:* Army Contracts Dept.; Assistant Director of Costings, War Office, 1917; Controller, Disposal Finance and Accounts, Ministry of Munitions, 1919. *Address:* 11, Blenheim Road, Bedford Park, W. 4. (O10594)

HEADLEY, Lieut. Arthur William Aimley, O.B.E., R.E. (T.F.).

HEADLEY, Robert Hollowell, M.B.E.

HEADS, John George, M.B.E.

HEADWARDS, Lieut. Horace, M.B.E., R.E.

HEAKES, Major Samuel Rigbye, O.B.E.

HEALD, Lieut.-Col. Charles Brehmer, C.B.E. Lieut.-Col. R.A.F.; Great War, 1914–19 (mentioned in despatches). (C862)

HEALD, Charles Ernest, O.B.E., b. 1870; s. of William Heald, of Mere, Cheshire; m. Ellen Mary Jeannette, d. of Thomas Garner Daniel, of Manchester. *Address:* Ventnor, Chislehurst. *Club:* Cavendish. (O10595)

HEALE, Capt. Robert John Wingfield, O.B.E.

HEALEY, Basil, O.B.E., b. 20 Jan. 1863; s. of William Healey, of Manchester; m. Catherine Anne, d. of J. Pickering, of Bedworth, Warwickshire. *Educ.:* Manchester; Barnet, Herts.; Bury Grammar School. District Goods Manager Lancs. and Yorks. Railway. *War Work:* Supervised the business connected with the Goods Department of the Lancs. and Yorks. Railway Co. at Liverpool during the years 1916–19 inclusive; weight of traffic dealt with, sixteen million tons, including seven million tons of Merchandise; one million tons of minerals (largely composed of steel billets from America for making shells), and eight million tons of coal, a considerable proportion of which was for the Admiralty and Government Transports; responsible for the movements of all traffic to and from the Aintree Munition Works, and Amatol Factory, from the date they were opened (June, 1916), to the date of the Armistice (total weight involved one million tons); also supervised the despatch of many trains dealt with at the Goods Stations with American Troops, and the unloading of trains of wounded soldiers returning to America; responsible for the working from Liverpool of horses and mules ex the United States intended for the Remount Depot at Ormskirk, no less than 213,000 animals being so conveyed over the Lancs. and Yorks Railway from Liverpool; finally, the Lancs. and Yorks. Company were called upon to deal at Aintree Station with 401 Ambulance trains containing 70,000 wounded soldiers.

HEALEY, Col. Coryndon William Rutherford, C.M.G., C.B.E.

HEALEY, Lieut. Harry, M.B.E.

HEALEY, John Edridge, M.B.E., M.B., Ch.B.

HEALEY, Sir Gerald Edward CHADWYCK-, 2nd Bart., C.B.E., Commander Crown of Italy, b. 16 May, 1873; s. of Sir Charles E. H. Chadwyck Healey, 1st Bart., K.C.B., of Wyphurst, Cranley; m. Mary Verena, d. of George A. Watson.

of East Court, Finchampstead. *Educ.:* Eton; Trinity College, Oxford. Chairman, "The Engineer," Ltd.; Chairman, A. G. Mumford, Ltd. *War Work:* Lieut. R.N.V.R., 1915; R.N.H.S. "Queen Alexandra"; Assistant to Controller, Admiralty, 1917; Director, of Materials and Priority, Admiralty, 1918–19. *Addresses:* Wyphurst, Cranley; 66, Warwick Square, S.W. *Clubs:* Windham; Garrick; Savile; Royal Automobile; Western; Glasgow. (C981)

HEALY, Lieut. Reginald Stafford, M.B.E.

HEAN, Walter John, M.B.E., *b.* July, 1873; *s.* of Henry John Hean, of London. *Educ.:* Haberdashers' Co. School, Hoxton, and King's Coll., London. *War Work:* Admiralty. *Address:* Paxtonia, Kent House Road, Beckenham. (M8420)

HEANLY, 2nd. Lieut. Wilfred Edward Graham, M.B.E., R.A.F.

HEAP, Edward Barlow, M.B.E., J.P., C.C.; *s.* of Edward Barlow Heap, of Ashton-under Lyne; *m.* Kate, *d.* of Dr. Schofield, M.R.C.S., L.S.A., Dukinfield, Cheshire. *Educ.:* Ashton-under-Lyne. *War Work:* Mayor of Ashton-under-Lyne, 1916–18; Chairman of Local War Pensions, Local Food Control, and War Savings Committees. *Address:* Stamford House, Ashton-under-Lyne, Lancashire. *Club:* Union, Ashton-under-Lyne. (M8421)

HEAP, Iris Evelina Margaret Campbell, M.B.E.

HEAP, Stephen, M.B.E.

HEAPS, James, M.B.E., *b.* Dec. 1861. *War Work:* With Ministry of Munitions, and then, on the inauguration of the Controller of Coal Mines, was appointed District Superintendent in the Lancashire, Cheshire, and West Cumberland Areas. *Address:* Springfield Street, Wigan. (M8422)

HEARD, Lieut. Charles Campbell, M.B.E., R.E.

HEARD, Lieut.-Col. Samuel Ferguson, O.B.E., A.P.D.

HEARN, Major Edward Michael William, O.B.E., R.A.F.

HEARN, Capt. and Qr.-Mr. George Henry Seymour, M.B.E., D.C.M., R.F.A. (T.).

HEARN, Lieut.-Col. Michael Leo, O.B.E.

HEARN, Phyllis, Mrs., M.B.E..

HEARN, Sir Walter Risely, K.B.E., *b.* 30 April, 1853; *s.* of William Hearn, of Buckingham; *m.* Edith Gertrude, (Order of the Reconnaissance Française and the Queen of Roumania's Red Cross Medal), *d.* of George W. Lawson, of Rio Grande do Sul, and granddaughter of the Visconde de Sao José do Norte, Brazilian Peerage. *Educ.:* France; Germany. Vice-Consul Christiania, 1883–1900; Consul at Rio Grande do Sul, 1890–95, at Cadiz, 1895–97 at Bordeaux 1897–1903,; Consul-General at Havre, 1903–07, at San Francisco, 1907–11, at Hamburg, 1911–14, and at Paris, 1914–19. *War Work:* Consul-General at Paris during the whole of War till signature of Peace; Chairman, Local Tribunal and Ambassador's Advisory Committee; President of the British Army and Navy Leave Club, Paris; Visiting member during War of the Hertford British Hospital (Red Cross); Sec. and Treas. of the Society for the Relief of the families of Devastated France,; Relief and supply of Homes to French Blinded soldiers. *Clubs:* National; Royal Yacht Squadron (Hon.). (K383)

HEARNDEN, Horace Richard, M.B.E.

HEARNE, Major Francis George, O.B.E., R.A.S.C.

HEARSEY, Dorothy Maud, Mrs., M.B.E.

HEARSEY, Lieut.-Col. Herbert Hyde Young, O.B.E.

HEARTLEY, Major Walter, O.B.E.

HEASLOP, Major Adair Colpoys, O.B.E., M.C., M.A., R.A., *b.* 9 Feb. 1875; *s.* of Col. C. P. Heaslop, R.M.A., of Salween, Ryde, I.W.; *m.* Sibyl Mary, *d.* of Henry Bromfield, of Newnham Hall, Daventry, Northamptonshire. *Educ.:* I.W. Coll., and Lincoln Coll., Oxford. *War Work:* B.E.F. France; actions, Aisne, Lys, 1st Battle of Ypres, Ploegsteert, Neuve Chapelle, Richbourg, Festubert, Givenchy, Ypres, June, 1915, to April, 1916; Hooge, Pilhem, Hooge, The Bluff, St. Eloi, Somme; M.E.F. Mesopotamia; Tekrit, Nov. 1917; Kifri, May, 1918; Fathah-Hawash, Oct. 1919; 3 times mentioned in despatches. *Address:* Westwood, Headley, Borden, Hants. (O6635)

HEASMAN, Capt. Albert Edward, O.B.E.

HEASMAN, Arthur William, O.B.E..

HEATH, Cuthbert Eden, O.B.E., *b.* 1859; *s.* of Admiral Sir Leopold Heath, of Anstie Grange, Holmwood (*see* BURKE's *Peerage*); *m.* Sarah C. Gore, *d.* of Charles Gore Gambier, of The Toft, Sharnbrook, Bedfordshire. *War Work:* Member of the Committee for drafting, and also for administering, the Gov. Aircraft Insurance Scheme; organised his country house, Anstie Grange, Holmwood, as a First Line Officer's Hospital, the Government grant being made over to Lady Dudley's Fund for invalid officers and men; trustee of Lloyd's Patriotic Fund. *Address:* Anstie Grange, Holmwood, Surrey. *Club:* Windham. (O10598)

HEATH, Major (ret.) Herbert Charles Selwyn, M.B.E., *b.* 2 Oct. 1869; *s.* of Com. G. P. Heath, R.N., of 24, Richmond Mansions, S.W. 5; *m.* Ethel Morton, *d.* of late Col. Morton Eden. *Educ.:* Sydney University, N.S.W. and R.M.C. Sandhurst; Joined Essex Regt. (2nd Battalion), Feb. 1894, retired as Capt. on Feb. 1907. *War Work:* Recalled to service as H.Q. Recruiting Officer 17th Regl. District, Aug. 1914; War Office Representative on Enlistment Complaints Committee, March, 1917; Deputy Assistant Inspector of Recruiting Northern Command, 1917; Transferred to Ministry of National Service, 1917; 2nd in command, 3rd Bn. Essex Regt. until 1918–19. *Address:* Hanover Court, Hanover Square, W. 1. *Clubs:* Naval and Military; Royal Automobile. (M530)

HEATH, John Henry, M.B.E.

HEATH, Meyrick William, O.B.E., *b.* 12 July, 1855; *s.* of Rev. William Mortimer Heath, of Lytchett Matravers, Dorset; *m.* Katharine Rose, *d.* of Rev. Joseph Mansfield, of Bournemouth. Retired Bank Manager. *War Work:* Accountant (Honorary), to the West of England Munitons Committee. *Address:* The Laurels, Cribbs Causeway, nr. Bristol. (O1455)

HEATH, Roland John, B.A., Mech.Sc., *b.* 15 Aug. 1892; *s.* of G. J. Heath; *m.* Muriel, *d.* of A. W. Hilling. *Educ.:*; Dulwich, and Pembroke Coll., Cambridge. *War Work:* Served with M.T., R.A.S.C., attached R.G.A. *Address:* Firgrove, Pinner, Middlesex. (M3131)

HEATH, Samuel, M.B.E.

HEATH, Capt. Sidney John, M.B.E.

HEATH, Major Thomas Arthur, M.B.E.

HEATH, Lieut. Walter Henry, M.B.E., M.C., *b.* 15 Oct. 1886; *m.* Ethel, *d.* of — Savory. *Educ.:* Wargrave School, Berks. *War Work:* Capt. Assistant Documents Officer, Repatriation Centre, Winchester. *Address:* Sunnyside, Norcot Road, Tilehurst, Berks. (M6649)

HEATHCOTE, Charles Francis, O.B.E.

HEATHCOTE, Capt. Gilbert Stanley, M.V.O., O.B.E. Sherwood Foresters; Great War, 1914–18 (despatches). (O5362)

HEATHCOTE, Lucy Lyttelton, Mrs. C. G., M.B.E.

HEATHER, Paymaster-Lieut.-Comm. Paul, O.B.E., R.N.

HEATLEY, Thomas Common, M.B.E., J.P., C.C., *b.* 30 Jan. 1862; *s.* of Capt. James Heatley, of Blyth, Northumberland; *m.* Hannah, *d.* of Capt. George Golder, of Blyth, Northumberland. *Educ.:* Blyth Public School. *War Work:* Enlisted, organised, and Commanded 500 Special Constables; recruited large numbers of soldiers; Chairman of Recruiting Committee, Military Advisory Committee, and Military Home-coming and Merit Committee. *Address:* 10, Bath Terrace, Blyth, Northumberland. (M8428)

HEATLEY, Major Thomas George, O.B.E., M.R.C.V.S., R.A.V.C. *b.* 1870; *s.* of Thomas Heatley, of Marton, Cheshire; *m.* Grace, A., *d.* of George Symonds, of Wortham, Suffolk. *Educ.:* King's School, Chester. *War Work:* Gazetted Lieut. R.A.V.C., June, 1915; went out with No 19 Hospital to Rouen; Home, sick, Dec. 1915; posted to 69th Div. May, 1916; served with various units in that Div. till Jan. 1917, when posted to Command Northumbrian Divisional Veterinary Hospital, Gosforth Park; remained in Command until July, 1919. *Address:* Marton Place, Woodbridge. (O7262)

HEATLEY, William Robertson, O.B.E., *b.* 6 June, 1861; *s.* of James Heatley, of Alnwick; *m.* Ella Bertha Louise, *d.* of — Christensen, of Copenhagen. *Educ.:* Alnwick; Glasgow Academy; Switzerland. Member of Newcastle-upon-Tyne City Council from 1910–19; member of Newcastle Chamber of Commerce Council. *War Work:* Member of Chamber of Commerce Committee to raise the commercial Battalions of the Northumberland Fusiliers in 1914; Chairman of the Dependents Committee of same; special Constable in 1915–16; a member of Military Tribunal in Newcastle 1916; H. M. Consul at Odense (Denmark) from Aug. 1916, to Dec. 1919; President of the Essen Office of the Inter-Allied Reparation Commission, under the Versailles Peace Treaty. *Address:* Union Club, Newcastle-upon-Tyne. (O1456)

HEATLY, Richard Fade Goff, M.B.E., *b.* 27 Oct. 1863; *s.* of Lieut.-Col. Charles Fade Heatly, late 68th Durham L.I.; *m.* Rose, *d.* of Jaques Léopold Weil, of Ribeauville, Alsace. *Educ.:* St. James' Collegiate School, Jersey; and St. Mark's School, Windsor. Staff Clerk, Board of Trade. *War Work:* Relief and repatriation of crews of merchant ships sunk by the enemy; three years and two months' service in Special Constabulary. *Addresses:* Finance Dept., Board of Trade, Great George Street, S.W. 1; Jhansi, 35, Freta Road, Bexley Heath, Kent. (M8429)

HEATON, Paymaster-Lieut.-Comm. Charles Howard, O.B.E., R.N.

HEATON, John, O.B.E.

HEATON, Mary, M.B.E.; *d.* of the late Rev. H. E. Heaton, of Plas Heaton, Trefnant, N. Wales. *War Work:* Pioneer work as Hon. Organiser and Founder of the Vale of Clwyd Rural Industries (established 1909), and obtained the sanction of Government as the first training centre on these lines for Disabled Sailors and Soldiers; raised upwards of £4000 to purchase and furnish a Hostel and erect and equip new workshops; was a member of Flintshire and Red Cross V.A.D. from its formation. *Address:* Arosfa, Trefnant, N. Wales. (M8430)

HEATON, Mary Meredyth, Lady, C.B.E.

HEATON, Margaret Elizabeth, Mrs., O.B.E.

HEATON, Trevor Braby, O.B.E., M.A., M.D., M.R.C.P., *b.* 9 Aug. 1886; *m.* 21 Dec. 1920, Constance Irene, *d.* of J. W. Wheeler-Bennett, C.B.E., J.P., of Ravensbourne, Keston, Kent. *Educ.:* Charterhouse; Christ Church, Oxford, and Guy's Hospital. Tutor of Christ Church, Oxford. *Address:* Christ Church, Oxford. (O8483)

HEAYBERD, Paymaster-Lieut. William Valentine, O.B.E.,R.N.R.,

HEBB, Florence Agnes, M.B.E., *b.* 10 Sept. 1872 Controller of Typists, Air Ministry. *Address:* 105, Narbonne Avenue, Clapham Common, S.W. (M531)

HEBB, Major John Harry, O.B.E., M.B., R.A.M.C., *b.* 21 June, 1878; *s.* of Rev. Harry Hebb, of Tunbridge Wells; *m.* Ethel Kathleen, *d.* of E. Wolfgang, of West Kirby. *Educ.:*

Kelly College, Tavistock; St. John's, Oxford; Westminster Hospital. Assistant Director Medical Services, Ministry of Pensions. *War Work*: Commissioned, 1915; M.O., 17 General Hospital, Egypt, 1915; H.M.H.S. "Essequibo," 1916; H.M.H.S. "Dongola," 1916; 107 Field Ambulance, B.E.F., 1916–18 as 2nd in command. *Address*: 10, Grey Coat Gardens, S.W. 1. *Club*: Royal Automobile. (O2559)

HEBBLETHWAITE, Reginald Sidney, M.B.E.

HEBDEN, Lieut.-Col. Sacheverell Arthur, O.B.E., R.A.F.

HEBERT, Major Charles, O.B.E.

HEBRON, Arthur Edward, M.B.E., D.C.M., *b.* 8 Sept. 1854; *s.* of Thomas Hebron, of Newcastle-on-Tyne; *m.* Sarah, *d.* of Robert Tuthill, of Bath. *Educ.*: Morpeth Grammar School, Northumberland. Mechanical Engineer. *War Work*: Appointed by War Office, Shipping Inspector of Royal Engineer Stores; served during the whole of the war at Southampton and London Docks. *Address*: 113, Worple Road, Wimbledon, London, S.W. 19. *Club*: Grosvenor. (M1880)

HEDDERWICK, Ethel Marian, Mrs., O.B.E., *b.* 23 May, 1867; *d.* of late Sir Alfred Apperly, of Rodborough Court, Gloucestershire; *m.* James David Hedderwick, LL.D., D.L., Glasgow, *s.* of Robert Hedderwick, of Glasgow. *Educ.*: Cheltenham Ladies College. *War Work*: Member of Territorial Nursing Service Committee; County of Glasgow Red Cross Committee; various Sub-committees; Convener of Red Cross Samaritan Committee of Scottish Branch, British Red Cross Society. *Address*: 2, Clairmont Gardens, Glasgow. *Club*: Kelvin Ladies', Glasgow. (O1458)

HEDDERWICK, Mary, M.B.E., *b.* 11 July, 1865; *d.* of James Hay Stuart, of Glasgow; *m.* Edwin Charles, *s.* of James Hedderwick, LL.D., of Glasgow. *War Work*: Hon. Sec. War Hospital Supply Depot, 22, Burnbank Terrace, Glasgow (County and City of Glasgow Branch, Scottish Branch, British Red Cross Society). *Address*: 17, Kew Terrace, Glasgow. (M8432)

HEDDLES, Lieut. Thomas Mann, O.B.E., R.N.R.

HEDGE, George Fullidge, O.B.E.

HEDGE, Henry Walter, M.B.E., *b.* 27 Jan. 1871. Foreman of Yard, H.M. Dockyard, Devonport. *War Work*: Appointed Admiralty Constructive Overseer in Charge of the Humber District soon after the commencement of hostilities, and whilst in charge refitted and fitted out innumerable Trawlers for mine sweeping; paddle Mine Sweepers; Cruisers and Torpedo-boat Destroyers, including the famous Cruiser "Chester," after the Jutland Battle. *Address*: 19, Mulgran Street, The Hoe, Plymouth. *Clubs*: Grimsby and County, Grimsby; Royal Plymouth Corinthian Yacht, Plymouth. (M8433)

HEDGES, Alfred James, M.B.E., *b.* 17 June, 1862; *s.* of George Hedges, Police Inspector, Ascot, Berks; *m.* Helen Louisa, *d.* of Supt. George Pocock, Berks Constabulary, Reading. *Educ.*: Stockcross School, Newbury, Berks. Deputy Chief Constable of Berkshire. *War Work*: Police administration during the war; specially recommended for recognition to the Secretary of State by Lieut.-Col. A. F. Poulton, Chief Constable of Berkshire, for the conspicuous ability he showed in carrying out his duties as Deputy Chief Constable during the absence of Lieut.-Col. Poulton on Active Service. *Address*: County Police Station, Reading. (M8434)

HEDGES, Lieut. Harold Edward, M.B.E., R.E.

HEDLEY, Capt. Edward Williams, M.B.E., M.D., B.C. R.A.M.C., *b.* 24 Oct. 1873; *s.* of John Hedley, M.D., of Middlesbrough; *m.* Winifred Agnes Gillott, *d.* of Theodore Hornung, of Middlesbrough. *Educ.*: Uppingham; King's Coll., Cambs.; St. Thomas's Hospital. Anæsthetist, St. Thomas's Hospital. *War Work*: Capt., 5th London General Hospital (T.); M.O., Officers' Hospital, 53, Cadogan Square, Gerstley-Hoare Hospital, Red Cross. *Address*: 10 Pont Street, London, S.W. (M10264)

HEDLEY, Mary Elizabeth, Mrs., O.B.E., *b.* 29 May, 1853; *d.* of Edward Williams, of Cleveland Lodge, Middlesbrough; *m.* John Hedley, J.P. *War Work*: Commandant Holgate Red Cross Hospital; Recruiting Commandant for North Riding, Yorkshire; Commandant V.A.D. Yorks 32; President Church of England Canteen for Sailors and Soldiers. *Address*: Cleveland, Lodge, Middlesbrough. (O3747)

HEDLEY, Oswald William Edward, O.B.E.

HEDLEY, Capt. Theodore Fenwick, M.B.E.

HEDLEY, Capt. and Qr.-Mr. Thomas, M.B.E., R.A.M.C.

HEDLEY, Col. Sir Walter Coote, K.B.E., C.B., C.M.G., *b.* 12 Dec. 1865; *s.* of the late Robert Hedley, of 44, St. George's Square, London; *m.* Anna Susan, *d.* of the late Colonel James Fellowes. *Educ.*: Marlborough. Retired from Army, 1 Sept. 1920. *War Work*: General Staff Officer 1st Grade at War Office. *Address*: The Hopps, nr. Horley, Surrey. *Club*: Army and Navy. (K321f)

HEEFS, James, O.B.E.

HEELEY, Lieut. Henry Norman, M.B.E., M.C.

HEELIS, Marion, M.B.E., *d.* of the Rev. John Heelis, Rector of Kirkby Thore, Westmorland. *War Work*: V.A.D. Nursing, 1915–16, at Raddon Court V.A.D. Hospital, Warrington, and B.R.C.S. Hospital at Netley; 1917–18, Commandant of Westmorland 12 V.A.D. Hospital at Appleby. (M3706)

HEFFORD, Eng.-Capt. Edward Owen, O.B.E., R.N.

HEGGIE, Amelia Young, M.B.E., *b.* 1855; *d.* of the late William Young, of Auchtermuchty, Fifeshire; *m.* Alexander, *s.* of James Heggie. *Educ.*: The Parish School, Auchtermuchty. *War Work*: Member of National Relief Fund Committee;

Local War Pensions Committee; Sailors' and Soldiers' Families Association; War Savings Committee. (M8435)

HELBERT, Lieut.-Col. Godfrey Gladstone, C.B.E.

HELDEN, Capt. Frederick, M.B.E., R.E.

HELE, Capt. Thomas Shirley, O.B.E., R.A.M.C. (T.F.)

HELLAWELL, Major Alfred Stanley, O.B.E., R.A.F.

HELLIER, Maurice, O.B.E.

HELLIWELL, Lieut.-Col. John Percival, C.B.E. T. Lieut.-Col. Special List; Great War, 1914–19 (mentioned in despatches). (C1611)

HELLYER, Capt. Ernest Palmer, M.B.E., F.C.A., *b.* 10 May, 1882; *s.* of Henry Hellyer, of Bristol; *m.* Elina, *d.* of James Teele, of Sligo. *Educ.*: Channel View School, Clevedon. Fellow of the Institute of Chartered Accountants in England and Wales; Hon. Auditor, Monmouthshire Local Representative Committee of the National Relief Fund. *War Work*: Paymaster, Royal Army Pay Department. *Address*: "Glencar," Fuller's Rd., Woodford, Essex. (M5338)

HELLYER, Flight.-Lieut. Francis Edgcombe, O.B.E., R.A.F., *b.* 1888; *s.* of the late Robert Edgcombe, of Farlington House, Havant. *Educ.*: Winchester, and Trinity Coll., Cambridge. *War Work*: Served in 9th Hants Regt., Aug. 1914, to Jan. 1916; served in R.F.C. and R.A.F., Jan. 1914, to Nov. 1918. *Club*: Oxford and Cambridge. (O8118)

HELM, Capt. William, M.B.E.

HELME, George Edgar, M.B.E., M.B., C.M.

HELMORE, George Reginald, O.B.E., *b.* 10 October, 1864; *s.* of George Helmore, of Woodlands, Shortlands, Kent; *m.* Edith Clara, *d.* of James William Hawes, of Great Yarmouth. *Educ.*: Eastbourne; Hamburg. Barrister-at-Law; Fellow of Institute of Chartered Accountants; Auditor of several Insurance Companies, and other public and private institutions. *War Work*: Sergeant of Special Constabulary "D" Division from August, 1914 to May, 1916; Military Representatibe before the Camberwell Tribunal July, 1916 to April, 1918; Assistant Director of National Service, South London and District Area, April, 1918 to March, 1919; Assistant Director of National Service for the Woolwich Area—all honorary. *Addresses*: Devonshire House, Shortlands, Kent; 185, Piccadilly, W. 1; 3, King's Bench Walk, Temple, E.C. 4. (O1459)

HELMORE, Heathcote George, M.B.E.

HELPS, Capt. Rowland Philip Arthur, O.B.E., M.C.

HELSHAM, Capt. Charles Howard, O.B.E., Aus. I.F.

HELY, Lieut.-Comm. Hamilton McMath, O.B.E., R.D., R.N.R.

HELYAR, Brig.-Gen. Arthur Beaumont, C.B.E., R.A. (retired), *b.* 3 March, 1858; *s.* of late Rev. H. Helyar, Combe Florey, Taunton, and Rector of Pendomer, Yeovil, Somerset. *Educ.*: Somerset College, Bath and Royal Military Academy. Served in the Tirah Expedition, 1897–98 (despatches, medal with two clasps); and in S. Africa, 1902 (Queen's medal, with four clasps). *War Work*: Formed the Divisional Artillery of the XIIIth Division and commanded it in Egypt in 1915; Commanded the Artillery of the Xth Division in operations in Greece and on the Bulgarian frontier, 1915–16. *Address*: 2, Ryder Street, St. James's, S.W. 1. *Club*: Army and Navy Club. (C839b)

HEMING, George Booth, C.B.E., J.P.

HEMING, Capt. Thomas Henry, C.B.E., R.N. Great War, 1914–19 (mentioned in despatches). (C1927)

HEMINGWAY, Charles Robert, C.B.E., J.P., *b.* 26 Sept. 1860; *s.* of James Hemingway, of Macclesfield. Member of National Council of Y.M.C.A.'s. *Address*: Penrhyn House, The Park, Nottingham; Park End, North Berwick. *Clubs*: Oriental; County, Nottingham; Borough, Nottingham. (C2670)

HEMINGWAY, Stennet, Mrs., M.B.E.

HEMPER, Lieut. and Qr.-Mr. John Richard, M.B.E.

HEMPHREY, Bernard, M.B.E., *b.* 4 March, 1868; *s.* of George Hemphrey, of Bridgford, Notts; *m.* Ada Eliza, *d.* of Henry Knight, of Dorking. Stationmaster, S. E. & C. Rly. *War Work*: Military Control, Aldershot District, S. E. & C. Rly., dealing with arrival and despatch of troop trains; arranging and regulating military stores and supply trains throughout whole war period. *Address*: Middleton, Lynchford Rd., Farnborough, Hants. (M8437)

HEMSLEY, Lieut. Alexander Guy, M.B.E.

HEMSLEY, Paymaster-Lieut.-Comm. Arthur Cyril, O.B.E., R.N.

HEMSLEY, 2nd Lieut. Noel, M.B.E., R.A.F.

HEMSTED, Rupert William, O.B.E.

HENDERSON, Capt. Alan Keith, O.B.E.

HENDERSON, Alexander, M.B.E. (M10355)

HENDERSON, Capt. Alexander Mitchell, O.B.E., R.A.

HENDERSON, Alice Craig, M.B.E.

HENDERSON, Capt. Hon. Arnold, O.B.E., *b.* 1 July, 1883; *s.* of Alexander, 1st Lord Faringdon, of Faringdon, Berks (*see* BURKE's *Peerage*); *m.* Helen Madeline, *d.* of Col. Alexander Evans-Gordon. *Educ.*: Wellington College. Stockbroker. *War Work*: Captain, Royal Wiltshire Yeomanry; served in France, 1915–1919; Staff Captain, 1918; mentioned twice in despatches. *Clubs*: Bachelors'; Bath. (O5363)

HENDERSON, Beatrice Elizabeth, Mrs., O.B.E. (O11786d)

HENDERSON, Charles Allan, M.B.E., J.P.

HENDERSON, Lieut. Charles Hender, M.B.E., R.E.

HENDERSON, Capt. Christopher Woodall, O.B.E.

HENDERSON, Duncan, O.B.E.

HENDERSON, Eveleen Mary, Mrs., O.B.E., *b.* 1858; *d.* of John Smith, of 27, Prince's Gate and Mickleham Hall,

Dorking; *m.* John, *s.* of Robert Henderson, of Randalls Park, Leatherhead. *Educ.:* At home. Vice-President, Leatherhead Division, Surrey Branch, B.R.C.S. *War Work:* Red Cross work generally in the Leatherhead Division; Commandant of the Red House Auxiliary Hospital, Leatherhead, Oct. 1917 to Feb. 1918. *Address:* Randalls Park, Leatherhead, Surrey. *Club:* The Ladies' Empire. (O3748)

HENDERSON, Freda Marguerita Dorothy, Mrs., M.B.E., *b.* 20 May, 1885; *d.* of Thomas Searancke Archer, of Hatfield; *m.* Charles James, *s.* of Henry Henderson. *Educ.:* Ursuline Convent, St. Trond, Belgium. *War Work:* Country Branch Sec. Women's Volunteer Reserve, 1914–16; Ministry of Munitions (Admin. Assist.), 1916–20. *Address:* 17B, Ladbroke Terrace, W. (M1882)

HENDERSON, Sir Frederick Ness, K.B.E., *b.* 23 Dec. 1862; *s.* of the late William Henderson, of Newfield, Ayrshire, and 11, Prince's Terrace, Glasgow; *m.* 24 Apr. 1888, Jessie Miller, *d.* of the late Alexander Strathern, Sheriff-Substitute of Lanark. Chairman of David and William Henderson & Co., Ltd,, Shipbuilders, of Glasgow; Vice Chairman of Iron Trades Employers' Insurance Association, Ltd.; and Director of North-West Bolt and Rivet Factory, of Glasgow; sometime member of the Admiralty Shipbuilding Council. *Address:* Crosbie House, Monkton, Ayrshire. *Clubs:* New (Glasgow); Royal Thames Yacht. (K79)

HENDERSON, Capt. Garnet Montgomery Hume, O.B.E., M.C.

HENDERSON, George, O.B.E.

HENDERSON, George, M.B.E.

HENDERSON, George Blake, M.B.E.

HENDERSON, Rev. Hamilton Dunstan, O.B.E., *b.* 15 May, 1891; *s.* of Hamilton Henderson, of Fishlake Vicarage, Doncaster. *Educ.:* Royal Kepier Grammar School (Houghton); Univ. Coll., Durham (B.A.); Bishop's Hostel, Lincoln. Curate of St. John's Parish, New Clee, Grimsby. *War Work:* Royal Army Chaplain's Department, 4th Class Chaplain (Temp.), Church of England; Egypt Exped. Force, 1916; Mesopotamian Exped. Force, 1917; mentioned in despatches, 1919. *Address:* 119, Stirling Street, New Clee, Grimsby. (O6636)

HENDERSON, Hon. 2nd Lieut. Harry Frederick, M.B.E., *b.* 24 Aug. 1877; *s.* of Duncan Henderson, of Leicester; *m.* Alice Mary, *d.* of B. B. Preston, of Leicester. *Educ.:* Wyggeston School, Leicester, and Privately; Matriculated, London Univ. Hon. Treas. and Vice-Chairman, Leicester City War Pensions Committee. *War Work:* Office organisation, and Financial Administration of Local War Pensions Committee; also served in the ranks and as subaltern in 1st Volunteer Batt. Leicestershire Regt. *Addresses:* Felday, Morland Avenue, Leicester; Laughton Cottage, Cromer. *Clubs:* Leicestershire, Leicester; Royal Cromer Golf. (M8439)

HENDERSON, Helen, M.B.E. (M10356)

HENDERSON, Henrietta Caroline, Lady, D.B.E.; *d.* of Henry R. Dundas; *m.* Lieut.-Gen. Sir David, K.C.B., K.C.V.O., D.S.O., *s.* of the late David Henderson, of Glasgow. *Address:* 22, Hans Crescent, S.W. 1. *Club:* Naval and Military. (D34)

HENDERSON, Henry Ludwig, O.B.E., Capt., Straits Settlements, Censorship. (O11790a)

HENDERSON, Capt. Herbert Purse, O.B.E., R.A.S.C.

HENDERSON, Capt. Hubert Douglas, M.B.E., M.A., *b.* 20 Oct. 1890; *s.* of John Henderson, of Glasgow; *m.* Faith Marian Jane, *d.* of Philip Bagenal, of Wimbledon. *Educ.:* Rugby School, and Emmanuel Coll., Cambridge. Fellow of Clare Coll., Cambridge; University Lecturer on Economics at Cambridge Univ. *War Work:* Temporarily employed in Board of Trade; Sec. to the Cotton Control Board, 1917–19; Sec. of Official Cotton Mission to United States, 1918. *Addresses:* Clare Coll., Cambridge; 45, Downshire Hill, Hampstead, N.W. 3. *Club:* 1917. (M3708)

HENDERSON, Capt. Ian Macdonald, M.B.E.

HENDERSON, John, M.B.E.

HENDERSON, Major John Acheson, D.S.O., O.B.E. Hon. Major in the Army; S. Africa, 1899–1902 (despatches, Queen's medal, with four clasps; King's medal with two clasps); Great War, 1914–18 (despatches thrice). (O7265)

HENDERSON, John Brownlie, O.B.E. (O11989)

HENDERSON, Major John Gilbert, O.B.E., M.C., R.E.

HENDERSON, John Hossell, O.B.E., *b.* 29 April, 1873; *s.* of George Henderson of Leghorn; *m.* Mary, *d.* of Dr. Byrom Bramwell, of Edinburgh. *Educ.:* George Watson's Coll.; Edinburgh Univ.; Balliol Coll., Oxford. Commercial Sec. to the British Embassy at Rome. *War Work:* Assistant to Commercial Attaché at Rome. *Address:* British Embassy, Rome. *Club:* Savile. (O10606)

HENDERSON, John Percy, M.B.E., *b.* 2 May, 1873; *s.* of John Henderson, of Shetland Isles; *m.* Jane Grace, *d.* of Thomas Cosser, of Newcastle-on-Tyne. Member Zetland County Council; Member Lerwick Town Council; Member Lerwick Parish Council; ex-Member Lerwick Harbour Trust; ex-Chairman, Public Health Committee of Zetland County Council; ex-Chairman, Landward Committee Lerwick Parish Council; Member T.F. Association; Director, Lerwick Gas Co.; Director, Lerwick Coal Co.; Director, Henderson & Sons, Ltd., Gateshead, etc. *War Work:* Patriotic services at Lerwick, Shetland Isles; Dental Treatment for men of the Royal Naval Reserve Forces and Navy at Lerwick, Shetland Isles; received the thanks of My Lords Commissioners of the Admiralty "for valuable services rendered," April, 1918. *Address:* Ellesmere House, Lerwick, Shetland. (M8440)

HENDERSON, Lieut.-Col. John Steill, O.B.E., J.P., *b.* 19 Sept. 1870; *s.* of William Henderson of Lawton, Perthshire; *m.* Anna Margaret, *d.* of Rev. R. Edgar, D.D., of Newburgh. *Educ.:* Dollar; Edinburgh University. *War Work:* On active service from August, 1914 to March, 1920; with Bn. in France till winter, 1915; Commanded 25th Division (Inf.) Base; Commanded group of Divisional Base Depots; Commanded General Base and Reinforcements of Rhine Army; Commanded Bn. H.L.I.; Commanded Demobilisation camps, Eastern Army; Commanded Demobilisation Camp of Western Army. *Address:* Seacliff, Ardrishaig, Argyll. *Club:* Scottish Conservative, Edinburgh. (O2563)

HENDERSON, John Wright, C.B.E. War Office Representative in India for Hides. (C1964)

HENDERSON, Kate, Mrs., O.B.E.

HENDERSON, Capt. Kenneth George, O.B.E.

HENDERSON, Laura Catherine, M.B.E.

HENDERSON, Mabel, Mrs., M.B.E.

HENDERSON, Marjorie Grace Seton, M.B.E., *b.* 24 May, 1886; *d.* of Hamilton Gerald Henderson, late R.F.A., of Truro, Cornwall. *Educ.:* Truro High School. *War Work:* Junior Administrative Assistant in the Department of the Director of Fortifications and Works, War Office. *Address:* 45, Morshead Mansions, London, W. 9. (M8441)

HENDERSON, Capt. Matthew Bolan, O.B.E., M.C., R.F.A. (T.).

HENDERSON, Robert Cron, O.B.E., J.P., *b.* 1860. *Educ.:* Sanquhar Public School; King's Coll., London. Bank Manager; Vice-President, League of Mercy (Epsom, Esher); Sutton Hospital (Chairman of Board); Sutton Petty Sessions (Vice-Chairman). *War Work:* Hon. Treas. British Red Cross Society, Sutton Division, and Sutton Red Cross Hospital; Member of Advisory Committee for Recruiting, Southern Area. *Address:* Nithsdale, Sutton, Surrey. *Clubs:* Caledonian; Surrey Magistrates'; Walton Heath Golf. (O10608)

HENDERSON, Rose Agnes, M.B.E.

HENDERSON, Violet, M.B.E.

HENDERSON, Lieut. Walter Salkeld, M.B.E.

HENDERSON, William Alexander Cruickshank, O.B.E., *b.* 5 Dec. 1876; *s.* of James Henderson, Archdeacon, of Northumberland; *m.* Pansy Viola, *d.* Bori Schürer. *Educ.:* King's School, Peterborough. Civil and Mechanical Engineer. *War Work:* Assistant Director, Outside Engineering Branch of Trench Warfare Supply Dept., and Director of Experimental Supplies Dept.; took Experimental Portable Ropeways to France. *Address:* c/o Sir John Jackson, Ltd., 53, Victoria Street, Westminster, S.W. 1. (O10609)

HENDERSON, Lieut.-Col. Thomas Maxwell Stuart MILNE-, O.B.E., R.E.

HENDIN, Alexander James, M.B.E.

HENDRIKS, Cecil Morgan, O.B.E. M.B.

HENDRIKS, Henry Leslie, O.B.E., *b.* 8 March, 1877; *s.* of the late Alfred Hendriks, of Worthing, Sussex; *m.* Viva, *d.* of Major James Penn, of Austin, Texas, U.S.A. *Educ.:* Cranleigh. Managing Director, Bradbury, Wilkinson & Co., Ltd. *War Work:* Chief Staff Officer, 2nd in command City of London Police Reserve. *Addresses:* The Old Well House, Calonne Road, Wimbledon Common; 25 & 27 Farringdon Road, E.C. 1. *Clubs:* British Empire; R.A.C. (O3749)

HENDRY, Capt. Alexander William, O.B.E., R.A.M.C.

HENDRY, Capt. Frank Coutts, O.B.E., M.C., I.A.R.O.

HENDRY, Major James, M.B.E.

HENDRY, John, O.B.E.

HENEAGE, Lieut.-Col. the Hon. George Edward, O.B.E., B.A., J.P., D.L., *b.* 3 July, 1866; *s.* of 1st Baron Heneage (*see* BURKE'S *Peerage*). *Educ.:* Eton; Trinity Coll. Cambridge. Lieut.-Col. commanding 10th (Service) Batt. Lincolnshire Regt. 1914–16; Vice-President of the Lindsey County Council, and Chairman of County Education Committee. *Address:* Hainton Hall, Lincoln. *Clubs:* Brooks's; Bachelors'; Hurlingham. (O7266)

HENESSEY, Dame Una Constance POPE-, D.B.E., Lady of Grace, St. John of Jerusalem in England; *d.* of Sir Arthur Birch, K.C.M.G.; *m.* Col. Richard Hubert Ladislaus (D.S.O.), *s.* of Sir John Pope-Hennessy, K.C.M.G., Knight of Malta, of Rostellan Castle, Co. Cork (*see* BURKE'S *Peerage*). *Educ.:* Privately. *War Work:* Prisoners' Department, Red Cross, 1915–16; Central Committee for Prisoners of War, 1916–18; Editor, "The British Prisoner of War"; organiser Ruhleben Exhibition Central Hall, Westminster, 1918; Member of Lord Justice Younger's Committee on the Treatment by the Enemy of British Prisoners of War. *Address:* 2, Albert Terrace, Regent's Park. (D47)

HENLEY, Lieut. Francis Antony Hoste, M.B.E., *b.* 11 Feb. 1884; *s.* of Anthony Alfred Henley, of Woodbridge, Suffolk; *m.* Margaret, *d.* of John Charrington, of The Grange, Shenley, Herts. *Educ.:* Forest School, and Oriel Coll., Oxford. Master, Ludgrove, New Barnet, Herts. *War Work:* 60th (London) Divl. Train, France, Salonica and Palestine. *Address:* Oriel Cottage, New Barnet. (M4682)

HENLEY, Major Frank Le Seu, D.S.O., O.B.E. Major Australian Army Ser. Corps; served in Great War, 1914–18 (mentioned in despatches). (O2844)

HENLEY, Sylvia Laura, Hon. Mrs., M.B.E.; 3rd *d.* of 4th Baron Sheffield (*see* BURKE'S *Peerage*); *m.* Brig.-Gen. the Hon. Arthur Anthony Morton Henley, C.M.G., D.S.O., 5th Lancers, 3rd *s.* of 3rd Baron Henley. (M3711)

HENLEY, Lieut.-Col. Sir Thomas, K.B.E., T.D., M.P. (N.S.W.), *b.* Wootton Bassett, Wilts, 4 Feb. 1860; *m. d.* of

Henn THE ORDER OF THE BRITISH EMPIRE.

Charles and Caroline Smith of Wiltshire. Builder and Contractor ; Alderman for Drummoyne since 1898 ; Mayor, 6 times ; amalgamated the Boroughs of Drummoyne and Five Dock into one municipality in 1902 ; served two terms in the City Council of Sydney ; Member of the Metropolitan Board of Water Supply and Sewerage since 1902, representing 68 municipalities and Shires ; Member of the New South Wales Parliament for Burwood ; elected in 1904 ; Honorary Organising Secretary and Relator in three actions at law against the Holman Government for what was known as the eviction of the Governor-General (Lord Denman) from Government House, Sydney, in 1912, after proceedings which lasted for nearly 3 years and cost £3,550, the proposal to use the building as a museum for antiquities was frustrated and the mansion remains the vice-regal home of the State Governor ; Member of the Board of the Western Suburbs Hospital ; his son, Captain Harold Leslie Henley, was killed in action in France, 1916. *War Work :* 4 years Commissioner Australian Comforts Fund in Egypt, France and England. *Clubs :* Commercial Travellers', Moore Street, Sydney ; Millions, Sydney. (K472)

HENN, Sir Sydney Herbert Holcroft, K.B.E., *b.* 4 Dec. 1861 ; *s.* of Rev. John Henn, Hon. Canon of Manchester ; *m.* Frances Amie Edith, *d.* of Frederick B. Shanklin, of Santiago de Chile. *Educ. :* Marlborough and Manchester. Retired South American Merchant. *War Work :* Director of Army Priority at the War Office, 1917–19 ; since then a Member of the Surplus Government Property Disposal Board. *Addresses :* Ixworth Court, Bedford ; Queen Anne's Mansions, S.W. 1. *Clubs :* City ; Royal Automobile. (K146)

HENNELL, Col. Sir Reginald, Knt. Bach., C.V.O., D.S.O., O.B.E., *b.* 11 June, 1844 ; *s.* of the late Robert George Hennell, of London. *Educ. :* Payne's, Leatherhead ; Knight's, Southsea. Lieut. of the King's Body Guard of the Yeoman of the Guard ; Hon. Col. 3rd Cadet Bn. of the Middlesex Regt. *War Work :* Abyssinian Expedition, 1867–68 (medal) ; Afghan Campaign, 1879–80 (services acknowledged by Government, medal) ; Burmese War, 1886–87 (medal, D.S.O., despatches). *Address :* 47, Coleherne Court, South Kensington, S.W. 5. *Clubs :* United Service ; National. (O7267)

HENNESSY, Major George Richard, O.B.E.
HENNESSY, Mary, Lady, C.B.E. ; *d.* of the late Michael Quenian, of Ballarat ; *m.* Sir David Valentine Hennessy, organiser, Victorian Branch of Australian Comforts Fund. (C360)

HENNESSY Lady Victoria, C.B.E.
HENNIKER, Lieut.-Col. Alan M., C.B.E., R.E., *b.* 1870. *War Work :* Served in France and Belgium from Aug. 1914, to Sept. 1919. *Address :* Carlinwark, Middleton Road, Camberley. *Club :* Junior United Service. (C1265)

HENNING, Gladys, Mrs., M.B.E. M10249e)
HENNINGS, William, M.B.E.
HENOCKSBURG, Josephine Norie, Mrs., M.B.E.
HENREY, Capt. James Osler, M.B.E.
HENRIQUES, Sir Philip Gutterez, K.B.E., J.P., D.L., C.C., *b.* 2 Nov. 1867 ; *s.* of Alfred G. Henriques, of Hove, Sussex ; *m.* Beatrice Rachael, *d.* of Sir George Faudel-Phillips, Bart., G.C.I.E., of Balls Park, Herts (*see* BURKE'S *Peerage*). *Educ. :* Wellington ; Trinity College, Cambridge. Barrister-at-Law ; Government Director of British Cellulose Co. Ltd. *War Work :* Deputy Director-General of Explosive Finance, Ministry of Munitions, 1915 ; also of Aircraft Finance from 1917 ; Assistant Financial Secretary, Ministry of Munitions, 1918–20. *Addresses :* 33, Grosvenor Place, London, S.W. ; Normandy Park, Guildford. *Clubs :* Carlton ; Athenæum. (K80)

HENROTIN, Jessie, Mrs., M.B.E., *b.* 13 March, 1859 ; *d.* of Frederick Feild Langstaff, of Andover, Hants ; *m.* Victor, *s.* of Joseph Henrotin, M.D., of Andover, Hants. *Educ. :* Ladies' Coll., Southampton. *War Work :* Opened tea shop for British soldiers on 11 Aug. 1914, in France at her own house, 34, Rue Gambetta, Sanvic ; voluntary worker in No. 4 Convalescent Camp, Havre, from June, 1915, to June, 1919, when the camp closed. *Address :* 34, Rue Gambetta, Sanvic, Seine Infre., France. (M8443)

HENRY, Lieut.-Col. Alfred Stanley, O.B.E.
HENRY, Alice Helen, Mrs., O.B.E., Officier de l'Instruction Publique, France, *b.* 12 Aug. 1881 ; *d.* of the late Sir Lauder Brunton, Bt. ; *m.* Augustine Henry. *Educ. :* France and Wycombe Abbey. *War Work :* Quartermaster, Sphagnum Department of the Irish War Hospitals Supply Organisation ; Royal College of Science for Ireland, acting as the Central Sphagnum Depot for Ireland. *Address :* 5, Sandford Terrace, Ranelagh, Dublin. (O3750)

HENRY, Major Hugh, O.B.E.
HENRY, Major James Douglas, C.B.E., D.S.O.
HENRY, Jane Selina, Mrs., M.B.E.
HENRY, John, M.B.E., 18 March, 1884 ; *s.* of James Henry, of Strathlea, Moffat, Dumfriesshire. *Educ. :* George Watson's College, Edinburgh. Secretary, Board of Trade Imports and Exports Consultative Council, 1918 ; Secretary, Canadian Mission in London, 1919 ; Secretary, Overseas Branch Dept. of Trade and Commerce of Canada, 1920. *War Work :* Private Secretary, War Trade Dept., 1915 to 1918 ; Member of Sub-Committee of Allied Blockade Committee ; Secretary of the Temporary Export Prohibitions Committee, War Trade Dept. *Addresses :* 15, Ashmount Road, N. 19 ; Strathlea, Moffat. (M535)
HENRY, Lieut. John Herbert Wallace, M.B.E., Aust. L.I.

HENRY, Margaret Jane, Mrs., M.B.E.
HENRY, Reginald George, M.B.E., *b.* 12 Sept. 1884 ; *s.* of the late T. A Henry, of Sutton. *Educ. :* Pocklington Grammar School, Yorks. H.M. Inspector of Taxes. *War Work :* H.M. Inspector of Taxes at Londonderry and Wigan (2nd district). *Addresses :* Cunard Buildings, Water Street, Liverpool ; 22, St. Malo Road, Wigan. (M8445)
HENRY, Florence Vaugham MITCHELL-, O.B.E., *b.* 20 1870 ; *d.* of Mitchell Henry, of Strathedon House, Rutland Gate, London. *War Work :* Organiser and Manager, Garrison Buffet, Dawson Street, Dublin, 1917–19. *Address :* Bannaboghee House, Letterfrack, Co. Galway. (O10612)
HENSHALL, Capt. Leonard, M.B.E., *b.* 3 Sept. 1891 ; *s.* of Louis Henshall, of Deganwy, North Wales. *Educ. :* Boteler Grammar School, Warrington. Ministry of Finance, Egypt, Customs Department. *War Work :* France, April, 1915, 4th Batt. South Lancs. Regt., T.F. ; severely wounded, June, 1915. at Hooge ; attached Royal Flying Corps, Sept. 1916, and served on Staff of R.A.F. until Sept. 1919. *Clubs :* R.A.F., London ; Union, Alexandria. (M5989)
HENSHAW, John Thomas, M.B.E., *b.* 27 Jan. 1876 ; *s.* of Charles Henshaw, of 1, York Place, Weston Street, Northampton ; *m.* Sarah Madeline, *d.* of Joseph Edward, of Northampton. *Educ. :* All Saints' Commercial School, Northampton. Served in the Army from June 1892 to Feb. 1920., *War Work :* Rejoined the colours from pension, and served as Regimental Sergeant-Major ; discharged from the Army of the Rhine, Feb. 1920. *Address :* 74, St. James's Road, Northampton. (M5340)
HENSHAW, Capt. Thomas, M.B.E., R.A.S.C.
HENSHAW, Thomas Arthur, M.B.E. ; *s.* of the late Thomas Henshaw, of The Hollies, Chester ; *m.* Lucy Mary, *d.* of Lawrence Booth, of Dingle Bank, Chester. *Educ. :* Stafford and Chester. Clerk to the Company of the Birmingham Canal Navigations. *War Work :* Canal transport ; Member of Canal Control Committee (Board of Trade) for Midlands ; also member of the Household Fuel and Lighting Committee for the City of Birmingham. *Addresses :* Daimler House, Paradise Street, Birmingham ; 52, Calthorpe Road, Edgbaston. (M8446)
HENSLOWE, Comm. Ernest, O.B.E., R.N.
HENSHILWOOD, George, M.B.E.
HENSON, George Herbert, C.B.E.
HENSON, John James, C.B.E.
HENSTIN, Jessie Mrs., M.B.E.
HENTY, Beatrice, C.B.E. Sec. of Australian Comforts Fund at Melbourne throughout Great War. *Address :* Melbourne, Australia. (C361)
HEPBURN, Thomas, M.B.E.
HEPENSTAL, Major Lambert John : *see* Dopping-Hepenstal.
HEPENSTAL, Lieut.-Col. Maxwell Edward Dopping, C.B.E. (C3090)
HEPPEL, Capt. Hugh Middleton, O.B.E., *b.* 5 April, 1893 ; *s.* of E. M. Heppel, of Somerset. *Educ. :* Blundell's School ; Sandhurst. *War Work :* Adjutant 11th, 12th, and 3rd Bns. Essex Regt. ; Staff Captain 5th Army and G.H.Q. ; D.A.A.G., Headquarters, L. of C. *Address :* Camerton, nr. Bath. *Club :* Junior United Service. (O2565)
HEPWORTH, Major Frank Arthur, O.B.E., M.B., F.R.C.S., R.A.M.C. (T.)
HERANO, Victor Carpenter, M.B.E.
HERAPATH, Major and Brevet Lieut.-Col. Lionel, C.B.E., *b.* 7 December, 1880 ; *s.* of Edwin John Herapath, of Blackheath, Barrister-at-Law ; *m.* Elsie Ellen, *d.* of Henry Hoyne Fox, Public Works Department (late Chief Engineer for Burma). *Educ. :* Charterhouse ; Cambridge. Fellow of Royal Geographical Society. *War Work :* France, 1915 ; East African Expeditionary Force, on Staff, 1917–19 ; Russia (Baltic States) with British Military Mission as A.A. and Q.M.G., 1919–20 ; Russian Order of St. Vladimir ; Chevalier of the Legion of Honour. *Address :* 4, Park Place, St. James's. (C2360a)
HERAPETH, Margaret Edith, Mrs., M.B.E.
HERAUD, Stanley Francis, Mrs., M.B.E.
HERBERT, Adelaide Jane, Mrs., O.B.E., *d.* of William Farrer Ecroyd, J.P., D.L., of Credenhill Court, Hereford ; *m.* Frederick William, *s.* of the late Francis William Herbert, of Hartleton, Ross. *Educ. :* Cheltenham Ladies' Coll. *War Work :* In charge of Soldiers' Recreation Hut, 1915–19, St. Thomas's Hospital, London. *Address :* 1, Barton Street, Westminster. (O10614)
HERBERT, Agnes Mary, M.B.E., V.A.D.
HERBERT, Sir Alfred Edward, K.B.E., *b.* 5 Sept. 1866 ; (*see* BURKE'S *Peerage*) ; 2nd *s.* of William Herbert, of Leicester ; *m.* 1st, Ellen Adela, *d.* of Thomas Ryley, of Coventry ; 2nd, Florence, widow of Lieut.-Col. H. F. E. Lucas, 2nd Dragoon Guards. *Educ. :* Stoneygate School, Leicester. Engineer ; Chairman and sole Governing Director of Alfred Herbert, Ltd., Coventry ; President, Société Anonyme Alfred Herbert, France ; President, Societa Anonima Italiana Alfred Herbert, Italy ; President of the Machine Tool Trades Association. *War Work :* Deputy Director-General, and subsequently Controller, of Machine Tools, Ministry of Munitions ; Officer of the Legion of Honour ; Order of St. Stanislaus, 2nd Class, Russia, with Star ; Officer of the Order of Leopold, Belgium. *Address :* Dunley, Manor, Whitchurch, Hants. *Club :* Fly Fishers'. (K23)
HERBERT, Lieut.-Col. Arthur Stanley, O.B.E.

HERBERT, Capt. Edward Dave Asher, O.B.E., R.G.A. (S.R.)

HERBERT, Brig.-Gen. Edward Sidney, C.M.G., C.B.E.

HERBERT, Lieut.-Col. Ernest Roland, O.B.E., T.D., J.P., *b.* 3 March, 1869 ; *s.* of John A. Herbert, J.P., of High Beach, Sheringham. *Educ.:* Privately. Landowner and Farmer. *War Work :* Commanded 1/1st Huntingdonshire Cyclist Batt. *Address :* Wereham Hall, Stoke Ferry, Norfolk. (O7269)

HERBERT, Capt. George, M.B.E., R.A.S.C.

HERBERT, Guy Frederick, M.B.E., R.N.

HERBERT, Capt. Harold, O.B.E.

HERBERT, Hellen Margaret, Mrs., M.B.E., *b.* 1867 ; *d.* of the late Col. W. R. M. Holroyd, formerly Director of Public Instruction, Punjab, India ; *m.* Lieut.-Col. Douglas, I.A., *s.* of late Major-Gen. Charles Herbert. *War Work :* With the Red Cross ; mentioned in the Gazette of India, July, 1919 ; received the war badge from the Government of India, and the thanks of H.E. the Commander-in-Chief in India, Aug. 1919. *Address :* Shillong, Assam, India. (M6160)

HERBERT, Lieut.-Col. Henry Carden, O.B.E.

HERBERT, Comm. Philip, O.B.E., R.N.V.R.

HERBERT, Group-Capt. Philip Lee William, C.M.G., C.B.E., *b.* 1882 ; *s.* of the late W. D. Herbert, of Civil Ser. Group-Capt. R.A.F. ; Great War, 1914–19, as Brig.-Gen. R.F.C. and R.F.A. (despatches, Order of St. Anne of Russia, Order of St. Saviour of Greece, Order of the Nile). (O418)

HERBERT, Rosalie Margaret, O.B.E., *b.* 29 Sept. 1868 ; *d.* of Horace A. Herbert, of London and India. *Educ. :* Kensington ; Richmond. Still serving for B.R.C.S., County of London ; Member of Victoria League ; Middle Class Union ; Primrose League. *War Work :* Service at Devonshire House ; Wounded and Missing ; Arlington Street, Norfolk House ; Commandant, London 216 B.R.C.S. ; Organiser and Administrator of Fairlawn Auxiliary Military Hospital, Forest Hill, Sept. 1915 to December, 1919 ; Jan. 1920, Commandant in Charge, Broad Street Clinic, B.R.C.S. Mentioned in Secretary of State's list. *Address :* B.R.C. Clinic, 57, Broad Street, W.C. 2. *Club :* V.A.D. Ladies'. (O1461)

HERBERT, Lady Victoria Alexandrina Mary Cecil, C.B.E., *b.* 1874 ; *d.* of 4th Earl of Carnarvon (*see* BURKE'S *Peerage*). *Address :* 5, Stratford Place, W. 1. (C982)

HERBERTSON, Capt. James John William, O.B.E.

HERBST, Major John Frederick, C.B.E.

HERCHMER, Major William Sinclair, O.B.E.

HERCUS, Major Charles Ernest, D.S.O., O.B.E. Major New Zealand Forces ; served in Great War, 1915–18 (mentioned in despatches). (O6339)

HERCY, Capt. Francis Hugh George, C.B.E., D.L., *b.* 14 May, 1868 ; *s.* of Thomas Joseph Hercy, B.A., D.L., J.P., of Cruchfield and Winkfield, Berks. *Educ.:* Woburn Park. Formerly Captain 3rd (Militia) Battalion, The Queen's R.W. Surrey Regt. *War Work :* Rejoined 5 August, 1914 ; appointed to Recruiting Staff at Headquarters, Whitehall, in charge of all special enlistments ; thanked for services by Earl Kitchener, and by Earl of Derby in 1915 ; D.A.A.G. at War Office during transfer of Recruiting to Civil Control ; transferred to Ministry of National Service and appointed D.D.N.S. London and South Eastern Region ; specially mentioned for services in connection with the War, 1917. *Address :* 80, South Audley Street, W. 1 ; *Club :* Junior Naval and Military.

HERD, Major Walter, O.B.E.

HERDMAN, Major Arthur Cochran, O.B.E.

HERDMAN, Maud Harriett, Mrs., M.B.E., J.P., *b.* 1 Sept, 1879 ; *d.* of Major-Gen. Clark-Kennedy, late of Camus, Strabane, Co. Tyrone ; *m.* Capt. John Clandius, D.L., *s.* of E. T. Herdman, D.L., late of Sion House, Sion Mills. *War Work :* Sec. and Commandant, V.A.D. Hospital, Strabane ; Sec. Strabane War Relief Committee ; Head of Sphagnum Moss Depot. *Address :* Sion House, Sion Mills, Co. Tyrone. (M8449)

HERDMAN, William Abbott, C.B.E., D.Sc., Hon. D.Sc., Harvard, Durham, Sydney and Western Australia, Hon. LL.D. Edin. : F.R.S., F.L.S., *b.* 8 Sept. 1858 ; *e. s.* of Robert Herdman, F.R.S.A. ; *m.* 1st Sarah Wyse Douglas, 2nd Jane Bandreth Holt. *Educ. :* Edinburgh Academy and University. Graduated, in 1879 ; Assistant to Sir Wyville Thomson in " Challenger " Expedition Office ; Demonstrator of Zoology in Edinburgh University, 1880 ; President, Zoological Section, British Association, 1895 ; General Secretary, British Association, 1903 ; President of Linnean Society, 1904 ; Foreign Secretary, Royal Society, 1916 ; has, along with others, established a Marine Biological Station at Port Erin, I. of M. and a Sea Fish hatchery at Piel near Barrow ; is Hon. Director of Scientific work to the Lancashire Sea Fisheries Committee ; was sent to Ceylon in 1901–2 to investigate the Pearl Oyster Fisheries for the Government ; President of the British Association, 1920 ; has published many scientific works. *Addresses :* Croxteth Lodge, Liverpool ; Rowany, Port Erin, Isle of Man. *Clubs :* Athenæum ; University, and Athenæum, Liverpool ; Royal Mersey Yacht. (C2674)

HERFORD, Caroline, M.B.E., M.A., J.P., C.C., *b.* 1 Nov. 1860 ; *d.* of W. H. Herford, of Manchester. *Educ. :* N. London Coll. School ; Newnham Coll., Cambridge. H.M. Ladybarn House School for boys and girls ; Lecturer and Tutor, Univ. Coll., Reading, and Manchester Univ. ; J.P. and City Councillor, Manchester. *War Work :* Commandant, Red Cross, E. Lancs. 194, assisted in organising part-time work of Univ.³ women undergraduates, *i.e.* meeting all trains of wounded arriving at

Mayfield Station, and serving them with refreshments (866 trains between May, 1915, and May, 1919). *Address :* 8, Oak Drive, Fallowfield, Manchester. *Clubs :* Univ. Club for Ladies ; Ladies', Manchester. (M3714)

HERIOT, William MAITLAND-, C.B.E., *b.* 1856 ; *s.* of Frederick L. Maitland-Heriot, of Ramornie, Fife ; *m.* Alice *d.* of John Bruce, of Edinburgh. *Educ. :* Abroad. *War Work :* Military Representative, afterwards National Service Representative on Dumfriesshire Local Tribunal ; Chairman of Dumfriesshire Local War Pensions Committee ; Member of Scottish Regional Director's Advisory Council. *Clubs :* Wellington ; New, Edinburgh. (C2675)

HERIVEL, Lieut. Sidney Peck, O.B.E., R.N.V.R.

HERMAN, Sur.-Lieut. Ashley Ernest, O.B.E., M.B., R.N.

HERMAN, Lena, Mrs., M.B.E.

HERN, William, O.B.E., M.R.C.S., L.D.S.

HERNE, Lieut.-Col. Arthur Cecil, O.B.E., *b.* 3 Aug. 1884 ; *s.* of Joseph Herne, of London ; *m.* Nora, *d.* of Joseph Ellis, of London. *Educ. :* King's Coll., London. Civil Service. *War Work :* Served in Volunteer and Territorial Forces for 10 years prior to outbreak of war ; mobilised with 13th (Kensington) Batt. London Regt., 4 Aug. 1914, and proceeded to France, Nov. 1914 ; invalided home 3 months later ; appointed Adjutant to 16th York and Lancaster Regt., Aug. 1916 ; promoted Lieut.-Col. to command same battalion, Dec. 1916 ; remained in command till July, 1918, then transferred to command of 16th South Lanc Regt., remaining with that unit until June, 1919. *Address :* H.M. Office of Works, Westminster, S.W. 1. (O7270)

HERNE, Capt. Edward, O.B.E., R.A.V.C.

HERON, Cyril Renton, M.B.E.

HERON, Lieut.-Col. George Wykeham, O.B.E., D.S.O., M.R.C.S., L.R.C.P., *b.* 1880 ; Major and Acting Lieut.-Col. R.A.M.C. ; served in Great War, 1914–16 (mentioned in despatches). (O6199)

HERON, Harold Hastings, O.B.E., *b* 1866 ; *s.* of Samuel Heron, of Garton, E. Yorks. *Educ. :* Commercial Travellers' School, Pinner. *War Work :* Transport *via* Scandinavia for Russia ; Member of Russian Government Committee, and connected with Norwegian Section, Ministry of Shipping. *Address :* 37, Tarrington Park, North Finchley. (O10615)

HERON, Brig.-Gen. Sir Thomas, K.B.E., C.B., *b.* 13 May, 1857 ; *s.* of William Heron, M.R.C.S.I., of Dublin ; *m.* Ethel Mary, *d.* of Richard Powis Monk, of Clapham Park. *Educ. :* Rathmines School, Dublin. Retired, Army Ordnance Department, Hon. Brigadier General. *War Work :* France, 1914–1917 D.D.O.S. L. of C. ; Member of Mr. Balfour's Mission to U.S.A. April, 1917 to July, 1917 ; W.O. representative at Franco-Hellenique Conference, Paris, on the reorganisation of Greek Army ; 1917 to 1919, W.O. special work as regards demobilisation &c. of war materials. *Address :* Round Croft, Cheshunt, Herts.

HERR, Helena, M.B.E., *b.* 23 March, 1873. *Educ. :* Privately. Financial Sec. British Congress on Tuberculosis, London, 1900–1 ; Gen. Sec. Church of England Women's Help Society, 1904–11 ; Member of Executive and Council, Westminster Social Welfare Association, 1907–11 ; Press Sec. National Union of Women's Suffrage, 1913–14. *War Work :* Recording Sec. Trained Nurses Dept., Joint War Committee, Order of St. John of Jerusalem and British Red Cross Society, Headquarters, 1915–19. *Address :* St. Barnabas Orphanage, Chislehurst, Kent. (M8451)

HERRICK, Capt. William, O.B.E., R.A.S.C.

HERRIDGE, Major George James, O.B.E., *b.* 24 Nov. 1858 ; *s.* of John Herridge, of Blewbury, Berks ; *m.* Constance Georgina, *d.* of John Lee, of Langham, Essex ; *Educ. :* Privately. Staff, 4th Army Corps and Eastern Command, 20 April, 1903, to 20 Feb. 1914. *War Work :* Attached to Headquarters, Eastern Command, from Aug. 1914, to Aug. 1919. *Address :* Harlington Towers, East Barnet, Herts. (O7271)

HERRING, Herbert Thomas, O.B.E., M.B., B.S., *b.* 1861 ; *s.* of John Barnwell Herring, of Esher ; *m.* Margaret, *d.* of T. Porter. *Educ. :* Brighton Coll. ; Univ. Coll. Hospital, London ; Coll. of Medicine, Newcastle-on-Tyne. *War Work :* Founder, Organiser, with Mrs. Herring and M.O. in charge Weymouth Street Auxiliary Hospital (A.), (54 Beds), 1914–19. *Address :* 50, Harley Street, W. 1. *Clubs :* Reform ; Garrick. (O11811)

HERRIOTT, Capt. William Malcolm, M.B.E., Aust. I.F.

HERRON, Capt. Robert Charles, O.B.E., R.A.S.C.

HERSCHELL, Lieut.-Col. Allan, O.B.E., M.C., R.E.

HERTSLET, Sir Cecil, K.B.E., J.P., *b.* 21 August, 1850 ; *s.* of Sir Edward Hertslet, K.C.B. ; *m.* Euphemia Sophia Dalway, *d.* of Rev. Alfred T. Lee, LL.D., D.C.L., Preacher at Gray's Inn. *Educ. :* King's College School ; King's College, London. Foreign Office, 1868–96 ; His Majesty's Consul-General at Havre, 1896–1903 ; His Majesty's Consul-General for Belgium 1903–19 ; His Majesty's Consul-General at Zurich, 1915–17 (during German occupation of Antwerp). *War Work :* at his post during the siege of Antwerp and the bombardment of the fortress from 4 August till 7 October, 1914, when he left, in view of the final bombardment by the German forces ; war work in Switzerland, 1915–17 ; returned to Antwerp, 30 November, 1918 ; retired 1 January, 1919. *Address :* The Vicarage, Ramsgate. *Clubs :* Royal Societies' ; Royal Yacht Squadron (hon.) ; Royal Yacht Club of Belgium (Membre d'Honneur). (K384)

HERVEY, Comm. Gerald Augustus Frederic, O.B.E., R.N.R.

HERVEY, Capt. Gerald Charles Irwin, O.B.E.

HERVEY, Comm. Richard George, O.B.E.

HESELTINE, Lieut.-Col. Christopher, O.B.E.

HESELTINE, Capt. Conrad Pelham, M.B.E.

HESKETH, Lieut.-Col. Rawdon John Isherwood, C.B.E., *b.* 3 February, 1872 ; *s.* of William Pemberton Hesketh, Captain, 42nd Royal Highlanders and 18th Hussars ; *m.* Grace, *d.* of Harry Holditch Marten, of Tunbridge Wells. *Educ.:* Privately. Ministry of Pensions. *War Work :* Commanding 7th Batt. the Royal Fusiliers in England from 4 August, 1914 ; France, July, 1916, till invalided end of May, 1917 ; Commanded 5th Batt. The Royal Fusiliers, January, 1918 till disembodied, November, 1919 ; joined Royal Fusiliers, 1900, served with Mounted Infantry, South Africa, Queen's Medal, 3 Clasps. *Address :* 58, Mount Ephraim, Tunbridge Wells. *Club :* Junior United Service. (C1614)

HESKETH, Capt. and Qr.-Mr. William Henry, M.B.E., R.G.A.

HESLOP, Major Alfred Herbert, D.S.O., O.B.E., M.B., B.S., *b.* 3 March, 1880 ; *s.* of late Rev. R. C. Heslop, M.A. *Educ.:* High School, Oxford ; University of Durham and St. Thomas' Hospital. Major, R.A.M.C. *War Work :* Deputy Assistant Director Medical Services, I. Corps and G.H.Q., B.E.F. *Address :* c/o Messrs Holt & Co., 3, Whitehall Place, S.W. (O5370)

HETCKE, Wilfred Fulleylove, M.B.E.

HETHERINGTON, Capt. Charles Goldby, M.B.E., R.A.F.

HETHERINGTON, Lieut. Graham, M.B.E., R.A.V.C.

HETHERINGTON, Roger Gaskell, M. Inst. C.E., *b.* 10 Feb. 1876 ; *s.* of William Lonsdale Hetherington, of Highgate ; *m.* Honoria, *d.* of Arthur Ranken Ford, of Highgate. *Educ.:* Highgate School and Trinity College, Cambridge. Engineering Inspector, Local Government Board and Ministry of Health. *War Work :* Lieut. Staff for R.E. Services ; Staff Officer, R.E., Eastern Command ; Secretary Works Construction Sub-Committee of War Cabinet Priority Committee. *Address :* 20, Hillside Gardens, Highgate, N. 6. *Club :* Oxford and Cambridge. (O1462)

HETHERINGTON, Major Thomas Gerard, C.B.E., *b.* 1886 ; *s.* of Thomas Hetherington, J.P., of Berechurch Hall, Colchester. Is Major, Hussars, and a Staff Officer R.A.F. with rank of Lieut.-Col. ; instrumental in origination of the Tanks. (C197)

HETHERINGTON, William Carruthers, M.B.E.

HETT, Janie, Mrs., O.B.E., *b.* 31 Jan. 1855 ; *d.* of George Turnbull, of Edinburgh and Melbourne ; *widow* of Frank Crowder (died 1918), *s.* of John Hett, of Brigg, Lincolnshire. *War Work :* Vice-President, Brigg District, North Lincolnshire Branch, British Red Cross Society. *Address :* The Limes, Brigg, Lincolnshire. *Club :* New Victorian. (O10616)

HETT, Reginald, O.B.E., *b.* 12 Feb. 1869 ; *s.* of Dr. Henry Nicholson Hett, of Lincolnshire ; *m.* Edith Mary Katharine, *d.* of Col. William Richardson, of Lincolnshire. *Educ.:* Epsom Coll. Head of Army Pay Department, Messrs. Holt & Co. *Address :* 3, Whitehall Place, S.W. ; 6, Montagu Gardens, Acton, W. 3. (O10617)

HEURTLEY, Walter, O.B.E. (O6479)

HEWAN, Elliot Dunville, O.B.E.

HEWELCKE, Theodore William, O.B.E.

HEWER, Basil, O.B.E., *b.* 7 March, 1865 ; *s.* of Robert Hewer, of Fair Green, Oxon ; *m.* Annie Elizabeth, *d.* of Joseph Hargroves, of Charterhouse Square, E.C. *Educ.:* High School, Swindon. Dean and Lecturer on " Y.M.C.A. History, Principles, and Methods," Training Coll., Mildmay, N. ; Sec. to the Anglo-American Y.M.C.A., Paris, 1890, Paddington Y.M.C.A., 1892, and Aldersgate Street, E.C., Y.M.C.A., 1897 ; National Staff of Y.M.C.A. as Sec. for London area and Religious Activities, 1908–12. *War Work :* Y.M.C.A., organising work among troops, N.E. England, 1914 ; Workers' Department, Y.M.C.A. Headquarters, 1915 ; Director of Y.M.C.A. Training School for war workers from Nov. 1915, to March, 1919. *Address :* Y.M.C.A. Training Coll., Mildmay Park, N. 1. (O10619)

HEWER, Cecil Mackenzie, O.B.E., F.R.C.S.

HEWER, Edward Septimus Earnshaw, O.B.E., F.R.C.S. Eng.), *b.* 7 Oct. 1875 ; *s.* of the late Dr. John Henry Hewer, of Highbury, London ; *m.* Lucy Margaret, *d.* of Canon Horace Newton, of Holmwood, Redditch. *Address :* Church House, Stratford-on-Avon. (O10621)

HEWER, Capt. John Radborn, O.B.E., R.A.V.C.

HEWETSON, John Torcliffe, M.B.E., R.N.

HEWETT, Arthur, M.B.E., M.C., R.A.S.C.

HEWETT, Lieut. Cecil Allan, M.B.E.

HEWETT, Lieut.-Col. Edward Vincent Osborne, C.M.G., D.S.O., O.B.E., late Royal West Kent Regt. *b.* 14 March, 1867 ; *s.* of Lieut.-Gen. E. O. Hewett, C.M.G., R.E., of Yyr Mar Ellis, Glamorganshire ; *m.* Brenda, *d.* of F. Platt-Higgins, J.P., M.P., of Homleigh, Bowdon, Cheshire. *Educ.:* R.M.C., Canada. Professor Strategy, Tactics, Military History, Staff Duties and Reconnaissance, B.M. College, Canada, 1900–5 ; Nile, 1885–96 ; N.-W. Frontier, 1896–97 ; mentioned in despatches. *War Work :* Sept. 1914, joined 8th K.W. Kents ; Feb. 1915, assumed command 6th South Wales Borderers ; March, 1918, commanded 3rd Royal West Kent Regt. ; reverted to retired pay, Sept. 1915 ; awarded C.M.G., D.S.O. for services in the Field ; thrice mentioned in despatches. *Addresses :* Kingston, Sandecotes Road, Parkstone, Dorset. (O7273)

HEWETT, Capt. George Stuart, C.B.E., *b.* 27 Dec. 1863 ; *s.* of Frank William Hewett, *g.s.* of Sir George Henry Hewett, 2nd Bart. (*see* BURKE'S *Peerage*) ; *m.* Maud Mary Brind, *d.* of Sur.-Gen. Henry Kendall, A.M.D. Capt. R.I.M. ; T. Comm. R.N. ; Deputy Director R.I.M., Calcutta ; J.P. and first-class Magistrate ; has Legion of Honour. (C2253)

HEWETT, James Henry, M.B.E., *b.* 3rd March 1868 ; *s* of George William, of Bristol ; *m.* Jane Julia, *d.* of Charles Briant, of Reading. Chief Prison Officer. *War Work :* Pensioned Qr.-Mr. Sergt., Royal Field Artillery ; served in the Zanzibar Defence Force throughout the War. *Address :* Central Prison, Zanzibar Protectorate. (M6449)

HEWETT, Charles Ernest, O.B.E., J.P.

HEWETT, Sir John Prescott, G.C.S.I., K.B.E., C.I.E., *b.* 1854 ; *s.* of Rev. J. Hewett, of Babbacombe ; *m.* Ethel (Lady of Grace of St. John of Jerusalem), *d.* of H. B. Webster, B.C.S. Entered B.C.S. (N.W. Prov. and Oudh), 1877 ; officiated as Priv. Sec. to the Viceroy in 1888 and 1892, and as Sec. to Government of India, Home Dept., March 1890 and Jan. 1892 ; Sec. 1895–1902 ; Magistrate and Coll. of Bareilly, 1893–5 ; Chief Commr. Central Prov. 1902–5 ; Member of Council of Gov.-Gen. of India, 1905–6 ; Lieut.-Gov. United Provinces of Agra and Oudh, 1907–12 ; Knight of Justice of St. John of Jerusalem. *Address :* 8, Cumberland Mansions, Upper George Street, W. 1. *Clubs :* Arthur's ; Oriental.

HEWETT, Comm. Paul, C.B.E., R.N. (ret.), *b.* 14 April, 1858 ; *s.* of Lieut.-Col. Philip George Hewett. *Educ.:* Stubbington. *War Work :* 1914, in Yacht " Sardonyx," carrying wounded between Paris and Rouen ; 1915–16, Sec. Local War Pensions Committee ; 1917–18 Commodore of Convoys between England and Gibraltar. *Address :* St. Anne's, Ryde, Isle of Wight. *Club :* Royal Victoria Yacht. (C1188)

HEWETT, Reginald, M.B.E.

HEWGILL, Edward Burnip, M.B.E. (M10357)

HEWGILL, Major William Herbert, O.B.E.

HEWINS, Harold Preece, O.B.E.

HEWISON, Robert, O.B.E.

HEWITT, Major Albert Claud, O.B.E., R.F., *b.* 13 Feb. 1882 ; *s.* of the late Stanley Hughes Hewitt. *Educ.:* Haileybury Coll. In Regular Army ; served in Egyptian Expeditionary Force. *Address :* 31, Cadogan Place, London, S.W. 1.. *Clubs :* Naval and Military ; Royal Automobile. (O8626)

HEWITT, Lieut.-Col. Alfred Scott, D.S.O., O.B.E., *b.* 1876 ; *s.* of the late Alfred Hewitt, of Lisle Court, Wootton, Isle of Wight. Major Roy. W. Kent. Regt. ; Dep. Provost Marshal with rank of Lieut.-Col. ; served in S. African War, 1900–2 ; Great War, 1914–18 (mentioned in despatches). *Address :* Lisle Court, Wootton, Isle of Wight. (O6379)

HEWITT, Lieut.-Comm. Brian Lifford, O.B.E.

HEWITT, Eileen Mabel, M.B.E., M.D., *b.* 1888 ; *d.* of James Hewitt, of Ballsbridge, Dublin. *Educ.:* Alexandra School and Coll., and Trinity Coll., Dublin. Assistant Medical Officer of Health, Stepney. *War Work ;* Medical Officer in charge, Women's Hospital, Royal Arsenal, Woolwich. *Address :* 33, High Street, St. John's Wood, N.W. 8. *Club :* Ladies' Univ. (M1887)

HEWITT, Lieut.-Comm. Heathcote George, O.B.E., R.N.

HEWITT, Major John Theodore, O.B.E.

HEWITT, Sarah, Mrs., M.B.E., *b.* 24 Dec. 1860 ; *d.* of the late Richard Suter, of Eastergate, Chichester, Sussex ; *m.* Francis Hewitt, of Leicester. *War Work :* Visiting and entertaining. *Address :* c/o F. O. Hewitt, Esq., Oaklands, Quorn, Leicester. (M8452)

HEWITT, Capt. Thomas, M.B.E.

HEWITT, Capt. Alfred A. T. LUDLOW-, O.B.E., *s.* of T. A. Ludlow-Hewitt, J.P., of Clancoole, Bandon, Co. Cork ; *m.* Margery, *d.* of late Professor H. W. Moseley, of Oxford. *Educ.:* Marlborough and Oxford University. Mentioned in Despatches. *Address :* Whitefield Court,·Deerhurst, Tewkesbury. (O5502)

HEWKIN, Edwin Percy, M.B.E., *b.* 9 Feb. 1872. Civil Servant. *War Work :* Head of Sugar Shipments Section, Ministry of Shipping. *Address :* 55, Hadleigh Road, Leigh-on-Sea, Essex. *Clubs :* National Liberal ; Essex Yacht ; Alexandra Yacht. (M3716)

HEWLETT, Beatrice, M.B.E., *b.* 22 June, 1888 ; *d.* of W. H. Hewlett, of Standish. *Educ.:* Eastbury House School, Northwood. *War Work :* Quartermaster at the 3rd Woodlands Military Auxiliary Hospital, Standish, Lancashire, from Nov. 1914 to Dec. 1917 ; Commandant and Quartermaster from Jan. 1918 to March, 1919, at the same hospital. *Address :* Strickland House, Standish, Lancashire. (M8453)

HEWLETT, Lieut.-Col. Francis Esme Theodore, O.B.E., D.S.O., R.A.F. Served in Directorate of Aircraft Production. (O1463)

HEWLETT, Major Kenelm, O.B.E., I.D.F.

HEWSON, Capt. Frank Lloyd, O.B.E., R.A.S.C., *b.* 8 Aug. 1885. *War Work :* Served in France, 1914–16, and 1918–19 ; N. Russia, March to Oct. 1919. *Address :* c/o A. Whitehead, Rougemont, Salisbury, Wilts. (O9718)

HEWSON, James Archibald, O.B.E., *b.* 26 Jan. 1863. Deputy Accountant and Comptroller-General, H.M. Customs and Excise. *War Work :* Official duties created by war conditions in connection with Prize, etc., New Revenue Duties ; Vice-Chairman and Ward Sec. Hornsey War Pensions Committee. *Address :* Heathdene, Cranley Gardens, Muswell Hill. (O10623)

HEXT, Lieut. Arthur Charles, M.B.E.

HEYCOCK, Lieut. Col. Charles Hensman, O.B.E., R.E.

HEYCOCK, Florence, Mrs., M.B.E.

HEYDE, Lieut. Douglas, O.B.E., R.E. (S.R.)

HEYER, Capt. George, M.B.E.

HEYLIN, Henry Brougham, O.B.E., M. Text. Inst., *b.* April, 1870; *s.* of Hy. B. Heylin, of Worsley; *m.* Annie Elizabeth, *d.* of Thos. Ball, of Manchester. Textile Expert under War Office. *War Work :* Advised on purchase and construction of textile materials for British War Office and Allies generally; substituted suitable cotton materials for various purposes in view of shortage of good flax materials; arbitrator in many cases for Board of Trade on behalf of Allied purchases; responsible for the inspection of textile materials generally in connection with Army Ordnance Supplies. *Address :* 8, Beechhill Road, Eltham, S.E. 9. (O10624)

HEYMAN, Frances Patton, Lady, M.B.E.; *d.* of Rev. William Impey, of Grahamstown; *m.* Sir Melville Heyman. *War Work :* Red Cross Work in Bulawayo, Rhodesia. *Address :* Bulawayo, Rhodesia. (M6450)

HEYMANN, Brevet-Major Frank Albert, O.B.E., *b.* 1 Sept. 1882; *s.* of Albert Heymann, of West Bridgford Hall, Notts; *m.* Elizabeth Rutherford, *d.* of John Oliver, of Lynnwood, Hawick. *Educ :* Haileybury. Regular Army. *War Work :* 1914–18, B.E.F.; 1919, Army of Occupation in Germany. *Address :* Lynnwood, Hawick, Scotland. (O5372)

HEYN, Capt. Richard Gustavus, O.B.E., R.A.F.

HEYNES, James Baylis, M.B.E., F.R.S.A., Cavaliere ufficiale della corona d'Italia, Knight of the Order of Wasa (Sweden), *b.* 1851; *s.* of James Heynes, of Bromsgrove, Worcestershire; *m.* Lilian, *d.* of late George Harper, J.P., of Southampton. *Educ :* St. John's College, Hurstpierpont. British Vice-Consul, Messina, Sicily; Lloyds' Agent, Messina, Sicily. *War Work :* Naval Intelligence Officer, Military Intelligence Officer; Port Transport Officer; Port Convoy Officer; Passport Control Officer, Messina. *Addresses :* British Vice-Consulate, Messina; Gazzi, near Messina. *Club :* National Liberal. (M538)

HEYWOOD, Ivy Lenore, M.B.E,

HEYWOOD, Lieut. Noel, O.B.E., R.A.S.C.

HEYWOOD, Major Thomas George Gordon, O.B.E., R.A.

HEYWORTH, Beatrice Hestietha Gundreda, M.B.E., Q.M.A.A.C.

HEZLET, Major and Brevet Lieut.-Col. Robert Knox, C.B.E., D.S.O., R.F.A., *b.* 21 Dec. 1879; *s.* of Lieut.-Col. R. J. Hezlet, of Bovagh, Aghadowey, Co. Londonderry, Ireland; *m.* Josepha Dorothy, *d.* of Andrew Arter, of Linden House, Ravenscourt Park, W. *Educ :* Clifton; Royal Military Academy, Woolwich. Regular Army, Royal Field Artillery, *War Work :* O.C. 19th Battery, R.F.A., France, 1915; mentioned in despatches; O.C. 9th Brigade, R.F.A., Mesopotamia, 1915–1916, mentioned in despatches; Member Ordnance Committee, Woolwich, 1916. *Address :* Bovagh, Aghadowey, Co. Londonderry. *Club :* Army and Navy. (C1615)

HEZLETT, Mary Kathleen, Mrs., O.B.E.

HIBBARD, Major Thomas, O.B.E., T.D., M.R.C.V.S., R.A.V.C., *b.* Mar. 1865; *s.* of Stephen Hibbard, of Gillingham, Kent; *m.* Fanny, *d.* of William George Fish, of Chingford. *Educ :* Doddington. Served in S. Africa, 1900. *War Work :* Mobilised, Aug. 1914; A.D.V.S. 56th (London) Division; A.D.V.S., 47th (London) Division. *Address :* Westcourt Cottage, Shepherdswell, Kent. (O5374)

HIBBERD, Henry George, M.B.E.

HIBBERD, Julia Florence, O.B.E., *b.* 12 Feb. 1873; *d.* of Tom Hibberd, of Dennington, Suffolk. *Educ :* Northwood Coll. *War Work :* Sandes Soldiers' Homes, India. (O9825)

HIBBERT, Lieut. George, O.B.E.

HIBBERT, Vice-Adm. Hugh Thomas, C.B.E., D.S.O., R.N., *b.* 1863; *s.* of Hugh Robert Hibbert, of Birkles Hall, Cheshire; *m.* 1892, Catherine Brownlow, *d.* of M. A. Butterfield. *Address :* Birtles Old Hall, Chelford. *Club :* Army and Navy. (C897)

HIBBS, Frank Edward, M.B.E.

HICK, Benjamin, O.B.E.

HICKES, Major Edward Weston, O.B.E.

HICKES, Major Lancelot Daryl, O.B.E., M.C., *b.* 30 May, 1884; *m.* Vera Newbury. *Educ :* Blundell's and Bedford School; R.M. Acadamy, Woolwich. Officer in Royal Artillery. Commissioned, Dec. 1903; W. Africa, 1908; *War Work :* Cameroons, 1914; Gallipoli, 1915; Egypt and France, 1916; France, 1917–18. *Address :* c/o Cox & Co (R.A. Dept.), 16, Charing Cross, London. *Club :* United Service. (O5376)

HICKEY, Capt. Jeremiah, M.B.E.

HICKEY, Major T.A., O.B.E.

HICKIE, Capt. George William Clement, O.B.E., R.A.S.C., *b.* 2 March, 1897; *s.* of the late Major W. B. Hickie, of S. & T. Corps. *Educ :* Cheltenham Coll., and Imperial Service Coll., Windsor. *War Work :* Served with B.E.F., France, 1915–16; E.E.F., Egypt and Palestine, 1916–18; British Military Mission, S. Russia, 1919–20; awarded 2nd Class Order of St. Stanislaus by Commander-in-Chief, Armed Forces, South Russia. *Addresses :* c/o Messrs. H. S. King & Co., 9, Pall Mall, S.W. 1; c/o Sir C. R. McGrigor, Bart., & Co., 39, Panton Street, Haymarket, S.W. 1. (O11800)

HICKIE, Capt. Henry Garnet, M.B.E., M.C., 1st Bn. Irish Guards, *b.* 29 Jan. 1872; *s.* of Capt. Henry Hickie, R.A.S.C.; *m.* Agnes, *d.* of John Cook, Bengal Fusiliers. *Educ :* Royal Hibernian Military School, Dublin. *War Work :* Served with

the Gordon Highlanders in the Tirah Campaign of 1897; wounded at the charge of Dargai; wounded with the Gordon Highlanders at Magersfontein; served throughout the Great War as Quartermaster of the 1st Batt. Irish Guards; awarded the Military Cross. (M6529)

HICKLEY, Alice, Mrs. Victor North, M.B.E.

HICKLEY, Sybil Louise, Mrs. NORTH-, M.B.E.; *d.* of Col. G. H. Trollope, of Cobham in Surrey. *War Work :* Organiser and Commandant of V.A.D. Hospital in Much Hadham Village, working under 1st E. G. Hospital, Cambridge, which started with six beds, Dec. 1914, was enlarged to 42 beds and closed Jan. 1919; Vice-President for district. *Address :* The Hill, Much Hadham, Herts. (M8455)

HICKLIN, Samuel, M.B.E.

HICKLING, Alice, Mrs., M.B.E.

HICKMAN, John Blair Smith, O.B.E., *b.* 22 Feb. 1861; *s.* of Charles Hickman, of Ravenscourt Park, Hammersmith, London; *m.* Lillian Alice, *d.* of Fleet Eng. R. T. Rundle, R.N., of Plymouth. *Educ :* Brackenburg House, Hammersmith, London, W. Superintendent of H.M. Victualling Yards, Malta; Sydney, N.S.W.; Royal Victorian Yard, Deptford, London; Royal Clarence Yard, Gosport. *War Work :* In charge of Naval Victualling Depot, Cape Town, 1900–1 (South African War). Supt. Royal William Yard, Plymouth 1913 to date. *Address :* Royal William Yard, Plymouth. *Club :* Malta Union. (O10626)

HICKMAN, Kenneth Claude Devereux, M.B.E., B.Sc., A.I.C., D.I.C., *b.* 4 Feb. 1896; *s.* of Claude A. Hickman, of Bromley, Kent. *Educ :* Hedden Court, Cockfosters; Royal Coll. of Science, S. Kensington. *War Work :* Research Chemist to Trench Warfare Dept.; Research Chemist at Chemical Projectile Laboratory, Wembley, under Chemical Warfare Dept.; Poison gas, Smoke screens, and flares. *Address :* Royal Coll. of Science, South Kensington. (M8457)

HICKS, Amy Maud, M.B.E., M.A.; *d.* of Charles Thompson Hicks, Gt. Holland Hall, Essex. *Educ :* North London Collegiate School, and Girton. *War Work :* Motor driver, Women's Reserve Ambulance; Canteen work in France; Higher Grade Clerk, Admiralty, 1916–17; Junior Administrative Assistant, War Office, 1917–19. *Address :* Runsell Green, Danbury, Essex. (M8458)

HICKS, Arthur Samuel, M.B.E., R.A.O.C.

HICKS, Corona, M.B.E.

HICKS, John William, M.B.E., F.R.A.S., *b.* 22 Oct. 1882; *s.* of John Hicks, of Lisburn, Belfast. *Educ :* Privately; Assistant to the Ballistic Officer, Ordnance Committee; "H" of "Arms and Explosives," and "The N.R.A. Journal"; "Balistica" of "The Rifleman." *War Work :* Preparation of Range Tables and other mathematical work in connection with Gunnery; Publications: "Vocations for our Sons" (Fisher Unwin, 1906); "The Theory of the Rifle and Rifle Shooting" (Griffin, 1919); *Addresses :* c/o The Royal Astronomical Society, Burlington House, W. 1; 27, Old Mill Road, Plumstead Common, S.E. 18. (M8459)

HICKS, Major Joseph Marmaduke, M.B.E.

HICKS, Lieut.-Col. Sir Maxwell, C.B.E., F.C.A., *b.* 20 March, 1878; *s.* of late Henry Hicks, of Plaistow Hall, Kent; *m.* Kate, *d.* of late John Giblett, of Woodside Park, Middlesex. *Educ :* Privately. Senior partner of firm of Maxwell Hicks & Co., Chartered Accountants. *War Work :* Commanded M.H.S., Accountants, a technical unit of R.A.S.C. dealing with the financial side of Expeditionary Force Canteens. *Addresses :* 6, Cadogan Gardens, S.W.; Lake Lodge, Wargrave, Berks. *Clubs :* Marlborough; Carlton. (C1266)

HICKS, Eng.-Lieut. Nicholas John, M.B.E., R.N., *b.* 26 Feb. 1867; *s.* of Henry Hicks, of St. Minver, Cornwall; *m.* Mary Jane, *d.* of Charles Hicks Harris, of Lostwithiel, Cornwall. *Educ :* Stoke Public Higher School, Devonport. *War Work :* Senior Eng. of H.M.S. "Blake"; repairs to destroyers of 11th Flotilla and attached destroyers at Northern bases. *Address :* 12, Mariston Avenue, Keyham, Barton, Devonport. (M1889)

HICKS, Thomas, M.B.E. (M10393)

HICKS, Thomas William, M.B.E., M.D. (Lond.), L.R.C.P. (Lond.) M.R.C.S. (Eng.), J.P. (Middlesex), *b.* 1869; *s.* of Richard Hicks, of Hull, E. Yorks.; *m.* Cicely Beatrix, *d.* of — Grylls. *Educ :* Hull and E. Riding Coll.; London Univ. Medical Officer and Public Vaccinator, 6th District, Barnet Union; Medical Officer, Finchley Cottage Hospital; Medical Officer, National Hospital (Finchley); Medical Officer, Summerton Hospital (Finchley). *War Work :* Mobilised and was Officer in Command Summerlee Auxiliary War Hospital, E. Finchley (100 Beds); Capt. Middlesex R.A.M.C. (V.); Capt. and Medical Officer of Eastern Command Volunteer Ambulance Convoy; Officer in Command, Middlesex V.A.D. 25. *Address :* Park House, E. Finchley, N.2. *Club :* Royal Automobile. (M1890)

HICKS, Comm. William Thomas, O.B.E., R.N.

HICKSON, Elizabeth, Mrs., M.B.E.; *d.* of Joseph Beck, of London; *m.* Frederick George, *s.* of George Hickson, of London. *Educ :* Univ. Coll., London. Co-Principal of "Oldfield " Co., Education School, Swanage. *War Work :* Quartermaster and later Assist. Commandant at Cluny Red Cross Auxiliary Hospital; Commandant of Dorset V.A.D. 36. *Club :* V.A.D. (M8460)

HICKSON, Major Gerald Robert Stedall, C.B.E., *b.* 1879. Major R.M.L.I.; served in Great War, 1914–19; mentioned in despatches. (C2288)

HICKSON, Major-Gen. Sir Samuel, K.B.E., C.B., B.A.,

M.B., B.Ch., L.M., Trinity Coll., Dublin; *b.* 14 Nov. 1859; *s.* of Capt. R. M. Hickson, J.P., of the Grove, Dingle, Co. Kerry; *m.* Aug. 1903, Elizabeth Constance, *y.d.* of the late Rev. Canon Bolsher, of Cork, and *w.* of R. Fry. Hon. Maj.-Gen. late R.A.M.C.; formerly Hon. Surgeon to the King; Inspector of Medical Services, War Office, 1914; and Asst. Director of Medical Services, B.E.F., 1914–17; served in S. Africa, 1896–7 (despatches, medal with clasp); in S. African War 1899–1902 (despatches, brevet, 2 medals with 4 clasps); and in the Great War (despatches). *Address:* White Lodge, Fleet, Hants. *Club:* Constitutional.

HICKSON, William Henry, O.B.E.

HIDE, Arthur, M.B.E.

HIDE, Constance, Mrs., M.B.E., *b.* 19 Oct. 1870; *d.* of Robert Redmayne, of The Hermitage, Bowness-on-Windermere; *m.* William Seymour, *s.* of T. C. Hide. *War Work:* Raising money for the East Riding Prisoners of War Fund; worked at the Riverside Quay, Hull, in connection with the Repatriated Prisoners. *Address:* Cottingham Grange, East Yorkshire. (M8461)

HIDE, Capt. Lewis, M.B.E., R.E.

HIGGIN, Elizabeth Philadelphia Lockhart, Mrs., M.B.E., *b.* 1866; *d.* of John MacMorland, of Roxburghshire; *m.* William, *s.* of William Higgin, of Rosgauna, Co. Antrim. *Educ.:* Privately. *War Work:* Soldiers' and Sailors' Families Association, and War Pensions. *Address:* Blackwoodhoure, Eaglesfield, Dumfriesshire. (M8462)

HIGGINS, Professor Alexander Pearce, C.B.E., M.A., LL.D., *b.* 24 April, 1865; *s.* of Alexander Higgins, of Worcester; *m.* Mina, *d.* of Simon MacLennan, of Glasgow. *Educ.:* Cathedral (King's) School, Worcester; Downing College, Cambridge, (Scholar). Whewell Professor of International Law, Cambridge; Professor of International Law, London. *War Work:* Adviser on International Law and Prize Law in the Departments of H.M. Procurator-General and Treasury Solicitor; Legal Adviser in International Law to the Admiralty for the Peace Conference at Paris. *Addresses:* 2, Pump Court, Temple, E.C.; 5, Salisbury Villas, Cambridge. *Club:* London University. (C198)

HIGGINS, Arthur Gordon, M.B.E., *b.* 18 Feb. 1871; *s.* of Thomas Dick Higgins, of Lewisham; *m.* Edith Alice, *d.* of Thomas Taylor, of Lewisham. *Educ.:* Roan School, Greenwich. Master of Belmont Institution. *War Work:* Acting Quartermaster during the occupation of the Institution as a Prisoners of War Hospital. *Address:* Belmont, Sutton. Surrey. (M8463)

HIGGINS, Lieut. Arthur Hall, M.B.E.

HIGGINS, Major Cecil Matthew, O.B.E., M.C.

HIGGINS, Capt. and Qr.-Mr. Charles Henry Pragnell, M.B.E.

HIGGINS, Edward John, C.B.E., *b.* 26 Nov. 1864; *s.* of the late Edward Higgins, of London; *m.* Catherine, *d.* of David G. Price, of Penarth. *Educ.:* Privately. Chief of Staff of Salvation Army. *War Work:* In charge of all Salvation Army work amongst the British Troops in Great Britain, France and Belgium. *Addresses:* 101, Queen Victoria Street, E.C.; Clovelly, Powys Lane, Palmers Green, N. 13. (C2676)

HIGGINS, Lieut. John, M.B.E.

HIGGINS, Major John Esmond Longuet, O.B.E., M.C.

HIGGINS, Lieut.-Col. and Qr.-Mr. Joseph Thomas, O.B.E., R.A.S.C.

HIGGINS, Capt. Robert Henry Constable, M.B.E., R.A.V.C., *b.* 13 June, 1889; *s.* of Lieut.-Col. Higgins, O.B.E., of Dublin; *m.* Phillis Edith, *d.* of C. R. Cook, of Wheathampstead. *Educ.:* St. Andrew's Coll., Dublin, and R.V. Coll. Ireland. *War Work:* With 3rd (Lahore) Division from India to France, Aug 1914, to May, 1915; posted to 46th Mobile Veterinary Section, Guards' Division, Aug. 1915, to Dec. 1915; proceeded to Mesopotamia, Dec. 1915, with No. 7 Field Vety. Section; appointed A.D.V.S. 14th (Indian) Division, May, 1916; transferred to U.K., Jan. 1919; proceeded to Archangel with Gen. Sadler Jackson's Brigade; appointed Commandant, Veterinary Training School, Archangel, until evacuated, with British Forces. *Club:* Junior Army and Navy. (M6964)

HIGGINS, Sir Sydney George, Knt. Bach., C.B.E., *b.* 26 Jan. 1867; *s.* of Warner Charles Higgins, of Portlane, Sunbury-on-Thames, late Receiver-Gen. H.M. Office of Woods and Forests; *m.* 27 Aug. 1890, Ida Blanche, *y. d.* of James Hollway, J.P., D.L., of Stanhoe Hall, Norfolk. Managing Director, William France Fenwick & Co., Ltd., Shipowners, London. *War Service:* Asst. Accountant-General and Ministry of Shipping, 1917–20. *Address:* Brooklands, Sunbury-on-Thames. *Club:* Union. (C518)

HIGGINS, Capt. Thomas Twistington, O.B.E., M.B., F.R.C.S.. R.A.M.C.

HIGGINS, William, O.B.E.

HIGGINS, Major William George, O.B.E., *b.* 4 May, 1883; *s.* of Charles Patrick; *m.* Adrienne Fannie, *d.* of Henry Higgins, of London and Paris. *Educ.:* Privately; on the Continent; Manchester University. *War Work:* Supplies, R.A.S.C.; Organiser and President, 3rd Army Purchase Board and Central Purchase Board, G.H.Q. France. *Club:* Thatched House. (O2568)

HIGGINSON, Charles James, C.B.E., *n.* 17 May, 1871; *s.* of Charles Frederick Higginson, of Hampstead. *Educ.:* Privately. Barrister-at-Law, (Inner Temple). *War Work:* From 1916 to 1919, Secretary to Restriction of Enemy Supplies Department; from February, 1919 to July 1919, Director of the Department. *Addresses:* 1, Paper Buildings, Temple;

54, Crediton Hill, Hampstead, N.W. 6. *Club:* Royal Societies'. (C2677)

HIGGON, Catherine Octavia, Mrs., M.B.E., J.P.; *d.* of Capt. C. W. Carden, 36th Regt.; *m.* Victor James, *s.* of Capt. J. D. G. Higgon, R.A., of Scolton, Pembrokeshire. *Educ.:* Privately. *War Work:* Commandant and Officer in charge, Cottesmore Auxiliary Hospital, Haverfordwest; Assistant County Director, B.R.C.S., for Pembrokeshire. *Address:* Treffgarne Hall, Pem. (M1892)

HIGGON, Victor James, M.B.E., J.P.; *s.* of J. D. G. Higgon, Capt., R.A., of Scolton, Pembrokeshire; *m.* Catherine Octavia, *s.* of C. W. Carden, Capt. 36th Regt. *Educ.:* Bradfield Coll., and Univ. Coll., Oxford. *War Work:* Territorial Force Association Sec. for the counties of Cardigan, Carmarthen and Pembroke, 1914–19. *Address:* Treffgarne Hall, Pembrokeshire. (M8464)

HIGGS, Charles James, M.B.E., *b.* 7 Oct. 1863. *War Work:* Services in connection with Food Control. *Address:* 6, Bigwood Avenue, Hove. (M8465)

HIGGS, Ernest Bertram, M.B.E.

HIGGS, Col. Frederick William, C.B.E., M.D., B.S., M.R.C.P., Army Medical Service, (T.F.), *b.* 18 May, 1881; *s.* of Augustus William Higgs, of Chelsea, sometime of E. Hagbourne; *m.* Dorothy Anderson, *d.* of John Walter Scott, of Chandler's Ford. *Educ.:* University of London; St. George's Hospital. A.D.M.S. 2nd London Division, Territorial Army; Medical Officer, Ministry of Health; late Physician, Belgrave Hospital for Children; Medical Registrar and Tutor, &c. St George's Hospital and Divisional Medical Officer L.C.C. Public Health Dept. *War Work:* 2nd in Command and Adjt. 1/2nd London C.C.S. (Home); O.C. No 8 Ambulance Train (Home); O.C., z/2nd London (No. 55) C.C.S. (Home and Abroad) A.D.M.S. 66th Division (Abroad). *Addresses:* Ministry of Health, Whitehall, S.W. 1; Dell-Quay, Sutton, Surrey. (C1267)

HIGGS, Lieut.-Col. Henry Joseph, O.B.E., A.M., M.I. Mech.E., A.M.I.C.E., B.A. (Cantab.); *s.* of Joseph Higgs, of Indiana, U.S.A.; *m.* Gladys Winifred, *d.* of James Rawlings, J.P., of Hartlepool. *Educ.:* St. Paul's School, and Magdalene Coll., Cambridge. Engineer, Managing Director, Ransome and Maries Bearing Co., Ltd., Newark; late Egyptian Civil Service (Irrigation Dept.). *War Work:* Served in 2nd Field Co., R.E., in France from Nov. 1914 to 1915; wounded, Neuve Chapelle; served G.H.Q. Staff in Palestine, 1917–19; given rank of Lieut.-Col.; thrice mentioned in despatches and awarded the Albert Medal in gold. *Address:* Southwell, Notts. (O6201)

HIGHAM, Lieut. Frank David, M.B.E.

HIGHET, Sir Robert Swan, C.B.E., M.I.C.E., *b.* 20 Mar. 1859; *s.* of late David Highet, of Ayr; *m.* Violet Gibson, *d.* of the late Charles Foegan, Towerhill, Ayrshire *Educ.:* Ayr Academy. Pupil and Assistant to John Skain, Civil Engineer, and Vice-Pres. Inst.C.E.; joined the East Indian Railway as Assist. Engineer, 1883; Chief Engineer, 1903; Agent, 1912–19; President Indian Railway Conference Association, 1918; Deputy Chairman East India Railway Co. *Address:* Cranley Lodge, Guildford. *Club:* Oriental. (C350)

HIGHFIELD, Comm. William, O.B.E., R.N.

HIGHMORE, Sir Nathaniel Joseph, G.B.E., K.C.B., *b.* 13 November, 1844; *s.* of William Highmore, M.D., of Sherborne, Dorset; *m.* Annie Louisa (Order of Mercy), *d.* of John Lane Cutcliffe, J.P., of Stoke Damerel, Devon. *Educ.:* Sherborne and Middle Temple. Barrister-at-Law; Assistant Solicitor of Inland Revenue and afterwards Solicitor for the Customs and Excise; Knighted 1907; retired 1913. *War Work:* Appointed, August 1914, by Treasury on Committee on Trade with the enemy; subsequently Secretary to the War Trade Department, Feb. 1915; and remained there until its close in March, 1919. *Address:* Harbybrowe, Worcester Park, Surrey. *Club:* Junior Carlton. (G52)

HIGHTON, Arthur Denys Salusbury, M.B.E., *b.* 20 Oct. 1880; *s.* of the late Rev. Edward Highton, of Tarrant Keynston, Dorset. *War Work:* Agent, Bank of Bengal, Lucknow, during flotation of the Government of India Loan of 1918, and a member of the United Provinces War Loan Committee. *Address:* Bank of Bengal, Lucknow. *Clubs:* East India United Service; Bengal, Calcutta; Royal Bombay Yacht. (M6162)

HIGHTON, William Thomas, M.B.E.

HIGMAN, Frank Sidney, M.B.E.

HIGMAN, Capt. Joseph Cresswell, M.B.E. *b.* 2 May, 1869; *s.* of the Rev. S. Higman, of Swansea, Glam. *Educ.:* Swansea Grammar School; Norton Coll. Principal Insurance Officer, Board of Trade (Wales). *War Work:* Assisted Ministry of Munitions, and Ministry of National Service; in charge Labour Supply (War Office), South Wales; Chairman, Road Transport Board, Wales; associated with Sir J. W. Courtes and Sir J. W. Beynon in raising two complete county corps Volunteers, R.A.S.C. *Address:* 68, Park Place, Cardiff. *Clubs:* Royal Automobile; National Liberal. (M8466)

HIGNETT, Alice, Mrs., M.B.E.

HIGNETT, Dorothy Eleanor Augusta, Mrs., M.B.E., Lady of Grace of St. John of Jerusalem; *d.* of Thomas Lawes Rogers, late Coldstream Guards, of Rainhill, Lancashire; *m.* Arthur Holland Hignett, *s.* of Thomas Hignett, of Cholmondeley, Cheshire. *Educ.:* At home. *War Work:* Deputy Head, Irish War Hospital Supply Depot; Hon. Organiser, South of Ireland Munition Makers' Canteens; Hon. Organiser, Irish National Waste Paper Collection and various other Red Cross activities. *Address:* 4, Shrewsbury Road, Dublin. (C2678)

HIGSON, Elizabeth Annie, Mrs., M.B.E.
HIGSON, Capt. Frank, O.B.E.
HIGSON, 2nd Lieut. Percy John, M.B.E., R.E.
HIGSON, Capt. William, M.B.E.
HILDYARD, Cicely Frances, M.B.E. ; d. of the late J. R. W. Hildyard, of Hutton Bonville, Yorkshire, and Horsley, Co. Durham. War Work : Hon. Sec. of the North Riding of Yorkshire Branch of the Incorporated Soldiers' and Sailors' Help Society ; Assistant Sec. and later Sec. of the North Riding of Yorkshire Local War Pensions Committee. Address : Hutton Bonville, Northallerton. Club : Ladies' Park.   (M8468)
HILDYARD, Gertrude Mary, Mrs. D'ARCY-, O.B.E., b. 28 Aug. 1870 ; Lady of the Manor of Colburn ; d. of J. E. Burdon, widow of Robert Maxwell, Capt. 68th D.L. Infantry, served Boer War (who died), s. of R. Thoroton-D'Arcy-Hildyard, Rifle Brigade, of Colburn Estate (see BURKE'S Landed Gentry). Educ. : Privately, and France. War Work : Organised at own expense Mrs. D'Arcy-Hildyard's Rest Home and Billet, The Quayside, Boulogne (250 beds) ; the Rest Home gave free beds and cooked rations for upwards of 250,000 men proceeding to and from the firing line ; holds 1914 Star, War and Victory medals ; mentioned in Gen. Haig's despatches, 1917. Addresses : 17, De Vere Gardens, W. 8 ; Colburn Manor, Catterick, Yorkshire. Club : Kennel.   (M3720)
HILES, Capt. Morton, O.B.E.
HILEY, Col. Ernest Haviland, C.B.E. New Zealand Forces ; served in Great War, 1915–19 ; mentioned in despatches.   (C1857)
HILEY, Sir Ernest Varvill, K.B.E., b. 11 Oct. 1868 ; s. of Charles Hiley, of Yeadon, Wharfedale, Yorks ; m. Edith Caroline, d. of James H. Beckingham, of Priestfield, Lintz Green, Co. Durham, and widow of Walter Whetstone, of Knighton. Solicitor ; Town Clerk of Birmingham, 1908–16 ; Chairman of Metropolitan Carriage, Wagon, and Finance Co., Ltd. ; Director, Vickers, Ltd. ; Vice-Chairman, Metropolitan Vickers Electrical Co., Ltd. ; Deputy Director-General of Natural Science, 1917. Address : 7, Chelsea Embankment, S.W. 3. Clubs : Carlton ; Conservative ; Union (Birmingham).   (K81)
HILEY, Mary, Mrs., O.B.E., b. 27 June, 1876 ; d. of John Freeman Chatwin, of Sleaford, Lincs ; m. George Archibald Wood, s. of William P. Hiley, of Skegness. Educ. : Sleaford, Lincs. War Work : Assisted in equipping and organising Sleaford Red Cross Hospital, 1914–19 ; Commandant from 1915. Address : 4, Ickworth Road, Sleaford, Lincs.   (O3253)
HILEY, Capt. Wilfrid Edward, O.B.E.
HILL, Alex, O.B.E., M.D., J.P., b. 1856 ; s. of John Hill, of the London Stock Exchange ; m. Emma Mary, d. of B. Woodward. Educ. : Univ. Coll. School, and Downing Coll., Cambridge. Sometime Master of Downing, and Vice-Chancellor of the Univ. of Cambridge. War Work : Served as Volunteer Medical Officer, H.M.S. Hospital Ship "Oxfordshire" ; lent Highfield Hall, Southampton, to British Red Cross for hospital (120 beds), 1914–19. Addresses : Highfield Hall, Southampton ; 50, Russell Square, W.C. 1. Clubs : Athenæum ; Royal Southern Yacht.   (O10629)
HILL, Alfred John, C.B.E., M.I.C.E., M.I.M.E., b. 1862 ; s. of Thomas Hill, of Peterborough ; m. 1892, Margaretta, d. of John Bressey, of Bournemouth. Whitworth Scholar, 1882. Engineer ; Chief Mechanical Engineer, Great Eastern Railway. Address : Pynes, Woodford Green, Essex. Club : Union.
HILL, Capt. Alfred Lyon, O.B.E., M.C., I.A.R.O.
HILL, Alfred Roland, M.B.E.
HILL, Professor Archibald Vivian, O.B.E., M.A., Sc.D., F.R.S. ; m. Margaret Neville, d. of John Neville Keynes, of Cambridge. Educ. : Blundell's School ; Trinity College, Cambridge. Professor of Physiology, Victoria University of Manchester ; Fellow of King's College, Cambridge ; sometime Fellow and Junior Dean of Trinity College, Cambridge ; University Lecturer in Physiology ; H. O. Jones University Lecturer in Physical Chemistry ; Governor of Blundell's School ; Chairman of Old Blundellian Club ; Member of Naval A.A. Gunnery Committee ; Associate Member of Ordnance Committee. War Work : Captain and Bt.-Major, 1st Bn. Cambs. Regt. T.F. ; Director of Anti-Aircraft Experimental Section Munitions Inventions Dept. ; Brevet Major ; Member of A. A. Equipment Committee, Ministry of Munitions ; Member of Air Inventions Committee. Addresses : 45, The Downs, Altrincham, Cheshire ; Trinity College, Cambridge ; King's College, Cambridge.   (O422)
HILL, Lieut. and Qr.-Mr. Arthur, M.B.E.
HILL, Arthur James, M.B.E.
HILL, Charles, M.B.E.   (M10394)
HILL, Lieut.-Col. Charles Henry, C.B.E., b. Aug. 1880 ; s. of Charles Henry Hill, of Southampton, Hants ; m. Francis Marie, d. of Hon. Edward H. Hawkes, of New York, U.S.A. Educ. : Woolstone College, Hants ; Handel College, Southampton, Hants. Banker, Colonial Bank of London, New York Agency. War Work : Oct. 1914 to March, 1916, Lieutenant, Royal Naval Division ; severely wounded at Gallipoli, May, 1915 ; March, 1916, transferred to Army, as Major, 2nd in Command 16th Yorks and Lancaster Regt. ; Dec. 1916, promoted to Lieut.-Col., raised and commanded 16th Battn. Scottish Rifles, Paisley, Scotland ; June, 1918, transferred to command 16th Battn., York and Lancaster Regt., Barnard Castle, Yorks. Address : c/o Colonial Bank of London, 22, William Street, New York, U.S.A.   (C1616)

HILL, Christopher John, O.B.E., B.A., b. 18 Sept. 1870 ; s. of Thomas Rowland Hill, of Broadwater Down, Tunbridge Wells ; m. Hilda Isabel, d. of Milner Moore, of Eastbourne. Educ. : Rugby and Trinity Coll., Cambridge. War Work : Chairman of Shell Band Committee, and Director of Department controlling the whole of the manufactured copper in the country. Address : Warley Mount, Brentwood, Essex. Clubs : New Univ. ; St. Stephen's ; Sports ; M.C.C.   (O10630)
HILL, Edith, O.B.E.
HILL, Capt. Ernest Edward, M.B.E., D.C.M., b. 29 Aug. 1870 ; s. of William Hill, of Littleport ; m. Agnes, d. of George Markall, of Southery. Educ. : Marham School, Norfolk. War Work : Adj. 2/1 Lincolnshire Yeomanry, and Garrison Adj., Canterbury. Address : Aberdeen, York Road, Herne Bay.   (M6654)
HILL, Elizabeth Ann, Mrs., O.B.E.
HILL, Emma Carey, Mrs., M.B.E.
HILL, Lieut.-Col. Francis Robert, C.B.E., T.D., M.B., C.M., b. 1873 ; s. of Laurence Hill, J.P., C.E., of Greenock. Educ. : Loretto. Chief Commissioner of Medical Services, London Region, Ministry of Pensions. War Work : Commanded 2/4th East Lancashire Howitzer Bde. R.F.A., 1915 ; Lieut.-Col. Commanding 331st Brigade R.F.A., 1915 to August, 1917 ; transferred to R.A.M.C., Aug. 1917 ; appointed D.A.D.G., A.M.S., at War Office ; transferred to Ministry of Pensions, April, 1919 ; Commissioner of Medical Services, West Midland Region, (Birmingham) till Jan. 1920, when he was appointed Director of Medical Services at Headquarters, which appointment he relinquished to become Chief Commissioner of the London Region in August, 1920. Address : 2, The Grove, Highgate Road, N.W. 5. Clubs : Caledonian ; Royal Society of Medicine.   (C1617)
HILL, Frank, M.B.E.
HILL, Lieut.-Col. Frank William Rowland, C.M.G., D.S.O., O.B.E., b. 1875 ; m. 1904, Queenie, d. of Col. Moutray Read, formerly of Oriel House, Folkestone. Entered Dorsetshire Regt. 1895 ; Capt. Roy. Fusiliers (City of London Regt.) 1901 ; transferred to Army Ordnance Depart. 1914 ; Brevet Lieut.-Col. 1915 ; Tirah Expedition, 1897–98 (medal with two clasps) ; S. Africa, 1899–1900 (despatches, Queen's medal with five clasps, King's medal with two clasps) ; Great War, 1914–17, as Ordnance Officer (despatches). Address : 30, Bramham Gardens, S.W.5.   (O7278)
HILL, Major Frederick George, O.B.E., b. 17 June, 1878 ; s. of Robert Hill-Littler, of Chichester Park, Belfast. Educ. : Royal Academy, Belfast. Official Assignee, Belfast Local Bankruptcy Court. War Work : O.C. R.G.A., Greypoint Batt., Helen's Bay, Co. Down, from Sept. 1914, to June, 1919 ; selected Military Officer, Belfast, Defences and in charge of Examination Service from Sept. 1914, to April, 1918 ; the Examination Anchorage, Belfast Lough, was one of the chief shelters for ships and convoys until late in 1918 ; responsible for identification and passing in of H.M. ships of all classes to the shipyards and docks for repairs. Address : Ballyvernett House, Bangor, Co. Down. Clubs : United Service ; Royal Ulster Yacht ; Bangor.   (O7278)
HILL, Lieut. Garrington Lewis Watson, M.B.E., R.G.A., S.R.
HILL, Lieut. George Alexander, D.S.O., M.B.E., M.C.
HILL, Major George Bernard, O.B.E., b. 1874 ; s. of James Duke Hill, of Terlings Park, Essex ; m. Frances Grace, d. of J. Heywood Johnstone, M.P., of Bignor Park, Sussex, and Trewithen, Cornwall. Educ. : Repton ; Pembroke College, Cambridge. Member of London Stock Exchange. War Work : Served 4 years in France in M.T., R.A.S.C. ; Commanded Fourth Army Mechanical Transport Company. Address : 37, Draycott Place, S.W. 3. Club : Wellington.   (O1468)
HILL, George Grayson, M.B.E.
HILL, George James, M.B.E., M.A. (Cantab.), F.C.I.S., b. 3 May, 1856 ; s. of Henry Hill, of Croft, Lincolnshire ; m. Emma Eleanor, d. of William Rhodes, of Antigua, West Indies. Educ. : Royal Coll. of Science, and Cambridge Univ. War Work : Hon. Sec. Cambridge War Savings Committee ; Member, Ministry of Labour ; Officers' Appointments Dept. Committee ; Officers' Univ. Mechanical Classes ; Private, 1st Vol. Batt. Cambridgeshire Regiment from May, 1917, to July, 1918. Addresses : 6, Pemberton Terrace, Cambridge ; Peterhouse, Cambridge. Club : Cambridge Union.   (M8471)
HILL, Lieut. Gerald Dudley, O.B.E., R.N.V.R.
HILL, Harry, M.B.E., b. 5 July, 1887. War Work : Executive Officer, Borough of Basingstoke Local Food Control Committee ; Hon. Sec. Church of England Soldiers' Institute ; Hon. Sec. National Service Local Committee ; Joint Hon. Sec. Y.M.C.A. Hut Week Committee. Address : Grove Cottage, Basingstoke.   (M8472)
HILL, Capt. Hedley, O.B.E., Can. A.P.C.
HILL, Helen Ogatha, M.B.E.
HILL, Henry Grenville, M.B.E.   (M10449)
HILL, Major Henry Leonard Gauntlett, O.B.E.
HILL, Major Herbert John, D.S.O., O.B.E.
HILL, Jessie, Mrs., M.B.E.
HILL, Capt. John, O.B.E., R.A.V.C.
HILL, Major John Arthur, O.B.E., R.A.S.C. (T.).
HILL, Capt. John Burrow, O.B.E., M.C., b. 27 Dec. 1885 ; s. of late Edward Burrow Hill, of Bristol ; m. Dorothy Muriel, d. of late Sir Lionel Darell, Bt. of Gloucestershire (see BURKE'S Peerage). Educ. : Winchester ; Magdalen College, Oxford. Land Agent ; Partner in firm of Messrs Whatley, Hill & Co., 24, Ryder Street, St. James's. War Work : Bucks Bn.,

Oxford and Bucks L. I. ; Staff Captain, 144 Infy. Bde. *Address :* 6, St. Leonard Terrace, Chelsea. *Club :* Windham. (O2481)

HILL, Major John Edgar, O.B.E., M.A., Oxon., *b.* 17 Aug.1886 ; *s.* of John Cathles Hill, of Highgate, London, N. *Educ. :* Felsted School ; Merton College, Oxford. *Address :* 9, Regent's Court, Hanover Gate, N.W. 1. *Club :* Oxford and Cambridge. (O2906)

HILL, Capt. Ledger Story, M.B.E.

HILL, Major Leslie Rowley, O.B.E., R.F.A., *b.* 28 Dec. 1884 ; *s.* of the late Lieut.-Col. R. R. C. Hill, 31st Foot ; *m.* Eileen Dorothy, *d.* of Col. J. B. Hutchinson, C.S.I., J.P., of Cambridge. *Educ. :* St. Ninians, Moffat, and Wellington. *War Work :* Sept. 1914, to June, 1916, France and Belgium ; Feb. 1917, to end of War, General Staff, War Office. *Address :* Cox & Co. (O8837)

HILL, Major Lionel Edward, O.B.E., M.C., R.E.

HILL, Rear-Adm. Marcus Rowley, C.B.E., *b.* 13 Mar. 1867 ; *s.* of late Rt. Rev. Rowley O. G., *g.s.* of Sir George Hill, 4th Bart. (*see* BURKE'S *Peerage*) ; *m.* Ellen Mabel, *d.* of Rt. Hon. J. W. Mellor, P.C., M.P. Is an officer of the Legion of Honour. *Club :* Naval and Military. (C2270)

HILL, Major Reginald Day Finch, O.B.E., *b.* 19 Jan. 1875 ; *s.* of Thomas Rowland Hill, of Tunbridge Wells ; *m.* Eugenie Marie, *d.* of L. Poudret, of France. *Educ. :* Clifton College. Chartered Accountant. *War Work :* R.A.S.C., Nov. 1914–April, 1919. *Addresses :* 10/12, Copthall Avenue, E.C. 2 ; "Tanagra," Brighton Road, Purley, Surrey. *Club :* City of London. (O2571)

HILL, Capt. Robert, M.B.E.

HILL, Robert, O.B.E.

HILL, Capt. Robert Charles, M.B.E.

HILL, Lieut.-Col. Robert Montague, C.B.E., R.G.A. (S.R.). Served in Great War, 1914–19 ; mentioned in des patches. (C1618)

HILL, Lieut. Thomas Edgar, M.B.E., R.A.S.C., *b.* 26 Jan. 1881 ; *s.* of Thomas Hill, of Moseley, Birmingham ; *m.* Mona Isobel, *d.* of G. A. J. Burr, of Douglas, Isle of Man. *Educ. :* King Edward VI. Grammar School, Birmingham. Cashier, Lloyds Bank, Ltd. (Final Institute of Bankers). *War Work :* Served with 2/5 Gloucesters, in France, 1916 ; with R.A.S.O., France and Belgium, Aug. 1917, to Sept. 1919 ; wounded, Sept. 1918. *Address :* St. Crantock, Wotton-under-Edge. (M4522)

HILL, Lieut.-Col. Thomas Eustace, O.B.E., M.A. (Durham), M.B., B.Sc. (Edin.), R.A.M.C. (V.), *b.* 1865 ; *s.* of Dr. Alfred Hill, F.R.S., of Birmingham ; *m.* Kate, *d.* of Edward Pritchard, of Kingswood, Warwickshire. *Educ. :* King Edward's High School, Birmingham, and Edinburgh University. County Medical Officer of Health, Durham, etc. ; Professor of Public Health, Durham University. *War Work :* Officer Commanding, Durham R.A.M.C. (V.). *Addresses :* Harewood Hill, Darlington ; Shire Hall, Durham. *Clubs :* County Durham ; Royal Societies'. (O1470)

HILL, Major Trevor Montague, O.B.E.

HILL, Lieut.-Col. Walter de Marchot, C.B.E., R.A.M.C., *b.* 12 Feb. 1877 ; *s.* of Major-Gen. William Hill ; *m.* Margaret Ethel, *d.* of Robert Reed, of Bristol. *Educ. :* Blairlodge, Scotland. Adviser in Special Military Surgery, Ministry of Pensions. *War Work :* Lieut. R.A.M.C., Nov. 1914 ; France, 1915, with 82nd Brigade, R.F.A. ; 1916–1918, Lieut.-Col., officer i/c Special Military Surgical Hospital, Shepherd's Bush ; 1918–1920, Assistant Inspector of Special Military Surgery, and Liaison Officer to Ministry of Pensions. *Addresses :* 31, Cadogan Gardens, S.W. ; 80, Grosvenor Street, W. *Club :* Wellington. (C1619)

HILL, Marjorie CROSBIE-, O.B.E.

HILL, Capt. Harold GARDINER-, M.B.E., R.A.F

HILL, Capt. Gerald Arthur SINCLAIR-, O.B.E., R.A.F.

HILL, Amy, Mrs. WOOD-, M.B.E.

HILLARY, Capt. Michael James, D.S.O., O.B.E. Lieut. and T. Capt. Australian Forces ; served in Great War, 1915–19 ; mentioned in despatches. (O6737)

HILLEARY, Major Edward Langdale, O.B.E.

HILLEARY, George Edward, O.B.E.

HILLIAR, Harry William, C.B.E.

HILLIAR, Robert James, M.B.E.

HILLIARD, Gladys Elizabeth Clark, M.B.E., *b.* Oct., 1880 ; *d.* of J. B. Hilliard, of Glasgow. *Educ. :* Glasgow ; Sunderland ; Brussels. Welfare Supt., The United Turkey Red Co., Ltd., Vale of Leven, Dumbartonshire, Scotland. *War Work :* Clothing and Despatch Dept., Glasgow (Scottish Branch British Red Cross Soc.) ; Canteen work in connection with Women's Volunteer Reserve (Glasgow Batt.) ; Lady Supt. Inspection Dept., Ministry of Munitions, Glasgow and West of Scotland Area. *Address :* 32, Athole Gardens, Kelvinside, Glasgow. *Club :* Lady Artists', Glasgow. (M1895)

HILLIARD, Capt. James Joseph, O.B.E., R.A.V.C.

HILLIARD, Robert, M.B.E.

HILLINGDON, Alice Marion, Lady, O.B.E., *b.* 1857 ; 2nd *d.* of 5th Baron Suffield (*see* BURKE'S *Peerage*) ; *m.* Charles William, 2nd Baron Hillingdon (died 1919) (*see* BURKE'S *Peerage*). *War Work :* Red Cross ; Middlesex Agricultural Women's Committee ; War Pensions ; Soldiers' and Sailors' Families Association. *Address :* Vernon House, 6, Park Place, St. James', S.W. 1. (O10633)

HILLKIRK, Evelyn Margaret, M.B.E.

HILLMAN, Capt. George Brown, M.B.E., L.M.S.S.A. (Lond.), L.S.A. (Lond.), R.A.M.C., *b.* 5 July, 1867 ; *s.* of Samuel David Hillman, of Ilkley, Yorkshire ; *m.* Christina

Gordon, *d.* of John Henderson, of Bradford, Yorks. *Educ. :* High School, Ilkley ; Yorkshire Coll. ; Leeds Univ. M.O.H. Whitwood Urban District ; Medical Referee, Ministry of Pensions ; Chairman, Local Medical and Panel Committees for W.R. of Yorkshire ; Chairman, Wakefield Division British Medical Association. *War Work :* Officer in charge " Spinola " and " Hamrun " Military Hospitals at Malta ; Medical Officer, Ledston Hall Auxiliary Hospital, Yorkshire ; Member of Recruiting Medical Boards, Pontefract. *Address :* 3, South Parade, Wakefield, Yorkshire. *Club :* Leeds and County Conservative. (M8475)

HILLS, Lieut.-Col. Charles Edward, O.B.E., R.A.S.C.

HILLS, Capt. Henry, M.B.E., R.E.

HILLS, Isabel Sinton, Mrs., M.B.E., M.A., *b.* 4 March, 1889 ; *d.* of William Thorburn, of Edinburgh ; *m.* Philip Cowlishaw, *s.* of W. A. Hills, M.Inst.M.M., of Barnes, London. *Educ. :* George Watson's Ladies' Coll., Edinburgh ; Edinburgh Univ. ; Women's Institute, Victoria Street, London. Asst. Sec. to the Natural Food Reform Assoc. ; Sec. to Messrs. E. W. Neems & Co., Gracechurch Street, E.C. *War Work :* Personal Assistant to Sir Arthur Dickinson, Chief Financial Adviser to the Controller of Coal Mines. *Address :* Thorhill, Denton, Kent. (M1898

HILLS, Major John Harris, O.B.E., R.A.F.

HILLS, Lieut. Loftus, M.B.E.

HILLS, Lucy, M.B.E., *b.* 1858 ; *d.* of John Hills, of Maidstone. *Educ. :* Privately. *War Work :* Responsible for sending boxes of food to Prisoners of War who belonged to Maidstone ; Hon. Business Manager to the Maidstone and District Central War Work Association ; Egg Controller for Maidstone, for sending eggs to the wounded. *Address :* Rock House, Maidstone. (M8476)

HILLS, Major Reginald Playfair, O.B.E., M.C.

HILLS, Capt. Reginald Thomas, M.B.E., *b.* 19 June, 1876 ; *s.* of Henry Hills, of Warwick ; *m.* Amy Lilian, *d.* of Robert Symington Gold, J.P., of Warwick. *Educ. :* Warwick School. Asst. Director of Education for County of Warwick. *War Work :* Served in France with 2/7th Batt. R. War. Regt. ; invalided Aug. 1916 ; on discharge from hospital, Aug. 1917, appointed to staff of L. S. Dept., Ministry of Munitions ; appointed Director, War Munitions Volunteer Enrolment Subsection of Ministry of Munitions, May, 1918. *Address :* Lane-borough, Leamington Spa. (M8477)

HILLS, Col. Edmond Herbert, GROVE-, C.M.G., C.B.E., *b.* 1 Aug. 1864 ; *s.* of Herbert A. Hills, of High Head Castle, Cumberland ; *m.* Juliet, *d.* of James Spencer-Bell, M.P., of Fawe Park, Keswick. Assumed by deed poll, 28 Oct. 1920, the additional name of Grove. *Educ. :* Winchester ; Royal Military Academy. Colonel, Royal Engineers. *War Work :* Assistant Chief Engineer, Eastern Command. *Address :* Campden Hill, W. 8. *Club :* United Service. (C1620)

HILLYARD, Capt. John William, O.B.E.

HILLYER, Herbert Keys, O.B.E.

HILTON, Evelyn, M.B.E. *War Work :* Hon. Sec., Soldiers' and Sailors' Families Association, Hampstead Division ; Hon. Sec., London War Pensions Committee, Hampstead ; Hon. Agent, Royal Patriotic Fund Corporation, Hampstead. *Address :* 52, Upper Park Road, Hampstead, London, N.W. 3. (M8478)

HILTON, George Grimmer, M.B.E., *b.* 1867 ; *s.* of Alderman George Hilton, of Chelsea ; *m.* Mary, *d.* of Henry Bayley, of Bleadon, Somerset. *Educ. :* City of London and City of Westminster Schools. Manager, Shipping Dept., Merchant's Office. *War Work :* Supervising Clerk, War Office ; Secretary, War Savings Association, M.S 4 T. Branch, War Office ; Treasurer, St. Mark's, Noel Park Institute War Savings Association. *Address :* 149, Lymington Avenue, Wood Green, London, N. (M3721)

HILTON, Mary, M.B.E., *b.* 24 May, 1848 ; *d.* of Capt. Thos. Hilton, of Sole Street, Faversham, Kent. *War Work :* Chiefly Canteen Work at West Station, Canterbury ; working for Blue Cross, horse bandages. *Address :* The Green, St. Stephen's, Canterbury. (M8479)

HILTON, Major R. S., O.B.E.

HINCHLIFFE, Capt. Arthur, M.B.E.

HINCHLIFFE, Robert, M.B.E., M.I.N.A., *b.* 28 July, 1874 ; *s.* of John Hinchliffe, of Newcastle-on-Tyne ; *m.* Elisabeth, *d.* of John T. Dove, of Newcastle-on-Tyne. *Educ. :* Rutherford Coll., Newcastle-on-Tyne. Assistant Naval Architect to Sir W. G. Armstrong, Whitworth & Co., Ltd., Newcastle-on-Tyne ; late Lecturer on Naval Architecture at Armstrong Coll., Univ. of Durham. *War Work :* Construction and repair of warships. (M1901)

HINCHLIFFE, Engineer-Capt., William Fryer, C.B.E. R.N. Served in Great War, 1914–19 ; mentioned in despatches. (C1928)

HINCKS, Capt. Henry, O.B.E., *b.* 10 June, 1879 ; *s.* of late Capt. T. C. Hincks, Royal Berks Regt. *Educ. :* Privately. Served York and Lancaster Militia Regt. during S. African War. *War Work :* Served in France ; appointed, under Ministry of National Service, Controller Profiteering Department. *Addresses :* Easterlands, Wellington, Somerset ; Howser, B.C., Canada. *Club :* Windham. (O3131)

HINCKS, William Edwin, O.B.E.

HIND, Capt. Arthur Mayger, O.B.E.

HIND, Capt. Leslie Glossop, M.B.E., *b.* 3 Jan. 1896 ; *s.* of Robert Anderson Hind, of Cheadle Heath, Cheshire. *Educ. :* Manchester Central High School. Assistant Chief of Police, Midland Railway. *War Work :* Served in France and

Belgium, 1914–20, as D.A.P.M. Railways, British Troops in France and Flanders. *Address:* Cleeve, Cheadle Heath, Cheshire; Glendale, Swinburne Street, Derby. *Club:* Derbyshire Conservative. (M6530)

HIND, Lieut. Norman Sinclair, O.B.E., R.N.V.R.

HIND, Robert William, M.B.E.

HIND, Wilhelmina Maria, Mrs., O.B.E., *b.* 29 May, 1859; *d.* of William Manfield, of Ixworth Thorpe, Bury St. Edmunds; *m.* Wheelton, *s.* of the Rev. W. M. Hind, LL.D., of Honington, Suffolk. *Educ.:* Privately. *War Work:* Vice-Pres. Red Cross Society, Stoke-upon-Trent Division; Hon. Commandant, V.A.D. Staffs 6; Sec. of Ladies' Committee (Stoke Branch), North Staffs Cripples' Aid Society; Initiator and Sec. Stoke upon-Trent Penny Fund from July, 1915, to Feb. 1919, which Fund realised nearly £1000 for Red Cross and Comforts for troops; Chairman and Sec. of Stoke-upon-Trent local Branch of Voluntary Organisation in the County Association of Staffordshire. *Address:* Roxeth House, Stoke-upon-Trent. (O10635)

HINDE, Lieut.-Col. Alfred Buckley, O.B.E., R.A.M.C. (ret.), *b.* 6 Nov. 1862; *s.* of Joshua Bryer Hinde, of Lancaster; *m.* Annie Jacoba, *d.* of Archibald McCallum, of Middelburg, Transvaal. *Educ.:* Elizabeth Coll., Guernsey; Middlesex Hospital, London. District Surgeon, De Lagers Drift, Middelburg; D.S., Carolina. *War Work:* India, N.W. Frontier, 1897, medal and clasp; South Africa, 1899–1902 (medal with five clasps; twice mentioned in despatches); A.D.M.S. German West Africa, Southern Force, 1914–15; O.C. 76th Field Ambulance, 25th Division, France, 1915–17 (mentioned in despatches); O.C. 31st General Hospital and 87th General Hospital (Egypt), 1917–19 (mentioned in despatches). *Address:* Carolina, Transvaal, South Africa. *Clubs:* Junior Naval and Military; Primrose. (O6202)

HINDE, Capt. Harold Montague, O.B.E., R.A.S.C., *b.* 24 Aug. 1895; *s.* of Lieut.-Col. W. H. Hinde, R.E. (ret.). *Educ.:* Blundell's School, and R.M.C., Sandhurst. *War Work:* Embarked with 6th Div. for France, Sept. 1914; invalided home, Aug. 1915; Home Service in Ireland, Jan. to May, 1916; embarked for France, June, 1916; with 30th Div., 1916–17; with Guards Div., M.T. Coy., till Jan. 1919; Hdqrs. 2nd Army and Rhine Army, Dec. 1919. *Club:* The Services. Heathcote, Wellington College, Berks. (O5382)

HINDE, Capt. Henry Thomas Langford, O.B.E.

HINDELL, Lieut. Harold Goodall, M.B.E., R.E.

HINDLEY, Edith Cairns, O.B.E., *d.* of Rev. W. Talbot Hindley. *War Work:* Warden of Bedford and Ingram House (Y.W.C.A.); Area Secretary, Boulogne (Clubs 2, Recreation Huts for the Q.M.A.A.C.). *Address:* 62, Gloucester Place, Portman Square. *Club:* Forum. (O3754)

HINDLEY, Major Frank Lawton, O.B.E., M.R., N.Z.O.F.

HINDLIP, Charles Allsopp, Lord, O.B.E., J.P., D.L., Junior Whip, House of Lords; *b.* 22 Sept. 1877; *s.* of 2nd Baron Hindlip (*see* BURKE'S *Peerage*); *m.* 1904 Agatha, *d.* of the late John C. Thynne. *Educ.:* Trinity Coll., Cambridge. Late Capt. 3rd Batt. Worcestershire Regt.; served in South African War, 1900 (medal, 3 clasps); A.D.C. to late Governor of Victoria; Capt. War Office Staff since Aug. 1914 (despatches). *Address:* Hindlip Hall, Worcester. *Clubs:* Carlton; Turf. (O8838)

HINDMARSH, Col. Edwin Andrew Cuthbert, M.B.E., V.D., F.R.C.S.E., *b.* 25 July, 1865; *s.* of John Hindmarsh; *m.* Mary Dorothea, *d.* of the late Thomas Gott Livingston, Vicar of Addingham, Diocese of Carlisle. *Educ.:* Univ. of Edinburgh. S.M.O., India Defence Force Medical Corps; M.D. 1st Bihar Light Horse; Civil Surgeon, Nuzaffarpur District; Superintendent, Nuzaffarpur Jail. *War Work:* Organised War Gifts Fund in Sept. 1914, acting as Hon. Sec. and Treasurer till 1919; lectured on the war; collected funds for "Our Day." *Address:* Nuzaffarpur, India. *Clubs:* Bengal; Junior Army and Navy; Royal Societies'. (M2762)

HINDMARSH, Capt. Harold Hammond, O.B.E.

HINE, Major Thomas Guy Macaulay, O.B.E., R.A.M.C.

HINE, Major Walter, O.B.E., *b.* 20 Nov. 1889; *s.* of Herbert Hine, of Essex. *Educ.:* Woodside. *War Work:* Served Egypt, Salonica and Constantinople continuously from 1915 to Feb. 1920. *Address:* 42A, Elsham Road, Kensington. (O8695)

HINES, Arthur Sidney, M.B.E.

HINES, Ernest Edward, M.B.E., F.C.I.I., *b.* 22 May, 1871; *s.* of Edward Hines, of Norwich; *m.* Mary Jane, *d.* of William Huddlestone, of Norwich. *Educ.:* King Edward VI. Commercial School, Norwich. Branch Manager, Commercial Union Assurance Co., Ltd., Norwich. *War Work:* Special Police, Commander No. 2 Company (Norwich). *Address:* 439, Unthank Road, Norwich. (M1902)

HINES, Major John Tatham, O.B.E., M.C., R.E.

HINGSTON, Lieut. Alfred, M.B.E., R.A.F.

HINGSTON, Capt. Alfred Joseph, O.B.E., R.E.

HINGSTON, Cicely Lamorna, M.B.E., *b.* 26 Aug. 1894; *d.* of Richard Hingston, of Liskeard, Cornwall. *Educ.:* Ladies' Coll., Cheltenham. *War Work:* Joint Committee V.A.D., proceeded to France 18 Aug. 1915; worked at Boulogne Rest Station (B.R.C.S.), attached to Gas Helmet Repair Depot, Abbeville, from Aug. 1915 to Feb. 1918; seconded to Queen Mary's Army Aux. Corps as Assist. Administrator, June, 1917; attached to Directorate of Ordnance Services, G.H.Q., Feb. 1918, and became Officer in charge, Central Registry at Directorate, April, 1918, till Nov. 1919 (mentioned in despatches).

Addresses: Liskeard, Cornwall; c/o Messrs Lloyds Bank, Ltd., St. James' Street, W. 1. *Club:* V.A.D. Ladies'. (M3133)

HINGSTON, Major Clayton Alexander Frances, O.B.E., I.M.S.

HINKS, Arthur Robert, C.B.E., M.A., F.R.S., Chevalier de l'Ordre de la Couronne (Belgium), *b.* 26 May, 1873; *s.* of Robert Hinks, of London; *m.* Lily Mary; *d.* of Jonathan Packman, of Croydon. *Educ.:* Whitgift Grammar School, Croydon, and Trinity College, Cambridge. Secretary of the Royal Geographical Society, and Gresham Lecturer in Astronomy. *War Work:* Geographical work for the General Staff, especially the 1/Million Map of Europe and the Near East, and the 1/Two Million Map of Africa. *Addresses:* 1, Percy Villas, Campden Hill, W. 8.; The White Cottage, Royston, Herts. (C2680)

HINKS, Lieut. Edward, M.B.E., R.A.V.C.

HINKS, Frederick George, O.B.E.

HINKS, Percy John, O.B.E.

HINKSON, Ernest Augustus, M.B.E.

HINNELL, Joseph Squier, O.B.E., M.D., B.C., B.A. (Cantab.), M.R.C.S. (Eng.), L.S.A. (Lond.), *b.* 16 April, 1862; *s.* of Geo. Jno. Hinnell, of Bury St. Edmunds; *m.* Emma Mary, *d.* of David Scott, of Cambridge. *Educ.:* Bury St. Edmunds Grammar School; Pembroke Coll., Cambridge; St. Thomas' Hospital, London. Senior Hon. Med. Officer, West Suffolk General Hospital, Bury St. Edmunds; Medical Officer and Public Vaccinator, 6th District of Bury St. Edmund's Union. *War Work:* Hon. Surgeon, Ampton Red Cross Hospital. *Address:* 62, Garland Street, Bury St. Edmunds. (O10636)

HINTON, Margaret Searle, M.B.E., *d.* of Thomas James Searle-Hinton, of Boundstone, Farnham. *Educ.:* St. John's, Oxford. *War Work:* Lady Supt. Separation Allowance Dept., Surrey Territorial Force Association, 1915–20. *Club:* Cartwright Gardens. (M8480)

HINTON, Lieut. William Henry, M.B.E., R.F.A.

HIPPISLEY, Major Arthur, O.B.E., late R.A., *b.* 1883; *s.* of Henry Edward Hippisley, J.P., of South Lawn, Ston-Easton; *m.* Cecily Louisa White Crawford, of Wyke Regis. *Educ.:* Wellington College, and R.M.A. *War Work:* France, Sept. 1914, 110 Heavy Battery; Egypt and France, Adjutant, 35 Heavy Artillery Group; Belgium and Italy, Commanding 197 Siege Battery, R.G.A.; Italy, Brigade Major, Heavy Artillery, British Force, in Italy. *Address:* South Lawn, Ston-Easton, nr. Bath. *Club:* Royal Automobile. (O2982)

HIPPISLEY, Comm. Richard John Bayntun, O.B.E., T.D., D.L., R.N.V.R.

HIPWELL, Rev. Richard Senior, O.B.E., M.A., B.D., *b.* 1881; *s.* of the late Abraham Hipwell, of Spring Gardens, Mountrath. *Educ.:* Patrician Brothers Schools, Mountrath; University of the Cape of Good Hope; Trinity Coll., Dublin. Curate-in-Charge of Oldcastle, Co. Meath. *War Work:* Temporary Chaplain to the Forces, 1915–20; served in Dardanelles, France, Egypt and Mesopotamia. *Address:* The Rectory, Oldcastle, Co. Meath. *Club:* Church Imperial, Westminster. (O6639)

HIRD, Frank, O.B.E., *b.* 16 Jan. 1873; *s.* of James Hird, R.N., of Lowmoor. *Educ.:* Privately. Assistant-Editor of the "Guardian." *War Work:* Voluntary service as porter and secretary in two Red Cross Hospitals in Tunbridge Wells. 1914–1916; voluntary service as Commissioner to the Third Army in France, and Assistant Chief Commissioner for France and Belgium, for the Church Army, 1916–1918. *Address:* 20, Redcliffe Gardens, S.W. 10. *Clubs:* Wellington; Odd Volumes. (O1475)

HIRD, Thomas Cullen, M.B.E.

HIRTZEL, Major Clement Henry Armitage, O.B.E., R.A.F.

HISCOX, George, M.B.E. (M10395)

HISLOP, James, O.B.E.

HISLOP, Margaret Mary Annie, M.B.E.

HITCH, Lilian, M.B.E.

HITCHCOCK, Eldred Frederick, C.B.E., Order of St. Stanislau (Russian), Order of the Crown (Belgium); *m.* Ethel May, *d.* of Adolph Lorie, of Horsham Downs, New Zealand. *Educ.:* Burford Grammar School, and Oxford University. Till Nov. 1919, Warden of Toynbee Hall, London. *War Work:* Deputy-Director of Wool Textiles, Department of Surveyor-General of Supply, War Office; Member of Board of Control of Wool Textile Industries, Wool Council, War Trade Department, Export Licences Committee, War Office Clothing Committee, etc.; Assistant Director of Raw Material. *Address:* 62, Cleveland Square, Hyde Park, W. 2. *Club:* Authors'. (C2681)

HITCHCOCK, Howard, O.B.E. (O11980)

HITCHCOCK, Katherine Elizabeth, M.B.E., *b.* 25 June, 1896; *d.* of Brooke Richard Brasier, J.P., of Bally Ellis, Mallow, Co. Cork; *m.* Frank C., *s.* of the Rev. F. R. Montgomery Hitchcock, D.D., of Kinnitty, King's Co. *Educ.:* French School, Bray; Northwood Hall, Hornsey, London. *War Work:* Manageress of the Mallow Free Buffet for Soldiers and Sailors from April, 1915, to Nov. 1918; organised entertainments for wounded soldiers. *Address:* c/o Lieut. F. C. Hitchcock, M.C., 1st Batt. the Leinster Regt., Fort St. George, Madras, India. (M8482)

HITCHCOCK, 2nd Lieut. Lawrence Hiron, M.B.E.

HITCHCOCK, Lieut. Percy Albion, O.B.E., M.C., R.E.

HITCHCOCK, Capt. Richard Howard, M.B.E.

HITCHCOCK, Capt. Roland George, M.B.E.

HITCHCOCK, Thomas Gilbert, O.B.E., *b.* 22 Nov. 1872;

s. of Albert Hitchcock, of Wellington, Somerset ; *m.* Jessie Maud, *d.* of Edward Parnell Vine, of London. *Educ.*: County School, Wellington, Som. *War Work*: Hon. Sec. Publicity Sub-Committee of Manchester War Savings Committtee. (O10637)

HITCHCOCK, Major Harry William Geddes BURNETT-, O.B.E.

HITCHEN, Ann Margaret, Mrs., M.B.E.,

HITCHINGS, Capt. Oswald Thomas, O.B.E.

HITCHON, Witham, M.B.E. *War Work*: Hon. Sec. War Savings Committee and Member of Food Control Committee, Denton ; Hon. Sec., Food Economy Committee. *Address*: 108, Hyde Road, Denton, Manchester. (M8483)

HIVES, Ernest Walter, M.B.E.

HIXSON, Francis William, O.B.E. (O11981)

HOAD, Capt. Lewis, O.B.E.

HOADLEY, Jane, C.B.E., R.R.C. Formerly Matron Queen Alexandra's Imperial Military Nursing Service. (C1621)

HOAR, Eng.-Lieut. Henry Samuel, O.B.E., R.N.

HOARE, Alfred Ernest, O.B.E., J.P., *b.* 29 Mar. 1861 ; *s.* of Francis Hoare, of 5, Buckingham Palace Gardens, S.W., and Cromer, Norfolk (*see* BURKE'S *Landed Gentry*) ; *m.* Edith Gertrude, *d.* of Richard Benyon, of Englefield House, Reading (*see* BURKE'S *Landed Gentry*). *Educ.*: Harrow, and Trinity College, Cambridge. County Councillor, West Suffolk ; J.P., Cambridgeshire and Suffolk. *War Work*: Hon. Secretary and Hon. Treasurer, British Red Cross Society, Suffolk Branch, Bury St. Edmunds. *Address*: Chelsworth Hall, Bildeston, Suffolk. *Clubs*: Boodle's ; County, West and East Suffolk ; Queen's. (O425)

HOARE, Capt. Charles, E., O.B.E. S.A.S.C.

HOARE, Brig.-Gen. Cuthbert Gurney, C.M.G., C.B.E., *b.* 1833 ; Major Indian Army ; Lieut.-Col. R.A.F. ; Brig.-Gen. ; served during Great War, 1914–19 ; mentioned in despatches. (C1896)

HOARE, Daisy, Mrs., M.B.E.

HOARE, Frances Louisa Gurney, M.B.E., ; *s.b.* 1875 of Richard Hoare, of Marden Hill, Hertford. *Educ.*: Privately. *War Work*: Commandant, Officers' Hospital, B.R.C.S., 53, Cadogan Square, S.W. *Addresses*: 40, Halsey Street ; North Cottage, Cromer. (M8487)

HOARE, Lieut.-Col. Francis Richard Gurney, C.B.E., R.A.F. Served in Great War, 1914–19 ; mentioned in despatches. (C863)

HOARE, Major and Brevet Lieut.-Col. Geoffrey Lennard, C.B.E., *b.* 10 April, 1879 ; *s.* of William Hoare, of Summerhill, Benenden, Cranbrook, Kent, late of Iden, Staplehurst. *Educ.*: Eton, and Christ Church, Oxford. Director, Artisans' and General Labourers Dwellings Co., Ltd., Foster and Dicksee, Ltd., Hoare, Gothard, and Bond, Ltd. *War Work*: Major and Brevet Lieut.-Col. Reserve of Officers (Spec. Res. R.F.A.) ; S. Africa, 1900–2 (Queen's Medal with three clasps) ; served in the Great War, 1914–18, General Staff Officer in charge of Economic and Miscellaneous Section of General Staff (directorate of Military Intelligence) ; served on various Government Committees ; awarded C.B.E.,(Mil.) 1918 ; Brevet Lieut.-Col., Chevalier of Legion of Honour. *Address*: Summerhill, Benenden, Cranbrook, Kent. *Club*: Travellers' ; M.C.C.(C520)

HOARE, Major Henry Noel, D.S.O., C.B.E., *b.* R.A.S.C. Served in Great War, 1914–18 ; mentioned in despatches. (O2983)

HOARE, Major Herbert, O.B.E.

HOARE, Margaret, M.B.E., *b.* 3 July, 1856 ; *d.* of John Gurney Hoare, of Cromer, Norfolk, Sidestrand Hall, and the Hill, Hampstead Heath (*see* BURKE'S *Peerage*). *Educ.*: Privately. Commandant, 114 London ; Lady Superintendent, St. John Brigade, N.D. 16 ; Hon. Nursing Sister of the Order of St. John of Jerusalem in London. *War Work*: Commandant, American Hospital, Caen Wood Towers ; Highgate ; Officers' Hostel, Oak Hill Lodge ; New End Military Hospital ; Manor House Hospital. *Address*: North End House, Hampstead Heath. N.W. (M8486)

HOARE, Robert Richard, O.B.E. (O11982)

HOARE, Lieut. Stephen Leonard, O.B.E., R.N.R.

HOARE, William Douro, C.B.E., J.P., M.A., *b.* 1 Aug. 1862 ; *s.* of Richard Hoare ; *m.* Ida Mary Lilian, *d.* of Lachlan Mackintosh Rate, of Milton Court, Dorking. *Educ.*: Winchester, 1875–80 ; Trinity College, Cambridge. Director, Bank of England ; Alliance Assurance ; Deputy Chairman, London and Brazilian Bank. *Addresses*: Gnessens, Welwyn, Herts ; North Lodge, Cromer ; 88, St. James Street, S.W. 1. ; and Pinner's Hut, E.C. 2. (C2682)

HOBART, Lieut.-Col. Claud Vere Cavendish, D.S.O., O.B.E., J.P., D.L., *b.* 1870 ; *o.s.* of Sir Robert Henry Hobart, Bart., K.C.V.O., C.B., of Langdown, Hants (*see* BURKE'S *Peerage*) ; *m.* Violet Verve, M.B.E., *d.* of late John Wylie, of West Cliff Hall, Hants. *Educ.*: Eton and Sandhurst. Retired Army Officer ; served in Grenadier Guards, 1890–1906 ; Commanded Princess Beatrice's I. W. Rifles (8th Bn. The Hampshire Regt.). 1908–1913 ; seconded for service in Uganda Protectorate, 1897–99 ; took part in operations in Naudi country and against Baganda rebels (D.S.O., Medal and clasp, mentioned in despatches) ; on Staff in South African War, 1899–1900, (Queen's Medal and clasp) ; on Staff British Forces in France and Flanders, 1914–19 ; Commandant First Army Railheads, 1915–19 ; three times mentioned in despatches ; O.B.E. (Mil.) ; 1914 Star ; British and Allied Medals. *Addresses*: West Cliff Hall, Hythe, Hants ; Standen House, Isle of Wight. *Club*: Travellers'. (O5384)

HOBART, Major Percy Cleghorn Stanley, D.S.O., O.B.E., M.C., *b.* 1885 ; *s.* of the late R. T. Hobart, I.C.S. *Educ.*: Clifton and R.M.A. Entered R.E. 1904 ; Capt. 1914 ; N.-W. Frontier of India, 1908 (medal with clasp) ; Great War, 1914–1919 as Gen. Staff Officer and Brig.-Maj. (despatches six times). *Club*: Junior Naval and Military. (O6203)

HOBART, Violet Verve, Mrs., M.B.E., *d.* of the late John Wylie, of West Cliff Hall, Hants ; *m.* Lieut.-Col. C. V. C. Hobart, D.S.O., O.B.E., *s.* of Sir R. H. Hobart, Bart, K.C.V.O. C.B., of Langdown, Hants (*see* BURKE'S *Peerage*). Vice-President, British Red Cross Society, Hampshire Branch. *War Work*: Donor and Commandant of West Cliff War Hospital, 1914–19 ; M.B.E. ; Queen Elizabeth Medal. *Addresses*: West Cliff Hall, Hythe, Hants ; Standen House, Isle of Wight. (M546)

HOBBINS, Capt. Thomas Phillips, C.B.E., R.E. Served in Great War, 1914–19, as Capt. and T. Lieut.-Col. ; mentioned in despatches. (C1400)

HOBBS, Herbert, C.B.E., *b.* 11 Oct. 1866 ; *s.* of Henry James Hobbs, of Falcons' Hall, Goldhanger, Essex ; *m.* Octavia Emily, *d.* of Edward Humphreys, of Maldon, Essex. *Educ.*: Bedford County School and privately. *War Work*: 2¼ years Deputy Food Commissioner, Northern Division, Ministry of Food. *Address*: Riding Mill, Northumberland. (O10638)

HOBBS, Irene Decima, M.B.E., B.A., *b.* 13 Aug. 1891 ; *d.* of James Hobbs, of Walton Hall, Felixstowe, Suffolk. *Educ.*: Ipswich High School, and Royal Holloway Coll. *War Work*: Overlooker in Small Arms Factory, Woolwich Arsenal, Sept. 1916, to April, 1917 ; Administrator in Q.M.A.A.C., Boulogne, Etaples, and Calais areas, June, 1917, to Jan. 1920. *Address*: Brampton Grove, Wangford, Suffolk. (M4523)

HOBBS, May Elliot, Mrs., M.B.E.

HOBBS, Major Reginald Arthur, O.B.E.

HOBBS, Walter Edward, O.B.E.

HOBDAY, John William, M.B.E.

HOBDAY, Kingsford George, O.B.E., *b.* 24 Oct. 1864 ; *s.* of Kingsford John Hobday, of Dover ; *m.* Alice Eleanor, *d.* of George Rymer, of Stepney. *Educ.*: Sheerness and London. Registrar of Births, Deaths, and Marriages for Poplar ; Member of Central Unemployed Body for London and Poplar Distress Committee. *War Work*: Hon. Sec. for all Voluntary Work in Poplar Borough in conjunction with the Mayor, 1914–19, including the War Hospital Supply Depot and all Flag Days. *Address*: 141, East India Dock Road, Poplar, E. 14. (O10639)

HOBDEN, Gideon, O.B.E., *b.* 5 Dec. 1872 ; *s.* of Edward Hobden of Ashburnham, Sussex ; *m.* Christina, *d.* of J. Tait, of " Dothan," Scotland. *Educ.*: Battle, Sussex, and Woolwich. Superintendent, The S ilors' Palace, Commercial Road, London. *War Work*: Dealing with the crews of torpedoed sailors in the Port of London, providing food, clothing, housing accommodation and entertainment ; feeding, sleeping, and entertainment of Naval Ratings in the Port of London ; in charge of large air raid shelter for 500 ; arranging work for Sea Scouts during air raids in the Dock Area. *Address*: The Sailors' Palace, 680, Commercial Road. (O3757)

HOBLEY, Alice Mary, Mrs. Charles William, M.B.E.

HOBSON, Arthur John, O.B.E.

HOBSON, Lieut. Bruce, M.B.E., Royal Berks. Regt., *b.* 1892 ; *s.* of Andrew Hobson. *War Work*: Served in France and Belgium, 1914 ; Prisoner of War in Germany 1915 ; served on Salonica Front, 1917–18, and subsequently in South Russia ; T. Capt. 1919 ; decorated for service in Russia. *Address*: 37, Connaught Street, Hyde Park, W. (M7013)

HOBSON, Charles Kenneth, M.B.E.

HOBSON, Dorothy, Mrs., M.B.E.

HOBSON, Rev. Edmund Joseph, O.B.E., *b.* 2 Dec. 1874 ; *s.* of Edmund J. Hobson. *Educ.*: Radcliffe Coll., Leicester ; Italy. Catholic Priest of the Institute of Charity. *War Work*: Army Chaplain, 4th Class, from Sept. 1916, to March, 1919 ; 2 years in Mesopotamia (twice mentioned in despatches). *Address*: St. Maries, Rugby. (O6640)

HOBSON, Hugh George, O.B.E. (O11946)

HOBSON, William Edward, M.B.E.

HOCKADAY, William Thomas, C.B.E.

HOCKING, Francis Almond, M.B.E., B.Sc. (Lond.), *b.* 12 June, 1869 ; *s.* of Francis Almond Hocking, of St. Ives, Cornwall ; *m.* Margaret, *d.* of Joseph Jones, of Cwmavon, South Wales. *Educ.*: Marylebone Grammar School ; King's and University Colleges, London Univ. Pharmaceuist to the London Hospital ; Lecturer on Materia Medica and Pharmacy, London Hospital Medical College ; Consulting Pharmacist to the Evelina and Western Ophthalmic Hospitals, and to the Hospital for Epilepsy, Maida Vale, W. ; Assistant Examiner to the Society of Apothecaries, London. *War Work*: Expert Adviser on Drugs and Chemicals to the Russian Government Committee and to the Russian Red Cross, from Sept. 1915, to May, 1917, in London ; Supply Officer for Drugs, etc., on the staff of the Commission Internationale de Ravitaillement from June, 1917, to March, 1919 ; Chevalier de l'Ordre de la Couronne (Belgium). *Addresses*: 32, Glenshiel Road, Eltham, S.E. 9 ; The London Hospital, Whitechapel, E. (M8489)

HOCKING, R. C., O.B.E.

HOCKING, William John, C.B.E., *b.* 10 Mar. 1864 ; *s.* of William Thomas Hocking ; *m.* Elizabeth Jane, *d.* of William Stokoe. *Educ.*: Privately. Superintendent, Operative Department, Royal Mint, E. 1. *War Work*: Coinage and Medal Work. *Address*: Royal Mint, E. 1. (C521)

HOCKING, William Stanley, M.B.E., *b.* 9 Nov. 1893 ;

s. of William John Hocking, of Royal Mint, London. *Educ.:* St. Olave's Grammar School, Southwark. Actuarial Assistant, Government Actuary's Department. *War Work:* War Trade Statistical Department, 1915–18. *Address:* The Royal Mint, London, E. 1. (M547)

HOCKRIDGE, Alfred George, M.B.E.

HODDER, Henry Charles, O.B.E., *b.* 13 July, 1861 *s.* of John Hodder, of London, England; *m.* Catherine, *d.* of John Fullerton, of London. Commissioner of The Salvation Army, New Zealand. *War Work:* Established Recreation Hutments and Hostels, one Hostel being especially for relatives of departed soldiers. accommodating upwards of 200, and patronised by thousands; raised £150,000 towards the comfort and benefit of men at home and abroad. (O2187)

HODES, Francis Percy, M.B.E.

HODGE, Alfred, M.B.E.

HODGE, John Mackey, D.S.O , O.B.E., R.N.

HODGE, Major Reginald Thomas Keble, O.B.E., *b.* 19 Aug. 1882; *s.* of the late Rev. W. H. Hodge, Vicar of Penwerris, Falmouth; *m.* Helen, *d.* of James A. Kellie, of Elgin, Scotland; and agent of Rohilkund and Kumaon Railway, India *Educ.:* Exeter School. *War Work:* Adjutant 4th D.C.L.I. from Aug. 1914 to Oct. 1916; Commanded 6th Loyal North Lancs. Mesopotamia, from Dec. 1916 until March 1917, during operations before Kut; served with 6th Loyal North Lancs. until end of war. *Address:* Messrs. Cox & Co., 16, Charing Cross, London, E.C. *Club:* Junior Army and Navy. (O6641)

HODGE, Rebecca Prince, M.B.E. *War Work:* The welfare of all Seaforth Highlanders in the field or as prisoners of war and their widows and dependants. *Address:* 1, Strathfillan Road, Edinburgh. (M8493)

HODGE, Lieut. Richard Henry, M.B.E. R.N.

HODGEN, Capt. Gordon West, M.B.E.

HODGENS, Lieut. John, O.B.E., R.N.V.R., *b.* Dec. 1869; *s.* of Edward Hodgens, of St. John's, N.B.; *m.* Katherine Maud, *d.* of Richard Parry Harries, of Kidwelly. *Educ.:* St. Andrew's College, and Lyceé de Coutances (France). Founder and Commodore, Swansea Naval Brigade. *War Work:* Hon. Naval Recruiting Officer for the area of Swansea, Carmarthen, Pembroke, and part of Breconshire; holds the record for one person, having enrolled over ten thousand naval ratings and six hundred boys, Ex-Brigade, during 1914–19. *Address:* South View, Sketty, Swansea. *Club:* Royal Corinthian Yacht. (O426)

HODGES, George Ernest, M.B.E.

HODGES, James Robert, M.B.E., *b.* 22 Aug. 1876; *s.* of James Joseph, of Yeovil, Somerset; *m.* Emma, *d.* of John Whitehead, of Stalybridge. *Educ.:* Forest Hill Coll.; Blankenberghe, Belgium. Deputy Chief Constable, Norwich City. *Address:* 8, Queen's Road, Norwich. (M8494)

HODGKINSON, Capt. Harry Drake, O.B.E., R.A.S.C.

HODGKINSON, Lieut.-Col. Robert Frank Byron, O.B.E., T.D., *b.* 27 March, 1876; *s.* of Robert Hodgkinson, of Newark; *m.* Isabel Freda, *d.* of the Rev. Frederick Vernon Russell, of Balderton, Notts. *Educ.:* Rugby. Solicitor. Registrar of Newark County Court. *War Work:* Mobilised and proceeded to France with 8th Sherwood Foresters (T.F.) (wounded); attached Headquarters, 3rd Line, North Midland Division; commanded 3/8 Sherwood Foresters (T.F.) until amalgamation with new Reserve Unit; President, Quartering Committee, Humber Garrison. *Address:* Trent View House, Mill Gate, Newark-on-Trent. *Club:* Junior Army and Navy. (O7286)

HODGKINSON, Thomas Thorpe, M.B.E., *b.* 30 June, 1874; *s.* of Thomas Clement Hodgkinson, of Melbourne, Victoria. *Educ.:* Rockhampton Grammar School, Queensland, Australia. Engineer. *War Work:* Returning from United States, Nov. 1915, joined temporary staff of Electrical Engineer's Department, Admiralty, initially to supervise work at Mudros; transferred to Invergordon Naval Base, N.B., March, 1916, for duties connected with the electrical equipment of the Repair Depot there, District Defences, and the Mining Bases at Dalmore and Glen Albyn, used by the U.S. Navy for assembly of mines for the Northern Barrage; resigned after termination of hostilities. (M8495)

HODGKINSON, Prof. William Richard, C.B.E., F.R.S.E., Ph.D., *b.* 1851; *s.* of Joseph Hodgkinson, of Hope. *Educ.:* Roy. Gram. Sch., Sheffield, and Roy. Sch. of Mines. Was Assist. Professor at Roy. Coll. of Chemistry; Professor of Chemistry and Metallurgy, Ordnance Coll., Woolwich; has made numerous inventions for War Office. *Address:* 89, Shooter's Hill Road, S.E.3. (C199)

HODGSON, Anthony, M.B.E., *b.* 8 Dec. 1863. Superintendent, Eastern Telegraph Co., Gibraltar. *Address:* Lamorna, South Gibraltar. (M6455)

HODGSON, Arthur John, O.B.E.

HODGSON, Benjamin, O.B.E., M.Sc., Ph.D., *b.* 1 July, 1882; *s.* of John Robson Hodgson, of Hylton; *m.* Margaret, *d.* of George Reay, of South Shields. *Educ.:* Armstrong Coll., Newcastle; Univ. of Göttingen. Lecturer in Physics, Bristol University. *War Work:* Experimental Officer, Signals Experimental Establishment, Woolwich. *Address:* The University, Bristol. (O10642)

HODGSON, Charles Courtenay, O.B.E., *b.* 3 Aug. 1860; *s.* of Rev. George Courtenay Hodgson, of Barton Vicarage, Westmorland. *Educ.:* Pocklington School, Yorkshire; University College, Durham, B.A., Hon. M.A. Oxon. Clerk of the Peace for Cumberland; Clerk of County Council;

Solicitor. *War Work:* Clerk to Appeal Tribunal for Cumberand and Westmorland, and the City of Carlisle, for whole period of its existence. *Addresses:* 1, Devonshire Terrace, Stanwix, Carlisle; The Courts, Carlisle. *Club:* Brooks's. (O427)

HODGSON, Lieut. Charles Edward, M.B.E., R.A.F.

HODGSON, Clement Gaukroger, O.B.E.

HODGSON, Edgar Stanley, O.B.E.

HODGSON, Edward Highton, O.B.E.

HODGSON, Elizabeth Odeyne, Hon. Mrs., O.B.E., *b.* 1861; *d.* of Thomas, 5th Lord Walsingham (*see* BURKE'S *Peerage*); *m.* Francis Henry; *s.* of Sir Arthur Hoagson, of Clopton, Warwickshire (*see* BURKE'S *Peerage*). *War Work:* Assistant Commandant, V.A.D. Hospital, Town Hall, Stratford-on-Avon; Commandant, Clopton War Hospital, Stratford-on-Avon. *Address:* Clopton, Stratford-on-Avon, Warwickshire. (O429)

HODGSON, Lieut.-Col. Greenwood, C.B.E. Capt. and T. Lieut.-Col. on Staff, S. African Forces. (C760)

HODGSON, Henry Michael, O.B.E.

HODGSON, John Alexander, O.B.E

HODGSON, Jonathan Wright, M.B.E.

HODGSON, Joseph Willoughby, O.B.E., M.D.. *b.* 30 March, 1857; *s.* of the Rev. John Willoughby Hodgson. *Educ.:* Brighton Coll.; Guy's Hospital. Radiographer and Electro-therapeutist to the Ministry of Pensions Hospital, Exeter. *War Work:* Special, Electrical Hospital for the Southern Command at Exmouth. (O1477)

HODGSON, Lillie, Mrs., M.B.E.

HODGSON, Malcolm Elliot, O.B.E., *b.* 1 Oct. 1877; *s.* of John Hodgson, of Nocton Hall, Lincoln; *m.* Mary Gwendolen Elizabeth, *d.* of Tom Mitchell, of Upwood, Bingley. *Educ.:* Tettenhall Coll. and abroad. Engineer. *War Work:* Chief Dilution Officer for North-Western area; worker in France for 9 months with the Croix Rouge Francaise. *Address:* Wyndgate, Scarboro'. *Club:* Reform. (O10644)

HODGSON, Comm. Oswald Tylston, O.B.E., R.N.

HODGSON, Capt. Patrick Kickman, O.B.E.

HODGSON, Capt. William Ewart, O.B.E

HODGSON, Capt. William, O.B.E., R.A.F.

HODKINSON, Frederick, M.B.E.

HODKINSON, John Alfred, O.B.E., *b.* 22 Feb. 1853; *s.* of George Hodkinson, of Preston; *m.* Anne, *d.* of George Bramwell, of Stockport. *Educ.:* Isherwood's Private School, Preston. *War Work:* District Goods Manager, Great Central Railway, Sheffield; supervising railway transit of important war material. *Addresses:* Gaythorn, Blyth Road, Worksop; The Cottage, Hutton, Lancashire. (O10645)

HODSDON, Sir James, K.B.E., J.P., M.D., F.R.C.S., *b.* 1858; *s.* of Francis Eve Hodsdon, of Pembroke, Bermuda; *m.* Joan Turnbull, *d.* of William Raffin, Edinburgh. *Educ.:* Sherborne School; Queen's College, Belfast; Edinburgh University. Senior Surgeon, Royal Infirmary, Edinburgh; Senior Lecturer on Clinical Surgery, University of Edinburgh; Member of General Medical Council. *War Work:* Major, R.A.M.C. (T.F.), 2nd Scottish General Hospital; Member of Scottish Medical Service Emergency Committee; Member for Scotland on the National Service Medical Advisory Board; Member of the Medical Advisory Council (Scotland), Ministry of Pensions; Member of Institutional Committee for Scotland, Ministry of Pensions; mentioned in despatches, 28 March, 1919, and 29 August, 1919; awarded C.B.E. (Mil.), dated 3 June, 1919. *Address:* 6, Chester Street, Edinburgh. *Clubs:* University, Edinburgh; Royal Societies'. (K385)

HODSMAN, Henry James, M.B.E., M.Sc., F.I.C., *b.* 24 Oct. 1886; *s.* of Joseph Hodsman, of York; *m.* Emily Muriel, *d.* of Walter Brayshay, of Leeds. *Educ.:* Archbishop Holgate's Grammar School, York; Leeds Univ.; Technical High School, Karlsruhe; La Sorbonne, Paris. Lecturer on Gas Chemistry, Univ., Leeds. *War Work:* Chief Assistant and Deputy of the Deputy Inspector of High Explosives (Leeds Area); in charge of the analysis and testing of tars and berzol produced in the gasworks of the counties of York and Lincoln, for Ministry of Munitions Department of Explosives Supply. *Address:* 2, Norwood Grove, Victoria Road, Headingley, Leeds. (M8497)

HODSON, Col. Frederick Arthur, C.B.E. N. Rhodesia Police. (C1882)

HODSON, Lieut. Leopold Percival, M.B.E.

HODSON, Thomas Stuart, M.B.E. A Deputy Chief Dilution Officer, Labour Supply Dept., Ministry of Munitions (M10258e)

HODSON, Violet, M.B.E., *b.* 1893; *d.* of Henry Algernon Hodson, of 23, Brunswick Square, Hove, Sussex. *Educ.:* Privately. *War Work:* Records Department, Prisoners of War, Dorset Guild of Workers. *Address:* Delphi Cottage, Parkstone, Dorset. (M8498)

HOFFMAN, Emilie, M.B.E., Secretary, Air Ministry Refreshment Club. *Address:* 66D, Prince's Square, W. 2. (M8499)

HOFFMANN, Anne Avery, Mrs., M.B.E., *b.* 1857; *d.* of James Law, of Bradford; *m.* Gustavus Julius James, *s.* of Achior Hoffmann, of Bradford. *Educ.:* Privately, and Versailles. *War Work:* Chairman of Soldiers' and Sailors' Dependents, Ladies' Committee, from Aug. 1914–19; collected privately £1500 for parcels to Prisoners of War and members of H.M. Forces; Member of War Pensions Committee. *Address:* Rookwood, Bradford. *Club:* Bradford Ladies'. (M3725)

HOFMAN, Capt. and Qr.-Mr. Augustus, M.B.E.

HOGAN, Arthur, M.B.E.

HOGAN, Lieut.-Col. Edward Vincent, C.B.E., Can. A.M.C. Med. Corps ; served in Great War, 1916–19 ; mentioned in despatches. (C1352)

HOGAN, Eva, Mrs., M.B.E.

HOGAN, Capt. Thomas, M.B.E., R.E.

HOGARTH, Major Archibald Harvey, C.B.E., D.C.M. Major, R.A.F. ; served in Great War, 1914–19 ; mentioned in despatches. (C2350)

HOGARTH, Frederick W., M.B.E.

HOGARTH, Major Lionel Brewer, O.B.E.

HOGARTH, Robert George, C.B.E., F.R.C.S. (Eng.), b. 18 May, 1868 ; s. of George Hogarth, of Eccles Tofts, Berwickshire ; m. Mabel Winifred, d. of D'Ewes Lynam, of Nottingham. Educ. : Felsted School, and St. Bartholomew's Hospital. Surgeon, General Hospital, Nottingham ; Consulting Surgeon, Childrens' Hospital, Nottingham. War Work : Consulting and Operating Surgeon to the Military Hospitals in and round Nottingham. Clubs : County, Nottingham ; Royal Automobile. (C1154)

HOGARTH, William, O.B.E., b. 9 Feb. 1868. Educ. : Rutherford College, Newcastle-on-Tyne. Civil Servant ; Superintendent, Royal Clarence Yard, Gosport. War Work : Superintendent, H.M. Victualling Yard, Malta ; Member of Control Board, Malta, and of Wheat Board, Malta. Address : Royal Clarence Yard, Gosport. Clubs : Sports ; Royal Albert Yacht (Southsea). (O1479)

HOGARTH, William Anthony, M.B.E.

HOGBEN, Lieut.-Col. George Justice, O.B.E., b. 6 May, 1879 ; s. of the Rev. Geo. Hogben, of Adelaide, S. Australia ; m. Maude Melita, d. of Wm. Bungay, of Cherryville, S. Australia. Educ. : Prince Alfred Coll., Adelaide. Acting Official Sec. to High Commissioner for Australia, London. War Work : Comptroller, A.I.F. Canteens ; General Auditor, A.I.F. Address : Australia House, London. Club : British Empire. (O7957)

HOGG, Lieut.-Col. Alexander Wilson, O.B.E.

HOGG, John Drummond, M.B.E.

HOGG, John Ewer Jefferson, O.B.E., M.A., J.P., D.L., b. 6 July, 1860 ; s. of John Hogg, M.A., J.P., F.R.S., Norton House, Co. Durham (see BURKE'S Landed Gentry) ; m. Lillie Grey, d. of Lieut.-Col. W. Williamson, of Whickham, Co. Durham. Educ. : Bath College ; Magdalen College, Oxford. Barrister-at-Law, Lincoln's Inn ; High Sheriff, Co. Durham, 1903 ; Deputy Lieutenant, Co. Durham ; J.P., Co. Durham, 1888 ; Alderman, and Mayor of Chelsea, 1920. War Work : Military Representative, Chelsea and Kensington ; Assistant Director, National Service, West London Area ; Sub-Inspector, Special Constabulary, "B" Division ; Hon. Secretary, Chelsea War Savings Committee. Address : 59, Elm Park Gardens. Club : Junior Carlton. (O3759)

HOGG, Margaret, C.B.E. Matron of Guy's Hospital. Terr. Force Nursing Service. Principal Matron 4th London General Hospital 1920. (C32)

HOGG, Major Robert Henry, O.B.E.

HOGG, 2nd Lieut. William, M.B.E.

HOILE, Lieut. George Vincent, M.B.E., R.A.

HOILE, William Henry, M.B.E., R.A.F.

HOLBERTON, Edgar Joseph, C.B.E. ; s. of John Ledstone Holberton, of Greenbank, Wordesley, Staffordshire ; m. 1911, Mary Renee, d. of Robert Ramsey Kane, of Dublin. Manager, Bombay-Burma Trading Corporation, Ltd., of Rangoon ; Member of Burma Legislative Council ; Consul for Siam at Rangoon ; Chairman, Burma Chamber of Commerce. Address : Kemendine Lodge, Rangoon, Burma. Club : Wellington. (C1079)

HOLBORN, Paymaster-Lieut. Arthur Savory, O.B.E., R.N.

HOLBROOK, Col. Sir Arthur Richard, K.B.E., V.D., J.P. for Portsmouth, D.L., Hants, M.P., Basingstoke Division of Hampshire, b 1850 ; s. of Richard Holbrook of Southsea ; m. Amelia Mary, d. of Alexander Parks, of Constantinople. Educ. : Portsmouth. President, Portsmouth Chamber of Commerce, 1907–12 ; President, Newspaper Society, 1913–14 ; Member, Admiralty, War Office, and Press Committee ; Fellow Institute of Journalists ; Deputy Prov. Grand Master, Mark Masons, Hampshire and Isle of Wight ; late Lieut.-Col., Commandant and Hon. Colonel, 3rd (Duke of Connaught's Own) Volunteer Battn, The Hampshire Regiment. War Work : Commanded Royal Army Service Corps, Salisbury Plain district 1914–1919. Address : Ashe House, Overton, Hants. Clubs : Constitutional ; Savage ; 1900 ; Unionist ; United. (K82)

HOLBROOK, Lieut.-Col. Claude Vivian, C.B.E.

HOLDEN, Rev. Albert Thomas, C.B.E. Hon. Chap. Australian Forces during Great War, 1915–19 ; mentioned in despatches. (C1842)

HOLDEN, Major Alexander Henry Shuttleworth, O.B.E., R.A.S.C., b. 8 March, 1884 ; s. of the Rev. James Shuttleworth Holden, of Aston-on-Trent ; m. Millicent Jeanie Lathom, d. of the Rev. Robert Charles Lathom Browne, of Hever, Kent. Educ. : Rossall. War Work : Served on the Western Front throughout the war. Address : c/o Sir C. R. McGrigor, Bart., & Co., 39, Panton Street, S.W. Clubs : Junior United Service ; Queen's ; United R.A.S.C. (O8590)

HOLDEN, Edge Anthony, O.B.E. (O11083)

HOLDEN, Major Ernest Frank, M.B.E.

HOLDEN, Ethel Mary, Mrs., M.B.E., b. 14 June, 1868 ; d. of Sir J. Benjamin Stone, of The Grange, Erdington, Warwickshire ; m. Robert Henry, s. of Sir Edward Holden, of Glenelg, Walsall. Educ. : Privately, and Germany. War Work :

Organising Sec. of Walsall B.R.C.S. Depot, and, together with Lady Holden, collected for an ambulance for France ; Member of Soldiers' and Sailors Committee, Rushall, Belgian and Walsall Hospitality to Soldiers' Committee ; Representative for Soldiers' and Sailors' Help Society. Address : Crandels, Walsall. Club : Three Counties', Birmingham. (M3727)

HOLDEN, Lieut. Fred, M.B.E., b. 4 Sept. 1888 ; s. of the late Richard Holden, of Burnley. War Work : Joined Army, Feb. 1915 ; served with R.A.S.C. in Gallipoli, Sept. 1915, to Jan. 1916 ; Egyptian Expeditionary Force, Jan. 1916, to June, 1919. Address : 496, Brunswick Terrace, Prestwich, Manchester. (M3182)

HOLDEN, Lieut. Frederick Morgan, M.B.E.

HOLDEN, John Edward, O.B.E.

HOLDEN, Norman Edward, O.B.E., LL.B., B.A., b. 30 Nov. 1879 ; s. of Sir Edward Holden, Bart. (see BURKE'S Peerage) ; m. Marion, d. of George S. Munro, of Wellington. Educ. : Lycee Condorcet, Paris ; Trinity Hall, Camb. Senior partner in Haes and Sons. War Work : Attached 18th Lancers, Indian Army, Aug. 1914–Jan. 1915 ; Gallipoli with Royal Naval armoured cars ; Deputy Director-General Mechanical Warfare Dept., Ministry of Munitions. Address : 6, Green Street, Park Lane, W. Clubs : Reform ; Cavalry ; Bath. (O430)

HOLDEN, Rev. Philip Giffard, O.B.E., M.A., b. 31 Oct. 1886 ; s. of Rev. A. M. Holden, of Kirkstead ; m. Margaret, d. of F. Rushworth, M.D., of London. Educ. : Coventry and Lincoln College, Oxford. Priest-in-Charge, St. Faith's Church, Parish of Portsea. War Work : Pte. in R.A.M.C., 1915 ; C.F., 1915–1919 to R.A. 2nd Div. ; mentioned in despatches. Address : 18, Wilberforce Road, Southsea. (O5385)

HOLDER, Rev. Albert Thomas, C.B.E., B.A.

HOLDER, Lieut. Alfred Edward, M.B.E., R.A.S.C.

HOLDER, Charles Howard, O.B.E.

HOLDER, Major Stanley Borwood, O.B.E., Aust. A.P.C.

HOLDERNESS, Barry Layton, M.B.E., b. 1877 ; s. of Henry Holderness, of Putney ; m. Emily, d. of F. Teale, of Richmond, Surrey. Educ. : St. John's High School, S.W. General Manager, The Peoples Refreshment House Association, Ltd. War Work : Central Control Board (Liquor Traffic). Club : Eccentric. (M8500)

HOLDFORTH, Harold, O.B.E., F.S.I., b. 26 Aug. 1881 ; s. of Henry Holdforth, of West Hartlepool ; m. Gladys, d. of J. Addison Smith, of Monkseaton, Northumberland. Educ. : Higher Grade School, and Municipal Technical Coll., West Hartlepool. Chartered Surveyor ; held appointments under the Corporations of West Hartlepool and Reading (Berks.), and Easington Rural District Council ; Established Valuer under the Board of Inland Revenue ; Acting District Valuer, Newcastle-upon-Tyne ; Diploma of the Royal Sanitary Institute. War Work : Hon. Sec. Tyneside Scottish Dependants' Aid Committee ; assisted in the recruitment of the Tyneside Scottish Brigade in 1914, and subsequently organised and controlled the machinery for affording relief in want, sickness, and distress of every kind, and the financial and other difficulties, consequent upon some 7000 men joining the colours. Address : 6, Granville Gardens, Jesmond, Newcastle-upon-Tyne ; 4, Mosley Street, Newcastle-upon-Tyne. Club : Valuers'. (O10646)

HOLDICH, Lieut.-Col. Thomas White, O.B.E.

HOLDICH, Capt. William Jeffkins, O.B.E.

HOLDSWORTH, Elizabeth Annie, Mrs., M.B.E.

HOLDSWORTH, Capt. John Evelyn, O.B.E., Reserve of Officers, late of 2nd Dragoon Guards (Queen's Bays), b. 1 May, 1883 ; s. of the late Capt. Walter Holdsworth, of Spring Hall, Halifax, Yorks. ; m. Emily Blanche, d. of Dr. W. H. L. Welchman, of Graaff Reinet, Cape Colony. Educ. : Clifton College, and Sandhurst. War Work : Served for first 18 months with 2nd Res. Regt. of Cavalry at Aldershot, then with Queen's Bays in France ; appointed A.P.M. of 17th Division in France from Sept. 1916 to the end of war. Address : Cavalry Club, Piccadilly, W. 1. Club : Cavalry. (O5387)

HOLDSWORTH, Major John Joseph, O.B.E., A.P.D.

HOLDSWORTH, William Godfrey, M.B.E.

HOLE, Edwin, M.B.E., R.N.

HOLFORD, Capt. Charles Frederick, D.S.O., O.B.E., late R.H.A., b. 2 Sept. 1879 ; s. of Thomas Holford, of Castle Hill, Dorchester ; m. Ursula Isobell, d. of R. C. Corbett, of 3, Cavendish Place, Bath. Educ. : Rugby. War Work : South Africa, 1898–1902 ; Southampton Docks, Embarkation Staff, Aug. 1914, to March, 1919. Address : Bircher Hall, Leominster, Herefordshire. (O7289)

HOLFORD, Lieut.-Col. Sir George Lindsay, K.C.V.O., C.I.E., C.V.O. C.B.E., b. 2nd June, 1860 ; s. of the late Robert Hayner Holford (see BURKE'S Landed Gentry) ; m. 17 July, 1912, Susannah West, e.d. of the late Arthur Wilson, D.L., of Tranby Croft, Yorks., and widow of John Graham Menzies. Late 1st Life Guards ; J.P. Co. Gloucester. Equerry to King Edward VII. 1892–1910, and to Queen Alexandra from 1910; Extra Equerry to King George V. from 1910 ; Esquire of the Order of St. John of Jerusalem in England ; Commander of the Order of Vasa of Sweden with Star. Addresses : Dorchester House, Park Lane, W. ; Weston Birt House, Tetbury. Club : Carlton.

HOLFORD, Mary Eleanor Mrs., Gwynne, C.B.E., b. 16 June, 1864 ; d. of P. R. Gordon Cannery, of Hartpeerz, Gloucester ; m. J. P. W. Gwynn Holford, J.P., D.L., of Buckland (see BURKE'S Landed Gentry). War Work : Initiated the work at Roehampton for supplying artificial limbs to Sailors and Soldiers who lost their limbs in the War. *Address :* Buckland, Bwlch, Breconshire.   (C522)

HOLGATE, Capt. Maurice James, O.B.E., I.M.S., M.B.

HOLLAND, Edith Clara, M.B.E., *b.* 12 June, 1862 ; *d.* of Joseph Holland, Superintendent of Whittingham County Asylum, Preston. *War Work :* Commandant of V.A.D. Cheshire 52, and Cheadle House Red Cross Hospital, Cheshire. *Address :* Cheadle, Cheshire.   (M552)

HOLLAND, Capt. Edgar Stopford, M.B.E.

HOLLAND, Capt. Francis, M.B.E.,

HOLLAND, Capt. Franklin, M.B.E., B.A., LL.B., *b.* 21 Aug., 1881 ; *s.* of Walter Holland, of Carnatic Hall, Liverpool ; *m.* Nancy, *d.* of the Rev. Canon Andrew Knox, of Birkenhead. *Educ. :* Rugby, and King's Coll., Cambridge. Barrister-at-Law. *War Work :* Served in Belgium and France with 10th King's Liverpool Regiment (Liverpool Scottish), 1st Batt. ; and served in England with Reserve Batt. 10th K.L.R. as Adjutant. *Address :* Edge House, Malpas, Cheshire.   (M3273)

HOLLAND, Henry, C.B.E., J.P., *b.* 1859 ; *m.* 1885, Jane, O.B.E., *d.* of — Eastwood. Member of Men's Executive of New Zealand Red Cross Soc. ; has been Mayor of Christchurch, New Zealand, since 1911. *Address :* Christchurch, New Zealand.   (C1995)

HOLLAND, Lieut.-Col. Henry William, D.S.O., O.B.E. Capt. (T.D.) Inns of Court Officers' Training Corps, and a Gen. Staff Officer with rank of Lieut.-Col. during Great War ; mentioned in despatches.   (O2595)

HOLLAND, Lieut.-Col. Henry William, D.S.O., O.B.E., T.D., *b.* 3 Jan., 1875 ; *s.* of Henry Holland, of Montrose. *Educ. :* Westminster. Capt. Inns of Court O.T.C. *War Work :* Attached Gen. Staff, B.E.F. ; subsequently Gen. Staff Officer, 1st Grade G.H.Q., France. *Address :* 28, Bramham Gardens, S.W.5. *Clubs :* Travellers' ; Wellington.   (O2575)

HOLLAND, Jane, Mrs., O.B.E.

HOLLAND, Julia, O.B.E., *b.* 28 Nov. 1873 ; *d.* of the late Rev. F. W. Holland, Vicar of Evesham. Guardian and D.C., Ledbury (Rural). *War Work :* Commandant of Brand Lodge Auxiliary Hospital, Colwall, Malvern, and of V.A.D. Worcester, 32. *Addresses :* Brand Lodge and Old Colwall, near Malvern.   (O431)

HOLLAND, Capt. Kenneth George, O.B.E., late R.A.S.C., *b.* 6 April, 1886 ; *s.* of S. George Holland, of 22A, Sussex Square, London, W. *Educ. :* Rugby, and Univ. Coll., Oxford. *War Work :* Served in R.A.S.C. from July, 1915, to July, 1919 ; service overseas with M.E.F. and E.E.F. from Sept. 1915, to July, 1919. *Address :* 38, Hyde Park Gate, S.W. 7. *Clubs :* Oxford and Cambridge ; Isthmian ; Ranelagh.   (O8628)

HOLLAND, Leonard Duncan, C.B.E., *b.* 16 Jan. 1874 ; *s.* of the late Rev. H. W. Holland ; *m.* Gertrude Mary, *d.* of John Conacher, Railway Manager. *Educ. :* Kingswood School, Bath, and Merton College, Oxford (late Classical Exhibitioner). Appointed to War Office, Oct. 1896 ; a principal clerk since 12 Jan. 1918. *Address :* 1, Gayton Crescent, Hampstead, N.W. 3.   (C2685)

HOLLAND, Mary Blanche, M.B.E., *b.* 19 June, 1862 ; *d.* of Francis Dermot Holland, of Cropthorne Court, Pershore. *Educ. :* Privately. *War Work :* Commandant, No. 14 Worcesters, Pershore Detachment, from 1914 ; inaugurated Work Depot at Pershore ; V.A.D. Nursing, June, 1915, to Dec. 1918 ; Assistant Commandant 2 years, and Commandant 1 year, Glos. 106 Detachment Red Cross at Naunton Park Auxiliary Hospital, Cheltenham, Gloucestershire. *Address :* Cropthorne Court, Pershore, Worcestershire.   (M8501)

HOLLAND, Robert Wolstenholme, O.B.E.

HOLLAND, Lieut. Ronald Morris, O.B.E., R.A.O.C. *y.s.* of the late William Holland of Brookside, Ashton-under-Lyne. Served in the Great War 1914–19.

HOLLAND, Thomas, M.B.E., J.P., *b.* 27 Dec. 1860 ; *s.* of Benjamin Holland, of Wigan ; *m.* Carry, *d.* of John Haigh Lister, of Manchester. *Educ. :* St. James', and Warrington Lane, Wigan. County Borough Councillor, serving on the following Committees : General Purposes, Local Pensions ; Byelaws and Charities, Education, Health, Housing, etc., Maternity and Child Welfare, Sewage Disposal, Fuel and Lighting, etc. ; Chairman of the Wigan Property Owners' Association ; Governor of the Wigan Grammar School, and Wigan and District Mining and Technical College. *War Work :* Hon. Administrator of all Local War Pensions work relating to allowances, adjustments, and payments of all kinds ; Hon. Treas. War Pensions Committee ; Hon. Treas. War Savings Committee ; Hon. Sec. and Treas. Lord Derby's Recruiting Committee, and Soldiers' and Sailors' Families Association ; a member of the Local Tribunal ; served on the following committees : National Service, War Aims, King's Fund, and Local Representation Relief. *Addresses :* Prudential Buildings, Wigan ; 31, Melling Road, Southport. *Club :* Conservative, Wigan.   (M8502)

HOLLAND, Capt. Thomas George, O.B.E., I.A.
HOLLAND, Capt. Theodore Samuel, O.B.E.
HOLLAND, Capt. Vyvyan Beresford, O.B.E., R.F.A.
HOLLAND, Major Wilfred, O.B.E.
HOLLANDER, Ethel Mary, Mrs., M.B.E.
HOLLANDER, John William, M.B.E.
HOLLANDS, Emily Hannah, Mrs., M.B.E.

HOLLEY, Alfred Ewart, O.B.E., *b.* 21 Aug. 1881 ; *s.* of Maurice Holley, of Calne, Wilts ; *m.* Emily, *d.* of Charles Turner, of Hastings. *Educ. :* Calne (Wilts) Grammar School. Chemical Engineer and Works Manager until July with Messrs. Chance and Hurt, Oldbury ; now commencing farming. *War Work :* Works Manager of H.M. Factory, Oldbury ; co-patentee of improved process for manufacturing T.N.T. in large quantities. *Address :* Huxton Grange, Sutton Scotney.   (O432)

HOLLEY, Capt. and Qr.-Mr. George, O.B.E.

HOLLICK, Frank, M.B.E., *b.* 15 April, 1879 ; *s.* of Henry Hollick, of Kenilworth ; *m.* Gladys May, *d.* of C. W. Sydney, of Coventry. *Educ. :* King Henry VIII. Grammar School, Coventry. Inspector of Naval and Military Guns at the works of Messrs. Cammell, Laird & Co., Ltd. *War Work :* Chief Inspecting Engineer of Tank construction for Mechanical Warfare Department, Ministry of Munitions, Eastern Area ; brought out several valuable improvements, and later acted as Divisional Liquidator for Disposal Board. *Addresses :* 88, Hewitt Road, Harringay, London, N. 8 ; 16, Gray's Inn Road, W.C. 1. *Club :* Rotary.   (M8504)

HOLLIDAY, Lieut.-Col. John Cecil Hamilton, O.B.E., I.A.

HOLLIDAY, Major Lionel Brook, O.B.E., T.D., M.F.H., 5th Duke of Wellington's West Riding Regt., *b.* 12 Jan. 1880 ; *s.* of Thomas Holliday, of Lunnclough Hall, Huddersfield. *Educ. :* Uppingham ; Bonn University. Master of the Derwent Foxhounds ; Chairman, L. B. Holliday & Co., Ltd., Aniline Dye Manufacturers, Huddersfield. *War Work :* Served in France with 49th Division ; mentioned in despatches, Sept. 1915 ; territorial decorations ; built and managed two Explosive Factories, making picric acid by new methods ; *Addresses :* Oaklands, Kirkburton, near Huddersfield ; Willersley, Scarborough. *Club :* Badminton.   (O1412)

HOLLIDGE, Lieut. Alec, M.B.E., R.A.S.C. (T.), *b.* 13 Jan. 1892 ; *s.* of Thomas Hollidge, of Hornsey Rise ; *m.* Dorothy Emily Durrant, *d.* of Alfred Francke, of Crouch End. *Educ. :* Tollington Park Coll. Supervisor of the testing department to Studebaker Motors, Ltd., London. *War Work :* Enlisted Artists' Rifles, Sept. 1914 ; Commission, Army Cyclist Corps, Aug. 1915 ; France, April, 1916, to Oct. 1919 ; transferred, 1917, to R.A.S.C., attached R.G.A. and M.T., Workshops. *Address :* 24, Elder Avenue, Crouch End.   (M4524)

HOLLINGDALE, Harold John, M.B.E., *b.* 23 July, 1875 ; *s.* of Eli Hollingdale, of Wivelsfield, Sussex ; *m.* Louisa Caroline, *d.* of Sergt. Thomas John Armstrong, 2nd Batt. Rifle Brigade, "Best Shot in the British Army," 1878–79. *Educ. :* St. John's, Penge, Surrey. Railway Stationmaster, L. B. & S. C. Rly. *War Work :* Control of Seaford Station, Sussex, 1914–20 ; transport arrangements of troops and stores from and to Seaford Military Camp, which was occupied successively by 22nd Division, 36th Ulster Division, West Indian Contingent, London Command Depot, 4th Reserve Infantry Brigade, and finally Canadian Training and Reserve Brigades ; Member of Seaford Local Coal Control Committee. *Address :* Station House, Seaford, Sussex.   (M8505)

HOLLINGS, Nina Augusta-Stracey, Mrs., O.B.E., *b.* 4 March, 1862 ; *d.* of Gen. J. H. Smyth, C.B., J.P., of Frimhurst, Frimley, Surrey ; *m.* Herbert J. B., J.P., D.L., Surrey, *s.* of John Holling, of Wheatly Hall, Yorks., and Watchetts, Frimley. Surrey. *War Work :* Ambulance driving, France, 1915 ; Joint Command of X-Ray Section Italian Front, 1915–17 ; *Addresses :* Watchetts, Frimley, Surrey ; Neuadd, Crickhowell, Brecknockshire. *Clubs :* Ladies' Empire ; Sesame. (O10647)

HOLLINGSWORTH, Howard, C.B.E., *b.* 1871 ; *s.* of Charles Hollingsworth, of Bilston. *Educ. :* St. James' School, Edgbaston, Birmingham, and Taunton School. Commander of the Order of the Crown of Belgium, 1916. *War Work :* Part donor of King Albert's Hospital, No. 1 ; and member of Executive Committee of King Albert's Hospitals ; Advisory Committee, Marylebone ; Pensions Committee, Marylebone. *Addresses :* Briar Clyffe, Lowestoft, and Oxford Street, London. *Club :* Royal Societies'.   (C523)

HOLLINGWORTH, Edward, C.B.E., J.P., *b.* 9 April, 1860 ; *s.* of James Hollingworth, of Dobcross ; *m.* Mary Alice, *d.* of William Radcliffe, Manufacturer, Greenfield. *Educ. :* Huddersfield Collegiate School. Engineer ; Chairman and Managing Director of Hutchinson, Hollingworth & Co., Ltd., Dobcross Loom Works, Dobcross ; Chairman of Directors, Chadwick Machine Co., Ltd., Cleckheaton ; Vice-Chairman, Henry Livesey. Ltd., Blackburn ; Director of Asa Lees & Co., Ltd., Oldham ; Director of the Gledhill-Brook Time Recorders, Ltd., Huddersfield. *War Work :* Chairman of Huddersfield District Munitions Committee, 1915 ; Member of Dr. Addison's Reconstruction Committee ; Chairman of Saddleworth War Agricultural Committee ; Vice-Chairman, Colne Valley Advisory Committee ; Divisional Commander of Special Constabulary ; Plant of Dobcross Works placed at disposal of Government for manufacture of bombs and hand-grenades, gearboxes for special tanks, and other experimental work, mine-sinkers, etc. *Address :* Moordale, Dobcross, Yorks. *Club :* Huddersfield.   (C2686)

HOLLINS, Beatrice Isabel, Mrs., M.B.E., *d.* of Charles Bircham Farnell, of The Elms, Acton Hill, W. ; *m.* Allatt Henry, of the Duke of Cornwall's Light Infantry, *s.* of Sidney Hollins, of Woodbank, nr. Stockport. *Educ. :* Privately. Married, 17 Feb. 1920. *War Work :* Quartermaster and Hon. Secretary of the Charing Cross Free Buffet for Sailors and Soldiers, Charing Cross Station, 1914–1918. *Address :* The Elms, Acton Hill, London, W. (M8049)

HOLLINS, Dora Emily, Lady, O.B.E.

HOLLINS, Edith Blanche, Mrs., O.B.E. *War Work ·* Founder and Organiser of Malvern Red Cross Depot and Comforts for Soldiers, including Recreation Rooms ; Organiser and Head of Malvern Red Cross Work Party, and of Branch of National Egg Collection ; Hon. Sec. Malvern Prisoners' of War Association under Central Committee ; served on the committees of the Red Cross and Order of St. John Hospitals, and the Malvern Urban District Council War Services. (O10648)

HOLLINS, Mary Clare, M.B.E., *b.* 18 June, 1879 ; *d.* of Edwin Francis Hollins, of Liverpool. *Educ. :* Chester Queen's School ; Liverpool High Schools. *War Work :* 4 years with the Y.M.C.A. in Rouen, France. *Address :* c/o Lloyds Bank, Lodge Lane, Liverpool. (M1909)

HOLLINS, Rotha Mary, M.B.E.,

HOLLIS, Alfred Claud, C.M.G., C.B.E., *b.* 12 May, 1874 ; *s.* of the late George Hollis, of West Worthing (formerly of Dartmouth Park, N.W.) ; *m.* Enid Mabel, *d.* of the late Valentine I. R. Longman, C.C., of Highgate. *Educ. :* Privately at Highgate and St. Leonards, and in Switzerland and Germany. Assistant Collector, East Africa Protectorate, 1897 ; Collector, 1900 ; Acting Vice-Consul for German East Africa, 1900–1901 ; Secretary to Administration, E.A.P., 1903 ; Secretary for Native Affairs and M.L.C., 1907–1912 ; Colonial Secretary, Sierra Leone, 1913 ; Secretary to Provisional Administration, German East Africa, 1916 ; Chief Secretary, Tanganyika Territory, 1919 ; Uganda Mutiny, 1897 ; Jubaland Expedition, 1900 ; Nandi Expedition, 1905–6 ; African General Service Medal and 2 clasps. *War Work :* As Secretary to the Provisional Administration of German East Africa assisted in the organisation on British lines of all departments of the administration of the former German Colony. *Address :* Dar-es-Salaam, Tanganyika Territory. *Clubs :* Oriental ; Sports. (C2020)

HOLLIS, John Walter, M.B.E.

HOLLIS, Lieut. Wilfred Norman, M.B.E.

HOLLOND, Henry Arthur, D.S.O., O.B.E., *b.* 14 Oct., 1884 ; *s.* of Edward Hollond, of Great Ashfield House, Bury St. Edmunds, and 5, Norfolk Crescent, London, W. 2. *Educ. :* Rugby ; Trinity Coll., Cambridge. Fellow and Lecturer of Trinity Coll., Cambridge, and Barrister-at-Law. *War Work :* Gazetted Lieut. in the Wessex (Hants.) R.G.A. (T.F.) in Oct. 1914 ; attached to the British Armies in France for duty as Court Martial Officer in Feb. 1916 ; appointed Staff Capt. at General Headquarters, France, in Aug. 1916, D.A.A.G., March, 1917 ; T. Major, March, 1918 ; mentioned in despatches, Dec. 1917, Dec. 1918, and June, 1919. *Address :* Trinity Coll., Cambridge. (O5392)

HOLLOWAY, Arthur Brissenden, M.B.E., *b.* 14 Nov., 1868 ; *s.* of William Henry Holloway, of Ealing ; *m.* Lizzie Frances Evelyn, *d.* of Edwin Mayo, of Basingstoke. *Educ. :* Ealing Coll. Great Western Railway, Principal Clerk, Chief Goods Manager's Office. *War Work :* Railway transport of Heavy Guns, Tanks, and general Munitions of War ; Supply of wagons for, and regulation of, movement of merchandise traffic over Great Western Railway. *Address :* 108, The Avenue, West Ealing. (M8508)

HOLLOWAY, Major Arthur Joseph, O.B.E., R.E.

HOLLOWAY, Arthur William, M.B.E.

HOLLOWAY, Capt. Ernest, O.B.E., R.A.F.

HOLLOWAY, Frank Herbert, M.B.E., *b.* 5 July, 1885 ; *s.* of Thomas Holloway, J.P., of Lavington, Wilts ; *m.* Helen Anne, *d.* of A. C. Bannister, of Bedford. *Educ. :* Queen's College, Taunton ; Crystal Palace School of Engineering. Proprietor Market Lavington Brick, Tile and Pottery Works ; Proprietor of Agricultural, Electrical and Motor Engineering Works. *War Work :* On Technical Staff of Ministry of Munitions and holding rank of Assistant Superintendent Engineer, North West Area. *Address :* Hill Cottage, Littleton Panell, Wilts. *Club :* Royal Automobile. (M553)

HOLLOWAY, Comm. Graham Charles, O.B.E., R.D., R.N.R.

HOLLOWAY, Henrietta Palfrey, Mrs., M.B.E.

HOLLOWAY, Herbert Benjamin, M.B.E., *b.* 9 March, 1881 ; *s.* of Joseph James Holloway, of Bristol ; *m.* Dora, *d.* of Robert Henry Bryans, M.I.E.E., of Sunderland. *Educ. :* St. Augustine's Upper Grade School, Kilburn, N.W. ; King's Coll., Strand. Acting Deputy Cashier, H.M. Dockyard, Invergordon. *War Work :* In charge of Cash Department of H.M. Dockyard, Invergordon, since the Dockyard Establishment was set up in September, 1914. *Address :* Mineral Bank, Saltburn, Invergordon. (M8509)

HOLLOWAY, Major Reginald, M,B.E., R.A.F.

HOLLOWAY, William Henry, O.B.E., *b.* 21 July, 1873 ; *s.* of W. Holloway, of Uley, Glos. ; *m.* Agnes, *d.* of George Waterfield, of Kingsthorpe. *Educ. :* Privately. Proprietor, "Northampton Independent." *War Work :* Founder and Hon. Treas. of the Northamptonshire Regimental Prisoners of War Fund ; Hon. Sec. of Northamptonshire Soldiers' Comforts Fund, and Northamptonshire Volunteer Regt. *Address :* Rosebank, Kingsley Park, Northampton. *Clubs :* Northampton ; Masonic, Northampton. (O10649)

HOLLWAY, Edith Blake, O.B.E., M.B., B.S. (Lond.) ; *d.* of William John Holloway, of Pinner. *Educ. :* London School of Medicine for Women, and Royal Free Hospital. *War Work :* Doctor attached Scottish Women's Hospital, Serbia and Corsica, 1914–16 ; and R.A.M.C., Malta, Salonica, Con-

stantinople, 1916–20. *Address :* R.A.M.C., Constantinople. (O8696)

HOLLWAY, Geoffrey Fynes, O.B.E.

HOLMAN, Lieut. Bernard Whelpton, O.B.E., R.E.

HOLMAN, Capt. Joseph Quest, M.B.E., M.C.

HOLMAN, Phyllis, O.B.E.

HOLMDEN, Sir Osborn George, K.B.E., J.P., D.L., London ; *b.* 24 Nov. 1869 ; *s.* of late George Holmden, of Shearnden, Kent ; *m.* 13 Oct. 1897, Mary Mildred, *d.* of John Swanston, of Marshall Meadows, Berwick-on-Tweed. Director of the Inter-Allied Chartering Executive during Great War ; has the Order of St. Olaf of Norway, and is Commander Order of the Crown of Belgium and Officer Legion of Honour. *Address :* Danes Hill, Oxshott, Surrey, *Clubs :* Conservative ; Bath ; City Carlton, and Ranelagh.

HOLME, Major Alfred Siegfried, O.B.E., R.E.

HOLME, T. Lieut. Charles Geoffrey, M.B.E., R.A.S.C.

HOLME, Ernest Rudolph, O.B.E. (O11984)

HOLME, Nellie, Mrs., M.B.E., *b.* 7 Oct. 1871 ; *d.* of the late Col. T. R. Cowie, I.A. ; *m.* Henry Edward, *s.* of Edward V. Holme, late of Naples, Italy. *War Work :* Hon. Sec. Red Cross, Bareilly, U.P., India ; Lady Manager, Monro Soldiers' Canteen, Bareilly. *Address :* Melrose, Hatherley Crescent, Sidcup, Kent. (M7103)

HOLMES, Capt. Alfred Henry Robert, M.B.E., R.E.

HOLMES, Annie Gertrude, Mrs., M.B.E., Hon. Serving Sister of the Order of St. John of Jerusalem, *b.* 18 September, 1861 ; *d.* of W. O. Quibell, J.P., of Newark-on-Trent ; *m.* Henry *s.* of Samuel Henry Holmes, J.P., of Hull. *Educ. :* Miss Janions, Harold House, Bayswater. Lady District Officer, No. VI District, St. John Ambulance Brigade. *War Work :* Organised Royal Naval Hospital, Hull ; County Commandant. Recruiting Commandant for the East Riding Yorkshire. *Address :* The Croft, Newark-on-Trent. (M554)

HOLMES, Lieut. Arthur Ernest, M.B.E., R.A.S.C.

HOLMES, Arthur William, C.B.E., *b.* 1877 ; *m.* 1905, Lottie, *d.* of the late Charles Wood, of Lewes, Sussex. Freeman of City of London ; Partner in the firm of Shipton, Anderson and Co., Grain Merchants, Leadenhall Street ; Director of Contracts, Roy. Commission on Wheat Supplies since 1916 ; appointed a Member of Royal Commission on Wheat Supplies, 1919. *Addresses :* Tytherley North, Surbiton Hill, Surrey ; Stokeley, Bognor, Sussex. *Clubs :* Athenæum, Royal Automobile ; Sports'. (C200)

HOLMES, Major Barnard, O.B.E., R.A.M.C., *b.* 31st July, 1876 ; *s.* of James Holmes, of Burnley ; *m.* Jane Alice, *d.* of John James Ashworth, of Burnley. *Educ. :* Fulledge Day School, Burnley, Lancs. Served in the R.A.M.C. from Sept. 1896 ; South Africa, 1899–1900 ; Malta, Crete, and India *War Work :* On mobilisation was appointed Warrant Officer in charge of the Clothing and Equipment Store at the Depot, R.A.M.C., Aldershot ; October, 1917, was appointed Quartermaster and proceeded to Woolwich for temporary employment in the Army Medical Reserve Store ; July, 1918, proceeded to North Russia as Officer-in-charge No. 15 Base Depot Medical Stores ; was brought to the notice of the Secretary of State for War for valuable services rendered whilst Warrant Officer-in-charge of the Clothing and Equipment Stores Depot, R.A.M.C., Aldershot ; in possession of Medal for Long Service and Good Conduct. *Address :* 3, Lark Street, Burnley, Lancashire. (O6813)

HOLMES, Constance Coote, O.B.E., *b.* 1883 ; *d.* of John S. Holmes, of Roborough, Barnstaple, formerly of Matahiwi, Masterton, Wellington, New Zealand. *Educ. :* New Zealand ; England ; Heidelberg, Germany. *War Work :* Organising Hon. Secretary to Belgian Refugee Food Fund, 1914–1915, (received Medal of Queen Elizabeth) ; Lady Welfare Inspector Army Pay Offices Female Staff, Jan. 1916–May, 1920. *Address :* Roborough, Barnstaple, N. Devon. *Club :* Forum. (O433)

HOLMES, Lieut. Dan Campbell, O.B.E.

HOLMES, Elsie May, M.B.E. (M10396)

HOLMES, Lieut.-Col. Gerard Robert Addison, C.M.G., O.B.E., D.Sc., *b.* 31 Aug. 1881 ; *s.* of Sir George Holmes, K.C.B., K.C.V.O., of Moycashel, Ireland (*see* BURKE'S *Peerage*). *Educ. :* Wellington, and Glasgow Univ Trained as a Naval Architect ; late with the Cunard Steam Ship Co., Ltd., now studying educational maters as a Schoolmaster. *War Work :* served as Lieut., Lieut.-Comm. and Comm. R.N.V.R., with naval forces from 1914–18 ; transferred to Royal Air Force as Lt.-Col. ; served in Cuxhaven Raid 1914, and Belgian Coast ; also Staff Appointments. *Address :* c/o Sir George Holmes, K.C.B., K.C.V.O., St. James' Club, Piccadilly. (O434)

HOLMES, Gertrude Eirene, M.B.E. South African Military Nursing Service. (M10258f)

HOLMES, Lieut.-Col. Gordon Morgan, C.M.G., C.B.E., M.D., F.R.C.P., B.A., *b.* 1876 ; *s.* of the late Gordon Holmes, of Dellin House, Castle Bellingham, Ireland. *Educ. :* Dublin Univ. Sometime Lieut.-Col. Roy. Army Med. Corps ; Physician to National Hospital for Paralysed and Epileptic ; Assist. Physician to Charing Cross Hospital ; served in Great War, 1914–19 ; mentioned in despatches. *Address :* 101, Harley Street, W. *Club :* Junior Athenæum. (C1268)

HOLMES, Brig.-Gen. Hardress Gilbert, C.M.G., C.B.E., J.P., *b.* 7 July, 1862 ; *s.* of Bassett William Holmes, J.P., D.L., of St. Davids, Nenagh ; *m.* Alice Maude Josephine, *d.* of John Lloyd, of Gloster, King's Co. Joined Yorkshire Regt., 1885 ; served N.W. Frontier, India, 1897–8 (Medal, 2 clasps) ; S. Africa, 1899–1902 ; Commanded M. I. Regt., and a Column (despatches twice, Bt.-Major, Queen's Medal, 5 clasps, King's Medal, 2 clasps), retired, 1908. *War Work:* Rejoined Army August, 1914; Commanded 9th Battn. Yorkshire Regt. and 8th Infantry Brigade in France also a Brigade in England; despatches 5 times, C.M.G., C.B.E., Bt. Lieut.-Colonel and Honorary Brigadier General; J.P., Co. Tipperary, High Sheriff, 1910. *Address:* St. Davids, Nenagh; *Clubs:* Naval and Military; Kildare Street, Dublin.   (C1623)

HOLMES, Henry Burvill, C.B.E., *b.* 1864; *s.* of the late Lieut.-Col. William Burvill Holmes, R.E.; *m.* Mabel de Freyne, *d.* of the late Victor Bertelsen, of the Indian Police. *Educ.:* Gram. School, Reading, and King William's Coll., Isle of Man. Lieut.-Col. and Hon. Col. Indian Defence Force (V.D.); entered Indian State Railway Depart. 1883; Dep. Traffic Sup. 1908; Traffic Sup. 1910; Agent Oudh and Rohilkund Railway, 1914. *Club:* United Service (Calcutta).   (C1080)

HOLMES, Henry Nicholls, O.B.E., F.R.G.S., *b.* 20 Sept. 1879; *s.* of Henry Holmes, of Adelaide, South Australia; *m.* Jeannette Elise, *d.* of the late Adam Knecht, of Dayton, Ohio, U.S.A. *Educ.:* Way College, South Australia. Secretary British National Council, Y.M.C.A. *War Work:* In 1915 organised the Y.M.C.A. with troops of General Botha in German South West Africa at Swakopmund; in 1916–17 in charge of Y.M.C.A. work with 2nd Army in France; in 1918 Field Secretary and Liaison Officer with British Y.M.C.A. France; and 1919 Chief Secretary of British Y.M.C.A. in France. *Address:* c/o Y.M.C.A., 13, Russell Square, London, W.C. 1.   (O1484)

HOLMES, Herbert Thomas, O.B.E., H.M.I., *b.* 6 Jan. 1876. *Educ.:* Merchant Taylors' School, London; St. John's Coll., Cambridge. H.M. Inspector, Technological Branch, Board of Education. *War Work:* Personal Assistant to Sir Glynn West, Controller of Shell Manufacture, Ministry of Munitions; Secretarial Officer, Materials Group, Ministry of Munitions. *Address:* 58, Rotherwick Road, Golders Green, London, N.W. 4.   (O10652)

HOLMES, Horace Gordon, O.B.E., F.C.A., *b.* 14 May, 1889; *s.* of Horace George Holmes, J.P., of Woodville, Brondesbury Park, N.W. 6.; *m.* Violet May, *d.* of Henry Parry, of Portmadoc and Aberystwyth, North Wales. *Educ.:* City of London School. During War held the rank of Honorary Temporary Captain. *War Work:* Assistant Commissioner and Financial Director to the British Red Cross and Order of St. John with the Mesopotamian Expeditionary Force, 1916 to 1918. *Address:* Copps Lodge, Northwood, Middlesex; 33, Paternoster Row, E.C. 4. *Clubs:* (Fellow) Royal Colonial Institute; Northwood Golf.   (O1485)

HOLMES, Major Hubert Jack, M.B.E., M.C.

HOLMES, Paymaster-Comm. John Dickenson, C.B.E., R.N.

HOLMES, Joseph Edward Leo, O.B.E.

HOLMES, Margaret Ann, Mrs., M.B.E.; *d.* of Ross Aldis, of Garstang, Lancashire; *m.* Ernest, *s.* of Henry Holmes, of Kilsby, Rugby. *Educ.:* Blackpool and Scarborough. Joined St. John Ambulance Brigade, 1897. *War Work:* Aug. to Nov. 1914, St. John Warehouse; Nov. to Dec. 1914, Nurse at Naval Hospital, Southend; Jan. to Dec. 1915, in charge of Gift Store, St. John's Warehouse; Jan. to May, 1916; Quartermaster, Lady Dane's Hospital, Southampton; May to Oct. 1916, Devonshire House; Oct. 1916, to July, 1917, No. 2 Red Cross Hospital, Rouen, France; Sept. 1917, to Dec. 1918, Acting Quartermaster, St. John's Depot, Belgrave Square; now working at V.A.D. Headquarters, Commandant of V.A.D. London 298, and Lady Supt. Temple Nursing Div., St. John's Ambulance Brigade. *Address:* 33, Sackville Gardens, Ilford. *Club:* V.A.D. Ladies'.   (M8510)

HOLMES, Major Maurice Gerald, O.B.E., R.A.S.C.

HOLMES, Capt. Reginald Valentine, O.B.E. R.A.S.C.

HOLMES, Lieut. Robert, M.B.E., R.N.

HOLMES, Col. Robert Blake Worsley, O.B.E.

HOLMES, Capt. Samuel Edward, O.B.E., R.A.V.C. (S.R.), *b.* 20 Feb. 1888; *s.* of John Holmes, of Co. Antrim, Ireland. *Educ.:* Ballymena Academy, Co. Antrim, Ireland. Veterinary Surgeon. *War Work:* Veterinary Officer with the 5th Division in France and Italy from August 1914 to May, 1919. *Address:* Warren Road, Reigate, Surrey.   (O2577)

HOLMES, William, O.B.E.   (O12058)

HOLT, Capt. Alec Horace Edward Litton. O.B.E.

HOLT, Constance, M.B.E., *b.* 19 May, 1897; *d.* of Edgar M. Holt, of East Sheen. *War Work:* Clerical work at the Admiralty. *Address:* 21, Richmond Park Road, East Sheen, Surrey.   (M2729)

HOLT, Sir Edward, Bt. C.B.E., *b.* 1850, (*see* BURKE's *Peerage*); *s.* of Joseph Holt, of Manchester; *m.* Elizabeth, *d.* of Joseph Brooks, of Manchester. *Educ.:* Privately. Chairman, Manchester Water Committee, Parliamentray Committee, Board of Overseers and War Pensions Committee. *War Work:* Chairman Manchester Local War Pensions since September, 1914. *Clubs:* Carlton; Clarendon; Constitutional.   (C2687)

HOLT, Edwin Brook, M.B.E., I.M.D.

HOLT, Frederick O.B.E.

HOLT, Frederick Appleby, O.B.E., *b.* May, 1888; *s.* of Edwyn Holt, of Hale, Cheshire; *m.* Rae Vera Franz, *d.* of Sir George Hutchinson, of 55, Pont Street, W., and Lyminster Court, Arundel. *Educ.:* Rugby, and King's Coll., Cambridge. *War Work:* 1916–19, Private Sec. to the Rt. Hon. H. W. Forster, M.P. (now Lord Forster of Lepe), Financial Sec. to the

War Office. *Address:* 28, Brechin Place, S.W. *Club:* Reform.   (O10655)

HOLT, Capt. Frederick William, M.B.E.

HOLT, Gertrude Mary, M.B.E.; *d.* of Vesey Weston Holt. *War Work:* Hon. Sec. to the Chelsea Workrooms and Depot of British Red Cross Society. *Address:* 14, Elm Park Gardens, London, S.W. 10.   (M8511)

HOLT, Lieut.-Col. Harold Edward Sherwin, C.B.E., F.R.C.S., *b.* 1862; *s.* of the late Major Joseph Holt, of Farnborough Grange, Hants; *m.* 1904, Lady Mary Florence Brabazon, *d.* of 12th Earl of Meath (*see* BURKE's *Peerage*). Formerly Major and Hon. Lieut.-Col. Hampshire Yeomanry; Major, attached R.A.F.; an Officer of Crown of Belgium; Lord of the Manor of Farnborough. *Addresses:* The Grange, Farnborough, Hants; Clashnardarroch, Aberdeenshire; *Clubs:* Wellington; Cavalry; Travellers'.   (C864)

HOLT, James Marston, M.B.E.

HOLT, Thomas, O.B.E., *b.* 25 Jan. 1873; *s.* of the late Thomas Holt, of Bolton and Leigh; *m.* Isabella, *d.* of the late Christopher Cook, of Preston and Leigh. *Educ.:* Bedford Church School, and Privately. Solicitor; Town Clerk, Deputy Clerk of the Peace, Clerk, Local Education Authority, and Clerk Old Age Pensions Committee, Winchester. *War Work:* Executive Officer. Local Food Control Committee; Member Recruiting Committee; Winchester Belgian Refugees Committee; Organising Sec. for Repatriation of Belgian Refugees; Member Winchester Soldiers' Club Committee; Clerk to the Local Tribunal, Winchester. *Address:* Westfield, Winchester.   (O10656)

HOLT, Thomas Herbert, O.B.E., *b.* 19 Nov. 1861; *s.* of the late R. B. Holt, of Whitby, Yorks; *m.* Edith Charlotte, *d.* of Walter King, of Frinton-on-Sea. *Educ.:* Fulneck School, Yorkshire. Head of Shipping Office, Crown Agents for the Colonies. *War Work:* Member of Overseas Prize Disposal Committee. *Addresses:* 13, Gt. St. Helens, E.C. 3; Aston, Bishop's Stortford. *Club:* Constitutional.   (O1487)

HOLT, Sir Vesey George Mackenzie, K.B.E., J.P., Kent, *b.* 23 Feb.1854; *s.* of the late Vesey Weston Holt, of Windsor Forest; *m.* Mabel Mary, *d.* of the late Walter Drummond (*see* BURKE's *Peerage*, Perth, E.). *Educ.:* Privately. Senior partner in firm of Holt & Co., Army Agents and Bankers; Chairman, London and Scottish Life Assurance Agency; of Scottish Metropolitan Insurance Co. Ltd.; of Anglo-American Debenture Corporation; and Director of New Zealand Loan and Mercantile Agency Co. *Addresses:* Mount Maseal, Bexley, Kent; 67, Cadogan Place, S.W. *Clubs:* Arthur's; Union.   (K458)

HOLT, Florence Annie, Mrs. LYSTER-, O.B.E.

HOLTON, Surgeon-Lieut. Ernest Charles, O.B.E. R.N

HOLYMAN, Honora, Mrs., M.B.E.   (M10397)

HOLYWOOD, Matthew, M.B.E., R.A.S.C.

HOME, Major George, O.B.E.

HOME, Lieut.-Col. George Archibald Swinton, O.B.E., D.S.O., *b.* 1875; *s.* of the late Rev. R. Home of Swinton, Berwickshire. *Educ.:* Privately. Major, 5th Dragoon Guards (ret.); Lieut.-Col. E. Africa Protectorate Forces; Resident at Soy; served during S. African War, 1899–1902 (Queen's medal with two clasps, King's medal with two clasps); has 2nd class of Order of Leopold of Belgium. *War Work:* Commandant East African Volunteer Forces; later, on Staff of East African Expeditionary Force and King's African Rifles. *Address:* Soy, Kenya Colony. *Clubs:* Cavalry; Naval and Military.   (O4148)

HOME, Col. James Murray, C.B.E. Lieut.-Col. and Hon. Col. R.A.F.; served in Great War, 1914–19; mentioned in despatches.   (C865)

HOME, Col. Robert Elton, C.B.E., D.S.O., *b.* 1869; *s.* of the late Col. Robert Home, C.I.E., R.E.; *m.* 1904, Delphine, *d.* of the late W. J. Etheridge. *Educ.:* Cheltenham Coll. Entered R.A. 1888; Capt. 1898; Major, 1908; Lieut.-Col. 1915; Brevet Col. 1917; served with Waziristan Expedition. 1894–95 (medal with clasp); Tirah Expedition, 1897–98 (medal with clasp); during S. African War, 1899–1902 (despatches three times, Queen's medal with five clasps, King's medal); appointed an Instructor at Ordnance Coll. 1906; Ordnance Officer, 1909; Ch. Instructor, Ordnance Coll. 1913; Comdt. 1918.   (C818)

HOME, Capt. Thomas Nathaniel, O.B.E., K.R.R.C.

HOME, Fleet-Surgeon William Edward, O.B.E., R.N., *b.* 1860. *Educ.:* Rugby; Edinburgh Univ. *War Work:* Major (A. Lieut.-Col.) R.A.M.C. Army Hospital Ships. *Clubs:* Naval and Military; Royal Naval, etc.   (O7291)

HOMER, Lieut.-Col. John Leonard, O.B.E., R.M.A.; *b.* 9 Oct. 1865; *s.* of T. Homer, J.P., of Witchampton, Wimborne, Dorset; *m.* Edith Frances, *d.* of Gen. Sir Henry Tuson, K.C.B., of The Poplars, Surbiton. *Educ.:* Cheltenham College. Assist. Gunnery Instructor, R.M.A., 1892–95; Gunnery Instructor, R.M.A., 1897–1902; Musketry Instructor, R.M.A., 1904–08; served H.M.S. "Swiftsure," 1889–90; H.M.S. "Camperdown," 1896–97; H.M.S. "Hannibal," 1902–4; "Prince George," 1908; "Duncan," 1908–09; "Exmouth," 1909–11; "Victory" (Staff of C.-in-C., Portsmouth), 1912–13; Paymaster, R.M.A., 1913–20. *Address:* Witchampton, Wimborne, Dorset.   (O9553)

HOMER, John Twigg, C.B.E., J.P., D.L. Co. Staffs, *b.* 24 June, 1865; *s.* of Frederick Augustus, J.P., of Sedgley, Staffs. *Educ.:* Wolverhampton Grammar School. Divisional Controller, West Midlands Division, Ministry of Labour; Alderman Staffordshire County Council; Member Staffordshire

Territorial Forces Association. *War Work :* Departmental Recruiting for Territorials. *Address :* Dormston, Sedgley, Staffs. *Club :* County, Stafford. (C2688)

HOMFRAY, Ernest Randolph Popkin, O.B.E., *b.* 12 Sept. 1860 ; *s.* of Charles Jeston Homfray, of Down Lodge, Wandsworth ; *m.* Gertrude Everard, *d.* of Dr. Richard Roe, of Eccles. *Educ.:* Privately. Sec. Appeal Committee, Guy's Hospital, London, S.E. *War Work :* Sec. H.M. Queen Mary's R.N. Hospital, Southend-on-Sea ; Commandant, 43rd Essex V.A.D. *Address :* Uckfield, Sussex. (O10657)

HOMFRAY, Lieut.-Col. John Robert Henry, C.B.E., R.M.A., (retired), *b.* 23 Oct. 1868 ; *s.* of Lieut.-Col. J. R. Mackenzie Homfray, of Indian Army ; *m.* Margaret Emily, *d.* of Captain Bonham Ward Bax, R.N. *Educ.:* R.N. Academy Gosport ; Portsmouth Grammar School. Now Master at Brighton College. *War Work :* 33 years in Royal Marine Artillery ; served in H.M.S. "King George V," 2nd Battle Squadron, Grand Fleet, 4 August, 1914 to 16 January, 1916 ; 2nd in command of R.M. Garrison, Cromarty ; O.C. Royal Marines, British West Indies, 1917–19. *Address :* Brighton College. (C2289)

HONEY, Annie Violet, O.B.E.
HONEY, Capt. William John, O.B.E.,
HONY, Capt. Henry Charles, M.B.E.
HOOD, David Wilson, C.B.E., *b.* 1874 ; *s.* of the late James Hood, J.P., of Lillesleaf, Roxburghshire. *Educ.:* Daniel Stewart's Coll., and Heriot Watt Coll., Edinburgh. Engineer-in-Chief to Trinity House. *Address :* 5, Beech Mansions, West Hampstead. (C983)

HOOD, Georgina, O.B.E.

HOOD, Grosvenor Arthur Alexander, Lieut.-Col. Viscount, O.B.E., *b.* 13 Nov. 1868 ; *s.* of 4th Viscount Hood (*see* BURKE'S *Peerage*) ; *m.* Primrose (who died, 1919), 3rd *d.* of Col. Hon. R. Stapleton Cotton (*see* BURKE'S *Peerage*, Combermere, V). *Educ.:* Eton, and R.M.A., Woolwich. 2nd Lieut. Royal Artillery, Feb. 1887 ; 2nd Lieut. Grenadier Guards, Sept. 1889 ; Lieut. 1893 ; Capt. 1899 ; Major 1905 ; on retired pay, 1907 ; Lieut.-Col. to Command 7th City of London Batt. T.F., 1912 ; retired owing to ill-health, Sept. 1914 ; Staff Officer L. of C. (at home), Oct. 1914 ; Defence Commander (T. Lieut.-Col.), Jan. 1916 ; retired (ill-health), April, 1920, with rank of Lieut.-Col. *War Work :* Commanded 7th City of London Batt., London Regt., Aug. to Sept. 1914 ; Staff Officer (D.A.A.G.), L. of C. (England), Oct. 1914 ; Defence Commander (T. Lieut.-Col.), Jan. 1916 ; Staff Capt., War Office, April, 1918. *Address :* 19, Upper Berkeley Street, London, W. 1. *Clubs :* Guards' ; Turf ; Carlton. (O7292)

HOOD, Joseph, M.B.E., M.A., F.E.I.S., *b.* 18 July, 1872 ; *s.* of William Hood, of Stirling, Scotland ; *m.* Louisa B. Wilson, *d.* of Thomas Wilson, of Douglas, Lanarkshire. *Educ.:* Glasgow Univ. Rector of Academy, Stranraer. *War Work :* Organised War Savings Associations in County of Wigtown, more especially in Schools, and assisted in various ways the Scottish War Savings Committee ; Chairman of Executive of War Savings Committee for Burgh of Stranraer ; Member of Stranraer Burgh Military Tribunal for upwards of 2 years. *Address :* The Rectory, Academy Street, Stranraer. (M8513)

HOOD, Margaret ACLAND-, M.B.E., *d.* of the late Sir A. Acland-Hood, Bt. (*see* BURKE'S *Peerage*). *War Work :* Organised large Central Clubs, Social and Educational, in various industrial towns, for working women and girls, some clubs having a membership of over 1000. *Address :* Erlands, Crondell, Hants. *Club :* The New Century. (M67)

HOOD, Lieut.-Col. Arthur FULLER-ACLAND-, O.B.E.
HOOK, Reginald Myles, M.B.E. (M10249g)
HOOKER, Edith, Mrs., M.B.E., *b.* 18 June, 1872 ; *d.* of Thomas Corsby, of London ; *m.* George Septimus, *s.* of William Thomas Hooker, of Hackney. *Educ.:* Privately. *War Work :* Class Sec., Quartermaster, and Assistant Commandant, Stechford Red Cross V.A.D. Hospital ; helped at Canteen work ; Leader of Sewing Circle for making garments for soldiers . *Address :* Finmarken, Lyttelton Road, Stechford, Birmingham. (M8514)

HOOKER, Lieut. Charles William Ross, O.B.E., R.N V.R.
HOOLEY, Lieut.-Col. Vernon Vavasour, C.B.E., *b.* 15 Mar. 1862 ; *s.* of William Hooley, of Ashton Lodge, Belmont Road, Southampton ; *m.* Mary, *d.* of Lieut.-Col. Thomas Maxwell, of Eshowe, Zululand. *Educ.:* South Hants College ; Privately. Shipping Manager. *War Work :* Formerly Shipping Manager at New York ; fitted out S.S. "Arcadian" and "Caribbean" which conveyed Canadian Troops from Quebec ; came to England, January, 1915 ; joined R.A.S.C. as Lieut. ; served at Deptford, Liverpool, France and Southampton until Nov. 1919. Commanded No. 2 Home Base Supply Dept. R.A.S.C. *Address :* Ashton Lodge, Belmont Road, Southampton. *Club :* United R.A.S.C. (C2121)

HOOPER, Major Alexander Francis Anderson, O.B.E.
HOOPER, Alfred, O.B.E., M.D., *b.* 18 May, 1848 ; *s.* of John Hooper, of Castle Gresley, Derbyshire ; *n.* Helen Louisa, *d.* of William Giles, of London. *Educ.:* Burton-on-Trent Grammar School, and Guy's Hospital. *War Work :* Civil Medical Officer to the Royal Air Force from May, 1917, to May, 1920. *Address :* The Manor House, Thurnby, near Leicester. (O10058)

HOOPER, Barrington, C.B.E.
HOOPER, Charles Stuart, M.B.E., *b.* 11 Aug, 1874 ; *s.* of Joshua Hooper, of Bridestowe, Devon ; *m.* Anne, *d.* of John Myatt, of Ilfracombe, Devon. *Educ.:* All Saints' Choir School, Clifton, Bristol. Assistant Accountant-General,

Ministry of Shipping. *War Work :* At Ministry of Shipping. *Address :* The Corner House, Greenhill, Sutton, Surrey. (M555)

HOOPER, Florence Mary Alice, M.B.E. ; *d.* of Sir Richard Mills, K.C.B., K.C.V.O., of Lindridge, Oxted, Surrey ; *m.* Godfrey, *s.* of George Hooper, of The Cedars, Mitcham Common. *War Work :* Commandant, V.A.D. Sussex 150 ; in charge of Red Cross Auxiliary Hospital, Lindfield, Sussex, from Nov. 1914, to Dec. 1918. *Address :* Lyndhurst, Lindfield, Sussex. (M8515)

HOOPER, Francis William, M.B.E.
HOOPER, Lieut. Geoffroy William Winsmore, O.B.E., R.N.
HOOPER, George Henry James, O.B.E., M.D.
HOOPER, Lieut.-Col. Harry Uppington, C.B.E. Col. R.E. (T.F.) ; served in Great War, 1914–19, in Balkans ; mentioned in despatches. (C1412)
HOOPER, Helen Elizabeth, M.B.E.
HOOPER, Capt. Herbert Ross, M.B.E., R.E.
HOOPER, John, M.B.E., *b.* 16 June, 1882 ; *s.* of Richard Streete Hooper, of London ; *m.* Elsie Angela, *d.* of Charles Vickers, of Enfield, Middlesex. Lecturer (Furniture, L.C.C.), 1903–11 ; Technical Assistant, H.M. Office of Works, 1911–19 ; appointed Deputy Controller, Furniture Section, Disposal Board, March, 1919, and Controller, March, 1920. In charge of special section at H.M. Office of Works, furnishing townships, including Gretna and Queensferry, hostels, hospitals, and furnishing services generally for the Ministry of Munitions, Air Ministry, Admiralty, and Ministry of Pensions. (M817)
HOOPER, Capt. Wallis Dawson, O.B.E.
HOPCRAFT, Capt. Harry Douglas, M.B.E., *b.* 26 Nov. 1892; *s.* of Alfred Hopcraft, of Deddington, Oxon. *Educ.:* Owen's School, Islington, N. *War Work :* Mobilised with 4th Oxf. and Bucks Infty (T.F.), Aug. 1914 ; France and Flanders, March, 1915, to Oct. 1915 ; invalided to England ; joined 4th Res. Batt. Oxf. and Bucks L. Infty ; posted to No. 12 O.C.B., April, 1917 ; Gazetted to 1/4th Oxf. and Bucks L. Infty, Sept. 1917 ; France and Italy, Oct. 1917, to March, 1919. *Address :* Fernleigh, Deddington, Oxon. (M4738)
HOPE, Capt. Arthur Clement, M.B.E., Scots Guards ; *o.s.* of Major Cecil Hope, late Inniskilling Dragoons. Served in the Great War, 1914–19. *Address :* The Deal House, West Lavington, Wilts. (M3183)
HOPE, Major Charles William Menelaus, O.B.E., R.A.M.C.
HOPE, Collingwood, C.B.E., K.C., J.P., D.L., *b.* 10 Nov. 1858 ; *s.* of Thomas Arthur Hope, of Bebington, Cheshire ; *m.* Alice Therese, *d.* of R. N. Dale, of Bromborough, Cheshire. *Educ.:* Rugby ; Oxford. Recorder of Bolton ; Deputy Chairman Quarter Sessions ; Chairman Essex District Wages Committee ; Chairman Agricultural Wages Board ; Chairman Profiteering Appeal Tribunal for Essex. *War Work :* 2 years Essex Territorial Association ; Chairman Military Appeal Tribunal for Essex ; Chairman Midland and S.E. Divisional Council ; Chairman District No. 9, Appointments Department, Ministry of Labour ; Volunteer and Special Constable. *Addresses :* Crix, Hatfield Peverel, Essex. *Club :* Windham. (C201)
HOPE, Edward William, O.B.E., M.D., D.Sc., *b.* 1856 ; *s.* of late R. W. Hope, formerly of War Office ; *m.* Charlotte Rennie, *d.* of John Bowring. of Newfoundland and Liverpool. *Educ.:* Royal School of Mines ; University of Edinburgh. Medical Officer of Health, Liverpool ; Professor of Public Health, University of Liverpool ; late Examiner in the Universities of Belfast, Cambridge, Edinburgh, Liverpool and Manchester. and Royal College of Physicians and Surgeons, London. *War Work :* Major, R.A.M.C. ; serving in connection with Port Sanitation, in regard to transport of Troops, Foodstuffs, etc. *Address :* Crow How, Rydal, Ambleside. *Club :* University, Liverpool. (O1492)
HOPE, Herbert George, M.B.E.
HOPE, John, M.B.E.
HOPE, Sir John Augustus O.B.E. (O7295)
HOPE, John Wilson, C.B.E., *b.* 1856 ; *s.* of William Hope, of Edinburgh ; *m.* Georgina, *d.* of William Lyon, of Edinburgh. *Educ.:* Edinburgh ; Brussels. Manufacturer. *War Work :* Ministries of Munitions, Food Control, and Reconstruction. *Address :* Drylaw, South Woodford, Essex. *Clubs :* British Empire ; Royal West Norfolk, Hunstanton ; Newquay Golf. (C202)
HOPE, Mabel Ellen, Mrs., O.B.E., *b.* 30 March, 1873 ; *d.* of Francis Riddell, J.P., of Cheeseburn Grange, Northumberland ; *m.* James Fitzalan, M.P., J.P. ; *s.* of James Hope Scott, Q.C., of Abbotsford, N B. *Educ.:* Privately. *War Work :* Chairman of the War Huts Committee of the Catholic Women's League, which equipped and ran thirty-five soldiers' Huts and Clubs in England, France, and Germany ; Mrs. Hope was given the Médaille de la Reine Elizabeth for Belgian Refugee work organised by the Catholic Women's League. *Address :* Herons Ghyll, Uckfield, Sussex. *Club :* Ladies' Athenæum. (O10660)
HOPE, Mary, Hon. Lady, O.B.E., *b.* 1877 ; *d.* of Lord Balfour of Burleigh, Kennet. Alloa (*see* BURKE'S *Peerage*) ; *m.* Lieut.-Col. Sir John, Bt., M.P., *s.* of the Rev. Canon Hope, and nephew of Sir Alexander Hope. *Educ.:* Privately. Chairman of Women's Sub-Committee of Edinburgh Labour Employment Committee. *War Work :* On various committees under the Ministry of Labour, dealing with recruiting for women's war services, substitution, re-settlement, and training, in Scotland. *Address :* Pinkie House, Musselburgh. *Club :* Queen's, Edinburgh. (O10661)

HOPE, Brevet Major (T. Lieut.-Col.) Percy Mirehouse, O.B.E., M.S.A., M.Inst., M.C.E., *b.* 17 July, 1886 ; *s.* of Joseph Fearon Hope, of Keswick ; *m.* Constance Maud, *s.* of Thomas William Mark, of Liverpool. *Educ.* : Keswick School ; King's College, London. *War Work* : With 4th Border Regt., Burma, 1914–15 ; Mesopotamia, 1915–18 ; Att. Royal Eng., firstly as o/c water supplies, then Deputy Assistant Director of Works at Baghdad on capture of that city ; then Deputy Assistant Director of Works Baghdad and Advanced Section on the advance beyond Baghdad ; then Assistant Director of Works (Engineer Field Parks), M.E.F. ; then Assistant Director of Works, L. of C., M.E.F., and lastly Assistant Director of Works, G.H.Q., M.E.F. ; Awarded O.B.E. ; Twice mentioned in despatches and promoted Brevet-Major for conspicuous service in the Field. *Addresses* : 39, Brundholme Terrace, Keswick ; 21, Station Road, Keswick. *Club* : Junior Army and Navy.   (O2278)

HOPGOOD, Francis George, M.B.E.

HOPKIN, Capt. Frank, O.B.E., M.R.C.V.S., *b.* July, 1879 ; *s.* of T. Hopkin, of Manchester ; *m.* Frances Shaw, *d.* of T. H. Forgan, of Northwich. *Educ.* : Rydal Mount, Colwyn Bay. Veterinary Surgeon. *War Work* : Joined R.A.V.C. on outbreak of war, Aug. 1914 ; served at home and with the Salonica Forces. *Address* : 15, New Bridge Street, Manchester.
(O6482)

HOPKINS, Charles James William, M.B.E.

HOPKINS, Rev. Father Charles Plomer, C.B.E., O.S.P., *b.* 7 March, 1861 ; *s.* of Charles Hopkins, of Bassein, Burmah. *Educ.* : Falmouth Grammar School ; Osnabrück, Germany. Superior General of the Order of St. Paul ; Hon. Trustee, National Sailors' and Firemen's Union ; Hon. Joint Sec., Sailors' and Firemen's Panel of the National Maritime Board. *War Work* : Co-operation with the Ministry of Shipping in matters appertaining to the *personnel* of the British Mercantile Marine. *Address* : The Priory, St. Mawes, Cornwall. *Club* : Royal Colonial Institute.   (C2690)

HOPKINS, Lieut. Francis Arthur, M.B.E.
HOPKINS, Frederick Friend, M.B.E.
HOPKINS, Major Gilbert Rivers, O.B.E.
HOPKINS, Harry, M.B.E., R.N.
HOPKINS, Harry Sinclair, O.B.E,
HOPKINS, James Francis Gordon, O.B.E. ; has 3rd Class Order of the Nile.
HOPKINS, Lieut. John Boyd, M.B.E.

HOPKINS, Lieut.-Col. Lewis Egerton, D.S.O., O.B.E., R.E., *b.* 1873 ; *s.* of the late Thomas Hopkins, of Limber Grange, Lincoln ; *m.* 1906, Carrie Estoteville, *d.* of Sir Peyton D'Estoteville Skipwith, 10th Bt. (*see* BURKE'S *Peerage*). Served during Great War, 1914–17 ; mentioned in despatches.
(O8487)

HOPKINS, Muriel Margaret, M.B.E., *d.* of J. W. W. Hopkins, M.P., of London. *Educ.* : St. Felix School, Southwold. *War Work* : Aug. 1914, to April, 1915, Local Branch of the Prince of Wales' Fund ; May, 1915, to Nov. 1915, secretarial work at the Westminster Red Cross Divisional Office ; Dec. 1915, to June, 1920, Secretarial work at Convalescent Homes for Officers Dept., B.R.C.S. *Address* : 80, Regent's Park Road, London, N.W. 1.   (M1915)

HOPKINS, Lieut.-Col. Percy Alfred, O.B.E.
HOPKINS, Capt. Raymond Beechey, O.B.E.
HOPKINS, Robert Hemiss Handasyd, O.B.E.
HOPKINS, Thomas, M.B.E., R.N.
HOPKINS, Thomas Edmund, O.B.E., J.P.
HOPKINS, Capt. Thomas Hollis, O.B.E., R.E.
HOPKINSON, Capt. Allen Haigh, M.B.E.
HOPKINSON, Gwendolin Blanche, O.B.E.
HOPKINSON, 2nd Lieut. Harold, M.B.E., R.A.S.C.

HOPKINSON, Col. (Lewa and Pasha Egyptian Army) Henry Charles Barwick, C.M.G., C.B.E., *b.* 6 Nov. 1867 ; *s.* of George Henry Hopkinson, late of Edgeworth Manor, Cirencester, Glos., and of Blanch Isabel Somerset ; *m.* Mabel Frances Lætitia, *d.* of Henry William Parnell 3rd Baron Congleton (*see* BURKE'S *Peerage*). *Educ.* : Winchester. Col., late Seaforth Highlanders ; Director-Gen. of the Municipality, Alexandria. *War Work* : Provost Marshal, D.A.A.G., E.E.F. *Address* : Downton House, Kington, Herefordshire. *Club* : Army and Navy.   (C1381)

HOPKINSON, Capt. Miles Staveley, O.B.E., *b.* 30 April, 1879 ; *s.* of the late George Henry Hopkinson, of Edgeworth Manor, Glos. ; *m.* Ellen Marion, *d.* of Henry Walter, of Ifield, Sussex. *Educ.* : Repton. Stockbroker. *War Work* : Served in France, 1915–17 ; Italy, 1917–19. *Address* : 23, Lansdowne Crescent, W. 11. *Club* : Royal Thames Yacht.   (O6381)

HOPKYNS, William Stenning, O.B.E.
HOPPER, James, M.B.E.
HOPPER, Percy Clarence, M.B.E.
HOPPERTON, 2nd Lieut. Henry Edward, M.B.E., R.E.
HOPPING, Sydney, O.B.E.
HOPPS, Walter, M.B.E.

HOPPS, William George, M.B.E., *b.* 30 April, 1871 ; *s.* of the late Thomas Hopps, of Lurgan, Ireland ; *m.* Eva May, *d.* of the late James Elsey, of Plumstead. *Educ.* : Lurgan Model School, and Privately. War Office Clerk. *War Work* : Employed in Quartermaster-General's Department of the War Office, during the whole period of war. *Address* : 4, Barnard Road, London, S.W. 11.   (M8521)

HOPWOOD, Eleanor Mary, O.B.E.

HOPWOOD, Capt. Geoffrey, C.B.E., R.N., *b.* 1877 ; *s.* of the late Rev. Canon Frank Edward Hopwood. Was Assist.

Director of Mobilisation, Admiralty, 1916–17 ; served in Great War, 1914–19 ; mentioned in despatches.   (C2271)

HORA, Capt. Hansord, M.B.E.
HORAN, Lieut. Preston, M.B.E.
HORDEN, Eva, Mrs., O.B.E.   (O11985)

HORDEN, Florence Julia, Mrs., M.B.E., *d.* of John B. Law, of Leamington Spa. ; *m.* Frederick Pilkington, *s.* of George Horden. *War Work* : Com. of Brynglas Red Cross Hospital, Newport (Mon). *Address* : 21, Bassaleg Road, Newport (Mon).   (M5 0)

HORDERN, Major Anthony, C.B.E., *b.* 1889 ; *s.* of Samuel Hordern, of Sydney, Australia ; *m.* Viola Sydney Bingham. Dep. Commr. Australian Red Cross Soc., Australian Imperial Forces.   (C417)

HORDERN, Rev. Arthur Venables Calveley, C.M.G., C.B.E., *b.* 12 April, 1866 ; *s.* of Rev. J. C. Hordern, late of R.N. ; *m.* Hilda Leigh, *d.* of Rev. F. Slater. *Educ.* : Privately. Retired Chaplain to the Forces, 1st Class ; now Rector of St. Peter's, Adderley, Market Drayton, Salop. *War Work* : Served in the South African War, 1899–1902 (including defence of Ladysmith), 2 Medals, 7 clasps, specially promoted and mentioned in despatches ; Principal Chaplain (Brig.-Gen.) in the campaigns of Gallipoli, Salonica, Sennusi, Egypt and Palestine, 1915–18 ; Asst. Chaplain Gen., Northern Command, 1918 to end of war ; mentioned in despatches 6 times. *Address* : Adderly Rectory, Market Drayton, Salop.   (C624)

HORDERN, Herbert Vivian, M.B.E.   (M10398)
HORDERN, Comm. Lionel Herbert, O.B.E., R.N.

HORE, Alexie, M.B.E., *b.* 29 June, 1882 ; *d.* of Charles, Clavell Hore, of Dulwich, Surrey. *Educ.* : Privately. *War Work* : Temp. Clerk in Officers Casualty Dept. (M.S. 3 Cas.), War Office, from Nov. 1915, to Sept. 1919. *Address* : The Corner House, Dulwich Common, S.E. 21.   (M3732)

HORE, Major Reginald Mitchell, O.B.E., Aust. A.V.C.
HORLICK, Major James Nockells, O.B.E., M.C.
HORN, Lieut. D'Arcy, O.B.E., R.A.S.C.

HORN, Gerald, M.B.E., *b.* 17 Feb. 1882 ; *s.* of the late George Horn, of Kempston, Bedford ; *m.* Marjorie Lilian, *d.* of H. S. Russell, B.Sc., of Hanwell, Middlesex. *Educ.* : Bedford Modern School. *War Work* : Was rejected for Military Service three times in Australia ; came home at own expense, and being rejected in England, entered Ministry of Munitions, in June, 1916 ; made assistant Director of Accounts, Oct. 1917 ; Section Director of Accounts, April, 1918 ; Deputy to Controller Non-Ferrous Raw Materials Dept., July, 1919 ; made Controller and Liquidator Non-Ferrous Raw Materials Dept., Oct. 1919 ; resigned Aug. 1920. *Address* : 2, Northcote Avenue, Ealing, W. 5.   (M8523)

HORN, Capt. Percy Sutherland, O.B.E., R.A.S.C.

HORN, Capt. Robert Victor Galbraith, D.S.O., O.B.E., M.C., *b.* 1886 ; *s.* of John Galbraith Horn (*see* BURKE'S *Peerage*). Capt. and Brevet Major, Royal Scots Fusiliers ; served in Great War, 1914–18 ; mentioned in despatches.   (O7247)

HORN, Major William Herbert Gascoine, O.B.E., R.A.S.C.

HORN, Edith Mabel FREEMAN-, M.B.E., *b.* 2 Oct. 1883 ; *d.* of W. Freeman-Horn, of Streatham. *Educ.* : East Putney High School, and Univ. Coll., London. Artist. *War Work* : British Red Cross Society ; on the Staff of the County of London Branch ; Organising Sec. of Collecting Box Department. *Address* : 27, Grosvenor Place, S.W. 1. *Club* : The Alliance.   (M8522)

HORNBLOWER, George Davis, O.B.E.
HORNBLOWER, William Crothers, O.B.E.

HORNBUCKLE, Thomas, M.B.E., B.Sc., Assoc. M.Inst. E.C. ; *s.* of Thomas Hornbuckle, of Barkestone, Leicestershire. *Educ.* : Univ. Coll., Nottingham. Electrical and works Inspector, Chief Mechanical Engineer's Dept., Midland Railway, Derby. *War Work* : Organising Manufacture of Fuses, Gun Parts, and Renovation of Cartridge Cases. *Addresses* : 6, Huntington Street, Derby ; Barkeston, Bottesford, Nottingham.   (M8524)

HORNBY, Capt. Henry Epton, O.B.E., R.A.V.C.
HORNBY, Anna, Mrs. PHIPPS-, M.B.E.

HORNE, Professor Alexander Robert, O.B.E., B.Sc., F.R.S.E., *b.* 8 March, 1881. *Educ.* : George Heriot's Hospital, Edinburgh. Professor of Engineering, Robert Gordon's Technical Coll., Aberdeen ; Lecturer in Engineering Fieldwork, in the Univ., Aberdeen. *War Work* : Engineer to North East Scotland Board of Management ; Manager, Aberdeen National Shell Factory. *Address* : 374, Gt. Western Road, Aberdeen.
(O10665)

HORNE, Andrew Coutts, M.B.E., J.P.
HORNE, Lieut. Charles Frederick, M.B.E., R.N.R.
HORNE, Col. Edward William, C.M.G., O.B.E.
HORNE, Rev. Edwin de Jersey, O.B.E., R.A.

HORNE, Frederic, O.B.E., J.P., *b.* 1863 ; *s.* of the late Charles Horne, M.A., of Newport, Salop ; *m.* Jean Picken, *d.* of Andrew Thomson, of Shifnal. *Educ.* : Adam's Grammar School, Newport, Salop. District Commissioner, Ministry of Agriculture and Fisheries. *War Work* : Commissioner, Food Production Dept., Board of Agriculture and Fisheries for the Counties of Somerset, Devon, and Cornwall. *Address* : Culloughmore, Exmouth. *Clubs* : Devon and Exeter ; National Liberal ; Farmers'.   (O437)

HORNE, Major Henry Hastings, O.B.E., *b.* 1872 ; *s.* of the late Henry Davidson, son of the late Sir William Horne, Attorney General, of Epping, Herts, and Margaret Hastings, granddaughter of the 11th Earl of Huntingdon (*see* BURKE'S

Peerage); *m.* Gladys, *d.* of Henry T. Toulmin, J.P., D.L., late of Childwickbury, Herts. *Educ.:* Clifton College. Acting Provincial Commissioner, Kenya Colony.· *War Work:* Political officer, att. 2nd Div., East African Campaign; Awarded Military O.B.E.,·for special services rendered on German East and Portuguese East African Borders. *Address:* Secretariat, Kenya Colony. *Club:* Sports. (O2319)

HORNE, Lieut. Henry Spence, O.B.E.

HORNE, John William, O.B.E.

HORNE, Lancelot Worthy, C.B.E., M.V.O., *b.* 8 April, 1875; *s.* of late Octavius Horne. *Educ.:* Shrewsbury. Superintendent of the Line London and North-Western Rly. *War Work:* Railway Transport. *Address:* The Manor House, Cheddington, Bucks. *Club:* Conservative. (C204)

HORNE, Leonard Thomas, C.B.E., *b.* 28 June, 1860; *s.* of Charles Horne, of Newport, Salop; *m.* Mary Fletcher, *d.* of M. I. Whibley, of Cambridge. *Educ.:* Newport Salop Grammar School; St. John's Coll., Cambridge. Late Assistant Sec., General Post Office. *War Work:* During 1916 in charge of the Disabled Soldiers Award Branch of the Ministry of Pensions, Chelsea. *Address:* Fairspeir, Totteridge, Herts. (C203)

HORNE, Marjorie, Mrs. M.B.E.; *d.* of George Miller-Cunningham, of Leithenhopes, Peebleshire (see BURKE'S *Landed Gentry)*; *m.* Edward William, *s.* of Major Horne, of Stirkuke, Caithness. *War Work:* Hon. Sec. Soldiers' and Sailors' Families Association, Caithness. *Address:* Stirkuke, Caithness. *Club:* Sesame. (M8526)

HORNE, Sir Robert Stevenson, P.C., G.B.E., K.C., M.P., General Officer of Crown of Italy, *b.* 28 Feb. 1871; *s.* of Rev. Robert S. Horne, of Stamannan, Stirlingshire. *Educ.:* University of Glasgow (M.A. with First-class Honours: LL.B.). Minister of Labour from Jan. 1919 till March, 1920; now President of Board of Trade. *War Work:* Deputy Director of Agriculture in National Service Dept.; Lieut.-Col. Royal Eng.; Assistant Inspector General of Transportation; Director of Materials at the Admiralty; Director of Labour at the Admiralty; Third Civil Lord and member of the Board of Admiralty *Addresses:* 59, Pall Mall, S.W.; 63, Northumberland Street. Edinburgh. *Clubs:* Carlton; Conservative. (G53)

HORNER, Frances, Lady, O.B.E., 4th *d.* of William Graham, M.P., *m.* Sir John Francis Fortescue Horner, K.C.V.O., J.P., D.L, (see BURKE'S *Peerage).* *Addresses:* Mells, Frome; 16, Lower Berkeley Street. *Club:* Bath. (O3762)

HORNER, Lieut. Harry, M.B.E.

HORNER, Major John FitzLloyd, O.B.E., J.P., *b.* 7 April, 1861; *s.* of John Horner, of Fitz Manor, nr. Shrewsbury; *m.* Maud, *d.* of Major-Gen. Hayward, of Crayford. *Educ.:* Malvern College; Christ Church, Oxford. *War Work:* Infantry Records, No. 4 District; Received thanks of Army Council. *Address:* Fitz Manor, nr. Shrewsbury. (O4275)

HORNIBLOW, Edith Marjory, M.B.E., Q.M.A.A.C.

HORNIBLOW, Emilie Hilda, C.B.E., *b.* 24 June, 1886; *d.* of F. T. Horniblow, of Reading. *Educ.:* Oxford High School for Girls; University College, Reading. Organising Training of unemployed Ex-service women. *War Work:* Deputy Commandant of Women's Legion (Military Cookery Section); after the absorption of this organisation into Q.M.A.A.C. was Area Controller for the Southern Command stationed at Salisbury; in 1918, was made Chief Controller of Q.M.A.A.C. att. to the American Expeditionary Force, and finally Chief Controller of the whole Corps. *Addresses:* 23, Hamilton Road, Reading; 8, Chaucer Mansions, Queen's Club Gardens, W. 14. (C1625)

HORNIBROOK, John Laurence, M.B.E.,

HORNIDGE, Capt. Edward Stewart, O.B.E., R.A.S.C.

HORNSBY, Bertram, C.B.E. Sub-Governor National Bank of the Nile; has 2nd Class Order of the Nile. (C2362)

HORNSBY, Major Frederick Middleton, O.B.E., M.B.E.

HOROBIN, Oliver William, O.B.E.

HORRIDGE, Herbert William, M.B.E.

HORSBRUGH, Florence Gertrude, M.B.E., *b.* 13 Oct., 1889; *d.* of Henry Moncrieff Horsbrugh, of Edinburgh. *Educ.:* St. Hilda's, Folkestone. *War Work:* Supervisor of Lady Lawrence Munition Canteen, Abbeywood, and Ministry of Munitions Canteen, Hotel Victoria; Supervisor of Chelsea National Kitchens. *Address:* 11, Belford Terrace, Edinburgh. (M8528)

HORSBURGH, Lieut.-Comm. Gordon Staveley, O.B.E., R.D., R.N.R.

HORSBURGH, Lambert Gordon, M.B.E.

HORSEY, Ada Noel, Mrs., M.B.E., W.R.N.S.

HORSEY, Lieut.-Comm. Frank Lankester, O.B.E., D.S.C. R.N.

HORSFIELD, Major George William, O.B.E., R.G.A. (T.F.).

HORSFIELD, Capt. James, M.B.E.

HORSFIELD, Robert Lund, M.B.E., *b.* 12 July, 1874; *s.* of Fairbank Horsfield, of Bradford; *m.* Susannah, *d.* of Timothy Lister Fisher, of Bingley, Yorks. *Educ.:* Public Elementary; Private; and Technical Institute, Bradford. General Manager, Cardiff City Tramways; Member of the Institute of Transport. *War Work:* Organising Munition Workers Transport; Sec. Local Advisory Committee No 4 Area Tramways ways (Board of Trade) Committee. *Address:* The Hayes, Cardiff. (M8531)

HORSLEY, Capt. Albert Beresford, C.B.E., F.R.G.S., J.P., *b.* 2 Jan. 1880 ; *s.* of George Horsley, J.P., of West Hartlepool ;

m. Ethel Rose, *d.* of the late Charles Cox, of Bristol. *Educ.:* Leys' School, Cambridge. *War Work:* Sec. to War Office Committee on Reorganisation of Recruiting Services, 1916–17; Deputy Director of Recruiting South Western Region; Deputy Director of Recruiting Wales. *Address:* Bradgate, West Hartlepool. *Club:* Arts. (C2692)

HORSMAN, Ernest George, M.B.E.

HORSTMANN, Gustav Otto Henry, M.B.E., *b.* 10 Feb., 1863; *s.* of Gustav Horstmann, of Bath; *m.* Eleanor Sarah, *d.* of Samuel Tarry, of Bath. *Educ.:* Privately. Engineer and Manufacturer of Automatic Lighting Apparatus and clocks. *War Work:* During the war The Horstmann Gear Co. of which the above is Chairman, was controlled under the Ministry of Munitions for the manufacture of hardened screw, plug, and ring gauges, and carried out the work with conspicuous success. *Address:* Forres, Newbridge Road West, Bath. (M1920)

HORSTMANN, Sidney Adolph, M.B.E.

HORTON, Ernest Charles, O.B.E., *b.* 25 Sept. 1865; *s.* of Benjamin Horton, of Lewisham, Kent; *m.* Ellen Louise, *d.* of George Burls, of Greenwich. *Educ.:* Privately; Margate College. Home Timber Merchant. *War Work:* Hon. Adviser on Home-grown timber matters to Timber Controller. *Address:* Eversleigh, Westerham, Kent. (O3736)

HORTON, Capt. Sydney Charles, O.B.E., *b.* 27 April 1895; *s.* of James Horton, of Whitchurch, Salop. *Educ.:* St. Martin's Grammar School, Scarborough. *War Work:* Served with Q.O. Oxfordshire Hussars, Sept. 1914, to March, 1915; R.A.S.C. March, 1915; Adjt. 7th Div. Train, France and Italy, Aug. 1917, to March, 1919. (O6382)

HORTON, Percy Thomas, O.B.E.

HORTON, Capt. Vernon Grove, M.B.E.

HORWICH, Lieut.-Col. David, O.B.E., S.A.M.C.

HORWOOD, Reuben, M.B.E.

HOSE, Capt. Walter, C.B.E., R.C.N.

HOSKEN, Major Courteney Charles, O.B.E., S.A.S.C.

HOSKEN, Capt. William Leslie, O.B.E.

HOSKING, Major Arthur, M.B.E.

HOSKING, Capt. Cyril William, M.B.E., Aust. A.S.C.

HOSKING, William Samuel Victor, M.B.E.

HOSKINS, Lieut. Wallace Edward, M.B.E., R.E.

HOSKYN, Brevet Lieut.-Col. John, C.B.E., D.S.O., Indian Army. *b.* 20 Dec. 1875; *s.* of Lieut. John T. Hoskyn, R.N.; *m.* Dorothy Mary, who died 1920, *d.* of Ffolliott Powell, of Allercombe, Devon. *War Work:* Staff Employ, India, Sept. 1914 to March, 1916; D.A.Q.M.G., General Headquarters, Mesopotamian Expeditionary Force, March, 1916 to Sept. 1917; A.A. and Q.M.G., 15th Indian Division, Mesopotamia, Sept. 1917 to May, 1918; G.S.O., First Grade, General Dunsterville's Force, Persia, May, 1918 to Oct. 1918; Military Attaché, British Legation, Tehran, Nov. 1918 to date. *Club:* United Services. (C1626)

HOSKYNS, Mabella Harriette Georgina, Mrs., O.B.E.; *d.* of Capt. Thomas Edward Whitby, of Creswell Hall, Stafford; *m.* Henry William Paget, *s.* of Henry William Hoskyns, of North Perrott Manor, Crewkerne, Somerset. Vice-President, Chard District, Somerset Branch, B.R.C.S. *War Work:* District Red Cross Work; District Representative Women's War Agricultural Committee, Somerset. *Address:* North Perrott Manor, Crewkerne, Somerset. *Club:* Ladies' Empire. (O1495)

HOSSACK, Lieut. James Davidson, O.B.E.

HOSTINGS, 2nd Lieut. James Walter, M.B.E., R.A.F.

HOTHERSALL, William Christian, M.B.E.

HOTSON, Capt. John Ernest Buttery, O.B.E.

HOUGH, Edwin Leadam, C.B.E., *b.* 22 Oct. 1852; *s.* of Edwin Hough of Carlisle; *m.* Emma Josephine, *d.* of Joseph Chambers, of Oxford, Lieut.-Col. H.M. Indian Army. *Educ.:* Rossall; Queen's College, Oxon. Late Senior Official Receiver in Bankruptcy, High Court of Justice. *Address:* Kildonan, Enfield. (C2693)

HOUGHTON, Elizabeth, Mrs., M.B.E.

HOUGHTON, Evelyn Francis, M.B.E.

HOUGHTON, Capt. Richard Johnson, O.B.E., B.A., M.A. Oxon., Cheshire Yeo., *b.* 14 June, 1876; *s.* of John Johnson Houghton, of Westwood, Neston, Cheshire; *m.* Margaret who died 1919, *d.* of Sir John Sutherland Harmood Banner, M.P., (see BURKE'S *Peerage).* *Educ.:* Eton; New College, Oxford. Master, Wirral Harriers from 1904. *War Work:* Served with Cheshire Yeomanry, Aug. 1914 to May, 1916, on East Coast and Egypt; Served with Imperial Camel Corps, May, 1916 to June, 1919, Egypt, Sinai, Palestine, and Western Desert. *Address:* Westwood, Neston, Cheshire. *Clubs:* Junior Carlton; Cavendish. (O2097)

HOUGHTON, Lieut. Sydney Charles, O.B.E., R.N.V.R.

HOUGHTON, Walter John, M.B.E.

HOULDSWORTH, Joseph, O.B.E.

HOURSTON, Charles Marshall, O.B.E.

HOURSTON, Margaret Anne, Mrs., O.B.E.; *d.* of James Patience, of Glasgow; *m.* John J. D. Hourston, C.A., J.P., *s.* of the late George Hourston, of Greenock. *Educ.:* High School, Inverness; Kilblain Academy, Greenock. *War Work:* From Aug. 1914, and during war devoted herself to the raising of money by organisation of War Relief Funds, thereby raising over £100,000; organised Italian Red Cross 1918; Scottish Churches Huts, 1917–18; Armenian Refugees, 1917; Jewish Refugees, 1916; Harry Lauder's Fund (Flag-day), 1918; Lewis Naval Disaster Fund, 1919; Toy Fair for Disabled Soldiers' and Sailors', 1915, and Maternity Hospital Flag Day,

1919; organised annually the Central areas of the City for Lifeboat Day, Heather Day, St. Andrews Ambulance Day, Red Cross Day, Y.M.C.A. Day, Limbless Hospital Day, Rose Day, and also acted similarly in the various Flag Days on behalf of Disabled Sailors' and Soldiers' Fund, French, Belgian, Serbian, and Montenegrin Relief Funds, Lord Roberts Memorial Funds, and Jocks' Box Funds; Hon. Treas. British and Foreign Sailors' Society, Ladies Guild, Glasgow Branch, and Vice-President of the National Society for the Prevention of Cruelty to Children. *Address:* Morangie, Larch Road, Dumbreck, Glasgow. (O10670)

HOUSDEN, James Anderson, O.B.E.

HOUSE, Charles Edward George, M.B.E., A.R.C.Sc. (Lond.), A.M.I.A.E., *b.* Sept, 1883; *s.* of John Charles House, of Chatham. *Educ.:* Mathematical School, Rochester; Royal Dockyard School, Chatham; Imperial College of Science and Technology, London. Senior Trade Officer, Dept. of Overseas Trade. *War Work:* Representative of Board of Trade and of Dept. of Overseas Trade, on the Priority Committee of the Ministry of Munitions of War, to advise the Committee as to applications for the supply of raw materials controlled by the Ministry of Munitions required for essential purposes not directly connected with the conduct of the war. *Address:* Beverley, Pollard Road, Whetstone, Middlesex. (M8534)

HOUSTON, Sir Alexander Cruikshank, K.B.E. (1918), C.V.O. (1919), M.B., D.Sc., *b.* 18 Sept. 1865; *s.* of the late Surgeon-Gen. John Houston, of I.M.S.; *m.* Ethel Mary, *d.* of the late William Hartley, of Catterall Hall, Settle. *Educ.:* Harborne Vicarage School; Merchiston Castle School; Edin. Univ. Director of Water Examination, Metropolitan Water Board; Examiner D.P.H. (Chemistry and Physics) Oxford University. *War Work:* Voluntary work for the Forces chiefly in connection with water supplies. *Addresses:* 19, Fairhazel Gardens, N.W. 6; 20 Nottingham Place, W. 1. *Club:* Royal Societies'. (K148)

HOUSTON, Major Alexander McLean, M.B.E.

HOUSTON, Henry James, O.B.E., *b.* 1885; *s.* of Henry Houston, of Deal; *m.* Lily, *d.* of Edward Hart, of Brandon. *Educ.:* Privately. *War Work:* Deputy Director, Printing Branch Ministry of Food, 1916–18; Director, Printing and Stationery Services Branch, Ministry of Food, 1918–20; Press and publicity work in France and with the Grand Fleet, 1917. *Addresses:* Rostherne, Bushey, Herts.; 8, Broad Court Chambers, Bow Street, W.C. 2. (O10672)

HOUSTON, Major Thomas, O.B.E., R.A.M.C.

HOUSTON, Thomas, M.B.E.

HOVELLS, Ernest William, M.B.E., R.N.R.

HOVEY, Major Gordon, O.B.E.

HOW, Ethel Mary Beatrice, Mrs., M.B.E.

HOW, Capt. Eustace Arnold, O.B.E.

HOW, Ellinor, Mrs. Trotter, O.B.E.

HOW, Willoughby, M.B.E.

HOWARD, 2nd Lieut. Alfred Thomas Stewart, M.B.E.

HOWARD, Annie, M.B.E.

HOWARD, Capt. Arthur Henry, M.B.E., M.C., Yorkshire Hussars Yeomanry, *b.* 20 March, 1885; *s.* of the Rev. Henry F. Howard, M.A., Rector of Brightwalton and Catmore, Carlisle Colls. (*see* BURKE'S *Peerage*). *Educ.:* Radley. *Club:* Junior Army and Navy. (M566)

HOWARD, Carter William, O.B.E., *b.* 10 Aug. 1861; *s.* of George Howard, of Eynesbury, Hunts.; *m.* Anne Cope, *d.* of Abraham Harrison, of Clonmore Co. Carlow. *Educ.:* King's Coll., London, and Univ. Coll., Dublin. Civil Servant; Director of Printing and Binding in H.M. Stationery Office; Director of British Delegation Press at Peace Conference, Paris. *Address:* Minvaude, Hampton-on-Thames. (O10673)

HOWARD, Catharine Meriel, Lady, M.B.E.

HOWARD, Major Cecil Harry St. Leger, O.B.E.

HOWARD, Major Charles Holmes, O.B.E.

HOWARD, Major Ernest James, O.B.E., R.A.F.

HOWARD, Helen Edith, Mrs., M.B.E.

HOWARD, Francis, M.B.E., *b.* 9 May, 1867; *m.* Sarah, *d.* of William Pickard, of Nottingham, and widow of William McQuade, of Sydney, N.S.W. Attached to the British Commission in Swaziland, 1889–90; official of the Imperial British East Africa Coy, 1890–93; private Sec. to Lord Currie, H.M. Ambassador, Constantinople and Rome, 1893–1903; and to Viscount Bertie of Thame, H.M. Ambassador, Rome and Paris, 1903–18. *Club:* Junior Constitutional. (M8536)

HOWARD, Lieut.-Col. Francis James Leigh, C.B.E., D.S.O., *b.* 1870. Lieut.-Col. Army Service Corps; Dongola Expedition, 1896 (despatches, medal); Nile Expedition, 1897–9 (despatches, medal with clasp); Great War, 1914–17. (C1627)

HOWARD, Frederick James, O.B.E., *b.* 24 Jan. 1883; *s.* of Frederick Thomas Howard, of Bedford; *m.* Nellie, *d.* of Chas. Hatfield, of Kimbolton, Beds. *Educ.:* Bedford Modern School; King's College, London. Civil Service. *War Work:* Loaned by War College to High Explosives Dept., Ministry of Munitions, Dec. 1914; Appointed Assistant Controller of Dept. Finance, 1918. *Address:* 4, Beech Walk, Mill Hill, N.W. 7. *Club:* R.A.C. (O440)

HOWARD, Helen Edith, Mrs., M.B.E.

HOWARD, Lieut. Henry Mowbray, O.B.E., R.N.V.R.

HOWARD, Major Henry Ralph Mowbray, O.B.E.

HOWARD, Holly, Mrs., M.B.E.

HOWARD, Capt. Hugh Roberts, O.B.E., R.A.S.C., *b.*

14 Sept. 1894; *s.* of S. Howard. *Educ.:* Dulwich; Brighton Technical College; Mechanical Engineer. *War Work:* Workshop Officer. R.A.S.C., M.T., France, 1914–19; Army of the Rhine, 1919; Army of the Black Sea, 1920. *Address:* Broadley Cottage, Grove Road, Bournemouth. *Clubs:* Alleyn; United R.A.S.C. (O5401)

HOWARD, John Palmer, M.B.E.

HOWARD, Joseph, O.B.E.

HOWARD, Lady Mabel, C.B.E.; 2 *d.* of 5th Earl of Antrim (*see* BURKE'S *Peerage*); *m.* 1878 Henry Charles Howard, of Greystoke, Cumberland (died 1914). *Address:* Greystoke Castle, Penrith. (C2694)

HOWARD, May, Mrs., M.B.E.

HOWARD, Robert, M.B.E., M.D.

HOWARD, Russell John, C.B.E., M.B., F.R.C.S., *b.* 1875. Sometime Senior Assist. Surg. London Hospital. *Address:* 40, Devonshire Place, W. (C1155)

HOWARD, 2nd Lieut. Septimus Carolus, M.B.E.

HOWARD, Major Stephen Goodwin, C.B.E., J.P., M.P.; *s.* of Stephen Howard, J.P., of Kirtling, Cambridgeshire; *m.* 1895, Mary Maude, *d.* of the late Henry Haily, of Clare, Suffolk. Comdg. a Batt. Cambridgeshire Vol. Regt.; County Alderman for Cambridgeshire and Chairman of its Appeal Tribunal; Sat as M.P. for Sudbury Div. of W. Suffolk since Dec. 1918. *Address:* The Moat, Upend, Newmarket. (C525)

HOWARD, Violet Angel, Mrs., M.B.E. (M10249)

HOWARD, Capt. William, O.B.E., R.A.O.C.

HOWARD, Capt. William Gilbert, C.B.E., R.N., *b.* 12 Mar. 1877; *s.* of Alfred John Harad, of Warton Hall, Isleworth (*see* BURKE'S *Peerage*, Carlisle, E.); *m.* Hon. Agnes Caroline Sophia Parnell, *d.* of 4th Baron Congleton (*see* BURKE'S *Peerage*). *Address:* Ernesettle House, St. Budeaux, S. Devon. (C1189)

HOWARD, William Henry Ker, O.B.E., *b.* 17 Sept. 1866; *s.* of Col. Howard, R.E.; *m.* Ethel Louisa, *d.* of Capt. C. E. Farquharson, late 21st Hussars. *Educ.:* Dulwich; Royal Indian Engineering College, Coopers Hill; Government of India; Public Works Dept. Railways. *War Work:* I.A.R.O. with Labour Corps in France. *Address:* c/o Messrs. Grindlay & Co., Parliament Street, S.W. *Club:* Junior Carlton. (O2057)

HOWARD, William James, O.B.E., *b.* 16 April, 1880; *s.* of John Howard, of Liverpool; *m.* Margaret Elsie, *d.* of John McDougall Kerr, of Seaforth, nr. Liverpool. *Educ.:* Liverpool Institute. Assistant General Manager, Union Cold Storage Co., Ltd. *War Work:* Director of Fish, Poultry, Game, and Egg Supplies for Ministry of Food; also Member of Fish Preservation Committee, Food Investigation Board, of the Department of Scientific and Industrial Research. *Address:* Santon, The Vale, Golders Green, N.W. (O10674)

HOWARD, Capt. Hon. Bernard Edward FITZALAN-, M.B.E., *b.* 10 May, 1885; *e.s.* of 2nd Baron Howard of Glossop (*see* BURKE'S *Peerage*); *m.* 1914 Baroness Beaumont (*see* BURKE'S *Peerage*). *Educ.:* Trinity Coll., Cambridge. *Address:* 15, Manchester Square, W.1. (M8535)

HOWARD DE WALDEN AND SEAFORD, Margherita Baroness, C.B.E. Maintained a hospital at her own expense in France, and allowed her own house in London to be used as a hospital. (C3138)

HOWARTH, Osbert John Radcliffe, O.B.E., *b.* 18 Nov. 1877; *m.* Eleanor Katherine, *d.* of Stephen Paget, F.R.C.S., of Limpsfield, Surrey. *Educ.:* Westminster and Christ Church, Oxford. Asst. Sec. Brit. Assoc. for Advancement of Science. *War Work:* Naval Intelligence Division. *Address:* Hawthorn Lodge, Sevenoaks. (O10675)

HOWARTH, William James, C.B.E., M.D., Medical Officer of Health, City of London. *Addresses:* Guildhall, E.C. 2; Hartley Grange, Longfield, Kent. (C1156)

HOWDEN, Lieut.-Comm. Jan, M.B.E., R.N.V.R.

HOWE, Capt. Albert Edward, M.B.E., Merchant Service, *b.* 2 Oct. 1871; *s.* of David Howe, of Bristol. *Educ.:* Bristol Cathedral School. *War Work:* Trooping, and Cross Channel Passenger Service to Havre and Channel Islands. *Address:* 37, Spring Road, Portswood, Southampton. *Club:* Carlyle. (M8538)

HOWE, Clarence Samuel, M.B.E., *b.* 3 Feb. 1865; *s.* of Capt. Benjamin Howe, of Brightlingsea, Essex; *m.* Catherine, *d.* of Capt. James Shaw, of Nairn, Scotland. *Educ.:* Brightlingsea. Shipmaster; went to sea at the age of 12; joined the Aberdeen Steam Nav. Co. in 1893; sailed in all capacities from A.B. to Master. *War Work:* Commanded the s.s. "City of London" between Aberdeen and London throughout the war; estimated distance through danger zone, 150,000 miles. (M8539)

HOWE, Francis Cecil, M.B.E.

HOWE, John Allen, O.B.E., B.Sc., F.G.S., M.Inst.M.M., *b.* 1869; *s.* of William Elliott Howe, of Matlock Bath; *m.* Isabel Sarah, *d.* of Thomas Bickley, of Barlaston, Staffs. *Educ.:* Privately, and Royal Coll. of Science, London. Curator and Librarian, H.M. Geological Survey and Museum of Practical Geology. *War Work:* Advisory duties in connection with Economic Geology and Mineralogy. *Addresses:* 28, Jermyn Street, London, S.W. 1; The Corner House, Dryburgh Road, Putney, S.W. 15. (O10676)

HOWE, Col. Randall Charles Annesley, C.B.E., *b.* 1858; *s.* of the late Randall Howe, J.P., of Richmond, Nenagh; *m.* Florence Maud, *d.* of the late W. J. Lewis, Fleet Surgeon, R.N. *Educ.:* Trinity College, Dublin. *War Work:* In

Command of 3rd Batt. York and Lancaster Regiment. *Address:* Stonepitts, Ryde, Isle of Wight. *Club:* Royal Victoria Yacht. (C1628)

HOWE, Major Thomas Harris Manners, O.B.E.

HOWE, Capt. William Tuxford, O.B.E., *b.* 5 Jan. 1892 ; *s.* of Alfred Jessie Howe, of Southsea. *Educ.:* Portsmouth High School. *War Work:* Mesopotamia, 1916–18 ; N. Persia, 1918–19 ; Palestine, 1920. *Address:* c/o Cox & Co., 16, Charing Cross, London. (O4218

HOWELL, Alban Berkley Butts, M.B.E.

HOWELL, Cecil Ingledew, M.B.E., R.N.R.

HOWELL, Charles Frederick, M.B.E., *b.* 27 July, 1854 ; *s.* of the late L. H. Howell, of Leatherhead, Surrey ; *m.* Maude, *d.* of Rev. H Power, of Bramley, Surrey. *Educ.:* Rugby. Member of the London Stock Exchange. *War Work:* Hon. Sec. and Hon. Treas. to the Eastleigh and District War Pensions Sub-Committee, Oct. 1916, to March, 1919 ; still Hon. Treas. *Address:* Wattles, Chandlers Ford, Hants. (M8541)

HOWELL, George, M.B.E. (M10249h)

HOWELL, Godfrey Valentine, O.B.E.

HOWELL, Major Hector Lionel, O.B.E., M.C., R.A.M.C., *b.* 1882 ; *s.* of Major R. H. Howell, of Rosherville, Kent; *m.* 8 Dec. 1920, Elsie Mary, *y.d.* of the late F. J. Batchelor and Mrs. Batchelor, O.B.E., of 10, Cumberland House, Kensington Road, W. 8. *Educ.:* Charing Cross Hospital. *War Work:* 1914, M.O. i/c 1st Sherwood Foresters; Oct. 1914 to June, 1915, France, 1914 star with clasp ; D.A.D.M.S., 18th Division, Sept. 1916 to Dec. 1918, Mesopotamia ; Three times mentioned in despatches: awarded M.C. in| France ; awarded O.B.E. in Mesopotamia. *Address:* 63, Leigham Vale, Streatham, London, S.W. *Club:* Junior Army and Navy. (O4219)

HOWELL, Lieut.-Col. Herbert Gwynne, D.S.O., O.B.E., R.F.A., *b.* 15 Nov. 1879 , *s.* of Marmaduke Gwynne Howell, of Llanelwedd Hall, Radnorshire, Wales ; *m.* Annable Dora, *d.* of Capt. Martin, late The Buffs, of Donmore House, Galway. *Educ.:* Privately. *War Work:* Bechuanaland, 1897 ; Le Fleur Rebellion, 1898 ; S. Africa, 1899–1902 (despatches twice) ; Nigeria, 1908 ; Great War, Cameroon Campaign (despatches three times, D.S.O.), Egypt and Palestine (despatches and O.B.E.). *Address:* Llanelwedd Hall, Radnorshire, Wales. *Clubs:* Army and Navy ; Sports. (O6210)

HOWELL, Ivor Morris, M.B.E.

HOWELL, John, C.B.E., M.B., B.S. (Lond.), F.R.C.S. (Eng.), *b.* 19 Sept. 1871 ; *s.* of William Griffith Howell, of Tynycymmer Hall, Porth, Glam. ; *m.* Ida, *d.* of Thomas Rees, of Newport, Pem. *Educ.:* Christ's College, Brecon ; Guy's Hospital, London. Hon. Surgeon, Cheltenham General Hospital ; Surgeon Cheltenham College ; Gen. Sec., Spa Medical Advisory Committee of Town Council. *War Work:* Consulting Surgeon, Cheltenham Auxiliary Hospital ; Hon. Sec. Medical Committee. *Address:* 7, Imperial Square, Cheltenham ; *Clubs:* New ; Steeplechase ; Polo, Cheltenham. (C2695)

HOWELL, Joseph, M.B.E.

HOWELL, Capt. Norman, O.B.E., R.F.A.

HOWELL, Major Owen Alfred, M.B.E., *b.* 12 April, 1862 ; *s.* of Frederick Howell. *Educ.:* King's Coll., London, and in Paris. *War Work:* O.C. B Squadron, 3rd Company of London Yeomanry, 1914 ; O.C. Depot. 3rd Co. and London Yeomanry, 1915–16 ; O.C. 368–369 Labour Co., 1917–19 ; and 686 Employment Co.; Military Representative of the Boro. of St. Marylebone. *Address:* 101, Sinclair Road, Kensington. *Clubs:* Junior Constitutional ; Royal Automobile. (M5359)

HOWELL, Lieut.-Col. Wilfred Russell, C.B.E., D.S.O.

HOWELLS, Capt. Wilfred Allen, O.B.E. ; *s.* of John Rowland Howells, of Franklyn House, Cardiff ; *m.* Ethel Mary, *d.* of Charles Davis, of Glossop, Derbyshire. Contributed cartoons to "Vanity Fair" over the name of "Owl." *War Work:* Joined the London Welsh Batt. (15th Royal Welch Fusiliers) in Oct. 1914 ; took Company to France in 1915 ; wounded on Somme, 1916 ; attached Camouflage School, Kensington Gardens, in 1917, as lecturer. *Addresses:* Parkdene, Glossop ; Larkhill, Wilts. *Club:* Chelsea Arts. (O7298)

HOWELLS, William Wallace, M.B.E.

HOWES, Arthur James, M.B.E., *b.* 8 Dec. 1864 ; *s.* of Charles Howes, of Norwich. *Educ.:* Presbyterian School, Norwich. Political Agent. *War Work:* Organiser, National Registration ; Hon. Sec. Derby Recruiting Scheme ; Hon. Sec. Advisory Committee, National Service ; Local Fuel Overseer ; Executive Officer, Local Food Control ; Special Constable. (M8545)

HOWES, Capt. William Thomas, M.B.E. (M10224)

HOWES, William Trotman, M.B.E., F.S.I., *b.* 3 April, 1870 ; *s.* of Joseph Tippett, of The Poplars, Kingswood, Bristol ; *m.* Eleanor Isabella, *d.* of William Sommerville, J.P., late of The Grange, Billon, Glos. *Educ.:* The Bristol Grammar School. Principal Valuer to the Ministry of Agriculture. *War Work:* Chief Executive Officer to the Wilts War Agricultural Executive Committee. *Address:* 21, Holwood Road, Bromley, Kent. *Club:* National. (M1924)

HOWIE, Capt. Adrian Morrison, O.B.E.

HOWIE, Christina Lamond, Mrs., M.B.E.

HOWIE, Leila Adeline, Mrs., M.B.E.

HOWKINS, Lieut.-Col. Cyril Henry, C.B.E., D.S.O., M.R.C.S., L.R.C.P., R.A.M.C. (T.) ; *m.* 1905, Annie, *d.* of the late Henry Shaw, of Birmingham. Hon. Dental Surg. to Birmingham Dental Hospital ; S. African War, 1901–12 as Civil Surg. (Queen's medal with four clasps) ; Great War,

1914–19 ; sometime Assist. Director of Med. Services to a Div. (despatches four times). *Addresses:* 3, York Road, Leamington Spa ; 83a, Edmund Street, Birmingham. (C1269)

HOWLETT, Charles Edgar, C.B.E., I.S.O., *b.* 16 Aug. 1854 ; *s.* of Henry Howlett, M.R.C.S., of Castlemaine, Australia ; *m.* Mary Sinkins, *d.* of the late J. Bayfield Clark, of Wingfield, Trowbridge. *Educ.:* Marlborough Grammar School. Formerly Joint Sec. Office of Woods and Forests. *War Work:* Home-grown Timber Committee, etc. *Address:* The Green, Maybury, Woking. *Club:* National. (C2696)

HOWLETT, Edmund Henry, C.B.E., *b.* 29 Sept. 1854 ; *s.* of the late Gen. Sir Arthur Howlett, K.C.B., late Indian Army ; *m.* Amy Lavinia, *d.* of Rev. R. Masters Hutchins, of Spilman's Court, Gloucestershire. *Educ.:* Cranbrook ; Eastbourne College. Surgeon ; Consulting Surgeon Hull Royal Infirmary ; M.O., G.P.O. and H.M. Prisons, Hull ; Radiographer, Hull Royal Infirmary. *War Work:* Radiographer to Royal Infirmary Naval Hospital, V.A.D. Hospital, Cottingham Road ; Surgeon, Naval Hospital and V.A.D. Hospital. *Address:* 4, Wright Street, Hull. (C2697)

HOWLETT, Frank, M.B.E., *b.* 28 May, 1884 ; *s.* of George Howlett, of Thame, Oxon. Assist. Sec. Church Army Social Centres. *War Work:* Stores and General Equipment Sec. of the Church Army, Naval and Military Dept., which opened over 2000 Huts and Centres for H.M. Forces during the war. *Addresses:* North Street, Thame, Oxon. ; Oaklands, Bramshill Road, Harlesden. (M1926)

HOWLETT, Capt. John Flemyng, M.B.E.

HOWLEY, Capt. James M., M.B.E.

HOWLEY, Richard Joseph, C.B.E., *b.* 1871 ; *s.* of Lieut.-Col. John Howley, D.L., of Rich Hill, Co. Limerick. *Educ.:* Oscott College. Vice-Chairman, Standing Joint Committee of Mechanical Road Transport Association ; Member of Institution of Civil Engineers. *War Work:* Member of Tramways (Board of Trade) Committee ; Member of Railways Priority Committee ; Ministry of Munitions. *Address:* 88, Kingsway, London, W.C.2. *Clubs:* Union ; St. Stephen's. (C2698)

HOWSE, Lieut. Gilbert, M.B.E., R.N.R., *b.* 10 Feb. 1858 ; *s.* of Richard Howse, M.A., of Newcastle-on-Tyne ; *m.* Alice Maud Mary, *d.* of George Mason, of Earsdon, nr. Newcastle-on-Tyne. *Educ.* Newcastle. Master Mercantile Marine. *War Work:* Admiralty Service, in s.s. "Gardenia" and "Clintonia." *Address:* "Allandale," Exeter Road, Exmouth, S. Devon. (M8546)

HOWSON, Capt. John, C.B.E., R.D. Comm. and Acting Capt. R.N.R. (R.D.) ; served in Great War, 1914–19, as Commodore of Convoys ; mentioned in despatches. (C1190)

HOYLAND, Lieut. Harold Allan Dilke, M.B.E.

HOYLAND, Lieut. Philip Charles, M.B.E., R.A.F.

HOYLE, Major, Edward Jonas, O.B.E., R.E.

HOYLE, Lieut.-Col. Emanuel, O.B.E., R.A.S.C. (T.).

HOYLE, George, M.B.E., M.D.. M.S.

HOYLE, George Herbert, M.B.E.,

HOYLE, John Philip, M.B.E., *b.* 28 June, 1876 ; *s.* of the late Caleb Hoyle, J.P., of Roomfield House, Todmorden, 1st Mayor of Todmorden ; *m.* Elizabeth, *d.* of Sugden Sutcliffe, J.P., of Prestwich. *Educ.:* Private School, Harrogate. Cotton Spinner and Manufacturer. *War Work:* Vice-Chairman' Todmorden Relief Committee ; Chairman, Labour Employment Committee ; Vice-Chairman, War Pensions Committee ; Chairman Disablement Committee. *Address:* Glenroyd, Todmorden. (M8548)

HUBAN, Capt. John Patrick, O.B.E. (O11745)

HUBBARD, John Francis, O.B.E.,

HUBBARD, Major Reginald Kirshaw, O.B.E., M.I.A.E., *b.* 6 April, 1887 ; *s.* of Robert Hubbard, of Worthing. *Educ.:* Bethany House School ; Goudhurst and Brighton Technical College. *War Work:* Employed in a civilian capacity by War Dept. Sept. 1914, at Avemouth in connection with the repair of a large number of impressed motor lorries which had broken down on their way to embarkation for France ; gazetted 2nd Lieut., Nov. 1914 ; Posted to 1st Indian Cavalry Supply Column which went over to France, Nov. 1914 ; commanded 1st Echelon of this unit, Aug. 1915 ; gazetted Capt. and transferred to 1st Base M.T. Depot, employed in connection with the technical stores for the Mechanical Transport in France ; responsible for the organisation of the Provision and Demands Office of that Depot ; Aug. 1917, gazetted Major and placed in charge of the whole of the Mechanical Transport Stores of the 1st Base M.T. Depot ; mentioned in despatches 4 times. *Address:* 8, New Parade, Worthing, Sussex ; c/o Primrose Club, 4, Park Place, St. James's S.W. *Club:* R.A.S.C. ; United. (O5403)

HUBBERSTY, William Philip Cantrell CANTRELL-, O.B.E., *b.* 24 Oct. 1877. *e.s.* of Col. Albert Cantrell Cantrell-Hubbersty, of Ragdale Hall and Ratcliffe Hall, co. Leicester. Reserve of Officers ; late Lieut. 15th Hussars ; Deputy Assistant Director of Remounts, Northern Command, 1905–10. (O2464)

HUBBERT, Oliver John, M.B.E., *b.* 9 Jan. 1886. *Educ.:* George Green's School, London. Staff Officer, Foreign Office. *Address:* Foreign Office, Downing Street, S.W. 1. (M8549)

HUBBLE, William Collister, M.B.E. (M10250a)

HUCK, Major John, O.B.E.. M.A., F.C.S., Border Regt., (T.), *b.* 17 May, 1872 ; *s.* of Richard Huck, of Leatherhead, Surrey ; *m.* Beatrice May, *d.* of T. E. G. Marley, of St. Bees, Cumberland. *Educ.:* High School, Dorking, Surrey ; Selwyn College, Cambridge. Headmaster, Stationers' Company's School, Hornsey, London, N. 8. *War Work:* In England and in France ; Mobilised with Territorial Force, 4 Aug. 1914 ;

Demobilised, 4 Feb. 1919; Mentioned in Sir D. Haig's despatches, March, 1919 (Gazette, 19 July, 1919). *Address :* 15, Clifton Road, Crouch End, London, N. 8.   (O5404)

HUDDART, Major Alfred Harry, M.B.E., A.S.C.

HUDDLESTON, Arthur James Croft, O.B.E.

HUDDLESTON, Capt. Ernest Whiteside, C.I.E. (1916), C.B.E. (1919), R.I.M., *b.* 18 Aug. 1874; *s.* of Major Graham Egerton-Huddleston, late c/o East Surrey Regt.; *m.* Elsie, *d.* of the late J. Barlow Smith, of Buenos Aires. Senior Marine Transport Officer, Bombay; Assistant Marine Transport Officer at Suakin 1896 (two medals); in China, 1901–2; in Somaliland, 1903–4; thanked by the Gov. of India, despatches thrice, and in Great War from 1914, despatches. *Club :* Royal Bombay Yacht.   (C2255)

HUDDLESTON, Lieut.-Col. Henry Batten, O.B.E.

HUDDLESTON, Col. Wilfrid Edward, C.M.G., C.B.E., D.S.O., *b.* 1872; *s.* of the late Col. Wilfrid Huddleston, Indian Army; *m.* 1908, Alice Maude Mary, *d.* of the late William Ferguson, W.S. Col. Army Med. Ser.; Nile Expedition, 1888 (medal); Great War, 1914–18; mentioned in despatches.   (C1270)

HUDDLESTONE, Frieda, Mrs., M.B.E., *b.* 7 April, 1871; *d.* of Joseph Ignac Kaczka, of Poland; *m.* John Richard, *s.* of John Huddlestone, of Rochdale. *Educ. :* Poland and France. Managing Director of the Blackpool Winter Gardens, Co. Ltd.; Chairman of the Board of Management of the Victoria Hospital Blackpool. *War Work :* In connection with Belgian wounded soldiers and refugees during the whole period of the war; President of Voluntary Aid Centre in Blackpool for providing comforts for British soldiers; awarded Palmes en Or de l'Ordre de la Couronne du Roi de la Belgique; Medaille de la Reine Elizabeth de la Belgique. *Address :* 5, Leopold Grove, Blackpool.   (M8550)

HUDLASS, Felix William, O.B.E.

HUDLESTON, Francis Josiah, C.B.E.

HUDSLON, Lieut. Alfred, M.B.E., R.E.

HUDSON, Albert Edward, M.B.E., F.S.I.A. M.R.San.Inst., *b.* 22 June, 1883; *s.* of Alfred Albert Hudson, of Halifax; *m.* Marie, *d.* of Augustus Oakes, of Halifax, Yorks. Chief Sanitary Inspector and District Food Officer. *War Work :* Executive Food Officer, Cheltenham; Area Organising Food Officer for Cheltenham and District; did a considerable amount of work (voluntary) in connection with Soldiers' Clubs, War Savings Certificates, National Registration, etc. *Address :* Southbourne House, Gloucester Road, Cheltenham.   (M8551)

HUDSON, Alfred, M.B.E., *b.* 7 Sept. 1876; *s.* of William Hudson, of Mayfield, Stafford; *m.* Edith Roberts, *d.* of Edward Draper, of Kirkheaton, Huddersfield, granddaughter of Professor John Beaumont of Leeds Univ. *Educ. :* Privately. Sec. to Hutchinson, Hollingworth & Co., Ltd., Dobcross Loom Works, Dobcross, Yorks. *War Work :* Works Accountant, Huddersfield National Shell Factory, 1915–19; Sec. Huddersfield N.S.F. War Savings Association. *Address :* Beulah House, Diggle, Dobcross; The Cottage, Kirkheaton, Huddersfield.   (M4793)

HUDSON, Capt. Charles, M.B.E.

HUDSON, Lieut.-Col. Charles, O.B.E., R.E.

HUDSON, Lieut.-Comm. Charles Edward, O.B.E.. R.D., R.N.R.

HUDSON, Major Ernest John, O.B.E.

HUDSON, Miss Fanny Marian, O.B.E., *b.* 4 Feb. 1850; *d.* of Capt. W. J. Hudson, of the 61st Regt. *War Work :* Utilised her own house as hospital for men class A; began with 20 beds, ended with a second house, as annexe, making 82 beds in all; was Officer-in-Charge. *Address :* Brabyns Hall, Marple Bridge, Cheshire.   (O1499)

HUDSON, George, M.B.E.

HUDSON, Harry Kynoch, C.B.E., *b.* 14 May, 1867; *s.* of Robert Hudson, of Lapworth; *m.* Emily Bright, *d.* of Henry Hammerton, of Coventry. *Educ. :* Ludlow Grammar School. Private Sec. to the late Rt. Hon. Sir Charles W. Dilke, Bart., M.P. *War Work :* Commissioner of the British Red Cross in Salonika, and in Russia, and Roumania. *Address :* Stratford Lodge, St. Peter's Road, Twickenham. *Clubs :* Union; Whitefriars.   (C526)

HUDSON, Lieut.-Col. Henry Victor, O.B.E., R.N.

HUDSON, Hilda Phoebe, O.B.E., M.A., Sc.D., A.F.R.Aë.S., *b.* 1881; *d.* of W. H. H. Hudson, late professor of mathematics at King's College, London. *Educ. :* Clapham High School; Newnham College, Cambridge. *War Work :* Technical Assistant, Aircraft Production Dept. *Address :* 34, Birdhurst Road, Croydon, Surrey.   (O1500)

HUDSON, Joe, M.B.E.

HUDSON, Eng.-Comm. John Augustine, O.B.E., R.N.

· HUDSON, J. H., M.B.E.

HUDSON, Kate, Lady, O.B.E.; *d.* of the late Major J. Hawkins, of 85th King's Light Infantry; *m.* Lt.-Gen. Sir Havelock Hudson, K.C.B., K.C.I.E., *s.* of the late Lt.-Gen. Sir John Hudson, K.C.B.   (O8261)

HUDSON, Sir Robert Arundell, G.B.E., Kt. Bach., J.P., *b.* 30 Aug. 1864; *s.* of the late Robert Hudson, of Lapworth, Warwickshire; *m.* Ada, who died 1895, *d.* of the late Henry Hammerton, of Coventry. *Educ. :* Stratford-on-Avon Grammar School and Ludlow Grammar School. Chief Agent of the Liberal Party since 1895; J.P., for the Counties of London and Suffolk; a trustee of Westminster Abbey Fund; Chevalier of the Legion of Honour. *War Work :* Chairman of the Finance Committee of the British Red Cross and Order of St. John; member of the Imperial

War Graves Commission. *Addresses :* 13, Dean's Yard, Westminster Abbey; Beach House, Felixstowe, Suffolk. *Club :* Reform.   (G27)

HUDSON, Major Robert Challis, O.B.E., T.D., *b.* 31 Dec. 1875; *s.* of Thomas Hudson, of Sunderland. *Educ. :* Rectory Park School, Bishopwearmouth. Hardware Dealer and Tool Merchant. *War Work :* Proceeded to France on 18 April 1915 in command of No. 3 Company, Army Service Corps, 50th Divisional Train; afterwards transferred to No. 2 Company, and finally to No. 1 (Headquarters) Company of the Train; was attached for about 6 months to Headquarters XIII. Corps as Demobilisation Officer; mentioned on three occasions in the Commander-in-Chief's despatches for distinguished service in the field; awarded the Order of the British Empire on 2 June 1919, and the Territorial Decoration on the 19 Aug. 1919; left Cambrai, 1 July, 1919, with the cadre of the Train for demobilisation. *Address :* 314, High Street West, Sunderland.   (O5406)

HUDSON, Lieut. Roland Cecil, M.B.E.

HUDSON, Russell, M.B.E., A.M.I.Mech.E., A.M.I.E.E., *b.* 9 May, 1880; *s.* of Joseph Hudson, of Whitby, Yorkshire; *m.* Rosa Amelia, *d.* of James Smith. *Educ. :* East London Technical Coll. (Univ. of London). Commercial Engineer. *War Work :* Technical Assistant to the Metropolitan Munitions Committee from its inception until Feb. 1917; transferred, by request of the Ministry of Munitions for War, to assist in the management of the Munitions Gauges Section of the Ministry; continued in this capacity with the rank of Section Director until March, 1919. *Address :* Ridgmont, James Lane, London, E. 10.   (M8555)

HUDSON, Samuel, M.B.E., F.A.I., *b.* 10 Dec. 1851; *s.* of George Hudson, of Burnley; *m.* Eliza Jane, *d.* of Thomas Calverley, of Burnley. *Educ. :* Burnley Grammar School, and Morton Banks, Keighley. Auctioneer and Valuer; Officer to the Sheriff of Lancashire since 1897. *War Work :* Commander of Special Constabulary from Oct. 1914, to Dec. 1919, Burnley. *Address :* Highmead, Piccadilly Road, Burnley, Lancashire.   (M8556)

HUDSON, Walter, O.B.E., J.P., *b.* 23 Jan. 1852; *s.* of Henry Courtley Hudson, of Richmond, Yorks; *m.* Catherine, *d.* of David Thomas, of Middlesbrough. *Educ. :* Richmond, (Yorks) National School. Trade Union Official. *War Work :* House of Commons Munitions Committee; visited front lines 1915 in France and Flanders; in charge of expert workers, on grenade. hand and rifle, and trench bombs; served on Executive Committee for relief of population in occupied Belgium and France; Military Service (Civil Liabilities) Committee, 4 years. *Address :* 22, Atherfold Road, Stockwell, S.W. 9.   (O27)

HUDSON, Major William, M.B.E., R.E., *b.* 6 March, 1885; *s.* of Wm. Wilmot Hudson, of Nottingham; *m.* Margaret Ellen, *d.* of John Michal Walsh, of Bristol. *Educ. :* Archbishop's Holgates, York; Bradford Grammar School. *Address :* Rose Bank, Park View Villas, Hove.   (M4302)

HUFFAM, Lieut.-Col. William Tyers Christopher, O.B.E., M.C.

HUGGARD, Capt. Rev. Richard, M.B.E.

HUGGETT, James, C.B.E. Served during Great War in Financial Sec's. Depart. War Office.   (C527)

HUGGINS, Amy Christine Adela, M.B.E.. *b.* 24 Feb. 1876; *d.* of William Huggins, of St. Vincent B.W.I. *Educ. :* Privately. *War Work :* Worked amongst, and for, the men of H.M.'s M. F.'s stationed in Trinidad, B.W.I., and to men of the Royal Navy and Merchant Service. during the War. Decorated by H.R.H. The Prince of Wales, at Govt. House. Trinidad, Sept. 1920. *Address :* "M. F. Cottage," 3, Warner Street, Port of Spain, Trinidad, B.W.I. *Club :* Sailors and Soldiers.   (M8554)

HUGGINS, Elizabeth Annie, Mrs., M.B.E.; *d.* of Charles Spencer Boorman, of Stanford-le-Hope, Essex; *m.* Henry, *s.* of Henry Huggins, of Gravesend. *Educ. :* Portland Avenue School, Chiswick. Mayoress of Gravesend, 1914–16. *War Work :* Hon. Sec., Treas., and Organiser of Gravesend Prisoners of War Fund; Organiser of Gravesend Disabled Sailors' and Soldiers' Fund; Founder of Gravesend Infant Welfare Centre. *Address :* 17, Clarence Place, Gravesend.   (M8558)

HUGGINS, George Frederick, O.B.E.

HUGGINS, Major Samuel John, O.B.E.

HUGHES, Agnes Eva, Mrs. Frederic Godfrey, O.B.E.

HUGHES, Albert, O.B.E.

HUGHES, Col. Alfred Mahony, C.B.E., D.S.O., *b.* 1867; *s.* of Edward Hughes, of Ellesmere, Burghersdorp, Cape Colony. S. Africa, 1899–1902, with Field Intelligence Dept.; twice mentioned in despatches. *Address :* Wonderpoort, Jamestown, Cape Province, S. Africa.   (C761)

HUGHES, Alfred Thomas, M.B.E., R.A.F.

HUGHES, Arthur, O.B.E.

HUGHES, Capt. Arthur Beckett, C.B.E., R.N. Served in Great War, 1914–19, with Ocean Escort; mentioned in despatches.   (C2313)

HUGHES, Arthur Joseph, O.B.E., *b.* 12 June, 1880; *s.* of Alexander Hughes, of London; *m.* Emma Elsie, *d.* of William Steven Grimwade, of Broughton Hall, Suffolk. *Educ. :* St. Dunstan's College. Marine Optician; Managing Director, H. Hughes & Son, Ltd., 59 Fenchurch Street. *War Work :* Invented and organised production of compasses for aeroplanes in immense quantities. *Addresses :* 19, Warren Road, Wanstead; Husim Works, Barkingside, Ilford. *Clubs :* Rotary; Cruising.   (O442)

HUGHES, T. Capt., **Bernard**, O.B.E., N. Stafford Regt., Service Batt. (O12063)

HUGHES, Charles, M.B.E., Medaille du Roi Albert, b. 21 Feb. 1881 ; s. of David Hughes, of Huntingdon ; m. Elsie Mary, d. of Wm. John Scarjeant, of Peterborough. Educ.: Privately. Organising Sec., Eastern Counties Liberal Federation. War Work : Hon. Sec., City of Peterborough Belgian Refugees Committee ; Hon. Sec., Mayor of Peterborough's Prince of Wales' Fund ; unpaid Private Sec. to Parliamentary Sec., Board of Agriculture, 1917–18 ; Hon. Organising Sec., Derby Recruiting Scheme, War Aims, etc. Addresses : 186, Lincoln Road, Peterborough. Club : National Liberal. (M8560)

HUGHES, Major Claud Gillan Erskine, O.B.E.

HUGHES, Surgeon-Comm. Cecil Hugh Myddleton, O.B.E., R.N.

HUGHES, Capt. Cyril Emerson, M.B.E.

HUGHES, Dulcie, M.B.E., b. 1882 ; d. of Jasper Hughes, of Medbourne, Swindon. Educ.: Privately. War Work : Quartermaster Cook in Red Cross Hospitals in France. Address : Medbourne, Swindon. (M8561)

HUGHES, Alderman Edward, M.B.E., J.P., b. 1862 ; s. of Joseph Hughes, of Llansilin, Denbighshire ; m. Margaret, d. of James Armstrong, of Liverpool. Educ.: Trefonnen and Oswestry. Mayor of Wrexham, 1906–7 and 1907–8 J.P., for County of Denbigh, 1908 ; Steward of the Crown Lordship of Bromfield and Yale since 1908 ; Member of Wrexham Town Council, since 1898 ; Alderman since 1907. War Work : Member of Wrexham Local Tribunal under Military Service Act ; Member of County Appeal Tribunal for Denbighshire ; Local Pensions Committee and Recruiting Committee ; and Local Food Control Committee ; Hon. Lieut. and Q.M. 2nd Vol. Batt. Royal Welsh Fusiliers. Addresses : Glyndwr, Wrexham, Denbighshire ; Frydlyn, Llansilin, nr. Oswestry. (M571)

HUGHES, Major Edward Locock, D.S.O., O.B.E., b. 21 Feb. 1880 ; s. of Dr. R. H. Hughes, M.A., M.B., of Plymouth ; m. Mary Tatham, d. of W. Tatham Hughes, late Assistant Secretary, Royal Hospital, Chelsea. Educ.: Kelly College ; Marlborough ; Clare College, Cambridge. War Work : Company Commander 1st Northamptonshire Regt. ; retreat from Mons ; wounded, Battle of Marne, 10 Sept. 1914 ; D.A.A. and Q.M.G. 3rd Canadian Division, 1916 ; A.A. and Q.M.G. 2nd Canadian Division, Jan. 1917 to May 1917 ; Base Commandant, Taranto, to July, 1918 ; Assistant to Brig.-Gen. i/c Administration Western Command, Aug. 1918 to May, 1920. Address : Richmond Barracks, Templemore. (O2249)

HUGHES, Capt. Edward Llewellyn, C.B.E. Com. and Acting Capt. R.N. ; served in Great War, 1914–19, as Commodore of Convoys ; mentioned in despatches. (C1191)

HUGHES, Elizabeth Phillips, M.B.E.

HUGHES, Capt. Ernest Cranmer, O.B.E., F.R.C.S., R.A.M.C. (T.).

HUGHES, Evan, C.B.E., b. 18 Jan. 1882 ; s. of Evan Hughes, of Llwydiarth Hall, Montgomeryshire ; m. Dora Mary, d. of Edward Brady Patching, of Brighton. Educ.: Deytheur School ; University College of Wales, Aberystwyth ; Gonville and Caius College, Cambridge. Director of External Organisation, National Savings Committee, (formerly University Lecturer in Economics). War Work : One of the chief promoters and organisers of the National War Savings Movement. Address : 5, Highfield Avenue, Hendon, N.W. 4. Club : National Liberal. (C528)

HUGHES, Capt. Evan Jukes, O.B.E., R.M.L.I.

HUGHES, Frances, M.B.E.

HUGHES, Frederick Richard, M.B.E., b. 9 Nov. 1869 ; s. of John Hughes, of Hampstead ; m. Lucy Marian, d. of Richard Hughes Evans, of Hampstead. Educ.: St. Paul's School. County Education Sec., West Suffolk County Council. War Work : Hon. Sec., Bury St. Edmunds and District War Savings Committee and Food Saving Campaign ; lectured to troops on " Belgium and France " ; lectures in Aid of Red Cross Funds ; Special Constable. Address : Hexham House, Bury St. Edmunds, Suffolk. Club : West Suffolk County. (M8562)

HUGHES, Major Frederick St. John, M.V.O., O.B.E., b. 22 Feb. 1866 ; s. of Capt. J. W. Hughes and grandson of the late Rev. Sir Collingwood Hughes, 8th Bart. (see BURKE'S Peerage) m. Mabel Jane, d. of David Evans, of Ffrwdgrech, nr. Brecon, S. Wales. Educ.: Winchester. Late Captain 1st S. Wales Borderers ; S. A. War Medal and 6 clasps ; mentioned in despatches ; A.D.C. to Sir F. Forestier-Walker, then to Gen. Sir Reg. Pole-Carew, afterwards to Lord Minto in Canada. War Work : Mounted Intelligence Corps, 1914 ; Adjutant, reinforcements, Havre to 1915 ; Camp Commandant 2nd Army to end of war ; Brevet Major M.V.O., Order of St. Maurice and Lazarus, Italy, O.B.E., twice mentioned in despatches. Address : Meon-Marsh, Titchfield, Hants. (O5407)

HUGHES, George, C.B.E.

HUGHES, George Wall Wall Bagot, M.B.E.

HUGHES, Gibbard Richard, M.B.E., b. 9 Feb. 1855 ; s. of Thomas John Hughes, Landscape Painter, of Hampstead ; m. Ethel Winifred, d. of Rev. William Farrer, LL.B., B.A., of New College, London. Educ.: Privately ; City of London Coll. War Work : Organising the production of articles of lamp-blown glass essential to the prosecution of the war, e.g. vaccine ampoules for inoculation, gas-antidote capsules, and mine-horns ; all these were required at short notice in enormous quantities, and belonged to a class of goods which this country had, with negligible exceptions, imported from enemy countries up to the date of the outbreak of war ; the mine-horns presented such peculiar technical difficulties that for several months the factory he controlled had the honour of being the only source of supply of this detail of the British defence against enemy submarines. Addresses : Hyposol, Limited, Wealdstone, Middlesex ; Great Hampden, Great Missenden, Bucks. (M3739)

HUGHES, Capt. H. H., M.B.E. Master of the s.s. " Franz Ferdinand."

HUGHES, Henry, O.B.E., b. 13 Oct. 1869 ; s. of Edward Thomas Hughes, of Barnes, Surrey. Educ.: Privately. Chief Surveyor, Department of Works and Buildings, Air Ministry. War Work : In connection with the construction of Aerodromes. Addresses : Air Ministry, Kingsway, London, W.C. 2 ; 11, Rutland Gardens, Hove, Sussex. Club : Golfers'. (O117868)

HUGHES, Rev. Hugh Michael, O.B.E., B.A. ; s. of Michael Hughes, of Llanllechid, Bangor ; m. Mary Anne, d. of Thomas Howell, of Aberystwyth. Educ.: Brecon Memorial, Aberystwyth, and Cardiff Univ. Colleges. Minister of Ebenezer Congregational Church, Cardiff ; Editor of " Y Tyst " ; Member of the Council and Court of Univ. Coll., Cardiff ; Member of the Court and of the Theological Board of the University of Wales ; Chairman of the Congregational Union of Wales, 1920–21 ; Vice-President of National Council of Public Morals (Wales). War Work : Chairman of Committee recruiting Temperance Companies for 3rd Welsh Regt., 1914–16 ; member of Cardiff Corporation Parliamentary Committee for Recruiting ; officiating Minister to Welsh-speaking troops in Cardiff and district ; only representative of Welsh Congregationalists on the United Navy and Army Board for selection of chaplains ; organised distribution of Welsh periodical literature in various camps. Address : 17, Glynrhondda Street, Cardiff. (O10678)

HUGHES, J. H., M.B.E. (M10323)

HUGHES Lieut. John Archibald, M.B.E.

HUGHES, Col. John Arthur, C.B. C.B.E., V.D., D.L., b. 14 June, 1860 ; s. of Dr. John Hughes, of Carmarthen. Educ.: Taunton ; Univ. College, London. Formerly Colonel Commanding Severn Div. R.E. (Submarine Miners) then C.R.E. Welsh Div., T.F. War Work : Recruiting Officer for Barry and Penarth Sub-area and also for Bridgend Sub-area ; also County Director of V.A.D's in Glamorgan, including charge of the administration of 47 hospitals providing over 3,100 beds. Club : National Liberal. (C529)

HUGHES, John Brierley, M.B.E., M.B., M.R.C.S., L.R.C.P.

HUGHES, John Gwilyar, M.B.E.

HUGHES, Lady, O.B.E.

HUGHES, Rev. Levi Gethin, M.B.E.

HUGHES, Phyllis May, Lady, O.B.E., b. 27 Sept. 1869 ; d. of tee late J. F. Edisbury J.P., of Wrexham, N. Wales ; m. Sir Thomas, Knt. Bach. (see BURKE'S Peerage) ; s. of the late Thomas Hughes, of Bridgend, Glamorgan. Educ.: Chester and Cassel (Germany). President of Cardiff City Collecting Guild ; Queen Victoria's Jubilee Institute for Nurses ; member of the Committee of the Cardiff Y.M.C.A. ; King Edward VII Hospital Needlework Guild and Cardiff War (Part time) Workers. War Work : Commandant, Munitions Canteen at National Shell Factory for two years ; Chairman of the Executive Committee ; organiser of the voluntary workers shifts of a local munition factory canteen. Address : Cardiff. (O1501).

HUGHES, Rev. Randolph, O.B.E.

HUGHES, Capt. Richard Lloyd, M.B.E.

HUGHES, Capt. Robert, O.B.E., R.A.S.C., (T.).

HUGHES, Lieut. Robert Edwarde Armour, M.B.E.

HUGHES, Sydney Herbert George, C.B.E., B.A., b. 14 July, 1879 ; s. of Geo. C. Hughes, of Folkestone ; m. Leonora Louise, d. of John James Carnon, of Southsea. Educ.: Alleyn's School, Dulwich and University College, London. Deputy Accountant-General, Ministry of Shipping ; Formerly held the appointments of Deputy Cashier, H.M. Dockyard, Portsmouth, 1902 ; Secretary and Cashier, H.M. Dockyard, Gibraltar, 1904–9 ; Accountant, National Health Insurance Commission, 1912. War Work : Navy and Army Insurance Fund ; Ministry of Shipping. Address : Thrale Hall, Streatham, S.W. 16. (C530)

HUGHES, Thomas, O.B.E., J.P., b. Aug. 1868 ; s. of the late William Hughes. Educ.: Brynhyfryd Board School, Swansea. Assist. District Sec., Tinplate Section, Dockers' Union. War Work : Chairman, Ward Committee, Prince of Wales' Fund ; member of Local Executive Committee ; Member, Swansea War Pensions Committee and Chairman of Training Committee ; Member and Vice-Chairman of South Wales Joint Disablement Committee and Chairman of Training Sub-Committee ; Member of Institutional Committee (Wales) ; Member of Swansea Local Employment Committee and of the National Employment Committee (Wales). Address : Y Dreflan, Landore, Swansea. (O10679)

HUGHES, Thomas John, M.B.E.

HUGHES, William, M.B.E., R.N.R.

HUGHES, William Henry, M.B.E.

HUGHES, Paymaster Comm. William Henry, O.B.E., R.N.

HUGHES, Major William Rawson, O.B.E., M.C., b. 1891 ; s. of the late W. H. Hughes, of Denbigh. War Work : Granted a commission at the beginning of the War served on the Staff of the 12th Division in France as D.A.Q.M.G. and later. at the end of the war, on the Staff of the 23rd Army Corps in England : and on the the Staff of the 2nd Army Corps in Germany ; mentioned in despatches three times.   (O2581)

HUGHES, Ethel Blanche, Mrs. PRICE-, O.B.E., *b.* 8 April, 1860 ; *d.* of Rev. James Cook, of Peopleton, Pershore, Worcestershire ; *m.* 1st, James Graham-Gilmour, and has issue, Herbert James, killed in action, 1914 ; Henry Reginald *d.* 1914, 2ndly. William Price-Hughes. *War Work* : Started a depot in Sept. 1914, for supplying comforts to the Worcestershire Regt. in France, and in 1915 a Red Cross Work Depot, British Red Cross and St. John of Jerusalem, for supplying all local hospitals and the headquarters in London and France ; continued this work for 6 years. *Address* : Red Hill, near Worcester. *Club* : Ladies' Army and Navy.   (O10677)

HUGHES, 2nd Lieut. Reginald THARLE-, M.B.E.

HUGHMAN, Capt. Gordon Stewart, O.B.E., Middlesex Regt., *b.* 1 Apr. 1885 ; *s.* of Capt. N. R. Hughman, of 120, Sinclair Road, London, W. 14 ; *m.* Catherine Muriel, *d.* of Daniel Woodruffe, of The Mount, Market Harboro. *Educ.* : Christ's Hospital. At present Adjutant 5th Bn. East Surrey Regt. (T.). *War Work* : M.G. officer 4/Middlesex Regt., Flanders, 1914–15 ; Adjutant and Asst. Instructor, Mersey School of Instructions for Young Officers, and O.C. Company 8th (Cadet) Bn., 1915–16 ; Staff Capt. (East Coast) 1916 ; D.A.A.G., 11th Division, B.E.F., 1917 ; D.A.A. and Q.M.G. Tees Garrison 1918 ; D.A.A.G. Woolwich Garrison 1919 ; D.A.A.G. G.H.Q. British Army of the Rhine, 1919–20. *Address* : 122, Pepys Road, Wimbledon, S.W. 19 ; Drill Hall, Wimbledon, S.W.19.   (O7304)

HUGILL, Engineer Lieut.-Com. Rene Charles, M.V.O., O.B.E. Entered R.N. 1905 ; Engineer Lieut. 1908 ; Engineer Lieut.-Com. 1916.   (O9432)

HUIE, Major Richard William, O.B.E., V.D., J.P. (ret.) R.G.A. (V.), *b.* 13 Aug. 1852 ; *s.* of the late Richard Huie, Banker, of Scarborough ; *m.* Mary Purvis, *d.* of the late Archibald Young, General Manager, Capital and Counties Bank, Ltd., London. *Educ.* : Clare Coll., Scorton, Yorkshire. Chairman of Directors, Edinburgh and Portobello Cemetery Co. (Piershill), Ltd., and New Edinburgh Investment Building Society ; Chairman, House Committee, Edinburgh Parish Council ; Chairman, Executive Committee, Church Army Labour Lodging Homes, Edinburgh ; Licensed Lay Reader, St. Columba's Episcopal Church, Edinburgh ; Member, Edinburgh District Board of Control ; Member, Edinburgh Distress Committee ; Justice of Peace for County and City of Edinburgh ; for many years Staff Officer and Member of Council, National Artillery Association. *War Work* : Recruiting Officer at Edinburgh ; Military Representative, Leith Tribunal ; Acting Anglican Chaplain. *Address* : 16, Findhorn Place, Edinburgh. *Clubs* : Duddingston Golf, Edinburgh ; Merchants of Edinburgh Golf ; Craiglockhart.   (O10680)

HUISH, Lizzie, Mrs., M.B.E., *b.* 18 Dec. 1880 ; *d.* of, Samuel Delderfield, of Northchurch, Herts ; *m.* Harry James, *s.* of John Huish, of Milton, Weston-super-Mare. *Educ.* : Berkhampsted. Staff Captain, Salvation Army, Argentine Republic, France, and Germany. *War Work* : Hut work at Etaples, France, and hospital visitation, June, 1915, to Jan. 1918 ; Cologne, Germany, with Army of Occupation, Jan. 1918, to May, 1920. *Address* : 10, Great Peter St., Westminster, S.W.   (M3740)

HULBERT, Capt. Harry, M.B.E., R.A.F.
HULBERT, Lieut. Leonard, M.B.E., I.A.R.O.
HULBERT, Major Thomas Ernest, O.B.E.
HULCATT, Helen Cornelia, M.B.E.
HULL, Charles, M.B.E.
HULL, Charles Robert Ingham, O.B.E.   (O2582)
HULL, Capt. Gordon Burnett Gifford, O.B.E., R.E.
HULL, Major Tom Grove, O.B.E., R.A.F.
HULLETT, Gertrude Cecilia, M.B.E.
HULME, Agnes Maud, O.B.E.
HULME, Gilbert Ratcliffe, M.B.E.
HULSE, Hilda Gertrude Overs, Mrs., M.B.E.
HULTON, Major John Meredith, C.B.E., D.S.O.
HULTON, William Arthur Hyde, O.B.E.
HUMAN, Arnold Henry, C.B.E.
HUMBERSETH, Lieut. John Johansen, M.B.E.

HUMBLEY, Cicely, Mrs., M.B.E., *b.* 1872 ; *d.* of the late Capt. W. H. Peel, of Trenant Park, Duloe, and Heronden, Tenterden ; *m.* William Wellesley, *s.* of Lieut.-Col. W. W. Humbley, of S. Neots, Hunts. *Educ.* : Privately. *War Work* : Commandant of the V.A.D. hospital, Tenterden, Kent, 1914–19. *Address* : Llais Afon, Llanddulas, nr. Abergele.   (M9273)

HUME, Alexander Walter, M.B.E.

HUME, Blanche, Mrs., O.B.E. ; *d.* of James Carr, of Belfast ; *m.* George Alexander, *s.* of George Alexander Hume, M.D., of Crumlin, Co. Antrim. *War Work* : Hon. Organising Sec., War Hospital Supply Depot, Belfast, under Queen Mary's Needlework Guild. *Address* : Dunvegan, Myrtlefield Park, Belfast.   (O10682)

HUME, Major Hugh Bliss Torriano, M.B.E.
HUME, Col. John Edward, C.B.E.
HUME, Col. John James Francis, C.B.E. Col. and Hon. Brig.-Gen. (ret.) ; Served in the Great War, 1914–19 ; mentioned in de- spatches.   (C1629)
HUME, William, M.B.E.
HUME, Lieut.-Col. Alexander ROSS-, O.B.E., R.A.F.
HUMFRESS, Flight-Lieut. Harold Tunmer O.B.E., R.A.F.

HUMFREY, John Charles Willis, O.B.E.
HUMPHREY, Capt. Bernard, O.B.E.
HUMPHERY, Major George Edward Woods, O.B.E., R.A.F.
HUMPHREY, Major John, O.B.E.
HUMPHREY, Comm. John Cave, O.B.E., R.N.
HUMPHREY, Comm. Percy Edward May, O.B.E., R.N.
HUMPHREY, Thomas Clements, M.B.E., *b.* 3 April, 1867 ; *s.* of Thomas Clements Humphrey, of Gosforth ; *m.* Frances Ann, *d.* of James Douglass Ridley, of Angerton, Morpeth. *Educ.* : Gosforth School. Station Master, York Station, N.E. Rly. *War Work* : Station Master at York Station during the whole of the war, being responsible for the conveyance of millions of troops, equipments, munitions, etc. ; carried out important work during mobilisation. *Address* : 26, Blossom Street, York. *Club* : York Conservative.   (M1931)

HUMPHREYS, Edith Louisa Sophia, M.B.E.
HUMPHREYS, Elizabeth Clement, O.B.E., R.R.C.
HUMPHREYS, George Oscar, M.B.E.
HUMPHREYS, George William, C.B.E., M. Inst. C.E., *b.* 1863 ; *s.* of T. W. Humphreys, of London ; *m.* Helen McGilliwie, *d.* of Robert Sinclair, of London. *Educ.* : Mill Hill School. Chief Engineer, L.C.C. *War Work* : Member, Vice-Chairman and Chairman of Munitions Works' Board, Ministry of Munitions. *Address* : 104, Drayton Gardens, S.W. 10. *Club* : Reform.   (C2702)

HUMPHREYS, Gilbert, O.B.E., *b.* 1880 ; *s.* of David Evan Humphreys, of Newport, Mon. ; *m.* Edith Louise, *d.* of I. Llewellin, of Newport, Mon. *Educ.* : Private Schools. Trained as an engineer ; successively Superintendent of Dockyard, Hong-Kong ; in business on own a/c as contractor in Montreal, Canada ; now Cologne manager, Inter-Allied Trade and Banking Corporation. *War Work* : Ministry of Munitions, as Director of shell and gun statistics ; Deputy Controller shell manufacture ; Deputy Liquidator projectile contracts. *Address* : 54, Windsor Road, Church End, Finchley, W. (O444)

HUMPHREYS, Harold Goundrill, M.B.E., *b.* 16 July, 1878 ; *s.* of the late John Goundrill Humphreys, O.B.E., of Birmingham and Liverpool ; *m.* Minnie Lindsay, *d.* of the late William Gerrard, of Liverpool. *Educ.* : High School, Liverpool Institute. Assistant Traffic Superintendent London N. W. Rly. Co., London District. *War Work* : Transport Department, Ministry of Munitions, 1915–1919 ; Sub. Section Director ; Director (Railways and Canals). *Address* : 2, Brockley Avenue, New Brighton, Cheshire.   (M574)

HUMPHREYS, Henry Herbert, O.B.E.   (O5410)
HUMPHREYS, Major Herbert, O.B.E., M.C., R.A.S.C.
HUMPHREYS, Capt. Percy Harry Illingworth, O.B.E.

HUMPHREYS, Richard, O.B.E., M.B., C.M. (Edin.), *b.* 9 May, 1860 ; *s.* of Humphrey Humphreys, of Llanfairtalhaiarn, N.W. ; *m.* Amy Mary, *d.* of John Dight, of Martock, Somerset. *Educ.* : Privately, and Edinburgh Univ. *War Work* : Medical Officer attached to the Mersey defences, and Assistant Embarkation Medical Officer. *Address* : 1, Cressington Park, Liverpool. *Club* : Fly Fishers'.   (O11813)

HUMPHREYS, Lieut. Robert Henry, M.B.E., R.A.F.
HUMPHREYS, Capt. and Qr.-Mr. Thomas, M.B.E.
HUMPHREYS, Walter Ebenezer, M.B.E., R.A.F.

HUMPHREYS, Lieut.-Col. William, O.B.E., V.D., 7th Batt. Lancashire Fusiliers (ret.), *b.* 10 July, 1858 ; *s.* of William Humphreys, of Didsbury. *Educ.* : Privately. *War Work* : Commandant, Manchester Group, Lancashire Volunteer Infantry Corps, which consisted of 8 battalions. *Address* : Lyndhurst, Eccles. *Club* : Union, Manchester.   (O7307)

HUMPHRIES, Albert, M.B.E.
HUMPHRIES, Lieut. Eric Beresford, M.B.E., M.C., R.A.S.C.
HUMPHRIES, Lieut. Henry Hurl, M.B.E., Can. A.S.C.
HUMPHRIES, 2nd Lieut. Hubert John, M.B.E.
HUMPHRYS, Col. Charles Vesey, C.B.E. Formerly W. Riding Regt. ; Col. in the Army ; S. Africa, 1899–1901 (despatches, Queen's medal with three clasps).   (C819)
HUMPHRYS, John Goundrill, O.B.E.
HUMPHRYS, Capt. Robert Arthur, M.B.E., B.Sc. (Lond.), A.M.I.C.E., R.A.S.C. (M.T.), *b.* 12 Oct. 1881 ; *s.* of Dr. Chas. B. Humphrys, of Eglinton, Clevedon, Somerset. *Educ.* : Malvern Coll. ; Univ. Coll., London. Engineer. *War Work* : O.C. 618 M.T. Co., R.A.S.C. ; B.E.F., E. Africa. *Address* : Eglinton, Clevedon, Somerset. *Clubs* : Public Schools ; United R.A.S.C.   (M3053)

HUNKIN, Rev. Joseph Wellington, O.B.E., M.C.
HUNLOKE, Sylvia, Mrs., O.B.E., *d.* of G. P. Heseltine, of 196, Queen's Gate ; *m.* Philip, *s.* of Perceval Hunloke. *War Work* : British Red Cross Stores Dept., Y.M.C.A. *Addresses* : Grenehurst Capel, Surrey, and 7, Sloane Street. *Club* : Empress.   (O1504)

HUNN, Lieut. John Alfred, O.B.E., R.N.V.C.
HUNN, Major Sydney Arthur, M.V.O., O.B.E., M.C. Capt. and T. Major, Australian Imperial Forces ; served in Great War, 1915–19 ; mentioned in despatches.   (O2846)

HUNT, Albert, C.B.E., *b.* 1863. *Educ.* : Horfield. Joined Donald Currie and Co., 1889 ; was Local Manager, Union-Castle Line at Southampton 1901–11 ; Freights Manager in London, 1911–12, since when he has been Joint Manager and Chairman of Managers, Union-Castle Mail Steamship Co., Ltd. ; Director of Bullard, King and Co., Ltd., and of the Durban Navigation Collieries, Ltd. ; Member of Executive Council of Chamber of Shipping, and of Shipping Federation ; Member of War Committee of Chamber of Shipping (submarine menace) ; inventor of numerous popular war

games ; assisted to organise Naval and Military Transport during S. African and European wars, especially despatch of original Expeditionary Force to France 1914. *Address :* 2, Oxford and Cambridge Mansions, N.W. *Club :* Constitutional.
(C531)

HUNT, Arthur Henry William, M.B.E., L.R.C.P., M.R.C.P.

HUNT, Dame Catherine Reeve, D.B.E., *b.* 22 Dec. 1854 ; *d.* of late Charles Henry Hawkins, J.P., of Maitlands, Colchester ; *m.* Edgar Atlee, J.P., *s.* of the late Josiah Hunt, of Westminister. Town Councillor of the Borough of Colchester ; Chairman of the Colchester Division Conservative and Unionist Women Workers' League. *War Work :* A Vice President and late Chairman of the Sailors' and Soldiers' Families Association ; Honorary Secretary of the Local War Pensions Committee, Colchester, 1914 to 1919. *Address :* Crouched Friars, Colchester.
(D48)

HUNT, Charles Henry, M.B.E.

HUNT, Francis Cecil, M.B.E., A.M.I.E.E., *b.* 27 Dec. 1885 ; *s.* of Edward Hunt, of Westminster ; *m.* Sarah Ann, *d.* of Alfred John Cooper, of Chelmsford. *Educ. :* Chatham Dockyard Schools and Battersea Polytechnic. First Assistant Electrical Engineer, H.M. Dockyard, Chatham. *War Work :* Installation of electrical equipment in warships, submarines, and mystery boats (special service ships). *Address :* 12, York Avenue, Gillingham, Kent.
(M8571)

HUNT, Lieut.-Col. Francis Dillon, O.B.E., A.V.C.

HUNT, Major Frederick Eckstein, D.S.O., O.B.E., *b.* 1879 ; *s.* of Arthur William Hunt, of Longlands, Lancaster ; *m.* 1908, Helen Ornis, *d.* of David McKaye Cassidy, M.D., F.R.C.S.E., of Lancaster Moor, Lancaster. Entered King's Own (Roy. Lancaster Regt.), 1901 ; Lieut. Indian Army, 1905 ; Capt. 1911 ; Major, 1917 ; served in S. Africa, 1900–1901 ; present at defence of Fish River Station (despatches twice).
(O8490)

HUNT, Col. Frederick Welsley, C.M.G., C.B.E., *b.* 1871 ; *s.* of Thomas Hunt, of Rockmount, co. Waterford ; *m.* 1910, Kathleen, *d.* of Col. Robert Frederic Williamson, C.B. Entered Army, 1895 ; Capt. Army Vet. Corps, 1902 ; Major, 1910 ; Lieut.-Col. 1915 ; Brevet Col. 1917 ; N.-W. Frontier of India, 1897–8 (medal with clasp) ; S. African War, 1899–1902 ; present at relief of Kimberly (Queen's medal with five clasps, King's medal with two clasps) ; Somaliland. 1908–10 (medal with clasp) ; Great War, 1914–19 (despatches) ; sometime Dep. Director of Vet. Sers.
(C1271)

HUNT, George, M.B.E., R.N.

HUNT, George Henry, C.B.E., I.S.O., *b.* 2 Jan. 1853 ; *s.* of late Henry Hunt, of Croydon ; *m.* Emily Mary, *d.* of the late George Hosegood, of Tiverton, Devon. *Educ. :* St. Olave's School. Appointed by open competition to Clerkship in Inland Revenue Department, Somerset House, February, 1872 ; appointed Assistant Accountant, H.M. Treasury, April, 1888 ; and Accountant, July, 1902 ; Created I.S.O., Nov. 1902, C.B.E., Jan. 1918. *Address :* 3, Bramley Hill, Croydon.
(C205)

HUNT, Geraldine, M.B.E.

HUNT, Gladys Muriel, Mrs., M.B.E., *b.* 20 Feb. 1892 ; *d.* of David George Ginn, of London ; *m.* Neville Greaves, *s.* of Neville Hunt, of Manchester. *Educ. :* Stamford Hill High School and Les Fauvettes, Dieppe, France. *War Work :* Secretarial work in the Women's War Relief Fund, Bombay ; Hon. Sec., National Service Bureau, War Purposes' Board, Bombay, and War Museum, War Purposes' Board, Bombay ; Red Cross searcher for three years. *Addresses :* Malabar Hill, Bombay ; 31, Weymouth Street, London, W.
(M6165)

HUNT, Lieut.-Col. Godfrey Massy Vere, C.B.E. Lieut.-Col. and Brevet Col. R.A.S.C. (ret.) ; served in Great War, 1914–19 ; mentioned in despatches.
(C1630)

HUNT, Capt. and Qr.-Mr. Henry Charles, M.B.E.

HUNT, Jesse Brookes, O.B.E.

HUNT, John, O.B.E.

HUNT, John Herbert, O.B.E., *b.* 4 April, 1885 ; *s.* of the late George Hunt, of Southampton. *Educ. :* Southampton. Organising Secretary, South Western Division of Y.M.C.A.'s. *War Work :* Organising Secretary for Y.M.C.A. with First Army, B.E.F., France, 1914–18. *Address :* 100, Union Street, Plymouth.
(O3766)

HUNT, Joseph, O.B.E., I.S.O., *b.* 12 Aug., 1854 ; *s.* of William Joseph Hunt ; *m.* Alberta, *d.* of Arthur Bown. *Educ. :* St. Olave's School, Southwark. Clerk in War Office, 1871 to 1890 ; Royal Ordnance Factories, 1890 to 1919. *War Work :* Deputy Civil Assistant to Chief Superintendent of Ordnance Factories, Woolwich Arsenal. *Address :* 3, St. Mildred's Road, Lee, S.E.
(O446)

HUNT, Joseph Henry, M.B.E., R.A.S.C., *b.* 1876 ; *s.* of Major J. Hunt, R.A.M.C., of "Woodville," Shooters Hill, Kent ; *m.* Elizabeth Mary, *d.* of Robert Frederick Seldon, of Barnstaple, Devon. *Educ. :* Taplow Grammar School. Government Clerk. From 1896 until the outbreak of war employed at the Supply Reserve Depôt, Royal Dockyard, Woolwich ; in 1914 moved to Deptford Cattle Market where he continued his duties, which consisted chiefly in providing provisions, etc., to British troops in every theatre of war ; attested under the " Derby Scheme," 1915, and exempted until July, 1918, when called up ; posted to Mechanical Transport and qualified as motor driver in Sept. 1918 ; posted to Cadet Co., R.A.S.C., Aldershot, and obtained a Temporary Commission in the R.A.S.C., March, 1919. *Address :* 51, Mayhill Road, Blackheath.
(M576)

HUNT, Lilian Hart, M.B.E., *b.* 23 May, 1889 ; *d.* of the late Col. W. H. Hunt, of Preston and Blackpool. *Educ. :* Southgate House, Devizes, and Fairhaven High School. *War Work :* V.A.D. Driver, Etretat and Tréport, France, Oct. 1916, to Dec. 1917 ; afterwards Commandant, Rouen Convoy, attached 41st Auxiliary Ambulance Car Co. ; later 21st V.R.P. M.T., R.A.S.C., 1917–20. *Address :* 22, Pollux Gate, Fairhaven, Lytham, Lancs. *Club :* V.A.D. Ladies'.
(M8572)

HUNT, Capt. Reginald Noel, M.B.E., *b.* 25 Dec. 1873 ; *s.* of Thomas Howard Hunt, of Glastonbury ; *m.* Lilian Mary, *d.* of Alfred Sidney. Joined the Army early in life. *War Work :* served with R.A.P.D. during the whole period of the war.
(M5364)

HUNT, Stanley Herbert, C.B.E.

HUNT, Stanley Percival, M.B.E.

HUNT, Thomas, M.B.E., R.A.

HUNT, Thomas, O.B.E., *b.* 5 April, 1867. Civil Servant ; Inspector of Schools, Board of Education. *War Work :* Registration Section of Recruiting Office (Ipswich) for the Derby Scheme and the Military Service Acts ; Hon. Sec. to the Suffolk County (East and West) War Savings Committees. *Address :* Bradgate, 102, Christchurch Street, Ipswich.
(O10684)

HUNT, William, M.B.E.

HUNT, William Wright, M.B.E., J.P.

HUNT, Major Thomas Edward CAREW-, D.S.O., O.B.E., Royal Berkshire Regt., *b.* 27 Nov. 1874 ; *s.* of H. T. Carew-Hunt, late H.M. Consul-General at New Orleans, U.S.A ; *m.* Ethel Emily, *d.* of the late C. J. L. Nicholson, of London. *War Work :* Proceeded with Royal Berkshire Regt. to France, 12 Aug. 1914 ; took part in battle of Mons, the Marne and the Aisne ; appointed Brigade Major, 146th Brigade, 49th Division, March, 1915 ; G.S.O.3, 10th Army Corps, April, 1916 ; G.S.O.2, 10th Army Corps, Aug. 1916 ; G.S.O.1, April, 1918 ; G.S.O.2, War Office, Sept. 1919 ; mentioned in despatches twice. *Address :* 22, Iverna Gardens, Kensington, London, W. 8. *Clubs :* United Service ; Royal Automobile. (O7308)

HUNTER, Major Albert, O.B.E.

HUNTER, Alexander, O.B.E., L.R.C.S.

HUNTER, Capt. Alfred Philip, M.B.E., R.E.

HUNTER, Campbell Murray, O.B.E.

HUNTER, Catharine Augusta, Mrs. Harry Osborne, M.B.E.
(M25)

HUNTER, Major Cecil Stuart, D.S.O., O.B.E.

HUNTER, David, O.B.E., *b.* 1863 ; *s.* of David Hunter, of Ayr ; *m.* Mary Louisa, *d.* of James Collier, of Musselburgh. *Educ. :* Glengarnoch and Glasgow. Shipping Agent. *War Work :* Five years' work among Belgian Refugees in Ilford, Essex ; organising allotments and vacant lands for cultivation. *Address :* Shandon, Holcombe Road, Ilford. (O10685)

HUNTER, David, C.B.E. Dep. Controller Coastal Shipping, Australia.
(C709)

HUNTER, Edith Lena, M.B.E.

HUNTER, Capt. Evan Austin, O.B.E., W.S., B.A. (Oxon.), R.A.S.C. (T.F.), *b.* 28 Sept. 1887 ; *s.* of Frank Hunter, W.S., of Edinburgh ; *m.* Jane Ritchie, of Hill of Ruthven, Perthshire ; *d.* of the late Thomas Smith Kay. *Educ. :* Fettes Coll., Edinburgh ; Christ Church, Oxford, and Edinburgh Univ. Writer to the Signet. *War Work :* 2nd Lieut. T. & S. Column, A.S.C. ; Scottish Horse Mounted Brigade (T.F.), 30 Sept. 1914 ; promoted Captain, Feb. 1915 ; O.C. 909 M.T. Co., R.A.S.C., March, 1917, in France ; Staff Captain, Q.M.G. 3, War Office, Dec. 1917 ; mentioned in despatches, March, 1919. *Addresses :* 7, York Place, Edinburgh ; Parkhill, Colinton, Midlothian. *Clubs :* New, Edinburgh ; Hon. Company Edinburgh Golfers, Muirfield ; Prestwick Golf ; Caledonian, London.
(O7309)

HUNTER, George Albert, M.B.E.

HUNTER, Sir George Burton, K.B.E., D.Sc., M.I.C.E., Member of Council, I.N.A., J.P., *b.* 19 Dec. 1845 ; *s.* of Thomas Hunter, of Sunderland ; *m.* Annie, *d.* of Charles Hudson, of Whitby, Yorks. *Educ. :* Private School. Shipbuilder. *War Work :* Shipbuilding. *Address :* The Willows, Jesmond, Newcastle-on-Tyne.
(K84)

HUNTER, Capt. George Noel, O.B.E.

HUNTER, Eng. Lieut. Harry, O.B.E., R.N.

HUNTER, Major Herbert Patrick, O.B.E.

HUNTER, Lieut.-Col. James, O.B.E., R.A., *b.* 30 May, 1868 ; *s.* of the late Major J. Hunter, of Cambridge ; *m.* Lilian Agnes, *d.* of the late William Vail, of Cambridge. *Educ.* Camden School. *War Work :* Command Artillery Defences, Simon's Bay, South Africa. *Address :* Commanding 3rd Div., Ammunition Column, R.F.A., Meerut, India.
(O8840)

HUNTER, Capt. James, O.B.E., *b.* July, 1863 ; *s.* of James Hunter, of Rosherville, Kent ; *m.* Gertrude, *d.* of William Skilleter, of Rosherville, Kent. *Educ. :* Gravesend. Commander, Eastern Telegraph Co. *War Work :* Repairing and laying submarine cables in Mediterranean and Atlantic during the War, 1914–20. *Address :* 8, Elliot Street, The Hoe, Plymouth, Devon.
(O10686)

HUNTER, Sir John, K.B.E., Officer of the Legion of Honour, Commander of the Order Leopold, Commander of the Order of the Crown of Italy, Member of the Order of St. Anne, with Diamonds, *b.* 1863 ; *s.* of John Hunter, of Montreal, Canada ; *m.* Catherine Finqland, *d.* of John Gardner, of Whitevale, Glasgow. Engineer ; Managing Director, Sir Wm. Arrol & Co., Ltd. ; Chairman, The North West Rivet, Bolt and Nut Factory, Ltd., Airdrie, and The Rivet, Bolt and Nut Co., Ltd., Glasgow ; Director, The Iron Trades Employers' Insurance

Association, Ltd. *War Work :* During the War was Director of Factory Construction and Director of Iron and Steel Production, Ministry of Munitions, from 1915 ; Member of the Air Ministry and the Council of the Ministry of Munitions. *Address :* Ravenscourt, Thorntonhall, Lanarkshire. *Clubs :* St. Stephen's ; Junior Carlton ; Ranelagh ; British Empire ; New, Glasgow. (K24)

HUNTER, 2nd Lieut. John, M.B.E., R.A.F.

HUNTER, Capt. John Francis Stuart, M.B.E., R.E. (T.).

HUNTER, John Henry, M.B.E., *b.* 28 April, 1881 ; *s.* of Harry Reed Hunter, of Newcastle-upon-Tyne ; *m.* Emma Frances, *d.* of Capt. Theodore F. Strand, of Brooklyn, N.Y. *Educ. :* Keyford School, Frome. Member of New York Produce Exchange ; Member of New York Maritime Exchange ; Member of the firm of H. W. St. John & Co., Forwarding Agents. *War Work :* Director British Ministry of Shipping in the U.S.A., and Liaison Officer between British Ministry of Shipping (in U.S.A.) and British Ministry of Shipping (in Canada) ; Liaison Officer between British Ministry of Shipping (in U.S.A.) and British Ministry of Food (in U.S.A.). *Addresses :* 1396, Carroll Street, Brooklyn, New York ; Riverside Drive, Red Bank, New Jersey. *Clubs :* Royal Automobile ; The Pilgrims ; British Schools and Universities ; St. George's Society ; Japan Society ; Crescent ; Staten Island Cricket and Tennis. (M3744)

HUNTER, Capt. John Leslie, M.B.E.

HUNTER, Margaret Bruce, Mrs., O.B.E., *b.* 21 March, 1863 ; *d.* of William Johnson, of Lerwick ; *m.* Robert Bruce, J.P., *s.* of Samuel Dunn Hunter, of Lerwick. *Educ. :* Privately and Anderson Institute, Lerwick. *War Work :* Acted as Hon. Treas. of the Shetland Branch of Queen Mary's Needlework Guild during the whole period of the war ; organised and superintended concerts, social evenings, processions, whist drives, competitions, etc., for the raising of War funds, and personally assisted in collecting and packing thousands of the celebrated Shetland hand-knitted and hand-spun articles of underclothing to be sent to the front. *Address :* Union Bank House, Lerwick, Shetland. (O10688)

HUNTER, Marion Janet, M.B.E.

HUNTER, Lieut. Col. Maurice, O.B.E., T.D., *b.* 28 Oct. 1863 ; *s.* of John Hunter, of Field Head House, Belper ; *m.* Agnes Mary, *d.* of Rev. J. Ford Simmons, of Hull. *Educ. :* Repton. Land Agent and Civil Engineer. *War Work :* Sept. 1914 to Jan. 1918. *Address :* Highfield, Belper. (O7311)

HUNTER, Philip Vassar, C.B.E., M.I.E.E., *b.* 3 Aug. 1883 ; *s.* of Josiah Hunter, of Emneth Hungate, Norfolk ; *m.* Helen Maud, *d.* of Charles Golder, of Finchley. *Educ. :* Wisbech Grammar School, and Faraday House, London. Member of Council of Institution of Electrical Engineers ; Member of Engineering Standards Association ; Member of the International Electrotechnical Commission. *War Work :* Engineer representing the Director of Experiments and Research in the Anti-Submarine Division of the Naval Staff, Admiralty. *Address :* Salcombe, Foxley Lane, Purley, Surrey. *Club :* St. Stephen's. (C2704)

HUNTER, Capt. Reginald Gordon Pulteney, O.B.E., R.E.

HUNTER, Summers, C.B.E., *b.* 12 July, 1856 ; *s.* of John Ranson Hunter, of Inverness ; *m.* Dora Elizabeth, *d.* of Joseph Elliott, of South Shields. *Educ. :* Royal Academy, Inverness ; Privately ; and Wedgwood Institute, Burslem. Chairman and Managing Director of The North Eastern Marine Engineering Co. Ltd., Wallsend and Sunderland ; Director of The Tyneside Tramways and Tramroads Co., Wallsend-on-Tyne. *War Work :* Vice-Chairman of North-East Coast Armaments Committee, which later became the Tyne and Wear Board of Management for Shell Production ; Member of Shipping Controller's Advisory Committee ; Admiralty Controller's Advisory Council ; Ministry of Munitions Advisory Committee *re* Labour ; Internal Combustion Engineering Sub-Committee of the Admiralty Board of Invention and Research ; Board of Trade Shipping and Shipbuilding Committee. *Address :* 1, Manor Terrace, Tynemouth, Northumberland. *Clubs :* Thatched House ; Union, Newcastle-on-Tyne. (C206)

HUNTER, Lieut.-Col. Thomas Anderson, C.B.E. Lieut.-Col. and Director of Dental Sers. New Zealand Forces. (C725)

HUNTER, Thomas Briggs, O.B.E.

HUNTER, Thomas Charles, O.B.E., M.Inst.C.E., *b.* 11 May, 1858 ; *s.* of the late William Danby Hunter, of Brighton ; *m.* Alice Jane, *d.* of Henry Gorham, of Folkestone. *Educ. :* Brighton. Civil Engineer ; late Assistant Director of Works. Admiralty. *War Work :* Responsible, under the Civil Engineer-in-Chief, Admiralty, for the War Emergency Works at the many Naval and Oil Fuel Bases on the East Coast of England and Scotland. *Address :* "Sliema," Effingham Road, Surbition. (O447)

HUNTER, William Robert, M.B.E.

HUNTER, Capt. John Eric ARROL-, O.B.E., R.A.F.

HUNTINGFORD, Lieut.-Col. Walter Legh, O.B.E., Major, R.M.A. ; served in Great War, 1914–19, as British Naval Liaison Officer, Mediterranean, with rank of Lieut.-Col. ; mentioned in despatches. (C2314)

HUNTINGTON, Major Herbert Francis Searancke, O.B.E., The Welsh Regt., *b.* 15 Jan. 1888 ; *s.* of Major H. Huntingdon, of 20, Abingdon Villas, Kensington, W. 8 ; *m.* Kathleen Mary, *d.* of Dr. Griffin, of Plymouth. *Educ. :* Felsted and Sandhurst. *War Work :* Served in France, 1916 to April, 1919 ; held appointments as Deputy Inspector of Physical Training, B.E.F., with Temporary rank of Lieut.-Col. *Addresses :* Hd. Qrs. Eastern Command ; 51, Queen's

Gardens, Bayswater, W.2. *Clubs :* Junior United Service ; Junior Army and Navy. (O5413)

HUNTLEY, Alfred Henry, M.B.E., M.C.I., *b.* 15 March, 1877 ; *s.* of Edmund Boyce Huntley, of Lowestoft ; *m.* Gertrude Amelia Florence, *d.* of Frederick Ernest William Resker, of Islington. *Educ. :* St. Mary's School, Walthamstow ; Science and Art School, South Kensington. Assistant Architect, H.M. Office of Works ; Member of the Concrete Institute. *War Work :* Special War Hospitals ; Chief Petty Officer, R.N.V.R., Anti-Aircraft Corps. (M8575)

HUNTON, Alfred William, O.B.E., M.R.C.S., L.R.C.P. (Lond.), *b.* 20 May, 1859 ; *s.* of Thomas Hunton, of Torquay ; *m.* Kate, *d.* of John Edwin Jones, of Breinton Herefordshire. *Educ. :* Owens College, Manchester. *War Work :* Manchester Infirmary ; Ancoats Hospital ; L'Hôpital Dames des Grèves, France ; the Lord Derby War Hospital, Warrington. (O4373)

HUNTON, Edgar Barton, O.B.E., B.Sc., *b.* Feb. 1877 ; *s.* of J. G. Hunton, J.P., of Stockton-on-Tees ; *m.* Sabina Booth, *d.* of John Graham, of Stockton-on-Tees. *Educ. :* High School, Stockton-on-Tees, and Durham Coll of Science, Newcastle-on-Tyne. H.M. Superintending Inspector of Taxes, Board of Inland Revenue. *War Work :* Arising out of the Administration of the Acts of Parliament imposing duties on Excess Profits and Munitions Exchequer payments. *Address :* Feilding, Egmont Road, Sutton, Surrey. (O10690)

HUNTON, Capt. and Brevet Major Thomas Lionel, O.B.E., Royal Marine Light Infantry, *b.* 30 Oct. 1885 ; *s.* of Theodore Hunton, of Clifton, Bristol ; *m.* Margaret Mary Frances, *d.* of Lieut.-Col. W. H. Steele, R.A.M.C., of Clifton, Bristol. *Educ. :* Clifton College. *War Work :* Mentioned in despatches, 1918 and 1919 ; Chevalier Order of Star of Roumania, April, 1919 ; Chevalier Legion of Honour, June, 1919 ; promotion to Brevet Major, 1 Jan. 1919, for distinguished service in the prosecution of war. (O9554)

HURCOMB, Cyril, C.B.E., *b.* 1883. *Educ. :* St. John's College, Oxford. An Assistant Secretary, Ministry of Transport. *War Work :* Deputy Director, and later Director, of Commercial Services, Ministry of Shipping. *Address :* 20, Cromwell Crescent, S.W. *Club :* Reform. (C209)

HURD, William Burton, O.B.E.

HURLE, Alfred Edward, M.B.E.

HURLSTON, William, M.B.E., *b.* 2 April, 1887 ; *s.* of Charles Hurlston, of Cheltenham and Birmingham. *Educ. :* King Edward VI. Grammar School, Birmingham. Finance Official, Birmingham Area, Ministry of Pensions. *War Work :* Joined Recruiting Staff, Birmingham, Aug. 1914 ; after being rejected for active service ; worked continuously under War Office until transferred to Ministry of National Service in November, 1917 ; afterwards transferred to Ministry of Pensions in April, 1919 ; appointed Finance Official and Secretary, Birmingham, in Feb. 1919. *Address :* 8, Montague Road, Handsworth, Birmingham. (M8577)

HURLEY, Charles Richard, M.B.E.

HURRY, Lieut. Sydney Charles, M.B.E., R.E.

HURSON, James, M.B.E., B.A., *b.* 1882 ; *Educ. :* Blackrock Coll., and Univ. Coll., Dublin. Private Secretary to the Vice-President of the Local Government Board for Ireland. *War Work :* National Relief Fund ; Measures for relief of distress occasioned by the war. (M8578)

HURST, Lieut.-Col. Arthur Reginald, D.S.O., O.B.E., *b.* 1867 ; *s.* of Robert Henry Hurst, of Horsham Park, Horsham ; *m.* Esther Winifred Mary, *d.* of Rev. E. Oldridge de la Hey of Bathealton. *Educ. :* Westminster, and Christ Church, Oxford. J.P. Oxfordshire ; retired Major 3rd Royal Sussex Regiment. *War Work :* Served with the 24th, 33rd, and 41st Divisions from 1914 to end of war ; organised, and went to France with, the Ammunition Column of 41st Division, and commanded it in Italy, Flanders and Germany. *Addresses :* Horsham Park, Horsham ; Little Barrington, Burford, Oxon. (O5414)

HURST, Christopher Salkeld, O.B.E. Appointed an Asst. Under-Secretary Mines Dept. Board of Trade. (O10691)

HURST, Major Godfrey Thomas, D.S.O., O.B.E., V.D.

HURST, John, O.B.E.

HURST, Capt. Jan., M.B.E.

HURSTHOUSE, Major William Richmond, M.B.E.

HUSKINSON, Col. Charles John, O.B.E., T.D., *b.* 28 Aug. 1867 ; *s.* of William Lambe Huskinson, of Epperstone, Notts. *Educ. :* Oakham School. *War Work :* 33 years Territorial Officer ; 1914–15, Lieut.-Col. Commanding 8th Battn. Sherwood Foresters (Notts and Derby Regt.) ; 1915 to 1919, Commanding Base Depôt at Etaples, France. *Address :* Newark, Notts. *Clubs :* County, Nottingham ; Bath. (O2583)

HUSKISSON, Major William Gordon, C.B.E., D.S.O., R.A.S.C., *b.* 23 Dec. 1877 ; *s.* of the late Colonel S. G. Huskisson, C.B., of S. Staffordshire and Middlesex Regts. *Educ. :* Privately. S. Africa, 1900–02 ; Somaliland, 1902–03 ; Egypt, Gallipoli, Palestine, 1914–18. *Address :* Home Mechanical Transport Depot, R.A.S.C. *Club :* Junior Naval and Military. (C1382)

HUSSEY, Annie, M.B.E.

HUSSEY, Lieut. Arthur Vivian, O.B.E., R.E.

HUSSEY, Capt. Henry, M.B.E., *b.* 1 Aug. 1869. Inspector of Army Schools. *War Work :* Officer in charge of the Central Casualty Bureau, Army Headquarters, India. (M5368)

HUSSEY, John Walton, O.B.E., F.A.I., *b.* 2 April, 1865 ; *s.* of John Richards Hussey, of Alphington, Devon ; *m.* Lily, *d.* of Thomas Andrew, J.P., of Exeter. *Educ. :* Malvern

College. *War Work:* Live Stock Control. *Address:* Matford Lodge, Exeter. *Club:* Northernhay, Exeter. (O10693)

HUTCHEON, Ada Mary, Mrs., M.B.E.; *d.* of Thomas Finer, of Tendring, Essex. *Educ.:* Privately. *War Work:* Chairman Soldiers' and Sailors' Families Association, Wimbledon Division; Vice-Chairman, Wimbledon War Pensions Committee; Member of Wimbledon Military Tribunal. *Address:* 113, Pepys Road, Cottenham Park, Wimbledon, S.W. 19. (M8580)

HUTCHESON, Alexander Byres, M.B.E.

HUTCHESON, Grace, M.B.E.; *d.* of John M. Hutcheson, of Greenock and London. *Educ.:* Highbury High School. *War Work:* Personal Secretary to Director of Intelligence, Mediterranean Naval Staff, Malta. *Address:* 55a, High Street, St. John's Wood, N.W. 8. *Club:* Ladies' Athenæum. (M8582)

HUTCHESON, Capt. and Qr.-Mr. John, M.B.E., Can. A.M.C.

HUTCHIN, Lieut.-Col. James William, C.M.G., C.B.E., A.P.C.

HUTCHINGS, Sir Alan, K.B.E. (1920), *b.* 9 May, 1880; *s.* of Alfred Blandford Hutchings, of Seaford. *Educ.:* Privately; Tonbridge School; Royal Agricultural College, Cirencester. *War Work:* Temporary Paymaster, Army Pay Department, 1914–15; Secretary to Department of Director-General of Voluntary Organisations (War Office), 1915–19; a member of several Government Committees in connection with the War. *Address:* 134, Westbourne Terrace, W. 2. *Clubs:* Carlton; Constitutional; Royal Thames Yacht. (K386)

HUTCHINGS, Charles Henry, O.B.E., K.C.

HUTCHINGS, Schoolmaster Lieut. Samuel Louis, O.B.E., R.N.

HUTCHINGS, Capt. W. F., M.B.E.

HUTCHINS, Arthur Edmund, M.B.E.

HUTCHINS, George D'Oyly, C.B.E., *b.* 15 Oct. 1866; *s.* of the late George Albert Hutchins, M.I.C.E., of Welshpool, N. Wales; *m.* Maude Emily, *d.* of Arthur Newman. *Educ.:* Bedford Grammar School. Secretary to Public Companies. *War Work:* Aug. 1915–Oct. 1916, Secretary, Munitions Inventions Dept., Ministry of Munitions; Oct. 1916–Aug. 1917, Secretary, the Advisory Committee, Ministry of Munitions; Aug. 1917–Aug. 1918, Chief Council Officer, Ministry of Munitions; Secretary to Co-ordinating Committee; Aug.—Nov. 1918, Aircraft Production Department (Personal Assistant to D.G.A.P.); Nov. 1918–Aug. 1919, Secretary to Liquidation of Aircraft Contracts Committee. *Addresses:* 70, Dukes Avenue, Chiswick, W. 4.; Pharaoh's Island, Shepperton-on-Thames. (C2705)

HUTCHINSON, Annie Irene, M.B.E.

HUTCHINSON, Arthur, O.B.E., M.A., Ph.D., *b.* 6 July, 1866; *s.* of George Hutchinson; *m.* Evaline Demezy, *d.* of Alexander Shipley, of Windsor. *Educ.:* Clifton College; Christ's College, Cambridge; and the Universities of Würzburg and Munich. Fellow and Tutor of Pembroke College, Cambridge; University Demonstrator of Mineralogy; Appointed Secretary to General Board of Studies, Cambridge. *War Work:* Chemical Work for the Admiralty. *Address:* Aysthorpe, Newton Road, Cambridge. *Club:* Royal Societies. (O449)

HUTCHINSON, Bertha Charlotte, Mrs., M.B.E.

HUTCHINSON, Beryl Butterworth, M.B.E. (M10250b)

HUTCHINSON, Frances Catherine Maude Haynes, M.B.E.; *d.* of Haynes Hanley Hutchinson. *War Work:* Recruiting; Statistics. *Clubs:* Roehampton; Royal North Devon Golf. (M3745)

HUTCHINSON, George Arnold, M.B.E., L.R.C.P. (Lond.), M.R.C.S. (Eng.), *b.* 7 Feb. 1870; *s.* of G. W. Hutchinson, of Barbados, W.I.; *m.* Helen Laura, *d.* of W. A. Young, of Bank of England, London. *Educ.:* St. Mary's Hospital, London. *War Work:* Civil Medical Practitioner attached to Seaforth Military Hospital, Liverpool. *Address:* Rosslyn, Crosby Road, N. Waterloo, Liverpool. (M10269)

HUTCHINSON, Major George Rowland, O.B.E.

HUTCHINSON, Henry Norton, O.B.E.

HUTCHINSON, Flight Lieut. Hubery Gerald, M.B.E., R.A.F.

HUTCHINSON, Lucy, Mrs., O.B.E.; *d.* of William Franks, of Liverpool; *m.* Edward Mason, *s.* of Edward Hutchinson, of Liverpool. *War Work:* Voluntary work daily from Aug. 1914; Liverpool Civic League, arranging working parties, ambulance classes for ladies, despatching parcels and comforts to troops at the front; British Red Cross Society (Liverpool Branch), Stock Room, receiving and packing clothing and surgical requisites for Military Hospitals, Liverpool, care of Ambulance equipment; riverside canteen for troops arriving and departing; founded "Inglefield" babies home, as a War Memorial. (O10694)

HUTCHINSON, Thomas Massie, O.B.E. (O5416)

HUTCHINSON, Capt. Thomas Herbert, M.B.E.

HUTCHINSON, Capt. Walter Ernest, O.B.E., R.N.H.

HUTCHINSON, Wilfred Leanold, O.B.E.

HUTCHINSON, Major William Gordon, O.B.E., *b.* 15 June, 1876; *s.* of Lt.-Col. J. B. Hutchinson, C.S.I., of Jhandraghat, Camberley; *m.* Kathleen Gordon, *d.* of Major-Gen. Alfred Denniss, R.A. *Educ.:* Wellington Coll. Govt. of India Political Dept. *War Work:* Political Agent Chaqai and in political charge of the Sarhad in Eastern Persia. *Address:* c/o Messrs. H. S. King & Co., 9, Pall Mall, S.W. *Club:* Junior Naval and Military. (O2068)

HUTCHINSON, Lieut.-Col. Coote Robert HELY-, O.B.E.

J.P., *b.* 6 Feb. 1870; *s.* of John Hely-Hutchinson, of Seafield, Donabate; *m.* Julia Hariet Vere, *d.* of William Browne-Clayton, of Brownes Hill, Carlow. *Educ.:* Harrow. *War Work:* Commanded 14th Royal Fusiliers, 1914–16; 31st Training Reserve Batt., 1916–18. *Address:* Lissen Hall, Swords, Co. Dublin. *Club:* Kildare Street. (O7264)

HUTCHISON, Agnes Hood, M.B.E., *b.* 4 Dec. 1876; *d.* of William Grant, of Dunoon, Argyllshire; *m.* William Hutchison, M.A., LL.B., *s.* of William Hutchison, of Greenock *Educ.:* Durham and Brussels. *War Work:* President of Soldiers' and Sailors' Families Association, Glasgow; President Women's Unionist (Bridgeton, Glasgow) Association Work Party and Clothing Department for Soldiers and Sailors from 1914 until War Pensions Committees were formed; afterwards local President of War Pensions and representative Unemployment Committee. *Address:* 22, Bute Gardens, Glasgow, W. *Club:* Glasgow Literary. (M8583)

HUTCHISON, Alexander, M.B.E.

HUTCHISON, Helen Duguid, M.B.E., *d.* of James H. Hutchison, of Newcastle-upon-Tyne. *Educ.:* Greenock and London. *War Work:* V.A.D. in R.A.M.C. Hospital, Jesmond Road, Newcastle-upon-Tyne, 1915–1916; V.A.D. St. John Ambulance Brigade Auxiliary Hospital, 6, Kensington Terrace, Newcastle-upon-Tyne; Commandant of same Hospital till May, 1919. *Address:* 131, Osborne Road, Newcastle-upon-Tyne. (M3746)

HUTCHISON, Col. James Alexander, C.B.E. Canadian Army Medical Corps; served in Great War, 1915–19; mentioned in despatches. (C1833)

HUTCHISON, Lieut. James Lawrie McKie, O.B.E.

HUTCHISON, Robert Oliphant, M.B.E., *b.* 1 Nov. 1880; *s.* of Henry William Hutchison, J.P., of Eastbank, Kirkcaldy; *m.* Rose Blenheim, *d.* of — Jupp. *Educ.:* Rugby and Oxford. Chief Magistrate and Rice Controller, Hong Kong. *War Work:* Work in Hongkiong in connection with Volunteers. *Address:* Thatched House, Eastbank, Kirkcaldy. *Club:* Hongkong. (M1271)

HUTCHISON, Lieut.-Col. Robert Schlesinger, C.B.E. Major and Brevet Lieut.-Col. Army Pay Depart.; served in Great War, 1914–19; mentioned in despatches. (C1127)

HUTCHISON, Sarah Hannah, Mrs., M.B.E., *b.* 1852; *d.* of John Key, of Kirkcaldy; *m.* Henry William, J.P., *s.* of Robert Hutchison, of Kirkcaldy. *Educ.:* Edinburgh. *War Work:* Chairman Disablement Committee, Kirkcaldy; Convenor 3rd Ward Pension Committee; President, Pattehead Tipperary Club for women; Member South Eastern District Committee for Scotland; Vice-President Nursing Association, and President Health Visitors, Kirkcaldy. *Address:* Eastbank, Kirkcaldy. (M8585)

HUTH, Bertha, Mrs. O.B.E., *b.* 10 Jan. 1862; *d.* of Edward Henry Moore, of Brighton, Sussex; *m.* Frank, *s.* of Edward Huth, J.P., of Huddersfield, Yorks. *Educ.:* Privately, and Royal Academy of Music. *War Work:* Ran a home for professional women affected by the War; organised concerts all over the country at camps for soldiers, and in hospitals; gave recitals in aid of Lord Roberts Memorial Fund and collected £28,000 thereby. *Address:* 29, Clarendon Road, Holland Park, London, W. 11. (O3767)

HUTSEL, Robert, O.B.E.

HUTSON, Capt. Henry Porter Wolseley, D.S.O., O.B.E. M.C., R.E.

HUTSON, Surgeon-Major John, M.B.E., M.B., C.M., D.P.H., J.P., Barbados Volunteer Force, *b.* 13 July, 1859; *s.* of Archdeacon Eyre Hutson, K.D., M.A., late of St. Thomas, Danish West Indies; *m.* Mary Ellen, *d.* of Archdeacon W. T. Webb, M.A., late of Codrington College, Barbados. *Educ.:* Codrington Coll., Barbados, and Edinburgh Univ. Senior Medical Officer Local Forces; Public Health Inspector and Poor Law Inspector; Medical Assessor and Member Gen. Board of Health, Barbados, W.I. *War Work:* Senior Medical Officer H. T. Magdalena for two voyages from W. I. to Egypt, 1916–17; employed as civil surgeon at Lakenham Military Hospital, Norwich; Ministry of Pensions, Chelsea, 1917; Appointed to be a member of the Legislative Council of the Island of Barbadoes. *Address:* Harmony Hall, Barbados, W.I. *Club:* Royal Societies'. (M2948)

HUTT, Alfred, M.B.E., B.Sc., *b.* 27 June, 1888; *s.* of George H. Hutt, of London. *Educ.:* Bedford Grammar School; Lycée Hoche, Versailles. *War Work:* Motor driver in France with British Red Cross, 1914 to 1915; Staff Lieut., Ministry of Munitions (Raw Materials Section), 1915 to 1919. *Address:* 52, Redcliffe Square, S.W. 10. (M582)

HUTT, John, M.B.E., *b.* 19 Jan. 1890; *s.* of George Harry Hutt, of Pietermaritzburg; *m.* Olive Villette, *d.* of W. H. Gillespie, of London. *Educ.:* Bedford Grammar School; Lycée Hoche, Versailles; Wöhler Realgymnasium, Frankfurt-am-Main. University College, London. Civil Servant (Class I.). *War Work:* In charge of Naval Supplies, Dunkerque, Dec. 1914 to June, 1916 (Lieut. R.N.V.R.); Woolwich Naval Ordnance Depot, 1916–18; Admiralty, 1918–19. *Address:* 5, Highmore Road, Blackheath, S.E. 3 *Club:* Junior Army and Navy. (M583)

HUTTON, Arnold William, M.B.E., *b.* 12 Sept. 1882; Organising Secretary, Hospitals Welfare Society; Member National Savings Assembly, 1919–20. *War Work:* Local War Savings work, War Loans, Food Economy Propaganda, National Service Recruiting, Red Cross work. *Address:* 11, Riseldine Road, Honor Oak Park, S.E. 23. (M8586)

HUTTON, Stamford, M.B.E. J.P.

HUTTON, William, O.B.E.

HUTTON, William Ross, M.B.E.

HUXFORD, Ernest Henry, M.B.E.

HUXLEY, Henry Scott, M.B.E.

HUXTABLE, 2nd Lieut. Geoffrey, M.B.E.

HUXTER, Muriel Kathleen, M.B.E.,

HUYSHE, Capt. Rowland Radcliffe, M.B.E., *b.* 17 Feb. 1881 ; *s.* of the Rev. Canon Huyshe, of Wimborne, Dorset. *Educ. :* Marlborough, and Oriel Coll., Oxford. Landowner and Farmer. *War Work :* Gazetted Lieut. in R.A.S.C. 1914 ; Capt. Dec. 1915. *Address :* The Manor, Clyst Hydon, near Exeter. (M5369)

HYATT, Major Percival Taylor, O.B.E.

HYDE, Charles, O.B.E.

HYDE, Lieut.-Col. Dermot Owen, C.B.E., D.S.O., B.A., M.B., B.Ch., B.A.O., D.P.H., Royal Army Medical Corps, *b.* 1877 ; *s.* of Brigade Surgeon Robert Hyde, late Army Medical Service ; *m.* Hilda Edith Richmond, *d.* of Lieut.-Col. F.R.M.C. de R. Mauduit, Indian Army. *Educ. :* Trinity College, Dublin. *War Work :* Deputy Assistant Director of Medical Services with 49th West Riding Territorial Division, and then with 5th Division, between Aug. 1914 and July, 1916 ; Officer Commanding 14th Field Ambulance during Battle of the Somme; Officer Commanding No 1 Casualty Clearing Station, Feb. 1917 to April, 1918 ; Assistant Director of Medical Services with 21st Division, April, 1918, to March, 1919 ; served in France from April, 1915, to March, 1919. (C1272)

HYDE, Ethel Vivian, Mrs., M.B.E., *b.* 12 March, 1880 ; *d.* of Frederick Dixon Taylor, of Tottenham ; *m.* Capt. John Sutherland, *s.* of Thomas Robert Hyde, of Tottenham. *Educ. :* Privately. *War Work :* Welfare Superintendent under Ministry of Munitions ; Unit Administrator Q.M.A.A.C., B.E.F. 1916–18. *Address :* 64, Anson Road, Tufnell Park, London, N. 7. (M3138)

HYDE, Lieut.-Col. James Reid, C.B.E. Major and Acting Lieut.-Col. Canadian Field Artillery ; served in Great War, 1915–19 ; mentioned in despatches. (C1139)

HYDE, Katharine Anne, Mrs., O.B.E.

HYDE, Capt. Richard, C.B.E., M.V.O., *b.* 1872 ; *s.* of the late William Hyde, of the Grange, Market Stainton. Entered R.N. 1886 ; Lieut. 1894 ; Com. 1905 ; Capt. 1912 ; and later Commodore (2nd class) ; Gambia Expedition, 1894 ; China, 1900 ; present at capture of Taku Forts ; Great War, 1914–19, with Ocean Escort ; mentioned in despatches. *Club :* Army and Navy. (C1192)

HYDE, Lieut.-Col. John Irvine LANG-, C.M.G., O.B.E., *b.* 1859 ; *s.* of William Lang, of Willowdale St. Mary's, Ontario, Canada ; *m.* 1895, Agnes Stanley, *d.* of the late Henry C. Hyde, of San Francisco, California. *Educ. :* R.M.C., Kingston, Canada Entered R.E. 1883 ; Capt. 1891 ; Major, 1900 ; Lieut.-Col. 1907 ; retired, 1912 ; A.D.C. to Inspector-Gen. of Fortifications, 1885–6 ; Boundary Commr. for delimitation of W. Frontier of Gold Coast Colony, 1891 ; Chief Engineer of proposed Railways Survey, Gold Coast, 1893 ; served on Staff during Attabubu Expedition, 1894 ; appointed British Commr. in connection with Niger Boundary, with temporary rank of Lieut.-Col. 1900. *Club :* Royal Societies'. (O3141)

HYLAND, Charles John, M.B.E.

HYMAN, Major Arthur Wellesley, O.B.E.

HYNARD, William George, O.B.E.

HYNES, Major Brian Mansfield, O.B.E., Royal Sussex Regt., *b.* 11 July, 1879 ; *s.* of John Hynes, Paymaster in-Chief Royal Navy. *Educ. :* Lancing Coll. *War Work :* Adjutant 6th Batt. Royal Sussex Regt. on outbreak of war ; subsequently 2nd in Command ; appointed to command 25th London Regt. May 1917 ; commanded Battalion in Waziristan 1917 and Afghan War 1919 ; mentioned in despatches. *Clubs :* Army and Navy ; Royal Cruising ; Royal Thames Yacht. (O8491)

HYSLOP, Francis, C.B.E. (C3095)

HYSLOP, Irene Murray, M.B.E., *d.* of Sir Murray Hyslop, of Beckenham. *Educ. :* Caldecote Towers, Bushey Heath. *War Work :* Secretary and Caterer of Crescent Road Soldiers' Club, Beckenham ; Worker at Grosvenor Gardens Y.M.C.A. Hut. *Address :* Cedar Lawn, Beckenham. (M8587)

HYSLOP, James, M.B.E.

HYSON, Herbert Augustine Henry, M.B.E.

IBBETSON, Alexander, O.B.E., *b.* 17 Nov. 1869 ; *s.* of Thomas Alexander, of London ; *m.* Jessie Madeline, *d.* of Benjamin Vibert, of Newport, I. of W. *Educ. :* United Westminster Schools. Chairman, Wholesale Tea Dealers' Section, Chamber of Commerce. *War Work :* Member of eight committees, assisting Ministry of Food in distribution of Tea ; Member of Tea Distribution Advisory Committee ; Gave Entertainments for wounded soldiers in hospitals. *Address :* 21, Oakdale Road, Streatham, S.W. 16. (O10699)

IBBITSON, Lieut. George, M.B.E., R.A.

IBBOTSON, Capt. Archie William, M.B.E,, M.C.. I.A.R.O.

IDLE, Percy, M.B.E.

IFOULD, Edwin, M.B.E.

IKIN, Lieut. Harry Claude, M.B.E., Aust. I.F.

ILBERT, Joyce Violet, O.B.E., *b.* 1890 ; *d.* of Sir Courtenay Ilbert, G.C.B., K.C.S.I., C.I.E., of Speaker's Court, Palace of Westminister (*see* BURKE'S *Peerage*). *War Work :* Secretary of the Collecting Box Dept. of the Collections Committee of the British Red Cross Society and Order of St. John ; and Member of the above Committee, 1915–19. *Addresses :* 24, Pelham Crescent, S.W. 7 ; Troutwells, Penn, Bucks. (O1509)

ILCHESTER, Giles Stephen Holland Fox-Strangeways, Earl of, O.B.E., *b.* 31 May 1874 ; *e.s.* of 5th Earl of Ilchester (*see* BURKE'S *Peerage*) and Mary, only *d.* of 1st Earl of Dartrey, K.P. (*see* BURKE'S *Peerage*) ; *m.* Lady Helen Stewart, only *d.* of 6th Marquess of Londonderry (*see* BURKE'S *Peerage*), late 2nd Lieut. Coldstream Guards. *Addresses :* Holland House, Kensington, W.8 ; Melbury House, Dorchester. (O8841)

ILES, Annie Christease, M.B.E., *b.* 18 June, 1867 ; *d.* of the late James Iles, J.P., of Binbrooke Hill, Lincolnshire. *Educ. :* Privately, and Sheffield High School. Dormitory Matron and Housekeeper, Guy's Hospital, S.E., 1896–1902. *War Work :* Housekeeper, Medical Officers' Mess, 2nd London General Hospital, Aug. 1914, to June, 1916 ; Lady Superintendent under Ministry of Munitions of the Ordnance Hostels for Girls, Coventry, Aug. 1916–18. *Address :* Castlemere, Nuneaton. *Club :* New Century. (M3748)

ILES, Surgeon-Lieut. Arthur Ernest, O.B.E., M.B., B.S. (Lond.), F.R.C.S.(Eng.), R.N., *b.* Aug. 1880 ; *s.* of Samuel Iles, of Bristol ; *m.* Amy Constance, *d.* of Frederick Wadmore, of Newport, Isle of Wight. *Educ. :* Clifton College ; University of Bristol ; St. Bartholomew's. Ophthalmic Surgeon ; Assistant Surgeon, Bristol Eye Hospital ; Ophthalmic Registrar, Bristol Royal Infirmary. *War Work :* Temporary Surgeon-Lieutenant, R.N., from Jan. 1915 to March, 1919. *Address :* 17, Victoria Square, Clifton, Bristol. (O3520)

ILES, George Ehret, O.B.E.

ILIFFE, Edward Mauger, C.B.E., *b.* 17 May, 1877 ; *s.* of William I. Iliffe, of Allesley, nr. Coventry ; *m.* Charlotte, *d.* of Henry Gilding, J.P., of Gateacre, nr. Liverpool. Managing Director, Iliffe and Sons, Ltd., proprietors of "The Autocar," "The Amateur Photographer," etc. *War Work :* Controller, Machine Tool Department, Ministry of Munitions. Has the Legion of Honour. *Addresses :* Allesley Hall, nr. Coventry ; 5, Portland Place, London, W. 1. *Clubs :* Royal Societies' ; Queen's. (C532)

ILSLEY, Arthur Frederick, M.B.E., *b.* 23 May, 1870 ; *s.* of Thomas Ilsley, of London ; *m.* Elizabeth Forbes, *d.* of James Wilson Robertson, of Rayne, Aberdeenshire. *Educ. :* Private School. *War Work :* Sec. (Hon.), Board of Trade Engineering Industries Committee ; Sec. (Hon.), Ministry of Munitions Financial Advisory Committee. *Address :* Thorndon Friars, Monken Hadley, Barnet, Herts. (M585)

IMISON, Herbert, M.B.E.

IMPEY, Frank, M.B.E.

IMPEY, Isabella Edith, M.B.E., *b.* 17 Aug. 1884 ; *d.* of Frederick Murray Impey, of Ottery St. Mary, Devon. *Educ. :* Tiffin's Endowed School, Kingston-on-Thames, and Christ's Hospital, Hertford. Civil Servant, 1st Class Clerk, London Telephone Service. *War Work :* Clerical and Accounting Work in connection with recruiting. *Address :* 36, Stanmore Road, West Green, N. 15. (M3749)

IMPEY, Lieut.-Col. Lawrence, C.S.I., C.I.E., C.B.E., *b.* 17 June, 1862 ; *s.* of Col. E. C. Impey, of Bengal Staff Corps. *Educ. :* Marlborough ; Sandhurst. Appointed to Notts and Derby Regt., 10 March, 1883 ; transferred to Indian Army, 1885 ; appointed to Indian Political Dept., Dec. 1887 ; C.I.E., 1911 ; C.S.I., 1917 ; C.B.E., 1920 ; retired in 1917. *War Work :* Sec. Central Prisoners of War Committee. *Club :* East India United Service. (C2706)

IMPSON, Herbert John, O.B.E., M.C.

IMRIE, George Blair, M.B.E., R.E. (T.).

IMRIE, May, Mrs., M.B.E., *b.* 28 Feb. 1873 ; *d.* of the late William John Bidfood, of Woolwich ; *m.* Henry John, *s.* of the late Henry William Imrie, of Plumstead, Kent. *Educ. :* Privately. *War Work :* Honorary, Y.M.C.A. Work (Canteen) at the Army Branch Y.M.C.A. of Jubbulpore, C.P., India. *Address :* 11, Mile End Lane, Stockport, Cheshire. (M6166)

IMRIE, Lieut.-Col. Hew Francis BLAIR-, C.M.G., O.B.E., J.P., *b.* 10 July, 1873 ; *s.* of Lieut.-Col. Henry Blair, R.E., of 21, Norfolk Crescent, Hyde Park ; *m.* Selina Gladys Eyre, *d.* of Brig.-Gen. Eyre Crabbe, C.B., of Glen Eyre, Southampton. *Educ. :* Wellington Coll. and Pembroke Coll., Cambridge. Landed Proprietor. *War Work :* Commanded 5th Batt. (T.F.) The Royal Highlanders (The Black Watch), and afterwards D.A.Q.M.G., Northern Command, York, until demobilisation ; twice mentioned in despatches. *Address :* Lunan House, Montrose. *Clubs :* United Service ; New (Edinburgh). (O6922)

IM THURN, Sir Everard, K.C.M.G., K.B.E., C.B. (*see* BURKE'S *Peerage*), *b.* 9 May, 1852 ; *s.* of J. C. im Thurn ; *m.* Hannah, *d.* of James Lorimer, Reg. Prof., of Edinburgh Univ. *Educ. :* Marlborough Coll., and Exeter Coll., Oxford. Civil Servant (ret.) ; late Governor of Fiji and High Commissioner of Western Pacific. *War Work :* Took charge of interests of Overseas Soldiers from the Crown Colonies, especially from Fiji ; Deputy Chairman of King George and Queen Mary's Soldiers' and Sailors' Club, Peel House ; Chairman of British West India Contingent Committee. *Address :* Cockenzie House, Prestonpans. *Club :* Athenæum. (K123)

IM THURN, Capt. John Knowles, C.B.E., R.N., *b.* 1881 ; *s.* of J. C. im Thurn. Served in the Great War, 1914–19 (despatches). (C2293)

INCE, Major Bernard Sidney, M.B.E.

INCE, Lieut. Eric Henry Philip Blundell, O.B.E.

INCH, Capt. Thomas Douglas, O.B.E., M.C., M.B.

INFIELD, Louis, O.B.E., *b.* 14 Oct. 1888 ; *s.* of Max Infield, of Methuen Park, Muswell Hill. *Educ. :* Owen's School, Islington, and Queens' Coll. Cambridge. Civil Servant, Ministry of Health. *War Work :* Secretary and Deputy

Controller, War Trade Statistical Department, Ministry of Blockade, Foreign Office, Dec. 1915 to April 1918; Director of Rationing and Distribution, Ministry of Food, April 1918, to Jan. 1921; British Representative, Essen Commission of Enquiry (Spa Protocol) 1920. *Address :* 5, Hinde House, Manchester Square, W.1. *Club :* Authors'. (O453)

INGHAM, Sybil, Mrs., M.B.E.

INGHAM, William Henry, O.B.E.

INGILBY, Lieut.-Col. John Uchtred Macdowall, O.B.E., late Gordon Highlanders, J.P., *b.* 28 Dec. 1874; *s.* of the late Sir William Ingilby, Bart. (*see* BURKE'S *Peerage*), of Ripley Castle, Harrogate; *m.* Marjorie Cecily (*q.v.*), *d.* of the late William Robert Phelips, of Montacute House, Somerset. *Educ. :* Charterhouse. J.P., West Riding, Yorkshire. *War Work :* Officer i/c Infantry Record Office, Perth. *Address :* North Deighton Manor, Wetherby. *Clubs :* Wellington, Yorkshire. (O4276)

INGILBY, Marjorie Cecily, Mrs., M.B.E.; *d.* of the late William Robert Phelips, of Montacute House, Somerset; *m.* Lieut.-Col. John Uchtred Macdowall (*q.v.*), *s.* of the late Sir William Ingilby, Bart. (*see* BURKE'S *Peerage*), of Ripley Castle, Harrogate. *War Work :* Was connected for 4½ years with the Perth War Dressings Organisation, and helped to found it; and for 2 years was Hon. Sec. and Organiser; was a member of the Executive Committee of the Perthshire Branch of the British Red Cross Society (Scottish Branch). *Address :* North Deighton Manor, Wetherby, Yorks. (M8593)

INGLE, Lieut. Harry Cyril, M.B.E.

INGLEFIELD, Rear Adm. Sir Edward Fitzmaurice, K.B.E., R.N. (ret.), *b.* 1861; *s.* of late Admiral Sir Edward Inglefield, K.C.B., D.C.L., F.R.S.; *m.* 1887 Julia Katherine Margaret (*q.v.*), *d.* of late J. Christopher Wilson, of 20, Charles St., Berkeley Sq., W., and Ambleside, Westmorland. *Educ. :* Privately. Entered R.N. 1874; served as Lieut. with Nile Expedition, 1884-85 (medal, clasp, and bronze star); Assistant Director of Naval Intelligence, 1901-5; Commanded H.M.S. Antrim 1905-6; A Younger Brother of Trinity House. *Addresses :* 49, Lennox Gardens, S.W.1; Burke House, Beaconsfield, Bucks. *Clubs :* United Service; City of London; Royal Yacht Squadron, Cowes (hon. mem.). (K200)

INGLEFIELD, Julia Katharine Margaret, Lady, O.B.E., and Medaille de la Reine Elizabeth; *d.* of Christopher Wilson, of Lownook, Westmorland; *m.* Admiral Sir Edward Inglefield (*q.v.*), *s.* of Admiral Sir Edward Inglefield (*see* BURKE'S *Peerage*). *Educ. :* Privately. President, Buckingham and Bedfordshire Lace Association. *War Work :* Hon. Sec. to the County Committee of Belgian Refugees, and had 2 hostels in London for distressed Belgian Lace and Lingerie makers; worked for 5 years for Local Government Board, London. *Addresses :* 49, Lennox Gardens, S.W.1; Burke House, Beaconsfield, Bucks. (O1070)

INGLIS, Major Alexander Francis, O.B.E., 1st King George's Own Gurkha Rifles, *b.* 16 Oct. 1881; *s.* of the late Col. David William Inglis, of 35th Sikhs; *m.* Anne Stirling, *d.* of Robert Houston, of Milliken Park, Renfrewshire, N.B. *Educ. :* Bedford School, and Royal Military Coll., Sandhurst. Commissioned, Sept. 1901 to 40th Regt. P.W.V., South Lancashire Regt., attached 82nd Regt. (2nd Batt.), India, 1902; transferred Indian Staff Corps, 1902, to 17th Bengal Infantry, Wana, Waziristan; attached 2nd King Edward's Own Gurkha Rifles; appointed 1st King George's Own Gurkha Rifles, Dharmsala, Punjaub, 1904; on duty with Indian Contingent for H.M. The King's Coronation, 1911; accompanied battalion Delhi Durbar, 1911; served Chitral (N.W.F.P.) and Gilgit as Military Assistant and Commandant Scouts, 1914-17. Proceeded to Egypt as Senior Special Service Officer to 1st Kashmir Imperial Service Infantry as Lieut.-Col.; commanded battalion in the line (Palestine), and in Gen. Allenby's final operations of Sept. 1918; participated in 10th Div. attack on Nablus with 30th Brigade; mentioned in despatches; O.B.E.; regiment received C.-in-C.'s congratulations, and was awarded 2 guns for its services in Sept., 1918. *Address :* c/o H. S. King & Co., 9, Pall Mall, London. *Club :* Junior Army and Navy. (O6212)

INGLIS, Capt. Alexander Reid, O.B.E.

INGLIS, Major Charles Edward, O.B.E., R.E.

INGLIS, Dorothy Winifred, Mrs., M.B.E.

INGLIS, Lieut. Henry Maxwell Burton, M.B.E.

INGLIS, Hugh, O.B.E.

INGLIS, Capt. John, O.B.E., R.A.M.C. (T.).

INGLIS, Kate, M.B.E., *b.* 5 Dec. 1873; *d.* of Frank Inglis, Capt., R.N. *Educ. :* St. Margaret's School for Naval Officers' daughters, Twickenham. Organiser and Speaker, Women's Unionist Assoc., 1906-14. *War Work :* British Red Cross Society (Headquarters), Aug. 1914 to July, 1918; France, Jan. 1915 to 15 July, 1918; mentioned in despatch from General Sir Douglas Haig, dated 13 Nov. 1916; joined Women's Royal Naval Service, July, 1918 to Dec. 1919. *Address :* 2, Elsham Road, Kensington, W. 14. (M587)

INGLIS, Walter George, M.B.E.

INGLIS, Capt. William Clarence, O.B.E.

INGLIS, Col. Russell TRACY-, C.B.E.

INGPEN, Capt. Arthur Lockyer, O.B.E.

INGRAM, Capt. Alexander Gordon, M.B.E.

INGRAM, Alfred Sydenham, M.B.E., *b.* 14 Sept. 1875; *s.* of Francis Thynne Ingram, of Salisbury; *m.* Kate, *d.* of George Janson, of Rio Janeiro. *Educ. :* Privately. *War Work :* In charge of all coaling of Naval ships and transports at Port Said until Oct. 1919; representative of Civilian Firms

on Labour Committee at Port Said, 1916-18. *Address :* The Square House, Bury St. Edmunds. *Club :* Road. (M8594)

INGRAM, Capt. Bruce Stirling, O.B.E., M.C., *b.* 5 May, 1877; *s.* of Sir William Ingram, Bart. (*see* BURKE'S *Peerage*), of Westgate-on-Sea; *m.* Amy, *d.* of John Foy, of London. *Educ. :* Winchester; Trinity College, Oxford. Editor of the " Illustrated London News," also of the " Sketch." *War Work :* Joined the Royal Garrison Artillery, Dec. 1915; fought in the first battle of the Somme, 1916, as second in command of 105 Siege Battery; joined the Staff of the Heavy Artillery 3rd Corps, with which he served during the first battle of Cambrai, for his service in which he received the M.C.; also during the Great Retreat, March, 1918, and the final victory of the Somme; he received his O.B.E. for services subsequent to the Armistice. *Address :* 65, Cromwell Road, London, S.W. *Clubs :* Bath; Burlington Fine Arts. (O5419)

INGRAM, Lieut.-Col. Charles Robert, D.S.O., O.B.E., *b.* 1882. Major, Royal W. Kent Regt.; A.Q.M.G. with rank of Lieut.-Col.; served in the Great War, 1914-18 (despatches). (O6643)

INGRAM, Hon. Capt. Edward Maurice Berkeley, O.B.E., M.A., *b.* 14 Dec. 1890; *s.* of Major Edward Russell Berkeley Ingram, of the Welsh Regiment. *Educ. :* Eton; King's College, Cambridge. 3rd Sec., H.M.'s Diplomatic Service. *War Work :* General Staff, War Office; Military Intelligence Directorate. *Address :* The Foreign Office, Downing Street. *Clubs :* Travellers'; Cavendish. (O453)

INGRAM, Major Francis Manning, O.B.E.

INGRAM, Capt. George Skinner, M.B.E.

INGRAM, Lieut.-Col. John O'Donnell, C.B.E., D.S.O., *b.* 1870; *s.* of Col. M. T. Ingram, of Littlehampton; *m.* Eileen, *d.* of J. C. Dunbar, of Ceylon. *Educ. :* Privately; Sandhurst. *War Work :* Served with 1st Gloucestershire Regt. in France till severely wounded, Nov. 1914; O.C. Depot, Gloucestershire Regt., 1916-20; O.C. Troops, Bristol, 1918-20; C.M.A., Gloucestershire and Bristol Counties. *Address :* St. Columba, Littlehampton. (C2122)

INGRAM, Joseph, O.B.E.

INGS, Lieut. George Benjamin, M.B.E.

INMAN, Arnold, O.B.E., *b.* 3 Nov. 1867; *s.* of T. F. Inman, of Bath; *m.* Margaret Amy Hope, *d.* of E. A. Le Mesurier, of Genoa. *Educ. :* Clifton, and Magd. Coll., Oxon. Barrister-at-Law. Commander X Division, Met. Special Constabulary. *Addresses :* Thorndyke, Hatch End, Middlesex; 5, Paper Buildings, Temple, E.C. *Club :* New University. (O10703)

INMAN, Cecil Daubeny, O.B.E.

INMAN, Ernest Stobart, M.B.E., J.P., *b.* 31 March, 1852; *s.* of William Inman, of Upton Manor, Birkenhead (*see* BURKE'S *Landed Gentry*); *m.* Rose, *d.* of the late Edward Foster, of London. *Educ. :* Repton. General Manager, River Weaver Navigation, 1892-1919. *War Work :* Member of Recruiting Committee, Military Tribunal, Local Government Labour Advisory Committee, and of Prince of Wales' Fund, War Pensions Committee; Hon. Treas. Queen Mary's Guild (Northwich Branch) Unemployment Committee. *Address :* Seaholm, Morlan Park, Rhyl, N. Wales. (M8595)

INNES, Capt. Arthur, O.B.E.

INNES, Lieut. Cameron Starr, M.B.E., R.E. (T.), *b.* 12 June, 1892; *s.* of George Innes, of Cults, Aberdeen; *m.* Christian Dempsey, *d.* of Henry Austin Robb, of Aberdeen. *Educ. :* Robert Gordon's Coll., Aberdeen. Civil Servant. *War Work :* With the Forces. *Address :* 44, Stanley Street, Aberdeen. (M3054)

INNES, Charles, O.B.E., B.Sc., A.M.I.C.E., *b.* 3 April, 1882; *s.* of Alexander Innes, of West Park, Dufftown, N.B. *Educ. :* Daniel Stewart's Coll., Edinburgh. Executive Engineer, Public Works Department, Burma. *War Work :* Opened communications to the Wolfram Mines, Tavoy, Burma. *Clubs :* Pegu, Rangoon; East India United Service. (O8262)

INNES, Major George Alexander, M.B.E.

INNES, James, O.B.E., *b.* 27 Aug. 1861; *s.* of David Innes, of Cupar-Fife and Coleraine, Ireland; *m.* Manuela, *d.* of Agustin Nava, of Albacete, Spain. *Educ. :* Model School, Coleraine, Co. Derry, Ireland. British Vice-Consul at Bilbao, Spain. *Address :* British Consulate, Bilbao; Las Arenas, Province of Biscay, Spain. *Club :* Overseas. (O10704)

INNES, Capt. James Oliver, M.B.E., M.C., R.N.

INNES, Capt. James William Guy, C.B.E., J.P., D.L., R.N., Chevalier of Legion of Honour, *b.* 1873; *s.* of Alexander Innes, J.P., D.L., of Raemoir Cowie and Dunnottar, Kincardineshire; *m.* Sheila, *d.* of Lieut.-Col. J. F. Forbes, J.P., D.L., of Rothiemay Castle, Banffshire. *Educ. :* H.M.S. " Britannia," and R.N. College Greenwich. Entered Royal Navy, 1887; Sub-Lieut. 1892; Lieut. 1895; Commander, 1906; ret. Captain, 1919. *Address :* Raemoir House, Banchory, Kincardineshire. *Club :* Royal Northern (Aberdeen). (C1165)

INNES, Jessie Dods, Lady, C.B.E., *b.* 1 Nov. 1860; *d.* of the late William Dods Pringle, of Lynedoch, Bedford, Cape Province; *m.* Sir James Rose Innes, P.C., K.C.M.G., *s.* of the late James Rose Innes, C.M.G., of Cape Town. *Educ. :* Good Hope Seminary, Cape Town. *War Work :* Committee, Field Force Comforts and Red Cross, Boer War; Chairman, National Council of Women's Defence Force Comforts; Chairman, Women's Committee Hospital Ship " Ebani "; Executive Committee, S. African Gifts and Comforts Association; Chair. Dept Committee; Member Voluntary Aid Committee, Red Cross of S. Africa, 1914-18. *Address :* Midwood, Newlands, near Cape Town. *Clubs :* Ladies' Empire; Alexandra, Cape Town. (C380)

INNES, Lieut. Robert, M.B.E., E.A.F.

INNES, Capt. Robert McGregor, O.B.E.

INNES, Capt. Cecil MITCHELL-, C.B.E. (ret.), *b.* 6 July, 1866 ; *s.* of Gilbert Mitchell-Innes, of Edinburgh ; *m.* Sarah Etheldreda, *d.* of the late Col. James Le Geyt Daniell. *Educ.:* Cheam School, Sutton, Surrey ; Fettes College, Edinburgh ; Royal Military College, Sandhurst. Gazetted to Prince of Wales' Lincoln Regt., 29 Aug. 1885 ; promoted to Capt., 23 Oct. 1893 ; transferred to 79th Queen's Own Cameron Highlanders, 1898 ; appointed Chief Constable of Lincolnshire, Oct. 1903. *Address:* High House, Leadenham, nr. Lincoln. *Club:* Junior United Service. (C2707)

INNES, Major Edward Alfred MITCHELL-, C.B.E., K.C., J.P., *b.* 21 Dec. 1863 ; *s.* of Gilbert Mitchell Innes, of 39, Inverleith Place, Edinburgh ; *m.* Annie Barbara, *d.* of Robert Laycock, of Wiseton, Bawtry, Yorks. *Educ.:* Wellington and Balliol Coll. Oxford. Barrister-at-Law ; K.C. 1908 ; Recorder of Middlesbrough, 1915 ; Bencher of Middle Temple, 1918 ; Deputy Chairman of Herts Quarter Sessions ; Member of National Assembly of Church of England ; Chairman of Consolidated Cambrian Ltd. ; and of Glamorgan Coal Co. Ltd. Ministry of Munitions ; Legal Adviser to British and Canadian Recruiting Mission in U.S.A., 1917–1918. *Address:* Churchill, Hemel Hempsted. *Clubs:* St. James' ; Garrick. (C1129)

INNS, Major Jeremiah, O.B.E., R.A.S.C.

INSKIP, Capt. Arthur Cecil, *b.* 7 Dec. 1892 ; *s.* of J. Inskip, of London ; *m.* Edith Annie, *d.* of E. C. Harper, of Brighton. *Educ.:* London. *War Work:* Served with Mediterranean Expeditionary Force in Gallipoli, and with British Expeditionary Force in France. *Addresses:* Adderbury, Egremont Place, Brighton ; Cawnpore, India. (O5420)

INSKIP, Grace Hampden, O.B.E.

INSKIP, Thomas Walker Hobart, C.B.E., K.C., J.P., M.P., *b.* 6 March, 1876 ; *s.* of the late James Inskip, of Clifton Park House, Bristol ; *m.* Lady Augusta Helen, 7th *d.* of Earl of Glasgow (*see* BURKE'S *Peerage*), of Kelburn. *Educ.:* Clifton ; King's College, Cambridge. King's Counsel ; Chancellor of Diocese of Truro ; M.P. for Central Bristol. *War Work:* Head of Naval Law Dept. of Admiralty. *Addresses:* 10, Eaton Square, S.W. 1 ; Knockinaam, Lochans, Wigtownshire. *Clubs:* Carlton ; United University ; Roehampton. (C2708)

INSKIPP, Major Percy Sidney, O.B.E., R.A.S.C.

INWOOD, Capt. Charles Herbert, O.B.E., M.C., Worcestershire Regt., *b.* 5 Feb. 1875 ; *s.* of George Inwood, of Leach, Herefordshire ; *m.* Sophia, *d.* of Christopher Evans, L.R.A.M., of London. *Educ.:* Edgbaston Commercial School, Birmingham. *Club:* Junior Army and Navy. (O6644)

IONIDES, Helen Euphrosyne, M.B.E., *b.* 7 April, 1871 ; *d.* of Constantine A. Ionides, of London. *Educ.:* Privately. *War Work:* Organised Gift Room at 2nd Eastern General Hospital ; Assistant to Controller of Q.M.A.A.C. in the Aldershot Command. *Addresses:* 23, Second Avenue, Hove ; 22, Prince Edward Mansions, Palace Court, W.2. *Club:* Albemarle. (M5374)

IRBY, 2nd Lieut. Gerald Howard Boteler, M.B.E.

IRBY, Lieut.-Col. Leonard Paul, O.B.E., *s.* of Leonard Howard Loyd Irby (*see* BURKE'S *Peerage*) ; *m.* Ethel Maud, *d.* of the late William John Casberd-Botelet, R.N., of Taplow (*see* BURKE'S *Landed Gentry*). *Educ.:* Eton. *War Work:* Commanded successively 15th Batt. Rifle Brigade, 24th Batt. King's Royal Rifles, and 16th Training Reserve Batt. ; subsequently served on lines of communication in Italy. *Address:* Evington, Ashford, Kent. *Clubs:* Army and Navy ; Windham. (O7315)

IREDALE, Lieut. Frederick Mitchell, M.B.E., R.A.F.

IREDALE, Joe, M.B.E., L.R.C.P., M.R.C.S.

IRELAND, Blanche, M.B.E., W.A.A.C.

IRELAND, Henry Ralph, M.B.E., *b.* 19 Nov. 1873 ; *s.* of J. Ireland, of Woodford. Bank Clerk. *War Work:* Services in connection with employment by Messrs. Morgan, Grenfell & Co., Merchants. *Address:* Norfolk Villa, St. Clements Avenue, Leigh-on-Sea, Essex. (M8597)

IRELAND, Herbert James, M.B.E.

IRELAND, Lieut. James Augustus, M.B.E., R.A.S.C.

IRELAND, Myrtle, De Courcy, M.B.E., *b.* 9 Aug. 1883 ; *t.* of the late John Lloyd, J.P., D.L. of Gloster, Roscrea, Kings Co. ; *m.* the late Wyndor Plunkett de Courcy, Lieut. Commander R.N. and R.N.A.S., *s.* of de Courcy Ireland, of Merton Hall, Borrisokane, Co. Tipperary. *Educ.:* Alexandra Coll., Dublin. *War Work:* Personal Assistant to the late Air Commodore R. M. Groves, C.B., D.S.O., A.F.C., during his appointments as Deputy Chief of Staff, Air Ministry, Deputy Controller, Technical Dept. Air Ministry, and Director Air Division, Admiralty, 1916–19. *Address:* Gloster, Roscrea, King's Co. *Club:* Empress. (M8598)

IRELAND, William Edward, O.B.E., M.I.M.E.

IREMONGER, Col. Edgar Assheton, C.B.E. Formerly Col. Durham L.I. ; served in the Great War, 1914–19 (despatches). (C1631)

IREMONGER, Capt. Ernest Lascelles, O.B.E.

IRISH, Elsie Celia, M.B.E.

IRON, Capt. Douglas, O.B.E., R.A.F.

IRON, Capt. John, O.B.E., *b.* 25 May, 1858 ; *s.* of Richard Iron, of Dover ; *m.* Annie, *d.* of H. Crundall, of Dover. *Educ.:* Dover College. Harbour Master and Surveyor to Lloyds Register. *War Work:* Salvage Officer for the District under the Admiral of the Dover Patrol. *Address:* 3, Maison Dieu Road, Dover. *Club:* Royal Cinque Ports Yacht. (O1511)

IRONS, Major Thomas William, M.B.E., R.A.O.C.

IRONSIDE, Catherine Mary, M.B.E., M.B.

IRONSIDE, Helen Maud BAX-, M.B.E.

IRVIN, Sir John Hannell, K.B.E., late Adviser to the Board of Trade and the Restriction of Enemies' Supplies Dept. on purchases of fish, etc., from Foreign Countries ; Joint Managing Director R. Irwin & Sons, Ltd. *Address:* 86, Queen's Road, Aberdeen. (K25)

IRVIN, Capt. William Dion, C.B.E., *b.* 1870 ; *s.* of David S. Irvin, of Bombay ; *m.* Winifred May, *d.* of C. H. Maxted, of Windermere. *Educ.:* Northern Institute, Liverpool. Comdr. and Acting Captain, R.N. *War Work:* 1914–19 ; present at the battle of Jutland ; at Zeebrugge ; and as Commodore of Convoy ; mentioned in despatches. *Club:* Naval and Military. (C1193)

IRVINE, Capt. Charles Alexander Lindsay, M.V.O., O.B.E.

IRVINE, Professor James Colquhoun, C.B.E., Ph.D., D.Sc., F.R.S., *b.* 9 May, 1877 ; *s.* of John Irvine, of Springburn, Glasgow ; *m.* Mabel Violet, *d.* of John Williams, of Dunmurry, Co. Antrim. *Educ.:* Allan Glen's School ; the Universities of St. Andrews and Leipzig. Professor of Chemistry and Dean of the Faculty of Science in the University of St. Andrews ; Director of the Chemical Research Laboratories in the United College, University of St. Andrews ; now Appointed Principal of the Univertity of St. Andrews. *War Work:* Devised new methods for the preparation of the Bacteriological Sugars required for the Navy and Army, and conducted their manufacture ; carried out investigations on gas-poisons, and acted as scientific adviser to various Government Departments. (C2709)

IRVINE, John Maitland, M.B.E., B.Sc., *b.* 29 Oct. 1878. *Educ.:* Robert Gordon's Coll., Aberdeen, and Aberdeen Univ. Schoolmaster, Headmaster, H.M. Dockyard School, Rosyth. *War Work:* Organised H.M. Dockyard School, Rosyth, in 1916 for the training of apprentices in Technical Education ; previously, Headmaster, H.M. Dockyard School, Pembroke Dock, South Wales. *Addresses:* H.M. Dockyard School, Rosyth ; 13, Stanley Street, Portobello, Edinburgh. (M8600)

IRVINE, Capt. Lionel Herbert, M.B.E.

IRVINE, Lieut. Matthew, O.B.E.

IRVINE, Margaret Elizabeth, Mrs. Charles Irvine DOUGLAS-, M.B.E.

IRVING, Henry Edward, M.B.E. Censor, Bloemfontein. (M10258g)

IRVING, Herbert Cavan, C.B.E., M.A., LL.M., *b.* 1854 ; *s.* of John Irving, of 94, Eaton Place, S.W. ; *m.* 1st, 1880, Mary Helen, who *d.* 1905, *d.* of the late John Johnstone, of Halbeaths ; 2nd, 1907, Jane Euphemia, *d.* of the late Robert Thorburn, of Romanby, Yorkshire. *Educ.:* Trinity Coll., Cambridge. Bar. Inner Temple, 1880 ; formerly Capt. and Hon. Major 3rd Batt. King's Own Scottish Borderers ; Chairman, Local Tribunals ; Convener, and J.P. for Dumfriesshire. *Address:* Burnfoot, Ecclefechan. *Clubs:* Windham ; New (Edinburgh). (C34)

IRVING, Irene Hazel, Mrs., M.B.E., *b.* 27 June, 1894 ; *d.* of the late Allan Bruce Maclean, C.M.G., of (*see* BURKE'S *Peerage*) ; *m.* Stanley Gordon, H.M. Commercial Diplomatic Service, *s.* of Charles Frederick Irving. *Educ.:* Godolphin School, Salisbury, and abroad. *War Work:* Voluntary confidential work at British Consulate-General, Valparaiso, Chile. *Address:* The Manor House, Oban, N.B. (M3823)

IRVING, John, M.B.E., *b.* 11 Sept. 1873 ; *s.* of William Lowther Irving, of Annan, N.B. ; *m.* Jessie Howatson Mitchell, *d.* of James Wyllie, of Elmbank, Dumfries. *Educ.:* Annan Academy ; Solihull Grammar School ; Edinburgh Univ. *War Work:* Hon. Sec. and Treas. Dumfries Burgh War Pensions Sub-committee. *Address:* The Summit, Dumfries, N.B. *Club:* Southern, Dumfries. (M8601)

IRVING, Capt. John Duckworth, O.B.E., M.C., *b.* 1890 ; *s.* of Martin Luther Irving, Rector of Bloxham, Lincoln. *Educ.:* St. John's, Leatherhead ; Lincoln School. *War Work:* Served in 23rd Division, 1916–17, France ; 1918 till conclusion of war in Italy. (O6385)

IRVING, Lieut.-Col. Lewis Allen, O.B.E., R.A.M.C. (ret. pay), *b.* 1850 ; *s.* of Major-Gen. A. Irving, of Royal Artillery. *Educ.:* Dublin and Germany. *War Work:* Member of the War Refugees Committee, with special charge of the Belgian Hostels in London. *Address:* 22, Westgate Terrace, Redcliffe Square, S.W. (O1512)

IRVING, Lieut.-Col. Miles, O.B.E.

IRVING, Lieut.-Comm. Robert Beaufin, O.B.E., R.D., R.N.R.

IRVING, Lieut.-Col. Andrew BELL-, D.S.O., O.B.E., *b.* 1855 ; *s.* of the late John Bell-Irving, of White Hill, co. Dumfries. Entered R.A. 1875 ; Capt. 1883 ; Major, 1891 ; Lieut.-Col. 1900 ; retired 1903 ; served in the Afghan War, 1878–80 ; present at battle of Kandahar (despatches, medal with clasp) ; S. Africa, 1900–2 (despatches twice) ; served in the Great War as D.A.A.G. 1914 ; Defence Commander, Lines of Communication, 1915–18. (O6895)

IRVING, Isabella, Mrs. BELL-, M.B.E.,

IRVING, Lieut.-Col. Richard BELL-, O.B.E.

IRVING, Major Alfred William Adamson, O.B.E., R.A.M.C.

IRWIN, Major Basil Herbert John, O.B.E.

IRWIN, Eric Barnby, M.B.E.

IRWIN, Capt. George Robert, C.S.I., O.B.E.

IRWIN, Jean Percival, Mrs., M.B.E.

IRWIN, Sarah, Mrs. Fitzjohn, M.B.E., *b.* 25 Feb. 1856 ; *d.* of A. A. Murray-Ker, J.P., D.L., of Newbliss ; *m.* the late Fitzjohn Robert, *s.* of John Irwin, of Carnagh. *War Work :* Commandant St. John V.A.D. 642 ; Head of Depot work under D.G.V.O. in Monaghan, Ireland ; Emergency Lecturer for F.A. and H.N., St. John Ambulance Association. *Address :* Beech Hill, Monaghan, Ireland. (M8603)

IRWIN, Lieut. Stanley, M.B.E.

IRWIN, Lieut.-Comm. Thomas Cuthbert, O.B.E., R.N.V.R.

IRWIN, Thomas James, O.B.E.

ISAAC, Charles, M.B.E.

ISAAC, John Edward, M.B.E.

ISAAC, John Raja Ratnam, M.B.E., B.A. (Madras), *b.* 20 Sept. 1881 ; *s.* of the Rev. Gurnbatham Isaac, of Palamcottah, S. India ; *m.* Dr. Mary Ratnamma (L.M.S., Madras), *d.* of Martin Luther, B.A., of Palamcottah. *Educ. :* C.M.S. Coll. Tinnevelly ; Madras Christian Coll. Gen. Sec. Y.M.C.A., Madras, Colombo, Bangalore. *War Work :* In Mesopotamia and Bangalore, among British and Indian troops. *Address :* Y.M.C.A., Bangalore. (M6168)

ISAAC, Joseph Charles, C.B.E.

ISAAC, Major Thomas Austin, O.B.E., T.D. R.E., (T.).

ISAAC, William Rudolph Vernon, M.B.E., M.C.

ISAACS, Capt. David Nathan, M.B.E., M.C.

ISAACS, Ellis, M.B.E., *b.* 1874 ; *s.* of Emanuel Isaacs, of Merthyr Tydvil, Wales. *Educ. :* Hutcheson Grammar School, Glasgow. President Jewish Representative Council, South Portland Street Synagogue, Hebrew Benevolent Loan Society, and Jewish Board of Guardians, Glasgow ; Member of the Board of Deputies of British Jews, London. *War Work :* Hon. Treas. Russian Jewish War Relief Fund ; Member Prince of Wales' Committee, Local Committee under Military Service Act, Food Committee, and Profiteering Committee. *Clubs :* Liberal, Glasgow ; Scottish Liberal, Edinburgh. (M8606)

ISAACS, Harry Michael, O.B.E., D.L.

ISAACS, Isaac Benjamin, O.B.E., *b.* 27 Feb. 1871. *Educ. :* Brighton Grammar School. Financier. *War Work :* Joined Wessex Divisional Train, Sept. 1914, and went to France with 27th Reserve Park, March, 1915 ; was given Command 1st Reserve Park, B.E.F., 1 June, 1915 ; promoted T. Major, Aug. 1915 ; joined 1st Cavalry Division as 1st Cavalry Divison Reserve Park, and remained with this Division until March, 1919, when the unit was broken up for Demobilisation ; mentioned in despatches, July, 1917. *Address :* 8, Jubilee Terrace, Southsea. (O2586)

ISAACS, Mariette, Mrs., O.B.E.

ISBISTER, Wlilliam James, M.B.E.

ISHAM, Lieut. Ralph Heyward, C.B.E., R.E.

ISHERWOOD, Col. Charles Edward Ramsbottom, C.B.E. T. Lieut.-Col. and Hon. Col. Special Reserve ; served in the Great War, 1914–19 (despatches). (C1310)

ISHERWOOD, Lieut.-Comm. Harold, O.B.E., R.N.V.R.

ISMAY, Capt. Charles BOWER-, C.B.E.

IVELL, Grace Mary, M.B.E. ; *d.* of William Ivell, of Birmingham. *Educ. :* Birmingham. Professional Singer. *War Work :* Concerts at the Fronts, for Miss Lena Ashwell, O.B.E., Feb. 1915, to Jan. 1916, France ; Feb. 1916, to Aug. 1916, Malta and Italy ; Aug. 1916, France ; Sept. 1916, to Jan. 1919, Egypt and Palestine ; Feb. 1919, to July, 1919, France and Germany. *Address :* 14, Observatory Road, East Sheen, London, S.W.14. (M8607)

IVERMEE, Lieut. Robert, M.B.E., R.N.

IVES, Lieut. William Henry Martin, O.B.E., *b.* 1 Sept. 1883 ; *s.* of Capt. J. F. Ives, M.C., of 65, Lincoln Road, Peterborough ; *m.* Annie, *d.* of Thomas Storrs, of Clayworth, Notts. *Educ. :* Army School (Elementary). Joined Royal Artillery, Jan. 1898 ; served through S. A. War, 1899–1902 (King and Queen's Medals with 7 clasps) ; Military Clerk, War Office, 1904–12 ; joined Staff of Committee of Imperial Defence, 1912 ; served with 2nd Cavalry Division in France, 1914–15 (1914 Star, British War Medal, and Victory Medal) ; War Committee Secretarial, 1915 ; Confidential and Chief Clerk, War Cabinet, 1916–19 ; Confidential and Chief Clerk Cabinet and Committee of Imperial Defence, 1919. *Address :* Chelstone, Waterden Road, Guildford. (O10709)

IVORY, Capt. Harold Frank, O.B.E., R.A.S.C.

IYOD, Edwin Gilbert, M.B.E.

IZARD, Major Arnold Woodford, O.B.E., M.C., M.D.

JABOTINSKY, Lieut. Vladimir, M.B.E.

JACK, Alexander Mackenzie, C.B.E., J.P., *b.* 1851 ; *s.* of Alexander Jack, of Avoch. Dep. Chairman of Hadfields, Ltd. *Address :* Brincliffe, Sheffield. (C2711)

JACK, Brig.-Gen. Archibald, C.B., C.M.G., C.B.E. ; Brig.-Gen. Great War, 1914–19 (despatches). *Address :* 13, Ladbroke Grove, W. 11. (C1632)

JACK, Douglas William, M.B.E.

JACK, Col. Herbert Rowett Henry, C.M.G., C.B.E., *b.* 1863 ; *s.* of Richard George Jack, M.D. Soudan Exp. 1884–5 (medal with two clasps, bronze star) ; S. Africa, 1899–1901, as Assist. Director of Supplies (despatches) ; Dep.-Director of Transport, 1914 ; Assist. Director of Supplies and Transport, 1915–19. (C820)

JACK, James Robertson, M.B.E.

JACK, Capt. John Gordon, O.B.E., Can. A.S.C.

JACK, John William, O.B.E.

JACK, Major Walter, O.B.E., Aust. A.O.C.

JACKA, Hilda Tyacke, M.B.E., M.A. *War Work :* Head of the Records and General Intelligence Section, Statistical Branch, Ministry of Food, 1918–19. (M8608)

JACKLING, Capt. Percival, O.B.E. *War Work :* Finance Officer, Machine Gun Corps, Machine Gun Training Centre, Headquarters, Grantham ; Controller and Hon. Treas. Machine Gun Corps Prisoners of War Relief Fund. *Address :* Lloyds Bank House, Hythe, Kent. (O10711)

JACKMAN, Lieut. Cornelius John Gershom, M.B.E., R.A.S.C., *b.* 5 Oct. 1888 ; *s.* of E. G. Jackman ; *m.* Laura Mary Dorothy, *d.* of Alderman Charles Farley, J.P., of Tenby. *Educ. :* Hillmartin Coll., London, N.W. Central Stores Department, Ministry of Munitions. *War Work :* Roads Officer, then Workshop Office, and finally O.C. 568 Co. R.A.S.C., attached 15th Motor Ambulance Convoy, France. *Address :* The Gables, Venner Road, Sydenham, S.E. 26. (M4529)

JACKMAN, Douglas Arthur John, M.B.E., *b.* 1 Jan. 1893 ; *s.* of A. D. Jackman, J.P. of Dorchester ; *m.* Nancy Oliphant, *d.* of H. W. Hutchison, J.P., of Kirkcaldy. *Educ. :* Dorchester Grammar School. *War Work :* 1914, V.A.D. Orderly) Feb. 1915 to May 1919, Sec. Y.M.C.A., Boulogne Base, B.E.F. *Address :* Equihen, Dorchester, Dorset. (M8753)

JACKS, Harold Benjamin, O.B.E.

JACKSON, Lieut.-Col. Alfred, O.B.E.

JACKSON, Alice Mabel Erskine, M.B.E., *b.* 29 Oct. 1873 ; *d.* of James Rawlinson Jackson, of the Indian Medical Service (Deputy Surgeon General), and of Kirkbuddo, Forfar, Scotland. *War Work :* Member of the East Scottish Branch Soldiers' and Sailors' Families Association (Forfarshire Branch) ; Member of the Dundee Local Committee ; Vice-Convener of the Disablements Department of that Committee ; Member of the Forfarshire Local Committee. *Address :* Kirkbuddo, Forfar, Scotland. (M591)

JACKSON, Aline Louise, Lady, O.B.E., *d.* of late William Wallace Cooper, of Dublin ; *m.* Sir Frederick John Jackson, K.C.M.G., C.B., Gov. and Com.-in-Chief of Uganda, 1911–17. *Address :* Evergreens, Lyndhurst, Hants. (O2356)

JACKSON, Andrew Eric, O.B.E., M.A., LL.D., *b.* 6 Aug. 1882 ; *s.* of Andrew Marvel Jackson, of Hessle, E. Yorks. *Educ. :* Hymers Coll., Hull ; Pembroke Coll., Cambridge. *War Work :* Procurator-General's Department dealing with Prize. *Addresses :* Beacongarth, Hessle, E. Yorks. ; Victoria Chambers, Bowlalley Lane, Hull. *Clubs :* Junior Constitutional, London ; Hull and East Riding, Hull. (O10713)

JACKSON, Arthur, M.B.E.

JACKSON, Sir Cyril, K.B,E., M.A., *b.* 1863 ; *s.* of the late Laurence Morris Jackson, of South Park, Bodiam, Sussex. *Educ. :* Charterhouse ; New Coll. Oxford. Barrister of the Inner Temple, 1893 ; Member of London School Board, 1891–96 ; Head of the Education Dept., West Australia, 1896–1903 ; Chief Inspector, Board of Education, 1903–6 ; Investigator on Unemployment in England and Ireland, and on Boy Labour, to the Royal Commission on the Poor Law, 1906 ; Member L.C.C., Limehouse Division, 1907–13 ; Alderman L.C.C. 1913–16 and 1919 ; Chairman L.C.C. 1915 ; Chairman of London Intelligence Committee on Unemployment Local Government Board, 1914 ; Chairman of Advisory Committee on National Register, 1915 ; Vice-Chairman War Pensions, etc., Statutory Committee, 1916–17 ; Member of Central Tribunal, 1915–16 and 1918–19. *Addresses :* Ballards Shaw, Limpsfield ; 12, St. James' Place, S.W.1. *Club :* Savile. (K26)

JACKSON, Daniel, C.B.E., partner in the firm of Denny Bros., shipbuilders, Dumbarton. *Address :* Dumbarton. (C209)

JACKSON, Daniel Noel, M.B.E., M.B., B.S., *b.* 25 Dec. 1871 ; *s.* of the late Daniel Jackson, of Bellister Castle, Haltwhistle-on-Tyne ; *m.* Catherine, *d.* of the late James Williamson, of Craigbarnet, Greenock. *Educ. :* Durham School, and Durham Univ. Medical Practitioner ; Poor Law Medical Officer ; Public Vaccinator. *War Work :* M.O. in charge 4th Northumberland Auxiliary Hospital, Dilston Hall, Corbridge ; M.O. in charge P. of W. Camp, Slaley, Northumberland. *Address :* Bridge House, Corbridge-on-Tyne. (M8609)

JACKSON, Dorothy Starr, Mrs., M.B.E.

JACKSON, Edward St. John, O.B.E.

JACKSON, Edward Siddall, M.B.E., M.D., C.M., *b.* 20 July, 1856 ; *s.* of William Jackson, M.R.C.S., of Bolton-le-Sands, Lancashire ; *m.* Nora, *d.* of John Vickers Stacey, of Sheffield. *Educ. :* Royal Grammar School, Lancaster, and Edinburgh Univ. Medical Officer of Health for Carnforth Urban District ; Poor Law Medical Officer for Lancaster Rural District Union, and for Luresdale Union ; Surgeon of Police ; Medical Officer for the Post Office. *War Work :* Medical Officer in Charge of Bleasdale House V.A.D. War Hospital ; Consulting Surgeon to the Wray V.A.D. War Hospital. *Address :* Robin Hill, Carnforth. *Club :* Carnforth Conservative. (M8610)

JACKSON, Capt. Francis Munton, M.B.E.

JACKSON, Freda Christelle, M.B.E.

JACKSON, Major George Erskine, O.B.E., M.C., T.D., J.P., *b.* 13 Mar. 1872 ; *s.* of James Rawlinson Jackson, Deputy Surgeon-General, I.M.D. *Educ. :* Haileybury Coll., and Corpus Christi Coll., Oxford (B.A., 1895 ; 2nd Class Honour Mods. ; 1st Class Honours Law). Writer to the Signet, 26, Rutland Square, Edinburgh ; Justice of the Peace, and Commissioner of Supply for the County of Forfar, late Major of

Fife and Forfar Yeoy. *War Work:* Served as Private in the C.I.V. (M.I.) in South African War (Queen's Medal, 3 Clasps), 1900; Staff Capt. Highland Mounted Brigade, Aug. 1914, to April, 1916; D.A.A. and Q.M.G. Western Force, E.E.F., June, 1916, to May, 1917; D.A.Q.M.G. Delta and Western Force, E.E.F., May, 1917, to July, 1917; D.A.A.G. Australian Mounted Division, E.E.F., July, 1917, to July 1919; Served in Gallipoli, including evacuation from Suvla; Egypt, Palestine, and Syria; took part with General Allenby's Mounted Troops in all the operations from the capture of Beersheba to the capture of Damascus; twice mentioned in despatches. *Addresses:* Kirkbuddo, Forfar; 26, Rutland Square, Edinburgh. *Clubs:* New, and Univ., Edinburgh; Caledonian, London. (O6214)

JACKSON, Lieut.-Col. George Scott, C.B.E., D.S.O., T.D., *b.* 1870; *s.* of the late Daniel Jackson; *m.* 1894, Maud, *d.* of the late C. Harrison Stanton. Major and Brevet Lieut.-Col. Northumberland Fusiliers (T.F.); served in the Great War, 1914–19 (despatches). *Address:* Alnwick, Northumberland. (C1273)

JACKSON, Gwendoline Doris, Mrs., O.B.E.
JACKSON, Comm. Harold Gordon, O.B.E., R.N.
JACKSON, Squadron-Leader Henry Leigh, C.B.E.
JACKSON, Herbert, M.B.E., I.A.
JACKSON, Professor Sir Herbert, K.B.E., F.R.S., *b.* 17 Mar. 1863; *m.* Amy, *d.* of James Collister. Assistant Professor, 1902; Professor of Organic Chemistry, King's Coll., 1905; Fellow of King's Coll. London, 1907; Director of Research; British Scientific Instruments Research Assoc.; Emeritus Professor of Chemistry, Univ. of London; Daniell Professor of Chemistry, King's Coll. London, 1914–18. *Address:* 49, Lansdowne Rd., Holland Park, W.11. *Clubs:* Athenæum; Savile. (K27)

JACKSON, Sir Herbert William, K.B.E., C.B., *b.* 5 Feb. 1861; *s.* of late W. H. Jackson, of Frowlesworth Hall, Leicester. Entered Army 1881; served Egyptian War, 1882 (medal and Khedive's Star); Sudan Expedition, 1884; joined the Egyptian Army, 1888; Nile Expedition, 1884–85; Dongola Expeditionary Force, 1896; Atbara, 1898 (clasp, despatches); battle of Khartoum (despatches, Br. Lt.-Col., clasp, British Nile Medal); Governor of Fashoda district and in command of forces at Fashoda during March and Mission incident; Nile Expedition, 1899; Governor of Berber Province, 1899–1900; Lt.-Gov. of the Sudan and Civil Secretary, 1900–2; mentioned in despatches, 1916, for administrative work connected with the situation in the Sudan created by the War. *Address:* Dongola, Egypt. (K325)

JACKSON, Capt. Hugh William, M.B.E.
JACKSON, Jessie Millicent, O.B.E., R.R.C., Q.A.I.M.N.S.R.
JACKSON, John, O.B.E., *b.* 1 Jan. 1865; *s.* of John Jackson, of Manchester; *m.* Amy A., *d.* of Samuel Beaumont, of Southport. *Educ.:* Broughton High School; Owens College, Manchester. Civil Servant. H.M. Superintending Inspector of Factories (Home Office) for the N.W. Division. *War Work:* Special work and enquiries in connection with the Factory Dept.; 1917, Commissioner for the N.W. Division, National Service Dept.; Technical Adviser to the Reserved Occupations Committee, and later to the Trade Exemptions Dept. of the Ministry of National Service. *Address:* Richmond Hill, Bowdon, Cheshire. (O457)

JACKSON, John William, O.B.E., *b.* 16 Sept. 1873; *s.* of William Jackson, of Pendleton, Manchester. *Educ.:* Manchester. Solicitor; Town Clerk of Grimsby and Clerk to the Enrolled Freemen of Grimsby since Jan. 1914; previously, Deputy Town Clerk of Salford. *War Work:* Member of the Board of Management, and Hon. Sec. to the Grimsby National Shell Factory; Clerk to the Local Military Tribunal; Member of the Recruiting Committee; Hon. Sec. to the War Emergency Committee; Sec. and Treas. to the Local War Pensions Committee; Executive Officer of the Food Control Committee, and Hon. Sec. to the Local Relief Committee. *Address:* The Mount, 8, Dudley Street, Grimsby. *Club:* County, Grimsby. (O10715)

JACKSON, Joseph Clough, M.B.E., *b.* 1 Dec. 1878; *s.* of Hornsby Jackson, of the Brownberries, Horsforth; *m.* Nora Wainman, *d.* of the late J. M. Fawcett, of Leeds. *Educ.:* Repton. Chartered Accountant. *War Work:* Hon. Sec., Lord Mayor of Leeds Belgian Refugees Committee. *Address:* Heathfield Cottage, Far Headingley, Leeds. *Club:* Leeds and County Conservative. (M594)

JACKSON, Laura, Mrs., O.B.E., *b.* 1867; *m.* George Frederick Jackson. *War Work:* Red Cross; Vice-President, Solihull Division, B.R.C.S., Warwickshire; Commandant, Springfield V.A.D. Hospital, Knowle. *Address:* Springfield House, Knowle, Warwickshire. *Club:* Three Counties, Birmingham. (O458)

JACKSON, Lieut. Leonard Edward Selmas, M.B.E. R.F.A. (T.F.).
JACKSON, Lillian May, Mrs., M.B.E., *b.* 11 Jan. 1895; *d.* of William Rogers, of Helston, Cornwall; *m.* Vincent Edmund, *s.* of E. B. P. Jackson, of Enfield. *War Work:* Service with Women's Voluntary Reserve, May, 1915, to July, 1917; service with Q.M.A.A.C. from Aug. 1917, to May, 1920. *Address:* 5, Hazelwood Lane, Palmers Green, N.13. (M1948)

JACKSON, Major Gen. Sir Louis Charles, K.B.E., C.B., C.M.G., *b.* 7 Mar. 1856; *s.* of late Sir Louis Stewart Jackson, C.I.E., B.C.S., of Hadleigh Hall, Suffolk; *m.* Bessie, *d.* of William Vivian, D.L. *Club:* United Service. (K85)

JACKSON, Mary, M.B.E.
JACKSON, Maud Mary, Mrs., M.B.E.
JACKSON, Capt. Max., O.B.E., *b.* 7 May, 1877; *s.* of Thos. H. Jackson, of the Manor House, Birkenhead; *m.* Lily, *d.* of Richard Stubbs, of Birkenhead. *Educ.:* Harrow. Farmer. *War Work:* Enlisted Public Schools Batt., R.N.D., Dec. 1914; Served with M.E.F. from May, 1915 to Dec. 1915; invalided home; commissioned as Transport Officer, 16th Batt., Sherwood Foresters (Chatsworth Rifles), June, 1916; served in France till Sept. 1916; invalided home; appointed M.A.R.O., Chester Area, May, 1917; Capt., Sept. 1917; Transferred to M.N.S. as D.D.N.L.S., Nov. 1917; Deputy Controller, Min. Lab., North-Western Division, from Jan. 1918 to Jan. 1919. *Address:* Upfield Farm, Brockweir, nr. Chepstow. (O3135)

JACKSON, Nellie, Mrs. Hilditch, M.B.E., *b.* 29 Dec. 1890; *d.* of Major John Pitt, of Hong Kong and Woolwich; *m.* Charles Hilditch, *s.* of Joseph Jackson, of Audley, Staffs. *Educ.:* Grosvenor House School, Wokingham, Berks. For eight years was engaged at the War Office, and during the War was in charge of the typing establishment, Park Buildings, War Office. *Address:* Glencairn, Forthbridge Road, Clapham Common. (M2291)

JACKSON, Sub.-Lieut. Norman, M.B.E., R.N.V.R. (M6853)

JACKSON, Major Oswald Egerton Orme, O.B.E.
JACKSON, Alderman Robert, O.B.E., J.P. Mayor of Todmorden for seven years. (O11907)

JACKSON, Major Robert Hugh Holmes, O.B.E., M.C., 3rd Batt. East Surrey Regt., *b.* 21 May, 1891; *s.* of Col. Sir Robert Whyte Melville Jackson, K.C.M.G., K.B.E., C.B. *Educ.:* Downside. *Address:* 50, Hurlingham Court, London, S.W.6. (O6485)

JACKSON, Col. Sir Robert Whyte Melville, K.C.M.G., K.B.E., C.B., *b.* 3 June 1860; *s.* of late Robert Jackson, Registrar-General of Shipping; *m.* Frances, *d.* of Capt. Hugh McTernan, J.P., D.L., of Heapstown House, Sligo. *Educ.:* Marlborough. Entered 2nd Batt. Royal Inniskilling Fusiliers, 1881; Army Ordnance, 1886; Capt. R. Inniskilling Fusiliers, 1890; Major, 1897; Lt.-Col., 1901; Col. 1907; Brig. Gen., 1915; served S. Africa, 1900–1 (despatches twice, brevet of Col., Queen's Medal, 3 clasps; King's Medal, 2 clasps, C.M.G.); Chief Ordnance Officer, Cape Colony, 1903–5; appointed Director of Ordnance for Mediterranean Expeditionary Force (despatches three times); Order of White Eagle, Serbia, 1916. *Address:* 50, Hurlingham Court, S.W.6. (K271)

JACKSON, Roland Octavius, M.B.E., *b.* 26 Mar. 1879; *s.* of Thomas Hughes Jackson, of the Manor House, Birkenhead. *Educ.:* Harrow; and Balliol Coll., Oxford. *War Work:* B.R.C.S. Transport Officer for Birkenhead and Wirral District. *Addresses:* The Manor House, Birkenhead; 2, Cockspur Street, London, S.W.1. *Clubs:* Bath; Denham Golf. (M1949)

JACKSON, Samuel, O.B.E., F.I.C., A.R.C.S., *b.* 20 March, 1871; *s.* of Joseph Jackson, of Keighley, Yorkshire; *m.* Maud Morison, *d.* of David Duncan, LL.D., of Aberdeen. *Educ.:* Yorkshire Coll. (now Leeds Univ.); Royal Coll. of Science, London. Superintending Chemist, Buckingham Mill Co., Ltd., Madras, and Camari Mill Co., Ltd., Madras. *War Work:* Chiefly engaged on Khaki Cloth for Indian Army (Army Clothing, Indian Munitions Board). *Address:* c/o Messrs. Binny & Co., Ltd., Madras, India. *Club:* Madras. (O8263)

JACKSON, Major Samuel, O.B.E., R.A.S.C. (T.).
JACKSON, Eng.-Lieut.-Col. Stanley, O.B.E., R.N.
JACKSON, Capt. Swinscho James, O.B.E. (Mil.), *b.* 19 Feb. 1868; *s.* of Swinscho Jackson, of Retford, Notts; *m.* Henrietta Elsie, *d.* of John Peters Richards, of Sharnbrook, Beds. *Educ.:* Privately. Served a number of years in the 14th (King's) Hussars, also in the 8th Royal Irish Hussars. *War Work:* Appointed (G.S.) General Service Officer on the outbreak of war and proceeded to Ireland; Commanded various detachments in Ireland and took part in the Rebellion, Dublin; took charge of the armoured cars, Royal Barracks, Dublin; afterwards proceeded to France with the 8th Batt. Royal Irish Regt., in the advance on Hindenburg lines; twice mentioned in despatches by Sir Douglas Haig. *Address:* 3, East Ascent, St. Leonards-on-Sea, Sussex. *Clubs:* Constitutional; Conservative (Hastings). (O5421)

JACKSON, Lieut. Thomas Edwin, O.B.E., R.N.V.R.
JACKSON, Capt. Thomas Eldridge, O.B.E.
JACKSON, Violet, Mrs., M.B.E.
JACKSON, Violette Mary, Mrs., M.B.E.
JACKSON, William Henry Congreve, M.B.E.
JACKSON, Ada Frances, Lady MATHER-, O.B.E., Lady of Grace St. John of Jerusalem, *b.* 17 March, 1861; *d.* of the late Gen. Edward Arthur Somerset, C.B., of Troy House, Monmouth; *m.* Henry Mather, *s.* of Sir Henry Mather-Jackson, Bart. (*see* BURKE's *Peerage*), of Llantillio Court, Abergavenny. Chairman of the Monmouth Board of Guardians; Sec. Monmouthshire Nursing Association; Member of the Maternity and Child Welfare Committee; C.C. *War Work:* Chairman of the Monmouthshire Land Army; Sec. of the Nursing Committee of the Manideff Court Auxiliary Red Cross Hospital, Abergavenny. (O10712)

JACKSON, Sir Henry MATHER-, C.B.E., J.P., D.L., *b.* 19 Oct. 1855; *m.* Ada, *d.* of late Gen. Somerset, C.B., Troy House, Monmouthshire. *Educ.:* Harrow; Trin. Coll. Cambridge. Barrister, Lincoln's Inn, 1881; Alderman; Chairman Quarter Sessions for Monmouthshire; Deputy Chairman of the Grand Trunk Railway of Canada. *Address :* Llantillio, Abergavenny; 56, Montagu Square, W.1. *Club :* Brooks's. (C533)

JACKSON, Lieut.-Col. Arnold Nugent Strode STRODE-, C.B.E., D.S.O., (Res. of Officers), *b.* 5 April, 1891 ; *s.* of the late Morton Strode-Jackson, I.S.O., of Addlestone, Surrey ; *m.* Dora Berryman, *d.* of the late William Allen Mooney, of Columbus, Indiana, U.S.A. *Educ. :* Malvern, and Brasenose College, Oxford. Barrister-at-Law (Middle Temple). *War Work :* Adjutant of 13th Bn. of the Rifle Brigade ; Commanded the 13th King's Royal Rifle Corps ; D.S.O. with 3 bars ; six times mentioned in despatches ; three times wounded ; temporarily lent to Foreign Office for duty with the British Delegation at the Peace Conference, Paris (C.B.E.). *Addresses :* Mead Cottage, Merstham, Surrey ; 93A, Linden Gardens, W. 2. *Club :* Junior Carlton. (C2712)

JACOB, Lieut.-Col. Arthur Leslie, C.I.E., O.B.E., *b.* 1870 ; *s.* of the late H. P. Jacob, Educational Depart., India ; *m.* 1896, Jenny Coke Mickleburgh. Entered Indian Army, 1891 ; Major, 1909 ; Lieut.-Col. 1917 ; appointed Assist. to Agent to Gov. Gen., Baluchistan, 1901 ; Assist. Political Agent, Zhob, 1903 ; Political Agent, Baluchistan, 1909 ; 1st Assist. Agent to Gov. Gen. 1909 ; Political Agent, Zhob, 1902. *Address :* Zhob, Baluchistan, India. (O843)

JACOB, Edmund Henry, O.B.E.

JACOB, Ven. John Attwood, O.B.E., M.A., *b.* 28 Sept. 1866 ; *s.* of Rev. Canon Jacob, of Horningsham, Wilts ; *m.* Alicia Barbara, *d.* of Rev. F. W. Maunsell, of Symondsbury, Dorset *Educ. :* Lancing College ; Keble College, Oxford. Archdeacon of Timaru and Westland ; Vicar of Timaru, New Zealand. *War Work :* Chaplain, New Zealand Expeditionary Force, 3rd class, July. 1916 Aug. 1919. *Address :* St. Saviour's Boys' Orphanage, Timaru, New Zealand. (O7998)

JACOB, John Hier, O.B.E., B.A. (Oxon.), *b.* 20 Feb. 1884 ; *s.* of the late Hier Jacob, Solicitor, of Abergavenny, Mon. and London ; *m.* Alice, *d.* of the late John Mortimer, of Ellands, Forres, N.B. *Educ. :* St. Paul's School ; Lincoln College, Oxford. Solicitor ; Principal Clerk, Legal Administrative side of the Public Trustee Office. *War Work :* Public Trustee's Office. *Addresses :* 15, Warwick Gardens, Kensington, London ; Callandraed, Cooden, Sussex. *Club :* Sudbrook Park Golf. (O3770)

JACOB, Rev. John Thomas, O.B.E., *b.* 1 Aug. 1859 ; *s.* of Philip Jacob, of Norwood ; *m.* Edith Mary, *d.* of Rev. Alfred Henry New, of Addiscombe. *Educ. :* Privately ; Cheshunt Coll. Cambs. ; Dublin Univ. Clerk in Holy Orders ; Vicar of Torquay ; Surrogate. *War Work :* Chaplain to the Torquay Town Hall Hospital for Wounded Soldiers, 1914–17 ; made 18 pr. shells in munition works in Torquay, 1914–17 ; Commissioned Chaplain Mar. 1917 to Mar. 1919 with H.Q. Heavy Artillery, 9th Corps, and after, with Fourth Army Artillery School, 27 Jan. 1918 to 13 July 1918 ; 71st Bde. H.A., 12 Aug. 1918 to 27 Aug. 1918 ; Fourth Army School of Musketry, 27 Aug. 1918 ; Instructor and Lecturer on History, Geography, and Photography in the 4th Army Young Soldiers' School, Namur ; mentioned in despatches ; held an Honorary Commission in the Army. *Address :* Tor Vicarage, Torquay. (O5422)

JACOBS, Dorothy Isabel, M.B.E.

JACOBS, Lieut. Jonathan, O.B.E., R.F.A. (T.).

JACOBS, Julius, O.B.E., J.P., *b.* 7 July, 1861 ; *s.* of David Jacobs, of Liverpool ; *m.* Hannah, *d.* of the late P. Hands, Banker, of Charing Cross, London. *Educ. :* Liverpool. Member of the Liverpool, Bootle, and District Advisory Committee, Ministry of Labour ; member of Committee of Employment Exchange ; member of Sub-Committee of the Local War Pensions Committee ; Visiting Justice, H.M. Prison, Walton ; Member of the Licensing Committee of Theatres and Public Entertainments. *War Work :* Hon. Sec. Liverpool and Birkenhead Branch of the National Association for Employment of ex-Soldiers. *Address :* Linwood, Sefton Park Road, Liverpool. *Clubs :* Conservative, Liverpool ; Press, Liverpool ; The Club, Harrogate. (O10717)

JACOBS, Louis, M.B.E., *b.* 26 Oct. 1891. *War Work :* Chief Accountant of the Trading with the Enemy Dept. *Address :* 57, Warrington Crescent, Maida Vale, W. (M8614)

JACOBSON, Ernest Nathaniel Joseph, C.B.E., *b.* 15 July 1877 ; *s.* of the late S. N. Jacobson, of 23, Woburn Square, London ; *m.* Gladys Welcome, *d.* of the late Walter Ellis, of 94, Portland Place, W. *Educ. :* City of London School. Member of firm of Guedalla, Jacobson & Spyer, Solicitors. *War Work :* Joined Metropolitan Special Constabulary, 1914 ; Chairman of Discipline Board from Oct. 1914 ; Assistant Staff Officer on Staff of Sir Edward Ward (Chief Staff Officer), Sept. 1914; Commandant and Chairman of Discipline Board of Metropolitan Special Constabulary Reserve. *Addresses :* Winchester House, Old Broad Street, E.C. 2 ; 63, Gloucester Portman Square, W. 1. *Clubs :* Reform ; Law Society ; Walton Heath Golf. (C35)

JACOBSZ, Lieut.-Col. Jan, O.B.E.

JACOMB, Major Frederick Basil Wood, O.B.E., I.A.

JACQUES, The Rev. George Henry Paul, M.B.E.

JAFFRAY, Rev. William Stevenson, Deputy Chaplain General to the Forces, C.M.G., C.B.E., D.D. (Edin.), *b.* 30 March, 1867 ; *s.* of the late William Stevenson Jaffray, of Greystones, Aberdeenshire ; *m.* Ethel Annie Duncan, *d.* of Major James Law, of Lauriston, Torphins, Aberdeenshire. *Educ. :* Edin-

burgh University. *War Work :* Senior Chaplain, 7th Division (1914–16), B.E.F. ; Assistant Principal Chaplain, 5th Army ; Principal Chaplain, British Salonica and Black Sea Forces ; Four times mentioned in despatches ; Awarded C.M.G., June, 1915 ; C.B.E., 1919 ; Knight Commander of Order of St. Sava, Serbia (St. Sava II Class). *Address :* Royal Army Chaplains' Dept., War Office. (C1413)

JAGGARD, Capt. George, O.B.E.

JAGGER, Major Hugh Cleivion, O.B.E., R.A.V.C. (T.).

JAGGER, Lieut. William, M.B.E., R.A.S.C.

JAIPUR, H.H. Maharajadhiraja Sir Sawai Madho Sing Bahadur of, G.C.S.I., G.C.I.E., C.V.O., G.B.E., *b.* 1861 ; *s.* of the Thakar of Isarda. Hon. Major-Gen. in the Indian Army; raised and maintains the Imperial Transport Corps for service of the British Govt.; raised a permanent Famine Relief Fund for India, 1900; attended Coronation of King Edward VII., 1902; entitled to salute of 21 guns. *Address :* Jaipur Palace, Rajputana India. (G20)

JAKEWAY, George, M.B.E.

JAMES, Lieut.-Col. Albert John Stanley, C.B.E., D.S.O. M.C. Major and Acting Lieut.-Col. Roy. Welsh Fusiliers; served in the Great War, 1914–18 (despatches). (C534)

JAMES, Alfred Henry, C.B.E.

JAMES, Arthur Godfrey, C.B.E., *b.* 22 Oct. 1876 ; *s.* of John Henry James, of Kingswood, Watford ; *m.* Helen, *d.* of Thomas Maitland, of Broughty Ferry, Scotland. *Educ. :* Eton ; Trinity Coll., Oxford. Solicitor. *War Work :* Lieut. R.A.S.C., 1915–16 ; Egypt, 1916 ; Staff Capt., D.A.A.G., War Office, 1916–17 ; Ministry of National Service, 1917–18. *Address :* 58, Rutland Gate, S.W. 7. *Clubs :* Union ; Burlington Fine Arts ; Leander. (C2713)

JAMES, Lieut.-Col. the Hon. Cuthbert, C.B.E., M.P., *b.* 29 Feb. 1872 ; *s.* of Walter Henry, 2nd Lord Northbourne (*see* BURKE'S *Peerage*), of Bettishanger, Eastry, Kent ; *m.* Florence Marion, *d.* of Hussey Packe, of Prestwold, Loughborough. *Educ. :* Harrow ; Magdalen Coll., Oxford. Lieut.-Col. (ret.). M.P. (Co.-U.) for Bromley, Kent, bye-election, Dec. 1919 ; formerly an officer in the East Surrey Regt., the Egyptian Army, holding appointments under the Sudan and Egyptian Governments. *War Work :* Joined up at outbreak of War ; Capt. 7th (s.) Batt. E. Surrey Regt. ; Major Nov. 1914 ; served in France and Flanders till early in 1916, relinquishing his commission owing to ill-health ; appointed to the Royal Marines, with rank of Major, as Inspector of Admiralty Motor Transport ; shortly after promoted Lieut.-Col. *Address :* 3, Ormonde Gate, S.W. 3. *Clubs :* Brooks's ; Garrick; Beefsteak; 1900, etc. (C1930)

JAMES, Major Dennis Cory, O.B.E., *b.* 1896 ; *s.* of late William Cory James, of Tafira, Grand Canary ; *m.* Florence Rose, *d.* of William Barr, of Naramine, Australia. *Educ. :* Hurstpierpont Coll. Sussex. Anglo-American Oil Co. *War Work :* Lieut., 2nd Worcestershire Regt. 1914–16 ; wounded ; transferred to Royal Flying Corps ; Staff Officer, Air Ministry, 1917–20 ; Staff Officer, 2nd Class and Sec. to R.A.F. Delegation to Peace Conference, Paris, 1920 ; Sec. to Technical sub-Commission on International Aerial Navigation, Paris, 1920. Legion of Honour. *Address :* 20, Woodville Gardens, Ealing, W. 5. *Club :* R.A.F. (O8124)

JAMES, Diana Lily, Mrs., M.B.E. ; *d.* of De Vere Beauclerk (*see* BURKE'S *Peerage*) ; *m.* Christian Hugh, *s.* of the late Thomas James, of Otterburn Towers, Northumberland (*see* BURKE'S *Landed Gentry*). *War Work :* Commandant, Holeyn Hall Hospital, Wylam-on-Tyne. *Address :* Rudchester, Wylam-on-Tyne. (M1951)

JAMES, Dudley William Henry, M.B.E., *b.* 1873 ; *s.* of William James, of Hampstead. *Educ. :* Univ. Coll. Chairman Income Tax Commissioners, St. Martin's Parish ; Chairman of Governors of St. Martin's High School. *War Work :* Sub-Inspector of Special Constabulary, H.Q.C. Division ; seconded for duty with Metropolitan Observation Service (Anti-Aircraft) ; Member of Advisory Committee to Tribunal, City of Westminster. *Address :* Under Ridge, Bourne End, Bucks. *Clubs :* Royal Automobile ; National Liberal. (M3755)

JAMES, Capt. Edward Lionel Lusombe, M.B.E.

JAMES, Major Edward Stewart, O.B.E., Aust. A.V.C.

JAMES, Eleanor Marian, M.B.E., W.R.N.S.

JAMES, Eric Ibbetson, O.B.E., M.A., *b.* 23 Sept. 1888 ; *s.* of the late Herbert James, of Hampstead ; *m.* Iris, *d.* of Charles Silburn Barber, of 12, Rivercourt Road, W. *Educ. :* St. Paul's School, and Corpus Christi Coll., Oxford. British Council Officer, Supreme Economic Council ; British Sec., Permanent Committee, Supreme Economic Council ; Sec., Interdepartmental Russian Trade Committee. *War Work :* Ministry of Food, 1917–19 ; Sec., Inter-Allied Oilseeds Executive, 1918–19 ; sometime British Sec. and acting representative, European Coal Commission. *Address :* 71, Talgarth Mansions, W. *Club :* Authors'. (O10718)

JAMES, Lieut.-Col. Eustace Lindsay Haweis, O.B.E., R.A.O.C.

JAMES, Major Frank Treharne, M.B.E., V.D., *b.* 9 Oct. 1861 ; *s.* of Frank James, of Merthyr Tydfil ; *m.* Agnes Grace, *d.* of William Powell, of Hirwain, Glamorganshire. *Educ. :* Clifton. Solicitor. *War Work :* Military Representative, O.C. 3rd V.B. Welsh Regiment. *Address :* Penydarren House, Merthyr Tydfil. *Clubs :* Sports ; Cardiff and County, Cardiff. (M8616)

JAMES, Major Frederick, C.B.E., R.A.S.C. Served in the Great War, 1914–19 (despatches). (C1633)

JAMES, Frederick Ernest, O.B.E.

JAMES, Frederick John, M.B.E.

JAMES, Capt. Fullarton, O.B.E.

JAMES, George Charles, O.B.E.

JAMES, Gwenyfred, Lady, O.B.E., J.P., *b.* 27 April, 1870 ; *d.* of Dr. Hearder, of Carmarthen, Wales ; *m.* Hon. Sir Walter Hartwell, K.C., of Perth, Western Australia (*see* BURKE'S *Peerage*), *s.* of Edward Senior James. *Educ. :* Carmarthen. *War Work :* Executive of Red Cross, Western Australia ; President, XI. Batt. Women Workers ; National Council of Women ; Y.M.C.A. *Address :* 69, Mount St., Perth, Western Australia. *Club :* Xanakatta, Perth.

JAMES, Gwilym Prosser, O.B.E., M.R.C.S.

JAMES, Henry Mannsell, M.B.E.

JAMES, Lieut.-Col. Herbert Ellison Rhodes, C.B., C.M.G., O.B.E., F.R.C.S., *b.* 20 Oct. 1857 ; *s.* of the late Rev. Herbert James, of Livermere, Suffolk. *Educ. :* Aldeburgh School ; Charing Cross Hospital. R.A.M.C., attached to General Staff, War Office, for training of Medical Units, O.T.C. *War Work :* Served in Egypt, Command of No. 15 General Hospital, 1915–18 ; Salonika, Command of Nos. 61 and 36 Gen. Hospitals, 1918–19. *Address :* c/o Messrs. Holt & Co., 3, Whitehall Place. *Clubs :* Junior United Service ; Flyfishers'. (O6486)

JAMES, Herbert William, M.B.E., *b.* 4 Dec. 1875 ; *s.* of the late Frederick James, of Twickenham ; *m.* Edith Mary, *d.* of the late Francis Millar, of Watford. *Educ. :* Watford Grammar School. Parliamentary Assistant, Solicitor's Office, L. and N.W.Ry., Euston Station, N.W. *War Work :* In charge of Legal Section, Timber Supplies Department, Board of Trade ; Assistant Controller of Timber Supplies, supervising administration of orders regulating the sale and purchase and distribution of home-grown timber and pitwood in England and Wales. *Address :* 4, Wiggenhall Road, Watford, Herts. (M3756)

JAMES, Iris Silburn, Mrs., M.B.E., *b.* Oct. 18 1892 ; *d.* of Charles Silburn Barber, of 12, Rivercourt Road, W. 6 ; *m.* Eric Ibbetson, *s.* of the late Herbert James. *Educ. :* Francis Holland School ; Ecole St. Pierre, Nancy. Official of the League of Nations. *War Work :* Voluntary work in connection with North Islington Welfare Centre ; organised registries in the Ministry of Food, M. and D. Divisions ; Sec. to Mr. J. I. Craig, Statistician, of the Ministry of Food ; organised Registries of the Supreme Economic Council ; loaned to the Reparation Commission for Inter-Allied Secretariat work. *Address :* 71, Talgarth Mansions, Barons Court, W. 14. (M1953)

JAMES, Ivor Lough, M.B.E.

JAMES, James Picton, M.B.E.

JAMES, Jenkin, O.B.E.

JAMES, Josephine Selina, Mrs., M.B.E. ; *d.* of Capt. Elisha Hitchins, of Falmouth ; *m.* Richard, *s.* of Richard James, of Tiverton. *War Work :* Hostel for Belgians ; Streatham War Hospital Supply Depot. (M1955)

JAMES, Katharine Margaret, M.B.E., W.R.N.S.

JAMES, 2nd Lieut. Maurice Jewison, M.B.E., R.A.F.

JAMES, Rev. Percival Walter, O.B.E.

JAMES, Lieut.-Col. Ralph Ernest Haweis, C.M.G., C.B.E., D.S.O., *b.* 1875. Major and Brevet Lieut.-Col. Loyal Regt. (N. Lancs.) ; served in China, 1900 (medal) ; and during Great War, 1914–18. *Address :* 47, Draycott Place, S.W.3. (C2354)

JAMES, Rebecca Green, Mrs., O.B.E., *b.* 1859 ; *d.* of William Davis, of Killeagh House, Co. Cork ; *m.* Charles Edward, *s.* of John James, of Butler House, Kilkenny. *War Work :* Hon. Sec. Soldiers' and Sailors' Families Assocn., " Friend " Soldiers' Help ; Hon. Sec. and Treas. Kilkenny Castle War Hospital Supply Depot, 1915–19 ; Assistant in Soldiers' Home ; Voluntary Recruiter for the Q.M.A.A.C., Member of Local War Pensions Committee. *Address :* Butler House, Kilkenny, Ireland. (O10722)

JAMES, Robert Percival, O.B.E.

JAMES, Sidney Frederick, O.B.E., *b.* 13 Sept. 1869 ; *s.* of E. James, of Liverpool ; *m.* Florence Gray, *d.* of J. E. Beer, of Liverpool. *Educ. :* Liverpool. Town Clerk ; Clerk to the Local Education Authority ; Clerk to the Higher Education Committee ; Clerk to the Burial Board, Ilkeston. *War Work :* Assist. Sec. Admiralty Labour Department ; Sec. Tramways (Board of Trade) Committee. *Address :* Town Hall, Ilkeston ; Roseneath, Ilkeston. (O10723)

JAMES, Rev. Canon Sidney Rhodes, C.B.E., V.D., *b.* May, 1855 ; *s.* of Rev. Herbert James, of Livermere, Suffolk ; *m.* Luida, *d.* of Henry Hoare, of Staplehurst, Kent. *Educ. :* Haileybury ; Trinity College, Cambridge ; Archdeacon of Dudley. Canon of Worcester Cathedral ; Examining Chaplain to Bp. of Worcester ; Select Preacher, Cambridge University, 1899, 1911, 1916 ; Formerly assistant master, Eton College, 1879–97, and headmaster, Malvern College, 1897–1914. *War Work :* Chaplain, (T.F.) First Class, 61st Division, 1915 ; Senior Chaplain Norwich, 1916 ; District Senior Chaplain, Thames and Medway Garrison (Chatham area), 1916–19. *Addresses :* The College, Worcester ; St. Denis, Bembridge, I. of W. *Clubs :* Worcestershire County ; Bembridge Sailing. (C1634)

JAMES, Thomas David, C.B.E., M.A., *b.* 3 April, 1871 ;

m. Pauline, *d.* of Sir Francis MacCabe, F.R.C.P.I., of Dublin. *Educ. :* Christ's College, Brecon ; Christ's College, Cambridge. Acting Deputy Accountant-General of the Navy. *Address :* 24, Queen's Gate Terrace, S.W. *Club :* Junior Carlton. (C2714)

JAMES, Thomas Qwynfab, M.B.E.

JAMES, Wilhelmina Martha, O.B.E. ; *d.* of Rev. Octavius James, of Clarghyll Hall, Alston, Cumberland. *Educ. :* At home. Literature. *War Work :* Canteen for Sick and Wounded under British Red Cross Society in Salonica, 1916–18 (2½ years) ; Canteens of the Church Army (after the Armistice) in Belgium, France and Germany ; also, Y.M.C.A. in All Welcome Hut, Victoria Station. *Address :* c/o Miss J. M. James, Summerfield, Malvern Wells, Worcestershire. *Club :* Ladies' Lyceum. (O1515)

JAMES, William Arthur, M.B.E.

JAMES, Eng.-Capt. William Henry, C.B.E., R.N.

JAMES, William Henry, O.B.E., *b.* 27 Sept. 1870 ; *s.* of William James, of Walsall ; *m.* Catherine Anne, *d.* of Rev. Griffith Williams, of Carnarvon. *Educ. :* Privately. Trained under the London and North Western Railway Co. at Crewe Works ; Civil Engineer on public works. *War Work :* Chief Investigation Officer, Northern Counties, investigating and adjusting industrial disputes in connection with wages, working conditions, etc. ; maintaining production by improving timekeeping and working conditions of the workers. *Address :* 30, Windsor Terrace, Gosforth, Newcastle-on-Tyne. *Club :* Rotary. (O10724)

JAMES, William Isaac, O.B.E.

JAMES, William John, O.B.E., *b.* 18 Oct. 1852 ; *s.* of the late John James, of Haven Street, nr. Hyde, I. of W. ; *m.* 1st, Sarah, *d.* of George Whale, late of Hampton Court, Middlesex, 2nd, Ethel Lucy, *d.* of W. H. Wooster, late of Bath. *Educ. :* Ryde, I. of W. Superintendent, Plymouth Post Office, 1885–90 ; Postmaster, Devonport, 1890–1900 ; Postmaster of Colchester, 1900–1 ; Postmaster of Middlesbrough, 1901–4 ; Postmaster of Oxford, 1904–7 ; Postmaster of Exeter, 1907–9 ; Postmaster of Southampton, 1909–18. *War Work :* Making up and receipt and disposal of mails to and from the armies overseas, and the great pressure of telegraph work relating to the various armies. *Address :* Westfield, Clifton Road, Southampton. (O1516)

JAMES, William Warwick, O.B.E., F.R.C.S., L.D.S.

JAMES, Williard Frank, O.B.E.

JAMES, Capt. Edward Hamilton CARKEET-, O.B.E., M.C., D.C.L.I., *b.* 15 June, 1893 ; *s.* of Charles Carkeet-James, of Westminster, S.W. *Educ. :* Cheltenham College ; R.M.C., Sandhurst. *War Work :* Served with the B.E.F., Dec. 1914 to May, 1915, and B.E.F., Nov. 1915 to May, 1919. *Clubs :* Junior United Service ; R.A.C. ; Roehampton. (O5075)

JAMES, Renel, Mrs. FULLARTON-, M.B.E.

JAMES, Capt. Charles Wilmot WANKLYN-, O.B.E. R.A.M.C.

JAMESON, Major Aaron, O.B.E.

JAMESON, Capt. David Napier, O.B.E., R.A.S.C.

JAMESON, Erskine Dawson, M.B.E., M.A., LL.B., *b.* 8 Feb. 1868 ; *s.* of James Jameson, of Elgin. *Educ. :* Aberdeen Grammar School ; Aberdeen and Edinburgh Universities. Solicitor and County Clerk of Moray. *War Work :* Hon. Treas. Red Cross Society, Morayshire Branch ; was instrumental in collecting large sums on behalf of Red Cross, French Relief Fund, Belgian Relief Fund, etc. ; largely responsible for success of War Savings movement in Elgin. *Clubs :* Elgin ; Scottish Conservative, Edinburgh. (M8619)

JAMESON, Capt. George Lionel, O.B.E., R.E.

JAMESON, Capt. William Storm, M.B.E.

JAMIESON, Adam James, M.B.E.

JAMIESON, Alexander, M.B.E.

JAMIESON, Major Alexander Harvey Morro, O.B.E., R.G.A.

JAMIESON, Charles Fleming, M.B.E.

JAMIESON, Major Edmund Charles Kean, M.B.E.

JAMIESON, Stanley Wyndham, C.B.E., *b.* 1885 ; *s.* of the late John Donaldson Jamieson, of Greenock ; *m.* Muriel Cartmel, *d.* of Rt. Hon. Lord Marchamley, of 29, Prince's Gardens, S.W. *Educ. :* Charterhouse. County Councillor, Gloucestershire ; Director, Duttons Brewery, Ltd. (Blackburn), and Burrow's Press, Ltd. (Cheltenham). *War Work :* Served Gloucestershire Regt. (1914–15) ; Private Sec. (unpaid), to Deputy Sec. of State for War (1916–19) ; Assistant (unpaid), to Controller of Inspection of Munitions (1919). *Addresses :* Thirlestaine Lodge, Cheltenham ; 103, St. George's Road, S.W. *Clubs :* Junior Athenæum ; New Cheltenham. (C984)

JAMIESON, Thomas Hill, M.B.E., *b.* 19 April, 1873 ; *s.* of Thomas Hill Jamieson, of Edinburgh ; *m.* Mary, *d.* of J. J. Milnes, of Huddersfield. *Educ. :* Arbroath High School, and Univ. of Edinburgh. Deputy Commissioner of Medical Services, Ministry of Pensions. *War Work :* Civilian doctor in charge of malaria wards, 4th London General Hospital. *Club :* Sports. (M13269)

JAMINSON, Samuel Jones, M.B.E.

JAMISON, Lieut. Robert Edward, M.B.E.

JAMMU AND KASHMIR, Lieut.-Gen. H.H. Maharaja Sir Pratap Singh Maharaja of, G.C.S.I., G.C.I.E., G.C.B., *b.* 14 July, 1850 ; *s.* of H.H. the late Maharaja, of Jammu and Kashmir, G.C.S.I. One of the Ruling Chiefs of India, with an area of 79,784 square miles and a population of three millions ; entitled to a salute of 21 guns. *Addresses :* Srinagar, Kashmir ; Jammu, Punjab. (G19)

JANES, Capt. Ernest, O.B.E., *b.* 10 Sept. 1879; *s.* of William James, of Long Crendon, Bucks.; *m.* Fanny Florence, *d.* of John Betts, of Long Crendon. *Educ.:* Long Crendon School. Quartermaster, R.A.M.C.; Commissioned from the ranks of the R.A.M.C. after 17 years' service in May, 1915. *War Work:* Employed at Headquarters of the Eastern Command, on the staff of the Deputy Director of Medical Services of that Command; from Jan. 1919, until May, 1920, held the appointment of Deputy Assistant Director of Medical Services, Eastern Command. *Addresses:* R.A.M.C. Record Office, Woking; Hilltop, Long Crendon, Bucks. (O7320)

JANION, Paymaster-Lieut.-Comm. Arthur Cyril Austin, O.B.E., R.N.

JANSON, Lieut. Frederick Ernest, M.B.E., R.A.O.C.

JAPP, George Allison, M.B.E., L.S.O., *b.* 18 Aug. 1865 *s.* of Alexander Japp. *Educ.:* Board School, Kirkcaldy, Scotland. Printer; now Salvation Army Officer. *War Work:* Assisted with Recruits at Cardiff early days of war; helped with reception of Belgian Refugees; work in Le Harve, Trouville and Rouen areas, from the spring of 1917, to Oct. 1919. *Address:* 84, Third Avenue, Heaton, Newcastle-on-Tyne. (M8622)

JAPP, Sir Henry, K.B.E., M.I.C.E., *b.* 6 June 1869; *s.* of James W. Japp, of Montrose; *m.* 1st, Elizabeth (died 1911), *d.* of David Hodge, Dundee; 2nd Kathie, *d.* of R. W. Sutherland, of Montreal. *Educ.:* Montrose Academy; Dundee Univ. Coll. Director and Managing Engineer S. Pearson & Son, Ltd., New York; President, S. Pearson, Son & Partners, Canada, Ltd., Montreal; with British War Mission in U.S.A.; Director in charge of Production. *Address:* 799, 17th St., Brooklyn, New York. *Club:* Bankers' (New York). (K149)

JARDIM, Antonietta Marcial, M.B.E.; *d.* of the late Antonio d'Almeida Jardim, of Funchal, Madeira. *Educ.:* Notre Dame de Sion, Worthing. *War Work:* Assist. Sec. at the King George Hospital, Stamford Street, London. *Address:* 5, Travessa do Arcipreste, Funchal, Madeira. (M8623)

JARDINE, Douglas James, O.B.E., M.A., *b.* 13 Oct. 1888; *s.* of James Jardine, M.D., of Richmond, Surrey. *Educ.:* Westminster; Trinity College, Cambridge. Assistant Secretary to the Government of Cyprus, 1910–16; Secretary to the Administration of British Somaliland, since 1916. *Address:* The Secretariat, British Somaliland. *Clubs:* New University; Royal Automobile. (O2226)

JARDINE, Ethel May, Lady, O.B.E.; *d.* of late Benjamin Piercy, of Marchwiel Hall Denbighshire, and of Macomer, Sardinia; *m.* 1894, Sir Robert William Buchanan Jardine, 2nd Bart. (*see* BURKE'S *Peerage*). *Addresses:* Castle Milk, Lockerbie, N.B.; 24, St. James's Place, S.W.; and the Kremlin, Newmarket. (O11787)

JARDINE, Capt. John, O.B.E., M.D., F.R.C.S.

JARDINE, Lieut. John, M.B.E., R.E.

JARDINE, Major William, O.B.E., T.D.

JARDINE, Capt. William Christopher, O.B.E., M.B., R.A.M.C.

JARMAN, Capt. Cecil Trevelyan, O.B.E., Aust. L.I., A.I.F.

JARMAY, Charlotte E., Lady, O.B.E.; *d.* of George Wyman, M.D., of Alcester; *m.* Sir John G. Jarmay, K.B.E. *War Work:* Vice-President Northwich Division, B.R.C.S.; Joint Officer in Charge, Auxiliary Hospital, The Ley, Northwich; and other war work for B.R.C.S. *Address:* Hartford Lodge, Hartford, Cheshire. (O10726)

JARMAY, Sir John Gustave, K.B.E., F.C.S., F.I.C., *b.* 31 Dec. 1856; *s.* of the late Gustav de Jarmay; *m.* Charlotte E., *d.* of late George Wyman, M.D. *Educ.:* Privately; Univ. of Zurich. Inventor of processes which are in use in several industries in England and abroad; special study in the Ammonia Soda Process with which industry he has been connected since its infancy; Technical Managing Director of Brunner, Mond & Co. Ltd., and Scientific Director of other Chemical Works in England and abroad. *Address:* Hartford, Cheshire. *Clubs:* Royal Societies'; Royal Automobile. (K86)

JARRATT, Elizabeth Lankester, Mrs., M.B.E., *b.* 17 May, 1887; *m.* William Theodore Jarratt, *s.* of William J. Jarratt, of Ealing. *Educ.:* Privately. *War Work:* Confidential clerk to the Controller of Shipping. *Address:* Ministry of Shipping, London. (M8624)

JARRETT, Herbert Ernest, M.B.E., R.A.S.C.

JARROLD, Alice Isabella, Mrs., M.B.E.

JARROTT, Major Charles, O.B.E., R.A.F.

JARRY, Rev. Frederick William, M.B.E., *b.* 25 Oct. 1871. Missionary in Orissa, India, for 25 years. *War Work:* Recruiting for Labour Corps in Mesopotamia. *Address:* Balangir, Orissa, India. (M4151)

JARVIS, Alfred William, M.B.E.

JARVIS, Lieut.-Col. Arthur Murray, C.M.G., C.B.E., *b.* 1863; *s.* of Arthur Murray Jarvis, of Osgoode Hall, Toronto; *m.* 1912, Gertrude Mary, *d.* of the late Capt. Lewis William Ord, 71st Highland L.I. Joined Canadian N.W. Mounted Police, 1880; retired, 1912; N.W. Rebellion, 1885 (medal); S. Africa, 1900–1, as Major, Strathcona's Horse (despatches), served in the Great War, 1914–19 as Assist. Provost Marshal, Canadian Forces with rank of Lieut.-Col; appointed Stipendiary Magistrate, Kootenay Co., British Columbia, 1897; to command out ports on Yukon River, 1902; Mackenzie River Dist. Police, Herschel Island, 1907; Magistrate of Alberta; engaged in farming and ranching. *Address:* Munson, Alberta, Canada. (C774)

JARVIS, Major Charles Francis Cracroft, O.B.E., *b.* 3 May, 1875; *s.* of Rev. Canon Jarvis (F.A.), of Burton-on-Stather Vicarage, Doncaster; *m.* Helen Constance, *d.* of Sir Edward Hunter Blair, Bart., of Blairquhan, Ayr, N.B. *Educ.:* Marlborough. Capt. (Ret. Pay), 19th Yorkshire Regt.; now Major, in 3rd Lincolns; Member of Lloyds. *War Work:* 1914–19, France; 1914 Star. *Addresses:* Doddington Hall, Lincoln; 8, Manson Place, Queen's Gate, S.W. *Club:* Boodles'. (O5425)

JARVIS, Enid Sybil, M.B.E., *b.* 29 April, 1899. *Educ.:* Bedford High School. *War Work:* Voluntary worker on National Registration and Recruiting; joined paid staff and held several responsible appointments, both under the War Office and Ministry of National Service, at Huntingdon, Watford, Hertford, and finally in London; on demobilisation of Ministry of National Service recommended to Home Counties Division, Ministry of Food; appointed Administrative Assistant in London and Home Counties Division, Ministry of Food. *Address:* 5, Kensington Gardens Square. (M8627)

JARVIS, Capt. Oswald Duke, O.B.E., M.D., R.A.M.C.

JARVIS, Capt. Thomas Stanley Wiles, O.B.E.

JARVIS, Capt. William Bertie, O.B.E.

JAY, Edward Aubrey Hastings, O.B.E., M.A., LL.B., *b.* 2 June, 1869; *s.* of the late Thomas Jay, of Clifton Villas, Putney; *m.* Isobel Violet, *d.* of Major P. G. Craigie, C.B., of Avenue House, Lympstone, Devon. *Educ.:* Winchester; and Trinity Coll., Cambridge. Member of London School Board, 1900–7; Assist. Sec. Royal Commission on Feeble Minded, 1905–7; London County Council, 1907–11; Chairman of L.C.C. Education Committee, 1910–11. *War Work:* Organising Sec. to Charity Organisation Society in East London, 1915–17; Chairman of Advisory Committee for Juvenile employment, Woolwich, 1914–15; also Chairman of Committee formed to organise hostels for boys employed in the Arsenal; Hon. Sec. Poplar War Savings Committee, 1916–17; Chairman of Whitechapel Local War Pension Committee, 1916–17; Ministry of Food, 1917–21. *Address:* Clifton Lodge, East Heath Road, Hampstead, N.W. 3. *Club:* Athenæum. (O10727)

JAY, Lieut. Stanley, M.B.E., K.R.R.C.

JAY, Major William Cunliffe Pickersgill, O.B.E. *Address:* White Lodge, Datchet, Bucks.

JAYNE, Major Arthur Alfred, O.B.E., D.S.O., M.C.

JAYNE, Ethel Basil, O.B.E., *d.* of the late Basil Jayne, J.P., of Breconshire. *Educ.:* St. John's College, St. Leonards-on-Sea. Founder and Director of the Little Laundries, Ltd. *War Work:* Women's Emergency Canteens for soldiers with the French 6th Army 1915; Organiser and Chief Superintendent of Welfare for Sir W. G. Armstrong Whitworth, Ltd., 1916–18; Capt. of the Elswick Co. of the Newcastle Women's Volunteer Reserve. *Address:* Kimscot, Stanmore, Middlesex. (O28)

JAYNE, Ronald Garland, O.B.E., *b.* 8 June, 1877; *s.* of F. J. Jayne, formerly Bishop of Chester; *m.* Mary Salkeld, *d.* of Thomas Salkeld Robinson, of Rochdale. *Educ.:* Privately. Managing Director of Garland, Laidley & Co., Ltd., Liverpool, Lisbon, Oporto, and Vigo; a founder of the British Hospital, Lisbon, and Lisbon Nursing Association; of the British Chamber of Commerce (Inc.) in Portugal; Chairman of Council of same since foundation; Member of the Navigation Committee of the Commercial Association, Lisbon. *War Work:* Director of British Press Bureau for Portugal and Colonies; Official representative of British Ministry of Information in Portugal and Colonies; Controller on behalf of the British Government at the Companhia Uniao Fabril, Portugal. *Address:* 65, Travessa de Cabral, Lisbon, Portugal. *Clubs:* R.A.C. and Junior Constitutional, London; Royal British, Lisbon; British, Oporto. (O10728)

JAZDOWSKA, Mary Margaret, M.B.E., *b.* 28 May, 1844; *d.* of John Jazdowska, of Aberdeen. *Educ.:* Aberdeen. *War Work:* Organising and running the British Sailors' and Soldiers' Club in Rome. *Address:* c/o Sir Charles McGrigor, Bart., & Co., 39, Panton Street, Haymarket, London. (M1956)

JEAL, George, M.B.E., *b.* 18 June, 1860; *s.* of Jeremiah Jeal, of Horsham; *m.* Charlotte, *d.* of Thomas Kent, of London. *Educ.:* Colgate, Sussex. Railway Station Superintendent. *Address:* 112, Buckingham Palace Road, S.W. 1. (M8628)

JEAL, Lieut. Joseph, M.B.E., R.A.S.C., *b.* 1 Aug. 1880; *s.* of Joseph Jeal, of Dorking, Surrey; *m.* Alice Annie, *d.* of Alfred Tickner, of Petworth. *Educ.:* Univ. School, Reigate. Shipping Agent. *War Work:* Special Police; 10th Surrey Volunteers as Platoon Commander and Musketry Officer, 1914–15; joined 3rd Batt. London Rifle Brigade, 1915, serving on Musketry Staff of that unit; commissioned 1918; served at Murmansk and Archangel; appointed A. Capt. May, 1919, while on the staff of D.D.S.T., Archangel Force. *Address:* Brook View, Wathen Road, Dorking. *Club:* United R.A.S.C. (M6968)

JEANS, Lieut.-Comm. George, O.B.E., R.N.

JEBB, Georgina Martha, Mrs., M.B.E., *b.* 1867; *d.* of Charles T. Tunnard, of Frampton House, Boston, Lincs. (*see* BURKE'S *Landed Gentry*); *m.* George S. W. Jebb, *s.* of John Joshua Jebb, of Norton House, Boston, Lincs. Sometime on the Board of Management, Bedford Co. Hospital; Sec., Bedford Habitation Primrose League; Mayoress of Boston, Lincs.; Vice-President, and Hon. Commandant of Lincs. 2/4 V.A.D.'s; on the Ely, Lincoln, and Hereford Councils of the Mothers' Union. *War Work:* Commandant Red Cross Auxiliary Hospital, Leintwardine, Herefordshire; Hon. Sec. of the Red Cross War Working Party; Registrar for the

Women's War Agricultural Work ; Hon. Sec. for the Fruit and Vegetable Depot at Leintwardine. *Address :* The Manor House, Meldreth, Nr. Royston, Herts. (M3758)

JEBB, Lieut.-Col. Gladwyn Dundas, C.M.G., C.B.E.

JEBB, Robert Russell Horsley, O.B.E.

JEEVES, Isabel Blanche, M.B.E.

JEEVES, William John, C.B.E., K.C., *b.* 20 Dec. 1864 ; *s.* of William Jeeves, of Hitchin, Herts. ; *m.* Elisabeth Blanche, *d.* of William Blinkhorn, J.P., of Sutton Grange, St. Helen's, Lancs. *Educ. :* Privately. Town Clerk of County Borough of St. Helens, 1891–99, and of the City of Leeds, 1899–1903. *War Work :* British Red Cross and Order of St. John ; Wounded and Missing Dept. ; Hon. Organiser of Searching for Information in all Provincial Hospitals in Great Britain and Ireland. *Addresses :* 3, Farrar's Buildings, Temple, E.C. 4 ; The Well House, Wimbledon. *Clubs :* St. Stephen's. (C2715)

JEFF, Capt. Robert Hunter, O.B.E.

JEFFERIES, Marguerite, M.B.E., B.Sc. (Lond.) ; *d.* of John Robert Jefferies, of Ipswich. *Educ. :* Ipswich High School, and Westfield Coll., London. Poor Law Guardian, Ipswich. *War Work :* Member of following Committees : Ipswich War Savings, Ipswich Communal Kitchen, of the Mayor's (Ipswich) War Relief Fund, of the Ipswich War Pensions, of East Suffolk Women's Agricultural. *Address :* 2, Park Road, Ipswich. (M3760)

JEFFERSON, Capt. Henry, C.B.E., R.N. ; *b.* 1865; *s.* of Henry Thomas Jefferson ; *m.* Violet Catherine, *d.* of late William Harrison, of Winscales, Cumberland. Dep. Naval Assistant Director of Transports. Great War 1914–19 (despatches). *Address :* Upton nr. Birkenhead. *Clubs :* Junior Army and Navy ; and Conservative, Liverpool. (C2256)

JEFFERSON, Capt. Herbert, O.B.E., R.A.S.C.

JEFFERY, Benjamin James Thomas, M.B.E., *b.* 31 Dec. 1870. *War Work :* Foreman of the Yard, H.M. Dockyard, Devonport, until July, 1917, then Senior Foreman of the Yard at H.M. Naval Base, Invergordon. *Address :* 28, Ford Hill, Devonport, Devon. (M8629)

JEFFERY, Florence Augusta, O.B.E., Medaille de la Reine Elisabeth ; *d.* of the late John Jeffery, of Broadmead, nr. Folkestone. *War Work :* In charge of Free Buffet for Soldiers and Sailors, Folkestone Pier, 1914–19. *Address :* Broadmead, nr. Folkestone, Kent. (O10729)

JEFFERY, Eng.-Comm.-Lieut. George Hoare, O.B.E., R.N.

JEFFERY, Major George Russell, O.B.E.

JEFFERY, Herbert Orthelstan, M.B.E.

JEFFERY, Major John, O.B.E., M.C.

JEFFERY, Margaret Ann, O.B.E., Medaille de la Reine Elisabeth ; *d.* of the late John Jeffery, Esq.. of Broadmead, nr. Folkestone. *War Work :* In charge of Free Buffet for Soldiers and Sailors, Folkestone Pier, 1914–19. *Address :* Broadmead, nr. Folkestone, Kent. (O10730)

JEFFERY, Lieut. Reginald, O.B.E., R.F.A.

JEFFERY, Surg.-Lieut.-Comm. Thomas Walter, O.B.E., R.N.

JEFFERYS, Capt. Arthur Harold, O.B.E., M.C.

JEFFERYS, Edward Compton, M.B.E., *b.* 19 Jan. 1877 ; *s.* of John Compton Jefferys, of Highgate. *Educ. :* Ushaw Coll., Durham. Secretary. *War Work :* Ministry of Munitions, Trench Warfare Dept., as Secretary to Sir Alexander Roger, 1915–17. *Address :* Swanmore, Hendon. *Club :* Royal Automobile. (M1957)

JEFFES, George Ernest, O.B.E.

JEFFREY, Edward James, M.B.E.

JEFFREYS, Charles Nicholas Theodore, M.B.E., *b.* 19 Nov. 1877 ; *s.* of the late Walter Powell Jeffreys, D.L., J.P., of Forde, Ludlow, Salop ; *m.* Ida Baines, *d.* of the late Sir Arthur Bower, of Forwood, Bart., P.C., M.P., of the Priory, Gateacre, Lancs. *Educ. :* Radley. Deputy Town Clerk of Brighton. *War Work :* Chief Superintendent, Brighton Force of Special Constables. *Address :* 7, Windlesham Gardens, Brighton. *Clubs :* New (Brighton) ; Leander R.C. (M601)

JEFFREYS, Capt. Henry Albert Gravious, O.B.E., A.P.C., E.A.F.

JEFFREYS, Hon. Brig.-Gen. Patrick Douglas, C.B., O.B.E., J.P., C.C., *b.* 29 July, 1848 ; *s.* of the late General E. R. Jeffreys, C.B. of Seafield House, Ryde, I. W. ; *m.* Maude Maynard, *d.* of the late Sir Richard C. Oldfield. *Educ. :* Marlborough Coll., and Royal Military Coll., Sandhurst. Entered 88th Regt. 1866 ; Captain 1878 ; Major, Connaught Rangers, 1881 ; Brevet Lieut.-Col. 1887 ; Brevet Col. 1891 ; Col. 1894 ; retired 1905 ; Brigade Major, Bengal, 1882–87 ; A.A.G. Sirhind Dist. 1887–88 ; A.A.G. Quetta Dist. 1889–94 ; A.A.G. at Headquarters in India 1894–98 ; in command of a 2nd Class District in India 1898–1903 ; Hon. Brig.-Gen. 1912 ; Zulu Campaign 1879 (Medal with clasp) ; Burmese Expedition 1886–87 as Brig. Maj. ; capture of Kemmendine Princes Camp (despatches, Medal with clasp Brev. of Lieut.-Col.) ; Zhob Field Force 1890 as A.A.G. (Despatches Brev.-Col.) ; in command of 2nd Brigade Malakand and Buner Field Forces on N.-W. Frontier of India 1897–98 (Despatches twice, Medal with clasp). *War Work :* Commanded East Group, Kent Volunteer Regiment, 1915–19. *Address :* Doddington Place, Sittingbourne, Kent. *Club :* United Service. (O7323)

JEFFRIES, Henry Charles, O.B.E.

JEFFRIES, Major Lewis Wibmer, D.S.O., O.B.E., M.B. B.S., *b.* 1884 ; *m.* 1917, Shirley Frances Singleton. *Educ. :*

Prince Alfred Coll., Adelaide ; Adelaide Univ. Australian Army Med. Corps ; Dep. Assist. Director of Med. Sers. ; served in the Great War, 1914–16 (despatches). (O1961)

JEFFRIES, Martha, O.B.E., *b.* 11 Aug. 1866 ; *d.* of William Harris, of Sydney, Australia ; *m.* Charles Henry, *s.* of William James, of London. *Educ. :* Australia. Officer, Salvation Army. *War Work :* Organised and directed women officers to visit wounded soldiers in 40 hospitals London and district, who distributed comforts, arranged accommodation for visiting relatives, communicated with friends, etc. *Address :* 200, Kilmarnock Road, Shawlands, Glasgow. (O10731)

JEHANGHIR, Cowasjee, O.B.E., C.I.E., J.P., *b.* Feb. 1879 ; *s.* of Sir Cowasjee Jehanghir, Bart. ; *m.* Hilla, *d.* of H. A. Hormarju. of Lowju Castle, Bombay. *Educ. :* St. Xavier's Coll. Bombay ; St. John's Coll. Cambridge. *Address :* Malabar Hill, Bombay. *Clubs :* Asian ; Willingdon ; Ripon ; Bombay. (O898)

JEKYLL, Agnes, Lady, D.B.E., *b.* 12 Oct. 1861 ; *d.* of William Graham ; *m.* Col. Sir Herbert Jekyll, K.C.M.G., R.E. Lady of Justice of the Order of St. John of Jerusalem Chairman of the Borstal Institution Visiting Committee, Aylesbury. *War Work :* Chairman, St. John and British Red Cross Hospital Supply Warehouse, St. John's Gate, Clerkenwell. *Address :* Munstead House, Godalming, Surrey. *Club :* Ladies' Empire. (D12)

JEKYLL, Annie, M.B.E.

JELLICOE, Brig.-Gen. Richard Carey, C.B.E., D.S.O.

JELLICORSE, Major Harold, O.B.E., J.P., late Royal Sussex Regt., *b.* 26 June, 1864 ; *s.* of E. J. B. Jellicorse, of Fallowfield, Lancashire ; *m.* Edith Emily, *d.* of Col. R. E. W. Garnham, of Densworth, near Chichester. *Educ. :* Dulwich Coll. *War Work :* Posting Officer for Sussex ; Posting Officer Army Trade Test Centre, Woolwich ; Hon. Organising Sec. of Committee formed by the Board of Admiralty, the Army Council, and the Air Ministry, to consider and report upon questions affecting the interests of those who have served and are serving in the Royal Navy, the Army, and Royal Air Force. *Club :* Naval and Military. (O7325)

JELLY, Lieut.-Col. Reginald Frank, O.B.E., R.E.

JEMMINSON, H., M.B.E.

JENKIN, Lieut.-Col. Charles Frewen, C.B.E., M.Inst.C.E., R.A.F., *b.* 24 Sept. 1865 ; *s.* of Henry Charles Fleeming Jenkin, of Edinburgh ; *m.* Mary Oswald, *d.* of Lord Mackenzie, of Edinburgh. *Educ. :* Edinburgh Academy ; Edinburgh University ; Cambridge University. Professor of Engineering Science, Oxford. *War Work :* Lieut.-Com., R.N.V.R., transferred to R.A.F. ; Director of Materials Section, Technical Dept., Air Ministry. *Addresses :* Engineering Laboratory, Parks Road, Oxford ; Brasenose College, Oxford ; 7, Fyfield Road, Oxford. (C1897)

JENKIN, Francis Charles, C.B.E. Dep. Sup. Hongkong Special Police Reserve. *Address :* Hongkong. (C395)

JENKIN, Henry Archibald, O.B.E.

JENKINS, Albert David, M.B.E.

JENKINS, Ann Nora, Mrs., O.B.E.

JENKINS, Frances Edith, M.B.E. *War Work :* Signal Division, Admiralty. *Club :* New Century. (M3762)

JENKINS, Brig.-Gen. Francis Conway, C.B.E., *b.* 25 Jan. 1888 ; *s.* of Edmund Ernest, of Westcliff ; *m.* Winifred Vera, *d.* of Thomas Cooper, of Worthing. *Educ. :* Privately. Managing Director, British Motor Trading Corporation, Ltd. *War Work :* Director of Aircraft Acceptance, Director of Parks and Depots, Air Ministry ; Pilot's Certificate, May, 1911 ; Second Class St. Stanislaus of Russia ; Commander Order of Redeemer of Greece. *Addresses :* Middle Fell, Whyteleafe, Surrey ; 25 Jermyn St., S.W. 1. *Clubs :* Badminton ; London Country ; R.A.F. (C536)

JENKINS, Lieut.-Col. Frederick Howard, O.B.E., C.M. *Address :* Micomi, Florida. (O8125)

JENKINS, Capt. George John, O.B.E., M.B., F.R.C.S., R.A.M.C. (T.)

JENKINS, Herbert George, O.B.E., *b.* 1873 ; *s.* of the late Capt. William Henry Jenkins, of Dublin. *Educ. :* St. Thomas's Church School, Seaforth. Master Mariner ; Master of the Ellerman Hall Line Steamer " Newby Hall " *en route* for Perim Island. *War Work :* Master of H.M.S. " Branksome Hall " employed in carrying Government Stores, etc., between England and France, principle loading port being Manchester ; H.M.S. " Denbigh Hall," which was sunk in May, 1918 when bound home from River Plata. *Addresses :* 40, Clarendon Road, Egremont, Cheshire ; Hall Line, Limited, Liverpool. *Club :* Mercantile Marine Service Association, Liverpool Lodge 594. (O1476)

JENKINS, Jenkin, M.B.E., *v.* 22 June, 1863 ; *s.* of Henry Jenkins, of New Quay, Cardiganshire ; *m.* Margaret, *d.* of Thomas Davies, of New Quay, Cardiganshire. Master Mariner. *War Work :* Commanding Naval Transport Collier. *Address :* Craig-y-mor, New Quay, Cardiganshire. (M3763)

JENKINS, Lieut.-Col. John Alexander, O.B.E.

JENKINS, Mary Ann, Mrs. *Address :* 30, Newland St., Barry, Glam. (M8632)

JENKINS, Brig.-Gen. Noble Fleming, C.M.G., C.B.E., *b.* 29 Oct. 1860 ; *s.* of D. J. Jenkins, M.P., of Penryn and Falmouth ; *m.* 1st, Mabel (who died 1918), *d.* of Maj.-Gen. J. F. Richardson, C.B. ; 2nd, Muriel, *d.* of Major L. B. Edgar. *Educ. :* Rugby and R.M.C. Sandhurst. Deputy Secretary, Society for the Propagation of the Gospel in Foreign Parts. *War Work :* Served in South African War ; in Great War as

Capt. with 2nd Border Regt. (7th Division) 1914; Lieut.-Col. 7th East Yorks, 1915; Infantry Brigade, 1916; Deputy Commander, Machine Gun Corps, 1917–18; three times mentioned in despatches. *Address:* 32, Greycoat Gardens, Westminster, S.W.1. (C1635)

JENKINS, Percy Fitzgerald, M.B.E., *b.* 3 Nov. 1883; *s.* of Watkin William Jenkins, of Aberdour, Cleveland Road, Paignton, South Devon; *m.* Florence Maude, *d.* of Alfred Syrett, J.P., of Sydenham, London. *Educ.:* Dudley Grammar School, and Lycée Lakanal, Sceaux, Paris. Director of Grainger & Smith, Ltd., Dudley. *War Work:* Hon. Sec. of Soldiers' and Sailors' Families Association, Dudley Branch; Hon. Sec. of Statutory Committee, then Naval and Military War Pensions Dudley Local Committee, and various Sub-committees and County Committees in connection with the same work; Member of Dudley Old Age Pensions Committee; Member of War Savings Committee. *Address:* Redlands, Stourbridge. (M8633)

JENKINS, Capt. Rees, M.B.E., *b.* 31 Aug. 1886; *s.* of Thomas Jenkins, of Blaencorrwg, Glamorganshire; *m.* Vera Muriel, *d.* of Herbert Selwood Sutton, of Neath, Glam. *Educ.:* Bath Coll., and Germany. *War Work:* Joined H.A.C. outbreak of war, afterwards commissioned in Welsh Regt.; transferred Intelligence Corps, then Aeronautical Commission of Control, Berlin. *Address:* 37, Gloucester Road, Kew, Surrey. (M1958)

JENKINS, Lieut. Stanley Evan, M.B.E., I.A.R.O.

JENKINS, Thomas Lewis, O.B.E.

JENKINS, Walter St. David, C.B., C.B.E. Director of Contracts, Admiralty; Order of Crown of Italy; Legion of Honour. (C211)

JENKINSON, Alfred James, O.B.E., *b.* 30 April, 1877; *s.* of the Rev. James Jenkinson, of Innellan, N.B.; *m.* Hilda Mary, *d.* of John Turner, of London. *Educ.:* Fettes Coll., Edinburgh, and Hertford Coll., Oxford. Fellow and Tutor of Brasenose Coll., Oxford. *War Work:* War Office, Armaments Output Committee, Intelligence Branch, May, 1915; Ministry of Munitions, Labour Department, July, 1915, to Dec. 1916, and Secretariat, Historical Records Section, Jan. 1917, to Sept. 1919. *Address:* Stamford House, Oxford. *Club:* Authors'. (O10735)

JENKINSON, Mark Webster, C.B.E., *b.* 1878; *s.* of Mark Jenkinson, of Sherwood, Kenwood Park Road, Sheffield. Chartered Accountant, 30, Cecil Chambers, Strand, W.C.; Controller of Factory Audits and Costs; Ministry of Munitions Chief Liquidator Munitions Contracts. *Clubs:* Royal Automobile; Authors'. (C537)

JENKINSON, Mary Adeline, M.B.E.

JENKINSON, Stanley Noel, M.B.E.

JENKINSON, Lieut.-Comm. Thomas Norman, O.B.E., R.N.V.R.

JENKINSON, William Russell, M.B.E.

JENKS, Capt. Herbert William, M.B.E., *b.* 2 June, 1878; *s.* of William Jenks, of Norwich. *Educ.:* Binfield Coll., Clapham. *War Work:* Officer in His Majesty's Army. (M5381)

JENNENS, Lenore Sybil, Mrs., M.B.E., *b.* 9 May, 1889; *d.* of Sir Gilbert Barling, Bart. (*see* BURKE'S *Peerage*); *m.* Capt. Keith Jennens. *War Work:* Motor Transport, V.A.D. Hospital, Highbury, Moor Green, Birmingham; Aero Engine Construction, Dumfries, Galloway Works; Ministry of Munitions, Dilution of Labour, Aero Section; Aeronautical Inspection Department, Engines. *Address:* 8, Glebe Place, Chelsea. *Club:* Writers'. (M8635)

JENNER, Major Lawrence Wynyard, O.B.E., R.A.S.C.

JENNEY, Col. Archibald Offley, C.B.E.; *b.* 1864; *s.* of late Arthur Henry Jenny, of Ditchingham Lodge, Norfolk (*see* BURKE'S *Landed Gentry*); *m.* Doreen Mary, *d.* of Col. Gerard Paul Townshend, Elcot Park, Hungerford; Col. Royal Scots, Great War 1914–19 (despatches). (C1274)

JENNINGS, Arthur Oldham, M.B.E., J.P., *b.* 15 July, 1855; *s.* of Frederick Jennings, of Framlingham, Suffolk; *m.* Mabel, *d.* of John Newnham Winter, of Brighton. Registrar of Brighton County Court; Chairman of Court of Referees for S. Sussex. *War Work:* Superintendent in Special Constabulary, Brighton. *Addresses:* 29, Adelaide Crescent, Hove; Chelwood Clump, Danehill, Sussex. *Club:* New, Brighton. (M8636)

JENNINGS, Lieut.-Col. Edward Charles, C.B.E., J.P., *b.* 17 July, 1877; *s.* of Richard Edward Jennings, D.L., J.P., of Gelli-deg, Kidwelly, S. Wales; *m.* Ethel Anita Dawes, *d.* of Thomas Teece Whitehurst, of The Mount, Shrewsbury. *Educ.:* Eton. J.P., Carmarthenshire; County Director, British Red Cross Society; Member, Territorial Association, Carmarthenshire; Commanding 6th Batt. (S.R.), Royal Fusiliers. *War Work:* 2nd in command, 6th Batt., Royal Fusiliers, from Aug. 1914; Commanded 6th Batt. (S.R.), Royal Fusiliers, from March, 1917; mentioned in despatches. *Clubs:* Army and Navy; Junior Constitutional. (C1636)

JENNINGS, Major George Leslie, O.B.E.

JENNINGS, Harry John, M.B.E.

JENNINGS, Ida, Mrs., M.B.E., *d.* of the Rev. A. Bennett, of Houghton-le-Spring, Co. Durham; *m.* Edward James, *s.* of Dr. E. Jennings, of Halifax, Nova Scotia. *Educ.:* Harrowden Hall, Wellingboro'; Glasgow; Hanover. *War Work:* Commandant Auxiliary Military Hospital, Abington Avenue, Northampton, 1915–19. (M3764)

JENNINGS, Capt. Leonard, O.B.E., *b.* 10 Nov. 1877; *s.* of S. Jennings, of Acton, Middlesex. *Educ.:* Privately. *War Work:* Enlisted in the Surrey Yeomanry, Sept. 1914; Com-

missioned 2nd Lieut. in the Northumberland Hussars, 21 Feb. 1915; Served in France and Belgium on the General Staffs of the 4th Army and the XIX Corps; mentioned in despatches. *Address:* 11, Cheyne Gardens, Chelsea, S.W.3. *Club:* Chelsea Arts. (O5428)

JENNINGS, Leonard William, M.B.E.

JENNINGS, Capt. Percy John, O.B.E., R.E.

JENNINGS, Col. Richard, C.B.E., M.D., late A.M.S., *b.* 2 Jan. 1858; *s.* of Martin Jennings, of Oldcourt, Creagh, Co. Cork; *m.* Mabel, died 13 July, 1919, *d.* of John Borthwick Paterson, late of Elmstone, Kent, and of Smyrna. *Educ.:* Privately; Queen's College, Cork. *War Work:* Administrative Medical Appointments in the Southern Command. *Address:* Chevrelle, Southsea, Hants. *Club:* Royal Albert Yacht, Southsea. (C281)

JENSEN, Major H. D., O.B.E., M.C.

JENSEN, W., Mrs.: *see* Gregory, W., Mrs. Gordon-.

JEPHCOTT, Susan, Mrs., M.B.E. *War Work:* Commandant V.A.D. Hospital, Alcester. *Address:* Hardwick House, Alcester. (M8640)

JEPHSON, Major, P.H.R., O.B.E.

JEPPE, Julius, C.B.E.; Services in connection with Hospitals and General War Work, Johannesburg, during Great War. (C3211)

JEREMY, Mary Ethel, O.B.E., M.B., B.Ch., *b.* 1864; *d.* of Daniel Davies Jeremy, of Dublin. *Educ.:* Alexandra College, Dublin; Privately; Royal Free Hospital School of Medicine. *War Work:* Medical Officer, University College Hospital, Southampton, July, 1916 to Jan. 1919. *Address:* Meadowside, Colehill, Wimborne. *Club:* Hants and Dorset Ladies' (Bournemouth). (O4314)

JERMAIN, Comm. Harry Bingham, O.B.E., R.N.

JERMYN, Ida Mary, O.B.E., W.R.N.S.

JERRAM, Frederick Horace Oldershaw, M.B.E.

JERRARD, Lieut.-Col. Augustus George Aimes, C.B.E. 3rd Batt. Somerset L.I. Served on the N.W. Frontier of India, 1897–98 (medal with clasp); Sierra Leone, 1898–99 (medal with clasp); S. Africa, 1900 (Queen's medal with four clasps); Great War, 1914–19 (despatches). (C1637)

JERRARD, Garnett Longsdon, M.B.E.

JERSEY, Margaret Elizabeth, Dowager Countess of, C.B.E., *b.* 29 Oct. 1849; *e.d.* of 2nd Baron Leigh (*see* BURKE'S *Peerage*); *m.* Victor Albert George, 7th Earl of Jersey, P.C., G.C.B., G.C.M.G. (d. 1915) (*see* BURKE'S *Peerage*). *War Work:* Red Cross Central Workrooms (Hon. Sec.). *Address:* 18, Montagu Square, W.1. *Club:* Ladies' Empire. (C2716)

JERVIS, Ethel Mary PARKER-, O.B.E., *d.* of W.R. Parker-Jervis, Meaford and Park Hall, Staffs. *War Work:* Commandant of Sandon Red Cross Hospital, 1915–19; Chairman of Stone War Refugees Committee, 1914–19; Medaille de la Reine Elizabeth. *Address:* Meaford Stone, Staffs. *Club:* Ladies' Army and Navy. (O631)

JERVOISE, Rear-Adm. Edmund Purefoy Ellis, C.B.E., R.N., *b.* 24 April, 1861; *s.* of F.J.E. Jervoise, of Herriard Park, Basingstoke, Hants; *m.* Alice J.M., *d.* of G. Christian, of Bighton Wood, Alresford, Hants. *Address:* Newton Valence Place, Alton, Hants. *Clubs:* Junior United Service. (C538)

JERVOISE, Edwyn, M.B.E., A.M.I.C.E., A.M.I.E.E., *b.* 13 June, 1884; *s.* of F.M.E. Jervoise, of Herriard Park, Basingstoke (*see* BURKE'S *Landed Gentry*); *Educ.:* Univ. Coll., London. Late Section Director, Ministry of Munitions, Gun Manufacture Dept. *Clubs:* Royal Societies'; Roehampton. (M8641)

JESS, Brig.-Gen. Carl Herman, C.M.G., C.B.E. D.S.O., *b.* 1884; *s.* of George Jess, of Bendigo, Victoria; *m.* Marjory, *d.* of D. McGibbon, of Melbourne. *War Services:* Great War, 1914–18, Gallipoli as Staff Capt., Brigade Major, and Commanding a Bn. and an Infantry Brig. (despatches thrice). *Addresses:* Montalto, Miller St., Fitzroy, Melbourne. *Clubs:* Naval and Military, Melbourne and Adelaide. (C3196)

JESSAP, Charles Townsley, M.B.E., *b.* 29 June, 1888; *s.* of Thomas Jessap, of Lincoln. Practising Accountant, Skegness; Member Urban District Council, Skegness; Fellow of Incorporated Secretaries' Association. *War Work:* 2½ years Adjutant of 4th Reserve Batt. The Lincolnshire Regt.; awarded M.B.E. for organising and administrative work in that capacity, and previously "mentioned" for the same work. *Address:* Gordon House, Skegness. (M5382)

JESSEP, Capt. Alfred James, M.B.E.

JESSIMAN, Major George Gaston, O.B.E.

JESSON, George Arthur Touchet, M.B.E., A.M.I.M.E., A.I.A.E., *b.* May 31, 1885; *s.* of Thomas Jesson, of Cambridge; *m.* Gwladys Bronwyn Violet, *d.* of A.J. Hunter, of Swinton, Lancs. *Educ.:* Felsted School. Governor and Hon. Sec. Manchester Children's Hospital; Director Messrs. Hale, Pearn & Co., Ltd., Manchester. *War Work:* Chairman of Grove House Red Cross Hosspital; of Pendleton B.R.C.S. "Smokes" Fund; of Pendleton B.R.C.S. Comforts Section; of Swinton Dist. Nat. War Savings Assocn.; of Irlams-o'-th'-Height Belgian Colony; Commandant Men's Detachment E. Lancs. No. 7. *Address:* Endsley, Swinton, Lancashire. *Clubs:* Constitutional, Manchester; Western, Eccles. (M8642)

JESSOP, Major Bernard, O.B.E., R.E.

JESSOP, Gertrude, M.B.E.

JESSOP, William, O.B.E.

JESTY, Ernest, M.B.E.

JEUNE, Charles Henry, M.B.E., *b.* 1877; *s.* of late Henry William Jeune. Purchasing Agent, Great Eastern

Railway Company. *War Work:* 1916–19, Sub.-section director, Railway Materials Department, Ministry of Munitions, War Office, Embankment Annexe; administered supplies of permanent way, rolling stock and other railway materials from Great Britain for France, Belgium, Italy and other allied countries both for military and civil requirements; Member of the Centralising Railway Committee of the Commission Internationale de Ravitaillement, and of the Railways Priority Committee of the Ministry of Munitions. *Address:* Liverpool Street Station, London, E.C.2. *Club:* Constitutional. (M8644)

JEWELL, Bertie, O.B.E., *b.* 6 July, 1881; *s.* of Thomas James Jewell, of London; *m.* Ethel Ada, *d.* of Henry Storry, of Southsea. *Educ.:* Wilson's Grammar School. Sec. H.M. Dockyard, Portsmouth. *War Work:* At Malta, Pembroke, Dover Dockyards, and R.N. Torpedo Factory, Greenock. *Address:* H.M. Dockyard, Portsmouth. (O10736)

JEWELL, Frank Ashton, M.B.E. J.P.

JEWELL, Henry James, M.B.E., *b.* 1 Aug. 1871; *s.* of Henry Jewell, of Torrington, N. Devon; *m.* Flora Alice, *d.* of George Charles Wickham, Kings Lynn. *Educ.:* Brompton School. Manager in United Kingdom B. and N. Line Norwegian Royal Mail Steamship; Director Haycock, Cadle and Graham, Ltd.; Director United Advertising Service, Ltd. *War Work:* Chairman and Divisional Officer, London and Home Counties Road Transport Board, Board of Trade. *Addresses:* The Poplars, Enfield Road, Southgate, London, N. 14; 179 and 353, Strand, London, W.C. *Club:* National Liberal. (O10737)

JEWELL, William Henry, O.B.E., M.D., D.P.H.

JEZZARD, Flying Officer Frank, M.B.E.

JICKLING, Major Charles Maurice, O.B.E.

JIMENEZ, Vivian Eustace, M.B.E.

JOANES, Capt. Walter, M.B.E.

JOB, Herbert Shipley, O.B.E.

JOBLING, Thomas, M.B.E., *b.* 28 Oct. 1861; *s.* of Thomas Jobling, of Wallsend-on-Tyne; *m.* Sarah Jane, *d.* of Robert Robson, of Newcastle-on-Tyne. *Educ.:* Walker Factory School. Foreman Blacksmith. *War Work:* Employed by Messrs. Swan, Hunter & Wigham Richardson, Ltd., Neptune Works, Newcastle-on-Tyne. *Address:* Rosalind, Appletree Gardens, Walkerville, Newcastle-on-Tyne. (M1961)

JODRELL, Mary Rennell, Lady COTTON-, O.B.E., *e.d.* of late Am. Rennell Coleridge, of Salston, Devon; *m.* 1878. Col. Sir Edward Thomas Davenant Cotton-Jodrell, K.C.B., T.D., J.P., D.L., of Reaseheath Hall, Cheshire (died 1917) (*see* BURKE'S *Peerage*). *Address:* 2, Portman Sq., W.1; Reaseheath Hall, Nantwich; Sallcross Manor, Whaley Bridge. (O10738)

JODRELL, Dorothy Lynch, Mrs. RAMSDEN-, C.B.E., *b.* 1879; *d.* of the late Sir E. T. S. Cotton-Jodrell (*see* BURKE'S *Peerage*, Combermere V.), of Reaseheath Hall, Nantwich, and Shallcross Manor, Whaley Bridge; *m.* Lt.-Col. Henry Ramsden, C.M.G. (who assumed the additional surname of Jodrell on his wife's succeeding to the Jodrell estate, 1920); *s.* of Capt. J. C. Ramsden (*see* BURKE'S *Peerage*), of Willinghurst, Guildford. *War Work:* Organiser of Y.M.C.A. Munitions Canteens. *Addresses:* Taxal Lodge, Whaley Bridge; 10, Stanhope Street, W. 2. (C2894)

JOEL, Capt. Herbert Cecil, O.B.E.

JOHN, Edwin, C.B.E. *Address:* Agra, United Provinces, India. (C197)

JOHN, Paymaster-Lieut. Henry Brynmor, M.B.E., R.N.

JOHN, Capt. Jordan Constantine, O.B.E., I.M.S., M.B.

JOHN, Major Nichol Shaw, O.B.E., R.A.S.C.

JOHNS, Arthur William, C.B.E. Assistant Director of Naval Construction, Admiralty. (C2717)

JOHNS, Lieut. Frederick, M.B.E., R.A.O.C.

JOHNS, Capt. Frederick Nelson, O.B.E., R.E.

JOHNS, Richard John, M.B.E.

JOHNS, Capt. William Alexander, M.B.E., R.E.

JOHNSON, Adela, Mrs., M.B.E., A.C.P.; *d.* of W. Howell Lambourne, of Oxford; *m.* the late Rev. Henry, *s.* of William Johnson. *Educ.:* Oxford and Cheltenham. Secretary. *War Work:* Superintendent of the Training Classes for Women Clerks, Aircraft Production Department, Ministry of Munitions. *Addresses:* The Rectory, South Hackney, E. 9; 59, Bainton Road, Oxford. (M8647)

JOHNSON, Agnes Norah, Mrs., M.B.E.

JOHNSON, Lieut. Albert, O.B.E., R.F.A., *b.* 8 Sept. 1889; *s.* of Charles Johnson, of Ashford, Kent; *m.* Miriam, *d.* of P. B. Newall, of Anerley, S.E. *Educ.:* Tonbridge, Kent. *War Work:* France and Flanders, 1914–18; Capt. Instructor in Gunnery, 1918–19, at Parkhurst, I. of W. *Addresses:* 54th A.A. Co. R.A., Dalmeny, N.B.; 43, Maple Road, Anerley, S.E. (O7331)

JOHNSON, Alfred Joseph, O.B.E., *b.* 7 Dec. 1873; *s.* of Joseph Johnson, of Harborne; *m.* Ida, *d.* of Frank Newman, of Sutton, Surrey. *Educ.:* New Hall Coll. Chairman and Governing Director of The Chad Valley Co., Ltd., of Harborne; Director of Chafen & Newman, Ltd., Riverside Engineers, London. *War Work:* Sub-Commissioner for National Service in Birmingham; Deputy Divisional Food Commissioner for Midland Counties. *Address:* The Oaklands, Knowle, Warwickshire. (O10739)

JOHNSON, Lieut. Alfred William, M.B.E.

JOHNSON, Major Arthur Ainslie, O.B.E.

JOHNSON, Arthur Henry, O.B.E.

JOHNSON, Capt. Cuthbert, M.B.E.

JOHNSON, Diana Mabel, M.B.E., *b.* 26 May, 1872; *d.* of the late Capt. F. Johnson, R.A., and of H.M. Prison Service. *Educ.:* Privately. Companion Governess. *War Work:* Canteen Work; Q.M.A.A.C. Official. *Address:* c/o Mrs. Kidd, Graylingwell, Chichester. (M4532)

JOHNSON, Dorothy, M.B.E.; *d.* of F. G. Johnson, of Clayton Hall, Newcastle, Staffs. *Educ.:* St. Leonard's School, St. Andrews, Fife. Hon. Sec. of the North Staffordshire Cripples Aid Society (Hanley Branch). *War Work:* Commandant of the Red Cross Hospital, The Hollies, Trent Vale, for troops in training (30 beds); Assistant Commandant of the Red Cross Hospital, Sandon Hall, Stafford (110 beds). *Address:* Clayton Hall, Newcastle, Staffordshire. (M3766)

JOHNSON, Lieut.-Col. Edgar David, O.B.E., R.A.V.C. (T.).

JOHNSON, Edith Clara, M.B.E., *b.* 12 April, 1864; *d.* of the Rev. Henry I. Johnson, Head Master of Royal Institution School, Liverpool, and formerly Rector of Trinity Church, Port Elizabeth, S. Africa. *Educ.:* Privately, and Ladies' Coll., Cheltenham. Teacher, Bolton High School for Girls and Clifton High School for Girls; Voluntary Social Economic work, Kensington. *War Work:* Hon. Sec. of the Kensington War Savings Local Central Committee, and various other movements for encouraging saving and general economy, both in Kensington and other parts of London. *Address:* 46, Campden House Court, Kensington, W. 8. (M3767)

JOHNSON, Edward Odlum, O.B.E., I.S.A.

JOHNSON, Edwin Thomas, M.B.E.

JOHNSON, Lieut. Edwin William, M.B.E.

JOHNSON, 2nd Lieut. Ernest Alfred, M.B.E., R.A.S.C.

JOHNSON, Ernest James, O.B.E., Fellow of the Institute of Municipal Treasurers and Accountants' (Incorporated), *b.* 24 Feb. 1879; *s.* of Edward Johnson, of Barking, Essex; *m.* Edith Sarah, *d.* of James Tully, of Brixton, Surrey. *Educ.:* Privately. Borough Treas., East Ham Corporation. *War Work:* Treasurer, East Ham War Pensions Committee, Local Committee for the Prevention and Relief of Civil Distress, the Soldiers' and Sailors' Families Association, Mayor's Belgian Relief Fund, and Mayor's Memorial to the Fallen Fund. *Address:* Bryn-Teg, 30, Lee Park, Blackheath, S.E. 3. (O10740)

JOHNSON, Major-Gen. (Hon.) Frederick Francis, C.B., C.B.E., D.L., *b.* 1 May, 1852; *s.* of the Rev. John Evans Johnson, D.D., of 70, Harcourt Street, Dublin; *m.* Bertha, *d.* of Henry Gotto, of New House Park, St. Albans. *Educ.:* Cheltenham; Trinity College, Dublin. Secretary, Territorial Force Association, County of Essex. *War Work:* Joined 69th Regt., 1874; transferred to 50th Regt., 1875; Adj. att. C. and T. Staff, 1881–89; Adj. transferred Army Service Corps, 1889; D.A.A.G., and Chief Staff Officer, Jamaica, 1887–90; D.A.A.G., Belfast District, 1891–94; A.A.G. N.E. District 1900–3; General Officer in Charge, Administration Southern Command, July, 1915 to Oct. 1916; Served in the Egyptian War (medal and clasp for Tel-el-Kebir, 4th class, Medjidieh, Khedive's star), South African War, 1899–1900 (medal and three clasps, C.B.); Decorated for services as Asst. Director of Supplies for South Africa, 1899–1900; promoted Hon. Major-Gen. for valuable services during the War, 3 June, 1917; County Commandant Essex Volunteer Corps, July, 1917 to Jan. 1920. *Address:* Hill House, Danbury, Chelmsford. *Clubs:* Army and Navy; United Service. (C2125)

JOHNSON, Frederick William, M.B.E.

JOHNSON, Major (A. Lieut.-Col.) Frederick William, O.B.E., T.D., R.A.M.C. (T.), *b.* 14 Oct. 1876; *s.* of the late Dr. William J. Johnson, of Bawtry, Yorkshire; *m.* Mary Irene, *d.* of Herbert Stephenson, of Slade Hooton Hall, Laughton, Yorks. *Educ.:* King Edward VI School, Retford; Leeds University. *War Work:* Served with 1st N. Midland Field Ambulance, R.A.M.C. (T.F.), from outbreak of War to May, 1917, in France and Belgium (six months in England); Commanded 2/2nd N. Midland Field Amb., R.A.M.C. (T.F.), in France and Belgium from May, 1917 to March, 1919. *Address:* Nearfield House, Bawtry, Yorkshire. (O5430)

JOHNSON, Lieut.-Col. George Hamilton, C.B.E. Canadian Forestry Corps; served in the Great War, 1915–19 (despatches). (C775)

JOHNSON, Rev. Gifford Henry, M.B.E., M.A., *b.* 30 Nov. 1859; *s.* of Henry Johnson; *m.* Katharine Frances Sinclair, *d.* of Fleet-Surgeon R. C. Scott, R.N. *Educ.:* Tonbridge School; Dover Coll.; Merton Coll., Oxford. *War Work:* B.R.C.S. orderly, Calais, Paris Plage, and Salonica. *Address:* 97, Park Lane, Croydon. (M8649)

JOHNSON, Lieut. Harold Cecil John, O.B.E., R.A.O.C., L.R.C.P., D.P.H.

JOHNSON, Harold Josse, O.B.E., M.B., M.R.C.S., L.R.C.P., L.S.A., D.P.H., R.A.M.C., *b.* 25 March, 1858; *s.* of George Noah Johnson, of Bishopgate, London; *m.* Emily Jane, *d.* of T. S. Foxwell, of Shepton Mallet. *Educ.:* Neuwied, Germany, and Univ. Coll., London. Chief Medical Officer, Gresham Assurance Societies; late House Surgeon, St. Bartholomew's Hospital; late Sen. Assist. Medical Officer, Co. Asylum, Gloucester. *War Work:* Resident Medical Officer (unpaid), Westminster Hospital, S.W. 1, Aug. 1914, to April, 1919. (O11816)

JOHNSON, Capt. Harry Bertram, O.B.E., M.C., R.A.O.C.

JOHNSON, Henry, O.B.E.

JOHNSON, Major Henry Campbell, M.B.E., M.V.O., K.O.Y.L.I., *b.* 13 May, 1879; *s.* of Col. C. H. Johnson, of Thorngumbald Hall, Hull; *m.* Marjorie Gooch, *d.* of J. A. Cottam, of Galmpton, Devon. *Educ.:* Repton. *War Work:*

S. African War, 1899–1902 ; France, 1916. *Address :* Thorngumbald Hall, near Burstwick, Hull. (O7332)

JOHNSON, Henry Langhorne, C.B.E., M.A., *b.* 30 Jan. 1874 ; *s.* of James Edwin Johnson, of Leeds ; *m.* Muriel Ada, *d.* of Worthington Church, of Salters Hall, Sudbury. *Educ. :* Leeds Grammar School ; Keble College, Oxford. Coal Factor, late Second Master, Hurstpierpoint College, Sussex. *War Work :* Chief Commissioner of the Church Army on the Western Front. *Address :* 12, Higher Drive, Purley, Surrey. (C539)

JOHNSON, Capt. Horace Swales, M.B.E.
JOHNSON, Hubert Lawrance, M.B.E.
JOHNSON, James, O.B.E.
JOHNSON, James, M.B.E., R.N.
JOHNSON, James William, M.B.E.
JOHNSON, Capt. John Ben, M.B.E., *b.* 11 Oct. 1867 ; *s.* of William Johnson, of Hatfield ; *m.* Henrietta Susannah, *d.* of Charles Jones, A.M.I.C.E., of Ealing. *Educ. :* St. Peter's Coll., Peterborough. Barrister-at-Law, and Director of Education for the Borough of Ealing. *War Work :* Commandant, Middlesex 7 V.A.D., and Capt. of No. 5 Co. of the Eastern Command Volunteer Ambulance Convoy ; Transport Officer, Southall V.A.D. Hospital. *Address :* 17, Madeley Road, Ealing, W. 5. (M3768)

JOHNSON, Lieut. Joseph Pratt, M.B.E.
JOHNSON, Margaret Lilian, M.B.E.
JOHNSON, Mary, Mrs., O.B.E., *b.* Oct. 1858 ; *d.* of John Rea, of Hull ; *m.* Hubert, *d.* of Christopher Johnson, of Boston, Lincs. *Educ. :* Kingston Academy, Hull ; Privately. *War Work :* 1915, organised Club for Soldiers' and Sailors' wives, with membership of 1400, and actively associated with this until its closing in March, 1919 ; in connection with St. John Ambulance, did rest station work, and from Sept. 1915, was closely connected with parcels for Prisoners of War, and organised workers for same ; 1917–18, Lady Mayoress of the City and County of Hull, during that period organised meetings for war savings, food economy, concerts for Serbian refugees, sewing meetings, and parcel packing for E. Yorks troops, comforts for E. R. Units, and was interested in all work that was for the benefit of the city and its people during that time. *Address :* St. Botolphs, The Park, Hull. (O3772)

JOHNSON, Mary Eliot, Mrs., O.B.E.
JOHNSON, Percy Faraday, M.B.E.
JOHNSON, Percy Richard, M.B.E.
JOHNSON, Lieut.-Col. Philip Henry, C.B.E., D.S.O.
JOHNSON, Capt. Raymond, O.B.E., M.B., F.R.C.S. R.A.M.C. (T.).
JOHNSON, Capt. Reginald, M.B.E., M.D., R.A.M.C., *b.* Sept. 13, 1888 ; *s.* of Prof. T. Johnson, D.Sc., F.L.S., of Dublin ; *m.* Agnes Faith, *d.* of Thomas McKeow, of King's Co , Ireland. *Educ. :* Archbishop Holgate's Grammar School, York ; Trinity Coll., Dublin. *War Work :* R.A.M.C. ; recommended for M.B.E. for work in connection with V.D. in the Army. *Address :* c/o Messrs. Holt & Co., Bankers, 3, Whitehall Place, S.W. (M5385)

JOHNSON, Brig.-Gen. Richard Francis, C.B., C.M.G., C.B.E., *b.* 12 July, 1852 ; *s.* of R. W. Johnson, D.L., of Worcestershire ; *m.* Mabel Edith Moreton, *d.* of Col. M. J. Wheatley, C.B., of Gwersylt, Denbighshire. *Educ. :* Rugby ; R.M.A. Joined Royal Artillery, Sept. 1872 ; Brig.-Major, R.A., Ireland, 1884–89 ; Court Defence Commander, 1906–9 ; S. African War, 1900–1. *War Work :* Garrison Com. Portland, 1915–17 ; Area Commandant, France, 1917 ; Examining Officer, Civil Liabilities Dept. (unpaid), 1917–18. *Address :* 6c, Montagu Mansions, W. 1. *Club :* Naval and Military. (C2127)

JOHNSON, Richard Spencer, M.B.E., F.R.G.S., *b.* 23 Oct. 1875 ; *s.* of Edward Killingworth. R.W.S., of Sible Hedingham, Essex ; *m.* Gertrude May, *d.* of Richard Forster, of South Hetton, Durham. *Educ. :* Dulwich Coll. Master Mariner ; Younger Brother of the London Trinity House. *War Work :* Master of S.S. " Hebburn," of London, under Admiralty requisition during war ; in July, 1918, whilst attached to H.M. ships on East Coast of Africa, sent landing party on shore, made up from crew of ship, to assist in defending the Portuguese town of Kilimane, which was threatened by German forces. *Address :* Englefield, West Ewell, Surrey. (M8653)

JOHNSON, Col. Robert Arthur, C.B.E., T.D., *b.* 20 Mar. 1874 ; *s.* of Rev. A. H. Johnson, of All Souls' College, Oxford ; *m.* Kathleen Eyre, *d.* of Sir Walpole Lloyd Greenwell, Bt., of Marden Park, Surrey. *Educ. :* Winchester ; New College, Oxford. Assistant Secretary in the Treasury. *War Work :* At the outbreak of War was in command of the 9th Cyclist Battalion, The Hampshire Regt. ; raised the 1/9th and 2/9th Battalions for foreign service, and commanded the 1/9th in India and Siberia till the conclusion of hostilities. *Address :* The Terrace House, Roehampton Vale, S.W. *Club :* Travellers'. (C2212e)

JOHNSON, Robert Stewart, O.B.E.
JOHNSON, Samuel, M.B.E.
JOHNSON, Lieut. Sidney, M.B.E., R.E.
JOHNSON, Sydney Frederick, O.B.E., *b.* 26 June, 1857 ; *s.* of C. J. Johnson, of Llangollen ; *m.* Eleanor Tracey, *d.* of J. Parker, of Reading. *Educ. :* Llangollen, North Wales. Railway Superintendent. *War Work :* Transport of Soldiers, Sailors, Ambulance, Stores, etc. *Address :* 52, Tennyson Road, Small Heath, Birmingham. (O10743)

JOHNSON, Lieut. Thomas Frank O.B.E., R.N.V.R.
JOHNSON, Violet Charlotte, Mrs., M.B.E.
JOHNSON, Violet Seymour, Mrs., M.B.E.

JOHNSON, Walter, O.B.E.
JOHNSON, Walter, M.B.E.
JOHNSON, Col. Walter Russell, C.B.E., D.S.O., *b.* 1888 ; *s.* of late Sir Walter Johnson, J.P. *Educ. :* Eastbourne and Sherborne. Served (1914–19) in Gallipoli, Egypt, and France, commanding a battalion ; and in N. Russia, commanding Lines of Communication (despatches). *Address :* Walton Hall, Purleigh, Essex. (C2359b)

JOHNSON, William, M.B.E., M.P.
JOHNSON, William Henry, M.B.E.
JOHNSON, Lieut. William Josiah, M.B.E.,
JOHNSON, Capt., Brev.-Major (T. Major, A. Lt.-Col.) William Frederick, O.B.E., Norfolk Regt., Spec. Res. and M.G.C. (O11945b)

JOHNSON, William Thomas, M.B.E. Genera Distribution Branch, Coal Mines Dept., Board of Trade. (M10258h)

JOHNSON, Winifred Farnell, O.B.E.
JOHNSON, Major Guy Allen Colpoys ORMSBY-, O.B.E., M.C., *b.* 25 May, 1886 ; *s.* of Frederick Colpoys Ormsby, of Lamorna, Weymouth ; *m.* Mary Isabella, *d.* of the late Col. B. G.Humfrey, of Cavanacor, Ballindrait, Co. Donegal. *Educ. :* Cheltenham Coll. Formerly Bedfordshire Regt., now Royal Army Pay Dept. *Address :* c/o Holt & Co., 3, Whitehall Place, S.W. *Club :* Junior United Service. (O7533)

JOHNSON, Dennis ROSS-, C.B.E., V.D., *b.* 1860 ; *s.* of the late H. C. Ross-Johnson, of Inner Temple, Barrister-at-Law ; *m.* Edith, *d.* of R. Restall, of Uitenhage, Cape Colony. *Educ. :* University College, London. Traffic Manager, Madras Railway, 1901–1906 ; Secretary, Indian Railway Conference Association, 1906–11 ; General Manager and Secretary, Bristol Corporation Docks, from 1911. *War Work :* Member of Board of Trade Advisory Committee on Congestion of British Ports ; Chairman, Bristol Port Labour Committee ; Secretary, Avonmouth Co-ordination Committee ; Member, Divisional Road Transport Board ; Member of Regional Shipping Committee appointed by Ministry of National Service ; Member of Panel of Experts appointed under the Ministry of Transport, Oct. 1919 ; Member of Association of Port Authorities' Executive Committee. *Address :* Clifton, Bristol. *Clubs :* Oriental ; Constitutional, Bristol. (C2718)

JOHNSON, Major Hugh SPENCER-, C.B.E., *b.* 7 Aug. 1871 ; *s.* of Matthew Spencer-Johnson, of Travancore, S. India. *Educ. :* King Edward's Grammar School, Birmingham. *War Work :* European War, 1914–17 ; 1917, Commissioner for the Army National War Savings Committee. *Club :* Junior Army and Navy. (C2719)

JOHNSON, Col. Alfred Edward WEBB-, C.B.E., D.S.O., M.B., F.R.C.S. ; *s.* of the late Samuel Johnson, of Stoke-on-Trent ; *m.* Cecilia Flora, *d.* of the late D. G. MacRae, of Norbiton, Surrey. *Educ. :* Manchester University and London. Surgeon to the Middlesex Hospital ; Surgeon to the Department of Urology ; Lecturer on Practical Surgery, and Dean of the Medical School ; Hunterian Professor of Surgery, Royal College of Surgeons of England ; Consulting Surgeon, Queen Alexandra Military Hospital, Millbank. *War Work :* Officer Commanding No. 14 General Hospital, and later Consulting Surgeon to the B.E.F., France ; mentioned in despatches three times ; C.B.E., D.S.O., Knight of Grace of the Order of St. John of Jerusalem in England. *Address :* 35, Grosvenor Street, W. 1. *Clubs :* Savage ; Roehampton. (C1345)

JOHNSON, Rosa WEBB-, M.B.E., *d.* of Dr. Samuel Johnson, of Stoke-upon-Trent. *War Work :* Vice-President, East Sheen Red Cross Depot ; Organising Sec. Y.M.C.A. Canteens, Richmond Park Camp. *Address :* Cricklewood, East Sheen, S.W. 14. (M8654)

JOHNSON, Annie Emily Blanche, Mrs., M.B.E., *b.* 4 March, 1878 ; *d.* of Major John Morton-Marshall, Military Knight of Windsor, late 9th Lancers and 3rd P. W. Dragoon Guards ; *m.* Archibald James, *s.* of J. Johnston. *Educ. :* Privately, and St. Anne's Diocesan Coll., Pietermaritzburg. *War Work :* May, 1915, to July, 1917, Home Sister at Sisters' Quarters, Military Hospital, Tidworth, Salisbury Plain ; Aug. 1917, to Oct. 1919, Unit Administrator in Queen Mary's Army Auxiliary Corps ; served at Etaples, First Army Infantry School, Vendroux, Montreuil, and Wimereux. *Address :* King Henry VIII. Gateway, Windsor Castle. (M3139)

JOHNSTON, Major Arthur Hammersley, O.B.E., M.R.C.S., L.R.C.P., Esquire Order St. John of Jerusalem, *b.* 4 Feb. 1862 ; *s.* of David Johnston, of Limerick, Ireland ; *m.* Blanche Amelia, *d.* of George James Jones, of Clapham, London, S.W. *Educ. :* Stamford House, Privately, and Guy's Hospital. Medical Practitioner ; M.O. Hull and Barnsley Rly. Co. ; M.O. Lees Rest Houses and various Insurance Societies. *War Work :* Assistant Commissioner (No. 6 Dist.) St. John Ambulance Brigade ; Assistant County Director, V.A.D., E. Riding T.F.A. ; Major i/c No. 1 Field Ambulance, E. Riding Forces R.A.M.C. (V.) ; Member Emergency Committee, Hull ; and in charge of air-raid ambulance arrangements ; Chairman Rest Station (Paragon Station) under Voluntary Aid Committee ; Member of Executive Peel House Voluntary Aid Committee ; Member Board St. John V.A.D. Hospital, Hull. *Address :* Lynton, 497, Anlaby Road, Hull. (O1522)

JOHNSTON, Augusta Rosalie, Mrs., M.B.E., Kaisr-i-Hind (2nd Class) ; *b.* 21 Aug. 1860 ; widow of the late Rev. S. H. Johnston. *War Work :* From Aug. 1914, to March, 1919. (M6171)

JOHNSTON, Capt. Benjamin James, O.B.E.
JOHNSTON, Major Bruce Campbell, O.B.E., R.E.
JOHNSTON, Charles Saint, M.B.E., M.R.C.S., *b.* 12 Sept .

1862; *s.* of James Johnston, M.B., of Birmingham; *m.* Marian, *d.* of Thomas Cattell, of Erdington. *Educ.:* Masons' Coll. *War Work:* Medical Officer to Gloucester Red Cross Hospital. *Address:* Rose Bank, Gloucester. (M8656)

JOHNSTON, Col. Sir Duncan Alexander, K.C.M.G., C.B., C.B.E. (*see* BURKE'S *Peerage*), *b.* 25 June, 1847; *s.* of Henry Johnston, of H.E.I.C.S.; *m.* Clara Millicent Mac-Kenzie (who died), *d.* of F. H. MacKenzie, of the U.S. Army. *Educ.:* Glenalmond, and Royal Military Academy, Woolwich. Director General Ordnance Survey, 1899–1905; Chairman Redistribution Committee, 1905; Member of Committee on Constitution of Transvaal and Orange River Colony, 1906; Chairman of Redistribution Commission Transvaal and Orange River Colony, 1906–7. *War Work:* Chairman Edinburgh Branch Soldiers' and Sailors' Help Society; Hon. Secretary, East Scottish Branch, Soldiers' and Sailors' Families Assoc.; Chairman Committee of Edinburgh Lord Roberts' Memorial Workshops; Member of Edinburgh and of Leith War Pensions Committee. *Address:* 8, Lansdowne Crescent, Edinburgh; *Clubs:* United Service; Caledonian United Service (Edinburgh); New (Edinburgh). (C2721)

JOHNSTON, Edith Alma, M.B.E.

JOHNSTON, Elizabeth Gairdner, M.B.E.

JOHNSTON, Lieut.-Col. Eric Archibald, C.B.E., R.E.

JOHNSTON, Major Ernest Henry, O.B.E., R.A.F.

JOHNSTON, Florence, Mrs., M.B.E., W.R.N.S.

JOHNSTON, T. Warrant Officer Francis, M.B.E. Royal Indian Marine.

JOHNSTON, Brig.-Gen. George Jamieson, C.B., C.M.G., C.B.E., *b.* 1869; *s.* of Charles Johnston, of Melbourne. Entered Australian Forces 1889; served in S. Africa, 1899–1900 (Queen's Medal with three clasps); 1815–17, Gallipoli, commanding a Division of Australian Artillery (despatches); and afterwards Administrator, German New Guinea. (C3197)

JOHNSTON, Col. Henry Halcro, C.B. (Mil.), 1902), C.B.E. (Mil., 1919), D.Sc., M.D., C.M., F.R.S.E., F.L.S., *b.* 13 Sept. 1856; *s.* of James Johnston, of Coubister, Orphir, Orkney. *Educ.:* Dollar Institution; Edinburgh Collegiate School, and Edinburgh University. Colonel, (retired pay), late Royal Army Medical Corps. *War Work:* Deputy Director of Medical Services, Gibraltar, 1915; Assistant Director of Medical Services, Western District, Scottish Command, Glasgow, 1916; Assistant Director of Medical Services, Headquarters, Northern Command, York, 1917–19. *Address:* Orphir House, Orphir, Orkney. (C1638)

JOHNSTON, Lieut.-Col. John, O.B.E., T.D., M.A., *b.* 16 Nov. 1883; *m.* Grace Nellie, *d.* of Alfred George Frost, of Royston, Herts. *Educ.:* Annan Academy and Edinburgh Univ. Educational (under Edinburgh Education Authority). *War Work:* Adjutant, 6th Bn. The Royal Scots, and 13th Leicesters, Aug. 1914 to May 1917; Adjutant, No. 39 Labour Group, B.E.F., May 1917 to March 1918; Assistant Labour Commandant on following staffs: 5th Corps, Fourth Army, Third Army, Fifth Army, March 1918 to June 1919; Deputy Controller of Labour, General Headquarters, France and Flanders; June 1919 to Aug. 1920; mentioned in despatches. *Addresses:* 1, Maitland Street, Edinburgh; The Cross, Royston, Herts. *Clubs:* Royal Scots (Edinburgh). (O5432)

JOHNSTON, John Ewing, M.B.E., M.R.C.V.S., *b.* 17 Aug. 1869; *s.* of Ronald Johnston, of Mullaghmore, Knox, Co. Tyrone; *m.* Hester, *d.* of Robert Corry, J.P., of Sandown, Belfast. *Educ.:* Gracehill Boarding School. Member of the War Pensions Committee; Member of the District Selective Committee; President of the North of Ireland Veterinary Medical Association; Member of the Council U.S.P.C.A.; Member of the Ulster Unionist Council. *War Work:* Veterinary Officer in charge of Remount Depot, Balmoral, Belfast, during the war; Veterinary Officer to a Government horse purchaser during mobilisation and during the war; Veterinary Officer in charge of Belfast Port during mobilisation. *Address:* Clarendon Place May Street, Belfast. (M3771)

JOHNSTON, Joseph Wilson, C.B.E., B.A., *b.* 1876; *s.* of the late Lieut.-Col. J. Wilson Johnston, formerly of Benmore, Oxton, Cheshire; *m.* 1900, Helen J. M., *d.* of Tomlin Campbell. *Educ.:* Rugby; Balliol Coll., Oxford. Bar. Inner Temple, 1899; Dep. Commr. Rawal Pindi, and Lieut. Indian Defence Force; Kaisir-i-Hind medal. *Address:* Rawal Pindi, Punjab. (C693)

JOHNSTON, Margaret Emmeline, Mrs. James Thomason, O.B.E.

JOHNSTON, Mary Ingham, Mrs., M.B.E.; *d.* of Joshua Rawlinson, J.P., of Burnley, Lancs.; *m.* George Minto, M.D., F.R.C.P.E., J.P.; *s.* of Thomas Johnston, of Leith. *Educ.:* Manchester High School for Girls, Paris, and Frankfurt. *War Work:* Hon. Sec. Families Sub-Committee, Leith War Pensions Committee; Member Leith War Pensions Committee; Hon. Sec. Leith Soldiers' Children's Committee; Hon. Sec. Soldiers' and Sailors' Families Association, Leith Branch; Member of Leith Committee of Veterans' Garden City Association. *Address:* 7, Wellington Place, Leith. (M3772)

JOHNSTON, Col. Osmond Moncrieff, C.B.E., *b.* 1848. Formerly Col. Army Pay Depart.; served in the Great War, 1914–19 (despatches). (C1639)

JOHNSTON, Capt. Percy Leo, O.B.E.

JOHNSTON, Reginald Fleming, C.B.E., M.A. (Oxon.), *b.* 31 Oct. 1874; *s.* of R. F. Johnston, of Scotland. Educ.: Magdalen Coll., Oxford. Assistant Colonial Sec. Hong Kong. Private Sec. to the Governor, Hong Kong; District Officer and Magistrate, Wei-hai-wei; Administered the Government of

Wei-hai-wei, 1917–18; Tutor to H.M. Hsuan Tung, ex-Emperor of China. *Club:* Peking, China. (C306)

JOHNSTON, Capt. Robert George, O.B.E., *b.* 5 Mar. 1878. *Educ.:* Berwick Grammar School. Solicitor, County Clerk of Berwickshire. *War Work:* County Red Cross Secretary for fourteen months after outbreak of War; Quartermaster with Field Ambulance on Western Front for three years: eighteen months with 39th Division and eighteen months with 51st (Highland) Division; mentioned in despatches. *Address:* Murray Place, Duns. (O5433)

JOHNSTON, Rosalie, Mrs., M.B.E.

JOHNSTON, Lieut.-Comm. William, O.B.E., R.N.

JOHNSTON, William Douglas, O.B.E.

JOHNSTON, Lieut.-Col. William James, C.B.E., R.E.

JOHNSTON, Winifred Blanche, Mrs., M.B.E.,

JOHNSTON, Hon. Winifred Mary, Lady, O.B.E., *b.* 18 Dec. 1871; *d.* of Florence, 5th Lord B ston, of Hedsor Bucks (*see* BURKE'S *Peerage*); *m.* Sir Henry Hamilton Johnston, G.C.M.G., K.C.B., *s.* of John Brooks Johnston, of Tudor House, Denmark Hill. *Educ.:* Privately. Guardian of the Poor; R.D.C., East Preston; Churchwarden, Poling Parish Church; Member Housing Committee, East Preston. *War Work:* Assistant Commandant, V.A.D. 122, Sussex, St. Wilfred's Auxiliary Hospital, Arundel; Hon. Sec. and Treas. Chichester Division, B.R.C.S.; Hon. Sec. and Treas. Soldiers' and Sailors' Families Association, Arundel District; Member of West Sussex Agricultural Selection Committee for Women's Land Army; Member Local Food Control Committee. *Address:* St. John's Priory, Poling, Arundel, Sussex. (O10745)

JOHNSTON, Sir George Lawson LAWSON-, K.B.E., *b.* 1873; *s.* of the late John Lawson-Johnston, of Kingswood, Kent; *m.* Hon. Edith Laura St. John, 5th *d.* of 16th Baron St. John of Bletsoe (*see* BURKE'S *Peerage*). *Educ.:* Privately. Chairman, Section B.2 (Raw Materials) under Surveyor-General of Supply (War Office); Chairman, East Indian Kip Committee (Raw Materials), War Office; Member of Council, British Empire League since 1897; Chairman, St. Marylebone Division, British Red Cross Society; Member of Committee, King Edward's Hospital Fund for London since 1902; Treas., Gt. Northern Central Hospital; Director of "Daily Express" from its foundation till 1917; Chairman, Bovril Ltd.; Director, Australian Mercantile Land and Finance Ltd. *Addresses:* 29, Portman Sq., W.1; Lavenham, Bury, Bedfordshire. *Clubs:* Devonshire; Bath; St. Stephen's. (K387)

JOHNSTON, Joseph WILSON-, C.B.E., I.C.S., *b.* 1876; *s.* of late Lieut.-Col. J. Wilson-Johnston, Indian Medical Service; *m.* Helen, *d.* of Tomlin Campbell. *Educ.:* Rugby and Balliol College, Oxford. Bar. Inner Temple, 1899; Dep. Commissioner, Rawal Pindi, and Lieut. Indian Defence Force; has Kaisir-i-Hind medal. *Address:* Rawal Pindi, Punjab. (C693)

JOHNSTONE, Alexander, M.B.E.

JOHNSTONE, Arthur Henry, M.B.E.

JOHNSTONE, Major Beresford Assheton, O.B.E., I.A.

JOHNSTONE, Major David Patrick, O.B.E., R.A.M.C.

JOHNSTONE, Ethel Rose, Mrs., M.B.E.; *m.* James Johnstone, F.R.C.S. *War Work:* Commandant, Hospital 307, Neuilly, Paris; Organiser and Superintendent of the Richmond War Hospital Supply Depot and Branch Depots. *Address:* Tudor House, King's Road, Richmond, Surrey. (M3773)

JOHNSTONE, Frances Lucy Schonswar, M.B.E.; *d.* of Vice-Admiral Charles Johnstone, of Graitney, Camberley, Surrey. *Educ.:* Privately, and Florence, Italy. *War Work:* British Consulate, Rotterdam; Neutral Propaganda, Dept. of Information, Wellington House, London; Enemy Propaganda, Crewe House, London; work in connection with the League of Nations. *Address:* Graitney, Camberley, Surrey. (M3774)

JOHNSTONE, Col. Hope, C.B.E., R.A.

JOHNSTONE, James Drummond, M.B.E., *b.* 24 July, 1890; *s.* of John Johnstone, of Glasgow. *Educ.:* Collegiate School, Glasgow. Shipping Agent. *War Work:* Assistant Administrative Officer in Cheese Section of Ministry of Food, Aug. 1917, to March, 1920; acted as Sec. to the Advisory Committee on Cheese, Ministry of Food; was rejected for the Army on health grounds. *Address:* Buxton, Pollok Road, Shawlands, Glasgow. *Club:* Royal Automobile. (M8658)

JOHNSTONE, Dr. James Glansey, O.B.E.

JOHNSTONE, Lieut. John Hamilton Lane, M.B.E.

JOHNSTONE, Joseph, O.B.E., F.R.C.S., J.P., M.P., *b.* 1860, *s.* of Robert Johnstone; *m.* Jane Clerk (who died 1917), *d.* of Alexander Muir, of Gateside, Beith. Cabinet Manufacturer; County Councillor and Vice-Convener for Renfrewshire; Liberal Member for E. Renfrewshire since 1918. *Address:* Calder House, Lockwinnoch Renfrewshire. *Clubs:* Liberal (Glasgow); Paisley. (O1523)

JOHNSTONE, Josephine, Mrs., O.B.E., *d.* of John Joseph Wells, of Bickley, Kent; *m.* John Heywood, *s.* of George Dempster, of Creed Rectory, Grampound, Cornwall. *Educ.:* At home. President of various Nursing Associations. *War Work:* Ran the Bignor Park Red Cross Hospital for four and a half years; Inaugurated Pulborough and Petworth platoon of the V.T.C. *Address:* Bignor Park, Pulborough, Sussex. (O1524)

JOHNSTONE, Robert William, C.B.E., M.A., M.D., F.R.C.S.E., *b.* 11 Aug. 1879; *s.* of Rev. Professor Robert Johnstone, D.D., United Free Church College, Aberdeen; *m.* Lucy Jane Christina, *d.* of the late George A. Gibson, LL.D.,

M.D., D.Sc., F.R.C.P.E., of Edinburgh. *Educ.:* George Watson's College, Edinburgh; University of Edinburgh, and studied in Dublin, Vienna and Prague. Lecturer on Midwifery and Gynæcology in, and Dean, of the School of Medicine of the Royal Colleges, Edinburgh; Assistant Physician to the Royal Maternity Hospital; Examiner in Midwifery in University of Aberdeen, to the Royal Colleges, and to the Central Midwives' Board for Scotland, etc. *War Work:* Surgeon-in-charge, Royal Victoria Red Cross Hospital, Edinburgh, 1914–16; Lieut. R.A.M.C. (Surgical Specialist, France), 1917; specially recalled by Minister of National Service, to act as Deputy Commissioner of Medical Services, Headquarters, Ministry of National Service, London; Commissioner, 1918–19. *Address:* 10, Alva Street, Edinburgh. *Club:* University (Edinburgh).
(C2722)

JOHNSTONE, Thomas White, M.B.E., A.R.C.Sc., D.I.C., *b.* 31 Aug. 1887. *Educ.:* South Kensington (Imperial and Royal Colleges of Science). Acting Chief Inspector of Factories, Bombay Presidency. *War Work:* In charge munition making, Guzerat, India; Priority Claims. *Address:* Custom House, Bombay, India.
(M4152)

JOHNSTONE, William Downs, C.B.E. *Address:* Hobart, Tasmania.
(C3198)

JOHNSTONE, Lieut.-Col. Charles Spread HOPE-, O.B.E., R.F.A.

JOLLIFFE, Capt. Arthur Henry, O.B.E., R.E.

JOLLY, Major Frank, O.B.E., R.A.F.

JOLLY, Major Henry, M.B.E.

JOLLY, Joan Vera Douglas, C.B.E., *b.* 20 May, 1887; *d.* of Alfred Ernest Learoyd, of Prince's Gate, London, S.W.; *m.* the late William Arnold, Barrister at Law of Lincoln's Inn and Williamstown Lodge, Whitegate, Co. Clare, *s.* of William Crucknell Jolly, formerly of Hampstead and Bath. *Educ.:* Wycombe Abbey, Bucks. *War Work:* Hon. Treasurer, East Norton Division (Leicestershire) of the Soldiers' and Sailors' Families Association from Aug. 1914–16; Clerical Staff V.A.D. Headquarters, Devonshire House, Piccadilly, W., from March, 1915 to November, 1916; Assistant Secretary, Women's Legion, Military, Cookery Section, Dec. 1916–March 1917; Assistant Controller of Administration, and afterwards Assistant Chief Controller, Q.M.A.A.C. from March, 1917 to November, 1919. *Address:* 21, Hereford Square, S.W. 7. *Clubs:* Ladies' Athenæum.
(C2128)

JOLLY, John, M.B.E., *b.* 30 Mar. 1881; *s.* of the late Rev. James Jolly, B.D., of the West Port Free Church, Edinburgh; *m.* Jean Hunter, *d.* of David Parker, of Kilmarnock. *Educ.:* Fettes College, Edinburgh. Civil Servant in the Admiralty. *War Work* In the Victualling Department of the Admiralty. *Address:* 46, Alba Gardens, Golders' Green, London, N.W. 4.
(M610)

JOLLY, Lieut.-Col. Thomas Riley, M.B.E., V.D., J.P., *b.* 23 Feb. 1849; *s.* of John Jolly, of Wrea Green; *m.* Catherine, *d.* of Richard Parkinson, of Longridge. *Educ.:* Kirkham Grammar School. Principal, Harris Institute and Victoria Technical School; Governor of Harris Orphanage, Preston. *War Work:* On declaration of War appointed O.C. West Lanc. National Reserve, Recruiting until Dec. 1915; then appointed Chief Military Representative for Preston Sub Area; in Jan. 1918, Chief Military Representative for the enlarged area of Preston, Blackpool, Fleetwood, St. Annes, Lytham, Kirkham, Chorley, Leyland, Longridge, and surrounding districts; retained the office until recruiting ceased. *Address:* Harris Orphanage, Preston. *Clubs:* Conservative; Winckley.
(M1966)

JOLLYE, Major Godfrey Herbert, O.B.E., R.M.A.

JONAS, Lieut.-Col. Harold Driver, O.B.E., *b.* 10 Sept. 1879; *s.* of Henry Jonas, of Portley Wood, Whyteleafe, Surrey. *Educ.:* Marlborough. Surveyor, Land Agent and Auctioneer. *War Work:* Directorate of Lands for War Office, Ministry of Munitions and Air Board. *Addresses:* 7, Charles Street, St. James's Square, S.W. 1; Ridgeway, Limpsfield, Surrey. *Club:* Junior Carlton.
(O464)

JONAS, Harry Marshall, C.B.E. Member of Advisory Committee on Controlled Establishments Branch, Ministry of Munitions. *Address:* St. Margaret's, Stevenage, Herts.
(C212)

JONES, Abel John, O.B.E., M.A. (Cantab.), B.Sc., Ph.D.; *s.* of D. R. Jones, of Tonypandy; *m.* Rhoda May (B.Sc.), *d.* of J. L. Williams, of Cardiff. *Educ.:* Aberystwyth Univ. Coll.; Clare Coll., Cambridge; Jena Univ., Germany. Inspector of Schools under the Board of Education; Author of "Eucken: A Philosophy of Life"; "Character in the Making"; "The Adolescent and the Continuation School"; "Deffro! Mae'n Ddydd"; "Chwedlau'r Deffro"; "Y Llyfrau Elfennol," etc. *War Work:* Hon. Organising Sec. for Glamorganshire under the National War Savings Committee; during tenure of office the number of Local Committees increased from 16 to 41, and the number of War Savings Associations from 700 to 1200. *Address:* 20, Connaught Road, Cardiff. *Clubs:* Cambridge Union; Hon. Soc. of Cymrodorion.
(O10746)

JONES, Rev. Albert, O.B.E., *b.* 26 Oct. 1886; *s.* of Edward Jones, of Rogerstone, Mon.; *m.* Gladys, *d.* of John E. Hirst, of Pastors Hill House, Bream, Gloucestershire. *Educ.:* Rogerstone; Maindee College, Newport; Handsworth Theological College, Birmingham; Wesleyan Methodist Minister. *War Work:* Chaplain, 4th Class, with Mesopotamian Expeditionary Force in Amara and Baghdad, two and three-quarter years. *Address:* Pennar House, Newbridge, Monmouthshire.
(O2280)

JONES, Alice Gray, Mrs., O.B.E.

JONES, Alice, Mrs. Lloyd, M.B.E.; *d.* of Frederick Ford-Smith, of Manchester; *m.* William Lloyd, *s.* of John William Jones, of Manchester. *Educ.:* Malvern. *War Work:* Commandant of Cheshire 74, British Red Cross Society, V.A. Detachment; Commandant of Hale Red Cross Hospital. *Address:* Wellfield, Hale, Cheshire.
(M678)

JONES, Aneurin, O.B.E., *b.* 3 Oct. 1873; *s.* of Thomas Jones J.P., C.C., of Hafod, Dowlais, S. Wales. *Educ.:* Llandovery School and Monmouth Grammar School. Solicitor. *War Work:* Secretary Priority Department of the Ministry of Munitions and of the Priority Committee. *Address:* 3, Glebeland Street, Merthyr Tydfil. *Club:* Hampden. (O1525)

JONES, Antoinette Manget, Mrs., M.B.E.

JONES, Arthur, O.B.E.

JONES, Arthur Dansey, O.B.E.

JONES, Arthur Llewelyn, O.B.E., M.C., Can. A.M.C.

JONES, Lieut. Arthur Melville, M.B.E.

JONES, Arthur Palm, M.B.E., *b.* 14 April, 1867; *s.* of Abraham Jones, of Newport, Mon.; *m.* Annie Maud Martha (Maud), *d.* of William Langmaid, of Newport, Mon. *Educ.:* Privately. Surveyor to Lloyd's Register of Shipping *War Work:* Special service surveying, repairing Admiralty transports, and French and general damaged ships and machinery at Marseilles and district, in the South of France during the whole period of the war. *Address:* 8, Rue de la Republique, Marseilles. *Club:* Société Nautique, Marseilles.
(M8659)

JONES, Capt. Benjamin Henry, C.B.E. Roy. Indian Marines.
(C2035)

JONES, Major and Qr.-Mr. Bernard Frederick, O.B.E., T.D., *b.* 17 Sept. 1874. *War Work:* From 22 March, 1915, to Jan. 1920, with 7th Royal Warwicks, 48th Division, in Belgium, France, Italy and Egypt. *Address:* Stoke, Coventry. (O2988)

JONES, Sir Bertram Hyde, K.B.E., *b.* 9 Jan. 1879 (*see* BURKE'S *Peerage*); *s.* of E. I. Jones; *m.* Constance Elizabeth, *d.* of W. J. Renshaw, of Putney, Surrey. *Educ.:* Privately. Member of Jones and Brown, London. *War Work:* May to November, 1916: at War Office organising Costing System, etc.; March, 1917 to Dec. 1918, Member of Weir Committee; Special Staff of Surveyor-General of Supply, War Office; Member of Mechanical Transport Board, War Office; Member of Board of Financial Control, Air Ministry; Civil Assistant, Controller-General of Equipment, Air Ministry; Special work for Secretary of State for Air; Member of various committees, War Office and Air Ministry, England and France. *Address:* Runwell, Wickford, Essex. *Clubs:* British Empire; Services.
(K388)

JONES, Bessie Lyon, Mrs., M.B.E.

JONES, Lieut. Brainard Arthur Robinson, M.B.E.

JONES, Cadwaladr Bryner, C.B.E. Welsh Secretary Board of Agriculture and Fisheries. *Address:* Ministry of Agriculture, Aberystwyth; 72, Victoria St., S.W. 1. *Club:* Farmers'.
(C2723)

JONES, Hon. C. F. Basil Dennis, O.B.E., M.A., F.R.G.S., *b.* 10 Aug. 1883; *s.* of Canon Arthur Jones, of Winlaton Rectory, Co. Durham. *Educ.:* Christ Church School, Oxford; Denstone College; Keble College, Oxford. Precentor and Chaplain of Trinity College, Cambridge; formerly at Hexham Abbey and Precentor, Minor Canon and Vicar of the Cathedral, Manchester. *War Work:* Chaplain to 29th Division, Gallipoli; Chaplain to 1st Brigade in East Africa; attached to Intelligence Dept., Palestine; Deputy Editor of "Palestine News," Army newpapers, etc. *Address:* Trinity College, Cambridge. *Clubs:* New Oxford and Cambridge; Imperial Church.
(O4155)

JONES, Cecil Barclay, M.B.E., *b.* 24 June, 1891; *s.* of Walter Henry, of Wimbledon; *m.* Eadith Beatrice, *d.* of Harry Bird, of Chingford. *Educ.:* City of London School. Admiralty from 1908–19; Assessor and Collector of Taxes for the Commissioners for the City of London, 1919. *War Work:* Admiralty; served in the Auxiliary Patrol Office from the inception of that service to end of war. *Address:* 20, The Drive, S.W. 6. *Clubs:* Royal Thames Yacht; Ranelagh Sailing.
(M8661)

JONES, Lieut. Charles, O.B.E., R.A.S.C., (T.F.).

JONES, Capt. Charles, O.B.E., T.F., *b.* 2 Apr. 1886. *War Work:* Granted commission in T.F., Sept. 1914; Service in France, Sept. 1916 to June 1919. *Address:* 141, Lord Street, Southport.
(O5434)

JONES, Capt. Charles Grey Peyton, O.B.E., R.G.A.

JONES, Charles Henry, C.B.E. (1918), *b.* 31 Mar. 1857; *m.* Isabel, *d.* of the late John Andrews. Registrar General of Shipping and Seamen since 1913. *Addresses:* General Register and Record Office of Shipping and Seamen, Tower Hill, E. 1.; 11, Emperor's Gate, S.W. 7.
(C213)

JONES, Lieut.-Col. Charles Hugh le Palleur, O.B.E.

JONES, Charles Leupolt, M.B.E., *b.* 11 April, 1859; *s.* of Samuel Simpson Jones, of Beccles, Suffolk; *m.* Elizabeth Augusta, *d.* of Joseph Ashlin, of Bromley, Middlesex. *Educ.:* Fauconberge School, Beccles, Suffolk. Civil Servant; Lecture Sec. Catholic Truth Society; Order *Pro Ecclesia et Pontifice* conferred by the Holy See, 1920. *War Work:* Statistical work, H.M. Custom and Excise, Custom House, London. *Address:* 283, Upton Lane, Forest Gate, London, E. 7.
(M8662)

JONES, Lieut.-Col. Cyril Vivian, C.B.E., *b.* 8 Feb. 1882; *s.* of John William Jones, of Dulwich. *Educ.:* Privately and in Germany. General Manager, Messrs. Peek, Frean & Co. Ltd. *War Work:* Commanded several R.A.S.C. Supply Depots;

mentioned four times by Secretary of State for War. *Clubs :* Junior Constitutional ; Royal Automobile.   (C1641)

JONES, Lieut. David Gwilym, O.B.E.. J.P., R.N.V.R.

JONES, David Marteine, M.B.E., *b.* 17 Feb. 1872 ; *s.* of late Thomas Davies Jones, of Bronwydd Arms, Carmarthenshire ; *m.* Mary Harriet, *d.* of the late Capt. William Williams, of Llanelly, Carmarthenshire. *Educ. :* Park-y-velvet Academy, Carmarthen. *War Work :* Chief Clerk of a branch of the Military Secretary's Department, War Office. *Address :* 8, Beaconsfield Road, Ealing, W. 5.   (M1969)

JONES, David Rocyn, C.B.E., M.R., C.M. Deputy co-Director Auxiliary Hospitals, Monmouthshire, during Great War. *Address :* Rhymney, Monmouthshire.   (C2724)

JONES, Paymaster-Lieut.-Comm. David Thomas, C.B.E., R.N.R., *b.* 10 June, 1866 ; *s.* of David T. Jones, of Greenhill, Gilfachgoch, Glamorganshire ; *m.* Alison Macmillan Beattie, *d.* of Robert Beattie, of Glenesk, Ineresk. *Educ. :* Public School and Long Ashton (Private School). Chairman, Fishery Board for Scotland. *War Work :* Various Government Committees dealing with food supplies and recruiting men engaged in fishing industry for Naval Reserve. *Address :* 12, Polwarth Grove, Edinburgh. *Clubs :* Caledonian (London) ; Caledonian, United Service (Edinburgh) ; President, Merchiston Tennis and Bowling.   (C985)

JONES, Edgar Anderson Averay, M.B.E., B.A. (Cantab.), *b.* 26 June, 1875 ; *s.* of the Rev. Alexander George Jones, of Barton House, Hereford. *Educ. :* Hereford School, and St. John's Coll., Cambridge. Magistrate and District Commissioner, Mweru-Luapula District, N. Rhodesia (B.W.A. Company Administration). *War Work :* In charge of Mweru-Luapula District, N. Rhodesia, during the greater part of the war ; organised the recruiting of Native Military Porters for the German East Africa Campaign. *Addresses :* Barton House, Hereford ; Livingstone, N. Rhodesia.   (M1273)

JONES, Sir Edgar Rees, K.B.E., M.P. (*see* BURKE'S *Peerage*), *b.* 27 Aug. 1878 ; *s.* of Morgan Humphrey, of Wattstown, Glamorgan ; *m.* Lillian Helena May, *d.* of George Brackley, of Westerham, Kent. *Educ. :* University of Wales. Member of Parliament for Merthyr Tydvil. *War Work :* Controller, Priority Department, Ministry of Munitions, 1915–18 ; *Address :* Jesmond Dene, Shepperton. *Club :* National Liberal.   (K871)

JONES, Capt. Edgar William, O.B.E., R.E. (T.).

JONES, Edith Muriel, M.B.E., *d.* of the late Adam Dugdale, of Griffin Lodge, Blackburn, and Gilmonby Hall, Bowes, Yorkshire ; *m.* William Edmund Jones. *War Work :* Quartermaster of Ellerslie Auxiliary Military Hospital, at Blackburn. *Address :* St. Croix, 72, Holly Walk, Leamington. *Club :* Ladies' Imperial.   (M8663)

JONES, Edmund Vaughan, M.B.E., *b.* 25 Feb. 1871 ; *s.* of William Jones, of Belfast ; *m.* Ethel, *d.* of Monkhouse Graham, of Great Ayton, Yorks. *Educ. :* Privately and Belfast Academy. Shipbuilder, tuition received at Harland and Wolff, Queen's Island, Belfast, and since been professionally employed in several of the principal shipbuilding firms in the kingdom. *War Work :* Employed in building all classes of war vessels with Cammell Laird, of Birkenhead, and employers' representative on Local Munition Tribunal and Court of Referees. *Address :* Normount, Cavendish Drive, Rock Ferry, Cheshire.
                                                        (M611)

JONES, Capt. Edward Denby, M.B.E., R.A.S.C.

JONES, Ernest Stephens, O.B.E., F.I.A., F.S.S., *b.* 15 Mar. 1880 ; *s.* of Rees Jones, of Brecon, S. Wales. *Educ. :* Owen's, Islington. Principal Clerk, National Debt Office, and Actuary to the Pensions Commutation Board ; Fellow of the Institute of Actuaries ; Fellow of the Royal Statistical Society ; *War Work :* Administration of Treasury Securities Deposit and Purchase Schemes at the American Dollar Securities Branch of the National Debt Office. *Addresses :* 23, Highbury Grange, London, N. 5 ; 19, Old Jewry, London, E.C. 2.

JONES, Ethel Mary, O.B.E., ; *d.* of H. E. Jones, J.P., Essex, of Marden Ash, Ongar, Essex. *Educ. :* Privately. *War Work :* Commandant Red Cross Hospital, Budworth Hall, Ongar, opened Oct. 1914, closed February, 1919. *Addresses :* Marden Ash, Ongar, Essex ; Windmill Cottage, Walberswick, Southwold, Suffolk. *Club :* Ladies' V.A.D.
                                                        (O1528)

JONES, Lieut. Francis Henry, M.B.E., R.E.
JONES, Rev. Francis Horace, O.B.E., B.A., R.N.
JONES, Frank Henry, M.B.E.
JONES, Lieut. Frank Murcheson, O.B.E., R.N.V.R.
JONES, Frederick Tobias, M.B.E., A.M.I.M.E., *b.* 29 Jan. 1884 ; *s.* of Henry I. Jones, of Summerfield Park, Edgbaston ; *m.* Lily. *d.* of William Smith, of Birmingham. *Educ. :* Barford Road Council School, and Birmingham Central Technical School. Engineer ; present Works Manager, John Marston, Ltd., Sunbeamland, Wolverhampton ; late Head of Engineering Dept., Aston Technical Coll., Birmingham. *War Work :* Organised Classes in Aston Technical Coll. for Training Munition Workers ; afterwards transferred to Ministry of Munitions to Equip and Organise Government Instructional Factory, Lancaster Street, Birmingham ; Works Manager there until end of war. *Addresses :* 11, Hunton Hill, Gravelly Hill, Birmingham ; Copthorne Road, Wolverhampton.   (M1972)

JONES, Frederick William, O.B.E., *b.* 7 April, 1867. *Educ. :* Nottingham Univ. Coll., and Royal Coll. of Science. Technical Chemist and Consulting Expert on Explosives ; Member of the Court of Assistants of the Gunmakers' Company ; Member of the Departmental Committee appointed by the

Home Office on the Heat Test of Explosives. *War Work :* Consultant to Manufacturers of Explosives and Small Arms Ammunition ; acted in consulting capacity (honorary) to the Trench Warfare and Munitions Designs Departments ; Technical Assistant (honorary) on the Staff of the Small Arms Ammunition Department of the Ministry of Munitions ; Member of a Commission sent to Russia on Small Arms Ammunition. *Address :* 25, Park Hill Rise, Croydon, Surrey.   (O10749)

JONES, George, M.B.E.
JONES, George Henry Walter, M.B.E.
JONES, Capt. Gerald Francis, O.B.E., R.E.
JONES, Gladys Alicia, Mrs., O.B.E.
JONES, Glynne, O.B.E.
JONES, Hannah, M.B.E.
JONES, Harold Edward, O.B.E.
JONES, Harold Spencer, M.B.E.
JONES, Capt. and Qr.-Mr. Harry Beresford, M.B.E., R.D.C.
JONES, Lieut. Harry Cardew, M.B.E., R.A.S.C.
JONES, 2nd Lieut. Henry, M.B.E., R.A.F.
JONES, Major Henry James, O.B.E., R.A.O.C.
JONES, Henry John Alfred, M.B.E.

JONES, Herbert Arthur, M.B.E., *b.* 24 May, 1882 ; *s.* of John Jones, of Ridgmont, Beds. ; *m.* Maud, *d.* of William Colston Powell, of Bristol. Inspector for Cornwall for the Employers' Liability Assurance Corporation, Ltd. *War Work :* Separation Allowance Department, War Office, Oct. 1914, to June, 1915 ; Assist. Sec. in charge of Separation Allowance Department, Cornwall Territorial Force Association, Truro, July, 1915, to July, 1919. *Addresses :* Silverdene, Perranwell Station, Cornwall ; Old Mansion House, Truro. *Club :* City, Truro.   (M8667)

JONES, Capt. Herbert Cavendish, O.B.E.

JONES, Herbert Charles, O.B.E., J.P., *b.* 1868 ; *s.* of Rufus Jones, of Nuneaton ; *m.* Ethel Mary, *d.* of John Ashworth, J.P., of Bury, Lancs. *Educ. :* King Edward VI.'s School, Nuneaton. *War Work :* Mayor of Nuneaton, 1915–18 ; Chairman, Nuneaton Recruiting Committee and Local Tribunal, and Food Control, Coal Control, War Pensions, War Savings, Local Employment Committees. *Address :* Attleborough Hall, Nuneaton. *Clubs :* Nuneaton ; National Liberal.
                                                        (O10751)

JONES, Capt. Herbert Oakes, M.B.E.

JONES, Major (T. Lieut.-Col.) Hubert Louis, O.B.E., R.M.L.I., *b.* 16 April, 1882 ; *s.* of George Thomas Jones, M.D., of Ludlow, Salop : *m.* Aimée Templer, *d.* of John Templer Horne, of Wynberg, Cape Colony. *Educ. :* Dulwich. District Intelligence Officer, The Nore. *War Work :* General Staff (Naval) Cape Town, Aug. 1914–March, 1918 ; General Staff Officer (Naval) Ponta Delgada, Azores, Aug. 1918 to Feb. 1919. *Address :* Commander-in-Chief's Office, Chatham.   (O3525)

JONES, Capt. Hugh Calvert Francis, M.B.E., R.A.
JONES, Lieut. Isaac, O.B.E., R.N.R.

JONES, James Stuart, M.B.E., *b.* 31 Aug. 1872 ; *s.* of James Jones, of Lima, Peru ; *m.* Emily, *d.* of Patrick Mackintosh, of Baileymawr, Penybont, Radnorshire. *Educ. :* The Academy, Forfar, Scotland. Inspector of Telegraph and Telephone Traffic, General Post Office. *War Work :* Air raid warnings, and other War emergency services involving the use of the public telephone and telegraph systems. *Address :* Secretary's Office, G.P.O., London, E.C. 1.   (M614)

JONES, John, M.B.E.   (M10250*d*)
JONES, John, M.B.E., L.R.C.P., J.P., D.L.
JONES, Lieut. John, O.B.E., R.A.O.C.

JONES, John, M.B.E., *b.* 20 Jan. 1874 ; *s.* of David Jones, of Garwdylau, Penderyn, Aberdare ; *m.* the late Rose, *d.* of Richard Cross, of Enstone, Oxon. *Educ. :* Ordinary Day School and private studies. Supt. Clerk, War Office. *War Work :* War Office Clerk, Aug. 1914, to Jan. 1916 ; Superintending Clerk, Training Branch, at G.H.Q. Home Forces, Jan. 1916, to Dec. 1919, all nominally War Office. *Address :* 525, Katharine Road, Forest Gate, E. 7. *Club :* Veterans'.
                                                        (M8668)

JONES, John Arnold, O.B.E., M.B., Ch.B., F.R.C.S. (Edin.), *b.* 7 May, 1879 ; *s.* of David Meredith Jones, of Manchester ; *m.* Jessie, *d.* of George Foxon, of Walthamstow. *Educ. :* Hulme Grammar School ; Manchester and Vienna Univs. Surgeon, St. John's Hospital for Diseases of the Ear, Manchester ; Surgeon-in-charge Ear, Nose, and Throat Dept., Manchester Children's Hospital. *War Work :* T. Major R.A.M.C. ; service in Macedonia, Nov. 1915, to Jan. 1919 ; Aural and Laryngeal Surgeon to the British Forces, Jan. 1917, to Jan.1919 ; mentioned in despatches, June,1919. *Addresses :* 20, St. John Street, Manchester ; 77, High Street, Whitworth Park, Manchester. *Club :* Brasenose, Manchester. (O6490)

JONES, John Colenso M.B.E.
JONES, Capt. John Fleming, O.B.E., D.S.C., R A.F.
JONES, John Francis, O.B.E.
JONES, Comm. John Herbert, O.B.E., R.N.
JONES, Capt. John Howard, O.B.E., R.A.V.C.. (T.).

JONES, John Hugh, M.B.E., *b.* 4 March, 1883 ; *s.* of William, of Ruthin, North Wales ; *m.* Ethel Agnes, *d.* of Joseph Southwood, of Hanwell, W. Manager, Sales Dept., English Margarine Works (1919), Ltd., Broad Green, Liverpool. *War Work :* Assistant Director, Oils and Fats Branch, Ministry of Food, Dec. 1917, to Feb. 1919. *Address :* 10, Mayville Road, Mossley Hill, Liverpool.   (M8671)

JONES, Major John Lloyd Charles, O.B.E., R.A.V.C. (T.).
JONES, John Phillips, O.B.E.
JONES, Capt. John Trevor Hughes, O.B.E., R.A.O.C.

JONES, Capt. John William, M.B.E.

JONES, Joseph, M.B.E., *b.* 9 March, 1857; *s.* of Owen Jones, of Colwyn, North Wales; *m.* Susan, *d.* of John Dodd, of Dartmouth, Devon. *Educ.:* National School, Colwyn. Stationmaster (Euston); general transportation work in connection with troops and machinery, etc.; Member of the Honourable Society of Cymmrodorion. (M8673)

JONES, Joseph, M.B.E., *b.* 21 May, 1880; *s.* of Evan Jones, of Cardiff; *m.* Hannah Gainor, *d.* of the Rev. J. P. Davies, of Cymmer, Porth. *Educ.:* Cardiff. City Librarian, Salisbury; Borough Librarian, Torquay. *War Work:* Army Pay Dept., June, 1915, to Dec. 1918; served in Egypt, Feb. 1917, to Sept. 1918. *Address:* 7, Gower Street, Swansea. *Club:* National Liberal. (M4687)

JONES, Llewellyn Thomas, M.B.E.

JONES, Major Lorne Fauntleroy, O.B.E., Can. A.M.C.

JONES, Malcolm Ludlow, O.B.E.

JONES, Margaret, O.B.E.

JONES, Margaret Ellen, M.B.E.

JONES, Mary, M.B.E., *b.* 1888; *d.* of John Jones, of Llangeitho, Cardiganshire, Wales. *Educ.:* Llangeitho School, and London. *War Work:* Administrator in Q.M.A.A.C. for 4 years; in charge of Staff College Mess at Sandhurst; also of Officers' Mess at Exeter, Winchester, etc. *Addresses:* Llangeitho, Llanio Road, Cardiganshire, S. Wales; 13, Canonbury Park South, Canonbury, London, N. 1. (M6661)

JONES, Capt. Oswell, M.B.E., *b.* 1883; *s.* of Coetmore Kendrick Jones, of North Wales; *m.* Molly, *d.* of William Henry Cook, of Hertford. *Educ.:* Hoffman's Coll., Nottingham. Electrical Engineer. *War Work:* Returned from Argentine in 1914 as a volunteer; obtained commission in Royal West Kents in Nov. 1914; went to France and Belgium with W. Kents; was seconded for duty with the R.E.'s, and attached to Tunnelling Company; wounded and returned to England in Dec. 1915. *Address:* 85, Clarence Gate Gardens, Regent's Park. (M5386)

JONES, Capt. Owen, C.B.E., R.D., R.N.R., *b.* 20 June, 1866; *s.* of Lieut.-Col. A. S. Jones, V.C., of 9th Lancers. *Educ.:* Grove Park School, Wrexham; and H.M.S. "Conway." Elder Brother, Trinity House. *Addresses:* Worplesdon Chase, Guildford; Trinity House, London, E.C. (C898)

JONES, Owen Thomas, M.B.E., L.R.C.P., M.R.C.S.

JONES, Patrick Nicholas Hill, O.B.E., *b.* 19 Sept. 1864; *s.* of Oswald Jones, of Bermuda. Late Director of Public Works, Gold Coast Colony, West Africa; M.Inst.C.E.; Consulting Engineer. *War Work:* Inspector of Gun Ammunition, Royal Arsenal, Woolwich, June, 1915–19. *Address:* 3, Victoria Street, Westminster, S.W. *Club:* Royal Societies'. (O467)

JONES Major Percival Walter Edwin, O.B.E., R.E.

JONES, Rev. Percy Herbert, C.B.E., M.A., R.N.

JONES, Capt. Reginald Vickers, M.B.E.

JONES, Lieut. Richard, M.B.E.

JONES, Richard Edward, O.B.E., J.P., C.C., Managing Director, William Jones and Son, Ltd., Maltsters, Shrewsbury. *War Work:* Chairman, County Distributing (Forage) Committee for Shropshire and Montgomeryshire; Chairman, Shrewsbury Employment Committee. *Addresses:* Oakley Grange, Shrewsbury; St. Davids, Fairbourne, Merionethshire. *Club:* Royal Automobile. (O10754)

JONES, Richard Evan, O.B.E., M.A. (Cantab.), J.P., *b.* 11 Sept. 1873; *s.* of the late Rev. Evan Jones, sometime vicar of the Metropolitan Welsh Church; *m.* Gertrude Helen, *d.* of Herbert Briddon, of Thorpe, Derbyshire. *Educ.:* Clare College, Cambridge. *War Work:* County Director of the British Red Cross Society; Military Representative, and afterwards National Service Representative, at Cardiganshire County Appeal Tribunal. *Address:* Borth, Cardiganshire. *Club:* Constitutional. (O1530)

JONES, Richard Nelson, O.B.E., M.R.C.S., L.R.C.P.

JONES, Sir Robert, K.B.E., C.B., LL.D. Aberdeen (Hon.), D.Sc. Wales (Hon.), M.Ch. Liverpool, F.R.C.S. Eng., Ire., Edin., F.A.C.S., D.S.M., U.S.A., *b.* 1858; *s.* of Robert Jones, of Rhyl; *m.* the late Susie Evans, *d.* of William Evans, of Southville, Bootle. *Educ.:* Sydenham Coll. Surgeon; Major-Gen. A.M.S.; Director of Military Orthopædics, A.M.S.; Member of Advisory Board, A.M.S.; Hon. Consultant on Orthopædics, Pensions Ministry; Director of Orthopædic Surgery (St. Thomas's Hospital); Surgeon to Royal National Orthopædic Hospital; Surgeon to various hospitals in Liverpool; Lecturer on Orthopædic Surgery to Liverpool Univ. *War Work:* Organised the Orthopædic Service for the War Office. *Addresses:* 11, Nelson Street, Liverpool; 9, Cavendish Square, London; 11, Belvedere Road, Liverpool. *Clubs:* Reform; Savile; Royal Automobile. (K295)

JONES, Capt. and Qr.-Mr. Robert, M.B.E., *b.* 5 Aug. 1863; *m.* Edis May, *d.* of Thomas Burleigh Peters, of Plymouth. Appointed Bandmaster, 2nd Black Watch, Jan. 1894; Quartermaster (Lieut.), 2/5th Sco. Rifles, Sept. 1914. *War Work:* Mobilised with 5th Sco. Rifles, Aug. 1914; Commissioned, Sept. 1914, in 2/5th Sco. Rifles as Lieut. and Qr.-Mr.; served with the 65th Division; also as Qr.-Mr. 2/1st County of London Yeomanry. *Address:* 105, Clarence Drive, Hyndland, Glasgow. (M5387)

JONES, Robert Arthur, M.B.E., Hon. Freeman of the County Borough of Southend-on-Sea, 20 Nov. 1849; *s.* of the late J. A. Jones, of Liverpool; *m.* Emma Julia, *d.* of the late T. Pedley, of Stoke-on-Trent. *Educ.:* Public School, Liverpool. Goldsmith and Diamond Merchant. *War Work:*

attendance upon the Naval and Military patients at Queen Mary's Naval Hospital and the Victoria Hospital, Southend-on-Sea, for over 2½ years. *Address:* Thamesmouth, The Cliffs, Southend-on-Sea. *Clubs:* Unionist, Southend and Southchurch; Naval and Military, Southend-on-Sea. (M8676)

JONES, Sir Roderick, K.B.E. (*see* BURKE'S *Peerage*), *b.* 1878; *s.* of Roderick Patrick Jones, of Manchester; *m.* Enid, *d.* of Col. Arthur Bagnold, C.B., C.M.G., of Shooters' Hill. *Educ.:* Privately. Chairman and Managing Director of Reuter's: succeeded the late Baron de Reuter as head of Reuter's in 1915. After acting as a Reuter correspondent in South Africa was appointed Reuter's South African Editor in London in 1902; returned to South Africa to take charge of Reuter's interests in South and Central Africa, end of 1905: came to London to succeed Baron de Reuter as Head of the Agency, and in control of its organisation throughout the world, after the Baron's death in 1915. Acted as Honorary Cable and Wireless Propaganda Adviser to the Foreign Office, 1915–17, and when the Ministry of Information was established in 1918, accepted the official invitation to become Director of Propaganda in Allied and Neutral Countries. *Address:* 51, South Street, Berkeley Square. *Clubs:* Windham; Hurlingham; Royal Automobile; Civil Service, Capetown. (K88)

JONES, Ronald Herbert, O.B.E., King Albert Medal, Reconnaissance Française, South African War Medal, *b.* 8 April, 1874. *Educ.:* South Africa. *War Work:* On the Commission for Relief in Belgium from its inception and throughout the war. (O10755)

JONES, Lieut.-Comm. Rupert Oswald, O.B.E., R.N.R.

JONES, Capt. Russell, O.B.E.

JONES, Samuel Glynne, O.B.E.

JONES, Major Seymour Whitworth, O.B.E., I.M.S.

JONES, Capt. Sydney Herbert, O.B.E.

JONES, Sydney Herbert, M.B.E., R.N.

JONES, Lieut. Theodore Warren, O.B.E., R.N.R., *b.* 26 Aug. 1887; *s.* of Charles H. Jones, Registrar General of Shipping and Seamen. Chief Officer, Shaw, Savill and Albion Company. *War Work:* Officer in Charge, London District, Defensively armed Merchant Ships, 1914–1919. *Address:* 11, Emperor's Gate, S.W. 7. *Club:* Junior Naval and Military. (O469)

JONES, Capt. and Qr.-Mr. Thomas, M.B.E., K.R.R.C.

JONES, 2nd Lieut. Thomas Cecil, M.B.E., R.F.A. (T.).

JONES, Thomas Hugh, O.B.E.

JONES, Paymaster Thomas Lionel, M.B.E.

JONES, 2nd Lieut. Thomas Pargeter, M.B.E., R.A.F.

JONES, Thomas Rees, C.B.E.

JONES, Tom Bruce, O.B.E.

JONES, Capt. Vincent Strickland, O.B.E. (O11747)

JONES, Walter Owen, M.B.E.

JONES, William, M.B.E.

JONES, Lieut. William, M.B.E., R.G.A. (att. R.A.O.C.), *b.* 6 May, 1880; *m.* Elizabeth, *d.* of W. J. Owen, of Kimbolton. *Educ.:* National School, Kimbolton. *War Work:* British East African Campaign in Jan. 1916, to end of war; engaged in salvage work until July, 1920. *Address:* Prospect Cottage, Stockton, nr. Leominster, Herefordshire. (M8677)

JONES, Capt. William, O.B.E.

JONES, Capt. William Edward, O.B.E., R.F.A.

JONES, William Henry, O.B.E., *b.* 25 Aug. 1873; *s.* of Henry Jones, of Cardiff; *m.* Bessie, *d.* of John Baker, of Brooklyn, N.Y., U.S.A. *Educ.:* Lewis School, Pengam, and Cardiff College. Director of the W. and C. T. Jones Steamship Co. Ltd., 1898–1916; Chairman of Directors, 1914–16; Vice-Chairman, Cardiff Shipowners Association, 1910; Director West of England Protection an Indemnity Association, 1906–14; on Executive of Shipping Federation, 1906–12; on Executive Chamber of Shipping of the United Kingdom, 1906–14. *War Work:* Served with the British Ministry of Shipping, New York, 1917–20, as Director of Transport Department and Deputy Director-General. *Address:* 854, President Street, Brooklyn, New York, U.S.A. (O10756)

JONES, Lieut. William Everard Tyldesley, M.B.E., R.G.A.

JONES, W. H., M.B.E.

JONES, Lieut. William Henry, M.B.E., Can. A.S.C.

JONES, Major William Henry, O.B.E., R.E.

JONES, William Henry, O.B.E.

JONES, Sir William John, K.B.E. (*see* BURKE'S *Peerage*), *b.* 31 Dec. 1866; *s.* of William Jones, of London; *m.* Emma, *d.* of George Hicks, of London. *Educ.:* Haberdashers' Company's Schools. Managing Director of The Woodall-Duckham Vertical Retort and Oven Construction Co. Ltd; Arthur Duckham and Co. Ltd; Director of Woodall, Duckan and Jones, Ltd.; Stourbridge Refractories Co. Ltd; British Magnesite Calcining Co. Ltd. *War Work:* Director of Refractory Materials, Iron and Steel Production Dept., Ministry of Munitions; British Representative, Inter-Allied Steel Commission; Deputy Controller, Iron and Steel Production Dept., Ministry of Munitions. *Address:* The Orchard, Warlingham, Surrey. *Club:* St. Stephen's. (K217)

JONES, William Tudor, M.B.E.

JONES, Lieut.-Col. Sir Robert ARMSTRONG-, C.B.E., M.D., J.P., D.L., R.A.M.C., Knight of Grace of the Order of St. John of Jerusalem, *b.* 1857; *s.* of Rev. Thomas Jones, of Eisteddfa, Criccieth; *m.* Margaret, *d.* of Sir Owen Roberts, M.A., D.C.L., J.P., D.L., of Henley Park, Guildford, Surrey, and Plas Dinas, Carnarvon, N. Wales. *Educ.:* St. Bartholomew's Hospital, London. Physician. *War Work:*

Consulting Physician in Mental Diseases to the London and Aldershot Commands. *Addresses :* 9, Bramham Gardens, London, S.W. 5 ; Plas Dinas, Carnarvon, N. Wales. *Club :* Athenæum. (C1447)

JONES, Herbert Thomas AVERAY-, M.B.E.

JONES, Reginald BENCE-, M.B.E., J.P., D.L., Co. Cork, *b.* 4 Nov. 1865 ; *s.* of William Bence-Jones, of Lisselan, Co. Cork ; *m.* Ethel, *d.* of D. C. Da Costa, of Barbados, West Indies. *Educ. :* Rugby, and St. John's Coll., Oxford. *War Work :* Industrial Reserve, the Ministry of Labour and subsequently Ministry of National Service. *Addresses :* Lisselan, Clonakilty, Co. Cork ; 15, Evelyn Mansions, Westminster, S.W. 1. *Clubs :* New Oxford and Cambridge ; County, Cork. (M3777)

JONES, Alice Pownall, Mrs. CATON-, O.B.E., *b.* 10 Dec. 1879 ; *d.* of Thomas Fielden, M.P. (*see* BURKE'S *Landed Gentry*), of Grimston Park, Tadcaster, Yorks ; *m.* Frederick William Caton, *s.* of Henry Jones, of Bianum, S. Australia. *War Work :* Private Canteen work in France. *Address :* Earlsdale, Pontesford, Salop. (O10748)

JONES, Capt. Elias Wynne CEMLYN-, M.B.E.

JONES, Col. William Fenton FENTON-, M.B.E., J.P., and Order of King Albert, Deputy Lieut. Co. of London, *b.* Nov. 1861 ; *s.* of Jno. Fenton-Jones, J.P., of 12, King Edward Road, Hackney ; *m. d.* of Robert Cain, of Douglas, Isle of Man. *Educ. :* Cheltenham and London. Mayor of Hackney, Coronation Year of King George ; Chairman Hackney Board of Guardians 1908-9 ; L.C.C. School Manager 9 years ; Military Representative during war time ; Chairman Advisory Committee Hackney Labour Exchange. *War Work :* Created National Reserves, Hackney, 10th Tenth Batt. the London Regt., Tenth County of London Cadet Corps ; Divisional Director British Red Cross, 4 detachments, Hackney ; Military Representative, Hackney, for Voluntary and Compulsory service ; on Recruiting Committee, Hackney, and Proposer of resolution which led to creation of 2 Artillery units. *Addresses :* Lezayre, Snakes Lane, Woodford Green, Essex ; 144, Mare Street, Hackney, E. 8.

JONES, Capt. Richard Reginald GLYNNE-, O.B.E.

JONES, Anne Laugharne Phillips GRIFFITH-, M.B.E., *b.* 15 April, 1891 ; *d.* of G. Griffith-Jones, Barrister-at-Law, of Aberystwyth. Welfare Supervisor (at Messrs. Baldwins, Ltd.) ; President of South Wales and Monmouthshire Association of Welfare Workers. *War Work :* Welfare Supervisor, Swansea National Shell Factory. (M3776)

JONES, Major Morgan Phillips GRIFFITH·, O.B.E., B.A., *b.* 1876 ; *s.* of Griffith Jones, Bar.-at-Law ; *m.* 1898, Violet Florence Gwendolen, *d.* of the late Buddle Atkinson, of Wooley Grange, Wilts. *Educ. :* Univ. Coll. Sch. ; Trin. Hall, Camb. Bar. Middle Temple, 1899 ; joined N.E. Circuit ; Major Durham L.I. (ret.) and Gen. List ; served in Great War, 1914-19 (wounded, despatches) ; appointed Pres. Pensions Appeal Tribunal, 1919. *Address :* Harpenden, Herts. *Clubs :* Arthur's ; Northern Counties'. (O4309)

JONES, Edgar HEATH-, O.B.E. Financial Sec., Central Prisoners of War Committee. (C986)

JONES, Lillie, Mrs. HIGHFIELD-, M.B.E., *b.* 23 Feb. 1863 ; *d.* of John Henry Storey, of Brooklands, Cheshire ; *m.* Benjamin Highfield, *s.* of Benjamin Jones, of Wolverhampton. *Educ. :* Wilton House, Edgbaston, Birmingham. *War Work :* Relief Committee ; Women's Unemployment Sub-Committee ; Capt. and Qr.-Mr. in Wolverhampton Branch of Women's Volunteer Reserve ; Special Policewoman. *Address :* Ash Hill, Compton, Wolverhampton. *Club :* Ladies', Wolverhampton. (M1974)

JONES, Major Robert HILTON-, O.B.E., R.A.F.

JONES, Lieut. Glyn Howard HOWARD-, O.B.E.

JONES, Llewelyn HUGH-, C.B.E., *b.* 27 Aug. 1863 ; *s.* of Ven. Archdeacon Hugh-Jones, late of Llanrwst, Denbighshire ; *m.* Clara, *d.* of William John Sisson, of Wrexham. *Educ. :* Grammar School, Llanrwst. Official Receiver in Bankruptcy for Chester and North Wales (1889) ; Clerk to Magistrates Bromfield Division of Denbighshire (1896) ; ditto, Overton Division of Flints (1910) ; Clerk to Commissioner of Taxes Maylor Division Flintshire (1915) ; Clerk to Lieutenancy Denbighshire (1917) ; Member of the Governing Body of the Welsh Church. *War Work :* Hon. Secretary S. and S. Families Association, Denbighshire ; Hon. Representative of Ministry of Pensions, North Wales ; Chairman, North Wales Joint Disablement Committee ; Member of the Institutional Committee for Wales. *Address :* Chevet Hey, Wrexham, N. Wales. (C2725)

JONES, Lieut. George LEGH-, M.B.E.

JONES, Frederick Archibald LESLIE-, C.B.E., M.A., *b.* 9 July, 1874 ; *s.* of the late Hudson Leslie-Jones, M.D., F.R.C.S.I. of Manchester ; *m.* Christiana Mary, *d.* of Rev. J. C. Baskett, of Donhead. *Educ. :* Bromsgrove School and Lincoln College, Oxford. Assistant Master, Marlborough College, 1897-1904 ; Principal Aitchison College, Lahore Panjab, 1904-1917 ; Principal Mayo College, Ajmer, Rajputana, 1917. *War Work :* President "Publicity," Ajmer-Merwara ; Hon. Editor "Ajmer-Merwara War Gazette." *Addresses :* c/o Thomas Cook, Ludgate Circus, London, and Mayo College, Ajmer, Rajputana, India. (C2386)

JONES, Lieut.-Col. Leycester Hudson LESLIE-, O.B.E., I.A.R.O.

JONES, Walter LINDLEY-, O.B.E.

JONES, Capt. Arthur Griffiths MAITLAND-, O.B.E., M.C., R.A.M.C.

JONES, Lieut.-Col. Albert Westhead PRYCE-, O.B.E., T.D., J.P., *b.* 26 May, 1870 ; 3rd *s.* of late Sir Pryce Pryce-Jones, of Newtown, Wales ; *m.* Rosina Ida, *d.* of William Gibson, of Roehampton. *Educ. :* Shrewsbury and Clare College, Cambridge. J.P. County of Montgomery ; J.P. Province of Alberta, Canada ; Member of Inner Temple ; Major 7th R.W.F. (T.F.R.). *War Work :* raised and commanded 113th Battn. Canadian Expeditionary Force ; served in France from Dec. 1916 to March, 1920 ; mentioned in despatches. *Address :* Calgary, Alberta, Canada. *Club :* (London). (O5696)

JONES, Brig.-Gen. Morey QUAYLE-, C.B., C.M.G., C.B.E., J.P., D.L. (Warwickshire), *b.* 8 Mar. 1855 ; *s.* of Charles William Jones, of Pakenham, Suffolk ; *m.* Isabel, *d.* of Maitland Dashwood. *Educ. :* Wellington Coll. Barrister-at-Law. *War Work :* Commanded 104th Brigade, 35th Division, 4th Army, 1914-16 ; County Director Auxiliary Hospitals and V.A.D. Detachments, 1914 ; Deputy President Warwickshire Branch British Red Cross Society ; National Service Sub-Commissioner. *Address :* Claverdon Hall, Warwick. *Club :* Army and Navy. (C2726)

JONES, Dorothea Adelaide Lowry PUGHE-, C.B.E., *b.* 23 June, 1874 ; *d.* of Robert Pughe-Jones, of Ynysgain, Criccieth. *Educ. :* Queen's Coll., London, and Somerville Coll., Oxford. *War Work :* Sept. 1915, to June, 1916, Red Cross work in France ; June, 1916, to Sept. 1918, V.A.D. Commandant, Hotel des Anglais, Le Touquet ; Sept. 1918, to May, 1919, Principal Commandant, V.A.D.'s in Salonica. *Address :* Ynysgain, Criccieth, N. Wales. (M1970)

JONES, Capt., William Henry STANLEY-, O.B.E.

JONES, Capt. Reginald TEAGUE-, M.B.E., I.A.R.O.

JONES, William James WALLIS-, M.B.E., *b.* 27 May 1873 ; *s.* of Evan Jones, of Alltywalis, Carmarthenshire (Woollen Manufacturer) ; *m.* Ethel Perrins, *d.* of James Perrins Carter, of Clifton. *Educ. :* Aberystwyth, University Coll. of Wales, and King's Coll., London. Solicitor ; Sec. and Registration Agent, Carmarthen Division Liberal Association ; Executive member Welsh National Liberal Council ; Clerk to the Visitors Joint Counties Mental Hospital, Carmarthen ; Clerk to the Newcastle Emlyn and Lampeter Unions Old Age Pensions Sub-Committees, etc. *War Work :* Branch Manager, Ministry of Labour (Employment Department) at Carmarthen ; Joint Sec. West Carm. Parliamentary Recruiting Committees and Aims Committee ; Hon. Recruiter R.N.D. and R.N.V.R. ; Clerk to N.C. Emlyn and Lampeter War Pensions District Committees, etc. ; author of "Welsh Characteristics" (1898), "The Welsh Regiment" (1900), etc. ; founded and Edited "Pencader and Llandyssul Guardian" in 1897. *Address :* Llys-yr-onen, Carmarthen. *Clubs :* Masonic, Carmarthen ; Law Society, London. (M8678)

JONES, Reginald John WALLIS-, O.B.E.

JOPP, Lieut.-Col. Stephen James Melville, O.B.E.

JORDAN, Alfred Charles, C.B.E., M.D., M.R.C.P. For work in connection with radiology at Queen Alexandra's Hospital. (C3150)

JORDAN, Charles William, M.B.E., *b.* 3 Dec. 1846 ; *s.* of John Jordan, of Moreton, Essex ; *m.* Hannah Jane Crosby, *d.* of Robson Hodgson, of Middlesbrough. *Educ. :* St. Michael's, Chester Square, London. Master Mariner of the s.s. "Claudia," *War Work :* Trading between France, Bergen, Norway, Leith, Tyne and Tees, and London, with cargo, provisions, and general stores. *Address :* Gordon Terrace, 148, Borough Road, Middlesboro', Yorks. *Clubs :* Tees Lodge 509, Stockton-on-Tees, Masonic ; Conservative, Middlesboro' ; Imperial Merchant Service Guild, Liverpool. (M8679)

JORDAN, Lieut. Harold George, O.B.E., R.E.

JORDAN, Herbert James, M.B.E.

JORDAN, John, C.B.E., J.P.

JORDAN, William Ezra, M.B.E.

JORDAN, William Henry, M.B.E.

JOSCELYNE, Major Frederic Percy, O.B.E., M.C., late R.A.M.C., *b.* 19 Jan. 1874 ; *s.* of the Rev. Henry Joscelyne, late Rector of Ibstone. *Educ. :* Felsted School. Medical Practitioner, M.D. (Brussels), D.P.H. (Oxon). *War Work :* Served with 2nd Sussex Regt. in France ; was Sanitary Officer in Albert, Poperinghe and Ypres ; D.A.D.M.S. of 5th Army ; awarded M.C. in 1915. *Address :* Mary St. House, Taunton. (O5440)

JOSEPH, Charles Henry, M.B.E.

JOSEPH, David, M.B.E.

JOSEPH, Major Ernest Martin, O.B.E.

JOSEPH, Capt. Francis L'Estrange, C.B.E., J.P., *b.* 31 July, 1870 ; *s.* of Thomas Joseph, of Liverpool ; *m.* Violet, *d.* of Joel Settle, of The Hill, Alsager, Cheshire. *Educ.* Caledonian Scottish School, Liverpool. Director, Settle, Speakman & Co. Ltd., Alsager, Liverpool, and London. *War Work :* Capt., Western Command ; transferred to War Office with staff rank ; Assist. Sec., Ministry National Service ; later Deputy Director, General National Labour Supply ; Member Port and Transit Executive Committee. *Address :* The Gables, Alsager, Cheshire. (C541)

JOSEPH, Janie, M.B.E.

JOSLIN, Capt. Evelyn Whyaid, M.B.E.

JOSLIN, William Joseph, M.B.E.

JOSS, Major Alexander WYNYARD-, O.B.E., Aust.A.S.C.

JOSSELYN, Col. John, C.M.G., D.S.O., O.B.E., T.D. (Reserve of Officers, Territorial Army), *b.* 28 Oct. 1872 ; *s.* of the late Frederic Josselyn ; *m.* Lilian Bella, *d.* of the late

Joughin THE ORDER OF THE BRITISH EMPIRE.

Venble. William Weston Elwes, Archdeacon of Madras. *War Work :* Served on Coast Defence with the 6th Batt. Suffolk Regt. from July, 1914, to Jan., 1915; appointed Brigade Major, 185 Infantry Brigade, Jan. 1915; Commanded 2/5th Bn. West Yorkshire Regt., May, 1916, to Dec. 1917; wounded in France in 1917; served in North Russia, June, 1918, to Oct. 1919; in Command of Dvina River Force, and afterwards as President, Claims Commission, North Russia; retained on duty in England to wind up finance, etc., of the North Russian Expedition till June, 1920. *Address :* 2, Whitehall Court, London, S.W. 1. *Club :* Junior Army and Navy; Ipswich; Madras. (O1534)

JOUGHIN, John Clague, M.B.E.

JOWITT, Frederick McCulloch, C.B.E.

JOY, Lieut.-Comm. Charles Edward, M.B.E., R.N.

JOY, Capt. George William, M.B.E., *b.* 27 June, 1863; *s.* of John Kinloch Joy, of Hull; *m.* Alice Maria, *d.* of John Jagger, of Hull. *Educ. :* Private Schools, Hull. Capt. Mercantile Marine. *War Work :* Transport Service. *Address :* 71, Park Road, Hull. (M3781)

JOY, Henry, O.B.E., *b.* 25 Aug. 1865; *s.* of Seth Joy, of Moss Side, Manchester; *m.* Martha, *d.* of Thomas Warnock, of Loughan, Coleraine. *Educ. :* Privately, and Askern, Doncaster. Controller, Post Office Savings Bank, March, 1899. *War Work :* In connection with the issue of Loans to finance the war. *Address :* Post Office Savings Bank, London, W. 14. (O3777)

JOY, Henry Holmes, O.B.E., B.A.; *s.* of John Holmes Joy, of Manor House, Tamworth, Staffs.; *m.* Clarie, *d.* of Stephen Stokes, of Hanch Hall, Lichfield. *Educ. :* Sherborne, and Trinity Hall, Cambridge. Barrister-at-Law, Inner Temple *War Work :* Assist. Sec. and Legal Adviser, Ministry of National Service; Metropolitan Special Constabulary, Kensington Division. *Address :* 37, Holland Park Avenue, London. (O10758)

JOY, Capt. and Qr.-Mr. Herbert Alfred, O.B.E., R.A.

JOY, Madeleine Jane, Mrs., M.B.E.; *d.* of Peter Blake, of Galway; *m.* Alexander Outhwaite, *s.* of George Outhwaite Joy, of Leeds. *Educ. :* Edinburgh. *War Work :* Donor with husband of the King's Cross Y.M.C.A. Hut, the Y.M.C.A. Hut at Amiens, one Church Army Hut in France, and was first Lady Superintendent of the King's Cross Hut. *Address :* Crown Hotel, Scarborough. (M8684)

JOY, Sydney Cooper, O.B.E.

JOYCE, Ellen, Hon. Mrs. James Gerald, C.B.E.

JOYCE, Lieut. Ernest Percy, M.B.E., R.A.S.C.

JOYCE, Lieut. Francis Matthew, M.B.E., M.B., R.F.A. (T.).

JOYCE, Francis Raoul, M.B.E.

JOYCE, Lieut.-Col. Pierce Charles, C.B.E., D.S.O., *b.* 23 June, 1878; *s.* of Pierce Joyce, D.L., of Mervue, Co. Galway, Ireland. *Educ. :* Beaumont Coll., Old Windsor. Governor Eastern and Southern Desert Province, Egypt. *War Work :* Gallipoli, 1915; Arabia, 1916–18; organised and served with Arab Army against the Turks up to date of Armistice. *Address :* Mervue, Galway, Ireland. *Club :* Army and Navy. (C2062)

JOYCE, Sterndale, M.B.E., R.A.O.C.

JOYCE, Capt. Thomas Athol, M.B.E., M.A., *b.* 4 Aug. 1878; *s.* of T. Heath Joyce, of Freshford, Somerset; *m.* Lilian Dayrell, *d.* of George Dayrell Reed, of Bromley, Kent. *Educ. :* Dulwich Coll.; Hertford Coll., Oxford. Assistant, British Museum. *War Work :* Military Enquiries Section, Official Press Bureau, 1915–16; Lieut. attached G.S., M.I.2.C. War Office, 1916–17; promoted Capt. 1917–19. *Address :* British Museum, W.C. (O471)

JOYNER, Capt. Cerdric Batson, O.B.E., M.A., *b.* 3 March, 1882; *s.* of the late Robert Batson Joyner, C.I.E., of Cheltenham, and Woody Bay, North Devon; *m.* Kate Evelyn, *d.* of the late George Marlow, of Arlington, Newbury. *Educ. :* Cheltenham Coll.; Emmanuel Coll., Cambridge (Honours, Mathematics and Science). Section Director, Training Dept., Ministry of Labour since Dec. 1918. *War Work :* Capt. 9th Essex Regt. (Sept. 1914), disabled by serious accident in Jan. 1915 at Shorncliffe; Administrative work in Labour Supply Department Ministry of Munitions from Aug. 1915 to Dec. 1918. *Address :* Fairmead, Station Road, Winchmore Hill, N. 21. *Club :* Badminton. (O10759)

JOYNSON, Margaret Beatrice Ethel, M.B.E.

JOYNT, Lieut.-Col. Richard Lane, O.B.E., M.D.

JUDD, Capt. Bertram Christopher, O.B.E.

JUDD, Harold Godfrey, C.B.E., C.A., *b.* 14 Dec. 1878; *s.* of Charles Henry Judd, of China; *m.* Constance Zoe, *d.* of William H. Hoyte, of Nottingham. *Educ. :* Collegiate School, Chefoo, China. Mann, Judd, Gordon & Co., Chartered Accountants; Deputy Controller of Contracts, Ministry of Munitions, since 1917; articled to John Mann and Son, C.A., Glasgow and London, 1894; assumed partner, 1905; entered Ministry of Munitions as assistant to Sir S. Hardman Lever (Financial Secretary), 1915; Deputy Director of Accounts (National Factories), 1916; Director of Contract Finance, 1917. *Addresses :* 8, Frederick's Place, E.C. 2; 61, Hampstead Way, N.W. 4. *Clubs :* New City; Authors'; Liberal, Glasgow. (C215)

JUDD, Capt. Henry Alexander, O.B.E.

JUDD, Leonard William, M.B.E.

JUDD, Thomas Langley, C.B.E., F.S.A.A. *Educ. :* Privately. *War Work :* Deputy Controller of Munition Accounts and Assistant Member of Council in the Ministry of Munitions. *Address :* Ridgway House, 40/42, King William Street, London,

E.C.; Littlebourne, Warren Road, Guildford. *Club :* New City. (C2729)

JUDGE, Lieut. Charles Edward Miller, M.B.E.

JUDGE, Lieut.-Col. and Qr.-Mr. Wybrants, M.B.E.

JUDSON, Capt. Daniel, O.B.E.

JUKES Alfred, M.B.E., R.A.F.

JULIAN, Maj.-Gen. Oliver Richard Archer, C.B., C.M.G., C.B.E., *b.* 1863; *s.* of Capt. Thomas Archer Julian, J.P., formerly 52nd Regt. Entered Roy. Army Med. Corps, 1887; Major, 1899; Brevet Lieut.-Col. 1908; Lieut.-Col. 1911; Col. Army Med. Ser. 1915; T. Maj.-Gen. 1918; served in S. Africa 1899–1902 (despatches); Zakka Khel and Mohmand Expeditions, 1908 (despatches); Great War, 1914–16 (despatches); appointed Physician and Surg., Royal Hospital, Chelsea, 1915. *Address :* Broomhill, Harford, Ivybridge. (C1642)

JUPP, Cecil May, Mrs., M.B.E., *b.* 1893; *d.* of Conway Morgan, of Stafford; *m.* 13 Oct. 1920, Major W. D. L. Jupp, O.B.E. *Educ. :* Rathgowry, Eastbourne. *War Work :* V.A.D. work from 1914, to Sept. 1915; started and managed Queen Mary Needlework Guild, Stafford, for a year; joined Queen Mary's Army Auxiliary Corps in Aug. 1917, as Assist.-Administrator, and crossed to France in Sept. 1917; promoted to Unit Administration in May, 1918, and given charge of one of the three largest camps in France, namely, Q.M.A.A.C. Camp, attached to E.R.S., R.A.F., France. *Address :* Queensville, Stafford. (M4556)

JUPP, Lieut.-Col. William Alfred, O.B.E.

JUPP, Major William Dallas Loney, O.B.E., R.A.F.

JURISS, Lieut. Maximilian, O.B.E., M.C., R.A.F.

JURY, Capt. Arthur Ernest, O.B.E., F.I.S.E., M.R.S.I., R.A.M.C. (T.), 2nd London Sanitary Co., *b.* 21 Jan. 1886; *s.* of Horatius Arthur Jury, of Southborough; *m.* Helen Dorothy, *d.* of D. W. Hopkins. *Educ. :* Privately, and Whitgift School. Sanitary Specialist; Housing Inspector, Ministry of Health; late Technical Secretary to Sir Alexander Houston, K.B.E., C.V.O. *War Work :* O.C. 32nd Sanitary Section, B.E.F.; Commandant III Army School of Sanitation, B.E.F.; Acting D.A.D.M.S. (San.) III Army, B.E.F.; Sanitary Officer Dover Garrison. *Addresses :* 59, Shelgate Road, S.W. 11; Saxondale, Orlando Drive, Carlton, Notts. *Club :* Nottinghamshire Masonic. (O2591)

JURY, Horatius Arthur, O.B.E. Chief Inspector, Public Health Dept., London County Council. (O11908)

JUSTICE, Charles Ernest William, M.B.E.

JUSTICE, Major Philip Welman, O.B.E., R.G.A.

JUTA, Helen Lena, Lady, O.B.E.

KAHL, Frederick, O.B.E.

KALKER, Emanuel, O.B.E.

KANE, Capt. John Leonard Kirkpatrick, O.B.E., I.A.

KAPPELE, Capt. John Logan, O.B.E., C.A.D.C.

KASTOR, Ella Marguerite, M.B.E. (M8686)

KAUFMAN, Louis, O.B.E.

KAUL, Sir Diwan Bahadur Dayer Kishan, K.B.E. (K330)

KAULBACH, Lieut.-Col. Henry Albert, O.B.E., The King's Own Royal Regt., *b.* 16 Feb. 1878; *s.* of the Ven. Archdeacon of Nova Scotia; *m.* Alice Mary, *d.* of Rev. A. J. Townend, C.F. *Educ. :* Collegiate School and King's Coll., Windsor, N.S., and R.M.C. Kingston, Ont. *War Work :* India, Aug. to Dec. 1914; Flanders, Jan. to March, 1915; D.A.A. and Q.M.G., Catterick Camp, Yorks, April, 1916, to end of war; wounded, Feb. 1915. *Address :* Royal Bank of Canada, Princes Street, London, E.C. 2. *Club :* United Service. (O7339)

KAUNTZ, Capt. William Henry, M.B.E.

KAUNTZE, Lieut.-Col. Bertram Charles, O.B.E.

KAVANAGH, Capt. Henry Richard, M.B.E., 2nd Batt. Princess Victoria's Royal Irish Fusiliers, *b.* 11 Aug. 1890; *s.* of Hope Kavanagh of Carlow, Ireland, late S. Police, United Provinces, India; *m.* Sylvia Eleanor, *d.* of Sir James Martin, M.B.E., J.P., of Bellair, Surbiton. *Educ. :* Queen Elizabeth Coll. Commissioned, Dec. 1910. *War Work :* France, 1914–16; Royal Air Force, 1917; Independant Air Force, France, Aug. 1918; Royal Air Force Staff, Cologne, 1919. *Address :* c/o Sir James Martin, Bellair, Surbiton, Surrey. *Club :* Services. (M5995)

KAXTON, Ella Marguerite, M.B.E.

KAY, Andrew Cassels, O.B.E.

KAY, David, M.B.E.

KAY, Edward, M.B.E.

KAY, Major Herbert Davenport, O.B.E.

KAY, Lieut.-Comm. Ivo James, O.B.E., R.N.R.

KAY, Mary Lees, Mrs., O.B.E.; *d.* of E. Moss, of Ravenscroft Hall, Middlewich; *m.* Christopher Kay, D.L., of Davenham Hall, Northwich. *War Work :* Vice President Red Cross Middlewich Division; Commandant of Red Cross Hospital, Middlewich; and of Ravenscroft Hall Annexe; President Soldiers' and Sailors' Families Association; and of Soldiers' and Sailors' Help Society. *Address :* Ravenscroft Hall, Middlewich. (O3778)

KAY, Sydney Entwisle, M.B.E.

KAY, Major William, O.B.E.

KAY, William Gimmell, O.B.E.

KAY, William Norrie, M.B.E., *b.* July, 1866; *s.* of the late William Norrie Kay, of Lorne Bank, Monifieth (Forfarshire); *m.* Margaret Gibson, *d.* of the late David Alexander Tealing, of Forfarshire. *Educ. :* Morgan Academy, Dundee. Chief Engineer Mercantile Marine. *War Work :* Chief Engineer of the steamers "Devona" and "Cairmona," Cairns-Thomson Line ; carried horses, munitions, and other stores from August, 1914, to the end of the war (from U.S.A. and Canada to France and U.K.). *Address* : Hillside, Monifieth, Forfarshire. (M8688)

KAYE, Lieut.-Col. Cecil, C.S.I., C.I.E., C.B.E., Indian Army, *b.* 27 May, 1868 ; *s.* of William Kaye, of the Indian Civil Service (retired) ; *m.* Margaret Sarah, *d.* of Rev. Thomas Bryson, of the London Missionary Society. *Educ.*: Winchester. Joined 2nd Batt. Derbyshire Regt. 1889 ; 21st Punjabas, 1892 ; served N.W. Frontier of India, 1897 ; General Staff Officer, Army Headquarters, India, 1907 ; Deputy Chief Censor, India, 1914 ; Director Central Intelligence, India, 1919. *War Work :* In charge of Censorship, both Cable and Postal, in India, from Oct. 1914 to Sept. 1919. *Addresses* : Simla (in the summer) ; Delhi (in the winter), India. (C2036)

KAYE, Evan, O.B.E.

KAYE, George William Clarkson, O.B.E., R.A.F.

KAYE, Sydney Herbert, O.B.E.

KAYE, Sir John Pepys LISTER-, Bt., O.B.E., *b.* 18 Feb., 1853 ; *s.* of Lister Lister-Kaye, and *g. s.* of Sir John Lister Lister-Kaye, 2nd Bt. (*see* BURKE'S *Peerage*), whom he succeeded in 1871 ; *m.* 5th Dec. 1881, Natica, 2nd *d.* of Senor Antonio Yznaga del Valle, of Ravenswood, Louisiana and Cuba ; late Lieut. Royal Horse Guards and Yorkshire Hussars, D.L. West Riding ; Groom-in-Waiting to King Edward VII., 1908–10. *Address* : Overton Lodge, nr. Wakefield, Yorkshire. *Clubs* : Carlton ; Marlborough. (O7393)

KAYE, Lieut.-Comm. Russell LISTER-, O.B.E., R.N.

KEALY, Florence Tempe, Mrs., M.B.E., *b.* 26 Oct. 1883 ; *d.* of Sir Charles Bayley, G.C.I.E., K.C.S.I., Secretary of State for India's Council (*see* BURKE'S *Peerage*) ; *m.* Edward Herbert, *s.* of the late John Robert Kealy, M.D. *War Work :* Hon. Sec. of the Ladies Branch of the British Red Cross Society and Order of St. John of Jerusalem in the North West Frontier Province, India. *Addresses* : c/o Grindlay & Co., London ; Little-hampton, Sussex. (M2695)

KEAN, Charles, M.B.E.

KEANE, Capt. Charles George Gordon, O.B.E., R.A.M.C., *b.* 5 Sept. 1891 ; *s.* of Major E. J. Keane, late of Indian Army ; *m.* Eva Constance, *d.* of F. A. Denny, of Wimbledon. *Educ.*: Bombay Univ. ; St. Mary's Hospital, London. *War Work :* With a Field Ambulance in France ; W.H.W.M.S., Syren Force, N. Russia. (O9719)

KEANE, Lieut.-Col. Richard Henry, C.B.E.

KEARN, Lieut. A. W., O.B.E., R.A O.C.

KEARNEY, Arthur Richard Kearney, M.B.E.

KEARNEY, Mother Superior Teresa Mary, M.B.E., O.S.F., *b.* 30 April 1876 ; *d.* of Michael Kearney, Arklow, Co. Wicklow, Ireland. *Educ.*: Convent of Mercy, Wicklow, Ireland. R.C. Mission Sister of the Order of Saint Francis. Worked in hospitals of the Mission of Mill Hill, in Nsambya, Uganda, for the native Carrier Corps and wounded brought from German East Africa Campaign until Nov. 1916. *Address* : Mill Hill Mission, Nsambya, Kampala P.O., Uganda. (M1274)

KEARNS, Haidee Ida, Mrs., M.B.E., *b.* 18 March, 1862 ; *d.* the late Henry Holmes, of Toronto, Canada ; *m.* the late Thomas Joseph, *s.* of Philip Kearns, of Portsmouth. *Educ.*: Privately. *War Work :* Camps Library, 1915 ; Welfare Supervisor, Navy and Army Canteen Board, Dec. 1916–18. *Address* : 14, Minnis Bay, Birchington-on-Sea. (M8689)

KEARNS, William Irving, O.B.E. (O11780)

KEARSEY, Major Alexander Horace Cyril, D.S.O., O.B.E. ; *b.* 17 Dec. 1877 ; *s.* of Francis Kearsey, of Burstow, Horley, Sussex ; *m.* Frances Mitford, *d.* of Lord Redesdale, of Batsford, Moreton-in-Marsh (*see* BURKE'S *Peerage*). *Educ.*: Rottingdean ; Clifton ; R.M.C. Commissioned, 1898. *War Work :* Staff Captain, Brigade Major, G.S.O. 1st Grade, Battalion Commander ; held rank during the war as Lieut.-Col. from Dec. 1915. *Address* : The Mount, Queen's Park, Bournemouth. *Clubs* : Army and Navy ; Queen's. (O9596)

KEARY, George, O.B.E., *b.* 8 July, 1859 ; *m.* Sarah Ann. *Educ.*: Ongar. Divisional Superintendent of Operations, London Division, Great Eastern Railway. *War Work :* Officer in charge of railway at night in connection with Transport and Air Raids. *Address* : Kingston, 8, Hempstead Road, Walthamstow, E. 17. (O1539)

KEARY, Margaret Alice, M.B.E.

KEATINGE, Reginald Heber, O.B.E., J.P., Co. Dublin, *b.* 25 April, 1874 ; *s.* of Joseph Francis Keatinge, J.P., of Dublin ; *m.* Florence, *d.* of L. C. Murphy, of Dublin. *War Work :* Hon. Sec., Irish War Hospital Supply Depot (Men's Section) ; Joint Hon. Sec., Ireland's "Our Day" Red Cross Fund ; Ast. County Director for the City of Dublin Branch Red Cross Soc. ; Corps Superintendent, St. John Ambulance Brigade. *Address* : Bramberg, Strand Road, Sutton, Co. Dublin. (O3779)

KEAY, James Donald, C.B.E., *s.* of David Keay. Engine Works Manager to Harland and Wolff (Limited). (C987)

KEAY, Lieut.-Col. John, C.B.E., M.D., F.R.C.P., R.A.M.C.

KEAYS, Capt. Cyril Arthur, O.B.E., R.A.S.C.

KEDDIE, Col. Herbert William Graham, C.B.E., D.S.O., *b.* 1873 ; Lieut.-Col. and T. Col. Army Ordnance Depart. ; served in S. African War, 1899–1902 (despatches, Queen's medal with two clasps) ; Somaliland, 1902–3 (medal with clasp) ; Great War, 1914–19 (despatches). (C1275)

KEEBLE, Frederick William, C.B.E., Sc.D., F.R.S., *b.* 2 March, 1870 ; *s.* of Francis Henry Keeble, of Tatsfield, nr. Westerham, Kent ; *m.* 1st, Mathilde Marie Cecile Marechal, who

d. 1915, and 2nd, 1920, Lillah, O.B.E. (*q.v.*), *d.* of J. McCarthy, of Cheltenham. *Educ.* : Alleyn's School, Dulwich ; Gonville and Caius College, Cambridge. Sherardian Professor of Botany, Oxford ; Scientific Adviser, "Gardener's Chronicle" ; formerly Assistant Sec., Ministry of Agriculture ; *War Work :* Controller of Horticulture, Ministry of Agriculture ; Member of Army Agricultural Committee. *Address* : Magdalen College, Oxford. *Club* : Savile. (C36)

KEEBLE, Lillah, Mrs. (Lillah McCarthy), O.B.E., *d.* of J. McCarthy, of Cheltenham ; *m.* 1920, Frederick William, C.B.E., Sc.D., F.R.S. (*q.v.*), *s.* of Francis Henry Keeble, of Tatsfield, nr. Westerham, Kent. Services in connection with the organisation of matinées and the collection of funds for the Queen Mary Fund in aid of the Star and Garter Hospital. *Address* : Magdalen College, Oxford. (O11913)

KEEFE, Capt. Ernest, M.B.E., *b.* 30 Nov. 1883 ; *s.* of Cornelius Keefe, of The Green, Bandon ; *m.* Gertrude, *d.* of John McMahon, of Castleconnel, Co. Limerick. *Educ.*: Rincurran, Summer Cove, Kinsale. *War Work :* served with 37th Field Bty., R.F.A., during retreat from Mons, Aug. 1914 ; wounded at Le Cateau, 1914 ; served as Adjt. to Training Brigades at home until Apr. 1919 ; now serving at Record Office, Woolwich. *Address* : 107, Shooter's Hill Road, Blackheath, S.E.3 *Club :* Conservative (Blackheath). (M5391)

KEEGAN, Capt. Michael, O.B.E., M.M., R.A.F.

KEEL, William Henry, O.B.E., *b.* 19 Dec. 1866 ; *s.* of William H. Keel, of Eastbourne ; *m.* Katherine Emily, *d.* of Joseph Watson, of Hampstead, N.W. *Educ.* : Privately. Retired Civil Engineer ; for ten years Resident Engineer, in Brazil, of the City of Santos Improvements Co., Ltd. *War Work :* For four years Head of the Men's Department, the St. Marylebone War Hospital Supply Depot, Cavendish Square, W. 1. *Addresses* : 41, Fellows Road, Hampstead, N.W. ; Budleigh Salterton, Devon. (O10764)

KEELING, Dorothy Clarissa, Mrs., M.B.E., *b.* 2 Dec. 1881 ; *d.* of Rev. W. H. Keeling, LL.D., Headmaster, Bradford Grammar School, 1872–1916. *Educ.*: Bradford Girls' Grammar School. Sec., Liverpool Personal Service Committee since 1918. *War Work :* Assistant Sec., Bradford City Guild of Help, 1907–17 ; Sec., National Association of Guild of Help, 1917–18 ; Joint Hon. Sec., Joint Com. of Social Service, 1917–18 ; Chairman, Bradford Women's Employment Workrooms Committee, 1914–15 ; Chairman, Bradford Tipperary Club, 1914–17 ; Chairman, Bradford Women Patrols, 1917–18. *Address* : 16, Huskisson Street, Liverpool. *Club :* Sandon Arts. (M3783)

KEEN, Katharine Elizabeth, Mrs., O.B.E., *b.* 26 July, 1846 ; *d.* of John Clutton, of Flanchford, Surrey ; *m.* Alfred Gunning, *s.* of Alfred Joyce Keen, of Buckland, Surrey. *Educ.* : Privately. *War Work :* Commandant of Hillfield Red Cross Hospital, Reigate, from opening in Nov. 1914, until closing, 31 Dec. 1918. *Address* : 8, York Road, Reigate. *Club :* Albemarle. (O10765)

KEEN, Lieut.-Col. William John, C.I.E., C.B.E., *e. s.* of the late Col. Sir Frederick John Keen, K.C.B. ; *m.* 1899, Marion Beatrice, *d.* of Col. A. McL. Mills, formerly Indian Army. *Educ.*: Haileybury, and R.M.C. Entered Royal Welsh Fusiliers, 1892 ; Indian Army, 1894. Served with the Chitral Relief Force, 1895 (medal with clasp), on N.-W. Frontier of India, 1908 (despatches, medal with clasp) ; during Afghan War, 1919. (C3096)

KEENAN, Major Augustine Henry, D.S.O., O.B.E.

KEENE, Henry Furse, O.B.E., *b.* 7 May, 1863. Asylums Officer, London County Council. *War Work :* As chief officer of the department was responsible for preliminary negotiations and subsequent administrative arrangements for the use of three of the L.C.C. mental hospitals as war hospitals, affording accommodation for 4000 sick and wounded soldiers. *Addresses* : 13, Arundel Street, Strand, W.C. ; 11, Creighton Avenue, Muswell Hill, N. (O10766)

KEENE, Capt. and Qr.-Mr. John James, O.B.E., R.A.S.C.

KEENE, Capt. John Limrick, O.B.E.

KEENE, Lieut.-Col. Thomas Mann, O.B.E.

KEENE, Lieut.-Col. Harry Lancelot RUCK-, D.S.O., O.B.E., *b.* 5 May, 1868 ; *s.* of Col. Edmund Ruck-Keene, of Swyncombe, Henley-on-Thames ; *m.* Awdry Frances, *d.* of William Henry Ashhurst, C.B.E., of Waterstock, Oxford. *Educ.*: Winchester and Sandhurst. Land Agent to the Rt. Hon. The Earl Fitzwilliam. *War Work :* July, 1917, Commandant Escort Prisoners of War, Proven nr. Poperinghe, att. H.Q., 5th Army ; Sept. 1917, Commandant Corps Troops, XIX Corps ; Nov. 1917, Commandant V Corps Reinforcement Training Camp ; May, 1918, Commandant V Corps Rest Camp ; June, 1918, Commandant "F" Infantry Base Depot, Etaples ; Feb. 1918, Commandant Base Depot, Camiers ; retired Aug. 1918, after thirty years' continuous service in the Oxford and Bucks Light Infantry (43rd and 52nd). *Address* : The White House, Armthorpe, Doncaster. *Clubs* : Naval and Military ; M.C.C. ; R.A.C. ; Doncaster. (O5139)

KEENLYSIDE, Rupert Hales Headlam, O.B.E.

KEEP, Major Thomas Bettsworth, O.B.E., *b.* 1884 ; *s.* of Alfred H. Keep, of Greenhithe ; *m.* Irene Alison, *d.* of Walter Heslop, of Margate. *Educ.*: Malvern College ; King's College, London. Engineer. *War Work :* In R.A.S.C. Mechanical Transport. *Address* : 29, High Street, Wimbledon, S.W. 19. (O5441)

KEEPING, Capt. Harold Balfour, M.B.E., *b.* 20 Sept. 1886 ; *s.* of Tom Jeffery Keeping. *Educ.*: Tonbridge School. Chartered Accountant. *War Work :* Private, 28th County of

London Regt., Sept. 1914, to Dec. 1914 ; Lieut. R.A.S.C., Jan. 1915, to Sept. 1915 ; Capt. R.A.S.C., Sept. 1915, to Jan. 1920 ; graded Staff F.F., July, 1919, to Jan. 1920. *Address :* 18–19, Ironmonger Lane, E.C. 2. (M5292)

KEER, Lieut. Raymond Wilfred Cordy, M.B.E.

KEERY, Lieut. and Qr.-Mr. William James, M.B.E.

KEESAU, Perdot Cuthbert, M.B.E.

KEESON, Peridot Clara Cuthbert, M.B.E., *b.* 1894 ; *d.* of Major C. Cuthbert Keeson, V.D. *Educ. :* Privately. *War Work :* H.R.H. Princess Beatrice's Surgical Depot, 2, Cavendish Square. *Address :* St. Cuthberts, Hampstead. (M8690)

KEEVIL, Capt. Ambrose, M.B.E., M.C.

KEIGHTLEY, Mary, M.B.E.

KEILY, Lieut.-Comm. Charles Joseph, O.B.E., R.N.R.

KEIR, William, M.B.E.

KEITH, Capt. Angus, O.B.E.

KEITH, Lieut.-Col. George Theodore Elphinstone, D.S.O., O.B.E., *b.* 22 May, 1882 ; *s.* of George Elphinstone, of 14, Hans Place, S.W. ; *m.* Catherine Julia, *d.* of J. Blease, of Liverpool. *Educ. :* Eton. Employed in France as a Regimental Officer from Aug. 1914 till wounded 22 Oct. ; Gazetted as Brigade Major, New Armies, 15 Feb. ; D.A.A.G., June, 1916 ; A.A. and Q.M.G., Nov. 1917 ; A.A.G., April, 1919. *Club :* Junior United Service. (O5442)

KEITH, Lieut. Gerald, O.B.E., R.A.O.C.

KEITLEY, Capt. Cyril Humby, M.B.E., *b.* 1891 ; *s.* of H. B. Keitley, of London ; *m.* Joyce Margaret, *d.* of Bernard Gibson, M.A., of London. *Educ. :* Shrewsbury School. *War Work :* Served with 12th Batt. The Sherwood Foresters ; 2nd Batt. The Manchester Regt. *Address :* The Torrs, South Norwood Park, London. (M5394)

KEKEWICH, Capt. Sydney, M.B.E., 21st Lancers, *b.* 17 June, 1893 ; *s.* of Lewis P. Kekewich, of 14, Adelaide Crescent, Brighton ; *m.* Madeline Elizabeth, *d.* of Rear-Admiral S. Gordridge, C.I.E., of Rudgwick Grange, Rudgwick, Sussex. *Educ. :* Eton. *War Work :* India (N.W.F.P.) wounded Sept. 1915 ; War Office, Jan. 1917, to Sept. 1919, as Staff Captain. *Club :* Cavalry. (M5394)

KELCEY, William FOORD-, O.B.E.

KELHAM, Bimbashi Arthur Robert Langdale, O.B.E., D.C.M., *b.* 25 Aug. 1865 ; *s.* of Augustus Kelham, of Chester ; *m.* Margaret Ethel, M.B.E., *d.* of Joseph Haselden, of Alexandria, Egypt. *Educ. :* Bedford Grammar School. Egyptian Police. *War Work :* Served in Dongola Expedit., 1896 ; Khartoum Campaign, 1897–98 ; thrice mentioned in despatches : D.C.M. ; Order of Medjieh and of Nile ; with Bikanir Camel Corps in Western Desert. *Address :* The Caracol, Sidi Gabor, Egypt. *Club :* Union, Alexandria. (O9864)

KELHAM, Margaret Ethel, Mrs., M.B.E., *b.* 17 Sept. 1876 ; *s.* of Joseph Haselden, of Alexandria, Egypt ; *m.* Major Arthur Robert Langdale Kelham, O.B.E., D.C.M., *s.* of Augustus Kelham, of Chester. *War Work :* Hospital Trains in Egypt, May to Aug. 1915 ; Red Cross Tea Kiosks on Alexandria Quays, 1914–18 ; Red Cross Librarian to March, 1920 ; despatches, June, 1917. *Address :* The Caracol, Sidi Gabor, Egypt. *Club :* Alexandria Sporting. (M8691)

KELL, Sir Vernon George Waldegrave, K.B.E., C.B., *b.* 21 Nov. 1873 ; *s.* of the late Major Waldegrave C. F. Kell ; *m.* Constance Rawdon, *d.* of James Scott, of Queenstown. *Educ. :* Sandhurst. *War Work :* First commissioned 1894 ; served China, 1900 (medal with clasp) ; has Order of St. Olaf (Norway) ; American Order of the Chinese Dragon ; Legion of Honour ; Order of St. Maurice and St. Lazarus. *Address :* 34, Argyll Road, W. 8. *Clubs :* Army and Navy ; Wellington. (K306)

KELLER, Lieut.-Col. Rudolph Henry, D.S.O., O.B.E.

KELLETT, Adelaide Maud, C.B.E., R.R.C. Matron Australian Army Nursing Staff during the Great War, 1915–19 (despatches).

KELLETT, Major and Qr.-Mr. James Albert, O.B.E., R.E.

KELLEWAY, Lieut. Percy Dixon, M.B.E., R.N.V.R.

KELLEY, Major Frederick Arthur, O.B.E., J.P., M.P., *b.* 6 May, 1863 ; *s.* of Ralph Kelley, of Heckmondwike ; *m.* Laura, *d.* of Charles Henry Pickles, of Heckmondwike. *Educ. :* Tettenhall College ; Giggleswick Grammar School. Managing Director, Messrs. Whitworth, Son and Nephew, Ltd., Wathon-Dearne ; Director, Messrs. Duncan Gilmour, Ltd., Sheffield. *War Work :* Raised Harrogate Pals Coy., recruited over 1000 men ; was O.C. R.D.C. Coy. *Addresses :* Holley Court, Harrogate ; Harcourt House, Cavendish Square, London. *Clubs :* Constitutional ; Junior Constitutional ; 1900. (O3138)

KELLNER, Lieut.-Col. Philip Travice Rubie, D.S.O., O.B.E., R.E., *b.* 19 Dec. 1872 ; *s.* of Edwin Welsh Kellner, C.I.E. ; *m.* Mabel Alicia, *d.* of Rev. Alfred Bourne, B.A. *Educ. :* Giggleswick Grammar School. Indian Finance Dept. ; now Ministry of Transport. *War Work :* In charge of Railway Stores, and later head of the Transportation Stores Dept., dealing with railways, roads, docks, and water transport, under the Dir.-Gen. of Transportation, B.E.F. ; served in France from Dec. 1914 to July, 1919. *Address :* The Oaks, Beaconsfield, Bucks. (O5444)

KELLY, Alfred Evans, O.B.E.

KELLY, Arthur Lindsay, O.B.E., *b.* 5 Sept. 1880. *Educ. :* Winchester ; University College, Oxford. *War Work :* Lieut., 6th Batt., King's Royal Rifle Corps ; Court Martial Officer ; Staff Captain. *Address :* Hockley Lands, Worplesdon, Guildford. *Club :* Carlton. (O5445)

KELLY, Edmund Walsh, M.B.E., F.R.S.A.I., J.P., *b.*

4 Oct. 1857 ; *s.* of Gerard Kelly, of Waterford ; *m.* Margaret, *d.* of Edward Slattery, of Carrick-on-Suir. *Educ. :* St. Stanislaus' Coll., Tullabeg. Hon. Life Member of the C.T.C. *War Work :* Co. Waterford War Pensions Committee ; Hon. Sec. Waterford Rural District Sub-Committee. *Address :* Bella Vista, Tramore, Co. Waterford. (M8692)

KELLY, Eleanor Sarah, M.B.E., R.R.C.

KELLY, Elisabeth Hariott, C.B.E., J.P., *b.* Jan. 1878 ; *s.* of the late Col. H. H. Kelly, R.M.A., of Southsea, and of Elisabeth Eleanor, *d.* of John Collum, Esq., of Bellevue, Co. Fermanagh. *Educ. :* The Hermitage, Southsea. Justice of Peace, Portsmouth ; Chairman of Sub-Committees, Portsmouth War Pensions Committee ; Member, Special Grants Committee, Ministry of Pensions ; Member of the Royal Patriotic Fund Corporation ; Chairman, Portsmouth Women's Employment Sub-Committee, Ministry of Labour ; Member of Portsmouth Insurance Committee. *War Work :* Joint Hon. Sec., S. and S. F.A., 1914–16 ; Hon. Org., Services' Children's Home ; Hon. Sec., Portsmouth Services' Committee, 1914–16 ; Hon. Sec. and Hon. Principal Officer, Portsmouth War Pensions Committee, 1916–20 ; Hon. Agent, R.P.F.C. ; Hon. Local Agent, S. & S.H.S. ; Member of Pensions and Grants Sub.-Com. Statutory Committee ; Member of Special Grants Committee, Ministry of Pensions ; Member, Portsmouth Employment Committee, Ministry of Labour ; Hon. Sec., Portsmouth Women's Patriotic League and United Service Clubs, 1914–19 ; Chairman, Children's Sub.-Com., Portsmouth War Pensions Committee ; Member National Relief Fund Com., Portsmouth ; Hon. Sec., Navy League Sub.-Com., Portsmouth, etc. *Address :* 2, Malvern Road, Southsea. *Clubs :* Sesame. (C2730)

KELLY, Col. Francis, C.B.E., *b.* 1868. Col. R.A.M.C. and Asst. Director of Med. Sers., Highland Div. during Great War, 1914–19 (despatches).

KELLY, Frank Arthur, M.B.E., *b.* 25 March, 1879 ; *s.* of Charles Kelly, of Newport, Mon. ; *m.* Irene Winifred, *d.* of William Lidwell Scoones, of Brixton. *Educ. :* Bancroft's School, Woodford Green, Essex. Principal Clerk to the Metropolitan Asylums Board. *War Work :* Provision of accommodation for, and maintenance of, War Refugees in London. *Address :* 262, Amesbury Avenue, Streatham Hill. (M626)

KELLY, Frederick Arthur, O.B.E., J.P., R.D.C., M.P.

KELLY, Helena Creed, Mrs., M.B.E., *b.* 8 Sept. 1888 ; *d.* of R. W. Phillips, of Dublin ; *m.* Joseph Angelo Kelly. *Educ. :* Kildare St. School, Dublin, and privately. Assistant Comptroller to the Lord-Lieutenant of Ireland. *War Work :* Was Private Sec. to Sir Cecil Partridge when Metropolitan Munitions started, and remained there till Dec. 1915 ; in 1916, when Irish Rebellion broke out, went to Ministry of Munitions and again returned to Dublin. *Address :* Vice-Regal Lodge, Dublin. *Club :* United Arts, Dublin. (M9293)

KELLY, Henry Titus, M.B.E.

KELLY, Hilda Margaret Catherine, O.B.E., *b.* Sept. 1875 ; *d.* of the late Col. H. H. Kelly, of Southsea. *Educ. :* The Hermitage, Southsea. Organising Sec., Charity Organisation Society. *War Work :* Sec. Officers' Families Fund, 1916–19 ; Member of local Com., Soldiers' and Sailors' Families Assoc., Soldiers' and Sailors' Help Society, and National Relief Fund ; Member of Women's Advisory Com., Central Control Board (Liquor Traffic), 1915–16. *Address :* 52, Lower Sloane Street, S.W. *Clubs :* Sesame ; Forum. (O1543)

KELLY, James, M.B.E.

KELLY, Eng.-Comm. John, O.B.E., R.N.

KELLY, Capt. Patrick Anselm, O.B.E., I.A.R. of O. (O11781)

KELLY, Lieut. Richard Cecil, O.B.E.

KELLY, Lieut. Thomas, M.B.E., A.P.D.

KELLY, Comm. Wm. H., C.B.E., D.S.O. ; Comm. and Acting Capt. R.N.R. Served during Great War, 1914–19, with Auxiliary Patrol (despatches).

KELMAN, John, O.B.E., M.A., D.D., *b.* 20 June, 1864 ; *s.* of Rev. John Kelman, B.D., of Edinburgh ; *m.* Ellin Runcorn, *d.* of William Hamilton Bell, of Edinburgh. *Educ. :* Edinburgh Royal High School ; Edinburgh University ; New College, and Ormond College, Melbourne. Minister of Peterculter United Free Church, 1892–97 ; New North United Free Church, Edinburgh, 1897–1907 ; St. George's United Free Church, Edinburgh, 1907–19 ; Fifth Avenue Presbyterian Church, New York, 1919. *War Work :* With Y.M.C.A. for six months, along whole British Front, engaged in lecturing on religious subjects, and also with a view to good understanding between British and American troops ; also four months' service under the British Foreign Office in the United States in 1917. *Clubs :* University Union, Edinburgh ; University, New York. (O477)

KELSEY, Lavinia Jano, M.B.E.

KEMBALL, Hattie, Lady, O.B.E. ; *d.* of Gilbert Elliot, I.C.S. ; *m.* Maj.-Gen. Sir George Vero Kemball, K.C.M.G., C.B., D.S.O. (O9827)

KEMBLE, Henry, M.B.E., F.R.G.S., *b.* 5 Sept. 1854 ; *s.* of Hon. H. F. Kemble, of Jamaica, West Indies. *Educ. :* Cheltenham College. Managing Director, Eastern Counties Branch of Lord Roberts' Memorial Workshops. *War Work :* Hon. Sec., Soldiers' and Sailors' Help Society, N. Essex ; Essex War Pensions Committee ; Colchester (Borough) War Pensions Committee. *Address :* West Bergholt, Essex. *Clubs :* Junior Carlton ; Sports. (M1982)

KEMBLE, Katherine Charlotte, M.B.E., *b.* 17 July, 1879 ; *d.* of Henry Kemble, of Wroughton, nr. Swindon. *War Work :*

Quartermaster, Asst. Commandant and finally Commandant at Struan House, Reading; V.A.D. Berks 52, from, 1914–19. *Address:* Newlands, Goodworth, Clatford, Andover. (M8693)

KEMBLE, Major Paul Berthon, O.B.E.

KEMBLE, Virginia Margaret, M.B.E., *d.* of the late Capt. H. F. Kemble, R.N., D.L., of St. Claydons, nr. Chelmsford. *War Work:* Commandant of Red Cross Hospital, Chelmsford, from 1915, when it opened until 1919, when it closed, during which time nearly 2000 patients passed through the hospital; mentioned in despatches, 1916. *Club:* Blue Triangle.

(M2782)

KEMM, Stephanie Lilian Septima, Mrs., O.B.E.; *d.* of Charles Piesse, M.R.C.S., D.P.H., Consul-General for Monaco, 1889–96; *m.* Thomas Kemm. *Educ.:* Putney College. *War Work:* Surrey Reserve Commandant; Assistant County Secretary, Surrey B.R.C.S., and other B.R.C.S. work. *Address:* 12, Deanhill Road, E. Sheen, S.W. 14. (O10767)

KEMP, Charles Richard William, M.B.E.

KEMP, Capt. Edgar Stephen, O.B.E.

KEMP, Herbert Edward, M.B.E., *b.* 17 Feb. 1867; *s.* of Edward Kemp, of Plumstead. *Educ.:* Plumstead High School and King's Coll., London. Senior Armament Supply Officer in the Armament Supply Department of the Admiralty and in charge of the Royal Naval Armament Depot at Crombie, N.B. *War Work:* Employed during the whole of the war at the Naval Ordnance Depot, Lodge Hill, supervising manufacture and supply of ammunition for the Fleet. *Address:* Ordnance House, Crombie, Dunfermline. (M8696)

KEMP, Joseph Horsford, C.B.E., B.A., K.C., *b.* 23 Dec. 1874; *s.* of P. Kemp, of Dublin; *m.* Mary, *d.* of P. Stuart, of London. *Educ.:* High School, Dublin; Cape Univ. Attorney-General, Hong Kong. *Address:* Hong Kong. (C397)

KEMP, Col. Sir Kenneth Hagar, Bt., C.B.E., B.A., *b.* 21 April, 1853; *m.* Henrietta, *d.* of Henry Hamilton, of Blackrock, Co. Leitrim, and Chilham, Kent. *Educ.:* Canterbury; Jesus Coll. Cambridge. Barrister and Banker; Col. Commanding 2nd Garrison Bn. Suffolk Regt. *Address:* Gissing Hall, Diss; Pentlow, Sheringham. *Club:* Carlton.

(C822)

KEMP, Omelia Susanna, Mrs., M.B.E.

KEMP, William, M.B.E.

KEMP, William Henry, M.B.E.

KEMPE, Charles Gilbert Burrington, O.B.E., M.D., B.S., M.R.C.S., L.R.C.P., *b.* 17 Feb. 1872; *s.* of Charles Marshall, of Chantry House, Shoreham-by-Sea; *m.* Ethel Maud, *d.* of George Rawlence, of Wilton, Wilts. *Educ.:* Brighton Grammar School; Durham University. Senior Hon. Surgeon, Salisbury Infirmary; Consulting Surgeon to Fisherton House, Laverstock House, Andover Hospital, Westminster Hospital, Shaftesbury, and G. W. Railway; Fellow of Royal Society of Medicine. *War Work:* In charge of Countess of Radnor's Hospital, Longford Castle; Consulting and Operating Surgeon to Countess of Pembroke's Hospital, Wilton House, Salisbury Infirmary, and Red Cross Hospitals. *Addresses:* 17, Endless Street, Salisbury; The Grange, Warminster, Wilts. (O4376)

KEMPER, Major Joseph, M.B.E.

KEMPLE, Major John Howard, O.B.E., 9th Lancers, *b.* 26 Aug. 1870; *s.* of John Howard Kemple, of Portumna, Co. Galway, Ireland; *m.* Edith Mary, *d.* of Francis Clarke, of Canterbury. *Educ.:* The Rectory, Brompton. *War Work:* Adjutant, 7th Reserve Cavalry Regiment, England; tour of Instruction, France and Belgium; attached 9th Lancers; Riding Master, 1st Reserve Cavalry Regt., Ireland. *Address:* 9th Lancers, Tidworth. (O8848)

KEMPSTER, James Charles, M.B.E.

KEMPSTER, Ruby, Mrs., M.B.E.

KEMPTON, Lieut.-Col. Charles Leslie, C.B.E., R.E. Served in the Great War, 1914–19 (despatches). (C1644)

KEMSLEY, John Chambers, M.B.E., *b.* 29 May, 1855; *s.* of the late John Chambers Kemsley, J.P., of Maidstone, Kent, and *g.s.* of late James Crawford, J.P., one of the British Settlers of 1820; *m.* Rachel Rogers, *d.* of Joseph Wesley Frost, of Port Elizabeth, and *g.d.* of late Joseph Wesley Frost, one of the British Settlers of 1820. *Educ.:* Grey Institute; High School, Port Elizabeth. Mayor, Port Elizabeth, Cape Province, South Africa, 1901–4, and 1915–18. *War Work:* Mayor of City; recruiting, organising and collecting Governor-General's Fund, etc.; Chairman, Governor-General's Fund; Chairman, Recruiting Committee, and Defence Committee. *Address:* 50, Park Drive, Port Elizabeth. *Club:* Port Elizabeth.

(M1222)

KEMSLEY, Kate Annie, Mrs., M.B.E. (M10450)

KENDALL, Beatrice, M.B.E.

KENDALL, Charlotte Emma Mabel, M.B.E., *b.* 28 Jan. 1894; *d.* of James Kendall, of Ellesmere, Shropshire. *War Work:* Quartermaster, Auxiliary Military Hospital, Ellesmere; Sec., Feb. to Dec. 1915; Q.M., Dec. 1915 to Feb. 1919. *Address:* Reevehurst, Ellesmere, Salop. *Club:* United Societies'.

(M1984)

KENDALL, Rev. George, O.B.E., S.C.F., *b.* 10 Oct. 1881; *s.* of Charles and Ann Kendall, of Burn Cross, Sheffield; *m.* Emily Mary, *d.* of John Nathaniel Lessware, of London. *Educ.:* Burn Cross Board School; Hartley College; Victoria University, Manchester. Primitive Methodist Minister; Sec. and President of the Windsor and District Free Church Council; Uxbridge and District; began ministry, Horncastle, 1906; Superintendent Minister of Shieldmuir, Wishaw, Scotland; Colnbrook and Uxbridge; Windsor. *War Work:* Commissioned as Chaplain to the Forces, 3 May, 1915, previously

officiated to the Troops in Windsor; served in France, Flanders, Salonica, and Germany, with 12th Division, 22nd Division, 59th Division, 38th Welsh Division, 17th Brigade, R.G.A., 50th Division; Senior Chaplain, Royal Naval Division; Northern Division; and to Forces in Belgium; Educational Officer to 17th Brigade, R.G.A., and Army of Occupation on the Rhine; mentioned in despatches. *Address:* Horncastle, Lincolnshire.

(O5446)

KENDALL, Rev. Henry Ewing, O.B.E., B.A., R.N.

KENDALL, Major John, O.B.E.

KENDALL, Lieut.-Col. John, O.B.E., Aust. A,V.C.

KENDALL, Major John Kaye, O.B.E., R.G.A.

KENDALL, Capt. John Murray, M.B.E. For work in connection with the Imperial War Museum. (M10324)

KENDALL, Joseph Abner, M.B.E., *b.* 3 Dec. 1883. Merchant. *War Work:* Red Cross work, and production of munitions. *Address:* Civil Lines, Cawnpore, India. (M6175)

KENDALL, Kathleen Addison, Mrs., M.B.E., *b.* 1874; *d.* of the late W. G. Izard, of Blackheath; *m.* Nicholas Fletcher, *s.* of F. R. Kendall. *War Work:* Joint Manager, Chiddingfold War Hospital Supply Depot (3 years). *Address:* Brookhurst, Chiddingfold, Surrey. (M8700)

KENDALL, Lieut. Ramsay George, M.B.E., R.E.

KENDALL, Major Sydney Robert Gordon, M.B.E.

(O11748)

KENDALL, William Henry, O.B.E., *b.* 12 Dec. 1858; *s.* of John Kendall, of Caterham; *m.* Alice, *d.* of Nathaniel Roberts, of Southwater, Sussex. *Educ.:* Private School and King's College, London. Secretary, Metropolitan Police Office, New Scotland Yard. *Address:* Claremont, Croham Road, South Croydon. *Club:* National Liberal. (O1544)

KENDALL, William Thomas, O.B.E.

KENDERDINE, Sir Charles Halestaff, K.B.E., *b.* 1866; *m.* Henrietta Florence, *d.* of the late Col. Vincent Bailey, Bedfordshire Regt. Secretary of the Land Union, 1910–17; Director Royal Insurance Company; Director of Artificial Limb Supplies for Disabled Sailors and Soldiers, Ministry of Pensions; one of the founders of Queen Mary's Convalescent Auxiliary Hospitals, Roehampton; The Queen's Hospital, Frognal, Sidcup; founder of Queen Mary's Workshops at the Pavilion, Brighton; Agent for the Earl of Romney and for the Lowndes Estates in Knightsbridge and Buckinghamshire. *Address:* 46, Thurloe Sq., S.W.7. *Club:* Union. (K89)

KENDRICK, Major Sydney John, O.B.E., 7th Batt. Indian Defence Force, *b.* 15 March, 1872; *s.* of John Kendrick, of Birmingham; *m.* Jessie, *d.* of John Masterman, of Hull. *Educ.:* Privately. Railway Engineer (Carriage and Wagon Supt. East Indian Railway). *War Work:* Superintendent of a large works in India manufacturing munitions of war and constructing rolling stock for the military railway in Mesopotamia. *Address:* Holmwood, Lillooah, Bengal, India. *Clubs:* St. Stephen's; Junior Army and Navy. (O4051)

KENELM, Capt. Francis, O.B.E.

KENNARD, Col. Henry Gerard Hegan, C.B.E., *b.* 1871; *s.* of Adam Steinovetz Kennard, of Belmore, Upham, Southampton; *m.* 1895, a *d.* of Col. Richard Poyser, D.S.O., F.R.C.V.S. Lieut.-Col. and Brevet Col. 5th Dragoon Guards; served in S. Africa, 1899–1902 (despatches, Queen's medal with four clasps, King's medal with two clasps); Great War, 1914–19 (despatches). (C1645)

KENNEDY Alexander, O.B.E., J.P.

KENNEDY, Lieut.-Col. Archibald Arrol, D.S.O., O.B.E., T.D., J.P.; *s.* of Thomas Kennedy, of Glasgow. *Educ.:* Albany Academy, Glasgow. Shipbroker. *War Work:* Mobilised 5 Aug. 1914; served in France and Flanders till 31 Dec, 1919; severely wounded High Wood, France, July 1916, when commanding the 5th Batt., The Cameronians (Scottish Rifles). *Address:* 1, Marchmont Terrace, Kelvinside, Glasgow. W. (O5448)

KENNEDY, Lieut.-Col. Charles Matheson, M.B.E., F.R.C.S. (Eng.), R.A.M.C. (T.), *b.* 25 June, 1884; *s.* of the late David Lithgow Kennedy, of Loughton, Essex; *m.* Mabel Maud, *d.* of Henry Hore, of Ware. *Educ.:* St. Edward's School, Oxford, and London Hospital. Assistant Surgeon, S. Devon and E. Cornwall Hospital; Consulting Surgeon to Paignton and District Hospital. *War Work:* Surgeon to Queen Mary's Hospital, Queensferry, Aug. and Sept. 1914; T. Lieut. R.A.M.C., Oct. 1914; Capt., 1915; A Major, Jan. 1918; served in France, Feb. 1915, to April, 1918, when invalided home after pneumonia; O.C. Charterhouse Military Hospital, May, 1918, to June, 1919. *Address:* 19, Lockyer Street, Plymouth. *Clubs:* Royal Western Yacht, Plymouth; Fellow Roy. Soc. Med. (M5397)

KENNEDY, David Henry, O.B.E., R.A.F.

KENNEDY, Lieut. Douglas Neil, M.B.E., R.D.C.

KENNEDY, Capt. Duncan, M.B.E., R.A.S.C.

KENNEDY, Helen, Mrs., M.B.E.

KENNEDY, Lieut. Horas Graham, M.B.E., R.A.S.C.

KENNEDY, Lieut. James, O.B.E., R.N.R.

KENNEDY, Capt. James Bowle, O.B.E., *b.* 29 Jan. 1867; *s.* of Admiral Kennedy, C.B., of 39, Onslow Square; *m.* Nina, *d.* of Sir George Lampson. *Educ.:* Rugby and Sandhurst. *War Work:* A.G.'s Branch, War Office, with rank of Staff Captain. *Address:* 54, Streatham Hill, S.W. *Club:* Naval and Military. (O1545)

KENNEDY, James Hutchinson, M.B.E.

KENNEDY, John Macfarlane, O.B.E., *b.* 12 Oct. 1879; *s.* of Sir Alexander B. W. Kennedy, Kt. Bach, of Λ7 The Albany, W. (*see* BURKE'S *Peerage*); *m.* Dorothy Farrer, *d.*

of the late Thomas Farrer. *Educ.:* University College School, and Cambridge University. Partner in firm of Kennedy and Donkin, Consulting Engineers, 17, Victoria Street, S.W. 1. *War Work:* Technical Assistant to Chief Engineer, Central Force, 1914–15; Chief Engineer on Construction, and subsequently Superintendent of Government Rolling Mills, Southampton, 1916–18. *Addresses:* 8, Bristol House, Southampton Row, W.C.; Blackheath, Chilworth, Surrey. *Club:* Athenæum. (O3782)

KENNEDY, John Morgan, M.B.E. (M10451)

KENNEDY, Rev. Samuel Hanna, M.B.E., B.A., D.D., *b.* 14 Nov. 1868; *s.* of James Kennedy, of Garryduff, Ballymoney, Ireland; *m.* Jennie Belle, *d.* of Josiah Dodds, of Topeka, Kansas, U.S.A. *Educ.:* Intermediate School, Ballymoney, and Queen's College, Belfast. Missionary, Irish and Scotch Reformed Presbyterian Mission, Syria. *War Work:* Y.M.C.A., Egypt. *Address:* Reformed Presbyterian Mission House, Alexandretta, Syria. (M2823)

KENNEDY, Major Stuart Samuel, O.B.E., R.A.F.

KENNEDY, Capt. Thomas Fuller, O.B.E., R.A.M.C., *b.* 12 June, 1892; *s.* of J. S. Kennedy, of Donnybrook, Dublin. *Educ.:* Royal University of Ireland. *War Work:* Joined R.A.M.C. Oct. 1914, and served abroad in Gallipoli, Serbia, Macedonia, and Palestine from July, 1915, until after Armistice. *Address:* c/o Messrs. Holt & Co., 3, Whitehall Place, London, S.W. 1. (O2913)

KENNEDY, Walter, M.B.E., *b.* 20 March, 1884; *s.* of Walter Kennedy, of Newcastle-on-Tyne; *m.* Olive Mansfield, *d.* of James Humphries, of Charlton, Kent. *Educ.:* Rutherford Coll., Newcastle-on-Tyne. Civil Servant. *War Work:* Navy and Army Insurance Fund. *Address:* 204, Pitshanger Lane, Ealing, W. *Club:* Hanger Hill Golf. (M8701)

KENNEDY, Lieut. Walter Stewart, M.B.E., R.F.A. (T.F.).

KENNEDY, Major William Nicol Watson, O.B.E., M.D., Ch.B., D.P.H., late R.A.M.C. (T.), *b.* 27 March, 1888; *s.* of the late Charles Kennedy, M.D., of Edinburgh; *m.* Mary Balfour, *d.* of John Alison, M.A., F.R.S. (Edin.), of Edinburgh. *Educ.:* George Watson's Coll., Edinburgh; Univ. of Edinburgh. Deputy Medical Officer of Health, County Borough of Croydon, Surrey. *War Work:* Specialist Sanitary Officer, France, Salonica, and North Wales; Deputy Assist. Director of Medical Services (Sanitation) for North Russian Expeditionary Force. *Address:* Town Hall, Croydon, Surrey. (O6801)

KENNEDY, Sir Charles Edward William MACKENZIE-, K.B.E., C.B., *b.* 6 July, 1860; *s.* of Rev. C. Le Poer M. Kennedy; *m.* Ethel May, *d.* of Major Fuller, I.A. *Educ.:* Canterbury and R.M.C., Sandhurst. Major-General Indian Army (retired). Burma 1885–87; Hazura, 1891; China, 1900–1; (Relief of Pekin). *War Work:* Commanded 26th Division, 1914–17; served in France and the Balkans. *Address:* c/o Grindlay & Co., 54, Parliament Street, S.W. 1. *Club:* United Service. (K3210)

KENNELL, Joseph, M.B.E., *b.* 24 May, 1874; *s.* of Charles Henry Kennell, of London. *Educ.:* Privately. Superintendent of Printing, Stationery and Stores in the Foreign Office. *War Work:* In charge of Government Secret printing work; attached to Peace Conference, Paris, 1919. *Addresses:* Foreign Office; Catford, London, S.E. (M8702)

KENNINGTON, Capt. Arthur James, O.B.E.

KENNY, Lieut. Louis, M.B.E., R.A.F.

KENNY, Lieut. Vincent Raymond, M.B.E., R.E.

KENNY, William James, M.B.E. Retired Civil Servant. *War Work:* Army Ordnance Department, Royal Arsenal, Woolwich. *Address:* Kenninghall, Attleborough, Norfolk. (M630)

KENRICK, Capt. Hubert Wynn, O.B.E., R.D., R.N.R., *b.* 9 July, 1863; *s.* of William Wynn, of Wynn Hall, Ruabon, Denbighshire; *m.* Alice Edith, *d.* of Charles Beal, J.P., of Mount Gellibrand, Victoria, Australia. *Educ.:* United States America; Cadet School-ship "Conway," Liverpool. Joined the P. and O. S. N. Co.'s service as a junior officer, in 1885; served in Hospital Transport "Malacca" in Benin Expedition and Cretan troubles, 1897; served in S.S. "Malta" conveying troops to South Africa in Boer War, 1899–1900; commanded Transport "Soudan," 1911–14, and mail steamer "India" during latter part of 1914. *War Work:* Reported at Chatham, Dec. 1914; appointed Trade Division Admiralty War Staff, Dec. 1914; as technical adviser in Mercantile Marine, and in March, 1916, was given additional appointment of Admiralty Shipping Intelligence Officer, Port of London. *Address:* 35, The Strand, Walmer, Kent. *Club:* Constitutional. (O478)

KENRICK, Sylvia, M.B.E.

KENSINGTON, Lieut.-Col. Guy Belfield, O.B.E., R.E.

KENT, Arthur Thomas, M.B.E.

KENT, Chris Shotter, C.B.E. Member of British War Mission to U.S.A. during the Great War. (C988)

KENT, Major Leslie Martin, O.B.E., R.E.

KENT, Rev. Norman Braund, O.B.E., R.N.

KENT, Eng.-Capt. Walter James, C.B.E., R.N. Engineer Overseer for Birmingham Dist. (C222)

KENT, Walter George, C.B.E., *b.* 1858; *s.* of George Kent, of Southwood, Highgate. *Educ.:* Private School, and London University. Manufacturing Engineer. *War Work:* Making and filling fuses of many natures for War Office, Ministry of Munitions, and Admiralty, gun directors, steering gears, mines, etc. *Address:* Ben Hale, Stanmore, Middlesex. *Club:* British Empire. (C216)

KENT, Capt. Wilfred Francis, O.B.E., R.E.

KENT, Paymaster-Lieut.-Comm. Arthur Clifton PELHAM-, O.B.E., R.N.

KENTISH, Hilda Mary, Mrs., M.B.E., *b.* 4 July, 1883; *d.* of Llewellyn Samuelson, Royal Thames Yacht Club; *m.* Major Leonard William, D.S.O., *s.* of George Kentish, of 12, Courtfield Gardens, South Kensington. *Educ.:* Holy Child Convent, St. Leonard's-on-Sea. *War Work:* Wycombe V.A.D. Hospital, Bucks, Nov. 1914 to Jan. 1919, Quartermaster, afterwards Commandant. *Address:* Hughenden Cottage, Hughenden, Bucks. *Club:* Ladies' V.A.D. (M3786)

KENTISH, Ida Clementina, M.B.E.; *d.* of John George Kentish, of Avening Court, Gloucestershire. *Educ.:* At home. *War Work:* Four-and-a-half years as Commandant, residing in Hospital (raised 20 beds to 54) Englethwaite AuxMilitary Hospital, Cumberland (Primary Hospital); with her detachment (24 V.A.D. Cumberland) served Red Cross trains, Carlisle Station, 1914–17; 1915–16 Commandant, Dalston Hall Hospital, Cumberland. *Address:* Whooff House, Carlisle. *Club:* V.A.D. (M3787)

KENWORTHY, Major Harold, O.B.E., R.E.

KENYON, Margaret Kilroy, Mrs., M.B.E., W.A.A.C.

KENYON, Milly Esther Innes, Mrs., M.B.E.

KENYON, Rose Alice, M.B.E.

KENYON, Thomas, M.B.E.

KENYON, Thomas Allan, M.B.E.

KENYOUMDJIAN, Manouk, M.B.E., B.C.A.

KEOGH, Capt. Joseph Wiseman, M.B.E., J.P., late Capt. 6th Brigade S. Irish Div., R.A.; *s.* of George Keogh, D.L., J.P., of Geevagh, Co. Sligo; Glencourt, Co. Wicklow; *m.* Ella Douglas, *d.* of Admiral Douglas Curry, of Shottery Hall, Warwickshire. *Educ.:* Oscott Coll.; Trinity Coll., Dublin. H.B.M. Consul for the Alpes Maritimes and Monaco. *War Work:* British representative at Nice. *Addresses:* Villa Barla, Nice; Geevagh, Co. Sligo. *Club:* Stephen's Green. (M631)

KEOUGH, Capt. and Qr.-Mr. Frederick, M.B.E., R.F.A.

KEPPEL, Capt. John Joseph Quiney, O.B.E., R.A.V.C. (S.R.).

KER, Col. Charles Arthur, C.M.G., C.B.E., D.S.O., *b.* 18 April, 1875; *s.* of Charles Buchanan Ker, of Clifton, Gloucestershire; *m.* Blanche, *d.* of Charles Bewes, of Gnaton Hall, Devon. *Educ.:* Clifton College; Royal Military Academy, Woolwich; Staff College, Camberley. Commissioned 2nd Lieut. Royal Artillery 15 June, 1895; promoted Brevet Major, 5 Aug. 1914; Brevet Lieut.-Col., 1 Jan. 1917; and Brevet Colonel 1 Jan. 1918; received the D.S.O. for his services in West Africa, 1898–9 (twice mentioned in despatches); served in the South African War, 1899–1902 (mentioned in despatches); served for four years in France during the Great War, rising to the rank of Brigadier-General, General Staff (four times mentioned in despatches), being awarded the C.M.G. and C.B.E.; is also Grand Officer of the Orders of Avis and Christo of Portugal. *Address:* War Office. (C1277)

KER, Helen Bethea, Mrs., M.B.E., *b.* 1855; *d.* of James Scott, of Woodside Place, Glasgow; *m.* Thomas Ripley, *s.* of Robert Ker, of Dougalston, Dumbartonshire. *War Work:* Vice Pres. Milngavie Red Cross Branch; Vice Pres. Sailors' and Soldiers' Families Association, New Kilpatrick, Dumbartonshire; President Local Pensions Committee for care of wives and dependants. *Address:* Dougalston, Milngavie, Dumbartonshire. *Club:* Kelvin (Glasgow). (M632)

KER, Major Hugh T., O.B.E., M.I.C.E., R.E. Served in the Great War, 1914–18 (despatches). (O4126)

KER, Major Thomas Reginald, O.B.E.

KER, Capt. (A. Lieut.-Col.) Douglas Rous EDWARDS-, O.B.E., R.E.; has Croix de Guerre of France (2nd Award). (O5231)

KERR, Allen Coulter, O.B.E., *b.* 28 Jan. 1875; *s.* of Thomas Coulter Kerr, of India Office. *Educ.:* Dulwich College. Late His Majesty's Chargé d'Affaires at Santiago, Chile; Local Rank of Second Secretary in His Majesty's Diplomatic Service. *War Work:* Foreign Office; Member of Special War Mission under Sir Maurice de Bunsen, Bart., G.C.M.G., which in 1918 visited the Republics of Brazil, Uruguay, Paraguay, Argentine, Chile, Peru, Bolivia, Ecuador, Pariama, Colombia, Venezuela, Cuba, and U.S.A. *Address:* 19, Collingham Road, S.W. 5. *Clubs:* St. James'; Beefsteak; R.A.C.; Addington Golf. (O1547)

KERR, Lady Anne, O.B.E., *b.* 27 April, 1857; *d.* of the 14th Duke of Norfolk (*see* BURKE'S *Peerage*); *m.* Maj.-Gen. Lord Ralph Kerr, K.C.B., late Col. 10th Hussars, who died 18 Sept. 1916, *s.* of the 7th Marquess of Lothian (*see* BURKE'S *Peerage*). *War Work:* County Director, Midlothian Red Cross Society; Chairman V.A.D. Selection Board for Scotland. *Address:* Woodburn, Dalkeith, Scotland. (O479)

KERR, Capt. Charles, O.B.E., M.B., R.A.M.C. (T.).

KERR, Errol, O.B.E.

KERR, Comm. Fairfax Moresby, O.B.E., R.N.

KERR, Harold, O.B.E., M.D., *b.* 1880; *s.* of Alexander Kerr, of Arran; *m.* Elsie, *d.* of Frank Dean, of Burgess Hill, Sussex. *Educ.:* Queen Elizabeth's School, Barnet; University of Edinburgh. Medical Officer of Health, City and County of Newcastle-upon-Tyne; Professor of Hygiene and Examiner, Durham University College of Medicine; Fellow of Society of Medical Officers of Health; of Royal Sanitary Institute. *War Work:* Medical Officer of Health, Newcastle-upon-Tyne. *Addresses:* Town Hall, Newcastle-upon-Tyne; 102, Moorside, Fenham, Newcastle-upon-Tyne. (O10771)

KERR, James Rutherford, C.B.E., Ch.M. (Glasg.), *b.* 14 June, 1878; *s.* of John G. Kerr, LL.D., of Glasgow; *m.* Nettie Russell, *d.* of Thomas Donald, of Glasgow. *Educ.:* Allan Glen's School, and University of Glasgow. Surgeon-in-charge of the Pilkington Special Hospital (Orthopædic and Limb-fitting Centre), St. Helens, Lancs. *War Work:* Chirurgien-chef, Hôpital de l'Alliance, Yvetot, France (awarded Médaille d'Honneur en Vermeil); Surgeon to the Pilkington Special Hospital; Surgeon to V.A.D. and Auxiliary Hospitals. *Address:* The Gables, St. Helens, Lancs.   (C2731)

KERR, Kenelm, O.B.E., *b.* 15 June, 1881; *s.* of W. R. Kerr, I.S.O. *Educ.:* Merchant Taylors' School, and Trinity Coll., Cambridge. Assistant to General Manager, North-Eastern Railway.   (O10772)

KERR, Martha, Mrs., O.B.E.

KERR, Maud, Mrs., M.B.E.

KERR, Muriel Constance, Mrs., O.B.E.

KERR, Major Norman Munroe, O.B.E.

KERR, Major Robert, D.S.O., O.B.E. Australian Forces; served in the Great War, 1915–18 (despatches).
                                                  (O6082)

KERR, Capt. Robert, M.B.E., R.A.O.C., *b.* 26 April, 1884; *s.* of James Kerr, of Edinburgh; *m.* Laura, *d.* of Samuel Smart, of Banbridge, Co. Down. *Educ.:* University Coll. and King's Coll., London. *War Work:* France, 1915; Royal Army Ordnance Depot, Weedon, 1915 to end of war. *Address:* Weedon, Northamptonshire. *Club:* Yorkshire Ramblers'.
                                                  (M5401)

KERR, Sybil Mary, M.B.E.

KERR, Walter Coke, M.B.E.

KERR, Capt. William Lord Coke, O.B.E., *b.* 30 Oct. 1887; *s.* of Lionel P. Kerr, J.P., of Mandeville, Jamaica, B.W.I.; *m.* Edith Maud, *d.* of J. Bowery, of Cheltenham. *Educ.:* Blackheath Prop. School, and Crystal Palace School of Engineering. Engineer. *War Work:* Served in France from 1 Sept. 1915 continuously in the R.A.S.C. (M.T.); was also in the march up to Germany.and served on the Rhine for 10 months; was then sent to join the Army of the Black Sea for 6 months in Salonica; held the appointment of Adjutant to a Siege Park for two and a half years.   (O2594)

KERR, Capt. William Munro, C.B.E., R.N.

KERR, William Warren, C.B.E., *b.* 1864; *s.* of the late John Wilson Kerr; *m.* 1887, Janie Buchanan, *d.* of the late Rev. Alexander Gosman, D.D., Congregational Min. of Hawthorn, Victoria, Australia. Managing Director of Richardson Kerr Property (Limited), insurance brokers, of Melbourne and Adelaide; President Australian Associated Chambers of Commerce; Dep. Commr. State Savings Bank of Victoria; Chairman Commonwealth War Savings Council and Victoria War Savings Committee; Chairman Congregational Union of Victoria, 1905–6; Mayor of Kew, 1907–8; Pres. Melbourne Chamber of Commerce, 1916–18. *Addresses:* Trenant, Kew, Melbourne, Australia; Crail, Upper Beaconsfield, Victoria, Australia.   (C710)

KERRISON, Lieut.-Col. Edmund Roger Allday, C.M.G., O.B.E., late R.A., *b.* 1855; *s.* of Roger Allday, Banker, of Norwich; *m.* Jessie, *d.* of Admiral Stapylton Greville, R.N. *Educ.:* Harrow, Repton, and R.M.A. *War Work:* Formed and commanded the 2/6 Norfolk Regiment. *Address:* Burgh Hall, Aylsham. *Club:* Army and Navy.   (O7347)

KERRY, Lieut. Arthur Henry Gould, M.B.E., R.E.

KERSEY, Winifred Esdaile, M.B.E.

KERSHAW, Abraham, O.B.E., F.Inst.P., F.O.S., *b.* 1861. Gov.-Director, A. Kershaw & Son, Ltd., Scientific Instrument Makers, Harehills Lane, Leeds. *War Work:* Organising on Optical Munitions. *Address:* Teddington Rise, Raincliffe Avenue, Scarboro'.   (O1548)

KERSHAW, Capt. Edward Bertram Hilton, O.B.E., B.A. (Cantab.), J.P., *b.* 17 May, 1870; *s.* of the late William Edward Evans, of Trefrie, Aberdovey, N. Wales; *m.* Alice Bleasdale Curling, *d.* of Edward Friend, of Southend, Essex. *Educ.:* Uppingham; St. John's Coll., Cambridge. Justice of the Peace for the County of Merionethshire; Vice Chairman of the Board of Conservators, Dovey, Mawddach, and Glaslyn rivers, N. Wales; Member of the Lancashire and Western Sea Fisheries Board; County Director, British Red Cross Society, Merioneth Branch; Sub-Commissioner of Pilotage, Aberdovey area; Barrister-at-law of the Inner Temple; author of "Brief Aids to the Criminal Law." *War Work:* County Director, B.R.C.S.; Member of County Appeal Tribunal; Special Constable; 2nd in Command 4th Vol. Batt., R.W.F. *Address:* Trefrie, Aberdovey, N. Wales.
                                                  (O1549)

KERSHAW, Comm. Frederick William, O.B.E., R.N.R.

KERSHAW, John Felix, O.B.E.

KERSLAKE Arthur Thomas, O.B.E.

KESTEVEN, Clement Percy, M.B.E.

KETT, George Robert, O.B.E.

KETTLE, Lieut. Harry Philip, O.B.E.

KETTELL, James Henry, M.B.E., *b.* 9 July, 1867; *s.* of Samuel Kettell, of Warmington, Cheshire. 1915, Deputy Mayor, Crewe; 1916 and 1917, Mayor; 1918, Deputy Mayor. *War Work:* Chairman, National Service Tribunal, Food Control, Profiteering Committee; Member of Agricultural War Committee; President of Allotment Association, and Rabbit and Poultry Society. *Address:* High Street, Crewe.
                                                  (M8706)

KETTLES, William, O.B.E.

KETTLEWELL, Arthur Bradley, C.I.E., C.B.E. *Educ.:*

Cheltenham, and New Coll. Oxford. Entered I.C.S. 1890; Political Officer, Wano, 1898; Deputy Commr. 1903; Sec. to Covt., Punjab, 1903; Officiating Ch. Sec. 1914; additional Sec. 1915; acted as Sec. to British Mission at Athens during the Great War.

KEW, John Charles, M.B.E., J.P., C.C. (Notts), Medaille du Roi Albert, *b.* 20 Jan. 1868; *s.* of John James Kew, of Newark; *m.* Annie, *d.* of Frederic Dixon, of Newark. *Educ.:* Newark. Mayor of Newark 1913–14, 1914–15; Chairman, Newark Board of Guardians; Chairman, Newark Rural District Council; Vice Chairman, Newark Education Committee; Member for Balderton Division, Notts County Council. *War Work:* Organised Belgian Relief Funds and placed refugees in scattered homes at Newark; raised £2500 for Prince of Wales' Fund; Chairman, Newark Division, Parliamentary Recruiting Committee; addressed recruiting meetings; organised War Savings effort in Newark R.D.C. area. *Addresses:* Magnus Street, Newark; Sunnyside, Sutton-on-Sea, Lincs.
                                                  (M1990)

KEWLEY, William Graham, M.B.E., R.A.F.

KEY, Benjamin Wm. Martin Aston, O.B.E., M.A., M.D. (Cantab.), *b.* 22 Aug. 1870; *s.* of Commander Benjamin H. Key, R.N., of Southsea; *m.* Edith, *d.* of Thomas Knowles, of Bradford. *Educ.:* Emmanuel College, Cambridge, and Guy's Hospital, London. Medical Referee to the Ministry of Pensions; Hon. Physician to Princess Christian's Home for Sailors and Soldiers, Portsmouth; Hon. Physician to United Services Children's Home, Southsea. *War Work:* Medical Officer in Cha.ge of R.A.M.C. Reception Hospital, Portsmouth, 1914–19. *Address:* Valetta, Clarendon Road, Southsea.   (O4377)

KEY, Lieut.-Comm. George, O.B.E., R.N.

KEY, Lieut.-Col. Robert Ellis, O.B.E., J.P., *b.* 21 Dec. 1882; *s.* of Capt. W. H. Key, J.P., of Water Fulford Hall (*see* BURKE'S *Landed Gentry*); *m.* Violet Mabel, *d.* of Lieut.-Col. C. Parker Jervis. *Educ.:* Richmond School, Yorks, and St. Peter's School, York. Sheriff of York, 1919–20. *War Work:* Major, 6th York and Lancaster Regt., 1914–16, Gallipoli campaign; Lieut.-Col. commanding 32 1d Royal Fusiliers, 1916–17 (despatches); Lieut.-Col. commanding 89th Training Reserve Batt., 1917–18; Lieut -Col. (special appointment), 1918–19. *Address:* Water Fulford Hall, York. *Clubs:* Naval and Military; Yorkshire.   (O7348)

KEYES, Lieut.-Comm. Adrian St. Vincent, C.B.E., D.S.O., *b.* 1882; *s.* of the late Gen. Sir Charles Patton Keyes, G.C.B.; *m.* 1916, Eleanor, *d.* of Lieut.-Col. Walter Campbell, of The Ivy House, Hampton Court. Entered R.N.; became Lieut. 1902; Lieut.-Com. (ret.), 1910; Acting Capt. on Staff of Com.-in-Chief, Plymouth; Dardanelles, 1915–16, in command of Canadian Submarines; present at landing at, and withdrawal from, Gallipoli (despatches twice).   (C2223)

KEYMER, Col. the Rev. Bernard William, O.B.E., R.A.F.

KEYMER, Daniel Thomas, O.B.E.; *e.s.* of late D. J. Keymer, of 1, Whitefriars, London. *Educ.:* City of London School. East India Merchant; Agent to the Government of Nepal; Hon. Treas. of Rev. Dr. Spurstowe and Bishop Wood's Charities; Hon. Treas. and Trustee, London Diocesan Church Schools Assoc.; Member of the Committee, Queen's Hospital for Children; was prospective Unionist candidate for Central Hackney, withdrew owing to Coalition; Ruling Councillor of the Cranborne Habitation of the Primrose League. *War Work:* Hon. Military Representative and Member of Advisory Committee; Chairman of Hackney Volunteers; Acting Chairman and Hon. Treas. 10th County of London Cadets; Chairman, Hackney and Stoke Newington Division, British Red Cross Society, and of Amhurst Park and Stormont House Hospitals, and Dalston Clinic; Member of the Belgian Refugees Committee; Member of the Hackney Recruiting Committee; on behalf of the Maharaja of Nepal, presented 31 machine-guns and equipment to H.M. the King in 1915. *Address:* 1, Whitefriars, London, E.C. 4. *Club:* Constitutional.   (O10777)

KEYSER, Maurice Max, O.B.E., *b.* 21 Nov. 1879; *s.* of Assur Keyser, of 29, Hamilton Terrace, London, N.W.; Butlers Green, Haywards Heath, Sussex; *m.* Margaret, *d.* of Mortimer Woolf, of London. *Educ.:* University Coll. School. *War Work:* Section Director, Priority Department, Ministry of Munitions. *Addresses:* 22, Greville Place, London, N.W. 6; 31, Throgmorton Street, E.C. 2.   (O10778)

KEYTE, Capt. Vincent John, O.B.E., *b.* 1872; *s.* of William John Keyte, of Westward Ho!, N. Devon. *Educ.:* Bideford Gram. Sch. *War Work:* Capt. Nyasaland Field Force; German East Africa, 1914–18; appointed Chief Transport Officer, Nyasaland Protectorate, 1911. *Address:* Zomba, Nyasaland, East Africa.   (O2228)

KIDBY, Capt. Edward William Brand, O.B.E.

KIDD, Lieut.-Col. Alexander Edward, O.B.E., R.A.M.C. (T.)

KIDD, Gladys Louise, M.B.E., *b.* 19 Dec. 1890; *d.* of John Kidd, C.M.G. *War Work:* Clerk in charge of Copying Department, H.M. Treasury, Whitehall, S.W. 1.   (M633)

KIDD, Lieut.-Col. Harold Andrew, C.B.E., R.A.M.C.

KIDD, Brevet Major James Dunlop, O.B.E., M.C., R.A.M.C., *b.* 4 April, 1883; *s.* of Thomas Kidd of Moniaive, Dumfriesshire. *Educ.:* Glasgow Academy, Glasgow Univ. *War Work:* East African Campaign, Oct. 1914, to Feb. 1919; served with various units and was A.D.M.S., G.H.Q. *Address:* c/o Messrs Holt & Co., 3, Whitehall Place, S.W. 1.   (O6753)

KIDDLE, Capt. John ,O.B.E., R.N.

KIDDLE, John Beacham, O.B.E.
KIDDLE, Capt. John Lindsay, M.B.E.
KIDDLE, Capt. Kerrison, C.B.E., R.N., *b.* 1876 ; *m.* 1909, Hjördis, *d.* of Consul-Gen. O. Holter, of Christiania. *War Work :* 1914–19 with 4th Destroyer Flotilla, with Dover Patrol, and Comdg. Depot Ship, Grand Fleet (despatches). *Club :* United Service. (C2224)
KIDLEY, Capt. Alexander John, O.B.E., R.A.S.C.
KIDNER, Samuel, O.B.E., J.P., C.C., *b.* 12 Aug. 1848 ; *s.* of William Kidner, of Milverton. *Educ. :* Taunton. Agriculture. *War Work :* On Advisory Committee, Board of Agriculture ; Central Advisory Committee, Food Control ; Central Advisory Forage Committee, War Office ; Chairman, County Forage Committee. *Address :* Milverton, Somerset. *Club :* Farmers'. (O480)
KIDSON, Arthur Frederic, O.B.E.
KIDSON, Edith Marian, M.B.E., *b.* 27 Jan. 1888 ; *d.* of J.C. Eyre Kidson, of Sittingbourne. *Educ. :* Woodford School, Croydon. *War Work :* Hon. Sec. of the Sittingbourne War Hospital Supply Depot, 1915–19. *Address :* Holy Trinity Vicarage, Sittingbourne, Kent.
KIDSON, Capt. Edward, O.B.E., R.E.
KIDSTON, Jessie Cecilia Brownlie, Mrs., M.B.E.
KILBY, Lieut. James Wheatley, O.B.E., R.E. (T.).
KILGOUR, Martin Hamilton, M.B.E., *b.* 1865 ; *s.* of John Stewart Kilgour, M.D., etc., of Cheltenham. *Educ. :* Privately in Cheltenham ; Fettes Coll., Edinburgh ; Finsbury and Central Technical Colleges, London ; School of Mines. Borough Electrical Engineer, Cheltenham, 1894–1905 ; *War Work :* Division Officer, R.E., Chelmsford, Jan. 1915, to May, 1919. *Clubs :* Promenade ; Union. (M8709)
KILLICK, John Spencer, C.B.E., M.Inst.C.E., *b.* 8 Sept. 1878 ; *s.* of William Cassam Killick, of Yalding ; *m.* Lizzie Sheldon, *d.* of Sir Henry Maybury, K.C.M.G., C.B., of Barnesfield, Greenhithe, Kent (*see* BURKE'S *Peerage*). *Educ. :* Cranleigh. Civil Engineer. Chief Engineer, Roads Dept., Ministry of Transport. *War Work :* Acting Manager and Chief Engineer of H.M. Road Board ; Chief Engineer, Joint Roads (W.O.) Committee. *Address :* Stone Park, Greenhithe, Kent. *Clubs :* R.A.C. ; Golfers'. (C2733)
KILLIN, Robert, C.B.E., *b.* 1870 ; *s.* of James Killin, of Rutherglen ; *m.* Jane Emily, *d.* of Peter Kerry, of Rutherglen. *Educ. :* Scott's School, Rutherglen. Superintendent of the Line, Caledonian Railway. *War Work :* Railway Transport. *Address :* Kingholm, Rutherglen, Scotland. (C217)
KILLMAYER, Flight-Lieut. Leon Joseph, M.B.E., R.N.
KILNER, Charles Scott, M.B.E., M.B., C.M., (Edin. Univ.), D.P.H. (Camb. Univ.), Fellow, Society of Medical Officers of Health, late President, East Anglian Branch, British Medical Association, J.P., *b.* 2 Oct. 1853 ; *s.* of John Kilner, F.R.C.S., of Bury St. Edmunds ; *m.* Lucy Ussher, *d.* of Strangman Davis-Goff, J.P., of Horetown House, Co. Wexford. *Educ. :* King Edward VI. School, Bury St. Edmunds, and Edinburgh Univ. Late Honorary Senior Medical Officer, West Suffolk General Hospital ; now Honorary Consulting Medical Officer, West Suffolk General Hospital : Medical Officer of Health, Thingoe Rural District. *War Work :* Senior Medical Officer, West Suffolk General Hospital, which received disabled men straight from the front ; Medical Officer, Northgate Red Cross Hospital, Bury St. Edmunds. *Address :* The Old Mill House, Bury St. Edmunds. *Club :* West Suffolk County. (M8710)
KILROY, Lieut. Willie Dickson, O.B.E., R.N.V.R.
KILVERT, Lieut. and Qr.-Mr. Charles Robert, M.B.E.
KILVERT, John Ellis, O.B.E., F.R.C.S., L.R.C.P.
KIMBER, Augustus Charles Edmund, O.B.E.
KIMBER, Lieut.-Col. Edmund Gibbs, C.B.E., D.S.O., T.D., late 13th Batt. (Princess Louise's Kensington Battalion) the London Regt., *b.* 6 Aug. 1870 ; *s.* of Edmund Kimber, of Shooter's Hill, Kent ; *m.* Maud, *d.* of William Bridekirk Wilson, of Manchester. *Educ. :* University College, London. Barrister-at-law ; called at Lincoln's Inn, 1892 ; also Member of Middle Temple, South-Eastern Circuit, Surrey and South London Sessions. *War Work :* Mobilised with 13th Batt. The London Regt. on 4 Aug. 1914 ; served in France with B.E.F., in 13th Batt. The London Regt., 25th Infantry Brigade, 8th Division ; present at Battles of Neuve Chapelle and Fromelles (wounded at latter battle on 9 May, 1915) ; awarded D.S.O. for services ; Prosecutor and Judge Advocate on standing Courts-Martial, Irish Rebellion, 1916 ; Staff Capt., War Office, 1917 ; D.A.A.G., War Office, 1918 ; A.A.G., War Office, 1919. *Addresses :* 6, Yale Court, West Hampstead, N.W. 6 ; 4, Pump Court, Temple, E.C. 4. *Club :* Junior Carlton. (C1646)
KIMBER, Ernest, M.B.E.
KIMBER, Florence Edith, M.B.E., *b.* 16 May, 1885. *Educ. :* Wesleyan Training Coll. School, Westminster. *Address :* 64, Foxbourne Road, London, S.W. 17. (M8711)
KIMBER, Thomas, M.B.E.
KIMBERLEY, Lieut. Harold William, M.B.E.
KIMBERLEY, Henry, M.B.E.
KIMBERLEY, Capt. Paul, O.B.E., *b.* 23 Nov. 1881 ; *s.* of Thomas Kimberley, of Langley, Birmingham ; *m.* Mabel Annie, *d.* of H. Knowles, of Isleworth. *Educ. :* St. John's, Paddington. Managing Director of Imperial Film Co., Ltd., also Director and Manager of Hepworth Picture Plays, Ltd. *War Work :* Started Training Scheme for Disabled Soldiers and Sailors, which was afterwards taken over by Ministry of Pensions, who formed National Cinema Trade Advisory Committee, and was appointed Hon. Technical Adviser on Methods

of Training ; also Capt. and Adjutant of County of London R.A.S.C., M.T. (V.). *Address :* Ivanhoe, 1, Pierrepoint Road, Acton, W. 3. *Clubs :* R.A.C. ; Eccentric. (O10779)
KIMMINS, James Charles Clegg, M.B.E., J.P., C.C., *b.* 31 July, 1850 ; *s.* of James Kimmins, of Stonehouse ; *m.* Isabel Maud, *d.* of Edward Hubbard, of London. *Educ. :* Privately. Chairman of Gloucestershire War Pensions Committee ; Vice Chairman of Gloucestershire Education Committee ; County Councillor for the Stonehouse Division of Gloucestershire ; Chairman of Stroud Rural District Council ; J.P. for the County of Gloucestershire ; Chairman of Stroud Rural District Tribunal and War Pensions Committee, and Gloucestershire War Pensions Committee. *Address :* Ryeford Hall, Stonehouse. *Club :* Bristol Liberal. (M1992)
KIMMITT, Lieut.-Col. Robert Robertson, O.B.E. ; *s.* of the late Rev. E. Kimmitt, of Knock, Co. Down ; *m.* Elizabeth Marie Rowand, *d.* of the late Charles Loudon, of Bank of Ireland, Belfast. *War Work :* Commanded the Reserve Batt. London Irish Rifles from its formation in April, 1915, until its disbandment in July, 1919. *Address :* 18, Mattock Lane, Ealing, W. 5. (O7349)
KIMPTON, Arthur Ernest, O.B.E.
KINAHAN, John, O.B.E., *b.* 6 April, 1866 ; *s.* of Fredk. Kinahan, of Low Wood, Belfast ; *m.* Eve, *d.* of Captain Thomas Sanders, D.L., Sallow Glen, Co. Kerry. *Educ. :* Repton. *War Work :* Hon. Superintendent of work of Soldiers Christian Association in France, 1914–19. *Address :* Lumville House, Curragh, Co. Kildare. *Club :* Junior Constitutional. (O1551)
KINAHAN, Major George Frederick HUDSON-, C.B.E.
KINCAIRD, James Scott, O.B.E.
KINDERSLEY, Ada Molesworth, M.B.E. ; *d.* of Capt. E. N. Molesworth Kindersley, of Sherborne, Dorset. *Educ. :* Privately. Head of Training Section, Women's Branch, Board of Agriculture. *War Work :* Hon. Sec. and Organiser of Queen Alexandra's Relief Fund for War Nurses ; head of Training Section, Women's Branch, Board of Agriculture. *Address :* 12, Graham Street, Eaton Terrace, S.W. 1. *Club :* Forum. (M8712)
KINDERSLEY, Capt. Guy, O.B.E.
KINDERSLEY, Katherine Emma, M.B.E.
KINDERSLEY, Sir Robert Molesworth, G.B.E., *b.* 1872 ; *s.* of Capt. E. N. M. Kindersley (*see* BURKE'S *Peerage*) ; *m.* Gladys Margaret, *d.* of Major-Gen. J. P. Beadle, R.E., of 6, Queen's Gate Gardens, S.W. *Educ. :* Repton. Chairman Lazard Bros. & Co., Ltd. ; Director of Bank of England ; Governor of the Hudson's Bay Co. ; Director of Eastern Telegraph Co. ; President of National Savings Committee ; Member of Court of Fishmongers' Company ; Lieutenant of City of London. *War Work :* Chairman of the National Savings Committee since its inception in 1916 until March, 1920. *Addresses :* 15, Charles Street, Berkeley Square, W. 1 ; Langley House, Abbots Langley, Herts. *Clubs :* Carlton ; Garrick ; Royal Thames Yacht. (G54)
KING, Capt. Albert Lewin, O.B.E.
KING, Alice Cicell, O.B.E., *d.* of James King, of Monkstown, Co. Dublin, Ireland. *Educ. :* Ladies' College, Cheltenham. *War Work :* Commandant of New Court Auxiliary Red Cross Hospital, Cheltenham, Gloucestershire ; opened the hospital on 21 Oct. 1914, and acted as Commandant till its close in Jan. 1919. *Address :* Lypiatt House, Cheltenham. (O3786)
KING, Capt. Basil, M.B.E., Royal Warwickshire Regt., *b.* 21 June, 1883 ; *s.* of the late George P. King, of Swindon, Wilts., *m.* Katherine Martha Woolford, *d.* of the late Henry John Brunsden, of Snodshill, Swindon, Wilts. *Educ. :* Privately ; Swindon Technical Coll. Accountant ; at present Manager and Accountant (Stores) Messrs. Doulton & Co., Sanitary Engineers, Lambeth, S.E. *War Work :* Served in the Wiltshire Regt. and Royal Warwickshire Regt. in the East and France in the Great War ; for the last twelve months of the War was Depot Manager, Birmingham, for the Central Stores Department, Ministry of Munitions. *Address :* Linden, Palace Road, East Molesey, Surrey. (M10250e)
KING, C. W., O.B.E., R.N.V.R.
KING, Col. Charles Dickson, C.B.E., *b.* 1860 ; Formerly Col. R.A. ; served with the Egyptian Expedition, 1882 ; present at Battle of Tel-el-Kebir (medal with clasp, bronze star) ; Great War, 1914–19 (despatches). (C1647)
KING, Capt. Charles John Stuart, O.B.E., R.E. (O11749)
KING, Capt. Colin, O.B.E., R.A.M.C.
KING, David Barty, O.B.E., M.B., M.R.C.P., R.A.M.C.
KING, Dame Ethel, O.B.E.
KING, Emma Ethel Maud Ford, M.B.E.
KING, Lieut.-Col. Frank, D.S.O. O.B.E.
KING, Capt. Frank, D.S.O., O.B.E., 4th Hussars. Served in the Great War, 1914–18 (despatches). (O5452)
KING, Capt. George, M.B.E., A.I.F.
KING, George William, M.B.E., R.E.
KING, Godfrey James, O.B.E., J.P., *b.* 29 Oct. 1870 ; *s.* of the late John Richard King, of St. Peter's Vicarage, Oxford ; *m.* Mary Francis, *d.* of Harcourt Capper, of Herefordshire. *Educ. :* Haileybury Coll., and Oriel Coll., Oxford. Registrar of Deeds Companies and Patents, Southern Rhodesia ; Civil Commissioner, Salisbury, Southern Rhodesia. *War Work :* Senior Censor, Southern Rhodesia. *Address :* Salisbury, Southern Rhodesia. *Club :* Salisbury. (O8394)
KING, Comm. Henry Douglas, C.B.E., D.S.O., M.P., *b.* 1877 ; *s.* of the late Capt. Henry Welchman King ; *m.* 1900, Margaret Elizabeth, *d.* of the late W. R. Swan, of S. Australia. Bar. Middle Temple, 1905 ; formerly in Mercantile Marine ;

Roy. Naval Reserve, 1893–1902 ; Inns of Court Rifles, 1902–4 ; Roy. Naval Vol. Reserve (VD.), 1904–14 ; served during the Great War, 1914–17, with Roy. Naval Div., with rank of Com. (despatches thrice, Croix de Guerre) ; appointed Parliamentary Private Sec. to Parliamentary Sec. to Min, of Shipping, 1919 ; unsuccessfully contested N. Div. of Norfolk, Jan. 1910, and Dec. 1910 ; elected therefor (C.-Ind.) Dec. 1918. *Address :* The Dales, Sheringham, Norfolk. *Clubs :* Junior Carlton ; Bath. (C1098)

KING, Henry Smails, O.B.E.

KING, Capt. James Edward, M.B.E., R.G.A.

KING, James Edward, C.B.E., B.A., *b.* 17 March, 1875 ; *s.* of Sir James King, Bart. (*see* BURKE'S *Peerage*), of Campsie and Carstairs ; *m.* Muriel May, *d.* of Capt. Frederick James Taylor, of Waddon, Surrey. *Educ. :* New Coll., Oxford. Barrister-at-Law, Inner Temple ; Second Secretary to the British Legation at The Hague. *War Work :* Attached to the Contraband Department, Foreign Office ; Sec. to the Allied Blockade Committee in London ; Hon. Sec. to the Borough of Stepney Committee for Production and Relief of Distress. *Addresses :* Monks' Alley, Binfield, Berks. ; British Legation, The Hague. *Clubs :* Travellers' ; Bath ; Hurlingham ; Oxford and Cambridge. (C2735)

KING, James Foster, C.B.E., Vice Pres. I.N.A., M.I.C.E., *b.* 1862 ; *s.* of James Foster King, of Longhaugh ; *m.* Margaret, *d.* of Douglas Turner. *Educ. :* Glasgow High School. Chief Surveyor to the British Corporation Registry of Shipping. *War Work :* In connection with the Admiralty programme of construction for their auxiliary fleet, and the Government programme of merchant ship construction, etc. *Address :* 14, Blythswood Square, Glasgow. *Club :* Royal Scottish Automobile. (C2736)

KING, Paymaster-Lieut. James Henry, O.B.E., R.N.

KING, John, M.B.E., *b.* 24 Aug. 1881 ; *s.* of Robert King, of Belfast ; *m.* Annie, *d.* of Thomas Gatensby, of Belfast. *Educ. :* Primary School ; Mercantile Coll., Belfast ; Royal Univ. of Ireland. Clerk in Secretary's Office, General Post Office. *War Work :* Head of Commercial Vehicles Section, Petrol Control Department, Board of Trade. *Address :* Lynsted, Hide Road, Harrow. (M8713)

KING, John Alexander, O.B.E., L.L.D.

KING, John Charles, O.B.E., M.R.C.S.

KING, Lieut.-Comm. Joseph, O.B.E., R.N.R.

KING, Major Lancelot Noel Friedrick Irving, O.B.E., R.E.

KING, Capt. Leonard Algernon Bertram, M.B.E.

KING, Capt. Malcolm Kirkwood, M.B.E., Argyll and Sutherland Highlanders, *b.* 7 Oct. 1886 ; *s.* of William King of Glasgow. *Educ. :* Strathbungo Public School. *War Work :* Returned from India with 1st Batt. Argyll and Sutherland Highlanders, Oct. 1914 ; joined Expeditionary Force, Dec 1914 ; served continuously in France and Flanders till Nov 1915 ; Macedonia, Nov. 1915 to Jan. 1919. *Address :* 6th Batt. Argyll and Sutherland Highlanders, 66, High Street, Paisley. (M4800)

KING, Mary Liddon, O.B.E. ; *d.* of Richard Poole King, J.P., of Brislington, Somerset. *War Work :* Commandant of Standish Red Cross Hospital ; a Vice President of Red Cross Society, Glos. Branch. *Address :* Newark Park, Wotton-under-Edge, Glos. *Club :* Empress. (O482)

KING, Nelly Maria, O.B.E. Acted for nearly there years as Hall Orderly at, and organised the voluntary work for Queen Alexandra's Hospital. (O11909)

KING, Nora, Mrs., M.B.E., *b.* 1883 ; *d.* of George and Frances McDonald, of Torquay ; *m.* James Malcolm, *s.* of James King, of D'Urbanville, S. Africa. *Educ. :* Herne Bay, and Tunbridge Wells. *War Work :* Red Cross work from (and since 1911) the commencement of War ; Commandant of Cambs. 26, and Matron of V.A.D. Hospital, Willingham, Cambs., from Jan. 1915, to April, 1919. *Addresses :* Willingham, Cambs. ; Lochgyle, Parsonage Road, Herne Bay. (M636)

KING, Sarah Hannah, Mrs., M.B.E.

KING, Rev. Thomas, M.B.E.

KING, Rev. Thomas Joseph, O.B.E.

KING, Rev. Vincent George Bryan, O.B.E.

KING, Capt. William Bernard Robinson, O.B.E., M.A., *b.* 12 Nov. 1889. *Educ. :* Uppingham, and Jesus College, Cambridge. Assistant to the Woodwardian Professor of Geology in the Univ. of Cambridge ; Fellow of Jesus College, Cambridge. *War Work :* Geologist to Engineer-in-Chief at G.H.Q., France, from July, 1915, to March, 1918. *Address :* 45, Barton Road, Cambridge. (O2596)

KING, William Frederick, O.B.E.

KING, Major William Henry, O.B.E., *b.* 13 Sept. 1871 ; *s.* of Capt. W. King, of Burridge, Chard ; *m.* May Violet, *d.* of J. O'Connor, of Halifax. Professor of Music. Inniskilling Dragoons, S. Africa, 1899–1902. *War Work :* Remounts, Ireland, 1914–15 ; Egypt, 1915–16 ; France, 1916–18. *Address :* 1, Duncairn Terrace, Bray, Co. Wicklow. *Club :* Kildare Street. (O7350)

KING, Capt. and Qr.-Mr. William Henry Daniel, O.B.E., M.G.C.

KING, William Samuel, M.B.E., *b.* 5 July, 1879 ; *s.* of the late Joseph William and Margaret King, of Clonmel, Ireland ; *m.* Evie Emily, *d.* of George Walton Abbott, of The Gables, Leytonstone, N.E. *Educ. :* Rockwell College, Ireland. Veterinary Surgeon. *War Work :* In sole veterinary charge of the 1st R.F. Artillery Officers' Cadet School horses. as well as being in sole veterinary charge of horses belonging to

many other units ; made collections which resulted in the accumulation of substantial sums of money for R.A.V.C. Comforts Fund. *Address :* 264, Burdett Road, Limehouse, E. 14. *Club :* National Sporting. (M1995)

KING, Dame Ethel LOCKE-, D.B.E. ; *d.* of Col. Sir Thomas Gore Browne, K.C.M.G., C.B. (who died 1887) ; *m.* Hugh Fortescue, *s.* of Hon. Peter John Locke-King, M.P., J.P., D.L. (who died 1885), of Brooklands. *Educ. :* At home. Assistant County Director, and Vice President, North Surrey Division, B.R.C.S. *War Work :* Raising V. A. Detachments ; organising and opening hospitals for sick and wounded in Surrey. *Address :* Brooklands, Weybridge. *Club :* Bath. (D14)

KING, Lieut.-Col. Francis John NEWTON-, O.B.E.

KINGDON, R.S.M. Albert Arthur, M.B.E., Norfolk Regt., *b.* 20 Jan. 1884 ; *s.* of the late E. Kingdon, of Thetford, Norfolk ; *m.* Maud, *d.* of the late James Calthrop, of Thetford. *Educ. :* Thetford Board School and Army School. *War Work :* Active Service, Mesopotamia, 1914–16 ; 13th (Transport Workers) Batt. the Bedfordshire Regt., 1917–19. *Address :* The Norfolk Regt. Depot, Britannia Barracks, Norwich. (M5404)

KINGHAM, Robert Dixon, O.B.E.

KINGHORN, Lieut. Douglas Charles, M.B.E., R.A.S.C.

KINGMAN, Capt. Abner, O.B.E.

KINGSBERRY, Lieut. William Henry, M.B.E., *b.* 11 Feb. 1897. *War Work :* commissioned Tempy. 2nd Lieut., 11th Bn. Loyal North Lancashire Regt., Mar. 1915 ; Commissioned 2nd Lieut. N. Lan. Regt., Feb. 1916 ; served with 6th Bn. Loyal North Lancashire Regt. Mes. Exped. Force, Dec. 1916 to Jan. 1919 ; Staff Capt. 34th Infy. Bde., Mesopotamia, since Jan. 1919. *Addresses :* c/o Messrs. Cox & Co., 16, Charing Cross, London, S.W.1 ; c/o Messrs. Cox & Co., Hornby Rd., Bombay. (M4887)

KINGSBURY, Kathleen, M.B.E. *War Work :* Ministry of Munitions, Central Stores Dept., Jan. 1916, to July, 1919. *Address :* 123, Herne Hill, S.E. 24. (M8714)

KINGSLAND, John Edward, M.B.E., *b.* 18 Nov. 1873 ; *s.* of William Gaylor Kingsland, of Canterbury ; *m.* Flora Kate, *d.* of Thomas Gambrill, of Crundale. Served with the 15th The King's Hussars at home and abroad, 1891–1909, and finished his military career with the East Kent Yeomanry. *War Work :* Employed at the War Office on work in connection with the transport of nurses to the various theatres of War, and was transferred to the Ministry of National Service in Dec. 1917, for duty with the Medical Department. *Address :* 38, Green Street, Cambridge. (M1997)

KINGSTON, 2nd Lieut. Alfred Thomas, M.B.E., D.C.M., R.E.

KINGSTON, Lieut. and Qr.-Mr. Charles, M.B.E., R.A.M.C.

KINGSTON, George Henry, O.B.E., *b.* 9 March, 1866 ; *s.* of Joseph Kingston, of Southsea ; *m.* Fanny Louisa, *d.* of Alfred George Croucher, of Southsea. Civil Servant, War Office. *War Work :* Assistant Director of Army Contracts, War Office and Ministry of Munitions ; Assistant Controller, Disposal Board, Ministry of Munitions. *Address :* 103, Streathbourne Road, Tooting Common, S.W. 17. *Club :* National Liberal. (O1555)

KINGSTON, Major John Rudolph, O.B.E., *b.* 8 July, 1882. *Educ. :* Hull Grammar School, and Hull Municipal Technical Coll. Civil Servant. *War Work :* Went to Belgium with Expeditionary Force in Oct. 1914, as officer in charge of Wireless Section of 4th Army Corps ; appointed Assist. Inspector of R.E. Stores at Woolwich in Sept. 1915, to complete design of new field wireless set ; promoted to Inspector, Dec. 1916 ; with British War Mission, U.S.A., Sept. to Dec. 1918. *Address :* Fern Bank, Colney Hatch Lane, Muswell Hill, London, N. *Club :* Junior Naval and Military. (O7351)

KINGSTON, Lieut.-Col. William, O.B.E., R.E.

KINGZETT, Norman Froggatt, M.B.E., *b.* 18 Nov. 1880 ; *s.* of Charles T. Kingzett, of Newlands, Weybridge, Surrey ; *m.* 1st, *d.* of T. B. Lightfoot, of Putney ; 2ndly, Cicely *y.d.* of Sir George Agnew, of Rougham Hall, Suffolk. *Educ. :* Royal Naval School, Eltham, Kent. Managing Director of Sanitas Co., Ltd. *War Work :* Member of Committee and Treas., Byfleet War Relief Committee, 1914–19 ; Chairman of Chertsey Rural Pensions Committee, 1916–19 ; Chairman of Chertsey with Egham War Pensions Committee from 1919 ; Treas. of Sanitas War Savings Assocn. *Address :* Karridale, West Byfleet. *Clubs :* Constitutional ; City Carlton ; R.A.C. (M8715)

KININMONTH, Lieut. Alec Marshall, M.B.E.

KINLOCH, Charles, M.B.E.,

KINLOCH, George, O.B.E.

KINLOCH, Sir George, Bart., O.B.E., J.P., *b.* 1 March, 1880 ; *s.* of the late Sir John G. S. Kinloch, 2nd Bart., of Kinloch, Meigle (*see* BURKE'S *Peerage*) ; *m.* Ethel May, *d.* of Major James Hawkins, of 85th Regt. *Educ. :* Charterhouse ; Trinity Coll., Cambridge (B.A.). *War Work :* Recruiting Officer, 42nd Area ; Lieut. T.F. Reserve ; Appeal National Service Representative for Perthshire. *Address :* Kinloch, Meigle, N.B. *Clubs :* New (Edinburgh) ; Caledonian. (O1556)

KINLOCH, Rev. Michael Ward, O.B.E., *b.* 18 Dec. 1865 ; *s.* of Charles Kinloch, of Harrow, Middlesex ; *m.* Ella Adria, *d.* of Percy C. Heath, Indian Army. *Educ. :* Harrow and Pembroke Coll., Camb. Rector of West Stafford, Dorset, 1896 ; Eccleston, Cheshire, 1904 ; Holy Trinity, Dorchester, 1911 ; Sarum St. Edmund, 1919; Prebendary of Salisbury Cathedral. *War Work :* Temp. C.F., Sept. 1914 ; Senior C.F., Portland Defences ; Mediterranean Expeditionary Force, May,

1915, Gallipoli, Mudros, and Egypt; Senior C.F., L. of C., Aug. 1915 to Feb. 1916; Senior C.F., 15th Army Corps, Feb. 1916 to July, 1916 (mentioned in despatches); C.F. Netley Hospital, Aug. 1916 to Nov. 1916; Senior C.F. Portsmouth, Nov. 1916 to Jan. 1919 (mentioned for Home Service). *Address:* St. Edmund's Rectory, Salisbury. (O7352)

KINNAIRD, Hon. Emily Cecilia, C.B.E.; *d.* of 10th Baron Kinnaird (*see* BURKE'S *Peerage*). *Educ.:* Privately. Acting Vice-President of the Y.W.C.A. of Great Britain, and Vice-President of the World's Y.W.C.A.; chairman of the Committee for Holiday Camps; member of the British Committee of the World Alliance for International Friendship among the Churches. *Address:* 4, Duke Street, Manchester Square, W. *Club:* Portman. (C2727)

KINNEAR, James Francis, M.B.E., *b.* 19 Nov. 1866; *s.* of James Kinnear, of Melrose; *m.* Beatrice Mabel, *d.* of late William Fred Vernon, of Kelso. *Educ.:* Edinburgh. Postmaster. *War Work:* Postal and Telegraphic Administration of Shetland from 1915–19; also War Savings Campaign. *Address:* Williamfield House, Stirling. (M8716)

KINNEAR, Thomas John, O.B.E., *b.* 19 Oct. 1870; *s.* of Alexander Kinnear, of Ballybay, Co. Monaghan, and Cremorne, Ballsbridge, Dublin. Barrister-at-law; Representative for Ulster of Industrial Department of Ministry of Labour. *War Work:* Sec. to Food Control Committee for Ireland; actively assisted Irish Recruiting Council, as voluntary organiser and speaker; assisted in Hospital Ship work as member of St. John's Ambulance Brigade. *Addresses:* Grand Central Hotel, Belfast; Holywood, Co. Down. (O10783)

KINNEAR, Sir Walter Samuel, K.B.E., B.A. (Hons.); *m.* Iris Mary, *d.* of Dr. W. Y. Orr, of Kenmore, Putney, S.W. Chairman of the Navy and Army Insurance Fund; Deputy Chairman of the National Health Insurance Commission (Ireland); Past President Insurance Institute of Ireland; Fellow Chartered Insurance Institute. *Addresses:* Cremorne, Ball's Bridge, Dublin; Wellington House, Buckingham Gate, S.W. *Club:* Stephen's Green (Dublin). (K150)

KINNERSLY, George Edward, M.B.E., *b.* 1869; *s.* of William Thomas, of Binfield Manor, Berks.; *m.* Mabel G., *d.* of Alan Broderick, of Broughton-Gifford. *Educ.:* St. Thomas' Hospital Medical School. Jurat, Royal Court of Guernsey. *War Work:* T. Capt., R.A.M.C., 1915–20. *Address:* St. Martin, Gurnsey, C.I. (M6664)

KINNERSLEY, Capt. William Harold, O.B.E., R.A.S.C.

KINROSS, Anne Mary, M.B.E., *b.* 25 Dec. 1887; *d.* of Henry Kinross, of Park Terrace, Stirling. *Educ.:* St. Leonard's School; St. Andrew's; Girton College, Cambridge. Teaching and lecturing. *War Work:* French Red Cross, 1915–16; France; Q.M.A.A.C. (Unit Administrator), France, May, 1917, to Oct. 1919. *Address:* 23, Park Terrace, Stirling. *Club:* St. Andrews House, W. 1. (M4535)

KINSMAN, Harry Jeoffrey, M.B.E.

KINSMAN, Major William Augustus Cecil, D.S.O., O.B.E.

KIPPEN, James William, M.B.E., K.O.S.B.

KIRALFY, Gerald Archibald, M.B.E.

KIRBY, Wing-Comm. Claude, O.B.E., R.A.F.

KIRBY, Major Edmund Bertram, O.B.E., R.F.A.

KIRBY, Capt. Edward William, M.B.E.

KIRBY, Lieut.-Col. F. H., V.C., *b.* 12 Nov. 1871; *s.* of William Henry and Ada Kirby; *m.* 1909, Kate Jolly. *Educ.:* Alleyne's School, Dulwich. Capt., Depot Comm., Squadron Comm. R.A.F.; enlisted in Royal Engineers, 1892; proceeded to S. Africa with Field Troops, Royal Engineers, on mobilisation 1899 (D.C.M. Bloemfontein, March, 1900; V.C. action East of Pretoria, June, 1900; Troop Sergt.-Major from Corporal for services in the field, July, 1901); Warrant Officer, Dec. 1906; commissioned from ranks, April, 1911; posted to Air Batt., Royal Engineers, South Farnborough; gazetted to R.F.C. 1912; served in the Great War, France, 1916–18; promoted to Capt. for services in the field, 1 Jan. 1917.

KIRBY, George, O.B.E., *b.* 6 Nov. 1845; *s.* of George Kirby, of Malton, Yorkshire; *m.* Hannah, *d.* of John Jackman, of Hardwick, Bucks. *Educ.:* Church of England School, Scampston. Curator of the City Art Gallery; Superintendent of the Exhibition Buildings, under the City of York Corporation, for 41 years. *War Work:* Local recruiting staff; Hon. Assist. Sec., National Service; Member of Publication Committee of the local Food Control Committee; organised and was for five years Hon. Sec. of the York Cheer and Comforts Committee for care of wounded soldiers. *Addresses:* 26, Clifton, York. *Club:* Comrades of the Great War, York. (O10784)

KIRBY, George Clarvis, M.B.E.

KIRBY, Marion Ellen, M.B.E.; *d.* of the late Alfred O. Kirby. *War Work:* Helped the Penny Fund for Sick and Wounded, collecting and organising the South Kensington Division; after was Joint Secretary of Lady Smith-Dorrien's Hospital Bag Fund from July, 1915, till it closed March, 1919. *Address:* 50, Burton Court, S.W. 3. *Club:* Albemarle. (M2000)

KIRBY, William, O.B.E., R.N.D.

KIRBY, Major William Lewis Clark, D.S.O., O.B.E.

KIRK, Col. Albert Edward, O.B.E., V.D.

KIRK, Capt. James Robert, M.B.E.

KIRK, Lieut.-Col. John Charters, C.B.E., R.F.A. (T.); *b.* 1868. *Educ.:* Wellington Coll. Lieut.-Col. Anti-Aircraft Defence, Home Forces.

KIRK, Mabel Cecil, Mrs., M.B.E.

KIRK, Norah, Mrs., O.B.E., *b.* 2 Jan. 1874; *d.* of Frederic

R. Rose, of Diss, Norfolk; *m.* John Lamplugh, *s.* of John Wright Kirk, of Hull. *Educ.:* Bromley (Kent) High School, andRoyal College of Music. *War Work:* Four years Commandant of V.A.D. Hospital, Hallgarth, Pickering, Yorks. *Address:* Houndgate, Pickering, Yorks. (O1558)

KIRKE, Sarah Elizabeth, Mrs., M.B.E.,

KIRKLAND, Lieut. James, O.B.E., R.A.O.C.

KIRKNESS, John Johnston, O.B.E.

KIRKNESS, Lieut.-Col. Lewis Hawker, D.S.O., O.B.E.

KIRKPATRICK, Cecil William, M.B.E.

KIRKPATRICK, Lieut.-Col. Charles, O.B.E., I.A.

KIRKPATRICK, Lieut.-Col. Ivone, C.B.E., *b.* 1860; *s.* of the late Alexander R. Kirkpatrick, of Donacomper, Celbridge, co. Kildare (*see* BURKE'S *Peerage*, Ashtown, B.); *m.* 1891, the Hon. Mary Hardinge, *d.* of the late Gen. the Hon. Sir Arthur Edward Hardinge, K.C.B., C.I.E. (*see* BURKE'S *Peerage*). Formerly Lieut.-Col. S. Staffordshire Regt.; Soudan Expedition, 1884–85 (medal with two clasps, bronze star); Great War, 1914–19 (despatches). (C1649)

KIRKPATRICK, John, M.B.E.

KIRKPATRICK, Mary Hawkins, Mrs., M.B.E.

KIRKPATRICK, Capt. and Qr.-Mr. Robert, M.B.E.

KIRKUS, Arthur Ernest, O.B.E., *b.* 30 Nov. 1875; *s.* of John Richard Kirkus, of Hessle, East Yorkshire; *m.* Mabel Mary Sergeant, *d.* of John Stow, J.P., of Hessle. *Educ.:* High School, Hornsea. Assistant Director of Statistics, Ministry of Transport. *War Work:* Head of Statistical Branch, Woolwich Arsenal, Oct. 1915 to June, 1917; Assistant to Director of Statistics, Admiralty, June, 1917, to Jan. 1919. *Address:* Oakhurst, Thicket Road, Sutton, Surrey. (O485)

KIRKWOOD, Major Andrew Samuel, O.B.E.

KIRKWOOD, Lieut.-Col. Andrew Torton, O.B.E., I.A.

KIRKWOOD, Ethel Kate, Mrs., M.B.E.; *m.* Montague Kirkwood. *War Work:* Hon. Sec. Soldiers' and Sailors' Families Association, Stepney and Mile End; Hon. Sec. of Sub-Committee London War Pensions for Stepney A. *Address:* 12, Egerton Gardens, S.W. *Club:* Lady Golfers'. (M8719)

KIRKWOOD, Richard Cameron, M.B.E.

KIRKWOOD, Major Thomas William, O.B.E., I.A.

KIRKWOOD, William Dennett, O.B.E., *b.* 1871; *s.* of William Kirkwood, of Glasgow; *m.* Isabella Robertson Stewart, *d.* of John Stewart, of Rutherglen. *Educ.:* Hutcheson's Grammar School, and Allan Glen's School. Engineer; appointed H.M. Inspector of Factories (Home Office), 1899, as Junior Inspector in Belfast and District Inspector in Aberdeen, then Lanarkshire. *War Work:* Transferred or lent to the Ministry of Munitions, June, 1915, acting as Superintendent Engineer till Feb. 1919, in Glasgow and West of Scotland Area, with responsibility for 27 direct, 82 indirect, contractors, and 5 National Projectile Factories; and latterly as Technical Assistant to the Director of Munitions in Scotland. *Address:* 11, Richmond Drive, Cambuslang, Glasgow. (O486)

KIRKWOOD, Lieut.-Col. William Love, O.B.E. Aust. A.M.C.

KIRSOP, Lieut. Alexander Kennedy, O.B.E.

KIRWAN, Florence Sydney Brudenell, M.B.E.

KIRWAN, Capt. Lionel Edward, M.B.E.

KIRWIN, Eng.-Comm. Joseph John, O.B.E., R.N.

KISCH, Brevet Lieut.-Col. Frederick Hermann, C.B.E., D.S.O., R.E., *b.* 23 Aug. 1888; *s.* of H. M. Kisch, C.S.I., of 56, Lexham Gardens, London; *m.* Jeanne Eleanor, *d.* of M. Philippe Colin, of Neuchâtel, Switzerland. *Educ.:* Clifton College, and R.M.A., Woolwich. *War Work:* Served in France and Mesopotamia in 1914, 1915, and 1916 with 3rd (Lahore) Division (thrice wounded); awarded D.S.O. and Croix de Guerre; served on the General Staff at the War Office from Sept. 1916 until the Armistice, and thereafter with the British Peace Delegation at Paris. *Address:* c/o Messrs. Cox & Co., 16, Charing Cross. *Club:* Bath. (C2133)

KISSANE, Matthew, O.B.E.

KISSOCK, William Henry, M.B.E.

KITCAT, Rev. Henry James, O.B.E., *b.* 12 March, 1860; *s.* of James Butler Kitcat, *m.* Ethelreda Sophie, *y.d.* of the late Sir Joseph Olliffe, Physician to the English Embassy in Paris. *Educ.:* St. Michael's Coll., Tenbury; Bradfield Coll.; Keble Coll., Oxford. Rector of St. Mary Stratford, Bow, E. 3, 1904; Rural Dean of Poplar, Nov. 1919; Senior Dean of Sion Coll., 1920; Councillor for Bow, South Ward, on Poplar Borough Council, Nov. 1919. *War Work:* Member of Soldiers' and Sailors' Families Association, Bow Committee; Chairman Poplar A. London War Pensions Sub-Committee; Member of Poplar Borough Air Raid Relief Committee; served in and chaplain to, the Local G.R. Volunteer Force. *Address:* The Rectory, Bow, E. 3. (O10785)

KITCAT, Capt. Henry Jeffreys de Winton, O.B.E., R.N.

KITCHEN, Preston, O.B.E.

KITCHIN, John William, O.B.E.

KITCHING, Lieut. Douglas Woolley, M.B.E., *b.* 28 Nov. 1880; *s.* of Albert George Kitching, of Enfield; *m.* Marjorie, *d.* of Morton Peto Betts, of Mentone. *Educ.:* Mill Hill School. *War Work:* Served with the Mesopotamian Expeditionary Force. *Address:* Holmbury, Keston, Kent. *Club:* R.A.C. (M4889)

KITCHING, Fanny Rushall, M.B.E. *War Work:* Controller of Typists, India Office. (M2004)

KITCHING, Lieut. Harold Edward, M.B.E.

KITCHING, Theodore Hopkins, C.B.E., *b.* 29 Dec. 1866;

s. of William Kitching, of Clevedon, Som.; *m.* Jane, *d.* of William C anshaw, of Southport. *Educ.:* Friends' School, Ackworth, Yorks. Secretary to General Bramwell Booth, of the Salvation Army. *War Work:* Was associated with General Bramwell Booth in organising the Salvation Army's work amongst His Majesty's forces in various parts of the Empire. *Addresses:* Ingleton, New Barnet, Herts; 101, Queen Victoria Street, London, E.C. 4.   (C2738)

KITSON, Lieut. Alan Kennedy, O.B.E., R.A.S.C., (T.).

KITSON, Albert Ernest, C.B.E. Director Gold Coast Geological Survey.   (C398)

KITSON, Major Alexander Wentworth, O.B.E., R.A.S.C., (T.).

KITSON, Lieut.-Col. Hubert Vernon, O.B.E., R.A.S.C' (T.), *b.* 9 April, 1883; *s.* of F. C. Kitson, of Leeds. *Educ.:* Forest School, Essex. Engineer; Director of Leeds Wheel and Axle Co., Ltd., Leeds. *War Work:* Aug. 1914, O.C. 2nd Brigade Co., West Riding Division T. and S. Column; Aug. 1914 to Nov. 1916, O.C. 49th Division Supply Column; Nov. 1916, appointed Deputy Assistant Director of Transport; Dec. 1918, Assistant Director of Transports. *Address:* Beamsley, Headingley, Leeds.   (O2599)

KITSON, Lieut.-Col. Paul Hengrave, O.B.E., *b.* 18 Jan. 1869; *s.* of Major G. P. Kitson, of Elm Lee, Winkfield; *m.* Ethel, *d.* of Hon. J. Meiring, of Bloemfontein. *Educ.:* L.I.C. Merton College. Served for thirty years in the Army and Police of Africa and India; through S. Af. War with S.A.L.H. and Roberts' Horse; gazetted Capt 1900; twice mentioned in despatches; commanded O.R.C. Police Force prior to it being taken over by S.A.C.; two medals and six clasps; on the outbreak of S.A. War, commanded two important districts; appointed J.P.; retrenched and returned to England on responsible government being granted; appointed to Indian Police. *War Work:* On the outbreak of European War was on leave; appointed for duty by War Office, Oct. 1914; organised and commanded three M.T. R.A.S.C. depots from 1915 to 1920; commanded Grove Park Depot (the largest in England) from 1918 until it was closed down in 1920; promoted Major 1915; Lieut.-Col. 1918, twice mentioned in despatches; during 'bus and railway strike assisted to organise lorry service; had command of 1000 men after the explosion at T.N.T. works Silvertown; organised and conducted the R.A.S.C., M.T. display at Naval and Military Tournament, Olympia, 1920; holds the Indian Durbar medal for special service during His Majesty's tour in India in 1912. *Club:* R.A.C.   (O7358)

KITSON, Major Walter Frederick Clifford, O.B.E., R.A.S.C., (T.).

KITTERMASTER, Harold Baxter, O.B.E.

KITTOE, Lieut -Col. Montagu Francis Markham Sloane, O.B.E., T.D., *b.* 1873; *s.* of late Capt. Markham Robinson Kittoe, late 106th (Durham) L.I.; grandson of late Major M. Kittoe, Bengal Native Infty., of Coddenham, Suffolk; *m.* Blanche Margaret Paton, *d.* of J. G. Scott, of Southport. *Educ.:* Chatham House, Ramsgate, and Middle Temple. Stockbroker. Some years on Essex County T.F. Association. *War Work:* Lieut.-Col. comdg. 1/10th London Regt., subsequently Director, R.M.L. Dept., Ministry of Munitions, and later Acting Controller, R.M. Disposal Dept., Disposal Board. *Addresses:* The Woodlands, Harrow-on-the-Hill; Newlands, Hook Heath, Woking. *Club:* Junior Army and Navy.   (O3789)

KLEIN, Major Adrian Bernard Leopold, M.B.E., *b.* 1 Sept. 1892; *s.* of Herman Klein, of 40, Avenue Road, Regent's Park, London; *m.* Angela Edith, *d.* of Admiral John Brackenbury, C.B., C.M.G. *Educ.:* Stevens' Institute of Technology, N.Y.; Horace Mann School, N.Y.; Slade School; London University. Artist and Scientist. Adviser on Colour Physics, the Calico Printers' Association, Manchester; Director, the Sheringham Daylight, Ltd., etc. *War Work:* Enlisted in Artists' Rifles Sept. 1914; received commission in 1st Batt. Norfolk Regt., June, 1915; wounded, Sept. 1915; Commanded Experimental Dept. the Camouflage School, R.E., 1916–19. *Address:* 32, The Pryors, East Heath Road, Hampstead. *Clubs:* Chelsea Arts; Art Workers' Guild.   (M3281)

KLEINENBERG, Maude Ellen, Mrs., M.B.E.

KLERCK, Major Willem Jan, O.B.E.

KLITZ, Wilfrid Robert, M.B.E., *b.* 16 May, 1883; *s.* of William Lawson Klitz, of Lymington, Hampshire; *m.* Dora Kathleen, *d.* of the late H. E. Welsh, of Wimbledon. *Educ.:* Gillingham Grammar School, Dorset; Byron House School, Ealing. Manager of Messrs. Eastwood and Holt's (Dunster House, Mincing Lane, E.C.) Fur Dept.; Brokers to the War Office for the purchase of goat and sheep skins and other fur and wool skins, etc., of which many millions were bought; subsequently acted in same capacity to Disposals Board for sale of surplus stock; originated the use of goatskin coats in the British Army; assisted in designing same; suggested various processes which were followed for adapting fur and wool skins to military uses. *Address:* Dorwil Cottage, Avenue Road, Epsom.   (M640)

KNAPP, Arthur Rowland, C.B.E., *b.* 10 Dec. 1870; *s.* of Lieut.-Col. C. B. Knapp; *m.* Florence Annie, *d.* of the late Dr. E. Moore, Canon of Canterbury. *Educ.:* Westminster and Christ Church. Indian Civil Service, 1891; served in Madras, Chief Sec. to Government and temporary member of Executive Council. *War Work:* In charge of the War Dept. of the Madras Government and organised the special war recruiting in the Madras Presidency. *Address:* Ootacamund, India. *Clubs:* Madras; East India United Service.   (C1974)

KNAPP, Lieut. E. C., M.B.E.

KNIBB, Frederick Charles, M.B.E.

KNIBBS, Lieut. Arthur Reginald, M.B.E.

KNIGHT, Capt. Alfred, M.B.E.

KNIGHT, Lieut. Alfred George, M.B.E., R.A.F.

KNIGHT, Lieut. and Qr.-Mr. Alfred James, M.B.E.

KNIGHT, Capt. and Qr.-Mr. Alfred John Hammond, O.B.E., R.A.M.C. (T.).

KNIGHT, Major Cecil Davenport, O.B.E.

KNIGHT, Lieut.-Col. Charles Louis William Norley, D.S.O., O.B.E.

KNIGHT, Christina Graham, M.B.E.

KNIGHT, Christopher Newman, O.B.E., B.A., *b.* 16 Feb. 1880; *s.* of John Cable Knight; *m.* Margaret Lawson, *d.* of John Follett. *Educ.:* Herne Bay College and Corpus Christi College, Oxford. Principal, Air Ministry. *Address:* The Birches, Durham Road, Bromley, Kent.   (O488)

KNIGHT, Enid Mary, M.B.E., *b.* 5 Jan. 1894; *d.* of the late Hugh Coleraine Knight, of Baron Grove, Mitcham; 2, South Square, Gray's Inn. *Educ.:* Wimbledon High School, Fontainebleau, Bournemouth, and abroad. Junior Administrative Assistant, Ministry of Health. *War Work:* Temporary Clerk, National Health Insurance Commission, 1915–17; Shipping Control Committee, 1917; personal clerk to Sir John Anderson, K.C.B. (Secretary, Ministry of Shipping), 1917–19; Ministry of Health, 1919. *Address:* 18, University Mansions, Putney, S.W. 15.   (M8721)

KNIGHT, Major Ernest, O.B.E., M.B. (Lond.), M.R.C.S., L.R.C.P., R.A.M.C.(T.). *b.* 29 April, 1870; *s.* of Jonas Knight, J.P., of Ashton-under-Lyne; *m.* Rachel, *d.* of William Jennison, of Manchester. *Educ.:* Manchester Grammar School, and Owen's College. Surgeon. *War Work:* Second in command of 1/3 West Lancashire Field Ambulance, 55th Division. *Address:* 45, Cross Street, Manchester. *Club:* Lytham; St. Anne's Golf.   (O5459)

KNIGHT, Ethel Corbet, O.B.E.

KNIGHT, Florence Mary, Mrs., M.B.E., *b.* 13 Feb. 1873; *d.* of Robert Dyson, of Rotherham; *m.* Henry Ernest, *s.* of Henry John Knight. *Educ.:* Westlands, Scarboro'; Royal Academy of Music. Rotherham Education Committee. *War Work:* Y.M.C.A. Munitions Canteen; Vice-Chairman, National Kitchen, Rotherham. *Address:* Brooklands, Rotherham.
                                                          (M8722)

KNIGHT, Frank, M.B.E.

KNIGHT, George, M.B.E.

KNIGHT, Lieut.-Col. Glen Alburn William James, O.B.E., Aust. A.M.C.

KNIGHT, Major James St. Pierre, O.B.E.

KNIGHT, John, M.B.E., *b.* 13 Oct. 1853; *s.* of John Knight, of High Wycombe, Bucks.; *m.* Martha Amelia, *d.* of George Kirlew, of Warthill, York. *Educ.:* National School, High Wycombe. Civil Servant, British Museum. *War Work:* Sailors' and Soldiers' Guide, Victoria Station, during the War giving 50 hours per week, meeting troop trains, conducting troops to the various railways and Rest Houses, performing innumerable other services to any soldiers or sailors passing through Victoria Station. *Address:* 111, Hughenden Road, High Wycombe, Bucks.   (M8723)

KNIGHT, 2nd Lieut. John Morgan, M.B.E., R.A.F.

KNIGHT, Capt. Robert Charles, M.B.E.

KNIGHT, Samuel Henry, M.B.E., R.N.

KNIGHT, Violet Hannah, M.B.E., *b.* 29 March, 1877, *d.* of the late George Edmunds, of Bethseda Place, Rogerstone, Mon.; *m.* the late Henry William Knight, *s.* of the late Thomas Knight, of Cliff House, Minster-on-Sea. *Educ.:* Grammar School, Pontlottyn, Glam. Matron-in-Chief and Superintendent Nurse, Union Workhouse and Infirmary, Hitchin, Herts. *War Work:* Two sick wards at the Infirmary were used for the military sick, containing 24 beds, from Feb. 1915 to March, 1919; during that period 2109 cases were admitted, medical and surgical; helped the medical officer with inoculations and vaccinations, and assisted at all sick parades and casualties during the day; in the absence of R.A.M.C. orderlies, undertook all duties until June, 1918, when the epidemic of influenza was raging, and R.A.M.C. orderlies were requisitioned.   (M8724)

KNIGHT, Capt. William Collins, O.B.E.

KNIGHTON, Thomas Spencer, M.B.E.

KNIGHTS, Capt. Alfred John Hammond, O.B.E., T.D., *b.* 1865; *s.* of John Hammond Knights, of Norfolk; *m.* Rose Maud, *d.* of Francis William Skipper, of London. *Educ.:* Wisbech, Cambs. *War Work:* Served with the 84th (2nd City of London) Field Ambulance, Aug. 1914 to Oct. 1919; with the 28th Division in Flanders, France, Egypt, Macedonia, Bulgaria, Turkey, and the Army of the Black Sea in Asia Minor; twice mentioned in despatches.   (O6493)

KNIGHTS, Capt. Henry Newton, M.B.E., J.P., M.P.

KNILL, Charles Henry, O.B.E., *b.* 1868; *s.* of Charles Knill, of Knighton. *Educ.:* Shrewsbury. Iron and Steel Manufacturer. *War Work:* O.C. Shrewsbury Remount Depot, Aug. 1914 to Sept. 1919. *Address:* Oak Lodge, Shrewsbury. *Clubs:* Shrewsbury, and Royal Automobile.
                                                          (O10788)

KNOCKER, George Stodart, M.B.E., M.I.Mech.E.' *b.* 1866; *s.* of Frederic Knocker, of Dover; *m.* Mary, *d.* of Francis Chamberlain, of Tottenham. *Educ.:* Haberdashers' School. Consulting Engineer. *War Work:* Volunteered

Oct. 1914 into Mechanical Transport, A.S.C. and served till Oct. 1915 in Flanders; joined Ministry of Munitions, Nov. 1915, and attached Area Office, Birmingham National Projectile Factory, Dudley, and in Dec. 1917, opened Area Office at Nottingham and appointed Superintending Engineer for East Midlands Area. *Clubs:* Royal Automobile; British Motor Boat. (M643)

KNOCKER, Reginald Edward, M.B.E., V.D., *b.* 13 Sept. 1870; *s.* of the late Sir E. W. N. Knocker, Kt., C.B., of Dover; *m.* Nora Violet, *d.* of W. W. Knocker, of Sevenoaks. *Educ.:* Dover College. Town Clerk of Dover; Registrar of the Cinque Ports. *War Work:* Duties as Town Clerk of Dover. *Address:* Cotswold, Kearsney, nr. Dover. *Club:* Royal Cinque Ports Yacht. (M2007)

KNOLLYS, Capt. the Hon. Edward George William Tyrwhitt ,M.B.E., D.F.C., 16th Bn. London Regt., *b.* 16 Jan. 1895; *e. s.* and heir of 1st Viscount Knollys, P.C., G.C.B., G.C.V.O., K.C.M.G. (*see* BURKE'S *Peerage*), Page of Honour to King Edward VII., 1904–10; Page of Honour to King George V., 1910–11; holds the Order of the Crown of Belgium. (M5999)

KNOLLYS, Ethelred Mary, Mrs., M.B.E.

KNOOP, Evelyn Elizabeth, M.B.E. (M8726)

KNOTT, Rev. Alfred Ernest, C.B.E., D.S.O., *b.* 1869. 1st Class Chap. to the Forces; served in the Tirah Campaign, 1897; France, 1914–15; Mesopotamia, 1916–19 (despatches twice). (C1109)

KNOTT, Major George Patrick, O.B.E., R.A.V.C.

KNOTT, Harry Ernest, O.B.E., J.P.

KNOWLAND, Capt. George Henry, O.B.E., I.A.

KNOWLES, Christine, O.B.E.

KNOWLES, Constance Mary, Lady, O.B.E., Lady of Grace, Order of the Hospital of St. John of Jerusalem, Nov. 1912; *d.* of James Augustus Elmslie, of 25, Norfolk Square, W.; *m.* Major-Gen. Sir Charles Benjamin, K.C.B., J.P., *s.* of John Knowles, of Trafford Bank House, Old Trafford. *War Work:* Commandant of Camberley Military Hospital, Camberley (130 Beds), Sept. 1914 to March, 1919, under the Aldershot Command; Vice-President Camberley and Windlesham Red Cross Division, and as such responsible for four women's and two men's detachments and for supervising the two Military Hospitals at Windlesham; served on County and Executive Committees and on all Sub-Committees throughout the War till Dec. 1919. *Address:* Eastfields, Camberley, Surrey. *Clubs:* Ladies' Athenæum. (O489)

KNOWLES, Charles James, M.B.E.

KNOWLES, Frank, C.B.E., *b.* 1865; *s.* of Joseph Knowles. War Office Meat Expert. *Address:* Shortlands, Kent. (C543)

KNOWLES, George Potter, M.B.E.

KNOWLES, George Shaw, O.B.E.

KNOWLES, Major James, O.B.E., 15th Hussars, *b.* 23 June, 1875; *s.* of Andrew Knowles, of Newent Court, nr. Gloucester (*see* BURKE'S *Landed Gentry*); *m.* Nancy, *d.* of William Hornibrook, of Bedford Square, London, W.C. *Educ.:* Eton. *War Work:* Assistant Military Secretary to G.O.C. Second Army, B.E.F., France; has Legion of Honour. *Address:* 31, Upper Hamilton Terrace, N.W. 8. *Clubs:* Cavalry; Army and Navy; Junior Carlton. (O2250)

KNOWLES, Kate Christine, O.B.E. *b.* 1890; *d.* of late Charles Julius Knowles, 17, Kensington Gore, and Linkenholt Manor, Hungerford, Berks. *Educ.:* At home. *War Work:* Founder and Hon. Treas. of British Prisoners of War Food Parcels and Clothing Fund, which started with 20 prisoners of war and at the date of Armistice had nearly 4,000 under its care; Founder and Chairman of Advisory After-Care Committee for British Prisoners of War; assisted ex-prisoners of war to find employment; visited cases in hospital; advanced sums of money pending Civil Liabilities Grants. *Address:* 17, Kensington Gore, London, S.W. 7. (O3791)

KNOWLES, Sir Lees, Bart., C.V.O., O.B.E., T.D., M.A., LL.M., D.L., Knight of Grace of St. John of Jerusalem, *b.* 16 Feb. 1857 (*see* BURKE'S *Peerage*); *s.* of John Knowles, D.L., J.P., of Westwood, Pendlebury; *m.* the Lady Nina, *y.d.* of the 10th Earl of Seafield (*see* BURKE'S *Peerage*). *Educ.:* Rugby School, and Trinity Coll., Cambridge. With his wife did much to alleviate the suffering of wounded soldiers; placed a large house at the disposal of a local doctor for hospital. endowed a bed at one of the hospitals in France, and also housed refugees; supplied a whole battalion with iodine capsules; canvassed for troops at the beginning of the war, and took special interest in the prisoners in camps in Germany; by correspondence, kept in touch with the Lancashire Fusiliers in all the camps, sending them supplies and cigarettes until that work was taken over by the Government. *Addresses:* Westwood, Pendlebury, and Turton Tower, Lancashire. *Clubs:* Carlton and Junior Carlton. (O10790)

KNOWLES, Thornton, O.B.E.

KNOWLING, Capt. Arthur Ernest George, O.B.E., M.A., *b.* 4 Feb. 1884; *s.* of Dr. E. M. Knowling, of Tenby; *m.* Ruth Geraldine, *d.* of the late Rev. Canon Mullins, of Grahamstown. *Educ.:* Cheltenham Coll.; New Coll., Oxford. Assistant Master at St. Andrews College, Grahamstown, S. Africa. *War Work:* Returned to England to join up, Dec. 1915; 2nd Lieut. R.A.S.C. May, 1916; attached D.D.S. and T.H.Q. 4th Army, 1917, France; Lieut. 1917; attached D.D.S. and T. 2nd Army, 1917–18, France and Belgium; Capt. 1918; mentioned in despatches. *Address:* St. Andrews College, Grahamstown, S. Africa. (O5462)

KNOX, Alice, Lady, M.B.E., *b.* 1855; 2nd *d.* of Sir Robert

Dundas, 1st Bart., of Arniston (*see* BURKE'S *Peerage*); *m.* Maj.-Gen. Sir William George Knox, K.C.B., who died 1916, *War Work:* Red Cross organisation. *Address:* 23, Cadogan Gardens, S.W. 3. (M2008)

KNOX, David Alexander, M.B.E.

KNOX, Capt. Errol Galbraith, M.B.E., Aust F.C., and R.A.F.

KNOX, Ethel Laura, Mrs. Stuart George, O.B.E.

KNOX, Brig.-Gen. Henry Owen, C.M.G., C.I.E., C.B.E., *b.* 1874; *s.* of the late Rt. Hon. Sir Ralph Henry Knox, P.C., K.C.B.; *m.* 1st, 1899, Muriel Lucy, who *d.* 1907, *d.* of the late Sir Owen Roberts, D.C.L., LL.D., F.S.A.; 2nd, 1910, Elsie Caroline, *d.* of the late Harry Harker, of Hurlingham Lodge, Hurlingham. Entered S. Staffordshire Regt. 1896; retired, 1914; Major Reserve of Officers, Army Ser. Corps; Hon. Brig.-Gen. Served in S. Africa, 1899–1901 (despatches, Queen's medal with four clasps); Great War, 1914–16; first in Flanders (despatches), and subsequently at Gallipoli, as A.Q.M.S., Australian and New Zealand Army Corps; Mesopotamia, 1916–17, as D.Q.M.G. (despatches), Order of St. Anne of Russia); Q.M.C., New Zealand Mil. Forces, 1911–14; joined Comdg. Engineer-in-Chief's Depart. Admiralty, 1918; became Chief of Staff, 1919. *Address:* Burwood, Upper Warlingham, Surrey. *Club:* United Service. (C2355)

KNOX, Lieut.-Col. James Stuart, O.B.E., late E. Yorks. Regt., *b.* 15 July, 1864; *s.* of Major James Knox, Governor of Wandsworth Prison; *m.* Ursula Mary Iremonger, *d.* of Francis Watts, of Newton Abbot. *Educ.:* King's School, Gloucester, and abroad. *p.s.c.*; Commander of a company of cadets at R.M.C.; now Inspector of H.M. Prisons. *War Work:* A.A. & Q.M.G., 41st Div., and after was A.A.G. with the A.I.F. *Address:* 106, Belgrave Road, S.W. 1. (O7360)

KNOX, Rev. John, O.B.E.

KNOX, Capt. John Frederick, O.B.E., R.N.

KNOX, Eng.-Lieut.-Comm. Robert G., O,B,E., R.N.

KNOX, Sara, M.B.E.

KNUDSEN, Sir Karl Fredrik, K.B.E.; *s.* of David Faye Knudsen, of Kristiania, Norway; *m.* Anne, *d.* of Alexander McArthur, of Kilmartin, Argyllshire. *Educ.:* High School, Kristiania, and Commercial College, Kristiania. Managing Director of H. Clarkson and Co., Ltd.; Director of British Bank of Northern Commerce; Member of Council and Past President of Norwegian Chamber of Commerce. *War Work:* During the war acted as unofficial intermediary between Norwegian shipowners and the Allies in concluding and executing shipping agreements; also presented the Allies' cause by writing in Norwegian Press and by public speaking in Norway. *Addresses:* 21, Queensberry Place, S.W. 7; Little Stoke Manor, North Stoke, Oxon. *Club:* National Liberal; Junior Athenæum. (K389)

KNUDSEN, Capt. Orric Joures, O.B.E.

KNUTFORD, Lilian May, Mrs. M.B.E. Had special charge of blinded men at St. Dunstan's who have also been crippled. (M10325)

KNUTHSEN, Major Louis Francis, O.B.E., R.A.M.C.

KNYVETT, Rev. Carey Frederick, O.B.E.

KNYFTON, Edith Mary, Mrs. GRAVES-, O.B.E.; *m.* late Major Reginald Benett Graves-Knyfton Somerset Light Infantry. *War Work:* Vice-President, B.R.C.S., in Weston-super-Mare district. *Address:* The Manor, Uphill, Weston-super-Mare. (O1561)

KOE, Col. Lancelot Charles, C.B.E., *b.* 1862; Formerly Lieut.-Col. and Brevet Col. R.G.A.; served in the Soudan Expedition, 1884–85 (medal with clasp, bronze star); Hazara Expedition, 1888 (medal with clasp); Benin Expedition, 1897 (severely wounded, medal with clasp); Great War, 1914–19 (despatches twice). (C1650)

KOHAN, Capt. Charles Mendel, O.B.E., B.A., F.S.S., *b.* 15 Nov. 1884. *Educ.:* Manchester Grammar School and Trinity Coll. Camb. Barrister-at-Law. *War Work:* Obtained commission in Royal Field Artillery, Sept. 1914; Adjutant, 291st Brigade R.F.A., Nov. 1917 to March, 1918; G.S.O. 3 H.Q. Fourth Army, Sept 1918 to March 1919. *Addresses:* 20, Albion Street, Hyde Park, W. 2; Farrar's Building, Temple, E.C. 4; Granby Lodge, Stanton-in-Peak, Derbyshire. *Clubs:* New Oxford and Cambridge; United. (O5465)

KONSTAM, Edwin Max, C.B.E., K.C., *b.* 10 June, 1870; *m.* Mary Beatrix, *d.* of Rev. Lewis Haig Loyd. *Educ.:* Marlborough; King's Coll. Camb. Indian Civil Service (Bengal, L.P.) 1890–1902. *War Work:* Hon. Sec. Shoreditch L. R. Committee, Prince of Wales' Fund, 1914; Hon. Sec. Shoreditch War Pensions Sub-committee, 1916; served in Food Production Dept. Board of Agriculture, from Jan. 1917; Director of Land Drainage, Ministry of Agriculture, Sept. 1918 to Dec. 1919. *Addresses:* 19, Chapel Street, Belgrave Square, S.W. 1; 2, Mitre Court Buildings, Temple, E.C. 4. *Club:* Oxford and Cambridge. (C2739)

KOPETZKY, Adolf, M.B.E. For services in connection with the Jewish War Refugees' Committee and the Russian Dependants' Committee. (M10326)

KOPPEL, Percy Alexander, C.B.E., *b.* 3 Nov. 1876. *s.* of B. Koppel, of 9, Wetherby Gardens; *m.* Dorothy, *d.* of J. C. im Thurn, of 5, Collingham Gardens. *Educ.:* Bradfield College; Magdalen Coll., Oxford. Inner Temple, called to Bar 1910, Northern Circuit; Law Clerk, National Health Insurance Commission (England), 1912; Prince of Wales's Fund, 1914; Wellington House Committee, 1914; News Dept. of Department of Information, 1917; Political Intelligence Dept. of Foreign Office, 1918; First Secretary in H.M. Diplomatic

Service and Foreign Office, 1920. *Address*: 5, Sumner Place, S.W. 7. *Clubs*: Oxford and Cambridge; Leander. (C2740)

KORN, George Ernest, M.B.E.

KOTAH, H.H. Maharo Sir Umed Singh Bahadur of, G.C.S.I., G.C.I.E., G.B.E.

KRABBE, Capt. Charles Frederick, O.B.E.

KRABBE, Capt. Clarence Brehmer, O.B.E., R.A.F.

KRANE, John, O.B.E.

KROHN, Alice, Mrs., O.B.E.; *d.* of Henry Moreing, of Braidwood, N.S.W.; *m.* Herman Alexander, *s.* of Nicolas Peter, of Grahamstown, S.A. Vice-President and Member of Executive Committee, Essex Branch, Royal Red Cross Society; Hon. Sec. for Victoria League (Essex Branch); Member of Demobilisation Committee, Essex Branch, Royal Red Cross Society. *War Work*: Lectured and examined for Red Cross and trained V.A.D.s; organised and ran River-court Hospital for 5 years; organised Red Cross Working Parties and collections for Our Day, for Comforts Fund for Essex troops, and for Jewel Fund. *Address*: Maldon Court, Maldon, Essex. *Clubs*: Ladies' Empire; Ladies' Service.
(O10792)

KROHN, Herman Alexander, C.B.E., J.P., D.L.; *s.* of Nicolas Peter Krohn, of Grahamstown, S. Africa; *m.* 1st, Amy Constance, *d.* of Col. Meadows Taylor, C.S.I.; 2nd, Alice, *d.* of Henry Moreing, of Braidwood, N.S. Wales. *Educ.*: Upping-ham and Cambridge. Vice-chairman, Essex Territorial Association, 1914–16; Chairman, Building and Ranges Com-mittee, since 1908; Alderman of Maldon, 1907 (Mayor 7 times); Assistant Director, Essex Branch, Royal Red Cross Society. *War Work*: Recruiting, etc., for Essex Territorial Association; Red Cross Hospital Management, etc.; Chairman, Maldon Military Tribunal; Member, Essex Committee, Prince of Wales' Fund. *Address*: Maldon Court, Maldon, Essex. *Club*: Thatched House.

KUHNE, Major Carl Hans, D.S.O., O.B.E., R.A.S.C., a Dep. Assist. Director of Transport; served in the Great War, 1914–19 (despatches). (O5466)

KUHNER, Charles Henry, M.B.E. Lately Hon. Sec. and Treasurer of Southminster and Denzil Hundred Sub-Committee of the Essex Local War Pensions Committee.
(M10327)

KUNNING, Arthur Blandford, M.B.E.

KYDD, Oswald Jensen, M.B.E. Master of s.s. "Austrat-ford." (M10250g)

KYLE, Phillip Kyle, O.B.E.

KYNOCH, Minnie, M.B.E.

LA BROOY, Amelia Fanny, Mrs., O.B.E., *d.* of Robert Johnston, of Sidcup; *m.* Justin Theodore, *s.* of Francis Frederick Theodore, of Ceylon. *Educ.*: Private Schools. *War Work*: Y.M.C.A. Canteens, Woolwich; Vice-President and Head of the Voluntary Workers Y.M.C.A. Emergency Canteen, Silvertown; Girls' Clubs, Woolwich; Member of the Woolwich Advisory Committee on Women's and Children's Welfare. *Address*: 20, Eldersllie Road, Eltham. (O10049)

LACEY, Ada, M.B.E.

LACEY, Ellen, M.B.E.; *d.* of Thomas Lacey, of Highbury, London, N. *Educ.*: Frances Mary Buss Schools. Late Matron, Heath Memorial Convalescent Home for Men, Llanfair-fechan, North Wales. *War Work*: Lady Superintendent in Army Pay Dept. at Dover, 1915–19; mentioned in despatches, Sept. 1917. *Address*: 21, Aubert Park, Highbury, London, N. 5. (M8728)

LACEY, Henry Cubitt, M.B.E.

LACEY, Capt. Samuel Barningham, O.B.E., Aust. A.S.C.

LACEY, Lieut.-Comm. Solomon James, O.B.E.

LACEY, William Henry Westwood, O.B.E. Manager, Checekan Oilfields, Baku. (O11790b)

LACK, Edwin, M.B.E., A.M.I.E.E., *b.* 12 Sept. 1865; *s.* of Robert West Lack, of Hull; *m.* Louisa, *d.* of George Blashill, of Hull. Assistant Staff Engineer, Engineer-in-Chief's Office, G.P.O., London. *Addresses*: General Post Office, London, E.C. 1; 61, Adelaide Road, Brockley, S.E. 4. (M644)

LACKIE, William Walker, C.B.E., *b.* July 1869; *s.* of David Lackie, J.P., of Montrose; *m.* Anne Robson, *d.* of William Robson, of Jarset House. *Educ.*: Montrose Academy; Grammar School, Aberdeen; University College, Dundee; University, Glasgow. Engineer and Manager, Glasgow Corporation Electricity Dept; Electricity Commissioner. *War Work*: Supply of electrical energy to munition works in the Clyde area; Princess Louisa Hospital, Engineering Equip-ment; Georgetown Shell-Filling Factory, Engineering Equip-ment. *Address*: Gwydyr House, Whitehall, London. *Clubs*: St. Stephen's; Conservative (Glasgow). (C989)

LACROIX, Capt. Lucien, O.B.E., Can. A.M.C.

LAFONE, Rear-Adm. Albert Sumner, C.B.E., F.R.Z.S., R.N. (ret.), *b.* 14 Oct. 1863; *s.* of the late Alfred Lafone, J.P., of Hanworth Park, Middlesex. *Educ.*: Privately; H.M.S. "Britannia." *Address*: Sherborne St. John, Hants. *Club*: Naval and Military. (C899)

LA FONTAINE, Capt. Edward Leonard, M.B.E.

LA FONTAINE, Capt. Frederick Charles, M.B.E.

LAGERWALL, Capt. Frank Alfred, M.B.E.

LAIDLAW, Lieut. John Brown, O.B.E., R.E.

LAIDLAY, Eileen, Mrs., M.B.E.; *m.* John E., J.P., *s.* of John Laidley, of Seacliff, North Berwick, East Lothian. *War Work*: Vice-President for Dirleton and Gullane, County of Hadding-

---

tonshire, East Lothian. *Address*: Inverell, Dirleton, Hadding-tonshire. *Club*: Queen's (Edinburgh). (M8730)

LAIDLEY, Ethel, Mrs., M.B.E.

LAING, Andrew, C.B.E. Director of Wallsend Slipway and Engineering Co., and of Newcastle and Gateshead Gas Co.; Dep. Chairman Walker and Wallsend Gas Co. *Address*: 15, Osborne Road, Newcastle-on-Tyne. (C38)

LAING, Major George, O.B.E., R.A.F.

LAING, George Smith, M.B.E.

LAING, Hugh, O.B.E.

LAING, John George, M.B.E.

LAIRD, Lieut. and Qr.-Mr. Frederick Nicholás, M.B.E., A.I.F.

LAIRD, Nellie, Mrs., M.B.E.

LAIRD, Roy Macgregor, C.B.E. Dist. Supt. of Ship Repairs, Liverpool and Manchester Dist., Ministry of Shipping.

LAIRD, William, C.B.E., L.R.C.P., L.R.C.S., *b.* 18 Nov. 1881; *s.* of Robert Laird, of Larkhall, Scotland; *m.* Mary, *d.* of Robert Mulholland, of Glasgow. *Educ.*: Glasgow University; St. Mungo's College, and Anderson's College, Glasgow. Surgeon-in-Charge, Orthopædic Annexe, and Artifi-cial Limbs Repair Depot (Ministry of Pensions); Dispensary Surgeon, Royal Infirmary, Glasgow. *War Work*: Lieut., R.A.M.C.; Surgical Specialist, 48th General Hospital, Salonica; Visiting Surgeon, Orthopædic Dept., Bellahouston Hospital; Visiting Surgeon, Springburn Red Cross Hospital, and Shakespeare Hospital, Glasgow. *Address*: 18, Royal Crescent, Glasgow, W. *Club*: Scottish Constitutional (Glas-gow). (C2743)

LAJOIE, Louis Patrick, M.B.E.

LAKE, Ada Louise, O.B.E.; *d.* of Henry G. Lake. *Educ.*: Privately. *War Work*: Lady Superintendent of the Sailors' and Soldiers' Free Buffet, Charing Cross Station; started as a worker Nov. 1914 and was made Lady Superintendent June, 1916. *Address*: 2, Greville Place, Kilburn Priory, N.W. 6. (O10705)

LAKE, Alfred Samuel, M.B.E.

LAKE, Lieut. Atwell Henry, O.B.E.

LAKE, Bruce Lancelot, O.B.E. (O9694)

LAKE, Lieut. Ernest, O.B.E., R.E.

LAKELAND, Capt. William John, M.B.E.

LAKER, Alfred, M.B.E.

LAKIN, Capt. Colin Arthur, O.B.E., I.A.R.O.

LAMAN, Capt. and Qr.-Mr. Ernest Kirkland, M.B.E.

LAMB, Andrew, O.B.E.

LAMB, Brydon, M.B.E.

LAMB, Major Claude Carnegie, O.B.E., Black Watch, *b.* 8 Jan. 1881; *s.* of David I. Lamb, of St. Andrews; *m.* Louise Harriet Mary, *d.* of Col. W. J. Parker, of Indian Staff Corps. *Educ.*: Trinity College, Glenalmond, and Sandhurst. *War Work*: Held Staff Appointments; Brigade-Major, South Mid-land Reserve Brigade and Light Reserve Brigade. *Address*: 6, Playfair Terrace, St. Andrews. *Club*: Royal and Ancient Golf (St. Andrews). (O8354)

LAMB, Lieut.-Col. David Ogilvy Wright, O.B.E., *p.s.c.,* 10th Lancers, *b.* 29 Jan. 1885; *s.* of D. I. Lamb, of St. Andrews, N.B. *Educ.*: Trinity College, Glenalmond, and R.M.C., Sandhurst. First commissioned Jan. 1904; appointed to Indian Army, April, 1905; Captain, Jan. 1913; Major, Feb. 1918; Asst. Instructor, Cav. School, 1913–14; Adjutant, Behar Light Horse, 1915; Brigade-Major, Allahabad, 1915; D.A.A.G., Army Headquarters, 1916 and in 1919; extra A.D.C. to Governor of Bengal, 1920. *War Work*: Served with 10th Lancers and as D.A.A.G., G.H.Q. Mesopotamia; D.A.Q.M.G. in Waziristan Expedition, 1917; Deputy Inspector-General of Communications, Khyber Line, in 3rd Afghan War. *Clubs*: Cavalry; Caledonian. (O4228)

LAMB, Dorothy, M.B.E.

LAMB, Edwin Daniel, M.B.E., R.N.

LAMB, Emily Frances Edith, M.B.E., *d.* of the late Edward Charles Lamb, of Bengal, India. *Educ.*: Privately; Cambridge (Higher) Certificate, Gold, Silver and Bronze Medals for Elocution. Private Secretary; Clerk to the Joint Council of the Order of St. John and the British Red Cross Society. *War Work*: Private Secretary to the Vice-Chairman and to the Organising Secretary of the British Red Cross Society since the commencement of the War; produced several plays in aid of the British Red Cross Society. *Address*: 103, Ebury Road, Rickmansworth, Herts. (M8734)

LAMB, Major Frank de Villiers, C.B.E., *b.* 1880; *s.* of John de Villiers Lamb, of Sydney, N.S. Wales. Hon. Major Australian Imperial Forces. *War Work*: Australian Branch of British Red Cross Soc. in Egypt, Malta, and England. (C362)

LAMB, Capt. Malcolm Henry Mortimer, O.B.E., M.C. (O1565)

LAMBERT, Arthur Bradley, C.B.E., *b.* 3 April 1858; *s.* of the late Henry Lambert, J.P., of Hampstead; *m.* Emma Matilda, *d.* of the late Charles Jones, M.I.C.E., of Ealing. *Educ.*: Privately. Original Member of Council and Executive Committee of Bribery and Secret Commissions Prevention League (Incorp.), 1906; Fellow of Royal Colonial Institute since 1909. *War Work*: Section Superintendent (Voluntary) Royal Army Clothing Department, 1914–18. *Addresses*: 18, Wood Street, E.C. 2; 232, St. James' Court, S.W. 1. *Clubs*: Junior Athenæum; Royal Automobile. (C37)

LAMBERT, Major Bertram, O.B.E., R.E.

LAMBERT, Blanche Sarah, M.B.E., 4th *d.* of Henry Lambert, late General Manager, Great Western Railway. *Educ.*: Princess Helena College, Ealing. Late Departmental

Secretary, Y.W.C.A. *War Work:* Secretary, War Workers' Welfare Committee of the Young Women's Christian Association. *Address:* 39, Biddulph Mansions, Elgin Avenue, W. 9. (M2012)

LAMBERT, Florence Barrie, C.B.E., M.B., B.S., D.P.H.; *d.* of Thomas Henry Lambert. *Educ.:* France, and London. School of Medicine for Women. Medical Officer, Ministry of Health. *War Work:* Inspector Military Massage and Electrical Services; Member, Electro-Medical Committe, War Office; Member of Electro-personnel Committee, War Office; Member of Joint War Office and Pensions Committee for Massage Personnel. *Address:* 10, Seymour Street, W. 1. *Club:* Forum. (C3080)

LAMBERT, Capt. Francis John, O.B.E., 9th D.L.I. (T.), *b.* 31 Aug. 1880; *s.* of Thomas Lambert, of Lintz Green House, Lintz Green, Co. Durham; *m.* Ena, *d.* of Wm. Patterson, J.P., of Blaydon-upon-Tyne. *Educ.:* Newcastle-upon-Tyne; Harrogate, and London. Solicitor to N.S.P.C.C.; Solicitor to Northumberland Division, Comrades of Great War. *War Work:* Mobilised 4 Aug. 1914; demobilised 31 March, 1919. *Address:* Lintz Green House, Lintz Green, Co. Durham. *Clubs:* Conservative; Pen and Pallet (Newcastle-upon-Tyne). (O3140)

LAMBERT, Major George Herbert, O.B.E.

LAMBERT, Henrietta Isabella, Mrs., M.B.E., *b.* 1873; *d.* of George Lowther, of Swillington House, Leeds, Yorks; *m.* Robert, *s.* of Robert Lambert, of Weston, Surrey. Commandant Shropshire 26, V.A.D. *War Work:* Mobilised, Jan. 1915 until March, 1919, and did whole-time work at her V.A.D. Hospital in Whitchurch, Salop. *Address:* Ash Grove, Whitchurch, Salop. (M8735)

LAMBERT, Surgeon-Lieut. John, O.B.E., R.N.

LAMBERT, Lieut.-Col. John Hamilton, O.B.E., R.M.L.I.

LAMBERT, Miriam Constance, M.B.E., *b.* 2 June 1884; *d.* of the late John Henry Lambert, of Aggard, Co. Galway. *Educ.:* Privately. *War Work:* Worked for Scottish Women's Hospitals for Foreign Service, 1916–17; Deputy Administrator, Q.M.A.A.C. (Overseas), 1917–20. *Address:* Redmount, Ballinasloe, Ireland. *Club:* Ladies' Caledonian (Edinburgh). (M3142)

LAMBERT, Octavius Edward, M.B.E.

LAMBERT, Olive Mary, Mrs., M.B.E.

LAMBERT, Lieut. Roger Uredale, M.B.E., R.F.A. (S.R.).

LAMBERT, Stanley Harrison, O.B.E.

LAMBERT, Major Thomas Erskine, M.B.E., R.A.S.C.

LAMBERT, Capt. William Clement, O.B.E.

LAMBERT, Major Arthur WARREN-, O.B.E., R.A.S.C.

LAMBIE, Lieut.-Col. George, M.B.E.

LAMBIE, Robert, O.B.E., *b.* 18 April, 1848. Member for Larkhall Division of Lanarkshire County Council, 1889–1919. *War Work:* Member of Naval and Military War Pensions Committee in Lanarkshire; Food Control Committee; Military Tribunal; took part in voluntary War Recruiting Campaign in Lanarkshire, 1915–16. *Address:* 446, Victoria Road, Queen's Park, Glasgow. (O10797)

LAMBOURN, Frank Harper, M.B.E., *b.* 27 March 1878; *t.* of George Lambourn, of Oxford; *m.* Eleanor, *d.* of R. V. Horsfall, of Slaithwaite. *Educ.:* Oxford High School. *War Work:* Superintendent of Royal Alexandra Navy Victualling Yard, Haulbowline, Ireland. *Address:* Midleton Park, Queenstown. *Club:* Royal Cork Yacht. (M3790)

LAMBOURN, Nora May, Mrs., M.B.E.; *b.* 2 Sept. 1880; *d.* of William Cox Brotherton, of Woodstock, Oxon.; *m.* George Ernest Lambourn. *War Work:* In Suri, Birbhum, Bengal and Dacca, Bengal; at the latter place Secretary to the Dacca Ladies' War Fund. (M7121)

LAMBOURNE, Christopher, M.B.E. (M10250h)

LAMBTEN, Dorothy, M.B.E.

LAMBTON, Brevet Lieut.-Col. George Charles, D.S.O., O.B.E., *b.* 10 Nov. 1872; *s.* of Lieut.-Col. Francis William Lambton. *Educ.:* Wellington. *War Work:* Commanded 2nd Worc. Regt., 29th R.F. (T.R.), 1st Norfolks (Temp.), 52nd Bn. Notts. and Derby and 11th Leicesters. *Address:* Brownstede, Pembroke. *Club:* Junior United Service. (O7365)

LAMING, Evelyn Hamar, Mrs., M.B.E.

LAMING, Major Henry Thornton, D.S.O., O.B.E., *b.* 28 July 1863; *s.* of the late James Laming, of Manor House, Richmond, Surrey; *m.* Ella Lœtitia, *d.* of the late Robert Cunliffe, D.L., of 17, Inverness Terrace. *Educ.:* Eton and Sandhurst. Served in 18th Hussars, 1883–1903. *War Work:* Second in Command, 11th and 5th Reserve Cavalry Regiments, Oct. 1914 to July 1919. *Address:* The Knoll, Barton-under-Needwood. *Clubs:* Naval and Military; Cavalry. (O7366)

LAMING, Richard Valentine, O.B.E., *b.* 30 Dec. 1887; *s.* of William Laming, of Rotterdam. *Educ.:* Gymnasium Erasmianum, Rotterdam, and Amsterdam University. Commercial Secretary, H.M. Legation, The Hague. *War Work:* Represented the Restriction of Enemy Supplies Department of the Ministry of Blockade in Holland. *Address:* 21a, Gavastraat, The Hague. (O10798)

LAMONT, Hellen, M.B.E. (M10452)

LAMONT, James, M.B.E.

LAMONT, John Macnab, M.B.E., J.P.

LAMPE, Capt. and Qr.-Mr. Frederick Nicholas, M.B.E., A.I.F.

LAMPSON, Curtis Walter, C.B.E., *b.* 18 Aug. 1875; *m.* 7 July, 1908, Hilda, *d.* of Sir David Baird, 3rd Bart., of Newbyth (*see* BURKE'S *Peerage*), B.A. Magdalen Coll. Oxford. *Address:* Hampton Lodge, Seale, Farnham. *Club:* Travellers'.

LANCE, Octavius, M.B.E., Chevalier of the Legion of Honour, *b.* 25 Dec. 1876; *s.* of W. H. Lance, of London; *m.* Mabel Elsie, *d.* of the late — Coleman, of Wisbech. *Educ.:* United Westminster School, Westminster. Officer of Accounts, H.M. Dockyard, Portsmouth. *War Work:* Employed in Admiralty Service. *Address:* 104, Palmerston Road, Southsea. *Clubs:* Union of Malta; Royal Portsmouth Corinthian Yacht. (M2013)

LAND, Col. William Henry, C.B.E., V.D.

LANDAU, Capt. Henry, O.B.E.

LANDAU, Herman, O.B.E.

LANDELLS, Helena Jane, M.B.E.

LANDER, Capt. Arthur, O.B.E.

LANDER, Capt. Edward Leonard, M.B.E., R.A.F.

LANDER, Richard Gilbert, M.B.E.

LANDER, Sidney Montem, M.B.E.

LANDON, Lieut. and Brevet Major Arthur Henry Whittington, O.B.E., M.C., Croix de Guerre, *b.* 13 Jan. 1889; *s.* of Major-Gen. Sir Frederick Landon, K.C.M.G., C.B., of 74, Gloucester Place, London, W. 1 (*see* BURKE'S *Peerage*); *m.* Elsie Mary, *d.* of J. Gillanders, of Drumlithie, Purley, Surrey. *Educ.:* Malvern; Worcester Coll., Oxford. Lieut. (Brevet Major) in the Royal Canadian Regt., Permanent Force of Canada. *War Work:* A.D.C. to Major-Gen. H. J. S. Landon, C.B., C.M.G., G.O.C. 9th (Scottish) Division, B.E.F., March, 1915; Staff Capt. 19th Infantry Bde., B.E.F., July, 1916; D.A.A.G. Headquarters, XVIIIth Army Corps, B.E.F., Jan. 1918; D.A.Q.M.G. at G.H.Q., Allied Forces, Archangel, July, 1919. *Addresses:* Wolseley Barracks, London, Ontario, Canada. *Club:* Junior Naval and Military. (O6017)

LANDON, Lieut.-Col. Cyril, O.B.E., M.C. (O11750)

LANDON, Paymaster Lieut.-Comm. Edward Cyril Turton, O.B.E., R.D., R.N.R., *b.* 31 Aug. 1877; *s.* of Frederic George Landon, M.A., of St. John's, S.E.; *m.* Daisy Herbert, *d.* of William Henry Evans, of Sheerness. *Educ.:* City of London School. Bank of England Clerk; Member of the Beddington and Wallington Urban District Council. *War Work:* On Naval Transport Staff at St. Nazaire, Dunkerque, Deptford and Copenhagen. *Address:* Glenlyon, Carew Road, Wallington, Surrey. (O9243)

LANDON, Lieut.-Col. Joseph Herbert Arthur, D.S.O., O.B.E., R.A.F. Served in the Great War, 1914–19 (wounded, despatches). (O8131)

LANDON, Capt. Joseph Whittington, M.B.E.

LANDON, Katharine Ann Brenda, M.B.E., *b.* 13 April 1879; *d.* of the late H. W. L. Landon, of Kenmore, Exmouth, Devon. *War Work:* Exmouth V.A. Hospital, 1914–19, as Quartermaster from Oct. 1914 and as Assistant Commandant (and Quartermaster) from April, 1917 to 1919. *Address:* Kenmore, Exmouth, Devon. *Club:* V.A.D. Ladies'. (M31)

LANDRY, Capt. Pierre Alfred, O.B.E., R.A.F.

LANE, Charlotte Jane, Lady Arbuthnot, M.B.E., Lady of Grace of St. John of Jerusalem; *d.* of J. Briscoe of London; *m.* Sir William Arbuthnot Lane, C.B., M.B., M.S. (Lond.), F.R.C.S. (Eng.). *Address:* 21, Cavendish Square, W. 1. (M2014)

LANE, Daniel de Moura, M.B.E.

LANE, Ernest, M.B.E.

LANE, Francis Lawrence, O.B.E., *b.* 1856; *s.* of John Lane, of The Limes, 27, Charnwood Street, Derby; *m.* 1885, Helen, *d.* of William John Horton, of Warrington. *Educ.:* Great Eastern Railway Mechanics' Institute. Engineer, and Managing Director Leeds Forge Co. (Limited). *Address:* Maryland House, Grosvenor Road, Leeds. *Clubs:* St. Stephen's; Constitutional; Royal Automobile. (O1566)

LANE, Major Frank Bernard, O.B.E., 8th Cavalry I.A.; *b.* 16 Aug. 1879; *s.* of Wilmot Lane, of Hove. *Educ.:* Shrewsbury School and Sandhurst. *War Work:* Mesopotamian Field Force. (O8725)

LANE, Lieut.-Col. Frederick, O.B.E.

LANE, Capt. Harold Arthur, O.B.E.

LANE, Capt. Harry James, O.B.E., Aust. A.S.C.

LANE, Harry Joseph, M.B.E.

LANE, Harry Philip Parnell, C.B.E., M.V.O., *b.* 1870; *s.* of the late Major Henry Eyre Wyatt Lane, R.M.L.I., of Seaton, Devon; *m.* 1903, Flora Emma, *d.* of the late Capt. Edmund Richard Peel, of Rock Ferry, Cheshire. Sometime in Essex, Devon, Kent, and Liverpool Police Forces; appointed Chief Constable of Lancashire, 1913. Has King's Police Medal. *Addresses:* Ellel Hall, Lancaster; County Constabulary Office, Preston. *Club:* County (Lancaster). (C544)

LANE, Helena, Mrs., M.B.E.

LANE, Capt. Henry Gerald Elliot, C.B.E., R.N., *b.* 1875; *m.* 1901, Rachel Elizabeth, *d.* of the late Adm. Sir John Reginald Thomas Fullerton, G.C.V.O. Served in the Great War, 1914–19.

LANE, Margaret, Mrs., M.B.E., Q.M.A.A.C.

LANE, Col. Samuel Wellington, C.B.E., R.A. (ret.) Served on the N.W. Frontier of India, 1897–98 (medal with clasp); S. Africa, 1900–2 (despatches, Brevet Lieut.-Col., Queen's medal with three clasps, King's medal with two clasps); Great War, 1914–19 (despatches). (C1652)

LANE, Lieut.-Col. William Byam, C.I.E., C.B.E., M.R.C.S. Eng., L.R.C.P. Lond.; *s.* of Edgar Henry Lane, of Antigua; *m.* 1896, Edith Kate Westlake Reindorp. Indian Med. Ser. Served with Hazara Expedition, 1891 (medal with clasp); Waziristan Expedition, 1894–95 (clasp); Chitral Relief Force, 1895 (medal with clasp); Mesopotamia, 1916–18, as Inspector of Disciplinary Labour Corps. (C1110)

LANE, Capt. Wilhelm Heinreich Christian Ahrens, M.B.E.

LANE, Col. William MOORE-, C.B.E., *b.* 1861 ; Formerly Col. R.A.O.C. ; served with the Hazara Expedition, 1888 ; Great War, 1914–19 (despatches). (C1704)

LANG, Flying Officer Albert Frank, M.B.E., R.A.F.

LANG, Charles Russell, C.B.E., *b.* 1862 ; *s.* of John Lang, engineer. Director of G. and J. Weir (Limited), of Cathcart, Glasgow. *Address :* Cathcart, Glasgow. (C545)

LANG, Col. Elliott Brownlow, C.B.E. Served in the Great War, 1914–19 (despatches). (C1426)

LANG, Capt. James, O.B.E., R.E.

LANG, Capt. James Arthur Maule, O.B.E., R.A.F.

LANG, John Henry, M.B.E.

LANG, Patrick Keith, C.B.E., *b.* 20 June, 1863 ; *s.* of Very Rev. J. Marshall Lang, C.V.O., LL.D., D.D., Principal of Aberdeen University ; *m.* Elizabeth Gentle Stevenson, of Ingliston, Ratho, Midlothian. *Educ. :* Privately and Glasgow University. Banker from 1881 to 1904 in India, Transvaal, Constantinople, and Egypt. Contested the Bridgeton Division of Glasgow as Unionist Candidate at the General Election of 1909–10. *War Work :* Commissioner (unpaid) for the organisation of Church Army Recreation Huts in the Area of the Second Army at the Western Front, 1916–17 ; Secretary (unpaid) of the Surplus Government Property Advisory Council, 1917–18 ; at the Ministry of Munitions 1919, under the Disposal Board, as Controller (unpaid) of Relations with the Governments of Dominions, British Colonies, Dependencies and Protectorates, and with Local Government Authorities. *Address :* Thorn Chace, Merrow, near Guildford, Surrey. *Clubs :* Oriental ; 1900. (C2745)

LANG, Stuart-Calvert Jackson, M.B.E., *b.* 4 July, 1888 ; *s.* of Dr. E. Jackson Lang, of London (Med. Supt. L. & S.W. Ry., Waterloo). *Educ. :* St. Dunstans, S.E. Commercial Representative : War Work : B.R.C.S., No. 2 M.A.C., Aug. 1914 to July, 1915 ; Aisne, Marne, Lys, Flanders, Ypres, etc. ; Advanced Stores, Southern Area, July, 1915, to April, 1919 ; Somme, Ancre, Marne, etc. *Address :* Rue Cambon 2 f., Paris. (M2015)

LANG, Lieut.-Col. William Henry, O.B.E., R.A.F.

LANGDALE, Lieut.-Col. Philip, O.B.E.

LANGDON, Capt. Charles Henry Clarke, C.B.E., R.N.

LANGDON, Major Henry Charles Theodore, O.B.E., R.A.F.

LANGE, Capt. Richard Charles, O.B.E.

LANGEBRINK, Col. Andries, O.B.E.

LANGER, Charles Frederick, M.B.E.

LANGFORD, Hon. Major Frederick Charles, M.B.E., V.D., M.B., M.R.C.S., L.R.C.P. (Lond.), R.A.M.C., *b.* 13 Mar. 1864 ; *s.* of Frederick George Langford, of Bristol ; *m.* Adelaide, *d.* of J. A. Marks, of East Dulwich, S.E. 22. *Educ. :* Royal Naval School, Devonport, and privately. *War Work :* Medical Officer in charge, Hanover Park Auxiliary Military Hospital ; Divisional Inspector, Camberwell Division, British Red Cross Society. *Address :* West Lodge, 142, The Rye, S.E. 22. (M8742)

LANGFORD, Lieut. Horace Trevor St. Ledger, O.B.E., R.N.V.R.

LANGLANDS, George, M.B.E.

LANGLEY, Capt. and Qr.-Mr. Albert Ernest, O.B.E., R.A.S.C., *b.* 3 Nov. 1876 ; *s.* of the late W. V. Langley, Fakenham, Norfolk ; *m.* Kathleen Leonie, *d.* of W. Eydmann, of Eastleigh. *Educ. :* Northampton. *War Work :* Proceeded to France as a warrant officer with Expeditionary Force in Aug. 1914 ; promoted to Lieut. and Qr.-Mr., Jan. 1915 ; proceeded to Egypt in March, 1915, and to Salonica in Oct. 1915, and served there until June, 1919 ; appointed T. Major (D.A.D.T.) Nov. 1918 ; relinquished appointment June, 1919. *Addresses :* Home M.T. Depot, Deptford, S.E. 8 ; 41, Eltham Road, Lee, S.E. 12. (O6494)

LANGLEY, Cecil Ernest Herrick, O.B.E. (O12050)

LANGLEY, Frank, M.B.E.

LANGLEY, George Johnson, M.B.E., M.D.

LANGLEY, Lieut. Gerald Maxwell Bradshaw, O.B.E., R.N.

LANGLEY, John, C.B.E. Under Sec. of State, Min. of Agriculture, Egypt. *Address :* Cairo, Egypt. (C1004)

LANGLEY, Col. John Penrice, C.B.E., late R.A., *b.* 17 April, 1860 ; *s.* of the late Gen. Sir G. C. Langley, K.C.B. *Educ. :* Cheltenham College. *War Work :* Commanding 6th Reserve Brigade, Royal Field Artillery. *Address :* Rowena, Westward Ho ! N. Devon. *Club :* Army and Navy. (C1653)

LANGLEY, Percy James, M.B.E., *b.* 1 June, 1877. Deputy Finance Officer, Ministry of Agriculture and Fisheries. *Address :* Whitehall Place, S.W. 1. (M2016)

LANGMAID, Ernest Richard, O.B.E.

LANGMAN, Thomas Witheridge, O.B.E.

LANGMEAD, Capt. Harold Francis, M.B.E.

LANGMUIR, Lieut. John William, M.B.E., R.A.F.

LANGRIDGE, Capt. and Qr.-Mr. Edwin Joseph, M.B.E., N. Stafford Regt., *b.* 11 Oct. 1876 ; *s.* of Edwin Joseph, of Portsmouth ; *m.* Margaret, *d.* of Thomas Duke, of Folkestone. *Educ. :* St. Mary's, Portsmouth. *War Work :* Served overseas Sept. 1914 to Aug. 1919 on Western Front. *Address :* St. Clair, Essex Road, Portsmouth. (M6002)

LANGRIDGE, Capt. Francis Barton, O.B.E.

LANGRIDGE, Harry Dickinson, M.B.E., *b.* 8 Aug. 1866 ; *s.* of William Langridge, of Manchester ; *m.* Constance Mary, *d.* of Edwin F. Prince, of Manchester. District Traffic Manager,

Great Central Railway, Manchester. *Address :* 24, Athol Road, Alexandra Park, Manchester. *Club :* Clydesdale (Manchester). (M8744)

LANGRIDGE, Herbert, M.B.E., *b.* 14 April, 1873 ; *s.* of Thomas Langridge, of Richmond, Surrey. *Educ. :* Richmond. Civil Servant, at present attached to the Department of Overseas Trade. *War Work :* During the whole course of the War engaged upon the staff of the Commission Internationale de Ravitaillement. *Address :* Llanrhos, Burnell Road, Sutton, Surrey. *Club :* Primrose. (M2017)

LANGRIDGE, William, O.B.E.

LANGSLOW, Lieut. Melville Cecil, M.B.E., Aust. A.P.C.

LANGSTAFF, William Henry, M.B.E.

LANGSTON, Jessie Eleanor, M.B.E., *b.* 3 Jan. 1891 ; *d.* of Henry Langston, late of Southwark and Upper Norwood. *Educ. :* Orford College and Sydenham High School. Ministry of Munitions, Nov. 1916 to March, 1918, Supervisor of Registrations of Contracts (Headquarters) ; Ministry of Labour, (Appointments Department) March, 1918, to date ; Supervisor and Organiser of system of registrations in regard to Demobilisation, Training of Serving Officers, Resettlement in Civil Life of ex-soldiers, Training and Appointments (Headquarters). *Address :* 27, Park Mansions, Prince of Wales Road, S.W. 11. (M3794)

LANGSTON, Lieut. and Qr.-Mr. William, M.B.E., R.A.M.C.

LANGTON, Albert Smith, M.B.E.

LANGTON, Capt. George Philip, O.B.E., B.A., *b.* 22 April, 1881 ; *s.* of F. A. R. Langton, of Danganmore, Co. Kilkenny ; *m.* Alice Mary Katherine, *d.* of D. F. Arthur Leahy, of Shanakiel, Co. Cork. *Educ. :* Beaumont, Stonyhurst, and New College, Oxford. Barrister-at-law. *War Work :* Served with Royal Garrison Artillery and in Military Intelligence Department of the War Office ; Deputy Controller (Military Service Branch) Labour Dept., Ministry of Munitions ; Special Commissioner, Labour Disputes, Ministry of Munitions ; Controller, Demobilisation of Services Branch, Demobilisation Dept., Ministry of Labour. *Address :* 26, South Eaton Place, London, S.W. *Clubs :* Athenæum ; Beefsteak. (O493)

LANGTON, Major Theobald Michael, O.B.E.

LANGTON, Major Francis Wilfred GORE-, O.B.E.

LANHAM, Laurence, M.B.E.

LANITIS, Vrasidas Demitriou, M.B.E.

LANSDOWN, Charles Ewbank, O.B.E., M.D.

LANSDOWNE, Maud Evelyn, Marchioness of, G.B.E., C.I., Lady of Justice of St. John of Jerusalem ; *m.* 1869 Henry Charles Keith Petty-Fitzmaurice, 5th Marquess of Lansdowne (*see* BURKE'S *Peerage*). *Addresses :* Lansdowne House, Berkeley Square, W. 1. ; Bowood Park, Calne, Wiltshire ; Derreen, Kenmare, Co. Kerry, Ireland. *Clubs :* Athenæum ; Brooks'. (DG30)

LAPAGE, Comm. Walter Neville, O.B.E., R.N.

LAPHAM, Major Robert John, M.B.E., A.S.C.

LAPRAIK, John, O.B.E., F.R.G.S., *b.* 28 Aug. 1877; *s.* of James Lapraik, of Muirkirk, Ayrshire ; *m.* Rachel, *d.* of Alfred Clark, late of the Bank of Bengal, Calcutta, and Gyalpore, Chittagong. Agent, Bank of Bengal, Bombay. *War Work :* War Loan propaganda as Agent of the Bank of Bengal, Cawnpore, and voluntary work as Hon. Treas. of various War Funds in the United Provinces, India. *Address :* Bank of Bengal, Elphinstone Circle, Bombay. (O9830)

LAPSLEY, Chief Engr. Claude Charles, O.B.E., R.N.R.

LAPSLEY, Major William, O.B.E., M.B., I.M.S.

LARACY, Patrick Joseph, M.B.E.

LARGE, Capt. Edwin R., D.S.O. O.B.E. Capt. in Mercantile Marine ; Lieut.-Com. Roy. Naval Reserve ; served in the Great War, 1914–19 (despatches). (O9144)

LARGE, Frederick George, M.B.E., *b.* 19 Mar. 1887 ; *s.* of Harry Large, of Thetford ; *m.* Florence, *d.* of James Piggott, of Birmingham. Adjutant, Salvation Army. *War Work :* Management of the Rest Huts and Hostels at Weedon, Ripon, Codford, Bulford, Calais, and Lille, 1914 to 1920. *Addresses :* 91, Boulevard Gambetta, Calais ; 10, B Terrace, Lawrence Street, Birmingham. (M8747)

LARGE, Robert James, M.B.E.

LARKE, William James, C.B.E., M.I.E.E., M.I.S.Inst. A.M.Inst. Mech. E., *b.* 26 April, 1875 ; *s.* of William James Larke, of London ; *m.* Louisa Jane, *d.* of James Tayler Milton, of Blackheath, Kent. *Educ. :* Colfe's School Technical College and Engineering Apprenticeship. Engineer ; Engineer and Manager of the Power Mining Dept. The British Thomson-Houston Co., Ltd., 1899 to 1912 ; Deputy to Chief Engineer, British Thomson-Houston Co., Ltd., 1912–15. *War Work :* Ministry of Munitions (Voluntary), July, 1915 to Feb. 1919 ; Director, Controlled Establishments Division, July, 1915 ; devised and introduced Priority of Work Order for regulation of production of Munitions and distribution of National resources, men and materials, Mar. 1916 ; re-organised and became Director Badges and Exemption Dept., June, 1916 ; re-organised and became Director, Dilution of Labour Dept., Jan. 1917 ; appointed Technical Adviser to Secretariat ranking as Assistant Secretary, Member Council Committee on Demobilisation and Reconstruction, Chairman of various Committees in connection therewith, Jan. 1918 ; Controller, D.B. 5 C. Miscellaneous Section, Disposal Board, Jan. 1919 ; appointed on Staff Ministry of Munitions, Feb. 1919 ; Chairman British Engineering Commission, visited the occupied territory of Germany, May, 1919 ; appointed Director-General of Raw Materials and Member of Disposal Board responsible for

Disposal of Ferrous and non-Ferrous Metals, Chemicals, and Explosives and warlike stores, June, 1919; in addition responsible for Disposal of Aircraft, Miscellaneous Stores and Factory Consumate Stores, May, 1920. *Addresses:* Ministry of Munitions, S.W.; Eastburn, Sidcup, Kent. *Clubs:* R.A.C.; Savile. (C2746)

LARKEN, Lieut.-Col. Edmund, C.B.E., Lincolnshire Yeo. Served in the Great War, 1914–19. (C1278)

LARKIN, Capt. Gerald Ross O.B.E., Can. A.S.C.

LARKIN, Herbert Benjamin George, C.B.E., *b.* 6 March, 1872; *s.* of George Edwin Larkin, of London; *m.* Annie Mary Frances, *d.* of Patrick McHugh, of Queensland, Australia. *Educ.:* Roan School, Greenwich. Commonwealth Government Shipping Representative and General Manager, Commonwealth Government Line of Steamers. *War Work:* Control and management in the United Kingdom of the Australian Naval Transport Department and Commonwealth Government-owned and controlled mercantile shipping throughout the War. *Addresses:* Australia House, Strand, London, W.C. 2; Kyarra, St. Kilda, Melbourne, Australia. *Clubs:* Royal Automobile; Australian. (C2747)

LARKING, Lieut.-Col. Reginald Nesbitt Wingfield, C.B.E., *b.* 5 Dec. 1868; *s.* of the late Col. Cuthbert Larking, of Layston Lodge, Buntingford, Herts.; *m.* Violet Campbell, *d.* of William Macbean Rankine, of Dudhope, Forfarshire, N.B. *Educ.:* Eton and Malvern. Joined Scots Guards Dec. 1891; placed on retired pay on account of ill-health, Dec. 1907; Active Service in South Africa, 1899–1900; Queen's Medal (2 clasps). *War Work:* Recalled to service with Scots Guards, Aug. 1914; attached General Staff, London District, to April, 1915; in April, 1915, appointed Deputy Assistant Adjutant-General, Headquarter Staff, War Office, and promoted Assistant Adjutant-General in July, 1917; New Years' Honours List, 1917, received Brevet Majority; in Birthday Honours, 1919, awarded C.B.E., also Order of the Crown of Belgium (Officer), awarded in 1918 by King of Belgium; Order of the Star of Roumania with Swords (Officer), awarded in 1920 by King of Roumania; Legion of Honour (Chevalier), awarded in 1920 by President of the French Republic; also holds Civil Medal, 1st class, and Order of Civil Merit, 1st class, awarded by King of Belgium in 1907 and 1914, respectively, for saving life. *Club:* Brooks'. (C1654)

LARKMAN, 2nd Lieut. Raymond, M.B.E., B.Sc., A.C.A., T.F. Reserve, *b.* 31 Oct. 1891; *s.* of Rev. C. S. Larkman, of Northampton. *Educ.:* Silcoates School and Manchester University. Chartered Accountant; at present Divisional Chief Accountant, Coal Mines Dept., Board of Trade. *War Work:* Coal Mines Dept. *Addresses:* 12, West Hill Road, Southfields, S.W.; 21, Birchfield Road, Northampton. (M8748)

LARNDER, Col. Eugene William, C.B.E., M.R.C.V.S. *b.* 1864; *s.* of the late George Philip Larnder; *m.* 1889, Mary, *d.* of the late Brake Marshall, M.R.C.S. Col. Army Vet. Ser.; served in the S. African War, 1899–1901, with 2nd Div.; Great War, 1914–19, in Salonica and France, as Asst. Director and Dept. Director Vet. Ser.; Afghan War, 1919, as Dept. Director Vet. Ser.; has been Dept. Director of Vet. Ser., Southern Command, India, since 1919. *Address:* Poona, Bombay. *Club:* Junior United Service.

LARNDER, Capt. Harold Frederick, O.B.E.

LARNER, Victor John, M.B.E.

LARPENT, Major Lionel William Peppe DE HOCHE-PIED-, O.B.E., Connaught Rangers, *b.* 10 Feb. 1877; *m.* 1907, Marion Lucy, *d.* of Lieut.-Col. G. F. A. Harris, M.D. (O8578)

LARSSON, Carl Alfred, M.B.E., *b.* 5 July, 1862; *s.* of B. C. Larsson, of Malmoe, Sweden; *m.* Eleanor Chambers, *d.* of J. C. Roe, of London. *Educ.:* Privately and Royal Technical High School, Stockholm. Engineer, Chief Designing Office, Machine Gun Dept., Vickers, Ltd. *War Work:* Responsible for designing, etc., of Vickers' Automatic guns and equipment used by the Allies. *Address:* 31, Oxford Road, Putney, S.W. (M8749)

LARTER, Alfred Tabois, M.B.E., B.Sc., *b.* 25 April, 1883; *Educ.:* St. Mark's College School; Finsbury Technical College; Central Technical College (now Imperial College of Science and Technology). *War Work:* Engaged at the Admiralty from Dec. 1914 to Feb. 1917, and at the Ministry of Munitions from Feb. 1917 to Jan. 1919, in connection with purchase of equipment for the Royal Naval Division, Royal Marine Artillery, Royal Naval Air Service, and Royal Air Force. *Address:* 5, Rookfield Avenue, Muswell Hill. (M10)

LARTER, Charles Seymour, M.B.E., R.N.R.

LARTER, Major Percy John, O.B.E.

LASCELLES, Edward Charles Ponsonby, O.B.E.

LASCELLES, Lieut.-Col. Edward ffrancis Ward, C.B.E. For services in connection with the Founding of Scholarships for Overseas Soldiers and Sailors. (C3151)

LASCELLES, Lieut.-Col. Ernest, O.B.E.

LASCELLES, Evelyn George, O.B.E., *b.* 22 June, 1853; *d.* of the Hon. George E. Lascelles, J.P. (died 1911), and Lady Louisa Lascelles, *d.* (died 1900) of 4th Earl of Mansfield (see BURKE'S *Peerage*), of Sion Hill, Thirsk, Yorks. *Educ.:* At home. Hon. Serving Sister the Order of St. John of Jerusalem. *War Work:* Appointed Commandant of St. John's V.A.D. 54, W.R. Yorks, 1911; Commandant of Grove House Aux. Mil. Hospital (Class A, 64 beds) from Nov. 1914, to April, 1919, when the Hospital was closed. *Address:* 19, Park View, Harrogate, Yorks. (O492)

LASCELLES, Lieut.-Col. George Reginald, O.B.E., *b.*

14 April, 1864; *s.* of Col. Walter R. Lascelles, J.P., D.L., of Norley, Cheshire; *m.* Beatrice, *d.* of Rev. R. Pulteney, of Ashley, Northants. *Educ.:* Marlborough. Exon. of the King's Body Guard. *War Work:* Commanded the 16th Batt. Royal Fusiliers, 1914–18; Area Commandant, Cavillon, Somme, France, 1919. *Address:* 6, Queen's Gate, S.W. *Club:* Army and Navy. (O7369)

LASCOT, Frank Leslie, O.B.E.

LASH, Major Ivor Richard de Warraine, O.B.E., R.A.O.C.

LASH, Major John Francis, O.B.E.

LASKEY, Major Walter William, O.B.E.

LASLETT, Eng.-Comm. Charles Frederick, M.B.E., R.I.M.

LATEY, William, M.B.E.

LATHAM, George, M.B.E., D.C.M.

LATHAM, Major John Ion, O.B.E., R.E.

LATHAM, Percy James, O.B.E., A.I.A., *b.* 2 Oct. 1880; 3rd *s.* of John Latham, of Tetsworth, Oxon., and Reading, Berks, and of Mrs. Latham, 34, Woodville Gardens, Ealing, Middlesex; *m.* Charlotte Cunningham (who died), *d.* of John Robert Greig, of Falkirk, Stirlingshire. *Educ.:* Brunswick House School, Reading; King's Coll., London, and privately. District Inspector, Ministry of Health (Insurance Department). *War Work:* Liaison Officer between the Navy and Army Insurance Fund, and the Inspectorate of the Insurance Department, Ministry of Health. *Addresses:* 34, Woodville Gardens, Ealing, Middlesex; Ministry of Health (Insurance Department); Brook House, Francis Street, London, W.C. 1. (O10808)

LATHBURY, Major Ernest Browning, O.B.E., R.A.M.C., *b.* 20 Oct. 1881; *s.* of F. R. Lathbury, of Chipperfield; *m.* Rhoda Matilda, *d.* of Bishop Fyson, of Hokkaido, Japan. *Educ.:* Aldenham, Epsom College, and St. Bartholomew's Hospital. *War Work:* Served with 3rd Cav. Field Amb., B.E.F., 1914–15; acting Lieut.-Col. Commandant Mile End Military Hospital, Southwark Military Hospital; S.M.O. Peace Concentration, Kensington Gardens; acting Lieut.-Col. Commandant 159 Field Amb., N. Russia Murmansk Relief Force; Commandant Hemel Hempstead and Warlingham Military Hospitals; Fellow of Royal Colonial Institute. (O7372)

LATIFI, Alma, O.B.E., M.A., LL.M. (Cantab.), LL.D. (Dublin), Battister-at-law, I.C.S., *b.* 12 Nov. 1879; *s.* of Kamaruddin Amiruddin Latifi, of Bombay; *m.* Nasima, *d.* of the late Hon. Mr. Justice Budrudin Tyabji, of Bombay. *Educ.:* Cambay (W. India); Zanzibar (W. Africa); Poona and Bombay; and later at Paris and Heildelberg. (Macmahon Law Studentship, St. John's Coll.; Degree of Honour, first division, of the Govt. of India for eminent proficiency in Arabic.) Joined the Indian Civil Service in Jan. 1903; Executive Judicial Officer in the Punjab; was on special duty to survey the industries of the Punjab in 1909–10; on special duty at the Press Camp, Coronation Durbar, Delhi, 1911–12; on deputation to the Hyderabad State (Deccan) as Director of Education, 1913–16. *War Work:* Sub-Divisional Officer (Rohtak District); Deputy Commissioner (Ludhiana and Hissar Districts); worked in connection with recruiting in the Punjab; commended for his success in keeping his district free from disturbances during the Punjab troubles in April–May, 1919; mentioned in the Government of India Gazette of 29 July 1919, for valuable services rendered in India in connection with the War awarded the recruiting badge and the badge for voluntary work in India. *Club:* Orient, Bombay. (O9831)

LA TOUCHE, Comm. George Henry Stransham, O.B.E., Royal Indian Marine, *b.* 10 April, 1872; *s.* of the late Gen. W. P. La Touche, of Wicklow, Ireland; *m.* Daisy Jerome, *d.* of Col. Julius Witkowski, of New York. *Educ.:* Cheltenham. *War Work:* Somaliland, 1902–4, medal and clasp; Persian Gulf Arms Traffic Operations, 1910–12, N.G.S. medal and clasp; 1914 Star, General Service, and Victory medals. *Address:* 33, Grange Road, Ealing. (O4055)

LATTER, Eva, M.B.E., *b.* 2 July, 1867; *d.* of Henry Joseph Latter, of Farnborough, Kent. *Educ.:* Privately. *War Work:* Hon. Sec. Battersea and Clapham War Hospital Supply Depot. *Address:* 12, Overstrand Mansions, Battersea, S.W. (M8750)

LATTER, Flora, M.B.E., *b.* 5 Nov. 1865; *d.* of Henry Joseph Latter, of Farnborough, Kent. *Educ.:* Privately. *War Work:* Soldiers' and Sailors' Families Association, Member of Committee, etc., from 1914; London War Pensions, Battersea Branch, Secretary (Hon.) and Member of Committee from inception; Soldiers' and Sailors' Help Society, Member of Committee. *Address:* 12, Overstrand Mansions, Battersea, S.W. 11. (M8751)

LATTEY, Jane Maude, M.B.E.

LATTINORE, Ralph, M.B.E.

LAUDER, Elizabeth Shaw, M.B.E.

LAUDER, William Beith, O.B.E., *b.* 13 July, 1874; William Lauder, of Glasgow; *m.* Ada, *d.* of Charles Goodley, of Nottingham. *Educ.:* Allan Glen's School, Glasgow; Glasgow and W. of Scotland Technical Coll.; and Glasgow Univ. His Majesty's Inspector of Factories and Workshops, Home Office. *War Work:* Prominent and active member of Tyneside-Scottish Committee, which in 1914 raised a full brigade of men; the committee was responsible for recruiting, housing, feeding, training and equipping the Tyneside-Scottish Brigade until taken over by the War Office; represented the Home Office on the N.E. Coast Armaments Committee, which was formed in 1915 for the purpose of increasing the production of munitions of war; the committee was formed with Lord

Kitchener's full approval and worked under the directions of War Office and Admiralty; National Service Commissioner for N. of England (appointed Jan. 1917); engaged at various times on special investigations for Home Office, War Office, Admiralty, and Ministry of Munitions. *Address:* 21, The Poplars, Gosforth, Newcastle-upon-Tyne.   (O10809)

LAUGHTON, Elvira Sibyl Marie, M.B.E., W.R.N.S.

LAUGHTON, Major Joseph Vinters, C.B.E. Quartermaster, T. Capt., and Acting Major, Lancers. Served with the Nile Expedition, 1898 (medal); Great War, 1914–19 (despatches).   (C764)

LAURENSON, Capt. George, M.B.E.

LAURIE, Annie Macpherson, Mrs., M.B.E.

LAURIE, Major Herbert, M.B.E., *b.* 4 April, 1874; *s.* of A. St. G. McAdam Laurie, J.P., of Rochdale, Sevenoaks, Kent. *Educ.:* Sherborne. Stockbroker. *Address:* Kingston Manor, near Lewes. *Clubs:* City of London; M.C.C.   (M653)

LAURIE, Capt. Rawdon Hastings St. Barbe, M.B.E.

LAURIE, T. Capt. Robert Douglas, O.B.E., M.B., R.A.M.C.

LAURIE, Capt. William, M.B.E., *b.* 5 Feb. 1868; *s.* of John Laurie, of Dunscore, Dumfriesshire; *m.* Agnes, *d.* of Alexander Gowdy, of Dublin. *War Work:* Chief Clerk, Headquarters, Southern Command, Salisbury, 1914–18; G.H.Q., Great Britain, London, 1918–19. *Address:* Thornhill, Dumfriesshire.   (M5410)

LAVENDER, Joseph, M.B.E. late F.R.I.B.A., *b.* 3 May, 1862; *s.* of Frederick Lavender, of Walsall; *m.* Emily, *d.* of Henry Farrington, of Walsall. *Educ.:* Privately. Private practice as an Architect in Wolverhampton for many years; retired 1910 on account of health. *War Work:* Chairman of 1st Prestatyn Belgian Refugee Relief Committee; Member of Local Tribunal during its existence; Hon. Sec. Local Committee for War Savings. *Address:* Plas Gwyn, Prestatyn.   (M8754)

LAVER, Samuel, M.B.E., *b.* 21 Sept. 1861; *s.* of George Laver. *Educ.:* All Saints' Coll., Hyderabad, Deccan. Merchant. *War Work:* Served on the Cantonment Committee of Secunderabad, and for two years ran a Cinema in the Cantonment Theatre; was also a member of the Protestant Orphanage Committee; frequently gave free shows at his theatre to wounded soldiers and for charitable purposes. *Address:* c/o The British India Corporation, Ltd., Cawnpore, U.P.   (M6189)

LAVERTON, Lieut.-Col. Henry Sanderson, O.B.E.

LAVERTON, Lieut.-Col. Herbert Curling, O.B.E., Reserve of Officers, the Black Watch, *b.* 26 March, 1875; *s.* of W. H. Laverton, D.L., J.P., of Leighton, Westbury. *Educ.:* Harrow. *Club:* Junior Army and Navy.   (O7373)

LAVERY, Capt. Andrew, M.B.E.

LAVILLE, Ellen, M.B.E.

LAVY, Rev. Ernest Edward, M.B.E.

LAW, Bertha, Mrs., M.B.E., *b.* 9 Jan. 1868; *d.* of James Robert Whitworth, of Weston Underwood, Bucks; *m.* Edward Ernest, *s.* of Thomas Law, of Leicester. *War Work:* Ran a Soldiers' Club for 208th Brigade, 69th Div., 1917–19, at Thoresby Camp, Doncaster, Welbeck Camp, Clipstone Camp, and Brocton Camp. *Address:* Sunnydene, Wellingborough.   (M18755)

LAW, Major David, O.B.E.

LAW, Laura Jessie, M.B.E., *b.* 26 April, 1860; *d.* of George Henry Law, of Northampton. *Educ.:* Anerley. Hon. Superintend of Balham and Streatham Nursing Division of St. John Ambulance Brigade. *War Work:* Secretary, St. John's Warehouse, Clerkenwell, for 5 years, under the Joint Committee of the British Red Cross Society and the Order of St. John of Jerusalem. *Address:* 58, Manville Road, Upper Tooting, S.W. 17.   (M3798)

LAW, Capt. Robert William Rowland, O.B.E., M.C.

LAWDER, Lieut.-Col. Cecil Edward, O.B.E., late R.F.A., and R.A.F., *b.* 6 May, 1877; *s.* of J. Ormsby Lawder, D.L., J.P., of Lawderdale, Co. Leitrim; *m.* Violet, *d.* of J. Basden Orr, of Irvine. *Educ.:* Shrewsbury. R.H.A. and R.F.A. 1900–8; R.H.A., R.F.A. and R.A.F. 1914–19; A.D.C. G.O.C. Eastern Dist. Cape Colony, 1902; A.D.C. Lieut. Governor Bengal, 1906–7; South Africa, 1900 to conclusion. *War Work:* Provost-Marshal, China Command, 1914–15; France and Home Service till April, 1919; Command of Battery R.F.A., M. of M., S.O.; R.A.F. Liaison Officer, Independent Air Force. *Addresses:* Lawderdale, Co. Leitrim; Tower House, West Dean, Salisbury. *Clubs:* Army and Navy; Bibury; Newbury Race.

LAWDER, Lieut.-Comm. Keith Macleod, O.B.E.

LAWES, Ernest Lingwood, M.B.E., *b.* 30 Aug. 18 ; *s.* of Tom Lawes, of Maidenhead, Berks; *m.* Edith Annie, *d.* of James Larrard, of Croydon. *Educ.:* Privately. Business Manager. *War Work:* Inspector, Police Reserve, Southend-on-Sea. *Address:* 39, Wenham Drive, Westcliff, Essex. (M654)

LAWFORD, Emma Ada, M.B.E.

LAWLER, Capt. Robert Edward, M.B.E.

LAWLESS, Major Thomas, O.B.E.

LAWLESS, Emily Anne, Lady CROOKE-, O.B.E.; *d.* of C. E. Lawless; *m.* 1894, Surgeon Lieut.-Col. Sir Warren Roland Crooke-Lawless, C.B., C.I.E., C.B.E., M.D. (*q.v.*). *Address:* Kilcrone, Cloyne, Co. Cork, Ireland.   (O1570)

LAWLESS, Surgeon Lieut.-Col. Sir Warren Roland CROOKE-, Kt., C.B., C.I.E., C.B.E., M.D., LL.D. (Hon. Caus.), late Surgeon to the Viceroy, *b.* 1863; *m.* 1894, Emily Anne, O.B.E. (*q.v.*), *d.* of C. E. Lawless. Joined the Army Medical Department, 1886; posted to the Coldstream Guards, 1892; given a commission in regiment as Surgeon-Major, 1898;

served throughout the South African War (despatches twice, promoted to rank of Surgeon Lieut.-Col.; Queen's Medal, 6 clasps; King's Medal, 2 clasps); retired 1911; D.L. Co. Cork; Knight of Grace, Order of St. John of Jerusalem, 1911. *Address:* House Governor Osborne, I.O.W.; Kilcrone, Cloyne, Co. Cork, Ireland. *Clubs:* Guards'; Albemarle. (O7990)

LAWLEY, Annie Allen, The Hon. Lady, G.B.E., Lady of Grace of St. John of Jerusalem; *d.* of Sir Edward Cunard, 2nd Bart.; *m.* 1885, Hon. Sir Arthur Lawley, 4th *s.* of 2nd Baron Wenlock (*see* BURKE's *Peerage*). *War Work:* Secretary to Queen Mary's Needlework Guild. *Address:* 9, Seymour Street, W. 1.   (DG1)

LAWLOR, Lieut. Leslie, O.B.E., R.N.R.

LAWN, James Gunson, C.B.E. Sometime Professor, Johannesburg School of Mines; Controller, Explosives Supply Dept. Ministry of Munitions, during the Great War.

LAWRENCE, Major Kenneth Edward, O.B.E.

LAWRENCE, Alexander Samuel, M.B.E., *b.* 7 Mar. 1876; *s.* of Surgeon-Captain James Lawrence, of Belgaum, Bombay Presidency, India; *m.* Florence Ethel, *d.* of — Brinkworth, of Simla. *Educ.:* Cathedral High School, Bombay. Superintendent, Home Department, Government of India. *War Work:* Dealt with all the war work in the Home Dept. of the Govt. of India, *i.e.* the civil side relating to internal India, Was mentioned on both occasions in the supplement to the Honors *Gazette* for good work done in connection with the war. *Addresses:* 22A, Goldstone Villas, Hove, near Brighton; Supt. Home Dept., Govt. of India, Simla.   (M4175)

LAWRENCE, Capt. Alfred, O.B.E., R.A.O.C.

LAWRENCE, Alfred Clive, C.B.E., *b.* 1876; *s.* of the Hon. Sir Alfred Tristram Lawrence. *Educ.:* Haileybury; Trin. Hall, Camb. Barrister Middle Temple, 1902; Revising Barrister, 1914; Director of Intelligence Branch, Procurator-Gen.'s Depart. since 1914. *Addresses:* 10, South Street, Mayfair, W.; 7, Fig Tree Court, Temple, E.C.; Bunce's Farm, Birch Grove, E. Grinstead. *Clubs:* Garrick; Oxford and Cambridge.   (C218)

LAWRENCE, Angel Lawrence, M.B.E., *b.* 1892; *d.* of Lieut.-Col. Henry J. Lawrence, of The Haven, Sandecotes, Parkstone, Dorset. *Educ.:* St. Leonard's; St. Andrews; Girton College, Cambridge, (1st Class Historical Tripos). Assistant Secretary, War Committee, British Medical Association, 1915; Intelligence Officer, British Medical Association, 1919; Vice-President, Women Clerks' Association. *War Work:* Work on Farm land, 1915, followed by War Committee of British Medical Association Assistant Secretaryship. *Address:* 16, St. Mary's Mansions, Paddington, W.   (M2019)

LAWRENCE, Aubrey Trevor, M.B.E.

LAWRENCE, Cecil John Rhodes, O.B.E.   (O6652)

LAWRENCE, Dora Muriel, M.B.E.

LAWRENCE, Dorothy Helen, Lady, C.B.E.; *d.* of the late Anthony Pemberton Hobson; *m.* Alexander Graham, 3rd Baron Lawrence, only son of 2nd Baron Lawrence (*see* BURKE's *Peerage*). *War Work:* Founded Munition Makers' Canteen Committee (President, May, 1915 to Jan. 1917); Adviser to Welfare Dept., Ministry of Munitions, May, 1917 to end of war. *Address:* Stanhope Park, Greenford, Middlesex. *Club:* Ladies' Imperial.   (C2749)

LAWRENCE, Elizabeth Mary Hilda, Mrs., M.B.E.; *d.* of the late William Sumner Rawcliffe, of Haigh, Lancashire; *m.* Edward, *s.* of the late James Lawrence, J.P., C.C., of Chorley, Lancashire. *Educ.:* Privately. *War Work:* Part Founder and Superintendent of the Wigan Work Room, British Red Cross Society, 1915–19. *Address:* Worthington Lodge, Worthington, near Wigan, Lancs.   (M2020)

LAWRENCE, Capt. Eric Nathan Samuel, M.B.E.,

LAWRENCE, Major Ernest Harry Thorne, O.B.E., *b.* 20 Feb. 1877; *s.* of A. F. Lawrence, of Brighton; *m.* Elaine Winning, *d.* of J. Cousins, of Brighton. Assistant Commissioner of Police, Uganda. Major Reserve of Officers, late 4th Connaught Rangers; served in S.A. War 1900–2; appointed Officer in Charge, Defence Measures, Uganda, Aug. 1914; Commandant, Uganda Volunteer Reserve; Provost-Marshal, Uganda; Commanded Uganda Police Service Battns. Dec. 1914 to Jan. 1917. *Address:* Uganda. *Clubs:* Junior Naval and Military.   (O6734)

LAWRENCE, Capt. Francis Henry, M.B.E., R.G.A.

LAWRENCE, Major Frederick George, D.S.O., O.B.E., *b.* 21 Aug. 1874; *s.* of the late Hugh Man Lawrence, of Brecon and Blackheath; *m.* Frances Mary, *d.* of the late Osborne Edward Mortimer, of Croydon. *Educ.:* Wellington Coll. South Wales Borderers. *War Work:* Served with 1st Batt. in France during the Retreat and afterwards; Commandant G.H.Q. Cadet School, France; D.A.Q.M.G. 33rd Div. and Fourth Army, France; A.Q.M.G. XV. Corps, France; and A.A.M.G., Southern Command, Salisbury. *Address:* 2nd Batt. South Wales Borderers, Jhansi, India. *Club:* United Service.   (O8856)

LAWRENCE, Lieut.-Col. Hervey Major, D.S.O.

LAWRENCE, Isaac, M.B.E., *b.* 5 Nov. 1863; *s.* of William Lawrence, of Stroud, Glos.; *d.* of Richard Banting, of Southsea. *Educ.:* National School, Stroud, Glos. Chief Clerk, General Staff, Headquarters, Southern Command; Pensioner Sergeant, Royal Marine Artillery, (served 21 years). *War Work:* Mobilised 4 Aug. 1914, with Royal Fleet Reserve. Returned to duty as Chief Clerk, General Staff, 26 August, 1914, and continued as Chief Clerk up to May, 1920. *Address:* 2, Queen Alexandra Road, Bemerton, Salisbury. *Clubs:* Portsmouth Masonic; Fisherton Liberal.   (M8758)

LAWRENCE, Capt. James, M.B.E.

LAWRENCE, John Henry, O.B.E.

LAWRENCE, Lister James Harvey, C.B.E. Reuter's Special Correspondent with British Fleet at Dardanelles, and with French Armies during the Great War.

LAWRENCE, Margaret Alice, Lady, M.B.E. ; *d.* of Joseph Jackson, of Southport, and widow of the late Sir Joseph, *s.* of the late Philip Lawrence, of Zante. *War Work :* Vice-President, Coulsdon and Purley B.R.C. Division War Hospital Supply Depot. *Address :* Oaklands, Kenley, Surrey.

LAWRENCE, Thomas David, M.B.E.

LAWRENSON, Thomas Alfred, O.B.E.

LAWRIE, Annie, Mrs. MACPHERSON-, O.B.E. ; *d.* of Rev. Samuel Johnson Smith, of Smithboro' and Orchard Vale, Co. Monaghan ; *m.* James Macpherson-Lawrie. *War Work :* Appointed Vice-President of Dorset Branch B.R.C.S. in 1911 ; organised and equipped four Red Cross Hospitals in Weymouth, complete and ready for duty with full medical and surgical staffs, on outbreak of war ; awarded decorations from the Czarina of Russia and King of the Belgians. *Address :* Greenhill, Weymouth, Dorset. (O3793)

LAWRY, Major Raymond Alexander Reid, O.B.E.

LAWRY, William, M.B.E., 29 Aug. 1879 ; *s.* of William Lawry, of St. Ives, Cornwall ; *m.* Kitty Lang, *d.* of William Lang Harry, of St. Ives, Cornwall. *Educ. :* National Schools, St. Ives, Cornwall. Organiser of Fisheries to Fisheries Organisation Society ; Secretary, Cornish Fishing Vessels Insurance Society ; Port Fishery Officer. *War Work :* Secretary, War Savings Association ; Organisation of Fishing Fleet under Protection, 1917–20 ; Sec. to St. Ives Fishermen's Society. *Address :* 35, Trenwith Place, St. Ives, Cornwall. (M8760)

LAWS, Ernest, M.B.E. Staff Clerk, Local Government Board (now Ministry of Health). *War Work :* Asst. Sec., London Intelligence Committee ; Asst. to Sec., National Register Committee ; Asst. in Military Service Tribunals Dept., Local Govt. Board. *Addresses :* Ministry of Health, Whitehall, S.W. 1 ; 158, Palmerston Road, Bowes Park, London, N. (M657)

LAWS, Major Frederick Charles Victor, O.B.E.

LAWS, Percy Charles Willoughby, O.B.E., M.A., L.M.S.S.A., *b.* 11 Jan. 1870 ; *s.* of Joseph Christopher Laws, of Brighton, Sussex. *Educ. :* University Coll. School, London ; Wadham Coll., Oxford ; St. George's Hospital, London. Formerly Lecturer in Bacteriology at the Durham Univ. Coll. of Medicine, Newcastle-on-Tyne ; now Pathologist to the War Pensions Hospital, Newcastle-on-Tyne. *War Work :* Held the post of Bacteriologist to No. 1 Area, Northern Command, for the investigation of Cerebro-spinal Fever amongst the troops, from Aug. 1915 to March, 1920 ; in addition was Bacteriologist to 1st Northern General Hospital, March, 1917, to June, 1919 ; Pathologist and Bacteriologist to the Northumberland War Hospital and Special Surgical Military Hospital, Newcastle-on-Tyne, May, 1919, to March, 1920. *Address :* 31, St. George's Terrace, Jesmond, Newcastle-on-Tyne. (O11819)

LAWSON, Sir Arnold, K.B.E., F.R.C.S. Eng., *b.* 4 Dec. 1867 ; *s.* of George Lawson, F.R.C.S. Eng., of 12, Harley Street, London, W. ; *m.* Helen Hargreaves, *d.* of Andrew Clark, F.R.C.S. Eng., of Cowley Grove, Uxbridge. *Educ. :* Merchant Taylor's School ; Middlesex Hospital Medical School. Senior Ophthalmic Surgeon and Lecturer on Ophthalmology Middlesex Hospital. *War Work :* For five years Hon. Surg. to St. Dunstan's Hostel for Blinded Sailors and Soldiers ; Hon. Ophthalmic Surgeon to many other War Hospitals, including Prince of Wales Hospital for Officers, King Edward VII. Hospital for Officers, the Duke of Rutland and Park Lane Hospitals for Officers ; twice mentioned in Secretary of State's Lists. *Address :* 12, Harley Street, London, W. *Clubs :* Royal Automobile ; Northwood Golf. (K459)

LAWSON, Emma Louisa, M.B.E.

LAWSON, Lieut.-Col. Eric St. John, O.B.E.

LAWSON, Capt. and Qr.-Mr. Ernest Evelyn Lister, O.B.E.

LAWSON, Major Francis Bernard, O.B.E., *b.* 22 July, 1861 ; *s.* of Rev. G. Lawson, of Upleadon, Gloucester ; *m.* Emilie Marian, *d.* of Rev. G. Garrett, of Kilmeague, Naas, Ireland. *Educ. :* Marlborough ; Sandhurst. Served in Northamptonshire Regt., Jan. 1880, to Jan. 1897. *War Work :* Recruiting. *Address :* 12, Wellington Court, Knightsbridge, S.W. *Clubs :* Junior United Service, Ranelagh, and Royal Automobile. (O1572)

LAWSON, Lieut. John Boyd, M.B.E., R.E. (T.).

LAWSON, Lieut. John Cuthbert, O.B.E., M.A., R.N.V.R.

LAWSON, Capt. John Hanson, O.B.E., R.E.

LAWSON, Mildred Zacyntha, Mrs., M.B.E.

LAWSON, Nellie Elizabeth, Mrs., M.B.E.

LAWSON, Noel John Cecil, M.B.E., *b.* 9 Dec. 1886 ; *s.* of F. W. Lawson, of Chelsea ; *m.* Edith Mathews, *d.* of Charles Dickey Monteith, of Exmouth. *Educ. :* St. Lawrence's Coll., Ramsgate ; and School Ship H.M.S. " Conway." In command of Eastern Telegraph Company's cable ship, laying and repairing submarine telegraph cables, etc. *Address :* 2, Carlton Hill, Exmouth. (M8762)

LAWSON, Capt. Wentworth Dillon, O.B.E., R.A.S.C.

LAWSON, William, M.B.E., N.D.A. (Hons.), N.D.D., C.D.A. (Glas.), *b.* 11 Aug. 1882. Organiser of Agricultural Education for West Sussex County Council. *War Work :* Chief Executive Officer, West Sussex Agricultural Executive Committee. *Address :* County Hall, Chichester. (M8763)

LAWSON, Lady Wilma, C.B.E., *d.* of the 5th Earl of

Radnor (*see* BURKE'S *Peerage*), and widow of Edward George, 2nd Earl of Lathom (*see* BURKE'S *Peerage*) ; *m.* 16 Nov. 1912. Lieut.-Gen. Sir Henry Meyrick, K.C.B., late A.D.C. *p.s.c.* R.E. ; *s.* of the late Rt. Hon. James A. Lawson, P.C., of Dublin. (C3106e)

LAWSON, Catherine Adah, Mrs. KERR-, O.B.E.

LAWTHER, James Alfred, M.B.E.

LAWTON, Frank Warburton, O.B.E., *b.* 26 Oct. 1881 ; *s.* of John Lawton, of Heaton Mersey ; *m.* Violet Miriam, *d.* of George Dickinson Savage, of Stratford-on-Avon. *Educ. :* Macclesfield and King's Coll., London. Solicitor ; Assistant in the Dept. of H.M. Procurator-General. *War Work :* Served as a trooper in the City of London (Rough Riders) I.Y. in South Africa, 1900 ; engaged on Prize Court work from Sept. 1914 onwards throughout the Great War. *Address :* 70, Bishops Mansions, S.W. 6. (O1573)

LAWTON, Major Frederick Donald Herbert Blois, O.B.E., Aust. A.M.C.

LAY, Capt. John Richard, O.B.E.

LAYARD, Major Arthur Raymond, O.B.E., R.A.F.

LAYLAND, Comm. Henry, O.B.E., R.N.R.

LAYTON, Maud Matilda, M.B.E., *b.* 1876 ; *d.* of William Layton, of London. *Educ. :* Folkestone and Germany. *War Work :* Head Masseuse in the Military Massage Service ; in charge of Massage and Electrical Departments at the 3rd London General Hospital, Wandsworth, 1915–20. *Address :* 55, West Side, Wandsworth Common, S.W.18 (M658)

LAYTON, Capt. Percival Norman, C.B.E., R.D., R.N.R. *War Work :* 1914–19, Commodore of Convoys (despatches). (C2316)

LAYTON, Walter Thomas, C.B.E., C.H., *b.* 15 Mar. 1884 ; *s.* of Alfred John Layton ; *m.* Eleanor Dorothea, *d.* of F. P. Osmaston. *Educ. :* King's Coll. School, London ; City of Westminster ; Trinity Coll., Cambridge. Fellow of Caius Coll., Cambridge ; University Lecturer ; Newmarch Lecturer, London University ; Assistant Editor " Economist " ; W. E. A. Lecturer for Portsmouth and Leicester. *War Work :* Director of Statistics at Ministry of Munitions ; Member of Munitions Council ; subsequently Director of Nat. Fed. of Iron and Steel Manufacturers ; temporarily Director of Economic Section of League of Nations. *Addresses :* Hillside, Weybridge, Surrey ; League of Nations Office, 16 Curzon Street. *Club :* National Liberal. (C39)

LAZARUS, Emanuel Samuel, O.B.E.

LAZENBY, Frederick George, C.B.E. Wounded and Missing Dept. British Red Cross, during the Great War.

LEA, Doris, M.B.E.

LEA, Hon. Capt. Frederick, O.B.E., D.Sc., M.Inst.C.E., M.I.M., A.R.C.S., Wh.Sc., R.A.F., *b.* 25 June, 1871 ; *s.* of Measham Lea, of Crewe ; *m.* Alice, *d.* of the Rev. W. R. Sunman. *Educ. :* Owens Coll. Manchester, and Royal Coll. of Science, London. Professor of Civil Engineering, Univ. of Birmingham. *War Work :* Served as Lieut. R.N.V.R., and Capt. R.A.F., and on Government Committees dealing with aircraft. Researches in connection with Aeroplanes and Rigid Airships. *Addresses :* Elmsdale, Mayfield Road, Moseley ; University, Birmingham. (O10813)

LEA, Capt. George Edward, O.B.E., Mercantile Marine, *b.* 2 Nov. 1878 ; *s.* of Joseph Lea, of Goole ; *m.* Edith Emma, *d.* of Charles D. Moore, of Goole. *Educ. :* Goole. Master Mariner. *War Work :* Captain of one of His Majesty's Military Transports, conveying munitions of war to France, 1914 to Nov. 1918. *Address :* 9, Cecil Street, Goole, Yorkshire. (O1575)

LEA, Measham, O.B.E., M.I.C.E., *b.* 3 July, 1869 ; *s.* of Measham Lea, of Crewe ; *m.* Annie, *d.* of Alfred Kingston, F.R.H.S., of London. *Educ. :* Crewe. Civil Engineer ; Chief Engineer to Municipality, City of Karachi, India ; Member Institution Municipal and County Engineers, of the Council and of the Examination Board, and Member, Royal Sanitary Institute. *War Work :* Engaged as Chief Engineer, Karachi, which city formed an important War base for troops for Mesopotamia, East Africa, and Europe ; received the special thanks of the military authorities. *Addresses :* Seafield Road, Karachi, India ; The Homestead, Sandford Road, Moseley, Birmingham. *Club :* Sind. (O9832)

LEACH, Arthur John, M.B.E.

LEACH, Charles Henry, M.B.E., J.P.

LEACH, Claude Pemberton, M.B.E., *b.* 1858 ; *s.* of Sir G. A. Leach, K.C.B., R.E. ; *m.* Mary Champain, *d.* of Thomas Leach, J.P., of Ryde, I.W. *Educ. :* Highgate School. Architect. *War Work :* Inventor of Leach's Trench Catapult ; Worker for Red Cross Hospital Supplies ; Inspector of Prisoners of War Parcels. *Address :* 21, Pelham Crescent, S.W.7. *Club :* Ranelagh (M8765)

LEACH, Dame Florence Edith Victoria, D.B.E., *b.* 9 Oct. 1874 ; *d.* of Colonel W. FitzA. Way ; *m.* Henry Edmund Burleigh, *s.* of Gen. Sir E. Leach, K.C.B. *Educ. :* Privately ; France ; Germany. *War Work :* Commandant Military Cookery Section, Women's Legion ; Controller-in-Chief Queen Mary's Army Auxiliary Corps. *Address :* 7, St. Leonard's Mansions, Chelsea, S.W. 3. (D32)

LEACH, Frank, M.B.E.

LEACH, Brig.-Gen. Harold Pemberton, C.B., C.M.G., D.S.O., late R.E., *b.* 14 April, 1851 ; *s.* of the late Sir George Archibald Leach, K.C.B., Royal Engineers. *Educ. :* Cholmeley School, Highgate, and Royal Military Academy. Afghan War, 1st Div. Khyber Field Force, 1878–79 (despatches), Kurram Valley, 1879–80 (despatches, thanks of Govt. of India, medal with clasp); Nile Expedition, 1884–85 (medal with 2 clasps, Bronze Star, Brevet of Major); Lushai Expedition, 1888–89 (Honourably mentioned, medal with clasp); Chin Lushai Expedition, 1889–90 (despatches, clasp, Brevet of Lieut.-Col., D.S.O. Birthday Gazette, 1891); Chitral Relief Force, 1895 (despatches, medal with clasp, C.B.). *War Work*: 1914–17, 1st Reserve Brigade (Secretary of State's list, C.B.E.). *Address*: 139, Gloucester Road, S.W. 7. *Clubs*: United Service; Ranelagh.   (C1655)

LEACH, Marian, Mrs., O.B.E.

LEACH, Mary Summer, M.B.E.

LEACH, Milton, M.B.E.

LEACH, Richard, O.B.E., *b.* March, 1863 · *s.* of William Leach, of Bradford, Yorks.; *m.* Elouise Annie, *d.* of R. J. Pearl, of Canonbury, N. Entered the Civil Service in Nov. 1881, and served successively in the Veterinary Dept. (Ireland), the Board of Trade, and the Ministry of Labour. Retired in Dec. 1918 on account of ill-health. *Address*: 22, Muswell Road, Muswell Hill, N.10.   (O1576)

LEACH, Major Richard Ernest Howell, O.B.E., M.A., M.D., B.Ch. (Oxon), M.R.C.S. (Eng.), L.R.C.P. (Lond.), R.A.M.C., *b.* 21 Nov. 1874. *Educ.*: Rugby; Merton Coll., Oxford; St. Thomas's Hospital. Deputy Commissioner of Medical Services, Ministry of Pensions. *War Work*: Served with E.E.F. 1915–19; Registrar 31st and 88th General Hospitals. *Address*: 16, Argyll Road, Kensington, London, W. 8. *Club*: Public Schools.   (O6221)

LEACH, William, M.B.E.

LEAHY, Lieut.-Col. Henry Gordon, O.B.E., J.P., R.A. (ret.), *p.a.c.*, Lefroy Gold Medal, *b.* 21 Jan. 1868; *s.* of the late Colonel Arthur Leahy, R.E., of Flesk, Killarney; *m.* Ellen Elizabeth, *d.* of William Johnson, formerly of Barnshill, Wavertree, Lancs. *Educ.*: Cheltenham Coll., and Royal Military Academy. *War Work*: Inspector of Guns and Carriages, 1914; Inspector of Guns 1914–15; Commanded 22nd Heavy Brigade, R.G.A., Aug. 1915; Commanded R.G.A. Sheerness, and No. 12 Fire Command, 1916–18. *Address*: Carriglea House, Killarney, Co. Kerry. *Club*: Army and Navy.   (O7376)

LEAHY, Eng.-Comm. James Palmer, O.B.E., R.N.

LEAHY, Lieut.-Col. John Patrick Daunt, C.B.E. New Zealand Med. Corps. Served in the Great War, 1915–19 (despatches).   (C1860)

LEAK, Daniel Arthur, O.B.E., I.S.O.

LEAKE, Major Claude Lancelot, O.B.E. M.C.

LEAKE, Frederick Osborne Simeon, O.B.E.

LEAKE, Sidney Henry, O.B.E., *b.* 31 May, 1892; *s.* of Henry Leake, of York. *Educ.*: Model School Training Coll., York. *War Work*: Secretarial Officer and Private Sec. to Secretary, Ministry of Munitions; Capt. on Special List whilst attached to Munitions Mission to Russia in 1917. *Address*: 13, Hermitage Road, Richmond, Surrey. *Club*: National Liberal.   (O10816)

LEAL, Winifred Marie Louise, M.B.E., *b.* 30 Dec. 1880; *s.* of late Charles Edward Leal, G.P.O. (S.B. Dept.). *Educ.*: North London Collegiate School. Salvation Army Officer. *War Work*: France, Jan. 1916 to Aug. 1917, Etaples, visiting and writing letters for the dangerously wounded; Sept. 1917 to Armistice, Le Tréport; Armistice to July 1919 with the Rhine Army working for the benefit of our troops. *Address*: 15, Taviton Street, Gordon Square, London, W.C.1. (M10251b)

LEAMY, Major Alfred, O.B.E.

LEAN, Janette Winifred, M.B.E., A.R.C.M., *b.* 17 Oct. 1893; *d.* of Lieut.-Col. W. W. Lean, late 5th Bengal Cavalry. *Educ.*: Redmoor, and Royal College of Music. *War Work*: Hon. Organising Sec. First Aid Nursing Yeomanry, Passport Dept., British Red Cross Society and Order of St. John of Jerusalem.   (M8767)

LEANE, Col. Edwin Thomas, C.B.E., Aust. A.V.C.

LEANING, William, M.B.E.

LEAPINGWELL, Major Louis Albert, M.B.E., R.E.

LEARMONT, Capt. John, O.B.E., J.P., D.L.

LEARMONTH, Rear-Adm. Frederick Charles, C.B., C.B.E., *b.* 1866; *s.* of the late Alexander Learmonth, M.P. Entered R.N. 1879; joined Hydrographic Service, 1891; has made surveys in all parts of the world (thrice thanked by Admiralty); became Superintendent of Charts at Admiralty, 1908; Hydrographer to the Navy, 1919; Director of Fixed Defences, 1918–19; Legion of Honour. *Address*: 87, Victoria Street, S.W. 1. *Clubs*: United Service; Junior Constitutional.   (C902)

LEARMONTH, Agnes Moore, Mrs., LIVINGSTONE-, C.B.E., M.D. Served in the Great War, 1914–19, with R.A.M.C. (despatches).

LEARMOUTH, Lieut. Archibald Thomas, O.B.E., R.N.R.

LEAROYD, Col. Charles Douglas, C.B.E.

LEAROYD, Joan Vera Douglas, O.B.E.

LEAROYD, Lieut. Leonard, O.B.E., R.N.V.R.

LEARY, Dennis Donald, M.B.E.

LEASK, Capt. James Bruce, O.B.E.

LEATHAM, Capt. Nigel Clere, O.B.E., M.B.E., R.A.S.C.

LEATHER, Lieut.-Col. Kenneth John Walters, C.B.E., *b.* 6 July, 1878; *s.* of the late Frederick John Leather, of Middleton Hall, Belford, Northumberland; *m.* Sybil Margarate, *d.* of Arthur Laing, of Sunderland. *Educ.*: Wellington Coll., and Trinity Coll., Cambridge. 2nd Lieut. 3rd (now 4th) Batt. Durham Light Infantry, March, 1898; 2nd Lieut. 1st Batt. Durham L.I., Sept. 1899; South Africa, Nov. 1899–1902

(5 clasps, Queen's Medal; 2 clasps, King's Medal); resigned commission and appointed Major and 2nd in Command 4th Extra Special Reserve Batt. Durham Light Infantry, March 1912; to Command, 22 March, 1918. *War Work*: 2nd in Command 4th Batt. Durham L.I. to Aug. 11, 1915; appointed to Command 20th Batt. (Wearside) Durham Light Infantry, which was raised by the Sunderland Recruiting Committee at the latter end of that month; went to France with the 41st Division at the end of April, 1916; severely wounded, July, 1916; attached Eastern Command Headquarters, March, 1917–18; appointed to command the 4th Extra Special Reserve Batt. Durham Light Infantry, March, 1918. *Address*: Whalton, Northumberland.   (C1656)

LEATHERBARROW, Edward John, M.B.E.

LEATHES, Major Carteret de Mussenden, O.B.E.

LEATHES, Major Herbert de Mussenden, O.B.E., *b.* 16 Nov. 1863; *s.* of Col. H. de Mussenden Leathes, of Herring-fleet Hall, Suffolk (*see* BURKE'S *Landed Gentry*); *m.* Agnes Isabel, *d.* of Mr. Justice Stephens, LL.D. *Educ.*: Haileybury, and Royal Agricultural Coll. Cirencester. Guardian to Rajah Sahib of Pooneh. *War Work*: Commanded 2/5th Yorks. Regt., and 15th Yorks. Regt.; 2nd in Command 13th Yorks. Regt., and 1st Gar. Batt. Scottish Rifles; Organising Sec. R.A.T.A., Simla; Provost Marshal, 2nd Rawalpindi Div. and Kashmir. *Address*: Kashmir House, Ajmer, Rajputana.   (O8496)

LEAVER, Frederick John, M.B.E., *b.* 1 March, 1872; *s.* of Frederick Leaver, of Newbury; *m.* Frances Elizabeth, *d.* of Richard Tomsett, of Bognor. *Educ.*: Newbury Grammar School. Raw Material Buyer in the Chocolate Dept. of Nestle, Anglo-Swiss Condensed Milk Co. *War Work*: Deputy Manager and Buyer for the Central Prisoners of War Committee of the British Red Cross Society. *Address*: Berstead, Purley Oaks Road, Sanderstead, Surrey.   (M3800)

LEAVER, Capt. Gray, M.B.E.

LEANER, Kate Rose, Mrs., M.B.E.

LEAVIS, Major Henry, C.B.E., *b.* 1 July, 1886; *s.* of the late James Hicks Leavis, of Cork; *m.* Josephine Rita, *niece* of the Earl of Reading. *Educ.*: Carmichael School; Presentation Coll., Cork; Private Study. Divisional Road Transport Officer, London and Home Counties Division. *War Work*: Enlisted Aug. 1914; Gazetted 2nd Lieut. R.A.S.C. Sept. 1914; promoted Major Feb. 1917; Mentioned in Despatches, 1919; awarded C.B.E., 1920; served in France, 1914–19. *Address*: 45, Bryanston Street, W. 1.   (C2752)

LE BRETON, Clement Martin, O.B.E., K.C., *s.* of the Very Rev. W. C. le Breton, M.A., Dean of Jersey. *Educ.*: Victoria Coll., Jersey, and Sandhurst. Recorder of Sudbury; Chairman of Trade Boards. *War Work*: Commissioner Civil Liabilities; Chairman of Trade Boards; Arbitrator in Industrial Disputes for Minister of Labour. *Clubs*: Reform; Orleans.   (O495)

LE BRUN, Paymaster-Comm. William Henry, C.B.E.

LEBUS, Herman Andrew Harris, C.B.E., *b.* 1 June, 1884; *s.* of Harris Lebus, of London; *m.* Ethel Hart Harris, *d.* of Charles Hart, of Chicago, Ill., U.S.A. Partner in Messrs. Harris Lebus, of Tabernacle Street, E.C. 2, and Tottenham, N. 17. *Address*: 6, Kensington Palace Gardens, London, W. 8. *Clubs*: Junior Constitutional; Royal Automobile. (C3106f)

LECHE, John Hurleston, O.B.E., Knight of Order of the Crown of Belgium, *b.* 21 Nov. 1889; *s.* of John Hurleston, of Carden Park, Chester (*see* BURKE'S *Landed Gentry*); *m.* Amy Violet, *d.* of Clement William Joseph Unthank, of Intwood Hall, Norwich. *Educ.*: Eton, and Sandhurst. 2nd Lieut. 12th Lancers, Feb. 1910 to Nov. 1913; Lieut. 12th Lancers Special Reserve; appointed 3rd Sec. Diplomatic Service, June, 1919. *War Work*: Served with 12th Lancers in France and Belgium, and on the Staff as General Staff Officer, 3rd Grade. *Addresses*: Carden Park, Chester; Stretton Hall, Malpas. *Clubs*: Carlton; White's.   (O5470)

LECK, William, M.B.E.

LECKIE, Col. John Edwards, C.M.G., C.B.E., D.S.O., B.Sc., *b.* 19 Feb. 1872; *s.* of the late Major Robert Gilmour Leckie. *Educ.*: Bishops Coll. School, Lennoxville; Royal Military Coll., Canada; King's Coll., Windsor, N.S. Mining Engineer. *War Work*: Lieut. Lord Strathcona's Horse, South Africa (Despatches and D.S.O.); Capt. 2nd Can. Mtd. Rifles, South Africa; Major, 2nd in Command 16th Batt. The Canadian Scottish, 1914; Lieut.-Col. and O.C. 16th Batt. 1915; Despatches and C.M.G.; Col. Commanding 2nd Can. Res. Brigade, 1917; Col. "Syren" Party, N.R.E.F. Murman Coast, 1918–19; Despatches, Croix de Guerre, Order of St. Vladimir. *Address*: Vancouver, B.C.   (C2359h)

LECKY, Col. John Gage, C.B.E., *b.* 19 July, 1872; *s.* of Col. George Lecky, late of the Indian Army; *m.* Ethelberta Theodosia, *d.* of Hunt Walsh Leech, of Castleroe, Coleraine, Co. Derry, Ireland. *Educ.*: Llandulas House (N. Wales); Repton School; Sandhurst. *War Work*: Senior Supply Officer (5th Division), B.E.F. Aug. 1914 to Dec. 1914 (Major); O.C. 5th Divisional Train, Dec. 1914 to Dec. 1915 (Lieut.-Col.); to United Kingdom as O.C. 40th Divisional Train (New Army), Dec. 1915 to May, 1916; O.C. 40th Divisional Train, B.E.F. June, 1916, to Oct. 1917; O.C. Base Supply Depot, Havre, Jan. 1918 to May, 1918; Assistant Director of Supplies, Base Ports, May, 1918 to Aug. 1918; Deputy Director of Supplies, Investigation Department, Aug. 1918 to July, 1919 (T. Col.); Deputy Director of Supplies, British Troops in France and Flanders, July to Dec. 1919 (T. Col.); Assistant Director of Supplies and Transport, British Forces on the

Rhine, Dec. 1919; Promoted Substantive Col. to date from Feb. 1919; mentioned in despatches four times. *Address:* Castleroe, Coleraine, Co. Derry, Ireland. *Club:* United Sports. (C1279)

LECOMBER, Capt. Harold Roger, O.B.E., R.A.F.

LECOURT, Rev. Gustave Alexander Vincent, M.B.E., O.S.M., *b.* 2 Sept. 1885; *m.* Gustave Alexander Lecourt, of Cork, Ireland. *Educ.:* England and Bologna, Italy. British Roman Catholic Chaplain in Brussels, from March, 1914, until Sept. 1919. *War Work:* Member of the various societies in Belgium for helping British subjects both civil and military in hiding, etc. *Addresses:* 264, Fulham Road, London, S.W.; The Priory, Clarence Road, Bognor, Sussex. (M8769)

LEDBURY, Rowland Egbert, M.B.E., *b.* 26 Aug. 1875; *s.* of Francis Rowland Ledbury, of Bradford-on-Avon, Wilts. Assistant Commissioner, Ministry of Food; Hon. Treas. Walsall General Hospital; Member, Walsall Naval Military War Pensions Committee; organiser of Weekly Entertainments for Wounded Sailors and Soldiers, Walsall and District, from Nov. 1914–18 (Honorary); organiser of Flag Days and other collections on behalf of the Mayor's Local War Fund, 1915–18. *Address:* Rochefort, Rushall, nr. Walsall. *Club:* Unionist, Walsall. (M8770)

LEDEBOER, Flight Lieut. John Henry, M.B.E., R.A.F.

LEDGARD, Reginald Armitage, O.B.E.

LEDGER, Sidney Seaward, M.B.E.

LEDINGHAM, Alexander, M.B.E., M.A., M.D., D.P.H., *b.* 15 Sept. 1872; *s.* of Rev. James Ledingham, of Boyndie, Banff; *m.* Louisa Lemmon, *d.* of William L. Stewart, M.D., of Falcon Avenue, Edinburgh. *Educ.:* Aberdeen Univ. Minister of the Parish of Boyndie; Medical Officer of Health of the County of Banff. *War Work:* County Director of the Banffshire Branch of the British Red Cross Society; Lance-Corporal of the Banff Company of the Banffshire Volunteer Battalion. *Address:* 43, High Street, Banff. (M8772)

LEDLIE, James Crawford, O.B.E., M.A., B.C.L., *b.* 29 April, 1860; *s.* of Alexander Holmes, late of Calcutta; *m.* Lily, *d.* of J. C. Ledlie, late of Endsleigh, Cork. *Educ.:* Heidelberg and Lincoln Coll., Oxford. Chief Clerk of the Judicial Department of the Privy Council Office, 1902–9; Chief Clerk of the Privy Council Office and Deputy-Clerk of the Council since 1909. *War Work:* In connection with the Privy Council Export Licence Department, 1914–15. *Addresses:* Privy Council Office, Whitehall, S.W.; The Garth, Cobham, Surrey. *Club:* Oxford and Cambridge Musical. (O49c)

LEDWARD, Lieut.-Col. Harold, O.B.E.

LEE, Lieut. Albert Victor, M.B.E.

LEE, Lieut. Alestair, M.B.E., R.A.F.

LEE OF FAREHAM, Col. The Right Hon. Arthur Hamilton, Lord, P.C., G.B.E., K.C.B., J.P., Knight of Grace of St. John of Jerusalem (*see* BURKE'S *Peerage*), *b.* 8 Nov. 1868; *s.* of Rev Melville Lee, of Bridport, Dorset; *m.* Ruth, *d.* of John Godfrey Moore, of New York, U.S.A. *Educ.:* Cheltenham; R.M.A. Woolwich. Minister of Agriculture and Fisheries; Col. General Reserve of Officers. *War Work:* Service with B.E.F. in France and Flanders, Sept. 1914, to Oct. 1915 as Colonel and Liaison Officer at G.H.Q. (1914 Star and clasp); Parliamentary Military Secretary, Ministry of Munitions, Nov. 1915, to July, 1916; Personal Mil. Sec. to Sec. of State for War (Mr. Lloyd George), July, 1916, to Dec. 1916; Director-Gen. of Food Production, Feb. 1917, to July, 1918. *Address:* 2, The Abbey Garden, Westminster, S.W. *Clubs:* Athenæum; United Service; Burlington Fine Arts. (G28)

LEE, Lieut.Col. Arthur Neale, D.S.O., O.B.E., T.D. Notts and Derby Regt.; Gen. Staff Officer; served in the Great War, 1914–19. (O2609)

LEE, Rear-Admiral Sir Charles Lionel, K.B.E., C.B., *b.* 27 Feb. 1867; *s.* of the late Vaughan H. Vaughan-Lee, of Dillington Park, Somerset; *m.* Rose, *d.* of Llewellyn Llewellyn, of Nethway, Devon. Entered the Royal Navy as Naval Cadet, 1880; served in the Egyptian War; Lieut. 1887; Commander 1889; Capt. 1904; Rear-Admiral 1915; Naval A.D.C. to the King, 1914. *Club:* Naval and Military. (K357)

LEE, Lieut. Emsley Mark, O.B.E., R.N.V.R.

LEE, Capt. Eric Alfred, M.B.E., Aust. I.F.

LEE, Brig.-Gen. Francis, C.B.E., *b.* 1866. Col. and Hon. Brig.-Gen. in the Army; served in Somaliland, 1903–4 (medal with two clasps); Great War, 1914–15 (despatches). (C1657)

LEE, Lieut.-Col. Frederick Reginald, M.B.E., V.D., M.A. (Oxon.), I.D.F. (ret.) *b.* 2 July, 1861; *s.* of the Rev. F. G. Lee, D.D., of Thame, Co. Oxon.; *m.* Mary Morwenna, *d.* of Lieut.-Col. C. E. Cardew, J.P., of Wadebridge, Cornwall. *Educ.:* King's Coll., London, and Oxford. For nearly 30 years an officer of the Indian Volunteer Service; before the war an active member of Lord Roberts' National Service League; author of "Practical Swordsmanship" and many articles on military subjects in the "Royal United Service Magazine, India." *War Work:* Served on the Burma Divisional Staff as Instructor in Pistol Shooting. *Address:* Taunggyi, S. Shan States, Burma. (M4178)

LEE, George, M.B.E., *b.* 23 Feb. 1880; *s.* of George Lee, of Portsmouth; *m.* Florence, *d.* of George Warren, of Portsmouth. *Educ.:* Chivers' Civil Service Academy, Southsea. Inspector, Electrical Engineers' Department, H.M. Dockyard, Portsmouth. *War Work:* Assistant Electrical Overseer, Glasgow and Newcastle District; from 1916 Electrical Overseer for Repairs, Liverpool District. *Addresses:* 334, Royal Liver Buildings, Liverpool; 79, Gorsefield Road, Birkenhead. (M8773)

LEE, Major George, M.B.E., R.A.

LEE, Harriet Louise, Mrs., M.B.E.

LEE, Henry Blott, M.B.E., *b.* 4 April, 1872; *s.* of John Lee, of Gt. Yarmouth. *Educ.:* Belle Vue House School, Eaton Park, Norwich. Managing Director and Secretary of Yarmouth Mercury, Ltd., Newspaper Proprietors. *War Work:* Divisional Leader, Gt. Yarmouth Special Constabulary. *Address:* 9, Gordon Road, Southtown, Great Yarmouth. (M8774)

LEE, Capt. and Qr.-Mr. Herbert Benjamin, O.B.E., R.A.M.C.

LEE, Herbert Newton, O.B.E.

LEE, Paymaster-Lieut. Herbert Victor, O.B.E., R.N.R.

LEE, Hugh Warren, O.B.E.

LEE, Jane Winfred, Mrs., M.B.E.

LEE, Capt. John Dalby, M.B.E.

LEE, John Robert, O.B.E., M.D., F.R.C.S., *b.* 1873; *s.* of William and E. J. Lee, of Victoria, Australia; *m.* Bertha Ethel, *d.* of John Butson, of Melbourne. *Educ.:* Melbourne. Surgeon. *War Work:* Officer-in-Charge of the Surgical Division, Fulham Military Hospital, Hammersmith, 1915–19. *Address:* 49, Harley Street, London, W. 1. (O7379)

LEE, John Thomas, M.B.E.

LEE, John William, O.B.E.

LEE, Major Lennie Henry, O.B.E., I.A.R.O.

LEE, Loraine, M.B.E.

LEE, Mabel Meyrick, Mrs., M.B.E., *b.* 2 April, 1892; *d.* of Capt. H. R. Fowler, of Hants Regt. (retired); *m.* Walter, *s.* of Frederick Lee, of Faversham. *Educ.:* Privately. *War Work:* General Service Section, British Red Cross Society, from July, 1915, to date; Chief Clerk to O.C. Cambridge Hospital, Aldershot, from Nov. 1915, to Nov. 1916; Chief Clerk, Queen's Hosp. for Facial Injuries, Sidcup, from opening in April, 1917 to date. *Address:* Frognal, Sidcup, Kent. (M8776)

LEE, Sarah Josephine, Mrs., O.B.E.

LEE, Very Rev. Canon William, M.B.E., *b.* 27 Sept. 1875; *s.* of Richard Lee, of Mitchelstown, Co. Cork. *Educ.:* St. Colman's, Fermoy; St. John's, Waterford; Oscott, Birmingham. Canon of Clifton, Bristol. *War Work:* Chairman of Belgian Refugee Committee, Bristol; Chaplain to R.C. Troops, Bristol. *Address:* Pro-Cathedral House, Clifton, Bristol. (M8777)

LEE, William Alexander, C.B.E., 31 May, 1886; *s.* of William Allan Lee, of Grantham; *m.* Edith Lydia, *d.* of William Henry Grimwood, of London. *Educ.:* Royal Grammar School, Newcastle-on-Tyne. Assistant Secretary to Mining Association of Great Britain. *War Work:* Secretary of Coal Mines Dept. of Board of Trade till end of 1919; is Officer of the Order of the Crown of Belgium. *Address:* 66, Rutland Park Mansions, London, N.W. 2. *Club:* St. Stephen's. (C2754)

LEE, William John, M.B.E., *b.* 30 April, 1856; *s.* of Rev. William Lee, D.D., Professor of Ecclesiastical History in the University of Glasgow; *m.* Amy Florence, *d.* of David Henry Lee. *Educ.:* Fettes Coll.; St. John's Coll., Cambridge. Barrister-at-law of the Inner Temple. *War Work:* Hon. Sec. and Treas. Roxburghshire Branch of the Scottish Branch, British Red Cross Society. *Address:* The Scaurs, Jedburgh, N.B. *Club:* United University. (M8778)

LEE, Major William Lauriston Melville, O.B.E., M.A., late Royal Warwickshire Regt., *b.* 8 Oct. 1865; *s.* of late Rev. Melville Lee, of Bridport, Dorset; *m.* Winifred Acton, *d.* of the late Henry Barter, D.L., of Worplesdon, Surrey, and Airlie Gardens, W. *Educ.:* Wellington Coll.; Magdalen Coll., Oxford; Sandhurst; Inner Temple. Sec. County of Oxford T.F. Assoc., Editor of "Industrial Peace." *War Work:* Territorial Army Administration; Ministry of Munitions; Food Production Department (Military Labour). *Addresses:* Stoke Place, Old Headington, Oxon.; 20, Magdalen Street, Oxford. *Clubs:* United Service; Royal Automobile; Oxford and County. (O1580)

LEE, Vaughan Alexander Edward HANNING-, D.S.O., O.B.E.

LEE, Vice-Adm. Sir Charles Lionel VAUGHAN-, K.B.E., C.B., *b.* 27 Feb. 1867; 3rd *s.* of the late Vaughan Hanning Vaughan-Lee, D.L., M.P., of Dallington Park, Somerset; *m.* 4 July, 1895, Rose Cecilia, *d.* of Llewellyn Llewellyn, of Nethway House, S. Devon. Admiral Supt. Portsmouth Dockyard, 1917–20; Naval A.D.C. to the King, 1914–15. Served in Egyptian War, 1882 (medal, bronze star); Great War, from 1914 (despatches); Commander Legion of Honour, Commander of the Order of St. Maurice and St. Lazarus of Italy, and 2nd Class Order of the Rising Sun of Japan. *Address:* Naval and Military Club.

LEE, Mary Ess WELSH-, Mrs., C.B.E. Sec. Pilgrims of Great Britain; Business Sec. American Officers' Club.

LEECH, Arthur John, M.B.E., *b.* 6 July, 1873; *s.* of Sir Bosdin T. Leech, of Manchester; *m.* Kathleen Maida, *d.* of William Cotton Rohde, of Folkestone. *Educ.:* Manchester Grammar School. Merchant. *War Work:* General War Work in Madras, principally in assisting the starting and running of a Soldiers' Club there. *Address:* The Palms, College Road, Madras. *Clubs:* Madras; Brazenose, Manchester. (M4176)

LEECH, Beatrice Ellen, Mrs., M.B.E.; *d.* of B. L. Nias; *m.* John Henry, *s.* of John Leech, of Gorse Hall, Cheshire. *War Work:* Hon. Sec. to Salisbury and District Prisoners of War Assoc., 1917–19. *Address:* Bretford Moat, Salisbury. (M8779)

LEECH, Samuel Chetwynd, O.B.E.

LEEDOM, Beatrice Lucy, M.B.E.. *b.* 17 Dec. 1895; *d.* of William James Tizard, of Weymouth, Dorset; *m.* Henry Stancliff, *s.* of William Leedom, of London. Shorthand Typist to the Secretary of the Ministry of Shipping. *Address:* Fire Station, Old Kent Road, London, S.E. 1.   (M8780)

LEEMAN, Walter Joseph, O.B.E., *b.* 2 Aug. 1858; *s.* of Commander J. Leeman, R.N.R., of Aberdeen; *m.* Ada Constance, *d.* of Thomas Gill, of the Manor of Treverbyn, Cornwall. *Educ.:* Aldenham, and Aberdeen. Member of the London Stock Exchange. *War Work:* As Acting Paymaster in the Army Pay Dept. from Aug. 1914, to Dec. 1918. *Address:* 39, Rusholme Road, Putney Hill, S.W. *Clubs:* Bath; Constitutional.   (O10820)

LEEPER, Alexander Wigram Allen, C.B.E., *b.* 4 Jan. 1887; *s.* of Alexander Leeper, LL.D., of Melbourne, Australia; *Educ.:* Church of England Grammar School, Melbourne; Trinity Coll., Univ. of Melbourne; Balliol Coll., Oxford. Second Secretary, Diplomatic Service, Foreign Office. *War Work:* Political intelligence work under the Foreign Office; subsequently at the Peace Conference. *Address:* 4, Palace Street, Westminster, London, S.W. 1. *Clubs:* New University; R.A.C.   (C2755)

LEEPER, Elizabeth Anne, Mrs., M.B.E.

LEEPER, Reginald Wildig Allen, C.B.E., *b.* 25 March, 1888; *s.* of Alexander Leeper, LL.D., of Melbourne, Australia; *m.* Margaret Primrose Dundas, *d.* of G. Boyce Allen, of 145, Woodstock Road, Oxford. *Educ.:* Melbourne Grammar School; Trinity Coll.; Melbourne Univ.; New Coll., Oxford. *War Work:* 1915–17, Press Work, News Department, Foreign Office; 1917–18, Intelligence Bureau, Department of Information; 1918–20, Political Intelligence Department, Foreign Office. *Address:* 9, Oxford and Cambridge Mansions, N.W. 1. *Club:* Wellington.   (C2756)

LEES, Lieut.-Col. Charles Archibald, C.B.E., R.A.M.C. (T.). Served in the Great War, 1914–18 (despatches). (C1658)

LEES, Ebenezer Antony, O.B.E., *b.* 1853; *s.* of Rev. W. Lees, of Glasgow, and Walsall; *m.* Alice Rose, *d.* of F. W. Woollard, J.P., of Stony Stratford. *Educ.:* Privately. Sec. of the Water Department, Birmingham Corporation (now retired). *War Work:* On the outbreak of war undertook the management of the Lady Mayoress's Depot, Birmingham, and was Chairman of the Executive and Finance Committee; Chairman of the Prisoners of War Fund from their inception until the end of the war. *Address:* 123, Oxford Road, Moseley, Birmingham.   (O1581)

LEES, Rear-Adm. Edgar, C.B.E., R.N., *b.* 1866; *s.* of the late James Lees, of Alkrington Hall, Lancashire; *m.* 1904, Mary Agnes, *d.* of Com. — Tucker, R.N.   (C901)

LEES, Major George, O.B.E., R.A.O.C.

LEES, Sir John McKie, K.B.E., M.A., LL.B. (Edin. Univ.), K.C., *b.* 1843; *s.* of Walter Lees, of Glasgow; *m.* Alice Susan, *d.* of James Clark, of Crossbasket, Lanarkshire. *Educ.:* Ayr and Edinburgh Academies and Edinburgh Univ. Sheriff-Principal of Forfarshire; Examiner for Degrees in Law to Edinburgh and Glasgow Universities; Scottish Bar, 1867; K.C. 1901; Sheriff-Substitute of Lanarkshire, 1872; Sheriff-Principal of Stirling, Dumbarton, and Clackmannan, 1891, and of Forfar, 1917; Convener of Sheriffs, 1907; Commissioner of Northern Lights, 1917. *War Work:* Chairman of Appeal, Military Tribunal of Stirling, Dumbarton, and Clackmannan Counties. *Address:* 4, Darnaway Street, Edinburgh. *Club:* University, Edinburgh.   (K218)

LEES, Kenneth Arthur, O.B.E., M.A., M.B., B.Ch. (Cantab.), F.R.C.S. (Eng.), *b.* 10 April, 1881; *s.* of the late David Lees, M.D., F.R.C.S., of 22, Weymouth Street, W. 1; *m.* Ivy Comyn, *d.* of J. Bastian Hill, of 55, Overstrand Mansions, S.W. 11. *Educ.:* St. Paul's School; King's Coll., Cambridge; St. Mary's Hospital, Paddington. Assistant Surgeon, Ear, Nose, and Throat Dept., St. Mary's Hospital; Surgeon, Ear, Nose, and Throat Dept., Queen's Hospital for Children, Hackney. *War Work:* Surgeon, Princess Club Military Hospital, Bermondsey; Temporary Asst. Surgeon at St. Mary's Hospital; Paddington Green Children's Hospital; Golden Square Throat Hospital; London Fever Hospital; Florence Nightingale Hospital. *Address:* 48, Harley Street, W. 1.   (O11820)

LEES, Lieut.-Col. Roderick Livingstone, D.S.O., O.B.E., V.D., Lancs Fusiliers, T.F., *b.* 17 Sept. 1864; *s.* of late James Lees, of Alkrington; *m.* Amy Constance, *d.* of William Jones, of Abberley Hall. *Educ.:* Eton Coll. *War Work:* Commanded 6th Batt. Lancashire Fusiliers in Gallipoli, Egypt, and France, 1914–17; Commanded 14th Batt. Suffolk Regt., 1917–19; mentioned three times in despatches. *Address:* c/o Manchester and County Bank, Manchester.   (O7380)

LEES, Dame Sarah Anne, D.B.E., LL.D., Lady of Grace of Order of St. John of Jerusalem, *b.* 13 Nov. 1842; *d.* of John Buckley, of Carr Hill, Mossley; *m.* Charles Edward Lees, *s.* of Eli Lees, of Werneth Park, Oldham. *Educ.:* Privately; and Wincobank Hall, Sheffield. Member of Oldham Town Council from 1907–19; First Freeman, 1910; Mayor, 1910–11; Alderman, 1913; Hon. LL.D., Manchester Univ., 1914. *Address:* Werneth Park, Oldham.   (D5)

LEES, Major Thomas Orde Hans, O.B.E., A.F.C., R.A.F.

LEES, William, O.B.E. Provost of Dunoon. Distinguished war service as municipal head of the Borough of Dunoon   (O11910)

LEES, William Clare, O.B.E., J.P., Hon. Serving Brother, Order of St. John, *b.* 9 Dec. 1874; *s.* of William Lees, of Birkdale; *m.* Kathleen, *d.* of John Nickson, of Liverpool, *Educ.:* Leys School, Cambridge. Director, Bleachers Association, Ltd.; Vice-President, the Manchester Chamber of Commerce; Assistant Commissioner, St. John Ambulance Brigade, No 4 District. *War Work:* 1915, Chairman, Building Committee, St. John V.A.D. Hospital (500 beds), Southport; 1917–19, Deputy Chief Executive Officer, War Department (Cotton Textiles), Manchester. *Address:* Etherow House, Hollingworth, Cheshire. *Clubs:* Constitutional; Clarendon, Manchester.   (O10821)

LEESE, Major Clive, M.B.E.

LEESE, Lieut.-Col. Neville, D.S.O., O.B.E., R.A.S.C., *b.* 23 March, 1872; 3rd *s.* of Sir Joseph Francis Leese, 1st Bart. (*see* BURKE'S *Peerage*); *m.* Matilda, *d.* of J. Saunders. (O6391)

LEESE, Vernon Francis, O.B.E.

LEESON, Gladys Mary, M.B.E.

LEETE, William Chambers, O.B.E.

LEETHAM, Ethel Mary, M.B.E., *b.* 1886; *d.* of Henry Ernest Leetham, J.P., of York. *Educ.:* The Mount School, York. *War Work:* Sec., and latterly Commandant, of the Training Coll. V.A.D. Hospital, York. *Address:* Aldersyde, Dringhouses, York.   (M8782)

LEFEBURE, Major Victor, O.B.E. Essex Regt.; has Legion of Honour.   (O7381)

LEFEURE, Capt. Frederick Charles, O.B.E.

LEFROY, Grace, C.B.E., *b.* 1848; *d.* of Rev. Anthony Cottrell Lefroy, of Church Crookham, Hants. *Educ.:* Privately. Hon. Sec. from 1886–1919 of the British Women's Emigration Association at the Imperial Institute, South Kensington. *Address:* 8, Launceston Place, Kensington, W. 8   (C2401)

LEFROY, Capt. Langlois Massey, O.B.E.

LEFTWICH, Charles Gerrans, C.B.E., B.A., I.C.S., *b.* 31 July, 1872; *s.* of late T. W. Leftwich, of E. Dulwich; *m.* Evadne, *d.* of H. W. Fawcus, of Alnmouth. *Educ.:* Christ's Hospital, and St. John's Coll., Cambridge. Indian Civil Service. *War Work:* Controller of Munitions, and Director of Civil Supplies, Central Provinces, India. *Address:* St. Aubins, Jersey, C.I. *Club:* Oxford and Cambridge. (C1975)

LEGARD, Lieut.-Col. Alfred Digby, C.B.E., *b.* 19 June, 1878; *m.* 19 Aug. 1902, Winifred, *o. d.* of Col. Sir William George Morris, K.C.M.G., C.B., R.E. Major and Brevet Lieut.-Col., late King's Royal Rifle Corps.   (C1659)

LEGAT, Kathleen, Mrs., M.B.E.

LEGG, Capt. Cecil Henry, O.B.E., *b.* 18 Nov. 1890; *s.* of H. P. Legg, of Leeds. *Educ.:* Eastbourne Coll. *War Work:* Mobilised with Yorks Hussars; served in France with the 49th (W.R.) Div. Train, R.A.S.C., 1915–19; Adjt. 1917–19. *Address:* 7, St. Mary's Road, Newton Park, Leeds. (O5474)

LEGG, Capt. Sir George Edward Wickham, K.B.E., M.V.O., Knight of Grace, Order of St. John of Jerusalem, Chevalier, Legion d'Honneur, *b.* 13 July, 1870; *s.* of Rev. William Legg, Rector of Hawkinge, Kent; *m.* Kathleen (Lady of Grace, Order of St. John of Jerusalem), *d.* of Col. Sir James Gildea, G.B.E., K.C.V.O., C.B. *Educ.:* Radley, Trinity Coll., Cambridge; Sandhurst. Joined South Staffordshire Regt. 1891; Capt. General Reserve of Officers, 1905; Member of the Council of St. Peter's Coll., Radley. *War Work:* Sec. Soldiers' and Sailors' Families Association. *Address:* 14, Pembroke Gardens, Kensington, W. 8. *Club:* Army and Navy.   (K390)

LEGGAT, Lieut.-Col. George Leggat, O.B.E., M.B.

LEGGATT, Capt. Charles William Stares, C.B.E., *b.* 1864 *s.* of the late Samuel Bethune Leggatt, of Crofton Manor, Fareham, Hants; *m.* 1900, Gertrude Elizabeth, *d.* of J. B. Walmsley, of Hartfield, Allerton, Liverpool. Formerly Capt. R.N.; joined Naval Transport Service, 1914; became Div. Naval Transport Officer, Devonport; served in the Great War, 1914–19 (despatches); Jubilee medal, 1897.   (C2259)

LEGGE, Capt. Edward Alder, M.B.E., D.C.M.

LEGGE, Major Francis Cecil, C.B.E., *b.* 14 Sept. 1873; *s.* of the late Charles Gounter Legge (*see* BURKE'S *Peerage*, Dartmouth, E.) District Superintendent, East India Railway, Calcutta; Hon. Major, Ind. Defence Force; Dep. Coal Controller, Bengal.   (C1976)

LEGGE, Brig.-Gen. Reginald Francis, C.B.E., D.S.O. Major and Brevet Lieut.-Col. Leinster Regt.; T. Brig.-Gen.; served in the S. African War, 1900–2 (Queen's medal with three clasps, King's medal with two clasps); Great War, 1914–17 (despatches; Legion of Honour).   (C1280)

LEGGE, Thomas Morison, C.B.E., M.D. Chief Med. Inspector of Factories.   (C547)

LEGGETT, Arthur, M.B.E.

LEGGETT, Major Edward James, O.B.E., R.A.O.C.

LEGGETT, Henry Anfrere, C.B.E. Principal Clerk in Ministry of Health.

LEGGETT, Lieut.-Col. Robert Anthony Clegthorn Linington, O.B.E., D.S.O., *b.* 1874; Major Reserve; Comdg. an Officer Cadet Batt. with rank of Lieut.-Col; served in the S. African War, 1899–1902 (Queen's medal with three clasps, King's medal with two clasps); Great War, 1914–19 (despatches).   (O7383)

LEGH, Major Frank Bertham, O.B.E., R.E. *Address:* 11, Salisbury Road, Edinburgh.   (O5475)

LEGH, Capt. the Hon. Piers Walter, O.B.E., Grenadier Guards, *b.* 12 Dec. 1890; *s.* of Lord Newton, of Lyme (*see* BURKE'S *Peerage*). *Educ.:* Eton. Equerry to His Royal Highness the Prince of Wales. *War Work:* A.D.C. to H.R.H. the Duke of Connaught from 1914–15; A.D.C. and

Military Sec. with the rank of Major to Gen. the Earl of Cavan, in France and Italy ; mentioned in despatches ; awarded the Croix de Guerre and the Italian Croce. *Addresses :* 75, Eaton Square, S.W. ; Lyme Park, Disley, Cheshire. *Clubs :* Guards' ; Bachelors'. (O6392)

LE GROS, Edith Katharine, Mrs., M.B.E., *b.* 22 Dec. 1878 ; *d.* of Peter Brotherhood, of 15, Hyde Park Gardens, W. ; *m.* John Alfred, *s.* of Philip Le Gros, J.P., of Frome, Somerset. *Educ. :* The Cliff, Eastbourne, and abroad. *War Work :* Supt. Knitting and Spinning Dept., British Red Cross and Order of St. John of Jerusalem, Central Workrooms, Burlington House. *Address :* Bury Court, Yapton, nr. Arundel. (M3686)

LEGROS, Lucien Alphonse, O.B.E., M.Inst.C.E., M.I. Mech E., M.I.E.E., M.I.A.E., M.desI.C.F., *b.* 1865 ; *s.* of Alphonse Legros, of Dijon, France. *Educ. :* Univ. Coll. School, and Univ. Coll. Member of Army Transport Advisory Board, War Office ; Member of Treasury Committee on Type Faces. *War Work :* 1915–16, Assistant Consulting Engineer to Admiralty Landship Committee, Tank Designing for Munitions Inventions Committee ; 1916–17, Chief Dilution Officer (Labour) Aircraft, Ministry of Munitions ; 1918, Chief Technical Assistant, Ministry of National Service. *Address :* 25, Cumberland Park, Acton, W.3. *Clubs :* Royal Automobile ; Royal Aero. (O3795)

LEHMANN, Henry David, M.B.E., R.A.F.

LEICESTER, Alice Emily, Countess of, D.B.E. ; *d.* of 2nd Baron Annaly (*see* BURKE'S *Peerage*) ; *m.* 1879, Thomas William Coke, G.C.V.O., C.M.G., 3rd Earl of Leicester, *e. s.* of 2nd Earl of Leicester, K.G. (died 1909) (*see* BURKE'S *Peerage*). *War Work :* President of the Norfolk Branch of the British Red Cross Society. *Address :* 44, Mount Street, W. 1 ; Holkham Hall, Wells, Norfolk. (D49)

LEIGH, Alan de Verd, M.B.E., B.A., *b.* 7 June, 1891 ; *s.* of the Rev. J. de V. Leigh, of Oatlands, Weybridge. *Educ. :* Marlborough, and Merton Coll., Oxon. Dept. Ass. Sec. London Chamber of Commerce. *War Work :* Accountant-General's Dept., Admiralty. *Address :* 88, Holland Road, W. 14. (M8783)

LEIGH, Charles Edward, M.B.E., M.A. (Cantab), *b.* 13 July, 1856 ; *s.* of the Rev. Charles Brian Leigh, J.P., of Goldhanger, Essex ; *m.* Constance Mary, *d.* of John Pickup Lord, J.P., of Hallow Park, Worcester. *Educ. :* Winchester ; Clare Coll., Cambridge. Assistant Land Agent to F. W. Greswolde Greswolde-Williams. *War Work :* Voluntary Ambulance Driver in France and Belgium, 1914–15 ; Hon. Sec. Leamington Local Central Committee for War Savings, 1916–18 ; Food Executive Officer, Leamington Food Control Committee, 1917–20. *Address :* Craiglea, Mount Hermon Road, Woking. (M8784)

LEIGH, Lieut.-Col. Geoffrey Hamilton, O.B.E.

LEIGH, Maxwell Studdy, O.B.E., I.C.S., *b.* 19 Oct. 1882 ; *s.* of Col. H. P. P. Leigh, C.I.E., of Bath ; *m.* Muriel Harriet, *d.* of James Whishaw, of Petrograd. *Educ. :* Newton Coll. ; Winchester Coll. ; New Coll., Oxford ; Univ. Coll., London. *Address :* c/o Civil Secretariat, Lahore. *Clubs :* East India United Services ; Punjab, Lahore. (O4056)

LEIGH, Norah Marjorie, Lady, C.B.E. ; *d.* of John Henry New, of Melbourne, Australia ; *m.* Sir John, 1st Bt., *s.* of John Leigh, J.P., of Brooklands, Cheshire. *War Work :* Equipped the John Leigh Memorial Hospital at Altrincham, which was presented by her husband to the British Red Cross Society for the use of wounded officers ; took a large share in the management and acted as officer in charge of the hospital, which contained 86 beds, and was opened in April, 1917, by Katherine, Duchess of Westminster ; received H.R.H. the Duke of Connaught when he inspected the hospital in June, 1918 ; responsible for the equipment and took an active interest in the John Leigh Memorial Hospital at Woodbourne, Brooklands, which her husband gave as a memorial to his father to the Ministry of Pensions for the treatment of shell-shock cases ; the hospital was opened by the Duke of Connaught on the occasion of his visit to Altrincham ; Member of the Board of Management of the Llandudno Hospital, to which her husband made a gift of £5000 in 1919 ; Member of the Council of the Beyond Seas Association, and took a warm interest in the work of the Canadian Officers' Club at 8, Chesterfield Gardens, which was established and maintained by her husband. (C2758)

LEIGH, Reginald Gerard, O.B.E.

LEIGHTON, Lieut.-Col. Gerald Rowley, O.B.E., M.D., *b.* 12 Dec. 1868 ; *s.* of the Rev. James Leighton, of Manchester ; *m.* Clara, *d.* of Bernard Gordon, of Manchester. *Educ. :* Nelson Coll., New Zealand ; Manchester Grammar School ; Edinburgh Univ. Late Professor of Pathology, Royal (Dick) Veterinary Coll., Edinburgh ; Medical Officer (Foods), Scottish Board of Health. *War Work :* Inspector of Army Food Contracts (Scotland) for War Office ; Inspector of Food Contracts for Admiralty (Scotland) ; Technical Adviser to National Salvage Council ; Administrative Adviser to Ministry of Food (Scotland) ; Member of Committee on Production and Distribution of Milk (Astor Committee) ; Member of Various Departmental Committees. *Address :* Scottish Board of Health, Edinburgh. *Clubs :* Authors' ; Scottish Conservative, Edinburgh. (O10823)

LEIGHTON, Jane Creagh, M.B.E., *b.* 11 April, 1865 ; *d.* of the late Rev. C. R. Leighton, of Charlton Kings, Gloucestershire. *Educ. :* Cheltenham. *War Work :* Sept. 1914, to May, 1915, as V.A.D. Nurse at Moorend, V.A.D. Hospital, Charlton Kings ; May, 1915, to Feb. 1919, as Quartermaster at Naunton V.A.D. Hospital, Cheltenham. *Address :* Menmuir Cottage, Charlton Kings, Gloucestershire. (M3801)

LEIGHTON, Comm. John Albert, C.B.E., D.S.O., R.N.R., Served in the Great War, 1914–18 (despatches, Order of Crown of Belgium). (C2258)

LEIGHTON, Thomas William, O.B.E., M.B., Ch.B., *b.* 18 Nov. 1877 ; *s.* of William Edward, of Blackburn, Lancs ; *m.* Florence, *d.* of John J. Stones, of Samlesbury, Lancs. *Educ. :* Ushaw, Durham, and Manchester Univ. District Med. Officer and Pub. Vaccinator, Chorley Union ; M.O. Post Office ; Member, U.D.C. Withnell. *War Work :* 1915–19, Capt. R.A.M.C. East Lancs Cas. Clearing Station Hospitals ; Med. Boards ; 2/2 Field Ambulance, France ; M.O. 2/7th Batt. Manchester Regt. France May, 1917, to March, 1918 ; taken prisoner, March, 1918 ; Rostatt-Mainz ; Med. Officer-in-charge Hospital, Wounded Allied Officers, Quedlenburg, Hartz, June to Dec. 1918. *Address :* Bury Lane, Brinscall, Lancashire. (O44889)

LEINSTER, Elsie Maude, M.B.E.

LEITCH, John, O.B.E. (O11987)

LEITCH, Walter, C.B.E. *War Work :* Director of Munitions, Australia. (C711)

LEITH, Major Alexander Robert, O.B.E., *b.* 22 Feb. 1878 ; *s.* of the late Major Thomas Leith and Lady Mary Leith, of Petmathen, Aberdeenshire (*see* BURKE'S *Peerage*, Carnwath, E.) ; *m.* Alexandra Gladys, *d.* of 1st Baron Swansea, of Singleton, Swansea (*see* BURKE'S *Peerage*). *Educ. :* Eton. Joined the King's Royal Rifle Corps, 1899, and rose to rank of Major ; S. African War (Queen's medal and five clasps) ; present at the Siege of Ladysmith. *War Work :* Served with 2nd Batt. K.R.R.C., in 1914 ; Staff Capt. Directorate of Movements, 1917–19 ; Order of White Eagle 4th class with swords (Serbia) ; Order of the Sacred Treasure 4th class (Japan) ; Order of the Wen Hu 4th class (China) ; Chevalier of the Legion of Honour (France) ; Croix de Guerre with palms (France). *Address :* Bishop's Sparkford, Winchester. *Club :* Wellington. (O8857)

LEITH, Capt. George Peacy, C.B.E. Com. and Acting Capt. R.N. *War Work :* 1914–19, with Ocean Escort (despatches). (C1194)

LEITH, Gordon, C.B., C.B.E., *b.* 10 March, 1879 ; *s.* of Walter Leith, of Manor House, Ashby-de-la-Zouch, Leicestershire. *Educ. :* Harrow and Trinity Coll., Cambridge. Banker, late partner of Messrs. Speyer Brothers. *War Work :* War Office Staff (Qr.-Mr.-General's Department) ; Chairman, Board of Management, Navy and Army Canteen Board ; Deputy Controller, Army Salvage Board ; rejoined Northumberland Yeomanry on outbreak of war ; Capt. 1914 ; Major 1916 ; Lieut.-Col. 1917 ; Colonel 1918 ; called to War Office, July, 1915. *Address :* 21, Portsea Place, Connaught Square, London. *Clubs :* Marlboro ; White's ; St. James'. (C1660)

LEITH, Major Thomas Geoffrey, O.B.E.

LELAND, Col. Francis William George, C.B.E., D.S.O., *b.* 1877 ; Major and Brevet Lieut.-Col. Army Ser. Corps ; Dep. Director of Supply and Transport, with rank of Col. ; served in S.Africa, 1901–2 (Queen's medal with four clasps) ; Great War, 1914–19 (despatches). (C1427)

LE MAISTRE, Charles, C.B.E. Adviser to Aircraft Production Department, Ministry of Munitions.

LEMAN, Lieut.-Col. George Edward, O.B.E.

LEMAN, Major George, O.B.E., *p.s.c., b.* 12 Sept. 1875 ; *s.* of George Downton Leman, of Madras Civil Service. *Educ. :* Charterhouse and Sandhurst. *War Work :* Served with 1st Batt. 6th Division to France ; wounded Armentiers, Nov. 1914 ; appointed General Staff Officer 10th Irish Division ; served with 10th Div. Dardanelles and Serbia, July 1915 to Dec. 1915, commanded 8th Ches. Regt. 13th Div. Dardanelles, Jan. 1916 ; transferred to command 7th N. Stafford Regt. Egypt, Mesopotamia, N W. Persia, Caucasus ; wounded Fallahiyah, April, 1916. *Address :* Raleigh, Bideford, N. Devon. *Club :* Army and Navy. (O8700)

LEMAN, Lt.-Col. Harry Charles, O.B.E., T.F. Reserve, *b.* 12 Sept. 1888 ; *s.* of Wiliam Edgar Leman, of Dulwich ; *m.* Florence Mary, *d.* of J. Fairer, of Dulwich. *Educ. :* St. Olaves, London. *War Work :* Served as O.C. 47th Div. Cycle Co. in France. March to June, 1915 ; Adjt. 3/25th Lond. Regt. Feb. to Aug. 1916 ; second-in-command 2/21st Lond. Regt. in France, Salonica, Egypt, Aug. 1916 to Oct. 1917 ; Prisoners of War Staff Egypt 1918–20. *Address :* Lancaster House, E. Dulwich Grove, London, S.E. *Clubs :* Services ; Junior Army and Navy. (O6224)

LE MARCHANT, Brig.-Gen. Edward Thomas, C.B.E., J.P., *b.* 21 Oct. 1871 ; 2nd *s.* of the late Sir Henry D. Le Marchant, Bart., of Chatham Place, Surrey ; *m.* Evelyn Brookes, *d.* of R. Millington Knowles, D.L., J.P., of Colston Bassett Hall, Notts. *Educ. :* Eton. Director of Messrs. Andrew Knowles & Sons, Ltd., Colliery Proprietors, Pendleby, Manchester, and the Griff Colliery Company. *War Work :* Brigade Commander 1915–16 attached Staff in France 1917. *Address :* Colston Bassett Hall, Bingham, Notts. *Club :* Naval and Military. (C1661)

LE MESURIER, Capt. Algernon George, O.B.E.

LE MESURIER, Major Edwin Philip, M.B.E.

LE MESURIER, Major James, C.B.E. Director of Small Craft Disposal, Ministry of Shipping.

LE MESURIER, Thomas Henry, O.B.E.

LEMON, Ernest John Hutchings, O.B.E.

LEMON, Major Guy Talbot, O.B.E., I.A.

LEMON, Margaretta Louisa, Mrs., M.B.E., M.B.O.U., F.Z.S., *b.* 22 Nov. 1860 ; *d.* of Capt. W. E. Smith, Royal Sherwood Foresters, of Moolpa, Australia, and Blackheath, Kent ; *m.* Frank Edward, *s.* of William George Lemon, J.P., of

Blackheath, Kent. *Educ.:* Belstead, near Ipswich. Hon. Sec. Watchers' Committee, Royal Society for the Protection of Birds ; Hon. Sec. East Surrey Branch R.S.P.C.A. ; Member of Reigate Board of Guardians ; School Manager. *War Work:* Commandant V.A.D. Surrey 108 ; 1914–15, Superintendent of Redhill War Emergency Clothing Depot ; 1915–17, Superintendent of Redhill Clinic for Treatment of Soldiers in Training ; 1917–19, Officer in charge of Redhill War Hospital. *Address:* Hillcrest, Redhill, Surrey. *Club:* V.A.D. Ladies'. (M8785)

LEMONIUS, Lieut.-Col. Gerald MacLean, C.B.E. Formerly Lieut.-Col. Liverpool Regt. ; served in the Great War, 1914–19 (despatches). (C1662)

LEMPFERT, Rudolph Gustav Karl, C.B.E., M.A., F.Inst.P., *b.* 1875 ; *s.* of the late Gustav Lempfert, of Manchester ; *m.* Marjorie Olive, *d.* of the late George Olive Hayward, Master Mariner, of London. *Educ.:* Manchester Grammar School ; Emmanuel Coll., Cambridge. Assistant Director, Meteorological Office. *War Work:* Superintendent Forecast Division of Meteorological Office through which weather reports and forecasts were supplied to H.M. Forces on land, sea, and in the air. *Address:* 54C, Redcliffe Square, S.W. 10. *Club:* Oxford and Cambridge Musical. (C220)

LEMPRIERE, Lancelot Raoul, O.B.E., B.A., M.B., *b.* 30 Aug. 1872 ; *s.* of Capt. P. R. Lempriere, R.A., of Ewell. *Educ.:* Haileybury Coll. ; Oxford ; Manchester Univ. Medical Officer, Haileybury Coll., Hertford. *War Work:* 13th Field Ambulance ; M.O. 1st Army H Q. *Address:* Haileybury Coll., Hertford. (O2610)

LENCH, Harry, O.B.E., J.P. for Staffordshire, *b.* 1868. *War Work:* Recruiting and other work as Chairman of the Rowley Regis Urban District Council. *Address:* Hazelmere, Blackleath, Staffordshire. (O1586)

LENCH, Major William F., M.B.E.

LENDEN, Mary Isabel, Mrs. O.B.E. (O11988)

LENDRUM, John Black, O.B.E., Hon. Assoc. Order of St. John of Jerusalem, M.D., C.M., *b.* 16 Feb. 1869 ; *s.* of the late George Lendrum, of Huddersfield, Yorks. ; *m.* Susan Edith, *d.* of the late John McGee MacCormac, M.D., of Belfast. *Educ.:* Huddersfield Coll. ; Aberdeen and Berlin Universities. Hon. Surgeon, Oldham Royal Infirmary ; Corps Surgeon, Oldham Corps St. John Ambulance Brigade ; C.M.P. 199th Ter. Force Depot, and 63rd Recruiting Area, Oldham ; Hon. Life Member, Brit. Red Cross Society. *War Work:* M.O.-incharge Woodfield Auxiliary Military Hospital, Oldham ; Lecturer to St. John Ambulance Assocn. and to British Red Cross Society. *Address:* 101, Manchester Street, Werneth, Oldham, Lancs. (O10824)

LENDY, Commissioned Mechanician Thomas, M.B.E., R.N.

LENEGHAN, Mary Esther Rishworth. M.B.E. ; *d.* of the late W. R. Leneghan, and *g.-d.* of the late Emmanuel Asquith, of Stubbing House, near Keighley, Yorks. Trained Nurse ; trained at Stockton and Thornaby Hospital ; afterwards Sister at the Children's Hospital, Mosely Hall, Birmingham ; Sister and Night Superintendent at Stockton and Thornaby Hospital. *War Work:* From Feb. 1915 to Dec. 1915 Sister at Lowfields War Hospital, Kirkby Lonsdale, Westmorland ; from Feb. 1916 to Feb. 1917 at the Urgency Cases Hospital for the French, near Bar-le-Duc ; April 1917 to April 1919, Unit Administrator Q.M.A.A.C. Depot, Aldershot Command. *Address:* Sutton-in-Craven, Yorks. (M3286)

LENG, Hilary Howard, C.B.E.

LENN, Paymaster-Commander Frank C.B.E., R.N., *b.* 7 Aug. 1868 ; *s.* of Charles Henry, of Launceston ; *m.* Lilian Maud, *d.* of W. F. World. *Educ.:* Greenwich Proprietory and Roan Schools. *War Work:* Chief Accountant Officer of the R.N.A.S. from its inception until amalgamation with R.F.C. as the R.A.F. *Address:* Wooda Bay, 87 Bristol Road, Weston-super-Mare. *Club:* Royal Aero. (C548)

LENNARD, Lieut.-Col. John BARRETT-, C.B.E., late Gen. List, *b.* 14 Dec. 1861 ; 3rd *s.* of Walter James Barrett-Lennard, and *g. s.* of Sir Thomas Barrett-Lennard, 1st Bart. (*see* BURKE'S *Peerage*) ; *m.* 20 Oct. 1887, Mary Emma, *e. d.* of J. Gardiner, of Richmond. Served in the S. African War and Great War. (C1450)

LENNOX, Agnes Margaret, Mrs., M.B.E.

LENNOX, Jessie Orr, Mrs., M.B.E.

LENNOX, Rev. John C. F., O.B.E.

LENNOX, Blanche, Lady Algernon GORDON-, D.B.E. ; *d.* of Col. Hon. Charles Maynard, of Easton Lodge, Dunmow, Essex (*see* BURKE'S *Peerage*) ; *m.* Algernon Charles, *s.* of Duke of Richmond and Gordon, K.G. (*see* BURKE'S *Peerage*). *War Work:* Attached 13th Stationary Hospital, B.E.F., throughout the war ; Director in France of H.R.H. Princess Victoria's Rest Clubs for Nurses. *Addresses:* 20, Queen Street, Mayfair, W. ; Monte San Michele, Capri, Italy. (D35)

LENTHALL, Lieut. Charles Bertram, O.B.E., R.N.V.R.

LEON, Capt. Joseph, O.B.E.

LEONARD, Capt. Guiseppe Stanley, M.B.E.

LEONARD, Major John Douglas, O.B.E.

LEONARD, Lieut. Thomas Goulton, M.B.E., R.G.A. (T.).

LEOROYD, Col. Charles Douglas, C.B.E. ; Lieut.-Col. and Brevet Col. R.E. Served in the Soudan, 1885 (medal with clasp, bronze star) ; Burma, 1885–6 (despatches, medal with clasp) ; S. Africa, 1900 (despatches, Queen's medal with four clasps, King's medal with two clasps, Brevet Lieut.-Col.) and in the Great War.

LEPORTIER, Lieut.-Comm. Theodore, O.B.E., R.N.R.

LEPPER, Elizabeth Herdman, O.B.E., M.D., R.A.M.C.

LERESCHE, Capt. Percy Vere, O.B.E., R.A.S.C. (T.).

LE ROSSIGNOL, Major H. S., O.B.E.

LE ROY, Donovan, M.B.E., R.A.O.C.

LERRY, George Geoffrey, M.B.E., *b.* 13 March, 1883 ; *s.* of Geo. H. Lerry, of Oswestry ; *m.* Bertha, *d.* of E. Schreiber, of Blackpool. *Educ.:* Oswestry Grammar School. Journalist; Editor of "Wrexham Leader"; Member of Welsh National Fund Executive ; Member of Ministry of Pensions Advisory Council (Wales). *War Work:* Secretary, Ministry of Pensions Joint Committee (North Wales) ; Secretary, Denbighshire War Pensions Committee. *Address:* 19, King's Mills Road, Wrexham. (M2031)

LERWILL, Capt. Francis William Henry, O.B.E., R.A.F.

LESCHALLAS, Capt. Henry PIGE-, M.B.E.

LESCHER, Thomas Edward, O.B.E., *b.* 12 June, 1877 ; *s.* of the late F. Harwood Lescher, of Devonshire Place, W. ; *m.* Ella Mary, *d.* of L. M. Casella, of Hampstead. *Educ.:* Stonyhurst College. Director, Evans Sons, Lescher and Webb, Ltd., Liverpool, London, and New York ; President The Drug Club ; Chairman Westminster Catholic Federation. *War Work:* As Hon. Sec. of The Drug Club rendered services in connection with supplies and control of Medical Drugs and Chemicals during the war ; Chairman Stonyhurst College War Memorial Council. *Address:* Eaglehurst, 10, Lyndhurst Gardens, Hampstead. *Clubs:* Conservative ; M.C.C. ; The Skating ; Northwood Golf ; Aldeburgh Golf. (O10825)

LESLIE, Arthur Trevor O'Bryen, M.B.E., *b.* May, 1868 ; *s.* of the late Capt. Thomas Leslie, of Kilmore, Co. Cavan ; *m.* Guendolen Amy (died 1912), *d.* of Sir Charles Rugge-Price, Bart., of Spring Grove (*see* BURKE'S *Peerage*). *Educ.:* Brighton Coll. Commandant "A" Division Metropolitan Police Special Reserve. *War Work:* Enlisted Special Constabulary "A" Division, 1914 ; served throughout the war on street and special duties. *Address:* 218, Adelaide Road, London, N.W. 3. *Club:* Royal Thames Yacht. (M3802)

LESLIE, Lieut.-Col. Bradford, O.B.E., R.E.

LESLIE, Capt. Charles William, M.B.E., R.A.S.C.

LESLIE, Emily Florence, Mrs., M.B.E. ; *d.* of Major Montagu Battye, of Hon. Corps Gentlemen-at-Arms (Royal Bodyguard) ; *m.* Arthur Cecil, *s.* of John Leslie. *War Work:* Assistant Commandant and Quartermaster under Mary, Lady Gerard, at Garswood Hall Auxiliary Hospital, Ashton-in-Makerfield, for 4½ years (Oct. 1914 to March 1919). *Address:* Newton-le-Willows, Lancashire. (M8786)

LESLIE, George, M.B.E.

LESLIE, Col. Sir John, Bart., C.B.E., D.L., late Royal Innis. Fus., *b.* 7 Aug. 1857 ; *s.* of the late Sir John Leslie, of Glaslough (*see* BURKE'S *Peerage*) ; *m.* Léonir Blanche, *d.* of the late Leonard Jerome, of N. York, U.S.A. *Educ.:* Eton. *War Work:* Raised and Commanded 12th Reserve Batt. R. Inn. Fus. ; Member of Council, Lord French's Irish Recruiting. *Address:* Glaslough, Ireland. *Clubs:* Guards' ; United Kildare St. (C1664)

LESLIE, Lewis Francis, O.B.E., M.R.C.S.

LESLIE, Sir Norman Alexander, K.B.E., *b.* 1870 ; *s.* of the late John Leslie ; *m.* 1898, Mimy Muriel, *d.* of the late James Gambier. Ministry of Shipping. *Address:* Birchwood, West Byfleet, Surrey. *Club:* Junior Carlton.

LESLIE, Lieut.-Col. Sir Norman Roderick Alexander David, 8th Bt., of Wardis, Co. Moray, C.B.E., *b.* 10 Jan. 1889 ; *s.* of Sir Charles Henry Leslie, 7th Bart. (*see* BURKE'S *Peerage*) ; *m.* 4 Oct. 1919, Betty Elise, *d.* of John Thomas Beadsworth Sewell, C.B.E. (*q. v.*) Major, King George's Own Central India Horse, Indian Army ; Squadron Leader R.A.F. ; G.S.O. (3rd grade) 1916 ; (2nd grade), 1917 ; Air Attaché British Embassy, Paris, 1918. *Addresses:* Goona, Central India ; c/o Messrs. Grindley & Co., 54, Parliament Street, S.W. 1. (C867)

LESLIE, Chief-Eng. Robert, O.B.E., R.N.R.

LESLIE, Major Robert Walker Dickson, O.B.E., R.A.M.C., *b.* 31 Jan. 1883 ; *s.* of the late T. C. Leslie, of Dungannon, Ireland ; *m.* Eleanor Violet, *d.* of Rear-Admiral F. L. Field, C.B., C.M.G., R.N., 3rd Sea Lord. *Educ.:* Michaelhouse, Natal, South Africa ; Royal College of Surgeons, Ireland. *Clubs:* Army and Navy ; Royal Automobile. (O5476)

LESLIE, Major Seymour Granger, O.B.E., R.A.O.C.

LESLIE, Theordore, O.B.E.

LESSER, Catherine Maud, Mrs., M.B.E., *b.* 21 Feb. 1878 ; *War Work:* Member of the Staff of the Officers' Clothing Branch, Officers' Families Fund, 2, Albert Gate, S.W. from Jan. 1915 to July 1919. *Address:* 90, Campden Hill Court, Kensington. (M8788)

LESSING, Lieut. Edward Albert, O.B.E.

LESTER, Eng.-Lieut.-Comm. Arthur Ellis, D.S.O., O.B.E. Entered R.N. 1900 ; became Engineer-Lieut. 1904 ; Engineer-Lieut.-Com. 1912 ; served in the Great War, 1915–19 ; present at landing at Gallipoli (despatches). (O3529)

LESTER, Horace Lenton, M.B.E.

LESTER, John Bingley Garland, M.B.E.

LESTER, Leontine Isabelle Emmeline, Mrs., M.B.E.

L'ESTRANGE, Major Henry Roland, O.B.E., R.A.M.C.

LETHABY, Major Tom, O.B.E.

LETHBRIDGE, Major Harold Octavius, M.B.E.

LETHBRIDGE, Marion Eva, C.B.E. *War Work:* Comdt. General Service V.A.D.'s, France. (C549)

LETHBRIDGE, Col. Robert Thomas Morland, O.B.E., A.P.D.

LETHBRIDGE, Lieut.-Col. Sydney, O.B.E., R.A.

LETT, Hugh, C.B.E., M.B., F.R.C.S., *b.* 17 April, 1876 ; *s.* of Richard Alfred Lett, of Wadingham, Lincs. ; *m.* Helen Buckston, *d.* of George Buckston Browne, of Wimpole Street. *Educ.:* Marlborough Coll. ; Leeds ; London Hospital. Surgeon to the London Hospital ; Vice-President Medical Society of London ; late President Hunterian Society. *War Work:* Surgeon to the Anglo-American Hospital, Wimereux, 1914–15 ; Surgeon to the Belgian Field Hospital, 1915 ; Major, R.A.M.C., Officer-in-charge Surgical Division. 31st General Hospital, Port Said, 1915–16 ; Consulting Surgeon to the Prince of Wales' Hospital for Officers, and other war hospitals, 1917–19. *Clubs:* Garrick ; Royal Automobile. (C3116)

LETTICE, Capt. and Qr.-Mr. William Henry, O.B.E.

LETTON, Charles Thomas, M.B.E., *b.* 25 March, 1878 ; *s.* of Charles W. Letton, of London ; *m.* Maud Annie, *d.* of Edward Barnes, of London. *Educ.:* London. Superintendent Government of India Printing Office, Simla, Punjab, India. *War Work:* Twice mentioned in Gazette of India for valuable services rendered in India in connection with the War. *Address:* Clarefield, Simla, Punjab. (M4179)

LETTS, William Malesbury, C.B.E., *b.* 1873. Managing Director of Crossley Motors (Limited), of Gorton, Manchester ; Governing Director of Charles Jarrott and Letts (Limited) ; Director of Carbic (Limited). (C550)

LETTY, William, M.B.E., *b.* 12 Dec. 1857 ; *s.* of William Joseph Millard Letty, of Portsmouth ; *m.* Susan, *d.* of Frederic Beck, of Southsea. *Educ.:* Privately. Principal Overseer Engineer-in-Chief's Department, Admiralty ; Steward in the Wesleyan Methodist Church. *War Work:* Inspecting and hastening manufacture and completion of machinery for war vessels. *Address:* 126, Wrottesley Road, Harlesden, London, N.W. 10. (M2033)

LE VACK, William, M.B.E., *b.* 4 Jan. 1862. Civil Servant ; Senior Clerk ; Statistical Office, H.M. Customs and Excise, London, E.C. 3. *War Work:* Lent by the Honourable Commissioners of H.M. Customs and Excise to organise and control a Statistical Branch of the War Trade Department, from March, 1915, to April, 1919. *Address:* 56, The Avenue, West Ealing, London, W. 13. (M2575)

LEVERETT, Frederick William, M.B.E.

LEVEY, 2nd Lieut. Bernard Alexander, M.B.E., R.A.F.

LEVEY, Lieut.-Col. Joseph Henry, D.S.O., O.B.E. Capt. and Brevet Major Gordon Highlanders ; Dep. Inspector of Training with rank of Lieut.-Col. ; served in the Great War, 1914–18 (despatches). (O5477)

LEVI, Louis, M.B.E.

LEVICK, Major Albert, O.B.E., R.A.F.

LEVICK, Sir Hugh Gwynne, K.B.E., *b.* 17 March, 1870 ; *s.* of John Musgrave Levick, of Burleigh, Cheshunt ; *m.* Agnes Burwell, *d.* of James D. Stout, of Hoboken, U.S.A. *Educ.:* Port Elizabeth, S.A. ; Malvern Coll. ; Hamburg. *War Work:* Treasury in an advisory capacity ; Chairman Russian Liquidation Committee ; Treasury Representative on London Exchange Committee ; Treasury Representative on Colwyn Committee on Contracts ; Deputy British Delegate to the Reparations Commission. *Addresses:* 7, Square Thiers, Avenue Victor Hugo, Paris ; The Manor, Castle Combe, Wilts. *Clubs:* St. James' ; City of London ; Algonquin, Boston, U.S.A. (K151)

LEVICK, Hon. Capt. Thomas Henry Carlton, O.B.E., *b.* 1867 ; *s.* of Frederick Levick, J.P., of Pinner, Middlesex ; *m.* Evelyn Constance, *d.* of the late Frederick Quinton, J.P. *Educ.:* London Univ. Coll. School, and France. *War Work:* Special Missions abroad for H.M. Foreign Office and Ministry of Shipping ; Capt. attached G.O.C. London Volunteer Regiments ; Capt. attached by H.M. War Office to Headquarters Staff of G.O.C. American Expeditionary Force, London. *Address:* 23, Palace Court, London, W. 2. *Clubs:* Royal Societies' ; Ranelagh. (O1592)

LEVICK, Capt. Vivian Mortimer KENNY-, M.B.E.

LEVIEN, Capt. Norman James, O.B.E.

LEVINGE, Edward George, M.B.E.

LEVITA, Lieut.-Col. Cecil Bingham, C.B.E., M.V.O., J.P. County of London, R.A., *b.* 1867 ; *s.* of the late E. Levita, of 27, Ennismore Gardens, London ; *m.* Florence Woodruff, *d.* of W. Robb, of Glasgow. *Educ.:* Royal Military Academy, Woolwich. Member of London County Council for N. Kensington ; Councillor of Hove ; Managing Committee of Brompton Hospital ; Member of Lloyds'. *War Work:* Matabele War, 1896 ; S. Africa, 1899, mentioned in despatches ; Lieut.-Col. Reserve of Officers, R.A. ; General Staff Officer, 1st Grade mentioned in despatches, 1917 ; thanked by Minister of National Service, 1919. *Address:* 6, Brunswick Square, Hove. *Clubs:* Carlton ; Garrick ; 1900. (C1665)

LEVITT, Capt. Robert Thorp, M.B.E., Cadet Batt. A.P.W.O. Yorkshire Regt., *b.* 18 June, 1870 ; *s.* of Joseph Levitt, of Kingston-upon-Hull ; *m.* Elizabeth, *d.* of Robert Morris, of. Kingston-upon-Hull. *Educ.:* St. John's Church School and West End Academy, Hull. Chief Clerk North Riding Territorial Force Association. *War Work:* Organisation, Clothing, Equipping, and Administration of Territorial and Volunteer Units raised in the North Riding of Yorkshire. *Address:* The Parade, Northallerton, Yorks. *Clubs:* Patriotic ; Conservative ; Comrades of the Great War. (M8790)

LEVY, Jeanne Athol, M.B.E.

LEVY, Joseph, M.B.E., R.A.M.C.

LEWARN, Harold Stanley, M.B.E., *b.* 9 June, 1883 ; *s.* of James Henry Lewarn, of Lydford, Devon. *Educ.:* Grey

Coat School, Plymouth. Sub-Conductor (Warrant Officer Class I). *War Work:* Served on the Staff of the Headquarters 4th Division B.E.F. from Aug. 1914 to May, 1919. *Addresses:* R.A.O.C., Army Inspection Buildings, Park Royal, London, N.W. 10 ; Rossmoyne, Lydford, Devonshire. (M4539)

LEWELLEN, Florence Beatrice, Mrs., M.B.E. ; *d.* of the late A. G. Kitching, J.P., of Enfield ; *m.* Ernest, *s.* of — Lewellen. *War Work:* Hon. Sec. of Finchley War Pensions Committee, and of Soldiers' and Sailors' Families Association, Finchley. *Address:* Coningsby, Duke's Avenue, Finchley. (M8791)

LEWER, Major Arthur John, O.B.E., *b.* 3 July, 1888 ; *s.* of John Lewer, of 7, Old Street, E.C. 1 ; *m.* Ada, *d.* of Edward Page, of Plumstead. *Educ.:* St. Thomas's ; Charterhouse. Bank Inspector ; Councillor, Islington Borough Council ; Chairman Finance Committee ; Major, T. F. Reserve ; stood in Labour interest (1918 General Election) for East Islington. *War Work:* Major, 11th London Regt. ; present at Suvla Bay, Aug. 1915 ; Recruiting Officer for Islington, 1916–17 ; substitution Officer for North London, 1917 ; Deputy Controller of Registration, Ministry of National Service, Dec. 1917, to Aug. 1918 ; Official i/c Propaganda, Irish Recruiting Council, Aug. 1918, to Nov. 1918. *Address:* 28, Aberdeen Park, N. 5. (O1593)

LEWERS, Lieut.-Col. Hugh Bennett, D.S.O., O.B.E. Assist. Director Australian Med. Ser. (O501)

LEWES, John Guy Robert, O.B.E. (O12051)

LEWES, Mary Louisa, M.B.E. ; *d.* of Major Price Lewes, R.A., J.P., D.L., of Tyglyn Aeron, Cardiganshire. *War Work:* Red Cross V.A.D. work ; organised and became Commandant of the Red Cross Auxiliary Hospital at Aberayron, Cardiganshire, July, 1916 to Jan. 1918. *Address:* Tyglyn Aeron, Cilian Aeron, Cardiganshire. *Clubs:* London ; New Century. (M8792)

LEWIN, Lady Ada Edwina Stewart, O.B.E., *b.* 28 March, 1878 ; *d.* of the late Field-Marshal 1st Earl Roberts, of Englemere, Ascot (see BURKE's *Peerage*) ; *m.* Col. Henry Frederick Elliott, R.A., *s.* of Commander W. H Lewin, R.N. *Educ.:* Privately. *Address:* Englemere, Ascot. (O502)

LEWIN, Isabella Marion, Mrs., M.B.E., *b.* 15 Oct. 1868 ; *d.* of the late James Brown Alston ; *m.* Lieut.-Col. Wilfred Hale Lewin, I.A. (retired), *s.* of the late Edward Bernard Hale Lewin. Quartermaster, V.A.D. Kent 54, 29 March, 1912 ; Commandant V.A.D. Kent 54. 30 April, 1913. *War Work:* Opened Red Cross Hospital at St. Mary's Church Hall, Bromley, Kent, on 14 Oct. 1914, which continued in operation until Dec. 1918 ; mentioned for War Services, Oct. 1917 and Aug. 1918 ; inscribed on Roll of Honourable Service, B.R.C.S. Oct. 1918. (M3804)

LEWIN, Percy Evans, M.B.E., F.R.Hist.S., *b.* 3 April, 1876 ; *s.* of Edward Christopher Lewin, of Boston, Lincolnshire ; *m.* Léontine Berthe, *d.* of John Dorman, of Cherbourg, France. *Educ.:* Boston Grammar School. Librarian, Royal Colonial Institute ; author of "The Germans and Africa" (1915) ; "The German Road to the East" (1916). *War Work:* Prepared a Report for the Foreign Office on German Administration in Africa ; employed in the Admiralty Intelligence Division (Geographical Section), 1918–19 ; Propaganda work. *Address:* Newholme, Coombe Lane, Wimbledon, S.W. 19. (M8793)

LEWIS, Alice Pansy Mary, M.B.E., *b.* 19 Feb. 1892 ; *d.* of Richard Lewis, of Tufnell Park. *Educ.:* Privately. *War Work:* Sec. at Ministry of Shipping (Transport Department) from Sept. 1915 to Dept. 1920. *Addresses:* 100, Huddleston Road, Tufnell Park, N. 7 ; 7, Impasse des Ormeant, Le Havre, France. (M8794)

LEWIS, Annie Caton, Mrs., O.B.E., *b.* 1 June, 1877 ; *d.* of the late Hugh Rose, of Edinburgh ; *m.* Frederick Gustav Lewis, C.B., C.M.G., T.D., of London. *Educ.:* The Grange House, Edinburgh. Assistant Hon. Sec. Kensington Division, B.R.C.S. ; Commandant, London V.A.D. 28. *War Work:* Commandant-in-charge Military Hospital, White City, Oct. 1914 to May, 1915 General Service Supervisor, 3rd London General Hospital, Aug. 1915 to March. 1916 ; Hostel Superintendent, No. 8 Red Cross Hospital, B.E.F. April, 1916, to Dec. 1917 ; P. of W. Central Committee, April, 1918, to Feb. 1919. *Club:* V.A.D. Ladies'. (O10821)

LEWIS, Benjamin Joseph, M.B.E.

LEWIS, Charles Henry, O.B.E., R.A.F.

LEWIS, Major Edward Trevor, O.B.E.

LEWIS, Edwin, M.B.E.

LEWIS, Elizabeth Tryphena, Mrs., O.B.E.

LEWIS, Ernest Harry, C.B.E.

LEWIS, Lieut.-Col. Ernest William, O.B.E., R.A.S.C.

LEWIS, Capt. Frank Oswald, C.B.E., R.N. (ret.), *b.* 1873 ; *s.* of the late Samuel Lewis, of Edgehill, Duffield, nr. Derby. Served in the Great War, 1914–19 (despatches twice). *Address:* Evancoyd, Walton, Radnorshire. *Club:* United Service. (C903)

LEWIS, Lieut. Frederick, M.B.E., R.A.S.C.

LEWIS, Capt. George Ernest, O.B.E., *b.* 20 April, 1872 ; *s.* of Lieut. W. Lewis, of Hereford. *Educ.:* Westminster and Cologne. *War Work:* Officer-in-charge Barracks and Camps in Dorset, Hants, Devon, and Cornwall. *Address:* 16J, Orchard Street, Westminster. (O7388)

LEWIS, George Frederick, O.B.E., *b.* 1889 ; *s.* of William Stephens Lewis, of Whitchurch, Glamorganshire. *Educ.:* Penarth County Coll. Commercial Manager. *War Work:* Joined Army Aug. 1914 ; proceeded France, 1915

Batt. Lewis Gun Officer, and IVth Corps Senior Lewis Gun Instructor; afterwards Company Commander; severely wounded during the taking of Eaucourt L'Abbeye (Somme) in the winter, 1916; joined Ministry of Shipping in 1917; appointed as Shipping Adviser on staff of Naval Commander-in-Chief, Mediterranean, and in this position visited all the Mediterranean ports. *Address:* Mayton, Whitchurch, Glam. (O10828)

LEWIS, Lieut.-Comm. Guy Perdell, O.B.E., R.N.R.

LEWIS, Helen, O.B.E. Attached to British Military Hospital British Military Mission, South Russia. (O11790c)

LEWIS, Col. Henry, O.B.E., V.D., J.P., D.L. Glamorgan, *b.* 21 July, 1847; *s.* of Henry Lewis, of Greenmeadow, Tongwynlois, near Cardiff; *m.* Rose Mabel, *d.* of Capt. Durham, Alderman Glamorgan County Council. *War Work:* Recruiting 4 years. *Address:* Greenmeadow, Tongwynlois, near Cardiff. *Club:* Chivalry. (O3796)

LEWIS, Major and Brevet Lieut.-Col. Henry Augustus, C.B.E., R.A., *b.* 20 Sept. 1879; *s.* of Major E. J. G. Lewis, Bengal Staff Corps; *m.* Mary Margaret, *d.* of P. A. Newton, of Westbourne. *Educ.:* Sedbergh School, Yorkshire. *War Work:* Deputy Supt. of Experiments, Shoeburyness, 1914–16; Siege Artillery Brigade Commander, France, 1917; Superintendent of Experiments, Shoeburyness, 1918. *Club:* United Service. (C2213e)

LEWIS, Herbert David William, O.B.E., M.I.E.E., Knight of Grace of the Order of the Hospital of St. John of Jerusalem, *b.* 25 Nov. 1872; *s.* of the Rev. David Lewis. V.D., M.A., R.D., of Briton Ferry; *m.* Kate, O.B.E., Deputy Lady Superintendent for Wales, Order of the Hospital of St. John of Jerusalem (*q.v.*) *d.* of Gomer Williams, of Aberlloch, Breconshire. *Educ.:* Rossall Coll., Lancashire, and Finsbury Technical Coll. Commissioner and Principal Secretary of the Priory for Wales. *Clubs:* Royal Automobile; Cardiff and County; M.C.C. (O503)

LEWIS, Lieut. James Charles, O.B.E., R.A.S.C.

LEWIS, Janet Marion Terry, M.B.E., *b.* 8 Oct. 1869; *d.* of the late Arthur James Lewis, of Moray Lodge, Campden Hill, Kensington. *Educ.:* Privately. *War Work:* Secretarial work Soldiers' and Sailors' Families Assocn., Sept. 1914, to Sept. 1915; Canteen work, Sept. 1915. to Sept. 1916; Ministry of Labour, 1916, to April, 1918; transferred to Ministry of Munitions as Section Director of Establishment, April, 1918, to April, 1919. *Address:* 16, Chapel Street, Belgrave Square, S.W. 1. (M665)

LEWIS, John, O.B.E.

LEWIS, John, M.B.E., J.P.

LEWIS, John, C.B.E., J.P., *b.* 14 Aug. 1851; *s.* of David Lewis, of Drefach Henllan; *m.* Anne, *d.* of Samuel Hullens, of Llysderi, Carmarthenshire. *Educ.:* Llangeler Nat. School; Trinity Chapel School, Penboyr. *War Work:* Member and Vice-Chairman of Local Tribunal; addressed meetings in connection with Agricultural Production; was a member of the Committee, the result of the Committee's efforts being an increase of 41 per cent. in acreage of land under corn; served on War Wool Allotment Committee for S. Wales; addressed meetings in connection with School Children's War Savings. *Address:* Meiros Hall, Defrach Henllan, S.O. Cardiganshire. (C991)

LEWIS, John, O.B.E., J.P., *b.* 5 Jan. 1863; *s.* of William Lewis, M.E., of Felinfoel; *m.* Eliza Anne, *d.* of the Rev. J. Jones, of Felinfoel. *Educ.:* Felinfoel School; Bangor Normal Coll. Headmaster of Ammanford School since 1892; Ex-Chairman Llandilo-Fawr Board of Guardians; Ex-Chairman Baptist Association; Hon. Sec. Sunday School Union. *War Work:* Hon. Sec. Recruiting Committee; Organiser of meetings in East Carmarthen Constituency. *Address:* Brynrhug, Ammanford. (O3797)

LEWIS, John Thomas, O.B.E. Probate Registrar, Oxford. (O11911)

LEWIS, Kate, Mrs., O.B.E.; *d.* of Gomer Williams, of Aberllech, Breconshire; *m.* Herbert David William, O.B.E., *q.v.*, *s.* of the Rev. David Lewis, M.A., R.D., of Briton Ferry, Glam. *Educ.:* Princess Helena Coll., Ealing; Zürich; Paris. Lady Superintendent for Wales (Priory for Wales), Order of St. John; Vice-President Young Women's Christian Association, S. Wales; Lady President Young Helpers League; Hon. Sec. Western Cardiff District, National Society for the Prevention of Cruelty to Children. *War Work:* Commandant V.A.D. 60, Glamorgen; Commandant of St. John Hospital, Porthcawl (200 beds); Supervising Commandant St. John Hospitals, Southerndown, Clydach, Pontardawe. *Address:* 61, Cathedral Road, Cardiff, Glamorgan. *Club:* V.A.D. (O10830)

LEWIS, Major Leonard Carey, O.B.E., R.A.O.C.

LEWIS, Llewelyn, O.B.E., M.D., J.P.; *s.* of William Lewis, of Neath; *m.* Lucy Maud, *d.* of James Kempthorne, of Wannceirch, Neath, and Westminster Hospital, London. *War Work:* Senior in Charge of Laurels Red Cross Hospital from beginning to end of war; Surgeon and Lecturer to Ambulance detachment of the V.T.C.; Lecturer and Examiner Red Cross Society. *Address:* Maesythaf, Neath. (O10831)

LEWIS, Lucas Reginald, C.B.E., Cavaliere of the Royal Crown of Italy, *b.* 8 Jan. 1883; *s.* of John Jenkins Lewis, C.E., of Llandaff; *m.* Daisy Maud, *d.* of the Ven. James Rice Buckley, B.D., Archdeacon of Llandaff. *Educ.:* Llandaff. Director of Lysberg, Ltd., Colliery Sales Agents, Coal Exporters, Shipbrokers, etc. A. M. McMillan & Co., Glasgow, Newcastle, and Hull; Chargeurs Belge, Antwerp, and Zambesia Mining Development, Ltd. *War Work:* In charge of Coal stemming

arrangements for British, French, Italian, Russian Navies, etc., from South Wales; afterwards acting as Direct Representative of the Coal Controller for all export from the whole of the Bristol Channel; resigned April, 1920, in order to devote more time to own business. *Address:* Ty-Gwyn, Llandaff, Glamorganshire. *Clubs:* British Empire; Cardiff Exchange. (C2759)

LEWIS, Margaret Blanche, O.B.E., M.A.; *d.* of John Rice Lewis, of Liverpool. *Educ.:* Liverpool High School; Newnham Coll., Cambridge. *War Work:* Sec. of the Liverpool Branch National Union of Women Workers (now National Council of Women), Liverpool Ladies' Sanitary Association, and Liverpool Enquiry and Employment Bureau for Educated Women, 1905–10; Supervising Clerk, Board of Trade Labour Exchanges, West Midlands Division, 1910; Organising Officer for Women's Work, Board of Trade Labour Exchanges, West Midlands Division, 1912; Chief Woman Officer, Ministry of Labour Employment Department, West Midlands Division, 1919. *Addresses:* 85, Oxford Road, Moseley, Birmingham; Divisional Office, 94, Corporation Street, Birmingham. *Club:* Three Counties', Birmingham. (O3798)

LEWIS, Capt. Orpheus William Henry, M.B.E., P.A.S.I., F.A.I., *b.* 7 Jan. 1882; *s.* of H. Stephen Lewis, of Chepstow, Mon. *Educ.:* Privately. Civil Servant. *War Work:* Lieut. E.R.R.G.A. (T.F.) Nov. 1915 to Dec. 1916; on Anti-Aircraft Duties and through all the Air Raids on Hull; General Staff, Dec. 1916, to Nov. 1919, on Anti-Aircraft Duties; Capt. General Staff, 1918; mentioned three times in despatches. *Address:* St. Maur, Hawthorne Avenue, Swansea. *Club* Constitutional, Hull; Masonic Lodge, Constitutional, 294. (M5420)

LEWIS, Rev. Percy, O.B.E., M.A., M.T.C.A., *b.* 12 Sept. 1882; *s.* of the Rev. L. O. Lewis, Vicar of Lindal-cum-Marton; *m.* Mabel Kathleen, *d.* of Frank Shrubsole, of Faversham. *Educ.:* Trent Coll.; Worcester Coll., Oxford. Curate, Christ Church, Ramsgate, 1906–12; Organising Sec. Chichester Diocesan C.E.T.S., 1912–15; Examiner, Oxford Local Examinations. *War Work:* Chaplain to the Forces, Egypt, 1915–17; Mesopotamia, 1917–19; Senior Chaplain, 18th Indian Division, 1918–19. *Address:* St. Alban's Lodge, Westgate-on-Sea. (O2286)

LEWIS, Reginald Jamieson, O.B.E. (O11989)

LEWIS, Ruth, Mrs., O.B.E., M.A., J.P., *b.* 1871; *d.* of the late William Sproston Caine, of Clapham Common; *m.* the Rt. Hon. J. Herbert Lewis, P.C., M.P., LL.D., Deputy Lieut. for Flintshire, *s.* of the late Enoch Lewis, of Mostyn Quay. *Educ.:* Clapham High School, and Newnham. Chairman of Women Clerks and Secretaries Friendly Society; Vice-President Women's Free Church Council; Member of Council of Aberystwyth Coll. *War Work:* Four years sec. and manager of Y.M.C.A. Canteen at Old Brewery, Earl Street, Westminster. *Addresses:* 23, Grosvenor Road, Westminster; Penucha, Caerwys, Flintshire. (O504)

LEWIS, Sarah Agnes Jane, M.B.E., *b.* 1860; *d.* of William Lynas, of Dungannon, Co. Tyrone; *m.* Milford John Knox, *s.* of Joseph Lewis, of Dublin. *Educ.:* Dublin. *War Work:* Amongst the soldiers at the Curragh Camp, Co. Kildare, Ireland. *Address:* St. Paul's Church Hut, Hare Park Military Camp, Curragh, Ireland. (M8797)

LEWIS, Thomas, C.B.E., M.D., D.Sc., F.R.C.P., F.R.S.; *s.* of Henry Lewis, J.P., of Cardiff; *m.* Alice Lorna Treharne, *d.* of Frank Treharne James, of Merthyr Tydfil. *Educ.:* Clifton Coll.; Univ. Coll., Cardiff; London. Physician of the Staff of Medical Research; Physician to Univ. Coll. Hospital, London. *War Work:* Hon. Consulting Physician in Diseases of the Heart, Ministry of Pensions; Director of Clinical Services, Military Heart Hospital, Hampstead and Colchester. *Address:* 10, Chesterford Gardens, N.W. 3. (C3117)

LEWIS, Thomas Henry, M.B.E., *b.* 26 June, 1882; *s.* of James Lewis, of Reading, Berks.; *m.* Vivian Mary, *d.* of Edmund Thatcher Birch, of Cape Town. *Educ.:* St. Thomas', Charterhouse, London. Compiled and Edited "*Women of South Africa*," and "*Children of South Africa*"; founded and was first editor of "*The Service*"; author of "*Germs from German East*"; at present Editor of "*Sales Management*," and lately Assistant Editor of "*Farm and Home*," and "*Gardening Illustrated*" (London). *War Work:* Served with 24th Batt. I. Yeomanry, South African War; Transvaal Mounted Rifles, Zululand Rebellion, 1906; South African Forces, East African Expeditionary Force, Great War (twice mentioned in despatches); seconded for service with the British Salvage Commission for East Africa, 1918, and appointed M.B.E. for conspicuous services with British Salvage Commission in East Africa. *Address:* 2, Bredon Gardens, West Ealing, W. 13. (M8798)

LEWIS, Capt. Thomas Percy, O.B.E., R.A.M.C.

LEWIS, W. H. P., O.B.E., J.P., *b.* 9 Feb. 1881; *e. s.* of the late Arthur Griffith Poyer Lewis (*see* BURKE'S *Landed Gentry*) and Annie Wilhelmine, *d.* of James Ellison, M.D., of Windsor, his wife; *m.* 29 July, 1908, Margaret Annie, *e. d.* of Sir John Eldon Bankes, K.C., a Judge of the High Court of Justice, of Loughton Hall, Flintshire (*see* BURKE'S *Landed Gentry*). *Address:* 1, Palace Road, Llandaff.

LEWIS, Capt. Wilfred Hubert Poyer, O.B.E.

LEWIS, William, M.B.E., R.N.R.

LEWIS, William John, M.B.E.

LEWIS, Lieut.-Col. William John, O.B.E., *b.* 5 Sept. 1868; *s.* of William John Lewis, of Bethnal Green; *m.* Alice, *d.* of John Staines, of Bethnal Green. *Educ.:* London School

THE ORDER OF THE BRITISH EMPIRE.

Board. Councillor, six years Mayor; Sec. North and East Branch Working Men's Club and Institute Union. *War Work:* Chairman Military Tribunal; Member of Russian Tribunal; Chairman of Local Council, Food Committee, Military Hospital Fund; Founder of Local Training Corp; interviewed Queen Mary upon Housing and escorted her round Brady Street, and other insanitary areas. *Address:* 35, St. Peter Street, E. 2. (O10832)

LEWIS, Wyndham, M.B.E.

LEWIS, Lieut.-Col. Arthur Francis OWEN-, D.S.O., O.B.E., *b.* 1868; *s.* of the late Henry Owen-Lewis, D.L. (formerly M.P. for Carlow), of 52, Cranley Gardens, S.W., and of Inniskeen, co. Monaghan; *m.* 1896, Kathleen, *d.* of the late William Henry, Chief Inspector, Roy. Irish Constabulary, of Tivoli, co. Dublin. *Educ.:* Beaumont Coll. Entered Princess of Wales's Own (Yorkshire Regt.) 1889; became Capt. 1900; retired, 1904; served in S. Africa, 1900 (despatches); Great War, 1914–19, as a Gen. Staff Officer and Hon. Major 4th Batt. Lancashire Fusiliers; an A.Q.M.G. with rank of Lieut.-Col. (despatches twice); Major, Gen. Reserve of Officers, and H.M. Inspector of Prisons, Ireland. *Address:* Willfield, Ballsbridge, Dublin. *Club:* Army and Navy. (O1594)

LEWIS, William REED-, M.B.E., *b.* 25 Nov. 1860; *s.* of Francis A. Lewis, of Philadelphia; *m.* Mary Balmain, *d.* of Lieut.-Col. Alex. Wynch, of Bath. *Educ.:* Philadelphia. *War Work:* Organiser E. Sussex Belgian Relief and Bexhill Belgian Refugee Committee. *Address:* The Library, Bexhill-on-Sea. (M2035)

LEWIS, Lieut. William John Duane REED-, O.B.E.

LEWTY, Mary, Mrs., M.B.E., *b.* 6 March, 1876; *m.* James Stanley Lewty. *War Work:* Commandant of Spondon V.A.D. Red Cross Hospital from Nov. 1914, to March, 1919 (40 Beds); Commandant, Spondon V.A.D. since inauguration in 1912. *Address:* Ingle Nook, Spondon, Derby. (M8800)

LEWY, Theodore Harold, M.B.E. (M5831)

LEY, Major Arthur Edwin Hale, O.B.E.

LEY, Major Cuthbert Hillyer, O.B.E.

LEY, Henry James, O.B.E., M.D., *b.* 1860; *s.* of Richard Ley, M.R.C.S., of South Molton, N. Devon; *m.* Nellie P., *d.* of Richard Norris, M.D., of Birmingham. *Educ.:* Epsom Coll., Edinburgh University, and London Hospital. Medical. *War Work:* Medical Services, Christchurch Auxiliary Hospital Hampshire. *Address:* 62, Herberton Road, West Southbourne, Bournemouth. (O11787c)

LEYCESTER, Capt. Philip Wrey, M.B.E., M.A., *b.* 16 Nov. 1894; *s.* of J. W. Leycester, D.L., of Ennismore, Cork. *Educ.:* Rugby School; Oriel Coll., Oxford. *War Work:* Served for 2 years with 1st Cavalry Division in France; later became attached to the R.F.C., and served with 10th Squadron, B.E.F.; after the Armistice, proceeded to British Military Mission, S. Russia, and was gazetted to the Staff. *Address:* Ennismore, Cork. *Club:* Carlyle. (M7014)

LEZARD, Herbert Lewis, M.B.E., A.R.S.M., J.P., *b.* 14 March, 1874; *s.* of Edward Joseph Lezard, of London; *m.* Isa, *d.* of Abraham Brown, of London. *Educ.:* Private Schools in London; Royal School of Mines. Mayor of Salisbury, 1914–15, 1916–17. *War Work:* Chairman, Rhodesian Soldiers Comforts Committee; Chairman, Mashonaland Central Fund. *Address:* P.O. Box 303, Salisbury. *Club:* Salisbury. (M6459)

LICKMAN, Major and Qr.-Mr. Harry Sylvanus, D.S.O., O.B.E.

LIDDELL, Lieut.-Col. Clive Gerard, C.M.G., C.B.E., D.S.O., Leicestershire Regt., *b.* 1 May, 1883; *s.* of John Liddell, of Huddersfield; *m.* 1st, Clare Lambert, *d.* of Lionel Lambert Roberts, of Haywards Heath; 2nd, Hilda Jessie Bisset, *d.* of Robert Gregg Kennedy, of Victoria, B.C. *Educ.:* Uppingham and Sandhurst. *War Work:* D.A.A. and Q.M.G., 1st Corps, France, 5 Nov. 1914, to 2 Jan. 1916; A.A. and Q.M.G., 55th (West Lancs.) Div., 3 Jan. 1916, to 9 Dec. 1916; A.A.G., W.O., 7 Feb. 1917, to 1 March, 1919; D.S.O., July, 1915; C.M.G., July, 1917; C.B.E., 1918; Bt. Lieut.-Col., Jan. 1917. *Clubs:* United Service; Royal Automobile. (C1666)

LIDDELL, Dorothy Mary, M.B.E., *b.* 24 Dec. 1889; eldest *d.* of John Liddell, of Sherfield Manor, Basingstoke. *Educ.:* Assumption Convent, St. Lawrence-on-Sea; Paris and Dresden. *War Work:* 1914–16, Commandant of the Sherfield Manor Auxiliary Military Hospital; 1916, Nurse at H.M. Queen of Belgian's Hospital, La Panne, Belgium; 1917, Nurse at Hospital Temporaire. Arc en Barrois, France; 1918, trained in Massage at Swedish Institute, London. *Address:* Sherfield Manor, Basingstoke, Hants. (M2037)

LIDDELL, Major Eric Manfre, O.B.E.

LIDDELL, Hilda Kathleen, O.B.E., *b.* 7 Feb. 1883; *d.* of Harry Liddell, J.P., of Garefield, Bodmin, Cornwall. *Educ.:* St. Nicholas' School, Bodmin. Certificated Teacher under the Cornwall Education Authority. *War Work:* Organiser of Hospitality Canteen at Bodmin G.W.R. Station; Christmas Parcels Fund to Bodmin Service men, 1914–18; Bodmin and District Beds (3), for the D.C.L.I. at the Queen Mary Convalescent Hospital, Roehampton; local Hon. Sec. of S.E. Cornwall Prisoners of War Fund; and local branch of the Cornwall Work Auxiliary of the British Red Cross. *Address:* Garefield, Bodmin, Cornwall. (O10833)

LIDDELL, Rhoda Caroline Anne, M.B.E., *b.* 1 July, 1859; *d.* of Henry George Liddell, D.D., of The Deanery, Ch. Ch., Oxford. *War Work:* Netley Red Cross Hospital, Orthopædic Splint Dept. *Address:* Hoseyrigge, Westerham, Kent. (M8801)

LIDDELL, Violet Constance, M.B.E., *b.* 9 March, 1864; *d.* of Henry George Liddell, D.D., of The Deanery, Christ Church, Oxford *War Work:* Netley Red Cross Hospital, Orthopædic Splint Dept. *Address:* Hoseyrigge, Westerham, Kent. (M8802)

LIDDERDALE, Alan Wadsworth, O.B.E., *b.* 1885; *s.* of the Rt. Hon Wm. Lidderdale. *Educ.:* Winchester; Balliol. Director of Nisbet & Co., Ltd., Publishers, 22, Berners Street, W. 1. *War Work:* Clerk in Contraband Dept., Foreign Office. *Address:* 1, Portsea Place, Connaught Square, W. 2. *Club:* New Univ. (O505)

LIDDERDALE, John Henry, O.B.E., R.A.F.

LIDDIARD, Edgar Stratton, M.B.E., I.C.S., *b.* 29 April, 1878; *s.* of the late W. B. Liddiard, of Lloyds'; *m.* Mabel Audrey, *d.* of H. R. Brooke, of Tonbridge. *Educ.:* Malvern and Worcester Coll., Oxford. Registrar, Judicial Commissioners Court, 1909–10; Settlement Officer, Etawah, 1911–14; District Magistrate, Jalaun, 1916–19; Etah, 1920. *War Work:* Raising recruits and organising investments in War Loan. *Address:* c/o Messrs. Grindlay & Co., 54, Parliament Street, London. (M7123)

LIDDIARD, Jessie, M.B.E., *b.* 31 July, 1870; *d.* of Edwin James Liddiard, of Thornton Heath. *Educ.:* Parkfield Coll., Forest Hill, S.E. Superintendent of Clerical Staff (Women), London Telephone Service. *War Work:* Assisting in organisation of Awards Branch, Ministry of Pensions, Chelsea, 1917. *Address:* 6, Norbury Avenue, Thornton Heath. *Club:* Forum. (M666)

LIDDINGTON, Ezra William Edmund, O.B.E.

LIDDLE, Capt. Dudley Mark Percy, O.B.E., *b.* 31 July, 1893; *s.* of the late Mark Anthony Liddle; *m.* Elinor Mary, *d.* of the late Frank Thomas Hill. *Educ.:* Mackenzie Park, Slough. Officer of the Merchant Taylors' Company. *War Work:* 4 Aug. 1914, Private (Transport) Artists Rifles; promoted Corporal, Nov. 1914; Sergt., Feb. 1915; gazetted 2nd Lieut., R.A.S.C., May, 1915; Lieut., Aug. 1915; Capt., Feb. 1916; appointed Adjutant, May. 1916; service with 56th Divisional Train in France, Feb. 1916, to June, 1919. *Address:* 4, Kingsmead Road. Streatham Hill, S.W. 2. (O5480)

LIDDLE, Thomas, M.B.E., J.P.

LIDIERTH, James Eugene, M.B.E.

LIENARD, 2nd Lieut. Walter, M.B.E., R.A.F.

LIGAT, John Mackinlay, M.B.E., *b.* 29 July, 1878; *s.* of John Ligat, of Glasgow; *m.* Winifred Mary, *d.* of John G. Miller, of Bramhall. *Educ.:* Hutcheson's Grammar School, Glasgow. *War Work:* In charge of the Comforts Depot, Manchester; British Red Cross Society, East Lancashire Branch, and Sec. to the Comforts Committee, 1914–18; Sec. to the Joint Committee of the Comforts Committee, B.R.C.S., East Lancashire Branch, and the Lancashire County War Association for the Manchester War Hospital Supply Workrooms, Dover House. *Address:* Kerry, Sylvan Avenue, Brooklands, Cheshire. (M3805)

LIGHT, Edgar William, M.B.E.

LIGHTBODY, Henry, M.B.E., J.P. *b.* 3 Oct. 1876; *s.* of Henry Nisbet Lightbody, of Wishaw, Scotland; *m.* Janet Littlejohn, *d.* of Wm. Christie, of Wishaw. *Educ.:* Berryhill School, Wishaw; Glasgow Athenæum; Birkbeck Coll., London. Gen. Sec. Scottish National Y.M.C.A. *War Work:* Convener, and afterwards Gen. Sec. of the Camp and Fleet Department, Scottish National Council of Y.M.C.A. *Addresses:* 118, George Street, Edinburgh; 7, Hermitage Drive, Edinburgh. *Clubs:* Scottish Liberal; Glasgow Liberal. (M668)

LIGHTFOOT, Georgina Flora, Mrs., M.B.E., *b.* 22 Sept. 1872; *d.* of George Nankivell, late of Kobe, Japan; *m.* Charles Herbert, *s.* of Frederick James, late of Esher, Surrey, England. *War Work:* A promoter and Hon. Sec. of the " Kobe British Women's Patriotic League," Japan, 1914–16; a promoter and Hon. Sec. of the " Shizuoka Allies League," Japan, 1916–18. *Address:* Shizuoka, Japan. (M3806)

LIGHTFOOT, Harriet, M.B.E., Q.M.A.A.C.

LIGHTFOOT, Major Kenneth, O.B.E., R.E.

LIGHTFOOT, Capt. Leslie Jabez, O.B.E., R.A.P.D., *b.* 11 April, 1889; *s.* of the late Col. Jabez Lightfoot, of Gorakapur, India. *Educ.:* Bedford School. *War Work:* Serving at Hamilton N.B. Army Pay Office on outbreak of war; in May, 1915, to Suvla Bay, Gallipoli, with Headquarters IX. Corps; left Suvla Bay during the evacuation in Dec. 1915; posted to Headquarters XIIth Corps at Salonica; left Salonica Force in April, 1919, for Constantinople; mentioned in despatches, 1917 and 1918. *Club:* Junior Army and Navy. (O6497)

LIGHTFOOT, Theresa Anne, M.B.E.

LIGHTWOOD, Francis Harry, M.B.E.

LILE, Henry John, M.B.E., J.P., *b.* 13 Sept. 1864; *s.* of William Lile, of Neyland, Pem, S. Wales; *m.* Kezin, *d.* of Isaac Chadwick, of Whitby, Yorks. *Educ.:* Pembroke Dock, S. Wales. Superintendent, Milford District, Trinity House Service. *War Work:* Admiralty Service connected with the Northern Barrage between Orkney Islands and Norway. *Address:* Trinity Wharf, Neyland, Pembroke, S. Wales. (M3807)

LILBURN, Bethea, Mrs., M.B.F.

LILLEY, Arthur Winfield, M.B.E., *b.* 8 Aug. 1884; *s.* of Alexander Wellington Lilley, of St. Paul, Minnesota; *m.* Kathleen Elsie, *d.* of Alfred Butterworth, of Cawnpore. *Educ.:* Public School of Minnesota, U.S.A. Director, British India

Corporation, Ltd.; Director, Alliance Advertising Association; Member Managing Committee, Upper India Chamber of Commerce, Cawnpore. *War Work:* Sec. of the Cawnpore Woollen Mills Co., which was engaged throughout the war exclusively in the manufacture of woollen wearing apparel for the Indian Army, and it was due to his efforts that the output of the mills was trebled during the emergency. *Addresses:* The Shieling, Cawnpore, India; 2174, Princeton Avenue, St. Paul, Minnesota, U.S.A. *Clubs:* Cawnpore; Minnesota, St. Paul, Minnesota. (M7125)

LILLEY, Kate, M.B.E., *b.* 4 Dec. 1873; *d.* of the late T. Lilley, J.P., of Clacton-on-Sea. *Educ.:* Privately and France. *War Work:* Hon. Sec. Soldiers' and Sailors' Families Association; Hon. Sec. War Pensions Sub-Committee, Clacton. *Addresses:* The Grange, Dovercourt; 213A, High Street, Kensington. (M8806)

LILLEY, Capt. Leonard Moore, O.B.E., R.A.F.

LILLICO, William Lionel James, C.B.E., *b.* 4 Oct. 1880; *s.* of William Lilico, J.P., of Croydon; *m.* Florence Mary, *d.* of George Eaton Goldsmith, of Bury St. Edmunds. *Educ.:* Aldenham Coll., Radlett, Herts. Grain Merchant; Partner of Wm. Lillico and Sons, 15, Seething Lane, E. 6. *War Work:* Director of Feeding Stuffs Supplies, Ministry of Food, for two years; gave his services gratuitously. *Clubs:* St. Stephen's; City Carlton. (C2760)

LILLINGSTON, Major Frederick Francis Innes, O.B.E. (O11746)

LILLICRAP, Charles Swift, M.B.E.

LILLICRAP, Herbert Richard, M.B.E.

LILLY, Walter Elsworthy, M.B.E., M.A., M.A.I., D.Sc., M.I.Mech.E., *b.* 1867. Lecturer in Mechanical Engineering, Trinity Coll., Dublin. *War Work:* Assistant Civilian Inspector, Woolwich. *Address:* 40, Trinity College, Dublin. (M10251c)

LIMB, Capt. Frank, O.B.E., R.A.S.C. (M.T.)

LIMERICK, May Imelda Josephine, Countess of, C.B.E., *d.* of Joseph Burke Irwin, of the Priory, Co. Limerick, and formerly Resident Magistrate, of Stulleson House, Drogheda; *m.* 1890, William Henry Edmond de Vere Sheaffe Pery, Earl of Limerick, late Capt. and Hon. Major, 5th Batt. R. Munster Fusiliers. *War Work:* Superintendent of the Free Buffet, London Bridge Station. *Address:* Dromore Castle, Pollaskerry, Limerick. (C3152)

LIMMING, William Thomas, M.B.E.

LINCOLN, Cecil Henning, O.B.E., M.B.E.

LINCOLN, John Bebrouth, C.B.E., B.A., B.C.L. (Oxon. LL.B. (Dublin), *b.* 29 Dec. 1875; *s.* of the late James Edward Lincoln; *m.* Harriett Ellen Irvine, *d.* of the late Joseph Arthur Beardmore. *Educ.:* King's Coll. School, and Corpus Christi Coll., Oxford. Barrister-at-Law of the Inner Temple, 1903; Civil Servant; Legal Department of the Board of Education, 1905–15. *War Work:* Assist. Sec. of the Central Control Board (Liquor Traffic), 1915. *Addresses:* 134, Piccadilly, Whithorn, Friern Lane, Whetstone, Middlesex. *Clubs:* Authors'; South Herts Golf. (O1595)

LINDESAY, Lieut.-Col. Frederick Sinclair, O.B.E.

LINDLEY, Hon. Francis Oswald, C.B., C.B.E., B.A., *b.* 12 June, 1872; 5th *s.* of the 1st Baron Lindley (*see* BURKE'S *Peerage);* *m.* 12 Jan. 1903, Hon. Ethelreda Mary Fraser, 3rd *d.* of Simon, 13th Lord Lovat (*see* BURKE'S *Peerage).* H.M.'s Envoy Extraordinary and Minister Plenipotentiary at Vienna from 1920. *Address:* The British Embassy, Vienna. *Clubs:* St. James's; Turf; Bachelors'; Brooks's. (C40)

LINDLEY, Tinsley, O.B.E., LL.D., B.A., *b.* 27 Oct. 1865; *s.* of the late Ald. Leonard Lindley, of Nottingham; *m.* Constance Agnes, *d.* of the late Sir Francis Burnand. *Educ.:* Nottingham High School; The Leys; Caius Coll., Cambridge. Barrister-at-Law; Law Lecturer, Nottingham Univ. Coll. *War Work:* Deputy Director, Notts. Territorial Association; Commissioner, Military Service (Civil Liabilities) Department; Commander, Nottingham City Special Constables; Assistant Notts Area, Remounts Department. *Addresses:* 14, Park Terrace, Nottingham; Lamb Buildings, Temple, E.C. *Clubs:* Notts County; Constitutional; Sports. (O506)

LINDLEY, Walter, M.B.E., J.P.

LINDLEY, William Burns, O.B.E.

LINDON, John Benjamin, O.B.E., M.A., LL.M., *b.* 14 Sept. 1884; *m.* Myleta Fenton, *d.* of Sir William Corry, Bart., of Norbury Park, Dorking; 118, Eaton Square, S.W. (*see* BURKE'S *Peerage).* *Educ.:* Harrow, and Caius Coll., Cambridge. Barrister-at-Law. *War Work:* Chief Intelligence Officer, War Trade Intelligence Department. *Addresses:* 23, Bryanston Square, W. 1; 11A, New Square, Lincoln's Inn. *Club:* Oxford and Cambridge. (O10835)

LINDOP, Capt. Patrick, M.B.E., A.P.D

LINDQUIST, Capt. Oskar, O.B.E., R.A.F.

LINDSAY, Lieut.-Col. Alexander Dunlop, C.B.E.; Capt. and A. Lieut.-Col. Gen. List. Served in the Great War, 1914–19 (despatches). (C1281)

LINDSAY, Alexander Harvey, M.B.E.

LINDSAY, Capt. Alfred Stewart, M.B.E., M.C., *b.* 15 March, 1887; *s.* of William Stewart Lindsay, of Timaru, New Zealand. *Educ.:* Christ Coll., Christchurch, New Zealand. *War Work:* Gallipoli; Patrol work in Egypt; has Croix de Guerre. *Address:* c/o John Stewart Robertson, Golf Park, Prestwick, Ayrshire. (M6551)

LINDSAY, Darcy, C.B.E., *b.* 1865; *s.* of the late David Baird Lindsay, of Dowhill, Kinross, N.B. Sec. Calcutta Branch of Royal Insurance Co., Ltd. *War Work:* Sec. 1917–18, War Loan Committee; organised war funds and collections for same. *Address:* 26, Dalhousie Square, Calcutta. *Clubs:* Sports; Bengal; New, Calcutta. (C1083)

LINDSAY, Eliza Hunter, M.B.E., *d.* of John Lindsay, of Lauder, N.B. *Educ.:* Lauder and Edinburgh; for many years Head Mistress of Lauder Public School (ret.). *War Work:* At the beginning of the war, as sister of the Provost of the Royal Burgh of Lauder, she devoted her time to the organising of schemes for the benefit both of local soldiers at home and abroad, as well as the soldiers in general, and through her initiative many comforts were made; Sec. of a Work Party of which the Viscountess Maitland, of Thirlestane Castle, Lauder, was President, and continued in the same capacity when the Work Party joined the Army Council Scheme under Sir Edward Ward, till the Association ended, 31 March, 1919, for which work she was mentioned in despatches in 1918. (M8808)

LINDSAY, Ernest Charles, C.B.E., M.B., F.R.C.S., *b.* 24 April, 1883; *s.* of the Rev. George Lindsay, of Southbridge, Canterbury, New Zealand. *Educ.:* Otago Univ., New Zealand. Assistant Surgeon, London Hospital, London, E.; Surgical Tutor, London Hospital Medical Coll. *War Work:* Surgical Specialist, 18 C.C.S., B.E.F.; Major, R.A.M.C., Officer in charge Surgical Division, 32 Stat. Hospital, B.E.F. *Address:* 46, Queen Anne Street, Cavendish Square, W. *Club:* Royal Automobile. (C1282)

LINDSAY, Eugenie Josephine, Mrs., C.B.E., *b.* 31 March, 1893; *d.* of Mr. and Mrs. Eugène Oudin, of London and New York; *m.* Peter Lindsay. *Educ.:* Queen's Coll., London. *War Work:* Before her marriage was Superintendent of Translation Bureau, War Office, 1914–17; private Sec. to Major-Gen. Sir George Macdonogh, Director of Military Intelligence, 1917–18; Private Sec. to Lieut.-Gen. Sir J. Macdonogh, Adjt.-Gen. to the Forces, 1918–19. *Address:* 21, Cadogan Gardens, S.W. (C2761)

LINDSAY, 2nd Lieut. Harry Robert, M.B.E.

LINDSAY, Harry Alexander Fanshawe, C.B.E., I.C.S.; *s.* of the late Alexander Martin Lindsay, C.I.E., of Bank of Bengal, Calcutta; *m.* 1909, Kathleen Louise Huntington. *Educ.:* St. Paul's School, and Worcester Coll., Oxford. Under Sec. Commerce and Industry Depart., India, 1912–15; Director-Gen. of Commercial Intelligence in India since 1916. *Address:* Calcutta. *Club:* Bengal (Calcutta). (C1977)

LINDSAY, Col. Henry Arthur Peyton, C.M.G., C.B.E., *b.* 1868; *s.* of the late Major Arthur Ferguson Lindsay, 8th Bengal Cav.; *m.* 1905, Charlotte Eliza Campbell, *d.* of the late Major A. F. Stewart, Worcestershire Regt. *Educ.:* Dulwich Coll. Entered W. Indian Regt. 1887, became Capt. Indian Army, 1898; Major, 1905; Lieut.-Col. 1913; served on the N.-W. Frontier of India, 1897–8 (medal with clasp); in the Great War, 1914–19 (despatches); Assist. Director of Transport, Rawal Pindi Concentration, 1905; Delhi Coronation Durbar, 1911; appointed to command Meerut Div. Train, 1912; Dep. Director of Supplies and Transport, 1916, with rank of Col. (C2037)

LINDSAY, Lieut.-Col. Henry Edith Arthur, O.D.E., J.P., *b.* 1866; *s.* of Lieut.-Col. the Hon. C. Lindsay, C.B.; *m.* Norah, *d.* of the Hon. E. Bourke (*see* BURKE'S *Peerage,* Mayo, E.). *Educ.:* Cheam, and Oxford Military Coll. *War Work:* Commission, B.R.F.S., Aug. 1914, to Aug. 1915; R.F.C. and R.A.F. to end of war. *Address:* The Manor House, Sutton Courtney, Abingdon. *Clubs:* Naval and Military; Royal Automobile. (O1597)

LINDSAY, James Brown, O.B.E.

LINDSAY, Major James Hawkins, O.B.E.

LINDSAY, The Lady Kathleen, O.B.E., *b.* 20 Dec. 1876; (*see* BURKE'S *Peerage,* Carrick, E.); *d.* of the late Earl of Carrick, of Mount Juliet, Thomastown, Co. Kilkenny; *m.* Walter Charles, *s.* of Col. Henry Gore Lindsay, of Glasnevin House, Dublin. *Educ.:* Privately. *War Work:* Sept. 1914, to April, 1916, Lady Superintendent of the Women Workers packing rations, etc., at the R.A.S.C. Supply Reserve Depot, Deptford; May, 1916, to June, 1919, Lady Superintendent of the Women Workers of the Inspection Department, Royal Arsenal, Woolwich. *Club:* Ladies' Athenæum. (O1598)

LINDSAY, Capt. Lionel Arthur, M.V.O., O.B.E.

LINDSAY, Major Norman James, O.B.E., Can. A.S.C. (M.T.)

LINDSAY, Capt. Peter, O.B.E., R.G.A.

LINDSAY, Capt. Walker Stewart, O.B.E., R.A.M.C., *b.* 1885; *d.* of M. M. Lindsay, of Halifax, Nova Scotia. *Educ.:* Dalhousie and Edinburgh Univs. Professor of Pathology and Bacteriology, Univ. of Saskatchewan. *War Work:* O.C. No 13 Mobile Laboratory. *Address:* The Univ., Saskatoon, Canada. (O5481)

LINDSAY, Major William George, O.B.E.

LINDSAY, William Joseph, M.B.E., M.A., M.D., B.C.; *s.* of the Rev. Thos. Lindsay, of Castle Ellis, Co. Wexford. *Educ.:* Epsom; Cambridge; Guy's Hospital. Ophthalmic appointments at Royal Eye Hospital, Southwark, and at other hospitals. *War Work:* Ophthalmic Surgeon, 4th London General Hospital, R.A.M.C. (T.). *Address:* 84, Herne Hill, S.E. 24. (M10270)

LINDSELL, Iris le Strange, M.B.E., *b.* 12 April, 1888; *d.* of the late Herbert Edward Lindsell, of Holme, Biggleswade, Beds. *War Work:* Sec. of Camps Library, 45, Horseferry Road, Westminster, for 5 years. *Address:* 35, Charleville Mansions, Kensington, W. 14. *Club:* New Century. (M3809)

LINDSELL, Capt. Reginald Stuart, O.B.E., R.A.F.

LINDSELL, Major Wilfred Gordon, D.S.O., O.B.E., M.C.,

R.A., *b.* 1884; *s.* of Gerald Charles Huntingdon Lindsell. Served in the Great War, 1914–18 (despatches, Croix de Guerre). (O2614)

LINDSEY, Rev. Charles Edward Chaloner, O.B.E.

LINEHAM, Samuel, O.B.E. Managing Director of Leigh, Lineham & Co., Ltd., Call Lane, Leeds. President of West Riding Provision Merchants and Wholesale Grocers Association, Ltd.; President, North Eastern Federation of Produce Merchants, Ltd.; Director of National Federation of Produce Merchants, Ltd.; Member of Bacon Advisory Committee at Ministry of Food, London; Member of the Council of the Leeds Chamber of Commerce. *Address :* 175, Chapeltown Road, Leeds. (O10837)

LINES, Lieut. Reginald Edward, M.B.E., I.A.R.O.

LINFIELD, Frederic Caesar, M.B.E., J.P.

LINFOOT, William Ernest, M.B.E., *b.* 10 Feb. 1872; *s.* of the late George Linfoot, of Spofforth; *m.* Florence, *d.* of the late John Stockdale, of Birstwith. *Educ. :* Rishworth Grammar School. Works Manager, The Campbell Gas Engine Co., Ltd., Halifax, Yorks. *War Work :* Organisation and manufacture of oil and steam engines for motor gunboats and trawlers; experimental paravanes, steam and electric winches for trawlers and kite balloons; air station installations, submarine engine components; for Army, shells, bombs of many varieties in large quantities, also many types of experimental chemical shells. *Address :* 28, Highfield Terrace, Halifax. (M8809)

LING, Robert, M B.E., R.N.R.

LING, Major Robert Walton, C.B.E., D.S.O., M.C., R.F.A., R.F.A., *b.* 29 March, 1886; *s.* of Christopher Ling, J.P., of Wandales, Wetheral, Cumberland; *m.* Mia Dorothy, *d.* of Thomas Reynell Lane, of London. *Educ. :* West Downs, Winchester; Bradfield Coll.; Royal Military Academy, Woolwich. *War Work :* Battery Commander, France, May, 1915, to Dec. 1917; Brigade Major, R.A., France, Dec. 1917, to March, 1919; Chief Artillery Liaison Officer with British Military to S. Russia, April, 1919, to July, 1920. *Address :* 2, Lassa Road, Eltham, Kent. *Club :* Junior United Service. (C3130)

LING, Lieut. Herbert Westwood, M.B.E.

LINGARD, Lieut. William, M.B.E., R.A.F.

LINK, Emily Ethel, M.B.E., *b.* 21 Jan. 1878; *d.* of John David Link, of Croydon. *Educ. :* Croydon High School. *War Work :* Hon. Sec. Wallacefield Auxiliary Hospital from Oct. 1914, until June, 1915; Commandant of St. Dorothy's Auxiliary Hospital from Jan. 1916, until June, 1919. *Address :* 21, Spencer Road, South Croydon. (M8810)

LINK, Major Willie Cresswell, O.B.E.

LINKLATER, Capt. George James, O.B.E., M.B., R.A.M.C. (T.).

LINLITHGOW, John Victor Alexander Hope, Marquess of, Earl of Hopetoun, Viscount Aithrie, Baron Hope, Baron Hopetoun, Baron Niddry, O.B.E., D.L., *b.* 24 Sept. 1887; *e.s.* of 1st Marquess and Hon. Hersey de Moleyns, 3rd *d.* of 4th Lord Ventry (*see* BURKE'S *Peerage*); *m.* Doreen Maud, 2nd *d.* of Sir Frederick Milner, Bt. (*see* BURKE'S *Peerage*). *Educ. :* Eton. *Addresses :* 91, Lancaster Gate, W. 2; Hopetoun House, Queensferry, Linlithgowshire. *Clubs :* Carlton; New, Edinburgh. (O7392)

LINNELL, Agnes Evelyn, Mrs., M.B.E.; *d.* of the Rev. E. T. Waters, of Highclere, Hants.; *m.* Dr. John Everard, M.B. (Cantab), D.P.H., *s.* of Forester Linnell, of Duddon Lodge, Tarporley. *War Work :* Assist. Commandant of V.A.D. Hospital, Sheringham. *Address :* The Point, Sheringham, Norfolk. (M671)

LINTHORNE, Richard Roope, O.B.E., *b.* Jan. 1864; *s.* of Richard Linthorne, of Poole, Dorset; *m.* Lizzie Gertrude, *d.* of Richard Gibbin, of Southampton. *Educ. :* Liverpool Coll. Solicitor; Town Clerk of Southampton since May, 1899. *War Work :* Hon. Sec. Southampton Representative Committee (Prince of Wales' Fund); Executive Officer for Southampton Food Control Committee; Clerk of Southampton Tribunal. *Addresses :* Municipal Offices, and 33, Westwood Road, Southampton. *Club :* Royal Societies'. (O10838)

LINTON, Major Adam Pearce, O.B.E.

LINTON, Col. Charles, O.B.E.

LINTON, Charles Astell George, M.B.E.

LINTON, Capt. George Purdie, O.B.E., M.C.

LINTOTT, Major John William, O.B.E., R.A.F.

LINTOTT, Walter, M.B.E., *b.* 6 July, 1868; *s.* of Samuel Lintott, of Lewes, Sussex. *Educ. :* Privately. Formerly Partner in the firm of Powell & Co., Land Agents, Lewes; Sec. Sussex County Agricultural Society, and Sussex Dairy Farmers' Association. *War Work :* Assisted in the organisation of the Lewes Company of the Volunteer Training Corps, and took a commission as Platoon Commander in the Company; resigned to take up command of the Lewes Company, Sussex Yeomanry Cadets, affiliated to the Sussex Territorial Force Association; in Aug. 1914, assisted in the arrangements for the establishment of Military Hospitals in Lewes; appointed Quartermaster and Treas. of the Military Hospital, Sussex 48, from the opening in May, 1915, and remained in office till demobilisation, 1919; acted as Sec. and Treas. to the Lewes Centre B.R.C.S., and as Treas. to the Mid-Sussex Branch, B.R.C.S.; on the outbreak of war assisted in the arrangement of the scheme for dealing with the population of Lewes in case

of emergency; has been Treas of the East Sussex War Pensions Committee, 1917–20; when the need of further food production throughout the country was realised, assisted the East Sussex War Agricultural Committee in the survey of certain parishes, and remained as Sec. to the Chailey Sub-Committee; Sec. and Treas. of the Agricultural Relief of Allies Committee. *Addresses :* 50, Osmond Road, Hove; St. Jean de Luz, B.P., France. *Clubs :* Constitutional; Royal Automobile; New, Brighton; Lewes and County, Lewes. (M8812)

LIPMAN, Samuel Niman, M.B.E.

LIPPOLD, Capt. and Qr.-Mr. Albert Arthur, M.B.E., R.A.M.C. (T.).

LIPSETT, Major Lewis Richard, O.B.E., R.A.S.C.

LISLE, Lieut. Arthur, M.B.E., R.E.

LISTER, Charles, M.B.E., *b.* 16 July, 1877; *s.* of Robert Lister, of Leeds. Textile Manufacturer; Director, Mysore Industrial Bank. *War Work :* Manufacture and Supply of Textiles for Indian Army. *Addresses :* Cubbon Hotel, Bangalore, India; Portland Terrace, Midvale Road, St. Heliers, Jersey. (M6192)

LISTER, Charles Ashton, C.B.E., *b.* 1871; *s.* of Sir Ashton Lister, C.B.E., M.P., of The Towers, Dursley, Gloucestershire; *m.* Laura Emmeline, *d.* of A. Browning, of The Homestead, Weston, Bath. J.P. for Gloucestershire; Chairman and Director of several engineering concerns; Member of W. of England Munitions Board of Management; Board of Management, Reconstruction Advisory Panel. *Address :* Sneyd Park House, Sneyd Park, Bristol. (C551)

LISTER, Brev.-Major Francis Vivian, O.B.E., A.I.C.E., M.R.San.I., F.R.G.S., *b.* 1871; *s.* of William Lister, of Great Crosby; *m.* Jessie Moseley, *d.* of Job Hamer, of Mexico. *Educ. :* Merchant Taylors'; France; U.S.A. *War Work :* Supt. Chemical Projectile Laboratory; Supt. of Design, Chemical Warfare Dept.; mentioned four times in despatches, 1915–19. *Clubs :* Devonshire and Ranelagh. (O508)

LISTER, Capt. George, M.B.E.

LISTER, Rev. Irvine, M.B.E., *b.* 9 Nov. 1883; *s.* of the late David Lister, of Hipperholme, Yorks; *m.* Jessie, *d.* of the late John Townsend, of Halifax, Yorks. *Educ. :* Hipperholme Grammar School; Manchester Univ.; United Coll., Bradford. Minister, Congregational Church, Uppermill, Yorks, 1909–14; Cairo Street Chapel, Warrington, 1914. *War Work :* Hon. Sec. Care Committee of the South Lancs. Regt. Prisoners of War; Hon. Chaplain, Whitecross Hospital, Military; Member of War Pensions Committee. *Addresses :* 9, Palmyra Square, Warrington; The Old Academy, Warrington. (M3810)

LISTER, Sir Robert Ashton, C.B.E., *b.* 4 Feb. 1845; *s.* of G. Lister, of Dursley; *m.* Frances Anne. *Educ. :* Dusseldorf; Versailles. Engineer and County Surveyor. *War Work :* County Chairman of War Savings Committee; Commissioner of War Savings for Wilts and Somerset. *Address :* The Towers, Dursley, Glioucestershire. *Clubs :* Reform; National Liberal; Gloucester. (C992)

LISTER, Thomas David, C.B.E., M.D., *b.* 30 Jan. 1869; *s.* of Francis Wilson Lister, of London; *m.* Louise Edna Bertha, *d.* of E. Ritter, of London. *Educ. :* Guy's Hospital; Senator of London Univ.; Consulting Physician to Royal Exchange Assurance, Friends' Provident Institution, North British and Mercantile; Visiting Physician to Mt. Vernon Hospital and Royal Waterloo Hospital. *War Work :* Was Consulting Physician for chest cases to the Prince of Wales' Hospital for Officers, Marylebone, with 800 beds (two epidemics of influenza and pneumonia), throughout its occupation as a hospital; and treated heart and gas cases, tuberculosis of the lungs, and other chest conditions. *Address :* 31, Harley Street, W.; Bockmer End, Medmenham, Bucks. *Club :* Royal Societies. (C3118)

LISTER, Lieut. William, M.B.E.

LISTON, Eng.-Comm. Andrew Graham, O.B.E., R.N.R.

LISTON, Mary Forbes, O.B.E., M.B., Ch.B.

LITCHFIELD, Capt. John Walter, M.B.E.

LITHIBY, Beatrice Ethel, M.B.E., A.R.M.A.A.C.

LITSTER, William James, O.B.E., *b.* 10 Feb. 1869; *s.* of Capt. Archie Litster, of Leslie, Fifeshire; *m.* Olivia Sarah Anne, *d.* of Thomas Bean, of Simla. *Educ. :* Bishop Cotton School, Simla, and Grammar School, Leslie, Fifeshire. Assist. Manager and Chief Accountant, Head Office of Alliance Bank of Simla, and later Secretary, Simla Municipality. *War Work :* Hon. Treas. Joint War Committee and St. John Ambulance Association, Headquarters for India. *Club :* United Service, Simla. (O4058)

LITTLE, Capt. Cuthbert Joseph Harwood, O.B.E., M.B., Ch.B., R.A.M.C., *b.* 13 June, 1889; *s.* of the Rev. J. Harwood Little, of Great Witcombe, Glos. *Educ. :* Dover Coll., and Switzerland. *War Work :* Served in India, Mesopotamia, Persia. *Address :* Great Witcombe, Gloucester. *Club :* Junior Naval and Military. (O4231)

LITTLE, Major D'Arcy Hunter, O.B.E., T.D., *b.* 3 Sept. 1874; *s.* of James Law Charles Hunter Little, late of Llanvair Grange, Monmouthshire. *Educ. :* Privately. Lord Chancellor's Department (Civil Service). *War Work :* Served with 56th and 58th Division, 1916–17; D.A.Q.M.G., Dunkerque, British Military Base Headquarters, 1918–19; Commandant British Troops, Dunkerque, with rank of Lieut.-Col., 1919–20. *Address :* Cawley Priory, Chichester. *Club :* Union. (O5483)

Spratton Hall, Northamptonshire. J.P. for Warwickshire ; Co. Director, Auxiliary Hospitals and V.A.D.'s, Warwickshire, during European War. *Address :* Newbold Pacy Hall, Warwickshire. *Club :* Junior Carlton.

LITTLE, James Mason, M.B.E.

LITTLE, James Raymond, M.B.E.

LITTLE, Lieut.-Col. John, O.B.E.

LITTLE, Brig.-Gen. Malcolm Orme, C.B., C.B.E., J.P., *b.* 28 Nov. 1857 ; *s.* of the late Gen. Sir Archibald Little, G.C.B., of Upton Tetbury ; *m.* Iris Hermione, *d.* of the late Albert Brassey, of Heythrop. *Educ. :* Wellington Coll. *War Work :* Inspector of Remounts, 1914 ; Commandant, Remount Brigade and Coast Defences, 1915–17. *Addresses :* Dunsmore, Rugby ; Garre, North Berwick. *Clubs :* Naval and Military ; Cavalry ; Arthur's.   (C1667)

LITTLE, Robert, O.B.E.   (O11990)

LITTLE, Lieut.-Col. William, O.B.E.

LITTLE, William, M.B.E., *b.* 29 Dec. 1858 ; *s.* of William Stewardson Little, of Holloway, London ; *m.* Eva Mary, *d.* of Walter Galton, of Winchester. *Educ. :* The British School, Sydenham. *War Work :* Railway Transport arrangements in connection with the original Army Mobilisation Scheme and similar subsequent work in connection with the Great European War. *Address :* Westerham, 4. Townley Road, E. Dulwich, S.E., 22. *Club :* Dulwich Conservative.   (M673)

LITTLEHALES, Capt. Joseph Thomas, M.B.E., R.F.A., *b.* 17 Sept. 1892 ; *s.* of William Littlehales, of Wolverhampton ; *m.* Elsie Olive, *d.* of George Reid, of Wolverhampton. *Educ. :* Wolverhampton. *War Work :* Service with North Russian Exped. Force ; Adjutant to Finnish Murman Legion. *Address :* 32, Stafford Road, Wolverhampton.   (M5015)

LITTLEJOHNS, Lieut. Alfred Edwin, M.B.E.

LITTLEWOOD, Eng.-Com. Alfred William, O.B.E., R.N.

LITTON, Major Marshal William, O.B.E., *b.* 1872 ; *s.* of Justice Litton, of Dublin. *Educ. :* Trinity Coll., Dublin. *War Work :* Served with the Royal Irish Fusiliers in France ; afterwards Staff Capt. at the War Office. *Clubs :* Irish Naval and Military ; Cork County.   (O7395)

LIVERPOOL, Annette Louise, Countess of, G.B.E., *d.* of 5th Viscount Monck ; *m.* Arthur William de Brito Savile Foljambe, 5th holder of title and 2nd holder of revived title of Earl of Liverpool, P.C., G.C.M.G., G.B.E., M.V.O., Governor-General of New Zealand. *Addresses :* Government House, Wellington, New Zealand ; 44, Grosvenor Gardens, S.W. 1 ; Hartsholme Hall, Lincoln.   (DG12)

LIVERPOOL, Arthur William de Brito Savile Foljambe, Earl of, P.C., G.C.B., G.C.M.G., G.B.E., M.V.O., Knight of Justice of the Order of St. John of Jerusalem, *b.* 27 May, 1870 ; *e. s.* of the 4th holder of the title and 1st holder of revived title of Earl of Liverpool, and Louisa Blanche, *e. d.* of Frederick John Howard (brother-in-law of 7th Duke of Devonshire) ; *m.* 1897, Hon. Annette Louise, G.B.E., *d.* of the 5th Viscount Monck (*see* BURKE'S *Peerage*). *Educ. :* Eton ; R.M.C. Sandhurst. 2nd Lieut. Rifle Brigade, 1891 ; Lieut. 1893 ; Capt. 1897 ; A.D.C. to Earl Cadogan, K.G., Lord Lieut. of Ireland, 1898–1900 ; formerly Major, The Rifle Brigade (Prince Consort's Own) ; Staff Capt., Dublin District, July 1900 to Dec. 1901 ; served South Africa, 1901–2 ; Major, 1907 ; State Steward and Chamberlain to the Earl of Aberdeen, K.T., Lord Lieut. of Ireland, 1906–8 ; Governor of New Zealand, 1912–17 ; Governor-General since 1917. *Addresses :* Government House, Wellington, New Zealand ; 44, Grosvenor Gardens, S.W. ; Hartsholm Hall, Lincoln. *Club :* Naval and Military.   (G37)

LIVESAY, Comm. Waterworth Bligh, O.B.E., R.I.M.

LIVESEY, Lieut.-Col. Everard Frederick Ernest, O.B.E.

LIVESEY, Geraldine Mary, M.B.E., *d.* of Reginald Livesey, *s.* of the late Joseph Livesey, of Stourton Hall, Lincolnshire. *Educ. :* Convent of the Sacred Heart, Brighton. *War Work :* Member of Gloucestershire V.A.D. at the Ghyll House Red Cross Hospital. St. Briavel's, Glos. ; Assist. Lady Superintendent Inspection Department, Royal Arsenal, Woolwich. *Address :* St. Briavel's, Gloucestershire.   (M674)

LIVESEY, Sir Harry, G.B.E., *b.* 30 May, 1860; *s.* of James Livesey, of 4, Whitehall Court, S.W. 1. *Educ. :* Privately. Civil Engineer. *War Work :* Deputy Director of Inland Waterways and Docks, War Office, Aug. 1916, to May, 1917 ; Director of Contracts, Admiralty. May. 1917, to Dec. 1918. *Address :* Watlands, Scaynes Hill, Sussex. *Clubs :* Reform ; Royal Thames.   (G55)

LIVESLEY, Edwin, O.B.E., *b.* 10 Dec. 1862 ; *s.* of the late Alderman Wm. Livesley, of Manchester ; *m.* Evelyn, *d.* of the late Philip Child, of Manchester. *Educ. :* Whalley Range High School, and Old Trafford School. Assistant Goods Manager, Great Central Railway ; Manager and Sec. Messrs. Thompson, McKay & Co. *War Work :* Deputy Controller of Horse Transport, Board of Trade, 1917–19. *Address :* Lynwood, 86, Green Lane, Northwood.   (O10839)

LIVINGSTONE, Dame Adelaide, D.B.E.

LIVINGSTONE, Capt. Alexander Frederick, M.B.E., K.R.R.C. and R.A.F.

LIVINGSTONE, Jessie Walker Shirriff, M.B.E. ; *d.* of Dr. James Livingstone, of Wishaw. *Educ. :* Charlotte Square Institution, Edinburgh, and Shandwick Place, Univ. of Edinburgh Classes. Hon. County Sec., Lanarkshire Red Cross ; Member of County of Lanark Insurance Committee. *War Work :* Organised Red Cross work in Lanarkshire and acted as Hon. Treas. ; over £91,000 being raised during the war. *Address :* 17. Hill Street, Wishaw, Lanarkshire.   (M8813)

LIVINGSTONE, Capt. and Qr.-Mr. John Stewart, O.B.E.

LIVINGSTONE, Lieut. Robert Heaton, O.B.E.

LIVINGSTONE, Marion Isabella Rose, Mrs. FENTON-, M.B.E., *b.* 1869 ; *d.* of Robert C. Traill, *y.s.* of George Traill, of Holland, D.L., Orkney ; *m.* George Frederick James Fenton-Livingstone, of Easter-Moffat, Lanarkshire (who died), *s.* of Thomas Livingstone Fenton-Livingstone, of Westquarter, and Bedlormie, Stirlingshire. *Educ. :* Privately. *War Work :* President, New Monkland Division Soldiers' and Sailors' Families Association, 1900–14 ; Vice-President, Airdrie and New Monkland Division British Red Cross Society, 1910–20 ; Assistant Sec. Lorn Division British Red Cross Society, 1913–15; Commandant, No. 1 V.A.D. Hostel, 2nd Scottish General Hospital, Hon. Sec. West Highland Sailors' and Soldiers' Rest, afterwards Petersen-Reynolds' Memorial Institute, Sailors' and Soldiers' Rest, 1916–20 ; ran a depot for comforts for Coast Watchers, 1914–16. *Address :* Glenroy, Oban, Argyll.

LLEWELLIN, Lieut. Charles Herbert, O.B.E., D.C.M., R.E.

LLEWELLYN, Clara Maud, M.B.E.

LLEWELLYN, Frederick Allen, O.B.E.

LLEWELLYN, Joseph Millro, O.B.E.

LLEWELLYN, Sir Leonard Wilkinson, K.B.E., J.P. for Glamorganshire, *b.* 1874 ; *s.* of the late Llewelyn Llewelyn, J.P., of King's Hill, Newport, Mon. ; *m.* Edith (died 1913), *d.* of the late Edward Jones, J.P., D.L., of Snatchwood Park, Pontypool, Mon. *Educ. :* Monmouth Grammar School, and Heidelberg. Coal Owner ; Consulting Engineer ; Director of several Coal, Iron, and Steel Companies ; High Sheriff Monmouthshire, 1920–21. *War Work :* Controller of Materials of Munitions Supply ; Chevalier and Officer of Legion of Honour ; Officer of Order of Leopold of Belgium ; holds the Order of St. Stanislaus, the Royal Humane Society's Silver Medal. *Addresses :* Malpas Court, Newport, Mon. ; 88, St. James's Street, London. *Clubs :* Bath ; Junior Carlton ; Sports ; National Sporting.   (K29)

LLEWELLYN, Comm. Llewellyn Evan Hugh, O.B.E.

LLEWELLYN, William Ewart, O.B.E., *b.* 4 Jan. 1880 ; *s.* of Joseph John Llewellyn, of Liverpool ; *m.* Lilian Annie, *d.* of Richard Hall, of Crouch End. *Educ. :* Liverpool Institute. Superintendent of Chart Issues, Admiralty ; Vice-Chairman, Admiralty Administrative Whitley Council. *War Work :* Superintendent of Chart Issues for Navy and Mercantile Marine. *Addresses :* 42. Cranbourn Street, W.C. 2 ; Wayfarers, Berkhamsted, Herts.   (O10841)

LLOYD, Albert Henry, C.B.E. Sec. Recreation Huts Department, Church Army.   (C993)

LLOYD, Amy Margaret Helen, M.B.E., *b.* 10 Dec. 1865 ; *d.* of the late Capt. E. W. C. Lloyd, Royal Fusiliers. *Educ. :* Privately. Secretary, United Arts Club, Dublin. *War Work :* May to Oct. 1915, V.A.D. at Fernleigh Hospital, Larkfield, Kent ; May, 1916, to Nov. 1917, V.A.D. (G. S. Section) Military Hospital, Newbridge, Co. Kildare ; Jan. 1918, Deputy Administrator W.A.A.C. Bedford ; Feb. 1918, to March, 1918, Deputy Administrator Scarborough ; March to May, Deputy Administrator, Q.M.A.A.C. Receiving Depot, Belfast ; May to Dec. Q.M.A.A.C. Residential Depot. Dublin ; March, to Dec. 1919, Unit Administrator Q.M.A.A.C. in charge of Q.M.A.A.C. Receiving Depot, Jury's Hotel, Dublin. *Address :* 16, Pembroke Park, Dublin.   (M6669)

LLOYD, Capt. Arthur Athelwold, D.S.O., O.B.E., *b.* 1864 ; 2nd surviving son of the late Pennant Athelwold Lloyd, of Pentrehobyn, Mold, and Craig Mair, Menai Bridge, N. Wales. Entered Northamptonshire Regt. 1885 ; Capt. 1894 ; ret. 1905 ; served in S. Africa, 1899–1902 (wounded, despatches twice) ; D.A.A.G. 5th Div. S. Command, 1902–5. *Club :* Army and Navy.   (O510)

LLOYD, Arthur Harold, M.B.E., B.Sc. (Lond.), *b.* 11 March, 1885 ; *s.* of Thomas Lloyd, of Lampeter ; *m.* Edith, *d.* of Joseph Pearson, of Coventry. *Educ. :* St. David's. Coll. School. Lampeter, and Univ. Coll. of Wales, Aberystwyth. *War Work :* Chief Tool Designer at Messrs. Alfred Herbert, Ltd., Coventry. *Address :* 33, Styvechale Avenue, Coventry. *Club :* Coventry and County.   (M8815)

LLOYD, Arthur Thomas, O.B.E.

LLOYD, Lieut.-Col. Charles, O.B.E., T.D.

LLOYD, Christopher, M.V.O., M.B.E.

LLOYD, Cyril Edward, O.B.E.

LLOYD, Capt. Daniel Charles, M.B.E., T.F., *b.* 13 Sept., 1879 ; *s.* of F. H. Lloyd, J.P. late of Lichfield ; *m.* Alice Hilda, *d.* of the Rev. C. N. Bolton, late of Lichfield. *Educ. :* Bilton Grange, and Repton. Steel Manufacturer. *War Work :* Joint Managing Director, F. H. Lloyd & Co., Ltd., James Bridge, Steel Works, Wednesbury, manufacturers of steel castings for all classes of war materials ; during the war manufacturers of naval shells. *Address :* Stechwell End, Tettenhall, Wolverhampton.   (M677)

LLOYD, Edmund, M.B.E., M.B. A Church Missionary Society Doctor in charge of relief and hospital work at Gaza,   (M1025)

LLOYD, Lieut.-Col. Ernest Herbert, O.B.E.

LLOYD, Ethel Vernon, Mrs., M.B.E., Q.M.A.A.C.

LLOYD, Frances, Mrs., M.B.E., *d.* of John Henry Darley, of Ferney, Co. Dublin ; *m.* Merrick Lloyd, J.P., D.L., *s.* of Guy Lloyd, J.P., D.L., of Croghan (*see* BURKE'S *Landed Gentry*). *War Work :* Vice-President, Boyle War Committee ; Manageress, Boyle War Hospital Supply Depot ; Vice-President, Boyle V.A.D. *Address :* Croghan House, Boyle, Ireland.   (M8817)

LLOYD, Francis Seymour, O.B.E., M.D. (Lond.), L.R.C.P.

(Lond.), M.R.C.S. (Eng.), *b*. 8 Oct. 1874 ; *s*. of the late Deputy Surgeon-Gen. E. Eyre Lloyd, of Wokingham, Berks. ; *m*. Constance Maud, *d*. of Thomas Sworder, of Holly Lodge, Luton. *Educ.*: Bedford School. Medical Officer to Bute Hospital, Luton, and to Children's Sick and Convalescent Home, Luton ; Certifying Surgeon (Luton District) ; Medical Officer to Luton Post Office ; Hon. Life Member, St. John Ambulance Association ; Hon. Commandant, British Red Cross Society, Luton Branch. *War Work :* Medical Officer to Wardown Auxiliary Hospital, and to Lady Wernher's Hospital for Convalescent Officers. *Address*: Homedale, Luton, Bedfordshire. (O10843)

LLOYD, Fred, M.B.E.

LLOYD, Col. Frederick Lindsay, C.M.G., C.B.E., *b*. 1860 ; Lieut.-Col. (ret.) ; T. Col. Reserve ; served in S. Africa, 1899–1900 (despatches, Queen's medal with three clasps). (C2136)

LLOYD, George Mayhey, M.B.E.

LLOYD, George William, O.B.E., I.S.O.

LLOYD, Lieut.-Col. George William David Bowen, O.B.E., J.P., Carmarthenshire, late Royal Welsh Fusiliers, *b*. Nov. 1866 ; *s*. of Charles Lloyd, of Brunant, Carmarthenshire ; *m*. Lilian, *d*. of D. C. Lloyd-Owen, of Vrondeg, Four Oaks, Warwickshire. *Educ.*: Privately ; St. Peter's Coll., Cambridge ; Sandhurst. Joined Royal Welsh Fusiliers, Feb. 1888, served with 1st and 2nd Batt. until June, 1913. *War Work :* 8th Batt. R.W.F. Aug. 1914 ; Commanded 11th Batt. R.W.F. 1915–16 (France and Salonica), invalided ; Rec. Officer, Southport ; Assist. Director of National Service, Carmarthenshire and Pembrokeshire, 1917–19 ; *Addresses :* Bronwerydd, Dyffryn, Merioneth ; Brunant, Pumpsaint, Llanwrda, R.S.O., S. Wales. *Clubs :* Army and Navy ; Carmarthen and County ; Royal St. Davids. (O7396)

LLOYD, Commissioned Gunner (T.) Harry Duncaff, M.B.E., R.N., *b*. 17 May, 1870 ; *s*. of James Rees, of Haverfordwest ; *m*. Elvina Mary, *d*. of James Beale, of Weymouth. *Educ.*: National School Bridgend, Glamorganshire. *War Work :* Special services in the Paravane Department. *Address :* 30, Fearon Road, North End, Portsmouth. (M2046)

LLOYD, Capt. Herbert Alan, M.B.E.

LLOYD, John, M.B.E.

LLOYD, Lieut.-Col. John Daniel, M.B.E., T.D., L.R.C.P., M.R.C.S. J.P.

LLOYD, Major John Daniel Stuart, O.B.E., M.C., T.D., *b*. 31 Dec. 1879 ; *s*. of Col. J. D. Lloyd, J.P., of Chirk ; *m*. Mabel, *d*. of the late Capt de Burgho-Hodge, 12th Lancers. *Educ.*: Shrewsbury. Served in Shropshire Yeomanry from 1902 until outbreak of war. *War Work :* Served in Royal Field Artillery and on the Staff in France, Belgium and Italy ; mentioned in despatches ; awarded the French and Belgian Croix de Guerre. *Address :* The Holt, Chirk, Denbighshire. *Club :* Raleigh. (O5489)

LLOYD, John William, M.B.E.

LLOYD, Paymaster Sub-Lieut. Leonard Wynne., M.B.E., R.N.R.

LLOYD, Major Llewellyn Hubert, O.B.E., R.A.S.C.

LLOYD, Nathaniel, O.B.E., *b*. 5 March, 1867 ; *s*. of John Lloyd, of Fox Hill Bank, Church, Lancashire ; *m*. Daisy, *d*. of Basil Field, of 36, Lincoln's Inn Fields, W.C. *War Work :* Hon. Recruiting Officer from Aug. 1914 ; Chief Military Representative, Chief National Service Representative, and Deputy Appeal N.S. Representative, Hastings Sub-Area ; also provided hospital accommodation (24 beds), staffed by Northiam V.A.D., in part of his residence during 3½ years. *Address :* Great Dixter, Northiam, Sussex. *Clubs :* Union ; Arts. (O1604)

LLOYD, Reginald William, M.B.E.

LLOYD, Lieut. Rowland Owen, O.B.E., R.N.

LLOYD, Samuel Cook, C.B.E., J.P. ; *s*. of David Turner Lloyd, of Dudley ; *m*. Emma Louisa, *d*. of George Boulton, of Allrighton. *Educ.*: Privately. Wholesale Draper. *War Work :* Chairman, Local Tribunal ; President, Local Volunteer Force and Recruiting Committee ; Chairman, War Pensions Committee ; Member Regional Advisory Committee (Birmingham Centre). *Address :* Woodleigh, Russell Street, Dudley. (C994)

LLOYD, Brig.-Gen. Samuel Eyre Massy, C.B.E., J.P., *b*. 1867 ; *e*. *s*. of Eyre Lloyd, Barr.-at-law ; *m*. 1890, Nancy, *d*. of E. Madoc Jones, of Glentworth, Oswestry. Major and Brevet Col. Suffolk Regt., and Brig.-Gen. ; served in S. Africa, 1899–1902 (despatches, Brevet Major, Queen's medal with three clasps, King's medal with two clasps) ; Great War, 1914–19 (despatches). (C1668)

LLOYD, Major Thomas Henry, O.B.E.

LLOYD, Thomas Joseph, M.B.E., *b*. 5 Feb. 1865 ; *s*. of Thomas Lloyd, of Pembroke ; *m*. Florence Mary, *d*. of James Thomas, of Pembroke. *Educ.*: Mr. Bowles' Seminary, Portsmouth. Foreman, Engineering Branch, His Majesty's Dockyard, Gibraltar. *War Work :* Supervising repairs, etc., of the Engineering Branch on refits of Grand Fleet Ships, Destroyers, etc., at Invergordon, Scotland. *Address :* 22, Tower Buildings, Gibraltar. (M8823)

LLOYD, William Reginald, M.B.E., *b*. 28 Feb. 1888 ; *s*. of Thomas Lloyd, of Lampeter ; *m*. Oliven Amey, *d*. of Hugh Jones, of Cardigan. *Educ.*: St. David's Coll. School. Solicitor. *War Work :* Executive Officer to the Lampeter Borough, Lampeter Rural District, and Llanybyther Rural District Food Control Committees. *Addresses :* Deri House, Lampeter ; Ty Ymberth, Lampeter. (M8824)

LLOYD, Frederick Propert JONES-, M.B.E., *b*. 8 Feb. 1865 ; *s*. of John Francis Jones-Lloyd, J.P., of Lancych Boncath, Pem. ; *m*. Martha Bissett, *d*. of James Watson, of Cluniter, Innellan, Argyll, N.B. *Educ.*: Privately, and Lycée de St. Omer, France. Solicitor and Notary Public, Commissioner for Oaths. *War Work :* Hon. Treas. Barry Division Red Cross Society and of two V.A.D. Hospitals (300 beds) ; also Hon. Sec. of Division and two Hospitals. *Address :* 33, Romilly Park, Barry, Glam. (M8818)

LLOYD, Lieut.-Col. Sir John Hall SEYMOUR-, K.B.E., C.M.G., *b*. 1873 ; *s*. of Richard Bowerman Lloyd ; *m*. Helen Kinnear Brown, *d*. of the late Very Rev. Samuel Prenter, D.D., LL.D., formerly Moderator of Presbyterian Church in Ireland. Called to Bar, Middle Temple, 1899 ; Practises at Parliamentary Bar ; Member of Executive Committee and Council Inns of Court Mission ; ex-President, Hardwicke Society. *War Work :* T. Lieut. R.A.S.C. Aug. 1915 ; Staff Capt. (T.) War Office, Nov. 1915 ; T. A.A.G. and Lieut.-Col. May, 1916 ; A. Dep. Director Recruiting, War Office, Feb. to Sept. 1917 ; on appointment as Director-General of Recruiting at Ministry of National Service, Sept. 1917, resigned Commission, granted rank of Lieut.-Col. ; resigned appointment, Dec. 1918, consequent upon cessation of hostilities. *Addresses :* Bentham Hill, Southborough, Kent ; 12, Victoria Street, Westminster, S.W. 1. *Clubs :* Carlton ; 1900. (K91)

LLYWARCH, Gerard, M.B.E., *s*. of John Edward Llywarch, of Llandysilio, Wales ; *m*. Margaret, *d*. of Thomas McPartland, of Boyle, Co. Roscommon. *Educ.*: Privately. Labour Superintendent, Slough Trading Co. *War Work :* Deputy Chief Labour Adviser to Government ; Sec. to Independent Advisory Committee on discharge of ex-service men. *Address :* 41, Matheson Road, West Kensington, W. 14. (M8825)

LOBB, Capt. William Stephen, M.B.E.

LOBBAN, Alexander Harper, O.B.E., *b*. 1855 ; *s*. of George Lobban, of Banff, Scotland ; *m*. Elizabeth, *d*. of George Grinslade. *Educ.*: Privately. Civil Service ; late Superintendent, H.M. Patent Office. *War Work :* Retired from Patent Office in June, 1914, and soon after outbreak of war returned to the Office and served 3½ years without remuneration ; also served as Private in the City of London National Guard from Jan. 1915, to Nov. 1919. *Address :* 55, Cromwell Avenue, Highgate. *Club :* Overseas. (O1605)

LOBJOIT, William George, O.B.E., J.P., *b*. 1 Oct. 1859 ; *s*. of William John Lobjoit, of Osterley Park Gardens, Middlesex ; *m*. Jane, *d*. of H. H. Speakman, of Woodham-Walter, Essex. *Educ.*: Putney Grammar School, and Halbrake School. Alderman, Middlesex County Council. *War Work :* Chairman, Agricultural Executive Committee, Middlesex ; Committee Middlesex War Hospital, Napsbury ; War Pensions Committee, Heston-Isleworth ; Recruiting Committee, Heston-Isleworth ; War Savings Committee, Heston-Isleworth, Food Control Committee, Heston-Isleworth ; and National Kitchen Committee, Heston-Isleworth. *Address :* Heston Farm, near Hounslow, Middlesex. *Clubs :* National Liberal ; Royal Automobile. (O10844)

LOBLEY, Major Owen Rickell, O.B.E.

LOBNITZ, Sir Frederick, K.B.E., Officer of Legion of Honour, France, D.L. and J.P. of Renfrewshire, *b*. 1863 ; *s*. of Henry C. Lobnitz, of Renfrew, and *g.s.* of Frederick Lobnitz, of Copenhagen ; *m*. Lizzie Georgina, *d*. of George Pearson, of Brickendonbury, Herts. *Educ.*: Abroad. Chairman of Lobnitz & Co., Engineers and Shipbuilders, Renfrew, Scotland. *War Work :* Director of Munitions for Scotland, 1917–19 ; Deputy Director Munitions for Scotland, 1915–16 ; received the Freedom of the Royal Borough of Renfrew, 1919. *Address :* Ross Hall, Crookston, Renfrewshire. *Clubs :* Reform ; Western, Glasgow. (K391)

LOBO, Diogo Xaiver, M.B.E. (M6193)

LOCH, Col. Edward Campbell, O.B.E.

LOCH, Emily Elizabeth, M.B.E., *b*. 14 April, 1848 ; *d*. of George Loch, Q.C. Lady-in-Waiting to H.R.H. Princess Christian. *War Work :* For 2½ years Manager of Y.M.C.A Hut in the Canadian Forestry Camp, Smiths Lawn, Windsor Park. *Address :* The Cottage, Bishopsgate, Englefield Green. *Club :* Ladies' V.A.D., 28, Cavendish Square. (M2049)

LOCH, George Richard Boycott, O.B.E.

LOCH, Ruth, O.B.E. ; *d*. of the late John Charles Loch. *Address :* 52, Onslow Square, London, S.W. *Club :* Albemarle. (O7606)

LOCHHEAD, James, O.B.E., M.A., M.D., B.Sc., F.R.C.S. (Edin.), *b*. 1878. Colonial Surgeon, Gibraltar. *War Work :* Services to merchant seamen ; also awarded by French Minister of Marine, the Médaille des Epidémies en Argent. (O8395)

LOCK, Capt. Arthur, O.B.E., R.A.S.C.

LOCK, Esther Georgina, Mrs., M.B.E.

LOCK, Lieut. James Steele, M.B.E., R.E.

LOCKE, Arthur, C.B.E., *b*. 14 Jan. 1872 ; *s*. of Edward Gordon Locke, of Newport, Isle of Wight ; *m*. Florence Mary Eastlake, *d*. of Rev. W. H. Eastlake, of Bradford, Yorks. *Educ.*: Elementary and Private Schools, Torquay. Civil Servant ; a Principal in the Home Office. *War Work :* Special services in addition to ordinary official duties. *Address :* Pyrlands, Maybury Hill, Woking. (C2763)

LOCKE, William, O.B.E.

LOCKETT, Emma, Mrs., O.B.E.

LOCKETT, Staff Paymaster Herbert Anthony, O.B.E., R.N.V.R.

LOCKHART, Comm. Murray MacGregor, O.B.E., R.N.

LOCKHART, Capt. Norman Charles, O.B.E.; *s.* of Norman Phillip Lockhart, of Albury, N. S. Wales, Australia. *Educ.:* Privately. Lawyer. *War Work:* Commissioned with Imperial Royal Artillery, Feb. 1915, 24th D.A.; Jan. 1917, appointed Staff Capt. 56th London Divl. Artillery; 1919, Staff Capt. R.A. VIth Corps, Army of Occupation, Cologne; Acting D.A.A.G. G.H.Q. Cologne; twice mentioned in despatches *Clubs:* Australian; Royal (Sydney); Sydney Golf.   (O5492)

LCCKIE, Major and Qr.-Mr. John, O.B.E.

LOCKINGTON, Comm. Arthur Esme, O.B.E., R.N.R.

LOCKINGTON, Lieut. Harry Aloysius, M.B.E,

LOCKYER, Frank Joshua, O.B.E., *b.* 2 May, 1865; *s.* of the late Augustus Walter Lockyer, of Shoreditch; *m.* Edith Mary, *d.* of the late Councillor Josiah Sutton, of Ilkeston. *Educ.:* Privately. Registrar of Births and Deaths for South-East Hackney. *War Work:* Member of War Pensions Sub-Committee for Hackney; Voluntary Clerical work Military Tribunal. *Address:* 80, Cassland Road, South Hackney, E. 9. *Club:* Junior Constitutional.   (O10846)

LOCKYER, Nicholas Colston, C.B.E., I.S.O., *b.* 1855; *s.* of the late Major Edmund Lockyer, formerly 57th Regt., Founder and first Comdt. of W. Australia; *m.* 1st, 1885, Queenie (who *d.* 1898), *d.* of the Hon. Geoffrey Eagar; 2ndly, 1901, Winifred Mary, *e. d.* of Sir Harry Newton Phillips Wollaston, K.C.M.G., I.S.O., LL.D. *Educ.:* Lyceum Acad., Sydney, N.S. Wales. Entered N.S. Wales Treasury, and became Revenue Receiver, 1891; Treasury Accountant, 1895; Ch. Commr. of Taxation and Collector of Customs, N.S. Wales, 1896; Comptroller-Gen. of Commonwealth Customs, 1911; Hon. Major, Australian Mil. Forces; Hon. Comptroller of Garrison Institutes and War Canteens; J.P. for N.S. Wales and Victoria; appointed a Member of Inter-State Comm., Commonwealth of Australia, 1913; and to supervise organisation of Australian Soldiers' Repatriation Depart. 1917 (thanked by Govt.). *Address:* Toorak, Victoria, Australia.   (C712)

LOCKYER, Comm. Sydney de Bohun, O.B.E., R.D., R.N.R.

LOCOCK, Katharine Beatrice, M.B.E., *b.* 9 Oct. 1869; *d.* of the late Col. Herbert Locock, R.E. *Educ.:* Privately; King's College for Women, London. Hon. Sec. Anti-Mendicity and Charity Organisation Society, Oxford. *War Work:* Hon. Sec. of Local Central War Savings Committee; Member of Mayor's War Relief Committee; Member of War Pensions Committee, Oxford. *Address:* 77, Banbury Road, Oxford.

(M8826)

LODER, Henrietta Mabel, Mrs., M.B.E.; *d.* of the late Col. James Poynter, 14th Hussars; *m.* Alfred Basil Loder (who died), *s.* of Sir Robert Loder, Bart. (*see* BURKE'S *Peerage*). *War Work:* Vice-President, Herts Branch British Red Cross Society, and Commandant of Rickmansworth Red Cross Hospitals, 1914–19 (44 beds). *Address:* 40, Beaufort Gardens, S.W. *Club:* Bath.   (M8827)

LODGE, Samuel Durham, O.B.E.

LODGE, Capt. Thomas, O.B.E.

LODGE, Capt. Thomas Arthur, O.B.E., A.R.I.B.A., F.S.I., *b.* 1888; *s.* of the late T. A. Lodge, of Thames Ditton; *m.* Vera Rose, *d.* of Harold J. Gayford, of 60, Drayton Gardens, S.W. *Educ.:* Epsom Coll. Architect. *War Work:* Served in France and Italy with 24th London Regt. Feb. 1915, to Nov, 1916; and with the 2nd Field Survey Batt. R.E., as Adjutant, Nov. 1916, to March, 1919; now Captain T.F. Res. *Address:* 1A, Grenville Place, S.W. 7.   (O2615)

LOFTHOUSE, Elizabeth Ann, Mrs., M.B.E.

LOFTIN, Florence Ann, Mrs., M.B.E.

LOGAN, Lieut.-Col. Francis Carleton Logan, O.B.E., late Loyal North Lancashire Regt. and Lancashire Fusiliers, *b.* 18 Dec. 1863; *s.* of the late Francis Logan, of Cliffeside, Bournemouth; *m.* Mabel Frances, *d.* of the Rev. James Heyworth, of Henbury Hill, Glos. *Educ.:* Wellington Coll. *War Work:* Commanding 11th Batt. Loyal North Lancashire Regt., etc. *Address:* 130, St. James' Court, Buckingham Gate, S.W. 1. *Clubs:* Naval and Military; Royal Automobile; Ranelagh.

(O7398)

LOGAN, Lieut. Frederick Robert, O.B.E., M.C. *War Work:* From outbreak of war to Dec. 1916, served with 1st Batt. Lancashire Fusiliers in Gallipoli, Belgium, and France; from Dec. 1916, to Armistice was successively Chief Instructor 4th Army Musketry Camp, Instructor G.H.Q. Small Arms School, Chief Instructor 5th Army Rifle Training School. *Address:* c/o Messrs. Cox & Co., 16, Charing Cross.   (O5494)

LOGAN, Lieut. James Henry, O.B.E., R.N.R.

LOGAN, Capt. Philip Norman, O.B.E., R.A.F.

LOGAN, Brevet Lieut.-Col. Robert Hector, O.B.E., *b.* 1877; *s.* of Robert Logan, of London; *m.* Gladys Gwenllian Crawford, *d.* of the Hon. G. H. Greene, M.L.C., of Australia. *Educ.:* Univ. Coll. School. *War Work:* Regular Army; 2nd Bn. the Loyal Regt. (North Lancashire). *Address:* 38, Chester Terrace, Regent's Park, N.W. 1. *Club:* Junior United Service.   (O2321)

LOGAN, William, M.B.E.   (M10358)

LOGAN, Major William, O.B.E., R.A.V.C.

LOGAN, William Malcolm, M.B.E.

LOHDEN, Lieut. Frederick Charles, O.B.E., *b.* at West Hartlepool 13 June, 1871; *s.* of J. Lohden, of Seaton Carew, Co. Durham; *m.* Margaret Emily, *d.* of Thomas Marshall, of Newbury. *Educ.:* Durham School; France; Germany. Northern Representative on the Lawn Tennis Association; Member of the Badminton Association; Member of the Baltic

Exchange; Fellow of the Institute of Chartered Shipbrokers. *War Work:* Commissioned as a Lieut. in 2/5th East Surrey Regt., 4th Nov. 1914; served until Sept. 1917, when entered Ministry of Shipping; had charge of the Standard Steamers, Oilers, Requisitioned Neutrals, Russian and Finns; left the Ministry in 1919. *Addresses:* Latchmere, Sutton, Surrey; Bury Street Chambers, Bury Street, E.C. 3. *Club:* Public Schools.   (O3802)

LOMAS, Hugh Arthur, O.B.E., I.C.S., *b.* 7 July, 1876; *s.* of John Lomas, of Territet, Switzerland; *m.* Florence Beatrix, *d.* of Frederick John Eyre, of St. John's Wood. *Educ.:* Bradfield; Lincoln Coll., Oxon. Major, N. Regt. U.P. Horse, I.D.F. *War Work:* Deputy Commissioner, Almora, U.P. *Address:* Cornborough, Abbotsham, N. Devon. *Club:* East India United Services.   (O4060)

LOMAX, Edith Annie, O.B.E.; *d.* of the late Rev. John Joseph Lomax, M.A., of Hereford. *War Work:* Controller of Women Staff, M.I. 5. War Office, Feb. 1915, to Aug. 1920. *Address:* 46, Jasper Road, Upper Norwood, London, S.E.

(O10848)

LOMAX, Frederick, M.B.E.

LOMAX, John, O.B.E., J.P., D.L.

LOMAX, Mabel Sarah, M.B.E., *b.* 13 Aug. 1875; *d.* of John Lomax, J.P., of Westwood, Brooklands, Cheshire. *Educ.:* Privately, and at Coed Coll., Chislehurst. *War Work:* Hon. Sec., Ashton-on-Mersey, Brooklands and Sale Township, Cheshire Branch B.R.C.S.; Officer-in-charge Linden Lea Aux. Mil. Hospital, Brooklands, Cheshire; Commandant, V.A.D. Cheshire 100. *Address:* Westwood, Brooklands, Cheshire. *Club:* V.A.D.   (M2053)

LOMBARD, Rev. Bousfield Swan, O.B.E., M.A., *b.* 25 Nov. 1866; *s.* of Graves Chamney Swan, Bedfordshire Regt.; *m.* Marian Alice, *d.* of the late Ferdinand Shaw, of Milford, Hants. *Educ.:* Berkhamstead Grammar School; Clare Coll., Cambridge. Vicar, All Hallows, North St. Pancras; Chaplain (British) British Factory and British Embassy, Petrograd; Rector of Cound, Shrewsbury. *War Work:* Acting Chaplain to Submarine Flotilla in the Baltic, 1914–18; Chaplain to British Military Mission, Petrograd; Hon. Chaplain to Anglo-Russian Hospital, Petrograd; C.F. 1919, Eastern Command; imprisoned and sentenced to death in the Fortress of SS. Peter and Paul, Petrograd, 1918. *Address:* Cound Rectory, Shrewsbury.   (O10849)

LOMER, Lieut.-Col. Sydney Frederick McIllree, O.B.E., late 60th Rifles, *b.* 21 May, 1880; *s.* of Cecil Wilson Lomer, of Old Colwall, Glos. *Educ.:* Rugby; Sandhurst. *War Work:* Adjutant, 1/6th Batt. Sherwood Foresters (France, 1914–15); Staff Sudan Administration (1916–17); 1st Commandant No. 2 O.T.T.W. of R.F.C., 1917–18; Commanded 52nd Graduated Batt. K.R.R.C. 1918–19. *Address:* Perrotts Brook House, near Cirencester, Glos. *Clubs:* Junior Naval and Military; Royal Automobile.   (O7400)

LONDON, Edgar Stanford, C.B.E., *b.* 1861; *s.* of Thomas London, of Bettws-y-Coed; *m.* Marion Fanny Pinnell, *d.* of Septimus Luff, of Parkstone. *Educ.:* Gloucester College School. Barrister-at-Law of Gray's Inn; entered Inland Revenue Dept., 1881, and became Chief Inspector of Stamps and Taxes, 1920; was Member of the Committee to Consolidate the Income Tax Acts, 1916–17. *Address:* Craigdarragh, Briar Walk, Putney. *Clubs:* Junior Athenæum; Ciro's.

(C223)

LONDON, Francis Henry, O.B.E., *b.* 31 Jan. 1865; *s.* of Alfred London, of Devizes; *m.* Mary Elizabeth, *d.* of John Downing Spencer, of Devizes. *Educ.:* Colston School. Assistant to General Manager, Great Northern Railway. *War Work:* Railway Transport. *Address:* Hartmoor, Chandos Avenue, Oakleigh Park, N. 20.   (O10850)

LONDON, William Shakespeare, O.B.E., J.P., *b.* 15 Dec. 1881. Councillor; Vice-Chairman, Southgate Urban District Council; Overseer of the Poor, Parish of Southgate; Chairman, General Purposes Committee, Southgate U.D.C. *War Work:* Hon. Sec. Middlesex War Pensions Committee; Vice-Chairman, Southgate War Pensions Committee; District Head, Soldiers' and Sailors' Help Society; Hon. Sec. Southgate War Savings Local Central Committee; formed 47 War Savings Associations, raised nearly £200,000; also Hon. Sec. of Southgate War Savings Committee. *Address:* Shakespeare House, Lakeside Road, Palmers Green.   (O10851)

LONDONDERRY, Dame Edith Helen, Marchioness of, D.B.E., J.P., *b.* 3 Dec. 1878; *d.* of Henry, 1st Viscount Chaplin (*see* BURKE'S *Peerage*); *m.* Charles Stewart Henry Vane Tempest Stewart, 7th Marquess of Londonderry (*see* BURKE'S *Peerage*). J.P. for County of Durham, and County Down, Ireland; President and Chairman, Women's Legion; Chairman, Service Women's Association, and South London Hospital for Women. *War Work:* Founded Women's Legion in 1915, first women employed in British Army, which eventually developed into existing Women's Services; Director, Londonderry House Hospital. *Address:* Londonderry House. *Clubs:* Bath; Ladies' Automobile.   (D1)

LONEY, Henry Frith, O.B.E.

LONG, Archibald Percy, O.B.E., B.A., Diploma of Agriculture and Diploma of Forestry (Cantab), *b.* 26 May, 1889; *s.* of Reuben Long, of Swaon, Cambs.; *m.* Annie Emily, *d.* of John Hunt, of Coton, Cambs. *Educ.:* The Perse, Cambridge, and St. John's Coll., Cambridge. Demonstrator in Forestry; Timber Research Officer; Cambridge Univ. School of Forestry (1912–14); Inspector Board of Agriculture and Fisheries (1914–19); Divisional Officer, Forestry Commission (Northern

Division), Sept. 1910. *War Work:* Divisional Officer-in-Charge, Board of Trade, Timber Supplies Department, Division X (Home Counties). *Address:* 22, Grosvenor Gardens, S.W. 1. (O10853)

LONG, Brig.-Gen. Sir Arthur, K.B.E., C.B., C.M.G., D.S.O., *b.* 26 Feb. 1866; *s.* of James and Elizabeth Long, of Henlow, Bedfordshire; *m.* Maud Eleanor, 2nd *d.* of Rev. Canon S. Davenport Kelly, of Manchester. *Educ.:* Modern School, Bedford. 1st Batt. Leinster Regt., 1887–90; Army Service Corps since 1890; served in defence of Ladysmith, Dec. 1890 to Mar. 1900 (special service); on Staff, Gen. Hunter's Division; Gen. Ian Hamilton's Division (despatches thrice; Queen's Medal, 4 clasps; King's Medal, 2 clasps, D.S.O.); commanding A.S.C., Egypt; Assistant Director Supplies, Army Headquarters, 1901–2; Assistant Director, Transport, S. Africa, 1903–4; Great War, 1914–19 (despatches eight times, K.B.E., C.M.G.); Director of Supplies and Transport, British Army in Macedonia and Black Sea since Jan. 1916. (K276)

LONG, Arthur Tilney, C.B.E. Union of S. Africa Agent, Lorenço Marques. *Address:* Lorenço Marques, British East Africa. (C2004)

LONG, Arthur William, M.B.E.

LONG, Capt. Edmund James, M.B.E.

LONG, Edward Ernest, O.B.E.; *s.* of Edward Long, of East Sutton; *m.* Mabel Edith, *d.* of Andrew Benjamin Leicester, of Singapore, Straits Settlements. *Educ.:* Sutton Valence School, and abroad. Editor " Rangoon Times," and " Indian Daily Telegraph,"; Special Correspondent of " The Times " in India; represented India at Conference of Overseas Journalists in London, 1910; Fellow, Institute of Journalists; now Officer-in-Charge, Eastern Section, News Department, Foreign Office. *War Work:* Lieut. Royal Field Artillery, Special Reserve; Seconded for special service with Foreign Office; organised propaganda in East and Far East; Director, Eastern Propaganda under Wellington House; Deputy Controller, Eastern Propaganda in Ministry of Information. *Address:* Lucknow, India. *Clubs:* Savage; United Service. (O3803)

LONG, Brig.Gen. George Merrick, C.B.E. Col. and T. Brig.-Gen. Australian Forces; served in the Great War, 1915–19 (despatches). (C1844)

LONG, Capt. Gerald Hanslip, O.B.E., *b.* 10 Sept. 1882; *s.* of Lawsell Long, of Brinkley, nr. Newmarket; *m.* Annie Frances, *d.* of A. R. Catchpole, of Lidgate Hall. *Educ.:* Privately. *War Work:* Served in Mercantile Marine for 3 years, and 2 years with Capetown Highlanders during S. African War, 1900–2; granted commission in that force and on termination of war granted hon. rank of Lieut. in C.C.F.; joined 5th Batt. Suffolk Regt. (T.F.) in 1913; appointed Adjutant and subsequently commanded 2/5 Batt. Suffolk Regt.; commanded 13th (S.) Batt. Yorkshire Regt., and invalided home after Spring offensive in 1918; commanded 2/1 Lothians and Border Horse in Ireland until demobilisation. *Address:* Fornham St. Martin, nr. Bury St. Edmund's. (O7401)

LONG, Hilda Charlotte, Mrs., M.B.E.

LONG, John Percy, M.B.E.

LONG, Katherine Ellis, Mrs., M.B.E.

LONG, Major Michael John, O.B.E., R.A., *b.* 16 Nov. 1854; *s.* of Michael Long, of County Cork, Ireland. *Educ.:* Privately. *War Work:* War Depot, Durham Light Infantry, Sept. 1914, to July, 1915; No 5 Territorial Royal Artillery School, July, 1915, to Feb. 1916; Anti-Aircraft Training Depot, Feb. 1916, to May, 1919; mentioned in despatches, 1916. *Address:* Fermoyle, Marine Parade, Gorleston-on-Sea, Suffolk. (O1607)

LONG, Lieut. Robert Claude, M.B.E., *b.* 2 May, 1887; *s.* of J. R. Long, of Saffron Walden; *m.* Dora Edith, *d.* of William Booth Reeve, M.B.E., J.P., of Margate. *Educ.:* King Edward Grammar School, Saffron Walden. *Address:* 48, Garden Avenue, Mitcham, Surrey. (M6670)

LONG, Capt. Sydney Herbert, O.B.E., R.E.

LONG, Capt. Walter, O.B.E., R.A.S.C.

LONG, Major Walter, M.B.E., M.C., R.F.A.

LONG, The Hon. Mrs. Walter, O.B.E.

LONG, Capt. William, M.B.E., *b.* 9 April, 1864; *s.* of Alexander Wearing Long, of Kendal, Westmorland; *m.* Margaret Voorhies, *d.* of F. O. Rhoades, of New York, U.S.A. *Educ.:* Stramongate School, Kendal; H.M.S. "Conway," Liverpool. Master Mariner; Manager of Steamship Line (Elders and Fyffes, Ltd., Gardon, Lancashire). *War Work:* As above and Salvage work in Ireland during the war. *Address:* 22, Western Drive, Grassendale, Liverpool. *Club:* Conway. (M2055)

LONG, Major William Dickson, O.B.E., R.A.F.

LONG, Lieut. William Edward, O.B.E.

LONG, Capt. William Edward, M.B.E., R.N.V.R.

LONGBOTHAM, Arthur Thompson, M.B.E., *b.* 2 Dec. 1864; *s.* of John William Longbotham, of Heath Bank, Halifax; *m.* Annie. *d.* of Arthur Barraclough, of Bright View, Halifax. *Educ.:* King William's Coll., Isle of Man. Solicitor; Clerk to Guardians; Clerk to Halifax Rural District Council; Clerk to several Urban District Councils in the neighbourhood of Halifax. *War Work:* Arranged transfer of St. Luke's Hospital, Halifax, as a War Hospital (700 beds); conducted financial operations in connection with Hospital throughout the war; acted as Clerk to several Military Service Tribunals. *Address:* Stafford Lawn, Halifax. *Club:* Halifax. (M682)

LONGBOTHAM, Capt. Charles Rawson, M.B.E.

LONGBOTHAM, Hugh Ashley, C.B.E., *b.* 28th Sept. 1880; *s.* of the late Jonathan Longbotham, Mining Engineer, of Sheffield; *m.* Muriel, *d.* of the late Harry Steel, of Sheffield. *Educ.:* King Edward School, Warwick, and St. Peter's, York. Chairman Rotherham Local Employment Committee; Vice-President North of England Coal Traders' Association. *War Work:* Sub-Commissioner for Rotherham and District under National Service Scheme; Author of Scheme for Employing Disabled ex-Service Men on a percentage basis. *Clubs:* Constitutional; St. Stephen's; Eccentric; Sheffield. (C2764)

LONGCROFT, Cecil James, M.B.E.

LONGCROFT, Gwendoline Mary, O.B.E., *b.* 24 March, 1881; *d.* of C. E. Longcroft, of Llanina, New Quay, Cardiganshire. *Address:* Llanina, New Quay, Cardiganshire. *Club:* New Century. (O10855)

LONGDEN, Capt. Henry John Leicester, O.B.E., A.E. Corps. (O7402)

LONGDIN, Lieut.-Col. Herbert William, O.B.E.

LONGDON, Arthur Frederick, O.B.E., J.P., *b.* 25 Aug. 1860; *s.* of the late Frederick Longdon, of Derby; *m.* Helen Mary, *d.* of the A. O. Francis, of Derby. *Educ.:* Derby School, and Bonn. Manufacturer. *War Work:* Chairman of Local Military Tribunal. *Address:* Highfield, Littleover Hill, Derby. (O10856)

LONGMORE, Col. John Constantine Gordon, C.B., C.M.G., C.B.E., D.S.O., *b.* 1870; *e. s.* of the late Surg.-Gen. Sir Thomas Longmore, C.B.; *m.* 1897, Anita, *d.* of the late Thomas Davis. Entered E. Lancashire Regt. 1892; Capt. Army Service Corps, 1898; Major, 1904; Lieut.-Col. 1913; Col. 1918; served in S. African War, 1899–1901, on Staff; present at actions of Belmont and Modder River (Queen's medal with five clasps); Great War, 1914–19 (despatches, Montenegrin gold medal for merit); Deputy Assist.-Director of Supplies and Transport, S. Command, 1910–13; appointed D.A. and Q.M.G. 1915; Assist.-Director Supplies and Transport, 1919; A.Q.M.G. 1919. (C1283)

LONGMORE, Philip Raynsford, O.B.E.

LONGMUIR, Percy, M.B.E.

LONGRIDGE, Michael, C.B.E., M.A. M.Inst.C.E., M.I.Mech.E., *b.* 29 July, 1847; *s.* of James Atkinson Longridge, M.Inst.C.E. (Inventor of the Wire Gun); *m.* Georgina Frederica Nepean, *d.* of Rev. Owen Lucas O'Neil, M.A., of Bishops Nympton, Devon. *Educ.:* Radley, and Trinity Coll., Cambridge. Past President Manchester Association of Engineers; Past President of the Institution of Mechanical Engineers. *War Work:* On Staff (unpaid) of the Munitions Inventions Department, and Member of the Advisory Panel of Scientific Experts; Member of the Advisory Council, Ministry of Pensions, Artificial Limbs Branch. *Address:* c/o Cyril Atkinson, K.C., 74, Oakwood Court, Kensington, W. 14. (C2765)

LONGRIDGE, Capt. Theodore Ernle, O.B.E., R.A.S.C., *b.* 29 Jan. 1894; *s.* of Theodore Longridge, of 3, Priory Parade, Cheltenham. *Educ.:* Wellington; Eastbourne; Sandhurst. *War Work:* Served from July, 1915, to Oct. 1919, with the Royal Flying Corps and Royal Air Force as Flying Officer and Staff Officer. *Address:* c/o Sir C. R. McGrigor, Bart., & Co., 39, Panton Street, Haymarket. *Clubs:* Badminton; Junior Army and Navy. (O3352)

LONGSTAFFE, Capt. John Walter, M.B.E., I.A.R.O.

LONGWORTH, Capt. Ernest Victor, M.B.E.

LONSDALE, Grace Cecilie Gordon, Countess of, C.B.E.; *d.* of Charles, 10th Marquess of Huntley (*see* BURKE'S *Peerage*); *m.* Col. Hugh Cecil Lowther, 5th Earl of Lonsdale, D.L. (*see* BURKES *Peerage*). *Address:* 14, Carlton House Terrace, S.W. 1; Lowther Castle, Penrith, Cumberland; Whitehaven Castle, Cumberland; Barley Thorpe, Oakham. (C2766)

LOONEY, Qr.-Mr. and Capt. Daniel, M.B.E. (M10227)

LORAINE, William George, O.B.E., J.P., *b.* 23 Aug. 1864; *s.* of Thomas Loraine, of West Hartlepool; *m.* Sarah Ann, *d.* of William Beedle, of West Hartlepool. *Educ.:* Elementary Schools. District Officer of the National Union of Railwaymen; Justice of the Peace for the Borough of Darlington; Councillor and Deputy Mayor for the County Borough of Darlington; 12 years a member of the Hartlepools' Board of Guardians; commenced to work at 13 years of age as a railway signal lamplighter (29 years' service with N.E. Railway). *War Work:* Member of the Local Military Tribunal; Member of the Food Control Committee; Chairman of the Darlington Labour Employment Committee. *Address:* 11, Milton Street, Eastbourne, Darlington. (O10858)

LORD, Arthur Ernest, M.B.E., *b.* 21 Dec. 1863; *m.* Ellen Phoebe, *d.* of C. J. Brown, of Bromley. Railway Station Supt. *War Work:* Transport, Charing Cross Station, S.E. and C.R. *Address:* 8, Beaufort Gardens, Lewisham, S.E. 13. (M8830)

LORD, Charles Ernest, M.B.E., *b.* 1863; *s.* of Stephen Watkin Lord, of London. *Educ.:* London and Paris. Banking. *War Work:* Principally in a professional capacity. *Address:* 86, rue Charles Laffitte, Neuilly-sur-Seine, France. (M2057)

LORD, Charles Lupton, O.B.E.

LORD, 2nd Lieut. Godfrey James, M.B.E., M.M.

LORD, Capt. Henry Hardman, O.B.E., R.A.V.C. (T.).

LORD, Lieut.-Col. John Robert, C.B.E., M.B., R.A.M.C. Served in the Great War, 1914–19 (despatches). (C1670)

LORD, Lieut.-Col. Percy Calvert, O.B.E.

LORD, William John, M.B.E.

LORIMER, Christian Gray, M.B.E., *b.* 16 Aug. 1885; *d.* of George Lorimer, of Edinburgh. *Educ.:* Edinburgh. Professional, D'Oyley Carte and Carl Rosa Companies. *War Work:* W.A.A.C.; Unit Administrator of 4 Camps. *Address:* 1, Elcho Terrace, Portobello, Edinburgh. (M4542)

LORIMER, Lieut. Duncan, O.B.E., M.B., F.R.C.S., R.N.V.R.

LORIMER, Hilda, Mrs., O.B.E.

LORIMER, Capt. James Vass, O.B.E., *b.* 30 June, 1889; *s.* of James Lorimer, J.P., of Aberdeen; *m.* Eleanor Rebecca, *d.* of the late George Atkins. *Educ.:* Aberdeen Grammar School. Boot and Shoe Manufacturer. *War Work:* Mobilised Aug. 1914, as Lieut. Highland Transport and Supply Column; promoted Capt. and appointed Adjutant 51st (Highland) Division Train, R.A.S.C., 26 Aug. 1914; proceeded to B.E.F., 30 April, 1915; wounded Sept. 1916; twice mentioned in despatches. *Address:* 24, Carlton Place, Aberdeen. (O5497)

LORNIE, Capt. Peter, O.B.E., M.D., *b.* 6 Oct. 1881; *s.* of the late Alexander Murray Lornie, of Newburgh-on-Tay, Scotland. *Educ.:* Perth Academy; Univ. of Edinburgh. Senior Assistant Medical Officer; Monmouthshire County Asylum, Abergavenny, Mon. *War Work:* Served with Medical and other units in France, Mesopotamia, Egypt, and Palestine. *Address:* Monmouthshire Asylum, Abergavenny, Mon. (O6229)

LORRAINE, Ellen Mary, M.B.E.

LOSCOMBE, Col. Arthur Russell, C.B.E., formerly W. India Regt. Lieut.-Col. and Brevet Col. in the Army. (C824)

LOTHIAN, James, O.B.E.

LOTT, Capt. Robert Elgin Lloyd, M.B.E., R.A.F.

LOUCH, Arthur Charles Innes, M.B.E.

LOUDON, Mary Sophia, Mrs., O.B.E., *b.* 1 Feb. 1869; *d.* of G. Wollen, of Normanhurst, Guildford; *m.* May Francis Arthur, late Administrator-General, Bombay, *s.* of William Loudon. *War Work:* Joint Commandant, Red Cross Hospital, Christchurch, from 1914–19. *Address:* Hengistbury House, Christchurch. *Club:* V.A.D. Ladies'. (O3804)

LOUDON, 2nd Lieut. Thomas, M.B.E., R.A.S.C.

LOUGH, Major Reginald Dawson Hopcraft, D.S.O., O.B.E., R.M.L.I., *b.* 1885. Served in the Great War, 1915–19 (despatches); has Croix de Guerre of France. (C2617)

LOUGHBOROUGH, Major Arthur Harold, O.B.E., R.A., *b.* 20 Feb. 1883; *s.* of the late Arthur Loughborough, Barrister-at-Law, of Lincoln's Inn; *m.* Norah Mary (who died), *d.* of the late Montague Alexis Pollard-Urquhart, Craigston Castle, Aberdeen, and Castle Pollard, Westmeath. *Educ.:* Bradfield Coll., Berkshire. Adjutant, Clyde R.G.A. (T.F.), 1913, to May, 1915; Assistant Superintendent of Experiments, 1918 and 1920. *War Work:* In the field, June, 1915, to end of 1917; wounded July, 1916; under Ministry of Munitions as above, 1918. *Address:* c/o Messrs. Cox & Co., 16, Charing Cross, London. *Club:* Sports. (O8863l)

LOUGHLIN, Francis James, M.B.E., *b.* 23 Sept. 1874; *s.* of Capt. James Loughlin, of Indian Ordnance Department; *m.* Ethel Berenice, *d.* of David Gantzer. *Educ.:* India. Postmaster, Simla, India. *War Work:* Political. *Address:* G.P.O., Simla, India. (M6194)

LOVATT, Major Harry Leslie Bache, O.B.E., M.C., *b.* Aug. 1886; *s.* of Thomas Wilson Lovatt, of Wightwick House, nr. Wolverhampton; *m.* Winifred Olive, *d.* of Frederick Theobald Langley, of Tettenhall, Wolverhampton. *Educ.:* Wellington Coll., Berks. *War Work:* Joined up Aug. 1914, and served until Armistice; served in 6th Batt. South Staff Regt.; transferred to Royal Engineers; awarded Military Cross and O.B.E. (Mil.), and mentioned in despatches. *Address:* Great Bents, Codsall, nr. Wolverhampton. *Club:* Junior Carlton. (O2618)

LOVATT, Capt. John Vincent Stratford, M.B.E., Royal Marines Engineers, *b.* 7 Sept. 1874; *s.* of Henry Lovatt, of Bushbury, Staffs; *m.* Margery Kate, *d.* of William Furniss Potter, of Ilkley, Yorks. *Educ.:* Rugby. *Club:* Royal Societies. (M6949)

LOVE, Capt. George William, M.B.E., I.A.R.O.

LOVE, Richard Archibald, C.B.E., *b.* 18 Oct, 1873; *s.* of the late Rev. Robert Love, M.A., Vicar Great Grosby, Lancs. *Educ.:* Merchant Taylors' School. Member of the Royal Commission on Wheat Supplies, London. *War Work:* Resident Commissioner in Australia for the Royal Commission on Wheat Supplies, London. *Address:* 55, Moor Lane, Gt. Crosby, nr. Liverpool. *Clubs:* Junior Athenæum; Conservative, Liverpool. (C2767)

LOVE, Ripeka Wharawhara, Mrs., O.B.E.

LOVEDAY, Arthur Frederic, O.B.E.

LOVEDAY, William Dunmore, O.B.E., M.R.C.S., L.R.C.P., J.P., *b.* 26 Sept. 1864; *s.* of William Loveday, of The Poplars, Northamptonshire; *m.* Lilian Emily, *d.* of the late Samuel Wix. *Educ.:* Privately, and Guy's Hospital. Retired from Medical Practice; Justice of Peace for County of Berks. *War Work:* Hon. Medical Examiner for Recruits; Medical Superintendent of St. Katherine Military Hospital; Inventor of the Wantage Adjustable Crutches, which became the Standard Army Crutch (100,000 made and used); Chairman of the Wantage Military Tribunal. *Address:* Beckett House, Wantage, Berks. (O1609)

LOVELACE, Major Peter Leo, M.B.E.

LOVELL, Elizabeth Isabel, Mrs., M.B.E. (M10430)

LOVELL, James, M.B.E.

LOVELL, Laura Mary, Mrs., M.B.E. For work in connection with the Imperial War Museum. (M10329)

LOVELL, Capt. William Day, M.B.E. (M10228)

LOVELL, William George, C.B.E., *b.* 16 May, 1865; *s.* of the late John Cary Lovell, of Tulse Hill, S.W. 2; *m.* Kate *d.* of the late George Arthur Ring, of Tulse Hill, S.W. 2. *Educ.:* Woking College. Director of Public Companies. *War Work:*

Divisional Commander, City of London Police Reserve, "A" Division; Director of Butter and Cheese Supplies, Ministry of Food; Member of Butter and Cheese Advisory and Butter and Cheese Import Committees, Ministry of Food; Member and Owner Driver, London Ambulance Column, Red Cross Society. *Address:* 144, Tulse Hill, S.W. 2. *Club:* Royal Automobile. (C2768)

LOVELOCK, Major Charles Prior, M.B.E., T.D., *b.* 10 Nov. 1864; *s.* of Thomas Lovelock, of Hemel Hempstead; *m.* Amelia, *d.* of George Kemp, of Chicago, U.S.A. *Educ.:* Privately. Clerk to Carshalton Urban District Council; founder and Hon. Sec. of the Carshalton District Hospital; much interested in the Volunteer and Territorial Force; Member of the Council of the Town Planning Institute; Joint Treasurer of the National Housing and Town Planning Council; Chairman of Carshalton Day Nursery; Member of Executive of National Baby Week Council; Chief Officer of Carshalton Fire Brigade; Chairman of Local Sub-Committees of the Surrey Education Committee. *War Work:* At outbreak of war took part in recruiting campaign; in Oct. 1914 joined 10th Batt. East Surrey Regt.; served until June, 1916, when invalided out; on recovery became Hon. Sec. of Local War Pension Sub-Committee; with the Carshalton Fire Brigade took part as Chief Officer in the defence of London during Air raids under a co-ordinated scheme with the London Fire Brigade.

LOVERIDGE, Capt. Cecil Hubert, O.B.E.

LOVERIDGE, Lieut. Frederick, M.B.E., R.A.F.

LOVEROCK, Major Robert Charles, D.S.O., O.B.E., *b.* 14 Dec. 1880; *s.* of James Bersalem Loverock, of Dublin; *m.* Margaret, *d.* of John Griffin, of Co. Cork. *Educ.:* Grammar School, Elphin, Co. Roscommon. Joined the ranks of the 1st Batt. Durham L.I., June, 1898; South Africa, 1899–1902, in the ranks of the 1st Batt. the Durham Light Infantry (King's and Queen's Medals, with 7 clasps. *War Work:* Commissioned from the rank of Colour-Sergt. to the 1st Batt., Oxford and Bucks L.I., Nov. 1914; Mesopotamia 1914–20, with the 1st Batt. the Oxford and Bucks Light Infantry; also Embarkation Staff Officer, Mesopotamia, from Sept. 1916. *Addresses:* c/o Messrs. Cox & Co., 16, Charing Cross, London, S.W.; Bombay, India. (O4232)

LOVETT, Clara Crofton, Lady, O.B.E.; *d.* of the late Major Charles Jamieson, Bengal S.C.; *m.* 10 Oct. 1893, Sir Sackville Harrington Hatton Verney, K.C.S.I., *s.* of the late Rev. Robert Lovett, rector of Caundle Bishop, Dorset. *Address:* Louvergrove, Oakfield Road, Ashtead, Surrey. (O2046)

LOVETT, T. Warrant Officer Arthur Harrison, Royal Indian Marine.

LOVETT, Frederic Reynolds, M.B.E., *b.* 15 Feb. 1880; *s.* of Rev. Richard Lovett, of Clapham, London. *Educ.:* St. Paul's School, and Magdalen Coll., Oxford. Civil Servant; Principal Clerk, Ministry of Health. *War Work:* Seconded to the Ministry of Munitions; worked from June, 1915, till Oct. 1918, in the Labour Supply Department, first at releasing skilled workmen from the Army and Navy, and later at the exemption and recruitment of Munition Workers, and the appeals of such workmen to Enlistment Complaints Committees. *Address:* 74, Victoria Road, Clapham Common, London, S.W. 4. (M686)

LOVETT, Rev. Canon Neville, C.B.E., M.A., *b.* 16 Feb. 1869; *s.* of Rev. Robert Lovett, of Bishops Caundle, Dorset (*see* BURKE'S *Landed Gentry*, Lovett of Liscombe, Bucks); *m.* Evelyn Janet, *d.* of Comm. Osmond de Beauvoir Brock, R.N. *Educ.:* Sherborne, and Christ's Coll., Cambridge. Rector and Rural Dean of Southampton; Chaplain to the King; Hon. Canon of Winchester; Proctor in Convocation; formerly Rector of Bishops Caundle, 1895–98; Vicar of S. Saviour's, Shanklin, I. of W., 1898–1908; Rector of Farnham, Surrey, 1908–12. *War Work:* Chairman of War Pensions Local Committee, Southampton, from inception; Hon. Chaplain Red Cross Hospital; Chairman of "Roberts Hall" Recreation Hut, Southampton Docks. *Address:* Deanery, Southampton. (C2769)

LOVETT, William Edward, M.B.E., R.A.S.C.

LOW, Alice, M.B.E., W.A.A.C.

LOW, Lieut.-Col., Charles Frederick Gemley, O.B.E., R.A.O.C.

LOW, Frederick Edward, M.B.E.

LOW, Capt. James Lawson, O.B.E.

LOW, Capt. and Qr.-Mr. James Lindsay, O.B.E. R.E.

LOW, John Spencer, C.B.E., B.Sc., M.B., Ch.B., D.P.H. Medical Supervisor of Army Meat Contracts in South America. (C3153)

LOW, Major Peter Dunstan, O.B.E., A.M.I.E.E., *b.* 29 Oct. 1891; *s.* of Peter Low. (O2288)

LOW, William, O.B.E.

LOW, Major Richard Marsden Marsden HUTCHINSON-, O.B.E., A.M.S., M.B. (took the name of Hutchinson by deed-poll, 1908); *s.* of William Low, of Roseneath, Wrexham; *m.* Emily Margaret Lavinia *d.* of Augustus Bayeley, of Liscard. *Educ.:* Privately. *War Work:* M.O., Cromwell Gardens P. of W. Detention Barracks. *Address:* 70, Philbeach Gardens, London. (O5499)

LOWE, Alice Mary, O.B.E.

LOWE, Major Andrew Alfred, O.B.E., R.E.

LOWE, Capt. Arthur Henry, M.B.E.

LOWE, Arthur Labron, C.B.E., M.A., LL.B., (Camb.), *b.* 17 Aug. 1861; *s.* of Henry Lowe, of Southfield, Norfolk Road, Edgbaston; *m.* Mary Letitia, *d.* of A. Bruce Mitchell, of Elmstead, Hagley Road, Edgbaston. *Educ.:* Clifton, and Clare Coll., Camb. Registrar of Birmingham County Court;

District Registrar of High Court of Justice, Birmingham District Registry; President Birmingham Law Society, 1916–18; President Association of County Court Registrars, 1910–20; Member of the Standing Committee for framing the Rules of the County Court. *War Work:* Chairman Birmingham Branch of the British Red Cross Society; Member of Committee appointed by the Lord Chancellor to review the staffs of military age of the County Courts, Registrars, High Bailiffs, Justices' Clerks and their assistants; Member of the City of Birmingham Local Tribunal. *Addresses:* 52, Westfield Road, Edgbaston; Monkspath Hall, Shirley, Warwickshire. *Club:* Union, Birmingham. (C995)

LOWE, Dorothy Ann Shelmerdine, M.B.E., *b.* 31 Dec. 1880; *d.* of Charles Lowe, of Stamford. *Educ.:* Newbury. Member War Pensions Committee, Chard; Member of the County Executive Committee of the Federation of Women's Institutes; Commandant Hinton House Hospital; Member Somerset County Agricultural Committee, Women's Section. *Address:* The Grange, Hinton S. George, Crewkerne, Somerset. *Club:* V.A.D. (M689)

LOWE, Capt. Edward Cronen, M.B.E., M.B., New Zealand A.M.C.

LOWE, Henry, M.B.E., *b.* Feb. 1887. *Educ.:* Alloa Academy. H.M. Inspector of Taxes, Inland Revenue Department. (M8833)

LOWE, Percy Roycroft, O.B.E., M.B.

LOWE, Major Sidney Joseph, D.S.O., O.B.E., *b.* 1880. Entered Royal Fusiliers (City of London Regt.), 1897; Capt. 1905; Major, 1915; served in the S. African War, 1899–1902, on Staff; present at relief of Ladysmith (Queen's medal with five clasps); Great War, 1914–19, as Brig.-Major on Staff (despatches, Legion of Honour, Croix de Guerre). (O6395)

LOWE, Capt. Stanley Philip, O.B.E., R.A.S.C., *b.* 17 Sept. 1883; *s.* of the late H. W. Lowe, of Walton-on-Thames; *m.* Elinor Constance, *d.* of — Partridge. *Educ.:* Westminster and Victoria Univ. Manchester. Civil, Chemical, Mechanical, and Mining Engineer; late Nitrate Mine Manager and Chemist, Chile, S. America. *War Work:* 375 M.T. Coy. R.A.S.C. 35th Div. Amm. Pack, France and Flanders, July, 1915, to Feb. 1917; April, 1917, "A" Corps Amm. Pack, Commanding 1040 M.T. Coy. R.A.S.C. Oct. 1917, to Aug. 1919, in Palestine and Egypt; twice mentioned in despatches. *Address:* Taito Estate, Songhor, B.E.A. (O6230)

LOWE, Lieut.-Col. Thomas Enoch, O.B.E., T.D., *b.* 2 Dec. 1860; *s.* of Isaac Lowe, of Lilleshall, Shropshire; *m.* Ellen Jane, *d.* of John Simon, of Market Drayton, Shropshire. *Educ.:* Newport Grammar School. Incorporated Accountant, F.S.A.A.. in practice since 1885. *War Work:* Mobilised 4 Aug. 1914; proceeded to France 28 Feb. 1915, as Second-in-Command of 6th South Staffordshire Regt., 46th Division; in action Neuve Chapelle, Armentieres, Messines Ridge, etc.; invalided home June, 1915; Home Service, attached R.E., acting C.R.E., Lincolnshire Coast, until demobilised April, 1919. *Address:* Oaken, nr. Wolverhampton. *Clubs:* Services; Conservative, Wolverhampton. (O7406)

LOWE, Capt. William Herbert, M.B.E., A.C.G.I., *b.* 11 Oct. 1884; *s.* of Frederick George Lowe, of London; *m.* Joanetta Marjorie, *d.* of Samuel Bruce, J.P., D.L., of Norton Hall, Campden, Glos. *Educ.:* The Leys School, Cambridge. *War Work:* 11th Batt. Royal Warwickshire Regt., 1914–16; Machine Gun Corps, 1916–17; Staff Captain in A.G.'s Dept., War Office, 1917–19. *Address:* 439, Grosvenor Avenue, Westmount, P.Q., Canada. *Club:* Junior Army and Navy. (M2059)

LOWIS, Horace Lake, O.B.E., M.B., C.M., *b.* 17 Sept. 1870; *s.* of Col. Ross F. Lowis, R.A.; *m.* Alice Christina Hogarth, *d.* of R. M. Ballantyne, of Harrow-on-the-Hill. *Educ.:* Edinburgh Univ. M.O. Frimley Cottage Hospital. *War Work:* M.O. Camberley Red Cross Military Hospital. *Address:* Underhill, Camberley. (O10861)

LOWMAN, Rose Frances, M.B.E.

LOWNDES, William Frederick Lowndes FRITH-, M.B.E., J.P., C.C., *b.* 1 July, 1871; *s.* of Henry Frith, of Shenstone House, Chalfont, Bucks; *m.* Ethel Maude, *d.* of the late Robert Sissons, of Newark House, Holmwood, Surrey. *Educ.:* Privately. *War Work:* Military Representative for Amersham and Chesham District; Capt. Chesham Company Special Constabulary. *Address:* The Bury, Chesham, Bucks. *Club:* Royal Automobile. (M8834)

LOWNDES, Major William SELBY-, O.B.E., T.D.

LOWREY, Sir Joseph, K.B.E., *b.* 14 Feb. 1859; *s.* of Joseph Lowrey, of Cocken, Durham; *m.* 16 Oct. 1917, Eleanor Octavia, *d.* of Edward Tuson Charnley, of Preston. Sec. London Salvage Association. *War Work:* Rendered special services in connection with the Ministry of Shipping and Shipping Casualties. *Address:* The Hermitage, Loughton, Essex. *Club:* Royal Societies'. (K153)

LOWRY, Frederick James Sharples, O.B.E.

LOWRY, Helen, Mrs., O.B.E.

LOWRY, Col. James, C.B.E., late A.P.D., *b.* 19 Feb. 1856; *s.* of Thomas Harvey Lowry, M.D., of West Malling, Kent. *Educ.:* Cheltenham. *War Work:* Command Paymaster, Scottish Commands. *Address:* Belmore, Wenlock Road, Shrewsbury. (C1671)

LOWRY, Thomas Martin, C.B.E., D.Sc., F.R.S., *b.* 26 Oct. 1874; *s.* of Rev. E. P. Lowry, H.C.F., of Aldershot; *m.* Eliza, *d.* of Rev. C. Wood. *Educ.:* Kingswood School, Bath, Central Technical Coll., South Kensington. Prof. of Physical Chemistry, Univ. of Cambridge; Associate Member of

Ordnance Committee. *War Work:* Director of Shell Filling. *Address:* Univ. Chemical Laboratory, Cambridge. (C2770)

LOWSLEY, Ethel Sarah, Mrs., M.B.E., *b.* 13 Dec. 1865; *d.* of Alfred Heasman, J.P., of Court Wick, Littlehampton, Sussex; *m.* Warin Asbel, *s.* of Luke Lowsley, of Hampstead-Morreys, Berks. *War Work:* President and Hon. Sec. Ladies Depot, Coimbatore, S. India. (M6195)

LOWSON, Kenneth John, O.B.E., M.A., LL.B. (Cantab.), *b.* 6 March, 1885; *s.* of the late David Lowson, M.D., of Hull. *Educ.:* St. Paul's School and Caius Coll., Cambridge. Solicitor: Exhibitioner of Caius College, Cambridge, 1904. *War Work:* Hon. Sec. Hull Refugees Committee; awarded La Médaille du Roi Albert, 1920. *Addresses:* Brough, East Yorks: 16, Bowlalley Lane, Hull. (O10864)

LOWTHER, Capt. the Hon. Lancelot Edward, O.B.E., J.P., *b.* 25 June, 1867; 4th *s.* of Henry, 3rd Earl of Lonsdale, of Lowther Castle, Penrith (*see* BURKE's *Peerage*); *m.* Guendoline Alice, *d.* of Sir Robert Sheffield, 5th Bart., of Normanby Park, Doncaster (*see* BURKE's *Peerage*); *Educ.:* Cheltenham Coll., and Magdalene Coll., Cambridge. J.P. for Rutland and Westmorland; formerly Capt. 3rd Batt. Border Regt.; *War Work:* Gen. Staff, War Office, 1914–19; War Office King's Messenger, 1914–19; awarded the 1914 Star; mentioned in despatches; awarded the Order of the Nile by Sultan of Egypt. *Address:* Ashwell Hill, Oakham. *Clubs:* Turf; White's; Orleans. (O8864)

LOWTHER, Mildred, O.B.E.

LOWTHER, Qr.-Mr. and Major Thomas Edwin, M.B.E., 2nd Batt. N. Staff. Regt. (M10229)

LOWTHIAN, Harold Douglas, O.B.E.

LOYD, Capt. Robert Lindsay, O.B.E., M.C., *b.* 16 Sept. 1887; *s.* of A. K. Loyd, K.C., of 21, Cadogan Square, S.W. 1, and Downs House, Steventon, Berks; *m.* Olive Mary, *d.* of J. E. Gladstone, of Bowden Park, Chippenham, Wilts. *Educ.:* Eton, and Magdalen Coll., Oxford. Gazetted 16th Lancers, Jan. 1911; promoted Lieut. March, 1913; Capt. Feb. 1919. *War Work:* Commanded 1st Signal Troop 1st Cavalry Brigade, Feb. 1914 to June, 1915, B.E.F.; Instructor Dunstable Signal Depot, 12 Dec. 1915, to 7 July, 1916; Inspecting Signal Officer, Southern Army, 7 July, 1916, to 15 Aug. 1916; attached 17th Corps Signals, Aug. 1916 to Nov. 1916; and attached 7th Corps Signals, Nov. 1916, to Jan. 1917; 2nd in command 4th Divisional Signals, Feb. 1917, to June, 1917, with rank of A. Capt.; Commandant 3rd Army Signal School, June, 1917, to March, 1918, with rank of A. Major; A. D. Signals, R.A.F., March, 1918, to June, 1918; Commandant 3rd Army Signal School, June, 1918, to Sept. 1918; Commanded Cadet Unit, Signal Service Training Centre, Sept. 1918, to Feb. 1919; 2nd in Command Haynes Park Signal Depot, Feb. 1919, to July, 1919. *Address:* 21, Cadogan Square, London, S.W. 1. *Clubs:* Cavalry; Conservative; Wellington. (O2620)

LUARD, Louise Henrietta, Mrs., M.B.E., *b.* 1873; *d.* of the Rev. Canon S. L. Smith, late Canon Residentiary of Hereford Cathedral; *m.* Lieut.-Col. E. B. Luard, D.S.O., who was killed commanding 1st Bn. K. Shropshire L.I., April, 1916. Elected Member of the Town Council of Hereford, 1919. *War Work:* Hon. Sec. and Treas. K. Shropshire L.I. Prisoners of War Fund; and 1st Bn. K. Shropshire L.I. Comforts Fund, 1914 to 1919. *Address:* South Bank, Hereford. *Club:* New Victorian. (M8835)

LUCAN, George Charles Bingham, 5th Earl of, K.B.E., C.B., T.D.; A.D.C. to the King; J.P., D.L.; Lord in Waiting from 1920; *b.* 13 Dec. 1860; *e. s.* of 4th Earl and Lady Cecilia Catherine Gordon-Lennox (d. 1910), *o. d.* of 5th Duke of Richmond, K.G.; *m.* Violet, *d.* of J. Spencer Clay, Ford Manor, Lingfield. *Educ.:* Harrow. Late Rifle Brigade, 1881–96; served Bechuanaland Expedition, 1884–85; Served in the Great War 1914–16; J.P. and D.L. Co. Mayo and Middlesex; High Sheriff Co. Mayo, 1902; Lieut.-Col. Commanding 1st London Volunteer Rifle Corps, 1901–8; 5th City of London Rifles (L.R.B.), 1908–12; Col. (T. Brig.-Gen.) commanding 1st London Infantry Brigade, 1912–16; Hon. Brig.-Gen. since 1916; M.P. (C.) Chertsey Div., Surrey, 1904–6; has Orders of St. Stanislaus of Russia (2nd Class) and Nile (3rd Class), 1916. *Addresses:* Laleham House, Staines; Castlebar House, Mayo; 10, Gloucester Place, W. 1. *Clubs:* Carlton; Turf. (K392)

LUCAN, Violet, Countess of, O.B.E., *o. d.* of J. Spencer Clay, of Ford Manor, Lingfield; *m.* George Charles Bingham, 5th Earl of Lucan, J.P., D.L. *Addresses:* Laleham House, Staines; Castlebar House, Mayo; 10, Gloucester Place, W. 1. (O10804)

LUCAS, Alfred, O.B.E., Egyptian Government. (O10941)

LUCAS, Capt. Armytage Anthony, C.B.E., R.N.

LUCAS, Arthur, C.B.E., I.C.S., *b.* 24 Jan. 1863; *s.* of Arthur Lucas, of Darlington; *m.* May Margaret, *d.* of F. Shore Bullock, late Assist. Commander Police, Scotland Yard. *Educ.:* Clifton Coll. *War Work:* Sec. Soldiers' and Sailors' Families Association, Sept. 1914 to June, 1915; Ministry of Munitions, Feb. 1916, to Sept. 1916; Board of Trade Import Restrictions, Oct. 1916, to April, 1919. *Address:* Edgemoor, Bovey Tracey, Devon. (C224)

LUCAS, Rev. Bernard, M.B.E.

LUCAS, Capt. Charles Alfred, O.B.E.

LUCAS, Capt. Charles Anthony Cecil, O.B.E., R.M.L.I.

LUCAS, Edward William, C.B.E. Managing Director, Bells, Hills and Lucas (Limited). (C553)

LUCAS, Major Frederick William, O.B.E., R.A.F.

LUCAS, 2nd Lieut., Gordon Tate, M.B.E., New Zealand M.G.C.

LUCAS, Mrs., M.B.E.

LUCAS, Major Reginald Hugh, O.B.E., *b.* 26 Sept. 1888 ; *s.* of Lieut.-Col. H. F. E. Lucas, of Dunchidcock House, near Exeter. *Educ. :* Repton, and Christ Church, Oxford. *War Work :* Supply Reserve Depot, Deptford, 1914–15 ; Supply Depot, Millwall Docks, 1915–17 ; War Office, 1917–20. *Address :* Holmbush, Ide, near Exeter, Devon. *Club :* Cavendish. (O7407)

LUCAS, Capt. Reginald Hutchinson, M.B.E., M.C., R.A.M.C.

LUCAS, Lieut. Reginald William Owen, M.B.E.. R.E. (T.F.)

LUCAS, Col. Thomas Woodwright, O.B.E., J.P., D.L., *b.* 22 May, 1959 ; *s.* of Lieut.-Col. C. Woodwright, of Golagh, Monaghan, Ireland ; *m.* Georgie (who died in 1894), *d.* of the late Sir James Godfrey, of Granville Manor, Jersey. *Educ. :* Trinity Coll., Dublin. Joined the 36th Foot, July 1878, Captain 1886, exchanged to 41st Regt. (Welsh) 1887 ; retired 1907. *War Work :* Area Commander Cardiff City Recruiting Area ; Sec. National Association for Employment of Reserve Soldiers, S. Wales ; Member Glamorgan Territorial Association ; Member Executive Committee of the Priory of the Order of St. John for Wales ; commanded Glamorgan and Monmouth Recruiting Area from Aug. 1914, to May, 1917 ; County Commandant and Commanding all Volunteers raised in the County of Glamorgan (6000 men). *Address :* Golagh, Roath Park, Cardiff. *Clubs :* Army and Navy ; Cardiff and County.

LUCAS, Terence, M.B.E.

LUCAS, Lieut. William, M.B.E., *b.* 24 May, 1872 ; *s.* of John William, of Oxon ; *m.* Katherine Elizabeth, *d.* of William Henry Smith, of Old Colwyn, Wales. *Educ. :* High School, Kensington. *War Work :* May, 1915, to Oct. 1916, Training Troops in England ; Nov. 1916, to Dec. 1917, with Gen. Allenby's Force, carrying supplies until they took Jerusalem, being held up owing to enemy shell fire on the road ; Jan. 1918, sent to take charge of all camel detachments on the Western Front, Hammam to Sollum, over 200 miles ; carried on without additional assistance during a serious outbreak of Spanish Influenza. *Addresses :* c/o Messrs. Peel & Co., Ltd., Alexandria, Egypt ; Northumberland House, Cleopatra, Ramleh, Egypt (M4693)

LUCAS, William Henry, C.S.I., C.B.E., *b.* 1867 ; *s.* of Arthur Lucas, of Bournemouth. *Educ. :* Clifton, and New Coll., Oxford. Entered I.C.S. 1888 ; Assist. Collector and Magistrate, Bombay, 1889 ; 1st Assist., Karachi, 1897 ; Dep. Commr. Thar and Parkar, 1900 ; Junior Collector and Collector of Salt Revenue, Bombay, 1904 ; Senior Collector, 1909 ; Ch. Sec. to Govt. in Revenue and Financial Depart. 1911–12 ; Commr. in Sind, 1912–16 ; ret. 1916. *Club :* East India United Service. (C2771)

LUCE, Emily Gertrude, O.B.E., *b.* 1871 ; *d.* of William Hollis Luce, J.P., of The Knoll, Malmesbury. *Educ. :* Privately. *War Work :* Commandant V.A.D. Wilts. 22, 1914 ; Worked at Countess of Suffolk's Red Cross Hospital, Charlton Park, Malmesbury, 1914–15 ; Commandant Red Cross Hospital, Malmesbury, 1916–19. *Address :* The Knoll, Malmesbury. (O1611)

LUCK, Ernest Bertram, M.B.E.

LUCK, Capt. Robert, M.B.E., *b.* 25 Nov. 1869 ; *s.* of Richard Luck, of Montreal and Liverpool ; *m.* Alice, *d.* of James Hartland, of Manchester. *Educ. :* Leeds High School. Sec. Cornwallis Road Hospital, London, N. 19. *War Work :* Assistant Commandant Prisoners of War Camp, under Home Office control, from June, 1915, to Nov. 1919 ; organised large number of interned enemy aliens to be of benefit to the State ; devoted considerable time to welfare of Belgian wounded by assisting in the management of King Albert's Hospital, Hazleville Road, N. *Address :* Shadwell House, Cornwallis Road, N. 19. (M690)

LUCK, Capt. Sidney Ivor, O.B.E., R.E.

LUCKHURST, Capt. Allen Edward James, M.B.E.

LUCY, Capt. John Charles Hampden, M.B.E., *b.* 11 Oct. 1879 ; *s.* of C. H. Lucy, of Hereford ; *m.* Frances Rose, *d.* of C. R. Seys, of Newport, Mon. *Educ. :* Hereford Cathedral School, and Univ. Coll., London. *War Work :* R.A.S.C. from Feb. 1915, to Feb. 1920. *Address :* Old Bank Chambers, Cheltenham. *Clubs :* Royal Automobile ; Cheltenham Race. (M5427)

LUDDINGTON, Leila Arthur, Mrs., M.B.E. ; *d.* of Major Henry Reginald Bate, of Bulford, Co. Mayo ; *m.* Henry Tansley, *s.* of Henry Luddington, of Littleport. *War Work :* Chairman of Sub-Com. of Prisoners of War (Isle of Ely) ; War Pensions ; Chairman Isle of Ely Women's War Agricultural Com. ; Chairman of Isle of Ely Women's Institutes Com. *Address :* Walton's Park, Ashdon, Saffron Walden, Essex. *Clubs :* Ladies' Army and Navy ; Forum. (M8839)

LUDFORD, George Frederick, M.B.E.

LUDLOW, Brig.-Gen. Edmund Ronald Owen, C.B., C.B.E., *b.* 5 Sept. 1864 ; *s.* of the late Col. E. S. Ludlow, I.A. *Educ. :* Privately. Served in S. African War ; Matabele War (1896) ; and in the Great War (1914–18) ; has Legion of Honour. *Club :* Junior Naval and Military. (C1672)

LUDLOW, Capt. Fred Ball, O.B.E., M.C.

LUDOVICI, Lieut. Anthony Mario, M.B.E., R.F.A.

LUFF, Brevet Lieut.-Col. Arthur Pearson, C.B.E., M.D., F.R.C.P.(Lond.), R.A.M.C. (T.), *b.* Nov. 1855 ; *s.* of Richard Luff ; *m.* Amy Annie, *d.* of George I. Leon. *Educ. :* Western Grammar School ; Royal Coll. of Science ; St. Mary's Hospital. Consulting Physician to St. Mary's Hospital. *War*

Work : In charge of Medical Division, 3rd London General Hospital ; served from 5 Aug. 1914, to 26 April, 1919. *Address :* Fairhurst, Peppard, Henley-on-Thames. (C1673)

LUFFMAN, Brooke Land, M.B.E.

LUFFMAN, John George Innes, M.B.E., *b.* 11 Feb. 1856 ; *s.* of Alfred Luffman, of London ; *m.* Marion Taylor, *d.* of W. Hawes, of Chelmsford. *Educ. :* Christ's Hospital. Confidential Clerk to Director of Naval Construction, Admiralty. *War Work :* Construction Department, Admiralty. *Address :* 4, Lancaster Road, Wimbledon, S.W. 19. (M8842)

LUGARD, Major Edward James, D.S.O., O.B.E., *b.* 23 March, 1865 ; *s.* of the late Rev. F. G. Lugard, M.A., of Norton, near Worcester ; *m.* Charlotte Eleanor, *d.* of the late Rev. G. B. Howard, B.A., of Worthing. *Educ. :* Rossall. 3rd Worcestershire Regt., 1885–86 ; 2nd Northumberland Fusiliers, 1886–88 ; Indian Army, 1888–1906 ; retired, 1906 ; served in the Burmah War, 1888–89 (medal with clasp) ; Chin-Lushai, 1889–90 (despatches, clasp, D.S.O.) ; Manipur, 1891 (slightly wounded, clasp) ; South African War, 1899–1900 (medal with 3 clasps) ; Expedition to Ngamiland, South-Central Africa, 1896–99 ; Political Assistant to the High Commissioner of Northern Nigeria, 1903–6 ; Secretary, Imperial Institute, 1908–12 ; Political Secretary to the Governor of Northern and Southern Nigeria, 1912–13, and to the Governor-General of Nigeria, 1914–15. *War Work :* In Naval Intelligence Department. *Address :* Othercote, Abinger Common, near Dorking. (O517)

LUGARD, Flora, Lady, D.B.E., 2nd *d.* of the late Major-Gen. George Shaw, C.B., R.A. ; *m.* 11 June, 1902, Rt. Hon. Sir Frederick John Dealtry, P.C., G.C.M.G., C.B., D.S.O., D.C.L., LL.D., *s.* of the Rev. F. G. Lugard. *Address :* Little Parkhurst, Abinger Common, Surrey. (D15)

LUKE, Alfred James, O.B.E., M.C.I., *b.* 24 Dec. 1867 ; *m.* Anne, *d.* of William Hall, of Co. Cork. Superintending Civil Engineer. Civil Engineer in Chief's Department, Admiralty. *War Work :* Execution of various Civil Engineering and Submarine Defence Works at Portsmouth ; Anti-Submarine and General Engineering work in connection with the Dover Patrol and S.E. Coast Naval Defences. *Address :* H.M. Dockyard, Haulbowline, Ireland. (O10865)

LUKE, Jacobina, Mrs., C.B.E., *d.* of the late H. A. McGregor, Govt. Inspector of Machinery, of New Zealand ; *m.* 1880, John Pearce Luke, C.M.G. Pres. British Red Cross, Women's Branch, and Member of Women's Red Cross Executive ; Pres. Countess of Liverpool War Fund ; Vice-Pres. St. John Ambulance Assocn.

LUKE, Brig.-Gen. Thomas Mawe, C.B.E., D.S.O., *b.* 1872 ; *s.* of Col. Henry Francis Luke ; *m.* 1901, Amy Elizabeth, *d.* of John Lamb, formerly of Burrel Green, Great Salkeld, Cumberland. *Educ. :* Privately, and R.M.A. Entered R.A. 1892 ; Capt. 1900 ; Major, 1913 ; Brevet Lieut.-Col. 1915 ; Lieut.-Col. 1917 ; served on the N.-W. Frontier of India, 1897–8 (medal with clasp) ; Tibet Mission Escort, 1903–4 (despatches, medal with clasp) ; Mohmand Expedition, 1908 (medal with clasp) ; appointed an A.A.G. on Head Quarters Staff, India, 1914 ; D.A.G. 1910, as Brig.-Gen. (C2038)

LUKE, William Joseph, C.B.E. Shipyard Director of John Brown and Co. (Limited), of Clydebank. *Address :* Clydebank, Scotland. (C225)

LUKER, Herbert William, M.B.E., *b.* 26 May, 1879 ; *s.* of the late G. H. Luker ; *m.* Ella Mathilde Henriette, M.A., *d.* of Rektor A. O. Hauch, of Copenhagen. *Educ. :* Privately. Director of Products and Equipment, Ltd. *War Work :* Personal Assist. to Controller of Munition Contracts, and also Secretary to the Interdepartmental Finance and Contract Committee of Admiralty, War Office, and Ministry of Munitions, 1915–18 ; Assist. Director of Engineering, Ministry of Food, 1918–19 ; Member of Munitions Priority Committee, 1918–19. *Addresses :* 125, Lower Thames Street, E.C. 3 ; 29, Glenmore Road, Hampstead, N.W. 3. (M2062)

LUMB, Norman Peace Lacy, O.B.E., *b.* 26 July, 1891 ; *s.* of J. W. Lumb, of Leeds. *Educ. :* London Univ. ; St. Thomas's Hospital, London. Consulting Surgeon. *War Work :* Capt. R.A.M.C. 1914–19, twice mentioned in despatches. *Addresses :* 42, Welbeck Street, W. 1 ; St. Cuthberts, Thurleigh Road, S.W. 12. (O5503)

LUMLEY, Capt. Charles Hope, M.B.E., *b.* 3 Oct. 1888 ; *s.* of Maitland Lumley, of 91, North Gate, N.W. 8 ; *m.* Kathleen Mary, *d.* of Justin Molyneux, of London. *Educ. :* Charterhouse. Engineer. *War Work :* Enlisted Aug. 1914 ; commissioned rank South Lancs. Regt., Sept. 1914 ; wounded, July, 1916 ; Head of Technical Section Ministry Munitions, Oct. 1916, to March, 1919 ; awarded Légion d'Honneur (Chevalier) ; Member of Special Mission to France to study French methods in Munition Factories, 1918. *Address :* 140, Sloane Street S.W. 1. *Club :* Junior Army and Navy. (M5429)

LUMLEY, Constance Ellinor, Mrs. Osbert, O.B.E. ; *e. d.* of the late Capt. Eustace John Wilson-Patten, 1st Life Guards, and Emily Constantia, *d.* of Rev. Lord John Thynne (she *m.* 2nd, 3rd Marquess of Headfort) ; *m.* Brig.-Gen. Hon. Osbert Lumley, *brother* and heir of the Earl of Scarbrough. *Address :* 50, Cadogan Square, S.W. 1. (O1612)

LUMLEY, Capt. Dudley Owen, O.B.E., *b.* 6 March, 1895 ; *s.* of the late Edward Warner Lumley, of Surbiton. *Educ. :* Sherborne ; Selwyn Coll., Cambridge. Assistant Principal (Higher Division), Secretary's Office, General Post Office. *War Work :* Served with 5th Batt. (Service) Wiltshire Regt., Gallipoli, 1915 ; employed on Recruiting Staff at Salisbury, Headquarters, Southern Command and at the War Office from Dec. 1915, to Oct. 1917 ; employed Ministry of National

Service, Oct. 1917, to March, 1919. *Address:* Woodlands, Adelaide Road, Surbiton. (O7409)

LUMLEY, Eva, M.B.E., *d.* of Capt. John Rutherford Lumley, Queen's Foreign Service Messenger. *Educ.:* Brussels, and Guild Hall School of Music, London. Junior Assistant Administrator, War Office. *War Work:* 5 years Clerical work in the German Section of the Military Intelligence Directorate, War Office. (M8843)

LUMLEY, Brig.-Gen. Francis Douglas, C.B., C.B.E., *b.* 13 Nov. 1857; *s.* of Colonel Frederick Douglas Lumley; *m.* the late Leonora Constance, *d.* of Arthur Kenyon. *Educ.:* Winchester Coll. Joined 77th Regiment, 1876; commanded 2nd Batt. Middlesex Regiment, 1901–5 (despatches, Queen's medal with 5 clasps, C.B.); commanded No. 10 District, 1907 to 1911; retired, 1911. *War Work:* Commanded Reserve Brigade at Chatham, 4 Aug. 1914, to 27 Dec. 1916; Special Service in France, 16 May, 1917, to 6 May, 1919 (despatches). *Address:* Blackwater House, Blackwater, Hants. *Club:* Naval and Military. (C825)

LUMLEY, Hon. Mrs. Osbert Victor George Atheling, O.B.E.

LUMPTON, Samuel, O.B.E.

LUMSDEN, Lieut. Charles Ernest, M.B.E., R.A.S.C. (T.), *b.* 18 Feb. 1882; *s.* of the late Henry Simson Lumsden, of Aberdeen. *Educ.:* Robert Gordon's Coll., Aberdeen. Merchant. *War Work:* On Staff of Supply Section R.A.S.C. Ripon Sub-District; appointed Supply Officer and Officer-in-charge Army Bakery, Ripon Camps. *Address:* 107, Desswood Place, Aberdeen. (M5430)

LUMSDEN, Sir John, K.B.E., D.L., Knight of Grace Order of St. John of Jerusalem, M.D., *b.* Nov. 1869; *s.* of John Lumsden, of Leeson Park, Dublin; *m.* Caro F., *d.* of the late Major Fitzhardinge Kingscote, of Galway. *Educ.:* Taunton Coll., and Dublin Univ. Chief Medical Officer to Guinness's Brewery; Senior Visiting Physician Mercer's Hospital, Dublin. *War Work:* Major R.A.M.C., 1917–18; Director-in-Chief B.R.C.S. and Order of St. John for Ireland; Commissioner St. John Ambulance Brigade for Ireland; Consulting Physician Red Cross War Hospitals; Chief Organiser of Red Cross, South of Ireland during war. *Addresses:* 4, Fitzwilliam Place, Dublin; Roslyn, Howth, Co. Dublin. *Clubs:* Friendly Brothers; Royal Irish Automobile; Royal Dublin Golf. (K154)

LUMSDEN, John Brown, M.B.E.

LUMSDEN, Lieut. Reginald Lewis, O.B.E.

LUMSDEN, Thomas, O.B.E.

LUMSDEN, Thomas William, M.B.E.

LUMSDEN, William Henry, M.B.E.

LUMSDEN, William Watt, M.B.E., F.I.C., *b.* 4 Nov. 1879; *s.* of Henry Lumsden, of Port Glasgow; *m.* Janetta Melville, *d.* of James Crichton, of Dumfries. *Educ.:* Royal Technical Coll., Glasgow. Assist. Manager, Arden Factory, Stevenston. *War Work:* Was Superintendent of the Manufacture of Military Explosives at Ardeen Factory, Stevenston, during the first three years of the war, and latterly Superintendent of H.M. Factory, Gwine. *Address:* 74, Caledonia Road, Saltcoats. (M3815)

LUND, Edmund, M.B.E.

LUND, Lieut. George Percy, O.B.E., M.C.

LUND, Janet, Mrs., M.B.E.; *d.* of the late Edward Hoyle, J.P., of Moorlands, Bacup; *m.* Frederick James, *s.* of the late James Lund, J.P., D.L., of Makis Hall, near Keighley. *War Work:* Jointly, with her husband, gave up her house, Beaulieu, in Harrogate and furnished it as an Auxiliary Military Hospital, of which she was the head, Oct. 1914, to April, 1919; Treasurer of the Aberford War Savings Association. *Address:* Becca Hall, Aberford, Yorks. (M2065)

LUND, Wilfred George, M.B.E. (M16251e)

LUNGLEY, George William, M.B.E., *b.* 26 Aug. 1863; *s.* of William Lungley, of Bradfield, Essex; *m.* Elizabeth, *d.* of Edward William Harrison, of St. George's East. *Educ.:* West Ham Model School. Manager, Builders' Merchant (Page, Calnan & Co., Ltd.); Past Chairman Hudson's Ward I. West Ham Unionist Association; District Administrator of Prince of Wales' and National Relief Funds; Member of West Ham War Pensions Committee; Chairman of Stratford District Disablement Committee; School Manager of West Ham Education Committee; Member of South West Ham Children's Convalescent Home Committee (in connection with Queen Mary's Hospital); Life Governor of West Ham Hospital. Member of West Ham Citizens Welfare Committee; Member of Committee for Apprenticeship of War Orphans. *Address:* 43, Crofton Road, Plaistow, E. 13. (M8846)

LUNN, Samuel, M.B.E. (M10400)

LUNN, John Reuben, O.B.E.

LUNN, William Henry, M.B.E., *b.* 6 Dec. 1876; *s.* of John Henry Lunn, of Boston; *m.* Louisa, *d.* of Edward Wright Edwards, of Barton. *Educ.:* Boston. Clerk to the Guardians; Clerk to Assessment Committee; Clerk to Boston District Old Age Pensions Committee; Sec. of Lincolnshire Standard, Ltd. *War Work:* Sec. War Pensions Committee, Boston District, 1916–20; voluntary worker in local war organisations. *Address:* Ranmoor, Carlton Road, Boston. (M8847)

LUPTON, Anne Muriel, M.B.E.

LUPTON, Charles, O.B.E., M.A. (Cantab), LL.D. (Leeds), J.P. and D.L. W. Riding of Yorks., *b.* 22 May, 1855; *s.* of Francis Lupton, J.P., of Beechwood, Roundhay, Leeds; *m.* Katharine, *d.* of Thomas Ashton, D.L. *Educ.:* Rugby, and Trinity Coll., Cambridge. Solicitor; Alderman of City of Leeds. *War Work:* Chairman of Military Appeal Tribunal

for North West Division of West Riding of Yorks.; Lord Mayor of Leeds, Nov. 1915, to Nov. 1916. *Address:* Carr Head, Roundhay, Leeds. *Club:* The Leeds. (O518)

LUPTON, Samuel, O.B.E., Member of the Institute of Journalists, *b.* 1 Dec. 1873; *s.* of the late James Oakey Lupton, of Ashton-under-Lyne, Lancs.; *m.* Gertrude, *d.* of the late Edward Greaves, of Heaton Chapel, near Stockport. *Educ.:* Manchester Grammar School. Editor of "*The Daily Gazette,*" Karachi, India. *War Work:* War Publicity work in Sind; edited "*Sindhi Junghi Akhbar*" (Sind War Journal), organ of the Sind Publicity Committee; received thanks of Indian and Bombay Governments for this and other voluntary war work, and was mentioned for valuable services rendered in India in connection with the war, in list published along with Commander-in-Chief's last despatch of July, 1919; received Souvenir War Badge. *Address:* "The Daily Gazette," Karachi, India. (O8272)

LUPTON, Walter James Edwin, O.B.E., I.C.S.

LUSCOMBE, Lieut.-Col. George Augustus, O.B.E.

LUSH, Lieut. Herbert, M.B.E.

LUTTRELL, Mary FOWNES-, O.B.E.

LUTTRELL, Eva FOWNES-, O.B.E., *b.* 18 Feb. 1858; *d.* of Henry Acland Fownes-Luttrell, of Badgworth Court. *War Work:* Red Cross Vice-President, and other Red Cross work. (O10867)

LUTWYCHE, Margaret Ruby, Mrs., M.B.E.

LUXMORE, Ethel, Mrs., O.B.E.

LUXON, Shipwright Lieut. George William, M.B.E., R.N.

LUXTON, Lieut. William John, M.B.E.

LYALL, Beatrix Margaret, Mrs., C.B.E. Member for Fulham, London County Council. (C3154)

LYALL, Charles Elliot, O.B.E.

LYALL, George, M.B.E.

LYALL, Lieut. George Henry Hudson, M.B.E., R.A.F.

LYALL, Mellicent, M.B.E.

LYALL, Capt. Peter Douglas Lorne, O.B.E., R.A.F.

LYALL, Lieut. William Hooker, M.B.E., R.A.F.

LYALL, Lieut. William James, O.B.E., R.F.

LYCETT, Capt. Cyril Vernon Lechmere, O.B.E., R.E., Spec. Res. (O1209a)

LYCETT, Edward Arthur, M.B.E.

LYDALL, Edward Wykeham, M.B.E.

LYDDON, Alfred Jonathan, O.B.E.

LYDDON, Katherine, M.B.E., *b.* 6 June, 1887; *d.* of William Croft, of Wood Green; *m.* Charles Henry, *s.* of George Lyddon, of Rading. *War Work:* 5 years with British and French Red Cross Societies; latterly Sub-Commissioner British Red Cross Society, Ismailia, Egypt. *Addresses:* White Rock, The Beach, Pevensey Bay, Sussex; Ismailia, Egypt. (M8849)

LYDE, Edith Mary, O.B.E., R.R.C.

LYEL, Percival Charles, M.B.E., *b.* 21 Feb. 1881; *s.* of Charles Lyel. Civil Servant, War Office. *War Work:* Served in the Lands Directorate of the War Office, Ministry of Munitions, and Air Ministry. *Address:* 127, Hampstead Way, Golders Green. (M8850)

LYELL, Col. David, C.M.G., C.B.E., D.S.O., R.E. Chief Railway Construction Engineer; served in the Great War, 1914–19 (despatches, Order of Leopold of Belgium, Croix de Guerre). (C1284)

LYELL, Maud Mary, M.B.E., *b.* 22 Oct. 1882; *d.* of George James Lyell, of Highlands, Heswall, Cheshire. *Educ.:* Privately. *War Work:* Member of V.A.D. Cheshire 106; served in France for 3½ years with the Liverpool Merchants' Mobile Hospital at Etaples, and afterwards at Trouville; 1915 Star; mentioned in despatches. *Address:* Highlands, Heswall, Cheshire. (M8851)

LYELL, Rosalind Margaret, Hon. Mrs., M.B.E., *b.* 13 Dec. 1891; *d.* of Vernon and Lady Margaret Watney, of Cornbury, Charlbury, Oxfordshire (*see* BURKE'S *Peerage*); *m.* the Hon. Charles Lyell (who died), *s.* of 1st Barton Lyell, of Kinnordy (*see* BURKE'S *Peerage*). *Educ.:* Privately. *War Work:* B.R.C.S., Wounded and Missing Dept., 1914–18. *Address:* 1, Cadogan Gardens, London, S.W. 3. *Club:* Queen's, Edinburgh. (M2069)

LYLE, Alexander McIntosh, M.B.E.

LYLE, Lieut.-Col. Arthur Abram, O.B.E.

LYLE, Major Arthur Nevin, O.B.E., R.E.

LYLE, Clare, Mrs., C.B.E.

LYLE, Col. Hugh Thomas, C.B.E., D.S.O., *b.* 1858; *e. s.* of the late Rev. John Lyle, of Knocktarna; *m.* 1886, Alice Fanny, *d.* of Sir Warren Hastings D'Oyly, 10th Bt. Entered Army, 1879; Capt. Royal Welsh Fusiliers, 1885; Major, 1896; Brevet Lieut.-Col. 1900; Lieut.-Col. 1903; Brevet Col. 1905 (ret. 1907); Commanded a Batt. Royal Irish Rifles, 1915; served with Burmah Expedition, 1885–86 (wounded), with Hazara Field Force, 1891 (despatches); S. Africa, 1901 (despatches, Brevet Lieut.-Col.); D.L. for co. Londonderry; was in command of a Territorial Force Brigade, 1909–10. *Address:* Knocktarna, Coleraine, co. Londonderry. (C1674)

LYLE, Lieut.-Col. J. C. V., D.S.O., O.B.E. Served in S. Africa, 1902, with 1st Kitchener's Fighting Scouts (despatches); during Great War, 1915–17; T. Lieut.-Col. Labour Corps. (O5505)

LYLE, Capt. Oliver, O.B.E.

LYLE, Samuel, C.B.E., M.B. Commr. Medical Services, Ministry of National Service during Great War. (C996)

LYMBURN, Mary Jane Dickie, M.B.E.

LYNA, Tryner, M.B.E., J.P.

LYNCH, Surg.-Lieut., O.B.E., M.B., R.N.

LYNCH, Lieut.-Col. David, C.B.E. Capt. and Brevet Lieut.-Col. Remount Service; served in the Great War, 1914–19 (despatches). (C1675)

LYNCH, Herbert Arthur, M.B.E., R.N.

LYNCH, James Challener, O.B.E.

LYNCH, Major Patrick, M.B.E., b. 15 Nov. 1856; s. of Michael Lynch, of Dublin. Educ.: The Monastery, Thurles, Co. Tipperary, Ireland; King's Coll., London. War Work: Controlling the exportation of merchandise from London. Addresses: 77, Windsor Road, Forest Gate, London, E. 3; Belgrave Park, Folkestone Road, Dover. Clubs: Devonshire; Alexandra Yacht, Southend-on-Sea; Wanstead Park Golf. (M2071)

LYNDE, Major Gilbert Somerville, O.B.E., R.E.

LYNDON, Arnold, O.B.E., M.D. (Lond.), b. 22 July, 1861; s. of George T. T. Lyndon, of Addlestone, Surrey; m. Charlotte, d. of the late William Rawson, J.P., of Hitchin. Educ.: Merchant Taylors' School; St. Bartholomew's Hospital; London Univ. Member of Public Health Committee, British Medical Association; Surgeon to Haslemere and District Cottage Hospital. War Work: Chairman Guildford Local Medical War Committee; Member of Central Medical War Committee; Medical Officer in charge, Grayshott Auxiliary Military Hospital. Address: Windwhistle House, Grayshott. Club: London Univ. (O10869)

LYNDON, Rev. Charles Henry Preston, O.B.E., M.A., b. 10 July, 1889; s. of the late Robert Lyndon, of Longford. Educ.: Masonic Boys' School, Dublin. Head of Trinity Coll. Mission, Belfast. War Work: Chaplain, 2nd Batt. Duke of Cornwall's Light Infantry; 1918, S.C.F., 27th Division; 1919, S.C.F. British Army of Black Sea. Address: Trinity Coll. Mission, Belfast. (O6502)

LYNE, Lieut. Edgar, M.B.E., R.A.F.

LYNE, Harry, O.B.E., b. 29 April, 1887; s. of Thomas Lyne, of Tingley, Yorks. Educ.: Lincoln. Gen. Sec. Y.M.C.A. War Work: 1914 to Oct. 1915, Sec. of Y.M.C.A. centres and areas in England; Nov. 1915, to Feb. 1917, Assist. Sec. Y.M.C.A., 2nd Army; Feb. 1917, to March, 1918, Gen. Sec. Y.M.C.A., 5th Army, B.E.F.; April, 1918, to May, 1919, Gen. Sec. Y.M.C.A., 4th Army, B.E.F.; Oct. 1919, to date, Gen. Sec. Y.M.C.A., Mesopotamia and Persia. Address: Y.M.C.A. H.Q., 13, Russell Square, London, W.C. 1. (O1613)

LYNE, Horace Sampson, M.B.E.

LYNN, Capt. William Davies Elliott, O.B.E., R.E.

LYNNE, Audrey, M.B.E.; d. of the late Walter Charles Cutbert Lynne. Educ.: St. Monica's School; Sisterhood of St. Deny's, Warminster, Wilts. War Work: Hon. Sec., Teignmouth Urban District Council's War Refugees Committee. Address: Clarina Cottage, Teignmouth, S. Devon. (M2072)

LYNOTT, Lieut. Michael Joseph, M.B.E., R.A.S.C.

LYON, Lieut.-Comm. Alexander, O.B.E., R.N.

LYON, Lieut. Francis Hamilton, M.B.E.

LYON, Isabella Romanes, Mrs., M.B.E., b. 25 June, 1859; d. of William Towers-Clark, of Wester Moffat, Lanarkshire; m. Walter Fitzgerald Knox (who died), s. of Lieut.-Col. G. Lyon, of Dalruscan, Dumfriesshire. Educ.: Chenies. War Work: President of the North Berwick Branch of the Voluntary War Workers' Association. Address: Tantallon Lodge, North Berwick. (M3816)

LYON, Kenneth, O.B.E., B.A. (Oxon.), b. 7 Feb. 1886; s. of William Lyon, of Birkenhead and London; m. Lucy, d. of Rev. J. M. Geden, of Burrough Rectory, Leicestershire. Educ.: Birkenhead School, and Merton Coll., Oxford. Civil Service; Higher division clerk, War Office, 1909–12. War Work: Private Sec. to Adjutant-Gen., War Office, 1912–16; Cadet, R.H.A., June, 1916; 2nd Lieut. R.F.A., Oct. 1916; B.E.F., France, Flanders, and Germany, Dec. 1916, to Jan. 1919, 13th Battery R.F.A.; Adjutant, 17th Brigade R.F.A.; Staff Captain 29th Divisional Artillery and Staff Captain 6th Divisional Artillery; mentioned in Secretary of State's List, Feb. 1917; despatches, Dec. 1918. Address: 58, Lansdowne Road, Holland Park, W. 11. (O5506)

LYON, Richard Charles, M.B.E., J.P., b. 8 Dec. 1864; s. of John Lyon, of Aberdeen; m. Margaret, d. of David Proudfoot, of Dundee. Educ.: Public Schools, Aberdeen. Carpenter and Joiner. War Work: Member of Local Appeal Tribunal during War period. Address: 44, Scott Street, Dundee. (M2073)

LYON, Violet Dorothy Agnes, M.B.E.

LYONS, Charles Michael, O.B.E.

LYONS, George Graham Percy, M.B.E.,

LYONS, Harry, M.B.E., b. 12 July, 1862; s. of David Lyon, of London; m. Mary Elizabeth, d. of J. Norman Rabjohns, of Newton Abbot. Educ.: City Middle Class School, Cooper Street, E.C. Theatrical and Vaudeville Manager. War Work: Arranging and conducting concerts for wounded soldiers in connection with the Hippodrome and Theatre Royal, Nottingham; Recruiting Concerts; Matinees for wounded soldiers. Address: 1, Chaucer Villas, Chaucer Street, Nottingham. Club: Vaudeville. (M8854)

LYONS, Major Henry Edward, O.B.E.

LYONS, Miriam Isabel, Mrs., C.B.E. Pres. Poona Women's Branch of War and Relief Fund, Bombay, during European War.

LYONS, Major Thomas, O.B.E.

LYSAGHT, Herbert Royes, O.B.E. (O11991)

LYSAGHT, William Rayse, C.B.E., b. 1858; s. of Thomas Royse Lysaght, of Mintinna, Co. Cork; m. 1890, Elizabeth, d. of the Rev. John Eddowes Gladstone, of Braunton, N. Devon. J.P. for Monmouthshire (High Sheriff, 1915); was Technical Adviser, Non-Ferrous Materials Dept. Ministry of Munitions during the Great War.

LYSTER, Surg.-Lieut., Ronald Guy, O.B.E., R.N.

LYTTELTON, Dame Edith, D.B.E.; d. of Archibald Balfour; m. Rt. Hon. Alfred Lyttelton, 8th s. of 4th Baron Lyttelton (d. 5 July, 1913) (see BURKE'S Peerage) (D4)

LYTTELTON, Stephen Clive, O.B.E., D.S.C.

LYTTON, Major Hon. Neville Stephen, O.B.E., b. 6 Feb. 1879; 4th s. of 1st Earl of Lytton; m. Judith Anne Dorothea (now Baroness Wentworth). Educ.: Eton. Major (General Staff); wounded in France, 1916; Amateur Tennis Champion and holder of the International Cup, Paris. Address: Crabbet Park, Poundhill, Three Bridges, Sussex. Clubs: Prince's; Queen's. (O8139)

LYWOOD, Oswyn George William Clifford, O.B.E., R.A.F.

MABEE, Major Oliver Hugel, O.B.E.

McADAM, Francis, Mrs., O.B.E.

MACADAM, Lieut. Ivison Stevonson, O.B.E., R.E. (T.).

MacAFEE, Annie Horner, M.B.E., b. 15 Sept. 1858; d. of Daniel Crowe, of Castleroe, Coleraine; m. Andrew, s. of Samuel MacAfee, of Ballymoney. Member of Committee of the Ulster Centre of St. John Ambulance Association; Member of Co. Tyrone War Pensions Committee; Member of Co. Tyrone Insurance Committee; Member of District Nursing Association; Member of Committee of the Women's National Health Association, Ireland. War Work: Organiser of sixteen V.A.D. Classes in Mid-Tyrone, and Lecturer on Home Nursing to fourteen of them; Recruiting Commandant for Co. Tyrone; Commandant No. 440 V.A.D., No. 2 War Office; Organiser for Red Cross in Mid-Tyrone; Head of Working Party No. 5317. Address: The Manse, Omagh, Co. Tyrone. (M8255)

McALISTER, Capt. Daniel Archibald, M.B.E., R.H.A. (T.).

McALISTER, Capt. John, M.B.E.

MacALISTER, Sir John Young Walker, O.B.E., F.S.A., F.R.G.S.; s. of Donald MacAlister, of Tarbert, Cantyre; m. Elizabeth, d. of George Batley. of Blackball, Edinburgh. Educ.: High School, Liverpool, and Edinburgh Univ. Editor of "The Library"; Sec., Editor, and Consulting Librarian, Roy. Soc. of Medicine; Member of the Institute of Journalists; Hon. Life Member of Savage Club; Sub-Librarian, Liverpool Library; Librarian, Leeds Library; founder and first Chairman of the University of London Press; Hon. Sec. Surgical Advisory Committee, War Office; Organiser and Hon. Sec. Emergency Aid Corps for Admiralty, War Office, and Metropolitan Police. Address: 33, Finchley Road, N.W. 8. Clubs: Garrick; Savage; Bath. (O10870)

MACALISTER, William Douglas, M.B.E.

MACALLAN, Arthur Ferguson, C.B.E., M.D.

MACALPINE, Lieut.-Col. Cyril Douglas Hughes, O.B.E.

McALPINE, George, O.B.E., b. 15 July, 1859; m. Margaret Ann, d. of David Brown. Educ.: Dalkeith High School. Secretary of the Church of Scotland Committee on Christian Life and Work. War Work: Hon. Sec. of the Scottish Churches Huts Committee, who carried on work among the troops in France and Germany; paid frequent visits to France and the Rhine Area in supervising the work; mentioned in despatches, March, 1919. Address: 22, Queen Street, Edinburgh. (O10871)

MACALPINE, Capt. Reginald John, O.B.E., M.C.

MACAN, Dorothy Vernon, M.B.E.; d. of the late Sir Arthur V. Macan, of 53, Merrion Square, Dublin (see BURKE'S Peerage). War Work: Y.W.C.A. Appeal Department. Address: Milford, Co. Donegal. (M8856)

McANALLY, Sibyl La Fontaine, M.B.E.

MACANDIE, George Lionel, C.B.E.

MACANDREW, Evan, M.B.E.

MACARDLE, Sir Thomas Callan, K.B.E., J.P., D.L., Louth County, b. 14 Jan. 1856; s. of Edward Henry Macardle, J.P., of Cambricville, Dundalk; m. Minnie, s. of Lieut.-Col. James Clarke Ross, late of Scots Greys. Educ.: St. Mary's College, Dundalk. High Sheriff, Louth County, 1917: Chairman, Dundalk and Newry Steampacket Co., Ltd.; Director, Macardle, Moore & Co., Ltd.; Director, Eagle, Star, and British Dominions Insurance Co. Ltd. (Irish Board). War Work: Chairman of the Louth Recruiting Committee; Pioneer of the Tillage Movement in Ireland, 1916. Address: St. Margaret's, Dundalk, Co. Louth, Ireland. Clubs: Stephen's Green, Dublin; The Dundalk. (K393)

McARTHUR, Lieut.-Col. Charles Joseph Edward Addis, O.B.E.

MACARTHUR, Major Donald Hector Colin, O.B.E., M.B., R.A.M.C.

McARTHUR, Gladys Forbes, M.B.E.; d. of the late Col. Edward McArthur, of Royal Marine Artillery, Eastney. Educ.: The Royal School for Officers' Daughters, Bath. (M8857)

McARTHUR, Capt. James, O.B.E., R.A.V.C. (T.).

McARTHUR, Capt. and Qr.-Mr. William James, O.B.E., R.A.V.C. (T.).

McARTHUR, William Lyon, C.B.E.

McARTHUR, Lieut.-Col. William Porter, D.S.O., O.B.E., M.B., B.Ch., M.R.C.P. Entered R.A.M.C. 1909 ; Capt. and Acting-Lieut.-Col. ; served in Great War, 1914–16 (mentioned in despatches). (O8867)

MACARTNEY, James, O.B.E.

MACASSEY Ethel, Constance Chapman, M.B.E.

MACASSEY, Sir Lynden Livingstone, K.B.E., M.A., LL.D., B.Sc., K.C. ; *s.* of the late L. L. Macassey, M.I.C.E., of Holywood, Co. Down ; *m.* Jeanne, *d.* of Robert M'Farland, of Melbourne. *Educ. :* Upper Sullivan School, Holywood, Bedford, and Trinity Coll., Dublin. Trained as an Engineer ; Assoc. Inst. C.E. ; Assoc. Surveyors' Inst. ; Assoc. Inst. of Patent Agents ; called to the Bar, 1899 ; Lecturer, Economics and Law ; School of Economics, London, 1901–9 ; Sec. to Royal Commission on London Traffic, 1903–6 ; Inspected on behalf of the Government, locomotion facilities in chief cities in U.S.A., 1914–16 ; Board of Trade Arbitrator in Shipbuilding and Engineering cases ; Member of many committees ; Director of Shipyard Labour, Admiralty, 1917–18 ; Member of War Cabinet Committee on Labour, 1917–18 ; on Women in Industry, 1918–19. *Addresses :* 16, Collingham Gardens, S.W. ; 3, Paper Buildings, Temple ; Palace Chambers, Westminster. *Clubs :* Athenæum ; Carlton ; Garrick ; St. Stephen's ; Ranelagh ; Royal Ulster Yacht. (K30)

McAUGHEY, John, O.B.E.

MACAULAY, Major Archibald Francis, O.B.E., Can. A.M.C.

MACAULAY, Lieut.-Col. Donald, O.B.E., R.A.M.C.

MACAULAY, Thomas Symington, O.B.E., *b.* 1847 ; *m.* Jen, *d.* of George Cowan. *Educ. :* Dumfries. Twice Provost of Dumfries ; Chairman Dumfries and Maxwelltown Water Commissioners, and of numerous other public bodies. *War Work :* Chairman Dumfries Recruiting Tribunal, Dumfries Burgh Food Control Committee, Joint Food Committee of Dumfriesshire, and Galloway, Fuel Control Committee, Prince of Wales Fund Committee, Burgh Branch Soldiers' and Sailors' Families Association ; Member of War Savings Committee and Red Cross Organisation ; did much work in connection with supplying comforts for troops ; for 35 years a Volunteer and a well-known shot, taking many prizes at Wimbledon and Bisley and at Edinburgh and Glasgow meetings. *Address :* Cherry House, Dock Park. (O521)

MACAULEY, Elizabeth Lusk, O.B.E.

MACAULEY, Brig.-Gen. Sir George Bohun, K.C.M.G., K.B.E., C.B., R.E., *b.* 25 Aug. 1869 ; *s.* of Col. G. W. Macauley. Entered R.E. 1889 ; Capt. 1900 ; Major, 1900 ; employed with Egyptian Army, 1896 ; ret. 1912 ; rejoined for Great War as T. Col. 1915 ; T. Brig.-Gen. 1917. Served Sudan Expedition, 1897 ; (mentioned in despatches, medal and clasp, 4th class Medjidieh) ; Khartoum Expedition, 1898 ; General Manager, Sudan Government Railways, 1898–1906 ; 2nd class Medjidieh, 1906 ; General Manager, Egyptian State Railways, 1906–19 ; Director of Railways, Egyptian Expeditionary Force, 1915–19 ; Adviser to Ministry of Communications, Egyptian Government, 1919. *Address :* Cairo, Egypt. (K321c)

McAULIFFE, Rev. Edmond, O.B.E.

M'AVITY, Lieut.-Col. Thomas Malcolm, C.B.E., D.S.O., *b.* 1889 ; *s.* of John M'Avity, of St. John, New Brunswick, Canada ; *m.* Frances Edith, *d.* of Sir Douglas Hazen, of St. John, N.B., Canada (*see* BURKE'S *Peerage*). *Educ. :* Rothesay Collegiate School ; Royal Military Coll. *War Work :* 1914, Junior Major, 26th N.B. Batt. (Canada) ; 1915, Bde. Major, 5th Can. Inf. Bdge. (England) ; France, Sept. 1915, to Oct. 1916 ; G.S.O.2, 2nd Can. Div. 1916 ; G.S.O.2, 3rd Can. Div. and Canadian Corps H.Q. 1917–18 ; G.S.O.1, Can. Corps H.Q., and of 4th Can. Div. 1919. *Address :* c/o T. M'Avity and Sons, St. John, N.B., Canada. *Club :* Union (St. John). (C2056)

McAVOY, Capt. John, M.B.E., *b.* 28 Dec. 1887 ; *s.* of John McAvoy, of Glasgow. *Educ. :* Duke of York's Royal Military School. Staff Captain at War Office since Aug. 1918. *War Work :* Kameruns ; France. (M5433)

McBAIN, Alexander Richardson, O.B.E., *b.* 22 April, 1887 ; *s.* of Alexander McBain, of Glasgow. *Educ. :* Glasgow High School. Civil Servant. *War Work :* Employed at War Office. *Address :* War Office. (O1617)

McBAIN, Lieut. Percival Alexander, M.B.E., Aust. F.C. and R.A.

McBARNET, Alexander Cockburn, O.B.E., 3rd Class Order of the Mejidieh, 3rd Class Order of the Nile, *b.* 6 Dec. 1867 ; *s.* of Lieut.-Col. A. C. McBarnet, formerly of Torridon and Attadale ; *m.* Elizabeth Mai, *d.* of the Hon. Augustus Erskine (*see* BURKE'S *Peerage*). *Educ. :* Fettes Coll., Edinburgh ; Balliol Coll., Oxford. Barrister-at-Law, Inner Temple, 1892 ; Lecturer, Khedivial School of Law, Cairo, 1904–1905 ; Judge of 1st Instance, Egypt, 1906–13 ; Judge of Court of Appeal 1913 ; Lieut.-Col. Southern Punitive Force, Egypt, 26 March, to 3 June, 1919 ; Legal Adviser, Police Court of Inquiry, Palestine, 18 April, 1920. *War Work :* Legal member, Permanent Arbitration Board, Egypt, Jan. 1914. *Addresses :* c/o H. Inglis Lindsay, W.S., 16, Queen Street, Edinburgh, N.B. ; 33c Khedivial Buildings, Sh. Emad-el-Deen, Cairo, Egypt. *Club :* Turf, Cairo. (O10872)

McBEATH, Sir William George, K.B.E. Chairman, Australia Defence Royal Commission. (K473)

MACBETH, Lieut. Allan, M.B.E., R.N.V.R.

MACBRAYNE, Lieut.-Comm. Laurence, O.B.E., R.N.V.R.

McBRIDE, John Corbet, M.B.E.

McBRIDGE, Capt. Stuart George, O.B.E., R.A.S.C.

McBRIGHT, David Samuel, M.B.E.

McBROOM, Lieut. Samuel, O.B.E.

McBRYDE, Tom Murray, M.B.E., *b.* 23 Oct. 1887 ; *Educ..* Rutherford Coll., Newcastle-on-Tyne. Technical Assistant, Board of Trade, Coal Mines Department (Shipping Branch). *War Work :* Sec., Newcastle and Gateshead Incorporated Chamber of Commerce, Military Committee—raisers of 16th, 18th, and 19th (Service), and 28th and 31st (Reserve) Battalions Northumberland Fusiliers ; organised motor outings and other entertainment for 35,000 wounded soldiers ; Member of Newcastle-on-Tyne War Pensions Committee. *Addresses :* 4, Mason Avenue, Whitley Bay, Northumberland ; 50, Beatrice Avenue, Norbury, London, S.W. 16. (M8859)

McCAFFERY, James, O.B.E.

McCALL, Amy Kerr, M.B.E., *b.* 21 Oct. 1895 ; *d.* of George Kerr McCall, of Trowbridge (Wilts). *Educ. :* High School for Girls, Bournemouth. *War Work :* Member of W.R.N.S. Private Sec. to the Rt. Hon. Eric Geddes, G.C.B., G.B.E., M.P. *Addresses :* 29, Francis Street, S.W. 1 ; The Orchard, Hilperton, Wilts. (M8860)

McCALL, Capt. Charles William Home, C.B.E., *b.* 22 Oct. 1877 ; *s.* of Charles McCall ; *m.* Dorothy Margaret, *d.* of Dr. Joseph Kidd. *Educ. :* Privately. Managing Director of the Ballantyne Press, 1908 ; Chairman, 1913. *War Work :* Liverpool Scottish, A. Adjutant, Norwich, Nov. 1915 ; Assistant Director, Small Arms Ammunition, March, 1916 ; Director, Non-Ferrous Rolled Metals, Nov. 1916 ; Deputy Controller Non-Ferrous Metals, 1917 ; Director of Officers' Technical Training Classes, 1917 ; Controller of the Appointments Department, March, 1918 ; Member of the Officers' Resettlement Committee and of the Officers' Univ. and Technical Training Committee. *Address :* Walberswick, Suffolk. (C997)

McCALL, David, M.B.E. Shipbuilding ; General Manager Ayrshire Dockyard Co., Ltd., Irvine. *War Work :* Shipyard Manager with Ayrshire Dockyard Co., Ltd., Irvine. *Address :* Fernlea, Irvine. (M734)

MACCALL, William Neil, M.B.E., M.D., C.M., *b.* 5 Nov. 1845 ; *s.* of John Campbell Maccall, of Largs (Ayrshire) and Glasgow ; *m.* Louisa Frances, *d.* of Thomas Tolmé, of Havana and London. *Educ. :* Glasgow Univ. Consulting Physician to the Northern Hospital for Women and Children, Manchester. *War Work :* Hon. Sec. and Member of Executive of Meols Hall Auxiliary Military Hospital, Southport, Feb. 1915, to March, 1920 ; Member of Recruiting Committee ; Member of Committee of Southport Branch of the British Red Cross Society ; Co-Treasurer, Carnival Fund in aid of local Military Hospitals ; Co-Treasurer, Southport Fund in aid of Scottish Women's War Hospitals. *Address :* 7, Argyle Road, Hesketh Park, Southport. (M8861)

McCALLUM, Capt. Alexander, M.B.E., A.I.F.

MacCALLUM, Archibald Donald, M.B.E.

McCALLUM, Dugald, M.B.E

McCALLUM, Lieut.-Col. Robert Towson, O.B.E., R.E. (T.).

MacCALLUM, Lieut. James Dalgleish KELLIE-, O.B.E., D.L., formerly Adjutant, 79th Queen's Own Cameron Highlanders, *b.* 7 June, 1845 ; *s.* of the late George Kellie-MacCallum, J.P., D.L., of Braco, Perthshire ; *m.* Eleanor Dora Margaret, *d.* of the late C. E. Fraser Tytler, of Aldourie, Inverness-shire. *Educ. :* Loretto and Glenalmond. Chief Constable of Northamptonshire and Liberty of Peterborough since 1881. *War Work :* Member of War Emergency Committee ; Soldiers' and Sailors' Families Association, Soldiers' and Sailors' Help Society, War Savings and War Pensions Committees. *Address :* Quinton Rising, Northamptonshire. *Club :* United Service.

McCALMONT, Col. Barklie Cairns, C.B., C.B.E., *b.* 22 Nov. 1860 ; *s.* of Rev. Thomas McCalmont, of Highfield, Southampton, and Abbeylands, Co. Antrim ; *m.* 1st, Madeline de Courcy, *d.* of Col. S. Stretton and Hon. Mrs. Stretton, (died 1911) (*see* BURKE'S *Peerage*) ; 2nd, Maud, *d.* of Rev. J. Phelps, of Iffley, Oxford. *Educ. :* Winchester Coll. Joined Army 1878 ; served in Royal Warwickshire Regt. till 1905 ; Commanded Battalion, South African War, 1900–2 ; mentioned in despatches, C.B., and medals ; retired 1905. *War Work :* Rejoined Army, Aug. 1914 ; raised, trained, and commanded 10th (Service) Batt. Royal Warwickshire Regt. 1914–15 ; invalided to Home Service ; appointed to General Staff, July, 1915 ; Commandant, Southern Command School of Instruction, 1915–17 ; Staff, London District, 1917 ; formed Volunteer Force ; County Commandant, County of London Volunteer Regt., 1918–20 ; mentioned in Secretary of State's List ; retired Jan. 1920. *Address :* 3, Lennox Gardens, S.W. 1. *Clubs :* Army and Navy ; Royal Yacht Squadron, Cowes, I.W. (C1676)

McCAMMON, Major Frank Alexander, O.B.E., M.C., R.A.M.C., *b.* 5 Nov. 1879 ; *s.* of the Rev. Francis McCammon, of Springvale, Co. Antrim ; *m.* Ethel, *d.* of James Franklin Bland, of Kerry, Ireland. *Educ. :* Queen's Coll., Belfast. *War Work :* With 4th Division, B.E.F. ; Officer Commanding No 3 Motor Ambulance Convoy ; Officer Commanding No 14 Field Ambulance ; Officer Commanding No 11 Convalescent Depot ; Officer Commanding No 14 Convalescent Depot ; Officer Commanding the Convalescent Depot, British Army of the Rhine. *Address :* Ballycastle, Co. Antrim, Ireland. (O2623)

McCAMMON, George William Richardson, M.B.E.

McCANCE, Capt. Henry Montray Jones, O.B.E.

McCANDLISH, Lieut.-Col. Patrick Dalmahoy, C.B.E.. D.S.O., *b.* 1871. Capt. and Brevet Lieut.-Col. Reserve ; N.-W. Frontier of India, 1897–98 (medal with clasp) ; Great War, 1914–19 (despatches) ; appointed A.Q.M.G. 1919. (C1385)

McCANN, John, O.B.E., *b.* 1869; *s.* of William McCann, of Hull. *Educ.:* Hull Grammar School. *War Work:* Fishery Captain, Port of Hull; Agent for Fisheries Department, Ministry of Food. *Address:* Delamore, Bridlington. (O561)

McCANN, Robert, O.B.E., *b.* 1856; *s.* of Hamilton McCann, of The Hill Farm, Killinchy, Co. Down; *m.* Minnie, *d.* of Dr. Bailey, of Castletown Conyers, Limerick. *Educ.:* Secondary School, Belfast. Sec. Naval and Military Department, National Council of Y.M.C.A. *War Work:* Welfare work of Y.M.C.A. in Home Camps and various fields of War Overseas; Anglo-Belge Committee for welfare work with Belgian troops; Committee of National Alliance of Employers and Employed; and League of Nations. *Addresses:* 42, Rotherwick Road, Hampstead Garden Suburb, N.W. 11; 13, Russell Square, W.C. 1. (O562)

McCARTHY, Dame Emma Maud, G.B.E., R.R.C., Legion d'Honneur (Chevalier); *d.* of the late William Frederick McCarthy, of Deepdene, Sydney, N.S. Wales. *Educ.:* Springfield Coll., Sydney. Matron-in-Chief, Territorial Force Nursing Service, War Office, 80, Pall Mall. *War Work:* Matron-in-Chief; British Armies in France. *Address:* 47, Markham Square, Chelsea, S.W. 3. (G20)

McCARTHY, Frank, C.B.E.

McCARTHY, Lieut. Henry, M.B.E., R.A.S.C., *b* 4 June, 1881. *War Work:* S. African War, Queen's Medal (4 bars); Mons Star, Victory and British War Medals, mentioned in despatches and awarded Meritorious Service Medal for Service in Field; mentioned S. of S. despatch service at home. *Address:* c/o Sir C. R. McGrigor, Bart., Haymarket, S.W. 1. (M6671)

McCARTHY, Ignatius James John, M.B.E., *b.* 26 Feb. 1875; *s.* of Ignatius McCarthy, of Camberwell; *m.* Alice, *d.* of Thomas Charles, of Dorchester. *Educ.:* St. Joseph's Secondary School, Camberwell. Civil Servant, late W.O. H.M. Forces. *War Work:* Employed on the Staff, Lieut.-Gen. E. C. Bethune, C.V.O., C.B., Director-General of the Territorial Force. *Address:* Southwood, Dunoon Road, Forest Hill, S.E. 23. (M23)

McCARTHY, Major James Joseph, C.B.E., D.S.O., M.C. Major, Rhodesian Police; served in Great War, 1914–18 (mentioned in despatches). (C1115)

McCARTHY, John William Henry, M.B.E.

McCARHTY, Lillah, *see* Keeble, Lillah, Mrs.

McCARTHY, May, Mrs., M.B.E.

McCARTHY, Sidney James, M.B.E., R.N.

MacCARTIE, Flora Theodosia, M.B.E., *b.* 1 Feb. 1859; *d.* of Joseph MacCartie, of Carrignavar, Cork. *War Work:* Hon. Sec., Soldiers' and Sailors' Help Society, Eastbourne and E. Sussex; Care of Invalided and Disabled Men at Sailors' and Soldiers' Home, Eastbourne; Hon. Sec. R. Sussex Regt. Prisoners of War Fund. *Address:* 59, Watts Lane, Eastbourne. (M8863)

McCAUSLAND, Gertrude, Mrs., M.B.E.

MacCAW, Vivian Hardy, O.B.E.; *s.* of W. J. M. MacCaw, of 103, Eaton Square, London. *Educ.:* Marlborough Coll., and Trinity Coll., Cambridge. *War Work:* Supervision of Enemy Aliens and Munitions. *Address:* Bengal Club, Calcutta, India. *Clubs:* Bachelors'; Bath. (O4062)

McCAY, Major-Gen. the Hon. Sir James Whiteside, K.C.M.G., K.B.E., C.B., V.D., M.A., LL.M., *b.* 21 Dec. 1864; *s.* of the Rev. Boyd McCay, D.D., M.A.; *m.* Julia Mary O'Meara. *Educ.:* Scotch Coll., Melbourne; Melbourne Univ. Barrister and Solicitor of High Court of Australia and Supreme Court of Victoria; Lieut. Victorian Volunteer Forces, 1886; Deputy Judge-Advocate, 1894; M.L.A. for Castlewaine, Victoria, 1895–99; Minister of Trades and Customs, and Minister of Education, 1899–1901; Member of the House of Representatives for Corinella, Australian Commonwealth Parliament, 1901–6; Minister of State for Defence, 1904–8; Col. Commanding Australian Intelligence Corps, and Director of Intelligence, Commonwealth Section, Imperial General Staff, 1909; Commanded 2nd Australian Infantry Brigade in Gallipoli, 15th Australian Division in Egypt and France, subsequently G.O.C. Australian Imperial Force, U.K.; Commander Legion of Honour. *Address:* 360, Colliers Street Melbourne. *Clubs:* Melbourne; Naval and Military (Melbourne). (K311)

McCHEANE, Lieut.-Col. Montague William Hiley, C.M.G., C.B.E., Order of the White Eagle, Serbia, Order of the Nahda, Hedjaz: *b.* 27 March, 1872; *s.* of the late Lieut.-Col. W. H. McCheane, R.M.L.I. *Educ.:* Portsmouth Grammar School, and Royal Military Academy, Woolwich. Late Royal Artillery; Royal Army Ordnance Corps; South African War, with Army Ordnance Department; mentioned in despatches. *War Work:* With Army Ordnance Dept., and Royal Army Ordnance Corps, from April, 1915, till end of war, in Egypt and Palestine; four times mentioned in despatches. *Club:* United Service. (C2063)

McCHRISTELL, Major Thomas, O.B.E., N.Z.A.O.C.

McCLEAN, Rev. Canon Richard Arthur, O.B.E. For services as Episcopalian Chaplain to the Forces in the War. (O11914)

McCLELLAN, Capt. Creighton William, M.B.E.

McCLELLAN, Frank Campbell, C.B.E.

McCLELLAN, Capt. Frederic Ewing, C.B.E.

McCLELLAN, Sarah Georgina Corbetta, M.B.E., *b.* 8 Aug. 1859; *d.* of Canon Griffiths of Machynlleth and Bangor; *m.* Rev. Edward James, *s.* of Captain James Creighton McClellan, of York. *Educ.:* St. Mary's Hall, Brighton. *War Work:* Hon. County Sec. (Breconshire) B.R.C.S.; Commandant,

Reserve County Detachment; organiser of "Our Day" Fund for Breconshire 1915–18; Assist. Administrator. Red Cross Hospital. *Address:* Llanhamlach Rectory, Brecon. *Club:* V.A.D., London. (M3819)

McCLELLAND, Andrew McClelland, M.B.E.

McCLELLAND, Sir Peter Hannay, K.B.E., *b.* 1856; *s.* of Thomas McClelland, of Wigtown; *m.* Aurora Amelia Violeta, *d.* of James Williamson, of Valparaiso (Chile). *Educ.:* Wigton Normal School; George Watson's Coll., Edinburgh. Merchant Banker; a Partner of Duncan Fox & Co., Liverpool and London; a Liveryman of the Girdlers' Guild; a Life Governor of the Royal Scottish Corporation; Director of the South American Export Syndicate, Ltd., the British Mexican Petroleum Co., Ltd., the British Union Oil Co., Ltd., and the Union Petroleum Products Co. Ltd. *Address:* Eaton House, 66A, Eaton Square, S.W. 1. *Club:* Royal Overseas Officers'; Argentine. (K95)

McCLELLAND, William, M.B.E., M.B., Ch.B.

McCLELLAND, William, O.B.E., M.I.E.E., *b.* 22 Oct. 1873; *s.* of the late William, of Ballybay, Clones, Ireland; *m.* Isabella, *d.* of James Whaley Shepherd, of Manchester. *Educ.:* Manchester. Member, Institution of Electrical Engineers; Associate Member of American Institute of Electrical Engineers. Director of Electrical Engineering, Admiralty. *War Work:* Responsible at Admiralty for administration of electrical engineering work at H.M. Dockyards, including electrical work in shipbuilding; also for electrical repairs to H.M. Ships of Fleet and Auxiliaries; also erection of electrical work at Shore Defences, War Factories, etc. *Address:* 62, York Mansions, London, S.W. 11. *Club:* St. Stephen's. (O563)

McCLIMENT, Rev. Robert James, O.B.E., B.A., *b.* 2 June, 1887; *s.* of R. J. McCliment, of Ardrossan. *Educ.:* St. Edmund's Coll., Old Hall, Ware. Professor, St. Edmund's Coll., Old Hall, Ware. *War Work:* Chaplain to the Forces; gazetted, Aug. 1914; proceeded to France, Dec. 1914; Italy, Nov. 1917. *Address:* St. Edmund's College, Old Hall, Ware. *Club:* Union, Cambridge. (O6397)

McCLINTOCK, Lucy Antonia, Mrs., O.B.E.: *d.* of Sir Anthony Cleasby (*see* BURKE'S *Peerage*); *m.* Frederick Robert, *s.* of Col. McClintock, of Drumcar. *War Work:* Breconshire War Hospital, Dec. 1915, to Feb. 1918. *Addresses:* Penogre, Brecon, S. Wales; 7, Ormonde Gate, Chelsea. (O1618)

McCLURE, Capt. George Buchanan, O.B.E., R.A.F.

McCLURE, Janet Mary, M.B.E., *b.* Oct. 1868; *d.* of Col. John McClure, of Stockport. *Educ.:* Laleham, London, and abroad. Commandant of the B.R.C.S. V.A.D. Cheshire 60, since commencement, 1910. *War Work:* Commandant of the Sir Ralph Pendlebury Auxiliary Hospital Stockport, Nov. 1914, to April, 1919; Masseuse to the above hospital and at Heysleigh Aux. Hospital; appointed to the Special Surgical Military Orthopædic Hospital, Newcastle-on-Tyne, June, 1919, as masseuse. *Address:* c/o Major W. R. McClure, Denby Lane Farm, Stockport. (M8864)

McCLURE, Mary, Lady, M.B.E., *b.* 18 Aug. 1860; *d.* of James Johnstone, of Holcombe, Lancashire; *m.* Sir John David (*see* BURKE'S *Peerage*), *s.* of John McClure, J.P., of Wigan. *Educ.:* Girls' High School, Saltaire. *War Work:* A Vice-President of the Middlesex Division of British Red Cross Society and Order of St. John; Head of Red Cross working party at Mill Hill, N.W. *Address:* Head Master's House, Mill Hill School, N.W. 7. (M2078)

McCLURE, Capt. Samuel, O.B.E., R.A.F.

McCLYMONT, Rev. James Alexander, C.B.E., V.D., D.D., *b.* 26 May, 1848; *s.* of Samuel McClymont, J.P., of Girvan, Ayrshire; *m.* Agnes, *d.* of Thomas Smith, J.P., of Dundee. *Educ.:* Girvan Grammar School; Ayr Academy; Edinburgh Univ. Deputy Clerk of the General Assembly of the Church of Scotland and Convener of Committee on Chaplains to H.M. Forces. *War Work:* Entrusted by the War Office with the duty of nominating several hundred Ministers of the Church of Scotland for appointment as Temporary Chaplains during the war; also served personally as a T.F. Chaplain for nearly five years; appointed Principal Chaplain, ranking as Brigadier-General, July, 1918; Moderator and Designate of the General Assembly, 1921. *Clubs:* Conservative, Edinburgh; Authors', London. (C22136)

McCLYMONT, Lillie Atkinson, M.B.E., *b.* 1 Jan. 1891; *d.* of Andrew McClymont, of Glasgow. *Educ.:* Glasgow. Sec. V.A.D. Committee, Scottish Branch, British Red Cross Society, Headquarters. *War Work:* Secretarial duties in connection with the administrative work of the Scottish Red Cross during the whole period of the war. *Address:* 61, Newlands Road, Newlands, Glasgow. *Club:* V.A.D., Glasgow. (M8865)

McCLYMONT, Lieut.-Col. Robert Arthur, C.B.E., D.S.O., *b.* 1874; Major, R.F.A.; S. African War, 1902 (Queen's medal with four clasps); Somaliland, 1904 (medal with two clasps); Great War, 1914–17 (despatches); appointed a Gen. Staff Officer at War Office, 1917; Mil. Attaché, 1918, with rank of Lieut.-Col. (C1677)

McCOLL, Col. George Guthrie, C.B.E. Australian Forces, Dep. Ch. Censor for Australia. (C714)

MACCOLL, Capt. Henry Hector, O.B.E.

McCOLL, Henrietta Sutherland, M.B.E., Q.M.A.A.C.

McCOLL, Hugh Ernest, O.B.E., M.B., Ch.B., R.A.M.C., *b.* 27 March, 1893; *s.* of Rev. John McColl, of Foveran, Aberdeenshire. *Educ.:* Paisley Grammar School, and Glasgow Univ. Junior Assistant Surgeon to Victoria Infirmary

Glasgow.¶ *War Work :* Sept. 1914, to March, 1915, Private, R.A.M.C., 3rd Scottish Gen. Hospital ; Nov. 1916, gazetted Lieut. ; Nov. 1917, Captain ; Dec. 1916, to June, 1918, service with Salonica Force, attached 2nd Buffs, 85th and 86th Field Ambulances, and 1st K.O.Y.L.I. ; July 1918, to Feb. 1919, service in France with 1st K.O.Y.L.I. ; March, 1919, to April, 1920, Bangour War Hospital, Edinburgh. *Addresses :* U.F. Manse, Foveran, Aberdeenshire ; c/o Adam, 5, Stanley Street, Charing Cross, Glasgow. (O2051)

McCOLL, Lieut.-Col. John Thomas, O.B.E., M.C., Aust. I.F.

McCONAGHY, Minnie Bevernand, O.B.E. Valuable services to the troops in Egypt. (O11790)

McCONKEY, Lieut.-Comm. Henry, O.B.E., R.N.R.

McCONNEL, Lieut.-Comm. William, O.B.E., R.N.V.R.

McCONNELL, William Alexander, O.B.E., F.C.I.I., *b.* 13 March, 1873 ; *s.* of the late James McConnell, of Dublin ; *m.* Ada Margaret, *d.* of the late Robert Morrow, of Dublin. *Educ. :* Dublin. Manager for Ireland, Friends' Provident and Century Life Office and Century Insurance Co., Ltd. ; Vice-President and Past President, Insurance Institute of Ireland. *War Work :* Joint Hon. Sec. National Savings Committee for Leinster, Munster, and Connaught. *Address :* Glenmalure, 11, Ailesbury Park, Merrion, Co. Dublin. *Club :* Rotary, Dublin. (O10874)

McCORKELL, Dudley Evelyn Bruce, M.B.E., B.A., J.P., Esquire of the Order of St. John of Jerusalem in England, *b.* 22 Feb. 1883 ; *s.* of David Browne McCorkell, J.P., D.L., of Ballyarnett, Londonderry ; *m.* Helen Elizabeth, *d.* of Francis James Usher, of Meadow Bank, Terenure, Co. Dublin. *Educ. :* Shrewsbury, and Pembroke Coll., Cambridge. *War Work :* County Director for British Red Cross and Order of St. John for City of Londonderry and County of Donegal ; War Pensions ; Recruiting. *Address :* Ballyarnett, Londonderry. *Club :* Univ. Dublin. (M2079)

MacCORMAC, Lieut.-Col. Henry, C.B.E., M.D., F.R.C.P., R.A.M.C. ; *s.* of John MacCormac, of Belfast (*see* BURKE'S *Peerage,* MacCormac, Bart.). *Educ. :* Edinburgh Univ. Physician for Diseases of the Skin, Middlesex Hospital, London ; Lecturer on Forensic Medicine in Medical School. *War Work :* Went to France, Jan. 1915, with French Red Cross ; then joined R.A.M.C. in June, 1915, as Lieut., finally becoming Consulting Dermatologist to B.E.F., France, in 1918, with rank of Lieut.-Col. ; twice mentioned in despatches. *Club :* Savile. (C1285)

McCORMACK, Arthur John, C.B.E.

McCORMACK, Major Carson Alexander Vivian, O.B.E.

McCORMICK, Gerald Bernard, M.B.E., R.N.

McCORMACK, Rev. John Bernard, M.B.E., E.A.F.

McCORMACK, Michael, O.B.E., M.C., *b.* 1 March, 1871 ; *s.* of Patrick McCormack, of Roscommon, Ireland ; *m.* Dulcie Evelyn, *d.* of T. T. Logan, late Indian Civil Service, of Bournemouth. *Educ. :* Elphin Grammar School, and privately in Dublin. Director of Companies. *War Work :* S. African War, 1899–1902, Capt. and Paymaster, Kitchener's Horse ; S.W. Africa, D.A.Q.M.G. to Gen. Botha's Force, with rank of Major ; subsequently attached to (Queen's) R.W. Surrey Regt. ; afterwards appointed for staff work, Mobilisation Dept. War Office ; transferred to National Aircraft Factories Dept., Ministry of Munitions, and appointed Assistant Controller of that Dept. *Addresses :* c/o Country Club, Johannesburg ; P.O., Box 1988, Johannesburg. *Clubs :* Rand ; Country ; Johannesburg Golf. (O7416)

McCORMICK, Lieut. Henry Charles Gordon, M.B.E., *b.* 20 July, 1888 ; *s.* of the Rev. Canon J. McCormick, D.D., of Roundstone, Co. Galway ; *m.* Eva, *d.* of Alexander Sim, J.P., of Collooney, Co. Sligo. *Educ. :* St. Lawrence Coll., Ramsgate. Solicitor. *War Work :* Served with 16th Irish Division, France, 1916, and with 28th Division, Macedonia, Serbia, Bulgaria, 1917–19 ; mentioned in despatches, March, 1919. *Address :* The Abbey, Collooney, Co. Sligo. (M4806)

McCORQUODALE, Norman, O.B.E., J.P., *b.* 24 Oct. 1863 ; *s.* of George McCorquodale, of Newton-le-Willows, Lancashire, and Gadlys, Isle of Anglesey (*see* BURKE'S *Landed Gentry*) ; *m.* Constance Helena, *d.* of E. C. Burton, of The Lodge, Daventry. *Educ. :* Harrow ; Pembroke Coll., Oxford. *War Work :* County Director for Buckinghamshire, St. John's and Red Cross. *Address :* Winslow Hall, Bucks. *Club :* Boodle's. (O10875)

McCOSH, Major Robert, O.B.E.

McCOWEN, Surg.-Lieut.-Comm. Gerald Roche, O.B.E., M.D., R.N.

McCOWEN, Oliver Hill, C.B.E., LL.B.

McCRACKEN, David Edenfield, O.B.E.

McCRACKEN, Major Frederic de Crez, O.B.E., late R.A.S.C. Special Reserve, *b.* 30 Jan. 1885 ; *s.* of Frank de Crez McCracken, of 14, Onslow Crescent, and 38, Queen Street, Cannon Street, E.C. *Educ. :* Switzerland (Lausanne) ; Arlington House, Brighton ; King's Coll., London. *War Work :* Attached headquarters 1st and 3rd British Armies in France, 1915–16 ; S.S.O., 12th Division in the field ; D.A.D.T. Headquarters, L. of C., France, Nov. 1917 to June, 1919. *Address :* 11, Wetherby Mansions, Earl's Court Square, London, S.W. 5. *Clubs :* Isthmian ; Travellers', Paris. (O5511)

McCRAE, Lieut.-Col. James, M.B.E., R.A.F.

McCRAKEN, John, M.B.E.

McCREA, Hugh Moreland, O.B.E., M.D., B.Ch., *b.* 4 March, 1877 ; *s.* of John McCrea, M.D., of Belfast ; *m.* Kate Rose, *d.* of Charles Hannen, late Commissioner Chinese Customs.

Educ. : Royal Academical Institution ; and Queen's Univ., Belfast. Assistant Physician to Out-Patients, Paddington Green Children's Hospital. *War Work :* Physician, City of London Military Hospital ; President, No. 2 Final Appeal Board ; organised and acted as Convener of the Emergency Surgical Aid Corps of Royal Society of Medicine. *Address :* 20, Devonshire Place, London, W. 1. (O11821a)

McCREERY, Emilie, Mrs., M.B.E.

McCRINDLE, Major James Ronald, O.B.E., M.C., R.A.F.

McCULLAGH, Capt. Francis, M.B.E.

McCULLAGH, Margaret Craig, Lady, C.B.E.; *d.* of William Brodie ; *m.* 1896, Sir Crawford, *s.* of Robert McCullagh, of Aghadee. *Address :* Niswara, Whiteabbey, Co. Antrim.

MACCULLAH, Major Albert, C.B.E., R.A.S.C.

McCULLOCH, John Smith, M.B.E., R.A.S.C.

McCULLOUGH, Capt. Robert Stuart, O.B.E., *b.* 18 April, 1883 ; *s.* of the late Wm. McCullough, of Omagh, Co. Tyrone, Ireland. *Educ. :* Portora Royal School, Enniskillen. *War Work :* Went to France, Dec. 1914, and served continuously with B.E.F. to end of war, with 3rd and 18th Divisions. *Address :* c/o Hartley Buckley, J.P., The Grange, Crawley Down, Sussex. *Clubs :* Constitutional ; United R.A.S.C. (O2624)

MACCULLUM, Alfred Erasmus Geoffrey, O.B.E., R.A.F.

McCURDY, David, O.B.E.

McCURDY, Major Donald Archibald, O.B.E.

McCUSKER, Ralph Henry John, M.B.E., R.N.

McCUTCHAN, Capt. William Charles, M.B.E., M.C.

McCUTCHIN, Sydney Cameron, M.B.E.

McDERMAID, Neil John, O.B.E.

McDERMENT, William, M.B.E., Can. A.D.C.

MACDERMOTT, Lieut.-Comm. Anthony Francis Joseph, O.B.E., R.N.

McDERMOTT, Lieut.-Col. John, O.B.E.

McDERMOTT, Lieut.-Col. Thomas, O.B.E., R.A.M.C.

McDERMOTT, Capt. William, O.B.E., *b.* 28 May, 1888 ; *s.* of T. McDermott, of Abbey Wood, Kent ; *m.* Kathleen Constance, *d.* of Jasper Geer, of Twickenham, Surrey. *Educ. :* Public School, London. *War Work :* Served in the Regular Forces in India and Mesopotamia, and commanded the 7th Cav. Bde., Ammunition Column, R.H.A., in Mesopotamia until Jan. 1919. *Address :* 42, The Vineyard, Richmond, Surrey. *Club :* Junior Army and Navy. (O6655)

MACDIARMID, Lieut.-Col. Peter, O.B.E., M.D., R.A.M.C.

MACDONA, Major Cuthbert Laud, O.B.E.

McDONALD, Capt. Alexander, M.B.E., R.G.A.

MACDONALD, Major Alexander, O.B.E.

MACDONALD, Allan McDonald, C.B.E.

MACDONALD, Capt. Allen Fraser, M.B.E., T.F. Res. (ret.).

MACDONALD, Amy Beatrice, Mrs., M.B.E., *b.* 12 July, 1880 ; *d.* of Rev. E. F. Cavalier, M.A., of Wramplingham, Norfolk ; *m.* Major Eric William, *s.* of John M. Macdonald, of Lombard Street, London. *Educ. :* St. Mary's Hall, Brighton. *War Work :* Organiser and Hon. Sec. of The King's Own (Scottish Borderers) Prisoners of War Fund, from 1914 to end of war. *Address :* Little Ote Hall, Burgess Hill, Sussex. (M8867)

MACDONALD, Major Andrew Edward, O.B.E.

MACDONALD, Rev. Angus, O.B.E.

MACDONALD, Capt. Angus G., O.B.E., M.D., R.A.M.C.

McDONALD, Eng.-Comm. Archibald Anthony, O.B.E.

MACDONALD, Archibald Campbell, C.B.E. Assist. Director of Agriculture E. Africa Protectorate, and a M.L.C. ; rendered services to E. African Expeditionary Force during Great War (mentioned in despatches). (C1145)

MACDONALD OF THE ISLES, Celia Violet Bosville, O.B.E., *b.* 28 Jan. 1889 ; *d.* of Sir Alexander Macdonald of the Isles, Bart., of Thorpe Hall, Bridlington (*see* BURKE'S *Peerage*). *Educ. :* Privately. *War Work :* Teaching (by request of the Chief Constable of the East Riding) a class of policemen Morse and Semaphore Signalling ; helping to found and run a Club at Farnborough for the girls of the clerical staff of the Aeroplane Factory ; helping the Countess of Harrowby in her work for Overseas Officers. *Address :* Thorpe Hall, Bridlington. (O8307)

MACDONALD, Charles, M.B.E., *b.* 1870. Manager, B Clearing House, Liverpool Docks Scheme, Ministry of Labour ; Manager of Bootle Employment Exchange. *War Work :* In connection with the inauguration of the 1st Dock Batt., K.L.R. *Address :* Inveresk, Ince Avenue, Great Crosby, Liverpool. (M8868)

McDONALD, Charles, O.B.E.

McDONALD, Major Charles James Lewis, O.B.E.

MACDONALD, Paymaster-Capt. David James, C.B.E. R.N. Served in Great War, 1914–19 (mentioned in despatches). (C2259)

McDONALD, 2nd Lieut. Duncan, O.B.E.

MACDONALD, Major Duncan, O.B.E., R.A.V.C.

MACDONALD, Comm. Duncan Finlayson, O.B.E.

MACDONALD, Elsie Hay, M.B.E., *b.* 8 June 1872 ; *d.* of D. J. K. Macdonald, of Sanda, Argyll. *War Work :* Hon. Sec. Soldiers' and Sailors' Families Association, Salisbury Div., from Aug. 1914 ; Member of Wilts. Local War Pension Committee from its formation, and Hon. Sec. of Salisbury Sub-Committee. *Address :* 23, The Close, Salisbury. *Club :* New Century. (M8869)

MACDONALD, Eva Flora Caroline, M.B.E., *b.* 27 Feb. 1892 ; *d.* of Alexander Macdonald, of Balranald, Lochmaddy, and Edenwood, Cupar, Fife. *Educ.*: Privately. *War Work*: 4 years coast watching for Admiralty, as District Head, and finally Head, Coast Watcher for Island of North Uist. *Addresses*: Balranald, Lochmaddy, North Uist; 19, St. Bernard's Crescent, Edinburgh. (M694)

MACDONALD, Lieut. Ewen William Charles, M.B.E., R.A.O.C.

MACDONALD, Flora Emma, Mrs., M.B.E.

MACDONALD, Florence, M.B.E., *b.* 23 Aug. 1869; *d.* of Rev. F. W. Macdonald, of London. *Educ.*: Clifton High School, and Handsworth Coll. Worker under the Young Women's Christian Association; leader of Girls' Clubs. *War Work*: Clerk in the Army Pay Dept. of the War Office; Superintendent of Y.W.C.A. Munition Workers' Club at Lancaster. *Addresses*: 18, Wellington Road, Bournemouth; Y.W.C.A. Club, Camberley, Surrey. (M695)

MACDONALD, Capt. Francis Caven, O.B.E., M.B., R.A.M.C.

MACDONALD, Lieut.-Col. George Frederic Handel, O.B.E., 1914 Star, G.S. Allied Medal, Volunteer Long Service Medal, Coronation Medal (King George and Mary), Order of the Nile, 3rd Class, 6th Essex Regt., *b.* 8 July, 1868; *s.* of Archibald McDonald, of Portsmouth; *m.* Mabel Annie, *d.* of Henry Hubbard Goodner, of Midhurst. *Educ.*: Portsmouth Grammar School (Stone Scholar). Associate of the Institute of Bankers; formerly Base Commandant, Suez; President of the Board of Control of Floating Craft and Labour, Port of Suez; thirty-five years' service in 17th North Middlesex Rifle Volunteers, London Scottish Rifle Volunteers, and Essex Regment; first commission, 8 April, 1898. *War Work*: Took part in the operations with the Mediterranean Expeditionary Force in the Islands of the Ægean Sea, Aug. 1915, to Jan. 1916; operations in Egypt, Jan. 1916, to March, 1916; operations with the Egyptian Expeditionary Force, March, 1916, to Oct. 1918; mentioned in despatches. *Address*: Emerson Park, Hornchurch, Essex. *Club*: Junior Army and Navy.

MacDONALD, George William, O.B.E., M.Sc., F.I.C.; *s.* of John MacDonald, of Casterton, Australia; *m.* Anne, *d.* of — Callender, of Birkenhead. *Educ.*: Melbourne Univ. Univ. of Londn. Analytical Chemist. *War Work*: Admiralty work in connection with Explosives. *Address*: 116, Belgrave Road, S.W. 1. (O523)

MACDONALD OF THE ISLES, Godfrey Meddleton Bosville, M.B.E., *b.* 25 Sept. 1887; *s.* of Sir Alexander Wentworth Macdonald Bosville Macdonald of the Isles, 14th Bart. of Sleat, in the Island of Skye, Co. Inverness (*see* BURKE'S *Peerage*); *m.* Rachel Audrey, *d.* of Colin Campbell (*see* BURKE'S *Peerage*, Harrowby E.). *Educ.*: Eton, and Magdalen Coll., Oxford. Barrister-at-law. *War Work*: Was in command B.R.C.S. Stores Transport Dept., Boulogne. *Address*: Scorborough Hall, Beverley. (M2082)

MACDONALD, Hector Munro, O.B.E.

MACDONALD, Herman Arthur, M.B.E.

MacDONALD, Lieut.-Col. Ian Thomas Alister, O.B.E., *b.* 14 April, 1883; *s.* of Rev. Alex. MacDonald; *m.* Ruby Josephine, *d.* of J. Boyd Love, J.P., of Outlands, Devonport. *Educ.*: Sherborne School; Univs. of Edinburgh and London. Ministry of Education, Egypt; Department of Supplies, Ministry of Agriculture. *War Work*: Lieut. A.S.C. and O.C.9 121st Co. A.S.C., attached 13th Division, Dardanelles; I.E.F. "D." Local Purchase Officer; Deputy Assist. Director and Assistant Director, Dept. of Local Resources, Mesopotamian Exped. Force; mentioned in despatches, Aug. 1918 and June, 1919; promoted Lieut.-Col., Jan. 1919. *Address*: Cereals Bureau, Alexandria, Egypt. *Club*: R.A.S.C. (O6656)

McDONALD, Capt. James, M.B.E., R.A.O.C.

MACDONALD, James, O.B.E.

MACDONALD, 2nd Lieut. James, O.B.E., K.O.S.B.

McDONALD, Major and Qr.-Mr. James, M.B.E.

McDONALD, James Gordon, O.B.E.

McDONALD, Major James Ratcliffe, O.B.E.

MACDONALD, Johanna Margaret, Mrs., M.B.E., Commandant S.C. Club, G.H.Q., France, ; *d.* of John Adam, of Indian Civil Service; *m.* Edward Ellice, late Rector of Hillhead High School, Glasgow. *War Work*: President of War Work Party for sending comforts to troops overseas, 1914–16; Commandant of Scottish Churches' Club, Montreuil S.M., France, and Wimereux, France, 1916–19. *Address*: Chapelton Terrace, Bearsden, Scotland. (M8870)

MACDONALD, Major John, O.B.E. Aust. A.M.C.

McDONALD, John, M.B.E. *Educ.*: George Heriot's School, Edinburgh. Manager of Hydropathic. *War Work*: Sec. Melrose War Savings Committee. *Address*: Waverley Hydropathic, Melrose. (M8872)

McDONALD, John, M.B.E.

MACDONALD, John, M.B.E., M.B., C.M., J.P., *b.* 23 Dec. 1860; *s.* of Archibald Macdonald, of Tobermory, Mull. *Educ.*: Tobermory School; Royal High School; Univ. of Edinburgh. Medical Officer, Parishes of Kembaek, Dairsie and Logie; Pensions Medical Referee for County Fife, etc.; Member Fife County Insurance Committee; Chairman Fife Panel Committee. *War Work*: Interim Red Cross Director for the County of Fife; Medical Officer in charge of Springfield V.A.D. Hospital; M.O. in charge troops, Cupar. *Address*: Marathon House, Cupar, Fife. (M8873)

MACDONALD, Major John Alexander, O.B.E.

MACDONALD, John Angus, M.B.E., J.P.

MACDONALD, Major the Rev. John Howard, C.B.E.,

D.D., F.R.G.S. Hon. Major Oversea Contingents; Assist. Director Chap. Sers. Canadian Forces. (C535)

MACDONALD, Major John Robert, O.B.E., Order of the Nile (4th Class), 17th London Regt., *b.* 19 June, 1879; *s.* of John Robert Macdonald, of Craigengower, Tighnabruaich; *m.* Marrion Elizabeth Evetts, *d.* of John Galloway Watson, of London. *Educ.*: Streete Court, Westgate-on-Sea. Barrister-at-law, Inner Temple (Nov. 1911); North-Eastern Circuit. *War Work*: Enlisted (London Scottish) Aug. 1914; B.E.F., Sept. 1914, to Sept. 1915; and June, 1916, to Dec. 1916; M.E.F. (Salonica), Dec. 1916 to June, 1917; E.E.F., June, 1917 to July, 1919; mentioned in despatches, June, 1919. *Address*: 3, Elm Court, Temple, E.C. 4. (O8631)

MACDONALD, Capt. Kenneth, O.B.E., *b.* 1883. Mercantile Marine, City Line. *War Work*: Commanded Admiralty Transports "Rufidji," "Huntscliff," and "Polglass Castle." *Address*: c/o The City Line, Bothwell Street, Glasgow. (O10880)

MACDONALD, Com. Malcolm Henry Somerled, O.B.E., D.S.O., R.N. Present at battle of Jutland, 1916; served at Peace Conference, 1919 (mentioned in despatches). (O9654)

MACDONALD, Margaret Clare, M.B.E.

MACDONALD, Marian Louie, M.B.E., W.R.N.S.

MACDONALD, Mina, M.B.E.

McDONALD, Niel, O.B.E., M.B.Ch.B., M.R.C.S., L.R.C.P., *b.* 29 July, 1886; *s.* of John McDonald, of Preston, Lancashire. *Educ.*: Preston Grammar School, and Manchester Univ. Hon. Anæsthetist, Royal Free Hospital, London. *War Work*: Medical Officer in charge of Royal Free Officers' Hospital, 1915–19. *Address*: 25, Gower Street, London, W.C. 1. *Club*: Royal Societies'. (O11822)

MacDONALD, Ranald, O.B.E., F.R.G.S., *b.* 8 April, 1868; *s.* of the late James MacDonald, of Lochmaddy, North Uist. *Educ.*: Lochmaddy and Glasgow. Comptroller of Customs and Magistrate, Nyasaland Protectorate. *War Work*: Served with, and in connection with, Nyasaland Field Force during the whole war. *Addresses*: Tigh-na-Creige, Lochmaddy, North Uist, N.B.; Port Herald, Nyasaland, Africa. *Club*: Caledonian. (O8398)

MacDONALD, Major Ranald, O.B.E., M.D., R.A.M.C. *b.* 1885; *s.* of W. J. MacDonald, M.A., F.R.S.E., of Edinburgh. *Educ.*: Daniel Stewart's Coll., and Edinburgh Univ. Doctor of Medicine. *War Work*: Egypt. *Address*: L.C. Mental Hospital, Colney Hatch, New Southgate. (O6232)

MACDONALD, Ranald, M.B.E., *b.* 25 April, 1895; *s.* of Ranald Macdonald, of Liverpool. *Educ.*: Liverpool Coll., and Queens' Coll., Cambridge. *War Work*: Served with the 15th and 9th Batt. "The King's" (Liverpool) Regt.; wounded at the Battle of Loos, Sept. 1915; Recording Office of 19 Squadron, R.A.F., France, 1917–18; Adjutant of the Royal Air Force School of Navigation and Bomb Dropping, at Andover, Hants. *Address*: 2, Belvidere Road, Prince's Park, Liverpool.

MACDONALD, Ranuld Macintosh, C.B.E. Rendered services during Great War to New Zealand War Contingent Assocn. in London. (C1996)

McDONALD, Rebecca Anne, M.B.E. (M10402)

MACDONALD, Major Reginald Henry, O.B.E., S. Lancs. Regt. (O11781)

MACDONALD, Rev. Robert Gordon, O.B.E., M.A., *b.* 12 Dec. 1885; *s.* of W. J. Macdonald, of Knockbreck House, Tain. *Educ.*: Tain Royal Academy; Aberdeen Univ.; Glasgow U.F.Coll. Scottish Sec., Student Christian Movement. *War Work*: Sec. Y.M.C.A., Third Army Area. *Address*: Knockbreck House, Tain. (O1623)

MACDONALD, Capt. Robert Parker, M.B.E.

MACDONALD, Sheena, Mrs., O.B.E.

MACDONALD, Wilfrid Frank, M.B.E.

MACDONALD, Lieut.-Col. William Marshall, C.B.E. New Zealand Med. Corps. (C848)

McDONELL, Major Aeneas Ranald, C.B.E., 21st Chief Glengarry (*see* BURKE'S *Perrage*), *b.* 8 Aug. 1875; *s.* of Æneas Ranald McDonell, 20th of Glengarry; *m.* Dorah Edith, *d.* of William H. Hartford, of Christchurch, Hants. *Educ.*: St. Paul's School. British Vice-Consul, Baku, S. Russia, 1907–17; British Consul, Tiflis, Caucasus, 1920. *War Work*: Joined Caucasus Military Mission in 1917; served in North Persia and Caucasus, 1918–19. *Address*: Foreign Office, London. *Clubs*: Badminton; Royal Automobile. (C2774)

MACDONELL, Lieut. Ian McLean, M.B.E.

MACDONNELL, Major Alister Maxwell, O.B.E., R.A.S.C.

MACDONNELL, Major Mervyn Sorly, O.B.E.

McDONNELL, Mysie, M.B.E.

MACDONNELL, Richard, M.B.E.

McDONNELL, Walter James, M.B.E.

MACDONOGH, George Frederick, M.B.E.

McDOUALL, Lieut.-Col. Robert, C.B., C.M.G., C.B.E., D.S.O., Officer of Legion of Honour, *b.* 3 Nov. 1871; *s.* of John McDouall, of Stranraer, Scotland; *m.* Mabel Constance, *d.* of Gen. Sir Charles Pennington, K.C.B. (*see* BURKE'S *Peerage*). *Educ.*: Felsted School, and R.M.C., Sandhurst. Joined the Buffs in 1892 and served on active service in the Chitral Relief Force; throughout the South African War; Relief of Kimberley, Paardeberg, etc.; twice mentioned in despatches, and D.S.O.; commanded 1st Batt. The Buffs in the Great War, and commanded an Infantry Brigade with the temporary rank of Brig.-Gen., from July, 1916, to the conclusion of hostilities; subsequently in command of the Base at Dunkirk; seven times mentioned in despatches, Brevet of Lieut.-Col. (C2049)

McDOUGALL, Agnes, Mrs., M.B.E.

McDOUGALL, Alexander Patrick, C.B.E.

McDOUGALL, Brig.-Gen. Alexander, C.B., C.B.E., *b.* 1878 ; *s.* of the late John Tom McDougall, C.M.G. Col. Canadian Forestry Corps, and a T. Brig.-Gen. ; served during Great War, 1915–18 ; Legion of Honour. (C999)

McDOUGALL, Lieut. Alfred, M.B.E., R.E.

McDOUGALL, Donald, M.B.E.

McDOUGALL, Edith, O.B.E.

MACDOUGALL, Major Frederick George, O.B.E., R.E. (I.W.T.)

McDOUGALL, Harold James, M.B.E., A.C.A., *b.* 5 Aug. 1878 ; *s.* of the late Walter McDougall, of Perrymead, Streatham, S.W. ; *m.* Helena Victoria Augusta, *d.* of the late Col. Eardley Maitland, C.B., of Westbourne Terrace, W. *Educ.*: Dulwich Coll. Chartered Accountant. *War Work*: Senior Clerk-in-charge, Vesting Orders Dept. of the Trading with the Enemy Dept., Public Trustee Office, Kingsway. *Address*: 5, St. John's Wood Park, N.W. 8. *Club*: The Drive. (M8878)

MACDOUGALL, Major Ian, O.B.E., *b.* 13 Sept. 1882 ; *s.* of the late Alexander Macdougall, of Fort William, Scotland ; *m.* Marjorie Elizabeth, *d.* of Hugh James McCubbin, of Millbank House, West Derby, Liverpool. *Educ.*: George Watson's Coll., Edinburgh. Farmer. *War Work*: Served in German South-West Campaign (Natal Light Horse) ; in France as Major, 2nd Regt. South African Infantry ; Adjutant, Reserve Batt. South African Infantry ; Commanding 2nd Res. Batt. South African Infantry ; Commandant, South African Contingent, Repatriation Depot, Harehall Hutments, Romford, Essex. *Address*: Catsfold, Henfield, Sussex. (O9016)

McDOUGALL, Major John McI, O.B.E., R.G.A.

McDOUGALL, Lieut.-Col. William Allan, D.S.O., O.B.E., *b.* 5th June, 1868 ; *s.* of John McDougall, of Jedburgh, Scotland. *Educ.*: The Nest Academy, Jedburgh ; New Veterinary Coll., Edinburgh. Appointed to a commission in Royal Army Veterinary Corps in June, 1893. *War Work*: Mobilised with 46th (North Midland) Division, T.F., as A.D.V.S. on outbreak of war ; served continuously with this Division until June, 1917 ; when he was appointed A.D.V.S. I. Corps and served with that Corps until the end of the war. *Address*: The Nest, Jedburgh, Scotland ; Morth Grange, Northlew, North Devon. (O5518)

MacDOUGALL, Alice Mary, Lady PATTEN-, O.B.E. ; *d.* of Major James Horne, of Stirkoke, Caithness ; *m.* Sir James Patten, who assumed the name of MacDougall on succeeding his mother in 1891 (*see* BURKE'S *Landed Gentry*), *s.* of John Patten, Writer to the Signet. *War Work*: President of Red Cross for Argyll ; Chairman of Soldiers' and Sailors' Families Association for North Argyll ; Chairman of Soldiers' and Sailors' War Pensions Committee for Lorn District, Argyll. *Address*: Gallanach, Oban. *Clubs*: Empress ; Queen's, Edinburgh. (O10881)

McDOWALL, Charles, O.B.E.

McDOWELL, Capt. Alexander, O.B.E., R.E.

McDOWELL, Lieut.-Col. Donald Keith, C.M.G., O.B.E., *b.* 16 Sept. 1867 ; *s.* of Col. Edmund Greswold McDowell, C.B., *m.* Bertha Kathleen Mary, *d.* of John Bailey, M.I.C.E. *Educ.*: Berkhampstead, and St. Thomas's Hospital. Late Principal Medical Officer, Federated Malay States. *War Work*: Lieut-Col. R.A.M.C., Aug. 1914, to Oct. 1919. *Address*: c/o Messrs. Holt & Co., 3, Whitehall Place, London, S.W. 1. *Club*: Wellington. (O7423)

McDOWELL, Major Samuel Johnson, O.B.E.

MACE, Comm. Frederick William, O.B.E., R.N.R.

MACE, William Ethrington, M.B.E., *b.* 26 Nov. 1881 ; *s.* of the late William Mace, of Marseilles and London ; *m.* Monica Helen Grace, *d.* of Richard Hemsley, of Montreal. *Educ.*: Durham ; Copenhagen. Investment Banker. *War Work*: Officer in charge Administration, Inspection Depot, Canada Imperial Ministry of Munitions, Ottawa, Canada, 1915–19. *Address*: 451, Mountain Avenue, Westmount, P.Q. *Clubs*: Montreal ; Royal St. Lawrence Yacht. (M3820)

McEACHARN, Capt. Niel Boyd Watson, M.B.E., D.L., K.O.S.B.

McELHONE, William Percy, M.B.E.

McELWAINE, Capt. Erick James Dalby, O.B.E.

MACEWEN, Capt. Andrew Kenneth, O.B.E., R.F.A. (T.); *m.* 27 Nov., 1920, Barbara Hussey Bowen.

McEWAN, Jean Margaret, M.B.E., W.R.N.S.

McEWAN, Lieut.-Comm. John Robert, O.B.E.

McEWEN, Frederick Charles, M.B.E.

MACEWEN, Hugh Allan, O.B.E., D.P.H. (Cantab.), F.R.S.E., *b.* 21 May, 1880 ; *s.* of Sir William Macewen, F.R.S., of 3, Woodside Crescent, Glasgow (*see* BURKE'S *Peerage*). *Educ.*: Univ. of Glasgow ; Univ. Coll., London ; Heidelberg. Medical Officer, Ministry of Health ; late Medical Officer of Health for Fife and Kinross ; Assistant Medical Officer of Health for Cumberland ; Lecturer on Hygiene, Cooper Medical Coll., San Francisco ; Resident Physician Belvedere Fever Hospital, Glasgow, etc. *Addresses*: Ministry of Health, Whitehall, S.W. 1 ; 5, Suffield Chambers, 79, Davies Street, W. 1. *Club*: Savage. (O3807)

McEWEN, Major James, O.B.E.

McEWEN, Major Robert James, O.B.E., Can. A.M.C.

McEWEN, Thomas, M.B.E.

MACEWEN, Capt. William, O.B.E., *b.* 2 July, 1886 ; *s.* of Sir William Macewen, C.B., F.R.S., Glasgow (*see* BURKE'S *Peerage*). *Educ.*: Glasgow ; London. Assistant Medical Officer, City of Exeter. *War Work*: O.C. No. 6 Mobile Laboratory (Hygiene), First Army, France, and No. 33 Mobile Laboratory (Hygiene), Third Army, France. *Address*: 5, Friars Walk, Exeter. (O5520)

McEWEN, William Fullerton, O.B.E., M.B.

MACEY, Josiah, M.B.E.

MacFADDEN, Cecil John Read, O.B.E., M.D., C.M.(Edin), *b.* 20 July, 1870 ; *s.* of James MacFadden, J.P., of Portadown, Co. Armagh ; *m.* May, *d.* of David Gibson, of Jonsered, Sweden. *Educ.*: Lurgan Coll., Ireland ; Edinburgh Univ. District Surgeon No. 1 District St. John Ambulance Brigade ; Divisional Surgeon Metropolitan Police ; Councillor, Hampstead Borough Council ; Chairman, Maternity and Child Welfare Committee for the Borough of Hampstead ; Hon. Treas. Hampstead Medical Society. *War Work*: M.O. in Charge Caenwood Towers Military Hospital, Highgate, Cedar Lawn Military Hospital, Hampstead ; M.O. Officers Hostel, Oak Hill Lodge, Hampstead ; Chief Surgeon, St. John Ambulance Brigade, London District Air Raid Organisation ; M.O. Sir Frederick Milner's Hostel for Neurasthenic Soldiers, and of Edith Cavell Home, Hampstead. *Address*: 30, Frognal, Hampstead, N.W. 3. (O4379)

McFADYEN, Lieut.-Col. Duncan, M.B.E., L.R.C.S.E., J.P., *b.* 5 June, 1846 ; *s.* of Duncan McFadyen, of Kilbride, Argyleshire ; *m.* Mary, *d.* of Walter Mundell, of Inverlaul. *Educ.*: Lochgilphead and Glasgow Univ. M.O. 3rd Cameron Highlanders ; M.O. Inverness Post Office ; M.O. for the Parish of Inverness ; Member of the Medical Staff of the Northern Infirmary, Inverness. *War Work*: Mobilised as M.O. 3rd Cameron Highlanders at Aldershot during the Boer War ; during the Great War acted as County Director for Inverness-shire under the British Red Cross Society, and is M.O. for the Highland Volunteers with rank of Captain. *Address*: 94, Academy Street, Inverness. (M8880)

MACFADYEN, Jessie, Mrs., M.B.E.

McFALL, Col. Albert William Crawford, O.B.E., *b.* 19 Feb. 1862 ; *s.* of Lieut.-Col. D. Chambers McFall ; *m.* Anne, *d.* of William Peter, of Glenloth. *Educ.*: Privately. *War Work*: Brigade Major 91st Infantry Brigade ; D.A.A. and Q.M.G. Southern Reserve Centre ; R.A.F. Disciplinary Branch, presiding on Courts Martial and instructing in Military Law. *Address*: The Manor House, Winterborne Zelstone, Blandford, Dorset. (O7426)

MACFARLANE, Capt. Alexander, O.B.E., *b.* 9 Oct. 1874 ; *s.* of Peter Macfarlane, of Port Glasgow ; *m.* Jean, *d.* of David Galloway, of Greenock. *Educ.*: Greenock Academy and Edinburgh Univ. Civil Service. *War Work*: Engaged in various Civil Service Departments. *Address*: 4, Devonshire Road, Davenport Park, Stockport. *Clubs*: National Liberal ; Davenport. (O10886)

McFARLANE, Andrew, O.B.E.

MACFARLANE, Edith Mary, Mrs., O.B.E.

MACFARLANE, Major Fane Andrew James, D.S.O., O.B.E., Capt. London Regt. ; D.A.Q.M.G. with rank of Major ; served during Great War, 1914–18 (mentioned in despatches). (O8594)

MACFARLANE, Hugh, O.B.E.

MACFARLANE, James Arthur Henderson, M.B.E.

MACFARLANE, James Colquhoun, O.B.E.

MACFARLANE, James Wallace, O.B.E.

McFARLANE, John Miller, O.B.E.

McFARLANE, Joseph, O.B.E.

MacFARLANE, Lauchlan Grant, O.B.E., *b.* 1 Jan., 1861 ; *s.* of Archibald MacFarlane, of Johnstone ; *m.* Helen Campbell Wylie, *d.* of John Wylie, of Largs. *Educ.*: Elderslie Wallace School, and Andersonian Coll., Glasgow. Manager of Submarine and Oil Engine Department, Cammell, Laird, Birkenhead. *War Work*: Submarines and Oil Engines. *Address*: 10, Princes Park Mansions, Liverpool. (O3609)

MACFARLANE, Malcolm, O.B.E.

MACFARLANE, Peter, O.B.E., J.P.

MACFARLANE, Stuart Gordon, M.B.E. (M10304)

MACFARLANE, Walter Mace, M.B.E.

MACFARLANE, Col. David James MASON-, C.M.G., C.B.E., T.D., M.D. (Edin. Univ.), 4th Seaforth Highlanders, *b.* 22 Nov. 1862 ; *s.* of David Mason, of Edinburgh, assumed by Royal Licence, 1909, Maternal Surname of MacFarlane ; *m.* Mary Blanche, *d.* of Francis Edmund Anstie, M.D.(Lond.), F.R.C.P.(Eng.), of London. *Educ.*: Edinburgh Institution and University of Edinburgh,. Practised as Physician in Maidenhead from 1888–1907 ; retired from practice on account of ill health, 1907 ; served in 4th Royal Berkshire Regiment from 1890–1913 ; rose from Subaltern to Major ; transferred Feb. 1913 to command 4th Batt. Seaforth Highlanders. *War Work*: Mobilised in Aug. 1914 ; commanded 4th Batt. Seaforth Highlanders and took the Batt. to France Nov. 1914 ; Dangerously wounded at battle of Neuve-Chapelle, March, 1915 ; received C.M.G. after the battle : in hospital for several months ; Feb. 1916 posted to command 4th Reserve Batt. Seaforth Highlanders, Commanded this Batt. until March, 1919, providing reinforcements for the 51st Division ; thrice mentioned in despatches. *Address*: Turin, Forfarshire, Scotland. *Clubs*: Arts ; Bath. (C1690)

McFERRAN, Lieut.-Col. Edwin Millar Gilliland, C.B.E. Lieut.-Col. 4th Batt. Royal Irish Rifles ; served in S. Africa, 1901–2 (Queen's medal with five clasps) ; during Great War, 1914–19 (mentioned in despatches). (C1678)

McFERRAN, Emily, M.B.E., *b.* 28 May, 1859 ; *d.* of Henry McFerran, J.P., of Newtown Hamilton, Co. Armagh, Ireland. *Educ.*: Privately. *War Work*: Head of Work Depot ; Organiser of Our Day Collections in Newtown Hamilton, Co. Armagh district during war ; also worked in Sphagnum Moss Depot. *Address*: Newtown Hamilton, Co. Armagh. (M2086)

McFERRAN, Helen Sarah, M.B.E.; *d.* of John McFerran, of The Barn, Carrickfergus, Co. Antrim. *War Work :* Commandant V.A.D. Auxiliary Hospital, Tickford Abbey ; Manager and Hon. Sec. North Bucks. War Hospital Supply Depot at Newport Pagnell. *Address :* Walton Manor, Bletchley, Bucks. (M8881)

McFERRAN, Howard Addison, O.B.E.

MACFIE, Mary Jane, Mrs., M.B.E., *b.* 22 Feb. 1855 ; *d.* of Charles Lloyd, of Waunifor, Maesycrugian, Carmarthenshire ; *m.* David Johnstone, *s.* of William Macfie, of Langhouse, Inverkip, Renfrewshire. *Educ. :* Privately. *War Work :* Chairman No. 1 Sub-Committee, Midlothian War Pensions ; Interviewer for Board of Agriculture (Women's Land Army for Border District) ; Chairman War Pensions Sub-Committee, Heriot and Stow ; Member of Midlothian Military Selection Board. *Address :* Borthwick Hall, Heriot, Midlothian. *Club :* Queen's. (M8882)

MACFIE, Major Ronald Bute, O.B.E., M.B., Ch.B., F.R.C.S.(Edin.), R.A.M.C., *b.* 28 June, 1887 ; *s.* of Daniel Macfie, of Edinburgh ; *m.* Monica Enid, *d.* of Rev. George R. Taylor, of Newcastle-on-Tyne. *Educ. :* George Watson's Coll., Edinburgh. Surgeon-in-charge, Orthopædic Clinic, St. Martin's, Cheltenham ; Medical Referee, Ministry of Pensions. *War Work :* Second Surgeon 36th C.C.S. France ; Surgical Specialist 55th C.C.S. France ; R.A.M.C., 1914 to 1919. *Address :* Segrave House, Cheltenham. (O5521)

McGAVIN, Lawrie Hugh, C.B.E., F.R.C.S.(Eng.), *b.* Nov. 1868 ; *s.* of John McGavin, of Calcutta, and Ayr, N.B. ; *m.* Edith Mary, *d.* of Horatio Beauchamp, of Melbourne. *Educ. :* Fettes Coll. ; R.M.C. Sandhurst ; Guy's Hospital. Consulting Surgeon ; Surgeon to the Dreadnought Hospital and to the Hospital for Women. *War Work :* Surgeon to the King George, Endsleigh Palace, Michie, R.A.F. and Farnborough Court Military Hospitals ; Member of the Emergency Surgical Aid Corps and Final Appea Board of Medical Assessors. *Addresses :* 32, Weymouth Street, W. 1 ; Moons Mill, Blackboys, Sussex. *Club :* Royal Automobile. (C3119)

McGAVIN, Maude, M.B.E.

MacGEAGH, Lieut.-Col. Henry Davies Foster, C.B.E., B.A., *b.* 21 Oct. 1883 ; *s.* of Foster MacGeagh, late of Hadlow Castle, Kent ; *m.* Rita, *d.* of the late William Kiddle, of Walbundrie, New South Wales. *Educ. :* St. Paul's, and Magdalen Coll., Oxford. Barrister-at-Law of the Middle Temple and South Eastern Circuit. *War Work :* 1st Batt. London Rifle Brigade ; Assist. Adjutant-General, War Office, since 1918 ; D.A.A.G., 1917 ; Military Assistant to the Judge Advocate-General, 1916–20 ; served in France and Belgium, 1914–15 ; mentioned in despatches ; Brevet-Majority, 1914 Star and clasp. *Addresses :* 29, Charles Street, Berkeley Square, W. 1 ; 2, Garden Court, Temple, E.C. *Clubs :* Arthur's ; Conservative ; Ranelagh ; Leander ; St. George's Hill Golf. (C826)

McGEORGE, Mary, Mrs., M.B.E., *b.* 7 May, 1867 ; *d.* of C. J. Bertram, of Newcastle on-Tyne ; *m.* David, *s.* of R. McGeorge, of Dumfries. *Educ. :* High School, Gateshead-on-Tyne. *War Work :* Commandant Dumfries Red Cross Auxiliary Hospital, 1914–19 ; Vice-President B.R.C.S. for Dumfries Burgh. *Address :* Dock Park House, Dumfries, Scotland. (M8883)

McGEOUGH, Alexander, O.B.E.

McGEVOR, Capt. John, M.B.E.

MACGIBBON, Mabel Jane, M.B.E.

McGIFFIN, Surg.-Lieut.-Comm. Robert Hunter, O.B.E., M.B., R.N.

McGILCHRIST, Thomas Brown, M.B.E.

McGILL, Alice Mary, Mrs., M.B.E.

McGILL, Edmund Allan, M.B.E.

MACGILL, George, M.B.E., L.R.C.S., L.R.C.P.

McGILL, Thomas Carlisle, M.B.E.

McGILLIVRAY, Lieut. Clifford, M.B.E.

MACGILLIVRAY, Capt. Gordon Leslie, O.B.E.

McGILLIVRAY, Major Percy Cranwell, O.B.E. Can. A.S.C.

McGILORAY James Anderson, M.B.E.

McGLINN, Brig.-Gen. John Patrick, C.M.G., C.B.E., Lieut.-Col. and T. Brig.-Gen. Australian Inf. ; S. Africa, 1900 (Queen's medal with six clasps) ; Great War, 1914–19, on Staff (despatches). (C845)

McGONIGAL, Margaret Dorothy, M.B.E.

McGOWAN, Sir Harry Duncan, K.B.E., *b.* 1874 ; *m.* Jean Boyle Young, of Paisley. Chairman and Managing Director, Nobel's Explosive Co., Ltd. ; Director of Canadian Explosives, Ltd., British Dyestuffs Corporation, Ltd., Dunlop Rubber Co., Ltd. *Address :* Abbotstall, Maxwell Park, Glasgow. *Clubs :* Bath ; Carlton ; Conservative (Glasgow). (K159)

McGOWAN, Capt. Henry Edward, M.B.E.

McGOWAN, James, O.B.E.

McGOWAN, James, O.B.E., *Educ. :* Dumfries Academy, and Durham Coll. of Science. Civil Servant ; formerly Surveyor of Taxes at Aberdeen, and Lands Valuation and Registration Assessor for the City of Aberdeen, and County of Kincardine ; now H.M. Superintending Inspector of Taxes at Somerset House. *Address :* 10, Woodland Gardens, N. 10. (O10889)

McGOWAN, Capt. James Alexander, O.B.E.

McGOWAN, Margaret Jane, Mrs., M.B.E., *b.* 18 Dec. 1877 ; *m.* Robert George McGowan. *Educ. :* Privately. *War Work :* Lady Superintendent of Shenstone House Auxiliary Hospital, Manchester. *Address :* 1, Thomas Street, Cheetham Hill, Manchester. (M8887)

McGRATH, Lieut. Harry Nisbet, O.B.E., R.N.V.R.

McGRATH, the Hon. Sir Patrick Thomas, K.B.E., LL.D., *b.* 16 Dec. 1868 ; *s.* of William McGrath. *Educ. :* Christian Brothers' Schools, St. John's, Nfld. Joined reporting staff of " Daily Herald " ; Acting Editor, 1893 ; Editor, 1894–1907 ; established " Evening Chronicle," 1912 ; held secretarial posts to various Government Commissions and Councils in Newfoundland ; Hon. Sec. Newfoundland Patriotic Fund, Newfoundland Regt. Finance Committee, and Newfoundland War Pensions Board, since Aug. 1914 ; Chairman, Cost of Living Commission, 1917. *Address :* 6, Gower Street, St. John's, Newfoundland. *Club :* B.I.S. (St. John's). (K121)

McGRATH, Lieut.-Comm. Redmond Walter, O.B.E., R.N.V.R.

McGRATH, Wellington Albert, M.B.E.

McGRATH, Lieut. William Henry, M.B.E., I.A.R.O.

McGREER, Rev. Arthur Huffman, O.B.E., M.C.

McGREGOR, Capt. Alexander Muir, O.B.E.

MACGREGOR, Major Alexander Stewart Murray, O.B.E., M.D., R.A.M.C. (T.).

MACGREGOR, Archibald Bow, M.B.E.

MACGREGOR, Capt. James St. Cuthbert, O.B.E., R.F.A,

MACGREGOR John, C.B.E., M.I.E.E. *Educ. :* Dollar. Managing Director Gloucester Railway Carriage and Wagon Co. ; Director Wagon Repairs, Ltd. *War Work :* Chairman Directing Board National Filling Factory No. 5 ; Member of Gloucester City Tribunal, Pensions Committee, and Labour Advisory Committee. *Address :* Falklands, Gloucester. *Club :* Gloucester. (C2775)

MACGREGOR, John, O.B.E.

MACGREGOR, John Alister, M.B.E., J.P., *b.* 27 Sept, 1874 ; *s.* of John Macgregor, of Balmenach, Cromdale, Morayshire ; *m.* Jemima Fanny, *d.* of William Ogilvy Cunningham, of Hillside, Broughty Ferry, Forfarshire. *Educ. :* Merchiston Castle, and Edinburgh Univ. *War Work :* Assistant County Director for the County of the City of Dundee ; Assistant to the Red Cross Commissioner for the Central Eastern District of Scotland. *Address :* Hurst Grange, Twyford, Berks. *Club :* Sports. (M8889)

MACGREGOR, John Julius, C.B.E., M.I.E.E.

McGREGOR, Lieut.-Col. John Robertson, O.B.E.

MACGREGOR, Joseph, M.B.E.

McGREGOR, Pura, Mrs., M.B.E.

MACGREGOR, Robert William, M.B.E., *b.* 9 May, 1886; *s.* of Alexander MacGregor, of Greenock ; *m.* Robina Garson, *d.* of James Scarth, of Birsay, Orkney. *Educ. :* Greenock Higher Grade, and Technical Schools. Chemical Engineers. *War Work :* Engineer for construction of Longparish Wood Distillation Factory ; appointed Superintendent when taken over by Ministry of Munitions. *Address :* 1237, Meridian Street, Fall River, Mass., U.S.A. (M2090)

McGRIGOR, Major Dalziel Buchanan, O.B.E., M.B., Ch.B., *b.* 20 Jan. 1885 ; *s.* of late James McGrigor, of Aberdeen, N.B. ; *m.* Dorothy Macgregor, *d.* of Alexander J. Macgregor Drysdale, of London Lieut. R.A.M.C. July, 1907 ; Capt. Jan. 1911 ; Major, July, 1919. Served in India, Sept. 1909 to Sept. 1914 ; France, Sept. 1914 to April, 1916 ; India, April, 1916 to Nov. 1918 ; D.A.D.M.S., Northern Command, York, Dec. 1918 to June, 1920. *Address :* Lag-Na-Ha, 17, Palace Road, Streatham Hill. *Club :* Caledonian. (O8869)

McGRIGOR, Margaret Anne Kay, Mrs., O.B.E., *b.* 2 March, 1865 ; *d.* of Sir John Muir, Bart., of Deanston House, Perthshire (*see* BURKE's *Peerage*) ; *m.* Alexander, *s.* of Alexander Bennett McGrigor, of Cairnoch. *War Work :* Organiser and Vice-President Argyll and Sutherland Highlanders Prisoners of War Fund and Stirlingshire Work Depot ; Vice-President Stirlingshire Branch British Red Cross Society ; Convener Stirlingshire V.A.D. Selection Committee. *Addresses :* Cairnoch by Cambusbarum, Stirling ; Beechwood, Stirling. *Clubs :* Queen's, Edinburgh ; Kelvin, Glasgow. (O3819)

MACGUCKIN, Charles John Graham, C.B.E., M.Inst.C.E., M.I.M.E., *b.* 26 Jan. 1884 ; *s.* of Neal MacGuckin, J.P., of Ballinderry, Co. Derry ; *m.* Anna, *d.* of James Malone, of Cookstown. *Educ. :* St. Mary's Coll., Dundalk. Local Director, Sir W. G. Armstrong, Whitworth & Co., Elswick Works, Newcastle-on-Tyne. *War Work :* In charge of Armstrong's Ammunition Factories from June, 1916, to end of war. *Address :* South House, Grainger Park Road, Newcastle-on-Tyne. *Club :* Junior Carlton. (C556)

McGUGAN, Capt. Donald, O.B.E., M.C.

McGUINESS, Mary Jane, M.B.E.

McGUINNESS, Capt. Charles Hamilton, O.B.E.

McGUINNESS, Ethel Theresa, M.B.E.

McGUINNESS, Nora Mary Ursula, M.B.E. ; *d.* of James McGuinness, of Felling-on-Tyne. *Educ. :* Convent of the Assumption, Richmond and France. *War Work :* Hon. Sec. of the Tyneside-Irish Brigade for two years ; Red Cross War Relief work ; nursed in France under the French Red Cross. *Address :* Shanid, Felling-on-Tyne, Co. Durham. (M8890)

MACGUIRE, Lieut. Edward Robert Mileson, M.B.E.

McGUIRE, Capt. George Patrick, O.B.E., *b.* 18 Dec. 1889 ; *s.* of George McGuire, of Ulverston ; *m.* Mabel Gladys, *d.* of Arthur Craven, of Hallas Hall, Cullingworth, Yorks. *Educ. :* Bradford Grammar School, and King William's Coll. Engineer. *War Work :* Joined R.N.A.S. Oct. 1914 ; transferred to 1/4th Duke of Wellington's (W.R.) Regt. Feb. 1915 ; active service in France, April, 1915, to Dec. 1919 ; Staff Capt.

G.H.Q. Jan. 1918; D.A.Q.M.G., G.H.Q. March, 1918, to Dec. 1919. *Address:* The Bungalow, Freshwater Bay, Isle of Wight. *Clubs:* Junior Army and Navy; English, Hurlingham Buenos Aires. (O2627)

McGUIRE, Major Michael, O.B.E.

McGUIRK, Lieut. Henry Francis, M.B.E.

McGUISE, T. Capt. Bernard Aloysius, O.B.E., R.A.V.C.

MACGURK, Capt. Nioll Austin, O.B.E., I.A.R.O.

MacGWIRE, Major and Brevet Lieut.-Col. John Edward, C.B.E., R.A.S.C., *b.* 14 April, 1878; *s.* of John Frederick Kane MccGwire; *m.* Jean Elizabeth, *d.* of Col. Henry Benjamin Naylor Adair, late Royal Engineers. *Educ.:* Privately. 2nd Lieut. 5th Batt. the Royal Fusiliers (Militia), 1900; served South African War, 1901–2 (Queen's S.A. Medal and 5 clasps); entered Army Service Corps, 1903; Lieut. 1905; Capt. 1912; T. Major, 1914; Major, 1916; T. Lieut.-Col. 1917–19; Brevet Lieut.-Col. 1918; served European War in France and Belgium, 1914; Staff Capt. at War Office, 1916; Deputy Assistant Director at War Office, 1917; entered the Middle Temple, 1911; called to Bar, 1917; 1914 Star and clasp, War Medal, and Victory Medal; thrice mentioned in Sec. of State for War's Lists. *Club:* Army and Navy. (C2139)

McHAFFIE, Major George Addison, O.B.E.

McHARDY, William, O.B.E.

MACHTIG, Eric, M.B.E.

McHUGH, Rev. Daniel John, O.B.E.

McHUGH, Harry Ralph, M.B.E.

MACHUTCHON, Capt. Edwin Gray, O.B.E., R.E. (T.).

McILROY, Anne Louise, O.B.E., M.D.

McILVENNA, James Graham, M.B.E.

MACILVENNA, Capt. John, O.B.E., R.A.V.C.

MACINDOE, Capt. James Douglas, O.B.E., M.C., Scots Guards, *b.* 31 Dec. 1888; *s.* of J. Black Macindoe, of Glasgow; *m.* Mary Margaret, *d.* of Capt. F. Hungerford Pollen, R.N., C.B.E., of Farley, Reigate. *Educ.:* Cayifield; Fettes; Sandhurst. *Address:* 43, Norfolk Square, Hyde Park. *Clubs:* Guards'; White's; Pratt's. (O7428)

MACINDOE, Major Robert Hall Forman, O.B.E., Aust. A.V.C.

McINERNEY, Margueratta, Mrs., O.B.E.

MacINNES, Mary, O.B.E.

MACINNIS, Major Carlyle William, O.B.E.

McINTOSH, Alexander, M.B.E., *b.* 13 Feb. 1873; *s.* of William McIntosh, of Tollomill. Inverkeithney, Banffshire; *m.* Agnes, *d.* of Andrew Howie, of Crosslet, Dumbarton. Banker. *War Work:* Sec. and Treas. of Naval and Military War Pensions and Dumbarton War Fund Committees. *Addresses:* Netherdale, Dumbarton; Commercial Bank, Dumbarton. *Clubs:* Dumbarton Philosophical Society; Dumbarton Bowling. (M8891)

McINTOSH, Alexander Hugh, M.B.E., *b.* 23 Aug. 1871; *s.* of David McIntosh, of Kirkwall; *m.* Isaline, *d.* of Pierre Dizins, of Albens, Savoie, France. *Educ.:* Kirkwall Burgh School, and Privately. War Office Clerk. *Address:* 9, Ruskin Walk, Herne Hill, S.E. 24. (M8892)

McINTOSH, Annie, C.B.E., R.R.C., Medaille d'Honneur (argent) l'assistance publique, Paris, 1914, *d.* of Donald McIntosh, J.P., of Bromyard, Herefordshire. *Educ.:* Wolverhampton High School for Girls. Matron and Superintendent of Nursing, St. Bartholomew's Hospital; Member of Committee of Nurses' Insurance Society; Nurses' Representative of Nurses' Policy Holders, National Pension Fund for Nurses; Member of College of Nursing (Limited). *War Work:* Was a member of Committee for Supply of Nurses by War Office, 1916; Member of Committee of Queen Alexandra's War Relief Fund for Nurses. *Address:* St. Bartholomew's Hospital, West Smithfield, E.C. 1.

MACINTOSH, John, O.B.E., M.D.

McINTOSH, John, M.B.E.

McINTYRE, Major Donald, M.B.E., M.B.Ch.B., F.R.C.S. Ed., L.M., *b.* 1891; *s.* of Donald McIntyre, of Greenock. *Educ.:* Glasgow Univ. Surgeon. *War Work:* Royal Army Medical Corps, Special Reserve; Active Service with Dardanelles Army and East African Forces; mentioned in despatches. *Address:* 36, Lansdowne Crescent, Kelvinside, Glasgow. (M5058)

McINTYRE, Donald Arderne, M.B.E., J.P., *b.* 6 July, 1857; *s.* of Malcolm McIntyre, of Glen Etive, Argyllshire, Scotland; *m.* Florence Maud Philipson, *d.* of Frederick Philipson Stow, of Nuneaton, Warwickshire. *Educ.:* Diocesan Coll., Rondebosch, Cape Province, S.Africa. Retired Civil Servant. O.C., Town Guard, George, in Boer War; Hon. Sec. Royal Automobile Club of South Africa. *War Work:* Hospital Transport work in connection with sick and wounded soldiers performed by the members of the Royal Automobile Club of South Africa during the War. *Address:* Park Road, Rondebosch, C.P., South Africa. *Club:* Civil Service, Cape Town. (M6363)

MACINTYRE, Capt. Duncan Charles, O.B.E., Order of the Sacred Treasure of Japan, R.N.R., *b.* 1864; *s.* of Ronald George Macintyre, of Glencoe, Inverness-shire, Scotland; *m.* Violet Frances, *d.* of Rev. G. Hesketh Biggs, Vicar of Ettington, Warwickshire. Port Officer. Harbour-master, and Marine Magistrate, Penang, Straits Settlement. *War Work:* Resident Naval Officer, Penang, H.M.S. "Tamar"; Member representing unofficial members Legislative Council on Military Tribunal; Resident Sec. at Penang, Govt. Control Shipping; Agent Food Control at Penang. (O8399)

MACINTYRE, Duncan Mackinnon, M.B.E.

MACKINTYRE, Lieut. Francis Peter, O.B.E., T. Major, 14th Hussars. (O11945c)

MACINTYRE, James Colin. M.B.E.

McINTYRE, James Lewis, O.B.E., M.A., D.Sc., F.E.I.S., J.P., *b.* 13 July, 1868; *s.* of the late James McIntyre, of "Scotsman," Edinburgh; *m.* Jane Russell, *d.* of the late Rev. Adam Ross, M.A., of U.F. Church, Rattray, Perthshire. *Educ.:* George Watson's Coll., Edinburgh; Univ. Edinburgh; Univ. Coll., Oxford; Freiburg i/B.; Berlin; Halle. Lecturer on Comparative Psychology, Aberdeen University, and Training Centre. *War Work:* Member of Aberdeenshire Branch B.R.C.S. Executive Committee, 1914; County Director of V.D. organisation, 1917; Volunteer, Special Constable, Munitions-worker; organisation work in connection with plot-holders' association; Member of the Advisory Committee, and of County Emergency Committee. *Address:* Abbotsville, Cults, Aberdeenshire. *Club:* Aberdeen Univ. (O10892)

MACINTYRE, John Andrew, O.B.E., B.Sc. (Lond.), *b.* 6 Sept. 1881; *s.* of Malcolm Macintyre, of Honolulu; *m.* Agnes, *d.* of Henry Bett, of Edinburgh. *Educ.:* Daniel Stewart's Coll.; Heriot Watt Coll.; Edinburgh Univ. Engineer. Senior Engineer, H.M. Office of Works. *War Work:* Engineering work in connection with National Filling Factories and other Munition Services. (O10893)

McINTYRE, Major Peter, O.B.E., R.A.V.C. (T.).

McINTYRE, Professor Ronald George, O.B.E., B.D., M.A.

McINTYRE, William, M.B.E.

MACIVER, Agnes Edith Stewart, M.B.E.

McIVER, Capt. Walter, M.B.E.

MACK, Peter, M.B.E.

MACKARNESS, Mildred Blankley, Mrs., M.B.E.

McKAY, Benjamin Thomas, C.B.E. Acting Manager, Australian Small Arms Factory. (C715)

MACKAY, Christian Frances Nora, M.B.E., Medaille des Epidémics, *b.* 30 May, 1887; *d.* of Col. J. F. Mackay, C.B.E., V.D., of Whitehouse, Cramond. *Educ.:* Bushey Heath, Herts; Edinburgh; Paris Universities. *War Work:* Attached S.W. Hospital, Abbaye de Royaumont, France, for 2½ years; Administrative and Executive posts as an official in the Q.M.A.A.C., from Aug. 1917 to Oct. 1919. *Address:* Whitehouse, Cramond Bridge, Midlothian. (M6672)

MACKAY, Daniel Sayre, O.B.E.

MACKAY, Capt. Donald Morrison, O.B.E., Can. A.O.C.

MACKAY, Capt. Frank Forbes, M.B.E.

McKAY, Hugh Victor, C.B.E., for services rendered to war industries during Great War. (C364)

MACKAY, Isobelle Mary Agnes, Mrs., M.B.E.

MACKAY, Col. and Hon. James Alexander Kenneth, C.B., O.B.E., F.R.G.S., *b.* 1859; *s.* of the late Alexander Mackay, of Wallendbeen, N.S. Wales; *m.* Mabel Katherine, *d.* of John Coppick White. *Educ.:* Camden Coll., and Grammar School, Sydney. Raised and Commanded 1st Australian Vol. Horse; raised W. Camden Light Horse; was a M.L.A. (Burrow Div.), 1898–9; Chief Staff Officer and A.A.G., Oversea Colonial Forces, Cape Town; served in S. Africa, 1900–1, as Col. 6th Imperial Bushmen (despatches); is a M.L.C. of N.S. Wales; Vice-Pres. of Executive Council; Chairman of Papuan Royal Commn. 1907; appointed |Brig. Australian Light Horse Brig. 1912; Director-Gen. Australian Army Reserve, 1916. *Address:* Wallandoon Station, Wallendbeen, N.S. Wales. *Clubs:* Australian and Imperial Service (Sydney). (O11992)

MACKAY, Lieut. James Eugene, M.B.E.

MACKAY, Lieut.-Col. and Hon. Col. James Francis, C.B.E., V.D., J.P. (Midlothian), R.G.A., Vol. and T.F., *b.* 6 April, 1855; *s.* of John Mackay, of Inveralmond, Cramond, Midlothian; *m.* Annie Alma, *d.* of David Croall, of Southfield, Midlothian. *Educ.:* Edinburgh Univ. Member of the Midlothian County Council. *War Work:* Commander of Artillery Depot, R.G.A., T.F.; also served on the recruiting Staff in Edinburgh, and latterly acted as military representative to the City of Edinburgh Tribunal. *Address:* White House, Cramond, Midlothian. *Club:* Northern, Edinburgh. (C2776)

MACKAY, John George, M.B.E.

McKAY, Mary, M.B.E.

MACKAY, Murdoch, M.B.E., *b.* 6 May, 1857. Chief Traffic Inspector, Highland Railway. *War Work:* Movement of Military and Naval Forces in the north of Scotland during the war. *Address:* Alfred Villa, 30, Union Road, Inverness. (M8895)

MACKAY, Neil, O.B.E.

MACKAY, Nora, O.B.E.

MACKAY, Rev. Patrick Robson, C.B.E.

MACKAY, Capt. Robert Henry Ramsay, O.B.E., R.N.

McKAY, Capt. Robert James, C.B.E., D.S.O., M.C. Capt. Argyll and Sutherland Highlanders; Great War, 1914–16 (mentioned in despatches). (C5443)

MACKAY, Robert John, C.B.E., *b.* 1859; *s.* of the late Robert Gordon Mackay, of Edinburgh; *m.* Edith Margaret Mary, *d.* of the late Henry Baxter, of Glasgow. *Educ.:* Edinburgh Institution School, Edinburgh Univ., and Univ. Coll., Oxford. Entered Sec.'s Office, Gen. Post Office, 1883, and became Principal Clerk, 1903; British Delegate to International Telegraph Conferences at Budapest, 1896; London, 1903; Lisbon, 1908; International Wireless Conferences at Berlin, 1903 and 1906; London, 1912; Knight of Order of Dannebrog of Denmark. *Address:* 1, Beulah Hill, Upper Norwood, S.E. (C557)

MACKAY, Capt. Robert Whyte, O.B.E., 1/7 Batt. The Gordon Highlanders, *b.* 24 March, 1874 ; *s.* of Robert Whyte Mackay, of 30, Albyn Place, Aberdeen ; *m.* Margarette Hyde, *d.* of Dr. T. W. H. Garstang, of Brit. Med. Assoc., London. *Educ.:* Aberdeen Grammar School ; Blairlodge School, Stirlingshire ; Heriot-Watt Coll., Edinburgh ; and Aberdeen Univ. Partner in the firm of Anderson and Thomson, Wholesale Woollen Merchants, Aberdeen, established in 1773. *War Work:* Served with the 7th Batt. Gordon Highlanders from 1914, until Feb. 1919 ; 4 years 8 months embodied service ; 3 years 4 months in France with the 51st (Highland) Division ; mentioned in despatches, April, 1919. *Address:* Alt-na-Braigh, Milltimber, by Aberdeen ; 103, Union Street, Aberdeen.
(O5524)

MACKAY, William George Scott, M.B.E., *b.* 15 Sept. 1889 ; *s.* of James Balfour Mackay, of Kinlochbervie, Sutherland ; *m.* Ella May, *d.* of William George Peacock, of Hyderabad, Deccan. *Educ.:* Cathedral High School, Bombay, India. Engineer, H.M. Mint, Bombay, India. *War Work:* Superintendent of Munitions Dept., H.M. Mint, Bombay, India. *Address:* 12, Kitteredge Road, Colaba Reclamation, Bombay, India.
(M6198)

McKAY, Major William Kirby, O.B.E., R.M.L.C.

MACKAY, Major William Murray, O.B.E., T.D., M.B., Ch.B., *b.* June 1875 ; *s.* of Alexander Mackay, J.P., of Black Hambledon and Crook, Durham ; *m.* Winifreda Jane Taylor or Mackay, *d.* of Rev. G. R. Taylor, of Byker, Newcastle-on-Tyne. *Educ.:* Durham School and Edinburgh Univ. Medical Officer to 6th Batt. Durham L.I. ; served 5 years in Edinburgh Univ. Corps, 1894–99 ; 2 year as Civil Surgeon to South African Field Forces (Medal and 4 clasps) ; continual service in volunteers and territorials during 23 years in R.A.M., C.T.F. *War Work:* Aug. 1914, to Dec. 1918, with various units as Major, R.A.M.C. (T.) ; wounded at Ypres, 1915 ; Territorial Officers' Decoration. *Address:* Wheatbottom, Crook, Co. Durham. *Clubs:* O.D.'s, Durham, and Crook Golf.
(O8870)

McKEARTAN, Mary, Mrs., M.B.E.

McKECHNIE, Capt. George, M.B.E.

McKECHNIE, Sir James, K.B.E., Director Vickers, Ltd., with control of their Naval Construction Works, Barrow-in-Furness ; Chairman of the Ioco Rubber and Waterproofing Co., Ltd., Glasgow ; Director of Contraflo Condenser and Kinetic Air Pump Co., Ltd. ; Vickers-Petters, Ltd. ; Canadian Vickers, Ltd. ; The Donaldson South American Line, Ltd., ; Centrifugal Separators, Ltd. ; The Isle of Walney Estates Co., Ltd. : awarded Grand Cross and Star as a Knight Commander of the Ancient Royal Order of Isabel la Catolica by the Queen Regent of Spain for work done whilst Engineer-in-Chief of Naval Works in Spain ; Member of Management Committee of the Engineering and the National Employers' Federation ; Member of Executive Council and Trustee of Foremen's Mutual Benefit Society ; Member of Council of Institution of Naval Architects ; Member of Institution of Civil Engineers ; Institution of Mechanical Engineers ; Liveryman of the Worshipful Company of Shipwrights ; Fellow of the Society of Antiquaries of Scotland ; has contributed several papers on technical subjects to Professional Societies. *War Work:* Responsible for the initiation and construction of the large extensions at the Barrow Works to meet the demands of the Naval, Military, and Air Forces ; under his direction the works produced complete all classes of war vessels, including battleships and submarines, mercantile ships, the largest types of naval gun mountings, airships, howitzers and projectiles of all types and sizes ; he was also responsible to the Ministry of Munitions for the erection and management of the National Projectile Factory, Lancaster, and the National Filling Factory, Morecambe. *Addresses:* 4, Whitehall Court, S.W. 1 ; The Abbey House, Furness Abbey, Lancashire. *Clubs:* Junior Carlton ; British Empire ; Royal Automobile ; Pilgrims'.
(K96)

MACKENSIE, Helen, C.B.E. Joint Sec. New Zealand War Contingent Assocn.
(C726)

MACKENZIE, Sir Alexander, K.B.E., *b.* 30 June, 1860 ; *s.* of Donald Mackenzie, of Kincardine, Canada ; *m.* May, *d.* of S. H. Blake, K.C., of Toronto, Canada. *Educ.:* Canada. Barrister and Solicitor ; President of various Public Utility Companies in Brazil. *Addresses:* 12, Hyde Park Place, W. 2 ; Avenida Atlantica 594, Rio de Janeiro, Brazil.
(K229)

MACKENZIE, Capt. Alexander, O.B.E., R.A.V.C., (T.), *b.* 1 Dec. 1885 ; *s.* of Alexander Mackenzie, of 115, South Street, St. Andrews. *Educ.:* Madras Coll. ; St. Andrews ; and Royal (Dick) Veterinary Coll., Edinburgh. Veterinary Surgeon. *War Work:* Attached Veterinary Hospital and in the Field with 51st, 55th, and 12th Divisions ; mentioned in despatches. *Address:* 115, South Street, St. Andrews.
(O5256)

MACKENZIE, Capt. Alexander Donald, O.B.E., R.E. (T.).

MACKENZIE, Major Colin, O.B.E., M.D., B.Ch. (Cantab.), F.R.C.S. (Eng.), R.A.M.C., *b.* 9 June, 1883 ; *s.* of Alexander George Mackenzie, of London ; *m.* Edith Annie, *d.* of David W. Rice, of Shaftesbury. *Educ.:* Eastbourne Coll. ; Emmanuel Coll., Cambridge ; Middlesex Hospital, London. Hon. Assistant Surgeon to the Royal Infirmary, Bradford. *War Work:* Mobilised Aug. 1914 ; served throughout the war in France and Flanders till March, 1919 ; Surgical Specialist and Officer in charge of Surgical Division, No. 14 General Hospital ; mentioned in despatches. *Address:* 1, Camden Terrace, Manningham Lane, Bradford.
(O5525)

MACKENZIE, Lieut.-Col. Colin Mansfield, D.S.O., O.B.E. Major and T. Lieut.-Col. London Regt. ; served in Great War, 1914–19 (mentioned in despatches).
(O7430)

MACKENZIE, Donald, M.B.E.

MACKENZIE, Dorothy Helen, Mrs., M.B.E.

MACKENZIE, Dorothy Rose, M.B.E.

MACKENZIE, Capt. Edward Montagu Compton, O.B.E., R.M.L.I.

MACKENZIE, Eric Francis Wallace, O.B.E., M.C. M.B., Ch.B., R.A.M.C., *b.* 1890 ; *s.* of Dr. F. Wallace Mackenzie, of Wellington, New Zealand. *Educ.:* Wellington, Coll., New Zealand ; Univ. of Edinburgh. Deputy Assistant Director-General, A.M.S. *War Work:* Medical Officer, 1/6th Gordon Highlanders, Depot R.A.M.C., and War Office. *Club:* Royal Automobile.
(O7431)

MACKENZIE, Finlay Matheson, O.B.E., L.R.C.P., J.P.

MACKENZIE, Frances Louisa, M.B.E., *b.* 26 Oct., 1849 ; *d.* of Kenneth Mackenzie, of 3rd Regt. of Foot. *War Work:* Soldiers' and Sailors' Families Association for Wolverhampton Rural (Representative Tettenhall Wood) and Seisdon S.C. ; Staffordshire War Pensions Committee. *Address:* Applecross, Tettenhall Wood, Staffs. *Club:* Ladies' Army and Navy.
(M889)

MACKENZIE, Helen, C.B.E.

MACKENZIE, Henrietta Mary, Lady, O.B.E. ; *d.* of the late Rev. Alex. Macquisten, D.D. ; *m.* as his 2nd wife, Col. Sir Robert Campbell, K.B.E., C.B., V.D., J.P., D.L. (*q.v.*) (*see* BURKE'S *Peerage*), *s.* of the late Walter Mackenzie, of Law and Edinbarnet. *Address:* Edinbarnet, Duntocher, Dumbartonshire.
(O10896)

MACKENZIE, James, O.B.E.

MACKENZIE, Jessie, M.B.E.

McKENZIE, John, M.B.E., J.P.

MACKENZIE, Major John William, O.B.E., M.D., R.A.M.C. (T.).

MACKENZIE, Kenneth Child, M.B.E.

MACKENZIE, Major Kenneth Davidson, O.B.E., *b.* 9 Aug. 1873 ; *s.* of H. D. Mackenzie, of Hattigor, Assam, India ; *m.* Lily Louise, *d.* of J. H. Croft, of 69, Redcliffe Gardens, London, S.W. *Educ.:* Uppingham School. *War Work:* Served in South Africa, 1900–1902 ; France, Flanders, East Africa, and North Russia, 1914–19. *Club:* Cavalry.
(O9698)

MACKENZIE, Malcolm Ayers, M.B.E.

MACKENZIE, Lady Marjorie Louise, C.B.E. ; *d.* of Viscount Stormont, *s.* of 4th Earl of Mansfield (*see* BURKE'S *Peerage*) ; *m.* Sir Kenneth John Mackenzie, 7th Bart. of Gairloch (*see* BURKE'S *Peerage*). *Addresses:* Conan House, Conan Bridge, Rosshire, N.B. ; Flowerdale, Gairloch, Rossshire ; 10, Moray Place, Edinburgh.
(C2777)

MACKENZIE, May, Lady, M.B.E., *b.* 31 May, 1870 ; *d.* of S. H. Blake, K.C., of Toronto, Canada ; *m.* Sir Alexander (*see* BURKE'S *Peerage*), *s.* of Donald Mackenzie, of Kincardine, Can. *Educ.:* Privately. *Addresses:* 12, Hyde Park Place, W. 2 ; 594, Avenida Atlantica, Rio de Janeiro, Brazil.
(M8899)

MACKENZIE, Millicent, Mrs., O.B.E.

MACKENZIE, Mina, M.B.E.

MACKENZIE, Lieut. Murdo, M.B.E.

MACKENZIE, Peter, M.B.E.

MACKENZIE, Col. Sir Robert Campbell, K.B.E., C.B., V.D., J.P., D.L., *b.* 1856 ; *s.* of the late Walter Mackenzie, J.P., C.A., of Law and Edinbarnet ; *m.* 1st Katherine Ellis, *d.* of David Richardson, of Hartfield ; 2nd, Henrietta Mary, O.B.E. (*q.v.*), *d.* of the Rev. Alex. Macquisten, D.D. *Educ.:* Glasgow Academy, Uppingham School, and Glasgow Univ. In business as Chartered Accountant ; Director, Scottish Board, Liverpool and London Globe Insurance Co. ; served as Lieut. and Capt. Glasgow Highland Regt. Volunteers, 1875–1889 ; Lieut.-Col. and C.O. 1st Vol. Batt. H.L.I. 1889–1906 ; Col. Commanding H.L.I. Brigade, 1906–11 ; 3rd Line Group Lowland Division, 1915 ; Chairman, T.F. Association of the County of the City of Glasgow ; Income Tax Commissioner, and Member Standing Joint Committee of Dumbartonshire of Licensing Appeal Committee in the County. *Address:* Edinbarnet, Duntocher, Dumbartonshire. *Clubs:* Bath ; Western (Glasgow).
(K308)

M'KENZIE, Hon. Robert Donald, O.B.E., *b.* 1 March, 1865 ; *s.* of Hugh M'Kenzie, J.P. ; *m.* Emma Mary, *d.* of James Widgery, of Sydney, N.S.W. *Educ.:* St. Paul's Grammar School, Melbourne. Went to Australia, 1892 ; a pioneer of Kalgoorlie ; largely interested in mining and commercial pursuits ; Senior Councillor of Kalgoorlie, afterwards Mayor ; Member of Legislative Council for N.E. Province since 1904 ; served on three Royal Commissions in connection with mining industries in W. Australia ; founded Kalgoorlie Chamber of Commerce ; elected first President ; Hon. Minister and Member of Executive Council of W. Australia. *Clubs:* Perth ; Hannans ; Kalgoorlie : Masonic (Perth).
(O3812)

MACKENZIE, Major Thomas Roderick, O.B.E.

MACKENZIE, Thomas William, O.B.E.

McKENZIE, William, O.B.E.

MACKENZIE, Capt. William, O.B.E.

MACKENZIE, Lieut.-Col. William Scobie, D.S.O., O.B.E., A.O.D. ; *m.* 1900, Geraldine, *d.* of the late Col. Francis Moore (*see* BURKE'S *Peerage*, Drogheda, E.). Served during Great War, 1914–18, as Lieut.-Col. (despatches).
(O8871)

MACKENZIE, Sir William Warrender, K.B.E., M.A., K.C., *b.* 1860 ; *m.* Lilian Bradbury. *Educ.:* Edinburgh Univ. ; Univ. Coll., London. President of the Industrial Court ; Chairman of National (Railway) Wages Board. *War Work:* Chairman of Commission on Industrial Unrest (South-Western District), 1917 ; Member of War Cabinet's Committee of Inquiry into position of Women in Industry, 1918–19 ; Chairman of Committee of Inquiry on Baking (Night Work),

1919; Chairman of Committee on Production, 1917–18; Chairman of Interim Court of Arbitration (Industrial), 1918–19; Arbitrator for Board of Trade and Minister of Labour. *Addresses:* 5, Old Palace Yard, Westminster; 3, Paper Buildings, Temple, London. *Club:* Reform. (K156)

MACKENZIE, Isabel BURTON-, O.B.E.

MACKENZIE, Beatrice Anna FRASER-, O.B.E., *b.* 28 Nov. 1862; *d.* of Capt. A. V. Mackenzie, of Ord; *m.* Robert Scarlett, *s.* of John Fraser, of Bunchrew. *War Work:* President Ross and Cromarty Red Cross, County Branch; Member Inverness-shire War Pensions Committee; Inverness-shire Food Production and Food Control Committee; Ross-shire Food Production Committee; Convener Inverness-shire and Ross-shire Women's Agricultural Committees, and Member Highlands (Inverness) Employment Committee (Women's Sub-Committee). *Address:* Allangrange, Munlochy, Ross-shire; Bunchrew, Inverness-shire. *Club:* Bath. (O10895)

MACKENZIE, John Hugh MUNRO-, O.B.E., J.P., *b.* 1 Sept. 1849; *s.* of John Munro-Mackenzie, of Mornish; *m.* Jeanie Helen, *d.* of Thomas Chalmers, of Tringcroft. *Educ.:* Edinburgh Univ. *War Work:* Head Coast Watcher, Isle of Mull; Appeal Tribunal. *Address:* Calgary, Isle of Mull. *Clubs:* Conservative, Edinburgh; Royal Highland Yacht, Oban. (O1625)

MACKENZIE OF SEAFORTH, Mary Margaret, Lady STEWART-, C.B.E.: *see* Seaforth, Mary Margaret, Lady.

McKEOWN, John James, O.B.E.

MACKEOWN, Surg.-Comm. Robert John, O.B.E.

McKEOWN, Col. Walter, C.B.E. T. Col. Canadian Army Medical Corps; served in Great War, 1915–19 (mentioned in despatches). (C1834)

McKERCHAR, James, M.B.E., M.A., F.S.A. (Scot.), *b.* 18 June, 1882; *s.* of James McKerchar, of Aberfeldy, Scotland; *m.* Nellie, *d.* of A. Murray Stewart, of Broughty Ferry, Scotland. *Educ.:* Breadalbane Academy, and Univ. of St. Andrews. Schoolmaster. *War Work:* Enlisted as a private in Seaforth Highlanders (Kitchener's Army) 1914; Commissioned into Army Service Corps, 1918; Officer in charge Supplies, Pechenga, 1918; O.C. R.A.S.C., Soroka, 1919 (North Russian Expeditionary Force); promoted A. Capt. April, 1919. *Address:* Kirkpatrick, Fleming, Lockerbie. (M5016)

McKERGOW, Lieut.-Col. Robert Wilson, O.B.E., T.D., M.F.H., *b.* 22 Sept. 1866; *s.* of Robert McKergow, of Burgess Hill; *m.* Jane Elizabeth Madelaine, *d.* of T. Baker, of Wilmington, Sussex. *Educ.:* Downing Coll., Cambridge. Lord of the Manor, Woodmancote, Sussex; Master of the Crawley and Horsham Foxhounds, 1919; Master of the Southdown Foxhounds, 1903–8; Joint Master of Crawley and Horsham Foxhounds, 1913–15. *War Work:* Raised the 3rd Line of Sussex Yeomanry in 1915, and commanded same till disbanded; then commanded the 4th Batt. Royal West Kent Regt. (Reserve) from 1917 to 1919; mentioned in despatches, 1917. *Clubs:* Badminton; Union and New, Brighton. (O7432)

McKERRELL, Lieut.-Col. Reginald L'Estrange, O.B.E., *b.* 5 March, 1860; *s.* of Robert McKerrell (*see* BURKE'S *Landed Gentry*—McKerrell of Hillhouse); *m.* Grace O'Brien, *d.* of The Hon. Henry O'Brien (*see* BURKE'S *Peerage*). *Educ.:* Hawtreys; Aldin House, Slough. Joined the Princess Louise's Argyll and Sutherland Highlanders 1879; retired, 1911. *War Work:* Deputy Provost Marshal, Scottish Command. *Address:* 94, Piccadilly. *Clubs:* Naval and Military; Wellington. (O7433)

McKERROW, Alexandrina, M.B.E.

McKERSIE, Marion, Mrs., M.B.E.; *d.* of the late Anthony McCall, of Ayr; *m.* William, *s.* of the late William McKersie, of Campbeltown. *Educ.:* Ayr Academy. *War Work:* Vice-President, Campbeltown Division, Argyllshire Branch, B.R.C.S. *Address:* Craigard, Campbeltown, Argyllshire. (M2099)

MACKESY, Lieut.-Col. Charles Ernest Ralph, C.M.G., C.B.E., D.S.O., *b.* 1861; *s.* of the late Major Mackesy. Lieut.-Col. New Zealand Mounted Rifles; Great War, 1915–18, in Gallipoli and Egypt (despatches); Mil. Gov. of Es-Salt-Amman Dist. E. of Jordan. (C1397)

McKEURTAN, Mary Mrs., O.B.E., *b.* 29 July, 1858; *d.* of William McFee, of Dundee, Scotland; *m.* John, *s.* of James McKeurtan of Gartmore, Scotland. *Educ.:* West End Academy, Dundee, Scotland. *War Work:* Meeting troops passing through Bulawayo to and from East Africa. *Address:* Box 189, Bulawayo. (O961)

McKEW, Rev. Robert, C.B.E., *b.* 1872; *s.* of John McKew, of Valencia, Co. Kerry. Chap. and Instructor-Comm. R.N.; Great War, 1914–19 (mentioned in despatches). (C1932)

McKEY, Capt. Charles, O.B.E.

McKIBBIN, Major Thomas, C.B.E.

McKICHAN, Lieut. John James, O.B.E., R.N.V.R.

MACKIDD, Barbara Winifred Logan, M.B.E.

MACKIE, Annie, M.B.E.

MACKIE, Major Frederick Percival, O.B.E., M.D., F.R.C.S., I.M.S.

MACKIE, George, M.B.E., *b.* 9 Nov. 1874; *s.* of George Mackie, of Leith; *m.* Margaret, *d.* of John Fraser, of Leith. *Educ.:* Leith Board School. Executive Officer, Leith Food Control Committee. *War Work:* Member of No. 1 Edinburgh V.A.D., B.R.C.S.; Member of Edinburgh Military Training Association, latterly Volunteers; Member of Local Volunteer Fire Brigade. *Address:* 33, Rychill Terrace, Leith. (M8904)

MACKIE, Lieut. George William, O.B.E., R.N.V.R.

MACKIE, Horatio George Arthur, C.B.E., *b.* 1868 Appointed Vice-Consul, 1895; Consul, 1905; Consul-Gen. at Buenos Aires, 1913; appointed H.M. Consul-Gen. for the Dept. of Seine, Seine-et-Marne, Marne, Seine-et-Oise, Oise, Eure-et-Loire, Loiret, Loir-et-Cher, Cher Indre, Meuse, Aube, Haute Marne, Yonne, Côte d'or, Aisnes and Ardennes, and to reside at Paris. *Address:* British Consulate-General, Buenos Aires. (C227)

McKIE, Lieut.-Col. John, C.B.E., D.S.O., *b.* 1857; *s.* of the late James McKie (formerly M.P. for Kirkcudbrightshire), of Bargaly; *m.* 1910, Violet, *d.* of Sir Oswald Mosley, 4th Bt., of Rolleston, Burton-on-Trent (*see* BURKE'S *Peerage*). *Educ.:* Harrow. Major and Hon. Lieut.-Col. (T.D.) King's Own Scottish Borderers; served in S. Africa, 1900–2, as Comdt. at Christiana and Modder River (despatches). *Address:* Ernespie, Castle Douglas, N.B. *Clubs:* Bachelors'; Boodle's. (C1680)

MACKIE, Mary A., Mrs. W. Campbell, M.B.E., M.B., Ch.B., *d.* of A. A. Noble, of Southport; *m.* Major William C. Mackie, R.A.M.C., *s.* of Dr. W. Mackie, of Helensburgh. *Educ.:* Glasgow Univ. Doctor of Medicine; Working under the Ministry of Health in Baghdad, Mesopotamia. *War Work:* Resident Surgeon, Royal Infirmary, Halifax, and Whitecross Military Hospital. *Address:* Baghdad, Mesopotamia.(M10273)

MACKIE, Thomas Callender Campbell, M.B.E., *b.* 1886; *s.* of Dr. Wm. Mackie, of Helensburgh. *Educ.:* Larchfield School; Glasgow School of Architecture; Glasgow School of Art. Artist and Decorative Architect. *War Work:* Organised for the Scottish Branch, British Red Cross Society, the Scottish Penny-a-week Fund for providing comforts for the Sick and Wounded; this Fund amounted to upwards of £53,000; was also official lecturer in Scotland for the Scottish Branch, B.R.C.S. (M2100)

MACKIE, Col. Tom Darke, C.M.G., O.B.E., M.I.M.E., R.A.F., *b.* 25 July, 1883; *s.* of the Rev. John Henry Mackie, M.A., Rector of Filton, Bristol; *m.* Constance, *d.* of Kilmister, of Edinburgh. *Educ.:* Sedbergh. Deputy-Director of Works and Buildings, R.A.F. *War Work:* Served as 2nd Lieut. in France, 1914; Dardanelles, 1915; France, 1916; Admiralty, end 1916, to March, 1918; Air Ministry, 1918–20, with rank of Colonel. *Address:* c/o The Air Ministry, London. *Club:* Wellington. (O1626)

MACKILLIGAN, Capt. Alister Pelham, O.B.E., R.A.F.

MACKILLIGAN, Capt. Robert Springett, O.B.E., M.C., R.E.

MACKILLOP, Edward Laurence, O.B.E., M.B.E.

McKILLOP, Margaret, Mrs., M.B.E., M.A., *b.* 22 Jan. 1864; *d.* of James Seward, of Liverpool; *m.* John McKillop. *Educ.:* Blackburne House, Liverpool; Somerville Coll., Oxford. Tutor Somerville Coll.; Lecturer Royal Holloway Coll.; Fellow and Lecturer of King's Coll. for Women, Univ. of London. *War Work:* Organiser for War Savings Committee, 1916; Head of Foreign Intelligence Section, Ministry of Food, till Jan. 1920. *Address:* 3, Stafford Mansions, Battersea Park, S.W. 11. (M8905)

McKIM, Major Frederick George, M.B.E., R.A.S.C. (M10230)

MACKINDER, Charles Henry, M.B.E., *b.* 14 Feb. 1871; *s.* of James Mackinder, of The Limes, Pitsmoor, Sheffield; *m.* Florence Edith, *d.* of Thomas Benbow Morrall, Burngreave Road, Sheffield. *Educ.:* Ashville Coll., Harrogate. *War Work:* As a Director of Kayser Ellison Co., Ltd., Steel Manufacturers, Sheffield, was concerned in the production of special steels for aircraft, motor transport, and more particularly armour-piercing bullets, and all steel aeroplane wings. *Address:* Somersby, 3, Endcliffe Grove Avenue, Sheffield. (M8906)

McKINERY, Lieut.-Col. John William Herbert, D.S.O., O.B.E., J.P., *b.* 1879; *s.* of the late John McKinery; *m.* Gertrude, *d.* of the late John Matthews, of Mossel Bay, S. Africa. Lieut.-Col. Canadian Forces; S. African War, 1899–1902 (despatches, King's and Queen's medals with five clasps); Great War, 1915–18 (despatches). *Club:* Beaufort. (O6023)

McKINLAY, Eng.-Comm. Alfred White, O.B.E., R.N.

McKINNA, Alexander, O.B.E.

MacKINNON, Major Alexander Dugald, O.B.E., V.D., J.P., *b.* 19 June, 1862; *s.* of Neil MacKinnon, of Tobermory, Island of Mull; *m.* Margaret Gertrude Harding, of Wetheral, near Carlisle. *Educ.:* Public School, Tobermory; George Watson's Coll., Edinburgh; Edinburgh Univ. Procurator-Fiscal Inverness-shire at Portree. Solicitor. *War Work:* Served in South African War, 1900–1, Capt. in command of Volunteer Service Company, Queen's Own Cameron Highlanders; granted rank of Hon. Capt.; Military Representative in Skye; National Service Representative in Skye and Outer Isles; Hon. Head Coast Watcher, Royal Navy, in Skye District of West Coast of Scotland. *Address:* 3, County Buildings, Portree. (O8872)

MACKINNON, Alister, M.B.E.

MACKINNON, Major Archibald Donald, C.M.G., O.B.E., M.D., J.P., *b.* 27 March, 1864; *s.* of the Rev. D. Mackinnon, D.D., of the Parish of Strath, Isle of Skye; *m.* Mary Henderson, *d.* of Harry Macdonald, of Portree. *Educ.:* Private school, and Aberdeen Univ. Physician (retired). *War Work:* Military duties. *Address:* Dunringell, Kyleakin, Isle of Skye. *Club:* Oriental, London; Highland, Inverness. (O7434)

MACKINNON, Capt. Cecil Gordon, O.B.E., Can. A.S.C.

MACKINNON, Eleanor Vokes Teby, Mrs., O.B.E.

MACKINNON, Lucy Vere, Mrs., O.B.E.

MACKINNON, Madeleine Frances, Lady, C.B.E.; *d.* of Col. Villiers Hatton, of Clonard, Wexford; *m.* General Sir

Henry (see BURKE's *Peerage*), *s.* of William Alexander Mackinnon, of Acryse Park, Kent. *War Work :* Chairman, City of London Red Cross, and Chester City Red Cross. *Address :* Evelyn Mansions, S.W. 1. *Club :* Ladies' Athenæum. (C2778)

McKINSTRY, Capt. Edward Robert, C.B.E., R.N.R. Great War, 1914–19, as Commodore of Convoys (despatches). (C1195)

MACKINTOSH, Alexander, M.B.E.

MACKINTOSH OF MACKINTOSH, Col. Alfred Donald, C.B.E., *s.* of the late Alexander MacKintosh of MacKintosh, *b*, 1851 ; *m.* 1880, Harriot Diana Arabella Mary, C.B.E. (*q.n.*), only child of the late Edward Priest Richards, of Plas Newydd, co. Glamorgan. Served in the Great War 1914–19 (despatches). *Addresses :* Moy Hall, Inverness ; Dunachton, Inverness ; Cattrell, Cardiff ; 8, Hill Street, Berkeley Square, W. 1. *Club :* Carlton. (C1681)

MACKINTOSH, Donald Grant, M.B.E., A.M.I.Mech.E., *s.* of George Andrews Mackintosh, of Aberdeen ; *m.* Louisa Humphrys, *d.* of Edwin John Lewis, of Reading. *Educ. :* King Edward VI. Grammar School, Birmingham. Works Manager, Messrs. Braithwaite & Co., Crown Bridge Works, West Bromwich. *Address :* Maney Villa, Birmingham Road, Sutton Coldfield. (M8908)

MACKINTOSH, Col. George, C.B., C.B.E., *b.* 28 Aug. 1860 ; *s.* of Eneas Mackintosh, J.P., D.L., of Balnespick, Inverness-shire ; *m.* Mary, *d.* of George Baynton Davy, of Spean Lodge, Inverness-shire, and Owthorpe, Notts. *Educ. :* Marlborough Coll. ; R.M.C. Sandhurst. Gazetted 78th Highlanders, May 1878 ; Commanding 2nd Batt. Seaforth Highlanders, 1904–9 ; Commanding No. 1 District, 1912. *War Work :* In command No. 1 District, and Col. in charge Records to March, 1919. *Address :* Clune, Tomatin, Inverness-shire. *Clubs :* Naval and Military ; New, Edinburgh ; Highland, Inverness. (C1682)

MACKINTOSH OF MACKINTOSH, Harriet Diana Arabella Mary, Mrs., C.B.E., *b.* 1859 ; *d.* of the late Edward Priest Richards, of Plas-Newydd, Co. Glamorgan ; *m.* Alfred Donald, The Mackintosh of Mackintosh, C.B.E. (*q.v.*). *War Work :* Supplied and entirely maintained during the war a private hospital at Inverness ; President, Inverness-shire Red Cross Association. *Addresses :* Moy Hall, Inverness-shire ; Cottrell, near Cardiff ; 8, Hill Street, Berkeley Square. *Clubs :* Alexandra ; Sesame. (C2779)

MACKINTOSH, Herbert Bannermen, M.B.E., F.S.A. (Scot.), *b.* 22 July, 1868 ; *s.* of Lachlan Mackintosh, of Old Lodge, Elgin. *Educ. :* Elgin Educational Institute ; West End School ; Elgin Academy. Hon. Sec. Moray and Nairn Unionist Association ; Hon. Sec. Elgin and Morayshire Literary and Scientific Association ; Curator of the Elgin Museum. *War Work :* One of the promoters in Aug. 1914 of the Elgin Volunteer Training Corps, and its Commandant during the two years of its existence ; Hon. Sec. and Organiser of the County of Moray War Work Association ; Organising Sec. for the 1918 County of Moray Red Cross Week ; a "socio perpetuo" of the Italian Red Cross ; Member of Committee of the Morayshire Seaforths Comforts Fund, and of the Elgin Y.M.C.A. Canteen. *Address :* Redhythe, Elgin. *Clubs :* Junior Constitutional ; Elgin. (M8909)

MACKINTOSH, James, O.B.E., *b.* 20 Nov. 1880 ; *s.* of James Mackintosh, of Coupar Angus, Perthshire, Scotland ; *m.* Margaret Guthrie Crawford, *d.* of John Ross, of Glasgow. *Educ. :* Glasgow and West of Scotland Agricultural Coll. Senior Lecturer in Agriculture, and Farm Director, South-Eastern Agricultural Coll., Wye, Kent ; Lecturer and Adviser in Dairy Farming, Univ. Coll., Reading ; in charge of Research in Dairy Husbandry, Research Institute in Dairying, Univ. Coll., Reading. *War Work :* Technical Adviser in Dairy Farming, Food Production Department ; Technical Adviser to Milk Section, Ministry of Food. *Addresses :* Univ. Coll., Reading ; Wolverscote, Addington Road, Reading. *Club :* Farmers'. (O10901)

MACKINTOSH, John, O.B.E. (O4380)

MACKINTOSH, Norna Susan, Mrs., O.B.E. ; *d.* of James Labouchere ; *m.* Charles Alexander Gordon Mackintosh. *War Work :* Canteen work at Rouen at Lady Mabelle Egerton's Rouen Station Coffee Shop ; founded the Church Army Club, Caudry, near Cambrai ; employed on special service during part of 1918 and 1919. *Addresses :* Gezira Gardens, Cairo ; 23, Chapel Street. London, S.W. (O10902)

MACKINTOSH, Capt. William Cameron, O.B.E.

MACKLIN, Capt. Alexander Hepburn, O.B.E., M.C., M.B., R.A.M.C.

MACKLIN, Barbara Emly, Lady, M.B.E. ; *d.* of A. M. Main, of Salisbury ; *m.* Sir James (see BURKE's *Peerage*), *s.* of James Macklin, of Harnham. *Educ. :* Privately. *War Work :* Chairman of the Q.M.N.G. Soldiers' Entertainment Committee ; Prisoners of War Committee ; Mayoress of Salisbury from 1913–19. *Address :* Harnham House, Salisbury. (M3821)

MACKLIN, Edward Lionel, O.B.E.

MACKROW, George Frank, M.B.E.

MACKWORTH, Col. John Dolben, C.B.E., B.A., *b.* 20 June, 1887 ; *s.* of Sir Arthur Mackworth, 6th Bart. (see BURKE's *Peerage*) ; *m.* Marianne Annette, *d.* of H. W. Sillem, of the Pines, Horsell. *Educ. :* Corpus Christi Coll., Oxford. Capt. late R. W. Surrey Regt., and Lieut.-Col. late R.A.F. ; has Legion of Honour. *Address :* Tudor House, Farnborough, Hants. (C558)

MACLACHAN, Morrison, M.B.E.

McLACHLAN, Lieut. Allan, M.B.E.

McLACHLAN, Arthur Cecil, O.B.E., *b.* 20 Nov. 1872 ; *s.* of James McLachlan, of Cheltenham. *Educ. :* Cheltenham, and abroad. *War Work :* Advisory Committee on Dutch and Dutch Colonial matters ; War Trade Intelligence Dept. *Address :* 51, South Street, Park Lane, W. 1. *Clubs :* St. James' ; Dutch. (O10904)

McLACHLAN, Donald McBrayne, M.B.E.

McLACHLAN, Gwendolen Mab, Mrs., M.B.E.

McLACHLAN, Isabella Brodie, Mrs., O.B.E., *b.* 12 Oct. 1877 ; *d.* of Col. Brodie-Mills ; *m.* Thomas Williamson McLachlan. *Educ. :* Orford Coll., Gipsy Hill, London. *War Work :* In England, Burma, Ceylon, and Aden, from 1914–20. *Address :* c/o The National Bank of India, 26, Bishopsgate, London. (O10905)

MacLACHLAN, James, M.B.E., T.D., M.B., C.M., J.P., *b.* 18 Oct. 1865 ; *s.* of David Ewing MacLachlan, of Alexandria, Dumbartonshire ; *m.* Christian, *d.* of John Fleming Cullen, M.D., of Alexandria. *Educ. :* Parish School ; Dumbarton Academy ; Glasgow Univ. Medical Officer of the Town and Parish of Dornoch since 1894 : Physician to the County Fever Hospital ; Factory Surgeon to the parishes of Criech and Dornoch ; Examiner of Recruits (Army) and several insurance companies ; represents Scottish Insurance Commissioners on County Committee ; Member of British Medical Association and Caledonian Medical Societies. *War Work :* Initiated and organised Recruiting Campaign in town and parish ; County Director and Hon. Sec. of Sutherland Branch, British Red Cross Society ; Member of Dornoch Tribunal Advisory Committee ; acted as M.O. to the 11th Service Batt. Gordon and Seaforth Highlanders ; Military Member of the County Territorial Association ; Member of Memorial Committee ; Medical Referee under Pensions Minister ; Combatant Officer (Lieut.), Sutherland Volunteer Regt. *Address :* Burnside, Dornoch, Sutherland. (O5527)

McLACHLAN, Major James, O.B.E.

McLACHLAN, Capt. James William Francis, O.B.E.

McLAGAN, Major Douglas Craig, D.S.O., M.B.E., T.D., *b.* 12 March, 1880 ; *s.* of the late Thomas Thompson McLagan, M.A., Edinburgh ; *m.* Jessie, *d.* of John Young-Scott, of Redford Hill, Peeblesshire. *Educ. :* Royal High School, Edinburgh, and Edin. Univ. *War Work :* Major, 5th Royal Scots, Gallipoli and France ; Deputy Controller of Stats., Ministry of National Service, Nov. 1917, to Feb. 1919 ; Ministry of Labour, Feb. 1919, to July, 1919. *Address :* 24, Queen Anne's Gate, London. *Clubs :* Junior Army and Navy ; Scottish Conservative, Edinburgh. (M8912)

MACLAGAN, Douglas Philip, M.B.E.

MACLAGAN, Eric Robert Dalrymple, C.B.E., B.A., Officier de l'Instruction Publique (French) ; Order of St. Saba, 5th Class (Serbian), *b.* 4 Dec. 1879 ; *s.* of the late William Dalrymple Maclagan, Archbishop of York ; *m.* Helen Elizabeth, *d.* of the Hon. Frederick Lascelles (see BURKE's *Peerage*), of Sutton Waldron, Dorset. *Educ. :* Winchester ; Christ Church, Oxford. Assistant-Keeper (Department of Architecture and Sculpture), Victoria and Albert Museum. *War Work :* Transferred to the Foreign Office (News Department), 1916, and later to the Ministry of Information ; in charge of Paris Bureau, 1917 ; Controller for France, 1918 ; attached to British Delegation (Foreign Office) at Peace Conference, 1919. *Address :* 15, Queen's Gate Place, S.W. 7. *Clubs :* Athenæum ; Burlington Fine Arts. (C1000)

McLAREN, Alexander Ernest, O.B.E. ; *s.* of Alick McLaren, of Edinburgh. *Educ. :* Merchiston, Edinburgh ; Trinity Coll., Oxford. 1st Class Clerk, Charity Commission. *War Work :* Enlisted in 16th Middlesex Regt., P.S.B., in Sept. 1914 ; 2nd Lieut., 6th North Staff. Regt. ; resigned commission in 1916, from ill-health due to service in the field ; served in Ministry of Food from Nov. 1916. *Address :* 43, Connaught Square, W. 2. *Club :* New University. (O1627)

McLAREN, Capt. Colin Temple, O.B.E., R.A.F.

McLAREN, Capt. Douglas, M.B.E.

MACLAREN, Major Geoffrey, O.B.E., *b.* 28 Feb. 1883 ; *s.* of James Maclaren, of Manchester ; *m.* Lily, *d.* of H. N. Suter. *Educ. :* Harrow. Civil Service. *War Work :* Served in Gallipoli, Egypt, Palestine. *Address :* Government House, Jerusalem, Palestine. (O8634)

McLAREN, Hon. Henry Duncan, C.B.E., M.P., *b.* 6 April. 1879 ; *s.* of Lord Aberconway, P.C., of 43, Belgrave Square, London (see BURKE's *Peerage*) ; *m.* Christabel Mary Melville, *d.* of Sir Melville Macnaghten (see BURKE's *Peerage*). *Educ. :* Eton and Balliol. Member of Parliament. *War Work :* Joined Staff of Ministry of Munitions, early in 1915, to assist in organisation of Munition Committees throughout the country to control groups of contractors and National Shell Factories ; subsequently appointed Director of Area Organisation, responsible for the work and output of these Committees, and also for all the local branches (Area Offices) of the Ministry. *Address :* 69, Eaton Place, London, S.W. *Clubs :* Brooks's ; Reform. (C244)

McLAREN, Sergt.-Major John, M.B.E., *b.* 4 Nov. 1852 ; *s.* of Duncan McLaren, of Killin ; *m.* Susan, *d.* of Robert Bell, of Edinburgh. *Educ. :* Duke of York's Royal Military School, Chelsea. Local General Manager, Lord Roberts' Memorial Workshops, Edinburgh Branch. *War Work :* Secretarial, The Incorporated Soldiers' and Sailors' Help Society. *Address :* 17, Morningside Gardens, Edinburgh. (M2105)

McLAREN, Lieut. John William, M.B.E., R.A.S.C. (T.).

McLAREN, Maurice Paterson, M.B.E., *b.* 12 Dec. 1878 ; *s.* of Robert McLaren, of Anie, Callander, Perthshire ; *m.*

Jean, d. of James Craik, of Dunbar. *Educ.:* George Watson's Coll., Edinburgh. Engineer, H.M. Office of Works. *War Work:* Engineering work in connection with various war services. *Address:* Chigwell, Harpenden, Herts. (M742)

McLAREN, Nellie Hessel, Mrs., M.B.E., *b.* 5 June, 1868; *m.* William McLaren, of Galashiels. *War Work:* Hon. Treas. Galashiels Local War Pensions Committee, and Convener of Finance and Claims Sub-Committee; Member of South-East of Scotland Joint Disablement Committee; Hon. Organiser and Manager of Galashiels Y.M.C.A. Canteen for Soldiers; Leader, War Dressings Work Party (Sphagnum Moss Depot). (M8913)

McLAREN, Capt. Richard, O.B.E.

McLAREN, Capt. Robert, M.B.E., A.P.D.

MACLAREN, Archibald Stuart Charles STUART-, O.B.E., M.C., A.F.C.

McLAUGHLAN, Henry Peter Marius, M.B.E., *b.* 25 Aug. 1871; *s.* of Philip Andrew McLaughlan, of Glasgow, Scotland; *m.* Elfrida Beatrice, *d.* of James Greenwood, of Nicosia, Cyprus. *Educ.:* Univ. of St. Joseph, and American Coll., Beyrout, Syria. Chief Clerk of the Chief Secretary's Office, Cyprus. Government. *War Work:* In charge of war official papers and Member of various Compensation Boards for purchase of transport animals and other supplies for the Army during the war. *Address:* Nicosia, Cyprus. *Club:* English, Nicosia. (M6466)

MacLAUGHLIN, Lieut.-Col. Arthur Maunsell, C.B.E., M.B., B.Ch., B.A.O., D.P.H., R.A.M.C.; *b.* 23 June, 1874; *s.* of Rev. Alex MacLaughlin, of Doon, Co. Limerick. *Educ.:* Trinity Coll., Dublin. *War Work:* A.D.M.S., 8th Division, Fifth Area, Boulogne District and British Troops in France and Flanders. *Club:* Junior Constitutional. (C1286)

McLAUGHLIN, Sir Henry, K.B.E., *b.* 21 March, 1876; *s.* of William Henry McLaughlin, D.L., of Macedon, Co. Antrim; *m.* Ethel Mary, *d.* of William S. Mollan, of Belfast. *Educ.:* Royal Academy, Belfast, and Mount Radford, Exeter. Chairman, McLaughlin and Harvey, Ltd., Contractors, Belfast, Dublin, and London; President, Dublin Building Trades Association, 1917; Chairman, Irish Advisory Council, Ministry of Labour, 1911–15. *War Work:* Hon. Director Irish Recruiting, 1915–16; organised first "Our Day" Red Cross Fund, Southern Ireland, raising £65,000; Vice-Chairman, City of Dublin Pensions Committee, 1917–19; Chairman since 1920; Member, Lord French's Recruiting Council, 1918. *Address:* Riversdale, Monkstown, Co. Dublin. *Club:* St. Stephen's Green, Dublin. (K222)

McLAUGHLIN, Hubert William Charles, M.B.E., M.A., *b.* 1 Sept. 1865; *s.* of Frederick Hubert McLaughlin, of the Indian Civil Service; *m.* Ida Evelyn, *d.* of Rev. E. H. Powell, of Hewish, Som. *Educ.:* Cheltenham Coll., and Christ's Coll., Camb. *Address:* Lockingarth, Corsham, Wilts. (M8914)

McLAUGHLIN, Patrick Joseph, M.B.E.

McLAUGHLIN, Major William Reginald, O.B.E.

MACLAVISH, Lieut. Herbert James, M.B.E., M.C., R.F.A. (S.R.).

MACLEAN, Agnes, O.B.E.

MCLEAN, Major Alan A., M.B.E., O.T.C. (T.).

McLEAN, Major Alexander Colin, O.B.E., J.P., *b.* 2 June, 1866; *s.* of Lachlan McLean, of Islay; *m.* Dora Georgina, *d.* of Sir Augustus Rivers Thompson, K.C.S.I. (*see* BURKE'S *Peerage*). *Educ.:* King's School, Canterbury. Chief Constable of Inverness-shire, late of The Black Watch and Cameron Highlanders. *Address:* Rossal, Inverness. *Clubs:* New and Military; New, Edinburgh. (O10907)

MACLEAN, Col. Archibald Campbell Holmes, C.B.E. Lieut.-Col. R.A.F.; served in Great War, 1914–19 (mentioned in despatches). (C868)

MACLEAN, Capt. Charles Allan, M.B.E.

MACLEAN, The Rt. Hon. Sir Donald, K.B.E., M.P., Hon. LL.D. (Cambridge); *s.* of the late John Maclean, of Kilmoluag, Tiree; *m.* Gwendolen Margaret, *d.* of Andrew Devitt, J.P., of Herontye, East Grinstead. *Educ.:* Privately. Solicitor. *War Work:* 1914–16, Member, Foreign Trade Debts Committee; Chairman, Enemy Debts Committee; Chairman, Local Government Reconstruction Committee; Chairman, London Appeal Tribunal for Military Service, 1916. *Address:* 6, Southwick Place, Hyde Park, London, W. 2. *Club:* Reform. (K2)

McLEAN, Esther Fanny, Mrs., M.B.E.; *d.* of Abraham Harris, of Southsea; *m.* William Richard James, *s.* of Richard Waters McLean, of Shoeburyness. *Educ.:* Privately. Commandant, B.R.C.S., V.A.D. London 154; Manager, Group of Council Schools, and Member of Care and After Care Committees; Member of Fulham Educational Council; Member of Children's Country Holiday Fund. *War Work:* 1914, Assisted husband to raise Fulham and Putney Division of B.R.C.S., and recruited and organised V.A. Detachment No. 154, County of London (1010 Members on Voluntary, Special and General Service); all these trained and placed in Hospitals and Institutions and many also mobilised on Air Raid Service under Commandant; provided Motor Ambulance for the Front and collected large sums for Head Quarters; also contributed over 14,000 articles to Hospitals, Institutions, and Head Quarters Stores, etc. *Address:* Queenscourt, Hurlingham Road, S.W. 6. (M743)

MACLEAN, Lieut. Harper, O.B.E., R.N.V.R.

MACLEAN, Henrietta Laura, Mrs., M.B.E.

McLEAN, Lieut.-Col. Henry John, C.B.E., M.D., M.B., F.R.C.S., *b.* 1868; *s.* of the late Duncan McLean, M.D. *Educ.:*

Edinburgh Univ. Lieut.-Col. New Zealand Med. Corps; Assist. Director of Med. Sers.; served in Great War, 1914–19, in Egypt, Gallipoli, and France (despatches). *Club:* Wellington (New Zealand). (C849)

McLEAN, Irene Hazel, M.B.E.

McLEAN, Isabel, M.B.E.

McLEAN, Capt. James, M.B.E.

MACLEAN, James Borrowman, C.B.E., *b.* 1881; *s.* of Lachlan Maclean, of Glasgow; *m.* Grace Isobel, *d.* of Duncan Macara, builder, of Glasgow. *Educ.:* Glasgow. Member of Institutes of Civil and Mechanical Engineers. *War Work:* Appointed Director of Shell Production, Ministry of Munitions, 1916; Controller of Gun Manufacture, 1917; Controller of Mechanical Warfare Depart.; Member of Munitions Works Board, and of Commn. of Enquiry on Woolwich Arsenal, 1918. *Club:* Royal Automobile. (C228)

MACLEAN, Col. James Reynolds, C.B.E., *b.* 1872; *s.* of John McLean, of Belfast; *m.* Margaret Emmie, *d.* of Laurence Steele, R.N., of Southampton. *Educ.:* Edinburgh and Cambridge Universities. Deputy Director-General of Recruiting. *War Work:* Work in connection with Recruiting. *Address:* Greenaleigh, Sydraw Road, Cardiff. *Club:* Junior Army and Navy. (C245)

McLEAN, John Hair Kirk, M.B.E.

McLEAN, Capt. John Reid, O.B.E., J.P.

McLEAN, Capt. Kenneth Hugh, O.B.E., R.N.V.R., R.A.F.

MACLEAN, Marion Louise, Mrs., M.B.E.; *d.* of Edward F. Davies, of Newport (Mon.); *m.* Neil J. Maclean. President, Milngavie Social Union; Sec. Milngavie Co. Girl Guides. *War Work:* Local Sec. New Kilpatrick War Pensions Committee (A); Sec. New Kilpatrick Branch of the Soldiers' and Sailors' Families Association. *Address:* The Meadows, Milngavie. *Club:* Literary. Glasgow. (M8918)

McLEAN, Matthew Adam, M.B.E.

McLEAN, Capt. Peter, O.B.E.

McLEAN, 2nd Lieut. Robert Knox, M.B.E., R.A.F.

MACLEAN, Thomas Finlay, M.B.E.

McLEAN, Col. William Richard James, C.B.E., T.D., Mus.B., *b.* 1858; *s.* of Richard Waters McLean, of Shoeburyness; *m.* Esther Fanny, M.B.E., *d.* of Abraham Harris, of Southsea. *Educ.:* Privately, and King's Coll., London; Graduated at Univ. of Durham. Late Assistant Adjutant-General and Inspecting Officer, Transport Workers' Battalions; previously Lieut.-Col. Commanding 2/13th (Princess Louise's) Kensington Battalion, London Regiment, and Lieut.-Col. Commanding 16th York and Lacaster Regiment; mentioned in despatches, 1917; Deputy Assistant County Director, Honorary Divisional Sec. and Treas., Fulham and Putney Division, B.R.C.S.; Grand Organist in Supreme Grand Chapter, 1905; in Grand Lodge, 1908; Past Deputy Grand Sword Bearer in Grand Lodge and Grand Chapter, 1919; Musical Director and Conductor of various Musical Societies; late Board of Education. *War Work:* Raised and trained two and a half Battalions; controlled twelve Battalions of Transport Workers; established and organised large Division of the B.R.C.S. *Address:* Queenscourt, Hurlingham Road, S.W. 6. *Club:* Senior Officers'. (C559)

MACLEAR, Major Ronald, O.B.E., M.C., R.A.S.C.

McLEISH, Lieut.-Col. Duncan, C.M.G., C.B.E., *b.* 1851; *s.* of Duncan McLeish, of Glenmore, Yea, Victoria. S. Africa, 1900, with Victorian Mounted Inf. and 2nd Batt. Australian Commonwealth Horse (despatches); is A.D.C. to Gov.-Gen. of Australian Commonwealth; Lieut.-Col. Australian Mounted Rifles. *Address:* Glenmore, Yea, Victoria, Australia. *Clubs:* Naval and Military; Stock Exchange (Melbourne). (C793)

McLEISH, Lieut. James, M.B.E., R.E.

McLELLAN, Capt. Charles Alexander, O.B.E.

McLELLAN, Lieut.-Col. William, C.B.E., R.M.

MACLELLAN, William Archibald, M.B.E.

MacLELLAN, William Turner, C.B.E., J.P., *b.* 1863; *s.* of Walter MacLellan, J.P., of Blairvaddick, Dumbartonshire; *m.* 1908, Lilias Mabel, *d.* of the late James Wylie Guild, of Glasgow. *Educ.:* Larchfield School, Helensburgh. Engineer. Dep.-Controller Iron and Steel Productions, Ministry of Munitions; Chairman of Bengal Iron and Steel Co.; has Legion of Honour and Order of Leopold of Belgium. *Address:* Mayford House, nr. Woking. *Clubs:* St. Stephen's; Ranelagh. (C229)

McLELLAND, Hugh, O.B.E.

MACLENNAN, Anna Buchanan, O.B.E.

McLENNAN, Prof. John Cunningham, O.B.E. F.R.S., Ph.D., LL.D., D.Sc., *b.* 14 April, 1867; *s.* of David McLennan, of Aberdeen, Scotland; *m.* Elsie Monro, *d.* of the late William Ramsay, of Bowland, Midlothian, Scotland. *Educ.:* Toronto and Cambridge. Professor of Physics, Univ. of Toronto; Member of the Advisory Council for Scientific and Industrial Research of Canada. *War Work:* Development of Anti-submarine measures during 1917–18; Scientific Adviser to Admiralty during 1919; development of large scale production of Helium for Airships, 1918–20. *Address:* 88, Prince Arthur Avenue, Toronto. *Clubs:* York, Toronto; Toronto Golf; Faculty Union, Univ. of Toronto. (O32)

McLENNAN, Capt. Kenneth, M.B.E.

MacLENNAN, William, O.B.E., J.P., *b.* 18 April, 1857; *s.* of the late John MacLennan, of Strathconan, Ross; *m.* Mary Joan Kennedy, *d.* of Capt. Allan Kennedy, of the Cunard Steamship Company, Ltd. *Educ.:* Royal Academy, Inverness. Chamberlain to the Marquis of Zetland in Orkney

Vice-Convener of the County of Orkney; Chairman of Orkney Harbours Commissioners, and a Governor of the North of Scotland College of Agriculture; Hon. Sheriff-Substitute of Caithness, Orkney, and Zetland; author of the "Flockmaster's Companion." *War Work:* Chairman of Local Military Tribunal; Chairman of the Agricultural Committee for Food Production and Vice-Chairman of Pensions Committee. *Address:* Grainbank, Kirkwall. *Club:* Scottish Conservative, Edinburgh.
(O533)

MacLEOD, Major Adam Gordon, D.S.O., O.B.E. Served in Great War, 1914-18 (mentioned in despatches). (O5328)

MacLEOD, Frederick Larkins, K.B.E., Chevalier de la Légion d'Honneur, *b.* April, 1858; *s.* of George MacLeod, of Glasgow; *m.* Jeanie Emma, *d.* of John Mackinlay, of Glasgow. *Educ.:* High School, Glasgow. Official Adviser as to Iron Ore, Ministry of Munitions. *Clubs:* Constitutional and New, Glasgow. (K394)

MacLEOD, Harold Hay Brodie, M.B.E., F.R.C.S. (Edin.), *b.* 25 Aug. 1865; *s.* of Donald Alexander MacLeod, of Dalvey Cottage, Forres, N.B.; *m.* Katherine, *d.* of William Harrison, of Aigburth. *Educ.:* Cheltenham Coll. Senior Surgeon, Royal Salop Infirmary, and Consulting Surgeon to other Shropshire Hospitals. *War Work:* Worked in the various regular Hospitals and emergency War Hospitals of Shropshire. *Address:* Clive House, Shrewsbury. (M8917)

MACLEOD, Herwald Byrne, M.B.E.

MACLEOD, Lieut. James Keith, M.B.E., R.F.A.

McLEOD, Capt. James Walter, O.B.E., M.B., R.A.M.C.

McLEOD, Major James William, O.B.E. A.S.C.

MACLEOD, Rev. John, O.B.E.

MacLEOD, Sir John Lorne, G.B.E., LL.B. (Edin.), *b.* 1873; *s.* of the late John MacLeod, formerly, R.A. *Educ.:* Arts and Law Classes at Edinburgh Univ. Admitted Member of Society of Solicitors, Supreme Courts of Scotland, 1895, and carries on legal practice in Edinburgh; Member of Edinburgh Town Council for Canongate Ward, 1905-19; City Treasurer, 1912-14; Lord Provost of Edinburgh, 1916-19: Ex-President of the T.F. Assocn.; Food Commissioner in Scotland, 1920; J.P. and D.L. of the County of the City; and J.P. for Argyllshire. *Address:* 72, Great King Street, Edinburgh. *Clubs:* National Liberal; University; Scottish Liberal (Edinburgh).
(G63)

McLEOD, Major Leonard Frederick, O.B.E., R.A.O.C.

MacLEOD, Major Murray, O.B.E., R.A., *b.* 9 Feb. 1886; *s.* of the late Admiral Angus MacLeod, C.V.O., of Holmisdal, Skye; *m.* Ethel Phillis, *d.* of William Boosey, of Streatley, Berks. *Educ.:* Privately. Army. *War Work:* At the Front, Aug. 1914, to Feb. 1915; present at battles of Mons, Le Cateau, the Marne, the Aisne, and Flanders; Inspection Dept., Woolwich Arsenal, 1915 to end of war. *Addresses:* Holmisdal, Glendale, Isle of Skye; Inspection Dept., Woolwich Arsenal. (O3814)

MACLEOD, Olive Moultrie, M.B.E.

MACLEOD, Col. Robert Lockhart Ross, C.B., C.B.E., M.D., R.A.M.C., *b.* 1863. *Educ.:* Glasgow Univ. (M.B. and C.M. 1884). S. African War, 1901-2 (Queen's medal with four clasps); Great War, 1914-19 (mentioned in despatches).
(C1287)

MACLEOD, Capt. Thomas, O.B.E., R.A.F.

MACLEOD, Lieut.-Comm. William Simon Fraser, O.B.E., R.N.

McLINTOCK, Charles Henry, O.B.E., C.A., *b.* 7 Nov. 1888; *s.* of Thomson McLintock, of Glasgow. *Educ.:* Glasgow Academy. *War Work:* Assistant Controller, Dept. of Factory Audit and Costs, Ministry of Munitions. *Address:* 42, Hamilton Drive, Pollokshields, Glasgow. (O531)

McLOUGHLIN, Lieut.-Col. Mark Wilson, D.S.O., O.B.E., *b.* 23 Sept. 1877; *s.* of Mark McLoughlin, of Londonderry; *m.* Mary Isabel, *d.* of James Macintosh, of Pretoria, S.A. *War Work:* S. African War, 1899-1902; Great War, 1914-20. *Address:* Box 6823 Johannesburg. *Club:* Pretoria. (O2386)

MACLURE, Lieut.-Col. Alfred Fay, O.B.E., Aust. A.M.C.

MACLURE, Harry Julius, M.B.E., *b.* 2 Feb. 1868; *s.* of H. Martyn Maclure, of Manchester; *m.* Edith, *d.* of Alfred Newell, of High Wycombe. *Educ.:* Privately. Inspector of Contract Depts., Telephone Branch, General Post Office. *War Work:* Occupied position of Section Director of Electrical Stores purchase Section of the Ministry of Munitions from the commencement of the work of the Ministry onwards. *Address:* 101, Airedale Avenue, Chiswick, London, W. 4. (M8918)

MACLURE, Margaret Eleanor, M.B.E., J.P., *b.* Aug. 1865; *d.* of Sir John W. Maclure, Bart., of Whalley Range, Manchester (*see* BURKE'S *Peerage*). J.P. for the County Palatine of Lancashire. *War Work:* Organiser of the Manchester War Hospital Supply Depot. *Address:* Brynderw, Oak Drive, Fallowfield, Manchester. (M2108)

McMAHON, Lieut. Albert James, M.B.E.

MacMAHON, Major Gerald Patrick Ruodh, M.B.E., A.G.R., *b.* 20 Feb. 1884; *s.* of Major George MacMahon, late Indian Staff Corps. *Educ.:* Wellington Coll. *War Work:* Proceeded overseas to France in Sept. 1914 with 1st Siege Brigade; joined Anti-Aircraft in June, 1915; Anti-Aircraft Instructor of Gunnery Shoeburyness from May, 1916, to May, 1918; acted as Anti Aircraft Defence Commander, Fifth Army, from May, 1918, to Armistice. *Address:* Anti-Aircraft Depot, Parkhurst, Isle of Wight. *Club:* Sports. (O5529)

McMAHON, Sir Horace Westropp, Bart., O.B.E., *b.* 28 Oct. 1863; *s.* of 3rd Bart. (*see* BURKE'S *Peerage*); *m.* Ellie Maude,

d. of Hon. H. Moses, M.L.C., Sydney, and widow of Capt. C. E. Bancroft, R.W.F. Joined Royal Welsh Fusiliers, 1885; Capt.1895; served S. Africa, 1896 (despatches, D.S.O., medal); Crete, 1898 (Brevet Major); S. Africa, 1899-1900; Croix de Guerre. *Address:* Southbroom House, Devizes, Wilts.
(O2242)

McMAHON, Lieut.-Col. Kellerman Eyre, O.B.E.

McMAHON, Michael, M.B.E., *b.* 1876; *s.* of Laurence McMahon, of Weymouth. *Educ.:* St. Augustin's, Weymouth; Kings Coll., London. Civil Servant; Irish Health Insurance Commission. *War Work:* In charge of Area Clearing Houses of the Ministry of Munitions; Section Director Dept. of Engineering; Section Director, Disposal Board. *Address:* Vernon Avenue, Clontarf, Dublin. (M8919)

MACMAHON, Major Neil Cullum Mildred, O.B.E., R.F.A. (T.).

McMANUS, Norman, O.B.E.

MCMASTER, Hugh, M.B.E., J.P.

McMASTER, Capt. Patrick Garnet Walsh McMaster, O.B.E.

McMATH, Capt. John, O.B.E.

McMENAMIN, Peter Paul, M.B.E.

McMENEMY, Capt. Frank, M.B.E., *b.* 22 Oct. 1853; *s.* of Capt. John McMenemy, of Campbeltown. *Educ.:* Grammar School, Campbeltown, Argyll. Master Mariner. *Address:* North Street, Houston, Renfrewshire. (M8921)

McMICHAEL, John Fisher, O.B.E.

McMICHAN, Capt. Walter Campbell, O.B.E., R.N.

MACMILLAN, Agnes Olive, O.B.E.; *d.* of John Macmillan, S.S.C., of Edinburgh. *Educ.:* Edinburgh and Germany. *War Work:* Chairwoman Forth R.G.A. Comforts Fund; Commandant in the Edinburgh American Welcome Club; Worker in Scottish Churches' Hut Canteen, London Road, Y.M.C.A. Canteen, St. Andrew's Square, and Regimental Canteen, Duddingston Camp, Edinburgh. *Address:* Newlands House, Bright Crescent, Edinburgh. (O10910)

MACMILLAN, Lieut.-Col. Alexander, O.B.E., T.D., R.G.A. (T), *b.* 17 Nov. 1871; *s.* of John Macmillan, S.S.C., of Edinburgh. *Educ.:* Royal High School, Edinburgh, and Edinburgh Univ. Solicitor Supreme Courts of Scotland. *War Work:* Lieut.-Col. commanding Forth R.G.A. (T.), C.R.G.A., Inner Forth Defences and Fire Commander; twice mentioned in Sec. of State for War's Lists. *Address:* Newlands House, Bright Crescent, Edinburgh. *Clubs:* Caledonian United Service; Scottish Conservative. (O532)

MACMILLAN, Capt. Archibald, O.B.E., L.R.C.P. & S. (Edin.), D.P.H. (Camb.), *b.* 1877. *Educ.:* Anderson's Coll., and Glasgow Univ. *War Work:* France and Mesopotamia, O.C. 19th Sanitary Sect., Basra. (O6659)

MACMILLAN, Archibald Macpherson, O.B.E.

McMILLAN, James, O.B.E. For many years Provost of Rothesay. (O11915)

MACMILLAN, Lieut. James Charles Newsome, O.B.E., R.N.

MACMILLAN, Rev. John Victor, O.B.E., *b.* 2 May, 1877; *s.* of the late Alexander Macmillan, Publisher, of London; *m.* Annie, *d.* of Maj.-Gen. Sir Frederick Maurice, K.C.B. *Educ.:* Eton Coll.; Magdalen Coll., Oxford. Vicar of Kew, Surrey; Hon. Chaplain to Archbishop of Canterbury. *War Work:* Temp. Chaplain to the Forces, 1915-16 and 1917-19; demobilised 3rd Class. *Address:* The Vicarage, Kew, Surrey. *Club:* Athenæum.

McMILLAN, Margaret, C.B.E., *b.* 1964; *s.* of James McMillan. *Educ.:* Inverness; Edinburgh; Geneva. Founded the first open-air nursery school. *Addresses:* 353, Evelyn Street, Deptford, S.E.; The Rachel McMillan Training Coll., 232, Church Street, Deptford, S.E. (C43)

McMILLAN, Sara Jane, Mrs., M.B.E., *b.* 6 Sept. 1874; *d.* of William Cameron, of Kilmarnock; *m.* Thomas, *s.* of James McMillan, of Galston. *Educ.:* Privately. *War Work:* Convener of Glasgow Corporation Committee for Belgian Refugees; Treas. for Glasgow Prisoners of War Care Committee. (M8929)

MACMILLAN, William, M.B.E.

McMILLAN, William Bentley, C.B.E., J.P.

McMORDIE, Julia, Mrs., C.B.E., J.P., *b.* 30 March, 1860; *d.* of Sir William Gray, D.L., of West Hartlepool; *m.* the late Robert James McMordie, M.A., M.P., *s.* of Rev. J. A. McMordie, of Seaford, Co. Down. *Educ.:* Chislehurst. Alderman in Belfast City Council; Lady of Grace of the Order of St. John of Jerusalem. *War Work:* President of Women's V.A. Detachments, Belfast; Head of large work parties for soldiers' comforts and Hospital requisites; Head of Depot for Ulster Joint Committee distributing materials. *Address:* Cabin Hill, Knock, Belfast. (C1002)

McMULLEN, 2nd Lieut. John Alexander, M.B.E., R.A.F.

McMULLEN, Capt. Kenrick James, M.B.E., R.E.

McMULLEN, Temp. Lieut. William Albert, M.B.E.

McMULLEN, William Halliburton, O.B.E., M.B., B.S., F.R.C.S., Fellow of the Royal Society of Medicine, *b.* 19 June, 1876; *s.* of William McMullen, of 40 Parliament Hill, Hampstead; *m.* Kate Constance, *d.* of G. Randall Higgins, J.P., of The Croft, Burcote, Oxon. *Educ.:* City of London School; King's Coll., London; King's Coll. Hospital. Ophthalmic Surgeon to the Great Northern Central Hospital, and to the Hospital for Sick Children, Great Ormond Street; Surgeon to the Royal Westminster Ophthalmic Hospital; Consulting Ophthalmologist to Ministry of Pensions, etc. *War Work:* Senior Ophthalmic Specialist to Central London Recruiting

Depot, Whitehall, 1916–18 ; Ophthalmic Specialist to London Pensions Medical Boards, 1918–19 ; Member of Advisory Committee on visual standards in The Army. *Addresses :* 133, Harley Street, W. 1. ; 30, Lyndhurst Road, N.W. 3.
(O1629)

McMUNN, Lieut.-Col. Andrew, O.B.E., R.A.M.C.

McMURDO, Archibald Hugh, M.B.E.

McMURRAY, Elizabeth Eleanor, Mrs., M.B.E.

MACMURRAY, James Hamish, C.B.E.

McMURRAY, William Hamilton, O.B.E., M.C.

McMURTRIE, Capt. Basil Flexman, O.B.E., R.F.A. (S.R.).

McNAB, James, O.B.E.

MACNAB, Margaret Grahame Bryce, M.B.E. *b.* 22 Aug. 1881 ; *d.* of William McNab, of Keithock, Brechin. *Educ. :* Haddington, Brechin, and Hampstead. Director and Member of House Committee Brechin Infirmary ; Member of Finance Committee, Brechin War Memorial ; District Commissioner Girl Guides ; Member of Black Watch Memorial Home Committee ; Member Executive and Organiser's Committees Forfarshire Unionist Association. *War Work :* Red Cross Commandant Brechin V.A.D. ; Worked in connection with Brechin Auxiliary Hospital ; organised entertainments to raise money for Red Cross and other War Funds ; organised and ran Brechin Red Cross Depot, 1914–19 ; Local National Egg Collection ; organised a large number of Flag Days in Brechin and District ; started a local Fund for Comforts for the 5th Black Watch on Active Service, and sent parcels from Nov. 1914 ; acted on Committees of Prince of Wales' Fund, Sailors' and Soldiers' Families Association, War Pensions, etc. *Address :* Keithock, Brechin, Forfarshire. (M2111)

MACNAB, Major Ronald Charles, O.B.E., R.A.O.C.

McNAB, Major Wallace John, O.B.E.

MACNAB, William, C.B.E., F.I.C., *b.* 1858 ; *s.* of William Macnab, Shipbuilder, of Greenock ; *m.* Jane *d.* of John Reid, of Glasgow. *Educ. :* Greenock Academy, Edinburgh Institution ; Glasgow Univ. *War Work :* Technical Adviser, Dept. Explosives Supply, Ministry of Munitions. *Address :* 10, Cromwell Crescent, S.W. *Clubs :* Bath ; Chemical Industry. (C2781)

McNABB, Surg.-Rear-Adm. Sir Daniel Joseph Patrick, K.B.E., C.B., *b.* 11 Oct. 1862 ; *s.* of Thomas McNabb, of Southsea : *m.* Kate Mayes, *d.* of Fysher Negus, of Southsea. *Educ. :* St. Cuthbert's Coll., Ushaw, Durham ; Durham Univ. ; London Hospital. Medical Officer Royal Navy ; Surgeon, 1886 ; Staff Surgeon, 1898 ; Fleet-Surgeon 1902 ; Surgeon Capt. 1914 ; Surgeon Rear-Admiral, 1919. *War Work :* Served as Deputy Director-General Medical Department, Admiralty, 1916–19 ; in command R.N. Hospital, Plymouth, since Nov. 1919. *Address :* R.N. Hospital, Plymouth. (K261)

MACNAGHTEN, Hon. Sir Malcolm Martin, K.B.E., M.A., K.C., *b.* 12 Jan. 1869 ; *s.* of Lord Macnaghten, G.C.B., G.C.M.G., of Runkerry, Co. Antrim (*see* BURKE's *Peerage*) ; *m.* Antonia Mary, *d.* of the late Rt. Hon. Charles Booth, F.R.S. *Educ. :* Eton, and Trinity Coll., Cambridge. Barrister, Lincoln's Inn, 1894 ; elected a Bencher, 1915 ; King's Counsel, 1919. *War Work :* Director of the Foreign Claims Office from 1915–19. *Addresses :* 28, Campden House Court, London, W. 8 ; Portballintrae, Bushmills, Co. Antrim. *Club :* United Univ. (K395)

MACNAGHTEN, Norman Donnelly, O.B.E.

MACNAGHTEN, Terence Charles, C.B.E.

McNAIR, Arnold Duncan, C.B.E., M.A., LL.M., *b.* 4 March, 1885 ; *s.* of John McNair, of Lloyd's, Royal Exchange, London ; *m.* Marjorie, *d.* of the Hon. Mr. Justice Bailhache, of Totteridge, Herts. *Educ. :* Aldenham School, and Gonville and Caius Coll., Cambridge. Fellow Tutor and Law Lecturer of Gonville and Caius Coll., Cambridge. *War Work :* Sec. to Coal Controller's Advisory Board ; Sec. to Coal Conservation Committee ; Sec. to Imperial Mineral Resources Bureau ; Sec. to Coal Industry Commission. *Addresses :* Gonville and Caius Coll. ; 4, Mortimer Road, Cambridge. (C561)

McNAIR, Arthur Wyndham, O.B.E., J.P., I.C.S., *b.* 23 Aug. 1872 ; *s.* of the late Major McNair, C.M.G., R.A., Brighton ; *m.* Elizabeth Eva Dawn, *d.* of the late David Charles Ballinger Griffith, Bedford. *Educ. :* St. Paul's School, and Balliol Coll., Oxford. Indian Civil Service ; Commissioner, Rohilkand Division, United Provinces, India. *Address :* Brentor View, Lewdown, North Devon. *Club :* East India United Service. (O4070)

McNAIR, Lieut. George Douglas, M.B.E., I.A.R.O.

McNAIR, Capt. Matthew Barr, M.B.E., R.A.S.C.

McNALTY, Lieut.-Col. Arthur George Preston, C.M.G., C.B.E., *s.* of the late Lieut.-Col. George William McNalty, C.B. *b.* 1871 ; *m. o.d.* of Harry de Windt, F.R.G.S.. Ent. Army Ser. Corps, 1901, and is Major and Brevet-Lieut.-Col. S. African War, 1899–1902 (Queen's and King's S.A. medals), Dardanelles, 1915–16 (wounded, despatches). (C1288)

MACNALTY, Mary, Mrs., M.B.E.

McNAUGHTAN, Capt. and Brevet Major William, O.B.E., M.B., R.A.M.C., *b.* 1887 ; *s.* of Major R. McNaughtan, of St. Fillans ; *m.,* 1920, Peggy, *d.* of C. Kinloch, of Corner House, Queensberry Road, Edinburgh. *Educ. :* Morrison's Academy, and Edinburgh University. *Address :* c/o Holt & Co., 3, Whitehall Place. (O6660)

McNAUGHTON, Capt. John Love, M.B.E., V.D., Order of the Crown of Belgium, *b.* 7 April, 1857 ; *s.* of John McNaughton, Kirkcowan, Wigtownshire ; *m.* Nellie Smith, *d.* of William Robert Duguid, M.D., J.P., of Buckie, Banffshire.

Educ. : Kirkbean Public School ; Edinburgh Univ. Solicitor ; Agent, Clydesdale Bank, Ltd. ; Clerk of the Peace for Banffshire ; Town Clerk of Buckie. *War Work :* Military Representative at 5 Local Tribunals ; Hon. Sec. County of Banff War Workers Association ; Hon. Sec. Buckie Belgian Fund ; Food Executive Officer for Burgh of Buckie ; Capt. " D " Coy. 1st Banffshire Volunteer Battalion. *Address :* Rosemount, Buckie, Scotland. *Club :* Scottish Conservative, Edinburgh. (M3824)

MACNEAL, Sir Hector Murray, K.B.E., '*b.* 8 Feb. 1879 ; *s.* of the late Frederick H. and grandson of the late George Macneal, of Ugadale, and Lossit, Argyllshire ; *m.* 9 Oct. 1912, Margery, *d.* of the late John Henderson. Rendered valuable voluntary service to Ministry of Shipping, principally in connection with the administration of tonnage for the United Kingdom and France. *Address :* 17, Queen's Gate, S.W. 7. *Clubs :* Caledonian ; Royal Societies' ; Conservative. (K396)

McNEICE, Capt. Arthur Charles Davenport, O.B.E.

McNEIL, T. Warrant Officer A., M.B.E. Royal Indian Marine.

McNEIL, Alice Hill, Mrs. Charles, O.B.E.

McNEIL, Charles, O.B.E.

McNEIL, Major James Howard, O.B.E.

McNEIL, Capt. Neil, O.B.E.

McNEILE, Mary Bridget, M.B.E., *b.* 4 Nov. 1896 ; *d.* of Lieut.-Col. J. McNeile, of Kippilan, St. Boswells, N.B. *Educ. :* Privately. *War Work :* Wounded and Missing Enquiry Department, British Red Cross, from 1915–18 ; Y.W.C.A. Canteen, The Hague, Holland, 1918. *Address :* 11, Embankment Gardens, Chelsea. (M3825)

McNEILL, Eileen Maud Mary, M.B.E., *b.* 14 July, 1893 ; *d.* of the late Duncan Alexander McNeill. *Educ. :* Francis Holland School, Eaton Square ; Queen Anne's School, Caversham, Reading. Sec. Foreign Office. for work abroad. *War Work :* Jan. 1916, to Jan. 1917, V.A.D. in Duncombe Park Hospital, Helmsley, Yorks ; Jan. 1917, to July, 1918, V.A.D. Sec. at No. 9 Red Cross Hospital (Millicent Sutherland Ambulance), France ; July, 1918, to Sept. 1919, Sec. Intelligence Section, War Office, for work abroad. *Address :* 130, Belgrave Road, London, W. (M8925)

McNEILL, Capt. Hector, O.B.E.

McNEILL, Rev. John Henry Horton, M.B.E., M.A., B.D., *b.* 12 Dec. 1872 ; *s.* of Alexander McNeill, J.P., of Glasgow ; *m.* Lilian Sophie, *d.* of Ronald Currie, M.D., J.P., of Skelmorlie. *Educ. :* Hutcheson's Grammar School and High School, Glasgow ; Madras Coll. ; St. Andrews, and Glasgow and Jena Univs. Indian Ecclesiastical Establishment. Officiating Presidency Senior Chaplain, Church of Scotland, Madras Presidency. *War Work :* 1914–15, with Indian Divisions in France ; 1916–17, in Mesopotamia (twice mentioned in despatches). *Address :* c/o Messrs. Cox & Co., Indian Dept., 16, Charing Cross, London, S.W. 1. (M3000)

MacNEILL, Malcolm, M.B.E., *b.* 22 June, 1871 ; *s.* of Hector MacNeill, of Ardlussa, Jura, Argyll ; *m.* Mary Helen, *d.* of John Sinclair, of Inveraray, Argyll. *Educ. :* Ardlussa Public School, Jura, Argyll. Sergt., Argyllshire Constabulary. *War Work :* In charge of the work of recovery and identification of American soldiers who lost their lives, off the coast of Islay, in the disasters to the Troopships " Tuscania " and " Otranto " on 5 Feb. and 6 Oct. 1918, respectively, and other equally important Police duties during the period of the Great War. *Address :* Argyllshire Constabulary, Bowmore, Islay. (M8926)

MACNEILL, William, O.B.E., J.P., *b.* 26 Feb. 1861 ; *s.* of William Macneill, of Muthill, Perthshire ; *m.* Janet Gardner MacGregor, *d.* of George Macgregor, of Motherwell. *Educ. :* Foulden, Berwickshire, ; Muthill, Perthshire. Provost of Motherwell, 1916–19. *War Work :* Chairman of Motherwell Tribunal, Motherwell War Savings Association, Motherwell Pensions Sub-Committee ; Committees of Motherwell Relief Fund, Belgian Relief Fund, Belgian Refugees Fund, Association of Voluntary Organisations (Comforts to Soldiers), Motherwell and District Nursing and Ambulance Association ; Member of Dalziel Auxiliary Hospital ; Member of County of Lanark Pensions Committee. *Address :* Dunira, Motherwell. (O10912)

McNICOLL, David, M.B.E.

McNISH, Col. George, C.B.E., T.D., J.P., *b.* 10 Sept. 1866 ; *s.* of Robert McNish, J.P., of Ardenlea, West Kilbride, Ayrshire ; *m.* Margaret, *d.* of William Frew, of Edinburgh. *Educ. :* Hutcheson's Grammar School, Glasgow, and Glasgow High School. *War Work :* In Command of 2/7th Batt. The Highland Light Infantry ; Officer in Charge Labour Corps Record Office. *Address :* 35, Falkland Mansions, Hyndland, Glasgow. *Club :* Junior Army and Navy. (C1118)

MACONACHIE, Capt. Charles Ogle, O.B.E., M.C., R.A.V.C.

MACONOCHIE, Charles Cornelius, C.B.E., K.C., *b.* 2 Jan. 1852 ; *s.* of Robert Blair Maconochie, of Gattonside House, Melrose ; *m.* Alice Mary, *d.* of R. Robertson, of Auchleeks, Perthshire. *Educ. :* Winchester ; Edinburgh Univ. Sheriff of the Lothians and Peebles, 1904–18. *War Work :* Chairman Appeal Tribunal of the Lothians and Peebles. *Address :* Avontoun, Linlithgowshire. *Clubs :* New Edinburgh ; Caledonian, London. (C232)

MACONOCHIE, Com. Charles Ernest, O.B.E., R.N.

MACONOCHIE, Robert Henry, O.B.E., *b.* 11 May, 1883 ; *s.* of C. C. Maconochie, of Avontoun, Linlithgow ; *m.* Laura

Patricia, *d.* of J. J. Cowan, of Westerlea, Murrayfield, Edinburgh. *Educ.:* Edinburgh Academy; Winchester; Univ. Coll., Oxford. Advocate, Edinburgh. *War Work:* Lieut., General List; Ministry of National Service. *Address:* 23, Northumberland Street, Edinburgh. *Clubs:* New, Edinburgh; Caledonian; Leander; Hon. Company of Edinburgh Golfers. (O381)

MACOUN, Capt. James, O.B.E.

MACOWAN, Capt. Norman James, O.B.E., R.A.S.C.

MACPHAIL, Capt. Agnew Main, M.B.E., *b.* 10th March, 1896; *s.* of S. Rutherford Macphail, Esq., M.D., of Rowditch, Derby. *Educ.:* The Glebe House, Hunstanton, Norfolk; Brighton Coll. Solicitor. *War Work:* Served with the 3rd Batt. Royal Berkshire Regt., Aug. 1914, to Nov. 1919; served in France attached to 1st Batt. King's Shropshire L.I. *Address:* 19, Portland Square, Carlisle. *Club:* Cumberland County, Carlisle. (M5450)

MACPHAIL, Major Sir Andrew, O.B.E.. M.A., M.D., M.R.C.S., *b.* 24 Nov. 1864; *s.* of William Macphail, of Orwell, Prince Edward Island, Canada; *m.* Georgina (d. 1902), *d.* of G. B. Burland, of Montreal. *Educ.:* Prince of Wales Coll.; McGill Univ.; London Hospital. Professor, History of Measure, McGill Univ. *War Work:* 6th Field Ambulance, 2nd Canadian Division, B.E.F.; Nov. 1914, to July, 1917; H.Q. Staff until April, 1919. *Address:* 216, Peel Street, Montreal. *Clubs:* Mount Royal, Univ., Montreal; Lotos, New York. (O7922)

MACPHAIL, Capt. Douglas Ross, O.B.E.

MACPHAIL, Dugald, M.B.E., *b.* 1869; *s.* of Angus Macphail, of Crinan, Argyllshire; *m.* Clara, *d.* of Joseph T. Wood, of Warrington, Lanc. *Educ.:* Bellanoch Public School. Ship master. *War Work:* Transport Service. *Address:* 96, Camphill Avenue, Langside, Glasgow. (M8928)

MACPHAIL, The Hon. Rev. Earle Monteith, C.B.E., *b.* 31 Jan. 1861; *s.* of the late Rev. Dr. J. C. Macphail, of Edinburgh; *m.* Mary, *d.* of the late James Meliss Stuart, of Eriska. *Educ.:* Edinburgh Academy; Edinburgh Univ; Universities of Jena, Tübingen, and Berlin; New Coll., Edinburgh. Missionary of the United Free Church of Scotland, Professor of History, and Acting Principal of the Madras Christian Coll.; Fellow of the Univ. of Madras; Member of the Legislation Council of the Governor of Fort St. George, Madras. *War Work:* Propaganda work; Chairman of the Publicity Board of the Madras Presidency. *Address:* Coll. Road, Madras; Benderloch, Kodaikanal, South India. *Club:* Madras. (C2387)

MACPHAIL, Major Hector Duncan, O.B.E., M.D., R.A.M.C.

McPHAIL, Lieut. Lachlan Rose, M.B.E.

McPHERSON, Lieut.-Col. Charles Duncan, O.B.E.

McPHERSON, Capt. Dougal Campbell, M.B.E., R.A.O.C.

MACPHERSON, Lieut.-Col. Duncan Gordon, C.B.E.,

MacPHERSON, Rev. Duncan Gordon, M.B.E., M.A., *b.* 12 Aug. 1879; *s.* of the late John MacPherson, of The Glebe, Penshurst. *Educ.:* Malvern Coll., and Gonville and Calus Coll., Cambridge. Formerly Warden of Calus Mission, Battersea, 1903–05; Curate in charge of Mission Church, St. Mary Redcliffe, Bristol, 1905–08; Vicar of Knighton, Rads. 1908–15; now Senior curate St. Mary Redcliffe, Bristol. *War Work:* Temp. Chaplain, 1915–17, with 16th Training Reserve Brigade; Commissioner Church Army, B.E.F., 1917; Messenger for C.E.M.S. to Troops in the East, 1917–18; Temp. Chaplain, M.E.F., 1918–19; Temp. Chaplain, Indian Ecclesiastical Establishment, 1919–20. *Addresses:* The Clergy House, Redcliffe, Bristol; c/o Grindlay & Co., 54, Parliament Street. (O6661)

MACPHERSON, Major Duncan Iver, O.B.E.

McPHERSON, Duncan Louis, M.B.E.

MACPHERSON, Rev. Eiven George Fitzroy, C.B.E., O.M.B.

MACPHERSON, Eleonora Thompson, Mrs., O.B.E.

MACPHERSON, Lieut.-Col. Ernest Ronald, O.B.E.

MACPHERSON, Rev. George Cook, O.B.E., M.A., B.D.

McPHERSON, Gilbert, O.B.E.

McPHERSON, Henry Alexander, C.B.E.

McPHERSON, Capt. Malcolm Munro, O.B.E., M.A., *b.* 1892; *s.* of Rev. Robert Macpherson, V.D., D.D., of Elgin, N.B. *Educ.:* Edinburgh Univ. *War Work:* Commissioned Oct. 1914, 6th Seaforth Highlanders (51st H.D.); Capt., 1916, Commanding 25th Labour Coy (Duke of Wellington's) 1917; Wounded; mentioned in despatches; 1914–15 Star. *Address:* The Manse, Elgin; Lipney, Lossiemouth, N.B. (O5532)

MACPHERSON, Margaret, Mrs., M.B.E.

MACPHERSON, Major Osborne Cluny, O.B.E., R.A.F.

MACPHERSON, Rev. Ranald, O.B.E., *b.* 1 Sept. 1871; *s.* of the late Charles Macpherson, of Edinburgh. *Educ.:* St. Paul's Cathedral School, London; Edinburgh Episcopal Theological Coll. Precentor, Ripon Cathedral. *War Work:* Chaplain, 1st W. Riding Brigade, till April, 1915; Senior C.E. Chaplain, Ripon, 1915–19. *Address:* The Cathedral, Ripon. (O7438)

McPHERSON, Capt. Stuart Mackintosh, M.B.E.

McPHERSON, Thomas, M.B.E.

MACPHERSON, Thomas, O.B.E.

McPHERSON, Thomas, M.B.E.

MACPHERSON, Violette, M.B.E.

MACPHIE, Major John James, O.B.E,

MACPHILLAMY, Verania, O.B.E.

McQUADE, William, M.B.E.

MACQUEEN, Frances Helen, Mrs., O.B.E., *b.* 17 Nov. 1886; *d.* of William Thomas Grant, M.D., of Broughty Ferry, Forfarshire; *m.* John Ellison Macqueen, Lieut.-Col., 6th Gordon Highlanders (killed in action at Loos, 25 Sept. 1915), *s.* of John Otto Macqueen, of Faemewell, Aberdeenshire. *Educ.:* St. Leonard's School, St. Andrews, Fife, and Paris. Member of Aberdeen Education Authority. *War Work:* Hon. Sec., Abderdeen War Dressings Depot; Member of Scottish Sphagnum Moss Committee; Director of Northern Area of Scottish Sphagnum Moss Committee; Member of various War Relief Committees in Aberdeen. *Address:* Thornlea, Seafield, Aberdeen. (O3821)

MACQUEEN, John, M.B.E.

MACQUEEN, Capt. Loudon Hope, O.B.E., R.A.V.C.

MACQUEEN, Margaret Marsden, M.B.E.

MACQUEEN, Major Robert Haldane, O.B.E.

McQUIBBAN, Lewis, O.B.E., *b.* 31 July, 1866; *m.* Constance Emma Lowd, *d.* of Arthur Jeffries, of London. *Educ.:* Grammar School, Old Aberdeen, and King's Coll., London. Senior Clerk, Scottish Education Department; Sec. Highlands and Islands Medical Service Board; Assist. Sec. Scottish Board of Health. *War Work:* Administration of medical and kindred services on the Highlands and Islands of Scotland. *Address:* 77, Morningside Park, Edinburgh. (O10913)

McQUILLEN, William, M.B.E., *b.* 31 Oct. 1863; *s.* of John McQuillen, of Newcastle-on-Tyne; *m.* Gertrude Evangeline, *d.* of John Storr, of West Hartlepool. *Educ.:* Bath Lane School; Rutherford Coll., Newcastle; Borough Road Coll., London. Headmaster, Park School, Whitley Bay. *War Work:* Hon. Sec. to the Schools' War Savings Committee of the Northumberland Education Authority; one of the pioneers of War Saving in public Elementary Schools. *Address:* Westward. St. George's Crescent, Monkseaton. (M2114)

McRAE, Alexander, M.B.E.

McRAE, Bessie, M.B.E.

MACRAE, Major Donald Macnaughton, O.B.E.

MACRAE, Elizabeth Nina, M.B.E., *b.* 30 Oct. 1893; *d.* of Linlay Alexander Macrae, of Warlingham, Surrey. *Educ.:* Tottenham High School; St. Hilda's Hall, Oxford. Extension Lecturer, London Univ. *War Work:* Welfare Department, Ministry of Munitions, 1916–17; National Savings Committee, 1917–18. *Address:* 60, Overstrand Mansions, London, S.W. 11. (M3827)

McRAE, Major Henry St. George Murray, D.S.O., M.B.E., 2/15 Sikhs. O11752)

MACRAE Herbert Alexander, M.B.E., M.A., *b.* 12 June, 1886. *Educ.:* Aberdeen Univ. His Majesty's Consular Service in Japan (Vice-Consul). *War Work:* Attached to British Legation, Christiania, for work in connection with Blockade. (M2116)

MACRAE, Lieut.-Col. Ian Macpherson, O.B.E., M.B.

MacRAE, Lady Margaret, O.B.E., J.P., *d.* of 3rd Marquess of Bute, K.T. (*see* BURKE'S *Peerage*); *m.* Major Colin William MacRae, of Feoirlinn, J.P., D.L., *s.* of Duncan MacRae, of Conchra, J.P., D.L. Lady of Grace of the Order of St. John of Jerusalem. *Address:* 22, Mansfield St., W. 1; Ascog Hall, Isle of Bute; Feoirlinn, Colintraive, Argyll. (O10914)

MACRAE, Lieut.-Col. Robert Scarth Farquhar, C.I.E., C.B.E., *b.* 1877; *s.* of the late John Macrae, Procurator Fiscal of Orkney; *m.* 1911, Beatrix Reed, *d.* of the late Andrew McGeoch, of Glasgow. *Educ.:* Glenalmond, and at St. Andrews Univ. Major and T. Lieut.-Col. Indian Police; Dist. Sup. of Police, Bihar and Orissa, and Commnr. of Police, Baroda, 1912–16; served in Somaliland, 1904–5 (medal with clasp); Mesopotamia, 1915–19, as Controller of Native Craft. *Address:* Grindelay, Orphir, Orkney. *Clubs:* Bengal United Service; Calcutta. (C1428)

McRAITH, John Warden, M.B.E.

MACREADY, Lieut.-Col. Gordon Nevil, D.S.O., O.B.E., M.C., *m.*, 1929, Elisabeth de Noailles, *y. d.* of the Duc de Noailles, of Mamheuan, Eure-et-Loire.

McREDDIE, Margaret, Mrs., M.B.E., *b.* 1 Nov. 1854; *d.* of Ralph Sillars Boyd, of Glasgow; *m.* George Dougal McReddie, *s.* of George King McReddie. *Educ.:* London. *War Work:* Hon. Sec. Soldiers' and Sailors' Families Association since 1900; Representative for Dartford Rural Division of War Pensions Sub-Committee. *Address:* Stone Court, Greenhithe, Kent. (M2117)

MACREDIE, Hastings George Cunningham, M.B.E.

McRITCHIE, Major Charles Bell, O.B.E., R.E.

McRITCHIE, Lieut. William MacPherson, O.B.E., R.N.R.

McROBBIE, David, M.B.E.

McROBERT, Sir Alexander, K.B.E. V.D., LL.D., F.R.G.S., *b.* 21 May, 1854; *s.* of John McRobert, of Downside, Tarland, N.B.; *m.* as his 2nd wife, Rachel, *d.* of Dr. William Hunter Workman, of Worcester, Massachusetts, U.S.A. *Educ.:* Public Schools, Newhills, N.B., and Royal Coll. of Science. Manager and Director of the Cawnpore Woollen Mills Co., Ltd., Cawnpore; before going to Cawnpore, in 1884, held appointment of Neil Arnott Lecturer in Experimental Physics, Mechanics' Institution, Aberdeen, and was Lecturer in Chemistry in Robert Gordon's Coll., Aberdeen; President of Upper India Chamber of Commerce for nine years, and five times Member of Legislative Council of the United Provinces of Agra and Oudh for periods of two years each ; Representative of the Chamber at the Congresses of Chambers of Commerce of the Empire at Montreal, 1903, London, 1906 and 1912, and Sydney, 1909 ; Fellow of the University of Allahabad ; Member of Committee, Government Engineering Coll., Roorkee ; Governor of Agricultural Coll., Cawnpore ; Lieut.-Col. Commanding Cawnpore Vol. Rifles, *Address:* The Shieling, Cawnpore. *Clubs:* Bath ; Oriental ; National Liberal (Cawnpore). (K331)

MacROBERT, William Graham, O.B.E. (O11993)

MACRORY, Lieut. Adam John Charles, M.B.E., R.F.A. (T.F.), *b.* 28 Oct. 1890 ; *s.* of L. G. F. Macrory, M.D., F.R.A.S., of Chesterfield, Worcester Park, Surrey ; *m.* Frances Mary, *d.* of E. H. Trotter, of Eastbourne. *Educ.:* St. Paul's School, Hammersmith. Late London Stock Exchange. *War Work:* 2nd London Brigade, R.F.A., Sept. 1914, to July, 1919 ; Active Service on Western Front with 36th and 56th Divisions. *Address:* St. Onge, Stoneleigh Drive, Worcester Park, Surrey. (M6673)

MACROSTIE, 2nd Lieut. Reginald David Gorrie, M.B.E., R.A.F.

MACROSTY, Henry William, O.B.E., B.A. (Lond.), *b.* 14 Jan. 1865 ; *s.* of the late Henry McRostie ; *m.* Edith Julia, *d.* of Hugh Bain, of Tain, Scotland. *Educ.:* Kirkcolm Public School, Wigtownshire, Scotland, and privately. Principal Staff Officer, Statistical Department, Board of Trade ; Author of "The Trust Movement in British Industry" (1907). *War Work:* Meat Supplies for the Allied Forces, and Control of Insulated Ships. *Address:* 29, Hervey Road, Blackheath, London, S.E. 3. (O533)

McSHEEHY, Lieut.-Col. Oswald William, D.S.O., M.B., B.S., L.R.C.P., M.R.C.S., *b.* 1884 ; *s.* of Surg.-Maj. E. L. McSheehy ; *m.* 1911, Carrie, *d.* of the late Col. H. Patterson, Indian Army. Entered Royal Army Med. Corps, 1909 ; Major and A. Lieut.-Col.: served during Great War, 1914–18 (despatches). (O8596)

MACSWINEY, Major John Charles, O.B.E.

MacSWINNEY, Elsie Trant, O.B.E., *b.* 1878 ; *d.* of R. F. MacSwinney, of the Inner Temple. *Educ.:* Privately. *War Work:* Nursing, Princess Beatrice Hospital, Hill Street, 1914–15 ; Commandant, V.A.D., London 198, May, 1915, to Jan. 1920 ; Officer-in-charge, Prisoner of War Parcels Census, July, 1916 ; Escort to Prisoners' Wives to Switzerland, Oct. 1916 ; Head of Motor Ambulance Department, V.A.D. H.Q., Devonshire House, July, 1916 onwards ; Head of Joint Committee Section V.A.D. H.Q., Sept. 1917, to May, 1919 ; Head of General Service Section, V.A.D. H.Q., May, 1919, to Dec. 1920 ; Divisional Sec., Paddington B.R.C.S., Jan. 1920 onwards. *Address:* 21, Sussex Square, W. 2. *Club:* Brancaster Golf. (O3822)

MacSWINNEY, Nora Kathleen, M.B.E., *d.* of R. F. MacSwinney, of 21, Sussex Square, W. 2. *Educ.:* Private School in London, and in Germany. Member of Paddington Borough Council. *War Work:* Quartermaster, Paddington Division B.R.C.S., Aug. 1914, to April, 1916 ; Quartermaster, Paddington V.A.D. Hospital, April, 1916, to July, 1919 ; mentioned by Secretary of State for War, Feb. 1919. *Address:* 21, Sussex Square, W. 2. *Club:* V.A.D. Ladies'. (M8931)

MACTAGGART, Lieut.-Col. John Norman, O.B.E., V.D., J.P. Valuable war services in the various local organisations in Kintyre. (O11916)

MACTIER, Henry Carter, M.B.E., B.A., M.B., B.Ch., B.A.O. (Dublin), *b.* 18 May, 1872 ; *s.* of James McTier, of Belfast and Castlebar ; *m.* Adeline Herbert, *d.* of Hugh Pierce, of Birkenhead. *Educ.:* Corrig School, Kingstown, Co. Dublin, and Dublin Univ. Hon. Surgeon, Wolverhampton and Mildand Counties Eye Infirmary ; Hon. Ophthalmic Surgeon, Royal Orphanage, Wolverhampton ; Member of Council British Medical Association ; Member Wolverhampton Insurance Committee. *War Work:* Member Wolverhampton Recruiting Board, 1914 –18 ; Member Pensions Board to May, 1919 ; Medical Referee, Ministry of Pensions, Feb. 1917, to Jan. 1920 ; in charge of wounded, Wolverhampton Eye Infirmary (auxiliary to 5th Northern Hospital) ; Hon. Sec. Local Medical War Committee, South Staffs. *Address:* 33, Tettenhall Road, Wolverhampton. (M8932)

McTURK, Major Alexander Gladstone, O.B.E., M.C.

McTURK, Isabel, Mrs., M.B.E., *d.* of John Marsh, of London. *Educ.:* London and Paris. Artist ; Exhibitor and Medallist. *War Work:* Queen Mary's Needlework Guild ; Head of Moss Dressings-room ; League of Remembrance, 1914–19. *Address:* 1 Marlborough Gate, W. 1. (M8933)

MACVEY, Major Thomas, O.B.E.

McVICAR, Neil, M.B.E.

McVITTIE, Lieut.-Col. Robert Henry, C.M.G., C.B.E.; *b.* 1872. Major and Brevet Lieut.-Col. Army Ordnance Depart.; N.-W. Frontier of India, 1897–98 (medal with two clasps) ; served in Great War, 1914–19 (mentioned in despatches). (C1429)

MacWATTERS, John Courtenay, M.B.E., M.R.C.S. (Eng.), L.R.C.P. (Lond.), *b.* 15 July, 1873 ; *s.* of David MacWatters, of Rudgeway, Glos. ; *m.* Ruth Ethel May, *d.* of Col. Stephen Bishop, of Clifton. *Educ.:* King Edward's School, Bath ; Bristol Univ. ; Medical School, R.U. Hospital, Bath ; Bristol Royal Infirmary ; St. Mary's Hospital, Paddington. Hon. Med. Off. Almondsbury Memorial Hospital ; Med. Off. P.O. Inspector of Factories for Almondsbury District ; Med. Off. Thornbury Union ; late Res. Obstetric Off. ; Assist. House Physician, and Clinical Assist. at Bristol Royal Infirmary.

War Work: In 1914, with the help of a committee, organised the Almondsbury Military Hospital (42 beds), (subsidiary to the 2nd S.G.H.), with his wife as Hon. Matron, and acted as Commandant and Hon. Med. Off. of this Institution till Jan. 1919 ; Hon. Med. Off. of the King's Weston Auxiliary Hospital (84 beds) : M.O. Prisoners of War Camp, Henbury ; M.O. Henbury I.W. and D. R.E., Camp. *Address:* The Copper Beeches, Almondsbury, Bristol. (M16274)

McWHAE, Col. Douglas Murray, C.M.G., C.B.E., M.D., B.S., *b.* 1884 ; *s.* of William Douglas McWhae. *Educ.:* Toorak and Melbourne Grammar Schools. Col. Australian Army Med. Corps ; Assist. Director of Med. Ses., Australian Imperial Forces Depots, Great Britain. (C846)

McWILLIAM, Andrew, C.B.E.

McWILLIAM, Dorothy, M.B.E.

MADDAMS, 2nd Lieut. William Samuel, M.B.E., R.E., E.A.F.

MADDEN, Frank Cole, O.B.E., M.D. (Melb.), F.R.C.S. (Eng.), *b.* 2 March, 1873 ; *s.* of Daniel Anthony Madden, of Sydney, Australia ; *m.* Madeline, *d.* of Dr. William Cox, of Winchcombe, Glos. ; *Educ.:* Scotch Coll., Melbourne ; Univ. of Melbourne ; St. Mary's Hospital, London. Professor of Surgery, Egyptian Govt. School of Medicine ; Senior Surgeon, Kasr-el-Ainy Hospital, Cairo ; Hon. Medical Adviser to H.E. the High Commissioner for Egypt. *War Work:* Civil Surgeon, Egyptian Expeditionary Force, with surgical charge of Surgical Division, Citadel Military Hospital, Cairo, Kasr-el-Ainy Hospital, as Military Hospital ; British Red Cross Hospital, Giza, near Cairo. *Address:* St. David's Buildings, Cairo, Egypt. *Club:* Authors'. (O4119)

MADDEN, Guy Ross, M.B.E., LL.B., *b.* 25 Sept. 1878 ; *s.* of the late Sir John Madden, G.C.M.G., LL.D., D.C.L., LL.D. (*see* BURKE'S *Peerage*) ; *m.* Doris Anne, *d.* of Charles Edward McEvoy, of Melbourne. *Educ.:* Crimloden ; Melbourne Univ. Solicitor ; Supreme Court of Victoria, High Court of Australia ; Member of the Firm of Woolcott, Drysdale, and Madden, Solicitors, Bank Place, Melbourne, Victoria, Australia. *War Work:* Captain in 52nd Infantry A.M.F.; employed on Embarkation and Training work, 1914– 17 ; Lieut. in R.A.S.C., O.C. 316 S.B.A.C., and 317 S.B.A.C., 1917–19, Italian Expeditionary Force. *Address:* Golden Quadrant, East Malvern, Victoria, Australia. *Clubs:* Melbourne ; Stock Exchange. (M4746)

MADDEN, Samuel Fitzgerald, O.B.E.

MADDEN, William Thomas, O.B.E.

MADDICK, Capt. Edmund Distin, C.B.E., F.R.C.S. ; Capt. on Special List, and Proprietor of the Scala Theatre. (C2783)

MADDISON, Charles Henry, M.B.E.

MADELEY, Edith Mary, Mrs., M.B.E., *b.* 1878 ; *d.* of John Watson, of Bolton ; *m.* James Welby, *s.* of James Chatburn Madeley, of Guildford. *War Work:* Red Cross, also social work for men on leave from Mesopotamia. *Addresses:* c/o London, County, Westminster, and Parr's Bank, Charing Cross ; Woodstock, Madras, S. India. (M6200)

MADGE, Gwendolen Mary Gladys, M.B.E.

MADGE, Henry Ashley, O.B.E.

MADGE, Capt. Quintus, O.B.E., B.A., M.R.C.S., L.R.C.P., R.A.M.C., *b.* 16 Nov. 1887 ; *s.* of Henry Woolley Madge, of Liverpool ; *m.* Janet Margaret Mathieson, *d.* of Alexander Boswell, M.D., of Ashbourne, Derbyshire. *Educ.:* Merchant Taylors' School, Crosby ; Emmanuel Coll., Cambridge. *War Work:* Served in East African Expeditionary Force from Aug. 1917. *Address:* Brookside, St. John Street, Ashbourne, Derbyshire. (O4158)

MADHAVLAL, Chinubhai, Lady, O.B.E., *d.* of Chunilal Khushalrai, of Ahmedabad ; *m.* as his 2nd wife, Sir Chinubhai Madhavlal (Runchorelal), C.I.E., 1st Bart. (*see* BURKE'S *Peerage*), who died 1916. *Address:* Shahpur House, Ahmedabad, India. (O8277)

MADIN, Charles Gilbert, O.B.E.

MADOC, Lieut.-Col. Henry William, C.B.E.

MAEERS, Frank, M.B.E.

MAER, Constance Muriel, Mrs. Astley, O.B.E.

MAFFEY, Dorothy, Mrs., O.B.E.

MAGEE, Thomas, M.B.E., *b.* 8 Feb. 1879. *Educ.:* Liverpool Institute. *War Work:* Assistant Commandant (now Commandant), Men's Detachment Cheshire 15, Wallasey Division, B.R.C.S. (M8936)

MAGEE, Arthur Fitzherbert, KING-, M.B.E., E.A.F.

MAGER, Sydney, C.B.E., *b.* 19 Dec. 1877 ; *s.* of the late Edmund Mager. *Educ.:* New Coll., Eastbourne. Chief Land Commissioner, Ministry of Agriculture and Fisheries. *War Work:* Chief Commissioner of Food Production Department of Ministry of Agriculture and Fisheries. *Address:* 12, Queen Anne's Gate, London, S.W. 1. *Clubs:* National ; Farmers'. (C562)

MAGGS, Agnes Mary, Mrs. O.B.E.

MAGGS, Percy Harold, O.B.E., *b.* 21 Jan. 1881. Director of Awards, Ministry of Pensions. *War Work:* Assistant Sec. Prince of Wales' National Relief Fund, 1914–16 ; Principal Clerk, War Pensions Statutory Committee, 1916–17 ; Director of Awards, Ministry of Pensions, 1917. *Address:* Belstone, Cromwell Avenue, Bromley, Kent. (O10916)

MAGILL, Ethel Mary, O.B.E., M.B., B.S., D.P.H., *b.* 1881 ; *d.* of James Magill, M.D., of Bovevagh, Co. Derry. *Educ.:* London School of Medicine for Women ; Royal Free Hospital. Examiner to the Chartered Society of Massage and Medical Gymnastics. *War Work:* Medical Officer in charge of the X-Ray, Medical Electricity, and Massage Departments at the Military Hospital, Endell Street, W.C. 1. *Address:* Gwelo, Southern Rhodesia. *Club:* Halcyon. (O11824)

MAGILL, Major Henry Patrick, O.B.E., Loyal North Lancashire Regt., *b.* 17 March, 1871 ; *s.* of James Macgillycuddy Magill, of Churchtown, Co. Kerry, Ireland ; *m.* Doris Cotterill, *d.* of George Harding Neame, of 6, Egerton Terrace, London, S.W. *Educ.:* Felsted School, and Trinity Coll., Dublin. *Address:* c/o Messrs. Holt & Co., 3, Whitehall Place, S.W. *Club:* Army and Navy. (O7440)

MAGINNESS, Edmond John, C.B.E., M.V.O., *b.* 1857 ; *s.* of the late John Maginness ; *m.* Jane, *d.* of Charles Augustus Bland, of Balmah Hall, Norfolk, and Melbourne, Australia. Sometime Constructive Manager, H.M. Dockyard, Chatham ; Member of Institute of Naval Architects. (C233)

MAGMAC, Brig.-Gen. Charles Lane, C.M.G., C.B.E.

MAGNAY, Capt. Christopher Robert Alexander, M.B.E.

MAGNIAC, Brig.-Gen. Charles Lane, C.M.G., C.B.E., *b.* 1873 ; *s.* of the late Maj.-Gen. Francis Lane Magniac, M.S.C. ; *m.* 1900, Letitia Anne, *d.* of T. H. W. Knowles, of Oatlands, Kinsale. Entered R.E. 1894 ; served in Great War, 1914–19 as Assist. Director of Railway Transport (despatches, Brevet Lieut.-Col, Legion of Honour) ; a Director of Railways in India with rank of Brig.-Gen. (C769)

MAGNUS, William Robert, M.B.E.

MAGOR, Edward Manuel, M.B.E., *b.* 29 Oct. 1877 ; *s.* of R. B. Magor, of Northfield, Minehead ; *m.* Olive Shirley, *d.* of J. E. Yerburgh, of 130, Oakwood Court. *Educ.:* Uppingham. Tea Broker. *War Work:* Supt. Essex Special Constabulary, Brentwood Division ; Chairman, Local Emergency Committee, Brentwood Area. *Address:* Long Ridings, Hutton. *Club:* Oriental. (M8937)

MAGRATH, Dr. Charles John, O.B.E., D.Litt., M.A., B.R. Hist. Soc., Belgian Croix de Guerre, *b.* 14 April, 1878 ; *s.* of the late Charles Frederick Magrath, of Bengal Civil Service. *Educ.:* Winchester Coll., and Oriel Coll., Oxford. Has held various educational appointments. *War Work:* Worked for B.R.C.S. and Y.M.C.A. 1915 ; Lieut., Gen. List, 1916 ; Capt., 1919. *Club:* Cavendish. (O1030)

MAGRUDER, Maryel Alpina, Mrs., M.B.E., *b.* 1875 ; *d.* of the late Rear-Adm. Sir Malcolm MacGregor of MacGregor, Bart., R.N. (*see* BURKE'S *Peerage*) ; *m.* Ernest Pendleton, A.M., M.D., Director of American Red Cross Unit 3, Serbia (died of typhus at Belgrade, April, 1915), *s.* of Caleb Clarke Magruder, of Glendale, Md., U.S.A. *Educ.:* Privately. *War Work:* Forewoman, Royal Naval Cordite Factory, Holton Heath, Dorset, 1916 ; Principal Forewoman, R.N.C.F. 1917. *Address:* c/o Lady Helen MacGregor of MacGregor, Edinchip, Balquhidder R.S.O., Perthshire. (M3288)

MAGUIRE, Emily Herbert, Mrs., M.B.E.

MAGUIRE, James Rochfort, C.B.E., *b.* 1853 ; *s.* of the Rev. JohnMaguire, Rector of Kilkeedy, Co. Limerick ; *m.* 1895, the Hon. Julia Beatrice Peel, *d.* of 1st Viscount Peel (*see* BURKE'S *Peerage*). *Educ.:* Cheltenham, and Merton Coll. Oxford. Bar. Inner Temple, 1883 ; M.P. for N. Donegal Div. of Donegal Co. (N.), 1890–92 ; and for W. Div. of Co. Clare, 1892–95 ; Ladies' Auxiliary Committee. *Address:* 3, Cleveland Square, St. James's, S.W. (C234)

MAGUIRE, Capt. Richard Kenneth Calton, M.B.E.

MAHON, Lilian Frances, O.B.E., *b.* 17 July, 1874 ; *d.* of the late John George Moore, I.C.S., of Onslow Square, London ; *m.* Foster MacMahon, *s.* of the late William Henry Cortlandt Mahon, of Dulwich. *Educ.:* Bedford ; Crescent House Schools. *War Work:* Commandant of the Close and Town Close V.A.D. Hospitals, Norwich. *Address:* Fernley, Newmarket Road, Norwich, Norfolk. *Club:* Forum. (O10917)

MAHONEY, Capt. and Qr.-Mr. Daniel, O.B.E.

MAHONY, Mary Ellen, M.B.E.

MAIDSTONE, Guy Montague George Finch Hatton, Viscount, O.B.E., D.S.C., Croix de Guerre, *b.* 28 May, 1885 ; *s.* of the Earl of Winchilsea, of Haverholme Priory, Sleaford (*see* BURKE'S *Peerage*) ; *m.* Margaretta Armstrong, *d.* of Anthony J. Drexel, of Philadelphia, U.S.A. *Educ.:* Eton, and Magdalen Coll., Oxford. Stockbroker. *War Work:* Served for 3 years with the Naval Siege Guns in Flanders, and for one year in the R.A.F. ; retired with hon. rank of Lieut.-Col. *Address:* 23, Manchester Square. *Clubs:* White's ; Bath. (O8143)

MAILE, Alfred Charles William, M.B.E., R.A.O.C., *b.* 3 Oct. 1881 ; *s.* of Alfred Maile, of Westminster ; *m.* Alice Ellen Amelia, *d.* of Walter Thomas Mack, of Southampton. *Educ.:* St. Stephens, Westminster. Chief Clerk, H.M. Gunwharf, Chatham. *War Work:* Director of Ordnance Services, Office General Headquarters, France, Aug. 1914, to March, 1920 ; mentioned in despatches, Feb. 1915 ; awarded Medal for Meritorious Service, Jan. 1917. *Addresses:* Rohilla, 12, Elm Avenue, Chatham ; 9, Portland Street, Southampton. (M4548)

MAILER, Ramsay, O.B.E.

MAIN, Ernest William, M.B.E., *b.* 23 March, 1879 ; *s.* of the late William Main, R.C.N.C. *War Work:* In charge of Admiralty Floating Dock at Harwich for the period of the war. (M8928)

MAIN, Melville Pownall, M.B.E.

MAIN, Lieut. William Smith, O.B.E., R.N.R.

MAIN, Capt. William Wright O.B.E.

MAINWARING, Rev. John, O.B.E.

MAINWARING, Mary Sibyl, Mrs., O.B.E., *b.* 1875 ; *d.* of Sir James Rankin, Bart., of Bryngwyn, Hereford (*see* BURKE'S *Peerage*) ; *m.* Charles Francis Kynaston, *s.* of Salusbury

Kynaston, of Oteley, Ellesmere (*see* BURKE'S *Landed Gentry*). *Educ.:* Privately. *War Work:* Commandant of V.A.D. Salop 36, and in charge of 3 Hospitals, Feb. 1915, to Feb. 1919. *Addresses:* Oteley, Ellesmere ; 19, Collingham Road, S.W. 5. (O535)

MAINWARING, Lieut.-Col. Watkin Randle Kynaston, C.B.E., J.P., *b.* 1875 ; *s.* of the late Salusbury Kynaston Mainwaring, of Oteley Park, Salop (*see* BURKE'S *Peerage*, Williams, Bart.) ; *m.* 1903, Violet Francis, *d.* of the late Sir Albert de Rutzen, Chief Metropolitan Magistrate. *Educ.:* Eton and Christ Church Coll. Oxford. Lieut.-Col. Denbighshire Yeomanry ; Hon. Capt. in the Army ; S. Africa, 1901–2 ; (present at action of Ladybrand, Queen's medal with clasps, King's medal with two clasps) ; Great War, 1914–19, as Brig.-Gen. (despatches) ; Serbian Order of the White Eagle. *Address:* Hafod-y-Coed, St. Asaph. *Club:* Junior Carlton. (C785)

MAINZ, Ernest, M.B.E.

MAIR, Jessy, Mrs., O.B.E.

MAIR, John Bagrie, O.B.E., M.V.O., J.P., *b.* 8 May, 1857 ; *s.* of John Mair, of Pitscurry, Huntly, Aberdeenshire ; *m.* Jessie, *d.* of Wm. Blackley, of High Blantyre, Lanarkshire. *Educ.:* Longhill School, and Privately. Chief Constable of Morayshire ; Inspector of Weights and Measures of Morayshire ; Burgh Prosecutor in the Burghs of Grantown-on-Spey, Rothes, and City of Elgin ; Manager of the scheme for clothing destitute children in Morayshire. *War Work:* Hon. Sec. of the Elgin section of the British Red Cross Society ; Commandant of No. 1 Men's Detachment ; Transport Officer for Morayshire, conveying all wounded soldiers arriving for the various V.A.D. Hospitals. *Address:* Maida View, Elgin. *Clubs:* Moray Golf ; Lossiemouth. (O10918)

MAIR, Robert, O.B.E.

MAITLAND, Sub.-Lieut. Arthur Albert, M.B.E., R.N.V.R.

MAITLAND, Edward Bellasis Wightman, O.B.E.

MAITLAND, Frederick Colin, Viscount, O.B.E., *b.* April, 1868 ; *s.* of 13th Earl of Lauderdale, of Thirlestane Castle, Lauder (*see* BURKE'S *Peerage*) ; *m.* Gwendoline Lucy, *d.* of Judge P. Vaughan-Williams, of Bodloufa. *War Work:* Served in the S. African War, and in the Great War. *Address:* Thirlestane Castle, Lauder, Scotland. *Clubs:* Naval and Military ; Bachelors' ; New (Edinburgh). (O7442)

MAITLAND, Jean Hamilton, M.B.E., *b.* 1890 ; *d.* of Robert Findlay, of Crossbasket, Lanarkshire ; *m.* George Ramsay, *s.* of Sir John Maitland (*see* BURKE'S *Peerage*). *War Work:* Work in connection with the B.R.C.S. *Club:* Empress. (M8941)

MAITLAND, Major Reginald Ferdinando, O.B.E., R.A.F.

MAITLAND, William Whitaker, O.B.E., *b.* 15 June, 1864 ; *s.* of the Rev. J. W. Maitland, of Loughton Hall, Essex ; *m.* Lindisfarne, *d.* of Ven. Geo. Hans Hamilton, Archdeacon of Northumberland, and Lady Louisa Hamilton (*see* BURKE'S *Peerage*). *Educ.:* Harrow, and Trinity Hall, Cambs. Sec. to the Government, Jersey, Channel Isles. *War Work:* The Government secretarial work was enormously increased by the war, and included much work outside the scope of ordinary duties. *Addresses:* Beau Désert, Jersey ; Loughton Hall, Essex. *Clubs:* Badminton ; Junior Carlton. (O1635)

MAJOR, Albany Featherstonehaugh, O.B.E., *b.* 3 Dec. 1858 ; *s.* of Charles Messenger Major, of Cromwell House, Croydon ; *m.* Margit, *d.* of Albert Grön, of Sandefjord, Norway. *Educ.:* Dulwich Coll. Principal, War Office (ret.) ; Hon. Sec. of the Committee on Ancient Defensive Earthworks, etc. (Congress of Archæological Societies) ; Hon. Sec. Viking Society, 1894–1903 ; Hon. Editor, 1904–09 ; Hon. Vice-President, 1918 ; President, Croydon Natural History and Scientific Society, 1919–20. *War Work:* Had charge of the Effects Branch of the War Office from Jan. 1915, to May, 1920. *Address:* Bifröst, 30, The Waldrons, Croydon. *Club:* Authors'. (O537)

MAJOR, Col. Charles Thomas, C.B.E., D.S.O.

MAJOR, Capt. William Reginald, O.B.E., R.E.

MAKALUA, Major Matthew James Manuia, O.B.E.

MAKEHAM, Rev. Edward, O.B.E., A.I.F.

MAKGILL, Lieut.-Col. Robert Haldane, C.B.E., M.D., *b.* 24 May, 1870 ; *s.* of Sir John Makgill, Bart. (*see* BURKE'S *Peerage*). Lieut.-Col. New Zealand Medical Corps. *Address:* Brackmont, Wamku, Auckland, New Zealand. (C1862)

MAKINS, Agatha Caroline, M.B.E., *d.* of Sir William Makins, Bart., of Rotherfield Court, Henley-on-Thames (*see* BURKE'S *Peerage*). *War Work:* Commandant, Auxiliary Military Hospital, Henley-on-Thames, Oct. 1914, to Nov. 1918 ; President, Red Cross Workrooms, Henley-on-Thames. *Address:* Paradise Farm, Henley-on-Thames. *Clubs:* Albemarle ; Bath. (M712)

MALAN, Charles Huntingford, O.B.E., I.C.S.

MALAN, Lieut.-Col. Leslie Noel, O.B.E., R.E.

MALBY, Henry Arthur, O.B.E.

MALCOLM, Lieut. Frederick Arthur, M.B.E., I.A.R.O.

MALCOLM, George, C.B.E., *b.* 6 Jan. 1876 ; *s.* of the late John Malcolm, F.E.I.S., of Blairgowrie, Perthshire ; *m.* Mary Sophia Lowden, *d.* of the late John Kelly Allan, of Dundee. East India Merchant, Messrs. Ralli Brothers. *War Work:* Controller of Raw Jute and Hemp, War Office and Ministry of Munitions. British Representation on Programmes Committee, Allied Maritime Transport Council ; Chairman of Commission of Enquiry into the condition of Jute Industry, appointed by the President of the Board of Trade 1919.

Addresses: Hartsfeld, Purley, Surrey; Bushbury, Blackboys, Sussex. (C235)

MALCOLM, George William, M.B.E., M.I.Mech.E., M.I.E.E., *b.* 5 May, 1870; *s.* of William Alfred Malcolm, of Twickenham, Middlesex, and Japan; *m.* Adelaide Marion, *d.* of William Maclachlan, of London. *Educ.:* St. Paul's School, London, and privately. Managing Director, Salt Union, Ltd., and Mersey Power Co., Ltd.; Member of Weaver Navigation Trust Board; Chairman, Local Juvenile Advisory Committee, Northwich. *War Work:* Superintendent, H.M. Magazine, Northwich; connected with construction and working of various Explosives Factories; Lieut., Cheshire Volunteer Regiment. *Address:* Davenham House, Northwich. (M8942)

MALCOLM, Harcourt Gladstone, O.B.E., K.C., J.P., *b.* 7 Feb. 1875; *s.* of the late Sir Ormond Drimmie Malcolm, K.C., Chief Justice of the Bahamas; *m.* Kathleen Helena Gray, *d.* of George Butler Adderley. *Educ.:* Privately. Barrister-at-Law; Private Sec. to the Governor of the Bahamas, 1892–99; member of the House of the Assembly of the Bahamas, 1900; Deputy Speaker, 1901; Acting Chief Justice of the Islands, 1913. *War Work:* Chairman, Bahamas War Relief Committee and Treas. "Our Day" Red Cross Fund; Senior Lieut. Bahamas Home Defence Fund; Bahamas delegate to Canada, West Indies, Conference at Ottawa; representative Bahamas House of Assembly at Tercentenary of Bermuda House of Assembly. *Address:* The Casuarinas, Nassau, Bahamas. *Clubs:* Royal Thames Yacht; Caledonian. (O1001)

MALCOLM, Jeanne Marie, Mrs., M.B.E.

MALCOLM, Major Pulteney William, O.B.E., R.M.L.I.

MALCOLM, William, M.B.E.

MALCOLM, Lieut.-Col. William Alister, O.B.E.

MALCOLMSON, Norman, O.B.E., *b.* 13 Oct. 1874; *s.* of George Forbes Malcolmson, of London; *m.* Edith Helen, *d.* of Thomas Du Buisson, of Betchworth, Surrey. *Educ.:* Eton and Cambridge. Private Banker and Merchant. *War Work:* Commanded D. Division, City Police Reserve. *Addresses:* Holmshurst, Burwash, Sussex; 19, Brechin Place, London, S.W. *Club:* Athenæum; Cavendish; Public Schools. (O10920)

MALDEN, Rev. Edward Elliott, M.B.E.

MALEHAM, George Edgar, M.B.E., *b.* 11 April, 1850; *s.* of Henry Maleham, of Sheffield; *m.* Edith, *d.* of John Yeomans, of Sheffield. *Educ.:* Wesley Coll., Sheffield. *War Work:* Hon. Sec. to the Soldiers' and Sailors' Families Association, Sheffield Division. *Address:* 88, Grove Road, Millhouses, Sheffield. *Club:* Athenæum, Sheffield. (M3829)

MALERBI, James Michael, M.B.E., Chevalier, Order of the Crown of Italy, Order Reconnaissance Francaise and the Russian Order Red Cross and Diplomas, *b.* 12 Jan. 1856; *s.* of Michael Angelo Malerbi, of Builth Wells, Breconshire; *m.* Blanche, *d.* of Percival Henry Fowler, of Essex Lodge, Watford. *Educ.:* Llanelwedd Schools, Builth Wells, Breconshire. Railway (Districts) Traffic Superintendent. *War Work:* Local Hon. Sec. National War Savings, Southampton; Joint Hon. Sec. Southampton American Welcome Committee; Organiser and Hon. Sec. of 58 Flag Days for Naval and Military Services, Local Hospitals, as well as the Red Cross and other activities in the town of Southampton. *Address:* Cranleigh, 26, The Polygon, Southampton. (M8943)

MALET, Sir Harry Charles, Bart., D.S.O., O.B.E., *b.* 21 Sept. 1873; *s.* of 5th Bart., *suc.* his nephew, the 6th Bart., 1918 (*see* BURKE'S *Peerage*); *m.* Mildred Laura, *d.* of Capt. H. S. Swiney, Gensing House, St. Leonards, Sussex, Lieut.-Col. (retd.). Formerly in Cape Mounted Rifles; Capt. 8th Hussars; served S. Africa, 1899–1902 (Queen's medal, 4 clasps, King's medal, 2 clasps). *Address:* Wilbury, Newton Tony, Salisbury. (O8597)

MALET, Major Robert James, O.B.E.

MALEY, 2nd Lieut. William John, M.B.E., R.A.F.

MALIM, Major Edward John, O.B.E., M.G.C.

MALIM, John Charles, M.B.E., A.M.I.C.E., *b.* 23 Aug. 1875; *s.* of Frederick John Malim, of Chichester; *m.* Brenda, Stirling, *d.* of William Frederick Robinson, of 53, Baker Street, W. 1. *Educ.:* Blackheath School, and Central Technical Coll., South Kensington. Civil Engineer in the Department of the Civil Engineer-in-Chief of the Admiralty. *War Work:* In charge of all engineering and building work at the Admiralty Establishments on the River Humber, including the Oil Fuel Storage Depot, and Air Station at Killingholme, the Naval Bases at Immingham, and Grimsby, and all similar work. *Address:* c/o Civil Engineer-in-Chief, Admiralty, London, S.W. 1. (M2124)

MALIM, Julia, Mrs., M.B.E., *d.* of Eccles Shorrock; *m.* Aubrey H., *s.* of Frederic Malim, of Grantham. *Educ.:* Queen's Coll., Harley Street, London. *War Work:* Sec. of large Soldiers' Home in connection with Belton Camp and Harrowby Camp, Grantham, Sept. 1914, to July, 1919. (M8944)

MALING, Nesta Gertrude, Mrs., M.B.E.

MALINS, Mary Selina Beatrice, O.B.E.

MALLALIEU, Vernon, M.B.E. Secretary, Lancashire Anti-Submarine Committee. (M10259b)

MALLEN, James, M.B.E., *b.* 28 July, 1882; *s.* of Joseph Mallen, of Galashiels; *m.* Barbara Mary, *d.* of John Thomas Smith, of Edinburgh. *Educ.:* Greenhill Public School; Glasgow Athenæum; Robertson's Coll., Glasgow. Sec. to General Manager, The Caledonian Railway; Traffic, etc., Assistant to the General Manager. *War Work:* Dealt with matters relating to traffic movement, especially in connection with urgent naval and military requirements. *Addresses:*

Rycroft, Selborne Road, Jordanhill, Glasgow; 302, Buchanan Street, Glasgow. (M8945)

MALLET, Lieut. Frank Charles, M.B.E., R.A.S.C.

MALLET, Matilde, Lady, C.B.E., *b.* 13 March, 1872; *d.* of Don G. de Obarrio, of Panama; *m.* Sir Claude Coventry (*see* BURKE'S *Peerage*), *s.* of Capt. Hugh Mallet, of Ash Hatherley, Devon. *Educ.:* Academy of the Sacred Heart, Manhattanville, New York; Convent du Sacré Cœur, Paris; Medaille de la Reine Elizabeth, Reconnaissance Francaise, Panama Red Cross. Lady Mallet is Founder and Life President of the Panama National Red Cross. *War Work:* Established branches of Queen Mary's Needle Work Guild and of the British Red Cross in Panama, Colon, Guayaquil (Ecuador), San José (Costa Rica), and other towns; forwarded to England clothing, blankets, chocolate, cigars, etc., and contributions of money, partly sent to France and Belgium,—of an approximate value of £10,000; collected funds to build three rooms at the Star and Garter Hospital, of which two are endowed; visited the Hospital Ships "Marama" and "Maheno" on all their journeys through the Panama Canal, and distributed on board the great number of gifts presented by the citizens of Panama for the wounded soldiers on their way to Australia and New Zealand. *Address:* 14, Seville Street, Lowndes Square, London, W.1. (C2785)

MALLETT, Capt. Henry Clifford, M.B.E., R.A.F.

MALLETT, John Moore, M.B.E.

MALLETT, Lieut. and Qr.-Mr. Thomas Robert, M.B.E.

MALLINS, Lieut.-Col. John Robert, O.B.E.

MALLINSON, Clarice Elsie, M.B.E., B.Sc., *b.* 21 Sept. 1894; *d.* of Samuel Mallinson, of Reedley, nr. Burnley. *Educ.:* Univ. Coll., Reading. Research Chemist; Research Department, Royal Arsenal, Woolwich, S.E. 18. *War Work:* Engaged in the Research Department, Woolwich, as Research Chemist from Sept. 1916, to the present time. *Addresses:* Holmleigh, Reedley, nr. Burnley, Lancs.; Research Department, Royal Arsenal, Woolwich, S.E. 18. (M10252a)

MALLINSON, Frederick, O.B.E., *b.* 23 Oct. 1880; *s.* of John Mallinson, of Birstall, near Leeds; *m.* Annie Eliza, *d.* of William Askew, of Norbury. *Educ.:* Batley Grammar School. *War Work:* Admiralty; Ministry of Shipping. *Address:* Swanfield, 107, Nimrod Road, Streatham Park, S.W. 16. (O10922)

MALLOCH, Ethel Josephine Victoria, Mrs., M.B.E., *d.* of William Oliver, of Highbury; *m.* George Reston, *s.* of John Malloch, J.P., of Elderslie, N.B. *Educ.:* Highbury High School, and Bad-Neuenahr. *War Work:* 1916–19, Sec. to Sir Ernest Michael Clarke, Director, Motor Ambulance Dept., B.R.C.S.'s Headquarters. *Address:* The White Cottage, Chingford, Essex. *Club:* Studio. (M8946)

MALMESBURY, Dorothy, Countess of, C.B.E., *b.* 5 Oct. 1885; *d.* of Augustus, 6th Lord Calthorpe (*see* BURKE'S *Peerage*); *m.* James Edward, 5th Earl of Malmesbury, *s.* of Edward James, 4th Earl of Malmesbury (*see* BURKE'S *Peerage*). *Educ.:* Privately. Lady of Grace of the Order of St. John of Jerusalem in England, and the Order of Mercy: President of Hampshire Branch B.R.C.S.; Member of Joint County Committee of Hampshire under Joint Council of the Order of St. John and B.R.C.S.; Divisional Commissioner of the Bournemouth Div. of Girl Guides; Rural District Councillor for the Parish of Hurn and Member of Board of Guardians. *War Work:* Donor and Organiser, Heron Court Auxiliary Hospital, Christchurch, Hants. *Address:* Heron Court, Christchurch, Hampshire. *Club:* Bath. (C2786)

MALONE, Cecil John l'Estrange, O.B.E., M.P., Order of the Nile, *b.* 7 Sept. 1880; *s.* of the Rev. Savile L'Estrange Malone, of Dalton, Yorkshire. *Educ.:* Ludgrove, New Barnet; Cordwalles, Maidenhead. Entered Royal Navy, 1905; served in H.M.S. "Isis," Sept. 1906, to Dec. 1906; in H.M.S. "Dreadnought," Jan. 1907, to Dec. 1908; H.M.S. "Duncan," 1908–9; in H.M.S. "Excellent"; H.M.T.B. No. 25 (Navigation School); H.M.S. "Vernon"; R.N. College, Greenwich, Jan. 1911, to May, 1911; H.M.T.B. No. 81; H.M.S. "Essex," 1911 to Dec. 1911; selected to undergo a flying course at Eastchurch, Dec. 1911; obtained R.A. Club's Pilot's certificate; appointed assistant of Air Department at the Admiralty on its formation, Nov. 1912. *War Work:* Aug. 1914, appointed in command of H.M.S. "Engadine"; Dec. 1914, in command of R.N.A.S. units during raid on Cuxhaven; 22 March, 1915, appointed to command H.M.S. "Ben-my-Chree"; served in Dardanelles campaign until final evacuation; Jan. 1916, commanded East Indies and Egypt seaplane squadron: Jan. 1917, employed at the Air Ministry; March, 1917, took command of Grain Air Station; May, 1917, to Jan. 1918, service in H.M.S. "Lion," flagship of the battle-cruiser "Force"; Dec. 1917, appointed Plans Division, Admiralty; Fellow of the Aeronautical Society; mentioned in despatches. *Clubs:* Reform; National Liberal; 1917; Royal Aero. (O3346)

MALONEY, William Donnellan, M.B.E., *b.* 29 July, 1868; *s.* of Patrick Maloney, of Nenagh, Ireland; *m.* Rosie Roberta, *d.* of William Wotton, of Exeter. *Educ.:* St. Brendan's Birr, Ireland. Assistant Sec. Territorial Force Association of the County of Lincoln. *War Work:* Served in Territorial Force. *Address:* The Old Barracks, Lincoln. (M8947)

MALONY, Edward, O.B.E.

MALPAS, Comdr. James Herbert, O.B.E., R.N.R.

MALTBY, William Graham, M.B.E., *b.* 6 June, 1882; *s.* of Ald. D. H. Maltby, J.P., of Mansfield. *War Work:* With the firm of Barringer, Wallis and Manners, Ltd., of Mansfield, in connection with the development and supply of Anti-Gas Equipment. *Address:* Coombhurst, Alexandra Avenue, Mansfield. (M8948)

MALYN, Capt. Donald Paton, M.B.E., R.A.S.C.

MALYON, Major Frank Haistone, O.B.E., I.A.

MAMOS, (Monsignore) John Baptist, M.B.E., Officer of Greek Order of Redeemer, Diplomé of University of Rome, *b.* 3 April, 1869; *s.* of Lorenzo Mamos, of Patras, Greece. *Educ.:* Urbanian Coll., Rome. Titular Bishop of the Papal Court; Vicar of the parish of St. Denis, Athens. *War Work:* Served in Balkan Wars as chaplain, during European War; has served on the British Refugee Committee, Athens. *Address:* Presbytery of Cathedral of St. Denis, Athens. (M8949)

MAN, Frederick Henry Dumas, O.B.E., *b.* 25 April, 1861; *s.* of Fredk. Man, of Beckenham, Kent; *m.* Catherine Fenwick, *d.* of — Wilson. *Educ.:* Charterhouse. Colonial Broker; Broker to Admiralty and War Office. *War Work:* Engaged in supplying the whole of the Rum used by both Navy and War Office; was a special constable. *Addresses:* 11, Hyde Park Terrace, W. 2; Mill House, Bransbury, Barton Stacey, Hants. *Clubs:* Cavendish; Royal Automobile; Royal St. George's Golf; Cinque Ports; Stoke Poges. (O538)

MAN, Lieut.-Col. Hubert William, C.B.E., D.S.O., *b.* 1876. Major and Brevet Lieut.-Col. Army Ordnance Depart.; Assist. Director of Ordnance Sers.; S. Africa War, 1899–1901 (Queen's medal with four clasps); Great War, 1914–19 (despatches). (C1289)

MAN. Capt. Joseph, O.B.E., C.M.G. Appt. Commander Order of Leopold of Belgium.

MANDER, Lieut. Albert, O.B.E.

MANDER, Capt. John Harold, O.B.E., *b.* 3 Aug. 1869; *s.* of Charles B. Mander, J.P., of The Mount, Compton, Wolverhampton; *m.* Elinor Lloyd, *d.* of the late J. P. A. Lloyd-Philipps, of Dale Castle, Pembrokeshire, and Mabys, Cardiganshire. *Educ.:* Rugby, and Trinity Hall, Cambridge. Lieut. 3rd N. Staffordshire Regt., 1888–90; Duke of Cornwall's L.I., 1890–1906; Adjutant, 4th V.B. Durham L.I., 1901–5; Brigade Major, D.L.I. Brigade, 1904–5; Chief Constable, Isle of Ely, 1906–19; Chief Constable, Norfolk, 1915. *War Work:* Chief Constable of Isle of Ely and Norfolk, 1915–19. *Address:* Thorpe Hurst, Thorpe St. Andrew, Norwich. *Club:* Naval and Military. (O10923)

MANDERSON, Major Robert Wardlaw, O.B.E.

MANICO, Capt. Arthur, M.B.E., *b.* 17 June, 1879. Fellow of the Auctioneers' and Estate Agents' Institute, and senior partner of the firm of Woolland, Son and Manico, Auctioneers and Estate Agents, Plymouth. *War Work:* Served with the Mechanical Transport Section of the R.A.S.C. *Address:* Kirknewton, Newton Abbot, S. Devon. *Club:* Plymouth.

MANIECE, William Christopher Henry, M.B.E.

MANIFOLD, Col. Sir Michael Graham Egerton BOWMAN-, K.B.E., C.B., C.M.G., D.S.O., R.E., *b.* 9 June, 1871; *s.* of the late Surg.-Gen. Manifold; *m.* Kathleen Cecilia, *d.* of the late Admiral Sir Thomas Brandreth, K.C.B. Entered Army, 1891; Dongola Exped. Force, 1896 (Khedive's Medal); Atbara, 1898; Khartoum; S. Africa, 1899–1901; Great War, Dardanelles, 1914–15; Egypt, 1917; has 4th Class Order of the Medjidieh, 4th Class Order of Osmanieh, is Officer of the Legion of Honour. *Club:* United Service. (K273)

MANIPUR, H.H. (Raja Chirra Chand Singh), Raja of, C.B.E. (C79)

MANLEY, Kate, O.B.E., H.M.I., *b.* 19 July 18,66; *d.* of Wm. Hewitt Manley, of Bridport, Dorset. His Majesty's Inspector of Schools, holding a Staff-Inspectorship under the Board of Education. *War Work:* Worked for the National War Savings Committee in their Food Economy Campaign; and later for the Ministry of Food. *Address:* 28, Chenies Street Chambers, W.C. 1. (O3823)

MANLEY, Major John Charles Medland, O.B.E., R.E.

MANLEY, Major William Edward, O.B.E., R.A.

MANN, Lieut.-Col. Algernon Edward, O.B.E., R.E.

MANN, David Barrie, M.B.E., *b.* 25 Dec. 1877; *s.* of George Mann, of Arbroath, Scotland. *Educ.:* Keptie School and High School, Arbroath, and Engineering College, Glasgow. Inspector of Factories, Governments of Bengal, Bihar and Orissa, and Assam. *War Work:* Engaged on Priority Work, Board of Industries and Munitions, 1916–19; appointed Government Arbitrator for steel plates, 1918; Member of the Priority Committees, Textiles and Engineering. *Clubs:* United Services (Calcutta); Barrackpore (Barrackpore, Bengal). (M4182)

MANN, Francis Oscar, O.B.E.

MANN, Frederick William, M.B.E.

MANN, Gerard Noel Cornwallis, M.B.E.

MANN, Grace, M.B.E., Q.M.A.A.C.

MANN, Surg.-Lieut. Harold Corry, O.B.E., M.D., M.R.C.P., R.N.

MANN, Major Harry Ainsley, O.B.E., M.C., R.E.

MANN, James Henderson, M.B.E.

MANN, Sir John, K.B.E., J.P., M.A., C.A., *b.* 8 April, 1863; *s.* of John Mann, of Glasgow; *m.* Margaret Anderson, *d.* of James Henderson, of Groomhill, Glasgow. *Educ.:* Glasgow Univ. *Addresses:* 8, Frederick's Place, Old Jewry, E.C.; Wrayfield, Reigate, Surrey. *Clubs:* Reform; Authors'; City; New, Glasgow. (K92)

MANN, Capt. Percival Ramsey, O.B.E.

MANN, Capt. Sydney Frederick, M.B.E.

MANN, Lieut. Thomas Clifford, M.B.E., R.E. (T.).

MANN, Walter George, M.B.E., *b.* 13 Aug. 1882; *s.* of

George T. Mann, of Faversham, Kent; *m.* Emily Elizabeth, *d.* of Henry Newton, of St. Albans. *Educ.:* Faversham, and Tunbridge Wells. Banker. *War Work:* Controlling Cable Iron, Chain Cable and Anchor Industries in connection with Department of Materials and Priority, Admiralty; Member of Admiralty Panel for Shipbuilding Supplies to U.S.A.; Member of Ministry of Munitions Sub-Committee on Forgings and Castings. *Address:* Newlands, Clarence Road, St. Albans. *Clubs:* Primrose; Verulam Golf, St. Albans. (M3830)

MANN, Lieut.-Comm. William Burridge, O.B.E., R.N.

MANN, William Henry, M.B.E., *b.* 14 March, 1872; *s.* of Henry Alfred Mann, J.P., of Cookstown, Co. Tyrone; *m.* Isabel Richmond, *d.* of Wm. Beer Lindsay, of The Lodge, Hilltown, Co. Down. *Educ.:* Cookstown Academy. Bank Manager. *War Work:* County Director for Tyrone British Red Cross and Order of St. John; Esquire of Order of St. John of Jerusalem. *Address:* Belfast Bank, Castle Place, Belfast. (M718)

MANN, Eng.-Comm. William Selwyn, O.B.E., R.N.

MANNERS, Capt. Charles Manners, O.B.E., R.E.

MANNERS, Lieut. James Benjamin, M.B.E., R.N.

MANNERS, Mildred Mary, Lady Robert, C.B.E.; *d.* of the late Rev. Charles Buckworth, of Sherborne; *m.* 1st, Major Henry Edward Buchanan Riddell, K.R.R.C., of Basingstoke, 2nd, the late Robert Manners William Orlando, C.M.G., D.S.O., K.R.R.C., *s.* of 7th Duke of Rutland (see BURKE's *Peerage*). *War Work:* Joint Sec. B.R.C.S., Central Workrooms. *Addresses:* The Red House, Knipton, Grantham; 20, Chester Street, S.W. (C2787)

MANNING, Albert John, M.B.E.

MANNING, Arthur Edward, M.B.E.

MANNING, Major Arthur Pitcher, C.I.E., O.B.E., M.C. Major Indian Army; Indian Telegraph Depart. (C2326)

MANNING, Charles Nicholson, O.B.E. (O12053)

MANNING, Edith Lindsay, O.B.E.; *d.* of the late Major-General Henry Dimsdale Manning. *War Work:* Head of the Surgical Department of Queen Mary's Needlework Guild at St. James's Palace, from Aug. 1914, to Feb. 1919. (O3824)

MANNING, Capt. Lionel John, O.B.E.

MANNING, Major Nathaniel Samuel, O.B.E., F.R.C.S.I., 6th Devon Regt., *b.* 1860; *s.* of George Manning, of Co. Cavan, Ireland; *m.* Winifred Alice, *d.* of Col. George Fleming, C.B., LL.D., Combe Martin, N. Devon. *Educ.:* Royal School Cavan, T.C.D.; Roy. Coll. Surgeons, Ireland. Med. Supt. City Hospitals, Birmingham; M.O. 8th District, Barnstaple. *War Work:* C.O. 2/6th Devons; transferred R.A.M.C., 1915; M.O. in charge Military Hospital and Camp, Wareham, Dorset; President, Recruiting Medical Board, Winchester; D.C.M.S. County Hampshire, M.N.S.; Chairman, Board of Medical Assessors, London, under L.G.B. (O10925)

MANNING, William, C.B.E. Dep. Commr. S. African Police; commanded Prisoners of War Camp, Pietermaritzburg, during Great War. (C2005)

MANNING, Brig.-Gen. Sir William Henry, G.C.M.G., K.B.E., C.B., *b.* 19 July, 1863; *s.* of Henry Manning. *Educ.:* Cambridge; R.M.C., Sandhurst. Governor and Commander-in-Chief of Ceylon. *War Work:* In connection with raising the Jamaica Contingent of the British West Indies Regiment, while Governor of Jamaica, and other War Work. *Addresses:* Queen's House, Colombo, Ceylon. *Clubs:* Naval and Military; East India United Services; Ranelagh. (K124)

MANSBRIDGE, Capt. Henry, O.B.E.

MANSEL, Charles John Linskill, O.B.E., M.D.

MANSELL, Arthur, M.B.E.

MANSELL, Rear-Adm. George Robert, C.B.E., M.V.O., *b.* 18 Feb. 1868; *s.* of the late Commander George Hope Mansell, R.N., of Westwood Park, Southampton; *m.* Lorna Sylvia Isabel, *d.* of Vice-Adm. George E. Richards, of Silverton, Devon. *Educ.:* The College, Southampton. Elder Brother of Trinity House, London. *War Work:* In command of the Royal Naval Coll., Keyham, Devonport; training Special Entry Naval Cadets. *Club:* United Service. (C906)

MANSELL, Lieut.-Col. Sir John Herbert, K.B.E., D.L., R.A., *b.* 20 Sept. 1864; *s.* of Capt. George Hope Mansell, R.N.; *m.* Jane Wilhelmina, *d.* of Major-Gen. W. J. Stuart, R.E. *Educ.:* Privately, and R.M.A., Woolwich. Commissioned in the Royal Artillery in 1883 and retired with rank of Lieut.-Col. in 1913; was Proof and Experimental Officer, Woolwich, 1901–1905; Supt. Research, 1906–10, and Chief Inspector, Woolwich, 1911–13; Director of the English Electric Co. *War Work:* Managing Director of the Coventry Ordnance Works. *Address:* The Chace, near Coventry. *Club:* United Service. (K223)

MANSELL, Capt. Reginald Anson, M.B.E., M.A., M.B., B.C. (Cantab.), R.A.M.C., *b.* 1 March, 1891; *s.* of Thomas Mansell, of Oxton, Cheshire. *Educ.:* Bradfield Coll., Berks.; Emmanuel Coll., Cambridge; St. Bartholomew's Hospital, London. *War Work:* Military Service. *Address:* c/o Messrs. Holt & Co., 3 Whitehall Place, London, S.W. (M3228)

MANSELL, Capt. Reginald Baynes, O.B.E., R.A.F.

MANSELL, Richard Vivian, O.B.E.

MANSELL, Rosalie, M.B.E.

MANSETH, Capt. William Alfred, M.B.E., S.A.S.C.

MANSFIELD, Sir Alfred, K.B.E., *b.* 17 May, 1870; *s.* of Edwin Mansfield, of Prenton, Cheshire. *Educ.:* Manchester. Managing Director, Olympia Mills, Selby; Managing Director, Mansfield and Sons, Ltd., Birkenhead. *War Work:* Director of Oils and Fats, Ministry of Food. *Address:* Bryanston Road, Prenton, Cheshire. *Club:* St. Stephen's. (K397)

MANSFIELD, Lieut.-Col. Henry Lattin, O.B.E.

MANSFIELD, Capt. and Qr.-Mr. James Walter, M.B.E.

MANSFIELD, Norman Polety, M.B.E., b. 12 March, 1869; s. of E. Mansfield, of Swansea; m. Rose Hannah, d. of B. Thomas, of Swansea. Educ.: Grammar School, Swansea. Station and Quay Superintendent, Fishguard Harbour; Member of the 1st Vol. Batt. Welsh Regt.; Member of "Our Boys" Committee; Chairman of Committee for assisting wives and dependents of soldiers; President of a St. John Ambulance Brigade; Vice-President of the District Horticultural Society. War Work: Transporting soldiers and war material to and from Rosslare, Cork, and Waterford, and a large quantity of high explosives in special steamers from Messrs. Kynochs', Arklow, to various ports of Great Britain. Address: Connaught House, Goodwick, Pem. (M8954)

MANSFIELD, Capt. Ralph Sheldon, O.B.E., R.E.

MANSFIELD, Thomas Edward, O.B.E., b. May, 1864; s. of the late James Mansfield, of Pointon Grange, Folkingham, Lincolnshire; m. Annie (who died), d. of the late John Thornton, of Bourne, Lincolnshire. Educ.: Spalding, Lincolnshire, and privately. Barrister-at-law, Northern Circuit and Lancashire Chancery Court. Chairman of Courts of Referees for North and East Lancashire under National Employment Act, 1911, and Chairman of Munition Tribunals for North and East Lancashire. War Work: In capacity as Chairman of Munition Courts as above; Sub-Commissioner, National Service for North and East Lancashire; Representative, Board of Trade on Port Labour Committees for Preston and Fleetwood; formed the Preston and District Chamber of Commerce, 1916; Member of the Council, Public Speaking for Recruiting, National War and Victory Loans. (O1641)

MANSFORD, Major Henry, O.B.E., b. 16 Feb. 1869. Educ.: Clifton. War Work: Commanded West London Recruiting Area, Sunderland Recruiting Area; Assist. Director of Recruiting and Assist. Director of National Service, Hampshire; Intelligence Department, War Office. Addresses: 39, Park Mansions, Knightsbridge, S.W.; Bouldnor Lodge, near Yarmouth, Isle of Wight. Clubs: Junior United Service; Royal Victoria Yacht; Solent Yacht; Bembridge Sailing. (O1642)

MANSON, Albert James, M.B.E.

MANTON, Arthur Woodroffe, O.B.E., B.Sc., M.I.C.E., M.Am.Soc.C.E., F.R.G.S., b. 2 July, 1866; s. of Sir Henry Manton, J.P., of Edgbaston, Birmingham; m. Alice Annie, d. of William Hooper Thorne, of Barnstaple. Educ.: Privately; Queen's Coll., Birmingham; Birmingham Univ., Birmingham. Civil Engineer. War Work: Sept. 1914, constructed south coast anti-submarine defences under Sir Ernest Moir, Bart., for the Admiralty; June, 1915, superintended machine-gun production for him at Ministry of Munitions, London; Sept. 1915, Res. Engr., under Sir Edward Pearson, J.P., at Gretna Explosives Factory, Scotland; Dec. 1915, appointed by Sir Ernest Moir (Chief of Ministry of Munitions in U.S.A.) to superintend production of machine-guns, shell components, raw materials, etc., in U.S.; and later in charge of a department for purchasing in the U.S. for the British War Mission, N.Y. Addresses: c/o S. Pearson & Son, Ltd., 10, Victoria Street, London, S.W. 1; Rowington, Norfolk Road, Edgbaston, Birmingham. (O540)

MANTON, John, M.B.E., b. 18 Oct. 1873; m. Alice Mary. Educ.: Birmingham Council School, Sparkbrook, Birmingham. Shorthand Writer, Staff College. War Work: Discharged to pension after 21 years' army service, 30 June, 1913; re-enlisted in response to the late Lord Kitchener's appeal to ex-N.C.O.s, Aug. 1914; served continuously in France and Egypt, May, 1915, to April, 1919; employed as superintending clerk; has Meritorious Service Medal, 1914–15 Star, War Medal, and Victory Medal; mentioned in despatches; served with Mohmand Field Force and Tirah Expeditionary Force; awarded India Medal, 1895, with clasps; Punjab Frontier, 1897–98; Tirah, 1897–98; in possession of G.C. Medal. Address: Norbury, The Flats, Blackwater. (M4547)

MANUEL, Stephen, C.B.E.

MANWELL, Capt. David Thomas William, M.B.E., Aust. F.C. and R.A.F.

MANWELL, Gertrude Thompson, M.B.E.

MAPLES, Major Edward William, O.B.E., LL.D.

MAPLES, Euretta Mary, M.B.E.

MAPLESDEN, Charles William, O.B.E.

MAQUIRE, Matthew Michael, O.B.E.

MARCH, Hilda Madeleine, Countess of, C.B.E.

MARCH, Joseph Ogdin, M.B.E., M.R.C.S., L.R.C.P., b. 18 Nov. 1866; s. of J. Ogdin March, of Emsworth, Hants; m. Grace Ellen, d. of H. J. Manning, of Laverstock, Salisbury. Educ.: Privately, and Trinity Coll., Cambridge. War Work: Red Cross Hospital, Bulford; Med. Off. Experimental Ground, Porton. (M8956)

MARCHAND, Isidore Henri Alphonse, M.B.E., J.P. for Herts and Middlesex, b. 16 Oct. 1860; s. of Charles Tony Marchand, of 14, Bentinck Street, London, W.; m. Annie Jane (who died 1894), d. of John James Heath, of New Barnet. Educ.: Privately, and abroad. County Councillor for Hertfordshire; Chairman, Barnet Local Old Age Pensions Committee, and Victoria Coll. Hospital, Barnet; Governor, Barnet Grammar School. War Work: Vice-President, Herts Branch, B.R.C.S.; Hon. Treas. St. James's V.A.D. Hospital, New Barnet; Visitor (under Herts War Pensions Committee) to Barnet War Hospital. Address: Orleans, Woodville Road, New Barnet. (M8957)

MARCHANT, 2nd Lieut. Alfred Palmer, M.B.E., D.S.M., R.A.F.

MARCHANT, Major Eric Lachlan, O.B.E., M.C.

MARCHANT, Frank, M.B.E., R.N.

MARCHANT, Lieut. Frederick James, M.B.E., R.A.P.C., b. 10 May, 1881; s. of Frederick Henry Marchant, of Ipswich; m. Beatrice, d. of Charles Henry Blackmore, of Exeter. Educ.: Halstead Grammar School, Essex. War Work: Was a member of the Army Pay Corps and Army Pay Department during the war; employed chiefly in connection with the organisation of the Army Pay Offices, R.H. and R.F.A., Blackheath, and Labour Corps, Nottingham; specially promoted to Assist. Paymaster, Army Pay Dept., from Staff Sergt.-Major, Army Pay Corps; and also specially mentioned by Secretary of State for valuable services in connection with the war. (M5455)

MARCHANT, Herbert George, M.B.E.

MARCHANT, Rev. James, C.B.E., LL.D., F.R.A.S., F.R.S., s. of the late John Marchant, b. 1867; m. 1895, Eleanor Jane, d. of George Gordon, of South Shields. Educ.: Privately. Minister of Exeter Street Independent Church, Director of National Council for Promotion of Race Regeneration, Sec. to Dr. Barnardo's Homes and Memorial 1905–6, and to National Birth Rate Commn. 1913–16. (C2789)

MARCHANT, Capt. William Francis, O.B.E.

MARCHBANK, Helen Millicent, M.B.E., b. 12 Dec. 1895; d. of Archibald Marchbank, of Dalbeattie, Scotland. Educ.: Mexico. Sec. to the British Consulate, Guayaquil, Ecuador. Address: c/o British Consulate, Guayaquil, Ecuador, S. America. (M720)

MARCY, Janie, O.B.E.; d. of George Nichols Marcy, of Chelmarsh Hall, Bridgworth, Shropshire; and 45, Oxford Terrace, Hyde Park, London, W. Educ.: Privately. War Work: March, 1915, to May, 1917, in the department of the R.N.A.S. Admiralty; May, 1917, to June, 1919, Junior Administrative Assistant, Ministry of Shipping. (O10926)

MARDALL, Col. George Stratford, O.B.E.

MARGACH, Capt. Lewis Grant, O.B.E.

MARGERISON, Laurence, C.B.E. Director of Administration of Local War Savings Committee. (C563)

MARGETSON, Florence Nys, Mrs., M.B.E., b. 16 Nov. 1846; d. of Edgar Lutwyche, of Streatham, Surrey; m. John Margetson, s. of John Stewart Margetson, of Streatham. War Work: President of Chislehurst and Bickley War Hospital Supply Depot. Address: Copley Dene, Chislehurst, Kent. (M8959)

MARGETTS, Surg.-Lieut. Horace Palmer, O.B.E., R.N.

MARIANS, Reginald Ingram, O.B.E. (O7448)

MARILLIER, Frank William, C.B.E., b. 29 Nov. 1855; s. of the Rev. J. F. Marillier, M.A. (Cantab.), of Hereford; m. Katherine Maud, d. of J. Brooke, of Marlborough, Wilts. Educ.: Bristol Grammar School. Engineer; Superintendent, Great Western Railway, Swindon, Carriage, Wagon, and Timber Departments. War Work: Chairman of the Technical Committee for Ambulance Trains in Great Britain, France, Lines of Communication, and the United States; also supervised the making of G.S. Wagons, Mark 5, Water Tanks, Leather Work for 4'5 Howitzer and 18-pounder Guns, Timber Trucks, Open Goods, Armoured Wagons, Bogie Wagons, for conveying Tanks, thousands of 6-inch Shells, Copper Bands. Address: Deva, Westlecott Road, Swindon, Wilts. (C2790)

MARINDIN, Lieut.-Col. Cecil Colvile, C.B.E., D.S.O., b. 1879; s. of Charles Randall Marindin, I.C.S.; m. Amy Victoria, d. of the late Rev. W. T. Richardson. Major and Brevet Lieut.-Col. R.A.; Tibet, 1903–4 (with clasp); Great War, 1914–18 (despatches, Italian Croce di Guerra). (C1898)

MARINDIN, Gertrude Florence Evelyn, Mrs., M.B.E., b. 11 Aug. 1876; s. of the late Edward Robert Erskine Wilmot Chetwode, of Woodbrook, Portarling, Queen's Co.; m. Arthur Henry, Brig.-Gen. C.B., D.S.O., s. of Henry Colvile Marindin. War Work: Soldiers' and Sailors' Families Association, East of Scotland; War Pensions Committee, Edinburgh (President, East. District). Address: The Constable's Tower, Dover. Club: Ladies' Imperial. (M8960)

MARJORIBANKS, Dudley Sinclair, C.B.E., b. 12 Feb. 1858; s. of Edward Marjoribanks, of Bushey Hall, Watford; m. Bertha, d. of the Rev. W. Featherstonhaugh, of Edmondbyers. Educ.: Eton, and King's Coll., London. Mechanical Engineer; Local Director and Controller of Labour, Sir W. G. Armstrong, Whitworth & Co., Elswick Works, Newcastle-on-Tyne. War Work: Civil War Workers' Committee; Chairman, National Trades Advisory Committee; Ministry of Munitions Advisory Committee; Ministry of Munitions Joint Consultative and Advisory Committee; Admiralty Advisory Committee; Tyne and Wear Board of Management for Munitions; Newcastle-on-Tyne Employment Committee; Chairman, Local Trade Advisory Committee for Newcastle-on-Tyne. Address: Shepherd's Bank, Riding Mill, Northumberland. Club: Northern Counties', Newcastle-on-Tyne. (C1004)

MARKBREITER, Charles Gustavus, C.B.E.

MARKHAM, Anna Elizabeth Daisy, Mrs., M.B.E.

MARKHAM, Brig.-Gen. Charles John, C.B.E., b. 1862. Col. and Hon. Brig.-Gen. (ret.); Manipur Expedition, 1891; Burma Expedition, 1891–2; served in Great War, 1914–19 (mentioned in despatches). (C1684)

MARKHAM, Surg.-Lieut.-Comm. Ernest Lacey, O.B.E.

MARKHAM, Lucy Bertram, Lady, C.B.E.; *d.* of Capt. Cunningham, R.H.A.; *m.* Arthur Basil, *s.* of Charles Markham, of Tapton House, Chesterfield. *War Work :* Converted her residence, Beechborough, near Folkestone, into the Queen's Canadian Military Hospital, and acted as Superintendent there for 18 months; collected £22,000 for the Wounded Allies' Relief Committee, including the proceeds of the sale of 11,000 tons of coal at the Caledonian Market; organised the Miners' Lamp Fund for Serbia, and collected £3000 for this fund; organised and worked the Women's Active Service Club in London through which 36,000 girls passed. *Address :* 47, Portland Place, W. 1.   (C2463)

MARKHAM, Theodora Chevallier, Lady, C.B.E.

MARKS, Lieut.-Col. Alexander Hammett, C.B.E., D.S.O., M.D., B.A., B.Ch., *b.* 1880; *s.* of the Hon. Charles Ferdinand Marks, M.D., of Brisbane, Queensland; *m.* 1907, Annie Georgina Rhodes, of Dublin. *Educ. :* Brisbane Grammar School and Dublin University. Lieut.-Col. Australian Army Med. Corps; served in Great War, 1914–19, as a Dep. Assist. Director of Med. Sers.; subsequently Comdg. a Field Ambulance (despatches).   (C1362)

MARKS, Major Edward Seaborn, O.B.E.

MARKS, Geoffrey, C.B.E., *b.* 15 Nov. 1864; *s.* of John George Marks, of Croydon; *m.* Alys Mary, *d.* of J. H. Bridges, of Ipswich. *Educ. :* Whitgift Grammar School. Actuary and Manager, National Mutual Life Assurance Society; Chairman of the Life Offices' Association, 1914–15; President of the Institute of Actuaries, 1918–20; ex-officio member of the Council of the Royal Patriotic Fund Corporation; Member of the Royal Commission on Decimal Coinage, 1918, and of the Royal Commission on Income Tax, 1919. *War Work :* 5 Aug. 1914, to Dec. 1916, Finance Officer, Metropolitan Special Constabulary, on the staff of Sir Edward Ward, Bart., K.C.V.O., K.C.B.; 1914–16, as Chairman of the Life Offices' Association, acted as intermediary between the Government and the Life Assurance Offices in negotiating the concessions in regard to Extra Premiums and other conditions of Assurance which Government wished to be abrogated in order to encourage recruiting; also conducted other negotiations in relation to questions arising out of the war, with the Treasury, Inland Revenue, and other Government Departments; Member of the Advisory Committee formed by the Insurance Offices and the Trust Companies at the request of the Treasury in order to promote the scheme for mobilisation of Dollar Securities; assisted in establishing and was for some time Chairman of the Disabled Officers' Home and Club, 46, Westbourne Terrace, W. 2; Dec. 1916, to July, 1919, lent to the Navy and Army Canteen Board—then the Army Canteen Committee—to act as Financial Adviser. This post was subsequently abolished, but on a formal request from the War Office (D.Q.M.G. Canteens) was lent as a whole time worker to the Navy and Army Canteen Board to act as Personal Assistant to the Controller, Lieut.-Col. Sir Francis Towle, C.B.E. All these services have been given in an honorary capacity, owing to disqualification for Military Service on account of age. *Address :* 8, Chesham Place, London, S.W. 1. *Clubs :* Union; M.C.C.; Royal St. George's.   (C2793)

MARKS, Sir George Croydon, C.B.E., J.P., M.P., *b.* 9 June, 1858; *s.* of the late William Marks, of Eltham; *m.* Margaret, *d.* of Thomas Maynard, of Bath. *Educ. :* Royal Arsenal School, Woolwich, and King's Coll., London. Consulting Engineer and International Patent Law Expert of London and New York. *War Work :* Member of Advisory Committee on Labour Dilution, Ministry of Munitions; Chief Commissioner for Dilution of Labour for Newcastle-on-Tyne district; Chairman of Commissioners for Unrest Enquiry, Midlands and E. Yorkshire; visited France on munition work during the war. *Addresses :* 58, Lincoln's Inn Fields, W.C. 2; Rothbury, Blackheath Park, S.E. 3; Penarvon, Bude, Cornwall. *Clubs :* National Liberal; Reform.   (C45)

MARKS, Henry, C.B.E., *b.* 1861; *s.* of the late Benjamin Marks, of Melbourne, Victoria; *m.* Annie Abrahams. Sometime Major, Fiji Vol. Force; Managing Director, Henry Marks and Co., Ltd., Merchants; M.E.C. and M.L.C. of Fiji; J.P. for Suva. *Address :* Suva, Fiji.   (C399)

MARKS, 2nd Lieut. Herbert Elton, M.B.E., D.C.L.I.

MARKS, Major John Barkly, O.B.E.

MARKS, Richard Harris, O.B.E. *War Work :* Chief Special Constable, Borough of Luton. *Address :* The Shanty, Leagrave Road, Luton. *Club :* R.A.C.   (O10927)

MARKWICK, Col. Ernest Elliott, C.B., C.B.E., R.A.O.C., *b.* 19 July, 1853; *s.* of William Markwick, of East Acton, Middlesex, W.; *m.* Amy, *d.* of F. M. Murton, of Pietermaritzburg, Natal. *Educ. :* Privately, and King's Coll., School. Entered late Control Dept. of the Army 1872; served Zulu War, 1879; Boer War, 1880–1881, including Siege of Pretoria; Bechuanaland Expedition, 1884–85, hon. mentioned and specially promoted, mentioned in despatches; Fellow of the Royal Astronomical Society, and past-president, British Astronomical Association. *War Work :* Assist. Director of Ordnance Services at G.H.Q., Dublin, during the whole period of the war. *Addresses :* The Knowle, West Moors, Dorset; c/o Sir C. R. McGrigor, Bart., & Co., 39, Panton Street, Haymarket, S.W. 1.   (C828)

MARLING, Lucia, Lady, C.B.E., *b.* 1883; *d.* of Major-Gen. Sir John Slade, K.C.B. (*see* BURKE's *Peerage*); *m.* Sir Charles Marling, K.C.M.G., C.B., H.B.M. Minister at Copenhagen, *s.* of Sir William Marling, Bart., Stanley Park, Stroud (*see* BURKE's *Peerage*). *War Work :* Looking after Belgian re-fugees at H.I.H. the Duchesse de Vendome Hostel at Wimbledon until 1915; raised a fund for comforts for the troops in Mesopotamia in 1915; in charge of arrangements for evacuation of women and children of British Colony from Tehran during Turkish advance in 1916; undertook organisation for repatriation of Prisoners of War and British civilians from Russia in March, 1920. *Addresses :* British Legation, Copenhagen; 8, Lowndes Street, S.W.   (C2794)

MARLOW, Major Arthur Lambert, O.B.E., *b.* 27 May, 1857; *s.* of Arthur Marlow, of Mullybrannon, Co. Tyrone; *m.* Sylvia Margaret, *d.* of E. B. Lewin Hill, C.B., J.P., of Kingston Hill. *War Work :* 1914–19, served with the Egyptian Expeditionary Force, and British Salonica Force. Twice mentioned in despatches. *Address :* 43, Rowan Road, W. 6. *Club :* Authors'.   (O6507)

MARLOW, Edmund George, O.B.E.

MARLOW, Capt. George William Augustus, O.B.E.

MAROCHETTI, George Charles Marie, Baron, M.V.O., O.B.E., Commander of the Order of the Crown of Italy, *b.* 1894. Lieut. 11th Hussars, 1916; Capt. Gen. Staff and Asst. British military representative, Vienna, 1919; naturalised in the United Kingdom, 1917; obtained a royal licence authorising him to bear the title of Baron in this country, 1918.

MARPLES, Capt. Morris Edgar, O.B.E., R.A.S.C.

MARQUAND, Alan Herbert, O.B.E.

MARR, Capt. David Murdock, O.B.E., R.A.M.C., (S.R.).

MARR, Major Hugh, O.B.E., M.C., *b.* 15 March, 1878; *s.* of Andrew and Sarah Marr, of Manchester; *m.* Emily, *d.* of William W. Rothero, of Brecon. *Educ. :* St. Clement's, Manchester. Enlisted private, Sept. 1899; Commissioned, Aug. 1914; South Africa, 1900–1904. *War Work :* Dardanelles and Mesopotamia, June, 1915, to March, 1920; Lieut.-Col. Commanding 18th (Indian) Machine Gun Batt.; Military Governor, Sulaimaniyah, Kurdistan; Brevet rank of Major on promotion to Capt.; five mentions in despatches. *Address :* The Watton, Brecon.   (M6664)

MARR, Sir James, Bart. C.B.E., *b.* 9 Sept. 1854; *s.* of Christopher Hall Matt, of Newcastle-on-Tyne; *Educ. :* Privately. Is the 1st Baronet (cr. 1919); is a shipbuilder; a Member of Shipping Controller's Advisory Committee; a Member of Shipbuilding Council at Admiralty; Chairman of Sir James Laing and Sons, of Sunderland, of Sunderland Forge Commrs., and of Lloyds Registry of Shipping; Managing Director of Joseph L. Thompson and Sons, of Sunderland; a Freeman of the City of London, and J.P. for Durham. *Address :* Parkside Roker, Sunderland. *Club :* Royal Thames Yacht.   (C237)

MARR, Lieut.-Col. John Lynn, O.B.E., T.D., R.G.A. (T.), *b.* 1877; *s.* of Sir James Marr, of Sunderland; *m.* May, *d.* of the late Robert Thompson, of Dinsdale, nr. Darlington. Forgemaster; Director of the Sunderland Forge and Engineering Co., Ltd., Sir James Laing and Sons, Ltd., T. W. Greenwell & Co., Lloyds British Testing Co., E. G. S., Ltd. *War Work :* Commanded the Durham Heavy Battery, R.G.A., from 1912; mobilised 14 Aug. 1914; in Flanders and France, 1916–17; recalled to British Admiralty, June, 1917; appointed Assist. Director, Merchant Shipbuilding Department to Armistice; O.C. 3rd Northumbrian Medium Brigade, R.G.A. (T.), April, 1920. *Address :* Aykleypeads, Durham. *Clubs :* St. Stephen's; National Sporting.

MARRACK, Philip Edward, O.B.E., *b.* 14 Aug. 1882; *s.* of John Reed Marrack, J.P., of Tiverton; *m.* Elizabeth Foster, *d.* of Roland Butler, Barrister, of Lincoln's Inn. *Educ. :* Blundell's School, and Trinity Coll., Cambridge. Admiralty Civil Servant. *Address :* Caer Eden, Lyonsdown Road, New Barnet. *Club :* United Univ.   (O3827)

MARRIOTT, Major Donald James, O.B.E., R.E.

MARRIOTT, Ethel Gertrude, Mrs., M.B.E.

MARRIOTT, Capt. Herbert, O.B.E.

MARRIOTT, Herbert, C.R.E., *b.* 1865. Chief Goods Manager of Lancashire and Yorkshire Railway; Traffic Sup. Dearne Valley Railway; Sec. S. Yorkshire Joint Line Committee and Axholme Joint Line. *Address :* Ellesmere House, Eccles.   (C564)

MARRIOTT, Surg.-Comm. Horace Bruce, O.B.E., R.N. (S.R.).

MARRIOTT, Brig.-Gen. John, C.B.E., M.V.O., D.S.O., *b.* 3 Nov. 1861; *s.* of John Marriott, of Stowmarket, Suffolk; *m.* Cordelia C. Nevers, of St. Johnsbury, Vermont, U.S.A. *Educ. :* King's Coll. School, London. *War Work :* Commanded the Surrey Infantry Brigade at outbreak of war; afterwards commanded the 112th Inf. Brigade in France; finally commanding the 221st Mixed Brigade on Coast Defences; served with the Norfolk Regt. during the South African War.   (C1685)

MARRIOTT, Major Samuel Warburton, O.B.E., R.A.V.C., 12 Sept. 1891; *s.* of S. J. Marriott, of Northampton. *Educ. :* Northampton Town and County School; Wellingborough School. *War Work :* Landed in France, Aug. 1914, with 34th Bde. R.F.A., 2nd Division; remained with B.E.F. France until the Armistice; commanded No. 2 Mobile Veterinary Section, 1st Division, and 2nd in command No. 5 Veterinary Hospital. *Address :* 55, Abington Street, Northampton.   (O5540)

MARRIOTT, Major William Mason, O.B.E., *b.* 23 Feb. 1889; *s.* of William Hall Marriott, of Hopton Grange, Mirfield Yorks; *m.* Violet Helen, *d.* of Percy Gordon. *Educ. :* Rugby. *War Work :* Served throughout war in 60th Rifles. *Addresses :*

Hopton Grange, Mirfield, Yorks ; The Manor School, Fermoy, Co. Cork. (O8877)

MARS, Lieut. Lionel Jackson, M.B.E., *b.* 31 Aug. 1896 ; *s.* of William Oswald, of Yorkshire. *Educ.:* Merchant Taylors' School. Yorkshire Hussars, and R.A.F. ; now studying for Commerce. *War Work :* Commissioned in Yorkshire Hussars, April, 1915 ; seconded to Royal Flying Corps, Sept. 1916. *Address :* 23, Mowbray Road, Brondesbury, London, N.W. 6. (M6003)

MARSACK, Col. Edward Lethbridge, O.B.E.

MARSDEN, Major Charles Howard, O.B.E., B.A., *b.* 1 March, 1876 ; *s.* of the late Rev. Maurice Howard Marsden, M.A., of Colliton, Dorchester ; *m.* Evelyn Grace Ida, *d.* of the late Adm. the Rt. Hon. Sir Astley Cooper-Key, P.C., G.C.B., D.C.L., F.R.S. (*see* BURKE'S *Peerage*), of 55, Elm Park Gardens, S.W. *Educ.:* Charterhouse, and Clare Coll., Cambridge. Reserve of Officers ; late Alexandra Princess of Wales's Own Yorkshire Regiment (1900-20). *Address :* Ingleton, Frensham, Farnham, Surrey. (O7451)

MARSDEN, Ethel, M.B.E. ; *d.* of Henry Marsden, J.P., of Manchester. *Educ.:* Manchester High School, and Bangor, N. Wales. *War Work :* Member of Committee of Soldiers' and Sailors' Wives and Mothers Relief Fund and Welfare, Work in connection with it ; Unit Administrator, Q.M.A.A.C. overseas Service, July, 1917, to Nov. 1919. *Address :* c/o Capt. Marsden, 165, High Street, Manchester, S.E. *Club :* Withington Golf, Manchester. (M4549)

MARSDEN, Frank, M.B.E.

MARSDEN, Herbert Harrison, M.B.E., M.R.C.S., L.R.C.P., *b.* 21 Sept. 1858 ; *s.* of Ellis Marsden, of Claughton, Birkenhead ; *m.* Edith Mary, *d.* of Robert Fisher Thompson, of Kendal. *Educ.:* Privately. Surgeon, Ormskirk Cottage Hospital ; Medical Officer, Post Office. *War Work :* Initiated the forming of the Ormskirk Cottage Hospital into an Auxiliary Hospital in 1914 for the treatment of sick and wounded soldiers ; Medical Officer in charge of personnel R.A.V.C. at Scarisbrick Hall. *Address :* The Hall, Ormskirk, Lancs. *Club :* Ormskirk Golf. (M8963)

MARSDEN, James Whittaker, O.B.E., *b.* 4 Nov. 1870 ; *s.* of Jeremiah Marsden, of Bolton, Lancs ; *m.* Maude, *d.* of John Cooper, of New Street, London, E.C. *Addresses :* Stock Exchange, London, E.C. ; St. David's, 29, Elmfield Road, Bromley, Kent. *Clubs :* Bromley and Bickley Golf ; Bromley County. (O10928)

MARSDEN, Lieut. John, O.B.E.

MARSDEN, Major John Henry Frederick, O.B.E., T.D.

MARSDEN, Sir Thomas Rodgerson, C.B.E., J.P. ; Managing Director of Platt, Brothers & Co., War Contractors, of Oldham ; Director and Member of Council of British Cotton-Growing Association. *Address :* Brookhurst, Alexandra Road, Oldham. (C238)

MARSDEN, William Allen, O.B.E.,

MARSDEN, Capt. William Murray, O.B.E.

MARSDEN, Winifrede, O.B.E., *b.* 9 March, 1882 ; *d.* of the late Rev. Maurice Howard Marsden, M.A., of Moreton Rectory, Dorchester. Commandant V.A.D. Dorset 92. *War Work :* Commandant of Colliton House V.A.D. Hospital from Nov. 1914, to May, 1919. *Address :* Colliton House, Dorchester. (O542)

MARSH, Constance Mabel Worsey, M.B.E., *b.* 14 July, 1887 ; *d.* of Col. Frank Marsh, C.B.E., of Birmingham. *Educ.:* Rippingale ; Eastbourne. *War Work :* Commandant of the Beeches Auxiliary Hospital, Bournville, 1915-19. *Address :* Quarry House, Northfield, Birmingham. (M8964)

MARSH, Major Cunliffe Hebbert, O.B.E., D.S.O., *b.* 1878 ; *s.* of the late Col. Hippisley Cunliffe Marsh, 18th Bengal Lancers, of Clarence Hill, Tunbridge Wells ; *m.* 1909, Nina Helen, *d.* of James George Smith, of Row, Dumbartonshire. *Educ.:* Repton School. Entered Prince of Wales Vol. (S. Lancashire Regt.), 1899 ; Capt. Indian Army, 1908 ; Major, 1915 ; served in S. Africa, 1899-1901 ; present at relief of Ladysmith (despatches, Queen's medal with seven clasps) ; Great War, 1914-17, as Lieut.-Col. Comdg. a Batt. Cameron Highlanders (despatches). (C8505)

MARSH, Ernest William, O.B.E.

MARSH, Col. Frank, C.B.E., M.Ch., M.B., F.R.C.S., R.A.M.C. (T.), D.L. (County of Warwick), *b.* 16 June, 1855 ; *s.* of Edward Marsh, of Tillington, near Stafford ; *m.* Annie Constance, *d.* of William Hooper, of Beechwood, Clapham Common. *Educ.:* King's Coll. and Hospital, London. Knight of Grace of the Order of St. John of Jerusalem in England ; Consulting Surgeon, Queen's Hospital, Birmingham ; Treas. ex-President Birmingham Medical Benevolent Society ; Vice-President, Birmingham Medical Institute ; commanding 1st Southern General Hospital and R.A.M.C. (T.), Birmingham Units ; Chairman, Recruiting Committee of Warwickshire Territorial Force Association. *War Work :* Officer Commanding 1st Southern General Hospital, Aug. 1914, to May, 1917 ; Assistant Director of Medical Services, Birmingham Area, Southern Command, June, 1917, to Sept. 1919. *Addresses :* Quarry House, Northfield, Birmingham ; 93, Cornwall Street, Birmingham. *Club :* Union, Birmingham. (C1686)

MARSH, Jane, Mrs. Earle, M.B.E.

MARSH, Malcolm Ready, O.B.E. (O11959)

MARSH, Major Octavius de-Burgh, O.B.E., B.A., M.B., B.Ch. (Cantab.), M.R.C.S. (Eng.), L.R.C.P. (Lond.), *b.* 1 Sept. 1885 ; *s.* of Lieut.-Col. Octavius Edward Bulwer Marsh, J.P., of Parkdale, Newport, Monmouthshire ; *m.* Elizabeth Mary, *a.* of the Rev. Canon S. Hemphill, D.D., Litt. D., of Drumbeg

Rectory, Dunmurray, Co. Antrim. *Educ.:* Epsom Coll. School ; Pembroke Coll., Cambridge ; London Hospital. Assist. Hon. Surgeon, Royal Gwent Hospital, Newport, Mon. *War Work :* Active service with R.A.M.C. in France, 1914-19 ; Staff appointment as D.A.D.M.S. 3rd Army and 3rd Area, B.E.F. during 1919. *Address :* Parkdale, Newport, Monmouthshire. *Club :* Monmouthshire, Newport, Mon. (O5543)

MARSH, Major William Lockwood, O.B.E., R.A.F.

MARSH, Esther Eleanora Mary, Mrs. CHISENHALE-, M.B.E. ; *d.* of Edward Byrom, D.L., of Culver, Exeter, and Kersal Coll., Lancashire ; *m.* William Swaine, D.L., J.P., Chairman, Essex County Council, *s.* of Thos. Coxhead Chisenhale-Marsh, of Gaynes Park, Epping. *War Work :* Essex Local Committee War Pensions. *Address :* Gaynes Park, Epping. (M8965)

MARSHALL, Capt. Albert Edward, M.B.E.

MARSHALL, Sir Arthur Harold, K.B.E., *b.* 1870 ; *s.* of the Rev. H. T. Marshall, D.D. ; *m.* Louise, *d.* of the late Joseph Hepworth, J.P., of Leeds, Torquay, and Harrogate. *Educ.:* Privately at Leeds and Halifax, and Yorkshire Univ. Barrister-at Law ; called to the Bar, 1904 ; Hon. Sec. of the Yorkshire Liberal Federation ; a Member of the Harrogate Corporation for six years ; a Director of the Legal Insurance Co., J. Hepworth and Son, Ltd., Kenneth Durward, Ltd., and the Harrogate Road Car Co. *Addresses :* 19, Wimborne Road, Bournemouth ; 1, King's Bench Walk, Temple, E.C. *Clubs :* Reform ; National Liberal ; Leeds and County Liberal. (K93)

MARSHALL, Lieut. Arthur James, O.B.E.

MARSHALL, Capt. Arthur Timothy, O.B.E.

MARSHALL, Lieut. Colin Andrew, O.B.E., R.A.S.C.

MARSHALL, David Gregory, M.B.E.

MARSHALL, Elizabeth Middleton, Mrs. Ord, C.B.E. ; *d.* of the Rev. R. S. Beloe, of Holton St. Mary, Suffolk ; *m.* William Ord Marshall. *Educ.:* Privately and abroad. Imperial Educational work ; Hon. Sec. League of Empire ; Member of many committees on Educational Subjects. *Address :* 124, Belgrave Road, S.W. (C737)

MARSHALL, Capt. Eric Stewart, C.B.E., M.C.

MARSHALL, Capt. Ethel Margaret, M.B.E.

MARSHALL, Capt. Frederick Herbert James, O.B.E.

MARSHALL, Capt. Frederick W., M.B.E.

MARSHALL, Capt. Geoffrey, O.B.E., R.A.M.C. (S.R.).

MARSHALL, Capt. George Sims, M.B.E.

MARSHALL, Flight-Lieut. Gerald Struan, O.B.E., M.R.C.S., L.R.C.P., L.D.S., Royal Air Force Medical Service. *War Work :* Served with R.A.M.C. in England and Mesopotamia. *Address :* c/o Messrs. Holt & Co., 3, Whitehall Place, S.W. (O4133)

MARSHALL, Gertrude Mary, Mrs., M.B.E. Donor of Pinner Auxiliary Hospital, Middlesex. (M10259c)

MARSHALL, Major Hannath Douglas, O.B.E., Indian Defence. (O9057g)

MARSHALL, Capt. and Qr.-Mr. Harry A., O.B.E., Can. A.M.C.

MARSHALL, Capt. Henry Edmund, O.B.E.

MARSHALL, Major Herbert Westmorland, O.B.E., R.E.

MARSHALL, Howard, O.B.E., M.A., M.B., B.C. (Camb.), *b.* 20 Dec. 1870 ; *s.* of John Ferrow Marshall, of Sunderland ; *m.* Florence Mary, *d.* of Charles E. Covey, of Alresford, Hants. *Educ.:* Elmham, Norfolk ; Caius Coll., Cambridge ; St. Bartholomew's Hospital, London, E.C. Surgeon. Surgeon to Cirencester Hospital. *Address :* Park House, Cirencester, Glos. *Clubs :* Royal Societies' ; East Gloucestershire, Cirencester. (O10930)

MARSHALL, Lieut. Hugh John Cole, O.B.E., R.E. (T.).

MARSHALL, Major Isa Carswell, O.B.E., R.A.M.C. (T.).

MARSHALL, James Currie, M.B.E., *b.* 27 May, 1855. Goods Superintendent, College Station, Glasgow and S.W. Railway, Glasgow. *War Work :* Transport of Equipment, Stores, etc. (M8967)

MARSHALL, Capt. James Frederick Stewart, O.B.E., M.C., Can. A.M.C.

MARSHALL, Janet Sophia, Mrs., M.B.E. ; *d.* of John Collis, of Wyre Hall, Penkridge, Staffordshire ; *m.* Charles Marshall. *Educ.:* Brighton and Oxford. Diction and Inspector of Military Hospital Kitchens and Food, under the War Office. *War Work :* Lady Supt. in charge of Patients' Kitchen at Chiseldon Camp Hospital, Sept. 1915, to Feb. 1917 ; Lady Supt. in Charge of Patients' Kitchen at the Red Cross Hospital, Netley, May, 1917, to June, 1919. *Address :* 33, Sinclair Road, West Kensington. *Club :* V.A.D. Ladies'. (M8968)

MARSHALL, John MacMillan, O.B.E.

MARSHALL, Kenneth McLean, C.B.E., B.A., LL.B., *b.* 16 May, 1874 ; *s.* of Francis Marshall, of Edinburgh ; *m.* Gladys Kathleen, *d.* of Charles Stonham, C.M.G., F.R.C.S., of London. *Educ.:* Rugby, and Trinity Coll., Cambridge. Deputy Judge Advocate. *Address :* 12, Chesham Place, S.W.1. *Clubs :* Union ; Savile. (C2795)

MARSHALL, Capt. Legh Richmond Herbert Peter, O.B.E., M.D., J.P., R.A.M.C., *b.* 29 June, 1874 ; *s.* of the late Henry Marshall, M.D., of Clifton, Bristol ; *m.* Frances Marion, *d.* of the late Charles Alexander Ainslie, Swinton Bank, Peebles. *Educ.:* Radley Coll. ; Univ. of Bristol (Engineering) ; Univ. of Edinburgh (Medical). Late Assist. Physician City Fever Hospital, Edinburgh ; House Surgeon and Physician, Deaconess Hospital, Edinburgh ; Clinical Assistant, Skin Dept., Edinburgh, Royal Infirmary. *War Work :* Hon. M.O. i/c Venlaw

Red Cross Auxiliary Hospital, Peebles, and Morelands Red Cross Hospital; M.O. i/c 14th Manchester Regt.; M.O. i/c European, Indian, West African and West Indian Wards, No 2. African Stationary Hospital, Voi, E.A.E.F.; M.O. i/c Sanitation, Voi Post May, 1916, to Jan. 1917, also Staff Surgeon, Voi Post; M.O. Native Details Hospital, Dar-es-Salaam; O.C. Prisoners of War Hospital, Dar-es-Salaam; S.M.O. Nakuru, and O.C. Command Camp Hospital, Nakuru; twice mentioned in despatches. *Address:* Peebles, Scotland. *Clubs:* Fellow Royal Colonial Institute, London; Fellow, Royal Medical Society, Edinburgh. (O4160)

MARSHALL, Major Mark Henry, O.B.E., *b.* 27 Dec. 1883; *s.* of the late Mark Bell Marshall, J.P., of Woodthorpe, Stroud, Glos.; *m.* Ethel, *d.* of J. Watson Kaye, of Mirfield, Yorks. *Educ.:* Harrow, and Christ Church, Oxford. *War Work:* 1914–16, served with R.A.S.C., 48th and 61st Divisions, B.E.F.; 1916–19, D.A.Q.M.G. at Chatham. *Address:* Heathfield, Brimscombe, Glos. *Clubs:* Junior Carlton; New Oxford and Cambridge. (O753)

MARSHALL, Capt. Oswald Percival, C.B.E., *b.* 1857; *s.* of the late Murray Marshall, of Godalming. Capt. Mercantile Marine; Elder Brother of Trinity House. (C907)

MARSHALL, Lieut. Reginald Ross, M.B.E.

MARSHALL, William, M.B.E.

MARSHALL, Major William Henry, O.B.E., Aust. A.D.S.

MARSHALL, William Lee, O.B.E.

MARSHALL, Major David Bannerman BURT-, D.S.O., O.B.E., Greek Order of the Redeemer, Seaforth Highlanders, *b.* 14 July, 1887; *s.* of the late J. Burt-Marshall, of Limcarty, Perthshire. *Educ.:* Ardvreck, Crieff; Rugby School; R.M.C. Camberley; Staff Coll., Camberley. *War Work:* Served throughout the war chiefly on the Staff in France, and latterly in Salonica; Wounded twice at Ypres and on the Somme; mentioned seven times in despatches. *Address:* Lumcarty, Perthshire. *Club:* Conservative. (O6446)

MARSHAM, George, C.B.E., J.P., D.L., *b.* 10 April, 1849; *s.* of the Rev. G. F. Marsham, Rector of Allington, Maidstone. *Educ.:* Eton and Merton Coll., Oxford. *War Work:* Entertained Lady Superintendent and nurses at a V.A.D. Hospital; also Chairman of Executive Committee of Lady Camden's Fund for the support of V.A.D. Hospitals in Kent. *Address:* Hayle Cottage, Maidstone. *Club:* Junior Carlton. (C2796)

MARSHAM, Joan, The Hon. Mrs. Sydney, O.B.E., *b.* Jan. 1888; *d.* of William Warry, I.S.O., of Shapwick, Somerset; *m.* Sydney Edward Marsham, *s.* of the 4th Earl of Romney (see BURKE'S *Peerage*). *War Work:* Hon. Supt. of the Bibisco Hut, Y.M.C.A., and the Queen Mary Club for Officers, Eaton Square. *Address:* 5, South Eaton Place, S.W. 1. (O544)

MARSHAM, Hon. Reginald Hastings, O.B.E., J.P., *b.* 19 Dec. 1865; *s.* of the 4th Earl of Romny, of The Mote, Maidstone (see BURKE'S *Peerage*); *m.* Dora Hermione, *d.* of Charles North, of Rougham, Norfolk. *Educ.:* Marlborough. *War Work:* Aug. 1914 to Jan. 1916, served on Remount Service in Canada and America; 1916–18, commanded Croft Spar Remount Depot. *Address:* Rougham, Kings Lynn. *Club:* Cavalry. (O1648)

MARSON, Capt. Thomas Bertrand, M.B.E., R.A.F.

MARTEN, Capt. Leslie Howard, O.B.E., *b.* 1886. Underwriter, Lloyds, E.C. *War Work:* Adjutant, 29th London Regt., Sept. 1914, to May, 1915; Staff Captain, 175th Infantry Brigade, May, 1915, to April, 1917; Headquarters, 58th Division, April to Oct. 1917; General Staff, 4th Army Headquarters, Oct. 1917, to Feb. 1918; General Staff, 2nd Army Headquarters, Feb. 1918, to Feb. 1919. *Address:* Maryon Lodge, Hampstead. *Club:* City of London. (O2633)

MARTER, Alice Eleanor, O.B.E., *d.* of the late Major-General R. J. C. Marter, of 1st Dragoon Guards, A.D.C. to Queen Victoria, 1883–88. *War Work:* Wounded and Missing Dept. B.R.C.S., and Order of St. John of Jerusalem. *Address:* Warblington House, Havant, Hants. (O10931)

MARTIN, Albert, O.B.E. (O11996)

MARTIN, Lieut. Alfred, O.B.E., R.N.V.R.

MARTIN, Alfred Andrew, M.B.E.

MARTIN, Alfred James, O.B.E.

MARTIN, Major Alfred Ridley, O.B.E., R.A.F.

MARTIN, Alfred Walter, M.B.E., *b.* 21 Feb., 1878; *s.* of John William Martin, of St. Helier, Jersey, C.I. *Educ.:* St. Helier's National School, Jersey. *War Work:* Conductor R.A.O.C.; served with British Expeditionary Force, France, from Aug. 1914, to June, 1920. *Address:* 2, Hospital Road, Colchester. (M4550)

MARTIN, Lieut. Andrew, O.B.E., R.N.R.

MARTIN, Arthur, O.B.E.

MARTIN, Beatrix Maria, M.B.E., *d.* of General William George Martin, of Hemingstone Hall, Ipswich (see BURKE'S *Landed Gentry*). *War Work:* Commandant of V.A.D. Suffolk, 14; Commandant of Shrubland Park Auxiliary Hospital, Suffolk. *Address:* Hemingstone Hall, Coddenham, Ipswich. (M722)

MARTIN, Major Charles James, O.B.E., T.D., R.A.M.C. (T.), *b.* 8 Nov. 1869; *s.* of Thomas Stanhope Walker Martin, of Ballygonnel, Wicklow, Ireland; *m.* Robina Elisabeth, *d.* of Major-General John A. Gildea, late 81st Regt. *Educ.:* Trinity Coll., Dublin. Late Anæsthetist Bolingbroke Hospital, London. *War Work:* M.O. 1/23rd Batt. London Regt.; D.A.D.M.S. 47th (London) Division; in charge of Medical Division, Medical Specialist, and in command, 35th General Hospital. *Club:* Royal Automobile. (O554)

MARTIN, Major Charles Jasper, O.B.E., M.C., R.A.S.C.

MARTIN, Charles Selwyn, O.B.E., *b.* 1 Feb. 1873; *s.* of Charles Martin, of Dartington, Devon; *m.* Cynthia Mildred, *d.* of Arthur Herbert Savory, of Merry Gardens, Burley, Hants. *Educ.:* Lancing Coll. *War Work:* Assistant Director Food Production Dept. (Horticulture); Director Fruit Production and Preservation Ministry of Food. *Address:* Hunsdon Mill House, Stanstead Abbotts, Herts. *Club:* Farmers'. (O545)

MARTIN, T.-Lieut. David, O.B.E., A.M.I.E.E., *b.* 12 Jan. 1874; *s.* of William Martin, of Glasgow; *m.* Margaret Marie Therese, *d.* of R. Macfie, of Rothesay and Glasgow. *Educ.:* Allan Glens School, and Royal Technical Coll., Glasgow. Late Works Manager, Messrs. Wm. McGeoch & Co., Ltd., Birmingham, Messrs. Mechans', Ltd., Scotstoun, Glasgow, and Messrs. Ferranti, Ltd., Manchester; now Scottish District Manager of Messrs. A. Reyrolle & Co., Ltd., Hebburn-on-Tyne, and St. Helens Cable and Rubber Co., Ltd., Warrington. *War Work:* In France and Belgium as Colour-Sergeant in 5th Scottish Rifles (T.F.) (The Cameronians), "1914" Star, and latterly, 1916–19, as Chief Investigation Officer to Ministry of Munitions into Industrial disputes. *Addresses:* 45, Hope Street, Glasgow; 149, Peveril Avenue, Shawlands, Glasgow. *Club:* Scottish Constitutional, Glasgow.

MARTIN, Lieut. Edward George, O.B.E., R.N.V.R.

MARTIN, Elizabeth Evelyn, Mrs., M.B.E.; *d.* of Richard Southon, of Port Elizabeth, S. Africa; *m.* Charles Beldam Martin, City Treasurer, Capetown, *s.* of the Rev. Henry Martin, of Cork, Ireland. *Educ.:* Port Elizabeth (S. Africa), and Cheltenham. *War Work:* Organiser and President Red Cross (Delicacies) No. 2 General Hospital, S. Africa; Member of Red Cross Committee, S. Africa. *Address:* Renfurley, Groot Schuur Avenue, Rondebosch, S. Africa. (M1223)

MARTIN, Ernest Charles, M.B.E.

MARTIN, Col. Ernest Edmund, C.M.G., C.B.E., F.R.C.V.S., *b.* 1869. Entered Army Vet. Corps, 1892; Lieut.-Col. 1915; served in S. Africa, 1902 (Queen's medal with two clasps); Great War, 1914–16 (despatches); Assist. Professor at Army Vet. School, 1902–6; Comdt. there April to Aug. 1914; Dep. Director-Gen. of Vet. Sers. with rank of Col. (C1687)

MARTIN, Francis Edward, M.B.E.

MARTIN, Artificer-Eng. Frank Lewis, M.B.E., R.N.

MARTIN, Frederick Barclay, O.B.E., *b.* 18 Jan. 1876; *s.* of G. W. K. Martin, Civil Engineer, P.W.D., India; *m.* Margaret, *d.* of John Lawson Kelly, of 3, Belvedere Terrace, Brighton. *Educ.:* St. Paul's School, and Messrs. Wren and Gurney's, of Bayswater. Civil Engineer, Indian State Railways. *War Work:* Thrice mentioned in despatches: General Sir A. Barrett's, operations against Mahsud, 1917; Government of India's, War against Germany, 1918; General Sir C. Munroe's, war against Afghanistan, 1919. (O4066)

MARTIN, Gaston Pacroe de, M.B.E. Assistant Censor, Hong Kong. (M10259d)

MARTIN, Capt. George Walter Howard, C.B.E., R.N., *b.* 1859; *s.* of George Peter Martin, C.B., R.N., J.P., of Highlands, Emsworth, Hants. *War Work:* Naval Transport Officer, Newhaven, Sussex; Divisional Naval Transport Officer "Thames," London, Devonport, and Plymouth. *Address:* Brockland, Saltwood, Hythe, Kent. *Club:* Cinque Ports, Hythe. (C566)

MARTIN, Capt. and Qr.-Mr. George William, M.B.E., R.A.S.C.

MARTIN, Gerald, O.B.E.

MARTIN, Lieut.-Col. Gerald Hamilton, C.M.G., D.S.O., O.B.E., *b.* 1879; *s.* of William John Martin; *m.* Mary Augusta, *d.* of the late George Banks Rennie (see BURKE'S *Peerage*, Anglesey, M.). Entered King's Royal Rifle Corps, 1898; Major, 1905; Brevet Lieut.-Col. 1917; S. African War, 1899–1902 (Queen's medal with four clasps, King's medal with two clasps); Great War, 1914–19 (despatches); appointed an A.Q.M.G. 1918. (O5548)

MARTIN, Capt. Gilbert Charles, M.B.E., *b.* 1887; *s.* of F. C. Martin, of Tewkesbury. *Educ.:* Dean Close Memorial School, Cheltenham. *War Work:* Joined 1916; commissioned March, 1917; service in Mesopotamia, May, 1917, until March, 1920; two mentions in despatches. *Address:* 103, High Street, Tewkesbury. (M4895)

MARTIN, Capt. Harrison, M.B.E., R.F.A. (T.).

MARTIN, Capt. Harry Cutfield, C.B.E., R.N. Served in Great War, 1914–19 (mentioned in despatches). (C2280)

MARTIN, Capt. Herbert Walter, O.B.E., Can. A.M.C.

MARTIN, Lieut.-Col. Horace, O.B.E., R.E.

MARTIN, Hubert Stanley, C.B.E., *b.* 12 Aug. 1879; *s.* of the late Capt. Ernest Martin, 31st Regt. *Educ.:* Huntingdon School, Teddington and King's Coll., London. Chief Passport Officer, Foreign Office. *War Work:* In charge of the British Passport Office throughout the war. *Address:* 43, Airedale Avenue, Chiswick, W. 4. *Club:* Cavendish. (C2747)

MARTIN, Hugh Grey, O.B.E. (O11753)

MARTIN, Sir James, M.B.E., J.P., *b.* 21 Sept. 1861; *s.* of William Butts Martin, of London; *m.* Sara, *d.* of Thomas James Firminger, of Honor Oak. *Educ.:* Christ's Hospital. Senior partner in firm of Martin Farlow & Co., Incorporated Accountants; Fellow, Hon. Member and Adviser to Council of the Society of Incorporated Accountants; Chairman of Council, London Chamber of Commerce. *War Work:* Chairman Surbiton Local Tribunal, 1916–19; Director of Contract Costing, Ministry of Munitions, 1917; Member of Companies

Acts Committee, 1918; Hon. Life Member of British Red Cross Society, 1918. *Addresses :* 50, Gresham Street, E.C. 2 ; Bellair, Surbiton. *Clubs :* Reform ; New City. (M8972)

MARTIN, Major James Cecil, O.B.E., *b.* 18 Aug. 1877 ; *s.* of John Martin, of Doncaster ; *m.* Jessie, *d.* of Henry Louis Creswell, late Secretary of H.M. Post Office, Ireland and Scotland. *Educ.:* Suffield Park School, Cromer ; and Thorpearch Grange, Yorkshire. Civil Engineer ; at present Chief Engineer National Shipyards, Chepstow. *War Work :* Retained by H.M. Post Office for construction of P.O. Tube Rly. ; trained at Richboro' Depot of R.E. ; seconded to Admiralty, Sept. 1917, for preparation of designs for National Shipyards ; officer-in-charge of Drawing Office at Admiralty until designs were completed ; transferred to site, June, 1918 ; appointed Deputy Chief Engineer by Sir Frank Baines, whose department H.M.O.W. took over the administration of the yards for the Ministry of Shipping in 1919 ; and promoted to Chief Engineer in July, 1920. *Address :* 7, Axholme Road, Doncaster. (O10934)

MARTIN, Lieut.-Col. James Fitzgerald, C.B.E., C.M.G., M.B., Ch.B., *b.* 1876 ; *s.* of Surg.-Col. W. T. Martin, formerly Army Med. Ser. ; *m.* 1908, Mary Latimer, *d.* of Col. Richard Stanley Hawke Moody, C.B. *Educ.:* Bath Coll. and Edinburgh University. Lieut.-Col. R.A.M.C. ; Dep. Assist. Director-Gen. Army Med. Ser. ; S. African War, 1900–1 ; present at actions of Poplar Grove and Driefontein (Queen's medal with four clasps, King's medal with two clasps) ; Great War, 1914–19 (despatches) ; Knight of Grace of Order of St. John of Jerusalem in England. (C1688)

MARTIN, Capt. James Seaton, M.B.E., N.Z.A.P.C.
MARTIN, Lieut. James Wright, M.B.E.
MARTIN, John Bentinck, M.B.E.
MARTIN, Capt. John Newton, M.B.E., R.A.M.C.
MARTIN, May Angela, Mrs., M.B.E.
MARTIN, Norman Macdonald, C.B.E. (C3179)
MARTIN, Capt. Robert, M.B.E., R.A.
MARTIN, Capt. Thomas, O.B.E., R.A.F.
MARTIN, Paymaster-Lieut. Thomas, O.B.E., R.N.R.
MARTIN, William, M.B.E., M.B., Ch.B., J.P.
MARTIN, Major William Lewis, O.B.E., T.D.
MARTIN, Surg.-Comm. William Ludgate, O.B.E., F.R.C.S.
MARTIN, Capt. Robert Fiennes WYKEHAM-, M.B.E., R.E.
MARTINDALE, Hilda, O.B.E.
MARTINE, Lieut. William Robert, M.B.E., H.L.I.
MARTINEAU, Edith, Mrs., M.B.E.

MARTINELLI, Alfred, M.B.E., *b.* 21 Feb. 1855 ; *m.* Florence Anne Fullwood, *d.* of Thomas Beach, of Derby. Late of the War Office. *War Work :* Confidential work under the Military Secretary. *Address :* Sidbank, Sidmouth. (M2137)

MARTYN, Major Anthony Wood, O.B.E., D.S.O.
MARTYN, Lieut. John, O.B.E.. R.N.R.

MARTYN, Major Samuel, O.B.E., R.A.M.C. (T.), *b.* 18 May, 1874 ; *s.* of David Martyn, J.P., of Airdrie ; *m.* Elizabeth Adam, *d.* of Robert Adam, J.P., of Bushyhill, Cambuslang. *Educ.:* Glasgow High School, and Glasgow Univ. Physician ; Medical Officer to Post Office and Board of Education (Scot.). *War Work :* 1914 to 1919 Medical Officer, 9th H. L. I. (Glasgow Highlanders) ; O.C. General Hospital, France. *Address :* Fullarton House, Airdrie, Lanarkshire. (O5550)

MARTYR, Richard Edward, C.B.E., I.S.O., *b.* 26 Aug. 1857 ; *s.* of Richard Barnard Martyr, of Paddington ; *m.* 1st, Beatrice, *d.* of W. H. Waring, of Westbourne Park (who died 1902), 2nd, Annie, *d.* of G. Garland, of Maida Vale. *Educ.:* St. James's School, Bayswater, and privately. Clerk, Board of Trade, 1873–1903 ; Sec., Ichthyological Research Committee, 1902 ; transferred with Fisheries work to Ministry of Agriculture and Fisheries, 1903 ; 1st class clerk and head of Fisheries Branch of that Office, 1907–1920 ; appointed on staff of Fishery Section, Maritime Service, Reparation Commission, 1920 ; awarded the Imperial Service Order, 1917. *War Work :* Had charge of administrative work connected with the regulation of Fishing operations, the issue of permits to Fish, chartering of fishing boats for naval purposes, recruitment of fishermen for the Navy and other war time activities of the Ministry of Agriculture and Fisheries, including control of Belgian fishing boats based at English ports, for which he was awarded the Decoration of Chevalier, Order of Leopold II. of Belgium. *Address :* 27, Dundonald Road, Brondesbury Park, N.W. (C2798)

MARWOOD, Brig.-Gen. Henry, C.B.E., *b.* 1864. Col. and Hon. Brig.-Gen. (ret.) ; Zululand, 1888 ; Dongola, 1896 (Brevet Major, 4th class Medjidie, Egyptian medal with clasps, medal) ; S. Africa, 1902 (Queen's medal with two clasps) ; served in Great War (despatches). (C1689)

MARX, Susannah Brandh, Mrs., O.B.E.
MASCALL, Major Maurice Edward, D.S.O., O.B.E., R.G.A.
MASHITER, Lieut. and Qr.-Mr. Thomas, M.B.E.
MASKALL, George Stephen, O.B.E.

MASKELL, Lieut.-Col. William Edward, O.B.E., *b.* 10 Feb. 1873 ; *s.* of the late Stewart Eaton Maskell, of London, W. ; *m.* Maria Cecilia, *d.* of Embert Brands, of Rotterdam. *Educ.:* Downside College. Managing Director, Devon and Genl. Assets, Ltd. *War Work :* Devon Regt., attached 42nd Division, Gallipoli, Egypt, and France ; commanded 1/7th Lancashire Fusiliers from Aug. 1916, to Sept. 1917. *Address :* 9, Kingsley Terrace, Westward Ho! N. Devon. (O7456)

MASKENS, Harry Frederick, M.B.E.
MASLIN, Charles James, O.B.E.
MASON, Mrs. Adeline, O.B.E.
MASON, Lieut.-Col. Albert Wilberforce, O.B.E., F.R.C.V.S., R.A.V.C. (T.).
MASON, Alexander Neil, O.B.E.

MASON, Alfred, O.B.E., M.C., *b.* 27 Sept. 1877 ; *s.* of the late Thomas Edward Mason, of Deal, Kent. *Educ.:* Epsom Coll. Surgeon and Agent, H.M. Admiralty ; Medical Officer of Health for Boro' of Deal ; Port Sanitary Medical Officer ; Asst. County Director British Red Cross Society. *War Work :* Medical Officer in charge St. Anselm's Red Cross Hospital ; two years on Active Service in Palestine and France. *Address :* The Limes, Deal. *Club :* Deal and Walmer Union. (O10935)

MASON, Major Alfred Sidell, O.B.E.
MASON, Capt. Algernon Montague Wilson, M.B.E.

MASON, Cecil Charles, O.B.E., M.A., *b.* 20 Nov. 1880 ; *s.* of Walter Mason, M.B.E., of Sydenham, London,. S.B.; *m.* Norah A., *d.* of — Evers. *Educ.:* Clifton Coll., and Trinity Hall, Cambridge. Joint Managing Director of the Cambridge, and Paul Instrument Co., Ltd. ; Director of Optical Manufacturers Mutual Insurance Association ; Member of Council, British Scientific Instrument Research Association. *War Work :* His Company was a controlled establishment ; he was also Technical Adviser to the Controller of Gun Ammunition at Ministry of Munitions ; Member of the panel Munition Invention Department ; Associate Member, Ordnance Committee, Woolwich. *Address :* Beverley, Cavendish Avenue, Cambridge. (O19936)

MASON, Capt. David, O.B.E., J.P., *b.* 11 May, 1862 ; *s.* of George Johnston Mason, of Glasgow ; *m.* Joan MacKintosh, *d.* of George Mylne, of Glasgow. *Educ.:* Queen's Park, Glasgow. Magistrate and Councillor of the City of the County of Glasgow ; Consul for Montenegro in Glasgow. *War Work :* Chairman of Glasgow Corporation Committee in charge of Recruiting, Equipping, and Training four Battalions of Infantry and one Brigade of Artillery. *Addresses :* Dykeneuk, Pollokshields, Glasgow ; 36, Queen Street, Glasgow. *Clubs :* Conservative ; Merchants', Glasgow. (O10937)

MASON, Lieut.-Col. Douglas Herbert Campbell, D.S.O., O.B.E., *b.* 16 Feb. 1883 ; *s.* of John Herbert Mason, of Toronto, Canada. *Educ.:* Ridley Coll., St. Catharines, Ont., and Univ. of Toronto. *War Work :* Served in 3rd Canadian Batt., Toronto Regt., Sept. 1914 ; France, Feb. 1915 ; wounded 2nd Battle of Ypres, April, 1915 ; Major, Feb. 1916 ; wounded June, 1916 ; 2nd in Command 3rd Batt. Toronto Regt., Dec. 1916 ; bar to D.S.O. 1918 ; wounded Sept. 1918 ; Lieut.-Col., April, 1919. *Address :* 295, Russell Hill Road, Toronto. *Clubs :* University, Toronto ; Royal Canadian Yacht ; Canadian Military Institute. (O6031)

MASON, Major Edward, O.B.E., R.A.S.C.
MASON, Lieut.-Col. Edward George, O.B.E., C.A.M.C.

MASON, Lady Evelyn Margaret, O.B.E., Lady of Grace of the Order of St. John of Jerusalem ; *d.* of James Ludovic, 26th Earl of Crawford, K.T. (*see* BURKE'S *Peerage*) ; *m.* James Francis Mason, J.P., *s.* of the late James Mason, J.P., of Eynsham Hall, Witney, Oxon. *War Work :* Donor and Administrator, Mason Hospital for Officers, 16, Bruton Street, W. 1, Oct. 1914, to Jan. 1919. *Addresses :* Eynsham Hall, Witney, Oxon. ; 16, Bruton Street, W. 1. (O10938)

MASON, Florence Irene, M.B.E.
MASON, Frank John, M.B.E., J.P.
MASON, Major Frederic Eugene, O.B.E., V.D.
MASON, Capt. Henry George, O.B.E.

MASON, Lieut.-Col. Henry Hyde Williamson, O.B.E., *b.* 8 March, 1857 ; *s.* of the late Major-Gen. John Mason, of Comrie House ; *m.* Florence, *d.* of Col. Alexander Hannay. *Educ.:* Harrow. Officer Commanding 2nd Batt. R.G.L.I. Militia ; 44th Regt. 1878–1905 ; appointed embarkation staff 1910 to command a Batt. R. Guernsey L.I. (Militia) 1913. *War Work :* Served in South Africa, 1899–1901 ; commanded the 2nd Res. Batt. R. Guernsey L.I. 1916–20. *Address :* Glencoe, St. Martins, Guernsey. *Club :* Public Schools. (O8892)

MASON, Herbert, M.B.E.
MASON, Lieut. Horace George, M.B.E., R.G.A.
MASON, Major James Ernest, O.B.E., R.A.S.C.
MASON, Major John Henry, O.B.E.

MASON, Major John Wright, M.B.E., M.B., C.M., D.P.H., M.R.C.S.E., late 2nd E.Y.V.A., *b.* 4 May, 1852 ; *s.* of George Draper Mason, of Marston, Grantham ; *m.* Annie, *d.* of Robert Johnson, of Westborough, Grantham. *Educ.:* Aberdeen Univ., and Guy's Hospital, London. Medical Officer of Health, City and Port of Hull ; Surgeon, City Police. *Address :* 78, Beverley Road, Hull. (M8978)

MASON, Joseph Warren Leets, O.B.E.

MASON, Major Laurence, O.B.E., M.C., Belgian Croix de Guerre, *b.* 27 Aug. 1886 ; *s.* of Herbert W. Mason, J.P., of Sproughton Manor, nr. Ipswich ; *m.* Margaret Menella, *d.* of the late Rev. H. P. Jollye, M.A., of Warwick. *Educ.:* Charterhouse ; Christ Church, Oxford. Indian Forest Service. *War Work :* Served in R.F.A., Oct. 1914, to Oct. 1919 ; twice mentioned in despatches ; served in France, Jan. 1915, to Feb. 1919. *Address :* c/o H. S. King & Co., 9, Pall Mall, S.W. *Club :* Cavendish. (O2636)

MASON, Mary Margaret, O.B.E., *b.* 20 July, 1872 ; *d.* of the late Rev. G. J. Blore, D.D., of St. Stephen's House, Canterbury ; *m.* the Rev. Arthur James Mason, D.D., Canon of Canterbury. *Educ.:* Privately. *War Work :* Chairman of the Executive Committee of the Canterbury and District War Work Depot. *Address:* The Precincts, Canterbury. (O10939)

MASON, Capt. Robert Wyllie, O.B.E., R.A.S.C.

MASON, Capt. Samuel, O.B.E.

MASON, Walter, M.B.E., Officer of the Order of the Crown, Belgium, *b.* 27 Dec. 1851; *s.* of Charles Mason, of Canterbury, Kent. *Educ.:* King's School, Canterbury; Continent, Germany and France. *War Work:* President, Belgian Refugees Committee, Sydenham; Vice-President, Belgian Government Schools, Sydenham; Treas. War Savings Committee, Sydenham. *Address:* Woodfield, Dacres Road, Forest Hill, S.E. 23. *Club:* City Carlton. (M8979)

MASON, William Thomas, M.B.E.

MASON, Major Godfrey Noel Grey MONCK-, O.B.E., A.I.

MASON, Rev. Richard Swann SWANN-, O.B.E., M.A., R.N.

MASSEY, Allen, Mrs., O.B.E.

MASSEY, Major Charles Montague Hamilton, O.B.E.

MASSEY, Christina Allen, C.B.E. (C371)

MASSEY, Major Everard Ernest, M.B.E., *b.* 1 Dec. 1880; *s.* of W. E. Massey; *m.* Annette Mabel, *d.* of — Gray. *Educ.:* Ascham; Eastbourne; City of London. *War Work:* Enlisted, Inns of Court, April, 1915; commissioned, R.A.S.C., July, 1915; Mesopotamia, 1916–19; twice mentioned in despatches. *Address:* Hampden Club, London N.W. 1. (M4896)

MASSEY, William Thomas, O.B.E.

MASSIE, Anne, M.B.E.

MASSIE, Major Robert, O.B.E., F.R.C.S., R.A.M.C., *b.* 15 Jan. 1871; *s.* of W. H. Massie, of Edinburgh. *Educ.:* George Watson's Coll., Edinburgh; Royal Coll. of Surgeons, Edinburgh. Hon. Surgeon, Royal Richmond Hospital. *War Work:* Served overseas with B.E.F., Salonica Exped. Force, and Rhine Army, Aug. 1915, to March, 1920; twice mentioned in despatches. *Address:* 75, Queen's Road, Richmond, Surrey. *Club:* Royal Automobile. (O5554)

MASSON, Professor Davies Orme, O.B.E., D.Sc., F.R.S., Professor of Chemistry, Melbourne University; *m.* Mary, C.B.E. *(q.v.)*, *d.* of the late Sir John Struthers, M.D., of Aberdeen. *Address:* The University, Melbourne.

MASSON, James Irvine Orme, M.B.E., D.Sc. *War Work:* Research Department, Woolwich. *Address:* University College, Gower Street, London, W.C. 1. (M2138)

MASSON, Mary, Mrs., C.B.E., *b.* 1862; *d.* of the late Sir John Struthers, M.D., of Aberdeen; *m.* 1886, David Orme Masson, O.B.E., D.Sc., F.R.S., Professor of Chemistry, Melbourne University *(q.v.)*. Rendered services to Victoria League, Australian Red Cross, and Australian Comforts Fund during Great War. *Address:* The University, Melbourne. (C365)

MASSY, Col. Percy Hugh Hamon, C.B.E., *b.* 1857; *m.* 1888, Rosamund Amabel Nora, *d.* of the late Sir Carey John Knyvett, K.C.B. Lieut.-Col. and Brevet Col. (ret.); Afghan War, 1879–80 (medal); Great War, 1914–19 (despatches). (C1691)

MASTER, Capt. Frederick Hill, O.B.E., R.E. (T.).

MASTER, 2nd Lieut. Archie George CHESTER-, M.B.E., R.A.S.C.

MASTERMAN, Air Commodore Edward Alexander Dimsdale, C.M.G., C.B.E., A.F.C., R.A.F., *b.* 15 April, 1880; *s.* of Edward Masterman, Jun., of Torquay; *m.* Heather Frances, *d.* of Rev. E. P. Gregg, of Torquay. *Educ.:* Evelyns, Uxbridge. President, Inter-Allied Aeronautical Commission of Control (Germany). *War Work:* Served in the Admiralty, and work in connection with Naval Airships. *Address:* The Firs, Hook, Basingstoke. *Club:* R.A.F. (C2347)

MASTERMAN, Lieut.-Col. Thomas Spry, C.B.E., J.P., *b.* 1866; *s.* of the late William Masterman, of Hampstead, N.W. S. African War (despatches thrice, King's and Queen's medals); joined British S. Africa Police, 1898, and is now Lieut.-Col.; Controller S. Rhodesian Defence Force. *Address:* Salisbury, S. Rhodesia. *Club:* Salisbury (Rhodesia). (C736)

MASTERS, Lieut. Albert Frederick, O.B.E., R.N.R.

MASTERS, Capt. Denis Macpherson, M.B.E., *b.* 2 Aug. 1893; *s.* of Gertrude Helen Masters, of Bowden, Cheshire. *Educ.:* Elstow School, Bedford. *War Work:* Served in the Army, 1915–19. *Address:* Elstow, Fermoy Road, Thorpe Bay, Essex. (M5457)

MASTERS, Rev. Thomas Heywood, C.B.E., M.A., *b.* 1865; *s.* of Heywood Masters, of Didsbury. *Educ.:* Christs' Coll. Cambridge. Vicar of E. Meon; Hon. 1st class Chap. to the Forces; served in Great War, 1914–19, as Staff-Chap. 4th Army, and Assist. Chap.-Gen. in France (despatches). *Address:* East Meon Vicarage. Petersfield. (C1290)

MASTERS, Wilfrid John, M.B.E.

MASTERSON, Major William, O.B.E.

MASTERTON, John, M.B.E., Div. Inspector of Mines.

MASTERTON, Rev. John, M.B.E.

MATCHAM, Lieut. Sydney Harold, M.B.E.

MATCHAM, Col. William, D.S.O., O.B.E.

MATCHETT, Lieut.-Col. Gerald Keith, O.B.E., *b.* 1 March, 1866; *s.* of Rev. H. H. Matchett, M.A., Rector of Stratton Strawless, Norfolk; *m.* Mary Virginia, *d.* of Percy Charrington, of Burys Court, Reigate. *Educ.:* Royal Naval School. Joined the Connaught Rangers as Lieut., Nov. 1886; retired Nov. 1909. *War Work:* Served in Sudan campaign, 1896–98; battle of Omdurman; mentioned in despatches; Brevet-Major (2 medals and 2nd Class Order of the Medjidieh); served in Egyptian Army with rank of Pasha; served through-

out European War on Staff of War Office and in France; twice mentioned in despatches; promoted Lieut.-Col. *Address:* Broadview, Petersfield, Hants. *Clubs:* Army and Navy; Royal Albert Yacht. (O5557)

MATHER, Alice, Mrs., M.B.E.; *m.* Charles Mather, for many years Assistant Manager Wigan Coal and Iron Co., who died 1919. *War Work:* Superintendent of St. John's Ambulance Div., St. John Ambulance Brigade; equipped nurses; organised three voluntary workrooms, St. John's and Red Cross joint centre, which despatched garments and medical articles to the front; worked on behalf of local War Pensions, Food Control, consumption cases, and raised much money for needs of local soldiers' families. *Address:* Hall Lane, Hindly, nr. Wigan. (M8981)

MATHER, Alice Lilian, M.B.E., *b.* 23 Nov. 1874; *d.* of Rev. F. A. Mather. *Educ.:* Cheltenham Ladies' Coll. *War Work:* Red Cross Enquiry Office for Wounded and Missing. *Address:* Highbury House, Hitchin, Herts. (M8982)

MATHER, Arthur Stanley, C.B.E., *b.* 13 May, 1842; *s.* of J. P. Mather, of Bootle Hall, Liverpool; *m.* Frances, *d.* of the late Thomas Court. *Educ.:* Rugby. Admitted Solicitor in 1865; retired 1916; is a J.P. and Alderman for Liverpool; Lord Mayor, 1915–16; Vice-President of Liverpool Convalescent Institution. *War Work:* Chairman of the Lancashire (West Derby Division) Military Appeal Tribunal, and of the Profiteering Appeal Tribunal. *Address:* Beechwood, Woolton, Liverpool. *Club:* Conservative, Liverpool. (C240)

MATHER, Joseph Louis, O.B.E.

MATHER, Capt. William Harold, O.B.E., R.E. (T.).

MATHERS, Lieut.-Col. David, D.S.O., O.B.E., *b.* 1870. Lieut.-Col. E. Yorkshire Regt.; Comdt. of a Rest Camp; Great War, 1914–19 (despatches). (O5558)

MATHERS, Rev. James, O.B.E.

MATHERS, John Jephson, M.B.E.

MATHERS, Mary Augusta, Mrs., O.B.E.

MATHESON, Capt. Edmund George, O.B.E., R.E.

MATHESON, Major Frederick William, M.B.E.

MATHESON, Capt. Ian McLeod Angus, O.B.E.

MATHESON, Ivy, O.B.E.; *d.* of Roderick Matheson, 3rd *s.* of the late Sir Alexander Matheson, Bart., of Lochalsh *(see BURKE'S Peerage)*. *War Work:* Hon. Sec., Ladies' Emergency Committee of Navy League; Divisional Director, Women's Royal Naval Service. *Address:* 11, Cresswell Gardens, S.W. 5. *Club:* Forum.

MATHESON, Percy Ewing, M.B.E.

MATHESON, Wilhelmina Jean, Mrs., O.B.E.; *d.* of Colonel James Waddell-Boyd, 56th Regiment; *m.* John Colin (Lieut.-Col., R.E.), *s.* of the Rev. John Matheson, M.A., Hampstead. *War Work:* Superintendent, Royal Engineers' Prisoners of War Fund; Queen Mary's Guild, War Hospital Supply Depot, Admiralty House; Chatham (mentioned by Sec. of State for War); Y.M.C.A., Gillingham, Kent (Order of Red Triangle and bar); War Pensions, Kent Local Committee. *Address:* c/o Messrs. Cox & Co., 16 Charing Cross. (O10941)

MATHEW, Charles James, C.B.E., K.C., *b.* 24 Oct. 1872; *s.* of Lord Justice Mathew; *m.* Anna, *d.* of James Cassidy, of Monasterevan, Co. Kildare, Ireland. *Educ.:* The Oratory School, Birmingham; Trinity Hall, Cambridge. *War Work:* Member of the Statutory Committee (Pensions); Chairman of the Special Grants Committee. *Addresses:* 76, Woodside, Wimbledon; 4, Old Square, Lincoln's Inn. *Club:* Athenæum. (C46)

MATHEW, Lieut. Felton Arthur Hamilton, O.B.E., M.C.

MATHEWS, Lieut. Charles Bernard, M.B.E., R.E.

MATHEWS, George Alfred, M.B.E., M.C., R.A.O.C.

MATHEWS, Major Henry Edmunds, O.B.E., T.D., F.R.I.B.A., *b.* 22 May, 1868; *s.* of J. Douglass Mathews, F.R.I.B.A., F.S.I., of Highbury, N.; *m.* Florence Mabel, *d.* of H. Jefferiss, of Sydenham. *Educ.:* Merchant Taylors' and Guilds of City of London Coll. Architect; Architect and Surveyor to St. Bartholomew's Hospital and London Estates, and also to Worshipful Company of Tallow Chandlers. *War Work:* Major in the 4th Batt. Royal Sussex Regt.; mobilised Aug. 1914; Headquarter Staff of London Command, March, 1915, to March, 1919. *Addresses:* 11, Dowgate Hill, E.C. 4; Anderida, Melville Avenue, South Croydon, Surrey. *Clubs:* Gresham; Church; Imperial. (O3150)

MATHEWS, Leslie, M.B.E. T. Commercial Assistant, Ministry of Shipping. (M10259e)

MATHEWS, Robert Gordon, O.B.E., Can. A.P.C.

MATHEWSON, Alfred Eugene, O.B.E., *b.* 14 March, 1875; *s.* of J. E. Mathewson, of Neosho, Wisconsin, U.S.A.; *m.* Constance Mary, *d.* of Charles Nickson, of Altrincham. *Educ.:* Sheffield; Sheffield Middle Class School; Sheffield Technical School; Firth Coll., Sheffield. Managing Director of Messrs. George Richards & Co., Ltd., of Broadheath, Manchester, Machine Tool Makers; also Managing Director of Messrs. Telghmans' Patent Sand Blast Co., Ltd., of Broadheath, near Manchester. *War Work:* Making of machine-tools for the manufacture of guns and sand-blast machinery for shells, steel, iron, and brass castings. *Address:* Woodheys, Sale, Cheshire. *Clubs:* Engineers, Manchester; Royal Mersey Yacht, Liverpool; Eccentric; R.A.C.; Constitutional. (O10942)

MATHIAS, Major James Herbert, O.B.E.

MATHIAS, Major Lewis James, O.B.E., R.F.A. Deputy-Lieut. for County of Cardigan, J.P. (Cardigan), Governor of Univ. Coll. of Wales, Member of Court of Welsh National Library, *b.* 1 Nov. 1861; *s.* of John Mathias, Aberystwyth *(see BURKE'S*

Peerage); *m.* Elsie Marion, *d.* of Edward Hooper, of Birmingham. *Educ.*: Aberystwyth Grammar School. Steamship Owner. *War Work*: In command of Cardiganshire Recruiting Area during the war. *Address*: Bronfadarn, Aberystwyth. *Club*: St. Davids, Aberystwyth. (C2801)

MATHIAS, Lieut.-Col. Oswald Llewellyn, O.B.E., *b.* Feb. 10, 1883; *s.* of the late Colonel H. H. Mathias, C.B., A.D.C., of 1st Batt. Gordon Highlanders; *m.* Violet Montgomerie, *d.* of the late James Williamson, of Tunbridge Wells. *Educ.*: Fettes. Late The Welsh Regt.; now Regional Director, Yorkshire Region, Ministry of Pensions. *War Work*: Served in South African War and European War, 1914–19; mentioned in "London Gazette" May, 1917. *Address*: Junior Army and Navy Club, Horse Guards Avenue, S.W. 1. *Clubs*: Junior Army and Navy; M.C.C. (O3151)

MATHIESON, Capt. William, O.B.E., R.A.M.C., *b.* 21 Sept. 1883; *s.* of the late John Mathieson. *Educ.*: Cambridge Univ., and St. Thomas's Hospital, London. *War Work*: Served in Gallipoli, Egypt, and Palestine, 1915–19. *Address*: c/o Holt & Co., 3, Whitehall Place, S.W. (O6243)

MATHISON, Mary Martin, Mrs., M.B.E. (M10505)

MATON, Lieut.-Comm. Reginald Foster Pitt, O.B.E., R.N., *b.* 30 May, 1886; *s.* of Leonard James Maton, of Sundial House, Kensington. *Educ.*: Rokeby, Wimbledon, and R.N. School, Lee-on-Solent. *War Work*: Gunnery Lieut. of H.M.S. "Duncan" Aug. 1914–15; Experimental Gunnery Officer H.M.S. "Excellent," March, 1915 till Armistice. *Club*: Junior United Service. (O1656)

MATON, William Clifford, M.B.E.

MATON, Lieut. William Henry George, M.B.E., R.A.

MATSON, James, O.B.E.

MATSON, Lieut.-Col. John, O.B.E., Mil. Farms Dept., I.A. (O11754)

MATTHEW, John Godfrey, O.B.E. (O11942)

MATTHEW, Ruth Mary, Mrs., M.B.E., *b.* 24 April, 1882; *d.* of James Ramsay, of Dundee, and Arbroath. *Educ.* Arbroath High School, and Harris Academy, Dundee. *War Work*: Hon. Organising Secretary for South Africa Lord Roberts Memorial Fund. *Address*: P.O., Box 60, East London, South Africa. (M8984)

MATTHEWS, Alice May, M.B.E., *b.* 1 May, 1889; *d.* of Colonel C. J. Matthews (late Middlesex Regt.), of Glenure House, Charlton Kings, Glos. *Educ.*: Badminton House, Clifton, Bristol. Assistant Radiographer. *War Work*: X-ray work, Cheltenham Red Cross Hospitals, 1914 to present date. *Addresses*: Glenure House, Charlton Kings; Ashfield, Bayshill Road, Cheltenham. (M8985)

MATTHEWS, Arthur, O.B.E.

MATTHEWS, Capt. Clement Norman, M.B.E.

MATTHEWS, Major Durham, O.B.E., J.P., *b.* 15 Jan. 1876; *s.* of the late T. B. Matthews, of Thorparch Hall, Yorkshire; *m.* Eileen, *d.* of Sir John Talbot Power, Bart., of Edermine, Co. Wexford, Ireland (*see* BURKE'S *Peerage*). 17th Lancers, R. of O. *War Work*: Served in France as a A.P.M., 16th (Irish) Division. *Addresses*: Clonsilla Grange, Co. Dublin, Ireland; 314, St. James' Court, London. *Club*: Army and Navy; Bachelors'; Kildare Street; Dublin. (O8879)

MATTHEWS, Major Edward, O.B.E., J.P., *b.* 4 May, 1864; *s.* of the late Joseph Matthews, J.P., of Foxbury, near Sevenoaks, Kent; *m.* C. I., *d.* of the late Lewis D. Wigan, J.P., of Oakwood Park, Maidstone. *Educ.*: Privately. 3rd Essex Militia. *War Work*: Joined, in Sept. 1914, 11th Batt. Essex Regt.; went to France, July, 1915; invalided home after the battle Hullock-Loos; joined 12th Essex Regt.; 2nd in command of 53rd T.S. Training Reserve Battalion until Feb. 1918; went to Gibraltar, joined as 2nd in command 1st S.B. Cheshire Regt.; disbanded Sept. 1919; mentioned in despatches, Jan. 1916. *Address*: Foxbury, near Sevenoaks, Kent. *Club*: Conservative. (O7460)

MATTHEWS, Edward Henry, M.B.E.

MATTHEWS, Lieut. Ernest Francis K., M.B.E.

MATTHEWS, Capt. Ernest James, O.B.E., *b.* 14 March, 1871; J. W. Matthews, of Ballinagore, Co. Westmeath; *m.* Henrietta Maud, *d.* of Alexander Eaton, of Carlow. *Educ.*: Knockdrin, Co. Westmeath. District Remount Officer, No. 3 District, 1 Circle, Western Command. *War Work*: Bechuanaland, 1896–97; South African Campaign, 1899–1902; Mafeking Siege, Operations in Transvaal and O.R.C.; Remount Department, Dieppe and Romsey, 1914–19. *Address*: 155, Burton Road, West Didsbury, Manchester. (O7461)

MATTHEWS, Florence, Mrs. Arthur Kennard, O.B.E.

MATTHEWS, Major Frank Melvin, O.B.E.

MATTHEWS, Lieut. Frederick Gwilliam, M.B.E.

MATTHEWS, Lieut. Harry, M.B.E., I.A.R.O.

MATTHEWS, Capt. Herbert, O.B.E., M.C., K.O.Y.L.I.

MATTHEWS, Major L:ewellin Washington, O.B.E.

MATTHEWS, Capt. Noel Lane, M.B.E., R.F.A.

MATTHEWS, Olive Harrington, M.B.E., *b.* 2 Aug. 1887; *d.* of Philip Walter Matthews, of Bankers' Clearing House, London. *Educ.*: Mary Datchelor School, Camberwell. *War Work*: Headquarters Camberwell Division V.A.D. Aug. 1914, to March, 1916; V.A.D. Headquarters Staff, March, 1916, to July, 1919; Commandant Detachment 228, Aug. 1914, to July, 1919. *Address*: 67, Sedlescombe Road South, S. Leonards, Sussex. (M8987)

MATTHEWS, Capt. Philip Edwin, M.B.E.

MATTHEWS, Robert Lee, M.B.E., *b.* 28 Aug. 1876; *s.* of William, late of Leeds; *m.* Ada, *d.* of John Parkinson, of Leeds. *Educ.*: Central High School, Leeds, and St. George's

School, Leeds. Assistant Chief Constable, Leeds City Police. *War Work*: Special assistance in emergency measures undertaken by police during the war. *Address*: Town Hall, Leeds. (M8988)

MATTHEWS, Major Robert Saxon, M.B.E., N.Z.A.P.C.

MATTHEWS, S. Emily, M.B.E., *d.* of John Matthews, J.P., of Trehinon, Amlwch, Anglesey. *Educ.*: Privately; Manchester School of Art. March, 1917, to Dec. 1919, Organising Sec. for Anglesey and Carnarvonshire Women's Branch, Board of Agriculture and Fisheries; Member of the Anglesey Education Authority; Hon. Sec. of Anglesey Nursing Committee, and of Anglesey Victoria Nursing Association; Hon. Sec. and Organiser of Anglesey Union of Village Halls and Societies (affiliated to V.C.A.); Member of Anglesey Employment Committee. (M8989)

MATTHEWS, Lieut. Thomas, M.B.E.

MATTHEWS, Thomas Leigh, O.B.E.

MATTHEWS, Lieut. Thomas Samuel, O.B.E.

MATTHEWS, Col. Valentine, C.B.E. (Mil. Div.), V.D., M.R.C.S., R.A.M.C., *b.* 14 Feb. 1855; *s.* of William Matthews, of Dulwich; *m.* Maude, *d.* of I. H. Garland. *Educ.*: St. Paul's School, and King's Coll., London. Associate of King's Coll., London; Hon. Life Member St. John Ambulance Association; 1st Iefe Hon. No. 3 Ambulance, Cruz Roja, Madrid; late Senior Surgeon, Westminster General Dispensary; T. Lieut.-Col. in Army; County Director, V.A.D., T.F. Association (County of London), 1909–17; Inspector of Rest Houses, London District; Medical Registrar and House Physician King's Coll. Hospital. *War Work*: County Director V.A.D. T.F. Association, County of London; Inspector of Rest Houses, London District; organised reception, distribution, transport, and food for soldiers on leave in, or passing through, London; also organised the Free Buffets at the seven London Termini. *Address*: 29, Onslow Square, S.W. 7. *Club*: Reform. (C241)

MATTHEWS, Major William John Richardson, O.B.E., J.P., Croice di Guerra (Italy), *b.* 1872; *s.* of William Matthews, of Llangollen, Denbighshire; *m.* Violet, *d.* of Arthur Labouchere, of Broome Hall, Surrey. Capt. Reserve of Officers, Manchester Regt.; South Africa, 1902 (Queen's Medal, 3 clasps). *War Work*: Staff Capt. in France, 1914–16; Staff Officer, Assistant Embarkation, 1916–17, Southampton; Deputy Assistant Director of Remounts, 1917–19, Italy; mentioned in despatches twice. *Address*: Admington Hall, Shipston-on-Stour. *Club*: White's. (O6399)

MATTHEWS, Lieut. William Reginald, M.B.E.

MATTHEWS, William Thomas, M.B.E.

MATTHEWS, Capt. Basil GARLAND-, M.B.E., *b.* 19 March, 1874; *s.* of Col. Garland-Matthews, of Manchester Regiment. *Educ.*: United Services Coll.; Westward Ho. *War Work*: Deputy Assist. Quartermaster-Gen. Australian Imperial Force Depots in United Kingdom. (M2144)

MATTHEWSON, Thomas, M.B.E., *b.* 31 Dec. 1854; *s.* of William John Matthewson, of Newcastle-on-Tyne; *m.* Ellen Mary, *s.* of William Lines, of Hertfordshire. *Educ.*: Royal Grammar School, and Dr. Bruce's Academy. Member of Newcastle-on-Tyne City Council; Vice-Chairman of War Pensions Committee; Chairman of the Executive and Cases Committees. *War Work*: Group Leader of Special Constables. *Address*: 3, Springbank Road, Newcastle-on-Tyne. (M8990)

MATTHEY, Percy, O.B.E., J.P.

MATTINSON, Major Arthur Bowman, O.B.E., M.C., F.R.C.V.S., R.A.V.C.

MATTINSON, Thomas Herbert, M.B.E., *b.* 9 July, 1879; *s.* of James Mattinson, of Kirkby Lonsdale, Westmorland; *m.* Marion Isobel, *d.* of William Armstrong, of Beverley, Yorks. *Educ.*: Grammar School, Kirkby Lonsdale. *War Work*: Assistant Director, and later Director, Fruit Supplies and Preservation Branch, Ministry of Food. *Address*: 19, New Walk, Beverley. (M2145)

MATTOCKS, Capt. Richard Mawson, O.B.E.

MATURIN, Capt. Hugh Geoffrey, O.B.E., I.A.

MAUD, Col. Harry, C.B.E., D.S.O. Major, Gen. List, A.Q.M.G. with rank of Col.; Great War, 1914–19 (mentioned in despatches). (C1291)

MAUD, Brig.-Gen. Philip, C.M.G., C.B.E., *b.* 8 Aug. 1870; *s.* of the late Rev. H. L. Maud, M.A. (Trinity, Camb.), of Embankment Gardens, Chelsea; *m.* Dorothy Louisa (who died 1920), *d.* of the Rev. J. M. Braithwaite, M.A. (Oxon.), late Vicar of Croydon. *Educ.*: Leamington Coll.; Royal Military Academy, Woolwich. Served in Royal Engineers from 1898 to 1910; appointed Chief Officer, L.C.C. Parks Department, 1911. *War Work*: Rejoined Army on mobilisation; served on General Staff, G.S.O. 2, and G.S.O. 1, till June, 1918; in charge of Anti-Aircraft Section, General Staff, Home Defence, from 1916 to June, 1918, when appointed Brig.-Gen. commanding Northern Air Defences. *Address*: 24, Egerton Terrace, S.W. 3. *Club*: Naval and Military. (C2141)

MAUDE, Major Charles Raymond, O.B.E.

MAUDE, Major Christian George, D.S.O., O.B.E., M.C., R.F., *b.* 4 Sept. 1884; *s.* of Lieut.-Col. Aubrey Maude, of 89, Eccleston Square, London, S.W.; *m.* the Hon. Patience, *d.* of Lord Rochdale, of Rochdale (*see* BURKE'S *Peerage*). *Educ.*: Rugby, and R.M.C., Sandhurst. *War Work*: Adjutant 24th London Regt. (The Queen's), T.F.; Staff-Capt. 13th Inf. Bgde.; D.A.A.Q.M.G. 1st Corps; A.Q.M.G. 21st Corps; A.A.Q.M.G. 52nd Division; A.Q.M.G. 9th Corps. *Address*: Bachelors' Club, London, W. *Clubs*: Bachelors'; White's; Pratt's; R.A.C.; Lord's. (O5563)

MAUDE, Christian George, O.B.E. (O5564)

MAUDE, Edith Caroline, Mrs., C.B.E. Hon. Sec., County of London Branch, Soldiers' and Sailors' Families Association. (C3156)

MAUDE, Jenny Maria Catherine, Mrs., O.B.E. Hon. Sec., Willesden Division, Soldiers' and Sailors' Families Association. (O11917)

MAUDE, Maude, Lady, O.B.E., *b.* of the late E. T. Atkinson, C.I.E., I.C.S.; *m.* Sir Walter, K.C.I.E., C.S.I., I.C.S. (*see* BURKE'S *Peerage*), *s.* of the late T. Y. Maude, of Highgate. *Educ.:* Zurich, Switzerland. *War Work:* Comforts for Troops, President Red Cross Committee, Province Behar and Orissa; Superintendent Convalescent Home for Soldiers, Ranchi. *Address:* Ranchi, Behar and Orissa, India. (O8278)

MAUDE, Major Ronald Edmund, O.B.E., *b.* 5 Nov. 1888; *s.* of Edmund Maude, J.P., of Leylands, Crowborough; *m.* Doris, *d.* of Kate Mary Lovett, of The Sun Dial, Sheringham. *Educ.:* Rugby. *War Work:* Capt. in 47th Div. Supply Column; later commanding 3rd Div. Ammunition Column; afterwards commanding 46th Divisional M.T. Company; mentioned in despatches, Jan. 1917. *Address:* 9, North Square, Hampstead Garden Suburb, N.W. 4. *Clubs:* Royal Automobile; Services. (O5565)

MAUDSLAY, Algernon, C.B.E., Commander Ordre de la Couronne de Belgique, Commander Order St. Sava of Serbia, and Serbian Royal Red Cross, *b.* 10 Jan. 1873; *s.* of Herbert Charles Maudslay, of Sea View, Isle of Wight. *Educ.:* Privately. *War Work:* Hon. Sec. War Refugees Committee; Hon. Director-General, British Committee of Russian Red Cross Fund; Chairman Managing Committee National Food Fund; Member of Polish Relief Fund, Serbian Relief Fund, and British Russian Relief Committees; Hon. Sec. Anglo-Belgian Union; Member of Committee Industrial Settlements for Soldiers and Sailors. *Address:* 34, Park Mansions, Knightsbridge, S.W. 1. *Clubs:* Wellington; Ranelagh; Royal Thames Yacht. (C47)

MAUDSLEY, Col. Sir Henry Carr, K.C.M.G., C.B.E., M.D. (Lond.), F.R.C.P. (Lond.),*b.* 25 April, 1859; *s.* of Thomas Maudsley, of Stainforth Hall, Settle, Yorkshire; *m.* Grace Elizabeth, *d.* of the Rev. John Stretch, of Maldon, Victoria. *Educ.:* Univ. Coll. London. Physician; Lecturer on Medicine, Univ. of Melbourne: Consulting Physician to the Melbourne Hospital, and to St. Vincent's Hospital, Melbourne. *War Work:* Colonel in the A.I.F.; Consulting Physician to the A.I.F. in Egypt, Gallipoli, and England, and the Imperial Forces in Cairo, 1915–16. *Address:* 8, Collins Street, Melbourne. *Club:* Melbourne. (C847)

MAUGER, Jean Adolphe, M.B.E.

MAULE, Capt. William Harry Fowke, D.S.O., M.B.E., B.A., *b.* 15 Dec. 1889; *s.* of the late Rev. W. Maule, of Privett Vicarage, Alton, Hants. *Educ.:* Winchester Coll.; Magdalene Coll., Cambridge. Loyal North Lancashire Regt. *War Work:* Served in France, 1915–18; despatches twice; attached British Military Mission to Poland, 1919. *Address:* 70, Cheyne Court, London, S.W. 3. *Club:* Cavendish. (M10363)

MAUND, Major Arthur Clinton, C.B.E., D.S.O., Lieut. and A. Major, Canadian Inf., and R.A.F.; served during Great War, 1914–18(despatches,Croix de Guerre with Palm). (C3180)

MAUND, Lieut. Ernest Ricardo, O.B.E.

MAUNSELL, Lieut.-Col. Francis Richard, C.M.G., C.B.E., *b.* 14 Feb. 1861; *s.* of Richard Maunsell, of Ballywilliam, Co. Limerick. *Educ.:* Cheltenham. Served in Royal Artillery; now Lieut.-Col. (retired); Military Attaché, British Embassy, Constantinople; Military Vice-Consul, Sivas, Trebizond, and Van, Turkey-in-Asia. *War Work:* Service for the Intelligence Division, War Office. *Club:* United Service. (C1692)

MAUNSELL, Mary Helen Maxwell, M.B.E., W.R.N.S.

MAUNSELL, Capt. Octavius Studdert, O.B.E., R.A.M.C.; *s.* of Major G. White Maunsell, J.P., of Fort Eyre, Co. Galway; *m.* Laura Eileen, 2nd *d.* of Major Sir Francis Synge, Bart., J.P., of Syngefield, Birr, King's Co., Ireland (*see* BURKE'S *Peerage*). *Educ.:* Kilkenny Coll.; Queen's Coll., Cork; Royal Coll. Surgeons, Edinburgh. Private practice, Kingstown, Co. Dublin; King and Queen's Medals South Africa; 1914–15 Star; General Service Medal; Allies' Medal; Medal Epidémie (French); mentioned in despatches; M.O. with Meerut Division (Artillery); M.O. 29 C.C.S. and No. 4 C.C.S.; M.O. 6 M.A.C.; Officer Commanding 20 M.A.C., Army of Occupation, Rhine. *Address:* 1, Clarinda Park, W. Kingstown, Co. Dublin. *Club:* Edward Yacht, Kingstown. (O5567)

MAUNSELL, Major Richard Edward Lloyd, C.B.E., R.E., *b.* 26 May, 1868; *s.* of John Maunsell, of Edenmore, Raheny, Co. Dublin; *m.* Edith Annie, *d.* of Thomas Pearson, of Bolton, Lancs. *Educ.:* Armagh Royal School, and Trinity Coll., Dublin. District Locomotive Supt., East Indian Railway; Works Manager, and subsequently Locomotive Engineer Great Southern and Western Railway, Ireland; Chief Mechanical Engineer, South Eastern and Chatham Railway. *War Work:* Railway work in England and France. *Address:* South Eastern and Chatham Railway Works, Ashford, Kent. *Clubs:* Constitutional; R.A.C. (C242)

MAUNSELL, Capt. Richard John Caswell, O.B.E.

MAUNSELL, Major Charles Henry WRAY-,O.B.E., J.P., Essex, *b.* 30 Sept. 1858; *s.* of the Rev. R. A. Maunsell, Canon of Kildare; *m.* Amy Charlotte, *d.* of George Matthey, F.R.S., of Cheyne House, Chelsea Embankment, and Rose Mount, Eastbourne. *Educ.:* Rossall. Served in East Yorkshire Regt., 1879–99 *War Work:* Afghan Campaign, 1878–80

(medal). *Address:* The Grove, Warley, Essex. *Club:* United Service. (O4277)

MAURICE, Lieut.-Col. David Blake, C.B.E., D.S.O., *b.* 1866; *s.* of the late Oliver Calley Maurice, of London Street, Reading, and Manton Grange, Marlborough; *m.* 1903, Cecilia Evelyn, *d.* of James Simonds, of Redlands, Reading. *Educ.:* Uppingham. Entered Princess Charlotte of Wales's (Roy. Berkshire) Regt. 1889; Capt. 1899; Major, 1908; Lieut.-Col. 1917; served in S. Africa, 1900–1, first with Composite Co. Mounted Inf., and subsequently on Railway Staff (despatches); Brig.-Major, 1914–15; Gen. Staff Officer, 1915–17. *Club:* Army and Navy. (C2142)

MAURICE, Col. George Thelwall Kindersley, C.M.G., C.B.E., M.R.C.S., L.R.C.P., *b.* 1867; *s.* of the late James Blake Maurice, F.R.C.S., J.P., of Marlborough, Wilts.; *m.* 1905, Olive, *d.* of Sir Henry Charles Burdett, K.C.B., K.C.V.O. (*see* BURKE'S *Peerage*). *Educ.:* Marlborough. Entered R.A.M.C. 1895; Capt. 1898; Major, 1907; Lieut.-Col. 1915; Brevet Col. and Col. Army Med. Ser. 1917; served during Great War, 1914–17 (despatches); appointed Assist. Director of Med. Sers. 1916. *Address:* The Elms, Burbage, Wilts. (C3098)

MAURICE, Major Lawrence Colley, O.B.E., R.E.

MAURICE, Thomas Cooper, M.B.E.

MAURICE, Walter Byron, M.B.E., M.R.C.S., L.R.C.P., J.P., Wilts, *b.* 5 Sept. 1872; *s.* of James Blake Maurice, of Lloran House, Marlborough; *m.* Caroline Edith, *d.* of Alec. C. Tosswill, of Garlands, Crowborough. *Educ.:* Marlborough. Surgeon Savernake Hospital; Town Councillor, Marlborough; Governor Marlborough Grammar School. *War Work:* M.O.-in-charge V.A.D. Hospital, Marlborough; M.O.-in-charge of various military units stationed in and about Marlborough; Medical Referee; Member Pensions Committee. (M8992)

MAUSELL, Lieut.-Col. Sir John H., K.B.E.

MAUVAN, Agnes Jessie, M.B.E.

MAVROGORDATO, Paul John, M.B.E.

MAWBY, Lieut. Arthur Wilders Montague, O.B.E., R.E. (T.).

MAWBY, Lilian Edith, M.B.E.; *d.* of George Edward Mawby, of Northampton. *Educ.:* Field House Coll., Manchester. Lady Corps Supt., Northampton Corps, St. John Ambulance Brigade, and Commandant V.A.D. 10; Visitor to the Northampton Crippled Children's Fund. *War Work:* Worked at Ambulance Headquarters, Northampton, 1914; with convoys, etc.; Milton Park V.A.D. Hospital, Peterboro', 2 months, 1915; Commandant of Dallington V.A.D. Hospital, Northampton, from Nov. 1915, to June, 1919. *Address:* 52, Billing Road, Northampton. (M3833)

MAWDSLEY, Lieut. James Buckland, M.B.E., Can. F.C. and R.A.F.

MAWLE, Sydney Joseph, M.B.E., *b.* 25 June, 1862; *s.* of the late John Mawle, of Banbury. *Educ.:* Banbury Academy, and High School, Weston-super-Mare. Agricultural Engineer and Seedsman; Hot Water Engineer. *War Work:* Commandant of Red Cross Hospital, Banbury; Officer-in-charge of Ambulance Trains, Rest Station at Banbury, providing refreshment for sick and wounded soldiers; Hon. Treas. for the Soldiers' and Sailors' Buffet at Banbury, supported entirely by voluntary contributions. *Addresses:* 22, High Street, and Chesterton House, Banbury. *Club:* Clarendon, Oxford; The Chestnuts Bowling, Banbury. (M2147)

MAWSON, Capt. William Willmott, O.B.E.

MAWSON, Sir Douglas, Kt. Bach., O.B.E., D.Sc., B.I., *b.* 5 May, 1882; *s.* of the late R. E. Mawson, of Otley, York, and afterwards of Sydney and New Guinea; *m.* 31 March, 1914, Paquita, *y. d.* of G. D. Delprat, of Amsterdam, Holland, and Melbourne. Head of Explosive and Chemical Section, Foreign Trade Dept.; Lecturer in Geology in Adelaide Univ.; Organiser and Leader of Australasian Antarctic Expedition, 1911–14; was Demonstrator of Chemistry, Sydney Univ. 1902; Lecturer at Adelaide Univ., 1905; engaged in geological investigation in Australia and New Hebrides Islands, 1904–7; on Staff of Shackleton Antarctic Expedition, 1908; T. Capt. whilst employed as Assistant Embarkation Staff Officer, 1916–18; Hon. Major specially employed, 1918–19; is officer of the Order of St. Maurice and St. Lazarus of Italy. *Address:* University, Adelaide. *Clubs:* Royal Thames Yacht; University (Sydney). (O11790e)

MAXSE, Marjorie, M.B.E.

MAXTED, Capt. Charles Stenteford, O.B.E.

MAXTONE, Robert Young, M.B.E., J.P., *b.* 1 May, 1870; *s.* of David Murray Maxtone, F.S.I., J.P., of Tighmamara, Campbeltown; *m.* Agnes, *d.* of Rev. G. W. Strang, M.A., of Campbeltown. *Educ.:* Royal High School, Edinburgh. County Treas., Collector, and Assessor for the County of Argyll. *War Work:* Hon. Treas. Soldiers' and Sailors' Families Association (So. Division); Registration of Voters Officer for the County of Argyll. Hon. Sec. for Venison Supply Committee for Argyll. *Address:* Tighnamara, Campbeltown. (M89913)

MAXWELL, Lieut.-Col. Alexander Gordon, O.B.E.

MAXWELL, Lieut. Charles Barker, O.B.E.

MAXWELL, Major Charles Henderson, O.B.E., T.D., J.P., *b.* 22 Jan. 1875; *s.* of C. C. Maxwell, of Dundee; *m.* Valérie, *d.* of George H. Lord, of Westbank, Dundee. *Educ.:* Dundee High School, and Edinburgh Univ. Town Clerk of the Burghs of Anstruther Easter, Anstruther Wester, Kilrenny, and Crail; Factor for Pitmilly and Balcomie Estates. *War Work:* Served in France with the 1/7th Black Watch; after being invalided home held important appointments under

Ministry of National Service. *Address:* Blair Lodge, Anstruther. *Club:* United Service, Edinburgh. (O1657)

MAXWELL, Major Edward Boyd, O.B.E., M.C., R.F.A.

MAXWELL, Lieut.-Col. Ernest Cassel, O.B.E., M.C., King and Queen's S.A. Medals, Order of the White Eagle with Swords, Officer of Royal Order of the Redeemer, Cross of the Order of Military Merit, *b.* 28 May, 1881 ; *s.* of Ernest Maxwell, of Leecarow, Cork ; *m.* Margaritha Albertina, *d.* of Mac-Calty-Morrogh, of Innishbeg, Co. Cork. *Educ.:* Privately. Officer of His Majesty's Land Forces ; employed as Lieut.-Col. since April, 1919, on the Allied Control of the Turkish Police, Constantinople (British member). *War Work:* Serving in India on declaration of war ; served in France with 2nd Batt. Cheshire Regt. as Co. Commander, from Jan. 1915, to Oct. 1915 ; Egypt, Oct. to Nov. 1915 ; Macedonia, Nov. 1915, to Nov. 1918 ; Turkey, Nov. 1918, to present date ; appointments held : Staff Capt., G.S.O. 3 Brigade ; Major and Command of 2nd Batt. the Cheshire Regt. from Jan. 18 to April, 1919 ; elected President of the International Boy Scout Council of Turkey, May, 1920. (O8703)

MAXWELL, Leslie Blyth, O.B.E., B.A. (Cantab.), M.R.C.S., L.R.C.P., *b.* 15 Feb. 1894 ; *s.* of late Frederick David Maxwell, Barrister-at-Law. *Educ.:* Radley, and Caius Coll., Cambridge. *War Work:* Hon. Capt. General List ; attached B.R.C.S. in command of the Friends' Ambulance Unit ; awarded also Order of St. John, Order of the Crown of Belgium, Croix de Guerre (French) : mentioned in British despatches. *Address:* St. Thomas's Hospital, S.E. 1. (O553)

MAXWELL, Marion Winefrid, M.B.E., *b.* 1893 ; *d.* of Comm. James Maxwell, R.N., of Paignton, Devon. *Educ.:* Privately. *War Work:* As V.A.D., 1914–16 ; then as Postal Censor ; and finally, for 4 years, as Junior Administrative Assistant in the Admiralty and Ministry of Shipping. *Address:* 2, Eton Villas, Hampstead, N.W. 3. (M3834)

MAXWELL OF DARGAVEL, Mary Alexandra, M.B.E., *b.* 1863 ; *d.* of late Gen. Alexander Maxwell, C.B., formerly 46th Regiment, Col. the Border Regiment (*see* BURKE'S *Landed Gentry*). *War Work:* Commandant, Drumpellier V.A.D. Hospital, Coatbridge, Lanarkshire. *Address:* c/o Donald & Co., 104, West George Street, Glasgow. *Clubs:* Sesame, London ; Kelvin, Glasgow. (M8995)

MAXWELL, Major Percy Alexander, O.B.E., I.A.

MAXWELL, Lieut.-Col. Raymond, O.B.E., M.C.

MAXWELL, Richard Cowdy, O.B.E., LL.D.

MAXWELL, Stephen John, M.B.E.

MAXWELL, Capt. Sir William, K.B.E., attached Imperial General Staff ; War Correspondent formerly of the " Standard " and the " Daily Mail " ; was with Lord Kitchener in the march on Khartoum, present at the Battle of Omdurman ; accompanied the Duke and Duchess of York in their tour through Australia, Canada, and the Colonies ; Russo-Japanese War ; joined " Daily Mail," 1905 ; accompanied the Prince of Wales on Indian tour ; present at Coronation of Shah of Persia ; present at Delhi Durbar, Chinese Revolution, Balkan War, Great War, on the Staff of the " Daily Mail " ; attached H.Q. Staff in Dardanelles. *Clubs:* St. James's ; Royal Automobile. (K224)

MAXWELL, William Blackley, M.B.E., *b.* 5 June, 1874 ; *s.* of John Maxwell, of Maxwelltown, Kirkcudbrightshire. *Educ.:* Nithside Academy, Dumfries, and Glasgow Univ. Solicitor. *War Work:* Hon. Sec. Hawick Burgh War Savings Central Committee ; organised in Hawick in 1918 an allied Fair to provide funds for the Y.M.C.A. Huts at the Front ; also organised War Weapons Week, and Tank Week, in connection with War Savings movement. *Address:* 3, Oliver Place, Hawick. *Club:* Border, Hawick. (M8996)

MAXWELL, William Jardine Herries, O.B.E., D.L.

MAXWELL, Adeline Helen, Mrs. HERON-, M.B.E., *b.* 1859 ; *d.* of Osgood Hanbury, of Holfield Grange, Coggeshall, Essex ; *m.* Col. William Henry Stopford, *s.* of Edward Heron Maxwell, of Teviot Bank, Hawick, and Penningham House, Newton Stewart. Member of War Pensions Committee for Roxburghshire ; Sec. and Vice President of Soldiers' and Sailors' Families Association ; Commandant of Hawick Voluntary Aid Detachment. *War Work:* The organisation of a Hospital for Troops quartered in Hawick during 1915–16. *Address:* Teviot Bank, Hawick, Roxburghshire. (M8994)

MAXWELL, Francis Jane, Mrs. Patrick HERON-, M.B.E.

MAY, Andrew, M.B.E., R.N.R.

MAY, Comm. Archibald Seaburne, M.V.O., O.B.E., R.N., *b.* 29 June, 1885 ; *s.* of Admiral of the Fleet Sir William May, G.C.B., G.C.V.O. (*see* BURKE'S *Peerage*), Bughtugg, Coldstream ; *m.* Mary, *d.* of Capt. E. Price, R.N., of Villa Frere, Malta. *Educ.:* H.M.S. " Britannia." *War Work:* Gunnery Officer of H.M.S. " Dominion " and " Valiant " with the Grand Fleet. *Club:* United Service. (O9397)

MAY, Capt. Arthur de Kewer Livius, C.B.E., R.N., *b.* 1875 ; *s.* of J. C. Frampton May, of Carvalion, Creech St. Michael, Taunton ; *m.* 1907, Henrietta, *d.* of the late William Bowley. Appointed Dep. Director, Operations Div. Naval Staff, 1918. *Club:* Naval and Military. (C2236)

MAY, Major Arthur Henry, O.B.E., R.E.

MAY, Capt. Arthur John, O.B.E.

MAY, Barry, C.M.G., C.B.E., *b.* 1869 ; *s.* of the late Staff Comm. D. J. May, R.N. ; *m.* Florence Thomson. *Educ.:* St. Saviour's Gram. Sch., and Diocesan Coll. Rondebosch. Appointed Govt. Sec. Bechuanaland, 1902 ; Dept. Resident Commr. and Treasurer, Basutoland, 1912. *Address:* Maseru, Basutoland. (C2802)

MAY, Bennett, C.B.E., M.B., F.R.C.S. (Lond.), *b.* 28 Aug. 1846 ; *s.* of Benjamin May, of Farnham, Surrey. *Educ.:* Edinburgh and Birmingham. Emeritus Professor of Surgery, Univ. of Birmingham ; Hon. Consulting Surgeon, Queen's Hospital, Birmingham (retired). *War Work:* Visiting Civil Surgeon at the First Birmingham War Hospital, Rubery, for 3 years. *Address:* 50, Frederick Road, Edgbaston, Birmingham. (C1157)

MAY, Major Charles Edward, O.B.E., N.Z.A.S.C.

MAY, Charlotte Dorothea, Mrs., M.B.E.

MAY, Mrs. Edith, M.B.E., *d.* of the late John Eliot Hodgkin, F.S.A. ; *m.* Walter May, R.N., M.Inst.C.E. *War Work:* Organising Sec. of the Woodford War Hospital Supply Workrooms, Sept. 1915, to March, 1919. *Address:* Brook House, Woodford Green. (M8997)

MAY, Eric Maurice, O.B.E.

MAY, Major Ernest, M.B.E., *b.* 18 March, 1881 ; *s.* of Horace Ray, of Tonbridge ; *m.* Emmie, *d.* of John Egan, of London. Boer War Medal with six clasps ; Staff Employment, Malay States Volunteer Rifles, 1912–1914. *War Work:* 1915–19, Mesopotamian Campaign ; after the fall of Kut, Staff Capt., and D.A.Q.M.G., Embarkation Staff Officer, 1917–18 ; Kut, 1918–19 ; Invalided Home, 1920 ; four times mentioned in despatches ; awards—Ordinul, Steaua, Romaniei, grade Cavaler. *Address:* Messrs. Cox & Co., 16, Charing Cross, London. (M4898)

MAY, Sir George Ernest, K.B.E., *b.* 1871. Sec. Prudential Assurance Co. ; Director, British Overseas Bank. *War Work:* Manager, American Dollar Securities Committee ; Chairman, Board of Management, Navy and Army Canteen Board ; Deputy Qr.-Mr.-General in charge Canteens, War Office ; Member Sugar Commission. *Address:* Bucknalls, nr. Watford. (K94)

MAY, Mrs. Harold, M.B.E.

MAY, Henry John, O.B.E.

MAY, Shipwright-Lieut.-Comm. James Rees, O.B.E., R.N.

MAY, Lieut. John Ivo Cecil, O.B.E.: *m.,* 1921, Ellen Evelyn Collins, M.B.E., *d.* of M. E. Collins, of Woodburn, Bucks.

MAY, Katharine Edith, Mrs., O.B.E., *b.* 24 Feb. 1873 ; *d.* of the late Robson Roose, M.D., of 45, Hill Street, Berkeley Square ; *m.* William Charles May. *Educ.:* Queen's Coll. School, Harley Street ; Germany and France. Commandant London 60 Red Cross V.A.D. *War Work:* Red Cross Divisional Sec.; Hampstead Division, when war broke out ; Commandant and administrator Cedar Lawn Auxiliary Hospital, Hampstead, from Nov. 1914, till June, 1919. *Address:* 13, Worsley Road, Hampstead, N.W. 3. *Club:* Ladies' V.A.D. (O555)

MAY, Lily Julia, Lady. O.B.E., *b.* 1879 ; *m.* Sir George Ernest May, K.B.E. (*see* BURKE'S *Peerage*). *War Work:* Worked at Ministry of Food, as deputy to Mrs. Pember Reeves (Co-Head of Women's section with Mrs. Peel, O.B.E., and afterwards Head of Education and propaganda section) from March, 1917, to March, 1920. *Address:* Bucknalls, nr. Watford. (O10945)

MAY, Major Noel Blankart, O.B.E., R.A.O.C.

MAY, Walter Baillie, M.B.E., *b.* 1 June, 1885 ; *s.* of Francis May, of York ; *m.* Edith Mabel, *d.* of Stephen Seal, of York. *Educ.:* Model School, attached St. John's Coll., York. Personal and Confidential Clerk to Sec. and Solicitor of the North Eastern Rly. Co., York, 1901–17. *War Work:* Personal and Confidential Clerk to Assist. Sec. (Board) Admiralty, Aug. 1917, to Dec. 1918 ; accompanied Naval Mission to America under Sir Eric Geddes (then First Lord of Admiralty) Oct. 1918 ; Sec., Co-ordination of Demobilisation Section of the War Cabinet, Dec. 1918, to March, 1919, and to Sec. and Solicitor (Designate) Ministry of Ways and Communications, April, 1919, to Aug. 1919 ; Private Sec. to Sec. and Solicitor, Ministry of Transport. *Address:* 4, Quadrant Road, Canonbury, London, N. (M3836)

MAY, William George, M.B.E.

MAY, Lieut.-Comm. William Henry, M.B.E., R.N.

MAY, Irene Harriet Bourne Seaburne BOURNE-, M.B.E. ; *s.* of J. W. S. Bourne-May, of 61, Eaton Place, S.W. 1. *Educ.:* Privately. *War Work:* Joint Hon. Sec. Lady Smith-Dorrien's Hospital Bag Fund, from Nov. 1915, to the end of the War. *Address:* 61, Eaton Place, S.W. 1. (M3835)

MAYBERY, Lucy Powys, Mrs., M.B.E., *b.* 1860 ; *d.* of J. R. Cobb, F.S.A., of Caldicot Castle, nr. Chepstow, and Nythfa Brecon ; *m.* Major Aveline Maybery. *Educ.:* The Manse, Malvern, and Munich. Governor of the Brecon County Schools ; Member of Breconshire Health Committee ; Sec. to the Mothers' Union in St. Davids diocese. Commandant at Penoyre Red Cross Hospital, 1915–19. *Address:* The Priory, Brecon, South Wales. (M731)

MAYBURY, Capt. Harry Percy, O.B.E., R.A.F.

MAYCOCK, Capt. Arthur Hubert, O.B.E., R.A.S.C.

MAYCOCK, Capt. Richard Beauchamp, O.B.E., R.A.F.

MAYCOCK, Thomas Langley, O.B.E.

MAYER, Major Garton, O.B.E., has Legion of Honour.

MAYER, John, M.B.E., J.P.

MAYES, Lieut.-Col. Henry George, M.B.E.

MAYES, Howard, M.B.E., *b.* 13 May, 1877 ; *s.* of Walter Mayes, of Southampton ; *m.* Margaret Anne, *d.* of Edward Stubbs, Capt. R.N., of Liverpool. *Educ.:* Westfields, Winchester. Engineer with the Buenos Aires and Pacific Railway Co., Argentina. *War Work:* Joined the Senior Assistant Inspector of Munition Areas, Woolwich Arsenal Inspection

Department, July, 1915. *Addresses:* Kelvedon, Leigh Road, Southampton, England; Threaber, Bella Vista, F.C.P., Buenos Aires, Argentina. (M9000)

MAYHEW, Sir Basil Edgar, K.B.E., F.C.A., Knight of Grace of the Order of St. John of Jerusalem, *b.* 9 Nov. 1883; *s.* of Thomas Edgar, of Ipswich; *m.* Dorothea Mary, *d.* of Stephen Paget, F.R.C.S. (*see* BURKE'S *Peerage*). *Educ.:* Worcester and Ipswich Schools. Member of firm of Blackburns, Barton, Mayhew & Co., Chartered Accountants; Member, Executive Committee, King Edward's Hospital Fund for London. *War Work:* Sec. of the Joint War Finance Committee and of the Central Demobilisation Board of the British Red Cross Society and the Order of St. John of Jerusalem; compiler of the Annual Accounts of the Auxiliary Military Hospitals in England, Wales, and Ireland, 1915-19. *Addresses:* 34, Kensington Park Gardens, W. 11; Alderman's House, Bishopsgate, E.C. 2. *Club:* Union. (K398(

MAYHEW, Major Mark James, O.B.E.

MAYMAN, Capt. Rupert Livingstone, O.B.E., A.I.F.

MAYNARD, Annie Evelyn, Mrs., M.B.E.; *d.* of the late Rev. H. A. Mitton, Master of Sherburn House, Co. Durham; *m.* Anthony Charles Hutton, *s.* of Anthony Lax Maynard, J.P., of Skinningrove, Yorks. *Educ.:* Privately. Diocesan (Ripon) Speaker for the Mothers' Union, and Member of the Diocesan Council; Hon. Organising Sec. for the Harrogate Branch Royal Society for the Prevention of Cruelty to Animals; Hon. Sec. Langthorpe Branch, Forest of Galtres Habitation of the Primrose League. *War Work:* Assisted in recruiting work; took charge of Belgian Refugees for some months in own house; worked for Northallerton Women Landworkers' Committee; also for Soldiers' and Sailors' Families Association and Northallerton War Pensions Committee; a Member of the North Riding Local Central Committee for War Saving, and organised and formed 17 War Savings Associations in the Rural Districts in the North Riding, Yorks; assisted in the Food Campaign in the North Riding while under the care of the War Savings Committee. *Address:* Langthorpe, Boroughbridge, Yorks. (M9001)

MAYNARD, Dudley Christopher, O.B.E., *b.* Nov. 27, 1874; *s.* of C. D. Maynard, of London; *m.* Mary Gertrude, *d.* of Robert Cockell, of Cheltenham. *Educ.:* Cambridge and Lausanne. Architect. *War Work:* Architect to Roehampton Hospital for Limbless Soldiers and Sailors, and Facial Hospital at Sidcup, Kent. *Address:* Broomlands, West Byfleet; 14, John St. Adelphi, W.C. *Club:* Constitutional. (O3830)

MAYNARD, Major George Darell, O.B.E.

MAYNARD, Harry Payne, O.B.E., B.A. Assistant Engineer, Great Western Railway. *Address:* 11, Addington Road, Reading. (O10947)

MAYNARD, Mildred, Mrs., M.B.E.

MAYNE, Surg.-Lieut. Cyril Frederick, O.B.E., R.N.

MAYNE, Capt. Jasper Graham, O.B.E., *b.* 9 April, 1859; *s.* of Col. Charles Otway Mayne, of Indian Staff Corps; *m.* Cecily Mary, *d.* of Sir Frederick Aloyeius Weld, G.C.M.G., of Chideock Manor, Dorset (*see* BURKE'S *Peerage*). *Educ.* Cheltenham. Late Royal Inniskilling Fusiliers; Chief Constable of East Suffolk. *War Work:* Hon. Sec. Suffolk Central Organising Committee. *Club:* Naval and Military. (O10948)

MAYNE, Olga Hermione Violet Mosley, O.B.E.; *d.* of Major Mosley Mayne. *War Work:* Soldiers' Club, Arquata Scrivia, Italy. *Address:* Hill Cottage, Slinfold, Sussex. *Club:* Writers'. (O3831)

MAYNE, Major Otway, O.B.E., D.L., *b.* 1855; *s.* of Major Henry Otway Mayne; *m.* Helena, *d.* of Ven. Archdeacon Nevill. *Educ.:* Wellington. Served in the Norfolk Regt.; Chief Constable of Bucks from 1896. *Address:* Walton Lodge, Aylesbury. *Club:* Naval and Military. (O1659)

MAYNE, William, O.B.E.

MAYNE, William, M.B.E.

MAYO, Henry Herbert Worsfold, O.B.E., *b.* 28 Oct. 1866; *s.* of Thomas Worsfold Mayo, of Swallowcliffe, Yeovil; *m.* Florence Bartlett, *d.* of Doctor — Fall, of Winfrith, Dorset. *Educ.:* Sherborne. Member of Yeovil Rural District Council and Board of Guardians; Vice-Chairman, East Coker Parish Council; Member of Somerset Local War Pensions Committee; Member of Yeovil and District War Pensions Sub-Committee. *War Work:* Hon. Sec. Soldiers' and Sailors' Families Association, Yeovil Division; Hon. Sec. Voluntary Help Association, Yeovil Division; Member, Soldiers' and Sailors' Help Society; Member of Advisory Committee at Yeovil; Holder of certificate issued under A.C.I. 1424 of 1916; Vice Chairman, East Coker Parish Council; Chairman, East Coker War Savings Association. *Address:* East Coker, Yeovil. (O10590)

MAYO, Lieut. Herbert Coates, O.B.E., R.N.

MAYO, Major Robert Hobart, O.B.E.

MAYOR, Lieut.-Col. Edgar William, O.B.E.

MEABY, Walter Alfred, M.B.E.

MEACHEM, Frank, M.B.E., R.N.

MEAD, Major Charles, O.B.E., R.A.S.C.

MEAD, Wing-Comm. John, C.B.E., M.C., R.A.F. Served in Great War (mentioned in despatches). (C2339)

MEADE, Francis Henry, C.B.E., *b.* 6 Dec. 1870; *s.* of the Hon. Sidney Meade, of Frankleigh House, Bradford-on-Avon (*see* BURKE'S *Peerage*); *m.* Beatrice Mary, *d.* Lord Esme Gordon, of Paxton Park, St. Neots (*see* BURKE'S *Peerage*). *Educ.:* Eton, and Magdalen Coll., Oxford. Barrister-at-law.

War Work: Sec. of the Official Press Bureau, Whitehall. *Address:* Overbury, Alton, Hants. (C2503)

MEADE, Capt. Harry Edward, O.B.E.

MEADE, Richard John Edward, O.B.E., B.A., *b.* 20 Aug. 1870; *s.* of Major Richard Raphael Meade; *m.* Helen Venetia Digby, *d.* of the Rev. G. D. Newbolt, late Rector of Sharnbrook, Beds. *Educ.:* Privately, and Clare Coll., Cambridge. Land Agent; Member of firm of Messrs. Edens; Agent to Capt. J. Windham Meade and others. *War Work:* Area Live Stock Commissioner, Eastern Division, Ministry of Food; Special Constable; Member of Emergency Committee. *Address:* Croxton, Norfolk; *Clubs:* Norfolk County; Oxford and Cambridge Musical. (O10951)

MEADOWS, Alice Margaret, O.B.E., M.B.E.

MEADOWS, Lieut.-Col. George Stephen, O.B.E., T.D., D.C.L.I., *b.* 15 Aug. 1864; *s.* of the late Major-Gen. Robert Wyatt Meadows, R.A.M.C., Fensalir, Saltash, Cornwall; *m.* Katherine Ellen, *d.* of the late William James Harris, of Halwill Manor, Beaworthy, Devon. *Educ.:* Privately. *War Work:* India, Aden, Palestine, with 1/4th Batt. D.C.L.I. as Capt. and Major, from Oct. 1914, till return to England in Dec. 1919, in command 2/4th Batt. D.C.L.I. *Address:* Belgrove House, Lamerton, Tavistock, Devon. *Club:* Junior Army and Navy. (O8508)

MEADOWS, Lieut. Henry George, M.B.E., R.A.O.C.

MEADUS, Engineer-Capt. Harry Howard, C.B.E., R.N. Repair Overseer, Tyne Dist. (C2225)

MEADUS, Engineer-Capt. William Henry, C.B.E., R.N. (ret.). Engineer Overseer, Birkenhead. (C3217)

MEAGHER, Major Denis John, O.B.E., I.A. (ret.); Chevalier Order of Leopold of Belgium.

MEAGHER, Major Henry Louis, O.B.E., T.D., R.F.A. (T.), *b.* 23 Jan. 1872; *s.* of Lieut.-Col. Henry Meagher, R.G.A., of Waterford. *Educ.:* Catholic Univ., Dublin. Engineer. *War Work:* Commanded 1st Northumbrian (250) Bgde. Ammunition Column, R.F.A., Aug. 1914. to May, 1916; Commanded "B" Echelon and S.A.A. Sections, 50th D.A.C., May, 1916, to April, 1919; Commanded 50th D.A.C., April, 1919, to Aug. 1919, when the unit was disembodied; twice mentioned in despatches. *Address:* Kilcairne Park, Navan, Co. Meath, Ireland. *Club:* Junior Army and Navy. (O5572).

MEAKIN, George Healey, M.B.E.

MEAKIN, Mary Ridgway, M.B.E., *b.* 1 May, 1875; *d.* of Jas. Meakin, of Darlaston Hall, Stone, Staffs. *Educ.:* Halliwich Manor, New Southgate. *War Work:* Commandant of Red Cross Auxiliary Hospital, Stone, from Feb. 1915, to May, 1919. *Address:* Darlaston Hall, Stone, Staffs. *Club:* V.A.D. Ladies'. (M3838)

MEANWELL, Gertrude Thompson, M.B.E.

MEARES, Lieut.-Col. Hugh Poynder, O.B.E., R.A., *b.* 14 May, 1872; *s.* of the late Hugh Meares, M.A., of Plas Llanstephan, Carmarthenshire, and Millfield, Ryde, I. of W.; *m.* Elsie Mary Mabel, *d.* of Major-Gen. Bertie-Clay. Commissioned Royal Artillery, Feb. 1893; retired May, 1909; rejoined at commencement of war. *War Work:* Overseas: special work, signallers; home: established and commanded S.C. Signal School, supplying all fronts with signallers; expert authority on higher branches of signalling, wireless, etc.; since Armistice, Military Sec. Southern Command, and Commandant Camp, Southampton. *Clubs:* Royal Automobile; Royal Western Yacht. (O90559)

MEARS, Grace Edith, M.B.E., *b.* 1 March, 1897; *d.* of the late William Thos. Mears, of East Ham. *Educ.:* East Ham Technical Coll. *War Work:* Foreign Office, since 1915. *Address:* 18, Dartmouth Park Avenue, N.W. 5. (M9002)

MEASOR, Henry Arthur, O.B.E., *b.* 16 July, 1855; *s.* of Edward J. Measor, of Exeter and London; *m.* Ellen Sophia Louisa, *d.* of Henry Boyer, of Bromley, Kent. *Educ.:* Barnet. Herts. Trinity House, London (ret.). (O3833)

MEASHAM, Capt. Richard John Rupert, O.B.E., R.E. (S.R.).

MEASURES, Lieut.-Col. Arthur Harold, O.B.E., R.A.F.

MEASURES, Benjamin, O.B.E.

MEASURES, Harry Bell, C.B.E., M.V.O., F.R.I.B.A., *b.* 1862; *s.* of Henry Measures, of Brighton. Director of Barrack Construction, War Office. *Address:* Kialama, West Byfleet, Surrey. (C247)

MEATH, Reginald Brabazon, 12th Earl of, P.C., K.P., G.B.E., H.M.L., St. John of Jerusalem Knight of Justice, J.P. (*see* BURKE'S *Peerage*), *b.* 31 July, 1841; *s.* of William, 11th Earl of Meath; *m.* The Lady Mary J. Maitland, *d.* of 11th Earl of Lauderdale, of Thirlestane Castle, Lauder, Scotland (*see* BURKE'S *Peerage*). *Educ.:* Eton, Germany, and Privately. Diplomatic Service; ex-Alderman London County Council; ex-Chancellor of Royal Univ. of Ireland; His Majesty's Lieutenant for the County and City of Dublin. *War Work:* Founded Recruiting Office in Dublin, and President of Recruiting Committee. *Addresses:* Kilbruddery, Bray, Ireland; Chaworth House, Ottershaw, Chertsey. *Clubs:* Travellers'; Kildare Street, Dublin. (G56)

MEDCALF, Capt. Herbert, M.B.E.

MEDCALF, William Harold, O.B.E. (O11787)

MEDCALFE, Capt. John Clarence, O.B.E., R.A.O.C.

MEDD, Jesse Simpson, M.B.E.

MEDD, Paymaster-Lieut.-Comm. Walter Hall, O.B.E., R.N.

MEDD, Wilfred, O.B.E.

MEDHURST, Major Charles Edward Hastings, O.B.E., M.C., R.A.F.

MEDLAND, James William, O.B.E.

MEDLEY, Major Edward Arnold, O.B.E., R.A.S.C., *b.* 22 Aug. 1873 ; *s.* of Edward Medley, of Chiswick, W. 4 ; *m.* Agnes Theresa, *d.* of James Dixon, of Liverpool. *Educ.:* Nottingham High School, Nottingham Univ., and City and Guilds of London Central Technical Coll., South Kensington. Works Manager of Richard Johnson and Nephew, Ltd., Bradford Iron Works, Manchester. *War Work :* enlisted in R.A.S.C. in May, 1915 ; 2nd Lieut., July, 1915 ; Lieut., March, 1916 ; Capt., 1916 ; Acting Major, 1917 ; Major (Temp.), April, 1918 ; Brevet Major, June, 1918 ; served with M.E.F. and E.E.F. from Sept. 1915, to May, 1919 ; D.A.D.T., G.H.Q., April, 1918, to May, 1919 ; employed in Q.M.G. 3, War Office, June, 1919, to Nov. 1919. *Addresses :* Roselea, Western Road, Flixton, Manchester ; Bradford Iron Works, Manchester.
(O6244)

MEDLICOTT, Capt. Richard Frederick Cavendish, O.B.E., M.C.

MEDROW, Walter Alfred, M.B.E.

MEDWIN, Gladys Leslie, M.B.E., *b.* 2 Dec. 1881 ; *d.* of the late Leslie Allen Medwin. *Educ.:* Privately. *War Work :* Voluntary Helper and Typist, Recruiting Office, Bournemouth, Oct. 1914, to April, 1918.
(M9002)

MEE, Oliver, M.B.E.

MEEHAM, Francis Edward, M.B.E., J.P.

MEEK, Flying Officer Kenneth Alexander, M.B.E., R.A.F., *b.* 1 May, 1896 ; *s.* of Herbert Denham Meek, of Hull. *Educ.:* Yardley Court, Tonbridge, and Eastbourne Coll. *War Work :* Enlisted as private, 2/5th R.W. Kents, Dec. 1914 ; commissioned March, 1915, 14th West Yorks ; overseas (France), 12th West Yorks, Oct. 1915, to June, 1916 ; Regimental Adjutant, Dec. 1915, to June, 1916 ; joined R.F.C., June, 1916 ; France, as Pilot, Oct. 1916, to Jan. 1917 ; Squadron R.O., Jan. 1917, to June, 1917, in France ; promoted Capt. and Wing Adjutant, April, 1918 ; Wing Adjutant, France, March, 1918, to June, 1918 ; Permanent Commission, R.A.F., Aug. 1918. *Address :* 21, Westbourne Avenue, Hull. *Club :* R.A.F.
(M6016)

MEEK, Elizabeth Muriel GRANT-, M.B.E., *b.* 25 May, 1877 ; *d.* of A. Grant-Meek, of Hillworth House. *War Work :* V.A.D. Devizes Auxiliary Hospital for 4 years ; Hon. Sec. Red Cross Needlework Association, Devizes, from Aug. 1914, to April, 1919. *Address :* The Hold, Manningford, Bruce, Marlborough, Wilts.
(M3840)

MEERES, Col. Charles Stuart, C.B.E., late R.A., *b.* 2 Jan. 1861 ; *s.* of Charles Meeres, M.R.C.S., of Sandown, I. of W. ; — *d.* of Robert Wilson, of India. *Educ.:* R.M. Academy, Woolwich. *War Work :* Staff work under War Office, and charge of all ammunition depots in England. *Address :* Colonnade House, Blackheath, S.E. *Club :* United Service.
(C1693)

MEESON, Paymaster-Comm. Charles Mortimore, O.B.E., R.N.

MEGLAUGHLIN, Barry, M.B.E., *b.* 5 Nov. 1886 ; *s.* of the late James Meglaughlin, of Gortmerron, Dungannon, Co. Tyrone ; *m.* Ethel, *d.* of the late Pierce Henry Crouch, of Woodford, Essex. *Educ.:* Royal School, Dungannon. Solicitor to Dungannon Urban and Rural Councils. *War Work :* In connection with the British Red Cross Society. *Address :* Gortmerron, Dungannon, Co. Tyrone.
(M2155)

MEIGGS, Mary Effie, M.B.E.

MEIGH, Edward, M.B.E., M.Sc., *b.* 26 Feb. 1886 ; *s.* of Edward Meigh, of Liverpool ; *m.* Elsie Elizabeth, *d.* of John Edward Draper, of Liverpool. *Educ.:* Liverpool Univ. Formerly Lecturer in Physics, Battersea Polytechnic, S.W., now Manager of the British Hartford-Fairmont Syndicate, Ltd., and Sec. of the Rockware Glass Syndicate, Ltd. *War Work :* Sub-section Director in the Optical Munitions, Glassware, and Potash Production Branch of the Ministry of Munitions ; member of the Inter-Departmental Glass Trades Committee, and of Inter-Departmental Advisory Committee on X-Ray and Electro-Medical Apparatus, and temp. Sec. of Glass Research Association. *Address :* 2, Upper Tooting Park Mansions, S.W. 17.
(M9007)

MEIGHAN, John McNair, O.B.E.

MEIKLE, Capt. John James, O.B.E., I.A.R.O.

MEINERS, Major Leo Udo Hugo, O.B.E., S.A.M.R.

MELANDRE, Joseph, M.B.E.

MELBA, Dame Helen (Nellie) Porter, D.B.E., Lady of Grace of St. John of Jerusalem, *b.* 19 May, 1865 ; *d.* of David Mitchell, of Doonside, Richmond, Australia. *Educ.:* Presbyterian Ladies' Coll., Melbourne. *War Work :* Gave concerts for Red Cross in Australia and Canada during the whole of the war. *Address :* Coombe Cottage, Coldstream, Australia. *Club :* Ladies' Athenæum.
(D22)

MELDON, Col. James Austin, C.B.E., R.M., *b.* 13 July, 1870 ; *s.* of the late Austin Meldon, D.L., of Merrion Square, Dublin ; *m.* Serena Letitia Hentrietta, *d.* of the late Rev. Canon Sadlier, D.D., of Dublin. *Educ.:* Pensionnat St. Michel, Brussels ; Clongowes Wood Coll., Kildare ; Trinity Coll., Dublin. Lieut.-Col. Commanding 4th Royal Dublin Fusiliers ; Resident Magistrate, Mayo. *War Work :* Commanded 4th Royal Dublin Fusiliers, May, 1915, to June, 1918 ; Commanded 1st Batt. Herefordshire Regt., Aug. 1918 ; Commanded 1st Royal Dublin Fusiliers, Oct. 1918, to Feb. 1919. *Address :* Rossmailley, Westport, Co. Mayo, Ireland. *Club :* Windham ; Sackville Street (Dublin).
(C1694)

MELHUIST, Lieut. John Barradale, M.B.E., R.E.

MELLAND, Norman, C.B.E., *b.* 12 Nov. 1865 ; *s.* of

Fredk. Melland, M.R.C.S., of Manchester ; *m.* Blanche, *d.* of Gerald Du Val, of Manchester. *Educ.:* Manchester Grammar School, Dresden, and Manchester Univ. *War Work :* Voluntary work, War Trade Dept. ; Chairman, Diamond Export Committee, etc. *Address :* Spey Lodge, Withington, Manchester. *Clubs :* Royal Automobile ; Queen's.
(C567)

MELLERSH, Arthur, C.B.E., *b.* 1857 ; *s.* of Henry Mellersh. Surveyor to Gen. Post Office.
(C1005)

MELLES, Lieut. Robert Ernest, M.B.E., R.G.A., *b.* 31 Dec. 1877. *Educ.:* St. Mark's Coll., Chelsea, S.W. Hea † Master, St. Luke's School, Chelsea, S.W. *War Work :* Officer Commanding A.A. Gun Section, Sutton Fields, Humber Garrison. *Address :* 58, Winchendon Road, Fulham, S.W.
(M6678)

MELLIAR, Capt. John Kenelm FOSTER-, M.B.E., *b.* 3 Aug. 1875 ; *s.* of Rev. Andrew Foster-Melliar, M.A., Rector of Sproughton, nr. Ipswich ; *m.* Phyllis Edrica, *d.* of Ralph Coker Adams Beck, of Cheam, Surrey. *Educ.:* Privately. *War Work :* Commissioned as Lieut. in 9th Batt. The Border Regt. 1914 ; proceeded to France, 1915 ; attached to G.H.Q. Staff, 1915–18 ; mentioned in despatches, 1917 ; recalled May, 1918, for duty as Staff Captain at the War Office ; Medals : 1914–15 Star, General Service and Victory Medal with Oak Leaves. *Address :* Catsfield Place, nr. Battle. *Club :* Badminton.
(M5267)

MELLING, Thomas William, M.B.E., *b.* 5 March, 1878 ; *s.* of William Melling, of Sheffield ; *m.* Alice, *d.* of Robert Broxham, of Sheffield. *Educ.:* Alexandroffsky English School, Petrograd, and Central Secondary School, Sheffield. Machine Shops Manager, Hadfields, Ltd., Hecla Works, Sheffield. *War Work :* Manufacture of all types of shell, gas and high explosive, for Army, from 6-pounder to 15-inch ; gas high-explosive, and Armour piercing shell for Navy, including the shell for the " Hush " boats, 6-inch trench howitzers, gun tubes, work for the Research Dept. training foremen for shell work. *Address :* Ashbrooke, Seagreave Road, Gleadless, Sheffield.
(M9009)

MELLIS, Lieut.-Col. William, O.B.E.

MELLONIE, Capt. Thomas Cyril, M.B.E., K.C.

MELLOR, Judge Francis Hamilton, C.B.E., K.C., *b.* 1854 ; *s.* of the Rt. Hon. Sir John Mellor ; *m.* Mabel Lucy, *d.* of — Knowles, of Barnagore, Calcutta. *Educ.:* Cheltenham Coll. ; Trinity Coll., Cambridge. Judge of County Courts, K.C., Chairman of the following Conciliation Boards : South Lancashire and North Staffordshire Coal Fields, the Lancashire and Yorkshire and the Cheshire Lines Railways. *War Work :* Chairman of S.E. Lancashire Appeal Tribunal and of the Bucklow Rural District and Knutsford Cheshire Local Tribunals ; Chairman of the Demobilisation Committee of the North-Western Area. *Address :* Heathfield, Knutsford, Cheshire. *Clubs :* New University ; M.C.C. ; Union (Manchester).
(C248)

MELLOR, John, M.B.E.

MELLOR, Lieut.-Col. John Seymour, O.B.E., M.C., Croix de Guerre (Étoile en Vermeil), *b.* 14 Sept. 1883 ; *s.* of James Mellor, of 51, Onslow Square, S.W. 7 ; *m.* Elizabeth Love, *d.* of the late Frederick A. Marquand, of New York, U.S.A. *Educ.:* St. Aubyns, Rottingdean, and Eton Coll. Was Adjutant Eton College O.T.C., 1911–14. Was granted one of Lord Roberts' free commissions after Boer War. *War Work :* Retreat from Mons with 2nd Batt. K.R.R.C. (wounded Sept. 1914) ; Instructor, R.M.C. Camberly, Dec. 1914 ; A.P.M. 29th Division, April, 1916 ; A.P.M. 18th Corps, Jan. 1917 ; D.P.M. Rhine Army, Cologne, Feb. 1919, to Oct. 1919 ; now reorganising Polish Police (Special Mission at Warsaw), five times mentioned in despatches. *Address :* 7, Vallance Road, Hove, Sussex. *Clubs :* Army and Navy ; M.C.C. ; Royal and Ancient (St. Andrews).
(O5575)

MELLOR, Juliet Vivian, M.B.E.

MELLOR, Major Robert Ramsden, C.B.E., T.F. Reserve. Served in Great War, 1914–19 (mentioned in despatches).
(C1695)

MELLOR, Major Thomas Reginald, O.B.E., Aust. F.A.

MELLOR, William Charles, M.B.E.

MELLOWS, Capt. Samuel, M.B.E.

MELLOWS, William Thomas, M.B.E., LL.B. (Lond.), *b.* 29 May, 1882 ; *s.* of William Mellows, Town Clerk, of Peterborough ; *m.* Beatrice Edith, *d.* of William Alfred Pitt, of Bristol. *Educ.:* Bishop's Stortford Coll. Solicitor, Town Clerk of Peterborough. *War Work :* Hon. Sec. Soke of Peterborough division Soldiers' and Sailors' Families Association, and Soldiers' and Sailors' Help Society ; Hon. Sec. County of Soke of Peterborough War Pensions Committee ; Hon. Sec. City of Peterborough Prince of Wales' Relief Committee. *Address :* Westleigh, Thorpe Road, Peterborough. *Clubs :* City and Counties ; Law Society.
(M9012)

MELLSOP, Capt. and Qr.-Mr. John Arthur, O.B.E.

MELLSTROW, Charles Gustav, M.B.E.

MELLY, George Henry, O.B.E., *b.* 5 March, 1860 ; *s.* of George Melly, of 90, Chatham Street, Liverpool ; *m.* Elizabeth, *d.* of Edward Edmonds, of London. *Educ.:* Rugby. Managing Director, Lamport and Holt, Ltd., Liverpool, London, Manchester, New York ; Director of Liverpool and London and Globe Insurance Co., Ltd., Thames and Mersey Marine Insurance Co., Ltd., Liverpool and London War Risks Insurance Association, Ltd., Liverpool and London Steamship Protection Association, Ltd., Archibald McMillan and Son, Ltd., Royal Mail Steam Packet Co. (Liverpool Board), and Excess Values (Liverpool and London) War Risk Insurance Association, Ltd. *War Work :* With the assistance of a few friends, financed the fitting up, equipping, and running for 3¼ years of the Myrtle Auxiliary Hospital, Liverpool, with all medical and surgical appliances of the most up-to-date description. *Address :* 3, Abercromby Square, Liverpool. *Clubs :* City of London ; Windham ; Palatine (Liverpool).

MELROSE, John, C.B.E., J.P., *b.* May, 1853 ; *s.* of John Melrose, of Hawick ; *m.* Grace French, *d.* of David Taylor, of Newhouses. *Educ. :* High School, Hawick. Town Councillor, 1898–1901 ; Bailie, 1901–2 ; Provost of Hawick, 1902–19 ; Governor of Hawick Savings Bank ; Chairman of Hawick Gas Light Co. *War Work :* Chairman of Belgian Relief Committee, War Savings Committee, Recruiting Tribunal, etc. ; number of contracts for Army Clothing Department. *Address :* Hopehill, Hawick. *Clubs :* Conservative (Edinburgh) ; Border (Hawick). (C2804)

MELSOM, Lieut. George Washington, O.B.E.

MELTRUISH, John Barradale, M.B.E. (M6677)

MELVILLE, Beresford Valentine, O.B.E., J.P., *b.* 1857 ; *s.* of Canon Melville, of Worcester ; *m.* Sydney, *d.* of the Rev. J. Garrett, of Kilgarron, Ireland. *Educ. :* Marlborough, and Brasenose Coll., Oxford. M.P. Stockport, 1895–1906. *War Work :* Press Bureau, Whitehall ; War Library, Surrey House. *Clubs :* Carlton ; Arthur's. (O10984)

MELVILLE, Capt. the Hon. David William, M.B.E., *b.* 1892 ; *m.* 1914, Susanna Elizabeth Johanna, *d.* of Francis Sleigh, of Cape Town, S. Africa. Late 10th Hussars ; served on Personal Staff during Great War ; has Order of the Redeemer of Greece, 5th class. (M3227)

MELVILLE, Lieut.-Col. Edward Patrick Alexander, C.B.E. Capt. and Acting Lieut.-Col. R.A.F. ; served in Great War, 1914–19 (mentioned in despatches). (C1899)

MELVILLE, Major George David, O.B.E., M.C.

MELVILLE, James, M.B.E.

MELVILLE, John Mitchell, M.B.E.

MELVILLE, William, O.B.E.

MELVILLE, William, M.V.O., M.B.E., J.P.

MELVILLE, Arthur Henry LESLIE-, O.B.E., J.P., *b.* 12 March, 1842 ; *s.* of the Hon. Alexander Leslie-Melville, of Branston Hall, Lincoln (*see* BURKE'S *Peerage*). *Educ. :* Brighton Coll. Banker. *War Work :* Treas. North Lincolnshire Branch, British Red Cross Society. *Address :* D'Isney Place, Lincoln. *Club :* Bath. (O1660)

MELVIN, Frank Widowfield, M.B.E., M.D., F.R.C.S.

MENARY, Thomas George, O.B.E.

MENDE, Lieut. Nickolas Edwin, M.B.E.

MENDL, Sir Sigismund Ferdinand, K.B.E., *b.* 2 Dec. 1866 ; *s.* of the late Ferdinand Mendl, of London and Shanklin, I. of W. ; *m.* Frances, *d.* of A. H. Moses, of London. *Educ. :* Harrow and Univ. Coll., Oxford. Merchant ; Chairman of National Federation of Corn Trade Association. *War Work :* Advisory Committee on Army Contracts, Oats Control Committee, Royal Commission on Wheat Supplies. *Address :* 17, Hyde Park Street, W. 2. *Clubs :* Reform ; New Univ. (K137)

MENSFORTH, Holberry, C.B.E., M.Sc., *b.* 1871 ; *s.* of Edward Mensforth, of Bradford, Yorkshire. Technical and Gen. Manager of Works of Metropolitan-Vickers Electrical Co. Ltd. ; Member of Manchester and Dist. Armaments Committee and National Shell Factory Board of Management during Great War. (C568)

MENZIES, Charles Duncan, M.B.E.

MENZIES, Capt. Donald, M.B.E., R.A.S.C. (M.T.).

MENZIES, Major Robert, C.B.E.

MENZIES, Thomas Graham, C.B.E., M.I.C.E., *b.* 1869 ; *s.* of Thomas Hunter Menzies, of Edinburgh ; *m.* Dorothy Frances, *d.* of Cornelius Horne, of Kew Gardens, Surrey. *Educ. :* Heriot Watt Coll., Edinburgh. Civil Engineer ; Director of Special Construction, Civil Engineer-in-Chief's Depart., Admiralty, 1917–19. *Addresses :* 11, West Park Road, Kew Gardens, Surrey ; Plockton, Ross-shire. (C1006)

MENZIES, Alexander James Pople, O.B.E., *b.* 6 July, 1863 ; *s.* of John Menzies, of Balloch, Dambartonshire ; *m.* Elizabeth Bannerman, *d.* of John Davidson, of Ravenswood, Inverness. *Educ. :* Royal Academy, Inverness ; Edinburgh, London, and Brussels Univs. Sheriff Substitute of Stirling and Dumbarton. *War Work :* Judicial and administrative at Lerwick, Shetland Isles, an important centre of the Fleet during the war. *Address :* County Buildings, Dumbarton. *Club :* Scottish Liberal. (O579)

MEPHAM, Capt. Charles Edward, C.B.E., R.A,O.C.

MERCER, 2nd Lieut. George Joseph, M.B.E.

MERCER, John Swan, O.B.E., *b.* 26 Aug. 1867 ; *s.* of the late James Mercer, J.P., of Southfield, Dalkeith, Midlothian ; *m.* Emily Maud, *d.* of the late James Maclean, of Wigtown. *Educ. :* Royal High School, and Edinburgh Univ. (B.L. Edinburgh) ; Advocate, Scotland, 1899 ; appointed Counsel for Crown as *ultimus hæres*, 1911 ; J.P. for Orkney, 1912 ; Sheriff Substitute of Caithness, Orkney, and Shetland at Kirkwall, since 1912. *War Work :* Chairman of the Orkney Appeal Tribunal (Military Service Acts) ; Chairman of Local War Pensions Committee ; Chairman of Agricultural Wages Committee for Orkney ; services in connection with voluntary recruiting, Food Economy, and War Savings. *Clubs :* Orkney (Kirkwall) : Scottish Liberal (Edinburgh). (O10956)

MERCER, William Ayerst, M.B.E.

MERCHANT, John Lewis, C.A., M.B.E., *b.* 22 April, 1864 ; *s.* of Charles Martin Merchant, of Tottington, Lancs. ; *m.* Elspeth Alexandra, *d.* of Alexander Stephen, of Belsize

Park, London. *Educ. :* Manchester Grammar School, and Owens Coll. Chartered Accountant. *War Work :* Hon. Sec. of Bury and District National Shell Factory and Clerk to the Bury and District Munitions Board. *Address :* Bankfield North, Bury, Lancs. ; Elspeth, Abbotsbrook, Bourne End. (M2159)

MERCHANT, Captain John Victor Jabez, M.B.E.

MEREDITH, Anne Maude, M.B.E., *Educ. :* Hampstead Collegiate School, and London Univ. Acting Editor of " The Englishwoman," 1911–12 ; assistant editor. of " The Common Cause," 1913–18. *War Work :* Administrative assistant in charge of Medical Section, Ministry of Food, Feb. 1918, to June, 1920. *Address :* 5A, Thackeray Street, Kensington Square. *Clubs :* Ladies' University ; To-morrow. (M9017)

MEREDITH, Capt. H. A., M.B.E.

MEREDITH, Major Henry Chase, O.B.E., T.D., *b.* 8 Oct. 1881 ; *s.* of the late Henry Hills Meredith, of Marton Hall, Baschurch, Salop ; *m.* Mary Leigh, *d.* of Sir Leigh Hoskyns, Bart., of 78, Cadogan Square, S.W. (*see* BURKE'S *Peerage*). *Educ. :* Eton and Christ's Church Coll., Oxford. Master of Ludlow Hounds, 1913–16, and 1919–20 ; Major in Shropshire Yeomanry. *War Work :* Mobilised with 1/1st Shropshire Yeomanry, Aug. 1914 ; transferred to 1/1st Leicestershire Yeomanry in France, July, 1915 ; remained with that Regt. until it was broken up in April, 1918, and then became A.D.C. to Major-Gen. Bridgford, and later to Major-Gen. T. S. Lambert ; twice mentioned in despatches. *Address :* Overton Lodge, Ludlow. *Clubs :* Cavalry ; M.C.C. (O5516)

MEREDITH, Hugh Owen, C.B.E.

MEREDYTH, Capt. Arthur Gwynn Moreton, C.B.E. Served in Great War, 1914–19, as Senior Naval Officer, Thurso. (C2298)

MEREDYTH, Paymaster-Capt. Charles Edward Hughes, C.B.E. ; *s.* of the Rev. T. E. Meredyth, R. and Rural Dean of Ightfield, Salop. Paymaster-Capt. R.N. ; served in Great War, 1914–19 (mentioned in despatches). (C1933)

MERIVALE, Capt. Bernard, O.B.E., B.A., LL.B., *b.* 15 July, 1882 ; *s.* of John Herman Merivale, of Togstone, Northumberland ; *m.* Cicely, *d.* of Richard Edwin Stuckey, of Eastbourne. *Educ. :* Sedbergh School, and St. John's Coll., Cambridge. *War Work :* Enlisted 9 Sept. 1914, in 13th West Yorks Regt. ; subsequently gazetted 2nd Lieut. to 8th London Regt. ; promoted Capt. ; incapacitated during Home Service ; appointed to command of Depot, 3rd London Regt. ; appointed Assistant Commissioner of Home Counties Division of Food Ministry and for Enforcement. *Address :* 27A, Notting Hill Gate, London, W. *Club :* Savile. (O10958)

MERMAGEN, Major Ernest Wallace, C.B.E.

MERRELLS, Thomas Arthur, C.B.E.

MERRETT, Capt. Francis George, M.B.E., R.E.

MERRICK, Frederick Thomas, M.B.E., R.E.

MERRICK, Frederick William, M.B.E.

MERRICKS, Frank, C.B.E., *b.* 11 March, 1866 ; *s.* of James Merricks, of Bodiam, Sussex ; *m.* Minnie, *d.* of Robert Thom, of Barremman, Dumbartonshire. *Educ. :* Privately and Royal School of Mines, London. Member of Geological Survey Board ; President of the Institution of Mining and Metallurgy, 1920–21. *War Work :* Hon. Mining Engineer, and in charge of Home Iron Ore and Limestone Development and Production, Iron and Steel Production Department, Ministry of Munitions, Sept. 1915, to Jan. 1919. *Address :* 47, Campden House Road, Kensington, W. 8. *Club :* Bath. (C2806)

MERRIEFIELD, Albert, M.B.E.

MERRILES, Alexander Horsburgh, M.B.E., *b.* 26 June, 1887. *Educ. :* George Watson's Coll., Edinburgh. Chartered Accountant. *War Work :* Production Department of British Ministry of Munitions in U.S.A. *Address :* 143, East 39th Street, New York. (M3841)

MERRIMAN, Major Frank Boyd, C.B.E., K.C. ; *m.* 1920, Olive McLaren Carver, M.B.E. (*q.v.*), *d.* of Frederick W. Carver.

MERRIMAN, Henry John, M.B.E.

MERRITT, Lieut.-Col. and Qr.-Mr. George, C.B.E.

MERRY, Paymaster-Lieut.-Comm. Colin Campbell, C.B.E., R.N.

MERRY, Capt. Edgar James, M.B.E.

MERRY, George Pitlow, O.B.E. (O11997)

MERRY, 2nd Lieut. Henry Edward, M.B.E.

MERRY, Henry Edward Dilke, M.B.E.

MERRY, William Joseph Collings, O.B.E., M.A., M.D., B.Ch. (Oxon), *b.* 29 June 1867 ; *s.* of W. W. Merry, D.D., Rector of Lincoln Coll., Oxford ; *m.* Eleanor Charlotte, *d.* of H. Kynaston, D.D., Canon of Durham. *Educ. :* Marlborough, and Magdalen Coll., Oxford, and St. Thomas' Hospital, London. Hon. Surgeon, Princess Alice Hospital, Eastbourne. *War Work :* Senior Surgeon, Auxiliary War Hospital, and Civil Surgeon, Military Hospital, Eastbourne. *Address :* 2, Chiswick Place, Eastbourne. *Clubs :* New University ; Royal Automobile. (O10959)

MERSTON, Ethel Gladys, C.B.E., W.R.N.S.

MERTON, Arthur Sidney, M.B.E.

MERVYN, Muriel Hermione Marion, M.B.E.

MESSEL, Lieut.-Col. Leonard Charles Rudolph, O.B.E., T.D., *b.* 19 Feb. 1872 ; *s.* of L. Messel, of Nymans, Hand Cross, Sussex ; *m.* Maud, M.B.E., *d.* of Linley Sambourne, of 18, Stafford Terrace, Kensington. *Educ. :* Eton, and Merton Coll., Oxford. *War Work :* Raised 3/4th Batt. The Buffs, and commanded this, and later the 4th Reserve Batt. The Buffs. T.F. *Address :* Nymans, Hand Cross, Sussex. *Clubs :* Arts ; Conservative. (O7472)

MESSEL, Maud Frances, M.B.E.; *d.* of Edward Linley Sambourne, of 18, Stafford Terrace, Kensington; *m.* Leonard C. R. *s.* of L. Messel, of Nymans, Handcross, Sussex. *War Work*: Commandant, V.A.D. Hospital, Balcombe, Sussex. *Addresses*: Nymans, Handcross, Sussex; 104, Lancaster Gate, W. *Club*: Ladies' Automobile. (M9019)

MESSER, Lieut.-Col. Arthur Albert, C.B.E., D.S.O., *b.* 1863; *s.* of the late John Messer, J.P. Served in Great War, 1914–19, in Graves Registration Section with rank of Lieut.-Col (mentioned in despatches); Legion of Honour. (C1120)

MESSER, Charles McIlvaine, O.B.E.

MESSITER, Lieut.-Col. Charles Bayard, D.S.O., O.B.E.

MESTON, Jeanie, Lady, C.B.E., Lady of Grace of St. John of Jerusalem; *d.* of the late James McDonald; *m.* Lord Meston of Agra and Dunottar (*see* BURKE'S *Peerage*). *War Work*: In the United Provinces of India. *Address*: Hurst, Cookham Dene, Berkshire. (C348)

METCALFE, Lieut. Bruce, O.B.E., R.N.R.

METCALFE, Claude, M.B.E., *b.* 29 Aug. 1866; *s.* of Robert Ives Metcalfe, of Beccles; *m.* Laura Marian, *d.* of the Rev. H. Windsor-Aubrey, Hale, Salisbury. *Educ.*: Fauconberge School, and Edinburgh Univ. General Manager, British Central Africa Co., Ltd., in Nyasaland, 1894–1917; Unofficial Member of First Nyasaland Legislative Council, 1908–1913. *War Work*: Nyasaland Volunteer Reserve, 1914–17 (Nyasaland Medal, 1915); Chairman and Divisional Road Transport Officer for North Midland Division Road Transport Board, 1918–19. *Address*: c/o Lloyds Bank, Bristol. *Club*: Notts County. (M9920)

METCALFE, Edith Minna, M.B.E., *b.* 3 Feb. 1863; *d.* of the late Frederick Metcalfe, Rector of Upper Hardres, Canterbury. *Educ.*: Protestant School, Orleans, France. *War Work*: Soldiers' and Sailors' Families Association, Chatham. *Address*: 22, Trinity Road, Gillingham, Kent.

METCALFE, Sir George, K.B.E., J.P., *b.* 1848; *s.* of the late John Metcalfe, of Leeds; *m.* Amy, *d.* of Capt. Alex. Grant, late 61st Regt. *Educ.*: Yorkshire Society's School. Member, Committee Stock Exchange, 1898–1909, and American Dollar Securities Committee. *Address*: Munster Lodge, Teddington. *Clubs*: Gresham; Royal Thames Yacht; National Liberal. (K399)

METCALFE, George Arthur, M.B.E.

METCALFE, Capt. Harold William, M.B.E.

METCALFE, Major Harry Francis, M.B.E., D.C.M., *b.* 1864; *s.* of Capt. T. Metcalfe, of Royal Fusiliers. *Educ.*: Canada, and St. Margaret's Coll. Served in S. Africa (D.C.M., and Meritorious Medal). *War Work*: 1914; served with the 6th Batt. Royal Fusiliers (twice mentioned in despatches). *Address*: Avoca, Thornbury Road, Osterley Park. (M5463)

METCALFE, Engineer-Capt. Henry Wray., C.B.E., R.N., *b.* 1864; *s.* of John William Metcalfe, M.D., of Geneva; *m.* 1893, Dora Henrietta, *d.* of the Rev. Frederick Metcalfe. *Educ.*: Hereford Cathedral School. Served with Anti-Submarine Div. during Great War. *Address*: Harbledown, Canterbury. (C908)

METCALFE, Lieut.-Col. Joseph Noel, O.B.E., D.S.C., R.E.

METCALFE, Capt. Percy Kynaston, M.B.E., R.A.S.C.

METCALFE, T. Warrant Officer Robert, M.B.E. Royal Indian Marine.

METCALFE, Thomas Edward, O.B.E..

METE, Erina, Mrs., M.B.E.

METFORD, Lieut.-Col. Francis Killigrew Seymour, O.B.E., V.D., D.L.

METHUEN, Lieut. Lionel Harry, O.B.E., M.C.

METHUEN, Mary Ethel, the Lady, C.B.E., *d.* of the late William Ayshford Sanford, of Nynehead Court; *m.* as his second wife, Field-Marshal Paul Sanford Methuen, 3rd Baron Methuen, G.C.B., G.C.M.G., G.C.V.O., J.P. *Address*: Corsham, Wilts. (C400)

METHVEN, John, M.B.E., *b.* 23 June, 1857; *s.* of William Methven, of Dundee; *m.* Emily Wilmot, *d.* of Alfred Boase, of Claverhouse, near Dundee. *Educ.*: Dundee and St. Andrews. *War Work*: Assistant Hon. Sec. Dundee Branch, B.R.C.S *Address*: 38, Magdalen Yard Road, Dundee. *Club*: Eastern (Dundee). (M755)

METHVEN, Lieut.-Col. Malcolm David, O.B.E., R.A.F.

METIVIER, Capt. Harry Vincent Mercer, O.B.E. B.Sc., M.R.C.V.S., *s.* of — Metivier, of Port of Spain, Trinidad; *m.*, 1920, Sylvia Kathleen, *e. d.* of S. H. Nye, of Loughton, Essex.

METSON, Capt. George, O.B.E., L.R.I.B.A., etc., *b.* 10 March, 1881; *s.* of George Metson, of Clapham Common, S.W.; *m.* Beatrice, *d.* of Capt. W. Mossop, of Burnley. *Educ.*: Upper Tooting High School, and privately. Area Surveyor, Midland Area, H.M. Office of Works. *War Work*: Capt. 1/19th Batt. London Regt., and later Headquarter Visiting Military Representative. *Address*: 39, Glasslyn Road, Crouch End, N. 8. (O580)

MEWBURN, Lieut.-Col. Frank Hamilton, O.B.E.

MEWETT, Major James Edward Hedley, O.B.E., M.C.

MEYNELL, Major Everard Charles, O.B.E., M.C., R.F.A. (T.).

MEYNELL, Capt. Robert Alexander Lindley, O.B.E.

MIALL, Frank Berger, M.B.E., *b.* 10 Sept. 1874; *s.* of the late Comm. Gover Miall, R.N., Portsmouth; *m.* Beatrice G., *d.* of W. J. Ruggier, late C.E. to H.M. Dockyard, Gibraltar. *Educ.*: Christ's Hospital. Chief Electrical Engineer, serving on cable ships of the Eastern Telegraph Company. *War Work*: Served in the cable ship "Sentinel II." in the Mediterranean during whole period of war, as Chief Electrician, for the maintenance of cable communications and the laying of temporary cables for naval and military purposes. *Address*: c/o Eastern Tel. Co., Electra House, Finsbury Pavement, E.C. (M9022)

MICHAEL, Lewis William, M.B.E.

MICHAEL, Rao Sahib., M.B.E.

MICHAELIS, Marie, M.B.E.

MICHELL, George Babington, O.B.E., H.M.B. Consul at Para, Brazil, *b.* 27 Aug. 1864; *s.* of the late George Dalton Michell, Capt. 19th Foot, of Milford, Surrey; *m.* Marion Fanny, *d.* of the late George Anstruther Harris, M.C.S., of Weston-super-Mare. *Educ.*: King's Coll. School, London. H.B.M. Consular Service since March, 1903; Vice-Consul successively at Casablanca, Morocco; Stanleyville, Congo Free State; Paris, 1908–11; H.M. Consul at Iquitos, Peru, 1911–12; H.M. Consul at Para since Feb. 1913. *War Work*: Carrying out the "Trading with the Enemy (Statutory List) Proclamation" and other Consular Duties; work for the Admiralty (searching the North-East Coasts of Brazil for Enemy Raiders), and for the War Office (Recruiting, etc.). *Addresses*: British Consulate, Para, Brazil; 8, Royal Park, Clifton, Bristol. *Club*: Para. (O581)

MICHELL, Major Herbert Arthur, O.B.E. R.A.F.

MICHELL, John Deeble, M.B.E., L.R.I.B.A., *b.* 1863; *s.* of the late Stephen Michell, formerly of Pednandrea, Redruth. Architectural Superintendent, War Office. *Address*: 7, Burnaby Crescent, London, W. 4. (M756)

MICHELL, Marie Louise, Mrs., O.B.E.

MICHIE, Lieut. and Qr.-Mr. Andrew, M.B.E.

MICHIE, Charles, C.B.E.

MICHIE, Capt. Henry Maurice, O.B.E.

MICHIE, James, C.B.E., M.I.Mar.E., *b.* 15 Aug. 1867; *s.* of the late James Michie, of Gaveney Cottage, Banff, N.B.; *m.* Louisa, *d.* of the late Joseph Monro, of Broomhill Farm, Aberdeen. *Educ.*: Grammar School, Banff, Scotland. Chief Engineer, s.s. "Ingoma," Messrs. T. & J. Harrison, of Liverpool and London (Harrison Line). *War Work*: Transporting troops from England to Egypt, Egypt to France, India to France, the Serbian Army from Corfu to Salonica, troops to Mesopotamia, on East and S. African coast troops for E. African campaign. *Addresses*: c/o Messrs. T. and J. Harrison, Dock House, Billiter Street, London, E.C.; 3, Alloa Road, Goodmayes, Essex. *Club*: Mercantile (Durban). (C2808)

MICHIE, Mary Agnes, Mrs. Coutts, C.B.E.

MICHIE, Major William Charles, O.B.E., R.A.F.

MICHOD, Lieut.-Col. Percy Douglas, O.B.E.

MICKLEM, Eva, M.B.E.; *d.* of the late T. M. Weguelin, M.P., of 44, Grosvenor Gardens, S.W.; *m.* Major-Gen. Edward Micklem, of Rosehill, Hurley, Berks. *War Work*: President, Local Branch Maidenhead Soldiers' and Sailors' Families Association; Member Berks War Pensions Committee; Vice-Chairman, Maidenhead Sub-Division War Pensions Committee. *Address*: Rosehill, Hurley, Berks. *Club*: Empress. (M9023)

MICKLETHWAIT, Francis Mary Gore, M.B.E.

MIDDLEMAS, Lieut. Percy, M.B.E., R.A.F.

MIDDLEMAS, Robert, O.B.E., *b.* 5 Aug. 1867; *d.* of Andrew Middlemas, of Kelso, N.B.; *m.* Blanche à Becket, *d.* of Thomas Rees à Becket Evans, of Berwick-on-Tweed. *Educ.*: Kelso, N.B. Import and Export business with Havana, Turkey, etc. *War Work*: National Service Representative at Ilford; planned the National Service scheme of land and other work for average and unfit men circulated by the Ministry as an example to be followed. *Address*: Cranham Court, Upminster. *Clubs*: Eccentric; Royal Automobile. (O10961)

MIDDLEMASS, Agnes Lizzie, Mrs., M.B.E., Q.M.A.A.C.

MIDDLEMISS, John, M.B.E.

MIDDLETON, Major Edward Meredyth, O.B.E., R.A.M.C., *b.* 10 Oct. 1880; *e. s.* of the late F. E. Middleton, M.A., of Hainford, Norfolk. *Educ.*: Privately, Toronto Univ., and St. Thomas's Hospital, London. Assistant Commandant, Royal Army Medical Coll., Millbank, London. *War Work*: On Active Service from Aug. 1914 to June, 1919, in France, Macedonia, and Palestine. *Address*: R.A.M.C. Mess, Millbank, London, S.W. *Club*: Junior Naval and Military. (O6245)

MIDDLETON, Lieut. Frederick George, M.B.E., R.E.

MIDDLETON, Capt. George, M.B.E., *b.* 8 Sept. 1864; *s.* of Samuel Middleton, of Gillingham, Kent; *m.* Fanny, *d.* of Thomas Forbes, of St. Heliers. Jersey. *Educ.*: Privately. Inspector, Army Schools Dept. (retired). *War Work*: Organising and Supervising Technical Military Education whilst Inspector of Army Schools, Eastern Command, during the whole period of the war. *Address*: Pevensey, Avondale Road, South Croydon. (M5465)

MIDDLETON, George Burnett, M.B.E.

MIDDLETON, George Francis, M.B.E.

MIDDLETON, Capt. Herbert Edgar, M.B.E., *b.* March, 1 1884; *s.* of Herbert George Middleton, of Leytonstone, Essex. *Educ.*: Privately. Finance Department, Shanghai Municipal Council, Shanghai, China. *War Work*: Served as a 2nd Lieut. in the Essex Regt. June, 1915, to Dec. 1915; transferred to the Machine Gun Corps, Dec. 1915; served with the M.G.C. in France and Belgium, Feb. 1916, to June, 1917, successively as Adjutant, 2nd in Command, and Acting C.O. of a M.G. Unit in the Field; promoted Lieut. July, 1916; wounded at Ypres, June, 1917; mentioned in despatches; attached General Staff (Staff Duties Branch) War Office, Nov. 1917, to Dec. 1918; promoted Acting Capt. and attached to British Military

Mission to Siberia, Dec. 1918, to Feb. 1920; granted the rank of Captain on completion of service, Aug. 1920. *Address :* Thatched House Club, St. James' Street. London, S.W. 1. *Club :* Shanghai (Shanghai, China). (M6771)

MIDDLETON, John, M.B.E., *b.* April, 1885; *s.* of John G. Middleton, of Sturton-by-Stow, Lincoln; *m.* Emily, *d.* of Seth Harrison, of Lincoln. *Educ. :* Queen Elizabeth's School, Gainsborough. Sec. Norfolk Mental Hospital, Thorpe, Norwich; Assist. Sec., Lincolnshire (Bracebridge) Mental Hospital, 1902–12. *War Work :* Secretary and Paymaster, Norfolk War (General) Hospital, Norwich, 1915–20, which Institution was the Norfolk Mental Hospital Converted into a hospital for sick and wounded officers and men. *Address :* Sturton Cottage, Thorpe. Norwich. (M9024)

MIDDLETON, Mary Katharine, Mrs. Hugh, O.B.E., *b.* 6 June, 1878; *s.* of the late Admiral S. Long, of Blendworth, Horndean, Hants; *m.* Hugh Jeffry Midaleton (who died), *s.* of Sir Arthur Middleton, Bart., of Belsay Castle, Northumberland (*see* BURKE'S *Peerage*). *Educ. :* Winchester High School. Chairman, Northumberland County Federation of Women's Institutes; County Commissioner Girl Guides; Member of Northumberland Agricultural Executive Committee, County Council Education Committee, and Castle Ward Rural District Council. *War Work :* Hon. Sec. Women's War Agricultural Committee; Chairman Red Cross Selection Committee. *Address :* Belsay Castle, Northumberland. *Club :* Ladies' Athenæum.

MIDDLETON, Sydney Albert, D.S.O., O.B.E.

MIDDLETON, Sir Thomas Hudson, K.B.E., C.B., *b.* 1863; *s.* of Alexander Allardyce Middleton, J.P.; *m.* Lydia Falconer Fraser Miller, *d.* of the late Prof. Davidson, of Adelaide Univ. *Educ. :* Merchiston Castle School, Edinburgh, and Univs. of Glasgow and Edinburgh. Professor of Agriculture, Saroda Coll., India, 1889–96; Lecturer on Agriculture, Univ. Coll. of Wales, Aberystwyth, 1896–99; Professor of Agriculture, Armstrong Coll., Newcastle, 1899–1902; Cambridge University, 1902–7; Assistant Sec., Board of Agriculture and Fisheries, 1906–19; Development Commissioner, 1919. *War Work :* Director and subsequently Deputy Director-General, Food Production Department. *Address :* 6A, Dean's Yard, S.W. 1; 3, Montpelier Avenue, W. 5. (K158)

MIDDLETON, Major Walter, O.B.E.

MIDDLETON, William Aberdein, O.B.E., *b.* 1 Feb' 1876; *s.* of William Aberdein Middleton, of Brechin, Forfarshire; *m.* Margaret Anne, *d.* of Robert Colvin Johnstone, of Edinburgh. Chartered Accountant (Edinburgh Society); Sec., National Insurance Audit Department, 3, Regent Street, S.W. 1. *Address :* 19, Criffel Avenue, S.W. 2. *Club :* National Liberal. (O3836)

MIDDLETON, Lieut.-Col. William Crawfurd, C.B.E., *b.* 1858. Major and Brevet Lieut.-Col. Remount Ser.; Sudan Expedition, 1884–5 (medal with clasp, bronze star); S. Africa, 1899–1902 (despatches, Queen's medal with seven clasps); Great War, 1914–19 (despatches). (C1698)

MIDGELEY, Lieut. Sam, M.B.E.

MIDGLEY, John William, M.B.E.

MIDMER, Thomas William, O.B.E.

MIDWINTER, Capt. Edward Colpoys, C.B., C.M.G., C.B.E., D.S.O., *b.* 1872; *s.* of the late Rev. Edward Adair Midwinter, Vicar of St. Paul's, Marylebone. *Educ. :* St. Paul's School, and R.M.A. Entered R.E. 1892; Capt. 1903; retired, 1907; Nile Expedition, 1897–1898; present at battle of Khartum (despatches, 4th class Medjidieh); El Lewa Pasha in Egyptian Army (3rd class Osmanieh); Gen. Manager of Sudan Govt. Railways; has 2nd class Order of the Nile. *Address :* Atbara, Sudan. *Club :* Army and Navy. (C1097)

MIDWOOD, Lieut.-Col. Harrison, C.B.E.

MIFSUD, Anne Gill, Mrs., M.B.E.

MIGNON, Edith Agnes Ida, Mrs., M.B.E.

MILBURN, Major Charles Henry, O.B.E., R.A.M.C.

MILBURN, Lieut.-Col. Thomas Alan, O.B.E., T.D., mentioned in despatches, *b.* 30 June, 1879; *s.* of Tom Milburn, of Portland Square, Workington; *m.* Maud Clarissa, *d.* of Col. A. J. Hopkins, of 78, Oxford Gardens, London, W. *Club :* Junior Army and Navy. (O7476)

MILBURN, William, M.B.E., F.R.I.B.A., J.P., *b.* 30 July, 1858; *s.* of William Milburn, of Sunderland; *m.* Julia Margaret, *d.* of John Wright Wayman, of Sunderland. *Educ. :* Private School, Sunderland. Architect and Surveyor. *War Work :* Chairman of Sunderland Recruiting Committee; Chairman of Sunderland Tribunal Advisory Committee; Chairman for Committees for raising 160th Brigade, R.F.A., and 20th D.L.I.; Assistant Controller of Registration (National Service) at Middlesbrough; Assistant Director of National Service for Newcastle-upon-Tyne Area. *Addresses :* 8, Thornhill Park, Sunderland; 17, Fawcett Street, Sunderland.

MILDMAY, Cecil Francis, Mrs. W. H. ST JOHN-, O.B.E.

MILDRED, Lieut.-Col. Spencer, C.B.E., D.S.O., R.E., *b.* 1872. Great War, 1914–17 (despatches); appointed to command R.E. of a Div. 1916. (C5581)

MILDREN, Capt. William, M.B.E.

MILES, Major Alfred George, M.B.E., R.E.

MILES, Alfred Henry, O.B.E.

MILES, Alfred, O.B.E., *b.* 1875; *s.* of the Rev. J. Miles, of Aberystwyth, Cardiganshire; *m.* Etheleen, *d.* of George Evans, of Pontypridd, Glam. *Educ. :* Privately; Univ. Coll., Wales, Aberystwyth; St. Bartholomew's Hospital, London. M.O. Post Office. *War Work :* 3 years Hon. M.O. and Officer-in-charge,

Dinas Powis Red Cross Hospital. *Address :* Glen View, Dinas Powis, Glam. (O10966)

MILES, Alice, Lady, C.B.E.. *d.* of the late Joseph Parker, of Brettenham Park, Suffolk; *m.* Lieut.-Gen. Sir Herbert Scott Gould Miles, G.C.B., G.C.M.G., K.C.B., G.B.E., C.V.O. M.V.O. Governor and Commander-in-Chief, Gibraltar (*q.v.*). *Address :* 22, Half Moon Street, W. 1. (C401)

MILES, Lieut. Cecil James, M.B.E., R.E. (S.R.)

MILES, Lieut.-Comm. Francis Nigel, O.B.E., R.N.

MILES, Rev. Frederic James, D.S.O., O.B.E., *b.* 1869; *s.* of the late Stephen Miles, printing machine manufacturer, of London; *m.* 1894, Isabella Killick, of N.S. Wales and Ceylon. *Educ. :* Privately. Baptist Minister and Senior Chaplain Australian Imperial Forces; served in Great War, 1914–17 (despatches); was Pres. of Christian Endeavour Union, W. Australia, Tasmania, and Victoria, 1900–14; Victorian Editor of "The Australian Baptist." *Addresses :* Lanka, Melbourne, Victoria; Knight's Hill, West Norwood, S.E. (O7965)

MILES, Lieut.-Col. George Edward, C.B.E., J.P., R.A.M.C.. *b.* 3 Feb. 1853; *s.* of George Daniel Miles, of Manchester, Jamaica, B.W.I.; *m.* daughter of the Rev. Richard King, of Prestwich, Manchester, Lancs. *Educ. :* Eastmans R.N. Academy, Southsea; Guy's Hospital. Previously Lunacy appointments in England; for 28 years Medical Superintendent, Lunacy Service, New South Wales, Australia. *War Work :* O.C Mental Division, R. V. Hospital, Netley; Mental Specialist, Southern Command. *Address :* c/o Bank of N.S.W., Threadneedle Street, E.C. *Clubs :* British Empire; Australian, Sydney. (C1699)

MILES, Harry Powell, O.B.E., M.Inst.C.E., M.Inst.T., *b.* 2 Dec. 1869. Assistant Engineer, Midland Railway. *War Work :* Work in connection with Railway Transport. *Address :* Edgerton, Duffield Road, Derby. (O10966)

MILES, Lieut.-Gen. Sir Herbert Scott Gould, G.C.B., G.C.M.G., G.B.E., C.V.O., *b.* 31 July, 1850; *m.* Alice, C.B.E. (*q.v.*), *d.* of the late Joseph Parker, of Brettenham Park, Suffolk. *Educ. :* Wellington, and R.M.C. Sandhurst. Entered Army. 1869; Col. 1893; A.A.G. Aldershot, 1893–98; Commandant Staff Coll. 1889–99; S. Africa (D.A.G.), 1899–1900; Commandant, Staff College, Camberley, 1900–3; G.O.C. Troops, Cape Colony, 1903; Director of Recruiting and Organisation H.Q. 1904; Q.M.G. to the Forces, 1908–12; Governor, Wellington Coll.; Grand Officer Legion of Honour, Grand Cross of the Crown of Italy, and of Isabella la Catolica of Spain; Governor and Commander-in-Chief, Gibraltar, 1913–18. *Address :* 22, Half Moon Street, W. 1. *Clubs :* Army and Navy; Marlborough; Arthur's. (G38)

MILES, Leopold, M.B.E.

MILES, Sybil Marguerite Goune, Mrs., O.B.E.

MILES, William, O.B.E.

MILES, Blanch Kate BEERE-, M.B.E.

MILEY, Major Arnold John, O.B.E., R.A.F.

MILFORD, Sydney William, O.B.E.

MILL, Capt. John Smith Tindal, M.B.E., R.E.

MILL, Lieut.-Col. Thomas, C.M.G., O.B.E., M.B., F.R.C.S.

MILLAR, Duncan Alexander, *b.* 29 Aug. 1870; *s.* of William Millar, of Kilmelford, Argyll; *m.* Mary Catherine, *d.* of Dr. M. F. O'Kelly, of Felling Lodge, Felling, Co. Durham. *Educ. :* Stirling High School, and Glasgow, and Univ. Durham. Pensions Referee; Poor Law M.O.; Corps Surgeon St. John Ambulance Brigade; Hon. Major R.A.M.C. (V.). *War Work :* M.O. Whinney House Hospital; Chief M.O. Sallwell Towers Hospital, Low Fell, Gateshead-on-Tyne; Major, R.A.M.C. (V.), No. 1, Durham F.A. *Address :* Felling Lodge, Felling-on-Tyne, Co. Durham. (O36)

MILLAR, Ella Morison, Mrs., M.B.E., *b.* 1869; *d.* of Sir Robert Kirk Inches, of Edinburgh (*see* BURKE'S *Peerage*); *m.* Thomas John, *s.* of Adam Millar, of Edinburgh. *Educ. :* Edinburgh. Town Councillor, Edinburgh. *War Work :* Red Cross; Prince of Wales' Fund; work for women; comforts for soldiers on active service; prisoners of War in Germany (Edinburgh Committee); Sailors' and Soldiers' Children's Home, etc. *Address :* 2, Strathearn Road, Edinburgh. *Club :* Ladies' Caledonian. (M759)

MILLAR, Major Exley Livingston, M.B.E.

MILLAR, Eng.-Lieut. Frank Ernest, C.B.E., R.N.

MILLAR, Capt. George McGregor, C.B.E., M.B.

MILLAR, Henry Horatio, M.B.E., J.P.

MILLAR, James, O.B.E., M.D., C.M., *b.* 30 Oct. 1849; *s.* of the late Christopher Millar, of Carmyllie, Forfarshire, N.B.; *m.* Kate, *d.* of Arthur Liberty, of Nottingham. *Educ. :* Aberdeen Univ. Late Assistant Demonstrator of Anatomy, Aberdeen Univ. *War Work :* M.O. in charge The Bowden Auxiliary Hospital, Nottingham, 1915–19; Member of Recruiting and Pensions Boards, 1915–19. (O10968)

MILLAR, Peter, M.B.E.

MILLAR, Rev. Peter Carmichael, O.B.E., B.D., *b.* 7 Aug. 1887; *s.* of James Millar, of Airdrie. *Educ. :* Airdrie Academy and Glasgow University. Minister of Balmerino, Fifeshire. *War Work :* Served as Chaplain with E.E.F., June, 1917, to June, 1919; mentioned in General Allenby's despatch of March, 1919. *Address :* Manse of Balmerino, Fife. (O6247)

MILLAR, William, C.B.E.

MILLARD, Claud John, M.B.E., R.A.S.C.

MILLARD, Ernest Alfred, M.B.E.

MILLARD, Col. Reginald Jaffray, C.M.G., C.B.E., M.B., Ch.M., *b.* 1868 ; *s.* of the late Rev. H. S. Millard, of Newcastle, N.S. Wales ; *m.* 1898, Margaret Alice Millard. *Educ.* : Sydney Univ. and Univ. Coll., London. Col. Australian Army Med. Corps ; appointed Med. Sup. Coast Hospital, N.S. Wales, 1908 ; Dep. Director of Med. Sers., Australian Imperial Force, Head Quarters, London, 1917 ; served during Great War, 1915–17, in Egypt and Gallipoli (despatches) ; N.S. Wales Lunacy Depart. 1892–1900 : Depart. of Public Health, 1900–14. *Clubs* : British Empire ; University (Sydney). (C1845)

MILLEDGE, Minnie, M.B.E., *b.* 6 Oct. 1872 ; *d.* of Alfred Milledge. *Educ.* : Privately. Deputy Superintendent, Insurance Dept., Ministry of Health. *War Work* : Work in connection with Benefits of Discharged Soldiers and Sailors under the National Health Insurance Act. *Address* : Keston, Weald Road, Brentwood. (M2169)

MILLER, Alexander, M.B.E.

MILLER, Lieut. Alfred, C.B.E.

MILLER, A. E., O.B.E.

MILLER, Brig.-Gen. Alfred Douglas, C.B.E., D.S.O., D.L., *b.* 1864 ; *s.* of Lieut.-Col. James Miller, of Shotover, Oxford. *m.* 1899, Ella, *d.* of the late John Fletcher, of Saltoun Hall, Haddington (see BURKE'S *Peerage*, Wemyss, E.). Entered Scots Greys, 1885 ; Capt. 1893 ; Major, 1902 ; Lieut.-Col. 1907 ; Col. 1911 ; Hon. Brig.-Gen. 1918 ; retired, 1914 ; S. Africa, 1899–1902, as D.A.A.G. ; Chief Staff Officer, Great War, 1914–18, on Staff (despatches) ; D.A.A.G. N.-E. Dist. 1903–5. *Addresses* : Shotover House, Wheatley, Oxfordshire ; 25, Great Cumberland Place, W. (C829)

MILLER, Major Allister Mackintosh, D.S.O., O.B.E. Served in Great War, 1914–19, with R.F.C. (mentioned in despatches). (O8147)

MILLER, Amy Bessie, Mrs., M.B.E. ; *d.* of the late William Dulley, of Wellingborough ; *m.* Hubert William, *s.* of the late William Walter, of Nottingham. *War Work* : Superintendent and Hon. Sec. of Exmouth Branch of the Surgical Requisites Association (Queen Mary's Needlework Guild). *Address* : 4, The Beacon, Exmouth. (N9628)

MILLER, Anne, O.B.E. ; *d.* of John Miller, of Scrabster. *Educ.* : Privately. *War Work* : V.A.D. Nurse, Divisional Sec., West of Caithness Red Cross Unit ; Member of several War Committees. *Address* : Scrabster House, Thurso, Caithness. *Club* : Ladies' National. (O10969)

MILLER, Annie, M.B.E., *b.* 6 May, 1870 ; *d.* of Sir Alexander E. Miller, of Ballycastle, Co. Antrim (see BURKE'S *Peerage*). *War Work* : Commandant of the Highlands Auxiliary Military Hospital, Shortheath, Farnham, Surrey, and of Surrey 74 V.A.D. *Address* : Corrymeela, Farnham, Surrey. (M670)

MILLER, Capt. Archibald Thomas, O.B.E., M.G.C.

MILLER, Arnold Henry, O.B.E., *b.* 1 Oct. 1865 ; *s.* of Henry Blake Miller, of Norwich ; *m.* Ella Constance, *d.* of Thornton Andrews, J.P., of Swansea. *Educ.* : King Edward VI. Grammar School, Norwich. Solicitor and Town Clerk, Norwich. *Address* : Woodlands, Norwich. (O583)

MILLER, Charles Cyril, O.B.E., *b.* 1870 ; *s.* of the late R. J. Miller, of London ; *m.* Lilian Jeanne, *d.* of E. A. Armstrong, of London. *Educ.* : City of London School. Collector of Customs and Excise, Port of Cape Town, and Shipping Master. *War Work* : Detaining Officer for the Admiralty ; Deputy-Controller of Imports and Exports, Cape Town ; Hon. Treas. Governor-General's Fund, Final Effort ; Organiser of Fairhaven Fund in aid of H.M. Navy and Mercantile Marine. *Address* : Custom House, Cape Town. *Club* : Durban.

MILLER, Capt. Charles Ernest Augustus, M.B.E., *b.* 27 Sept. 1872 ; *s.* of Charles Miller, of Alexandra, Victoria ; *m.* Martha Maria, *d.* of the late Joseph Berry, of Creswick, Victoria. *Educ.* : Public School and privately. 25 years on Postal Service as Telegraphist and Postmaster (Victoria) ; 9 years Department of Home Affairs, 1st as Clerk-in-charge Victorian Commonwealth Electoral Department, and later as Divisional Returning Officer for Melbourne. *War Work* : London, March, 1918, to Nov. 1919, had charge of Records of all Australian Munition Workers, and Australian War Workers overseas, and in addition did the correspondence between the London office and the Department of Defence, Melbourne, in connection with the above. *Addresses* : 31, Collins Street, Melbourne ; 14, Tantram Avenue, East St. Kilda, Victoria, Australia. (M9029)

MILLER, Col. Charles Hewitt, C.B.E. T. Major and T. Col. R.A.M.C. ; served in Great War, 1914–19 (mentioned in despatches). (C1292)

MILLER, Capt. Charles Thomas Nanamore, M.B.E.

MILLER, Capt. David Simpson, M.B.E., R.D.

MILLER, Edith Mary, Mrs., M.B.E. ; *d.* of A. S. Graves, of Rock Ferry, Cheshire ; *m.* William, *s.* of Thomas Miller, of Rock Ferry. *Educ.* : Elmhurst, Rock Ferry, Cheshire. *War Work* : Commandant of Cheshire 90 V.A.D., and had charge of the Chalet V.A.D. Hospital, Hoylake, Cheshire, from Feb. 1915, to Feb. 1919. *Address* : Drummond Road, Hoylake, Cheshire. (M2171)

MILLER, Edmund Josiah, M.B.E., *b.* 5 March, 1880 ; *s.* of J. W. Miller, of Portsmouth ; *m.* Catherine, *d.* of Charles Chiverton, of Portsmouth. *Educ.* : Mr. Napier's, Portsmouth. *War Work* : Served in Secretary's Department of Admiralty. *Address* : Montbrison, Blakehall Road, Carshalton. (M9032)

MILLER, Lieut.-Col. Edward Darley, C.B.E., D.S.O., *b.* 1865 ; *s.* of Edward Miller, of Hartsfield, Betchworth ; *m.* Irene Helen, *d.* of the late Col. Langtry, 8th Hussars. *Educ.* :

Harrow ; Trinity Coll., Cambridge. Joined 17th Lancers, 1886 ; served in South African War with Imperial Yeomanry ; mentioned in despatches. *War Work* : Northamptonshire Yeomanry in France, 1914–16 ; in Command of 2/1st Pembroke Yeomanry, 1916–17 ; Corps Horse Adviser, 15th Corps, 1918–19. *Address* : Spring Hill, Rugby. *Clubs* : Cavalry ; Hurlingham ; Ranelagh ; Roehampton ; Rugby Polo. (C1293)

MILLER, Ernest Charles, M.B.E., D.S.C., R.N.

MILLER, Major Frank Edwin, O.B.E., I.O.D.

MILLER, Frank Lawrence, O.B.E., *b.* 1872 ; *s.* of Daniel Miller, of Biggleswade, Beds. ; *m.* Tryphosa Amelia, *d.* of John Bonney, of Chigwell. *Educ.* : Thames Nautical Training Coll. ; H.M.S. "Worcester." Civil Service. *War Work* : Ministry of Munitions ; London Shipowners and Transport Workers Military Service Committee ; Signalling Instruction (voluntary), City of London National Guard. *Address* : Ivel Bury, Swanley, Kent. (O584)

MILLER, Lieut. Frederick William, M.B.E.

MILLER, Paymaster-Comm. Grenville Acton, C.B.E., R.N., *b.* 30 July, 1876 ; *s.* of the late Comm. Wm. E. Miller, of Southampton ; *m.* Clara Ainslie, *d.* of Eric H. Mackay, of Queensland, Australia. *War Work* : Paymaster Commander of H.M.S. "Vindictive" ; successively Sec. to Commander-in-Chief, North America and West Indies, Vice-Admiral Commanding Fourth Battle Squadron, Grand Fleet and Allied Naval Armistice Commission. *Address* : Northwood House, Fareham, Hants. *Clubs* : Junior United Service ; Royal Naval, Portsmouth. (C1166)

MILLER, Harold Tibbatts, M.B.E.

MILLER, Col. Hugh de Burgh, C.B.E., D.S.O., *b.* 1874 ; *s.* of the late Thomas de Burgh Miller, Adviser to Maharajah of Burdwan ; *m.* 1906, Una M. I., *d.* of Col. Andrew Wilson Baird C.S.I., of Palmers' Cross, Elgin. *Educ.* : Brighton Coll., and at R.M.A. Entered R.A. 1894, Capt. 1901, Major 1911, Brevet Lieut.-Col. 1915, Lieut.-Col. 1916, and Brevet Col. 1917 ; served in S. Africa, 1899–1901 (despatches) ; was Officer in charge of Danger Buildings, Woolwich, 1911–13 ; appointed 2nd Assist. Sup. Roy. Laboratory there, 1913, Assist. Sup. 1914, an A.A.G. at War Office 1915, and a Dep. Director there, 1919. *Address* : Royal Laboratory, Woolwich. (C1700)

MILLER, Irene Helen, Mrs., O.B.E.

MILLER, Lieut. James, M.B.E.

MILLER, Capt. James Cousins, O.B.E., R.A.V.C.

MILLER, 2nd Lieut. John Alfred Tennant, O.B.E.

MILLER, Rev. John Harry, C.B.E., D.D., *b.* 4 Nov. 1869 ; *s.* of John R. Miller, Ironfounder, of Glasgow ; and of Georgina Caird, of Dundee ; *m.* Marie Sophie, *d.* of Henri Alexis de Joannis, of Touraine, France. *Educ.* : Albany Academy ; Glasgow Univ. ; Glasgow Free Church Coll. Minister of United Free Church of Scotland, first at Elie, Fife, then Roseburn, Edinburgh ; now Warden of New Coll. Settlement, Edinburgh ; Coll. tutor in Practical Training at New Coll., and Minister of Pleasance Church ; Hon. degree of D.D. conferred by Edinburgh Univ. in 1919 ; Chaplain to 5th Batt. Royal Scots, 1909–20 ; Chaplain to Univ. of Edinburgh O.T.C. 1920 onwards. *War Work* : 1915, June to Sept., Chaplain in Forth Defence Area, Scottish Command ; 1915–17, Chaplain at Etaples Base ; June to Sept. 1917, 19th Corps H.Q. ; Dec. 1917, to Sept. 1918, Assist. Principal Chaplain, with rank of Colonel, at Rouen ; Oct. 1918, to April, 1919, as Principal Chaplain, with rank of Colonel, 2nd Army H.Q. at Roubaix, and with Army of Occupation on Cologne. *Address* : Warden's Lodge, Mound Place, Edinburgh. (C2050)

MILLER, Lieut.-Col. John Lawrence, C.B.E. Lieut.-Col. Canadian Forestry Corps ; served in Great War (mentioned in despatches). (C776)

MILLER, Joseph, M.B.E. (M21025b)

MILLER, Lieut. Joseph Charles, M.B.E., R.A.O.C.

MILLER, Joseph Edward, M.B.E., *b.* 19 Nov. 1863 ; *s.* of the late Stephen Peter Miller, of St. Leonard's-on-Sea ; *m.* Isabella Miller, *d.* of Nicholas Duckworth, of Hove. *Educ.* : St. Mary's School, Woolhampton, Berks, and St. Edmund's Coll., Ware. Assistant Sec. to the Brighton Education Committee. *War Work* : Hon. Sec. to the Brighton Central War Savings Committee ; Special Constabulary 5¼ years, with rank of inspector. *Address* : 35, Florence Road, Brighton. (M9035)

MILLER, Sir Leslie Creery, C.B.E.

MILLER, Margaret Julia, Lady, O.B.E.

MILLER, Mary Elizabeth, Lady, O.B.E., *b.* 1856 ; *d.* of Henry Darlot, of Melbourne, Australia ; *m.* Sir Edward Miller (see BURKE'S *Peerage*) ; *s.* of Henry Miller, of Melbourne, Australia. *Educ.* : Melbourne. *War Work* : Head of Red Cross Depot, Melbourne, for 6 years. *Address* : Glynn, Toorak, Melbourne. *Clubs* : Ladies' Empire (London) ; Alexandra (Melbourne). (O926)

MILLER, Sidney James, M.B.E., *b.* 18 May, 1870 ; *m.* Ethel, *d.* of Tomsett, of Osborne Lodge, Tulse Hill, London, S.W. *Educ.* : Univ. School, Hastings. Solicitor. *War Work* : Military Representative and National Science Representative for the Borough of Cambridge. *Address* : St. Ronans, Station Road, and 20, St. Andrew's Street, Cambridge. (M9036)

MILLER, Thomas Lodwick, O.B.E., M.I.C.E., M.I.M.E., M.I.E.E., *b.* 21 March, 1860 ; *s.* of Thomas Miller, of Plymouth and Liverpool ; *m.* Annie Sophia, *d.* of John Wyles, of Kirkcaldy, N.B. *Educ.* : Royal Institution School, Liverpool. Acted as Consulting Engineer to a large number of local authorities and companies, both at home and abroad, including work for Nepaul (India), Antofagasta (Chili), Hong Kong

(China), etc. ; Past-President, Liverpool Engineering Society ; Past-Chairman, Manchester Section of the Institution Electrical Engineers. *War Work :* General Manager and Sec. Liverpool Munitions of War Committee ; responsible for equipment and running of 6 National Factories (including National Shell Forging and Cartridge Case Pressing Factory), and some 60 firms of contractors ; also responsible for electrical and heating installations, and plant equipment at No. 2 Filling Factory, and No. 2 Amatol Factory, Aintree, Liverpool. *Addresses :* 316, Royal Liver Building, Liverpool ; Danehurst, Prenton, Birkenhead. (O1667)

MILLER, Thomas Maskew, M.B.E.

MILLER, Major Walter, O.B.E.

MILLER, Major William Charles Walmer, O.B.E., *b.* 19 Nov. 1870. Indian Service of Engineers. *War Work :* Indian Army Reserve of Officers ; called up Oct. 1914, released Jan. 1919 ; Mesopotamia, April, 1916 to Dec. 1916 ; mentioned in "Gazette" of India, dated 29 July, 1919, for valuable services rendered in India in connection with the war, 1914–19 ; War badge as souvenir and mark of appreciation. *Club :* Punjab, Lahore. (O8279)

MILLER, Capt. William Duncan, O.B.E.

MILLER, Ellen, Mrs. CAMERON-, O.B.E., *b.* 30 May, 1865 ; *d.* of Ewen Cameron, of Ness Park, Inverness ; *m.* John James Miller (who died). *Educ. :* Liverpool ; France ; Germany. *War Work :* Matron in charge of Convalescent Hospital at Allerton Beeches, Liverpool, 1914–15 ; Superintended No. 17 Hospital Kitchen, Alexandria, 1915–16 ; Matron in charge, British Red Cross Convalescent Hospital for Officers (No. 1), Alexandria. *Addresses :* c/o Lloyd's Bank, Bold Street Branch, Liverpool ; Tomanbuidh, Pitlochry. (O3838)

MILLICAN, Lieut.-Col. Harry Cyril, O.B.E., T.D., *b.* 6 July, 1882 ; *s.* of Richard Henry Millican, J.P., of Newcastle-upon-Tyne ; *m.* Deborah, *d.* of John Putney, of London *Educ. :* Durham School. Company Director and Merchant. *War Work :* Recruited and trained 2nd Line, Northumbrian Divisional Train ; commanded 54th Divisional Train ; O.C. A.S.C., Portsmouth District ; commanded 27th Divisional Train in Macedonia and the Caucasus. *Address :* New Market Street, Newcastle-upon-Tyne. *Clubs :* Junior Army and Navy ; Royal Army Service Corps ; Pen and Palette. (O7477)

MILLIGAN, Edward Thomas Campbell, O.B.E., *b.* 1886 ; *s.* of E. Milligan, of Victoria ; *m.* Josie, *d.* of P.B. Moore. *Educ. :* Ormond College, Melbourne Univ. Hon. Surgeon, Dreadnought Hospital ; and to Weir Hospital. *War Work :* Surgical Specialist, France, 1914–18. *Address :* 13, Harley Street, W. (O5583)

MILLIGAN, George, M.B.E.

MILLIGAN, Helena Mary, Mrs., M.B.E., *b.* 1875 ; *d.* of the late Wm. Clarke, J.P., of The Hermitage, Gateshead-on-Tyne ; *m.* Fredk. P., *s.* of the late Very Rev. Professor Milligan, of Aberdeen University. *Educ. :* St. Leonard's School, St. Andrew's, Fife. *War Work :* From May, 1916, to July, 1919, was Hon. Sec. of the Ladies' Committee of Boys' Brigade Rest Hut for Sailors and Soldiers, The Mound, Edinburgh ; this hut was open day and night for 3 years and entirely staffed by voluntary workers. *Address :* 1, Moray Place, Edinburgh. (M3850)

MILLIGAN, John Arthur, M.B.E., *b.* 18 May, 1875 ; *s.* of the late John Milligan, of Whitehaven, Cumberland ; *m.* Amy, *d.* of Frederick Fielding, of Oldham. Head of Section, Office of Supt. of the Line, L. & N.W. Rly., Euston ; Head of the New Works Section under the Supt. of the Line, L. & N.W. Rly., Euston. *War Work :* Owing to having previously been Indoor chief of the "Goods Trains" Section under the Supt. of the Line at Euston, was temporarily returned for the period of the war to that section to take indoor control from Euston of the transit of important Government stores, Admiralty coal, etc. *Address :* 113, Ramuz Drive, Westcliff-on-Sea. *Club :* Conservative, Watford. (M9037)

MILLIGAN, Major Robert Arthur, O.B.E., M.D.

MILLIKEN, Lieut. Ernest Norman, M.B.E., R.A.S.C.

MILLIKEN, Gertrude Andrews, O.B.E. ; *d.* of William Andrews, of Belfast, Ireland ; *m.* John, *s.* of Hugh Milliken, of Whitepark, Co. Down, Ireland. *Educ. :* Victoria Coll., Belfast ; Swanley Horticultural Coll., Kent. *War Work :* Head of first Depot in Ireland for making Sphagnum Moss Dressings ; afterwards head of the Belfast Depot, Ulster Sphagnum Moss Association, which under the D.G.V.O. sent many thousands of dressings to all theatres of war at home and abroad, Sept. 1915, to Sept. 1919. (O1668)

MILLINGER, Capt. Thomas, M.B.E.

MILLINGTON, Eng. David, O.B.E., *b.* 7 Aug. 1877 ; *s.* of Thomas Millington, of Dundas, Ontario, Canada ; *m.* Lila Thompson, *d.* of John Lawrence Stutt, of West Flamboro', Ontario. *Educ. :* Dundas Schools. Inventor and representative for Ludw. Loewe & Co., Ltd., Berlin, Germany, and Manager for Alfred Herbert, Ltd. Coventry, in Germany ; General Works Manager, W. & T. Avery, Soho Foundry, Birmingham. *War Work :* Interned Ruhleben, 1914–16 ; Liaison Officer, M. of M., and Deputy General Manager for Bean & Son, of N.P.F., Dudley ; Organised and started National Fuse Factory, Tipton, Staffs. ; Officer in V.T.C. *Address :* The Hollies, Oakham, Dudley, Worcs. (O10971)

MILLINGTON, Herbert Ashlin, O.B.E.

MILLINGTON, John Price, M.B.E., M.A., *b.* 21 Aug. 1879 ; *s.* of John Millington, of Ketley, Salop. *Educ. :* Christ's Coll., Cambridge. *Address :* 18, Cadogan Court, S.W. 3. *Clubs :* Savile ; United University. (M9039)

MILLMAN, Major Francis Henry, O.B.E.

MILLMAN, Lieut. William Henry Ennor, O.B.E.

MILLS, Arthur, M.B.E., *b.* 19 June, 1876 ; *s.* of Joseph Mills, of Great Yarmouth ; *m.* Gertrude Helen, *d.* of William Allen, of Thelma, Hamworthy, Dorset. *Educ. :* St. Edmund's, Sheffield. *War Work :* Invalided out of Army, May, 1917 ; commenced duties in Nov. 1917 as Works Manager at No. 7 National Sawmilling Factory, Hamworthy, Dorset, subsequently as General Manager, producing case-boards for munitions. *Address :* 58, Myddelton Street, Clerkenwell, London, E.C. 1. (M9040)

MILLS, Arthur John, C.B.E., *b.* 11 Feb. 1886. *s.* of Alfred C. Mills, of Streatham ; *m.* Margaret, *d.* of Geo. Hay, J.P., of Snaresbrook. *Educ. :* Bishopsgate School. Produce Agent ; late Chairman Home and Foreign Produce Exchange, and Provision Trade Benevolent Institution ; Member, Butter and Cheese Import Board (Ministry of Food). *War Work :* Chairman, Pricing Committee for Provisions (Provision Exchanges of U.K.) to fix Maximum prices for Ministry of Food ; Representative of Ministry of Food, New York and Montreal. *Address :* Holly House, Buckhurst Hill, Essex. *Club :* Constitutional. (C2810)

MILLS, Capt. Charles, O.B.E., A.I.F.

MILLS, Charles Augustus, M.B.E., *b.* 1850 ; *s.* of C. A. Mills, of Leyton, Essex. *Educ. :* Charterhouse, and R.I.E.C. Cooper's Hill. P.W.D., India. *War Work :* Propaganda work in Italy. *Clubs :* East India United Service ; Savage. (M2172)

MILLS, Lieut. Charles Egerton, M.B.E.

MILLS, Lieut. Charles James, O.B.E., R.N.V.R.

MILLS, Sir Charles William, Bart., O.B.E.

MILLS, Capt. Eric, O.B.E.

MILLS, Capt. Ernest James, O.B.E., M.A., *b.* 6 Feb. 1886 ; *s.* of Rev. J. Mills, B.A., of Hale, Cheshire. *Educ. :* Burton-on-Trent Grammar School ; Univ. Birmingham ; St. John's Coll., Cambridge. Mathematical Master, Coatham Grammar School, Redcar ; Tutor, Training Coll., Chester, etc. ; Clerk, Ramsbottom Tottington and Turton Education Committees, Lancs Education Committee. *War Work :* Lieut. and Capt. 5th Earl of Chester's Batt., Cheshire Regt. (T.F.) ; Capt. and Adjutant, 39 Army Batt. M.G.C. ; Education Officer (Hospitals) London District ; 2½ years with the B.E.F., France ; mentioned in despatches. *Address :* 50, Westgate Hall, Cheshire. (O2642)

MILLS, Esther Mary, M.B.E., *b.* 1885 ; *d.* of Francis Mills, of Pillerton, Warwick. *Educ. :* Crescent House Coll., Bedford. Welfare Supervisor, Ordnance Survey. *War Work .* Unit Administrator, Q.M.A.A.C., attached Overseas Branch Ordnance Survey. *Address :* Manor House, Pillerton, Warwick. (M4555)

MILLS, Florence Leyland, M.B.E., *b.* 27 June, 1886 ; *d.* of James Leyland Mills, of Liverpool. *Educ. :* Girton House, Liverpool. *War Work :* Assist. Hon. Sec., Liverpool Centre St. John Ambulance Association ; Commandant, West Lancs Reserve V.A.D. ; Lady Divisional Supt., Abercromby Nursing Div. St. John Ambulance Brigade Service, from Aug. 1914. *Address :* 88, Sheil Road, Liverpool. (M2173)

MILLS, Capt. Geoffrey Horner, O.B.E., R.A.S.C. (T.).

MILLS, Lieut. Gerald Edgell, O.B.E., R.N.V.R.

MILLS, Capt. Harry Sturgess, M.B.E., L.C.P., R.A.

MILLS, Major Henry Percival, O.B.E.

MILLS, Major James Jesse, O.B.E., R.A.O.C.

MILLS, Janet Melanie Ailsa, M.B.E., *b.* 1 April, 1894 ; *d.* of Harry Mills, of Mitcham. *Educ. :* 54, Kensington Gardens Square, London, and Beauregard, Vevey, Switzerland. *War Work :* Directorate of Military Operations, War Office, for 4 years. *Address :* 91, Clapham Road, S.W. 9. (M3851)

MILLS, John Edwin, M.B.E.

MILLS, Capt. Paul Hubert, O.B.E., Can. F.A.

MILLS, Robert Clarkson, M.B.E.

MILLS, Samuel, M.B.E.

MILLS, Comm. Tom Lakin, O.B.E., R.D., R.N.R.

MILLS, Hon. Violet Louisa, M.B.E., *b.* 12 Feb 1872 ; *d.* of Charles Henry, 1st Baron Hillingdon, of Wildernesse, Sevenoaks (*see* BURKE'S *Peerage*). *War Work :* Commandant Wildernesse V.A.D. Hospital. *Address :* The Grey House, Leat, Sevenoaks. *Club :* Ladies' Empire. (M9042)

MILLS, Major Walter Henry, O.B.E.

MILLS, William Henry, M.B.E.

MILLS, Zae, M.B.E.

MILLSON, George, O.B.E., M.R.C.S., L.R.C.P., *b.* 1844 ; *s.* of E. Millson, of Donington, Lincolnshire ; *m.* Sarah Ellen, *d.* of W. Butlin, of Duston House, Northampton. *Educ. :* Boston and St. Mary's Hospital, Paddington. Medical Officer of Health of the Metropolitan Borough of Southwark. *War Work :* General Health work and the Examination of all food-stuffs for the government. *Address :* 90, Angell Road, Brixton, S.E. (O10972)

MILLTON, James Dothie, M.B.E.

MILLWARD, Lieut.-Col. Harry Dacres, O.B.E.

MILLWARD, Richard Tudor, M.B.E.

MILLWARD, Thomas, M.B.E., *b.* 9 April, 1865 ; *s.* of the late John Millward, of Cardiff ; *m.* Margaret Clare, *d.* of John Coughlan, of Clashmore and Youghal. *Educ. :* Privately. *War Work :* Superintending Clerk R.A.S.C. Records. *Address :* 76, Wood Street, Woolwich, S.E. 18. (M4343)

MILMAN, Capt. Hugh, O.B.E., R.A., and R.A.F.

MILNE, Alice Stuart, Mrs., M.B.E.

MILNE, Lieut.-Col. Charles, O.B.E., M.B., I.M.S

MILNE, Claire Marjoribanks, Lady, M.B.E., *b.* 10 July, 1885 ; *d.* of Sir John N. Maitland, Baronet, of 8, Grassington Road, Eastbourne ; *m.* Gen. Sir George Francis, *s.* of George Milne, of Westwood, Aberdeen. *Educ.:* Wycombe Abbey, Bucks. *War Work:* Secretarial work, G.H.Q., in France. *Address:* 4, Thurloe Court, S.W. 3. *Club:* Empress. (M9045)

MILNE, Lieut. Edward Arthur, M.B.E., R.N.V.R.

MILNE, Florence, Mrs., M.B.E., *b.* Sept. 1864 ; *d.* of J. W. Barclay, of Glenbuchat, Aberdeenshire ; *m.* George, *s.* of James Milne, of Kinaldie. *War Work:* Commandant, V.A.D., Aberdeen 34 ; County Director Aberdeenshire Red Cross, Convener Aux. Hospital, Drumrossie, 1914–19 ; Chairman, Ladies' Needlework Guild, 1st Scottish General Hospital, 1914–19. *Addresses:* Logie, Pitcaple ; Glenbuchat, Aberdeenshire. (M9046)

MILNE, George, M.B.E.

MILNE, George Torrance, O.B.E., *b.* 9 Aug. 1862 ; *s.* of Peter Milne, of Edinburgh ; *m.* Betty, *d.* of John Golby, of Thorpe Mandeville, Northants. *Educ.:* Privately, and George Watson's Coll.; Edinburgh Univ. 1911–12, Special Commissioner of the Board of Trade in Central America, Colombia and Venezuela ; 1913–18, H.M. Trade Commissioner in Australia ; 1918–19, H.M. Senior Trade Commissioner in Canada and Newfoundland ; 1919–20 H.M. Commercial Sec. of Legation at Havana. *Address:* Dept. of Overseas Trade, 35, Old Queen Street, S.W. *Club:* British Empire. (O3840)

MILNE, Lieut.-Col. George Wardlaw, C.B.E., D.S.O., R.A.M.C.

MILNE, Isabella Steele, M.B.E., Q.M.A.A.C.

MILNE, James William, O.B.E., *b.* 6 Nov. 1869 ; *s.* of James Milne, of Aberdeen ; *m.* Jeanie McGavin, *d.* of James Kinghorn, J.P., of Aberdeen. *Educ.:* Aberdeen Grammar School and University. Chartered Accountant ; Partner in the firm of Cooper Brothers & Co., London and Liverpool. *War Work:* Accountant, Munition Levy Dept., Ministry of Munitions Sept. 1915, to Jan. 1918 ; Director, Contract and Prices Section, Machine Tool Dept., Ministry of Munitions, Jan. 1918, to Nov. 1918 ; Liquidator, Machine Tool Dept., M. of M., Nov. 1918, to June, 1919. *Address:* 25, Balls Road, Oxton, Birkenhead. *Clubs:* Aberdeen University ; Royal Aberdeen Golf. (O11787g)

MILNE, John Alexander, C.B.E., J.P., *b.* 11 Aug. 1872 ; *s.* of late Rev. John Milne, M.A. (Senior Chaplain, H.M. Forces); *m.* Isabel Mary, *d.* of the late Theobald Theobald, J.P., M.F.H., of The Abbey, Sutton Courtenay, Berks. *Educ.:* Rathmines School, Dublin, and privately. Member Berkshire County Council, 1904–07; J.P. for Berkshire. *War Work:* Served R.N.A.S., 1914–15 ; Member, Admiralty Committee War Trade Dept. 1915–16 ; Chairman, Linen and Silk Committee, W.T.D., 1916–19 ; Member Flax Control Board, 1917–20 ; Member Consultative Council Imports and Exports, 1918–19 ; conducted Special Missions to Paris in connection with blockade, on behalf of Foreign Office, 1916–17. *Addresses:* Lennox Wood, Windlesham, Surrey ; 25, Portland Court, London, W. *Clubs:* Carlton ; Caledonian. (C569)

MILNE, John Archibald Douglas, O.B.E.

MILNE, John F., M.B.E. *Educ.:* Daniel Stewart's Coll., Edinburgh. Constructional Engineer, Anglo-Persian Company, London. *War Work:* Defences of London and various Munition Factories, amongst which were Hereford and Lancaster. (M764)

MILNE, Rev. John Lloyd, O.B.E., B.A., *b.* 30 Dec. 1889 ; *s.* of John Martyn Milne, of London. *Educ.:* Monkton Combe School, Bath ; and Wadham Coll., Oxford. Assistant Curate St. Anne, Limehouse. *War Work:* Chaplain to Forces, 4th Class ; organised Canteens on Doiran Front, Salonika, and Dedeagatch. *Address:* Limehouse Rectory, E. 14. (O6510)

MILNE, John Robertson, M.B.E.

MILNE, Kenneth John, C.B.E., *b.* 1 Sept. 1880 ; *s.* of John Vine Milne, of St. Andrew's, Burgess Hill, Sussex ; *m.* Maud Lilian, *d.* of the late John Innes, of Weymouth, Dorset. *Educ.:* Westminster School. Assistant Sec., Ministry of Pensions ; Admitted Solicitor, 1903 ; entered Civil Service (Estate Duty Office, Somerset House), 1904. *War Work:* Ministry of Pensions as Private Sec. to Sir Matthew Nathan, G.C.M.G., 1918 ; appointed Assistant Sec., Ministry of Pensions, 1920. *Address:* 8, Avondale Road, South Croydon. (C2811)

MILNE, Margaret Smith, M.B.E.

MILNE, Lieut.-Col. William Harcourt, O.B.E.

MILNER, Sarah Elizabeth, Mrs., O.B.E., *b.* 1857 ; *d.* of Samuel Roberts ; *m.* William Aldam, *s.* of W. P. Milner. *War Work:* Vice-President Derbyshire Branch, B.R.C.S. *Address:* Totley Hall, Derbyshire. (O1671)

MILTON, Major James Clymo, M.B.E., East Lancashire Regt., *b.* 19 May, 1869 ; *s.* of John Penn Milton, of Penzance, Cornwall ; *m.* Lilian Mary, *d.* of late Andrew Baird, of Plymouth, Devon. *Educ.:* Blundell's School, Tiverton. Solicitor. Member of Town Council Chorley (Lancs) ; Commissioner for Oaths ; Officer Volunteer Force, June, 1887, to Jan. 1901; at present Staff Officer at War Office. *War Work:* Raised Company (New Army) at Chorley in Sept. 1914 ; served in United Kingdom, Egypt, Sinai Peninsula, and France ; Regimental and Staff Employment ; at present on staff at G.H.Q., Ireland ; Capt. Sept. 1914 ; Major Jan. 1915. *Address:* Russell Square, Chorley, Lancs. *Club:* Old Rectory, Manchester. (M5471)

MILWARD, Eliza Margaret, M.B.E.

MILWARD, Major Robert Spencer, O.B.E.

MINCHIN, Arthur, M.B.E., *b.* 27 May, 1876 ; *s.* of Benjamin Minchin, of Binfield, Berks ; *m.* Alberta Emily, *d.* of W. Ardley, of South Kensington, S.W. and Castle Hedingham, Essex. *Educ.:* Privately. Civil Servant War Office. *War Work:* On the Headquarter Staff dealing with the Administration of War Department property at home and abroad ; the requirements of the Army, and Ministry of Munitions and Air Ministry, threw a heavy strain on the department which was formed into a comprehensive Directorate of Lands with Sir Howard Frank, Bart., as Director-General ; also received mention in Secretary of State's list, 1918. *Address:* 23, Observatory Road, East Sheen, Surrey. (M9048)

MINCHIN, Lieut.-Col. Frederick Frank, C.B.E., D.S.O., M.C., *b.* 1890 ; *s.* of Maj.-Gen. Frederick Falkner Minchin, C.B. Major R.A.F. ; served in Great War, 1914–18 (mentioned in despatches). (C181)

MINETT, Capt. Francis Colin, M.B.E.

MINGARD, Herbert Samuel, M.B.E., *b.* 1 July, 1871 ; *s.* of John Thomas Mingard, of London ; *m.* Nelly, *d.* of Edwin Charles Miles, of London. *Educ.:* City of London School. Fellow of Chartered Institute of Secretaries ; partner in A. Moir & Co., 1, London Wall, Buildings E.C. 2. *War Work:* Lectured on behalf of Belgian Refugee Funds during winter of 1914–15 ; joined High Explosives Dept. of War Office (subsequently Explosives Dept. of Ministry of Munitions), Jan. 1915 ; became Assistant Director, Sub-Section Director, and finally Section Director of Contracts Section ; continued till Dec. 1919 as Director of Sales in Explosives and Chemicals Section of Disposal Board. *Address:* Denham, 27, Fitzwarren Gardens, Highgate, N. 19. *Club:* New City. (M766)

MINNS, Lieut. Alfred, M.B.E.

MINSON, Herbert, M.B.E., I.C.S.

MINTER, Capt. George Ash, M.B.E., R.A.S.C.

MINTER, Lieut. Joseph Alfred, O.B.E., R.N.

MINTER, Percy, C.B.E., *b.* 3 March, 1866 ; *s.* of John Minter, of Norwood Green, Southall, Middlesex ; *m.* Mary, *d.* of Charles West, of Pangbourne, Berks. *Educ.:* Philological School, Marylebone. Deputy Director of Navy Contracts, Admiralty. *War Work:* Supervision of patents for Naval inventions ; negotiation and administration of contracts for torpedoes, mines, wireless telegraph apparatus, clothing, textile materials, provisions, and various other stores and appliances for the Navy. *Address:* Staddleswood, St. Mary's Platt, Sevenoaks. (C2812)

MINTON, Richard Caldwell, O.B.E.

MINTY, Major Thomas William, O.B.E. I.M.S.

MIREHOUSE, 2nd Lieut. Henry William, M.B.E.

MIRRLEES, Major Arthur, O.B.E., T.D., *b.* 21 Aug. 1873 ; *s.* of late James Buchanan Mirrlees, of Redlands, Glasgow ; *m.* Anna Fraser, *d.* of late Col. John Kennedy, of Brookside, Sandbach, Cheshire, and Kirkland, Thornhill, Dumfriesshire. *Educ.:* Loretto School, and Trinity Coll., Cambridge. *War Work:* Served with Sherwood Rangers Yeomanry in Gallipoli, Serbia, Macedonia, Egypt, Palestine, and Commandant Prisoners of War Camps, Kantara, Egypt. *Address:* Hingham, Attleborough, Norfolk. *Club:* Bath.

MITCHELL, Albert Ernest, O.B.E.

MITCHELL, Alexander, M.B.E.

MITCHELL, Lieut. Alfred Henry, M.B.E., M.C., Dorsetshire Regt., *b.* 27 Aug. 1888 ; *s.* of Alfred Mitchell, of Rocky Lane, Liverpool ; *m.* Selina Doris, *d.* of Wm. Jones, M.D. and H.B., of Liverpool. *Educ.:* Brae Street Science School, Liverpool. *War Work:* France and Belgium, Feb. 1915, to June, 1918 ; wounded twice ; served with 6th Batt. King's Liverpool Regt. (in ranks), and 6th Dorsetshire Regt. in commissioned ranks and as Adjutant ; Staff Capt. March 1919 to May, 1920. *Addresses:* 22, Bridgecroft Road, Wallasey, Cheshire, and 14, Denbigh Road, Bayswater, W. 11. (M6679)

MITCHELL, Lieut.-Col. Arthur Brownlow, O.B.E., R.A.M.C.

MITCHELL, Arthur Martin, O.B.E., M.D., B.Ch., D.P.H.

MITCHELL, Major Charles, D.S.O., O.B.E. Grenadier Guards and a D.A.A.G. during Great War, 1914–18 (mentioned in despatches). (O6400)

MITCHEL, Lieut. Donald Robert, M.B.E., R.A.F.

MITCHELL, Eliza Fraser, Mrs., O.B.E. Rendered services to Australian Branch of British Red Cross Soc. during Great War. (C366)

MITCHELL, Elizabeth Duff, M.B.E.

MITCHELL, Capt. Frank Brigham, O.B.E., *b.* 16 Dec. 1870 ; *s.* of Ald. C. T. Mitchell, J.P., of Clitheroe, Lancashire. *Educ.:* Clitheroe Royal Grammar School. Mentioned in despatches. *War Work:* Recruited Clitheroe Co. for 2/4th (Reserve) Batt. E. Lancs Regt. T.F. ; (M.E.F.) Gallipoli, 1915, with 4th Lancs Regt. ; wounded ; (E.E.F.) Egypt to Feb. 1917 ; (B.E.F.) France, to Nov. 1917 ; Medical Board declared unfit for front line, (I.E.F.) Italy to Jan. 1919. *Address:* Almonds, Clitheroe, Lancashire. (O2922)

MITCHELL, Frank Carlyle, O.B.E.

MITCHELL, Frank Herbert, C.B.E., *b.* 13 June, 1872 ; *s.* of R. A. H. Mitchell, of Eton ; *m.* Grace Penelope, *d.* of Thomas Maffey, of Rugby. *Educ.:* Eton and Oxford. Press Secretary, Buckingham Palace. *War Work:* Assistant Director, Official Press Bureau, 1915–19. *Address:* Forest House, Crowborough, Sussex. *Clubs:* Union ; M.C.C. (C249)

MITCHELL, George Bennett, M.B.E., F.S.I., F.I.S.A., J.P., D.L., *b.* 27 Nov. 1865 ; *s.* of Thomas Mitchell, Shipmaster, of Aberdeen ; *m.* Margaret A., *d.* of James Angus, of Mauritius. *Educ.:* Aberdeen. Architect. *War Work:* Transport Officer for B.R.C.S. in North East of Scotland, and other

Red Cross work. *Addresses:* 148, Union Street, Aberdeen; Cean-na-coil, Aboyne, Aberdeenshire. *Club:* Royal Scottish Automobile. (M767)

MITCHELL, Hélène Penelope Doris, M.B.E., *b.* 15 Nov. 1888; *d.* of John Louis Mitchell, Barrister-at-law, of Inner Temple. *Educ.:* Privately; Germany; France. Was Sec. to Greek Delegation during the Balkan Peace Conference in London, 1912. *War Work:* Sub-section Director, Dept. of Foreign Aircraft Services, Dept. of Aircraft Production (Ministry of Munitions); Resident Managing Sec. of the Bushey Heath Belgian Refugees Home, Oct. 1914, to April, 1916; Peace Conference, Paris, Dec. 1918, to May, 1920. *Address:* 82, St. George's Square, London, S.W. 1. (M9051)

MITCHELL, Col. Hugh Henry Gordon, O.B.E.

MITCHELL, James, O.B.E., J.P.

MITCHELL, Capt. and Qr.-Mr. James, M.B.E.

MITCHELL, James Knight, M.B.E.

MITCHELL, John Adamson, M.B.E.

MITCHELL, John Edwin, O.B.E., J.P., *s.* of late Henry Mitchell, of Edgbaston; *m.* Bertha, *d.* of late Joseph Moore, of Hagley House, Worcestershire. Barrister-at-law of the Middle Temple. *War Work:* Purchased horses for the Army; Chairman of South Staffordshire Appeal Tribunal; Chairman of Labour Advisory Committee; Member of Local Road Transport Committee; appointed representative of Bar Council on Committee for demobilised Officers, etc. *Address:* Firrwood, Rowington, Warwick. (O10974)

MITCHELL, Major John Malcolm, O.B.E., M.C.

MITCHELL, Capt. John Marsters, O.B.E., M.B., R.A.M.C.

MITCHELL, John Methven, M.B.E., L.A., *b.* 21 Dec. 1887; *s.* of John Mitchell, of 4 Prospect Place, Dundee; *m.* Ruth Ina, *d.* of William D. Patrick, of Arden, Cupar. *Educ.:* Dundee High School, and Univ. of Edinburgh. Joint County Clerk of Fife; Joint Clerk to Cupar District Committee; Joint Clerk to Fife and Kinross Sanatorium Board; Clerk to Income Tax Commissioners for Cupar District. *War Work:* Sec. and Treas. to Fife War Pensions Committee; Executive Officer to Fife Food Control Committee; Sec. to Cupar District War Savings Committee; Sec. to Cupar and St. Andrews Military Service Tribunals; Sec. to Fife Central Agriculture Committee and Cupar District Profiteering Committee. *Address:* St. Helens, Cupar, Fife. (M9052)

MITCHELL, Capt. John Mitchell, O.B.E., R.A.F.

MITCHELL, Capt. John Phimister, O.B.E., M.B., R.A.M.C. (S.R.)

MITCHELL, Capt. Lachlan Martin Victor, O.B.E., M.B., R.A.M.C. (T.).

MITCHELL, Lawrence Yuille, M.B.E., *b.* 28 Oct. 1870; *s.* of George Mitchell, of Glasgow; *m.* Marie Helen Lilla Hall, *d.* of James Arthur Campbell, of Irvine. *Educ.:* High School, Glasgow. Assistant City Assessor, Glasgow. *War Work:* Reception of and arranging Hospitality to Belgian refugees in Scotland under the auspices of the Corporation of the City of Glasgow. *Address:* Umtata, Newlands, Glasgow. *Club:* Palette, Glasgow. (M9053)

MITCHELL, Margaret Florence, M.B.E., *b.* 5 May, 1893; *d.* of James Mitchell. *Educ.:* Clapham High School. Instructress of Domestic Economy. *War Work:* Assistant cook in Women's Legion working in the Infantry Barracks, York. Nov. 1916, to April, 1917; Assistant Superintendent Women's Legion, Cookery Section, at Rest Camps, Folkestone, May, 1917, to Oct. 1917, when this section of the Women's Legion was absorbed by Q.M.A.A.C.; promoted Unit Administrator Q.M.A.A.C., Rest Camps, Folkestone, March, 1918, to Aug. 1919. *Address:* 3, Magdalen Road, Wandsworth Common, London, S.W. 18. (M5472)

MITCHELL, Mary Birch, M.B.E., *b.* 29 July, 1884; *d.* of Charles Thomas Mitchell, Barrister-at-law, Lincoln's Inn. *Educ.:* Notting Hill High School; University Coll., London. Clerk, Foreign Office. *War Work:* Sept. 1915, to Jan. 1916; Friends' War Victims Relief Committee, Udenvluchtoord, Holland; June to July, 1916, Herb collecting near Windermere; Oct. 1916, Clerk, Foreign Office. *Address:* 50, Platt's Lane, N.W. 3. (M9054)

MITCHELL, Percival Ambler, O.B.E.

MITCHELL, Rev. Percy Robert, O.B.E.

MITCHELL, Lieut.-Col. Peter, O.B.E., R.A.M.C. (T.).

MITCHELL, Peter, O.B.E., Medaille du Roi Albert, *b.* 29 Oct. 1880; *s.* of Andrew Mitchell, of Tudhoe, Co. Durham; *Educ.:* Tudhoe C.E. School, and privately. First Class Clerk in the Office of the Clerk of the Peace for Northumberland. *War Work:* Hon. Sec. Northumberland Belgian Relief Fund. *Address:* The Moothall, Newcastle-upon-Tyne. (O3052)

MITCHELL, Peter Chalmers, C.B.E., F.R.S., D.Sc.- LL.D., *b.* 23 Nov. 1864; *s.* of Rev. Alex. Mitchell, D.D., of Dunfermline, N.B.; *m.* Lilian Bessie, *d.* of Rev. Charles Pritchard, D.D., F.R.S., of Oxford. *Educ.:* Aberdeen and Oxford. Sec. Zoological Society of London; Editorial Staff "The Times." *War Work:* Attached Directorate Military Intelligence, War Office; Liaison Officer, Directorate Military Intelligence and British War Mission and Air Ministry. *Address:* Zoological Society, Regrent's Park, N.W. 8. *Club:* Reform. (C1007)

MITCHELL, Capt. Richard Galbraith, O.B.E., R.A.F.

MITCHELL, Robert, M.B.E., M.D., C.M., *b.* 23 Jan. 1867; *s.* of John Mitchell, of Denhill, Fynie, Aberdeenshire, N.B. *Educ.:* King's Coll., Old Aberdeen, and Aberdeen Univ. District Medical Officer and Public Vaccinator to the Doncaster Union. *War Work:* M.O. for Hooton-Pagnell Hall Auxiliary Military Hospital (No. 134), Doncaster, from Nov.

1914, to March, 1919; M.O. for Belgian soldiers and refugees at Hickleton, Doncaster. *Address:* The Elms, Pickburn, Doncaster. *Club:* Doncaster. (M9055)

MITCHELL, Major Robert, C.B.E., J.P., *b.* 1855. Sometime Director of Training, Min. of Pensions. (C250)

MITCHELL, Lieut.-Col. Spencer, O.B.E.

MITCHELL, Thomas John, M.B.E.

MITCHELL, Walter, M.B.E.

MITCHELL, Lieut. William Alfred James, M.B.E., R.G.A. (T.).

MITCHELL, 2nd Lieut. William Boyd, M.B.E.

MITCHELL, Major Wright, O.B.E., B.A., B.Ch., B.A.O., M.B., R.A.M.C. *Educ.:* St. Andrews Coll., and Trinity Coll., Dublin. *War Work:* Served with Exped. Forces in France, East Africa, and Italy. *Address:* 31, Ann Street, Edinburgh, Scotland. (O4488h)

MITCHELMORE, Shipwright-Lieut. Augustus John, M.B.E., R.N.

MITCHIE, Henry Maurice, O.B.E. (O6509)

MITCHISON, Mary Emeline, Mrs., O.B.E.; *d.* of the late Thomas Russell, C.M.G., of Normanswood, Farnham, Surrey; *m.* Arthur Maw Mitchison, *s.* of the late W. A. Mitchison, of The Manor House, Sunbury-on-Thames. *War Work:* Organised, financed, and maintained a hospital for Officers with 30 beds, from April, 1915 to end of the war; the Hospital was known as Mrs. Mitchison's Hospital, Clock House, Chelsea Embankment. *Address:* 10, Eaton Gate, Eaton Square, S.W. 1. (O10976)

MITFORD, Dorothy Frances, M.B.E.; *d.* of Edward Mitford, of Northumberland (*see* BURKE'S *Landed Gentry*). *War Work:* Ordinary Member of Filey V.A.D. 1915–17; Deputy Commandant of another hospital opened at Filey for 45 patients, 1917–19. *Address:* Hunmanby Vicarage, Yorkshire. (M9057)

MITTELL, Lieut. Richard William, O.B.E., R.N.V.R.

MITTON, Col. George Jones, C.B.E.

MIZEN, Frederick George, M.B.E.

MOAT, Major William, O.B.E., T.D., J.P., D.L. *b.* 9 Oct. 1867; *s.* of Robert Moat, of Johnson Hall, Staffs; *m.* Sibyl Frances, *d.* of William Francis Spencer, of 26, Sloane Court, S.W. *Educ.:* Exeter Coll., Oxford. *War Work:* Assistant Food Commissioner, Midland Division. *Address:* Johnson Hall, Eccleshall, Staffs. *Club:* Wellington. (O10976A)

MOBBS, Arthur Noel, O.B.E.

MOBERLY, Lieut. James Edward, M.B.E.

MOCATTA, Major Valentine Elkin, O.B.E.

MOCK, William John, O.B.E., F.S.A.A.; *s.* of William Mock, of St. Austell; *m.* Nora Louise, *d.* of William Gale, of St. Austell. *Educ.:* St. Austell School. County Accountant for Cornwall. *War Work:* Hon. Sec. Cornish Fishing Vessels Insurance Society, Ltd.; Hon. Accountant and Auditor Cornwall War Agriculture Executive Committee; Hon. Auditor, Cornwall War Pensions Committee; Hon. Auditor, Cornwall Patriotic Fund; Hon. Auditor, Cornwall Lord Lieutenant's Land Settlement Committee. *Address:* Elmwood. Truro, Cornwall. (O10977)

MOCKETT, Capt. Vere, M.B.E.

MODLIN, Isaac Gibson, O.B.E., M.D., B.S., L.S.A., Esquire of Order of St. John, *b.* 24 Oct. 1865; *s.* of Thomas Modlin, of Sunderland; *m.* Gertrude Jane Alice, *d.* of William Harrison Smith, of London. *Educ.:* Durham School; Univ. of Durham Coll. of Medicine, Newcastle-on-Tyne. Hon. Surgeon to Monkswearmouth Hospital, Sunderland; Chairman Health Committee; Chairman Housing Committee, Sunderland Corporation. *War Work:* Commandant and Hon. Surgeon to No. IV. Co. Durham V.A.D. Hospital, Jeffrey Hall, Sunderland. *Address:* 148, Roker Avenue, Sunderland. (O10978)

MOELLER, Winnifred, Mrs., M.B.E.

MOENS, Lieut.-Col. Seaburne Godfrey Arthur May, C.I.E., C.B.E., Knight of St. John, *b.* 25 Sept. 1876; *s.* of the late Seaburne May Moens, I.C.S. *Educ.:* Charterhouse, and "Wrens." Headmaster, Down House, Rottingdean. *War Work:* Member of 1st British Red Cross Motor Ambulance Unit in Italy, 1915; Red Cross Commissioner in Mesopotamia and in Persia, 1916–19. *Address:* Down House, Rottingdean, Sussex. *Club:* Windham. (C570)

MOFFAT, Capt. Elijah James, M.B.E. Master of s.s. "Ipu."

MOFFAT, Paymaster-Lieut.-Comm. George, M.B.E., R.N.R.

MOFFAT, James, O.B.E., J.P., Provost of Royal Burgh of Forfar since 1907, La Médaille du Roi Albert for assisting the Belgians, *b.* 1848; *s.* of John Moffat, of Forfar; *m.* Margaret, *d.* of James Lemon, of Huntly, Aberdeenshire. *Educ.:* Forfar. Hon. Sheriff Substitute for Forfarshire; Chairman of the Forfarshire Educational Authority; Chairman of the Forfarshire Insurance Committee. *War Work:* Member of Appeal Tribunal and Territorial Association for Forfar, and also Vice-President of the Forfarshire Red Cross Branch. *Address:* Mount Feredith, Forfar. (O586)

MOFFAT, John, C.B.E.; *s.* of John Moffat. *Educ.:* Cheam, Eton, and Cambridge. Chevalier of Legion of Honour; Commander Order Leopold II.; Medaille d'Academie; Commander Order St. Sava (of Serbia); Knight Commander of Crown of Italy; contested Elgin Burghs for House of Commons. *War Work:* Charge of actual Distribution of Propaganda in printed form in U.S.A. for Production Dept. of Information Bureau of British Foreign Office; Member Advisory Committee of British and Canadian Recruiting

Mission ; Chairman Direct Appeal Committee of British and Canadian Patriotic Fund ; Chairman National Allied Commission in U.S.A., which raised fifty millions for Allied Relief ; Vice-President, Federation American Agencies for Relief in France ; President, International Reconstruction League ; Executive Chairman, French Heroes Lafayette Memorial Fund Inc. ; Chairman, French Tuberculous Children's Fund ; Chairman Belgian Prisoners of War Fund ; Chairman of American Tribute to Italy. *Address* : Ritz-Carlton Hotel, New York. *Club* : Coffee House, N. Y.   (C1008)

MOFFAT, Rennie John, M.B.E.

MOFFATT, Alexander George, M.B.E.

MOGER, Walter Henry, O.B.E.

MOGG, Major Graham Beauchamp Coxeter REES-. O.B.E., R.A.V.C.

MOGGRIDGE, Harry Weston, O.B.E.   (O2645)

MOHR, Capt. Reginald Harry, M.B.E., Aust. A.P.C.

MOHR, Major Stanley Melbourne, O.B.E., M.C., M.I.E.E., *b.* 7 July, 1885 ; *s.* of M. Mohr, of Hampstead, London ; *m.* Marjorie, *d.* of Ernest Joseph, of Hampstead, London. *Educ.* : Univ. Coll. School, and London Univ. Electrical Engineer ; General Sales Manager, Micanite and Insulators Co., Ltd., Empire Works, Walthamstow, London. *War Work* : Served with 12th Service Batt., Sherwood Foresters, B.E.F. France, Aug. 1915, to Aug. 1918 ; served with North Russian Expeditionary Force, Archangel Front, as General Staff Officer (Intelligence), Sept. 1918, to Oct. 1919 ; received Order of St. Stanislaus and of St. Anne, 2nd Class with Swords. *Address* : 9, Albemarle Mansions, Heath Drive, Hampstead, London, N.W. 3. *Clubs* : Royal Automobile ; Road.   (O6803)

MOILLET, Major Hubert Mainwaring Keir, O.B.E., R.E.

MOIR, Alexander, O.B.E.

MOIR, Alexander Penrose David, M.B.E. ; *s.* of the Very Rev. Dean Moir, of Jedburgh, Roxburghshire. *Educ.* : Hest Academy, Jedburgh, and Sutton House, Dartford. *War Work* : Hon. Auditor to Scottish War Savings Committee, and other war work. *Address* : Linkslea, Musselburgh, Midlothian.   (M2179)

MOIR, Capt. Archibald Patrick, M.B.E.

MOIR, Charles Robert, O.B.E. ; *s.* of Andrew Moir, of Aberdeen and London ; *m.* Elizabeth, *d.* of C. J. Bond, of Blackheath. Army Auditor for Scotland. *Address* : Westerlea, Esslemont Road, Edinburgh.   (O10980)

MOIR, Capt. George, O.B.E., F.R.C.V.S., *b.* 19 April, 1875 ; *s.* of Robert Moir, of Cluny, Aberdeenshire ; *m.* Elsie Anita, *d.* of William Harvey Wellington, of Penzance. *Educ.* : Gordon's Coll., Aberdeen ; Royal Veterinary Coll., Edinburgh. Government Veterinary Surgeon, Perak, Federated Malay States. *War Work* : 1916, No. 11 Veterinary Hospital ; later, attached 1st Brigade, R.F.A. ; 1917, Vet. Bacteriologist, B.S.F. ; 1918, Officer in charge Base Veterinary Laboratory, B.S.F. *Address* : Taiping, Perak, Federated Malay States.   (O3053)

MOIR, Ian, O.B.E.

MOIR, John Watson, M.B.E.

MOIR, Margaret Bruce, Lady, O.B.E. : *d.* of John Pennycock, of Ravelston and Dalmeny ; *m.* Sir Ernest William, 1st Bart., *s.* of Alexander M. Moir, of Hampstead. *War Work* : War Savings Women's Advisory Committee (Treas.), Salisbury Square, and organised women for week-end relief work in Munition Factories. *Addresses* : 41, Cadogan Square, S.W. ; Whitehanger, Marley Common, Fernhurst, Sussex.   (O10981)

MOIR, Capt. Thomas, M.B.E

MOIR, William Robertson. M.B.E.

MOIR, Capt. William Mitchell, C.B.E., *b.* 1873 ; *s. o.* the late James Moir, of Bedford Place, Alloa ; *m.* 1905, Edith, *d.* of the late J. A. Bailey, J.P., of Riverview, Alloa. Chief Staff Officer Harwich Destroyer Flotilla during Great War.   (C2231)

MOLD, Lieut. Leonard Ernest, O.B.E., R.E.

MOLE, Charles Johns, M.B.E., A.R.I.B.A., *b.* 6 Feb. 1886 ; *s.* of Charles Mole, of Broadhempston, Totnes ; *m.* Annie, *d.* of Richard Hugh Martin, of Whibble Hill House, Compton, Plymouth. Assistant Architect in H.M. Office of Works. *War Work* : In connection with the erection of buildings urgently required during the war, which were undertaken by H.M. Office of Works. *Address* : Glenlyn, Bowes Road, Walton-on-Thames.   (M9062)

MOLE, Ernest, M.B.E., *b.* 15 Nov. 1875 ; *s.* of William Mole, of Milton-Ernest, Bedford ; *m.* Jessie, *d.* of James Henderson, of Aberdeen. *Educ.* : Commercial School, Bedford. Inspector (Special Service Branch) Criminal Investigation Department, Metropolitan Police. *War Work* : Intelligence Department, Headquarters Staff, Dover Garrison ; in charge of Metropolitan Police attached to British Peace Delegation, Paris, Versailles, and St. Germain, for the signing of German and Austrian Treaties. *Address* : 33, The Chase, Clapham Common, S.W.   (M9063)

MOLESWORTH, Col. William, C.I.E., O.B.E., Y.H.S., *b.* 30 Dec. 1865 ; *s.* of the late Lieut.-Col. Molesworth, R.A., of Cruicksfield, Berwickshire ; *m.* Winifred, *d.* of the late T. E. Weekes, J.P., of Haseldean, Co. Cork. *Educ.* : At Redland Hill House, Clifton, and Durham Univ. *War Work* : Commander-in-Chief's Despatches, Simla, 1918. *Address* : Cruicksfield, near Duns, Berwickshire.   (C747)

MOLINEUX, Capt. George, M.B.E., R.A.S.C.

MOLL, Frederick William, M.B.E.

MOLLER, Major Oden, M.B.E.

MOLLER, Wilhelmina Nancy, Mrs., M.B.E.,

MOLLISON, William Mayhew, C.B.E., M.A., M.Ch., F.R.C.S. For voluntary services at St. Dunstan's.   (C3157)

MOLLOY, Lieut.-Col. Gerald Macleay, O.B.E.

MOLLOY, Gwendolen Beatrice Sanchai May, Mrs., M.B.E., *b.* 1876 ; *d.* of Col. W. T. Markham, of Becca Hall, Yorks ; *m.* 1st, Major Harry Francis Pakenham, 60th Rifles (died 1905), 2ndly. Brian Molloy (King's Messenger, 1902-12), Queen's Own Oxfordshire Hussars, killed in action 1 Nov. 1914. *War Work* : Hon. Sec. Officers' Clothing Branch, Officers' Families Fund. *Address* : 13, Oxford Square, W. 2.   (M9064)

MOLLOY, Major Leonard Greenham Star, C.B.E., D.S.O., M.M., M.A., *b.* 1861, *s.* of the late Richard Molloy, of Rathgar, co. Dublin. *Educ.* : Trin. Coll., Dublin ; is. Major Yeo. Territorial Force Reserve ; served during Great War 1914-17 (despatches) ; *Address* : 3, Brighton Parade, Blackpool : *Club* : Cavalry.   (C1086)

MOLONY, Capt. Brian Charles, O.B.E.

MOLONY, Edmund Alexander, C.B.E., *s.* of Edmund Weldon Molony, *b.* 1866 ; *m.* Ethel Blanche, *d.* of the late Herbert Smith, of Barla, Aligarh Dist., India. *Educ.* : Marlborough ; Emmanuel Coll., Camb. ; entered I.C.S. 1886 ; Commr., Agra Div., United Provinces 1915-19 ; retired 1919 ; sometime a M.L.C., United Provinces of Agra and Oudh ; author of a *Manual of Irrigation Wells.*   (C1086)

MOLONY, Lieut.-Col. Francis Arthur, O.B.E., R.E.

MOLONY, John Barre de Winton, O.B.E., I.M.S., M.B.

MOLONY, Rev. John Patrick, O.B.E., M.C., *b.* 6 Oct. 1875 ; *s.* of Michael Molony, Civil Service. *Educ.* : St. Edward's Coll., Liverpool, and St. Joseph's Coll., Upholland. Senior Chaplain and Vicar-General, Mesopotamian Expeditionary Force. *War Work* : Aug. 1914, to May, 1915, with 2nd Cav. Div. France ; June, 1915, to Sept. 1915, with 2nd Leinsters R.C., 6th Div. ; Sept. 1915, wounded ; Feb. 1916, went to Salonica, on Hospital Ship "Massilia" ; July, 1916, on Somme with 8th L.N.L. ; rejoined 2nd Leinsters, Sept. 1916 ; wounded at Messines, 1917 ; May 5 to present time in Mesopotamia. Awarded M.C., 1915. *Address* : 2, Elmhurst Road, Bruce Grove, N. 17.   (O6672)

MOLYNEAUX, Thomas, M.B.E.

MOLYNEUX, Caroline Elizabeth, Hon. Mrs. Caryl, M.B.E., *b.* Jan, 1848 ; *d.* of 2nd Baron Wenlock, of Escrick Park, York (see BURKE'S *Peerage*) ; *m.* Lieut.-Col. the Hon. Caryl Craven (died 1912), *s.* of 3rd Earl of Sefton, of Croxteth, Liverpool (see BURKE'S *Peerage*). *War Work* : County Sec. Oxfordshire Soldiers' and Sailors' Families Association ; Member Executive Committee, County Red Cross ; President Banbury War Hospital Supply Depot, Queen Mary's Needlework Guild. *Address* : The Red House, Bodicote, Banbury.   (M9065)

MOLYNEUX, Lieut. Edward Arthur, M.B.E., R.A.F.

MOLYNEUX, Rev. Frederick Merivale, M.B.E., M.A., *b.* 10 May, 1885 ; *s.* of Rev. F. E. Molyneux, Rector of Martyrworthy. *Educ.* : Rossall School ; Keble Coll., Oxford ; Cuddesdon Coll. Hon. C. F. (4th Class) ; Vicar of High Wycombe ; and lately Chaplain of Cuddesdon College. *War Work* : C.F., Woolwich, 1916 ; embarked for Mesopotamia, Nov. 1916 ; Chaplain, 40th British General Hospital, Mesopotamia, Jan. 1917, to May, 1917 ; Chaplain 23rd British Stationary Hospital and Isolation Hospital, Baghdad, May, 1917, to Nov. 1917 ; Chaplain, Gen. Headqrs., Mesopotamia Exped. Force, Nov. 1917, to May, 1919 ; mentioned, 1917. *Address* : High Wycombe Vicarage, Bucks.   (M3002)

MOLYNEUX, Thomas Fell, O.B.E.

MONCK, Louise Emilia, M.B.E.

MONCKTON, Lieut.-Col. Thomas Anthony, O.B.E., M.A. (Cantab.), R.A.F., *b.* 22 Oct. 1885 ; *s.* of E. P. Monckton, M.A., J.P., of Fineshade Abbey, Stamford. *Educ.* : Haileybury ; Trinity Coll., Cambridge. Royal Mint, Ottawa, Canada ; Dobel's Metal and Munitions, Birmingham ; Messrs. Johnson and Sons, Refiners, London ; on Chemical, Engineering and Inspection work. *War Work* : Design, invention, and supply of all Hydrogen and Hydrogen-making machinery for British airships and kite balloons throughout war, and in sole charge of that department. *Club* : Junior Carlton.   (O1676)

MONCKTON, William Leopold, O.B.E., *b.* 1865 ; *s.* of Rev. Inglis George (died 1899). Divisional Engineer (London), Great Western Railway. *War Work* : Great Western Railway. *Address* : 19, Upton Road, Slough, Bucks.   (O10982)

MONCRIEFF, John, O.B.E., *b.* 1874 ; *s.* of John Moncrieff, of Perth ; *m.* Marion Isobel, *d.* of — Dunlop, of Glasgow. *Educ.* : Perth Academy, and Switzerland. *War Work* : Establishment of Scientific and Chemical Glassware production in this country ; also services to the Glass Industry generally. *Address* : Summerbank, Perth. *Club* : Caledonian. (O10984)

MONCRIEFF, Lieut.-Col. John Mitchell, C.B.E., M.I.C.E., late R.E., *b.* 8 March, 1865 ; *s.* of the late Mitchell Moncrieff, of South Shields ; *m.* Elizabeth, *d.* of the late P. Allan. Consulting Engineer. Director of Engineering Work, Dept. of Controller-General of Merchant Shipbuilding, Admiralty, July, 1917, to May, 1918. *Address* : 33, Old Jewry, E.C. 2. *Clubs* : St. Stephen's ; New City ; Union (Newcastle-on-Tyne).   (C571)

MONCRIEFF, Capt. Malcolm Matthew, M.B.E.

MONCRIEFF, Major Roger Murray, O.B.E. ; *s.* of the

late Col. Sir Alexander Moncrieff, K.C.B. *Address:* 9, Moore Street, Cadogan Gardens, S.W. 3. *Club:* Bachelors'. (O5587)

MONCRIEFF, Jane Mary SCOTT-, O.B.E., *d.* of the late Major Alexander Pringle Scott-Moncrieff, Bengal Staff Corps. *War Work:* Originator of Canteens at Railway Stations, Aug. 1914; also ran Soldiers' Hostel and Institute at Strensell Camp, York. *Addresses:* Strensall Camp, York; The Castle, Elie, Fife, Scotland. (O10983)

MOND, Violet Florence Mabel, Lady, D.B.E., ; *d.* of the late James Henry Gortze; *m.* Rt. Hon. Sir Alfred Moritz Mond, P.C., M.P., 1st Bart. (*see* BURKE'S *Peerage*), *s.* of the late Ludwig Mond, Ph.D., F.R.S., of 20, Avenue Road, St. John's Wood, and Winnington Hall, Northwich. *Address:* 35, Loundes Square, S.W.; Ffynone, Swansea. (D59)

MONEY, Sir Arthur Wigram, K.C.B., K.B.E., C.S.I., *b.* 23 Oct. 1866; *s.* of the late Gilbert Pocklington Money, of Bengal Civil Service; *m.* Euphemia Mabel, *d.* of the late George James Drummond, of Swaylands, Penshurst, Kent. *Educ.:* Charterhouse, and R.M.A. Woolwich. Major-Gen., General Staff, Mesopotamia, 1916–17; Chief Administrator of Palestine, 1918–19; retired, March, 1920. *Address:* Levington Hall. Ipswich. *Clubs:* United Service; Wellington. (K270)

MONEY, Major Kenneth Robertson, M.B.E.

MONEY, Mildred Catherine, Mrs., O.B.E., *b.* 22 July, 1868; *d.* of William H. FitzHugh; *m.* Col. George Alfred, *s.* of Wigram Elliot Money, I.C.S., Brighton. *War Work:* Commandant, Sussex 66, B.R.C.S., and later Commandant, Sussex Reserve Division. *Address:* Westmeston Place, Hassocks, Sussex. (O10985)

MONEY, Lieut.-Comm. Norman Angel Kyrle, O.B.E., R.N.

MONEY, Col. Robert Cotton, C.M.G., C.B.E., *b.* 1881. Col. (ret.); served in Great War, 1915–19 with Canadian Force (mentioned in despatches). (C1294)

MONEY, Major Rowland, O.B.E.

MONEY, Capt. Wigram Seymour Elliot, O.B.E.

MONEYPENNY, Sir Frederick William, C.B.E., M.V.O., *b.* 6 Feb. 1859; *s.* of Joseph Moneypenny, of Belfast. City Chamberlain, Belfast, and private secretary to the Lord Mayor of that City. *War Work:* Conspicuous service throughout the war. *Address:* Wyncote, Strandtown, Belfast. (C2814)

MONFRIES, Major Charles Babington Smith, C.B.E. special List, Finance Sec. to Commn. Internationale de Ravitaillement; has Order of Crown of Italy. (C572)

MONK, Capt. Errol Francis, O.B.E., R.A.F.

MONK, Geoffrey, M.B.E., *b.* 28 Nov. 1881; *s.* of George H. Monk, of Blackheath. *Educ.:* Stratheden House School, Blackheath; Roan School, Greenwich; King's Coll., Civil Service Dept. Staff Clerk, War Office. *War Work:* In connection with administration of Royal Army Chaplains' Dept. *Address:* 191, Shooters Hill Road, Blackheath, S.E. 3. (M9066)

MONK, Capt. John Bird, M.B.E., H.A.C., *b.* 1883; *s.* of the late Thomas Henry Monk, of Horsell, Surrey, and Toronto. Member of the London Stock Exchange. *War Work:* Proceeded overseas with 1st Batt. H.A.C., in Sept. 1914; Adjutant of Tower of London, 1917–18; Staff Capt., 3rd London Reserve Brigade, 1918–19. *Addresses:* Elm Cottage, Church Road, Hanwell; 62, London Wall, E.C. *Club:* Devonshire. (M5477)

MONK, Owen, M.B.E.

MONK, William Alfred, M.B.E.

MONK, William Dusar, M.B.E., *b.* 23 March, 1882; *s.* of James William Monk, of Isle of Sheppey; *m.* Maud, *d.* of William Henry Savage, of London. Poor Law Administration for 24 years. *War Work:* Quartermaster, Lewisham Military Hospital. *Address:* Summerhill, Leaves Green, Kent. (M775)

MONKHOUSE, John Parry, O.B.E.

MONKHOUSE, Marjorie Mary, O.B.E., W.R.N.S.

MONKHOUSE, Olive Eleanor, M.B.E., B.A.

MONKS, Major Kelson Charles Harley, O.B.E.

MONKS, Lieut. Thomas Vernon, M.B.E.

MONRO, Rev. and Capt. Alexander James Falconer, O.B.E., M.A. (Hon.), *b.* 22 Jan. 1885; *s.* of Alexander Monro, of Fraserburgh, Aberdeenshire. *Educ.:* Aberdeen Grammar School; Aberdeen Univ. Clergyman ordained to U.F. Church, Ancrum, Roxburghshire, Scotland; commissioned 4th Batt. Gordon Highlanders; transferred to 9th West Riding Regt.; Sec. Social Welfare Association of London; Sec. Central Charities Committee; Sec. War Relief Trustees. *War Work:* Left his parish at outbreak of war and joined Gordon Highlanders; commissioned 4th Batt. Gordon Highlanders in France, May, 1915; wounded; transferred 9th West Riding Regt.; invalided out 1918; took charge of repatriation of all British civilian prisoners of war and refugees, under Ministry of Health. *Addresses:* Auchreddie, New Deer, Aberdeenshire; 26, Rosebery Street, Aberdeen. *Club:* Rhymour, Edinburgh. (O10987)

MONRO, Major John Duncan, O.B.E., R.E.

MONRO, Hon. Mary Touneley, Lady, D.B.E., ; *d.* of 1st Baron O'Hagan (*see* BURKE'S *Peerage*); *m.* Gen. Sir Charles Carmichael Monro, G.C.M.G., G.C.B., G.C.S.I., Commander-in-Chief, India (*see* BURKE'S *Peerage*). *Address:* 20, Eccleston Square, S.W. (D38)

MONSELL, Caroline Mary Sybil EYRES-, Mrs., C.B.E., *b.* 1881. *d.* of the late Henry William Eyres, of Dumbleton Hall, Worcestershire; *m.* Bolton Meredith Eyres Monsell, M.P. for S. Div. of Worcestershire. Donor and Administrator of Annexe to King Edward VII. Hospital. *Addresses:* 19, Belgrave Square S.W.; Dumbleton Hall, Evesham. (C573)

MONTAGU, Col. Edward, C.B.E., *b.* 23 Nov. 1861; *s.* of the late General Sir Horace William Montagu, K.C.B., of the Royal Engineers (*see* BURKE'S *Peerage*); *m.* Charlotte Eva, *d.* of Edward Kemble, formerly a Judge of the Supreme Court, Jamaica. *Educ.:* Wellington Coll.; Sandhurst; Staff College. 30 years in Suffolk Regiment; commanded 1st Batt., 1908–1912; Staff Capt., Alexandria, 1898–1903. *War Work:* Hazara Expedition, Burmah, 1888 (medal and clasp); Chin-Lushai Expedition, India, 1889–90 (clasp); European War, 1914–18, first as A.A. and Q.M.G. in France, and afterwards as A.A. and Q.M.G. at Plymouth; twice mentioned in despatches, C.B.E.; 1914 Star, British War Medal, and Allied Victory Medal. *Address:* Holmwood, Swaffham, Norfolk. *Club:* United Service. (C1701)

MONTAGU, Capt. Frederick James Osbaldeston, M.C., *b.* 9 Feb. 1878; *s.* of James Montagu, J.P., of Milton Park, Doncaster (*see* BURKE'S *Landed Gentry*); *m.* Louisa St. Aubyn, *d.* of W. Collier St. A. Angove, of London. *Educ.:* Eton. *War Work:* South Africa, 1899–1902; France, 1915–19. *Address:* Lynford Hall, Norfolk. *Clubs:* Guards'; Travellers'; Naval and Military; Carlton. (O5591)

MONTAGU, Major St. John Edward, O.B.E., Chevalier de la Légion d'Honneur, late Capt. Northumberland Fusiliers, *b.* 26 Jan. 1878; *s.* of the late Right Hon. Lord Robert Montagu, P.C. (*see* BURKE'S *Peerage*). *Educ.:* Charterhouse. Director of Public Companies. *War Work:* South African War, 1899–1902 (mentioned in despatches, Queen's medal and four clasps, King's medal and two clasps); European War, 1914 to end (mentioned in despatches, 1914 Star, General Service, and Victory Medals. *Address:* 27, Austin Friars, E.C. 2. *Club:* Army and Navy. (O5592)

MONTAGU, Capt. Vivian Charles, O.B.E., *b.* 28 July, 1885; *m.* Terese Maria, *d.* of — Donovan. *Educ.:* Cheltenham Coll. *War Work:* Served with Honourable Artillery Company. *Address:* 10, Kensington Court Place, W. 8. *Club:* R.A. (O5593)

MONTAGUE, Capt. Charles Edward, O.B.E.

MONTAGUE, Major Stewart Francis, O.B.E.

MONTEFIORE, Capt. Claude Emanuel, O.B.E.

MONTEFIORE, Captain Leonard Nathaniel, O.B.E.

MONTEFIORE, Edmund SEBAG-, C.B.E., *b.* 2 Nov. 1869; *s.* of Sir Joseph Sebag-Montefiore, of East Cliffe Lodge, Ramsgate; *m.* Alice, *d.* of Col. Lysaght. *Educ.:* Clifton. *War Work:* Home Office. *Clubs:* Bath; Wellington. (C49)

MONTEFIORE, Capt. Geoffrey Edmund SEBAG-, M.B.E., 21st Lancers, *b.* 12 April, 1893; *s.* of Edmund Sebag-Montefiore, of London. *Educ.:* Eton; Sandhurst. *War Work:* 2nd Lieut. attached 9th Lancers, Aug. 1914, to Oct. 1914; Adjutant, Sidi Bishr Camp, Alexandria, Dec. 1915, to April, 1916; Assistant Provost-Marshal, Alexandria, April, 1916, to June, 1917; Assistant Provost-Marshal, Palestine Lines of Communication, June, 1917, to May, 1919. *Address:* Bath Club, Dover Street. *Clubs:* Bath; Cavalry. (M2182)

MONTEITH, Capt. Hugh Glencairn, D.S.O., O.B.E., R.A.M.C., *b.* 1883; *s.* of the late Rev. J. C. Monteith, of Glencairn, Dumfriesshire; *m.* Dorothy Huntly, *d.* of Owen Robert Dunell, of Garboldisham Manor, Norfolk. Great War, 1914–19 (despatches). *Addresses:* 59, Catherine Street, Westminster, S.W.; Moniaive, Dumfriesshire. (O5595)

MONTFORD, Eleanora, M.B.E.; *d.* of Edward Montford, of Ivy House, Church Stoke, and Pentreheyling, Shropshire. *Educ.:* The Cedars, Clapham. *War Work:* Commandant of Broadway House Hospital for four years. *Address:* Ivy House, Church Stoke, Montgomeryshire. (M777)

MONTGOMERY, Lieut.-Col. Alexander, C.B.E., *b.* 4 Nov. 1882; *s.* of Hugh Montgomerie, of Rothesay, Scotland; *m.* Willena Blanche, *d.* of Hugh Mackay, of Trenton, Nova Scotia. *Educ.:* Halifax, Canada. Manager for Nova Scotia and Newfoundland for Furness, Withy & Co., Ltd., Steamship Owners. *War Work:* District Officer Commanding Newfoundland; Deputy Registrar, Military Service Act; Member, Military Service Board; Member, Militia Council; Member Executive and Finance Committees, Newfoundland Patriotic Association. *Address:* Rosemont, Jubilee Road, Halifax, Nova Scotia. *Clubs:* Halifax; City; Waegwaltic, Halifax. (C1884)

MONTGOMERIE, Isabella Macallister, M.B.E., *b.* 27 Sept., 1879; *d.* of John C. Montgomerie, of Dalmore, Stair, Ayrshire. *Educ.:* Privately. *War Work:* Sec. to the Mauchline Division of the Naval and Military War Pensions Committee. *Address:* Dalmore, Stair, Tarbolton Station R.S.O., Ayr. (M778)

MONTGOMERIE, Major Victor, O.B.E., 2nd Life Guards (Reserve of Officers), *b.* 1887; *s.* of Rear-Admiral R. A. J. Montgomerie, C.V.O., C.B., C.M.G.; *m.* Mildred Mary, *d.* of W. Dalglish-Bellasis, of Sundorne Castle, Shrewsbury. *Educ.:* H.M.S. "Britannia." *War Work:* Exped. Force, France, 1914–18. *Address:* Hunsdon House, near Ware, Herts. *Clubs:* Conservative; Junior United Service; Royal Automobile. (O7487)

MONTGOMERIE, Capt. William Dunn, M.B.E., *b.* 3 Jan. 1892; *s.* of J. C. Montgomerie, of Dalmore, Stair, Ayrshire. *War Work:* Joined the Army as a private in the 7th Batt. Cameron Highlanders, Sept. 1914; active service in France, 1915 and 1916, as 2nd Lieut. with 8th Batt. Black Watch; active service in Mesopotamia, 1917–19, as 2nd Lieut. with 2nd Batt. Black Watch, also as Lieut. and Staff Capt. with Army Headquarters. (M4280)

MONTGOMERIE, Mary MOLINEAUX-, M.B.E.

MONTGOMERY, Col. James Alexander Lawrence, C.S.I.,

C.B.E., J.P., D.L., b. 1849; s. of the late Sir Robert Montgomery, G.C.S.I., K.C.B., of New Park, Moville, Ireland; m. 1st, 1876, Jessie Alice, d. of the late Sir Douglas Forsyth, K.C.S I., C.B.; 2nd, Katharine Mary, d. of Col. F. J. Millar, Indian Army. Educ.: Harrow. Entered Gordon Highlanders, 1867; Capt. Indian Army, 1879; Major, 1887; Lieut.-Col. 1893; Hon. Col. 1916; was Assist. Commr. and Settlement Officer, Punjab, 1870–85; Director of Settlement and Revenue Records, 1885–7; appointed Dep. Commr., 1887; Settlement Commr., 1897; Commr. and Sup., 1899; Financial Commr., Punjab, 1904; retired. 1905; was a Member of Indian Police Commn., 1902–3; Commr. of Lands, British E. Africa, 1906–10; High Sheriff for co. Donegal, 1915; British Red Cross Commr. E. Africa Expeditionary Force, 1916–19, with rank of Col. (despatches); Knight of Grace of Order of St. John of Jerusalem in England. Address: St. Columb's, Moville, Londonderry. Club: Junior United Service. (C252)

MONTGOMERY, Major James Thomas, O.B.E.

MONTGOMERY, John, M.B.E.

MONTGOMERY, Samuel, M.B.E., b. 27 May, 1882; s. of Samuel Montgomery, of Park Hall, Antrim, Ireland. Educ.: Model School, Ballymena, Ireland. Hon. Lieut. A.I.F. Dairy Expert. War Work: Enlisted for active service in the Australian Imperial Force, Feb. 1915; obtained commissioned rank, May, 1915; served in Egypt and Gallipoli; disabled and invalided to 3rd London Gen. Hospital, Dec. 1915; returned to Australia, Sept. 1916, and invalided from the Army, Dec. 1916; volunteered again for service in any capacity; returned to England, June, 1917; served in civil capacity in Milk Section, Ministry of Food, until 30 June, 1919. Address: c/o Durban Club, Durban, Natal. (M9071)

MONTGOMERY, Walter Ernest, M.B.E., R.N.

MONTGOMERY, William, M.B.E.

MONTGOMERY, Major William Alexander, C.B.E., D.S.O. Is Capt. and Acting Major, Roy. Irish Rifles; served during Great War, 1914–18 (mentioned in despatches). (C2815)

MONTGOMERY, William Barr, O.B.E.

MONTGOMERY, William Hugh, O.B.E. Assist. Director of Base Records in New Zealand. Address: Wellington, New Zealand. (C1999)

MONTGOMERY, Walter Basil GRAHAM-, O.B.E., J.P., D.L., County of Kinross, b. 20 Aug. 1881; s. of Sir Basil Graham Montgomery, Bart., Stanhope and Kinross House, Kinross. Educ.: Eton Coll., and Trinity Hall, Cambridge. War Work: County Director, Clackmannan and Kinross Voluntary Aid Detachments; Military Representative under M.S.A. and National Service Representative, Kinross-shire Tribunals; Sec. part time Labour Committee, under Ministry of National Service; County Commissioner, Boy Scouts' Association. Addresses: Kinross House, Kinross, Scotland; 25, Bruton Street, London, W. 1. Clubs: Turf; Bachelors'. (O10988)

MONTGOMERY, Mary Maud, Mrs. NURVIS-RUSSELL-, M.B.E.

MONTIETH, David Taylor Monteith, O.B.E.

MONTIETH, Major Joseph Basil Lawrence, O.B.E.

MONTROSE, Violet Hermione, Duchess of, G.B.E.; d. Sir Frederick Graham, 3rd Bart. of Netherby, Cumberland (see BURKE'S Peerage); m. Douglas Beresford Malise Ronald Graham, K.T., 5th Duke of Montrose (see BURKE'S Peerage). Address: Buchanan Castle, nr. Glasgow. (DG10)

MOOD, Major John Muspratt, O.B.E., M.C.

MOODIE, Adam Wilson, O.B.E.

MOODY, Lieut.-Col. Arthur Hatfield, C.B.E., F.J.I., C.C. for Worcestershire, b. 21 Jan. 1875; s. of George Moody, of Stourbridge; m. Mary, d. of C. Holroyd-Doveton, of London. Educ.: King Edward VI.'s Grammar School, Stourbridge, and Wolverley. Journalist and Newspaper Proprietor; Alderman of Borough of Stourbridge. War Work: Selected in 1914 for service under the Forage Committee, War Office; became successively D.P.O.S., Berks and Oxford; Deputy Administrator Eastern Area; Administrator of Eastern Area, Administrator of Northern Area, Administrator of West Midland Area; twice mentioned (Brevet-Major, C.B.E.). Address: Norton Close, Stourbridge. Club: Press. (C2142)

MOODY, Charles Harry, C.B.E. Organist at Ripon Cathedral for 20 years. For war services in Ripon. (C3158)

MOODY, Major Edward Thomas, O.B.E., M.C., b. 1890; s. of Thomas Moody, of Finchley; m. Glady Harriet, d. of Arthur Flint, of Finchley. Educ.: Privately, and Christ's Coll. War Work: Served in Territorial Force with 7th Middlesex Regt. (Company Commander) in Gibraltar and France until end of 1916; then as Staff Capt. to 23rd Bgde. and 214th Bgde.; D.A.A.G. 23rd Corps early in 1918; from Aug. 1918, until June, 1920, D.A.A.G. G.H.Q. Palestine and Egypt. Address: Underwood, Finchley. Club: Junior Army and Navy. (O8635)

MOON, Lieut.-Col. Alfred, C.M.G., O.B.E., b. 1861; s of the late W. H. Moon, of Sheffield; m. 1907, Christina Elsie McLennan. Educ.: Grammar Sch., Farnsworth. A general merchant in Brisbane; Lieut.-Col. Army Ser. Corps, Australian Imperial Force; served during Great War, 1914–16, commdg. a Div. Supply Column (despatches); was a Trustee of Commercial Travellers' Assoc. of Queensland, 1906–14; Pres. Merchants Assoc., Brisbane, 1910–12; a Trustee of United Sers. Institution, Queensland, 1909–14. Address: Brisbane, Queensland. (O7966)

MOON, Capt. Jasper, O.B

MOON, Malinda Ann, M.B.E.; d. of the late Thomas

Moon, of Barlby House, Selby. Educ.: Riversdale, Boston Spa, Yorks. First Class Diplomée, Yorks School of Cookery and Domestic Science, Leeds. War Work: Supervisor, Gasshell Filling Factory for Russian Munition Supply; Deputy Cashier at the Selby Branch of Yorks Dyeware and Chemical Co., Ltd.; ordered and distributed food and stores for Sailors and Soldiers' Canteen, N.E. Railway Station, Selby. Address: West Lynne, Selby. (M9072)

MOON, Rosa, O.B.E.; d. of the late Charles Moon, of Anerley. Educ.: Privately. Gen. Sec. of the London Division of the Young Women's Christian Association. War Work: Organising girls' clubs in districts which for the time were military centres; organising canteen for girls employed in Pension Office; arranging for accommodation for British refugees on arrival in England from the enemy countries. Address: 75, Croydon Road, Anerley, S.E. (O10990)

MOONEY, Alexander Patrick, M.B.E., M.D., J.P.

MOONEY, Lieut. Cecil Douglas, M.B.E., M.C., R.A.S.C.

MOONEY, Rev. George Elderkin, M.B.E., M.A., b. 28 Feb. 1860; s. of William Mooney, of Huntingdon, Hunts; m. Clara, d. of Thomas Booth Wilkinson, of Sale, Cheshire. Educ.: Trinity Coll., Dublin. Chaplain of St. Edmund's Church, Christiania, and Hon. Chaplain to H.M. Legation, Christiania. War Work: Voluntary services rendered on work connected with the war for H.M. Legation, Christiania; work for the Red Cross, and also for British seamen interned in Norway. Address: 45, Nils Juels Gate, Christiania, Norway. (M9074)

MOONEY, Sir John Joseph, K.B.E., B.L., J.P., b. 1874; s. of J. G. Mooney, of Dublin; m. Ethel, d. of E. Macmillan, M.D., of Hull. Educ.: Belvedere, Dublin; Ushaw; T.C.D. M.P., Dublin County, 1900–6, Newry Borough, 1906–18. War Work: Aliens Advisory Committee and Defence of the Realm Advisory Committee. Address: 11, Allen House, Kensington, W. 8. Clubs: National Liberal; Royal Automobile. (K400)

MOOR, Marjorie, M.B.E., b. 1 Dec. 1894; d. of the Rt. Hon. Sir Frederick Moor, P.C., K.C.M.G., D.Ch., LL.D., M.L.A., of Greystone, Estcourt, Natal (see BURKE'S Peerage). Educ.: Dykeham School, Pietermaritzburg, Natal, S. Africa. Organiser. War Work: Sept. 1914, to Feb. 1916, work for Soldiers' and Sailors' Families Assocn., Leith; Feb. 1916, to Nov. 1916, work on land Argylleshire, N.B.; Nov. 1916, to Sept., 1917, with Scottish Women's Hospital, Abbaye de Royaumont, France; Oct. 1917, to Dec. 1919, Unit Administrator, Q.M.A.A.C. Clubs: Forum; International Franchise. (M5478)

MOORE, Eng.-Comm. Albert John Campbell, O.B.E., R.N.

MOORE, Lieut.-Col. Alfred William, O.B.E., M.B., b. 1881. s. of the Rev. W. T. Moore, of Norwich; m. Dorothy, d. of Rev. F. Lane. Educ.: Norwich; Emmanuel Coll., Cambridge; St. George's Hospital, London. Commissioner of Medical Services, West Midland Region, Birmingham, Ministry of Pensions. War Work: Commanded 10th Cavalry Brigade Field Ambulance in Palestine and Syria, and acting A.D.M.S. 4th Cavalry Division; thrice mentioned in despatches. Address: Hampton-in-Arden, Warwickshire. Club: Junior Army and Navy. (O6252)

MOORE, Annie, Mrs., M.B.E.

MOORE, Arthur Frederick, M.B.E., b. 22 Dec. 1859; s. of Edwin Moore, M.D., of Preston; m. Bessie Haslam, d. of George Galloway, J.P., of Preston. Educ.: Preston Grammar School, and Privately. Solicitor. War Work: On various committees connected with the safety and welfare of the town of Birkenhead; Member of the 2nd Batt. Cheshire Volunteer Regt.; Superintendent of the Birkenhead Special Constabulary. Address: 10, Devonshire Place, Claughton, Birkenhead. Club: Birkenhead Constitutional. (M8075)

MOORE, Capt. Arthur Thomas, O.B.E., R.A.F.

MOORE, Col. Arthur Trevelyan, C.B.E., b. 1866. Col. R.E.; Izanzai Expedition, 1892; served in Great War, 1814–19 (mentioned in despatches). (C1702)

MOORE, Capt. Cecil Arbuthnot St. George, M.B.E.

MOORE, Charles Henry, O.B.E.

MOORE, Christina Turnbull, M.B.E.

MOORE, Rev. David Keys, C.B.E., M.A., b. 1854; s. of Rev. Hugh Moore, of Donegal, Ireland. Educ.: Trinity Coll., Dublin. Senior Moderator (Modern Literature); British Chaplain at Lille, France, 1913–20; Vicar of St. James's, Hull, 1887–1913; Member of Hull School Board for 6 years, twice Mayor's Chaplain. War Work: In connection with the British Colony at Lille, and for wounded British and French soldier prisoners; Member of two French Red Cross Societies. Address: Heatherlea, Hessle, E. Yorks. (C2816)

MOORE, Decima, C.B.E.: see Guggisberg, Decima.

MOORE, Ernest Reginald, M.B.E.

MOORE, Evelyn, O.B.E.

MOORE, Lieut.-Col. Francis, D.S.O. O.B.E., b. 22 Dec. 1879; s. of the late Col. Francis Moore, 8th Regt. (see BURKE'S Peerage, Drogheda, E.); m., 1916, Annie Early, d. of William Van Wyck, of New Jersey, U.S.A. Roy. Fusiliers. Served in S. African War, 1900–1901 (Queen's medal with four clasps); and in Great War. (O6804)

MOORE, Lieut.-Col. Francis Hamilton, C.B.E., D.S.O., b. 1876. Entered Roy. Berkshire Regt., 1896; became Major, 1915; served during S. African War, 1899–1902 (Queen's medal with three clasps, King's medal with two clasps); during Great War, 1914–18, as a Gen. Staff Officer with rank of Lieut.-Col. (despatches). (C2145)

MOORE, Lieut. Frederick Ernest, M.B.E.

MOORE, Eng.-Comm. Gerald, O.B.E., R.N.

MOORE, George Frederick, M.B.E.

MOORE, Lieut. George James, O.B.E., M.C.

MOORE, 2nd Lieut. Gordon, M.B.E., R.A.F.

MOORE, Harold, O.B.E., B.Sc., F.I.C., F.Inst.P., b. 5 Jan. 1878 ; s. of the late William Moore, of Middlesbrough ; m. Grace Dora, d. of the late R. J. Read, of Norwich. Metallurgist ; Director of Metallurgical Research, Research Department, Woolwich ; Associate Member of the Ordnance Committee. War Work : Carrying out and directing metallurgical research work in connection with the manufacture of guns, ammunition, and other war supplies for the Navy and Army. Addresses : Lindsey House, Blackheath, S.E. 3 ; Research Department, Royal Arsenal, Woolwich, S.E. 18.   (O593)

MOORE, Lieut.-Col. Harold Arthur, C.B.E., M.C. Major and Acting Lieut.-Col., R.A.F. ; served in Great War, 1914-19 (mentioned in despatches).   (C869)

MOORE, Major Harold Mead, M.B.E., R.A.S.C.

MOORE, Capt. Harry Formby, M.B.E.

MOORE, Major Harry Francis Beauchamp Seymour, O.B.E., R.E.

MOORE, Comdr. Hartley Russell Gwennap, O.B.E., R.N., b. 18 April, 1881 ; s. of the late John Gwennap Dennis Moore, of Garlenick, Cornwall : m. Lenore, d. of Col. Ewing Crawford, D.L., of Auchentroig, Stirlingshire. Entered H.M.S. " Britannia," 1895. Comm. R.N., 1914 ; served on the Staff of the Admiral ; 2nd in Command, Grand Fleet ; subsequently on Naval Staff at the Admiralty ; in command of H.M.S. " Nairana," Jan. to Nov. 1919, operating with North Russian Expeditionary Force in the White Sea. Address : Gartinstarry, Bucklyvie, Stirlingshire.   (O3543)

MOORE, Henry Byron, O.B.E.

MOORE, Herbert Joseph, M.B.E.

MOORE, Major Herbert William, O.B.E., R.G.A.

MOORE, Capt. James Horatio, O.B.E., M.C., R.A.S.C., b. 17 Feb. 1870 ; s. of George Horatio Moore, of Liverpool ; m. Margaret Francis, d. of John McNevin, of Birr. Educ. : Privately. War Work : Base Supply Officer, France, Aug. 1914, to Oct. 1914 ; Chief Clerk to Qr.-Mr.-General to the Forces in France and Flanders, Oct. 1914, to Sept. 1919 ; five times mentioned in despatches ; Chevalier of the Order of Crown of Roumania. Address : c/o Sir C. R. McGrigor, Bart., 39, Panton Street, Haymarket, S.W. Clubs : Conservative, Liverpool.   (O5598)

MOORE, Capt. James Stuart Hamilton, O.B.E.

MOORE, Capt. James York, O.B.E., R.A.M.C.

MOORE, John, M.B.E., b. 20 Nov. 1856 ; s. of John Moore, of Liverpool ; m. Isabella A., d. of William Thompson, of Liverpool. Educ. : Commerical and Mathematical School, Chesham, Bucks. Assistant Collector, H.M. Customs and Excise, Port of Liverpool (ret.). War Work : Carrying out the war regulations in connection with the above office as regards the prohibitions and restrictions on goods imported and exported ; also the special facilities granted for the admission into this country of goods free of duty, which would be otherwise liable, for deposit in approved depots for use of Empire troops, and for shipment to the front. Address : 22, Penkett Road, Wallasey, Cheshire.   (M9076)

MOORE, John George, M.B.E., b. 6 Jan. 1863 ; s. of William Moore, of Portsmouth ; m. Sarah, d. of John Archer, of Leek Wooton, Warwick. Educ. : Bowlesc' Academy, Portsmouth. Chief Supt. of Portsmouth Constabulary. War Work : Second in command of the Portsmouth Police Force during the war ; arranged for billeting of the 1st Army Corps on mobilisation ; assisted the Army and Navy commands to deal with exceptional circumstances arising from the war. Address : 3, The Square, Milton Road, Portsmouth. Club : Waverley, Southsea.   (M9077)

MOORE, Capt. and Qr.-Mr. John Sarel, M.B.E., b. 29 Oct. 1872. Accountant. War Work : Mesopotamia from July, 1916, to May, 1919 ; Afghan War, May, 1919, to Oct. 1919. Address : 18, Nansen Road, Clapham Common, S.W. 11.   (M4903)

MOORE, John Thomas, M.B.E., b. 2 Feb. 1859 ; s. of John Moore, of Jedburgh, N.B. ; m. Elizabeth Jane, d. of William Taylor, of Bridgwater. Educ. : H.M. Army Schools, and Privately. Surveyor, H.M. Customs and Excise. War Work : Detention and seizure of enemy cargo in the port of London. Address : 23, Chadwick Road, Leytonstone, E. 11.   (M9078)

MOORE, Margaret, M.B.E., d. of Alex. Moore, C.A., of Glasgow Educ. : Glasgow. War Work : Town Canteen, Comforts for soldiers (laundry and mending) ; Red Cross workparty ; superintending Concerts, Sales, Games, for various funds and for soldiers. Address : Deanville, Bridge of Allan, Stirlingshire.   (M9079)

MOORE, Margaret Stuart, Mrs., M.B.E., b. 18 Jan. 1889 ; d. of D. Percival Whitcombe, of 69, Queen's Gate ; m. John Roland, s. of — Moore. Educ. : Queen's Coll., Harley Street. War Work : Head of the Bread Section Dept. at the Central Prisoners of War Committee, Thurloe Place. Address : 41, Rosary Gardens, S.W. 7. Club : Bembridge Sailing.   (M9080)

MOORE, Muriel, Mrs., M.B.E., b. 29 April, 1879 ; d. of Frank Burton, of Gt. Yarmouth ; m. John Lee Moore, s. of John Robert Moore, I.S.O., of Bromley, Kent. Educ. : Privately. Commandant, V.A.D. Norfolk 2. War Work : Commandant, Gt. Yarmouth Red Cross Auxiliary Hospital,

Feb. 1915, to Jan. 1920. Address : 200, Lowestoft Road Gorleston.   (M9081)

MOORE, Capt. Nithsdale Carleton Atkinson, C.B.E., R.N., b. 1874 ; s. of Joseph Fletcher Moore, of Manor Kilbride, co. Dublin. Served in Great War, 1914-19, as Port Convoy Officer and Senior Naval Officer, Lamlach (despatches). Club : United Services.

MOORE, Pye, M.B.E.

MOORE, Capt. and Qr.-Mr. Richard William, M.B.E., b. 29 Dec. 1858 ; s. of Richard Moore, of London ; m. Louisa, d. of Arthur James Smith, of London. Educ. : Spa Fields. War Work : Served with Norfolk Regt. in Gallipoli, 1915 ; invalided home ; posted to 4th Res. Batt. Norfolk Regt., Quartermaster ; disembodied 14th June, 1919 ; 1914-15 Star, B.W. Medal, Victory, King George Coronation, L.S.G. Conduct Medal. Address : 30, Neville Street, Norwich.   (M5480)

MOORE, Robert Foster, O.B.E., M.A., B.C. (Cantab.), F.R.C.S., b. 1878 ; s. of Edward Moore, of Cambridge ; m. Sophie Elizabeth, d. of Thomas Attridge, of Mallow. Educ. : Christ's Coll., Cambridge ; St. Bartholomew's Hospital. Assistant Ophthalmic Surgeon, St. Bartholomew's Hospital ; Surgeon, Moorfields Eye Hospital. War Work : In charge of Ophthalmic Centre, Etaples, France. Address : 91, Harley Street, W. 1.   (O5600)

MOORE, Brevet-Col. Robert Reginald Heber, C.B.E., M.D., R.A.M.C., b. 8 April, 1858 ; s. of Rev. Thomas Moore, of Midleton, Co. Cork ; m. Christina Turnbull, d. of Lewis Bilton, W.S., of Edinburgh. Educ. : Midleton Coll., Co. Cork ; T. C. Dublin. War Work : Assist. Director of Medical Services at Headquarters of Eastern Command. Address : Painswick Lodge, Cheltenham.   (C1703)

MOORE, Brevet-Major Thomas Cecil Russell, C.B.E., b. 16 Sept. 1886 ; s. of John Watt Moore, of Fintona, Co. Tyrone, Ireland. Educ. : Portora Royal School, Enniskillen, and privately. Deputy Assist. Director of Supplies and Transport, Ireland, June, 1916, to Sept. 1918, and Assist. Director of Supplies and Transports, " Syren " Force, North Russian Exped. Force, during operations in North Russia ; Order of the White Eagle 4th Class. Address : 7, Park Place, St. James's, London. Clubs : Junior Naval and Military ; Golfers' ; Stephen's Green ; Dublin and Royal Irish Yacht, Kingstown, Ireland.   (C2359e)

MOORE, Thomas Edwin, M.B.E., s. of James Moore, of Styal, Cheshire ; m. Annie, d. of William Brown, of Melchbourne, Beds. Superintendent and Deputy Chief Constable, Stockport Borough Police Force. War Work : Personally making inquiries of a secret and confidential nature for the authorities at the War Office, Home Office, and other Government Departments, and being successful generally in supplying the required information. Address : 143, Chapel Street, Stockport.   (M9082)

MOORE, Thomas Warren, C.B.E., F.R.G.S., Hon. Lieut. R.N.R., b. 20 April, 1872 ; s. of the late Captain John Grant Moore, of Bebington. Educ. : Privately. Sec., Imperial Merchant Service Guild ; Joint-Chairman, Navigating Officers' Panel of the National Maritime Board ; Vice-Chairman, Seafarers' Joint Council ; Hon. Sec., Fryatt Memorial Fund. War Work : Voluntary Services to the Admiralty, War Office, India Office, and other Government Departments, who, through his hands, secured over 6000 experienced certificated Seafarers who were appointed for war service with officers' commissions in either the Naval or Military Forces, and other confidential business in respect to the work of these Departments ; service on the National Maritime Board as a representative of the Navigating Officers of the Merchant Service ; a member of the Admiralty Transport Arbitration Board ; Organiser of the Imperial Merchant Service Guild War Fund, and of the Captain Fryatt Memorial Fund ; Member of the Committee on the Release of Ruhleben Prisoners of War. Address : Dixon House, Lloyd's Avenue, London. Clubs : Royal Mersey Yacht ; Royal Automobile ; Conservative, Liverpool. (C2817)

MOORE, Major William, O.B.E., T.D., A.C.I.S., b. 25 Feb. 1886. Sec. of Public Companies. War Work : Aug. 1914 to Nov. 1916, 4th London Regt., England, Malta, France, and Belgium ; Nov. 1916, to May, 1918, Royal Welsh Fusiliers, England ; May, 1918 to Jan. 1920, D.A.Q.M.G., 69th Division, England. Club : Junior Army and Navy.   (O7489)

MOORE, William Arthur, M.B.E.   (M5481)

MOORE, Lieut.-Col. William Gale, O.B.E., b. 16 Oct. 1881 ; m. William Turle Moore, late of Stock Exchange. Educ. : Felsted School, Essex. War Work : At outbreak, Capt. in Kent Cyclist Batt. on coast defence duties ; Batt. changed to infantry and sent to India, March, 1916 ; became second in command ; obtained command in May, 1916 ; Campaigns : Waziristan, 1917 ; Baluchistan, 1918 ; Afghanistan, 1919. Address : 133, Finchley Road, London, N.W. Clubs : Junior Army and Navy ; Royal Temple Yacht.   (O8514)

MOORE, William Gunn, M.B.E., Ex-Provost of Dornoch, b. 1 Dec. 1867 ; s. of Sinclair Moore, of Acharry ; m. Hellen, d. of Robt. Sutherland, of Plancey. Educ. : Larachan Public School. Clothier. Provost of Dornoch, 1913-19. War Work : Chairman, Local Tribunal ; Chairman, Red Cross ; Chairman, War Savings Association, the Royal Burgh of Domoch ; was successful in winning the Victory Loan Flag, and had the honour of receiving same at the hands of H.R.H. The Princess Mary on board the Royal Yacht at Aberdeen. Address : St. Clair House, Dornoch.   (M9083)

MOORE, William Struthers, M.B.E., M.D., Ch.B.

MOOREHOUSE, Jessie Matilda, Mrs., O.B.E.

MOORES, Major Frank Gerald Guise, O.B.E., R.A.S.C., *b.* 15 Nov. 1884; *s.* of Col. S. Moores, late Devon Regt. *Educ.:* Cheltenham Coll., and Royal Military Academy, Woolwich. *Club:* R.A.S.C. (O6816)

MOOREHEAD, Harold Percival, O.B.E. (O11998)

MOORHEAD, Major Charles Andrews, O.B.E.

MOORHOUSE, Col. William Henry Septon, M.B.E.

MOORS Florence Donald. M.B.E.

MOORSHEAD, Engineer-Capt. Herbert Brooks, C.B.E., R.N. Served in Great War 1914–19 (mentioned in despatches). (C1934)

MOORSOM, Comm. Winstanley Robert Coverdale, O.B.E., R.N.

MORAN, Capt. John William, O.B.E., B.A., B.A.I., A.M.I.C.E.I., R.A.S.C. (S.R.), *b.* 12 Aug. 1888; *s.* of the late Gerald A. Moran, of 61, Elm Park Gardens, S.W. *Educ.:* Lausanne; Clongowes Wood Coll.; Dublin Univ. T.C.D. Civil Engineer; Dublin Port and Docks Board. *War Work:* Mobilised, Aug. 1914; proceeded overseas (France), 1915, with 16th Division and served with 16th Divisional Train, until disembodied, in July, 1919; twice mentioned in despatches. *Address:* 5, De Vesci Terrace, Kingstown, Co. Dublin. (O5601)

MORAN, Mrs. Selina, M.B.E., *b.* 22 Jan. 1877; *d.* of James Henderson, of Newcastle; *m.* John Moran, *s.* of Francis Moran, of Durham. Eight years member of Hebburn Education Committee; member of National Insurance Committee. *War Work:* Member of Prince of Wales' Committee; Local War Relief, Local Pensions, Food Control, and Soldiers' and Sailors' Dependants Committees. *Address:* 30, Frederick Street, Hebburn Colliery, Co. Durham. (M9084)

MORANT, Lydia Louisa, O.B.E. Hon. Sec., Bermondsey Division, Soldiers' and Sailors' Families' Association. (O11918)

MORANT, William George, O.B.E., D.L., *b.* 1862; *s.* of late Alfred William Morant, M.Inst.C.E., F.S.A., F.G.S., of Leeds. *Educ.:* Privately. Chief Constable of the County of Durham. *War Work:* General and assisting Naval and Military Authorities. Awarded the Cross of Chevalier of the Order of Leopold II. for services rendered to Belgian Government; Hon. Serving Brother, the Grand Priory of the Order of the Hospital of St. John of Jerusalem in England. *Address:* 23 Old Elvet, Durham. *Club:* County, Durham. (O10991)

MORCOM, Lieut.-Col. Reginald Keble, C.B.E. Major and Acting Lieut.-Col., R.E.; served in Great War, 1914–19, in Balkans (mentioned in despatches). (C1414)

MORDEY, Thomas, M.B.E.

MORE, Comm. George Irwin Sanctuary, O.B.E., R.N.

MORE, Jasper Frederick, O.B.E., *b.* 23 June, 1876; *s.* of the late Robert Jasper More, M.P., of Linley Hall, Bishops Castle, Shropshire; *m.* Rosamond Winifred, *d.* of W. Morton Philips, of Heybridge, Tean, Staffs. *Educ.:* Westminster School. Barrister-at-law, Lincoln's Inn, 1903; Principal Clerk, Chancery Registrar's Office. *War Work:* Military Intelligence Department, War Office, Aug. 1914, to July, 1919. *Address:* The Old Vicarage, Ware, Herts. *Club:* Travellers'. (O594)

MORE, Lieut.-Col. Paxton St. Clair, O.B.E., M.B., I.M.S.

MORE, Richard Edwardes, O.B.E.

MORE, Brig.-Gen. Robert Henry, C.M.G., C.B.E., *b.* 1875; *s.* of the late Robert Jasper More, M.P. for S., or Ludlow Div. of Shropshire, of Linley, Bishop's Castle, Shropshire; *m.* 1919. Phyllis Blanche, *d.* of the Hon. Francis Parker (*see* BURKE's *Peerage,* Macclesfield, E). Hon. Lieut.-Col. Reserve in the Army; T. Col. R.A.F.; Dep. Director Air Personal Ser., with rank of Brig.-Gen.; S. African War, 1900–2 (Queen's medal with three clasps, King's medal with two clasps); Great War, 1914–19 (Order of St. Maurice and St. Lazarus). *Address:* 17, South Eaton Place, S.W. *Club:* Wellington. (C1900)

MORE, Lieut. Thomas, M.B.E., Cameron Highlanders, *b.* 12 April, 1885; *s.* of the late Francis More, of Edinburgh. *Educ.:* Edinburgh Academy; Gonville and Caius Coll., Cambridge. *War Work:* B.E.F., France; attached G.H.Q., Great Britain, for Anti-Aircraft work; attached General Staff, War Office, Directorate of Military Intelligence. *Addresses:* 76, St. George's Road, Warwick Square, S.W. 1; 4, Royal Circus, Edinburgh. *Club:* Leander. (M6681)

MORE, Thomas Jasper Mytton, O.B.E., J.P.

MORE, Sir James, Bart., C.B.E.

MORELAND, Major Harold, O.B.E.

MORELL, Major Roy, D.S.O., O.B.E., *b.* 18 May, 1889; *s.* of James Harris Morell, of Sydney, N.S.W.; *m.* Frances Ioné, *d.* of Charles E. Pole-Carew, of Totnes, Devon. *War Work:* Enlisted as trooper, Sept. 1914, 6th Aust. L. H. Regt.; Egypt, 1915; Gallipoli, May, 1915, to Nov. 1915; Lieut. Aug. 1915; Capt. March, 1916 (in command 13th Aust. M.G.C.); France, June, 1916; Staff Capt. Oct. 1916 (13th Aust. C.M.G.C.); Staff Major, March, 1917 (13th Aust. C.M.G.C.); July, 1918, Corps M.G. Officer. *Address;* Morval, Maxwelton, North Queensland. (O6087)

MORESBY, Walter Halliday, C.B.E., M.A., LL.B. (Cantab.), *s.* of Admiral John Moresby, of Fareham; *m.* Mary Graham, *d.* of Capt. Oswald Niven, R.N., of Torquay. *Educ.:* Westminster School, and St. John's Coll., Cambridge. Barrister-at-law; Legal Adviser, War Office; Hon. Legal Adviser, Chevrons Club. *War Work:* Legal Adviser, Special Intelligence Department, War Office. *Addresses:* 2, Hare Court Temple; 11, Pembroke Road, Kensington. *Club:* Caledonian. (C2818)

MORETON, Capt. Arthur Ernest, M.B.E., K.O.S.B., *b.* 28 Feb. 1882; *s.* of Joseph Moreton, of Winchester; *m.* Violet Waldie, *d.* of James Cruden, of West Ferry, N.B. *Educ.:* Privately. *War Work:* Served with the 2nd K.O.S.B. in the Great War, 1914–18; mentioned in despatches, July, 1915; wounded (gassed), April, 1915. *Address:* c/o Cox & Co., Army Agents. (M5482)

MORETON, Loftus B., O.B.E., J.P., D.L., *b.* 1859; *s.* of John Moreton, of Moseley Court, Wolverhampton; *m.* Grace, *d.* of Joseph Underhill, Q.C., of London. *Educ.:* Clifton Coll. Chairman, Wolverhampton Local Employment Committee. *War Work:* Chairman of Tribunal; Territorial Force Association. *Address:* Moseley Hall, Wolverhampton. *Club:* Conservative; Gresham. (O1677)

MORGAN, Col. Alexander Braithwaite, C.B.E., *b.* 1866. Lieut.-Col. and T. Col., Army Pay Dept.; Hazara Expedition, 1888 (medal with clasp); S. Africa, 1899–1902 (Queen's medal with five clasps, King's medal with two clasps); Great War, 1914–19 (despatches). (C1705)

MORGAN, Amy Helena Margaret, M.B.E., *d.* of William Fairbank, C.V.O., O.B.E.(*q.v.*), of Windsor; *m.* 5 Feb. 1921, Benjamin Howell Morgan, *s.* of late Benjamin Morgan, of Ferryside. Asst.-Sec. British Empire Producers' Organisation. *War Work:* Canteen Work, 1914; Shell Department, Vickers, Erith, 1915–16; Deputy Chief Woman Dilution Officer, Ministry of Munitions, 1917; Chief Woman Technical Assistant, Ministry of National Service, 1918. *Address:* Moulsey House, Windsor. *Clubs:* Forum; Roehampton. (M3634)

MORGAN, Lady Anne Lalande, M.B.E. Responsible for the welfare of blinded officers, St. Dunstan's. (M10331)

MORGAN, Arthur Richard, M.B.E., R.E.

MORGAN, Capt. Bernard Donald Crawford, O.B.E.

MORGAN, Bessie, M.B.E.; *d.* of James Morgan of Pembrokeshire and Liverpool. *Educ.:* Merchant Taylors' School for Girls, Great Crosby; Switzerland, Germany, and Italy. *War Work:* Joined the Postal Censorship in Dec. 1914; Censor in charge of the Female Staff of the Liverpool Branch, 1915–19. *Address:* 62, Hough Green, Chester. (M2189)

MORGAN, Cecil May: *see* JUPP, Cecil May, Mrs.

MORGAN, Lieut.-Col. Charles Langbridge, C.B.E., M.I.C.E., R.E., *b.* 1855; *s.* of the late William Morgan, of Tower House, Beacon Hill, Bath; *m.* 1883, Mary, *d.* of William Watkins. *Educ.:* Privately in Australia, and Bath. Civil Engineer; a Director of London Brighton and S. Coast Railway (Chief Engineer, 1896–1917); sometime a Member of Hon. Advisory Valuation Committee, Min. of Munitions. *Address:* Woodhurst, Kenley, Surrey. *Club:* St. Stephen's. (C253)

MORGAN, 2nd Lieut. David, M.B.E., R.F.A. (T.).

MORGAN, Lieut.-Col. David Watts, C.B.E., D.S.O., M.P., *b.* 1867; *s.* of Thos. Morgan, of Neath, Glam.; *m.* Blanche Amy, *d.* of George Moon, of Shepton Mallet. *Educ.:* Elementary School, Meath. Mining Engineer and Miners' Agent; Rescue work after Explosions; Research work Govt. Depts. Raised 8 Infantry Battalions; Welsh Army Corps; 2 Labour Battalions; Cambrai Pick and Shovel Labour Corps. (C2819)

MORGAN, Edith Lilian, M.B.E., *b.* 21 Nov. 1876; *d.* of Charles Morgan, 5th son of the late Giles Chapman Morgan, of Macknade, Kent. *Educ.:* King Edward's High School, Birmingham; Birmingham Univ. *War Work:* King Edward's School Belgian House, Treas. and Sec. (Hon.); Organiser (Hon.) King Edward's School Canteen, at Messrs. Bulpitt & Sons, Birmingham. 1915–16; Supervisor of Canteens at National Projectile Factory, Dudley, 1916–18; at National Fuse Factory, Tipton, 1917–18; and at National Projectile Factory, Templeborough, Sheffield, 1918. *Address:* 22, Hallewell Road, Edgbaston, Birmingham. *Clubs:* Birmingham Girls' Old Edwardian; Three Counties, Birmingham. (M9085)

MORGAN, Edward Barcham, M.B.E.

MORGAN, Edward Lleurwg, O.B.E.

MORGAN, Effie Blanche, Mrs., O.B.E., *b.* 20 Jan. 1866; *d.* of Charles Noon, of Knighton, Leicester; *m.* Conway, *s.* of John Morgan, of Forebridge, Stafford. *War Work:* Equipped and organised " Soldiers' Welcome Club " in Stafford, which was open from Jan. 1915, to May, 1919. Three members of her family received the D.S.O., D.S.C., and M.B.E. respectively. *Address:* Queensville, Stafford. (O10994)

MORGAN, Eileen Cynthia Marjorie, M.B.E., *b.* 5 June, 1897; *d.* of Robert Upton Morgan. *Educ.:* Camden School for Girls. *War Work:* Divisional Superintendent, Pension Issue Office, Ministry of Pensions. *Address:* Woodside, Baring Road, Beaconsfield. (M9086)

MORGAN, Eleanor Elizabeth Bamlet, Mrs., O.B.E. (O11787g)

MORGAN, Ethel Marion, M.B.E., *b.* 4 Dec. 1882; *d.* of Albert C. F. Morgan, of 135, Oakwood Court, London, W. *Educ.:* Kensington Park High School, London, W. *War Work:* Central Prisoners of War Committee of the British Red Cross Society; Head of the Civilian Dept. of the above and Sec. of the Repatriated British Civilians Help Committee. *Address:* 135, Oakwood Court, London, W. (M9087)

MORGAN, Col. Frederick James, C.M.G., C.B.E., *b.* 21 June, 1862; *s.* of Dr. J. L. Morgan, of London; *m.* Elizabeth Agnes, *d.* of W. H. Johnston, of Dumfriesshire. *Educ.:* University Coll. School and Westminster Hospital. Served in Army Medical Service (ret.) in Egypt (Nile Expedition), 1889, as Colonel, and in South Africa, 1900–1902; mentioned in despatches; received thanks of C.-in-C.; Queen's medal with three clasps: King's medal with two clasps. *War Work:* Served in France and Flanders, 1914–19; O.C. No. 2 Clearing Hospital; O.C. No. 5 General Hospital, 1914; A.D.M.S. 38th (Welsh) Division, 1915–17; D.D.M.S. Cavalry Corps, 1917–19; mentioned in despatches. *Address:* 5, Ravenna Road, Putney, S.W.   (C1296)

MORGAN, George, C.B.E., I.S.O., Chevalier de l'Ordre de Léopold, *b.* 15 April, 1853; *s* of William Morgan, of Alton, Hants; *m.* Annie E., *d.* of Joseph Feltham, of Canonbury. *Educ.:* Wanstead, Essex; City of London College; Birkbeck Institute; Finsbury Technical College. Controller of the Post Office Stores Department (Embracing Factories and Stamps); Member of the Fair Wages Advisory Committee; Official Adviser to the Central Committee on Women's Employment during the War. *War Work:* Largely of a technical and confidential nature, connected with the supply of material for the Imperial Forces in the Field and at Home as well as for the Allies, and for many of the special organisations established during the War. *Address:* Downings, Wallington, Surrey.   (C1009)

MORGAN, Capt. George Urquhart, O.B.E., R.E.

MORGAN, Gilbert Thomas, O.B.E., F.R.S., D.Sc. Professor of Chemistry Unversity of Birmingham. *War Work:* Associate Member, Chemical Warfare Committee. *Address:* The University, Edgbaston, Birmingham.   (O10995)

MORGAN, Capt. Griffith Benjamin, M.B.E.

MORGAN, Harold Roland, M.B.E

MORGAN, Sir Herbert Edward, K.B.E., *b.* 11 Sept. 1876; *s.* of the Rev. A. R. Morgan. *Educ.:* In U.S.A. General Adviser in printing and advertising to W. H. Smith & Sons; a Director of A. and F. Pears; Vice-chairman, Mac Fisheries, Ltd.; worked in connection with War Refugees' Committee, Serbian Relief Fund, Polish War Victims' Relief Fund, and Queen Alexandra's Field Force Fund; Hon. Organiser of the Union Jack Club Fund since 1919; in charge of Inspection, etc., Intelligence Dept., Ministry of Labour, 1919; Adviser in Propaganda, Housing Dept., Local Government Board; acted in an advisory capacity to Parliamentary War Savings Committee, Labour Dept., Ministry of Munitions, Imperial Munitions Board of Canada, Labour Organisation; President of many public societies and clubs. *Address:* 1B, King Street, St. James's Square, S.W. *Clubs:* Savage; Reform; American; Royal Automobile; Thames Punting; Rye; Walton Heath; Gullane.   (K31)

MORGAN, Brig.-Gen. Sir Hill Godfrey, K.B.E., C.B., C.M.G., D.S.O., *b.* 20 June, 1862; *s.* of the late Capt. Hill Faulconer Morgan, 28th Foot; *m.* Fanny, *d.* of the late J. Bonsfield, of Grassmere, Craneswater Park, Southsea. Joined 1st Gloucestershire Regt. 1883 from the Militia as Lieut. and transferred to R.A.S.C. as Capt. 1888; Major, 1898; served Dongola, 1896–98; Nile Expedition, Khartoum, mentioned in despatches, D.S.O., 4th class Medjidieh. 4th class Osmanieh, Khedive medal, and British medal with two clasps; Director of Supplies, Natal, 1899–1900, S. Africa, 1900–2, five times mentioned in despatches; C.B.; Brevet Lieut.-Col.; Queen's medal with six clasps; King's medal, two clasps; Lieut.-Col. 1904; Brevet Col. 1917; retired 1906; Assist.-Director of Supplies, Central Force, Home Army, 1914; Mil. Member Organising Committee Farmer's County Committees, 1914; Administrative Member Forage Committee, 1916; T. Brig.-Gen. 1917; mentioned for valuable services in connection with the war (C.M.G., K.B.E., and medal). *Residence:* 9. Manson Place, Queen's Gate, S.W. 7. *Clubs:* Junior United Service; Ranelagh.   (K304)

MORGAN, Hopkin, C.B.E., J.P., *b.* 1849; *s.* of Morgan Morgan, of Neath; *m.* Hannah, *d.* of David Griffiths, of Neath. *Educ.:* Neath Academy. Alderman of Glamorgan County Council, and also of Neath Town Council; President of Welsh Education Committees; Member of Court of Welsh University; Member of Central Welsh Board for Secondary Education; Member of Welsh Council of Music; Chairman of Board of Governors Neath County Schoool; Chairman of Neath Education Committee. *War Work:* Addressed Meetings for Recruiting purposes; Chairman of County Appeal Tribunal (Western); addressed Meetings *re* War Loan. *Address:* Bryn Clydach, Neath. *Club:* Neath Liberal.   (C254)

MORGAN, Capt. Hugh, M.B.E.

MORGAN, Paymaster-Lieut. James Walwyn Gynlais, M.B.E., R.N.R.

MORGAN, John, M.B.E.

MORGAN, Capt. John Hamilton, O B.E., R.M.

MORGAN, Lieut. John Scrammell, M.B.E.

MORGAN, Major Kenyon Pascoe Vaughan, O.B.E., R.A.S.C.

MORGAN, Margaret Alice Agnes, Mrs. Conway, M.B.E.

MORGAN, Capt. Percival Robert, M.B.E., R.I.M.

MORGAN, Capt. Phillip Sydney, M.B.E., R.A.V.C. (T.).

MORGAN, Robert Henry, M.B.E.

MORGAN, Robert Upton, M.B.E.

MORGAN, Lieut. Stanley Herbert, O.B.E., R.E.

MORGAN, Major Sydney Cope, M.B.E., M.A., *b.* 25 Oct. 1887; *s.* of G. E. Morgan, of Hampstead, N.W. *Educ.:* Tarnton and Trinity Coll., Cambridge. Entered Middle Temple, Jan. 1919. *War Work:* Commanding A Coy. 6 S.W.B. from formation Sept. 1914, till wounded in Somme Battle, 1916; Company Commander and 2nd in Command of Garrison Officer Cadet Batt., Cambridge; called to the Bar, Middle Temple, 1921. *Club:* United University.   (M5486)

MORGAN, Thomas, M.B.E.

MORGAN, Major Thomas Henry, O.B.E.

MORGAN, Tom Henry, M.B.E.

MORGAN, Walter Llewellyn, M.B.E.

MORGAN, Capt. William, M.B.E., R.E.

MORGAN, Capt. William Harold, M.B.E., *b.* 27 Aug., 1884; *s.* of J. P. Morgan, of Peterstow, Ross. *Educ.:* Dean Close School, Cheltenham. Merchant. *War Work:* Enlisted in Herefordshire Regiment, Sept. 1914; Commissioned to Welsh Divisional Train (R.A.S.C.) July, 1915; Mesopotamia, March, 1917, to July, 1919. *Address:* Peterstow, Ross, Herefordshire.   (M4901)

MORGAN, William Henry, O.B.E.

MORGAN, William Richard, M.B.E., *b.* 10 March, 1879; *s.* of John Morgan, of Abernant-y-groes, Cwmbach, Aberdare. *Educ.:* Grammar School, Pontypridd. Solicitor; Clerk to Aberdare Urban District Council; Deputy Registration Officer, Aberdare Division, Parliamentary Boro of Merthyr Tydfil. *Address:* Abernant-y-groes, Cwmbach, Aberdare. (M9090)

MORGANS, Lieut.-Col. Godfrey Ewart, O.B.E., R.E.

MORGON, Lieut.-Comm. James Kendle, O.B.E., R.N.

MORICE, George Farquhar, C.B.E., Public Security Dept.   (C3184)

MORISON, Albert Edward, O.B.E., M.B., F.R.C.S.

MORISON, Capt. Ernest, O.B.E.

MORISON, Sir Theodore, K.C.S.I., K.C.I.E., C.B.E., M.A., *b.* 9 May, 1863; *s.* of James Cotter Morison; *m.* Margaret, *d.* of the Rt. Hon. Arthur Cohen, K.C. *Educ.:* Westminster, and Trinity Coll., Cambridge. Tutor to the Maharajas of Chhaturpur and Charkhari, Central India, 1885; joined Staff of Muhammadan Coll. of Eligarh, 1889; Principal, 1899–1905; Additional Member of Viceroy's Legislative Council, 1903–4; Member of the Council of India, 1906–16; now Principal of Armstrong College; 2nd Lieut Cambridgeshire Regt. (T.), 1915; Political Staff, E. African Force, 1916; D.P.O. Moslie, 1916–17; Hon. Major attached to Belgian Forces, 1917; Senior Political Officer in charge of Southern Area, G.L.A., with hon. rank of Lieut.-Col. 1917–18; T. Lieut.-Col. G.S.O. 1. *Address:* Principal's Lodge, Armstrong College, Newcastle. *Clubs:* United University; Northern Counties.   (K743)

MORISON, Capt. William Roger, O.B.E.

MORISONS, Jules Louis, O.B.E.

MORKEL, Paul Andrew, M.B.E.

MORKETT, Hugh Brooke, O.B.E.

MORKILL, William Lucius, C.B.E.

MORLAND, Lieut.-Col. Algernon, O.B.E., A.P.D.

MORLE, Major Denzil Adair Bartlett, O.B.E., R.A.F.

MORLE, Helena Francis, M.B.E.

MORLEY, Arthur, O.B.E., M.A., *b.* 19 Nov. 1881; *s.* of William James Morley, of Heaton. Bradford; *m.* Dorothy Innes Murray, *d.* of the late William Forest, of Bank of Australia. *Educ.:* Bradford School and Christ Church. Oxford. Barrister-at-Law, Middle Temple; Practising London and N.E. Circuit. *War Work:* Administration Officer, Royal National Orthopædic Hospital Military Section; Hon. Sec. and Administration Officer, Lady Evelyn Mason's Hospital for Officers. *Address:* 4, Harcourt Buildings, Temple. *Club:* United University; Union.   (O10996)

MORLEY, Lieut. Cornelius Cecil, O.B.E., R.N.V.R.

MORLEY, George, C.B.E., B.C.L. (Oxon.), *b.* 17 Nov. 1873; *s.* of William James Morley, F.R.I.B.A., of Heaton, Bradford; *m.* Agnes, *d.* of Joseph Tetley Milnes, of Hillside House, Bradford, and Brookside, Bishops Lydeard. *Educ.:* Worcester College, Oxford. Chief Constable of Hull; a Governor of the Hull Savings Bank; a Co-opted Governor of Hymer's College, Hull. *Clubs:* Oxford and Cambridge; National.   (2820)

MORLEY, Ida Rose, Mrs., O.B.E., *b.* 1857; *d.* of Stephen Seaward Tayler, of Streatham, London; *m.* Henry Forster, *s.* of Prof. Henry Morley, LL.D., of Hampstead, and Carisbrooke, Isle of Wight. *Educ.:* Bedford College, London, and Royal Academy Art Schools, London. *War Work:* Organiser of the Rosslyn Depot, Hampstead, Queen Mary's Needlework Guild. *Addresses:* 5, Lyndhurst Road, Hampstead, N.W.; Midhurst, Sussex.   (O10997)

MORLEY, James Wycliffe HEADLAM-, C.B.E., *b.* 24 Dec. 1863; *s.* of Rev. Canon Headlam, of Whorlton Hall, Barnard Castle; *m.* Else *d.* of Dr. A. Sonntag, of Lüneburg. *Educ.:* Eton (Scholar); King's College, Cambridge (Fellow). Historical Adviser to the Foreign Office. *War Work:* 1914–17, Co-operated in work of Propaganda; and numerous other articles and pamphlets; 1917–1918, Assistant Director of Political Intelligence Bureau in the Department of Information; 1918–20, Assistant Director of Political Intelligence Department in the Foreign Office; 1919, Member of Political Section of the British Delegation to the Peace Conference at Paris. *Address:* 1, St. Mary's Road, Wimbledon. *Club:* Oxford and Cambridge.   (C2821)

MORLEY, Lieut.-Col. Lyddon Charlris, C.B.E. Legion of Honour.

MORNEMENT, Col. Edward, C.B.E., R.E.

MORNEMENT, Surg.-Comm. Robert Harry, O.B.E., R.A.F.

MORPHY, Arthur, O.B.E., *b.* 7 Nov. 1876; *s.* of William Morphy, of Patras, Greece and London; *m.* Gwendolyn, *d.* of Lewis Pilcher, of London. *Educ.:* Whitgift Grammar School and Louvain. Ship agent and owner. *War Work:* Foreign Office (F.T.D.) from beginning of 1916, till Feb. 1919.

Address : Moorsfort, East Sheen, S.W. 140. *Clubs :* Royal Automobile ; Roehampton. (O10998)

MORRELL, Alfred, C.B.E., *b.* 15 Aug. 1865 ; *s.* of George Morrell, of Liverpool ; *m.* Edith Alice, *d.* of Frederick Simmons, of Birmingham. *Educ. :* Turton Hall College, nr. Leeds. Managing Director, John Morrell & Co., Ltd., Merchants, Liverpool. *War Work :* At Ministry of Food in Voluntary capacity as Director of Bacon Section from July, 1917, to April, 1919. *Address :* Balholm, Blundellsands Liverpool. *Clubs :* Junior Constitutional ; Exchange Club, Liverpool ; West Lancashire, and Formby Golf. (C2822)

MORRELL, Capt. Arthur Claude, O.B.E., M.C.

MORRELL, Capt. Henry, O.B.E., R.A.S.C.

MORREY, Lieut. Percy, M.B.E.

MORRIS, Major Alfred Samuel, O.B.E., R.A.F.

MORRIS, Lieut. Archibald John, M.B.E.

MORRIS, Arthur, M.B.E., *b.* 1875 ; *s.* of Sir Lewis Morris, of Penbryn, Carmarthen ; *m.* Margaret Christina, *d.* of George A. Sanford, J.P., of Hertfordshire. *Educ. :* Westminster and Royal Naval College, Greenwich. Armstrong Naval Yard, Newcastle-on-Tyne. *War Work :* Assistant to General Manager, Armstrong Naval Yard, Newcastle-on-Tyne. *Addresses :* The Lea House, Riding Mill, Northumberland ; Penbryn, Carmarthen. (M2194)

MORRIS, Col. Arthur Hugh, C.B.E. Served in Great War, 1914–15 (mentioned in despatches). (C1430)

MORRIS, Basil Arthur, M.B.E.

MORRIS, Cecilia Margaret, M.B.E.

MORRIS, Charles Edward, M.B.E.

MORRIS, Surg.-Comm. Claude Woodham, O.B.E., R.N.

MORRIS, Cynthia Gertrude, Mrs, O.B.E.

MORRIS, Edward, M.B.E.

MORRIS, Capt. Edward Gilbert, O.B.E., B.A., East African Forces, *b.* 15 July, 1884 ; *s.* of William Morris, M.I.C.E., of Brockley, Kent ; *m.* Mary Grave, *d.* of Frank Grave Morris, M.I.C.E., of Brentford, Middlesex. *Educ. :* Bedford School, and Hertford Coll., Oxford. District Commissioner, Uganda ; District Political Officer, Tanganyika. *War Work :* Assisted organisation food and transport Uganda Forces, also for Belgian troops advancing Tabora ; District Commissioner in charge Aukole District on German border. *Address :* Kampala, Uganda. *Clubs :* Constitutional, Isthmian. (O8402)

MORRIS, Edward Robert, C.B.E. Was a Member of Newfoundland War Contingent Assoc. in London. (C2009)

MORRIS, Major Edwin Logie, O.B.E., M.C., R.E. ; 2nd son of late Dr. Clarke Morris, J.P., and Mrs. Clarke Morris.

MORRIS, Elza Mary Jane Mrs. M.B.E.

MORRIS, Ernest William, C.B.E., *b.* 1865 ; *s.* of the Rev. William Edward Morris, of Market Harborough ; *m.* Mary, *d.* of John Ashton Knight, of Walthamstow. *Educ. :* Privately. House Governor of the London Hospital, E. 1. *War Work :* The London Hospital was the first to organise for the reception of wounded, and did admit, at the request of the War Office, the first wounded sent to this country, on Aug. 30, 1914 (350) ; from this date onward, the Hospital admitted Officers and Men throughout the war (about 7000) ; loaned by the Hospital to the War Office during the early part of the War to assist in the work of equipping the hospitals at the Front. *Address :* The Elms, Winchmore Hill, N. 21. (C2823)

MORRIS, Etheldreda Elizabeth. M.B.E. ; *d.* of late Sir Lewis Morris, poet, of Penbryn. *War Work :* Qr.-Mr., Red Cross Hospital, Carmarthen, 1914–16 ; Chief Welfare Superintendent, National Filling Factory, Pembrey, 1916–20. *Address :* Penbryn, Carmarthen, S. Wales. (M2196)

MORRIS, Florence Muriel, O.B.E., M.D. ; *d.* of John Edward Morris, of Bishop's Stortford. *Educ. :* Tremaith School ; Bedford College ; London School of Medicine for Women. Medical Officer, Paignton and District Hospital ; Medical Officer, Infant Welfare Centre, Paignton. *War Work :* Commandant, Devon 104 and Medical Officer in Charge, The Larches, V.A. Hospital, Paignton. *Address :* 4 Queen's Park, Paignton. (O10999)

MORRIS, Francis Joseph, O.B.E., K.C.

MORRIS, Frank, M.B.E., *b.* 9 March, 1893 ; *s.* of William Walter Morris, of Bolton. *Educ. :* Sandbach Grammar School. Member of Cheshire County Horticultural Sub-Committee, and Bee Sub-Committee. *War Work :* County Horticultural Organiser and Sec. Horticultural Sub-Committee (Cheshire) ; Hon. Sec. County Bee Sub-Committee (Cheshire). *Address :* The Limes, Middlewich. (M9091)

MORRIS, Major Frederick, O.B.E., M.C., R.A.O.C.

MORRIS, Major Frederick Herbert, M.B.E., *b.* 2 June, 1872 ; *s.* of I. Morris, of Wellington, Shropshire ; *m.* Evaline Morris, *d.* of H. Harrison, of Fairfield, Manchester. *Educ. :* St. Paul's Coll., Cheltenham. Headmaster, Whitfield School, Glossop. *War Work :* Major in 3/6 Batt. Cheshire Regt. ; Supervising Officer of Recruits Training, attached 204th Infantry Brigade ; Commandant, N.C.O.'s School of Instruction, 204th Infantry Brigade. *Address :* Hill Crest, Glossop, Derbyshire. (M5488)

MORRIS, Capt. Frederick Montague Augustus, M.B.E.

MORRIS, Major George Philip O.B.E., I.A.

MORRIS, Harold Spencer, M.B.E., *b.* 21 Dec , 1876 ; *s.* of Sir Malcolm Morris, K.C.V.O. of 11, Marlborough Place, N.W. ; *m.* Olga, *d.* of Emil Teichmann, of Sitka, Chislehurst. *Educ. :* Clifton Coll., and Magdalen Coll., Oxford. Barrister. *War Work :* 1915–16, Special Constable ; June, 1916, Commission Coldstream Guards ; Oct. 1916, went to France and served

with 1st Battalion ; Sept. 1917, A.D.C. to Maj.-Gen. Sir Geoffrey Feilding G.O.C. Guards Division ; June, 1918, Staff Appointment with R.A.F. with rank of Major ; Feb. 1919, left France. *Address :* 28, Chester Square, S.W. 1. *Clubs :* Reform ; Guards'. (M6018)

MORRIS, Harry, M.B.E.

MORRIS, Henry, O.B.E.

MORRIS, Capt. James Hulbert, O.B.E., R.E.

MORRIS, Jean Anderson, M.B.E.

MORRIS, John, M.B.E., *b.* 2 Nov. 1868 ; *s.* of Charles, of Winkfield, Berkshire ; *m.* Alice Barber, *d.* of Andrew Thomson, of Edinburgh. *Educ. :* Winkfield, Berkshire. Retired non-commissioned officer from Regular Army, after 21 years' service. *War Work :* Superintending clerk in a Military Branch of the War Office during the whole period of the Great War. *Address :* 93, Oliphant Street, London, W. 10. (M9094)

MORRIS, John William, M.B.E.

MORRIS, Jorwerth, M.B.E.

MORRIS, Surg.-Lieut.-Comm. Leslie Miles, O.B.E., R.N.

MORRIS, Lieut. Max Cyril, M.B.E.

MORRIS, Rev. Patrick Joseph, M.B.E.

MORRIS, Lieut. Rhys Hopkin, M.B.E.

MORRIS, Lieut.-Col. Richard John, C.B.E., T.D., M.D., M.R.C.P., M.R.C.S., L.S.A., R.A.M.C. (Retired), *b.* 23 July, 1860 ; *s.* of John Beamish Morris, of Corron, Leap, Co. Cork ; *m.* Martha A., *d.* of Joseph Benn, of Hortan Grange, Bradford, and Willaston, Harrogate. *Educ. :* Queen's Univ., Ireland ; Queen's Coll., Cork ; St. Bartholomew's Hospital, London. Gazetted to 1st V.B. (King's Own) Royal Lancaster Regt. July, 1888 ; Capt. 5 Sept. 1891 ; transferred to Surg.-Lieut. July, 1900 ; passed School, Aldershot, July, 1900 ; appointed Surg.-Capt. 8 Aug. 1903 ; Territorial decoration, May, 1909 ; Hon. Surg.-Major May, 1909, ante-dated March, 1908 ; retired July, 1910. *War Work :* T. Lieut.-Col. 18 Oct. 1915 ; appointed Medical Officer in Charge Northern Command Depot, North Camp, Ripon ; on demobilisation of this Depot was appointed Medical Officer in Charge of Malarial Concentration Centre, No. 17 Camp, Ripon ; mentioned in Sec. of State's list for War Services Feb. 1917. *Address :* Southfield, York Place, Harrogate. *Clubs :* Royal Cork Club, Queenstown ; Royal Automobile, London. (C2214a)

MORRIS, Lieut.-Col. Thomas Henry, C.B.E., J.P., D.L., *b.* 3 Feb. 1848 ; *s.* of William, of The Lodge, nr. Halifax, York ; *m.* Florence Ethel, *d.* of Richard Crompton, of Bury, Lancs. *Educ. :* Rugby. *War Work :* Public and local services as Chairman of the West Riding Standing Joint Committee, Special Constables, and Advisory Committee for Recruiting. *Address :* Bolton Lodge, Bolton Percy. Yorks. *Club :* Union. (C574)

MORRIS, Lieut. Thomas Robertson, O.B.E., R.N.R.

MORRIS, William Anthony, M.B.E.

MORRIS, William Hardwick Grant, M.B.E.

MORRIS, Lieut. and Qr.-Mr. William Henry, M.B.E.

MORRIS, Lieut. William Henry, M.B.E., R.A.S.C., *b.* 3 Nov. 1886 ; *s.* of Mr. W. H. Morris, of Darwen, Lancs. ; *m.* the *d.* of J. W. Faulkner, of Rugby. *Educ. :* Darwen Secondary School. Engineer. *War Work :* Enlisted Nov. 1915 ; trained at Marlborough, Bulford, and Bath ; France, May, 1916 ; Lorry driver in Bethune sector ; later drove an ambulance car in same area ; Rouen in 2nd Heavy Repair Shops as designer and technical engineer for 1 year ; came home for Commission Dec. 1917 ; Commd. Feb. 1918 ; was first at Norwood Depot, and then at London M.T. Repair Depot in charge of Drawing Office and Engine Test Dept. for 1 year. *Address :* 40, Woodlands Park Road, Kings Norton, Birmingham. (M4558)

MORRIS, William Richard, O.B.E.

MORRIS, Lieut.-Col. Thomas Anselan POLLOK-, O.B.E.

MORRIS, Lieut.-Col. Alfred Drummond WARRINGTON-, O.B.E., R.A.F.

MORRISON, Agnes Brysson, C B.E., *b.* 24 March, 1867 ; *d.* of Thomas Inglis, of Edinburgh ; *m.* Arthur Mackie, *s.* of John Morrison, of Glasgow. *Educ. :* Edinburgh ; London ; Leipzig. *War Work :* Raising of Funds for War Charities ; Originator and initiator of the Flag Day movement ; Organised Union Jack Day in Glasgow, on 5 Sept. 1914, which was the first Flag Day ever held ; the total sum collected in the United Kingdom by Flag Days amounts to over £15,000,000 ; personally organised, in Glasgow, Flag Days which resulted in the collection of over £30,000, and in addition organised 344 Flag Days in other centres ; has taken a keen interest in philanthropic and social work, especially in that pertaining to Child Welfare ; identified with the Glasgow Branch of the Scottish Children's League of Pity for a great number of years, being President of that Branch for seven years ; organised many Charity Matinees, the first of these being held on 31 March, 1900, on behalf of the Lord Provost of Glasgow's Fund for sufferers in the South African War. *Address :* Merchiston, 8, Freeland Road, Ealing, London, W. 5. (C2827)

MORRISON, Lieut. Archibald Cameron, O.B.E., M.A., LL.B., 4th Batt. Gordon Highlanders, *b.* 29 July, 1870 ; *s.* of John Morrison, of Logie Pert, Forfarshire ; *m.* Agnes Sproul Nicolson, *d.* of John Nicolson, of Paisley. *Educ. :* Logie Pert School ; Royal High School, Edinburgh ; St. Andrews and Glasgow Universities. Advocate in Aberdeen ; Lecturer in Conveyancing in the Univ. of Aberdeen. *War*

Work: Service at Home with Gordon Highlanders; Military Representative at Appeal Recruiting Tribunal for 175th Recruiting Area Counties of Aberdeen, Kincardine, and Banff. *Address:* 54, Rubislawden North, Aberdeen.   (O11001)

MORRISON, Florence Mildred, Mrs., M.B.E.

MORRISON, Henry St. John, Indian Police; *s.* of Malcolm Brown Morrison, of Bhagalpur, India; *m.* Winifred Alice, *d.* of — de Almeida, of Calcutta, India. *Educ.:* St. Xaviers College, Calcutta, India. *War Work:* Helping to raise the 133rd Behar and Orissa Regiment; helping to preserve order at a time of unusual unrest in the Province; assisting in the control of cloth, coal, and other products. *Address:* Bhagalpur, Behar and Orissa, India.   (M6211)

MORRISON, James Augustus, M.B.E.; *s.* of James Morrison, of Edinburgh; *m.* Grace, *d.* of John Mark, of Enfield. *Educ.:* St. Mary's School, Edinburgh. Master, Princess Christian Homes and Workshops, Bisley; late Staff Qr.-Mr.-Sergt., Brigade of Guards; served in the Kaffir and Zulu War, 1877–9 (Medal and clasp), Nile Expedition, 1884–5 (Medal and clasp) and Khedive of Egypt's Bronze Star; The Long Service Medal. *War Work:* Was in charge of The Princess Christian Convalescent Hospital for Wounded Soldiers and Sailors during the War, and responsible for maintenance, general comfort, recreation, and amusement from 1914–19. *Address:* Princess Christian Homes, Bisley, Surrey. (M2201)

MORRISON, Col. John, M.V.O., O.B.E., J.P.

MORRISON John, O.B.E.

MORRISON, John, M.B.E.

MORRISON, John, O B E.

MORRISON, John, M.B.E.

MORRISON John Dow, O.B.E.

MORRISON, Lieut. John Fraser, O.B.E., R.A.O.C.

MORRISON, Major John Norman, O.B.E., *b.* 20 Aug. 1889, *s.* of John S. Morrison, of Galashiels. *Educ.:* Heidelberg and Hanover. Farmer in England and the Argentine. *War Work:* Four and a half years with Army Remount Service in England, Egypt, and Salonica. *Addresses:* Southmoor House, Kingston-Bagpuize, Berks; Rowanlea, Galashiels, Scotland.   (O6512)

MORRISON, John Tertius, O.B.E., F.R.C.S., late Major, R.A.M.C., *b.* 1888; *s.* of Rev. John Morrison, M.A., D.D., of Yester, Lady Road, Edinburgh; *m.* Eliza Mary, *d.* of William Wrigley, of Wesley Villa, Rawtenstall, Lancs. *Educ.:* Fettes Coll., Edinburgh, and Edinburgh Univ. Surgical Registrar, Royal Southern Hospital, Liverpool; Demonstrator of Anatomy, Univ. of Liverpool. *War Work:* Surgeon i/c Surgical Research Unit, Etaples (2 years); Officer i/c Surgical Division, General Hospital, B.E.F., France. *Address:* 5, St. James' Road, Rodney Street, Liverpool. *Club:* Univ. Liverpool.   (O5607)

MORRISON, Julia Minnie, C.B.E.; *d.* of John Hamilton Whitcroft, of Kilree House, Co. Kilkenny; *m.* Beamish Austin, *s.* of W. B. A. Morrison, of Queenstown, Co. Cork. *Educ.:* Kilkenny. *War Work:* Organising Soldiers' and Sailors' Buffet at Kingstown, Ireland. *Address:* 3, Arkendale Road, Glenageary, Co. Dublin.   (C2825)

MORRISON, Kate, M.B.E., Principal Women's Training College.   (M10359)

MORRISON, Sidney William, O.B.E.

MORRISON, Major William Geekie, O.B.E., Can. A.P.C.

MORRISSEY, Paymaster-Lieut. Patrick Henry, M.B.E., R.N.

MORRISSEY, William, M.B.E., R.N.

MORROW, Charles Thomas, M.B.E.   (M10244)

MORROW, George Andrew, O.B.E., *b.* 28 Oct. 1877; *s.* of J. M. Morrow, of Toronto, Canada; *m.* Phoebe C., *d.* of J. C. Graham, of Toronto, Canada. *Educ.:* Collegiate Institute, Peterboro, Toronto, Canada. Financier; President, Imperial Life Assurance Coy., Toronto, Canada. *War Work:* Director of Aviation for Canada during years 1917–18, under Imperial Munitions Board (Canada). *Address:* 26, King St. East, Toronto. *Clubs:* York; Toronto.   (O599)

MORROW, Major John Smythe, O.B.E., M.D., R.A.M.C.

MORSE, Capt. Leopold George Esmond, M.B.E.

MORSE, Major Thomas Ricketts, O.B.E., *b.* 3 Oct. 1858; *s.* of Richard Morse, of Aivre, Glos.; *m.* Janie Williamson, *d.* of Henry Scott, of Winterton Holmes, Lincoln. *Educ.:* Cheltenham. *War Work:* 5½ years during late war; Active service in France and Serbia; 2nd in Command 9th Border Regt.; Commanded 27th Div. Base Depot, Salonica and Egypt; Commanded 4th Convalescent Depot, Salonica. *Address:* North House, Northam, N. Devon.   (O8887)

MORSLEY, Major John William, O.B.E., R.A.

MORSON, Surg.-Lieut. Albert Clifford, O.B.E., F.R.C.S., R.N.

MORSON, Arthur, M.B.E.

MORT, Arthur, O.B.E., *b.* 15 Sept. 1873; *s.* of William Mort, of Manchester; *m.* Florence Ann, *d.* of Rev. J. Court, Rector of Widdington, Essex. *Educ.:* Central School, Manchester, and Royal Coll. of Science, Dublin; B.Sc. London University. Mining engineer. *War Work:* Was on Govt. Mining service in Baluchistan, India. *Addresses:* Quetta, India; 34, Central Road, West Didsbury, Manchester.   (O4075)

MORT, Lieut. John William, M.B.E.

MORT, Mary Laidley Marjorie, O.B.E.   (O11999)

MORTEN, Lieut.-Col. Raymond Laroche Alexander Burdett, O.B.E., R.A.S.C.

MORTIMER, Capt. Frederick George Crofton, O.B.E., R.A.O.C.

MORTIMER, Joseph, O.B.E.

MORTIMER, Capt. Leslie, O.B.E., R.A.S.C.

MORTIMER, Muriel Ida, Mary, M.B.E., *b.* 22 April, 1871; *d.* of Alfred Thomas, J.P., of Frodsham, Cheshire; *m.* Harry Percival, *s.* of William Mortimer, J.P. *Educ.:* Privately. *War Work:* Official Searcher, Enquiry Department for Wounded and Missing, British Red Cross Society. *Address:* Crofton Lodge, Kingsley, Cheshire.   (M9097)

MORTIMER, Ralph George Elphinstone, O.B.E., M.A., J.P., Hon. Capt. 1st (Vol.) Batt. Northumberland Fusiliers. *b.* 7 July, 1869; *s.* of William Brook Mortimer, of Hay Carr, nr. Lancaster; *m.* Violet, *d.* of Major E. W. Stokes, of King's Own Regt. *Educ.:* Elstree; Harrow; Trinity Coll., Cambridge. Chairman, Castle Ward Board of Guardians; Member Castle Ward Rural District Council; Vice-Chairman, House Committee, Royal Victoria Infirmary, Newcastle-upon-Tyne; J.P. Northumberland; Chairman, Northumberland County Cricket Committee; District Commissioner, East Castle Ward, Boy Scouts. *War Work:* Commandant Belsay V.A.D.; Group Leader Castle Ward Special Constables; Private, and later commission, 1st (Vol.) Batt. Northumberland Fusiliers; National Service Sub-Commissioner; Assistant Commissioner for Food, Northumberland; Chairman Castle Ward Local Tribunal (Military Service Act), and Local Food Control Committee. *Address:* Milbourne Hall, Higham Dykes, Northumberland. *Clubs:* Sports; Northern Counties (Newcastle-upon-Tyne); County (Lancaster).   (O11006)

MORTIMER, Hon. Lieut. Reginald Mortimer Higgs, M.B.E., M.A., J.P., for Herts County, *b.* 2 April, 1861; *s.* of the Rev. Mortimer Lloyd Mortimer, of Norton Vicarage, Durham; *m.* Gertrude Mary, *d.* of Rev. E. Norgate, of Bartlow Rectory, Cambs. *Educ.:* Harrow and Cambridge. Divisional Director of Industrial Training for Disabled Soldiers. *War Work:* Helped to raise and train a Company of the Herts (V.) Regt.; Military Representative N. Herts., 1915–17; Assistant Director of National Service for Hertfordshire. *Address:* Molesworth, Hitchin. *Club:* Carlton.   (M9098)

MORTIMER, Robert Richardson, M.B.E.

MORTIMER, William Alfred, M.B.E.

MORTIMORE, Lieut. Clifford Charles, M.B.E.

MORTISHED, Paymaster Lieut.-Comm. John, M.B.E., R.D., R.N.R., *b.* 16 June, 1861; *s.* of P. Mortished, of Limerick. Collector, H.M. Customs and Excise, Middlesbrough; Superintendent Mercantile Marine; Registrar Royal Naval Reserve; Admiralty Marshal's Substitute. *War Work:* Mobilisation of District Forces of the Royal Naval Reserve; official supervision of control of imports and exports of the port of Middlesbrough; receipt and disposal of Naval Prize Cargoes. *Address:* Marton, Cleveland, Yorks.   (M0099)

MORTON, Capt. Alfred, M.B.E., *b.* 1886; *s.* of Sir Alpheus C. Morton, of London. *Educ.:* Merchant Taylors' School. *War Work:* Army, 1914–1920, Bedford Regt., Staff Capt. Jan. 1919, to April, 1920. *Address:* 47, Ganden Road, S.W. 4. *Club:* Junior Constitutional.   (M6682)

MORTON, Major Arthur William, O.B.E., Can. A.S.C., R.A.S.C.

MORTON, Professor Charles Alexander, O.B.E., F.R.C.S. *b.* 10 Sept. 1860. *s.* of John Morton, of Indian Medical Service. *Educ.:* Bristol, and St. Bartholomew's Hospital, London. Professor of Surgery in University of Bristol, Senior Surgeon to the Bristol General Hospital; Consulting Surgeon to the Bristol Children's Hospital. *War Work:* Surgeon to the Beauford War Hospital, Bristol, for 4 years, and District Consulting Surgeon for Gloucester and Somerset in the Southern Command. *Address:* 14, Vyvyan Terrace, Clifton, Bristol.   (O8889)

MORTON, Lieut.-Col. Edward, C.B.E., the Cheshire Regt., *b.* 28 April, 1871; *s.* of the late Robert Morton, Col., Royal Artillery; *m.* Adeline Louise, *d.* of the late Rev. R. Langshaw, Rector of West Grinstead. *Educ.:* Privately. *Club:* Junior Army and Navy.   (C1706)

MORTON, Capt. Edwin Ralph Maddison, O.B.E., M.A., *b.* 7 Dec. 1891; *s.* of Edwin Morton, M.A., M.D., D.P.H.; of Christ Church, Oxford. *Educ.:* Magdalen Coll. School, Queen's Coll., Oxford. *War Work:* France and Belgium, Aug. 1914, to March, 1919; Germany, Nov. 1919; Adjutant, Sept. 1917, to Nov. 1919. *Addresses:* Chaucer's House, Woodstock; United Service Institution.   (O5608)

MORTON, Elsie Eleanor, M.B.E.; *d.* of Sir Alpheus C. Morton, M.P. for Sutherland, 1906–18; Chairman of Deptford Association of Care Committees; Member of London Insurance Committee; Member of London Old Age Pensions Committee; Chairman of Old Age Pensions Committee for Southwark and Bermondsey. *War Work:* Hon. Org. Sec. of workrooms for unemployed women and girls in the City of London and in Deptford; Hon. Organising Sec. of Deptford War Hospital Supply Depot; Member of London Committee for allocating allowances to soldiers' dependants; work on Sundays as relief hand at munition factory, Bermondsey. *Addresses:* 47, Gauden Road, Clapham, S.W.; The Home Farm, Pattersen Court, Redhill, Surrey.   (M2206)

MORTON, Lieut. George Bowen, M.B.E., R.F.A., *b.* 25 March, 1888; *s.* of Rev. T. E. F. Morton, of Princess Anne, U.S.A.; *m.* Beatrice Louisa, *d.* of J. Oxford, of Brookwood, Surrey. *Address:* c/o Cox & Co., 16, Charing Cross, London, S.W. 1.   (M5491)

MORTON, Hugh, O.B.E.

MORTON, Lieut.-Col. Hugh Murray, C.B.E., D.S.O., M.B., R.A.M.C., *b.* 1873. *Educ.:* Edinburgh Univ. (M.B. and C.M.

1896). S. Africa, 1900–2, present at relief of Ladysmith (Queen's medal with five clasps) ; served in Great War in Mesopotamia, 1915–19 (mentioned in despatches). (C1431)

MORTON, Lieut. John Darnley Mitford, M.B.E.

MORTON, Capt. Robert, O.B.E.

MORTON, Capt. Robert Connell, M.B.E., R.E.

MORTON, William Cuthbert, C.B.E., M.A., M.D., *b.* 1 March, 1875 ; *s.* of Rev. John Morton, D.D., of Trinidad, B.W. Indies. *Educ.* : Royal Coll., Trinidad ; Edinburgh Univ. Hon. Demonstrator in Anatomy, Univ. of Leeds. *War Work* : Captain, R.A.M.C., in charge of Department for Muscle Re-education, 2nd Northern General Military Hospital (Orthopædic). *Address* : 34, Headingley Lane, Leeds. (C1158)

MORWOOD, 2nd Lieut. Arthur, O.B.E.

MOSCRIP, Holbourn Jackson, M.B.E., *b.* 5 May, 1869 ; *s.* of Holbourn James Moscrip, of Boston, Lincolnshire ; *m.* Margaret, *d.* of Thomas Lowes, of Newcastle-upon-Tyne. *Educ.* : Boston Grammar School. Committee Clerk, Tyne Improvement Commission, Newcastle-upon-Tyne. *War Work* : Services in connection with the maintenance of the flow of traffic in the port of Tyne. *Address* : 35, Balmoral Terrace, Gosforth, Newcastle-upon-Tyne. (M9100)

MOSCROP, Andrew, O.B.E., J.P., *b.* 1863 ; *s.* of the late William Jobson Moscrop, of Saltburn-by-Sea ; *m.* Annie Chapman, *d.* of Eccles Haigh. Land Agent ; Member of Agricultural Wages Board, Council of Yorkshire Agricultural Society ; Chairman of Yorkshire Fat Stock Society ; President of Yorkshire Coach Horse Society. *War Work* : Member, Central Agricultural Advisory Council, and Advisory Council on Food Production under four successive Presidents of Board of Agriculture ; Chairman of Local Tribunal, Local Food Control Committee. *Address* : Thorganby Hall, York. *Club* : Farmers'. (O1685)

MOSELEY, Arthur Herbert, M.B.E.

MOSELEY, Lieut. Edward James, O.B.E., R.N.V.R.

MOSELEY, Louise, M.B.E. ; *d.* of the late Joseph Moseley, J.P., of Cringle Hall, Levenshulme. *War Work* : Drove motor cars and ambulances for the East Lancashire Branch of the B.R.C.S. from Aug. 1914, to 11 May, 1919 ; assisted in the direction of the Cringle Hall Convalescent Home, Levenshulme, from Oct. 1914, to Jan. 1919. *Address* : Pendyffryn, Penmon, Beaumaris, Anglesey. *Clubs* : Royal Anglesey Yacht ; Empress. (M9101)

MOSELEY, Mary, M.B.E.

MOSELEY, Miriam Louise, Mrs., O.B.E.

MOSES, Capt. and Qr.-Mr. Joseph Henry Gronow, M.B.E.

MOSEY, Paymaster Lieut.-Comm. James Yeoman, O.B.E., R.D., R.N.R., *b.* 1857 ; *s.* of Philip Stephen Mosey, of London ; *m.* Frances, *d.* of S. Clarke Tolbutt, of Sussex. *Educ.* : Privately and City of London Coll. Chief Superintendent, Board of Trade Mercantile Marine Office, London District. *War Work* : Mobilisation of R.N.R. and despatching men to Depot ; recruitment in large numbers of Merchant Seamen for Ministry of Shipping for Admiralty Auxiliary Reserve ; promptly refitting crews of torpedoed vessels and generally assisting in the work of keeping the Merchant Service going during the war. *Address* : Beachfield, Leigh-on-Sea, Essex. *Club* : P.M. L.R. All Saints' Lodge of Freemasons. (O11009)

MOSS, Enoch, M.B.E., M.D.

MOSS, Lieut. Frederic William, M.B.E., M.C., M.G.C.

MOSS, George Sinclair, M.B.E., *b.* 26 April, 1882 ; *s.* of Charles Davis Moss, of Cirencester and Yokohama ; *m.* Gladys Lucy, *d.* of G. A. Moore, of Liverpool. *Educ.* : Privately and King's Coll., London. H.M. Vice-Consul in China. *War Work* : District Officer and Magistrate, Weihaiwei, 1914–15 ; employed in the Foreign Office, 1916 ; Principal Assistant to the War Office Representative for the Recruitment of Chinese Labour, 1916–18 ; appointed War Office Representative, 1918–20. (M787)

MOSS, Henry, M.B.E., A.M.I.M.E.

MOSS, Lieut. (T. Capt.) Kenneth Neville, O.B.E., A.M.Inst.C.E., M.Sc., R.E. (T.), *b.* 30 May, 1891 ; *s.* of William Moss, of Gairloch, Penns, Warwickshire ; *m.* Dorothy, *d.* of Professor R. Warington, F.R.S., M.A., of Harpenden and Oxford. *Educ.* : Queen Mary's School, Walsall, and Birmingham Univ. Mining Engineer ; Assistant Professor of Coal Mining, Birmingham Univ. ; Tyndall Scholar of the Royal Society, 1920. *War Work* : Joined S. Staffs. Regt. as a 2nd Lieut., Feb. 1915, transferred to Royal Engineers, T.F., in May, appointed Adjutant to 59th Divisional R.E. in Nov. 1915 ; served in Ireland during the Rebellion, April, 1916, to Jan. 1917 ; served in France, Feb. 1917, to Jan. 1919, as Adjutant to 59th Div. R.E. ; twice mentioned in despatches. *Address* : Gairloch, Penns, Warwickshire. (O5610)

MOSS, Margaret, Mrs., O.B.E., W.R.A.F.

MOSS, Thomas, O.B.E.

MOSS, Wilfred, M.B.E. ; Chairman of Advisory Committees under the Derby Scheme and Military Service Acts. (M10339)

MOSSES, William, O.B.E.

MOSTYN, Mary Florence Edith, Lady, O.B.E. ; *s.* of the 4th Earl of Leitrim (*see* BURKE'S *Peerage*) ; *m.* Llewellyn Nevile Vaughan, 3rd Baron Mostyn, *s.* of the Hon. Thomas Edward Lloyd-Mostyn (and *g.s.* of 1st Baron ; *see* BURKE'S *Peerage*) and Lady Henrietta Augusta Nevile, *d.* of 4th Earl of Abergavenny (*see* BURKE'S *Peerage*). *Address* : Mostyn Hall, Holywell, Flint. (O3846)

MOSTYN, Pamela Georgina, Hon. Mrs. LLOYD-, M.B.E. ;

d. of the 2nd Lord Penrhyn (*see* BURKE'S *Peerage*) ; *m.* the Hon. Henry Richard Howel, J.P., D.L., Lieut.-Col. Commanding 17th Batt. R. W. Fusiliers, *s.* of the Hon. Thomas E. Lloyd-Mostyn, and brother of the 3rd Baron Mostyn. *Address* : Bodysgallen, Llandudno. (M9102)

MOTH, Rev. John Charles, O.B.E.

MOTHERWELL, Capt. Gavin Black Loudon, O.B.E.

MOTHES, 2nd Lieut. Frederick William, M.B.E.

MOTT, Sir Frederick Walker, K.B.E., F.R.S., M.D., *b.* 23 Oct. 1853 ; *s.* of Henry Mott, of Brighton ; *m.* Georgiana Alexandra, *d.* of G. T. Soley, of Liverpool. *Educ.* : University Coll., London. Consulting Physician, Charing Cross Hospital ; Director, Pathological Laboratory, L.C.C. Asylums. *War Work* : Neurological Specialist, Maudsley Neurological Clearing Hospital, Denmark Hill, with rank of Brevet Lieut.-Col. ; mentioned in despatches. *Address* : 25, Nottingham Place, London, W. *Club* : Savage. (K294)

MOTT, Owen Edward, O.B.E., Ph.D.

MOTTRAM, Capt. Francis Henry, M.B.E., R.E., *b.* 24 April, 1891. *Educ.* : Felsted School, Essex. Mechanical Engineer. *War Work* : Joined R.E. (T.F.) 5 Sept. 1914 ; served abroad in Egypt, Gallipoli, Balkans, Caucasus (South Russia), June, 1915, to Aug. 1919. *Address* : 23, Westbourne Road, Birkdale, Lancs. (M6579)

MOTTRAM, Thomas Harry, C.B.E. Chief Inspector for Mines, and Chairman of Colliery Recruiting Courts, Yorkshire and N. Midlands Div. (C255)

MOUAT, Basilina Ninian, M.B.E., W.R.N.S.

MOUAT, Lieut. Charles George KAY-, O.B.E., 1/70 Burma Rifles. (M9057e)

MOULD, Capt. and Qr.-Mr. John Alfred, O.B.E.

MOULDEN, Capt. Arnold Meredith, O.B.E.

MOULLIN, Brevet. Col. Charles William MANSELL-, C.B.E., M.A., M.D., F.R.C.S., R.A.M.C. (T.), *b.* 24 Oct. 1851 ; *s.* of James Mansell-Moullin, of Porchester Terrace, W. 2 ; *m.* Edith Ruth, *d.* of D. C. Thomas, of Hove. *Educ.* : Pembroke Coll., Oxford ; St. Bartholomew's Hospital. Consulting Surgeon, London Hospital ; formerly Vice-Pres. and Member of Council of Royal College of Surgeons ; Radcliffe's Travelling Fellow, Oxford ; Examiner in Surgery, Universities of Oxford, Cambridge, Glasgow. *War Work* : Col. in charge of Surgical Division, 2nd London (City of London) General Hospital, Chelsea. *Address* : 28, Victoria Road, Kensington, W. 8. (C1707)

MOULTON, Major John Coney, O.B.E.

MOULTON, John Fletcher, Baron, P.C., G.B.E., K.C.B., *b.* 1844, 3rd *s.* of the Rev. James Egan Moulton ; *m.* 1875, Clara, widow of R. W. Thompson, of Edinburgh. M.A. (Cantab.), Senior Wrangler and First Smith's Prizeman, 1868 ; Bar.-at-Law. Chairman, Med. Research Committee, National Insurance Act ; Director-General of Explosives, Ministry of Munitions ; Grand Officer, Order of " Etoile Noire," Comm. Legion of Honour and Order of Leopold of Belgium. *Addresses* : 57, Onslow Square, S.W. ; Forest Green, Bank, near Lyndhurst, Hants. *Clubs* : Athenæum ; Reform ; Savage ; Garrick ; Royal Automobile. (G4)

MOUNSEY, George Augustus, O.B.E.

MOUNSEY, Major John, O.B.E.

MOUNSEY, Major Roland James, O.B.E., R.A.F.

MOUNT, Lieut.-Col. Alan Henry Lawrence, C.B.E.

MOUNT, Hilda Lucy Adelaide, Mrs., O.B.E., *b.* 25 May, 1875 ; *d.* of Malcolm Low, of Clatto, Cupar, Fife ; *m.* William Arthur, *s.* of William George Mount, of Wasing Place, Berks. *War Work* : Hon. Sec. Royal Berks Regt.. Prisoners of War Committee. *Address* : Wasing Place, Berks. *Club* : Ladies' Imperial. (O11010)

MOUNT, William Arthur, C.B.E., B.A., J.P., M.P., *b.* 1866 ; *s.* of the late William George Mount, of Wasing Place, Berks ; *m.* 1899, Hilda Lucy Adelaide, *d.* of Malcolm Low, of Clatto, Cupar, Fife, and 22, Roland Gardens, S.W. *Educ.* : Eton and New Coll. Oxford. Called to the Bar, Inner Temple, 1893 ; Assist. Private Sec. 1895–1900 ; Parliamentary Private Sec. 1900–1, to Chancellor of the Exchequer, 1902 ; Civil Member of Claims Commn. War Office, 1916–17 ; Member of Council of Duchy of Lancaster, and an Officer of Legion of Honour ; appointed Second Church Estates Commr. 1919 ; sat as M.P. for S. or Newbury Div. of Berkshire, 1900–6, and 1910–18 ; elected for Berks, Newbury Div. Dec. 1918. *Address* : Wasing Place, near Reading. *Clubs* : Oxford and Cambridge ; Carlton. (C256)

MOUNTFORD, Lewis James, C.B.E., *b.* 1871 ; *s.* of Henry Mountford, of West Dulwich, S.E. *Educ.* : Dulwich Coll. and Pembroke Coll. Camb. Entered I.C.S. 1890 ; appointed Collector of Sholapur, 1907 ; Satara, 1911 ; Poona, 1913 ; Commr. since 1916 ; Member of Standing Committee of Bombay Provincial Recruiting Board, 1917 ; Additional Member of Viceroy's Legislative Council, 1919. *Address* : Belgaum, Bombay Presidency, India. *Clubs* : East India United Service ; Royal Automobile. (C690)

MOUNTGARRET, Robinia Marion, Viscountess, O.B.E., Lady of Grace of Order of St. John of Jerusalem, *b.* 25 Aug. 1874 ; *d.* of Col. E. Hanning-Lee, 2nd Life Guards, of Brighton, Alresford, Hants ; *m.* Henry Edmund, 14th Viscount (died 1912), *s.* of Henry Edmund, 13th Viscount Mountgarret (*see* BURKE'S *Peerage*). *War Work* : Vice-President of No. 4 District W.R. Yorkshire, St. John Ambulance Association ; for four years Commandant and Matron, Officers' Hospital at 18, Cadogan Gardens, London. *Address* : Nidd Hall, Ripley, Harrogate. *Club* : Ladies' Athenæum. (O11011)

MOUNTIFIELD, Engineer-Capt. James, C.B.E., *b.* 1871 ; *s.* of Alfred Mountifield ; *m.* 1908, Maud, *d.* of William Phillips. *Educ.* : R.N. Engineering Coll., Keyham, and R.N. Coll., Greenwich. Professional A.M.I.C.E. 1902 ; Assist. Engineer-Manager at Chatham, 1900–6 ; at Hong Kong, 1908–9 ; at Devonport, 1910–13 ; and at Portsmouth, 1915–17 ; since when he has been Chief Engineer, Sheerness Dockyard ; served in Great War, 1914–15, present at battle of Dogger Bank. *Address* : H.M. Dockyard, Sheerness. (C2318)

MOUNTJOY, John Percy, O.B.E., F.C.A., *b.* 18 May, 1881 ; *s.* of J. Fursman Mountjoy, of Bideford, North Devon ; *m.* Alice, *d.* of Major Rees Thomas, J.P., of Pyle, Glam. *Educ.* : Cardiff Municipal Secondary School ; Chartered Accountant in practice at Cardiff. *War Work* : Divisional Accountant, Coal Mines Department, Board of Trade ; Hon. Auditor, National Relief Fund, County of Montgomery. *Addresses* : 5, Plasturton Avenue ; 27, High Street, Cardiff. (O1688)

MOUNT STEPHEN, Giana, Baroness, D.B.E., Lady of Grace of St. John of Jerusalem, *b.* Aug. 1862 ; *d.* of the late Capt. George Tufnell, R.N. ; *m.* George Stephen, 1st Baron Mount Stephen, G.C.V.O. (*see* BURKE'S *Peerage*), *s.* of William Stephen, of Dufftown, Banff. *War Work* : Queen Mary's Needlework Guild, St. James' Palace ; Vice-President, British Red Cross in County of Hertfordshire. *Addresses* : 17, Carlton House Terrace ; Brocket Hall, Hatfield, Herts. (D36)

MOUNTSTEPHENS, Lieut. Richard, O.B.E., R.N.

MOUSLEY, Arthur, M.B.E.

MOWAT, Brig.-Gen. Magnus, C.B.E., T.D., R.E., M. Inst. C.E., M.I.M.E., *b.* 1875 ; *s.* of the late Hon. Magnus Mowat. *Educ.* : King's Coll., London (Asso. Honours in Engmeering). Was administrative Officer for Roads and Bridges at War Office, 1919–20 ; served in Great War 1914–19 as Staff Officer to Ch. Engineer Comdg. R.E. of a Div. and Director at War Office. (C2214*f*)

MOWAT, Annie Angus, M.B.E.

MOWBRAY, George, M.B.E.

MOWBRAY, Lieut.-Col. John Arthur Clark, O.B.E., Can. A.P.C.

MOXON, Hon. Major Francis Henry, O.B.E., M.B., B.S., R.A.M.C., *b.* 22 Aug. 1879 ; *s.* of Dr. Benjamin Howard Hoxon, of Hull, Yorks ; *m.* Alice Esther (d. 25 May, 1914), *d.* of I. M. Gilford, of Redhill, and Evelyn Anna, widow of B. P. Eykyn, and *d.* of J. L. Patton, of U.S.A. *Educ.* : Ockbrook Moravian School, and Durham Univ. Hon. Ophthalmic Surgeon, St. Marylebone General Dispensary ; Chief Clinical Assistant, Moorfields Eye Hospital ; Oculist, Medical Boards, Ministry of Pensions. *War Work* : Gazetted Temp. Lieut., Aug. 1914 ; Officer in charge, Ophthalmic Centre, Havre Base ; Officer in charge, Ophthalmic Centre, St. Omer Area ; Officer in charge, Ophthalmic Centre, First and Fifth Armies ; Officer in charge, Spectacle Depot at Arques for all the Armies at the Front (1st, 2nd, 3rd, 4th, and 5th) ; Officer in charge, Ophthalmic Centre, Trouville Hospital Centre ; Officer in charge Ophthalmic Centre, Boulogne Base ; Officer in charge, Surgical Division, No. 14 Stationary Hospital. *Addresses* : 4, Bentinck Street, Cavendish Square, W. 1. ; Barham Cottage, Wimbledon Common, S.W. 19. (O5611)

MOXON, Lieut.-Col. Herbert William, O.B.E.

MOXON, John, O.B.E., *b.* 17 Oct. 1864 ; *s.* of John Moxon, of Baghill House, Pontefract ; *m.* Annie Henrietta Helena Louisa, *d.* of Philip Ebzury Purdon, of Kilcooley, Co. Meath, Ireland. *Educ.* : St. Peters, York, and The Leys, Cambridge. Chairman Newport Electricity and Tramways Undertakings ; late Chairman, Newport Harbour Commissioners ; Alderman of Newport Corporation. *War Work* : Secretary, the Newport National Shell Factory. *Addresses* : The Lodge, Malpas, Newport, Mon. *Clubs* : Constitutional ; County, Newport. (O1689)

MOYLAN, John FitzGerald, C.B.E., *b.* 16 June, 1882 ; *s.* of the late Edward Kyran Moylan, of Rangoon, Burmah ; *m.* Ysolda Mary Nesta, *d.* of the late Hon. J. D. FitzGerald, K.C. *Educ.* : Bedford School and Queen's Coll., Cambridge. Receiver for Metropolitan Police District. *War Work* : Home Office. *Address* : 24, Stafford Terrace, W. 8. *Club* : Oxford and Cambridge. (C575)

MOYLES, John George, M.B.E., M.B., B.Ch., B.A.O., J.P., *b.* 24 Feb. 1864 ; *s.* of Robert Moyles, of Queen's County, Ireland ; *m.* Evelyn Mary, *d.* of Charles D. Phillips, London. *Educ.* : Dublin Univ. Liverpool City Councillor for 17 years ; Created an Alderman of the City Council, Liverpool, 1920 ; Chairman of the Port Sanitary and Hospital Committee. *War Work* : Medical Officer in charge of Westminster Road Aux. Military Hospital (250 beds) for 4½ years ; Medical Referee, Ministry of Pensions ; Medical Officer in charge, Walton Recruiting Station, 1914–15. *Address* : 2, Bedford Road, Walton, Liverpool. *Club* : Conservative, Liverpool. (M10277)

MOYSES, Harry John Swenson, O.B.E.

MOZLEY, William, O.B.E.

MUDD, Edith Emily, M.B.E. ; *d.* of Barrington Richard Mudd, of Storrington, Sussex. *Educ.* : Privately. Lady Almoner, St. George's Hospital ; District Organiser of Children's Care Work (L.C.C.). *War Work* : Superintendent of Canteen, Park Royal Inspection Buildings. *Clubs* : Sesame ; Ladies' Alpine. (M2210)

MUDGE. Jenny, M.B.E. ; *d.* of Arthur Thomas Mudge, of Sydney Plympton, S. Devon. *War Work* : Quartermaster, V.A. Hospital, Plympton, S. Devon ; Superintendent, Sec. of Plympton War Hospital Supply Depot ; Manager of Plympton Local Work Party. *Address* : Sydney, Plympton, S. Devon. (M9104)

MUDIE, Annie Bertha, Mrs., O.B.E., *b.* 13 March, 1861 ; *d.* of the late William Milner, of Hampstead ; *m.* Ernest Robert, *s.* of George Ritchie Mudie. *War Work* : President of the Executive Committee of the Muswell Hill War Hospital Supply Depot, a Surgical Branch of Queen Mary's Needlework Guild. *Address* : 34, Queen's Avenue, Muswell Hill, N. 10. *Club* : Highgate Golf. (O3847)

MUDIE, Capt. Robert Francis, O.B.E.

MUDGE, Capt. Albert Edward Phayre, O.B.E.

MUECKE, Lieut.-Col. Francis Frederick, C.B.E., M.B., B.S., F.R.C.S., *b.* 1879 ; *s.* of the Hon. H. E. Muecke, M.L.C., of Adelaide ; *m.* 1905, Ada, *d.* of the late Edward Wallis Crossley. *Educ.* : Adelaide Univ. Assist. Surg. London Throat Hospital ; Assist. Aural Surg. London Hospital, Member of British Med. Assocn. ; served in Great War, 1914–19, as Lieut.-Col. R.A.F. (despatches). *Address* : 59, Queen Anne Street, W. (C870)

MUGGERIDGE, Capt. Charles Ernest, O.B.E., M.C.

MUGLISTON, Francis Hugh, O.B.E., B.A., Bar.-at-Law ; Chevalier de l'Ordre de la Couronne, *b.* 7 June, 1886 ; *s.* of Thomas Crichton Mugliston, M.R.C.S., L.R.C.P., etc., Colonial Medical Service (ret.); *m.* Amy Phyllis Keigwin, *d.* of the late Thomas Henry Keigwin, of Sydney, New South Wales. *Educ.* : Rossall School, and Pembroke Coll., Cambridge. Home Civil Service ; appointed H.M. Superintending Aliens Officer in Jan. 1917 ; H.M. Deputy Inspector under the Aliens Act in July, 1918, and H.M. Superintending Inspector, Aliens Branch, Home Office, in June, 1920. *War Work* : Gazetted 2nd Lieut. 6th Batt. (Service), Duke of Cornwall's Light Infantry, 43rd Brigade, 14th Light Division, in Sept. 1914 ; seriously wounded at Ypres in June, 1915 ; 1916, did voluntary work for the Government Committee on the Treatment by the Enemy of British Prisoners of War, and for the Central Tribunal, National Service Department ; invalided out of the Army in Sept. 1918, on account of ill-health caused by wounds. *Address* : 15, Cornwall Gardens, S.W. *Clubs* : Cavendish ; M.C.C. ; Free Foresters C.C. ; Corinthian Football ; Oxford and Cambridge Golfing Society. (O11013)

MUIR, Major Allan Stanley, O.B.E.

MUIR, Lieut. Allan Thompson, O.B.E., R.N.R.

MUIR, Major Archibald Huleath Huntley, O.B.E.

MUIR, Dorothy Coward, M.B.E., R.A.F.

MUIR, Lieut.-Col. George, O.B.E., R.E. (S.R.)

MUIR, Major James Ernest, O.B.E., R.E.

MUIR, Capt. John, O.B.E., R.A.M.C. (T.).

MUIR, John, O.B.E., J.P.

MUIR, Lieut.-Col. Robert Bunten, O.B.E.

MUIR, Major Wingate Wemyss, O.B.E.

MUIRHEAD, Essa Gemmell, Mrs., M.B.E. ; *d.* of Andrew G. Ronald, late of Oak Hill Park, Liverpool ; *m.* David James, *s.* of David Muirhead, late of Shanghai, China. *Educ.* : Privately, and Villa Marie Louise, Paris. *War Work* : Hon. Sec. of Local War Savings Committee, Woking, Surrey, from Dec. 1916 ; Hon. Sec. and Organiser of the local War Loan Campaigns, also the Food Control Committee of 1917. *Address* : Sturry House, Weybridge, Surrey. (M9105)

MUIRHEAD, Frank Stirling, O.B.E.

MUIRHEAD, Capt. James Calder, M.B.E.

MUIRHEAD, John, O.B.E.

MUIRHEAD, Hon. Mrs. Katherine Charlotte Elizabeth Stewart, M.B.E., *b.* 1861 ; *d.* of the 17th Baron Semphill, of Craigievar, Aberdeenshire (*see* BURKE'S *Peerage*) ; *m.* George Muirhead. *War Work* : Vice-President of the Fochabers and Garmouth Branches of the Morayshire Red Cross Society ; Convenor of the House Committee of the Gordon Castle Auxiliary Hospital (100 beds) ; Member of the Finance Committee connected with that hospital ; started and helped to carry on a large and successful Red Cross Work Party ; assisted in equipping and carrying on a Red Cross Hospital of 30 beds at Spey Bay, Morayshire, for wounded Belgian soldiers. *Address* : Speymain, Fochabers, Morayshire. *Club* : Ladies' Park, Knightsbridge, London, S.W. (M3858)

MUIRHEAD, Lieut.-Col. William Henry, O.B.E.

MULCAHY, James Hamilton, M.B.E., *b.* 25 July, 1878 ; *s.* of the late William Mulcahy, a Mutiny veteran holding the Mutiny Medal, Long Service and Good Conduct Medal, of Tipperary, Ireland ; *m.* Emily Ada, *d.* of George Turnage, of London and B.I.S.N. Co., India. *Educ.* : St. George's School, Hyderabad, Deccan, India, and Ootacamund Laurence Asylum, India. Assistant Commissioner of Police Criminal Investigation Department. *War Work* : In charge of the German and Austrian subjects (civil) during the war ; rounding up of enemy subjects, supervision of enemy correspondence ; tracing spies, suppressing illegal trading and checking of passports during the whole period of the war ; general supervision in Calcutta. *Address* : 18, Lall Bazaar, Police Office, Calcutta, India. (M7132)

MULES, Sir (Horace) Charles, Knt. Bach., C.S.I., M.V.O., O.B.E., *b.* 23 March, 1856 ; *s.* of Lieut. W. M. Mules, 1st Bombay European Fusiliers, of Honiton, Devon ; *m.* Jane Lee, *d.* of M. G. Luck, of Campden Hill, Kensington. *Educ.* : Wellington Coll., Berkshire. Sind Commission ; Chairman Port Trust, Karachi Sind, from Nov. 1909, to May, 1920 ; now retired. *War Work* : Chairman of the Karachi Port Trust throughout the war ; was actively concerned in the embarkation and disembarkation of troops and stores. *Address* : 29, Bramham Gardens, S.W. 5. *Clubs* : Sind (Karachi) ; East India United Service. (O4076)

MULHALLEN, Vivian BREW-, M.B.E.

MULHERION, George Frederick, D.S.O., O.B.E.

MULHOLLAND, Capt. the Hon. Charles Henry George, D.S.O., O.B.E., 11th Hussars, *b.* 19 Aug. 1886 ; eldest surviving *s.* of 2nd Baron Dunleath, of Ballywalter, Co. Down (*see* BURKE's *Peerage*) ; *m.* Sylvia, *d.* of the late Sir Douglas Brooke, of Colebrooke, Co. Fermanagh. *Educ.* : Eton and Sandhurst. Military Sec. to Lord-Lieutenant of Ireland. *War Work* : Adjutant 11th Hussars with original Exped. Force ; severely wounded at Messines, Oct. 1914 ; twice mentioned in despatches ; 1916–18, Home Service and Brigade-Major, 3rd Cyclist Brigade. *Address* : Ballywalter Park, Ballywalter, Co. Down. *Club* : Cavalry. (O7500)

MULLAN, Capt. Henry Felix, M.B.E., R.A.M.C.

MULLAN, Rev. Father John, M.B.E., M.C.

MULLARD, Capt. Stanley Robert, M.B.E., R.A.F.

MULLENEUX, Capt. Hugh Bowring, C.B.E., R.N. Served in Great War, 1914–19, as Chief of Staff, N. America and W. Indies Station, and as Liaison Officer, Navy Depart. Washington (mentioned in despatches). (C1198)

MULLER, George Herbert, C.B.E., V.D.

MULLER, Lilian, Mrs., M.B.E.

MULLER, Percy MAXWELL-, M.B.E.

MULLICK, Sarat Kumar Bose, C.B.E., M.D., M.B., C.M., *b.* 1870 ; *s.* of O. C. Mullick, Bar.-at-law ; *m.* 1903, Shishir Kumarie, *d.* of the late Hon. Larbmohun Ghose. *Educ.* : St. Xavier's Coll. Calcutta ; Edinburgh Univ. ; Univ. Coll. London ; and in Paris. Founded National Med. Coll. India, and King's Hospital, Calcutta ; Hon. Sec. Bengalee Regt. Committee ; All-India Med. and Indian Health Assocns. ; Member of Provincial Recruiting Board, Bengal Publicity Board, and Calcutta Corporation. *Club* : Calcutta. (C700)

MULLIGAN, Lieut. Clifford Victor, M.B.E.

MULLIGAN, Capt. William Percival, O.B.E.

MULLINEAUX, John, M.B.E.

MULLINGS, Major Joseph Randolf, O.B.E. R.F.A.

MULLINS, Alfred James, M.B.E. Chief Cable Censor, Malta. (M10259*f*)

MULLINS, Arthur, C.B.E.

MULLINS, George William, M.B.E., M.Inst.Met., *b.* 1867 ; *s.* of the late William Mullins, of Birmingham ; *m.* Jane Elizabeth, *d.* of the late Samuel Francis, of Birmingham. *Educ.* : King Edward's School, Birmingham. Commercial Manager ; Director, Cold Rolled Brass and Copper Association, Birmingham. *War Work* : With the King's Norton Metal Co., Ltd., Birmingham, both before and through the war ; then concerned in ammunition production and in metal trades work for munition purposes. *Address* : King's Heath, Birmingham. (M2213)

MULLINS, Capt. (A. Lieut.-Col.) James Finbarr, O.B.E.

MULLINS, Rev. William, O.B.E.

MULLINS, Capt. Henry Rubert, O.B.E.

MULOCK, Lieut.-Col. Redford Henry, C.B.E., D.S.O., R.A.F., *b.* 1886 ; *s.* of W. R. Mulock, K.C. Served in Great War, 1914–19 (mentioned in despatches, Legion of Honour). *Address* : 557, Wellington Crescent, Winnipeg, Canada. (C1901)

MUMFORD, Agnes, Mrs., M.B.E.

MUMFORD, Charles Allan, O.B.E., J.P., I.C.S., *b.* 4 Feb. 1874 ; *s.* of Charles Mumford, of Wisbech ; *m.* Hilda, *d.* of F. Manser, of Tunbridge Wells. *Educ.* : Oundle School and Peterhouse (Camb.). Deputy Commissioner of Naini Tal in the United Provinces of India. *War Work* : Collector of Bulandshahi district (U.P.), which had 15,018 combatants and 5952 non-combatants in the Indian Army at the conclusion of the Armistice. *Address* : Aberfoyle, Naini Tal, India. (O4077)

MUMFORD, Capt. Harry George, M.B.E.

MUMFORD, Hilda, Mrs., M.B.E.

MUMFORD, Capt. Wilfred George, O.B.E., M.B., F.R.C.S., R.A.M.C.

MUMMERY, John Howard, C.B.E., D.Sc. (Penn.), M.R.C.S., L.D.P. (Eng.), *b.* 18 Jan. 1847 ; *s.* of John Rigden Mummery, of Cavendish Place, London ; *m.* 1st, Mary Lily, *d.* of Dr. Lockhart, of Shanghai, 2nd, Lillian, *d.* of Thomas Parker, of Nottingham. *Educ.* : Univ. Coll., London. Late Examiner in Dental Surgery, Royal Coll. of Surgeons ; late Lecturer on Bacteriology, Royal Dental Hospital of London. *War Work* : Commandant and Medical Superintendent to Maxillo-Facial (War) Hospital, Kennington. *Address* : 79, Albert Bridge Road, S.W. 11. (C2827)

MUNBY, Mary Forth, O.B.E., *b.* 8 July, 1859 ; *d.* of John Forth Munby, of Clifton, York. *Educ.* : Clewer Sisters' School of St. John Baptist, London. Hon. Branch Sec. Girls' Friendly Society, York and Ainsty Branch, and other social work. *War Work* : Hon. Sec. York Station Canteen for Soldiers and Sailors. (O11016)

MUNDAY, Major and Qr.-Mr. Alfred, M.B.E., R.A.S.C.

MUNDAY, John Augustus, O.B.E., *b.* 21 Oct. 1863 ; *s.* of John Munday, R.N., of Thanet, Kent ; *m.* Mary Elizabeth, *d.* of J. W. Cripps, of London. *Educ.* : Privately, and St. John's Coll., Battersea, S.W. Commissioner National Savings Committee ; Headmaster (1) Hartfield School, Sussex, (2) Abingdon N. Boys' School, Berks ; Organising Inspector of Schools, Diocese of Winchester (1891–98) ; States Inspector and Sec. of Education, Guernsey (1898–1914). *War Work* : Joint Hon. Organiser for War Savings, West Riding of Yorkshire ; established War Savings Local Committees and Associations throughout the W. Riding ; assisted in " Tank " and

other Loan Campaigns in Leeds, Bradford, Halifax, Huddersfield, Dewsbury, Harrogate, and other towns and localities. *Address* : 17, Claremont Drive, Headingley, Leeds. (O11017)

MUNDAY, Lieut. William Thomas, M.B.E.

MUNDAY, Major Henry Clement PAUNCEFORT-, O.B.E.

MUNDY, Major Robert Godfrey, O.B.E., *b.* 21 Oct. 1875; *s.* of Lieut.-Col. Herbert G. Mundy, Colonial Office ; *m.* Dorothy, *d.* of Capt. F. Phillips, J.P., of Bydown, North Devon. *Educ.* : Eastbourne and Clifton. Formerly Private Sec. to Permanent Under Sec. to Colonies ; served in the Border Horse, South African War. *War Work* : Commanded Headquarter Co. 17th Div. Train, R.A.S.C., 1914–19 ; wounded, March, 1918 ; twice mentioned in despatches. *Address* : Raleigh House, Barnstaple, North Devon. (O5614)

MUNDY, William Charles, M.B.E.

MUNDY, Catherine Lousia, Mrs. MILLER-, O.B.E., *b.* 24 May, 1863 ; *d.* of the late Sir John W. Cradock Hartopp, Bart. ; *m.* E. Miller-Mundy, of Shipley Hall, Derby (who died). *War Work* : Vice-President of Ilkeston Division (Derbyshire) B.R.C.S. (O3848)

MUNFORD, Alfred James, M.B.E., R.E.

MUNFORD, Frank Jago, M.B.E., *b.* 12 April, 1868 ; *s.* of Francis Munford, of Leytonstone ; *m.* Catharine Ann, *d.* of William Plumsted, of Norwich. *Educ.* : Leytonstone, Essex. *War Work* : War Office (Recruiting Department) and Statistical Department, Ministry of National Service. *Address* : 19, Westbourne Street, Ebury Street, London, S.W. 1. (M788)

MUNGALL, Walter Heggie, M.B.E., B.Sc., *b.* 1867 ; *s.* of the late James Mungall, of Transy, near Dunfermline ; *m.* Mary Catherine, *d.* of William Simpson, of Dunfermline. *Educ.* : Dollar Academy, and Glasgow Univ. Provost of Crieff from 1913 ; Chairman, Crieff and District Cottage Hospital ; a Governor of Morrison's Academy, Crieff. *War Work* : Chairman of Crieff Belgian Refugee Committee, Derby Recruiting Committee, Local Tribunal for Burgh of Crieff, Dependants Allowances Committee, Lady Burghclere's Prisoners of War Fund, Crieff Food Control Committee and Crieff District War Savings Committee ; Member of Executive Committee, British Red Cross Society (Perthshire Branch). *Address* : Croftweit, Crieff. *Clubs* : Scottish Conservative, Edinburgh ; Unionist, Crieff ; Royal Scottish Automobile, Glasgow. (M9110)

MunGAVIN, George Walter, M.B.E., *b.* 6 June, 1857 ; *s.* of James St. John MunGavin, of Castle Connel, Ireland ; *m.* Ella, *d.* of David Harold Sykes, of Yorkshire. Late Engineer and Electrician, Indo-European Telegraph Dept., Karachi, India. *War Work* : Attached War Office (Ms. 3), Jan. 1917, to Dec. 1919. *Address* : c/o Messrs. T. Cook & Sons, Ludgate Circus. (M9111)

MUNKHOUSE, Alfred Frederick O'GORMAN-, O.B.E., F.R.G.S., F.R.C.I., *b.* 28 April, 1856 ; *s.* of Edmund Thomas O'Gorman-Munkhouse, of Winton, Westmorland ; *m.* Mary Anne, *d.* of Henry Rourke, of Melbourne, Aust. *Educ.* : Privately. Acting British Vice-Consul at San Francisco, California ; during 14 years' residence in Australia was Justice of Peace, Queensland and Northern Territory of South Australia. *War Work* : Voluntary Services to British Consulate-General, San Francisco. *Address* : British Consulate-General, San Francisco ; 972, Bush Street, S.F. (O11018)

MUNN, Capt. Leonard, O.B.E.

MUNRO, Flight-Lieut. David, O.B.E., R.A.F.

MUNRO, Donald, O.B.E.

MUNRO, Major Edward Brodie, O.B.E., M.D., I.M.S.

MUNRO, Hugh George, O.B.E.

MUNRO, Rev. James Lorimer, O.B.E.

MUNRO, John Edward, O.B.E.

MUNRO, Col. Lewis, C.B.E. (retired pay), late Hampshire Regt., *b.* 25, July, 1859 ; *s.* of the late Capt. Lewis Munro, of Hon. East India Company's Service ; *m.* Maud, *d.* of C. B. Eynaud, of Malta. *Educ.* : Clifton Coll ; Sandhurst. Joined 37th Foot as 2nd Lieut., 14 Jan. 1880 ; Lieut. Hampshire Regt., 9 April, 1881 ; Adjutant, Hampshire Regt., Nov. 1882, to Oct. 1886 ; Captain, July, 1886 ; Major, Sept. 1896 ; Lieut.-Col., Jan. 1905 ; Brevet Col., Jan. 1908 ; Col., June, 1909 ; Bgde. Major, Gibraltar, Dec. 1891, to Dec. 1894 ; Bgde. Major, Inf. Bgde., Aldershot, Jan. 1898, to Oct. 1899 ; Bgde. Major, Inf. Bgde., S. Africa, Oct. 1899, to Dec. 1899 ; D.A.A.G., S. Africa, Dec. 1899, to Mar. 1900 ; Hon. Staff Officer, graded as D.A.A.G., S. Africa, Mar. 1900, to Nov. 1900 ; D.A.A.G. for Colonial Forces, H.Q., S. Africa, Dec. 1900, to June, 1901 : retired, Jan. 1909. *War Work* : From commencement of War to Feb. 1918, Assistant Major-Gen. in charge Administration and A.Q.M.G., Eastern Command ; Feb. 1918, to June, 1919, employed under Air Ministry as S.O. 1 R.A.F. *Club* : Army and Navy. (C2333)

MUNRO, Sir Thomas, G.B.E., J.P., D.L., *b.* 10 June ; 1866 ; *s.* of Thomas Munro, of Moorfarm House, Tain ; *m.* Jean Russell, *d.* of James Smart, of Balgreen, Hamilton. *Educ.* : Privately ; Milne's Institution, Fochabers ; Edinburgh Univ. County Clerk and Treas. of Lanarkshire ; Clerk and Treas. Lanarkshire Education Authority ; Clerk and Treas. Lanark District Board of Control, and other public appointments in Lanarkshire ; Chairman of Consultative Council on Local Health Administration and General Health Questions, Scottish Board of Health ; Chairman of Lanarkshire Local Advisory Committee, Ministry of Labour ; Chairman appointed by Government of National Industrial Provisional Joint Committee (1919–20). *Addresses* : Avongrange, Hamilton ; 53,

Manor Place, Edinburgh. *Clubs:* National; Caledonian; Univ., Edinburgh. (G57)

MUNROE, Lieut.-Col. Hugh Edwin, O.B.E., Can. A.M.C.

MUNTON, Lieut. Horace Munton BAKER-, M.B.E., M.C., R.A.F.

MUNTYER, George Frederick, O.B.E.

MURCH, John, M.B.E.

MURCHESON, Lieut.-Comm. Frank, O.B.E., R.N.V.R.

MURCHIE, Archibald, O.B.E., M.A., B.L., *b.* 30 Jan. 1890; *s.* of Capt. Archibald Murchie, of Ardrossan, Scotland.; *m.* Marianne, *d.* of Brooklyn Birks, of Manchester. *Educ.:* Ardrossan Academy, and Glasgow Univ. *War Work:* June, 1915, to May, 1919, Supervising Accountant of the Y.M.C.A. with the British Armies in France and Belgium. *Address:* Welbeck, Waterloo Park, Liverpool. (O3849)

MURDOCH, Comm. Hugh Campbell, O.B.E., R.C.

MURDOCH Major Robert, O.B.E., J.P., Tipperary, *b.* 24 Nov. 1871; *s.* of Sidney Murdoch, M.D.; *m.* Florence Maude Mary, *d.* of John Alexander, M.A., Dean of Ferns. *Educ.:* Uppingham; Trinity, Dublin. *War Work:* Major, R.A.S.C., Motor Transport, in France. *Address:* Kilcoran, Cahir, Co. Tipperary. *Club:* Royal Automobile. (O5616)

MURDOCH, Major-Gen. John Francis BURN-, C.B., C.M.G., C.B.E., J.P., *b.* 26 March, 1859; *s.* of the late Rev. Canon Burn-Murdoch, of Greenyards; *m.* Alice, *d.* of J. Burn-Murdoch, J.P., of Gartincaber. *Educ.:* Eton. Hon. Major-Gen. (ret.); Col. The Royal Dragoon. *War Work:* Commanded a mounted division until March, 1918; then Staff Officer for Volunteer Services, Northern Command. *Address:* The Manor House, Normanton-on-Soar, Loughborough. *Clubs:* Cavalry; Naval and Military; New, Edinburgh. (C1491)

MURDOCH, Major Ian BURN-, O.B.E., *b.* 1 Nov. 1885; *s.* of Thomas Monck Burn-Murdock, F.R.C.P. (E.), M.B., C.M. (Edin.), of Edinburgh (*see* BURKE'S *Landed Gentry*), 1/32nd Sikh Pioneers. (O11945a)

MURDOCH, Regiaulde de Maule, Mrs. T. BURN-, M.B.E., *b.* 23 Oct. 1856; *d.* of Capt. Urmston, R.N., Knight, Legion of Honour; *m.* Thomas Monck, *s.* of John Burn-Murdoch, of Gartincaber, Doune, Perthshire. *Educ.:* Privately. *War Work:* Assistant County Director, Edinburgh; worked at forming and training Voluntary Aid Detachments in Edinburgh and Midlothian; assisted with staffing and equipping Auxiliary Hospitals; served on several Red Cross Committees in Edinburgh and Glasgow, both before and during the war. *Address:* Gartincaber, Doune, Perthshire. *Club:* Ladies' Caledonian, Edinburgh. (M196)

MURE, Emily May, M.B.E.; *d.* of J. B. Innes, W.S., of Edinburgh; *m.* William John, *s.* of David Mure. *Educ.:* Privately. Vice-President, Scottish Red Cross Society, East Lothian Branch. *Addresses:* St. Ann's, North Berwick; 39, Lennon Gardens, S.W. 1. *Club:* Queen's, Edinburgh. (M9112)

MURFITT, Major Charles Joseph, O.B.E., R.A.F.

MURGATROYD, Dorothy Sarah, Mrs., M.B.E., B.A. Hons. (Lond.), 24 Sept. 1890; *d.* of the late Frederick John Cox, of Nottingham. *Educ.:* Mundella Secondary School, and Univ. Coll., Nottingham. Assistant Mistress, Secondary Schools. *War Work:* Deputy Administrator, Q.M.A.A.C.; afterwards Acting Unit Administrator; organised work under 67th Division, attached to Divl. Train. *Address:* 30, Oxford Terrace, Hyde Park, W. 2. (M5495)

MURGATROYD, William John, M.B.E., *b.* 11 Nov. 1876. *Educ.:* The Old British School, Castle Street, Kendal. President, Kendal Adult School; Vice-President, Kendal Y.M.C.A.; Chairman, W.P.C., N.S.P.C.C.; District Sec. Alliance of Honour; Sec. Kendal Savings Committee; Cir. Steward, Primitive Methodist Church. *War Work:* Sec. of Local War Savings Committee; succeeded in establishing 65 War Savings Associations, together with Local Agencies in a wild and scattered area. *Addresses:* 5, Parr Street, Kendal; 26, Stricklandgate, Kendal. (M9113)

MURISON, Annie Alice, Mrs., O.B.E., *b.* 26 Jan. 1869; *d.* of Peter Crombie, Dental Surgeon, of Aberdeen; *m.* William Murison, County Clerk of Aberdeenshire. *Educ.:* Aberdeen, and Privately. *War Work:* Hon. Quartermaster, Aberdeen and District Prisoners of War Bureau. *Address:* 67, Forest Road, Aberdeen; County Buildings, Aberdeen. (O11022)

MURISON, William, O.B.E.

MURLEY, Rev. James Reginald de Courcy O'Grady, O.B.E., *b.* 19 April, 1882; *s.* of John James Murley, Vicar of St. Erth, Cornwall; *m.* Florence Annie, *d.* of Reuben O'Neill Pearson, of Tanley, Cartmell. *Educ.:* Malvern Coll., and Pembroke Coll., Oxford. 1906, Curate, St. Mary, Hornsey; 1911, Curate, St. George's, Hanover Square; 1920, Vicar of Dunstall; 1920, Rector of Lanreath. *War Work:* T.C.F. 4th Class, 1916; T.C.F. 3rd Class, 1917; Assistant Principal Chaplain, British Salonica Force, and Army of the Black Sea, 1917–19; mentioned in despatches, 1918 and 1919; Officer of the Serbian Order of St. Sava, 4th Class, 1920. *Address:* Lanreath Rectory, Duloe, R.S.O., Cornwall. (O6513)

MURPHY, Rev. Charles, M.B.E., A.I.F.

MURPHY, Capt. and Qr.-Mr. Clarence Robert, M.B.E.

MURPHY, Ellen Theodora, Lady, M.B.E., *d.* of the late Henry S. King; *m.* 1880, Sir Shirley Foster Murphy, *s.* of the late George Murphy. *Address:* 9, Bentinck Terrace, Regent's Park, N.W. (M3861)

MURPHY, Major Francis Philip Sidney, M.B.E., *b.* 22 July, 1882; *s.* of Francis Murphy, Solicitor, of Liverpool. *Educ.:* Privately, and Liverpool Univ. Solicitor; Member of

the firm of F. Murphy and Son, 2, Hatton Garden, Liverpool, Solicitors. *War Work:* Major, 8th (Irish) Batt. The King's Liverpool Regt.; mobilised at outbreak of War; assisted to recruiting 2nd Batt.; served with Expeditionary Force in France, 1915; invalided; appointed Appeal Representative to the Salford National Service Hundred Appeal Tribunal, 1917. *Address:* Walton Park, Liverpool. (M5496)

MURPHY, Lieut. Frank, M.B.E., R.A.F.

MURPHY, Hannah, Mrs., M.B.E.

MURPHY, Henry Palmer, M.B.E., *b.* 24 July, 1861; *s.* of William John Murphy, of Plumstead, Kent; *m.* Susan, *d.* of George Copsey, of Gosfield, Essex. *Educ.:* Privately. Retired Civil Servant; entered the Royal Arsenal, Woolwich, July 1879; transferred to Inspection Department, March, 1888; Chief Clerk to successive Chief Inspectors of Ordnance until June, 1915; when appointed Special Assistant to Chief Inspector of Munitions, Woolwich; personal Assistant to Director-General of Inspection of Munitions at Ministry of Munitions from April, 1916, to Feb. 1920. *Address:* 64, Genesta Road, Plumstead. (M789)

MURPHY, Major James, M.B.E.

MURPHY, James, M.B.E., F.R.C.S.E.; *s.* of John Murphy, of Midleton, Co. Cork. *Educ.:* Queen's Coll., Cork, and Edinburgh. Hon. Surgeon, Albert Infirmary, Winsford; Hon. Surgeon, Cottage Hospital, Tarporley. *War Work:* M.O. in charge Hôpital Hotel Notre Dame des Grèves, Paramé, 1914–15; M.O. in charge Auxiliary Home Hospital, Middlewich, 1915–19. *Address:* The Beeches, Middlewich (M9114)

MURPHY, Jerome Bernard, M.B.E.

MURPHY, Capt. John, O.B.E.

MURPHY, Maurice Michael, M.B.E., L.R.C.P., L.R.C.S. *Educ.:* Ireland, and Edinburgh. Hon. Physician, Borough Hospital, Birkenhead; Med. Officer to Post Office. *War Work:* Medical Officer-in-charge, Hemingford Street Military Hospital; Physician, Boro' Hospital, Birkenhead; Medical Officer, 19 T Branch of Red Cross. *Address:* 77, Woodchurch Road, Birkenhead. *Club:* Birkenhead Constitutional. (M10278)

MURPHY, Lieut. Peter Kevin, M.B.E., A.I.F.

MURPHY, Capt. and Qr.-Mr. Reginald William, M.B.E., A.I.F.

MURPHY, Sir Shirley Forster, K.B.E., F.R.C.S.; *s.* of the late George Murphy; *m.* Ellen Theodora, M.B.E. (*q.v.*), *d.* of Henry S. King. *Educ.:* Univ. Coll. School; Guy's Hospital. Lieut.-Col. R.A.M.C. (T.); Vice-President, Royal Sanitary Institute; Society of Medical Officers of Health and Epidemiological Section, Royal Society of Medicine; Fellow Royal Statistical Society; Deputy Chairman of Tailoring and Shirt Making Trade Boards; late Examiner in Public Health, Royal Colleges of Physicians and Surgeons; Bisset Hawkins Medallist, Royal College of Physicians; late Medical Officer of Health Administrative County of London; Member of Royal Commission on Tuberculosis. *Address:* 9, Bentinck Terrace, Regent's Park, N.W. 8. *Clubs:* Athenæum; Savile. (K288)

MURPHY, Rev. Thomas Carlyle, O.B.E.

MURPHY, Rev. William, C.B.E. Is in Holy Orders of Church of Rome; Chap. to the Forces; served in Great War, 1914–19 (mentioned in despatches). (C1709)

MURRANT, Ernest Henry, M.B.E.

MURRAY, Lieut.-Col. Alan Sim, O.B.E.

MURRAY, Alexander, O.B.E., *b.* 25 May, 1868; *s.* of Daniel Murray, Inspector of Poor, Carluke; *m.* Jessie Helen *d.* of Gavin Muter, of Stonehouse. *Educ.:* Carluke Public School, and Hamilton Academy. Assessor and Registration Officer for the County of Lanark. *War Work:* Organised recruiting meetings throughout the county; had charge of National Registration, Local Tibunal annt War Pension work; acted as Assistant Hon. Sec. of Lanarkshire War Relief Fund. *Address:* Balintore, Stewarton Drive, Cambuslang. *Club:* County, Hamilton. (O1696)

MURRAY, Sir Alexander Robertson, Knt. Bach., C.B.E. Senior Partner, Messrs. Duff & Company, Calcutta; President, Chamber of Commerce.

MURRAY, Amelia Henrietta, Mrs., M.B.E.

MURRAY. Amy H., Mrs., M.B.E., *b.* 13 Nov. 1870; *d.* of Andrew J. Johnston, of Dublin; *m.* Albert E. Murray, R.H.A., F.R.I.B.A., *s.* of William George Murray, of Dublin. *Educ.:* Alexandra School, Dublin; France; Alexandra Coll., Dublin. *War Work:* for some time Chairman Women's Branch Royal Dublin Fusiliers; 1916–19, Organiser and Hon. Treas. of the Soldiers' Club, Ball's Bridge, Dublin, and of Military Canteen at Bombing School, Irish Command; this club was a great success: the proceeds, £229, were given to the Dummond Institute of Orphan Daughters of Soldiers. (M945)

MURRAY, Arthur John Layard, D.S.O., O.B.E., R.N.

MURRAY, Lieut.-Col. Charles Frederick Kennan, O.B.E., M.D., F.R.C.S.I., J.P., *b.* 27 Sept. 1848; *s.* of Thomas Davis Murray, of Co. Wicklow; *m.* Caroline, *d.* of Sir John Charles Molteno, K.C.M.G., of S. Africa. *Educ.:* Queen's and Royal Univ. of Ireland. President Colonial Medical Council, S. Africa; Consulting Medical Officer of Somerset Hospital, Cape Town; Consulting Surgeon Wynberg Hospital. *War Work:* Surgeon, Royal Navy, 1869; served in Ashantee War, 1873; mentioned in despatches; awarded Ashantee War Medal; served as Lieut.-Col. S.A.M.C.; Medical Officer in charge of Convalescent Hospitals at Wynberg and Newlands, S. Africa, 1915–18. *Addresses:* Kenilworth, C.P., South Africa; Palmiet P.O., Elgin, C.P., S. Africa. (O8359)

MURRAY, Capt. Charles Geoffrey, O.B.E., R.M.

MURRAY, Edith, Mrs., M.B.E.; *d.* of Robert McKerchar, M.B., Ch.B., Newton House, Dalbeattie, Scotland; *m.* Lieut. Matthew Randolph, R.E., *s.* of M. D. Murray. *Educ.:* Geo. Watson's Coll., Edinburgh. *War Work:* Hon. Sec. to the Local War Pensions Committee. (M9116)

MURRAY, Edward, M.B.E. (M10457)

MURRAY, Lieut.-Col. Eric Madden C.B.E., A.P.D., *b.* 3 March, 1869; *s.* of the late Col. J. W. Murray, of Walmer; *m.* Mary Elizabeth, *d.* of the late Surgeon-Major P. H. Roe, of Coolfinn, Ireland. *Educ.:* United Services Coll., Westward Ho! Joined Royal Warwickshire Regt., 9 April, 1892; seconded for service under the Foreign Office and served as District Commissioner, H.B.M.'s Niger Coast Protectorate, 1896–1900; rejoined regiment, Jan. 1900; transferred from Royal Warwickshire Regt. to Royal Army Pay Department, June, 1900. *War Work:* Served in Command Pay Office, Dublin, Aug. 1914, to Sept 1915; Regimental Pay Office, Perth, Oct. 1915, to Dec. 1916; Regimental Pay Office, Chatham, Dec. 1916, to Feb. 1918; in charge of Regimental Pay Office, Woking, Feb. 1918, to date. *Address:* c/o Messrs. Cox & Co., 16, Charing Cross, London. *Club:* Junior Army and Navy. (C1710)

MURRAY, Evelyn, Hon. Mrs. Ronald Thomas Graham, O.B.E.; *d.* of Sir David Baird, 3rd Bart. (*see* BURKE'S *Peerage*); *m.* Major Hon. Ronald Thomas Graham, *s.* of the 1st Baron Dunedin, Capt. 3rd Batt. Black Watch. *Address:* 13, Cheyne Place, Chelsea, S.W. 3. (O994)

MURRAY, Everitt George Dunne, O.B.E., M.A. (Cantab.), L.M.S.S.A.; *s.* of G. A. E. Murray, M.B., F.R.C.S., of 24, Plein Street, Johannesburg, S. Africa; *m.* Winifred Hardwick, *d.* of T. Hardwick Woods, of Blundeston Hall, Suffolk. *Educ.:* St. John's Coll.; Johannesburg Coll.; Transvaal Univ. Coll.; Christ's Coll., Cambridge; St. Bartholomew's Hospital, London. Late Senior Demonstrator of Pathology, St. Bartholomew's Hospital, London; in charge of the Medical Research Councils, Serology Laboratory, Cambridge. *War Work:* On the Staff of the Central Cerebro-Spinal Fever Laboratory, London; served at Basra, Mesopotamia; on the Staff of the Vaccine Department of the R.A. Medical Coll., London; Member of the War Office Committee on Bacillary Dysentery. *Address:* The Univ. of Cambridge Field Laboratories, Milton, Cambridge. *Club:* Fly Fishers'. (O7503)

MURRAY, Dr. Flora, C.B.E. Doctor-in-Charge of Mil. Hospital, Endell Street, W.C. (C50)

MURRAY, Frederick, M.B.E.

MURRAY, Sir George, K.B.E., *b.* 12 Aug. 1865; *s.* of Lieut.-Col. Charles Murray, 42nd Black Watch (Royal Highlanders); *m.* Lily Gwendoline, *d.* of Walter Mayhew, J.P., of Duxbury Park, Chorley, Lancs. *Educ.:* Weston-super-Mare. *War Work:* Territorial Officers' Casualty Dept. War Office,, 1915–17; Statistical Department, War Office, 1917–20; Secretary of Ferguson Committee, War Office, 1918. *Address:* 37, Kensington Park Gardens, W. 11. *Clubs:* Junior Carlton; Baldwin. (K401)

MURRAY, Eng.-Capt. George William, C.B.E., R.N.

MURRAY, Gertrude Margaret, Mrs., O.B.E.; *d.* of W. Mills Baker, of Stoke Bishop; *m.* John, *s.* of John Murray, of Dublin. *Educ.:* Clifton High School; Laleham; The London Hospital. *War Work:* The Central Depot (H.R.H. Princess Beatrice's), 2, Cavendish Square. *Address:* 110, Harley Street, W. 1. (O11025)

MURRAY, Helen Mary, Hon. Lady, C.B.E., Lady of Grace, Order of St. John of Jerusalem, *b.* 18 Oct. 1857; *d.* of 1st Baron Dunleath, of Ballywalter Park, Ireland (*see* BURKE'S *Peerage*); *m.* Rt. Hon. Sir George Herbert, P.C., G.C.B., *s.* of the Rev. George Murray, of Southfleet. *War Work:* Founder of No. 10 B.R.C. Hospital, Le Tréport, France, a hospital for British Officers from June, 1916, to Feb. 1919 (previously for French wounded, from Dec. 1914, to June, 1916), for which she received the Médaille de la Reconnaisance Francaise. *Address:* 15, Cadogan Square, S.W. (C1010)

MURRAY, Capt. Howard, O.B.E., *b.* 19 Feb. 1875; *s.* of Edward Murray, of Halifax, N.S.; *m.* Ida Gertrude, *d.* of Alex. J. Ritchie, of Halifax, N.S. *Educ.:* Halifax County Academy. Financier; Vice-President, Aldred & Co., Ltd., Investment Bankers; Vice-President, The Shawinigan Water and Power Co.; Member, Council of Public Instruction for Province of Quebec. *War Work:* Chairman, Explosives Committee, Imperial Munitions Board, directing production of Explosives and Propellents in Canada, including erection of National plants; directed development of Canadian Electro Products Co. plant producing acetic acid and acetone. *Address:* 51, Belvedere Road, Westmount, P.Q.; Ivesleigh, Stanstead County, P.Q. *Clubs:* St. James'; Beaconsfield Golf; Hermitage Country; Royal St. Lawrence Yacht. (O602)

MURRAY, Hugh, C.I.E., C.B.E., J.P., *b.* 1861; *s.* of the late Lieut.-Col. Charles Murray, 42nd Highlanders; *m.* 1st, Gwendoline Mabel Langridge (who died); 2nd, Dorothy Christine, *d.* of the late Rt. Hon. Sir William Mather, P.C., of Bramble Hill Lodge, New Forest, Hants. Entered India Forest Ser. 1882; Dep. Conservator, 1887; Conservator, 1905; retired as Senior Conservator of Forests, Bombay, 1911; appointed Dep. Controller of Timber, 1907; Assist. Commr. Forestry Commr. for England and Wales, 1919. *Address:* Graylands, Wimbledon Park, S.W. (C576)

MURRAY, Janet, M.B.E.

MURRAY, James, O.B.E., J.P., *b.* 2 Aug. 1854; *s.* of David Murray, of East Grinstead, Sussex; *m.* Fannie, *d.* of

Henry Hall, of East Grinstead, Sussex. *Educ.:* East Grinstead. Farmer. *War Work:* Chairman of the Surrey War Agricultural Executive Committee. *Address:* Headley Grove, Epsom, Surrey. (O604)

MURRAY, Lieut. James Edward, M.B.E.

MURRAY, James Robertson, M.B.E., *b.* 9 Feb. 1886; *s.* of the late James Robertson Murray; *m.* Helen Brooks, *d.* of Dr. F. M. Wilson, of Bridgeport, Conn. U.S.A. *Educ.:* Privately. H.M. Consul at Lille. *War Work:* Acting Consul, Colon, Panama. *Address:* H.M. Consulate, Lille. *Club:* Royal Automobile. (M791)

MURRAY, John, O.B.E., *b.* 12 May, 1871; *s.* of Alexander Murray, of Gartymore, Sutherlandshire. *Educ.:* Dr. Coke's School, Brecon. Superintendent of Freight trains, Midland Railway. *Address:* 52, Hartington Street, Derby. (O11027)

MURRAY, Major John, O.B.E., R.A.M.C. (T.), *b.* 5 Feb. 1871; *s.* of Alexander Murray, of Glasgow; *m.* Elizabeth Craig, *d.* of W. S. Miller, J.P., of Brecon. *Educ.:* Hutchesons Grammar School, and Glasgow Univ. President of the Shropshire and Mid-Wales Branch of the British Medical Association; M.O.H. Llandrindod Wells Urban District; Senior Medical Officer Llandrindod Wells Hospital. *War Work:* M.O-in-charge Auxiliary Hospital, Llandrindod Wells. *Address:* Havod Awen, Llandrindod Wells. *Club:* Royal Societies'. (O11026)

MURRAY, Engineer-Capt. John Adam, C.B.E., R.N. (ret.). Emergency Repair Overseer, Aberdeen, during Great War. (C2319)

MURRAY, Capt. and Qr.-Mr. John Francis Stuart, M.B.E., M.C., Aust. A.M.C.

MURRAY, Josephine, M.B.E.; *d.* of P. J. Murray, late Manager National Bank, Galway. *Educ.:* Sacred Heart Convent, Carlisle, and Calais. *War Work:* Hon. Treas. and Sec., Irish War Hospital Supply Sub-Depot, Galway; Hon. Treas., Galway War Fund Association; Soldiers' and Sailors' Help Society Friend. *Address:* Eglinton House, Galway. (M9118)

MURRAY, Major Kenneth A., O.B.E.

MURRAY, Capt. Lennox Biggar, O.B.E.

MURRY, Mary Stewart, O.B.E.

MURRAY, Lieut. Neil Smith, O.B.E., R.N.R.

MURRAY, Major Patrick Moncreiff, O.B.E., M.C., *b.* 8 April, 1884; *s.* of Patrick Murray, W.S., of 7, Eton Terrace, Edinburgh; *m.* Margaret, *d.* of the late W. Holms-Kerr, of Largs, Ayrshire. *Educ.:* The Edinburgh Academy, Edinburgh. Tea Planter. *War Work:* Joined the Lothians and Border Horse Yeomanry, Sept. 1914; Commissioned 2nd Lieut. 7th Batt. the Seaforth Highlanders, Dec. 1914; France, May, 1915; invalided to U.K. Oct. 1915; attached H.Q. 75th Inf. Bgde., France, as Staff Capt. 124th Inf. Bdge., March, 1917; Italy, Nov. 1917; D.A.A.G. 48th South Midland Division, March, 1918; D.A.A.G., G.H.Q. Italy, March to July, 1919. Has Italian Croce di Guerra; twice mentioned in despatches. *Addresses:* Brownlow Estate, Maskeliya, Ceylon; 7, Eton Terrace, Edinburgh, Scotland. *Club:* The Hill, Nuwara Eliya, Ceylon. (O2993)

MURRAY, Phoebe Henrietta, Mrs., O.B.E. (O12052)

MURRAY, 2nd Lieut. Reginald Myrie, M.B.E.

MURRAY, Richard, O.B.E., M.V.O., *b.* 19 June, 1865; *s.* of Richard Murray, of Portsmouth; *m.* Isabella, *d.* of the late Thomas Sagar, Fleet Engineer, R.N. *Educ.:* Privately. Technical Assistant Naval Store Dept., Admiralty, S.W. *Address:* 14, Oakington Avenue, Wembley Park, Middlesex. (O11029)

MURRAY Robert Alexander, O.B.E., M.D., J.P. *Educ.:* Edinburgh Univ.; Paris. Consulting Surgeon (Hon. Surgeon for 25 years); Alderman, County Borough of Stockport; Chairman, Old Age Pensions Committee. *War Work:* Took active part in organising and was A. Medical Officer to School, and Military Hospitals, and Brinnington Neurological Hospital, Stockport (over 60,000 cases treated). *Address:* Apsley, Stockport, Cheshire. (O11828)

MURRAY, Robert Alexander, M.B.E., *b.* 5 June, 1864; *s.* of the late John Murray, of Grongar Bank, Kilmarnock; *m.* Jessie Kerr, *d.* of Gordon Kerr, of Helensburgh. *Educ.:* Grongar School; Wigtown School; Crookedholm School; Kilmarnock Academy and School of Art. Bank Agent; Actuary Bathgate Savings Bank; House Factor and Insurance Agent; Sec. Bathgate Agricultural Association and Farmers' Union; Sec. St. Andrews' Ambulance Association Bathgate Centre. *War Work:* Commandant of No. 1 Linlithgow V.A.D. serving at Bangour War Hospital on arrival of all convoys of wounded from the front; Sec. of Bathgate Red Cross Society, and latterly of Linlithgowshire Branch. *Address:* National Bank House, Bathgate. (M9119)

MURRAY, Major Robert William, O.B.E., R.A.M.C. (T.), F.R.C.S.

MURRAY, Hon. Mrs. Ronald Thomas Graham, O.B.E.

MURRAY, Stuart, O.B.E., M.B., Ch.B., M.R.C.S., L.R.C.P., F.R.G.S., *b.* 1880; *s.* of Richard Murray, of Manchester; *m.* Constance Mary, *d.* of T. C. Orton, of Nottingham. *Educ.:* Manchester Univ. Medical Officer, Ministry of Pensions. *War Work:* T. Capt., R.A.M.C. *Address:* King's Lancashire Convalescent Centre, Blackpool. (O6675)

MURRAY, Susan Ann, Mrs., M.B.E.; *d.* of Robert Stephen, of Peterhead, Scotland; *m.* Donald David Coghill Murray, D.S.O., *s.* of the late John Jolly Murray, of Castletown, Caithness, Scotland. *Educ.:* Church of Scotland Training Coll., Aberdeen, Scotland. Hon. Organising Sec. of the

Victoria League of South Africa (Orange Free State Section); Hon. Sec. of the South African Red Cross Society in the Orange Free State; Chairman of the Orange Free State Committee of the South African Soldiers' Graves Association. *War Work:* Hon. Organising Sec. of the Provincial War Relief Committee of the Victoria League of South Africa (Orange Free State Section), which acted as the O.F.S. Branch of the Queen Mary's Needlework Guild, the South African Gifts and Comforts Organisation, and the South African Red Cross Society, with headquarters at Bloemfontein. *Address:* Haldon, nr. Bloemfontein, Orange Free State, S. Africa. *Clubs:* Ramblers (Bloemfontein); Alexandra (Capetown); Associate of the Royal Colonial Institute, London. (M1225)

MURRAY, Thomas Roberts, O.B.E., *b.* 9 Feb. 1862, *s.* of James Murray, of Hendon; *m.* Annie Storrier Bain, *d.* of Peter Bain, of Fountville, Woodside, Aberdeen. *Educ.:* Chanonry House School, Old Aberdeen. Joint Managing Director to Messrs. Spencer & Co., Ltd., Engineers of Melksham, Wilts. *War Work:* Engaged in development and production of war and munition work, explosive paravanes. *Address:* Keverstone, Bath. *Clubs:* Bath and County; Royal Automobile; British Empire. (O605)

MURRAY, Col. Sir Valentine, K.B.E., C.B., C.M.G. (late R.E.), *b.* 13 Feb. 1867; *s.* of George Murray, of Lincoln's Inn; *m.* Flora Constance, *d.* of Ralph Entwistle Peters, of Eastington, Glos. *Educ.:* Malvern Coll., and R.M.A. Woolwich. Lieut. R.E., 1886; Capt. R.E., 1896; Brevet Major, 1900; Major R.E., 1904; Lieut.-Col. R.E., 1912; Colonel, 1916. *War Work:* South African War, 1899–1902; Queen's Medal, with 3 clasps, King's Medal, 2 clasps; Despatches; Brevet Majority; European War, 1914–18, employed as Deputy Director of Railways, France, Oct. 1914, to Feb. 1917; Director of Transportation and Railway Traffic, with rank of Brig.-Gen. Feb. 1917, to June, 1919; despatches 5 times; Knight of Grace St. John of Jerusalem; Commandeur Legion d'Honneur. *Address:* 10, Cumberland Terrace, Regent's Park, N.W. 1. *Club:* United Service. (K267)

MURRAY, Violet, O.B.E.
MURRAY, Major Walter, O.B.E., M.C., R.E.
MURRAY, William, M.B.E.
MURRAY, William, O.B.E., J.P.
MURRAY, Major William, O.B.E., M.P., *b.* 31 Oct. 1865; *s.* of Capt. John Murray, R.N., of Murraythwaite, Ecclefechan, N.B.; *m.* Evelyn, *d.* of John Bruce, of 13, Ainslie Place, Edinburgh. *Educ.:* Privately, and Magdalen Coll., Oxford. M.P. Dumfriesshire, 1918. *War Work:* Deputy Assistant Inspector of Recruiting H.Q. Scottish Command, 1915–18; Competent Military Authority, Forth Garrison Command, 1918–19. *Addresses:* Murraythwaite, Ecclefechan, N.B.; 98, Park Street, Mayfair, W. 1. *Clubs:* Carlton; New Edinburgh. (O1697)

MURRAY, Major William Alexander Kininmount, O.B.E.
MURRAY, William Alfred, O.B.E., *b.* 1865; *s.* of Dr. J. Ivor Murray, of Hong Kong, and Scarborough; *m.* Edith Mary, *d.* of Rev. J. Sturton, of Woodboro', Wilts. *Educ.:* Tonbridge School; Queen's Coll., Cambridge; St. Bartholomew's Hospital; Aberdeen Univ. D.C.M.S. (Tropical diseases) Ministry of Pensions, Yorkshire Region. *War Work:* Civil Surgeon, Chittagong, Bengal, 1915–16; R.A.M.C., 1917–18; M.O. 43 Stadantwerpen; M.O.-in-charge Tropical Diseases Section, 4th London General Hospital; War Office, as assistant to Consultant in Malaria. *Addresses:* c/o National Bank of India, Bishopsgate Street, E.C.; c/o C.M.S. Ministry of Pensions, 7, Boar Lane, Leeds. *Club:* Public Schools. (O7404)

MURRAY, Major William Cochrane, O.B.E., M.B., R.A.M.C. (T.).
MURRAY, Major Robert Alan ERSKINE-, O.B.E.
MURRAY, Clarisse Maria Guthrie RIGBY-, Mrs., O.B.E., *d.* of Capt. C. W. Reynolds; *m.* George Rigby, *s.* of B. Rigby Murray, of Parton. *War Work:* In charge of Y.M.C.A. Hut in Military Surgical Hospital, Shepherd's Bush, London. *Address:* Parton, Galloway, Scotland. (O11023)

MURRAY, Emma Cecilia, Lady WYNDHAM-, O.B.E., *d.* of E. Walker; *m.* Col. Sir Charles Wyndham, K.C.B., *s.* of the late Rev. T. B. Murray, Prebendary of St. Paul's. *Addresses:* 10, Rutland Gate, S.W. 7; Winton House, Richmond, Surrey. (O5235)

MURRELL, Capt. Henry Francis, M.B.E.
MURRELL, Major Percy Murray John, O.B.E., R.A.F.
MURRY, John Middleton, O.B.E., *b.* 6 Aug. 1889; *s.* of John Murry, of Wandsworth, London; *m.* Kathleen, *d.* of Harold Beauchamp, of Wellington, N.Z. *Educ.:* Christ's Hospital; Brasenose Coll., Oxford. Editor of the " Athenæum." *War Work:* Editor of the " Daily Review of the Foreign Press." *Address:* 2 Portland Villas, Hampstead. (O11031)

MURSELL, Col. Henry Temple, O.B.E.
MURTON, Alice Hope, Mrs., M.B.E.; *d.* of the late William Hardwick Bradbury, Proprietor of "Punch"; *m.* Charles Duncan, *s.* of Sir Walter Murton, C.B., of Langton, Kent. *War Work:* Commandant of the Aux. Mil. V.A.D. Hospital, Cranbrook. Kent, from Oct. 1914, to Jan. 1919. *Address:* Cranbrook Lodge, Cranbrook, Kent. *Club:* Halcyon. (M9121)

MURTON, Capt. Ivo Murray, M.B.E.
MURTRIE, David James, O.B.E., I.S.O.
MUSGRAVE, Lieut. Arthur Stanley Gordon, M.B.E., R.E.

MUSGRAVE, Lieut.-Col. Bernard, O.B.E., M.I.M.E., *b.* 4 April, 1877; *s.* of Walter Martin, of Bolton, Lancashire; *m.* Ellen Susan, *d.* of Thomas Symes, of Yeovil. *Educ.:* Uppingham, and Neuwied, Germany. Late Director of Messrs. John Musgrave & Sons, Ltd., Bolton, Lancashire. *War Work:* Commanded the 2/12th The Loyal North Lancashire Regt. in England, the 1/4th K.O.Y.L.I. in France; left for Russia North Expd. Force, June, 1918, returned Nov. 1919; mentioned three times in despatches. *Addresses:* Glenwood, Amersham Common, Bucks; Valparaiso, Chili. (O9701)

MUSGRAVE, Catherine Wares Rittie, Mrs., M.B.E., *b.* 19 July, 1864; *d.* of James Bremner, of Kirkhill, Wick, Caithness; *m.* Edgar Musgrave, *s.* of Benjamin Musgrave. *Educ.:* Wick; Edinburgh; London; Germany. Manageress, Prince's Hotel, Hove. *War Work:* Care of invalid officers, who through the generosity of the Directors of Prince's Hotel were given free hospitality. *Address:* Prince's Hotel, Hove. (M9122)

MUSGRAVE, Capt. Francis Peete, M B.E., I.A.R.O.
MUSGRAVE, Henry, O.B.E.
MUSGRAVE, Capt. William Newcome, O.B.E., R.A.S.C.
MUSGRAVE, William Noel SAGAR-, M.B.E., *b.* 18 Jan. 1876; *s.* of J. M. Sagar-Musgrave, of Red Hall, Shadwell, Leeds. *Educ.:* Cheltenham Coll. *War Work:* Assist. Commander, " C " Division, the Metropolitan Special Constabulary. *Address:* 30, St. James' Square, Pall Mall, S.W. 1. *Clubs:* Junior Carlton; Royal Automobile. (M9123)

MUSGRIN, William Charles, M.B.E.
MUSKER, Capt. Herbert, O.B.E.
MUSPRATT, Horace, O.B.E., *b.* 31 Dec. 1875; *s.* of Edmund K. Muspratt, of Seaforth Hall, Seaforth, Lancashire; *m.* Rose Mary, *d.* of Hugh Verdon, of Llanerchydol Hall, Welshpool, Montgomery. *Educ.:* Lockers Park; Clifton Coll.; Paris; Wiesbaden. Director of the United Alkali Co., Ltd. *War Work:* Hon. Sec. Liverpool Local Central Committee for War Savings, which was instrumental in collecting more money for War Bonds, Loans, and War Savings Certificates than any other provincial city. *Address:* 15, Alexandra Drive, Sefton Park, Liverpool. *Clubs:* Racquet, Liverpool; National Liberal. (O1698)

MUSSON, Arthur, M.B.E.
MUSTARDE, John Clark, M.B.E.
MUTEE, Rohera Muriwair, Mrs., O.B.E. (O2193)
MUTTLEBURY, Stanley Duff, O.B.E.
MYATT, Agnes Rose, M.B.E., *b.* 15 July, 1891; *d.* of the late Frederick Myatt. *Educ.:* Green Secondary School, Isleworth. *War Work:* Chief of Women's Staff, War Trade Statistical Dept.; Member of Women's Legion. (M2216)

MYATT, Major Arthur Egbert, O.B.E.
MYDDLETON, Lieut.-Col. Cornelius William, O.B.E., R.A.M.C.
MYERS, Arthur Wallis, C.B.E., *b.* 24 July, 1878; *s.* of the late Rev. John Brown Myers, of Watford, Herts.; *m.* Lilian Agnes, *d.* of the late Captain George Gentry, of Maldon, Essex. *Educ.:* Watford; The Leys, Cambridge. *War Work:* Attached Department of Information (Foreign Office); Director of Publications, National War Aims Committee. *Address:* Berrow, Epsom. *Clubs:* Royal Automobile; Queen's. (C2828)

MYERS, Charles Samuel, C.B.E., F.R.S., *b.* 13 March, 1873; *s.* of Wolf Myers, of London; *m.* Edith, *d.* of I. Seligman, of London. *Educ.:* City of London School; Gonville and Caius Coll., Camb.; St. Bartholomew's Hospital. Director of the Psychological Laboratory, Cambridge; Fellow of Gonville and Caius Coll.; Editor of the " British Journal of Psychology "; Member of the Industrial Fatigue Research Board. *War Work:* Consultant Psychologist to the British Armies in France; Inspector of Neurological Hospitals for the War Office; Advisor to the Anti-Submarine Division of the Admiralty in selection tests for hydrophone operators. *Addresses:* 30, Montagu Square, London, W. 1; Birchwood, Porlock, Somerset. *Clubs:* Athenæum; Savile; Oxford and Cambridge Musical. (C2051)

MYERS, Dudley Borron, O.B.E., *b.* 23 Feb. 1861; *s.* of the late Thomas Borron Myers, J.P., of Porters Park, Shenley, Herts; *m.* Anna Frances, *d.* of the late Major Thomas William Hilton, of H.M. Indian Army. *Educ.:* Eton. Late President in India of European Association of India. *War Work:* 1914, organising centres for Voluntary Social Service Bureau for Men; also voluntary work, Queen's Work for Women Fund; 1915, voluntary work, Government Commission for Providing Occupation for Belgian Refugees; 1915–19, Hon. Sec. Employment Bureau, Queen Mary's Convalescent Auxiliary Hospitals, Roehampton; Member Committee Queen Mary's Workshop, Pavilion Military Hospital, Brighton. *Address:* Junior Carlton Club. *Clubs:* Junior Carlton; Orleans; Royal Automobile; Hurlingham. (O1699)

MYERS, Lieutenant Harry Cecil, M.B.E.
MYERS, Horace, M.B.E.
MYERS, James Eckersley, O.B.E., D.Sc., A.I.C., *b.* 24 June, 1890; *s.* of William Myers, of Bolton, and Cheadle, Hulme; *m.* Elsie, *d.* of John Ingram, of Colwyn Bay. *Educ.:* Manchester Grammar School, and Manchester Univ. Senior Lecturer in Chemistry, and Science Tutor Univ. of Manchester. *War Work:* Research on various chemical problems, including poison gases, for H.M. Ministry of Munitions. *Address:* The University, Manchester. (O11033)

MYERS, Lancelot Brainard, M.B.E., L.D.S., R.C.S. (Eng.), *b.* 1 May, 1870. *Educ.:* St. Albans Grammar School; Middlesex and Nat. Dental Hospitals. Dental Surgeon. Hon.

Dent. Surgeon, Cornelia Hospital, Poole; Dental Surgeon, Poole School Clinic. *War Work:* Hon. Sec., Poole Local War Pensions; Hon. Dental Surgeon, Poole Red Cross Hospital; Member of the Red Cross. *Address:* The Pines, Parkstone Road, Longfleet, Poole, Dorset. *Clubs:* Poole Yacht; Dorset Golf. (M9123)

MYERS Leopold,, O.B.E.

MYERS, Lieut. Nathan Coleman, M.B.E., I.A.R.O.

MYERS, Vera Anita, Mrs., O.B.E.

MYLCHREEST, Thomas, M.B.E.

MYLES, Lieut.-Col. Charles Duncan, O.B.E., M.B., R.A.M.C.

MYLES, Capt. Robert Boulton, O.B.E., M.B., R.A.M.C. (O11756)

MYLES, Surg.-Comm. Thomas William, C.B.E., M.D., B.A., B.A.O., B.Ch., F.R.C.S., R.N , *b.* 27 May, 1878 ; *s.* of Thomas W. Myles, M.D., of Howth, Co. Dublin, Ireland. *Educ.:* High School, Dublin ; Trinity Coll., Dublin ; Royal Coll. of Surgeons, Edinburgh. Officer of Crown of Italy ; Officer of Order George I. of Greece ; Greek Order of Military Merit. *War Work:* Medal and clasp for operation in the Persian Gulf, H.M.S. "Hyacinth," flagship, Rear-Admiral Sir F. Slade, 1909–11 ; S.M.O. H.M.S. "Sapphire" 1914–16 ; employed on Dover Patrol, North Sea, and in the landing at Y. Beach, Gallipoli, 2d April, 1915 ; May, 1915, to Oct. 1916, attached to the Italian Light Cruiser division in the Adriatic, Dec. 1916–20, S.M.O. 3rd Royal Marine Batt. attached to the Salonica Field Force ; afterwards S.M.O. Royal Marine Garrison, Ægean Islands, and Royal Naval Hospital, Mudros, and Russian Refugee Camps at Mudros. *Address:* c/o Admiralty, London. *Club:* Royal Societies'. (C3215)

MYLES, Capt. Walter Andrew, O.B.E., *b.* 18 Sept. 1892; *s.* of Capt. Walter Myles, of the Mercantile Marine. *Educ.:* Holy Trinity School, Formby, Lancashire. Entered Liverpool cotton firm (Continental Dept.), 1910 ; enlisted T.F. (Scottish Batt.) May, 1912, and subsequently won many shooting prizes ; mobilised Aug. 1914, and went to France Oct. same year ; wounded, Ypres, 1915, and Somme, 1916 ; to Prisoners of War Camp in France, 1917 ; promoted Capt., 1918 ; to command 189 Prisoners of War Co. ; relinquished this on being appointed Staff Lieut., G.H.Q., and later Staff Capt., G.H.Q. (Prisoners of War Section) ; after all Prisoners of War repatriated from France in 1919, transferred to War Office to wind up Prisoners of War affairs. *Address:* St. Brelades, Lakehouse Road, Wanstead, Essex. (O5619)

MYLINS, Wilhelmina Leonie, M.B.E.

MYLNE, Katharine Isabel, O.B.E. ; *d.* of the Rev. Townsend Webb Mylne. *War Work:* Headquarters, St. John Ambulance Brigade. *Address:* 42, Bullingham Mansions, Kensington. (O11035)

MYLREA, Doctor Charles Stanley Garland, O.B.E.

MYLREA, Maynard, Mrs., M.B.E. ; *d.* of the Rev. Charles Matheson, of St. Edmunds School, Canterbury ; *m.* Col. William Percy Mylrea (who died 1915). *Educ.:* Privately. *War Work:* Nurse at Woodhouse Hospital, Essex ; four years in charge of Y.M.C.A. Hut for N.Z. troops at Sling Camp, Salisbury Plain. *Address:* Hospytts Hall, Gt. Horkesley, Colchester. (M792)

MYOTT, John, M.B.E., R.N.

MYRES, Lieut.-Comm. John Linton, O.B.E., R.N.V.R.

MYSORE, H.H. Maharaja Sur Krishnaraja Wadijat, Bahadur of, G.B.E. (G17)

NADIN, Joseph, O.B.E., F.R.S.A., *b.* 2 Jan. 1860 ; *s.* of John Nadin, of Salford ; *m.* Hannah Jane, *d.* of William Oldham, of Oldham. *Educ.:* Privately. Co-opted member of Oldham Education Committee ; a Governor of the Municipal Secondary School ; a Trustee of the United Charities ; Member of Council of Social Welfare. *War Work:* Hon. Sec. of Local Representative Committee of National Relief Fund ; Hon. Sec., Soldiers' and Sailors' Families Association ; District Head Incor. Soldiers' and Sailors' Help Society ; the Oldham Representative on the Lancashire County Appeals Tribunal ; District Representative Women on Land ; Chairman, Oldham War Pensions, etc., Local Committee, and member Lancashire and Westmorland Advisory Committee, Belgian Refugees Hospitality Committee, War Savings Committee, Allies General Relief Fund Committee, Oldham, and Middleton Labour Advisory Committee, and Executive Council of Oldham Branch League of Nations Union. *Address:* 11, Nadin Street, Oldham. *Club:* Reform, Oldham. (O11036)

NAEF, Conrad James, C.B.E., *b.* 28 July, 1871 ; *s.* of Conrad Naef, of Hausen am Albis, Switzerland. *Educ.:* City of London School, and Merton Coll., Oxford. Civil Servant ; Deputy Accountant-Gen. of the Navy. *Addresses:* Admiralty, London, S.W. ; 32, Strawberry Hill Road, Twickenham. *Clubs:* United Univ. ; Royal Societies'. (C257)

NAGGS, 2nd Lieut. Leonard Bertram, M.B.E.

NAIRN, Capt. Douglas Gordon, O.B.E., R.A.S.C. (T.).

NAIRN, Major George Alexander Stokes, M.B.E.

NAISH, Lieut. Francis Clement Prideaux, M.B.E., R.E.

NAISH, Harold Walter, M.B.E.

NALDER, Leonard Fielding, C.I.E., C.B.E., T. Major (T. Lieut.-Col.), Special List. (C3185a)

NANCARROW, Charlotte Alice, Mrs., M.B.E.

NANCE, Sir Arthur Stanley, K.B.E., C.B., J.P., R.N., *b.* 27 May, 1860 ; *s.* of James Nance, F.R.C.S., of Eccleshall, Staffs. ; *m.* Janet Besnard, *d.* of William Newburgh Tisdall,

of Donemark, Bantry. *Educ.:* Trent Coll.; St. Bart's. Hospital. *War Work:* Naval Medical Transport Officer for Scotland, and later Principal Medical Transport Officer at the Admiralty ; temporarily employed Ministry of Pensions, London. *Address:* Donemark House, Bantry, Co. Cork. *Club:* Junior Army and Navy. (K262)

NANCE, Thomas Pierce Hains, M.B.E. (M10408)

NAPIER, Capt. Arthur Lenox, O.B.E., *b.* 3 Dec. 1863 ; *s.* of the late Rev. J. W. Napier-Clavering, of Axwell Park, Blaydon-on-Tyne ; *m.* Marianne, *d.* of the late Louis Valentine, of Belfast. *Educ.:* Rossall School, and R.M. Coll. Lieut. Alexandra P.W.O. Yorks. Regt., 1882 ; Capt. 1892 ; retired, 1904 ; Assistant to Col. in charge Records Border Grouped Regt. District, 1905 ; Sec. Northumberland T.F. Association, 1908. *War Work:* Sec. Northumberland T.F. Association, Northumberland Local War Pensions Committee, Committee of Northumberland Prisoners of War Organisation. *Address:* Abbey Cottage, Alnwick, Northumberland. *Club:* Army and Navy. (O606)

NAPIER, Cecilia Jane, Mrs., C.B.E. ; *d.* of Charles John Harper, of Canterbury, N.Z., and *gr. d.* of the Right Rev. H. J. C. Harper, D.D., first Bishop of Christchurch, N.Z., and Primate of New Zealand ; *m.* Arundel Berkeley Napier, second *s.* of Edward Berkeley Napier, of Penward House, Shepton Mallet. *War Work:* Hon. Sec. British Red Cross, Bath 1914–19 ; Commandant V.A.D., Somerset 120, since 1915 ; Hon. Sec. Bath War Hospital Committee, 1915–20 ; Commandant Bath Rest Station, 1916–19 ; Hon. Sec. Bath Red Cross Soldiers' Comforts, 1916–19 ; Commandant Bathampton Red Cross Hospital for Limbless Soldiers, 1917–19 ; Organising Sec. Bath Flag Days, 1916–19 ; Joint Sec. Bath Red Cross Fete, 1917. *Address:* 26, St. James' Square, Bath. (C2829)

NAPIER, Major Charles James, O.B.E.

NAPIER, Major Francis, O.B.E.

NAPIER, 2nd Lieut. James Roos, M.B.E., M.C.

NAPIER, Lieut.-Col. John Steward, O.B.E., R.A.S.C.

NAPIER, Norman Wilson, M.B.E.

NARBETH, John Harper, C.B.E., M.V.O., R.C.N.C., M.Inst.N.A., *b.* 26 May, 1863 ; *s.* of John Harper Narbeth, of Pembroke Dock, South Wales ; *m.* Aquila Elizabeth, *d.* of William Anstey, of Portsmouth. *Educ.:* National School, Pembroke Dock ; Mathematical School, Pembroke Dockyard ; Royal Naval Coll., Greenwich. Chief Constructor, Royal Corps of Naval Constructors; Member Inst. of Naval Architects; Member of various committees and sub-committees of British Engineering Standards Association ; Member of Joint Aeronautical Technical Committee of Admiralty and Air Ministry. *War Work:* Design and construction of immense numbers of vessels for auxiliary services, such as Oil Tank Steamers for fleet services and ocean transports ; conversion of passenger and cargo steamers for same purposes ; mine sweeping vessels, such as Single Screw Sloops of Flower Class and Paddle Steamers of Ascot Class ; Submarine hunting vessels ; Seaplane and Aircraft Carriers, such as "Ark Royal," "Engadine" and "Campania." *Addresses:* Ferndale, Grove Road, Sutton, Surrey ; Admiralty, Whitehall, London, S.W. 1. (C2830)

NARES, Lieut. Ramsay Llewellyn Ives, M.B.E.

NARRACOT, Isabella Frances, M.B.E., Q.M.A.A.C.

NASH, Agnes Kathleen Mary, Lady, M.B.E. ; *e.d.* of the late James Harran, J.P., of Limerick ; *m.* Sir Vincent Nash, Knt. Bach., J.P., D.L., who, in 1909, was created Knight Commander of the Order of St. Gregory the Great by His Holiness Pius the 10th. *Address:* Shannon View House, Kilmurry, Co. Limerick.

NASH, Alice Emma, M.B.E., *b.* 24 Jan. 1857 ; *d.* of William Nash. *War Work:* Divisional Sec. B.R.C.S., Lambeth, from 1916 ; (Special Work) Air Raid Organisation. *Address:* 17, Barrington Road, Brixton, S.W. 9. (M9133)

NASH, Blanche Thompson, M.B.E. ; *d.* of the late Thompson Nash, of 14, Highbury Terrace, N. ; The Old House, Geldeston, Norfolk. *Educ.:* Privately ; Highbury and Islington High School. Lady Superintendent, Mersey Dock and Harbour Board. *War Work:* Welfare Supervisor, Ministry of Shipping, from Aug. 1916, to Nov. 1919. *Address:* 38, Brooke Road, Blundellsands, near Liverpool. (M2220)

NASH, Dorothea, M.B.E. ; *d.* of Walter Nash, of Hampton-in-Arden. *Educ.:* Privately. *War Work:* Commandant of V.A.D. Warwick 52, and of the Auxiliary Hospital, Hampton-in-Arden, opened in Dec. 1914. *Address:* Glenthorne, Hampton-in-Arden. *Clubs:* Three Counties', Birmingham ; V.A.D. Ladies'. (M9134)

NASH, Elizabeth Lily, Mrs., M.B.E.

NASH, Elsie Kathleen, M.B.E.

NASH, Capt. Francis Joseph, M.B.E., A.C.A., A.P.D., *b.* 17 Aug. 1884 ; *s.* of William Joseph Nash, of Breamore, Combe Down, Bath ; *m.* Louisa Theresa Aubrey, *d.* of the late Robert Maclauchlan Brandreth, D.C.L., of Woodcombe, Minehead, Somerset. *Educ.:* St. George's School, Southampton ; Prior Park Coll., Bath. *War Work:* Acting Paymaster, Army Pay Office, Preston, 1915–18 ; Paymaster, Army Pay Office, Preston, Feb. 1918 to date. *Address:* Breamore, Combe Down, Bath. (M5497)

NASH, Lieut. Frank Horace Elliott, M.B.E., R.N.V.R.

NASH, George Howard, C.B.E., M.I.E.E., *b.* 1881 ; *s.* of George Nash, of 45, Clifton Gardens, W. ; *m.* 1914, Florence Clarice, *d.* of Edward Mills, Mus. B. Electrical Engineer ; Chief Engineer, Western Electric Co., Ltd., since 1911 ; Technical Adviser to Admiralty Experimental Station, Portland, since 1918. *Club:* Royal Dorset Yacht.

NASH, Henry, M.B.E.

NASH, Lilian Mary Hamel, M.B.E. ; *d.* of the Rev. Canon T. A. Nash, M.A., Hon. Canon of Norwich. *War Work :* Superintendent of Girl Messengers at Air Ministry, March, 1917, to 30 Sept. 1919 ; previously Assist. Supt. of Girl Messengers at War Office, Jan. 1916, to March, 1917. (M9136)

NASH, Capt. Ryder Percival, O.B.E., R.A.M.C. (T.).

NASH, Comm. Walter Macdonald, O.B.E., R.N.

NASH, William, O.B.E., *b.* 18 Nov. 1889. *Educ. :* Cleaves School, Yalding. Civil Servant, Ministry of Labour ; upon demobilisation from Navy in Dec. 1918, was loaned to Ministry of Food, and appointed Sec. to the Flour Mills Control Committee ; still so employed. *War Work :* 1914–15, Receiving Officer for Board of Trade, of Belgian refugees at Tilbury and Folkestone Harbour ; 1915–17, Personal Assistant to Director-General of National Labour Supply, Ministry of Munitions ; subsequently Sec. to National Labour Advisory Board, Ministry of National Service ; 1918, Sub-Lieut. R.N.V.R. Southern Patrol (Anti-Submarine Division) ; decorated by Belgian Government with Medaille du Roi Albert avec rayure. *Address :* United Sports Club. (O607)

NASH, Capt. William, M.B.E., *b.* 4 Aug. 1892 ; *s.* of W. G. Nash, of St. Paul's Cray, Kent. *Educ. :* The Leys School, Cambridge. *War Work :* Served with 1/4th Royal West Kent Regt., Aug. 1914, to June, 1918 ; as G.S.O. 3 with Special Military Mission to Meshed and Russian Turkestan, July, 1918, to Jan. 1919 ; mentioned in despatches. *Address :* St. Paul's Cray, Kent. *Club :* Conservative. (M6499)

NASH, Capt. William John Charles, O.B.E., R.N.R. (ret.), *b.* 28 Dec. 1866 ; *s.* of William Nash, of Dublin ; *m.* Mabel Louise, *d.* of Francis Tozer Kinsman, of Eccles. *Educ. :* Bridge House, Chester. Marine and Dock Superintendent, London and North-Western Railway Company, Holyhead. *War Work :* In command of Auxiliary Cruiser attached to Grand Fleet, Aug. 1914, to Aug. 1915 ; in command Hospital Ship, Aug. 1915, to March, 1916. *Address :* Bryn-y-mor, Holyhead. *Club :* Holyhead Golf. (O1701)

NASMITH, Major George William, O.B.E., *b.* 11 July, 1888 ; *s.* of John William Nasmith, of Barlochan, Dalbeattie, N.B. ; *m.* Mary Frew, *d.* of John M. Robertson, of Glasgow. *Educ. :* Manchester Univ. Engineer, Vickers, Ltd. *War Work :* Regimental Duty, 7th Batt. Manchester Regt., T.F. ; seconded to R.E. Salonica ; attached to 16th Corps H.Q. on Struma Front, in charge Light Railways for British Troops, afterwards instructing and handing over to Greek troops ; after Armistice, with Bulgars, duty with Light Railways in Bulgaria, and Standard Gauge, Adrianople ; one of the four members of Inter-Allied Military Railway Commission for the Near East. *Address :* Norwood, Heaton Mersey, Manchester. *Club :* Junior Army and Navy. (O6515)

NASON, Lieut.-Col. Henry Hyde Williamson, D.S.O., O.B.E., *b.* 8 March, 1857 ; *s.* of the late Major-Gen. John Nason, of Comrie House, Comrie, Perthshire ; *m.* Florence Hannay, *d.* of Col. Alexander Hannay. *Educ. :* Harrow. O.C. 2nd Batt. R. Guernsey L.I. (Militia) Embarkation Staff, 1910–13. *War Work :* O.C. 2nd Reserve Batt. R. Guernsey L.I., 1916–20. *Club :* Public Schools. (O8892)

NATHAN, Capt. Arthur Frederic, O.B.E.

NATHAN, Capt. Edward Jonah, O.B.E.

NATHAN, Col. Sir Frederic Lewis, K.B.E., Knt. Bach., late R.A., *b.* 10 Feb. 1861 ; *s.* of Jonah Nathan, of 11, Pembridge Square, London ; *m.* Adeline Edith, *d.* of E. F. Sichel, of London. *Educ. :* Privately ; Royal Military Academy, Woolwich. Entered Royal Artillery, 1879 ; Capt.1887 ; Major, 1897 ; Lieut.-Col. 1905 ; Brevet Col. 1908 ; Capt. Inspector, Royal Laboratory, 1886–88 ; 2nd Assist. to the D.O. of Ordnance Factories, 1888–92 ; Officer-in-charge of Danger Buildings, Royal Gunpowder Factory, 1892–99 ; Assist. Superintendent, R.G.P.F. 1899–1900 ; Superintendent, 1900–9 ; Works Manager, Nobel's Explosives Co., Ardeer Factory, 1909–15. *War Work :* Adviser to the Admiralty on Cordite Supplies, 1915 ; Director of Propellant Supplies, Ministry of Munitions, 1915–19. *Address :* 37, Cornwall Gardens, S.W. 7. *Club :* Army and Navy. (K159)

NATHAN, Lieut.-Comm. George Emanuel, O.B.E., R.N.V.R.

NATHAN, Lieut. Stanley John, M.B.E., R.E.

NATHAN, Sybil Caroline, M.B.E.

NAUGHE, James, O.B.E.

NAUGHTON, Lieut. Thomas Henry, M.B.E., Mily. Works, I.A.

NAWANAGAR, Lieut.-Col. H.H. Shri Sir Ranjitsinhji Vibhaji Jam Sahib, G.B.E., K.C.S.I. (G45)

NAWTON, Daisy, M.B.E., *b.* 6 Jan. 1868 ; *d.* of Thomas Court, of Winchcombe, Gloucestershire ; *m.* Charles William, *s.* of George Nawton ; of Kirby-Moorside, Yorks. *Educ. :* Winchcombe Private School. *War Work :* Searching for Missing at King George Hospital, S.E. 1, for 4 years ; air raid duty, and general V.A.D. work as Section Leader L/258, B.R.C.S. ; now doing voluntary work for L.C.C. Children's Care Committee. *Address :* 28, Canterbury Road, Brixton, S.W. 9. (M9137)

NAYLER, Joseph, M.B.E.

NAYLOR, Rev. Capt. Alfred Thomas Arthur, O.B.E., M.A. (Cantab.), hon. C.F., *b.* 27 Dec. 1889 ; *s.* of the Rev. A. J. Naylor, of Tunbridge Wells. *Educ. :* King Edward's School ; Emmanuel Coll., Ridley Hall, Cambridge. Domestic Chaplain, Wemyss Castle ; Chaplain, Wemyss Coal Company. *War Work :* B.E.F., France, 1914 15 and 1916–19 ; mentioned in

despatches, Nov. 1917, Dec. 1918. *Address :* Chaplain, Wemyss Castle, Fife, Scotland. *Clubs :* Conservative, Edinburgh ; Arts, Glasgow. (O2654)

NAYLOR, Henry William Letts, O.B.E., *b.* 1873 ; *s.* of Capt. Henry Thomas Naylor, late Cavalry Depot, Canterbury. Office of the Crown Agents of the Colonies. *War Work :* Army Contracts ; Assistant Director of Raw Materials and Assist. Controller of Salvage ; Chevalier de l'Ordre de la Couronne (Belgian) 1918. *Addresses :* 4, Millbank, Westminster ; 50, Aldrington Road, Streatham Park. *Club* Royal Automobile. (O11038)

NAYLOR, William James, M.B.E.

NEALE, Clara, M.B.E., *d.* of George Antrim, of Gloucester. *Educ. :* Privately. Missionary in Portuguese East Africa. *War Work :* Queen Mary's Army Aux. Corps, Unit Administrator. *Address :* 242, Pitt Street, Sydney, Australia. *Club :* Belgrave. (M3146)

NEALE, Major John Arnold, O.B.E., *b.* 9 April, 1894 ; *s.* of Arnold Ferrers Neale, of Dulwich, Surrey. *Educ. :* C. B. Coll., St. Kilda, Australia. Officer of Commonwealth of Australia Public Service. *War Work :* Lieut. 14th Batt. Aus. Inf. ; Capt. 3rd Echelon, Egypt ; Major and O.C. Base Records, A.I.F., London. *Address :* 16, Mayfield Street, St. Kilda East. (O8995)

NEALE, Major William Walter Raymond, O.B.E., R.A.V.C.

NEAME, Ada Grace, Mrs., M.B.E., *b.* 1860 ; *d.* of James Sant, C.V.O., R.A., Principal Painter in Ordinary to the late Queen Victoria ; *m.* Laurence, *s.* of George Harding. *War Work :* Commandant of Christchurch V.A.D. Hospital, Beckenham, for 4 years (130 beds). *Address :* Woodfield, Southend Road, Beckenham. *Club :* V.A.D. (M796)

NEAME, Major Arthur Lawrence Cecil, O.B.E., R.E., and R.A.F.

NEAME, Lieut. George Austin, M.B.E.

NEAME, Maud Kathleen Frances, Mrs., M.B.E., *b.* 1874 ; *d.* of Francis Marsden Cobb, of Margate ; *m.* Harry Sidney, *s.* of Percy Beale Neame, of Faversham. *Educ. :* Brussels. *War Work :* Commandant at The Mount Hospital, Faversham ; Vice-President of the Clothing Branch, Soldiers' and Sailors' Families Association ; packed for the Faversham Branch of the Prisoners of War. *Address :* Alfred House, Faversham, Kent. (M3862)

NEAME, Thomas, M.B.E., M.A., *b.* 23 Dec. 1885 ; *s.* of Frederick Neame, of Luton, near Faversham. *Educ. :* Cheltenham ; Caius Coll., Cambridge. *War Work :* Served in Gallipoli with 9th Batt. Worcestershire Regt. ; Manager of Brass and Spelter Departments with Messrs. Stewarts and Lloyds, Ltd. *Address :* Colkins, Faversham. (M797)

NEASHAM, Lieut. John Robert, M.B.E., R.N.V.R.

NEATE, Capt. Alfred, O.B.E., *b.* 19 Feb. 1873 ; *s.* of Charles Neate, of Bristol. *War Work :* Served as Quartermaster with 1st Batt. P.A. Somerset L.I. throughout the war. *Address :* Palace Barracks, Holywood, Co. Down. (O5621)

NEATE, Lieut. Frederick Harry, O.B.E., R.E.

NEAVE, Major Charles Alexander, O.B.E., R.A.S.C.

NEAVE, John Sime, M.B.E.

NEEDHAM, Major Alfred Owen, O.B.E., M.C.

NEEDHAM, James Easthorpe, O.B.E.

NEEDHAM, James Ernest, C.B.E., *b.* 30 April, 1875 ; *s.* of Edward Moore Needham, of Duffield, Derbyshire ; *m.* Dorothy, *d.* of Graham R. Lynn, of Karachi. *Educ. :* Rugby. *Clubs :* Royal Automobile ; Oriental ; Byculla ; Royal Bombay Yacht ; Bombay, India. (C2831)

NEEDHAM, James Henry, M.B.E.

NEEDHAM, John Hewson, O.B.E.

NEEDHAM, Col. Joseph George, D.S.O., O.B.E., T.D., *b.* 2 Sept. 1876 ; *s.* of the late John Needham, of Eccles, Lancs. *Educ. :* Privately, and Owens Coll. Steel and Iron Merchant, partner, John Needham and Sons, 15, Cross Street, Manchester. *War Work :* Mobilised and Commanded 42nd (East Lancashire) Divisional Train ; embarked for Egypt, Sept. 1914 ; remained in command till Feb. 1918 ; Command 60th (London) Divl. Train until April, 1919 ; mentioned in despatches four times. *Addresses :* 15, Cross Street, Manchester ; Ranighar, Didsbury. *Clubs :* Clarendon, Manchester ; United R.A.S.C. (O6258)

NEEVE, William, M.B.E.

NEIGHBOUR, Capt. Sidney William, O.B.E., T.D., Artists Rifles, *b.* 4 Aug. 1875 ; *s.* of W. F. Neighbour, F.S.I., of 56, Chancery Lane, W.C. ; *m.* Gwenydd Joyce, *d.* of the late Edward Prentis, of Tunstall, Kent. *Educ. :* Privately. *War Work :* Mobilised, Aug. 1914 ; proceeded to France Oct. 1914 ; served in France until 1918 ; served with 1st Batt. Artists Rifles and on Staff of 102nd and 12th Infty. Bdes. ; North Russia, 1918–19, served on Staff of Dwina Force. *Address :* 56, Chancery Lane, W.C. (O6702)

NEIL, Capt. George London, O.B.E., R.A.M.C.

NEILD, Capt. Ralph, O.B.E., I.A.R.O.

NEILEY, Major B₃yard Lamont, O.B.E., Can. A.D.C.

NEILL, Capt. Eric Vansithart Ernest, M.B.E.

NEILL, Col. James William SMITH, C.B.E., J.P. Bucks and Ayrshire, late Scots Guards, *b.* 6 March, 1865 ; *s.* of the late Capt. W. J. Smith-Neill, late R.H.A., of Swindugenum, Ayrshire. *Educ. :* Wellington. Joined Scots Guards 1888. retired 1903 ; Member of Bucks County Council, 1901–7 ; Sec. Renfrewshire Territorial Force Association, 1907–14 ; rejoined the Army for service during the war ; appointed D.A.Q.M.G. London District, Nov. 1914 ; appointed G.S. 2, London District, 1915 ; appointed Lieut.-Col. commanding

Scots Guards, March, 1916, to end of war; appointed comptroller and equerry to H.R.H. Princess Louise, Duchess of Argyll, April, 1919. *Address:* Doonbrae, Alloway, Ayr. *Club:* Guards'; Arthur's. (C1767)

NEILL, Capt. Joseph, O.B.E., R.G.A.

NEILL, William Reid, M.B.E.

NEILSON, Capt. George Clement, O.B.E.. M.B., R.A M.C.

NEILSON, Major Henry John, C.B.E., M.D., *b.* 30 Dec. 1862; *s.* of Matthew Gilmour, of Glasgow; *m.* Annie Keil, *d.* of John Tullis, of Glasgow. *Educ.:* Glasgow High School; Univs. of Glasgow, Vienna, and Berlin. Chief Commissioner of Medical Services, London Region, Ministry of Pensions. *War Work:* Major, R.A.M.C., in medical charge of Scottish Command Depot, Randalstown, Ireland; Deputy Chief Commissioner of Medical Services, Ministry of National Service. *Address:* Shandon, St. George's Hill, Weybridge, Surrey. *Club:* Royal Automobile. (C830)

NEILSON, Major John Fraser, C.B.E., D.S.O., 10th Royal Hussars, *b.* 27 June, 1884; *s.* of William Neilson, of Arnewood, Kelvinside, Glasgow; *m.* Helen Vera. *d.* of Wm. Cazalet, of Moscow. *Educ.:* Uppingham; Sandhurst. *War Work:* Attached Russian Armies in the Field, Aug. 1914, to end of war; attached Russian Armies in the Field in Siberia, Sept. 1918, to Oct. 1919; ret. 1920. *Club:* Cavalry. (C2212h)

NEILSON, Katherine Helen, M.B.E., *b.* 1852; *d.* of Daniel Neilson, of Hundhill Hall, Yorkshire. *War Work:* Founder and Chief Supporter of Flounders College Auxiliary Hospital, Ackworth, Yorkshire. *Address:* Hundhill Hall, Pontefract, Yorkshire. (M3863)

NEILSON, Capt. Ronald Braco Stenhouse, O.B.E.

NEILSON William Hardcastle, O.B.E., M.A., M.A.I. (Dublin), M.I.C.E., M.I.M.E., *b.* 21 Feb. 1875; *s.* of Henry Charles Neilson, of Dublin; *m.* Ethel Maud, *d.* of Frank Phillips, of Plymouth. *Educ.:* Mr. Strangways' School; Trinity Coll., Dublin. Chief Engineer, Karachi Port Trust, India; Member of Concrete Institute, American Society of Civil Engineers, Council of the Institution of Engineers (India). *War Work:* Controller of Munitions, Karachi Circle, Indian Munitions Board, 1917; Member of the Priority Committee, Karachi Circle, Indian Munitions Board, 1917–18; Karachi being the base of operations for the campaign in Mesopotamia, a large amount of work was undertaken by the Karachi Port Trust for the Military Authorities. *Clubs:* Oriental; Sind, Karachi. (O9837)

NEISH, Major Colin Graham, O.B.E.

NEISH, Elizabeth Oliver, M.B.E.

NEL, Charles Paul Leonard, M.B.E.

NELIGAN, Comm. Eric Claude, O.B.E., R.N.

NELSON, Major Arthur, O.B.E.

NELSON, Arthur Edward, O.B.E., J.P., I.C.S., *b.* 17 April, 1875. *Educ.:* Newcastle High School, and Magdalen Coll., Oxford. Chief Sec. C.P. and Berar Administration. *War Work:* Secretary of Provincial Red Cross Fund. *Address:* Nagpur, C.P., India. *Club:* East India United Service. (O4078)

NELSON, Charlotte Mabel, M.B.E. *b.,* 21 Jan. 1877; *d.* of Alline James Nelson, of Fulneck, Leeds. *Educ.:* Ockbrook; Bedford; Brighton; Switzerland. *War Work:* Appointed Quartermaster of V.A.D. 2 Derby, at its commencement, in 1910; became Commandant in April, 1914; detachment equipped a Sunday School lent for a hospital in Autumn, 1914, in Ockbrook; received 20 British patients on Dec. 23, 1914; after which date patients were received till Feb. 27, 1919, when the hospital was closed. *Address:* Hillside, Ockbrook, Derby. (M9142)

NELSON, Major and Qr.-Mr. David, M.B.E., D.C.M., *b.* 25 Oct. 1866. *War Work:* Served with 2/1st Lothians and Border Horse Yeomanry from its formation in September, 1914, until disbanded in Sept. 1919; D.C.M. awarded for services in South African War, 1900. (M5498)

NELSON, Brig.-Gen. Edgar Forbes, C.B.E., *b.* 1859. Col. and Hon. Brig.-Gen; Served in S. Africa, 1899–1902 (Queen's medal with three clasps, King's medal with two clasps); Great War, 1914–19 (despatches). (C1712a)

NELSON, Lieut.-Col. Henry, O.B.E.

NELSON, Bt.-Lieut.-Col. James Owen, O.B.E.

NELSON, Joe, M.B.E. (M4748)

NELSON, Capt. John Joseph Harper, O.B.E., M.C., M.D., F.R.C.S., I.M.S.

NELSON, Capt. Maurice Henry Horatio, C.B.E., R.N. (ret.); *s.* of the late Rear-Admiral Hon. M. H. Nelson. *Educ.:* Royal Academy, Gosport. *War Work:* Employed at Devonport Dockyard as assistant to the Captain of the Dockyard. *Address:* Summer House, Hamble, Southampton. (C2320)

NELSON, Col. Percy Reginald, C.B.E., *b.* 9 Sept. 1884; *m.* Helen Cicely, *d.* of the late Edward Willett, of Bromley, Kent. *War Work:* Served with Expeditionary Force Canteens in France from Jan. 1915, to April, 1919; twice mentioned in despatches. *Club:* Union. (C1298)

NELSON, Eng.-Comm. Robert Douglas, O.B.E., R.N.

NELSON, Lieut.-Col. William, O.B.E.

NELSON, William, O.B.E., M.A., *b.* 16 June, 1862; *s.* of Joseph Nelson, of Appleby, Westmorland; *m.* Annie, *d.* of Dr. Charles Read, of London. *Educ.:* Elmfield Coll., York; King's Coll., London. Headmaster, Royal Schools for the Deaf, Manchester; Registrar, National Coll. of Teachers of the Deaf. *War Work:* Sec. Special Aural Board, Ministry of Pensions. *Address:* Royal Schools for the Deaf, Old Trafford, Manchester. (O7704)

NELSON, William, M.B.E.

NELSON, William Ernest, O.B.E., M.A., M.R.C.S., L.R.C.P., *b.* 7 Nov. 1870; *s.* of the late Rev. William Nelson, M.A., of Arden House, Henley-in-Arden; *m.* Rosa Gertrude, *d.* of the late A. J. Tompkins, of 10, Park Terrace, Cambridge. *Educ.:* Haileybury Coll.; Clare Coll., Cambridge; St. Thomas' Hospital, London. Medical Practitioner at Henley-in-Arden, Warwickshire; also partner with Oswald Nelson, at Arden House, Henley-in-Arden, Preparatory School for Boys. *War Work:* Commandant and Medical Officer of the V.A.D. Auxiliary Hospital, Henley-in-Arden (82 beds); Medical Director, B.R.C.S., for the County of Warwickshire. *Address:* Arden House, Henley-in-Arden, Warwickshire. *Club:* Sports. (O41)

NELTHORPE, Major Robert Nassau SUTTON-, O.B.E., J.P., D.L., late 8th Hussars, *b.* 13 May, 1850; *s.* of the Rev. Robert Sutton, of Scawby Hall, Lincs.; *m.* the Hon. Dulcibella Eden, *d.* of William George, 4th Baron Auckland (*see* BURKE'S *Peerage*). *Educ.:* Eton. Formerly County Councillor and Alderman of the Lindsey County Council; Chairman of Education and Finance Committees; Chairman of Governors, Brigg Grammar School. *War Work:* Chairman of the Emergency Committee for the River Trent, from Nottingham to the Humber. *Address:* Scawby Hall, Brigg, Lincs. *Club:* Oriental. (O1705)

NEOBARD, Capt. Harold John Cooke, O.B.E.

NESBIT, Capt. George, O.B.E., M.C.

NESBITT, Lieut. Thomas Hunter, M.B.E., R.A.F

NESBITT, Edward John BEAMONT-, O.B.E., H.M.L. King's County, *b.* 20 Nov. 1860; *s.* of Rev. T. G. Beaumont, formerly Rector of Chelmondiston, Suffolk; *m.* Helen (died 1918), *d.* of Frederick Freeman Thomas, of Ratton, Sussex. *Educ.:* Winchester and Oriel Coll., Oxford. *War Work:* Parliamentary Dept., Foreign Office. *Addresses:* Tubberdaly, Edenderry, Ireland; 56, Rutland Gate, S.W. *Clubs:* Travellers'; Kildare Street, Dublin. (O11040)

NESS, Bertha, Mrs., M.B.E. Worker in Catholic Soldiers' Club. Abbeville. (M10259g)

NESS, Helen Dorothy Parker, M.B.E., *b.* 10 March, 1886; *d.* of G. Parker Ness, Barrister-at-Law, J.P., of 19, Porchester Terrace, London. *Educ.:* Bedford Coll. *War Work:* Quartermaster, Westbourne Hospital, Porchester Terrace. *Address:* 19, Porchester Terrace, London. (M9143)

NETHERSOLE, Harrison Ralph, M.B.E.

NETTLEFOLD, Robert, M.B.E.

NETTLESHIP, William Sharp, M.B.E.

NEVATT, Capt. Christopher George, O.B.E., R.A.F.

NEVE, Col. Edward John, C.B.E., *b.* 1870. Lieut.-Col. and T. Col. Army Pay Corps; served in the Great War, 1914–19 (despatches). (C1712b)

NEVE, Col. Edward John, O.B.E., A.P.D.

NEVILE, Maria Elizabeth, M.B.E., *b.* 1861; *d.* of Canon Nevile, of Lincoln. *War Work:* Member of Lincolnshire Military Appeal Tribunal; Chairman, Women's Relief Committee. (M2225)

NEVILL, Major Cosmos Charles Richard, D.S.O., O.B.E., *b.* 1873. Entered Roy. Warwickshire Regt. 1900; Major, 1915; served in the S. African War, 1902 (medal); Great War, 1914–19 (despatches). (O7514)

NEVILL, Euphan, Mrs., M.B.E,

NEVILL, Florence Mary, Lady George, C.B.E., Lady of Grace of St. John of Jerusalem; *d.* of the late Temple Soanes, of Brenchley House, Kent; *m.* 1882, Lord George Montacute Nevill, J.P., D.L., 3rd *s.* of the 1st Marquess of Abergavenny, K.G., J.P. (*see* BURKE'S *Peerage*). *War Work:* Deputy President of B.R.C.S., Brighton, Hove, Preston, and Patcham Division. Is Commandant of the Lady George Nevill Hospital, now in conjunction with the Ministry of Pensions. *Addresses:* 22, Palmeira Square, Hove, Sussex; 7a, Eaton Square, S.W. (C2832)

NEVILL, Lieut.-Col. Henry Rivers, O.B.E.

NEVILL, Major Stanley Sharp, O.B.E., R.A.F.

NEVILL, Capt. Walter Elphinstone, O.B.E.

NEVILLE, Lieut. Maurice Michael, O.B.E., R.A.S.C.

NEVILLE, Ralph, O.B.E. (O11787h)

NEVILLE, Sir William Henry, K.B.E.

NEW, Lieut. Arthur Henry, O.B.E., R.N.V.R.

NEW, Major Claud E., O.B.E.

NEW, Evelyn Helen Johnston, M.B.E.

NEWAL, Lieut.-Col. Frederick William Monk, O.B.E.

NEWALL, Group-Capt. Cyril Louis Norton, C.M.G., C.B.E. Dep. Director R.A.F.; served in the Great War, 1914–19 (despatches). (C1902)

NEWALL, Ethel Nest, Mrs. Geoffrey Stirling, O.B.E.

NEWALL, John Walker, M.B.E.

NEWALL, Capt. Norman Dakeyne, O.B.E.. R.A.F.

NEWALL, Helen Frances, Mrs. STIRLING-, M.B.E., *d.* of John Deakin Heaton, M.D., F.R.C.P., LL.D., J.P., of Claremont, Leeds; *m.* Frederick Stirling, *s.* of Robert Stirling Newall, F.R.S., D.C., J.P. *War Work:* Sec. and Organiser of the Wylam Hospital Supply Depot, which made 200,000 articles for every part of the fighting zone; meetings were held partly at Castle Hill and partly at a village institute; responsible for buying, warehousing, and raising the Fund of £2000; judge of the soldiers needlework at the Military Hospital, Cox Ledge, Newcastle-on-Tyne. *Address:* Castle Hill, Wylam-on-Tyne. *Club:* Empress. (M9144)

NEWBERRY, Percy Edward, O.B.E., M.A., *b.* 23 April, 1869; *s.* of Henry James Newberry, of Ealing; *m.* Essie

Winifred. *d.* of William Johnston, of Bromborough, Cheshire. *Educ.:* King's Coll. School, and King's Coll., London. Brunner Professor of Egyptology in the Univ. of Liverpool, 1906–19; Hon. Reader in Egyptian Art University of Liverpool 1919: Fellow of King's Coll., London. *War Work:* Police work and organising help for Belgian refugees, 1914–15; enrolled as a War Munitions Volunteer, 1916; employed first in shell-turning, and during the whole of 1917 on gauge-making; Assist. Sec. to the Director of National Service, London and South-Eastern Region, 1918–19. *Address:* Oldbury Place, Ightham, Kent. *Clubs:* Constitutional; University, Liverpool. (O11041)

NEWBERY, Capt. James Wilfred Trevor, O.B.E., M.C., R.F.A.

NEWBOLD, Col. Ambrose William, O.B.E.

NEWBOLD, Major William, O.B.E., M.A., F.R.A.S., F.R.G.S., R.G.A., *b.* 17 June, 1878; *s.* of William Newbold, of Tunbridge Wells and the City of Mexico. *Educ.:* Uppingham, and Magdalen Coll., Oxford. Assist. Master, Tonbridge School, 1902–14; H.M. Inspector of Schools (Secondary Branch), 1919. *War Work:* Commissioned Lieut., R.G.A., Dec. 1, 1914; served with B.E.F. France, Jan. 1915, to March, 1919; 119th Heavy Battery, R.G.A., Feb. 1915, to Jan. 1916; attached 3rd Field Survey Batt., R.E., Jan. 1916, to Nov. 1918; attached Maps Section, General Staff, G.H.Q., Nov. 1918, to March, 1919; thrice mentioned in despatches. *Address:* c/o Board of Education, London. *Club:* Royal Automobile. (O2658)

NEWBOLT, George Palmerston, C.B.E., M.B., F.R.C.S. (Eng.), *b.* 15 March, 1863; *s.* of Kosciusko Kent Newbolt, of Weymouth; *m.* Lila, *d.* of John Elliot, of Canonbie. *Educ.:* Weymouth Coll.; Thompson's, Jersey; St. Bartholomew's Hospital; Univ. of Durham. Consulting Surgeon; Hon. Surgeon, Royal Southern Hospital, Liverpool; Leasowe Children's Hospital. *War Work:* Operating Surgeon, Royal Southern Hospital, Myrtle Auxiliary Hospital, Croxteth Hall Officers' Hospital, and Leasowe Children's Hospital. *Address:* 5, Gambier Terrace, Liverpool. *Club:* Hoylake and Wallasey Golf. (C2833)

NEWBY, Albert Ernest, M.B.E.

NEWBY, Gervase Edward, O.B.E., F.R.C.S.

NEWBY, Styan, O.B.E.

NEWCASTLE, Kathleen Florence May, Duchess of, O.B.E.; *d.* of the late Major Henry Augustus, 9th Lancers, and Hon. Mrs. Candy, *d.* of the 3rd Baron Rossmore (*see* BURKE'S *Peerage*); *m.* 1889, Henry Pelham Archibald Douglas Pelham-Clinton, 7th Duke of Newcastle (*see* BURKE'S *Peerage*). *Addresses:* Clumber Park, Worksop, Notts; Forest Farm, Windsor Forest; 11, Berkeley House, Hay Hill, W. 1. (O11042)

NEWCOMB, Major Neville, O.B.E.

NEWCOMBE, Major Harold Kenzie, O.B.E.

NEWEL, Rose Alice, Mrs., M.B.E.

NEWELL, Frank, O.B.E.

NEWELL, Lieut.-Col Leopold Monk, O.B.E., T.D., R.A.S.C. (T.).

NEWELL, Lieut.-Col. Stanley Monk, D.S.O., O.B.E., R.E. (T.). Served in the Great War, 1914–18 (despatches). (O4240)

NEWELL, 2nd Lieut. Will, M.B.E.

NEWEY, Capt. Frank, O.B.E. R.A.M.C. (T.).

NEWHAM, Major William Henry, O.B.E., M.B.E.

NEWITT, Leonard, O.B.E., M.I.E.E., *b.* 10 Aug. 1865; *s.* of Edward Newitt, of Westbury, Bucks; *m.* Ethel, *d.* of William Scott, of Glasgow. *Educ.:* Magdalen Coll. School, Brackley, Oxford. Electrical Engineer, M.H. Dockyard, Chatham. *War Work:* Engaged in supervising the repairs and installation of electrical gear on H.M. Ships. *Address:* H.M. Dockyard, Chatham. (O610)

NEWLAND, Col. Edmund Walcott, C.B.E., A.P.D., *b.* 11 Jan. 1858; *s.* of Capt. Charles Frankland Newland, R.N., of Midhurst, Sussex; *m.* Ellen Charlotte, *d.* of Charles Hornby, of Dalton Hall, Lancs. *Educ.:* King Edward VI. School, Bruton, and Sidney Coll., Bath. *War Work:* Command Paymaster, Western Command, Aug. 1914, to Jan. 1916; Command Paymaster, Gibraltar, Jan. 1916, to end of war. *Address:* c/o Messrs. Cox & Co., Charing Cross. (C1713)

NEWLAND, Lieut.-Col. Henry Simpson, C.B.E., D.S.O., M.B., B.S., M.S., F.R.C.S., Australian Army Med. Corps, *b.* 1873; *s.* of Simpson Newland, of The Terraces, Adelaide, S. Australia; *m.* 1910, Ellen Mary, *d.* of James Hemery Lindon. *Educ.:* St. Peter's School, Adelaide, and Adelaide Univ. Assist. Surg. Adelaide Hospital; Senior Surg. Children's Hospital, Adelaide; Surg. Australian Section, Queen's Hospital, Served during European War, 1914–18, in Egypt, Gallipoli, and France (despatches); Surg.-Registrar, London Hospital, 1901. *Address:* Strangways Terrace, North Adelaide, Australia. *Club:* Adelaide. (C2194)

NEWLAND, Major Victor Marra, O.B.E., M.C.

NEWLANDS, Capt. Alexander, M.B.E.

NEWLANDS, Alexander, C.B.E., M.I.C.E., F.R.S.A., *b.* 11 Jan. 1870; *s.* of Alexander Newlands, of Elgin, Morayshire; *m.* Bessie Hamilton, *d.* of the Rev. John MacGilchrist, of Bowmore, Islay. *Educ.:* West End School, and Privately. Engineer-in-Chief, Highland Railway Co., Inverness; Member of the Board of Trade Water Power Resources Committee; Member of the Conjoint Board of Scientific Societies, Royal Society Water Power Sub-Committee; Deputy Chairman of Inverness (Highlands) Local Advisory Committee. *Addresses:* Highland Railway; Caol-Ila, Inverness. (C2834)

NEWLANDS, Archibald, O.B.E.

NEWLANDS, John, C.I.E., C.B.E., *b.* 1857; *s.* of the late John Newlands, of Galashiels, Selkirkshire; *m.* 1881, Cecilia Catherine, *d.* of the late John Wicks, dentist, of Edinburgh. *Educ.:* Jedburgh and Edinburgh. Entered Postal Telegraph Ser. Edinburgh, 1870; Controller, Telegraph Depart. 1898; Traffic Manager, Sec.'s Office, Gen. Post Office, London, 1901; Dep. Controller, Central Telegraph Office. 1905; Controller, 1910; retired, 1919; reorganised Traffic Depart. Indian Telegraphs, 1907–9; has Order of Crown of Belgium. *War Work:* Inlan d and Foreign Telegraph work. *Address:* Bemersyde, Farnham Royal, Bucks. (C578)

NEWMAN, Comm. Edward John Kendall, C.B.E., R.N. Div. Naval Transport Officer; served in the Great War, 1914–9. (despatches). (C2260)

NEWMAN, Capt. and Qr.-Mr. Frederick Herbert, O.B.E.

NEWMAN, Henry Charles, M.B.E., R.N.

NEWMAN, Lieut. Herbert John Greatrex, M.B.E., R.A.F.

NEWMAN, Lieut. James Benjamin, O.B.E., R.N.

NEWMAN, Lieut. James Colin, M.B.E.

NEWMAN, Capt. John Campin, O.B.E., M.B., F.R.C.S., R.A.M.C. (T.).

NEWMAN, Capt. Leslie, O.B.E., R.A.F.

NEWMAN, Major Richard Ernest Upton, O.B.E., M.C., R.A.M.C.

NEWMAN, Capt. Vincent Chester, O.B.E., R.M.

NEWMAN, William, O.B.E

NEWMAN, William, M.B.E., *b.* 11 Jan. 1868. *Educ.:* National and Collegiate Schools. Superintendent, Metropolitan Police. *War Work:* Intensive police work in the central (Metropolitan) bombed areas. *Address:* 1, Queen Street, Hammersmith, London, W. 6. (M9147)

NEWMAN, William Augustin, M.B.E. (M10409)

NEWMARCH, Bernard James, C.M.G., C.B.E., V.D., M.R.C.S. (Eng.), L.R.C.P., *b.* 28 April, 1856; *s.* of the late John Newmarch, Barrister-at-Law, of the Inner Temple; *m.* Blanche Edith, *d.* of the late John Heathcote, R.N., of Canley Vale, N.S.W. *Educ.:* Cholmondeley School, Highgate; Buston and Sherborne; King's Coll., London. Hon. Consulting Surgeon, Sydney Hospital, and Royal North Shore Hospital, North Sydney. *War Work:* O.C. 1st Australian Field Ambulance; O.C. 1st and 3rd Australian General Hospitals (1914–19). *Address:* 193, Macquarie Street, Sydney. *Clubs:* Imperial Service (Sydney); Automobile Club of Australia. (C2195)

NEWMARCH, Capt. Edward, M.B.E., *b.* 1880; *s.* of Joseph Newmarch, of South Shields; *m.* Margaret Bone, *d.* of Henry Holland, of South Shields. Master Mariner; Master, s.s. "War Grange." *War Work:* White Sea, Russian Expedition. *Address:* 70, Julian Avenue, South Shields. (M9148)

NEWMARCH, Henry Clarence, M.B.E., R.N.

NEWNHAM, Charles, M.B.E., *b.* 23 May, 1850. *Educ.:* Munslow National School (Salop). Hon. Licensed Lay Reader, Diocese of Exeter; late Conductor, Ordnance Store Corps (Egyptian Medal and Star, 1882). *War Work:* Superintendent, Separation Allowance Section, Worcester Territorial Force Association, Dec. 1914, to March, 1920. *Address:* Broadhempston, Totnes, Devon. (M9149)

NEWNHAM, John Montague, O.B.E., V.D., D.L.

NEWPORT, Lieut. and Qr.-Mr. George Charles, M.B.E., *b.* 15 Oct. 1881. *War Work:* Joined the Rifle Brigade, afterwards receiving Commission in Royal Fusiliers; served with 39th Royal Fusiliers (Jewish Batt.) from their formation, proceeding to Egypt and afterwards to Palestine; was present with Battalion in the Jordan Valley, also taking part in the offensive, Sept. 1918, in the advance on Es Salt and Ammar. (M4697)

NEWSOM, Col. Augustus Charles, C.M.G., C.B.E., R.A.V.C., *b.* 1866. Dep. Director of Vet. Sers.; served with the Chitral Relief Force, 1895 (medal with clasp); in S. Africa, 1899–1900, present at defence of Ladysmith (Queen's medal, with clasp); Great War, 1914–19 (despatches). (C1299)

NEWSOME, Capt. Charles Todd, O.B.E., *b.* 8 Aug. 1888; *s.* of Mark Newsome, of Dewsbury; *m.* Elsie Mary, *d.* of J. M. Hay, of Wallasey. *Educ.:* Harrogate and Rossall. Motor Engineer. *Address:* Myton Bury, Warwick. *Club:* Junior Army and Navy. (O5629)

NEWTON, Alice C., Mrs., M.B.E.; *d.* of Duncan Henderson, J.P., of Leicester. *War Work:* Commandant of Knighton V.A.D. Hospital, Evington, Leicester, Sept. 1915, to Feb. 1919. *Address:* Bridport, Great Malvern. (M532)

NEWTON, Alice Elizabeth Maud, Mrs., M.B.E.

NEWTON, Charles Wemyss, M.B.E.

NEWTON, Elizabeth Louisa, O.B.E., Médaille de S.M. la Reine Elisabeth; *d.* of the late General W. S. Newton, of 43, Lowndes Street. *War Work:* Worked for the War Refugee Committee, General Buildings, Aldwych, from Sept. 1914, to the end of May, 1919. *Address:* 43, Lowndes Street, S.W. 1. (O11045)

NEWTON, Ernest, C.B.E., R.A., *b.* 12 Sept. 1856; *s.* of Henry Newton, of Bickley, Kent; *m.* Antoinette Johanna, *d.* of William Hoyack, of Rotterdam, Holland. *Educ.:* Private School, Blackheath; Uppingham. *War Work:* Hon. Director Building Licences Section; Chairman, Building Labour Committee, Ministry of Munitions; transferred in March, 1918, to Ministry of National Service. *Clubs:* Athenæum; Arts. (C2835)

NEWTON, Florence Mai Shedlock, Mrs., M.B.E., R.A.F.

NEWTON, Lieut.-Col. Frank Graham, C.B.E., D.S.O. Australian Gen. List; served in the Great War, 1915-19 (despatches). (C794)

NEWTON, Capt. Frederick, M.B.E., *b.* 23 July, 1858; *s.* of John Newton, of Warrington; *m.* Margaret Annie Maitland. *Educ.:* Public School. Master Mariner. *War Work:* On Salvage Work, Admiralty Service, United Kingdom and Belgian Coasts. *Addresses:* Macuan, The Ards, Holyhead; Liverpool Salvage Association, The Exchange. (M9150)

NEWTON, George Burns, M.B.E.

NEWTON, Sir (George) Douglas Cochrane, K.B.E.; *s.* of the late George Onslow Newton, and of the late Lady Alice Newton, of Croxton Park, Cambs. (*see* BURKE'S *Landed Gentry*); *m.* Muriel, *d.* of the late Colonel Jemmett Duke, of Newpark, Co. Sligo. *Educ.:* Eton, and Trinity Coll., Cambridge. High Sheriff of Cambs. and Hunts, 1910; Chairman of the Cambridgeshire County Council, 1919-20; before that, Vice-Chairman of Cambridge County Council. *War Work:* Assistant Sec. at the Ministry of Reconstruction; also at the Ministry of Munitions. *Address:* Croxton Park, Cambridgeshire. *Clubs:* Bachelors'; Carlton; Boodle's. (K225)

NEWTON, Lieut. Giles Fendall, M.B.E., R.A.

NEWTON, Major Harry Kottingham, O.B.E.. M.A. (Oxon.), M.P., *b.* 2 April, 1875; *s.* of Sir Alfred James Newton, Bart., of 17, Cumberland Terrace, Regent's Park; *m.* Myrtle Irene, *d.* of W. W. Grantham, J.P., of Balneath Manor, Sussex; *Educ.:* Rugby, and New Coll., Oxford. M.P., Harwich Division of Essex since Jan. 1910 (Unionist); One of His Majesty's Lieutenants for the City of London. *War Work:* A.D., S. and T. Thames and Medway Defences, 1914-15; D.A. Director Supplies and Transport, Eastern Command, 1915-19; acting Hon. Sec. C.I.V. Regiment, South African War. *Address:* 4, Lower Sloane Street, S.W. 1. *Clubs:* Junior Carlton; Bath; Garrick. (O3160)

NEWTON, Lt.-Col. Henry, C.B.E., D.S.O., *b.* 24 Feb. 1880; *s.* of Thomas Newton, of The Hollies, Quarndon, nr. Derby; *m.* Beryl Bertha, *d.* of Earnest Augustus Barford, of Luton. *Educ.:* Derby School. Director of Newton Brothers (Derby), Ltd. *War Work:* Commanded a company 5th Notts and Derby Regt. (T.F.) 46th N. Mid. Division, 1914 up till May, 1915; was the founder of and Officer Commanding II Army R.E. Workshops, May, 1915, to Dec. 1917; Member of Trench Warfare Committee, Deputy Controller Trench Warfare Dept., and chief design officer Mechanical Traction Dept., Dec. 1917 until March, 1919; Inventor of the Nos. 107 and 110 "Newton" fuses (the first wire-cutting fuses ever used by British troops); Inventor of the "Newton" 6-inch Trench Mortar; Inventor of the "Newton" Trench Mortar bomb used for British Trench Mortars; Inventor of the "Newton" Pippin rifle grenade; Inventor of the "Ring charge" for the Stokes Mortar which increased the range from 300 yards to 800 yards and reduced "prematures;" Inventor of the "Newton Universal Military Tractor" among many other minor devices, whilst serving with Infantry, Royal Engineers, and Artillery services. *Address:* Mile Ash House, Darley, nr. Derby. *Clubs:* St. Stephen's; Royal Automobile. (C22149)

NEWTON, John Charles, M.B.E., J.P., *b.* 29 May, 1869; *s.* of Thomas Newton, of Liverpool; *m.* Emma Casson, *d.* of Thomas Rogers, of Liverpool. *Educ.:* Liverpool Institute. Unofficial Member of the Legislative Council of Sierra Leone; Justice of the Peace of the Colony of Sierra Leone. *War Work:* As Manager for Elder Dempster & Co., Ltd., and The Sierra Leone Coaling Company, had charge, under Admiralty direction, of all Coaling and Transport Operations on the Sierra Leone Station, which was the base for the 9th Cruiser Squadron. (M2228)

NEWTON, Capt. Robert Henry, C.B.E., *b.* 8 April, 1864; *s.* of Robert Newton, of Liscard, Cheshire; *m.* Catherine, *d.* of William Jones, of Holyhead. *Educ.:* The Northern Institute, Liverpool. *War Work:* Capt. of R.M.S. "Ulster," carrying H.M. mails, despatches, troops, and civilian passengers between Holyhead and Kingstown. *Address:* Homelea, Walthew Avenue, Holyhead. (C2836)

NEWTON, Major Stephen Guy, O B E., *b.* 18 March, 1889; *s.* of John Vernon Newton, of Chesterfield; *m.* Maud, *d.* of A. J. Forsdike, of Sheffield. *Educ.:* Worcester Coll. *War Work:* Gazetted 2nd Lieut. Sept. 1914; appointed to K.O. Yorks. Light Infantry; Capt. and Adjutant, May, 1915; Major, May, 1916; served with Mediterranean Expeditionary Force, 1915 to March. 1916; France, 1916 to First Battle of Somme; In command of Leeds Recruiting Area, 1917; appointed to Lord French's Irish Staff for special duties, 1918. *Address:* Knaresboro' Road, Millhouses, Sheffield. *Club:* Athenæum, Sheffield. (O7512)

NEWTON, Susan, M.B.E.; *d.* of James Lafferty, of Parsonstown, Ireland; *m.* George Daniel, *s.* of George Newton of Burton, Lincolnshire. *War Work:* Commandant of V.A.D. 176 East Lancs., raised Aug. 1914; Organiser and Commandant-in-Charge of Britannia and Hartley Coll. Hospitals, Manchester, from Dec. 1915 to April, 1919. *Address:* 36, Manley Road, Whalley Range Manchester. (M3865)

NEWTON, Major Thomas Cochrane, D.S.O., O.B.E., R.A., *b.* 1 Jan. 1885; *s.* of G. O. Newton, of Croxton Park, St. Neots, Hunts. *Educ.:* Wellington, and Royal Military Academy, Woolwich. *War Work:* Service in France and Belgium. *Club:* Army and Navy. (O7513)

NEWTON, Zoe Ellesmere Davidson, Mrs., M.B.E.

NEYLAN, Daniel, C.B.E., *b.* 1866; *s.* of the late James Neylan, of Dysart, Co. Clare. Sometime Financial Adviser to Salonica Expeditionary Force; Director of Finance, War Office. (C258)

NGATA, Aritia Kane, Mrs., M.B.E.

NIAS, Lieut. Herbert John, M.B.E.

NIBLETT, Capt. and Qr.-Mr. Harry Edwin Newton, O.B.E., D.C.M.

NIBLETT, Lieut.-Col. Herbert, C.B.E., D.S.O., R.A.S.C. Dep. Assist. Director at War Office with rank of Lieut.-Col.: Member of the Mechanical Transport Advisory Board, War Office; served in the Great War, 1914-19 (despatches). (C1714)

NICHOLAS, Alice Jane Winifred, M.B.E.

NICHOLAS, Lieut.-Col. Edward Hall, O.B.E., R.A.M.C.

NICHOLAS, Lieut. Ernest, O.B.E., R.N. (ret.).

NICHOLAS, Lieut.-Col. John, O.B.E., R.A.V.C.

NICHOLAS, T. Lieut. Samuel William, O.B.E., R.E.

NICHOLAS, Major Tressilian Charles, O.B.E., M.C., M.A., R.E., *b.* 17 Aug. 1888; *s.* of Charles Alfred Nicholas, of Canterbury (late of London Stock Exchange); *m.* Emily Lothian, *d.* of the late John Buchanan, of Wishaw. *Educ.:* Berkhamsted, and Trinity Coll., Cambridge. Fellow and Lecturer of Trinity Coll., Cambridge; Fellow of the Geological Society of London. *War Work:* Drawing, printing, and issue of Maps with the 5th Field Survey Batt., R.E., B.E.F., 1916-19; att. Gen. Staff for Map work, Dardanelles, 1915, and Egypt, 1916. *Address:* Trinity Coll., Cambridge. (O2661)

NICHOLL, Capt. Charles Carlyon, O.B.E., F.I.A., F.F.A., *b.* 10 May, 1879; *s.* of David Charles Nicholl, of Wisbech, Cambs. *Educ.:* Le Collège, Vevey; Sedberly; Cambridge. Actuary to Great Eastern Life Assurance Company, Singapore. *War Work:* Served in R.A.S.C. Investigation Dept.; France, Dec. 1915, to Feb. 1918; Italy, Feb. 1918, to April, 1919. *Address:* Great Eastern Life Assurance Co., Singapore. *Club:* Singapore. (O6404)

NICHOLL, David Arthur, O.B.E., M.A., LL.M., *b.* 1868; *s.* of Rev. David Nicholl, M.A., of Edwin Loach Rectory, Herefordshire; *m.* Hilda Maud, *d.* of J. Chalmers-Hunt, of Chadwell, Ware, Herts. *Educ.:* St. John's Coll., Cambridge. Solicitor; Town Clerk of Wandsworth; Election Registration Officer of Wandsworth, etc. *Address:* 36, St. John's Road, Putney Hill, S.W. *Clubs:* Oxford and Cambridge; Albemarle. (O42)

NICHOLL, Major Earle McKillop, O.B.E., R.A.V.C.

NICHOLL, Lieut. Edwin McKillop, M.B.E., I.A.

NICHOLL, Major Hazleton Robson, O.B.E., R.A.F.

NICHOLL, Allan HUME-, C.B.E., *b.* 12 March, 1866; *s.* of Hume Nicholl, of Usk. Monmouthshire; *m.* Annie Rosalie, *d.* of W. H. Thornton, of Minster. *Educ.:* Cordwallis; Maidenhead; King's Coll. Mayor of Lewisham, 1914-19; Alderman of Lewisham, 1911 to date; Div. Commander City of London Police Reserve, B Div.; Governor Lewisham Grammar School; Div. Inspector Lewisham Red Cross V.A.D.; Chairman, Profiteering Committee; Chairman Lewisham War Pensions; trustee Crystal Palace; Governor, St. Dunstan School; Chairman, Red Cross, Lewisham Div., War Loan, War Savings, Tribunal, Food Control. *Address:* Hillsboro', Sydenham. *Club:* Junior Carlton. (C2837)

NICHOLLS, Ada Casterton, Mrs., M.B.E.

NICHOLLS, Arthur Burleigh, M.B.E., Cavaliere della Corona d'Italia, *b.* 8 July, 1876; *s.* of William Henry, of Burleigh House, Sutton, Surrey; *m.* Nell Duncan, *d.* of Ronald D. Doulton, of Surbiton. *Educ.:* Merchant Taylors' School; France and Germany. Merchant, Milan, Italy. *War Work:* Head of Metal Department, Commission Internationale de Ravitaillement, India House, Kingsway. *Address:* Rovera, Mahiate pior. di Como, Italy. (M9152)

NICHOLLS, Lieut.-Comm. Arthur Sydney Moir, O.B.E., R.N.R.

NICHOLLS, Major Edward Alfred, O.B.E.

NICHOLLS, Evelyn, M.B.E.

NICHOLLS, Frederick Lucius, O.B.E., *b.* 29 Dec. 1859; *s.* of Lucius Nicholls, and Amy Nicholls, *nee* Pigott, of the family of Abington Pigott, of Cambridgeshire and grandson of Major John George Bell; *m.* Margaret Jesse Bance, *d.* of William Albert James, of the family of James, of Chilcompton, Somerset. *War Work:* Medical Officer to Auxiliary Hospital; Medical Attendance to the wives and families of soldiers and sailors, and assistance to Belgian Refugees. *Address:* Fulbourn, nr. Cambridge. (O11046)

NICHOLLS, George, O.B.E., J.P., *b.* 25 June, 1864; *Educ.:* Privately. Chief Organiser for Agricultural Organisation Society, on the Allotments and Small Holdings Section. *War Work:* Lecturing for Recruiting Campaign, for War Savings; Mayor of Peterborough, 1916-18; Chairman of a number of Committees for War purposes; Member of Agricultural Wages Board; Member of the recent Royal Commission on Agriculture; was M.P. for N. Northamptonshire, 1906-10. *Address:* Kimberley Lodge, 162, Lincoln Road, Peterborough. *Club:* National Liberal. (O11047)

NICHOLLS, George Thomas, M.B.E.

NICHOLLS, Major Gregory Basil Treglisson, O.B.E., R.A.O.C.

NICHOLLS, Helen, LADY, O.B.E., *v.* 13 Oct. 1879; *d.* of Chas. P. Sprent, late Surveyor-General of Tasmania; *m.* Sir Herbert Nicholls, Chief Justice of Tasmania, *s.* of Henry Richard Nicholls, of Ballarat, Victoria, and Hobart, Tasmania. *Educ.:* Friends' High School, Hobart. *War Work:* Vice-President, Tasmanian Red Cross Society during the war, and Member of executive committee and organiser and head of a

Red Cross Circle, formed to collect money and make garments for Australian Red Cross; Member of Australian Comforts Fund Committee. *Address:* Dionnan, Pillinger Street, Hobart, Tasmania. (O2166)

NICHOLLS, Capt. James Edward, O.B.E.

NICHOLLS, Capt. Reginald Latham, O.B.E., I.A.R.O.

NICHOLLS, Richard Howell, C.B.E.; Supt. of the Line, Great Western Railway. (C2838)

NICHOLLS, Thomas, M.B.E.

NICHOLLS, Capt. William, M.B.E.

NICHOLS, Charles Lee, C.B.E. Hon. Auditor of British Red Cross Society and Order of St. John of Jerusalem. (C1011)

NICHOLS, Dorothea Marian, M.B.E.

NICHOLS, Lieut. Frederick William, M.B.E.

NICHOLS, John Alexander, M.B.E., *b.* 23 Jan. 1880; *s.* of H. Norman Nichols, of Wantage; *m.* Agnes Mabel, *d.* of J. A. George, Auctioneer, of Newport, Mon. *Educ.:* King Alfred's Grammar School, Wantage. *War Work:* Founded and organised the Wantage and District Territorial Comforts Fund which sent out many comforts to the men; it also maintained Prisoners of War; Hon. Sec. of the Wantage and District War Savings Committee, the first committee in the county to form a War Savings Association in every village in its district; the savings per head of the population and per head per member were highest in the county; also Hon. Sec. of the Wantage War Savings Association. (M9156)

NICHOLS, Col. Joseph Cowie, C.B.E., *b.* 1859; *s.* of Charles Nichols, of Dunedin, New Zealand; *m.* 1900, Helen Hunter, *d.* of R. M. Ayre, of Benduck Station, Hay, New South Wales. *Educ.:* Boys' High School, Otago; Christ's Coll. Christchurch; Jesus Coll. Cambridge. Sheep farmer; Director of N. Otago Farmers Co-operative Association, Ltd.; Col. New Zealand Mounted Rifles, Comdg. Otago Dist.; J. P. for New Zealand; appointed an A.D.C. to Gov.-Gen. 1913. *Address:* Kuriheka Station, New Zealand. *Club:* Otago (Dunedin). (C707)

NICHOLS, Capt. Thomas George, M.B.E.

NICHOLSON, Capt. Bernard John, M.B.E., R.A.F.

NICHOLSON, Catherine, Mrs., O.B.E.

NICHOLSON, Christabel, M.B.E., W.L.

NICHOLSON, David Walter, O.B.E.

NICHOLSON, Evelyn Johanna, Mrs., M.B.E.; *d.* of Thomas H. Jackson, of The Manor House, Birkenhead; *m.* Charles M. Nicholson, *s.* of Hugh H. Nicholson, of Spital Hall, Spital. *War Work:* Quartermaster, Vernon Institute Red Cross Hospital, Sanghall, Chester. *Address:* Mollington, nr. Chester. (M801)

NICHOLSON, Florence Isabel, Mrs., M.B.E., *b.* 12 July, 1881; *d.* of Thomas Rothwell, of Rockfield, Kells; *m.* John Hampden, *s.* of Christopher Armytage, of Babrath Burry, Kells. *War Work:* Commandant of Kells Auxiliary Hospital, May, 1917, to Feb. 1919. *Address:* Babrath Burry, Kells, Co. Meath. *Club:* Automobile, Dublin. (M2231)

NICHOLSON, George Gibb, C.B.E. (C3201)

NICHOLSON, Major Henry Scoble, O.B.E.

NICHOLSON, Ivor Percy, C.B.E., *b.* 1891; *s.* of the late Rev. Thomas Nicholson, of London. *Educ.:* Mill Hill School. *War Work:* Ministry of Information, 1916–18, Pictorial Propaganda Dept., Officer-in-Charge of Periodicals; Department of Overseas Trade, 1918–19, Assistant Private Sec. to Sir Arthur Steel-Maitland, Bart., M.P., and in charge of Press Dept. under Rt. Hon. Sir Hamar Greenwood, K.C., M.P.; Victory Loan Campaign, 1919, Assistant Director to Mr. Sydney Walton, C.B.E. *Address:* 18, Queensthorpe Road, Sydenham, London, S.E. 26. *Club:* Whitefriars. (C2839)

NICHOLSON, Col. John Sanctuary, C.B., C.M.G., C.B.E., D.S.O., *b.* 1863; *s.* of William Nicholson, of Basing Park, Alton, Hants, and 2, South Audley Street, W. Entered Hussars, 1884; Capt. 1891; Major, 1899; Brevet Lieut.-Col. 1900; Lieut.-Col. (h.-p.) 1903; Brevet Col. 1905; Col. 1907; deputed to take over guns, arms, etc., of British S. Africa Co., subsequent to Dr. Jameson's raid into Transvaal, 1896; served during Matabele War, 1896–97 (despatches); S. Africa, 1900–2 (despatches, Brevet Lieut.-Col.); served during the Great War, 1914–17, on Staff (despatches, Order of Leopold of Belgium, Legion of Honour, Croix de Guerre); raised British S. Africa Co.'s Police, of which he was appointed Comdt. North of Zambesi, 1897; Comdt.-Gen. Rhodesia Protectorate, 1898; sometime Inspector-Gen. S. African Constabulary; Comdt. at Base, 1914–19, with rank of Brig.-Gen. 1917; Vice-Chairman of Hants Territorial Force Assoc.; unsuccessfully contested Stafford (C.), Dec. 1910. *Addresses:* Bordean House, Langrish, Petersfield; 2, South Audley Street, W. *Clubs:* Naval and Military; Cavalry. (C579)

NICHOLSON, Capt. John Steel, M.B.E.

NICHOLSON, Lieut.-Col. Malcolm, M.B.E., R.A.F., *b.* 30 Jan. 1888; *s.* of Sir Arthur Nicholson, of Highfield Hall, Leek, Staffs.; *m.* Kathleen Gertrude, *d.* of Cornelius Chambers, of Moseley, Birmingham. *Educ.:* Private School, and Trinity Hall, Cambridge. Barrister-at-Law. *War Work:* Joined Army as 2nd Lieut. R.F.A., Oct. 1914; transferred to R.F.C., March, 1916; served overseas, France; transferred to Royal Air Force Staff at the Horse Guards as Staff Officer, 1st Class, on the London Air Defences. *Address:* Calluna, Heathside Road, Woking, Surrey. *Club:* Royal Automobile. (M2232)

NICHOLSON, Capt. Norwood, M.B.E., *b.* 4 May, 1880; *s.* of Rev. Thomas Nicholson, of Birkdale; *m.* Eileen Hilda, *d.* of the late F. G. Myers, of Rotherham. *Educ.:* Rotherham Grammar School. Chartered Accountant. *War Work:*

Accounts, Home Base Supply Depot (No 3). *Address:* Edale, Moorgate, Rotherham. (M5502)

NICHOLSON, Reginald, M.B.E., M.P. for Doncaster; *s.* of William Norris Nicholson, of 43, Phillimore Gardens, London; *m.* Natalie, *d.* of Frederick S. Pearson, of New York. *Educ.:* Charterhouse. Assist. Traffic Manager, Bengal Nagpur Railway, 1894; Manager of "The Times," 1909–15. *War Work:* Central Prisoners of War Committee, Food Production Department. *Address:* 61, Park Mansions, Knightsbridge; Hurley, Gt. Marlow; Tretheake Mill, Tregoney, Cornwall. *Clubs:* Queens; Princes. (M2233)

NICHOLSON, Major Richard Granville, O.B.E.

NICHOLSON, Robert Beattie, O.B.E., *b.* 17 April, 1848; *s.* of James Nicholson, of Carlisle; *m.* Sarah Jane, *d.* of Joseph Pattinson, of Carlisle. *Educ.:* Privately. Town Clerk; Clerk to the Education Committee, Port Sanitary, and Burial Authorities. *War Work:* Hon. Sec. Conference of East Coast Watering Places, Local Canadian Fund Committee, Local National Relief Fund Committee; Special Constable; Sec. to Emergency Committee, Local Tribunal, Naval and Military War Pensions Committee, Fuel Control Committee; Joint Executive Officer Food Control Committee. *Address:* Kirklinton, Lowestoft. *Clubs:* Northern Counties; Lowestoft Golf. (O7708)

NICHOLSON, Major Roger Brighouse, O.B.E., I.M.S.

NICHOLSON, Samuel Thomas, M.B.E., *b.* 10 Dec. 1850; *s.* of William Nicholson, of Crowle, Lincs. Insurance Manager. *War Work:* Member of Home Office Shops Committee; Organised and became Hon. Sec. to the National Chamber of Trade in support of the Camps Library, and other Voluntary Assistance. *Address:* Chaseley, Holderness Road, Hull. *Club:* Literary; Hull Exchange. (M2234)

NICHOLSON, Major Stephen William, O.B.E., M.C., R.A.

NICHOLSON, Sybil Helen, Lady, O.B.E., *d.* of the late Sir Herbert Croft, 9th Baronet; *m.,* 1902, Sir John Rumney Nicholson, Knt. Bach., C.M.G., M.I.C.E., Chief Eng. for Docks N. E. Rly. *Address:* 20, Nevern Mansions, S.W. 5. (O1003)

NICHOLSON, Capt. Thomas, M.B.E.

NICHOLSON, Major Thomas Brinsley, O.B.E.

NICHOLSON, Capt. and Qr.-Mr. William Henry, O.B.E., M.B.E.

NICHOLSON, Capt. and Qr.-Mr. William James, O.B.E., Can. M.G.C.

NICOL, Charlotte, M.B.E.; *d.* of Alexander Nicol, of Belfast. *Educ.:* Belfast Mercantile Coll. *War Work:* Joined Ministry of Munitions in July, 1916, as Sec. to representative of the Ministry at Lancaster National Projectile Factory; transferred to Headquarters in Feb. 1917; returned to Lancaster Factory in July, 1917, as Chief Assistant to representative of the Ministry, and remained there until Oct. 1919. *Address:* 20, Hopefield Avenue, Belfast. *Club:* Anglo-French Society. (M9158)

NICOL, Lieut. George, O.B.E.

NICOL, Rev. George Erskine, O.B.E., *b.* 15 July, 1868; *s.* of George Nicol, of Clackmannan; *m.* Isabella Bowman Geddes, *d.* of George Geddes, of Dysart. *Educ.:* Edinburgh Univ.; United Presbyterian Theological Hall. Minister, at Muswell Hill, Presbyterian Church. *War Work:* Three years' service as Chaplain, mostly with Fourth Army on the Somme; attended sick and wounded in Casualty Clearing Stations; conducted Recreation Rooms and Canteens for the troops; provided equipment for football teams, and concert parties' and acted as billeting officer. *Address:* 31, Church Crescent, Muswell Hill, N. 10. (O5634)

NICOL, Capt. John, O.B.E., V.D.

NICOL, John Strathdee, M.B.E., *b.* 12 April, 1869; *s.* of M. Nicol, of Cumnock, Ayrshire; *m.* Jeannie Rae, *d.* of Jas Breckemidge, of Cumnock. *Educ.:* Cumnock Public School, and Ayr Academy. Explosives Factory Manager; Chairman, Pitsea Drainage Board; Member Southend L.A.C.; Ex-Chairman of Pitsea Parish Council. *War Work:* Manufacture of Propellants (Cordite). *Address:* 44, Kilworth Avenue, Southend-on-Sea. (M803)

NICOL, Quintin Anderson, M.B.E., *b.* 1876; *s.* of Edward Douglas Nicol, of Arbroath; *m.* Cisse, *d.* of Ralph Wilks Herbert, of Sunderland. *Educ.:* Arbroath and Sunderland. Assistant County Director V.A.D.; District Officer for Transport, St. John Ambulance Brigade; Hon. Serving Brother of the Order of St. John of Jerusalem in England; Corps Transport Officer, Royal Naval Medical Transport Corps. *War Work:* Organised and controlled all Ambulance and Hospital Transport work in Durham County for Military and Naval purposes during the period of the War, 1914–18. *Address:* The Hermitage, Roker, Sunderland. *Clubs:* Royal Automobile; Road. (M2235)

NICOL, Capt. Randall James, O.B.E., *b.* Aug. 1882; *s.* of William Edward Nicol, of Ballogie. *Educ.:* Eton and Christ Church, Oxford. *War Work:* Capt. (T. Major) Argyll and Sutherland Highlanders; Camp Commandant VII Corps H.Q. *Address:* Ballogie, Aboyne, N.B. *Club:* Junior Carlton. (O5635)

NICOL, Robert Gordon, O.B.E., J.P.

NICOL, Sir Thomas Drysdale, K.B.E., *b.* 16 Feb. 1878; *s.* of Thomas Nicol; *m.* Jean Henderson, *y.* *d.* of Robert Simpson. *Educ.:* High School, Glasgow, and Univ. Glasgow. *War Work:* Financial Adviser to the Ministry of Munitions; Controller of Aircraft Contracts; Chairman of Liquidation of

Aircraft and Mechanical Transport Contracts Committee; Special Commissioner for Disposal of Surplus Government Property in the Occupied Area of Germany. *Address:* 28, Park Lane, London, W. 1. *Club:* Royal Automobile.
(K402)

NICOL, Major Brev. Lieut.-Col. William Hutton, O.B.E., R.A.V.C.

NICOLL, Capt. Frederick Alan Benson, O.B.E.

NICOLL, Lieut.-Col. Peter Strachan, C.B.E., T.D., J.P., D.L., *b.* 21 Nov. 1864; *s.* of Robert Nicoll, of Dundee; *m.* Jane, *d.* of James Rutherford, of Dundee. *Educ.:* Dundee High School. Colliery and Shipping Agent; Lord Dean of Guild, City of Dundee. *War Work:* served with 1/5th Black Watch; raised and commanded 2/5th Black Watch; commanded 9th (Res.) Argyle and Sutherland Highlanders, and 2/7th Northumberland Fusiliers, E.E.F., and Sudan; Order of the Nile, 3rd Class; mentioned in despatches 3 times. *Addresses:* 65, Trades Lane, Dundee; Eaglemount, Carnoustie. (C1386)

NICOLL, Thomas Alexander, M.B.E.

NICOLL, William Harry, M.B.E.

NICOLLE, Capt. John MacArthur, O.B.E., R.A.F.

NICOLLS, Edward Hugh Dyneley, O.B.E.

NICOLLS, Heloise Scott, M.B.E., Q.M.A.A.C.

NICOLSON, Joseph, Henry, O.B.E.

NIELD, Faerie Edith Lilian, M.B.E., L.L.A.; *d.* of Edward Whalley, of Liverpool; *m.* Charles E. Nield. *War Work:* Hon. Treas. Soldiers' and Sailors' Families Assocn. (Southport Branch); Member of War Pensions Committee; Member of Birkdale Surgical Aid Association; Queen Mary's Needlework Guild. *Address:* 16, Oxford Road, Birkdale, Lancashire. *Club:* Formby Ladies' Golf. (M9160)

NIGHTINGALE, Capt. and Qr.-Mr. Thomas George Hull, M.B.E., R.A.

NIGHTINGALE, Thomas Herbert, M.B.E

NIGHTINGALE, William Joseph Edward, M.B.E., R.N.

NIGHTINGALE, William Maxwell, M.B.E.

NIMMO, Sir Adam, K.B.E., Vice-President, Mining Association of Great Britain; Chairman of the Scottish Coal Trade Conciliation Board; Managing Director, James Nimmo & Co., Ltd.; Director, Fife Coal Co., Ltd.; Scottish Boiler Insurance and Engine Inspection Co., Ltd.; Yorkshire Insurance Co., Ltd.; The Shotts Iron Co., Ltd. *Address:* 21, Bothwell Street, Glasgow. (K160)

NIND, Capt. Henry James, O.B.E., R.A.

NISBET, Henry Kingscote, O.B.E., *b.* 21 Sept. 1875; *s.* of Rev. Canon John Marjoribanks Nisbet, formerly Canon of Norwich, and Rector of St. Giles in the Fields. *Educ.:* Eton, and Balliol Coll., Oxford. General Inspector Local Government Board. *War Work:* Ordinary and War Work of the Local Government Board. *Address:* Purton, Wilts. *Clubs:* Athenæum; Union. (O3851)

NISBET, Robert, M.B.E.

NIVEN, Charles Bain, M.B.E.

NIVISON, William, M.B.E.

NIX, Major Charles George Ashburton, O.B.E.

NIXON, Herbert Thomlinson, M.B.E., M.D., Ch.B., F.R.C.S.E., *b.* 17 Dec. 1869; *s.* of John Nixon, of Aintree, Liverpool. *Educ.:* Royal Institution School, Liverpool Univ. Coll., and Royal Infirmary, Liverpool. *War Work:* Medical Officer, Venice Street Auxiliary Military Hospital, Liverpool. (M10279)

NIXON, Margaret Eva, M.B.E.

NIXON, Capt. Sydney, O.B.E., R.A.F.

NOAL, Frederick Worth, M.B.E.

NOAL, Comm. Richard John, O.B.E., R.N.R.

NOBLE, Alexander, M.B.E., R.N.

NOBLE, Major Bertram Wilfrid, O.B.E., H.A.C., *b.* 3 July, 1881; *s.* of Chas. Rossiter Noble, of Athol House, Sidcup, Kent. *Educ.:* Sidcup Coll., Kent. Chairman, B. W. Noble, Ltd., Incorporated Insurance Brokers and Managers, 78–79, King William Street, E.C. 4. *War Work:* served 1914–17, H.A.C. Infantry in France and Belgium and in England, 1917–19; attached XIII. Corps H.Q., as Chief Instructor XIII. Corps Infantry Schools. *Address:* Crossways, Bickley Park, Kent. *Clubs:* New City; Exchange, Liverpool. (O5637)

NOBLE, Major Crawford, M.B.E., *b.* 13 Oct. 1880; *s.* of Crawford Noble, of Aberdeen; *m.* Elizabeth Kathleen, *d.* of the late Richard Reade, of Ballycayne, Co. Wicklow. *Educ.:* Aberdeen Univ., and Ecole des Eaux et Forets, Nancy, France. Assist. Principal Forest Officer, Cyprus. *War Work:* 2/1 Suffolk Yeomanry, A.P.M., 27th Division, and afterwards in charge of all Military Police in the Caucasus. *Address:* Nicosia, Cyprus. (M4817)

NOBLE, Capt. George Anderson, M.B.E.

NOBLE, John, M.B.E., M.B., J.P.

NOBLE, Capt. Richard, O.B.E.

NOBLETT, Brevet Lieut.-Col. Louis Hemington, C.B.E., R. of O. Royal Irish Rifles, *b.* 15 Jan. 1869; *s.* of H. S. Noblett, of Cork; *m.* Edith Mary, *d.* of George Bennett, late of Little Rissington Manor, Glos. *Educ.:* Bath Coll. Joined Royal Irish Rifles, Aug. 1888; served in S.A. War as Company Commander in "Lumsden's Horse"; mentioned in despatches and awarded Brevet Majority. *War Work:* Employed as Embarkation Staff Officer from Aug. 1914, to May, 1919 at Liverpool and Folkestone; mentioned. *Address:* Ashton, Chaffcombe, Chard, Somerset. *Club:* Junior Army and Navy.
(C1715)

NOEL, Hon. Charles (Hubert Francis), O.B.E., Capt.,

1st Batt. Coldstream Guards, *b.* 22 Oct. 1885; 2nd *s.* of the 3rd Earl of Gainsborough (*see* BURKE'S *Peerage*); *m.* May, *d.* of Brig.-Gen. Douglas Dick, C.B. of Pithkerro. *Address:* Campden House, Gloucestershire. *Clubs:* Guards'; Naval and Military. (O5638)

NOEL, Charlotte, M.B.E.

NOEL, Major Frances Arthur Gerard, O.B.E.

NOEL, Capt Kenneth Hugh, O.B.E., I.A.

NOEL, Martial Louis Auguste, C.B.E. Registrar-Gen. of Mauritius. *War Work:* Acted as Food Controller and Controller of Exports. *Address:* Port Louis, Mauritius.
(C2021)

NOLAN, Elizabeth Florence Mary, M.B.E., *b.* 11 Aug. 1887; *d.* of John Nolan, of Sawbridgeworth, Herts., and Monaghan, Ireland. *Educ.:* Privately, and at Sacred Heart Convent, Deal. *War Work:* Sec. to Principal Clerk and Supervisor of Women's Staff, Public Trustee Office. *Address:* St. Kilda's, Worcester Park, Surrey. (M9164)

NOLAN, Robert Howard, C.B.E. Hon. Sec. New Zealand Soldiers' Club. (C372)

NOON, Major Charles, O.B.E., F.R.C.S., R.A.M.C.

NORBURY, Major Frank Hubert, O.B.E., R.A.S.C. (T.).

NORBURY, Capt. Lionel Edward Close, O.B.E., M.B., B.S.(Lond.), F.R.C.S.(Eng.), R.A.M.C., *b.* 9 Jan. 1882; *s.* of Sir H. F. Norbury, K.C.B., K.H.S., of St. Margaret's, Eltham, Kent; *m.* Grace, *d.* of A. W. Rogerson, of The Avenue, Lewes. *Educ.:* Merchant Taylors' School, and St. Thomas's Hospital. Surgeon Belgrave Hospital for Children; Assistant Surgeon, St. Mark's Hospital; Assistant Surgeon Mildmay Mission Hospital; Consulting Surgeon, Isleworth Infirmary; Demonstrator of Anatomy St. Thomas's Hospital. *War Work:* Surgeon British Red Cross Hospital, Netley, from Oct. 1914, to May, 1919, with temp. hon. rank of Capt., R.A.M.C. *Address:* 25, Harley Street, London, W. 1. (O3852), R.N.

NORCOCK, Comm. Charles Vernon Lowcay, O.B.E., R.N.

NORIE, Grace, Mrs., O.B.E.

NORIE, Capt. Thomas, M.B.E.

NORMAN, Major Edward Hubert, D.S.O., O.B.E., The Queen's Own (R.W.K.) Regt., *b.* 5 Nov. 1880; *s.* of Philip Norman, of 45, Evelyn, Gardens, London, S.W.; *m.* Isabel Helen, *d.* of J. W. Philip, of Johannesburg, South Africa. *Educ.:* Eton. *Club:* Army and Navy. (O5339)

NORMAN, Florence Priscilla, Hon. Lady, C.B.E.; *d.* of Charles Benjamin Bright M'Laren, 1st Baron Aberconway (*see* BURKE'S *Peerage*); *m.*, 1907, as his 2nd wife Rt. Hon. Sir Henry Norman, Knt. Bach., P.C., M.P. (L.) for Blackburn, 1910. *War Work:* Established and superintended the British Hospital, Wimereux, 1914–16; was mentioned in the Commander-in-Chief's despatches; has the 1914 Star, British War Medal and Victory Medal; was member of the General Committee, Chairman of Women's Work Sub-Committee; and is a trustee of Imperial War Museum. *Addresses:* The Corner House, Cowley Street, S.W. 1; Honeyhanger, Hindhead, Surrey. (C51)

NORMAN, Frank Arthur, O.B.E., Commander of the Order of Leopold II. of Belgium, *b.* 14 Dec. 1883; *s.* of Frank E. B. Norman, late of Kingsley Road, Kings Norton, Birmingham; *m.* Ethel Frances Lucy, *d.* of H. F. Austen Peck, of Earls Court Road, S.W. *Educ.:* King Charles I. Grammar School, Kidderminster. Acting Principal Clerk, Establishments Dept., Ministry of Labour. *War Work:* Belgian Refugee work in England and Holland with special reference to the question of employment; Chief Labour Officer of the Ministry of Munitions for the London and South Eastern Division, 1916; special work for Ministry of Labour and London War Pensions Committee in connection with the employment and training of disabled sailors and soldiers; received La Medaille du Roi Albert avec Rayure from the King of the Belgians. *Address:* 5, Manor Road, Merton Park, S.W. 19. *Club:* Emerson.
(O1710)

NORMAN, Herman Cameron, C.S.I., C.B.E., B.A., *b.* 1872; *s.* of the late Charles Loyd Norman, of Bromley Common, Kent. *Educ.:* Eton, and Trinity Coll. Cambridge. Appointed Attaché, 1894; 3rd Sec. in the Diplomatic Service, 1896; 2nd Sec. 1900; 1st Sec. 1907; Counsellor of Embassy, 1914 Min. Plen. 1919; Secretary British Delegation at Peace Conference at Paris, 1919. *Clubs:* Marlborough; Travellers'; St. James's; Beefsteak; Royal Automobile. (C52)

NORMAN, Jennie Gilkinson, Mrs., M.B.E.

NORMAN, Percy George, O.B.E.

NORMANBY, Gertrude Stansfeld, Marchioness of, O.B.E.; *d.* of Johnston J. Foster, of Moor Park, Ludlow, Shropshire; *m.* the Rev. Constantine Charles Henry Phipps, 3rd Marquess of Normanby (*see* BURKE'S *Peerage*). *War Work:* Jointly with her husband, equipped and maintained for 4½ years the hospital in Mulgrave Castle for wounded Soldiers, which was opened in Dec. 1914, first with an accommodation of 30 beds, and later on with 40 beds; the hospital was closed in May, 1919; was Commandant of the Mulgrave Detachment of V.A.D., North Riding, Yorkshire; President and Chairman of the Whitby Women's League of Help for the War; Voluntary Organiser of the Whitby Strand Sub-Depot of the Voluntary Workers' Association; Chairman of the Naval and Military War Pensions, Whitby Local Sub-Committee. *Addresses:* Mulgrave Castle, Whitby, Yorkshire; 90, Eaton Square, S.W.
(O11051)

NORMINGTON, Arthur Edward, M.B.E., M.B., Ch.B (Vict.), J.P., *b.* 11 Jan. 1872; *s.* of Joshua Normington, of

Keighley, Yorkshire; *m.* Edna Mabel, *d.* of Edmund Lea, M.R.C.S., L.R.C.P., of Manchester. *Educ.:* Grammar School, Keighley; Victoria Univ., Manchester Surgeon Nelson Brigade St. John Ambulance Assocn.; Representative Burnley Division British Medical Assocn.; Surgeon Reedyford Hospital, Nelson; Hon. Sec. Nelson Medical Society. *War Work:* Medical Officer in Charge of Reedyford Auxiliary Military Hospital, Nelson, from Oct. 1915, to May, 1919. *Address:* Remony House, Nelson, Lancashire. (M9167)

NORNABELL, Major Henry Marshall, D.S.O., O.B.E., R.F.A., *b.* 16 Oct. 1877; *s.* of the late M. Nornabell, of Nafferton and Bridlington; *m.* Catherine Van Dyke, *d.* of the late George Van Dyke, of New York and Detroit, U.S.A. *Educ.:* Wellington (Salop). *War Work:* Served in France, Aug. 1914, as Adjutant, 39th Brigade, R.F.A., 1st Division; Indian Corps, 18th Brigade, R.F.A. (3 times despatches). *Clubs:* Junior United Services; Junior Naval and Military. (O7522)

NORRIE, Beatrice, Mrs., C.B.E.; 2nd *d.* of the late Andrew Stephen, of 58, Queen's Gate Terrace; widow of Major G. M. Norrie. *War Work:* Lady President of the London Bridge Y.M.C.A., also of Ciro's Y.M.C.A., Orange Street, Leicester Square; organised Y.M.C.A. Free Buffet at Cannon Street Station, for Repatriated Prisoners of War, where 20,000 prisoners were received and welcomed; organiser of Y.M.C.A. canteens in Hyde Park during railway strike in Oct. 1919. *Address:* 62, Queen's Gate, S.W. *Club:* Ladies' Park. (C2840)

NORRIE, Capt. Forster Heddle Brown, O.B.E., M.B., R.A.M.C. (O1175a)

NORRIS, Francis Edward Boshear, C.B.E., F.G.S., F.R.G.S., *b.* 17 May, 1885; *s.* of Francis Boshear Norris; *m.* Nancy Rosalind Mary, *d.* of Frank W. Jenkins. *Educ.:* Rugby, and Corpus Christi Coll., Oxford. Superintendent, Seismographic Observatory, Guildford (now closed). *War Work:* County Director and Hon. County Sec. for Surrey, British Red Cross. *Address:* Ockwells, East Molesey, Surrey. (C2841)

NORRIS, Capt. Harold, M.B.E.

NORRIS, Henry, C.B.E., *b.* 1852; *s.* of Robert Norris. Dock and Warehouse Manager, Port of London Authority. (C580)

NORRIS, Capt. William Albert, M.B.E., I.A.R.O.

NORRISH, Edith Gladys Barrett, M.B.E.; *d.* of George Roper Norrish, of Upper Norwood. *Educ.:* Privately, and Crystal Palace Art School. *War Work:* Registrar, Restriction of Enemy Supplies Dept., Ministry of Blockade, Foreign Office. *Address:* Hawley House, Upper Norwood. (M9168)

NORTH, Lieut.-Col. Edward, O.B.E., R.E. (T.).

NORTH, Frank, M.B.E., *b.* 19 Oct. 1880; *s.* of Joseph North, of Bracebridge, Lincoln; *m.* Gertrude Annie, *d.* of Charles Bugg, of Lincoln. *Educ.:* Lincoln. Sec. Lincoln Unionist Association; Sec. Lincoln and Rutland Provincial Division, National Unionist Association. *War Work:* Hon. Sec. Lincs Regt. Tobacco Fund; Hon. Sec. Lincs. Regt. Plum Pudding Fund; Hon. Sec. Special Effort for Lincs. Regt. Prisoners of War Fund; assisted other War Charities, including Red Cross Society, altogether raising about £14,000; Hon. Sec. Lincoln Sailors' and Soldiers' Reception Committee, which entertained 4000 returned service men. *Address:* 11, Albert Crescent, Lincoln. *Club:* Constitutional, Lincoln. (M9169)

NORTH, Rev. Frank, C.B.E.

NORTH, Rev. Frank William, C.B.E., M.A., A.K.C., *b.* 20 June, 1872; *s.* of George William North, of Salisbury; *m.* Margaret Caird, *d.* of John Birse, of Blairgowrie. *Educ.:* King's Coll., London, and Durham Univ. British Chaplain, Moscow, Russia; Temp. Chaplain to H.M.'s Legation at Helsingfors. *War Work:* The care of British Officers and men who were prisoners of war in Moscow, together with civilian prisoners and destitute members of British Moscow Colony. *Address:* c/o The Russia Company, 17, St. Helen's Place, Bishopsgate, E.C. *Club:* Church Imperial. (C2842)

NORTH, Major John Tom, O.B.E., *b.* 17 Jan. 1884; *s.* of Gamble North, of Silverlands, Eridge, Sussex; *m.* Paula Elizabeth (Betty), *d.* of Julius William Petersen, of Chicago, U.S.A. *Educ.:* Rugby. *War Work:* Rejoined 2nd Dragoon Guards in 1914, as Capt.; invalided April, 1916; worked with the R.F.C. in London, as S.O.2, Headquarters 6th Brigade, R.F.C.; Promoted to Major. *Address:* Silverlands, Eridge, Sussex. *Club:* Cavalry. (O3381)

NORTH, Margaret Caird, Mrs., C.B.E., *b.* 30 Sept. 1879; *d.* of John Birse, of Petrograd, Russia; *m.* Frank William, *s.* of William North, of London. *Educ.:* Petrograd. *War Work:* Worked in connection with aid to Prisoners of War in Moscow. *Address:* 20, Pembridge Villas, London, W.11. (C3160)

NORTHAM, James, M.B.E.

NORTHAM, Walter Arthur, O.B.E., *b.* 26 May, 1881; *s.* of Walter Tooze Bryant Northam, of Bristol; *m.* Ethel Elizabeth, *d.* of James Brown, of Bristol. Printer, and an Ex-President of the Master Printers' Association of South-East London; now connected with the Cinematograph Trade and an ex-Member of the Council of the Kinematograph Manufacturers' Association. *War Work:* General Manager of the Cinematograph Department of the Ministry of Information. *Addresses:* 8, Waverley Road, Redland, Bristol; 199, Piccadilly, London, W.1. *Club:* The Road. (O3853)

NORTHBROOK, Florence Anita, Countess of, C.B.E.; *d.* of Eyre Coote, of West Park, Hants (*see* BURKE'S *Peerage*), and *w.* of Sir Robert John Abercromby, 7th Bt. (*see* BURKE'S *Peerage*); *m.* Francis George Baring, 2nd Earl of Northbrook (*see* BURKE'S *Peerage*). *War Work:* Organised Red Cross Hospital, Winchester, opened Aug. 1914; President and Chairman, Women's War Agricultural Committee, and of Women's Land Army; President Hants Federation of Women's Institutes; Member of County Nursing Association, and of County Hospital Committee; Member of Agricultural Education Committee, and Spareholt County Council Farm School; President Girls' Patriotic Club, and Chairman of Winchester War Clothing and Prisoners Fund Depot. *Address:* 36, Great Cumberland Place, W.1. (C2843)

NORTHCLIFFE, Mary Elizabeth, Viscountess, G.B.E., R.R.C., Lady of Grace of the Order of St. John of Jerusalem in England; *d.* of Robert Milner, of Kidlington, Oxford, and St. Vincent, West Indies; *m.* Alfred Charles William Harmsworth, 1st Viscount Northcliffe (*see* BURKE'S *Peerage*). *War Work:* Donor and Administrator of The Lady Northcliffe Hospital for Officers; Member of the Joint War Committee, Red Cross. *Addresses:* 1, Carlton Gardens, S.W.1; Buckthorn Hill, Crowborough, Sussex. (DG11)

NORTHCOTE, Alice, Lady, D.B.E., C.I., adopted daughter of the 1st Baron Mount Stephen, G.C.V.O.; *m.* 1873, 1st and last Baron Northcote, P.C., G.C.M.G., G.C.I.E., C.B., Governor-General of Australia, 1903–8 (d. 1911); Lady of Grace of St. John of Jerusalem. *Address:* 25, St. James's Place, S.W.1; Eastwell Park, Ashford, Kent. (D41)

NORTHCOTE, Evelyn Maude, The Hon. Mrs. George, O.B.E., *b.* 5 Feb. 1872; *d.* of 1st Baron Waleran, of Bradfield, Devon; *m.* George Russell, *s.* of the Rev. Henry Moubray Northcote, of Monk Okehampton, Devon. *War Work:* Commandant V.A.D. Motor School, 1916–17; Divisional Director, Women's Royal Naval Service, 1917–19. *Address:* 10, Collingham Road, London, S.W.5. (O4899)

NORTHCOTE, Lieut. Harry Peter, M.B.E., R.A.F.

NORTHCOTE, Jabez Charles, M.B.E.

NORTHCOTE, Major James Alfred, M.B.E.

NORTHCOTT, George Henry Ashplant, M.B.E., *b.* 3 Sept. 1876; *s.* of William Northcott, J.P., of Buckfastleigh, Devon. *War Work:* Divisional Sec. in charge of Y.M.C.A. War work throughout East Anglia. (M806)

NORTHCOTT, Capt. Harold James, O.B.E., R.A.S.C. (S.R.).

NORTHCROFT, George, O.B.E., D.D.S., L.D.S., *b.* 8 July, 1869. *Educ.:* The Leys. Hon. Dental Surgeon, London Hospital. *War Work:* Jaw Injuries Depts. of various hospitals. *Address:* 115, Harley Street, W.1. *Club:* Savile. (O11880)

NORTHEN, Capt. Frank, O.B.E., R.D.C.

NORTHERN, Lieut.-Col. Arthur, C.B.E., D.S.O., R.A.S.C., *b.* 1873 Served in the S. African War, 1899–1902 (Queen's medal with three clasps, King's medal with two clasps); Great War, 1914–17 (despatches, Brevet Lieut.-Col.). (C2147)

NORTHEY, Henry John, M.B.E., R.N.

NORTHOVER, Major Harry Robert, O.B.E., M.C.

NORTHUMBERLAND, Alan Ian Percy, 8th Duke of, C.B.E., M.V.O., Hon. Col., Tyne Electrical Engineers, *b.* 17 April, 1880; *e. surv. s.* of the 7th Duke and Lady Edith Campbell (d. 1913) (*see* BURKE'S *Peerage*), *d.* of the 8th Duke of Argyll (*see* BURKE'S *Peerage*); *m.* 1911, Lady Helen Gordon-Lennox (*q.v.*), *y.d.* of the 7th Duke of Richmond (*see* BURKE'S *Peerage*) Capt. Grenadier Guards (Spec. Res.); served South Africa, 1901–2 (Queen's Medal, 4 clasps); Soudan, 1908 (Egyptian Medal and clasp); Great War, 1914–16 (despatches). *Addresses:* 17, Princes Gate, S.W.7; Albury Park, Guildford; Alnwick Castle, Northumberland; Syon House, Brentford; Kielder Castle, North Tyne; Stanwick, Darlington. (C1716)

NORTHUMBERLAND, Helen Magdalen, Duchess of, C.B.E.; *y.d.* of the 7th Duke of Richmond (*see* BURKE'S *Peerage*); *m.* Alan Ian Percy (*q.v.*), 8th Duke of Northumberland, C.B.E., *e. surv. s.* of the 7th Duke and Lady Edith Campbell (d. 1913) (*see* BURKE'S *Peerage*), *d.* of the 8th Duke of Argyll (*see* BURKE'S *Peerage*). *Addresses:* 17, Princes Gate, S.W.7; Albury Park, Guildford; Alnwick Castle, Northumberland; Syon House, Brentford; Kielder Castle, North Tyne. (C2544)

NORTON, Eleanor Millicent, M.B.E., R.R.C. (2nd class), *b.* 4 Oct. 1893; *d.* of the Rev. F. C. Norton, of Ditchling. *Educ.:* Eastbourne, and Freiburg in Baden. *War Work:* Commandant V.A.D. Hospital at Ditchling for 4 years; the hospital was given by the Rev. F. C. Norton. *Address:* Ditchling Vicarage, Sussex. *Clubs:* New Century. (M3869)

NORTON, Ethel Ada, Mrs., O.B.E.

NORTON, Grace Madeleine, Mrs., O.B.E.

NORTON, Herbert John, O.B.E.

NORTON, Jessie Jane Jardine, Mrs., M.B.E.

NORTON, Robert Frederick, C.B.E., V.D., B.A., LL.D., K.C., *b.* 1854; *s.* of the late Frederick Norton, Principal Clerk in Chancery Taxing Office. *Educ.:* City of London School and London University. Barrister, Lincoln's Inn, 1879; sometime Hon. Legal Adviser to Foreign Trade Depart., Foreign Office. *Addresses:* 36, Inverness Terrace, W.; 11, Old Square, Lincoln's Inn, W.C. (C581)

NORTON, Robert Henry, O.B.E.

NORTON, Thomas, C.B.E., J.P., D.L., *b.* 28 Oct. 1845; *s.* of George Norton, of Bagden Hall; *m.* Jessie Jardine, M.B.E., *d.* of Donald Blacklock. *Educ.:* Privately. Deputy-Chairman, Quarter Sessions, and Chairman West Riding, Staincross Petty Sessions; Chairman (local) Income Tax Commissioners. *War Work:* Chairman East Central Appeal Tribunal, West Riding of Yorkshire; assisted with recruiting, and connected with prominent war charities. *Address* : Bagden Hall, near Huddersfield, Yorks. (C259)

NORWOOD, Major Charles John, O.B.E.

NOSEDA, Capt. Paul Rodolfe, M.B.E.

NOTLEY, Comm. Sir Franke Bartlett Stuart, K.B.E., R.D., R.N.R. (ret.), *b.* 7 Jan. 1865 ; *s.* of A. Franke Notley, of Hove ; *m.* Jane Elizabeth Lang, *d.* of the Rev. George Chambers, of West Putford, Devon. *Educ.* : Private Schools, Rochester, and Cork. Went to sea in sail, March, 1879 ; joined P. & O. S. N. Ltd., June, 1886 ; in command June, 1905 ; made Marine Superintendent, London, Dec. 1916 ; Younger Brother Trinity House, May, 1906 ; Associate Institute Naval Architects, March, 1918 ; R.N.R. Service, 1894–1919. *War Work* : In command R.M.S "Medina," India and Australia Mail Service ; came on shore, 28 Dec. 1916 ; superintending fitting of P. & O. ships for Transport work and Hospital work, etc. ; Medals—S. Africa Transport, 1901 ; R.D., 1910 ; Coronation Medal, 1911 ; Mercantile Marine War Medal, 1914–19 ; M. M. General Service, 1914–19. *Address* : Borealis, Essex Road, Gravesend. (K403)

NOTLEY, Leslie Richard, M.B.E.

NOTT, Harry Augustus, M.B.E.

NOTT, Marjorie, M.B.E., B.Sc., *b.* 1 June, 1894 ; *d.* of Francis Robert Nott, LL.B., J.P., of Highgate, N. *Educ.* : Channing House School, Highgate, and London School of Economics and Political Science. Assist. Sec. International Committee for Relief Credits. *War Work* : Statistical and Administrative work for Royal Commission on Wheat Supplies, Inter-Allied Scientific Food Commission, Inter-Allied Food Council, and Supreme Economic Council. *Address* : 42, South Grove, Highgate, N. 6. (M9171)

NOTTIDGE, Major George, O.B.E., R.E.

NOTTINGHAM, William, M.B.E. (10459)

NOVAR, Helen Hermione, Viscountess, G.B.E., J.P.; *d.* of Frederick Temple, 1st Marquess Dufferin and Ava ; *m.* Col. Right Hon. Sir Ronald Craufurd Munro-Ferguson, P.C., G.C.M.G., 1st Viscount Novar, Gov. Gen. of Commonwealth of Australia 1914–20. *Addresses* : Raith, Kirkcaldy ; Novar, Ross-shire. (DG21)

NOVIS, Lieut. William Herbert, M.B.E., *b.* 26 June, 1872 ; *s.* of Richard Novis, of St. Leonards-on-Sea ; *m.* Amy Edith, *d.* of Joseph Watford, of Lewes. Unionist Agent and Organising Sec. late Northern (or Newport) Division of Shropshire Unionist Association, now organising Sec. West Essex Central Unionist Association (Epping Division). *War Work* : Hon. Sec. to the Shropshire Voluntary Aid Detachment which controlled the County of Shropshire from Jan. 1915, to June, 1919 ; Joint Hon. Sec. of the Parliamentary Recruiting Committee under Lord Derby's Scheme for the Northern (or Newport) Division of Shropshire ; also Munition Area Recruiting Officer for the Shrewsbury Area from the commencement of the scheme. *Address* : West View, Broomhill Road, Woodford, Essex. (M2238)

NOURSE. William John Chichele, O.B.E., F.R.C.S (Edin.), *b.* 5 Dec. 1855 ; *s.* of the late William Edward Charles Nourse, F.R.C.S., of Brighton ; *m.* Emily Lucy, *d.* of the late Charles Snape, M.D., of Wiveliscombe. *Educ.* : Tonbridge ; Berkhamsted. Consulting Surgeon, Central London Throat, Nose, and Ear Hospital. *War Work* : Surgeon, Throat, Nose, and Ear Wards, Fulham Military Hospital. *Address* : 20, Weymouth Street, London, W. 1. (O11831)

NOWITSKY, Lieut. Vladimir, M.B.E.

NOYCE, Frank, C.B.E., I.C.S.

NOYES, Alfred, C.B.E., Litt.D., *b.* 16 Sept. 1880 ; *s.* of Alfred Noyes ; *m.* Garnett, *d.* of Col. B. G. Daniels, U.S. Army and Consular Service, of Washington. *Educ.* : Exeter Coll., Oxford. Author of " Drake : an English Epic," Collected Poems (three volumes) ; " The Forest of Wild Thyme," " The Elfin Artist " ; gave the Lowell Lectures in America, 1912 ; elected Visiting Professor of English Literature, Princeton Univ., 1914. *Address* : Cadogan Gardens, S.W. *Club* : Arts. (C582)

NOYES, Capt. Edwin Brownrigg, M.B.E.

NUGENT, Lieut.-Col. George Roubiliac Hodges, O.B.E., R.A., *p.s.c.,* *b.* 4 March, 1873 ; *s.* of Peter Nugent-Hodges Nugent ; *m.* Violet Stella, *d.* of Capt. Sheppard. *Educ.* : Malvern Coll. *War Work* : On the Staff in France ; very severely wounded serving with the artillery in the Somme fighting, 1916 ; on returning to duty was appointed A.A.G. Southern Command. *Clubs* : Junior Army and Navy. (O7523)

NUGENT, Major Hector Alexander, D.S.O., O.B.E. *b.* 1887 ; *s.* of William Burnett Nugent. Australian Army Ser. Corps ; served in the Great War, 1915–19 (despatches). (O6089)

NUGENT, Lieut.-Col. Walter Vyvian, C.B.E., D.S.O., R.A., *b.* 3 Dec. 1880 ; *s.* of Nicholas Nugent of Sowerby, Yorkshire ; *m.* Dorothy Florence, *d.* of J. Selwyn Ranson, J.P., of Sowerby, Yorkshire. *Educ.* : Pocklington School, York ; Royal Mil. Academy, Woolwich ; Staff Coll., Camberley. Employed as General Staff Officer, First Grade, to the Director of Military Operations, War Office, 1919–20. *War Work* : Staff Officer for Topographical duties at G.H.Q., Dardanelles Campaign, 1915 ; Chief of Field Intelligence at G.H.Q., Egypt and Palestine, under Sir E. Allenby, 1917–18 ; in charge of Eastern Operations Section, War Office, 1919. *Address* : Sowerby Bridge, Yorkshire. *Clubs* : Junior Naval and Military. (C1717)

NUGENT, Brevet Lieut.-Col. Frank Henry BURNELL-, D.S.O., O.B.E., M.A. (*Hon. Causa*), Rifle Brigade, *b.* 1880 ; *s.* of the late Albert Nugent, of Beacon Lodge, Christchurch, Hants ; *m.* Ellen Coke, *d.* of T. Coke Burnell, of St. Cross Grange, Winchester ; assumed additional surname of Burnell, in 1916. *Educ.* : Horris Hill ; Winchester Coll. ; Royal Military Coll., Camberley. Joined the Rifle Brigade in 1899 ; served with Mounted Infantry in S. Africa, 1901 (dangerously wounded, medal with 4 clasps). *War Work* : Wounded in 1914, in retreat from Mons ; Commanded 2nd Batt. Rifle Brigade, 1915–16, and 167th and 182nd Infantry Brigades, with temp. rank of Brig.-Gen. (despatches). *Address* : 6, Cadogan Court, London, S.W. 3. *Clubs* : Army and Navy. (O6961)

NUNBURNHOLME, Florence Jane Helen, Lady, O.B.E., *e.d.* of Col. Wm. Henry Charles Wellesley, 10th Foot, and widow of Charles Henry, 1st Baron Nunburnholme, J.P., D.L. *Addresses* : Warter Priory, Pocklington, York ; 9, Cadogan Place, S.W. (O612)

NUNN, Surg.-Lieut.-Comm. Gerald, O.B.E., R.N.

NUNNELEY, Major Frederick Pitcairn, O.B.E., M.A., M.D. (Oxon.), *b.* 24 Feb. 1877 ; *s.* of the Rev. Dr. F. B. Nunneley of Leicester House, Leamington ; *m.* Lyonella, *d.* of the Rev. R. W. L. Tollemache, of South Witham, Grantham (*see* BURKE'S *Peerage,* Dysart, E.). *Educ.* : Marlborough Coll. ; Brasenose Coll., Oxford ; St. George's Hospital. Hon. Physician, Llandrindod Wells Hospital. *War Work* : B.E.F. France, Nov. 1914, to April, 1915 ; O.C. Central Military Hospital for Officers, Brighton, Nov. 1915, to March, 1920. *Address* : Derrymore, Llandrindod Wells. *Club* : Oxford and Cambridge. (O11056)

NUSSEY, Lieut.-Col. Albert Henry Mortimer, C.B.E. D.S.O., Union Defence Force (Hon. Brig.-Gen. Imperial Army), *b.* 11 July, 1880 ; *s.* of the late Joab Nussey ; *m.* Bridget *d.* of P. Kelly, of Bloemfontein, O.F.S. *Educ.* : Privately. Orange Free State Civil Service, 1894 ; Field Cornet on General de Wet's Staff, 1899–1902 ; Staff Adjutant, Military Act No. 3, Union Defence. 1913 ; District Staff Officer, Dist. No. 10, 1914. *War Work* : Brigade Major 1st S.A. Mounted Brigade ; G.O.C. 1/2nd Division, East Africa ; Brig.-Gen. 1st S.A. Mounted Brigade, East Africa ; Dist. Staff Officer, No. 3 Military District, 1918 ; District Staff Officer, No. 7 Military District, 1920. *Addresses* : c/o Defence Headquarters, Potchefstroom ; c/o Union Defence Headquarters, Pretoria. *Clubs* : Potchefstroom ; S.A.P., Johannesburg. (C1434)

NUTSFORD, Major Henry Charles, M.B.E., N.Z.S.C.

NUTT, Francis George, O.B.E., B.A., *b.* 11 Sept. 1878 ; *s.* of George Nutt, of Rugby. *Educ.* : Winchester and Oxford. Civil Servant, 1st Division Clerk, Admiralty, 1901 ; Assistant Principal, Admiralty, 1906 ; Principal, Air Ministry, 1918. *Address* : 142, Adelaide Road, N.W. 3. *Club* : Royal Societies'. (O613)

NUTT, Mary Ann Margaret, O.B.E.

NUTT, Walter Frederick, O.B.E.

NUTTALL, Edmund, M.B.E., 14 Aug. 1868 ; *s.* of James Nuttall, of Haslingden, Lancashire. Conservative and Unionist Agent. *War Work* : Sec. Tonbridge Division Recruiting Committee, Tonbridge Division Lord Derby's Scheme, and Tunbridge Wells Advisory Committee ; Military and National Service Representative, Maidstone, Tunbridge Wells, and other tribunals. (M9172)

NUTTALL, Maria, Mrs., M.B.E.

NUTTALL, May, Mrs., O.B.E., *b.* 31 July, 1877 ; *d.* of William Hartley, J.P., V.D., of Heywood, Lancs. ; *m.* John Stafford, *s.* of John William Nuttall, of Bowdon, Cheshire. *Educ.* : Privately. *War Work* : Vice-President, Oldham Division, East Lancashire Branch, British Red Cross Society ; also Commandant of V.A.D. 70, East Lancashire. *Address* : Broomhurst, Werneth, Oldham, Lancs. (O3855)

NUTTALL, Thomas Downham, C.B.E., *b.* 1877 ; *s.* of James Nuttall, of Bury, Lancs. *Educ.* : Bury Grammar School. Engineer. Director of Bentley and Jackson, Ltd., Bury, Lancs. *War Work* : Chairman, Bury Munitions Board of Management. *Address* : Park View, Bury, Lancs. *Club* : Palatine, Bury. (C583)

NUTTALL, William, M.B.E., A.C.A., *b.* 4 Sept. 1889 ; *s.* of late John Nuttall, J.P., of Farnworth, Bolton. *Educ.* : Leys School, Cambridge. *War Work* : Hon. Accountant at Head quarters of East Lancashire Branch, British Red Cross Society, 1915–19. *Address* : Wellington House, Farnworth, Bolton. (M9173)

NUTTALL, Capt. William Ewart, M.B.E., R.A.F.

NUTTER, Alfred Barrett, O.B.E., M.A., *b.* 18 May, 1870 ; *s.* of John Frederick Nutter, of Caldwell Priory, Bedford. *Educ.* : Bedford School, and Brasenose Coll., Oxford. Barrister-at-Law, Lincoln's Inn. *War Work* : R.N.V.R. (Anti-Aircraft Division) A.B., Dec. 1915, to Feb. 1918 ; Superintending Clerk at Admiralty (Accountant-General's Dept.), June, 1918, to Sept. 1919. *Address* : 15, Old Square, Lincoln's Inn, W.C. ; 15 Barkston Gardens, South Kensington, S.W. 5. *Clubs* : New Univ. ; Leander. (O11057)

NYE, Wing-Comm. Alfred Thomas Larcom, O.B.E., R.A.F.

NYE, Capt. Arthur Field, O.B.E.. *b.* 16 Nov. 1867 ; *s.* of the late Charles Nye. *Educ.* : Christ's Hospital. Member of London Stock Exchange. *War Work* : Army Pay Department ; served in France and Murmansk, North Russia. *Address* : Stock Exchange, E.C. (O6817)

NYE, Violet Mary, M.B.E., Q.M.A.A.C.

OAKDEN, Ralph, O.B.E., J.P., I.C.S.; *s.* of Rev. Roger Oakden, late Rector of Bramshall, Uttoxeter, Staffs.; *m.* Rosa Mary, *d.* of the late P. A. Eagles, Meophams Bank, Hollington, St. Leonards-on-Sea. *Educ.*: Cranbrook, and Hertford Coll., Oxford. District Magistrate of Aligarh, and Commissioner of Lucknow. *War Work*: Recruiting for Indian Army, and stimulating war loans. *Address*: Windley, Beaconsfield, Bucks. *Club*: East India United Service.
(O4079)

OAKELEY, Capt. Henry Echley Herbert, M.B.E.

OAKES, James, C.B.E., J.P., *b.* 23 July, 1858; *s.* of Charles Henry Oakes, of Riddings, Alfreton. *Educ.*: Harrow and Trinity Coll., Oxford. Alderman, Derbyshire County Council. *War Work*: Chairman of County Appeal Tribunal. *Address*: Riddings House, Alfreton, Derbyshire. *Club*: United Univ.
(C2845)

OAKES, Col. Richard, C.B.E., R.E. Served in the Great War, 1914–19, in Mesopotamia (despatches).
(C1111)

OAKESHOTT, Capt. Claude Albert, M.B.E.

OAKESHOTT, Frances Maude, Mrs., M.B.E.; *d.* of G. T. Hellicar, of Stoke Newington; *m.* Joseph Francis Oakeshott. Hon. Sec. Harpenden District Nursing Association. *War Work*: Commandant, St. John Ambulance Brigade, V.A.D.; Commandant and Organiser, Rosemary V.A.D. Auxiliary Hospital, March, 1917, to March, 1919; special mention for hospital work (1919), to the Secretary of State for War for valuable services in connection with the establishment, organisation, and maintenance of hospitals. *Address*: Chelsfield, Harpenden.
(M9176)

OAKESHOTT, Reuben, M.B.E.

OAKLEY, Alice Annette, Mrs., M.B.E.

OAKLEY, Harry Ekermans, O.B.E., M.Inst.C.E., *b.* 1 Feb. 1866; *s.* of Harry Oakley, of London; *m.* Alice Isabel, *d.* of Dr. Samuel Woodman, Ramsgate. Civil Engineer; Deputy Director of Works, Air Ministry. *War Work*: Superintending Civil Engineer, Chatham Dockyard; Director of Marine Works, Air Ministry. *Address*: 10, Russell Road, Kensington, W. 14. *Clubs*: Royal Societies'; West Middlesex Golf.
(O1712)

OAKLEY, Lieut. Harry Lawrence, M.B.E.

OAKLEY, Lieut. John Gretton, O.B.E.

OAKLEY, Winifred, Mrs., M.B.E.

OAKSHETT, Owen James, M.B.E.

OAKSHOTT, Julia Maud, M.B.E.; *d.* of the late Thos. W. Oakshott, of Liverpool and Rock Ferry. *Educ.*: Rock Ferry; Paris; Dresden. President of the Birkenhead District Nursing Society. *War Work*: Commandant, V.A.D. Cheshire 126, B.R.C.S.; Officer-in-Charge, Auxiliary Hospital, Abbotsford, Rock Ferry. *Address*: Derby House, Rock Ferry, Cheshire.
(M9177)

OAKSHOTT, Ronald Stanley, O.B.E.

OATES, Lieut. Frank, M.B.E., R.E.

OATES, Major William, O.B.E., R.E. (S.R.).

OATES, Major William Henry, O.B.E., *b.* 29 July, 1884; *s.* of George Oates, of Dewsbury; *m.* Annie Elizabeth, *d.* of James Wood, of Stalybridge. *Educ.*: Leeds. Engineer. *War Work*: Officer-in-charge Group 4, County of London R.A.S.C. (M.T.). *Clubs*: Royal Automobile; B.A.R.C.
(O11059)

OBORN, Capt. and Qr.-Mr. Joseph, M.B.E., M.G.C.

OBRÉ, Henry, C.B.E., J.P., *b.* 17 April, 1855; *s.* of Henry Obré, of Queenstown, Co. Cork; *m.* Emma Eveline Wynn, *d.* of Lieut. A. R. Wilby, of Gloucestershire Regt. *Educ.*: Privately, and at Queen's Coll., Cork. Merchant; a Director of the Baltic Mercantile and Shipping Exchange. *War Work*: War Chairman of the Baltic and Corn Exchange Hospital at Calais, Paris Plage, and Boulogne, from 1914–19. *Address*: The Manor House, Knebworth, Herts. *Clubs*: Union; Royal Thames Yacht; City of London.
(C1012)

O'BRIAN, Herbert Edgar Whitehead, O.B.E., *b.* 14 April, 1873; *s.* of John Maurice O'Brian, of Poona, India; *m.* Camilla Mary, *d.* of Milton Hoogewerf, of Travancore, India. *Educ.*: Bishop's High School, Poona, India. Accountant, Military Accounts Department, India. *War Work*: Field Disbursing Officer (British Troops), Mesopotamian Expeditionary Force; Fixed Centre Disbursing Officer (Infantry); Deputy Field Controller of Military Accounts. *Address*: 138, Croxted Road, West Dulwich, London.
(O8285)

O'BRIEN, Lieut.-Col. Aubrey John, C.I.E., C.B.E., *b.* 5 Dec. 1870; *s.* of Edward O'Brien, of Leitrim; *m.* Winifred, *d.* of James D'Arcy, of Kew. *Educ.*: Dover Coll., and Sandhurst. Deputy Commander in the Punjab; Political Agent, Bahawalpur. *War Work*: Recruiting in Gujranwala, Punjab. *Address*: c/o Messrs. H. S. King & Co., 9, Pall Mall. *Club*: East India United Service.
(C1088)

O'BRIEN, Beatrice Jane, O.B.E.

O'BRIEN, Charles Henry William, M.B.E., *b.* 5 July, 1863; *s.* of Charles Bartholomew O'Brien, of Nassau, N.P. Bahamas; *m.* Amy, *d.* of William John Wingate, of Portsmouth. *Educ.*: The Grammar School, Nassau, N.P. Bahamas. Civil Service; Board of Education, 1883–1912; National Insurance Audit Department, 1912. *War Work*: Registrar and Clerk of Accounts, Prisoners' of War Information Bureau, Sept. 1914, to June, 1920. July 1920, Maritime Service of the Reparation Committee. *Address*: Hazel Bank, Priory Road, Hornsey, N. 8.
(M9178)

O'BRIEN, Brig.-Gen. Edmund Donough John, C.B., C.B.E., late 14th Hussars, *b.* 19 Aug. 1858 · *s.* of the late Col.

Sir J. T. N. O'Brien, K.C.M.G., Governor of Heligoland and Newfoundland; *m.* Florence Harriet, *d.* of Frederick Wheeler, of Worcester Park House, Worcester Park, Surrey. *Educ.*: Felsted, and Royal Military Coll. *War Work*: Supt. Remounts, Redhill, 1914–15; Commanded Yeomanry Brigade, 1915–17; Commanded Labour Group, France, 1917–19. *Address*: The Rectory, Buxted, Sussex. *Club*: United Service.
(C1718)

O'BRIEN, Eugene Herbert, M.B.E., R.N.

O'BRIEN, Florence Mary, Mrs. Vere, M.B.E., *d.* of W. D. Arnold, and adopted daughter of the Rt. Hon. W. E. Forster; *m.* Robert Vere, *s.* of the Hon. Robert O'Brien. *Educ.*: Privately. *War Work*: Helped as Hon. Sec. of Hostel for Belgian Refugees in Ennis, Co. Clare, for 3 years; also as head and Hon. Sec. Ennis War Hospital Supply Sub-Depot. *Address*: Ballyalla, Ennis, Co. Clare.
(M9180)

O'BRIEN, Herbert Charles, M.B.E., F.R.C.I., *b.* 30 June, 1869; *s.* of J. O'Brien; *m.* Helen Louise, *d.* of Arthur Foy. *War Work*: Finance Department, Government of India, 1914–15; Ministry of Munitions, London, Finance Department, 1916–17; Department of Factory Audit and Costs, as Director, 1917–19; Stores Auditor, 1920 to date. *Address*: Royal Colonial Institute, Northumberland Avenue, W.C. 2.
(M9179)

O'BRIEN, Capt. James Matthew, M.B.E., M.C.

O'BRIEN, Major John, O.B.E.

O'BRIEN, Major Joseph, O.B.E., I.A.R.O.

O'BRIEN, Lennox Brett, O.B.E.

O'BRIEN, Richard Alfred, C.B.E., M.D.

O'BRIEN, Rev. Thomas Francis, O.B.E., C.S.Sp., *b.* 23 Feb. 1871; *s.* of Thomas O'Brien, of Mullinahone, Co. Tipperary. *Educ.*: Rockwell Coll., Cashel; Univ. Coll., Blackrocks, Dublin; Paris. Member of the Foreign Missionary Order of the Holy Ghost (C.S.Sp.); worked in Lima (Peru), Trinidad (B.W.I.), Ireland, and England. *War Work*: Served as Capt. R.A.Ch.D. (R.C.), to 67th Brigade, 22nd Division, Salonica, E.F., from Dec. 1917, to March 1919; mentioned in despatches, June, 1919. *Address*: St. Mary's, Rathmines, Dublin.
(O6518)

O'BRIEN, William John, O.B.E.

O'BRYEN, Lieut.-Col. Charles William, O.B.E., I.A.

O'BYRNE, John, M.B.E.

O'CALLAGHAN, Rev. James, O.B.E.

O'CALLAGHAN, Major Richard Grainger Denis, M.B.E., J.P., *b.* 30 June, 1879; *s.* of the late Denis Richard, of Killenleagh, Kanturk, Co. Cork, and Brackenstown House, Swords, Co. Dublin; *m.* Jessie Gwendoline Mary, *d.* of the late George Frederick Insole, of The Court, Llandaff, S. Wales. *Educ.*: St. Columba's Coll., and Dublin Univ. *Addresses*: Brackenstown House, Swords, Co. Dublin; Stephen's Green, Dublin. *Clubs*: Roehampton; Royal Automobile; Junior Army and Navy.
(M3873)

O'CARROLL, Col. Joseph Francis, C.B.E., M.D.

O'CONNELL, Cormac John, M.B.E., *b.* 14 March, 1881. War Office, 1896–1912; National Health Insurance Commission (Ireland), 1912–19; Assistant Local Accountant, Ministry of Labour, 1919. *War Work*: Transport Dept. of the Admiralty, and Ministry of Shipping 1916–19.
(M9181)

O'CONNOR, Henry, M.B.E., *b.* 19 Jan. 1871; *s.* of Henry O'Connor, of Dublin. *Educ.*: St. Patrick's Knights Endowed School. Y.M.C.A. Divisional Sec., Mid-Ireland Representative Governor Morgan's School, Castleknock Dublin; Member General Synod, Church of Ireland; Member various Religious and Philanthropic Committees, Dublin. *War Work*: Organised and controlled 33 War Y.M.C.A. Centres for men of H.M. Forces in the Midlands of Ireland from 1914–19. *Addresses*: Bedite, Charleston Road, Rathmines, Dublin; 43, Upper Sackville Street, Dublin.
(M9182)

O'CONNOR, James Lynch, O.B.E.
(O4241)

O'CONNOR, Lieut.-Comm. Thomas Reginald Gill, O.B.E., R.N.

O'CONOR, Sir John, K.B.E., M.A., M.D., B.Ch., *b.* 21 Dec. 1863; *s.* of Abraham O'Conor, of Carrick-on-Shannon; *m.* Grace Beatrice Richmond, *d.* of James Oxley, of Frome. *Educ.*: Armagh, and Trinity Coll., Dublin. Senior Medical Officer, British Hospital, Buenos Aires. *War Work*: Chairman British Patriotic Administrative Committee, Argentine Republic; Chairman, Local Military Commission, 1918. *Addresses*: 1042, Avenida Mayo, Buenos Aires; Mayfair, Freshwater Bay, Isle of Wight. *Clubs*: Jockey, Buenos Aires; Royal Albert Yacht, Southsea; Devonshire.
(K443e)

O'CONOR, Maude, Mrs. Edmond, O.B.E.

O'DELL, Capt. Edward Seymour, M.B.E.

ODELL, Major Oswald Facer, O.B.E.

ODLUM, Major Benjamm Alexander, O.B.E., R.A.M.C., *b.* 9 Aug. 1882; *s.* of B. R. Odlum, of Ballamooney House, Geashill, King's Co.; *m.* Carlotta Carmen, *d.* of Andre Delpech de Cocujac, of Biarritz. *Educ.*: Arlington House, Portarlington, Queen's Co. *War Work*: A.D.M.S. German South-West African Campaign; O.C. 26th M.A.C., France; D.A.D.M.S., 39th Division; D.A.D.M.S. Mediterranean, L. of C.; O.C. 1st Field Ambulance, 1st Division; 4 mentions in despatches. *Address*: Ard House, Geashill, King's County.
(O2663)

O'DONEL, Capt. John, M.B.E., D.L.

O'DONEL, Major Manus Basil Hugh, O.B.E., R.E.

O'DONEL, Edith, Mrs., M.B.E.

O'DONNELL, James Rodney, O.B.E.

O'DONNELL, Lieut.-Col. and Qr.-Mr. John, O.B.E.

O'DONNELL, John David, M.B.E.

O'DONOGHUE, Mary, M.B.E.; *d.* of John O'Donoghue, of His Majesty's Customs and Excise. *Educ.*: Waverley Road Secondary School, Birmingham; St. Paul's High School, Edgbaston. Junior Administrative Assistant, Ministry of Shipping. *War Work*: In charge of a section of women staff, and responsible for the recruiting, drafting, and promotion of 50,000 Mercantile Marine Reserve ratings employed on commissioned ships during the war. *Address*: 17, Hornsey Lane Gardens, Highgate, N.   (M9184)

O'DONOGHUE, Lieut.-Col. Montague Ernest, C.B.E. Lieut.-Col. and Brevet Col. Indian Army; served in the Afghan War, 1880 (medal); Burma Expedition, 1887 (medal with two clasps); Great War, 1914–19 (despatches).   (C1720)

O'DONOVAN, William James, O.B.E., M.D., M.R.C.P., *b.* 20 Sept. 1886; *s.* of P. O'Donovan, of Ardfield, Co. Cork; *m.* Ethel Kate, *d.* of Edgar Charles Smith, of Woodford, Essex. Dermatologist and Syphilologist to London Hospital. *War Work*: Chief Medical Officer, Ministry of Munitions; Member T.N.T. Committee; Member Dentists' Tribunal. *Address*: 30, New Cavendish Street, W.   (O11060)

O'DWYER, Dame Una Eunice, Lady, D.B.E., Lady of Grace of St. John of Jerusalem, *b.* 1872; *d.* of the Rev. Antoine Bord, of Castres, France.; *m.* Sir Michael Francis, *s.* of John O'Dwyer, of Barronstoun, Tipperary. *Educ.*: Privately. *War Work*: Inaugurated Lady O'Dwyer Punjab Comfort Fund, 1914–19; Comforts for troops in Europe, British East Africa, Egypt, Persia, Mesopotamia, and Palestine; also St. John Ambulance Association for Punjab, providing all Indian and English hospitals with comforts, 1915–19. *Address*: 26, Brechin Place, S.W. 7.   (D39)

O'FARRELL, Rev. Francis, O.B.E., L.D., *b.* 14 May, 1869; *s.* of James O'Farrell, of Ordnance Survey, Southampton. *Educ.*: St. Edmund's Coll., Ware; English Coll., Rome; Gregorian Univ., Rome. Rector of St. Patrick's, Woolston, Hants., 1897–1902; Rector of St. Joseph's, Aldershot, 1902 to date; Member, Aldershot Education Committee, 1903 to date; Poor Law Guardian (Farnham Union), 1904 to date. *War Work*: R.C. Chaplain, Netley Hospital, during South African War, 1900–2; Senior Chaplain (R.C.) Aldershot Command, 1914–18; Assistant and Principal Chaplain (R.C.), Aldershot Command, 1918–19. *Address*: St. Joseph's, Aldershot.   (O8898)

OFFICER, Major Keith, O.B.E., M.C., A.I.F.

OFFORD, Alfred James, M.B.E., *b.* 4 Jan. 1878; *s.* of William Offord, of Hadleigh, Suffolk; *m.* Olive Ellen, *d.* of the late George Peacock. *Educ.*: St. Peter's School, Bury St. Edmunds, and National School, Lavenham. Essex County Constabulary as Superintendent and Chief Clerk. *War Work*: Various public duties arising out of Office, including close liaison with the military authorities for the defence of the Realm. *Address*: Springfield Court, Chelmsford.   (M2239)

OFFORD, Frederick George, M.B.E.

OGDEN, Alice, M.B.E.

OGDEN, Major Charles Percy, O.B.E., R.A.F.

OGG, Major Arthur Charles, D.S.O., O.B.E., I.A., *b.* 1878; Gen. Staff Officer at War Office; served during the Great War, 1914–16 (despatches).   (O2350)

OGIER, Capt. L. L'H., O.B.E.

OGILVIE, Capt. Alan Grant, O.B.E.,

OGILVIE, Alec, C.B.E., *b.* 1882; *s.* of the late Arthur Graeme Ogilvie, of 8, Grove End Road, St. John's Wood. *Educ.*: Rugby; Trinity Coll., Cambridge. Consulting Aeronautical Engineer; Member of Aeronautical Research Committee. *War Work*: 1915, in charge of R.N.A.S. Training School, Eastchurch; 1916, in charge of Repair Depot, R.N.A.S., Dunkirk, France; 1917–18, in charge New Design Branch, Technical Department, Aircraft Production. *Address*: 3, Hans Crescent, Sloane Street, S.W. 1. *Clubs*: Royal Aero; Royal Air Force; Bath; Royal Societies'.   (C871)

OGILVIE, Lieut.-Col. Alexander, M.A., T.D., R.E. (T.).

OGILVIE, Col. Sir Andrew Muter John, K.B.E., C.B., *s.* of Robert A. Ogilvie, C.B. Assist. Sec. of Post Office, 1907; Third Sec., 1911; Joint Second Sec., 1914–19. *War Work*: Director of Army Signals (Home Defence), 1913–19. *Addresses*: 7, Sheffield Terrace, W. 8; Golf Cottage, St. John's, Woking. *Clubs*: Union; Albemarle.   (K97)

OGILVIE, Col. Edward Collingwood, C.M.G., C.B.E., R.E., *b.* 1867. Served with the Miranzai Expedition, 1891 (medal with clasp); Chitral Relief Force, 1895 (medal with clasp); Mesopotamia, 1915–19 (despatches).   (C2040)

OGILVIE, Helen Leslie, M.B.E., *b.* 6 June, 1879; *d.* of Joseph Ogilvie, LL.D. *Educ.*: Aberdeen; Paris; London. *War Work*: British Red Cross Society (Scottish Branch), Aberdeen County Branch, Aug. 1914, to Nov. 1917; British Red Cross Society (Scottish Branch), N.E. District Depot, Supervisor of Garment Department from May, 1917, to May, 1919. *Address*: 4, Queen's Terrace, Aberdeen.   (M810)

OGILVY, Diana Elizabeth Maria, M.B.E.; *d.* of Rev. C. W. N. and Hon. Mrs. Ogilvy. *War Work*: Commandant of Battenhall Auxiliary Hospital, Worcester, 1915–19. *Addresses*: Bishops House, Worcester; Villa Victoria, 2, Via le Principe Umberto, Florence, Italy. *Club*: V.A.D.   (M2241)

OGILVY, Harry Lort Stephen Balfour, M.B.E.

OGILVY, Walter, M.B.E.

OGLE, Major Arthur Bertram, O.B.E., R.E.

OGLE, Pay-Sub.-Lieut. John, M.B.E., R.N.R.

O'GORMAN, Rev. John Joseph, O.B.E.

O'GORMAN, Hon. Lieut. Count Robert Jean Marie Gaspard, M.B.E,

O'GORMON, Flora, Mrs., O.B.E.   (O11788a)

O'GRADY, Capt. J. J., M.B.E.

O'GRADY, Capt. Robert Louis, O.B.E.

OGSTON, Walter Henry, O.B.E., *b.* 29 Nov. 1873; *s.* of Sir Alexander Ogston, K.C.V.O., of Aberdeen; *m.* Josephine Elizabeth, *d.* of W. H. Carter, of London. *Educ.*: Bedford School, and Aberdeen Univ. East India Merchant. *War Work*: Railway Transport, and Embarkation Staff Officer. Manager, Ministry of Shipping, Russian Shipping Section, Liverpool. *Addresses*: Mendip Cottage, Kingston Hill, Surrey; Balnastraid, Dinnet, Aberdeenshire.   (O11061)

O'HARA, Major Charles Kean, O.B.E., *b.* 10 Dec. 1860; *s.* of C. W. O'Hara, D.L., J.P., of Annaghmore and Coopershill. *Educ.*: Eton. His Majesty's Lieut. and. Custos Rotulorum, Co. Sligo. *War Work*: Appointed purchaser of remounts at outbreak of war; President, Local Recruiting Committee and County Controller of Recruiting; President, Soldiers' and Sailors' Help Society; Chairman, Local Distress Committee, and Local Sec. and Treas. Prince of Wales' Fund; Local Sec. and Treas. Prisoners of War Fund; Chairman, Sligo War Pensions Committee; Local Sec. and Treas. of Irish National War Memorial. *Address*: Annaghmore, Collooney, Co. Sligo, Ireland. *Clubs*: Kildare Street, Dublin; Royal St. George Yacht, Kingstown; Junior Constitutional; County and Constitutional, Sligo; and County, Roscommon.   (O11062)

O'HARA, Capt. and Qr.-Mr. Ernest, O.B.E., R.A.M.C.

O'HARA, Ethel, Mrs., M.B.E., *b.* 15 Jan. 1870; *d.* of Archibald Fisken, of Lal-Lal, Victoria, Australia; *m.* Richard Edward, *s.* of Charles William O'Hara, D.L., J.P., of Annaghmore, Co. Sligo. *Educ.*: Privately. *War Work*: Representative of Sligo Pension Committee for districts of Ballymote and Riverstown; organiser of two weekly sewing parties for Red Cross Work, and Voluntary Workers' Association in Sligo, and for local men serving at the Front; organiser of 5 concerts in aid of Star and Garter Hospital, London, French Red Cross, Belgian Red Cross, and the Irish County Hospital. *Address*: New Park, Ballymote, Co. Sligo.   (M9186)

O'HARA, John Wesley, O.B.E.

OKE, Sophy, Mrs., O.B.E.

OKEDEN, Violet PARRY-, O.B.E.; *d.* of Lieut.-Col. Parry-Okeden, of Turnworth, Dorset. Poultry Farming. *War Work*: Commandant, Norfolk V.A.D. 76; Matron, Auxiliary Hospital, Walsingham, Norfolk; Scoutmaster, Walsingham Troop of Boy Scouts; Vice-President, North Greenhoe Division, Norfolk, B.R.C.S. *Address*: The Poultry Farm, Pilford, Wimborne.   (O1714)

O'KEEFE, James George, C.B.E. Financial Representative, War Office; Ministry of Munitions in U.S.A.   (C1013)

O'KEEFFE, Capt. Francis Stephen LANIGAN-, M.B.E., *b.* 10 July, 1891; *s.* of the late S. M. Lanigan-O'Keeffe, of Glenagyle, Co. Tipperary, and Delville, Glasnevin, Co. Dublin; *m.* Sylvia Isabelle, *d.* of Col. A. J. Hogg, V.D., of Abbotsford, Eastbourne. *Educ.*: Mount St. Mary's Coll., Chesterfield, and Sandhurst. *War Work*: Served in Gallipoli, April, 1915, and France, Feb. 1917; specially employed at War Office, Oct. 1918, to Dec. 1919. *Club*: Junior Naval and Military.   (M5408)

O'KELLY, Capt. Edward Joseph, M.B.E.

O'KELLY, Major John William, O.B.E., R.A.V.C., *b.* 1882; *s.* of W. H. O'Kelly, of Monkstown Castle, Co. Dublin; *m.* Mary, *d.* of Laurence Rorke, J.P., of Floraville, Clondalkin, Co. Dublin. *Educ.*: St. Vincent's Coll., Castleknock, and St. Joseph's Coll., Dumfries. First Commissioner, Royal Army Veterinary Corps, 1907; served in England, Egypt, and India; appointed to the Indian Remount Department in 1911, and served with Remount Dept. till end of 1916. *War Work*: On leave from India, beginning of war, recalled to India and served with Remount Department till end of 1916; returned to England beginning of 1917, and appointed A.D.V.S., 11th Division, served in France and Belgium with 11th Division till its break up in 1919; appointed A.D.V.S., Northern Division, and subsequently A.D.V.S., Rhine Garrison; served in Germany till Feb. 1920 as A.D.V.S., Rhine Garrison. *Address*: Kildangan, Kinnegad, Westmeath. *Club*: Junior Army and Navy.   (O5646)

OLDEN, Capt. and Qr.-Mr. George William, O.B.E.

OLDERSHAW, Albert William, M.B.E., B.Sc. (Edin.), N.D.A., *b.* 2 March, 1883; *s.* of John Oldershaw, of Costock, Nottinghamshire; *m.* Elizabeth, *d.* of William Smeeton, of Bunny, Nottingham. *Educ.*: Loughborough Grammar School; Univ. Coll., Nottingham; Midland Agricul. Coll., Edinburgh Univ. Agricultural Organiser for East Suffolk. *War Work*: Assisted in the Food Production Campaign, especially with regard to organising the sale of Artificial Manure to Farmers, in order to increase crop yields; acted as Hon. Sec. to East Suffolk War Agricultural Committee. *Address*: 24, Cardigan Street, Ipswich.   (M39)

OLDERSHAW, Lieut.-Col. William James Norman, C.B.E., V.D., *b.* 1856; *s.* of the late William Oldershaw. Australian Forces; Rifle Shooting Expert; Sugar Controller of Australia. *War Work*: Rendered services to Australian Commonwealth Shipping Board. *Address*: Melbourne, Australia.   (C367)

OLDFIELD, Lieut.-Col. Christopher George, C.M.G., C.B.E., R.A.O.C., *b.* 1863.

OLDFIELD, Geraldine, Mrs., M.B.E.

OLDFIELD, T. Major John William, O.B.E., M.C.

OLDFIELD, Norman, M.B.E.

OLDHAM, Alfred, O.B.E.

OLDHAM, Rev. Gordon Miles Staveley, O.B.E., M.A., *b.* 28 Jan. 1885 ; *s.* of Thomas Staveley Oldham, of London ; *m.* Hilda Georgina Susan, *d.* of Major the Hon. W. H. Curzon, of London. *Educ.* : Westminster, and Christ Church, Oxford. Hon. Claphain to the Forces. Vicar of St. James', Clapton, London. *War Work* : C. F. attached 1st Batt. Welsh Guards. B.E.F. *Address* : St. James' Vicarage, 58, Kenninghall Road, Clapton, London, E. 5. (O5647)

OLDHAM, Hugh Falconer, M.B.E., M.D., B.Ch., J.P.

OLDHAM, Reta, O.B.E.

OLDHAM, Comm. Ronald Wolseley, O.B.E.

OLDMEADOW, George Edward, M.B.E.

O'LEARY, Lieut. Michael George, M.B.E.

O'LEARY, Brig.-Gen. T. Evelyn, C.B., C.M.G., C.B.E., *b.* 1862 ; *s.* of the late Surg.-Gen. Thomas Conor O'Leary ; *m.* 1894, a *d.* of Maj.-Gen. Francis William Ward, C.B. Served with Miranzai Expedition, 1891 (Medal with clasp) ; Isazai Expedition, 1892 ; Chitral Relief Force, 1895 (medal with clasp) ; S. Africa, 1899–1902 (Queen's medal with six clasps, King's medal with two clasps). Dardanelles, 1915 ; Mesopotamia, 1916 (despatches twice) ; Dep. Director at War Office, 1917–19. *Address* : West End, Haslemere. *Club* : Army & Navy. (C1721)

OLIPHANT, Capt. Andrew John, M.B.E.

OLIPHANT, John Ninian, M.B.E.

OLIPHANT, William Elwin, O.B.E., M.B.E., *b.* 31 March. 1860 ; *s.* of John Elwin Oliphant, of Maxton, Kent ; *m.* Célestinn Cornélie, *d.* of Ferdinand Schoch-de-Ravalet, of Apeldorn, Holland. *Educ.* : Dover Private School ; Seminary St. Omer ; London Univ. Divinity Coll., and Friedrich Wilhelm Univ., Berlin. Commissioner of the Salvation Army. Curate, North London. Curacy, St. Paul's, Onslow Square, S. Kensington, London, 1882 ; joined Salvation Army, 1884 ; Private Sec. to the present General Booth, 1886 ; Commissioner for work in Holland, Sweden, Germany, Switzerland, and United Territory, respectively. *War Work* : Opened , Home and Tea-rooms at Chateau d'Oex and Leysin and Switzerland, for English prisoners of war ; established research bureau for lost and missing British officers and soldiers at Geneva (Head Office, Berne) ; met trains conveying prisoners of war to various destinations, and of various nationalities, with an organising committee to distribute necessities, comforts, and literature ; opened three homes for Italian soldiers in Naples and Florence ; sheltered many hundreds of Serbians for over a year in Rome ; distributed over one million of liras among Italian refugees after Caparetto from Milan to Palermo ; opened Foyer for French Soldiers at Milan, and a large Foyer at Arquarta, the British Base in Italy, where many thousands of British Soldiers received food and help of all kind. *Address* : Chalêt d'Erlach, Spièz, Switzerland. (O11064)

OLIVE, Annie Gordon, Mrs., M.B.E., *b.* 26 Aug. 1860 ; *d.* of Rev. Wm. Guard Price, of Newtownards, Co. Down, Ireland ; *m.* Eustace John Parke, *s.* of Eustace Henry Olive, of Northampton. *Educ.* : Privately. *War Work* : Four years commandant of Holmdene Auxiliary Hospital, Leamington, Warwickshire. *Address* : Avon Royd, Leamington. (M2244)

OLIVE, Eustace John Parke, O.B.E., M.D. (Cantab), F.R.C.S. (Eng.), *b.* 1862. *Educ.* : St. John's College, Cambridge and St. Bartholomew's Hospital, London. Surgeon. *War Work* : Medical Officer, Holmdene Auxiliary Hospital, Leamington. *Address* : Avon Royd, Leamington. (O11065)

OLIVE, James William, C.B.E., Chevalier Legion d'Honneur, *b.* Nov. 1857 ; *s.* of the late James Olive, of Uxbridge, Middlesex. *Educ.* : Privately. Assistant Commissioner, Metropolitan Police, New Scotland Yard. *War Work* : General administration in connection with duties devolving upon London Metropolitan Police under laws and regulations passed during the period of the war. *Address* : 9, Brooksville Avenue. *Clubs* : National. (C284)

OLIVE, May Winifred, M.B.E. ; *d.* of William Hayes, of Tyndales Park, Clifton, Bristol. *Educ.* : Privately. *War Work* : A voluntary worker on the Belgian Relief Committee, 1914–15 ; subsequently joining the British Inquiry Bureau, a voluntary organisation for the Assistance and Entertainment of wounded soldiers ; working at the 2nd S. Gen. and Beaufort War Hospitals until the closing of the Hospitals in 1919. (M9188)

OLIVER, Arthur Maule, O.B.E., *b.* 25 Aug. 1871 ; *s.* of William Atkinson Oliver, Solicitor, of Sunderland ; *m.* Emily Margaret, *d.* of Samuel Horsfield, J.P., of Hyde, Cheshire. *Educ.* : Eastbourne Coll. Solicitor ; Town Clerk and Clerk of the Peace of Newcastle-upon-Tyne. *War Work* : Executive Officer, Newcastle Local Food Control Committee ; Clerk to Local Tribunal ; Sec. to Local War Pensions Committee, and to Northern Counties Joint (Disablement) Committee. *Address* : West House, Cleadon, Co. Durham. *Club* : Union. Newcastle. (O3858)

OLIVER, Bertie Cecil, M.B.E.

OLIVER, Dame Beryl Carnegy, Lady, D.B.E., R.R.C., *b.* 20 Aug. 1882 ; *d.* of Mrs. Carnegy, of Lour, Forfar ; *m.* Vice-Admiral Sir Henry Oliver, K.C.B., K.C.M.G., M.V.O., LL.D., *s.* of Robert Oliver, of Lockside, Roxburghshire. Lady of Justice, Order of St. John of Jerusalem ; holds Coronation Medal (King George), and Order of Mercy. *Address* : 20, South Eaton Place, London, S.W. 1. (D51)

OLIVER, Charles Augustus, C.B.E., Order of the Rising Sun (3rd class), *b.* 16 Oct. 1861 ; *s.* of Admiral R. A. Oliver ; *m.* Hilda. *d.* of Lieut.-Col. Woollcombe-Adams, of Anstey Hall, Warwickshire (*see* BURKE'S *Landed Gentry*). *Educ.* : Winchester

and abroad. Entered Admiralty, 1885 ; appointed Assist. Director of Navy Contracts, 1904. *War Work* : Acted as Director of Contracts, 1915–17 ; Member of the Disposal and Salvage Boards. *Address* : 1, Addison Gardens, Kensington. *Clubs* : Union ; Albemarle. (C1015)

OLIVER, Charles Thomas, M.B.E.

OLIVER, Charlotte, M.B.E., *b.* 13 Sept. 1862 ; *d.* of Charles Thomas Gostenhofer, J.P., of Birkenhead, Cheshire. *War Work* : Hon. Sec. Soldiers' and Sailors' Families Association, Birkenhead Division ; since 1885, Soldiers' and Sailors' Help Society, Birkenhead ; Member of Local Committee, Statutory Committee and War Pensions. *Address* : Sandycroft, West Kirby, Cheshire. (M3875)

OLIVER, Wing Commander Douglas Austin, D.S.O., O.B.E., R.A.F., *b.* 9 Dec. 1887 ; *s.* of Rev. Austin Oliver, Latton, Essex ; *m.* Sheila Laura. *d.* of Capt. Grant-Suttie, R.N., of Preston Grange, North Berwick. *Educ.* : The Grange, Folkestone, and H.M.S. "Britannia." *War Work* : As Flight-Comdr., R.N.A.S., Cuxhaven Raid, Dec. 25, 1914 ; mentioned in despatches ; promoted to Squadron-Comdr., Jan. 1915 ; awarded D.S.O. for attack on German Battle Cruisers on 25 April, 1916 ; promoted to Wing-Comdr. July, 1917 ; mentioned in despatches, Jan. 1919, for services in Adriatic ; awarded Italian War Cross. *Address* : Latton Vicarage, Harlow, Essex. *Club* : Junior Naval and Military. (O8160)

OLIVER, Capt. Edward Victor, O.B.E., R.A.O.C.

OLIVER, John David, M.B.E.

OLIVER, John Penry, M.B.E., *b.* 24 Jan. 1861 ; *s.* of the Rev. Henry Oliver, B.A., of Llanfynydd, Carmarthenshire ; *m.* Laura Beatrice, *d.* of Edwin Brown, of Leamington. *Educ.* : Congregational School, Caterham Valley. Barrister-at-law ; Temp. Chief Examiner at Passport Office. *War Work* : Chief Inspector, X Div., Metropolitan Special Constabulary ; Chairman of Harrow-on-the-Hill Military Tribunal Advisory Committee. *Addresses* : 6, Pump Court, Temple, E.C. ; Bellevue, Sudbury Hill, Harrow-on-the-Hill. (M9190)

OLIVER, John William Lambton, C.B.E.,

OLIVER, Matthew William Baillie, O.B.E., M.B., B.C., F.R.C.S. ; *s.* of Robt. B. Oliver, of Strathwell, Whitwell, Isle of Wight. *Educ.* : Cheltenham Coll. ; Trinity Coll., Cambridge. Assistant Surgeon to the Central London Ophthalmic Hospital ; Ophthalmic Surgeon to the Queen's Hospital for facial injuries, Sidcup. *War Work* : Service in France and Belgium with the British Expeditionary Force from the commencement of the war in 1914 until May, 1919 ; service with several units, and from 1917–1918 as Surgical Specialist to the 15th Casualty Clearing Station. *Address* : 128, Harley Street. *Clubs* : New Univ. ; Royal Automobile. (O5649)

OLIVER, Percy Lane, O.B.E., *b.* 11 April, 1878 ; *s.* of Edward Lane Oliver, of Peckham ; *m.* Ethel Grace, *d.* of Joseph Hebden, of Peckham. *Educ.* : Peckham Wesleyan School. Municipal Clerk, Camberwell Borough Council. *War Work* : Hon. Sec., Camberwell Division, Brit. Red Cross Society, throughout War ; Assistant Transport Officer, War Refugees Committee, 1914–15 ; Leading Aircraftsman, Royal Naval Air Service, 1916–18 ; Sergeant, Royal Air Force, 1918–19. *Address* : 44, Talfourd Road, S.E. 15. (O1715)

OLIVER, Philip Milner, C.B.E., B.A., *b.* 30 Aug. 1884 ; *s.* of John R. Oliver. *Educ.* : Bowdon Coll. ; Manchester Grammar School ; Corpus Christi, Oxford. *War Work* : Hon. Sec. British Red Cross Society, East Lancashire Branch, *Addresses* : 41, John Dalton Street, Manchester ; High Croft, Bowdon. *Club* : Reform, Manchester. (C2849)

OLIVER, Capt. and Qr.-Mr. Richard, M.B.E., D.C.M.

OLIVER, Rev. Richard John Deane, C.B.E., M.A., *b.* 22 June, 1863 ; *s.* of Richard Charles Deane Oliver, of Rockmills House, Co. Cork. *Educ.* : Coll. of St. Columba, Co. Dublin, and Trinity Coll., Dublin. Private Sec. to Lord Plunket, Archbishop of Dublin, 1886 ; Domestic Chaplain, 1888 ; Chaplain to the Forces, 1892 ; Assistant Chaplain-General, Eastern Command, 1915 ; retired, 1920. *War Work* : Co-Founder with C. B. Combes, of Sandgate, Kent, of the Church of England Clubs for soldiers in the Shorncliffe Training Area (22 clubs in the Federation). *Address* : 4, Wellington Terrace, Sandgate, Kent. *Club* : Church Imperial. (C1722)

OLIVER, Col. William James, C.B.E., R.A.O.C.

OLIVIER, Edith Maud, M.B.E. ; *d.* of Rev. Canon D. Olivier, of Wilton, Wilts. *Educ.* : St. Hugh's Coll., Oxford. *War Work* : Hon. Sec. and Organising Sec. to Wilts Women's War Agricultural Committee. *Address* : Fitz House, Teffont Magna, Salisbury. *Club* : Ladies' Athenæum. (M9191)

OLLEY, Capt. Arthur Edward, O.B.E., R.A., *b.* 1884 ; *s.* of Henry R. Olley, of Llangollen, North Wales ; *m.* May, *d.* of James Evans, of Manchester. *Educ.* : Privately ; Ulver's Mount School, Scarborough ; County School, Llangollen. Journalist. *War Work* : After one year in 12th Heavy Baty., R.G.A., 60-pounders, was made Artillery Liaison Officer with R.A.F. squadrons working from time to time with 3rd Corps ; twice mentioned in despatches. *Address* : 6, Kenyon Mansions, West Kensington, W. 14. (O5656)

OLLIVANT, Major Rupert Charles, O.B.E., R.F.A. (T.).

O'MAHONEY, Major Charles Carleton SAUNDERS-, O.B.E., R.A.S.C.

O'MAHONY, Pierce de Lacy (THE O'MAHONY), C.B.E., D.L. Co. Wicklow, *b.* 9 June, 1850 ; *s.* of Pierce Kenefick Mahony, of Kilmorna, Co. Kerry (*see* BURKE'S *Landed Gentry*) ; *m.* Helen Louise, *d.* of Maurice Collis, of Coohane, Co. Tipperary. *Educ.* : Rugby ; Magdalen Coll., Oxford ; Agricultural Coll., Cirencester

(Haygarth Gold Medal). Hereditary Chieftain of the O'Mahony Sept, M.P., North Meath, 1886 to 1892. *War Work :* Recruiting in Ireland, 1915. *Addresses :* Grange Con, Co. Wicklow ; Mucklagh, Aughrim, Co. Wicklow.   (C2850)

O'MALLEY, Capt. David Vincent, O.B.E., M.B., R.A.M.C.

OMAN, Sir Charles William Chadwick, K.B.E., M.P., F.B.A., Hon. LL.D. (Edin.), *b.* 12 Jan. 1860 ; *s.* of Charles Philip Austin Oman, of Hatauri, Bahar, India ; *m.* Mary Mabel, second *d.* of General Robert Maclagan, R.E. 1 son 2 daughters. *Educ. :* Winchester Coll., and New Coll., Oxford. Fellow of All Souls Coll., Oxford, 1883 ; Chichele Professor of Modern History, Oxford, 1906 : Hon. LL.D., Edinburgh, 1910 ; M.P. for Oxford Univ., 1919 ; President of Royal Historical Society, 1917 ; President of Royal Numismatic Society, 1919 *War Work :* Censorship, Sept. 1914 to Dec. 1916 ; Foreign Office, Jan. 1917 to Jan. 1919. *Clubs :* Athenæum ; Burlington.   (K404)

O'MEAGHER, Col. John Kevin, C.B.E., B.A., late Royal Munster Fusiliers, *b.* 24 June, 1866 ; *s.* of the late J. O'Meagher, M.R.I.A., Officier d'Académie Française. *Educ. :* Prior Park Coll., Bath ; Royal Univ., Ireland ; Sandhurst. *War Work :* 1914, raised and commanded 8th Service Batt. Royal Munster Fusiliers ; 1915, raised and commanded with rank of Col. 3rd Line Groups, 2nd London Division (T.F.) until their abolition in Sept. 1916 ; raised and commanded 3rd Res. Garrison Batt. Royal Irish Fusiliers ; despatches, 1914 Star, General Service Medal and Victory Medal. *Address :* 25, Wellington Road, Dublin. *Club :* Army and Navy.   (C1723)

O'MEARA, David John, M.B.E., R.N.

O'MEARA, Lieut.-Col. Eugene John, O.B.E., I.M.S.

O'MEARA, Lieut. Michael Aloysius, M.B.E., R.A.S.C.

OMMANNEY, Lieut.-Col. Charles Vernon, C.B.E., *b.* 1872 ; *s.* of the late Col. Edward Lacon Ommanney, C.S.I. ; *m.* 1904, Honoria Catherine, *d.* of the late Dr. H. Cripps Lawrence. Lieut.-Col. Indian Army. Served in the Great War as Administrator, Kamaran Island, and in Palestine, 1918, with 2/30th Punjabis, which he raised (despatches, 1914–15 Star, two medals) ; Afghan War, 1919 (despatches, medal with clasp) ; Waziristan, 1919.   (C3099)

OMMANNEY, Adm. Sir Robert Nelson, K.B.E., C.B., R.N. (ret.), *b.* 31 Jan. 1854 ; *s.* of Octavius Ommanney, of Bloxham, Oxon. ; *m.* Ethel Mary, *d.* of the Rev. Lawrence Harrison, of Mortlake and East Sheen. *Educ. :* Worthing House, Worthing, and Temple Grove, East Sheen. Admiral Superintendent, H.M. Dockyard, Chatham, 1909–12. *War Work :* Chairman of Mining Committee, 1915 ; War Staff for Mining duties, 1915–17 ; Superintendent of Fitting Minelayers, 1917–18. *Address :* c/o Messrs. Holt & Co., 44, Charing Cross, S.W. 1.   (K199)

OMMANNEY, Capt. Walter Montagu, O.B.E.

O'NEILL, Major Arthur, O.B.E., M.R.C.S., R.A.M.C.

O'NEILL, Sir Arthur Eugene, K.B.E., *b.* 17 Dec. 1877 ; *s.* of Capt. Owen O'Neill ; *m.* Edith Frances, *d.* of William Hopkins Tomson. *Educ. :* St. Edmund's Coll., Old Hall, Ware. Partner, Frank C. Strick & Co., Ltd. *War Work :* Admiralty and Ministry of Shipping. *Address :* The Moorings, The Avenue, Bushey, Herts. *Club :* Junior Carlton. (K405)

O'NEILL, Capt. Charles Sefton, O.B.E., M.D., R.A.M.C.

O'NEILL, Herbert Charles, O.B.E.

O'NEILL, Leo Francis, M.B.E.

ONSLOW, Brig.-Gen. Cranley Charlton, C.M.G., C.B.E., D.S.O., *b.* 1869 ; only *s.* of Hamilton Cranley Onslow, Madras S.C. (d. 1874) ; *m.* Sydney Alice H., younger *d.* of Sir Benjamin Franklin, K.C.I.E. Served with the Isazai Expedition, 1892 ; Chitral Relief Force 1895 ; Lieut.-Col. Bedford Regt. from 1916 ; Brigade Commander (T. Brig.-Gen.) 1916 ; awarded the Croix de Guerre.   (C1724)

ONSLOW, Harriet Katharine, O.B.E.

ONSLOW, Richard William Alan Onslow, 5th Earl of, O.B.E., J.P., D.L., F.R.H.S., F.Z.S., *b.* 23 Aug. 1876 ; *e.s.* of the 4th Earl and Hon. Florence Coulston Gardner, *d.* of the 3rd Lord Gardner ; *m.* 1906, Hon. Violet Maria Catherine Warwick Bampfylde, Lady of Grace of Order of St. John of Jerusalem (*q.v.*), *d.* of the 3rd Lord Poltimore. *Educ. :* Eton ; New Coll., Oxford. Attached H.M. Diplomatic Service, 1901 ; appointed Madrid, 1902 ; Tangier, 1903 ; granted allowances for knowledge of Arabic and International Law ; 3rd Sec. Petrograd ; Private Sec. to Rt. Hon. Sir C. Hardinge and Rt. Hon. Sir A. Nicholson, 1904–6 ; 2nd Sec. Berlin, 1907 ; Secretary-in-Charge of Commercial Affairs at Berlin, 1908 ; Assistant Private Secretary to Sir Edward Grey, 1909 ; Clerk in the Foreign Office, 1910 ; Private Secretary to the Permanent Under-Secretary of State for Foreign Affairs, 1911 ; Assistant Clerk, Foreign Office, 1913 ; resigned 1914 ; appointed a Civil Lord of the Admiralty, 1920 ; Staff Lieut. in Army, 1915 ; served in Great War (despatches twice) ; Captain, 1916 ; G.S.O. 2nd Grade, Dec. 1916 ; Major, May, 1918 ; Hon. Lieut.-Col. 3rd Vol. Bn. Queen's Roy. West Surrey Regt. ; Col. G.S.O. 1st Grade, G.H.Q., B.E.F. France 1918 ; Knight of Grace, St. John of Jerusalem ; Knight of Legion of Honour. *Addresses :* 107, St. George's Square, S.W.1 ; Clandon Park, Guildford. *Clubs :* Carlton ; Beefsteak ; Turf ; Travellers' ; M.C.C. ; Guildford County.   (O619)

ONSLOW, Violet Marcia Catherine Warwick, Countess of, C.B.E., A.R.R.C., Lady of Grace, Order of St. John of Jerusalem ; only *d.* of 3rd Baron Poltimore, of Poltimore Park, Exeter (*see* BURKE'S *Peerage*) ; *m.* William Alan Richard, *s.* of William Hillier, 4th Earl of Onslow, of Clandon Park, Guildford (*see* BURKE'S *Peerage*). Lady District Officer for

Surrey, St. John Ambulance Brigade. *War Work :* Commandant, Clandon Park Primary Military Hospital, 1914–19 ; Commandant, Broom House Auxiliary Red Cross Hospital, 1915–19 ; Vice-President, Surrey Branch B.R.C.S., 1914–20 ; Commandant, Women's V.A.D. Surrey 86, 1914–20. *Addresses :* Clandon Park, Guildford ; 107, St. George's Square, S.W. 1.   (C2852)

ONSLOW, Henry HUGHES-, C.B.E., *b.* 3 Jan. 1871 ; 5th *s.* of the late H. J. Hughes-Onslow, of Balkissock, Co. Ayr (*see* BURKE'S *Peerage*, Onslow, E.). *Educ. :* Eton. Master of the Supreme Court of Judicature. *War Work :* Organised the examination of witnesses for the Government Committee on the Treatment by the Enemy of British Prisoners of War, etc. *Addresses :* 8, Cavendish Place, Cavendish Square, W. 1 ; Royal Courts of Justice, W.C. 2. *Clubs :* Carlton ; Marlborough ; White's ; Bath.   (C1016)

ONSLOW, Marion, Mrs. Denzil HUGHES-, C.B.E. ; *d.* of George Oliver, of Laggan, Ayrshire ; *m.* Denzil, Major 6th Dorsets (killed in action, July, 1916), *s.* of Henry John Hughes-Onslow, of Balkissock, Ayr (*see* BURKE'S *Peerage*, Onslow E.). Donor and Resident Commandant of Laggan House Red Cross Auxiliary Hospital, Ballantrae, Ayrshire, which hospital (50 beds) she maintained at her own expense, free of all Government or other grants, from 1916 till its close in 1919 ; she also, with her husband, the late Major Denzil Hughes-Onslow, handed over her English residence, Colliton House, Dorchester, as a Red Cross Auxiliary Hospital (200 beds) from 1914 till 1919 ; Commandant of Ayr (50) V.A.D. of the Red Cross ; President of the Ballantrae District Sailors' and Soldiers' Families Association till merged into the Sailors' and Soldiers' Help Association and Pensions Committee ; President of the Ballantrae War Work Party and of the Ballantrae District Committee's Campaign for promoting employment of women on the land. *Addresses :* Laggan House ; Balkissock Lodge, Ballantrae, Ayrshire ; Colliton House, Dorchester. *Club :* Ladies' Athenæum.   (C2851)

OPENSHAW, Edith Newbold, M.B.E. *Educ. :* Ladies' Coll., Cheltenham. *War Work :* Voluntary Worker, Bury War Pensions Committee. *Address :* Brooklands, Wilson Street, Bury, Lancs.   (M9193)

OPENSHAW, Florence, Mrs., M.B.E., *b.* 3 June, 1872 ; *d.* of Henry Grey, of Herne, Kent ; *m.* Lawrence Græme, *s.* of Thomas Openshaw, of Middleton Cheney Rectory. *Educ. :* Herne Bay. *War Work :* Commandant of V.A.D. Detachment, Kent 90 ; in charge of Auxiliary Hospital, Herne Bay, from 1914–18. *Address :* The Haven, Exton-in-Exeter. *Club :* New Century.   (M9194)

OPENSHAW, Lieut. George Arthur, M.B.E.

OPENSHAW, James, O.B.E., M.A., J.P., D.L. (Lancs), *b.* 13 April, 1871 ; *s.* of the late Frederick Openshaw, of Hothersall Hall, Ribchester ; *m.* Muriel Ellen, *d.* of the Rev. W. J. Melville, of Ashton-in-Makerfield. *Educ. :* Harrow, and Trinity Coll., Cambridge. Chairman, Lancashire Quarter Sessions (Preston Division). *Address :* Hothersall Hall, Ribchester, near Preston.   (O11066)

OPPENHEIM, Major Arthur Edwin, O.B.E., I.A.

OPPENHEIM, Lieut.-Col. Robert William, O.B.E.

ORAM, Major Harry, O.B.E.

ORAM, Capt. Matthew Henry, M.B.E.

ORAM, Dame Sarah Elizabeth, D.B.E., R.R.C. Principal Matron, Queen Alexandra's Imp. Mil. Nursing Service. (D40)

ORANGE, George James, C.B.E. Joint Hon. Organiser for Official Agents, National War Savings Committee. (C2853)

ORANGE, Lionel, M.B.E.

ORCHARD, Alfred John, C.B.E. Chairman of War Pensions Committee, Rhondda.   (C2854)

ORCHARD, Lieut. Edward Henslow, M.B.E., R.G.A.

ORCHARD, Lieut.-Comm. Edwin Harold, O.B.E., R.N.R.

ORCHARD, Jonathan, C.B.E., B.Sc. (Lond.), *b.* 4 Dec. 1853 ; *s.* of Jonathan Orchard, of Southampton ; *m.* Charlotte Sophia, *d.* of J. Pitt, of Southampton. *Educ. :* Private School, Lowestoft ; Mason's Coll., Birmingham. Late Chief Inspector of Customs and Excise, Custom House, London, E.C. *War Work :* In connection with administration of Customs and Excise Dept. *Address :* 319A, Brixton Road, S.W. 9. (C1017)

ORCHARD, Hon. Richard Beaumont, C.B.E. Minister for Recruiting, Commonwealth of Australia, during the Great War.   (C3202)

ORD, Lieut. Benjamin, M.B.E.

ORD, Evelyne Mary, O.B.E. ; *d.* of the late Richard Ord, of Sands Hall, Co. Durham. *Educ. :* Privately ; Bedford Women's Coll. President, Sedgefield District, Soldiers' and Sailors' Families Association ; President of other local societies. *War Work :* Founder, organiser, and Hon. Sec. of the British and Allies Comforts and Victims of War Fund ; assisted directly over 10,000 individuals, not counting the thousands helped indirectly by goods sent in bulk ; received the Order of the Serbian Red Cross ; also Order of Montenegrin Red Cross. *Address :* Sands Hall, Sedgefield, Co. Durham.   (O11067)

ORD, Mark Curry, M.B.E.

ORD, William Wallis, O.B.E., M.D.

O'REILLY, Arthur, M.B.E.

O'REILLY, Major Brefney Rolph, O.B.E., M.D., R.A.F.

O'REILLY, Isabella, Mrs., M.B.E.

O'REILLY, Rev. James, O.B.E.

O'REILLY, Major Thomas Leslie, O.B.E.

ORFORD, Lieut.-Col. Herbert John, O.B.E.

ORFORD, John, M.B.E., M.R.C.S., L.R.C.P., L.S.A., *b.* 22 March, 1857 ; *s.* of John Orford, of Brookes Hall, Ipswich ;

m. Fanny Florence, *d.* of Thomas Sorby, of Sheffield. *Educ.:* St. Thomas' Hospital. Surgeon. *War Work:* Medical Officer in charge Stapleton, Darrington and Swillington War Hospitals. (M9197)

ORFORD, Capt. William Oswald, O.B.E., R.F.A. (T.).

O'RIORDAN, Lieut. Henry Michael, O.B.E.

ORLOFF, Capt. Eugene, M.B.E., R.E.

ORMAN, Frederick Brook, M.B.E., *b.* 9 Oct. 1869; *s.* of Henry Orman of Portsmouth, Hants; *m.* Amy Drew, *d.* of John Gapes, of Portsmouth, Hants. *Educ.:* Gorsuch's Academy, and Dockyard School, Portsmouth. Surveyor of Stores. H.M. Dockyard, Rosyth. *War Work:* Aug. 1914 to Feb. 1918, Principal Hull Overseer in the Tyne District for emergency repairs to H.M. ships, and during this period dealt with the repairs to several of H.M. vessels damaged by enemy action, besides attending to the general maintenance and refitting of many vessels of the Grand Fleet. *Address:* 4, Fingal Place, Edinburgh. (M3876)

ORME, Capt. Frederick George, O.B.E., 7th Bn. Middlesex Regt. (T.), *b.* 1874; *s.* of George Hill Orme, of Bayswater; *m.* Minnie, *d.* of John Rutgers, of Amsterdam. *Educ.:* St. Paul's School. Fellow of the Chartered Institute of Secretaries. *War Work:* Held rank of Inspector in the Inspection Dept., Royal Arsenal, Woolwich, High Explosives Directorate. *Address:* 3, Fairfax Mansions, Hampstead, N.W. 3. *Club:* Royal Automobile. (O1716)

ORME, Marie, Mrs., M.B.E., L.R.C.P.I., L.R.C.S.I; *d.* of John Goodwin, of Matlock, Derbyshire; *m.* Albert L'Estrange, *s.* of Robert Orme, of Owenmore, Co. Mayo. *Educ.:* Privately. Resident Physician, Matlock Hydro, Matlock; Hon. Physician, Derby and Derbyshire Convalescent Home, Matlock, and the Sheffield Works Association Convalescent Home for Women. *War Work:* M.O. Royal Air Force Hospital for Officers, Rockside; M.O. Red Cross Auxiliary Hospital, Darley, near Matlock: Commandant, Derby 22 R.C. V.A.D., which, conjointly with Derby 34 R.C. V.A.D., organised and ran the Darley Auxiliary Red Cross Hospital for wounded soldiers, over 2000 cases being admitted; served as Member of the Matlock Belgian Relief and War Relief Committees. *Address:* Rockside, Matlock. (M9198)

ORME, Thomas Charles Rushmer, O.B.E., *b.* 11 March, 1861. *Educ.:* Park House Academy, Southampton. Assistant Marine Manager, London and South-Western Railway Co. *War Work:* Transport. *Address:* Blair Athol, Alma Road, Southampton. (O11069)

ORMEROD, Annie, M.B.E.

ORMEROD, Marion Grace, O.B.E., *b.* 12 June, 1872; *d.* of the Rev. Canon J. G. Alford, C.B.E., of Bristol (*q.v.*); *m* Henry Lawrence Ormerod, M.D., *s.* of Henry Ormerod, Surgeon, of Westbury-on-Trym. *Educ.:* Privately. *War Work:* Commandant Bristol 8; Rest Station work, Sept. 1914, to April, 1919; also on County Director's Selection Board. *Address:* 2, Henleaze Road, Westbury-on-Trym. (O11070)

ORMISTON, Capt. Thomas Maclay, O.B.E., R.A.M.C. (T.), *b.* 30 July, 1889; *s.* of Robert Ormiston, of Alloa, Scotland; *m.* Winifred Ethel Douglas, *d.* of the Rev. John Ross, M.A., of Garnethill Parish, Glasgow. *Educ.:* Alloa Academy. *Address:* 375, Sauchiehall St., Glasgow. (O5653)

ORMOND, Bt. Major Arthur William, C.B.E., F.R.C.S., *b.* 8 Dec. 1871; *s.* of Maurice Ormond, of London; *m.* Mary Charlotte, *d.* of E. H. P. Eason, of London. *Educ.:* Guy's Hospital. Ophthalmic Surgeon, Guy's Hospital; Lecturer in Medical School. *War Work:* Officer in charge Ophthalmic Department, 2nd London General Hospital, Chelsea; Ophthalmic Specialist, London Area; Hon. Ophthalmic Surgeon, St. Dunstan's Hostel for Blinded Sailors and Soldiers. *Address:* 7, Devonshire Place, W. (C2151)

ORMSBY, Surg.-Comm. William Edwin, O.B.E., M.B.

ORMSTON, John Maurice, M.B.E.

O'RORKE, Major George Mackenzie, C.I.E., M.B.E.

O'RORKE, Gertrude Isabel, Mrs., M.B.E., *d.* of the late Rev. Canon William Wayman Hutt, of Hockwold Rectory, Brandon, Norfolk; *m.* Ashley Robert Howard, *s.* of the late Rev. Henry O'Rorke, of Feltwell Rectory, Brandon, Norfolk. *War Work:* Commandant, and later Qr.-Mr. and Sec. of Pontyclun Red Cross Auxiliary Hospital, Pontyclun, Glamorgan, S. Wales, July, 1915, to Jan. 1919. *Address:* Tal-y-garn, Pontyclun, Glamorgan, S. Wales. (M9199)

ORPEN, Major Anthony Shroeder, O.B.E.

ORPEN, Ida Grace Victoria, M.B.E., *b.* 31 March, 1887; *d* of Richard Hugh Millerd, of Ardtully, Kenmare, Co. Kerry, Ireland. *Educ.:* Privately. *War Work:* Lady Superintendent, H.M. Inspection of Munition Areas, Sheffield, Liverpool, and North Wales for 2 years; District Lady Superintendent, H.M. Central Stores Dept., Birmingham and the Midlands. (M3877)

ORPEN, Sybil Margaret, Hon. Mrs., O.B.E.; *d.* of 1st Baron Plumer (*see* BURKE'S *Peerage*); *m.* 1916, Maj. Anthony S. Orpen, E. Lancs. Regt. *Address:* 10, Old Court Mansions, S.W. 8 (O11071)

ORPEN, Sir William Newenham Montague, K.B.E., R.A., *b.* 1878; *s.* of Arthur Herbert Orpen, M.A. (of Oriel), of Stillorgan, Co. Dublin; *m.* Grace, *d.* of Walter John Knewstub, of Highgate. *Addresses:* 8, South Bolton Gardens, S.W.10; 11, Royal Hospital Rd., Chelsea, S.W.3. *Clubs:* Garrick; Savile; Arts. (K161)

ORR, Charles Roger, C.B.E.

ORR, Major Frank George, C.B.E., R.F.A. (T.).

ORR, Lieut. George, M.B.E., *b.* 24 July, 1884. *Educ.:*

Hutcheson's Grammar School. Cooperage Proprietor. *Address:* 431, Victoria Road, Queen's Park, Glasgow. (M3007)

ORR, Major Harold, O.B.E., Can. A.M.C.

ORR, James Peter, C.S.I., C.B.E., I.C.S.

ORR, John, M.B.E., J.P. Kimberley; *b.* 7 Jan. 1858; *s.* of Dixon Orr, of Benburb, co. Tyrone, Ireland; *m.* Mary Ellen, *d.* of Henry ——, of Staffordshire. *Educ.:* National School and private tuition. Merchant, Kimberley, Durban, Johannesburg, etc. *War Work:* Was for three years Mayor of Kimberley, S. Africa, during the war period 1916–19, and during that time was Chairman of the local Recruiting Committee and of the various patriotic organisations—notably that of the Governor-General's Fund—for which an amount of nearly £30,000 was raised at the "Kimberley War Market." President, Kimberley Branch of Navy League of S. Africa. *Club:* Kimberley. (O11072)

ORR, John, O.B.E., M.B., C.M., late Capt. R.A.M.C. (T.), *b.* 17 Jan. 1861; *s.* of the late Major-General James Orr, of 27th Regt. N.I. (India); *m.* Annie Isabel; *d.* of the late Thomas Jones, of Woodcroft, Windermere. *Educ.:* St. Andrews (Fife), and Edinburgh Univ. Medical Referee to Board of Education; Medical Referee to Ministry of Pensions; M.O. to Post Office. *War Work:* Officer in charge of Elm Bank Hospital (Red Cross), and Eccles and Patricroft Hospital, Patricroft; M.O. to both hospitals. *Address:* 3, Clarendon Road, Eccles, Lancs. (O11072)

ORR, John, O.B.E., B.Sc., M.I.C.E., M.I.Mech.E., *b.* 25 April 1870; *s.* of late Henry Orr, of Westcraigs, Lanarkshire, Scotland; *m.* Janet Louise, *d.* of F. J. Quinton, of Johannesburg. *Educ.:* Royal Technical College, Glasgow, and Glasgow University. Professor of Mechanical Engineering at Univ. College, Johannesburg (University of South Africa); Past President S.A. Institution of Engineers; Past President S.A. Association for the Advancement of Science; Member Union Government Advisory Board of Industry and Science (1917–20); Chairman British Engineering Standards Association (S.A. Branch); Dean of Faculty of Engineering, Univ. of South Africa (1918–21). *War Work:* Chairman of Witwatersrand Disabled Soldiers Board; Member of Central Executive of the Governor-General's Fund and of Administrative Committee Governor-General's Fund (Johannesburg Branch). *Address:* P.O. Box 1176, Johannesburg. *Clubs:* Rand (Johannesburg); Kimberley (Kimberley). (O4361)

ORR, William James, C.B.E., *b.* 26 Jan. 1874; *s.* of James Orr, of Manchester; *m.* Kathleen Marguerite, *d.* of the late Sir Joseph Leigh, of Stockport. *Educ.:* Pembroke House School; Switzerland and Germany. *War Work:* Textile Adviser to the Director of Army Contracts, and later Chief Executive Officer of the War Dept. Cotton Textiles Office, Manchester; Chevalier Order of the Crown of Belgium. *Addresses:* Empire House, Charlotte Street, Manchester; Barton Grange, near Preston. *Club:* Clarendon, Manchester. (C2855)

ORRIN, Herbert Charles, O.B.E., F.R.C.S., *b.* 1878; *s.* of the late Henry Orrin; *m.* Beth A., *d.* of the late Rev. T. W. Gibson, M.A. *Educ.:* Privately. Surgeon, Ministry of Pensions Board. *War Work:* 1914–20, Medical Officer in charge, Earl of Onslow's Hospital, Clandon Park; Medical Officer in charge, Kensington Red Cross Hospital, London; Surgeon attached 3rd London General Hospital. *Address:* 150, Harley Street, W. 1. (O4382)

ORTON, C. J., M.B.E.

ORTON, Comm. John Henry, O.B.E., R.N.

ORTON, William, M.B.E.

OSBORN, Catherine Augusta, Mrs., M.B.E., *d.* of Andrew Cusin, of Kirkcaldy, Fife; *m.* Harry, *s.* of William Edward Osborn, of Kirn, N.B. *Educ.:* Convent of Notre Dame, Liverpool. *War Work:* Quartermaster at Hoole House Auxiliary Mil. Hospl. Chester, Aug 1915 to June 1919; Nursing Duties at Richmond House Aux. Mil. Hospl. Chester, 1914–15. *Address:* 18, Castle Street, Chester. (M25)

OSBORN, Capt. Howard Harry, M.B.E.

OSBORN, Capt. Tom Douglas Hamilton, M.B.E., R.A.F.

OSBORN, William Albert, M.B.E., R.N.

OSBORNE, Albert Alfred, O.B.E., M.R.C.S., L.R.C.P.

OSBORNE, Major David, M.B.E., V.D., J.P., *b.* 15 Feb., 1846; *s.* of Robert Osborne, of Thorntonhall, Lanarkshire; *m.* Robina Wilson, *d.* of William Duncan, of Cupar, Fife. *Educ.:* Glasgow High School, and Glasgow Univ. County Treasurer of Fife. *War Work:* Sec. and Treas. Fife Branch of Scottish Branch of British Red Cross Society: raised and commanded Company of Fife Volunteers. *Address:* Belmore, Cupar. *Club:* Scottish Conservative, Edinburgh. (M3878)

OSBORNE, Frederick William, O.B.E. Principal Assistant, London County Council Stores Department. *War Work:* Sec. Anti-Gas Committee; Director, Anti-Gas Contracts; Superintendent H.M. Anti-Gas Factory, Watford; largely responsible for the design and production of components required to produce Anti-Gas apparatus. (O11073)

OSBORNE, Lieut.-Col. George Henry, O.B.E., *b.* 1 Dec. 1858; *s.* of W. M. Osborne, of Cowes, I. of W.; *m.* Annie, *d.* of J. O'Neill, of Aldershot. *Educ.:* Privately. *War Work:* Service in India and Arabia. *Address:* 50, Latchmere Road, Kingston-on-Thames. (O8522)

OSBORNE, Lieut. Henry William, M.B.E.

OSBORNE, Capt. John Warde, C.B.E., R.N.

OSBORNE, Major John William, O.B.E., R.A.M.C., *b.* 23 Feb. 1867; *s.* of Ed. Osborne, of Ramsey St. Mary, Herts; *m.* Emily Ann, *d.* of G. Cudlipp, of Hitchin, Herts.

Educ.: Ramsey and Peterborough. Commissioned in 1908. *War Work:* Proceeded to France with a General Hospital on 12 Aug. 1914, and continued to serve in France throughout the war till 26 May, 1919, with various units and formations. *Addresses:* 46, Wimpole Road, Colchester; c/o Holt & Co.
(O5654)

OSBORNE, Margaret, O.B.E. Superintendent, Londonderry North-West Sphagnum Moss Depot. (O11790*f*)

OSBORNE, Rosabelle, C.B.E. Principal Matron Army Nursing Service. *War Work:* Rendered services in connection with military operations in Salonica. (C1124)

OSBORNE, William Henry, M.B.E. (M10410)

OSBURN, Lieut. Harold, O.B.E.; R.N.V.R.

OSGERBY, Isabel, Mrs., M.B.E.

OSGOOD, Frederick Stanley, C.B.E., M.V.O.

OSLER, Capt. James Bell, O.B.E., *b.* 6 July, 1889; *s.* of James Bell Osler, of Coupar Angus. *Educ.:* Dundee High School; Royal Technical Coll., Glasgow. Engineer. *Address:* 49, Ridgmount Gardens, W.C. 1. *Club:* Royal Automobile.
(O5655)

OSMAN, Hon. Lieut.-Col. Alfred Henry, O.B.E., *b.* 12 July, 1864; *s.* of John Jonas Osman, of the Civil Service; *m.* Ada Gertrude, *d.* of Edward Jones, of Tonbridge. *Educ.:* Edmonton Grammar School. *War Work:* (voluntary) Organised the Carrier Pigeon Service; enlisted men for this service after examination; obtained, free of cost to the country, thousands of carrier pigeons to maintain the service on all fronts; was in command of the Carrier Pigeon Service G.H.Q. Great Britain; bred and supplied large numbers of birds from his own lofts. *Address:* Apsley House, Cambridge Park, Leytonstone, E. 11. (O1717)

OSMASTON, Col. Cecil Alvend FitzHerbert, C.B., C.B.E. late R.M. Artillery, *b.* 24 July, 1866; *s.* of John Osmaston, of Osmaston Manor; *m.* Minnie Buckley, *d.* of General Sir Henry Tuson, late R.M. Artillery. *Educ.:* Winchester. Adjutant, R.M. Artillery; Adjutant, Sligo Artillery; Instructor of Gunnery, R.M. Artillery (ret.); Member, Ordnance Board; Member, Ordnance Committee; Assistant Controller, Munitions Inventions Department. *War Work:* Commanded Brigade of Artillery in France. *Club:* United Service. (C2281)

OSMASTON, Sophie Florence Lothrop, C.B.E.

OSMOND, Lieut.-Col. Edward, C.B.E., R.A.F. Served during the Great War, 1914–19 (despatches). (C1903)

OST, Lieut. Henry John, M.B.E., R.E.

OST, Lieut. William Lewis, M.B.E., R.N., *b.* 5 Feb. 1859. June, 1915, appointed to H.M.S. " Colleen," as assistant to Officer in charge of Anti-Submarine Boom Defence, Queenstown Harbour; Aug. 1917, took over charge of Boom Defence, Queenstown, from Comdr. E. L. Hughes, R.N., and continued in charge until the end of the Great War. *Address:* 3, Ardnalee, Crosshaven, Co. Cork, Ireland. (M2250)

OSTLE, Helen Muriel, M.B.E., *b.* 18 May, 1883; *d.* of the late Rev. Wm. Ostle of the Vicarage, S. Bartholomew's Hospital, E.C., and Haydon Vicarage, Sherborne, Dorset. *Educ.:* St. Mary's Hall, Brighton; City of London High School; and Wiesbaden. Emigration work in connection with the S. African Colonisation Society and British Women's Emigration Association; L.C.C. Care Committee work; In charge of Employment Department for Debenham's, Ltd. *War Work:* Administrative Assistant in Gun Ammunition Filling Dept., Ministry of Munitions, Dec. 1915, to March, 1919. *Address:* 5, Smith Street, Chelsea, S.W. 3. *Club:* Efficiency. (M9201)

OSTLER, Major Francis Edward, O.B.E., N.Z.A.S.C.

OSTREHAN, Lieut.-Col. Francis George Rodney, O.B.E., I.A.

OSTREHAN, Capt. Malcolm, M.B.E.

O'SULLIVAN, Col. Daniel, C.B.E., *b.* 1853. Col. Army Med. Depart. (ret.); served during the Great War, 1914–19 (despatches). (C1726)

O'SULLIVAN, Gerald Hendon, M.B.E., *b.* 6 Jan. 1888; *s.* of John O'Sullivan, of Aberavon, South Wales. *Educ.:* Privately, and at Broadstairs. *War Work:* Acted as Admiralty Sub-agent at Port Talbot, 1914–19, and as Transport Officer during most of the time. *Address:* St. Cuthbert's, Port Talbot, South Wales. (M2251)

O'SULLIVAN, Cadet Lieut.-Col. Hugh Dermod Evan, C.B.E., Royal Marines, *b.* 11 Sept. 1874; *s.* of Lieut.-Col. Eugene O'Sullivan, Royal Artillery; *m.* Flora, *d.* of Hugh Campbell, of Eden Lodge, Beckenham. *Educ.:* Wimborne, and Royal Naval Coll. Royal Marines L.I. 1892; attached Egyptian Army, 1901; and Sudan Government, 1903; Governor and O.C. Troops, Upper Nile Province, 1909–11; Senior Officer, Royal Marines, East Indies Naval Command, 1912–14; Orders: Osmanieh, the Medjidieh, and the Nile. *War Work:* Senior Officer, Royal Marines, East India and Egypt, 1914–15; Intelligence Officer to Naval C.-in-C., East Indies and Egypt, 1915; General Staff Officer (1st Grade), Special Service on Staff of Naval C.-in-C., East Indies and Egypt, 1916, and of Mediterranean, 1917; Naval Political Officer (G.S.O. 1), Egypt, 1918–19. *Address:* Royal Marines, Stonehouse, Plymouth. *Club:* United Service.

O'SULLIVAN, Major Patrick, O.B.E., R.A.

O'SULLIVAN, Capt. Richard Benjamin, O.B.E.

OSWALD, Lieut.-Col. Christopher Percy, O.B.E.

OSWALD, Surg.-Sub.-Lieut. David James Tosh, M.B.E., R.N.V.R.

OSWALD, Ethel Margaret Oswald, M.B.E.

OSWALD, Maude, Mrs., O.B.E., *b.* 18 June, 1849; *d.* of

James H. Smith Barry, of Marbury Hall, Cheshire; *m.* Richard, *s.* of George D. Oswald, of Auchincruive, Ayr. *War Work:* Vice-President, Red Cross; Convener, Carrick House, and Seafields Auxiliary Hospitals; Vice-President Pensions Committee, Soldiers' and Sailors' Families Association. *Address:* Auchincruive, Ayr. (O11074)

OSWALD, Percy Cunningham, O.B.E.

OSWALD, Lieut.-Col. Robert James William, O.B.E., R.A.M.C. (T.).

OTTAWAY, John, M.B.E.

OTTEWILL, James Thomas, M.B.E.

OTTLEY, Capt. Robert Bruce Hamilton, M.B.E., R.A.S.C.

OTTMAN, Amelia Gertrude, M.B.E.; *d.* of Hugo Ottman, of Glasgow. *Educ.:* Park School, Glasgow; Brussels, and Dresden. *War Work:* Joined Q.M.A.A.C., Jan. 1918; proceeded overseas and was posted to Camp 3, Abbeville; in Sept. 1918, was put in charge of War Workers' Parties at Gezaincourt Chateau, under G.H.Q., till work closed there at end of Jan. 1919; returned to Camp 3, Abbeville, and remained there as Deputy Administrator till demobilised in Nov. 1919. *Address:* 13, Glenan Gardens, Helensburgh, Scotland. (M4566)

OUDIN, Eugenie Josephine, O.B.E.

OUGHTON, Ernest, O.B.E.

OUSELEY, Capt. Joseph William Glynn, O.B.E.

OUSELEY, William, M.B.E.

OUTERBRIDGE, Capt. and Qr.-Mr. Herbert A., M.B.E.

OUTRAM, Major Francis Davidson, O.B.E., M.I.C.E., M.I.M.E., late R.E.; *b.* 4 Aug. 1867; 2nd *s.* of Sir Francis Boyd Outram, of Clach-na-faire, Pitlochry, N.B. (*see* BURKE'S *Peerage*); *m.* 1st, Maud Charlotte, *d.* of the late J. P. Kitchin, of the Manor House, Hampton-on-Thames (died 1913), 2nd, Isabel Mary, *d.* of late H. C. Berry, of Birmingham. *Educ.:* Haileybury, and R.I.E.C., Coopers Hill. 2nd Lieut. Royal Engineers, Nov. 1889; Lieut. Nov. 1892; retired, 1897; Consulting Engineer at 28, Victoria Street, S.W., until 1911. *War Work:* Staff Capt., Directorate of Fortifications and Works, War Office, Dec. 1914, to July, 1917; Deputy Assistant Director of Fortifications and Works, War Office, July, 1917, to April, 1919. *Address:* Lyss-na-greyne, Aboyne, Aberdeenshire. *Club:* National. (O7537)

OUTRAM, Haidee Maria, Mrs., M.B.E., *b.* 23 July, 1873; *d.* of H. F. Beaumont, of Whitley Beaumont, Huddersfield; *m.* William, *s.* of Sir Francis B. Outram, Bart., of Clach-na-faire, Pitlochry (*see* BURKE'S *Peerage*). *War Work:* Commandant of Kirkburton Military Hospital, 1915–18; Sec. for the Kirkburton Belgian Refugees, 1914–19. *Address:* Stubbings Vicarage, Maidenhead. (M2252)

OUTRAM, Wing-Comm. Harold William Sydney, C.B.E., R.A.F. Served in the Great War, 1914–19 (despatches).
(C2340)

OUVRY, Lieut.-Col. Ernest Carrington, M.B.E., *b.* 2 July, 1866; *s.* of The Rev. Peter Thomas Ouvry, M.A., J.P., of Wing, Bucks., and East Acton, Middlesex; *m.* Elinor Southwood, *d.* of Charles Lee Lewes, L.C.C., of 3, Cambridge Terrace, Regent's Park. *Educ.:* Marlborough Coll.; Wadham Coll., Oxford. Senior partner, Ellis & Ellis, Solicitors, Westminster; Steward of the Manors of, and Solicitor to, New Coll., Oxford; a Director of French Protestant Hospital, Victoria Park; a Governor and Hon. Sec. Westminster French Protestant School; Trustee French Church, Soho; Sec. French Protestant Church of the Savoy; Fellow of the Huguenot Society. *War Work:* South African War, 1900–1; 34th Co. Middlesex Imperial Yeomanry (medal, 4 clasps); Veterans' Corps, Hon. Artillery Co.; raised and C.O. 1st Cadet Batt. Hon. Artillery Co.; Member, City of London Territorial Cadet Committee; Sec. National Association of Cadet Training. *Addresses:* 10, Little College Street, Westminster; 15, Sussex Gardens, Hyde Park; Crockham Hill, Kent. *Clubs:* St. Stephen's; Public Schools. (M9204)

OUZMAN, William Charles, M.B.E.

OVANS, Capt. Charles Phipps John, O.B.E.

OVANS, Major Hugh Lambert, C.B.E. Ministry of National Service. (C3161)

OVEN, Capt. Richard Trevor Tudor, M.B.E.

OVENS, Lieut. Alexander Rutherford, M.B.E., R.A.F.

OVENS, Jean Broomfield Weir, M.B.E.; *d.* of Walter Ovens, of Torr, Castle Douglas, N.B. *War Work:* Joined Women's Legion, Sept. 1916; in charge of kitchen at Summerdown Camp, Eastbourne, for 10 months; superintendent of an Officers' Mess in same town, Aug. 1917; transferred to Q.M.A.A.C., Oct. 1917; Unit Administrator at Officers' Command Depot, Eastbourne, Nov. 1917, to Jan. 1919, and at Grove Park, Feb. 1919, to Dec. 1919. (M5509)

OVERELL, Major Percy William, O.B.E.

OVERHEAD, William Henry, M.B.E., R.N.

OVERMAN, Henry, C.B.E., J.P.

OWEN, 2nd Lieut. Bertram Maurice, O.B.E., M.C., R.E.

OWEN, Edward Tudor, O.B.E.

OWEN, Frederick William, M.B.E., *b.* 1 Dec. 1879; *s.* of George Owen, of Williton, Somerset; *m.* Edith Eveline, *d.* of Alfred Woodmansey, of Harpham, Yorkshire. *Educ.:* Westminster. *War Work:* Cabinet Staff. *Address:* 96, Norbury Court Road, Norbury, Surrey. (M3880)

OWEN, Gladys, O.B.E.

OWEN, Griffith Ellis, M.B.E., *b.* 25 July, 1855; *s.* of Ellis Owen, of Craflwyn, Beddgelert; *m.* Gwen, *d.* of Rees Edwards, of Barmouth. *Educ.:* Beddgelert. Member of various local and county committees. *War Work:* Member of Food Control and Fuel Committees; also Sec. of the Barmouth War Refugees Committee, 1914–18; awarded Medaille du Roi Albert. *Addresses:* Greenwich House, Barmouth; Wern, Barnouth, N. Wales.   (M9205)

OWEN, Major Herbert Charles, O.B.E., M.C., *b.* 18 Aug. 1877; *s.* of Col. G. P. Owen, J.P., of Folkestone; *m.* Mabel Elvira, *d.* of the late Right Hon. Sir Samuel Walker, Bart., Lord Chancellor of Ireland. *Educ.:* Marlborough Coll., and Sandhurst. Resident Magistrate in Ireland; stationed at Donegal. *War Work:* Deputy Assistant Adjutant-Gen., 23rd Division; served in France and Italy, 1917–18; Gen. Staff Officer, Chatham, 1915–16; four times mentioned in despatches; awarded Croce di Guerra. *Address:* Magherabeg, Donegal, Ireland.   (O2996)

OWEN, John, O.B.E., *b.* 3 Feb. 1858; *s.* of William Owen, of Trefriw, N. Wales; *m.* Sarah Ann, *d.* of Benjamin Powell, of Mold. *Educ.:* Llanrwst Grammar School. Small Holdings Commissioner, under Board of Agriculture and Fisheries, for Wales and Monmouth; District Commissioner, Food Production Department; Superintending Commissioner for Land Settlement and Small Holdings for Wales and Monmouth, under Ministry of Agriculture and Fisheries. *War Work:* Superintending the work of War Agricultural Executive Committees in Wales; Recruiting Labour for Agriculture. *Address:* Whitehouse, Bersham, Wrexham. *Club:* National Liberal; Farmers'.   (O1720)

OWEN, John Albert, M.B.E.

OWEN, Langer, C.B.E., K.C. Barrister, Lincoln's Inn, 1888. *War Work:* Rendered services in connection with Information Bureau, N.S. Wales Div., Australian Red Cross. *Address:* Sydney, N.S. Wales.   (C717)

OWEN, Percy Thomas, O.B.E.   (O12001)

OWEN, Capt. Reginald Charles Lloyd, O.B.E., R.N.

OWEN, Capt. and Qr.-Mr. Richard A., O.B.E., R.A.V.C., *b.* 9 Aug. 1871; *s.* of A. Owen, of Springfields, Wolverhampton, Staffs.; *m.* Helen Maud Mary, *d.* of Horatio W. Pearce, of Cosham, Hants. *Educ.:* St. Mary's, Wolverhampton. Served through ranks from 1889–1920. *War Work:* Assist.-Deputy Director of Vety. Services, Aldershot Command, 1914–18 (despatches, M.B.E., 1916); service in Salonika, and South Russia as D.A.A.G. to Denikin's Mission (despatches, 1920). *Address:* Sutton Scotney Hants. *Club:* H. and H.E., Farnham. (O9747)

OWEN, Lieut.-Col. Roger Carmichael Robert, C.M.G., O.B.E., F.R.G.S.

OWEN, Capt. Robert David, O.B.E., *b.* 9 Aug. 1870; *s.* of Robert Owen, of Fourcrosse; *m.* Elizabeth Catherine, *d.* of David Evans, of Bay View, Nevin. *Educ.:* Edeyrn National School. Master Mariner; Master of T.S.S. "Nestor" (15,000 tons), Messrs. Alfred Holt & Co., of Liverpool (Blue Funnel Line). *War Work:* In command of the "Nestor" at the commencement of trooping in Aug. 1915; she was then taken over by the Australian Government, and since that time has carried over 55,000 soldiers, including Australians, Imperials, South Africans, and Americans; she was unsuccessfully attacked by submarine—twice with troops on board, and three times without; the largest complement she carried on one trip was 2930 Americans from New York to Liverpool, and on that occasion she established the record of arriving without one single case in hospital. *Addresses:* Bay View, Nevin, Carnarvonshire; 70, Farrar Road, Bangor, North Wales.   (O11076)

OWEN, Thomas, M.B.E., *b.* 15 Dec. 1872. Manager of Llanelly Employment Exchange, Ministry of Labour. *War Work:* Assisted in recruiting labour for three large munition factories; Member of Executive Committee of Llanelly Borough War Relief Fund for dependants of sailors and soldiers.   (M3881)

OWEN, Lieut.-Col. William Hugh, C.B.E., R.E.; *s.* of the late Thomas Owen, of Holyhead, N. Wales; *m.* 1919, Enid Strathearn, *d.* of Col. the Hon. Sir John Strathearn Hendrie, K.C.M.G., C.V.O. (*see* BURKE's *Peerage*). Served in the Great War, 1914–19 (despatches).   (C1727)

OWEN, Frederick Philip Lewis CUNLIFFE-, C.B.E., *b.* 30 Jan. 1855; *s.* of Sir Philip Cunliffe-Owen, K.C.B., K.C.M.G., etc.; *m.* Marguerite Isaure, *d.* of Jules de Godart, Comte du Planty et de Sourdis, France. *Educ.:* Lancing, Sussex. Vice-President of the Pilgrims' Society of the United States; Chairman of the France America Society; of the American and Hellenic Society; Chairman of the American Committee of Queen Alexandra's Lord Kitchener Memorial Fund; Officer of the Order of the Legion of Honour, and of the Instruction Publique of France; Grand Commander of the Greek Order of the Redeemer, the Order of Charles III. of Spain, the Osmanieh; Commander of the Italian Order of the Crown, of the Serbian Order of the White Eagle, and several other foreign orders. *Address:* 248, Central Park West, New York. *Clubs:* New York Yacht; Garrick.   (C2857)

OWEN, Major Alfred LLOYD-, O.B.E., M.C., R.E., *b.* 10 Feb. 1884; *s.* of the late Dr. A. Lloyd-Owen, M.D., of Southsea; *m.* Marion Elizabeth, *d.* of late Joseph Hayward Jervis, late Chief Constable of Warwickshire. *Educ.:* Portsmouth Grammar School; Royal Military Academy, Woolwich. *War Work:* Served with B.E.F. in France, Aug. 1914, till the Armistice; Commanded 11th Corps Signal Company, and 3rd Army Signal Company; subsequently to the Armistice was in command of the Signal Depot, B.E.F., with acting rank of Lieut.-Col. for a period of five months. *Address:* The Cot, Hayling Island, Hampshire.   (O1718)

OWEN, Muriel Mary, Mrs. TUDOR-, M.B.E., *b.* 24 Aug. 1876; *d.* of Henry J. Musgrave Croley; *m.* William Courtenay. I.C.S., The Abbey, Denbigh, *s.* of Edward Tudor-Owen. *Educ.:* Privately. *War Work:* Organised working party and raised £6000 funds for War purposes at Wadhwan and Gohelwad Prant; worked in connection with Convalescent Officers' Home at Palitana, from 1916–18. *Address:* c/o Messrs. Cox and Co., Bankers, Bombay.   (M7167)

OWENS, Lieut. John Daniel, O.B.E., R.N.R.

OWENS, Lieut. Joseph Hubert, C.I.E., M.B.E.

OWENS, Col. Robert Leonce, C.B.E., R.M., late The Royal Irish Regt., *b.* 3 Oct. 1862; *s.* of Robert Ivers Owens, of Limerick; *m.* Helen Mary Winifred, *d.* of Lieut.-Col. F. G. Shaw, late of Heathburn Hall, Riverstick, Co. Cork. *Educ.:* Privately. Commissioned May 1887, Bedford Regt.; promoted Capt., The Royal Irish Regt., Jan. 1895; retired Major, The Royal Irish Regt., March, 1908; promoted Lieut.-Col. 3rd Batt., April, 1913. *War Work:* Served in Dublin from Aug. 1914, and Commanded Batt. at top of Sackville Street, during Rebellion of 1916; despatches, London Gazette, Brevet of Col.; from March, 1918, until Oct. 1919, Commanded the troops in the following disturbed areas: Co. Clare, West Cork, North Tipperary, Westport, Co. Mayo, and Co. Tipperary; promoted Substantive Col., Jan. 1919; appointed Resident Magistrate, March, 1920. *Address:* Spring Gardens, Mallow, Co. Cork. *Clubs:* Kildare Street; County, Cork.   (C1728)

OWENS, William, M.B.E.

OWTRAM, Lieut.-Col. Herbert Hawkesworth, O.B.E.

OXBURGH, Lieut. George Stanley, M.B.E.

OXLAND, Capt. Thomas Benjamin, M.B.E.

OXLEY, Major Frederick John, O.B.E., R.A.M.C.

OXLEY, John Stewart, C.B.E.; *s.* of the late John Stewart Oxley, of Fen Place, Turners Hill, Sussex; *m.* Helen Charlotte, *d.* of the late Charles D. Cumming, of Hayling, Epsom. *Educ.:* Charterhouse; Trinity Coll., Cambridge. Barrister-at-Law, and General Inspector, Ministry of Health. *Address:* Monks, Balcombe, Sussex. *Club:* Conservative.
                                                          (C585)

OXLEY, Alfred James RICE-, C.B.E., M.D., M.R.C.P., J.P., Member of the Order of Isabella the Catholic, *b.* Jan. 1856; *s.* of George Oxley, of Yorkshire; *m.* Eva Augusta, *d.* of C. E. Amos, C.E., of Clapham. *Educ.:* Doncaster Grammar School; Balliol Coll., Oxford; The London Hospital. Physician-in-Ordinary, H.R.H. Princess Beatrice; Mayor of the Royal Borough of Kensington; President, Kensington Council of Social Service; President, West London Medico-Chirurgical Society; Chairman, Council Society of Yorkshiremen in London; late Member Central Council British Medical Association. *War Work:* Hon. Medical Director and Acting Physician, H.R.H. Princess Beatrice's Auxiliary Hospital for Wounded Officers, and Dorchester House Hospital for Wounded Officers, during whole period of war; mentioned for valuable services in connection with war. *Address:* 5, Prince of Wales' Terrace, Kensington. *Club:* Roehampton.   (C1160)

OYLER, Cadet-Col. Alexander Wilfred, O.B.E., *b.* 19 Sept. 1884; *s.* of David Jonathan Oyler, of The Laurels, Millfield Lane, Highgate, N. 6. *Educ.:* St. Andrew's School, Eastbourne; Winchester Coll. Managing Director, Oylers, Limited, tyre manufacturers and Rapson Automobile Patents, Limited; Member London District Council of National Joint Industrial Rubber Council; Cadet-Col., Chief Staff Officer, London Division, Church Lads' Brigade; Member of Committee, London Diocesan Council for Welfare of Lads, and Seaside Camps for London Working Boys; Chairman, St. Pancras Juvenile Welfare Committee, and London Joint Council of Juvenile Organisations Committees, Board of Education. *Address:* The Laurels, Millfield Lane, Highgate, N. 6. *Clubs:* Cavendish; Royal Automobile; M.C.C.
                                                          (O11078)

OYSTON, William Fletcher, M.B.E., M.B., Ch.B., *b.* 26 Oct. 1873; *s.* of the Rev. George Oyston, B.A., of 116, Union Road, Sheffield; *m.* Florence Caroline, *d.* of Robert Marshall, J.P., Pontefract. *Educ.:* Kingswood School, Bath. M.O. Friends School, Ackworth; M.O. and Public Vaccinator, Hemsworth, R.D.C. *War Work:* M.O., Flounders Coll. Auxiliary Hospital, Ackworth, near Pontefract (100 beds). *Address:* High Ackworth, near Pontefract.   (M9207)

PACKARD, Major and Qr.-Mr. Joseph Thomas, O.B.E., R.A.M.C.

PACKE, Lieut.-Col. Edmund Christopher, D.S.O., O.B.E.

PACKE, Sir Edward Hussey, K.B.E., *b.* 6 Jan. 1878; *s.* of the late Hussey Packe, of Prestwold Hall, Leicestershire (*see* BURKE's *Landed Gentry*); *m.* the Hon. Mary Sydney Colebrooke, *d.* of Edward, 1st Lord Colebrooke (*see* BURKE's *Peerage*). *Educ.:* Eton. J.P. and D.L. for the County of Leicester; High Sheriff, 1911 : a member of the County Council, 1908–19; Assistant Priv. Sec. to Sec. of State for War (Marquis of Landsowne), 1900; Assist. Private Sec. to First Lord of the Admiralty (the Earl of Selborne), 1901–5, and to the Earl of Cawdor, 1905; a Government Director of the Anglo-Persian Oil Co., since 1919. *War Work:* Attached to the Civil Staff of the Admiralty, 4 Aug. 1914, as Assistant to the Permanent Sec. of the Admiralty; appointed Assistant Private Sec. to the First Lord of the Admiralty (the Right Hon. A. J. Balfour), 1915–16, to Sir Edward Carson, 1917; Private Sec. to Sir

Eric Geddes, 1917–19, and to the Right Hon. Walter Long, 1919. *Addresses:* Prestwold Hall, Loughborough; 41, Charles Street, W. *Clubs:* Brooks's; Turf. (K406)

PACKE, Lieut.-Col. Frederick Edward, O.B.E., *b.* 12 May, 1879; *s.* of William Packe, of 1, Cavendish Square. *Educ.:* Marlborough. *War Work:* France, 1914, very severely wounded; France, 1915, very severely wounded; France, 1916. *Clubs:* Army and Navy; Arthur's. (O7540)

PACKER, Rev. George Francis, O.B.E.

PACKER, Henry Walter Percy, M.B.E.

PACKFORD, Lieut. Charles William, O.B.E., R.A.O.C.

PADDEY, Major John Elliott, O.B.E., *b.* 24 March, 1870; *s.* of George Paddey, of Wolverhampton; *m.* Edith Fanny, *d.* of Thomas Malpas, of Codsall. *Educ.:* St. Mary's, Wolverhampton. Superintendent Telegraphs, Post Office. *War Work:* Joined as subaltern in the R.E. in Dec. 1914; served in France, Macedonia, and Turkey; mentioned in despatches, 25 Oct. 1917 and 1 Nov. 1918; awarded the Medaille d'Honneur. *Address:* Allen Road, Wolverhampton. (O3055)

PADDISON, William Perceval, M.B.E.

PADDLE, Lieut. Albert, M.B.E.

PADDON, 2nd. Lieut. John Locke, M.B.E., R.A.S.C.

PADFIELD, Capt. Cecil James Carpenter, M.B.E., *b.* 4 July, 1893; *s.* of Joseph Webb Padfield, of Coleford, Somerset; *m.* Olga, *d.* of John Terlezky, of Vladivostok. *Educ.:* Halstow School; privately. *War Work:* Enlisted Sept. 21 1914; commissioned Sept. 27, 1915; gazetted Capt. Oct. 14, 1916; Hong Kong, 1916–18; Russia, 1918–19; Hythe Certificate (Distinguished) Musketry, 1915. *Addresses:* 24, Humber Road, Blackheath; 12, Markelovski, Vladivostok. (M6773)

PADFIELD, Major Frederick Henry, O.B.E.

PADWICK, Francis Herbert, C.B.E., J.P., *b.* 21 March, 1856; *s.* of Frederick Padwick, of West Thorney, Sussex; *m.* Mary Grace, *d.* of Rev. Thos. P. Boultbee, LL.D., Principal of London Coll. of Divinity, of Highbury, N. *Educ.:* Tonbridge School; Corpus Christi Coll., Camb.; Inner Temple. Barrister at law, and Agriculturist. *War Work:* Served on the Agricultural Consultative Committee, appointed by Lord Lucas (President of Board of Agriculture), and continued to serve under Lord Selborne and Lord Crawford; on Mr. Prothero's (Lord Ernle) Advisory Committee on Food Production; on Central Agricultural Advisory Council (appointed to advise President of Board of Agriculture and Ministry of Food); on Departmental Committee appointed by the President of Board of Agriculture to consider the Settlement and Employment on the land, in England and Wales, of discharged sailors and soldiers; Chairman of the West Sussex County War Agricultural Committee; Chairman of West Sussex County War Agricultural Executive Committee; Chairman of the West Sussex County National Services Committee (Neville Chamberlain's Scheme); served on West Sussex County Distress Committee; served on West Sussex County War Savings Committee; served Chichester Petty Sessional Division Emergency (Invasion) Committee; served Westbourne Local Tribunal; Chairman Westbourne Rural District Food Control Committee; Chairman Westbourne Rural District War Savings Committee; Chairman Westbourne Rural District Distress Committee. *Address:* The Red House, West Ashling, Chichester. *Club:* Farmers'. (C54)

PAFFARD, Paymaster-Lieut.-Comm. Reginald Douglas, O.B.E., R.N.

PAGE, Agnes Margaret, Mrs., M.B.E.

PAGE, Charles Herbert, O.B.E.

PAGE, Edward, M.B.E., *b.* 6 Feb. 1860; *s.* of Thomas Page, of Hastings; *m.* Elizabeth Caroline, *d.* of James Gregory, of New Zealand. *Educ.:* Church School, Hastings. Chief Fishery Officer under the Sussex Sea Fisheries. *War Work:* In connection with Board of Agriculture and Fisheries, and with the Admiralty. *Address:* 61, Tamworth Road, Hove, Sussex. (M821)

PAGE, Ethel Augusta, M.B.E.

PAGE, Capt. Francis James, O.B.E.

PAGE, Frederick Handley, C.B.E., *b.* 1885. Managing Director of Handley Page, Ltd., Aeroplane Manufacturers. (C586)

PAGE, Frederick James, O.B.E., *b.* 19 Dec. 1920; *s.* of Sidney John Page, of Yatton, Somerset; *m.* Margaret, *d.* of Henry Casswell, of Boston, Lincolnshire. *Educ.:* Castle Hill School, Ealing. Engineer; Locomotive and Carriage Supt. of Bombay-Baroda Central India Rly. *War Work:* Railway work in moving material and troops; manufacture of munitions and war material in railway shops; Member of Bombay Government Munitions Committee, and later of Advisory Committee to Munitions Board. *Club:* Royal Yacht (Bombay). (O4168)

PAGE, Lieut.-Col. Frederick William, O.B.E., Aust. A.O.C.

PAGE, George Albert, M.B.E.

PAGE, Capt. Harold James, M.B.E., B.Sc. (Lond.), A.I.C., R.F.A. (S.R.) (ret.), *b.* 29 May, 1890; *s.* of James William Page, of Carshalton, Surrey; *m.* Gladys Isabel, *d.* of Edward Easton Shepperd, of Knockholt, Kent. *Educ.:* Southend-on-Sea High School, and Univ. Coll., Univ. of London. Head of Soil Chemistry Department to Lawes Agricultural Trust, Rothamsted Experimental Station, Harpenden. *War Work:* Served in France in R.F.A. from 1914–16; twice mentioned in despatches; wounded July, 1916; served under Ministry of Munitions at Research Department, Royal Arsenal,

Woolwich, from 1917–19. *Address:* Rothamsted, Harpenden, Herts. (M5510)

PAGE, Howard John, M.B.E., *b.* 23 March, 1856, *s.* of John Page, Supt. of Constabulary, Dorking; *m.* Florence Helena, *d.* of John Guttridge Burry. *Educ.:* Mr. Hooke's School, at Dorking, Surrey. *Address:* Epsom Road, Guildford, Surrey. (M9210)

PAGE, James, M.B.E., Esquire of the Order of St. John of Jerusalem, Town Councillor, *b.* 21 June, 1864; *s.* of Thos. A. Page, of South Shields; *m.* Frances Charlotte Mary, *d.* of Edward Smith, of Quebec, Canada. *Educ.:* Smoults Academy. Architect. Hon. Sec. St. John Ambulance Association, South Shields Centre, 30 years; Capt. South Shields Volunteer Life Brigade (Rocket Life Saving Apparatus); Capt. South Shields Golf Club. *War Work:* Assistant County Director Durham V.A.D.'s; District Staff Officer, St. John Ambulance Brigade; Chief Staff Officer, Royal Naval Medical Transport Corps; Assistant Commandant, No. 2 V.A.D. Hospital, South Shields. *Address:* South View, South Shields. (M3882)

PAGE, Jessie Ellen, Mrs., M.B.E.

PAGE, John Foulger, M.B.E.

PAGE, Capt. Reginald, M.B.E., *b.* 10 Oct. 1881; *s.* of William John Page, of Dulwich, London; *m.* Margaret Helena, *d.* of William Parkinson, of Princes Park, Liverpool. *Educ.:* Liverpool Institute. *War Work:* Served in the Rifle Brigade, 1915–19. *Address:* 107, Kingsley Road, Princes Park, Liverpool. (M9212)

PAGE, Robert Palgrave, C.B.E., *b.* 29 Nov. 1867; *s.* of the late Samuel Page. *Educ.:* Harrow, and Trinity Hall, Cambridge. *War Work:* Intelligence Staff, War Office. *Address:* 33, Dover Street, W. 1. *Clubs:* Travellers'; Orleans. (C2858)

PAGE, Rev. Walter Sutton, O.B.E., B.A., B.D.

PAGE, William Charles, M.B.E.

PAGE, William Morton, C.B.E., *b.* 1883; *s.* of George Charles Page, of Ashby-de-la-Zouch; *m.* 1911, Nora Margaret, *d.* of W. H. Harsant, of Clifton. *Educ.:* King's Coll. Cambridge (B.A. 1905, M.A. and Fellow, 1908). H.M. Inspector of Schools; an Officer of Order of St. Maurice and St. Lazarus of Italy; Chevalier of Legion of Honour; Assist. Sec. for Requirements and Statistics, Ministry of Munitions, since 1917. *Address:* Minster Yard, Lincoln. (C587)

PAGET, Major Eden Wilberforce, C.B.E., *b.* 9 Sept. 1865; *s.* of Rev. Edward Heneage Paget (*see* BURKE'S *Peerage,* Anglesey, M.), Vicar of Hoxne, Suffolk, and Hon. Emma Mary, 3rd *d.* of Robert, 3rd Lord Auckland, Bishop of Bath and Wells (*see* BURKE'S *Peerage*); *m.* 4 Dec. 1898, Gertrude Amy, *d.* of the late William Maudesley Charnley, of Preston. (C588)

PAGET, Lieut.-Comm. Henry Edward Clarence, C.B.E., J.P., R.N.V.R., *b.* 20 March, 1860; *s.* of the Rev. Edward and Hon. Mrs. Paget (*see* BURKE'S *Peerage*); *m.* Maria Caroline, *d.* of the late Thomas Simon Bolitho, of Trengwainton (*see* BURKE'S *Landed Gentry*). Late Commissioner of Police, Calcutta. *War Work:* Naval Intelligence Departments, and afterwards organised and commanded the Metropolitan Observation Service. *Address:* 31, Bryanston Square, London, W. 1. *Club:* Boodle's. (C1018)

PAGET, Louisa Margaret Leila Wemyss, Lady, G.B.E.

PAGET, Lady Muriel Evelyn Vernon, O.B.E., *b.* 19 Aug. 1876; *d.* of 11th Earl of Winchilsea and Nottingham (*see* BURKE'S *Peerage*); *m.* Sir Richard Arthur Surteus, *s.* of the late Rt. Hon. Sir Richard Paget, Bart., P.C. (*see* BURKE'S *Peerage*). *Educ.:* At Home. *War Work:* 1914–15, invalid Kitchens of London; 1915–18, inaugurated Anglo-Russian Hospitals; served at intervals in Russia, in Petrograd, and on Southern Fronts, and in Roumania; organised allied civil relief in Kiev, 1918; 1919–20, organised relief missions, Czecho-Slovakia, Crimea and Dvinsk. *Addresses:* Cranmore Hall, Shepton Mallet; 1, Devonshire Terrace, Lancaster Gate, W. 2. *Club:* Ladies' Athenæum. (O43)

PAGET, Rosalind Margaret, Mrs., O.B.E., *b.* Feb. 1856; *d.* of Peter Northall Laurie, Pax Hill Park, Lenchfield, Sussex; *m.* William Henry, *s.* of Lord William Paget, R.N. *War Work:* Organised and superintended Westminster War Hospitals Supply Depot for 4 years; Y.M.C.A. Canteen Work throughout the war. *Address:* 12A, Evelyn Mansions, Carlisle Place, Victoria Street, S.W. *Club:* Forum. (O11079)

PAIN, Dorothy Alice, O.B.E. Superintendent of Class Rooms in which inmates of St. Dunstan's learn Braille. (O11920)

PAIN, Lieut.-Col. Edgar, O.B.E., B.E., A.R.S.M., M.I.M.M., *b.* 21 Oct. 1882; *s.* of Leopold Pain, of Welwyn, Herts.; *m.* Mary Millicent, *d.* of R. D. Prior. Came from Africa. R.E. April 1916; joined 170th Coy. R.E., in France as 2nd Lieut.; transferred to H.Q. 1st Army on Q. Staff, July 1916; D.A.D.G.T. 1st Army, Dec. 1916, with rank of Capt.; promoted Major, Oct. 1918; A.D.G.T. 1st Army, July 1918, with rank of Lt.-Col.; transferred to Div. G.H.Q. Ipa., Dec. 1918, and to Army of the Rhine. Jan. 1919. *Address:* The Gables, Cleveland, Transvaal. *Club:* Rand. Johannesburg. (O5561)

PAIN, Brig.-Gen. Sir George William HACKET-, K.B.E., C.B., J.P., *b.* 1855; *s.* of the late George Pain, formerly in the 11th Hussars; *m.* Saidee, *d.* of S. Merton, of Sidney, N.S. Wales. *Educ.:* Elizabeth Coll., Guernsey, and privately. Divisional Commissioner of Royal Irish Constabulary for Ulster, and Justice of Peace for every county in the province; late 2nd Worcester Regt., formerly Queen's Royal Regt., Comdg. No. VII Dist., 1908–11; ret. 1912. Served in the Soudan,

1888, action of Gamaizah, capture of Tokar (horse shot, medal with clasp, bronze star with clasp, 3rd class Medjidieh, 3rd class Osmanieh); with Dongola Expedition 1896 (horse shot, despatches, medal with two clasps, Brevet Lieut.-Col.), with Nile Expedition, 1897–8 (medal); in S. African War, 1899–1902 (despatches), two medals, five clasps, C.B. *War Service:* Raised and commanded 108th Infantry Brigade. Ulster Division, in 1914; served in France; awarded 1915 star, Victory and Allies' Medals; commanded Northern District Ireland, 1916–20. *Clubs:* United Service; Kildare Street: Automobile. (K301)

PAINTER, Paymaster-Lieut. Arthur Collett, O.B.E., R.N.

PAINTER, Thomas Abbott, M.B.E., *b.* 11 Nov. 1864; *s.* of J. Painter, of Launceston, Cornwall; *m.* Selina Ann, *d.* of Thomas Holmes, of Edensor, Derbyshire. *Educ.:* Wesleyan Schools, Doncaster, Yorkshire. Assistant District Manager, G.N.R., King's Cross, London. *War Work:* Commandant of No. 44 Middlesex V.A.D.; Assistant County Director, Middlesex (N. E. District); Organising and Training Detachments; attending convoys of wounded trains, and air raid duties. *Address:* 47, Elvendon Road, Palmers Green, London, N. 13. (M3884)

PAINTING, Helen, M.B.E,

PAISH, Leonard Alfred, O.B.E.

PAKEMAN, John Robert, C.B.E., *b.* 22 July 1860; *s.* of Robert Pakeman, of Highgate; *m.* 1st, Florence, *d.* of Major Drerer, 2nd, Charlotte Isobel, widow of Capt. Julian Spencer-Mitchell. *Educ.:* Private School. Solicitor. *War Work:* Chairman of Section B, London Appeal Tribunal, and Chairman of other War Committees in the City of London; also Advisory Member of the American Leather Mission. *Addresses:* 25, Victoria Road, Kensington, W. 8; 16, Ironmonger Lane, E.C. *Clubs:* Constitutional; Royal Automobile; Guildhall. (C1019)

PAKINGTON, Hon. Mary Augusta, M.B.E., *b.* 21 June, 1878; *d.* of Herbert Perrott Murray Pakington, 3rd Baron Hampton, of Westwood and Hampton Lovett (*see* BURKE'S *Peerage*). *War Work:* Hon. Sec. Worcestershire Women's War Agricultural Committee; Member of Hartlebury V.A.D. *Address:* Waresley Court, near Kidderminster. (M9213)

PALAEOLOGUS, Harriett Oatman, O.B.E. (O11788b)

PALFREMAN, Eng.-Lieut. Edwin, O.B.E., R.N.

PALIN, Helen Grace, M.B.E.

PALIN, Major Randle Harry, O.B.E., I.A.

PALING, Vincent, M.B.E., *b.* 1882. *s.* of Robert Paling; *m.* Lily Gertrude, *d.* of William Ranger, of Stroud. *Educ.:* Birmingham. Secretary. *War Work:* Sec. to Controller of Gun Manufacture, Ministry of Munitions, being associated with Ministry from inception in 1915 to June, 1919. *Address:* Mossend, Lanarkshire, Scotland. (M2259)

PALLIN, Sydney David, M.B.E.

PALLIN, Major (T. Col.) William Alfred, C.B.E., D.S.O., *b.* 6 June, 1873; *s.* of William Pallin, of Athgarvan Lodge, Curragh Camp, Co. Kildare, Ireland; *m.* Agnes Marie Marthé, *d.* of Emile de Lenclos, of Aubyn St. Vaast, France. *Educ.:* Aravon, Bray, Co. Wicklow, Ireland; Cheltenham Coll., England. Major (T. Col.) Royal Army Veterinary Corps; Fellow of the Royal Coll. of Veterinary Surgeons; Fellow of the Royal Society of Edinburgh; Deputy Director-General R.A.V.S. *War Work:* Vet. Officer-in-charge, Royal Horse Guards, 1914–15; Assist. Director of Veterinary Services, 37th Division, 1915–16; D.D.V.S., L. of C., Northern B.E.F., 1916–17, and H.Q. Third Army, B.E.F., 1917–19. *Address:* 36, Buckingham Gate, London, S.W. 1. *Club:* Junior Army and Navy. (C1300)

PALLIS, Lieut. Andreas, M.B.E.

PALMER, Capt. Alexander Croyden, O.B.E., F.R.C.S., R.A.M.C.

PALMER, Major Archibald James, O.B.E.

PALMER, Major Basil Owen, M.B.E., 1st Border Regt., *s.* of the late Edward Palmer, of Froddington House, Southsea. *Educ.:* Vickerys Coll. Joined the Army in 1899; served in the S. African War, 1900–2; took part in the operations in the Transvaal, 30 Nov. 1900, to 31 May, 1902 (Queen's medal with 3 clasps, and King's medal with 2 clasps). *War Work:* Employed on Recruiting at Whitehall. *Address:* 96, Piccadilly. *Club:* Junior Naval and Military. (M5511)

PALMER, Paymaster-Lieut. Bennet, O.B.E., R.N.R.

PALMER, Major Charles Ernest, O.B.E., R.E.

PALMER, Major Charles William Gustavus, O.B.E., T.D., *b.* 14 Jan. 1875; *s.* of W. J. Palmer, of Bournemouth; *m.* Ethel Blanche, *d.* of the late C. W. Keep, of Bournemouth. *Educ.:* Private Schools. Wine Merchant. *War Work:* Left 1/7th Hampshire Regt. in Sept. 1914; helped form 2/7th Hampshire Regt.; proceeded with that unit to India in 1914; stationed at Trimulgherry (Deccan), Jubbulpore, Subathu, and Deolali; regiment ordered to Mesopotamia in 1917; stationed at Azizieh, Amara, and the Jabal Hamdin; twice mentioned in despatches. *Address:* 25, Richmond Park Crescent, Bournemouth. (O6682)

PALMER, Clara Adeline, M.B.E.

PALMER, Lieut.-Col. Claude Bowes, C.B.E., J.P., D.L., Knight of Grace, Order of St. John of Jerusalem, *b.* 29 March, 1868; *s.* of Sir Charles Mark Palmer, 1st Bart., M.P., of Grinkle Park, Yorkshire (*see* BURKE'S *Peerage*); *m.* Marian, O.B.E., A.R.R.C., Lady of Grace, Order of St. John of Jerusalem (*q.v.*), *d.* of Edward Charlton Ramsey, of South Shields, and widow of Edmund Charles Jenkins. *Educ.:* Cheltenham Coll., and Royal School of Mines, Freiberg, Saxony. Com-

missioner, Northumberland, Durham, North and East Yorkshire, St. John Ambulance Brigade; County Director, V.A.D., Northumberland and Durham; Member of Durham Territorial Force Association; Member of Durham County Licensing Committee; is a J.P. and D.L., Co. of Durham; Lieut., late Army Motor Reserve of Officers. *War Work:* Had charge of all Red Cross work of the Order of St. John and British Red Cross Society in Northumberland and Durham; raised and commanded (Lieut.-Col.) Northumberland R.A.M.C. (V.); raised and commanded Royal Naval Medical Transport Corps; raised two Volunteer Field Ambulances in Durham; took contingents of men of the St. John Ambulance Brigade to France, 1914–15; inspected, on behalf of the French Red Cross, over 200 French Hospitals in France; in charge of Auxiliary Medical Arrangements for Coast Defences of Tyne and Tees Garrisons; had charge of 47 Auxiliary Hospitals in Northumberland and Durham. *Addresses:* Wardley Hall, Pelaw-on-Tyne; 28, Lexham Gardens, W. 8. *Clubs:* Royal Automobile; County, Durham; Union, Newcastle-on-Tyne. (C261)

PALMER, Capt. Creighton Ross, O.B.E., A.P.C.

PALMER, Lieut. Edward George, M.B.E.

PALMER, Capt. Edward Henry Banks, O.B.E., R.A.F.

PALMER, Comm. Edwin Mansergh, O.B.E., R.N.

PALMER, Ellen Amelia, Mrs., M.B.E., Q.M.A.A.C.

PALMER, Major Eric Barton, O.B.E.

PALMER, Capt. Ernest Henry, O.B.E., R.A.O.C.

PALMER, Florence Mary, M.B.E.; *d.* of the late Samuel Palmer, of Northcourt, Hampstead. *War Work:* Joint organiser of Belgian Refugee Hostel, followed by club for same, Sept. 1914, to July, 1915; joint organiser of Hampstead War Hospital Supply Depot, July, 1915, to March, 1919. *Address:* 1, Compagne Gardens, N.W. (M9214)

PALMER, Capt. Gilbert, M.B.E., R.A.F.

PALMER, Lieut.-Col. Herbert James Leslie, O.B.E., R.A.O.C.

PALMER, Horace Frank, M.B.E.

PALMER, Lieut. Hubert Leslie, M.B.E.

PALMER, Major John Harald Gore, O.B.E., I.A.

PALMER, Surgeon-Major John Irwin, O.B.E. (V.M.S. ret.); *s.* of John Palmer, of Eliot Place, Blackheath; *m.* Alice Scott, *d.* of Charles Wild, of Hampton Wick. *Educ.:* Guy's Hospital. Surgeon; Visiting Medical Officer, Special Surgical Neurological Hospital, Church Lane, S.W. *War Work:* Visiting Surgeon, Tooting Military Hospital and Mile End Military Hospital; attached Special Orthopædic Hospital, Ducane Road, W.; Medical Officer, Special Surgical Neurological Hospital, Ministry of Pensions, Tooting, S.W.; Member and Hon. Sec. Marylebone Medical War Committee. *Address:* 31, New Cavendish Street, Harley Street, W. (O11832)

PALMER, Surg.-Lieut. Comdr. John Ramsey, O.B.E., L.D.S., R.N.V.R.

PALMER, Capt. Leonard Edgcombe, O.B.E., R.A.F.

PALMER, Louise Madeleine, Mrs., O.B.E.

PALMER, Marian, Mrs., O.B.E., Royal Red Cross, 2nd Class; *d.* of Edward Charlton Ramsey, of South Shields; *m.* Lieut.-Col. Claude Bowes, C.B.E., D.L. (*q.v.*), *s.* of Sir Charles Mark Palmer, 1st Bart., M.P., of Grinkle Park, Yorkshire (*see* BURKE'S *Peerage*). Formerly Lady District Superintendent, Northumberland, Durham, North and East Yorkshire St. John Ambulance Brigade; late Lady Assistant, County Director Voluntary Aid Detachments, Co. of Durham. *War Work:* Commandant, 1st Durham V.A.D. Hospital (110 beds), Whinney House, Gateshead; and St. John Ambulance Brigade Hospital (50 beds), Saltwell Towers, Gateshead; as Lady Assist. County Director (Durham) had supervision of 8 Auxiliary Hospitals; mentioned by Secretary of State for valuable services rendered; late Lady Superintendent, Royal Naval Medical Transport Corps. *Addresses:* Wardley Hall, Pelaw-on-Tyne, Co. Durham; 28, Lexham Gardens, W. 8. *Club:* Ladies' Army and Navy. (O625)

PALMER, May Blanche, Mrs., M.B.E., *b.* 6 Jan. 1876; *d.* of Alexander Place, of Halifax; *m.* Edward, *s.* of James Edward Palmer, Major, Indian Army, of Deccan, Hyderabad, India. *Educ.:* Privately. Lady Superintendent of Liptons, Ltd. *War Work:* Lady Superintendent of the munition workers colony at Slades Green, Kent, from 1916–19. *Address:* Tigarah, 11, St. Mary's Rd., Highbury, London, N. (M824)

PALMER, Nellie Hurcomb, M.B.E., *b.* 27 Oct. 1889; *d.* of William Henry Palmer, of Nottingham. *Educ.:* Lichfield High School; Birmingham Women's Settlement. Organising Sec. National Union of Women's Suffrage Societies, 1912–14. *War Work:* Senior Lady Superintendent, both technical and welfare, Army Pay Dept.; stationed at Exeter Army Pay Office. *Address:* Nadderwater, Exeter. *Club:* Exeter Ladies'. (M3885)

PALMER, Philip, O.B.E.

PALMER, Lieut. Reginald Howard, O.B.E., R.N.V.R.

PALMER, Robert Edward, O.B.E., B.Sc., M.Inst.M. & M., *b.* 16 Dec. 1865; *s.* of Charles Palmer, K.C., of Prince Edward Island, Canada; *m.* Mary Helen Constance, *d.* of Charles Maitland Leonard, of Canada. *Educ.:* Prince of Wales' Coll., P.E. Island; McGill Univ., Montreal. Consulting Mining Engineer, Rio Tinto Co., Ltd. *War Work:* Sectional Director, Dept. of Iron and Steel Production, Ministry of Munitions, London. *Addresses:* 3, Lombard Street, London, E.C.; 55, Iverna Court, Kensington, W. 8. *Club:* Mining and Metallurgical. (O11082)

PALMER, Rosa Jane, M.B.E.

PALMER, Sydney Joseph, M.B.E., M.D., *b.* 1863 ; *s.* of Joseph Tett Palmer, of Seaton, Devon ; *m.* Florence, *d.* of Dr. William Palmer Rowe, of Liverpool. *Educ.* : Framingham Coll. ; St. Bart.'s Hospital ; Durham Univ. Member Special Medical Board, Ministry of Pensions ; late Surgeon Liverpool Police ; Hon. Medical Officer, Liverpool Penitentiary and Magdalen Home, Liverpool. *War Work* : M.O. in charge Netherfield Road Auxiliary Military Hospital, Liverpool. *Address* : 15, Oxford Street, Liverpool. (M10281)

PALMER, Capt. Vivian Trestrail Dampier, O.B.E., J.P., *b.* 29 Dec. 1876 ; *s.* of the late Col. James Dampier Palmer, M.P. of Herondon Hall, Tenterden ; *m.* Melita, *d.* of Fairless Harrison, of Newcastle-on-Tyne. *Educ.* : Marlborough Coll. Served in S. African War, 1899–1900 ; Hon. Lieut. in the Army, 1900 ; Capt. 3rd Batt. E. Kent Regt., 1904–7 ; late 2nd Lieut. Coldstream Guards ; C.C. Kent (on roll for High Sheriff, 1920) *War Work* : Capt. (temp.), 1914–19 ; Recruiting Staff Officer, 3rd Regimental District ; Sec. South-Eastern Region, Ministry of National Service, and Private Sec. to Sir Cecil Beck, M.P. (Parliamentary Sec., Ministry of National Service). *Address* : Herondon Hall, Tenterden, Kent. *Club* : Junior Carlton.
(O1724)

PALMER, Capt. Walter Benjamin, O.B.E.
PALMER, Lieut. William, O.B.E., R.N.
PALMER, Capt. William, M.B.E.
PALMER, William Harold, O.B.E.
PALMER, William Henry, M.B.E.
PALMER, Lieut.-Col. Frederick Carey Stukeley SAMBORNE-, C.B.E.

PAM, Major Albert, O.B.E., Legion d'Honneur, Croix de Guerre ; *m.* Maude le Clerc (*q.v.*), *d.* of the late Gen. J. G. Faugh K.H.S. (O5660)

PAM, Lieut.-Col. Edgar, O.B.E.

PAM, Maude Le Clerc, Mrs., O.B.E., and mentioned in despatches ; *d.* of the late Gen. J. G. Faught, K.H.S. ; *m.* Major Albert Pam, O.B.E., Legion d' Honneur, Croix de Guerre. While waiting for Hospital to be used, worked at Canteen in charge of shift of 30, and Red Cross working parties. *War Work* : Lent own house, fully equipped for 120 beds, as Auxiliary Hospital, and personally organised and administered same as Commandant and Quartermaster from March, 1916, to March, 1919 ; raised detachment Herts 48 to work hospital ; Vice-President, B.R.C.S. for Wormley and Broxbourne ; raised substantial sums to send to headquarters of the B.R.C.S. *Address* : Wormley Bury, near Broxbourne, Herts. *Club* : Ladies' Imperial. (O1726)

PANCHAUD, Lieut.-Col. Harry George Louis, O.B.E.

PANCKRIDGE, William Panckridge, O.B.E., M.B., *b.* 14 March, 1874 ; *s.* of Francis Panckridge, of Broadwell, Oxon ; *m.* Maria, *d.* of — Waiting of Johannesburg. *Educ.* : Forest School ; Middlesex Hospital. Hon. Surgeon, Petersfield Cottage Hospital ; M.O. Petersfield Isolation Hospital Committee. *War Work* : M.O. Adhurst St. Mary, Clayton Court, and Heath Lodge Auxiliary Red Cross Hospitals. *Address* : Winton House, Petersfield. *Club* : Royal Automobile.
(O11083)

PANNELL, Charles Thomas, M.B.E.
PANTER, Lieut. George William, M.B.E., R.A.F.
PANTHER, Helen Annie, Mrs., M.B.E.
PANTLING, Frederick, M.B.E., R.N.
PAPE, Comm. Percy John, O.B.E., R.N.R., R.D.
PAPE, William George, O.B.E.
PAPWORTH, Frederic William, O.B.E., F.S.A.A., Assistant Accountant-General, Admiralty. *War Work* : At Admiralty. *Address* : 7, Whitefriars Crescent, Westcliff, Essex. (O11085)
PARAMOUR, Capt. Frank Richard, M.B.E.
PARDOE, Major Edward Percy Hamilton, O.B.E.
PARDOE, Winnie, Mrs., O.B.E.
PARDON, Eva, Mrs., M.B.E.
PARES, Sir Bernard, K.B.E., *b.* 1 March, 1867 ; *s.* of the late John Pares, J.P., of Westfield, Southsea ; *m.* Margaret Ellis, *d.* of E. A. Dixon. *Educ.* : Harrow, and Trinity Coll., Cambridge. Professor of Russian in the Univ. of London ; formerly Professor in the Univ. of Liverpool, 1908–17. *War Work* : Attached as official correspondent of H.M. Government to the Russian forces ; later attached to H.M. Ambassador in Petrograd ; attached to the Russian Red Cross ; Soldiers' Cross and Medal of St. George ; gave addresses at many meetings in Russia and in the chief towns of Siberia. *Addresses* : Westfield, Adelaide Road, Surbiton ; King's Coll., London, W.C 2 *Club* : Univ., Liverpool. (K226)
PARGITER, David Scott, C.B.E. Chairman of S. African Shipping Committee for Homeward Loading. (C729?)
PARIS, William Richard, M.B.E., R.N.
PARISH, Arthur John, C.B., C.B.E., *b.* 1861 ; *s.* of the late Rev. William Samuel Parish, Rector of Freckenham, Suffolk ; *m.* 1911, Helen Mary, *d.* of William Griffiths, C.E., of 61, Sinclair Road, Kensington, W. *Educ.* : King's Sch., Ely, and St. Peter's Coll., Camb. (B.A., 26th Wrangler, 1884 ; M.A. 1887). Appointed a Naval Instructor, R.N., 1886 ; Dep. Sup. of Naval Examination, 1909 ; Chief Naval Instructor, 1917 ; Dep. Adviser on Naval Education, 1919 ; retired, 1919. *Address* : The Red Gable, Cleardown, Woking. (C1199)
PARISH, Henry, M.B.E., *b.* 27 May, 1862 ; *s.* of Henry Parish, of The Hollies, Halesowen, Worcestershire ; *m.* Florence Kate, *d.* of Edward Dutton, of Oldbury, Worcestershire. *Educ.* : Townshend House School, Kidderminster, and Cambridge House School, Birchfields, Birmingham. Sec. of Women Unionists War Savings Association ; Member of District

Nursing Association, and Civic Recreation Committees ; a Foundation Manager, Correspondent, and Hon. Treas. of Christchurch Schools ; Member of Lichfield Diocesan Council ; Member of Stanley Trust. *War Work* : From the commencement of the war did a lot of useful and important work as District Head of the Incorporated Soldiers' and Sailors' Help Society, and as a member of the Local War Pensions Committee ; Chairman of Enquiries and Grants Sub-Committee ; Member of Finance and General Purposes Sub-Committee, and Disablement Sub-Committee ; represents Local War Pension Committee on Ministry of Labour, Employment Department, and on Association of Local War Pension Committees. *Address* : Hafod, 8, Grange Road, West Bromwich. (M9219)

PARISH, Brevet Lieut.-Col. Woodbine, C.B.E., *b.* 21 Sept. 1862 ; *s.* of Frank Parish, of London ; *m.* Frances Helen, *d.* of George Brittain, of Tunbridge Wells. *Educ.* : Cheltenham Coll. Director of several Railways. *War Work* : D.A.D.M War Office Staff. *Address* : 2, Stanhope Street, Hyde Park. *Clubs* : St. Stephen's ; Argentine ; Ranelagh ; Royal St. George's ; M.C.C. (C1988)

PARISOTTI, Rev. Albert, O.B.E., C.F., *b.* 8 May, 1885 ; *s.* of L. Parisotti. *Educ.* : Old Hall, Ware. (O6265)

PARK, Ernest William, M.B.E.
PARK, Major Frank Stewart, O.B.E., Can. A.M.C.
PARK, James Harvey Williamson, O.B.E.
PARK, Thomas, O.B.E.
PARK, Major William, O.B.E., R.A.F.
PARK, Rev. William Robert, C.I.E., O.B.E.
PARKER, Arthur Claude, M.B.E.
PARKER, Capt. Arthur Stanley, O.B.E., *b.* 12 May, 1894 ; *s.* of Favor Parker, of Mildenhall, Suffolk. Served with 5th Batt. Suffolk Regt. *Addresses* : Mildenhall, Suffolk ; Soy P.O., Kenya Colony. (O6266)
PARKER, Major Beltran William, O.B.E., R.A.S.C.
PARKER, Bertha Theodore England, M.B.E.
PARKER, Charles, M.B.E.
PARKER, Lieut. Charles Anson, M.B.E.
PARKER, Capt. Charles Percival, O.B.E.
PARKER, Charles Thomas, C.B.E., J.P., *b.* 6 Jan. 1859 ; *s.* of John Francis Parker, Osbournby, Lincs ; *m.* Mary Ann, *d.* of Charles Hunt, of North Hykeham. Entered City Council, 1901 ; Mayor, 1909–10. *War Work* : Chairman, Local Military Service Tribunal throughout its existence ; Mayor, 1915–16, 1916–17, 1917–18, 1918–19 ; first Chairman, Local Food Control Committee ; Chairman, Watch Committee ; took great interest in organisation of Special Constabulary in arrangements for dealing with enemy aerial attack. (C2859)
PARKER, Major and Qr.-Mr. Edward Augustus, O.B.E. M.C., D.C.M.
PARKER, Major Edwin Charles Lewis, O.B.E., R.A.S.C., *b.* 8 Jan. 1874 ; *s.* of the Rev. Fredk. Wm. Parker, M.A., of Cheltenham, formerly of Montgomery, N. Wales. *Educ.* : Winchester. Solicitor. *War Work* : Gazetted Lieut., R.A.S.C. April, 1915 ; Capt., Aug., 1915 ; Major, Aug. 1917 ; Mesopotamia, 1917–19 ; thrice mentioned in despatches. *Address* : Salisbury. (O6684)
PARKER, Edwin Thorley, O.B.E.
PARKER, Capt. Ernest Edward, O.B.E., R.N.
PARKER, Ethel Elizabeth, M.B.E., *b.* 27 Jan. 1886. *Address* : Charlwood, Harrow View, Harrow. (M9221)
PARKER, F., Mrs., O.B.E.
PARKER, Frances Mary, O.B.E. M.B.E., W.A.A.C.
PARKER, Major Frank Woolmer, O.B.E.
PARKER, Surg.-Comm. Frederick William, O.B.E., R.N.
PARKER, George Phillips, O.B.E., J.P.
PARKER, Haydon, O.B.E.
PARKER, Lieut. Henry Charles, M.B.E., R.E.
PARKER, 2nd Lieut. Hugh Love, M.B.E.
PARKER, James George, M.B.E., *b.* 15 Jan. 1864 ; *s.* of the late David Parker, of London ; *m.* Rosina Anne (who died), *d.* of the late William Jones, of Barnstaple, Devon. *Educ.* : Privately. Assist. Commander H. Div. Metropolitan Special Constabulary (now retired) ; Assistant Town Clerk, Metropolitan Borough of Stepney ; Liveryman of the City of London (Basketmaker's Company). *War Work* : Assistant organising officer of the Stepney National Reserve since May, 1911 ; King's Coronation Medal, 1912 ; enrolled as a Special Constable on 4 Dec. 1914 ; promoted to Inspector on the Headquarter Staff, and Assistant Commander in May, 1915 ; carried out the administrative duties, and also the reorganisation of the Force ; paid special attention to recruiting, serving until 1 Nov. 1919 (Special Constabulary Medal) ; enlisted in the Volunteer Force in 1881 ; resigned on account of official duties in 1902 (Volunteer Long Service Medal) ; one of the promoters and first Capt. of the Stepney Municipal Staff Miniature Rifle Club. *Address* : Fern Cottage, 82, Chetwynd Road, Dartmouth Park, London, N.W. 5. (M9222)
PARKER, John, O.B.E.
PARKER, 2nd Lieut. John, M.B.E.
PARKER, John Joslin, M.B.E., R.A.S.C.
PARKER, Rev. Joseph, O.B.E.
PARKER, Capt. Leslie Clive, O.B.E., A.I.F.
PARKER, Mary Jeannette, M.B.E.
PARKER, Owen, C.B.E., J.P. for County of Northampton, *b.* 21 Aug. 1860 ; *s.* of the late Alderman Charles Parker, J.P., of Higham Ferrers ; *m.* Kate Annie, *d.* of the late G. F. Packwood, of Rushden. *Educ.* : Chichele Grammar School. Boot and Shoe Manufacturer ; President of the Incorporated Federated Associations of Boot and Shoe Manufacturers of

Great Britain and Ireland; Churchwarden of the Parish Church; Member of the Northants Territorial Force Association. *War Work:* Technical Adviser to the War Office (Raw Material Dept.); Controller of War Time Boot Scheme; Member of the Leather Control Board. *Address:* Ivy House, Higham Ferrers. *Clubs:* Junior Constitutional; Northampton County. (C2860)

PARKER, Capt. Percy Frank, M.B.E., R.A.O.C.

PARKER, Reginald Barcroft, O.B.E., *b.* 1855; *s.* of the Rev. Edward Parker, Vicar of Waddington, Yorks; *m.* Margaret Anne, *d.* of Col. T. G. Parker, D.L., of Browsholme, Yorks. *Educ.:* Rossall. *War Work:* Organised Soldiers' and Sailors' Canteen at Selby Station,1915–19, which provided food for upwards of 1,000,000 men; Military Representative on two tribunals, twice commended in 1917 by Recruiting Service Bulletin for his appeals for withdrawal of Exemption Certificates held by young men, to enable them to take the place of soldiers, who, after being wounded, were sent back to the trenches. *Address:* Milford Hall, S. Milford, Yorks. (O11088)

PARKER, Capt. Reginald Frank, O.B.E., M.C.

PARKER, Capt. Robert Derwent, O.B.E.

PARKER, Capt. Ronald Francis, M.B.E., *b.* 26 Jan. 1883; *s.* of Hon. Francis Parker (*see* BURKE'S *Peerage*, Macclesfield, E.). *Educ.:* Eton; R.M.A., Woolwich. *War Work:* Commander, Metropolitan Special Constabulary, R.H. and R.F.A. (1914 Star). *Clubs:* Bachelors'; Pratt's. (M9223)

PARKER, Major Sidney Ernest, M.B.E., A.F.C., R.A.F.

PARKER, Lieut. Sidney James, O.B.E.

PARKER, Capt. Thomas Mayor, M.B.E., R.A.V.C.

PARKER, Capt. Walter Henry. C.B.E., R.D., R.N.R., *War Work:* As Commodore of Convoys (despatches). (C1200)

PARKER, Capt. Wilfrid Watson, M.B.E., T.D., *b.* 13 June, 1869; *s.* of the late Sir Henry Watson Parker, Kt., of Hampstead; *m.* Frances Charlotte, *d.* of the late Alfred Purssell, of Hampstead. *Educ.:* Beaumont Coll., Old Windsor. Solicitor. *War Work:* Musketry Staff appointment. *Addresses:* 35, Bloomsbury Square, London; Hethe, near Bicester, Oxon. (M5516)

PARKER, William Edwin, O.B.E. (O11788c)

PARKER, Sir William Lorenzo, 3rd Bt., O.B.E., *b.* 1889; *s.* of Sir William Biddulph Parker, 2nd Bt. (*see* BURKE'S *Peerage*); *m.* 1915, Ruth Margaret, only *d.* of A. B. Hanbury Sparrow (*see* BURKE'S *Landed Gentry*). *Address:* Blackbrook House, Fareham, Hants. (O9048)

PARKER, Engineer-Capt. William Ramsey, C.B.E., R.N. *War Work:* In charge of Repair Work, E. Coast of Scotland. (C2226)

PARKES, Lieut. Alfred John, O.B.E., R.N.

PARKES, Major Charles Herbert, O.B.E., R.A.F.

PARKES, Colin Egbert, M.B.E.

PARKES, Dorothy Phoebe, Mrs., M.B.E., Q.M.A.A.C

PARKES, Edward, O.B.E., *b.* 19 Jan. 1864; *s.* of the late Capt. Harry Parkes, R.A., of Southampton; *m.* Florence E., *d.* of E.J. Hastler, of Shirley, Southampton. *Educ.:* Privately, Fareham, Hants. Assistant Librarian of the Foreign Office; Editor of British and Foreign State Papers. *Address:* Foreign Office, Whitehall, S.W. (O1728)

PARKES, Edwin, M.B.E.

PARKES, Lily Beatrice, Mrs., M.B.E.

PARKES, Surg.-Lieut. Oscar, O.B.E., M.B., R.N.

PARKES, Capt. William Ashley, O.B.E., R.A.S.C.

PARKES, Col. William Henry, C.M.G., C.B.E., M.B., F.R.C.S., *b.* 1864; *s.* of the late William Parkes, of Christchurch, New Zealand. *Educ.:* Edinburgh Univ. New Zealand Forces; served during the Great War, 1915–16, comdg. a New Zealand Gen. Hospital, and subsequently as Dep. Director of N.Z. Expeditionary Med. Services (despatches, promoted Col.). *Address:* Marinoto, Symonds Street, Auckland, New Zealand. (C589)

PARKHOUSE, Lieut.-Col. John Bardsley, O.B.E.

PARKHOUSE, Capt. Stanley Ernest, O.B.E., R.E.

PARKIN, Fanny Ida, Mrs., M.B.E., *b.* 19 Nov. 1877; *d.* of Lieut.-Col. T. C. McKenzie, of Caldra, Duns, N.B.; *m.* Lieut.-Col. Francis Hearle Parkin, O.B.E. (*q.v.*) *Educ.:* Brighton. *War Work:* Hon. Sec. Families' Benevolent Fund, Aldershot Command, and Aldershot Branch, Soldiers' and Sailors' Families Association; Member of Aldershot and Farnborough War Pensions Committees; Representative of Aldershot Command on Hampshire County War Pensions Committee. *Address:* Academy House, Coldstream, N.B. (M9227)

PARKIN, Lieut.-Col. Francis Hearle, O.B.E., *b.* 16 Aug. 1872; *s.* of the late Capt. J. B. Parkin, R.A., of Woolwich. *Educ.:* Privately. South Staffordshire Regt. (ret.). *War Work:* Commanded 28th (R.) Batt. Middlesex Regt., and afterwards 53rd (Y.S.) Batt. Middlesex Regt. *Address:* Academy House, Coldstream, N.B. *Club:* Wellington. (O7545)

PARKIN, Major Herbert Denis, O.B.E., M.C. R.A.S.C.

PARKIN, Major James Edward, M.B.E., R.A.F.

PARKIN, Joseph Henry, M.B.E.

PARKINSON, Albert Ernest, O.B.E., *b.* 7 March, 1869; *s.* of Joseph Parkinson, of Shipley; *m.* Mary Margaretta, *d.* of Charles Henry Wilkinson, of Keighley. *Educ.:* Bingley Grammar School. Machine Tool and Small Tool Maker. *War Work:* Chairman of Board of Management, Bradford National Munitions Factory. *Address:* High Close, Shipley. *Club:* Royal Automobile. (O44)

PARKINSON, Major Arthur Charles Cosmo, O.B.E.

PARKINSON, Frederick Henry, M.B.E., *b.* 26 Sept. 1887; *s.* of William Henry Parkinson, of Preston; *m.* Laura, *d.* of

Edward Heenan, of Bolton. *Educ.:* Bolton. Accountant. *War Work:* Joint Hon. Sec. Bolton Local War Savings Committee; Hon. Sec. Bolton Food Economy Committee; Executive Officer, Bolton Local Food Control Committee. (M9229)

PARKINSON, James, M.B.E.

PARKINSON, Janet, M.B.E., *b.* 12 Aug. 1887; *d.* of Thomas Parkinson, of Norden, near Rochdale. *Educ.:* North Manchester High School for Girls. Secretary. *War Work:* Soldiers' and Sailors' Families Association, and War Pensions work. *Address:* Brook House, Norden, Rochdale. (M9230)

PARKINSON, John Frederick Main, M.B.E., *b.* 25 March, 1861; *s.* of the late John F. Parkinson, of Portsmouth. Senior Examiner of Marine Engine Work, Engineer-in-Chief's Department. Admiralty. *War Work:* Preparation and Examination of the designs of machinery for war vessels. etc., for the past 22 years, in the Engineer-in-Chief's Department Admiralty. *Address:* 48, Montholme Road, New Wandsworth, London, S.W. (M9231)

PARKINSON, Lieut.-Col. Percival George, O.B.E., R.A.O.C.

PARKINSON, Walter, M.B.E.

PARKS, Major Ernest William, O.B.E.. R.A.V.C. (T.).

PARKS, Lieut.-Col. John Hegan, O.B.E., *b.* 21 Dec. 1874; *s.* of John Hegan Parks, of St. John, N.B., Canada; *m.* Ethel Louise, *d.* of G. W. Burpee, of Vancouver, B.C. *Educ.:* Royal Military Coll.; Kingston, Ont., Canada. Civil Engineer. *War Work:* Served in France in the Infantry (Canadian) till Dec. 1915; seconded to Royal Engineers and served with Adriatic Mission to Serbs, in Macedonia and Italy till end of war. *Clubs:* Constitutional; Vancouver, Vancouver, B.C. (O2252)

PARKYN, Major Harry Gordon, O.B.E.

PARKYNS, Thomas Samuel, M.B.E.

PARLBY, Joshua, O.B.E.

PARLETT, Harry Edgar, C.B.E., M.I.N.A., *b* 15 Nov. 1865; *s.* of Henry Thomas Parlett, of Portsmouth. Deputy Director Technical Services, Transport Dept., Admiralty. *War Work:* Arranging, planning, fitting, etc., of merchant ships taken up for transport service, hospital ships, horse and infantry transports; visited U.S.A. in connection with transport of American troops. *Address:* 70, Geraldine Road, Wandsworth Common, S.W. (C2861)

PARMELEE, Major James Grannis, O.B.E., Can. A.S.C.

PARMITER, Major Charles Lister, O.B.E.

PARNABY, John Murray, M.B.E., F.S.A.A., *b.* 13 June, 1857; *s.* of John Parnaby, of Middlesbrough (Congregational Minister). *Educ.:* Wakefield, and privately. Borough Accountant of Middlesbrough. *War Work:* Hon. Sec. Local War Savings Committee; Hon. Treas. Local War Pensions Committee. *Addresses:* Municipal Buildings, Middlesbrough; Dalry, the Avenue, Marton, Middlesbrough. (M9233)

PARNELL, Comm. Gerald Langton, D.S.O., O.B.E., R.N. *War Work:* 1914–18, with Destroyer and Torpedo Boat Flotillas (despatches, Croix de Guerre). (C9672)

PARNELL, John William, O.B.E. (O12002)

PARNIO, Alfredo, O.B.E., LL.D.

PARR, Capt. Cecil William Chase, O.B.E.

PARR, Col. Clements, C.B.E.; *b.* 1865; Major, Brevet Lieut.-Col. and T. Col., Oxford and Buckinghamshire L.I. (ret.); served with the Tirah Expeditionary Force, 1897–8 (medal with two clasps); and in the Great War, 1914–19 (despatches). (C1729)

PARR, George Herbert Edmeston, M.B.E.

PARR, Robert John, O.B.E., *b.* 12 April, 1862; *s.* of John Parr, of Torquay; *m.* Louie, *d.* of William A. Goss, of Torquay. *Educ.:* Torquay. Director, N.S.P.C.C. since 1905. *War Work:* Undertook at the request of the War Office to inquire into and assist the cases of children of soldiers; from Oct. 1914, to the date of the Armistice 81,079 children were helped by the N.S.P.C.C. *Addresses:* 3, Philbeach Court, S.W. 5; 40, Leicester Square, W.C. 2. (O45)

PARR, Major Sydney Charles, O.B.E., R.A.F.

PARR, William Henry, M.B.E., R.A.M.C.

PARROTT, Arthur Hughes, O.B.E., M.D.S. (Birm.), L.D.S., R.C.S. (Eng.), *b.* 8 June, 1876; *s.* of Thomas Dancer Parrott, of Birmingham; *m.* Annie Edith Maude, *d.* of Richard Cable Taylor, of Birmingham. *Educ.:* Privately and Mason Coll., Birmingham. Hon. Dental Surgeon, Birmingham Dental Hospital; Clinical Lecturer, Birmingham Univ.; Hon. Dental Surgeon to Protestant Dissenting Charity School; Hon. Dental Surgeon to the Crippled Children's Home, Northfield; President of the Central Counties Branch British Dental Association; Past President of Birmingham Dental Students' Society; Demonstrator and House Surgeon, Birmingham Dental Hospital; Member of Royal Society of Medicine (Odontological Section), and of the British Dental Association. *War Work:* Hon. Consulting Dental Surgeon in charge of Centre for Jaw and Facial Injuries of the Southern Command, at 1st and 2nd Southern General Hospitals, Birmingham, where over 2000 cases passed through; Active Member of 1st Volunteer Batt. Royal Warwickshire Regt. from its formation. *Addresses:* 87, Cornwall Street, Birmingham; Delaware, The Lickey, Bromsgrove. *Club:* Birmingham Univ. (O11833)

PARRY, Capt. Arthur Haydon, O.B.E.

PARRY, Charles de Courcy, C.B.E., *b.* 29 Nov. 1869; Capt. F. J. Parry, of Stonehouse, Glos.; *m.* Gwendoline Mary, *d.* of G. W. Wilkinson, J.P., of Risca, Mon. *Educ.:* Repton

School. Late Chief Constable of Cumberland and Westmorland (retired July, 1920). *Address :* Earnslaw, Malvern. *Club :* Junior Carlton.   (C2862)

PARRY, Major Edward Cecil Morgan, O.B.E.

PARRY, Lieut. Gladwyn, O.B.E., R.N.

PARRY, Lieut.-Col. Henry Jules, C.B.E., D.S.O., M.B.. M.R.C.S. (Eng.), L.R.C.P. (Lond.), *b.* 1867 ; *m.* 1899, Helen Dorothea Elizabeth Cockburn, *d.* of the late Robert Pitcairn, Barrister-at-Law. *Educ. :* Durham Univ. Entered Royal Army Med. Corps, 1890 ; retired, 1910 ; served in S. Africa, 1900 (despatches) ; and in the Great War, 1914–19 (Brevet Lieut.-Col.) ; formerly Surg. at Roy. Infirmary, Newcastle-on-Tyne.   (C1730)

PARRY, Eng.-Comm. Herbert Lyell, O.B.E., R.N.

PARRY, Hugh Lloyd, O.B.E.

PARRY, Joan Brunner, Mrs., M.B.E., *b.* 12 March, 1896 ; *d.* of Major T. W. and Mrs. Buckley, of Clopton Manor, Thrapston ; *m.* Major Rey Griffith Parry, D.S.O., R.A.F. *Educ. :* Winchester School for Girls and Geneva University. *War Work :* Entered War Office, Military Intelligence Directorate, Nov. 1915 ; appointed Junior Administrative Assistant, July, 1918 ; private secretary to Deputy Director of Military Intelligence Sept. 1918, until July, 1919 ; mentioned in Gazette, Aug. 1918. *Address :* The Gables, Turvey, Beds. *Club :* Halcyon.   (M7541)

PARRY, John, O.B.E., *b.* 20 June, 1858 ; *s.* of William Parry, of Penmon, Anglesea, N. Wales ; *m.* Elizabeth, *d.* of Robert Lloyd, of Geltic Farm, Nerquis, N. Wales. *Educ. :* Penmon National School. Master of S.S. " Dronian," Messrs. F. Leyland & Co., Ltd., 27, James Street, Liverpool ; 11 March, 1906, rescued crew of " British King " in a heavy gale in mid-Atlantic ; received the British Government's plate, Shipwrecked and Humane Society's gold medal, Emile Robinson's award for the most meritorious act of the year 1906 ; the New York Life Saving Benevolent Society's gold medal. *War Work :* From Aug. 1914, to April, 1915, in Expeditionary Force, in command of transport " Georgian " ; afterwards on Mediterranean Auxiliary Fleet Force, from May, 1915, to March, 1917 ; carrying wounded from Gallipoli, Aug. and Sept. 1915 ; mentioned in despatches, May, 1916 ; made 4 voyages up to Busara and relieving garrisons in Red Sea ; on the Shireff of Mecca's Expedition, 1916 ; from Jan. 1917, to March, 1917, trooping between Alexandria and Salonica ; torpedoed in the Ægean Sea with large number of Greek and British troops on board, lost 37 men in all ; 26 April, 1918, attacked by an enemy submarine off coast of Ireland, saved the ship and escaped ; 6 Feb. 1920, rescued the crew of S.S. " Bradboyne " in a strong gale in mid-Atlantic ; awarded the Shipwrecked and Humane Society's silver medal, silver mounted prism binoculars, and illuminated address ; 13 Aug. 1920, awarded the British Government's plate. *Address :* 10, Exeter Road, Bootle, Liverpool.   (O11090)

PARRY, Col. Llewelyn England Sidney, C.B.E., D.S.O., T.D., D.L., J.P., *b.* 1856 ; *s.* of Richard Parry, of Royal Scots Greys ; *m.* Mary Sophia, *d.* of Sir R. Price Puleston, of Emral, co. Flint. *Educ. :* Rugby, and Trinity Col., Oxford. *War Work :* Lieut.-Col. Commanding 2/1 Denbighshire (Hussars) Yeo. ; Staff appointment in France. *Address :* Pengwern, Rhuddlan *Clubs :* United Univ. ; Cavalry.   (C1731)

PARRY, Mary Evelyn, M.B.E.

PARRY, Lieut.-Col. Percy Edward Langworthy, D.S.O., O.B.E. Major (ret.). Great War, 1914–19 (despatches).   (O7368)

PARRY, Capt. William Francis Vaughan, M.B.E.

PARRY, William John, C.B.E., F.C.A., *b.* 28 Sept. 1842 ; *s.* of John Parry, of Bethesda, North Wales ; *m.* Mary, *d.* of Samuel Horne, of Kingswinford. *Educ. :* National ; British Schools, and Grammar School, Llanrwst. Chartered Accountant ; Ex-Chairman of Carnarvon County Council, and Carnarvonshire Standing Joint Police Committee, and Bethesda District Council ; Alderman of the County ; one of the original members of the National Liberal Club. *War Work :* Hon. Auditor of Carnarvonshire and Anglesey Soldiers' and Sailors' Association Fund ; Chairman of the Bethesda Tribunal, and of the Bangor Pension Committee. *Address :* Coetmor Hall, Bethesda. *Club :* National Liberal.   (C2863)

PARRY, Major Ernest GAMBIER-. O.B.E., J.P., late Royal Welsh Fusiliers, and 1st R. Devon Yeomanry, *b.* 25 Oct. 1853 ; *s.* of Thomas Gambier-Parry, J P., D.L., of Highnam Court, Gloucester ; *m.* Hon. Evelyn, *d.* of Lord Haldon, of Haldon Exeter. *Educ. :* Eton. *War Work :* Served in the Eastern Sudan 1885 ; Major for services, medal and clasp, and Khedive's Star ; ran a hospital during the Great War, 1914–18, largely at his own expense. *Address :* Highnam Court, Gloucester. *Club :* Naval and Military.   (O1730)

PARSLEY, Major Walter, M.B.E., M.C.

PARSONS, Arthur Ambrose, M.B.E.

PARSONS, Capt. Arthur Edward Broadbent, O.B.E., 52nd Sikhs.   (O11762)

PARSONS, Bertha Adelaide, Mrs., M.B.E., *b.* 10 March, 1879 ; *d.* of George Pellew Paul ; *m.* Ronald Cleeve. *War Work :* With the Delhi—Simla work-party, 1914–19 ; also with the Monro Canteen. *Addresses :* Hyde Vale, Simla, India ; 9, Cavalry Lines, Delhi, India.   (M7143)

PARSONS, Charles O'Connor, M.B.E., L.R.C.P.S. (Edin.), L.F.P.S.G., *b.* 20 July. 1863 ; *s.* of Daniel Walter Parsons, of Liverpool ; *m.* Isabel Elizabeth, *d.* of Edward Kidman, of Shefford, Brds. *Educ. :* Liverpool, and Tullabeg, Ireland. Medical Officer, Ecclesall and Bierlow Union. *War Work :*

Medical Officer, St. John's Red Cross Hospital, Dore, and Carter Knowle Hospital, Sheffield ; Medical Examiner Recruiting Station, Sheffield. *Address :* Totley Brook Road, near Sheffield. *Club :* Athenæum, Sheffield.

PARSONS, Christopher Thackray, O.B.E., M.D. (Lond.), *b.* 7 Aug. 1870 ; *s.* of Abram Parsons, of London ; *m.* 1st Amy Elizabeth (who died), 2nd daughter of James Hunter, of Liverpool ; 2ndly, 3 Jan. 1921, Annie Burgess, *w.* of Archibald Hugh Payon Downay, F.R.C.S. *Educ. :* St. Mary's Hospital, Univ. of London. Physician ; Med. Supt. Fulham Infirmary, W. 6. *War Work :* Capt. R.A.M.C. with Mesopotamian Expeditionary Force M. O. 40th General Hospital ; M.O. Tigris Transport ; M.O. 112th Indian Field Ambulance ; Lieut.-Col. R.A.M.C. officer-in-charge Fulham Military Hospital. *Address :* Fulham Infirmary, W. 6.   (O7552)

PARSONS, Major Edward Howard Thornbrough, C.B.E., late R.A., *b.* 1868 ; *s.* of Capt. Edward Thornbrough Parsons, R.N. ; *m.* Marion Marjorie Winifred Glen, *d.* of Sir Thomas Glen-Coats, Bart., C.B. (*see* BURKE'S *Peerage*), of Ferguslie Park, Paisley. *Educ. :* Clifton. Royal Artillery, and Metropolitan Police. *War Work :* As Chief Constable, Metropolitan Police. *Address :* 5, Prince's Gardens, London, S.W. 7. *Clubs :* Army and Navy ; Cavalry.   (C262)

PARSONS, Col. Frederick George, D.S.O., O.B.E.

PARSONS, Joan Dorothea Langton, M.B.E.

PARSONS, John Edward Hocking, M.B.E., B.A. (Cantab.), M.R.C.S. (Eng.), L.R.C.P. (Lond.), *b.* 12 Nov. 1870 ; *s.* of Thomas Parsons, of Whiteleaf, Prince's Risborough, Bucks ; *m.* Cecilia Emela A. Drummond Parsons, *d.* of the late John Sale Barker, of Palace Gardens Terrace, London. *Educ. :* Cambridge and Guy's Hospital. Poor Law Medical Officer, and Public Vaccinator No. 4 District, Chipping-Norton Union. *War Work :* Bruern Abbey V.A.D. Hospital ; Shipton Court Auxiliary Hospital for Officers ; Chipping-Norton V.A.D. Hospital ; Medical Charge of Guard of Leafield Wireless Station. *Address :* The Cottage, Shipton-under-Wychwood, Oxon.   (M9237)

PARSONS, John Herbert, C.B.E., D.Sc., F.R.C.S., *b.* 1868 ; I. J. Parsons, of Bristol. *Educ. :* Bristol. Ophthalmic Surgeon ; Ophthalmic Surgeon to Univ. Coll. Hospital, London ; Surgeon to the Royal London (Moorfields) Ophthalmic Hospital. *War Work :* Colonel, A.M.S. ; Consulting Ophthalmic Surgeon to the Forces. *Address :* 54, Queen Anne Street, Cavendish Square, London, W. 1.   (C1732)

PARSONS, Paymaster-Lieut.-Comm. Oswy Lonsdale, O.B.E., R.N.

PARSONS, Rachael Fannie, Mrs., O.B.E.

PARSONS, Ronald, M.B.E.

PARSONS, Paymaster-Lieut. Stanley Seymour Conway, O.B.E., R.N.

PARSONS, Capt. and Qr.-Mr. William Henry, M.B.E.

PARSONS, Eng.-Capt. William Roskilly, C.B.E., *b.* 1865. Engineer-Capt. R.N. (ret.).   (C590)

PART, Lt.-Col. Dealtry Charles, O.B.E., R. of O. 21st Lancers, *b.* 1882 ; *s.* of Charles Thomas, D.L., J.P., of Aldenham Lodge, Radlett, Herts ; *m.* Edith Mary, *d.* of the late Wakefield Christie Miller, of Britwell Court, Burnham, Bucks. *Educ. :* Harrow. *War Work :* Deputy Assist. Director of Remounts Indian Cavalry Corps, 1915–16, and commanded a Remount Depot. *Address :* Houghton Hall, Dunstable, Beds. *Club :* Cavalry.   (O7550)

PARTINGTON, Charles Frederick, O.B.E., J.P., *b.* 17 Jan. 1858 ; *s.* of Thomas Ashton Partington, of Liverpool ; *m.* Olivia Gertrude, *d.* of Julius Lowenthal, of London. *Educ. :* Liverpool Institute. Produce Broker, Hibernia Chambers, London Bridge, S.E. 1 ; Chairman Provision Trade Benevolent Institution ; Chairman Amalgamated Trades Association ; Vice-Chairman London Savings Bank. *War Work :* Ministry of Food, Butter and Cheese Import Committee ; Surveyor of Provisions to the Board of Trade ; Lambeth Recruiting Tribunal ; Lambeth Local Food Committee. *Addresses :* Hibernia Chambers, London Bridge, S.E. 1 ; The Forest, Felpham, Sussex.   (O11091)

PARTINGTON, Lieut. James Riddick, M.B.E.

PARTINGTON, Mary Alice, Mrs., M.B.E.

PARTINGTON, Thomas, M.B.E., *b.* 30 May, 1872 ; *s.* of Frederick Partington, of Manchester ; *m.* Emily Agnes, *d.* of Alfred West Battey, of Hanwell. *Educ. :* Manchester. (M4819)

PARTINGTON, Willie Percival Hindley, M.B.E., *b.* 12 Aug. 1883 ; *s.* of John Frederick Partington, of Atherton, Lancashire ; *m.* May Caroline, *d.* of Amos Gutteridge, of London. *Educ. :* Bury Grammar School. *War Work :* Sub-Section Director, Machine Gun Section, Small Arms and Machine Gun Dept., Ministry of Munitions.   (M9239)

PARTRIDGE, Sir Cecil, K.B.E., *b.* 1873 ; *s.* of R. W. Partridge, of Worcester ; *m.* Ada I., *d.* of the late David William Palmer, of Doddington House, St. Margarets-on-Thames. *Educ. :* Privately. Chairman and Managing Director, Kirk and Randall, Ltd. ; Chairman, South African Carbide and By-Products Co., Ltd. ; Chairman Ambrose Shardlow & Co., Ltd. ; formerly, General Manager of the Central London Railway. *War Work :* General Manager of the Metropolitan Munitions Committee. *Address :* 24, Grosvenor Place, S.W. 1. *Club :* Constitutional.   (K32)

PARTRIDGE, Major Edward Henry William, O.B.E., R.A.S.C. (M.T.), *b.* 22 April, 1882 ; *s.* of Charles Edward Partridge, of Damemora, Beaminster ; *m.* Margie, *d.* of E. Marshall, of London. *Educ. :* Uppingham. Engineer, M.I.M.E., M.I.A.E. *War Work :* enlisted as private, Aug. 1914 ; served in France from Aug. 1914, till date; five mentions in despatches. *Address:* 147, Shooters Hill Road, Blackheath, S.E. (O2670)

PARTRIDGE, Comm. Reginald Montague O.B.E., R.D., R.N.R.

PARTRIDGE, Lieut.-Col. Sydney George, C.B.E., *b.* 1881; *e. s.* of Arthur George Partridge, formerly of Painswick, Gloucester; *m.* 1912, Elsie, *d.* of E. Judson Mills. *War Work:* Director of Army Printing and Stationery Services, General Headquarters in France during 1914–18, with rank of Col. (despatches twice). (C411)

PARTRIDGE, Sydney John, M.B.E., *b.* 19 Jan. 1877; *s.* of William Dickens Partridge, of Dunstable, Beds.; *m.* Blanche Cordelia. *Educ.:* Richmond. Deputy Accounts Officer, Admiralty. *Address:* Lodore, 65, Earlsfield Road, Wandsworth Common, S.W. 18. (M9240)

PASCOE, Lieut. Claud Alfred Leonard, O.B.E., London Regt. (O11883)

PASCOE, Frederick Richard, M.B.E., J.P.

PASKE, Major Edward Lake, O.B.E.

PASS, Ralph, M.B.E.

PASSINGHAM, Edith Laura, Mrs., O.B.E.

PASSINGHAM, Major Robert Townshend ANWYL-, O.B.E., J.P., *b.* 16 Oct. 1867; *s.* of Robert Townshend Anwyl-Passingham, of Bryn-y-groes, Bala (*see* BURKE'S *Landed Gentry*); *m.* Charlotte Angie Bigoe, *d.* of Capt. R. Bigoe Williams, of late 4th Dragoon Guards. *Educ.:* Sandhurst. *War Work:* Recruiting Officer 23rd Recruiting Area; afterwards Assistant Director of National Service for North Wales. *Address:* Bryn-y-groes, Bala, N. Wales. *Club:* Junior United Service. (O1731)

PASSINGHAM, Lieut.-Col. Augustus Mervyn Owen Anwyl ANWYL-, O.B.E.; Officer of the Order of the Crown of Italy.

PASSMORE, Capt. Herbert, M.B.E.

PATCH, Capt. James, O.B.E.

PATCHETT, Capt. Arthur Nesbit, O.B.E., R.A.S.C.

PATE, George, O.B.E.

PATENALL, Clara Poynton, Mrs., M.B.E.; *d.* of S. J. Joll, of Waddington, Lincs.; *m.* Thomas, *s.* of James Patenall, of Higham Ferrers. *War Work:* Four years as Commandant in the Higham Ferrers V.A.D. Hospital. *Address:* Bron Dinas, Rushden, Northants. (M2268)

PATERSON, Clifford Copland, O.B.E., M.I.C.E., M.I.E.E., *b.* 17 Oct. 1879; *s.* of Frederick Paterson, of River House, Woodberry Down, N.; *m.* Eleanor Daisy, *d.* of William Thomas Ogden, of 93, Clapton Common, N *Educ.:* Mill Hill School. Director of the Research Laboratories of the General Electric Co., London; formerly in charge of the Electro-technical Dept. at the National Physical Laboratory. *War Work:* Range-finding apparatus in connection with Anti-Aircraft Gunnery, and other research and standardisation work at the National Physical Laboratory and the Engineering Standards Association. *Addresses:* Research Laboratories of the General Electric Co., Ltd., 67. Queen Victoria Street, London; 10, Walpole Gardens, Twickenham. (O633)

PATERSON, Daniel Gavin, O.B.E. (O12003)

PATERSON, Doris Hirst, M.B.E.

PATERSON, Florence Lavinia, Mrs., O.B.E.

PATERSON, Herbert John, O.B.E., R.N.R.

PATERSON, Herbert John, C.B.E., M.C., M.A., M.B. (Cantab.), F.R.C.S. (Eng.), *b.* 1868; *m.* Tempé Langrish, *d.* of the late Geo. H. Faber, Beckenham, M.P. for Boston. *Educ.:* Trinity Coll., Cambridge. Senior Surgeon London Temperance Hospital; Medical Hon. Sec. Royal British Nurses' Association; Joint Hon. Sec. Fellowship of Medicine. *War Work:* Commandant and Honorary Surgeon-in-charge Queen Alexandra's Hospital for Officers; Hon. Surgeon to King Edward the VII. Hospital for Officers. *Address:* 9, Upper Wimpole Street, London, W. *Clubs:* M.C.C.; Berkhamstead and Machinhanish Golf. (C3120)

PATERSON, James Graham, O.B.E.

PATERSON, Capt. John, O.B.E.

PATERSON, John Wilson, M.B.E.

PATERSON, Louise, Mrs., O.B.E.

PATERSON, Mary Agnes, Mrs., M.B.E.; *d.* of the Rev. John McNeill, of Rutherglen; *m.* James Bain, C.A., J.P., *s.* of James Paterson, M.D., L.R.C.P. & S. (E.), of Partick. *Educ.:* Chalmers' and Dick's School, Claremont Terrace, Glasgow. *War Work:* President of Partick West, Whiteinch and Scotstoun Division of the Soldiers' and Sailors' Families Association and Member of the Partick Local Sub-Committee of the Glasgow War Pensions Committee. *Address:* 6, Bowmont Terrace, Kelvinside, Glasgow. (M9244)

PATERSON, Mary Muirhead, C.B.E. National Health Insurance Comm., Scotland. (C2864)

PATERSON, Capt. Matthew Wallace, O.B.E., M.C., R.A.M.C. (S.R.).

PATERSON, Lieut.-Col. Robert Ormiston, O.B.E., R.M.A.

PATERSON, Col. Stanley, C.B.E., *b.* 1860. Col. (ret.). Served in the Great War, 1914–19 (despatches). (C1733)

PATERSON, 2nd Lieut. Thomas, O.B.E., R.A.

PATERSON, Thomas, M.B.E., *b.* 1 July, 1861; *s.* of Thomas Paterson, of Lugar, Ayrshire. *Educ.:* Irvine Academy and Ayr Academy. Master, Merchant Service. *War Work:* Master of H.M. Transport "Hunsgate." *Address:* 39, Ashgrove Street, Ayr. (M3887)

PATIALA, Maj.-Gen. H. H. (Maharajah of), G.C.S.I., G.C.I.E., G.B.E. One of the Ruling Chiefs of India; Chief of

Patiala States; Hon. Col. Patiala Inf. and an Hon. Maj.-Gen. in the Army; served with the Indian Expeditionary Force during the Great War, 1914 (Grand Cordon of the Order of the Nile, Grand Cross of the Order of Leopold of Belgium, and Legion of Honour); appointed a Member of Council of Gov. of Punjab 1917; represented India at Special War Conference, 1918. (G22)

PATMAN, Frederick, O.B.E., M.Inst.T., *b.* 7 Nov. 1869 *s.* of the late John Richardson Patman, of Gosberton, near Boston, Lincs.; *m.* Bertha, *d.* of the late John Nicholson, of Nostell, Wakefield, Yorks, *Educ.:* Tankersley, near Barnsley, Yorks. District Traffic Manager (Eastern Division) Great Central Railway. *War Work:* Transportation; in charge of troop movements under Northern Command, to and from camps at Humberstone, Weelsby, Grimsby, Riby, Stallingboro, Brocklesby, Lincoln, and Clipstone Camp, Mansfield; Naval and Military requirements at Humber ports; East Coast Air Raid arrangements. *Addresses:* The Royal Grimsby Docks; 1, Grosvenor Crescent, Grimsby. (O11094)

PATON, Sir Alfred Vaughan, K.B.E., *b.* 18 Nov. 1861; *s.* of the Rev. Dr. J. B. Paton, of Nottingham. *Educ.:* Clifton Coll., and Trinity, Oxford. Retired merchant. *War Work:* As President of the Liverpool Cotton Association, 1917–18, served as Chairman of Committees acting on behalf of the Board of Trade and Ministry of Shipping in connection with the cotton trade, and in Oct. 1918, went to Washington, D.C., for the Board of Trade as chairman of a Cotton Mission. *Address:* West Kirby, Cheshire. *Club:* Univ., Liverpool. (K407)

PATON, Benjamin Lewis, O.B.E., B.A. (Lond.), M.D. (Edin.), D.P.H. (Camb.), Fellow of Royal Institute of Public Health, *b.* 22 Dec. 1860; *s.* of Robert Paton, of Highbury, London; *m.* Janet Cowan Scott, *d.* of John William Macfie, of Rowton Hall, Chester. *Educ.:* Univ. Coll., London, and Edinburgh Univ. Medical Officer, Rugeley District Hospital; M.O. to Post Office. *War Work:* M.O. Ravenhill Auxiliary Military Hospital; Member of Medical and Pension Assessment Board, Walsall; Part-time M.O. Rugeley Camp. *Address:* Rugeley, Staffs. (O11094)

PATON, Daniel Shaw, M.B.E., *b.* 31 Dec. 1877; *s.* of George Fisher Paton, of Paisley; *m.* Florence, *d.* of Joseph Glazier Fillingham, of Bourne. *Educ.:* John Neilson Educational Institution, Paisley. Surveyor in H.M. Customs and Excise Department. *War Work:* As Hon. Sec. Bourne District, British Red Cross Society. *Addresses:* Custom House, E.C. 4, and Bourne, Lincolnshire. (M9245)

PATON, Mary Emma, O.B.E.

PATRICK, Lieut. and Qr.-Mr. John McDonald, M.B.E.

PATRICK, Neil James KENNEDY-COCHRAN-, O.B.E., B.A. (Cantab.), LL.B. (Edinburgh), J.P., D.L., (Ayrshire), *b.* 18 Aug. 1866; *s.* of John Kennedy, of Underwood; *m.* Eleonora Agnes, *d.* of Robert William Cochran-Patrick, J.P., LL.D., of Woodside and Ladyland. *Educ.:* Edinburgh Academy; Monkton Combe; Cambridge Univ.; Edinburgh Univ. Advocate; contested the Unionist interest the constituency of Stirling Burghs at the General Election of Jan. 1910, and the County of Roxburghshire, Dec. 1910. *War Work:* Joined 2/4th Royal Scots Fusiliers in Oct. 1914, with rank of T. Capt.; in March, 1916, appointed Appeal Military Representative for the Counties of Renfrewshire and Bute, and acted as such until the Armistice. *Address:* Ladyland, Beith, Ayrshire. *Clubs:* New, Edinburgh; County, Ayr. (OM2269)

PATRON, Joseph Armand, C.M.G., O.B.E.

PATTEN, Alan Stewart, M.B.E.; *b.* 6 Oct. 1894; *s.* of Lieut.-Col. Patten, of Clone Aughrim, Co. Wicklow. *Educ.:* Wellington Coll. *Address:* Clone, Aughrim, Co. Wicklow. (M4571)

PATTENSON, Lieut.-Col. Edwin Cooke TYLDEN-, D.S.O., O.B.E. (O11770)

PATTERSON, Lieut. D. H., M.B.E., R.A.S.C. (M.T.).

PATTERSON, Major Daniel Wells, O.B.E., M.B., R.A.M.C. (T.).

PATTERSON, Eng.-Comm. George, O.B.E., R.N.R.

PATTERSON, Capt. Harold Dorman, O.B.E.

PATTERSON, Comm. Julian Francis Chichester, O.B.E., R.N.

PATTERSON, Major Lamont, O.B.E., M.D.

PATTERSON, Robert George, O.B.E., J.P.

PATTERSON, Robert Hogarth, M.B.E.

PATTERSON, Walter, M.B.E., J.P.

PATTERSON, William Baker, M.B.E.

PATTINSON, Lieut. Edward Harold, M.B.E., R.A.S.C. (T.).

PATTINSON, Major George Hedworth, O.B.E., M.C., R.E.

PATTINSON, Henry, O.B.E., *b.* 28 Nov. 1865; *s.* of John A. Pattinson, of Liverpool; *m.* Kate Alexandra, *d.* of Hugh James Galbraith, of Kenley. *Educ.:* Harrow. *War Work:* Chairman, Liverpool Raw Cocoa Grading Committee. *Address:* 8, Fulwood Park, Liverpool. *Club:* Liverpool Racquet. (O11097)

PATTISON, Annie Maitland, M.B.E., *b.* 7 Feb. 1887; *d.* of Fred. L. Maitland Moir, of 16, Kensington Gate, Glasgow, W.; *m.* Major James William Henry Pattison, *s.* of James Pattison, of Drimnamona, Kilmacolm, Renfrewshire. *Educ.:* St. Leonard's School, St. Andrews, Fife. *War Work:* Hon. Sec. Ladies' Auxiliary Committee of Scottish Y.M.C.A. (M772)

PATTLE, Cecil Frederic, M.B.E.

PATTLE, Capt. Rupert James Hartwell, M.B.E., S.A.S.C.

PATTRICK, Emma, Mrs., M.B.E.

PATTULLO, James Burleigh, O.B.E., Can. A.P.C.

PAUL, Lieut.-Col. Denis, C.M.G., C.B.E. Army Ordnance Dept.; sometime Chief Inspector of Ordnance Machinery; served during S. African War, 1899–1902 (despatches, Queen's medal with two clasps, King's medal with two clasps); and during the Great War, 1914–16 (despatches). (C591)

PAUL, Brig.-Gen. Ernest Moncreiff, C.B., C.B.E., Order of the Nile, Associate Institution of Civil Engineers, *b.* 2 Sept. 1864; *s.* of Henry Moncreiff Paul, late of 12, Lansdowne Crescent, London, W.; *m.* Katherine Harriette Coldstream. *Educ.:* King's Coll. School, London; Marlborough Coll., Wilts; Royal Indian Engineering Coll., Coopers Hill; School of Military Engineering, Chatham. Lieut. Royal Engineers, 6 Jan. 1886; Colonel, 15 Oct. 1915, and Brig.-Gen. 23 Nov. 1915; 35 years' Army Service (Home 18 years, foreign, 17 years, India, Gibraltar, Ceylon, Egypt); selected six times to carry out special service for Government, 1900–6; Member of Executive Committee, Palestine Exploration Fund, also Anglo-Russian Literary Society; Assessor for War Office to Advisory Council for Scientific and Industrial Research; Military Interpreter, Russian; author of " Road Construction and Maintenance "; has travelled extensively in different parts of the world, viz. nearly every country in Europe, also India, Burma, Russian Central Asia, Caucasus, China, West Indies, Venezuela Panama, Morocco, Egypt, Macedonia, Ægean, and Palestine. *War Service:* Served from 1914–19, without a break in following theatres : East Indies, Gallipoli, Salonica, Egypt, Sinai, and Palestine; awarded C.B. (1915) for Distinguished Service in the Field (Gallipoli), and C.B.E. (1919) for work in Palestine and Egypt; 4 times mentioned in despatches; officiated as Engineer-in-Chief to Field Marshal Viscount Allenby in Palestine for four months, 1917–18; as Director of Works, Mediterranean, Gallipoli, Egypt, Sinai, and Palestine for almost the whole war, had full responsible control of all expenditure on Works, Air Buildings, Aerodromes, Engineer Stores and Workshops, with attendant finance and management involving some millions of money; conserved the economy of the Public Purse, meriting special commendation from Viscount Allenby, War Office, etc. *Address :* 26, Campden Hill Court, Kensington, W. 8. *Clubs :* Army and Navy; Senior Officers'. (C1387)

PAUL, Eveline Alice Wanda, Lady, O.B.E.

PAUL, Capt. Henry William Moncreiff, O.B.E., M.C., Legion of Honour, Middlesex Regt., *b.* 20 Jan. 1894; *s.* of Brig.-Gen. Ernest Moncreiff Paul, C.B.E., of 26, Campden Hill Court, Kensington (*q.v.*). *Educ.:* Hartford House, Winchfield; Wellington Coll. (Berks); Royal Military Coll., Sandhurst. 2nd Lieut. Feb. 1914; Capt. Aug. 1916 *War Work :* Full period, 1914–19. without a break in following theatres : France, B.E.F., Dardanelles, Egypt, Salonica; awarded M.C. for gallantry in action, 1916; O.B.E., Jan. 1919; Legion of Honour, March, 1919; thrice mentioned in despatches; held General Staff appointment G.S.O. 3; Brigade Major, G.S.O. 2; served with Royal Air Force, Oct. 1917, to Nov. 1918; subsequently with Army of Occupation; A.D.C. to Lord Horne during tour with Lord Kitchener in the East. *Address :* 26, Campden Hill Court, Kensington. *Clubs :* Army and Navy; Royal Air Force. (O3385)

PAUL, Janie Ramsbottom, Mrs., M.B.E.

PAUL, Minnie, Mrs., M.B.E.

PAUL, Engr.-Capt. Oliver Richard, C.B.E., R.N. *War Work :* 1914–19, Senior British Naval Officer in Italy (despatches). (C2272)

PAUL, Ruth Ethel, Mrs., M.B.E.

PAUL, Lieut.-Col. Walter Reginald, C.B.E., R.F.A., *b.* 28 April, 1882; *s.* of the late Charles Paul, of Clifton, Bristol; *m.* Eileen, *d.* of the late Col. J. W. H. Potts, R.H.A., of New Court, Athlone. *Educ.:* Clifton Coll. *War Work :* Experimental Establishment, Shoeburyness. *Address :* The New Ranges, Shoeburyness, Essex. (C2153)

PAUL, Walter Wyatt, O.B.E., *b.* 21 April, 1864; *s.* of Walter Paul, of Bradford Abbas, Sherborne, Dorset; *m.* Sarah Elizabeth, *d.* of Daniel Ewens Biddlecombe, of Bridport, Dorset. *Educ.:* Privately at Wallingford, Berks. Farmer and Landowner; Lord of the Manor of Bradford Abbas. *War Work :* As Chairman of the Local Advisory Committee and Member of Central Committee of Flax Branch under the Board of Agriculture and Fisheries, gave assistance in the development of the Flax industry as a war measure rendered necessary through failure of supplies and the particular need to safeguard sufficient seed. *Address :* The Manor, Bradford Abbas, Sherborne, Dorset. (O11098)

PAUL, William Francis, O.B.E., *b.* 11 Feb. 1850. Merchant; Justice of the Peace for the Borough of Ipswich and the County of Suffolk. *War Work :* Equipped and maintained Broadwater Hospital, Ipswich, 50 beds, 1914–19. *Address :* Orwell Lodge, Ipswich. *Club :* Reform. (O3865)

PAULL, Catherine Swan, Mrs., M.B.E., *b.* 21 July, 1864; *d.* of James Drysdale, of Devonside, N.B.; *m.* Alan, J.P.; *s.* of H. J. Paull, of London. *Educ.:* Dollar Academy; Thornbeck House, Darlington. *War Work :* Commandant of Willesden District Military V.A.D. 1st Line Hospital, from Dec. 1914, to Dec. 1918. *Address :* Kylecote, North Wembley, Middlesex. (M830)

PAULL, Emily Anne, Mrs., M.B.E.

PAULL, James George, O.B.E., *b.* 4 Nov. 1870; *s.* of the Rev. William Paull, of Tullynessle, Aberdeenshire; *m.* Charlotte Rose, *d.* of Charles Duncan, of Deebank, Aberdeen.

Educ.: Aberdeen Univ. Advocate. *War Work :* Soldiers' and Sailors' Families Association (Hon. Sec.) and Local War Pensions Committees for Aberdeen (City) and Aberdeenshire (County). *Address :* Danestone House, Woodside, Aberdeenshire. *Clubs :* Royal Northern; Scottish Conservative. (O11100)

PAULL, Lieut.-Col. James Ratley, O.B.E., T.D., *b.* 15 April, 1863; *s.* of Joseph Paull, of Ilminster; *m.* Elizabeth Agnes Barry, *d.* of Lieut.-Col. F. A. Smyth, of Weymouth. *Educ.:* Ilminster Grammar School, and Fullands School, Taunton. Has filled the offices of Guardian of the Poor, Grammar School Governor, Chairman of School Board, Churchwarden (Vicar's), Capt. of Ringers, Capt. Cricket Club, Capt. Fire Brigade, Superintendant Sunday School, Treas. Provident Club, Sec. Allotments Trustees, Member of Diocesan Board, and W.M. 3 times, Nyanza Lodge, and P.P.G. S.W. Somerset. *War Work :* Mobilised on Salisbury Plain when war broke out; was 2nd in Command of 5th Batt. Somerset L.I.; appointed to Command Reserve Batt. 5th Somerset L.I. 3 Oct. 1914; took Batt. to Burma on 12 Dec. 1914; transferred to India, May, 1917; stayed in India until Oct. 1919. *Address :* Summerlands, Ilminster. (O8525)

PAUS, Christopher Lintrup, C.B.E.

PAVY, Dorothea, Mrs., C.B.E., D.Sc., B.A., *d.* of the late Cornelius Proud, of Blackwood, S. Australia; *m.* 1917, Capt. Gordon Augustus Pavy, Australian Imperial Forces. Obtained Certificate of Social Ser. (Honours), Adelaide, 1912; first Catherine Helen Spence Scholar for S. Australia, 1912–15; Diploma of Social Science (Honours), London, 1914; D.Sc. (Economics), London, 1916; has been in Welfare and Health Section, Ministry of Munitions, since 1915; author of *Welfare Work.* (C58)

PAWLE, Capt. Hanbury, O.B.E.

PAWLEY, Katharine Alice, M.B.E., *b.* 1887; *d.* of Tom Edward Pawley, of Bromley, Kent. *Educ.:* Tonbridge, Kent; Dresden, Germany. *War Work :* Commandant of Church House V.A.D. Hospital, Bromley, Kent, 1915–19. *Address :* Yardley Dene, Bromley, Kent. (M9252)

PAWSON, Herbert Alfred James, M.B.E.

PAXMAN, Major William, O.B.E., T.D., *b.* 28 May, 1866; *s.* of James Paxman, of Colchester; *m.* Mildred Evelyn, *d.* of Major John Barnett Barker, late 5th Fusiliers, of Birkenhead. *Educ.:* Privately, and Univ. Coll. London. Engineer; Director of Davey, Paxman & Co., Ltd. *War Work :* Company Commander in the London Rifle Brigade from 16 Jan. 1915, to 10 Feb. 1919. *Address :* Colchester. *Club :* Junior Naval and Military. (O7557)

PAYN, Thomas, O.B.E.

PAYNE, Hon. Lieut. Arthur, M.B.E., *s.* of John Buxton Payne, of Knutsford, Cheshire; *m.* Ethel Maud, *d.* of Henry Dalton, of Stella, Northumberland. *Educ.:* Royal Grammar School, Newcastle-on-Tyne. Hon. Serving Brother of the Order of St. John of Jerusalem; Fellow of the Chemical Society of London; Fellow of the Royal Photographic Society of Great Britain. *War Work :* Administrator, 7th Northumberland V.A. Hospital, Whitley Bay, Northumberland; Commandant, V.A.D. Northumberland 41; Lieut. Northumberland R.A.M.C.(V.); Div. Supt., Whitley Bay and Monkseaton Division St. John Ambulance Brigade; Charge of Air and Sea raid ambulance dressing stations at Whitley Bay. *Address :* 5, Saltwell View, Gateshead, Northumberland. (M9253)

PAYNE, Charles, C.B.E., J.P. Shipbuilder; Managing Director, Harland and Wolff, Ltd., Belfast. *War Work :* Managing Director, National Shipyards. *Address :* Verona, Malone Park, Belfast. *Club :* Automobile (C2866)

PAYNE, Major and Qr.-Mr. Charles, O.B.E., R.E.

PAYNE, Capt. Christopher Russell, C.B.E., *b.* 1874; *s.* of the late Rev. S. W. Payne, LL.D., R.N., Rector of Delamere, Cheshire. Capt. and Commodore (2nd class), R.N.; served in the Great War, 1914–19 (despatches); is Com. Legion of Honour, and has 3rd class of Japanese Order of Rising Sun. (C1170)

PAYNE, Capt. Clifford, O.B.E.

PAYNE, Ellen, M.B.E.

PAYNE, Rev. Francis Reginald Chassereau, O.B.E., M.A., *b.* 17 June, 1876; *s.* of the Rev. William John Payne, of Brighton; *m.* Ethel Annie, *d.* of John Ambrose Cope, of Derby. *Educ.:* Saffron Walden; Keble Coll., Oxford. Vicar of St. Margaret's, Leicester; Chaplain, H.M. Prison, Leicester. *War Work :* Ward Sec. for Relief to Soldiers' Wives, 1914–15; Hon. Sec. Leicester, Leicestershire, and Rutland Prisoners of War Committee. *Address :* St. Margaret's Vicarage, Leicester. (O11103)

PAYNE, Capt. George, M.B.E., R.G.A., *b.* 8 Aug. 1876; *s.* of George Payne, of Wandsworth, Surrey; *Educ.:* Council Schools, London, and Army. *War Work :* Organisation and control of Ammunition Depot under Royal Army Ordnance Corps. *Addresses :* The Nook, Harwell, Steventon, Berks; Ordnance, Didcot, Berks. (M2270)

PAYNE, Hazel Vivienne, M.B.E.

PAYNE, Herbert, M.B.E.

PAYNE, Col. Herbert Chidgey Brine, C.M.G., C.B.E., *b.* 12 Oct. 1862; *s.* of the late Col. James Payne. *Educ.:* Harrow. *War Work :* Chief Paymaster, British Salonica Force. *Club :* Junior United Service. (C1415)

PAYNE, Janet, Mrs., M.B.E.

PAYNE, Joseph, O.B.E.

PAYNE, Joseph Lewin, O.B.E., L.R.C.P. (Lond.), M.R.C.S.,

L.D.S. (Eng.), *b.* 1872 ; *s.* of William Payne, of The Guildhall, London ; *m.* May Castine, *d.* of Charles J. D. Derry, of The Hall, Cliffs' End. *Educ. :* City of London School, and Guy's Hospital. Dental Surgeon and Lecturer in Dental Surgery to Guy's Hospital ; External Examiner in Dental Subjects to the Universities of Birmingham and Leeds. *War Work :* Hon. Consulting Dental Surgeon attached to London Military Hospitals ; treated cases suffering from jaw injuries at The Hampstead Military Hospital, Southwark Military Hospital, Richmond Military Hospital and Belmont Hospital for prisoners of war ; Hon. Dental Surgeon to the Maxillo Facial Hospital at Kennington. *Address :* 18, Portland Place, London, W. *Clubs :* Royal Automobile ; London University.   (O11737)

PAYNE, Lily, M.B.E.

PAYNE, Percy John, M.B.E.

PAYNE, Richard Alfred Ernest, O.B.E.

PAYNE, Stephen, M.B.E., R.G.N.G., *b.* 8 July, 1886 ; *s.* of Jabez Payne, of Portsmouth ; *m.* Mireille Antonia, *d.* of Dr. Peirre Dorey, of Vienne, Isère, France. *Educ. :* Royal Naval Engineering Coll., Keyham ; Royal Naval Coll., Greenwich. Assistant Constructor, Devonport Dockyard and Admiralty ; Airship Constructor, Cardington, Bedford. *War Work :* Constructor in charge of construction, H.M.S. " Aurora " ; Designed calculations of H.M.S. " Renown " and " Repulse " ; Chief Airship Overseer, R31, R32, R37, and R38. *Address :* 21, Devon Road, Bedford.   (M9257)

PAYNE, Sylvia May, Mrs., C.B.E., M.B., B.S., *b.* 1880 ; *d.* of the Rev. Edwin William Moore, of Wimbledon, S.W. ; *m.* 1908, John Ernest Payne, M.B., B.C., F.R.C.S. Comdt. and Med. Officer in charge, Torquay Auxiliary Hospital. *Address :* 57, Carlisle Road, Eastbourne.   (C592)

PAYNE, Tom, M.B.E., R.A.O.C.

PAYNE, Walter, O.B.E., *b.* 26 June, 1874 ; *s.* of George Adney Payne, of London. *Educ. :* City of London School ; Heidelberg University. Barrister-at-Law ; Director of Public Companies. *War Work :* Director of Outside Organisation (Labour Regulation and Munitions Tribunals), Ministry of Munitions ; Chief Resettlement Officer, Demobilisation and Resettlement Dept. ; Deputy-Controller, Military Service (Civil Liabilities) Department. *Address :* 16A, New Cavendish St., Portland Place, W.1. *Club :* Bath.   (O638)

PEABODY, Kathleen, O.B.E.

PEACE, Edwin, O.B.E.

PEACE, John William, M.B.E.,; *s.* of Joseph Peace, of Leeds ; *m.* Clara Foster, *d.* of Joseph Broadbent, of Leeds. *Educ. :* Morley Collegiate School, Morley, near Leeds. Goods Agent, Midland Railway Co. *War Work :* Loaned by Midland Rly. Co., and acted as Divisional Road Transport Officer, Ministry of Food, North-Eastern Division ; Member of N.E. Divisional Road Transport Board, Road Transport Board, Board of Trade ; Munitions, Inland Transport Officer, No. 3 Area, Ministry of Munitions, Leeds. *Address :* 41, Church Hill, Northfield, Birmingham.   (M9258)

PEACH, Major Benjamin Neave, O.B.E., R.F.A.

PEACH, Lieut. Leonard Thomas, O.B.E., R.A.S.C., S.R.

PEACH, Capt. Robert STEPHENSON-, M.B.E., R.A.F.

PEACHEY, George Wyatt, O.B.E., F.R.H.S., *b.* 26 Feb. 1864 ; *s.* of George Charles Peachey, of Barrow, Suffolk. *Educ. :* Privately, and in France. Councillor of Borough of Fulham since 1903. *War Work :* Military Representative of Fulham Area and National Service Official under National Service Ministry. *Address :* Rose Villa, Fulham Park. *Clubs :* Royal Automobile ; Fulham Unionist and Conservative.   (O11104)

PEACHEY, Rev. Robert William, M.B.E., *b.* 1865 ; *s.* of Robert Peachey, of Halesworth, Suffolk ; *m.* Lydia, *d.* of James Barber, of Stoven, Suffolk. *Educ. :* Church Missionary Society's Coll., Islington, N. C.M.S. Sec., Madras, South India ; formerly C.M.S. Missionary, Beywada, Telugu Mission. *War Work :* Recruiting principally labourers for Mesopotamia Railway Corps, Porter Corps, etc. ; Joint Sec. District Soldiers' Committee. *Address :* C.M. House, Vepery, Madras, South India.   (M7148)

PEACHEY, Lieut.-Col. William Ellis, O.B.E.

PEACOCK, Alice Evelyn, M.B.E., *b.* 30 Jan. 1864 ; *d.* of Mark Beauchamp Peacock, of Springfield Place, Essex. *Educ. :* Germany and France. *War Work :* National Registration, Aug. 1915, and the Brighton Recruiting Office till Dec. 1918. *Address :* 157, Marine Parade, Brighton.   (M2273)

PEACOCK, Rev. Charles Alfred, C.B.E., *b.* 1868 ; *s.* of the late Rev. E. Peacock, Vicar of Netherexe, Devon ; *m.* Annie Kathleen, *d.* of the late Capt. W. E. Rendle, of 10th Lincolnshire Regt. *Educ. :* Oxford (M.A. (Oxon.), 1897). Chaplain to the Forces, 1st Class ; Assistant Chaplain-General, Irish Command, since July, 1917. *War Work :* S.C.F., Woolwich District, 1914–17 ; A.C.G., Irish Command, 1917. *Address :* Glen Lodge, Park Gate, Dublin. *Clubs :* Phyllis Court, Henley-on-Thames ; Royal St. George's Yacht, Kingstown.   (C1734)

PEACOCK, Major Gerald Selwyn, O.B.E., R.A.F.

PEACOCK, George John, O.B.E., M.D., F.R.C.P.I.

PEACOCK, Major Henry, O.B.E.

PEACOCK, Capt. Henry Kartchkal, M.B.E., R.G.A.

PEACOCK, May Beauchamp, M.B.E., *b.* 12 Jan. 1868 ; *d.* of Mark Beauchamp Peacock, of Springfield Place, Essex. *Educ. :* Germany and France. *War Work :* National Registration, Aug. 1915 ; Secretarial work at Brighton Recruiting Office to Dec. 1918. *Address :* Belgrave House, 157, Marine Parade, Brighton.   (M2274)

PEACOCKE, Aungier, M.B.E., *b.* 6 Oct. 1869. Station-master, G.E. Railway, Cambridge. *War Work :* Transport of troops and material. *Address :* Morcambe House, Mill Road, Cambridge.   (M9259)

PEACOCKE, Ethel Helen, Mrs., M.B.E.

PEACOCKE, Lieut.-Col. Goodricke Thomas, O.B.E., *b.* 8 Sept. 1865 ; *s.* of Goodricke Thomas Peacocke, of Carraigna-Greine, Dalkey, Co. Dublin ; *m.* Maud Mary, *d.* of A. R. Cobbett, of Woburn Chase, Addlestone, Surrey. *Educ. :* Harrow, and Sandhurst Coll. *War Work :* Officer-in-charge Infy. Records, Lichfield. *Address :* Argyll Lodge, Lichfield, Staffs. *Club :* Army and Navy.   (O8904)

PEACOCKE, Reginald Christopher, O.B.E., M.D., *b.* 5 April, 1871 ; *s.* of the Most Rev. Joseph Ferguson Peacocke, D.D., late Archbishop of Dublin ; *m.* Evelyn Clair, *d.* of the late Wm. Hyde, of Bangor, Co. Down. *Educ. :* Corrig School, Kingstown ; Trinity Coll., Dublin. Medical Officer, Post Office ; Hon. Anæsthetist, Monkstown Hospital ; Member of Council, B.M.A. *War Work :* Medical Officer, Corrig Castle Red Cross Hospital ; Anæsthetist, Special Military Surgical Hospital, Blackrock ; Assistant County Director, Co. Dublin Branch, British Red Cross Society. *Address :* Blackrock Lodge, Blackrock, Co. Dublin. *Club :* Royal Automobile, Dublin.   (O4383)

PEAD, Winifred, M.B.E.

PEAK, William Herbert, O.B.E., *b.* 27 Oct. 1879 ; *s.* of William Henry Peak, of Belper ; *m.* Kate Beatrice, *d.* of Harry Sedgwick Sever. *Educ. :* Manchester Grammar School. Chief Accountant, Imperial Tobacco Co., Ogden Branch ; also Wm. Cory and Son, Ltd., London ; Sec. and Chief Accountant, Jurgens, Ltd., London. *War Work :* Chief Financial Representative, H.M. Factory, Gretna. *Address :* 14, Kensington Crescent, Kensington, W. 14.   (O1736)

PEAKE, Major Edward Gordon, O.B.E.

PEAKE, Emily M., Mrs., M.B.E., *b.* 14 June, 1863 ; *d.* of E. J. B. Jellicorse, of Fallowfield, Manchester ; *m.* Arthur Copson, *s.* of Edward Copson Peake, of Pinner. *Educ. :* Privately. *War Work :* Diocesan President, Girls' Friendly Society, Ripon Diocese ; Recreation Hut at Catterick Camp, Yorkshire, for the Q.M.A.A.C., and its finance, for which £2700 was raised within three months. *Address :* Underbank, Elstree, Herts.   (M9261)

PEAKE, Lieut.-Col. Walter King, O.B.E.

PEAKE, Wilfred Stevenson, O.B.E. Staff Engineer Grade I., Wireless Telegraphy Staff, H.M. Signal School, Portsmouth.   (O11921)

PEAKER, Alfred, O.B.E.

PEAL, Major Edward Raymond, C.B.E., D.S.C. Major R.A.F. ; served in the Great War, 1914–19 (despatches).   (C2347)

PEARCE, Agnes Isobel, M.B.E., V.A.D.

PEARCE, Col. Charles Marshall, C.B.E., V.D. Indian Defence Force. Gen. Traffic Manager, E. India Railway, Bengal.   (C1090)

PEARCE, Lieut.-Col. Cyril Harvey, C.B.E., T.D., T.F.R., *b.* 19 July, 1878 ; *s.* of Thomas Pearce, of Hull ; *m.* Martha, *d.* of Martin Henry Cross, of Hull. *Educ. :* Denstone Coll. *War Work :* 5th Yorkshire Regt., France and Belgium ; Capt., 1914 ; Major, 1915 ; Lieut.-Col., 1916 ; Commanded 5th Yorkshire Regt. in France, until wounded in autumn, 1917 ; Commanded 7th (R.) West Yorkshire Regt. and East Riding Yeomanry in Ireland until Feb. 1920 ; battles of Ypres, Hooge, Loos, Somme, Arras.   (C1235)

PEARCE, Capt. Edward Oscar, O.B.E., R.E.

PEARCE, Ernest Alfred John, O.B.E.

PEARCE, Herbert Cecil, M.B.E., *b.* 19 Dec. 1884 ; *y.s.* of the late William Pearce, of South Hampstead, London, and Mrs. Pearce, of Ardun, Howard Road, Bournemouth ; *m.* Katharine, *d.* of Walter Hooker, of Beech House, Croydon. *Educ. :* Privately, Margate ; Blois, France ; Brunswick, Germany. *Address :* Sydney, N.S.W, Australia.   (M4572)

PEARCE, James, M.B.E.

PEARCE, John, M.B.E.

PEARCE, Major and Qr.-Mr. John Wesley, O.B.E., R.E.

PEARCE, John William, M.B.E., *b.* 22 June, 1873 ; *s.* of the late Robert Frederick Pearce, of Bristol. Public Works Contractor, Contractor to H.M. Government. *War Work :* Divisional Officer for Board of Trade, Timber Supplies over Yorkshire, Nottingham, and Lincolnshire ; Authority on Housing ; at present engaged on large development scheme for Housing on Tees-side, Cleveland. *Address :* 14, Prudential Buildings, Doncaster.   (M9263)

PEARCE, Capt. Joseph, O.B.E., R.A.F.

PEARCE, Kathleen, M.B.E., W.R.A.F.

PEARCE, Standen Leonard, C.B.E., M.Sc., M.I.C.E., M.I.M.E., M.I.E.E., *b.* 1873 ; *s.* of the late Rev. Standen Pearce, of Crewkerne, Somerset. *Educ. :* Bishop's Stortford Coll. and Finsbury Technical Coll. Chief Engineer and General Manager Manchester Corporation Electricity Dept. ; Past Pres. Incorporated Municipal Electrical Assoc. *Address :* 15, Edge Lane, Chorlton-cum-Hardy, Lancashire.   (C1020)

PEARCE, Thomas, O.B.E. Superintending Inspector of Customs and Excise.   (O11106)

PEARCE, Capt. Wallace George James, O.B.E.

PEARCE, Major William, O.B.E., R.E.

PEARCE, William Sidney, M.B.E.

PEARMAN, Ernest Albert, M.B.E., A.C.I.S., A.M.Inst.T., F.L.A.A., *b.* 2 Nov. 1874 ; *s.* of John Pearman, of Leyton, Essex ; *m.* Jessie Letitia, *d.* of John Embleton Smith, of

Wanstead. *Educ.:* Leyton. Accountant and Traffic Supt. Sunderland District Electric Tramways, Ltd.; Assistant Overseer to the Parish of East and Middle Herrington. *War Work:* Member of the Durham County Committee for War Savings; Hon. Sec. Houghton and Sunderland Rural Local Committees for War Savings. *Address:* 9, Ryhope Village, Co. Durham.   (M9264)

PEARS, Vice-Adm. Sir Edmund Radcliffe, K.B.E., C.B., *b.* 25 April, 1862; *s.* of the late Lieut.-Col. A. C. Pears, of Bath; *m.* Jeanie Mayhew, *d.* of J. H. Innes, of Vancouver Island. *Educ.:* Clifton Coll. Entered Royal Navy 1875; Captain, 1904; Rear-Adm., 1914; Vice-Adm., 1920. *War Work:* Acting Sub-Lieut. of "Ruby" in Egyptian War, 1882 (Egyptian Medal, Khedive's Star); 1st Lieut. of "Forte" in Benin Expedition, 1897 (Benin Medal); Commander of "Perseus" in Expeditions against Mullah, 1902–3 (Somaliland Medal); Rear-Admiral Commanding Cromarty Naval Base, 1914–20; *Address:* 1958, Ogden Avenue, Vancouver, B.C.   (K201)

PEARSALL, Lieut. Richard Montague Stack, M.B.E.

PEARSALL, Capt. and Qr.-Mr. Sidney James, O.B.E.

PEARSE, Capt. Claude Alwin Rombulow, C.B.E., R.N. Served in the Great War, 1914–19, at Mudros Base (despatches).   (C3359a)

PEARSE, Eleanor, M.B.E., B.Sc., F.L.S.; *s.* of William Henry Pearse, M.D., of Plymouth. *Educ.:* High School for Girls, Plymouth; Bedford Coll.; Univ. of London. Science Mistress, Mary Datchelor School, Camberwell; Lecturer in Science, L.C.C. Furzedown Training Coll. *War Work:* Recorder, Chemical Warfare Committee, Ministry of Munitions. *Club:* Univ. of London.   (M9265)

PEARSE, Paymaster-Sub-Lieut. Hender Trevenen, M.B.E., R.N.R.

PEARSE, James, C.B.E., M.D. Inspector of various factories manufacturing foodstuffs in the United Kingdom for the consumption of the troops.   (C3162)

PEARSE, Lieut. Robert Bernard, M.B.E.

PEARSON, Arthur Frederick, M.B.E., J.P., *b.* 1 July, 1855; *s.* of Thomas Pearson, formerly of Torquay. High Sheriff of Anglesey, 1914–15. *War Work:* Lieut. R.N.V.R., 1915–19; Assistant in the Isle of Anglesey to the Divisional Officer for Coast Watching Services; Deputy Superintendent of Ship Repairs for Holyhead District of the Mersey Division, 1917–19. *Address:* Soldiers Point, Holyhead, Anglesey. *Club:* Conservative.   (M9266)

PEARSON, Capt. Basil Lancelot, O.B.E., B.A., *b.* 1 June, 1892; *s.* of the Rev. Henry Pearson, of Lambley Rectory, Notts; *m.* Ruby, *d.* of William J. Holmes, of British Consulate St. Gall, Switzerland. *Educ.:* Oundle School, Northants, and Sidney Sussex Coll., Cambridge. Capt. in Royal Army Service Corps, Regular Army. *War Work:* First Commission, Sept. 1914; served in France, April, 1915, to Feb. 1919. *Address:* 3, Hammelton Road, Bromley, Kent. *Club:* Junior Army and Navy.   (O5672)

PEARSON, Burton, O.B.E., *b.* 1872; *s.* of Samuel Pearson, of Wolverhampton. *Educ.:* Wolverhampton Grammar School and Birmingham Univ. Assistant Gen. Manager, Egyptian State Railways, Cairo. *War Work:* As Divisional Traffic Superintendent (graded Major, locally), assisted in supervising military transport on E.S.R., in connection with operations in Egypt, Sinai and Palestine, 1914–18. *Address:* Gezira North, Cairo. *Clubs:* Constitutional; Turf (Cairo).   (O2132)

PEARSON, Charles Child, C.B.E., *b.* 19 Nov. 1875; *s.* of John Wyse Pearson, of Waterloo, Liverpool; *m.* Ada Mavis, *d.* of William Powell, of Allerton, Liverpool. *Educ.:* Cambridge House, Seaforth, nr. Liverpool, and Privately. Member of the firm of Andrew Callender & Co., Victoria Street, Liverpool, Produce and Provision Importers, Brokers and Commission Agents; Official Brokers to the Marshal of the Admiralty, the Navy and Army Canteen Board, the War Office, and other Government Departments; Chairman of the Liverpool Produce Exchange Benevolent Guild in 1916; Vice-President, 1916–17, of the Liverpool Produce Exchange and Provision Trade Association, Ltd., resigned Presidency upon joining the special War Food Mission to the United States of America, which left England on 23 Sept. 1917; remained in U.S.A. from Oct. 1917, to Nov. 1918, as Director of Allied Provisions Export Commission; Liaison Officer of same at Washington, D.C., between British Ministry of Food in U.S.A. and the United States Food Administration which was set up by the U.S. Government under Mr. Herbert C. Hoover, the American Food Controller, and as such conducted negotiations with Mr. Hoover regarding all American Food supplies (other than cereals and sugar) for Great Britian, France, Italy, and Belgium; Official representative at Washington; D.C., of the British Ministry of Food; Director of Purchases in U.S.A. of all Packing House Products (other than fresh and frozen meat) for Great Britain, and all European Allies, including British and Allied Army food requirements, also edible oils and fats for margarine supplies; personally negotiating and supervising in one year purchases exceeding one hundred and forty millions sterling, which sum does not include very large purchases made to cover the monthly requirements of France, Italy, and Belgium; Nov. 1918, joined the Ministry of Food in London, in advisory capacity, and conducted negotiations between the British Ministry and Mr. Hoover, and the United States Food Mission then resident in London; in March, 1919, proceed to Holland, and made preliminary arrangements for flow of necessary relief food

supplies to Germany through Rotterdam, and the setting up of a permanent British Commission to deal with these matters; conducted conferences at Rotterdam with British and German delegates, and concluded commercial agreement with the latter to govern all matters relating to payment, sales, and deliveries of certain foodstuffs to Germany in accordance with the undertaking entered into at the Allied Peace Conferences at Trèves, Spa, and Brussels; upon completion of Mission to Holland, resigned position with Ministry of Food, and returned to business in private capacity. *Address:* Greenfields, Blundellsands, Lancashire. *Clubs:* Conservative, Liverpool; Formby Golf; West Lancashire Golf; West Lancashire Ladies' Golf.   (C2867)

PEARSON, Capt. Charles Edmund, O.B.E.

PEARSON, Sir (Cyril) Arthur, Bart., G.B.E. (*see* BURKE'S *Peerage*), *b.* 24 Feb. 1866; *s.* of the Rev. Arthur Cyril Pearson, of Springfield, Essex; *m.* Dame Ethel Maud, D.B.E. (*q.v.*), *d.* of William John Fraser, of Cromartie, Herne Bay, Kent. *Educ.:* Winchester. Chairman of C. Arthur Pearson, Ltd., Principal proprietor of various monthly and weekly publications; and founder of many well-known publications; newspaper proprietor until complete failure of eyesight in 1914. *War Work:* Organised measures for the relief of Blinded Soldiers and Sailors, with headquarters at St. Dunstan's, Regent's Park; Joint Hon. Sec. of the Collecting Committee of the National Relief Fund. *Address:* 15, Devonshire Street, W. 1. *Clubs:* Carlton; Bath; Travellers' (Paris).   (G10)

PEARSON, Dora Alexandrina, Mrs., M.B.E., B.Litt. *d.* of George Pearson, of London. *Educ.:* St. Leonards School; St. Andrew's, Fife; Durham Univ. *War Work:* Four years on V.A.D. Headquarters Staff, Devonshire House, W., and 53, Grosvenor Gardens, Oct. 1915, to Aug. 1919. *Address:* P.O., Box 265, Benoni, Transvaal.   (M1549)

PEARSON, Ethel Maud, Lady, D.B.E., *d.* of William John Fraser, of London; *m.* Sir Cyril Arthur, Bart., G.B.E. (*q.v.*), *s.* of Rev. Arthur Cyril Pearson, of Springfield, Essex. *War Work:* Hon. Treas. Queen's Work for Women Fund; also closely connected with her husband, Sir Arthur Pearson, in his work for St. Dunstan's and the Soldiers and Sailors blinded in the War. *Address:* 15, Devonshire Street, London, W. 1.   (D60)

PEARSON, Geoffrey Hope, O.B.E.

PEARSON, Lieut.-Col. George Thomson, C.B.E., R.F.A. Served in the Great War, 1914–19 (despatches).   (C1736)

PEARSON, Capt. Gilbert Livermore, O.B.E., Can. A.S.C.

PEARSON, Capt. Henry John, M.B.E., R.A.S.C.

PEARSON, Lieut.-Col. Hugh Frederick Archie, O.B.E.

PEARSON, Major John Barrington, O.B.E., R.E.

PEARSON, John Howard, M.B.E.

PEARSON, Louis Frederick, C.B.E., *b.* 1863; *s.* of the late John Royston Pearson, Chilwell House, Notts.; *m.* Gertrude, *d.* of the late Thomas Potter, of Bramcote, Notts. *Educ.:* Grosvenor School, Nottingham. Engineer. *War Work:* Chairman of Nottingham and Notts Shell Factory, and of Munition Board of Management, 1915–19. *Address:* Lenton Grove, Nottingham. *Clubs:* Carlton; Notts County.   (C1021)

PEARSON, Lieut.-Col. Maurice Grey, O.B.E., M.B., F.R.C.S.

PEARSON, Capt. Richard William, O.B.E., R.A.S.C.

PEARSON, Robert James, M.B.E.

PEARSON, Robert John Addison, O.B.E.

PEARSON, Major Robert Stanley, O.B.E.

PEARSON, Brig.-Gen. Walter Bagot, C.M.G., C.B.E., *b.* 1872; *m.* 1919, Ielena, *d.* of Louis Wensten, of Paris. Served with the Nile Expedition, 1898, and in S. Africa, 1899–1902 (Queen's medal with three clasps, King's medal with two clasps). *Address:* Kirkby Lonsdale.   (C1301)

PEARSON, Wesley Marshall, M.B.E.   (M10413)

PEARSON, William Henry, M.B.E., *b.* 11 April, 1857; *s.* of Henry Pearson, of Wakefield, Yorks.; *m.* Mary Booth, *d.* of John Fowler, of Lytham, and Blackpool. *Educ.:* Mechanics' Institute, Manchester. Railway Official. *War Work:* Railway Transport. *Address:* 8, Stanley Grove, Heaton Moor, Stockport.   (M9268)

PEART, Lieut. Charles, M.B.E.

PEASE, Ella, O.B.E.

PEASE, Capt. Ernest Hubert, O.B.E.

PEASE, Evelyn Ada, O.B.E., *b.* 10 Nov. 1876; *d.* of Arthur Pease, M.P., of Cliff House, Marske-by-the-Sea; 2, Princes Gardens and Hummersknott, Darlington. *War Work:* Commandant, Richmond Auxiliary Military Hospital; Vice-President, Gilling West Division B.R.C.S. *Address:* Hill House, Richmond, Yorkshire. *Clubs:* Ladies' Empire; Ladies' V.A.D.   (O641)

PEASE, Joseph Gerald, C.B.E., *b.* 1863; *s.* of the late Thomas Pease, of Cote Bank, Westbury-on-Trym; *m.* Winifred, *d.* of Col. Josiah Hudleston, of the Madras Staff Corps. *Educ.:* Univ. Coll., London. Barrister-at-Law; Lecturer on Law at the Inns of Court; Chairman of Court of Referees, London. *War Work:* Treasury Solicitor's Department; Chairman, Munitions Tribunal, Cambridge; Deputy Chairman, Munitions Tribunal, London. *Address:* 36, Downshire Hill, Hampstead. *Clubs:* Athenæum; Savile; Royal Cruising.   (C2868)

PEASE, Lucy Victoria, Mrs., O.B.E., *d.* of the late W. Browne-Clayton, of Browne's Hill, Carlow, Ireland; *m.* Claud Edward, *s.* of Arthur Pease, of Cliff House, Marske-by-the-Sea. *Educ.:* At home. *War Work:* Commandant of Yorks. (8)

N. Riding Hospital at Redcar, open Jan. 1915, to June, 1919. *Address:* Selaby Hall, Darlington.   (O642)

PEAT, Sir Harry (William Henry), K.B.E., M.A., F.C.A., *b.* 4 May, 1878 ; *s.* of Sir William Barclay Peat, Kt. Bach., of Wykeham Rise, Totteridge, Herts ; *m.* Alice Evelyn, *d.* of the late Lieut.-Col. John Eustace Jameson. *Educ.:* St. Paul's School, and Trinity Coll., Oxford. Partner in firm of W. B. Peat & Co., Chartered Accountants, 11, Ironmonger Lane, London, E.C. 2, and other towns in Great Britain ; Member of Corporation of City of London since 1915 ; Financial Sec. and Accounting Officer to Ministry of Food, 1917–20. *Address:* Hillside, Bushey, Herts. *Clubs:* United Univ. ; Gresham.   (K460)

PEATT, Capt. Ernest Snowden Wallace, O.B.E., F.R.C.V.S., R.A.V.C., *b.* 16 March, 1895 ; *s.* of J. W. Peatt, M.R.C.V.S., of Leominster. *Educ.:* Kilkenny Coll. *War Work:* Commissioned 11 Sept. 1916 ; served British Salonica Force, Oct. 1916, to July, 1919, and Army of Black Sea, July, 1919, to Aug. 1920. *Address:* Marsh House, Leominster, Herefordshire.   (O6250)

PEATTIE, Lieut. Alexander Bonnie, O.B.E., R.N.V.R.

PEATTIE, 2nd Lieut. Donald Munroe, O.B.E.

PECK, Elfrida Mary, M.B.E., *b.* 4 March 1893 ; *d.* of late Oswald Peck, of Wigan. *Educ.:* Bedford High School. Road Transport Officer, Bedford Area, formerly operating under Board of T4ade, now acting under Ministry of Food, Road Transport Department. *War Work:* Appointed chief clerk . in the Bedford Boro' Food Control Office, 1917 ; appointed Road Transport Officer for Bedfordshire, 1918, working under the Board of Trade, and afterwards under the Ministry of Food, despatching during Railway Strike, 1919, for carriage of foodstuffs to and from Bedford Area. *Addresses:* 60, Bushmead Avenue, Bedford ; Town Hall, Bedford.   (M9269)

PECK, Capt. Frederick George, M.B.E., *b.* 22 July, 1862 ; *s.* of John Peck ; *m.* Jemima Delia, *d.* of James Somerville, of Beyrout. *Educ.:* Furness Collegiate School. Master Mariner ; Marine Superintendent for Khedivial Mail Line. *War Work:* Acting as Pilot for Ports and Lights for 3½ years without pay, working day and night ; housing and feeding soldiers before the Commissariat was organised ; acting as train despatcher at night-time. *Address:* c/o Khedivial Mail Line, Port Tewfik. *Club:* Union, Port Tewfik.   (M9270)

PECK, Margaret Catherine, O.B.E. *War Work:* Charge of Comforts for Troops Depot, Folkestone, three years ; Red Cross work (certificate gained) ; Work for Refugees coming into Folkestone ; war work for G.F.S. ; Chairwoman of Committee for placing girls on land, two years. *Address:* 5, Kingsnorth Gardens, Folkestone.   (O3867)

PECK, Lieut. Richard Hallam, O.B.E., R.A.F.

PECK, Lieut. Victor Newton, M.B.E.

PECKITT, Reginald Godfrey, C.B.E., *b.* 1868 ; *s.* of Lieut.-Col. R. W. Peckitt ; *m.* Mary Amelia, *d.* of Dr. M. F. Kirkbride, of Philadelphia, U.S.A. *Educ.:* King William's Coll., and Wadham Coll., Oxford. Chief Mechanical Engineer, Egyptian State Railways. *War Work:* Construction of armoured trains, hospital trains, pontoons and service carts, spares for machine-guns and for heavy guns and carriages, hand grenades, repairs and upkeep of rolling stock for Palestine military railways. *Address:* Cairo, Egypt. *Clubs:* St. Stephen's ; Turf, Cairo ; Sultan Hussein, Alexandria.   (C412)

PEDDELL, Lieut. Thomas Arthur, M.B.E., R.A.F

PEDDER, Sir John, K.B.E., C.B., *b.* 27 Jan. 1869 ; *s.* of the Rev. John Pedder, of Lancaster and Durham ; *m.* Frances Evelyn, *d.* of W. Arthur Sharpe, of Highgate. *Educ.:* Somersetshire Coll., Bath ; Bath Coll. ; Oriel Coll., Oxford. Assist. Sec. Home Office ; Member of Central Control Board (Liquor Traffic). *War Work:* Head of the Division of Home Office dealing with the Control of Aliens, Nationality questions, etc. ; Regulation of the sale and supply of Intoxicating Liquor. *Address:* 20A, Cheyne Walk, Chelsea, S.W. 3. *Club:* Athenæum.   (K227)

PEDDIE, Francis Grove, M.B.E.

PEDDIE, Capt. John Ronald, M.B.E.

PEDDLE, Cyril James, M.B.E., D.Sc., F.I.C., F.C.S., *b.* 1 Feb. 1887 ; *s.* of John Peddle, of Cudworth, Yorkshire ; *m.* Hilda Augusta, *d.* of Charles Ridal Hampshire, of Holmfirth. *Educ.:* Barnsley Grammar School ; The Univ., Sheffield. Head of Research Department, Messrs. Wood Bros., Ltd., Barnsley, and Derby Crown Glass Co., Ltd. *War Work:* Assisted in Development of Optical Glasses ; worked out formulæ for over 70 different types, including most of the important glasses of pre-war days, together with several new types not hitherto available. *Address:* Ravenscliffe, Turnditch, near Derby.   (M9272)

PEDLEY, Major Oswald Henry, O.B.E., J.P., *b.* 8 July, 1860 ; *s.* of Thomas Humphrey Pedley, of Chesterfield ; *m.* Josephine, *d.* of the late A. Porral, C.M.G., I.S.O., of Gibraltar. *Educ.:* Eastbourne Coll. ; Royal Military Coll., Sandhurst. Vice-Consul, La Linea, Spain. Expedition to Dongola, 1896 ; Nile Expedition, 1897–99 ; despatches twice ; 4th Class Medjidieh, Egyptian Medal with 2 clasps, Medal, Brevet of Major ; S. African War, 1901–2 ; despatches ; Queen's Medal with 2 clasps, War, 1914–19, O.B.E. *Address:* Gibraltar. *Clubs:* Army and Navy ; Mediterranean, Gibraltar.   (O3163)

PEEBLES, Capt. Arthur Charlesworth, O.B.E., R.E. (T.).

PEECH, James, C.B.E., *b.* 1878 ; *s.* of Henry Peech, formerly of Roehampton ; *m.* 1912, Winifred Wyndham. *Educ.:* in France. Steel Manufacturer ; a partner in the firm of Steel, Peech and Tozer, of Rotherham ; Adviser on Shell

Steel, Ministry of Munitions. *Addresses:* Abbey Mead, Bourne End, Bucks ; 44, Hans Mansions, S.W. ; Beaulieu, Hants.   (C263)

PEEK, William Heath, M.B.E.

PEEL, Cicely, M.B.E.

PEEL, Dorothy Constance, Mrs., O.B.E. : 2nd *d.* of Capt. and Mrs. Richard Lane Bayliff ; *m.* S. C. Peel. *Educ.:* At home. Editor of " Hearth and Home " and " Woman," and Managing Director of Beeton & Co., Ltd., 1903–6. *War Work:* Director of Women's Service, Ministry of Food ; Departmental Editor " Daily Mail," 1918–20. *Address:* 7, Alexander Square, London, S.W. 3. *Club:* Forum.   (O643)

PEEL, Dorothy Mary Grace, Mrs. John Graham, M.B.E., *d.* of Lieut.-Gen. Horatio Shirley Morant, of Blendworth Lodge, Horndean, Hants. ; *m.* John Graham, *s.* of the late Gerald Peel, J.P., of Parkfield, Swinton. *War Work:* Donor and Officer-in-Charge of Private Military Hospital, at Colshaw Hall, Over Peover (60 beds), from April, 1915, to Feb. 1919. *Addresses:* Peover Hall, Knutsford, Cheshire ; Colshaw Hall, Cheshire. *Club:* Albemarle.   (M92748)

PEEL, Col. Herbert Hawarth, C.B.E., *b.* 1866 ; *s.* of Frederick Peel, of Highlands, East Bergholt, Suffolk ; *m.* Monica, *d.* of the Rev. J. E. Coulson, of Long Preston, Yorkshire. *Educ.:* Wellington Coll. *War Work:* Served in European War, 1915–20. *Addresses:* Highlands, East Bergholt, Suffolk ; 1A, Queen's Gate, S.W. 7.   (C1130)

PEEL, Major Robert, O.B.E.

PEEL, Walter, O.B.E., J.P., County of Chester, *b.* 7 Sept. 1868 ; *s.* of Capt. Edmund R. Peel, of Rock Ferry, Cheshire ; *m.* Helen Margaret (died Dec. 1897), *d.* of John H. Hubback, of New Ferry, Cheshire. *Educ.:* Malvern. District Registrar of the High Court of Justice, Liverpool. *War Work:* Chairman, Disablement Sub-Committee, Liverpool War Pensions Committee ; Hon. Sec. Liverpool Branch Soldiers' and Sailors' Help Society ; Hon. Director, Lord Roberts' Memorial Workshops, Liverpool ; Hon. Sec. Prince of Wales' Fund, Liverpool ; Member of Committee in Liverpool of Red Cross Society, Lord Mayor's Silver Badge Fund, and Prisoners of War Fund. *Address:* The Shrublands, Chester. *Clubs:* Fly Fishers' ; Public Schools'.   (O11109)

PEEL, William Robert Wellesley, 2nd Viscount, P.C., G.B.E., *b.* 7 Jan. 1867 ; *e.s.* of 1st Viscount Peel (*see* BURKE'S *Peerage*) ; *m.* Hon. Ella Williamson, *e.d.* of 1st Baron Ashton (*see* BURKE'S *Peerage*). *Educ.:* Harrow ; Baliol Coll., Oxford. Under Sec. of State for War since 1919 ; called to the Bar, Inner Temple, 1893 ; member of Royal Commission for the Port of London ; Leader of the Municipal Reform Party, 1908–10 ; Chairman of L.C.C., 1914 ; J.P., D.L. Bedfordshire ; Governor of Victoria University, Manchester ; Col. of the Bedfordshire Yeomanry 1912–15 ; Chairman of Committee on detention of Neutral Vessels, 1916 ; Joint Parliamentary Sec. to National Service Dept., 1917 ; acted as " Daily Telegraph " Correspondent during Græco-Turkish War ; M.P. (U.), Southern Division of Manchester, 1900–6 ; Taunton, 1909–12 ; contested Harrow Division, 1906 ; Officer Legion of Honour. *Addresses:* 52, Grosvenor St., W.1 ; The Lodge, Sandy, Bedfordshire ; Coombe Cross, East Meon, Petersfield. *Clubs:* Carlton ; Brooks's ; Garrick.   (G42)

PEET, Howard, M.B.E.

PEGG, Capt. Thomas Edgar, M.B.E., R.A.S.C.

PEGRUM, Major Abraham William, M.B.E., R.A.O.C.

PEILE, Henry, C.B.E., D.Sc. (Durham), *b.* 1862 ; *s.* of George Peile, of Shotley Bridge, Co. Durham ; *m.* Eva Ethel, *d.* of J. H. Beckingham, of Newcastle-on-Tyne. *Educ.:* Queenwood Coll., Hampshire ; Owens' Coll., Manchester ; Zurich, Switzerland. Managing Director of the Priestman Collieries, Ltd. ; Chairman of the Newcastle Alloy Co., Ltd. ; Chairman of the Newcastle Benzol Co., Ltd. ; Director of the Newcastle Graphite Co., Ltd. ; Director of the Priestman Power Co., Ltd. *Club:* Royal Societies'.   (C2869)

PEIRCE, Richard Gall, M.B.E.

PEIRSE, Florence Ida, Mrs., M.B.E.

PEIRSE, Admiral Sir Richard Henry, K.C.B., K.B.E., M.V.O., *b.* 4 Sept. 1860 ; *s.* of the late Lieut.-Col. C. H. Peirse, of Minster Yard, York ; *m.* Blanche Melville, *d.* of the Rev. E. J. Wemyss Whittaker, of Bath. *Educ.:* H.M.S. " Britannia." Joined Royal Navy, 1873 ; specially promoted Lieut. for meritorious examinations, 1881 ; as Lieut. of " Inflexible," 1882 ; was present at the bombardment of Alexandria, and during Egyptian War (Medal with clasp, Khedive's Star) ; commanded " Barracouta " during South African War, 1900 (Medal, and promoted Capt.) ; became a member of the Ordnance Board, 1907 ; A.D.C. to King Edward, 1908–9 ; Inspector of Target Practice, 1909–11 ; Commanded 1st Battle Squadron, Home Fleet, 1911–12 ; Commander-in-Chief, East Indies Station, 1913–16. *War Work:* On outbreak of war was Commander-in-Chief, East Indies Station ; in 1914, conducted Convoy of Indian Expeditionary Force from India to Suez ; Headquarters transferred to Egypt in Dec. 1914, and was in charge of Naval operations during attack on Suez Canal in Feb. 1915 ; commanded squadron which bombarded Smyrna forts in March, 1915 ; on return to England on termination of appointment in 1916, became Naval Member of Central Committee of Board of Invention and Research ; is a Grand Officer of the Legion of Honour and has Grand Cordon of Order of the Nile ; was first naval officer to receive the K.B.E. *Address:* Fiesole, Bathwick Hill, Bath. *Clubs:* United Service ; Bath and County.   (K162)

PEIRSE, *Capt.* Arthur Cecil Proctor de la Poer BERES-
FORD-, M.B.E.

PEIRSE, Henrietta Lady BERESFORD-, O.B.E., only *d.* of
Sir Matthew Smith-Dodsworth, 4th Bt. ; *m.* Sir Henry Monson
de la Poer Beresford Peirse, 3rd Bt. *Address :* The Hall,
Bedale, Yorkshire. (O1741)

PELHAM, Admiral Frederick Sidney, C.B.E., *b.* 25 Oct.
1854 ; *s.* of Rear-Admiral the Hon. F. T. Pelham, C.B. ; *m.*
Louise Elizabeth, *d.* of Major-Gen. Wm. J. Chads, C.B. *Educ. :*
Brenchby, Kent. Entered Royal Navy, 1868 ; Capt. 1898 ;
Rear-Admiral, 1907 ; retired, 1916 ; A.D.C. to H.M. The King,
1906–7 ; served Somaliland, 1904 (despatches) ; Admiral
Superintendent, Gibraltar, 1909–12. *War Work :* B.R.C.S.,
County Director for Sussex during the War. *Club :* United
Service. (C1022)

PELHAM, Louisa, Hon. Mrs. Thomas, O.B.E. ; *d.* of the late
William Bruce, of Kennet, N.B. ; *m.* Thomas Henry William,
C.B., M.A. (who died), *s.* of the 3rd Earl of Chichester (*see*
BURKE'S *Peerage*). *War Work :* Chairman of Wandsworth,
Putney, and Roehampton War Hospital Supply Depot.
Address : 24, Brechin Place, S.W. 7. (O11111)

PELHAM, Maud Katherine, O.B.E., *b.* 20 Sept. 1887 ;
d. of the late Hon. Thomas Pelham, C.B., *s.* of 3rd Earl of
Chichester (*see* BURKE'S *Peerage*), Assistant Sec. Board of Trade.
War Work : Y.W.C.A., War Department. *Address :* 24, Brechin
Place. S.W. 7. (O1742)

PELHAM, T. Capt. Alfred ANDERSON-, O.B.E., R.F.A.

PELHAM, Major Cecil Henry ANDERSON-, O.B.E.,
b. 25 Jan. 1874 ; *s.* of Hon. E. A. Pelham, of St. Lawrence,
I. of W. (*see* BURKE'S *Peerage*, Yarborough, E.) ; *m.* Hon.
Georgina Hamilton (*q.v.*), 2nd *d.* of the 1st Lord Holm Patrick,
of Abbotstown, Co. Dublin (*see* BURKE'S *Peerage*). D. A.
Director of Remounts, Horse Guards from 1916 ; was Brigade
Major N. Midland Infantry Brigade (T.), 1908–12, and
Deputy Director of Remounts at Headquarters, Northern
Command, 1912–15 ; late Capt. and Hon. Major, Northampton-
shire Yeomanry, formerly 12th Lancers ; served in the S.
African War, 1899–1902. *Addresses :* Cedar House, Castor,
Peterborough ; The Cottage, St. Lawrence, I. of W. *Club :*
Cavalry. (O6669)

PELHAM, Georgina, Hon. Mrs. ANDERSON-, O.B.E., *b.*
2 Nov. 1880 ; 2nd *d.* of Ion Trant Hamilton, 1st Baron Holm
Patrick, of Abbotstown, Co. Dublin, Ireland ; *m.* Cecil Henry
(*q.v.*), *s.* of Hon. Evelyn Anderson-Pelham, of St. Lawrence,
Ventnor (*see* BURKE'S *Peerage*, Yarborough, E.). *War Work :*
Hon. Sec. York Military Division Soldiers' and Sailors' Families
Association, 1914–15 ; Canteen work, Joint Women's V.A.D.
Department, 1917–20. *Addresses :* Cedar House, Peter-
borough ; 1, Mount Street, W. 1. (O11110)

PELL, Henry William, O.B.E.

PELLATT, Capt. Hamilton Francis Moore, M.B.E.,
M.C.

PELLEREAU, Capt. John Cyril Etienne, O.B.E., R.A.,
b. 30 May, 1891 ; *s.* of H. E. Pellereau, late P.W.D., India ;
m. Aileen Nora Vidal, *d.* of General R. M. Betham, of Indian
Army. *Educ. :* Harrow, and R.M.A., Woolwich. *War Work :*
France and Belgium, Oct. 1914, to March, 1916, and Feb. 1917,
to Jan. 1919, serving with 7th (Meerut) Div., 49th (W.R.) Div.,
57th (W.L.) Div., and 1st Army Troops. *Address :* c/o Messrs.
Cox & Co., Charing Cross. *Club :* Junior United Service.
(O5675)

PELLEW, Capt. Edward Irving Pownel, O.B.E.,
R.A.M.C.

PELLING, Charlie, M.B.E.

PELLY, Lieut. Evelyn, M.B.E., R.A.S.C.

PEMBERTON, Capt. Edward Gerald, M.B.E., M.C.

PEMBERTON, Eleonora Blanshard, O.B.E., *b.* 19 July,
1885 ; *d.* of Busick E. Pemberton, of Messrs. Lee and Pemberton's 44, Lincoln's Inn Fields, and Cokes Green, Chalfont
St. Giles, Bucks. *Educ. :* St. Felix School, Southwold, Suffolk,
and Paris. *War Work :* V.A.D. under Joint Committee
British Red Cross and Order of St. John of Jerusalem in France,
Oct. 1914–17 ; Divisional Sec. Paddington Division, B.R.C.S.,
1917–20. *Address :* Cokes Green, Chalfont St. Giles, Bucks.
Clubs : Ladies' V.A.D. ; Portsmouth. (O11112)

PEMBERTON, Capt. Francis Seaton, O.B.E., M.C.

PEMBERTON, Lieut. William, O.B.E., R.N.R.

PEMBROKE AND MONTGOMERY, Beatrice Eleanor,
Countess of, C.B.E., *b.* 22 June, 1883 ; *y.d.* of the late Lord
Alexander Paget, and sister of present Marquis of Anglesey
(*see* BURKE'S *Peerage*) ; *m.* Reginald, 15th Earl of Pembroke and
Montgomery (*see* BURKE'S *Peerage*). *War Work :* Com-
mandant, Wilton House Hospital, 1915–19 ; Chairman,
Women's Sub-Committee, Wilts War Agricultural Committee ;
Vice-President and Chairman, Salisbury and South Wilts Div.
B.R.C.S. ; Hon. Treas. Royal Horse Guards European War
Fund. *Addresses :* Wilton House, Salisbury ; 6, Belgrave
Square, S.W. (C1023)

PENBERTHY, Major Philip Pearce Clay, O.B.E., *b.* 22
Oct. 1895 ; *s.* of F. Penberthy, of Hampstead, London. *Educ. :*
St. Paul's ; France ; Germany. Motor Business ; Sales
Manager Messrs. R. E. Jones, Ltd., London, Cardiff, Swansea,
Bristol, and Exeter. *War Work :* Enlisted Royal Fusiliers,
University and Public School Brigade, on Formation, Aug.
1914 ; Gazetted 2nd Lieut. K.S.L.I. Oct. 1914 ; promoted
Lieut. Dec. 1914 ; A. Adjut. 9th K.S.L.I. ; Musketry Officer,
9th K.S.L.I. ; transferred R.F.C. Jan. Sept. 1916 ; appointed
Flying Officer Pilot, Feb. 1917 ; Adjt. 4 C.A.R.D. Chelsea ;
Staff Capt. and Staff Major, June, 1918, to April, 1919 ; served

overseas, France, with R.F.C. Mentioned in the New Year's
Honours List, 1919. *Address :* 2, Canfield House, Finchley
Road, Hampstead, London, N.W. 3. *Clubs :* R.A.F. ; Public
School. (O8165)

PENDARVES, Alice Louisa, Mrs., O.B.E., *b.* 2 Dec. 1857 ;
d. of Henry Richard Farrer, of Green Hammerton Hall, York ;
m. William Cole, *d.* of John Wood, of Martock, Somerset. *War
Work :* Deputy-President, B.R.C.S. Cornwall Branch ; organiser
of "Our Day," 1916–18, in Cornwall. *Addresses :* Pendarves
Camborne, Cornwall ; 40, Cadogan Square, London, S.W. 1.
(O644)

PENDER, Major James, C.B.E., J.P., T.D., of Ardnadam,
Argyll, *b.* 1860 ; *s.* of James Pender, of Clober, Stirling ; *m.* Janet
Helen Maud, *d.* of Thomas Geils, of Geilston, Ardmore, and Ar-
dardan, Dumbartonshire. *Educ. :* Larchfield Academy ; Edinburgh Univ. Lately Member of County and Parish Councils,
and of School and Parochial Boards ; served as Capt. during
South African War, 1900–2. *War Work :* Major 8th Argyll
and Sutherland Highlanders, 1914–15 ; Commanding Depot,
Dunoon, and Military Representative for Cowal and Dunoon,
1916–17 ; Assistant Food Commissioner for Glasgow and West
of Scotland, 1918–20. *Address :* 14, Polwarth Terrace,
Edinburgh. *Club :* Caledonian ; R.A.C.A. (C2870)

PENDER, Lieut. William Stanhope, M.B.E., I.A.

PENDER, William Edmonstone, O.B.E., Eastern Telegraph Co. (O11943)

PENDER, Sir John DENISON-, G.B.E., K.C.M.G., J.P.,
b. 10 Oct. 1855 ; 3rd *s.* of the late Sir John Pender, G.C.M.G.,
M.P., of 18, Arlington Street, S.W. 1, and Foots Cray Place,
Kent ; *m.* Beatrice Katherine, only child of Cuthbert Ellison.
Educ. : Eton. Chairman and Managing Director of Associated
Cable Companies, Electra House, E.C. 2 ; Knight Commander
of Dannebrog ; Grand Cross Order of Lady Conception,
Portugal ; Grand Cordon Osmanieh, Turkey ; Double Dragon,
Second Division, China ; decorated for services in connection
with South Africa and China. *War Work :* In connection with
above Telegraph Cable Companies. *Address :* 6, Grosvenor
Crescent, S.W. 1. *Clubs :* Reform ; R.Y.S. (G58)

PENFOLD, Comm. Marchant Hubert, C.B.E., R.N.

PENFOLD, William Cowan, M.B.E.

PENFOLD, Paymaster-Capt. William George Edward,
C.B.E., *b.* 1852. Entered R.N., 1869 ; present during forcing
of Dardanelles, 1878 ; was Sec. to Commodore, Jamaica,
during Yellow Fever epidemic ; served in the Great War,
1914–19 (despatches) ; is Sec. Royal Naval and Marine Orphan
Home, Portsmouth. *Clubs :* Portsmouth ; Sports ; Royal
Naval (Portsmouth) ; Royal Corinthian Yacht. (C1935)

PENHALE, Capt. Richard Hugh, O.B.E., *b.* 5 June, 1894 ;
s. of William Penhale, of Holsworthy, Devon ; *m.* Lilian Mary,
d. of G. P. Dymond, M.A., of Plymouth. Veterinary Surgeon.
War Work : East Coast and Salonica Force. *Addresses :*
Penbode, Holsworthy, Devon ; 6, Lockyer Street, Plymouth.
(O6251)

PENGELLY, Major George Hastings, O.B.E., S. and T.
Co., I.A.

PENHORWOOD, Lieut.-Col. Sydney Lewis, M.V.O.,
O.B.E.

PENKETH, Major James, O.B.E.

PENMAN, 2nd Lieut. Victor Robert, M.B.E., R.A.S.C.

PENN, Lieut. Henry Albert, O.B.E., R.A.O.C.

PENNEFATHER, Major Edward Cyril, M.B.E.

PENNEFATHER, T. Capt. John Broderick, O.B.E.

PENNELL, Charles Waldegrave, M.B.E., J.P. Chairman,
Wm. Foster & Co., Ltd., Engineers ; Chairman, Lindsey and
Kesteven Chemical Co., Ltd. ; Chairman, City of Lincoln Public
Library. *War Work :* Chief Superintendent, Special Constabu-
lary. *Address :* 12, Lindum Terrace, Lincoln. *Club :* Royal
Automobile. (M2277)

PENNELL, Dorothy, Mrs., M.B.E. ; *d.* of Sir Herbert
Thirkell White, K.C.I.E. (*see* BURKE'S *Peerage*) ; *m.* Charles
Stuart, *s.* of the Rev. James Pennell. *Educ. :* Abroad. *War
Work :* President from Jan. 1915 till the end of the War of the
Prome Centre of the Burma Branch of the Indian Red Cross
Society. *Address :* Bassein, Burma. (M4199)

PENNELL, Frederick, M.B.E.

PENNEY, Mary Bentley, M.B.E. ; *d.* of the late D. J. E.
Penney, of Edinburgh. *Educ. :* Sherborne. *War Work :* Commandant's Head Clerk and Treas. V.A. Hospital, Exmouth
(Special Electrical Treatment Centre), from 1914–19. *Address :*
2, Morton Crescent, Exmouth, S. Devon. (M9257)

PENNEY, Peter John, O.B.E.

PENNING, Walter, M.B.E.

PENNY, Capt. Cyril John, O.B.E., R.A.M.C. (S.R.), *b.*
16 Sept. 1892 ; *s.* of Thomas S. Penny, J.P., of Taunton ;
m. Muriel Mercer, *d.* of Dr. A. B. Kenworthy, of Southport.
Educ. : Mill Hill School ; Jesus Coll., Cambs. ; Middlesex
Hospital. *War Work :* Surgeon Probationer, R.N.V.R.
H.M.T.B. "Liberty," Harwich Flotilla, 1915 ; R.A.M.C.
Mesopotamia and India, 1917–19. *Address :* Knowls, Taunton.
(O4242)

PENNY, Surgeon-Capt. Herbert Lloyd, O.B.E., R.N.,
b. 13 Jan. 1867 ; *s.* of Rev. E. G. Penny, M.A. (deceased), of
Gloucester ; *m.* Elizabeth, *d.* of Rev. F. E. Drummond Hay,
of Bath. *Educ. :* Christ's Coll., N.Z. ; Rossall School, Lancs. ;
London Hospital, E. Surgeon-Capt., R.N. Barracks, Chatham
Address : 20, Sion Hill, Bath. (O3548)

PENNY, Richard, M.B.E.

PENOYRE, John, M.A., C.B.E. ; *s.* of the Rev. Slade
Baker Penoyre, of Clifton-on-Teme (Worcs.). *Educ. :*

Cheltenham Coll.; Keble Coll., Oxford. Sec. to the Society for the Promotion of Hellenic Studies; Sec. to the British School at Athens. *War Work:* Manager of Lord Roberts' Field Glass Fund: organiser of a movement for supplementing the supply of sweaters to the Forces; manager of the organisation devised by Sir Edward Ward, D.G.V.O., for the provision of Games for the Forces. *Addresses:* 8, King's Bench Walk, Inner Temple, E.C. 4; 19, Bloomsbury Square, W.C. 1. (C593)

PENROSE, Major Edward Samuel, O.B.E.

PENROSE, Emily, O.B.E., M.A., *b.* 18 Sept., 1858; *d.* of Francis Cranmer Penrose, F.R.S., of Colebyfield, Wimbledon. *Educ.:* Somerville Coll. Principal of Bedford Coll., 1893–98; Principal of the Royal Holloway Coll., 1898–1907; Principal of Somerville Coll., since 1907; Member of the Senate of the Univ. of London, 1900–7; Member of Advisory Committee on Univ. Grants, 1911–19; Member of the Royal Commission on Univ. Education in Wales, 1916; Member of the Royal Commission on the Univs. of Oxford and Cambridge, 1919. *Address:* Somerville Coll., Oxford. *Club:* Albemarle. (O646)

PENROSE, Katharine St. Aubyn, O.B.E. (O4900)

PENROSE, Nevill Coghill, O.B.E., M.B., Ch.B., *b.* 1884; *s.* of James E. Penrose, of Woodhill, Co. Cork, Ireland; *m.* Nellie, *d.* of the late A. C. Osler, of Birmingham. *Educ.:* Haileybury Coll.; Birmingham Univ. Hon. Surgeon, Horton Infirmary, Banbury. *War Work:* Commandant, Oxford V.A.D. 30; M.O. Banbury Auxiliary Hospital; M.O. Banbury Rest Station. *Address:* South Bank, Oxford Road, Banbury, Oxon. (O11113)

PENSON, Sir (Thomas) Henry, K.B.E., M.A., *b.* 1864; *s.* of late John Whiteman Penson, of Oxford; *m.* Sigrid, *d.* of Dr. T. A. Säve, K.V.O., R.N.O., late member of the First Chamber of the Swedish Riksdag. *Educ.:* City of London School; Worcester Coll. Oxford Lecturer and Tutor in Modern History and Economics, Pembroke Coll., Oxford; Lecturer and Examiner for the Oxford Diploma in Economics and Political Science; Chairman of the Trade Clearing House (War Trade Dept.), 1915; Chairman of the War Trade Intelligence Dept., since 1916. *Addresses:* War Trade Intelligence Dept., 1, Lake Buildings, St. James' Park, S.W.1; 104, Oakley St., Chelsea, S.W. *Club:* New University. (K98)

PENTLAND, Lady Marjorie Adeline Gordon, K.T., Lady of Grace of St. John of Jerusalem, only *d.* of 7th Earl of Aberdeen, K.T., P.C., G.C.M.G. (*see* BURKE'S *Peerage*); *m.* (1904) John Sinclair, 1st Baron Pentland, P.C., G.C.I.E., G.C.S.I. (D6)

PENTON, Sir Edward, K.B.E., *b.* 18 June, 1875; *s.* of Edward Penton, of 9, Cavendish Square, W. 1; *m.* Eleanor, 2nd *d.* of William Arthur Sharpe, of Broadlands Road, Highgate. *Educ.:* Rugby, and New Coll., Oxford. Mayor of Metropolitan Borough of St. Marylebone, 1912–13; Alderman, 1913; Chairman of Executive Committee of Boot Trade Benevolent Society; Member of Board of Management of Cordwainers' Coll.; Member of Weekly Board of Middlesex Hospital. *War Work:* Superintendent of Royal Army Clothing Department (Boot Section), and afterwards Deputy-Director from November, 1914, to May, 1919. *Addresses:* 2, Cambridge Terrace, Regent's Park, N.W. 1; Ashwick, Dulverton, Somerset. *Clubs:* Brooks's; Garrick; Oxford and Cambridge; Reform. (K99)

PEPLER, Capt. Seth Bernard, M.B.E., M.C.

PEPLOE, Alfred, O.B.E.

PEPLOE, Rev. Howard Melville WEBB-, O.B.E., M.A., C.F. 2nd Class, *b.* 12 Feb. 1870; *s.* of the Rev. Prebendary H. W. Webb-Peploe, of London. *Educ.:* Brighton Coll.; Neuwied on the Rhine; Pembroke Coll., Cambridge. Curate St. Paul's, Onslow Square, S.W., from 1894–1902; Acting Chaplain to the Forces, S. African War, 26 May, 1900, to 8 Oct. 1901; Chaplain to the Forces, 15 July, 1902 (Portsmouth, Shorncliffe, Roberts' Heights, Harrismith, Aldershot, Caterham). *War Work:* C.F. 19th Infty. Bgde. B.E.F., Aug. 1914, to Aug. 1915; S.C.F. 6th Div. Jan. 1915, to April, 1915; S.C.F. 16th Div. Sept. 1915, to June, 1916; S.C.F. 1st Corps June, 1916, to Nov. 1916: went to Salonica, Jan. 1917; S.C.F. C. of E., 16th Corps, and B.S.F., Nov. 1917, to Dec. 1918. Chaplain to R.M.S.M. Kneller Hall and Hounslow Barracks. *Address:* 31, Lampton Road, Hounslow. (O3069)

PEPPE, Caroline Marion, Mrs., M.B.E.; *d.* of Charles Henry Pope, of Bath, and late of Tirhoot, India, and Bengal; *m.* Arthur Tosco, *s.* of Thomas Fraser Peppé, of Chota Nagpur. *Educ.:* Cheltenham. *War Work:* Hon. Treas. of the Red Cross Society for the province of Bihar and Orissa, from 28 Aug. 1914, to April, 1915; Hon. Treas. for the same Society of the same province, excluding the Patna Branch, from 1 Jan. 1916, to 25 April, 1919. *Addresses:* Ranchi, B.N. Railway, Chota Nagpur, India; Apthorpe, Weston Road, Bath. (M7146)

PEPPER, Major Arthur Llewellyn, O.B.E., M.C.

PEPPER, Colonel Charles, M.B.E., J.P., D.L., Hon. Colonel of the 5th Bn. Leinster Regt., *b.* 1 Nov. 1845; *s.* of Col. Charles Pepper, Ballygarth Castle, Julianstown, Co. Meath. *Educ.:* Harrow; Trinity Coll., Cambridge (M.A.). *War Work:* County Director, Co. of Meath. *Address:* Ballygarth Castle, Julianstown, Drogheda. *Clubs:* Carlton; Kildare Street; Sackville Street, Dublin. (M9277)

PEPPER, Major Henry, O.B.E., I.A.

PEPPER, Major Thomas Oswald, O.B.E., R.E.

PEPPER, William James, M.B.E., *b.* 18 March, 1875; *s.* of the late S. H. Pepper, of Peterborough; *m.* Audrey Devonald, *d.* of Devonald Edwards, of Haverfordwest. Principal Clerk in office of General Manager of the Great Northern Railway. *Address:* York Road, New Barnet, Herts. (M9278)

PEPPERCORN, Capt. Geoffrey Arthur, M.B.E., M.C., A.M.I.C.E.

PERCEVAL, Col. Charles Cecil, C.B.E., R.E.

PERCEVAL, Brevet-Major Francis Westby, O.B.E., B.A., *b.* 21 Jan. 1882; *s.* of Sir Westby Perceval, K.C.M.G., of Southdown, Wimbledon, S.W. (*see* BURKE'S *Peerage*); *m.* Dorothy Anne Cecilia, *d.* of George Thornton, of Fairlawn, Eltham, Kent. *Educ.:* Wimbledon Coll.; Stonyhurst Coll.; Balliol Coll., Oxford. Barrister-at-Law, Inner Temple, 1907. *War Work:* Joined Royal Army Ordnance Corps as Lieut., 1915; Officer-in-charge Army Clothing Depot, Dewsbury, 1916; Assistant to A.D.O.S. (Clothing) War Office, 1916–18; appointed Deputy Assistant Director of Equipment and Ordnance Stores (Q.M.G. 7B), 1918; finally in charge of Q.M.G. 7B directly under D.E.O.S.; Q.M.G. 7B was inaugurated to deal with unserviceable and part-worn army clothing, and the laundry arrangements for the troops in the United Kingdom; four times mentioned for valuable services rendered in connection with the war, and promoted Brevet Major. *Address:* Dunclutha, North Park, Eltham, Kent. *Clubs:* Royal Automobile; Royal Wimbledon Golf; All England Tennis; Eltham Golf. (O7567)

PERCH, William John, M.B.E., R.A.M.C. (T.).

PERCIVAL, Capt. Alexander Philip, M.B.E.

PERCIVAL, George Henry, O.B.E., M.B. (Lond.), M.R.C.S., *b.* 23 Feb. 1848; *s.* of William Percival, of Northampton; *m.* Alice, *d.* of William Martin, of Paul's Grove, Cosham. *Educ.:* Aylsham, Norfolk. Consulting Surgeon to the Northampton General Hospital; Police Surgeon; Surgeon to L. & N.W.R. and Midland Railway (Northampton District). *War Work:* Consulting Surgeon to War Hospital, Duston, Northampton. *Address:* 20, Kingsley Road, Northampton. *Club:* Northampton Town and County. (O4384)

PERCIVAL, Surgeon-Lieut. Harold Fey, O.B.E., R.N.

PERCIVAL, Col. Harold Franz Passawer, C.M.G., C.B.E., D.S.O., *b.* 1876; *s.* of E. P. Percival, LL.D., of Vienna; *m.* 1904, Constance Lilian, *d.* of J. Meyrick, formerly of The Grange, Medling. *Educ.:* Christ Church, Oxford. Entered Sherwood Foresters, 1898; became Capt. Army Ser. Corps, 1904; Major, 1914, and Brevet Lieut.-Col. 1918; served in S. Africa, 1899–1902, with Mounted Inf.; during the Great War, 1914–18, D.A.Q.M.G. at Gen. Headquarters (despatches twice, Order of White Eagle, Legion of Honour, Brevet Lieut.-Col., Order of Crown of Italy); appointed a Staff-Capt. at Headquarters, 1910; a D.A.Q.M.G., Staff Coll., 1912; Assist. Director at War Office, 1915; a Dep. Director, 1917, and A.Q.M.G., 1919, with rank of Col.; was British Representative Silesian Plebiscite Commn., 1919. (C2155)

PERCIVAL, Mary, Mrs., M.B.E.

PERCIVAL, Lieut. Philip Mason, M.B.E.

PERCY, Gladys May Heber, M.B.E.

PERCY, Brig.-Gen. Sir John Samuel Jocelyn, K.B.E., C.B., C.M.G., D.S.O., East Lancs Regt., *b.* 1871; *s.* of the late Edward Jocelyn Baumgartien Percy, J.P. County of Huntingdon; *m.* Inez D'Aguilar, *d.* of Col. Alister William Jameson, of Indian Army. *Educ.:* Queen Elizabeth's School, Sevenoaks; Royal Military College, Sandhurst. Served, Chitral, 1895 (medal with clasp); South African War, 1899–1902 (despatches, Bt. Major, Queen's Medal, 4 clasps; King's Medal, 2 clasps); Great War, 1914–18 (despatches, Bt. Lieut.-Col., C.B., C.M.G., D.S.O.). *Club:* Army and Navy. (K446a)

PERCY, Col. Lord William Richard, C.B.E., D.S.O., *b.* 1882; 5th *s.* of the 7th Duke of Northumberland. Barrister, Inner Temple, 1906; Capt. (Brevet Major, 1919), Grenadier Guards from 1916; Dep. Judge-Advocate-General (T. Major), 1915–18; A.A.G. (T. Lieut.-Col.), 1918–19; Assistant Director at War Office 1919. *Club:* Travellers'. (C2156)

PERDUE, Florence Louise Sophia, M.B.E., A.R.R.C., *b.* 30 Dec. 1876; *d.* of William James, of Lethbridge, Alberta, Canada. *Educ.:* Brighton. Special Surgical training (Orthopædic and Massage); General training, Hertford British Hospital and St. Mary's Highgate Hill; Fever, Haverstock Hill. *War Work:* Attached private Nursing Co., Paris, from 1903–14, when she joined French Red Cross, Aug. 1914, again joined Private Nursing Co. from 1919; Sister Scottish Women's Hospital, Claridge's Hotel, Oct. 1914; attached French Army, Dec. 1914; Sister, St. Valey Hospital, Dec. 1915; Sister at Frevent Military Hospital, Assistant Matron, 1st Field Ambulance, 1915; Tenedos, Oct. 1915; Matron at Imbros, 1916 (Royal Naval Division); Sister, Royal Naval Hospital at Mudros, 1916–18. *Addresses:* 33, rue Greuze, Paris; Royal National Pension Fund, 15, Buckingham Street, Strand. (M9280)

PEREIRA, T. Warrant Officer Vincent Manoel Francis, M.B.E. Royal Indian Marine.

PEREZ, Mary, Mrs., M.B.E.

PERFECT, Capt. Herbert Mosley, C.B.E., R.N.

PERKIN, Frederick Mollwo, C.B.E., D.Sc. Rendered valuable services to various departments of State. (C3163)

PERKIN, Herbert, O.B.E., M.I.Min.E., F.S.I., *b.* 17 Aug. 1876; *s.* of John Perkin, of Leeds; *m.* Emily Elizabeth, *d.* of Richard Brooks, of Leeds. *Educ.:* Leeds Univ. Head of Technical Section, Production Division, Coal Mines Dept. Board of Trade; sometime Mining Engineer to the Great Central Railway; joint author "Electricity as applied to Mining"; formerly engaged in management of collieries and lecturer in the Mining Dept., Leeds Univ. *War Work:* On the invitation of Sir Guy Calthrop, then Controller of Coal Mines, joined the Staff of the Coal Mines Dept. in July, 1917, being loaned by the Great Central Railway Co.; rendered valuable service in a technical capacity on mining engineering questions arising in the control of the Mining Industry. *Addresses:* 17, Welldon Crescent, Harrow; Hotel Windsor, Victoria Street, S.W. (O11115)

PERKINS, Major Albert Augustus, O.B.E., T.D.
PERKINS, Charles Cliffarde, M.B.E.
PERKINS, Col. Edwin King, C.B.E., D.L.
PERKINS, Frederick William, C.B.E.
PERKINS, 2nd Lieut. Harry Dunbar, M.B.E.
PERKINS, Lieut.-Col. Hugh Marsham, C.B.E.
PERKINS, 2nd Lieut. James, M.B.E., R.E.
PERKINS, Capt. Lewis Arthur, M.B.E.
PERKINS, Lieut.-Col. Hugh Wharton, C.B.E. On Special List, and Dep. Assist. Director of Railway Transport, S. Command. (C1739)
PERKINS, Sydney, M.B.E.
PERKINS, Capt. William Hughes, O.B.E., R.E.
PERKINS, Capt. William Jackson, O.B.E., M.C.
PERKINS, Alys Mary, Mrs. BERTIE-, O.B.E.; *d.* of Thomas Sandbrook, of Swansea; *m.* Albert Auguste, *s.* of Christian Henry Perkins, of Swansea. *Educ.:* Swansea High School for Girls. *War Work:* Hon. Sec. and District Commandant, B.R.C.S., Swansea Division; Hon. Recruiting Commandant for County of Glamorgan under the General Service Scheme. *Address:* Rhyd yr helyg, Skett, Glamorgan. (O743)
PERKINS, Major Alfred Horace Steele STEELE-, O.B.E., R.A.F.
PERKINS, Winifred Mary, Mrs. WARD-, M.B.E., *b.* 1885; *d.* of J. R. Hickman, of Bromley, Kent; *m.* Bryan Ward-Perkins. *War Work:* President Amherst District Red Cross Society, 1916–18; Member of Friends' War Victims Relief party in France, 1915; V.A.D. work in England, 1914–15. *Address:* c/o B. Ward Perkins, E.I.C.S., Burma. (M4200)
PEROT, Louise Pauline, M.B.E.
PERRETT, Lieut.-Col. Thomas Edwin, O.B.E.
PERREY, Albert Victor George, M.B.E., *b.* 9 Nov. 1881; *s.* of Charles Henry Perrey, of Plymouth, Devon; *m.* Annie Beatrice, *d.* of John Glasson, of Truro, Cornwall. *Educ.:* Stoke Public High School, Devonport, Devon. Staff Officer of Ministry of Labour, formerly engineer in service of Admiralty. *War Work:* As Manager of Ministry of Labour Employment Exchange assisted in administering various war-time measures; recruited labour for armament work; recruited for H.M. Forces, Women's Land Army, Q.M.A.A.C., W.R.N.S., etc.; also assisted Minister of Munitions, as skilled investigator, in the release of men from H.M. Forces for munitions work; suffered severe and permanent breakdown in health as result of work during the war. *Addresses:* 46, Abbotsbury Road, Weymouth; 176, Whiteladies Road, Bristol. (M10252e)
PERRIER, Capt. John William O.B.E.
PERRIN, Alfred William, M.B.E., *b.* 5 July, 1853; *s.* of Samuel James Perrin; *m.* Emily Elizabeth (who died 1913), *d.* of James Finch, of Sudbury, Suffolk. *Educ.:* National School; Evenings: Spurgeon's Coll., East London; Regent St. Poly.; Tottenham Poly., in Art, Physiology, Chemistry and Common Law. Works Overseer; Tottenham U.D. Councillor; Member of Finance Committee; Vice-Chairman War Pensions and Chairman Disablement Committees; Chairman of Trustees of War Services Inst.; Member of Education, Higher Education and Health Committees; Chairman of Finance Committee of Maternity and Child Welfare, etc. *War Work:* Tottenham Naval and Military War Pensions Committee; Chairman of Disablement Committee, Middlesex and Essex Joint N. and M. War Pensions Committee; London Technical Trades N. and M. War Pensions Committee; Prince of Wales' Distress Committee; Promoter and Chairman of a Works War Savings, resulting in raising £9,600; Promoter and Chairman of Principals and Employees Special Appeals Fund, distributing £2,500; Promoter and Chairman of Tottenham War Services Inst.; through Mr. Percy Alden, M.P., sent to Special Committee of House of Commons; suggested additions to the Workmen's Compensation Act relative to employment of partially disabled soldiers; advised the training of men on Fancy Leather Goods and served on sub-committee; Member of the Walthamstow Memorial Y.M.C.A.; Member of Tottenham Raising Committee for Training and Equipping Local troops; Member of the Committee of 7th Bn. Middlesex Volunteers, and of Middlesex and Tottenham Comforts Committee, providing comforts for Middlesex and local troops; Vice-Chairman of Fete Committee for St. Dunstan's, realising £1700, and numerous committees for whist drives, fetes, etc., to raise funds for War Charities; Member of Executive of Tottenham War Savings Committee; shared service at Casualty Air Raid Centre with Medical Officer and Nurses; taken by motor at syren signal day or night; commissioned by Warrant to administer to distressed through air raids in the locality; Member of Executive, London Branch of Welfare Workers; Vice-President of two Allotment-holders' Associations; Vice-President of Juvenile After-care, and of Juvenile Employment Bureau; Member of National Council V.D.; Member of Tottenham Coal Supply Committee; Chairman Extra Ration Committee, and of Tottenham Labour Advisory Committee; Chairman Labour Advisory Women's Committee. *Address:* 62, Tynemouth Road, Tottenham, N. 15. (M9282)

PERRIN, Flight Lieut. Eugene Courtenay, O.B.E., B.A., LL.B. (Cantab)., R.A.F., *b.* 13 Dec. 1885; *s.* of John Edward Perrin, M.B.E., of Hoylake, Cheshire, *q.v.*; *m.* Katherine Arthur Mary Violet, *d.* of the late Arthur Percy Hickman, of Hagley, Worcs. *Educ.:* Mostyn House School, Parkgate, Cheshire; Shrewsbury School; Peterhouse, Cambridge (Classical Scholar). Barrister-at-law; called to the Bar, Inner Temple, Jan. 1912; gazetted to a Regular Commission in R.A.F., 1 Aug. 1919; previously held a commission in 4th Batt. the Cheshire Regt., T.F.; first commissioned, May, 1911. *War Work:* Mobilised with the 4th Batt. Cheshire Regt., 4 Aug. 1914, and served with Regt. until transferred to R.F.C., 5 Aug. 1915; proceeded to France with No. 12 Sqdn., R.F.C., as observer, Sept. 1915, returning to England, Jan. 1916; injured in aero accident, April, 1916, and subsequently Adjutant to various R.F.C. units; on Staff, H.Q., Western Group, R.F.C., Nov. 1917; S.O. 2, H.Q., Midland Area, R.A.F. April, 1918; gazetted O.B.E., Jan. 1919. *Address:* 15, St. Mark's Road, Leamington. *Club:* Isthmian. (O3388)
PERRIN, Rev. Howard Nasmith, O.B.E., M.A., *b.* 1873; *s.* of the late Henry Story Perrin, of Old Change. London; *m.* Katharine Meta Fairfax, *d.* of the late Edward Fairfax Taylor, of Ewell. *Educ.:* Clifton Coll.; King's Coll., Cambridge; Auckland Castle. Curate of St. John's, Darlington, 1898–1903; Member of Oxford Diocesan Society of Mission Clergy, 1903–7; Domestic Chaplain to the Bishop of Oxford, 1907–11; Vicar of Runcorn, 1911 to date. *War Work:* Donor and Hon. Commandant of Runcorn Vicarage Hospital (150 beds). *Address:* The Vicarage, Runcorn, Cheshire. (O3868)
PERRIN, John Edward, M.B.E., *b.* 11 June, 1858; *s.* of Eugene Henry Perrin, of Wicklow; *m.* Mary Theophila, *d.* of Courtenay Cruttenden, of Macclesfield. *Educ.:* Birkenhead School. General Produce Broker; Senior Partner in the firms of E. H. Perrin & Co., Liverpool, and of Nickoll & Knight, London. *Addresses:* The Paddock, Hoylake, Cheshire; D9, Exchange Buildings, Liverpool; 65, London Wall, London, E.C. 2. *Club:* Royal Liverpool Golf. (M9283)
PERRIN, Capt. and Qr.-Mr. William Andrew, M.B.E.
PERRIN, Capt. William Gordon, O.B.E., R.A.F.
PERRY, Ada Stair, M.B.E.
PERRY, Edward Verdon, O.B.E., L.R.C.P.L., M.R.C.S., J.P., Norfolk, *b.* 29 March, 1852; *s.* of Charles Henry Perry of Reepham, Norfolk. *Educ.:* Gresham School, Holt, Norfolk; Royal Medical Coll., Epsom. Medical Officer and Public Vaccinator, No. 1 District, Aylsham Union; Gt. Witchingham District, St. Faith's Union, and Sparham District, Mitford and Launditch Union. *War Work:* Medical Officer, Red Cross Hospitals, Reepham, Cawston Manor, and Felthorpe Hall; Prisoners of War Camp, Whitwell, Norfolk. *Address:* Reepham, Norfolk. (O11116)
PERRY, Major Ernest Middleton, C.B.E., T.D., F.R.C.V.S., *b.* 1878; *s.* of Samuel Perry, of Croydon; *m.* Gladys L., *d.* of S. H. Weston, of Eastbourne. *Educ.:* The Whitgift School; Royal Veterinary Coll., London. Veterinary Surgeon; D.A.D.V.S., 1st London Division, T.A. Joined Volunteers, 1901, in 2nd Sussex R.G.A.; transferred into Territorial Force R.F.A.; commanded 6th Sussex Battery until 1912; transferred to R.A.V.C. (T.F.); mobilised 4 Aug. 1914; organised and commanded Home Counties Veterinary Hospital, Aylesford; proceeded overseas April, 1915, as A.D.V.S., 51st (Highland) Division; June, 1917, appointed A.D.V.S. 15th Corps with temporary rank of Lieut.-Col.; appointed A.D.V.S. Advanced G.H.Q. and subsequently to No. 4 Area, returning home Oct. 1919; now appointed D.A.D.V.S., 1st London Division (T.A.); awarded C.B.E., and gained the T.D.; thrice mentioned in despatches. *Address:* Sutherlands, Sunnyside, Wimbledon. (C1302)
PERRY, George Albert, M.B.E.
PERRY, George Henry, O.B.E.
PERRY, Major Henry Marrian, O.B.E., R.A.M.C., *b.* 1884; *s.* of John Perry, of Ireland; *m.* Mary Eleanor, *d.* of Edward Griffith Brewer, of Cornwall. Assistant Professor, Royal Army Medical Coll., London; late Assistant Adviser in Pathology to B.E.F. *War Work:* France, Aug. 1914, as Regimental Medical Officer; later commanded Field Ambulance; in latter part of war, Assistant Adviser in Pathology to British Expeditionary Force. *Address:* 26, Carlisle Mansions, Carlisle Place, S.W. 1. (O5678)
PERRY, Capt. Joseph Charles, M.B.E.
PERRY, Muriel, O.B.E., *b.* 5 March, 1886; *d.* of George William Perry, of Clifton. *Educ.:* Home. *War Work:* Sept. 1914, worked with Belgian Refugees, Victoria Station; three years Quartermaster, Free Buffet, Victoria Station; April, 1918, went to Italy with British Pioneer Motor Kitchen and Ambulance Unit, attached to 3rd Army on Italian Front; 1916, awarded Elizabeth Reine des Belges medal; June, 1918, decorated by the King of Italy during the Piave attack with Al Valore Militaire medal for Ambulance work; despatches, 1919; received Croce di Guerra with two bars, Red Cross Order of Merit Silver medal, British Service medals, Victory medal; 1920, received the O.B.E. for work with the British and Italian Armies in Italy. *Address:* 13, Eccleston Street, Eaton Square, London, S.W. (O11116)
PERRY, Sir Percival Lea Dewhurst, K.B.E., *b.* 18 March, 1878, 3rd *s.* of Alfred Thomas Perry. *Educ.:* King Edward School, Birmingham. President, Motor Trade Association, 1914–16; Director, Machinery Dept. and Food Production Dept., 1916; Director, Machinery Branch, Agricultural Machinery Dept. Ministry of Munitions, 1917–18; Deputy

Controller, Mechanical Warfare Dept. and Director of Traction, Ministry of Munitions, 1918–19. *Address:* Ewell Place, Ewell, Surrey. *Clubs:* Reform; National Liberal; Royal Automobile. (K163)

PERRY, Robert Grosvenor, C.B.E. Rendered service in production of explosives during European War. (C56)

PERRY, Violet, M.B.E.

PERRY, William, M.B.E.

PERRYER, Lieut. Harold William, M.B.E., R.E.

PERRYMAN, Percy Wilbraham, M.B.E.

PERTWEE, Wwenlliam, Mrs., M.B.E., W.R.A.F.

PESCOD, Joseph Hind, M.B.E.

PESKETT, Leonard, O.B.E.

PETAVEL, Sir Joseph Ernest, K.B.E., D.Sc., F.R.S., M.I.Mech.E.; A.M.I.C.E., *b.* 14 Aug. 1873; *s.* of the late Rev. E. Petavel, D.D. *Educ.:* Univ. Coll., London. Scientific research at the Royal Institution and at the Davy-Faraday Laboratory, 1896–98; John Harling Fellow of the Owens Coll., Manchester, 1900–3; Director, National Physical Laboratory since 1919; Professor of Engineering and Director of the Whitworth Laboratories, the University, Manchester, 1908–19; Member of the Aeronautical Research Committee. *Address:* National Physical Laboratory, Teddington. *Clubs:* Athenæum; Primrose; Royal Automobile. (K408)

PETCH, Lieut. Frederick, M.B.E., R.A.F.

PETERKIN, Major Charles Duncan, C.B.E., M.A., LL.B., *b.* 14 June, 1887; *s.* of the late Henry Peterkin, of Aberdeen; *m.* Netta Macgregor, the adopted daughter of Sir Thomas Jaffrey, Kt., of Aberdeen. *Educ.:* Aberdeen Grammar School, and Aberdeen Univ. Advocate in Aberdeen; 2nd in command, 4th Batt. The Gordon Highlanders (T.A.). *War Work:* Served continuously, 5 Aug. 1914, to 13 Dec. 1919; 3 years and 10 months with B.E.F. and Army of the Rhine; wounded 25 Sept. 1915; twice mentioned in despatches; C.B.E., 1914–15 Star, General Service medal, and Victory medal. *Addresses:* 21, Golden Square, Aberdeen; 71, Fountainhall Road, Aberdeen. (C1303)

PETERKIN, Lieut.-Col. Montagu James Grant, O.B.E.

PETERKIN, Lieut. William, O.B.E., R.N.R.

PETERS, Alice, Mrs., M.B.E.

PETERS, Arthur, C.B.E., J.P., *b.* 18 July, 1867; *s.* of James Peters, of Brighton; *m.* Annie, *d.* of Alfred Lowe, of Blakeney, Glos. *Educ.:* Brighton Commercial School. Deputy Housing Commissioner (Ministry of Health); Member Croydon Borough Council; Member Croydon Borough Magistrates. *War Work:* Joint Hon. Sec. Parliamentary Recruiting Committee; Joint Hon. Sec. War Aims Committee; Deputy Chairman, Croydon Food Control Committee. *Address:* The Hawthorns, Pollards Hill West, Norbury, S.W. 16. (C594)

PETERS, Bernard Richard, M.B.E.

PETERS, Cecil James Razzell, M.B.E., *b.* 3 March, 1889; *s.* of James Peters, of Purley, Surrey; *m.* Rita Gertrude, *d.* of Charles Cooke, of Westcliff-on-Sea, Essex. *Educ.:* Privately, and King's Coll., London. *War Work:* Entered Civil Service, May 1908; serving in War Office at outbreak of war; transferred to Ministry of Munitions, May, 1915; and served in the Explosives Dept. of that Ministry until Jan. 1919; since March, 1917, as Assistant Director of Propellant Supplies under Col. Sir F. L. Nathan, K.B.E., Director; transferred to Ministry of Labour, Jan. 1919; present official rank, Deputy Assistant Accountant-General, Finance Dept., Ministry of Labour, St. Ermins, Westminster, S.W. 1. *Address:* 15, Edith Road, South Norwood, S.E. 25. (M841)

PETERS, Capt. Gordon, O.B.E.

PETERS, Herbert John, M.B.E.

PETERS, Henry Robert, M.B.E., *b.* 13 Oct. 1888; *s.* of the late Robert John Peters, of Oakley, Hants.; *m.* May, *d.* of the late Charles Dudley West, of Downton, Wilts. *Educ.:* Queen Mary's Grammar School, Basingstoke. Assistant to Sec., Railway Executive Committee, Board of Trade. *War Work:* General railway administration; arrangements in connection with the conveyance of heavy guns, troops, and all kinds of explosives; air raid control arrangements so far as the railways were concerned. (M9286)

PETERS, Major John Weston Parsons, D.S.O., O.B.E., R. of O., 7th Dragoon Guards. *Educ.:* Winchester; R.M.C., Sandhurst. Served Chin Lushai Expedition, 1889–90 (medal with clasp); Hazara Expedition, 1891 (clasp); S. African War, 1900–2 (Queen's medal, 4 clasps, King's medal, 2 clasps); Great War, 1914–16 (despatches thrice, D.S.O.). *Address:* 5, Palmer Street, Westminster, S.W. 1. *Club:* Naval and Military. (O8907)

PETERS, Sir Lindsey Byron, K.B.E. Chairman, Engineer and Works Supply Committee, War Office; Director of G. D. Peters & Co., Ltd.; Burma Development Syndicate, Ltd. *Address:* Windlesham Moor, Windlesham, Surrey. (K164)

PETERSEN, Sir William, K.B.E., F.R.A.S., F.R.G.S., *b.* 29 May, 1856; *m.* (1889) Flora McKay (died 1918), *e.d.* of George Sinclair, J.P. of Aberdeen. *Educ.:* Roskelde and Copenhagen. Chairman of Petersen & Co., Ltd., London, Shipowners; Founder and Director of London-American Maritime Trading Co., Ltd., and Director of several other shipping companies; Founder of the Royal and Oraneum Passenger Lines to Canada and U.S.A.; Chairman of the British Committee of the International Shipping Registry, Bureau Veritas (nominated by the Board of Trade); Proprietor of the Hebridean Islands, Eigg; owns over 18,000 acres.

Address: 80, Portland Place, W. 1.; Herons Ghyll, Uckfield, Sussex; The Lodge, Eigg, Inverness-shire. *Clubs:* Junior Carlton; Constitutional; Royal Societies'; Ranelagh. (K409)

PETERSON, Major Guy Lansbury, O.B.E., R.A.S.C.

PETHERICK, Wallace, M.B.E., *b.* 22 Jan. 1858; *s.* of J. W. Petherick, Solicitor, of Exeter; *m.* Gertrude Elizabeth, *d.* of Richard Moxon, of Pontefract. *Educ.:* Privately. General Medical Practitioner. *War Work:* Surgeon to Garboldisham Auxiliary Hospital for four years. *Address:* Hopton, Attleborough, Norfolk. (M9287)

PETIT, Joyce Jbhangir, Mrs., M.B.E. (M7148)

PETO, Dorothy Olivia Georgiana, O.B.E., *b.* 15 Dec. 1886; *d.* of Morton Kelsall and Olivia G. E. Peto (*nee* Maude), of Old House, North Cheriton, Somerset, lately of Littlecroft, Lyndhurst, Hants. *Educ.:* At home. Director of the Bristol Training School for Policewomen and Patrols from May, 1915, to present time. First began patrol work, Nov. 1914; as Director of Bristol School trained and supplied a number of policewomen and patrols, besides training all the patrols for Q.M.A.A.C. and the first of those for the W.R.A.F. *Address:* Old House, North Cheriton, Somerset. (O11119)

PETO, Capt. Geoffrey Kelsall, C.B.E., Wilts Yeomanry, *b.* 8 Sept. 1878; 2nd *s.* of William Herbert Peto, of Dunkinty, Elgin, and *g. s.* of Sir Samuel Morton Peto, 1st Bart. (*see* BURKE'S *Peerage*); *m.* 1 July, 1903, Pauline, *d.* of the late William Quirin, of Boston, U.S.A., and widow of Lieut.-Col. R. Cokayne-Frith, 15th Hussars. (C1024)

PETRE, Francis Loraine, O.B.E., *b.* 22 Feb. 1852; *s.* of the late Hon. Edmund Petre; *m.* Maud Ellen, *d.* of Rev. W. C. Rawlinson, of Chedburgh, Suffolk. *Educ.:* Oscott College. Indian Civil Service (retired), and Ministry of Munitions (Finance Dept.). *War Work:* Ministry of Munitions, Finance Dept., 1915–20, and previously worked for Soldiers' and Sailors' Families Association. *Address:* Bekyngton, Farnham Royal, Bucks. *Clubs:* East India United Service; Hurlingham. (O11120)

PETRE, Col. Henry Cecil, C.M.G., O.B.E., *b.* 27 Oct. 1861; *s.* of Sir George Glynn Petre, K.C.M.G., C.B., of Dunkenhalgh, Lancashire; *m.* Marjorie Elizabeth, *d.* of the late R. H. Seymour, of Boxley Abbey, Maidstone. *Educ.:* Oratory School, Edgbaston; Harrow; Royal Military Coll., Sandhurst. Commanded 3rd Bn. Rifle Brigade from 1909–1913. Served in India, Burmah and Egypt, and in S. African War. *War Work:* Appointed to command Rifle Depot, Winchester, 1 Sept. 1914; left Winchester 12 Sept. 1914, to take over command of 11th Bn. Rifle Brigade on its formation at Aldershot; took 11th Bn. Rifle Brigade to France, 21 July, 1915, occupying the line at Laventie; moved afterwards to Ypres with the Bn.; mentioned in despatches twice; returned to England, 31 Jan. 1916; commanded 14th and 15th Bns. K.R.R.C. at Seaford and Northampton; demobilised Jan. 1919; O.B.E., 5 June, 1919; C.M.G., 3 June, 1916. *Addresses:* Charlton Hawthorne House, Sherborne; 19, Park Mansions, Knightsbridge. *Clubs:* Travellers'; Naval and Military. (O7670)

PETRIE, David, C.I.E., C.B.E., *b.* 9 Sept. 1879; *s.* of Thomas Petrie, of Inveraven, N.B.; *m.* Edris Naida, *d.* of Capt. H. Elliston Warrall. *Educ.:* Aberdeen Univ.; M.A., 1900. Entered Indian Police, 1900; Adjutant, Samana Rifles, Punjab; Assistant Director, Criminal Intelligence. Govt. of India; on special duty under Home Department since 1915. *War Work:* Suppression of Indian and Indo-German revolutionary plots in India, Burma, Siam, and the Far East. *Address:* c/o Messrs. King, King & Co., Bombay. *Club:* East India United Service. (C1091)

PETRIE, Helen Young, Mrs., M.B.E.

PETRIE, Major James, M.B.E.

PETRIE, Major John Campbell Eggar, O.B.E., I.A.R. of O. (O11783)

PETRIE, Thomas Alexander, O.B.E., M.I.Mech.E., *b.* 1877. *War Work:* On Technical Staff of the Coventry Ordnance Works; General Manager of the Basford National Ordnance Factory, Nottingham. *Address:* 10, Caledon Road, Sherwood, Nottingham. (O11211)

PETTEN, Eliza, Mrs., M.B.E.

PETTER, Edith Mary, Mrs., O.B.E., *b.* 3 June. 1869; *d.* of the late James Hutchinson Robson, of Darlington; *m.* Walter, *s.* of the late Henry Petter, of Minehead. *Educ.:* Scarborough. *War Work:* Commandant Durham 6th V.A. Hospital, Woodside, Darlington, 1914, to July, 1919. *Address:* Netherlaw, Darlington.

PETTET, Walter Bell, M.B.E. (O1750)

PETTIFOR, William, O.B.E.

PETTIT, Isobel Helena Courtney, Mrs., M.B.E.

PETTIT, Major William Haddon, M.B.E.

PETTYFER, Percy William, M.B.E., *b.* 26 Dec. 1868; *s.* of the late J. Pettyfer, of Penshurst and Oxford; *m.* Louisa Maude, *d.* of Joseph Pettyfer, of Ringwood, Hants. *Educ.:* Privately. Station Superintendent, S.E. and C. Rly., Canterbury. *War Work:* Transportation of troops, war material, etc.; receipt and despatch of wounded; also receipt and despatch of repatriated prisoners of war. *Address:* 28, St. Dunstans, Canterbury. (M9288)

PEUCH, Capt. Albert Gottlieb, O.B.E., V.D.

PEYTON, Guy Wynne, C.B.E.

PEYTON, Capt. William de Malet, O.B.E., M.B.

PHARASYN, Godfrey Norris, O.B.E.

PHAYRE, Lieut.-Col. Richard, O.B.E., J.P., D.L.; *s.* of General Sir Robert Phayre, G.C.B.; *m.* Frances Anne, *d.* of the late John Jasper Leigh Bayly, of Alderley, Gloucestershire.

Educ.: Marlborough Coll. Lieut.-Col. (ret.), Alexandra, Princess of Wales' Own Yorkshire Regt. Served in Afghan War, 1880, Medal, mentioned in despatches. *Address:* Belgaum, Woking. *Club:* Junior United Service. (O1752)

PHELPS, Fanny Elizabeth, M.B.E.

PHELPS, Major Joseph Bryan William, O.B.E., *b.* 16 Jan. 1879; *s.* of Rev. and Mrs. J. F. Phelps, of St. Johns, Newfoundland; *m.* Agnes Muriel, *d.* of Dr. Evans, of Edgbaston. *Educ.:* Rossall. Civil Engineer; South Africa, South America. *War Work:* 9th Div. Amm. Park; 613 M.T. Co. R.A.S.C., Western Command; 7th Div., Amm. Sub-Park, France; 613 M.T. Co., Western Command, England; Jan. 1915, to May, 1919. *Address:* Grimsdell Cottage, Amersham Common, Bucks. *Clubs:* English, Buenos Aires; Argentine, London: Racquet, Liverpool. (O11122)

PHELPS, Capt. Joseph Harold, O.B.E., *b.* 1874; *s.* of the late J. L. Phelps, of Water Park, Castleconnell, Ireland. *Educ.:* Harrow, and Magdalen Coll., Oxford. Sec. to H.H. The Maharajah of Karhmir's Game Reserves. *War Work:* 1915–17, with Col. A. J. Barry's Unit of B.R.C.S., serving with French Army, Champagne, 1915, Verdun, 1916 (Croix de Guerre, 2 citations), 1917, to end of War; in Mesopotamia as Director of Motor Launches, B.R.C.S. (mentioned in despatches). *Clubs:* Windham; Wellington. (O11123)

PHELPS, Maude Marion, Mrs., M.B.E.

PHELPS, Lieut. Seth Arthur Rose, M.B.E., R.E.

PHEYSEY, Capt. Frederick Cecil, M.B.E., R.A.S.C.

PHILIP, Alexander John, M.B.E., *b.* 18 April, 1879; *s.* of Thomas Philip, of New Aberdour; *m.* Yvonne, *d.* of Breton de Plunivez, of Bordeaux. Borough Librarian, Gravesend; Compiler of International Bibliography of the War; Author. *War Work:* Executive Officer, Food Control; Hon. Searcher for missing; Hon. Sec. War Savings Committee; Author "Rations, Rationing, and Food Control." *Address:* Bendula, Old Road West, Gravesend. (M3896)

PHILIP, Eng.-Comm. Arthur Edward, O.B.E., R.N.R.

PHILIP, Elsie Green, Mrs., M.B.E., *b.* 24 March, 1856; *d.* of James Cumming, of Keith, Banffshire, Scotland; *m.* Peter, *s.* of James Philip, of Insch, Aberdeenshire. *Educ.:* Private School and Grammar School, Keith. *War Work:* President, Div. 13, Soldiers' and Sailors' Families Association, Glasgow; an official visitor at Stobhill Military Hospital under Red Cross; later, Member of Gorbals and Tradeston Local War Pensions Committee. Glasgow. *Address:* 16, Braemar Street, Langside, Glasgow. (M9289)

PHILIP, Fullarton Bell, M.B.E.

PHILIP, Professor James Charles, O.B.E., D.Sc., *b.* 12 Feb. 1873. Professor of Physical Chemistry at the Imperial Coll. of Science and Technology, South Kensington; Sec. of the Chemical Society. *War Work:* Research work in connection with defence against poison gas. *Addresses:* Imperial Coll. of Science, S.W. 7; 5, Queen Anne's Gardens, Bedford Park, W. 4. (O1753)

PHILIP, Major James Porter, O.B.E., M.D., C.M., D.P.H., *b.* 15 Oct. 1865; *s.* of the late Rev. G. F. J. Philip, of New Deer, Aberdeenshire. *m.* Susan Kinnear, *d.* of the late John Fleming, J.P., of Aberdeen. *Educ.:* Aberdeen Univ.; King's and Marshall's Coll. Private practice in Morpeth; M.O.H. Morpeth Rural District; Medical Referee to Northumberland Pensions Committee. *War Work:* M.O. i/c 6th Northumberland V.A. Hospital since Aug. 1914, until April, 1919; Temporary M.O. i/c 3/6th D.L.I.; M.O. i/c Whalton Auxil. Hospital; M.O. i/c all troops in Morpeth Area; Major, Permanent rank granted O.C. of C. Section Volunteer Ambulance R.A.M.C. *Address:* Bon-Accord House, Morpeth, Northumberland. (O11830)

PHILIP, Bimbashi (Major) John, M.B.E., D.C.M., *b.* 3 Jan. 1873; *s.* of Thomas Philip, of New Pitsligo, Aberdeenshire; *m.* Annie Grace Park, *d.* of James Barnet, of Ugiebrae, Old Deer, Aberdeenshire. Enlisted 1st Gren. Guards, June, 1886; Services lent to Egyptian Army as Sergt. Instructor, Feb. 1897; present with 3rd Batt. E.A. at Battles of Abu Hamed 1897, Atbara and Khartoum, 1898; granted Medal for Distinguished Conduct in the Field (D.C.M.) at latter engagement; Khedive's Medal with 5 clasps, Queen's Sudan Medal, Long Service Medal; joined Egyptian Civil Police as Capt. Oct. 1907; granted 4th Class Order of the Nile by H.H. The Sultan of Egypt in 1916; assisting British Army by working with Military Police, in Civil Police capacity, in all work where soldiers and civilians were concerned during the war. *Address:* Esbekieh Caracol, Cairo City Police, Cairo. (M7036)

PHILIP, Katherine Laura, Mrs., M.B.E., *b.* 26 June, 1861; *d.* of the late Rev. Dr. Cruickshank, of Turriff, Aberdeenshire; *m.* James Allan, *s.* of the late Dr. James Philip, of Aberdeen. *War Work:* Canteen worker, at the British Soldiers' Institute, Boulogne-sur-Mer, from its opening in Oct. 1914, to its finish in Jan. 1920. *Address:* 95, Grande Rue, Boulogne-sur-Mer. (M9290)

PHILIPE, George William Vitalli de Rhe, O.B.E.

PHILIPE, Mary Catharine Catharine, Mrs. de Rhe, M.B.E. (M6223)

PHILIPPIDES, Messib Cleanthes, M.B.E., Legal Dept. (M10360)

PHILIPPS, Mai Alice Magdalen, Lady, C.B.E., Lady of Grace of St. John of Jerusalem; co-heiress of the late Thos. Morris, D.L., of Coomb, Carmarthenshire; *m.* (1902) Sir Owen (Cosby) Philipps, G.C.M.G., D.L., M.P. (U.), Chester, since 1916; Knight of Justice of St. John of Jerusalem in England; 3rd

s. of the Rev. Canon Sir Jas. Erasmus Philipps, 12th Bart., and Hon. Lady Philipps, sister of 5th Baron Wynford (*see* BURKE'S *Peerage*). *Addresses:* Amroth Castle, Pembrokeshire; Coomb, Llangain, Carmarthen; Trevallyn Rossett, Denbigh; Chelsea House, Cadogan Place, S.W. 1. (C2874)

PHILIPPS, Marian Isobel (Mabel), Lady, O.B.E.: *y.d.* of late J. B. Mirrlees, of Redlands, Glasgow, wife of Major-General Sir Ivor Philipps, K.C.B., D.S.O., M.P. *War Work:* Organiser and Hon. Sec. Welsh Regiment Prisoners of War Association; Vice-President, Pembrokeshire Branch British Red Cross Society. *Addresses:* Cosheston Hall, Pembrokeshire; Chantrey House, Eccleston Street, S.W. 1. (O11125)

PHILIPS, Edward Mark, O.B.E., *b.* 25 April, 1879; *s.* of Rev. E. Philips, of Hollington, Tean, Staffs; *m.* Diana O'Carrol, *nee* Darby. *Educ.:* Shrewsbury. Managing; Director of J. & N. Philips & Co. Ltd., Manchester; Director of the Lancashire and Yorkshire Bank. *War Work:* Hon. Sec. and Organiser of East Lancs Homes for disabled Sailors and Soldiers. *Address:* Colshaw Hall, Over Peover, Cheshire. *Clubs:* Union; Clarendon, Manchester. (O11124)

PHILIPS, Enid, Mrs., M.B.E.

PHILIPS, Capt. Harry Vaughan, M.B.E.

PHILIPS, Helena Adelaide Sara, Mrs., M.B.E., *b.* 24 Feb. 1870; *d.* of the late Col. B. G. Davies-Cooke, of Colomendy, Mold; *m.* Basil Edwin Philips, J.P., D.L., of Rhual, Mold, Lieut.-Col. Commanding 5th Bn. R.W.F. (Flintshire Territorials), killed in action, Gallipoli, Aug. 10, 1915. *Educ.:* Privately. *War Work:* Vice-President, Soldiers' and Sailors' Families Association, Mold and district, Flintshire War Pensions Committee, Flintshire Women's War Agricultural Committee; Head of Working Party B.R.C.S. (Gwernaffield Branch); work for Girls' Friendly Society War Emergency Committee, particularly in organising Canteen for Munition Workers at Wrexham. *Address:* Rhual, Mold, Flintshire. *Club:* Alexandra. (M9291)

PHILIPS, Col. Lewis Francis, C.M.G., C.B.E., D.S.O., *b.* 1870; *s.* of the late John William Philips, of Heybridge Staffordshire; *m.* 1909, Margaret Aline, *d.* of the late Lieut.-Col. Augustus Henry Macdonald-Moreton (*see* BURKE'S *Peerage*, Ducie, E.). *Educ.:* Winchester, and at R.M.C. Entered King's Roy. Rifle Corps, 1890; became Capt. 1898; Brevet Major, 1902; Lieut.-Col. 1915; served in the S. African War, 1899–1902; present at actions of Colenso and Spion Kop, and at relief of Ladysmith (despatches, Brevet Major); in the Great War, 1914–19, as a Brig.-Com. with rank of Brig.-Gen. (despatches). *Address:* Darts Cottage, Bembridge, Isle of Wight. *Club:* Naval and Military. (C770)

PHILLIBROWN, George Ernest, M.B.E.

PHILLIMORE, Ethel Maud, M.B.E. *War Work:* Quartermaster, Standish Aux. Military Hospital. 1915–19. *Address:* Stonehouse, Glos. (M3895)

PHILLIMORE, Capt. Valentine Egerton Bagot, C.B.E. D.S.O., *b.* 1875; *s.* of the late Sir Augustus Phillimore, K.C.B. (*see* BURKE'S *Peerage*, Fortescue, E.); *m.* 1st, 1908, Mary Kathleen, who died 1909, *d.* of the late George Robinson, of Overdale, Skipton-in-Craven, Yorkshire; 2nd, 1910, Inés Agnes Geraldine, *d.* of 15th Baron of Castel Cicciano. Entered R.N. 1888; became Lieut. 1896; Com. 1906; Capt. 1913; served in China, 1900. *Club:* United Service. (C3185)

PHILLIP, William Littlejohn, O.B.E.

PHILLIPS, Acton, O.B.E., *b.* 29 May, 1877; *s.* of Maberly Phillips, F.S.A. J.P., of Enfield, Middlesex; *m.* Marion, *d.* of George William Fail, of Netherton, Northumberland. *Educ.:* Privately. Chartered Accountant. *War Work:* After being totally rejected on Medical grounds for Active Service took charge under the Joint Finance Committee of the British Red Cross and Order of St. John of the Accounts and Statistics of over 1000 Auxiliary Hospitals; after the Armistice was Assist. Sec. to the Central Demobilisation Board. *Addresses:* Avenue House, Frinton-on-Sea; 28, Basinghall Street, E.C. (O11126)

PHILLIPS, Paymaster-Lieut. Algernon Wynn Pendennis, O.B.E., R.N. (ret.).

PHILLIPS, Cecilia L. M.B.E.; *d.* of James Phillips, of Clifton. *Educ.:* Ellenborough House School, Clifton. Head mistress, The Grammar School for Girls, Thetford, Norfolk; Girl Guide Commissioner, S.W. Division of Norfolk. *War Work:* Vice-President, British Red Cross Society, Thetford Division; Member of Norfolk County Executive Committee B.R.C.S. *Addresses:* The Girls' Grammar School, Thetford; Glenholme, Sheringham. (M2283)

PHILLIPS, Major Charles Edmund Stanley, O.B.E.

PHILLIPS, Major Charles Keith, O.B.E., M.A., *b.* 1 Dec. 1880; *s.* of Alfred Phillips, of 57, St. George's Square, S.W. 1. *Educ.:* Merchant Taylors' School; St. Catharine's Coll., Cambridge. Land and Legal Adviser, Imperial War Graves Commission. *War Work:* Feb. 1915, 2nd Lieut. Royal Irish Rifles; Feb. 1917, Staff Capt. H.Q.; 2nd Army; Aug. 1918, D.A.A.G., G.H.Q. British Forces in Italy. *Address:* 57, St. George's Square, S.W. 1. *Club:* New Oxford and Cambridge. (O6407)

PHILLIPS, Major Charles Kendall, O.B.E.

PHILLIPS, Capt. Cyril Charles, O.B.E., R.G.A.

PHILLIPS, David, M.B.E.

PHILLIPS, Edith Helen, Mrs., O.B.E., R.R.C., *b.* 1871; *d.* of the late Alfred Coxon; *m.* Llewellyn Powell, M.A., M.D., F.R.C.S., F.R.C.P., *s.* of James Mathias Phillips, M.D., of Cardigan, S. Wales. *War Work:* Hon. Matron, Duchess of Westminster's Hospital, Le Touquet, 1914–15; mentioned in despatches (F.M. Sir John French); Hon. Matron in Chief for Egypt. Brit. Red Cross Society, Matron of Giza Hospital, 1915–18; mentioned in despatches (Gen. Sir J. Maxwell); twice mentioned in despatches (Gen. Sir A. Murray); Lady Superintendent and Inspector Women's Internment Camps, Prisoners of War from Palestine and Hedjaz (Egypt); twice mentioned in despatches (F.M. Viscount Allenby). *Addresses:* 8, Sharia Suliman Pasha, Cairo, Egypt; 17, De Vere Gardens, London, W. (O11127)

PHILLIPS, **Elizabeth Miller, Mrs.**, O.B.E.
PHILLIPS, **Emily, Mrs.**, M.B.E.
PHILLIPS, **Eric Taylor, M.B.E.**
PHILLIPS, **Ernest Harold**, O.B.E., *b.* 8 April, 1881; *s.* of H. T. Phillips, of Wolverhampton. *Educ.:* Wolverhampton Grammar School, and Sidney Sussex Coll., Cambridge. Civil Service; Principal, Ministry of Health. *War Work:* Private Sec. to Parliamentary Sec. and to Permanent Sec. of Local Government Board. *Address:* Dalry, Heathside Avenue, Woking. (O1754)

PHILLIPS, **Ernest Thomas Adams**, M.B.E., *b.* 22 May, 1878; *s.* of Thomas Adams Phillips, of Bromley, Kent. *Educ.:* Eastbourne Coll., and Emmanuel Coll., Cambridge (LL.B. degree). Solicitor; Assistant Official Receiver, Companies Liquidation Dept. *War Work:* England, Artists' Rifles; France, 296 Siege Battery, R.G.A. (S.R.); Anti-Gas Schools, Havre, attached R.E. *Address:* Beech Corner, Chipstead, Surrey. (M4576)

PHILLIPS, **Lieut. Ernest William**, O.B.E., R.G.A.
PHILLIPS, **Ernest William**, O.B.E.
PHILLIPS, **Lieut. and Qr.-Mr. Francis Hardwick**, O.B.E., A.I.F.
PHILLIPS, **Eng.-Lieut.-Comm. Frederick Brown**, O.B.E.
PHILLIPS, **Frederick Solomon**, O.B.E., *b.* 21 Nov. 1860; *s.* of Barnet S. Phillips, of 59, Queen's Gardens, Hyde Park; *m.* Lily Adeline, *d.* of R. Hall, of Brighton. *Educ.:* University Coll., School. *War Work:* Hon. Asst. Sec. to the St. John Ambulance Association from Oct. 1914, till end of War. *Addresses:* Sunnyside, Holmwood, Surrey; 14, Marina Court Avenue, Bexhill-on-Sea. *Clubs:* Badminton; Albemarle; Royal Automobile. (O1756)

PHILLIPS, **Brig.-Gen. Geoffrey Francis**, C.B.E., D.S.O., *b.* 1879; *s.* of J. H. Phillips. *Educ.:* Wellington Coll. Entered Duke of Cornwall's L.I. 1900; Capt. 1910; Major, 1915; Brevet Lieut.-Col. 1917; serving with King's African Rifles, with rank of Brig.-Gen; served in Somaliland, 1908–10 (medal with clasp); Great War, 1914–19, on Staff (wounded, despatches, Brevet Lieut.-Col., Order of SS. Maurice and Lazarus of Italy). (C1099)

PHILLIPS, **Lieut.-Col. George Ingleton**, C.B.E. T. Major and Brevet Lieut.-Col. in the Army; served in the Great War, 1914–19 (despatches) (C1740)

PHILLIPS, **Major George Lort**, M.B.E., *b.* 7 March, 1891; *s.* of George Gordon Owen Phillips, M.D., F.R.C.S., F.R.C.P., of Warwick, Queensland, Australia, late of Milford Haven, Pembrokeshire, Wales; *m.* Lilian, *d.* of the late John Ansell, of Inverell, N.S.W. *Educ.:* Church of England Grammar School, Melbourne, Victoria, Australia. Confidential Sec. to Australian Diplomatic Service; Freeman of County of Haverfordwest, Wales. *War Work:* Served in Australian Imperial Forces from Aug. 1914, in 2nd Battn. A.I.F.; Active Service, Egypt and Gallipoli; wounded severely latter theatre, "Lone Pine," and repatriated to England; afterwards Adjutant, Australian Command Depot, Salisbury Plains; A.D.C. to G.O.C., A.I.F.; Camp Commandant, A.I.F. Depots in U.K.; Commandant, A.I.F. Detention Barracks, Lewes, Sessex; C.O. Australian Graves Services in all theatres. *Address:* Australia House, Strand, London. *Club:* Royal Automobile. (M2284)

PHILLIPS, **Lieut.-Col. George Percy Achilles**, O.B.E.,
PHILLIPS, **Lieut. Harold Lionel**, M.B.E., R.F.A. (T.)
PHILLIPS, **Harry Joseph**, M.B.E.
PHILLIPS, **Helena Creed**, M.B.E.
PHILLIPS, **Henry Archibald Allen**, M.I.M.E., *b.* 13 Oct 1871; *s.* of William Henry Medland Phillips, of Edge Hill House, Mitcheldean, Glos.; *m.* Madeleine, *d.* of John E. Thomas, of Aberdare. *Educ.:* Colston School, Bristol, and Llandovery Coll. Mining Engineer, practising at Swansea; District Inspector under the Coal Mines Department for South Wales, Mon., Somerset. and Glos.; Consulting Engineer to several Collieries, and Mineral and Estate Agent. *War Work:* District Inspector as above; Executive Officer, Pitwood Department for South Wales; Member, and acted Sec., of the South Wales Pitwood Allocation Committee; Member of Commission appointed to inquire into short time worked in South Wales Collieries, 1918. *Address:* Westmancote, Uplands Terrace, Swansea. (O11128)

PHILLIPS, **Henry Dixon**, M.B.E., J.P.
PHILLIPS, **Henry Percy**, O.B.E., *b.* 26 July, 1869; *s.* of Edwin Phillips, of Machen, Mon.; *m.* Lucy Edith, *d.* of John Pritchard, of Beaumaris. *Educ.:* Private School, and Commercial Coll., Neuchatel, Switzerland. Colliery Shipping Agent (played half-back under the Rugby code for Newport, Mon., 1889–93, and for Wales, 1891–93). *War Work:* Hon. Sec. for Belgian Refugee Committee at Newport and Monmouth shire (for which was made "an Officer of the Order of the Crown" by the King of the Belgians); voluntary munition worker making Shells; voluntary work in Recruiting Office; Member of the Port Labour Committee for organising Dock

Work during the War; Member of the Committee for the arrangement of Export of Coal to France and Italy during the War. *Address:* Rose..laul, 19, Fields Park Road, Newport, Mon. *Club:* Monmouthshire. (O1758)

PHILLIPS, **Henry Thomas**, M.B.E.
PHILLIPS, **Herbert**, O.B.E.
PHILLIPS, **Capt. Herbert Thomas**, M.B.E., A.I.F.
PHILLIPS, **Capt. Horace Stock**, M.B.E., R.E.
PHILLIPS, **Lieut. James Charles Joseph**, M.B.E., R.A.S.C.
PHILLIPS, **James Falkner**, M.B.E.
PHILLIPS, **John Henry**, M.B.E.
PHILLIPS, **John Robert**, O.B.E., *b.* 28 May, 1871; *s.* of the late John Foster Phillips, of Brixton, Surrey; *m.* Lydia Redfarn, *d.* of the late Henry Smith, of Hay's Wharf, and St. John's, S.E. *Educ.:* Haberdashers' School; Birkbeck Coll. Civil Servant; Boy Clerk, Money Order Dept., G.P.O., 1887–90; Second Divion Clerk and Examiner, 1890–1914; Accountant General's Dept., 1914–19; Accounting Officer, National (War) Savings Committee, 1917; Director of Accounts National (War) Savings Committee, 1919. *War Work:* Special duties in G.P.O., 1914–16; seconded to National (War) Savings Committee, May, 1916; appointed Accounting Officer, March, 1917. *Address:* 11, Slaithwaite Road, Lewisham, S.E. 13. (O3870)

PHILLIPS, **Major John Robert Parry**, O.B.E., R.A.S.C.
PHILLIPS, **John Ruskin**, M.B.E.
PHILLIPS, **Lilian Marion Estelle, Mrs.**, O.B.E.; *d.* of the late Edward Savile, of Okehampton. Devon; *m.* Capt. Lionel C. W., *s.* of Charles Phillips, of Unsted Park, Godalming. *War Work:* Vice-Pres., Surrey B.R.C.S.; Commandant Thorncombe Military Hospital, Bramley, Surrey. *Address:* Unsted Park, Godalming, Surrey. *Club:* Bath. (O1759)

PHILLIPS, **Margaret, Mrs.**, M.B.E.
PHILLIPS, **Marion Isabel, Lady**, O.B.E.
PHILLIPS, **Major Percival**, O.B.E.
PHILLIPS, **Sir Percival**, K.B.E., *b.* 2 July, 1877; *s.* of Hibbard Samuel Phillips, M.D., of Canonsburgh, Pennsylvania, U.S.A. *Educ.:* Pittsburgh, Pennsylvania, U.S.A. Associated continuously with daily newspapers in America 1895–1901; with Greek Army in War against Turkey, 1897; Spanish-American War, 1898; War Correspondent, "Daily Express" in Russo-Japanese War, 1904; Jamaica earthquake, 1907; Balkans, 1909; revolution in Catalonia, 1909; revolution in Portugal, 1910; Champagne riots, Northern France, 1911; with Italian Expedition in Tripoli 1911; Coronation Durbar at India, and Imperial tour through India, 1911–12; other Royal tours at home and abroad; funeral of King Frederick of Denmark, 1912; with Bulgarian Army in first Balkan campaign, 1912–13; with Belgian Field Army from declaration of War, August, 1914, until fall of Antwerp; one of the first five accredited war correspondents with British Armies (Western Front), May, 1915; representing "Daily Express" and "Morning Post"; and served in this capacity until the Armistice, 1918; with the advance into Germany, and attached British Army of the Rhine until conclusion of Peace; accompanied Prince of Wales on Canadian Tour, 1919; in Egypt, then Syria and Palestine during Arab rising, 1919–20; in Constantinople until signing of Peace with Turkey: and Athens during Greek Crisis, 1920; Chevalier of the Legion of Honour. *Clubs:* Royal Aero; Savage; Royal Automobile. (K410)

PHILLIPS, **Capt. Rees**, O.B.E., M.D., D.P.H. (London), *b.* 1878; *s.* of Richard Phillips, of Great Molleston, Narberth, Pembrokeshire; *m.* Ida Gladys, *d.* of Walter Sheard, of Leeds. *Educ.:* Univ. Coll., Aberystwyth; Middlesex Hospital, Univ. of London. Medical Practitioner. *War Work:* Section Commander in 1/2nd East Anglian Field Ambulance; served in Gallipoli, Egypt, and Palestine, 1915–18; mentioned in despatches twice. *Address:* 62, Upper Kennington Lane, S.E. 11. (O6269)

PHILLIPS, **Paymaster-Comm. Richard Hood Grant**, O.B.E., R.N.
PHILLIPS, **Lieut.-Col. Thomas Brocklehurst**, O.B.E.
PHILLIPS, **Thomas Williams**, C.B.E., *b.* 1883; *s.* of Thomas Phillips, of Schoolhouse, Cemmaes, Montgomeryshire; *m.* 1913, Alice Hair Potter. *Educ.:* Jesus Coll., Oxford. Barrister, Gray's Inn, 1913; entered Board of Trade, 1906; became Principal Officer, Employment Depart. 1916; appointed Acting Director, Employment Depart., Ministry of Labour, 1918; Assist. Sec. 1918; also a Member of its Departmental Council, 1919. *Club:* Royal Societies'. (C595)

PHILLIPS, **Wallace Henry**, M.B.E.
PHILLIPS, **Walter John**, M.B.E.
PHILLIPS, **Major William Albert**, O.B.E.
PHILLIPS, **Major William Austin**, M.B.E.
PHILLIPS, **William James**, M.B.E., *b.* 16 April, 1892; *s.* of John W. Phillips, of Chelsea. Incorporated Accountant Superintending Accountant, Admiralty. *War Work:* Work for Admiralty. *Address:* 56, Delaford Street, Fulham, London, S.W. 6. (O8019)

PHILLIPS, **Capt. William James**, O.B.E.
PHILLIPS, **Capt. and Qr.-Mr. William John**, O.B.E., R.A.
PHILLIPS **Capt. William John**, O.B.E., *b.* 5 July, 1867; *s.* of the late William Beal Phillips, of Brentford and Chelmsford; *m.* Emily, *d.* of John Cooksey, late of Aldershot. *Educ.:* Liskeard County School, and Military School. Capt. and Qr.-Mr. Royal Horse Artillery. *War Work:* Instructor in

Gunnery and Artillery to the 9th, 12th, 14th, 17th, 23rd, and 37th Division, R.A.; Instructor and Camp Staff Officer, Okehampton Artillery Camp, 1915–16; Instructor at St. Johns Wood and Mansfield Park, Officer Cadet Schools; Instructor in Artillery to Young Officers, No 6C Reserve Bde., R.F.A. *Address :* Ash Bank, Ash Vale, Aldershot. (O7547)

PHILLIPS, William Lambert Collyer, O.B.E.

PHILLIPSON, Major John, O.B.E.

PHILLPOTTS, Bertha Surtees, O.B.E., Litt.D.; *d.* of James Surtees Phillpotts, B.C.L., formerly Head Master of Bedford School. *Educ.:* Girton Coll., Cambridge. Principal of Westfield Coll. (Univ. of London); previously Lady Carlisle Research Fellow, Somerville Coll., Oxford. *War Work :* Private Sec. to H.B.M. Minister at Stockholm. *Address :* Westfield College, London, N.W. 3. *Club :* Univ. for Ladies.
(O1761)

PHILLPOTTS, Lillian Lestella Elizabeth Georgina, M.B.E., Q.M.A.A.C.

PHILLPOTTS, Owen Surtees, O.B.E., *b.* 9 Oct. 1870; *s.* of James Surtees Phillpotts, of The Ousels, Tunbridge Wells. *Educ.:* Bedford; Worcester Coll., Oxford. H.B.M. Commercial Sec. to H.B.M. Legation in Vienna; formerly H.M. Consul in Vienna. *War Work :* Commercial Attaché to H.M. Legation at Stockholm. *Club :* National Liberal. (O652)

PHILPOT, Lieut. Albert John, O.B.E., R.E.

PHILPOT, David, D.S.O., O.B.E.

PHILPOT, Harold Percy, M.B.E., F.C.I.S., *b.* 28 March, 1878; *s.* of Percival Philpot, of Lewisham; *m.* Jessie, *d.* of George Henniker, of Wandsworth Common. *Educ.:* East Dulwich Coll. (now dissolved). Director, Canned Goods Importers. *War Work :* In charge of Canned Fish Section, Ministry of Food, until 1 Jan. 1920. *Address :* 47–51, King William Street, E.C. 4. (M3849)

PHILPOT, Joseph Henry, M.B.E., M.D. (Lond.), M.R.C.P. (Lond.), *b.* 14 July, 1850; *s.* of the Rev. Joseph Charles Philpot, formerly Fellow of Worcester Coll., Oxford; *m.* Isaline, *d.* of Joseph Needham, of New Inn, W.C. *Educ.:* King's Coll., London. *War Work :* Chairman of Committee, War Refugees' Dispensary; awarded the Médaille du Roi Albert, by the King of the Belgians. *Address :* 61, Chester Square, S.W. 1. *Club :* Savile. (M9297)

PHILPOT, Thomas, M.B.E., J.P.

PHILPOTT, Capt. Henry Goschen, O.B.E., R.N.

PHILPS, Evelyn Chapman, M.B.E.

PHILSON, Lucy, Mrs., M.B.E.

PHIPPS, 2nd Lieut. Charles William, M.B.E., R.A.F.

PHIPPS, Capt. Frederick Reginald, O.B.E., R.E.

PHIPPS, Capt. Henry Croly, M.B.E.; *s.* of the late Charles Hare Phipps, M.A., of South Cregg, Fermoy, Co. Cork; *m.* Dorothy Emily Mary, *d.* of the late George Masters Pyne, of Ballyvolane, Fermoy, Co. Cork. *War Work :* Royal Army Service Corps. *Club.:* Royal Irish Yacht, Kingstown.
(M5535)

PHIPPS, Capt. Paul Campbell, M.B.E.

PHIZACKERLEY, George Thompson, O.B.E., M.Inst.T., *b.* 22 Oct. 1858; *s.* of Edmund Phizackerley, of Lancaster; *m.* Margaret, *d.* of William Kench, of Chipping Norton, Oxon. *Educ.:* Privately. District Goods Manager (for Liverpool and Birkenhead), L. & N.-W. Railway. *War Work :* Transport of Munitions of War, Foodstuffs, and Military Equipment of Canadian-American troops through Liverpool; Member of several local Government Committees in connection with transport, etc. *Address :* 25, Highfield South, Rock Ferry, Cheshire. *Club :* Exchange, Liverpool. (O11129)

PHŒNIX, Herbert Ray, M.B.E., *b.* 19 May, 1873; *s.* of Joseph Phœnix, late of Inland Revenue Dept., Ipswich; *m.* Lucy Maud, *d.* of Joseph Summers, of Wood Green, N. *Educ.:* Berners House School, Ipswich; Ipswich Middle School. Chief Registrar, Ministry of Labour. *War Work :* Reorganisation and control of Registry Branch, Labour Departments, Ministry of Munitions; organisation and control, Registry Branch, Department of Demobilisation and Resettlement; co-ordination and control of Registries of Ministry of Labour. *Addresses :* Laleham, Barnard Hill, Muswell Hill, N. 10; Ministry of Labour, Whitehall, S.W. 1. (M9298)

PHOTIADES, Lieut. Nicolas John, M.B.E.

PHYTHIAN, Thomas Ewart, M.B.E.

PICKARD, Henry, M.B.E.

PICKEN, Capt. Andrew, O.B.E., M.B., R.A.M.C. (S.R.).

PICKEN, Anna Craig, Mrs., M.B.E.

PICKEN, 2nd Lieut. Richard Nelson, M.B.E.

PICKERILL, Major Henry Percy, O.B.E., M.D.

PICKERING, Alice Mabel, Mrs., M.B.E., A.R.R.C. *b.* 1860; *d.* of the Rev. Michael Henry Simpson, of Tow Law, Durham; *m.* William Henry, H.M. Chief Inspector of Mines, *s.* of James Pickering, of Gathurst, Wigan. *Educ.:* St. Peter's School, York. *War Work :* Commandant of the Arnold Auxiliary Military Hospital, Doncaster, 1914–19; hospital began 25 beds, increased to 150; over 3000 patients were treated in hospital; 2000 out-patients were treated; £2000 handed over to the local infirmary when hospital closed. *Address :* Ridgehome, Bentley, Doncaster. (M849)

PICKERING, Lieut. Edwin Fitzgerald Samuel, M.B.E.

PICKERING, Fred, M.B.E., J.P., *b.* Sept. 1866; *s.* of George Pickering of Batley, Yorkshire; *m.* Emma Louisa, *d.* of George Wright Grinstead, of Leeds. *Educ.:* Batley Grammar School. J.P., Bradford; Managing Director, Fred Pickering & Son, Ltd., Umbrella and Stick Manufacturers; Sec. and Director, John W. Hill, Ltd., Cloth

and Yarn Manufacturers; Hon. Sec. of Bradford Chamber of Trade for 14 years until 1919; President National Chamber of Trade 21st Conference at Bradford, 1919, now Hon. Sec. again; North of England and North Wales Organiser And Adviser under the One-Man Business Preservation Scheme of the Ministry of National Service and the Local Government Board; Vice-President of the West Yorkshire Federated Chambers of Trade of the National Chamber; was the Organiser and Hon. Sec. of the Bradford Traders' War Fund, which raised nearly £9,000 in weekly collections from traders; joint Hon. Sec. of the Lord Mayor's War Fund (raised £200,000); Hon. Sec. and Organiser of the Bradford Sailors' and Soldiers' Children's Christmas Fund, which entertained some 80,000 youngsters each war-time Christmas; Hon. Sec. of the local Belgian Pure Water Fund and the Serbian Fund of a similar nature; Organiser of egg shows which resulted in thousands of fresh eggs being collected for the military hospitals; Organiser of a traders' contribution to the Y.M.C.A. funds for a new Bradford centre; local Hon. Sec. for the Farmers' Red Cross Fund; a Member of the local Military Service Tribunal; Trader's Representative on the Bradford Citizens' Army League, which raised three " Pals " battalions and recruited for other units; Chairman of the local Committee administering the Retail Businesses Licensing Order; Member of the local Labour Advisory Committee; Vice-Chairman of Directors of the Yorkshire branch of the 'Lord Roberts' Memorial Workshops for disabled Service men; Member of the Council of the Bradford Army Veterans' Association and of the local Committee of the Navy and Army War Pensions Committee; Member of the Interviewing Board, Appointments Committee, Ministry of Labour; Member of the local Advisory Committee, Ministry of Labour. *Address :* Fagley House, Bradford. (M9302)

PICKERING, Lieut.-Com. Frederick, O.B.E., R.N.R., R.D.

PICKERING, Capt. John Russell, M.B.E., F.L.A.A., *b.* 7 July, 1884; *s.* of J. C. Pickering, of Scarborough; *m.* Dora, *d.* of A. W. Hilling, of Chorley Wood. *Educ.:* Ancaster House, St. Leonards, and King's. *War Work :* With the Royal Army Service Corps. *Addresses :* Balham Court, London, S.W. 12; The Point, Exmouth. *Clubs :* Farmers'; United R.A.S.C. (M5536)

PICKERING, Percy, M.B.E.

PICKERING, Comm. William Alfred, O.B.E., R.N.

PICKERSGILL, William, C.B.E., J.P., W.Sch., *b.* 1 March, 1861; *s.* of John Gaukrodger Pickersgill, of Crewe; *m.* Mary, *d.* of James Hope, of Jamulpur, India. *Educ. :* Public School and Academy, Crewe; Finsbury College; and Birkbeck Institute, London. Locomotive, Carriage, and Wagon Superintendent, Caledonian Railway Company; Member of Engineers and Shipbuilders Institute of Scotland; Member of Institute of Locomotive Engineers (President, 1920); Member of Association of Railway Locomotive Engineers of Great Britain and Ireland (President, 1912). *War Work :* Manufacture of ambulance trains for France for British Troops; supplied locomotives to France; manufacture of general service waggons, fuses, torpedoes, gun mountings, mines, transport waggons, railway waggons for armoured trains, sterilising tanks, etc. (C2875)

PICKETT, Capt. Alfred Cleveland, O.B.E., R.A.M.C.

PICKFORD, Hind, M.B.E.

PICKIN, Major William David, O.B.E.

PICKLES, Edward Llewellyn, M.B.E.

PICOT, Henrietta Sybil Douglas, M.B.E.

PICOT, Lieut.-Col. Henry Philip, C.B.E., late Indian Staff Corps, Officer of Legion of Honour, *b.* 29 April, 1857; *s.* of Phillip Henry Picot, of Brisbane, Australia; *m.* Frances Mary Douglas, *d.* of Major-Gen. Douglas Scott, of Erin Lodge, Weybridge. *Educ.:* Thomsons' School, Jersey; R.M.C. Sandhurst. Lieut., 21 Sept. 1874, Duke of Wellington's Regt.; retired as Lieut.-Col. 4 Nov. 1903; Afghanistan, 1878–80 (twice mentioned in despatches); Zaimusht Expedition (mentioned in depatches); Black Mountain Expedition; Military attaché, Teheran 1893–1900; Oriental Secretary, H.M.'s Legation Teheran, 1898–1900. *War Work :* Military Attaché, Berne, Switzerland, 1914–16; Officer in Charge of British Interned in Switzerland, 1916–18; President of the British Legation, Red Cross Organisation in Switzerland (Interned Branch) 1916–18; Member of Committee of Berne Bread Bureau (affiliated to Central Prisoners of War Committee, London), 1915–16. *Address :* 33, Onslow Gardens, S.W. 7. *Club :* Junior United Service. (C596)

PICTON, Lionel James, O.B.E., M.A. Oxon., M.B. Oxon., B.Ch., L.R.C.P., M.R.C.S., *b.* 20 Feb. 1874; *s.* of William Henry Picton, of Bebbington, Cheshire, and Liverpool; *m.* Mary Emma, A.R.R.C., *d.* of Charles Hibbert Binney, of Ilford. *Educ.:* Merchant Taylors' School, Crosby; Merton Coll., Oxford, and St. Bartholomew's Hospital, London; Surgeon, Albert Infirmary, Winsford; M.O.H. Winsford; Hon. Sec., Cheshire Medical and Panel Committee. *War Work :* Surgeon and Registrar Baltic and Corn Exchange Hospital, Calais; Surgeon in charge of St. John Auxiliary Hospital, Somerford Park, Congleton, and Witten House Hospital, Northwich; Surgeon, Holmes Chapel Divisions, St. John Ambulance Brigade. *Addresses :* Holmes Chapel, Cheshire; B.M.A. 429, Strand, W.C.; Liverpool Medical Institution.
(O11130)

PICTON, Col. Reginald Ernest, C.B.E. Formerly Col. R.E.; served in Somaliland, 1890; and in China, 1900 (medal with clasp). (C2041)

PIDGEON, Major Geoffrey Denzie, O.B.E., R.A.

PIENAAR, Felippus Fowrie, O.B.E. (O12054)

PIERCE, Elsie Louisa, Mrs., M.B.E., b. 23 March, 1895; d. of John Robert Dines, of Grays, Essex; m. Ernest Vernon, s. of Ellis Pierce, of Rainham, Kent. *Educ.:* Palmer's Coll., Grays, and the Convent of La Ste. Union des Sacrés Cœurs, Grays, Essex. *War Work:* Member of Sir Auckland Geddes' Personal Secretariat during his tenure of office as Minister of National Service; President of the Board of Trade, Minister of Reconstruction, and President of the Local Government Board. *Address:* New Road, Grays, Essex. (M9305)

PIERCE, Helen, O.B.E.

PIERCE, Thomas John, M.B.E.

PIERCE, Major William Robertus, O.B.E., R.A.M.C., T.F., b. 15 Aug. 1883; s. of Hugh Pierce, of Llanrwst; m. Leta Rogers, d. of T. Rogers Jones, J.P., C.C., of Llanrwst. *Educ.:* Wesley Coll., Sheffield; Univ. of Liverpool. Hon. Anæsthetist David Lewis Northern Hospital, Liverpool. *War Work:* Served in 2nd West Lancs Field Ambulance, 34 Casualty Clearing Station, and 41st Stationary Hospital in France, 1915–18. *Address:* 34, Princes Avenue, Liverpool. *Clubs:* Lyceum; University. (O5682)

PIERCY, Mary Louisa, Mrs. William, O.B.E.

PIERCY, William, C.B.E., Officier de l'Order de Leopold II, b. 7 Feb. 1886; s. of Edward Piercy; m. May Louisa, d. of Hon. T. H. W. Pelham, of Deene House, Putney Hill, S.W. (see BURKE'S *Peerage,* Chichester, E). Lecturer at the London School of Economics and Political Science. *War Work:* Principal Assistant C.E. Division, Ministry of Munitions; Associated Secretarial Officer of Inland Revenue, Member of Allied Provisions Export Commission, U.S.A.; Director of British Ministry of Food in U.S.A. *Address:* 12, The Grove, Boltons, London, S.W. *Club:* National. (C1025)

PIERPOINT, Major Harry William, O.B.E., F.R.C.S. I.M.S.

PIERPOINT, Marie Eugenie, Mrs., M.B.E.

PIERSON, Reginald Kershaw. M.B.E.

PIETER, Sir John George, O.B.E.

PIGGOTT, His Honour Judge Sir George Bettesworth, K.B.E., F.R.G.S., J.P., b. 30 April, 1857; s. of Fraser Piggott, J.P., of Fitz-Hall, Sussex; m. 1st, Amy (di.d 1909), d. of Major Harvey Spiller. 2nd, Madine Sophie, d. of the late Sir Reginald Proctor Beauchamp, 5th Bart. and Lady Violet, d. of 5th Earl of Roden (see BURKE'S *Peerage*). *Educ.:* Westminster School. Student, Middle Temple, 1884; called to Bar, 1888; Judicial Officer and Vice-Consul of the British Central Africa Protectorate 1896; Chief Judicial Officer, 1898; Assistant Judge for Zanzibar, 1900; Senior Judge 1901–4; Assistant Judge H.M.'s Supreme Consular Court, Sublime Ottoman Porte, 1904–12, and Acting Judge; retired, 1911; sat in Appellate Jurisdiction as Pres. of H.M. Appeal Court for Eastern Africa; also sat as Judge in Arab matters on the highest judicial tribunal of H.M. the Sultan of Zanzibar; was legal member of the East Africa Protectorate Council; Member of the Appeal Tribunal for the County of London under the Military Service Act, and Deputy Chairman and Secretary to that tribunal. *Address:* 24, Cliveden Place, Eaton Square, S.W. *Clubs:* Carlton; St. James's; Wellington. (K228)

PIGGOTT, Henry Howard, C.B., C.B.E., b. 13 Sept. 1871; s. of the late Rev. Henry James Piggott, of Villino Belloni, Via Mondoni, Rome, Italy; m. Mary Edith Frederica, d. of the late Rev. Routh Tomlinson, of Finchampstead, Berks. *Educ.:* Kingswood School, Bath, and Corpus Christi Coll., Oxford. Assistant Master, Bradfield College, Berks, 1895–1902; H.M. Inspector of Schools, Board of Education, 1902–15. *War Work:* Ministry of Munitions, 1915–19; Private Sec. to Rt. Hon. C. Addison and to Rt. Hon. Winston Churchill, when Ministers of Munitions, 1916–17; Assistant Secretary to the Ministry of Munitions, 1917–19. *Address:* 74, Cheyne Court, Chelsea, S.W. 3. (C265)

PIGHTLING, Garnet, M.B.E.

PIGOTT, Major Henry Lionel, O.B.E., Lieut.-Comm. R.N., retired, b. 6 Sept. 1877; s. of Edmund Pigott, of Trentham Staffs.; m. Mary Gwendolyn, d. of Walter Palmour, of Preston. *Educ.:* Stubbington. Chief Land Agent, Southern Command. *Address:* The Red House, Durrington, Wilts. *Club:* Sports. (O1762)

PIGOTT, Capt. John Glyn, O.B.E.

PIGOTT, Capt. St. John Renwick, O.B.E.

PIGOTT, Richard, C.B.E., J.P., b. 1 April, 1861; s. of Richard Pigott, of London; m. Mary Richards, d. of Edward Mountford, of Shipston-on-Stour. *Educ.:* Mill Hill School. Wholesale Tea and Coffee Merchant. *War Work:* Hon. Director of Tea Supplies at the Ministry of Food. *Address:* 1, Earlsfield Road, Wandsworth Common, London. *Clubs:* Reform; New City. (C1026)

PIGOTT, Lieut.-Col. Wellesley George, O.B.E., C.M.G., b. 20 April, 1861; s. of the Rev. W. Pigott, of Bemerton, Salisbury; m. Helen Louise, d. of Captain T. Donaldson, of Cheswardine, Salop, 3rd Hussars. *Educ.:* Eton. Rifle Brigade 1881–97; 1900–1, 1914–19; Adjutant 3rd Batt. Rifle Brigade, 1884–89; Adjutant, Rifle Depot, 1889–92; Adjutant, 3rd V.B. Essex Regt. 1892–1897; Adjutant, Royal Rifle Reserve Regt., 1900–1. *War Work:* Rejoined for service, Sept. 1914; served with 12th Batt. Rifle Brigade, and Commanded it at the Battle of Loos; Commanded 15th Batt. Rifle Brigade from May, 1916, to Feb. 1919, and 25th Batt. Rifle Brigade from Feb. to June, 1919. *Address:* The Weirs, Brockenhurst. *Club:* Army and Navy. (O7576)

PIKE, Lieut.-Col. Cuthbert Joseph, C.B.E., D.L., Cornwall, b. 5 June, 1868; s. of Walter Pike, m. Dorothy Margaret Mary, d. of the late Daniel O'Connell (deceased). *Educ.:* Oscott Coll. Commanding 3rd Batt., Duke of Cornwall's Light Infantry. *Addresses:* 1, Douro Terrace, St. Helier, Jersey; Porkellis, nr. Helston, Cornwall. (C1741)

PIKE, Emma, M.B.E., b. 5 May, 1861. Trained Nurse. *War Work:* District Nursing at Ramsgate. *Address:* Langdon House, The Elms, Ramsgate. (M9310)

PIKE, Paymaster-Lieut. Evan Cuthbert, M.B.E., R.N.R.

PIKE, John, O.B.E., M.Inst.T., b. 1868; s. of John Pike, of Knightsbridge; m. Laura Edith, d. of Adolphus Pursell Patten, of Rickmansworth. *Educ.:* City of London School. Director of Rates and Charges, Ministry of Transport. *War Work:* Assistant Goods Manager, L. and N.W.Rly.; represented Railway Companies on Port and Transit Executive Committee, and Home Trade Transport Control Committee. *Address:* Cromdale, Marlborough Hill, Harrow. *Club:* Junior Constitutional. (O11131)

PIKE, T. Major Montague Headland, O.B.E., M.C.

PIKE, Robert, O.B.E.

PILCHER, Cecil Westland, M.B.E., b. 15 Oct. 1870; s. of W. J. Pilcher, F.R.C.S., of Boston; m. Evelyn Mary, d. of Clement Southam F.S.A., of Shrewsbury. *Educ.:* Bath Coll.; Oxford Univ.; St. Thomas's Hospital. *War Work:* Medical Officer in charge of troops, 1914–18; Commandant V.A.D. (men); Capt. Lincs. R.A.M.C. (V). *Address:* Boston, Lincolnshire. (M9311)

PILCHER, Col. Edgar Montagu, C.B., C.B.E., D.S.O., M.B., B.A., B.C., F.R.C.S., b. 1865; s. of Col. Jesse G. Pilcher, F.R.C.S., Indian Med. Ser.; m. 1899, Lilias, d. of the late Capt. Henri Campbell, I.S.C. *Educ.:* Clifton, and Clare Coll. Camb. Entered Army, 1892; Capt. R.A.M.C. 1895; Major, 1904; Brevet Lieut.-Col. 1913; Lieut.-Col. 1914; Brevet Col. 1916; Col. Army Med. Ser. 1917; served with Tirah Expedition, 1897–98 (medal with two clasps); S. Africa, 1900 (despatches, Queen's medal with five clasps, King's medal with two clasps); appointed Professor of Mil. Surg., Roy. Army. Med. Coll. 1910; Hon. Surg. to H.M. 1918. *Club:* Constitutional. (C1304)

PILCHER, Richard Bertram, O.B.E., F.C.I.S., b. 23 March, 1874; s. of Herbert Edward Pilcher, of Patrixbourne, Kent; m. Violet Frances, d. of George Alfred Sims, of Upper Winchendon, Bucks. *Educ.:* B.O.A., and King's Coll., London. Registrar and Sec. of the Institute of Chemistry of Great Britain and Ireland; Member of Council, Chartered Institute of Secretaries, 1st President of the Chartered Secretaries' Students, Society (London); a Vice-President, Association of Men of Kent and Kentish Men; Sec. of the Glass Research Committee of the Institute of Chemistry, promoting the production of scientific glassware, etc., co-operating with the Department of Scientific and Industrial Research and the Department of Optical Munitions and Glassware Supply, Ministry of Munitions; assisted in securing the services of chemists (1) for the Admiralty, especially for the R.N. Experimental Station, Stratford, (2) for the War Office, especially in connection with Gas Warfare (offensive and defensive), and Royal Army Ordnance Corps, (3) for the Royal Air Force (Hydrogen Officers, Kite Balloon Section, Aeronautical Inspection Department and Royal Aircraft Factory), (4) for the Ministry of Munitions, Department of Explosives Supplies. (5) for other Government Departments, (6) for Controlled Establishments producing various materials of war, etc.; joined Special Constabulary, Aug. 1914; Dep. Insp.1920; Member of the Officers' Resettlement Committee, Ministry of Labour, 1918–20; Civilian Advisory Board (France), 1919; Member of the Grants Committee, Appointments Department, Ministry of Labour, 1919–20; Resettlement of Ex-Service Chemists in civil appointments. *Addresses:* 9, Westbury Road, Woodside Park, Finchley, London, N. 12; 30, Russell Square, W.C. 1. *Club:* Chemical Industry. (O11133)

PILDITCH, Eng.-Lieut. Cyril Harold Lee, O.B.E., R.N.

PILGRIM, Ida Helen, Mrs., O.B.E., b. 27 April, 1869; d. of Alfred Ernest Hawley, of Leicester; m. Walter John, s. of Stephen Pilgrim, of The Castle Hill, Hinckley. *War Work:* Hon. Sec. for the Hinckley and Market Bosworth Division of the Soldiers' and Sailors' Families Association; Organiser and Joint Hon. Sec. Hinckley Area War Pensions Committee; Organiser and Hon. Sec. Hinckley and District Prisoners of War Relief Fund. *Address:* The Priest Hills, Hinckley, Leicestershire. (O11134)

PILKINGTON, Lieut. Dennis Fielden, M.B.E., R.A.S.C.

PILKINGTON, Lieut.-Col. Herbert Edward, C.B.E. New Zealand Forces; served in S. Africa, 1900 (Queen's medal with four clasps); Great War, 1915–19 (despatches). (C1864)

PILKINGTON, Leonard Garnier, M.B.E.

PILKINGTON, Percy, M.B.E.

PILLAI, Hannah Sargon, Mrs., M.B.E.

PILLER, Sir John George, O.B.E.

PILLERS, Major Robert Kingsley, O.B.E., R.A.F.

PILLING, Henry, M.B.E., b. 13 July, 1867; s. of William Pilling, of Bolton; m. Sarah, d. of Miles Gerrard, of Bolton. *Educ.:* Manchester Grammar School. General Manager of Galloways, Ltd., Engineers, Manchester. *War Work:* Steam Boilers, Rolling Mill Engines, Blast Furnace Gas Engines; Shell Forgings, Floating Mines, Aerial Torpedoes, Tank Hulls, Machined Shells, etc. *Address:* Glenderwyn, 20, Manchester Road, Chorlton-cum-Hardy. *Clubs:* Engineers'; Reform, Manchester. (M850)

PILLOW, Capt. Frederick William, O.B.E.

PILTER, Sir John, O.B.E., Knight of Legion of Honour, and Commander of the Order of Nicliam Iftikhae, *b.* 17 March, 1848 ; *s.* of Thomas Pilter, of Paris ; *m.* Emily, *d.* of James Bowman, J.P., of Halifax. *Educ.*: Privately. Retired from business ; Hon. President, British Chamber of Commerce, Paris. *War Work*: Chairman of Committee of Hertford British Hospital, Paris ; Hon. Sec. and Treas. British Charitable Fund, Paris ; Member of Committee of Paris British Recruiting Committee ; Member of Military Local Tribunal and Ambassador's Advisory Committee on Exemption ; Hon. Treas. of Corner of Blighty for soldiers on leave in Paris ; British Vice-President of Union des Colonies Etrangères in Paris for the re-education of mutilated soldiers ; Member of Council of Association France—Great Britain. *Address*: 48, Rue Michel Ange, Paris. *Clubs*: St. James's ; Interallied (Paris). (O11135)

PIM, James Howard, C.B.E. Chairman, Cost of Living Commn., S. Africa, during the Great War. (C2006)

PIM, Major John, O.B.E.

PIM, Violet May, Mrs., O.B.E. ; *d.* of J. G. Thompson, of Grantham ; *m.* John, *s.* of Joshua Pim, of Killiney, Co. Dublin. *Educ.*: Grantham Ladies' Coll., and Baker Street High School. *War Work*: Commandant V.A.D. No 12, Lincs. and Red. Cross Hospital, The Barracks, Grantham (60 beds), Non. 1914, to Feb. 1919. *Address*: Norman Leys, Grantham. (O1765)

PIN, Violet Constance Letitia Mary, M.B.E. *Educ.*: St. Martin's-in-the-Fields High School. Private Sec. to The Hon. Sir Arthur Stanley, G.B.E., Chairman, Joint Council British Red Cross Society and Order of St. John. *Address*: 6, Sandringham Buildings, Charing Cross Road, London, W.C. 2. (M9312)

PINCHARD, Rev. Arnold Theophilus Biddulph, M.B.E., Chevalier de l'Ordre de la Couronne (Belgique), *b.* 30 June, 1860 ; *s.* of John Henry Biddulph Pinchard ; *m.* Maud Sophia Julia, *d.* of John Matthew Butler, M.D., of Woolwich. *Educ.*: Shrewsbury School, Durham Univ. Sec. to the English Church Union. *War Work*: Vice-Chairman and Sec. to the War Refugees Committee, Birmingham ; Chairman, Civic Recreation League, Birmingham. *Address*: 31, Russell Square, W.C. 1. *Club*: Authors'. (M851)

PINCHES, Nora, Mrs., M.B.E.

PINCHIN, Lieut. John Fitzmaurice, O.B.E., R.N.R.

PINCHING, Charles James, O.B.E., M.B., B.Ch. Oxon, *b.* 12 April, 1875 ; *s.* of Charles John Pinching, of 76, New, Road, Gravesend ; *m.* Gertrude, *d.* of John Russell, of Gravesend. *Educ.*: Tonbridge School ; Oxford Univ. ; Guy's Hospital. Surgeon Gravesend Hospital. *War Work*: M.O. in charge of Military Hospital, Gravesend ; Consulting Surgeon Great Hermitage Auxiliary Hospital ; Surgeon Military Red Cross Gravesend Hospital ; Surgeon, Thames Section Thames and Medway Defences. *Address*: 76, New Road, Gravesend. (O4385)

PINCKNEY, Capt. David Ward, M.B.E., R.A.F.

PINCKNEY, John Robert Hugh, C.B.E., *b.* 11 May, 1876 ; *s.* of Erlysman Pinckney, of Highbury, Warminster ; *m.* Winifred, *d.* of James Ledger Hill, of Combe Grove, Bath. *Educ.*: Wellington College, and Trinity College, Cambridge. Director of various Public Companies. *War Work*: War Trade Intelligence Department (acting Deputy Chairman). *Address*: Hidden Cottage, Hungerford. *Clubs*: Carlton ; Oriental. (C2876)

PINCKNEY, Capt. Leonard Durnford, O.B.E., *b.* 21 Sept. 1869 ; 2nd *s.* of John Pinckney, of The Manor House, Great Durnford, Salisbury. *Educ.*: Dr. Burney's, Gosport ; Training Ship "Conway." Capt. P. and O.Co. *War Work*: Capt. of P. and O. s.s. "Somali" in Aug. 1914 ; "Somali" at outbreak of war was fitted as troopship and carried troops to India and back ; carried troops to Gallipoli ; at Malta was fitted as H.M. Hospital ship under Admiralty ; all through the Campaign was carrying wounded from Gallipoli to Malta and Alexandria ; was present at both evacuations and finally brought wounded to England, when he was transferred to P. and O. s.s. "Kyber" acting as H.M. Troopship ; carried troops twice to Montreal and back ; after Armistice was for six months in North Sea taking Belgians from Hull to Antwerp, and bringing back English Prisoners of War from Rotterdam to Hull. *Address*: Eastmount, Salisbury. *Club*: Golfer's. (O11136)

PINCOMBE, Arthur, M.B.E., *b.* 18 Jan. 1869 ; *s.* of John Pincombe, of Cardiff ; *m.* Annie Jane, *d.* of Cornelius James Gullyes, of Cardiff. *Educ.*: Privately. Solicitor and Clerk to the Mountain Ash Urban District Council ; Clerk to Mountain Ash Burial Board, and Legal Adviser to Mountain Ash Education Committee. *War Work*: Hon. Sec. of Local Representative Committee of National Relief Fund ; Hon. Sec. of Local Belgian Refugees Committee ; Clerk to Local Tribunal under the Military Service Acts ; Hon. Sec. of Local Food Control Committee. Hon. Sec. Local War Pensions Committee. *Address*: The Town Hall, and Glanpennar, Mountain Ash. (M9313)

PINDER, Lieut. Arthur William, M.B.E.

PINDER, Charles Ralph, C.B.E., *b.* 1866 ; *s.* of the late Frederick Pinder of Exeter ; Construction Manager at H.M. High Explosives Factories since 1915. (C266)

PINDER, Lieut. Francis William Stanley, O.B.E.

PINE, Capt. Charles, O.B.E., R.A., *s.* of Thomas Pine, of Westbury-on-Trim, Gloster.; *m.* Emily, *d.* of Joseph Brace, of St. Neots, Bedfordshire. *Educ.*: Birmingham. For 30 years in the Royal Regiment of Artillery through every grade from Gunner to Captain ; *War Work*: Instructor in Gunnery Coast Artillery School, Golden Hill, and Portsmouth Garrison, 1914–20. *Address*: Tremelbye, Afton Road, Freshwater, Isle of Wight. (O8910)

PINE, Lieut. John Henry, M.B.E.

PINHEY, Eustace Townley, O.B.E., M.B., Ch.M., *b.* 1877 ; *s.* of W. H. Pinhey, of Strathfield, Sydney, Australia. *Educ.*: Sydney Univ. Senior Medical Officer, Hackney Infirmary, London. Awarded Silver Medal of Royal Humane Society of New South Wales, 1908, for conspicuous bravery in saving two lives from drowning. *War Work*: Regimental Medical Officer attached 78th Brigade, Royal Field Artillery ; twice mentioned in despatches ; Surgeon, Military Hospital, Bethnal Green, London. (O11837)

PINHORN, Col. Henry Quinten, C.B.E., Retired Pay, *b.* 11 Dec. 1862 ; *s.* of the late C. H. Pinhorn, and grandson of Joseph Pinhorn, of Vale End, Southsea. Late Royal Army Pay Department, formerly East Lancashire Regiment. *War Work*: served throughout the war, T. Col. and Chief Paymaster, 11 Dec 1916 ; mentioned in despatches, 7 Aug. 1917 and C.B.E. (military Division), 3 June, 1919 ; promoted substantive Colonel on retirement. *Address*: Barkston Gardens Hotel, Earl's Court, S.W. 5. *Club*: Junior Army and Navy. (C1742)

PINK, Wing-Comm. Richard Charles Montague, C.B.E., R.A.F. Served in the Great War, 1914–19 (despatches).

PINKERTON, 2nd Lieut. James Morton, M.B.E. R.A.F.

PINKHAM, Lieut.-Col. Charles, O.B.E., J.P., D.L., M.P., Alderman, Middlesex County Council, *b.* 24 Oct. 1853 ; *s.* of Philip Pinkham, of Plympton, Devon. *Educ.*: Plympton, Devon. Builder and Contractor (ret.). *War Work*: Recruiting Chairman, War Service Tribunal ; Member, Middlesex Profiteering Appeal Committee ; Member, Munition Court, N.W. District ; Chairman, Willesden Military Hospital. *Address*: Linden Lodge, Winchester Avenue, Brondesbury, N.W. 6. *Club*: St. Stephen's. (O11137)

PINKNEY, Major Samuel Renny, O.B.E., T.D., *b.* 28 Oct. 1873 ; *s.* of Thomas Pinkney, of Sunderland and Sleights, Yorks. ; *m.* Evelyn Mary, *d.* of J. Bourdas, of London and Whitby, Yorks. *Educ.*: England ; Germany. *War Work*: Military Representative at Tribunals ; Recruiting Officer ; Assistant Director in Ship Purchase Department of Ministry of Shipping. *Address*: Eskholme, Ashbrooke Crescent, Sunderland. *Clubs*: Royal Societies'; Sunderland. (O3871)

PINNIGER, Capt. Albert Edward, O.B.E., R.A.M.C.

PINNINGTON, Francis Stanilaus, O.B.E.

PINSENT, Capt. Arthur, M.B.E., R.E.

PIPE, Nellie, Mrs., M.B.E.

PIPER, Capt. Arthur, M.B.E., *b.* 20 Jan. 1866 ; *s.* of late Austin Piper, of Norwich ; *m.* Maude Monemia, *d.* of Charles Dennison, of Eltham. *Educ.*: Dulwich College. Stockbroker. *War Work*: Royal Army Pay Department. *Address*: Herongate Common, nr. Brentwood, Essex. *Club*: New Hampton Court. (M853)

PIPER, George, O.B.E.

PIPER, Oliver James Southwell, O.B.E.

PIPON, Comm. James Murray, M.V.O., O.B.E., R.N.

PIPPARD, Alfred John Sutton, O.B.E., M.A., D.Sc., *b.* 6 April, 1891 ; *s.* of the late Alfred William Pippard, of Yeovil, Somerset. *Educ.*: Bristol University. Consulting Engineer. *War Work*: Technical Staff, Admiralty Air Department and Air Ministry. *Address*: 41A, Penywern Road, S.W. 5. (M854)

PIRIE, Lieut.-Col. Duncan Vernon, O.B.E., J.P., D.L., M.P. for N. Aberdeen, 1896–1918 ; *b.* 22 March, 1858 ; *s.* of Gordon Pirie, of Waterton, Aberdeenshire ; *m.* Hon. Evelyn Courtenay Forbes-Sempill, *d.* of 18th Baron Sempill (*see* BURKE'S *Peerage*), of Craigievar, Aberdeenshire. *Educ.*: Glenalmond College, Perthshire, and Clifton College. *War Work*: M.L.O. Boulogne, Marseilles, Havre, 1914–16 ; Suffolk Regt. attached D.L.I. Salonica ; Commandant of the Likovan area in Macedonia, 1917 ; promoted to rank of Lieut.-Colonel and given command of the forces at Corfu, 1917–18. *Address*: Chateau de Varennes, Savennieres, France. *Club*: Bachelors'.

PIRIE, Major William Rattray, O.B.E., R.A.M.C. (T.), *b.* 15 Aug. 1868 ; *s.* of J. K. Pirie, of Aberdeen ; *m.* Ella Gordon, *d.* of George Collie, of Balnagarth. *Educ.*: Universities of Aberdeen, Leipzig, and Vienna. Physician ; Hon. Physician, Aberdeen Royal Infirmary ; Lecturer in Clinical Medicine Aberdeen Royal Infirmary, etc. *War Work*: Attached to 1st Scottish General Hospital, 1914–16, thereafter mainly employed in Recruiting, Medical Boards, and Pension Boards. *Address*: 20, Bon-Accord Square, Aberdeen. (O7577)

PITCHER, Albert John, O.B.E.

PITCHER, Brig.-Gen. Duncan Le Geyt, C.M.G., C.B.E., *b.* 1877. Major and Brevet Col. Indian Army ; Brig. Com. R.A.F. with rank of Brig.-Gen. ; Great War, 1914–18 (despatches). (C1904)

PITKEATHLY, Col. James Scott, C.V.O., C.B.E., D.S.O., *b.* 1882 ; *s.* of James Pitkeathly ; *m.* 1913, Eleanor Mary, *d.* of Henry Haines, of Astley, Worcestershire, and Tipton, Staffordshire. Electrical Inspector to Govt. of United Provinces, India ; Electrical Engineer, Coronation Durbar, Delhi, 1911 ; T. Major on Special List ; Dep. Director of Works (Electrical and Mechanical) in Mesopotamia with rank of Col. (C1112)

PITMAN, Arthur James, M.B.E.

PITMAN, Arthur Joseph, O.B.E.

PITT, Arthur George, M.B.E., *b.* 1880, of London ; *m.*, Ethel, *d.* of R. T. Woods, of London. *Educ.*: London, Assoc

Member Institution Mechanical Engineers; Member, Inst. Automobile Engineers; Chief Designer (Engines) Royal Aircraft Establishment. *War Work*: Designing motor ambulances, and field workshops at Messrs. D. Napier & Sons, superintending design of aero engines and experimental apparatus at Royal Aircraft Establishment. *Address*: Borfield, Fellows Road, Farnborough, Hants. (M9316)

PITT, Major Bernard, O.B.E.

PITT, Charles Peniston, M.B.E.

PITT¹ Capt. and Qr.-Mr. George John, O.B.E.

PITT, George John, O.B.E., *b.* 17 Jan. 1868; *s.* of Malcolm Bruce Pitt, of Stroud, Glos.; *m.* Alice Caroline, *d.* of William Neale, of London. *Educ.*: Birkbeck Schools, London. Costings Accountant. *War Work*: served with the 1st Batt. Manchester Regt. in South African Campaign; was besieged in Ladysmith (medal and 5 clasps); served with 12th (Duke of Lancaster's Own Yeomanry) Batt. the Manchester Regt. in the Great War in Fance and Flanders for 4 years; 4 times mentioned in despatches. *Address*: Ikona, North Road, Parkstone, Dorset. *Club*: Overseas. (O2675)

PITT, Major George Newton, O.B.E., M.D., R.A.M.C. (T.).

PITT, George Philip, M.B.E., R.N.

PITT, Harry Arthur, O.B.E.

PITT, Inez Mary, Mrs., M.B.E., *b.* 15 June, 1867; *d.* of the late William Mitchell Innes, of Ayton Castle, Ayton, Berwickshire; *m.* Brig.-Gen. Thomas Morton Stanhope, *s.* of the late Colonel Thomas Pitt, deceased, of Hayle Place, Maidstone, Kent. *Educ.*: Privately. *War Work*: Commandant of Charing Cross V.A.D. Hospitals for 4 years. (M9317)

PITT, Marion, Mrs., O.B.E; *d.* of J. Hanson-Walker, *m.* Sydney Pitt. *War Work*: Was one of the first to take a Canteen out to France in 1914, working there for 3½ years. *Addresses*: 12, Hyde Park Gate, S.W.; The Islands, Cookham, Berks. (O1767) (M2291)

PITT, Nellie Flora, M.B.E.

PITTS, Capt. Joseph, C.B.E., M.C.

PITTS, Mary, Mrs., C.B.E., *b.* 1843; *d.* of Alexander Mackay; *m.* the Hon James S. Pitts, C.M.G. (who died). A Vice-Pres. of Newfoundland Women's Patriotic Assoc. *Address*: St. John's, Newfoundland. (C2010)

PITTS, Comm. Percy, C.B.E., R.N.

PITTS, Robert Henry, O.B.E.

PIXLEY, Major Stewart Aitken, O.B.E.

PLACKETT, James William, O.B.E.

PLAGE, John Philip, O.B.E.

PLAISTER, Major William Edward Plaister, M.B.E.

PLANT, Hon. Major David Thomas, M.B.E.

PLANT, Major Eric Clive Pegus, D.S.O., O.B.E., Australian Forces; *s.* of Lieut.-Col. C. F. Plant, Brisbane; *m.* Oona, *d.* of the late J. Hunter Brown. Served in the Great War, 1914–18. *Address*: Thornton, Pinner. (O6092)

PLATT, Capt. Claude Bernard Meister, M.B.E.

PLATT, Isaiah, O.B.E.

PLATT, 2nd Lieut. Oswald Gordon, M.B.E., M.C.

PLATT, Capt. Sydney Frank, M.B.E.

PLATT, William Alexander, M.B.E.

PLATT, William Charles, M.B.E.

PLATT. Lieut. William Percival, M.B.E.

PLATTEN, Samuel Henry, M.B.E., J.P., *b.* 26 Feb. 1857; *s.* of William Platten, of Sudbury, Suffolk; *m.* Rebecca Elizabeth, *d.* of John Martin Coward. *Educ.*: Privately. Ministry of Food. *War Work*: Chairman of Tribunal (Local) Distribution of Food. *Address*: 20, Latymer Road, Edmonton. *Club*: Edmonton Conservative. (M9320)

PLATTS, Capt. Matthew George, O.B.E., M.C.

PLAYER, William John Percy, M.B.E.

PLAYFAIR, Caro, Mrs., M.B.E.

PLAYFAIR, Brevet.-Major Charles Murray, O.B.E.

PLAYFAIR, Wing-Comm. Frederick Hope Grant, C.B.E., R.A.F. Served in the Great War, 1914–19 (despatches).

PLAYFAIR, Thomas Alfred Jack, O.B.E. (O6091)

PLAYFORD, Major Elliott Frank, O.B.E.

PLEDGE, Henry, C.B.E. Assist. Director of Naval Construction, Admiralty. (C267)

PLEDGER, Charles Russell, M.B.E.

PLENDER, Sir William, G.B.E., Kt. Bach., J.P. Kent, Knight of Grace of the Order of St. John of Jerusalem in England, *b.* 20 Aug. 1861; *s.* of William Plender, of The Oaks, Dalston, Cumberland; *m.* Marian, *d.* of John Channon, of Woodford Green. Advised the Government in connection with the Port of London Bill, 1908; Member of Committee on Irish Finance, 1911; Member Royal Commission on Railways, 1913; Commissioner (unpaid) under the Welsh Church Act, 1914; Senior Partner in firm of Deloitte, Plender, Griffiths & Co., of London, United States, Canada, Argentine, Brazil, and South Africa; President of Institute of Chartered Accountants, 1910–12. *War Work*: Treasury Controller German, Austrian, and Turkish Banks, 1914–18; Member of Foreign Trade Debts Committee, of Enemy Debts Committee, of Liquor Trade Finance Committees (2); Government Representative on Metropolitan Munitions Committee; Chairman of Panels Military Service (Civil Liabilities) and Ministry of Labour Grants Committee; Member of Committee, Company Law Amendment and of Public Trustee Organisation Inquiry; Hon. Financial Adviser to the Board of Trade; Chairman, Advisory Committee Clearing Office (Enemy Debts), etc. *Addresses*: 51, Kensington Court, W. 8; Ovenden, Sundridge, Sevenoaks. *Clubs*: Reform; Garrick; City of London; Arts; Burlington Fine Arts; Ranelagh. (G29)

PLENDERLEATH, Capt. Claude William Manners, C.B.E., R.N. *War Work*: 1914–19, as Commodore of Convoys (despatches). (C1201)

PLEVIN, Mary Jean, M.B.E.

PLEWS, Capt. and Qr.-Mr. Harry, O.B.E.

PLOWMAN, Lieut.-Col. William Albert, M.B.E

PLUCKNETT, 2nd Lieut. Frederick, O.B.E.

PLUMER, Annie Constance, Lady, O.B.E.; *d.* of the late George Goss, of Park Crescent; *m.* 1st Baron Plumer (Field Marshal Sir Herbert Charles Onslow Plumer, G.C.B., G.C.M.G., G.C.V.O.) (*see* BURKE'S *Peerage*). *Addresses*: The Palace, Valetta, Malta; 22, Ennismore Gardens, S.W. 7. (O657)

PLUMMER, Arthur Bertram, M.B.E.

PLUMMER, John Robert, M.B.E.

PLUMMER, Wilfred Henry Coates, O.B.E., *b.* Jan. 1877; *s.* of H. J. Plummer, of Oxford; *m.* Elizabeth Silvester, *d.* of F. T. Harrison, of Kensington. *Educ.*: Oxford High School. Director, Soldiers' Awards Branch, Ministry of Pensions. *War Work*: Acting Assistant Sec. Royal Hospital, Chelsea; Director, Soldiers' Awards Branch, Ministry of Pensions. *Address*: 62, Hazlewell Road, Putney, S.W. 15. (O11146)

PLUNKETT, Lieut.-Col. Edward Abadie, C.B.E., *b.* 28 July, 1870; *s.* of Lieut.-Col. G. T. Plunkett, of Belvedere Lodge, St. Mary's Road, Wimbledon; *m.* Grace Mary, *d.* of Lieut.-Col. Morgan Martin, of Sydney, Australia. *Educ.*: Dover Coll. *War Work*: Military Staff work. *Address*: 108, Brompton Road, S.W. *Club*: Junior United Service. (C1743)

PLUNKETT, Capt. James Joseph, O.B.E., R.A.V.C.

PLYMOUTH, Robert George Windsor-Clive, Earl of P.C., G.B.E., C.B., Officer of the Legion of Honour (France), *b.* 27 Aug. 1857; *s.* of The Hon. Robert Windsor-Clive, M.P. (*see* BURKE'S *Peerage*); *m.* Alberta Victoria Sarah Caroline, *d.* of Sir Augustus Paget, P.C., G.C.B. (*see* BURKE'S *Peerage*). *Educ.*: Eton, and St. John's Coll., Cambridge. Lord-Lieutenant of the County of Glamorgan, Sub-prior of the Order of St. John of Jerusalem in England; High Steward of the Univ. of Cambridge. *War Work*: Joint Committee of the Order of St. John and the British Red Cross Society; Hon. Treas. of the Serbian Relief Fund. *Addresses*: 2, Great Cumberland Place, W.; Hewell Grange, Redditch; St. Fagan's Castle, Cardiff. *Clubs*: Carlton; Travellers'; Marlborough. (G34)

POATE, Herbert, M.B E.

POCHIN, Edmund Arthur Norman, M.B.E.

POCHIN, Harold Nichols, M.B.E.

POCKLINGTON, Amy Jane, Mrs., M.B.E., *b.* 28 March, 1863; *d.* of the late John Hargreaves, of Maiden Erlegh, Reading; *m.* Harry Evelyn Stracey, Capt. 15th Hussars (died 1903), *s.* of the late Colonel H. G. Pocklington, of Chelsworth, Suffolk (died 1908). *War Work*: Hon. Sec. of Kashmir Red Cross. *Address*: Srinagar, Kashmir, India. *Club*: Ladies' Army and Navy. (M6224)

POCOCK, Dorothy Martha, M.B.E., *b.* 10 July, 1891; *d.* of Edward Henry Samuel Pocock, of Marlborough, Wilts. *Educ.*: Drapers' Coll., Tottenham. Canteen Supervisor Associated Equipment, Walthamstow. *War Work*: Battersea Canteen, Eagle Hut; Ponders End Shell Works. *Address*: 97, Philip Lane, Tottenham. (M2295)

POCOCK, Capt. Elisha John, M.B.E., *b.* 20 July, 1869; *s.* of Elisha Pocock, of Boldre, Lymington; *m.* Sarah, *d.* of William Anstey, of Dyrham, Chippenham. *Educ.*: Taplow Grammar School. *Address*: Army Pay Office, Hounslow. (M5543)

POCOCK, Capt. Herbert Cheyney, O.B.E., R.N.

POCOCK, Capt. James Charles, O.B.E.. R.E.

POCOCK, Major Sydney Elsdon, O.B.E., LL.B., *b.* 19 Aug. 1880; *s.* of Sydney Pocock, of Chase Lodge, Clapham, S.W. *Educ.*: City of London School, and King's Coll., Cambridge. *War Work*: Royal Army Service Corps. *Addresses*: 2, The Sycamores, Crooked Billet, Wimbledon Common; 1, Harcourt Buildings, Temple, London. (O7581)

POË, Muriel Gladys, M.B.E., Lady of Grace of the Order of St. John of Jerusalem; *d.* of Capt. Poë, R.N., of Santry Court, Co. Dublin. *Educ.*: Privately, and Cheltenham Ladies' Coll. *War Work*: Administrative Work as District Officer St. John Ambulance Brigade; member of Irish Joint V.A.D. Selection Board; Assist. County Director, etc.; also nursed in France as a V.A.D. *Address*: Santry Court, Co. Dublin. (M9323)

POETT, Major-Gen. Joseph Howard, C.B., C.M.G., C.B.E., *b.* 16 Oct. 1858; *s.* of Joseph Henry Poett, of San Mateo, California; *m.* Julia Caswell Poett, *d.* of Edward Thompson Caswell, of Providence, Rhode Island, U.S.A. *Educ.*: Beaumont Coll. Gazetted 39th Regt. Sept. 1876; passed Staff Coll. 1890; retired, March, 1911; 1879, Afghan War, medal; 1884–85, Bechuanaland Expedition; 1899–1902, S. African War, Headquarters Staff, A.A.G., C.B., King's and Queen's Medals, five clasps, Brevet Lieut.-Col., and twice mentioned in despatches. *War Work*: 1914–19, Staff; promoted Hon. Major-General; five times mentioned in despatches, C.M.G., C.B.E., Order of St. Anne, 3rd class, 1915 Star, General Service, and Victory Medals. *Address*: Rhode Bungalow, Up Lyme, Devon. *Club*: Naval and Military. (C771)

POIGNANT, Lieut.-Col. Axel Jonas Alfred, O.B.E., M.C., West Yorks Regt., *b.* 23 Nov. 1876; *s.* of E. Poignant, late Lieut.-Governor of Gotland, Sweden; *m.* Annie Lake, *d.* of H. Ferraby, of Cottingham, Hull. *Educ.*: Naval Coll.,

Stockholm, Sweden. *War Work :* Joined 15th West Yorks, Sept. 1914 as Lieut.; gazetted Capt., Sept. 1914 ; France, Sept. 1916, to Oct. 1917 ; Major, Sept. 1917 ; Lieut.-Col., Dec. 1918, on going to North Russia ; Commanded Vaga Column, Archangel Force, Jan. 1919, to June, 1919 ; Commandant Advanced Base, Bereznik, June to Sept. 1919 ; mentioned in despatches. *Address .* Stockholm, Sweden. (O9703)

POINTING, T. Warrant Officer Albert E., M.B.E.

POLE, 2nd Lieut. Wellesley Tudor, O.B.E.

POLEHAMPTON, Lieut. John, O.B.E., R.N.R.

POLLARD, Lieut.-Col. Arthur Erskine St. Vincent, O.B.E., *b.* 30 July, 1869 ; *s.* of Rear-Adml. E. J. Pollard, R.N., D.L., of Haynford Hall, Norwich ; *m.* Enid, *d.* of W. H. Wilson, of Ootacamund. *Educ. :* Repton Oriel Coll., Oxford ; R.M.C. Sandhurst. S. African Campaign, 1899–1902 ; Queen's Medal with five clasps, King's Medal, two clasps. *War Work :* D.A.A.G. India, Aug. 1914, to July, 1915 ; Commanded 1st Border Regt., Gallipoli Campaign, July, 1915, to evacuation, and in Egypt and France to May, 1916 ; Commanded 3rd Border Regt. Jan. 1917, to end of war. *Address :* Quetta, Sarlsdown Rd., Exmouth. *Club :* Naval and Military. (O7582)

POLLARD, Charles, M.B.E., *b.* 3 April, 1868 ; *s.* of Eli Pollard, of Waddesdon, Bucks ; *m.* Emma Jane, *d.* of G. Hillesdon, of Waddesdon. Deputy Chief Constable and Chief Clerk Buckinghamshire Constabulary. *War Work :* Administrative work in Headquarters Office of County Constabulary. *Address :* St. Mary's Villa, Aylesbury. (M9324)

POLLARD, Major Frederick Ernest, M.B.E., A.R.C.S., A.F.R.Ae.S., R.A.F. (ret.), *b.* 29 Sept. 1880 ; *s.* of John Pollard, of Eastwood, Notts. *Educ. :* Royal Coll. of Science, South Kensington. H.M. Inspector of Factories. *War Work :* On Technical Staff of R.N.A.S., Admiralty, Air Board, and Air Ministry. *Address :* Eastwood, Notts. (M3906)

POLLARD, Capt. Pedr, M.B.E., C.A.I.B.(Eng.). The Loyal Regt. (North Lancashire). *b.* 29 Aug. 1894 ; *s.* of Benjamin Pollard, of Highfield, Davenport Park, Stockport. *Educ. :* Manchester Grammar School. Controller of Stores and Supervisor of Workshops, Ministry of Pensions Hospital, Blackrock, Co. Dublin, Ireland. *War Work :* From Cadet to Capt. ; Musketry, Physical Training, Bayonet Fighting, and Bombing Instructional work from time to time ; A.R.T.O. ; District Salvage Officer, Dublin District ; Assistant Staff Capt., Dublin Castle ; Administrative work generally ; Officer-in-charge Workshops for Disabled in Ireland ; overseas twice; invalided home once. *Addresses :* Arbutus, Monkstown, County Dublin ; Highfield, Davenport Park, Stockport, Cheshire. *Club :* Sackville Street, Dublin. (M6692)

POLLEN, Capt. Francis Gabriel Hungerford, C.B.E., R.N. (ret.), *b.* 25 Mar. 1862 ; 4th *s.* of John Hungerford Pollen, M.A., formerly Fellow of Merton College, Oxford, and *g.s.* of Sir John Pollen, 1st Bart. (*see* BURKE'S *Peerage*) ; *m.* 4 Nov. 1890, Flora Mary, *d.* of the late James Logan Donolly. Served in the Soudan, 1884–85 (medal with clasp) ; Burmah, 1886 (medal) ; Great War as S.N.O., Grimsby. *Address :* Langham Mansions, Earl's Court. *Club :* Naval and Military. (C911)

POLLOCK, Capt. Arthur Jocelyn Coleman, O.B.E.

POLLOCK, Catherine Hentig, M.B.E., *b.* 28 Oct. 1884; *d.* of the late James Gibson Pollock, of Oatlands, Stillorgan, Co. Dublin, Ireland. *Educ. :* St. Margaret's Hall, Dublin. Masseuse at the Special Surgical Neurological Hospital, Church Lane, Tooting, S.W. *War Work :* Nov. 1914 to March, 1917, King George V. Hospital, Dublin ; March, 1917, to Aug. 1917, Military Orthopædic Hospital, Blackrock, Co Dublin ; Aug. 1917, to March, 1919, 8th Stationary Hospital, B.E.F., France. is a diplomée I.S.T.M. ; Masseuse of the A.P.M.M.C. (M9325)

POLLOCK, Col. Charles Edward, C.B.E., D.S.O., A.M.S., *b.* 1868 ; *s.* of Alexander R. Pollock, J.P., of Greenhill, Paisley ; *m.* Winifred, *d.* of C. E. H. Jay, of Felixstowe. *Educ. :* Wellington Coll. ; Guy's Hospital. *War Work :* A.D.M.S. 15th Division ; D.D.M.S., 4th Corps and 6th Corps, B.E.F. *Club :* Junior United Service. (C1305)

POLLOCK, Lieut. Douglas Warren, M.B.E., R.E.

POLLOCK, Sir Ernest Murray, K.B.E., K.C., J.P., M.P., *b.* 25 Nov. 1861 ; *s.* of George Frederick Pollock, of Hanworth, Middlesex ; *m.* Laura Helen, *d.* of Sir Thomas Salt, Bart., of Weeping Cross, Stafford (*see* BURKE'S *Peerage*). *Educ. :* Charterhouse (Scholar), and Trinity Coll. Cambridge. Barrister-at-Law, Inner Temple, 1885 ; K.C. 1905 ; Solicitor-General, 1919 ; J.P. for Hertfordshire. *War Work :* Chairman of Contraband Committee, Nov. 1915, to Jan. 1917 ; Controller of Foreign Trade Department of the Foreign Office from Jan. 1917, to Jan. 1919 ; made an Officer of the Legion of Honour by President of French Republic and Officer of the Order of St. Maurice and St. Lazarus by the King of Italy for services rendered as above during the war. *Addresses :* 40, Thurloe Square, S.W. ; Northaw, Herts. *Clubs :* Athenæum ; Carlton ; Oxford and Cambridge. (K33)

POLLOCK, Col. Evelyn, C.B.E., *b.* 28 Jan. 1861 ; 3rd *s.* of the late George David Pollock, and *g.s.* of Sir George Pollock, 1st Bart. (*see* BURKE'S *Peerage*) ; *m.* 16 July 1890, Mary, *d.* of the late Henry Jeffard Tarrant. Lieut.-Col. and Brevet Col. late R.H.A. : Lieut.-Col. Comdg. Jersey Artillery ; Commandant Lines of Communication, 1914. *Address :* 40, Gledstairs Road, W. *Club :* Army and Navy. (C786)

POLLOCK, Lieut.-Col. Evelyn Hay, O.B.E., T.D.

POLLOCK, Surg.-Lieut. J. Donald, O.B.E., M.D.

POLLOCK, John Wilson, M.B.E., *b.* 9 Aug. 1854 ; *s.* of Alex. Pollock, Junr., J.P., of Paisley ; *m.* Marion Shaw, *d.* of

John Brunton, M.A., M.D., of London. *Educ. :* Paisley Grammar School. Civil Servant ; Ministry of Labour, Employment Dept. ; Manager of Govan Labour Exchange. *War Work :* Special work of various kinds for the War Office, Ministry of Munitions, and Ministry of Labour. *Address :* Lyndhurst, Hawkhead Road, Paisley. (M9326)

POLLOCK, Samuel Alexander, O.B.E.

POLLOK, Major Allan Bingham, O.B.E.

POLLOK, Robert, O.B.E., M.I.N.A., M.I.E. & S., *b.* 6 April, 1859 ; *s.* of Robert Pollok, of Mearns, Renfrewshire ; *m.* Louise Augusta, *d.* of George Baker, of Southampton. *Educ. :* Paisley Grammar School ; High School of Glasgow. General Shipyard Manager. *War Work :* In charge of all Admiralty Shipyard work at Messrs. Vickers, Ltd., Barrow-in-Furness. *Address :* Cavendish Park, Barrow-in-Furness. *Club :* Barrow County. (O1771)

POLLOK, Major Robert Valentine, C.B.E., D.S.O., Irish Guards, *b.* 14 Feb. 1884 ; *s.* of John Pollok, of Lismany, Ballinasloe, Co. Galway ; *m.* Sylvia Bettina, *d.* of George Fellows, of Barrow-on-Soar, Loughborough. *Educ. :* Eton, and R.M.C. *Clubs :* Guards' ; Cavalry ; Kildare Street, Dublin. (C1306)

POLSON, Col. Sir Thomas Andrew, K.B.E., C.M.G., T.D., M.P., *b.* 28 Aug. 1865 ; *s.* of the late Thomas Andrew Polson, of Dublin and Tuam, Co. Galway ; *m.* Elizabeth *d.* of John Lindsay, of Edinburgh. *Educ. :* Dublin. Joined the Middlesex Yeomanry Cavalry (now the 1st County of London Yeomanry) in 1896, transferred to the City of London Yeomanry, Rough Riders, 1901, and was mainly responsible for recruiting that regiment ; in command of " A " Squadron at outbreak of war, and was subsequently appointed to command of the depot, during which appointment he raised the first second line of a yeomanry regiment raised in the war ; 1916 gazetted to the Royal Army Ordnance Corps, and appointed Chief Inspector of Clothing with the rank of Col. ; lent to the Air Ministry for three months end of 1917, and did valuable reorganisation work for that Ministry as well as representing it on the Army Agricultural Committee ; also served on the Expenditure of Stores and Supplies Committee set up by the Surveyor-General of Supply ; is a Trustee of the R.A.O.C. Memorial Fund ; elected M.P. for Dover, Jan., 1921. *Address :* 18, Sussex Place, N.W. *Club :* Cavalry. (K229)

POLWARTH, Walter George Hepburne-Scott, Baron, C.B.E., V.D., J.P., D.L., *b.* 7 Feb. 1864 ; *s.* of Walter Hugh, Lord Polwarth, of Mertoun St. Bonvello (*see* BURKE'S *Peerage*) ; *m.* Edith Frances, *d.* of the late Sir T. Fowell Buxton, Bart., of Warlies, Essex (*see* BURKE'S *Peerage*). *Educ. :* Eton, and Trinity Coll., Cambridge. Chairman Prison Commissioners for Scotland. *War Work :* Lieut.-Col. Commanding 3rd Reserve Bn. 8th Royal Scots, Jan. 1915, to Dec. 1915 ; Col. Commanding Lowland Reserve Brigade, Dec. 1915, to Sept. 1916 ; Col. on Gen. Staff, Scottish Command ; Staff Officer for Volunteer Services, Sept. 1916, to April, 1918. *Address :* Humbie House, Humbie. *Clubs :* New, Edinburgh ; National, London. (C1612)

POLWHELE, Arthur Carne, O.B.E., J.P., *b.* 20 Feb. 1864 ; *s.* of the late Thomas Roxborough Polwhele, of Polwhele, Truro (*see* BURKE'S *Landed Gentry*) ; *m.* Eva Florence, *d.* of William Nassau Gordon, of Mullingar. *Educ. :* Tavistock, and Cooper's Hill. Superintending Engineer, India Public Works Dept., retired, 1912 ; present occupation, Farmer. *War. Work :* County Director Cornwall Voluntary Aid Organisation. *Address :* Polwhele, Truro. (O11148)

POLYBLANK, Major William Joseph, O.B.E., R.A.F.

POMARE, Miria Woodbine, Mrs, O.B.E.

POMEROY, Amy, Mrs., M.B.E.

POMEROY, Lieut. Arthur William Jobbins, M.B.E.

POMEROY, Major the Hon. Ralph Legge, O.B.E., J.P., *b.* 1869 ; *s.* of the 6th Viscount Harberton (*see* BURKE'S *Peerage*) ; *m.* Mary Katherine, *d.* of Arthur Leatham, J.P., of Smallfield Place, Surrey. *Educ. :* Charterhouse, and Balliol Coll., Oxford. Major late 5th Dragoon Guards ; J.P. for Northamptonshire. *War Work :* Served with the Reserve Regiment of Dragoons, affiliated to the 5th Dragoon Guards from Aug. 1914, to March, 1919. *Address :* Southfields Place, Towcester. *Club :* Cavalry. (O3166)

POMFRET, Edith Mary, Mrs., M.B.E., *b.* 2 Jan, 1877; *d.* of John Carrick, of Southborough, Tunbridge Wells ; *m.* Charles Denne, *s.* of Benjamin Pomfret, of Tunbridge Wells. *Educ. :* Ashburnham House School, Southborough. *Sec.* (Organising) Women's Reform Club, and National Service Fund, Johannesburg. *War Work :* With National Service Fund (amongst wives and children of soldiers, etc.). *Addresses :* Kintore, Melrose, Johannesburg ; Eden, Simon's Town, Cape. *Clubs :* Women's Reform ; Phœnix, Johannesburg. (M1319)

POND, Ethel Augusta, Mrs., M.B.E.

PONSONBY, Hon. Cyril Walter, O.B.E., *b.* 8 Sept. 1853 ; *s.* of 7th Earl of Bessborough, of Bessborough, Piltown, Ireland (*see* BURKE'S *Peerage*) ; *m.* Emily Harriet, *d.* of the Rev. H. Addington, of Henlow, Beds. *Educ. :* Harrow. *War Work :* Head of Station Guides, Victoria Station ; Sergeant, 7th Section H.Q.C.D. ; Founder and Manager of St. Valentine Hostel for Married Soldiers, 37, Eccleston Square. *Address :* 53, Draycott Place, Cadogan Gardens, S.W. (O11409)

PONSONBY, Diamond, M.B.E., *d.* of Hon. Mrs. Arthur Ponsonby, of London. *Educ. :* Wantage. *War Work :* Aug. to Oct. 1915, Land Work, Wiverton Hall, Norfolk ; Nov. 1915, to June, 1918, Red Cross Work, V.A.D. Nurse at The Wier Hospital, Balham, London ; June, 1918, Ministry of

Food, London. *Addresses :* 55, Cambridge Street, Hyde Park ; Hotel Bristol, Vienna, Austria. (M9328)

PONSONBY, Hon. Mrs. Maurice George Jesses, O.B.E.

PONTIN, Capt. and Qr.-Mr. William James Henry, M.B.E., R.A.M.C.

POOL, Augustus Frank, O.B.E., *b.* 14 Aug. 1872 ; *s.* of the late Lieut. William Pool, R.N., of Blackheath, S.E. ; *m.* Harriette Maude Mary, *d.* of the late Oliver Smith, of Greenwich. *Educ. :* The Academy, Lowestoft, and King's Coll., London. Assistant Chief Inspector of Taxes, Inland Revenue Department. President of the Association of Tax Surveying Branch in 1917–18. *Address :* Kenmuir, Manor Way, Beckenham, Kent. (O659)

POOLE, Arthur Reginald, M.B.E., *b.* 24 March, 1885. Member of Staff of Ministry of Agriculture and Fisheries. *War Work :* Administration of the purchases of Standing Timber by Timber Supply Department of Board of Trade. (M2296)

POOLE, Major Francis Garden, D.S.O., O.B.E., Reserve of Officers, *b.* 24 June, 1870 ; *s.* of the late Rev. S. W. Poole, M.D., of St. Mark's, Cambridge ; *m.* Madeline Leyland, *d.* of Alfred Bright, of Windy Gap, Formby, Lancashire. *Educ. :* Cambridge, and Royal Military Coll., Sandhurst. *War Work :* With 3rd Middlesex Regt., Ypres Salient, Jan. 1915, to Feb. 1915 (invalided) ; Commandant, Officers' School of Instruction, 1915–16 ; General Staff Officer, 2nd Grade, 1916–17, mentioned in despatches ; returned British Exp. Force, 1917–19 ; Batt. Commander and General Staff Officer, 2nd Grade, 2nd Army and War Office ; mentioned in despatches ; Mil. O.B.E. *Address :* 18, Great College Street, S.W. 1. *Clubs :* Travellers' and United Service. (O5688)

POOLE, Major-Gen. Sir Frederick Cuthbert, K.B.E., C.B., C.M.G., D.S.O., *b.* 3 Aug. 1869 ; *s.* of the late Rev. R. H. Poole, of West Rainton, Durham ; *m.* Alice Maude, *d.* of Sir Charles A. Hanson, Bart., M.P., of Fowey Hall, Cornwall (*see* BURKE'S *Peerage*). *Educ. :* Durham School, and R.M.A., Woolwich. Joined Royal Artillery, 15 Feb. 1889. Served in Tirah Expedition, 1897–98 ; S. African War, 1899–1902 (3 times mentioned in despatches, D.S.O.) ; Somaliland Exp. 1903–4 (mentioned in despatches). *War Work :* 1914–18, seven times mentioned in despatches ; C.M.G., C.B., K.B.E., Officier de la Legion d'honneur (France), Grand Officer de la Couronne de Rumanie (Rumania), Grand Cross St. Anne and St. Stanislaus (Russia), St. Vladimir, 2nd Class (Russia). *Addresses :* Cotswold House, Fowey, Cornwall ; Lane End, Danchurch, Rugby. *Club :* Army and Navy. (K284)

POOLE, Capt. George Arthur Evered, M.B.E.

POOLE, George Francis, M.B.E., *b.* 6 Aug. 1874 ; *s.* of George Poole, of Crowle, Lincolnshire ; *m.* Lily, *d.* of George Banks, Birkdale, Lancs. *Educ. :* Epworth, Lincolnshire. Director of English Margarine Works (1919), Limited. *War Work :* Organised and controlled the Inspectors' Department of the Margarine Clearing House under the Ministry of Food. (M9329)

POOLE, Major Henry Reynold, D.S.O., O.B.E., *b.* 1877 ; *s.* of Henry Skeffington Poole, of Halifax, Nova Scotia. Entered R.A. 1899 ; became Major, 1914 ; served during the Great War, 1914–16 (despatches, Legion of Honour). (O7585)

POOLE, Herbert Richard, M.B.E., *b.* 27 Dec. 1872 ; *s.* of John Westbrook Poole, of London ; *m.* Mary Anne, *d.* of Charles Wyman, of Edmonton. *Educ. :* Latymer's School, Edmonton. Accountant, Office of Accountant and Comptroller General, Customs and Excise, Custom House, London. *Addresses :* Custom House, London, E.C. 3 ; Clevedon, 48, Foxley Lane, Purley, Surrey.

POOLER, Major John Read, O.B.E., M.B., B.Ch., R.A.M.C. (T.), *b.* 23 Nov. 1875 ; *s.* of Henry Pooler, of Wellington, Shropshire ; *m.* Florence Beatrice, *d.* of William Parker Pigcott, of Bishopsgate, E.C. *Educ. :* Adam's Grammar School, Newport, Salop ; Birmingham Univ. Bachelor of Medicine, Bachelor of Surgery, Univ. of Birmingham ; Licentiate in Medicine, Surgery, and Midwifery ; Society of Apothecaries, London ; Deputy Commissioner of Medical Services, Ministry of Pensions. *War Work :* Civil Surgeon, South African Field Force, 1901–2 ; Lieut.-Col. Commanding 1/3rd East Anglian Field Amb., 54th Division, and 10th Cavalry Brigade Combined Field Ambulance, 4th Cavalry Division in Gallipoli, Egypt, Palestine, and Syria, 1914–20. *Address :* Stonebroom, nr. Alfreton, Derbyshire. (O6271)

POOLE, Capt. John Sanderson, D.S.O., O.B.E., *b.* 1896. Capt. King's Roy. Rifle Corps ; Staff-Capt. ; served during the Great War, 1914–17 (despatches). (O6807)

POOLE, Comm. Richard Hayden Owen LANE-, O.B.E., R.N.

POOLES, Capt. Mark, O.B.E., R.A.S.C.

POOLEY, Arthur Milnes, M.B.E.

POOLEY, Capt. Robert, O.B.E., *b.* 6 Feb. 1874 ; *s.* of Robert Pooley, of Wimbledon ; *m.* Adie Emma, *d.* of Robert Lawes, of Aldershot. *Educ. :* City of London, and King's Coll. London Representative, Shelton Iron, Steel, and Coal Co., Ltd. *War Work :* Joined Inland Waterways Dept. of War Office, Dec. 1916, and loaned to Admiralty in May, 1917, as personal assistant to Sir Harry Livesey, Director of Navy Contracts. *Addresses :* Tregonwell, Teddington ; 122, Cannon Street, E.C. (O11150)

POOLEY, Warner Lake, O.B.E., *b.* 28 Dec. 1878 ; *s.* of the late Rev. J. G. Pooley, R.D., J.P., of Stonham Aspal, Suffolk ; *m.* Ethel Dora, *d.* of Francis Ince, of The Hermitage,

Jarvis Brook, Sussex. *Educ. :* Haileybury Coll. Chief Accountant of the Navy and Army Canteen Board. *War Work :* In relation to canteens through the following bodies : Canteen and Mess Co-op. Society, Ltd. ; Expeditionary Force Canteens ; Army Canteen Committee ; Navy and Army Canteen Board. *Address :* The Leyslands, Radlett, Herts. *Clubs :* Union ; Cavendish. (O11151)

POPE, Capt. Andrew Noble, O.B.E., R.F., *b.* 14 Nov. 1881 ; *s.* of J. N. C. Pope, of Clifton, Bristol ; *m.* Marjory Lorna, *d.* of John Shute, of Bristol. *Educ. :* Harrow and Magdalen Coll., Oxford. *War Work :* Served with 9th Battn. Royal Fusiliers from formation till Sept., 1915, in France ; attached H.Q. 6th Corps from Sept. 1915, until appointed Camp Commandant, 6th Corps, in June, 1916 ; resigned appointment Sept. 1919, to join 4th Battn. Royal Fusiliers. *Addresses :* 7, Princes Buildings, Clifton, Bristol ; 5, Addison Mansions, London, W.14. (O5690)

POPE, Frances Madge, M.B.E., *b.* 11 July, 1893 ; *s.* of John Madge Pope, of Copplestone. *Educ. :* At home, and Sandecotes School, Parkstone, Dorset. *War Work :* Clerk on the County Director's Staff of the Devonshire Branch, British Red Cross Society, later promoted to Head Clerk ; Assistant Sec. to the County Director and Commandant Devon Reserve 16, and in May, 1919, Sec. to the County Director. *Address :* Copplestone House, Copplestone, N. Devon. (M9331)

POPE, Major Seymour Fell, O.B.E., *b.* 1 Feb. 1880 ; *s.* of William Pope, of Okefield, Crediton ; *m.* Helen Caroline, *d.* of George Sinclair-Smith, of Coombe, Copplestone. *Educ. :* Winchester Coll., and Univ. Coll., Oxford. Solicitor. *War Work :* D.A.Q.M.G., Base Headquarters, Basra, Mesopotamia ; D.A.Q.M.G., Refugee Camp, Baquba. *Address :* Forches Corner, Crediton. *Clubs :* Devon and Exeter ; Leander. (O4243)

POPE, Lieut.-Col. William Henry, O.B.E., R.A.F.

POPE, Professor Sir William Jackson, K.B.E., F.R.S., M.A. (Cantab.), D.Sc. (Melbourne), LL.D. (St. Andrews), *b.* 31 March, 1870 ; *s.* of William Pope, of Chiswick. *Educ. :* London. Professor of Chemistry, Univ. of Cambridge ; President of the Society of Chemical Industry ; lately President of the Chemical Society. *War Work :* Member of the Chemical Warfare Committee ; Member of Lord Fisher's Panel, Board of Invention and Research. *Address :* The Chemical Laboratory, Cambridge University. *Clubs :* Savile ; Savage ; Chemical Industries. (K230)

POPHAM, Henry Bradshaw, M.B.E.

POPPLESTONE, Capt. William Gilbert, M.B.E.

POPPLEWELL, Violet May, M.B.E., *b.* 27 Jan. 1892 ; *d.* of Arthur Popplewell, of Sydney, N.S.W., Australia. *Educ. :* Groveley Manor Coll., Boscombe, Hants. *War Work :* 2¼ years as V.A.D. in 6th Australian Auxiliary Hospital in London ; 15 months with the Home Defence Comforts Fund (being transferred from the former) at Tollesbury, Essex, on the East Coast, being in charge of an emergency station there, sometimes working single handed, and for which work received the order of M.B.E. *Address :* Craigie Lodge, St. Lawrence, Isle of Wight. (M9332)

PORDAGE, Anna, Mrs., M.B.E., *b.* 22 April, 1873 ; *d.* of Christopher Richardson, of Camerton, Somersetshire ; *m.* Frederick *s.* of John Pordage, of Faversham. Certified Midwife ; trained general nursing Royal Infirmary, Bradford, afterwards appointed sister same institution ; night sister Rochester Hospital ; nursing sister Uganda Administration ; Matron Victoria Hospital, St. Lucia, B.W.I. *War Work :* Nursing of military patients from Royal Canadian Garrison Artillery ; emergency pneumonia patients from troopship " Grantully Castle," and other ships ; instruction to members of the local V.A.D. *Address :* c/o The National Bank of India, Ltd., 26, Bishopsgate, E.C.2. (M6476)

PORGES, Major Edmund Daniel, O.B.E.

PORITT, Hannah Mary, Mrs., M.B.E.

PORTAL, Florence Elizabeth Mary, Lady, C.B.E., Order of Mercy, Lady of Grace of St. John of Jerusalem, *b.* 17 June, 1858 ; *d.* of the late Hon. St. Leger Glyn (*see* BURKE'S *Peerage*, Wolverton, B.) ; *m.* William Wyndham, *s.* of the late Sir Wyndham Portal, Bart., of Laverstoke (*see* BURKE'S *Peerage*). *War Work :* Commandant of Laverstoke Red Cross Hospital from Sept. 1914, to July, 1919. *Addresses :* Laverstoke House, Whitchurch, Hants. ; 12 Grafton Street, W. 1. *Club :* Ladies' Automobile. (C2877)

PORTAL, Lady Louise Rosemary Kathleen Virginia, M.B.E., *b.* 1889 ; *d.* of 2nd Earl of Cairns (*see* BURKE'S *Peerage*) ; *m.* (1909) Lieut.-Col. Wyndham Raymond Portal, M.V.O., D.S.O., *e.s.* of Sir William Wyndham Portal, 2nd Bart. (*see* BURKE'S *Peerage*). *Address :* Kingsclere House, nr. Newbury. (M3907)

PORTEOUS, Capt. Lawrence Victor, M.B.E.

PORTEOUS, Major Percy Guynedd, O.B E. R.E.

PORTER, Amy, Mrs., M.B.E.

PORTER, Lieut. Edward Ernest, M.B.E., D.C.M.

PORTER, Elizabeth Allison, Mrs., M.B.E., *b.* 12 May, 1865 ; *d.* of Turnbull James, of Plumstead ; *m.* William Henry, *s.* of Thomas Porter, of Plumstead. *War Work :* Y.M.C.A. Munition Workers' Canteens, Royal Arsenal and Drill Hall, Woolwich ; Voluntary worker, full time (Purple Ladies) ; Caterer (voluntary) for Munition Girls' Club, held at Royal Arsenal ; Reference Library, dealing with, on an average, two hundred girls each evening ; packing of parcels for Prisoners of War of the Royal Regiment of Artillery. (M9333)

PORTER, Frank, O.B.E., M.A., *b.* 23 Nov. 1878; *s.* of William Porter, J.P., of Boston, Lincolnshire; *m.* Marjorie Lillian, *d.* of the late James Pascall, J.P., of Southwark and Croydon. *Educ.:* Boston Grammar School; Caius Coll., Cambridge; Worcester Coll., Oxford. Entered Admiralty (Accountant-General's Department), 1902; Superintending Clerk, 1911; Assistant Accountant-General, 1919. *War Work:* Admiralty. *Address:* 3, Fryston Avenue, Croydon. *Club:* National Liberal. (O11152)

PORTER, Herbert, O.B.E., *b.* 1 Jan. 1880; *s.* of Rev. John Robinson Porter, M.A., of Wartling, Sussex; *m.* Evelyn Cecile Mary, *d.* of Richard David Sanders, of Blackheath. *Educ.:* Tonbridge School. Fellow of the Institute of Chartered Accountants. *War Work:* Squadron Q.M.S., Inns of Court O.T.C. (T.F.), Aug. 1914 to Aug. 1915; Assistant Director Finance Department, Ministry of Munitions, Aug. 1915, to March, 1919. *Address:* Struan, Beaconsfield Road, Blackheath, S.E. *Club:* Constitutional. (O660)

PORTER, Major Herbert Charles Vivian, O.B.E.

PORTER, Major James Douglas, O.B.E.

PORTER, John Fletcher, C.B.E., M.B., J.P.

PORTER, Joseph Francis, O.B.E., M.D., M.R.C.S.

PORTER, Ludovic Charles, C.S.I., C.I.E., O.B.E., *b.* 27 Nov. 1869; *s.* of Ludovic Porter, of Cockington, Devon. *Educ.:* Eton; Trin. College, Cambridge. Commissioner, United Provinces India (I.C.S.). Joined Indian Civil Service, 1889; at present Commissioner and Member Legislative Council, U.P. *War Work:* Executive Council, Lady Lansdowne's Fund; Ministry of Munitions, 1916-18 (Director, Release from the Colours Section); attached Sir John Hewett's mission to Mesopotamia, 1918. *Address:* Lucknow, U.P. *Clubs:* Bath; Oriental. (O11153)

PORTER, Major Mansel Loudon, O.B E., King's Royal Rifle Corps, *b.* 1869; *s.* of Capt. Henry Porter, 60th Rifles, of Birlingham, near Pershore, Worcestershire. *Educ.:* Harrow. Joined King's Royal Rifle Corps, 1892; promoted Capt. 1900; served in S. Africa, 1899-1902 (Queen's medal with 6 clasps); Major, 1915 (Reserve of Officers); appointed Sec. Berkshire Territorial Force Association, Sept. 1913. *Club:* Army and Navy. (O661)

PORTER, Comm. Robert Milne, O.B.E., R.N.R.

PORTER, Col. Sir (Harry Edwin) Bruce BRUCE-, K.B.E., C.M.G., M.D., *b.* 5 Feb. 1869; *s.* of the late Capt. J. Porter, R.A.; *m.* Agnes Sinclair, *d.* of the late Rev. David Bruce, D.D., of Auckland, N.Z., and widow of the late J. H. Honeyman, M.D., of Auckland, N.Z. *Educ.:* London; Brussels, etc. Physician; is Knight of Grace of St. John of Jerusalem. *War Work:* Commanded 3rd London Gen. Hospital, Wandsworth; commanded 40th Gen. Hospital, I.E.F.D., Mesopotamia; Medical Member of Mission to Italy, 1915; served 1914-19; despatches. *Addresses:* 6, Grosvenor Street, W. 1; New House Farm, Chobham, Surrey. *Clubs:* Royal Automobile; Pilgrims'. (K198)

PORTER, Capt. Samuel LOWRY-, M.B.E.

PORTERS, Lieut. Robert Halstead, M.B.E.

POST, Capt. Donnell Shepard, M.B.E.

POST, Lieut. George Henry Draper, M.B.E., R.A.S.C.

POSTLETHWAITE, Major Francis John Marshall, O.B.E.

POSTLETHWAITE, Lieut. Frederick Hartley, M.B.E., R.A.F.

POSTLETHWAITE, John Rutherford Parkin, M.B.E., *b.* 26 Nov. 1883; *s.* of John William Postlethwaite; *m.* Ellen Anna, *d.* of Col. Caddell, of Dublin. *Educ.:* Haileybury Coll. District Commissioner, Uganda. *War Work:* Recruiting for King's African Rifles in the Northern Province of Uganda; Hon. Lieut. on Staff of Western Command during leave from Uganda. *Club:* Constitutional. (M6477)

POSTLETHWAITE, William Taylor, O.B.E., L.L.B.

POTIER, George Charles, M.B.E., *b.* 1 June, 1867; *s.* of George Potier, of London; *m.* Nellie, *d.* of — Leedham, of Dudley. *Educ.:* St. Giles, Camberwell. Chief Clerk, Staff Coll., Camberley, Surrey; served in Matabeleland 1896 (medal), and South Africa, 1899-1900 (medal and 3 clasps); Long Service and G.C. medal). *War Work:* B.E.F. from May, 1915, to May, 1920; mentioned in despatches; meritorious service medal, 1914-15 Star, G.S. and Victory medals. *Address:* Amblecote, Frogmore, Blackwater, Hants. (M4580)

POTT, Evelyn Mabel, M.B.E.; *d.* of the late Robert Pott, of Bentham Hill, near Tunbridge Wells. *War Work:* Member of V.A.D. Kent 74; worked at the Auxiliary Hospital, staffed by that detachment, Oct. 1914, to Feb. 1919; awarded Silver War Badge, 1917. *Address:* Paveys, Langton Green, Kent. (M9334)

POTT, Gladys Sydney, M.B.E., *b.* 1867; *d.* of Alfred Pott, Archdeacon of Berkshire. *Educ.:* Privately. *War Work:* Hon. Sec. National Relief Fund, Berkshire, 1914-16; Hon. Sec Women and Farm Labour Committee, Berkshire, 1914-17; travelling Inspector to Board of Agriculture (Women's Branch), 1917-20; Sec. to Agricultural Sub-Committee of Reconstruction Dept, 1919; Woman Commissioner under Overseas Settlement Committee (Colonial Office), 1919; Chairman of Society for Overseas Settlement of British Women, 1920. *Addresses:* 3, Cleveland Gardens, W.; Little Place, Clifton Hampden, Abingdon. *Club:* Forum. (M9335)

POTT, Katharine Frances Wilson, M.B.E., *b.* 4 Oct. 1867, *d.* of Francis Pott Rector, of Northill, Beds. *Educ.:* Privately. *War Work:* .Commandant V.A.D. Kent 74, Speldhurst and District, Bidborough Court Hospital, Oct. 1914, to Aug. 1916;

Nevill Park Hospital, Tunbridge Wells, Oct. **1916,** to Feb. 1919. *Address:* Birchetts, Speldhurst, Kent. (M3908)

POTT, Walter, O.B.E., F.R.I.B.A., F.S.I., *b.* 23 Feb. 1864. Late Principal Architect in H.M. Office of Works (ret.). *War Work:* Architectural services in connection with the provision of buildings for Government Departments during the war. *Address:* Warren Garth, Belmont, Surrey. (O1772)

POTTER, Major Benjamin Henry, O.B.E., M.C.

POTTER, Major Cyril Charlie Hamilton, O.B.E.

POTTER, Edith Madelene, M.B.E.

POTTER, Edith, Mrs., O.B.E., *b.* 1870; *d.* of Robert Roberts, C.E., of Chester, and widow of Arthur Randal Flint, of Chester; *m.* Charles John Potter, *s.* of Lieut.-Col. Addison Potter, C.B., of Heaton Hall, Newcastle-on-Tyne. *War Work:* Food distribution for the Counties of Northumberland and Durham V.A.D. Hospitals; Commandant of Detachment Reserve T.F.A. in the County of Northumberland. *Address:* Heaton Hall, Newcastle-on-Tyne. (O11154)

POTTER, Edmund, C.B.E., *b.* 1853; *s.* of Robert Potter, of Shepherdswell, Dover; *m.* 1880, Edith Isabel Loud, *d.* of Henry Loud Harrisson, formerly of Blackheath. Assist. Solicitor, Board of Trade. *Address:* Chester Lodge, 78, Gleneldon Road, Streatham, S.W. (C597)

POTTER, Francis Martin, M.B.E., B.Sc., A.R.C.S., F.I.C., *b.* 1887. *Educ.:* City of London, Hameln Weser, Germany, and Royal Coll. of Science, London. Member of Council, Institute of Chemistry. *War Work:* Served with London Scottish, 1914-15; Superintendent H.M. Factory, Penrhyndendraeth, N. Wales, 1915-18. *Club:* Chemical Industry. (M859)

POTTER, Major Frank Thomas, O.B.E., M.C., R.A.O.C.

POTTER, Capt. Frederick Effingham, M.B.E.

POTTER, Major and Brevet Lieut.-Col. James Archer, C.B.E., T.D., *b.* 27 March, 1875; *s.* of Wm. Hy. Potter, of Leicester. *War Work:* 4th Leicester Regt. (T.) and served on the Staff. *Address:* Meadowcourt Road, Leicester. (C2157)

POTTER, John Alexander, C.B.E. A member of Military Service Committee, Ministry of Munitions during the Great War. (C2879)

POTTER, Mary Ann, Mrs., M.B.E.

POTTER, Capt. and Qr.-Mr. Thomas, O.B.E., D.C.M.

POTTER, Major Thomas James, O.B.E., R.A.M.C.

POTTS, Alan Calder, M.B.E., *b.* 14 Aug. 1869; *s.* of George Calder Potts, of Newcastle-on-Tyne. *Educ.:* Privately. Mechanical Engineer; Superintendent Steamers Works, Sudan Govt. Railways and Steamers Dept. *War Work:* Construction and upkeep of fleet of Sudan Government steamers and barges employed in military and other transport in the Sudan. (M1152)

POTTS, Capt. and Bt. Major Charles, O.B.E.

POTTS, Dorothy Feilden, Mrs., M.B.E., *b.* 22 Nov. 1887; *d.* of Arthur Cuthbert Alport, of Herne Bay, Kent, England. *m.* William Edward Herbert, *s.* of Thomas Moodie Potts, of Newcastle-on-Tyne. *Educ.:* Rocklands High Schools, Cradock, C.P., and Normal Coll., Pretoria, Transvaal. *War Work:* Organised, equipped, and conducted a Rest Hut for troops engaged in the German East Campaign, in the town of Chinde, at the mouth of the Zambesi River, in Portuguese East Africa. *Address:* St. Andrews Road, Yeoville; Johannesburg, Box 3410. (M9336)

POTTS, George Louis, M.B.E., *b.* 9 Feb. 1865; *s.* of George Potts, of Louth, Lincolnshire; *m.* Lina Fanny, *d.* of James Jeanneret, of Neuchatel. Director, Messrs Apperly, Curtis & Co., Ltd., Dudbridge Mills, Stroud, Glos.; Vice-President, British Chamber of Commerce in Belgium. *War Work:* Head of Textiles, Commission Internationale de Ravitaillement, India House, Kingsway; Officer Order of Leopold II. *Clubs:* Junior Constitutional; Eccentric; Cercle Artistique (Bruxelles). (M9337)

POTTS, Reginald, O.B.E.

POTTS, Lieut. Thomas Moffett, O.B.E., R.N.R.

POTTS, Thomas Worthington, O.B.E.

POTTS, William Thomas, C.B.E. A J.P. for Essex; Director of Port Forwarding Depart., Ministry of Munitions, during the Great War. *Address:* The Hall, Southminster, Essex. (C2880)

POUGNET, Lieut. John Maurice Barbes, O.B.E., R.N.R.

POULTNEY, Edward Cecil, M.B.E.

POULTNEY, Samuel Levi, M.B.E.

POULTON, Lieut.-Col. Arthur Faulconer, C.B.E., *b.* 28 July, 1858; *s.* of Dep. Surgeon-General C. W. Poulton, of Cricklade, Wiltshire; *m.* Susan Edith, *d.* of W. E. Grimston, of Earls Colne, Essex. *Educ.:* Royal Navy (1871-77), and Royal Military Coll., Sandhurst (1878-79). Served in Suffolk Regt., 1879-99; Afghan War, 1879-80 (medal); Chief Constable of West Suffolk, 1899-1902; Chief Constable of Berkshire from 1902. *War Work:* Area Administrative Officer, Southern Area, R.A.S.C., Forage Dept, 1915-18; granted rank of Lieut.-Col. *Address:* Highgrove, Reading. *Clubs:* Wellington; Berkshire County. (C1744)

POULTON, E. L., O.B.E.,

POULTON, Capt. Faville Clement, O.B.E., R.A.O.C.

POUNTNEY, Arthur Meek, C.B.E. Treasurer of Straits Settlement. *Address:* Singapore, Straits Settlements. (C2022)

POUPART, William John, M.B.E.

POVER, Eng.-Comm. Thomas Pierce, O.B.E., R.N.R.

POWELL, Arthur, O.B.E., J.P., V.D., B.A., M.B., M.S., *b.* 1864; *s.* of the late John Donor Powell, of Dublin. *Educ.:* Trinity Coll., Dublin; Royal Coll. of Surgeons, Dublin;

Queen's Univ., Belfast. Physician; late Professor of Medical Jurisprudence, Bombay Univ.; Pathologist to Coroner, Bombay; Physician in charge, Northcote Hospital; Consulting Physician, St. George's Hospital, Bombay; Consulting Physician Tropical Diseases, Ministry of Pensions. *War Work:* Served as Captain, Indian Mounted Infantry (Lumsden's Horse), S. African War, 1900–1; Lieut.-Col., O.C. Byculla Officers' Hospital, Bombay, 1915–19. *Addresses:* 9, Harley Street, W. 1; The Firs, Worcester Road, Sutton. *Clubs:* Oriental; Byculla; Royal Societies'; W. India Turf. (O9846)

POWELL, Benjamin Henry, M.B.E., *b.* 20 Aug. 1863; *s.* of Benjamin Powell, of Newport, Salop. *War Work:* Hon. Sec. Eastry Rural District Local War Savings Committee; Hon. Sec. Betteshanger War Savings Association; Head Special Constable for Betteshanger Parish; Voluntary Work Eastry Rural Food Office. *Address:* Betteshanger, Eastry, Kent. (M9340)

POWELL, Clare Carew, Mrs., M.B.E.
POWELL, David, M.B.E., J.P.
POWELL, Lieut.-Col. Douglas, C.B.E., *b.* 8 July, 1874; *s* of Sir Richard Douglas Powell, Bart., K.C.V.O. (*see* BURKE'S *Peerage*); *m.* Muriel Albinia, *d.* of W. F. Powell, of Sharow Hall, Ripon, Yorkshire (*see* BURKE'S *Peerage*). *Educ.:* Clifton; Magdalen Coll., Oxford. *War Work:* Served in France in Royal Welsh Fusiliers. *Address:* 9, West Eaton Place, S.W. 1. *Club:* Naval and Military. (C872)

POWELL, Edith, Mrs., M.B.E.
POWELL, Major Enoch, O.B.E., R.A.F.
POWELL, Major Eric Walter, O.B.E., R.A.F.
POWELL, Ernest Robert, M.B.E.
POWELL, Bimbashi Felix Edmund, Bey, M.B.E.
POWELL, Frank Grove, M.B.E., *b.* 26 July 1860; *s.* of James Powell, of Chichester; *m.* Rosa Edwina, *d.* of Edward Smith, of Richmond, Surrey. *Educ.:* Prebendal School, Chichester, and Cheltenham Coll. Barrister-at-law, Journalist. *War Work:* Organised Richmond Detachment, Met. Special Constabulary, Aug. 1914, to April, 1915; Assistant Commander (2nd in command) V Div. Met. Spec. Const., April 1915, to June, 1919, in acting command 2 years. *Address:* 1, The Little Green, Richmond, Surrey. (M9344)

POWELL, Lieut. Frank James Bickley, M.B.E., R.A.F.
POWELL, George Allan, C.B.E.; *s.* of the late R. D. Powell; *m.* Jeannie Jack, *d.* of Dr. W. Marshall, of Inellan. Bar., Gray's Inn, 1907; Officer-in-charge of Govt. War Refugees Camp, Earl's Court, during the Great War; is an officer of Order of Leopold of Belgium, and a Chevalier of Order of Crown of Italy. (C2881)

POWELL, George Henry, M.B.E., F.R.H.S., *b.* 25 Jan. 1867; *s.* of George John Powell, of London Corn Exchange; *m.* Caroline Martha, *d.* of Thomas Elliott, of Monaghan, Ireland. *Educ.:* Church Schools and City of London Coll. Hon. Sec. Soldiers' and Sailors' Families Association (Hendon Division); District Head, Soldiers' and Sailors' Help Society (Hendon Division); Hon. Treas. Tonic Solfa Association. *War Work:* Recruiting work under Lord Derby's scheme; Member of Local Advisory Committee (Mil. Service), Hendon Tribunal; Hon. Sec. Hendon Local War Pensions Committee (Central Ward Sub-Area); Member of Hendon National Service Committee. *Address:* Monaghan, 87, Sunny Gardens, Hendon, N.W. 4. *Club:* Alexandra (Hendon). (M9345)

POWELL, Lieut.-Col. George Robert, O.B.E.
POWELL, Major Harold Haines, O.B.E., *b.* 19 Oct. 1868; *s.* of Thomas Powell; *m.* Margaret Jane, *d.* of Philip Crampton, M.D. *Educ.:* Privately, and Royal Military College, Sandhurst. Joined 2nd Batt. East Yorkshire Regt., Sept. 1889, and served with the regiment at home and abroad, and when war broke out accompanied it to France as 2nd in Command; wounded at the 2nd Battle of Ypres in May, 1915; in Sept. 1915, was appointed General Staff Officer, 2nd Grade, and held this appointment until the end of 1917; later was employed for 2 years and 3 months in Intelligence Directorate at the War Office. *Address:* 54, Gordon Mansions, Gower Street, W.C.1. *Club:* Junior Army and Navy. (O8911)

POWELL, Harry James, C.B.E., B.A., *b.* 1853; *s.* of Nathanael Powell, J.P., D.L., of Buckhurst Hill, Essex; *m.* Emma, *d.* of Major W. S. Stuart, R.E., of Chigwell, Sussex. *Educ.:* Rugby, and Trinity Coll., Oxford. Glass-maker, 1873–1919, Whitefriars Glass Works, London; Member for Dulwich of first and second London County Councils; Co-opted Member of London Technical Education Board; Member of Art Workers' Guild, from 1890; Member of Arts and Crafts Society; Governor of Dulwich Coll., from 1889; served on Board of Education Committee to advise on rearrangement of Art Collections in Victoria and Albert Museum; Member of Board of Education Committee for Advice on Education in Art. *War Work:* Manufactured many special glasses for clinical and high-temperature thermometers, X-ray bulbs, and glass for the projecting " horns " of marine mines. (C2882)

POWELL, Hugh Falkenberg, M.B.E., M.D., M.R.C.S., L.R.C.P., *b.* 14 Aug. 1880; *s.* of the late Wm. Powell, M.R.C.S., of Cheltenham; *m.* Ethel Mary, *d.* of the late S. Arnott, of Topcliffe, Yorks. *Educ.:* Cheltenham Coll. and Univ. Coll. Hospital, London. Medical Practitioner; Hon. Anæsthetist, Cheltenham General Hospital; Senior Hon. Obstetric Surgeon, Victoria Home, Cheltenham; Deputy Coroner, Upper Division, Gloucestershire, etc. *War Work:* Temp. Capt. R.A.M.C.; Transport Officer and Consulting Anæsthetist V.A. Hospitals, Cheltenham Area. *Address:* Belle Vue House, Cheltenham. *Club:* New. (M3909)

POWELL, James Ablitt Pasifull, O.B.E.
POWELL, Col. James Leslie Grove, C.B.E., V.D., T.D., J.P., and D.L. Surrey (ret.), *b.* 26 April, 1853; *s.* of James Powell, of Chichester, Sussex; *m.* Harriette Charlotte (who died 1908), *d.* of Henry Huish, M.D., Surgeon-Major 3rd (King's Own) Hussars). *Educ.:* Cheltenham Coll. Solicitor; Alderman Surrey County Council, Hon. Col. 6th Batt. East Surrey Regt.; Lieut.-Col. and Hon. Col. Commanding, 1898–1909. *War Work:* Raised and commanded 2/6th Batt. East Surrey Regt., 1914–15; Recruiting Officer and Sub-Area Commander, East Surrey Regimental District; Military and National Service Representative before Tribunals, Richmond, Barnes, and Mortlake, and Appeal Tribunal Kingston-on-Thames. *Address:* Tapton House, Richmond, Surrey. *Clubs:* St. Stephen's; Royal Automobile. (C598)

POWELL, Lieut.-Col. John, O.B.E., V.D., J.P. (ret.), *b.* 16 Jan. 1856; *s.* of Francis Powell, of London; *m.* Edith May, *d.* of Frederick Bradshaw Hopkins. *Educ.:* Daniel Stuarts Institution, Edinburgh. Hon. Magistrate, 1st Class J.P.; Lieut.-Col. (ret.), Punjab Light Horse; Member, Punjab Legislative Council; Vice-Chairman, Town of Murnee, Punjab, India; served on Sir J. Willcocks' Staff, Delhi Durbar (Medal); also received the Kaisir-i-Hind Medal in 1914 for public services. *War Work:* Hon. Sec. Rawal Pindee War Fund; assisted in recruiting; in command of School for training officers and men, P.L. Horse, Rawal Pindee. *Clubs:* Junior Army and Navy; Rawal Pindee. (O4082)

POWELL, Joseph, O.B.E., *b.* 25 April, 1875; *s.* of Alfred William Powell, of London. *War Work:* Elected by the interned British civilians at Ruhleben Camp, Germany, as Captain of the Camp and their leader; carried on this work from the first day of internment till the last day (Nov. 1914 to Nov. 1918). (O11156)

POWELL, Kate Haidee, Mrs., O.B.E., *b.* 16 April, 1857; *d.* of S. C. Hemming. *Educ.:* Brighton. *War Work:* Commandant of the Bowden Hospital for 4 years. *Address:* Mapperley Hill, Nottingham. (O1775)

POWELL, Lieut. Malcolm Cecil, O.B.E., R.N.R.
POWELL, Margaret Joyce, O.B.E., M.A., *b.* 1888; *d.* of Arthur C. Powell, of Bencomb, Dorking. *Educ.:* Newnham Coll., Cambridge. Director, Messrs. James Powell and Sons (Whitefriars), Ltd., Glass manufacturers. *War Work:* Assistant Administrative Officer, Ministry of Food. *Address:* Bencomb, Dorking. *Club:* Ladies' University. (O3873)

POWELL, Lieut.-Col. Philip Lionel William, C.B.E., D.S.O., *b.* 1882; Major and Brevet Lieut.-Col. Welsh Regt. and an A.A.G. at War Office; served in the S. African War, 1899–1902 (Queen's medal with two clasps); Great War, 1915–19 (despatches). (C1745)

POWELL, Lieut.-Col. Samuel Arthur, O.B.E., V.D.,M.B.
POWELL, Thomas Percy Prosser, M.B.E., *b.* 26 Dec. 1869; *s.* of Rev. T. P. Powell, of Dorstone, Herefordshire; *m.* Evelyn Lucy Alice, *d.* of J. H. Arkwright, of Hampton Court, Herefordshire. *Educ.:* Charterhouse and Oriel Coll., Oxford. Barrister-at-law; County Councillor for Herefordshire. *War Work:* Joined Montgomeryshire Yeomanry, Sept. 1914; appointed A.D.C. to G.O.C. 10th Division, Feb. 1916; served in Macedonia, Palestine, and Egypt in that appointment till July, 1919. *Address:* Aylestone Cottage, Hereford. *Club:* New University. (M3190)

POWELL, Lieut. Wilfred Monsell, M.B.E.
POWELL, Capt. William Clive, M.B.E.
POWELL, William Wallace, O.B.E., B.A., I.C.S., *b.* 14 Nov. 1882; *s.* of Richard Powell, of Dublin. *Educ.:* The High School, Dublin. Indian Civil Service. *War Work:* Service in connection with recruiting in the Punjab. *Address:* 17, Lawrence Road, Lahore. *Clubs:* East India United Service; Punjab. (O8389)

POWELL, Winifred, Mrs., O.B.E., W.R.A.F.
POWELL, Herbert James BINGHAM-, O.B.E., M.Inst. C.E., M.I.Mech.E., M.Amer.Soc.C.E., F.R.San.I., A.C.G.I., *b.* 23 March, 1878; *s.* of Col. Bingham Powell, of London; *m.* Laura Mary, *d.* of John Joseph Clarke, of New York and Peru. *Educ.:* Burgess Park, Imperial Coll. of Science, London. Civil and Mechanical Engineer; Consulting Engineer to the Governments and principal Municipalities of Peru and Bolivia; Engineer of the Peruvian Corporation, Ltd. *War Work:* With the British War Mission to the United States from 1915 to 1918; district Inspection Officer; afterwards Officer in charge of the combined department of Gauges and Standards of the Mission, and of the Bureau of Aircraft Production of the U.S. War Dept.; Liaison Officer between the American Authorities and the British Engineering Standards Association; inventor of several precision measuring machines used in U.S.A. during war. *Address:* Quilca 315, Lima, Peru, South America. (O1776)

POWER, Lieut. Charles Louis, M.B.E., R.N.V.R.
POWER, Sir D'Arcy, K.B.E., F.R.C.S. (Eng.), *b.* 1855; *e. s.* of Henry Power, F.R.C.S. (Eng.), of Bagdale Hall, Whitby, Yorkshire; *m.* Eleanor, *y. d.* of George Haynes Fosbroke, M.R.C.S. (Eng.), of Bidford-on-Avon, Warwickshire. *Educ.:* Merchant Taylors' School, London; New and Exeter Coll., Oxford; St. Bartholomew's Hospital. Consulting Surgeon to St. Bartholomew's Hospital; member of the Council of the Royal College of Surgeons of England. *War Work:* Lieut.-Col. R.A.M.C. (T.) attached First London General Hospital (T.F.); Officer in charge of First London General Hospital, 1916–17; Consulting Surgeon, Fishmongers' Hall War Hospital and the Elstree War Hospital, Bromley, Kent; representative of the

Royal College of Surgeons on the Statutory Committee of Reference 1915. *Address :* 10A, Chandos Street, Cavendish Square, W. 1. *Club :* Oxford and Cambridge. (K289)

POWER, Capt. Frank Trevor, M.B.E.

POWER, George, M.B.E.

POWER, Lieut. George Teevan, M.B.E.

POWER, Lieut. Gerald Hugh, M.B.E., 9th Royal Warwick Regt., *b.* 9 Sept. 1888 ; *s.* of Harry Shakespeare Power, J.P., of Mid Illoro, Natal ; *m.* Ella, *d.* of Petros Mamikonyane, of Baku, Russia. *Educ. :* Bedford Grammar School. Farming. *War Work :* South-West African Campaign, and from there to Europe ; then India, Mesopotamia (Baghdad to Baku march), and Russia. *Address :* Monoughmore, Ladysmith, Natal. (M4912)

POWER, James Augustine, M.B.E., *b.* 16 June, 1856 ; *s.* of James Power, of Salford, Lancashire ; *m.* Amelia Rose, *d.* of John William Hall, of Fulham, London. *Educ. :* St. John's School, Salford, Lancs. *War Work :* Superintending Clerk at War Office. *Address :* 38, Kyrle Road, Clapham Common S.W. 11. (M9346)

POWER, Leila, M.B.E.

POWER, Margaret, O.B.E. Matron of St. Dunstan's, No. 11 House. (O11923)

POWER, Margaret Mary, Mrs., M.B.E.

POWER, Capt. Richard Pascal, O.B.E., *b.* 27 May, 1886 ; *s.* of Pierce Power, of Limerick, Ireland ; *m.* Dorothy Lyle. *d.* of Robert Allan Wilson, of Londonderry. *Educ. :* Privately. *War Work :* Served with Royal Irish Fusiliers from Aug. 1914, to Feb. 1916 ; served on the staff in various appointments from Feb. 1916, to 1918. *Club :* Junior United Service. (O2678)

POWLETT, Rear-Adm. Frederick Armand, C.B.E., R.N. Chief of Staff to Vice-Adm. Comdg. E. Coast during the Great War. (C2238)

POWNALL, Lieut.-Col. Assheton, O.B.E.

POWNE, Leslie, M.B.E., M.R.C.S., *b.* 8 Oct. 1859 : *s.* of William Powne, of Swindon ; *m.* Jessie, *d.* of Barnes Wimbush, of London. *Educ. :* Leamington. Medical Officer of Health, Crediton Rural District. *War Work :* O.C. V.A.D. Hospital, Crediton. *Address :* 52, High Street, Crediton. (M2299)

POWNEY, Lieut.-Col. Cecil Du Pre Penton, M.B.E., F.R.G.S., F.L.S., M.R.I., J.P., *b.* 21 Aug. 1862 ; *s.* of Edward Penton Powney, formerly Judge of Supreme Court of Madras, of Fyfield House, Andover ; *m.* Ethel Mary, *d.* of Col. Norton Knatchbull, of Onelton, Andover. *Educ. :* Eton, and Trinity Coll., Cambridge. Lieut. Grenadier Guards, 1884–94 ; served in the Soudan, 1885 (Medal with Clasp, Khedive's Star) ; Director Liberian International Corpn. *War Work :* Commanded 3rd Hants. Regt., 1914–16 ; Commander B. Div. Metropolitan Special Constabulary, 1917–19. *Addresses :* 41, Wilton Crescent, S.W. 1 ; Lenham Court, near Maidstone. *Clubs :* Bachelors' ; Guards'. (M3910)

POYNTER, Vernon Hamilton, M.B.E.

POYNTER, William Dyke, M.B.E.

POYNTON, Hon. Alexander, O.B.E. (O12004)

POYNTON, John William, O.B.E.

POYNTON, Joseph William, O.B.E., *b.* 11 Dec. 1861 ; *s.* of Joseph Poynton, of Dublin, Ireland ; *m.* Ada Edmonds, *d.* of John Macgregor, of Christchurch. *Educ. :* Privately. Barrister-at-law ; Stipendiary Magistrate, 1895–1900 ; Public Trustee, 1900–10 ; Secretary to the Treasury, 1910–13 ; at present Stipendiary Magistrate, Auckland, N.Z. *War Work :* Chairman, No. 2 Wellington Military Service Board, 1916–18. *Address :* Court House, Auckland, N.Z. (O8335)

POYSER, Capt. John, O.B.E., *b.* 17 July, 1883 ; *s.* of Thomas John Poyser, of Wirksworth, Derbyshire. *Educ. :* Westminster School. Barrister, Middle Temple ; is a Civil Servant (Ministry of Health). *War Work :* Served with R.A.S.C. in France, 1915–18 ; despatches twice. *Club :* Wellington. (O5691)

PRAEGER, Capt. and Qr.-Mr. Isouard Paul, M.B.E., *b.* 6 Sept. 1871 ; *s.* of Isouard Praeger, of Warrington ; *m.* Emily Spencer, *d.* of William Wright, of Farnham. *Educ. :* People College, Warrington. *War Work :* Served in S. Africa, 1899–1902 (Queen's Medal and 7 clasps, King's medal and 2 clasps), and in Great War from Sept. 1914, to Aug. 1919 (despatches). *Address :* 12, Church Street, Edgemont, Liverpool. (M4366)

PRAGNELL, Lieut. D. W. Alan, M.B.E., *b.* 17 May, 1895 ; *s.* of Arthur Pragnell, of London. *Educ. :* Kent College, Canterbury ; College de la Très Saint Trinité, Louvain. Commercial Agent for Messrs. Cook, Son & Co., London. *War Work :* Enlisted in Inns of Court O.T.C. ; afterwards went through the Grove Park O.T.C. for M.T., R.A.S.C. ; gazetted 2nd Lieut. May, 1917 ; served in Mesopotamia, 1917–19, with 971 M.T. Ford Company, operating with 15th Div. on the Euphrates, and 1st Corps on the Tigris. *Address :* The Hutch, Herne Bay. (M4910)

PRANCE, Capt. Basil C., O.B.E.

PRANCE, Geoffrey Hammett, O.B.E., M.D., C.M. (Edin.), *b.* 1868 ; *s.* of Courtenay Connell Prance, of Cheltenham ; *m.* Annie Rosalie, *d.* of Theo. Sandeman, of 21, Bolton Gardens, S. Kensington. *Educ. :* Cheltenham Coll., and Edinburgh Univ. Hon. Med. Officer, Childrens' Convalescent Home, Weston-super-Mare ; Mem. B.M.A. ; Hon. Obst. Surg. Vict. Home and Cheltenham Nursing Assocn. ; Hon. Surg. Cheltenham Gen. Hospital. *War Work :* Recruiting Medical Officer ; Medical Officer in charge troops in Weston-super-Mare ; Medical Officer, Ashcombe House Military Hospital ; Commandant, V.A.D. Somerset 94. *Address :* Belvedere, Weston-super-Mare (O11157)

PRATER, Capt. and Qr.-Mr. George, O.B.E.

PRATT, Charlotte Anyand Powys, Mrs., M.B.E.

PRATT, Edith Helen, O.B.E., B.A. ; *d.* of John Marchant Pratt, of Pratshayes, Exmouth. *Educ. :* Southlands School, Exmouth ; (Exhibitioner of) Girton Coll., Cambridge. Formerly Lecturer in Philosophy, Ladies' Coll., Cheltenham. *War Work :* 1915–17, Inspector of the National Filling Factories, Ministry of Munitions (first Woman Inspector appointed at the Ministry) ; 1917–18, Deputy Chief Controller of Q.M.A.A.C. with the British Armies in France ; 1918, Deputy Commandant Women's R.A.F. *Address :* Pratshayes, Exmouth, Devon. *Club :* Ladies' University. (O48)

PRATT, Lieut.-Comm. Edwin, O.B.E., R.N.

PRATT, Elizabeth Worth, M.B.E., L.L.A. *Educ. :* Privately and at Brighton Coll. Divisional Sec., B.R.C.S., Bermondsey. *War Work :* Served with British Red Cross Society in connection with Hospitals and Air Raids duty in the borough. *Address :* 12, Rebecca Terrace, Southwark Park, S.E. 16. (M9349)

PRATT, Frances Margaret Ethel, Mrs., M.B.E.,; *d.* of Major-Gen. C. N. Martin, R.E., of Mount Long, Castle Cork ; *m.* Lieut.-Col. H. A. Pratt, R.A., *s.* of Col. H. Pratt, of King's County, Ireland. *Educ. :* Privately ; S. Kensington School of Art ; Julian's, Paris. Exhibited at Salon, Paris. *War Work :* Commandant, British Red Cross from 1911 ; Commandant Dorset 66, which has four hospitals to its credit ; in 1914 eqipped and staffed Cornelia Hospital, Poole Red Cross wards (for direct overseas cases) ; also Forest Holme Hospital, and Naval Base Hospital, Poole ; staffed Grata Guies Hospital, Bournemouth ; organised and coached Red Cross lectures for 2,000 people ; raised funds for entertainments and comforts for troops for over four years ; Member of Committee of East Dorset Guild of workers ; mentioned 3 times. *Address :* The Castle, Parkstone, Dorset. *Club :* Forum. (M9350)

PRATT, Frank, M.B.E. *War Work :* Member of M.C.A.Y. War Emergency, Finance, and Trading and Equipment Committees ; organised Y.M.C.A. work for troops billeted in Watford, and acted as Hon. Sec. and Treasurer. *Address :* The Cottage, Upton Road, Watford. (M9351)

PRATT, Frank Herbert, M.B.E., *b.* 21 Oct. 1877 ; *s.* of James Frederick Pratt, of S. Lambeth, London ; *m.* Beatrice, *d.* of Edward Wyer, of S. Lambeth. *War Work :* In charge of Printing Establishment of Messrs. Harrison & Sons. Ltd., at the War Office throughout the war. *Address :* 29, Teevan Road, Lower Addiscombe Road, Croydon. (M9352)

PRATT, Henry Francis, O.B.E.

PRATT, Hilda Gertrude Van Hecke, M.B.E., *b.* 20 Dec. 1893 ; *d.* of Benjamin Pratt, of Leeds ; *m.* Jules, *s.* of Van Hecke, of Eecloo (Belgium). *Educ. :* Privately. *War Work :* Assistance to prisoners of War during the German occupation in Ghent, 1914 18 ; secret service work from 1915–18. *Address :* Chateau de Bierbais, Mt. St. Guibert. Belgium. (M9353)

PRATT, Capt. James Davidson, O.B.E., M.A., B.Sc., *b.* 13 Aug. 1891 ; *m.* Kathleen Winifred Jean Marsden, *d.* of William Summers, M.I.N.A., of Southampton. *Educ. :* Drumoak Public School ; Robert Gordon's Coll., and Aberdeen Univ. *War Work :* Embodied Aug. 1914 as colour-sergeant of the University Company of the 4th Bn. Gordon Highlanders (T.) ; promoted Company Sergt.-Major ; commissioned March 1915 ; Lieut. (temp.) June 1915 ; on active service in France, Feb. to Sept. 1915 ; wounded three times ; Aug. 1916 appointed Assistant Sec. and later Sec. to the Chemical Advisory (afterwards the Chemical Warfare) Committee of the Ministry of Munitions, while unfit for foreign service ; promoted Capt. (temp.) June 1918, and Staff Capt. on July 1919. *Address :* 3, Leinster Gardens, W. 2. *Club :* Junior Army and Navy. (O7593)

PRATT, May, Mrs., M.B.E.

PREECE, George, O.B.E., F.L.A., *b.* 30 July, 1866 ; *s.* of Richard Preece, of Wotherton, Shropshire ; *m.* Florence Julia Beatrice, *d.* of Henry Honour, of Spring Hill, Birmingham. *Educ. :* Chirbury School, Shropshire. Librarian and Clerk to the Committee, Stoke Newington Public Library ; Assistant Librarian, Barrow-in-Furness Public Library, 1882–88 ; Branch Librarian Chelsea Public Library, 1888–1893 ; Acting Town Clerk (temp.) Stoke Newington, in 1913 ; Fellow of the Library Association, and Member of the Council (1915–19). *War Work :* Executive Officer to the Stoke Newington Food Control and National Kitchens Committee ; Member of Local War Savings Committee, and Hon. Sec. of Branch War Savings Association. *Address :* 158, Church Street, Stoke Newington, London, N. 16. (O11158)

PREEDY, Capt. Clement, O.B.E., R.E.

PRENDERGAST, Comm. Edmund James, O.B.E., R.N.

PRENDERGAST, Surg.-Lieut. John Arnoux, O.B.E., R.N.

PRENDERGAST, Maud Dora Josephine, M.B.E. ; *d.* of General Sir Harry Prendergast, V.C., G.C.B., R.E., of Richmond. Commandant of Surrey 4 Red Cross Detachment. *War Work :* Organiser and Commandant of Red Cross Hospital, Richmond, Surrey, 1914–19. *Address :* Heron Court, Richmond, Surrey. *Club :* V.A.D. (M3911)

PRENDERGAST, Col. Theodore John Warrender, C.B.E., *b.* 1858 ; Col. R.E. (ret.) ; served in China, 1900 (medal) ; and in the Great War, 1914–19 (despatches). (C1746)

PRENTICE, Joseph, M.B.E., *b.* 17 July, 1877. Director of Railway Transport, Ministry of Food. *War Work :* Loaned by Great Central Rly. Co. to War Office as Assistant in Directorate of Movements to control working of Military Stores

to and from the ports. *Address :* 3, Axholme Road, Doncaster.
(M9354)

PRENTICE, Capt. William Francis, M.BE., R.A.F.

PRENTICE, William Hogg, M.B.E., M.D.

PRESCOTT, Charles Clark, M.B.E.

PRESCOTT, Charles William Beeston, O.B.E.

PRESCOTT, Constance Alice, M.B.E.

PRESCOTT, Lieut.-Col. John Joseph Whitworth, D.S.O., O.B.E., V.H.S., *b.* 5 Sept. 1875 ; *s.* of George Prescott, of Merrion, Dublin. *m.* Mabel, *d.* of Robert Simpson, of Dublin. *Educ.:* High School, Dublin, Dublin Univ., and R.C.S.I. Officer commanding 34 General Hospital, Deolali, India. *War Work :* Embarkation Medical Officer No. 3 Base, France ; O.C. No. 17 Stationary Hospital, Gallipoli ; O.C. Taj Mahal War Hospital, Bombay ; organised and commanded the Northumberland War Hospital, Newcastle-on-Tyne, Cumballa War Hospital, Bombay ; Alexandra War Hospital, Bombay ; and the Princess Mary War Hospital, Bombay ; at present Commanding 34 (the Welsh) General Hospital, India ; appointed Hon. Surgeon to His Excellency The Viceroy, Nov. 1918. *Address :* c/o Messrs. Holt & Co., 3, Whitehall Place, London, S.W. *Club :* Royal Bombay Yacht. (O857)

PRESCOTT, Major William Henry, C.B.E., J.P., M.P., M.Inst.C.E., R.E., *b.* 26 March, 1874 ; *s.* of John Prescott, of Blackburn, Lancashire ; *m.* Bessie Smith, *d.* of Mark Stanley, of Ambleside. *Educ.:* Privately. M.P. (Co. U.) N. Tottenham ; J.P. Middlesex ; Governor, Prince of Wales' General Hospital ; Member of Middlesex Territorial Force Association, Middlesex County Council, London Water Board, Grand Council Primrose League, and Govt. Roads Advisory Committee ; Barrister-at-law ; M.Inst.C.E. ; M.I.Mech.E. ; Past-President Institute of Sanitary Engineers ; Hon. Mem. Institution of Municipal and County Engineers. *War Work :* Hon. Organiser for the raising and training of the 33rd Division (Tottenham) Royal Engineers, which was attached to the 1st Army in France, comprising the 212th, 222nd, and 226th Field Cos., R.E., and 33rd Signal Co., R.E. ; also acted as the Hon. Organiser for the raising of the 230th Army Troops Co., R.E. ; served in France in 1915 in command of the 222nd Field Co., R.E., and was invalided home. *Address :* Allington House, Tottenham. *Club :* St. Stephen's. (C2883)

PRESLAND, Claud William, M.B.E. ; *s.* of the Rev. William A. Presland, of Camden Road, London, N. *Educ.:* Tollington Park Coll., London. *War Work :* Assistant Works Manager, National Projectile and Ordnance Factory, Nottingham. *Addresses :* 5, Annington Road, Fortis Green, London, N. 2 ; Dumsey Deep, Shepperton. (M9357)

PREST, Ellen Gertrude, M.B.E. (10252g)

PRESTON, Arthur, C.B.E. Hon. Sec. Indian Soldiers' Fund Committee. (C1980)

PRESTON, Arthur Sansome, O.B.E., LL.B.

PRESTON, Lieut.-Col. Eyre Evans, O.B.E.

PRESTON, Sir Frederick George Panizzi, K.B.E., J.P. Berks. *b.* 23 July, 1867 ; *s.* of R. T. Preston, of Hayes Court, Kent ; *m.* Ethel Mary, *d.* of Rev. T. Peters, of Taunton. *Educ.:* Blackheath School. Chairman of Messrs. J. Stone & Co., Ltd., Engineers, London. *War Work :* Undertook Special Mission for H.M. Government to Italy and Spain. *Address :* Landford Manor, Salisbury ; 14, Pall Mall, S.W. *Clubs :* Carlton ; Union ; Boodle's ; Royal Yacht Squadron. (K100)

PRESTON, George Frederic, C.B.E., M.I.E.E. ; *s.* of John Lovesay Preston ; *m.* 1889, Catherine Elizabeth, *d.* of John Bacon, of Taunton. Controller, London Telephone Service ; served in Bechuanaland Field Force, 1884–85 ; commanded 1st Vol. Bn. E. Surrey Regt., 1916–20. *Address :* Stanhope House, Surbiton. (C2885)

PRESTON, Herbert James, O.B.E.

PRESTON, Mark Rushworth, M.B.E.

PRESTON, Capt. Marvin James, O.B.E Can., A.V.C.

PRESTON, Sidney, C.B.E., *b.* 10 Sept. 1850 ; *s.* of Joseph Thomas Preston, of London ; *m.* Amelia, *d.* of Alexander O'Driscoll Taylor, of Belfast. *Educ.:* Univ. Coll. School, and King's Coll., London. Appointed Public Works Dept. Govt. of India, 1870 ; served in Irrigation Dept. of Punjab and United Provinces till 1902, when appointed Sec. to Govt. of India and Inspector-General of Irrigation ; retired Sept. 1905 ; served from Dec. 1906 to April, 1914, in Gwalior State, Central India, as Chief Engineer for Irrigation. *War Work :* Chairman, Canal Control Committee, from April, 1917 ; Technical Adviser to Ministry of Agriculture and Fisheries, from Nov. 1918. *Address :* 5, Cleveland Road, Ealing, W. 13. *Clubs :* Royal Automobile and Union (Ealing). (C2886)

PRESTON, William Edward, M.B.E., *b.* 3 Jan. 1883, *s.* of A. E. Preston, of Leicester ; *m.* Georgette Aline, *d.* of Georges Victor Gautier, of Paris. *Educ.:* Roan's School, Greenwich. Grain Salesman. *War Work :* With Ministry of Food. *Address :* 4, Emmanuel Road, Balham, S.W. (M2302)

PRESTON, Lieut.-Col. William John Phaelim, D.S.O., O.B.E., *b.* 11 June, 1873 ; *s.* of the late Surgeon-Gen. A. F. Preston, K.H.P., A.M.S., of Co. Meath, Ireland ; *m.* in 1912, Christina, *d.* of the late the Right Hon. Sir Christopher Nixon, Bart., P.C., M.D., of 2, Merrion Square, Dublin. *Educ.:* St. Helen's Coll., Southsea ; R.M.C. Sandhurst. Commandant 1/97th Infantry, Indian Army. *War Work :* Served on the Indian Frontier, 1914–15 ; in Mesopotamia, 1915–16 ; severely wounded at the action of Skaikh Saad, despatches, D.S.O., Afghanistan and North West Frontier, 1919. *Addresses :* 34, Carlisle Mansions, Victoria Street, S.W. ; c/o H. S. King

& Co., 9, Pall Mall, S.W. *Clubs :* Junior United Service ; Hurlingham ; Queen's. (O8529)

PRESTON OF ARDCHATTAN, Mary Augusta Margaret Nicol, Mrs. CAMPBELL- M.B.E. ; *d.* of the late Augustus Thorne, of 22, Gt. Cumberland Place, W. ; *m.* Robert William Piggott Clarke-Campbell-Preston, *s.* of Rev. William Colin Clarke Preston, of Valleyfield, Perthshire (died 1870). *Address :* Ardchattan Priory, Taynuilt, Argyllshire. (M9358)

PRESTON, Capt. Alistair HOUSTON-BOSWELL-, C.B.E.

PRETTY, Margaret Emily, Mrs., M.B.E.

PRETTY, Lieut.-Col. William Tertius, O.B.E., T.D., J.P., D.L., M.F.H., *b.* 1866 ; *s.* of William Pretty, of Ipswich ; *m.* Mabel Hewett, *d.* of R. S. Paul, of Ipswich. *War Work :* Commanded 1/6th Suffolk Regt, 1911–18, (despatches twice). *Address :* Goldrood, Ipswich. (O7595)

PRETYMAN, Lady Beatrice Adine, O.B.E., *b.* 1870 ; *d.* of the Earl of Bradford (*see* BURKE'S *Peerage*) ; *m.* Ernest George, *s.* of Canon F. Pretyman. *War Work :* Commandant of Hospital. *Address :* Orwell Park, Ipswich. (O3874)

PRETYMAN, Wing-Comdr. George Frederick, D.S.O., O.B.E., R.A.F., *b.* 8 Sept. 1891 ; *s.* of the late Major-Gen. Sir Geo. Pretyman, K.C.M.G., C.B. ; *m.* Maureen Kate, *d.* of Col. E. S. Heard, of Rossdohan, Co. Kerry, Ireland. *Educ.:* Wellington Coll., and Sandhurst. *War Work :* Served in France with R.F.C. from Aug. 1914, to Dec. 1917 ; Air Ministry, March, 1918, to conclusion of hostilities. *Address :* c/o Messrs. Cox & Co., 110, St. Martin's Lane, W.C. 2. *Clubs :* United Service ; R.A.F. ; Royal Aero. (O3394)

PREWER, Major William Henry Russell, O.B.E., *b.* 16 Feb. ; *s.* of William Prewer, of Horringer, Suffolk ; *m.* Isabel Susannah, *d.* of Samuel Lister, of Plumstead, S.E. 18. Major in the Royal Regiment of Artillery. *War Work :* Adjutant, Ordnance Coll., Woolwich. *Address :* c/o Messrs. Cox & Co., 16, Charing Cross, S.W. (O7596)

PRICE, Annie Vincent, M.B.E., M.M.S., *b.* 18 Sept. 1862 ; *d.* of Walter Price, of Bristol. *Educ.:* Privately. *War Work :* Four years at Netley, three under the Almeric Paget Massage Corps, and one under the Military Massage Service. *Address :* Sisters' Quarters, British Red Cross Section, Royal Victoria Hospital, Netley, Hants. (M9360)

PRICE, Bernard, O.B.E. (O12055)

PRICE, Capt. and Qr.-Mr. Cecil Stanley, M.B.E., Aust. A.M.C.

PRICE, Lieut.-Col. Charles Weaver, O.B.E., M.C., *b.* 12 June, 1876 ; *s.* of C. E. Weaver Price, of North House, Brecon ; *m.* Rhianedd Mary Gwendolen, *d.* of Gwilym Jones, of Pwllhelig, Llanwonno, Glamorgan. *Educ.:* Christ's Coll., Brecon. Clerk to Commissioners of Taxes. Agriculturist. *War Work :* Enlisted in South Wales Borderers, Sept. 1914 ; transferred to Motor Machine Guns, Nov. 1914 ; went to France as Battery Sergt.-Major of 12th Motor Machine Gun Battery, 13 July, 1915 ; Commissioned, Dec. 1915 ; transferred to Heavy Branch (Tanks), March 1916 ; Staff Capt. Tank Corps (H.Q.), June 1917 ; Commanding Tank Corps, Dec. 1919 to June 1920. *Address :* Ashgrove, Brecon. (O5693)

PRICE, Major Columbus Leigh, O.B.E., A.I.F.

PRICE, Cyril Oliver Rose, M.B.E.

PRICE, Edward French, M.B.E.

PRICE, Edwin Lessware, O.B.E., B.A. Oxon., Bar.-at-Law, *b.* 1874 ; *s.* of E. A. Price, of London ; *m.* 1st, Hilda Dorothy (who *d.* 1913), *d.* of F. Wright, J.P., of Lenton Hall, Notts ; 2nd, Kathleen Mary, *d.* of R. P. Earle, Barrister, Brisbane, Australia. Merchant. *War Work :* Assessor, Transport Claims Committee, India, 1915 ; Member, Government of Bombay, War Purposes Board, Sind Publicity Committee, and Karachi Sub-Committee Government Hides ; President, Karachi Division, War League of India ; Agent Consulaire de France à Karachi ; elected Member Indian Legislative Assembly for Bombay European Constituency, 1920. *Address :* Chartered Bank Buildings, Karachi, India. *Clubs :* Berkshire (Reading) ; Sind (Karachi). (O9847)

PRICE, Emily Annie, M.B.E. Hon. Sec. of the Lewisham and Blackheath Division Soldiers' and Sailors' Families Association. (M16333)

PRICE, Ernest, M.B.E., *b.* 14 Dec. 1879. Civil Servant ; India Store Depot, India Office. *War Work :* Shipment of war stores to India. *Address :* 5, Beechhill Road, Eltham, S.E. 9. (M864)

PRICE, T. Major Frank, O.B.E., R.A.S.C.

PRICE, George, M.B.E.

PRICE, Henry Gilbert, O.B.E.

PRICE, James Ben, M.B.E.

PRICE, John Glanville, M.B.E., *b.* 1876 ; *s.* of David Griffith Price, of Penmark (Glam.) ; *m.* Harriet, *d.* of George Telford. *Educ.:* Collegiate School, Penarth, Wales. Architect. *War Work :* Building of munition workers' huts and hostels at Woolwich ; Depot Manager for Central Stores Department of the Ministry of Munitions. *Address :* Sandford House. Luton Avenue, Broadstairs. (M9363)

PRICE, Joseph Thomas, M.B.E.

PRICE, Julian Hugh, M.B.E.

PRICE, Percy Howard, O.B.E.

PRICE, Col. Sir Rhys Howell, K.B.E., C.M.G., *b.* 1872 ; only *s.* of Sir Thomas Rees Price, K.C.M.G., of Johannesburg ; *m.* Constance Mary, 3rd *d.* of John M. Peacock, of Queenstown, Cape of Good Hope. Served in S. African War, 1899–1902, with Kaffrarian Rifles, and commanding Border Light Horse (three times mentioned in despatches ; Queen's medal, 4 clasps ;

King's medal, 2 clasps) ; Officer Commanding Union Expeditionary Base, Capetown, Sept. 1914 ; Col., April 1915 ; Director of War Recruiting, Nov. 1916. *Address :* Artillery Barracks, Pretoria, S. Africa. (K191)

PRICE, Richard, M.B.E., *b.* 6 June, 1867 ; *s.* of Richard Price, of Northumberland ; *m.* Louisa Ellen, *s.* of John Lane, of Larkfield. *Educ. :* Scotch School, Woolwich. *War Work :* Director Inspection of Optical Supplies. *Address :* 23, Wrottesley Road, Plumstead, S.E. 18. (M3913)

PRICE, Sydney Reginald, M.B.E. Technical Assistant, H.M. Contracts Section, Explosives Supply Dept., Ministry of Munitions. (M10259h)

PRICE, Lieut.-Comm. Thomas Slater, O.B.E., R.N.V.R.

PRICE, Violet Amelia, Mrs., M.B.E.

PRICE, Capt. Walter Dennis, O.B.E., *b.* 2 Oct. 1895 ; *s.* of W. J. Price, of Bournemouth. *Educ. :* Abingdon. Director of E. Price and Sons, Ltd., Pianoforte Dealers. *War Work :* Mobilised with special service section of Territorial Force, July, 1914 ; served throughout the war with the 1/9th Hampshire Regt. in England, India, and Siberia. *Address :* Handel House, Bournemouth. (O9049)

PRICE, Brig.-Gen. William, C.B., C.M.G., C.B.E., V.D.. *b.* 1864 ; *m.* 1891, Mary, *d.* of the late George Middleton, of Culiss, Ross-shire. Hon. Major in the Army, and Lieut.-Col. R.E. ; sometime Major and Hon. Lieut.-Col. 8th Battn. City of London Regt. ; served in S. Africa, 1899–1902, with Army Post Office Corps (despatches) ; Great War, 1914–18, on Staff (despatches) ; appointed Assist. Private Sec. to Postmaster-Gen. (Rt. Hon. S. C. Buxton, M.P.), 1907 ; Private Sec. to Postmaster-Gen. (Rt. Hon. H. Samuel, M.P.), 1910 ; Director of Army Postal Services, 1913, with rank of Brig.-Gen. *Address :* 21, Emperor's Gate, S.W. (C599)

PRICE, Lieut. William, M.B.E., A.I.F.

PRICE, Lieut. William Alfred, O.B.E., R.N.

PRICE, Lieut. William Edward, O.B.E., T.F.

PRICE, Gertrude, Mrs. STANLEY-, M.B.E. ; *d.* of Dossey Wightman, of Unstone Grange, Derbyshire. *War Work :* Wynberg Base Hospital, Cape Colony ; Superintendent of Vickers' Canteen, Weybridge, Surrey, of Ordnance Hostels Canteen, Coventry, and of Edgewood Hostels, Kent. *Address :* ᵀInstone Grange, Derbyshire. (M3912)

PRICHARD, Alice Maud, Mrs., M.B.E. ; *d.* of J. T. Dugdale, of Ivy Bank, Barnley, Sezincote, Moreton-in-Marsh. *War Work :* Commandant of Red Cross Detachment Glos. 58, which detachment staffed a hospital. *Address :* Donnington Manor, Moreton-in-Marsh. (M2305)

PRICHARD, Lt.-Col. Hubert Cecil, C.B.E., *b.* 1865 ; *s.* of the late Charles John Collins Prichard, of Clifton, Bristol (*see* BURKE's *Landed Gentry*) ; *m.* 1905, Nora Diana, *d.* of Arthur Piero, of 31, Sefton Park Rd., Liverpool. Major and Hon. Lieut.-Col. Glamorganshire Yeomanry ; a J.P. for Glamorgan, and Lord of the Manor of Colwinston. Served in the Great War as Lieut.-Col. (despatches). (C2158)

PRICHARD, Mabel Henrietta, Mrs., M.B.E.

PRICHARD, Richard John, M.B.E., *b.* 28 Sept. 1862 ; *s.* of Richard Prichard, of Holyhead ; *m.* Matilda (who *d.*), *d.* Robert Seed, of Preston. *Educ. :* Beaumaris Grammar School. Chief Engineer, Merchant Service. *War Work :* Aug. 1914, to July, 1915, Engineer-Lieut. R.N.R. H.M.S. "Cambria" attached to Grand Fleet, North Sea ; Aug. 1915, to Oct. 1916, Hospital Ship "Cambria," Englano to various French Ports ; Oct. 1916, to March, 1919, Chief Engineer, Transport "Greenone." *Address :* Llanfair Bach, Holyhead. (M3914)

PRICHARD, Captain Samuel David, M.B.E.

PRICKETT, Major Frederick Cecil, O.B.E., M.C., *b.* 19 Feb. 1895 ; *s.* of William Prickett, of Haverfordwest, Pembrokeshire, South Wales. *Educ :* Sir John Cass's Foundation, in the City of London, E.C. Fruit grower in Victoria and Western Australia ; Freeman of the City of London. *War Work :* Enlisted Aug. 1914, as Rifleman 1/6th Batt. City of London Rifles (T.F.) ; Commissioned Jan. 1916, Durham Light Infantry ; seconded to Command the 93rd Light Trench Mortar Battery from Aug. 1916, to March, 1919 ; proceeded to the British Military Mission, South Russia (General Denikin's Forces), April, 1919, as Chief Instructor Light Trench Mortars ; Evacuated (Typhus), March, 1920 ; thrice mentioned in despatches ; awarded the Russian Order of St. Anne, 2nd and 3rd Class, with Swords ; twice wounded. *Addresses :* c/o Australian Farms, Ltd., 99, King's Street, Melbourne, Australia ; Royal Colonial Institute, Northumberland Avenue, London, S.W. (9748)

PRIDDEN, Edith Mary, O.B.E., W.A.A.C.

PRIDE, Herbert Charles, M.B.E.

PRIDEAUX, Constance Mary, Mrs., O.B.E.

PRIDEAUX, Frank Winckworth Austice, O.B.E.

PRIDEAUX, George Edward, M.B.E., R.N.

PRIDHAM, Lieut.-Col. Geoffrey Robert, D.S.O., O.B.E., C.R.E., *b.* 4 Oct. 1872 ; *s.* of Colonel F. Pridham, of Instow, North Devon ; *m.* Mignonne Muriel Maude, *d.* of C. L. B. Cumming, I.C.S. *Educ. :* Marlborough Coll. ; R.M.A., Woolwich. *War Work :* Service in Gallipoli and France. *Club :* United Service. (O7597)

PRIEST, James Dainer, M.B.E., M.R.C.S.

PRIEST, Joseph, M.B.E., *b.* 9 June, 1874 ; *s.* of Thomas Priest, of Birmingham ; *m.* Agneta Elizabeth, *d.* of William Rowland, of Redhill, Surrey. *Educ. :* Birmingham. Director of F. and C. Osler, Ltd., Birmingham, and late Chairman of the Electricity Committee (Reigate Borough Council). *War*

Work : Engaged in Manufacture of Small Tools for Filling Factories, Aeroplane Parts, etc. ; Member of the Reigate Food Control Committee. *Address* Hatchlands, Redhill, Surrey. (M9368)

PRIESTLEY, Beatrice Ada, O.B.E. Q.M.A.A.C.

PRIESTLEY, Robert Chambers, O.B.E., M.A., M.B. (Camb.), J.P. Bucks., *b.* 1857 ; *s.* of Sir William O. Priestley, of London ; *m.* Ida Mary, *d.* of T. Eustace Smith, M.P., of Newcastle-on-Tyne. *Educ. :* Harrow, and Trinity Coll., Cambridge. *War Work :* Medical Officer, Wycombe V.A.D. Hospital. *Address :* Terriers House, High Wycombe, Bucks. *Clubs :* United University ; Royal Automobile. (O11160)

PRIETLYS, Major William, O.B.E.

PRIME, Capt. Frederick Charles, M.B.E., *b.* 11 Feb. 1869 ; *s.* of the late John Prime, of Needham Market, Suffolk ; *m.* Emma Bessie Fox, *d.* of James Richard Smithson Barnicott, of Sheerness. *Educ. :* Army Schools. late R.A. *War Work :* Served with No. 1 Depot Royal Garrison Artillery, Aug. 1914, to May, 1915 ; joined the Inspection Department, Woolwich, May, 1915, as Assist. to the Director of Inspection of High Explosives, and served in the Dept. until the end of the war. *Address :* 30, Vambery Road, Plumstead Common, London, S.E. 18. (M866)

PRIMROSE, Capt. Alexander Ferguson, O.B.E., R.E. (T.).

PRINCE, Major Charles Edmond, O.B.E., *b.* 9 July, 1874 ; *s.* of the late Rev. E. B. Prince, ot Witham Friary, Bath ; *m.* Amélie Ella Violet, *d.* of C. A. Verner, of War Coppice, Caterham. *Educ. :* Clifton Coll., Faraday House. Technical Manager, Aircraft Dept. Marconi's Wireless Telegraph Co. *War Work :* Originator of the application of Wireless Telephony to aeroplane work, and designer of most of this apparatus used in the war ; seconded from Westmorland and Cumberland Yeomanry to R.A.F., in 1915, for wireless work, and, on formation of Air Force, appointed Officer-in-charge Experimental Section, Wireless Experimental Establishment, R.A.F. *Addresses :* Stubbings Manor, Burchetts Green, Berks. ; 63, Drayton Gardens, S.W. (O3395)

PRINCE, Constance Perrott, M.B.E.

PRINCE, Edwin James, M.B.E., *b.* 1 Oct. 1859 ; *s.* of John Prince, of Romsey, Hampshire ; *m.* Ida Isobella, *d.* of Isaac Mouland, of Nether Wallop. *Educ. :* Privately. Station Superintendent, Waterloo Station, L. & S. W. Rly. *War Work :* Dealt with all Naval and Military traffic in connection with the war. *Address :* Delapre, 2, Howard Road, New Malden, Surrey. (M2307)

PRINGLE, Col. David, C.B.E., T.D. Col. New Zealand Forces ; served in the Great War, 1915–19 (despatches). (C1865)

PRINCE, George, M.B.E., R.N.

PRING, 2nd Lieut. John Nathaniel, M.B.E., R.A.O.C.

PRINGLE, Arthur Young, O.B.E. M.R.C.S., L.R.C.P.

PRINGLE, Lieut.-Col. Charles Herford, O.B.E., A.P.D.

PRINGLE, Ethel Louise, Mrs., M.B.E.

PRINGLE, George Cossar, M.B.E., *b.* 10 Dec. 1858 ; *s.* of George Pringle, of Greenlaw, Berwickshire ; *m.* Annie Hay, *d.* of James Douglas, of Edinburgh. *Educ. :* Greenlaw, and Edinburgh Univ. Late Rector of Peebles Burgh and County High School ; now Organising Sec. Educational Institute of Scotland. *War Work :* Convener of Thrift Sub-Committee of the Educational Institute of Scotland, the Secondary Education Association of Scotland, and the Scottish Class Teachers' Federation ; Member of the Scottish War Savings Committee, and Convener of its Schools Sub-Committee till 1918. *Addresses :* 47, Moray Place ; 120, Polwarth Terrace, Edinburgh. *Club :* Liberal (Edinburgh). (M43)

PRINGLE, James Scott, O.B.E.

PRINGLE, Lieut.-Col. Seton Sidney, O.B.E., R.A.M.C.

PRIOLEAU, Major Lynch Hamilton, M.B.E.

PRIOR, Paymaster-Comm. Cunningham, O.B.E., R.N.

PRIOR, Lieut.-Col. Harold Astley Somerset, O.B.E., D.S.O. Major and T. Lieut.-Col. Comdg. a Battn. Yorkshire Regt. ; served in the Great War, 1914–19 (despatches). (O7602)

PRIOR, Capt. William Henry, M.B.E.

PRISMALL, Lieut.-Col. Edwin, O.B.E., T.D.

PRITCHARD, Charles William, M.B.E., *b.* 1 May, 1870 ; *s.* of Thomas Pritchard, of Sheffield ; *m.* Amy Bell, *d.* of Thomas Braithwaite, of Selby. *Educ. :* Pitsmore, and Sheffield. Surveyor, Loddon and Clavering Rural District Council, Norfolk ; late Resident Engineer to Road Board. *War Work :* Resident Engineer for Construction of Military Camp Road ; Executive Officer, Food Control Committee ; Night Orderly at Local Military Red Cross Hospital. (M9370)

PRITCHARD, Paymaster-Capt. Francis Burnett, C.B.E., R.N. Accountant Officer at Liverpool ; served in the Great War, 1914–19 (despatches). (C2262)

PRITCHARD, Henry Ambrose, O.B.E.

PRITCHARD, Herbert Alfred, M.B.E., F.S.I., *b.* 20 Aug. 1872 ; *s.* of Alfred John Pritchard, of London. *Educ. :* Privately, and St. Paul's. Surveyor ; District Valuer, Cardiff District, Valuation Department, Inland Revenue. *War Work :* Secretary Glamorgan War Agricultural Executive Committee. *Address :* 30, Marlborough Road, Cardiff. (M44)

PRITCHARD, Henry Gibbon, O.B.E.

PRITCHARD, Hugh John Mostyn, O.B.E.

PRITCHARD, Isabel, Mrs., O.B.E. ; *d.* of Henry Leigh Lace, of Cardiff. *War Work :* Served in Women's Legion as Superintendent, April, 1916 ; as Administrator in Women's

Army Auxiliary Force, April, 1917; promoted Controller in Irish Command in Queen Mary's Army Auxiliary Force attached to G.H.Q., Aug. 1917; with demobilised, Dec. 1919. *Address:* The Great House, Llanblethian, Cowbridge, Glam. (O9796)

PRITCHARD, Flight-Lieut. John Edward Maddock, O.B.E., A.F.C., R.A.F.

PRITCHARD, Capt. John Mervyn, O.B.E., *b.* 19 May, 1895; *s.* of John Arthur Pritchard, of London. *Educ.:* Charterhouse, and Oxford. *War Work:* Commissioned, Aug. 1914, 5th R.W. Kent Regt.; India, Dec. 1914, to Dec. 1917; Mesopotamia, Dec. 1917, to Feb. 1919; T. Capt., Sept. 1915; Capt., June, 1916; T. D.A.Q.M.G. 18th Div. Mes. Exp. Force, May and June, 1918; Staff Capt. 51st Inf. Bgde. 17th Div. Mes. Exp. Force, Sept. to Dec. 1918; demobilised, March, 1919. *Address:* c/o Messrs. Grindlay & Co., 54, Parliament Street, S.W. 1. (O6687)

PRITCHARD, Mary Ellen, Mrs., M.B.E., *b.* 18 Feb. 1876; *d.* of Alderman W. Eifl Jones, of Pwllheli; *m.* Hugh Pritchard (who died), Solicitor, Ex-Mayor of Pwllheli. *Educ.:* Pwllheli and Ladies' Collegiate School, Stafford. *War Work:* Hon. Sec. and Hon. Treas. Soldiers' and Sailors' Families Association; Co.-Sec. Pwllheli War Relief Association; Hon. Sec. Pwllheli War Entertainments Committee; Member of Local War Pensions and North Wales Joint Disablement Committees. *Address:* Mount Pleasant, Pwllheli. (M9371)

PRITCHARD, Major Richard Graham, O.B.E., R.E.

PRITCHETT, Theodore, O.B.E.

PRIVETT, Eng.-Lieut. George John, O.B.E., R.N.

PROBERT, Col. William Godfrey, O.B.E., R.A.S.C. (T.).

PROBST, John Charles, O.B.E., *b.* 20 Dec. 1865; *s.* of Peter E. Probst, of Caterham Valley. *Educ.:* St. John's School, Wandsworth. *War Work:* Sub-Commissioner, British Red Cross Society, 1914–20, Havre district. *Address:* Cercle François, Havre. (O11165)

PROBYN, Emily, Lady, O.B.E., *b.* 1867; *d.* of G. Davies, of Bristol; *m.* Sir Leslie, Governor of Jamacia, *s.* of E. Probyn, of Huntley. *Educ.:* Privately. Specially interested in organisations which aim at securing the welfare of young women. *War Work:* Work in connection with the Prince of Wales' National Relief Fund, Queen Mary's Fund, King George's Fund for Sailors, and "The Shower of Gifts." *Address:* King's House, Jamaica. (O1006)

PROCTER, Charles James, O.B.E., J.P., *b.* 5 March, 1850; *s.* of Robert Procter, of Liverpool; *m.* Bertha Evaline, *d.* of William H. Fitz-Hugh, of Liverpool. *Educ.:* Liverpool Coll. Corn Merchant; Freeman of City of Liverpool; J.P. for Liverpool; Director of Liverpool Grain Storage Co.; Director of State Assurance Co.; President Wirral Children's Hospital; President Birkenhead Y.M.C.A. *War Work:* One of initiators of Y.M.C.A. Army work, and actively engaged throughout war in North-Western District; Chairman of Merseyside Dock Canteen Work. *Address:* Boscobel, Oxton, Birkenhead. *Club:* Exchange (Liverpool). (O663)

PROCTER, Capt. Edward, O.B.E., R.E.

PROCTER, George Henderson, O.B.E., J.P.

PROCTER, Helen Matilda, Lady, C.B.E.; *d.* of Lieut.-Col. T. A. Freeman, East Surrey Regt.; *m.* Henry Edward Edleston, *s.* of Charles E. Procter, of Macclesfield. *Educ.:* Cheltenham Ladies' Coll. *War Work:* Chairman of the War Work Department of the Young Women's Christian Association, responsible for the Blue Triangle Hostels, Clubs, Rest and Recreation Rooms and Canteens for Women Workers in England and France. *Addresses:* Ware Hill, Great Amwell, Herts; 15, New Cavendish Street, London, W. 1. (C269)

PROCTER, Sir Henry Edward Edleston, Knt. Bach., C.B.E., *b.* 30 April, 1866; *s.* of Charles Edward Procter, of Macclesfield; *m.* Helen Matilda, *d.* of Lieut.-Col. T. A. Freeman. *Educ.:* Birkenhead School. East Indian Merchant. *War Work:* Hon. Treas. Y.M.C.A. *Address:* Ware Hill, Great Amwell, Herts. *Clubs:* Oriental; Royal Automobile; Byculla (Bombay). (C600)

PROCTOR, Doris Brownsword, M.B.E.

PROCTOR, Sir Philip Bridger, K.B.E., *b.* 1870; *s.* of the late Philip Francis Proctor, of Nightingale Lane, S.W.; *m.* Nellie, *d.* of H. B. Shaul. *Educ.:* St. Paul's. *War Work:* Director of Meat Supplies, Ministry of Food. *Address:* Tilehurst, Furze Hill, Purley. *Club:* St. Stephen's. (K461)

PROCTOR, Capt. Roger Cecil, M.B.E.

PROCTOR, Vernon, M.B.E.; *s.* of the late Robert Proctor, of Sheffield; *m.* Lilian Agnes, *d.* of John Kirby, of Purley, Surrey. *Educ.:* Grammar School, Sheffield. Steel Manufacturer and Merchant. *War Work:* Manufacture of gun forgings and armour plates for tanks, etc. *Address:* Ecclesall, Sheffield. *Club:* Athenæum (Sheffield). (M3916)

PROGER, Harriett Gertrude, Mrs., M.B.E., *b.* 8 Nov. 1865; *d.* of John Waldron, of Moulsford, Berks.; *m.* Thomas William, *s.* of John Guy Proger. *War Work:* Commandant of St. Fagan's V.A.D. Hospital for 4 years. *Address:* Llanmaes, St. Fagan's, near Cardiff. (M2308)

PROSSER, Ernest Albert, C.B.E. General Manager of Taff Vale Railway. (C2887)

PROSSER, Thomas Gilbert, O.B.E., M.R.C.S.

PROSSER, Walter Byron, O.B.E.

PROTHERO, Sir George Walter, K.B.E., Litt.D., LL.D., F.B.A., *b.* 14 Oct. 1848; *s.* of the Rev. Canon Prothero, of Whippingham, I. of Wight; *m.* Mary Frances, *d.* of the Right Rev. Dr. Butcher, Bishop of Meath. *Educ.:* Eton, and King's Coll., Cambridge. Tutor of King's Coll., Camb., 1878–94; Professor of History in the Univ. of Edinburgh, 1894–9;

Editor of the "Quarterly Review" since 1899; Editor of the Camb. Historical Series, and co-Editor of the Camb. Modern History. *War Work:* In conjunction with Henry Cust, founded the Committee for National Patriotic Organisation; wrote three pamphlets concerning the war, and a book "German Policy before the War" (1916); Director of the Historical Section in the Foreign Office, 1917–19; attended the Peace Conference as Historical Adviser to the British Delegation, Feb. to April, 1919. *Address:* 24, Bedford Square, W.C. 1. *Clubs:* Athenæum; Alpine; Rye Golf. (K411)

PROTHEROE, Major Arthur Havard, O.B.E., M.C., R.A.S.C.

PROUD, Lieut. and Qr.-Mr. William, M.B.E.

PROUT, Lieut.-Col. William Thomas, C.M.G., O.B.E., M.B.

PROUT, Major Reginald ADDENBROOKE-, O.B.E., M.C., R.A.F.

PROWER, Ernest Edward, M.B.E., *b.* 4 Au g. 1877; *s.* of John Alfred Prower, of Devon; *m.* Mabel, *d.* of W. G. Sudbury, of Halstead, Essex. Quantity Surveyor. Performed valuable organisation work in connection with the Great War. *Addresses:* Weeton, New Malden, Surrey; 13, South Square, Gray's Inn, W. C. 2. (M867)

PROWSE, Albert Edward, M.B.E., *b.* 5 Feb. 1880; *s.* of Albert Edward Prowse, of Aston Manor, Birmingham; *m.* Annie Marguerite Clare, *d.* of John Alfred Darby, of Sutton Coldfield. *Educ.:* Aston Manor. Fellow of the Surveyors' Institution; Associate of the Auctioneers' Institute; Chevalier de l'ordre de Leopold. *War Work:* Local Representative of the Ministry of Munitions at the temporary village of Elizabethville, built and equipped for the housing of Belgians engaged on Munition Work at the National Projectile Factory, Birtley, Co. Durham. *Addresses:* Lambton House, Birtley, Co. Durham; Ministry of Munitions Estate Offices, Birtley, Co. Durham; and Scotswood, Newcastle-upon-Tyne. (M2309)

PROWSE, John Skardon, M.B.E., B.A., M.B., B.C. (Cantab.), L.M.S.S.A. (London), *b.* 5 May, 1861; *s.* of the late William Prowse, M.R.C.S., of Clifton, Bristol; *m.* Cecilia, *d.* of the late George Cartwright, of Kirmington, Lincs. *Educ.:* Perse School, and Fitzwilliam Hall, Cambridge, and St. Mary's Hospital, London. Physician and Surgeon; Senior Hon. Physician, Hulme Dispensary, Manchester; Hon. Medical Officer, Hulme Day Nursery. *War Work:* Hon. Medical Officer of Basford House Auxiliary Military Hospital, Old Trafford, and of Willow Bank Red Cross Hospital, Moss Side; Anæsthetist, Clyne House Military Hospital, Old Trafford; Member of Manchester Medical War Committee; Recruiting and Pensions Medical Board work throughout the war. *Address:* Oker House, Moss Lane East, Manchester. (M9373)

PRUNELL, Rev. William Alfred, O.B.E., Hon. C.F., *b.* 5 Jan. 1874; *s.* of William Prunell, of Kidderminster; *m.* Hannah Louise, *d.* of Jabez Mather, of Hobart Town, Tasmania. *Educ.:* Didsbury Coll. Wesleyan Minister. *War Work:* Sept. 1915, to Aug. 1916, Senior Chaplain (Wesleyan) at Le Havre, B.E.F.; Aug. 1916, to March, 1918, attached 1st Guards Brigade (Battle of the Somme, 3rd Battle of Ypres, Arras, Cambrai, and advance to Maubeuge, with Guards' Division to Cologne); despatches twice. *Address:* Eastcott House, Swindon. (O2682)

PRUST, Major Robert Bateman, O.B.E.

PRYCE, Major Walter John Dakyns, O.B.E., D.C.M.

PRYCE, Major Wilfred Harry, O.B.E.

PRYN, Sir William Wenmoth, K.B.E., C.B., R.N., *b.* 21 Oct. 1859; *s.* of William Pryn, of Tredown, Saltash; *m.* Isabella Kate, *d.* of Major John Cotter, of The Buffs. *Educ.:* Blundell's School, Tiverton, and Guy's Hospital, London. Surgeon Rear-Admiral (retired). *War Work:* Deputy Surgeon-Gen. in charge of Royal Naval Hospital, Gibraltar, 1912–16; Surgeon Rear-Admiral in charge of Royal Naval Hospital, Plymouth, 1917–19. *Address:* Yeoland, Yelverton, S. Devon. (K258)

PRYNNE, Col. Harold Vernon, C.B.E., D.S.O., F.R.C.S., A.M.S., *b.* 1869. Served in China, 1900 (medal with clasp); Great War, 1914–17 (despatches). (C1307)

PRYOR, Ethne Philippa, Mrs., M.B.E., *b.* 19 Jan. 1886; *d.* of Sir Norman Moore, Bart., M.D., of 67, Gloucester Place, London, W., and Hancox, Battle, Sussex; *m.* Lieut.-Col. Walter Marlborough Pryor, D.S.O., of Weston Stevenage; of the late Marlborough Robert Pryor, of Weston. *Educ.:* Privately. *War Work:* Hon. Sec. Royal Air Force Prisoners' Fund, 1915–19. *Address:* Weston, Stevenage, Herts. *Club:* Empress. (M2310)

PRYOR, Capt. William, M.B.E.

PRYSE, Nina Katherine Webley PARRY-, O.B.E.

PRYTHERCH, Henry James, M.B.E.

PUCKLE, Emily Alice, M.B.E.

PUDDEY, Henry, M.B.E.

PUDDICOMBE, John, M.B.E.

PUGH, Col. Archibald John, O.B.E.

PUGH, Capt. George Wilfred, O.B.E., R.A.O.C.

PUGH, Prof. William John, O.B.E., *b.* 28 July, 1892; *s.* of John Pugh, of Westbury, Shrewsbury; *m.* Manon Clayton, *d.* of J. Davies Bryan, of Alexandria, Egypt. *Educ.:* Univ. Coll. of Wales, Aberystwyth. Professor of Geology, Univ. Coll. of Wales, Aberystwyth. *War Work:* Served with 4th (Reserve) Batt. Royal Welsh Fusiliers, 2nd Batt. Royal Welsh Fusiliers, and later attached to General Staff, 2nd and 4th Army H.Q.; has French Croix de Guerre; twice mentioned in despatches. *Address:* Geological Department, University College of Wales, Aberystwyth. (O2683)

PUGH, 2nd Lieut. William Peter Boulton, M.B.E., R.A.F.

PULFORD, Major Conway Walker Heath, O.B.E. R.A.F.

PULFORD, William John, O.B.E.

PULHAM, Capt. Frederick Bygrave, O.B.E. R.A.F.

PULLAR, Major George Douglas, O.B.E., T.D., b. 6 Feb. 1883 ; s. of Alfred Pullar, M.D., of Edinburgh. *Educ.*: Dulwich Coll. *War Work*: Served in France and Belgium with the 6th Batt. Black Watch (R.H) in the 51st (Highland) Division, and subsequently on the staff of the 61st Division. *Address*: Lyndhurst, Oakcroft Road, Blackheath, S.E. 13.
(O5697)

PULLAR, Capt. John Lindsay, O.B.E.

PULLIBLANK, Engineer-Comm. John, D.S.O., O.B.E., R.N., b. 1879 ; s. of the late Rev. Canon Joseph Pulliblank, Rector of Rampisham, Dorset. *War Work*: 1914–19, with Dover Patrol, and at Vladivostock (despatches twice). (O9572)

PULLING, Rev. Edward Herbert, O.B.E., b. 1859 ; s. of lthe Rev. F. W. Pulling, Vicar of Pinhoe, Devonshire ; *m.* Emily Frances, *e.d.* of Oswald Cornish Arthur, and Mrs. Arthur, of Wellsbourne, Compton Gifford, Plymouth. *Educ.*: Royal Academy, Gosport ; Oxford Univ. ; Salisbury Theological Coll. Vicar of Morgan's Vale. *War Work*: Senior Chaplain, Portsmouth Command ; Senior Chaplain, Humber Garrison and Lincolnshire Coast Defences ; Y.M.C.A. work. *Address*: The Vicarage, Morgan's Vale, Salisbury. *Club*: Church Imperial.
(C1747)

PULLINGER, Dorothee Aurelie Marianne, M.B.E., b. 13 Jan. 1894; *d.* of T. C. W. Pullinger, C.B.E., J.P., (q.v.) of Dumfries. *Educ.*: Loughborough High School, and in France. Engineer. *War Work*: Lady Supt., Messrs. Vickers, Ltd., Barrow-in-Furness, during the whole period of the war. *Address*: The Brae, near Dumfries, Scotland. (M9377)

PULLINGER, Thomas Charles Willis, C.B.E., J.P., b. 1867 ; s. of Fleet-Paymaster Thomas Pinfold Pullinger, R.N., of Wyvenhoe, Dartford ; *m.* 1893, Aurélie Bernice Sitwell, of St. Nicholas, D'Aliumont, Seine Inférieur, France. Managing Director, Arrol Johnston (Limited) of Dumfries, and a Director of Galloway Engineering Co., of Tougland, Kirkcudbright. *Address*: The Brae, nr. Dumfries. *Clubs*: Royal Automobile ; Royal Scottish Automobile ; Royal Clyde Yacht ; Conservative (Glasgow). (C2888)

PULLMAN, Major Gerald Cozens, O.B.E., M.A. (Oxon.), b. 10 May, 1885 ; s. of Henry Pullman, J.P., of 64, Oakwood Court, Kensington, W. 19. *Educ.*: Uppingham, and St. John's Coll., Oxford. Solicitor ; Member of the firm of Nicholson, Graham, and Jones, Solicitors, 24, Coleman Street, E.C. ; served in 6th Batt. East Surrey Regt. (T.A.) *War Work*: Mobilised with Territorial Force, Aug. 1914 ; served with Regiment in India, Dec. 1914, to July, 1916 ; with Aden Field Force, March, 1917, to April, 1919. Staff Appointments : Acting G.S.O. (2nd Grade), 2nd (Rawal Pindi) Division, India ; Acting Brigade Major, Rawal Pindi (Infantry Brigade) ; Staff Capt. and Acting Brigade Major, Aden (Infantry)Brigade ; D.A.A.G. Aden Field Force ; twice mentioned in despatches. *Addresses*: 64, Oakwood Court, Kensington, W. 14 ; 24, Coleman Street, E.C. 2. *Club*: Junior Army and Navy.
(O6823)

PUNCHARD, John Alfred, O.B.E., b. 2 Sept. 1858. Cashier, South Eastern and Chatham Railway. *War Work*: Organised and was in charge of the exchange of foreign money during the war for British, Colonial, and Belgian troops arriving at Victoria Station on leave ; the total exchange amounted to nearly £15,000,000 ; this work was undertaken in addition to ordinary duties as cashier of S.E. & C. Rly. *Address*: Bramble Tor, South Croydon. (O11168)

PUNTIS, Major Walter Ernest, O.B.E.

PURCELL, Col. Matthew Henry, O.B.E., R.E. (retired), b. 15 July, 1845 ; s. of Admiral Edward Purcell, of 13, Camden Crescent, Bath ; *m.* Caroline Mary, *d.* of Richard Westmacott, R.A., of 1, Kensington Gate, London, S.W. *Educ.*: Bath, and Royal Military Academy, Woolwich. Employed on Ordnance Survey of Great Britain from April, 1877, to April, 1883 ; Professor of Fortification and Geometry at Royal Military Academy, Woolwich, 1890 to 1893 ; Acting Colonial Engineer at Gibraltar, 1896–97. *War Work*: Worked for Westminster Division of the Soldiers' and Sailors' Families Association from Aug. 1914, to July, 1916, and for Admiralty in the Elswick Works, Newcastle-on-Tyne, as Temporary Assistant Inspector of Steel from Dec. 1917, to May, 1919. *Address*: The White House, Ferring, Goring-on-Sea, Sussex. *Club*: Junior United Service. (O11169)

PURCELL, Capt. Thomas Edwin, M.B.E.

PURCHAS, Frederick Hayden, M.B.E., b. 1861 ; s. of William Henry Purchas, of Wakefield ; *m.* Mary, *d.* of Robert Gilliat, of Oldham and Eccles, Lancashire. *Educ.*: Wakefield. Journalist, formerly proprietor "Dewsbury District News," and "Batley News," now Editor "Country Gentleman's Estate Magazine " and " Estate Book " ; Manager Land Agency, Farm Management, and Farm Accountancy Departments for the Country Gentleman's Association, Limited. *War Work*: Senior Stores Officer, Bolton Shell Inspection Board ; subsequently made Superintendent of the Manchester-Barrow area in charge of all the Bonds and Stores ; Organiser of School for Stores Officers, School for lady clerks ; inventor of shell painting machines. *Address*: 26, Balaclava Road, Surbiton. *Clubs*: Cocoa Tree ; Farmers'. (M869)

PURDIE, Rev. Albert Bertrand, O.B.E., b. 27 Aug. 1888 ;

s. of Arthur Purdie, of London. *Educ.*: St. Edmund's, Old Hall, and Christ's Coll., Cambridge. *War Work*: Joined Army in Aug. 1914 ; served in France and Balkans, 1915–19 ; Senior R.C. Chaplain of British Salonika Force ; Order of St. Sava (3rd class) ; mentioned in despatches. *Address*: St. Edmund's House, Cambridge. (O3059)

PURDOM, John Ritchie, O.B.E., J.P., Capt. late Border Rifle Volunteers, Roxburghshire, b. 27 Sept. 1862 ; s. of the late Thomas Purdom, of Hawick, Scotland ; *m.* Annie Hume (who died), *d.* of the late Alexander Rutherford Turnbull, of Hawick. *Educ.*: Privately, and Edinburgh Univ. Solicitor and Banker ; Joint Town Clerk of Hawick ; Chairman Local War Pensions Committee ; President of Council of Juvenile Organisations. *War Work*: Local Recruiting Officer (unpaid) and Clerk to Local Recruiting Tribunal ; Hon. Sec. and Treas. to many local War Charities ; Hon. Sec. War Memorial. *Address*: Langheugh, Hawick, Scotland. *Club*: Border.
(O11170)

PURDON, Lieut. Alick, O.B.E., R.N.R.

PURDON, Lieut. Henry Maurice Chidley, O.B.E., R.N.

PURDON, Col. Richard Ireland, C.B.E. Lieut.-Col. in the Army during the Great War, 1914–19. (C2052)

PURDUE, Lieut. Harry Roy, M.B.E., b. 9 Sept. 1887 ; s. of George Henry Purdue, of Surbiton ; *m.* Edith Annie, *d.* of the late F. Dexter, of Northampton. Sec. Imports and Transport Board, Ministry of Food. *War Work*: Joined 21st County of London Regiment 10 Aug. 1914; won Commission in the Field, Aug. 1916 ; served in France, Belgium, Salonika, and Serbia ; relinquished commission, March, 1918 ; appointed Assist. Sec., Inter-Allied Meat and Fats Executive, and afterwards Sec., Imports and Transport Board, Ministry of Food. (M9379)

PURDY, Col. James Robert, C.B.E., V.D. Col. New Zealand Forces ; served in the Great War, 1915–19 (despatches).
(C1866)

PURDY, William Frank, O.B.E.

PUREFOY, Adm. Richard Purefoy, C.B.E., M.V.O., J.P., b. 26 May, 1862 ; s. of Richard Purefoy FitzGerald ; *m.* Mary Lillias, *d.* of the Rev. F. G. Sandys Lumsdaine, of Blancrue Edronn, Berwickshire, N.B. *Educ.*: Royal Navy. J.P., Co. Bucks, and Co. Southampton. *War Work*: Naval Service, 1914–15 ; Naval Attaché, The Hague, 1916–18 ; Special Service (Convoy), 1918–19. *Address*: Shalstone Manor, Buckingham. *Club*: Army and Navy. (C1202)

PURNELL, Edward Kelly, M.B.E., M.A., F.R.Hist.Soc., b. 1849 ; s. of the late W. A. Purnell, Physician General, Bombay Army ; *m.* Elizabeth, *d.* of C. J. Geldard, of Settle. *Educ.*: Wellington and Cambridge. Assist. Master, Wellington Coll. *War Work*: Served at Admiralty, Foreign Office, and Ministry of Shipping ; Sec., Greek Ships Committee, and temp. Assist. Master Eton Coll. *Address*: North Hill, Windlesham, Surrey. *Club*: United Univ. (M9380)

PURNELL, William Ralph, O.B.E., A.L.C.M., b. 11 Nov. 1885 ; s. of H. A. Purnell, of Edinburgh and Glasgow ; *m.* Elizabeth Hogg, M.A., *d.* of Robert Hogg Miller, of Glasgow. *Educ.*: Glasgow. *War Work*: 1914–15, Chief Draughtsman with the Glasgow Steel Roofing Co., Ltd., engaged on steel construction for the several Government departments ; 1915–16, Superintending Engineer for same firm, erecting large airship sheds ; 1916–17, Confidential Assistant to Managing Director of same firm, engaged wholly upon Government work ; Jan. 1918–19, Chief Engineer in charge of Administration and Control of Construction on Marine Stations, Air Ministry, in Great Britain, Ireland, Northern France, and the Mediterranean. *Address*: 46, Kersland Street, Glasgow. (O11171)

PURSER, Major Arthur William, O.B.E., R.F.A. *Educ.*: Marlborough, and R.M. Academy. *War Work*: Served in the R.F.A. (O7605)

PURSER, Francis C., O.B.E. *Educ.*: Galway, and Dublin Univ. *Address*: 32, Fitzwilliam Place, Dublin. *Club*: University (Dublin). (O7606)

PURSLEW, Samuel, M.B.E.

PURSSELL, Francis William, M.B.E.

PURSSELL, Richard Stanley, O.B.E.

PURVES, Major Thomas Fortune, O.B.E., R.E.

PURVIS, Bertha Maud Isabella, M.B.E. ; *d.* of Gilbert Purvis, of Walliscote, Torquay. *Educ.*: Privately. *War Work*: Hon. organiser and head of the War Hospital Supply Depot, Torquay, from its commencement, July, 1915, till its close in Dec. 1918, which included 600 members and supplied over 100 hospitals at home and abroad. *Address*: Walliscote, Torquay. (M9383)

PURVIS, Isabelle Marie, Mrs., M.B.E.

PURVIS, Col. John Spottiswoode, C.B.E., R.E., b. 1864 ; Served in S. Africa, 1900–1 (Queen's medal with two clasps ; King's medal with two clasps) ; Great War, 1914–19 (despatches). (C1748)

PURVIS, William Frederick, M.B.E.

PUTNAM, William Clarke, M.B.E.

PUTT, Paymaster-Comm. William Pearce, O.B.E., R.N.

PUTTOCK, Muriel, Mrs., M.B.E., B.A. (Hons. Lond.), b. 16 Sept. 1888 ; *d.* of the Rev. John Wilson, M.B.E., D.D., of Woolwich ; *m.* Harold, s. of George S. Puttock, of Exmouth. *Educ.*: Greenwich and Bedford Coll., London. *War Work*: Superintendent of the staff of 900 women at the office of the Public Trustee, including the section engaged in the Trading with the Enemy Dept. ; also worked for Y.M.C.A. and Munition Girls' Club. *Address*: Desswood, Oakes, Huddersfield.
(M9385)

PYBUS, Percy John, C.B.E., b. 1880; s. of John Pybus, of Kingston-on-Hull. Electrical Engineer and Joint Managing Director of English Electric Co., Ltd., of Bradford; rendered services to Labour Supply Depart. Ministry of Munitions, during the Great War; author of various pamphlets on educational and social subjects. Addresses: Bradford, Yorkshire; 9, Whitehall Court, S.W. 1. Clubs: Cavendish; Royal Automobile. (C59)

PYGALL, Frank Thomas, M.B.E.

PYKE, Cyril Cameron, O.B.E.

PYKE, Harold Reason, O.B.E., LL.D., b. 29 Sept. 1887; s. of Joseph Pyke, of Reading; m. Theodora Vera, d. of the late Edward William Austin, of Bridgnorth. Educ.: Christ's Hospital, and King's Coll., London. Solicitor; Commissioner for Oaths. War Work: Temporary Clerk at the Foreign Office (Ministry of Blockade), 1916–19; Author of "The Law of Contraband of War" (Oxford Univ. Press, 1915). Addresses: Bankside, Upper Tooting Park, S.W. 17; 218, Strand, W.C. 2; 240, Lavender Hill, S.W. 11. (O11173)

PYKE, Capt. William Thomas, M.B.E.

PYLE, Lieut.-Col. George-Elliot, O.B.E.; s. of T. T Pyle, J.P., of Earsdon, Northumberland; m. Lurline, d. of Col. J. E. Varty-Rogers, of H.M. Bodyguard. War Work: Commanded Territorial Batt. 1914–19. Address: 19, Onslow Gardens, S.W. Club: Junior United Service. (O7608)

PYM, Major Charles Evelyn, O.B.E.

PYM, Major Frederick Harry Morris, C.M.G., O.B.E.

PYMAN, Elizabeth, M.B.E., b. 9 Nov. 1892; d. of F. H. Pyman, of 82, Fitzjohn's Avenue, Hampstead. Masseuse. War Work: Assisted in running Hawkstone Park Convalescent Hospital for Officers, April, 1916, to July, 1918; trained as masseuse and worked in that capacity during the year 1919, both in London and West Hartlepool. Address: 82, Fitzjohn's Avenue, Hampstead, N.W. (M9387)

PYNE, Capt. Frederick Dennis, O.B.E., R.E. (T.)

QUARMBY, Herbert Henry, O.B.E., b. 9 Jan. 1883; s. of Charles Quarmby, of Horbury, Wakefield; m. Jessie Symes, d. of the late Christopher James Fry. Educ.: Spalding Grammar School, First-Class Establishment and Accounts Officer, Foreign Office. War Work: Responsible for establishments dealing with the carrying out of the Blockade. Address: Parkhurst, 38, Bridport Road, Thornton Heath, Surrey. (O11174)

QUANN, John James, M.B.E.

QUARTLEY, Lieut. Arthur Gilbert, M.B.E.

QUASS, Phineas, O.B.E., b. 6 Aug. 1891; s. of Michael Quass. Educ.: Univ. Coll. School, and St. John's Coll., Cambridge. Barrister-at-Law; sometime Macmahon Law Student, Whewell Scholar in International Law in the Univ. of Cambridge, and holder of the Bar Studentship. War Work: Served in Admiralty and Ministry of Shipping, and later in Ministry of Food, successively as Assistant Director of Statistics, Director of Requirements, and Assistant Legal Adviser. Address: 2 Paper Bldngs., Temple, London, E.C. 4. (O11175)

QUAYLE, Lieut.-Col. Edwin, M.B.E., R.A.M.C.

QUAYLE, John, O.B.E., b. 30 Aug. 1876; s. of Thomas Quayle, of Peel, Isle of Man, and Liverpool; m. Jane, d. of Joseph Pattinson, of Maryport (Cumberland), and Liverpool. Educ.: Liverpool. Chief Engineer, Mercantile Marine. War Work: Employed as Chief Engineer in the following vessels of the Elder and Fyffe Steamship Company during whole of war period, viz: "Barranca," "Reventazon," "Aracataca," "Matina," "Manzanares," and thus completing forty-one Atlantic voyages between Aug. 1914, and the Armistice, in these ships. Address: Canonby, 8, Oxford Avenue, Bootle, Liverpool. (O3875)

QUELCH, Arthur Temple, O.B.E., B.Sc. (Lond.), M.I.Mech.E., A.M.I.N.A., b. 28 Nov. 1874; s. of Robert James Quelch, of London; m. Wilhelmina Alice, d. of John Ball, of Swansea. Educ.: City of London School, and Univ. Coll., London. Works Manager, The Manganese Bronze and Brass Co., Ltd. War Work: The production of propellers for ships of His Majesty's Navy, and many other special castings in manganese bronze. Addresses: 41, Breakspears Road, Brockley, S.E. 4; St. David's Wharf, Westferry Road, Millwall, E. 14. (O1784)

QUENNELL, Robert William, O.B.E., M.R.C.S.

QUEST, Arthur Charles, O.B.E.

QUICK, Lieut. Abraham, M.B.E.

QUICK, Eliza Ellen, Mrs., M.B.E.

QUICK, Henry James, M.B.E.

QUICK, Sidney Curtis, M.B.E.

QUILTER, Major Eustace Cuthbert, O.B.E.

QUILTER, Joseph Rogers, M.B.E., F.C.I.S., b. 1865; s. of William Quilter, of Chelmsford, Essex. Educ.: Chelmsford. Chartered Secretary. War Work: Assisted variously in Government departments. Addresses: 104–6, Newgate Street, London, E.C.; Lerryn, Sutton, Surrey. (M871)

QUIN, Major Charles Frederick Talbot Wyndham, O.B.E.

QUINAN, Major Edward Pellew, O.B.E., 27th Punj., I.A. (O11764)

QUINCEY, George, M.B.E., R.N.

QUINN, George Edwin Walter, M.B.E.

QUINN, Major John James, M.B.E., b. 9 Aug. 1875; s. of John James Quinn; m. Geraldine Winifred, d. of Richard

George Moore. Educ.: St. Fidelis's School, Mussoorie, India. Major, Royal Army Service Corps. War Work: At Profession; also specially employed on the introduction of Automatic Machine Bakeries into the Army. Club: The United R.A.S.C. (M5753)

QUIRK, Capt. Edward John Joseph, M.B.E.

QUIRKE, Capt. Raymond Fitzwilliam, O.B.E., R.G.A. (S.R.), Professional Associate of Surveyors' Institution, F.R.H.S., b. 10 April, 1889; s. of William Michael Quirke, of Clonmel, Co. Tipperary, Ireland, and Hove, Sussex, England. Educ.: Privately. Surveyor to the Wick Estate, Hove, Sussex; Assistant Quantity Surveyor on the Staff of the Ministry of Agriculture and Fisheries. War Work: Enlisted 2/1st Sussex Yeomanry, Sept. 1914; transferred to Inns of Court O.T.C., Aug. 1915; Commissioned R.G.A. (S.R.) on July, 1916; R.G.A., Sheerness, 1917–18; carried out experimental flying tests with R.A.E., Farnborough, and R.A.F.; appointed Liaison Officer with the R.A.F. and attached to General Staff G.H.Q., Great Britain, 22 Aug. 1918; Addresses: 5, Shepherd Market, Curzon Street, Mayfair, W.; 22, Compton Avenue, Brighton, Sussex. (O7610)

RABAGLIATI, Major Duncan Silvestro, O.B.E., B.Sc. M.R.C.V.S., R.V.S., b. 31 July, 1880; s. of A. C. F. Rabagliati, of Bradford, Yorkshire; m. Lucy Evershed, d. of the late Thomas Dale, or Scoughall, North Berwick. Educ.: Bradford Grammar School, and Edinburgh Univ. Director, Serum Institute, Ministry of Agriculture, Egyptian Government. War Work: Capt. R.A.V.C., Feb. to Aug. 1916; Major, R.A.V.C., Aug. 1916, to July, 1919; O.C. No. 1 Camel Veterinary Hospital, E.E.F. Address: Fidra, Zeitoun, Egypt. Club: Turf, Cairo; and Silvesto Rabagliati. (O6274)

RABAN, Brig.-Gen. Sir Edward, K.C.B., K.B.E., late R.E., b. 8 Aug. 1850; s. of Major-Gen. H. Raban, of Bengal Staff Corps; m. Edith, e.d. of Col. H. W. P. Welman. Educ.: Sherborne; R.M.A., Woolwich. Address: 35, Elm Park Gardens, S.W. 10. Club: United Service. (K302)

RABBIT, Edward Joseph, O.B.E.

RABINO, Hyacinth Louis, O.B.E., b. 17 July, 1877; s. of Joseph Rabino (di Borgomale). H.B.M. Consul, Casablanca, Morocco. Address: 33, St. George's Road, Eccleston Square, London, S.W. 1. (O1177)

RACKHAM, Lieut. George John, M.B.E.

RACTLIFFE, Dorothy Mary, M.B.E., b. Dec. 1890; d. of William Ractliffe, of Preston, Cirencester. War Work: Assistant Commandant and Qr.-Mr. at the Cirencester Red Cross Hospital for two years; was in Salonika for ten months with the British Red Cross as Invalid Cook; afterwards joining the Scottish Women's Hospital (Dr. Elsie Inglis Unit) and going with them to Macedonia and Serbia for one year. Address: Preston, Cirencester, Glos. (M9388)

RADCLIFF, Capt Arthur Samuel, O.B.E., R.A.S.C., S.R.

RADCLIFFE, Major Arthur S., O.B.E.; s. of W. P. Radcliff, of Hurdlestown, Kells. War Work: Gazetted 2nd Lieut., Aug. 1914 (Special Reserve); served overseas, France, from Dec. 1914, to May, 1920; mentioned in despatches, Dec. 1918; awarded O.B.E., Jan. 1919 (Military Division). (O2685)

RADCLIFFE, Cecily, Mrs., O.B.E.

RADCLIFFE, Frank, O.B.E., M.B., Ch.B.

RADCLIFFE, Lieut.-Col. Frederick Walter, C.M.G., C.I.E., C.B.E., p.s.c., commanding 2nd Bn., The Dorsetshire Regt., b. 25 Jan. 1873; s. of Gen. G. T. Radcliffe, of Leamside, Leamington, Warwickshire; m. Mabel Gertrude, d. of Frederic Steward, of Lincoln's Inn. Educ.: Leamington Coll.; R.M.C. Sandhurst. 2nd Lieut., the Dorsetshire Regt., March, 1894; Chief of Police, Crete, 1898–99; S. African War, 1899–1902, on Staff; held several Staff appointments; Lieut.-Col. 2nd Dorsetshire Regt., Oct. 1918. War Work: Mesopotamia, 1914–15; commanded 2nd Dorset Regt.; severely wounded at capture of Kut-el-Amara, Sept. 1915; G.S.O. 2 and G.S.O. 1, 58th Division; Assist. Commandant, R.M.C., 1916–17; France, 1917–19; Brig.-Gen.; Officier Legion of Honour (France). Addresses: The Bourne, Camberley; c/o Cox & Co., Charing Cross. Clubs: Junior Army and Navy; Cecil. (C1308)

RADCLIFFE, John, M.B.E.

RADCLIFFE, Robert, M.B.E., b. 28 Oct. 1868; s. of Capt. R. Radcliffe, of St. Agnes, Cornwall; m. Johannah, d. of Leonard Rogers, of St. Agnes. Educ.: St. Agnes, and Culham Coll., Oxford. Schoolmaster; Ex-President, N.U.T. (Cornwall County Association); Representative to the National Assembly; Member of the Hayle Urban District Council; Advanced Liberal; ardent Wesleyan. War Work: Sec. of the Local War Savings Association, Hayle; Member of Hayle Tribunal; E.O. of Local Food Control Committee. Address: 16, Penpol Road, Hayle, Cornwall. (M9389)

RADCLIFFE, Major Seymour Arthur DELME-, O.B.E.

RADCLYFFE, Major Charles Raymond, C.B.E., D.S.O., R.A.S.C. (C3125)

RADFORD, Beatrice Letitia May, Mrs., O.B.E.

RADFORD, Dorothy, Mrs., M.B.E., b. 8 Sept. 1887; d. of Capt. J. A. H. Green, C.B.E., of Nottingham; m. William Ernest, s. of F. R. Radford, of Nottingham. Educ.: Privately. War Work: Hon. Qr.-Mr. General Hospital, Nottingham (300 beds), from Oct. 1914, to March, 1919. Address: 35, Lucknow Drive, Nottingham. (M2317)

RADFORD, Joseph Charles, M.B.E.

RADFORD, Lily Anne, Mrs., M.B.E.

RADNOR, Jacob, Earl of, C.I.E., C.B.E., T.D., additional

A.D.C. to the King, J.P., *b.* 8 July, 1868 ; *s.* of William, 5th Earl of Radnor ; *m.* Julian Eleanor Adelaide, *d.* of Charles Balfour, of Newton Don. *Educ.:* Harrow ; Trinity Coll., Cambridge. Alderman, Wilts County Council ; Chairman, Wilts Standing Joint Committee ; Chairman, Wilts T.F. Association. *War Work:* Commanded 4th Batt. Wilts Regt., 1914 ; Col. Dehra Dun Bde., India, April, 1915, to April, 1917 (Brig.-Gen.) ; Commanding 52nd Grad. Batt. Notts and Derby Regt., 1917 ; Director Agricultural Production, B.E.F., Jan. 1918–19. *Addresses:* Longford Castle, Salisbury ; Cliff House, Sandgate, Kent. *Clubs:* Carlton ; St. Stephen's. (C1309)

RADSTOCK, Granville George, Lord, C.B.E., *b.* 1 Sept. 1859 ; *s.* of 3rd Baron Radstock, of Castletown (*see* BURKE'S *Peerage*). *Educ.:* Repton School ; Trinity Coll., Cambridge. *War Work:* With Y.M.C.A. during the War. *Address:* Mayfield, Woolston, Hants. *Club:* National. (C601)

RAE, Alexander Frederick, M.B.E.

RAE, Major James Gordon, O.B.E., I.A.

RAE, Sir James Robert, K.B.E. Master Mercantile Marine. *Address:* 73, Caledonia Road, Saltcoats, Scotland. (K412)

RAEBURN, Sir Ernest Manifold, K.B.E., *b.* 13 Dec. 1878 ; *s.* of Sir W. H. Raeburn, M.P., of Woodend, Helensburgh, N.B. ; *m.* Greta Mary Alison, *d.* of Eng.-Capt. James H. Watson, R.N., *Educ.:* Kelvinside Academy. Shipowner. *War Work:* Advisory capacity, Transport Dept., 1915 ; Private Sec. Shipping Controller, 1916 ; Advisory capacity, Washington, 1917 ; Assistant Director, British Ministry of Shipping, New York, 1918 ; Director-General, British Ministry of Shipping, New York, 1919–20. *Address:* Auchengower, Helensburgh, Dumbartonshire. *Clubs:* Caledonian ; Royal Societies' ; Conservative, Glasgow. (K413)

RAEBURN, Ernest Manifold, C.B.E. Director of Transport Depart. Ministry of Shipping. (K413)

RAEBURN, William Norman, C.B.E., M.A., LL.B., K.C., *b.* 1877 ; *s.* of Sir William H. Raeburn, M.P., of Woodend, Helensburgh, N.B. ; *m.* Mary Irene, *d.* of Frederick Lennard, of Hove. *Educ.:* Kelvinside Academy, Glasgow ; Uppingham School ; Glasgow Univ. Barrister. *War Work:* Served as assistant to H.M. Procurator-General, and Treasury Solicitor. *Addresses:* 5, Paper Buildings, Temple, E.C. ; The Mount, St. John's, Woking. *Clubs:* Union ; Woking Golf. (C2890)

RAFFETY, Harold V., O.B.E.

RAFFLES, Capt. Stamford Cecil, O.B.E., R.A.F.

RAFTER, Charles Haughton, C.B.E.

RAGLAN, George FitzRoy Henry Somerst, Lord, G.B.E., C.B., J.P., D.L., *b.* 18 Sept. 1857 ; *s.* of Richard, 2nd Lord Raglan (*see* BURKE'S *Peerage*) ; *m.* Lady Ethel Ponsonby, *d.* of Walter, 7th Earl of Bessborough (*see* BURKE'S *Peerage*). *Educ.:* Eton ; Sandhurst. Page of Honour to Queen Victoria, 1868–74 ; late Capt. Grenadier Guards ; late Lieut.-Col. R. Monmouthshire R.E. Militia ; now Hon. Col. R. Monmouthshire R.E., Special Reserve ; Under Sec. of State for War, 1900–02, *War Work:* Lieut.-Governor, Isle of Man. *Addresses:* Cefntilla Court, Usk ; 24, Sloane Gardens, S.W. 1. *Clubs:* Guards ; Carlton ; Royal Automobile. (G43)

RAHILLY, Major John Maurice Bisdec, O.B.E., M.B., R.A.M.C.

RAIKES, Ernest Barkley, O.B.E.

RAIKES, Francis Edward, M.V.O., O.B.E.

RAIKES, Henry St. John Digby, C.B.E., J.P., D.L., *b.* 23 Dec. 1863 ; *s.* of The Right Hon. Henry Cecil Raikes, M.P., of Llwynegrin Hall, Flintshire ; *m.* Annie Lucinda, *d.* of Gen. D. H. MacKinnon, of 16th Lancers. *Educ.:* Charterhouse ; Trin. Coll., Cambridge. Recorder of King's Lynn ; Chairman of Derbyshire Quarter Sessions. *War Work:* Chairman, Derbyshire War Savings Committee ; Chairman, Div. II., Derbyshire Military Appeal Tribunal ; Member Coal Supplies Committee for Midlands. *Addresses:* 10, Eccleston Square, S.W. 1 ; 4, Paper Buildings, Temple, E.C. 4 ; Makeney Lodge, Derbyshire ; Llwynegrin Hall, Flintshire. *Club:* Carlton. (C2892)

RAIKES, Hilda, Mrs., M.B.E.

RAIKES, Hilda Taunton, M.B.E.

RAIKES, Capt. Kenneth Cochrane, O.B.E., *b.* 9 May, 1889 ; *s.* of Francis Walter Raikes, J.P., of Malpas. Newport, Mon. ; *m.* Sybil, *d.* of the late William Slater Boddington, of Manchester. *Educ.:* Shrewsbury School, and Keble Coll., Oxford. Barrister-at-law (not practising) ; Assistant Works Manager, Cordes (Dos Works), Ltd., Newport, Mon. *War Work:* Capt., 1st Monmouthshire Regt., France ; Staff Capt. and D.A.Q.M.G., General Headquarters, France. *Address:* Ferncliffe, Stow Park, Newport, Mon. *Club:* Vincent's, Oxford. (O2686)

RAIKES, Lieut.-Col. Richard, O.B.E., Can. A.M.C.

RAIKES, Capt. Robert Cecil Montague, O.B.E., R.A.

RAIKES, Lieut. Wm. Oswell, O.B.E., R.A.F.

RAILTON, James, C.B.E., *b.* 10 May, 1863 ; *s.* of the late James Railton, of Malpas, Mon. ; *m.* Margery, *d.* of Llewellyn Wood, J.P., of Gardenhurst, Penarth. *Educ.:* Privately. Director of Topham, Jones and Railton, Ltd. ; Alto Parana Development Co., Ltd. *War Work:* Submarine defence at Scapa Flow ; Erection of Explosive Factories, etc. ; various works in France. *Address:* St. Leonards, Windsor. *Clubs:* Union ; St. Stephen's. (C270)

RAINBOW, Wm. Thomas, O.B.E.

RAINE, 2nd Lieut. John Charles, M.B.E., R.A.F.

RAINE, William Stephenson, M.B.E., *b.* 10 Jan. 1880 ; *s.* of William Raine, of Newcastle-on-Tyne ; *m.* Eleanor Annie,

d. of E. A. Bance, of Woolton Hill, Newbury. *Educ.:* High School, Stockton-on-Tees. Engineer and Surveyor to the Hungerford District Counicl. *War Work:* Hon. Executive Officer to Hungerford and District Food Control Committee ; Propaganda work in connection with Economy and other War Emergency Committees. *Address:* Hillside, Hungerton. (M9304)

RAINEY Major John Wakefield, C.B.E.

RAINFORD, Thomas, M.B.E.

RAINIER, Gladys Mary, M.B.E.

RAINSFORD, Lieut. George, O.B.E.

RAIT, Lieut. Alexander Macpherson, M.B.E. (T.), R.F.A.

RAIT, Helen, C.B.E., R.R.C., Chief Lady Superintendent, Q.A.M.N.S. for India. *War Work:* France, Oct. 1914, to Dec. 1915 ; Mesopotamia, 1916, to 1917 ; C.B.E., Sept. 1919 ; twice mentioned in despatches ; 1914 Star ; awarded Royal Red Cross, Dec. 1915 ; Kaisir-i-Hind Medal, 1911. *Address:* c/o Messrs. Grindlay & Co., 54, Parliament Street, London, England. (C2042)

RAIT, Robert Sangster, C.B.E., *b.* 10 Feb. 1874 ; *s.* of David Rait, of Aberdeen ; *m.* Ruth Edith Mary, *d.* of John C. E. Bridge, of Peverel Court, Aylesbury. *Educ.:* Aberdeen Univ. ; New Coll., Oxford. Historiographer Royal for Scotland since 1919 ; Fellow of New Coll., Oxford, 1899–1913, and Tutor 1903–13 ; Professor of Scottish History and Literature in the University of Glasgow since 1913. *War Work:* Served in the War Trade Intelligence Department from Aug. 1915, to Dec. 1918 ; Sec. of a Departmental Committee of the Department of Information, 1917–18. *Address:* 31, Lilybank Gardens, or The University, Glasgow. *Club:* Athenæum. (C602)

RAITT, Charles Palmer, M.B.E., M.Inst.J.E., *b.* 12 Dec. 1878 ; *s.* of Daniel Raitt, of Worcester. *Educ.:* Secondary School, Dockyard Apprentices' School, Municipal Coll., Portsmouth. Inspector of Engine Fitters, H.M. Dockyard, Malta. *War Work:* Inspection of Machinery Repairs on H.M. ships at Portsmouth Dockyard till May, 1915, and then in Liverpool District to Nov. 1919. *Addresses:* 137, St. Augustine Road, Southsea, Hants ; 14, Strada Macina, Senglea, Malta. (M9395)

RALEY, Lieut.-Col. William Ensley, O.B.E.

RALPH, Alexander, M.B.E., R.N.R.

RALSTON, Andrew Agnew, O.B.E.

RALSTON, Capt. Gavin, M.B.E., R.A.F.

RALSTON, Helen Ripley, Mrs., M.B.E.

RAMAGE, Capt. George, M.B.E., R.A.F.

RAMAGE, Capt. William, O.B.E., R.A.S.C.

RAMSAY, Alexander, O.B.E.

RAMSAY, Arthur Dennys Gilbert, O.B.E.

RAMSAY, Capt. Arthur Douglas, O.B.E.

RAMSAY, Arthur George, M.B.E.

RAMSAY, Eleanor, Mrs., M.B.E. ; *d.* of J. T. Hopwood, of Ketton Hall, Stamford ; *widow* of the late Herbert Murray Ramsay. *War Work:* For four years Quarter Master and Hon. Sec. of V.A. Detachment Wilts 22 ; one year at the Countess of Suffolk's Hospital, Charlton Park, Malmesbury ; three years at the Red Cross Auxiliary Hospital, Malmesbury. *Address:* The Beeches, Malmesbury, Wilts. (M9297)

RAMSAY, Ermyntrude Sidwell, Mrs., O.B.E.

RAMSAY, Francis Graham, M.B.E.

RAMSAY, Capt. Graham Colville, O.B.E., M.B., R.A.M.C.

RAMSAY, Helen Margaret, M.B.E.

RAMSAY, James, M.B.E., *b.* 14 Dec. 1851 ; *s.* of the late John Ramsay, Ward of Turin Rescobie, Forfarshire ; *m.* Isabella, *d.* of Duncan Gilchrist, of Chirnside, Berwickshire. *Educ.:* Newtyle, Couparangus, and Dundee, Forfarshire. Since 1893, Works Manager at Vickers' Gun Works, Erith. *War Work:* Manufacturing guns, gun mountings, gun carriages, shells of various sizes and types ; machine guns, etc., and sights for all sizes of guns. *Address:* Park Crescent House, Erith, Kent. (M3918)

RAMSAY, James, O.B.E., *b.* 14 Aug. 1868 ; *s.* of James Ramsay, of Perth, Scotland. *Educ.:* Perth. *War Work:* Wagon supplies for traffic arising on Caledonian Railway. *Address:* 15, Florida Street, Mount Florida, Glasgow. *Clubs:* Gleneagles, Perthshire ; Caldwell Golf, Renfrewshire. (O1787)

RAMSAY, Lieut.-Col. James Gordon, D.S.O., O.B.E., *b.* 1880. Cameron Highlanders, and an A.A. and Q.M.G. with rank of Lieut.-Col. ; served in S. Africa, 1901–2 (Queen's medal with five clasps, King's medal with two clasps) ; Great War, 1914–18 (despatches, Croix de Guerre). (O86014)

RAMSAY, Capt. Jeffrey, O.B.E., M.D., R.A.M.C. (I.).

RAMSAY, John Maclean, O.B.E., M.A. (Glas.), B.A. (Oxon.), *b.* 3 Nov. 1875 ; *s.* of G. A. Ramsay, of Greenock ; *m.* Florence Mary, *d.* of George Smith, of London. *Educ.:* Greenock Academy ; Glasgow Univ. ; Oxford. Superintendent of Statistics and Intelligence, Board of Agriculture for Scotland, 29, St. Andrew Square, Edinburgh. *War Work:* Official work. *Address:* 10, Merchiston Gardens, Edinburgh. (O3877)

RAMSAY, Major Kenneth Alan, D.S.O., O.B.E. Canadian Forces ; served in the Great War, 1915–18 (despatches). (O6042)

RAMSAY, Margaret, Lady, O.B.E., *b.* 1868 ; *d.* of the late Frederick Henvey, of Indian Civil Service ; *m.* Sir John, K.C.I.E., C.S.I., *s.* of General Sir H. Ramsay, K.C.S.I., C.B. *War Work:* Raised and administered a fund called Lady Ramsay's Fund for Comforts for Troops in Baluchistan, India, from 1915–18. *Address:* c/o Messrs. King & Co., 9, Pall Mall. *Club:* Kent County. (O71)

RAMSAY, Margaret Evelyn, M.B.E., *b.* 16 March, 1898 ; *d.* of the Rev. A. Ramsay, D.D., of Highgate. *Educ.:* North London Collegiate School. *War Work:* Junior Administrative Assistant, Ministry of Shipping. (M9399)

RAMSAY, Major Ronald Arthur, O.B.E.

RAMSAY, William, C.B.E., J.P., *b.* 22 Oct. 1847 ; *s.* of Alexander Laing Ramsay, of Elgin.; *m.* Amelia Stirling, *d.* of the Rev. James Reid, of Auldearn, Nairn. *Educ.:* Elgin Academy. Hon. Sheriff Substitute for Inverness, Moray, and Nairn ; Justice of the Peace for Moray ; Lord Provost of the City of Elgin, 1913–19. *War Work:* Chairman of War Savings and of Local Tribunal Committees. *Address:* Longmorn House, Longmorn, Moray, Scotland. *Club:* Elgin. (C2893)

RAMSBOTHAM, Major Herwald, O.B.E.

RAMSBOTHAM, Lieut. Richard Bury, M.B.E., I.A.R.O.

RAMSBOTTOM, Edmund Cecil, M.B.E., *b.* 30 |Sept. 1881 ; *s.* of E. Ramsbottom, of Manchester. *Educ.:* Manchester Grammar School. Ministry of Labour. *War Work:* Board of Trade ; Ministry of Food ; Ministry of Labour ; Sec. of Departmental Food Prices Committee. *Address:* 58, Blenheim Gardens, Cricklewood, N.W. 2. (M2321)

RAMSBOTTOM, James, O.B.E., M.B., Ch.B., D.P.H., *b.* 3 Feb. 1884 ; *s.* of Rev. G. F. Ramsbottom, of Thornham, Lancs. *Educ.:* Middleton Grammar School, and Manchester Univ. Medical Officer of Health to the Tendring Rural District Council ; Assistant County Medical Officer of Health for Essex. *War Work:* Served in German East Africa, 1917–19, as Sanitary Officer for the Tabora area. *Address:* Thornham House, Castleton, Manchester. (O6523)

RAMSBOTTOM, Lieut. John, O.B.E., R.A.M.C.

RAMSDALE, Capt. James Ellwood, M.B.E.

RAMSDEN, Dorothy, Mrs., C.B.E.

RAMSDEN, Major Eugene, O.B.E.

RAMSDEN, Col. Herbert Frecheville Smyth, C.B.E., J.P. (Sussex). *b.* 6 March, 1856 ; *s.* of the Rev. C. H. Ramsden, of Chilham, Kent ; *m.* Hon. Edwyna S. E., *d.* of 17th Baron Saye and Sele (*see* BURKE'S *Peerage*), of Broughton Castle. Oxon. *Educ.:* Felsted School, and R.M.C., Sandhurst. Indian Army (ret.) ; Military Accountant-General, India, 1905–8. *War Work:* Re-employed as Pay Officer, Indian Troops in England, Dec. 1914, to March, 1916 ; Field Controller of Military Accounts, Indian Force in France, Feb. 1918 to Oct. 1919 ; despatches, C.B.E. (Mil.), 1919. *Address:* Mostham House, Wadhurst, Sussex. (C1311)

RAMSEY, Arthur George, M.B.E., B.Sc. (Eng.), A.M.I.C.E. A.M.I.E.E., F.R.S.A., *b.* 16 Dec. 1890 ; *s.* of Arthur James Ramsey, of London, W. 4 ; *m.* Bertha Elizabeth, *d.* of the late John Turner Emmett, of Manchester. *Educ.:* Emmanuel School, S.W. ; Xaverian Coll., Cressier, Neuchatel, Switzerland ; Privately at Bonn, Germany ; Day Technical Coll. (Univ. of London) ; Battersea Polytechnic, S.W. Electrical and Mechanical Engineer ; 1910–14, with the British Westinghouse Electric and Manufacturing Co., Ltd., Manchester ; 1914–19, Scottish District Engineer, H.M. Office of Works (Headquarters, Edinburgh) ; 1919–20, Assistant Engineer, H.M. Office of Works, London, S.W. 1 ; 1920, Engineer, H.M. Office of Works, London, S.W. 1. *War Work:* Design and installation of general and process plant in National Shell Filling Factories, Munition Inspection Bonds, National Sawmills, Government Industrial Mills, plant and Electro-Medical apparatus in hospitals : in addition, the inspection, testing, and purchase of locomotives, cranes, general mechanical and electrical plant for war purposes. *Address:* H.M. Office of Works, Engineering Division, Westminster, S.W. 1. (M9400)

RAMSEY, Florence Edith, Mrs., M.B.E.

RANDALL, Alec Walter George, O.B.E., 3rd Secretary H.M.'s Diplomatic Service.

RANDALL, Lieut.-Col. Charles Russell Jekyl, C.B.E., R.A.F. Served in the Great War, 1914–19 (despatches). (C873)

RANDALL, Lieut.-Comm. James, O.B.E., *b.* 9 May, 1876 ; *s.* of Col. Randall. *Educ.:* Sedbergh School. Merchant. *War Work:* Intelligence Division, Admiralty. *Address:* 6, Pelham Place, S.W. 7. *Clubs:* Reform ; M.C.C. (O671)

RANDALL, Capt. Richard Walter Kimbal, M.B.F., A.P.D.

RANDELL, Capt. Alan Summers, O.B.E.

RANDELL, Reginald Maurice Henry, M.B.E., M.D.(Lond.), M.R.C.S. (Eng.), *b.* 26 April 1862 ; *s.* of Surg.-Major Henry Lloyd Randell, P.M.O. Straits Settlements. *Educ.:* Wellington Coll. ; Guy's Hospital. 27 years Member of Beckenham Urban District Council ; Chairman in 1902 and 1919 ; 20 years Chairman Bromley and Beckenham Joint Hospital Board. *War Work:* M.O., Balgowan Hospital, Kent V.A.D. 96 ; Capt., Kent R.A.M.C.(V.) ; awarded King Albert's Medal for services to Belgians. *Address:* 10, Copers Cope Road, Beckenham, Kent. *Club:* Constitutional. (M9401)

RANDOLPH, George Boscawen, O.B.E., J.P., *b.* 28 Oct. 1864 ; *s.* of the late Rev. Leveson Cyril Randolph, of Hill House, Streatham Common, S.W. *Educ.:* Marlborough Coll. J.P. (Oxfordshire) ; Chairman of the Education Committee of the Oxfordshire County Council, 1919–20. *War Work:* National War Savings work in the County. *Address:* Steeple Aston, Oxon. (O11182)

RANDOLPH, Thomas Henry, O.B.E.

RANKEN, Cadet Capt. Charles Ernest, M.B.E., *b.* 27 Feb. 1867 ; *s.* of Samuel Ranken, of Chelsea. *Educ.:* Western Grammar School. London District Sec., The Boys' Brigade, Joint Council London J.O.C. (Board of Education). *War Work:*

Leader, the Boys' Brigade Recreation Huts Base Camp (France) Visitation 2nd London General Hospital. *Addresses:* 3, Gressenhall Road, S.W. 18 ; 34, Paternoster Row, E.C. 4. (M9402)

RANKEN, Wing-Comm. Francis, O.B.E., R.A.F.

RANKIN, Alexander Donald, O.B.E.

RANKIN, Lieut.-Comm. Francis James, O.B.E., R.D., R.N.R.

RANKIN, Major Frederick Powlett, O.B.E., R.A.M.C.

RANKIN, George William, M.B.E.

RANKIN, Capt. Henry Charles Deans, O.B.E., M.B., Ch.B., R.A.M.C., *b.* 16 Sept. 1888 ; *s.* of Henry C. D. Rankin, of Skelmorlie, Ayrshire ; *m.* Edith Watson, *d.* of James Gardner, of Skelmorlie, Ayrshire. *Educ.:* Stanley House, Bridge of Allan ; Glasgow Academy ; Glasgow Univ. *Address:* Briarfield, Skelmorlie, Ayrshire. *Club:* Junior United Service. (O8601b)

RANKIN, Hugh Fraser, O.B.E., F.E.I.S., *b.* 10 Nov. 1868 ; *s.* of Andrew Rankin, of Stratherrick ; *m.* Margaret Elizabeth, *d.* of William Ramsay, of Glasgow. *Educ.:* Fort William Public School ; Edinburgh Univ. ; Caen (France). Civil Servant in Ministry of Food, formerly Principal, Anglo-Chinese Coll., Amoy. *War Work:* Inspecting Schools in Scotland, 1916 ; making Munitions in Royal Scottish Museum Edinburgh, for 2 months ; in Ministry of Food since Jan. 1917 ; at present, Sec. of Butter and Cheese Import Committee. *Addresses:* 30, Moston Terrace, Edinburgh ; Ruskin Manor, Denmark Hill (London). *Clubs:* Overseas ; Moray House. (O672)

RANKIN, John Arthur, M.B.E.

RANKIN, Mary Ellen, Mrs., M.B.E., *b.* 28 Aug. 1880 ; *d.* of William Macdonald, of P. W. Department, India ; *m.* James Thomson, *s.* of James Rankin, of Carluke. *Educ.:* Privately. *War Work:* Vice-President, St. John's Ambulance War Gift Dept., Darjeeling ; worked for Soldier's Club, Darjeeling ; worked for Lady Carmichael's Bengal Women's War Fund in Calcutta and Darjeeling ; organised Howrah Fete, 1917. *Address:* c/o Messrs. Grindlay & Co., Calcutta and London. (M6229)

RANKIN, Major Thomas, O.B.E.

RANKIN, Lieut. William Robert Theodore, M.B.E., and Order of St. Stanislav of Russia, *b.* 14 June, 1881 ; *s.* of Hamilton Rankin, late of The Stock Exchange, London ; *m.* Florence, *d.* of Charles Stevens, of Barnet, Herts. *Educ.:* Privately. Member of the London Stock Exchange. *War Work:* Temporary Commission in Royal Army Service Corps ; served in France and North Russia ; was O.C. R.A.S.C., Onega, from Sept. 1918, to July, 1919, and was awarded Order of St. Stanislav (3rd class) with swords and ribbons, by the Archangel Government. *Address:* Wimpson Farm, Millbrook, Southampton. (M6979)

RANKINE, Professor Alexander Oliver, O.B.E., D.Sc., *b.* 1881 ; *s.* of Rev. John Rankine, of Guildford ; *m.* Ruby Irene, *d.* of Samuel Short, of Reading. *Educ.:* Guildford Grammar School ; Univ. Coll., London. Professor of Physics in the Imperial Coll. of Science and Technology, South Kensington. *War Work:* Chief Research Assistant, Admiralty Experimental Station, Harwich, 1917–18 : Deputy Resident Director of Research, Admiralty Experimental Station, Dartmouth, 1918. *Addresses:* Imperial Coll. of Science and Technology S.W.7 ; 9, Birch Grove, Acton W. 3. (O3878)

RANKINE, Surg.-Lieut.-Comm. Roger Aiken, O.B.E., M.B., R.N.

RANKINE, William, M.B.E.

RANN, Major Alfred Edward, O.B.E., M.C.

RANSOM, Herbert Charles, M.B.E.

RANSOME, Edward Coleby, O.B.E., J.P., *b.* 1 Sept. 1864 ; *s.* of late James Edward Ransome, of Holmewood, Ipswich ; *m.* Florence Mitford, *d.* of the late Rev. J. J. Smith, of Loddon, Norfolk, sometime tutor of Caius Coll., Cambridge. *Educ.:* Haileybury and Pembroke Coll., Cambridge. Chairman, Ransomes, Sims and Jefferies Ltd. *War Work:* Member of Advisory Committee of the Agricultural Machinery Department, Ministry of Munitions. *Address:* Highwood, Ipswich. *Clubs:* British Empire ; County Club, Ipswich. (O11183)

RANSON, Capt. Joseph Barlow, O.B.E.

RANSON, Lieut. Percy, O.B.E., R.N.R.

RAPER, Major Ernest Charles, O.B.E.

RAPER, Lieut.-Col. Henry Stanley, C.B.E., R.E. Served in the Great War, 1914–19 (despatches). (C1749)

RAPHAEL, Effie, Mrs., M.B.E. ; *d.* of John Galloway, of Kilmeny, Ardrossan ; *m.* Robert Walker, *s.* of John Raphael, of Ballymena, Co. Antrim. *Educ.:* Glasgow and London. *War Work:* In the Huts of Soldiers' Christian Association at Convalescent Camps at Rouen and Buchy, at 5 different periods between 1915 and 1919 ; returned from France in Feb. 1919, when the Camps and Huts were closing down. *Address:* Kincaid House, Milton-of-Campsie, Stirlingshire. *Club:* Kelvin, Glasgow.

RAPKIN, Paymaster-Lieut.-Comm. Geoffrey Jennings, O.B.E., R.N.

RAPLEY, Lieut. William Sydney, M.B.E., R.E.

RASHBROOK, Engr.-Capt. Henry Samuel, C.B.E., R.N. On Staff of Rear-Admiral, Falmouth. (C2227)

RASHLEIGH, Capt. Vernon Stanhope, C.B.E., R.N., *b.* 1897 ; *s.* of George Vernon Rashleigh ; formerly of Lustleigh. Devon ; *m.* 1909, Dorothy Richendra, *d.* of John Cooper Wilkinson, M.B., of Ashford, Kent. *Educ.:* Christ's Hospital. *War Work:* 1914–19, with Ocean Escort (despatches). *Address:* Erskine House, Erskine Hill, N.W. *Club:* Junior United Service. (C1203)

RASMUSEN, Capt. Charles Francis, O.B.E., R.A.F.
RATCLIFF, Major Charles John, O.B.E.
RATCLIFF, Constance Lilian, O.B.E., b. 30 April, 1877 ; d. of Richard Ratcliff, of Stanford Hall, Loughborough. War Work : Commandant, Race Course Hospital, Cheltenham, from Oct. 1914, to March, 1919 ; Address : Southam Delabere, Prestbury, Glos. Clubs : Ladies' Park ; V.A.D. Ladies'. (O674)
RATCLIFF, Sidney, M.B.E., R.N.
RATCLIFFE, Lieut. Charles Plummer, M.B.E., R.E.
RATCLIFFE, Henry Stephenson, O.B.E.
RATCLIFFE, Herbert Coakley, M.B.E.
RATCLIFFE, Lieut. Herbert James, O.B.E.
RATHBONE, Capt. Charles Arthur, O.B.E.
RATHBUN, Aileen, Mrs., M.B.E., R.A.F.
RATSEY, Major Harold Edward, C.B.E., D.S.O.
RATTEY, Eng.-Comm. William, O.B.E., R.N.
RATTRAY, Francis Cochrane, O.B.E.
RATTRAY, Col. Paul Robert BURN-CLERK-, C.B.E., J.P., D.L., b. 1859 ; s. of the Rev. John Alexander Higgins Burn-Murdoch, of Neuch, Larbert, Stirlingshire ; m. 1910, Ferelith, d. of Sir James Henry Ramsay, 10th Bart. (see BURKE'S Peerage). Educ.: R.M.A. Formerly Col. R.E. ; served in S. Africa, 1899–1902 (despatches twice) commanded R.E., Highland Dist. 1914–18 ; assumed by deed poll, 1910, the surname of Burn-Clerk-Rattray, in lieu of his patronymic. Address : Craighall-Rattray, Blairgowrie. Clubs : United Service ; New (Edinburgh). (C803)
RATTRAY, Robert Sutherland, M.B.E.
RAVEN, Lieut. Norman Vincent, M.B.E.
RAVEN, Sir Vincent Litchfield, K.B.E., M.I.C.E., M.I.M.E. Engineering pupil with the Chief Engineer, N.E.R., afterwards holding many positions with N.E.R., until appointed Chief Assist. Mech. Eng. 1902, in charge of wagon, engine and carriage building, and repairing establishments ; Chief Mechanical Engineer, North Eastern Railway Co., since 1910 ; Chief Superintendent, Royal Arsenal Factories, Woolwich, 1915–17 ; Controller of Armament Production, Admiralty, since 1917 ; returned to N.E.R. in previous capacity, 1919. Address : Chief Mechanical Engineer, North Eastern Railway, Darlington. Club : Wellington.
RAVENSCROFT, Capt. and Asst.-Paymaster John Arthur, O.B.E., A.P.D.
RAVENSHAW, Rose Constance, Mrs. Hurdis Secundus Lalande, O.B.E.
RAW, Rev. Albert Edward, O.B.E., C.F., b. 24 May, 1862 ; s. of Rev. N. Raw, Wesleyan Minister ; m. Gertrude Maria, (died Dec. 24, 1919), d. of the late Francis Bretherton, of Tunbridge Wells. Educ.: Kingswood School, Bath. Wesleyan Minister. Temp. Chaplain 4th Class. War Work : Chaplain to Forces, Salisbury Plain, Aug. 1914 to Oct. 1918 (mentioned) ; A.P.C., S. Command, Oct. 1918, to March, 1919 ; A.P.C., E. Command, March, 1919, to Aug. 1920. Address : No. 3/65 Elgin Crescent, Notting Hill, W. (O7613)
RAWBONE, Annie Christine, Mrs., O.B.E. (O12056)
RAWES, Stanley, O.B.E., b. 31 Dec. 1873 ; s. of the late James Rawes, of Lisbon ; m. Amy Jane, d. of Errington Dawson, O.B.E., of Lisbon. Educ.: Dover College. Partner in James Rawes & Co., Lisbon. War Work : Providing office accommodation for British Intelligence Department and Senior Naval Transport Officer. Address : c/o James Rawes & Co., 47, Rua do Corpo Santo, Lisbon. Clubs : Royal British, Lisbon ; Lisbon Cricket ; Espinho Golf ; Constitutional, London. (O11184)
RAWLES, Kate Eleanor, Mrs., M.B.E.
RAWLING, Lieut.Com. Henry Bernard, O.B.E., R.N. For valuable services to the British Military Mission to Poland. (O11946a)
RAWLINGS, Capt. Geoffrey Nares, O.B.E.
RAWLINGS, Herbert Henry, M.B.E., R.N.
RAWLINS. Lieut.-Col. Arthur Kennedy, C.I.E., C.B.E., D.S.O., b. 15 May, 1868 ; s. of the late Major-Gen J. S. Rawlins. Educ.: Haileybury College. Army Officer. War Work : Served throughout the war with the Egyptian Expeditionary Force, in charge of the Bikaner Camel Corps. Address : Bahawalpur, India. (C797)
RAWLINS, Lieut. Frank William, M.B.E.
RAWLINS, Capt. Howard St. George, O.B.E., R.A.S.C.
RAWLINS, Louisa Geraldine, Mrs., O.B.E., b. 1869 ; d. of Colonel A. F. Connell, R.A. ; m. Thomas George, s. of Adolphus Fredrick Connell, of Longford, Co. Longford, Ireland. Educ.: Ladies' Coll., Guernsey, and Hanover. War Work : Commandant and Matron Eccleston Hospital for Officers, 26, Eccleston Square, 1916–19. Addresses : 30, St. George's Road, Eccleston Square S. W. 1 ; Melrose College, Pirlington. Clubs : Albemarle ; Ladies' V.A.D. (O11185)
RAWLINSON, Alfred, C.B.E. (C2072)
RAWLINSON, Lieut. Arthur Richard, M.B.E.
RAWLINSON, Rev. Bernard Stephen, C.M.G., O.B.E., b. 27 June, 1865 ; s. of Thomas Rawlinson. Educ.: Downside School. Head of Catholic Settlement in Bermondsey from 1910–14. War Work : Acting Chaplain to the Forces from Sept. 1914, to July, 1920 ; Assistant to Principal Chaplain, B.E.F., France, from 1915–20 ; Senior (R.C.) Chaplain, B.E.F., from 1916–20. Address : Downside Abbey, near Bath. Club : Royal Societies. (O1790)
RAWLINSON, Leonard, M.B.E., b. 11 Jan. 1876 ; s. of Henry Rawlinson, of St. Helens ; m. Louisa Eleanor, d. of Mrs. Glover, of Eccleston Park, Prescot. Educ.: Cowley Schools, St. Helens. Town Clerk, Leamington ; Clerk, Local

Education Authority, Leamington ; Clerk, Local Pensions Committee, Leamington ; Clerk, Further Education Committee for Warwick and Leamington. War Work : Clerk to Local Tribunal ; Hon. Sec. War Emergency and National Service Committees. Address : 21, Adelaide Road, Leamington Spa. (M2327)
RAWLINSON, Ralph George Joynson, O.B.E., b. 13 June, 1877 ; s. of the late Ralph Rawlinson, of Eltham, Kent ; m. Muriel Domville, d. of late Thomas Cooper, of Bedford. Educ.: Aldenham, and Keble Coll., Oxford. Divisional Commandant (R. Division), since July, 1919 ; Metropolitan Special Constabulary Reserve. War Work : Metropolitan Special Constabulary, Aug. 1914, to July, 1919 ; Assistant Divisional Commander, Sept. 1914, to Feb. 1915 ; Divisional Commander (R. Div.), Feb. 1915, to July, 1919. Addresses : Roselands, Mottingham Lane, Eltham, S.E. 9. (O3879)
HAWNSLEY, Col. Claude, C.M.G., C.B.E., D.S.O., R.A.S.C. (ret.), b. 4 Aug. 1862 ; s. of Lieut.-Col. Thomas Joseph Rawnsley ; m. Lilian Maude, d. of the late Fred. Augustus Percy Wood, R.M.L.I., and Receiver-General of the Gold Coast. Educ.: Queen Elizabeth's School, Cranbrook ; Royal Military Academy, Woolwich. Joined Royal Artillery, 1882 ; transferred to A.S.C. as Capt., 1889 ; promoted Lieut.-Col. 1901, and Brevet-Col., 1904 ; retired, 1906 ; served S. African War, 1899–1902, first as D.A.A.G., and afterwards as A.A.G. (despatches, Queen's medal, 3 clasps, King's medal, 2 clasps, D.S.O.) War Work : European War in France, Aug. 1914, to April, 1919 ; in command of the R.A.S.C. Section G.H.Q., 3rd Echelon (despatches 4 times, 1914 Star, G.S. medal, Victory medal, C.M.G., 1917, C.B.E. (1919).) Sec. Arthur's Club, St. James's Street, S.W., 1907–14 ; Sec. Brooks's Club, St. James's Street, since July 1919. Address : 26, Nevern Mansions, Warwick Road, S.W. 5. (C1312)
RAWNSLEY, Helen Maud, Mrs. W. H., O.B.E., F.R.G.S., F.R.H.S., F.R.Z.S.: d. of Lieut.-Col. R. F. Chaplin, of Louth, Lincolnshire ; m. Major Walter Hugh Rawnsley, J.P. Vice-President, B.R.C.S. of South Lindsey, N. Lincs. Branch ; County Commissioner Girl Guides ; Chairman, Local War Pensions Committee ; Ruling Councillor, Culworth Division Primrose League ; Chairman, Women's Coalition Association, S. Lindsey, Lincs. War Work : Vice-President, B.R.C.S. ; Superintendent of Y.M.C.A. Hut in France ; Superintendent, C. A. Club, Calais ; Chairman of two local committees ; W.W.A.C., Chairman, War Pensions Committee. Addresses : Well Vale, Alford, Lincolnshire ; 4, Eaton Mansions, S.W. (O11186)
RAWS, Col. William Lennon, C.B.E., Australian Forces, b. 1878 ; s. of the Rev. John G. Raws, of Adelaide, S. Australia ; m. 1905, Elsie, Cecilia, d. of the late William Rogers, of Adelaide. Chairman, Australian Metal Exchange. Address : Wurssna, Martin Street, Elsternwick, Victoria, Australia. Clubs : Naval and Military ; Australian. (C718)
RAWSON, Lieut. Geoffrey, O.B.E.
RAWSON, Major Geoffrey Grahame, O.B.E., M.C., R.E.
RAWSON, Harry, C.B.E., J.P., D.L., b. 30 Jan. 1862 ; s. of William Rawson, of Halifax, Yorkshire ; m. Laura Emily, d. of Robert John Turner, of Ipswich, Suffolk. Educ.: Park Field House ; Beeston Hall, Ripponden (Yorks.). Chairman, Edinburgh Territorial Army Association ; Deputy Lieutenant of the City and County of Edinburgh ; J.P., Peeblesshire. War Work : Devoted whole time during the war to above association (Honorary) ; clothing and equipping 36,000 troops ; attending to general welfare of all troops under his association. Addresses : 19, Royal Terrace, Edinburgh ; St. Romains Wells, Innerleithen, N.B. Clubs : Scottish Conservative ; Forth Corinthian Yacht. (C2711)
RAWSTORNE, Maria Harriet, M.B.E. ; d. of the late Rev. Canon Rawstorne. Educ.: At home and abroad. Social work of various kinds. War Work : Hon. Sec. Soldiers' and Sailors' Families Association, and London War Pensions Committee, Wandsworth B., 1914–20 ; Member of L.W.P. Committee ; Member of British Red Cross Society ; Vol. Aid. Detachment, London 286. Address : 50, Keswick Road, E. Putney, S.W. (M9408)
RAY, Helen MacLaine, M.B.E., b. 31 Aug. 1879 ; d. of Richard Ray, Rector of Killyleagh, Co. Down. Educ.: Privately. War Work : Ulster Women's Gift Fund for Prisoners of War. Address : 27, Rosetta Avenue, Ormeau Road, Belfast. (M9409)
RAYLEIGH, Kathleen Alice, Lady, O.B.E., b. 25 Jan. 1886 ; d. of John C. Straker, of Stagshaw, House ; m. 1st, Capt. J. H. Cuthbert, D.S.O. (who was killed in action) ; 2nd, Robert John, 4th Baron Rayleigh (see BURKE'S Peerage). War Work : Assistant County Director of the B.R.C.S. for Northumberland ; President and Sec. of the Corbridge Branch, B.R.C.S. Addresses : Beaufront Castle, Hexham ; Terling Place, Essex ; 69, Cadogan Square. (O276)
RAYMENT, Instructor-Comm. Guy Varley, C.B.E., b. 1878 ; s. of Henry Rayment, of Sidcup ; m. 1911, Laura Frances, d. of George Ingram, of Sidcup. Educ.: Trin. Coll. Camb. (B.A. 1900). Instructor-Comm. R.N., Intelligence Div. Address : Sidcup. Club : Cocoa Tree. (C1147)
RAYMOND, Comm. (retired) Eben Lindsay, O.B.E., R.D., R.N.R., b. 17 April, 1867 ; s. of the late Lieut.-Col. Robert Peel Raymond, of Sydney, N.S.W. ; m. Sara Jane, d. of William Dunlop Anderson, of London. Educ.: Coreen Coll., Sydney, N.S.W. War Work : Joined 6th Manchester Regt. (T.) as Major, Sept. 1914 ; transferred to 19th Bn. The Rifle Brigade (T.), Nov. 1915 ; embarked for Egypt, Dec. 1915, and served with E.E.F. until May, 1919 ; second in

command of Batt. from April, 1916, till May, 1919; mentioned in despatches (Gen. Allenby's), April, 1918 and March, 1919. *Address:* The Glen, Swaythling, Hants. *Clubs:* Trojans, Southampton. (O6278)

RAYMOND, Major Harold, O.B.E., M.C., M.A., *b.* 24 July, 1887; *s.* of the late Cuthbert Raymond, of Rose Lawn, Worcester; *m.* Vera Frances Ethel, *d.* of the late Rev. T. M. Everett, of Ruislip, Middlesex. *Educ.:* King's School, Worcester, and Pembroke Coll., Oxford. *War Work:* Temp. Commission 10th (Service) Batt. Worcestershire Regt., Sept. 1914; Capt., June, 1915; France, July, 1915; Staff Capt., 58th Brigade, Sept. 1916; D.A.A.G., 19th Division, March, 1918; demobilised, July, 1919; mentioned in despatches, Jan. 1917, June, 1917, and June, 1918. *Address:* 99, St. Martin's Lane, W.C. 2. *Club:* New Oxford and Cambridge. (O5704)

RAYMOND, Captain Hugh Philip, O.B.E., R.A.S.C., *b.* 15 Feb. 1889; *s.* of the Rev. P. F. Raymond, M.A., K.H.C., of Middleton, Essex; *m.* Gwendolen Hilda, *d.* of J. H. Clare, of Farnham, Surrey. *Educ.:* Berkhamsted, and R.M.C., Sandhurst. Gazetted from R.M.C., Sandhurst, into Royal Army Service Corps, Sept. 1908; promoted to Lieut. Sept. 1911; promoted Capt. Oct. 1914; granted temporary Majority, Nov. 1914. *War Work:* Went to France with original B.E.F. in Aug. 1914; served through retreat from Mons with 4th Division; four years' service in France and Germany. *Address:* Farlands Croft, Farnham, Surrey. (O5705)

RAYMOND, Mary, Mrs., M.B.E.

RAYNE, T. Major Henry, M.B.E.

RAYNER, Eng.-Capt. Alfred, O.B.E., R.N.

RAYNER, Capt. Arthur Ernest, O.B.E., M.D., R.A.M.C.

RAYNER, Eva Alexina Snoad, Mrs. (Hugh), O.B.E., *d.* of J. H. Taylor, of 6, Montagu Mansions, W. 1; *m.* Surgeon Lieut.-Col. Hugh, Royal Horse Guards, *s.* of Lloyd Rayner, of Liverpool. *Educ.:* Privately. *War Work:* Ran a troop of Boy Scouts (2nd Barnes) for 4 years as Scoutmaster whilst the S.M. was on active service; drove own Ambulance for the Prince of Wales' Hospital, and on duty all Air Raids, 1915–18, as an officer in the Boy Scout Movement, with the ambulance. *Club:* Writers', Strand. (O11187)

RAYNER, Capt. George Henry, O.B.E.

RAYNER, Major Ralph Herbert, M.B.E., Sig. Service. (M102 36)

RAYNER, Harry, M.B.E., M.C., R.A.S.C.

RAYNER, Capt. Oswald Theodore, M.B.E.

RAYNER, Lieut. Walter John, M.B.E.

RAYNOR, Capt. Robert Osmond, M.B.E., *b.* 17 July, 1887; *s.* of Frank Charles Raynor, of King's Lynn; *m.* Constance Stewart Campbell, *d.* of — Samson, of Sanquhar. *Educ.:* Privately. Engineer. *War Work:* Army from 5 Aug. 1914, to 1 Nov. 1919. *Address:* The Red House, Walton-on-Thames, Surrey. *Club:* Junior Army and Navy. (M2329)

REA, Paymaster-Lieut. Basil Soame, M.B.E., R.N.

REA, Lieut. Donald, M.B.E., M.A., *b.* 7 April, 1894; *s.* of the Rev. Thomas Rea, of Flyford Flavel, Worcester. *Educ.:* St. John's School, Leatherhead; Downing Coll., Cambridge. *War Work:* Service with 1st Garrison Bn. The Suffolk Regt.; 3rd, 7th, and 11th Bn. The Suffolk Regt. *Addresses:* Theological College, Chichester; Flyford Flavel Rectory, Worcester; Downing College, Cambridge. (M6539)

REA, George Grey, C.B.E., B.A., C.A., J.P., *b.* 1858; *s.* of George Rea, of Middleton and Berrington, Northumberland; *m.* Mary, *d.* of G. A. Grey, D.L., J.P., of Milfield, Northumberland. *Educ.:* Shrewsbury School, and Jesus Coll., Cambridge. *War Work:* Member of Agricultural Sub-Committee of Reconstruction Committee; Advisory Committee on Purchase of Wool; President of Board of Agriculture's Advisory Committee; Central Agricultural Advisory Council; Cereals Committee; Agricultural Wages Board; County War Agricultural Committee, etc. *Address:* Doddington, Wooler, Northumberland. *Clubs:* New University; Northern Counties. (C2727)

REACH Lieut. Alexander Robertson, O.B.E., R.A.S.C. (T.)

REACH, Capt. David Mackinlay Potter, M.B.E.

READ, Capt. Alfred, M.B.E.

READ, Capt. Archibald Hugh, O.B.E., North Staffordshire Regt., *b.* 25 April, 1891; *s.* of Edward Bruce Read, of Bisley, Surrey; *m.* Joan, *d.* of the late Lieut.-Col. E. H. Montrésor, of Royal Sussex Regt. *Educ.:* Rugby. Reserve of Officers. *Address:* Dovercourt, Hurworth-on-Tees, Durham. (O7615)

READ, Francis Edward, O.B.E., *b.* 25 Oct. 1864. Electrical Engineer; Member of Stafford Town Council. *War Work:* Chairman, Local War Pension Committee, Military Advisory Committee, Food Profiteering Committee, and Siemens Bros. Dynamo Works War Savings Committee, etc. *Address:* 1, Salt Avenue, Stafford. (O11188)

READ, George Daniel, M.B.E.,

READ, Lieut. Geoffrey Jervis, O.B.E., R.A.F.

READ, George William, M.B.E., *b.* 1879; *s.* of Charles Walter Read, of Weston-super-Mare; *m.* Agnes, *d.* of Albert Batty, of Brighton. *Educ.:* The Coll., Weston-super-Mare. Chief Assist. Rate Collector to Urban District Council of Weston-super-Mare. *War Work:* Hon. Sec. Weston-super-Mare Local Central War Savings Committee and Food Economy Committee. *Address:* 34, Uphill Park Road, Weston-super-Mare. (M9410)

READ, Major Hector, O.B.E.

READ, Capt. John Victor, M.B.E., R.AF.

READ, Mary Ada Alice, M.B.E.; *d.* of Samuel Counsell, of Blackburn; *m.* Frederick Morgan, *s.* of Morgan Read. *Educ.:* Science and Art School, Blackburn. *War Work:* Member of the Leyton Education, Maternity and Child Welfare, Profiteering, Queen's Work for Women, and Food Control Committees; President Leyton Women's Union; Voluntary worker investigating Exemption Claims for Tribunal; Hon. Sec. War Pensions Local Committee; Soldiers' and Sailors' Families Association Representative. (O9412)

READ, Mary Amy, M.B.E. Hon. Sec. of the Bolton Division, Soldiers' and Sailors' Families Association. (M10334)

READ, Major Philip Austin Ottley, O.B.E., T.D., *b.* 1882; *s.* of the late Rev. Philip Read, of Bolton; *m.* Margaret Agnes, *d.* of Arthur T. Crook, of Bolton. *Educ.:* Haileybury Coll., Hertford. Solicitor. *War Work:* 1/5th Loyal North Lancs., France, Feb. 1915, to Feb. 1916; No. 2 Infy. Records, Preston, Aug. 1916, to March, 1920. *Address:* 34, Somerset Road, Bolton. (O4278)

READ, Lieut. Sidney, M.B.E., M.C.

READ, Capt. Edward Harry HANDLEY-, M.B.E., *b.* 18 March, 1870; *s.* of Harry Read, of Lincoln; *m.* Eva Mary, *d.* of Charles Handley, of Brighton. *Educ.:* Western Grammar School. Artist, R.B.A. *War Work:* Organised Army Studio; invented new methods of teaching Machine Guns, etc.; Camouflage Expert, and Lecturer to Machine-Gun Corps. *Addresses:* 2, Harley Place, Harley Street, W. 1.; 16, Hill Road, St. John's Wood. *Clubs:* Chelsea Arts; Langham Sketching; St. John's Wood Arts.

READ, Major Hugh Arthur MOUTRAY-, M.B.E., *b.* March 15, 1876; *s.* of Col. J. Moutray-Read, late of Newport Hall, Herefordshire, and Sandford Dene, Cheltenham; *m.* Florence Jane, *d.* of Edwin Islip, of Brighton. *Educ.:* Cheltenham Coll. Auctioneer, Coy. Director, etc.; late 2nd New Zealand Mounted Rifles, Boer War, 1899–1900; Supt. Transvaal Mounted Constabulary, 1900–3; Chief of Pretoria Fire Brigade, 1900–3. *War Work:* Trooper, 2nd King Edward's Horse, 1914–15; Lieut. A.S.C., France, 1915; Staff Capt. at War Office, 1916–19; Chief Inspector of Fire Services for War Office, 1916–19; under Major-General Bond, Director of Quartering, was responsible for six hundred million pounds worth of Government property in the United Kingdom; compiled Army Fire Manual, 1917–18–19. *Addresses:* 23, St. Aubyn's Road; 32, Church Road (Read's Mart.), Upper Norwood, S.E.

READ, Lilian, Mrs. RUDSTON-, M.B.E., *b.* July 8, 1863; *d.* of Frederick Cox, of Messrs. Cox & Co., Bankers; *m.* Harry Rudston-Read. *War Work:* Commandant of Stanswood Auxiliary War Hospital, Fawley, Southampton, from Oct. 1914, to Dec. 1918. *Address:* The Orchard, Fawley, Southampton. (M9411)

READE, Surg.-Lieut. Arthur George Lawrence, O.B.E., R.N.V.R.

READER, Capt. and Qr.-Mr. Ernest John Ward, O.B.E.

READER, Thomas, M.B.E., *b.* 10 Dec. 1867; *s.* of Thomas Reader, of Maidstone, Kent; *m.* Ellen Annie Louisa, *d.* of Thomas George Tiller, of Indian Ordnance Dept., Trimulgherry, India. *Educ.:* Westbourne Park. Late Staff Sergt. the Welsh Regt.; Superintending Clerk, War Office. *War Work:* Reinforcements for all dismounted officers, including Australian, New Zealand, Canadian and South African Contingents for all theatres of War; total number of Officers placed under orders from Sept. 1914, to Nov. 1918, 148,790, reinforcements only, not including divisions or units. *Addresses:* Wennington, 93, Howarth Road, Bostall Hill, Plumstead, Kent; A.G.2(O), War Office, Embankment Annexe, S.W. 1. (M2330)

READING, Alice Edith, Countess of, G.B.E., 3rd *d.* of the late Albert Cohen, of London; *m.* 1887, Sir Rufus Isaacs, P.C., G.C.B., K.C.V.O., Earl of Reading (*see* BURKE'S *Peerage*). *Address:* 32. Curzon Street, Mayfair, W. (DG31)

READING, Harry Thomas, O.B.E.

READING, Joseph William, M.B.E.

READMAN, Annie Bradley, Mrs., M.B.E.

READY, Lieut.-Col. Basil Tobin, O.B.E.

REAKES, Col. Charles John, C.B.E. New Zealand Forces; served in the Great War, 1915–19 (despatches). (C1867)

REAKS, Sidney Hugh, M.B.E.

REAN, Major William Henry, O.B.E., R.N. (S.R.).

REASON, Lieut.-Col. Clifford Hamilton, D.S.O. O.B.E., Canadian Army Med. Corps; served in the Great War, 1914–19 (despatches). (O6643)

REAVELL, Lieut.-Col. George, O.B.E., T.D., *b.* 31 Jan. 1865; *s.* of George Reavell, of Alnwick; *m.* Eliza Anna, *d.* of the late John Bolam, of Bilton House. *Educ.:* Alnwick Grammar School, and privately; Architect; F.R.I.B.A. *War Work:* Commanded 2/7th Northumberland Fusiliers and 35th Northumberland Fusiliers. *Address:* Alnwick, Northumberland. (O7616)

REAVILL, Ernest Alfred, M.B.E.

REAY, Col. William Thomas, C.B.E., *b.* 9 Nov. 1858; *s.* of E. W. Reay, of Melbourne, Australia; *m.* Lucinda, *d.* of G. Broadbent, of Melbourne, Australia. *Educ.:* Melbourne, Australia. Editor of "Melbourne Herald," afterwards London correspondent of that paper; Col. (ret.) in Australian Force. *War Work:* Inspector-General for the Metropolitan Special Constabulary. *Address:* 134, Portsdown Road, London, W. *Club:* National Liberal. (C2895)

RECKITT, Lieut. Charles Edward Hay, O.B.E., R.E.

RECKITT, Philip Bealby, O.B.E.

REDDIE, Constance Katharine Mary, Mrs., O.B.E.

REDDISH, George Joseph, M.B.E., *b.* 6 Oct. 1872 ; *s.* of A. W. Reddish, of Warwick ; *m.* Frances Kate, *d.* of William Cox, of Marlow-on-Thames. *Educ.:* Westminster Training College. L.B. and S.C. Rly, appointed Oct. 1886· *War Work:* Stationmaster, Crowborough and Jarvis Brook L.B. and S.C. Rly., June, 1915. *Address:* Station House, Jarvis Brook, Sussex. (M9413)

REDDOCK, Capt. John Simpson, O.B.E.

REDFERN, Major Arthur Edward, O.B.E., M.C., *b.* 1888 ; *s.* of Canon Thomas Redfern, of Denbigh, North Wales ; *m.* Rita, *o.d.* of John Bamford, J.P., of Oldfields Hall, Uttoxeter. *Educ.:* Pocklington. *War Work:* Served with Royal Welsh Fusiliers and Headquarters 9th (Scottish) division in France and Belgium from 1915 ; joined 16th Royal Welsh Fusiliers as private soldier ; awarded Belgian Croix de Guerre. (O5767)

REDHILL, Samuel, M.B.E.

REDL, Mary Beatrice, Mrs., M.B.E.

REDLICH, Capt. Stefan, M.B.E. R.G.A., mentioned in despatches ; *s.* of Rudolf Redlich, of Russia. *Educ.:* St. John's Coll., Cambridge. Member of Stock Exchange, London. *Address:* 65, Upper Berkeley Street, W. 1. *Club:* Royal Automobile. (M5561)

REDMAN, George Herbert, O.B.E., *b.* 21 Sept. 1882 ; *s.* of Rev. G. O. Redman, of Withnell ; *m.* Fanny Ethel, *d.* of Eli Crook, of Hoghton. *Educ.:* Rivington Grammar School, and Owen College, Manchester. Managing Director, J. E. Baxter & Co., Ltd., Leyland. *War Work:* Consultant to Government Depts. including the Anti-Gas Department. *Address:* Levens Lodge, Leyland. *Clubs:* Royal Automobile ; Engineers'. (O11191)

REDMAN, Major Henry Gordon, O.B.E., T.F.R., *b.* 12 Nov. 1884 ; *s.* of T. E. Redman, of The Knoll, Shawford, Winchester. *Educ.:* Repton. Solicitor, Bournemouth. *War Work:* Territorial, 4th Wiltshire Regt. Oct. 1914, to Aug. 1917 ; India and N.W. Frontier, Aug. 1917, to March, 1920 ; Mesopotamia, Machine Gun Corps. *Address:* Holmdale, 38, Branksome Wood Road, Bournemouth. (O6690)

REDMAN, Capt. Sidney George, O.B.E.

REDMOND, Capt. Henry Joseph, M.B.E.

REDPATH, Robert, C.B.E., M.Inst.C.E., *b.* 1871 ; *s.* of Robert Redpath, of Newcastle-on-Tyne. *Educ.:* Newcastle Grammar School. Chief Designer, Coventry Ordnance Works Ltd. *War Work:* Designer of 4·5-inch Q.F. Field Howitzer, 15-inch B.L. Howitzer and other Field and Naval war material ; Member of Board of Invention and Research, and Guns and Ammunition, and Sights and Rangefinders Panels of Munitions Inventions Department. *Address:* Twyford House, Leamington. (C2896)

REDSTONE, Lilian Jane, M.B.E., B.A. (Lond.), *b.* 1885 ; *d.* of V. B. Redstone, of Woodbridge, Suffolk. *Educ.:* Ipswich High School. Historical Research. *War Work:* In Historical Records Branch of the Ministry of Munitions. *Address:* 125, Alderney Street, London, S.W. 1. *Club:* London Univ. (M3920)

REED, Alice Clay, Mrs., M.B.E., *b.* 11 July, 1865 ; *d.* of John Geach Rowe, J.P., of Polmenna, Weymouth ; *m.* Arthur Farnell Graham ,*s.* of Col. William Reed, Deputy Lieut., Middlesex, of St. Mary's, Bedfont, Middlesex. *Educ.:* Privately. *War Work:* Commandant, Kent 62 V.A.D. Hospital, Sidcup, from its opening, Dec. 1914, to Feb. 1919. *Address:* Barcaldene, Sidcup, Kent. *Club:* V.A.D. Ladies'. (M3921)

REED, Lieut. Baron Noel, M.B.E., R.O.A.C.

REED, Edwin, M.B.E.

REED Frank William, O.B.E., *b.* 1860 ; *s.* of William Reed, of Manchester ; *m.* Florence, *d.* of George Gill, of Manchester. *Educ.:* Manchester Technical School, and Owens College. Mechanical Engineer ; Director of Messrs. Craven Brothers (Manchester), Ltd., Reddish Stockport, manufacturers of machine tools, cranes, etc. ; President of Manchester Association of Engineers, 1916–17. *War Work:* Engaged in the production of machine tools, cranes, etc., for the manufacture of all classes of guns, shells, etc. *Addresses:* Craven Bros. (Manchester), Ltd., Reddish, Stockport ; The Grange, South Reddish, Stockport. (O677)

REED, Capt. George Stanley, O.B.E., M.C.

REED, Major George Washington, M.B.E.

REED, Harbottle, M.B.E.

REED, John Arthur, O.B.E., M.B., Ch.B.

REED, Major John Arthur Wemyss, O.B.E., R.A.S.C.

REED, Col. John Ranken, C.B.E.

REED, Leah Lewis, Mrs. Walter, M.B.E. ; *m.* Walter Reed, Solicitor. *War Work:* Working member of the following Committees : War Pensions, Local Relief, and the Employment Committee, Hull.

REED, Margaret Haythorne, M.B.E., *b.* 26 Sept. 1893 ; *d.* of the late Mrs. T. Haynes Reed, of Hampstead. *Educ.:* Allen-Olney School, Hampstead. *War Work:* Air Division and Plans Division of Admiralty ; Earl Roberts' Rest House, King's Cross and Hampstead War Hospital Supply Depot ; Naval Section of Peace Conference, Paris. *Address:* 117, Finchley Road, London, N.W. (M9415)

REED, Sir Stanley, K.B.E., LL.D., *b.* 1872 ; *m.* Lilian,

d. of John Humphrey, of Bombay. Editor of the "Times of India," since 1907 ; joined staff of "Times of India" 1897 ; special correspondent in famine districts of India, 1900 ; Prince and Princess of Wales' tour, 1905–1906 ; Amir's visit, 1907 ; Persian Gulf, 1907 ; Joint Hon. Sec., Bombay Presidency, King Edward and Lord Hardinge Memorials ; Lieut.-Col. commanding Bombay Light Horse, and Hon. A.D.C. to Viceroy ; represented Western India at Imperial Press Conference, 1909 ; Vice-President, Central Publicity Board, 1918 ; *Addresses:* 99, Shore Lane, E.C. ; "Times of India," Bombay. *Clubs:* Byculla ; Royal Bombay Yacht ; Orient ; Willingdon ; Bombay Sports. (K247)

REED, Capt. Thomas, M.B.E.

REED, Thomas Danby, O.B.E., J.P., *b.* 12 May, 1871 ; *s.* of Thomas Reed, of Beeford Grange, Driffield ; *m.* Alice Maud, *d.* of Lamplugh, of Dringhoe. J.P. for the East Riding of Yorkshire ; Alderman of E.R. of Yorkshire County Council. *War Work:* Chairman, East Riding of Yorkshire War Agricultural Executive Committees ; Representative of the Board of Agriculture before the East Riding of Yorkshire Military Service Appeal Tribunal. *Address:* Beeford Grange, Driffield, East Yorks. (O11192)

REED, William, O.B.E.

REED, Major William Louis Lindsay, O.B.E., V.D.

REED, Lieut. John Seymour BLAKE-, O.B.E., R.N.V.R.

REEDER, Capt. and Qr.-Mr. Robert John, M.B.E., R.E.

REEKIE, William Maxwell, O.B.E., *b.* 26 April, 1869 ; *s.* of John Reekie, of Manchester ; *m.* Mary Helen, *d.* of D. R. Paterson, of Bowden, Cheshire. *Educ.:* Manchester Grammar School, and Victoria Univ. Chairman Manchester Royal Institution ; Governor of Whitworth Institute ; Vice-President Manchester Athenæum ; Ex-President Manchester Graphic Club ; Chairman Manchester Branch of The Designs and Industries Association ; co-opted Member of Art Gallery Committee. *War Work:* Member of Local Tribunal ; Deputy Leader Manchester Special Police ; Chairman West Didsbury Belgian Relief Fund ; President Athenæum Rifle Club ; Chairman and Corps Treas. St. John Ambulance Brigade, which along with Special Police raised £10,000 for St. John Hospital in France. *Addresses:* Rowsley, West Didsbury, Manchester ; Orient House, Granly Row, Manchester. *Clubs:* Reform ; Athenæum. (O679)

REEKS, Lieut.-Col. James Albert, O.B.E., *b.* 9 Aug. 1860 ; *s.* of C. F. Reeks, F.R.I.B.A. ; *m.* Elwena Grace Norie, *d.* of F. Norie Miller, J.P., of Cleeve, Perth, Scotland. *Educ.:* Westminster. *War Work:* Commanded Depot, Sherwood Foresters, and the 45th Regt. District Recruiting Area. *Address:* Beechcroft, Epsom, Surrey. *Club:* Junior United Service. (O680)

REEKS, Reginald Rupert, M.B.E.

REEP, William, O.B.E.

REES, Major Blethyn Treharne, O.B.E., Croix de Guerre, *b.* 11 Oct. 1878 ; *s.* of the late Togarmah Rees, of Newport, Mon.; *m.* Edith Mary, *d.* of Edward Phillips, of Newport, Mon. *Educ.:* Clifton Coll. Civil Engineer ; Engineer to H.M. Commissioners of Sewers for Monmouthshire ; Member of Newport Harbour Commissioners. *War Work:* Commanded Reserve Batt. of the Monmouthshire Regiment ; served in France from 1916 to termination of war ; from end of 1917 acted as A.L. Commandant 13th Corps. *Address:* Cwon-y-wiwer, Caerleon, Mon. *Club:* County, Newport, Mon. (O5708)

REES, Catherine Mary, Mrs., M.B.E.

REES, David, C.B.E.

REES, David John, M.B.E.. J.P.

REES, 2nd Lieut. David Morris, M.B.E., R.A.F.

REES, Major David Valentine, O.B.E.. T.D., J P., and D.L. (Breconshire), 1st. Brecknock Batt. S.W.B. (ret.), *b.* 21 July, 1853 ; *s.* of Valentine Rees, of Carmarthen ; *m.* Florence, *d.* of John North, J.P., of Brecon. *Educ.:* Llandovery Coll., and London Hospital. Surgeon, Senior Surgeon Brecknock County Infirmary. *War Work:* Operating Surgeon, Breconshire V.A.D. Hospitals ; Chairman Brecon Recruiting Medical Board. *Address:* Cantie Selyff, Brecon. *Club:* County, Brecon. (O3881)

REES, Ernest Wilmot, M.B.E.

REES, Capt. Frederick William, M.B.E.

REES, Major George Martin Treherne, O.B.E., R.A.F.

REES, Lieut. Harry, M.B.E., R.A.

REES, Henry, M.B.E., *b.* 1 Nov. 1880 ; *s.* of George Rees, of Lampeter ; *m.* Rachel, *d.* of Elias Davies, of Rhydcymerau. *Educ.:* Llandyssul. Journalist, and Sec. to the Cardiganshire Liberal Association. *War Work:* Joint Sec. to Cardiganshire Parliamentary Recruiting Committee ; Sec. and Organiser to Cardiganshire National Service and National War Aims Committees. *Address:* Argoed, Lampeter. (M2334)

REES, Major Herbert, O.B.E.

REES, Henry Bernard, M.B.E.

REES, Howell, C.B.E., J.P., *b.* 1847 ; *s.* of William Rees, of Maesteg. *Educ.:* Univ. Coll., London. *War Work:* District Head Soldiers' and Sailors' Help Society ; Chairman of Local War Pensions, and Member of four sub-committees, and Welsh National Fund ; Member of Glamorgan Red Cross Society. *Address:* 190, Newport Road, Cardiff. (C2897)

REES, James Daniel, O.B.E., *b.* 22 April, 1860 ; *s.* of Griffith Rees, of Swansea. *Educ. :* Swansea Grammar School. Appointed to Exchequer and Audit Department, 1878. *War Work :* Audit of war expenditure Admiralty, and Ministry of Shipping. (O681)

REES, John, M.B.E., *b.* 7 June, 1869 ; *s.* of John Rees, of Glanmo Terrace, Llanelly ; *m.* Anna Jane, *d.* of Benjamin Bowen, of Hermon, Llanfyrnach, Pembs. *Educ. :* Pentrepoth School. Carmarthen ; Normal Coll., Bangor. Headmaster of Clydey Tegryn Council School, Llanfyrnach, Pembs. ; Executive Officer Llanfyrnach Food Committee. *War Work :* Clerk to Llanfyrnach Rural Tribunal since inception ; Executive Officer of Llanfyrnach Food Committee ; Hon. Sec. of Tegryn War Savings Association (£5000) ; Hon. Sec. of Llanfyrnach District War Savings Committee. *Addresses :* Tegryn Council School ; Glynhefin, Llanfyrnach, Pembs. (M9418)

REES, Engineer-Capt. John David, C.B.E., R.N. Served in the Great War, 1914–19 (despatches). (C1936)

REES, Joseph Cook, O.B.E., *b.* 1870 ; *s.* of J. Cook Rees, of Neath ; *m.* Eleanor Jane, *d.* of the late J. Bevan Davies, J.P., of Neath. *Educ. :* Neath. Architect and Surveyor at Neath. *War Work :* In charge of detraining of wounded at Neath, 3rd Western General Hospital at Neath ; Assistant County Director, Red Cross Society, Div. 15, Glam. ; later as County Director, Glamorganshire. *Address :* Glanffrwd, Neath. *Club :* Neath Constitutional. (O3882)

REES, Wing-Comm. Lionel Wilmot Brabazon, V.C., O.B.E., M.C., A.F.C., R.A.F., *b.* 31 July, 1884 ; *s.* of Col. C. H. Rees, V.D., of Carnarvon. *Educ. :* Eastbourne Coll., and R.M.A., Woolwich. Wing-Comm., R.A.F. *War Work :* With R.F.C. in France. *Address :* R.A.F. Cadet College, Cranwell, Lincs. *Club :* R.A.F. (O8173)

REES, Thomas Edgar, M.B.E.

REES, Capt. William Arthur, O.B.E., R.A.M.C.

REEVE, Lieut. Arthur William Simms, O.B.E., R.N.R., *s.* of W. H. Simms Reeve, and *g. s.* of the late Simms Reeve, J.P. and D.L. for Norfolk, *m.*, 11 Sept. 1920, Marguerite Frances, *d.* of the late Antonie Middlemore Sergeant, of New Milton. (O4443)

REEVE, Georgina Ruth, M.B.E.

REEVE, Joan Leslie, Mrs., M.B.E.

REEVE, William Booth, M.B.E., J.P., *b.* 11 Dec. 1861 ; *s.* of John Reeve, of Canterbury, Margate. *Educ. :* Canterbury, Margate. *War Work :* Mayor of Margate, 1913–19, during whole period of war. *Clubs :* Cliftonville and Margate. (M2336)

REEVES, Capt. Edward Charles, M.B.E.

REEVES, Lieut.-Comm. George, M.B.E., R.N.

REEVES, Lieut. John Horace, M.B.E., R.G.A.

REEVES, John James, O.B.E., *b.* 5 April, 1857 ; *s.* of E. B. Reeves, R.N., of Portsmouth ; *m* Annie Jane, *d.* of T. Marshall, of Portsmouth. *Educ. :* Portsmouth. 48 years' service in the Constructive, Accounts, and Naval Ordnance Depts. of the Admiralty. *War Work :* Senior Naval Ordnance Store Officer, Naval Ordnance Dept., Gibraltar, throughout the war. *Address :* The Haven, Park Road, Hythe, Kent. (O11194)

REEVES, Mary Sybil, M.B.E., *b.* 11 May, 1885 ; *d.* of Edmund Whitelock Reeves, of 48, Argyll Road, W. 8. *Educ. :* London ; Folkestone ; Paris. *War Work :* V.A.D., London, 50 ; West End Hospital for Nerves (Shell Shock wards for soldiers), 1915 ; Westminster Hospital (Military wards), 1915–16 ; 1st British Ambulance Unit for Italy, B.R.C.S. Clearing Station for 2nd Army, Italian Front, 1917 ; original railhead canteen for British troops on entering Italy, 1917. *Address :* 48, Argyll Road, London, W. 8. (M9419)

REEVES Capt. Patrick John, O.B.E., *b.* 13 Oct. 1888 ; *s.* of Col. John Reeves, C.B., of Royal Irish Fusiliers. *Educ. :* Charterhouse, and Royal Military Coll., Sandhurst. The Royal Berkshire Regt. *Club :* Army and Navy. (O7617)

REEVES, Lieut. William, M.B.E., *b.* 14 Sept. 1873 ; *s.* of Clifford Reeves, of Birmingham, England. *War Work :* With Royal Newfoundland Regiment. *Address :* P.O. Box, 404, St. John's, Newfoundland. (M5902)

REEVES, William Harvey, O.B.E., Knight of Grace, Order of St. John, *b.* 6 Sept. 1871 ; *s.* of the late William Whittle Reeves, of St. Albans ; *m.* Patty, *d.* of the late Joseph Douglas, of Northampton. *Educ. :* Northampton Grammar School. Member of Northampton Town Council ; Mayor, 1912–13, and 1920–21 ; Assist. Commissioner, St. John Ambulance Brigade ; Hon. County Sec. Northants Red Cross Society, and an Assist. County Director, Northants V.A.D. ; President, Northampton Branch of the Royal Life Saving Institute ; Chairman, Northampton Branch, National Lifeboat Institution ; on Committee of Northampton Cripple Children's Fund, Northampton Amateur Operatic Society, etc. ; Past Master of Kingsley Lodge, Freemasons. *War Work :* Gave whole time for 5 years to Red Cross Work in Northamptonshire ; was presented with oil painting of self by members of the Northants V.A.D., as was also Mrs. Reeves, who gave whole time to the work, as well as other presentations ; Mrs. Reeves was awarded A.R.R.C. and money was collected in the town to endow a cot at the Northampton General Hospital to commemorate her work ; she is also a Lady of Grace of the Order of St. John. *Address :* Spencer Parade, Northampton. *Club :* County, Northampton. (O1794)

REFALO, His Honour Sir Michael Angelo, Knt. Bach., C.B.E., B.A., LL.D., *b.* 1876. Appointed Professor of Commercial Law and History of Legislation, Malta Univ. 1908 ;

Assist. Crown Advocate, Malta, 1910 ; Crown Advocate, 1915 ; Chief Justice and Pres. of Court of Appeal, 1919 ; Member of Control Board, Malta. *Address :* Malta. (C738)

REGAN, Comm. Maurice Ambrose, O.B.E., R.N.V.R., *b.* 1863 ; *s.* of T. A. Regan, of Maryport. *Educ. :* Privately. *War Work :* Naval Transport Officer for the Humber, and Admiralty Agent. *Address :* The Avenue, Hull. *Club :* Hull and East Riding, Hull. (O682)

REGAN, Percy Raphael, M.B.E., M.M., R.E.

REGAN, Robert Henry, M.B.E., R.N.

REHM, Eveline Lucy, M.B.E.

REID, Andrew, M.B.E.

REID, Sir Archibald Douglas, K.B.E., C.M.G., *b.* 14 July, 1871 ; *s.* of Dr. Douglas A. Reid, J.P., of Tenby ; *m.* Annie Allan, *d.* of John Clapperton, of Greenock. *Educ. :* Bradford Coll., and King's Coll. Hospital. Consulting Radiologist ; Superintendent of X-Ray Dept., St. Thomas' Hospital. *War Work :* Capt. (T. Lieut.-Col. R.A.M.C.), R.A.M.C. (T.F.), President, War Office X-Ray Committee, 1915–19. *Address :* 30, Welbeck Street, London, W. 1. (K296)

REID, Beatrice, Mrs., O.B.E.

REID, Charles, O.B.E., *b.* 5 Nov. 1865 ; *s.* of David Reid of Aberdeen ; *m.* Ada Mary, *d.* of Frank Weston, of Stafford. *Educ. :* Aberdeen Univ. Medical Practitioner ; Hon. Physician, Staffordshire General Infirmary ; Staff Surgeon, Staffordshire County Police. *War Work :* County Medical Director, Staffordshire Branch, Red Cross Society ; Commandant, 5th Staffs V.A.D. *Address :* The Diglake, Stafford. *Club :* Stafford County. (O3883)

REID, Major (ret.) Charles Clements, M.B.E., *b.* 30 Aug. 1861 ; *s.* of the late Major-Gen. James Reid. *Educ. :* Edinburgh Academy ; Edinburgh Institution ; Sandhurst. *War Work :* Hon. Sec. and Treas. Clackmannan and Kinross Branch, British Red Cross Society. *Address :* Whinfield, Kinross. (M878)

REID, David Alexander, M.B.E.

REID, Capt. Eric, M.B.E.

REID, Florence, Lady, G.B.E. ; *d.* of Lieut.-Col John Mahony, C.M.G. ; *m.* Sir George Archdall O'Brien, K.B.E., M.B., C.M., F.R.S. (*see* BURKE'S *Peerage*), *s.* of Capt Charles Auguste Reid, 20th Bengal Native Infantry. *Address :* 9, Victoria Road South, Southsea. (DG3)

REID, Lieut.-Col. Frederic James, C.B.E., D.S.O., R.A.S.C., *b.* 1877. Served in the S. African War, 1900–2 (Queen's medal with three clasps, King's medal with two clasps) ; Great War, 1914–19 (despatches). (C1313)

REID, Frederick William, M.B.E.

REID, George, O.B.E., M.D., D.P.H., *b.* 22 Jan. 1854 ; *s.* of David Reid, of Aberdeen ; *m.* Grace Estelle, *d.* of J. H. D. G. Goldie, of Richmond. *Educ. :* Aberdeen Grammar School, and Aberdeen Univ. Medical Officer of Health, Staffordshire County Council ; Examiner in Public Health, Cambridge Univ. *War Work :* Divisional Sanitary Officer, North Midland Division, T.F. *Address :* Broc Hill, Milford, Stafford. County, Stafford. (O683)

REID, Sir George Archdall O'Brien, K.B.E., M.B., C.M., F.R.S.E., *b.* 7 April, 1860 ; *s.* of Capt. Charles Auguste Reid, of 20th Native Infantry, H.E.I.C. ; *m.* Florence Pollard, *d.* of Col. John Mahony, C.M.G., of 24th Regt. *Educ. :* Privately. *War Work :* Four years Medical Officer-in-charge of troops. *Address :* 9, Victoria Road South, Southsea. (K231)

REID, Lieut.-Col. Harold Avery, M.B.E.

REID, Lieut.-Col. Hector-Gowans, C.M.G., C.B.E., D.S.O., A.S.C. Served in South Africa, 1901–2 (Queen's medal with five clasps) ; Great War, 1914–18 (despatches). (C3176)

REID, Lieut.-Col. Hugh, C.B.E., V.D., LL.D., M.Inst.C.E., J.P., D.L., *b.* 9 Feb. 1860 ; *s.* of James Reid, M.Inst.C.E., of Auchterarder, Perthshire ; *m.* Marion, *d.* of John Bell, Shipowner, of Craigview, Prestwick, Ayrshire. *Educ. :* Glasgow High School, and Glasgow Univ. Retired in 1903 from 1st Lanark Royal Engineers (Vols.) with rank of Lieut.-Col. ; Dean of Guild, Glasgow, 1917–18 ; received the Hon. Freedom of the City of Glasgow, 1917 ; Member of the Royal Company of Archers, King's Body Guard for Scotland ; Chief Managing Director of the North British Locomotive Co., Ltd. ; Director, Clydesdale Bank, Ltd. *War Work :* 1908–20, Vice-Chairman, Glasgow Territorial Force Association ; Member, War Executive, Scottish Branch, British Red Cross Society ; Member of Management Committee, Glasgow and West of Scotland Armaments Board. *Address :* Belmont, Springburn, Glasgow. *Clubs :* Royal Societies' ; Junior Army and Navy ; Western, Art, Glasgow. (C273)

REID, Capt. Isaac William, M.B.E., R.E.

REID, Isabella Elizabeth, M.B.E.

REID, James, M.B.E., D.L.

REID, Lieut. James, M.B.E., R.A.O.C.

REID, Paymaster-Lieut. Joseph Alfred, O.B.E., R.N.R.

REID, Lieut. Lionel, O.B.E., R.N.V.R.

REID, Maria Jane, Mrs., M.P.E.

REID, May, C.B.E., *b.* 1 May, 1882 ; *d.* of the late Edward Jervis Reid. *War Work :* Acting County Sec. County of London Branch, British Red Cross Society. *Address :* 137, Ladbroke Road, London, W. *Club :* V.A.D. Ladies'. (C2898)

REID, Pauline, Mrs., O.B.E. (O12009)

REID, Lieut.-Col. Percy Lester, O.B.E., *b.* 20 Nov. 1882 ; *s.* of Percy T. Reid, of Mill Hall, Cuckfield ; *m.* M. E. Fergusson. *Educ. :* Eton. One of the first regular officers to receive the order. *War Work :* Joined B.E.F. in 1914 ; Commanded 2nd Batt. Irish Guards, and end of war was at G.H.Q., France ;

four times mentioned in despatches. *Address:* Thorpe Mandeville Manor, Banbury. *Clubs:* Guards'; Bath. (O1795)

REID, Robert, O.B.E.

REID, Capt. Robert Alburne, O.B.E., R.A.F.

REID, Robert Whyte, C.B.E., *b.* 25 Feb. 1885; *s.* of William Paton Reid, C.B.E., of Belmont Crescent, Glasgow retired Loco Supt., North British Railway; *m.* Frances Mary, *d.* of Edward McInnes, of The Old Hall, Littleover, Derby. *Educ.:* Dundee High School, and Royal Technical Coll., Glasgow. Trained as an Engineer in Glasgow and elsewhere; joined Midland Railway, 1909, as Assistant Works Manager, Carriage and Wagon Dept.; held progressive positions until appointed Carriage and Wagon Supt., Midland Railway, May, 1919. *War Work:* Acted as Carriage and Wagon Supt. during the absence of D. Bain, C.B.E., in the Ministry of Munitions, and was responsible for special rolling stock required in connection with war purposes in this country and overseas. *Address:* South Avenue, Littleover, Derby. (C2894)

REID, Thomas, M.B.E.

REID, Thomas Ebenezer, M.B.E., J.P., *b.* 1869; *s.* of Thomas E. Reid, of Armagh; *m.* Annie Margretta, B.A., *d.* of Robert Mann, of Hockley. *Educ.:* Armagh. Sec. to County Council, and Clerk to the Local Authority for the County of Armagh *War Work:* Hon. Sec. Comforts Fund, Royal Irish Fusiliers; Hon. Sec. Co. Recruiting Committee; Hon. Sec. to Reception Committee for Irish Canadian Rangers, Irish Fusiliers, and Irish Guards; Hon. Sec. Distress Committee for Co. Armagh; Hon. Sec. Belgian Relief Committee, Armagh District. *Address:* County Court House, Armagh; Little Castledillon, Armagh. *Club:* Armagh City. (M10252*h*)

REID, Capt. Thomas Morley, O.B.E.

REID, Major Walter Clarke, O.B.E., I.A.

REID, Major Sir William, Knt. Bach., M.B.E., J.P., *s.* of the late William Reid, of Glenhead, Lenzie, Provost of Largs, 1915–18; Chairman, Royal Glasgow Asylum for the Blind, 1918–21; Vice-Chairman of Advisory Committee to the Scottish Board of Health on the care and supervision of the Blind, 1918–21 *Address:* Hutton Park, Largs, Ayrshire. *Clubs:* National Liberal; Scottish Liberal (Edinburgh); Liberal (Glasgow); Royal Scottish Automobile; Royal Gourock Yacht. (M9427)

REID, William, M.B.E.

REID, William Macdonald, M.B.E., *b.* 27 Sept 1873; *s.* of William Reid, of Dungarvan; *m.* Jane Coulter Amelia, *d.* of Samuel Gilmore, M.D., of Castleblayney. *Educ.:* Royal School, Cavan. Solicitor. *War Work:* Recruiting Services. *Address:* Church Street, Cavan. *Club:* Co. Cavan. (M9428)

REID, William Paton, C.B.E., *b.* 8 Sept. 1854; *s.* of Robert Reid, of Glasgow. Locomotive Superintendent, North British Railway. *War Work:* Gun Mountings, Transport Wagons, etc. *Address:* 15, Belmont Crescent, Glasgow. (C2900)

REID, Dame Clarissa GUTHRIE-, D.B.E.; *d.* of Wm. Harnett Blanch; *m.* James Guthrie Reid. *Educ.:* Privately. *War Work:* Founder and Hon. Sec. of the Anglo-South American Central Depot and Club. *Address:* 2, Queen's Gate, S.W. 7. (D29)

REILLY, Major Bernard Rawdon, O.B.E.

REILLY, Professor Charles Herbert, O.B.E., M.A (Cantab.), F.R.I.B.A., *b.* 1874; *s.* of Charles Reilly, of High House, Upminster, Essex; *m.* Dorothy Gladys, *d.* of James Jerram Pratt, of Bournemouth. *Educ.:* Merchant Taylors' School, and Queens' Coll., Cambridge. Professor of Architecture, Univ. of Liverpool; Vice-Chairman, Liverpool Repertory Theatre Co.,; Member of Board of Architectural Education, R.I.B.A.; late Member of Council of the Royal Institute of British Architects. *War Work:* H.M. Inspector, Munitions Areas, Liverpool and N. Wales. *Address:* Univ. Liverpool. *Club:* Univ. Liverpool. (O11195)

REILLY, Lieut. Charles Oliver Calcott, M.B.E., I.A.

REILLY, Major James Myles Townsend, O.B.E., J.P., *b.* 23 April, 1855; *s.* of the late Capt. J. M. T. Reilly, of Scarva, Co. Down, Ireland; *m.* Frances Isabel, *d.* of Dr. S. Spranger. Major, Royal Inniskilling Fusiliers (ret.). *War Work:* Sub-Area Commander for Recruiting from Aug. 1914–18. *Address:* 18, Royal Crescent, Bath. *Clubs:* Junior United Service; Bath and County. (O8961)

REILLY, Capt. and Qr.-Mr. Thomas, M.B.E.

REISS, Lieut.-Col. Alexander, C.B.E., J.P., *b.* 27 March, 1871; *s.* of Frederick Reiss, of 42, Pont Street, London, S.W.; *m.* Angélique Constance, *d.* of William Candy, of 183, Ashley Gardens, London, S.W. *Educ.:* Winchester. *War Work:* Interpreter, Sept. 1914; joined Cheshire Regt. (new Army), Oct. 1914; 2nd in command 12th (S.) Batt. March, 1915, transferred to R.A.F. 1 April, 1918; Assist. Controller, Aircraft France and Salonica; later, Deputy Assist. Director, W.O.; transferred to R.A.F. 1 April, 1918; Assist. Controller, Aircraft Production Dept., attached to Ministry of Munitions, 1 Jan. 1918. *Address:* 30, Hans Mansions, London, S.W. 1. *Clubs:* Cavalry; Hurlingham; M.C.C. (C2348)

REISS, Charles, C.B.E., B.A. (Oxon.), *b.* 7 Sept. 1873; *s.* of F. Reiss, of 42, Pont Street, S.W. 1; *m.* Esmé, *d.* of A. P. MacEwen. *Educ.:* Harrow-on-the-Hill, and Christ Church, Oxford. *War Work:* Sec. to the Liner Requisition at the Ministry of Shipping. *Address:* 22, Hans Place, London, S.W. 1. *Club:* Oxford and Cambridge. (C1028)

REISS, Phyllis Emily, Mrs., M.B.E.

REITH, Alexander Murray, O.B.E., M.S.A., J.P., *b.*

18 Sept. 1885; *s.* of Wm. Reith, of Aberdeen. *Educ.:* Aberdeen, and Edinburgh. Partner in firm of Richardson and Cruddas, Engineers, Bombay and Madras. *War Work:* Deputy Sec. to Government, Bombay, in charge of War Resources in 1918; one of the founders of the "Bombay Scottish." *Clubs:* Royal Bombay Yacht; Caledonian. (O8292)

REITH, Jan Stuart, M.B.E.

RELPH, John William, M.B.E.

RELTON, Arthur John, C.B.E., F.C.I.I., *b.* 4 Nov. 1856; *s.* of the late Francis Boyer Relton, of St. Leonards-on-Sea; *m.* Geraldine Victoria, *d.* of Daniel Thomas Lyons Clanchy, of Charleville, Co. Cork. *Educ.:* Chatham House, Ramsgate, and Oberlahnstein-am-Rhine; Fellow of Chartered Institute of Insurance; Member of Aircraft Insurance Committee; Manager of Fire and other Departments, Guardian Insurance Co., 1888–1915. *War Work:* Member of War Risks Insurance Committee (Govt.). *Clubs:* Junior Athenæum; Sandy Lodge Golf. (C274)

REMINGTON, Alfred Arnold, O.B.E., M.I.MechE., M.I.A.E., A.F.Ae.S., *b.* 25 April, 1877; *s.* of John Remington, of Birmingham. Past-President, Institution of Automobile Engineers; Technical Director Karrier Motors, Ltd., Huddersfield. *War Work:* Engineer in connection with production of Aeronautical Engines. *Address:* Overdale, Wylde Green. *Club:* Royal Automobile. (O11196)

REMINGTON, Capt. Percy Thordon, M.B.E.

REMNANT, Lieut.-Col. Sir James Farquharson, Bart., C.B.E.; *m.* Frances Emily, *d.* of late Robert Gosling, of Hassebury, Bishop-Stortford. *Educ.:* Harrow, and Magdalen Coll., Oxford. Called to the Bar, 1886; M.P. for Holborn since 1900; Member L.C.C. for Holborn, 1892–1900. *Address:* The Grange, Twyford, Berks. *Clubs:* Constitutional; United. (C1750)

RENAUD, Lieut.-Col. Ernest James, O.B.E.

RENDALL, Percy John, O.B.E., M.D., *b.* 26 July, 1861; *s.* of John Rendall, of Inner Temple; *m.* Edith, *d.* of E. Watson, of Buckhurst Hill. *Educ.:* Repton; King's Coll., London; St. Bartholomew's Hospital. Medical Officer, Special Clinics at Royal Surrey County Hospital, Guildford, and Victoria Cottage Hospital, Woking, under Surrey County Council. *War Work:* Lieut. R.A.M.C.; Clin. Apt. Skin Dept. Middlesex Hospital; M.O.-in-charge Special Clinic, Royal Herbert Hospital, Woolwich; mentioned in despatches, Feb. 1919. *Address:* 28A, Moorgate Street, London, E.C. (O11841)

RENDALL, Capt. Thomas Shuttleworth, O.B.E.

RENDEL, Major Richard Meadows, O.B.E., R.A.

RENDEL, 2nd Lieut. William Vincent, M.B.E.

RENDELL, Robert George, C.B.E. Organised Newfoundland Cadet Corps. (C2011)

RENDELL, Lieut.-Col. Walter Frederick, C.B.E.

RENDLE, Evangeline Annette Harriett, Mrs. (Eva), M.B.E., *b.* 1855; *d.* of Thomas Saunders Cave, of Brancliffe Grange, Yorkshire, and Rossbrin, Co. Cork, Ireland; *m.* Arthur Edgcumbe, *s.* of William Edgcumbe Rendle, London. *Educ.:* England and France. *War Work:* Superintendent of Indexing Staff of Prize Court Branch of Treasury Solicitor's Dept. Law Courts, for 5¼ years. *Address:* 28, Lebanon Park, Twickenham. (M3927)

RENDLE, Lieut. William Edgcumbe, O.B.E.

RENFREW, Lieut. Robert, M.B.E.

RENNET, Major and Brevet Lieut.-Col. David, M.B.E., M.D., D.P.H., R.A.M.C. (T.), *b.* 19 Jan. 1866; *s.* of David Rennet, LL.D., of Aberdeen; *m.* Elizabeth, *d.* of — Foggo, of Braemar. *Educ.:* Grammar School; Univ. Aberdeen. Medical Officer of Health, City of Chester. *War Work:* Specialist Sanitary Officer, Western Command, Sept. 1914, to March, 1919. *Address:* Cluny, Queen's Park, Chester. (M5568)

RENNICK, Major Denis Kingston, M.B.E., I.A.

RENNIE, Comm. Alexander, O.B.E., R.N.R.

RENNIE, Capt. Andy Gerald, M.B.E.

RENNIE, Lieut. George, M.B.E.

RENNIE, (Cadet) Lieut.-Col. Horace Watt, C.B.E., *b.* 6 May, 1866; *s.* of the late James Rennie, of Edgbaston; *m.* Margaret Maude, *d.* of Robert Dixon, of Truro, Cornwall. *Educ.:* K.E. High School, Birmingham; Mason's Science Coll. Trained as Metallurgical Chemist and Mining Engineer; Metallurgist to Pahang Corporation, Ltd. (Malay States); at present partner in firm of James Rennie & Co., Metal Merchants, Birmingham (founded 1868). *War Work:* Not passed for active service, being over age; joined Warwickshire Rifle Corps, Sept. 1914; received Cadet Commission, May, 1915; later appointed County Staff Officer for Cadets, Warwickshire, to supervise organisation and training of the 60 Cadet Companies under command of Brig.-Gen. W. R. Ludlow, C.B., T.D.; still hold this appointment, and granted C.B.E. for services rendered during the war. *Addresses:* The Gable House, Hazelwell, Birmingham; 54, Exchange Buildings, Birmingham. *Club:* Old Edwardians'. (C2901)

RENNIE, Capt. William Hoyles, M.B.E.

RENOUF, Lieut. Cyril Percival, O.B.E.

RENSHAW, Lieut. John William, M.B.E., R.N.

RENSHAW, Samuel Henry, O.B.E., J.P.

RENTON, Capt. and Qr.-Mr. William Clifford, O.B.E., R.A.M.C.

RENWICK, Sir Harry (Benedetto), K.B.E., *b.* 13 June, 1861; *s.* of Andrew Renwick, of Windscr; *m.* Frederica Louisa, *d.* of Robert Laing, of Stirling, N.B. *Educ.:* Brunswick

House, Windsor, and Privately. Chairman and Managing Director of the County of London Electric Supply Co. Ltd., of the Bournemouth and Poole Electricity Supply Co., Ltd., of the South London Electric Supply Co., Ltd., of the Richmond (Surrey) Electric Light and Power Co., Ltd., of the Coatbridge and Airdrie Electric Supply Co., Ltd., of the Lower Thames Land and Power Co., Ltd.; Director of the South Metropolitan Electric Supply Co., Ltd.; Chairman of the Provincial Electric Supply Committee of the United Kingdom, and other companies; Member of the Institute of Electrical Engineers. *War Work:* Director of Feeding Stuffs, Ministry of Food, 1917–18; and served on several Government Committees. *Address:* Burnham, Chartfield Avenue, Putney Hill, S.W. *Club:* City of London; Gresham; St. Stephen's; Automobile. (K414)

RENWICK, Capt. John, O.B.E., R.A.M.C.

REPTON, Guy George, M.B.E., *b.* 16 Aug. 1861; *s.* of George William John Repton, late M.P. Warwick, and Lady Jane Repton, daughter of third Duke of Leinster (*see* BURKE'S *Peerage*); *m.* Marion Emily, *d.* of John James Knight. *Educ.:* Eton and Oxford. *War Work:* Metropolitan Special Constabulary; now Commandant " G " Division. *Addresses:* 29, Curzon Street, Mayfair, W.; Winchfield House, Winchfield, Hants. *Clubs:* Carlton; Bachelors'. (M9431)

RESIDE, Capt. David Alexander. M.B.E.

RESTALL, Walter Tapley, O.B.E., *b.* 10 Dec. 1858; *s.* of Robert Restall; *m.* Edith Jessie, *d.* of William Pugh. Senior Clerk in H.M. Exchequer and Audit Department; served as Private Secretary to Sir John A. Kempe, K.C.B., late Compt. and Auditor-General, and to Sir Henry J. Gibson, K.C.B., Compt. and Auditor-General. *Address:* Rothesay, 14, Parkside, Hampton Wick. (O1798)

RESTLER, Squadron-Leader James Douglas Kendall, O.B.E., R.A.F.

RETALLACK, Major John Ley, O.B.E.

REVELL, Alfred Edgar, O.B.E. (O11788)

REVILLON, 2nd Lieut. Joseph Whistler, O.B.E., R.E.

REVNELL, Rev. Arthur Jesse, O.B.E., *b.* 24 Feb. 1877; *s.* of William Fry Revnell, of London; *m.* Alice Louisa. *d.* of Henry Gould Barker, of Dover. *Educ.:* Martyr Memorial School, and Richmond Coll. Superintending Wesleyan Chaplain in India. *War Work:* Chaplain to the Forces in Mesopotamia. *Address:* Abbeyfeale Lodge, Simla. *Club:* United Service (Simla). (O4246)

REW, Lieut.-Col. Charles Edward Daliel Oldham, O.B.E.

REYNARDSON, Lieut.-Col. Arthur ACLAND-HOOD-, O.B.E., J.P., *b.* Dec. 1859; *s.* of Sir Alexander Acland-Hood, Bart., of St. Audries, Somerset; *m.* Miriam Anne, *d.* of Col. Birch-Reynardson, of Holywell Hall, Stamford. *Educ.:* Eton. Retired, 1906—as a Major in the Rifle Brigade. *War Work:* 1914; Intelligence (Home); 1915, Camp Commandant to T.I.G.C., B.E.F., Mediterranean; 1916–19, Commanded a Batt. of Cheshire Regt. *Address:* Ranworth Hall, Norwich. *Club:* Travellers'. (O7172)

REYNAUD, Capt. Edward Henry, M.B.E., R.M.A., *b.* 8 Oct. 1874; *s.* of Henry Frederick Reynaud, of Valetta, Malta. *Educ.:* Lyceum, and Malta Univ. Acting Staff Capt., No. 1 Section, Malta. *War Work:* Orderly Officer to G.O.C., No. 1 Section, on Staff since 1917; Acting Staff Capt., No. 1 Section and twice acted as Staff Officer to the General commanding No. 1 Section. Malta, and A.O. Royal Artillery. *Address:* 2, Sda. Molini, Valetta, Malta. *Club:* Casino Maltese. (M6695)

REYNISH, Capt. James Bruce, M.B.E., B.A., B.Sc., H.M.I., *b.* 14 April, 1879; *s.* of the late James Reynish, of Poole, Dorset; *m.* Aileen, *d.* of the Rev. F. W. Aveling, M.A., B.Sc., of Twickenham, Middlesex. *Educ.:* London Univ., and St. John's Coll., Oxford. H.M. Inspector of Schools, Board of Education. *War Work:* Capt. R.E. Chemical Warfare, Anti-Gas Section; Officer-in-charge Inspection Depots. *Address:* 712, Chester Road, Stretford, Lancs. (M5569)

REYNOLDS, Lieut. Andrew Bishop, M.B.E., R.N., *b.* 1 Feb. 1870. Divisional Officer of Coastguard. *War Work:* Examining Officer (N.E.S.), Berehaven, 1914–17; Assistant King's Harbour Master and Coaling Officer, Berehaven, 1917–19; Divisional Officer of Coastguard, Castletown Division, 1919–20. *Address:* 49, Blenheim Street, Hull, Yorkshire. (M10487)

REYNOLDS, Comm. Arthur, M.B.E., *b.* 30 Oct. 1866; *s.* of Matthew Reynolds, of Hucknall Torkard, Notts; *m.* Elizabeth Francis, *d.* of James Aellens, of Hastings. *Educ.:* Hucknall Torkard, Notts. Over 33 years' service as a Salvation Army Officer. *War Work:* Manager of the Salvation Army Hut, Shorncliffe, 6 months, the Salvation Army Naval and Military Chatham Home, for three years, and the Salvation Army Naval and Military Home, Dover, for one year. *Address:* 130A, Snargate Street, Dover. (M9433)

REYNOLDS, Arthur Charles, M.B.E., *b.* 13 April, 1875; *s.* of R. C. Reynolds, R.N., of Portsmouth; *m.* Edith, *d.* of James Brewtey, of Windsor. *Educ.:* Christ's Hospital, Newgate Street, E.C. Master Mariner, Trinity House Steam Vessel Service. *War Work:* General sea work in the Harwich area throughout the whole period of the war; for Trinity House and Admiralty, maintaining the war channel; locating and surveying wrecks; buoying mine fields, etc. *Address:* 1, Alexandra Road, Dovercourt, Essex. (M3929)

REYNOLDS, Clement Unsworth, M.B.E.

REYNOLDS Lieut.-Col. Edgar Hercules, O.B.E., *b.*

20 Oct. 1878; *s.* of Capt. R. H. Reynolds, of Sydney; *m.* Frances Lucy, *d.* of Francis Adams, of Sydney. *Educ.:* St. Aloysius Coll., and Univ. of Sydney. Seconded from the Royal Australian Artillery to the General Staff; now G.S.O., 1st Grade, at Dist. H.Q., Sydney. *War Work:* Director of Military Operations at Army H.Q. (Melbourne, Australia), Aug. 1914 to March 1916 organised the Australian Flying Corps and commanded the 1st Squadron; appointed at War Office, May 1916, to organise the A.F.C. and act as Liaison Officer; served on Australian H.Q. in France as G.S.O.2 until appointed Staff Officer Australian Flying Corps; appointed Director of Military Art, R.M.C., Duntroon, Oct. 1918. *Address:* Victoria Barracks, Sydney. *Club:* New South Wales (Sydney). (O1800)

REYNOLDS, Capt. Ernest Brayley, O.B.E., M.R.C.V.S., R.A.V.C., *b.* 3 Jan. 1879; *s.* of James Henry Reynolds, of Daventry. Veterinary Surgeon; Professor at Royal Veterinary Coll., London. *War Work:* Served through South African War; served in France, then in Mesopotamia, commanding the veterinary hospital at Baghdad, and later on the North-West Frontier, India. *Address:* Royal Veterinary College, Camden Town, London. (O6692)

REYNOLDS, Ethel Maude, M.B.E.

REYNOLDS, Col. Frank Romilly, O.B.E., R.F.

REYNOLDS, Harold Bulkely, O.B.E.

REYNOLDS, Harriet Sarah, Mrs., M.B.E.

REYNOLDS, Henry George, M.B.E., *b.* 1873; *s.* of the late Henry Niblett Reynolds, of Bristol; *m.* Beatrice Elizabeth, *d.* of the late Henry Fisher, of Bristol. *Educ.:* British School, Bedminster, Bristol. Secretary: appointed Divisional Sec. South Midland Division, Young Men's Christian Association, 1916. *War Work:* Organising Sec. for military work in the counties of Northamptonshire, Bedfordshire, Buckinghamshire, and Hertfordshire. *Address:* 144, Birchfield Road, Northampton. (M3930)

REYNOLDS, Major Herbert James Blakemore, M.B.E., *s.* of John James Reynolds, of Manchester. *Educ.:* Sedbergh. Mining Engineer (private practice). *War Work:* Officer of the R.A.S.C. (T.F.); O.C. R.A.S.C., Cyprus, 1914–15; Mediterranean Exped. Force, Gallipoli, 1915; Egyptian Exped. Force, 1916; Mesopotamian Exped. Force, commanding 596 Co. R.A.S.C., M.T., 1916–19. *Addresses:* Parr's Bank Buildings, 3 York Street, Manchester; 16, Knowsley Road, Southport, Lancs. (O2295)

REYNOLDS, (late Major) Louis George Stanley, O.B.E., (T.F. and R.A.F.), *b.* 23 Dec. 1883; *s.* of the late Col. E. Swatman Reynolds, of Indian Staff Corps. *Educ.:* Bradfield, and Balliol. Civil Servant; Private Sec. to Under Sec. of State for War (Col. Seely), Jan. to June, 1912; Private Sec. to Q.M.G. to the Forces (Sir J. S. Cowans), July, 1912, to Aug. 1916. *War Work:* Private Sec. to Q.M.G., War Office, outbreak of war till Aug. 1916; Aeronautical Contracts Dept., Aug. 1916, to May, 1917; R.F.C. and R.A.F. (Flying Officer and Flight Comm.), May, 1917, to March, 1919; S.O.2, Air Ministry, April to May, 1918. Chevalier Legion d'Honneur. *Address:* 2, Stanhope Gardens, S.W. 7. *Clubs:* St. Stephen's; R.A.F. (O7621)

REYNOLDS, Margaret Maude, Mrs., M.B.E., Q.M.A.A.C.

REYNOLDS, Capt. Philip George, M.B.E., R.A.S.C.

REYNOLDS, Capt. Reginald Carey, O.B.E., M.Inst.T., A.C.I.S., *b.* 9 Feb. 1883; *s.* of Herbert Reynolds, of London; *m.* Rosa Stella, *d.* of Powell S. Tripp, of Manchester. *Educ.:* Borden Grammar School, Kent. *War Work:* Chairman of Advisory Committee; Chairman of Divisional Board, and Divisional Road Transport Officer; Road Transport Board, North Western Division; various transport undertakings and contracts for H.M. Government. *Address:* Dunedin, Albert Road, Whalley Range, Manchester. *Club:* Arts, Manchester. (O11198)

REYNOLDS, Col. Reginald Philip Nesi, C.B.E. R.E. (ret.).

REYNOLDS, Lieut.-Col. Sidney Latimer, O.B.E., R.A.S.C.

REYNOLDS, Lieut. Walter Deveson, M.B.E., R.E.

REYNOLDS, Capt. Walter Philip Kearns, O.B.E., R.A.S.C. (T.F.)

REYNOLDS, William, M.B.E., *b.* 5 July, 1871; *s.* of the late James Reynolds, of Truro, Cornwall, and latterly of King's Heath, Birmingham; *m.* Mary Ann Rennell, *d.* of George Shears, of Churchill, nr. Salcombe, South Devon. *Educ.:* St. John's Collegiate School, Truro, Cornwall. Began journalistic work in 1889 as member of Staff of " Western Morning News," Plymouth; appointed Sub-Editor of " The Midland Daily Telegraph," Coventry, 1894; has been Editor of " Midland Daily Telegraph " since 1914. *War Work:* The journal of which he is Editor took active part in support of cause of National Service and in the promotion of recruiting and other war activities, including assisting Red Cross and similar work. *Address:* 12, Ellys Road, Coventry. (M9434)

REYNOLDS, Capt. William Charles Noel, O.B.E.

REYNOLDS, William Howe, M.B.E.

RENAUD, Lieut. Edward Henry, M.B.E.

RHIND, Sir Thomas Duncan, K.B.E., T.D. *b.* 1871; *s.* of late John Rhind, Sculptor, A.R.S.A.; *m.* Mary Elizabeth, *d.* of late W. Mathews Gilbert, of Edinburgh. *Educ.:* George Watson's Coll., Edinburgh. Served with the Royal Scots; Statistical Advisor Ministry of Pensions. *Club:* Junior Naval and Military; Scottish Conservative (Edinburgh). (K232)

RHIND, William Alexander, M.B.E., R.N.

RHODES, Arthur Edgar Gravenor, O.B.E.

RHODES, Campbell Ward, C.B.E., b. 17 Jan. 1874; *s.* of Francis Rhodes, M.D.; *m.* Eleanor Wemyss, *d.* of A. G. Reid, J.P. *Educ.*: Manchester Grammar School, and Owens Coll. Chairman, Hoare, Miller & Co., Ltd., Calcutta and Bombay; Member of the Bengal Legislative Council. *Address*: 10, Loudon Street, Calcutta. *Clubs*: Bengal; Calcutta; Oriental. (C2392)

RHODES, Caroline Maud, Mrs., M.B.E; *d.* of Robert Griffin, J.P., of Court Garden, Marlow; *m.* Hubert Victor (Major, O.B.E.), *s.* of J. W. Rhodes, J.P., D.L., of Hennerton, Henley-on-Thames. *War Work*: Served in France, Jan. 1915, Commandant V.A.D. Berks. 58, B.R.C.S., and opened Woodclyffe Auxiliary Hospital, Wargrave, in 1915; was Commandant of that until it closed in 1919; holds British War Medal, and Victory Medal; mentioned in despatches. *Address*: Ash Tree House, Wargrave, Berks. *Club*: Empress. (M3931)

RHODES, Edward Hugh, O.B.E., b. 3 Jan. 1874; *s.* of Edward Hawksley Rhodes, late Deputy-Keeper of the Land Revenue Record Office; *m.* Patricia, *d.* of W. H. Scrymgour, of Millstrood, Whitstable. *Educ.*: Clare Coll., Cambridge. Principal Clerk, Ministry of Health; Barrister-at-law. *War Work*: In charge of War Refugees Department, Local Government Board, during war. *Address*: 8, Belsize Lane, N.W. 3. (O11199)

RHODES, Ellen Laura Amy, Mrs., O.B.E.

RHODES, George Edward, O.B.E.

RHODES, Capt. and Brevet-Major Godfrey Dean, C.B.E., D.S.O., R.E., also Officier Legion d'Honneur, *b.* 18 July, 1886; *s.* of H. Rhodes, of Vancouver, B.C., Canada; *m.* Marion Jessie, *d.* of the late W. Topping, London. *Educ.*: Trinity Coll. School, Port Hope; Royal Military Coll., Kingston. Royal Engineers; Indian State Rlys. (P.W.D.) *War Work*: O.C. Rly. Construction Co., 1915–16; Asst. Director of Rlys. (Construction), Salonika, 1916–17; ·Director of Rlys. Salonika, 1917–18; Constantinople, 1918–20; has held the rank of Brig.-Gen. *Address*: c/o Cox & Co., 16, Charing Cross. *Club*: Junior United Service. (C1416)

RHODES, Major Hubert Victor, O.B.E., b. 20 Aug. 1873; *s.* of the late John William Rhodes, J.P., D.L., of Co. Berks., and Hennerton, Henley-on-Thames; *m.* Caroline Maud, *d.* of Robert Griffin, J.P., Co. Bucks., of Court Garden, Marlow. *Educ.*: Winchester Coll. Army (retired), Reserve of Officers; late The Sherwood Foresters; served in India, China, South Africa, Malay States, Mediterranean; War Service; South Africa, 1899–1903 (Queen's Medal, 4 clasps; King's Medal, 2 clasps; despatches); European War, 1914–19; 1914 Star, Allied Victory Medal, British War Medal, Despatches, O.B.E.; served on Staff throughout the war. *Addresses*: Ash Tree House, Wargrave; Messrs. Cox & Co., 16, Charing Cross. *Clubs*: Army and Navy; M.C.C.; Phyllis Court. (O7624)

RHODES, Sir Robert Heaton, K.B.E., M.A.; *s.* of late Robert Heaton Rhodes, Christchurch; *m.* Jessie Cooper, *d.* of late Walter Clark, of Clenara, Victoria. *Educ.*: New Zealand; Brasenose Coll., Oxford. Barrister-at-law, Inner Temple, 1887; Member of House of Representatives for Ellesmere since 1899; served S. African War with 8th N.Z. Contingent, commanding the Canterbury Mounted Rifles Brigade of New Zealand Territorial Force; Postmaster-General and Minister for Public Health, Hospitals and Tourists Resorts, 1912–15; N.Z. Red Cross Commissioner, London, 1917; Special Commissioner, London, 1917; Special Commissioner to Egypt and Gallipoli to report on conditions of N.Z. troops, 1915. *Address*: 125, High Holborn, W.C.; Otahuna, Tai Tapu, Canterbury, N.Z. (K235)

RHODES, Major Stanislas Matthew Hastings, O.B.E.

RHONDDA, Sybil Margaret, Viscountess (Dowager), D.B.E., b. 25 Feb. 1857; *d.* of George Augustus Haig, of Pen Ithon; *m.* David Alfred Thomas, 1st Viscount Rhondda (see BURKE'S *Peerage*). *Educ.*: Home. *War Work*: Chairman, Women Advisory Committee, National War Savings Committee. *Addresses*: Llanwern Park, Newport, Mon.; 122, Ashley Gardens, Westminster. *Clubs*: Lyceum; Forum. (D52)

RIACH, George, M.B.E.

RIALL, Major Malcolm Brown Bookey, O.B.E.

RICARDO, Brig.-Gen. Ambrose St. Quintin, C.M.G., C.B.E., D.S.O., b. 21 Nov. 1866; *s.* of Henry David Ricardo, of Gatcombe, Minchinhampton, Gloucestershire; *m.* Elizabeth Alice, *d.* of Emerson T. Herdman, of Sion Mills, Co. Tyrone. *Educ.*: Winchester Coll. J.P. *War Work*: Served Tirah Expedition. 1897–8; S.A. War, 1899–1902; Great War, 1914–19. *Address*: Sion Mills, Co. Tyrone. *Clubs*: Ulster, Belfast; Friendly Brothers House, Dublin.

RICARDO, Col. Francis Cecil, C.V.O., C.B.E., b. 1852; *s.* of the late Percy Ricardo, of Bramley Park, Guildford; *m.* Marie Annie, who *d.* 1907, *d.* of J. Littlefield. Entered Grenadier Guards, 1872; Capt. 1884; Major, 1890; Lieut.-Col. 1897; Col. 1903 (h.p. 1905); retired, 1909; Adj. at School of Instruction for Auxiliary and Reserve Forces, Wellington Barracks, 1877–80; A.D.C. to Lord-Lieut. of Ireland, 1880; Brig. Major, Home Dist. 1885–90; A.A.G. Home Dist. 1900–4; acted for 11 years as Hon. Sec. to Royal Military Tournament; Chief Constable of Berks, 1915–18; J.P. for Berks (High Sheriff, 1913); received Coronation medal, 1902. *Address*: Lullebrook Manor. Cookham. (C2902)

RICARDO, Katherine Alice, O.B.E., b. 22 Dec. 1879; *d.* of Frank Ricardo, of Bure Homage, Christchurch, and Bromesberrow Place, Gloucester. *Educ.*: Privately. *War Work*: Commandant, Red Cross Hospital, Sept. 1914, to Feb.

1919, Christchurch, Hants. *Address*: Berghmote, Wimborne, Dorset. *Club*: Empress. (O3884)

RICCARD, Major John Stanley, O.B.E., R.G.A.

RICE, Major Arthur Henry, O.B.E.

RICE, Arthur John, M.B.E., R.N.

RICE, Bernard, O.B.E., M.D, M.R.C.S., b. 8 July, 1860; *s.* of Bernard Rice, of Stratford-on-Avon; *m.* Lilian Hyde, *d.* of William Hannay, of Leamington. *Educ.*: King Edward's School, Stratford-on-Avon, and St. Bartholomew's Hospital. Consulting Surgeon (late Surgeon), Warneford Hospital; Consulting Surgeon, Midland Counties Home for Incurables, and Leamington Provident Dispensary. *War Work*: Surgeon to Warneford Auxiliary Military Hospital; Surgeon-in-charge, The Warren V.A.D. Hospital. *Address*: Westrock House, Leamington Spa. (O4388)

RICE, Lieut.-Col. Cecil Edward, C.B.E., D.S.O. Comdt. of a School of Instruction with rank of Lieut.-Col.; served in S. Africa, 1901–2; Great War, 1914–19 (despatches, with Bar). (C1388)

RICE, Fabian Arthur Besant, O.B.E.

RICE, Helen Sarah, Hon. Mrs., O.B.E. J.P.; *d.* of Sir Arthur Godley, G.C.B., 1st Baron Kilbracken (see BURKE'S *Peerage*); *m.* Henry Edward Harcourt, *s.* of the late Adm. Sir E. Rice, K.C.B., of Dane Court (see BURKE'S *Landed Gentry*). *Address*: Dane Court. Dover, Kent. (O11200)

RICE, Lieut.-Comm. James, O.B.E., M.V.O.

RICE, Percy Christopher, M.B.E., b. 21 Feb. 1877; *s.* of John Norman Rice, of West Dulwich; *m.* Edith Beatrice, *d.* of Ernest Colman, of Wimbledon. *Educ.*: King's Coll., London. Passed a competitive examination, 16 May, 1895, and appointed a Second Division Clerk in the Foreign Office, 30 Dec. 1895; promoted to be a Staff Officer, 16 Jan. 1916; appointed a Member of the Order of the British Empire, 1 Jan. 1918; appointed Finance Officer in the Department of Overseas Trade, 1 April, 1919; assistant Editor of the "Foreign Office List" since 1 Oct. 1915. *Address*: Kildare, Worple Road, Wimbledon, London, S.W. 19. (M884)

RICE, Lieut.-Col. Sidney Mervyn, C.I.E., C.B.E., b. 1873; *s.* of Lewis Rice, C.I.E., of Greenhalgh, Harrow-on-the-Hill. *Educ.*: Reading and R.M.C. Lieut.-Col. Indian Army; A.Q.M.G. S. Command, India. *Address*: Poona, India. *Clubs*: East India United Service; Junior Army and Navy. (C3101)

RICE, Major William Henry, M.B.

RICE, Dame Margaret, VAUGHAN-PRYSE-, D.B.E., b. 17 July, 1869; 2nd *d.* of late Capt. James Stewart, D.L., of Alityrodyn, Cardiganshire (see BURKE'S *Landed Gentry*); *m.* 27 Sept. 1887, John Carberry Pugh Vaughan-Pryse-Rice, D.I.., *o. s.* of late John Pugh Vaughan-Pryse, D.L., of Bwichbychan, Cardiganshire (see BURKE'S *Landed Gentry*). President Carmarthenshire British Red Cross Society, which she organised in 1910. *Address*: Llwyn-y-Brain, Llandovery, Carmarthenshire. (D16)

RICH, Major Theodore, O.B.E., R.E. (T.)

RICHARDS, Albert Edwin George, C.B.E., R.C.N.C., b. 11 Aug. 1856; *s.* of George Richards, of Pembroke, Pembroke shire; *m.* Hannah Elizabeth, *d.* of George Tucker, of Sheerness, Kent. *Educ.*: Royal Naval Coll., Greenwich. Naval Constructor, Admiralty; Assistant Director of Naval Construction, Royal Corps Naval Constructors. *War Work*: Design of Warships. *Address*: Morlands, Rueford Road, Streatham, London, S.W. 16. (C2903)

RICHARDS, Lieut.-Col. Arthur Carew, O.B.E., b. 20 Feb. 1865; *s.* of the late Rev. W. H. Richards, of Westridge, Ryde, Isle of Wight; *m.* Gwaldys Penelope, *d.* of the late Major-Gen. C. J. Richards, of Indian Army. *Educ.*: Eton and Cambridge. *War Work*: Railway Transport Officer, Woolwich, 4 Aug. 1914, to 17 May, 1916; Commandant Prisoners of War Camps, 16 June, 1916, to 12 Jan. 1920. *Address*: Westridge, Ryde, Isle of Wight. *Clubs*: M.C.C.; Free Foresters. (O891)

RICHARDS, Paymaster-Lieut. Augustus Gluckstein, O.B.E., R.N.

RICHARDS, Eng.-Lieut. Edward, O.B.E., R.N.

RICHARDS, Eleonora Kathleen, Mrs.. O.B.E.. b. 24 Dec. 1881; *d.* of Thomas Gulston-Wollaston, M.D., of Liverpool; *m.* Henry Edward Sutherland (Doctor of Medicine), *s.* of the late John Richards, of Co. Wexford, Ireland. *Educ.*: Liverpool High School, and Dresden. Hon. Commandant of the British Red Cross Society. *War Work*: Recruiting Commandant for the County of London Branch of the British Red Cross Society; three and a half years' service on the staff of the County Director; raised personally a V.A.D. of 1000 personnel, and recruited a further 2000 women into other detachments. *Address*: 6, Grosvenor Place, London, S.W. 1. *Club*: The Forum.

RICHARDS, Francis Bartlett. M.B.E.

RICHARDS, Frances Maud Lyster, Lady, O.B.E.; *d.* of late Henry M. Smythe, of Barbavilla, Co. Westmeath; *m.* Sir Henry George, K.B.E.. K.C., M.A. (see BURKE'S *Peerage*); *s.* of late John Henry Richards, *g. s.* of late Rt. Hon. John Richards, Baron, of Court of Exchequer in Ireland. *Address*: The Yarrows, Church Hill, Camberley. (O8273)

RICHARDS, Gertrude Mary, C.B.E. Matron Queen Alexandra's Imperial Mil. Nursing Ser. (C1751)

RICHARDS, Capt. Harold, O.B.E.

RICHARDS, Sir Harvey George, K.B.E., K.C., M.A.; *s.* of late John Henry, and *g. s.* of late Rt. Hon. John Richards, Baron of Court of Exchequer in Ireland; *m.* Frances Maud

Lyster, *d.* of late Henry M. Smythe, of Barbaville, Westmeath. *Educ.:* Trinity Coll., Dublin. Called to Irish Bar, 1883; joined Connaught Circuit; practised in Irish Courts; Senior Crown Prosecutor for Counties of Roscommon and Mayo; Puisne Judge, High Court of Judicature for the New Provinces of India, 1905–11; Chief Justice, 1911; retired 1919. *Address:* The Yarrows, Church Hill, Camberley. *Club:* University (Dublin). (K246)

RICHARDS, Sir Henry George, K.B.E., Knt. Bach., M.A., T.C.D.; *b.* 21 Sept. 1860; *s.* of John Henry Richards, late County Court Judge of Co. Mayo; *m.* 20 Aug. 1891, Frances Maud Lyster, O.B.E., *y. d.* of late Henry Matthew Smythe, of Barbavilla, Co. Westmeath. Called to Irish Bar, 1883; K.C. 1901; Judge of High Court of Judicature, N.W. Provinces, 1905–11: Chief Justice, 1911–19; Vice-Chancellor of Univ. of Allahabad, 1909–12. *Address:* University Club, Dublin. (K248)

RICHARDS, Major Henry Meredyth, O.B.E., J.P., D.L., *b.* 30 Jan. 1870; *s.* of Richard Meredyth Richards, of Caerynwch; *m.* Mary Alice Ellinor, *d.* of Frederick Stokes, of Knowle Hurst, Lichfield. *Educ.:* Winchester Coll.; R.M.C., Sandhurst. Landowner. *War Work:* Served as 2nd in-command of 16th Batt. Royal Welsh Fusiliers, 1914–17; afterwards 2nd-in-command, 53rd Batt. Welsh Regt., 1918–19. *Address:* Caerynwch, Dolgelley. *Clubs:* Naval and Military; Junior Carlton. (O7627)

RICHARDS, Jane Wilson, Mrs., M.B.E.

RICHARDS, John, O.B.E.

RICHARDS, Engineer-Capt. John Arthur, C.B.E., R.N. Served in the Great War, 1914–19 (despatches). (C2273)

RICHARDS, Lieut. John Osment, O.B.E., R.N.R.

RICHARDS, John Samuel, M.B.E.

RICHARDS, John Thomas, O.B.E.

RICHARDS, Lieut. Malcolm John, O.B.E., *b.* 19 Feb. 1897; *s.* of G. E. Richards, of Stour Lodge, Wimborne, Dorset. *Educ.:* Marlborough Coll. Lieut., Royal Garrison Artillery. *War Work:* Army. *Address:* Stour Lodge, Wimborne, Dorset. *Clubs:* United Service; Pall Mall; Royal Automobile. (O5713)

RICHARDS, Lieut. Percival Stanley, M.B.E.

RICHARDS, Province Wellesley, M.B.E.

RICHARDS, Lieut. R. M., M.B.E.

RICHARDS, Rupert Peel, C.B.E., *b.* 6 April, 1871; *s.* of James Richards, M.A., Clerk in Holy Orders, late Vicar Newbold, Rochdale, Lancashire; *m.* Helen, *d.* of John Pilling, J.P., of Deeplish Hall, Rochdale. *Educ.:* Middleton School, Bognor, Sussex; Premium App. in Crewe, Pupil of the late F. W. Webb, C.E., Loco. Sup. L.N.W.R. Inspecting Engineer, under Sir A. M. Rendle, K.C.I.E., 1897–99; Assistant Manager to the Vulcan Foundry, Ltd., Newton-le-Willows, Lancs., from 1899–1904; Works Manager, 1904–14; Assistant Gen. Manager 1914–17; Gen. Manager, 1917 to present time. *War Work:* Engaged at the above works on Admiralty guns, gun mountings, sights, paravanes, tanks for Tank Dept., War Office, breech mechanism for the Admiralty, locomotives for the Ministry of Munitions. *Address:* Holly House, Wargrave, Newton-le-Willows, Lancashire. (C2904)

RICHARDS, Capt. Samuel Charles, O.B.E., A.V.C.

RICHARDS, Rev. Sydney William Letcher, O.B.E., M.A., D.C.L., *b.* 21 Oct. 1878; *s.* of the late James Richards, of Mellanoweth, Cornwall; *m.* Evelyn Mary, *d.* of the late Frank Holman, of Bristol. *Educ.:* Privately, and Univ. of Durham (Hatfield Coll.). Vicar of Cricklade, Wilts. *War Work:* Chaplain to the Forces, 1915–20; in France, 1915–19; Senior Chaplain, North Camps Area, Rouen, B.E.F., 1916–18; Senior Chaplain Repatriation Centre, Winchester, 1918–20. *Address:* The Vicarage, Cricklade, Wilts. (O8918)

RICHARDS, William, C.B.E., *b.* 19 April, 1863; *s.* of William Richards, of Springfield, Upper Clapton, N.E.; *m.* Marion Montgomerie, *d.* of William Lang, of Glengorm, Isle of Mull. *Educ.:* Marlborough Coll. *War Work:* Member of the first Committee appointed by the Government on the outbreak of the Great War, being then appointed to organise and carry on the Government War Risks Insurance Scheme, and Joint Manager of its Claims Department throughout the War. *Addresses:* 39, Cleveland Square, London, W. 2; 70, Gracechurch Street, London, E.C. 3. *Club:* City of London. (C2905)

RICHARDS, Major John Charles FIELD-, O.B.E., *b.* 10 May, 1878; *s.* of the late Rev. Frederick Field-Richards, of Newlyn, Cornwall. *Educ.:* Privately, and Keble Coll., Oxford. *War Work:* 2nd Batt. Hampshire Regt., France, 1914; Commandant, Officers' School of Instruction and Training Company, Chatham, 1915; Staff Capt. and President, Central Quartering Committee, Harwich Garrison; 2nd Batt. Yorkshire Regt., France, 1916; Staff Capt., Military Secretary's Branch, War Office, 1917–20; retired April, 1920. *Address:* Maison Amitié, Jersey. *Clubs:* Carlton; Junior Carlton; Royal Western Yacht; Junior Constitutional; R.A.C.; Cruising Association. (O7628)

RICHARDS, George Cobley SMYTH-, O.B.E.

RICHARDSON, Surg.-Lieut. Alan Harvey, O.B.E., R.N.

RICHARDSON, Capt. Albert Angus, O.B.E.

RICHARDSON, Rev. Albert Thomas, M.B.E., M.A., *b.* 20 Feb. 1862; *s.* of J. C. Richardson, of Lichfield; *m.* 1st, Annie Hurt, *d.* of E. W. Barnsley, of Edgbaston; 2nd, Muriel, *d.* of the Rev. Robert Taylor, Vicar of Warthill, Yorks. *Educ.:* Queen Mary's School, Walsall; Hertford Coll., Oxford. Vicar of Bradford-on-Avon; formerly Vicar of Langrish, and Vicar

of Keevil. *War Work:* Founder and Sec. of Bradford-on-Avon War Loan Syndicate. *Address:* The Vicarage, Bradford-on-Avon. (M2340)

RICHARDSON, Sqdn.-Leader Albert Victor John, O.B.E., R.A.F.

RICHARDSON, Sir Albion Henry Herbert, Knt. Bach., C.B.E., *b.* 1874; *s.* of the late James Henry Richardson. Barrister, Gray's Inn, 1912; M.P. for Peckham from 1910; Chairman, Law Society; Sec. London Appeal Tribunal. *Address:* 5, Portman Mansions, York Place, W. *Clubs:* Eighty; Reform. (C603)

RICHARDSON, Alderman David, M.B.E., J.P., *b.* 27 June, 1867; *s.* of W. H. Richardson, of North Shields. *Educ.:* Union British School, South Shields. Ex-Mayor; Vice-Chairman South Shields Education Committee. *War Work:* Chairman Local Parliamentary Recruiting Committee; Chairman Local War Emergency Committee; Superintendent South Shields Special Constabulary; Chairman Local Red Cross Motor Ambulance Fund; South Shields Representative National Committee for Relief of the Belgians. *Address:* Bodavon, St. Aidan's Road, South Shields. *Clubs:* South Shields Liberal; Newcastle Farmers'. (M9439)

RICHARDSON, Annie Bertha, Mrs., M.B.E., *b.* 18 May, 1867; *d.* of John Lumby, of Eversley, Bournemouth; *m.* Arthur, *s.* of Thomas Martinson Richardson, B.C.L. (Camb.), of Croxton, Lincolnshire. *Educ.:* Privately. Commandant 8 and R. Oxon. V.A.D.; Assistant County Director, B.R.C.S.; Hon. Sec. Oxford Women's Ambulance Society. *War Work:* B.R.C.S. as above. *Address:* 187, Banbury Road, Oxford. *Club:* V.A.D. Ladies. (M2341)

RICHARDSON, Bernhard Herrmann, O.B.E., *b.* 28 May, 1877. *Educ.:* George Watson's Coll., Edinburgh, and Edinburgh Univ. Acting Chief Accountant, War Office. *War Work:* Army Auditor, Salonika, and Mediterranean Expeditionary Forces (temporarily); Acting Financial Adviser, Egyptian Expeditionary Force, April, 1915, to Sept. 1917. (O11203)

RICHARDSON, Lieut.-Comm. Charles Dene, O.B.E., R.N.

RICHARDSON, Lieut.-Col. Charles William, O.B.E.

RICHARDSON, Capt. Colin Spencer, M.B.E., R.A.F.

RICHARDSON, Dunsford, O.B.E., *b.* 23 Dec. 1863; *s.* of John Richardson, of Gledhow, Leeds; *m.* Jeanie, *d.* of Henry Walton Whitehead, of Leeds. *Educ.:* Leeds Grammar School. Commission Agent; Chief Distribution Officer, and Assistant Commissioner for N.E. Division, Yorkshire. *War Work:* Hon. Treas. Moortown War Fund, raised about £700 in village house-to-house collections. *Address:* Holly Bank, Moortown, Leeds. (O11204)

RICHARDSON, Lieut.-Col. Edwin Hautonville, O.B.E.

RICHARDSON, Florence Ellen, Lady, O.B.E.; *d.* of the late Fleetwood Williams; *m.* Lieut.-Gen. Sir George Richardson, K.C.B., C.S.I., C.I.E. *War Work:* Ulster Prisoners of War; War Pensions. *Address:* Hyde Court, Chalford, Gloucestershire. *Club:* Ladies' Army and Navy. (O11205)

RICHARDSON, Comm. Francis Joseph, O.B.E. R.N.V.R.

RICHARDSON, Capt. and Qr.-Mr. Frederick, O.B.E. R.A.M.C.

RICHARDSON, Major Frederick, O.B.E.

RICHARDSON, Capt. Frederick, O.B.E.

RICHARDSON, George Alexander, O.B.E.

RICHARDSON, George Herbert, M.B.E., *b.* 1858; *s.* of William Richardson, of Dewsbury, Yorks; *m.* Mary, *d.* of Thomas Spedding, of The Aldams, Dewsbury. *Educ.:* Batley Grammar School; Oundle, Northants; Yorkshire Coll. of Science, Leeds. Examiner of Cloth, Alipore, India, 1889–90; Inspector of Cloth, Royal Army Clothing Department, London, 1891–1920; retired (after 28¼ years' service), 31 Jan. 1920. *War Work:* In connection with provision and examination of cloth supplies for the British Army and for armies of our Allies. *Address:* Horton Bank, 20, Grosvenor Road, Scarborough. *Club:* Ganton Golf. (M885)

RICHARDSON, Brig.-Gen. George Stafford, C.B., C.M.G., C.B.E., New Zealand Staff Corps, *b.* 1869. *War Work:* 1915–16 as D.A. and Q.M.G.; New Zealand Representative at the War Office; Comdt. New Zealand Forces in England, with rank of Brig.-Gen (despatches, Legion of Honour). (C850)

RICHARDSON, Capt. Harry, O.B.E., M.C., R.E. (T.).

RICHARDSON, Harry, M.B.E.

RICHARDSON, Lieut. Harry, O.B.E., 1st Vol. Bn. R. Warwicks. Regt., *b.* 7 Feb. 1865; *s.* of Samuel Richardson, of Birmingham; *m.* Ida Ellen, *d.* of H. M. Stevenson, of Birmingham. *Educ.:* King Edward's, Birmingham, and privately. Civil Engineer; Chief Assistant Engineer and Surveyor, City of Birmingham. *War Work:* Executive Officer of Food Control, City of Birmingham; introduced first Food Rationing Scheme, 1917–18. *Address:* Handsworth Wood, Birmingham. (O3886)

RICHARDSON, Helen Morewood, Mrs., O.B.E.

RICHARDSON, Herbert Lindsley, O.B.E., B.A. (Cantab.), M.I.C.E.; *s.* of William Richardson, of Bishop Downs Grange, Tunbridge Wells; *m.* Sybil Ursula, *d.* of R. C. A. Beck, of Cheam. *Educ.:* Marlborough Coll. and Trinity Co l., Cambridge. Partner in Messrs. Richardson and Cruddas, Engineers, Bombay. *War Work:* Section Director, Gun Ammunition Fillings Department, Ministry of Munitions of War. *Address:* Southfield, Southborough, Kent. *Clubs:* Royal Bombay Yacht; Byculla, Bombay. (O11206)

RICHARDSON, Capt. Henry William Arbuckle, O.B.E.

RICHARDSON, Paymaster Lt.-Comm. Hugh Maclean, O.B.E., R.N.

RICHARDSON Major and Qr.-Mr. James, O.B.E., R.A.S.C.

RICHARDSON, James Birrell, O.B.E.; *s.* of John, of Dryfedalegate, Lockerby; *m.* Anna Arundel, *d.* of Geo. Bourn, of Ryton-on-Tyne. *Educ.:* Royal Grammar School, Newcastle-on-Tyne. Managing Director, Brown, Lerox & Co., Ltd.; Chairman, Brown, Lerox & Co. (London), Ltd. *War Work:* Warship production, chain cables and gear, anchors, harbour moorings. *Address:* Llonblethion House, Cowbridge, Glamorgan. *Club:* British Empire. (O11211)

RICHARDSON, Jerusha Davidson, Mrs. Aubrey, O.B.E.; *d.* of Richard Hunting, of Holmdale, Priory Road, N.W.; *m.* Aubrey, *s.* of Sir Benjamin Ward Richardson, M.D., F.R.S., F.R.C.P., LL.D. *Educ.:* Privately, and Boarding School; studied piano with Otto Goldschmidt. Clerk to the Chadwick Trustees, and Sec. Chadwick Public Lectures; Hon. Sec. and Founder of the Phœbe Girls' Club, Kilburn. *War Work:* In 1914, formed, under the Presidency of Her Grace the Duchess of Bedford, and with a committee of ladies interested in social work among women and girls, the Kilburn Girls' Auxiliary for Nursing and General Service with the St. John V.A.D.; all members of the Auxiliary were officers or members of the Phœbe Girls' Club, or Kilburn Company of the Church Nursing and Ambulance Brigade; the Auxiliary was posted by the County Director, Middlesex, to the first Willesden War Hospital at St. Matthew's Institute, Harlesden, in Nov. 1914, and it formed a nucleus for V.A.D. Middlesex 58, which was registered with Mrs. Aubrey Richardson as Commandant in Aug. 1915; Mrs. Richardson had previously served as Assist.-Quartermaster and Quartermaster at Harlesden; V.A.D. Middlesex 58 was appointed to the charge of Dollis Hill House Auxiliary Military Hospital in Oct. 1915, and the Hospital was opened for patients Feb. 1916, Mrs. Richardson being Commandant of the hospital until its demobilisation as a War Hospital, March, 1919; beginning with 23 beds, the hospital had 72 at the close, and received in all 2416 patients. *Address:* St. John's Vicarage, Kilburn, N.W. 6. *Club:* Victoria Ladies'. (O11207)

RICHARDSON, John William, M.B.E., *b.* 25 Sept. 1882; Chairman of Conference of Executive Officers of Local War Pensions Committees in the Northern Section of the North Western Region; for nineteen years with the Town Clerk of Blackburn, now Sec. Blackburn Local War Pensions Committee; Hon. Sec. Blackburn Local Subscription Committee, Lord Kitchener Memorial Homes, Lowestoft; Assistant Hon. Sec. Local Branch of Imperial Association for assisting disabled Naval and Military Officers. *War Work:* Dependants' Separation Allowance Claims, 1914–19; War Relief Work, 1916–20; War Pensions Work, 1916 to date. *Address:* Red Lodge, Pleasington, near Blackburn. (M9441)

RICHARDSON, Kathleen Rayner, O.B.E.

RICHARDSON, Lewis, C.B.E. *War Work:* Rendered services in connection with Gov.-Gen. of S. Africa's Fund and Returned Soldiers. (C2007)

RICHARDSON, Mabel, M.B.E.

RICHARDSON, Maria Isabel, Mrs., M.B.E., *b.* 27 Dec. 1868; *d.* of Wm. S. Spivey, of Carmarthen; *m.* William, *s.* of Luke Richardson, of Willington-on-Tyne, Northumberland. *Educ.:* High School, Carmarthen, and Whitelands Coll., Chelsea. Member of Northumberland County Education Committee; Wallsend Borough Education Committee; Treas. of District Nursing Association. *War Work:* Founder and Hon. Sec. of Wallsend Borough Branch of the Soldiers' and Sailors' Families Association; Hon. Sec. of Wallsend Borough War Pensions Committee; Guardian to Motherless Children. *Address:* Field Head, Willington-on-Tyne, Northumberland. (M9442)

RICHARDSON, Mary Anita, Mrs., M.B.E.

RICHARDSON, Percy, O.B.E., *b.* 28 Feb. 1878; *s.* of John Gadd Richardson, of Nottingham; *m.* Patricia Annie, *d.* of John Bain, of Dublin. *Educ.:* Nottingham. Late Managing Director of the Sheffield-Simplex Motor Works, Ltd., of Tinsley, Sheffield. *War Work:* Supervised design and construction of Armoured Motor Cars; directed reorganisation and extensions of the works of the Sheffield-Simplex Co. for execution of following work: Experimental work on power units for large and small airships for Admiralty and aero engines for Air Board; produced large quantities of shells, hand grenades, aero engines, aero bombs, paravanes, and other war material. *Address:* The Pebble, Bexhill-on-Sea. *Clubs:* Royal Automobile; Royal Aero; Road; London Flying. (O11209)

RICHARDSON, Peter, M.B.E., *b.* 23 Sept. 1878; *s.* of James Richardson, of Stockport; *m.* Lucy, *d.* of Samuel Arnold, of Prestbury. *Educ.:* Stockport. Goods Agent, L. & N.W. Rly. Co., London Road Station, Manchester. *Address:* 7 Erlington Avenue, Rye Bank Road, Old Trafford, Manchester. (M9443)

RICHARDSON, Peter, M.B.E., *b.* Sept. 1860; *s.* of the late James Richardson, of Dumbarton; *m.* Mary Connell. *Educ.:* Grammar School, Dumbarton. Blacksmith; Member of Dumbartonshire Territorial Force Association. *War Work:* Was a Member of the Military Appeal Tribunal for the Sheriffdom of Stirling, Dumbarton, and Clackmannan, also the Profiteering Appeal Tribunal for the same areas. *Address:* 25, Castlegreen Terrace, Dumbarton. (M886)

RICHARDSON, Lieut.-Col. Philip Wigham, O.B.E.

RICHARDSON, Capt. Rosslyn James Dilyell, O.B.E. I.A.R.O.

RICHARDSON, Comm. Sidney Sherlock, O.B.E., R.D., R.N.R., *b.* 4 March, 1877; *s.* of the late George Richardson, of Halewood, Lancs.; *m.* Margaret, *d.* of the late Thomas Brakell, of Blundellsands, Liverpool. *Educ.:* The College School, Huyton, Liverpool, and H.M.S. " Conway." Master Mariner. *War Work:* Naval Officer in charge of Defensive Arming of Merchant Ships, Liverpool. *Address:* 23, Regent Road, Gt. Crosby, Liverpool. *Clubs:* Northern and " Conway." (O1806)

RICHARDSON, Capt. Thomas, O.B.E.

RICHARDSON, Major Thomas William, O.B.E., R.A.S.C., *b.* 24 Feb. 1895; *s.* of T. W. Richardson, M.R.C.S. (Eng.), of Norwich; *g.s.* of Major-Gen. A. T. Ethridge, C.S.I., Indian Army. *Educ.:* Norwich, and R.M.C., Sandhurst. Regular Officer. *War Work:* Adjutant 3rd Divisional Train; O.C. 37th Divisional M.T. Company; O.C. 4th Army Troops, M.T. Company; twice mentioned in despatches. *Address:* Eaton Cottage, Eaton Hill, Norwich. *Club:* Junior Army and Navy. (O2694)

RICHARDSON, William, M.B.E., *b.* 20 Jan. 1863; *s.* of the late Joseph Richardson, of Springfield, Lisburn, Co. Antrim; *m.* Laura Emily, *d.* of the late John Richardson, J.P., of Lambeg House, Lisburn. *Educ.:* Hitchin, Herts. *War Work:* Hon. Treas. Waterford County Division of Soldiers' and Sailors' Families Association and Waterford County War Pensions Committee. *Club:* County, Waterford. (M9444)

RICHARDSON, Capt. William Augustus, O.B.E., Can. A.M.C.

RICHARDSON, Capt. William WIGHAM-, M.B.E.

RICHES, Henry, O.B.E.

RICHMOND, Alice Jane Maud, Mrs., O.B.E.; *d.* of the late J. J. de Rozario, of the Provincial Judicial Service; *m.* the Hon. Thomas Richmond, B.A., Barrister-at-law, *s.* of Francis Edward, late of Mannantoddy, Wynaad, Southern India. *War Work:* Almost from the beginning of the War till long after the conclusion of the Armistice, Mrs. Richmond worked indefatigably in assisting Her Excellency, Lady Pentland, in the enormous Ladies' War Work inaugurated and managed with much success by Her Excellency. *Address:* Linden Towers, Nungumbankum, Madras, India. (O8295)

RICHMOND, Annie Catherine Mary, M.B.E.

RICHMOND, Capt. Arthur Eaton, O.B.E., R.A.M.C., *b.* 28 Feb. 1892; *s.* of Richard Richmond, M.D., of Wimbledon; *m.* Margaret Mary, *d.* of W. Kelly, of Cool Park, Tuam, Ireland. *Educ.:* Oundle School; London Univ.; St. Thomas' Hospital. *War Work:* Medical Transport work in Ægean Sea; Assistant Embarkation Medical Officer, Alexandria; Deputy Assistant Director of Medical Services, Alexandria District; Field Ambulance, 75th Division, Palestine; D.A.D.M.S. Headquarters Force, Egypt; D.A.D.M.S. 20th Corps; D.A.D.M.S., G.H.Q., E.E.F. *Address:* c/o Messrs. Holt & Co., London. (O8644)

RICHMOND, Daniel, O.B.E., *b.* 18 Jan. 1868; *s.* of Hugh Richmond, of Kilraughts, Co. Antrim; *m.* Helen Mary, *d.* of John Harper, of Seaham Harbour. *Educ.:* Ballymoney; Queen's Coll., Belfast; Glasgow Univ.; Manchester University, E.C. Surgeon; Senior Surgeon, Rochdale Infirmary. *War Work:* Chief Surgeon and M.O. in charge, St. John's Ambulance Drill Hall, V.A.D. Hospital, Rochdale, 350 beds. *Address:* Buckley Hill House, Milnrow, Rochdale. (O11210)

RICHMOND, Major John Duncan, D.S.O., O.B.E., M.B., Ch.B., R.A.M.C., *b.* 14 Oct. 1877; *s.* of William Richmond, of Glasgow. *Educ.:* Allan Glen's School, Glasgow, and Glasgow Univ. *War Work:* D.A.D.M.S., Headquarters Scottish Command; D.A.D.M.S. 12th Infantry Division, O.C. 65th Field Ambulance, D.A.D.M.S. Rouen, D.A.D.M.S. Headquarters L. of C., France; O.C. 173 Indian Cavalry Field Ambulance, Afghan War, 1919. *Address:* c/o Messrs. Holt & Co., 3, Whitehall Place, London. (O5715)

RICHMOND, John Ritchie, C.B.E., J.P., *b.* 1869; *s.* of John Richmond, of Kilmarnock; *m.* Isabella Macintyre, *d.* of Thomas Davidson, of Cambuslang. *Educ.:* Glasgow High School, and Glasgow Univ. *War Work:* Managing Director, G. & J. Weir, Ltd., Glasgow. *Addresses:* 7, Blanefield, Kirkoswald, Ayrshire; 14, Hamilton Drive, Pollokshields, Glasgow. *Clubs:* New, Conservative, and Art, Glasgow; St. Stephen's, London. (C276)

RICHMOND, Lieut.-Col. Thomas Heyliger, O.B.E., M.B., Ch.B., *b.* 2 April, 1879; *s.* of (Dr.) Thomas Richmond, of Glasgow; *m.* Stuart, *d.* of Alexander Mories, of Greenock. *Educ.:* Glasgow High School, and Glasgow and Edinburgh Univs. Capt. R.A.M.C. (T.F.): Surgeon, Longton Hospital, Stoke-on-Trent. *War Work:* M.O. 23rd North Midland Brigade, R.F.A.; Officer in charge Surgical Division, Fargo Military Hospital, Salisbury Plain; O.C. 85 General Hospital, Archangel, N. Russia. *Address:* Chaplin House, Normacot, Stoke-on-Trent. *Club:* Royal Automobile.

RICHMOND, Lieut.-Col. Vincent Crane, O.B.E., B.Sc., A.R.C.Sc., A.F.R.Ae.S., *b.* 21 Jan. 1893; *s.* of Joshua Richmond; *m.* Florence Mary, *d.* of Capt. H. C. Hodder, of Preston, N. Shields. *Educ.:* Royal Coll. of Science, London. *War Work:* R.N.A.S., Mar. 1915, to April, 1918; Lieut. and Lieut. Com. R.N.V.R., Airship Flying and Construction; R.A.F., April, 1918, to Sept. 1919; Major and Lieut.-Col.; O.C. Royal Airship Works, White City, London, Sept. 1919; Inter-Allied Aeronautical Commission of Control, Germany. *Address:* 5 Peterborough Rd., Harrow-on-the-Hill.

RICKARD, Barbara, M.B.E., *b.* 24 Oct. 1894 ; *d.* of the late Rev. Thomas Rickard, of Kemendine, Rangoon, Burma. *Educ.:* Queen Anne's School, Caversham, Reading, and Manchester Univ. *War Work :* Woman Clerk in Accountant-General's Department, Admiralty, from July, 1915. *Address :* 25, Blenheim Park Road, South Croydon, Surrey.   (M9445)

RICKARD, late Lieut.-Comm. Charles Ernest, O.B.E., M.I.Mech.E., *b.* 31 May, 1880 ; *s.* of Thomas William Rickard, of Dorchester. *Educ.:* Univ. Coll., London. Late Inspector-General and Technical Adviser in Radiotelegraphy to Chilean Navy ; Chilean Delegate Plenipotentiary to International Radio-telegraph Conference, London, 1912 ; at present Deputy Chief Engineer, Marconi's Wireless Telegraph Co. *War Work :* Valuable services to H.M. Navy in South America. *Address :* 5, Baldwyn Gardens, Acton, W. 3. *Club :* Junior Constitutional.   (O4212)

RICKENBACH, Frieda, M.B.E., *d.* of the late Edward Rickenbach, of London, and Milan, Italy. *Educ.:* Clifton High School. *War Work :* Commandant V.A.D., Sussex, 106, B.R.C.S. ; V.A.D. Hospital, Claytons, Mayfield, 1915–19. *Address :* Airlie Cottage, Mayfield, Sussex.   (M9446)

RICKETT, Alfred Charles James, M.B.E.

RICKETT, Capt. Gerard Russell, O.B.E., M.D., R.A.M.C. (T.).

RICKETT, Hubert Cecil, O.B.E.

RICKETT, Capt. Joseph, M.B.E., R.E.

RICKETTS, Capt. Walter, M.B.E., R.A.F.

RICKMAN, Capt. Arthur Patrick William, O.B.E.

RICKMAN, Major Graham Egerton, O.B.E., *b.* 10 May, 1869 ; *s.* of the late Lieut.-Gen. W. Rickman ; *m.* Florence, *d.* of the late B. Piercy, of Marchwiel Hall, Wrexham. *Educ.:* Winchester. *Address :* 79, Knightsbridge. *Club :* Naval and Military.   (O3169)

RICKMAN, Mary Charlotte Murray, M.B.E.

RIDDELL, Major Brownlow, O.B.E., M.D., R.A.M.C. (T.).

RIDDELL, Capt. Douglas Errington, M.B.E., A.F.R.Ae.S., *b.* 26 March, 1892 ; *s.* of Charles Scofield Riddell, of Edgbaston, Birmingham ; *m.* Nancy Westropp, *d.* of Joseph Thompson, of Bournemouth. *Educ.:* Oundle. Technical Officer, Directorate of Research, Air Ministry. *War Work :* Capt. 5th Batt. Royal Warwickshire Regt. (T.F.), France and Belgium, 48th Division, March to Dec. 1915 ; invalided and sick till Oct. 1916 ; Oct. 1916, to Dec. 1916, Reserve Battalion ; Dec. 1916, to May, 1919 ; Design Dept., Ordnance Factories, Woolwich Arsenal. *Address :* 8, Chester House, Eccleston Place, S.W. 1. *Club :* Royal Automobile.   (M5573)

RIDDELL, Col. Edward Vansittart Dick, C.B.E., D.S.O., R.G.A., *b.* 30 Mar. 1873 ; *s.* of the late Col. Robert Vansittart Riddell, R.E. (*see* BURKE'S *Peerage*) ; *m.* 10 Feb. 1902, Edith Mary, *d.* of Maj.-Gen. E. P. Bingham-Turner, R.A. Served in the S. African War, 1900–02 (Brevet, two medals, four clasps) ; Great War from 1914 (despatches five times). (C2168)

RIDDELL, Major John Balfour C.B.E., D.S.O.

RIDDELL, Col. John Scott, C.B.E., M.V.O., T.D., M.A., M.B.C.M., Hon. LL.D., A.M.S. (T.) (ret.), *b.* 10 April, 1864 ; *s.* of John Scott Riddell, of Aberdeen ; *m.* Jean Grindlay, *d.* of John Gordon, J.P., of Arabella, Ross-shire. *Educ.:* Grammar School, and Univ. of Aberdeen. Consulting Surgeon, Aberdeen Royal Infirmary ; Hon. Medical Director Aberdeen Orthopædic Annexe ; Member of Council of British Red Cross Society (Scottish Branch) ; Assessor on Aberdeen Univ. Court ; Univ. Representative on City of Aberdeen Territorial Army Assoc. ; Chairman of Joint (Disablement) Committee of North of Scotland ; Member of Joint Institutional Committee for Scotland (Ministry of Pensions). *War Work :* Consulting Surgeon to Royal Navy ; Red Cross Commissioner, North Eastern District of Scotland ; Surgeon-in-charge of Naval Wards, Aberdeen Royal Infirmary.   (C292)

RIDDELL, William George, O.B.E.

RIDDING, Capt. Reginald, M.B.E.

RIDEAL, Capt. Eric Keightley, M.B.E., D.Sc., M.A., Ph.D., F.I.C., M.R.I., *b.* 11 April, 1890 ; *s.* of Samuel Rideal, of Elstead, Surrey. *Educ.:* Oundle, Northants ; Trinity Hall, Cambridge ; Bonn, Germany. Late Visiting Professor of Physical Chemistry, Univ. of Illinois, U.S.A. *War Work :* Captain, R.E., Service in France ; Anti-Gas, and Munitions Inventions Dept. *Addresses :* 94, Queen's Gate, S. Kensington ; The Old Cottage, Elstead, Surrey.   (M2344)

RIDEHALGH, Gertrude Mary, M.B.E. ; *d.* of James Ridehalgh, of Lancashire. *War Work :* Ambulance Driver for the Red Cross, East Lancs. Branch. *Address :* Shawe Hall, Flixton, near Manchester.   (M9447)

RIDER, Douglas, O.B.E.

RIDER, Graham Stanley, M.B.E.

RIDER, Lewis Herbert, O.B.E., *b.* 8 Jan. 1877 ; *s.* of James Carter Rider, of Chertsey ; *m.* Gertrude, *d.* of Richard F. Cooper, of Chobham. *Educ.:* Highfield School, Chertsey, and King's Coll., London. Civil Servant, Board of Inland Revenue. *War Work :* Finance Branch, Ministry of Shipping, where he was head of one of the Finance Divisions ; he was lent by the Revenue to the Transport Dept., Admiralty, in Sept. 1914, having had previous experience in that Dept. during the S. African War ; the Transport Dept. became the Ministry of Shipping. *Address :* Calais Cottage, Chertsey, Surrey.   (O11215)

RIDER, Lieut. William Rider, M.B.E.

RIDGES, Lieut. Robert Vigurs, M.B.E.

RIDGWAY, Lieut.-Comm. Bertram Henry Akroyd, O.B.E., R.N.R.

RIDGWAY, Lieut. Robert Edward, O.B.E., R.G.A. (T.).

RIDINGS, Major Cecil, C.B.E., D.S.O., *b.* 1876 ; *s.* of the late Surg.-Maj. James Sadleir Ridings. Entered Roy. Inniskilling Fusiliers, 1896 ; Capt. 1904 ; Major, 1915 ; served in Dardanelles, 1915 (despatches) ; Brig.-Maj.   (C8919)

RIDLAND, Capt. Charles Forbes, M.B.E.

RIDLER, Lieut. Arthur James, M.B.E.

RIDLEY, Capt. Albert, M.B.E.

RIDLEY, Rev. Charles Lawrence, O.B.E.

RIDLEY, Most Rev. Archbishop Charles Owen Leaver, O.B.E.   (O12010)

RIDLEY, Cecil Guy, C.B.E., *b.* 21 June, 1885 ; *s.* of Right Hon. Sir Edward Ridley, of 48, Lennox Gardens, S.W. 1. *Educ.:* Harrow ; New Coll., Oxford. Barrister-at-law. *War Work :* Private Sec. to Sir Edward Ward, Bart., G.B.E., etc., from Aug. 1914, to Dec. 1914 ; Staff Officer to Metropolitan Special Constabulary (under Sir E. Ward), from Dec. 1914, to Feb. 1918 ; from Feb. 1918, to Dec. 1920, in the Ministry of Labour. *Address :* 48, Lennox Gardens, S.W. 1. *Clubs :* Oxford and Cambridge ; Burlington Fine Arts.   (C604)

RIDLEY, Clarence Oliver, O.B.E., M.I.C.E., M.I.Mech.E., M.N.E.C.I.E. & S., *b.* 9 Aug. 1869 ; *s.* of the late Oliver Matthew Ridley, of Charminster, Dorset ; *m.* Gertrude Henrietta, *d.* of Henry Houseman. *Educ.:* Harrow. *War Work :* Manager of Engine Works Department, Elswick, for Sir W. G. Armstrong, Whitworth & Co. ; also in Ministry of Munitions, Hydraulic Machinery Section. *Addresses :* Lancaster Lodge, Putney, S.W. ; Australia House, Strand. *Clubs :* St. Stephen's ; New, Glasgow.   (O11216)

RIDLEY, Ernest Rupert, M.B.E., I.A.

RIDLEY, Ethel Blanche, C.B.E., R.R.C.

RIDLEY, Eustace, M.B.E., M.I.E.E., *b.* 26 Jan. 1873 ; *s.* of Percy Ridley, of Morden, Surrey ; *m.* Annie, *d.* of Joseph Ridgway, of Hartshill, Stoke-on-Trent. Engineer, London County Council (Fire Brigade). *War Work :* Sec. to Ministry of Munitions, Fire Protection Advisory Committee. *Address :* Morden, Burcott Road, Purley, Surrey.   (M9449)

RIDLEY, Capt. Geoffrey William, O.B.E., A.R.I., B.A., *b.* 13 March, 1887 ; *s.* of William and Mary Ridley, of London ; *m.* Ursula Mary, *d.* of J. Godwin King, J.P., of West Hoathly, Sussex. *Educ.:* Charterhouse. Architect. *War Work :* Territorial Force pre-war, and Active Service in Gallipoli, Egypt, and Palestine. *Address :* West Hoathly, Sussex.   (O6281)

RIDLEY, Major the Hon. Jasper Nicholas, O.B.E., B.A., *b.* 6 Jan. 1887 ; *s.* of Sir Matthew White Ridley, 5th Bart., created Viscount Ridley and Baron Wensleydale of Blagdon and Blyth, Northumberland (*see* BURKE'S *Peerage*) ; *m.* Countess Nathalie, *d.* of H. E. the late Count Benckendorff. *Educ.:* Eton, and Balliol Coll., Oxford. Called to the Bar, Inner Temple, 1913 ; Major of Yeomanry and a D.A.A.G. ; served during European War, 1914–18 ; mentioned in despatches. *Address :* 31, Gloucester Place, Portman Square, W. *Clubs :* Carlton ; Travellers'.   (O5716)

RIDLEY, John Henry Llewellyn, O.B.E.

RIDLEY, Mary Constance, M.B.E. ; *d.* of the late J. H. Ridley, of Park End, Northumberland, and Mrs. Ridley, of Little Park End. *War Work :* Organised and acted as Hon. Sec. to the War Information Office, Newcastle-on-Tyne, from Sept. 1914, till June, 1919 ; this office was run as a department of the Newcastle-on-Tyne War Relief Fund. *Address :* Little Park End, Wark-on-Tyne. *Club :* Ladies' Park.   (M9450)

RIDLEY, Mary Stephanie, Mrs. Henry Matthew, O.B.E.

RIDLEY, Major Richard Cooke, O.B.E., R.A.S.C.

RIDLEY, Rosamond Cornelia Gwladys, Viscountess, D.B.E. ; *d.* of 1st Baron Wimborne (*see* BURKE'S *Peerage*) ; *m.* 2nd Viscount Ridley (who died 1916) (*see* BURKE'S *Peerage*). *Addresses :* Blagdon, Cramlington, Northumberland ; 10, Carlton House Terrace, S.W.   (D17)

RIDOUT, Col. Sir Dudley Howard, K.B.E., C.B., C.M.G., *b.* 15 Jan. 1866 ; *s.* of late Lieut.-Col. Joseph Bramley Ridout ; *m.* Maud Elizabeth, *d.* of C. H. Hutton, of Middleburg, Cape Province. *Educ.:* Christ's Hospital, Kingston Collegiate Institute, R.M.C., Canada. Entered Army, 1885 ; Capt. 1894 ; Major, 1902 ; Lieut.-Col. 1910 ; Col. 1914 ; T. Brig.-Gen. 1915 ; T. Maj.-Gen. 1916 ; War Office Staff, 1888–89 ; S. Africa Intelligence Office and Cavalry Brigade, 1900–2 ; mentioned in despatches ; Great War, Singapore Command, 1914–18 ; mentioned in despatches ; Member of Executive and Legislative Council, 1915–19. *Club :* United Services. (K282)

RIDSDALE, Sir Edward Aurelian, G.B.E., J.P., *b.* 23 Feb. 1864 ; *s.* of Edward Lucas Jenks Ridsdale, of Rottingdean, Sussex ; *m.* Susan Stirling, *d.* of John Ritchie Findlay, of Aberlour, Banffshire. *Educ.:* Univ. Coll. School, and Royal School of Mines. For some years member of the London Stock Exchange, retired 1904. *War Work :* Chairman and Deputy Chairman of the Executive Committee of the British Red Cross Society, and organising and administrative work in connection therewith at home and abroad ; also member of the Commission appointed to investigate the breakdown of the Medical Services in Mesopotamia in 1916. *Addresses :* 14, Ennismore Gardens, London, S.W. ; Waterwynch, Tenby, Pembrokeshire. *Clubs :* Reform ; Brooks's ; Bath   (G59)

RIDSDALE, Herbert Wheatley, M.B.E.

RIDYARD, Lieut. Arnold, O.B.E., R.N.R.

RIGBY, Major James Charles Alexander, O.B.E., M.B.

RIGBY, Lieut. Robert Stacey Marks, M.B.E., M.G.C.

RIGDEN, Major William Percy, O.B.E., T.D.

RIGG, Hubert MacMullen, M.B.E.

RIGG, Major Richard, O.B.E., T.D., J.P.

RIGG, Rowland William, O.B.E.

RILEY, Edmond John, O.B.E.

RILEY, George Willis, M.B.E., *b.* 8 March, 1871 ; *s.* of Abraham Raby Riley, of Wolverhampton ; *m.* Jessie Elizabeth, *d.* ¦of Peter Mitchell, of Wolverhampton. *Educ. :* Wolverhampton. Chief Examiner of Printers' Accounts, H.M. Stationery Office, Westminster. *War Work :* Control of the examination of a tremendously increased number of accounts and contracts involving constant late work over several years. (M9452)

RILEY, Lieut.-Comm. Gerard Brook, O.B.E., R.N.

RILEY, Henry, M.B.E., *b.* 3 March, 1874 ; *s.* of Henry Riley, of Widnes ; *m.* Florence Jane, *d.* of John Gratrix, of Manchester. *Educ. :* Widnes West Bank Board School. District Inspector, Rolling Stock Dept., L. & N. W. Rly. *War Work :* Providing stock and seeing all troop trains marshalled correctly as required by Transport Officer, and despatching same to loading point from commencement of the war up to date. *Address :* 259, Smithdown Road, Sefton Park, Liverpool. (M10253)

RILEY, Joseph Albert, O.B.E.

RILEY, Richard, M.B.E.

RIMER, Alfred Henry, M.B.E.

RIMINGTON, Frederick James, M.B.E.

RIND, Walter Lockhart, O.B.E., *b.* 28 May, 1876 ; *s.* of the late Col. M. M'Neill Rind, of Royal Sussex Regt. ; *m.* Lalla, *d.* of the Hon. G. Hollier Griffiths, I.S.O. *Educ. :* Rossall, and Univ. Coll., Oxon. Civil Servant. Colonial Civil Service, 1900–11 ; 1911, National Health Insurance Committee ; Private Sec. to Mr. Charles Roberts and Sir E. Cornwall ; 1917, Ministry of Pensions, Deputy Assist. Sec. ; 1918–20, Ministry of Munitions. *War Work :* Belgian Refugees (is Officier de l'Ordre de la Couronne) ; Ministry of Pensions ; Ministry of Munitions. *Address :* 23, Buxton Gardens, Acton, W. 3. *Clubs :* M.C.C. ; Northwood Golf. (O687)

RING, Major James Sinclair Henry, O.B.E., I.A.

RINGLAND, Major Thomas Hazlett, M.B.E.

RINTOUL, William, O.B.E.

RIORDAN, John McMahon, O.B.E.

RIORDAN, Patrick, M.B.E.

RIORDAN, Thomas Mortimer, M.B.E.

RIPLEY, Lieut.-Col. Blair, C.B.E., D.S.O., Canadian Forces. Served in the Great War, 1915–19 (despatches). (C1354)

RIPLEY, Capt. Edward Guy, O.B.E., R.A.S.C.

RIPLEY, Lieut. Horace Stephens, M.B.E., R.E. (T.).

RIPON, Rt. Rev. Thomas Banks Strong, Bishop of, G.B.E., D.D., *b.* 24 Oct. 1861 ; *s.* of Thomas Banks Strong, of 1, Priory Grove, West Brompton, S.W. *Educ. :* Westminster School ; Christ Church, Oxford. Bishop of Ripon. *War Work :* Administration of University of Oxford as Vice-Chancellor, 1914–17. *Address :* The Palace, Ripon. *Club :* Athenæum. (G35)

RIPPON, Joseph, O.B.E.

RIPPON, Squadon-Leader Thomas Stanley, O.B.E., R.A.F., *b.* 19 Sept. 1883 ; *s.* of the Rev. Thomas Rippon, of Gateshead-on-Tyne ; *m.* Dorette Adeline, *d.* of Louis Roche, of Napier Avenue, Hurlingham. *Educ. :* Bristol Univ., and London Hospital. M.R.C.S. (Eng.), L.R.C.P. (Lond.), 1911. *War Work :* Temp. Com. R.A.M.C., 1915 ; served in France with 38th (Welsh) Div. and was in the Arras attack with 30th Div. (98th Field Ambulance), attached R.F.C., 1917 ; transferred to R.A.F., 1918 ; promoted Squadron-Leader, 1919 ; contributed "The Essential Characteristics of Successful and Unsuccessful Aviators," *Lancet*, 1918 (Rippon and Manuel) ; on staff of H.Q. R.A.F. in India, 1920. *Address :* H.Q., Royal Air Force, Ambala, India. (O8174)

RISELEY, Arthur Henry, O.B.E., *b.* 7 July, 1874 ; *s.* of Henry Lorymer Riseley, J.P., of Bristol ; *m.* Gertrude Edith, *d.* of Marcellus Purnell Castle, M.V.O., J.P., of Brighton. *Educ. :* Privately. Barrister-at-law (Middle Temple), Western Circuit, and Fellow of the Corporation of Insurance Brokers. *War Work :* 1914–17, Assistant to Recruiting Officer, Bristol ; 1918, Sec. Ministry of National Service, South Western Region ; 1914–19, Hon. Sec. Bristol Citizens' Recruiting Committee. *Addresses :* 4, Princes Buildings, Clifton, Bristol ; 33, Corn Street, Bristol. (O3887)

RISELEY, John William, M.B.E. (M10462)

RISHWORTH, Lieut.-Col. Albert Henry, O.B.E., *b.* 30 Sept. 1858 ; *s.* of Henry Rishworth, of Keighley, Yorks. ; *m.* Melicent Estcourt, *d.* of Nathaniel Bradley, J.P., F.C.S., of Manchester. *Educ. :* Pannal Coll., Harrogate. Vice-President, St. John Ambulance Association. *War Work :* Organising Officer ¦National Reserve ; assisted in training three Battalions of New Army, Aug. 1914, to Jan. 1915 ; commanded 2nd Vol. Batt. E.Y.R., Jan. 1915, to May, 1920 ; Special Constable Commander, Jan. 1915, to May, 1920 ; Military Representative, Skirlaugh Tribunal ; Member of Committee Territorial Force Association, E. Yorks. *Address :* 59, Park Avenue, Hull. *Club :* Constitutional, Hull. (O11220)

RISHWORTH, Major Norman John, M.B.E.

RISING, Comm. Francis Simon, O.B.E., R.N.

RISK, Capt. Richard Henry Little, C.B.E., R.N. Assist. to Senior Naval Officer, Liverpool. (C2221)

RITCHIE, Alice Maude, M.B.E. ; *d.* of Sir James Thomson Ritchie, Bart. *War Work :* Recruiting Commandant

St. John Ambulance Brigade, County of London. *Address :* 72, Queensborough Terrace, Hyde Park, London, W. 2. (M9455)

RITCHIE, Major Blyth, O.B.E.

RITCHIE, Charles John, M.B.E., J.P., D.L., City of London, *b.* 12 Jan. 1871 ; *s.* of Sir James Ritchie, Bart., of London ; *m.* Ethel Beatrice, *d.* of David Bruce, of Dundee. *Educ. :* Westminster School. *War Work :* Assistant Commander, Metropolitan Special Constabulary, Aug. 1914, to July, 1919. Chairman, All Saints' Hospital ; Member of City of London Committee for National Service. *Address :* 141, Gloucester Terrace, Hyde Park, London. *Clubs :* Carlton ; Royal Thames Yacht ; Royal Automobile. (M9456)

RITCHIE, Hugh, O.B.E., *b.* 19 Sept. 1864 ; *s.* of the late John Ritchie, of H.M. Customs ; *m.* Clara Amelia, *d.* of Robert Blow, of Grimsby. Assistant, Treaty Department, Foreign Office. *Address :* Dover House, Painswick, Glos. (O688)

RITCHIE, Sir James William, Bart., M.B.E., *b.* 1868 ; *s.* of the late Sir James Thomson Ritchie, of Dundee ; *m.* Edna Muriel, *d.* of J. Emerton, of Cheltenham. *Educ. :* Westminster School ; Lincoln Coll., Oxford. Deputy Lieutenant, City of London. *War Work :* Commander " D " Division, Special Constabulary, since Sept. 1914. *Addresses :* 26, Melcombe Court, Dorset Square, N.W. 8 ; Crick Manor, nr. Rugby. *Clubs :* Garrick ; Carlton. (M892)

RITCHIE, Lieut. John, M.B.E.

RITCHIE, Marie Isabel, Mrs., M.B.E., *b.* 28 Aug 1893 ; *d.* of Frederick Finch, of Wembley ; *m.* Alexander Gordon, Capt. R.A.O.C., *s.* of Alexander Ritchie. *Educ. :* St. Paul's Girls' School ; Univ. Coll., London. *War Work :* Assistant to Lieut.-Col. Fulcher, Deputy Assistant to Director of Artillery, for 3 years until Feb. 1919. (M1716)

RITCHIE, Mary, Mrs., M.B.E., *b.* 1853 ; *d.* of William Harvey, of 10, Park Terrace, Glasgow ; *m.* James, *s.* of David Ritchie, of 29, Park Circus, Glasgow. *Educ. :* Edinburgh, and Glasgow Univ. On committees for social and philanthropic Work. *War Work :* Hon. Sec. City of Westminster War Savings Committee. *Address :* 28, Victoria Street, S.W. 1 ; Women's Institute, 92, Victoria Street, S.W. 1. (M3935)

RITCHIE, Major Michael, Balfour Hutchison, D.S.O., O.B.E., M.B., Ch.B., *b.* 1882 ; of the late Rev. R. Ritchie, of St. Mary's, Inverurie ; *m.* 1910, Sydney D'Abzac, *d.* of the late Rev. Addison Crofton (*see* BURKE's *Peerage*). *Educ. :* Aberdeen Univ. Entered R.A.M.C. 1905 ; Capt. 1909 ; Major, 1915 ; served on N.-W. Frontier of India, 1908 (despatches, medal with clasp) ; Great War, 1914–16, as a D.A.D.M.S, (despatches).

RITCHIE, Capt. Robert Linton, O.B.E., R.A.M.C.

RITCHIE, Major Thomas Clark, O.B.E., M.D., B.Sc., *b.* 26 Oct. 1886 ; *s.* of James Ritchie, M.D., F.R.C.P. (Edin.), F.R.C.S. (Edin.), of Edinburgh ; *m.* Isobel, *d.* of Mrs. Dobie, of Leytonstone, Essex. *Educ. :* Edinburgh Academy, and Edinburgh Univ. Medical Practitioner, Prospect House, Malpas, Cheshire. *War Work :* Temporary commission as Lieut. R.A.M.C., July, 1915 ; served in France as Medical Specialist to 30 C.C.S., R.A.M.C. from Sept. 1915, to March, 1919, when demobilised as Major ; T. Capt. July, 1916 ; A. Major, Jan. 1918. *Address :* The Groves, Malpas, Cheshire. (O2690)

RITCHIE, Major William, O.B.E., *b.* 11 Nov. 1867 ; *s.* of James Ritchie, Textile Manufacturer, of Glasgow. *Educ. :* The Western Academy, Glasgow ; Allan Glen's School, Glasgow. *War Work :* Served with Egyptian Expeditionary Force. *Address :* 137, Stockwell Street, Glasgow. (O2926)

RITCHIE, William Thomas, O.B.E., *b.* 1873 ; *s.* of Robert Brown Ritchie, of Edinburgh. *Educ. :* Edinburgh Academy, and Edinburgh Univ. M.D., F.R.C.P. (Edin.) ; Physician to the Deaconess Hospital ; Assistant Physician, Edinburgh Royal Infirmary ; Lecturer on Clinical Medicine in the Univ. of Edinburgh. *War Work :* Capt. (A. Major) R.A.M.C. (T.). *Address :* 14, Rothesay Place, Edinburgh. *Club :* University, Edinburgh. (O6282)

RITCHINGS, Mary Thompson, M.B.E., M.B., Ch.B.

RITSON, Major Cuthbert Ward, O.B.E.

RIVERS, Lieut. Arthur Thomas, O.B.E., *b.* 28 May, 1882 ; *s.* of Thomas Rivers, of Brockley ; *m.* Ethel Emma, *d.* of James William Bowery, of Reading. *Educ. :* Westbourne Schools. Member of the Executive Committee of the Junior Imperial League. *War Work :* Hon. Treas. Overseas Reception Committee which dealt with over one million oversea troops, attached as Lieutenant, Headquarters, Overseas Military Forces of Canada. *Addresses :* 41, Burnaby Gardens, Gunnersbury, W. 4 ; 1, Sanctuary Buildings, Gt. Smith Street, S.W. 1. (O11221)

RIVERS Capt. and Qr.-Mr. Walter Samuel, O.B.E., R.A.M.C. (T.).

RIVERS, Capt. Arthur Joseph DE CARRARA-, O.B.E., R.G.A. Called to the Bar, Inner Temple.

RIVET, Albert Robert, M.B.E., *b.* 28 Jan. 1879 ; *s.* of Pierre Rivet, of Brixton and Paris. *Educ. :* Privately, England and France. Manager (Lead Manufacturers). *War Work :* Director of Materials, Non-Ferrous Material Supplies, Ministry of Munitions, Northumberland Avenue, Jan. 1917, to 31 Dec. 1918. *Address :* Sardis, Meteor Road, Westcliff-on-Sea, Essex. (M9457)

RIVETT, Flying Officer Wilfred John CARNAC-, M.B.E.

RIVIERE, Capt. Eugene Gonzague, M.B.E., M.C.

RIVIERE, Evelyn, O.B.E., *b.* 22 Feb. 1876 ; *s.* of Briton Riviere, R.A., D.C.L. ; *m.* Joan, *d.* of Hugh J. Verrall, of

Brighton. *Educ.*: St. Paul's School, and Balliol Coll., Oxford. Barrister. *War Work*: Legal Assistant, Ministry of Munitions, from Sept. 1915 to, April, 1919. *Addresses*: 11, Old Square, Lincoln's Inn; 10, Nottingham Terrace, York Gate. *Club*: Athenæum.   (O11222)

RIX, Capt. Dudley Gerald, M.B.E.

RIX, Lucy, Mrs., M.B.E.; widow of Septimus Rix, of Buenos Aires. *War Work*: Head of Splint Room, Surgical Branch Q.M.N. Guild, 2, Cavendish Square; Canteen work at Shakespeare Hut, New Zealand Y.M.C.A., 1915–20. *Addresses*: 14, Chaucer Mansions, Queen's Club Gardens, Kensington, W. 14; Remembrance League, 1, Marlborough Gate, W. *Club*: Overseas.

ROAD, Alfred, M.B.E.

ROADS, Edith Mary, O.B.E. *War Work*: Controller of Typists in the War Office. *Address*: 42, Craigen Avenue, Addiscombe, Croydon.   (O2888)

ROAF, Major James Richardson, O.B.E.

ROARK, John, M.B.E.

ROB, Joseph William, O.B.E., M.D. (Cantab.), *b.* 14 Oct. 1876; *s.* of Joseph Dresser Rob, of The Hall, Skipton-on-Swale, Yorkshire; *m.* Alice Maud, *d.* of the Rev. Canon Granville Smith, of Little Fransham. *Educ.*: St. John's Coll., Cambridge; St. Thomas' Hospital, London. Medical Officer to Junior Masonic School for Girls, and to the Walton-on-Thames Hospital; formerly House Surgeon St. Thomas' Hospital, London. *War Work*: M.O. to the St. George's Hill Hospital, 1914–19. *Address*: Oatlands Park, Weybridge.   (O11223)

ROBB, Capt. James Jenkins, O.B.E., M.D.

ROBB, John McLorinan, O.B.E., M.I.E.E., *b.* 17 Oct. 1859; *s.* of Gawn Robb, of Belfast; *m.* Charlotte, *d.* of John Johnston, of Garvagh, Co. Londonderry. *Educ.*: Privately. Superintending Engineer, Post Office Engineering Dept., South Midland District. *War Work*: Provision of Telegraph and Telephone Lines for Admiralty, War Office, and anti-aircraft purposes. *Address*: Ardmore, Wokingham Road, Reading.   (O3889)

ROBBINS, Sir Edmund, K.B.E., *b.* 4 April, 1847; *s.* of Councillor R. Robbins, of Launceston, Cornwall; *m.* Jeannette, *d.* of William Pearson, of Plymouth. *Educ.*: At Priory House Academy, and Eagle House Academy, Launceston. Journalist; connected with the Press Association for nearly 50 years; Chief Sub-Editor, 1870–74; Sec. and Assistant Manager, 1874–80; Chief of the Staff, 1878–80; Manager, 1880–1917; Sec. of the Provincial Newspaper Society, 1870–81; Chairman of the Liberator Relief Fund until transferred to the Public Trustee; Vice-President of the Newspaper Press Fund. *War Work*: Sec. of the Admiralty, War Office, and Press Committee from its formation. *Address*: 168, Peckham Rye Common, S.E. 22.   (K36)

ROBBINS, Gertrude Florence Eveline, Mrs., M.B.E.

ROBBINS, Rowland Richard, C.B.E., J.P., *b.* 24 Dec. 1872; *s.* of Rowland Robbins, of Willersey, Hounslow, Middlesex; *m.* Estella May, *d.* of Charles Centurier Harris, of St. John's Wood, N.W. *Educ.*: Taunton School and private School at Maidenhead; Member Middlesex County Council; Vice-President National Farmers' Union; Income Tax Commissioner (General); Justice of the Peace, Middlesex; Member Royal Commission on Agriculture, (1919); Member Agricultural Wages Board (England and Wales). *War Work*: Chairman of the following committees: Staines Rural District Military Service Tribunal, Staines Rural District Naval and Military Pensions, Staines Rural District Food Control, and Cultivation and Machinery, Middlesex Agricultural Executive Committee. *Address*: Hollycroft, Sipson, Middlesex. *Clubs*: National Liberal; Farmers'.   (C2906)

ROBBINS, William Henry, M.B.E., R.N.

ROBERTON, Margaret, Mrs., M.B.E., L.L.A.; *d.* of the Rev. Thomas Hill, of Dundee; *m.* Nigel Craig, *s.* of the Rev. Thomas Roberton, of Dunipace, Stirling. *Educ.*: Privately. Hon. Sec. of the Q.V.J. Nursing Association, Wick; Member of the Education Authority of Caithness. *War Work*: Sec. of the Wick and East of Caithness Branch of the Red Cross Society, Aug. 1914, to March, 1919. *Address*: Central United Free Church Manse, Wick, Caithness. (M9461)

ROBERTS, Adeline, O.B.E., Q.M.A.A.C.

ROBERTS, Aileen Mary, Countess, D.B.E., *b.* 20 Sept. 1870; *d.* of 1st Earl Roberts, *S.* father, 1914. Founder of Field Glass Fund; Hon. Sec. of Officers' Families Fund, and a member of War Pensions Committee. *Address*: Englemere, Ascot.   (D30)

ROBERTS, Lieut.-Col. Alexander Fowler, C.B.E.; New Zealand Forces. *War Work*: Director of Field Artillery and Senior Embarkation Officer.   (C1869)

ROBERTS, Alfred Henry, O.B.E., *b.* 1872; *s.* of Charles Digby Roberts, of Bath. *Educ.*: Bedford Grammar School. Supt. and Engineer, Leith Dock Commission; Member-Institution of Civil Engineers; Fellow of Royal Society of Edinburgh. *War Work*: Advisory and other Committees on Port and Labour questions.   (O1810)

ROBERTS, Alfred Jabez, O.B.E.

ROBERTS, Lieut.-Comm. Arthur Cecil, O.B.E., R.N.

ROBERTS, Sir Arthur Cornelius, K.B.E., *b.* 15 Sept. 1869; *s.* of Stephen Arthur Roberts, of Clapham Park; *m.* Madeline Rose, *d.* of F. C. Brown. *Educ.*: New Coll., Eastbourne. Chartered Accountant; Senior Partner in firm of A. C. Roberts, Wright & Co., 9–10, Pancras Lane, Queen Street, E.C. 4; L.C.C. Member for Streatham. *War Work*:

Assist.-Director-Gen. Royal Army Clothing Department, and Chairman, Clothing Committee, Contracts Department, War Office, 1916; Chairman, Board of Financial Control, and Chief Auditor of Works Accounts, Air Ministry, 1917–18. *Address*: Copthorne, 29, Aldrington Road, Streatham Park, S.W. 16. *Clubs*: British Empire; New City.   (K35)

ROBERTS, Arthur Harry, M.B.E., *b.* 12 March, 1865; *s.* of Charles Roberts, of Exeter; *m.* Cora, *d.* of Samuel Cornish, of Bradninch, Devon. *Educ.*: Exeter Training Coll., Practising School. Executive Engineer, G.P.O., A.M.I.E.E. *War Work*: Establishment of communications in North Russia. *Address*: 17, Foyle Road, Blackheath, S.E. 3.   (M9462)

ROBERTS, Lieut.-Col. Arthur Henry, O.B.E., D.S.O., R.A.S.C., *b.* 1876. Served in the S. African War, 1900–2 (Queen's medal with seven clasps); Great War, 1914–19 (despatches).   (C3001)

ROBERTS, Major Arthur Neil Stewart, O.B.E.

ROBERTS, Col. Arthur Noel, C.B.E., R.A.S.C. (ret.), *b.* 1860. Served in S. Africa, 1899–1902 (Queen's medal with our clasps); Great War, 1914–19 (despatches).   (C1752)

ROBERTS, Capt. Cecil Henry Woolcott, O.B.E.

ROBERTS, Charles Abraham, C.B.E., *b.* Nov. 1855. *Educ.*: Northleach Grammar School; Gloucestershire. Joined service of Great Western Railway Co. in 1871; was Goods Manager for Gloucester District from 1893 to 1896, and for Bristol District from 1896 to 1904; Assistant Chief Goods Manager, 1904–1912, and from that date Chief Goods Manager; Chairman of Goods Manager Conference at Railway Clearing House during year 1918. *Address*: Fair Leigh, Windsor Road, Slough.   (C2907)

ROBERTS, Major Charles Cecil Gwynedd, O.B.E.

ROBERTS, Charles Herbert, M.B.E.

ROBERTS, Paymaster-Sub-Lieut. Charles John, M.B.E., R.N.V.R.

ROBERTS, David Richard, M.B.E., *b.* 12 March, 1879; *s.* of Richard Roberts, of Rhydyfelin, Aberystwyth; *m.* Gwen Ellen,)*d.* of David Griffith, of Portmadoc. *Educ.*: Clark's Coll. Civil Service: Intermediate. *War Work*: 4 years at Ministry of Munitions of War; Director in the Central Stores Department. *Address*: 2, The Chestnuts, Adelaide Road, Surbiton, Surrey.   (M2348)

ROBERTS, Edward Coleridge, O.B.E., M.R.C.S., J.P.

ROBERTS, Ernest, O.B.E.

ROBERTS, Evan, M.B.E.

ROBERTS, Florence Alice, M.B.E.

ROBERTS, Major Geoffray Dorling, O.B.E.

ROBERTS, George Augustus, C.B.E., F.R.C.S. (Eng.), *b.* 30 May, 1875; *s.* of The Rev. A. J. Roberts, of Tidebrook, Sussex; *m.* Florence Muriel, *d.* of Col. A. McMill, of Indian Army. *Educ.*: Marlborough Coll., and King's Coll. Hospital. Hon. Surgeon Royal Hants. County Hospital, Winchester. *War Work*: Surgeon to the Red Cross Hospitals, Winchester. *Address*: Walcote, Winchester.   (C2908)

ROBERTS, Major George Fossett, O.B.E., J.P., *b.* 1 Nov. 1870; *s.* of David Roberts, of Aberystwyth; *m.* Mary, *d.* of John Parry, of Glanpaith, Cardiganshire. *Educ.*: At Cheltenham (Private School). *War Work*: Embarkation Staff Officer, Aug. 1914 to June, 1919. *Address*: Laura Place, Aberystwyth.   (O7638)

ROBERTS, George James, M.B.E.

ROBERTS, George Quinlan, C.B.E., M.A., *b.* Feb. 1860; *s.* of G. V. Roberts, of Hobart, Tasmania; *m.* Mary Louise, *d.* of Henry Waters, of Chisell Hall. *Educ.*: Hutchins School, Hobart; Hertford Coll., Oxford. Formerly House Governor, London Hospital; since 1903 Sec. and Receiver, St. Thomas' Hospital. *War Work*: Sec. St. Thomas' Hospital; Huts built; St. Thomas' was constituted 5th London General Hospital (520 military beds); took active part in arrangements for treatment of wounded and war prisoners. *Clubs*: Leander; Royal Automobile.   (O1029)

ROBERTS, Capt. George William Pearson, M.B.E., B.Sc., R.A.S.C., *b.* 1893; *s.* of Gervase Henry, of Lee, S.E. *Educ.*: Univ. Coll. School, and City and Guilds Coll., S. Kensington. Engineering Student at Royal Arsenal, Woolwich. *War Work*: Joined R.A.S.C., Dec. 1915; commissioned, May, 1916; served with B.E.F., June, 1916, to July, 1917; demobilised, Oct. 1919. *Address*: 79, Burnt Ash Hill, Lee, S.E. 12.   (M5577)

ROBERTS, Gervase Henry, C.B.E., M.Inst.C.E.; *s.* of Alderman G. H. Roberts, J.P., Mayor of City of Wakefield *Educ.*: Stanley Hall, and Leeds Univ. Civil Engineer. *War Work*: Chief Mechanical Engineer, Royal Arsenal, Woolwich. *Address*: 3, Blessington Road, Blackheath, S.E. 13.   (C277)

ROBERTS, Gomer, M.B.E., J.P., *b.* 18 April, 1852; *s.* of John Roberts, of Tyddyn Uchaf, Corwen; *m.* Margaret, *d.* of William Jones, of Maesmor Farm, Denbighshire. *Educ.*: Glanrafon and Corwen British Schools. Temp. Valuer under the Board of Inland Revenue, 1914–15; Market and Crop Reporter for the Ministry of Agriculture since 1904; appointed sub-commissioner by the same on the North Wales area, 1919. *War Work*: Took up the appointment of Chief Executive Officer for Denbighshire, 1917–19, under the Ministry succeeded in increasing the cultivable area of the county by 32,000 acres, under the Cultivation of Lands Order, 1917; Member of the County Tribunal under the Lord Derby Scheme, to which he devoted much time. *Address*: 1, Llanfair Villas, Llanfair, D.C., Ruthin.   (M2349)

ROBERTS, Capt. Hamilton Walter, O.B.E., Royal Artillery, b. 10 Aug. 1884; s. of the late Lieut.-Col. Francis Roberts, R.A., of Wimbledon. Educ.: Dulwich Coll., and Royal Military Academy, Woolwich. Regular Officer. War Work: A.D.C. to G.O.C. Troops, Sierra Leone, West Africa, Aug. 1914. to Sept. 1915; France and Belgium with 82nd Siege Battery, R.G.A.; commanded 104th Siege Battery, R.G.A., in Belgium; and 82nd Siege Battery, R.G.A.; twice mentioned in despatches; wounded at Ypres, Dec. 1916. Address: 10, Lauriston Road, Wimbledon, S.W. Club: Naval and Military. (O8912)

ROBERTS, Henry David, M.B.E., b. 6th Feb. 1870; s. of the late Henry Wm. Roberts, of H.M. Civil Service; m. Margaret Cuthbertson, d. of the late James Mackintosh, of Glasgow and Buenos Aires. Educ.: Worcester Cathedral King's School (King's Scholar) and Old Elvet School, Durham. Director of the following: Public Library, Museums and Art Galleries; Publicity Department, and Royal Pavilion Estate, Brighton. War Work: Hon. Sec. Brighton National Service Committee; Hon. Sec. to committee for recruiting for W.A.A.C. and for female munition workers; Hon. Sec. Inter-Allied Exhibition on Disablement (Ministry of Pensions), 1918; Member of Brighton Special Constabulary; Officer local Volunteers; Chevalier of the Order of the Crown of Italy (1919); Chevalier of the Order of the Crown of Belgium (1920) "for valuable services rendered to these countries during the war." Address: Royal Pavilion, Brighton. Clubs: Brighton and Hove Rotary; Brighton Arts. (M2350)

ROBERTS, Lieut.-Col. Rev. Henry George, O.B.E., M.A. Educ.: Headingley Coll., Leeds. War Work: Assistant Principal Chaplain, E.E.F.; mentioned in Lord Allenby's despatches, 1919; appointed by G.H.Q.. E.E.F., Lecturer on Morals and Ethics to the troops in E.E.F. Address: Central Buildings. Westminster, London, S.W. 1. (O8645)

ROBERTS, Capt. Herbert Charles, M.B.E., b. 21 Oct. 1872; s. of Henry William Roberts, of Worcester; m. Alice Jane, d. of John Beer, of Stoke-in-Teignhead, S. Devon. Educ.: Bede Coll., Durham. War Work: 1914–15, teaching first aid under London County Council; V.A.D. work wth British Red Cross Society, No. 1 County of London, 1916–17; Stores Manager with British Red Cross Society's commission to East Africa (Mombasa and Dar-es-salaam), 1917–19; Stores Manager (Medical Dept.), B.R.C.S., London. Address: 15, High Street, Bognor, Sussex. (M2351)

ROBERTS, Lieut.-Col. Hugh Bradley, O.B.E., R.A.

ROBERTS, Major Hugh Denison, O.B.E., b. 5 Nov. 1891; s. of Rev. A. C. Roberts, of Havenstreet, near Ryde. I. of W.; m. Hilda Frances, d. of W. A. Buckenham, of Stoke Ferry, Norfolk. Educ.: Reagill House School, Bath, and Bath College. War Work: Enlisted Aug. 1914; commissioned 2nd Lieut. Sept. 1915; Lieutenant, May, 1916; Captain, Oct. 1917; Major, Nov. 1918. Address: Osborne House, Stoke Ferry, Norfolk. (O8920)

ROBERTS, Irene Helen, Mrs., M.B.E.

ROBERTS, Capt. J., C.B.E., D.S.O., R.D. R.N.R. War Work: 1914–19, with Auxiliary Patrol (despatches); Commodore of Convoys (despatches). (C1204)

ROBERTS, Major James Ernest Helme, O.B.E.

ROBERTS, Lieut.-Comm. John, M.B.E., R.N., b. 26 Nov. 1852; s. of William Henry Roberts, of Plymouth; m. Mary, d. of Michael Flynn, of Kinsale, Ireland. Educ.: St. German's Grammar School, Cornwall. Royal Navy. War Work: Admiralty Mail Officer, R.N. Barracks, Chatham, from Feb. 1915, to April, 1919. Address: 1, Beresford Terrace, Peverell, Plymouth. (M2352)

ROBERTS, Maria Theresa, Hon. Mrs. A. Phillips, d. of William Henry John North, 11th Baron North (see BURKE'S Peerage); m. Arthur Phillips Roberts, J.P., D.L., who died 1911. (O11226)

ROBERTS, Lieut.-Col. Montgomery Browne, O.B.E.

ROBERTS, Major Norcliffe, O.B.E., M.B., R.A.M.C.

ROBERTS, Capt. Norman Stanley, M.B.E., b. 20 Aug. 1893. War Work: Joined B.E.F., France, Nov. 1914; wounded, April, 1915, to April, 1916; served in France and Salonica with Rifle Brigade until Jan. 1919; R.T.O. Tiflis, Jan. 1919, to Sept. 1919; Staff Capt., Railways, S. Russia, Nov. 1919, to July, 1920. Address: The Birches, Adswood, Cheadle Hulme, Cheshire.

ROBERTS, Reginald, O.B.E., B.A., b. 17 April, 1862; s. of Edward Roberts, of Berden Hall, Bishops Stortford, Herts.; m. Edith Vining, d. of Arthur Baker, of Henbury Hill House, Henbury, Bristol. Educ.: Monkton Combe School, Bath, and St. John's Coll., Cambridge. War Work: Transport work at the Reading War Hospital. Address: Alton Priors, nr. Pewsey, Wilts. (O11227)

ROBERTS, Major Richard Cowan, O.B.E.

ROBERTS, Capt. Richard Gilbert, O.B.E.

ROBERTS, Ronald Cleave, M.B.E.

ROBERTS, Talbot Vivian Waymen, M.B.E., M.C.

ROBERTS, His Honour Judge Sir Walworth Howland, Knt. Bach., C.B.E., J.P., b. 30 Aug. 1855; s. of Sir Thomas Howland Roberts, Bart.; m. Katherine, d. of John Gibson Thomson, of Aitechnan, Ardrishaig, Argyleshire, N.B. Educ.: Highgate School; King's Coll., London. Judge of the Marylebone County Court; J.P. Staffs.; Member (Chairman) of County Courts Ruffe Committee; Member of Lord Chancellor's County Courts Staff Committee, 1919–20; formerly in succession Judge of County Court Circuits, 25, 37, and 41. War Work: A Chairman of Committee on Production and of the Interim Court of Arbitration. Address: 16, Palace Gardens Terrace, Kensington, W. 8; Club: Savile. (C2909)

ROBERTS, William, O.B.E.

ROBERTS, Capt. William Ivor, M.B.E.

ROBERTS, Winifred Eyre, Mrs. CROMPTON-, M.B.E.

ROBERTS, Major Kenneth Farquharson FARQU-HARSON-, O.B.E., R.A.O.C.

ROBERTS, Col. Prescott Anson PRESCOTT-, O.B.E., R.A.S.C.

ROBERTS, Capt. Arthur Edward STOKES-, O.B.E., M.C.

ROBERTSHAW, Robert Henry, M.B.E.

ROBERTSON, Lieut. Adam McCall, M.B.E., R.F.A., (T.).

ROBERTSON, Capt. Alexander Smith, M.B.E., R.E.

ROBERTSON, Capt. Alfred Leopold, O.B.E., R.A.M.C.

ROBERTSON, Capt. Andrew, O.B.E., R.A.M.C. (T.).

ROBERTSON, Lieut. Andrew Clark, O.B.E., R.A.S.C. (T.).

ROBERTSON, Ann Margaret, M.B.E.

ROBERTSON, Annie, M.B.E., b. 1890; d. of the late William Robertson, of Elgin, Scotland. Educ.: Elgin Academy, Blackheath High School, and Newnham Coll., Cambridge. Welfare Supervisor for the Ebbw Vale Steel, Iron, and Coal Co., Ltd. War Work: Member of the 24th Morayshire V.A.D. Detachment; in charge of both outdoor and indoor women workers employed by the Ebbw Vale Steel, Iron, and Coal Co., from 1916 until end of the war. Address: Linkwood, Elgin, N.B. Club: Social, Ebbw Vale. (M3937)

ROBERTSON, Archibald Campbell, M.B.E., J.P.

ROBERTSON, Arthur Hurle, M.B.E., M.I.M.E., b. 23 Oct. 1871; s. of James Robertson, of Dundee; m. the late Thirza Ann, d. of Thomas Costello, of London. Educ.: Private Schools. Marine Engineer. War Work: Chief Engineer on Admiralty Transport Services trading between London and the French Ports. Address: 413, Romford Road, Forest Gate, London. Club: Member of the Institute of Marine Engineers. (M9467)

ROBERTSON, Capt. Charles, O.B.E., Mercantile Marine Service, b. 19 June, 1859; s. of Capt. Charles Robertson, of Glasgow; grandson of Capt. Chas. Robertson, Port Glasgow, and Capt. James Malcolm of St. Johns, N.B.; m. Emma Jane, d. of W. J. Flower of Southampton. Educ.: Liverpool Institute, Liverpool. Member of Newport Town Council, and Overseer; Chairman, Secondary Education Committee, etc. War Work: Chairman, National Relief Fund (Prince of Wales' Fund), locally; 1914, Soldiers' and Sailors' Families Association, daily work; Chairman, Local War Pensions, etc., Committee, since formation; Member, Executive Welsh National Fund, and of Local Employment Committee (Ministry of Labour). Address: 19. Morden Road. Newport, Mon. (O11228)

ROBERTSON, Major Charles Bruce, O.B.E., b. 25 Nov. 1890; s. of the late C. J. P. Robertson, M.I.E.E., of London. Educ.: Trent Coll., and Kensington Coaching Coll. Ministry of Food, Road Transport Dept. War Work: Artists' Rifles, and R.A.S.C. (M.T.); served overseas 4½ years, Belgium, France, Italy, Egypt, Mesopotamia, and Persia. Club: Royal Automobile. (O11229)

ROBERTSON, Charles George, O.B.E.

ROBERTSON, Lieut.-Col. Charles MacIver, O.B.E., R.A.F., and R.F.A.

ROBERTSON, Charlotte, Lady, C.B.E.; d. of late W. Young, of Londonderry; m. Sir Benjamin, K.C.S.I., K.C.M.G., C.I.E., LL.D., Indian Civil Service (see BURKE'S Peerage), s. of late B. Robertson, of Dungstail, Morayshire. Address: Nagput, Central Provinces, India. (C685)

ROBERTSON, Lieut.-Col. Colin John Trevelyan, M.C., M.A., b. 20 Nov. 1877; s. of the late Charles Robertson, J.P., D.L., of Kindeace, Delny, Ross-shire. Educ.: Cambridge Univ. Joint Headmaster of Shirley House Preparatory School, Old Charlton, S.E. War Work: Nov. 1915, to June, 1918, D.A.D.O.S., 5th Div., B.E.F.; June, 1918, to Oct. 1918, A.D.O.S. Independent Air Force, France; Feb. 1919, to Oct. 1919, A.D.O.S. Murmansh Exp. Force; demobilised, April, 1920, with rank of Lieut.-Col. Address: The Cedars, Old Charlton, Kent. (O9724)

ROBERTSON, Lieut.-Col. David Stephen, O.B.E.

ROBERTSON, Duncan John, O.B.E., b. 14 Jan. 1860; s. of James Robertson, Sheriff-Substitute of Orkney; m. Margaret Keir, d. of Archibald Garden, J.P. for Morayshire. Educ.: Edinburgh Academy, and Edinburgh Univ. J.P., Clerk, and County Clerk for Orkney; Vice-Consul for Denmark, Norway, and Sweden; author of "Waith and Wrack" (Longmans, Green & Co.). War Work: National Registration, Food Control, Agricultural Executive Committee, Local Tribunal, War Pensions Committee, and other work. Address: Crantit House, St. Ola, Orkney. Club: Orkney, Kirkwall. (O1813)

ROBERTSON, Lieut. Frederick William, M.B.E., R.A.F. (T.)

ROBERTSON, Capt. Frederick William, O.B.E., R.F.A., F.I.A., b. 22 April, 1883; s. of Thomas Robertson, I.S.O., of Edinburgh; m. Marjory Forster, d. of Gervas Woodhouse, B.A., of York. Educ.: Edinburgh Academy. Employed at Head Office of the Scottish Widows' Fund Life Assurance Society, Edinburgh. Address: 29, Inverleith Gardens, Edinburgh. (O5723)

ROBERTSON, Lieut.-Col. Frederick, O.B.E.

ROBERTSON, George, M.B.E.

ROBERTSON, Major George Whiteside, O.B.E.

ROBERTSON, Major Hector Murdoch Maxwell, O.B.E., M.C., R.F.A., *b.* 27 May, 1888; *s.* of Col. H. Maxwell Robertson, of Eastbourne; *m.* Emilie Marie Edouard, *d.* of Monsieur Auguste Gillard, Secretaire-General de la Société de la Vieille Montagne, of Liège, Belgium. *Educ.:* Wellington Coll., Berks. Substantive Major, R.F.A. *War Work:* A.D.C., G.O.C., R.A., 2nd Div., France, Aug. 1914, to Nov. 1914 (wounded, Ypres); March, 1915, to Nov. 1915, 118th Bde. R.F.A., 1st Canadian Division, France (invalided); March, 1916, to France as O.C. A/184 Bty, 39th Div.; 1918, G.S.O., R.A.F., home, and Germany. *Addresses:* Moorland House, Westmount Rd., Eltham; R.M.A. Woolwich. *Clubs:* M.C.C.; Free Foresters'. (O8176)

ROBERTSON, Herbert James Duncan, M.B.E.

ROBERTSON, Col. Herman Melchoir, C.B.E. Canadian Army Med. Corps; served in Great War, 1915–19 (despatches). (C1835)

ROBERTSON, Capt. Hugh Given, O.B.E., M.B. R.A.M.C.

ROBERTSON, James Alexander, O.B.E.

ROBERTSON, Paymaster-Lieut.-Comm. James Anderson Brown, O.B.E., R.N.

ROBERTSON, James Constable, M.B.E., J.P.

ROBERTSON, Col. James Currie, C.M.G., C.I.E., C.B.E., M.B., B.Sc., D.P.H., *b.* 1870; *s.* of Alexander Robertson, J.P.; *m.* 1903, Catherine Jones. Entered Indian Med. Ser. 1896; Capt. 1899; Major, 1907; Lieut.-Col. 1915; served with Dongola Expedition, 1896 (medal, Khedive's medal); S. Africa, 1902, on special duty (despatches, Queen's medal with two clasps); appointed Dep. Sanitary Commr., United Provinces, India, 1901; Sanitary Commr. Govt. of India; 1912; Additional Member of Council of Gov.-Gen. of India; Assist. Director of Med. Services with rank of Col. *Address:* Delhi, India. (C1401)

ROBERTSON, Lieut.-Col. James Herbert Graham, C.B.E. New Zealand Med. Corps; served in the Great War (despatches). (C1870)

ROBERTSON, Capt. and Qr.-Mr. James Sin, M.B.E.

ROBERTSON, Major James Stewart, O.B.E.

ROBERTSON, Janet, M.B.E.

ROBERTSON, Jean Dewar, M.B.E.

ROBERTSON, John, O.B.E., M.D.

ROBERTSON, John, M.B.E.

ROBERTSON, Hon. Lieut.-Col. John, C.M.G., O.B.E., M.D., B.Sc., R.A.M.C., *b.* 1862. *Educ.:* Edinburgh Univ. Medical Officer of Health, Birmingham; Professor of Public Health, Univ. of Birmingham. *War Work:* Served on Army Sanitary Committee, 1914–19. *Address:* The Council House, Birmingham. *Club:* Union, Birmingham. (O691)

ROBERTSON, Major John, C.B.E. T. Capt. and Brevet Major, R.E.; served in the Great War, 1914–19 (despatches). (C1316)

ROBERTSON, John, C.B.E. *War Work:* Provost of Paisley; Chairman of Local National Service and Food Control Committees; Member of Appeal Tribunal. *Address:* Paisley. (C278)

ROBERTSON, John Argyll, O.B.E., *b.* 26 Sept. 1871; *s.* of John Hutchinson Robertson, of Singapore, S.S.; *m.* Sarah Lilian Pitt, *d.* of W. G. Healing, of Tewkesbury. *Educ.:* George Watson's Coll., Edinburgh. Agent, Chartered Bank of India, Australia, and China, Kuala Lumpur, F.M.S. *Address:* Thatched House. (O8408)

ROBERTSON, Capt. John Hercules, C.B.E., R.N. *War Work:* 1914–19, Naval Centre Officer at Invergordon and Devonport. (C2299)

ROBERTSON, Capt. John William, O.B.E., M.B., F.R.C.S., R.A.M.C.

ROBERTSON, Kate Ann, Lady, O.B.E.; *d.* of Thomas Morris-Banks, of Liverpool; widow of Sir Helenus Robert, *s.* of James Hunter Robertson, of Greenock. *War Work:* Organised scheme for providing free board and lodging for relatives of dangerously ill or wounded soldiers who had been summoned to their bedside; on all War Committees in Chester; started one of the first Belgian Refugee Homes in Cheshire. *Address:* Netley Park, Gomshall, Surrey. (O11231)

ROBERTSON, Major Kenneth Struan, O.B.E.

ROBERTSON, Major Malcolm, O.B.E., M.C.

ROBERTSON, Margaret Agnes Josepha, M.B.E., *b.* 2 Nov. 1869; *d.* of Vincent Stuart Robertson. *War Work:* V.A.D. Nurse, St. John's Ambulance Brigade, at 16th General Hospital, Le Tréport, France, then 13th General Hospital, Boulogne, subsequently 4th Northern General Hospital, Lincoln, and two V.A.D. Hospitals for short periods; Q.M.A.A.C. Administrator, Jan. 1918, to May, 1919; Q.M.A.A.C. Records, and U.A., R.H.G., Regent's Park Barracks; Quartermistress, British Com. French Red Cross at Vitry-en-Artois, June, 1919, to April, 1920. *Address:* South Lodge, Enfield Chase, Middlesex. *Club:* Q.M.A.A.C. Old Comrades Association. (M5580)

ROBERTSON, Margaret Ida, M.B.E. (M10253)

ROBERTSON, Margaret Hill, Mrs., M.B.E.

ROBERTSON, Mary Elizabethe, M.B.E.

ROBERTSON, John, Philadelphia Nina, O.B.E., *d.* of the late Very Rev. John D. Robertson, of Melbourne, Victoria, Australia. *Educ.:* Presbyterian Ladies' Coll., Melbourne. Secretary-General of Australian Red Cross Society. *War Work:* Since 1915 has acted in above capacity at Head-

quarters of Australian Red Cross Society, Federal Government House, Melbourne, working under Her Excellency Lady Helen Munro Ferguson, G.B.E., President of the Society. *Address:* c/o Australian Red Cross Society, Federal Government House, Melbourne. (O929)

ROBERTSON, Richard, M.B.E.

ROBERTSON, Richard Frederick, M.B.E.

ROBERTSON, Sir Robert, K.B.E., M.A., F.R.S., *b.* 17 April, 1869; *s.* of Dr. John A. Robertson, of Cupar, Fife; *m.* Kathleen *d.* of the late Professor Hugh Hutton Stannus, F.R.I.B.A., of Hindhead. *Educ.:* Madras Academy, Cupar, Fife; St. Andrews Univ. (M.A. 1890, D.Sc. 1897). Director of Explosives, Research Dept., Woolwich; Associate Member, Ordnance Committee; Vice-President, Institute of Chemistry, 1918. Principal Government Chemist. *War Work:* In charge of Research on Explosives at Research Dept., Woolwich, from which emanated many processes and new explosives adopted into the Service and used on the largest scale during the war. *Addresses:* Research Dept., Woolwich; 29, Charlton Road, Blackheath, S.E., 3. *Club:* Chemical Industry. (K102)

ROBERTSON, Robert, O.B.E., *b.* 26 Jan. 1879; *s.* of John Sinclair Robertson, of Kinross, Scotland; *m.* Elizabeth, *d.* of James Patterson, of Highgate. *Educ.:* Waterloo School, Oldham; and at Kinross. Borough Accountant, Lowestoft. *War Work:* Hon. Treas. and Financial Adviser to East Coast towns; for the Inhabitants the sum of £473,379 was obtained, and for the Municipalities, £290,000, a total of £763,379; Hon. Treas. War Pensions Committee; Hon. Treas. War Savings Committee; Hon. Treas. and Administrator, Canadian Relief Fund, and also of Mayor's Relief Fund. *Address:* Town Hall, Lowestoft. (O11232)

ROBERTSON, Capt. Robert Charles, O.B.E., R.A.M.C.

ROBERTSON, Major Russell Butler, O.B.E., Can. A.M.C.

ROBERTSON, Lieut.-Col. Struan Gordon, C.B.E. Canadian Forces. *War Work:* Officer in Charge of Estates Branch, Overseas Military Forces of Canada. (C605)

ROBERTSON, Stuart Duncan, O.B.E., *b.* 12 June, 1884; *s.* of Murray Robertson. *Educ.:* King's School, Ely, and elsewhere. Deputy Traffic Manager, Great Indian Peninsula Railway, Bombay, India. *War Work:* In charge of all military traffic during last 3 years of war on Great Indian Peninsula Railway, Bombay, which was main base for all Indian Expeditionary Forces and the G.I.P.R. carried the bulk of the traffic. *Address:* Co.'s Offices, G.I.P.R., Bombay. *Club:* Royal Bombay Yacht. (O8297)

ROBERTSON, Major Thomas Alexander, O.B.E., D.C.M., R.A.M.C.

ROBERTSON, Major Thomas Edward, O.B.E., R.A.F.

ROBERTSON, Lieut. Walter Allan, M.B.E., Aust. A.P.C., A.I.F.

ROBERTSON, Walter Thomas, M.B.E.

ROBERTSON, Capt. William, M.B.E.

ROBERTSON, William, O.B.E., *b.* 23 April, 1856; *s.* of James Robertson, J.P., of Brighton; *m.* Edith Grace, *d.* of N. Salamon, of London. *Educ.:* Weymouth Coll., and privately. *War Work:* Royal Army Pay Department, Chatham and Hounslow Pay Offices. *Address:* 43, Mount Park Crescent, Ealing. (O11233)

ROBERTSON, Lieut.-Col. William, V.C., O.B.E., *b.* 27 Feb. 1865; *s.* of John Robertson, of Dumfries; *m.* Sarah, *d.* of Samuel Ferris, of Belfast. Enlisted in Gordon Highlanders, Dec. 1884; Commissioned during S.A. War, May, 1900; promoted Lieut.-Col. for services in connection with the war, April, 1917. *War Work:* Recruiting Staff Officer, Edinburgh, and afterwards Assistant Director of National Service for Edinburgh and Lothian and Peebles Area under Ministry of National Service; was awarded V.C. in S.A. War as a combatant. *Addresses:* 5, St. Andrew Square, Edinburgh; 21, Lee Crescent, Portobello. (O692)

ROBERTSON, Capt. William Adam, O.B.E., Can. A.V.C.

ROBERTSON, William Eugene, M.B.E.

ROBERTSON, William Nathaniel, C.B.E. (C3203)

ROBERTSON, William St. Leonards, O.B.E.

ROBERTSON, Winifred Agnes Florence, M.B.E.

ROBERTSON, Major James Archibald St. George FITZWARRENNE-DESPENCER-, O.B.E., *b.* 1888; *s.* of the late Sir Helenus Robertson. *Educ.:* Eton, and New Coll., Oxford. *War Work:* Mil. Sec. to Gen. Sir Henry Mackinnon, G.C.B., Nov. 1914, to March, 1916; attached to War Office, March, 1916, to April, 1916; attached to Western Command, April, 1916, to May, 1918; Mil. Sec. Western Command, May, 1918, to April, 1919. *Address:* Netley Park, Gomshall, Surrey. *Club:* Bath: Leander. (O7150)

ROBERTSON, Hon. Major James STEWART-, O.B.E., late 3rd Bn. The Black Watch, *b.* 14 Nov. 1856; *s.* of James Stewart Robertson, of Edsadynate, Strathtay, Perthshire; *m.* Janet Beatrice, *d.* of T. W. Murray Allan, of Glenfeochan, Kilmore, Argyll. *Educ.:* Loretto and privately. *War Work:* Local War Pensions Committee for Perthshire; Joint (Disablement) Committee for Central Scotland; Local Tribunal, Highland Area and Highland Agricultural Committee; Food Control Committee for County. *Address:* Edradynate, Strathtay, Perthshire. *Club:* New, Edinburgh. (O11230)

ROBEY, George, C.B.E., *b.* 20 Sept. 1869; *m.* Ethel, *d.* of — Haydon. Comedian; made first appearance, 1891; has appeared at the Alhambra Theatre and the Hippodrome and all the principal variety theatres in London and the

Provinces. Worked in connection with various war charities, raising money, organising, and giving his services for theatrical performances. *Address:* 3, Cadogan Place, S.W. *Clubs:* Eccentric; M.C.C.

ROBIN, Alexander Gibson, O.B.E.

ROBIN, Maggie, M.B.E.

ROBIN, Matthew, O.B.E., *b.* 30 Jan. 1867; *s.* of Robert Robin, of Hamilton and Glasgow; *m.* Mabel Mylius, *d.* of Surgeon-Gen. W. G. Don, of London. *Educ.:* Gilbertfield, Hamilton, and Glasgow Univ. Engine Builder (Marine), retired; late Managing Director, Muir and Houston, Ltd., Glasgow. *War Work:* Special Constable, Central Division, Glasgow; Constable to Inspector to Superintendent of Central Division, Canteen, Central Station, Glasgow; *Address:* Lanfine, Dumbreck, Glasgow. *Clubs:* Royal Scottish Automobile; Scottish Constitutional, Glasgow. (O11236)

ROBINOW, William, M.B.E., M.C., M.A., *b.* 8 Nov. 1882; *s.* of the late Max. Emil Robinson, of Manchester. *Educ.:* Rugby School, and Christ Church, Oxford. Called to the Bar, 1908. *War Work:* Sec. East Lancashire Branch, British Red Cross Society; private in Royal Fusiliers to Capt. 3rd Batt. Tank Corps. *Address:* Hawthornden, Green Walk, Bowdon, Cheshire. *Club:* Clarendon, Manchester. (M9472)

ROBINS, Harry George, M.B.E.

ROBINS, Eng.-Comm. Leslie, O.B.E., R.N.

ROBINS, Lieut. Veral Glen, M.B.E.. R.E.

ROBINSON, Major Alexander Augustus Edmund, O.B.E., R.A.F.

ROBINSON, Major Alick Christopher, O.B.E., R.A.F.

ROBINSON, Andrew, C.B.E., M.V.O., F.R.S.A., *b.* 17 Feb. 1858; *s.* of George Robinson, of Ballytweedy, Muckamore, Co. Antrim; *m.* Robina, *d.* of James Hutton Salmond, of Perth, Scotland. *Educ.:* Belfast. Principal Architect, Office of Public Works, Dublin; Inspector of Ancient and National Monuments in Ireland. *War Work:* Special services rendered in connection with naval, military, and Royal Air Force operations, wireless and hydrophone stations and munitions works; also services rendered to the United States Navy Department. *Addresses:* 116, St. Lawrence Road, Clontarf, Dublin; Ballytweedy, Muckamore, Co. Antrim. (C606)

ROBINSON, Major Augustus Francis, O.B.E., *b.* 1883; *s.* of the late Frederick King Robinson, of London.; *m.* Doris Isabel, *d.* of the late Thomas Chas. Cloud, of Malden, Surrey. *Educ.:* King's Coll., Strand, W.C. Chartered Secretary. *War Work:* On the outbreak of war was mobilised with the 19th London Regt., and drafted to France as part of the 47th (London) Division on 9 March, 1915; served with the battalion until after the Battle of Loos, Sept. 1915, when he was appointed Acting Staff Capt. to the 141st Infantry Brigade; was Adjutant of the 47th Divisional School of Instruction until Oct. 1916, when Divisional Schools were abolished; he was then sent to Divisional Headquarters to understudy "Q" Branch; also organised laundry service for division, being mentioned in despatches in 1917; in Oct. 1917, was sent to Headquarters 2nd Army, and organised laundries for the whole of the 2nd Army; mentioned in despatches, 1918; continued as Laundry Adviser, G.H.Q., British Army of the Rhine. *Address:* 120, Castellain Mansions, Maida Vale, London, W. 9. *Club:* Junior Army and Navy. (O5725)

ROBINSON, Beatrice Evelyn Eugenie, Mrs., M.B.E.

ROBINSON, Lieut. Bernal, M.B.E., R.A.S.C.

ROBINSON, Lieut. Charles, O.B.E., I.A.R.O.

ROBINSON, Charles, M.B.E.

ROBINSON, Major Charles Walter, O.B.E., Aust. A.S.C.

ROBINSON, Major Charles Wilson, O.B.E.

ROBINSON, Major Cyril Ellett, O.B.E., late R.G.A., *b.* 3 Sept. 1889; *s.* of Charles Robinson, of Willesden Lane, N.W.; *m.* Bertha Marie. *d.* of William T. Bashford, of Cricklewood, N.W. *Educ.:* Kilburn Grammar School. Engineer. *War Work:* Served with Royal Garrison Artillery, 1914–19; commanded 13th Heavy Battery. *Address:* 293, Willesden Lane, London, N.W. (O6525)

ROBINSON, Doris Firth, M.B.E., *b.* Feb. 1892; *d.* of Thomas A. Robinson, of North Ferriby, East Yorks. *War Work:* Organising work in St. John Ambulance Brigade; Quartermaster-in-charge, Sculcoates V.A.D. Hospital, Hull; 1917–19, Registrar and Quartermaster, St. John V.A.D. Hospital, Hull (450 beds). *Address:* Ferriby House, North Ferriby, East Yorks. (M9475)

ROBINSON, Dorothy Eyre, O.B.E., *b.* 6 Jan. 1889; *d.* of Herbert Sylvester Robinson, of Wilmslow, Cheshire. *Educ.:* Privately. *War Work:* Hon. Assist. County Sec. B.R.C.S., Cheshire Branch, April, 1915, to Dec. 1917; Hon. Acting County Sec. B.R.C.S., Cheshire Branch, Dec. 1917, to date. *Address:* Hill Crest, Wilmslow, Cheshire. *Club:* V.A.D. Ladies'. (O1815)

ROBINSON, Dorothy Faith, M.B.E. (M10253e)

ROBINSON, Edward, M.B.E.

ROBINSON, Edwin, O.B.E.

ROBINSON, Elizabeth Street, Mrs., M.B.E., *b.* 12 Oct. 1857; *d.* of J. B. Plumb, of Niagara, Canada; *m.* Christopher, *s.* of Sir John Beverley Robinson, Bart., of Toronto. *War Work:* Lady Superintendent, Canadian Convalescent Home for Officers, Dieppe and Trouville, France, from Oct. 1915, to Jan. 1919. *Address:* A, Sultan Street, Toronto, Canada. *Club:* Toronto Ladies', Toronto, Canada. (M3940)

ROBINSON, Lieut.-Col. Ernest, O.B.E., R.E.

ROBINSON, Eric Gascoigne, V.C., O.B.E., R.N,

ROBINSON, Frederick Anthony, M.B.E., *b.* 12 Jan. 1852; *s.* of the late George Robinson, of Northampton. *Educ.:* Northampton Grammar School. Accountant to the Northants County Mental Hospital, Berry Wood, near Northampton. *War Work:* Accountant at the Northants War Hospital at Duston, near Northampton. *Address:* Duston, Northampton. (M9477)

ROBINSON, Frederick Field, O.B.E., L.D.S., *b.* 28 March, 1858; *s.* of Thomas Field Robinson, of Richmond· (Yorks); *m.* Florence Elizabeth, *d.* of Francis E. Anneveld, of London. *Educ.:* Doncaster Grammar School. Dental Surgeon, Hertford British Hospital, Paris. *War Work:* Senior Dental Surgeon to the following: British Red Cross Society, Paris Branch, No. 4 General Hospital, Versailles, B.R.C.S. Auxiliary Hospital, Hotel Astoria, Paris, and to the British Army in Paris District from Oct. 1914, to June, 1919. *Address:* 9, Boulevard Malesherbes, Paris.

ROBINSON, George Fox, M.B.E.

ROBINSON, George Lovely, M.B.E.

ROBINSON, Lieut. George William, M.B.E.

ROBINSON, Lieut. Harold, M.B.E., R.G.A.

ROBINSON, Paymaster-Capt. Harry, O.B.E., R.N.

ROBINSON, Sir Harry Perry, K.B.E., Knt. Bach., Chevalier, Legion d'Honneur, *b.* 30 Nov. 1859; *s.* of Rev. Julian Robinson, Chaplain in Hon. East India Co.'s service; *m.* Florence Anne, *d.* of Joseph Tester, of Surbiton, Surrey. *Educ.:* Westminster (Capt. of the School), and Christ Church, Oxford. For many years on the Staff of the "Times." *War Work:* War Correspondent for the "Times" from Aug. 1914, in Belgium; in 1915, in Serbia; 1916 to Armistice, in France and Belgium; then to Cologne, etc. *Address:* The "Times" Office. *Club:* New University. (K415)

ROBINSON, Major Henry, O.B.E., F.R.C.S. R.A.M.C.

ROBINSON, Henry William Bradley, M.B.E.

ROBINSON, Horace Astell Lynn, O.B.E., *b.* 22 Sept., 1870. Superintendent, the Eastern Telegraph Co., Ltd. *War Work:* Valuable services rendered to the Government of India, 1914–18. *Address:* Electra House, Finsbury Pavement, E.C. 2. *Clubs:* Royal Bombay Yacht, Bombay; Exiles'. (O4084)

ROBINSON, Capt. James, M.B.E., R.A.F.

ROBINSON, James Thomas, M.B.E.

ROBINSON, Surgeon James, C.B.E., *b.* 1867; *s.* of Richard Robinson, of Portadown; *m.* Harriet Agnes, *d.* of Thomas Bevan, of Abergavenny. *Educ.:* Dundalk, Galway, Belfast, and Dublin. Physician and Surgeon. *War Work:* Chairman of Executive Committee, Welsh National Hospital, Netley. *Address:* Hillside, Penylan, Cardiff. (C2910)

ROBINSON, John, C.B.E.

ROBINSON, John Alexander, M.B.E., LL.D., J.P., *b.* 29 June, 1862; *s.* of the late Rev. E. J. Robinson, of Weston-super-Mare; *m.* Flora Louisa, *d.* of the late Joseph Hayward Taylor, of Carbonear, Newfoundland. *Educ.:* Victoria Coll., Jersey; New Kingswood, Bath; Manchester Grammar School. Journalist. "Daily News and Free Press," St. John's (Robinson & Co., Ltd.). *Address:* 14, Cathedral Street, St. John's, Newfoundland. *Clubs:* City, St. John's; Masonic, St. John's. (M6401)

ROBINSON, John George, C.B.E., M.Inst.C.E., M.Inst.M.E., *b.* 30 July, 1856; *s.* of Matthew Robinson, of Bristol; *m.* Mary Ann, *d.* of Richard Hildyard Dalton. *Educ.:* Chester; Engineering training received in the Great Western Rly. Works, Swindon, Wilts. Locomotive and Carriage and Wagon Supt. to the Waterford, Limerick, and Western Railway of Ireland, 1888 to 1900; joined the Great Central Railway Company in July, 1900, as Chief Mechanical Engineer. *War Work:* Member of the Railway War Manufactures Sub-Committee, and superintended the Manufacture of Gun Carriages, 6-inch High Explosive Shells, Cartridge Cases, etc., at the Company's Gorton Works; also the building of Ambulance Trains at Dukinfield Works; his design of 2-8-0 Locomotive Engine was adopted by the War Office as standard for service in France; Inventor of the "Robinson Superheater," the "Intensifore Lubricator," and of apparatus for burning Pulverised Coal, Oil, and Colloidal Mixtures as applied to Locomotive and Marine work. *Address:* Mere Bank, Fairfield, near Manchester. (C2912)

ROBINSON, Katharine Haigh, O.B.E.

ROBINSON, Lieut.-Comm. Leonard, O.B.E., R.N. (ret.)

ROBINSON, Leonard Bainbridge, O.B.E., *b.* 26 April, 1888; *s.* of Samuel Robinson, O.B.E., of Sheffield; *m.* Jessie Barnes, *d.* of Benjamin B. Brown, of Sheffield. *Educ.:* Derwent House School, and Sheffield Univ. Manager, Machine Shops, W. Beardmore & Co., Ltd., Parkhead, Glasgow. *War Work:* Manufacture of guns of all sizes, 15-inch to 6-pounders, with breech mechanisms, ships' castings, and machinery. *Address:* Inniemore, Blairbeth Road, Burnside, Glasgow. (O11238)

ROBINSON, Lieut. Leonard Mould, O.B.E., R.N.V.R.

ROBINSON, Hon. Lieut.-Col. Leonard Nicholas, C.B.E., M.D. (Edin.), M.D. (Paris), R.A.M.C., *b.* 24 Nov. 1869; *s.* of Samuel Henry Robinson, of Howrah, Bengal; *m.* Victoria, *d.* of D. Hoef. *Educ.:* Malvern Coll., and Univs. of Edinburgh and Paris. Senior Physician, Hertford British Hospital, Paris; Senior Member, Paris Board, Egyptian Government Medical Commission; Chairman, Executive Committee, Paris Branch, Overseas Club and Patriotic League; Chairman, Executive Committee, Imperial Club, Paris. *War Work:* President,

Paris Branch, B.R.C.S., from Sept. 1914 ; gazetted Commission, Hon. and T. Lieut.-Col. R.A.M.C., June, 1915 ; mentioned in despatches, May, 1917 ; Chevalier de la Legion d'Honneur. *Address*: 28, rue de Ponthieu, Paris VIIIe. *Clubs*: Travellers' ; Imperial, Paris. (C2913)

ROBINSON, Maurice Alexander, O.B.E.

ROBINSON, Norah Gertrude, M.B.E., W.R.N.S.

ROBINSON, Lieut. Percy Gilbert, M.B.E.

ROBINSON, Hon. Lieut. and Qr.-Mr. Percy, Holland, M.B.E., R.A.M.C. (V.), Lancs., *b.* 16 July, 1873, *s.* of Edward M. Robinson, of Liverpool ; *m.* Mary Elizabeth, *d.* of Rowland Allen, of New Hall, West Derby, Lancs. *Educ.*: Breck House Coll., Liverpool. Insurance Manager. *War Work*: Quartermaster of British Red Cross Society and West Lancs T.F.A. ; Voluntary Aid Detachment, No. 27, having charge on arrival of all sick and wounded both from overseas and by rail in the port and city of Liverpool ; received commission as Lieut. and Qr.-Mr. in Lancs R.A.M.C. (V.), Liverpool Field Ambulance, for assisting to raise that corps, and various other duties such as the training of nurses for France in stretcher drill, etc. *Address*: 53, Mayville Road, Mossley Hill, Liverpool. (M9481)

ROBINSON, Lieut.-Col. Richard Stirling, O.B.E., R.A.F.

ROBINSON, Lieut.-Col. Robert Hervey St. Clair, M.B.E.

ROBINSON, Roy Lister, C.B.E., B.A. (Oxon.), B.Sc., *b.* 8 March, 1883 ; *s.* of Wm. Robinson, of South Australia ; *m.* Charlotte Marion, *d.* of — Bradshaw, of Torquay. *Educ.*: St. Peter's Coll., South Australia ; Adelaide and Oxford Univs. (Rhodes Scholar). Forestry Commissioner. *War Work*: Explosives Department, Board of Agriculture and Fisheries. *Address*: 22, Grosvenor Gardens, S.W. (O694)

ROBINSON, Samuel, C.B.E.

ROBINSON, Rev. Samuel Fairbrother, O.B.E., *b.* 19 March, 1879 ; *s.* of Robert Edward Robinson, of Rochdale ; *m.* Ada, *d.* of Henry Broughton, of Rochdale. *Educ.*: Congregational Institute, Nottingham. Sec. and Treas. Macclesfield Local War Pensions Committee ; Free Church Minister, Cheshire County Asylum, Parkside, Macclesfield. *War Work*: Vice-Chairman, Cheshire Joint (Disablements) Committee ; Hon. Sec. Macclesfield Borough Division, Soldiers' and Sailors' Families Association ; Hon. Sec. War Pensions Committee, Macclesfield. *Address*: Brierfield, Chester Road, Macclesfield. (O11230)

ROBINSON, Sir Thomas, K.B.E., J P., C.C., *b.* 23 Jan. 1855 ; *s.* of John Robinson, of Cleethorpes ; *m.* Cornelia Agnes, *d.* of George Wheeler, of Cleethorpes. *Educ.*: Humberstone Grammar School. Steam Trawler Owner ; Director of several companies. *War Work*: Technical Adviser to the Fish Food Committee, Board of Agriculture and Fisheries ; Member of the Cured Fish Committee, Ministry of Food ; Technical Adviser to the Dept. of Fisheries. *Address*: Southlands, Cleethorpes. (K34)

ROBINSON, Sir Thomas, O.B.E., J.P., M.P., *b.* 2 Jan. 1863 ; *s.* of Peter Robinson, of Stretford ; *m.* Emma, *d.* of William Lowe, of Chorlton, Manchester. *Educ.*: Stretford. Dyer ; Director, Bradford Dyers' Association, Ltd. ; for 25 years Member of the Stretford Urban District Council, and thrice Chairman ; Chairman of the County Licensing Committee, Salford Hundred ; Manchester Port Sanitary Authority ; of the Allied Trades, Bleaching, Dyeing, and Printing Industries, Lancs., Cheshire, and Yorks. *War Work*: Chairman of the Stretford Red Cross Society, and Hospitals Committee ; M.P. for the Stretford Division of Lancashire, since 1918. *Address*: The Hawthorns, Edge Lane, Stretford. *Clubs*: National Liberal, London ; Reform, Manchester. (O3892)

ROBINSON, Thomas, C.B.E.

ROBINSON, Lieut.-Col. Sir Thomas Bilbe, K.C.M.G., K.B., *b.* 1853 ; *s.* of Robert William Robinson, of Nelson Dock, Rotherhithe ; *m.* Rosa Hannah, *d.* of W. Cowell, of Broadstairs. Agent-General for Queensland, 1910–20. *War Work*: Purchaser and Director of meat supplies for the Allied Armies in all theatres of war ; purchaser and director of army and civilian imported cheese supplies from 1915, until relieved from this duty by the Ministry of Food ; Chairman of Refrigerated Ships' Tonnage Control Committee ; Officer Legion of Honour, Commander Crown of Italy, Crown of Belgium. *Addresses*: 7, Cambridge Gate, Regent's Park ; North Foreland, Broadstairs. *Clubs*: Oriental ; Reform ; Queensland ; Chelsea Arts.

ROBINSON, Thomas Ingle, M.B.E., *b.* 13 Aug. 1878 ; *s.* of John Robinson, of Over, Cambs. ; *m.* Gertrude, *d.* of Thomas Page, Ockley, Surrey. *Educ.*: Privately, and Military. Civil Servant. *War Work*: Civil Service duties at War Office. *Address*: Glen-Derup, 29, Derwent Road, Palmers Green, N. 13. (M2355)

ROBINSON, William, C.B.E. Financial Sec., India Office. (C279)

ROBINSON, Col. William Arthur, C.B., C.M.G., *b.* 1864 ; *s.* of the late George Robinson, of Réunion, Mauritius ; *m.* 1906, Florence Helen, *d.* of the late Wentworth L. Cole. *Educ.*: Eton, and R.M.A. Entered R.A.. 1884 ; became Capt. 1893 ; Brevet Major, 1899 ; Lieut.-Col. 1910 ; Col. 1913 (h.-p., 1919) ; served with the Niger Expedition, 1897–98 (despatches, medal with clasp, Brevet Major) ; in the S. African War, 1899–1900 ; present at actions of Paardeberg and Poplar Grove (Queen's medal with five clasps) ; in the Great War, 1914–19, as Brig.-Gen. on Staff (despatches). *Address*: 6, Albert Gate Court, Knightsbridge, S.W. 1. *Club*: Naval and Military. (C280)

ROBINSON, Sir William Arthur, K.C.B., C.B., C.B.E., *b.* 9 Sept. 1874 ; *s.* of late William Robinson, of Saunders House, Long Marton, Westmorland ; *m.* 24 Oct. 1910, Jean Pasley, 2nd. *d.* of C. Mitchell. Served in Colonial Office, 1897–1912 ; First-Class Clerk, 1905 ; Asst. Secretary, Imperial Conference, 1907 and 1911 ; Secretary Dominions Royal Commission, 1911–12 ; Asst. Secretary H.M. Office of Works, 1912–18 ; Permanent Secretary to the Air Council, 1918–20 ; First Secretary, Ministry of Health, from 1920. *Address*: 12, Albion Street, Hyde Park, W. (C280)

ROBINSON, William Charles, M.B.E., *b.* 18 Oct. 1855 ; *s.* of William Robinson, of Peckham, S.E. ; *m.* Mary Ada Allen, *d.* of Henry Taylor, of Bow, E. *Educ.*: Wesleyan Training Coll., Horseferry Road, Westminster, S.W. Superintendent of "V" Division, Metropolitan Police (ret.) ; Member of the Richmond Borough Council. *War Work*: In charge of a large area of London during the air raids of the war. *Address*: Melvin, High Park Avenue, Kew Gardens, Surrey. *Club*: National Liberal. (M900)

ROBINSON, William Cornforth, O.B.E., J.P., *b.* 12 July, 1861 ; *s.* of Mary Ann Smith, of Burnley ; *m.* Martha Ann, *d.* of Dennis Booth, of Burnley. *Educ.*: Burnley. Trade Union Sec. *War Work*: Red Cross (Sir Dennis Bayley's Committee) ; County Tribunal, re Recruiting. *Address*: 237, Manchester Road, Bury. (O52)

ROBINSON, Capt. William Edward, M.B.E.

ROBINSON, William Henry, C.B.E.

ROBINSON, Major William Henry, O.B.E., Can. A.S.C., has Croix de Guerre of France (2nd Award).

ROBINSON, Lieut. William Henry, M.B.E.

ROBINSON, Major-Gen. William Henry Banner, C.B., C.B.E., *b.* 1863 ; *s.* of the late Capt. Vallancy Robinson, R.N. ; *m.* 1905, Elsie Marian, *d.* of W. Deane Butcher, M.R.C.S., of Holyrood, Ealing, W. Entered Indian Medical Service, 1888 ; became Major, 1898 ; Lieut.-Col. 1900 ; Col., 1914, and Maj.-Gen., 1918 ; served with the Burma Expedition, 1885–89 (despatches, medal with two clasps) ; Waziristan Expedition, 1894–95 (clasp) ; Chitral Relief Force, 1895 (medal with clasp) ; Tirah Expedition, 1897–98 (clasp) ; in the Great War, 1914–15 (despatches) ; appointed an Hon. Surg. to H.M., 1919. (C2914)

ROBINSON, Lieut.-Col. William Pasley, D.S.O., O.B.E., R.A.S.C., *b.* 1877. An Assist. Director of Transport with rank of Lieut.-Col. ; served in the S. African War, 1900–2 (Queen's medal with four clasps, King's medal with two clasps) ; in the Great War, 1914–17 (despatches). (O8533)

ROBINSON, William Walter, M.B.E.

ROBINSON, Capt. Cecil BOWES-, M.B.E., R.A.S.C.

ROBLEY, Lieut. Vernon Edward, M.B.E.

ROBSON, Major Archibald, O.B.E.

ROBSON, Constance Evelyn, Mrs., M.B.E.

ROBSON, Helene, Mrs., M.B.E.

ROBSON, Sir Herbert Thomas, K.B.E., *b.* 17 Nov. 1874 ; *s.* of the Rev. Canon W. H. F. Robson, of Claughton, Birkenhead ; *m.* Gladys Meredith, *d.* of J. G. Apthorp, of Brough, Yorks. *Educ.*: Birkenhead School ; Trinity Coll., Cambridge. Chairman, Karachi Chamber of Commerce, 1910–11 ; additional Member, Bombay Legislative Council 1910–11 ; Chevalier of the Legion of Honour, Sept. 1919. *War Work*: Member Royal Commission on Wheat Supplies, 1917 to date ; Chairman, Wheat Export Co., Inc., New York, Official Agents to Allied Wheat Executive, 1917 to date. *Address*: Westalls, Burnham, Bucks. (K401)

ROBSON, James, M.B.E., *b.* 5 Oct. 1871 ; *s.* of George Robson, of Hexham ; *m.* Margaret Alice, *d.* of Andrew Leithead, of Newcastle-on-Tyne. *Educ.*: Elswick. Engineer. *War Work*: Design of heavy gun mountings for H.M. Services, and special adaptations of heavy naval guns for use in the field. *Address*: 61, Earlsdon Street, Coventry. *Clubs*: C.F.A., Coventry ; Hearsal. (M901)

ROBSON, Capt. John, O.B.E.

ROBSON, Lieut. John Wintour, O.B.E.

ROBSON, Philip Warwick, O.B.E.

ROBSON, Lieut. Thomas Buston, M.B.E., R.G.A. (T.)

ROBSON, William Tuke, M.B.E.

ROBSON, Col. Sir Arthur William. MAYO-, K.B.E., C.B., C.V.O., Knight of Grace Order of St. John of Jerusalem, D.Sc., F.R.C.S., *b.* 17 April, 1853 ; *s.* of J. B. Robson, of Filey ; *m.* Florence, *d.* of Wm. Walker, of Osmondthorpe Hall, Yorkshire. *Educ.*: Wesley Coll., and Yorkshire Coll., Victoria Univ. Hon. Consulting Surgeon, King Edward VII. Memorial Hospital, Windsor, also of Leeds General Infirmary ; Emeritus Professor of Surgery, Univ. of Leeds ; Member of Council, Royal Coll. of Surgeons of England, 1893–1909 ; Vice-President, 1902–3, and 1904–5 ; Hunterian Professor, R.C.S., 1897, 1900, 1904 ; Bradshaw Lecturer, R.C.S., 1905 ; late Hon. Surgeon, Dreadnought Hospital, and Lecturer, London School of Clinical Medicine ; Hon. President, 15th International Congress of Medicine at Lisbon, 1906 ; Hon. President, Surgical Section, 13th International Medical Congress, Paris, 1903 ; Past President of Leeds and W.R. Med. Chir. Soc. ; Hon. Fellow American Surgical Soc. ; Hon. Member Soc. de Chir., Paris ; Hon. Member, Royal Soc. de Medic., Ghent ; Governor and Member of Council, Imperial Service Coll., Windsor ; Chairman, Managing Committee, Home of Recovery, Cobham ; Author of several works on Surgery and Allied Subjects, and of numerous articles in Medical Journals ; Joint Editor of "Surgery, Medicine and Gynæcology," Philadelphia. *War Work*: Col. A.M.S. ; served 6 months in 3rd

London General Hospital; Feb. 1915, lent by War Office at request of French Military Sec. to Instal Urgency Cases Hospital for the French in the Argonne; April, 1915, recalled to help instal Reading War Hospital (3000 beds); May, 1915, sent to Egypt; served through Dardanelles Campaign; at Suvla Landing; mentioned twice in despatches, Egypt and Dardanelles; later in France; awarded C.B. (Mil.), and K.B.E. (Mil.); 1917–20, Consulting Surgeon, Southern Command; Member of Council of Consultants at War Office; Inspector of Special Military Surgical Hospitals, Southern Command. *Address:* Broadoak, Seale, Surrey. *Clubs:* Athenæum; Bath; Royal Societies'; Ranelagh. (K292)

ROCH, Col. Horace Sampson, C.M.G., C.B.E., D.S.O., *b.* 1876; *s.* of the late Dep. Surg.-Gen. Sampson Roch, of Woodbine Hill, co. Waterford; *m.* 1919, Marjorie, who died, 1919, *e. d.* of the late Robert Henry Power, of Cliff House, Ardmore, co. Waterford (*see* BURKE's *Peerage*). Lieut.-Col. R.A.M.C.; Assist. Director of Med. Sers. of a Div. with rank of Col.; served in the S. African War, 1899–1902; present at relief of Ladysmith (Queen's medal with six clasps, King's medal with two clasps); in the Great War, 1915–18 (despatches). (C3177)

ROCH, Eng.-Comm. Sydney George, O.B.E., R.N.

ROCHDALE, Lady Beatrice Mary, M.B.E., *b.* 5 Nov. 1871; *d.* of 3rd Earl of Ellesmere (*see* BURKE's *Peerage*); *m.* George Kemp, 1st Baron Rochdale (*see* BURKE's *Peerage*). *Educ.:* Privately. *War Work:* Commandant Convalescent Hospital for officers and men. *Address:* Lingholm, Keswick. *Club:* Ladies' Athenæum. (M9485)

ROCHE, Capt. Alfred Lyttleton, M.B.E.

ROCHE, A. W., O.B.E. (O11788*f*)

ROCHE, Lieut.-Col. Benjamin Robert, O.B.E., *b.* 3 Feb. 1865; *s.* of T. Roche, J.P., of Annakisha House, Killavullen, Co. Cork; *m.* Blanche, *d.* of W. Jones, of Manor House, Finchley, N. *Educ.:* The Abbey, Tipperary. *War Work:* Served in France from Nov. 1914 to Feb. 1916; home from Feb. 1916 to Sept. 1919. *Address:* Dorset Lodge, Killiney, Co. Dublin. *Club:* Royal Irish Yacht. (O7645)

ROCHE, Elizabeth Jane, M.B.E. *War Work:* For three years from 1916–19, organising Sec. of the Ealing War Dressings Association, 2, Grange Road, Ealing, W. *Address:* 16, St. Stephen's Road, Ealing, W. 13. (M3943)

ROCHE, Francis Patrick, M.B.E.

ROCHE, Lieut.-Col. Nelson Joseph, O.B.E., R.A.F.

ROCKETT, Capt. Herbert Charles, O.B.E., M.R.C.V.S., *b.* 12 Aug. 1892; *s.* of F. Rockett, of Paignton; *m.* Florence Beatrice, *d.* of W. R. Greenwood, of London. *Educ.:* Allhallows School, Honiton, and Queen's Coll., Taunton. Veterinary Surgeon. *War Work:* Royal Army Veterinary Corps (attached 34th Division). *Address:* 14, Claremont Road, Tunbridge Wells. (O5727)

ROCKEY, Willie, O.B.E.

RODD, Surg.-Comm. Montague Louis Bouchier, O.B.E., R.N.

RODDA, George Charles, M.B.E.

RODDAM, Lieut.-Col. Roddam John, O.B.E., J.P., D.L., *b.* March, 1857; *s.* of Roddam John Roddam, of Roddam; *m.* Helen Fredericka, *d.* of Capt. A. T. Goldie, R.N., of The Hermitage, Douglas, Isle of Man. *Educ.:* Clare Coll., Cambridge. Commandant, 3rd Batt. Northumberland Fusiliers (Special Reserve) from 1909. *War Work:* Raised and commanded 15th Batt. Northumberland Fus. in 1914 till Sept. 1916; Military Member of Travelling Medical Board; went overseas in May, 1917, and was attached to 2nd Anzac Corps (afterwards the 22nd Corps). *Address:* Roddam Hall, Wooperton Station, Northumberland. (O696)

RODDIS, Lieut. Ernest, M.B.E., *b.* 16 July, 1885; *s.* of Thomas Roddis, of Rotherham; *m.* Daisy Lilian, *d.* of Alfred C. Taylor, of Warwick. *Educ.:* Grammar School, Rotherham. Civil Servant. *War Work:* Royal Engineers (Signals), Dec. 1914, to Oct. 1919; France, Salonica, E.E.F. *Address:* Alpha Cottage, 16, Cherry Street, Warwick. (M4701)

RODERICK, Dr. Henry Buckley, O.B.E., T.D., M.A., M.Ch., M.D. (Cantab.), M.R.C.S., L.R.C.P. (Lond.), D.P.H. (Camb.), *b.* 19 Aug. 1874; *s.* of William and Maria Roderick, of Llanelly; *m.* Hilda Mary, *d.* of John Clay, of Cambridge. *Educ.:* Bath Coll.; Emmanuel Coll., Cambridge; St. George's Hospital, London. Surgeon; Univ. Demonstrator of Surgery; Surgeon to Addenbrooke's Hospital, Cambridge. *War Work:* Lieut.-Col. R.A.M.C. (T.F.), commanding Medical Unit of Cambridge Univ. O.T.C.; M.O. to Univ. Board for Commissions; Surgeon to first Eastern General Hospital; Officer commanding No. 55 General Hospital, B.E.F., France; twice mentioned in despatches. *Address:* 17, Trumpington Street, Cambridge. (O5728)

RODERICKS, John FISHER-, M.B.E., *b.* 12 July, 1866; *s.* of George Rodericks, of Madras. Postmaster of some of the largest Post Offices in India and in chief charge, as Presidency Postmaster, of Madras and Calcutta; now Postmaster-General and Deputy Director-General Posts and Telegraphs, Indian Empire. *War Work:* Hon. Sec. of the Publicity Committee (Calcutta Branch) of the Great War Loan raised in India. *Address:* Alipore Park Place, Calcutta. (M6283)

RODET, Engr.-Capt. Ernest William, C.B.E., R.N. Served in the Great War, 1914–19 (despatches). (C1937)

RODGER, Alexander, O.B.E.

RODGER, James Allison, M.B.E.

RODGERS, Charles, O.B.E.

RODGERS, Major Frederick Millar, O.B.E., M.D., R.A.M.C.

RODGERS, Capt. Rivers Thomas, M.B.E., I.M.D., *b.* 13 Sept. 1872; *s.* of Thomas Rodgers, of Chunar; *m.* Elizabeth Idee; *d.* of W. J. Brinkworth, of Simla. *Educ.:* Boys' High School, Allahabad, India, and privately. Assistant Health Officer, Simla, 1899; Civil Surgeon, Buldona, Berars, 1906–11; Superintendent, Central Jails, Rajpur, Nagpur, Jubbulpore, India, from 1911–20. *War Work:* In Medical and Executive charge of the Jubbulpore Central Jail; the custody of certain special prisoners, and the manufacture of Textile Munitions for British and Indian troops. *Address:* c/o Inspector-General of Prisons, Central Provinces, India. *Club:* Nerbudda, Jubbulpore, C.P. (M6234)

RODHAM, Paymaster-Comm. Cuthbert Halliburton, O.B.E., R.N.

RODHAM, Robert, M.B.E.

RODHOUSE, Alfred Edward, M.B.E., *b.* 13 Nov. 1871; *s.* of Charles Rodhouse, J.P., of Daventry, Northants; *m.* Amy Ellen, *d.* of John Matthew Ambler. *Educ.:* Daventry Grammar School. Leather Factor. *Address:* Lugano, The Drive, Northampton. (M9487)

RODICK, Lieut. William, O.B.E.

RODLIFFE, Capt. Thomas, O.B.E., R.A.O.C.

RODNEY, Corisande, Baroness, C.B.E.

RODWAY, Barron John, O.B.E., L.D.S.

RODWAY, George Frederick, M.B.E., R.N.

RODWELL, Major Francis John, O.B.E., T.D., *b.* 1886; *s.* of John Kirby Rodwell, of Cambridge; *m.* Florence Catherine, *d.* of Frederick Brown, I.S.O., of Malvern. *Educ.:* Dulwich Coll. Solicitor; Clerk to Halesworth District Council; Clerk to Burial Board, etc. *War Work:* Volunteer, 1903; Active Service, Aug. 1914–19. *Address:* Castle House, Halesworth, Suffolk. (O3172)

RODWELL, Major James Theodore, O.B.E., R.A.F.

ROE, Alliott Verdon, O.B.E., *b.* 26 April, 1877; *s.* of Edwin Hodgson Roe, of Manchester; *m.* Mildred, *d.* of Samuel Kirk, of Derby. *Educ.:* St. Paul's, Hammersmith. *War Work:* Pioneered and developed the Avro Aeroplanes; during the latter part of the war about one-third of the total timber supply for aircraft was absorbed by the Avros, according to a speech made by Lord Weir. *Address:* High Firs, Bursledon, Hants. *Club:* Royal Aero. (O697)

ROE, Flight-Lieut. Robert Lloyd, O.B.E., M.B., R.A.M.C.

ROEBER, William Carl Trorey, O.B.E., M.C., Capt. (T.F. Res.), *b.* 25 Sept. 1887; *s.* of the late Oscar Julius Hugo Roeber; *m.* Dorothy, *d.* of Charles Goode, of Wandsworth Common. *Educ.:* Sir Walter St. John's School. *War Work:* Served at home and B.E.F. France, in the ranks, 1914–17; Civil Service Rifles and Army Cyclist Corps; later at No. 8 O.C.B., Lichfield; commissioned, March 1918, to Civil Service Rifles; served for winter campaign, North Russia, Sept. 1918, to June, 1919; mentioned in despatches, and received Order of St. Stanislaus (2nd Class) with swords, and Order of St. Anne (3rd Class) with swords. *Address:* 5, Broomwood Road, Wandsworth Common, S.W. *Club:* Civil Service Rifles. (O6808)

ROEBUCK, Samuel, M.B.E., J.P.

ROFFE, John, M.B.E., *b.* 16 March, 1857; *s.* of William Henry Roffe, of Tunbridge Wells; *m.* Mary Sophia, *d.* of Thomas Palmer Machin, of Beddington, Surrey. *Educ.:* St. James' School, Tunbridge Wells. Station Superintendent, Central Station, Brighton, L.B. & S.C. Rly. *War Work:* In connection with movement of troops, ambulance trains conveying wounded, etc. *Address:* Station House, Shaftesbury Place, Brighton. (M9488)

ROGAN, Rev. Peter, O.B.E.

ROGER, Herbert Campbell, M.B.E.

ROGERS, Capt. Alfred George, M.B.E., The King's Liverpool Regt., *b.* 5 July, 1878; *s.* of the late Tom Rogers; *m.* Emily Alice. *Educ.:* Army Schools. Joined the Army at the age of 15, and passed through the various ranks from Boy to Capt. (27 years service). *War Work:* Commanded The Depot, The King's Liverpool Regt., Peshawar, during the Frontier Risings, Aug. to Dec. 1915; commanded the Attached Section and Rest Camps, Bombay, 1916–19; awarded M.B.E., June, 1919, for work in connection with accommodating large numbers of troops at very short notice and making them comfortable compatible with the circumstances; also accommodating large numbers prisoners of war. *Addresses:* 2, Westgate Gardens, Ealing, W. 13; c/o Messrs. Cox & Co., 16, Charing Cross. (M6512)

ROGERS, Arthur Burden Campbell, C.B.E., M.I.C.E.

ROGERS, Lieut.-Col. Charles Herman, O.B.E.

ROGERS, Dorothy Heyward, M.B.E.

ROGERS, Rev. Edgar, O.B.E., M.A., *b.* 26 Feb. 1873; *s.* of John Frederick Rogers, of Liverpool; *m.* Alice Buckley, *d.* of James Smith, of Wigan. *Educ.:* Liverpool Coll.; St. John's Coll., Oxford. Chaplain-General and Sec. of Church Lads' Brigade (K.R.R.C.) Cadets; late Vicar of St. Sepulchre, London, Middlesex. *War Work:* Cadet service, joint raiser of 16th (S.) Batt. K.R.R.C. (C.L.B.). *Address:* 5, Essex Villas, Kensington, W. (O11242)

ROGERS, Edith Louisa Julie, Lady, C.B.E., Lady of Grace of St. John of Jerusalem, *b.* 21 Nov. 1861; *d.* of Major Frederick Sykes, of 3rd Bombay Cavalry; *m.* John Godfrey, *s.* of the late G. Handel Rogers. *Educ.:* London. *War Work:* Seventeen months nursing as V.A.D. in Red Cross Hospital,

Cairo, Egypt; section leader of detachment executive; on committees for convalescent outings, Nurses (Red Cross) Club, Rea Cross Work Rooms; President of Committee running permanent canteen for troops, and railway canteens. *Address*: Whitelands, Edenbridge, Kent. (C607)

ROGERS, Fergus Carstairs, M.B.E.

ROGERS, Florence Crichton, Mrs., M.B.E.; *d.* of G. T. Jenkins, of Franklands, Burgess Hill, Sussex; *m.* Col. G. W. N. Rogers, late the Royal Irish. *War Work*: Six years' work for wives and families of soldiers and sailors with Soldiers' and Sailors' Families Assoc., and War Pensions; and Chairman of sub-committees, etc. *Address*: 25, Albany Villas, Hove, Sussex. (M9490)

ROGERS, Frederick Henry, M.B.E., *b.* 16 May, 1884; *s.* of F. H. Rogers, Councillor of Teignmouth; *m.* May Edith, *d.* of Thomas Lay, of Stockwell, S.W. *Educ.*: Ashburton Grammar School, South Devon. Staff Clerk, Air Ministry, Kingsway. *War Work*: Assisted in the organisation of the Prisoners of War Bureau, Wellington Street, Strand; from 1916 onwards engaged upon compiling the records and arranging the distribution and despatch of correspondence of the whole Air Ministry; also acted as custodian of files of an extremely confidential nature. *Address*: 1, Linden Avenue, Thornton Heath. (M9491)

ROGERS, George James Nicholas, M.B.E.

ROGERS, Lieut. George Wase, M.B.E.

ROGERS, Lieut. Gilbert, M.B.E.

ROGERS, Lieutenant Gilbert, M.B.E.

ROGERS, Capt. and Qr.-Mr. Harry George, M.B.E., M.C., *b.* 14 Feb. 1873; *s.* of George Rogers, of Essex; *m.* Alice Emily, *d.* of Frederick Kemp, of Essex. *Educ.*: London. *War Work*: Quartermaster 1st Batt. R.W. Kent Regt., British Expeditionary Force, Aug. 1914, to Aug. 1916. *Address*: 87, Tonbridge Road, Maidstone. (M6700)

ROGERS, Henry, M.B.E., *b.* 9 Sept. 1862; *s.* of George Rogers, of Cheddleton, Staffs; *m.* Georgina, *d.* of John Foster, of Cheltenham. *Educ.*: Cheddleton School. Metallurgist and Works Manager. *War Work*: Production of High Class Non-ferrous alloys for Ammunition. *Address*: 75, Blenheim Road, Moseley, Birmingham. *Clubs*: Member of Institute of Metals; Fellow of the Royal Society of Arts. (M2360)

ROGERS, Paymaster-Lieut.-Comm. Henry, O.B.E., R.N.

ROGERS, Henry Montague, M.B.E., *b.* 22 Aug. 1885. Chief Clerk, Government Office, Isle of Man; Private Sec. to the Lieutenant Governor. *War Work*: Chiefly in connection with Alien's Detention Camps. *Address*: Maybank, Eastfield, Douglas, Isle of Man. (M3944)

ROGERS, Capt. Henry Waters Lyttleton, M.B.E.

ROGERS, Herbert Edwin Wright, O.B.E., J.P., *b.* 30th June, 1864; *s.* of Herbert Wright, of London; *m.* Ellen Maud Bickley, *d.* of Benjamin Bickley Rogers, M.A., D.Litt., of Strawberry Hill, Middlesex. *Educ.*: Charterhouse and Trinity Coll., Cambridge. M.A., LL.B., Barrister-at-Law. *War Work*: Member of Discipline Board, Metropolitan Special Constabulary; Member of Committee of Royal Air Force Hospitals. *Addresses*: Yarlington, Somerset; Old Bracondale, Cromer, Norfolk; 57, Cleveland Square, London, W.2; 11A, New Square, Lincoln's Inn, London, W.C.2. *Clubs*: Reform; Royal Automobile; Cromer. (O1819)

ROGERS, Comm. Hugh Hext, O.B.E., R.N.

ROGERS, Hugh Innes, O.B.E., M.I.E.E., *b.* 1872; *s.* of Jonh Innes Rogers, of Bournemouth; *m.* Beatrice Elizabeth, *d.* of Charles Hunton, of Bath. *Educ*: Temple Grove; Marlborough; King's Coll., London. President Bristol Association of Engineers, 1913–15; Chairman Western Centre Institution of Electrical Engineers, 1918–19; Member of Council Institution of Electrical Engineers, 1918–20. *War Work*: Member West of England Munitions Committee; as Chairman of Brecknell, Munro and Rogers, Ltd., Bristol, organised and extended their works which became the biggest producer of shells in the West of England. *Address*: Heathfield, St. Stephen's Road, Bath. (O11243)

ROGERS, James George, M.B.E., R.N.

ROGERS, Joan, M.B.E., *b.* 2 July, 1894; *d.* of Arthur Edmond Rogers, of London. *Educ.*: St. Paul's Girls' School. *War Work*: Lady Superintendent, Royal Army Pay Department, 3 years 8 months; also for two years worked on the National Land Council, training and placing women on the land. *Address*: 24, Charleville Road, W.14. (M2363)

ROGERS, John, O.B.E.

ROGERS, John, O.B.E.

ROGERS, John Henry, O.B.E., *b.* 15 Feb. 1867; *s.* of John Rogers, of Birmingham; *m.* Nellie Coulson, *d.* of Edward Smith, of Birmingham. *Educ.*: Privately. Chartered Accountant. *War Work*: Hon. Sec. Birmingham Joint V.A.D. Committee; Hon. Sec. Birmingham Local Centre, St. John Ambulance Association; Knight of Grace of the Order of St. John. *Address*: Calthorpe Fields, Edgbaston, Birmingham. *Club*: Clef. (O3893)

ROGERS, Kenneth, O.B.E., M.D. (Lond.) 1894, M.R.C.S., L.R.C.P. (1893), *b.* 17 March, 1870; *s.* of John Innes Rogers, of Knyveton Court, Bournemouth; *m.* Elizabeth Hope, *d.* of Archibald Parker, of Camden Wood, Chislehurst. *Educ.*: Temple Grove School; Marlborough Coll.; St. Bartholomew's Hospital; and Vienna. House Physician, St. Bart.'s Hospital, 1895–96; author of "Musings of a Medico" (verse). *War Work*: Physician on staff of the Brook War Hospital, Woolwich, 1915–19. *Address*: 16, Upper Park Road, Bromley, Kent. *Clubs*: Walton Heath; Sundridge Park Golf. (O4389)

ROGERS, Lilian May, M.B.E., Q.M.A.A.C.

ROGERS, Capt. Lincoln Coslett, O.B.E., R.A.O.C.

ROGERS, Mary Georgiana Helen, Mrs., M.B.E., *b.* 27 Jan. 1871; *d.* of Capt. Duncan McNeill, of Oransay Priory, Argyllshire; *m.* 1st, J. F. Tarlatt, of Ellary, Argyll; 2nd, Rev. Henry Rogers, *s.* of the late Richard Rogers, of Coltishall Hall, Norwich. *War Work*: Hon. Organising Officer of Women's Recruiting for Lowestoft Area under Ministry of Labour; was member of Divisional Council of Ministry of Labour for S. Midlands and Eastern Division; Member of Lowestoft Local Employment Committee; Chairman of Women's Sub-Committee; Chairman of Main L.E.C. from March, 1920. *Addresses*: Ellary, Ardrishaig, Argyll; Clarendon, Lowestoft.

ROGERS, Richard Hawke, M.B.E.

ROGERS, Rose Sophia, M.B.E., *b.* 8 June, 1852; *d.* of John Rogers, of Holt Hall, Norfolk. *Educ.*: At home. Member of Board of Guardians. *War Work*: Hon. Sec. Red Cross Mutford and Lothingland District, Suffolk; Quartermaster Suffolk 48 V.A.D.; Member of Local Tribunal and Food Committee; Collector of Red Cross Work for three parishes. *Address*: The Lodge, Belton, Gt. Yarmouth. *Club*: Alexandra Ladies'. (M3945)

ROGERS, Major Tanner Montagu, O.B.E.

ROGERS, Thomas Edward, M.B.E.

ROGERS, Major Thomas Leslie, O.B.E., A.P.D.

ROGERS, Timothy, M.B.E., *b.* 3rd Sept. 1862; *s.* of John Rogers, of Scariff, Co. Clare. Surveyor of Customs and Excise. *War Work*: Deputy to the Admiralty Marshal in work associated with the Blockade. (M9494)

ROGERS, Lieut. William Aldrich, M.B.E., R.A.S.C.

ROGERS, Muriel Augusta G., Mrs. COLTMAN-, C.B.E.; *d.* of Major Fred. B. Chapman, of 14th Hussars; *m.* Charles Coltman, *s.* of the Rev. John Rogers. *Educ.*: Privately. Member Local Education Authority, Co. Radnor; County Nursing Committee; President B.R.C.S., Radnor. *War Work*: Commandant Knighton Auxiliary Hospital (100 beds); Chairman Radnor Women's War Agricultural Committee; Member County Appeal Tribunal. *Addresses*: Stanage Park, Brampton-Bryan, Radnorshire; Llagnaby Priory, Spilsby, Lincolnshire. (C2915)

ROGERS, Capt. Henry Waters LYTTELTON-. O.B.E., *b.* 1878; *s.* of Capt. J.H. Lyttelton-Rogers, of Co. Longford, Ireland; *m.* Eleanor Frances, *d.* of Major H. W. Reeve. *Educ.*: Abroad. *War Work*: Service in France, June, 1916, to Feb. 1919. *Address*: 25, Hill Street, Knightsbridge, London, S.W. (O5729)

ROGERSON, Albert Chorley, C.B.E., M.Inst.C.E., M.I.Mech.E., *b.* 13 June, 1860; *s.* of William Chorley Rogerson, of Manchester; *m.* Eleanor Blanche, *d.* of Arthur Hambleton, of Manchester. *Educ.*: Privately, and Manchester School of Technology. General Manager of Messrs. Beyer Peacock & Co., Ltd. Locomotive Engineers and Machine Tool Makers, Manchester; Member of the Institute of Civil Engineers, Institute of Mechanical Engineers, and Executive Committee of the Manchester Engineering Trades Employers' Association. *War Work*: Field Artillery; 18-Pounder Gun Carriages; Howitzer Carriages and Equipments, and Gun Director Towers for Battleships. *Addresses*: Gorton, Manchester; Malvern, Allerton Road, Hesketh Park, Southport. (C2916)

ROGERSON, Capt. John Edwin, O.B.E.

ROGERSON, William Henry, M.B.E.

ROLFE, Capt. Charles Bertram, M.B.E., *b.* 21 April, 1884; *s.* of Francis Rolfe, of Wendon Lofts. *Educ.*: Perse School, Cambridge. Surveyor; Sec. The Farmers' Club. *War Work*: Hon. Artillery Company, Aug. 1914, to March, 1915; Sec. The Forage Committee, War Office, March, 1915, to April, 1919. *Address*: The Farmers' Club, 2, Whitehall Court, S.W.1. *Club*: R.A.S.C. (M5586)

ROLFE, Ethel Blanche, M.B.E.

ROLFE, Richard Alfred, M.B.E.

ROLFE, Sybil Katherine, Mrs. NEVILLE-, O.B.E.

ROLLAND, Lieut.-Col. Charles Edward Tulloch, C.B.E., R.G.A.

ROLLASON, Walter Herbert, O.B.E., *b.* 1868. *Educ.*: Leamington Coll., and Caius Coll., Cambridge. *War Work*: Hon. Executive Officer, Llandudno Food Control Committee, and other clerical work. *Address*: Wynberg, Carmen Sylva Road, Llandudno. (O11244)

ROLLESTON, Major Arthur George, O.B.E., R.H.A., and R.F.A., *b.* 11 Oct. 1883; *s.* of T. W. Rolleston, of Glasshouse, Shinrone, King's Co.; *m.* Susan Agnes, *d.* of Baron Clarina, of Elm Park, Clarina, Limerick (*see* BURKE'S *Peerage*). *Educ.*: St. Columba's Coll., Rathfarnham, Co. Dublin. Army (Regular). *War Work*: Served with R.H.A. and R.F.A. in Belgium, France, Egypt, and Italy; Commandant of Artillery School in Italy, 1918, with rank of Lieut.-Col. *Address*: Elm Park, Clarina, Limerick. *Club*: Cavalry. (O6412)

ROLLESTON, C. E. Maud, Lady, C.B.E., *b.* Sept. 1859; *d.* of Col. the Hon. Robert Dalzell, C.B. (*see* BURKE'S *Peerage*); *m.* Sir Lancelot, K.C.B., D.S.O., *s.* of Col. Lancelot Rolleston, of Watnall Hall, Notts. (*see* BURKE'S *Landed Gentry*). *Educ.*: At home. President of the City and County of Nottingham Women's Police Court Association. County Sec. Soldiers' and Sailors' Families Association; Member of County War Pensions Committee. *Address*: Watnall Hall, Notts. (C1013)

ROLLESTON, Iris Brenda, Mrs., C.B.E. Organised and was Matron of Taumaru Hospital (N.Z.) for wounded and

Convalescent Soldiers. *Address:* Taumaru, Lowry Bay, New Zealand. (C1998)

ROLLESTON, Lieut.-Col. Lancelot William, C.B.E., M.B., R.A.M.C.

ROLLIN, Ambrose, O.B.E., *b.* 5 July, 1871; *s.* of William Chas. Rollin, of Plymouth; *m.* Eva Maria Edwinia, *d.* of Edwin Smithbirt, of Plymouth. *Educ.:* Stoke Public School, Devonport; King's Coll., London. *War Work:* Served as Cashier, H.M. Dockyard, Devonport, throughout the war, with a turnover of several millions of money each year. *Address:* Pentillie House, 23, Ford Park Road, Plymouth. (O3894)

ROLLING, Lieut.-Col. Bernard Ismay, D S.O., O.B.E., R.E. (T.), *b.* 31 May, 1883; *s.* of George Miller Rolling, of The Grove, Penistone, near Sheffield; *m.* Edith Annie, *d.* of W. H. Bourne, of Stourbridge. *Educ.:* Wheelwright Grammar School, and Victoria Univ., Leeds. Engineer, Igranic Electric Co. *War Work:* Commanding 2nd Lowland Field Co., R.E., 29th Division, 1915; took part in original landing in Gallipoli, April, 1915; commanding 412 Field Co., 1916–18, in Egypt, Palestine, and France; C.R.E. 8th Corps, Oct. 1918, to June, 1919; awarded Brevet Majority, and 4 times mentioned in despatches. *Addresses:* 9, Craignulla Road, Langside, Glasgow; Maybank, Auchamore Road, Dunoon, Argyllshire. *Club:* Constitutional, Glasgow. (O2699)

ROLLINGS, William George Benjamin, M.B.E.

ROLLINSON, Capt. Harry Duggan, O.B.E., R.A.M.C. (S.R.).

ROLLO, William John, M.B.E.

ROLO, Robert, O.B.E.

ROLT, Frederick Henry, M.B.E. (London), B.Sc., A.C.G.I., A.M.I.Mech.E., *b.* Nov. 1888; *s.* of Frederick James Rolt, of Wimbledon; *m.* Florence Mary, *d.* of Samuel Edwards, of Wimbledon. *Educ.:* Rutlish Science School, Merton; Central Technical Coll., Univ. of London. Senior Assistant in Metrology Dept. of The National Physical Laboratory. *War Work:* Supervision of Gauge-Testing Work for Munitions. *Address:* National Physical Laboratory, Teddington. (M9499)

ROME, Francis John de, M.B.E. Assistant Censor, Hong Kong. (M10260a)

ROME, Capt. Samuel Greenlees, O.B.E., M.B.

ROMER, Capt. Charles Robert Ritchie, O.B.E.

ROMER, Lieut. Frederick, O.B.E., R.N.V.R.

ROMER, Leila Harriette, Mrs., M.B.E., *b.* 29 Aug. 1864; *d.* of John Harding Robinson, late Examiner Standing Orders, House of Lords; *m.* Thomas Ansdell, late Senior Chancery Master, *s.* of Thomas Romer. *War Work:* Started and ran Y.M.C.A. Hut, Kensington, from Oct. 1914 till July, 1919. (M2354)

ROMER, Lieut.-Col. Malcolm, O.B.E., *b.* 13 April, 1882; *s.* of Col. F. C. Romer; *m.* Evelyn Louisa, *d.* of General Sir Reginald Gipps. *Educ.:* Eton. 2nd Lieut. Scots Guards, Jan. 1901; Lieut. 1903; Capt. 1906; Adjutant, 1st Batt. Dec. 1910, to April, 1914; Major, Sept. 1915; A. Lieut.-Col. Sept. 1917; retired on retired pay, with rank of Lieut.-Col., July, 1919. *War Work:* Served with 2nd Batt. Scots Guards, Sept. 1914. to Nov. 1914, B.E.F.; Adjutant 3rd Batt., Jan. 1915, to Jan. 1916; Regimental Adjutant, May, 1916, to July, 1917; Commanded 1st Batt. B.E.F., Aug. 1917, to March, 1918; Commanded 3rd Batt., Aug. 1918, to July, 1919; mentioned in despatches, June, 1918, and June, 1919. *Address:* Addington Manor, Thrapston, Northamptonshire. *Clubs:* Guards'; Turf; Boodle's; Arthur's. (O8927)

ROMER, Robert Leslie, O.B.E., M.R.C.S.

ROMER, Capt. Robert Wolfgang, O.B.E., R.F.A., *b.* 16 Feb. 1895; *s.* of Robert W. W. Romer, of Reigate, Surrey. *Educ.:* Bedford School. Shaw Wallace & Co., Calcutta. *War Work:* Joined H.A.C. in Aug. 1914; proceeded with "B" Battery to Egypt and Aden; returned as Sergeant, May, 1916; received commission in R.F.A., Aug. 1914; proceeded to France, Feb. 1917; wounded and gassed at Armentiers, July, 1917, and sent to Manchester, Convalescent; returned to France, Nov. 1917; promoted to Capt. and appointed Instructor of French Mortar School at St. Omer; was specially mentioned in despatches. (O5732)

ROMILLY, Capt. Herbrand Alan, M.B.E.

ROMNEY, William, M.B.E., *b.* 22 June, 1865; *s.* of William Romney, of Barfrestone, Kent.; *m.* Clara, *d.* of Richard Coleman, of Langdon Court, nr. Dover. *Educ.:* Deal School. Continental Agent, Folkstone Harbour (S.E. and C. Ry. Co.). *War Work:* At Folkestone Harbour, Passenger and Goods, Troops and Military Stores, during whole period of War. *Address:* 5, Wear Bay Crescent, Folkestone. (M905)

RONALD, George, O.B.E. (O6784)

RONALD, James, M.B.E.

RONALD, Capt. Reginald Stanley, O.B.E., R.A.S.C. (T.F.).

RONALDSON, Thomas Percy, M.B.E., *b.* 17 June, 1865; *s.* of the late Thomas Ronaldson, of Bickley, Kent, late of Bournemouth; *m.* Christine, *d.* of S. V. B. Asser, J.P., of Windlesham. *Educ.:* Privately. Formerly engaged in shipping business both in London and Antwerp; was residing at the latter place when war broke out. *War Work:* At War Trade Intelligence Department from Feb. 1915, to April, 1916; at Censorship (War Office) from April, 1916, to Aug. 1919 (as Censor, then Assistant Chief Censor). *Address:* 34, St. Mary's Mansions, W. 2. *Club:* Thatched House. (M9504)

RONALDSON, Thomas Sheriff, O.B.E.

RONAN, Capt. Walter Joseph, O.B.E., M.B., R.A.M.C., *b.* 19 April, 1890; *s.* of Walter B. Ronan, of Cork, Ireland.

Educ.: Stonyhurst Coll. and Dublin Univ. Surgeon. *War Work:* Capt., R.A.M.C., 1914–19. *Address:* 47B, Welbeck Street, Cavendish Square, W. 1. *Club:* Constitutional. (O5733)

RONCA, James Francis, M.B.E.

ROOK, Major William Robert, O.B.E., T.D., *b.* 18 Nov. 1877. *War Work:* France, 1915–18. *Address:* Edwalton, Notts. (O5134)

ROOKE, Lieut.-Col. Alfred Shipton, O.B.E.

ROOKE, Capt. John Wentworth, O.B.E.

ROOME, Engr.-Capt. George William, C.B.E., R.N., *b.* 1865; *s.* of Henry Roome, formerly Sup. Clerk, Admiralty; *m.* 1895, Catherine Aaderson, Stewart, of Newbury, Fife. *Educ.:* Aske Sch., Hatcham, S.E. Assist. Instructor Roy. Naval Coll., Greenwich, 1895–98 and 1906–11, and to Chief Engineer, Devonport Dockyard, 1898–1901; Malta, 1901–2, and Devonport, 1902–5; Chief Engineer, Dockyard, Hong Kong, 1912–15, and Pembroke, 1915. (C913)

ROOSE, Capt. Gerald Unna Bond, O.B.E.

ROPE, Irene Mary, M.B.E., W.R.N.S.

ROPER, Brig.-Gen. Alexander William, C.B., C.B.E., *b.* 3 July, 1862; *s.* of Sir Henry Roper. *Educ.:* Marlborough and Royal Military Academy, Woolwich. *War Work:* Chief Engineer, Eastern Command, Jan. to Feb. 1915; attached to G.H.Q., Mediterranean Expeditionary Forces, March, to Oct. 1915; Inspector of Royal Engineers, Nov. 1915, to Dec. 1919. *Address:* 21, Arlington Road, Eastbourne. *Clubs:* Army and Navy; M.C.C.; Sussex (Eastbourne); Royal Eastbourne Golf. (C1755)

ROPER, Ann, Mrs., O.B.E.

ROPER, Lieut. George Orchard, M.B.E., R.A.F.

ROPER, John Gregson, O.B.E.

RORISON, George Henry, M.B.E., *b.* 13 Dec. 1883; *s.* of James of Liverpool. *Educ.:* Birkenhead. Cargo and Lighterage Expert. *War Work:* Lighterage Control Board at Port Said. *Club:* Union (Port Said, Egypt). (M9502)

ROSCOE, Major Harry, O.B.E., R.G.A. (T.), *b.* 31 March, 1886; *s.* of Walter Roscoe, of Worsley, Manchester; *m.* Elizabeth Annie, *d.* of J. C. Schofield, of Hanley. *Educ.:* St. Mark's, Worsley, and Salford Royal Tech. Institute. Surveyor, Stafford, Coal and Iron Co., Ltd. *War Work:* Mobilised with 1/1 North Midland (Staffs) R.G.A. (T.F.), Aug. 1914 (Lieut.); Captain, July, 1915; transferred to 2/1 N.M. (Staffs.) R.G.A., April, 1915 (owing to injury); posted to command 2/4 Staffs R.F.A. Bty. Oct. 1915; served in Irish Rebellion, April, 1916; transferred to R.G.A., Woolwich July, 1916; commanded 187 Hy. Bty., Sept. 1916, to Jan. 1917; Capt. 188 Hy. Bty., R.G.A., 60-Pdr., 17 Feb.; served with 188 Hy. Bty., Macedonia, April, 1917, to Jan. 1919, being in Command from Feb. 1918; first 60-Pdr. Bty. to enter Bulgaria, Sept. 1918; invalided home, Jan. 1919; demobilised. May, 22, 1919. *Address:* Primrose Hill, Hanford, Stoke-on-Trent. (O6528)

ROSE, Lieut.-Col. and Qr.-Mr. Ambrose George, O.B.E., R.A.S.C.

ROSE, Lieut. Clifford, I.A.

ROSE, Edith, O.B.E., *d.* of the late John Rose, of Norwich. Liverpool and District Secretary of the National Vigilance Association. *War work:* Honorary Secretary to the Liverpool Reception Committee for Belgian Refugees and other Allies. *Address:* 16, Daulby Street, Liverpool. (O11247)

ROSE, Edward Armstrong, O.B.E., *b.* 4 Oct., 1868; *s.* of Edward Rose, of Wyton Grange, Huntingdon. *Educ.:* Cowper House School, Huntingdon. Alderman of Huntingdon County Council and Chairman of County Small Holding and Allotment Committee. *War Work:* Active Member of County War Agricultural Executive Committee. (O11248)

ROSE, Lieut.-Col. Ernest Albert, C.B.E., R.A.S.C. Served in the Great War, 1914–19 (despatches). (C1402)

ROSE, Felix, O.B.E., J.P., *b.* 1867. *Educ.:* Royal Institution, Liverpool. Barrister-at-Law. *War Work:* Hon. Director, Purchases Department, Board of Trade; Hon. Assessor Cotton Claims, Board of Trade, from June, 1915, to July, 1920. *Address:* 66, Portland Place, London, W. 1. *Club:* Reform; Walton Heath Golf. (O53)

ROSE, Hannah Catherine, M.B.E.

ROSE, Harold Greenwell, M.B.E., Assoc. M. Inst. C.E., *b.* 16 April, 1878; *s.* of John Thompson Rose, of Roker, Sunderland; *m.* Margaret, *d.* of Thomas Leeman of Geneva, Switzerland. *Educ.:* Bede Collegiate School, Sunderland. Civil Engineer; Managing Director of the Provincial Construction Co., Ltd., Public Works Contractors, Sunderland *War Work:* Design of Sewerage and Sewage disposal works for many Camps; Resident Engineer, Kinmel Park Camp, Rhyl; Chief Assistant Drainage Engineer to the Air Ministry. *Address:* 39, West Sunniside, Sunderland. (M9504)

ROSE, Major Harold Oldham, M.B.E., R.E., *b.* 13 Dec. 1880; *s.* of Henry Rose, of Bishop Auckland. *Educ.:* Durham. Overseer, G.P.O. Sunderland. *War Work:* R.E. Signals, France, Salonica Force, Army of the Black Sea. *Address:* 25, Grindon Terrace, Sunderland. (M4821)

ROSE, Ivor Sainte Avix, O.B.E.

ROSE, Major James, M.B.E., *b.* 24 Aug. 1875; *s.* of James Rose, of Lodsworth Manor, Sussex; *m.* Margaret Sophia, *d.* of Alfred Leighton, of Pelton, Co. Durham. *Educ.:* Midhurst Grammar School. Enlisted at age of 18 years in the Royal Garrison Artillery. *War Work:* Served in Sierra Leone from outbreak of war till Nov. 1915; organised and managed the Ordnance Depot attached to No 1 National Filling Factory

BIOGRAPHIES. **Rostron**

nr. Leeds. *Address:* 5, Marshall Avenue, Cross Gates, nr. Leeds. (M2365)

ROSE, Lieut. Norman Frank, M.B.E., M.G.C.

ROSE, Capt. Thomas Whateley, M.B.E., M.C., *b.* 10 May, 1876; *s.* of Frederick Rose, J.P., of Westminster; *m.* Isabel Emma, *d.* of Frederick Savage, of Marden, Kent. *Educ.:* Westminster School. Solicitor, England; Barrister and Solicitor, Western Australia; Solicitor, New South Wales. *War Work:* Returned from Western Australia, Dec. 1914; rejoined 5th Batt. The Royal Sussex Regt., 18 Feb. 1915; Served in France, Belgium, and Italy, June. 1915, to April, 1919; mentioned in despatches; awarded Italian Silver Medal for Valour. *Address:* Katoomba, New South Wales. *Club:* Imperial Service (Sydney). (M3214)

ROSEVEARE, Major Leslie, O.B.E., M.Inst.C.E., *b.* 12 May, 1876; *s.* of Edwin Roseveare, J.P., of Plymouth. *Educ.:* Wycliffe College. Civil Engineer. *War Work:* Deputy Assistant Director of Roads, 1 Corps, France, 1916–19. *Address:* 2, Wilmington Square, Eastbourne. (O5735)

ROSEVERE, Eng.-Comm. Edward James, O.B.E., R.N.

ROSHER, Noel Burn, O.B.E., M.I.E.E., *b.* 6 Dec. 1875; *s.* of George Rosher, of Higham, Kent; *m.* Madeline, *d.* of Rev. Canon Cayley, of Toronto. *Educ.:* Repton School and King's Coll. Consulting Engineer; Vice-Chairman, Midland Centre of the Institution of Electrical Engineers. *War Work:* Inspector of Munitions Areas under Ministry of Munitions. *Address:* 48, Fountain Road, Edgbaston, Birmingham. *Club:* Union Club (Birmingham). (O700)

ROSKROW, Albert Cyril, M.B.E.

ROSKRUGE, Engr.-Comm. Francis John, D.S.O., O.B.E., R.N., *b.* 1871. Served in S. Africa, 1899–1900 with Naval guns, and in E. Africa, 1914–18 (despatches). *Club:* Services. (O3557)

ROSLING, 2nd Lieut. Cecil, M.B.E., R.E.

ROSS, Lieut. Alexander Jacob Meyer, M.B.E., R.A.F.

ROSS, 2nd Lieut. Alexander Joseph, M.B.E.

ROSS, Capt. Alexander Lewis, M.B.E., R.A.S.C.

ROSS, Alice Constance, Mrs., O.B.E., *b.* 31 July, 1870; *d.* of Major-Gen. T. Bland Strange, of Geraghmeen, Camberley; *m.* John, *s.* of Hon. John Ross, of Toronto, Ontario. *War Work:* Hon. Divisional Sec. for Westminster Division, British Red Cross Society. *Address:* The Steps, Playden, Sussex. *Club:* Victoria, for Ladies. (O11249)

ROSS, Major Andrew Alexander, O.B.E., R.A.F.

ROSS, Capt. Angus, O.B.E.

ROSS, Archibald John Campbell, C.B.E., *b.* 1867; *s.* of the Rev. Alexander Johnstone Ross, D.D.; *m.* 1896, Marion *d.* of the late Col. — Gousieff. *Educ.:* Marlborough. Shipbuilder and Engineer; a Member of Shipbuilding Council, Admiralty. *War Work:* Member of Advisory Committee on Merchant Shipbuilding, Ministry of Shipping, and to Admiralty Controller, 1917. *Clubs:* Royal Societies'; Royal Automobile. (C282)

ROSS, Lieut. Charles Arthur, M.B.E., R.E. (T.).

ROSS, Capt. and Qr.-Mr. Charles Thomas, O.B.E., R.A.M.C. (T.).

ROSS, Clara Louise, O.B.E., R.R.C., A.I.F.

ROSS, Major Conrad, O.B.E., R.A., *b.* 25 Nov. 1884; *s.* of Col. W. H. Ross, Indian Staff Corps, of Bournemouth; *m.* Helen, *d.* of Martin Cormac, of Eltham. *Educ.:* Downside School, Wimbledon Coll., and R.M.A., Woolwich. Officer in the Royal Garrison Artillery. *War Work:* Research Department, Woolwich Arsenal. (O7649)

ROSS, 2nd Lieut. Duncan, O.B.E., R.E.

ROSS, Lieut.-Col. Edward Henry, O.B.E.

ROSS, Capt. Findlay McKay, M.B.E., M.C.

ROSS, Frederick Alexander, O.B.E.

ROSS, Gladys Ethel, M.B.E.

ROSS, Lieut.-Col. Henry, O.B.E., *b.* 29 June, 1877; *s.* of William Ross, of Leeholme, Cork; *m.* Betty, *d.* of Christopher Mitchell, of Weymouth. *Educ.:* Queen's Coll., Cork. Indian Medical Service. *War Work:* Hospital Ship "Joorkha," Oct. 1914, to April, 1916; Assistant Director-Gen. Indian Medical Service, April, 1916, to end of War; Commandant, Lady Chelmsford Convalescent Home for Officers, Simla, from 1916–19; Hon. Sec. Indian Joint War Committee for periods aggregating three years during war. *Address:* The Crags, Simla. *Clubs:* East Indian U.S.; U.S. (Simla). (O8928)

ROSS, Lieut.-Col. Hew Dalrymple, O.B.E., *b.* 22 Sept. 1871; *s.* of Gen. Sir John Ross, G.C.B.; *m.* Kathleen Emma Mabel, *d.* of Col. Rt. Hon. Sir Albert Hime, P.C., K.C.M.G. *Educ.:* Eton and Sandhurst. Rifle Brigade. *War Work:* Home, France, and Flanders with Service Battalions of the Rifle Brigade, 1914–16; Rifle Records Office, Winchester, 1916–20. *Addresses:* c/o Messrs. Cox & Co.; Hill House, Winchester. *Clubs:* Hampshire County; Greenjackets Cricket. (O8929)

ROSS, Hugh Henderson, O.B.E.

ROSS, Capt. James Maxwell, M.B.E., F.R.C.S.

ROSS, James Stirling, M.A., C.B.E., *b.* 3 Aug. 1877; *s.* of John Ross, of Edinburgh; *m.* Christina MacDonald, M.A., *d.* of John Ross, M.A., of Arbroath. *Educ.:* Royal High School, Edinburgh; Edinburgh Univ.; and Balliol Coll., Oxford. Appointed to War Office Staff, 1900; now Director of Finance (for Personnel), Air Ministry. *War Work:* Chief Accountant for Q.M.G's finance, War Office, and Deputy to the Assistant Financial Secretary, Air Ministry. *Address:* Chumleigh, Nether Street, Finchley, London, N.3. (C1032)

ROSS, John David McBeath, M.B.E.

ROSS, Comm. John Kenneth Leveson, O.B.E.

ROSS, Millicent Ellen, M.B.E.

ROSS, Roderick, C.B.E., M.V.O., *b.* 1865; *m.* Eliza beth Esther, *e. d.* of Henry Mills, of Folkestone. *Educ.:* Helmsdale. Chief Constable of Ramsgate, 1895–97, and of Bradford, 1898–99; Chief Constable of Edinburgh City since 1899; author of "City of Bradford Constabulary Code," and "City of Edinburgh Constabulary Code." *Address:* Bual, Helmsdale, Sutherlandshire. (C2917)

ROSS, Stella M. Dalrymple, M.B.E.; *d.* of Gen. Sir John Ross, G.C.B., formerly of Stone House, Hayton, Carlisle. *War Work:* Hon. Sec. Southfield Red Cross Hospital, Duns; Hon. Sec. and Treas. County Local War Pensions Committee. *Address:* Oxendean, Duns, Berwickshire. *Clubs:* New Victorian; Queen's (Edinburgh). (M2368)

ROSS, Stewart Buckle Carne, O.B.E. Censor-in-Charge, Hong Kong. (O11790g)

ROSS, Pilot Officer Tascar Alan, M.B.E., R.A.F.

ROSS OF CROMARTY, Brig.-Gen. Sir Walter Charteris, K.B.E., C.B. C.M.G., J.P., D.L., *b.* 5 Aug. 1857; *s.* of Col. G. W. H. Ross of Cromarty, Cromarty House, Cromarty; *m.* Gertrude May Gathorne, *d.* of Charles Hill, of Clevedon Hall and Hazel Manor, Compton Martin, Somerset, England. Served with Durham Light Infantry in Afghan War (mentioned); S. Africa (3 mentions and C.B. 1900); dangerously wounded 1899 at Botheville, S. Africa; Military Sec. C. in C., Punjab, India, 1898–99. *War Work:* Commanded 1st Highland Brigade, France, 1914–16, and 228th Brigade, Salonica Force, 1916–18 (4 mentions); Greek Order of Redeemer, Greek Military Medal, Star of Roumania. *Address:* Cromarty House, Cromarty. *Club:* Naval and Military.

ROSS, Major William, O.B.E.

ROSS, Major William David, M.A., O.B.E., *b.* 15 April, 1877: *s.* of John Ross, M.A., of Edinburgh; *m.* Edith Helen, *d.* of John Ogden, of Manchester. *Educ.:* Royal High School, Edinburgh; Edinburgh Univ.; Balliol Coll., Oxford. Fellow, Tutor, and Librarian of Oriel Coll., Oxford. *War Work:* Secretary, N.E. Coast Armaments Committee, 1915–16; Administrative Officer, Inspection Dept., Royal Arsenal, Woolwich, 1916–17; Deputy Director of Inspection, Ministry of Munitions, 1917–18; Deputy Assistant Secretary, Ministry of Munitions, 1918–19. *Address:* Oriel College, Oxford; 6, Charlbury Road, Oxford. (O1823)

ROSS, William Henry, O.B.E., *b.* 19 June, 1862; *s.* of the late John Ross, of Dalkeith; *m.* Annie Gilmour Pollok, *d.* of the late David Dalglish, of Manchester. *Educ.:* George Watson's Coll., Edinburgh. Managing Director of the Distillers' Company, Ltd., Edinburgh, also director of several other public and private companies. *War Work:* Member of Advisory Committee on Alcohol supplies. *Address:* Stanmore, Davidson's Mains, Midlothian. *Clubs:* Devonshire; Royal Automobile; Scottish Conservative (Edin.). (O1824)

ROSS, Major William John, O.B.E., F.R.G.S., R.E., *b.* 20 Aug. 1881; *s.* of Donald Ross, of Inverness, N.B.; *m.* Laura, *d.* of Jonathan Brown, of Horley, Surrey. *Educ.:* Royal Academy, Inverness, N.B. Before war, Chief Engineer, Dorada Railway Ropeway Extension, Colombia, S.A.; formerly General Manager Bahia S.W. Railway, Brazil, and Construction Engineer, Uruguay, E.C. Railway; served in S.A. War with 1st Cam. Highs. 1900–1. *War Work:* 1915–16, Lieut. 110th Co. R.E., B.E.F., France; 1916–17, Capt. 110th Co. R.E., B.E.F., France; O.C. 110th Co. R.E., France; 1917–19, O.C. 266th Co. R.E., Palestine; 1919–20 Major R.E. Chief Engineer, Palestine Military Railways. *Address:* c/o Cox and Co. Charing Cross, London. (O6285)

ROSS, Winifred Margaret, O.B.E., M.B., Ch.B.

ROSSALL, Jane, M.B.E.

ROSSER, Thomas Newland, M.B.E.

ROSSITER, Capt. Frederick Norman Chambers, M.B.E., M.C., R.A.

ROSSITER, Capt. Thomas Frederick, M.B.E.

ROSSMORE, Mittie, The Lady, O.B.E., *d.* of Richard Christopher Naylor, Hooton Hall, Cheshire; *m.* Derrick Warner William, 5th Baron Rossmore, who died 31 Jan. 1921 (*see* BURKE'S *Peerage*). *War Work:* Red Cross and Canteen. *Addresses:* Rossmore, Monaghan; The Steed House, Hampton Court. (O11250)

ROST, Lieut.-Col. Ernest Reinhold, O.B.E., I.M.S.

ROSTERN, Joseph, C.B.E., M.Inst.T., *b.* 4 Oct. 1862; *s.* of Philip Rostern, of Manchester; *m.* Clara, *d.* of John Walkden, J.P., C.C., of Manchester. *Educ.:* Privately. Assistant to General Manager, Great Central Railway, 1899–12; Chief Goods Manager, G.C.R. since 1912; Chairman of Goods Managers' Conference, 1916; a member of Sub-Committee of Board of Trade Railway Conference, 1908–9; Foundation Member of Institute of Transport, 1920. *War Work:* Served on Railway Executive Committee and various Sub-Committees, 1914–19; Member of the Treasury Committee on Staffs, re Staffing of Government Offices, 1918; Member. Road Transport Board, 1918; Member, War Cabinet Strike Committee (Traffic Emergency Committee), 1919; Member, War Cabinet Committee (Congestion at Ports), 1919; Member, Storage and Transit Committee, 1919; Member, Standing Committee Government Departments and Railways, 1915–19 (Chairman, 1916). *Address:* Prestwych, Northwood, Middlesex. (C2981)

ROSTRON, Comm. Arthur Henry, C.B.E., R.D., R.N.R.

ROSTRON, Major Philip Simpson, O.B.E.

ROTH, Major Albert Alexander, O.B.E., *b.* 11 Nov. 1889 ; *s.* of Charles Roth. *Educ.:* Privately and London Univ. Accountant ; now Partner in firm of Roth and Gibson, Importers and Exporters of China and Glass. *War Work :* Obtained commission in R.A.O.C. from London Univ. Officers' Training Corps, Feb. 1915 ; appointed to command a company of R A.O.C. in April, 1915 ; took it to France in June, 1915; appointed D.A.D.O.S. of the 50th Division (Northumbrian), Dec. 1915 ; made Captain, Jan. 1916 ; Major, 1918 ; three times mentioned in despatches. *Address :* 1–3 Red Lion Court, Watling Street, E.C. *Clubs :* Royal Automobile.　(O2700)

ROTHERA, Capt. Percy O.B.E., I.A.

ROTHSCHILD, Capt. Sydney Henry, O.B.E., *b.* 1875 ; *s.* of the late Alfred A. Rothschild, of 80, Lancaster Gate, W. ; *m.* Helen Jane, *d.* of the late W. Taylor, of Felstead Essex. *Educ.:* Clifton College. Stockbroker. *War Work :* Enlisted 18th Royal Fusiliers, Sept. 1914 ; 2nd Lieut. R.A.S.C., May, 1915 ; 31st Div., 52nd Div., 4th Cavalry Div., Egypt, Palestine, Syria, 1915–19 ; twice mentioned in despatches. *Address :* 20, York Buildings, Adelphi W.C. *Club :* Bath.　(O6286)

ROTHWELL, James Herbert, C.B.E., *b.* 7 July, 1881 ; *s.* of John Rothwell, of Southport ; *m.* Evelyn Mary, *d.* of Chas. R. Johnson, of Sheffield. *Educ.:* Southport Modern School. Solicitor ; Town Clerk, Chesterfield. *War Work :* Director of Local Rationing Schemes, and later Director and Deputy Assistant Secretary, Rationing Division, Ministry of Food. *Address :* Crossfield House, Chesterfield. *Clubs :* Law Society ; East Derbyshire.　(C2920)

ROTHWELL, Thomas James, O.B.E.　(O12011)

ROTHWELL, William Edward, O.B.E.　(O2701)

ROTTER, Godfrey, O.B.E., D.Sc., F.I.C., *b.* 3 Sept. 1879 ; *s.* of Charles G. Rotter, of Croydon and Fowlmere ; *m.* Gertrude Elizabeth, *d.* of George Plank, of Clapton. *Educ.:* City of London School, and Univ. Coll. of North Wales. Chemist, Research Department, Royal Arsenal, Woolwich. *War Work :* Part inventor of new process for making trotyl, of cordite R.D.B., and of the No 106 Fuse, also occupied with general research in connection with service explosives and ammunition. *Address :* 2, Parkhill Road, Sidcup, Kent. *Club :* Chemical Industries.　(O9702)

ROTTON, Letitia, M.B.E., *b.* 4 May, 1896 ; *d.* of J. R. C. Rotton, of 45, Hamilton Terrace, London, N.W. *Educ.:* Francis Holland School, Clarence Gate, N.W. *War Work :* Clerk in the Ministry of Shipping. *Address :* 45, Hamilton Terrace, London, N.W. 8.　(M3948)

ROUGUETTE, Gladys Howard, Mrs., M.B.E.

ROUND, Arthur, O.B.E., *b.* 20 March, 1875 ; *s.* of Benjamin John Round, J.P., of Nithsdate, St. Mary's Road, Leamington ; *m.* Gertrude Elizabeth, *d.* of Mark Lawton, of Handsworth, Birmingham. *Educ.:* King Edward's School, Aston. Solicitor ; Commissioner for Oaths. *War Work :* Regional Officer for Civilian National Service, West Midlands Division ; Assistant Clerk to the Military Tribunal, Birmingham. *Addresses :* 21, Waterloo Street, Birmingham ; Nithsdale, St. Mary's Road, Leamington.　(O11251)

ROUNDELL, Lieut. Christopher Foulis, C.R.E., *b.* 11 July, 1876 ; *s.* of the late Charles Savile Roundell ; *m.* Lady Maude, *d.* of the 4th Earl of Leitrim (*see* BURKE'S *Peerage*). *Educ.:* Harrow ; Balliol. General Inspector, Ministry of Health ; Barrister-at-Law. *War Work :* In charge of Transport arrangements for Refugees and Allied Recruits, Local Government Board War Refugee Department, and of Jewish Refuges and Refugees ; Member of Special Government Tribunal (Military Service Conventions with Allies) ; Inspector, Quartermaster-General's Department, War Office and Eastern Command ; Commissioner, National Salvage Council. *Address :* 54 Rutland Gate, London, S.W. 7. *Clubs :* Travellers' ; Brooks's ; Windham ; Garrick.　(C2921)

ROUSE, Capt. Alfred Corrie, O.B.E., *b.* 28 Oct. 1886 ; *s.* of Alfred Rouse, of Carvedras, Truro ; *m.* Elizabeth Jane Marian Drewe, *d.* of T. E. Thriscutt, of Newquay. *Educ.:* Christ's Hospital, and King's Coll. Secretary and Land Agent. *War Service :* Commissioned in 1914 ; served with B.E.F. France, July, 1915, to Feb. 1919, with 19th Division ; O.C. No. 1 Co., 19th Div. Train ; twice mentioned in despatches. *Address :* Treburthes, Newquay, Cornwall. *Clubs :* Junior Army and Navy ; Hurlingham (B. Aires).　(O2703)

ROUTLEDGE, Robert, M.B.E., R.G.A., *b.* 5th July, 1868. Clerk (War Office).　(M9510)

ROUSE, Alfred Robert, M.B.E.

ROUSE, Lieut. William Sydney, M.B.E.

ROUTH, Lieut.-Col. Jason Rudolph, O.B.E.

ROUNTREE Capt. Arthur Noel, O.B.E., R.A.S.C. *Address :* Glenrise, Parkstone, Dorset.

ROUNTREE, Capt. Arthur Fitzgerald, O.B.E., I.A.R.O.

ROW, Bessie Rose, O.B.E.

ROWAN, Major Robert Houston, O.B.E., T.D., R.E., *b.* 19 July, 1875 ; *s.* of Thomas B. Rowan, of Greenock ; *m.* Betty, *d.* of George Macdonald, of Greenock. *Educ.:* Blairlodge School, Polmont. Chartered Accountant. *War Work :* O.C. Clyde Electric Light Defences, Coast Defence ; Intelligence Officer, Clyde Defences. *Address :* 22, Esplanade, Greenock. *Club :* Greenock.　(O7652)

ROWBOTHAM, Capt. Farnel, O.B.E., R.A.O.C.

ROWBOTHAM, James MacKean, M.B.E.. M.I.C.E.

ROWBOTTOM, Lieut. Wilmos William Boxall, M.B.E., R.E. (I.W.T.).

ROWCLIFFE, Clementina Elizabeth Hope, Mrs , O.B.E. ,

and Order of Mercy ; *d.* of the late Gen. Sir Edward Williams, K.C.I.E. ; *m.* Edward Lee, *s.* of the late William Rowcliffe, of Northbrook, Farnham, Surrey. *War Work :* Commandant and Administrator of Oaklands Red Cross Hospital, Cranleigh, Surrey, for 3 years, 1915–18 ; Vice-President, Cranleigh Division, Surrey, Branch of the B.R.C.S., 1910–20. *Addresses :* Hall Place, Cranleigh, Surrey ; Stovolds Hill, Cranleigh, Surrey ; 70, St. James's Court, Buckingham Gate, S.W. 1. *Club :* The Ladies' Empire.　(O3897)

ROWDEN, Major Arthur Roger, O.B.E.

ROWDEN, Capt. Ernest George, O.B.E.

ROWE, Lieut. Alfred Edward, M.B.E., *b.* 24 Feb. 1893 ; *s.* of the late Josiah Rowe, late of Birmingham ; *m.* Ada, *d.* of E. Rawlings, of Shirley, Birmingham. *Educ.:* Waverley Road Secondary School, Birmingham ; matriculated at Birmingham Univ. Incorporated Accountant, holding appointment as Assistant Local Accountant under Ministry of Labour. *War Work :* Assistant Chief Accountant to British Red Cross and Order of St. John in France and Belgium, Jan.–May, 1917 ; and Chief Accountant in the Balkans, June, 1917, to June, 1919 ; mentioned in despatches, Nov. 1918. *Address :* 27, Westfield Road, Acock's Green, Birmingham.　(M9511)

ROWE, Capt. Arthur Alfred, M.B.E., R.E. and R.A.F.

ROWE, Arthur William, M.B.E.

ROWE, Major Charles William, M.B.E.

ROWE, George John, O.B.E.

ROWE, Capt. and Qr.-Mr. George Richard, M.B.E., R.A.S.C.

ROWE, Capt. Henry Gordon, O.B.E., R.A. (T.).

ROWE, Capt. James Stewart, M.B.E., R.A.S.C., *b.* 6 Feb. 1880 ; *s.* of the late Robert Rowe, South Kensington ; *m.* Anna Gray, *d.* of William Ernest Good, M.R.C.S. (Lond.), of Dorchester, Dorset. Director, Burton, Rowe and River, Ltd. *Address :* The Avenue, Surbiton Hill. *Club :* City Carlton.　(M5590)

ROWE, John William, M.B.E.

ROWE, Mabel Ruth, Mrs., M.B.E. ; *m.* Thomas Bradley. *Educ.:* Exeter High School. *War Work :* Mayoress of Exeter's Depot from 1914 till 1919. *Address :* Lafrowda, Exeter.　(M2370)

ROWE, Capt. Wilfred Aubrey, M.B.E.

ROWE, William George, M.B.E.

ROWE, Lieut.-Col. William Hugh Cecil, C.B.E., *b.* 19 July, 1883 ; *s.* of tne late William Hugh Rowe, Assist. Paymaster, Supreme Court of Justice, of London. *Educ.:* St. Paul's School, London, and Jesus Col., Cambridge. *War Work :* Served in R.A.S.C., 8th Aug. 1914, to 30 June, 1919 ; B.E.F. France, 14 Aug. 1914, to 9 Dec. 1917 ; Italian E.F., 10 Dec. 1917, to 8 June, 1919 ; Ministry of Munitions, June, 1919, to May, 1920. *Address :* 32, Victoria Road, Kensington, London, W. 8. *Club :* Junior Constitutional.　(C1403)

ROWE, Lieut.-Col. Herbert Mayow FISHER-, C.B.E., T.F.R., *b.* 1870 ; *s.* of the late Edward Rowe Fisher-Rowe, of Thorncombe, Surrey ; *m.* 1901, Maud, *d.* of the late Alfred Seymour. of Hollybrook, Southampton (*see* BURKE'S *Peerage*, Hertford, M.). Served in the Great War, 1914–19 (despatches).　(C1563)

ROWELL, Capt. Charles, O.B.E.

ROWELL, Henry Snowden, O.B.E.

ROWELL, Sir Herbert Babington, K.B.E., J.P., M.Inst.C.E., M.I.N.A. ; *b.* 24 Nov. 1860 ; *s.* of Robert Rowell, of Newcastle-on-Tyne ; *m.* Mary Dobree, *d.* of John N. Robin, of Naples. *Educ.:* Mill Hill ; Switzerland ; Glasgow Univ. Chairman of R. and W. Hawthorn Leslie & Co., Ltd., Newcastle-on-Tyne, Shipbuilders, Marine and Locomotive Manufacturers ; President of Shipbuilding Employers' Federation, 1912–14 ; President of N.E. Coast Institution of Engineers and Shipbuilders, 1915–17 ; Vice-President of Federation of British Industries ; Member of Northumberland Territorial Force Association ; Member of Council, Institution of Naval Architects ; Member of Council, Armstrong College ; Member of Lloyd's Technical Committee ; Member of Board of Trade Shipping Advisory Committee ; Member of Council, Industrial Welfare Society. *War Work :* Served on the following Government Committees : Board of Trade Committee on Engineering Trades after the War ; Advisory Committee to Admiralty Shipyard Labour Department ; Committee of Enquiry into Government Labour Embargo Scheme ; Admiralty Shipbuilding Council ; Advisory Committees to Ministry of Munitions, Ministry of Labour, and Ministry of Reconstruction ; Standing Council on Post-War Priority. *Addresses :* The Manor House, Jesmond, Newcastle-on-Tyne ; Reedsmouth House, Northumberland ; 242, St. James's Court, London, S.W. 1. *Clubs :* Royal Automobile ; Royal Societies.　(K103)

ROWELL, Capt. William Henry, O.B.E. R.A.M.C. (T.).

ROWLAND, Arthur Margaret, M.B.E.

ROWLAND, Frank Mortimer, C.B.E., M.D., B.Ch., B.A. (Cantab.), M.R.C.S. (Eng.), L.R.C.P. (Lond.), *b.* 19 April, 1866 ; *s.* of William Samuel Rowland, of Wolverhampton and Lichfield ; *m.* Cornelia Isabel, *d.* of the Rev. W. H. A. Truell (*see* BURKE'S *Peerage*, E. of Moray), Clonmannon, Co. Wicklow. *Educ.:* Repton ; Caius Coll., Cambridge ; Univ. Coll., London ; Birmingham. County Hon. Treas. and Assistant County Director (Staffs Branch) B.R.C.S. ; Medical Referee, Ministry of Pensions ; Medical Referee, Workmen's Compensation Act (County Court Circuits 25 and 26) ; Medical Officer, Police, Post Office, Workhouse, Girls' High School, King Edward VII. School, Girls' Industrial School, Boys' Short Term Industrial

School. *War Work:* Medical Officer, Freeford Hall V.A.D. Hospital; Medical Officer, Ward in own private house; Organised Red Cross Transport locally; Chairman, Mid-Staffs Local Medical War Committee. *Address:* 26, St. John Street, Lichfield.   (C2922)

ROWLAND, Frederick, O.B.E., F.C.I.S., *b.* 13 April, 1871; *m.* Maud Mary, who was a member of the Natal Volunteer Nursing Service, and served through siege of Ladysmith (mentioned in despatches, Queen's Medal). Sec. South African Red Cross Society; Assist. Sec. Institute of Land Surveyors of the Transvaal. *War Work:* Boer War—assisted in formation of irregular Corps in Natal, Oct. 1899; subsequently Lieut. Bethune's Mounted Infantry on formation; promoted Capt., Dec. 1900 (Queen's Medal, 6 clasps; King's Medal, 2 clasps); Great War—Hon. Sec. South African Red Cross Society. *Addresses:* African Board of Executors Building, Sauer and Fox Streets, P. O. Box 3266; Barkly Road, Parktown West, Johannesburg. *Tel. Add.:* "Red Cross," Johannesburg.   (O8363)

ROWLAND, John, C.B.E., M.V.O., J.P., *b.* 1 June, 1877; *s.* of John Rowland, of Tregaron, Cardiganshire; *m.* Mair, *d.* of David Lewis, of Aberystwyth. *Educ.:* Technical Coll., Cardiff, and Univ. Coll., Aberystwyth. Member of Welsh Board of Health. *War Work:* Commissioner for National Service in Wales. *Addresses:* 166, Cathedral Road, Cardiff; City Hall, Cardiff; and Penbontfach, Tragaron.   (C283)

ROWLAND, Joseph Samuel, M.B.E., J.P.

ROWLAND, Margaret Lilian, O.B.E.; *d.* of Thomas Bushby, of Trevor, Llangollen; *m.* Sir Leonard Bromfield Rowland, Kt., *s.* of William Rowland, of Wrexham. Mayoress of Wrexham, 1915–18. *War Work:* Chairman and Organiser of R. W. F. Comforts Fund, and Wrexham Municipal War Work Committee; Member, Women's Land Army Committee, Q.M.A.A.C. Committee, Q.M. Needlework Guild, Y.M.C.A. local committee, Pensions Committee, Food Committee, etc. *Address:* Whybro House, Wrexham.   (O1827)

ROWLANDS, Capt. Archibald, M.B.E., A.C.C.

ROWLANDS, Richard Alun, O.B.E., M.D., B.S., B.Sc., M.R.C.P., *b.* 12 Sept. 1885; *s.* of Richard Rowlands, of Bryngwran, Anglesey. *Educ.:* Beaumaris Grammar School; Univ. Coll. of North Wales; London Hospital. Physician; Assistant Physician to the London Hospital; Physician to Poplar Hospital; Medical Tutor and Demonstrator of Physiology, London Hospital Medical College. *War Work:* Civil and Military Medical Work at the London and Poplar Hospitals. *Address:* 58, Queen Anne Street, Cavendish Square, W. 1.   (O11843)

ROWLANDS, Capt. Robert Pugh, O.B.E., M.B., F.R.C.S., R.A.M.C. (T.).

ROWLANDSON, Major Herbert Wynyard, O.B.E., I.A.

ROWLATT, Capt. Charles James. M.B.E., M.A., *b.* 24 Aug. 1894; *s.* of The Hon. Mr. Justice Rowlatt, Q.C. *Educ.:* Eton and Univ. Coll., Oxford. Assistant Master at Eton College. *War Work:* Oct. 1914, gazetted 2nd Lieut. 13th Batt. Rifle Brigade; March, 1916, promoted Lieut.; July, 1916, wounded in the 1st Battle of the Somme; Feb. 1918, appointed General Staff Officer (3rd Grade) in the Intelligence Directorate, War Office. *Address:* Eton College, Windsor. *Clubs:* Oxford and Cambridge; Leander Rowing.

ROWLATT, Capt. Frederick George, M.B.E.

ROWLATT, Sir Frederick Terry, K.B.E., *b.* 10 Feb. 1865; *s.* of late A. H. Rowlatt; *m.* Edith May, *d.* of J. E. Cornish, C.M.G. *Educ.:* Fettes Coll., Edinburgh. Fellow, Inst. of Bankers, London; Grand Cordon of the Medjidieh and of the Nile; Governor, National Bank of Egypt; President, Agricultural Bank of Egypt; President, Bank of Abyssinia. *Address:* National Bank of Egypt, Head Office, Cairo, Egypt. (K324)

ROWLATT, Lieut. John Henry, M.B.E., R.A.S.C.

ROWLEDGE, Arthur John, M.B.E.

ROWLEY, Amy Isabel, Lady, O.B.E., *b.* 21 Oct. 1867; *d.* of William Forster Batt, of Cae Kenfy, Abergavenny; *m.* George Charles Erskine (3rd Baronet) (*see* BURKE'S *Peerage*), *s.* of Major George Rowley, of Bombay Light Cavalry. *War Work:* Vice-President Guildford Division, B.R.C.S., 1910–20; Commandant Hill House Hospital, Guildford; Staff Commandant, Red Cross Annexe, Royal Surrey County Hospital, Guildford. *Address:* Eastfield Lodge, Guildford. *Club:* V.A.D. Ladies.   (O704)

ROWLEY, Capt. Charles Donovan, M.B.E., R.A.

ROWLEY, Capt. Howard Fiennes Julius, C.B.E., R.N. (ret.), *b.* 14 Aug. 1868; *4th s.* of the Rev. Julius Henry Rowley, M.A., rector of South Ockendon, Essex (*see* BURKE'S *Peerage*); *m.* 27 Mar. 1900, Alice Udall, *d.* of the late William Paterson Muir, of Melbourne, Victoria. Served in the Great War; has American Distinguished Service Medal. *Address:* The Ingle, Weybridge. *Club:* United Service.   (C1167)

ROWLEY, Mary Mildred, M.B.E.; *d.* of Smith Howlett Rowley, J.P., Histon, Cambs. *Educ.:* Cambridge. *War Work:* Commandant, Histon Red Cross Hospital, 1914–19. *Address:* Histon, Cambs.   (M911)

ROWLINSON, George Henry, M.B.E., J.P., *b.* 24 July, 1852; *s.* of Samuel Rowlinson, of Walsall; *m.* Sarah, *d.* of John Lane, of Cheltenham. Late Miners' Agent for Forest of Dean; Chairman of East Dean Rural District Council; Vice-Chairman, Westbury-on-Severn Board of Guardians; Chairman, Forest of Dean Group of Council Schools. *War Work:* Chairman of War Savings Committee (East Dean); Chairman of Local Recruiting Committee Vice-

Chairman of East Dean Recruiting Tribunal; Chairman, Belgian Refugees Committee; Chairman, East Dean Meritorious War Fund, etc. *Address:* Prospect House, Cinderford, Gloucestershire. *Club:* Gloucester Liberal.   (M912)

ROWLLINGS, Major Alfred Lefevre, O.B.E., *b.* 1869; *s.* of Edward Rowllings, of Corby, Lincolnshire; *m.* Elizabeth, *d.* of Stephen Wilkinson, of Lindley, Yorkshire. *Educ.:* Corby Grammar School, and Edinburgh. Marine Superintendent. *War Work:* Mesopotamia, 1917 to 1918; Egypt, 1918 and 1919; mentioned in despatches 3 times. *Addresses:* 28, Park Mansions; 2, Clive Ghat Street, Calcutta; Ash Vale, Surrey.   (O2296)

ROWNTREE, John Harvey Wodville, M.B.E.

ROWORTH, Harry James, M.B.E., *b.* 25 April, 1870; *s.* of Thomas Roworth, of London; *m.* Emily Ellen, *d.* of A. MacDonald, of London. *Educ.:* St. Thomas, Charterhouse (Goswell Road), and Birkbeck Institute. Railway Accountant; Head of Division, Railway Clearing House. *War Work:* Ministry of Munitions, June, 1915, to June, 1920; Statistical work for Gun Ammunition Dept. until Armistice; then appointed Section Director in charge of Records and Statistics for Liquidator of Projectile Contracts. *Address:* 94, Duke's Avenue, Chiswick, W. 4.   (M913)

ROWS, Lieut.-Col. Richard Gundry, C.B.E., M.D.

ROWSE, Arthur Albert, M.B.E.

ROWSELL, Comm. Clarence Ralph, C.B.E., R.N. A Div. Naval Transport Officer; served in the Great War, 1914–19 (despatches).   (C2263)

ROXBURGH, Eleanor Mary Ann, Lady, C.B.E.; *d.* of the late Sir Thomas Chambers, Q.C.; *m.* 1888, as his second wife, Sir Francis Roxburgh, Q.C., who *d.* 1891. *Addresses:* 12, Devonshire Place, W.; Glenisla, Felixstowe, Suffolk.   (C60)

ROXBURGHE, Annie Emily, Duchess of, V.A., O.B.E., *d.* of 7th Duke of Marlborough (*see* BURKE'S *Peerage*), and widow of 7th Duke of Roxburghe (*see* BURKE'S *Peerage*). Was Mistress of the Robes to H.M. Queen Victoria, 1883; extra Lady of the Bedchamber to H.M. Queen Victoria, 1895–97; and a lady of the Bedchamber to H.M. Queen Victoria, 1897–1901. *Address:* Broxmouth Park, Dunbar.   (O3899)

ROXBY, Lieut.-Col. Francis Maude, O.B.E., D.F.C., R.A.F.

ROY, Jotindra Nath, O.B.E., I.C.S.

ROY, Thomas, O.B.E.

ROYALL, William, M.B.E., R.N.

ROYCE, Elizabeth Lilian, M.B.E.

ROYCE, Frederick Henry, O.B.E., M.I.M.E., M.I.E.E., *b.* 27 March, 1863; *s.* of the late James Royce, Corn Miller, of Allwalton, nr. Peterborough. *Educ.:* Croydon; City Guilds' Technical Coll., London. Mechanical and Electrical Engineer; one of the Founders and Directors of Royce, Ltd., Manchester, and Rolls-Royce, Ltd., Derby and London. *War Work:* Responsible for the design and manufacture of the aero engines made by the Rolls-Royce Company, and other firms, known as the "Eagle," "Falcon," "Hawk," and "Condor"; also airship gearing, etc. *Address:* Elmstead, West Wittering, nr. Chichester.   (O705)

ROYDEN, Ethel Martha, O.B.E.

ROYDS, Lieut.-Col. Albert Henry, O.B.E., *b.* 7 April, 1876; *s.* of Edmund Albert Nuttall, of Failinge, Lancs.; *m.* Adeliza Beatrix, *d.* of George James Drummond, of Swaylands, Penshurst, Kent. *Educ.:* Eton. Lieut.-Col. (retired) Scots Guards; joined Scots Guards, 1899; Capt. 1904; Major, 1914; Lieut.-Col. 1919; served in S. African War, 1900–2 (Queen's Medal with 3 clasps; King's Medal with 2 clasps), *War Work:* Served in France from Aug. 1915, to Dec. 1918, as Commandant Guards Divisional Base Depot; mentioned twice in despatches. *Addresses:* Brownhill, Rochdale; Kenegil, Gulval, nr. Penzance. *Clubs:* Guards'; Carlton; United Service.   (O2705)

ROYDS, Annie Bourne, M.B.E.

ROYDS, Lieut.-Col. Edmund, O.B.E., M.P.

ROYDS, Margaret Ada, Mrs., M.B.E.; *d.* of Charles Everard, of Cawthorpe, nr. Bourne, Lincs.; *m.* Charles Cradock Twemlow, *s.* of Charles Twemlow Royds, of Heysham, Lancs. *War Work:* A private Hospital at Heysham Rectory. *Address:* Heysham Rectory, Lancs.   (M9515)

ROYLANCE, Ethel Manford, Mrs., O.B.E. *War Work:* Officer-in-charge, Auxiliary Military Hospital, Assembly Rooms, Bowdon, Cheshire.   (M9516)

ROYLE, Capt. Ernest Rupert, O.B.E.

ROYLE, Sir George, O.B.E., F.R.G.S., J.P., *b.* 3 Nov. 1861; *s.* of the late George Royle, Bury, Lancs.; *m.* Rosetta, *d.* of W. Wilford, of Northants. *Educ.:* Clarke Street Schools, Bury, and Privately. Mayor of Bedford, 1903; Chairman of Bedfordshire National Health Insurance, and National Savings Committees. *War Work:* Hon. Recruiting Officer Army, appointed 1914; Navy, appointed 1915; Hon. Gen. Sec. Derby Scheme; National Service Representative to two Tribunals; Chairman of Belgian Refugees Committee, Bedford; Chairman of the War Savings and War Loan Committee, Bedford, etc. *Clubs:* National Liberal; Eighty; Bedford De Pary's.   (O11252)

ROYLE, Leonard, M.B.E., *b.* 15 Feb. 1883; *s.* of Booth Royle, of Manchester. *War Work:* Commandant, East Lances. 77 Voluntary Aid Detachment, British Red Cross Society. *Address:* 3, St. James's Square, Manchester. (M9517)

ROYLE, Thomas Wright, M.B.E., A.M.I.T., *b.* 27 Sept. 1882; *s.* of T. W. Royle, of Manchester; *m.* Mary Ellen, *d.* of Charles Elliott, of Manchester. *Educ.:* Manchester. Assistant

Superintendent of the Line Lancashire and Yorkshire Railway, and Associate Member Institute of Transport. *War Work:* Railway work in connection with Railway Executive Committee. *Address:* 12, Hawkshead Street, Southport, Lancs.
(M915)

ROYTHORNE, Herbert, M.B.E.

ROZARIO, Michael Anthony, M.B.E.

RUBENSTEIN, Vera Rachel, Mrs., M.B.E., W.R.N.S.

RUBIE, Major John, O.B.E., R.A.F.

RUBY, Anna Colburn, M.B.E.; *d.* of the Rev. James Smith Ruby, M.A., of Murragh Rectory, Bandon, Co. Cork, Ireland. *Educ.:* At private schools, Clifton (England), and Dublin. *Address:* Bride Park, Ovens, Co. Cork. (M9519)

RUCK, Capt. Richard Conyers, O.B.E., I.A.

RUCK, Major-Gen. Sir Richard Matthews, K.B.E., C.B., C.M.G., *b.* 1851; *s.* of the late Laurence Ruck, of Newington Manor House, Kent. Entered R.E., 1871; Capt., 1883; Major, 1889; Lieut.-Col., 1896; Brevet Col. 1901; Col., 1904; Maj.-Gen. 1908; retired, 1912; Assist. Instructor in Telegraphy, Sch. of Mil. Engineering, 1881–85; Assist. Inspector Submarine Mining Defences 1886-91, Inspector Mining Defences at Headquarters, 1891–96; Dep. Inspector-Gen. of Fortifications, 1902–4; Director of Fortifications and Works, 1904–8; Maj.-Gen. in charge of Administration, E. Command, 1908–12 and 1915–16; was a Chief Engineer 1914–15. *Address:* 44, Thurloe Square, S.W. (K417)

RUCKER, Reginald Wynn, C.B.E., *b.* 27 Dec. 1854; *s.* of the late Daniel Henry Rucker, of Errington, Clapham Park; *m.* Frances Mary, *d.* of the late Henry Harrod, F.R.S.A., of Aylsham, Norfolk. *Educ.:* Clifton Coll., B.N.C., Oxford. Partner in Henry Rogers, Sons & Co., of 85, Gracechurch Street, E.C., Metal Merchants; Chairman of Committee of London Metal Exchange, 1897–1901, and 1916–19. Director of Messrs. P. H. Muntz & Co., Ltd., West Bromwich, Yellow Metal Manufacturers; Director of British Metal Corporation, 3, Abchurch Yard, E.C. *War Work:* Ministry of Munitions, 1916, to Sept. 1919 (Copper Committee, Assistant Controller of Non-Ferrous Materials, Supply Dept.); Feb. to Sept. 1919, Controller and Liquidator of Non-Ferrous Materials. *Address:* 113, Kenilworth Court, Putney. (C2923)

RUDD, Lieut.-Col. Hubert, O.B.E.

RUDD, Col. Thomas William, C.B.E., R.A.V.C. Served on the N.-W. Frontier of India, 1897–98 (medal); in the Great War, 1914–19 (despatches). (C1318)

RUDDEN, Capt. Bernard, M.B.E., *b.* 10 March. 1877; *s.* of Charles Rudden, of Armagh; *m.* Mary, *d.* of John McGrath, of Carlisle. *Educ.:* Private School. Enlisted Border Regt., Aug. 1894; Lieut., British West Indies Regt., Nov. 1916; Capt., Dec. 1918. *War Work:* Served in the Field—Egypt, Belgium, France, and Italy. *Address:* 11, Peter Street, Carlisle. (M2972)

RUDDER, Capt. Charles Joseph, O.B.E.

RUDDICK, John, M.B.E.

RUDDIN, John Henry, M.B.E., *b.* 1 Nov. 1871; *s.* of James Ruddin, of Liverpool; *m.* Ethel Mary, *d.* of Thomas Hamson, of Liverpool. *Educ.:* Ampleforth Coll., Yorkshire. *War Work:* Technical Adviser to Ministry of Food. *Address:* 12, Sutton Court Road, Chiswick, London, W. (M9521)

RUDDLE, Frank William, O.B.E.

RUDDLE, George, M.B.E.

RUDDOCK, Thomas Emerson, C.B.E., *b.* 1873; *s.* of the late Thomas Ruddock, of Gosforth, Newcastle-on-Tyne; *m.* 1899, Elizabeth, *d.* of the late William English, of Newcastle, on-Tyne. *Educ.:* Privately. Shipowner and Coal Exporter; Head of Norwegian Section, Ministry of Shipping, since 1917; Principal Coal and Shipping Adviser to Mins. in Christiania, Stockholm and Copenhagen, 1916–17. *Address:* Kingswood, Gosforth, Newcastle-on-Tyne. *Clubs:* Junior Constitutional Northern Conservative (Newcastle-on-Tyne). (C608)

RUDGARD, Henry John, O.B.E., M.I.C.E., *b.* 1 Dec. 1866; *s.* of J. R. Rudgard, of Lincoln. *Educ.:* Malvern Coll., and St. Peter's, York. Assistant Engineer (Maintenance), North Eastern Railway, York. *Address:* Aldeen, St. Peter's Grove, York. (O11254)

RUDGE, Louise Alice, M.B.E.

RUDGE, Florence Mrs., HAYNES-, C.B.E.; *d.* of the late Charles Fox; *m.* 1st, Edward Charles Rudge, J.P., of Abbey Manor, Evesham, Worcestershire, who died; 2ndly, 1916, Capt. Leonard Haynes, Worcestershire Yeo., who assumed the additional surname of Rudge. *War Work:* Comdt. and Donor Abbey Manor Auxiliary Hospital, Evesham, during European War. *Address:* Evesham, Worcestershire. (C1033)

RUDKIN, George Drury, O.B.E., B.A., *b.* 22 Jan. 1879; *s.* of G. M. A. Rudkin, of Teignmouth; *m.* Heather Kathleen, *d.* of F. E. Little, of Teignmouth. *Educ.:* Blundells School and Balliol Coll., Oxford. Indian Civil Service; Revenue and Finance Member of Council, Bikaner, India. *War Work:* President of War Board, Bikaner. *Addresses:* Bikaner, Rajputana, India; c/o Cox & Co., 16, Charing Cross, London, S.W. *Clubs:* E. I. United Service. (O4087)

RUDKIN, Major Hugh Ernest, O.B.E.

RUDLAND, Paymaster-Lieut. Henry Alfred, O.B.E., R.N.R.

RUDOLF, Col. Robert Dawson, C.B.E., M.D., F.R.C.P., *b.* 1865; *s.* of William Norman Rudolf; *m.* 1894, Rosa Marguerite Danson. *Educ.:* Birkenhead School and Edinburgh Univ. Canadian Army Med. Corps; Professor of Therapeutics in Toronto Univ.; sometime Consulting Physician, Canadian Forces. *Addresses:* 100, College Street, Toronto;

147, Farnham Avenue, Toronto. *Club:* York (Toronto).
(C284)

RUEGG, Alfred James, M.B.E.

RUFFELL, Frederick, O.B.E., *b.* 10 Feb. 1872; *s.* of J. Ruffell, of Watford Gap, Northamptonshire; *m.* Lillian Ellena, *d.* of B. Attwell, of Somerset. *Educ.:* Privately; Rugby. Superintendent of Rolling Stock, L. & N. W. Rly., Crewe. *War Work:* Responsible for preparation of troop trains, etc.; Also provision of stock for all Munitions of War, etc., and was one of those responsible for scheme and working of common user of waggons on the railways. *Address:* Oak Lodge, Penkridge, Staffs. (O11255)

RUFFER, Ferdinand Robert, M.B.E.

RUFFLE, Capt. William Harry, M.B.E., R.A.M.C., *b.* 14 Dec. 1872; *s.* of George William Harry Ruffle, of London; *m.* Annie Elizabeth Emma, *d.* of Arthur Prickett, of Maidstone. *Educ.:* London. Capt. R.A.S.C.; South Africa, 1901–2. *War Work:* Curragh, 1914; England and France, 1915, as O.C L. of C. Units, 32nd Division; German East Africa, 1916–1 as O.C. Imperial Section, East African Expeditionary Force, graded as Staff Capt. *Address:* Curragh Camp, Co. Kildare, Ireland. (M3066)

RULE, Alexander, M.B.E., D.Sc., Ph.D., F.I.C., *b.* 15 Aug. 1880; *s.* of Alexander Rule, of Liverpool. *Educ.:* Merchant Taylors' School, Crosby; Victoria Univ., Univ. of Jena. Lecturer in Chemistry, Univ. of Liverpool. *War Work:* Superintendent of Wood Distillation Factories, and Administrative Officer of Wood Distillation Factories, Ministry of Munitions. *Address:* 33, Melling Road, Southport, Lancs. *Clubs:* University, Liverpool; Chemical Industry, London (M3949)

RULE, Lieut.-Col. John Allan, O.B.E., *b.* 29 July, 1878; *s.* of J. A. Rule, of Cincinnati, Ohio, U.S.A. *Educ.:* Public Schools, U.S.A. *War Work:* Dardanelles, May to Aug. 1915; wounded, Aug. 1915; Egypt, Oct. 1915, to Sept. 1916; Salonica Force, Sept. 1916 to Dec. 1918, except Sept. to Oct. 1917, when served in France and Italy; Russia, Transcaucasia, Dec. 1918, to July, 1920; Turkey, July to Aug. 1920. Four times mentioned in despatches. *Clubs:* Thatched House; Canton (China); Constantinople.

RUMBOLD, Etheldred Constantia, Lady, C.B.E., *b.* 3 July, 1879; *d.* of Sir Edmund Fane, K.C.M.G., of Boyton Manor, Wilts; *m.* Rt. Hon. Sir Horace, Bt., P.C., K.C.M.G., M.V.O., *s.* of Sir Horace Rumbold, G.C.B. *War Work:* President of Prisoners of War Bread Bureau at Berne, 1916–19, and of British Legation Red Cross in Switzerland, 1916–19. *Address:* British Legation, Warsaw, Poland. (C2924)

RUMBOLL, Arthur Charles, C.I.E., O.B.E.

RUMFORD, Dame Clara Ellen BUTT-, D.B.E., *b.* 1 Feb. 1873; *d.* of Capt. H. A. Butt, of Bristol; *m.* Robert Kennerley, *s.* of Joseph Kennerley Rumford, of London. *Educ.:* Royal College of Music. Singer. *War Work:* Gave over £80,000 by means of concerts and pageants to various war charities. *Address:* 7, Harley Road, London.

RUMMINS, Major Henry, O.B.E.

RUNCIMAN, Henry Weir, M.B.E.

RUNDALL, Col. Frank Montagu, C.B., D.S.O., O.B.E., *b.* 1851; *s.* of the late Gen. Francis Hornblow Rundall; *m.* 1876, Emily Rosa, *e. d.* of the late Rt. Rev. Edward Henry Bickersteth. Served Burma War (medal with clasp); Chin-Lushai Expedition (despatches, clasp); Chin Hills, Commanding Column as Political Officer (despatches); was A.A.G. 9th Div. S. Command, India; Commanding Group A, City of London Vol. Regt. (mentioned). *Address:* 25, Porchester Square, Bayswater, W. (O7660)

RUNDELL, Comm. Matthew Adkins, C.B.E., *b.* 1856; *s.* of Matthew Rundell, of Devonport; *m.* Susan, *d.* of W. W. Rundell, of Liverpool. *Educ.:* Plymouth Grammar School. *War Work:* Govt. Representative on London Group of War Insurance Associations (Ships), and also on Fishing Vessels War Insurance Association. *Address:* Grove Park, Kent. *Club:* London University. (C285)

RUNDLE, Brevet Lieut.-Col. Claude, O.B.E., M.D., R.A.M.C. (T.), *b.* 1873; *s.* of the late J. P. Rundle, of Saltash, Cornwall; *m.* Florence Maltby, *d.* of William Kerruish, of Isle of Man. *Educ.:* Plymouth Grammar School. Superintendent, Fazakerley Hospitals and Sanatorium, Liverpool; Lecturer, Univ. of Liverpool. *War Work:* Registrar, 1st Western General Hospital, Liverpool; Officer Commanding, Berrington War Hospital, Shrewsbury; Officer Commanding, No. 54 General Hospital, France Expeditionary Force. *Address:* Fazakerley Hospital, Liverpool. *Club:* University (Liverpool).

RUNDLE, Comm. Henry John Montague, O.B.E., R.N., Chevalier of the Legion of Honour, *b.* 29 Oct. 1874; *s.* of the late Robert Rundle, of Stoke, Devonport; *m.* Alida, *d.* of the late Rev. J. P. Jourdan, of Victoria West, South Africa. *Educ.:* Stubbington House, Fareham, and H.M.S. "Britannia." Served in Royal Navy, 1890–1919. *War Work:* Intelligence Officer on Staff of Commander-in-Chief, Coast of Scotland, Aug. 1914, to March, 1917; Assistant Director of Minesweeping, Naval Staff, Admiralty, March, 1917, to Oct. 1919. *Club:* Junior Army and Navy. (O1830)

RUNGE, Norah Cecil, Mrs., O.B.E.; *d.* of Lawrence Hasluck; *m.* Julius Joseph Runge. *War Work:* Superintendent Sailors' and Soldiers' Free Buffet, Paddington Sattion. *Address:* 24, Westbourne Terrace, W. 2. (O708)

RUNTZ, Sidney Westwood, C.B.E., F.C.A., *b.* 1875; *s.* of Sir John Runtz, of Tunnel Woods, Watford. *Educ.:* Uppingham. *War Work:* Financial Adviser to the Coal Mines

Department of Board of Trade. *Address:* Tunnel Woods, Watford. *Club:* City Carlton. (C2925)

RUSH, Frederick Charles, O.B.E. (O7933)

RUSH, Engineer Thomas Arthur Edwin, M.B.E., R.N., *b.* 19 April, 1869; *s.* of Thomas Rush, of Floore, near Weedon, Northamptonshire; *m.* Elizabeth, *d.* of William Jackson, of Northampton. *Educ.:* Weedon Grammar School. Commissioned Engineer, R.N. *War Work:* Artificer Engineer in H.M.S. "Hogue" until Torpedoed; next H.M.S. "Actæon"; to Torpedo Boat No. 3, for escort duty from Newhaven to France (night work for 2 years); and to H.M.S. Destroyer "Pigeon," for escort and patrol duties from Buncrana, North of Ireland, until Oct. 1919. *Addresses:* R.N. Depot, Immingham; 39, Linden Road, Gillingham, Kent. (M2377)

RUSH, Major John Shipman, O.B.E.

RUSH, Lieut. William, M.B.E.

RUSHALL, Richard Boswell, M.B.E., *b.* 6 March, 1865; *s.* of Benjamin Rushall, of Braunston, Northamptonshire; *m.* Charlotte Sarah, *d.* of Charles Trype, of Rangoon. *Educ.:* National School, Braunston. Sole proprietor of Rushall & Co., Stevedores, Rangoon. *Address:* Post Office Box, 197, Rangoon; Lyndene, Clifton Road, Rugby. (M9524)

RUSHTON, Capt. Leveson, M.B.E.

RUSHWORTH, Mary, M.B.E., Q.M.A.A.C.

RUSSELL, Major Alexander, O.B.E., M.C.

RUSSELL, Alexandra Alberta, M.B.E., *b.* 10 Jan. 1883; *d.* of Major-Gen. John Cecil Russell, C.V.O., Extra Equerry to King Edward VII., and Col. of 12th Royal Lancers, of Barton Court, Canterbury. *War Work:* Commandant, Dane John Hospital, Canterbury, V.A.D. Kent 186. *Address:* Barton Court, Canterbury, Kent. (M3950)

RUSSELL, Lieut. Arthur Edward Jan Montague, M.B.E.

RUSSELL, Rev. Cecil Edward, M.B.E., *b.* 18 June, 1889; *s.* of W. H. Russell, of Muswell Hill; *m.* Cicely Cherry, *d.* of A. J. Squire, of Ealing. *Educ.:* Owens School, and King's Coll., Univ. of London. Priest, St. Saviour, Ealing, 1913–18; Vicar of Manston, near Leeds, 1919. *War Work:* Assistant to Sec., Clergy National Service Committee, then Assistant to Sec., Boy Labour Section, National Service Dept.; finally in charge of Boy Labour Section, Ministry of National Service. *Address:* Manston Vicarage, Cross Gates, nr. Leeds. *Club:* Scouts'. (M3951)

RUSSELL, Delia Constance, Mrs., O.B.E. (O12013)

RUSSELL, Diana, M.B.E.

RUSSELL, Major Edmond Cecil, O.B.E.

RUSSELL, Comm. Edward Holden, O.B.E., R.N.

RUSSELL, Edward John, O.B.E., F.R.S., D.Sc., Officer of the Order of the Crown of Belgium, *b.* 1872; *s.* of the late Rev. E. T. Russell, of Glasgow; *m.* Elnor, *d.* of the late Walter Oldham, of Singapore and Manchester. *Educ.:* Univ. Coll. of Wales, Aberystwyth; Victoria Univ., Manchester. Director of the Rothamsted Experimental Station, Harpenden. *War Work:* Technical Adviser, Food Production Dept.; Member of the Munitions Inventions Panel and of the National Salvage Council, 1917. *Address:* Laboratory House, Harpenden, Herts. *Club:* Savile. (O709)

RUSSELL, Capt. Ernest Gordon, O.B.E., R.A.S.C.

RUSSELL, Ethel, Mrs., M.B.E.

RUSSELL, Frederick Vernon, C.B.E., *b.* 7 May, 1870; *s.* of Henry Vernon Russell, R.N., of Warwick; *m.* Gladys, *d.* of — Sala, of Carcassone. *Educ.:* Christ's Hospital. Superintendent of Operation, Great Eastern Railway. *War Work:* Railway Operating, Military and Civil; public safety precautions, especially in connection with the East Coast; protection of the public and railway, etc., in connection with hostile aircraft. *Address:* 17, Teesdale Road, Leytonstone, E. 11. (C2926)

RUSSELL, George Dearie, O.B.E.

RUSSELL, George Shipton, M.B.E., *b.* 8 Feb. 1878; *s.* of Herbert Russell, of Lichfield; *m.* Ella Maud, *d.* of Robert Colegate, of Sutton, Surrey. *Educ.:* Rossall. Solicitor; Under-Sheriff of the City of Lichfield. *War Work:* As an amateur mechanic constructed a four-stretcher ambulance, and maintained and drove it over 25,000 miles without a breakdown. *Address:* Gaialands, Lichfield. (M9527)

RUSSELL, Major Harry William, O.B.E., M.D., R.A.M.C. *b.* 31 March, 1877; *s.* of the late Rev. Canon E. J. Russell, of Todmorden. *Educ.:* Rossall and Manchester. Major, R.A.M.C. *War Work:* O.C. 8 B.F.A., France and Mesopotamia; O.C. Officers' Hospital, Baghdad; O.C. Military Hospital, Mosul. *Address:* c/o Holt & Co., 3, Whitehall Place, Westminster, S.W. (O6697)

RUSSELL, Lieut.-Comm. Harold David Watts, O.B.E., R.N.R. R.D.

RUSSELL, Henry Alexander, M.B.E.

RUSSELL, Capt. Henry Hartley Aloysius, O.B.E.

RUSSELL, Herbert Ernest Henry, O.B.E.

RUSSELL, Sir Herbert William Henry, K.B.E., *b.* 28 March, 1869; *s.* of W. Clark Russell, of Bath; *m.* Lucie Marion, *d.* of Charles Meech, of Beaminster, Dorset. *Educ.:* Royal Grammar School, Newcastle-on-Tyne, and privately. Reuter's War Correspondent. *War Work:* Gallipoli, June to Sept. 1915 (invalided home with dysentery); France, Dec. 1915, to Nov. 1918; received Order of Chevalier of the Legion of Honour from French Government; gave first news to the world of opening of Somme offensive, capture of Bapaume, and fall of Lille. *Address:* Plymouth. *Club:* Royal South-Western Yacht. (K418)

RUSSELL, Janie, M.B.E.; *d.* of John Russell, of Middlefield, Cupar, Fife, and Helen McLaren, Castle Hill, Perthshire. *Educ.:* Madras Coll. *War Work:* Canteening with the French Army in war zone, 1916; assisted in Chester Gate Canteen, Regent's Park; decorated for work in connection with the repatriation of civilian prisoners. *Address:* 6, Grosvenor Place, S.W. 1. *Club:* Forum. (M9529)

RUSSELL, John, M.B.E., *b.* 25 May, 1857; *s.* of John Russell, of Newcastle-on-Tyne; *m.* Eleanor Jane, *d.* of Robert Bunn, of Gateshead-on-Tyne. *Educ.:* Kidman's Academy, Newcastle-on-Tyne. Certified Sanitary Inspector; Chief Inspector to the Tyne Port Sanitary Authority. *War Work:* Voluntary Services rendered in the transport of sick and wounded naval patients during the period of the war. *Address:* Port Sanitary Offices, Mill Dam, South Shields. (M9530)

RUSSELL, John, O.B.E., Major 5th N. Staffs. Regt. (ret.), *b.* 30 July, 1862; *s.* of John Russell, of Insch, Aberdeenshire; *m.* Alice, *d.* of the late Peter Whyte, of Streatham, London. *Educ.:* Aberdeen Univ. Hon. Physician, N. Staff. Infirmary. *War Work:* Assistant Director, British Red Cross Society, N. Staffordshire; Physician, Stoke-on-Trent War Hospital. *Address:* Bleak Hill House, Burslem, Stoke-on-Trent. (O711)

RUSSELL, Mary Ruth, Lady, M.B.E., *b.* 8 Jan. 1859; *d.* of the late Capt. George Boyes Prior, R.A.; *m.* Sir James A., LL.D., *s.* of the Rev. Alex. Fraser Russell, M.A. *War Work:* Convener, Ladies' Committee, Boys' Brigade, Y.M.C.A. Rest Hut, 1915–19. *Address:* Woodville, Canaan Lane, Edinburgh. (M9531)

RUSSELL, Mildred, M.B.E., *b.* 1866; *d.* of Capt. Andrew Hamilton Russell, of The Heath House, Petersfield. *Educ.:* Lausanne. *War Work:* Divisional Sec., Petersfield British Red Cross Society. *Address:* The Heath House, Petersfield, Hants. (M3952)

RUSSELL, Rachel Augusta, M.B.E., *b.* 20 Nov. 1888; *d.* of Champion B. Russell, of Stubbers, North Ockendon, Essex. *War Work:* Ministry of Munitions, July, 1915, to June, 1919; Private Sec. to the Sec. Ministry of Munitions, Sept. 1917, to June, 1919. *Address:* 258, King's Road, Chelsea, S.W. 3. (M2379)

RUSSELL, Lieut.-Col. Reginald Edmund Maghlin, C.B.E., D.S.O., *b.* 1870; *s.* of E. M. Russell, of Milford House, Limerick; *m.* 1918, Dorothy, *d.* of the late Major E. B. Crake, Rifle Brig. *Educ.:* Cheltenham Coll. Entered R.E., 1898; became Capt., 1907; Major, 1915; Brevet Lieut.-Col., 1918; served in S. Africa, 1901–2 (despatches, Queen's medal with five clasps); with Anuak Expedition, 1912 (medal, Order of Medjidieh); and during the Great War, 1914–15, on Suez Canal Defences, and subsequently on Gen. Staff, Headquarters, Cairo (despatches, Order of the Nile and of SS. Maurice and Lazarus of Italy, Brevet Lieut.-Col.); attached to Egyptian Army, 1905–15; was a Gen. Staff Officer, 1916; and a Chief Engineer, 1917–19. *Club:* Naval and Military. (C1905)

RUSSELL, Capt. Thomas, O.B.E., R.A.M.C. (T.).

RUSSELL, Thomas Wentworth, O.B.E.

RUSSELL, Lieut.-Col. the Hon. Victor Alexander Frederick Villiers, O.B.E., B.A., *b.* 27 June, 1874; *s.* of Lord Odo William Russell, 1st Lord Ampthill (*see* BURKE's *Peerage*); *m.* Annora Margaret Bromley, *d.* of late George Edward Martin, of Ham Court, Worcester (*see* BURKE's *Peerage*). *Educ.:* Wellington New Coll., Oxford. Barrister-at-law; Lieut.-Col. 5th Batt. Bedfordshire Regt. *Address:* 17, Hornton Street, W. *Club:* Brooks's. (O8183)

RUSSELL, William Archibald, M.B.E.

RUSSELL, Wm. John, O.B.E., J.P., D.L., *b.* 1853; *s.* of Rear-Admiral John Russell, of Maulside, Ayrshire; *m.* Jessie Blake, *d.* of Robert Finnie, of Newfield, Kilmarnock. Deputy Chairman, Lanarkshire and Ayrshire Railway, and Deputy Chairman, Ardrossan Harbour Co. *War Work:* Convener of County of Ayr during period of the War, and therefore connected with various war associations, and war work in the county. *Address:* Maulside, Glengarnock, Ayrshire. *Clubs:* County (Ayr); New (Edinburgh). (O11256)

RUSSELL, William Sidney, M.B.E.

RUSSELL, Capt. William Sydney Kemp, O.B.E., *b.* 14 Dec. 1895; *s.* of W. J. Russell, of Hayes House, Hayes, Kent; *m.* Dorothy, *d.* of W. Durran, of 30, Vereker Road, W. *Educ.:* St. Vincents, Eastbourne; Shrewsbury; and Pembroke Coll., Cambridge. *War Work:* 2nd Lieut. Royal Sussex Regt., 1914; served in France with K.R.R.C. 1916–18; Censorship and Publicity Section, General Staff, G.H.Q., France, 1918–19. *Address:* South Lodge, Grange Road, Eastbourne. (O5741)

RUSSELL, Hon. Eustace Scott HAMILTON-, O.B.E., J.P., *b.* 7 Feb. 1878; *s.* of Gustavus Russell, 8th Viscount Boyne, D.L., J.P.; *m.* Olive Mary, *d.* of Francis Alexander Woolryche-Whitmore, J.P., of Dudnaston, Salop (*see* BURKE's *Landed Gentry*). Late Lieut. 5th Batt. Northumberland Fusiliers. *Address:* Stoke Lodge, Ludlow. *Club:* Junior Carlton. (O3900)

RUST, John. M.B.E., M.R.C.S., L.R.C.P.

RUST, Capt. Percy, M.B.E.

RUSTON, Henry Thomas, M.B.E.

RUSTON, John Albert Edgar, M.B.E.

RUTHEN, Sir Charles Tamlin, O.B.E., *b.* 22 Oct 1871; *s.* of the late John Ruthen, of South Shields; *m.* Matilda Jane, *d.* of the late William Bondfield Westlake, of Swansea. *Educ.:* Public School, South Shields, and privately. Fellow of the Royal Institute of British Architects; President of the Society of Architects; Member of the Council of the Institute of Arbitrators and of the London Society; Fellow of the Royal

Society of Arts ; Member of the Concrete Institute, Grants Committee of the Ministry of Labour, and General Advisory Committee of the Empire Timber Exhibition, 1920 ; *War Work :* Inspector, War Cabinet Committee on Accommodation, 1917–18 ; Chief Inspector and Deputy Controller for London Area, 1918–20 ; now Consulting Chief Inspector of Accommodation, H.M. Office of Works (honorary appointments) ; Capt. R.A.S.C., M.T. (V.) ; Special Constabulary (Motor Ambulance), County Borough of Swansea. *Addresses :* Dderwen-fawr, Blackpyl, Swansea ; Bank Chambers, Heathfield Street, Swansea ; 44, Bedford Row, London, W.C. 1. *Clubs :* National Liberal ; Swansea Liberal ; Swiss Alpine. (O1832)

RUTHERFORD, Ernest Victor Buckley, O.B.E., C.C., *b.* 1871 ; *s.* of James Buckley Rutherford, of London ; *m.* Alice Maud Julia, *d.* of Wm. Oliver, of Hove. *Educ. :* Westminster. Adviser on wines and spirits to War Office. *War Work :* Sub-Inspector, Special Constabulary, F Div. ; Adviser to War Office on wines and spirits. *Address :* 29, Orsett Terrace, Hyde Park, W. *Clubs :* Junior Carlton ; Ranelagh. (O11257)

RUTHERFORD, Eva Lydia, Mrs., O.B.E.

RUTHERFORD, Capt. Percival Thomas, O.B.E., *b.* 21 Nov. 1884 ; *s.* of John James Rutherford, M.D., of Rock Villa, Shipley, Yorks ; *m.* Lilian, *d.* of John Greenwood, of Highfield, Ravensbourne Park, S.E. *Educ. :* Salts Schools, Saltaire, Yorks. *War Work :* 2nd Lieut. 4th London How. Bgde., R.F.A., 1st London Division ; Medical Officer, 4th London How. Bgde., R.F.A., 56th Division ; M.O. 283rd Bgde., R.F.A., 56th (London) Division ; Second-in-Command, 2/3rd London Field Ambulance, 56th (London) Division ; Lieut.-Col. Commanding 2/3rd West Riding Field Ambulance, Highland Division, British Army of the Rhine ; Lieut.-Col. Commanding 2/3rd Wessex Field Ambulance, 57th Division. (O5742)

RUTHERFORD, Capt. the Hon. Charles Edward Stewart HUE-, O.B.E., *b.* 21 April, 1940 ; *s.* of William Hue-Ruthven and *g. s.* of Mary Elizabeth Thornton, Baroness Ruthven (*see* BURKE'S *Peerage*) ; *m.* Mariana, *d.* of Col. Edward Robert Wood, of Southall, Co. Glamorgan. Late Lieut. 51st Regt. and Capt. Quebec Artillery ; J P., Breconshire. *Address :* Vaynot House, Cefn Coed, Merthyr Tydfil. (O11258)

RUTLAND, George Henry, M.B.E., A.K.C., A.M.Inst.N.A., *b.* 16 March, 1884 ; *s.* of George Rutland, of Conduit Street, London, W. ; *m.* Daisy Florence Mary, *d.* of William Henry Roberts, of Lowestoft. *Educ. :* Tiffin School, Kingston-on-Thames, and King's Coll., Univ. of London. Late Chief Draughtsman, Warship Department, Messrs. R. and W. Hawthorn, Leslie & Co., Ltd., Newcastle-on-Tyne. *War Work :* Design and construction of vessels for H.M. Navy. *Address :* The College, Loughborough. (M2382)

RUTTAN OF FREELAND, Lieut.-Col. Charles Millidge, C.B.E. Canadian Army Service Corps · served in the Great War, 1915–19 (despatches). (C1836)

RUTTER, Herbert Llewellyn, M.B.E., F.R.C.S., M.D.

RUTTER, Joseph Gatt, M.B.E.

RUTTER, Richard Golden, M.B.E.

RUTTLE, Lieut. Jacob Sutcliffe, M.B.E., R.A.F.

RUTTLEDGE, Lieut.-Col. Thomas Geoffrey, O.B.E. M.C.

RUXTON, Major Robert Minturn Clarges, O.B.E.

RUXTON, Lieut. William Mill, O.B.E., R.N.R.

RYALL, Sir Charles, Knt. Bach., C.B.E., F.R.C.S., *b.* 1870 ; *s.* of Edward C. Ryall, M.R.C.S., 18th and 86th Regts. ; *m.* Frances Mary, *d.* of Thos. Collier, J.P., of Alderley Edge. *Educ. :* Dublin, Paris, Westminster, and King's Coll. Hospital. Member of Council of the Royal College of Surgeons ; Senior Surgeon to Cancer Hospital and to Bolingbroke Hospital ; Consulting Surgeon to London Lock Hospital, Gordon Hospital for Diseases of Rectum, and Leatherhead Cottage Hospital. *War Work :* Assessor-in-Charge of the Appeal Board of Medical Assessors to the Appeal Tribunals of England and Wales ; Member of National Service Advisory Medical Board, and of Committee of Reference for recruiting doctors and seeing to needs of Metropolitan Hospitals ; Surgeon to King George's Hospital and Lady Carnarvon's Hospital for Officers ; formerly Member of the Special Medical Appeal Board under Army Council. *Addresses :* 62, Harley Street, W. ; Aldenham Corner, Radlett, Herts. *Clubs :* Ranelagh ; Reform. (C1609)

RYAN, Brig.-Gen. Charles Montgomerie, C.M.G., C.B.E., D.S.O., Officier Legion d'Honneur, France, *b.* 12 Aug. 1867 ; *s.* of the late Col. Edward Moody Ryan, of Bengal Staff Corps, Indian Army. *Educ* Winchester Coll., and Jesus Coll., Cambridge. Retired List (Reserve of Officers) ; Commissioned 22 Aug. 1888, to 29 Aug. 1919. *Address :* c/o Sir C. R. McGrigor, Bart., & Co., 39, Panton Street, Haymarket, London, S.W. *Clubs :* United Service ; Sports. (C610)

RYAN, Major-Gen. Sir Charles Snodgrass, K.B.E., C.B., C.M.G., V.D., *b.* 20 Sept. 1853 ; *s.* of Charles Ryan, of Darriwait, Upper Macedon, West ; *m.* Alice Elfrida, *d.* of The Hon. Theo Sumner, of Stony Park, Brunswick. *Educ. :* Church of England Grammar School, Edinburgh ; Paris ; Bonn ; Vienna. Surgeon ; Cons. Surgeon, Melbourne Hospital ; Cons. Surgeon, Children's Hospital ; late Surgeon in Turkish Army during the Servo-Turkish and Russo-Turkish Wars of 1876–8. *War Work :* A.D.M.S., 1st Australian Division, at Anzac, France, and England ; Consulting Surgeon to the Australian Imperial Force. *Clubs :* Oriental ; Melbourne. (C61)

RYAN, Rear-Adm. Frank Edward Cavendish, C.B.E. Rear-Adm. (ret.), and Capt. R.N.R. ; served in the Great War, 1914–19 (despatches). (C1938)

RYAN, (late Capt.) Hugh Kaye, O.B.E., M.A., LL.M., *b.* 25 Jan. 1875 ; *s.* of the late Vicar of St. Barnabas, Hessle, Yorks ; *m.* Anne Campbell, *d.* of John Cooke, M.D., of St. Leonards. *Educ. :* Privately, and Corpus Christi Coll., Cambridge. Barrister-at-Law of the Inner Temple ; well-known platform speaker ; author of various works. *War Work :* Took prominent part in establishing the extensive recruiting organisation of the Inns of Court O.T.C., thereby furnishing many thousands of officers for training ; then did secret work for the military authorities ; afterwards joined Directorate of the Inland Waterways and Docks, War Office, and rendered special services, for which he was mentioned and later recommended for distinction. *Addresses :* 2, Crown Office Row, Temple, E.C.4 , 37, Craven Terrace, Hyde Park, London, W. 2 ; Bugsell, Robertsbridge, Sussex. (O7663)

RYAN, Isabel, Mrs., M.B.E.

RYAN, John, O.B.E.

RYAN, Mervyn Frederick, C.B.E. *War Work :* Director of Munition Gauges. (C611)

RYAN, Capt. Pierce Neimeyer, O.B.E., R.N.R.

RYAN, Lieut. Thomas Philip, O.B.E., R.N.R.

RYAN, Lieut. Walter Thomas, O.B.E., R.N.R.

RYAN, Victor Herbert, O.B.E. (O12015)

RYAN, Rev. William, O.B.E., *b.* 8 Dec. 1887 ; *s.* of Daniel and Mary Ryan, of Tramore, Co. Waterford. *Educ. :* St. John's Coll., Waterford. Was Curate in St. Mary's, Greenock, in the Archdiocese of Glasgow. *War Work :* Served with the 49th Division in France from 11 May, 1915, and with the 2nd Royal Munster Fus. (wounded, Dec. 1916) ; appointed S.C.F. 30th Division, and assistant to A.P.C. Boulogne ; twice mentioned in despatches. *Addresses :* R.E. Officers' Mess, Bulford Camp, Wilts ; Marine View, Tramore, Co. Waterford. (O5746)

RYAN, Lieut.-Col. William John, C.B.E., R.A.F. Served in the Great War, 1914–19 (despatches, M.B.E., O.B.E.). (C1906)

RYCROFT, Lieut. Albert, M.B.E., R.A.

RYCROFT, Capt. Frederick, M.B.E., R.A.

RYCROFT, Percy Edward, M.B.E.

RYDER, Edward Northern, M.B.E.

RYDER, Lieut.-Col. Charles Frederick, O.B.E.

RYDER, Lady Frances, C.B.E., *b.* 7 Aug. 1888 ; *d.* of 5th Earl of Harrowby, of Sandon Hall, Stafford (*see* BURKE'S *Peerage*). *War Work :* Nursed in military hospitals in England and France ; organised Hospitality Scheme for Overseas Officers since Feb. 1917. *Addresses :* Sandon Hall, Stafford ; Norton House, Campden, Glos. (C2023)

RYDER, George Thomas, O.B.E., J.P.

RYDER, Lady Mary Maud Anson, O.B.E ; 3rd *d.* of 2nd Earl of Lichfield (*see* BURKE'S *Peerage*) ; *m.* Hon. Edward Alan Dudley, *s.* of 5th Earl of Harrowby (*see* BURKE'S *Peerage*). *Address :* 46. Cadogan Square, S.W (O11259)

RYLAND, Edith, Mrs. SMITH-, M.B.E. ; *d.* of the late W. F. Richards, of Folkestone ; widow of Charles Alston Smith-Ryland, of Barford Hill, Warwick. *War Work :* Hon. Treas. British Red Cross Society, Warwickshire County ; Commandant, Barford Hill Auxiliary Hospital, March, 1916, to Dec. 1918. *Address :* Chobham Park, Chobham, Surrey. *Clubs :* Empress ; Forum. (M3954)

RYLE, Herbert, O.B.E.

RYLES, Major Charles, O.B.E., M.B., R.A.M.C.

SABESTON, Robert, O.B.E., A.I.F.

SABINE, Dorothy Gladys, M.B.E., *b.* 10 Aug. 1898 ; *d.* of Henry George Sabine, of London. *War Work :* Joined British Red Cross Society on the outbreak of the war and served at the Royal Herbert Hospital, Woolwich, from 1915–16 ; until cessation of hostilities was available for Red Cross Ambulance duty during air raids on London ; War Office Staff, 1916 till present date. (M9534)

SACKETT, Rev. Alfred Barrett, O.B.E.

SADLER, Annie, O.B.E.

SADLER, Henry, M.B.E.

SADLER, James, O.B.E., *b.* 4 Jan. 1858 ; *s.* of Charles Sadler, of Tattenhall Lanes, Chester ; *m.* Emma, *d.* of Edward Dod, of Hampton, Malpas ; *Educ. :* British School, Tattenhall, Chester. Member of County Agricultural Committee ; Sec. to Cheshire Milk Producers' Association, Cheshire Chamber of Agriculture, Cheshire Dairy Farmers' Association, Cheshire Milk Producers' Depots, Ltd., Cheshire Rural Workers' Friendly Society, Nantwich Farmers' Club. *War Work :* Sub-Commissioner to Food Production Department ; Sec. to Local War Agricultural Committee, Supplies Sub-Committee, and Committee for Supply of Forage to His Majesty's Forces ; Representative of Board of Agriculture on Local Tribunal. *Address :* Holmleigh, Wistaston, Nantwich, Cheshire. (O11261)

SADLER, Lieut.-Col. Leslie, O.B.E.

SAER, John, M.B.E., *b.* 12 Jan. 1864 ; *s.* of the late John Saer, of Newhouse, St. Clears ; *m.* Sarah, *d.* of David Lewis, of Bridgend. Clerk to the Carmarthen Rural District Council ; and to Guardians of Carmarthen Union. *War Work :* Executive Officer, Carmarthen Rural Food Control Committee ; Clerk to Local Tribunal ; Member of Local Committee Soldiers' and Sailors' Families Association. *Address :* Glannant House, Carmarthen. (M9535)

SAFFORD, Stella Fanny, O.B.E.

SAGE, Arthur Reginald, M.B.E.

SAGE, Molyneux Baxter Sage, M.B.E.

SAIES. Rev. Father Lorenso, M.B.E.

SAINSBURY, Charles, M.B.E., *b.* 10 Nov. 1885; *s.* of Edward Sainsbury. *Educ.:* Clifton Coll. Stock Exchange. *War Work:* Ministry of Munitions. *Address:* 35, Upper Gloucester Place, London, N.W. 1. (M45)

SAINSBURY, Edgar John, O.B.E.

SAINSBURY, Lieut. Eric John, M.B.E., R.F.A. (S.R.)

SAINSBURY, Flora Gregory, M.B.E., *b.* 6 April, 1883; *d.* of Richard Henry Sainsbury, of Trowbridge. *Educ.:* Hawkesbury, Clevedon, Somerset. Teacher of Domestic Science; and Organising Inspectress in Domestic Subjects under Norfolk County Council. *War Work:* Administrator in Q.M.A.A.C. at Boyton and Chiseldon Camps, and Preston Barracks. *Address:* 3, Bradley Road, Trowbridge, Wilts. *Club:* Women's Active Service. (M6702)

SAINSBURY, Harrington, O.B.E., M.D., F.R.C.P., *b.* 1853. Consulting Physician to the Royal Free Hospital and the City of London Hospital for Diseases of the Chest, Victoria Park; Examining Physician, Royal National Hospital, Ventnor. *War Work:* At the Richmond Military Hospital and subsequently at the Bermondsey Military Hospital. *Addresses:* 52, Wimpole Street, W. 1; 12, Woburn Square, W.C. 1. (O11844)

SAINT, Major Charles Frederick Morris, C.B.E., M.B., F.R.C.S., R.A.M.C. Served in the Great War, 1914–19 (despatches). (C1319)

SAINT, Rosa Charlotte, M.B.E.; *d.* of the late John James Heath Saint, Recorder of Leicester. *Educ.:* St. Mary's Convent, S. Ascot, Berks. *War Work:* Clerk at the War Office. *Address:* 6, Lisgar Terrace, W. 14. (M9537)

ST. AUBYN, Brevet.-Major Guy Stewart, O.B.E.

ST. AUBYN, Ingeborg Alfhild Lady MOLESWORTH-O.B.E.; *d.* of I. V. Sigvald Muller, of Beaucliffe House, Newquay, Cornwall; *m.* the late Sir St. Aubyn Hender, *s.* of Hender Molesworth-St. Aubyn, of Pencarrow, Cornwall. *Educ.:* Privately. President of Cornwall County Federation of Women's Institutes; Vice-Chairman of County Horticultural Committee; Member of the Statutory Agricultural Committee for Cornwall, and County Agricultural Executive Committee; Delegate to the National Federation of Agricultural Executive Committee. *War Work:* Chairman, Cornwall War Service for Women Committee; President of Cornwall Women's Agricultural Council; Chairman of its Executive Committee; Vice-Chairman of the National Federation of Women's Agricultural Committees; Chairman of Allotments and Horticultural Committee during the Food Production Campaign; Member of County Appeal Tribunal (Military Service). *Address:* Atlantic House, Newquay, Cornwall. *Clubs:* County of Cornwall Ladies'; Women's Institute, Newquay. (O11263)

ST. BARBE, Henry, M.B.E.

ST. CLAIR, Frank Verity, O.B.E., *b.* Sept. 1858; *s.* of Francis Robert, of Addingham; *m.* Mary Adelaide, *d.* of William Fox, of Poynton. *Educ.:* Dr. Kerrs, Wharfedale. Executive Committee, V.A.F. and M.H.A. Benevolent Funds; Provincial Delegate, Variety Artistes Federation. *War Work:* Organising War Charities and Concerts for Wounded; devoted all profits from the sales of his compositions: "Follow The Drum," "When the Boys Come Home," and other patriotic songs; received fourteen thousand post-cards from the trenches, and three thousand from British prisoners for comforts his songs sent out. *Address:* The Chalet, Prees Heath, Salop. *Club:* Vaudeville. (O11264)

ST. CLAIR, Hon. Lockhart Matthew, C.I.E., O.B.E., M.Inst.C.E., *b.* 25 July, 1855; *s.* of 14th Baron Sinclair (*see* BURKE's *Peerage*); *m.* Ellen Mary Margaret, *d.* of the late Surgeon-Major-Gen. W. R. Rice, C.S.I., M.D. *Educ.:* Wellington Coll., and Royal Indian Engineering Coll., Cooper's Hill. Joined the Indian Public Works Department, Oct. 1876; served as Assistant Engineer in the Saugor Road, and Executive Engineer in Charge of Nagpur and Jubbulpur Divisions, 1881–85; State Engineer to the Nepal Government, 1889–92; Executive Engineer, Lower Assam, 1894–95; Executive Engineer, Hoshungabad Division, Central Provinces, 1895–97; Under Sec. to the Government, Central Provinces, in the Public Works Department, 1897–99; in charge Nagpur Division Buildings, Roads, Waterworks, and Famine Relief Works, Oct. 1899, to March, 1900; Superintendent of Works for all works 8 Southern Districts of the C.P.; in Nov. 1900, appointed Superintending Engineer and Sec. to the Government, Central Provinces, in the P.W.D.; as such had professional responsibility for, and administrative control of, all Public Works in the Provinces, including roads, buildings, waterworks, railways, mines, irrigation works, relief works, etc.; designed and superintended the building of many waterworks in India, for which he received the thanks of the Imperial Government; C.I.E., 1902; retired from the Public Service, 1904. *War Work:* Joined the Metropolitan Special Constabulary, Aug. 1914; appointed Chief Inspector of the Sutton Sub-Division; appointed Assistant Commander, Sept. 1914; Acting Commander of the "W" Division, Oct. 1914; Commander, Nov. 1914, which post he has since held. *Address:* Derriana, Mayfield Road, Sutton, Surrey. *Clubs:* Junior Carlton; Royal Automobile. (O3964)

ST. HELIER, Susan Mary Elizabeth, Lady, C.B.E.

ST. JOHN, Lieut.-Col. Henry Beauchamp, C.I.E., C.B.E., Indian Army, *b.* 26 Aug. 1874; *e. s.* of Sir Oliver Beauchamp Coventry St. John, K.C.S.I., R.E. (*see* BURKE's *Peerage*); *m.* 6 Feb. 1907, Olive Amy, 2nd *d.* of Col. Charles Herbert,

Resident at Jaipur, Rajputana. Assist. Sec. to the Government of India. *Address:* Foreign Department, Simla. (C1303)

ST. LAWRENCE, Bertha, Mrs. GAISFORD-, M.B.E.; *d.* of Francis Riddell, of Cheeseburn Grange, Northumberland; *m.* 1889, Julian Charles, *s.* of Thomas Gaisford-St. Lawrence, of Offington, and Lady Emily St. Lawrence, *e. d.* of 3rd Earl of Howth. *Address:* Howth Castle, Co. Dublin. (M9539)

ST. MAUR, Nina Mabel Mary, Mrs., M.B.E.

ST. QUINTIN, Lieut.-Col. Arthur Newton, O.B.E., late Naval Ordnance Department, *b.* 9 April, 1854; *s.* of William St. Quintin, of Bengal Civil Service; *m.* Mary Leaper, *d.* of Charles Edmund Newton, of Mickleover Manor, Derby (*see* BURKE's *Landed Gentry*). *Educ.:* Blackheath School. Sec., Lloyds Patriotic Fund. *War Work:* Admiralty, 1914–15; Special Constable, 1915–19; Member London War Pensions Committee from formation, 1916; Hon. Sec. Princess Christian Home, Portsmouth. *Addresses:* 36, Moore Street, Chelsea; Lattice House, Bracknell, Berks. *Club:* National. (O11265)

SALBERG, Capt. Frank James, M.B.E., I.A.R.O.

SALCOMBE, Capt. Ernest Walter, O.B.E.

SALE, Major Arthur Bromwich, O.B.E., M.C., M.A., *b.* 17 Nov. 1884; *s.* of William Hanson Sale, J.P., of Atherstone; *m.* Dorothea Lucy, *d.* of Walter Bicknell, of Henley-in-Arden. *Educ.:* St. Peter's School, York, and Pembroke Coll., Oxford. Schoolmaster. *War Work:* Served with 13th Batt. R. Warwickshire Regt., at home, and 9th Batt. R. Warwickshire Regt. in Mesopotamia, India, Persia, Turkestan, Trans-Caspia, Caucasus, Turkey, and in Salonica; 2nd in command, 9th R. Warwickshire Regt., July, 1916, to Jan. 1917, and Jan. 1919, to Sept. 1919 (disbandment of battalion); commanded 7th R. Berkshire Regt., Aug. to Sept. 1919, in Caucasus. *Address:* Arden Hill, Atherstone. (O8710)

SALISBURY, Francis, C.B.E., I.S.O., J.P., *b.* 13 June, 1850; *s.* of the late Francis Salisbury, of the General Post Office; *m.* Ann Catherine, *d.* of the late Dr. Hugh R. Hughes, J.P., of Bangor, Carnarvonshire. *Educ.:* Stockwell Grammar School, London. District Surveyor and Postmaster, General Post Office; Postmaster Surveyor at Liverpool, Jan. 1896, to June, 1913. *War Work:* Took charge of the North Midland Postal District, April. 1915, to April, 1919; employed as Postal Adviser to British Delegate to Marienwerder Inter-Allied Plebiscite Commission, Jan. 1920, to Aug. 1920. *Address:* Athenæum, Liverpool. (C612)

SALLIS, Major Daniel, O.B.E., T.D.; *s.* of George Sallis, of Malvern; *m.* Sarah, *d.* of John Davis, of Chaddesley Corbett. *Educ.:* Army Schools. Sec., War Pensions Committee. *War Work:* Mobilised with 1/8th Batt. the Worcestershire Regt., 5 Aug. 1914; served in France, Belgium, and Italy; mentioned in despatches twice, and awarded higher rate of pay for service in the field. *Address:* 28, Hill Avenue, Worcester. (O7664)

SALMON, Hedley, O.B.E.

SALMON, Major Isidore, C.B.E., D.L., L.C.C., *b.* 10 Feb. 1876; *s.* of B. Salmon. *Educ.:* Privately. Managing Director of Public Company; Member of London County Council; Vice-Chairman of London War Pensions Committee; Chairman City of London Employment Exchange (Ministry of Labour). *Address:* 30, Holland Villas Road, Kensington, London, W. 14. (C2928)

SALMON, Joseph Harold, M.B.E.

SALMON, Lieut. Ronald Martin, M.B.E., R.E.

SALMON, William John Cecil Redford, M.B.E., *b.* 5 June, 1876; *s.* of Chas. Salmon, M.I.C.E., J.P., R.N., of Riversfield, Erith; *m.* Lilian Harriet Augusta, *d.* of Capt. John Prittie Bayly, R.N., of Ballyre, Co. Cork, Ireland. *Educ.:* Privately, and Univ. Coll., London. Mechanical Engineer, 1898–1910; Assist.-Manager Messrs. Vickers, Ltd., 1908–1913; held commission in 4th Home Counties Howitzer Bde.; resigned commission as Battery Leader whilst in Australia. *War Work:* Returned to England, Oct. 1915; joined Inspection Dept. at Woolwich as Assist.-Inspector of Carriages; went to America, U.S.A., for special work on guns, carriages, and shells, etc., Jan. 1918; appointed Assist.-Inspector Carriages, Manchester; resigned March, 1919; joined the firm of Sir W. G. Armstrong, Whitworth & Co. *Address:* Riversfield, Erith, Kent. *Clubs:* Royal Automobile. (M9541)

SALMOND, Elaine Marguerite, Mrs., O.B.E., *b.* 1870. *War Work:* London War Pensions Committee. *Address:* 36, Brunswick Square, W.C. 1. (O11266)

SALMOND, Mary Augusta Compton, Mrs., O.B.E., *b.* 12 Sept. 1858; *d.* of William Compton Smith, of Wandsworth, Surrey; *m.* Walter, *s.* of Col. J. Salmond, of Waterfoot, Cumberland, and Langton Hall, near Alfreton (*see* BURKE's *Landed Gentry*). *Educ.:* Privately. Song writer; Hon. County Sec. for Derbyshire of the Soldiers' and Sailors' Help Society for nearly 20 years; Member of Lord Roberts' Memorial Workshops Committee (East Midlands); Lady Almoner of Regimental Homes of the Sherwood Foresters (Notts. and Derby Regt.); Member of four War Pensions Committees; Hospital visitor in three counties, and voluntary pianist in hospitals. *Addresses:* Newton Old Hall, near Alfreton, Derbyshire; and Folkestone. (O1835)

SALMOND, Robert Williamson Asher, O.B.E., M.D., *b.* 1883; *s.* of Robert Salmond, of Aberdeen; *m.* Amelia Maud, *d.* of J. Thomlinson, of Headcorn. *Educ.:* Grammar School, and Marischal Coll., Aberdeen. Physician and Radiologist; Hon. Radiologist, Univ. Coll. Hospital, London; and Lecturer in Radiology. *War Work:* Deputy Consulting Radiologist,

British Armies in France. *Addresses:* 51, Welbeck Street, London, W. 1; 4, Brendon House, Great Woodstock Street, W. 1. *Club:* Aberdeen Univ. (O8602)

SALMOND, Comm. Kenneth GOFTON-, O.B.E., R.N., *b.* 17 July, 1880; *s.* of Robert Gofton-Salmond, and *g.s.* of Robert Salmond, Capt. R.N., of H.M.S. "Birkenhead"; *m.* Maud Alice, *d.* of Col. W. H. Lyster, of Indian Army. *Educ.:* Dulwich, and Royal Naval School, Eltham. Member of British Naval Mission to Greece, 1910–12; Director of Naval Ordnance, Royal Hellenic Navy; Naval Sec. to the Navy League, 1913–14; Capt.-Supt. of the Sea Cadet Corps, 1919–20; Director of Organisation, British Commonwealth Union, from 1919; awarded Royal Humane Society's Bronze Medal, 1904; and Order of the Redeemer of Grace by the late King George of Greece, in 1912, for valuable services rendered. *War Work:* Aug. 1914, to May, 1915, Gunnery Officer of H.M.S. "Amphitrite," Atlantic Patrol Flagship of Vice-Admiral de Roebeck; May, 1915, to Jan. 1916, Second-in-Command, and Gunnery Officer, of H.M.S. "Grafton," Dardanelles and Gallipoli; invalided as unfit for sea service; Jan. 1916, to Feb. 1919, Naval Experimental Officer at Experimental Establishment, New Ranges, Shoeburyness. *Address:* The Nook, Kingswood Road, Upper Norwood, S.E. 19. *Clubs:* Junior Army and Navy; Royal Navy Club. (O9165)

SALSBURY, Albert Edward, M.B.E., D.C.M.

SALTER, Albert Hugh, M.B.E. (M10465)

SALTER, William Henry, M.B.E., M.A., LL.B., *b.* 19 March, 1880; *s.* of W. H. Gurney Salter, of 66, Ladbroke Road, W.; *m.* Helen Woollgar de Gandrion, *d.* of Prof. A. W. Verrall, of Cambridge. *Educ.:* St. Paul's School; Trinity Coll., Cambridge. Barrister-at-Law. *War Work:* Ministry of Munitions (Labour Supply, Legal Departments, and Secretariat). *Addresses:* Crown House, Newport, Essex; 3, New Square, Lincoln's Inn. *Club:* United Univ. (M2384)

SALVIDGE, Sir Archibald Tutton James, K.B.E., Knt. Bach., J.P., *b.* 1863; 2nd *s.* of Archibald Tutton Salvidge; *m.* 1885, Alice Margaret, *d.* of late Thomas McKernan. *Educ.:* Liverpool Institute. Managing Director, Bent's Brewery Co., Ltd.; Liverpool Alderman; Chairman Liverpool Men's Conservative Assocn.; of Council National Unionist Assoc.; of Conservative and Liberal Unionist Organisations, 1913; of Canvassing Sub-committee; Liverpool Recruiting Committee; of Liverpool Advisory Committee; declined Lord Mayoralty (Liverpool), 1910; Leader of City Council and of Unionist Party in Liverpool. *Address:* Braxted, Hoylake. *Clubs:* Constitutional; Conservative; Royal Golf, Liverpool. (K419)

SAMBLE, Read, O.B.E., *b.* 4 Dec. 1876; *s.* of the late Read Samble, of Burton-on-Trent; *m.* Rowena, *d.* of the late Alderman John Yeomans, of Burton-on-Trent. *Educ.:* Burton-on-Trent Grammar School. Solicitor; Chairman of Higher Education Committee. *War Work:* Sec. to War Pensions Committee, Burton-on-Trent; Hon. Sec. to Burton-on-Trent Parish Belgian Refugees Committee. *Address:* Marchington House, Stanton Road, Burton-on-Trent. (O11627)

SAMBRIDGE, William, M.B.E.

SAMMUT, Mrs., M.B.E.

SAMPLE, Charles Herbert, O.B.E., B.A., F.S.I., *b.* 22 Nov. 1862; *s.* of Thomas Sample, of Bothal Castle, Morpeth, and Carrycoats Hall, Northumberland; *m.* Maria Florence, *d.* of John Greene, of Gateshead. *Educ.:* Edinburgh Academy and Cambridge Univ. Alderman Northumberland County Council; Chairman of Small Holdings Committee, and of Committee of Management of Cockle Park Experimental Station; Land Agent for several estates in Northumberland and Durham. *War Work:* From Feb. 1917, to Feb. 1919, District Commissioner for four Northern Counties for Board of Agriculture and Fisheries (Food Production Department). *Addresses:* Shildon Grange, Corbridge; 29, Grainger Street West, Newcastle-on-Tyne. *Clubs:* Union and Farmers', Newcastle; Farmers', London. (O1836)

SAMPLE, Capt. Leslie, M.B.E.

SAMPSON, Alexander Whitehead, C.B.E., *b.* 13 Oct. 1859; *s.* of the late Thomas Sampson, of Greenock; *m.* Jane (who died), *d.* of John Tait, of Greenock. *Educ.:* Normal School, Edinburgh. Shipbuilder; late Director and Shipyard Manager of the Fairfield Shipbuilding and Engineering Co., Ltd., Glasgow. *War Work:* Director of Auxiliary Vessels, at the Admiralty, and responsible for the ordering and completion of all Auxiliary War Vessels. *Address:* Bonington, Bellahouston, Glasgow. *Club:* Royal Scottish Automobile. (C1034)

SAMPSON, George Frederick, O.B.E., *b.* 21 Feb. 1883; *s.* of John Sampson, of Stanley, near Wakefield; *m.* Gerda, *d.* of E. A. Hedin, of Gefle (Sweden). *Educ.:* Wakefield Grammar School; Berlin Univ. Archivist at British Embassy, Berlin, till 1914; Assistant Commercial Attaché to British Legation, Stockholm, during war. *Address:* 66, Sinclair Road, West Kensington. *Clubs:* National Liberal; New City. (O11268)

SAMPSON, Henry William, O.B.E.

SAMPSON, Major Herbert Henry, O.B.E., M.C., M.B., B.Ch., F.R.C.S. (Eng.), *b.* 4 Oct. 1886; *s.* of the late Frederick Sampson, of Sutton Coldfield. *Educ.:* Birmingham Univ.; London Hospital. Consulting Surgeon; Assistant Surgeon, General Hospital, Birmingham, and Children's Hospital, Birmingham. *War Work:* France, 69th Field Ambulance, 1915; 26th Field Ambulance, 1916; Surgeon-in-charge of Special Abdominal Hospital, Bac St. Maus, 1915–16; 6 Casualty Clearing Station, 1916, surgeon; 19 Casualty Clearing Station; Surgical Specialist, 1916 to end of war. *Addresses:*

47, Newhall Street, Birmingham; Ferndale, Manor Road, Sutton Coldfield. *Clubs:* Conservative; Clef, Birmingham. (O5757)

SAMPSON, Lieut. Howard, M.B.E.

SAMPSON, John, C.B.E., M.I.C.E., M.I.N.A., *b.* 1859; *s.* of John Sampson, of Hayle, Cornwall; *m.* 1890, Lucy Elizabeth, *d.* of John Pearce Sawyer, of Filham House, Ivybridge, Devon. A Director of John Brown and Co. (Limited), of Sheffield and Clydebank, and other steel production, shipbuilding, engineering, electricity and ordnance Cos.; a Member of Financial Facilities Committee; sometime British Representative on Anglo-Russian Sub-Committee in New York. *Addresses:* Queen Anne's Mansions, S.W.; Folkestone, Kent. *Clubs:* Athenæum; Reform. (C613)

SAMPSON, Leslie Norman, O.B.E.

SAMSON, Sir Edward Marlay, K.B.E., K.C., *b.* 27 March, 1869; *s.* of Louis Samson, of Scotchwell, Haverfordwest. *Educ.:* Harrow; Trinity Coll., Oxford. Recorder of Swansea; Chancellor, St. David's Diocese; Chairman, Court of Quarter Sessions, Haverfordwest; Vice-Chairman, Court of Quarter Sessions, County of Pembroke. *War Work:* Chairman, South Wales and Monmouth Disablement Committee; Vice-President, Association of War Pensions Committees; Chairman, Institutional Committee (Wales): Hon. Sec. Welsh National Fund. *Address:* Scotchwell, Haverfordwest. *Clubs:* Carlton; United Univ. (K420)

SAMSON, Major Felix Rumney, O.B.E., R.A.F.

SAMSON, Howard Lewis, M.B.E.

SAMSON, Lieut.-Col. Louis Lort Rhys, C.M.G., C.B.E., *b.* 1866; *e.s.* of Louis Samson, J.P., D.L., of Scotchwell, Haverfordwest; *m.* Gertrude Maud, *d.* of the late Edwin Williams. *Educ.:* Harrow, and R.M.C. Entered Army, 1886; Capt. Lancashire Fusiliers, 1894; Major King's Own (Roy. Lancaster Regt.), 1905; Brevet Lieut.-Col. 1916; served in S. Africa, 1900–2 (Queen's medal with two clasps, King's medal with two clasps); was Consul at Adrianople, 1906–14; appointed a Gen. Staff Officer, 1916; J.P. for Pembrokeshire. *Club:* Junior Army and Navy. (C2161)

SAMUEL, Casmire, Mrs., M.B.E.

SAMUEL, Rt. Hon. Sir Herbert Louis, P.C., G.B.E., M.A., (M.P. Cleveland Division, N. Riding, Yorks. 1902–18), *b.* 6 Nov. 1870; *s.* of the late Edwin L. Samuel and Clara Yates; *m.* 1897 Beatrice, *y. d.* of the late Ellis A. Franklin. *Educ.:* Univ. Coll. School; Balliol Coll., Oxford. First Class Honours, Oxford, 1893; contested South Oxfordshire as a Liberal 1895, and 1900; Parliamentary Under-Sec. Home Dept. 1905–9; Privy Councillor 1908; Chancellor of the Duchy of Lancaster (with a seat in the Cabinet) 1909–10, and 1915–16; Postmaster-General, 1910–14, and 1915–16; President of the Local Government Board, 1914–15; Secretary of State for Home Affairs 1916; Chairman, Select Committee on National Expenditure, 1917–18; British Special Commissioner to Belgium, 1919; appointed High Commissioner for Palestine, 1920. *Address:* Government House, Jerusalem, Palestine. (G65)

SAMUEL, Sir John Smith, K.B.E., F.R.S.E., F.S.A. (Scot.), J.P., D.L., Knight of the Swedish Royal Order of Vasa (1st class), Commander of the Belgian Order of the Crown, Chevalier of the Order of the Legion of Honour, Cavalier of the Italian Order of the Crown, Order of St. Sava of Serbia, Imperial Order of the Russian Red Cross, Officier de l'Academie of France, Officer of Order of Prince Danilo of Montenegro, *b.* 2 April, 1870; *s.* of Hugh Samuel, of Glasgow. *Educ.:* Glasgow Univ. Official Sec. to the Lord Provosts of Glasgow; Clerk of Lieutenancy for the County of the City of Glasgow, and to the Visiting Committee of H.M. Prison, Barlinnie; Hon. Sec. Glasgow Branch of the Soldiers' and Sailors' Help Society; Joint Hon. Sec. of the Pr ncess Louise Scottish Hospital for Limbless Sailors and Soldiers; Hon. Sec. of the Prince Albert Workshops for the Training of Disabled Sailors and Soldiers; Member of the Glasgow War Pensions Committee, and Chairman of Springburn District War Pensions Committee; Member of the City of Glasgow Branch of the Red Cross Society. *War Work:* Was identified with all the most important War organisations in Glasgow from the commencement of hostilities in 1914 till the signing of the Armistice in 1918; has held the office of Hon. Sec. of the Glasgow Branch of the Soldiers' and Sailors' Help Society since 1901, and personally interviewed and assisted most of the discharged service men belonging to Glasgow for 16 years; during the late war, the Society was placed upon a permanent footing, and an Acting Sec. was appointed to take over the work hitherto discharged voluntarily by him; one of the promoters and is Joint Hon. Sec. of the Princess Louise Scottish Hospital for Limbless Sailors and Soldiers at Erskine, on the Clyde; one of the promoters and Hon. Sec. of the Prince Albert Workshops for the training of disabled sailors and soldiers at Possilpark, Glasgow; his most important War work was the raising and collecting of War Funds under the auspices of successive Lord Provosts of Glasgow; Hon. Treas. of a great variety of such funds, including the Prince of Wales' National Relief Fund, for which the enormous sum of £270,000 was subscribed; one of the first 43 Knight Commanders to receive the accolade which was conferred upon him by H.M. the King at an open-air Investiture held in Glasgow on 18 Sept., 1917. *Addresses:* City Chambers, Glasgow; 13, Park Circus, Glasgow. *Clubs:* Caledonian and Road, London; Art and Literary, Glasgow. (K37)

SAMUEL, Dame Victoria Louise, O.B.E. A founder of War Refugees Committee during Great War. (D54)

SAMUEL, Thomas John, M.B.E.

SAMUELSON, Lieut.-Col. Cecil Llewellyn, O.B.E., *b.* 7 June, 1882 ; *s.* of Llewellyn Samuelson, of Cookham, Berks. ; *m.* Norah, *d.* of Henry Richardson, of Kirklevington, Yorks. (*see* BURKE'S *Landed Gentry*). *Educ.:* Cheltenham Coll. Member of London Stock Exchange. *War Work :* Served in Royal Army Service Corps. *Address :* 6, Sumner Terrace, London, S.W. 7. *Club :* Bath.   (O9725)

SAMUELSON, Sybil Charlotte Eleanor, Mrs., O.B.E., *b.* 27 Feb. 1876 ; *d.* of the late Hon. Walter Harbord, *s.* of 3rd Baron Suffield (*see* BURKE'S *Peerage*) ; *m.* Herbert Walter, *s.* of the late Rt. Hon. Sir Bernhard Samuelson, Bart., P.C., F.R.S. (*see* BURKE'S *Peerage*). *War Work :* Gave her residence, 58, Grosvenor Street, London, W. 1, for Hospital for Officers for 4½ years, to which officers were sent direct from abroad ; the hospital contained 14 beds, and about 520 patients were treated there. *Address :* 58, Grosvenor Street, London, W. 1. (O11269)

SAMWAYS, William Henry, M.B.E., R.N.

SANDARS, Major Edmund Thomas, O.B.E., R.A.S.C.

SANDARS, Gertrude Marian, Mrs., O.B.E., *b.* 23 July, 1863 ; *d.* of William Wingate, of Ludford, Lincolnshire ; *m.* George Edward Sandars, *s.* of John Edward Sandars, of Sandsfield, Gainsboro'. *War Work :* Head of small voluntary needlework party at the 4th Northern General Hospital, Lincoln ; Red Cross visitor to Australians and Americans at above hospital, and latterly Chairman of the Territorial Force Nursing Service Committee. *Address :* Scampton, Lincolnshire.   (O11270)

SANDBACH, Ina, Hon. Mrs. Arthur Edmund, O.B.E., 5th *d.* of 2nd Baron Penrhyn (*see* BURKE'S *Peerage*) ; *m.* (1902) Arthur Edmund, 3rd *s.* of the late H. R. Sandbach, of Hafodunnos, Co. Denbigh, and Elizabeth, *d.* and co-heir of Martin Williams, of Bryn Gwyn, Co. Montgomery. *Address :* Bryn Gwyn, Bwlch-y-Cibau, Montgomeryshire.   (O1837)

SANDBERG, Christer Peter, C.B.E., M.I.C.E.

SANDBERG, Judith Mary, M.B.E., Q.M.A.A.C., *d.* of the late Rev. Francis Sandberg, Indian Government Chaplain, and Mrs. Sandberg, 3, Wellington Mansions, Queen's Club Gardens, W. 14.

SANDBERG, Nils Percy Patrick, C.B.E., *b.* 1881 ; *s.* of Christian Peter Sandberg ; *m.* 1911, Rina Mary Stewart, *d.* of Com. Samuel Ewing, R.N. *Educ.:* Dulwich Coll., and in Brussels. Civil Engineer, and a partner in the firm of C. P. Sandberg, consulting engineer, of 40, Grosvenor Gardens, S.W. ; was Director of Inspection of Steel (Land Ser.), Min. of Munitions during the Great War. *Address :* 6, West Eaton Place, S.W.   (C287)

SANDBERG, Oscar Fridolf Alexander, O.B.E.

SANDELS, T. Lieut. Cecil Arthur ANGLESEA-, M.B.E., M.C., R.F.A.

SANDELSON, Capt. David Isambard, M.B.E., B.A., B.C.L., *b.* 6 Oct. 1889 ; *s.* of the Rev. Rabbi Y. M. Sandelson, of Newcastle-on-Tyne ; *m.* Dora, *d.* of Victor Lightman, J.P., of Roundhay, near Leeds. *Educ. :* Durham Univ. Solicitor. *War Work :* 1915–17, Acting Paymaster, Northern Command ; 1917–18, War Office Representative at Tsingtau, North China, for recruitment of Chinese Labour for France ; 1918–19, Financial Adviser to British Military Mission to Siberia. *Address :* Chistlehurst, Street Lane, Roundhay, Leeds. *Clubs :* Law Society ; National Liberal.   (M6775)

SANDEMAN, Major Alfred Patrick, O.B.E.

SANDEMAN, David Alexander Stewart, O.B.E.

SANDEMAN, Ella Victoire Glas, M.B.E., *b.* 1863 ; *d.* of John Glas Sandeman, of Whin-Hurst, Hayling, Island (*see* BURKE'S *Landed Gentry*). *War Work :* Commandant, V.A.D. Hospital, Hants, 32, Hayling Island, 1915–19. *Address :* Whin-Hurst, Hayling Island, Hants. *Club :* Sesame. (M922)

SANDEMAN, Isabella Emma, Mrs., O.B.E. ; *d.* of John Henry Willock, I.C.S. *Educ.:* Privately. *War Work :* Deputy President, Brighton, Hove and Preston Division of British Red Cross Society, from 1910–18. *Address :* 14, Second Avenue, Hove. *Clubs :* Sesame ; Royal Colonial Institute.   (O1838)

SANDEMAN, Ronald Leighton, O.B.E.

SANDEMAN, William Wellington, M.B.E.

SANDERCOCK, Lieut. Archie, M.B.E., R.G.A. (T.).

SANDERS, Surg.-Lieut.-Comm. Arthur Addison, O.B.E., M.B., R.N.

SANDERS, Sir Charles John Ough, K.B.E., *b.* 14 July, 1865 ; *s.* of James Charles, of Devonport ; *m.* Agnes Jessie, *d.* of Howell Hughes, of Neath and Llanelly. *Educ. :* Privately, and King's Coll., London. Chairman, Conference and Works Board, Shipbuilding Employers' Federation. *War Work :* In charge of Merchant Shipbuilding, Board of Trade, 1914–16 ; Director of Shipbuilding Work, Ministry of Shipping, 1916–17 ; Assistant to Deputy Controller of Auxiliary Shipbuilding, Admiralty, 1917 ; Assistant to Controller-General of Merchant Shipbuilding, 1917–18 ; Member of several Departmental and Inter-Departmental War Committees ; is Commander of the Order of the Crown of Italy. *Addresses :* 9, Victoria Street, Westminster, S.W. ; Lyndhurst, Northbrook Road, Lee, S.E. 13. *Clubs :* Royal Societies' ; National Liberal.   (K421)

SANDERS, Major Douglas Brooking, O.B.E., R.A.F.

SANDERS, Grace Louise, O.B.E., *b.* 30 Jan. 1888 ; *d.* of James Harris Sanders, of London. *Educ.:* Privately. Civil Servant, Ministry of Labour. *War Work :* National Relief Fund and National Registration, Stepney ; Lord Derby's Recruiting Canvas, Edmonton ; Clerk, War Trade Dept. and Admiralty ; served in Q.M.A.A.C. June, 1917, to Oct. 1919,

overseas ; Controller, H.Q. Northern Command. *Address :* 406, Fulham Road, S.W. 6.   (O8932)

SANDERS, Hilda, Mrs., M.B.E. ; *d.* of Francis H. Beaumont, of Buckland Court, Betchworth, Surrey (*see* BURKE'S *Landed Gentry*) ; *m.* Robert Massy Dawson, *s.* of Thomas Sanders, of Charleville Park, Co. Cork (*see* BURKE'S *Landed Gentry*). *War Work :* Hon. Sec. Charleville War Pensions Sub-Committee. *Addresses :* Charleville Park, Co. Cork ; 259, St. James' Court, London, S.W. *Club :* Ladies' Automobile.   (M9546)

SANDERS, Lewis Samuel, O.B.E.   (O12016)

SANDERS, 2nd Lieut. Percy Alan, O.B.E.

SANDERS, Major Samuel George, O.B.E.

SANDERS, Capt. William Stephen, C.B.E. Sec. British Section, International Socialist Party.   (C289)

SANDERSON, Lieut. Francis Robert, O.B.E., Chevalier of the Order of King George of Greece.

SANDERSON, Capt. William Lauchlan, O.B.E., M.C., *b.* 23 Oct. 1890 ; *s.* of W. J. A. Sanderson, of New Zealand and India. *Educ.:* Scotch Coll., Western Australia. Irrigation and Drainage Engineer ; at present engaged in pastoral pursuits. *War Work :* Embarked from Western Australia with the Australian Light Horse, and served on Gallipoli, taking part in their famous charge on the 7th August, 1915, against " The Nek " ; was wounded at Hill 60, Gallipoli, and after the evacuation, transferred to the 4th Australian Divisional Artillery, and served with them in France and Flanders from June, 1916, till the termination of the war ; French Croix de Guerre ; mentioned in despatches. *Addresses :* Claremont, Western Australia ; Kooline Station, *via* Onslow, W.A. *Club :* Naval and Military (Western Australia).   (O1855)

SANDES, Major Charles William Wallace, O.B.E.

SANDES, Elizabeth, C.B.E., *b.* 1851 ; *d.* of Stephen Sandes, of Sallowglen, Co. Kerry (*see* BURKE'S *Landed Gentry*). *Educ.:* The French School, Bray. *War Work :* Originator of Soldiers' Homes in Ireland and India, and for fifty years Hon. Supt. of Soldiers' Homes, which now number thirty. *Address :* Sandes Soldiers' Home, Curragh Camp, Ireland.   (C2930)

SANDES, Lieut.-Col. Thomas Lindsay, O.B.E., M.A., M.D. (Dublin), F.R.C.S. (Eng.), F.R.C.S. (Ireland), *b.* 1882 ; *s.* of Thomas Sanders, S.A.M.C., of County Dublin, Ireland ; *m.* Evelyn Bell, *d.* of — Metcalf, of Cradock, Cape. *Educ. :* Privately ; Trinity Coll., Dublin Univ. ; Berne Univ., Switzerland. Surgical Specialist, Wynberg Military Hospital, Cape. *War Work :* Capt. S.A.M.C., Surgical Specialist, Wynberg Military Hospital, Cape, 1914 ; Major, R.A.M.C., with South African Military Hospital, France, 1915–16 ; Lieut.-Col., S.A.M.C., Surgical Specialist, South African Military Hospital, Richmond, Surrey, 1917–20. *Clubs :* Civil Service, Capetown ; Union of South Africa.   (O1841)

SANDFORD, Lieut.-Comm. Cecil Stanley, O.B.E., R.N.

SANDFORD, Elizabeth Ada, M.B.E., R.R.C.

SANDFORD, Thomas Frederick, M.B.E.

SANDHURST, Eleanor Mary Caroline, Viscountess, O.B.E., *d.* of Matthew Arnold and *widow* of Hon. Armine Wodehouse ; *m.* (1909) William Mansfield, 1st Viscount Sandhurst, P.C., G.C.V.O., G.C.S.I., G.C.I.E., J.P., Lord Chamberlain. *Address :* 60, Eaton Square, S.W. 1.   (O3906)

SANDIESON, Eng.-Lieut. John, O.B.E., R.N.

SANDISON, David, O.B.E.

SANDISON, Capt. John Forbes William, O.B.E., M.C., M.B., R.A.M.C.

SANDLANDS, Paul Ernest, O.B.E., *b.* 25 May, 1878 ; *s.* of Rev. J. P. Sandlands, late Vicar of Brigstock, Northants ; *m.* Laura, *d.* of the late B. E. West, of Flore Grange, Weedon. *Educ.:* Trinity Coll., Cambridge. Barrister-at-Law, Recorder of Newark-on-Trent. *War Work :* S. Africa, 1900, Queen's Medal and 5 clasps ; C.I.V. (Mounted Infantry) ; Commander B. Division, Special Constabulary, Birmingham ; Member of the Committee of Queen's Hospital, Birmingham, during the War. *Addresses :* 16, Emperor's Gate, S.W. 7 ; 2, Harcourt Buildings, Temple, E.C. 4. *Club :* Oxford and Cambridge Univ.   (O11272)

SANDON, Capt. James Francis, O.B.E., *b.* 20 April, 1885 ; *s.* of Charles Albert Sandon. *Educ.:* Stratheden House, Blackheath ; Munich, Bavaria ; Neuchatel, Switzerland. Employed with General Merchants and Shippers. *War Work :* Volunteered and obtained commission in R.F.A. in Nov. 1914 ; Demobilised Oct. 1919, as Staff-Capt. G.H.Q., Army of the Rhine (Cologne).   (O5749)

SANDS, Charles Edward Walker, O.B.E.

SANDS, Robert Sydney, M.B.E.   (M10414)

SANDS, T. Major Robert William Philip, O.B.E., A.P.D.

SANDWELL, Percy William, M.B.E.

SANFORD, Lieut.-Col. George Batthyany, O.B.E., I.A.

SANGSTER, Major Thomas Alexander Gardner, M.B.E.

SANGUINETTI, Major William Roger, O.B.E., M.C., late R.E., *b.* 31 Oct. 1871 ; *s.* of Edmund Sheddon Sanguinetti, of Jamaica ; *m.* Helen, *d.* of W. S. Kirsopp, of Hexham. *Educ. :* Privately. Civil Engineer ; Public Works Department, Colonial Civil Service, Federated Malay States. *War Work :* Singapore, during Mutiny of 5 B.L.I. and until 15 April, 1915 ; England, training R.E. New Army, 2nd in command 222nd Field Co. and O.C. 230th A. T. Co., R.E. ; proceeded to France, January, 1916 with latter Co. ; Field Engineer 17th Corps, and 3rd Army as Officer-in-charge Water Supply ; Staff Officer to C.E , and later C.R.E., Paris ; twice mentioned

in despatches. *Address:* Public Works Department, Kuala Pilah, Federated Malay States. *Club:* Junior Army and Navy.
(O5750)

SANKEY, Henry John, M.B.E., *b.* 1 Dec. 1868; *s.* of the late John Sankey, of Plumstead, *m.* Mary, *d.* of the late Joseph Farley, of Plumstead. *Educ.:* Victoria Collegiate School, Erith, Kent. Assistant to Director of Inspection of Guns, Inspection Department, Royal Arsenal, Woolwich. *Address:* 10, Vambery Road, Plumstead, S.E. 18. (M2389)

SANKEY, Sir John, G.B.E., M.A., K.C., *b.* 1866; *s.* of Thomas Sankey. *Educ.:* Lancing and Oxford. Chairman of Coal Industry Commission. *Address:* 28, Dean's Yard, Westminster Abbey, S.W. 1. *Clubs:* Athenæum; Garrick; Oxford and Cambridge. (G11)

SANKEY, Capt. Matthew Henry Phineas Riall, C.B., C.B.E., *b.* 1853; *s.* of the late William Sankey, C.B., of Bawnmore, co. Cork; *m.* Elizabeth, *d.* of Maj.-Gen. Pym. Formerly R.E. (C2931)

SANSOM, William Campbell, M.B.E.

SARCHET, Rev. William Henry, O.B.E., M.C., *b.* 4 Dec. 1862; *s.* of Thomas John Sarchet, of Guernsey; *m.* Emily Victoria, *d.* of Major S. Deacon, of 1st Batt. Royal Berks. Regt. *Educ.:* Richmond Coll., Surrey. *Assistant Principal Chaplain* (Wes.), Southern Command. *War Work:* Mobilised with B.E.F. Aug. 1914; attached No. 3 General Hospital; Dec. 1914, posted to 2nd Division, 6th Brigade, No. 6 Field Ambulance; Feb. 1917, posted to Hdqrs. 13th Corps, as D.A.P.C.; March, 1919, posted to Hdqrs. Southern Command, A.P.C. *Address:* Hamilton House, Tidworth, Hants. *Club:* Officers', Tidworth. (O5751)

SAREL, Comm. Colin Alfred Molyneux, O.B.E., R.N.

SAREL, William Samuel, C.B., C.B.E., *b.* 18 Aug. 1861; *s.* of Samuel Sarel, of Edith Terrace, West Brompton; *m.* Alice Mary, *d.* of the late George Henry Chatwin, of St. Leonards-on-Sea. *Educ.:* Privately. Deputy Accountant General of the Navy. *Addresses:* 18, Hazlewell Road, Putney, S.W. 15; Admiralty, S.W. 1. (C290)

SARGANT, Francis William, O.B.E., Cavaliere Corona d'Italia, *b.* 10 Jan. 1870; *s.* of Henry, of Lincoln's Inn. *Educ.:* Rugby, and New Coll., Oxford. Sculptor. *War Work:* Voluntary driver, ambulance, Belgium and France, 1914–15; Italy (with Italian Army), 1915–18; Commandant 2nd Unit, B.R.C.S. Italy, Feb. 1916. *Address:* 17, Boundary Road, N.W. 8. *Clubs:* Albemarle; Florence, Italy. (O11273)

SARGEAUNT, Bertram Edward, M.V.O., O.B.E., *b.* 4 Dec. 1877; *s.* of the late Capt. Frederic A. Sargeaunt, R.N. and Alice Caroline, sister of first Baron Fisher of Kilverstone (*see* BURKE'S *Peerage*); *m.* Kathleen Hamilton, *d.* of Robert Thornewill, of Craythorne, Burton-on-Trent. *Educ.:* Bedford School. Civil Servant; Assist. Sec. R.U.S.I. Whitehall, S.W. 1899–1910; Government Sec. and Treas., Isle of Man, since 1910. *War Work:* Work in connection with the administration of the prisoner of war camps in the Isle of Man and duties attaching to general war conditions in the Island. *Addresses:* Eaglehurst, Isle of Man; Government Office, Isle of Man. *Club:* Isthmian. (O717)

SARGENT, Frederick Albert, O.B.E., *b.* 10 March, 1858; *s.* of Charles Sargent, of Watford; *m.* Annie Maria, *d.* of John Green, of Watford. *Educ.:* Privately. Railway Officer, L. & N.W.Ry. *War Work:* Served on following Government Sub-Committees; Inter-Departmental Advisory Committee of Board of Agriculture (Fruit and Vegetables), Army Service Corps (Motor Transport Section), attached to Railway Companies, Chairman of Committee of Transport Workers Labour Battalion (London district north of Thames), Port and Transit Committee (Home Trade Transport Section). *Address:* Clovelly, Upton Road, Watford, Herts. *Clubs:* Watford Conservative; West Herts Club and Ground, West Herts Golf. (O11274)

SARGENT, Major-Gen. Harry-Neptune, C.B., C.B.E. D.S.O., *b.* 1886; *s.* of the late Maj. Gen. E. W. Sargent; *m.* 1st, 1897, Ethel, who *d.* 1915, *d.* of the late Daniel Twomey, of Kolor, Penshurst, Australia; 2nd, 1918, Olive Tufnell-Fordine, *d.* of Col. W. Nevill Tufnell, of Langleys, Chelmsford. Entered Devonshire Regt. 1886; Army Service Corps, 1890; Capt. 1892; Brevet Major, 1898; Lieut.-Col. 1906; Brevet Col. 1909; Col. 1911; Hon. Maj.-Gen. (ret.), 1919; served with the Nile Expedition, 1898; present at battle of Khartum (despatches, medal with clasp, Khedive's Star, Brevet Major); in S. Africa, 1899–1902, as D.A.A.G.; present at relief of Ladysmith and actions of Spion Kop, Vaal Krantz, Tugela Heights, Pieter's Hill, and Laing's Nek (despatches thrice, Queen's medal with six clasps, King's medal with two clasps); Great War, 1914–19, on Staff, with rank of Brig.-Gen. (despatches thrice, Legion of Honour); was Dep. Assist.-Director of Supplies and Transport, Irish Command, 1903–6; in command of Army Service Corps, Dublin, 1906–8; of Service Cos., Army Service Corps, Aldershot, 1908–11; Officer-in-charge of Army Service Records, Woolwich, 1912; Assist.-Director Supplies and Transport, Aldershot, 1913–14. (C1320)

SARGENT, Walter Anthony, M.B.E., A.M.I.T., *b.* 7 July, 1876; *s.* of Anthony Sargent, of Derby; *m.* Ellen Ann, *d.* of Henry Ellis, of Derby. *Educ.:* Privately. Superintendent of Operations, Assistant, Midland Railway, Derby. *War Work:* In charge of special arrangements on the Midland Railway for the transport of Naval and Military Forces. *Address:* 195, Upper Dale Road, Derby. (M924)

SARGINT, Olga Joyce Forbes, Mrs., M.B.E., *b.* 4 Aug.

1887; *d.* of Sir William Schooling, K.B.E., of London (*q.v.*); *m.* Herman John Jeffers, *s.* of Richard Sargint, of Zante, Greece. *Educ.:* Kensington High School. *War Work:* Work in connection with the Library for wounded men at the Fulham Military Hospital; worked at War Office for a few months in 1915; and at the National Savings Committee from its inception, both at their headquarters and on the Hammersmith Local Committee. *Address:* 36, Brook Green, London, W. 6. (M2390)

SARJEANT, Frederick Arthur, C.B.E., J.P., *b.* 13 July, 1861; *s.* of Thomas Sarjeant, of Sheffield; *m.* Charlotte, *d.* of Thomas Brown, of Piddington, Oxon. *Educ.:* Privately. Solicitor. *War Work:* Mayor of Reading, 1916–17 and 1917–18; Chairman of Food Control Com., Fuel and Lighting Com., National War Savings Com., Unemployed Com., and Y.M.C.A. Com. for War Work; Hon. Treas. Navy and Army Pensions Com., and member of several other war committees. (C2932)

SARJEANT, Lieut. Leonard James, O.B.E.

SARSON, Col. John Edward, O.B.E., V.D., D.L., *b.* 7 Dec. 1844; *s.* of John Sarson, of Kibworth; *m.* Emily, *d.* of James Vipan Vipan, of Constantia, Cape of Good Hope. *Educ.:* Kettering Grammar School. *War Work:* Commanded National Reserve (afterwards Royal Defence Corps) at outbreak of war; raised 4th (Reserve) Battalion Leicestershire Regt. and commanded 1915–16; County Commandant Leicestershire Volunteer Regt., Dec. 1916, to demobilisation. *Address:* Corrie, Woodland Avenue, Leicester. *Club:* Leicestershire County. (O7667)

SASSOON, Capt. Arthur Meyer, O.B.E., M.C.

SASSOON, Louise, Mrs. C.B.E., *b.* 5 May, 1854; *d.* of Achille Perugia, of Trieste; *m.* Arthur, *s.* of David Sassoon. *War Work:* Officers' Families Clothing Branch. *Address:* 2, Albert Gate, S.W. 1. (C2933)

SATCHWELL, Lieut.-Col. Ernest, O.B.E., *b.* 11 Aug. 1876; *s.* of Thomas Satchwell, of London; *m.* Marie Pauline. *Educ.:* Highgate School, and Zehlendorf (Germany). Jute Merchant. *War Work:* Officer in charge of Coal Supply, B.E.F., in liaison with French Coal Controller. *Address:* 23, Rue de Choiseul, Paris. *Club:* Junior Naval and Military. (O5752).

SATOW, Major Graham Francis Henry, O.B.E., *b.* 26 Dec. 1886; *s.* of Henry W. Satow, of Bangor, N. Wales; *m.* Evelyn Mary, *d.* of Charles S. Moore, of Foochow, China, and Bushey, Herts. *Educ.:* Blackheath School, and Liverpool Univ. Engineer. *War Work:* Lieut. 8th Border Regt., France, 1914; Capt. 75th Bgde.; Machine Gun Officer, France, 1915; Major, Instructor M.G.T.C. 1916–17; M.G. Officer, 2nd Corps, France, 1918; G.S.O. (2nd Grade) Machine Guns, G.H.Q. France, 1918; mentioned in despatches, 1918 and 1919; 1st Staff Officer appointed to M.G.C. in France. *Addresses:* Corfe Cottage, Bushey, Herts; 1, Albemarle Street, W. 1. *Club:* Royal Automobile. (O5753)

SATOW, Harold Eustace, O.B.E.

SATOW, Major Hugh Ralph, C.B.E.

SATOW, Capt. Lawrence De Wahl, C.B.E., R.N. Div. Naval Transport Officer, Port Said; served in the Great War, 1914–19 (despatches). (C2264)

SATTERLY, Charles Skinner, O.B.E., *b.* 21 July, 1878. Appointed Assistant Inspector of Schools to the Board of Education, 1913. *War Work:* Acted as County Secretary for War Savings, War Loans, etc., in Lincolnshire, 1916–18, and in 1919 was appointed Commissioner to the National Savings Committee for the North-Eastern Division of England. *Address:* Eastgate, Sleaford, Lincs. (O1843)

SATTERTHWAITE, Major Clement Richard, O.B.E., R.E

SAUL, Lieut. Joseph, M.B.E., R.G.A. (T.), *b.* 26 June, 1884; *s.* of Cuthbert Saul, of Newcastle-on-Tyne; *m.* Florence Eveline, *d.* of William Marshall Cox, of Newcastle-on-Tyne. *Educ.:* Rutherford Coll., Newcastle-on-Tyne. Deputy Bank Manager with Lloyds Bank, Ltd. *War Work:* Awarded M.B.E. (Mil. Division) for conspicuous bravery and devotion to duty in connection with a fire which broke out in a shell magazine at Tynemouth Castle, Oct. 1918. Entered magazine with a sergeant and gunner after two explosions had taken place and brought out burning boxes of H.E. and Shrapnel Shell. *Address:* 31, Eastbourne Gardens, Monkseaton, Northumberland. (M3311)

SAUNDERS, Lieut. Alan Arthur, O.B.E., R.E. (T.)

SAUNDERS, Lieut.-Comm. Arthur Patrick, O.B.E., R.N.

SAUNDERS, Sqdn.-Leader Edgar Stopford, R.A.F.

SAUNDERS, Edward, M.B.E., J.P.

SAUNDERS, Elsie, O.B.E.

SAUNDERS, Major Ernest Howie, D.S.O., O.B.E.

SAUNDERS, Major Ernest Victor, O.B.E., *b.* 30 April, 1865. *Educ.:* National Schools. *War Work:* Routine, in connection with Royal Army Medical Corps. *Address:* 9, Church Hill, Aldershot. (O8670)

SAUNDERS, Florence Margaret, M.B.E. (M10415)

SAUNDERS, Capt. Frank Veall, O.B.E., Aust. A.S.C.

SAUNDERS, Lieut. Frederick, M.B.E., R.E.

SAUNDERS, Frederick James, O.B.E.

SAUNDERS, George, O.B.E., B.A., LL.D.; *s.* of the late D. H. Saunders, J.P., of Dundee and Craigmill, Blairgowrie; *m.* Gertrude, *d.* of Herr Oskar Hainauer, of Berlin. *Educ.:* Universities of Glasgow; Bonn; Göttingen; Balliol Coll., Oxford. 1888–97, Berlin Correspondent of " Morning

Post "; 1897–1908, Berlin Correspondent of "Times"; 1908–14, Paris Correspondent of "Times"; 1915–18, Political Intelligence Work; 1918–20, Political Intelligence Department of the Foreign Office. *Address:* Pontsam, Woking. *Club:* St. James's. (O11275)

SAUNDERS, Lieut.-Col. George Muskett, O.B.E., R.E., 2nd *s.* of H. J. Saunders, of Tongaat, Bath; *m.* 13 Sept. 1920, Mary Ryan, of Courtsfold, Haslemere, *d.* of the late Rev. G. B. Ryan, of Stranford, Co. Down.

SAUNDERS, George William, O.B.E., *b.* 10 Nov. 1883; *s.* of George William Saunders, of Eton; *m.* Dallas Eveline, *d.* of Thomas William McCulloch, of Kenilworth. *Educ.:* Tiffin's School, Kingston-on-Thames. Shipbroker. *War Work:* Ships Requisitioning Branch, Ministry of Shipping, from Dec. 1914, and Member of Ships Licensing Committee till July, 1920. *Address:* The Manor, Abbess Roding, Fyfield, near Ongar. (O3907)

SAUNDERS, Capt. Harry Francis, M.B.E.

SAUNDERS, T. Lieut. Henry Hume, M.B.E., R.E.

SAUNDERS, Ina, Mrs., V.A.D.

SAUNDERS, Capt. John Augustus, O.B.E., R.A.S.C.

SAUNDERS, Lilian Beatrice Anna, M.B.E.

SAUNDERS, Maude Irene, M.B.E.

SAUNDERS, Molly, M.B.E., Q.M.A.A.C.

SAUNDERS, Capt. Percy Tunstall, O.B.E., M.R.C.V.S., R.A.V.C. (S.R.), *b.* 8 Sept. 1884; *s.* of Major R. Saunders, R.A. of Hull. *Educ.:* Carlisle and Edinburgh. Served in the S. African War, 1901–2 (medal and five clasps). *War Work:* Went to France 19 Aug. 1914 with 4th Division; in Retreat, Marne, and Aisne; 2nd Indian Cavalry Division, Feb. 1915; 1st Indian Cavalry Division, Dec. 1915; 2nd Indian Cavalry Division (later 5th Cavalry Division, Dec. 1916, till its dissolution, March, 1919); in France till March, 1918, and later Egypt, Palestine, Syria, etc., till Sept. 1920. *Address:* 16, Sunny Bank, Hull. *Club:* Sports. (O8649)

SAUNDERS, Samuel Edgar, O.B.E.

SAUNDERS, Thomas Arthur, M.B.E., *b.* 22 Aug. 1873; *s.* of Charles Thomas Saunders, of London; *m.* Ethel Marion, *d.* of Robert Self, of Eye, Suffolk. Staff Clerk General Register Office, Somerset House, W.C. 2. *War Work:* At General Register Office: Central Register of War Refugees, National Register (under National Registration Acts, 1915 and 1918); at Ministry of National Service: Registration at Recruiting Offices. *Address:* 16, Redcliffe Gardens, Ilford, Essex. (M928)

SAUNDERS, Thomas Edward, M.B.E., *b.* 21 Feb. 1874; *s.* of Thomas R. Saunders, of Folkestone; *m.* Sarah Jane, *d.* of Richard A. G. Bailey, of Whitstable. *Educ.:* Wesleyan Elementary School, Folkestone. Collector of Fishery Statistics; Shipwright and Boatbuilder; Fisherman; Proprietor of Motor Boats. *War Work:* Acting under orders of Local S.N.O. and Captain of Trawler Patrols at Dover in directing fishing operations; dealing with mines landed by fishing vessels; Salving aviator; rendering assistance to aviators at sea; salving planes and other Crown property. *Address:* Froghole Boat Yard, Folkestone. *Clubs:* Free and Accepted Masons, Castle Lodge 1436, and Amhurst Lodge 266. (M9349)

SAUZIER, Emile, O.B.E., K.C.

SAVAGE, Capt. James Edmund, M.B.E., Aust. A.S.C.

SAVAGE, Major John Clifford, M.B.E., R.A.F., *b.* 23 Oct. 1891; *s.* of William Brown Savage, of Leslie House, Ryde, I. of W.; *m.* Pauline Elisabeth, *d.* of Richard Stafford, of Liverpool. *Educ.:* Sandown, and Privately. Aeronautical Engineer and Company Manager; technical contributor to "Flight" and "Scientific American" 1911–13; Commercial Manager of British Aerial Transport Co., Ltd., 1919. *War Work:* Production, storage, and supply of all kite balloon gear to British Naval and Military units and to some Allied Forces; design of special K.B. winch and hydrogen gear. *Addresses:* 38, Conduit Street, W. 1; Leslie House, Ryde, I. of W. *Clubs:* Royal Aero; Press; London Sketch. (M2392)

SAVAGE, Joseph, M.B.E.

SAVAGE, Lieut.-Col. Morris Boscawen, C.B.E., D.S.O.

SAVAGE, Lieut.-Col. Cecil Francis HEYWORTH-, O.B.E., *b.* 3 March, 1864; *s.* of G. F. Heyworth, of 96, Lancaster Gate, London; *m.* Mary Clarissa, *d.* of W. Gillilan, of 6, Palace Gate, London. *Educ.:* Wellington Coll., and Sandhurst. Late Royal Fusiliers. Burmese Campaign, 1886–87; S. African War, 1899–1902; Great War, 1914–18. *Address:* Toddington Grange, Winchcombe, Glos. *Clubs:* Naval and Military; Prince's; Royal Automobile. (O5373)

SAVILE, Major Clare Ruxton Uvedale, D.S.O., O.B.E., *b.* 5 Dec. 1881; *s.* of Brig.-Gen. Walter Clare Savile, C.B., D.S.O.; *m.* Katherine Gladys, *d.* of the Rev. G. M. St. M. Ritchie, Ch. Forces. *Educ.:* Wellington Coll., and Sandhurst. Royal Fusiliers. *War Work:* Staff Capt. Cameroon Campaign, 1914–16; Brigade Major, France, 1917; Assist. Adj. and Qr.-Mr. General, Malta Command (T. Lieut.-Col.), 1918–20. *Club:* Junior Army and Navy. (O7671)

SAVILE, Col. George Walter Wray, C.B.E. D.S.O.

SAVILE, Major (T. Lieut.-Col.) Robert Vesey, C.B.E., (R. of O.), *b.* 31 Dec. 1873; *s.* of the late Col. H. B. O. Savile, C.B., of Clifton, Bristol; *m.* Evelyn Gertrude, *d.* of Robert L. Hunter, of 17, Stratton Street, W. 1. *Educ.:* Clifton Coll., and R.M.C. Sandhurst. Gazetted 2nd Lieut. The Sherwood Foresters, 1893, promoted Lieut. 1896, and Captain 1900; seconded for service with the Egyptian Army, 1899, and entered Sudan Civil Service, 1901; retired from the Army, 1909; Assist. Civil Secretary, Sudan Government, 1907; Governor

Bahr el Ghazal Province, 1908; Governor Kordofan, 1909; Governor Darfur, 1917; promoted Major in Reserve of Officers, 1915; T. Lieut.-Col. 1st Jan. 1917; 3rd Class Medjidieh, 1905; 3rd Class, Nile, 1916; O.B.E., 1918; C.B.E. (Mil.) 1919. *Address:* El Fasher, Darfur, Sudan. *Clubs:* Army and Navy; Sports. (C1389)

SAVILL, Edwin, O.B.E.

SAVILLE, Paymaster-Lieut. Cyril Arthur, M.B.E., R.N.R.

SAVILLE, Daniel Benjamin Sheriff, M.B.E., *b.* 25 Sept. 1866; *s.* of Daniel Saville, of Thaxted, Essex; *m.* Georgina, *d.* of Stephen Kingston, of Lower Heyford, Northants. *Educ.:* Charlton, Dover; St. Paul's, Canterbury. Marine Engineer; Chief Engineer, H.M. Submarine Cable Ships. *War Work:* Work in connection with the laying and repairing of submarine cables. *Address:* 98, Catford Hill, Catford, S.E. 6. (M3959)

SAVILLE, Francis Ernest, O.B.E., *b.* 28 Dec. 1876; *s.* of John James Walker Saville, of Leeds; *m* Beatrice Olive, *d.* of Francis Long, of Chichester. *Educ.:* Barnsley Grammar School; Leeds High School; Yorkshire Coll. Managing Director, Leech and Sinkinson, Ltd., Cotton Yarn Merchants and Exporters, Leeds and Oldham. *War Work:* Chief Administrator, Leeds Special Constabulary. *Address:* 23, Kelso Road, Leeds. (O720)

SAVONA, Major William, M.B.E.

SAW, Lieut.-Col. Athelstan John Henton, O.B.E., Aust. A.M.C.

SAWARD, Capt. Frank Robert, M.B.E., R.E.

SAWDAY, Albert Edwin, O.B.E., F.R.I.B.A., J.P., *b.* 21 Dec. 1851; *s.* of George Sawday, of Sidmouth, Devon; *m.* Elizabeth Hannah, *d.* of Dr. Thomas Brown, of London. *Educ.:* Binfield House School, Stockwell, London. Architect; Alderman and Ex-Mayor of Leicester; Chairman of Estate Committee. *War Work:* Chairman of Leicester Tribunal. *Addresses:* Briarwood, Springfield Road, Leicester; 56, London Road, Leicester. *Clubs:* Leicester Liberal; Leicestershire. (O721)

SAWDON, Frank Reginald, M.B.E., M.B., Ch.B., *b.* 13 Aug. 1879; *s.* of Richard Ainsworth Sawdon, of Turncroft, Lytham; *m.* Winifred Gertrude, *d.* of Tom Cunliffe, of Ardwick, Manchester. *Educ.:* Rugby School, and Victoria Univ., Manchester. Councillor, Buxton Corporation; Hon. Physician, Devonshire Hospital, Buxton. *War Work:* Capt. (Hon.) Canadian Army Medical Corps; Commandant, Buxton V.A.D. (No. 8 Derby). *Address:* Grafton House, Buxton. *Club:* Union (Buxton). (M9550)

SAWERS, Major John Boothman, O.B.E., A.I.F

SAWYER, Col. Charles Edward, C.B.E., *b.* 21 Sept. 1848; *s.* of the late Lieut.-Col. C. R. J. Sawyer, Chevalier de la Couronne de Chine; *m.* Florence Wroughton, *d.* of the late Rev. F. L. M. Anderson, of North Berwick. *Educ.:* Wellington Coll. and Sandhurst. Late Loyal North Lancashire Regt. *War Work:* Afghan Campaign, 1878–80 (medal with clasp); Great War, 1914; Commandant 3rd Line Northumbrian Division (T.). *Address:* Brentwood, North Berwick, N.B. (C1758)

SAWYER, Geo. Alex., C.B.E. Rendered services in connection with War Charities during Great War. (C2924)

SAWYER, Hedley, M.B.E.

SAWYERS, William Henry, M.B.E., R.N.R.

SAXON, Amy, Mrs., M.B.E.

SAXTON, Amy Harriette, M.B.E., *b.* 7 Feb. 1867; *d.* of Major-General G. H. Saxton, late of Madras Staff Corps. *War Work:* Managing Director of the Woking War Hospital Supply Depot (Woking Branch of Queen Mary's Needlework Guild, Surgical Branch). (M9553)

SAY, Lieut. Geoffrey Baldwin, M.B.E., R.N.V.R.

SAY, Lieut.-Comm. Richard, O.B.E., F.C.I.S., R.N.V.R. *Educ.:* Berkhamsted. General Secretary of the Grand Fleet Fund; held the appointment of Fleet Mail Officer (1915–19) to the Grand Fleet. *Addresses:* 11, Regent Street, S.W.; 30, Regent's Park Road, N.W. *Club:* Royal Thames Yacht. (O1846)

SAYER, Major George William, O.B.E., R.E.

SAYER, Harold Edward, M.B.E.

SAYER, Lieut.-Col. Maxwell Barcham, C.B.E.

SAYER, Thomas Lewes, M.B.E., *b.* 16 Nov. 1865; *s.* of Charles James Sayer, of West Kensington, and Beccles, Suffolk; *m.* Lilian May, *d.* of Frank Christie, of Ipswich. *Educ.:* Philological School, Marylebone. Official of the Corporation of the City of London since 1881. *War Work:* Chairman of Committee of the Local War Distress Fund; City of London National Guard, 1915; Chairman Wallington Recruiting Committee; Member of Local Advisory Committee and Tribunal and Local Victory Loan Association; Chairman of Local Agricultural and Allotments Committee; Member of Local Food Committee, Peace Celebration and War Memorial Committees. *Addresses:* Guildhall, E.C.; The White House, Wallington, Surrey. (M9555)

SAYERS, Joseph, O.B.E.

SAYERS, Josiah, O.B.E.

SAYERS, Major Raymond Cecil, O.B.E., R.A., *b.* 27 March, 1884; *s.* of Robert Cecil Sayers; *m.* Lucy Antoinette, *d.* of the late Rev. Jocelyn Barnes, of S. Breage Vicarage, Cornwall. *Educ.:* St. Paul's School, and Royal Military Academy. Commissioned in Royal Garrison Artillery, Dec. 1903; 1st Lieut. Dec. 1906; Capt. Oct. 1914; Major, Oct. 1918; at present Staff Capt. in the War Office. *War Work:* Active Service in France; 1914, in 115th Heavy Battery,

R.G.A.; 1915, Commanding 22nd Anti-Aircraft Section, R.A.; 1916–17, Commanding 109th Siege Battery, R.G.A. *Address:* 54, Overstrand Mansions, S.W. 11. (O7673)

SCAIFE, Comm. John Andrew Hanson, O.B.E., R.N.

SCALE, Major John Dymoke, C.B.E., D.S.O., Indian Army, *b.* 1882. Gen. Staff Officer; served during Great War, 1914–17 (despatches); has Orders of St. Vladimir and St. Anne of Russia, Order of Star of Rumania, and Legion of Honour. (C9533)

SCALES, George Herbert, M.B.E.

SCANDRETT, Capt. James Herbert, M.B.E., M.C., R.A.F.

SCANLEN, Emilie, Mrs., M.B.E.

SCANLON, Leonard Edmund, M.B.E., M.R.C.S., L.R.C.P.

SCANNELL, James Berchmans, M.B.E., *b.* 30 Jan. 1879; *s.* of the late J. A. Scannell, of Cork. *Educ.:* Presentation Coll., Cork. Admiralty Civil Service; Officer-in-charge of Expense Accounts, H.M. Dockyard, Pembroke, 1904–12, and H.M. Dockyard, Gibraltar, 1912–19. *Addresses:* H.M. Dockyard, Chatham; Dockyard Accounts Dept., Admiralty, S.W. (M9567)

SCARFE, Fred, M.B.E.

SCARFF, Capt. Frederick William, M.B.E., R.A.F.

SCARLETT, Albert Edward, M.B.E.

SCARR, George, O.B.E., M.B., L.R.C.S.I., J.P., C.C., *b.* 1 Jan. 1853; *s.* of Lodge Scarr, of Bainbridge, Yorkshire; *m.* Sidney Jane, *d.* of Matthew Wright, of Dunganstown, Co. Wicklow. *Educ.:* Tramore Boarding School, and Trinity Coll., Univ. of Dublin. Physician and Surgeon. *War Work:* Organised St. John Auxiliary Military Home Hospital, Radcliffe, Lancashire, in Ambulance Drill Hall, which opened on 28 Nov. 1914, with 20 beds, and closed on 15 March, 1919, with 66 beds; 1066 patients passed through: Medical Officer in charge and Commandant during that period; Member of War Savings and Hon. Treas. of War Pensions Committees. *Address:* Beech House, Radcliffe, Lancashire. *Club:* Rectory (Manchester). (O11277)

SCATTERTY, Agnes, Mrs., M.B.E.; *d.* of John Morrison, J.P., of Kennethmont, Aberdeenshire; *m.* Lieut.-Col. William Scatterty, R.A.M.C.; *s.* of John Scatterty, of Kennethmont. *Educ.:* Huntly, and London. *War Work:* Commandant Keighley Ambulance Hospital. *Address:* Highfield House, Keighley, Yorks. (M2396)

SCAWIN, Major Harold Willis, O.B.E., M.R.C.S., L.R.C.P., *b.* 25 Aug. 1884; *s.* of W. Scawin, of York; *m.* Maud, *d.* of T. W. Taylor, of London. *Educ.:* St. Peter's School, York; King Edward VII. School, Retford; St. Bartholomew's Hospital, London, E.C. Medical Officer, Iver Cottage Hospital. *War Work:* R.A.M.C., temporary commission, France, June, 1915, to March, 1919. *Address:* York Cottage, Iver, Bucks. (O5755)

SCHARLIEB, Dr. Mary Ann Dacomb, C.B.E., M.D., M.S., *b.* 1845; *d.* of William Candler Bird, of The Hollies, Manchester; *m.* 1865, William Mason Scharlieb, who *d.* 1891. *Educ.:* London School of Med. for Women. Physician and Surg.; Consulting Surg., New Hospital for Women (sometime Senior Surg.), and to South London Hospital for Women; Consulting Gynæcologist Roy. Free Hospital; rendered services in social work during the Great War; author of "The Seven Ages of Woman," etc. *Address:* 149, Harley Street, W. (C61)

SCHAVERINE, Lieut. Samuel, M.B.E., L.F.I., *b.* 6 Jan. 1887; *s.* of Joseph Schaverine, of London; *m.* Daisy May, *d.* of Benjamin Francis Augustus Hodgson, of London. *Educ.:* Hindle Coll. General Insurance Expert; Special Representative to Prudential Assurance Co., Ltd. *War Work:* 2nd York and Lancaster Regt., with regiment until Cambrai, 1918; Commandant, Prisoners of War, 1st Army, B.E.F., May, 1919, to Nov. 1919; Commandant, Repatriated Prisoners of War, B.E.F., Nov. 1919, to Aug. 1920. *Address:* 140, Fairview Road, Stamford Hill, N. 15. (M4588)

SCHIERWATER, Charles Adolf, M.B.E., *b.* March, 1880; *s.* of Amandus Schierwater, of Liverpool; *m.* Dora, *d.* of John Fothergill, of Liverpool. *Educ.:* Privately. Managing Director of Pastimes, Ltd., exporters of jewellers' sundries; Senior Partner, Schierwater & Lloyd, Diamond Merchants; Senior Partner, Charles Schierwater & Co., Wholesale Merchants. *War Work:* Commandant in command of fifty motor ambulances attached to Liverpool; Member of the Finance Committee, Management Committee, and Joint Ambulance Committee of the British Red Cross Society, Liverpool. *Address:* The Octagon, Princes Road, Liverpool. *Clubs:* Liverpool Racquets; Liverpool Exchange. (M9558)

SCHIFF, Ernst, M.B.E.

SCHIFF, Otto, M.B.E.

SCHLESINGER, Surg.-Lieut. Edward Gustave, C.B.E., M.B., F.R.C.S., R.N.

SCHLESINGER, Richard Alphonse, M.B.E., *b.* 12 Sept. 1861; *s.* of Bernhard Schlesinger, of Frankfort-on-Main; *m.* Estella, *d.* of Alexander Ellinger, of Manchester. *Educ.:* Frankfort-on-Main, and London. Member of London Stock Exchange. *War Work:* Member of Jewish War Refugees Committee. *Address:* 15, Fitzjohn's Avenue, London, N.W. (M9560)

SCHOFIELD, Lieut.-Comm. James Rimmer, M.B.E., *b.* 5 Nov. 1869; *s.* of Edward Schofield, of Rochdale, Lancs.; *m.* Emily *d.* of Charles Whilwork, of Rochdale. *Educ.:* Public School, Rochdale. Principal and Managing

Director, Wireless Training Colls., Cardiff and Bristol, also Founder of Glanhurst Shipping Co., Ltd. *War Work:* Sent over 750 Trained Wireless Operators to the Services, also founded a Naval Vol. Training Corps. *Address:* Marconi, Penciselr Rd., Cardiff. *Clubs:* Junior Army and Navy. (M2397)

SCHOFIELD, Joseph, M.B.E., *b.* 14 Sept. 1879; *s.* of Samuel Schofield, of Chadderton; *m.* Annie, *d.* of John Henry Mercer, of Oldham. *Educ.:* Waterloo Higher Grade School, Oldham. Clerk of the Urban District Council of Chadderton; and of the Chadderton, Royton and Crompton Joint Hospital Board. *War Work:* Hon. Sec. and Treas. Chadderton Local War Pensions Committee, and of Chadderton War Relief Committee; Hon. Sec. Soldiers' and Sailors' Families Association, and Hon. Sec. and Treas. Sailors' and Soldiers' Help Society. *Address:* Hope House, Chadderton, near Oldham. (M9561)

SCHOFIELD, Major William Ernest, O.B.E., R.A.V.C., *b.* 4 Jan. 1878; *s.* of W. G. Schofield, J.P., of Pontefract; *m.* Winifred Isabel De Courcy, *d.* of Surgeon-Gen. Tippetts, of Army Medical Service. *Educ.:* King's School, Pontefract, Yorks. *War Work:* Military duties in India and at home. *Addresses:* D.A.D.V.S., G.H.Q., British Forces on the Rhine, Cologne; c/o Messrs. Holt & Co., 3, Whitehall Place, S.W. *Club:* Junior Army and Navy. (O7675)

SCHOLEFIELD, Cotterill, O.B.E., J.P., D.L., *b.* July, 1855. *Educ.:* Harrow, and Exeter Coll., Oxford. *War Work:* Assist. County Director, Cumberland and Westmorland Territorial Force Association, and Assist. C. D. of Cumberland Branch British Red Cross Society; Administration of Hospitals and Transport during the war. *Address:* Newbiggin Hall, Carlisle. (O11278)

SCHOLEFIELD, George Edward, M.B.E., M.D., C.M. (Edin.), D.P.H. (Vict.), *b.* Sept. 1856; *s.* of William Scholefield, of Sowerby Bridge, Yorks; *m.* Sarah Roseline, *d.* of William Dyer, of Halifax. *Educ.:* Privately, and Edinburgh Univ. Medical Officer of Health, West Lancashire Rural District Council, and Ormskirk Urban District Council; Examiner, St. John Ambulance Association. *War Work:* Organised and acted as Commandant and Medical Officer of the V.A.D. Auxiliary Military Convalescent Hospital, Aughton, Lancashire (West Lancs. 62); served on the Local Committee for the Prince of Wales' Fund, and West Lancashire Food Control Committee. *Address:* Ormskirk, Lancashire. (M9562)

SCHOLEFIELD, Guy Hardy, O.B.E.

SCHOLEFIELD, Lieut. Maurice Theodore, M.B.E.

SCHOLES, Lieut. George Ernest, M.B.E., R.E. (T.)

SCHOLES, Joseph, O.B.E.

SCHOLES, Capt. Walter Nevelle, O.B.E., R.E.

SCHOLEY, Harry, C.B.E. London Member of Clyde Anti-Submarine Committee during the Great War. (C2925)

SCHOLFIELD, Brig.-Gen. George Peabody, C.M.G., C.B.E., Deputy Chief Engineer. *b.* 1868. Entered R.E. 1887; became Brevet Maj. 1902; Lieut.-Col. 1914; Brevet Col. 1918; Col. 1919; served in the S. African War, 1899–1902, on Staff, present at relief of Ladysmith (Queen's medal with five clasps, King's medal with two clasps, Brevet Major); Great War, 1914–19; appointed a Chief Engineer, 1918, with rank of Brig.-Gen. (despatches); has French Croix de Guerre. (C1759)

SCHOLFIELD, Herbert, M.B.E.

SCHOLFIELD, William Farrar, O.B.E., *b.* 12 May, 1885; *s.* of John Scholfield, of Eccleston Park, Prescot, Lancs. *Educ.:* Liverpool Coll., and Trinity Coll., Cambridge. Principal Clerk, H.M. Office of Works. *Address:* 46, Norfolk Square, Hyde Park, W. 2. *Club:* New Oxford and Cambridge. (O3909)

SCHOLTE, Lieut.-Col. Frederick Lewellen, O.B.E., A.M.I.A.E., *b.* 1890; *s.* of Frederick P. Scholte, of Hampstead; *m.* Hilda May, *d.* of James Gardner, of Skelmorlie, Ayrshire, N.B. *Educ.:* Highgate School. Engineer. *Address:* 1, Burgess Hill, Hampstead, N.W. *Club:* Royal Automobile. (O3410)

SCHOLTZ, Capt. Edmund John, O.B.E.

SCHOLTZ, Capt. Ellis Keith, O.B.E., *b.* 14 April, 1886; *s.* of Dr. Wm. C. Scholtz, M.D., B.Sc., of Cape Town, South Africa. *Educ.:* St. George's Grammar School, Cape Town; King's Coll., London Univ.; Camborne School of Mines, Cornwall. Mining Engineer. *War Work:* 1/1 West Kent (Q.O.) Imperial Yeomanry; R.A.S.C.; I.A.R.O.; served in Egypt, Gallipoli, France, Flanders; mentioned in despatches. (O5756)

SCHONLAND, Capt. Basil Ferdinand Jamieson, O.B.E., B.A. (Cape and Cantab.), *b.* 5 Feb. 1896; *s.* of Dr. S. Schonland, M.A. Ph.D., etc., of Grahamstown, South Africa. *Educ.:* St. Andrew's Coll., Grahamstown, and Gonville and Caius Coll., Cambridge. Scientific Research (Physics). *War Work:* Signals Officer, R.E., B.E.F., France, 1916–19; Staff Officer (Wireless) to Chief Signal Officer, 1st Army, B.E.F., France, 1918. *Addresses:* Gonville and Caius Coll., Cambridge; Oatlands, Grahamstown, S. Africa. (O5757)

SCHOOLING, Sir William K.B.E., F.R.A.S., *b.* 16 Dec. 1860; *s.* of Henry Schooling, of Notting Hill Gate; *m.* Sarah Jessie, *d.* of Thomas Forbes. *Educ.:* Elizabeth Coll., Guernsey, and Private Schools. Author and Journalist. *War Work:* Originally Hon. Sec. and now a Vice-Chairman of the National Savings Committee. *Address:* 36, Brook Green, W. 6. *Club:* Devonshire. (K422)

SCHREIBER, Capt. Arthur Thomas, O.B.E.

SCHULTZE, Alfred Cecil Dunbar, O.B.E.

SCHUSTER, Lieut.-Col. George Ernest, C.B.E., M.C., *b.* 25 April, 1881; *s.* of Ernest Schuster, LL.D., of London;

m. Hon. Gwendolen, *d*. of Lord Parker of Waddington, of Aldworth, near Haslemere (*see* BURKE'S *Peerage*). *Educ.*: Charterhouse and New Coll., Oxford. Barrister-at-Law and director of various companies before the war. *War Work*: Joined Queen's Own Oxfordshire Hussars, Sept. 1914; served with regiment in France till March, 1916; afterwards Staff Capt. H.A. 1st Corps, B.E.F.; Staff Officer R.A., 1st Army, B.E.F.; and from Jan. 1919, A.A. and Q.M.G., North Russian Expeditionary Force, Murmansk; 4 times mentioned in despatches. *Addresses*: Nether Worton House, Steeple Aston, Oxon; 3, Barton Street, Westminster. *Clubs*: New Univ.; Cavendish. (C2359f)

SCHWABE, Capt. Charles Parker, O.B.E.

SCICLUNA, Corinna, Marchesa, O.B.E.

SCINDHIA OF GWALIOR, H.H. Maharaja Sir Madho Rao Bahadur, G.B.E. (G18)

SCLATER, Charlotte Seymour, Mrs. C.B.E., R.R.C.; *d*. of the late William Proctor Mellen, of New York and Colorado, U.S.A.; *m*. William Lutley, M.A. (Oxon.), F.R.G.S., F.Z.S., *s*. of Philip Lutley Sclater, of Odiham Priory, Hants. During the South African War created an organisation, " The Field Force Fund," for providing comforts for the soldiers in the field, for this was decorated by H.M. King Edward with the Royal Red Cross; at the commencement of the Great War revived the organisation under the direct patronage of H.M. Queen Alexandra, under the name of Queen Alexandra's Field Force Fund for the same purpose, acting as Hon. Sec. of both organisations; was awarded C.B.E. at the first institution of the Order. *Address*: 10, Sloane Court, S.W. 1. (C62)

SCLATER, Edith Harriet, Lady, D.B.E.; *d*. of the late Col. Rt. Hon. Sir Walter Barttelot, C.B., of Stopham, Sussex (*see* BURKE'S *Peerage*); *m*. Gen. Sir Henry Crichton Sclater, G.C.B., G.B.E., *s*. of the late James Henry Sclater, J.P., D.L., of Newick Park, Sussex. *War Work*: Organiser and President of Lady Sclater's Workrooms for Soldiers' Hospitals, both at home and abroad; President of the Fund for Smokes for Wounded Soldiers and Sailors; President of the Salisbury Branch of the Prisoners of War Packing Association, and of Soldiers' and Sailors' Families Association at Central Hackney, and of the Salisbury Plain Pensions Committee. *Address*: Holmwood, Edenbridge, Kent. *Club*: Ladies' Imperial. (D18)

SCLATER, Eliza, Mrs., M.B.E.

SCLATER, Capt. Frank Arthur, O.B.E., M.C., R.E., (S.R.)

SCLATER, Gen. Sir Henry Crichton, G.C.B., G.B.E., Col.-Comm. Royal Artillery, *b*. 5 Nov. 1855; *s*. of James Henry Sclater, of Newick Park, Sussex; *m*. Edith Harriet, *d*. of Col. the Rt. Hon. Sir Walter Barttelot, Bart., C.B., M.P., of Stopham, Sussex (*see* BURKE'S *Peerage*). *Educ.*: Cheltenham Coll. Entered R.A. as Lieut. 28 Jan, 1875; Captain, Dec. 1883; Brevet Major, June, 1885; Major, Oct. 1891; Lieut.-Col. July, 1900; Brevet Col. Nov. 1900; Col. Nov. 1902; Maj.-Gen. Oct. 1906; Lieut.-Gen. June, 1911; Gen. Nov. 1919; held many staff appointments at home and in Egypt, S. Africa, and India, from Feb. 1885 to Nov. 1908; Div. Comdr. India, Nov. 1908 to Nov. 1912; Adj.-Gen. to the Forces (2nd Mil. Member, Army Council) April, 1914 to Feb. 1916; G.O. Comdg.-in-Chief S. Command, Mar. 1916 to May, 1919. *Address*: Holmwood, Edenbridge, Kent. *Club*: Naval and Military. (G39)

SCOBIE, Grace Locke, O.B.E.

SCOBLE, Capt. Walter Alfred, M.B.E., R.A.F.

SCORER, Frank, M.B.E., M.R.C.S., L.R.C.P., *b*. 16 June, 1868; *s*. of Alfred Scorer, of London; *m*. Violet Eleanor, *d*. of Alfred Norris, of London. *Educ.*: Highgate School, and St. Bartholomew's Hospital. Hon. Anæsthetist, Royal Victoria and West Hants Hospital; Medical Officer, Sunday School Union Convalescent Home, Bournemouth. *War Work*: Received Belgian wounded soldiers in private house, 1914–15; M.O. in charge, Crag Head Red Cross Auxiliary Hospital. *Club*: Bournemouth. (M9563)

SCORGIE, Lieut.-Col. Norman Gibb, O.B.E.

SCOTLAND, T. Capt. Alexander Patterson, O.B.E.

SCOTT, Adam, O.B.E.

SCOTT, Capt. Albert Charles, C.B.E., R.N., *b*. 1872; *s*. of the late Maj.-Gen. Charles Scott, R.E. Served in the Great War, 1914–18; present at battle of Jutland; appointed Capt. Portsmouth Dockyard, 1918; has Legion of Honour. *Address*: H.M. Dockyard, Portsmouth. (C2322)

SCOTT, Alexander Thomas, M.B.E. M.R.C.S., M.R.C.P

SCOTT, Alice Mary, O.B.E., *b*. 20 Sept. 1848; *d*. of John Scott, Barrister, Inner Temple. Red Cross worker. *War Work*: Four years' work at Private Canteen in Vauxhall Bridge Road, S.W. *Address*: 55, Elm Park Mansions, Chelsea, S.W. (O11280)

SCOTT, Andrew, C.B.E.

SCOTT, Archibald, M.B.E., A.R.I.B.A., *b*. 17 Oct. 1882; *s*. of Archibald Scott, of Glasgow; *m*. Dora, *d*. of George Taggart, J.P., of Glasgow. *Educ.*: Whitehill School, Glasgow; Glasgow and West of Scotland Technical Coll. Architect, in H.M. Office of Works. *War Work*: Government Building work; Hospitals, Housing, Factories. *Address*: 18, Sandwell Mansions, West Hampstead, N.W. 6. (M9565)

SCOTT, Lieut. Arthur Frank, M.B.E., *b*. 23 Dec. 1873; *s*. of Charles Scott, of Newport, Isle of Wight; *m*. Emily

Rowena. Enlisted into 5th Royal Irish Lancers, May. 1890; discharged to pension, as Acting R.S.M. Lincolnshire Yeomanry, Dec. 1915; Commissioned in Lincolnshire Yeomanry, Dec. 1915; served with 5th R.I. Lancers in India, 1891–98; South African War (Queen's Medal and 5 clasps, King's Medal, and two clasps). *War Work*: Mobilised with Lincolnshire Yeomanry, Aug. 1914; proceeded to Egypt, Oct. 1915; appointed Assist. Instructor, Imperial School of Instruction, Zeitoun, Egypt, June to Nov. 1916; returned to England, Dec. 1916; appointed Assist. Instructor, Cavalry School, Netheravon, March, 1917, to Feb. 1919; mentioned in despatches; attached for duty with Cavalry Record Office, York, from Feb. 1919, to March, 1920. *Address*: 57, Westgate. Lincoln. (M5603)

SCOTT, Charles, C.B.E.

SCOTT, Lieut.-Col. Charles McAdam, O.B.E., Can. A.S.C.

SCOTT, Charles Robert, O.B.E., M.B.

SCOTT, Lieut.-Col. David Jobson, O.B.E., M.C., M.D., *b*. 7 July, 1881; *s*. of the late Rev. Dr. Robert Scott, D.D., of Craig, Forfarshire; *m*. Isabel Mary, *d*. of — Collins, of Melbourne. *Educ.*: Edinburgh and St. Andrews Univs. Deputy Commissioner of Med. Services, Ministry of Pensions. *War Work*: Gazetted Sept. 1914, Lieut. 2/1st London Field Ambulance; appointed D.A.D.M.S., 56th (London) Division, B.E.F., D.A.D.M.S. XVIII. Corps, B.E.F., and Acting Lieut.-Col. and O.C. 1/2nd Lowland Field Ambulance, B.E.F. *Address*: c/o Messrs. Holt & Co., 44, Charing Cross, S.W. (O5759)

SCOTT, Capt. Donald Charles, O.B.E., R.A.M.C.

SCOTT, Elizabeth Mabel, M.B.E., M.A., *b*. 18 Aug. 1892; *d*. of Wm. Scott, M.B.C.M., J.P., of Ruthwell, Dumfriesshire. *Educ.*: Dumfries Academy, and Edinburgh Univ. Junior Administrative Assistant, Board of Trade. *Addresses*: Ruthwell, Dumfriesshire; 8, North Villas, Camden Square, N.W. 1. (M9566)

SCOTT, Elvise Irene, M.B.E.

SCOTT, Ernest Alexander, O.B.E.

SCOTT, Major Eustace Lindsay, O.B.E., M.C.

SCOTT, Lieut. Eustace Edward, M.B.E., R.A.V.C., *b*. 9 July, 1889; *s*. of Edward Henry Scott, of Leyton, Essex; *m*. Winifred Mabel, *d*. of John Waltam, of Leytonstone, Essex. *Educ.*: St. Mark's Coll., Chelsea; Friends School, Saffron Walden; Veterinary Coll., London. Veterinary Student. *War Work*: Continuous service at sea, Sept. 1914, to Feb. 1918, as Officer-in-Charge of horses from America and Canada, and also from England to Eastern theatres of war. *Address*: 727. High Road, Leyton, Essex. (M5604)

SCOTT, Surg.-Lieut. Evelyn Dennis, O.B.E., R.N.

SCOTT, Finlay Forbes, C.B.E., *b*. 21 Dec. 1858; *s*. of John Scott, of Hassocks, Sussex. *Educ.*: Ardingly Coll., Sussex. Superintendent of the Line, L.B. & S.C. Railway. *War Work*: Railway Transport. *Address*: Clydesdale. 2, Altyre Road, Croydon, Surrey. *Club*: Croydon. (C291)

SCOTT, Flora Murray, M.B.E., M.A., B.Sc., *b*. 6 Sept, 1891; *d*. of the Rev. Robert Scott, D.D., of Craig Manse, Montrose. *Educ.*: Montrose Academy; United Coll., St. Andrews Univ. Carnegie Research Scholar in Botany, 1914–15. *War Work*: Assist. Forewoman, Cap and Detonator Factory, Royal Arsenal, Woolwich, 1916–17; Worker, Assist. Administrator, and Unit Administrator, Q.M.A.A.C., B.E.F., France, 1917–19. *Address*: c/o Messrs. Johnstone, Simpson, and Thomson, Solicitors, 87, Commercial Street, Dundee, Forfarshire. *Club*: International Franchise Club, 9, Grafton Street, W. 1. (M3151)

SCOTT, Florence Oswald, Mrs., O.B.E. Opened and organised a Red Cross Depot over which she acted as Commandant all through the War. (O11924)

SCOTT, Lieut. Frank, O.B.E., R.E.

SCOTT, Frank Stanley, M.B.E.

SCOTT, Frederick Emelius, O.B.E.

SCOTT, Capt. George Alfred, M.B.E.

SCOTT, Capt. George Edward, O.B.E., Indian Def. Force. (O9058a)

SCOTT, Major George Herbert, C.B.E., R.A.F. Commanded Airship R34 on first voyage across Atlantic to U.S.A. and back, 1919. (M2305)

SCOTT, Gladys Mary, M.B.E., *b*. Nov. 1881; *d*. of Lieut. Col. A. Scott, of 2nd Queen's R.W. Surrey. *Educ.*: Bath High School, and Bath School of Cookery. 1st Class Diplômé Cookery, Laundry, . *War Work*: Bath War Hospital, and Lady Superintendent of Red Cross Kitchens, Salonica, 1916–17. *Address*: Polperro, Cornwall. (M2599)

SCOTT, Ina Lochhead, M.B.E.

SCOTT, Isabel Mary Gordon, M.B.E., *b*. 5 Oct. 1892; *d*. of H. Gordon Scott, of Melbourne, Australia. *Educ.*: Notre Dame and Presentation Academies, Berkley, California. *War Work*: Connected with Sir Connop Guthrie's Staff, British Ministry of Shipping, New York; thereafter sent in the capacity of Private Secretary to Sir Thomas Royden, Bart., to Washington, D.C., and served with his successor, Sir Ernest Raeburn, until demobilisation; also associated wth Sir Thomas Fisher, British Embassy, Washington, D.C. *Address*: 252, East 40th Street. Norfolk, Virginia, U.S.A. (M9568)

SCOTT, Isabella, M.B.E. *War Work*: Commandant of Mayfield, V.A. Hospital, Jarrow-on-Tyne. *Address*: 36, Bede Burn Road, Jarrow-on-Tyne. (M9569)

SCOTT, Major Ivor Buchanan Wyndham, O.B.E., *b.* 10 Nov. 1894; *s.* of Col. Sir Buchanan Scott, K.C.I.E., R.E., of 2, Belvedere Grove, Wimbledon (*see* BURKE'S *Peerage*). *Educ.*: Winchester Coll., and Royal Military Academy, Woolwich. *War Work*: Served R.F.A., and as Divisional Observer for R.F.C. in Gallipoli; afterwards Pilot, R.F.C.; attached G.H.Q., Eastern Command, 1916–17; Staff Officer at G.H.Q. Forces in Great Britain, for Anti-Aircraft and Air Defence Training as G.S.O., 3rd Grade; 1917–18 Sec. Camouflage Committee; promoted G.S.O., 2nd Grade, 1918; mentioned in despatches. *Addresses*: 2, Belvedere Grove, Wimbledon; 86, York Street, Westminster, S.W. *Club*: Junior United Service.   (O7676)

SCOTT, James, M.B.E., *b.* 1855; *s.* of John Scott, of Hawick; *m.* Joanna Ross, *d.* of John Ross, of Roslin. *Educ.*: Maxwelltown Burgh School, Dumfries. Formerly, sea-going Engineer, holding 1st B.O.T. Certificate, and latterly an Engineering Business for nearly 30 years at Denny, Stirlingshire. *War Work*: For 3½ years at the works of Messrs. G. and I. Weir & Co., Glasgow, and A. V. Roe & Co., Ltd., Manchester, under the Aeronautical Inspection Directorate, London, and Examiner-in-Charge at the Sheffield Simplex Motor Works, Ltd., Sheffield. *Club*: Possilpark Bowling.   (M2400)

SCOTT, Major and Qr.-Mr. James, O.B.E., D.C.M.

SCOTT, Lieut. James, C.I.E. M.B.E.

SCOTT, Lieut.-Col. James Edward, O.B.E., I.A.R.O.

SCOTT, Major James Harry, O.B.E.

SCOTT, James Reid, M.B.E.

SCOTT, Capt. John, M.B.E., *b.* 29 Dec. 1852; *s.* of John Scott, of Shetland; *m.* Joan, *d.* of J. Jamieson, of Shetland. *Educ.*: Privately. Shipmaster. *War Work*: Commander R.M.S. " St. Rognvald " during whole period of the war, and safely carried mails, passengers, and cargo. *Address*: Adelaide, King Harold Street, Lerwick.   (M3961)

SCOTT, John, M.B.E., *b.* 13 Oct. 1867; *s.* of J. Gillespie Scott, of Falkirk; *m.* Margaret, *d.* of John Green, of Glasgow. *Educ.*: John Neilson School, Paisley. Postmaster Surveyor. *War Work*: Joint Sec. Sheffield War Savings Association. *Address*: G.P.O. Birmingham.   (M2401)

SCOTT, John Archibald, O.B.E.

SCOTT, Major John Creagh, D.S.O., O.B.E., *b.* 18 Nov. 1879; *s.* of Captain James Creagh Richard Scott, of Crevagh and Kildysert; *m.* Sybil, *d.* of Col. Sir Henry Oldham, K.C.V.O. (*see* BURKE'S *Peerage*), of Cannington, Boscombe. *Educ.*: Radley Coll. Adjutant 1st Argyll and Sutherland Highlanders, 1911–14; Inspector of Recruiting, Scotland, 1914, to Jan. 1915; Staff Capt., G.H.Q., France; D.A.A.G., France; D.A.A.G. 15th Corps, France; D.A.A.G. Aldershot Command. *War Work*: Inspector of Recruiting, Scotland, Aug. 1914 to Jan. 1915; Commanded a company, 2nd A. and S. H. Jan., 1915, to July, 1910; Staff G.H.Q., July, 1915, to April, 1916; 2nd in Command 10th A. & S.H., April, 1915, to May, 1915; Commanded 5/6 R.S. Fus., May, 1915, to June, 1915 Commanded 2nd A. and S.H., June, 1916, to Aug. 1916; Commanded 2nd A. and S.H., Jan. 1916, to April, 1916; Staff, May, 1916, to end of war; French Croix de Guerre avec Etoile d'or; 1914–15 Star; Victory Medal; Allied Medal; twice wounded during the war; mentioned in despatches several times. *Clubs*: Army and Navy; Royal Automobile. (O5762)

SCOTT, Major John Philip, O.B.E., *b.* 6 June, 1891; *s.* of Francis Oliver Scott, of Hawkwell, York. *Educ.*: Sedbugh School. *War Work*: For 2 years served on the Western Front, and for 2 years served on Palestine, Salonika, and Black Sea Fronts; twice mentioned in despatches. *Club*: Junior Army and Navy.   (O8712)

SCOTT, Katherine, Mrs., M.B.E.

SCOTT, Capt. Keith Stanley Malcolm, M.B.E., B.Sc., R.E. (T.).

SCOTT, Louisa Leslie Florence, Mrs., O.B.E., *d.* of the late Henry Strickland Bryant, Privy Council Office; *m.* Capt. Arthur Frances Scott, late Rifle Brigade, and 5th Lancers. Commandant Roxburgh 4 V.A.D. since 1911. *War Work*: Joint Women's V.A.D. Department, Devonshire House, 1915–19. *Address*: Langlee, Jedburgh, N.B.   (O1848)

SCOTT, Maitland Bodley, O.B.E., F.R.C.S.E., Order of St. Anne, Russia, 1916, Order of St. Stanislaus, 1916, *b.* 18 Feb. 1878; *s.* of Dr. T. Bodley Scott, of Bournemouth; *m.* Hilda, *d.* of A. Durancé George, of High Cliff. *Educ.*: Marlborough Coll., and St. Bartholomew's Hospital, London. Assistant Surgeon, Royal Victoria and West Hants Hospital, Bournemouth; Surgeon-in-charge of Orthopædic Dept., Hants Hospital, Bournemouth. *War Work*: Surgeon-in-charge of Red Cross Hospital, St. Malo; Surgeon, R.N.; Major, R.A.M.C. *Address*: Shiplake, Bournemouth.   (O4249)

SCOTT, Capt. Hon. Michael, O.B.E.

SCOTT, Muriel Elena, M.B.E., Q.M.A.A.C.

SCOTT, Nora Carlyle, M.B.E.

SCOTT, Capt. Percy Alexander, O.B.E.

SCOTT, Robert, M.B.E., *b.* 14 May, 1868; *s.* of James Scott, of Dalkeith, Scotland. *Educ.*: Alloa, Scotland. *War Work*: At the Admiralty in the Military Branch.   (M9571)

SCOTT, Robert, M.B.E.

SCOTT, Major Robert Hamilton, D.S.O., O.B.E. Roy. Inniskilling Fusiliers; a D.A.A.G.; served in the Great War, 1914–19 (despatches).   (O2929)

SCOTT, Sidney, C.B.E., *b.* 1863; *s.* of the Rev. Charles Scott; *m.* 1897, Margaret, *d.* of John McKittrick. Collector of Customs and Excise, Glasgow.   (C2937)

SCOTT, Sophie Beatrix Mary, Lady, C.B.E., *b.* 1874; *w.* of George, 5th Earl Cadogan, K.G. (*see* BURKE'S *Peerage*); *m.* Sir Samuel Scott, Bart., M.P., *s.* of Sir Edward Scott, Bart. (*see* BURKE'S *Peerage*). *War Work*: Head of the Gifts Department at the British Red Cross Stores Headquarters, 83, Pall Mall. *Addresses*: 78, Mount Street, W. 1; Westbury Manor, Brackley, Northants. *Club*: Bath.   (C63)

SCOTT, Thomas John, M.B.E.

SCOTT, Capt. Walter, M.B.E., A.I.F.

SCOTT, Lieut. Walter Nedham, M.B.E.

SCOTT, William, M.B.E., R.A.M.C.

SCOTT, William, O.B.E.

SCOTT, William Harding, O.B.E., M.I.E.E., *b.* 13 May, 1862; *s.* of James Scott, of Wimbledon Founder and a Managing Director of Laurence Scott & Co., Ltd., Electrical Engineers, Norwich; Managing Director of Norwich Components, Ltd., Norwich. *War Work*: A Member of the Board of Management of the East Anglian Munitions Committee; the design and manufacture of electrical machinery for H.M. Navy; and of special plant for the making of high explosive and shrapnel shells, which produced a large number of these shells with great efficiency and accuracy. *Address*: Oaklands, Thorpe, Norwich. *Club*: Royal Automobile. Chemical Industry.   (O11283)

SCOTT, Major Archibald Malcolm HENDERSON-, C.B.E.

SCOTT, Capt. David John MONTAGU-DOUGLAS-, O.B.E., *b.* 1887; *m.* 1918, Dorothy Charlotte, *d.* of the late Cecil George Assheton Drummond. Capt. 3rd Bn. Royal Scots (Lothian Regt.). Served in Great War, Chevalier Legion of Honour.   (O8885)

SCOTT, Lieut.-Col. Lord George William MONTAGU-DOUGLAS-, O.B.E., *b.* 31 Aug. 1866; 2nd *s.* of the 6th Duke of Buccleugh (*see*, BURKE'S *Peerage*); *m.* Lady Elizabeth Manners, *y. d.* of the 7th Duke of Rutland (*see* BURKE'S *Peerage*). *Educ.*: Eton; Christ Church, Oxford. Lieut.-Col., 2/1 Lothians and Border Horse Yeomanry. Entered 10th Hussars, 1889; Capt. 1897; served South Africa 1899–1900; left the Army 1902. *Address*: Kirklands, Ancrum, N.B. *Clubs*: Turf; Naval and Military; New (Edinburgh).   (O7485)

SCOVELL, Lieut.-Col. George Julian Selwyn, C.B.E., *b.* April, 1881; *s.* of Capt. G.T. Scovell, late 79th Highlanders. *Educ.*: Bruton and Osborne's; Haileybury; Sandhurst. *War Work*: General Staff Officer, 2nd Grade, Headquarters Northern Command, 1914–16; Assist. Adjutant-General at War Office, 1916–17; Deputy Director-General of Recruiting, Ministry of National Service, 1917–18; Demobilisation Section, War Cabinet Secretariat, 1918–19. *Address*: c/o Messrs. Holt & Co., Whitehall Place, S.W. 1. *Clubs*: Brooks'; Army and Navy; Royal Automobile; New, Edinburgh.   (O831)

SCRATCHLEY, Lieut.-Col. Victor Henry Sylvester, D.S.O., O.B.E., *b.* 1870; *s.* of the late Maj.-Gen. Sir Peter Henry Scratchley, K.C.M.G., R.E.; *m.* 1901, Anna Clementina, *d.* of the late John Harvey, of Mayfield, Shooters Hill, S.E. Entered King's Royal Rifle Corps, 1891; Capt. 1899; ret. 1907; served with Isazai Expedition. 1892; Chitral Relief Force, 1895 (medal with clasp); S. Africa, 1899–1900 (despatches); was a Superintendent of Gymnasia, 1901–4; is Lieut.-Col. Territorial Force. *Club*: Naval and Military.   (O3176)

SCRATTON, Capt. Edward William Howet Blackburn, O.B.E.

SCREECH, Alfred Leonard, O.B.E.

SCREECH, George Ernest, M.B.E., *b.* 9 June, 1868; *s.* of Samuel Thomas, of West Wittering, nr. Chichester, Sussex; *m.* Thyra, *d.* of Joseph Thomson, of Croydon. *Educ.*: Privately. L.C.C. Official (Dept. of the Education Officer). *War Work*: Attached to War Office with rank of Chief Examiner; dealt chiefly with questions of recruiting and labour. *Address*: 111, Croydon Road, Anerley, S.E. 20.   (M9574)

SCRIMGEOUR, Major Frederic John, O.B.E.

SCRIMGEOUR, Lieut. James, M.B.E.

SCRIMSHAW, Ellen Mary, Mrs., M.B.E.

SCRIVEN, Charles, O.B.E., LL.B., *b.* 16 April, 1871; *s.* of Charles Scriven, of Leeds, Mechanical Engineer; *m.* Annie, *d.* of Henry Edwin Bown, of Harrogate, Architect. *Educ.*: Leeds Grammar School, and Leeds Univ. Solicitor. Sen. partner, Peckover, Scriven & Co., 5, Greek Street, Leeds; Commissioner for Oaths; also Commissioner for Oaths in the Provinces of Ontario and Quebec, Canada; Hon. Sec., Leeds Law Society, and Yorkshire Board of Legal Studies. *War Work*: Voluntary Appeal National Service Representative on the Appeal Tribunal, West Riding of Yorkshire (Northern District); Leeds and Bradford Tribunals; Chief Inspector, Leeds Special Constabulary. *Addresses*: Aros, Allerton Park, Leeds; 5, Greek Street, Leeds, and at Harrogate. *Clubs*: Leeds and County Conservative; Junior Constitutional.   (O11286)

SCRIVENER, Capt. Harry Stanley, M.B.E., M.A. (Oxon.), *b.* 1 Oct. 1865; *s.* of the late Col. T. P. Scrivener, V.D., J.P., of Kingston-on-Thames; *m.* Janet Frances, *d.* of John Bowbrick, of Southwark. *Educ.*: St. Paul's School, and Magdalen Coll., Oxford. Journalist and Member of the Bar. *War Work*: Commissioned R.A.S.C., M.T., 15 May, 1916; Lieut., 15 Nov. 1917; A. Capt., 15 Aug. 1918; Demobilised, 5 March, 1919:

served during the whole of this period at M.T. Depot, Bulford Camp, Salisbury Plain ; Assistant to D.A.D.T. (Headquarters) from Dec. 1916 to date of demobilisation ; mentioned in Gazette, Mar. 1919, for valuable services in connection with the War. *Addresses :* 4, Crown Office Row, Temple, E.C. ; 14, Stanley Road, Wimbledon, S.W. 19. *Clubs :* All England Lawn Tennis ; Queen's.   (M5608)

SCRIVENER, Wm. Charles, O.B.E.

SCRUBY, Capt. Frank Sutherland, M.A., O.B.E., *b.* 25 July, 1881 ; *s.* of Theodore Robinet Scruby, of Hatherley, Saffron Walden ; *m.* Lucretia Mary, *d.* of Arthur Edward Chaplin, of Cambridge. *Educ. :* King Edward's School, Saffron Walden, and Selwyn Coll., Cambridge. H.M. Inspector of Industrial Schools, Home Office. *War Work :* Chemical Adviser to the Southern Army, Home Defence ; Gas Officer, H.Q. 17th Division, B.E.F. *Addresses :* 62, Hallowell Road, Northwood ; Home Office, London.   (O5763)

SCRUBY, Major William Sidney James, O.B.E., I.A.

SCUDAMORE, Sybil Frances, Mrs. Lucas, M.B.E.

SCUDAMORE, Lieut. William George, M.B.E., R.E.

SCULLY, James Donald, M.B.E.

SCULLY, Lieut.-Col. Vincent Marcus Barron, D.S.O., O.B.E., Border Regt., *b.* 1881 ; *s.* of Vincent Scully, of Mantlehill House, Golden, Co. Tipperary. Served in the Great War, 1914–19 (despatches thrice).   (O1849)

SCULOCK, Daniel, M.B.E.

SEABROOK, Eng.-Lieut. James Alfred, O.B.E., R.N.

SEAFORTH, Mary Margaret, Lady, C.B.E., Lady of Grace of the Order of St. John of Jerusalem ; *d.* of the late Edward Steinkopff ; *m.* Col. Jas. Alex. Stewart-Mackenzie of Seaforth, D.L., J.P. (*see* BURKE's *Peerage*, Galloway, E.), who was raised to the Peerage in Jan. 1921 as Baron Seaforth, of Brahan in Urray. *War Work :* Organised and was First President of Scottish Red Cross in Ross-shire, in 1909 ; Donor and Commandant of the Seaforth Red Cross Hospital, Conon Bridge, and the Seaforth Annexe, Strathpeffer ; Superintendent of Seaforth Surgical War Dressings Party and Hon. Sec. of the Ross-shire Prisoners' of War Fund and Seaforth Weaving Industry for disabled Soldiers and Sailors. *Addresses :* Lydhurst, Sussex ; Brahan Castle, Ross-shire ; 47, Berkeley Square, London, W.   (C307)

SEAGER, John Renwick, C.B.E., J.P., *b.* 10 May, 1849. For many years member of the Head Quarters Staff of the Liberal Party, prior to retirement in 1916. *War Work :* Member of Department of Central Parliamentary Recruiting Committee from Sept. 1914, to April, 1916. *Address :* Esplanade House, Clevedon, Som. *Club :* National Liberal. (C618)

SEALE, Major Edward Wilmot, O.B.E., R.E.

SEALY, Capt. Philip Temple, O.B.E., B.A., R.A.S.C., *b.* 7 Sept. 1888 ; *s.* of Rev. W. B. Sealy, M.A., of Harmondsworth, Middlesex. *Educ. :* St. Lawrence Coll., Ramsgate ; Peterhouse, Cambridge. Commissioned 3 Feb. 1911. *War Work :* Embarked with the Expeditionary Force, Aug. 1914, and after commanding various units in the field, assisted in the clearing up of Mechanical Transport in France ; Gazetted T. Capt., 30 Nov. 1914 ; Capt. 3 Feb. 1917. *Address :* c/o Sir Charles R. McGrigor, Bart. & Co., Ltd., 39, Panton Street, S.W. 1. *Club :* United R.A.S.C.   (O5765)

SEARIGHT, Lieut.-Col. James Gerald Lamb, O.B.E.

SEARLE, Capt. Arthur Mackenzie, M.B.E., R.E.

SEARLE, Emma Jane, Mrs., O.B.E., *b.* 17 Sept. 1863 ; *d.* of Frederick York St. Leger, of Cape Town ; *m.* Malcolm William (Judge of Supreme Court, Cape Town), *s.* of Walter Searle, of Cape Town. *Educ. :* St. Cyprian's, Cape Town ; Miss Werner's School, Tonbridge, Kent, England. Member of Peace Time Committee of the British Red Cross Society. *War Work :* With the Red Cross at the Military Hospital, Wynberg ; Governor-General's Fund ; and on Advisory Board of Official Visitors to Military Hospitals under Defence Force. *Address :* Highlands, Wynberg, Cape. *Clubs :* Services ; Alexandra, (Cape Town).   (O8364)

SEARLE, Col. Frank, C.B.E., D.S.O., Tank Corps, Chief Mechanical Engineer, with rank of Col. ; served during the Great War, 1914–19 (despatches).   (C1322)

SEARLE, Susan Margaret, O.B.E.

SEARLE, Lieut.-Comm. Sydney, O.B.E., R.N.V.R.

SEARLES, Sydney William, M.B.E.

SEARS, John Edward, C.B.E., M.A., A.M.I.C.E., *b.* 18 Sept. 1883 ; *s.* of John Edward Sears, J.P., F.R.I.B.A., of Westover, Cromwell Road, Teddington, Middlesex ; *m.* Kathleen Lucy, *d.* of Edward Wadsworth, of 19, Nicoll Road, Harlesden, N.W. 10. *Educ. :* Mill Hill School, and St. John's Coll., Camb. Supt. Metrology Dept., The National Physical Laboratory, Teddington, Middlesex. *War Work :* Organised and controlled the testing of engineers' gauges of all kinds, for the Ministry of Munitions. *Address :* Twyford, 22, Gloucester Road, Teddington, Middlesex.   (C2938)

SEARS, Nell, Mrs., M.B.E.

SEATLE, John Bridson, O.B.E., *b.* 25 March, 1858 ; *s.* of Henry Seatle, of Ulverston ; *m.* Emma, *d.* of George Holloway, of Stroud, Glos *Educ. :* Privately. Solicitor and Commissioner for Oaths. *War Work :* Assisted the T. V. Dept. of the War Office in the organisation and carrying on of the Volunteer Force Record Office from May, 1917, to Feb. 1919, for which services was mentioned in Home Despatches. *Address :* Fairfield, Putney, S.W. *Clubs :* Junior Carlton ; Royal Automobile.   (O3911)

SEATON, Peter, M.B.E.

SECCOMBE, Lieut. Edward Arthur John, O.B.E.,R.N.V.R.

SECCOMBE, Major John William Smyth, O.B.E., R.A.M.C. *b.* 1876 ; *s.* of Paymaster-Capt. J. W. Seccombe, of Royal Navy ; *m.* Beatrice Martha, *d.* of Capt. H. B. Lang, R.N., of Hartrow Manor, Somerset. *Educ. :* St. George's Hospital Medical School, London. Military Surgeon. *War Work :* Served as an Officer of the Royal Army Medical Corps, with the Mediterranean Exped. Force, and Egyptian Expeditionary Force, being mentioned in despatches for services rendered. *Address :* c/o Messrs. Holt & Co., Army Agents, 3, Whitehall Place, London, S.W. 1.   (O6291)

SECRETAN, Hubert Arthur, O.B.E., *b.* 8 Aug. 1891 ; *s.* of Walter Bernard Secretan, of Croydon. *Educ. :* Wellington ; Balliol Coll., Oxford. Temporary appointment Admiralty, 1915–17 ; Ministry of Shipping, 1917–19, *Address :* Coignafearn, Croydon, Surrey.   (O11288)

SEDDON, Harry Sterratt, C.B.E., *b.* 30 Dec. 1881 ; *s.* of William Seddon, of Bolton, Lancashire. *Educ. :* Miles Platting Institute, Manchester. *War Work :* Chairman of Lancashire County War Comforts Association ; Treas. of Manchester Regiment Prisoners of War Care Committee ; Accountant, Ministry of Munitions (Explosives Department). *Address :* Laurel Bank, Queen's Park, Manchester. *Clubs :* Reform, Manchester ; National Liberal, London ; Liberal, Newcastle-upon-Tyne.   (C1035)

SEDDON, James, M.B.E.

SEDDON, Thomas, M.B.E., *b.* 29 Sept. 1861 ; *s.* of Edward Seddon, of Ringley, Lancs. ; *m.* Sarah Elizabeth, *d.* of Samuel Barlow, of Stoke Albany, Northants. *Educ. :* Ringley Grammar School, Manchester. Managing Director of Seddon & Arlidge Co., Ltd., and Chairman of Directors Chairman Food Control, County Road Transport, War Pensions, Prisoners of War, Joint Hospital Board, St. John Ambulance, Motor Ambulance, and Coal Control Committees ; a Member of Kettering Urban District Council. *Address :* The Nook, Rockingham Road, Kettering.   (M9582)

SEDGWICK, Richard Rommy, M.B.E.   (M10253 *f*)

SEDGWICK, Susie, M.B.E.

SEELEY, Rev. John, M.B.E., *b.* April, 1852 ; *s.* of William Seeley, of Ireland ; *m.* Emmeline, *d.* of Archibald Carruthers, of Manchester. *Educ. :* Pastors Coll., London. *War Work :* Chaplain in Woolwich Garrison ; work in Recreation Clubs, Y.M.C.A., etc. *Address :* 51, Wrottesley Road, Woolwich, S.E. 18.   (M5611)

SEGAR, John, O.B.E.

SEGRAVE, Capt. Thomas George, C.B.E., R.I.M., *b.* 26 May, 1864 ; *s.* of Capt. T. Segrave, R.M., of Mallow, Co. Cork ; *m.* Harriet Rose Gertrude, *d.* of Baron Dunsandle, of Dunsandle, Co. Galway (*see* BURKE's *Peerage*). *Educ. :* St. Charles' Coll., and H.M.S. "Conway." Shipping Surveyor, and Adviser and Director India Office Shipping. *War Work :* Transport work in connection with the India Office, and Ministry of Shipping, and Technical Adviser, Ministry of Shipping. *Address :* White Cottage, Shenfield, Essex. *Club :* East India United Service.   (C2939)

SEGRUE, Ship't. Lieut. Comdr. George Edward, M.B.E., R.N. (Ret.)

SELBIE, Robert Hope, C.B.E., *b.* 31 Jan. 1868 ; *s.* of Rev. R. W. Selbie, of Manchester ; *m.* Florence, *d.* of E. Heyworth, of Blackburn. *Educ. :* Manchester Grammar School, and Victoria Univ. General Manager of Metropolitan Railway Coy., and Director of various Land and Development Companies. *War Work :* Controller of Horse Transport, and Member of Army Forage Committee. *Addresses :* Baker Street Station, N.W. ; The Orchard, Chorley Moor, Herts. *Club :* Reform.   (C1036)

SELBY, Edmond Wallace, O.B.E., M.D., B.S., F.R.C.S., *b.* 1869. Medical Officer to the Ministry of Health (1920). *War Work :* M.O. in charge Arnold Auxiliary Hospital, Doncaster. *Address :* Crescent House, Hillary Place, Leeds. (O11200)

SELBY, Major Edward James, O.B.E., M.A. (Camb.), M.R.C.S. (Eng.), L.R.C.P. (Lond.), *b.* 21 July, 1890 ; *s.* of J. Selby of Nottingham. *Educ. :* Cambridge Univ. *War Work :* Major, R.A.M.C. ; Service in France. *Address :* Sidmouth Lodge, S. Ealing Road, Ealing, W. 5.   (O5766)

SELBY, Elizabeth Mary Alice, Mrs., M.B.E., *b.* 3 June, 1867 ; *d.* of Rev. J. H. Eastty, of Oxford ; *m.* Prideaux G., O.B.E., *s.* of Prideaux Selby, of The Bank of Australasia, and Croydon. *Educ. :* Wellington House, Great Malvern. *War Work :* Commandant Kent 72 V.A.D. and Glovers V.A.D. Hospitals, Sittingbourne. *Address :* Teynham, Kent. *Club :* V.A.D.   (M9584)

SELBY, Capt. Ernest, O.B.E., R.A.F.

SELBY, Francis James, C.B.E., M.A., *b.* 8 Aug., 1867 *s.* of the late Edward Selby, of Ravensbourne Park, Catford, S.E. ; *m.* Mary Florence, *d.* of the late John Child, of Holland Villas Road, Kensington. *Educ. :* Univ. Coll., London ; Trinity Coll., Cambridge. Sec., National Physical Laboratory, and Advisory Committee for Aeronautics. *Address :* 30, Hampton Road, Teddington. *Club :* R.A.C.   (C2940)

SELBY, Prideaux George, O.B.E., M.R.C.S., L.R.C.P., *b.* 6 Aug. 1865 ; *s.* of Prideaux Selby, of Koroit, Croydon ; *m.* ElizabethnMary Alice, *d.* of Rev. J. H. Eastty, of Worcester Coll., Oxon. *Educ. :* Bedford Grammar School ; St. Bartholomews Hospital. Hon. Major, R.A.M.C. ; Medical Officer of Health (Faversham Rural District) ; Assistant Commissioner St. John Ambulance Brigade. *War Work :* Surgeon to Glovers V.A.D. Hospital, Sittingbourne ; C.O. 1st Sect. Field Ambulance, R.A.M.C. (Kent Volunteers) ; Divisional County Director, Kent, V.A.D. ; Associate Order of St. John of Jerusalem in

England. *Addresses:* Beaugill, Lynsted ; Brusons, Teynham, Kent. (O3913)

SELBY, Thomas James, M.B.E.

SELBY, Rev. William John, C.B.E., T.D., M.A., *b.* 26 Jan. 1858 ; *s.* of Henry Slby ; *m.* Elizabeth Ann, *d.* of John Goold, of Wotton Lodge, Gloucester. *Educ.:* St. Marylebone and All Souls' Grammar School ; London Univ. Hon. Missioner and Public Preacher, Diocese of Gloucester ; formerly Vicar of Churcham-with-Bulley, Glos. *War Work:* S.C.F. 48th and 61st Div. ; S.C.F. Res. (Terr.) Bge. Glosters ; M.G.C., Grantham, Colchester Garrison, Northern Army (H.D.), Plymouth Garrison ; D.S.C.F. Sussex and Surrey ; Dep. Chaplain-in-Chief, Mid. Area, R.A.F. ; at present Chaplain (Class I.) T.F., and Hon. Chaplain, R.A.F. *Address:* Weland Lodge, Cheltenham. (C1760)

SELL, Edith Lilian, Mrs., M.B.E.

SELLERS, Frederick Custance, O.B.E., *b.* 11 Jan. 1879 ; *s.* of Frederick William Sellers, of Oporto, Portugal ; *m.* Beatrice Emily, *d.* of Charles R. Adam. *Educ.:* Philberd's School, Maidenhead, and Deal Coll. Managing Director of Vacuum Oil Company of New York for Portugal, Morocco, and West Coast of Africa ; Managing Director of Vacuum Oil Coy., of Canary Islands, S.A.E. and of the Gibraltar Petroleum Coy., Ltd. *War Work:* Before America came into the war responsible for the ultimate destination of all petroleum products in above territories and afterwards continue to take the same precautions and give such information as might be of interest to the British Government. *Address:* Palacio Condeixa, Lisbon. *Clubs:* Royal British ; Club Tauromachico ; Sociedade Hippica Portugueza ; Automovel de Portugal. (O11291)

SELLERS, Rev. Harold Gordon, O.B.E., H.C.F., *b.* 12 Aug. 1889 ; *s.* of Rev. W. E. Sellers, of Wesley Manse, Walsall ; *m.* Mary Stuart, *d.* of the late Alexander Murray, Alford, Aberdeenshire. *Educ.:* Ed. VI Royal Grammar School, Guildford, and Handsworth Theological Coll., Birmingham. *War Work:* Acting Scout Master, Inverurie Troop, Boy Scouts ; enlisted in 2/6 Gordon Highlanders ; Commissioned as Chaplain 18 Sept. 1916 ; posted to General Hospital (Skin Diseases) Manoel from Nov. 1916, to July, 1917, in Malta and to 85th Infantry Bge, 28th Div. Aug. 1917, Salonica ; to 79th Bge (Inf.) 26th Div. 1918 ; in advance to Strumitza, to Mustafa Pasha, to Roustchouk ; posted 27th Div. Batoum, Army of Black Sea ; Demob. Aug. 1919 ; mentioned in despatches, Nov. 1918. *Address:* Wesley Manse, Knaresborough, Yorks. (O5631)

SELLERS, Lieut. and Qr.-Mr. Harry, M.B.E.

SELLICK, Major Alfred James, O.B.E.

SELLS, Arthur Freakish, M.B.E.

SELLS, Charles de Grave, O.B.E., *b.* 1856 ; *s.* of Charles Sells, of Lambeth and East Twickenham. *Educ.:* King's Coll. School and King's Coll., London. Vice-Chairman of the British Chamber of Commerce for Italy at Genoa. *War Work:* Chief Commissioner of the Church Army for the British Troops in Italy ; Member and Hon. Sec. of the Committee for the Importation of High Speed Steel Instituted by the British and Italian Governments ; British Admiralty Inspector for the submarine engines built in Italy. *Addresses:* Cornigliano, Ligure ; "Buon Riposo," London. *Clubs:* Constitutional ; Union (Genoa) and British-American (Milan). (O11292)

SELLS, Julia, Mrs. Perronet, O.B.E. ; *d.* of Thomas Wall ; *m.* Edward Perronet, *s.* of Edward Perronet Sells, of Croydon. *War Work:* Chairman of the Highgate War Hospital Supply Depot. (O3914)

SELLS, Lieut. Martin Perronet, O.B.E., R.E.

SELWIN, Paymaster-Lieut. Percy, O.B.E., R.N.R.

SELLWOOD, Major Frank Greaves, O.B.E., M.C., B.A., *b.* 3 Feb. 1893 ; *s.* of Frank Sellwood, of Cullompton. *Educ.:* Dean Close School, Cheltenham, and Emanuel Coll., Cambridge. Tanner ; Director, Sellwood Bros., Ltd., Cullompton. *War Work.:* Served in R.A.S.C. 14 Nov. 1914, to 17 Dec. 1919, in Dardanelles, Egypt, Salonica, and Mesopotamia. *Address:* Cullompton, Devon. (O6699)

SELOUS, Gerald Holgate, M.B.E., H.B.M. Vice-Consul, *b.* 14 July, 1887 ; *s.* of Edmund Selous of Wyke Castle, nr. Weymouth, Dorset. *Educ.:* Cheltenham Coll., and Pembroke Coll., Cambridge. Acting Vice-Consul at Tangier, 1910–13 and at Sajfie in 1913 ; Acting Consul, Fez, 1911 ; in 1913 Brit. delegate on the Comité Spécial and Commission General des Travaux Publics at Tangier ; Acting Interpreter at Tangier, 1913–16 ; attached to Consulate at Casblanca, Oct. 1916, to May, 1917 ; Acting Vice Consul at Laioicke, 1917, to Aug. 1917, and at Tetuan from Nov. 1917. *War Work:* Special work in Spanish zone of Morocco during the war. *Address:* c/o Foreign Office, Whitehall, London, S.W. 1. (M9587)

SELOUS, Capt. William Boyd, O.B.E., R.G.A., *b.* 23 July, 1889 ; *s.* of John Selous, of "Berea," Willifield Way, Golder's Green. *Educ.:* City of London School and King's Coll., London. With Messrs. Jardine Skinner & Co., 4, Clive Row, Calcutta. *War Work:* With Volunteers India 1914–15 ; Cadet at St. John's Wood, F.R.A., Cadet School, Jan. 1916 ; Commissioned June, 1916 ; went to France with 152 Siege Battery, Aug. 1916 ; Adjutant, 42 Heavy Artillery Brigade Feb. 1917 ; appointed to Sir Charles Fergusson's Staff as Staff Captain 17th Corps Heavy Artillery, April, 1918 ; in battles of Ancre, Messines, Passendaele, retirement in March, 1918, from St. Quentin and advance from Arras to Mons, July,

to Nov. 1918 ; made a Freeman of City of London, Dec. 1018. *Address:* 4A, Russell Street, Calcutta. *Clubs:* Royal Automobile ; Bengal, Calcutta. (O5768)

SELWAY, Cornelius James, C.B.E., *b.* 28 July, 1875 ; *s.* of James Selway, of Shepton Mallet. *Educ.:* United Westminster School. Supt. of Line, Great Northern Railway. *War Work:* Transport work in connection with G.N.R. *Address:* "Tankerville," 21, Queenswood Avenue, Highgate, N. 10. (C619)

SELWIN, Paymaster-Lieut. Percy, O.B.E., R.N.R.

SEMMENS, James Michael, O.B.E.

SEMMONS, Lieut. Foster James, M.B.E.

SEMPLE Major Robert, O.B.E., M.D.

SENIOR, Albert, C.B.E., *b.* 1867 ; *s.* of the late Alderman George Senior. Head of the firm of G. Senior and Sons (Limited), of Sheffield, and a J.P. *Address:* Forsbacka, Ivy Park Road, Sheffield. (C293)

SENIOR, George Gaunt, O.B.E., M.Inst.T., *b.* 27 April. 1861 ; *s.* of W. Henry Senior, of Barnsley, Yorkshire ; *m.* Hannah, *d.* of F. J. Butler, of Barnsley. *Educ.:* Robinson's Academy and Grammar School, Barnsley. Assistant to General manager, Lancashire and Yorkshire Railway. *War Work:* Railway Executive Committee Staff and Labour. *Address:* Kingswood, Victoria Crescent, Eccles, nr. Manchester. (O1850)

SENIOR, Hellen Stuart, Mrs. WALLER-, M.B.E., *b.* 18 Oct. 1861 ; *d.* of Henry Blunt, Magistrate, of North India ; *m.* Robert, *s.* of Robert Waller-Senior. *Educ.:* Woodstack Coll., Mussoorie, India. *War Work:* Member of St. John's Ambulance Committee, Bangalore Branch, from Dec. 1914 ; organised a Fund and forwarded through St. J. A. A. garments to Destitute Belgian Children, also money to the National Committee for Relief in Belgium ; visited Military Hospitals during the war, and for 2 years was worker at the "Blighty" Temperance Federation Tea Rooms for soldiers. (M6266)

SENN, Charles Herman, O.B.E.

SERGEANT, Capt. and Qr.-Mr. Archibald Joseph, M.B.E., R.E. (T.)

SERGEANT, Lieut. Herbert Lee, M.B.E., R.E. (T.)

SERJEANT, Lieut.-Col. Theophilus Hengist, O.B.E.

SERGEANT, Wilfred Oswald Faithfull, M.B.E., *b.* 27 March, 1871 ; *s.* of the Rev. O. P. Sergeant ; *m.* Ethel Maude, *d.* of R. C. Hamilton. *Educ.:* Winchester Coll. *War Work:* Hon. Sec. Soldiers' and Sailors' Families Association, Winchester (Military Division), 1914–16 ; Joint Hon. Treas Hampshire War Pensions Local Committee, 1916–20 ; Chairman and Hon. Treas. Winchester Sub-Committee of Hampshire War Pensions. *Address:* The Mount, Winchester. (M9589)

SERJEANTSON, Major Cecil Myles, O.B.E.

SEROCOLD, Comm. Claud PEARCE-, O.B.E., R.N.V.R., *b.* 5 July, 1875 ; *s.* of Charles Pearce-Serocold, of Taplow, Bucks. (*see* BURKE'S *Landed Gentry*). *Educ.:* Eton and Oxford. *War Work:* Personal Assistant to Director of Naval Intelligence, Admiralty War Staff, 1914–19 ; Officer of Legion of Honour ; Order of Leopold, St. Maurice and Lazarus ; 3rd Class, Sacred Treasure, of Japan, and 3rd Class, St. Anne of Russia. *Address:* 25A, North Audley Street, W. *Clubs:* St. James' ; Garrick ; Beefsteak ; Royal Yacht Squadron. (O640)

SEROPIAN, Lieut. Charles Dickron Oliver Deodat, O.B.E., R.N., *b.* 15 Oct. 1894 ; *s.* of Seropé Bemen Seropian ; *m.* Hilda Marion, *d.* of Sir Robert Glanfield. *Educ.:* Eastman's Royal Naval Coll., and H.M.S. "Conway." *War Work:* Joined H.M.S. "London," June, 1914 ; through Dardanelles campaign ; H.M.S. "Bristol," 1916 ; in action against 3 Austrian Light Cruisers, 15 May, 1917 ; H.M.S. "Caroline," Jan. 1918 ; from March, 1918, till Jan. 1919, Commanded H.M.T. "Charles Hammond," in anti-submarine Flotilla, Northern Patrol Force. *Address:* 1, Dingwall Gardens, Golder's Green. London, N.W. 4. (O4413)

SETTLE, Agnes Hannah, Mrs., M.B.E., *b.* 31 May, 1865 ; *d.* of the late Joseph Walker, of Revesby, Lincs. ; *m.* Joseph William Grundy, *s.* of Joseph Settle, of Horncastle, Lincs. *Educ.:* West End House, Wellingboro', Northants. *War Work:* Commandant of Horncastle Auxiliary Hospital, staffed by V.A.D. *Address:* Sunnyside, Horncastle, Lincs. (M2406)

SEVERN, Margaret Annie, Mrs., M.B.E. ; *d.* of the late Professor T. Lowndes Bullock, of Oxford ; *m.* Claud Severn, C.M.G., *s.* of Walter Severn, of 9, Earls Court Square, London, S.W. *Educ.:* Oxford High School, and Girton Coll., Cambridge. *War Work:* Clerk in Recruiting Office. (M3548)

SEWARD, Alfred Charles, M.B.E.

SEWELL, Capt. Douglas Arden Dalrymple, O.B.E., Chevalier of the Crown of Italy, *b.* 11 Oct. 1895 ; *s.* of Edward Humphrey Dalrymple Sewell. *Educ.:* Bedford School. *War Work:* Served with 2nd Batt. Oxfordshire and Buckinghamshire Light Infantry, Feb. 1915, to May, 1915, and Oct. 1915, to Dec. 1915 ; Adjutant, 14th Infty. Base Depot, Feb. 1916, to Nov. 1916 ; Staff Capt. War Office, March, 1917, to Dec. 1918 ; Staff Capt. G.H.Q., France, Dec. 1918, to May, 1919 ; Deputy Assist. Military Sec. (G.H.Q. France), May, 1919, to Feb. 1920 ; Staff Capt. War Office, Feb. 1920, to date. *Club:* Junior United Service. (O8604)

SEWELL, Capt. and Qr.-Mr. John, O.B.E., *b.* 12 Nov. 1872. *War Work:* British Expeditionary Force, France, Aug. 1914, to Nov. 1915 ; Egyptian Expeditionary Force, Egypt and Palestine, Dec. 1915, to June, 1919. *Address:* 12, Penwortham Road, Streatham, S.W. 16. (O6292)

SEWELL, Sqdn.-Leader, John Percy Claude, O.B.E., R.A.F.

SEWELL, John Thomas Beadsworth, O.B.E., M.A., LL.D., *b.* 1858; *s.* of John Sewell, of Uppingham; *m.* 1890, Madeleine Mayer, of St. Germain-en-Laye. *Educ.:* Uppingham, and Downing Coll., Cambridge. Admitted Solicitor, 1884; has been Solicitor to British Embassy, Paris, since that year. *Addresses:* 54, Faubourg St. Honoré, Paris VIIIe; 47, Boulevard Lannes, Paris. *Clubs:* Travellers' (Paris); Automobile (Paris); Cercle du Bois de Boulogne. (C620)

SEXTON, Major Eric James, O.B.E.

SEXTON, James, C.B.E., M.P., *b.* 1856. *Educ.:* Low House School, St. Helen's. Is a J.P.; Gen. Sec. of National Union of Dock Labourers; elected a Member of Parliamentary Committee, 1900; President Trades Union Congress, 1905; has sat as M.P. for St. Helen's (Lab.) since Dec. 1918. *Address:* Birks House, Gateacre, Liverpool. (C64)

SEXTON, Walter, C.B.E.

SEYBOLD, Lieut. John Clifford, M.B.E., Can. A.P.C.

SEYFANG, Eveline Mary, M.B.E.; *d.* of W. L. Seyfang, of St. Leonards-on-Sea, late Secretary and General Manager of the Kent Fire and Life Insurance Companies. *Educ.:* Privately. *War Work:* Worked in Filsham Park Red Cross Auxiliary Hospital (Sussex 16) from its opening (Oct. 1914) until its close (May, 1919), as V.A.D. orderly and nurse from Oct. 1914, until March, 1917, and as Secretary and Quartermaster from March, 1917, becoming Commandant of the Detachment on 1 Jan. 1919. *Address:* Craiglea, St. Leonards-on-Sea. (M9550)

SEYMOUR, Arthur George, M.B.E., *b.* 7 Nov. 1862; *s.* of the late J. B. Seymour, of Slough; *m.* Mary Grace, *d.* of the late Samuel Lyle, of Liverpool. *Educ.:* Westminster Training Coll. Accountant, Household Staff, Windsor Castle; Hon. Sec. Windsor and Eton Scientific and Archæological Society, and Windsor Branch, Royal Society of St. George. *War Work:* Hon. District Sec. Windsor War Savings Committee. *Address:* 23, Park Street, Windsor. (M9551)

SEYMOUR, Cynthia, M.B.E.; *d.* of Sir Horace Seymour, K.C.B. (*see* BURKE'S *Peerage*). *Educ.:* City of London School for Girls. Private Sec. to Sir George Clerk, British Legation, Prague, Czecho-Slovakia. *War Work:* At the Foreign Office on Lord Robert Cecil's Secretarial Staff, and at Peace Conference, Paris, on Mr. Balfour's Secretarial Staff. *Address:* 19, Chesham Road, Brighton. *Club:* Sesame. (M9592)

SEYMOUR, Major Edward, D.S.O., M.V.O., O.B.E., *b.* 10 Feb. 1877; *s.* of the late Lieut.-Col. Leopold Richard Seymour, Grenadier Guards (*see* BURKE'S *Peerage*, Hertford, M.); *m.* 29 July, 1905, Lady Blanche Frances Conyngham, *e. d.* of the 4th Marquess Conyngham (*see* BURKE'S *Peerage*). Comptroller to H.R.H. the Duchess of Albany, 1908; G.S.O., 2nd grade, from 1916; served in the Nile Expedition; S. Africa; Great War (despatches). *Address:* Broom Hill, Esher. *Clubs:* Brooks's; Guards'. (O7681)

SEYMOUR, Brig.-Gen. Sir Edward Hamilton, K.B.E., C.B., C.M.G., *b.* 19 May, 1860; *s.* of the late Rev. Francis Payne Seymour, Rector of Havant; *m.* Rowena, *d.* of the late George Wall, of Colombo, Ceylon. *Educ.:* Blundell's School, Tiverton, and Royal Military Coll., Sandhurst. *War Work:* Was Deputy Director of Equipment and Stores, War Office, 1914–18; Inspector of Army Ordnance Services, 1918–20; retired, 1920. *Address:* Ivy House, Lymington, Hants. (K280)

SEYMOUR, Major Evelyn Francis Edward, D.S.O., O.B.E., *b.* 1 May, 1882; *s.* of Brig.-Gen. Sir Edward Hamilton Seymour, K.B.E., C.B., C.W.G. (*see* BURKE'S *Peerage*, Somerset, D.); *m.* 3 Jan. 1906, Edith Mary, *o. d.* of the late William Parker, J.P., of Whittington Hall, Derbyshire. Served in the S. African War, 1901–2 (medal, five clasps); Aden, 1903; Great War (despatches). *Address:* Ebberley House, Bedford, S.O., N. Devon. (O7682)

SEYMOUR, Frank, M.B.E.

SEYMOUR, Frederick Powell, M.B.E.,

SEYMOUR, Lettice, M.B.E.

SEYMOUR, Capt. Lionel, O.B.E., *b.* 24 Feb. 1889; *s.* of the late Lieut.-Col. Leopold Seymour, of Brockham Park, Betchworth, Surrey; *m.* Catherine, *d.* of William Wooding, of Rugby. *Educ.:* Eton, and New Coll., Oxford. Barrister-at-Law; now at the Foreign Office. *War Work:* Inns of Court O.T.C., 1914–15; Herts R. (T.F.), 1915; Deputy Assistant Military Sec. to G.O.C., Eastern Command, 1916–19. *Address:* Long Edge, East Molesey, Surrey. *Club:* United University. (O7683)

SEYS, Roger Cecil, O.B.E. (O7684)

SHACKLADY, Thomas George, M.B.E.

SHACKLETON, Capt. and Qr.-Mr. Alfred George, O.B.E.

SHACKLETON, Sir Ernest (Henry), Knt. Bach., C.V.O., O.B.E., F.R.G.S., F.R.A.S.; Explorer, *b.* 15 Feb. 1874; *e.* of Henry Shackleton, M.D., of Kilkee; *m.* Emily Mary, 2nd *d.* of the late Charles Dorman. *Educ.:* Dulwich Coll. Went to sea in the Merchant Service; formerly Lieut. R.N.R.; 3rd Lieut. National Antarctic Expedition, 1901; Sec. and Treas. R. Scottish Geographical Society, 1903–6; contested Dundee (U.) 1906; commanded British Antarctic Expedition, 1907–9. which reached within 97 miles of the South Pole, also Antarctic Expedition, 1914–16: a Younger Brother of Trinity House; Special Gold Medallist and Silver Medallist, R.G.S.; King's Polar Medal (2 bars); Gold Medal, Geographical Societies of Scotland, Denmark, Belgium, France, Antwerp, Italy, America, City of Paris, and Russia; Commander of Orders of Dannebrag of Denmark, Pole Star of Sweden, St. Olaf of Norway, Officier Legion d'Honneur, Crown of Italy, St. Anne of Russia,

etc. *Address:* 14, Milnthorpe Road, Eastbourne. *Clubs:* Savage; Royal Belgian Yacht; Marlborough. (O682)

SHACKLETON, Capt. Herbert Park, O.B.E., R.A.M.C.

SHACKLETON, Kathleen, M.B.E., *d.* of Henry Shackleton, M.D., of Sydenham and Kilkea, Co. Carlow. *Educ.:* Privately. Journalist and Artist; Editor, Women and Children's Pages, and Artist on "Montreal Daily Star." *War Work:* Appointed Establishment Officer to the Coal Mines Department, Board of Trade, when that Dept. was first created in 1917; promoted chief women's Establishment Officer at Board of Trade Headquarters, Jan. 1918. *Address:* c/o Bank of Montreal, Waterloo Place, S.W. (M2409)

SHACKLETON, William, M.B.E. (M10253h)

SHACKLOCK, Henry Stephen, O.B.E., *b.* 11 Sept. 1875; *s.* of Henry Stephen Shacklock, of Meadow House, Mansfield; *m.* Minnie Annie Elizabeth, *d.* of William John Wadge, of Taunton. *Educ.:* Trent Coll. Solicitor; Conservative Agent, Mansfield Division; Hon. Sec. Incorporated Soldiers' and Sailors' Help Society, Notts County; Sec. Sutton-in-Ashfield War Pensions Sub-Committee. *War Work:* Chairman, Sutton-in-Ashfield Prince of Wales' Relief Fund; Deputy Chairman, Patriotic Fair Committee; Joint Hon. Sec. Mansfield Division Recruiting and Advisory Committees; Branch Hon. Sec. to Soldiers' and Sailors' Families Association, Soldiers' and Sailors' Help Society, and Statutory Committee; Member of Nottinghamshire Local Committee, Lord Roberts' Workshops. *Addresses:* Bathwood Cottage, Sutton-in-Ashfield; 49, Forest Street, Sutton-in-Ashfield. *Clubs:* Notts Golf; Mansfield and Sutton-in-Ashfield Conservative. (O11293)

SHADDICK, Rev. Henry George Hastings, O.B.E., *b.* 19 April, 1883; *s.* of John Jones Shaddick, of Barnstaple; *m.* Ellen Lilian, *d.* of John Cawsey, of Barnstaple. *Educ.:* Durham Univ. Curate of Stanhope since 1910. *War Work:* Appointed Chaplain, 6th Durham L.I. (T.), 1912; mobilised, 1914; proceeded abroad with Battalion, April, 1915; Chaplain No. 9 C.C.S., 1916; G.H.Q., Italy, 1917; Assistant to Principal Chaplain, and S.C.F., Italy, 1918–19; twice mentioned in despatches. *Address:* The Curatage, Stanhope, Co. Durham. (O6415)

SHADFORTH, Capt. Harold Anthony, O.B.E., M.C., *b.* 1892; *s.* of Major G. A. Shadforth, of Rye. *Educ.:* Bedford and Sandhurst. Royal Dublin Fusiliers, attached Egyptian Army. *Address:* c/o G.P.O., Khartoum. *Club:* Naval and Military. (O4286)

SHADWELL, Lieut. Lancelot Horace Augustus, O.B.E., R.N.V.R.

SHADWELL, Rev. Col. Leonard Julius, O.B.E., *b.* 5 Dec. 1860; *s.* of the late Rev. Julius Shadwell; *m.* Gertrude Ellen, *d.* of Col. George Milman, of Exeter, Devon. *Educ.:* Winchester Coll., and Académie de Lausanne. Suffolk Regiment and Lancashire Fusiliers; lent by War Office to S. African Union Government, 1907–15; Col. 1919; Clerk in Holy Orders since 1919. *War Work:* Headquarters, Southern Command, Sept. 1915, to Oct. 1919. *Address:* 5, Mont le Grand, Exeter. *Club:* Army and Navy. (O7685)

SHAFTESBURY, Anthony Ashley Cooper, 9th Earl of, K.P., K.C.V.O., C.B.E., *b.* 31 Aug. 1869; *s.* of the 8th Earl and Harriet, *o. d.* of the 3rd Marquess of Donegall, K.P.; *m.* Lady Constance Grosvenor, *e. d.* of the late Earl Grosvenor, and *g. d.* of the 1st Duke of Westminster. *Educ.:* Eton; Sandhurst. H.M. Lieut. Co. Dorset; Brig.-Gen. Commanding 1st South West Mounted Brigade, 1913–16; and 3rd Cyclist Brigade, till 1919; retired with the Hon. rank of Brig.-Gen.; Lord Chamberlain to the Queen, 1910; Commissioner of Congested Districts Board for Ireland, 1902–14; Chancellor of Queen's University of Belfast; H.M. Lieutenant for Co. of Antrim, 1911–16; Grand Officer Legion of Honour. Entered Army, 10th Hussars, 1890; Lieut. 1891; Capt. 1898; resigned commission, 1899; A.D.C. to Governor of Victoria, Lord Brassey, 1895–98; commanded North Irish Horse, 1902–12; H.M. Lieutenant, Belfast, 1904–11; Lord Mayor of Belfast, 1901. *Addresses:* St. Giles House, Salisbury, Dorset; Belfast Castle, Belfast. *Clubs:* Travellers'; Marlborough. (C1761)

SHAFTO, Helena Rosa, Mrs. DUNCOMBE-, O.B.E.

SHAIRP, Gertrude Ethel, Mrs., M.B.E.

SHAIRP, Major Henry Frank, O.B.E., I.A.

SHAKERLEY, Hilda Mary, Lady, C.B.E., *o. d.* of Henry Hodgson, of Currarevagh, Co. Galway; *m.* 7 Jan. 1885, Sir Walter Geoffrey Shakerley, 3rd Bt. *q.v. War Work:* Vice-President, Congleton Div. B.R.C.S., Cheshire; Quartermaster and Sec. St. John Aux. Mil. Hospital, Somerford Park, 1914–19; Lady of Grace of the Order of St. John of Jerusalem; Médaille de la Reine Elizabeth. *Address:* Somerford Park, Congleton, Cheshire. (C2942)

SHAKERLEY, Sir Walter Geoffrey, Bart., C.B.E., T.D., *b.* 26 Nov. 1859; *s.* of Sir Charles Watkin Shakerley, 2nd Bt., K.C.B., J.P., D.L. (*see* BURKE'S *Peerage*); *m.* 7 Jan. 1885, Hilda Mary (*q.v.*), *o.d.* of Henry Hodgson, of Currarevagh, Co. Galway. *Educ.:* Harrow. Cheshire Regt. Hon. Col. (commanded 1891–1909) 7th Batt.; Vice-Chairman, Cheshire Territorial Force Association. *War Work:* Acting Chairman, Cheshire Territorial Force Association; Lieut.-Col. Command-ing 2/7th Batt. Cheshire Regt. 1914–16; lent to Joint Committee, B.R.C.S. and St. John, as Auxiliary Military Hospital, Somerford Park, Congleton, 1914–19; Officer-in-charge of Hospital, 1916–19. *Address:* Somerford Park, Congleton. (C1762)

SHAKESPEAR, Dame Ethel Mary Reader, D.B.E., D.Sc., F.G.S., *b.* 17 July, 1871; *d.* of the Rev. Henry Wood, of Biddenham, Bedfordshire; *m.* Gilbert Arden, *s.* of John Shakespear, of Copston, Warwickshire. *Educ.:* Bedford High School, and Newnham Coll., Cambridge. *War Work:* Hon. Sec. Birmingham War Pensions Local Committee and Citizens' Committee, and of the Association of Local War Pensions Committee; Member of Special Grants Committee, Ministry of Pensions. *Address:* 21, Woodland Road, Northfield, Birmingham. *Club:* Three Counties (Birmingham).   (D55)

SHALLCRASS, Robert William, M.B.E.

SHALLIS, Major Boydell, M.B.E., R.N.

SHAND, Major David Brett, M.B.E.

SHAND, Lieut. George, M.B.E.

SHAND, Eliza Eveline KYNOCH-, M.B.E.

SHANN, Lilian Alice, Mrs., O.B.E., *b.* 1877.: *d.* of John Ernest Weekes, of Kensington, W.; *m.* Charles John Harold, *s.* of Charles Shann, of York. Sec. Suffolk Branch of British Red Cross Society. *Address:* 15, Crown Street, Bury St. Edmunds. *Club:* Ladies' Army and Navy.   (O11295)

SHANNON, Frank Ernest, M.B.E., R.N.

SHANNON, Major and Qr.-Mr. John, O.B.E.

SHANNON, Capt. Richard, M.B.E., R.G.A.

SHANNON, Col. the Rev. William Floyd, O.B.E.

SHANNON, William Fry, O.B.E.

SHANNONS, Frederick Alfred, M.B.E.

SHAPLEY, George William Thomas, M.B.E.

SHAPLEY, William Gilbert, O.B.E.

SHARE, Paymaster-in-Ch. Sir Hamnet Holditch, K.B.E., C.B., *b.* 1864; *s.* of the late Holditch Share; *m.* 1918, Alfreda Caroline Mary, *d.* of the late Rear-Adm. Walter B. Bridges, of Trawalla, Victoria, Australia. Entered R.N. 1880; became Paymaster, 1898; Staff-Paymaster, 1902; Fleet-Paymaster, 1906; Paymaster-in-Chief, 1917; served during Egyptian War, 1882 (medal, bronze star); Great War, 1914–18, as Sec. to Com.-in-Chief of Grand Fleet (despatches); has Russian Order of St. Anne, Legion of Honour, and Order of Rising Sun of Japan.   (K447)

SHARLAND, Lieut. Ernest John, M.B.E.

SHARLES, Lieut. Frederick Francis, M.B.E.

SHARMAN, Col. Charles Henry Ludovic, C.M.G., C.B.E., *b.* 29 Sept. 1881; *s.* of C. C. Sharman, of Trefula, South Woodford; *m.* Mabel, *d.* of J. Bershen, of Regina, Canada. *Educ.:* St. Lawrence Coll., Ramsgate. Canadian Civil Service, and Sec. Canadian Artillery Association. *War Work:* France, Feb. 1915, with 1st Brigade Canadian Field Artillery; wounded, second Battle of Ypres, and evacuated; returned to France with 2nd Canadian Division, commanded 4th Brigade, C.F.A., 1917, Chief Gunnery Instructor, Canadian School of Gunnery, 1918, Commandant, Canadian Reserve Artillery; 1918–19, C.R.A. Dvina Force, North Russian Exped. Force. *Address:* 18, Woodlawn Avenue, Ottawa. *Club:* Laurentian.   (C621)

SHARP, Alphonse, C.B.E.

SHARP, Major Aubrey Temple, O.B.E., M.G.C.

SHARP, Ernest Hamilton, O.B.E., M.A., B.C.L., K.C.; *s.* of Edmund Hamilton Sharp; *m.* Sarah, *d.* of Roger Cunliffe, of Tunbridge Wells, Kent. *Educ.:* Lincoln Coll., Oxford. Barrister-at-Law of the Inner Temple. *War Work:* Chairman of Executive Committee of War Charities, Hong Kong, 1916–18; of Military Service Commission, Hong Kong, 1917; and of General Military Service Tribunal, Hong Kong, 1918. *Addresses:* Great Bookham, Surrey; 5, Stone Buildings, Lincoln's Inn, W.C. *Club:* Junior Carlton.   (O1011)

SHARP, Major Frederic Joseph, O.B E.

SHARP, Lieut.-Col. George Edward, O.B.E., *b.* 13 March, 1871; *s.* of Henry Sharp, of Newbrook, Atherton, Lancashire; *m.* Hilda Gratrix, *d.* of Thomas Claye-Shaw, M.D., of Claremont Lodge, Cheltenham. *Educ.:* Rugby and Sandhurst. Bursar of Rugby School. *War Work:* Served in South African War as Capt. in East Lancashire Regt. (Queen's Medal with 3 clasps, King's Medal with 2 clasps); served during late war in R.A. Pay Department, France, March, 1916, to Nov. 1917; Italy, Nov. 1917, to June, 1919; latterly as Command Paymaster in Italy (mentioned, O.B.E.). *Address:* Rugby. *Clubs:* Wellington; Fly Fishers'.   (O6416)

SHARP, Major Gerald Whittaker, M.B.E.

SHARP, James, M.B.E., *b.* 30 Aug. 1870; *s.* of Henry Sharp, of Bromley, Kent, and Wingfield, Suffolk; *m.* Helen, *d.* of Richard Smith, of Highbury, N., and Badingham, Suffolk. *Educ.:* Privately. Member, Eton Board of Guardians and Rural District Council. *War Work:* Chairman, Eton Rural District Food Committee, and Assist. Commissioner, Ministry of Food, South Midland Division; Hon. Sec. and Treas. Incorporated Soldiers' and Sailors' Help Society for County of Bucks; Bucks County Relief Committee, Eton Rural Military Tribunal, and Bucks County Profiteering Appeal Tribunal; Vice-Chairman, Burnham (Bucks) War Pensions Committee; Bucks County Special Constabulary (Sergt.); Sergt.-Instr. Musketry, 1st Vol. Batt. Oxford and Bucks L.I. *Address:* Green Alley, Farnham Common, Bucks.   (M9596)

SHARP, Capt. Rowland, D.S.O., R.E. (T.).

SHARP, Major Wilfred, O.B.E., R.E. (T.).

SHARP, Lieut. William, M.B.E.

SHARPE, Major Alfred Gerald Meredith, D.S.O., O.B.E., Royal Berkshire Regt., *b.* 1884. Served in the Great War, 1914–18 (despatches, Croix de Guerre).   (O8935)

SHARPE, Daniel Crawford, M.B.E., *b.* 11 June, 1862; *s.* of Daniel Sharpe, of Greenock; *m.* Annie Isabel, *d.* of Frank Cox, of Liverpool. *Educ.:* Liverpool Institute. Provision

Merchant; Director and Vice-President (1919–20), Liverpool Provision Trade Association; Member of the firm of Clampitt and Sharpe, 46, Harrington Street, Liverpool. *War Work:* Administrative Head in charge of Clerical Staff, Imports Branch, Bacon Division, Ministry of Food, Dec. 1917, to Nov. 1919. *Addresses:* 13, Waverley Road; 46, Harrington Street, Liverpool.   (M9597)

SHARPE, Capt. Frederick William, M.B.E., D.C.M., R.A.M.C., *b.* 1872; *s.* of Charles Sharpe, of London. *Educ.:* Privately. *War Work:* South African Campaign, 1900–2; France and Belgium, 1914–15; Balkans, 1916–18; and South Russia, 1919–20. Chevalier of the Order of King George I of Greece. *Address:* 21st Stationary Hospital, Ferevaki, Constantinople.   (M7017)

SHARPE, Lieut.-Col. Gerald Whittaker, O.B.E., *b.* 30 Aug. 1878; *s.* of Edmund Sharpe, of Halton Hall, Lancaster; *m.* Margaret Annie, *d.* of the late Rev. C. S. Hope, of Southport. *Educ.:* Harrow and Cambridge. Director of Storey Bros. & Co., Ltd., Oil Cloth Manufacturers, Lancaster. *War Work:* Mobilised with 5th King's Own Royal Lancaster Regt., Aug. 1914; France with 5th K.O.R.L.R. Feb. 1915; commanded 2/5th K.O.R.L.R. Aug. 1915, to April, 1917; France with 2/5th K.O.R.L.R. Feb 1917; Senior Danger Building Officer, under Ministry of Munitions, White Lund, Morecambe, from Aug. 1917, to June, 1918; France, Sept. 1918, attached 63rd Div.; disembodied, March, 1919; now commanding 5th K.O.R.L. Regt. (T.F.); mentioned in despatches. *Address:* Shefferlands, Halton, Lancaster, *Clubs:* Royal Automobile; County; Conservative (Lancaster).   (O5771)

SHARPE, James Edward, M.B.E.

SHARPLES, Lieut. Frank Deeks, O.B.E., R.A.S.C. (T.F.).

SHARPLES, George Bertrand, O.B.E.

SHARPLES, Lieut. John Butterfield, M.B.E., R.A.F.

SHARPLES, Richard William, O.B.E., *b.* 4 Aug. 1867; *s.* of William Sharples, of Ledsham, near Chester. Director of C. Czarnikow, Ltd., 29, Mincing Lane, E.C., Guardian Assurance Co., Ltd., and Reliance Marine Insurance Co., Ltd. *War Work:* Three years' voluntary work as Assistant Director of the Overseas Transport Department of the Ministry of Munitions. *Address:* 12, Hyde Park Place, London, W. 2. *Clubs:* Royal Thames Yacht; Palatine (Liverpool).   (O1852)

SHARPLEY, Edward Burgess, O.B.E.

SHARROCK, Alice Edith, M.B.E.

SHATFORD, Rev. Allan Pearson, O.B.E., M.A., D.C.L., *b.* 9 May, 1873; *s.* of James E. Shatford, of St. Margaret's Bay, N.S.; *m.* Elizabeth, *d.* of James Macfarlane, of Bridgewater, N.S. *Educ.:* King's Coll., Windsor, N.S. Rector, Church of St. James the Apostle, Montreal, Canada; Canon of Christ Church Cathedral, Montreal, Canada. *War Work:* Chaplain, 24th Batt. C.E.F., 1914–15, Canada, England, and France; Chaplain, Canadian Hospitals, France, 1916; Corps Chaplain, France, 1917–18; Senior Chaplain, 4th Canadian Division, 1918–19; retired as Hon. Major. *Address:* 697, St. Catherine Street W., Montreal, Canada.   (O6049)

SHAUGHNESSY, Edward Herbert, O.B.E.

SHAW, Adela Constance Alexandrina, Mrs., O.B.E.

SHAW, Major Arthur Godfrey, O.B.E.

SHAW, Lieut. Cyril Hay, M.B.E.

SHAW, David Nairn, M.B.E.

SHAW, Donald Stuart, M.B.E., *b.* 1867; *s.* of Donald Shaw, of Tomintoul; *m.* Belle Louise, *d.* of F. G. Barnard, of Edinburgh. *Educ.:* St. Mungo's Academy, Glasgow. Provost of Fort William. *War Work:* Chairman, War Savings, Fuel and Lighting, and Profiteering Committees; Member of Burgh Tribunal, and of Burgh and County Food Control Committees. *Address:* Dalnahaine, Fort William.   (M3962)

SHAW, Edward Harry, M.B.E., *b.* 13 July, 1888. *Educ.:* Luton Higher Grade School, and King's Coll., London. *War Work:* Organiser, Church Army War Work in Egypt, 1914–15; Assistant Sec. Naval and Military Dept., Church Army, London, 1916–19. *Address:* 55, Bryanston Street, Marble Arch, W.   (M9600)

SHAW, Elsie Marie, M.B.E., *d.* of Col. G. J. Shaw, Indian Army (ret.). *Educ.:* Privately. *War Work:* Sec. to the Commandant, Indian Military Depot, Milford-on-Sea, Hants; V.A.D. Lymington War Hospital, Hants; Countess of Stradbroke's Hospital at Henham Hall, Suffolk; No. 9, Red Cross Hospital, Calais, France; also 2 years War Office, Jan. 1917–19. *Address:* 12, Tavistock Road, W. 11.   (M3963)

SHAW, Surg.-Comm. Ernest Albert, O.B.E., M.D., B.A., R.N.

SHAW, Lieut. Francis Blewett, O.B.E., R.N.V.R.

SHAW, Major Francis Stewart Kennedy, C.B.E., Remount Service. Served in S. Africa, 1900 (Queen's medal with two clasps); Great War, 1914–19 (despatches).   (C1323)

SHAW, Lieut.-Col. Frederick Arthur, O.B.E.

SHAW, George Ernest, O.B.E.

SHAW, Gertrude Powell, M.B.E., *b.* 3 Jan. 1873; *d.* of James W. Shaw, of Liverpool. *Educ.:* Edge Hill Training Coll., Liverpool. L.C.C. Full Time Responsible Mistress; Health Visitor and School Nurse. *War Work:* Organised Woolwich Canteens, Y.M.C.A.; Supt. Coventry Colony (Government); Organised and Inspected Canteens and Hostels, (Gov. and Y.M.C.A.). *Address:* 94, Abbey Road Mansions, St. John's Wood, N.W.   (M2413)

SHAW, Gwendoline Mary, O.B.E.; *d.* of the late William Henry Shaw, of Fernwood, Clapham Common, S.W. *Educ.:*

St. Leonards-on-Sea. *War Work:* Hon. Sec. of the Ipswich War Hospital Supply Depot. *Address:* Redlands, Warrington Road, Ipswich. *Club:* New Century. (O3917)

SHAW, Capt. Harry Turner, O.B.E., R.A.F.

SHAW, Helen, Mrs., M.B.E., *b.* 28 Sept. 1896 ; *d.* of Clarkson Henry Tredgold, of Salisbury, Rhodesia ; *m.* Arnold Bramwell, *s.* of George Henry Bramwell Shaw, of Grahamstown, S.A. *Educ.:* Girls' High School, Wynberg, Cape Province. *War Work:* 1915 and 1916, represented the Rhodesian Comforts Committee in Cape Town ; attended to all comforts for Rhodesians in Hospital ; visited the hospitals and arranged outings for the soldiers ; returned to Salisbury, Rhodesia, and did the same work for men in hospital there ; met all troop trains passing to and from East Africa. *Address:* Governor's Kop, Grahamstown, S.A. (M6486)

SHAW, Helen Brown, Mrs., M.B.E. ; *m.* Major D. P. Shaw, 6th Cameronians, killed in action, June, 1915. *War Work:* President, Soldiers' and Sailors' Families Association (local branch) ; Member of Local Committee War Pensions Committee ; Representative of Women on Local Food Control Committee ; Convener, Care Committee, 6th Cameronians Prisoners of War. *Address:* Merchiston, Uddingston, Lanarkshire. (M9601)

SHAW, Herbert, M.B.E., M.I.C.E.

SHAW, Herbert Hunley, M.B.E.

SHAW, Isabella Mackintosh, M.B.E.

SHAW, Lieut. James Henry Montague, O.B.E.

SHAW, Lieut. and Qr.-Mr. James William, M.B.E., *b.* 21 June, 1868 ; *s.* of John Shaw, of Plymouth ; *m.* Harriet, *d.* of Maurice Slade, of Portland. *Educ.:* Privately R.Q.M.Sgt., 8th Batt. Rifle Brigade ; Lieut. and Qr.-Mr., 24th Batt. Royal Fusiliers, and 23rd Middlesex Regt. *War Work:* R.Q.M.Sgt. of 8th Batt. Rifle Brigade, 20 Aug. 1914 ; Batt. B.E.F., France, 18 May, 1915 ; Commissioned as Lieut. and Qr.-Mr. 24th Batt. Royal Fus., 20 Aug. 1917, and attached to 23rd Batt. Middlesex Regt., Rhine Army, 28 Feb. 1919, as Lieut. and Qr.-Mr. *Address:* 49, Nuns Road, Winchester. (M5617)

SHAW, Katharine, Mrs., M.B.E.

SHAW, Mary Charlotte, Mrs., M.B.E.

SHAW, Mary Margaret, M.B.E.

SHAW, Capt. Peter, O.B.E.

SHAW, Lieut. Reginald Frank, M.B.E.

SHAW, Richard Holgate, M.B.E., M.R.C.S., L.R.C.P., *b.* 28 Feb. 1868 ; *s.* of Richard Holgate Shaw, of Leeds, Yorks ; *m.* Louisa Marion, *d.* of Francis Boynton-Lee, F.R.C.P., of Yorkshire. *Educ.:* Leeds School of Medicine. Divisional Police Surgeon, Metropolitan Police, Golder's Green, N.W. *War Work:* Medical Officer in charge of the Hampstead Garden Suburb Auxiliary Military Hospital. *Address:* Crantock, Finchley Road, Golder's Green, N.W. (M9604)

SHAW, Capt. Richard James Herbert, C.B.E.

SHAW, Lieut. Robert John, M.B.E., R.N., *b.* 10 Feb. 1900 ; *s.* of the Rt. Rev. E. D. Shaw. Bishop of Buckingham, of Beaconsfield, Bucks. *Educ.:* Osborne, and Dartmouth. *War Work:* Naval service in Grand Fleet, 1915–18 ; Battle of Jutland. *Address:* The Bishop's House, Beaconsfield. (M6864)

SHAW, Lieut. Robert, O.B.E.

SHAW, Thomas, C.B.E., J.P., M.P., *b.* 9 April, 1878 ; *s.* of Ellis Shaw, of Colne. *Educ.:* Technical Schools, Colne. Sec. International Textile Workers. *War Work:* Recruiting Campaign, Adviser to National Service Ministry ; Director of Recruiting and National Service for five counties of West Midlands. *Address:* 243, Keighley Road, Colne, Lancs. (C1037)

SHAW, Major Thomas Alfred, O.B.E., R.E.

SHAW, Flying Officer Walter Langston, M.B.E., R.A.F.

SHAW, William Barbour, C.B.E., M.I.C.E., *b.* 13 Sept. 1868 ; *s.* of William B. Shaw, of Glasgow ; *m.* Adeline, *d.* of Alexander Ewing, of Fordyce. *Educ.:* Gordon's Coll., Aberdeen. Partner in firm of Babtie Shaw and Morton, Civil Engineers, Glasgow. *War Work:* Joined Staff of Ministry of Munitions, in 1915, under Sir John Hunter, K.B.E., as Deputy Director, and afterwards Director, of Factory Construction. *Address:* Cruach, Bearsden, Dumbartonshire. *Club:* Scottish Constitutional (Glasgow). (C1038)

SHAW, William Vernon, O.B.E., M.D.

SHAW, Lisa Rebecca, Mrs. GRESHAM-, O.B.E. ; *d.* of S. Fisher, H.E.I.C.S., and widow of C. Pierre Shaw, of New York. *Educ.:* Privately. *War Work:* H.Q. Westminster Div. Red Cross ; Red Cross worker in Prince of Wales' Hospital, Tottenham, Edmonton, and Rugeley Camp Hospitals ; Commandant of Red Cross Hospital for Facial Injuries, Norfolk Street, W. 1. *Address:* Alexandra Hotel, Hyde Park Corner, S.W. 1. *Club:* Forum. (O11298)

SHAW, Josephine, Mrs. RAWSON-, M.B.E., *b.* 14 Jan. 1865 ; *d.* of Joseph Crook, of Oakfield, Bolton, Lancs. ; *m.* William, *s.* of Thomas Shaw, J.P., D.L., M.P., of Halifax. *War Work:* Assist. Commandant, Mil. Auxiliary Hospital (A) at Littlehampton, 1914–16, and Commandant, 1916–19. *Address:* Slindon, Arundel, Sussex. *Club:* Albemarle. (M9602)

SHAWCROSS, George Nuttall, M.B.E., F.R.Hist.S., M.I.Mech.E. *Educ.:* Rivington School. Assistant Works Manager, Horwich Locomotive Works, L. & Y. Rly. Co. ; Chairman of Governors, Educational Endowment, Rivington and district. *War Work:* Acting Works Manager, Horwich, 1914–19. *Address:* Lakelands, Rivington, Lancs. (M2416)

SHAWE, Lieut.-Col. Charles, C.B.E., *b.* 15 Nov. 1878 ; *s.* of late Henry Cunliffe Shawe, of Weddington Hall, Nuneaton ; *m.* Christabel Nattle, *d.* of John Grigg, of Longbeach, New

Zealand. *Educ.:* Eton and R.M.C., Sandhurst. Served in the Rifle Brigade, 1898–1913 ; R. of O., Rifle Brigade, since 1913. *War Work:* With the New Zealand Expeditionary Force, 1914–15 ; present with this force in Egypt and at the landing at Anzac, Gallipoli, on 25 April, 1915 ; served in War Office, end 1915 to 1919, in Directorate of Military Operations. *Club:* Army and Navy. (C1763)

SHEAN, Major and Qr.-Mr. Walter, M.B.E., R.A.

SHEARBURN, Major and Qr.-Mr. Alan Darvil, O.B.E., R.E.

SHEARME, Paymaster-Capt. Edward Haweis, C.B.E., R.N. (ret), *b.* 21 June, 1876 ; *s.* of John Shearme, of Bude, N. Cornwall ; *m.* Angela Anne, *d.* of the Rev. Preb. R. H. Barnes, of Heavitree, Exeter. *War Work:* Assistant Chief Censor, Admiralty. *Address:* 30, Campden House Chambers, Sheffield Terrace, Kensington, W. 8. *Club:* Junior United Service. (C2945)

SHEARER, David, M.B.E.

SHEARER, James, O.B.E.

SHEARMAN, Montague, M.B.E.

SHEARMAN, Richard, O.B.E.

SHEARWOOD, Capt. and Qr.-Mr. Thomas, M.B.E.

SHEATH, Major William Archibald Sidney, O.B.E.

SHEAT, William James Oliver, O.B.E., J.P., *b.* 13 Feb. 1864 ; *s.* of the late James Sheat, of San Francisco, U.S.A. ; *m.* Susannah, *d.* of the late John Back, of Limehouse. *Educ.:* Limehouse Grammar School. Member of the Stock Exchange. *War Work:* Chairman, Ilford Urban District Council, 1914–15, War Emergency Committee for Ilford, Belgian Refugee Committee for Ilford, and Ilford Local Employment Committee under Ministry of Labour ; Member of Essex County Appeal Tribunal (Military Service Act) ; Hon. Treas. Ilford War Pensions Statutory Committee. *Address:* 120, Cranbrook Road, Ilford, Essex. (O11301)

SHEDDEN, Lewis, C.B.E., J.P., *b.* 9 June, 1870 ; *s.* of the late Lewis Shedden, of Glasgow ; *m.* Minnie Knox Burnett, *d.* of the late Robert Allan, of Glasgow. *Educ.:* Glasgow. Sec. Scottish Unionist Association (Western Divisional Council) and Glasgow Unionist Association. *War Work:* From the outbreak of war until the coming into operation of the Military Service Act was actively engaged in the work of recruiting for the New Armies, as Joint Hon. Sec. of the Central Recruiting Committee for West of Scotland. From that time until the Armistice the work varied as occasion arose : War Savings, Joint Hon. Sec. Scottish War Savings Committee, West of Scotland ; National Service, Joint Hon. Sec. Committee arranging meetings, also Deputy Commissioner, Agricultural Section ; Member of Committee Scottish Y.M.C.A. (Admiralty) Hostel Board ; and finished as Joint Hon. Sec. Scottish War Aims Committee, West of Scotland ; in Dec. 1915, was one of a deputation to visit the lines of the British Army in Flanders. *Address:* Mossgiel, Haggs Road, Maxwell Park, Glasgow. *Clubs:* Conservative (Glasgow) ; Scottish Constitutional (Glasgow). (C2946)

SHEDDEN, Lieut.William St. John, M.B.E., R.A.S.C. (T.).

SHEE, Comm. Richard John, O.B.E., R.N.

SHEEDY, Capt Frederick John, M.B.E.

SHEEDY, Capt. Thomas, O.B.E., *b.* 1884 ; *s.* of the late John Sheedy, of Cork ; *m.* Claire, *d.* of the late William Nicolle, of Guernsey. *Educ.:* Clongowes Wood Coll., Co. Kildare, and Queen's Coll., Cork. Medical Profession ; Civil Servant. *War Work:* R.A.M.C. 1914–20, and Staff Capt., War Office. *Address:* 12, Arundel Mansions, S.W. 6. (O7688)

SHEFF, Lieut. John, M.B.E., D.C.M.

SHEEN, Col. Alfred William, C.B.E., T.D., M.S., F.R.C.S., *b.* 30 April, 1869 ; *s.* of Alfred Sheen, M.D., of Cardiff ; *m.* Christine, *d.* of J. P. Ingledew, J.P., of Cardiff. *Educ.:* Guy's Hospital. Consulting Surgeon, King Edward VII.'s Hospital, Cardiff, and other hospitals. *War Work:* Officer Commanding Welsh Hospitals ; Consulting Surgeon, War Hospitals, India ; Surgeon, Imperial Yeomanry Field Hospital, S. Africa, 1900. *Address:* 69, Wimpole Street, W. 1. (C748)

SHEFFIELD, Joseph, O.B.E., J.P., *b.* 7 Oct. 1854 ; *s.* of Amos Sheffield, of Quorn, Leicestershire ; *m.* Emily, *d.* of Thomas Lupton, of Knaresboro'. *Educ.:* High School, Loughborough. Elected Councillor, Borough of Harrogate, 1901 ; Elected Ald. and Mayor, Nov. 1913–14 ; Re-elected Mayor, Nov. 1914–15 ; J.P. for Harrogate ; Member National Unionist Association for Ripon Division for 20 years. *War Work:* Recruiting, establishing numerous war funds ; Chairman of Tribunal ; organised reception and provision for Belgian refugees, founded fund for relief of returned sailors' and soldiers and their dependants. *Address:* Quorn House, Harrogate. *Club:* Conservative (Harrogate). (O11302)

SHEFFIELD, Julia, Lady, O.B.E., L. G. St. J.J. ; *e. d.* of Baron de Tuyll of the Hague ; *m.* 19 July, 1904, Sir Berkeley Digby George Sheffield, 6th Bt. (*see* BURKE'S *Peerage*). (O11303)

SHEFFIELD, Mary Edith, M.B.E., *d.* of Frederick Sheffield, solicitor, of London. *Educ.:* Privately. Social Worker. *War Work:* Welfare Worker in explosives filling station ; relief worker with Friends' War Victims Relief among refugees in France. *Address:* 1, Spring Mansions, Gondar Gardens, N.W. 6. (M2417)

SHEFFIELD, Mary Katherine, Lady, C.B.E., *d.* of Sir Lothian Bell, 1st Bt. of Washington, Durham (*see* BURKE'S *Peerage*); *m.* 6 Feb. 1873, Sir Edward Lyulph Stanley, Baron Sheffield (*see* BURKE'S *Peerage*).

SHEFFORD. Capt. Alan Douglas Edward, M.B.E.

SHEILDS, Francis Ernest WENTWORTH-, O.B.E., M.I.C.E., *b.* 16 Nov. 1869 ; *s.* of F. Wentworth-Sheilds, M.I.C.E., of Westminster ; *m.* Mary, *d.* of the late Right Rev. Bishop Boyd Carpenter, K.C.V.O., D.D., of Riversea, Kingswear. *Educ.* : St. Paul's School, and Owen's Coll., Manchester. Manchester Ship Canal (Salford Docks, 1888–91) ; Assist. Engineer, Dock Extensions, Southampton, 1892–96 ; Resident Engineer, N. Cornwall Rly. Extension, 1896–99 ; Resident Engineer, Bakerloo Tube, 1899–1901 ; Resident Engineer, Trafalgar Graving Dock and Deep Water Quays, Southampton, 1901–5 ; Resident Engineer, Isna Barrage. Egypt, 1905–7 ; Chief Engineer for Design and Construction of White Star Dock and the widening of Trafalgar Dock, Southampton, 1907–12 ; appointed Docks Engineer to London and South Western Rly., 1909 ; President of Concrete Institute, 1916–18 ; Bronze Medal of Concrete Institute, 1916 ; George Stephenson Gold Medal of Institution C.E., 1914 ; Member of Engineering Standards Association (Portland Cement Committee) ; Member of the Reinforced Concrete Com. of Inst. C.E. ; Chairman of Joint Committee (on Research work) of the Concrete Inst. 1916–18 ; visited Calcutta, 1919–20, at request of Port Commissioners to advise and report on lay-out of New Docks at Calcutta. *War Work* : Designed and erected various structures for war purposes at Southampton and elsewhere. *Addresses* : Docks Engineer's Office, Southampton ; 28 London Road, Southampton. *Club* : St. Stephen's. (O11304)

SHELDON, Hanah, M.B.E.
SHELDON, Thomas Alfred, M.B.E.
SHELDRAKE, Col. Edward Nodin, C.B.E., *b.* 1858 ; *s.* of the late James Sheldrake ; *m.* Imogen Mary Duncan, *d.* of Brigade Surgeon Lieut.-Col. A. B. R. Myers, Brigade of Guards. *Educ.* : Univ. Coll., London. Late Surgeon Lieut.-Col., Grenadier Guards. *War Work* : S. African War, 1899–1902 (mentioned in despatches) ; Queen's Medal and 6 clasps, King's Medal and 2 clasps ; the Great War : War Office Medical Board. *Address* : 15, St. George's Square, London, S.W. 1. *Clubs* : Guards' ; Arthur's ; Army and Navy. (C2164)

SHELDRAKE, Comm. John William, M.V.O., M.B.E.
SHELMERDINE, Lieut.-Col. Francis Claude, O.B.E., R.A.F.
SHELMERDINE, Capt. Henry Neal, M.B.E., M.C., *b.* 21 July, 1891 ; *s.* of Anthony Shelmerdine, J.P., of Liverpool ; *m.* Mary Blanche Reeve, *d.* of Lyle Rathbone, J.P., of Liverpool. *Educ.* : Liverpool Coll. Engineer. *War Work* : Capt. R.F.A. ; 2 years in France, finally appointed to Shoeburyness Gunnery Staff as Capt. Instructor of Gunnery. *Address* : High Birks, Gateacre, near Liverpool. (M5620)
SHELSWELL, Oscar Berridge, O.B.E., *b.* 23 Oct. 1857, *s.* of Thomas Henry Shelswell, of Sibford, Banbury ; *m.* Anne Elizabeth Lucy, *d.* of the Rev. T. H. Wilkinson, of Coatham, Yorks. *Educ.* : St. Anne's School. *War Work* : Medical Officer to Holborn Military Hospital, Mitcham. *Address* : Sibford, Mitcham. (O11845)
SHELTON, Lieut. Frederick Soltau, O.B.E.. R.N.V.R.
SHELTON, Lieut. Harry Gordon, M.B.E., R.A.S.C.
SHELTON, Robert Melvin, O.B.E.
SHEPHERD, Col. Arthur Edmund, C.B.E., D.S.O. Australian Army Med. Corps. Served in the Great War, 1915–19 (despatches). (C1363)
SHEPHERD, Charles Edward, M.B.E.
SHEPHERD, Lieut. Charles Herbert, M.B.E., *b.* 7 June, 1888 ; *s.* of W. M. Shepherd, of Cardiff. *Educ.* : Cardiff High School. Coal Salesman to the South Wales Collieries controlled by the late Lord Rhondda. *War Work* : Gazetted as 2nd Lieut. in Welsh Regt. in May, 1915 ; served with this regiment until July, 1916, then attached to the Duke of Wellington's Regt. for service in France, returning incapacitated in Oct. 1917 ; promoted Lieut. July, 1917 ; seconded for service with the Ministry of Food from Nov. 1917 to April, 1919, and acted as Secretary to the Freight Dept. of the Food Section of the Supreme Economic Council. *Address* : Wilton, Marlborough Road, Roath Park, Cardiff. (M9607)
SHEPHERD, Lieut. and Qr.-Mr. Cornelius, M.B.E.
SHEPHERD, Frederick Hawkesworth Sinclair, M.B.E., *b.* 26 Feb. 1877, *s.* of the Rev. F. Shepherd of Stoke-under-Ham, Somerset. *Educ.* : Rugby, and Corpus Christi Coll., Oxford. Artist. *War Work* : Sub-section Director, Ministry of Munitions ; Chevalier de l'Ordre de la Couronne. *Address* : 7, Trafalgar Studios, Manresa Road, Chelsea. *Clubs* : Chelsea Arts ; Oxford and Cambridge Musical. (M9608)
SHEPHERD, Flight-Lieut. George Granville, O.B.E., R.A.F.
SHEPHERD, Harry, M.B.E.
SHEPHERD, John Dawson, O.B.E., Egyptian Ministry. (O11944)
SHEPHERD, John Ernest, M.B.E., R.N.R.
SHEPHERD, Joseph Wilfrid, C.B.E., *b.* 29 March, 1885 ; *s.* of Richard Shepherd, of Preston, Lancs ; *m.* Gertrude Mary, *d.* of F. J. Ainsworth, of Blackpool. Fellow of the Society of Incorporated Accountants and Auditors. *War Work* : Sec of the Manchester Belgium Refugees Committee. *Addresses* : 78, King Street, Manchester ; Kilronan, Whalley Range, Manchester. *Club* : Arts, Manchester. (C2948)
SHEPHERD, Major Percy Edward, O.B.E., A.M.I.C.E. R.E., *b.* 8 Aug. 1878 ; *s.* of Edward Shepherd of 2, Cornwall Road, Westbourne Park, W. 11 ; *m.* Ella, *d.* of Joseph Roome, of Wolverton, Bucks. *Educ.* : Buxton Coll. Chief Engineer, National Shipyards. *War Work* : 2nd in command Train

Ferry Terminal, Southampton, 1917 ; Commanding National Shipyard, No. 3, Portbury, 1918. *Address* : The Old Vicarage, Beachley, near Chepstow. *Club* : Engineers', Manchester. (O11305)

SHEPHERD, Philip William, M.B.E., R.A.S.C.
SHEPHERD, Capt. Walter Isaac, O.B.E., I.A.R.O.
SHEPHERD, Walter Rider, O.B.E.
SHEPHERD, Col. William Constable, O.B.E., T.D.
SHEPPARD, Alfred Edwin, M.B.E.
SHEPPARD, Amy, O.B.E., M.B., D.P.H. *Educ.* : London Royal Free Hospital School of Medicine for Women. Ophthalmic Surgeon to the Elizabeth Garrett Anderson Hospital, Euston Road, N.W., and the Clapham Maternity Hospital, S.W. ; Consulting Ophthalmic Surgeon to the Women's Settlement Hospital, Plaistow, E. *War Work* : Member of Women's Hospital Corps, 1914 ; Ophthalmic Surgeon to the Military Hospital, Endell Street, W.C. 2, and to the Q.M.A.A.C. Hospital, Isleworth. *Address* : 17, Harley Street, Cavendish Square, London, W. 1. *Clubs* : Lyceum ; International Women's Franchise. (O11846)
SHEPPARD, Capt. Eric William, O.B.E., M.C., *b.* 14 July, 1890 ; *s.* of the Rev. W. K. Sheppard, of Ripon, Yorkshire ; *m.* Kathleen, *d.* of Dr. E. J. Ryan MacMahon, of Cheltenham. *Educ.* : Trent Coll., Derbyshire ; Hertford Coll., Oxford. Capt. Regular Army ; General Staff, War Office. *War Work* : Service in France and Near East. *Address* : Hell Fire Corner, Horley Row, Horley, Surrey. *Club* : Junior Army and Navy. (O7689)
SHEPPARD, Frank, O.B.E.
SHEPPARD, Helen Mildred, O.B.E., Q.M.A.A.C.
SHEPPARD, Herbert St. John, M.B.E.
SHEPPARD, John Tresidder, M.B.E.
SHEPPARD, Mary Constance, M.B.E., *d.* of Dr. W. J. Sheppard, of Putney. Private Secretary. *War Work* : 3 years at Aircraft Production Dept., Ministry of Munitions ; Woman Staff Officer, and Junior Administrative Assistant. *Address* : 235, Upper Richmond Road, Putney. (M9610)
SHEPPARD, Walter, M.B.E.
SHEPPERD, Walter Henry, O.B.E., *b.* 30 June, 1872 ; *s.* of the late Henry J. Shepperd, of London ; *m.* Taisie Steuart, *d.* of the late William F. C. S. Corry, of Belfast. *Educ.* : Methodist Coll., Belfast. Director and Sec. William Corry & Co., Ltd., Belfast. *War Work* : Paymaster, Army Pay Department. *Address* : Tyneholme, Bangor, Co. Down. (O3918)

SHERA, Major Louis Murray, O.B.E.
SHERBROOKE, Margaret Macdonald, Mrs., O.B.E., Médaille de la Reine Elisabeth, *b.* 18 July, 1849 ; *d.* of Alexander Graham, J.P., of Dunclutha, Argyll ; *m.* Commander William Sherbrooke, R.N., of Oxton, Notts (who died) ; *s.* of Henry Sherbrooke, of Oxton Hall, Notts. (see BURKE'S *Landed Gentry*). *Educ.* : Privately. President of the Assocn. for the Return of Women Guardians ; Lancashire Poor Law Guardian, Ormskirk Union, Lancs ; and Upton-on-Severn, Worcestershire. *War Work* : Organised, April, 1915, at the request of General, Eastern Command, and through O.C. Shorncliffe Military Hospital, " Welfare Wounded," Folkestone, which was closed Dec. 1920 ; was Hon. Sec. of the same. *Address* : Oxton Hall, Southwell, Notts. *Club* : Lyceum, Piccadilly. (O11306)
SHERER, Lieut.-Col. John Corrie, O.B.E., I.A.
SHERIDAN, Lieut. Norman Charles, M.B.E.
SHERINGTON, Major Guy, O.B.E.
SHERLOCK, Capt. David Thomas Joseph, M.B.E., B.A., *b.* 6 Sept. 1881 ; *s.* of Thomas T. Sherlock, of Dublin ; *m.* Augusta Anna, *d.* of Sir Francis Cruise, D.L., of Dublin. *Educ.* : Downside Coll. ; Dublin Univ. Barrister-at-Law ; appointed Judicial Commissioner British North Borneo, 1920. *War Work* : Served in Gallipoli and Egypt, 1915–19. *Address* : 20, Upper Mount Street, Dublin. *Club* : University, Dublin ; Limerick County. (M4704)
SHERMAN, Comm. Carlton Collingwood, O.B.E., R.N., *b.* 1 Jan. 1884 ; *s.* of Charles Belli Bivar Sherman, of Holland House, Albury Heath, Surrey ; *m.* Francesca Isabella, *d.* of Comm. J. Honner, R.N. *Educ.* : Cheltenham Coll., and H.M.S. " Britannia." London Manager of Robey & Co., Ltd., Engineers, Lincoln. *War Work* : 1914, Mine Sweeping ; 1915–16, Assistant to Director of Naval Ordnance, Admiralty ; 1917–18, Deputy Director of Production for Mines, Torpedoes, and Anti-Submarine Weapons, Admiralty. *Address* : Woodville, Ashtead, Surrey. (O1858)
SHERRALL, Alice Georgina, Mrs., M.B.E.
SHERREN, Col. James, C.B.E., F.R.C.S., *b.* 1872. Surgeon, London Hospital ; Consulting Surgeon Poplar Hospital for Accidents and Stanmore Cottage Hospital ; Hunterian Professor and Member of Council, Royal College of Surgeons ; Examiner in Surgery Univ. of London. *War Work* : Consulting Surgeon attached to War Office ; rank of Col. A.M.S., Surgeon King Edward VII. Hospital for Officers ; Consulting Surgeon Yarrow Military Hospital, Broadstairs. *Address* : 6, Devonshire Place, W. 1. *Club* : Union. (C1764)
SHERWOOD, Montague Earle, M.B.E.
SHEWAN, Major Robert Ernest TOMLIN-MONEY-, O.B.E.
SHEWELL, Surg.-Comm. Herbert Wells Bayly, O.B.E., M.B., M.A., R.N.
SHIELD, Capt. John Gilson, M.B.E
SHIELDS, Capt. Oswald Clive Graeme, M.B.E., M.B., R.A.M.C.
SHIELDS, Lieut. William Cecil, M.B.E., R.N.V.R.

SHIFFNER, Elsie, Lady, O.B.E., Lady of Grace of the Order of St. John of Jerusalem ; *b.* 23 Sept. 1872 ; *d.* of O. H. Burrows, of Newport, U.S.A. ; *m.* Sir John Shiffner, 5th Bart. (who died 5 Apr. 1914), *s.* of Sir G. C. Shiffner, 4th Bart., of Coombe, Lewes, Sussex (*see* BURKE'S *Peerage*). *War Work :* Two years at Newick Red Cross Hospital as V.A.D., and two years at Pavilion Hospital, Brighton, as V.A.D., making temporary plaster-of-Paris peg-legs for men before being fitted with artificial legs. *Address :* Coombe Place, Lewes, Sussex.
(O11308)

SHILLAKER, James Frederick, M.B.E.

SHILLINGTON, Elizabeth Mildred, M.B.E.

SHILSON, Major Bernard William, O.B.E. R.A.S.C.

SHILSTON, Capt. Walter Richard, M.B.E.

SHILTON, Capt. Frederick Walton, O.B.E.

SHINE, Major Eugene Percy Forrest, O.B.E., I.A.

SHINGLETON, Major Leslie, O.B.E., *b.* 9 July, 1878 ; *s.* of Frederick Shingleton, M.V.O., of 67, Cornwall Gardens, S.W. ; *m.* Edith Frances, *d.* of the late John Williams, J.P., of Paddington. *Educ. :* King William's Coll., Isle of Man. *War Work :* Served in Royal Engineers in France and Greece from Sept. 1915 to June, 1919 ; Act. Lieut.-Col., Assistant Director of Works ; Medaille d'Honneur avec glaives en vermeuil ; 1914–15 Star. *Address :* 66, Comeragh Road, W. (O3061)

SHIPLEY, Sir Arthur Everett, G.B.E., *b.* 10 March, 1861 ; *s.* of the late Alexander Shipley, of the Hall, Datchet, Bucks. *Educ. :* Univ. Coll. School ; St. Bartholomew's Hospital ; Christ's Coll., Cambridge. Deputy Vice-Chancellor of Cambridge Univ. ; Master of Christ's Coll., Cambridge ; Reader in Zoology in the Univ. of Cambridge, 1908 ; late Vice-President of the Linnæan Society ; Chairman of the Council of the Marine Biological Association ; Member of the Central Medical War Committee ; Foreign Member American Association of Economic Entomologists and of the Helminthological Society of Washington ; Hunterian Trustee ; Tancred Trustee ; Beit Trustee ; Member of the Royal Commission on the Civil Service and the Departmental Enquiry into Grouse Diseases ; sent on a mission by Colonial Office to investigate a plant disease in the Bermudas, 1887 ; Sec. of the Museums and Lecture Rooms Syndicate, 1891 ; Member of the Council of the Senate. *Publications : Zoology of the Invertebrata,* 1893 ; *Pearls and Parasites,* 1908 ; ' *J.,*' *A Memoir of John Willis Clark,* 1913 ; *The Minor Horrors of War ; More Minor Horrors,* 1916 ; *The Voyage of a Vice-Chancellor,* 1919 ; part translator of *Weismann on Heredity,* 2 volumes, 1889–92 ; *Studies in Insect Life,* 1916 ; (with A. Schuster, *q.v.*); *Britain's Heritage of Science,* 1917 ; joint-editor and part-author of the *Camb. Natural History ; Grouse in Health and in Disease :* editor of the *Pitt Press Natural Science Manuals,* Biological Series ; and of the *Fauna of British India* series ; part author and editor of *A Text-book on Zoology ;* and *Handbook to Natural History of Cambridgeshire ;* author of articles in the *Encyclopœdia Britannica,* the *Encyclopœdia of Sport, Allbutt and Rolleston's Systems of Medicine,* and the *Encyclopœdia Biblica ;* formerly co-editor of *Parasitology,* and of the *Journal of Economic Biology,* and author of numerous zoological papers in various scientific journals. *Addresses :* Christ's College Lodge, Cambridge ; The Manor Cottage, Englefield Green, Surrey. *Clubs :* Athenæum ; United University ; Pitt, Cambridge. (G60)

SHIPLEY, Walter Henry Foster, M.B.E.

SHIPMAN, Lieut. Frederick L., O.B.E., R.N.V.R.

SHIPP, Capt. Frederic Edgar, O.B.E., *b.* 9 July, 1892 ; *s.* of C. W. Shipp, of Cadenham Manor, Chippenham, Wilts ; *m.* Rita Minnie, *d.* of A. T. Candy, of Bath. *Educ. :* Kingsholme, Weston-super-Mare, and Bath. H.M. Regular Commission. *Addresses :* Cadenham Manor, Chippenham, Wilts. ; McGrigor's, Panton Street. *Club :* R.A.S.C. (O5777)

SHIPTON, Lieut.-Comm. Francis Henry Eldred, O.B.E.

SHIRER, Rev. William, O.B.E.

SHIRRES, Christian, M.B.E. ; *d.* of William Shirres, of Aberdeen. *Educ. :* Aberdeen, Bournemouth, and Paris. *War Work :* Sec. War Dressings Depot, North-eastern District, Scotland, British Red Cross Society ; and Official Red Cross Searcher for the Missing, Albyn Place Hospital, Aberdeen. *Address :* 15, Bonaccord Crescent, Aberdeen. (M9613)

SHIRTCLIFFE, George, O.B.E.,

SHOETENSACK, Major Edgar Leonard, O.B.E., *b.* 26 Oct. 1888 ; *s.* of George Shoetensack, of Hampstead ; *m.* Nora Wallis, *d.* of John Lancaster, of Manchester. *Educ. :* Boston Grammar School ; Univ. Coll. School. Called to the Bar (Middle Temple), 1910 ; entered Home Civil Service, 1912 ; 1912–14 at the National Health Insurance Commission (England) ; 1919, Ministry of Health. *War Work :* Commissioned R.A.O.C. Feb. 1915 ; after serving at Haulbowline, Ireland, held positions of Ordnance Officer, Selby, and Ordnance Officer, York ; subsequently proceeded to Italy, and served, first as Ordnance Officer, Base Depot, then as D.A.D.O.S. 7th Division ; was with 7th Division during the advance from the Piave to the Tagliamento ; decorated by H.M. the King of Italy with the Croce di Guerra. *Address :* Stoke Hall, Althorne, Maldon, Essex. (O6417)

SHORE, Capt. Alfred George, M.B.E.

SHORE, Capt. George William, O.B.E., M.B., B.S., *b.* 10 March, 1888 ; *s.* of J. G. Shore, of 30, Mount Nod Road, Streatham, London, S.W. 16. *Educ. :* Dulwich Coll., and King's Coll., Univ. of London. Assistant Medical Officer, Surrey Education Committee. *War Work :* At outbreak of war served with 4th London General Hospital ; later, went to Mesopotamia as Ophthalmic Surgeon, No. 40 British General Hospital ; on being invalided home, became Assistant Registrar, and later, Registrar, 4th London General Hospital. *Address :* 30, Mount Nod Road, Streatham, London, S.W. 16. (O7690)

SHORE, Lewis Erle, O.B.E., *b.* 1863 ; *s.* of T. W. Shore, of Southampton ; *m.* Agatha Catherine, *d.* of R. Gresley Hall, of Upton House, Bitton. *Educ. :* Southampton Grammar School ; St. John's Coll. Camb. ; St. Bartholomew's Hospital ; Breslau Univ. Fellow and Junior Bursar, St. John's Coll., Cambridge ; Lecturer on Physiology, Cambridge Univ. *War Work :* Neurologist and M.O. i/c Electrical Dept., 1st Eastern General Hospital. *Address :* 8, Madingley Road ; St. John's College, Cambridge. (O4392)

SHORE, Thomas William, O.B.E., M.D.

SHOREY, Percy Thomas, M.B.E., *b.* 29 June, 1887 ; *s.* of Thomas Shorey, of London. Clerk, Board of Trade and Treasury Solicitor's Department ; Confidential Clerk, Home Office, 1910–20 ; now Private Sec. to Sir John Baird, Bart., C.M.G., D.S.O., M.P., Parliamentary Under-Secretary of State for the Home Department. *Address :* 9, Highbury Quadrant, London, N. 5. (M938)

SHORLAND, Elizabeth Freeman, Mrs., M.B.E., *b.* 9 Dec. 1868 ; *d.* of George Ager, of Holloway ; *m.* Harry Frederick Shorland, *s.* of Robert Philip Shorland, of New Southgate. *Educ. :* West Holloway High School. Hon. Sec. Teddington Branch, Church of England Waifs and Strays Society (Children's Union Branch). *War Work :* Principal Commandant (Women's Detachments), Percy House Auxiliary Military Hospital, Isleworth, and Commandant of Middlesex 22 Women's Voluntary Aid Detachment ; Member of the Committee of the Middlesex Centre of the St. John Ambulance Brigade. *Address :* Haslemere, Waldegrave Park, Strawberry Hill, Middlesex. *Clubs :* Ladies' Forum ; V.A.D. ; Fulwell Golf. (M9614)

SHORNEY, Lieut. and Qr.-Mr. Frederick William M.B.E.

SHORT, Lieut.-Col. Ernest William George, M.B.E.

SHORT, Capt. Henry, M.B.E.

SHORT, Major Hugh, O.B.E

SHORT, John, M.B.E.

SHORT, John, M.B.E.

SHORT, Oswald Murton, O.B.E.

SHORTER, Albert Edward, M.B.E.

SHORTO, Major Harry George, O.B.E., T.D., R.A.S.C (T.). *War Work :* Gallipoli Expedition, Senior Supply. Officer, 29th Division ; O.C. R.A.S.C., Lough Swilly Sub-District, Irish Command ; served Aug. 1914, to Jan. 1920. *Address :* Rochester House, Alton Road, Plymouth. (O7691)

SHORTO, Henry Ralph Trenchard, O.B.E., *b.* 2 July, 1874 ; *s.* of Henry Ralph Shorto, of Dorchester ; *m.* Helen Frances, *d.* of Henry Francis Harding, of Ireland. *Educ. :* Canterbury. Merchant ; for many years a Manager of the London and River Plate Bank, Ltd. *War Work :* War Commercial Intelligence Dept. ; Red Cross Work in Sao Paulo, Brazil ; one of the founders of the British Chamber of Commerce in that City, founded during the war, and Vice-President of the Allied Commercial Congress in Sao Paulo, Brazil, during years 1915–18 ; also Vice-President of the Brazilian Chamber of Commerce, 1917–18. *Clubs :* Junior Athenæum ; Automobile (Sao Paulo) ; International (Pernambuco). (O11310)

SHORTO, William Alfred Thomas, C.B.E., *b.* 30 June, 1876 ; *s.* of the late Henry Ralph Shorto, of Maiden Newton, Dorset ; *m.* Alice Léonide, *d.* of the late George Alexander Seymour, of Barnes. *Educ. :* Simon Langton School, and King's School, Canterbury. Civil Servant ; Principal Clerk, Secretary's Dept., Admiralty. *War Work :* Secretary's Dept., Admiralty ; Civil Assistant to Director of (Naval) Air Services ; and Sec. of Department of Controller-Gen. of Merchant Shipbuilding. *Address :* 24, St. Thomas's Mansions, Westminster Bridge, S.E. 1. (C2949)

SHORTRIDGE, Guy Chester, M.B.E., M.A., R.A.F.

SHOTTON, Charles, M.B.E., *b.* 1 Dec. 1860 ; *s.* of Henry Shotton, of Birmingham ; *m.* Rose, *d.* of William May, of Sheffield. *Educ. :* Privately. Ironfounder and Pawnbroker. *War Work :* Alderman and Deputy-Mayor (for one year) for the Borough of Smethwick ; Tribunal, Naval and Military Pensions Committee ; Chairman, Estates Committee (Allotments). *Address :* The Oaks, South Road, Smethwick. (M9616)

SHOULDER, Lieut. Henry, M.B.E.

SHOVE, Lieut.-Col. Cyril Ambrose, O.B.E., R.A.F.

SHOWELL, Lieut. and Qr.-Mr. Charles Frederick, M.B.E., R.G.A.

SHOWERS, Capt. Edward Maclean, O.B.E., *b.* 10 Dec. 1846 ; *s.* of Major E. S. G. Showers, of Madras Horse Artillery ; *m.* Georgina Hester Cornelia (Countess d'Epineuil), *d.* of Col. Henry Capel Somerset, of Gloucestershire. *Educ. :* Wellington Coll. Late 95th Regt., and late Chief Constable of Essex. (O11311)

SHREEVE, Lieut. Arthur William, M.B.E., R.A.M.C., *b.* 1874. *War Work :* Soudan Campaign, 1898 (British Soudan Medal, Khedive's Medal, Clasps for Atbara and Khartoum) with Queen's Own Cameron Highlanders ; left for France Aug. 1915, with the R.A.M.C., 65th Field Ambulance ; with 21st Div. for Battles of Loos, Somme, and Vimy Ridge operations ; Salonica, 1917 ; Egypt, 1918–19. *Address :* 1, Pimhill Street, Princes Park, Liverpool. (M3192)

SHUBRICK, Eleanor Mary, *War Work :* Organised and superintended two Soldiers' Homes and Tea Rooms at Rouen from March, 1915, to June, 1920 ; and a Soldiers' Home

at Woolwich. *Address:* Elvaston Place, London, S.W. 7.
(M9617)

SHUCKBURGH, Honor Zoe, Lady, O.B.E., *b.* 18 Aug. 1886; *d.* of the late Neville Thursby, of Harlestone, Northampton; *m.* Sir Gerald Francis Stewkby, 11th Bart., *s.* of Sir George Shuckburgh, of Shuckburgh, 9th Bart. (*see* BURKE'S *Peerage*). *War Work:* Vice-President, Southam Division, Warwickshire Branch, B.R.C.S.; Commandant of V.A.D. Warwick 60, and of Southam Auxiliary Hospital. *Address:* Shuckburgh, Daventry. *Clubs:* Bath; New Century.
(O11312)

SHURMUR, Lieut. Stanley Emberick, M.B.E., R.A.S.C.

SHUTE, Charles William, O.B.E.

SHUTE, Lieut.-Col. Cyril Aveling, C.B.E., I.A.

SHUTER, James Percy, O.B.E., *b.* 4 Oct. 1866. *Educ.:* Merchant Taylors' School. Town Clerk, Fulham. *Address:* Town Hall, Fulham. (O1862)

SHUTTLEWORTH, Lieut.-Col. Digby Inglis, C.B.E., D.S.O., Indian Army. Served in the Great War, 1914-19, in the Balkans (despatches, Brevet Lieut.-Col.). (C1417)

SIBBALD, Capt. Arthur Trevitt, M.B.E., *b.* 5 Dec. 1866; *s.* of Adam Sibbald, of Liverpool; *m.* Gertrude, *d.* of Martin Cavanagh, of Willenhall, Staffs. *Educ.:* Liverpool Coll., and Kirkcudbright Academy, N.B. Commander in Merchant Service; awarded in 1900 the U.S. Gold Medal for life-saving at the destruction of Galveston, Texas. *War Work:* Commander of H.M. Ammunition Transport "Clapham," in which made 115 consecutive voyages between England and France; commended by Admiralty for successfully extinguishing a serious fire amongst ammunition in his ship, June, 1918. *Address:* 122, Manor Lane, Lee, Kent. (M9618)

SIBLEY, Edith Waters, Mrs., O.B.E., 24 April, 1873; *d.* of John Robinson, of Clohes, Co. Monaghan; *m.* William, *s.* of Robert George, of Binstead, I. of W. *War Work:* Howth War Work Party, 1914-18; Belgian Refugees, 1915-16; Soldiers' and Sailors' Free Buffet, Amiens Street, Dublin. *Address:* The Burrow, Sutton, Co. Dublin. (O11313)

SIDDALS, Paymaster-Comm. John, O.B.E., R.N.

SIDDELEY, John Davenport, C.B.E., *b.* 1866. Managing Director. *War Work:* Construction of Aircraft Engines; Member of Civil Aerial Transport Committee. *Addresses:* Crackley, Kenilworth; 12, Old Burlington Street, W. 1. *Club:* Conservative. (C294)

SIDDLE, Robert, M.B.E.

SIDDON, Emily Frances, M.B.E., J.P., Order of Queen Elizabeth of Belgium; *d.* of Samuel Siddon, of Pleasley Hill, Notts. *Educ.:* Privately. *War Work:* President, Soldiers' and Sailors' Families Association (Huddersfield Branch); Member, War Pensions Committee; Vice-Chairman, Local War Relief Fund, Soldiers' Comforts Fund, and Prisoners of War Fund. *Address:* Honley House, Honley, Huddersfield. *Club:* Ladies' Athenæum. (M2419)

SIDEBOTTOM, Herbert, M.B.E.

SIDEBOTTOM, Capt. John Kercheval, O.B.E., R.E.

SIDEBOTTOM, Samuel, M.B.E., *b.* 9 July, 1865; *s.* of Samuel Sidebottom, of Castleton House, Rochdale; *m.* Maude Peternel, *d.* of the Rev. James Richards, of Newbold, Rochdale. *Educ.:* Shrewsbury School. *War Work:* Director of Army Contracts and Head of Army Remount Depot, at Macclesfield. *Address:* Littleton Hall, Chester. *Clubs:* Grosvenor (Chester): Constitutional (Manchester). (M3967)

SILGREAVES, Major Arthur Frederick, O.B.E., R.A.F.

SIDGWICK, Major Harry Christopher, O.B.E., M.B., M.R.C.S., L.R.C.P., B.A., R.A.M.C., *b.* 7 Dec. 1877; *s.* of the Rev. J. B. Sidgwick, of Strathmore, Stoke Abbott Road, Worthing; *m.* Marjorie Molyneux, *d.* of Robert Miller, of Wimbledon. *Educ.:* Lancing Coll., Clare Coll., Cambridge. and St. Bartholomew's Hospital. 1913-14, Surgical Specialist, Royal Herbert Hospital, Woolwich; and 1920, Surgical Specialist, 6th (Poona) Division, India. *War Work:* France, B.E.F.: 1914-15, in charge of Surgical Division, No. 12 General Hospital; 1915-16, O.C. No. 10 Stationary Hospital; 1916-18, O.C. No. 83 General Hospital; and 1918-19, O.C. No. 22 C.C.S. *Address:* c/o Messrs. Holt & Co., 3, Whitehall Place, S.W. *Club:* Junior United Service. (O8605)

SIDNEY, Edward, C.B.E. (C2360e)

SIDNEY, Capt. Ernest Hemming, O.B.E., D.C.M., *b.* 1 Aug. 1868; *s.* of Edwin Alfred Sidney, of Gillingham, Kent; *m.* Sara Maude, *d.* of James Williams, of Dublin. *Educ.:* Claremont School, Gillingham. Royal Army Ordnance Corps. Served in S. African War, 1899-1902 (twice mentioned in despatches and awarded Distinguished Conduct Medal). *War Work:* Served in Malta, 1914; Greek Macedonia, 1915-18; Caucasus, 1918-20 (Batoum and Baku); Anatolia, 1920 (mentioned in despatches). *Address:* 135, Kinveachy Gardens, Charlton, S.E. (O8714)

SIDNEY, Leicester Philip, M.B.E., *b.* 27 March, 1871; *s.* of Capt. Philip Sidney, R.M.L.I., of Yarmouth, and *g.s.* of the late Admiral F. W. Sidney, of Southsea. *Educ.:* Brighton, and at Boulogne-sur-Mer Communal Coll. Assistant Sec. since 1904, Iron and Steel Institute; formerly Chief Chemist at the Shelton Iron, Coal, and Steel Company, Stoke-on-Trent, and subsequently Sub-Editor of the "Iron and Coal Trades Review." *War Work:* Served with Ministry of Munitions Aug. 1915, to Dec. 1918; in control of all printed and manifolded communications, and of issue of all permits to visit munitions and explosives factories and stores from 1916-18; Ministry Representative on Control Orders Sub-Committee of

War Priorities Committee, and on Defence of the Realm Regulations Committee. *Addresses:* 76, York Mansions, Battersea Park, S.W.; 28, Victoria Street, S.W. (M9619)

SIEBER, John Frederick, O.B.E.

SIEVWRIGHT, 2nd Lieut. Andrew George Hume, M.B.E., I.A.R.O.

SIGRIST, Capt. Edward, O.B.E., R.A.O.C.

SIGRIST, Frederick, M.B.E.

SIKES, Major Charles William Booth, O.B.E., R.A.V.C., *b.* 6 Aug. 1875; *s.* of George William Sikes, of Retford, Notts. *Educ.:* Atherstone Grammar School, and Royal Veterinary Coll., Camden Town. Veterinary Surgeon. *War Work:* Went to France with 41st Division in April, 1916; took command of 52nd Mobile Veterinary Section through Battle of Somme, 1916; was appointed D.A.D.V.S. of 41st Division in 1917, and served with this division in France, Belgium, Italy, and Germany, during which period was mentioned in despatches four times. *Address:* Castle Street, Warwick. (O8606)

SILBURN, Lieut.-Col. Percy Arthur Baxter, C.B.E., D.S.O., *b.* 1876; *s.* of Arthur Silburn, of Durban, Natal; *m.* 1901, Marie Antoinette, *d.* of the late J. T. Riley Hartley. *Educ.:* Privately. Served in S. Africa, 1899-1902, present at relief of Ladysmith (despatches, medal with five clasps, promoted Major); joined Cape Mounted Rifles, 1891, and is Major and T. Lieut.-Col.; appointed Gunnery Instructor Natal Forces; was Secretary Natal Defence Commn. 1902-4; elected a M.L.A., Natal, for Alfred co. Div. 1906; S. African Parliament (for Durban), 1910. *Address:* Mitchell Park, Berea, Durban, Natal. (C739)

SILK, Paymaster-Capt. Ernest Edwin, C.B.E., R.N., *b.* 1862; *s.* of the late Edward Silk; *m.* Isabel Maud, *d.* of the late Capt. E. C. Wilford, 96th Regt. Served in the China War, 1900 (medal); Great War, 1914-19 (despatches). (C1939)

SILLAR, Arthur Molyneux, M.B.E., M.I.C.E., *b.* 1865; *s.* of T. F. Sillar, of London and Shanghai; *m.* Leslie, *d.* of Robert Graham, of Inverness. *Educ.:* Shrewsbury. Formerly partner in firm of Lacey, Sillar and Leigh, Consulting Engineers to many local authorities and companies for electrical power generation and distribution, light railways and tramways; amongst these are Batley, Belfast, Blackburn, Bournemouth, Bury, Colchester, Middleton, Radcliffe, Rawtenstall, Rochdale, Salford, and Swindon, the Lancashire Power Co., Trafford Power Co., and L. and N.-W. Railway Co.; at present Consulting Engineer to the Post Office London Railway, and, amongst others, to the electricity supply systems at Peking and Tientsin. *War Work:* Ministry of Munitions, 1915-19, as Assistant Superintending Engineer, Metropolitan Area, and of South-East England; Superintending Engineer, East Anglia and South-East Midlands; and Director of National Gauge Factories. *Address:* 104, Victoria Street, S.W. *Clubs:* St. Stephen's; Royal Automobile. (M941)

SILLEY, Major Edward Charles, O.B.E.

SILLEY, John Henry, O.B.E.

SILTZER, Violet, Mrs., O.B.E., *b.* 1873; *d.* of Henry Stourton, J.P., of Holme Hall, York; *m.* Francis Siltzer. Sec. to Rt. Hon. Walter Long, M.P. *War Work:* Red Cross Stores Dept., Pall Mall; also Nurse at the Hospital, Charing, Kent. *Address:* 8, Chester Street, Belgrave Square, S.W. 1. (O3919)

SILVER, Lieut.-Col. John Payzant, C.B.E., D.S.O., B.A., M.B., C.M., R.A.M.C., *b.* 17 May, 1869; *s.* of W. C. Silver, of Halifax, Canada; *m.* Louie Mabel, *d.* of William Drake-Brockman, of Cheriton, Bournemouth. *Educ.:* Univ. of Windsor, Nova Scotia; Univ. of Edinburgh. *War Work:* O.C. 17th Field Ambulance, 6th Division, B.E.F. Aug. 1914, to Feb. 1916; Assistant Director of Medical Services, 12th Division, B.E.F., Feb. 1916, to March, 1919; present at seven battles; retired totally disabled from illness contracted at the Front. *Address:* Lloyds Bank, 72, Lombard Street, E.C. (C1324)

SILVER, Rear-Adm. Mortimer L'Estrange, C.B.E., R.N. (ret.). Sometime Capt. of the Dockyard, Dept. Supt., and King's Harbour Master, Chatham. (C2239)

SILVERTHORNE, Major James William Bradford, O.B.E.

SILVESTER, Colin Joseph, O.B.E.

SIM, James, M.B.E.

SIM, Capt. James, O.B.E., *b.* 13 Jan. 1864; *s.* of David Sim, of Dundee; *m.* Veronica, *d.* of Patrick McNamara, of Limerick. *Educ.:* Public School. Mercantile Marine. *War Work:* Commanded a ship carrying troops from Australia to Egypt, France, and England, 1915; taken over by Imperial Government and continued as a hospital ship and continued as such until sunk by a Hun submarine in Aug. 1918. *Address:* Warilda, Bannerman Street, Cramorne, Sydney, N.S.W. (O11314)

SIM, John, O.B.E.

SIMCOCK, James, M.B.E., M.D., *b.* 5 June, 1866; *s.* of Caleb Simcock, of Knutsford; *m.* Jean, *d.* of John Ward, of Manchester. *Educ.:* Commercial School, Knutsford; Victoria Univ., and Royal Infirmary, Manchester. *War Work:* Assistant County Director, East Lancashire Branch (Heaton Chapel Division), British Red Cross Society; Medical Officer-in-Charge, Heaton Mersey Auxiliary Hospital, and Reform Club Hospital, Heaton Moor; Recruiting Medical Officer, Stockport; Chairman, Neurological Pensions Board, Manchester. *Address:* Stoneleigh, Heaton Moor, Stockport. (M3968)

SIMCOX, William, M.B.E., J.P.

SIME, Major W. Malacca, O.B.E.

SIMEY, Alma Margaret, Mrs., M.B.E., *b.* 1873 ; *d.* of Forster Alleyne, of Clifton, Bristol ; *m.* Athelstane Iliff, *s.* of Ralph Simey, J.P., D.L., of Durham. *Educ.:* Clifton High School. *War Work:* Commandant of V.A.D. Warwick 40, and of Te Hira Section of Rugby Town V.A. Hospital, Auxiliary of 1st Southern General Hospital, Birmingham. *Address :* St. John's. Rugby. (M9622)

SIMKINS, Helen, Mrs., O.B.E.

SIMMETT, Capt. William Edward, M.B.E., R.E.

SIMMONDS, Charles, O.B.E., F.I.C., F.C.S., *b.* 19 Dec. 1861 ; *s.* of William Simmonds, of Stourbridge, Worcs. ; *m.* Edythe Aurelia, *d.* of Thos. Henry Dunne, late of Indian Civil Service. *Educ.:* Royal Coll. of Science, London. Superintending Analyst, Department of the Government Chemist, London. *War Work :* Analysis of anæsthetics, drugs, and other medicines for the use of H.M. Forces. *Addresses :* 32, Woodside, Wimbledon ; Government Laboratory, London. (O11315)

SIMMONDS, Frederick Victor, M.B.E.

SIMMONDS, Herbert John, C.B., C.B.E., Asst.-Sec. Board of Education ; sometime Sec. to Advisory Committee of Civil Liabilities (Mil.) Committee. (C2039)

SIMMONDS, Percy, M.B.E.

SIMMONDS, Major Roy, C.B.E.

SIMMONS, Edward Walpole, O.B.E., M.D.

SIMMONS, Frederick, M.B.E., *b.* 6 Jan. 1880. *Educ.:* Christ's Hospital. Engineer. *War Work :* War Priorities Committee. *Address :* Queen Anne's Chambers, Westminster, S.W. *Club :* Royal Automobile. (M3969)

SIMMONS, Frederic Vital, M.B.E., *b.* 28 May, 1874 ; *s.* of Frederick Simmons, of Oxford ; *m.* Louise, *d.* of James Keeves, of Stamford Hill. Insurance Manager. *War Work :* Commandant London Ambulance Column, Aug. 1914, to March, 1919. *Address :* Waverley. Gayton Road, Harrow. (M9624)

SIMMONS, Engr.-Capt. George Thomas, C.B.E., R.N. Served in the Great War, 1914–19 (despatches). (C1940)

SIMMONS, John Barnett, O.B.E.

SIMMONS, Capt. Stanley Hall, O.B.E.

SIMMONS, Sir William Anker, K.B.E., J.P., Berks., *b.* 5 Oct. 1857 ; *e. s.* of Charles Simmons of Crandem Gate, Henley-on-Thames ; *m.* Edith Nora, *o. d.* of Edward Smith Beddome, of Lloyds. *Educ.:* Privately ; Henley Old Grammar School. Fellow of Surveyors' Institute ; Senior Partner of Simmons & Sons, Chartered Surveyors, of Henley-on-Thames, Reading, and Basingstoke ; an authority on Agricultural and Land Questions ; Agricultural Adviser, from its formation, to the Ministry of Food ; Past Chairman of the Farmer's Club ; Alderman and Senior Member of Henley Town Council (35 years) ; four times Mayor of Henley ; five times P.M. ; was invited to stand as Agricultural candidate for S. Oxon, 1918. *Address :* Bird Place, Henley-on-Thames. *Clubs :* Junior Athenæum : Farmers'. (K423)

SIMON, Paymaster-Lieut. Arnold, O.B.E., R.N.R.

SIMON, Emily Anne, Mrs., O.B.E., *b.* 27 April, 1858 ; *d.* of E. M. Stock, of Manchester and Alderley Edge ; *m.* Henry, *s.* of Gustav Simon, of Brieg in Silesia. *Educ.:* Privately *War Work :* Gave her home as a Red Cross Hospital ; Hon. Commandant of Lawnhurst Hospital ; Vice-President of Didsbury and Withington Division ; Member of Belgian Refugees Committee. *Address :* Lawnhurst, Didsbury. *Club :* Ladies' Athenæum. (O11317)

SIMON, Rt. Hon. Sir John (Allsebrook), P.C., K.C.V.O., Knt. Bach., O.B.E., M.P. (L.) Walthamstow Div. Essex, 1906–18 ; Bencher, Inner Temple, 1910 ; late standing Counsel to Oxford Univ., *b.* 28 Feb. 1873 ; *o. s.* of the Rev. Edwin Simon, Congregational Minister, and Fanny Allsebrook ; *m.* 1st Ethel Mary Venables (d. 1902), 2nd Kathleen Manning. *Educ.:* Fettes Coll., Edinburgh ; Wadham Coll., Oxford (Scholar, Hon. Fellow) ; Fellow of All Souls Coll., Oxford ; President, Oxford Union Society, 1896 ; Barstow Law Scholar, 1898 ; called to Bar, 1899 ; K.C. 1908 ; one of the Counsel for British Government in Alaska Boundary Arbitration, 1903 ; Chairman of Departmental Committee on Street Trading, 1909 ; Member of Royal Commission on Justices of the Peace, 1910 ; Solicitor-General, 1910–13 ; Attorney-General with seat in Cabinet, 1913–15 ; Secretary of State for Home Affairs ; 1915–16 ; Major in Royal Air Force, serving in France, 1917–18. *Addresses :* Fritwell Manor, Banbury ; 1, Temple Gardens, E.C. 4. *Clubs :* Reform ; Garrick ; National Liberal ; Eighty ; Royal Automobile. (O3412)

SIMON, Col. Maximilian St. Leger, C.B.E., R.E., *b.* 28 March, 1876 ; *s.* of Dr. Maximilian Frank Simon, C.M.G., of Singapore, S.S. ; *m.* Mabel Louise, *d.* of T. Hastings Lees, of Guilsborough, Northamptonshire. *Educ.:* Blundell's School, Tiverton, and R.M. Academy. 1909–10, Assistant Director of Engineer Services, Canada ; 1911–15, Staff Captain, War Office (Fortifications and Works). *War Work :* 1916, Engineer Officer in charge construction of London Anti-Aircraft Defences ; 1917–18, Commander, London Anti-Aircraft Defences ; 1918, Commander, Anti-Aircraft Defences, Independent Force, R.A.F. ; 1919, Belgian Coast, Inter-Service Mission (A. A. Defences) ; 1920, General Staff, War Office. *Address :* Redlands Cottage, Holmwood, Surrey. *Club :* United Service. (C2166)

SIMOND, Charles Francois, C.B.E., *b.* 28 Dec. 1872 ; *s.* of François Frédéric Simond ; *m.* 1st, Lilian Edith, *d.* of Frederick Octavius Crump ; 2nd, Adgie, *d.* of Hugh Inglis Gray, of Uddingstone. *Educ.:* London International College

and Switzerland. *War Work :* Manager of Nestlé and Anglo-Swiss Condensed Milk Co. ; responsible for practically entire demand of condensed milk for British Forces ashore and afloat ; acted on numerous committees appointed by Food Ministry in connection with milk and condensed milk and assisted in administration of condensed milk orders. *Address :* 4, Mulberry Walk, Chelsea, S.W. 3. *Clubs :* Sports ; Queen's ; All England. (C2950)

SIMONDS, Cecilia Elizabeth Beatrice, Mrs., O.B.E., *b.* 30 March, 1854 ; *d.* of Col. Daniel (late Rifle Brigade) ; *m.* James Simonds (who died), *s.* of Charles Simonds, of Reading. *War Work :* Vice-President, Soldiers' and Sailors' Families Assoc. ; Almoner of Soldiers' and Sailors' Help Society, Reading ; Member of War Pensions Committee since formation, and of Disablement, etc., Cases Committee ; Executive Committee ; also on the Unemployment Committee. *Address :* Redlands House, Reading. (O11318)

SIMONDS, Col. Robert Henville, O.B.E., V.D., J.P., D.L., 15 Nov. 1852 ; *s.* of Robert Withington Simonds, of Winchester ; *m.* Winifred May, *d.* of Henry Stilwell, of Steepleton, Dorset. *Educ.:* Winchester Christ Church Coll., Oxford. Vice-Chairman, Dorset County Council ; Chairman, Dorchester Rural District Council. *War Work :* Sec. Territorial Force Association of the County of Dorset. *Address :* Winterbourne Abbas, Dorchester. *Club :* Hampshire. (O734)

SIMONIS, Henry, C.B.E.

SIMONSON, Capt. Paul William, O.B.E.

SIMPKIN, Oswald Richard Arthur, C.B.E..

SIMPKINS, Ernest Charles, M.B.E., *b.* 9 Aug. 1870 ; *s.* of John Simpkins, of Newton St. Loe, Bath ; *m.* Lily, *d.* of William Booth, of Swindon, Wilts. *Educ.:* Swindon. *War Work :* Transportation. *Address :* Trenance, Shakespeare Road, Hanwell, W. (M9625)

SIMPSON, Lieut.-Col. Alexander, C.B.E., M.D., R.A.M.C.

SIMPSON, Col. Alexander Petrie, O.B.E., T.D., *b.* 28 Sept. 1867. *Educ.:* Merchiston Castle, Edinburgh, and Edinburgh Univ. Writer to the Signet, Linlithgow. *War Work :* Commanding 1/10th (Cyclist) Batt. Royal Scots, 24th Labour Group, France, No. 4 Salvage District, France, Somain Sub-. District, France, and No. 1 District, France, Aug. 1914, to Oct. 1920. *Address :* Annet House, Linlithgow, Scotland. (O2715)

SIMPSON, Alfred, M.B.E., *b.* 3 Dec. 1885 *Educ.:* Castleford Technical and Evening Schools. Coal Miner ; Clerk to Great and Little Preston Parish Council and Assistant Overseer, also Hon. Sec. of the Kippax District Local Savings Committee. *War Work :* Mobilised as a Territorial in the 5th Batt. King's Own Yorkshire Light Infantry, Aug. 1914 ; embarked to France, April, 1915 ; whilst at an Auxiliary Hospital near Manchester carried out a successful local munition volunteering campaign ; organised production of sandbags, and forwarded them to Army Ordnance Depot ; worked in shell factory as clerk. *Address :* 24, Hill Street, Bowers Rows, Woodlesford. (M9626)

SIMPSON, Annie Louise, O.B.E., *b.* 20 April, 1891. Civil Servant. *War Work :* Assist. Sec. to Sir Herbert Llewellyn Smith, G.C.B., Permanent Sec. to Board of Trade, June, 1915, to Dec. 1916 ; Personal Clerk to Prime Minister, Jan. 1917 ; Dec. 1919, attached Economic Section, Peace Conference, Paris, Jan. 1920, to July, 1920. *Address :* 108, Brownlow Road, New Southgate, N. (O11319)

SIMPSON, Lieut.-Col. Arthur William Woodman, O.B.E., T.D., *b.* 3 April, 1873 ; *s.* of Walter Simpson, of Longhurst, Haigh. *Educ.:* Christ's Coll., Cambridge. Director of several Colliery Companies ; Member of the Governing Body of the Church Lads' Brigade Cadets (King's Royal Rifle Corps) ; commanding 5th Batt. the Manchester Regt. *War Work :* Mobilised with 5th Batt. Manchester Regt. ; left England for Egypt, Sept. 1914 ; left Egypt for Dardanelles, May. 1915, subsequently returning to Egypt ; appointed Inspector, Prisoners of War Camps, E.E.F., attached G.H.Q., Egypt ; mentioned five times in despatches, and 3rd Class Order of the Nile. *Address :* 78, The Promenade, Southport ; South House, Cresswell, Morpeth, Northumberland. *Club :* Constitutional. (O2930)

SIMPSON, Clement Pearson, O.B.E., *b.* 13 June, 1869 ; *s.* of John Simpson, of 59, Claverton Street, S.W. *Educ.:* Wellington Coll., and Trinity Coll., Cambridge. Director of West Surrey Water Company. *War Work :* Head Coast Watcher for Drumbeg District of Sutherland, N.B. *Addresses :* Oldany, Lochinver, Lairg, N.B. ; 59, Claverton Street, London, S.W. 1. *Club :* New University. (O11320)

SIMPSON, Rear-Adm. Cortland Herbert, C.B.E. Capt. and Commodore (2nd Class), R.N.R. ; (ret.) served in the Soudan, 1884–85 ; Great War, 1914–19, as Senior Officer, W. Indies Auxiliary Patrol (despatches). (C1205)

SIMPSON, Capt. David, M.B.E., *b.* 10 July, 1872 ; *s.* of David Simpson, of Southwold, Suffolk ; *m.* Margaret Taylor, *d.* of Edward Taylor Wigg, of Southwold. *Educ.:* Southwold and London. Merchant Service. *War Work :* On Transport M.F.A. "Wandby," 1288. *Address :* 50, Fair Close Road, Beccles, Suffolk. (M3970)

SIMPSON, Major Edward Herbert, O.B.E., M.C., F.R.G.S. *Educ.:* King's School, Pontefract, and Edinburgh Univ. Barrister-at-law of the Middle Temple. *War Work :* Served S. African War, 1899–1902 ; two medals and 8 clasps ; Served Great War in France and Flanders from Sept. 1914, to Nov. 1919 ; on Staff as D.A.A.G. Headquarters 3rd Army, June, 1915, to March, 1916 ; G.H.Q. Staff. March, 1916, to

Nov. 1919; four times mentioned in despatches; 1914 Star, Order of St. John, and French Life Saving Medal. *Address:* 1, The Cloisters, Temple, E.C. 4. (O5779)

SIMPSON, Major Geoffrey Hugh, M.B.E., *b.* 23 Jan. 1886; *s.* of James Simpson, General Manager, Bank of Africa, Ltd., Capetown. *Educ.:* Blundell's School, Tiverton; Diocesan Coll., and South African Coll., Capetown. Solicitor and Public Notary, South Africa, till 1914; appointed Assistant Manager, Trinidad Leasehold, Ltd., Trinidad, B.W.I., Feb. 1920. Commissioned R.A.S.C., 4 June, 1915; Gallipoli, Oct. to Dec. 1915; O.C. Main Supply Depot, Kantara, Egypt, Sept. 1917, to Sept. 1918; appointed Deputy Assistant Director of Supplies, G.H.Q., E.E.F., Sept. 1918. *Address:* c/o Trinidad Leasehold, Ltd., 1, London Wall Buildings, London; Pointe à Pierre, Trinidad. *Club:* Union (Trinidad). (M2421)

SIMPSON, Capt. George Charles Edward, O.B.E., M.B., F.R.C.S., R.A.M.C., *b.* 10 March, 1881; *s.* of Edward James Simpson, of St. Helens, Lancs; *m.* Elwina Constance, *d.* of J. C. Horobin, of Homerton Coll., Cambridge. *Educ.:* Mill Hill; St. John's Coll., Cambridge; St. Bartholomew's Hospital. Hon. Surgeon, David Lewis Northern Hospital, Liverpool; Associate Professor of Human Anatomy, Univ. of Liverpool; Lecturer in Clinical Surgery, Univ. of Liverpool; Hon. Cons. Surgeon, Children's Rest, Liverpool, and Leasowe Hospital for Children. *War Work:* Mobilised with 2nd West Lancs Field Ambulance (98th and 63rd Field Ambulances); served in France as Surgical Specialist and as Lieut.-Col., commanding 34th (West Lancashire) Casualty Clearing Station, 1915–18; Surgeon in Military Wards, David Lewis Northern Hospital, Liverpool. *Address:* 15, Rodney Street, Liverpool. *Clubs:* Athenæum; Medical Institution (Liverpool). (O5780)

SIMPSON, George Clarke, C.B.E.

SIMPSON, Capt. Gilbert, O.B.E., R.A.S.C. (O11884)

SIMPSON, Lieut. George Wilmot Rae, M.B.E.

SIMPSON, Capt. Herbert, M.B.E., M.C., *b.* 20 July, 1880; *s.* of Joseph Frederick Simpson, of Wakefield; *m.* Henrietta Augusta, *d.* of H. A. Rattray, of London. *Educ.:* The Academy, Wakefield. Personal Assistant to Deputy Chief of the Imperial General Staff, War Office. *War Work:* Headquarters of Cavalry Division and Cavalry Corps, France and Flanders. *Address:* 15, Cedars Road, Beckenham. (M2422)

SIMPSON, Hubert Ashton Laselve, O.B.E.

SIMPSON, Lieut.-Col. James, O.B.E.

SIMPSON, Major James Bertie, O.B.E., T.D., M.D., J.P., D.L., *b.* 9 Dec. 1863. Surgeon, Lawson Memorial Hospital, Golspie; Member, Consultative Council, Scottish Board of Health. *War Work:* Major, R.A.M.C. attached 5th Seaforth Highlanders, 1914–15; afterwards Surgeon, Royal Navy, Adriatic, Suez Canal, and Mediterranean, 1916–18. *Club:* The Hollies, Golspie, Sutherland. *Club:* Conservative (Edinburgh). (O11321)

SIMPSON, Jane, Mrs., M.B.E.

SIMPSON, Jean, Mrs., M.B.E.

SIMPSON, Jeanie Nelson Taylor, Mrs., M.B.E., *b.* 5 March, 1871; *d.* of James Taylor, of Wheatholm Bakery, Rawyards, Airdrie; *m.* David M. Simpson, M.A., F.E.I.S., *s.* of James Simpson, of Rawyards, Airdrie. *Educ.:* Rawyards Public School, Albert School, Airdrie, and City Girls' School, Glasgow. *War Work:* Joint Hon. Sec. Soldiers' and Sailors' Families Association, Newmonkland Division; President of Red Cross Work Party, Wellwynd U.F. Church; Airdrie British Women's Temperance Association, Red Cross Work Party; Member of Lanarkshire War Pensions Committee and three of its Sub-Committees; Hon. Sec. and Treas. of Airdrie War Pensions Sub-Committee. *Address:* Colwyn, Airdrie, Lanarkshire. (M9627)

SIMPSON, John Leonard, M.B.E.

SIMPSON, John William, M.B.E.

SIMPSON, Joseph, C.B.E., I.S.O.

SIMPSON, Col. Lightly Stapleton, C.B.E., D.S.O., R.E.; Chief Mechanical Engineer with rank of Col.; Head of Mechanical Engineering Depart. Ministry of Transport, 1919; Great War, 1914–19 (despatches). (C1325)

SIMPSON, Lieut. Malcolm Macrae, M.B.E., R.A.S.C.

SIMPSON, Mary Helen, M.B.E., *b.* 23 April, 1875; *d.* of W. Hirst Simpson, C.B.E., of Chelveston. *Educ.:* Privately. Member, Northamptonshire War Pensions Committee, Soldiers' and Sailors' Families Association, Public Health Committee, Agricultural Executive Committee, and Northamptonshire and Peterborough Agricultural Wages Board; Sec. Northamptonshire District Nursing Association; Hon. Sec. and Treas. Wellingboro' Rural District Soldiers' and Sailors' Families Association; Hon. Sec. Rushen and Higham Ferrers Urban District, and Belgian Relief Committees; Organising Sec. Board of Agriculture and Fisheries, Women's Land Army, and National Federation of Women's Institutes. *Addrses:* Chelveston, Higham Ferrers. *Clubs:* Northamptonshire Ladies' (Northampton); Women's Farm and Garden. (M9629)

SIMPSON, Col. Robert Mills, C.B.E., D.S.O. Canadian Army Med. Corps. Served in the Great War, 1914–19 (despatches). (C1537)

SIMPSON, Major Selwyn George, O.B.E., *b.* 11 March, 1882; *s.* of Rev. G. A. K. Simpson, of Worcester. *Educ.:* King's School, Worcester; Sidney Sussex Coll., Cambridge; Lille Univ.; The Sorbonne, Paris; Heidelberg Univ. Major in Army; Member of the Council of the Bristol Branch of the Royal Colonial Institute. *War Work:* Sept. 1914, went to France as interpreter with the 2nd Life Guards; for two years was Deputy Assistant Director of the Requisition,

billeting and hiring services in France; for 18 months was G.S.O. 2 on the Staff of the Fifth Army in France as Education Officer. *Address:* 80, Pembroke Road, Clifton, Bristol. *Club:* United Univ. (O5781)

SIMPSON, Thomas Young, C.B.E., M.D., M.S., F.R.C.S., L.R.C.P., *b.* 9 Jan. 1875; *s.* of John Simpson, of Dungannon, Co. Tyrone, Ireland; *m.* Rosalie Florence, *d.* of Silas Thomas Tall, of Glenholme Mannamead, Plymouth. *Educ.:* Bristol Grammar School; London and Middlesex Hospitals; Univs. Durham and Edinburgh. Consulting Surgeon, Plymouth Borough Hospital; Military Families Hospital, Devonport; Surgical Referee, Ministry of Pensions. *War Work:* Chief Surgeon, English Hospital, 249 bis St. Rambert, Lyons, Rhone, France; attended wounded after Verdun, 1916; Surgeon, 4th Southern General Hospital, Devonport. *Address:* 5, Windsor Villas, Lockyer Street, Plymouth. (C1161a)

SIMPSON, Lieut.-Comm. William, O.B.E., R.N.V.R.

SIMPSON, William Arthur John, M.B.E.

SIMPSON, William Hirst, C.B.E., B.A., *b.* 8 March, 1847; *s.* of Rev. William Hirst Simpson; *m.* 1st, Helen Granger, *d.* of Rev. Joseph Clark, 2nd, Katharine Maud, *d.* of Thomas Evans. *Educ.:* Uppingham School, and St. John's Coll., Cambridge. County Councillor, Northamptonshire. *War Work:* Chairman of the Committee of Management of the Duston War Hospital, County of Northampton. *Address:* Chelveston, near Higham Ferrers, Northampton. *Clubs:* Bath; Cambridge Union. (C2954)

SIMPSON, Capt. William Slessor, O.B.E.

SIMPSON, Winifred Elizabeth Louise, Mrs., M.B.E., *b.* 29 March, 1887; *d.* of Charles Samuel Hunting, J.P., of Slaley Hall, Slaley Riding Mill, Northumberland; *m.* John Andrew Simpson, *s.* of Capt. Robert P. J. Simpson, R.N., of Liverpool. *Educ.:* Privately. *War Work:* Organising Sec. India's Fund for St. Dunstan's since 1918; Head of Work Rooms, Bengal Women's War Depot; Official Adviser, Officers' Family Fund, Calcutta; President Soldiers' and Sailors' Families Association; Presidency Brigade, 1916–20; organised and acted as Sec. Calcutta War Seal Fund; Commandant of the Light Horse Section of St. John's Ambulance; worked in St. John's Nursing Sisters' Convalescent Home as Masseuse, winter of 1916–17. *Address:* 10, Middleton Row, Calcutta. *Clubs:* Ladies' Army and Navy; Saturday (Calcutta). (M6243)

SIMS, Alfred James, O.B.E.

SIMS, Lieut.-Col. John Henry Lang, O.B.E., T.D., *b.* 9 Jan. 1866; *s.* of the late Samuel Sims, of Blackheath; *m.* Dorothy Blanche, *d.* of the late Col. E. Baldwin Wake, of 21st Lancers. *Educ.:* Privately. Vice-Chairman, Herne Bay Urban District Council, and Chairman, Public Health Committee; Chairman, Herne Bay War Pensions Committee; Member of the British Olympic Council, and other public bodies; Life Governor of the City of London Hospital for Diseases of the Chest, Victoria Park. *War Work:* Entered 1st Royal Sussex Regt., 1886; Hazara Campaign, 1887–88 (medal and clasp); Cape Colonial Forces, Bechuanaland Campaign, 1897–98 (medal and clasp); 1st Manchester Regt., Siege of Ladysmith (Queen's medal, and 4 clasps; King's medal, and 2 clasps; 4th Batt. The King's (Liverpool Regt.), European War, Battle of Neuve Chapelle (medals: 1914–15, General Service, and Victory); raised and commanded a battalion of the Loyal North Lancashire Regt., and commanded 11th Batt. Bedford Regt. *Address:* Victoria Park, Herne Bay, Kent. *Club:* Junior United Service. (O7693)

SIMS, John William, M.B.E.

SIMS, Comm. William, O.B.E., R.N.

SIMSON, Major Arthur Fraser, O.B.E., R.M.A. (ret.), *b.* 22 Sept. 1878; *s.* of Arthur Theodore Simson; *m.* May Frances, *d.* of the late John Stafford Bucknall. *Educ.:* Dulwich Coll. 2nd Lieut. R.M.A., 1896; Capt. 1902; Major, 1915; Recruiting Staff Officer, R.N. and R.M., Southampton District, May, 1920. *War Work:* Belgium and Land Defences, Scapa Flow. *Address:* Pollards Moor Farm, Cadnam, Southampton. *Club:* Royal Automobile. (O9315)

SIMSON, Lieut.-Col. Harold, O.B.E., R.A.M.C.

SIMSON, Lena, Mrs. Henry John Forbes, O.B.E.

SIMSON, Richard Arbuthnot, C.B.E., *b.* 11 Dec. 1871; *s.* of Herman Simson, of 36, Montagu Square, London, W. *Educ.:* Marlborough Coll., and Cheltenham Coll. Commandant, Metropolitan Special Constabulary. *Address:* 36, Montagu Square, London, W. *Clubs:* Oriental; Royal Thames Yacht. (C2955)

SIMSON, Lieut.-Col. Robert, O.B.E.

SIMSON, Capt. Rupert, O.B.E., *b.* 20 Aug. 1884; *s.* of the late Alfred Simson, of 32, Brompton Square, S.W. 3; *m.* Dorothy Maud, *d.* of Francis Jerome Palmes. *Educ.:* Eton Coll., and Royal Military Coll., Camberley. 4th Cavalry Indian Army; joined H.M. Land Forces 18 Jan. 1905, and invalided out of the Service on 11 June, 1914. *War Work:* General Staff, War Office, Sept. 1914, to Nov. 1918. *Address:* Cavalry Club, Piccadilly, W. (O3179)

SINCLAIR, Andrew Gibson, M.B.E.

SINCLAIR, Andrew Macgregor, O.B.E.

SINCLAIR, Barbara Margaret Anne, O.B.E.

SINCLAIR, Capt. Donald Boase, O.B.E., B.A., LL.B., *b.* 16 May, 1886; *s.* of Robert Sinclair, M.D., LL.D., of Dundee; *m.* Margaret Richardson, *d.* of Lieut. Col. James Arnott, I.M.S., of Wyseby, Kirtlebridge, Dumfries-shire. *Educ.:* Fettes Coll., Edinburgh; Univ. Coll., Oxford. Writer to the Signet. *War Work:* Gazetted 2nd Lieut. 9th Royal Scots, Oct. 1914; appointed Staff Capt. at the War Office, March, 1917; Sec.

of the London and South-Eastern Region, Ministry of National Service, Feb. 1918. *Address:* Parkhill, Leven, Fife. (O3925)

SINCLAIR, Edward, M.B.E.

SINCLAIR, Ellen Lowry, M.B.E.

SINCLAIR, Elizabeth Brown, Mrs., M.B.E., *b.* 8 Dec. 1893 ; *d.* of Wm. Fairbairn, of Netherwood, Linlithgow, N.B. ; *m.* James, *s.* of John Sinclair, J.P. of Sligo. *Educ.:* Linlithgow Academy. *War Work:* Joined Women's Legion, Sept. 1915 ; transferred to Q.M.A.A.C. as Deputy Administrator, on Sept. 1917 ; served in France from Oct. 1918 to July, 1919, as Unit, Administrator ; attached American Expeditionary Force. *Address:* 34, Knox Street. Sligo. (M6633)

SINCLAIR, George Fraser, M.B.E.

SINCLAIR, George Greig, M.B.E.

SINCLAIR, Col. Hugh Montgomerie, C.B., C.M.G., C.B.E., late R.E., *b.* 23 Feb. 1855 ; 5th *s.* of the Rev. William Sinclair, M.A. (*see* BURKE'S *Peerage,* Sinclair of Ulbster) ; *m.* 4 July, 1905, Rosalie Sybil, 2nd *d.* of the late Sir John Jackson, M.P., LL.D., of Henley Park, Henley. O.C. Railway Troops, R.E., from 1915 ; sometime Chief Engineer, Scottish Command. *Address:* Barming House, Maidstone. *Clubs:* Junior United Service ; Wellington. (C1985)

SINCLAIR, James Donald, O.B.E., M.R.C.S., L.R.C.P., *b.* 2 Jan. 1874 ; *s.* of James Sinclair, of Derby ; *m.* Ethel Monypenny Grant, *d.* of Rev. Charles Grant Forrester, of Port Elizabeth, S. Africa. *Educ.:* Derby and Edinburgh Univ. Hon. Radiologist and Hon. Assistant Physician, Darlington Hospital. *War Work:* Medical Officer, 6th Durham V.A.D. Hospital, Woodside Darlington ; Medical Officer in charge of troops, Darlington. *Address:* Wellington Cottage, Grange Road, Darlington, (O11325)

SINCLAIR, John, C.B.E., M.D., M.R.C.P., M.R.C.S., L.S.A., *b.* 5 July, 1860. Civil Servant ; late Chief Medical Officer to the Post Office ; Hon. Associate of the Order of St. John of Jerusalem in England ; late President of the Post Office Centre of the St. John Ambulance Association. *War Work:* Chief Medical Officer to the Post Office ; Medical Officer in charge of the Post Office Hospital, Kensington Palace Gardens, W. *Club:* Royal Societies'. (C3121)

SINCLAIR, John Houston, C.M.G., C.B.E., *b.* 6 Dec. 1871 ; *s.* of William Houston Sinclair, of Morton, Brading, I. of W. ; *m.* Muriel Eveleen Kathleen, M.B.E., *d.* of Col. C. Cockburn, late of Black Watch. *Educ.:* I. of Wight Coll. Chief Sec. to Government, Zanzibar. *War Work:* Commanded the Zanzibar Volunteer Defence Force ; assisted in organising various carrier corps for service in German East Africa. *Clubs:* Wellington ; Zanzibar. (C2024)

SINCLAIR, Muriel Eveleen Kathleen, Mrs. John Houston, M.B.E.

SINCLAIR, Capt. Robert Albert Dunbar, M.B.E.

SINCLAIR, Robert John, M.B.E., B.A., *b.* 29 July, 1893 ; *s.* of R. H. Sinclair, J.P., of Glasgow ; *m.* Mary Shearer, *d.* of R. S. Barclay, of Randfontein, S.A. *Educ.:* Glasgow Academy and Oriel Coll., Oxford. Assistant Sec. Imperial Tobacco Co. (Gt. Britain and Ireland), Ltd. *War Work:* Commissioned 5th K.O.S.B., Aug. 1914 ; Gallipoli, 1915 ; mentioned in despatches, 1916–19 ; Administrative Work in Inspection Dept. Ministry of Munitions (Woolwich Arsenal, and latterly Hotel Metropole). *Address:* Rock Cottage, Cleeve, Yatton, Somerset. *Club:* New Univ. (M5628)

SINCLAIR, Russell, O.B.E. (O12019)

SINCLAIR, Capt. Samuel Christiana, M.B.E.

SINCLAIR, Lieut.-Col. Sir Walrond Arthur Frank, K.B.E. Controller of Registration, Ministry of National Service. *Address:* Registration Dept., Ministry of National Service, Victoria Street, S.W. 1. (K166)

SINCLAIR, Lieut.-Col. Walter, O.B.E., R.M.L.I., *b.* 2 June, 1880 ; *s.* of William Sinclair, of New York, near Lincoln, England ; *m.* Clara Annie, *d.* of G. H. Schofield, J.P., of Bridlington, Yorkshire. *Educ.:* Bradfield Coll. Served in Intelligence Division of the Admiralty War Staff throughout the war ; Assistant Director of Naval Intelligence ; joined Royal Marines, 1898 ; Capt. 1908 ; Major, 1916 ; T. Lieut.-Col. 1918 ; distinguished in musketry at Hythe ; qualified as wireless expert and served as such under Admiral Lowry in 2nd Cruiser Squadron ; qualified as interpreter in Russian, French, Italian, and Spanish ; at present serving on the War Staff of the Commander-in-Chief, North America and West Indies Station. *Address:* Royal Marine Barracks, Gosport, Hants. (O4330)

SINCLAIR, Stroma ALEXANDER-, M.B.E., *b.* 8 Nov. 1899 ; *d.* of Rear-Admiral Edwyn S. Alexander-Sinclair, of Freswick (*see* BURKE'S *Landed Gentry*). *War Work:* Head Coast Watcher, Royal Navy ; district that work was carried out, 20 miles of coast between Wick and Berriedale in Caithness ; principal duties, signalling messages and receiving reports from H.M. ships, and keeping general look-out for submarines, mines, etc. *Address:* Dunbeath Castle, Caithness, Scotland. (M75)

SINFIELD, Capt. and Qr.-Mr. Alfred, M.B.E., R.A.M.C. (T.)

SINFIELD, Major Thomas, M.B.E., R.A.S.C.

SINGER, Aline Madeleine, Lady, O.B.E., *b.* 9 Feb. 1877 ; *d.* of Etienne Pilavoine, of Biarritz, France ; *m.* Sir Mortimer Singer, K.B.E., *s.* of Isaac Merrit Singer, the inventor of the Singer Sewing Machine, of Yonkers, U.S.A. *Educ.:* By Les Sœurs de la Croix, Ustaritz, Basses-Pyrénées. *War Work:* Matron-in-Chief of Milton Hill Section Hospital, Steventon, Berks., for 220 N.C.O.'s and men, owned, organised, and

administered by Sir Mortimer Singer, K.B.E. *q.v.* ; opened 27th Aug. 1914, and ran continuously throughout the war, *Addresses:* Milton Hill, Steventon, Berks ; 3, Harcourt House. Cavendish Square, W. 1. (O11326)

SINGER, Major Charles Archibald, C.B.E., R.E.

SINGER, Lieut. and Qr.-Mr. David Charles, M.B.E., R.E.

SINGER, Sir Mortimer, K.B.E., J.P., *b.* 25 July, 1863 ; *s.* of Isaac Merrit Singer, inventor of the Singer Sewing Machine, of Yonkers, U.S.A. ; *m.* 1st, Mary Maund, *d.* of John Oxley, of Maldon, Yorks, 2nd, Aline Madeleine, O.B.E., *q.v., d.* of Etienne Pilavoine, of Biarritz, France. *Educ.:* Cambridge. Justice of the Peace for Berks. *War Work:* Owner, organiser, and administrator of Milton Hill Section Hospital, Steventon, Berks, for 220 N.C.O.'s and men ; opened 27th Aug. 1914, and run continuously throughout the war ; Matron-in-chief, Lady Singer, O.B.E. *Addresses:* Milton Hill, Steventon, Berks ; 3, Harcourt House, Cavendish Square, W. 1. *Clubs:* Junior Carlton ; Royal Thames Yacht ; Royal Automobile ; Royal Aero ; Royal Western (Plymouth). (K424)

SINGLETON, Albert Henry, M.B.E., R.N.

SINGLETON, Capt. Henry, C.B.E.

SINGLETON, James Edward, O.B.E., *b.* 20 May, 1855 ; *s.* of Joseph Singleton, of Mirfield, Yorks. ; *m.* Sarah Jane, *d.* of John Henderson, of Crosby, Maryport. *Educ.:* Westminster Tr. Coll. Sub-Inspector of Schools, Board of Education. *War Work:* Hon. Sec. Cumberland County Committee for War Savings. *Address:* 8, Spencer Street, Carlisle. (O3924)

SINKINSON, Major Alfred Peveril Le Mesurier, O.B.E., B.A., *b.* 1 July, 1889 ; *s.* of Edward James Sinkinson, LL.D., I.C.S., of Kendal. *Educ.:* Univ. Coll. School, and Wadham Coll., Oxford. *War Work:* D.A.A.G., G.H.Q., France. *Address:* 49, Haverstock Hill, N.W. 3. *Clubs:* Junior Naval and Military ; Authors'. (O8608)

SINNATT, Capt. Frank Sturdy, M.B.E.

SINNOTT, John, O.B.E., *b.* 24 June, 1867 ; *s.* of Thomas Sinnott, of Roscrea, Co. Tipperary ; *m.* Henrietta, *d.* of Thomas Higgins, of Dublin. *Educ.:* Erasmus Smith's School, Roscrea. Staff Engineer, G.P.O. Engineering Dept., London ; Member Inst. Electrical Engineers, and of Inst. Railway Signal Engineers. *War Work:* Designed several types of signal cables used by the Forces abroad and at home ; carried out special investigations for the Admiralty in the detection of submarines ; designed several special items used abroad in aerial line construction carried out by the various signal corps, R.E. *Address:* Struan, East End Road, East Finchley, N. 2. (O11327)

SIPPE, Major Sidney Vincent, D.S O., O.B.E., R.A.F., *b.* 24 April, 1889 ; *s.* of H. Sippé, of Beckenham, Kent ; *m.* Mabel Frances, *d.* of — d'Arcy, of Dublin. *Educ.:* Dulwich Coll. Engineer. *Address:* Quenta, Birchington, Kent. *Clubs:* R.A.F. ; R.A.C. (O3414)

SIRE, Henry Alphonse, C.B.E., *b.* 1864 ; *s.* of the late Alfred Sire, M.V.O. Goods Manager, London, Brighton, and South Coast Railway. (C2956)

SISSONS, Major Henry Arnott, C.B.E., R.E.

SITTERS, Percy Henry Smart, O.B.E., *b.* 2 April, 1883 ; *s.* of George Sitters, of Plymouth ; *m.* Kathleen Margaret, *d.* of Rev. Edward Bell, M.A. Travelling Sec. National Council Y.M.C.A. *War Work:* Organising Sec. Y.M.C.A. with B.E.F., also Organising Sec. Y.M.C.A. with the Belgian Army ; made Chevalier Ordre Leopold II. by King Albert for services to Belgian Army during the war. *Address:* 13, Russell Square, London, W.C. 1. (O3925)

SITWELL, William Sacheverell, M.B.E., *b.* 18 Dec. 1870 ; *s.* of Rev. Canon Degge Wilmot Sitwell, of Leamington, Hastings, Warwickshire ; *m.* Dorothea Mary, *d.* of Thomas Roxburgh Polwhele, of Polwhele, Cornwall (*see* BURKE'S *Landed Gentry*). *Educ.:* Rugby. Solicitor ; Clerk to the Lieutenancy for Cornwall ; Registrar for Archdeaconry of Cornwall ; Under Sheriff for Cornwall, 1920–21. *War Work:* Clerk to Cornwall Appeal Tribunal ; Hon. Sec. Cornwall Patriotic Fund, 1914–19, and Cornwall War Memorial Committee. *Addresses:* Elm Cottage, Truro ; 2, Prince's Street, Truro. (M945)

SKAIFE, Major Eric Ommanney, C.B.E.

SKEATS, Major Thomas George, O.B.E., Legion of Honour.

SKEELS, Lewis Serecold, C.B.E.

SKEENS, Frederick, M.B.E., R.C.N.C., *b.* 9 Jan. 1867 ; *s.* of the late Henry Christopher Skeens, of Southsea ; *m.* Maria Elizabeth, *d.* of the late Joseph Thomas Pearce, of Southsea. Assistant Naval Constructor, Admiralty. *War Work:* 1914, Engaged in converting merchant ships into mock battleships ; 1915, worked on mine defence gear for ships and armament designs for tanks ; Feb. 1916, Assistant Naval Constructor at Ministry of Munitions ; invented new type of gun-mounting, Dec. 1916 ; Director of Armament Section, Mech. Warfare (Tanks) Dept., Oct. 1918. *Address:* 34, Kingscliffe Gardens, Wimbledon Park, S.W. 19. (M9684)

SKEET, Major Arthur Robert, O.B.E., *b.* 2 June, 1876 ; *s.* of Robert Henry Skeet, of Rushmere, Ipswich ; *m.* Ellen, *d.* of Lewis Wright, of Bristol. *Educ.:* Palace School, Enfield, and Channel View, Clevedon, Somerset. Owner, W. H. Childe & Co., Ltd., Bradford, Yorks. *War Work:* Joined Optimist Volunteer Corps, Sept. 1914, and assisted with transport of Belgian Refugees ; founded and organised North London Squadron National Motor Volunteers, 1915 ; appointed Squadron-Commander of same by Robert, Marquis of Crewe, Jan. 1916 ; gazetted Major and Adjutant Middlesex R.A.S.C., M.T. (V.), 31 Oct. 1917 ; still hold this appointment ; while holding these positions assisted with Squadron in meeting convoy trains of wounded soldiers, and also conveying troops on leave across London at night in conjunction with Y.M.C.A., who presented him with Order of the Red Triangle and Bar. *Addresses :* Melford Lodge, Muswell Hill, London, N. ; 48, Fore Street, London, E.C. (O11328)

SKEGGS, James Buteux, C.B.E.

SKELLY, Henry Wilfred, M.B.E.

SKELSEY, Richard Robert, M.B.E., *b.* 3 Feb. 1887. Sec. of Public Companies. *War Work :* Railway Materials Department, Ministry of Munitions. *Address :* 38, Castleton Road, Walthamstow. (M9635)

SKELTON, Lieut. Allan, M.B.E.

SKELTON, Engr.-Comm. Reginald William, O.B.E., D.S.O., R.N. Served at battle of Jutland, 1916 (despatches) ; Archangel, 1919 ; has Russian Order of St. Stanislaus. (C2337)

SKELTON, William Simmonds, M.B.E., J.P., *b.* 24 Oct. 1858 ; *s.* of Sir Charles T. Skelton, J.P., of Sheffield ; *m.* Mary Elizabeth, *d.* of Edwin Moore, of Sheffield. *Educ. :* Ackworth. *War Work :* Local Advisory Committee ; Small Tools Advisory Committee ; Surplus Stock Small Tools Disposal Committee. *Address :* Meadow Bank, Sheffield. *Clubs :* National Liberal ; Reform (Sheffield). (M2426)

SKENE, Lillias Margaret, Mrs., M.B.E.

SKENE, Lieut.-Col. Philip George Moncrieff, O.B.E. (*see* BURKE'S *Landed Gentry*), *b.* 18 July, 1880 : *s.* of the late William Baillie Skene, of Hallyards and Pitlour ; *m.* Dorothea Lucy, *d.* of the late Charles Maitland Pelham Burn. *Educ. :* Eton and Christchurch, Oxford. J.P. Fife. *War Work :* Mentioned in despatches, G.S.O. 1, North Russian Expeditionary Force ; invalided from service, July, 1919 ; awarded Croix de Guerre avec Palmes and St. Stanislaus, 2nd Class. *Address :* Pitlour, Strathmiglo, Fife. *Clubs :* Royal and Ancient ; Hon. Company : M.C.C. ; New Club (Edinburgh). (O735)

SKENTELBERY, George Arthur, O.B.E.

SKERMAN, Oscar, M.B.E.

SKETCH, Samuel Bolt, O.B.E., J.P.

SKEVINGTON, Frank, M.B.E., *b.* 27 May, 1884 ; *s.* of Charles Samuel Skevington, of Nottingham ; *m.* Catherine Annie, *d.* of Edmund Damon, of Yeovil. *Educ. :* High Pavement School, Nottingham. Civil Servant ; Principal, Treasury. *Address :* Arundale, Anglesea Road, Kingston-on-Thames. (M9637)

SKIFFINGTON, Donald McLean, M.B.E.

SKILBECK, Mary Alethea, Mrs., M.B.E. ; *d.* of James Appleby Longden, of Sunderland ; *m.* Charles Thornton Skilbeck, *s.* of George Thornton Skilbeck, of St. Petroe, Cornwall. *Educ. :* Durham High School, and Bedford Physical Culture Coll. *War Work :* Qr.-Mr. Chipstead V.A.D. Hospital, Oct. 1914, to Oct. 1916 ; Commandant, Oct. 1916, to March, 1919. *Address :* The Quarry, Brasted, Kent. (M9638)

SKINNER, Lieut.-Col. Alexander Baird, D.S.O., C.B.E., Indian Cav., *b.* 1879. Served in the Great War, 1914–19 (despatches). (O8559)

SKINNER, Christian Laing, M.B.E., *b.* 1881 ; *d.* of Henry Skinner, of Auchtermuchty. *Educ. :* St. George's High School, Edinburgh. *War Work :* Canteen work in France with the Scottish Churches' Huts from 1917–19, chiefly at the Scottish Soldiers' Club, Boulogne. *Address :* 9, Hatton Place, Edinburgh. (M9639)

SKINNER, Capt. Donald Chipman, O.B.E.

SKINNER, Edward John, M.B.E.

SKINNER, Lieut.-Col. Ernest William, O.B.E., M.D., J.P., R.A.M.C., *b.* 4 Nov. 1861 ; *s.* of Robert Vaile Skinner, of Winchelsea ; *m.* Isobel Katherine, *d.* of George Mallows Freeman, K.C., of Winchelsea. *Educ. :* Dulwich Coll., and Univ. of Edinburgh. *War Work :* Temp. Major, R.A.M.C., attached 3/5th Royal Sussex Regt. ; M.O. Cottonera Mil. Hospital, Malta ; O.C. Floriana Military Hospital, Malta (local Lieut.-Col.) ; 65th General Hospital, Salonika (Ac. Lieut.-Col.), and 65th British General Hospital, Mesopotamia. *Address :* Mountsfield, Rye, Sussex. (O6700)

SKINNER, Col. Frederick St. Duthus, C.B.E. ; Canadian Reserve of Officers ; served in the Great War, 1915–19 (despatches). (C1837)

SKINNER, Lieut. Herbert Fenton, M.B.E.

SKINNER, Major Robert Bruce, O.B.E., R.E.

SKINNER, Paymaster-Lieut.-Comm. William Shelford, O.B.E., R.N.

SKIPPER, Henry Hubert, M.B.E.

SKIPWITH, Richard Edward, M.B.E.

SKIPWITH, Sophia Flora, Mrs. Grey Townsend, O.B.E.

SKIPWORTH, George Philip, O.B.E.

SKIRROW, Florence, M.B.E., *b.* 22 May, 1860 ; *d.* of the late Walker Skirrow, of London. *Educ. :* London. *War Work :* Hon. Sec. of Torquay War Savings Committee, under the National War Savings Committee. *Address :* Sunshine, 15, Broadmead Road South, Babbacombe, S. Devon. (M9641)

SKURRAY, Ernest Clement, M.B.E., J.P., *b.* 19 Sept. 1865 ; *s.* of Francis, of Reading ; *m.* Susan Mary, *d.* of William Forty, of Weston Lodge, Weston-super-Mare. *Educ. :* Reading. *War Work :* Tractor Representative for County of Wilts. *Address :* West Lodge, Swindon. (M2429)

SLADDEN, Lieut. Robert John, M.B.E., D.C.M., R.A.F.

SLADE, Edward Charles, M.B.E., *b.* 10 March, 1895 ; *s.* of E. Arthur Slade, of 19, Bride Lane, E.C. 4 ; *m.* Nellie M., *d.* of Joseph Millard. Acting Class A Ex-soldier Clerk, War Office. *War Work :* Enlisted Aug. 1914, 6th London Regt. ; discharged unfit (consequent on service), Aug. 1916 ; employed

at War Office, Sept. 1916, subsequently becoming Supervising Clerk of Section of Officers' Casualties Dept. *Address :* 3, Ivy Lane, Crofton Park, Lewisham. (M9642)

SLADE, George Frederick, M.B.E., J.P.

SLADE, Mary Elizabeth, M.B.E.

SLADEN, Mary, Mrs., M.B.E.

SLADEN, Lieut.-Comm. Sir Sampson, K.B.E., R.N., *b.* 1868 ; *s.* of Lt.-Col. Joseph Sladen, late of Ripple Court, Kent (*see* BURKE'S *Landed Gentry*). *Educ. :* Privately and H.M.S. "Britannia." Served in Royal Navy, 1882–99 ; resigned on receiving appointment in London Fire Brigade ; promoted Chief Officer, 1909 ; resigned, 1919 ; Area Commissioner (London), Ministry of Transport, 1920. *War Work :* As Chief Officer London Fire Brigade was responsible for special arrangements made for coping with fires caused by enemy action in Greater London ; also during the war inaugurated London Ambulance Service, and acted as Chairman of Fire Protection Advisory Committee, Ministry of Munitions, 1916–17. *Address :* 75, Victoria Street, S.W. 1. *Clubs :* United Service ; Roehampton. (K425)

SLANEY, Major Charles Wynne, O.B.E., R.M.L.I., *b.* 20 Nov. 1855 ; *Educ. :* Privately. Sec. to Surgeon Rear-Admiral. *War Work :* Acted in above capacity during the war. *Address :* R.N. Hospital, Chatham. (O3565)

SLANEY, Lieut.-Col. F. G. KENYON-, C.B.E., Lieut.-Col. Reserve of Officers, late Durham L.I., *b.* 1858 ; *s.* of William Kenyon-Slaney, J.P. ; *m.* 1892, Edith Mary Sherwin, *d.* of Major Joseph Holt. *Address :* Ayton Hall, Shifnal. *Clubs :* Wellington ; Junior United Service. (C2131)

SLATER, Alexander, M.B.E.

SLATER, Alexander Frederick, M.B.E.

SLATER, Alexander Ransford, C.M.G., C.B.E., B.A., *b.* 1874 ; *s.* of the late Rev. C. S. Slater, of Plymouth ; *m.* 1906, Dora Waterfield, *d.* of H. T. S. Ward, sometime Director of Irrigation, Ceylon. *Educ. :* King Edward School, Birmingham, and Emmanuel Coll., Camb. Entered Ceylon Civil Service, 1898 ; 2nd Assist. Postmaster-Gen. Ceylon, 1900 ; Acting 2nd Assist. Colonial Sec. 1901 ; Clerk to Legislative Council, 1904 ; Dist. Judge, Badulla, 1906 ; Additional Assist. Colonial Sec., and Clerk to Legislative Council, 1907 ; Acting Principal Assist. Colonial Sec. 1909 ; Dep. Collector of Customs, Colombo, 1910 : Principal Assist. Colonial Sec. 1912, and Colonial Sec. Gold Coast, 1914 (has acted as Gov.). *Addresses :* Accra, Gold Coast ; Claremont Avenue, Woking. *Club :* Royal Societies'. (C403)

SLATER, Edward, M.B.E.

SLATER, George, C.B.E.

SLATER, George Frederick, M.B.E.

SLATER, 2nd Lieut. James Henry, M.B.E., R.A.F.

SLATER, Lieut. John Alan, M.B.E. R.A.F. (S.R.),

SLATER, John Gladstone, M.B.E., *b.* 16 April, 1872; *s.* of John Slater, of Yeadon, Yorks. ; *m.* Hannah Mary, *d.* of Henry Teale, of Yeadon, Yorks. *Educ. :* Privately. Schoolmaster. *War Work :* Assisted in National Registration; Sec of Lord Derby Recruiting (Local) Committee ; Sec. of Local Savings Committee, and Local War Memorial Committee ; also acted as Sec. in all local War Bond campaigns ; Hon. Sec. of two War Savings Associations ; Special Constable ; Member of Belgian Relief Committee, Food Control Committee, Local War Pensions Committee ; organised Flag Days, and local Y.M.C.A. Canteen. *Addresses :* 41, Titchfield Street, Hucknall ; Butler's Hill Boys' School, Hucknall ; Y.M.C.A. Hucknall. (M9646)

SLATER, Quintin Fleming, M.B.E.

SLATER, Flight-Lieut. Leonard Horatio, O.B.E., D.S.C., D.F.C.

SLAUGHTER, Lieut. Ernest William, M.B.E., R.A.O.C.

SLAUGHTER, Leonard Lansdell, M.B.E., *b.* 17 Jan. 1892 ; *s.* of the late Richard Slaughter, of 12, Courtfield Road, S.W. ; *m.* Doris, *d.* of Ernest E. Wastall, J.P., of Durlock Grange, Minster, Thanet. *Educ. :* Westminster. *War Work :* Joined Public School Mounted Corps, Sept. 1914 ; appointed Troop Commander, " D " (Thanet) Troop, East Kent Mounted Constabulary, June 1916 ; and Squadron-Commander and Supervisor of East Kent Mounted Constabulary, Sept. 1918. *Address :* 87, Queen's Gate, S.W. ; Mundy Bois, Egerton, Kent. (M3974)

SLAYTER, Capt. John Howard, M.B.E.

SLEE, Capt. John Ambrose, C.B.E., R.N. ; *m.* 1919, Sybil Mary, *d.* of the late R. J. Sissons. Served in the Great War. (C1168)

SLEEMAN, Lieut.-Col. James Lewis, C.B.E. ; New Zealand Forces ; served in the Great War, 1915–19 (despatches). (C1871)

SLEIGH, Constance, Mrs., M.B.E.

SLEIGHT, Major Ernest, O.B.E., T.D. ; *s.* of Sir Geo. F. Sleight, Bart. (*see* BURKE'S *Peerage*), of Weelsby Hall, Grimsby; *m.* Margaret, *d.* of C. F. Carter, J.P., of Grimsby. *Educ. :* Rugby. *Address :* The Crossways, Stallingborough, Lincolnshire. (O1867)

SLEITH, Thomas, M.B.E.

SLESINGER, Edward G., O.B.E., M.B., B.Sc. (Lond.), F.R.C.S. (Eng.), Croix de Guerre *b.* 17 March, 1888 ; *s.* of the late Gustave Schlesinger, of Blakemore Lodge, Shoot-up-Hill, London ; *m.* Gladys Eleanor, *d.* of the late Arthur W. Trench, of Brooklyn, N.Y. T. Surg.-Lieut. R.N. 1914–19 ; Hunterian Professor of Royal College of Surgeons, 1918–19 ; Research Scholar, Brit. Med. Assocn. 1919 ; Assistant Surgeon, Guy's Hospital ; Fellow Royal Society of Medicine ; Member, British

Orthopædic Society, has Croix de Guerre of France. *Address* : 2, Devonshire Place, W.1. *Club* : Junior Army and Navy. (O9494)

SLESSOR, Lieut.-Col. Herbert, O.B.E., R.M.A.

SLINGSBY, Lieut. Charles Richard, M.B.E.

SLOAN, David, M.B.E. (M10465)

SLOAN, Robert Patrick, O.B.E., M.I.E.E., *b.* 1874 ; *s.* of John Morrison Sloan, of Edinburgh ; *m.* Inda, *d.* of David Ellis, late of Santos, Brazil. *Educ.* : Glasgow and Edinburgh. Director and Manager of Newcastle-upon-Tyne Electric Supply Co., Ltd., and several other Electric Power Supply Companies ; Member of National Joint Industrial Council (Electricity Supply Industry), and of Council of Incorporated Association of Electric Power Companies. *War Work* : Engaged upon supply of electrical power to Munition Manufacturers, shipbuilders, etc., on North-East Coast. *Address* : Craiglea, Gosforth, Newcastle-upon-Tyne. *Clubs* : Devonshire ; Union (Newcastle) ; Cleveland. (C1040)

SLOCOMBE, Frank Edwin, O.B.E.

SLOPER, Capt. John Smith, O.B.E., R.A.M.C.

SLOWAN, Capt. William John More, O.B.E., M.D., *b.* 9 Aug. 1869 ; *s.* of Wm. Slowan, of Glasgow ; *m.* Jeannette, *d.* of David Macdonald, M.D., of Edinburgh. *Educ.* : Univ. of Glasgow. Assistant Medical Officer, L.C.C. *War Work* : O.C. 2nd London Sanitary Co.; Sanitary Officer, London District. *Address* : 68, South Croxted Road, Dulwich, S.E. 21. (O8937)

SLYNE, Denis, C.B.E. Receiver-Gen. and Chairman of Committee for Winding-up Alien Enemies' Estates, Trinidad. *Address* : Port of Spain, Trinidad. (C2025)

SMAIL, James Cameron, O.B.E., *b.* 1880 ; *s.* of the late Adam Smail, of Edinburgh ; *m.* Florence Louisa, *d.* of Alexander Davidson, of Winnipeg. *Educ.* : Daniel Stewart's Coll. ; Heriot Watt Coll., Edinburgh ; Royal Coll. of Science, London. Assistant Education Officer, L.C.C. Education Department ; Inspector of Technical Instruction, Department of Agriculture, and Technical Instruction, Ireland, 1902–11. *War Work* : District Manager, Metropolitan Munitions Committee, 1915–18 ; Manager of Gaugemaking and Munitions Training for L.C.C., 1915–18. *Club* : Caledonian. (O3927)

SMALE, Bertram Haylock, M.B.E.

SMALE, Samuel, M.B.E., *b.* 24 June, 1881 ; *s.* of William Smale, of Devon ; *m.* May, *d.* of Edward Henry Nethercliff, of Nottingham. *Educ.* : Tollington Park Coll., London, and St. John's Coll., Westcliff. *War Work* : Voluntary Red Cross and Canteen Work, 1914–16, and head of night staff and member of the Paris Committee of the Women's Emergency Canteens, Sept. 1916, to June. 1919. *Address* : 8, Rue d'Enghien, Paris. (M9647)

SMALL, Elsie Mary, O.B.E.

SMALL, Frederick Trouton, O.B.E.

SMALL, George James, M.B.E.

SMALL, Hannah, Mrs., M.B.E.

SMALL, John, M.B.E., *b.* Oct. 1844 ; *s.* of John Small, of Sunderland ; *m.* Mary Elizabeth, *d.* of Robert Lowe, of Sunderland. *Educ.* : Privately. Master Mariner ; Master's Certificate, 1873 ; took command in steam, 1882 ; intended retiring in 1914, at the age of 70, after being at sea since the age of 11, but on outbreak of war decided to carry on in his own line ; Admiralty took over ship in Jan. 1916, for transport work in cross-Channel service ; was obliged to leave the ship in Feb. 1919, by the doctor's orders. *Address* : 311, Spring Bank West, Hull. (M9648)

SMALL, Capt. Victor, M.B.E.

SMALL, Lieut. William, M.B.E.

SMALL, William Keane, M.B.E., *b.* 21 Nov. 1884 ; *s.* of William Fraser McPherson Small, of Washington, D.C. Univ. of Toronto, Canada ; Georgetown Univ., and St. John's Coll., Washington, D.C. British Vice-Consul, St. Louis, Missouri, U.S.A. ; Barrister, specialising in the law of patents, trade-marks, copyrights, and unfair competition. *Address* : 605, Granite Building, corner 4th and Market Streets, St. Louis, Missouri. *Club* : Forest Park Golf, St. Louis. (M9649)

SMALLBONES, Robert Townsend, M.B.E., *b.* 19 March, 1884 ; *s.* of Paul Bromfield Smallbones, of Castle Velm ; *m.* Inga, *d.* of — Gjertsen, of Kin. *Educ.* : Trinity Coll., Oxford. H.M. Consular Service. *War Work* : H.B.M. Vice-Consul, Itavanger, Norway. *Address* : c/o Foreign Office. *Club* : Isthmian. (M2432)

SMALLMAN, Lieut.-Col. Arthur Briton, D.S.O., O.B.E., M.D., Ch.B., *b.* 1873 ; *s.* of S. Smallman, Rowley Barton, Torquay ; *m.* 1916, Alice Florence, *d.* of R. G. Duncan, of Lindens, Farnborough, Hants. *Educ.* : Grammar School, Manchester, and Owens Coll. Manchester. Entered R.A.M.C. 1902 ; Capt. 1906 ; Brevet Major, 1913 ; Major, 1914 ; served in the S. African War 1900–2 (Queen's medal with three clasps, King's medal with two clasps) ; Balkan Campaign, 1912–13, with Turkish Forces ; Great War. 1914–19 (despatches twice) ; Assist. Director-Gen. Army Medical Services. (C2168)

SMALLWOOD, Arthur William, C.B.E. Assist. Director of Contracts, Admiralty. *Address* : The Admiralty, Whitehall, S.W. (C296)

SMALLWOOD, Elinor Katharine, Mrs., M.B.E., *b.* 15 Dec. 1896 ; *d.* of the late Lovell Drage, M.D. (Oxon.), of Hatfield, Herts ; *m.* Matthew Edmund Smallwood, M.D., *s.* of the late Warren Charles Smallwood, of Witley, Cheshire. *Educ.* : The Manor House, Brondesbury, N.W. *War Work* : 1914, to Aug. 1916, worked at Herts Red Cross and County Regiment Depot (Hon. Sec. from May, 1915) ; from Oct. 1916, to Dec. 1918, V.A.D. at Royal Free Hospital, with an interval of three months (awarded red efficiency stripe after thirteen months service) ; from Jan. 1919, to Sept. 1919, local representative for Herts War Pensions Committee. *Address* : Wheathampstead, Herts. *Club* : V.A.D. Ladies'. (M7936)

SMALLWOOD, George Clarence, O.B.E., *b.* 18 May, 1882 ; *s.* of George Thomas, of London ; *m.* Ruby Hautot, *d.* of Arthur Thomas Winson. *Educ.* : Christ's Hospital, and King's Coll., London. Civil Servant. *War Work* : Loaned by Board of Trade to Ministry of Munitions ; Secretarial Officer to Chemical Group of Munitions Council ; Sec. Lord Crewe's Committee on Fuel Oil from Home Sources ; Sec. Chemical Trades Committee, Reconstruction Ministry. *Address* : Kingston-on-Thames. (O1868)

SMALLWOOD Henry Sankey, M.B.E.

SMALLWOOD, Richard Coningsby, C.B.E., *b.* 14 July, 1879 ; *s.* of the late Rev. Warren C. Smallwood, of Whitley, Cheshire ; *m.* Evelyn Mary Leadam, *d.* of E. Leadam Hough, C.B.E. (*q.v.*), of Enfield, Middlesex. *Educ.* : St. Edmund's School, Canterbury. Member of London Stock Exchange. *War Work* : Ministry of Munitions Finance Department ; Financial Adviser, Ministry of Reconstruction ; Sec. to Financial Facilities Committee, and Committee on Financial Risks attaching to the Holding of Trading Stocks. *Address* : West View, Enfield, Middlesex. (C2958)

SMART, Annie Wilhelmina, Mrs., M.B.E.

SMART, Capt. Archibald Guelph Holdsworth, M.B.E., M.B., R.A.M.C. and R.A.F.

SMART, Lieut. Harold Nevil, C.M.G., O.B.E. *Address* : 29 Mincing Lane, E. C.

SMART, Herbert Samuel, M.B.E., *s.* of William Smart, of Yatton, Somerset ; *m.* Margaret, *d.* of William Henry Daniel, of Truro, Cornwall. *Educ.* : Ardingley Coll., Haywards Heath, Sussex. Sec. Y.M.C.A., Weston-super-Mare, 1900–4 ; Derby, 1904–7 ; Swansea, 1907–14 ; Y.M.C.A. National Council Staff, 1914. *War Work* : Liverpool and Cheshire ; Leader of Y.M.C.A., Crystal Palace, London, 1914–16 ; Italy, Greece, and Mediterranean, 1916–17 ; Director of Financial Campaigns for Y.M.C.A. throughout Midland Counties, Lancashire, Cheshire, Westmorland, and Cumberland ; Leader of Liverpool Campaign for Red Cross in 1918. *Addresses* : 26, Heathfield Road, Wavertree, Liverpool ; 230, Deansgate, Manchester. (M9550)

SMART, John Manson, M.B.E.

SMART, Capt. Thomas Fraser Mackenzie, O.B.E.

SMARTT, Sybil Annie, Lady, O.B.E.

SMEAL, Joseph, C.B.E. Goods Manager, London and S. W. Railway. (C2959)

SMEDDLE, Major John Henry, O.B.E., T.D.

SMEDLEY, Capt. Charles Frederick, M.B.E., *b.* 14 April, 1889 ; *s.* of Frederick Bingham Smedley, of Oriental Parade, Wellington, N.Z. ; *m.* Ruth Gladys, *d.* of Jonathan Fletcher, of Makeney Old Hall, Milford, Derby. *Educ.* : Belper Grammar School, Belper ; Palmer's Coll., Grays, Essex. Five years' active service with the New Zealand Expeditionary Force. *Address* : Makeney, Opuawhanga, North Auckland, New Zealand. (M2434)

SMEDLEY, William Henry, M.B.E.

SMEDLEY, Olive Truda MARSDEN-, M.B.E.

SMEETON, Charles William, O.B.E., M.R.C.S., L.R.C.P., *b.* 24 July, 1865 ; *s.* of William Smeeton, of Leeds ; *m.* Ethel Isabel, *d.* of William Kendall, of Ness Hall, Nunnington. *Educ.* : Leeds Grammar School. Medical Officer and Public Vaccinator, Hovingham District, Malton Union. *War Work* : Commandant and Medical Officer-in-charge, Hovingham Hall Red Cross Hospital ; Capt. commanding " A " Coy., 2nd V.B. Alexandra P.W.O. Yorkshire Regt. *Address* : Hovingham, Malton. (O11332)

SMELLIE, James, M.B.E, F.R.S.A., J.P., *b.* 31 May, 1861 ; *s.* of William Smellie. *Educ.* : Hutton Hall Academy. Councillor, County Borough, Dudley ; Chairman of Dudley Education Committee ; Governor of Grammar School, Girls High School, and Training Coll. ; Representative Governor of Birmingham Univ. *War Work* : National Service Representative for Dudley and Member of Pensions Committee, and Chairman of Ward Committee. *Address* : Comberton House, Kidderminster. (M9651)

SMELLIE, Lieut.-Col. John Hugh, D.S.O., O.B.E. Railway Corps, Uganda. (O2338)

SMELLIE, Lieut. William Thomas, O.B.E.

SMETHURST, Sir Thomas, K.B.E., J.P., *b.* 26 May, 1860 ; *s.* of George Smethurst, of Middleton ; *m.* Amelia, *d.* of A. Bottoms, of Chadderton. *Educ.* : Crayford. Chartered Accountant, and Director of Manchester Ship Canal and other Companies ; Member of Manchester City Council since 1896 ; 10 years Deputy Chairman, Water Committee. *War Work* : Lord Mayor of Manchester, Feb. 1916, to Nov. 1917 ; Chairman, Manchester War Savings Committee, and other War Emergency Committees and Charitable Organisations. *Addresses* : 26, Pall Mall, Manchester ; Erlesmere, Lytham. *Clubs* : Constitutional (Manchester) ; Lytham and St. Anne's Golf. (K426

SMETHURST, Lieut.-Col. William Wintringham, O.B.E., R.F.A. (T.).

SMILES, Samuel, O.B.E., D.Sc., F.I.C., F.R.S., *b.* 1877 ; *s.* of Samuel Smiles. *Educ.* : Marlborough Coll. ; Univ. Coll., London ; Univs. of Paris and Jena. Daniell Professor of Chemistry, King's Coll., London ; Vice-President of the Chemical Society. *War Work* : Advisory Chemist to the Small Arms Ammunition Committee, Ministry of Munitions. *Address* : King's Coll., London. (O1869)

SMILES, Lieut. Stephen Hudson, O.B.E.. R.N.R.

SMILEY, George Kennedy, O.B.E., *b.* 1870; *s.* of Joseph Smiley, of Lisardahla, Londonderry; *m.* Constance Nina Somerset, *d.* of Capt. L. Dod Sampson, R.N. *Educ.*: Belfast and Dublin. Late Surgeon, Londonderry Eye, Ear, and Throat Hospital. *War Work*: O.C. Military Hospital, Derby; S.M.O., Derby; M.O.-in-charge Temple House V.A.D. Hospital, Derby; Hon. Sec. Local Medical War Committee. *Address*: Examiner Buildings, Strutt Street, Manchester.
(O4847)

SMITH, Capt. Alan Rae, O.B.E.

SMITH, Albert, M.B.E.

SMITH, Capt. Albert, O.B.E., M.P.

SMITH, Lieut.-Col. Albert Alexander, O.B.E.

SMITH, Capt. Albert Augustus, O.B.E.

SMITH, Lieut. Albert George, O.B.E., R.E.

SMITH, Albert William, C.B.E., *b.* 24 April, 1863; *s.* of John Joseph Smith, of Manor House, Eaglescliffe, Co. Durham. *Educ.*: Yarm Grammar School. Solicitor; Chairman, Darlington Courts of Referees, Unemployment Insurance; Sec., Tees Fishery Board; Clerk to Justices and Commissioners of Taxes, Gilling East Division, N.R., Yorks. *War Work*: Chairman, Tees and Darlington Local Munitions Tribunal. *Addresses*: Greencroft East, Darlington; 6, Church Row, Darlington.
(C622)

SMITH, Alfred, O.B.E.; *s.* of Henry Smith, of Skipton-in-Craven; *m.* Ann Elizabeth; *d.* of Richard Longden Hattersley, J.P., Keighley. *Educ.*: Allesley Park Coll. *War Work*: In connection with Ministry of Munitions. *Addresses*: Woodworth, Keighley; Hoff Bank, Appleby. *Clubs*: British Empire; National Liberal.
(O738)

SMITH, Lieut. Alfred Charles, M.B.E., R.N.

SMITH, Alexander, M.B.E.

SMITH, Alexander Glegg, M.B.E., M.C., R.A.F.

SMITH, Alic Halford, C.B.E. Sometime Senior Clerk, Scottish Office.
(C2960)

SMITH, Sir Allan MacGregor, K.B.E., M.A., LL.B., M.P. Chairman of the Managing Committee Engineering Employers' Federation. Solicitor. *Address*: 9, Oakhill Avenue, N.W. 3.
(K167)

SMITH, Major Allison Eugene, O.B.E., M.C., R.G.A.

SMITH, Alwyn Dudley, O.B.E.

SMITH, Anne Beadsmore, C.B.E., R.R.C., *b.* 24 March, 1869; *d.* of William Smith, of Highbury. Matron-in-Chief, Queen Alexandra's Imperial Military Nursing Service. *War Work*: Served in South African War on the Staff of the Military Hospitals, 1899–1902; served with the B.E.F., in France, 1914–17; Administration work at War Office since 1917; has Legion of Honour. *Addresses*: 40, Audley House, Margaret Street; Beaumont Manor, Wormley, Herts.
(C1765)

SMITH, Anne Huntingdon Melville, Mrs., M.B.E.

SMITH, Annie Hansley, M.B.E., *b.* 1874; *d.* of Alfred Robert Smith, of Clapham. *Educ.*: Privately. *War Work*: Clerical and other work at St. John Ambulance Association, St. John's Gate, Clerkenwell; forming First Aid and Home Nursing Classes, and assisting at same under St. John Ambulance Association; Nursing in hospitals; on the Staff of J.W. V.A.D. Headquarters from May, 1916, to Nov. 1917, as clerical member; Head of Filing and Registry Dept., J.W. V.A.D. Headquarters from Nov. 1917. *Address*: The Hollies, Park Hill, Clapham, S.W.
(M2438)

SMITH, Annie Margaret Keeble, Mrs., M.B.E.

SMITH, Arthur Croxton, O.B.E.; *s.* of the late William Croxton Smith, of Huntingdonshire; *m.* Ada Frances, *d.* of the late Frederick Stimpson, of Northampton. *Educ.*: Privately. Journalist; Director of Publicity, Ministry of Food. *Address*: Burlington House, Wandle Road, Upper Tooting, S.W. 17. *Clubs*: Kennel; National Liberal.
(O11334)

SMITH, Major Arthur Henderson, O.B.E.

SMITH, Arthur Herbert, O.B.E.

SMITH, Arthur Ives, M.B.E.

SMITH, Capt. Arthur William, O.B.E.

SMITH, Capt. Arthur William, O.B.E., R.G.A.

SMITH, Aubrey Golding, M.B.E., *b.* 1 Dec. 1886; *s.* of Christopher Smith, of Wellington, New Zealand. *Educ.*: Wanganui Collegiate School, N.Z. *War Work*: Ambulance work with the British Red Cross in France and Italy; received Italian decorations of Al Valore Militare in Bronze; Order of the Crown of Italy, and Croce di Guerra. *Address*: Rocklands, Oriental Bay, Wellington, New Zealand.
(M2439)

SMITH, Capt. Augustus William, O.B.E.

SMITH, T. Lieut.-Col. Bertram Gilbert, O.B.E.

SMITH, Capt. Bertram Hornsby, C.B.E., R.N., *b.* 1874; *s.* of Francis E. Smith, of Gen. Post Office; *m.* Lucy M. Wyatt. Served in the Great War, 1914–18, in Dardanelles and on Naval Staff at Admiralty (Legion of Honour, Order of Crown of Belgium); appointed Director of Mercantile Movements, Naval Staff, 1919. *Club*: United Service.
(C2323)

SMITH, Lieut. Cecil Edward Bartholomew, M.B.E.

SMITH, Charles, O.B.E., *b.* 5 Dec. 1858; *s.* of Emmanuel Smith, of Portsmouth. *Educ.*: Birkbeck Coll. Civil Servant 1877–1919 (ret.), late Principal Clerk in H.M. Paymaster-General's Department, Whitehall. *War Work*: Payments in respect of Army and Navy Services, including pensions, etc., of Military and Naval Officers and their dependants; also pensions and allowances awarded by the Ministry of Pensions to Officers and to their widows and dependants; a Commis-

sioner of Income Tax from 1913–19. *Address*: Hazelwood, Sidcup, Kent.
(O739)

SMITH, Comm. Charles Appleton, C.B.E., R.D., R.N.R.

SMITH, Charles Bowtell, M.B.E.

SMITH, Major Charles Edward, O.B.E.

SMITH, Lieut. Charles Frederick Tate, M.B.E.

SMITH, Major Charles Gainer, O.B.E., R.A.F.

SMITH, Capt. Charles Harold, O.B.E., I.M.S.

SMITH, Lieut. Charles Hodgkinson, M.B.E., R.A.F.

SMITH, Lieut. Charles Newbald, M.B.E.

SMITH, Lieut. Charles Probyn, M.B.E., R.E.

SMITH, Capt. Charles Valentine, C.B.E., R.N., *b.* 14 Feb. 1854; *s.* of C. W. Smith, of Penn Road, London, N.; *m.* Josefa Francis, *d.* of the Hon. Robert Butler, of Nassau, Bahamas. *Educ.*: H.M.S. "Britannia." Royal Navy. *War Work*: Employed at the Admiralty as Superintendent of Sailing Directions, Hydrographic Department. *Address*: 17, Woodfield Road, Ealing.
(C916)

SMITH, Very Rev. Monsignor Charles William, C.B.E., D.S.O., *b.* 1873; *s.* of Frederick A. Smith, of Oxford. 1st Class Chaplain to the Forces, and Assist. Principal Chaplain to an Army in France during the Great War, 1915–19 (despatches thrice); appointed Private Chamberlain to Pope Benedict XV. 1917.
(C1326)

SMITH, Capt. Charles William, O.B.E., M.B., F.R.C.S., R.A.M.C.

SMITH, Capt. and Qr.-Mr. Charles William Gates, M.B.E., R.A.S.C.

SMITH, Cicely, Mrs., O.B.E., *b.* 24 Oct. 1881; *d.* of Charles Frank Forster, of Southill, Plawsworth, Co. Durham; *m.* Clarence Dalrymple, *s.* of Thomas Eustace Smith, of Gosforth House, Newcastle-on-Tyne. *Educ.*: Privately. *War Work*: Organiser and Hon. Sec. of the Hexham War Hospital Supply and Clothing Depot; Member of the Northumberland Belgian Relief Committee, and Hon. Sec. of Hexham Branch; awarded the Medaille de la Reine Elisabeth. *Address*: Loughbrow, Hexham, Northumberland.
(O11335)

SMITH, Clarence Dalrymple, O.B.E., J.P., *b.* 16 May, 1868; *s.* of Thomas Eustace Smith, of Gosforth House, Northumberland; *m.* Cicely, *d.* of Charles Frank Forster, of Southill, Co. Durham. *Educ.*: Privately. Managing Director, Thos. and Wm. Smith, Ltd.; Chairman, British Wire Rope Manufacturers' Association; Director, Smith's Dock Co., Ltd.; Chairman of the Consett Iron Co., Ltd., the Consett Spanish Ore Co., Ltd., the Newcastle Local Board, Royal Insurance Co., and of the Tynemouth Unionist Association. *War Work*: Chairman of Executive Committee, Northumberland Belgian Relief Fund; Member of National Committee for Relief in Belgium; Chairman of the Care, Training, and Employment Sub-Committee of the Northumberland War Pensions Committee; Chairman of the Newcastle Chamber of Commerce Committee for the employment of ex-officers, and Hon. Assist. District Director of the Appointments Department; Chairman of the Ropemakers' Advisory Committee to the Air Ministry; *Address*: Loughbrow, Hexham, Northumberland. *Clubs*: Carlton; Windham.
(O11336)

SMITH, Major Clarence Gorton Ross, O.B.E., A.P.D.

SMITH, Comm. Clifford Edward Heathcote, O.B.E., R.N.V.R.

SMITH, Constance Isabella Stuart, O.B.E.; *d.* of the late Rev. Hinton Castle Smith, Vicar of Marston Meysey, Wilts. *Educ.*: King's Coll., London. His Majesty's Senior Lady Inspector of Factories, Factory Department, Home Office. *War Work*: Special work in connection with Factory Department; Sec., Committee on Employment of Women, Ministry of Reconstruction. *Address*: 26, Victoria Road, Withington, Manchester.
(O11337)

SMITH, Major Daniel Rowland, O.B.E., M.C., R.A.O.C.

SMITH, Major David Joseph, O.B.E.

SMITH, Dempster, M.B.E.

SMITH, Lieut. Dennis William, M.B.E.

SMITH, Denton, M.B.E., R.F.A., *b.* 4 April, 1881; *s.* of William Smith, of Sunderland; *m.* Jeanie, *d.* of William Nichol, of Skinburness, Silloth. *Educ.*: Privately. *War Work*: France, 1914, in Lahore Division, La Basse Front; England, 1915; joined 23rd Division, France, Aug. 1915, Armentières; Arras, Feb. 1916; Vimy Ridge, April, 1916; Somme, July, 1916; Ypres, Dec. 1916, to Nov. 1917; Italy, Dec. 1917; Montello Front, Asiago Mountains, April, 1918; Lower Piava, Oct. 1918; crossed lower Piava, Nov. 1918; Acting R.S.M. from Nov. 1915, to May, 1919.
(M4752)

SMITH, Capt. and Qr.-Mr. Donald Woodford, M.B.E., R.G.A.

SMITH, Eng.-Comm. Edgar Charles, O.B.E., R.N.

SMITH, Edith Flora, Mrs., O.B.E., *d.* of Smith Howlett Rowley, J.P., of Histon, Cambs.; *m.* Frank, *s.* of the late Thomas Hayden Smith, of Standon, Herts. *Educ.*: Privately. *War Work*: Commandant V.A.D., Cambs. 16; Hospital opened for Belgian wounded, 15 Nov. 1914; received British wounded, June, 1915. *Address*: Chilford Hall, Linton, Cambs.
(O1138)

SMITH, Edith Mabel, Mrs., M.B.E.

SMITH, Edith Marion Drummond, Mrs., M.B.E.

SMITH, Col. Edmund Robinson, C.B.E., V.D.; New Zealand Forces; served in the Great War, 1915–19 (despatches).
(C1872)

SMITH, Capt. Edward Percival Allman, O.B.E., M.C., R.A.M.C.

SMITH, Capt. Edwin Thomas, M.B.E.

SMITH, Elizabeth Dorothea, Mrs. Hyde, M.B.E.

SMITH, Elizabeth Frances Jane Oke, M.B.E., *b.* 4 Jan. 1856 ; *d.* of Francis Edward Smith, of Crediton, Devon. *War Work :* Quartermaster, V.A. Hospitals, Crediton, Devon. *Address :* Greystone, Crediton, Devon. (M9655)

SMITH, 2nd Lieut. Eric Payton, M.B.E.

SMITH, Ernest Alfred, M.B.E., R.A.M.C.

SMITH, Ernest Arthur, M.B.E.

SMITH, Ernest Wentworth, O.B.E., A.M.I.M.E., *b.* 1885 ; *s.* of Herbert Smith, of Canonbury, London ; *m.* Ruby Ethel, *d.* of Edward William Hatton, of Brixton, London. *Educ. :* Essex County Coll. General Manager (Steel Dept.), Harris & Sheldon, Ltd., Birmingham. *War Work :* Deputy Director of Gauges, Ministry of Munitions, 1915–19, and Member of British Engineering Standards Committee. *Addresses :* 46, Cannon Street, E.C. 4 ; Highfield, The Chase, Coulsdon, Surrey. (O740)

SMITH, Ernest William, M.B.E., *b.* 18 Dec. 1880 ; *s.* of Samuel William Smith, of Birmingham. *Educ. :* Birmingham. Railway Official. *War Work :* Board of Trade, Coal Mines Department, Household Fuel and Lighting Branch ; Retail Coal Prices Section. *Address :* Fernhill, Warwick Road, Acocks Green, Birmingham. *Club :* Hampden. (M9657)

SMITH, Eva Agnes, M.B.E.

SMITH, Capt. Felix Patrick, O.B.E. Assistant Provost-Marshal at Cologne. *Address :* The Bowling Green, Castle Bellingham, Co. Louth. (O5786)

SMITH, Frances Mary, O.B.E.

SMITH, Major Frank, M.B.E., *b.* 17 Feb. 1881 ; *s.* of Thomas Smith, of Axford ; nr. Marlborough, Wilts ; *m.* Fanny, *d.* of Charles Flippance, of Mildenhall, nr. Marlborough, Wilts. *Educ. :* Kintbury. *War Work :* Served in 6th Regt. of Mounted Infantry during South African War, as corporal ; commissioned 5th Dorset Regt. Dec. 1914 ; took part in landing at Suvla Bay, Aug. 1915 ; wounded ; promoted Lieut. Aug. 1915 ; invalided home ; promoted Capt. and appointed Adjutant in 19th Hampshire Regt., May, 1916 ; France, May, 1916 ; promoted Major, Dec. 1917 ; invalided home, Oct. 1918, mentioned in despatches 1918. *Address :* Florence Villa, Wimborne Road, Poole, Dorset. (M6707)

SMITH, Frank, O.B.E.

SMITH, Frank Edward, O.B.E., F.R.S., *b.* 14 Oct. 1876 ; *s.* of Joseph Smith, of Birmingham ; *m.* May, *d.* of Thomas B. King, of Birmingham. *Educ. :* Royal Coll. of Science, London. For 19 years Superintendent of Electrical Department, National Physical Laboratory, Teddington ; since Feb. 1920, Director of Scientific Research, Admiralty, also Sec. of Physical Society of London. *War Work :* Confidential work for Admiralty and War Office. *Address :* Redcot, St. James's Avenue, Hampton Hill. *Club :* Physical Society. (O741)

SMITH, Frank Robinson, M.B.E., R.A.S.C.

SMITH, Frank William, M.B.E.

SMITH, Frederick, C.B.E. Assist. Director of Materials and Priority, Controller's Depart. Admiralty. *Address :* Admiralty, Whitehall, S.W. (C270)

SMITH, Capt. Frederick Crawford, O.B.E., *b.* 20 Aug. 1870 ; *s.* of Thomas Smith, of Leith ; *m.* Grace, *d.* of Albert Edward Beeton. *Educ. :* Silligs, Vevey, Switzerland ; Institution, Edinburgh. *War Work :* Shellmaker, Vickers, Erith ; B.R.C.S. Voluntary Driver ; O.C., Etaples, 1916 ; O.C., Boulogne, 1917–18 ; and Deputy Director Transport. *Address :* Chimney Corner, Walton-on-the-Hill. *Clubs :* Royal Automobile ; Argentine. (O3931)

SMITH, Major Frederick H., O.B.E., R.M.

SMITH, Major Frederick Hargreaves, O.B.E., R.A.S.C., *b.* 17 April, 1869. *Educ. :* Shrewsbury, Univ. of London. *War Work :* Served in His Majesty's forces from March, 1915 ; twice mentioned in despatches. *Address :* Silcuri, Lancing, Sussex. (O7703)

SMITH, Frederick Herbert, M.B.E.

SMITH, Frederick Robertson, M.B.E.

SMITH, Major Fred John, M.B.E.

SMITH, Capt. Geoffrey Lionel, O.B.E.

SMITH, Lieut. George, M.B.E.

SMITH, Lieut. George Clarke, M.B.E., R.E.

SMITH, Capt. George Edward, O.B.E.. R.A.F.

SMITH, George Foster, M.B.E., Lecturer. (M10316)

SMITH, George Frederick, M.B.E., *b.* 1875 ; *s.* of J. Smith, of Leeds. *Educ. :* Leeds Univ. Engineer ; Works Manager, Kitson & Co., Ltd., Leeds. *War Work :* Superintending construction of tanks, 6-inch howitzers carriages, 4·5 shells, trench guns, and locomotives for transport in France. *Address :* 82, Stratford Terrace, Leeds. (M9660)

SMITH, Lieut.-Col. George Frederick, O.B.E., R.A.S.C. (T.)

SMITH, 2nd Lieut. George Geoffrey, M.B.E.

SMITH, Major G. Graham, O.B.E.

SMITH, George Henry Cheverton, O.B.E., *b.* 19 March, 1866 ; *s.* of the late Francis Smith, of Isle of Wight ; *m.* Ada Mary Cheverton, *d.* of John William Tuckett, of Worthing, Sussex. *Educ. :* Grammar School, Newport, Isle of Wight. Clerk at the Admiralty from 1885 to 1900 ; Assistant Cashier at H.M. Dockyards, Devonport, Sheerness, Gibraltar, Portsmouth, and Dover from 1900–14 ; Deputy Cashier at H.M. Dockyard, Devonport from 1914–15 ; Sec. and Cashier at H.M. Dockyard, Pembroke Dock, from June, 1915. *War Work :* Sec. and Cashier at H.M. Dockyard, Pembroke Dock. *Address :* Backmark Farm, Rosyth, Scotland. (O742)

SMITH, Lieut. George Henry Gould, M.B.E., R.E.

SMITH, Col. the Hon. George John, C.B.E., New Zealand Forces, *b.* 1862 ; *s.* of John Smith, of Consett, England ; *m.* 1887, Eleanor S. B., *d.* of Robert Dawson, of Brucefield, Christchurch, New Zealand. General Merchant ; Comdg. a New Zealand Inf. Brig. ; elected a M.L.A. New Zealand, 1893, 1896 and 1901 ; M.L.C. 1907 ; Member of Port of Lyttelton (N.Z.) Harbour Board, 1903–7 ; Board of Govs. of Canterbury Coll. (Univ. of N.Z.), 1903–7 and 1913–18. *Address :* Riverland, Opawa, Christchurch, New Zealand. (C298)

SMITH, George Milner, M.B.E.

SMITH, Major George Rainier De Herriez, O.B.E., I.A.R.O.

SMITH, George Scoby, C.B.E., J.P.

SMITH, George William, O.B.E., M.B., Ch.B., *b.* 29 April, 1876 ; *s.* of Rev. John Smith, of Corstorphine, Midlothian ; *m.* Sylvia Rose Margaret, *d.* of Frederick Elliot Blackstone, of London. *Educ. :* George Watson's Coll., Edinburgh ; and Edinburgh Univ. T. Major, R.A.M.C. ; D.A.D.M.S., Rouen Base, B.E.F. *Address :* Chiswick House, Chiswick, London, W. 4. (O5787)

SMITH, Major George Wilson, O.B.E., K.O.S.B.

SMITH, George Wishart, O.B.E.

SMITH, Gladys Augusta, M.B.E., *b.* 27 Feb. 1893 ; *d.* of C. J. R. Smith, of Sutton. *Educ. :* Sutton High School, and Neuchatel, Switzerland. *War Work :* Served as V.A.D. nurse at Sutton Red Cross Hospital, June, 1915, to July, 1917 ; joined British War Mission to United States, July, 1917, to July, 1918 ; Private Sec. to A. Chairman of British War Mission in New York ; Junior Administrative Assistant at Ministry of Shipping. *Address :* Holland House, Sutton, Surrey. (M952)

SMITH, Harold, M.B.E.

SMITH, Capt. Harold Howard, M.B.E. ; *s.* of Howard Alfred Smith, of Birmingham. *Educ. :* Birmingham. Painter and Author ; served for several years before the war in City of London Yeomanry ; subsequently obtained a commission in the Horse Transport Branch of the Royal Army Service Corps. *War Work :* Served for 3 years overseas with the British Salonica Force ; Commanded the Macedonian Mule Corps ; volunteered for service in Russia and served there as Staff Capt., and personal Staff Officer to the G.O.C. (M7019)

SMITH, Lieut. Harold James, M.B.E.

SMITH, Harold Robert, M.B.E.

SMITH, Capt. Sir Harry, K.B.E., R.A.S.C., M.T. (V.), *b.* 27 Sept. 1874 ; *s.* of James Smith, of Netherwood, Keighley ; *m.* Evangeline, *d.* of Pearson Atkinson, of Beechroyd, Keighley. *Educ. :* Pannal Coll., Harrogate. *War Work :* Chairman, Board of Management, H.M. National Shell Factory, Keighley ; Area organisation Committee, Ministry of Munitions, London. *Address :* Yew Bank, Keighley. *Club :* Royal Automobile. (K104)

SMITH, Lieut. Harry Cyril, O.B.E., M.C., R.E. (T.).

SMITH, Helen Nora, Mrs., M.B.E.

SMITH, Sir Henry Babington, G.B.E., K.C.B., C.S.I., C.H., *b.* 29 Jan. 1863 ; *s.* of Archibald Smith, F.R.S., of Jordanhill, Renfrewshire (*see* BURKE'S *Landed Gentry*) ; *m.* Lady Elisabeth Mary, *d.* of 10th Earl of Elgin, K.G., of Broomhall, Dunfermline (*see* BURKE'S *Peerage*). *Educ. :* Eton ; Trinity Coll., Cambridge. Deputy Governor, British Trade Corporation ; formerly Sec. to the Post Office. *War Work :* Member of Financial Mission to the United States, 1915 ; Chairman, Enemy Debts Committee, Foreign Trade Debts Committee, and other Government Committees ; Assistant Commissioner for Great Britain in the United States, 1918–19. *Addresses :* Vineyards, Saffron Walden ; 121, St. James' Court, S.W. *Club :* Brooks's. (G61)

SMITH, Henry John, O.B.E., *b.* 29 Jan. 1865. *Educ. :* City of London School. Manager, National Provincial and Union Bank of England, Cardiff. *War Work :* Hon. Treas. and Chairman of Disablement Sub-Committee of War Pensions Committee ; Chairman of War Savings Committee ; Hon. Treas. Palace V.A.D. Hospital ; additional member appointed by Minister of Labour of Local Employment Committee, all of Gloucester. *Address :* Meadowside, Llandaff, Glam. *Club :* Cardiff and County. (O11340)

SMITH, Capt. Henry Joseph Cecil, M.B.E., R.A.F.

SMITH, Capt. Henry Surridge, M.B.E., R.E.

SMITH, Henry Watson, O.B.E., M.D., *b.* 6 Feb. 1879 ; *s.* of the late Alexander Henry Smith, of Aberdeen, Scotland ; *m.* Bertha Ada, *d.* of John Moseley Greatwich, of Wednesbury, Staffs. *Educ. :* Aberdeen Univ. Late House Surgeon, West Suffolk General Hospital, Bury St. Edmund's ; Assistant Medical Officer, Peckham House Asylum, and Durham County Asylum. *War Service :* Civil Prisoner of War in Turkey ; Director Lebanon Hospital for Mental Diseases, Asfuriyeh, Beyrout, Syria ; kept hospital (Anglo-American) open throughout war ; received letter of appreciation and thanks from Gen. Allenby. *Address :* Lebanon Hospital for Mental Diseases, Asfuriyeh, Beyrout, Syria. (O11341)

SMITH, Henry White, C.B.E., Chevalier Legion d'Honneur, 1919, *b.* 6 July, 1878 ; *s.* of the late W. G. Smith, of Bristol ; *m.* Winifred, *d.* of the late James Kirkpatrick. *Educ. :* Privately. Director of the Bristol Aeroplane Co., Ltd. ; Chairman, Society of British Aircraft Constructors, Ltd., the representative body of the British Aircraft Industry, since its foundation ; Member of Government Advisory Committee on Civil Aviation, and of Government Committee on Aeronautical Research and Education ; was Commercial Delegate representing the British Aircraft Industry on the International Air Convention of the Peace Conference, occupying position of Vice-Chairman to Legal and Commercial Sub-Commission ; was Member of Government Civil Aerial Transport Committees ;

Member of Executive Committee of the Federation of British Industries ; Chairman of West of England Association of Controlled Establishments. *Address :* Winterbourne House, Winterbourne, Glos. *Clubs :* St. Stephen's ; Royal Automobile ; Royal Aero.; Bristol Constitutional. (C626)

SMITH, Herbert Edwin, M.B.E.

SMITH, Herbert Francis, O.B.E., *b.* 1 March, 1873 ; *s.* of Septimus Francis, of Clapham ; *m.* Evelyn Fanny, *d.* of Charles Butler, of Surbiton. *Educ. :* Malvern Coll. Secretary, Crown Agents for the Colonies. *War Work :* Equipment of troops in East and West Africa. *Addresses :* Bramerton, West Byfleet ; 4, Millbank, S.W. 1. *Club :* Royal Automobile. (O11342)

SMITH, Herbert Melville, C.B.E. General Manager, King's Norton Filling Factory, Abbey Wood, Ministry of Munitions, during Great War. (C2062)

SMITH, Herbert Parker Hastings, M.B.E.

SMITH, Major Isaac Claude Victor, O.B.E., R.A.S.C.

SMITH, James, M.B.E.

SMITH, James, M.B.E.

SMITH, James Alfred, M.B.E., *b.* 15 Aug. 1871 ; *s.* of the late William Smith ; *m.* Kate, *d.* of Charles Fowler Bacon. *Educ. :* Haberdashers' Schools, Hoxton ; King's Coll., London. Civil Servant ; Staff Clerk in the Colonial Office. *War Work :* Administrative work, more particularly in connection with the defence of the Colonies, and carrying out of war measures by the several Colonial Administrations. *Address :* 26, Broomfield Avenue, Palmer's Green, London (M955)

SMITH, 2nd Lieut. James Albert, M.B.E.

SMITH, James Cruickshank, C.B.E., M.A., *b.* 1867 ; *s* of James Smith, of Dun, Forfarshire ; *m.* 1896, Edith, *d.* of William Philip, J.P. *Educ. :* Edinburgh Univ. and Trin. Coll. Oxford. Chief Inspector for Training of Teachers in Scotland ; Director of Supplementary Rations, Ministry of Food ; Chairman, Central Classification Committee ; Director, Wages Section, Ministry of Munitions, 1915–17 ; Vice-Chairman, Ministry of Munitions, Special Arbitration Tribunal on Women's Wages, 1917–18. *Address :* Murrayfield Avenue, Edinburgh. (C627)

SMITH, Capt. James Drummond, O.B.E., R.A.F.

SMITH, Major James Haig, O.B.E., *b.* 8 Nov. 1884 ; *s.* of James Stuart Smith, of Carluke and Glasgow ; *m.* Daisy Kydd, *d.* of James William Haig, of Edinburgh. *Educ. :* George Heriot's School, Edinburgh. Assistant Surveyor, General Post Office. *War Work :* Deputy Assist.-Director Postal Services, 19th Corps, H.Q., France, 1918, and G.H.Q., N. Russian Exped. Force, Archangel, 1918–19 ; mentioned in despatches ; Order of St. Stanislaus, 2nd Class with swords ; Hon. Sec. and Treas., G.H.Q. Winter Sports Committee, to provide exercise and amusement for the troops operating from Archangel during winter of 1918–19. *Address :* 12, Comely Bank Terrace, Edinburgh. (O9706)

SMITH, Lieut. James Hampstead, M.B.E.

SMITH, Col. James Irvine, C.B.E. ; S. African Forces ; served in the Great War in German S.-W. Africa, 1914–15 (despatches). (C756)

SMITH, Capt. and Qr.-Mr. James William, M.B.E., R.A.S.C.

SMITH, John, M.B.E.

SMITH, Capt. John, M.B.E., R.A.O.C.

SMITH, John Arthur, O.B.E.

SMITH, John Llewellin, M.B.E.

SMITH, John William, O.B.E.

SMITH, Capt. and Qr.-Mr. John William, O.B.E.

SMITH, Joseph Alfred Punton, M.B.E.

SMITH, Joseph Kent, O.B.E.

SMITH, Lieut.-Col. Julian Carter Carrington, O.B.E., M.B., I.M.S.

SMITH, Sir Keith Macpherson, K.B.E. Lieut. late R.A.F. ; made the successful flight from England to Australia in 1919, with Capt. Sir Ross Macpherson Smith, K.B.E., M.C., D.F.C., A.F.C. (K327)

SMITH, Launcelot Eustace, C.B.E., *b.* 1868. Chairman and Managing Director of Smith's Dock Co., Ltd., of High Docks, S. Shields ; Director of Smith's Dock Trust Co., Ltd., and of N.E. Railway Co. *Address :* Piper Close, Corbridge-on-Tyne. *Clubs :* Northern Counties ; Union (Newcastle-upon-Tyne). (C299)

SMITH, Lancelot Grey Hugh, C.B.E., *b.* 4 Aug. 1870 ; *s.* of the late Hugh Colin Smith, of Mount Clare, Roehampton (*see* BURKE'S *Landed Gentry*). *Educ. :* Eton ; Trinity Coll., Cambridge. *War Work :* Lieut., Westminster Dragoons (2nd County of London Yeomanry) ; principal delegate, British Mission to Sweden, 1915 ; Chairman, Tobacco and Matches Control Board ; Chairman several Board of Trade Restriction Imports Committees ; also served on Inter-departmental Oil Committee at the Admiralty ; Norwegian Fish Purchase Committee at Board of Agriculture, and Contraband Committee. (C65)

SMITH, Capt. Leslie Harcourt, O.B.E.

SMITH, Lewis William, M.B.E., *b.* 28 July, 1862 ; *s.* of William Smith, of Newburn-on-Tyne ; *m.* Caroline, *d.* of Foster Dobson, of Throckley. *Educ. :* Newburn Manor School. *War Work :* Engaged in the manufacturing of Naval and Howitzer guns ; also worked on the manufacture of guns for all the big navies of the world. *Address :* 4, Albany Gardens, Springboig, Shettleston, Glasgow. (M3978)

SMITH, Lillie Edith, Lady, O.B.E., *d.* of J. A. Mashew; *m.* 9 Oct. 1890, Sir Frederick William (*see* BURKE'S *Peerage*), *s.* of William James Smith. *Address :* c/o Messrs. Smith, Webster and Co., Capetown, S.A.

SMITH, Lilly Mary, Mrs., M.B.E.

SMITH, Lucie McDuff, Lady, C.B.E. ; *d.* of the late, W. W. Cargill, of Lancaster Lodge, Kensington ; *m.* Sir George, K.C.M.G., C.M.G., *s.* of the late Hugh Smith, of Darvel, Ayrshire. Invested with the C.B.E. for services in connection with the Nyasaland Relief Fund, and other charitable funds, Nyasaland Protectorate. *Address :* Government House, Zomba, Nyasaland. (C740)

SMITH, Sir Malcolm, K.B.E., J.P., *b.* 1856 ; *s.* of Peter Halcrow Smith, of Hoswick and Lerwick, Shetland ; *m.* Jane Tod, *d.* of Thomas Dickson, of Edinburgh. *Educ. :* Anderson Institute, Lerwick. Provost of Leith, 1908–1917 ; Member of Fishery Board for Scotland since 1911 ; J.P. for Midlothian ; Treas. Edinburgh Merchant Co. *War Work :* Chairman of Local Recruiting Committee, Appeals Tribunal, War Pensions Committee, National Relief Committee, Belgian Refugees Relief Committee, and Home for Disabled Men Committee ; Member of Munitions Board, East of Scotland ; Board of Trade Representative on Port Labour Committee. *Address :* Clifton Lodge, Trinity, Leith. *Clubs :* Scottish Liberal ; Northern ; Royal Forth Yacht ; Leith Merchants'. (K427)

SMITH, Margaret Newbigging, M.B.E., *b.* 1873 ; *d.* of the late Joseph Newbigging Smith, of Glasgow. *Educ. :* Privately. *War Work :* Sec. Central Committee, Paisley, for Sailors' and Soldiers' Comforts ; Supervisor Renfrewshire Red Cross Depot, Paisley ; parcels for Prisoners of War, 5th, 6th, and 16th Argyll and Sutherland Highlanders ; comforts for Renfrewshire Territorials. *Address :* Medwyn, Castlehead, Paisley. (M9668)

SMITH, Marshall King, O.B.E., *b.* 22 June, 1867 ; *s.* of Michael Henry Smith, *m.* Mary, *d.* of Capt. Robert Gray. *Educ. :* Privately. Sec. of Trinity House. *War Work :* In connection with the Lighthouse Service of England and Wales. *Address :* Trinity House, E.C. *Clubs :* Constitutional ; Alpine. (O3932)

SMITH, Mary Amelia, M.B.E. ; *d.* of Thomas Smith, of Liverpool. *Educ. :* England and Switzerland. Formerly Lady Superintendent of The Aberdeen School of Domestic Science. *War Work :* May, 1917, to Oct. 1919, Unit Administrator, Q.M.A.A.C. in Military Hostels in the Aldershot Command. *Address :* The Training School of Cookery, Colquitt Street, Liverpool, (M5635)

SMITH, Mary Euphemia Roseborough, Mrs., M.B.E.

SMITH, Mary Isobel Barr, Mrs., C.B.E. *War Work :* Rendered services in connection with Red Cross movement in S. Australia. (C719)

SMITH, Mathew, M.B.E.

SMITH, Major Maurice Castle, O.B.E.

SMITH, Maye Alice Pressley, M.B.E.

SMITH, Lieut. Miles Staniforth Cator, M.B.E.

SMITH, Noel William Kelland Isbister, M.B.E.

SMITH, Percival, M.B.E.

SMITH, Capt. Percy, M.B.E.

SMITH, Percy Campbell, O.B.E. ; *s.* of Alfred William Smith, of Stamford Hill, London ; *m.* Edith Caroline, *d.* of Charles Heane, of Derby. *Educ. :* Privately. *War Work :* Served in France, Commissioned rank, with Northumberland Fusiliers ; wounded at Arras, April 1917 ; later appointed Assistant Accountant, General Ministry of Shipping. *Addresses :* 44, Duke Street, St. James, Piccadilly ; Whitemeads, Hatch End, Middlesex. *Club :* Royal Automobile. (O11345)

SMITH, Lieut.-Col. Peter Caldwell, C.B.E., R.A.M.C. (T.). Served in the Great War, 1914–19 (despatches). (C1766)

SMITH, Major Philip Albert, O.B.E.

SMITH, Capt. Ralph William, M.B.E., *b.* 7 Sept. 1877 ; *s.* of Ralph Smith, of Camberwell ; *m.* Blanche Maud, *d.* of George Murray, of Balham. *Educ. :* St. Saviour's School. *War Work :* France, 1914–15 ; Mesopotamia, 1915–19, with Manchester Regt. *Address :* 45, Dalkeith Road, West Dulwich. (M4926)

SMITH, Surg.-Lieut. Reginald Eccles, O.B.E., M.B., F.R.C.S., R.N.

SMITH, Major Richard Stephenson, O.B.E.

SMITH, Capt. Robert Adam, O.B.E., J.P., *b.* 22 April, 1875 ; *s.* of Archibald Smith, J.P., late of Kirriemuir, Forfarshire ; *m.* Katie Adeline, *d.* of Frederick Stedman, M.D., of Leighton Buzzard, Bedfordshire. *Educ. :* Webster's Seminary, Kirriemuir ; High School, Dundee ; Univ. of Edinburgh. Town Clerk of Kirriemuir ; Sec. to the Territorial Force Association of the County of Forfar ; Hon. Sec. and Treas. Forfarshire Branch, British Red Cross Society ; Local Agent, Ministry of Labour. *War Work :* Acted as Sec. of the Territorial Force Association of the County of Forfar ; as Hon. Sec. and Treas. of the County Branch of the British Red Cross Society, and associated with the County Committee under the Presidency of the Dowager Countess of Airlie, G.B.E., in raising large sums of money for the Red Cross ; and as Clerk to Local Tribunals. *Address :* Wellbank, Kirriemuir. (O11346)

SMITH, Major Robert Hunter, O.B.E., R.A.S.C.

SMITH, Robert James, O.B.E., M.B., B.Ch.

SMITH, Robert John, C.B.E., C.A., F.S.S., *b.* 1866 ; *s.* of Robert Burns Smith, of Glasgow ; *m.* Kate Dinwoodie, *d.* of Rev. Alexander Linn, of Glasgow. *Educ. :* Norland House, and Pollokshields. Chartered Accountant ; Sec. of the Royal Scottish Automobile Club. *War Work :* Member of Executive and Chairman, Transport Committee, Scottish Branch British Red Cross Society ; Director, Scottish Filling Factory, Georgetown ; Chevalier Legion of Honour. *Address :* 2, Redlands Road, Kelvinside, Glasgow. *Clubs :*

Royal Automobile; Royal Scottish Automobile; Troon Golf; Royal Clyde Yacht. (C629)

SMITH, Capt. Robert Melville, M.B.E., R.E.

SMITH, Rodnoy, M.B.E.

SMITH, Capt. Ronald Maskeleyn, O.B.E.

SMITH, Capt. Sir Ross Macpherson, K.B.E., M.C., D.F.C., A.F.C., Australian Flying Corps. Made the successful flight from England to Australia with Sir Keith Macpherson Smith, K.B.E.; has the Order of Nahda of Hedjaz, 4th Class. (K326)

SMITH, Capt. S., O.B.E.

SMITH, St. Osyth Mahala Eustace, O.B.E.

SMITH, Lieut.-Col. Samuel Boylan, D.S.O., O.B.E., M.D. B.A., R.A.M.C., b. 1872. Served on the N.-W. Frontier of India, 1908 (medal with clasp); Great War, 1914–19 (wounded, despatches). (C5789)

SMITH, Sarah Helen, O.B.E., b. 15 May, 1872; d. of Major-Gen. William Smith, R.A., of Balcarras House, Charlton Kings. Educ.: Sydenham High School. War Work: Commandant of The Priory Hospital, Cheltenham, V.A.D. Glos. 30. Address: Balcarras House, Charlton Kings, Cheltenham. (O3933)

SMITH, Sarah Louisa, Mrs., M.B.E.; d. of Richard Winter Kempson, of Barnet, Herts.; m. Frederick William Smith, s. of John Smith, of Bristol. Educ.: Barnet Coll. War Work: Red Cross work as Quartermaster Bristol/2, and Sec. County Selection Board; Sec., St. John Ambulance Brigade, Nursing Division; Member of Red Cross since 1909. Address: 6, Cambridge Park, Durdham Down, Bristol. (M9670)

SMITH, Col. Sidney Ernest, C.B.E., R.A.F. Served in the Great War, 1914–19 (despatches, O.B.E.). (C1907)

SMITH, Capt. Sidney James, O.B.E.

SMITH, Major Soloman Charles Kaines, M.B.E.

SMITH, Capt. Stanley, O.B.E., R.A.S.C. (T.).

SMITH, Major Stanley Alwyn, D.S.O., O.B.E., M.D., M.Ch., F.R.C.S.E., R.A.M.C., b. 1882; s. of Col. T. J. Smith, V.D., of Rushton Spencer, Staffordshire. Educ.: Repton School and Edinburgh Univ. Orthopœdic Surg. to Gen. Hospital and Children's Hospital at Winnipeg; served during the Great War 1914–15 (despatches). (O8939)

SMITH, Col. Stanley George Drew, M.B.E., late R.A., b. 31 May, 1858; s. of Surg.-Gen. George Smith, M.D., of Indian Medical Service; m. Louisa Marian (who died), d. of James Edmunds, M.D., of London. Educ.: Privately in Edinburgh, and Germany; Royal Military Academy, Woolwich. Military Service in Royal Artillery, afterwards in Departmental Services of the Indian Ordnance Department Factory Branch. War Work: Appointed Assistant Inspector, Woolwich Inspection Department, Oct. 1915; promoted Inspector, Oct. 1917, until Sept. 1919; previous to the above was Ordnance Officer in charge of Kurram Ordnance Field Park, Afghan War of 1878–80. Address: 33, Sussex Square, Brighton. Clubs: United Service; Royal Automobile. (M959)

SMITH, Lieut. Stanley Oscar, M.B.E.

SMITH, Stanley William, M.B.E.

SMITH, Sydney, M.B.E., M.I.M.E.

SMITH, Sydney Edwin, O.B.E., b. 15 June, 1884; s. of Frederick Edward Smith, of Westcliffe-on-Sea. Incorporated Accountant; partner in firm of Hoale, Smith and Field, Cross Keys House, Moorgate Street, E.C. War Work: May, 1916, to Feb. 1919, held following appointments at Ministry of Munitions; Assistant Director of Finance, Assitsant Controller of Accounts, Member of Accounts Board, Member of Control of Materials Committee, and Deputy Assistant Financial Sec. Address: Cross Keys House, Moorgate Street. (O1873)

SMITH, Sydney George, M.B.E., D.C.M., R.E.

SMITH, Major Sydney William, O.B.E., R.A., and R,A.F.

SMITH, Lieut. Thomas, M.B.E.

SMITH, Capt. and Qr.-Mr. Thomas, M.B.E., R.E.

SMITH, Thomas Armstrong, M.B.E.

SMITH, Thomas Blampey, O.B.E.

SMITH, Lieut. Thomas Harold, M.B.E., R.E.

SMITH, Sir Thomas James, K.B.E., J.P. Inspector-General of the Royal Irish Constabulary. (K492)

SMITH, Capt. and Qr.-Mr. Thomas Joseph, M.B.E.,

SMITH, Capt. Thomas Sinclair, M.B.E.

SMITH, Thomas William, C.B.E., b. 1881; s. of Walter Reeve Smith. Asst. Sec. Ministry of Munitions. (C2963)

SMITH, Victor Vyvian Cuthbertson, O.B.E.

SMITH, Major Vincent, O.B.E., R.A.S.C.

SMITH, Capt. Walter William, O.B.E., R.A.O.C.

SMITH, Col. Walter William Marriott, C.B.E., R.A. (ret.), b. 21 Dec. 1846; s. of the Rev. Henry Curtis Smith, rector of Rushton, Dorset (see BURKE'S Peerage, Smith-Marriott, Bt.); m. 8 Aug. 1874, Alice Mary, 2nd d. of John H. Ley, of Trehill, Devon. Address: Dcwnside, Winchester. (C750)

SMITH, William Brownhill, O.B.E., J.P.

SMITH, William Charles Clifford, O.B.E.

SMITH, Capt. William Edwin, O.B.E., R.A.F.

SMITH, Col. William Frank, O.B.E.

SMITH, William George, O.B.E. Educ.: Privately. War Work: Assistant Commissioner, St. John Ambulance Brigade (No 12 District); Assistant County Director, British Red Cross Society and Order of St. John, City and County of Dublin. Addresses: The Bungalow, Butterfield Ave., Rathfarnham. Co. Dublin.; 40, Merrion Square, Dublin. (O11350)

SMITH, Brig.-Gen. William Hugh Usher, C.B., C.B.E., D.S.O., b. 1869; s. of the late Rev. Francis Smith, rector of Atherstone, Stratford-on-Avon; m. 1897, Amy, e. d. of Lieut-

Col. F. Hall, formerly Connaught Rangers. Educ.: Trinity Coll. Stratford-on-Avon. Entered R.A. 1888; Capt. 1898; Major Army Ordnance Depart. 1904; Lieut.-Col. 1907; Col. 1914; served in S. Africa, 1899–1902, with Army Ordnance Depart. (despatches); Great War, 1915–19, as Director of Ordnance Services, with rank of Brig.-Gen. (despatches, Order of Redeemer of Greece). (C1418)

SMITH, William James, O.B.E.

SMITH, William Joseph, M.B.E.

SMITH, Flight-Lieut. William Percy, O.B.E., R.A.F.

SMITH, Lieut.-Col. William Stanley, O.B.E., b 21 Aug. 1868; s. of Edward Smith, of Chedleton, Leck, Staffs.; m. Constance Vining, d. of Philip H. George, of Barrow Gurney, Som. Educ.: King's Coll., London; Munich; Copenhagen. War Work: France, Belgium, Mediterranean, N. African Coast (Salvage, Royal Flying Corps), Lieut., Capt., R.F.C., and G.S.O.I. (Assist. Controller of Salvage, War Office) Aug. 1915, to Nov. 1919. Address: 33, Compton Road, Wimbledon, S.W. 19. (O7708)

SMITH, William Sydney, O.B.E.

SMITH, Lieut.-Col. Chilton Lind ADDISON-, O.B.E.

SMITH, David BAIRD-, C.B.E., LL.B., M.A., Hon. LL.D., Chevalier de la Légion d'Honneur, b. 1877; s. of the late John Baird-Smith, of Glasgow; m. Jessica Duncan, d. of the late Thomas Duncan Jameson, of Burma Police. Educ.: Glasgow Univ. Solicitor; General Editor, Scottish Text Society; Hon. Sec. Franco-Scottish Society. War Work: Member of War Executive, Scottish Branch, British Red Cross Society, and of British Committee, Croix Rouge Française. Address: 6, Woodlands Terrace, Glasgow. Club: Western (Glasgow). (C9261)

SMITH, Constance Brightman, Mrs. BARRETT- M.B.E.

SMITH, Capt. Wm. BOWDEN-, C.B.E., Capt. R.N. Great War, 1914–19, with Grand Fleet in Dardanelles, Ocean Escort, and as Senior Naval Officer on the Tyne (despatches). (C1179)

SMITH, Major Philip William Lilian BROKE-, D.S.O., O.B.E., R.E.

SMITH, Percy Pyne CALDECOLT-, O.B.E., F.S.I.

SMITH, Maude Ellefred, Mrs. Hugh CASTLE-, M.B.E.

SMITH, Ella Gertrude CASTLEMAN-, M.B.E., b. 1860; d. of Edwin A. Smith, Letton, Blandford. Hon. Sec. and Treas. of Dorset County Nursing Association; appointed Member of Dorset District Wages Board; Member of County Insurance Committee and of Local Advisory Committee (Western Counties) for the Blind; Poor Law Guardian, etc. War Work: Chairman of Executive Committee of Dorset Women's War Agricultural Committee, Hon. Treas. War Savings Association; Member of War Pensions Committee; Local Food Control Committee, and Profiteering Committee; Hon. Sec. of Working Party for Soldiers, etc. Address) The Close, Blandford. (M9656:

SMITH, Wyke CATTERSON-, M.B.E.

SMITH, Major Percy George DARVIL-, C.B.E., b. 1880; s. of George Smith; m. 1911, Ethel Kathleen, e. d. of the late Thomas Henry Biss. Educ.: Wesley Coll. Dublin. Hon. Major, late R.A.M.C. (Vol.); Sec. St. John Ambulance Brigade: Asst. Commr. for Bucks; Sec. Terr. Branch St. John Ambulance Assocn.; Organising Sec. Middlesex Voluntary Aid Organisation, 1911–14, and Co, Div. Aux. Hospitals and V.A.D.'s, Middlesex, 1914–18; served in the S. African War (Queen's medal and four clasps). Address: Orchard Cottage, Prestwood, near Great Missenden. (C628)

SMITH, Major Percy William DAYER-, O.B.E., R.A.V.C. (T.).

SMITH, Capt. and Qr.-Mr. Harry Launcelot ETHERINGTON-, O.B.E., R.A.M.C.

SMITH, Major Cyril McLaurin EUAN-, O.B.E., M.C. b. 1878. Educ.: St. Paul's School, and Germany. War Work: Served with R.G.A. in France, May, 1915, to April, 1919; on Relief Mission in Turkey and Armenia, April to Aug. 1919, under Supreme Economic Council. Address: White Rigg, Starcross, Devon. Club: Royal Societies'. (O2510)

SMITH, Lieut. William GLEGG-, O.B.E. R.N.V.R.

SMITH, Olive Frances, Mrs. GUTHRIE-, M.B.E., b. 1883; d. of Col. S. C. F. Peile, Indian Army; m. the late Major W. M. Guthrie-Smith, 10th Gurkha Rifles, s. of Sheriff Guthrie-Smith, of Edinburgh. War Work: In charge of Electro-therapeutic dept. of London Command Depot, Seaford, Sussex, and at Shoreham, Sussex. Address: 106, Cromwell Road, S.W. 7. (M493)

SMITH, Izz Constance, Lady HADDON-, O.B.E., d. of the late Col. B. Hodson, of Bath; m. Sir George Basil Smith, K.C.M.G., C.M.G., Governor and Commander-in-Chief, Windward Islands. Address: Government House, Grenada, Windward Islands. (O8386)

SMITH, Lieut. Norman HAMILTON-, M.B.E., B.A., LL.B., b. 10 March, 1884; s. of the late William Smith, of Melbourne, Australia; m. Shirley Roughton, d. of Henry Roughton Hogg, of 23, Hornton Street, W. 8. Educ.: Tonbridge School; Trinity Hall, Cambridge; Inner Temple. Barrister-at-Law; Director, A. L. Elder & Co. (1915), Ltd.; London Director of Sands and McDougall Ppy. Ltd., Melbourne, Australia. War Work: Commissioned R.G.A. (S.R.), June, 1915; active service in France and Italy. Addresses: 7, St. Helen's Place, E.C. 3; Dormy House, Sunningdale. Melbourne (Australia). (M4713)

SMITH, Major Ralph Henry HAMMERSLEY-, O.B.E.

SMITH, Sir Thomas Rudolph HAMPDEN-, Bart.,

C.B.E., M.A., M.B. (Camb.), L.R.C.P. and F.R.C.S. (London), b. 1869 ; s. of Sir Thomas Smith, Bart., of London (see BURKE'S Peerage) ; m. 14 June, 1897 Ann Ellen, d. of Joseph William Sharp. War Work : Worked in Hospitals. (C3122)

SMITH, Theodore Edward HART-, O.B.E.

SMITH, William HAYNES-, M.B.E., b. 4 Nov. 1870. Educ. : Eton, and Trinity Coll., Cambridge. Address : Turleigh Mill, Bradford-on-Avon. Club : White's. (M9675)

SMITH, Christine Louise HERBERT-, Mrs., M.B.E.

SMITH, Frank HOLGATE-, M.B.E.

SMITH-, Elizabeth Dorothea, Mrs. HYDE-, M.B.E., b. 9 Oct. 1886 ; d. of Archibald Dunlop, M.D., of Holywood, Co. Down ; m. Major Herbert Charles, D.S.O., Scottish Rifles, s. of Sergison Hyde-Smith. Educ. : Cheltenham Ladies' Coll. War Work : Helped to start, and ran a club for soldiers in Rouen, France, Oct. 1915, to Nov. 1919. Address : St. Helen's, Holywood, Co. Down. (M3619)

SMITH, Capt. Valentine Gardner HYDE-, M.B.E.

SMITH, Annie Margaret, Mrs. KEEBLE-, M.B.E. b. 23 July, 1886 ; d. of John Francis Burnett, of Hurst Manor, Slimbridge, Glos. ; m. George Digby Keeble-Smith, s. of George Keeble-Smith. Educ. : Down End, Clifton. Trained nurse. War Work : Staff Nurse at Cedar Lawn Military Hospital, and at Caen Wood Towers Hospital ; Welfare Superintendent at the Aston Construction Co. Address : 46 Eagle Wharf Road, N. 1. (M624)

SMITH, Frances Louise, Mrs. KYRLE-, O.B.E.

SMITH, Harold LEA-, O.B.E., b. 13 July. 1873 ; s. of John Lea-Smith, of 41, Bryanston Square, London, W. ; m Adele, d. of T. C. Brandon, of Sandgate, Kent. Educ. : Rugby. War Work : Actively engaged in Volunteer work ; Member of London Coal Committee of Board of Trade ; Divisional Officer, Metropolitan Area, Household Fuel and Lighting Order Branch, Board of Trade. Address : Woodhouse, Wimbledon Park, Surrey. Clubs : Royal Automobile ; Royal Wimbledon Golf. (O11339)

SMITH, Capt. Lindsay LINDSAY-, M.B.E., R.A.O.C., s. of the late F. A. Lindsay-Smith, J.P., C.C., and Lady Polson, of 18, Sussex Place, Regents Park ; m. 12 Jan. 1921, Eleri, d. of John Bilbie, M.I. Mech. E., C.C., of Purley, and 106, Queen Victoria St., E.C. (M6668)

SMITH, John LLEWELLIN-, M.B.E., L.R.I.B.A., b. 14 June, 1873 ; s. of David Smith, M.E., of Aberdare, Glam. ; m. Mabel Millicent, d. of Frederick W. Mander, J.P., of Aberdare, Glam. Educ. : Wycliffe Coll., Stonehouse. Architect and Estate Agent. War Work : Member and Hon. Treas., Aberdare War Pensions Committee ; Vice-Chairman, Training Sub-Committee of South Wales Joint Disablement Committee ; Chairman, Local Employment Committee (Ministry of Labour) ; Hon. Sec., Belgian Relief Committee, Aberdare. Address : Fernleigh, Aberdare, Glam. Club : Aberdare Valley Golf. (M9665)

SMITH, Capt. John Alfred LUCIE-, O.B.E.

SMITH, Lieut.-Col. Bertram METCALFE-, C.B.E. Special List ; served in S. Africa, 1900–2 (Queen's medal with two clasps, King's medal with two clasps) ; Great War, 1914–19 (despatches). (C1696)

SMITH, Hilda Mary MONCRIEFF-, Mrs., O.B.E.

SMITH, Robert Earl MONTEITH-, O.B.E.

SMITH, Lieut.-Col. Arthur MURRAY-, C.B.E., b. 25 April, 1868 ; s. of the late Rev. I. Gregory Smith, LL.D. ; m. Rebe Mabel, d. of Thomas Marlow of Aldridge, Staffs. Educ. : Marlborough Coll. ; R. M. Academy. War Work : Aug. 1913 rejoined the Reserve of Officers as Brigade Major R.A., of the 1st South Midland (48th) Division T.F. ; France, March, 1915 ; invalided home, June, 1915 ; passed as fit for Home Service only ; R.M. Academy, Woolwich, Sept. 1915, as Chief Instructor in Artillery ; served in this appointment until Dept. 1919. Club : Army and Navy. (C1711)

SMITH, Montague Bentley Talbot PASKE-, O.B.E.

SMITH, Major Douglas Cyril PERCY-, D.S.O., O.B.E.

SMITH, Lieut.-Col. Hugh Bateman PROTHEROE-, O.B.E.

SMITH, Capt. Edward RAWDON-, O.B.E., b. 2 July, 1890 ; s. of F. Rawdon-Smith, J.P., of Eastfield, Ironbridge, Salop ; m. Agnes Cottam, d. of John Brayton, of Hindley, Lancs. Educ. : St. Edward's School, Oxford ; Queen's Coll., Oxford. Barrister-at-law ; Company Sec. War Work : Served in Rifle Brigade ; War Office Recruiting Department ; Ministry of National Service, Assistant Sec. ; Sec. of Labour Sub-Committee of War Cabinet. Address : 41, Circus Road, St. John's Wood ; 2, Central Buildings, Westminster. Club : Conservative. (O3929)

SMITH, Capt. Eric RIVERS-, M.B.E.

SMITH, Capt. Stanley RIVERS-, O.B.E.

SMITH, Paymaster-Capt. Charles ROACH-, C.B.E., R.N. (Ret.), b. 10 Aug. 1860 ; s. of John Smith, of Landguard, Isle of Wight ; m. Catherine Frances, d. of the late Paymaster-in-Chief Edward Robinson, R.N. Educ. : St. Helen's Coll., Southsea. War Work : H.M.S. President's Office for Shore and Special appointments, R.N.R., R.N.V.R. Address : Landguard, Sawbridgeworth, Herts. (C623)

SMITH, Mabel ROUSE-, M B E

SMITH, George SCOBY-, C.B.E., J.P., b. 21 Nov. 1848 ; s. of Joseph Smith, of Middlesbrough ; m. Harriet Coates, d. of William Burdon. Company Manager, Bolckow, Vaughan & Co. ; Chairman of Directors, Brit. Basic Slag, Ltd., Director of Brit. Magnesite Calcining Co., and Steetley Lime Co. War Work : Member of Lord Balfour's Committee on

Trade after the War, Pig-iron Control Committee, and of the Provisional Advisory Council of the Board of Trade ; Chairman of the Committee appointed by the Board of Trade on the Iron and Steel Trades after the War, and of the Ministry of Munitions N.E. Coast Pig-iron Control Committee. Addresses : Lyndhurst, Roman Road, Linthorpe, Middlesbrough. Clubs : Constitutional and Royal Automobile, London ; Cleveland, Middlesbrough. (C625)

SMITH, Lieut. Henry Edward Goves SCOTT-, O.B.E., R.N.R.

SMITH, Capt. Keith John SETH-, O.B.E., R.F.A.

SMITH, Edward Shrapnell SHRAPNELL-, C.B.E., F.C.S., M.Inst.T., b. 1875 ; s. of Edward Charles Smith, of Liverpool (compounded mother's maiden name, Shrapnell, with surname in 1912) ; m. Sarah Rosalie, d. of the late Major-Gen. R. Temple Godman, of Highden, Sussex. Educ. : Liverpool Royal Institution School, and Liverpool Univ. Coll. Director of Transport Companies and Chemical Engineer ; Director-General London Housing Bonds Campaign. War Work : Chairman, Standing Joint Committee, Mechanical Road Transport Associations, 1914–18 ; Hon. Sec. and Treas. Comforts Fund for R.A.S.C., M.T., 1914–17 ; Chief Economy Officer and Deputy Director (Technical Investigations) on H.M. Petroleum Executive, 1917–19. Address : Hound House, Shere, Surrey. Clubs : Royal Societies' ; Royal Automobile. (C624)

SMITH, Lieut.-Col. Richard Talbot SNOWDEN-, C.B.E.. R.A.S.C.

SMITH, Lieut. Charles TYSOE-, M.B.E., I.A.R.O., R.E.

SMITH, Helen, Mrs. WILLOUGHBY-, M.B.E.

SMITH, Constance Maitland WILSON-, Mrs., M.B.E., b. 19 Oct. 1862 ; d. of Lieut.-Col. F. Maitland Wilson, of Stowlangtoft Hall, Bury St. Edmunds (see BURKE's Landed Gentry) ; m. Henry Wilson Smith, s. of W. A. Smith, of Colebrooke Park, Tonbridge. War Work : Commandant, V.A.D. Kent 14 ; Hayle Place Hospital, Maidstone, Oct. 1914, to Jan. 1919. Address : Colebrooke Park, Tonbridge, Kent. Club : Empress. (M2440)

SMITH, Constance Evelyn WINWOOD-, M.B.E.

SMITHE, Ida Elizabeth, Mrs., C.B.E., b. 24 Dec. 1872 ; d. of Capt. John Hampden Waller, M.V.O., Royal Body Guard, of Lee Place, Charlbury, Oxon. ; m. Bevil Granville Smithe. War Work : Vice-President British Red Cross Society ; Hon. Sec. Rye Div. ; Commandant V.A.D. Sussex. Address : Burnt Wood, Battle, Sussex. Clubs : V.A.D. Ladies'. (C631)

SMITHERS, Hubert, O.B.E, b. 23 Feb. 1885 ; s. of Sir Alfred Waldron Smithers, of Knockholt, Kent. Educ. : Charterhouse. Member London Stock Exchange. War Work : Mobilised with 4th Batt. Royal West Kent Regt (T.F.) ; 2nd in command and subsequently commanded 2/4th Batt. R.W. Kent Regt. at landing, Suvla Bay ; later employed at Cairo as D.A.D.R.T. till end of war. Address : Knockholt, Kent. Club : Royal Automobile. (O2933)

SMITHERS, Sub-Lieut. Walter Gilbert, M.B.E., R.N.V.R.

SMITHERS, Lieut. William Henry Grant, O.B.E., R.N.R.

SMITHETT, Major Henry Cecil East, O.B.E., b. 25 Oct. 1860 ; s. of the late Capt. M. E. Smithett, R.N. ; m. Coralie Charlotte, d. of T. F. Harrington, of London. Educ. : Cheltenham Coll. Regular Army (ret.). War Work : Employed at home, Aug. 1914, to Aug. 1920, in various capacities, Staff and Regimental. Address : 12, Haleswelle Road, Golders Green, N.W. (O7709)

SMITHSON, Lieut.-Comm. Alfred Edward, O.B.E., R.N.V.R.

SMITHSON, Lieut. Edward, M.B.E.

SMITHSON, John George, O.B.E.

SMITHSON, Brig.-Gen. Walter Charles, C.B.E.. D.S.O.. b. 26 Jan. 1860 ; s. of Samuel Smithson, J.P., of Lentran, Inverness ; m. Anne Charlotte Le Gendre, d. of John Piers Chamberlain Starkie, of Ashton Hall, Lancaster. Educ. : Faithfull's, Storrington. Joined the Militia, 1877 ; Commissioned 13th Hussars, 7 Jan, 1880 ; served with this regiment, East Indies, 1880 ; Afghanistan, 1880–81 ; East Indies 1881–84 ; S. Africa, 1884–85 ; appointed A.D.C. to the late F.M. Visct. Wolseley, K.P., 1891–1905 ; promoted Major, 1896 ; served in Boer War, 1899–1902 ; Commanding the regiment from Aug. 1901 ; present at the relief of Ladysmith, Colenso, Spion Kop, Vaal Krantz, Tugela Heights, and Pieters Hill (severely wounded, Queen's Medal, 5 clasps ; King's Medal, 2 clasps ; mentioned in despatches). War Work : appointed to the 2/6th Gordon Highlanders, Oct. 1914 ; promoted Officer in Command Northern Cavalry Depot, Scarborough, Nov. 1914, to Feb. 1915 ; placed in command of 2/1 Yorkshire Mounted Brigade, Feb. 1915, to Nov. 1916 ; mentioned in Sec. of State's List, Feb. 1917. Address : Invery, Banchory. Clubs : Army and Navy ; Roehampton. (C1768)

SMITHWICK, Major Standish George, O.B.E., b. 21 Jan. 1878 ; d. of the Rev. Chancellor S. P. Smithwick, of Monasterevan, Co. Kildare ; m. Dora Louisa, d. of Charles Webb, J.P., of Park Place Tashinny Co. Longford. Educ. : Corrig School Kingstown and Trinity Coll., Dublin. Major, 2nd battalion Royal Dublin Fusiliers ; South African War, 1899–1902 (Queen's Medal, 3 clasps ; Kings Medal, 2 clasps). War Work : 1914–18, 1914 Star, G.S., and Victory medals ; wounded. mentioned in despatches ; still serving with regt. in Constantinople. (O7710)

SMY, Capt. Alfred, M.B.E.

SMYLY, Luiet.-Col. Frederick Philip, O.B.E.

SMYLY, Major Richard Josiah, O.B.E.

SMYTH, Barbara, Mrs. Ross, O.B.E.; *d.* of the late Andrew Hepburn, of Dunallan, Crieff ; *m.* John, *s.* of the late George Gillie Smyth, of Edinburgh. *Educ.:* Morrison's Academy, Crieff. Convener, Soldiers' and Sailors' Families Association, Perth City Branch, and of Dependants' Committee, Perth Local War Pensions Committee. *War Work:* Aug. 1914, joined Mrs. John Berrington, in reconstituting Perth City Branch of Soldiers' and Sailors' Families Association, and succeeded her as Convener ; July, 1916, when local War Pensions Committees were organised, appointed Convener of Dependants' Committee. *Address:* Laggan, Clyde Place, Perth. (O11352)

SMYTH, Major Benjamin, M.V.O., O.B.E.

SMYTH, Capt. Bernard Owen, O.B.E.

SMYTH, Ethel Downing, Mrs., M.B.E., *b.* 1870 ; *d.* of James Leonard Wilson, of Wimbledon ; *m.* Percy Meliss Smyth. *Educ.:* St. Helen's, Clifton. *War Work:* In connection with National Relief Fund in Hackney, and Hon. Sec. Hackney Local Central Committee for War Savings. *Address:* 21, Elm Park Gardens, London, S.W. 3. (M3980)

SMYTH, Francis Watson, M.B.E.

SMYTH, Major Frederick Wilkinson, O.B.E.

SMYTH, George Edward, O.B.E.

SMYTH, Major Humphrey Etwall, D.S.O., O.B.E., *b.* 1884 ; *s.* of Col. Etwall Walker Smyth, C.B. *Educ.:* R.M.A. Entered R.G.A. 1902 ; Major, 1917 ; transferred to R.A.O.C. 1918 ; served in the Great War, 1914–19 (despatches). (O6418)

SMYTH, Jane Robinson, Mrs., M.B.E. *Educ.:* Edinburgh. *War Work:* President of Soldiers' and Sailors' Families Assoc., Bambridge Area ; Member, Co. Down War Pensions Local Committee. *Address:* Brookfield, Banbridge, Co. Down. (M9677)

SMYTH, John Cecil, M.B.E., M.D.

SMYTH, John George, O.B.E., *b.* 4 Aug. 1876 ; *s.* of Capt. T. Smyth, late of 1st Gloucestershire Regt. Asst. Accountant-General, Ministry of Shipping, and Superintending Inspector of Taxes, Inland Revenue. *War Work:* Worked at Ministry of Shipping (Finance Branch). *Address:* 30, Barrowgate Road, Chiswick, W. 4. (O11354)

SMYTH, Vice-Adm. Morris Harry, C.B.E., R.N. Lieutenant employed on the Indian Marine Survey ; served with the Naval Brigade during the Burma Annexation War, 1885–86 (mentioned in despatches) ; India Medal, Burma, 1885–87, clasp ; Cross of the Order of Naval and Military Merit (Spain) ; Rear Admiral (retired) Nov. 1908 ; Vice-Admiral, April. 1914. (C1941)

SMYTH, Vice-Adm. Morris Henry, C.B.E., R.N.R.

SMYTH, Brig.-Gen. Robert Napier, C.B.E., D.S.O. (late 21st Lancers), *b.* 26 June, 1868 ; *s.* of Maj.-Gen. J. H. Smyth, C.B., of Frimhurst, Frimley, Surrey. *Educ.:* Wellington Coll. D.A.A.G., Intelligence, 1900–1902 ; Staff Officer, South African Constabulary, 1902–1905 ; G.O.C., Fermoy, Ireland, 1919. *War Work:* Egyptian Campaign, 1898 ; South African War, 1899–1902 ; G.S.O., G.H.Q. France, 1914–15 ; Brigade Commander, 1915–18. *Clubs:* Naval and Military ; Cavalry. (C1769)

SMYTH, Lieut.-Col. Robert MILNER-, O.B.E., S.A.M.C.

SMYTH, Barbara, Mrs. ROSS-, O.B.E.

SMYTHE, Altamont, O.B.E.

SMYTHE, Lieut. Frank Oldham, M.B.E.

SMYTHE, Major Harry Alexander, O.B.E., R.A.S.C., *b.* 8 July, 1885 ; *s.* of Henry G. Smythe, of Herne Hill, London. *Educ.:* Dulwich Coll. *War Work:* Served in France from Sept. 1914, to May, 1916 ; in Ireland, Aug. 1916, to Aug. 1918 ; in Macedonia, Sept. 1918, to Nov. 1918 ; and in Turkey, Nov. 1918, to Nov. 1919. (O6532)

SMYTHE, Capt. Patrick Cecil. *Educ.:* Charterhouse, and Christ Church, Oxon. Served in Army. *Address:* Braco, Isla Road, Perth. (O5791)

SMYTHE, Capt. Theodeor Wm., O.B.E.

SMYTHE, Lieut.-Col. William Ross, C.B.E. Canadian Forestry Corps ; served in the Great War. (C841)

SMYTHE, Albert Charles BUTLER-, M.B.E., F.R.C.S.

SNAGGE, Sir Harold Edward, K.B.E., *b.* 28 Dec. 1872 ; *s.* of the late Sir Thomas Snagge, K.C.M.G., Judge of County Courts ; *m.* 1901, Inez Alfreda, *d.* of the late Alfred Lubbock, of Par, Cornwall. *Educ.:* Eton Coll., and New Coll., Oxford. East India Merchant, and Banker ; Director of Barclays Bank, Ltd., The British Trade Corporation, and other companies partner in firm of Edward Bonstead & Co., London ; an Additional Commissioner of Taxes in the City of London. *War Work:* Sec. (unpaid) to the Ministry of Information. *Address:* Sandhills, Bletchingley, Surrey. *Clubs:* Travellers' ; Wellington ; Beefsteak ; Garrick. (K428)

SNAITH, Adam Currie, M.B.E., *b.* 9 May, 1877 ; *s.* of George Snaith, of Darlington ; *m.* Marie, *d.* of William Morris, of Maryport. *Educ.:* Chester Coll. Headmaster, Eaglescliffe Junction School, and North Brancepeth School, Co. Durham. Inspector of Schools, Durham County Council. *War Work:* Hon. Sec. Brandon and Byshottles War Savings and Food Economy Committee ; and Executive Officer, Food Control Committee ; Hon. Sec. Langley Moor (East Ward) Relief Committee. *Address:* Whitwell Villas, Langley Moor, Co' Durham. (M2451)

SNAPE, Major Albert Edward, O.B.E., R.A.F.

SNAPE, Henry Lloyd, O.B.E., D.Sc., Ph.D., F.I.C., *b.* 20 April, 1861 ; *s.* of the late Alderman Thomas Snape, J.P., of Liverpool ; *m.* Maud Mary, *d.* of the late John Bonfield Allen. of Norwich. *Educ.:* Liverpool Institute ; Owens Coll., Manchester ; Univ. Coll., Liverpool ; Univ. Coll., London ; Univs. of Berlin and Göttingen. Formerly held the appointments of Demonstrator of Chemistry, Univ. Coll., Liverpool ; Head of Department of Chemistry and Physics, Manchester Technical School ; Professor of Chemistry, Univ. Coll., Aberystwyth, Univ. of Wales ; Public Analyst for Cardiganshire, and Director of Education to the Lancashire County Council. *War Work:* Chairman of Education Committtee which organised, for the Counties of Lancashire and Westmorland, courses of Technical Instruction for disabled sailors and soldiers. *Address:* Fernlea, Torquay. (O11355)

SNELGAR, Capt. John Thomas, M.B.E., *b.* 8 Aug. 1887 ; *s.* of Hugh Snelgar, of Redlynch, Wiltshire ; *m.* Verona Rebecca, *d.* of William Russell, of Wimbledon. *Educ.:* Bournemouth School, and London Univ. Administrative Officer in the L.C.C. Education Service. *War Work:* Gazetted to Wilts Regt. Feb. 1915, and served in France with 1st Wilts. from June, 1915, to July, 1916 ; mentioned in despatches for gallantry at Hooge ; twice wounded on the Somme ; served in Mesopotamia with 5th Wilts, March. 1917, to March, 1919 ; Staff work round Kirkuk whilst Adjutant, July, 1918, to Sept. 1919 ; Commanded a company in No. 2 Special Batt. in India during riots and Afghan rising, 1919. *Address:* 12, Kitchener Road, Thornton Heath. (M4928)

SNELL, John Beddome, O.B.E., *b.* 2 March, 1864 ; *s.* of Frederick William Snell, of Kenley. Surrey ; *m.* Susan Emily, *d.* of Theodore Howard, of Bickley, Kent. *Educ.:* Merchant Taylors' School. Alderman of Tunbridge Wells ; Solicitor (1st Class Honours), and Notary Public. *War Work:* Hon. Executive Officer, Food Control Committee, Tunbridge Wells, 1917–20, and Executive Officer, Ticehurst Food Control Committee, 1919–20 ; Chairman of Tunbridge Wells Recruiting Committee, Military Advisory Committee, War Savings Committee, Economy Campaign, and National Service Committee. *Address:* Bramdean, Stonegate, Ticehurst, Sussex. (O11356)

SNELL, Philip William, M.B.E., R.N.

SNELLING, Major Leonard Fowler, O.B.E., R.A.O.C., *b.* 18 July, 1877 ; *s.* of James William Snelling, of Winchester ; *m.* Ethel Marion, *d.* of the Rev. H. A. Burrowes, of Ireland. *Educ.:* Alleyn's, Dulwich. Served in the Great War. Mentioned in despatches, 13 Mar. 1918. *Address:* The Garrison, Purfleet, Essex. *Club:* Sundridge Park Golf. (O7712)

SNELLING, Lieut.-Comm. Norman George Fowler, O.B.E., R.N.V.R.

SNEPP, Major John Wansey, O.B.E.

SNIDER, Col. Irvine Robinson, O.B.E., *b.* 1 Jan. 1864 ; *s.* of Edwy Snider, of Toronto, Canada ; *m.* Ellen, *d.* of Thomas Swales, of Portage la Prairie. *Educ.:* Toronto. Farmer. *War Work:* Commanded the 27th City of Winnipeg Batt. from Nov. 1914, until April, 1916 ; served in Belgium and France ; commanded 14th Canadian Reserve Batt., Shorncliffe, Jan. 1917, to Feb. 1918, and 10th Canadian Garrison Batt., Winnipeg, until Feb. 1919. *Address:* Portage la Prairie, Manitoba, Canada. (O1877)

SNODGRASS, Burns, M.B.E.

SNODGRASS, William Wallace, M.B.E.

SNOW, Daisy, Mrs., M.B.E.

SNOW, Hilda Gertrude, M.B.E,

SNOW, T. Lieut. William, M.B.E., R.A.S.C.

SNOWDEN, Hon. Major Arthur de Winton, C.B.E., M.A., M.D., B.C. (Cantab), M.R.C.S., L.R.C.P., *b.* 12 Sept. 1872 ; *s.* of John Hampden Snowden, Prebendary of St. Paul's Cathedral ; *m.* Elizabeth Cecil, *d.* of Capt. Cecil George Assheton Drummond, of Enderby Hall, Leicester. *Educ.:* St. Paul's School, Cambridge, and St. George's Hospital. South African War, Civil Surgeon, 1899–1901. *War Work:* Major, R.A.M.C., Great War, 1914–19. *Address:* Broomy Hurst, Ringwood.

SNOWDEN, Cyril Ralph, C.B.E. Controller, Finance Section, Ministry of Blockade, during the Great War. (C2965)

SNOWDEN, Florence Mary, Mrs., O.B.E.

SNOWDEN, Frederick Cousins, M.B.E.

SNOWDON, John Henry Reed, M.B.E., *b.* 6 April, 1890 ; *s.* of John William Snowdon, of Gateshead-on-Tyne. *Educ.:* Gateshead-on-Tyne. *War Work:* Private Sec., Director of Experiments and Research, Admiralty. *Address:* 12, Overdale Road, W. 5. (M9681)

SNOWIE, James, M.B.E.

SOAMES, Capt. Arthur Granville, O.B.E., *b.* 12 Oct. 1886 ; *s.* of the late Harold Soames, of Lilliput, Dorset ; *m.* Hope Mary Woodbyne, *d.* of Charles Woodbyne Parish, of 58, Ennismore Gardens, London, S.W. 7. *Educ.:* Eton and Sandhurst. Coldstream Guards, 1905–19 ; Retired, Dec. 1919. *War Work:* Staff Capt., 4th Guards Brigade, 1914 ; Brigade Major, 119th Infantry Brigade, 1915–16, and 12th Infantry Brigade, 1917 ; G.S.O. II., 58th Division, 1917 ; G.S.O. II., Australian Imperial Force Depots in U.K., 1917 ; Brigade Major, 23rd Reserve Brigade, 1917–19. *Address:* Ashwell Manor, Penn, Bucks. *Clubs:* Guards' ; Arthur's. (O7714)

SOAMES, Capt. Gerald, O.B.E.

SOAMES, Mabel Janet, Mrs., M.B.E., *b.* 4 Nov. 1875 ; *d.* of the late Capt. J. T. Wetherall, of Loddington House, near Kettering. *War Work:* Sec. Red Cross Hospital ; Joint Manager, War Hospital Supply Depot ; Sec. Trowbridge Div. British Red Cross Society. *Address:* Hilperton, Trowbridge. (M3982)

SOAMES, Una, Mrs, M.B.E.
SOAMES, Major Walter Field, O.B.E.
SOANE, Ely Banister, C.B.E. Political Officer, Mesopotamia Exped. Force, during Great War. (C746)
SOLLY, Henry Wilkinson, M.B.E.
SOLLY, Lieut. and Qr.-Mr. William, M.B.E., R.E.
SOLOMAN, Edward, M.B.E.
SOLOMON, Lieut.-Col. Harold Josiah, O.B.E., M.C., R.A.S.C.
SOLOMON, Capt. Joseph, M.B.E., b. 3 Dec. 1872; s. of Joseph Lewis Solomon, of Lewes, Sussex; m. Alice, d. of William Groves, of Edenbridge, Kent. Educ.: Lewes, and Army Schools. War Work: Army Pensioner; re-enlisted, Sept. 1914; commissioned, July, 1915; served continuously in France and Flanders with 8th Royal Sussex and on the Rhine with Army of Occupation, 53rd Royal Sussex, until March, 1920; thrice mentioned in despatches. Address: Olinda, Gibauderie, Guernsey. (M6450)
SOLTAU, Col. Alfred Bertram, C.M.G., C.B.E., T.D., M.D., M.R.C.P., F.R.C.S., b. 21 March, 1876; s. of George Soltan, of Plymouth; m. Edith Mary, d. of William Watts, of Plymouth. Educ.: London Hospital. Hon. Consulting Physician for Gassed cases, Ministry of Pensions; Hon. Physician, S. Devon and E. Cornwall Hospital, and Devon and Cornwall Ear and Throat Hospital; Member of Plymouth Borough Council, and Chairman, Public Health Committee. War Work: Commanded 25th Field Ambulance from April, 1908, to Aug. 1916; Consulting Physician to 1st and 2nd Armies, Nov. 1916, to Sept. 1918; Consulting Physician, War Office, Oct. 1918, to April, 1919; despatches 4 times; 1914 Star and Clasp, Croix de Guerre, Commander Order of Aviz. Address: 1, The Crescent, Plymouth. Club: Royal Western Yacht. (C1121)
SOMAN, Mariette, M.B.E., b. 2 June, 1889; d. of A. E. Soman, of Norwich, Norfolk. Educ.: Norwich High School; Girton Coll.; Sorbonne. Docteur de l'Université de Paris. War Work: Translator in Secret Intelligence Dept., Admiralty; Sec. in Naval Section, Paris Peace Conference. Address: The Book House, Norwich. (M9083)
SOMERLEYTON, Phyllis, Lady. C.B.E.; d. of the late Gen. Sir H. P. de Bathe, Bart., K.C.B., of Knightstown, Co. Meath; m. Savile Brinton Crossley, 1st Baron Somerleyton, P.C., K.C.V.O. (see BURKE'S Peerage). War Work: Equipped, maintained, and was Matron of a Primary Auxiliary Military Hospital, from Aug. 1914, to June, 1917, when this hospital was closed owing to the doctors being called up for military service abroad; went as V.A.D. Nurse to Sir Douglas Shields Hospital, 17, Park Lane, from Aug. 1917, to Feb. 1919. Addresses: Somerleyton Hall, Suffolk; 7, Deanery Street, Park Lane, W. 1. Club: Ladies' Automobile. (C632)
SOMERS, Charles Dudley, O.B.E., M.B., B.Ch., M.R.C.S., L.R.C.P., b. 25 Sept. 1869; s. of J. B. S. Somers, of Belsize Park, Hampstead; m. Lilian Ethel, d. of Tansley Witt, M.V.O. of Teddington. Educ.: Malvern; Pembroke Coll., Cambridge; and St. Thomas' Hospital. Medical Officer of Health to Aldeburgh Corporation; Public Vaccinator; Naval Surgeon and Agent. War Work: Medical Officer in charge of troops stationed at Aldeburgh (100th Provis. Batt., 2/4th Welsh Fusiliers, 2/4th Shropshire L. Infantry, 56th S. Wales Borderers, 2/7th Devonshires). Address: Shelley, Aldeburgh, Suffolk. Clubs: Leander; Cavendish. (O4394)
SOMERS, Capt. Frank, O.B.E.
SOMERS, Major John Percy, O.B.E.
SOMERSET, Capt. Somers, O.B.E.
SOMERTON, Carolina Augusta, M.B.E.
SOMERVELL, T. Major Arnold Colin, O.B.E., R.A.S.C.
SOMERVILLE, Capt. Donald Bradley, O.B.E.
SOMERVILLE, Lieut. George Aytoun, M.B.E.
SOMERVILLE, Col. John Arthur Goghill, C.M.G., C.B.E., b. 26 Mar. 1872; s. of Lieut.-Col. T. H. Somerville, J.P., D.L., of Drishane, Skibbereen Co. Cork; m. Vera Cooper, d. of C. W. Aston Key, of 52, Cambridge Terrace, W.2. Educ.: Bedford Grammar School and Royal Military College, Sandhurst. Commandant, Royal Military School of Music. War Work: Military Attaché, British Embassy, Tokyo; afterwards attached to Staff of Maj.-Gen. Sir A. W. F. Knox, K.C.B., in Siberia. Address: Kneller Hall, Twickenham. Club: Naval and Military. (C2170)
SOMERVILLE, Capt. Thomas Victor, O.B.E., M.C., R.A.M.C.
SOMMERVILLE, James, O.B.E.
SOMERVILLE, John, M.B.E.
SOMOLY, William Henry. O.B.E.
SONCHON, Hippolyte Norris Wiehe du Condray, C.B.E., Representative in London of the Mauritius Chamber of Agriculture. Address: 4, Blenheim Street, W. 1. (C404)
SONGHURST, Major Fred Hibbard, M.B.E., R.A.F., b. 18 Dec. 1894; s. of Alfred Songhurst, of Bexhill-on-Sea, Sussex; m. Kathleen Vera, d. of Augustus Blackiston, of Horsham, Sussex. Educ.: Collier's School, Horsham. Mechanical Engineer. War Work: Enlisted in Sussex Yeomanry, 1914; received a commission in the R.F.C., Nov. 1915; posted to Force "D," Mesopotamia, July, 1916; arriving shortly after the first relief of Kut; was posted April, 1917, to the Salonica Expeditionary Force and mentioned in General Milne's despatch, Nov. 1917; acted as King's messenger in 1918 between Salonica and London; subsequently attached to Home Establishment for duty at York Address: 1, Honey Hill, Hillingdon, Uxbridge. (M2452)

SOPWITH, Thomas Octave Murdoch, C.B.E., b. 18 Jan. 1888; s. of Thomas Sopwith, M.I.C.E.; m. Beatrix, d. of Lord Ruthven of Gowrie (see BURKE'S Peerage). Educ.: Cottesmore, Brighton, and Seafield Engineering Coll. Member of Civil Aerial Transport Committee, 1919. War Work: Chairman, Sopwith Aviation and Engineering Co., Ltd., Kingston-on-Thames. Address: Horsley Towers, East Horsley, Surrey. Clubs: Carlton; Royal Aero; Royal Automobile; Royal Southampton Yacht. (C300)
SORBY, Gertrude Vera, M.B.E.
SORENSEN, Capt. Michael, M.B.E.
SORLEY, Major Gerald Merson, O.B.E.
SORRELL, Lieut. Herbert Alfred George, M.B.E.
SOTHAM, Louise Victoria Gisela, Mrs., M.B.E.
SOUNDRY, William Henry, O.B.E.
SOUNDY, Sir John Thomas, C.B.E. Acted as Food Controller at Windsor for two years. Rendered much honorary service during the war. (C3165)
SOUTAR, Charles, M.B.E., b. 30 Jan. 1873; m. Helen Mary, d. of Alexander Agnew. Solicitor; Session Clerk and Kirk Treas. of the Parish of Dundee; Sec. Dundee Area, Road Transport Department, Ministry of Food; Deputy-Procurator Fiscal of Forfarshire (Dundee District). War Work: Capt. C (University) Co., No. 1 Batt., Dundee V.T.C.; Assistant Distribution Officer, Ministry of Food; Sec. Dundee Area, Road Transport Board. Addresses: 11, Whitehall Street, Dundee; Seacraig House, East Newport, Fife. (M9685)
SOUTH, Major Thomas, O.B.E., T.D., Order of St. Aine, 3rd Class, Russia, b. 20 Feb. 1877; s. of Thomas South, of Southsea; m. Florence Annie, d. of the late Samuel Collinge, of Leeds. Educ.: Privately. Manager of Barclays' Bank, Ltd., Esher, 1905-14, now Manager of Barclays' Bank, Ltd., Ascot. Served in the S. African War. War Work: Served with 8th Bn. Middlesex Regt. in M. and E.E.F.'s until Oct. 1916; D.A.A.G., B.S.F., Oct. 1916, till Nov. 1918; D A.A. and G.M.G., Constantinople Base, Nov. 1918, to Dec 1918; D.A.A. and Q.M.G., Batoum, 27th Division Army of Black Sea, Dec. 1918, to Dec. 1919. Address: Old Bank House, Ascot, Berks. Clubs: Junior Army and Navy; Royal Ascot Golf. (O6523)
SOUTHAM, Arthur H. Ridgway, M.B.E., b. 25 March, 1876; s. of J. Downes Southam, C.C. of Shrewsbury. Educ.: Shrewsbury School. Vice-President of Battersea Juvenile Organisations Council and Battersea National Reserve O.C. Association; Chairman of Territorial Cadet Officers' Institution, and the Borough of Fulham Scout Council; Life Member of Old Salopian Club; Member of London Scout Council, Executive Committee, County of London Branch, British Red Cross Society; and Executive Committee, Shropshire Society in London. War Work: Officer at Belgian Refugee Depot, 1914; raised and appointed Lieut.-Col. Commanding a Cadet Batt. in 1915; retired in 1919 with permission to wear uniform; awarded the Silver Service Medal, Order of St. John of Jerusalem, 1916; placed on Roll of Honourable Service, 1918, British Red Cross Society. Addresses: The Cottage, Cannon Lane, Pinner, Middlesex; St. George's House, 193, Regent Street, W. 1. (M9686)
SOUTHAM, Frederick Neil, O.B.E. War Work: With Imperial Munitions Board, Canada; associated with others in charge of shell production. Address: Montreal, Canada. (O749)
SOUTHAM, Thomas Frank, M.B.E., M.D., L.R.C.P. & S. (Edin.), b. 20 Jan. 1862; s. of Thomas Southam, LL.D., of Bentcliffe, Eccles, Manchester; m. Marian, d. of James Syddall, of Harden Park, Alderley Edge, Cheshire. Educ.: Bowdon Coll., Cheshire; Edinburgh High School; Edinburgh Univ. Consulting Physician (ret.). War Work: Hon. Resident Medical Officer in charge Roby Street Branch of Manchester Royal Infirmary for wounded soldiers; Hon. Medical Officer in charge Hale Auxiliary Red Cross Hospital, Cheshire. (M9687)
SOUTHAMPTON, Charles Henry Fitzroy, Baron, O.B.E., b. 11 May, 1867; s. of Charles, 3rd Baron Southampton (see BURKE'S Peerage); m. 9 July, 1892, Lady Hilda Mary Dundas, e. d. of Lawrence, 1st Marquis of Zetland (see BURKE'S Peerage).
SOUTHEE, Capt. Ethelbert Ambrook, O.B.E., R.A.S.C.
SOUTHERN, John Acton, O.B.E., M.R.C.S., L.R.C.P.
SOUTHEY, Lieut.-Col. John Henry Willes, O.B.E., b. 5 Oct. 1861; s. of the late Rev. H. W. Southey, Vicar of Woburn, Beds.; m. Laura Hamilton, d. of Robert Gillan, of Ayr. Educ.: Clifton Coll. War Work: Infantry Record Office, Warwick. Address: 18, Clarendon Square, Leamington. Club: Army and Navy. (O1880)
SOUTHEY, Lieut. Maurice Edward, M.B.E.
SOUTHGATE, Charles Joseph, O.B.E.
SOUTHON, Major Charles Edward, O.B.E., M.B., M.S.
SOUTTAR, Major Henry Sessions, C.B.E., M.Ch., F.R.C.S., b. 1875; s. of Robinson Souttar; m. 1904, Catharine, d. of Professor Clifton, F.R.S., of Oxford. Educ.: Queen's Coll. Oxford. Consulting Surg.; Hon. Major R.A.M.C.; Assist. Surg. London and W. London Hospitals; served in the Great War, 1914-19, as Surgeon Field Hospitals; has Order of Crown of Belgium. Address: 46, Queen Anne Street, W.1. Club: Thatched House. (C832)
SOWDEN, Capt. Felix Musgrave, O.B.E., Can. A.S.C.
SOWERBY, Lieut.-Col. Edward Chaytor, O.B.E., b. 2 Sept. 1872; s. of Thomas C. I. Sowerby, of Snow Hall, Darlington; m. Muriel Evelyn, d. of I. Gardiner Muir, of Farming Woods Hall, Northants. Educ.: Wellington Coll.

Land Agent. Served in the South African War (mentioned in despatches). *War Work*: 1915, attached to Sir Horace Smith-Dorrien's Staff; 1916–19, Staff of Western Command Headquarters; Senior Inspector, Quartermaster-General's Services; twice mentioned in despatches. *Address*: Uppington House, Wellington, Salop. *Club*: Bath. (O7716)

SOWMAN, Lieut. Ulric Doncaster, M.B.E., R.A.S.C.

SPADACCINI, Henry, M.B.E.

SPAFFORD, Lieut. Arthur Owen, O.B.E. R.E. (T.).

SPAFFORD, Capt. Percy Lionel, O.B.E., R.A.S.C.

SPAIGHT, James Molony, O.B.E., LL.D., *b.* 17 Oct. 1877; *s.* of Robert Spaight, J.P., of Co. Clare, Ireland; *m.* Constance Elizabeth, *d.* of Col. W. F. Spaight, R.E., J.P., of Union Hall, Co. Cork, and Ardnatagle, Co. Clare. *Educ.*: T.C.D. Civil Servant, Air Ministry. *War Work*: Civil Servant, War Office, 1914–18; Air Ministry, 1918. *Address*: Inglemere, Smitham Downs Road, Purley, Surrey. (O1881)

SPAIN, Major Gerald DIXON-, O.B.E.

SPAIN, Major John Edward DIXON-, O.B.E.

SPALDING, Major William Burrington, O.B.E.

SPALL, Lieut. Leslie Alan, O.B.E.

SPARKES, Henry, O.B.E.

SPARKES, Stanley, M.B.E.

SPARKS, Sir Ashley, K.B.E., *b.* 23 March, 1877; *s.* of John Ashley Sparks, of Sutton, Surrey; *m.* Mina Jane, *d.* of James Roberts, of New York. *Educ.*: Barnet Grammar School; Denstone Coll.; Hurstpierpoint. Resident Director and General Agent, Cunard Line in U.S.A.; President and Director, Funch Edye & Co., Inc., New York; Director, Commonwealth and Dominion Line; President and Director, The Twenty-five Broadway Corporation, and 2nd Vice-President, St. George's Society, New York. *War Work*: Representative, Shipping Controller-in-charge Shipbuilding programme in U.S.A., 1917; Member British War Mission Oil Committee, 1917; attached Mr. Balfour's Mission to Washington as Advisor, 1917; Director-General, British Ministry of Shipping in U.S.A., 1918–19; Chairman, Patriotic League of Britons Overseas, New York Branch. *Address*: Northaw, Syosset, Long Island, N.Y., U.S.A.; 130, East 67th Street, New York. *Clubs*: Racquet and Tennis, N.Y.; Riding; Bankers'; and India House, Piping Rock, Baltusrol Golf, Blind Brook, Golf. (K233)

SPARKS, Charles Pratt, C.B.E., *b.* 13 May, 1866. *Educ.*: Repton School. Consulting Engineer. *Address*: Blackfriars House, New Bridge Street, London, E.C. 4. *Clubs*: City of London; Junior Carlton. (C2966)

SPARKS, James Noel, O.B.E., B.A. (Cantab.), *b.* M.Inst.C.E., *b.* 25 Dec. 1869; *s.* of Col. John Barnes Sparks, of Bengal Staff Corps; *m.* Bessie Ellen Randall, *d.* of Middleton Rayne, M.Inst.C.E. *Educ.*: United Services Coll., Westward Ho!; King's Coll., London; Jesus Coll., Cambridge. Consulting Civil and Metallurgical Engineer; took a prominent part as Member of Council in the organisation of the Imperial Services Coll., Windsor (formerly the United Services Coll., Westward Ho!), designed to afford facilities for the education, at reasonable rates, of the sons of Officers in the Imperial Services. *War Work*: Engaged at Foreign Office (Contraband Dept.) in administration of the Blockade; and advising the Contraband Committee in technical matters and in questions relating to metals, minerals. *Address*: Church House, Rodmersham, Sittingbourne, Kent. (O11359)

SPARROW, Guy, M.B.E.

SPARROW, Major Walter Augustus, O.B.E., F.S.A.A., R.E. (T.), *b.* 7 Dec. 1877; *s.* of Walter Sparrow, of Eastbourne; *m.* Florence, *d.* of William Banner, of London. *Educ.*: Eastbourne. Borough Accountant of Eastbourne. *War Work*: On outbreak of war, Capt. and second-in-command, 1st H.C. Field Co., R.E.; Nov. 1914, Command 2/1st H.C. Field Co., R.E.; April, 1915, promoted Major; Sept. 1915, Staff Capt., 9th Provisional Brigade; Dec. 1915, Brigade-Major, 9th Provisional Brigade; Nov. 1916, Brigade Major, 218th Infantry Brigade; Feb. 1918, second-in-command, 5th Reserve Batt. R.E., and R.E. Training Centre, Christchurch, Hants.; Sept. 1918, Command 5th Reserve Batt. R.E., and R.S. Training Centre, Christchurch. *Address*: 12, Hartfield Road, Eastbourne. *Club*: Junior Army and Navy. (O7718)

SPARROW, Lieut.-Col. and Qr.-Mr. William George, O.B.E., R.M.A. (ret.).

SPARSHOTT, Margaret Elwin, C.B.E., R.R.C. T.F. Nursing Service. (C1770)

SPEAR. 2nd Lieut. Richard William, M.B.E., R.E.

SPEAR, Wilfrid Guy, O.B.E., *b.* 8 April, 1875; *s.* of the late Rev. John Williams Spear, of Yorktown, Surrey; *m.* Gertrude Leah, *d.* of Alfred Batchelor, of Clifton, Glos. *Educ.*: Kingsbridge, S. Devon. Superintending Clerk, Dept. of the Accountant-General of the Navy, Admiralty. *Address*: 4, Park Way, Ruislip, Middlesex. (O3935)

SPEARMAN, Jessie Aubrey, Mrs., M.B.E., *b.* 31 Dec. 1863; *d.* of the Rev. Cadwallader Corker, of Oxfordshire; *m.* Commander Alexander J. C. M. Spearman, R.N., *s.* of Alexander Spearman. *War Work*: Superintendent of Linen League for Devon, V.A.D. *Address*: Parks, Crediton, Devon. (M3985)

SPEARS, Brig.-Gen. Edward Louis, C.B., C.B.E., M.C., *b.* 1886; formerly Capt. and Brevet Lieut.-Col. 11th Hussars (ret.). Served in the Great War, 1914–19; Comm. Legion of Honour, Orders of Star of Roumania with Swords, and White Eagle of Serbia with Swords. (C1771)

SPEDDING, Belle, M.B.E.

SPEDDING, Lieut.-Col. Edward Wilfred, C.M.G., O.B.E., *b.* 1867; *s.* of John James Spedding, of Keswick; *m.* 1898, Georgiana Victoria, *d.* of Sir John Wrixon-Becher, 3rd Bt. Entered R.A. 1887; Capt. 1897; Major, 1903; Lieut.-Col. 1914; S. Africa, 1902 (Queen's medal with two clasps); Great War, 1914–18, as a Brig.-Gen. R.A. (despatches). *Address*: Windebrowe, Keswick. (O2722)

SPEED, Capt. Douglas Charles Leyland, O.B.E., *b.* 8 Oct. 1893; *s.* of Major Elmer Speed, of Knowlton Court, near Canterbury; *m.* Myrtle, *d.* of Sir Henry Dering, Bart., of Surrenden, Dering, Kent. *Educ.*: Eton and Oxford. *War Work*: 1st commission, King's Royal Rifle Corps, 23 Jan. 1914; Lieut., Dec. 1914; Capt., July, 1916; seconded to R.F.C., April, 1916; Flight-Comm. in R.F.C., Aug. 1916; A. Major, Royal Air Force, May, 1918, to May, 1919; restored to establishment, K.R.R.C., Sept. 1919; served in France with K.R.R.C., Nov. to Dec. 1915, and with K.R.R.C., May to Aug., 1916. *Addresses*: Knowlton Court, near Canterbury; 23, Princes' Gate, S.W. *Clubs*: Naval and Military; Bath. (O8194)

SPEED, Capt. Ralph Henley, O.B.E., R.A.S.C.

SPEKE, Capt. Herbert Benjamin, O.B.E., *b.* 18 Feb. 1877; *s.* of the Rev. Benjamin Speke, of Wakehill, Ilminster, Somerset; *m.* Sybil, *d.* of Charles Archibald Percival Reed, of Aydon, Corbridge-on-Tyne. *Educ.*: Marlborough Coll. Stockbroker; Partner of Wise, Speke & Co., 28, Collingwood Street, Newcastle-on-Tyne. *War Work*: Served with 1/4th Northumberland Fusiliers (T.F.), France, April, 1915; wounded, April, 1915; joined Batt. again in Sept. 1917; transferred to 2nd Army Headquarters, March, 1918, to March, 1919, as Assistant Camp Commandant. *Address*: Pigdon, Morpeth, Northumberland. *Club*: Oriental. (O5794)

SPELLAR, William David, M.B.E.

SPENCE, Alexander, O.B.E., J.P., D.L.

SPENCE, Lieut.-Col. Alexander Hierom Ogilvy, C.I.E., C.B.E., I.A., *b.* 23 May, 1869; *s.* of Alexander Ogilvy Spence, of Edinburgh; *m.* Hon. Christina Philippa Agnes, O.B.E., *y.d.* of 11th Baron North, of Wroxton Abbey, Oxon, and Kirtling Tower, Newmarket (*see* BURKE's *Peerage*). *Educ.*: The Leys, Cambridge. *Clubs*: Cavalry; Royal Automobile. (C2043)

SPENCE, Alfred, M.B.E., *b.* 8 Sept. 1892; *s.* of Charles Spence, of Bedford Park, W.; *m.* Violet Rose, *d.* of the late Arthur Herbert Duncan. *Educ.*: Christ Church School, Waterloo, Liverpool; King's Coll., London. *War Work*: Officer-in-Charge of Printing Section, Ministry of Information. *Address*: Timahoe, Grove Road, North Finchley, N. 12. (M3987)

SPENCE, Capt. and Qr.-Mr. Andrew, M.B.E., M.C.

SPENCE, Caroline Mary, Mrs., M.B.E.

SPENCE, Christina Philippa Agnes, Hon. Mrs., O.B.E., Lady of Grace of the Order of St. John of Jerusalem, Kaisir-i-Hind (gold medal), *b.* 27 Dec. 1869; *d.* of 11th Baron North, of Wroxton Abbey, Banbury, Oxon, and Kirtling Tower, Newmarket, Cambridgeshire (*see* BURKE's *Peerage*); *m.* Lieut.-Col. Alexander Hierom Ogilvy, C.I.E., C.B.E., I.A., *s.* of Alexander Ogilvy Spence, of Edinburgh. *War Work*: Red Cross and other War Work from 1914–19, in India. *Address*: 8, Clarendon Crescent, Edinburgh. (O8306)

SPENCE, James Beveridge, O.B.E., M.D., M.Ch.

SPENCE, Major John Charles, M.B.E.

SPENCE, Capt. Lockhart James, M.B.E., M.B., R.A.M.C.

SPENCE, Mary Denham, Mrs., M.B.E.

SPENCE, Major Richard Bennett, O.B.E.

SPENCER, Blanche Mary, Mrs., M.B.E.

SPENCER, Col. Charles Louis, C.B.E., D.S.O., T.D., *b.* Nov. 1870; *s.* of John Spencer, of Glasgow. *Educ.*: Kelvinside Academy, Glasgow; Coll. Chaptal, Paris. Engineer. *War Work*: Mobilised with Highland Division, Aug. 1914; B.E.F., France, May, 1915, to March, 1919. *Address*: 5, Great Western Terrace, Glasgow. *Clubs*: New, Glasgow; Caledonian, London. (C1327)

SPENCER, Christopher John, O.B.E.

SPENCER, Edith, M.B.E.

SPENCER, Lieut. Fred, O.B.E.

SPENCER, Capt. Gerald Theodosius Leigh, M.B.E., B.A., LL.B., *b.* 4 Oct. 1882; *s.* of the Rev. G. Leigh Spencer, of Hereford; *m.* Mary Beatrice, *d.* of R. Edward Couchman, of Birmingham. *Educ.*: Rossall School, and Trinity Coll., Cambridge. Solicitor. *War Work*: Enlisted 10 Sept. 1914, in 14th Service (1st Birmingham) Batt. Royal Warwickshire Regt.; appointed to commission in same Batt. Dec. 1914; Lieut. in April 1915; Adjutant, June 1915; served with Batt. in France as Adjutant from Nov. 1915 to Aug. 1916; subsequent service in England with 51st Devon Regt. from Nov. 1916 to March; 1919; in Germany as Brigade Education Officer with 3rd Southern Infantry Brigade, Rhine Army, from April, 1919, to Nov. 1919. *Address*: 3, Richmond Hill, Bath. (M5642)

SPENCER, Gladys Marion, M.B.E., *b.* 28 May, 1882; *d.* of Charles Spencer, of Warwickshire. *Educ.*: Orford Coll., and Hanover. Child Welfare Worker. *War Work*: Ministry of Information, Photographic Section. *Address*: 93, St. George's Road, S.W. 1. (M3988)

SPENCER, Lieut.-Col. Harold Ernest, O.B.E. R.E.

SPENCER, Lieut.-Col. Harrison, O.B.E.

SPENCER, Capt. Harry, M.B.E., M.C., Royal Fus., *b.* 18 March, 1875; *s.* of W. H. Spencer, of Godalming, Surrey; *m.* Fanny, *d.* of George Wiltshire, of Devizes. *Educ.*:

Privately. Manager, Letchworth Hall Hotel, Letchworth, Herts ; April, 1916, commissioned to 23rd R.F. from 1st K.R.R.C. *War Work :* Served throughout the S.A. War (Siege of Ladysmith ; King and Queen's S.A. medals, 8 clasps) ; served throughout the Great War without a break (Victory medal, G.S. medal, 1914 Star, Long Service Medal, 6 times mentioned in despatches). *Address :* Letchworth Hall Hotel, Letchworth, Herts. (M4601)

SPENCER, Henry, M.B.E.

SPENCER, Henry Bath, M.B.E.

SPENCER, Rev. Henry Thomas, O.B.E.

SPENCER, Major Herbert Eames, O.B.E.

SPENCER, John Hayward, M.B.E.

SPENCER, Martha, Mrs., M.B.E.

SPENCER, Mary Gertrude Catherine Hitchcock, O.B.E., *Educ. :* Coed-bel, Chislehurst. Sec. to Central Bureau for the Employment of Women ; Managing Director of Women's Employment Publishing Co., Ltd. *War Work :* In connection with the National Relief Fund and its administration to cases of distress among professional women. *Address :* 5, Princes Street, Cavendish Square, W. *Club :* Ladies' University. (O751)

SPENCER, Thomas, M.B.E., *b.* 3 May, 1856 ; *s.* of Leonard Spencer, of Ipswich ; *m.* Elizabeth, *d.* of John Salter, of Alnwick. *Educ. :* Union British School. Engineer. *War Work :* War Pensions Committee ; Prince of Wales' Fund Committees ; National Maritime Board ; Engineers' Panel. (M9691)

SPENCER, Sir Thomas Harris, K.B.E., J.P., *b.* 22 May, 1863 ; *s.* of Thomas Spencer, J.P., of West Bromwich ; *m.* Ada Burgess, *d.* of Henry Cross, of Cambridge. *Educ. :* St. James' Grammar School, Almonbury, near Huddersfield. Managing Director, John Spencer, Ltd., Wednesbury ; Director of Birmingham Rly. Carriage and Wagon Co., Ltd., George Salter & Co., Ltd., and J. E. and S. Spencer, Ltd., London ; Member Institution of Mechanical Engineers, and Iron and Steel Institute ; President Birmingham Engineering and National Employers Federations. *War Work :* Chairman Birmingham Board of Management ; Chairman No. 4 Munitions Area Committee ; Member of Board of Management Executive ; Member of Employers Advisory Committee. *Address :* Summersfield Court, West Bromwich. *Clubs :* St. Stephen's, Westminster ; Union and Conservative, Birmingham ; Engineers'. Manchester. (K168)

SPENCER, Major Walter George, O.B.E., M.B., F.R.C.S., R.A.M.C. (T.).

SPENCER, Major William Arthur, M.B.E., *b.* 22 Feb. 1860 ; *s.* of Thomas Spence, of Headingley, Leeds ; *m.* Emma, *d.* of Edward Stephen Gurton, of London. *Educ. :* Privately. Civil Establishment of the War Office. *War Work :* Late 4th V.B. East Surrey Regt. (now 23rd London Regt.) ; Officer in charge of General Enquiry Department, and enquiries concerning Officers' casualties, War Office. *Addresses :* Wanstead, Essex ; and Eastbourne. (M3989)

SPENDER, Arthur Francis, O.B.E., *b.* 28 Nov. 1870 ; *Educ. :* Cambridge. Director of the British Institute of Florence, founded by H.M. Government during the war as a centre of intellectual and political influence in Italy. *Address :* 3, Via dei Conti, Florence. *Clubs :* Royal Societies', London ; Leonardo da Vinci, Florence. (O11364)

SPENS, Capt. Archibald Borthwick, O.B.E., C.A., *b.* 11 Nov. 1879 ; *s.* of William George, of Edinburgh ; *m.* Diana, *d.* of D. Mallory. *Educ. :* Trinity Coll., Glenalmond. Scottish Sec. to Automobile Association ; Chartered Accountant. *War Work :* 1915, Essex Regt., transport Officer ; 1916, Divisional Transport Officer, 2nd Cyclist Division ; subsequently transferred R.A.S.C. ; Q.M.G. 3 (Women's Motor Car Section, Women's Legion), War Office, Statistical Section. *Address :* 8, Howe Street, Heriot Row, Edinburgh. *Clubs :* Caledonian, London ; Caledonian United Service, Edinburgh. (O7722)

SPENS, Major John Ivan, O.B.E., *b.* 22 Feb. 1890 ; *s.* of John A. Spens, of 25, Park Circus, Glasgow. *Educ. :* Rugby. Chartered Accountant. *Address :* 30, St. James's Square, S.W. 1. (O7723)

SPENS, Will, C.B.E., *b.* 31 May, 1920 ; *e. s.* of John A. Spens, LL.D. of Glasgow ; *m.* Dorothy Theresa, *d.* of the late J. R. Selwyn, D.D., Bishop of Melanesia, and subsequently Master of Selwyn Coll., Cambridge. *Educ. :* Rugby, and King's Coll., Cambridge. Fellow and Tutor of Corpus Christi Coll., Cambridge. *War Work :* Temp. Clerk in the Foreign Office, Sept. 1915 ; Priv. Sec. to the Controller of the Foreign Trade Dept. of that Office, Jan. 1916, and Sec. to the Foreign Trade Dept., Feb. 1917 ; Chevalier of the Legion of Honour ; Officer of the Order of the Crown of Italy. *Address :* Corpus Christi Coll. Cambridge. *Clubs :* Carlton ; United Universities ; Cambridge, County. (C301)

SPENS, Capt. William Patrick, O.B.E.

SPENSLEY, James Calvert, O.B.E., *b.* 13 Dec. 1869 ; *s.* of Rev. James Spensley, of Reeth, N. Yorks ; *m.* Eleanor, *d.* of Samuel Foster, of Northgrove, Queen's Co. *Educ. :* Kingswood School, Bath. Assistant valuer to the London County Council ; Member of the Council of the Royal Statistical Society, F.S.I. *War Work :* Principal Assistant Director of Statistics, Ministry of Food. *Address :* Chalcots, England's Lane, Hampstead, N.W. 3. (O11365)

SPERANZA, Capt. Victor Ernest, O.B.E., R.D., R.N.R. (ret.), *b.* 5th Oct. 1867 ; *s.* of Col. Joseph Speranza, R.M.A., of Malta ; *m.* Florence, *d.* of Charles Johnson, of Southport. *Educ. :* Savona's Grammar School ; Lyceum ; Univ. of Malta.

Marine Superintendent, Pacific Steam Nav. Co. *War Work :* During war was British Vice-Consul, Valparaiso ; British Consul, Punta Arenas ; Assistant Naval Attaché, West Coast S. America, and Naval Intelligence Officer for same ; Naval Member of Sir Maurice De Bunsen's Mission to South America in 1918 ; commanded H.M.T. " Clacton " early in the war, engaged in the Fleet sweeping section and parol duties ; organised the Intelligence Service on the West Coast of S. America ; took over part of the German vessels laid up in Chilean waters after the Armistice. *Address :* The Pacific Steam Navigation Co., Valparaiso, Chile ; 34, Bullingham Mansions, Church Street, Kensington, W. 8. (O1883)

SPICER, Sir Howard Handley, K.B.E. ; *s.* of the late James Spicer, of Eltham ; *m.* Muriel, *d.* of the Rev. S. B. Handley. *Educ. :* Leys School, Cambridge, and privately abroad. Paper Merchant ; Manufacturer ; Partner in firm of James Spicer & Sons ; Technical Adviser to the War Office ; Co-Founder of Boys' Empire League. *Address :* Long Cross House, nr. Chertsey, Surrey. *Clubs :* Reform ; Devonshire ; Eighty ; Kennel ; Royal Automobile. (K169)

SPICES, Alfred, M.B.E.

SPIERS, Brig.-Gen. Edward Louis, C.B.E. 11th Hussars, T. Brig.-Gen. ; served in the Great War, 1914–19 (despatches). (C1771)

SPIERS, Frederick Solomon, O.B.E., B.Sc. For services in the Ministry of Munitions in connection with synthetic nitrogen. (O11925)

SPIERS, Gavin, M.B.E.

SPILLANE, Richard, M.B.E., R.A.O.C.

SPILLER, Edward Francis, M.B.E.

SPILLER, John Wyatt, M.B.E.

SPILLER, Lieut.-Col. Lionel Wallace, C.B.E., 3rd Bn. Duke of Edinburgh's Wiltshire Regt., *b.* 1873 ; *s.* of the late Charles Spiller. *Educ. :* Privately. *War Work :* Served in South African War ; served in Gallipoli Campaign (despatches), and Palestine Campaign (despatches). *Address :* Ashcroft, Shalford, Surrey. *Club :* Junior Constitutional. (C2171)

SPINK, Capt. Bertram John William, O.B.E.

SPINKS, Lieut.-Col. Charlton Watson, D.S.O., O.B.E., R.A., *b.* 1877 ; *s.* of John Charlton Spinks, of Victoria, British Columbia ; *m.* 1915, Marguerite Stuart Coleman. Comdt. Artillery, and Director of Ordnance, Egyptian Army ; served in N. Nigeria, 1903 (despatches, medal with clasp) ; 1903–4 (despatches, clasp) ; Sudan, 1912 (medal with clasp) ; Great War, 1914–19, in Gallipoli and Egypt (despatches). *Club :* United Service. (O6295)

SPINKS, Capt. Edwin Gardiner, M.B.E., R.A.O.C.

SPINNEY, Capt. Thomas George, M.B.E., R.E.

SPINS, Armande, Mrs., M.B.E.

SPITE, Eva Harvey, M.B.E.

SPITTAL, Capt. Charles Edward, M.B.E., Aust. A.P.C.

SPITTAL, John Kerr, M.B.E., *b.* 2 Jan. 1883 ; *. g. s.* of the late Sir James Spittal, of Edinburgh. *Educ. :* Edinburgh Academy. Ranching, Mining, and Smelting, 1900–14. *War Work :* Joined R. A. Sept. 1914 ; Commissioned, Oct. 1914 ; served six months with 113th Batt., R.F.A., 1st Division, France ; commanded No. 4 Depot, Recruits, Woolwich, May, 1916, to June, 1917 ; joined Staff of Royal Gun and Carriage Factory, Woolwich Arsenal, June, 1917. *Addresses :* 2049, Granite Street, Oak Bay, Victoria, B.C. ; 5, Shawfield Park, Bromley, Kent. *Clubs :* Royal Automobile ; Foreign Mexico. (M5645)

SPITTELER, Major Alfred, O.B.E., I.M.S.

SPITTLE, Edward Alfred, M.B.E., R.N.

SPITTLE, Major John Trevor, O.B.E., R.A.F.

SPIVEY, Lieut. Charles Henry Hughes, M.B.E.

SPOONER, Rev. Harold, M.B.E., M.C.

SPOOR, Benjamin Charles, O.B.E.

SPOOR, Capt. Sidney George, O.B.E., R.A.S.C. (T.).

SPOTTISWOODE, Col. Robert Collinson D'Esterre, M.B.E., late 10th Royal Hussars, *b.* 24 Dec. 1841 ; *s.* of Major-Gen. Arthur Cole Spottiswoode, Bengal Army ; *m.* Anne Elizabeth Burrell, *d.* of Patrick Turnbull, 34, India Street, Edinburgh. *Educ. :* Edinburgh Academy ; Merchiston Castle ; Clapham Grammar School. Joined H.E.I.C. European Cavalry in 1858 ; transferred to 21st Light Dragoons (afterwards 21st Hussars) in 1862 ; exchanged to 10th Hussars, 1874 ; promoted H.P. Lieut.-Col. 1887 ; served on Cork District Staff from 1887 to 1890, when he retired ; served in Afghanistan, 1878–79 ; was a Special Service Officer, Souakim Field Force, 1885, and received Brevet of Lieut.-Col. for his services in 1885. *Address :* Glenburn, Glanmire, Cork. *Club :* Army and Navy ; County, Cork ; New, Edinburgh. (M9693)

SPRAGUE, Major Daniel Emes, O.B.E.

SPRANGER, Major Francis Jeffries Spranger, O.B.E., R.A.O.C.

SPRATLEY, Capt. Thomas James, O.B.E., R.A.M.C., *b.* 14 Oct. 1868 ; *s.* of James Edward Spratley, of South Lambeth ; *m.* Edith, *d.* of Alexander Farquharson, of Edinburgh. *Educ. :* Belmont Coll., South Lambeth. Assistant Sec. to City of London Branch of British Red Cross Society. *War Work :* Quartermaster of 2nd London General Hospital, St. Mark's College, Chelsea, 1914–19 ; re-posted to Cherryhinton Military Hospital, Cambridge. *Address :* 82, Seaforth Avenue, New Malden, Surrey. (O8943)

SPRATT, Laura Gertrude, Mrs., O.B.E., *b.* 30 March, 1869 ; *d.* of the late Edward Jarvis, of Union Bank of London ; *m.* Thomas Oswald, *s.* of the late Thomas Spratt of Sloane Square, S.W. *Educ. :* Haberdashers' Girls' School, and Lady

Holles' School, Hackney. Head Mistress, Queen's Head Street Senior Girls' L.C.C. School, South Islington, N.1. *War Work :* Representative of primary schools ; the school organisation, collection, and distribution of funds and materials in response to the various appeals for help in connection with the war ; the aggregate funds distributed through the medium of the primary schools of London are estimated at £91,400, exclusive of large consignments of socks, gloves, mittens. *Address :* 60, Park Avenue, Palmers Green, N. 13. (O11366)

SPREAD, Major Eustace John William, O.B.E., M.C., Loyal North Lancashire Regt., *b.* 19 May, 1884 ; *s.* of the late Henry Fenton Spread, of Grayswood Beeches, Haslemere, Surrey ; *m.* Norah Nell, *d.* of — Hotblack. Gazetted 2nd Lieut. in 1st Batt. Loyal North Lancashire Regt., 6th Aug. 1906. *War Work :* Proceeded to France with 1st Batt. Loyal North Lancashire Regt. Aug. 1914 ; present in retreat from Mons, Battles of the Marne and Aisne ; severely wounded, Sept. 1914 ; mentioned in despatches ; received Military Cross ; Adjutant Motor Machine Gun Corps ; Staff Capt. and D.A.A.G. Headquarters, Northern Command ; D.A.A.G. War Office. *Address :* 10, Mulberry Walk, Chelsea, S.W. 3. *Club :* United Service.

SPRECKLEY, Herbert William, C.B.E. Chairman, Worcester Branch, Sailors' and Soldiers' Families Assocn. (C2967)

SPRIGGS, Paymaster-Comm. Harold James, Duthoit, O.B.E., R.N.

SPRING, Capt. George Conrad, O.B.E.

SPRING, Capt. and Qr.-Mr. George Robert, M.B.E., R.A.M.C.

SPRINGATE, Lieut. Albert Edward, M.B.E., R.A.

SPRINGATE, Edward Tom, M.B.E.

SPRINGER, Samuel, M.B.E., *b.* 29 Sept. 1883 ; *s.* of Maurice Springer, of London. *Educ. :* Central Foundation School ; King's Coll., London. Assistant Director, Federation of British Industries. *War Work :* Clerk in Foreign Office ; Head of General Department of the Foreign Trade Department of the Foreign Office ; Head of General Section, Overseas Dept. of the Department of Overseas Trade. *Address :* Glenmore, Alcester Crescent, Clapton, London. *Club :* Royal Automobile. (M968)

SPRINGHALL, Capt. and Qr.-Mr. John Winchester, O.B.E.

SPROTT, James, O.B.E., *b.* 16 Aug. 1846 ; second *s.* of late Wm. Sprott, of Dromore, Co. Down, Ireland. *Educ. :* Privately. Retired Linen Manufacturer. *War Work :* Sept. 1914, to Jan. 1919, conducted a War Hospitals Supply Depot, Old Town Hall Buildings, Belfast, as one of the joint acting secretaries (Hon.) for the supply of extra comforts to the men of the Navy and Army at the Front ; also gave large grants of hospital requisites to many hospitals at home, and in the different war areas. *Address :* Melfort, 40, Adelaide Park, Belfast. (O11367)

SPROTT, Right Rev. Thomas Henry, O.B.E., D.D.

SPROULE, Major Harper, O.B.E.

SPROULE, Capt. James Chambers, O.B.E., R.A.M.C., *b,* 28 Aug. 1887 ; *s.* of A. H. R. Sproule, J.P., of Fintona, Tyrone ; *m.* Clare Stewart, *d.* of George F. Aldous, F.R.C.S. (Edin.), of Charlton House, Plymouth. *Educ. :* Royal School, Raphoe ; Royal Coll. of Surgeons, Ireland. *War Work :* France, Aug. 1914, to Jan. 1920. *Address :* c/o Holt & Co., 3, Whitehall Place, London, S.W. (O8609)

SPRY, Lieut.-Col. Daniel William Bigelows, O.B.E.

SPRY, Henry Ernest, C.B.E. Chief Establishment Officer, Aircraft Production Dept., Ministry of Munitions. (C3107d)

SPURGEON, Charles Herbert, O.B.E.

SPURLING, Lieut. Charles George, M.B.E., R.A.F.

SPURLING, Major Dennis, O.B.E., R.F.A., *b.* 21 Aug. 1872 ; *s.* of the late Henry John Spurling, of the Stock Exchange, London, and Denmark Hill, S.E. ; *m.* Edith Nellie, *d.* of James Reid, of Dorchester. *Educ. :* Dulwich College. *War Work :* May, 1915, formed 33rd Divisional Ammunition Column, R.F.A., Lieut. ; Capt. Oct. 1915 ; France, Dec. 1915, commanding No. 3 Sec., 33 D.A.C., R.F.A. ; Feb. 1917, commanding 14th Army Brigade Ammunition Column, R.F.A. ; Major, Nov. 1917 ; to Italy, commanding 48th Divisional Ammunition Column until Feb. 1919 ; then to England ; continuous service supplying ammunition to 18-pounders in France and Italy from Dec. 1915 to Feb. 1919 ; holds South African War Medal with five clasps. *Address :* 27, Weihurst Gardens, Sutton, Surrey. (O3003)

SPURLING, Salisbury Stanley, O.B.E., appointed Member of the Executive Council of the Bermudas for a further term of 3 years. (O1013)

SPURRIER, Alfred Henry, C.M.G., O.B.E., L.R.C.P.

SPURRIER, Lieut.-Col. George Stretton, D.S.O., O.B.E. Royal Army Service Corps ; served in the Great War, 1914–19 (despatches). (O6421)

SPURWAY, Major John Edward, O.B.E., R.A.S.C.

SPYER, Major George, O.B.E.

SQUANCE, Muriel Mary, M.B.E.

SQUAREY, Robert Thomas, O.B.E.

SQUIRE, Rose Elizabeth, O.B.E., *b.* May 19, 1861 ; *d.* of the late William Squire, M.D., F.R.C.P., of London. *Educ. :* Privately. H.M. Deputy Lady Inspector of Factories, Home Office. *War Work :* Member of Health of Munition Workers Committee, Ministry of Munitions ; Hours of Labour Committee, Ministry of Munitions, and Substitution of Women for Men in Distributing Trades Committee, Home Office ; Director of Women's Welfare, Ministry of Munitions ; Head of

Women's Training Branch, Ministry of Labour. *Addresses :* Home Office, S.W. 1 ; 23, Clifton Hill, N.W. 8. (O752)

SQUIRE, Major Walter Ernest, M.B.E., R.A.M.C.

SQUIRES, Ernest Edward William, C.B.E., General Manager, Metropolitan Carriage, Wagon, and Finance Co., Ltd., of Birmingham. (C302)

SQUIRES, Capt. Thomas L., O.B.E.

SQUIRRELL, Joseph Cooper, M.B.E.

STABB, Ethel, Mrs., M.B.E.

STABB, Sir Newton John, Knt. Bach., O.B.E. Chief Manager of the Hong-Kong and Shanghai Banking Corporation, Hong Kong. (O1014)

STACEY, Fanny, M.B.E. ; *d.* of Charles Stacey, of Wickham Hall, Bishop Stortford. *Educ. :* Privately. *War Work :* Commandant of Herts 12 V.A.D. Hospital. *Address :* Wickham Hall, Bishop Stortford. (M970)

STACK, Paymaster-Comm. Alan Edward Stack, O.B.E., R.N.

STACK, Rev. Father James, O.B.E., C.S.S.R., *b.* 30 July 1880 ; *s.* of Richard Stack, of Drumcollogher, Co. Limerick, Ireland. *Educ. :* Jesuit Coll., Limerick, and Redemptorist Seminary, Mautern, Austria. *War Work :* Commissioned in Sept. 1914 as Temp. 4th Class Chaplain ; stationed at Fort Matilda, Greenock, for 2 months ; proceeded to France, Nov. 1914 ; promoted 2nd Class Chaplain, with rank of Lieut.-Col. Jan. 1917 ; appointed Deputy Assistant Principal Chaplain of 11th Corps ; wounded on Somme in Sept. 1916 ; mentioned in despatches four times. *Address :* St. Mary's, Kinnoull, Perth, Scotland. (O5798)

STACK, Major-Gen. Sir Lee Oliver Fitzmaurice, K.B.E., C.M.G., *b.* 15 May, 1868 ; *s.* of the late Oliver Stokes Stack ; *m.* Flora Center, *d.* of the late Edwin Ramsay Moodie. *Educ. :* Clifton Coll., and R.M.C. Sandhurst. R. of O., Sirdar of the Egyptian Army, and Governor-General of the Soudan ; formerly Capt. Border Regt. ; employed with Egyptian Army, 1899 ; D.A.A.G. 1900 ; A.A.G. 1901 ; Assist. Mil. Sec. to Sirdar, 1903 ; and subsequently Civil Secretary to the Sudan Government ; served in Sudan in command of Shambe Field Force, 1900–2 (medal with clasp) ; Order of Osmanieh, 4th class ; Order of the Nile, 1st class ; and Order of El Nahda of Hedjaz. *Address :* The Palace, Khartoum. *Club :* United Service. (K115)

STACK, Norah Blake, M.B.E., Q.M.A.A.C.

STACK, Susan, Mrs., M.B.E. ; *d.* of John Hanbury Masfen, of Bole Hall, Tamworth, Warwickshire ; *m.* Edward Churchill, *s.* of Charles Maurice Stack, late Lord Bishop of Clogher. *Educ. :* Privately. Poor Law Guardian ; Member of War Pensions Committee. *War Work :* Hon. Sec. Rurton Branch Comforts for Troops Fund. *Address :* The Soho, Burton-on-Trent. (M3990)

STACKE, Capt. Hedley Herbert, O.B.E.

STACPOOLE, Lieut.-Col. George William Robert, D.S.O., O.B.E., *b.* 27 May, 1872 ; *s.* of Richard John, of Eden Vale, Ennis. *Educ. :* St. Columbus, and Cheltenham Coll. *War Work :* A.P.M. successively of No. 1 Base, 2nd Division, and 5th Corps ; D.P.M., L. of C. Area. *Address :* Abbeyville, Groom, Co. Limerick. *Clubs :* Co. Limerick ; Kildare Street ; Army and Navy. (O2727)

STACY, Lieut.-Col. Valentine Osborne, O.B.E., Aust. A.M.C.

STADDON, Kate Elizabeth, Mrs., M.B.E.

STAFFORD, Lieut. Edward, M.B.E., *b.* 7 May, 1875 ; *s.* of William Stafford, of Sunderland ; *m.* Charlotte, *d.* of Edward Cooper, of Brentford. *Educ. :* Army Schools. Expert in Physical Exercises ; Instructor in Swimming and Life Saving. *War Work :* Draft Conducting Officer to 16th Durham L.I. in 1915 ; specially selected by Col. H. E. Deane, Commandant of the Croydon War Hospital, and placed in charge of the gymnasium to carry out his system of restoring function to the disabled limbs of wounded men. *Address :* 11, Bensham Manor Road, Thornton Heath, Surrey. (M5649)

STAFFORD, James William, M.B.E.

STAFFORD, John, M.B.E.

STAFFORD, Major Percy Beaumont, O.B.E.

STAFFORD, Lieut. Reginald Vernon, M.B.E.

STAFFORD, Capt. Waddington, O.B.E., R.A.S.C.

STAFFORD, Salvador GUATTARI-, O.B.E., *b.* 30 Dec. 1875 ; *s.* of Augustus Guattari. His Britannic Majesty's Consul at Savona, Italy. *War Work :* In charge of the British Vice-Consulate, Spezia, Italy ; work in connection with Transports. *Address :* British Vice-Consulate, Spezia, Italy. (O11368)

STAGG, Arthur George, M.B.E.

STAGG, Major George Ernest, M.B.E., R.A.F.

STAGG, Major Montague, O.B.E., R.E.

STAINFORTH, Gladys Margaret, M.B.E.

STAINFORTH, Capt. Rowland John, O.B.E.

STAINLAND, Alfred Edward, O.B.E., J.P.

STAINTHORP, Amy, M.B.E., *b.* 4 Nov. 1889 ; *d.* of Henry Stainthorp, of Nosterfield. *Educ. :* Mowbray House School, Northallerton. *War Work :* County Secretary British Red Cross Society, N. R. Yorks. Branch. *Address :* Northallerton, Yorkshire. (M9697)

STAINTHORPE, William Waters, O.B.E., M.D., J.P., *b.* 10 May, 1844 ; *s.* of Thomas G. Stainthorpe, of Hexham. *Educ. :* Hexham and Newcastle. Medical Officer of Health (retired). *War Work :* National Service Representative, Guisborough U. Council ; Member of Consultative Committee, North Riding War Saving Committee ; Organised War Savings Associations throughout the East Langbaurgh Petty Sessions Division ; assisted in obtaining recruits under Lord Derby's scheme ; advised and assisted the Military Authorities in matters connected with the sanitation of billets and camps, and with the health of the troops stationed in East Langbaurgh. *Address :* 15, Stirling Road, Bournemouth. (O11369)

STALKER, Lieut. John, O.B.E., R.E.

STALKER, John, M.B.E., *b.* 5 Oct. 1848 ; *s.* of George Stalker, of Blair Drummond ; *m.* Margaret, *d.* of William Stewart, of Strathbraan. *Educ. :* Kincardine-in-Menteith Parish School, and E. C. Training Coll., Glasgow. Schoolmaster in Logiealmond for 38 years (retired). *War Work :* Member of Soldiers' and Sailors' Families Association, and of various Committees connected therewith ; Member of local War Pensions Committee for County of Perth, of Disablements Sub-Committee for Central Scotland, and of Pensioners Aid Society. *Address :* Bella Vista, Scone, Perthshire. (O8716)

STALLAN, Capt. Herbert Alfred, M.B.E., R.A., *b.* 21 Feb. 1875 ; *s.* of Alfred Stallan, of Sawston, Cambridge ; *m.* Carrie, *d.* of John Walker, of Norwich. *Educ. :* Cambridge. *War Work :* Mainly on the Staff of the War Office. *Address :* Bayfield, Mill Hill, Hadham, Herts. (M3316)

STALLARD, Lieut.-Col. Robert Humphry, O.B.E., R.E.

STALLARD, Lieut.-Col. Sidney, D.S.O., O.B.E. London Regt. ; served in S. Africa, 1901–2 (Queen's medal with five clasps, King's medal with two clasps) ; Great War, 1914–19 (despatches) ; has Legion of Honour. (O5803)

STALLEY, Ernest Alfred, M.B.E.

STALLYBRASS, William Teulon Swan, O.B.E., M.A., *b.* 22 Nov. 1883 ; *s.* of William Swan Stallybrass, of 20, Linden Gardens, London, W. 2. *Educ. :* Westminster, and Christ Church, Oxford. Barrister-at-Law ; Fellow and Vice-Principal of Brasenose Coll., Oxford ; Hon. Treas. Oxford Univ. Cricket Club ; Lecturer in Jurisprudence at Oriel and Lincoln Colleges, Oxford ; Examiner in the Honour School of Jurisprudence, 1915, 1918–20. *War Work :* 1915, Badges Department, Ministry of Munitions ; 1916–18, Section Director, Priority Department, Ministry of Munitions. *Address :* Brasenose College, Oxford. *Clubs :* Royal Automobile ; Frilford Heath Golf. (O1885)

STAMBERG, Major Arthur Clement, O.B.E., M.D., R.A.M.C.

STAMER, Arthur Cowie, C.B.E., M.I.M.E., *b.* 7 March, 1869 ; *s.* of the late Rt. Rev. Sir L. T. Stamer, Bt., Bishop of Shrewsbury ; *m.* Everilda Mary, *d.* of the late G. Thompson, of Terrington Hall, York. *Educ. :* Rugby. Assistant Chief Mechanical Engineer, North Eastern Railway. *War Work :* Acting Chief Mech. Engineer for N. E. Rly. for 3½ years ; responsible for production of shells, gun carriages, and other munitions of war in addition to usual duties of Chief Mech. Engineer of a Railway Co. *Address :* Faverdale, Darlington. *Club :* Yorkshire. (C2968)

STAMFORD, Emma Pauline, Mrs., O.B.E.

STAMFORD, Penelope, Countess of, O.B.E. ; 3rd *d.* of the Rev. Canon Charles Theobald, Rural Dean of Lasham, Hants ; *m.* William, 9th Earl of Stamford (d. 1910) (*see* BURKE'S *Peerage*). *War Work :* Vice-President for Altrincham Division of B.R.C. from 1911 ; President of Prisoners of War Packing Centre, and President of Union Jack Club in Altrincham for wounded soldiers ; Commandant of Stamford Hospital for wounded men, at Dunham Massey Hall. *Address :* Dunham Massey Hall, Altrincham. *Club :* Ladies' Empire. (O11371)

STAMMERS, Capt. Frederick Gunning, O.B.E.

STAMMERS, Lieut.-Col. George Elliott Frank, O.B.E., R.A.M.C. (retired), *b.* 13 Feb. 1873 ; *s.* of the late Lieut.-Col. R.T.F. Stammers, 10th Foot ; *m.* Constance Louisa, *d.* of the late Dr. J. R. Clarke, of Derrycappagh, Mount Mellick, Queen's Co., Ireland. *Educ. :* Bath Coll., and Bristol Univ. Deputy Director, Wellcome Bureau of Scientific Research, 25–27, Endsleigh Gardens, Gordon Square, N.W. 1. *War Work :* With the British Military Mission to the Serbian Army for preventive work against Typhus Fever ; A.D.M.S. (Sanitation) with P.D.M.S., Eastern Mediterranean ; A.D.M.S. (Sanitation), G.H.Q., Salonika Expeditionary Force ; D.A.D.M.S. (Sanitation), Alexandria District, Egypt ; A.D.M.S. (Sanitation), G.H.Q., Egyptian Expeditionary Force. *Address :* c/o Messrs. Holt & Co., 3, Whitehall Place, S.W. 1. (O2934)

STAMP, Major Arthur Frederick, O.B.E., R.F.A.

STAMP, Sir Josiah Charles, K.B.E., D.Sc., *b.* 21 June, 1880 ; *s.* of Charles Stamp, of Sidcup ; *m.* Olive Jessie, *d.* of Alfred Marsh, of Grove Park. *Educ. :* London Univ. (Cobden Prizeman, 1912 ; Hutchinson Research Medallist, 1916 ; Guy Medallist, Royal Statistical Society, 1919). Assist. Sec. Inland Revenue, resigned March, 1919 ; Sec. to Explosives Trades, Ltd., 1919 ; Joint Hon. Sec. and Editor Royal Statistical Society ; Newmarch Lecturer on Statistics, London Univ. ; Examiner in Public Finance, etc., to London Univ. ; Examiner in Economics and Statistics to Soc. of Incorp. Accts. and Auditors. *War Work :* Official duties in Parliament upon all the Budgets, especially in relation to the Excess Profits Duty, and also Coal Mines Control ; Member of the Committee upon Financial Risks attaching to Trading Stocks, and member of the Royal Commission upon the Income Tax. Evidence before various commissions, including the Coal Commission and War Wealth Taxation Committee. *Address :* Passeys House, Eltham, S.E. 9. *Clubs :* Junior Athenæum ; London Univ. (K462)

STAMPE, Bernard Coatsworth, M.B.E.

STANBURY, Lieut. Ernest Borland, M.B.E., Aust. E.

STANBURY, George Crocker, M.B.E.

STANDAGE, Capt. Henry Edmund, O.B.E.

STANDEN, Oona, Mrs., O.B.E.

STANDING, Comm. Sir Guy, K.B.E., R.N.V.R., *b.* 1873 ; *s.* of James Herbert Standing, of London and Los Angeles, U.S.A. ; *m.* Dorothy Frances, *d.* of Joshua Plaskitt, F.R.C.S. *Educ. :* Eltham Coll. Served with R.N.V.R., 1914–16 ; has been attached to Naval Intelligence Div. since 1916. *Address :* 21, Greycoat Gardens, S.W. 1. *Clubs :* Garrick ; Royal Automobile. (K234)

STANDISH, Major William Percy, O.B.E.

STANFORD, Major Frederick Owen, O.B.E., R.E.

STANFORD, Col. the Hon. Sir Walter Ernest Mortimer, K.B.E., C.B., C.M.G., *b.* 2 Aug. 1850 ; *s.* of the late William Stanford, of Buck Kraal, Fort Peddir, Cape Colony ; *m.* Alice, *d.* of Joseph Walker. *Educ. :* Lovedale, Cape Province. Senator of S. Africa since 1910 ; Garlika War, 1877–78 ; Col. Commanding Forces in East Griqualand, S. African War, 1899–1902 ; Member of Native Laws and Customs Commission, 1880–82 ; employed special service in Pondoland, 1884 ; Chief Magistrate Griqualand East, 1885 ; Sec. Native Affairs Dept., Capetown, 1897 and 1903–7, when he retired ; Chief Magistrate of Transkeian Territories, 1902–3 ; Member for Tembuland in Cape House of Assembly, 1908 ; Delegate from Cape Colony to] S. African National Convention, 1908–9. *War Work :* Director of War Recruiting and Committee for Returned Soldiers, Feb. 1918, to July, 1919. *Address :* Lindaric, Stellenbosh, S. Africa. *Club :* Civil Service (Cape Town). (K316)

STANFORD, Major William, O.B.E., R.F.A.

STANGER, Ernest William, O.B.E.

STANHOPE, Cicely, M.B.E., Q.M.A.A.C.

STANHOPE, Lieut. Colin Lundin, O.B.E.

STANHOPE, Adele, Hon. Mrs. Charles Hay SCUDAMORE-, O.B.E., *b.* 7 Jan. 1863 ; *d.* of the late Sir Robert Hay, Bart., of Haystoun ; *m.* Charles Hay, 6th *s.* of 9th Earl of Chesterfield (*see* BURKE'S *Peerage*). *War Work :* Chairman War Workers Committee, Y.W.C.A. ; Nat. Vice-President, Y.W.C.A. *Address :* 64, Queen's Gate, S.W. (O1887)

STANIER, William Henry, O.B.E., J.P. Wilts, *b.* 28 April, 1849 ; *s.* of Thomas Stanier, of Wolverhampton ; *m.* Susan Sophia, *d.* of Thomas Harris, of Calne. *Educ. :* Privately. Retired Stores Superintendent, Great Western Railway ; Alderman Wilts Co. Council. *War Work :* Assisted Railway Executive in distribution to British Rlys. of Timber and other controlled materials. *Address :* South Place, Calne, Wilts. *Club :* Nat. Liberal. (O11372)

STANION, Oliver Bown, O.B.E., *b.* 13 May, 1856 ; *s.* of the late Rev. Thomas Stanion, of Gt. Berkhamstead ; *m.* Mary, *d.* of William Stanyon, of Leicester. Yarn Merchant, Leicester. Chairman of The Eiderwear Co., Ltd., Leicester ; Director of The Leicester Permanent Building Society. *War Work :* Chairman Labour Advisory Committee, Leicester ; Member South Midlands and Eastern Divisional Council ; Chairman (Hon. Vice-President) Leicester Chamber of Commerce. *Address :* Norlands, Victoria Park Road, Leicester ; The Royal Colonial Institute, London. *Club :* The Leicestershire. (O11373)

STANISTREET, Col. (T. Major-Gen.) Sir George Bradshaw, K.B.E., C.B., C.M.G., B.A., M.B., B.Ch., Trin. Coll., Dublin, *b.* 13 May. 1866 ; *s.* of late Richard Stanistreet, M.D., of Malahide, Ireland. Joined R.A.M.C., 1891 ; Major 1903 ; Lieut.-Col. 1913 ; Col., 1917 ; T. Major-General, 1918 ; Personal Assistant to P.M.O., Punjab Command, 1896–1901. Staff Officer to P.M.O., Southern Command, 1906–10. *War Work :* Dep. Assist. Director-Gen., A.M.S., War Office, 1913–17 ; Assist. Director-Gen. 1917–18 ; Dep. Director-Gen. from 1918 ; Commander of Order of the Crown of Italy ; Esquire of the Order of St. John. *Club :* Junior United Service. (K285)

STANLEY, Hon. Sir Arthur, G.B.E., C.B., M.V.O., J.P., D.L. ; 3rd *s.* of 16th Earl of Derby (*see* BURKE'S *Peerage*). *Educ. :* Wellington Coll. Treas. St. Thomas's Hospital ; Chairman British Red Cross and St. John Ambulance. *War Work :* Red Cross. *Address :* Treasurer's House, St. Thomas's Hospital, S.E. *Clubs :* Royal Automobile ; Carlton ; Turf. (G8)

STANLEY, Arthur, M.B.E.

STANLEY, Beatrix Taylour, Lady, C.B.E. Hon. Sec., Lancashire Branch of the Soldiers' and Sailors' Families Association. (C3166)

STANLEY, Lieut. Ernest Raymond, O.B.E.

STANLEY, Capt. Herbert Vernon, M.B.E., M.C., R.A.M.C.

STANLEY, Major James, O.B.E.

STANLEY, Sir John, K.C.I.E., C.B.E., Q.C., J.P., *b.* 22 Nov. 1846 ; *s.* of the late John Stanley, of Armagh, Ireland ; *m.* Annic. *d.* of the late James Norris, of Bletchingley, Surrey. *Educ. :* Armagh Royal School ; Trinity Coll., Dublin. Barrister-at-Law ; Queen's Counsel, 1892 ; Bencher, King's Inns, Dublin, 1892 ; Hon. Bencher, 1898 ; Puisne Judge of High Court at Calcutta, 1898–1901 ; Chief Justice of High Court of N. W. Province, 1901–1911 ; Knight of Grace Order of St. John. *War Work :* Convener of Comforts Committee and afterwards Vice-Chairman of Indian Soldiers Fund, 1914–19. *Address :* 19, Gledhow Gardens, London, S.W. *Clubs :* Junior Carlton ; Ranelagh ; Univ. Dublin. (C1092)

STANLEY, Lieut.-Col. Joseph Henry, C.B.E., F.R.G.S., J.P., *b.* 16 May, 1864 ; *s.* of John Stanley, J.P., of Calcutta. *Educ. :* Privately. Deputy Commissioner, British Red Cross,

Mesopotamia; Vice-President, Church Army. *War Work:* Served in France, Oct. 1914–16, and in Mesopotamia from Jan. 1917. to March, 1919. *Club:* Royal Societies'. (C634)

STANLEY, Leonard, M.B.E.
STANLEY, Capt. and Qr.-Mr. Robert, M.B.E.
STANLEY, Capt. Robert Vinin Stanley, O.B.E., R.A.S.C.
STANLEY, Rowland John, M.B.E.
STANLEY, Capt. William Blakeney, M.B.E.
STANLEY, Olivia Elizabeth, Mrs. SLOANE-, O.B.E.
STANNARD, Lieut. Frank Charles, O.B.E., D.C.M., R.F.A. (T.)
STANNUS, Lieut.-Col. Gerald Walter James Fitzgerald, O.B.E.
STANSFIELD, Lieut.-Col. Cyril Grey, O.B.E.
STANSFIELD, George Sutcliffe, O.B.E., M.R.C.S., L.R.C.P., *b.* 29 Oct. 1849; *s.* of James Stansfield, of Bacup; *m.* Oceana, *d.* of Capt. E. Graham, of Birkenhead. *Educ.:* Privately, and Manchester Royal School of Medicine. Consulting Surgeon, Birkenhead Boro' Hospital; late Superintendent Birkenhead Union Infirmary. *War Work:* M.O.-incharge Tranmere Military Hospital, 420 beds, with full equipment for operative and X-ray work. (O11849)
STANSFIELD, Capt. Harold, M.B.E., R.A.F.
STANSFIELD, Col. James Rawdon, C.B., C.B.E., *b.* 11 Aug. 1866; *s.* of the late Lieut.-General T. W. Stansfeld, of Indian Staff Corps; *m.* Eleanor Susan, *d.* of the late William Martineau, M.I.C.E. *Educ.:* Cheltenham Coll., R.M. Academy. Royal Artillery; Instructor and Chief Instructor Ordnance College, 1901–4; Assistant Inspector, Inspection Department, 1904–5; Inspector, 1905–6, and 1908–12; Chief Inspector, Woolwich, 1913. *War Work:* Chief Inspector, Woolwich, till April, 1916; Deputy Director-General, Ministry of Munitions, 1916–19. *Address:* c/o Messrs. Cox & Co., Charing Cross. *Club:* United Service. (C1722)
STANSFIELD, John Firth, M.B.E. (M10254)
STANSFIELD, Louis Donald, M.B.E.
STANSFIELD, Lieut.-Col. Thomas Edward Knowles, C.B.E., M.B., *b.* 1862; *s.* of Thomas Stansfield; *m.* 1908, Mary Caroline, *d.* of James Dever. Resident Physician and Superintendent of London County Mental Hospital at Bexley; Hon. Lieut.-Col. R.A.M.C. *Address:* Baldwin's Park, Bexley. *Club:* Royal Automobile. (C1773)
STANTON, Charles Butt, C.B.E., J.P., M.P. for Aberdare. (C3164)
STANTON, Ernest William, M.B.E., *b.* 7 June, 1872; *s.* of George Stanton, of Remenham, Berks.; *m.* Ethel, *d.* of William John Stuart, of Upper Warlingham. *Educ.:* Henley School. Manager, The National Provincial and Union Bank of England, Limited, Hythe, Kent. *War Work:* Hon. Sec. Hythe War Savings Committee; Hon. Auditor, local War Pensions Committee. *Address:* The Hut, Hythe, Kent. *Club:* Hythe. (M9702)
STANTON, Capt. Frederick William, M.B.E., A.S.C.
STANTON, Harold Westwood, O.B.E., B.A. Hons. (Lond.), *b.* 2 Nov. 1882; *s.* of James Stanton, of Tipton, Staffordshire. *Educ.:* King Edward's School, Birmingham, and London Univ. Solicitor; Deputy Town Clerk of Woolwich; Deputy Executive Officer to the Woolwich Food Control Committee. *Address:* Town Hall, Woolwich, S.E. 18. (O11375)
STANTON, Helen, M.B.E., *d.* of the late John Underwood Stanton, of Northampton. *Educ.:* Bedford. *War Work:* Member of Committee of Soldiers' and Sailors' Families Association, and Local War Pensions. *Address:* 4, Billing Road, Northampton. (M9703)
STANTON, Capt. Reginald, O.B.E., Gen. List. (O11885)
STANTON, Major Reginald William Starkey, O.B.E., late K. O. Yorks. L.I., *b.* 28 Aug. 1877; *s.* of the late Gen. Sir Edward Stanton, K.C.B., K.C.M.G.; *m.* Margaret Ursula, *d.* of the late Lieut.-Col. H. F. Hill, Essex Regt. *Educ.:* Marlborough and Sandhurst. *War Work:* Served with 2nd K. O. Yorks L.I. in France, Sept. to Oct. 1914, including Battle of Aisne; severely wounded, Oct. 1914; 7th K.O. Yorks L.I., April to June, 1915; D.A.A. and Q.M.G. Plymouth Garrison, June, 1915, to Jan. 1916; D.A.A.G. 59th Division, Jan. 1916, to Nov. 1918, including Sein Fein Rebellion, 1916; B.E.F. France, Feb. 1917, to Nov. 1918; D.A.A.G. 17th Corps, B.E.F., Nov. 1918, to Dec. 1918; D.A.A.G. Military Governor, Cologne, Dec. 1918, to Feb. 1919; three times mentioned in despatches. *Address:* Kittoes, Bishops Teignton, S. Devon. *Club:* Army and Navy. (O2731)
STANTON, Thomas Ernest, C.B.E., D.Sc., F.R.S., *b.* 12 Dec. 1865; *s.* of Thomas Stanton, of Atherstone; *m.* Martha Grace, *d.* of John Child, of London. *Educ.:* Owen's Coll. Manchester. Superintendent of Engineering Department, National Physical Laboratory. *Address:* St. Lucia, Hampton Road, Teddington. *Club:* Royal Automobile. (C2969)
STANWORTH, James, M.B.E.
STAPLE, Rev. Richard, M.B.E., M.A., *b.* 22 Jan. 1879; *s.* of the late W. W. Staple; *m.* Hyacinth Margaret Louisa Finch Hatton, *d.* of the late Hugh Fraser, of Achnagairn, J.P., D.L., Inverness-shire. *Educ.:* Privately, and Magdalen Coll., Oxford. Vicar of Lympne with West Hythe. *War Work:* Head Special Constable, Canterbury, 1914–18; Hon. Recruiting Officer, Canterbury, 1915–16; Military Representative, Canterbury Sub-Area, 1916–17; Hon. Sec. Canterbury War Pensions Committee, 1917–18. *Address:* Lympne Vicarage, Hythe, Kent. (M974)
STAPLEDON, Reginald George, M.B.E.

STAPLETON, Capt. Edward Parker, O.B.E., R.A.F.
STAPLETON, Frederick, M.B.E.
STAPLETON, May COTTON-, M.B.E. In 1917 took entire charge of Ministry of Pensions correspondence upon individual cases of tuberculosis. (M10355)
STAPLEY, Frank Robert, O.B.E.
STAPYLTON, Capt. Martyn Frederic, O.B.E., R.N.
STAPYLTON, Lieut.-Col. Miles John, O.B.E.
STAR, Surg.-Comm. Paul Hohling Mills, O.B.E.
STARBUCK, Thomas William Charles, M.B.E., *b.* 7 Feb. 1890; *s.* of Walter Starbuck, of Doncaster; *m.* Lily, *d.* of David Piggott, of Sheffield. *Educ.:* Doncaster. Ensign Salvation Army. *War Work:* Control of S.A. Hostels at Dunkerque, Paris, and with 4th Army in Belgium. *Addresses:* Rockley, near Retford, Notts; Spansyke Street, Doncaster. (M3992)
STARK, Frank Tapscott, M.B.E.
STARK, James, O.B.E.
STARK, John, O.B.E.
STARK, John, O.B.E.
STARKEY, Capt. Dickinson, O.B.E., R.A.V.C.
STARKEY, Henry Samuel Crichton, O.B.E., R.A.M.C. (T.).
STARKEY, Capt. Herbert James, O.B.E., R.E.
STARKEY, Margaret, Mrs., M.B.E., Q.M.A.A.C.
STARLING, Lieut.-Col. John, O.B.E., R.A.F.
STARLING, John Henry, O.B.E.
STARNES, Major Fred, D.S.O., O.B.E.
STARR, Lieut. Frank John, O.B.E.
STARR, Major Frederick Newton Gisborne, C.B.E., R.A.M.C. Served in the Great War, 1914–19 (despatches). (C1328)
STARR, Col. William Henderson, C.B., C.M.G., C.B.E., *b.* 1861, Waziristan Exped. 1894–5 (medal with clasps); China, 1900 (medal); Mesopotamia, 1915–19 (despatches). (C1433)
STARRATT, Lieut. Harry Joseph, M.B.E., Can. C.C.B.
STARTIN, Lieut. Robert Arthur, O.B.E., A.M., R.N.
STATHAM, Col. John Charles Baron, C.M.G., C.B.E., *b.* 1872. Entered R.A.M.C. 1896; Capt. 1899; Major, 1907; Lieut.-Col. 1915; Col. Army Medical Service, 1917; N.-W. Frontier of India, 1897–98 (medal with clasp); Great War, 1914–19, as A.D.M.S. (despatches). (C1239)
STATHAM, Reginald Samuel Sherard, O.B.E., *b.* 11 March, 1884; *s.* of the Rev. S. P. H. Statham, of Pendleton, Lancs.; *m.* Annie Maitland, *d.* of Rupert Sherwin, of Worcester. *Educ.:* Bradfield Coll., Berks.; Westminster and Bristol Medical Schools. Doctor of Medicine; Hon. Assist. Gynaecologist, Bristol Royal Infirmary; Demonstrator of Obstetrics, Bristol Univ. *War Work:* Mobilised, Aug. 1914, 3rd Field Amb., 1st Division; M.O. to 2nd Royal Munster Fusiliers, Oct. 1914, to May, 1915; Surgical Specialist, 5th Gen. Hospital, 1916–18; in charge Surgical Div., 6th Gen. Hospital, Aug. 1918, to Dec. 1919. *Address:* Ormlie, Clifton Down Road, Clifton, Bristol. (O8804)
STAUNTON, George Sydney, M.B.E.
STAUNTON, Capt. Hugh Geoffrey, C.B.E., R.D., R.N.R., *b.* 1892; *s.* of Henry Staunton, of Snelston Hall, Derbyshire. *War Work:* 1914–19, as Commodore of Convoys (despatches). (C1206)
STAVERT, Sir William Ewen, K.B.E., *b.* 9 April, 1861; *s.* of Robert McCall Stavert, of P. E. Island, Canada; *m.* Alma Kate, *d.* of Samuel Thomson, of Newcastle, N.B., Canada. *Educ.:* Summerside; P. E. Island Grammar School. Retired Banker. *War Work:* Canadian Red Cross, and later Director of Finance in Ministry of Information, London, England. *Address:* 33, Macgregor Street, Montreal, Canada. *Clubs:* Mount Royal, and St. James's, Montreal. (K251)
STAVERS, Lieut.-Col. John, M.V.O., O.B.E.
STAWELL, Roldolph de Salis, O.B.E., M.B., F.R.C.S.
STAYNER, Capt. Richard Winslow, C.B.E., D.S.O., M.C., Canadian Forces, *b.* 1877; *s.* of the late Rev. Thomas Laurence Stayner; *m.* 1911, Winifred Elga Russell. *Educ.:* Marlborough. Served in S. Africa, 1899–1901; Great War, 1915–18 (despatches) (C2213)
STEAD, Capt. Norman, M.B.E.
STEAD, William, M.B.E.
STEARNS, Major Cyril Ernest, O.B.E., K.R.R.C. (S.R.)
STEBBING, Henry Mark, M.B.E.
STEDMAN, Albert Douglas, M.B.E.
STEDMAN, Major Ernest Walker, O.B.E., R.A.F.
STEDMAN, Isabel Margaret, O.B.E.
STEEDS, Ethel Mary, M.B.E.
STEEGMANN, Surg.-Lieut.-Comm. Edward John, O.B.E., M.B., D.P.H., R.N.V.R.
STEEL, Alexander, O.B.E., J.P.
STEEL, Alfred Ernest, O.B.E.
STEEL, Capt. Charles Walter, M.B.E., *b.* 14 Feb. 1878; *s.* of John Henry Dixon Steel, of Blackheath and Lowestoft; *m.* Dorothy Margaret, *d.* of the late James Calban, of Greenwich. *Educ.:* Gt. Yarmouth Grammar School. Hon. Sec. Norwich Division, British Red Cross Society; Assist. Hon. Sec. Norwich Univ. Extension Society. *War Work:* O/C Transport, Norwich British Red Cross Society; Adjutant of Norfolk R.A.M.C. Volunteers. *Address:* 19, Cecil Road, Norwich. *Clubs:* Red Cross, and Masonic, Norwich. (M2475)
STEEL, Capt. Frank, O.B.E., R.A.F.
STEEL, Lieut. Gabriel, O.B.E., R.E.
STEEL, Air Commodore John Miles, C.M.G., C.B.E., *b.*

11 Sept. 1877; *s.* of Col. J. P. Steel, R.E. (ret.); *m.* Laura Kathleen, *d.* of the late William Sinclair Thomson, M.P. *Educ.:* Stubbington House, Fareham, and H.M.S. "Britannia." Late Capt. R.N. *War Work:* Royal Navy, Grand Fleet, 1914–17; Royal Naval Air Service, 1917–18; transferred to Royal Air Force, April, 1918; mentioned in Naval Despatches (Jutland). *Address:* Brook House, Chislehurst. *Club:* Junior Naval and Military. (C874)

STEEL, Major John Valentine, O.B.E., R.A.F.
STEEL, Lieut.-Col. Thomas Heron, O.B.E.,
STEELE, Alfred Lilburn, M.B.E.
STEELE, Arnold Francis, M.B.E.
STEELE, Major Charles Edward Beevor, O.B.E.
STEELE, Major Henry Squire, O.B.E.
STEELE, Major Gerald, O.B.E., *b.* 6 April, 1874; *s.* of Matthew Steele, of Frodsham, Cheshire; *m.* Maud, *d.* of William Mackinlay, of Wynard, S. India. *War Work:* France, 1914–17; North Russia, 1918–19. *Address:* 22, Emperor's Gate, S.W. 7. *Club:* Boodle's. (O3077)
STEELE, Lieut. Matthew Garvan, M.B.E., R.F.A.
STEELE, Reginald Johns, M.B.E., *b.* 25 Aug. 1881; *s.* of G. H. Steele, of Stroud, Glos.; *m.* Alice Mary, *d.* of T. A. Roberts, of Bradford. *Educ.:* Marling School, Stroud, and Leeds Univ. Head Chemist to Yarn Branch of the Bradford Dyers Association. *War Work:* Acted as Director of Textile Section of the Ministry of Food; this Department controlled the use of all edible starches and flours needed by the Textile and Adhesive Industry. *Address:* 2, Whetley Grove, Bradford. (M3994)
STEELE, Lieut. Thomas, M.B.E.
STEELE, W. H., C.B.E. Assist. and Acting Traffic Manager, Chinese Govt. Railways, Peking-Mukden Line. *Address:* Peking, China. (C635)
STEEN, Minnie, Mrs., M.B.E.
STEEN, Major Royston Dunbar, M.B.E., R.A.S.C.
STEER, Charles Robert, M.B.E.
STEER, Frank, M.B.E.
STEER, George Patrick, M.B.E., R.A.M.C.
STEGGALL, Capt. and Qr.-Mr. Robert Ernest, M.B.E.
STEIN, Charles, O.B.E., M.C.
STELLING, Lieut. Carl David, M.B.E.
STEMP, Major Charles Hubert, C.B.E.
STENHOUSE, James Wilson, M.B.E., M.B., M.R.C.S., L.R.C.S.
STENHOUSE, Lieut. Joseph Russell, O.B.E.
STENNING, Lieut.-Col. Henry Alexander, O.B.E., T.D.
STENNING, Jessie, M.B.E., *b.* 30 March, 1869; *d.* of Edward Stenning, of Beckenham, Kent. *Educ.:* Worcester Park, Surrey. Commandant Kent 86 V.A.D., B.R.C.S. *War Work:* British Red Cross Society, 1914–19; Acting as Qr.-Mr. at Christ Church V.A.D. Hospital, Beckenham (auxiliary to the Royal Herbert Woolwich), Oct. 1914, to July, 1918; Commandant of same until Jan. 1919. *Address:* Taversham House, Beckenham, Kent. (M9708)
STENNING, Lieut.-Col. John Frederick, C.B., C.B.E. T.D., *b.* 1868; *s.* of the late Edward Stenning, of Beckenham, Kent; *m.* Ethelwynne, *d.* of W. H. Alexander, of Oxton, Cheshire. Univ. Lecturer, Fellow, Tutor, Dean, and Librarian of Wadham Coll. Oxford; Lieut.-Col. Comdg. an Officers' Training Corps. (C1774)
STENNING, William Lees, M.B.E., J.P., *b.* 4 July, 1865; *s.* of William Stenning, of Redhill; *m.* Mary Elizabeth, *d.* of the Rev. James Schofield, of Westgate, Co. Durham. *Educ.:* Repton School. *War Work:* Divisional Officer under Timber Supply Department of Board of Trade. *Address:* Ranmore, Redhill, Surrey. (M3995)
STENSON, George Routledge, O.B.E.
STEPHEN, Major George Andrew, O.B.E., *b.* 15 April, 1879; *s.* of James A. Stephen, Solicitor and Bank Manager, Keith. *Educ.:* Blairlodge School, Stirlingshire; Aberdeen and Edinburgh Universities. Solicitor and Bank Manager, Keith, Banffshire. *War Work:* Mobilised Aug. 1914; Active Service, France, Nov. 1914, to Dec. 1915, in 1/6 Gordon Highlanders (T.F.); Instructional Staff, Machine Gun Corps; Commanding No. 2 (Res.) Batt. M.G.C. *Address:* Union Bank House. Keith. Banffshire. (O7737)
STEPHEN, Lieut.-Col. Guy Neville, O.B.E., R.A.M.C.
STEPHEN, Henry, O.B.E.
STEPHEN, Capt. Henry Brown Torrie, M.B.E.
STEPHEN, Henry Buckingham, M.B.E.
STEPHEN, Nancy Consett, M.B.E.
STEPHENS, Adelaide Charlotte Edith, Mrs., M.B.E., *b.* 3 Dec. 1880; *d.* of George Simpson, of Wray Park, Reigate; *m.* Peter Stuart, *s.* of Thomas Walls Stephens, of Downe House, Richmond. *Educ.:* Allenswood, Wimbledon Park. *War Work:* Sec. Soldiers' and Sailors' Families Association, Merstham; Member, Reigate Rural District Food Control Committee; Representative for Merstham for Women's Land Army; Vice-Chairman and subsequently Chairman of the Reigate Rural District War Pensions Committee. *Address:* Coppice Lea, Merstham, Surrey. *Club:* Halcyon. (M9709)
STEPHENS, Albert, M.B.E. (M10254f)
STEPHENS, Amy Frances Caroline, M.B.E., *b.* 2 July, 1879; *d.* of the late William Henry Stephens, R.N. *Educ.:* Leamington High School. Junior Administrative Assistant, Accountant-General's Dept., Admiralty, Whitehall. *War Work:* Assisted at Farnborough Court Red Cross Hospital; Canteen; and Prisoners of War Parcels Packing Depot, Farnborough. *Address:* Lincroft, Farnborough, Hants. (M2477)

STEPHENS, Charles Hoak, O.B.E.
STEPHENS, Edwin, M.B.E., *b.* 12 Feb. 1856; *s.* of the late John Stephens, Shipbuilder, of Carnon Yard, Feock, Cornwall; *m.* Jane Crozier, *d.* of William Cornish, Warrant Officer, R.N., of Devonport. 1878, joined the Government Service at Keyham Dockyard, Devonport, and after 17 years' in the drawing-office, Chief Engineer's Dept., selected for special duty at the Admiralty in connection with designs for foreign (extension works) for Gibraltar, Malta, etc.; after 4 years' service at Admiralty, appointed, March, 1901, Foreman of Engineering Branch H.M. Dockyard, Devonport; had charge under Chief Engineer, of Yard of new construction work, fitting out battleships and cruisers, such as "Lion" and other ships that fought in the Jutland Battle; on attaining the age of 60, owing to the war, was reappointed by the Admiralty to serve a further period during the war, and on retirement was awarded the Imperial Service Medal. *Address:* 10, St. John's Terrace, Devoran, Cornwall. (M9710)
STEPHENS, Einna Gwendolen, M.B.E.
STEPHENS, Major Francis Trant, O.B.E.
STEPHENS, Major Frank Harold, O.B.E., R.A.F.
STEPHENS, Surg.-Lieut.-Comm. Horace Elliot Rose, O.B.E., M.B., D.P.H., R.N.
STEPHENS, Lieut. Hubert Stanley, O.B.E., H.A.C. (T.F.)
STEPHENS, Capt. John Kyle, M.B.E., R.E.
STEPHENS, Lackhart, C.B.E., M.R.C.S., D.L.
STEPHENS, Major Leslie Nalder, O.B.E., R.A.
STEPHENS, Engr.-Capt. Lindsay James, C.B.E., R.N. Served in the Great War, 1914–19 (despatches). (C1942)
STEPHENS, Lieut. Sidney Francis Hood M.B.E., R.F.A., (S.R.)
STEPHENS, William Edgar, O.B.E., *b.* 31 Dec. 1871; *s.* of Thomas James Stephens, of Roath, Cardiff; *m.* Mary Elsie, *d.* of John Bevington, late of Barlaston, Staffs. *Educ.:* Monkton House School, Cardiff; South Wales Univ. Coll. Solicitor; Town Clerk, Great Yarmouth, Registrar; Borough Court of Record; Registration Officer; Hon. Clerk Distress Committee, Great Yarmouth. *War Work:* Clerk to Great Yarmouth Local Tribunal; Divisional Secretary Soldiers' and Sailors' Families Association, and Soldiers' and Sailors' Help Society; Hon. Clerk to Local War Pensions Committee; Member of East Anglian Joint Disablement Committee; Hon. Sec. and Organiser Great Yarmouth Vol. War Workers Association; Hon. Clerk Local Emergency Committee; Member Norfolk Emergency Committee; Hon. Clerk and Organising Sec. Local Committee for the Prevention and Relief of Distress; Special Constable; Member War Savings Committee. *Addresses:* The Greylands, Gorleston, Suffolk; The Town Hall, Great Yarmouth. *Clubs:* The Great Yarmouth Conservative; Great Yarmouth and Caister Golf. (O11382)
STEPHENS, William John, M.B.E., *b.* 15 March, 1882; *s.* of John Stephens, of Rhyddings, Neath; *m.* Ethel May, *d.* of Daniel Davies, C.E., of Neath. *Educ.:* Neath. Member of the Neath Rural District Council and the Board of Guardians. *War Work:* Acted for the Ministry of Munitions Labour Dept. as Chief Executive Officer for Wales. *Clubs:* Swansea and Counties. (M9712)
STEPHENSON, Major Basil, O.B.E., M.C., *b.* 14 April, 1880; *s.* of Reuben Stephenson, of Devonport; *m.* Joyce Edith, *d.* of Frederick William Higgins, of Chittagong, India. *Educ.:* Plymouth Coll., Plymouth. Banker, Imperial Bank of India and Bank of Bengal. *War Work:* Royal 1st Devon Yeomanry, Gallipoli, Egypt, Palestine, and L. of C. Palestine, E.E.F. *Addresses:* c/o Coutts & Co., London; Bank of Bengal, India. (O0298)
STEPHENSON, Gertrude, Mrs., M.B.E.
STEPHENSON, John, O.B.E.
STEPHENSON, Joseph, O.B.E., F.S.A.A., *b.* 9 May, 1882; *s.* of the late George Frederick Stephenson, of Harrogate; *m.* Emmeline Louise, *d.* of A. N. Bailey, of Peterboro'. *Educ.:* Privately. Fellow of the Society of Incorporated Accountants and Auditors; Elective Auditor City of Peterborough. *War Work:* Hon. Sec. and Treas. Soke of Peterboro' Red Cross and Voluntary Organisation Committees; Hon. County Sec. Soke of Peterborough National War Savings Committee; Executive Officer, Peterboro' and District Joint Executive Food Control Committee; Sec. of the Provincial Feeding Stuffs Committee for Peterboro' Area; Special Constable. *Address:* The Hollies, Eastfield, Peterboro'. *Clubs:* Junior Constitutional; Royal Automobile; City and Counties (Peterboro'). (O11383)
STEPHENSON, Marjory, M.B.E.
STEPHENSON, Philippa Anna Frederica, Mrs., O.B.E., *d.* of the late Colonel Gordon Watson, of 8, Cadogan Gardens, and Wydford House, Ryde; *m.* Major-Gen. Theodore Edward, C.B., *s.* of the Rev. Canon Stephenson, of St. Johns, Weymouth. Artist. *War Work:* Sec. of the Essex Regt. Prisoners of War Fund (collected £28,000); on Executive Committee of Soldiers' and Sailors' Help Society. *Address:* 75, Carlisle Mansions, S.W. 1. *Clubs:* Lyceum; Ladies' Army and Navy. (O3939)
STEPHENSON, Richard Henry, O.B.E.
STEPHENSON, Lieut.-Col. Robert, C.B.E., D.S.O.
STEPHENSON, Stanley George, O.B.E.
STERICKER, Capt. John, M.B.E., R.E.
STERICKER, Major Stanley, O.B.E.
STERLING, Thomas Smith, M.B.E.
STERN, Sir Albert Gerald, K.B.E., C.M.G. Lieut.-Col. Machine Gun Corps; was Commander Mechanical Warfare (Overseas and Allies) Dept. 1917–19. (K170)

STERN, Major Frederic Claude, O.B.E., M.C.

STERNDALE, Hilda, M.B.E. *War Work:* Deputy Administrator in Q.M.A.A.C., attached 40 Q.M.A.A.C. Depot Hostel, Handsworth Coll., Birmingham, as Company Commander; later, in charge of a Unit attached to Tractor Depot, Avonmouth. *Address:* The Green, Seaton Carew, County Durham. (M6710)

STERRY, Major John, O.B.E., M.R.C.S., L.R.C.P., R.A.M.C. (V.), *b.* 9 Jan. 1870; *s.* of John Sterry, of Nutfield, Surrey; *m.* Beatrice, *d.* of William Allen, of Leek, Staffordshire. *Educ.:* St. Bartholomew's Hospital. Fellow Royal Medical Society; F.Z.S.; Medical Officer of Holmesdale Cottage Hospital, and Sevenoaks Hip Hospital. *War Work:* Served abroad as Lieut. R.A.M.C.; Assistant County Director, Kent V.A.D.; Medical Officer, St. John's V.A.D. Hospital, Sevenoaks; Major R.A.M.C. (V.), Kent Field Ambulance. *Address:* Suffolk Place, Sevenoaks, Kent. *Clubs:* Royal Automobile; Flyfishers'. (O11384)

STERRY, Wasey, C.B.E., *b.* 1866; *e. s.* of the Rev. Francis Sterry, of Fort Hill, Barnstaple. *Educ.:* Eton, and Merton Coll. Oxford. Called to the Bar, Lincoln's Inn, 1892; appointed a Judge in Sudan, 1901; Chief Justice, 1905–17; Legal Sec. Sudan Govt. 1917; has 3rd class Medjidie; 2nd class of Order of the Nile. *Addresses:* Khartum, Sudan; Fort Hill, Barnstaple. *Club:* Savile. (C355)

STERT, Mabel, M.B.E., *b.* 9 April, 1866; *d.* of the late Rev. Arthur Richard Stert, of Cheltenham. *Educ.:* Ladies' Coll., Cheltenham. *War Work:* In Aug. 1914, helped to arrange homes for and to look after Belgian Refugees; worked for the Soldiers' and Sailors' Families Association and the Frome War Depot; in Oct. 1917, was appointed Hon. Sec. and Treas. to the War Pensions Sub-Committees, Frome, and held the post 2½ years. *Address:* Chosen House, Charlton Kings, Cheltenham. (M9713)

STEUART, James, O.B.E., M.A., J.P., *b.* 7 Sept. 1860; *s.* of Archibald Steuart, W.S., Edinburgh; *m.* Agatha, *d.* of Canon Francis Coulman Royds. *Educ.:* Edinburgh Academy, and Edinburgh Univ. Royal Company of Archers (King's Bodyguard for Scotland); Writer to the Signet; Senior Partner of J. C. and A. Steuart, W.S., 25, Rutland Street, Edinburgh; Director Eagle, Star, and British Dominions Insurance Co., Limited (Edinburgh Board); Member of London Committee of Zafra and Huelva Railway Company. *War Work:* Commander Edinburgh City Special Constables (Foot Section). *Addresses:* Crossways, Murrayfield, Midlothian; 25, Rutland Street, Edinburgh. *Club:* Caledonian United Service (Edinburgh). (O11385)

STEUART, Maud Anne Sophia, Mrs., M.B.E.; *d.* of Leut.-Gen. Chas. S. Steward, I.A.; *m.* Murray Babington, *s.* of George Steuart, Brig.-Gen. Royal Coy. of Archers, of Edinburgh. *War Work:* Hon. Sec. Kirkcudbright Local War Pensions Sub-Committee until a paid secretary was appointed; Representative in Kirkcudbright of the Soldiers' and Sailors' Families Association previous to and during the war. *Address:* Oakley, Kirkcudbright. (M9714)

STEVENI, Major Leo, O.B.E.. M.C.

STEVENS, Arthur Michael Bygholm, M.B.E., C.E., *b.* 2 March, 1872; *s.* of William Stevens, late of Bygholm, Denmark and London; *m.* Helga, *d.* of Balthazar Worm, of Aalborg, Denmark. *Educ.:* Crystal Palace Practical School of Engineering. Administrator Flax Supplies Committee, Belfast; Assist. and District Engineer Assam-Bengal Rly., India; Resident Engineer-in-charge, Barsi Light Rly., India; Engineer at Ironhirst Peat Works, Dumfries, Scotland. *War Work:* Senior Assist. Inspector of Munitions Areas, Ministry of Munitions; Engineer-in-Charge, Bettisfield Camp-Hutments, for Messrs. J. Norton Griffiths, Contractors for War Office. *Address:* c/o Messrs. Grindlay & Co., 54, Parliament Street, London. *Club:* Union (Belfast). (M9715)

STEVENS, Engr.-Capt. Charles, C.B.E., R.N., *b.* 1869; *s.* of the late James Stevens, of Moseley, near Birmingham. Served in the Great War, 1914–19 (despatches) (C1943)

STEVENS, Clement Henry, C.B.E., *b.* 1870; *s.* of the late G. J. B. Stevens, M.R.C.S., L.R.C.P., of Wadhurst House, Newington Green, S.E. Deputy Director of Shell Manufacture, June to Sept. 1917; Controller of Gun Ammunition since that date. (C66)

STEVENS, Edith, Mrs., O.B.E., *b.* 1873; *d.* of the late Rt. Hon. Sir Daniel Dixon, Bart, P.C., M.P., D.L., of Ballymenoch, Co. Down; *m.* Lieut.-Col. F. Stevens, C.B.E., D.L. *War Work:* Commandant of Aux. Hospital, 1914–19; organiser of Our Day (Bedford), 1915–16; a Lady of Grace of the Order of St. John of Jerusalem in England. *Address:* Clairmont, Shakespeare Road, Bedford. *Club:* Ladies' V.A.D. (O1889)

STEVENS, Major Edward James, O.B.E., R.A., Chevalier of the Legion of Honour. (O5807)

STEVENS, Lieut.-Col. Frank Augustus Douglas, C.B.E., *b.* 1877; *s.* of Col. F. E. Stevens, of Marlow; *m.* 1890, Edith, O.B.E., *d.* of the Rt. Hon. Sir Daniel Dixon, P.C., M.P., 1st Bt. Chief Constable of Beds; County Director and a D.L. for Bedfordshire; Chairman of its Territorial Force Association; Esquire of Order of St. John of Jerusalem in England. *Address:* Claremont, Shakespeare Road, Bedford. *Club:* Junior United Service. (C036)

STEVENS, Capt. Frank Douglas, O.B.E., M.G.C., E.L.

STEVENS, Frederick, O.B.E.

STEVENS, Frederick Charles, M.B.E., *b.* 9 Oct. 1876; *s.* of Frederick Stevens, of Hitchin; *m.* Florence Louisa, *d.* of Isaac Ivory, of Stevenage. *Educ.:* Hitchin Grammar School.

Printer and Stationer. *War Work:* Served with Bedfordshire Regt., also on the Staff of the War Cabinet, and the Staff of the Cabinet Offices. *Address:* 78, High Street, Stevenage, Herts. (M9716)

STEVENS, Major Frederick John, O.B.E., *b.* Feb. 6, 1883; *s.* of Lieut.-Col. S. J. Stevens, 16th Lancers, of Chiltley, Liphook, Hants. *Educ.:* King's College, London; Messrs. Adams and Millard, Freiburg, Barden, Germany. Farming. *War Work:* Was in the Special Reserve before the War; mobilised 4 Aug. 1914, and joined 4th Batt. P.W.O. West Yorkshire Regiment; served at home and on the Western Front; demobilised, 22 April, 1919. *Address:* Chiltley, Sopley, Christchurch, Hants.

STEVENS, Capt. George, O.B.E., R.A.F.

STEVENS, George Douglas, M.B.E., *b.* 6 May, 1858; *s.* of Henry George Stevens, of Islington, London, N.; *m.* Mary Ann Elizabeth, *d.* of Robert Keyte, of Tottenham, N. *Educ.:* Deal Coll. Formerly Assist. Manager and later Manager for the Chilworth Gunpowder Co., Ltd., at Chilworth, Guildford, Surrey, for 35 years. *War Work:* The manufacture of explosives for the Services. *Address:* Hill Top, Fort Road, Guildford, Surrey. (M0996)

STEVENS, Capt. Gordon. M.B.E., C.E., R.E., *b.* 19 Sept. 1893; *s.* of J. G. Stevens, of Hawkesbury, Upton; *m.* Kate, Alice, *d.* of Robert Street, of Northfleet. *Educ.:* Colston School, Bristol. Articled to H. T. Chapman, late County Surveyor of Somerset. *War Work:* Joined Inns of Court O.T.C., Dec. 1915; Commissioned R.E., Chatham, Sept. 1916; Salonica, Jan. 1917, to Dec. 1919. *Address:* Oldbury, Bower Mount Road, Maidstone. (M3235)

STEVENS, Harold Blythen, O.B.E.

STEVENS, Ida Kathleen, O.B.E.

STEVENS, James Algernon, C.I.E., O.B.E.

STEVENS, Engr.-Capt. John Greet, C.B.E. Served in the Great War, 1914–19 (despatches). (C1944)

STEVENS, Leonard Cording, O.B.E., *b.* 23 Nov. 1890; *s.* of the late Robert Stevens, of Timberscombe, Taunton; *m.* Nancy Lorna, *d.* of Col. H. N. V. Harington, I.M.S., of The Arrow Lakes, British Columbia. *Educ.:* Wellington, and London Univ. Schoolmaster and Tutor, Commanding 229th (Sussex) Battery, R.F.A. (T.). *War Work:* France (Sept. and Oct. 1914); India, Mesopotamia (1916–17); organised India's "Own Day," 1918, which brought £825,000 to Red Cross Funds; organised and carried out India's War Propaganda Campaign, 1918–19. *Address:* Chelmsford Hall, Eastbourne, Sussex. (O8307)

STEVENS, Patrick William Joseph, O.B.E.

STEVENS, Lieut. Reginald, M.B.E., R.E.

STEVENS, Lieut. Thomas Harry Gouldsworthy, O.B.E., R.E., I.A.R.O.

STEVENS, Walter William Spencer, M.B.E., R.N.

STEVENSON, Arnold, M.B.E.

STEVENSON, Capt. Bertrand James, O.B.E.

STEVENSON, Capt. Douglas Stuart, M.B.E., R.A.F.

STEVENSON, Eileen, Mrs., M.B.E., *b.* 28 May, 1870; *d.* of the late Charles Haugh, of Portlaw, Co. Waterford; *m.* David, *s.* of Hugh Stevenson, of Northland House, Londonderry. *Educ.:* Dublin. *War Work:* Hon. Co-Sec. Londonderry War Hospital Supply Depot, under Dir -Gen. Voluntary Organisations; Executive Committee Soldiers' and Sailors' Families Association, and Military and Naval War Pensions Committee, representing this committee on Regional Directors Court, Belfast; Sailors' and Soldiers' Free Buffets, etc. *Address:* The Collon House, Londonderry. (M9717)

STEVENSON, Comm. Ernest, O.B.E., R.N.

STEVENSON, Florence Johanna, Mrs., M.B.E.

STEVENSON, Frances Louise, C.B.E. Secretary to Prime Minister (Rt. Hon. D. Lloyd George, M.P.). (C305)

STEVENSON, Capt. George Henderson, O.B.E., M.C. R.A.M.C. (S.R.)

STEVENSON, Col. Harry Daniel Muhldoroff, O.B.E., M.C., I.A.

STEVENSON, Herbert Given, M.B.E.

STEVENSON, Hilda, M.B.E., *d.* of L. R. Stevenson, late 3rd Hussars. *War Work:* Second-in-charge of Red Cross Work Depot, Birkenhead; organiser and Head of Red Cross Gift House, Birkenhead. *Address:* 31, Beresford Road, Birkenhead. *Clubs:* Halcyon; Forum. (M9718)

STEVENSON, Rev. Hugh, M.B.E., M.A., *b.* 16 Feb. 1864; *s.* of Andrew Stevenson, of Belth, Ayrshire; *m.* Eleanor, *d.* of William Kennedy, M.A., LL.D., of Glasgow. *Educ.:* Tollcross Public School, Glasgow Univ., and Glasgow Free Church Coll. Minister, United Free Church, Dunblane; Member of the Parish Council of Dunblane and Lecroft; Member of the School Management Committee of the parishes of Ardoch and Dunblane and Lecroft. *War Work:* Patriotic Services in Scotland, specially in Recruiting, Derby Scheme, Military and National Service Representatives, and War Savings Campaigns. *Address:* East Manse, Dunblane. (M9719)

STEVENSON, Lieut. Ian Teacher, O.B.E., R.N.V.R.

STEVENSON, Major James, M.B.E., B.L., R.E. (T.), *b.* 2 March, 1883; *s.* of William Stevenson, of Glasgow; *m.* Suphronia Reynolds, *d.* of Richard Gleeson, of Toronto, Canada. *Educ.:* Kelvinside Academy, Glasgow. Advocate. *War Work:* Signals, R.E. *Address:* 20, Heriot Row, Edinburgh. (O2734)

STEVENSON, James Maxton, O.B.E.

STEVENSON, James Verdier, C.B.E., M.V.O., *b.* 1858;

Chief Constable of Glasgow; District Inspector, Royal Irish Constabulary, 1884–1902. (C637)

STEVENSON, John Horne, M.B.E., M.A., K.C., *b.* 1855; *s.* of the Very Rev. Robert Horne Stevenson, of St. George's Parish, Edinburgh. *Educ.:* Edinburgh. Unicorn Pursuivant; Knight of Justice, Order of St. John of Jerusalem in England; Member of the Royal Company of Archers (King's Body Guard for Scotland); Member of Educational Authority, Edinburgh. *War Work:* With the Red Cross, and as a Munition worker. *Address:* 9, Oxford Terrace, Edinburgh. *Clubs:* Caledonian; Conservative (Edinburgh). (M2479)

STEVENSON, John Proctor, M.B.E., *b.* 29 Dec. 1882; *s.* of John Powell Stevenson, of Cardiff; *m.* Ellen, *d.* of A. Rowe. *Educ.:* Priory Upper Grade School, Gt. Yarmouth, and City Municipal Secondary School, Cardiff. Accountant, H.M. Stationery Office. *War Work:* As Deputy Supt. of Stores, H.M. Stationery Office, Member of Treasury Committee on office machinery, and one of H.M.S.O. members on Staff of British Delegation at Peace Conference, Paris. *Address:* 4, Hillbrow, New Malden, Surrey. (M9720)

STEVENSON, May Margaret, O.B.E.

STEVENSON, Major Robert, O.B.E., M.C., R.A.O.C.

STEVENSON, Capt. Robert Little, M.B.E., R.A.F.

STEVENSON, Samuel, M.B.E., J.P·

STEVENSON, Thomas Henry Craig, C.B.E., *b.* 1870; *s.* of James Stevenson, of Strabane, Co. Tyrone; *m.* Ella Louise, *d.* of Samuel Sillifant, of Cardiff. *Educ.:* Univ. Coll., London. Superintendent of Statistics, General Register Office; Fellow (Guy gold medallist) and formerly Hon. Sec. of the Royal Statistical Society; Fellow of Univ. Coll. *War Work:* Member of Reserved Occupations and Enemy Personnel Committees; employed on National Register and recruiting statistics. *Address:* General Register Office, Somerset House, W.C. 2. (C306)

STEVENSON, Major Walter Ormond, O.B.E., Aust, A.S.C.

STEVENSON William King, O.B.E., B.A., *b.* 10 Nov. 1891; *s.* of the late Samuel Brown Stevenson, of Glencregagh, Belfast. *Educ.:* Methodist Coll., Belfast, and Trinity Coll. Dublin. *War Work:* Engaged during the first half of 1916 in recruiting work in the Northern Area of Ireland; Sept. 1916, appointed Hon. Treas. of the Ulster Women's Gift Fund for Men on Active Service and Prisoners of War; this Fund, which, apart from its activities on behalf of Men on Active Service, was responsible for the support of some 4000 Prisoners of War, reached a total of £120,000. *Address:* Glencregagh, Belfast. (O11388)

STEVENSON, William March, C.B.E., *b.* 31 March, 1864; *s.* of W. H. Stevenson, of Millside House, Dorking; *m.* Cecilia Violet, *d.* of Arthur S. Hanson, M.D., of Titchfield, Hants. *Educ.:* Queen Elizabeth's Grammar School, Southwark. General Managers' Assistant, Lloyds Bank, Limited. *War Work:* Financial Adviser, Finance Section, Ministry of Blockade, 1916–17; attached to British Embassy, Washington, in advisory capacity, 1917–18. *Address:* Rookwood, Dorking, Surrey. (C638)

STEVENSON, Stansmore Leslie Dean, Mrs. MACAULAY- M.B.E.; *d.* of A. D. Dean, of Glasgow; *m.* Robert, *s.* of John Stevenson, of Glasgow. *War Work:* Ran the Scottish Hut at G.H.Q., Montreuil-sur-Mer. *Addresses:* Robinsfield-by-Milngavie, Glasgow; Montreuil-sur-Mer, France. (M3998)

STEWARD, Alexandrina Ryrie, O.B.E.

STEWARD, Lieut. Charles Arthur Cholmley, M.B.E., M.C.

STEWARD, Major Edward Merivale, O.B.E., S. and T. Co. (O11767)

STEWARD, Col. Godfrey Robert Viveash, C.B.E., D.S.O., *b.* 1881; *s.* of Maj.-Gen. Edward Harding Steward, C.M.G. *Educ.:* Wellington Coll., and R.M.C. Entered Roy. Inniskilling Fusiliers, 1899; became Capt. 1905; Major, 1915; Brevet Lieut.-Col., 1917; served in the S. African War, 1899–1902; present at relief of Ladysmith (severely wounded, Queen's medal with three clasps, King's medal with two clasps); in the Great War, 1914–19 (severely wounded, despatches, Brevet Lieut.-Col.); appointed to command a Labour Batt., 1918, with rank of Col. *Club:* United Service. (C1330)

STEWARD, Lieut.-Col. Reginald Holden, O.B.E., *b.* 12 Feb. 1866; *s.* of the Rev. Charles Holden Steward, of Northway House, near Tewkesbury; *m.* Alexanduria Ryrie Steward, *d.* of James Scott Rome, of West Dingle, near Liverpool. *Educ.:* Haileybury Coll. *War Work:* Commanding Troops, Devizes. *Address:* Rockley House, Devizes. *Club:* Primrose. (O7743)

STEWARD, William Arthur Briault, M.B.E., A.M.I.Mech.E., *b.* 7 Nov. 1881; *s.* of William Steward of London; *m.* Louisa Ada, *d.* of Joseph Risley, of London. *Educ.:* East London Coll. Engineer; before the war attached to Chief Mechanical Engineer's Dept., Midland Railway, Derby; now London Manager, Société Genevoise d'Instruments de Physique, Geneva. *War Work:* Section Director, Gun Ammunition Manufacture Dept., Ministry of Munitions of War, London. *Addresses:* 95, Queen Victoria Street, London, E.C. 4; 14, Chester Rd., Southend-on-Sea, Essex. (M9721)

STEWARD, Lily Mrs. GORDON-, M.B.E.

STEWART, Agnes Paterson, Mrs., M.B.E.

STEWART, Lieut.-Col. Albert Fortescue, C.M.G., O.B.E., Suffolk Regt., *b.* 30 March, 1868; *s.* of Sir John Marcus Stewart 3rd Bt., D.L. (*see* BURKE'S *Peerage*); *m.* 3 July, 1902, Rita, 3rd *d.* of the late Right Hon. Jonathan Christian, Lord Justice

of Appeal in Ireland Served in S. Africa, 1901–2 (despatches medal with clasp); in the Great War, from 1914 (despatches, brevet); Chevalier of the Order of Leopold of Belgium. (O7744)

STEWART, Lieut.-Col. Alexander Brodie Seton, O.B.E., R.A.M.C. (T.).

STEWART, Alice Margaret, Lady, O.B.E., *b.* 1863; *d.* of John Christie, of Cowden, Perthshire; *m.* Sir Robert King, *s.* of R. Stewart, of Murdostoun. Vice-President, Franco-Scottish Society. *War Work:* Deputy Chairman, Lanarkshire Red Cross Committee; Commandant, Hartwoodhill Auxiliary Hospital (opened Dec. 1914, closed 1919); Member Scottish Branch War Executive and V.A.D. Committees. *Address:* Murdostoun Castle, Newmains, N.B. *Clubs:* Empress; Queen's (Edinburgh); Kelvin (Glasgow). (O766)

STEWART, Angus, O.B.E., J.P., C.C., *b.* 17 Sept. 1852; *s.* of John Stewart, of Drumchork, lately Westar Tempar, Rannoch, Perthshire. *Educ.:* Parish School, Gairloch. Farmer, Estate Factor, County and Parish Works, and Piermaster at Aultbea, where the Admiralty established a Naval Base, at the outbreak of the war. *War Work:* Chairman of the Western District Committee of Ross and Cromarty and Sub-Committee of the Local War Pensions Committee; Member of Food Control Committee, Western Ross Tribunal and Health Insurance, and Governor of the North of Scotland Coll. of Agriculture. *Address:* Zetville, Aultbea, Ross-shire. (O11389)

STEWART, Major Angus Matheson, M.B.E., R.E.

STEWART, Comm. Archibald Thomas, O.B.E., R.N., *b.* 10 Jan. 1876; *s.* of Col. T. B. Stewart, 30th Regt. and A.S.C., retired; *m.* Agnes Herbert, *d.* of the late James B. Thorpe, of The Hut, Port Erin, Isle of Man, and Sandywood, Pendlebury, Lancs. *Educ.:* Dover Coll., and H.M.S. "Britannia." *War Work:* H.M.S. "Cornwallis," 1914–17; served throughout Dardanelles Campaign, Egypt, and Eastern Mediterranean; Staff of S.N.O., Malta; appointed Port Convoy Officer and British S.N.O. at Bizerta, 1917–19; Chevalier Legion d'Honneur; Commander of the Order of the Nichan Iftikar (Tunis); 1914–15 Star, General Service Medal, Victory Medal. *Address:* Heathfield, Winchmore Hill, Middlesex. (O1890)

STEWART, Capt. Arthur Courtenay, C.B.E., R.N. (ret.), *b.* 1 May, 1871; *s.* of Charles Patrick Stewart, of Silwood Park, Sunningdale, Berks (*see* BURKE'S *Peerage*, Galloway, E); *m.* 18 Jan. 1911, Gwendolyn Marion, *d.* of Waldo Story, of Rome. *Address:* Ashby Manor, Box, Wilts. (C2274)

STEWART, Athole Chalmers, O.B.E., *b.* 25 June, 1879; *s.* of the late George Stewart, of Grange Park, Ealing; *m.* Ellen Frances, *d.* of the late Gen. W. S. Hatch, R.A. *War Work:* Entered Foreign Office, April, 1915, as temporary clerk; head of Telegram Section of the Parliamentary Dept. on his retirement, Dec. 1918. *Address:* 6, Coulson Street, Chelsea, S.W. 3. *Clubs:* Beefsteak; Garrick. (O767)

STEWART, Major Aubrey George Battersby, O.B.E., R.A.O.C.

STEWART, Lieut.-Col. Charles, O.B.E.

STEWART, Charles, O.B.E.

STEWART, Charles, M.B.E., *b.* 2 Aug. 1881; *s.* of William Stewart, of Carnoustie; *m.* Jessie Ferguson, *d.* of William Ducat, of Warslap, Arbroath. *Educ.:* St. Salvador's School, Dundee. Chartered Accountant, holding public appointments under Scottish Office and Board of Public Health; Registrar for the Diocese of Brechin. *War Work:* Treas. Red Cross Society and Transport Officer in Charge of Personnel. *Addresses:* 234, Ferry Road, Dundee; 2, Union Street, Dundee. *Clubs:* New (Dundee); Elliott and Caledonia Golf. (M9723)

STEWART, Sqdn.-Leader Charles John, O.B.E., R.A.F.

STEWART, Sir Charles John, K.B.E., *b.* 28 June, 1851; *s.* of J. Vandeleur Stewart, of Rockhill, Co. Donegal; *m.* Lady Mary Catherine, *d.* of 3rd Earl of Norbury (*see* BURKE'S *Peerage*). *Educ.:* Harrow. Barrister-at-Law; Official Receiver Companies; Clerk of the London County Council; Public Trustee. *War Work:* Custodian of Enemy Property; Member of Enemy Debts Committee; Assisted in War Savings Movement and Economy Campaign and Exhibitions; assisted formation of and appointed by War Office, member of Central Committee of Volunteers. *Addresses:* 24, Eccleston Square, S.W. 1; Rockhill, Co. Donegal, Ireland. *Club:* Junior Carlton. (K105)

STEWART, Capt. Charles Ravenscroft, O.B.E., R.A.M.C.

STEWART, Donald Alexander, M.B.E., *b.* 30 Sept. 1877; *s.* of Ewen Stewart, J.P., of Kinlochiel; *m.* Jeannie, *d.* of the Rev. Donald MacMaster, of Islay. *Educ.:* Kinlochiel and Fort William Schools. *War Work:* Acted from Jan. 1916, till April, 1920, under the Home-Grown Timber Committee (Board of Agriculture and Fisheries), War Office, and the Board of Trade (Timber Supply Department) as Superintendent of Works in Scotland. *Addresses:* St. John's House, Oban, Kinlochiel, Inverness-shire. (M9724)

STEWART, Major Donald Maciver, O.B.E., R.E., Officer of the Order of Leopold of Belgium.

STEWART, Duncan, M.B.E., V.D., L.R.C.P., L.R.C.S.

STEWART, Sir Edward, K.B.E., M.D., J.P., D.L., *b.* 16 Feb. 1857; *s.* of William Edward Stewart, F.R.C.S., late of 16, Harley Street, W.; *m.* Lady Philippa, *d.* of Henry Granville, 14th Duke of Norfolk (*see* BURKE'S *Peerage*). *War Work:* Surgeon to S. African Field Force in Boer War (Queen's Medal with 3 clasps); Medical Assessor to Joint Commission (Red Cross and St. John of Jerusalem); France, 1914–18 with rank of Hon. Lieut.-Col. R.A.M.C. *Address:* 34, Connaught Square, London, W. 2. *Club:* Junior Carlton. (K38)

STEWART, Edward Pakenham, M.B.E., *b.* 18 April, 1870; *s.* of the Rev. John Alexander Stewart, M.A., T.C.D., of Clooney, Co. Derry; *m.* Amy Eliza, *d.* of W. Postill, of Painswick, Glos. *Educ.:* Royal School, Armagh, and privately. Civil Servant in Directorate of Movements and Quartering. *War Work:* Movements of troops by sea, including all shipping arrangements (in conjunction with Admiralty) connected with Dardanelles Expedition; later conveyance of stores and ammunition to and from all stations abroad other than cross-Channel. *Address:* 5, St. George's Mansions, London, S.W. 1. (M3999)

STEWART, Elizabeth Woodhead, Mrs., M.B.E., V.A.D.

STEWART, Ellen Frances, Mrs., C.B.E., *d.* of Gen. W. S. Hatch, R.A.; *m.* Athole Chalmers, *s.* of Geo. Stewart. *Educ.:* Privately. *War Work:* 14 Aug. 1914, Hon. Sec. to Matron, Charing Cross Hospital; 1915–17, Temp. Organising Officer, Ministry of Labour; April, 1917, to April, 1920, Superintendent, Women's Forage Corps, R.A.S.C. *Address:* 6, Coulson Street, London, S.W. 3. *Club:* Forum. (C2972)

STEWART, Ethel, M.B.E. *War Work:* Took an active part in The Durham Light Infantry Prisoners of War Fund from its establishment in 1915. *Address:* 3, South Hill Crescent, Sunderland. (M9726)

STEWART, Rev. Frank White, C.B.E., M.A., *b.* 23 Sept. 1867; *s.* of John Stewart; *m.* Maggie Josephine, *d.* of — Murray. *Educ.:* Perth Academy, and Edinburgh Univ. *War Work:* Chaplain to the Forces, France, Belgium, and Germany, August, 1914, to Dec. 1919. *Address:* c/o Sir C. R. McGrigor, Bart., & Co., London. (C1331)

STEWART, Lieut.-Col. George Herbert, O.B.E., M.B., I.M.S.

STEWART, Gertrude, O.B.E., Q.M.A.A.C.

STEWART, Helen Osmer, Mrs., O.B.E.

STEWART, Lieut.-Col. Herbert Arthur, D.S.O., O.B.E., *b.* 1878; *s.* of Arthur Stewart, formerly I.C.S.; *m.* 1907, Janet Bertha, *d.* of the late Frederick Macleay Passow. *Educ.:* Portsmouth Grammar School. Entered Suffolk Regt., 1899; transferred to Army Service Corps, 1900; became Capt., 1902; Major, 1914; Lieut.-Col., 1916; served in the S. African War, 1899–1902; present at operations in Transvaal, Orange River, and Cape Colonies (Queen's medal with three clasps, King's medal with two clasps); in the Great War, 1914–19, on Staff. (despatches); is a Member of Cruising Assoc. *Address:* Beke Hutte, Billingshurst, Sussex. (C2735)

STEWART, Hugh Henry Boyd, M.B.E., F.R.C.I., *b.* 22 May, 1875; *s.* of the late John Stewart, of Breda Park, Belfast; *m.* Mary Selene, *d.* of the late Honoratus Leigh Thomas of Chester. On the outbreak of war was engaged in Central Africa on Engineering development work. *War Work:* Attached to Directorate of Works and Buildings, Air Ministry. *Address:* 18, Goldington Avenue, Bedford.

STEWART, Isabella Forbes, M.B.E., *b.* 1877; *d.* of the late Very Rev. Principal Stewart, D.D., of St. Andrews, Scotland. *Educ.:* Aberdeen, and Univ. of St. Andrews. Lady Warden of Residential Club under the Church of Scotland (1919). *War Work:* In Scottish Churches' Huts, 1916–17, and from July to Oct. 1917, at the Base Camp of Etaples; Oct. 1917, to May, 1919, Lady Commandant of the Scottish Club in Rouen. *Address:* Lister House, The Mount, Edinburgh. *Club:* St. Margaret's (Edinburgh). (M4000)

STEWART, Major Jack, O.B.E.

STEWART, James, O.B.E.

STEWART, James, O.B.E.

STEWART, James, M.B.E.

STEWART, Major James, O.B.E., M.Inst.C.E. (retired pay), *b.* 18 Feb. 1861; *s.* of the late Capt. J. Stewart, 16th Lancers, of Williamwood, Renfrewshire, N.B.; *m.* Frederica, *d.* of the late L. Lablache, of London. *Educ.:* Cheltenham Coll. Engineering Inspector, Ministry of Health. *War Work:* Re-employed, 1915–18, on Headquarter Staff, Aldershot Command. *Address:* 90, Coleherne Court, S.W. 5. *Club:* East India United Service. (O7748)

STEWART, Lieut.-Col. James Allan, O.B.E.

STEWART, James King, C.B.E., *b.* 24 April, 1863; *s.* of James Stewart, Postmaster of Leith; *m.* Margaret, *d.* of James Law, East Mains, Broxburn, Linlithgowshire. *Educ.:* Edinburgh Institution. Comptroller of Stamps and Taxes for Scotland. *War Work:* Immediate supervision and administration or H.M. Inland Revenue in Scotland, including the new duties on Excess Profits, Excess Mineral Rights Coal Levy, and Income Tax on weekly wage earners. *Address:* Craig Urrard, Northfield Liberton, Midlothian. (C2973)

STEWART, Jean Carruthers M.B.E.

STEWART, Col. John, C.B.E., Can. A.M.G.

STEWART, John, M.B.E., *b.* 7 Jan. 1878; *s.* of John Stewart, of Laggan, Strathyre; *m.* Margaret Bell, *d.* of William R. Watson, of Edinburgh. *Educ.:* McLaren High School, Callander, and Univ. of Edinburgh. Solicitor and Notary Public; District Clerk; Depute Clerk of the Peace; Clerk Balquhidder Parish Council; Cashier County Savings Bank; Clerk Leeropt Heritors; Sec. Dunblane Agricultural Society. *War Work:* Sec. for West Perthshire District Agricultural Committee; Clerk, West Perthshire County Tribunal; Sec. Lord Derby Recruiting Scheme; Sec., District Food Control Committee. *Address:* Westholm, Dunblane. (M973)

STEWART, John, O.B.E., J.P., S.S.C., *b.* 1866; *s.* of James Stewart, of Nairn; *m.* Eliza Jane, *d.* of James

Clark, of Golford, Nairnshire. *Educ.:* Forres Academy, and Edinburgh Univ. Chief Education Officer to the Education Authority of the City of Edinburgh, and a Solicitor to the Supreme Courts of Scotland; a Justice of the Peace for the County of the City of Edinburgh. *War Work:* Supervisor for National Registration, National Service, and for Recruiting for the City of Edinburgh; as Executive Officer organised the Food Control for the City, and assisted in organising the Volunteer Movement, holding a Commission in the Royal Scots Volunteer Regiment for Edinburgh. *Address:* 14, Murrayfield Road, *Club:* Northern, Edinburgh. (O3941)

STEWART, Lieut.-Col. John Douglas Reginald, O.B.E.

STEWART, Capt. John Henry George, M.B.E., *b.* 17 Nov. 1883; *s.* of A. G. Stewart, of Wimbledon Park; *m.* Florence Edith Maud, *d.* of G. White, of Wimbledon Park. *Educ.:* Archbishop's School, Lambeth. Civil Servant (G.P.O.). *War Work:* Army Postal Service, 1915–19 (Royal Engineers, Special Reserve). *Address:* 69, Durham Road, Wimbledon, S.W. 19. (M5655)

STEWART, Lieut.-Col. John Mitchell Young, C.B.E., D.S.O., Australian Forces. Served during Great War, 1915–18 (despatches). (C219)

STEWART, Lieut. Keith Lindsay, M.B.E.

STEWART, Louisa Mary, C.B.E., R.R.C., *b.* 11 Aug. 1861; *d.* of the late Major-Gen. Robert Cross Stewart, C.B., of Palmeira Mansions, Hove, Sussex. *War Work:* Matron in Queen Alexandra's Imperial Military Nursing service, 1889–1919. *Address:* Marsh Cottage, Queens Road, Minehead, Somerset. (C1119)

STEWART, Mary Downes, O.B.E.

STEWART, Mary Jane Finlay, M.B.E., *b.* 1894; *d.* of William Stewart, of Glasgow. *Educ.:* Eastbourne and Paris. *War Work:* Superintendent, Surgical Dressings Department; Red Cross Central Workrooms, Burlington House. *Address:* 46, Palace Gardens Terrace, Kensington. *Clubs:* Halcyon; Mid-Surrey Golf. (M2481)

STEWART, Maude, Mrs., M.B.E.

STEWART, Lieut.-Col. P. A. V., C.B.E., D.S.O., *b.* 1875; *s.* of Lieut.-Gen. John Mackie Stewart; *m.* 1911, Mildred Annie Ferrars, *d.* of the late Tom Ferrars Guy. Served in Great War, 1914–19, on Staff (despatches Brevet Lieut.-Col., Belgian Croix de Guerre). *Club:* Naval and Military. (C1779)

STEWART, Percy Malcolm, O.B.E., J.P., *b.* 9 May, 1872; *s.* of Halley Stewart, of The Red House, Harpenden, Herts; *m.* Beatrice Maud, *d.* of the late Joseph B. Pratt, of Brenchley, Kent. *Educ.:* Univ. School, Hastings, and Royal High School, Edinburgh. Cement Manufacturer. *War Work:* At Ministry of Munitions; Director of the Government Rolling Mills, Southampton. *Address:* 4, Templewood Avenue, Hampstead, N.W. 3. *Clubs:* Reform; Royal Automobile. (O1891)

STEWART, Capt. Percy Peter James, O.B.E., F.R.C.S., M.B., R.A.M.C.

STEWART, Major Peter Donald, O.B.E., Can. A.M.C.

STEWART, Robert, M.B.E.

STEWART, Sir Robert King, K.B.E., J.P., D.L., Co. Lanark, *b.* 1853; *s.* of Robert Stewart, J.P., D.L., of Murdostoun; *m.* Alice Margaret, *d.* of John Christie, of Cowden. *Educ.:* Glasgow and Oxford Universities. Vice-Lieut. and Convener of County of Lanark. *War Work:* County Director, Lanarkshire Branch of Red Cross Society; Vice-Chairman of War Pensions Committee; Member of Prince of Wales' War Fund, Scottish Committee; Chairman of Lanarkshire Food Control Committee. *Address:* Murdostoun Castle, Newmains, Lanarkshire. *Clubs:* New, Edinburgh; Oxford and Cambridge. (K171)

STEWART, Major Robert Neil, O.B.E., M.C.

STEWART, Surg.-Comm. Robert William Glennan, O.B.E., M.D., R.N.

STEWART, Capt. Valentine Peter Beardmore, C.B.E., 5th Highland Light Infantry, *b.* 14 Feb. 1882; *s.* of Duncan Stewart, of Glasgow; *m.* Goldie, *d.* of the Rev. A. M. Maclean, C.M.G., D.D., of Paisley Abbey. *Educ.:* Kelvinside and Eastbourne. Local Director, William Beardmore & Co., Ltd., Glasgow. *War Work:* Gallipoli, 1915; Director National Factories, Glasgow, 1916; Deputy Director of Gun Manufacture, 1917; Controller of Gun Manufacture, 1918. *Clubs:* Junior Carlton; Junior Constitutional. (C2974)

STEWART, Walter Grahame, M.B.E., M.B., B.S.(Lond.), M.R.C.S., L.R.C.P., *b.* 5 Oct. 1874; *s.* of the late Robert Stewart, Standard Bank, South Africa; *m.* Rebecca C. Stewart, *d.* of Maj.-Gen. F. F. Daniell, late of Gordon Highlanders. *Educ.:* Dulwich Coll., and Guy's Hospital. Vice Chairman, Hertfordshire Pensions Board; Medical Superintendent, Hertford and Ware Joint Hospital; Medical Officer, Herts Reformatory, Ltd., Ware Board of Guardians, and Ware Post Office. *War Work:* Medical Officer and Commandant, Ware V.A.D. Hospital (Herts 14), March, 1915, to Dec. 1918; Medical Officer, Poles Convalescent Home for Officers, annexe of Ridley House, Carlton House Terrace; Medical Officer to Local Troops and Anti-Aircraft Stations; Member of Herts Recruiting Board, and Special Constable. *Address:* Baldock House, Ware, Herts. (M9728)

STEWART, William, M.B.E., F.R.I.B.A., *b.* 14 Nov. 1867; *s.* of Charles Henry, of South Woodford, Essex; *m.* Maud M. A. E. (who died), *d.* of W. J. Jarrow, of Finsbury Park. *Educ.:* Chigwell Grammar School. Architect and Surveyor. *War Work:* Joint Military Representative, Wanstead, Essex, Tribunal; National Service Representative,

Islington *Addresses :* Grove Park, Wanstead, Essex; Newlyn House, Aldgate, London, E. 2. *Club :* Constitutional. (M9730)

STEWART, William Alexander, M.B.E., J.P.

STEWART, William Allison, O.B.E.

STEWART, Lieut.-Col. William Archibald, O.B.E., Middlesex Reg., *b.* 8 Dec. 1880 ; *s.* of the late Major Alexander Stewart, of Scone, N.B. ; *m.* Hilda Hilton, *d.* of the late Col. Charles Briggs, J.P., D.L., of Hylton Castle, Durham. *Educ. :* Sandhurst. *War Work :* Served in South African War with Middlesex Regiment and Mounted Infantry, including battle of Spion Kop and other engagements for relief of Ladysmith ; D.A.A. and Q.M.G. Burma Division ; Commandant, British General Depot, Basra ; D.A.A. and Q.M.G., and A.A. and Q.M.G Mesopotamian Expeditionary Force ; Despatches three times. *Address :* Bagdad, Mesopotamia. *Club :* Junior United Service. (O6706)

STEWART, T. Capt. William Hendry Burgess, O.B.E., R.E.

STEWART, Capt. and Qr.-Mr. William Henry, O.B.E., (R.E.)

STEWART, Brig.-Gen. William Robert, C.B., C.B.E. (late R.E.), *b.* 20 July, 1862 ; *s.* of the late Stair A. Stewart, M.I.C.E., 2nd son of Stair Hathorn Stewart, of Physgill and Glasserton, N.B. ; *m.* Ethel, *d.* of the late Rev. F. T. Salmon, late of Gittsham Rectory, Devon. *Educ. :* Blairlodge School, Polmont, N.B. ; R.M.A., Woolwich. Regular Officer, R.E., from 1 Oct. 1882, to 19 Aug. 1919, when placed on retired list. *War Work :* Assistant Director Fortifications and Works, War Office, 1913–16 ; Chief Engineer, Scottish Command, 1916–19. *Address :* c/o Messrs. Cox & Co., 16, Charing Cross. *Clubs :* Junior United Service. (C1776)

STEWART, Brig.-Gen. Charles, GORDON-, C.B.E. (ret.). Served in the Great War, 1914–19 (despatches). (C1585)

STEWART, Lily, Mrs. GORDON-, M.B.E.

STEWART, Lady Alice Emma SHAW-, C.B.E., *b.* 27 Jan 1864 : *e.d.* of John, 4th Marquess of Bath (*see* BURKE'S *Peerage*) ; *m.* Sir Michael Hugh, 8th Bart., *s.* of the late Sir Michael R. Shaw-Stewart (*see* BURKE'S *Peerage*). *War Work :* Commandant, Ardgowan Auxiliary Hospital ; Lady President Renfrewshire Committee, British Red Cross Society ; Member of Greenock Local War Pensions Committee ; Member of Renfrewshire Local War Pensions Committee. *Address :* Ardgowan, Inverkip, Renfrewshire. (C2971)

STEWART, Sir Hugh SHAW-, Bart., C.B.E.

STEWART, Mary Beatrice, Mrs. SHAW-, O.B.E., *b.* 19 Aug. 1865 ; *d.* of Sidney Leveson Lane, of Manor House, Great Addington, Northants, and Mary Isabel, Viscountess Downe (*see* BURKE'S *Peerage*) ; *m.* Walter Richard, *s.* of the late Sir Michael Shaw-Stewart, of Ardgowan, Renfrewshire. *War Work :* Commandant of Tisbury V.A.D. Auxiliary A Hospitals. *Addresses :* Hays, Shaftesbury, Wilts ; Villa Shaw-Stewart, Ajaccio, Corsica. *Club :* The Victoria. (O11391)

STEWART, Walter Richard SHAW-, M.B.E., J.P., D.L., C.C. for Wilts, *b.* 27 June, 1861 ; *s.* of the late Sir M. R. Shaw-Stewart 7th Bart., of Ardgowan, Greenock, N.B. (*see* BURKE'S *Peerage*) ; *m.* Mary Beatrice Sydney, O.B.E. (*q.v.*), *d.* of the late S. L. Lane, J.P., D.L., of Great Addington, Northants. *Educ. :* Harrow. Formerly Capt. 4th Argyle and Sutherland Highlanders, and Capt. 1st Wilts Vol. Rifle Corps. *War Work :* In charge of T.F. Officers Casualty Dept., 1915–17, at the War Office. *Addresses :* Hays, Sedgehill, nr. Shaftesbury ; Villa Shaw-Stewart, Ajaccio, Corsica. *Club :* Junior Carlton. (M9729)

STICKINGS, Capt. Ralph William Ewart, O.B.E., B.Sc., D.I.C., A.I.C., R.A.M.C. (T.), *b.* 20 March, 1895 ; *s.* of John Stickings, of Mitcham, Surrey ; *m.* Dora Sybil, *d.* of Charles Sayers, of Mitcham, Surrey. *Educ. :* Rutlish School, Merton ; King's Coll.. London ; Royal Coll. of Science, South Kensington. Research Chemist ; Fellow of Chemical Society. *War Work :* 1914–15, Manufacture of Synthetic Drugs at Imperial College of Science ; 1915–16, organisation of First Water Tank Co. for France ; 1916–19, Senior Chemist, No. 1 Water Tank Co., employed in providing drinking water for troops on Western Front, principally during advances. *Address :* The Rowans, Ravensbury Park, Mitcham, Surrey. (O5813)

STICKLAND, John Northover, O.B.E., *b.* 1 March, 1854 ; *s.* of Jasper Stickland, of Milborne Port, Somerset ; *m.* Bessie, *d.* of Alfred Reynolds, of Milborne Port. Late Superintending Inspector of Customs and Excise. *War Work :* Member of Advisory Committee (Customs and Excise) dealing with the restrictions on the delivery of wine and spirits from bond ; controlled the Committee's staff. *Address :* 19, Mayford Road, Wandsworth Common, S.W. 12. (O3942)

STICKNEY, Evelyn Mary, M.B.E., *b.* 17 April, 1876 ; *d.* of the late Walter Meynell Stickney, of Beverley. *Educ. :* The Westlands School, Scarborough. *War Work :* Hon. Div. Sec., Soldiers' and Sailors' Families Association ; Member of Executive County Relief Committee, Local Relief Committee, and Local War Pensions Committee ; appointed Assistant Sec. and later Administrative Officer of Pensions Committee. *Address :* 44, Westwood Road, Beverley. (M9731)

STIFFE, Lieut.-Col. Archibald Francis Everitt, O.B.E., Royal Artillery (ret.), *b.* 5 July, 1867 ; *s.* of Capt. A. W. Stiffe. *Educ. :* Marlborough. *Club :* East India United Service. (O8549)

STIFFE, Norman Cecil, O.B.E., I.C.S.

STIGGER, Horace Charles, M.B.E., *b.* 8 Nov. 1867; *s.* of James Stigger, of Sevenoaks ; *m.* Emily, *d.* of William Stevens, of Exeter. *Educ. :* St. Stephen's, Paddington, W.; King's Coll., London. Paper Room Clerk. Home Office. *War Work :* In connection with Police Service. *Address :* 263, Fulham Palace Road, S.W. 6. (M9732)

STILEMAN, Rear-Adm. Sir Harry Hampson, K.B.E., *b.* 1860 ; *s.* of the late Major-Gen. William Croughton Stileman, of Brighton ; *m.* Emma Frances, *d.* of the late Major-Gen. Richard Oldfield, R.A. *Educ. :* Eastman's R.N. Academy, and H.M.S. " Britannia." Entered Royal Navy, 1882 ; ret. 1909 ; Senior Naval Officer at Liverpool during the whole period of the war ; Rear-Admiral, 1914 ; Director of Dr. Barnardo's Homes. *Address :* 18, Stepney Causeway, E. 1. *Club :* National. (K332)

STILES, Sir Harold Jalland, K.B.E., M.B., C.M., F.R.C.S., Ed., *b.* 1863 ; *s.* of Henry T. Stiles, M.D., J.P., of Spalding, Lincs ; *m.* Cecilia Norton, *d.* of David Law, of Glasgow. *Educ. :* Totteridge Park ; Edinburgh Univ. ; Berne. Surgeon ; Regius Prof. of Clinical Surgery, Univ. of Edinburgh, and Surgeon to the Royal Infirmary, Edinburgh ; Consulting Surgeon to Royal Edinburgh Hospital for Sick Children and to Chalmers' Hospital, Edinburgh ; Hon. Fellow of the American Surgical Association ; Hon. Member of the Amer. Medical Association and of the British Orthopædic Association ; President of the Association of Surgeons of Great Britain and Ireland. *War Work :* T. Col., A.M.S. (Brevet Lieut.-Col.) ; Assistant Inspector of Special Military Surgery, and Chief Surgeon Special Military Surgery, the Edinburgh War Hospital, Bangour ; Consulting Surgeon, Scottish Command ; Member of Army Medical Advisory Board, and of Council of Consultants. *Addresses :* 9, Great Stuart Street, Edinburgh ; Whatton Lodge, Gullane. *Clubs :* Savile, and University ; Caledonian, and United Service, Edinburgh. (K321h)

STILL, Ernest Henry, M.B.E.

STILL, Capt. James, O.B.E., Can. A.P.C.

STILL, Marjorie, M.B.E., *b.* 7 Jan. 1886 ; *d.* of E. Robert Still, of Leatherhead. *Educ. :* Privately. *War Work :* Hon. Sec. Soldiers' and Sailors' Families Association, and War Pensions Sub-Committee for Brixton, S.W., Aug. 1914–20. *Address :* Windfield, Leatherhead. *Club :* Ladies' Army and Navy. (M2482)

STILL, William Chester, C.B.E., *b.* 1878 ; *s.* of William Mudd Still, late of Winchmore Hill ; *m.* Maud Ellen, *d.* of Edward Bullock, of Dulwich. *Educ. :* Cowper Street Schools. Engineer ; Managing Director of W. M. Still and Sons, Ltd. *Address :* Aberfoyle, Broad Walk, Winchmore Hill, N. 21. (C308)

STILL, Alicia Frances Jane LLOYD-, C.B.E., R.R.C.; *d.* of the late Henry Lloyd-Still, Ceylon Civil Service, of Walton-by-Clevedon. *Educ. :* Privately. Matron, St. Thomas's Hospital, and Superintendent of Nightingale Training School. *War Work :* Principal Matron T.F.N.S. No. 5 London (City of London) General Hospital, St. Thomas's Hospital. *Address :* Matron's House, St. Thomas's Hospital. (C67)

STILLWELL, Gloria Ethel Ada, M.B.E., Q.M.A.A.C.

STILWELL, George Robert Fabris, O.B.E., M.B., M.R.C.S.

STIRK, Rufus, O.B.E.

STIRLING, Hon. Mrs. A., O.B.E.

STIRLING, 2nd Lieut. Charles Frederick, M.B.E.

STIRLING, Lieut. Charles McKidd, M.B.E., R.A.S.C.

STIRLING, Sir George Murray Home, 9th Bart., C.B.E., D.S.O., J.P., D.L., of Glorat (Nova Scotia Baronetcy, A.D. 1666), *b.* 4 Sept. 1869 ; *s.* of Sir Chas. Elphinstone Fleming, Bart., of Glorat, Stirlingshire (*see* BURKE'S *Peerage*) ; *m.* Mabel Elizabeth, *d.* of Sir Alexander Sprot, Bart., C.M.G., of Stravithie, M.P. for East Fife ; 2 sons, 3 dau. ; heir, Charles Alexander Sprot Home Stirling. *Educ. :* Eton, Sandhurst. Is a J.P. and D.L. for the County of Stirlingshire, and a Member of the King's Bodyguard for Scotland (Royal Company of Archers) ; served thirty years in the Essex Regt. (now retired) ; served in Chitral, 1895 ; Tirah, 1897 ; South African, 1900–2 ; Somaliland, 1903–4 ; European (1915–18) ; Campaigns, Commanded in turn both regular battalions of the Essex Regt. during the Great War. *Address :* Baldoran, Milton of Campsie, Stirlingshire. *Clubs :* Army and Navy ; New, Edinburgh ; Stirling County. (C1332)

STIRLING, Capt. Hugh William, M.B.E.

STIRLING, John O.B.E., *b.* 28 Aug. 1863 ; *s.* of the late James Stirling, of Whitehill, Aberdeenshire ; *m.* Barbara Anne, *d.* of Alexander Cruickshank, of King-Edwards, Aberdeenshire, *Educ. :* Cairnbanno, Madras Public School. Chief Constable of the County Borough of Grimsby, and Chief Officer of the Grimsby Corporation Volunteer Fire Brigade. *War Work :* On the outbreak of war organised a body of Spcial Constables, including a signalling section and observation posts, to cope with any emergency ; took stringent measures to have the town thoroughly darkened. *Address :* Craigston, Abbey Road, Grimsby. (O11393)

STIRLING, Capt. John, M.B.E.

STIRLING, Major John, M.B.E.

STIRLING, John Featherstone, Rev., O.B.E.

STIRLING, Sir John Lancelot, K.C.M.G., O.B.E., B.A., LL.B., J.P., M.L.C., *b.* 5 Nov. 1849 ; *s.* of Hon. Edward Stirling M.L.C., of Adelaide, S. Australia ; *m.* Florence Marian, *d.* of Sir William Milne, of Adelaide, S. Australia (*see* BURKE'S *Peerage*). *Educ. :* St. Peter's College, Adelaide, and Trinity Coll., Cambridge. Barrister-at-Law ; Pres. of the Legislative

Council, S. Australia ; sheep farmer. *War Work :* Work in connection with the Red Cross ; Member of Finance Committee, S. Australian Branch, Red Cross. *Address :* The Lodge Strathallyn, S. Australia. *Clubs :* New University ; Adelaide (Australia). (O2172)

STIRLING, Margaret Mary, Hon. Mrs., O.B.E., J.P., *b.* 25 June, 1881 ; *d.* of 13th Baron Lovat (*see* BURKE'S *Peerage*) ; *m.* Brig. Gen. Archibald Stirling, *s.* of Sir William Stirling Maxwell, of Keir and Pollok. *Educ.* : Privately. *War Work :* Hospital and War Pensions and Red Cross Work. *Address :* Keir, Dunblane. *Club :* Queen's (Edinburgh). (O11394)

STIRLING, Major Patrick Douglas, O.B.E., M.C.

STIRLING, Comm. Thomas Willing, O.B.E., R.N.

STIRLING, William, O.B.E., M.D. (Vict.), *b.* 6 March, 1889 ; *s.* of Prof. W. Stirling, M.D., D.Sc., LL.D., of Manchester ; *m.* Florence Fleming, *d.* of Peter Watson, J.P., of Drumsuie, of Red House, Ayr. *Educ.* : Victoria University of Manchester. Ophthalmic Surgeon ; Assist. Hon.-Surgeon, Manchester Royal Eye Hospital ; Consulting Ophthalmic Surgeon, Ancoats Hospital, Manchester ; Ophthalmic Surgeon, Ministry of Pensions (N.W. Area). *War Work :* Joined R.A.M.C., Dec. 1915 ; M.O. i/c 9th York and Lancaster Regt. ; Ophthalmic Surgeon i/c 4th Army ; Ophthalmic Surgeon, Etaples ; Ophthalmic Surgeon, Camiérs ; Sept. 1916, to March, 1919, Ophthalmic Surgeon i/c Calais and Dunkirk areas. *Addresses :* 4, St. John Street, Manchester ; 55, Mauldeth Road, Withington, Manchester. (O5815)

STIRLING, Comm. George Harry MILLER-, O.B.E., J.P., and D.L. for Stirlingshire, *b.* Aug. 1853 ; *s.* of James Black Miller, of Muirshiel, Renfrewshire ; *m.* Caroline Frances, *d.* of Major Charles Campbell Graham Stirling, of Craigbarnet, *War Work :* Hon. Sec. W. of Scotland Branch of the Soldiers' and Sailors' Families Association. *Address :* Craigbarnet, Campsil Glen, N.B. *Clubs :* Western, Glasgow ; Stirling County. (O11392)

STIRRETT, Lieut.-Col. Albert Newton, O.B.E., M.C., Can. A.S.C.

STITT, Iza, M.B.E., Q.M.A.A.C.

STOBART, Bessie, Mrs., O.B.E., *b.* 6 Jan. 1874 ; *d.* of Frederick H. Brydges, of Victoria, B.C., Canada ; *m.* Henry Gerdas, *s.* of William Stobart, of Pepper Arden, Yorkshire. *War Work :* Chairman, War Agricultural Executive Committee and of the Home for Convalescent Sailors under the Admiralty ; President of Durham Federation of Women's Institutes. *Address :* Bedale Hall, Bedale. *Clubs :* Ladies' Empire ; Forum. (O11395)

STOBART, Frederick William, O.B.E., *b.* 27 Jan. 1859 ; *s.* of the late William Stobart, of Pepper Arden, Northallerton ; *m.* Margaret, *d.* of the late C. J. Brydges, of Winnipeg, Canada. *Educ.* : Wellington College, and Jesus Coll., Cambridge. *War Work :* Purchased supplies in Canada and United States for the War Office. *Address :* Wispers, Midhurst, Sussex. *Clubs :* Wellington ; Wyndham ; Manitoba, Winnipeg. (O773)

STOBART, Lieut.-Col. George Herbert, C.B.E., D.S.O., J.P. (R.A.), *b.* 18 Feb. 1873 ; *s.* of W. C. Stobart, of Spellow Hill, Yorks ; *m.* Mary Alexandra, *d.* of Rev. H. J. Kinnear, of Copgrove Rectory, Yorks. *Educ.* : Aysgarth School Yorks ; Harrow School, and Woolwich. Lieut.-Col. Commanding 6th Durham Light Infantry (Territorials). Entered Army, 1894 ; Major, 1911 ; retired 1911 ; served S. Africa, 1899–1900 (Queen's Medal, with clasp) ; European War, 1914–15 (despatches, D.S.O., Brev. Lieut.-Col., C.B.E.), J.P., Co. Durham. *Address :* Harperley Park, Co. Durham. *Club :* Army and Navy. (C1777)

STOBART, Harriet Katie, M.B.E., *b.* 26 Aug. 1870 ; *d.* of Alfred Conyers Haycraft, of London ; *m.* Louis Walter, *s.* of William Stobart. *Educ.* : Privately. *War Work :* Commandant, Somerset/80 (Women's) Red Cross Detachment ; Commandant of the Red Cross (Primary) Hospital at Baptist Schools, Yeovil, Som. *Address :* Flat 2, 19, Second Avenue, Hove, Sussex. (M5733)

STOBART, Henry John Scott, O.B.E., *b.* Aug. 1867, *s.* of Rev. Henry Stobart, of Warkton Rectory, Kettering ; *m.* Frances Geraldine, *d.* of W. Culley Stobart, of Spellow Hill, Yorks. *Educ.* : Haileybury and Pembroke College, Cambridge. *War Work :* Managing Director of Messrs. Chance Brothers & Co., manufacturers of Optical glass for war purposes. *Address :* Church House, Belbroughton, nr. Stourbridge. *Clubs :* Oxford and Cambridge. (O1892)

STOBART, Lieut.-Col. Hugh Morton, C.B.E., D.S.O., *b.* 1883 ; *s.* of the late Frank Stobart, of Selaby, Gainford-on-Tees ; *m.* 1910, Esmée Violet Helen, *d.* of Alfred James Bethell. Served during Great War, 1914–18 (despatches). *Address :* Biddick Hall, Fence Houses, Durham. (C1041)

STOBART, Jessica Octavia, Mrs., O.B.E., Lady of Grace of the Order of the Hospital of St. John of Jerusalem in England, *b.* 13 July, 1872 ; *d.* of Francis George Butler, of Cross Hall Lodge, St. Neots, Hunts. ; *m.* William Ryder, *s.* of William Culley Stobart, of Spellow Hill, Knaresboro'. *War Work :* Commandant of 17th Durham V.A. Hospital, Etherley, Bishop Auckland, from March, 1915, to April, 1919. *Addresses :* Mazonet, Stoke Gabriel, Totnes. S. Devon ; Bragleenbeg, Kilninver, Oban, Argyllshire. (O1893)

STOBIE, Major Harold Ramsay, O.B.E.

STOBIE, Capt. William, O.B.E., R.A.M.C. (T.)

STOCK, Enid Amy, Mrs., M.B.E.

STOCK, Capt. Ernest Elliot, M.B.E., E.A.F.

STOCK, Col. Philip Graham, C.B., C.B.E., M.B., *b.* 1878 ;

s. of Granger Stock, of Clifton, Bristol ; *m.* 1913, Dorothy, *d.* of Herbert Oxley, of Hans Crescent, S.W. *Educ.* : Clifton and Bristol Univ. Director of Med. Ser., Union of S. Africa ; a J.P. for S. Africa ; served in S. Africa, 1899–1902 (Queen's medal with three clasps, King's medal with two clasps) ; in German S.-W. Africa, 1914–15 (despatches) ; France, 1915–18. *Address :* 45, Wetherby Mansions, S.W. *Clubs :* Pretoria ; Rand. (C1883)

STOCKER, Edward Barlow, O.B.E. *b.* 4 Feb. 1877 ; *s.* of William Jeffrey Stocker, of Pendower, Nottingham ; *m.* Florence Harriett, *d.* of Arthur C. Brown, of Nottingham. *Educ.* : Nottingham High School. *War Work :* County Director, Notts V.A.D. ; Transport Officer, responsible for all the Transport of the Nottingham Military and V.A.D. Hospitals. *Club :* Borough, Nottingham. (O11396)

STOCKER, Eng.-Comm. Percy, O.B.E., R.N.

STOCKINGS, Major Arthur Perry, C.B.E., F.R.G.S. *b.* 3 Jan. 1880 ; *s.* of George Stockings, of Topcroft, Bournemouth ; *m.* Dorothy, *d.* of Richard England, of Rumney Court, St. Mellons, Cardiff. *Educ.* : Privately ; Germany (Marburg). Chief Engineer and general manager of several important British companies in South America, principally in Bolivia ; earlier work of a similar nature in South Africa. *War Work :* Hon. Sec. to the Joint War Committee of the Order of St. John and British Red Cross ; Sub-Commissioner British Red Cross at Malta ; subsequently granted a commission in the 2/2 London Regt. Royal Fusiliers (T.) and fought in the Dardanelles after service in Malta and Egypt ; placed on light duty ; appointed Director of supply section in the Trench Warfare Dept., Ministry of Munitions ; finally appointed Director of Stores and Sub-Commissioner for the British Red Cross for Italy ; after the Armistice appointed B.R.C. Commissioner for Italy to carry out demobilisation. *Address :* Aragon, Letchmore Heath, nr. Watford. *Club :* Constitutional. (C2975)

STOCKLEY, Major Henry Hudson Fraser, O.B.E., R.M.L.I., *b.* 30 Oct. 1878 ; *s.* of Col. George W. Stockley, J.P., R.E., of West Malling, Kent ; *m.* Ismay Madeleine, *d.* of Dacre M. A. Hamilton, J.P., D.L., of Cornacassa, Monaghan. *Educ.* : Haileybury Coll. 2nd Lieut.R.M.L.I., 1897 ; Sword of Honour Royal Naval Coll., Greenwich, 1897 ; Lieut. R.M.L.I. 1898 ; H.M.S. " Niobe," during South African War ; H.M.S. " Ophir," during tour of T.R.H. the Duke and Duchess of Cornwall and York, 1901 ; Capt. R.M.L.I. 1903 ; A.D.C. to the Governor of the Straits Settlements, 1904–10. *War Work :* Served with Portsmouth Batt. R.M.L.I., France and Flanders, 1914 ; Gallipoli, 1915 ; severely wounded, 1915 ; mentioned in despatches, Major, 1915 ; Lord Chamberlain's Department, 1916. *Address :* 8, Charles Street, Knightsbridge, S.W. 7. *Club :* Sports. (O11397)

STOCKS, Andrew Denys, O.B.E., *b.* 2 Dec. 1884 ; *s.* of the Ven. John Edward Stocks, Archdeacon of Leicester. *Educ.* : Loretto School. Lieut. Coldstream Guards, S.R. ; Assistant Solicitor and Legal Adviser, Ministry of Agriculture and Fisheries. *Address :* 8, Old Square, Lincoln's Inn, W.C. 2. *Club :* Union. (O3945)

STOCKS, George, M.B.E., A.M.Inst.T., *b.* 6 March, 1875 ; *s.* of George Stocks, of Doncaster ; *m.* Annie Gertrude, *d.* of William Chambers, of Bulwell, Notts. 28 years in the service of the Great Central Railway Co. in various capacities and eventually transferred to the General Manager's Department. *War Work :* In August, 1916, transferred to the Railway Executive Committee, and appointed to deal with matters relating to transport of traffic, enlistment, and demobilisation of railwaymen ; in charge of operations affecting railways during hostile air raids. *Addresses :* 35, Parliament Street, Westminster, S.W. 1 ; 25, Hughenden Road, High Wycombe, Bucks. (M9734)

STOCKWELL, Major Hugh Charles, O.B.E.

STODDARD, Major Ernest Algernon, M.B.E.

STODDARD, Lieut. John Wilkie, M.B.E.

STODDARD, Reginald Thomas, M.B.E.

STODDART, Capt. Guy, O.B.E., I.A.

STODDART, George Frederick, O.B.E.

STODDART, Capt. Kenneth Bowring, C.B.E., *b.* 1877 ; *s.* of Laurence Stoddart, of Liverpool ; *m.* Constance, *d.* of John W. West, of Newfoundland. *Educ.* : Liverpool Coll. *War Work :* Capt. 18th King's Liverpool Regt., 1914–16 ; President, Wheat Export Co., Canada ; Vice-President, Wheat Export Co., New York ; Member Royal Commission on Wheat Supplies, 1916–20. *Address :* c/o Samuel Sandy & Co., Holland House, Bury Street, London, E.C. (C2976)

STODDART, Swinton, M.B.E.

STOKER, George Herbert, O.B.E., B.A., India Office, *b.* 12 Feb. 1874 ; *s.* of George Naylor Stoker, F.I.C., E.R.M.S., late of the Government Laboratory ; *m.* Florence Margaret, *d.* of the Rev. Henry Cotton. *Educ.* : City of London School, and Corpus Christi Coll., Oxford. *War Work :* War and demobilisation accounts connected with India and Home Government. *Address :* 41, Westwell Road, Streatham Common. *Club :* Oxford and Cambridge Musical. (O1894)

STOKER, Gilbert, O.B.E., A.M.I.C.E, *b.* 1869 ; *s.* of Gilbert J. Stoker, of Birmingham ; *m.* Marion, *d.* of Charles Flint, of Birmingham. *Educ.* : King Edward VI. High School, Birmingham. Civil Engineer. *War Work :* Assistant Controller and Engineer-in-charge of Works. and Maintenance of the Central Stores Department, Ministry of Munitions of War. *Address :* Cornwall House, Waterloo Bridge Road, London. (O1895)

STOKES, Capt. Adrian, D.S.O., O.B.E., M.D., B.Ch.,

F.R.C.S.I., M.R.C.S., R.A.M.C., *b.* 1862 ; *s.* of H. S. Stokes, formerly I.C.S. *Educ.:* Trinity Coll., Camb., and Dublin Univ. Served in the Great War, 1914–19 (despatches, Order of Crown of Belgium). (O5818)

STOKES, Lieut.-Col. Claude Bayfield, D.S.O., O.B.E., C.I.E., *b.* 1875 ; *s.* of the Rev. Arthur Stokes, of 10, Canfield Gardens, N.W. ; *Educ.:* St. John's School., Leatherhead, and R.M.C. Major and Brevet Lieut.-Col., Indian Cav. ; served on N.-W. Frontier of India, 1897, as Lieut. The Buffs ; was Military Attaché, Teheran, 1907–11, and on Gen. Staff. Headquarters, India, 1912–17 ; served in the Great War, 1917–19, in Mesopotamia, Persia, and Caucasus (Brevet Lieut.-Col.), as Lieut.-Col. on Gen. Staff. *Clubs:* Junior Naval and Military ; United Service. (O6536)

STOKES, Edith Nellie, Mrs., C.B.E. Hon. Organiser, Surgical Requisities Assoc. (C68)

STOKES, Major Edward, O.B.E., R.A.F.

STOKES, Major Francis Maurice Collins, O.B.E.

STOKES, Sir Frederick Wilfrid Scott, K.B.E., M.I.C.E., *b.* 9 April, 1860 ; *s.* of Scott Nasmyth Stokes ; *m.* Irine Theadora, *d.* of Luke Ionides. Engineer ; Chairman and Managing Director, Messrs. Ransomes and Rapier, Ltd. *War Work:* Chairman, East Anglian Munitions Committee and Board of Management ; Member of 4 committees, Munitions Inventions Dept. ; Chairman, London and Eastern Counties Controlled Establishment Association ; Chairman, Ipswich and District Employers Association ; Member of Executive Committee, Board of Management Representative Committee. Inventor of the "Stokes" gun and shell. *Addresses:* 7, Park Lane, W. 1 ; Millwater, Ripley, Surrey. *Clubs:* St. Stephen's ; Arts. (K39)

STOKES, Major George Edward, O.B.E., *b.* 4 Dec. 1882 ; *s.* of George Stokes, of Brentford, Middlesex. Civil Servant ; Exchequer and Audit Dept., Victoria Embankment, E.C. 4 *War Work:* Served with the 15th Batt. London Regt. (Prince of Wales's Own Civil Service Rifles), Nov. 1901, to Aug. 1920 ; twice mentioned in despatches. *Address:* 4, Hamilton Road, Brentford. (O2737)

STOKES, Capt. Henry, O.B.E., R.A.M.C.

STOKES, Capt. Hubert Francis, O.B.E., R.A.M.C., *b.* 16 Jan. 1887 ; *s.* of Col. A. H. Stokes, of Tralee, Ireland ; *m.* Marjorie, *d.* of G. A. Duff, of Folkestone. *Educ.:* Cheltenham Coll. *War Work:* Regimental duty with B.E.F., France, 1914 ; Adjutant R. Newfoundland Regt., 1915 ; Regt. duty with B.E.F., France, 1916 ; G.S.O., 23rd Army Corps, 1917–18 ; *Address:* 34, Linden Road, Bedford. *Club:* Junior United Services. (O7750)

STOKES, Major Hugh Gabriel, O.B.E., I.A.R.O.

STOKES, Irene Mary, O.B.E.

STOKES, Capt. Leslie Eric Sheldon, O.B.E., R.F.A.

STOKES, Madel Louise, M.B.E.

STOKES, Ralph Shelton Griffin, D.S.O., O.B.E., M.C., *b.* 31 July, 1882 ; *s.* of Francis Griffin Stokes, of Highgate, London. *Educ.:* Pennington Hall, Southborough, Kent. Mining engineer ; Assistant General Manager (Mines Dept.), De Beers Consolidated Mines, Ltd., Kimberley, South Africa. *War Work:* With Royal Engineers in France and North Russia from 1914 to 1919. *Address:* Hotel Belgrave, Kimberley, S. Africa. *Clubs:* Saville ; Kimberley (Kimberley). (O3078)

STOKES, Richard Albert, M.B.E.

STOKES, Robert Day, M.B.E., L.R.C.P., L.R.C.S.

STOKES, Sarah Shelton, Mrs., M.B.E., *b.* 14 Aug. 1853 ; *d.* of the Rev. Maurice Shelton Suckling, of Shipmeadow Rectory, Beccles ; *m.* Francis Griffin, *s.* of Thomas Stokes, of Hean Castle, Pembrokeshire. *Educ.:* Privately. *War Work:* Hon. Organising Sec. of the Red Cross Depot, Muswell Hill, N., from Sept. 1914, to Feb. 1919 ; organiser of Flag Days for " Our Day " and other War Charities. *Address:* 41, Talbot Road, Highgate, N. 6. (M9737)

STOKES, 2nd Lieut. William Henry, M.B.E., D.C.M., M.G.C.

STOKES, William Noel, O.B.E., D.S.C., R.A.O.C.

STOMM, Major P. W. J. A., C.B.E. Major (ret.), R.F.A. (Special Reserve). Great War, 1914–19 (despatches). (C2172)

STONE, Major Alan Getheng, O.B.E., M.C., I.A.

STONE, Benjamin Garne, M.B.E., *b.* 31 Aug. 1857 ; *s* of Edmund Stone, of Aldsworth, Gloucestershire ; *m.* Ellen, *d.* of Alfred Bourne, of Louth, Lincs. *Educ.:* Public Elementary Schools. Estate Agent. *War Work:* Chairman, Louth and District Emergency Committee ; Sec. to War Agricultural Committee (Louth District) ; Member Local Military Tribunal. *Address:* Elkington Estate Office, Louth, Lincs. (M9738)

STONE, Eng.-Comm. Charles Edward, O.B.E., R.N.

STONE, Ernest Stacey, M.B.E., R.N.

STONE, Henry, M.B.E., F.C.I.S., *b.* 26 Feb. 1872. Clerk to Rural District Council of Basford, Local Tribunal, Food Control (Executive Officer), Superintendent Registrar. *Address:* 8, Alexandra Street, Sherwood Rise, Nottingham. *Club:* Constitutional, Nottingham. (M9739)

STONE, Rev. Henry Cecil Brough, C.B.E., M.A., Hon. C. F., 2nd Class, *b.* 14 Aug. 1873 ; *s.* of Very Rev. W. H. Stone, Dean of Kilmore ; *d.* of the Rev. C. Faris, M.A., of St. Patrick's Cathedral, Armagh. *Educ.:* Trinity Coll., Dublin. Senior Chaplain, Indian Ecclesiastical Establishment. *War Work:* Senior Chaplain to the Forces (C. of E.), Mesopotamian Expeditionary Force, 1917–19. *Address:* c/o Bank of Madras, Madras. (C1113)

STONE, Isaac, M.B.E., *b.* 27 April, 1867 ; *s.* of Robert Stone, of Kilburn ; *m.* Annie Eliza, *d.* of Joseph Stone, of Watford, Herts. *Educ.:* St. Andrews, Watford, Herts. Builder's Manager. *War Work:* Factory Construction : Chilwell, Notts, Shell-Filling Factory, Northwich, Cheshire ; Soda Nitrate, National Aircraft Factory, Waddon, Croydon ; Anglo-American Tank Assembly Factory, Chateauroux, Indre, France. *Address:* 113, Boundaries Road, Balham, S.W. 12. (M2485)

STONE, John William, C.B.E., *b.* 9 Aug. 1852 ; *s.* of John William Stone, of London ; *m.* Catherine Jane (*d.* 1918), *d.* of the late John Edwards, of Llangefni, Anglesea. *Educ.:* Privately. Chief Surveyor of Lands, Civil Engineer-in-Chief Dept. Admiralty. *Address:* Plas Isa, 126, Breakspears Road, Brockley, S.E. 4. *Clubs:* Reform ; National Liberal. (C309)

STONE, Lieut. Leslie Norman Waldegrave, M.B.E.

STONE, T. Lieut. Philip Arthur, O.B.E., R.A.S.C.

STONEHAM, Allen Henry Philip, O.B.E., *b.* 22 Nov. 1855 ; *s.* of Allen Stoneham (Financial Secretary, Board of Trade) ; *m.* Florence Marie Louise (M.B.E.), *d.* of John C. Garrett, of Montreal. *Educ.:* City of London School, and King's Coll., London. *War Work:* Aug. to Dec. 1914, Red Cross and Canteen Work ; Dec. 1914, suggested to Lord Kitchener formation of camp at Etaples or Le Touquet (and offered land for the purpose) in place of camp on Salisbury Plain ; result Etaples adopted ; helped to lay out first camp at Etaples, and acted as Interpreter ; in 1915–18 gave land for camps for 3rd Cavalry Division, Lewis Gun School, Hotchkiss School, Trench Mortar School, Motor Transport, Veterinary Lines, G.H.Q., L. of C., and was constantly at disposal of officers requiring local information ; in 1916, suggested that troops at bases should be utilised to grow food for the Army, with result that an Agricultural Department of the Army was created ; awarded British War Medal and Allied Victory Medal. *Address:* Le Manoir, Le Touquet, Etaples, Pas-de-Calais. *Clubs:* Carlton ; 1900 ; Royal Automobile ; Travellers', Paris. (O11398)

STONEHAM, Edgar Cooper, O.B.E.

STONEHAM, Florence Marie Louise, M.B.E., *b.* 14 Sept. 1875 ; *d.* of John C. Garrett, of Montreal ; *m.* Allen Henry Philip Stoneham, O.B.E., *s.* of Allen Stoneham. *Educ.:* Villa Marie Convent at Montreal. *War Work:* Started canteen at Etaples Station, Sept. 1914, being first canteen in north of France ; this canteen fed some 300,000 British and French soldiers passing through to the battlefields ; received thanks of British and French Generals ; early in 1915, finding nothing being done for comfort of officers, started first officers' club and library, and continued this till early in 1918 ; suggested and organised first ceremonies at military cemeteries at Le Touquet and Etaples in honour of the fallen ; mentioned in Sir Douglas Haig's despatches, 1918. *Address:* Le Manoir, Le Touquet, Pas-de-Calais. *Club:* Ladies' Empire. (M9740)

STONEHAM, Capt. Hugh Frederic, O.B.E., *b.* 30 July, 1889 ; *s.* of F. W. Stoneham, of Reigate, Surrey. *Educ.:* King's Coll. School ; Sandhurst. Joined 1st Batt. East Surrey Regt. (31st Foot) from Sandhurst, April, 1910 ; Member of British Ornithologists' Union, and Fellow of the Entomological Society of London. *War Work:* Served in France with regiment from outbreak of war ; East Africa, 1916–17 ; Mesopotamia, 1917–19 ; mentioned in despatches. *Addresses:* Stoneleigh, Reigate, Surrey ; Trans-Nzoia, Kenya Colony. *Clubs:* Army and Navy ; British Ornithologists'. (O6710)

STONEHOUSE, Lieut.-Comm. Andrew Woodhouse, O.B.E., R.N.R.

STONEMAN, John Oliver Veysey, M.B.E., *b.* 15 May, 1866 ; *s.* of Edward Elliott Stoneman, of Kingsbridge ; *m.* Clara, *d.* of James Willcox, of Bath. *Educ.:* Kingsbridge Grammar School. Member, Kingsbridge Urban District Council ; President, Kingsbridge Town Association ; Hon. Sec. Kingsbridge Choral, and Operatic Societies ; Chairman, Kingsbridge Horticultural Society. *War Work:* Hon. Sec. National War Savings Committee, and of War Memorial Committee. *Address:* Beethoven House, Kingsbridge, South Devon. *Club:* Constitutional, Kingsbridge. (M9741)

STONES, Frederick, O.B.E.

STONES, John, M.B.E.

STONESTREET, George William, C.B.E., *b.* 1863 ; *s.* of Ephraim Stonestreet, formerly of Maidstone ; *m.* 1899, Alice Elizabeth, *d.* of Thomas Sanford, formerly of Exeter. *Educ.:* King's Coll., London. Appointed Director of Stamping, Inland Revenue, 1917. *Address:* 13, Hillcroft Crescent, Ealing, W.5. (C1042)

STONEY, Florence Ada, O.B.E., M.D., B.S. (Lond.), *b.* 1870 ; *d.* of George Johnstone Stoney, M.A., Sc.D., F.R.S., of Dublin. *Educ.:* Privately ; London School of Medicine for Women. Hon. Medical Officer to the Electrical Department, Royal Victoria and West Hants Hospital, Bournemouth. *War Work:* Head of Imperial Service League Hospital, Antwerp, 1914, and Anglo-French Hospital, No. 2, Cherbourg, 1914–15 ; Head of Electrical Department, Fulham Military Hospital, London, 1915–19. *Address:* Ardvoulan, 29, Poole Road, Bournemouth. *Club:* Lyceum, London. (O4395)

STONEY, Col. Ralph Durrant Sadleir, C.B.E., *b.* 1873 ; *s.* of Lieut.-Col. Francis Sadleir Stoney, formerly of Little Heath, Kent ; *m.* 1900, Amy, *d.* of the Rev. W. Moore Morgan, Canon of Armagh. Lieut.-Col., R.A.F. ; served in the Great War, 1914–19, as Col. (despatches). (C875)

STONHAM, Edwin Earle, O.B.E., *b.* 16 July, 1867 ; *s.* of Edwin John Stonham, of New Romney, Kent ; *m.* Louise

Edith, d. of the late E. E. Lucas, R.N. *Educ.*: Sheerness, and King's Coll., London. Collector of H.M. Customs and Excise for Port and District of Bristol. *War Work*: Was responsible for seeing that all restrictions as to shipping, imports, and exports were observed in Bristol and district, and in capacity of Substitute for the Marshal of the Admiralty Court, was in charge of all Prize Goods brought to the Port. *Address*: 37, Regent Street, Clifton, Bristol. *Club*: Constitutional, Bristol. (O11399)

STOODLEY, Lieut. Fred, M.B.E.

STOPFORD, Annette Hilda, M.B.E.; d. of Capt. Walter James Stopford, C.B. *War Work*: Clerk in Honours Department, War Office, from July, 1916. *Address*: 19, Belgrave Road, London, S.W. 1. (M9743)

STOPFORD, James Richard Neville, Viscount, O.B.E., b. 1877; s. of James Walter Milles Stopford, 7th Earl of Courtown (see BURKE'S *Peerage*); m. 1905, Cicely Mary, y. d. of the late John Arden Birch, D.L. Co. Wexford. T. Major (Gen. List), Staff Capt. War Office, 1916–18; D.A.A.G. War Office from 1916. Served in S. African War, 1900–1 (medal); Great War (despatches). *Address*: Wendover House, Beaconsfield, Bucks. *Club*: Royal Automobile. (O7751)

STOPFORD, John Sebastian Bach, M.B.E., M.D.

STOPHER, Arthur James, O.B.E., Whitworth Scholar, b. 23 June, 1862; s. of Thomas Stopher, of Winchester; m. Cecilia Bernardine, d. of William Baker, of Halifax, Nova Scotia. *Educ.*: Trafalgar House School, Winchester; Nottingham Univ. Coll. Served apprenticeship as mechanical engineer in Manchester and Nottingham; gained Whitworth Scholarship in 1885. *War Work*: Served as cable engineer-in-charge of Messrs. Siemens Bros. & Co.'s cable ship " Faraday," which in 1915 and 1918 carried out important deep-water repairs and renewals to various Atlantic Cables, and in 1917 laid a telegraph cable from Murmansk to Archangel, and a telephone cable across the White Sea; was also engaged in cable work for the Admiralty in connection with hydrophones for the detection of submarines. *Address*: 1, Bell Rock, Mycenae Road, Blackheath, London, S.E., 3. (O11400)

STORDY, Col. Robert John, C.B.E., D.S.O., Army Vet. Corps. Dep. Director of Vet. Sers. with rank of Col.; served in E. Africa, 1914–17, as Chief Veterinary Officer (despatches); France, 1918 (wounded). (C1778)

STOREY, Capt. Alan Thomas Trevor, O.B.E.

STOREY, Ethel Mary Hutton, O.B.E.

STOREY, Florence Lizzie, M.B.E.

STOREY, George Alexander, M.B.E.

STOREY, Henry, M.B.E. R.N. (ret.), b. 8 Jan. 1857; s. of John Storey, of Sheffield; m. Jane, d. of Robert Linch, of Southampton. *Educ.*: Holy Rood School, Southampton. Collector of Fishery Statistics for Ministry of Agriculture and Fisheries. *War Work*: Raising Men for R.N.R. and R.N.V.R. *Address*: 48, Beresford Road, Lowestoft. (M2486)

STOREY, John, M.B.E., F.R.A.S.

STOREY, Lieut.-Col. John Colvin, O.B.E., Aust. A.M.C.

STOREY, Lieut. John William, M.D.E.

STOREY, Lieut. Joseph Kearon, O.B.E., R.N.R., b. 23rd Jan. 1891; s. of John Storey, of Arklow, Ireland; m. Chrissie, d. of David Bunyan, of Haddington, Scotland. *Educ.*: Private Tuition and Skerry's. Master Mariner. *War Work*: Belgian coast; special service (for Restriction of Enemy's Supply Dept.) in Finland. *Addresses*: Hall Line, Ltd., Tower Building, Liverpool; 73, Spottiswoode Street, Edinburgh; Crosby Hall, Durban, S. Africa. (O11402)

STOREY, Mary Gladys, O.B.E.; d. of the late Professor G. A. Storey, R.A., of the Royal Academy of Arts, London. and 39, Broadhurst Gardens, London, N.W. *Educ.*: Privately. Stage; played first at the age of 15; acted at principal London Theatres and on tour; in 1914 played " Georgette " (the ingénue part) in Henry Bernstein's play " The Attack," with the late Sir George Alexander, at St. James's Theatre, London; temporarily gave up stage career in 1914 for war work; first joined Recruiting Staff, Whitehall. *War Work*: Organised and ran single-handed a fund (Nov. 1914) for providing free Bovril to British troops in every theatre of war (personal letters of appreciation from Field-Marshals French and Haig, and all the Army Commanders, and hundreds of letters from the trenches; gifts sent also to the French, Belgian, and American soldiers (letters from Marshal Foch, M. Vandervelde, and General Pershing); in 1916 the Army Council allocated 500 guineas to the fund; H.M. The King gave five times to the fund; personal contributions also from H.R.H. Prince of Wales, H.M. Queen Alexandra, H.R.H. the Duke of Connaught, the Prime Minister, etc.; organised matinee at Palladium, lent free by the management, which realised over £1181; at the request of the G.O.C., supplied the whole of the British Mission in S. Russia with free Bovril through the winter of 1920. *Addresses*: Hougoumont, 39, Broadhurst Gardens, South Hampstead, London; Pootings, Edenbridge, Kent. (O11403)

STOREY, Major Robert, O.B.E., R.A.S.C.

STOREY, Sir Thomas James, K.B.E., b. 1851; s. of the late Capt. Wm. Storey; m. 1877, d. of the late Fearnley Bannell. Member of the Committee and Chairman of the Classification Committee of Lloyds' Register of Shipping. *Address*: 24, Cambalt Road, Putney Hill, S.W. (K106)

STOREY, Lieut. Wilfred Robinson, M.B.E.

STORR, Capt. Francis Holland, O.B.E.

STORRAR, George Ronald, M.B.E., b. 2nd Aug. 1876; s. of Richard A. Storrar. Assistant Engineer, Sudan Government Railways. *War Work*: Remained in Sudan Govern-

ment Service throughout the war; took part in operations against the Sultan of Darfur; mentioned in despatches, and decorated with 4th Class Order of the Star of the Nile. *Address*: Atbara, Sudan. *Club*: Sports. (M2825)

STORRIE, John Hay Atwall, M.B.E., b. 15 Dec. 1871; m. Euphemia Graham McBeth. *Educ.*: Privately, and Public Schools, Greenock and Glasgow. District Manager, Post Office Telephone Service, Aberdeen; held similar appointments at York and at Kirkcaldy (Fife). *War Work*: Chairman of Y.M.C.A., York, during war. *Address*: Telephone House, Bon-Accord Street, Aberdeen. (M9746)

STORRS, Col. Ronald, C.M.G., C.B.E.,!b. 19 Nov. 1881; s. of the Very Rev. John Storrs, Dean of Rochester. *Educ.*: Temple Grove, Charterhouse; Pemb. Coll., Cambridge. Ministry of Finance, Cairo; Oriental Sec. British Agency, later Residency, Cairo. *War Work*: Political Liaison, Baghdad and Arab Movement; Secretariat, War Cabinet; Military Governor, Jerusalem, Dec. 1917, to June, 1920; Acting Chief Administrator, Palestine, Dec. to March, 1919; Governor, Jerusalem District, 1 July, 1920. *Address*: Governorate, Jerusalem. *Club*: Travellers'. (C788)

STORRY, Sir Thomas James, K.B.E., b. 1851; s. of the late Capt William Storry; m. a d. of the late Fearnley Bonnett, of Bradford, Yorks. Member of Managing Committee, and Chairman of Classification Committee, Lloyds Register of Shipping. *Address*: 24, Cambalt Road, Putney Hill, S.W. (K106)

STORY, Major Robert Douglas, C.B.E. Major, Indian Army, and Agent to Shipping Controller, India, during Great War, 1914–19 (despatches). (C2212a)

STORY, Adm. Wm. Oswald, C.B.

STOTHERT, Sir Percy Kendall, K.B.E., M.Inst.C.E., J.P., b. 21 June, 1863; s. of John Lum Stothert, of Bath; m. Violet Ellen, d. of Col. H. S. E. Reeves, C.B., of East Sheen. *Educ.*: Clifton Coll. Chairman, Bath Gas Co., Clevedon Gas Co., Clevedon Water Co.; Director, Stothert and Pitt, Ltd., Bristol Gas Co. *War Work*: Chairman, West of England Munitions Committee. *Address*: 1, Lansdown Place West, Bath. *Clubs*: Windham; Bath and County, Bath. (K107)

STOTHERT, Major William, O.B.E., C.di.G., M.R.C.V.S., F.E.V.M.S., b. 1868; s. of Richard Stothert, of Atherton; m. Nellie, d. of John Charnley, of Blackburn. *Educ.*: Ilkley and Edinburgh. *War Work*: Commanding Veterinary Hospitals at Swaythling and Winchester, 1914–16; D.A.D.V.S. in France and Italy, 1916–19. *Address*: Bregner, Bournemouth. (O3005)

STOTT, Lieut.-Col. Herbert, O.B.E., J.P., b. 20 Jan. 1874; s. of Thomas F. Stott, of Manchester; m. Lily Gertrude, d. of Thomas G. Russell, of Manchester. *Educ.*: Manchester. Cotton Manufacturer, Empire Mill, Congleton, Cheshire, and 4, Minshull Street, Manchester. *War Work*: Mobilised, Aug. 1914; recruited and raised 3/6th Cheshire Regt., and Commanded until Aug. 1916; appointed to command 14th Loyal North Lancs. Sept. 1916, to Oct. 1917; Deputy Commander, Comrades of the Great War, Cheshire Division. *Address*: The Grange, Cheadle Hulme, Cheshire. *Club*: Reform (Manchester). (O7752)

STOTT, Capt. Hugh, O.B.E., M.B., I.M.S.

STOTT, Capt. James Robert, O.B.E., R.A.M.C.

STOTT, William Harle, O.B.E., late Major R.A.M.C., b. 17 Jan. 1871; s. of the late Rev. Jonas Stott, M.A., of Manchester; m. Evelyn Marguerite, d. of Louis Hervey d'Egville, of London. *Educ.*: Manchester Grammar School; Owens Coll., Manchester. Medical Officer to the Harborough and Uppingham Unions. *War Work*: Medical Referee, War Pensions; M.O. 4th King's Liverpool Regt. (France), and 89th Field Ambulance, 29th Division (Gallipoli); O.C. Troops, H.M.A.T., St. David, and H.M.A.T., Panama; Humane Society's Certificate for saving lunatic patient in the sea at Salonica, 1916. *Address*: Hallaton, Market Harboro'. (O7753)

STOUGHTON, Maud Eleanor, M.B.E.

STOURTON, Major Herbert Marmaduke Joseph, O.B.E., b. 30 Dec. 1873; s. of the late Hon. Albert Stourton; m. Frances Mary Winifrede, d. of the late Viscount Southwell. *Educ.*: Beaumont Coll. *War Work*: France, Oct. 1914, to Nov. 1915; Salonica, as A.M.L.O., Nov. 1915, to August, 1917; M.L.O. Hea, Oct. 1917, to Jan. 1918; A.M.L.O. Salonica, Feb. 1918, to Aug. 1918; M.L.O. Dedeagatch, Oct. 1918, to Nov. 1918; M.L.O. Constantinople, Nov. 1918, to April, 1920; O.B.E. (military), 1914 Star, Greek Order of Merit, Medaille d'honneur avec glaives vermeils; mentioned in despatches. *Clubs*: Boodle's; Constantinople. (O6539)

STOUT, Capt. Percy Wyfold, D.S.O., O.B.E., Mounted Machine Gun Corps. Served in the Great War, 1914–19 (despatches). (O2937)

STOUT, Major Thomas Duncan MacGregor, D.S.O., O.B.E., M.S., F.R.C.S., L.R.C.P., b. 1885; s. of the Hon. Sir Robert Stout, K.C.M.G., Ch. Justice of New Zealand. *Educ.*: Wellington Coll., New Zealand. New Zealand Med. Corps. *War Work*: 1914–17, as Div. Surgical Officer, New Zealand Gen. Hospital, No. 1, in Port Said, Salonica, and France (despatches). (O9011)

STOVELL, Lieut. Frederick, M.B.E.

STOVOLD, Herbert William, O.B.E., b. 29 Jan. 1871; s. of Thomas Stovold, of Croydon; m. Jessie Edith, d. of W. Sterndale Scarr, of Westcombe Park, S.E. *Educ.*: Whitgift Grammar School. Croydon. Entered the service of the London County Council. 1891; appointed Assistant Comptroller, Jan.

1920, and Deputy Comptroller, May, 1920. *War Work:* Loaned by the London County Council to the Ministry of Food for the purpose of undertaking the financial arrangements in connection with Local Food Control Committees; entered the service of the Ministry in Sept. 1917, and received the title of Assistant Director of Finance; recalled by the London County Council, Dec. 1918. *Address:* Lanhydrock, Addiscombe Road, Croydon. *Club:* Royal Societies'. (O1897)

STOW, Alexander Montagu, O.B.E.

STOW, Major David Fenwick, O.B.E., R.A.S.C.

STOW, Capt. George, O.B.E., R.E., Wh. Ex. A.M.I.C.E., A.M.I.M.E., *b.* 11 July, 1876; *s.* of Thomas Stow, of Shoreham, Sussex; *m.* Mary Florence,'*d.* of Edwin Snewin, of Littlehampton. *Educ.:* Hayle's Private School. Public Works Contractor. *War Work:* Adjutant, C.R.E., 2nd Army, B.E.F.; thrice mentioned in despatches. *Addresses:* Lyndale, Llanthewy Road, Newport, Mon.; Station Chambers, Cambrian Road, Newport, Mon. (O5821)

STOW, Major Harry Vane, O.B.E., V.D., *b.* 13 Jan. 1852; *s.* of Edward Stow. *Educ.:* Privately, and City of London School. Hon. Assist. Sec. and Organiser, Royal Military Tournament (1885–96); Hon. Sec. National Artillery Association. *War Work:* Sec. Newspapers for the Fleet Committee, for providing free reading matter for the Grand Fleet; 20 million books and papers, etc., despatched, about £26,000 subscribed and disbursed in expenses. *Address:* 69, Philbeach Gardens, Earl's Court, S.W. *Club:* Junior Army and Navy. (O775)

STOWE, Richard Walter, M.B.E.

STOWELL, Capt. George Christopher, M.B.E.

STOWELL, Harold Joseph, M.B.E.

STOWELL, Vere Arthur, O.B.E., *b.* 12 Sept. 1873; *s.* of the Rev. H. A. Stowell, of Breadsall, Derbyshire. *Educ.:* Rossall School, and C.C.C., Oxford. Indian Civil Service, 1896–1920, Magistrate and Collector, 1st Grade. *War Work:* Sec. United Provinces War Board, 1917–19; Sec. U.P. Joint War Committee, 1917–19; Sec. U.P. Soldiers' Board, 1919. *Address:* Jaunpur, U.P., India. *Club:* East India United Service. (O2052)

STOYLE, Capt. William, O.B.E., R.F.A.

STRACHAN, Lieut. Charles John, M.B.E.

STRACHAN, Major Ernest Frederick, O.B.E., M.C.

STRACHAN, James, M.B.E., *b.* 31 July, 1857; *s.* of Peter Strachan, of Perth; *m.* Isabella Wallace, *d.* of — Morrison, of Dundee. *Educ.:* Sharpe's Institution, Perth. Acting Works Manager, L. & N.W. Railway Carriage Works, Wolverton, Bucks. *War Work:* Work in connection with Ambulance Trains, Transport Wagons, Munitions. *Address:* The Hawthorns, Wolverton, Bucks. (M2489)

STRACHAN, John, M.B.E., *b.* 7 Dec. 1890; *s.* of Alexander Strachan, of Glasgow; *m.* Kate, *d.* of Peter Ewing, F.L.S., of Uddingston, Lanarkshire. *Educ.:* Privately. Surveyor, City Assessor's Office, City Chambers, Glasgow. *War Work:* In connection with the Belgian Refugees sent to Scotland. *Address:* 11 St. James Terrace, Kilmacolm, Scotland. *Club:* Athenæum, Glasgow. (M9748)

STRACHAN, Robert, M.B.E., M.B.

STRACHEY, Amy, Mrs. O.B.E., *b.* 5 May, 1866; *d.* of Charles Turner Simpson, of London; *m.* John St. Loe, *s.* of Sir Edward Strachey, Bart., of Sutton Court, Somerset (*see* BURKE'S *Peerage*). *Educ.:* Privately. Governor, King's Coll., Chelsea Polytechnic. Sec. Welfare Department, B.R.C.S. Headquarters. *War Work:* Commandant Newlands Corner Hospital, Merrow Downs, Guildford; Vice-President, Albury and Shire Division, Surrey Branch, B.R.C.S.; Commandant, V.A.D. Surrey 10. *Address:* Newlands Corner, Merrow Downs, Guildford. *Clubs:* V.A.D. Ladies'; Ladies' Empire. (O776)

STRADBROKE, Col. George Edward John Mowbray Earl of, K.C.M.G., C.B., C.V.O., C.B.E., V.D., A.D.C., J.P., D.L., *b.* 19 Nov. 1862; *s.* of John, 2nd Earl of Stradbroke, of Henham, Suffolk (*see* BURKE'S *Peerage*); *m.* Helena Violet Alice, O.B.E., *d.* of the late Lieut.-Gen. Keith Fraser, C.M.G., of Ledclune and Morar, N.B. *Educ.:* Harrow and Cambridge. Chairman, East Suffolk County Council; Chairman, Suffolk County Territorial Association; President, National Sea Fisheries Protection Association; President, Central London Ophthalmic Hospital; President of the Council of the National Art Association; Pro Grand Master Mark Masons; Prov. Grand Master Suffolk Freemasons; appointed by His Majesty to be Governor of Victoria, Aug. 1920. *War Work:* Served in England, France, Egypt, and Palestine from July, 1914, to July, 1920, as Col. Comm. 3rd East Anglian R.F.A. Brigade, the 272nd, 172nd, and 191st, R.F.A. Brigades; C.R.A., 54th Div. Aug. 1916, to Nov. 1916. in Egypt; Comm. Kantara Area, 1919 and 1920. *Address:* Henham Hall, Wangford, Suffolk. *Clubs:* Carlton; Royal Yacht Squadron; Royal Thames Yacht; Bachelor's. (C1779)

STRADBROKE, Helena Violet Alice, Countess of, O.B.E., *d.* of Major-Gen. Keith Fraser, C.M.G.; *m.* Col. George Edward John Mowbray, 3rd Earl of Stradbroke, C.B., C.V.O., A.D.C., Governor of Victoria (*see* BURKE'S *Peerage*). *War Work:* In 1914 organised and equipped Henham Hall as hospital, 100 beds, for direct convoy first-line cases; personal work as V.A.D. after training in a General Hospital; afterwards acted as Superintendent; also organised and managed for short time large hostel, 500 beds, in London, for soldiers and sailors on leave; equipped and organised soldiers' club and tea rooms in country. *Address:* Henham Hall, Wangford, Suffolk. (O1898)

STRADLING, Capt. Alfred Eric Hugh, O.B.E., *b.* 9 May,

1892; *s.* of Mrs. F. M. Stradling, of Crowthorne. Gordon Highlanders, and Royal Air Force, Staff Officer (personnel). *War Work:* 1914–16, France and Flanders with Gordon Highlanders; 1917–19, France and Germany with Royal Air Force. *Addresses:* 7, Harley Street, London; 1, Pilgrims' Lane, Hampstead; Pinegrove, Crowthorne. *Club:* Royal Air Force. (O8200)

STRADLING, Capt. Charles Austice, M.B.E.

STRAHAN, Sir Aubrey, K.B.E., Sc.D. (Camb.), Hon. LL.D. (Toronto), F.R.S., *b.* 20 April, 1852; *s.* of William Strahan, of Sidmouth; *m.* Fanny Evelyn Margaret, *d.* of Edward Roscoe, of Chester. *Educ.:* Eton, and St. John's Coll., Cambridge. Late Director of the Geological Survey of Great Britain, and Museum of Practical Geology. *Address:* Fairfield, Goring, Reading. *Club:* Athenæum. (K235)

STRAHAN, Capt. Geoffrey Cartaret, O.B.E., I.A.

STRAIN, James Bruce, C.B.E., *b.* 13 July, 1866. *War Work:* Deputy Controller in the Gun Ammunition Filling Dept. of the Ministry of Munitions (Voluntary). *Addresses:* 27, Leadenhall Street, E.C. 2; Stone House, Reigate, Surrey. *Clubs:* Bengal; Oriental; Constitutional; Ranelagh. (C1043)

STRAIN, Lieut.-Col. Lawrence Hugh, O.B.E., D.S.C.

STRANG, Alexander Ronald, C.B.E., J.P., late Capt. 7th V.B., Argyll and Sutherland Hrs., *b.* 23 Nov. 1848; *s.* of Robert Strang, of Alloa, N.B.; *m.* Agnes, *d.* of Alexander Begg, of Paisley. *Educ.:* The Academy, Alloa. Provost of Alloa, 1913–16. *War Work:* Chairman of Tribunal; Chairman of Recruiting Committees; Chairman of Prince of Wales Fund Committee; Member of War Pensions and various Relief Committees; Chief Special Constable. *Address:* North Park, Alloa, N.B. (C2977)

STRANG, Duncan, O.B.E., J.P. Valuable local and public services in Ardrishaig throughout the war. (O11926)

STRANG, Matthew Smellie, M.B.E.

STRANG, William, M.B.E., *b.* 2 Jan. 1893; *s.* of James Strang, of Croydon; *m.* Elsie Wynne, *d.* of J. E. Jones. *Educ.:* Palmer's Endowed School; Univ. Coll., London; Univ. of Paris. Appd. 3rd. Sec. H.B.M. Legation, Belgrade, Sept. 1919. *War Work:* With 4th Batt. Worcestershire Regt., 1916–18; with 29th Division, Army of Occupation on the Rhine, 1918–19. *Address:* c/o Foreign Office, Downing Street, S.W. *Club:* University of London. (M4608)

STRANGE, Lieut.-Col. Edward Fairbrother, C.B.E., T.D., *b.* 8 Oct. 1862; *s.* of the late Richard Fairbrother Strange; *m.* Margaret Elisabeth, *d.* of the late Walter Scott Coward, H.M.I. *Educ.:* Worcester Cathedral School; Kidderminster Grammar School. Keeper of Woodwork, Victoria and Albert Museum. *War Work:* Major, 1/15 Bn. The London Regt., Aug. 1914, to Dec. 1915; Commanded 2/15 Bn. The London Regt., May, 1915, to May, 1916; Commanded 13th Reserve Bn. The London Regt., June, 1916, to Sept. 1917; joined Ministry of Food, Sept. 1917; Deputy Director, Butter and Cheese Supplies, 1917; Controller, Margarine Rationing Scheme, 1918; Assist. Sec. 1918; Food Commissioner with British Army on the Rhine, and British Member of Inter-allied Military Food Commission, 1919; Member of Food Council, 1919; Deputy Chairman, Wholesale Markets Committee, 1919; Chairman of Fair Trading Councils for Fish, Fruit, Vegetable, and Jam Trades, 1920. *Address:* 14, Hayes Way, Parklangley, Beckenham. *Club:* Arts. (C640)

STRANGE, Lieut. Jack Ronald Stewart, O.B.E., R.N.R.

STRANGE, John, M.B.E., R.A.O.C.

STRATFORD, Lenna Mary, M.B.E., B.A., *b.* 1877; *d.* of the late Capt. Robert Stratford, Royal Warwickshire Regt. *Educ.:* Notting Hill High School, London. Chief Inspectress of Schools, Punjab. *Addresses:* Chief Inspectors Schools; Nedrons' Hotel, Lahore. (M6256)

STRATFORD, Rosalind Isabel, Mrs. WINGFIELD-, M.B.E., *b.* 7 Nov. 1857; *d.* of the late Rev. Hon. Edward Vesey Bligh, of Fartherwell, W. Malling, Kent (*see* BURKE'S *Peerage*, Darnley, E.); *m.* Brig.-Gen. Cecil Vernon, C.B., C.M.G., *s.* of John Wingfield-Stratford, of Addington Park, Kent (*see* BURKE'S *Peerage*, Powerscourt, V). *War Work:* Commandant, Kent V.A.D. 150; in charge of West Malling Auxiliary Hospital, 1914–19. *Address:* Fartherwell, West Malling, Kent. *Clubs:* Empress; Lady Golfers'. (M9749)

STRATHCLYDE, Alexander Ure, Lord, P.C., G.B.E., *b.* 1853; *s.* of John Ure, Sometime Lord Provost, of Glasgow; *m.* Margaret McDowall, *d.* of the late Thomas Steven, of Helensburgh. *Educ.:* Larchfield Academy, Helensburgh, and Glasgow Univ. Formerly Lord Justice-General and Lord President of the Court of Session. *War Work:* Chairman of the Scottish War Savings Committee; Addressed Meetings in all parts of Scotland on National Thrift. *Addresses:* 31, Heriot Row, Edinburgh; Cairndhu, Helensburgh. *Clubs:* Reform; Western (Glasgow); University (Edinburgh); Royal Northern Yacht.

STRATHEARN, Capt. John, O.B.E., M.D., F.R.C.S., R.A.M.C. (T.).

STRATTON, Capt. Howard Wallace, O.B.E.

STRATTON, Lieut. James Phillips, M.B.E., R.A.S.C. (T.).

STRATTON, Percy Montague, M.B.E.

STRATTON, Robert, M.B.E.

STRAUS, Blanche, M.B.E., *d.* of Albert Dux, of Manchester; *m.* Percy, *s.* of Ralph Straus, of Manchester. *Educ.:* Ellerslie, Victoria Park, Manchester. *War Work:* Worked at the Red Cross Hospital (Abbey Lodge), Chislehurst;

afterwards at the St. Marylebone War Hospital Supply Depot (later H.R.H. Princess's Beatrice's); appointed head of the Surgical Dressings Dept. in that Depot. *Address:* Hatton Cottage, Chislehurst, Kent. *Clubs:* Ladies' Athenæum; Chislehurst Golf. (M9752)

STRAW, Arthur Roger, M.B.E.

STRAWN, Frances May, Mrs., M.B.E. (M10254g)

STREATFEILD, Evelyn Olive, Mrs., O.B.E., b. 21 Sept. 1871; *d.* of Pim Cherry, of Co. Waterford, Ireland; *m.* Major Hugh Sidney, J.P. (late R.F.A.), *s.* of the late Capt. Sidney R. Streatfeild, R.N. *War Work:* Asst. County Director Co. Durham, and Commandant 12th Durham V.A.D. and 3rd Durham Auxiliary Hospital, from Aug. 1914, to Feb. 1919; organised and ran this Hospital, Hamerton House, Sunderland, during the War. *Addresses:* Ryhope Hall, Co. Durham; Barlay. Balmaclellan, Kirkcudbrightshire, N.B. (O777)

STREATFEILD, Capt. Granville Edward Stewart, D.S.O., O.B.E., R.E., b. 1869; *s.* of the late Rev. William Champion Streatfeild, of Chart's Edge, Kent, and Selina Frances Diana, 3rd *d.* of William, Titsey Place, Surrey (*see* BURKE's *Peerage,* Sutherland, D.); *m.* 1911, Lucy Anne Evelyn, *d.* of the late Col. Bonar Deane. Served in the Great War, 1914–17 (despatches). (O5822)

STREATFEILD, Lucy Anne Evelyn, Mrs., C.B.E., *d.* of the late Col. Bonar Millet Deane; *m.* 1911, Granville Edward Stewart Streatfeild. Member of Soldiers' Dependants Assessment Appeals Committee. (C210)

STREATFEILD, Mary Cormande, O.B.E.

STREET, Lieut.-Col. Arthur, O.B.E., R.A.S.C.

STREET, Capt. Cecil John Charles, O.B.E.. M.C., b. 3 May, 1884; *s.* of Major-Gen. A. J. Street, C.B. *Educ.:* Wellington Coll. and R.M.A., Woolwich. *Club:* Authors'. (O7755)

STREET, Capt. Charles Edmund, O.B.E. Professional Asistant in the former Dept. of tne Controller-General of Merchant Shipping. (O11927)

STREET, Clare, Mrs., O.B.E.

STREET, Joseph Mansfield, M.B.E., b. 11 Sept. 1877; Assistant to Director of Inspection of Gun Ammunition (Technical), Royal Arsenal, Woolwich; President, War Departments Writers' Association; Chairman, Club No 62B Royal Arsenal Branch of National Savings Association; Member of V.D. Committee of Council of Public Welfare, Woolwich. *Address:* 2, Heavitree Road, Plumstead, S.E. 18. (M9754)

STREETER, Gertrude, M. H., Mrs., M.B.E., Q.M.A.A.C.

STREIGHT, Major Samuel James, O.B.E., Can. A.M.C.

STREVENS, Irene, M.B.E.

STRIBLING, Lieut. William James Leonard, M.B.E., R.A.S.C.

STRICKLAND, Major Guy Tyrone, O.B.E., R.F.A.

STRICKLAND, Mary Constance Elizabeth Christine, M.B.E.. W.R.N.S.

STRICKLAND, William Henry, O.B.E., b. 10 May, 1863; *o.* of William Strickland, of Southsea; *m.* Caroline Sophia, *d.* of William Ash, of Southsea. *Educ.:* Privately. *War Work:* Senior Visiting Inspector, Contract Department, Admiralty; Outdoor organisation in connection with the supplies of stores required by H.M. Navy, both on a peace and a war footing; inspection of factories and workshops with a view to determining the standing and suitability of the firms for admission to the Admiralty List of Contractors; investigation of industrial disputes and settlement of complaints arising out of the interpretation of the Fair Wages Clause in Admiralty contracts. *Address:* Ashleigh, 23, Tenbury Road, King's Heath, Birmingham. (O11404)

STRIEDINGER, Col. Oscar, D.S.O., O.B.E., Army Ser Corps., *b.* 1875. Served in S. Africa, 1899–1902 (Queen's medal with five clasps, King's medal with two clasps); in the Great War, 1914–19 (despatches twice). (O2073)

STRINA, Capt. Gerard Lionel, M.B.E., b. 28 Nov. 1881; *s.* of Julius Strina, of Cardiff. *Educ.:* Harlow. Journalist. *War Work:* With 718 W. Tank Co. till Nov. 17; went to Italy to the British Military Mission in Naples until Feb. 1919; acted as Sec. to Disposal Board (Italy) to July, 1919, then went out with the Relief Exp. force to North Russia (Murmansk front); returned to U.K. Oct. 1919; served three months in Ireland; and March, 1920, proceeded to Mesopotami attached to G.H.Q. and L.A.M. Brigade. *Address:* Villa Strina, Arquata Scrivia, Italy. *Club:* Royal Automobile. (M4753)

STRINGER, Ernest Edward, M.B.E.

STRINGER, Col, Frederick, M.B.E., J.P. Worcestershire; *b.* 28 Feb. 1844; *s.* of William Stringer, of New Bromley Kent; *m.* Eliza Laura, *d.* of Nathan Dyer, of Bridon Manor. *Educ.:* Royal Naval School, New Cross, and Royal Military Coll., Sandhurst. D.A.A.G., Western District, 1880–87. *War Work:* Hon. Sec. Worcestershire Branch Soldiers' and Sailors' Families Association. *Address:* The Old Mansion, Bridon, Tewkesbury. *Club:* Cheltenham. (M9755)

STRINGER, Lieut. Herbert Alfred, M.B.E., R.A.O.C.

STRINGER, Capt. Hubert Leslie, M.B.E.. R.E.

STRINGER. Lieut.-Comm. Reginald Heber, O.B.E., R.D., R.N.R.

STRODE, Edward David Chetham, C.B.E., b. 1 Sept. 1871; *s.* of Capt. Augustus Chetham Strode, R.N., C.B. *Educ.:* Charterhouse; Trinity Coll., Cambridge. Barrister-at-law; Legal Adviser Clearing Office (Enemy debts) *War Work:* Legal assistant, Ministry of Munitions, from July, 1915, to Dec. 1919. *Address:* 7, Stafford Terrace, Kensing-

ton, London, W. 8. *Clubs:* Union; Oxford and Cambridge Musical. (C2978)

STRODE, Major George Sydney Strode, O.B.E.,J.P.,D.L., C.C. (Devon), *b.* 29 Jan. 1861; *s.* of Admiral Arthur Lowe, of Stoke Danurell, Devonport; *m.* Anna Fielding, *d.* of Thompson Boyd, of Edinburgh. *Educ.:* Privately. High Sheriff Devon, 1906–07; Capt. and Hon. Major, 3rd Batt. Devon Regt. (ret. 1897). *War Work:* Recruiting Officer in charge Plymouth area, 1915–17; Commandant V.A. Hospital, Plymouth, May, 1917, to July, 1919. *Address:* Newnham Park, Plympton, S. Devon. *Clubs:* Royal Western Yacht; Devon and Exeter; Junior Constitutional. (O11405)

STROMEYER, Charles Edmond, O.B.E., b. 28 April, 1856; *s.* of Charles Stromeyer, of London; *m.* Alma Karin, *d.* of Director H. Lindsten, of Skara, Sweden. *Educ.:* London and Air-la-Chapelle. Chief Engineer, Manchester Steam Users' Association for the Prevention of Boiler Explosions. *War Work:* Inspection of War Office boilers. *Addresses:* 9, Mount Street, Manchester; Lancefield, West Didsbury. *Club:* Brasenose (Manchester). (O11406)

STRONACH, 2nd Lieut. John Grant McKenzie Martin, M.B.E.. R.A.F.

STRONACH, Brig.-Gen. Robert Summers, C.B.E.

STRONG, Capt. Cecil Alfred, O.B.E., M.C., 3/1 Gurkha Rifles. (O11768)

STRONG, John, C.B.E., b. 1868; *s.* of Joseph Strong, of Barrow-in-Furness; *m.* 1899, Ethel May, *d.* of Alfred Knapton Dobson, of Newton Lodge, Roundhay, Leeds. Hon. LL.D., St. Andrews. Professor of Education in Leeds Univ.; was Pres. Educational Institute of Scotland, 1917–18; Rector of Montrose Acad., 1900–1914; Rector of Roy. High School, Edinburgh, 1914–19. (C641)

STRONG, Major Robert Henry, O.B.E., M.B.

STRONG, Rt. Rev. Thomas Banks, C.B.E., D.D. *See* Ripon, Bishop of.

STRONG, William Henry, M.B.E.

STRONG, Col. William James, C.B.E., T.D., New Zealand Forces. Served in the Great War, 1915–19 (despatches).

STRONGHILL, Mabel Anna, O.B.E., R.R.C.

STROUD, Arthur, M.B.E., b. 8 May, 1889; *s.* of David Stroud, of Canterbury; *m.* Louisa Marjorie, *d.* of Bernard John Howard, of Canterbury. *Educ.:* St. Dunstans, Canterbury. Church Army Officer. *War Work:* Erected and managed Munition Canteen at the Docks, Middlesbrough; opened and managed the Buckingham Palace Hotel Soldiers' and Sailors' Hostel, and the King's Hostel in Buckingham Palace Grounds for Overseas troops on leave from the various fronts; opened and organised accommodation for 3000 troops per night in the Maida Vale District, 1½ million troops being accommodated. (M9756)

STROUD, Arthur May, M.B.E., b. 10 March, 1878; *s.* of James May Stroud, of Highbury; *m.* Elsie Violet, *d.* of Arthur John Davis, of Pagham, Sussex. *Educ.:* Merchant Taylors' School. *War Work:* Sec. to Non-Ferrous Metals Committee, Dec. 1916, to Dec. 1018. *Address:* 87, Highbury Hill, London, N. *Clubs:* Sports; Australasian. (M9757)

STROUD, George John, M.B.E., R.A.F.

STROUD, George Thomas, M.B.E., R.A.F.

STROTHER, Lieut. Cyril John, M.B.E., R.A.F.

STROVER, Henry William Martyn, O.B.E., M.B., Ch.B. *b.* 18 March, 1876; *s.* of Major Gen. Henry Strover, of Lansdowne, Bath; *m.* Margaret Ann, *d.* of James Gillanders, of Aberdeen. *Educ.:* Bath Coll., and Aberdeen Univ. Hon. Associate Order of St. John of Jerusalem in England. *War Work:* Medical Officer V.A.D. Garrison Hospital, West Hartlepool (Bombarded by German Navy); Medical Officer-in-charge troops West Hartlepool Tees Garrison; Lieut. R.A.M.C., service in France. *Addresses:* Dudley House, West Hartlepool; 24, Gloucester Rd., Bristol. (O11851)

STRUBEN, Major Arthur, O.B.E., R.A.F.

STRUBEN, Lieut. Charles Frederick William, O.B.E., R.N.V.R.

STRUBEN, Capt. Robert Henry, O.B.E.

STRUTHERS, John, M.B.E. Member of the War Information Committee at Tokio. Secretary of the Tokio Branch of Patriotic League of Britons Overseas. (M10336)

STRUTT, Lieut.-Col. Edward Lisle, C.B.E., D.S.O., Royal Scots (Lothian Regt.), *b.* 8 Nov. 1874; *s.* of the late Hon. Arthur Strutt, of Milford House, Derby (*see* BURKE'S *Peerage,* Belper, B.); *s.* of the late John Hollond, of Wonham, Bampton, Devon. *Educ.:* Beaumont Coll., and Christ Church, Oxford. *War Work:* Served in South African War (despatches, Queen's Medal and 4 clasps, King's Medal and 2 clasps); European War, 1914–19, severely wounded; despatches four times; 1914 Star and clasps; Legion of Honour, "Chevalier," 1915; Legion of Honour, "Officier," 1917; Croix de Guerre with 4 palms; Order of Leopold, "Chevalier," 1915; Star of Rumania, "Officier," 1919. *Address:* 117, St. James's Court, S.W. 1. *Clubs:* Travellers'; White's; Alpine; New (Edinburgh). (C1780)

STRUTT, Emily Mary Charlotte, Mrs., O.B.E.

STRUTT, Capt. Geoffrey St. John, C.B.E., b. 1888; *s* of the Hon. Richard Strutt, of The Court, St. Catharine, Bath (*see* BURKE'S *Peerage,* Rayleigh, B.); *m.* Sybil Eyre, *d.* of the late Sir Walpole Greenwell, Bart., of Marden Park, Surrey. *Educ.:* Winchester, and Magdalen Coll., Oxford. Private Sec. to Ministry of Blockade and Pensions. *War Work:* Enlisted Sept. 1914; Commissioned Nov. 1914; served in

France; invalided out, 1918. *Address:* Glenwood, Wolding-ham, Surrey. *Club:* Bath. (C2979)

STRUVE, Kenneth Chetwood Price, O.B.E.

STUART, Sir Campbell, K.B.E., *b.* 5th July, 1885; *s.* of Ernest Stuart, of Montreal. *Educ.:* Privately. Deputy Chairman of The Times Publishing Company; Director of the Associated Newspapers, Ltd.; Director of the Anglo-New-foundland Development Company. *War Work:* Represented the Headquarters Staff of the Canadian Army on the occasion of the visit to Ireland of the Duchess of Connaught's Own Irish Canadian Rangers, Jan. 1917, which battalion he recruited in the Province of Quebec for service in the European War; Assistant Military Attaché, British Embassy, Washington, March, 1917; Vice-Chairman of the London Headquarters of the British War Mission to the United States of America, Jan. 1918; Deputy Director of Propaganda in Enemy Countries, May, 1918. *Addresses:* Printing House Square, E.C. 4; 20, Eaton Square, S.W. 1 (Victoria 5148). *Clubs:* Sunning-dale Golf; Marlborough; St. James' (Montreal); York (Toronto). (K109)

STUART, Charles Edward, M.B.E.

STUART, Lieut.-Comm. Charles Joseph Stuart, O.B.E.

STUART, Lieut.-Col. Donald Mackenzie, O.B.E.

STUART, Capt. Donald Richard, M.B.E.

STUART, Major Edward John, O.B.E., A.M.I., Mech.E., *b.* 2 May, 1882; *s.* of Charles Edward William Stuart, of London. *Educ.:* Cranleigh School. Engineer. *War Work:* Assisted in raising Public School Brigade, Royal Fusiliers; gazetted to 20th S. Bn., Royal Fusiliers; 1916, attached to Ministry of Munitions and transferred to General List. *Address:* 16, Wolverton Gardens, Ealing, W. 5. *Clubs:* New Oxford and Cambridge. (O1899)

STUART, Fairless, Mrs., M.B.E.

STUART, Florence Louise, Lady, M.B.E., *b.* 20 Feb. 1867; *d.* of the late Henry Harmond Gudge, Barrister-at-law; *m.* Sir Simeon Henry Lechmere Stuart, 7th Bart., of Hartley, Mandit. *War Work:* Sec. to Procurator-General's Intelligence Branch. *Address:* 87, Northgate, N.W. 8. *Clubs:* Ladies' Army and Navy. (M2492)

STUART, Major Frederick Joshua, O.B.E., R.A.M.C.

STUART, George Barclay, M.B.E.

STUART, John, C.B.E.

STUART, Major John, O.B.E., Black Watch (ret.), *b.* 27 Feb. 1863; *s.* of William Stuart, of Feddal, Perthshire; *m.* Katharine Yseult, *d.* of E. H. J. Craufurd, of Auchenames. *Educ.:* Clifton Coll. *War Work:* Recruiting Officer, 42nd Regimental District; Recruiting Staff Officer, No 1 Highland District; Assistant Inspector of Recruiting, Scottish Command. *Clubs:* Naval and Military; New (Edinburgh). (O780)

STUART, Thane Charles, M.B.E. (M3075)

STUART, George Eustace BURNETT-, C.B.E., *b.* 1876; *s.* of Eustace Robertson Burnett-Stuart, J.P., D.L., of Crichie, Stuartfield, Aberdeenshire. *Educ.:* Repton, and Oxford Univ. Director of Personnel, Ministry of Interior, Egypt, since 1910. *Club:* Oxford and Cambridge. (C356)

STUART, Major Charles KENNEDY-CRAUFURD-, C.B.E., D.S.O., 127th Baluchis, *b.* 29 Aug. 1879; *s.* of Robert Stuart, of Rye, Sussex; *m* Amelia Rumsey, *d.* of Samuel Wheeler, of Bridgeport, Connecticut, U.S.A. *Educ.:* Merchant Taylors' School. Military Secretary to the Viceroy of India, Lord Reading. Entered Army from Militia, April, 1900; South African War, 1900–1902 (2 Medals); Transferred to Indian Army, 1903; served in Burma, 1908–14; received thanks of Burmese Government, 1919, for capturing a band of murderers in unad-ministered territory. *War Work:* 1915, served in Gallipoli as Commandant, Head Batt., Royal Naval Division; served in Sudan, in Special service, 1916–17 (received thanks of Sudan Government); served in America, 1918–20, Private Sec. to Earl of Reading and Viscount Grey; Order of George 1st of Greece. *Clubs:* Carlton; Travellers'; United Service; Royal Thames Yacht; New (Edinburgh). (C2980)

STUART, Major (Bt. Lieut.-Col.) John Patrick VILLIERS-, D.S.O., O.B.E. (O11771)

STUART, Lieut.-Col. William VILLIERS-, C.B.E., *b.* 11 April, 1872; *s.* of Col. Villiers-Stuart, formerly of Castle-town, Carrick-on-Suir, Ireland. *War Work:* Raised and commanded 9th Labour Brigade; raised and commanded 3rd Batt. Q.V.O. Corps of Guides Infantry; Commanded 1/5th Gurkha Rifles, temporarily; Superintending Officer, Nepalese Allied Contingent; Commandant Mountain Warfare School, India; Inspector of Infantry (North) India. *Addresses:* Castlane, Carrick-on-Suir, Ireland; Abbottabad, N.W.F.P. India. *Club:* Junior Naval and Military. (C2044)

STUBBINGTON, Ruby, M.B.E.

STUBBS, Arthur, O.B.E., M.I.Mech.E., M.I.A.E., F.R.S.A. *Educ.:* Privately; Lincoln High School; Polytechnic, and King's Coll. (Univ. of London). Managing Director, Smethwick Stamping Co., Smethwick. *War Work:* Technical Adviser, Stampings and Castings Dept., Ministry of Munitions; Assist. Director (Forgings), and Assistant Controller (Forgings and Castings), Ministry of Munitions. *Address:* Sennocke Lodge, Four Oaks, Sutton Coldfield. (O11407)

STUBBS, George, C.B.E., *b.* 1864. Supt. Analyst Dept. of Govt. Chemist; Vice-Pres. Institute of Chemistry. (C2981)

STUBBS, Capt. Harry, M.B.E., R.A.S.C., Ret., *b.* 1st Oct. 1861; *s.* of Charles Stubbs, of Ashton, Bishops Stortford; *m.* Janet, *d.* of John Frost, of Stafford. *Educ.:* Wolvesey Diocesan School, Winchester. *War Work:* Ashanti Expedi-tion, 1895–96 (Bronze Star); South African War 1899–1902

(Queen's Medal, 3 clasps; King's Medal, 2 clasps); The Great War, on Staff Head Quarters Western Command; mentioned in despatches; British War Medal. *Address:* Prescott, Bishops Waltham, Hants. (M5659)

STUBBS, 2nd Lieut. Shirley Graham, O.B.E., I.A.R.O.

STUBBS, Lieut.-Comm. Sydenham Ernest, O.B.E., R.N.R.

STUBBS, Winefrid Marjory, Lady, C.B.E., *b.* 6 Feb. 1889; *d.* of Frederick Womack, M.B., of St. Bartholomew's Hospital; *m.* Sir Reginald Edward Stubbs K.C.M.G. (*see* BURKE'S *Peerage*); *s.* of late Right Rev. William Stubbs, Lord Bishop of Oxford. *Educ.:* South Hampstead High School. *War Work:* Vice-President in Ceylon of Queen Mary's Needlework Guild. *Address:* Government House, Kong Kong. (C2026)

STUCKEY, Capt. Edward Joseph, O.B.E., B.Sc., M.B., B.S., *b.* 29 Sept. 1875; *s.* of Joseph James Stuckey, M.A., A.I.A., of Adelaide, South Australia; *m.* Frances Helen, *d.* of James Maitland Campbell, of Melbourne. *Educ.:* Adelaide Univ., South Australia. Medical Missionary of London Missionary Society, 1905; Siaochang, North China, 1909; Principal of Union Medical Coll., Peking, 1920; Medical Officer, Peking University, Peking. *War Work:* Medical Officer to Batts. V. and VI. of Chinese Labour Corps, from Weihaiwei to France; Eye Specialist to Chinese General Hospital, B.E.F., France; Medical Officer on Ambulance Transport of A.I.F., from Liverpool to Melbourne. *Address:* London Mission, West City, Peking, China. (O5823)

STUCKEY, Ellen Elizabeth, M.B.E.

STUDD, Major John Edward Kynaston, O.B.E., *b.* 26 July, 1858; *s.* of Edward Studd, of 2, Hyde Park Gardens, W. 2; *m.* Hilda, *d.* of Sir Thomas Proctor-Brauchamp, Bart., of Langley Park, Norwich. *Educ.:* Eton, and Trinity Coll., Cambridge. President and Chairman of the Polytechnic, 309, Regent Street, London, W. 1. *War Work:* Recruiting and Training men in the Polytechnic for the Army and R.F.C. Wireless Operators, and Munition work; Training of Disabled Soldiers; started and commanded Polytechnic Volunteer Training Corps, Sept. 1914; Commander 21st Batt. County of London Volunteer Regiment, 1916–18; Commanded West London Volunteer Group, July, 1918, to 1920. *Address:* 67, Harley Street, London. W. 1. (O3947)

STUDDART, Isabel, Mrs. Naniton, M.B.E.

STUDDERT, Frederick Naunton, O.B.E., D.L. for Co. Clare, *b.* 18 June, 1866; *s.* of Major Geo. S. Studdert, of Moy House, Lahinch, Co. Clare; *m.* Isabel Millar, *d.* of Hugh Ballingall, D.L., of Dundee. *War Work:* Chairman, Co. Clare War Pensions Committee. (O11407)

STUDHOLME, Lieut.-Col. John, C.B.E., D.S.O., M.A., J.P., *b.* 1863; *s.* of John Studholme, of Merivale, Christchurch, New Zealand; *m.* 1st, 1897, Alexandra *d.* of the late Most Rev. (William Thomson) Lord Archbishop of York; 2ndly, 1909, Katherine G., *d.* of the late Hon. Sir Charles Christopher Bowen, K.C.M.G. *Educ.:* Christ's Coll., Christchurch, New Zealand, and Christ Church, Oxford. J.P. for New Zealand; Major and T. Lieut.-Col. New Zealand Mounted Rifles, and A.A.G. Head-quarters, New Zealand Expeditionary Force; twice unsuc-cessfully contested Ashburton (N.Z.) in interest of Reform Party; sometime Member of Ashburton (N.Z.) County Council *Clubs:* Oxford and Cambridge; Christchurch (N.Z.). (C1874)

STUNT, Edith Melba, Mrs., O.B.E., *b.* 2 March, 1870; *d.* of William Howells Rix, of Tunbridge Wells; *m.* George Norwood, *s.* of George Stunt, of Kenley. *Educ.:* Princess Helena Coll., Ealing, and Holloway. Joined V.A.D. Sussex 92 in 1910; Commandant V.A.D. Sussex 92 from 1912, and Vice-President Rye Division Sussex Branch B.R.C.S. *War Work:* Commandant and Officer-in-Charge of St. Mark's Military Auxiliary Hospital, Tunbridge Wells, from Oct. 1914, to Dec. 1918. *Addresses:* Fernet, Frant, Sussex; Abbot Park, Greenodd, Ulverston, Lancashire. *Club:* V.A.D. Ladies.' (O1901)

STURDEE, Arthur Hope, M.B.E.

STURDEE, Surg.-Lieut. Edwin Lawrence, O.B.E., R.N.

STURDEE, Lieut.-Col. Vernon Ashton Hobart, D.S.O., O.B.E., *b.* 1890; *s.* of Col. Alfred Hobart Sturdee, C.M.G.; *m.* 1913, Edith Georgina, *d.* of F. J. Robins, of Melbourne. *Educ.:* Church of England Grammar School, Melbourne. Served during the Great War, 1914–19, in Gallipoli, Egypt, and France (despatches). (O2857)

STURDY, Lieut. A. E., M.B.E.

STURDY, Edward Vyse, O.B.E.

STURGEON, Robert Wallace, M.B.E.

STURGESS, Capt. Charles, M.B.E.

STURMAN, Major Albert Edward, C.B.E. Major, S. Africa Field Post and Telegraph Corps, German W. Africa, 1914–15 (despatches). (C757a)

STURMAN, Lieut. Charles, M.B.E., A.I.F.

STURMAN, Major Edward, C.B.E., S. African Field Post and Telegraph Corps. Served in German W. Africa, 1914–15 (despatches). (C757a)

STURT, Ethel Harriette, Mrs., M.B.E.

STYLE, Col. Sydney Richard, M.B.E.

STYLES, Paymaster-Comm. Edward Goggin, O.B.E., R.N.

SUART, Capt. Montagu Wemyss, C.B.E.

SUDBURY, Evelyn Mary, M.B.E.

SUDDS, Lieut.-Col. William Benjamin, C.B.E., R.A.O.C.

SUDHAL, Deo Raja, C.B.E. Feudatory Chief of Bamra. *Address:* Bamra, Bihar and Orissa, India. (C1072)

SUFFERN, Lieut.-Col. Alexander Canning, O.B.E., R.A.M.C.

SUFFIELD, Lieut. **William Joseph,** M.B.E.

SUGDEN, Capt. **John Leslie,** O.B.E., Can. A.S.C.

SULIVAN, Col. **Ernest Frederic,** C.B.E., b. 12 May, 1860 ; s. of Rev. Filmer Sulivan ; m. Florence Mary, d. of James Houldsworth, of Coltness. Educ.: Harrow and Sandhurst. War Work: Commanded 3rd and 10th Batt. East Surrey Regt., and 30th and 116th Training Reserve Batt. Club: Travellers'. (C1781)

SULIVAN, Capt. **Lionel Michael Patrick,** O.B.E., R.E. and R.A.F.

SULLIVAN, Daniel, M.B.E.

SULLIVAN, Dorothy Evelyn, Mrs., M.B.E.. b. July, 1890 ; d. ot I. A. Hattersley, of 14, Blomfield Road, London, W. ; m. Bernard Ponsonby, Commercial Diplomatic Service, s. of the Rev. P. A. M. Sullivan, of Rangeworthy, Gloucestershire. Educ.: Maida Vale High School, and Le Chatelard School, Vevey, Switzerland. War Work: Clerk, Foreign Office. Address: British Embassy, Brussels. (M9761)

SULLIVAN, Major George Kingston, O.B.E., M.C., b. 6 June, 1878 ; s. of Thomas K. Sullivan, of Bandon, Co. Cork ; m. Frances Helen, d. of the late Col. G. T. Skipwith, Loversal Hall, Doncaster. Educ.: Privately. Comdg. Depot, K.O.Y.L.I., Pontefract. War Work: Proceeded to France as Adjutant of 5th (Territorial) Batt., K.O.Y.L.I., April, 1915 ; later Commanded 1/4th Duke of Wellington's Regt. ; severely wounded near Ypres, Nov. 1915 ; appointed Brigade Major, 175th Infantry Brigade, June, 1916 ; returned to France in Jan. 1917 ; Commanded 2/4th London Regt., April, 1917 ; employed as Instructor Senior Officers School, 1918 ; held rank of Lieut.-Col., April, 1917, to March, 1919 (Temp.). Address: The Barracks, Pontefract. Club: United Service. (O7757)

SULLIVAN, John Andrew, M.B.E.

SULLIVAN, Joseph, M.B.E., J.P., b. 8 Sept. 1866 ; s. of Bernard Sullivan, of Bellshill ; m. Winlers, d. of Thomas Winters, of Uddingston. Educ.: Bellshill. County Councillor ; Member of Educational Authority for County of Lanark. War Work: Pensions Food Committee and Recruiting. Addresses: 5, Westcraigs Road, Harthill, Lanarkshire ; Miners Office. Cadgow Street, Hamilton. (M2496)

SULLIVAN, Richard, M.B.E., R.N.

SULLIVAN, Robina Olive, Mrs., M.B.E.

SULMAN, Helena Catharine, M.B.E., A.R.R.C., b. April, 1874 ; s. of the late Benjamin Sulman, The Chestnuts, Tottenham. Educ.: North Middlesex High School. War Work: Commandant Kempston Red Cross Hospital, Eastborne, March, 1915, to 1919 ; joined Red Cross, Autumn, 1909. Address: 40, The Goffs, Eastbourne. (M9765)

SUMMERS, Ada Jane, Mrs., M.B.E.

SUMMERS, Edward Joseph, M.B.E.

SUMMERS, Patrick Joseph, O.B.E., K.C.

SUMMONS, Col. **Walter Ernest,** O.B.E., Aust., A.M.C.

SUMNER, Harold, O.B.E., J.P., County of Lancaster, b. 2 Feb. 1869 ; s. of William Sumner, of Butt Hall, Prestwich, Lancs ; m. Nina Mary Hazel, d. of Ven. Archdeacon Fletcher, of Chorley. Educ.: Clifton Coll. War Work: Assistant County Director, British Red Cross Society, Wigan Division, comprising 6 V.A.D. Detachments, 3 Hospitals, and 4 Workrooms ; Officer-in-Charge of the three Woodlands Auxiliary Military Hospitals, 1914–19. Address: Ashfield House, Standish, Lancs. Clubs: Isthmian ; Clarendon (Manchester). (O11409)

SUMNER, Flight-Lieut. James Arthur Chester, M.B.E., R.A.F.

SUMNER, Leonard, O.B.E.

SUMNER, Capt. **Orlando,** O.B.E., R.E.

SUMNER, Capt. **Berkeley HOME-,** C.B.E.. R.N.

SUNDERLAND, Major Brian Gresley Elton, O.B.E., R.A., b. 15 Dec. 1883 ; s. of the Rev. James Sunderland, of Egginton Vicarage ; m. Violet, d. of George Wright Mumford, of Oakfield Gateacre. Educ.: Sherborne, and Royal Military Academy, Woolwich. War Work: Sept. 1914, to Oct. 1915. 3rd Siege Battery, France ; Oct. 1915, to April, 1917, Staff Capt., Director of Artillery's Dept., War Office ; April, 1917, to date, Deputy Assistant Director of Artillery, Director of Artillery Department, War Office. Address: Egginton Vicarage, Leighton Buzzard. Club: Junior Army and Navy. (O782)

SURTEES, Capt. **Robert Lambton,** O.B.E.

SUSANS, Lieut. **Frank,** M.B.E., R.A.F.

SUTCLIFFE, Frances Edith, O.B.E., b. 30 Dec. 1860 ; d. of Edward Sutcliffe, of Mirfield. Educ.: Culcheth Hall, Bowden. War Work: Belgian Refugee work under W. R. Committee ; Sec. Buxton Refugees Committee, 1914–19 ; responsible for fund for V.A.D. Hospital for wounded Belgian soldiers, to which the public responded generously ; Medaille de la Reine Elizabeth, 1916. Address: 9, Hartington Road, Buxton. (O11410)

SUTCLIFFE, John Hamer, O.B.E., F.B.O.A., b. 1867 ; s. of Robert Sutcliffe ; m. Margaret, d. of James Emery. Educ.: Rochdale High School ; Owen's Coll., Victoria Univ., Manchester. 1895, Sec., British Optical Association ; Editor "Dioptric Review," 25 years ; President, Optical Society, 1907–1909 ; Superintendent, Army Spectacle Depot, 1916–20 ; Librarian to Optical Society, 1909–21 ; at present Superintendent Optical Appliances Depot (Ministry of Pensions). War Work: Head of dept. for supply of all spectacles and ophthalmological requirements to the Army. Address: Clifford's Inn Hall, Fleet Street, E.C 4. (O11411)

SUTCLIFFE, Surg.-Comm. Percy Temple, O.B.E., M.B., M.A., R.N.

SUTCLIFFE, William Greenwood, O.B.E., F.R.C.S. (Eng.), b. 14 Aug. 1866 ; s. of William Greenwood Sutcliffe, of London ; m. Kathleen Elizabeth Mary, d. of J. T. Sayers, of London. Educ.: St. Thomas's Hospital, London. Surgeon. War Work: Lieut.-Col. R.A.M.C. (T.) Surgical Specialist, and O.C. 32 C.C.S., 1914–19. Address: Margate, Kent. (O2741)

SUTER, George Edward, M.V.O., O.B.E., R.C.N.C., b. 8 Dec. 1869 ; s. of Philip James ; m. Eva, d. of Hugh Hicks. Educ.: R. N. Coll., Greenwich. Constructive Manager, H.M. Dockyard, Portsmouth, 1919 ; Acting Constructive Manager H.M. Dockyard, Rosyth, 1918. Address: 2, The Parade, H.M. Dockyard, Portsmouth. (O783)

SUTHERLAND, Alexander, M.B.E., b. 22 Jan. 1867 ; s. of Charles Sutherland, of St. Helens, Lancashire ; m. Elizabeth, d. of Andrew Murray, of St. Helens, Lancashire. Educ.: Windle School. Assistant to the District Traffic Superintendent and Dock Master, L. & N.W. Rly. Co., Garston Docks, Liverpool. War Work: Two years with the Controller of Coal Mines, London, attached to secretariat and dealt with all questions relating to the pit and export prices of coal. Address: 2 Garston Old Road, Grassendale, Liverpool. (M4009)

SUTHERLAND, Capt. **Arthur Henry Carr,** O.B.E., M.C., The Black Watch, b. 3 April, 1891 ; s. of Sir George H. Sutherland, of 36, Upper Brook Street ; m. Ruby, d. of the late Capt. W. G. P. Miller, of Thisleton Lodge, Lancashire. Educ.: Eton, and Sandhurst. War Work: Employed regimentally, and on the Staff. Clubs: Naval and Military ; Caledonian ; New (Edinburgh). (O2742)

SUTHERLAND, Sir Arthur Munro, K.B.E., J.P., b. 2 Oct. 1867 ; s. of Benjamin John Sutherland, of Newcastle-upon-Tyne ; m. Fanny Linda, d. of Robert Hood Haggie, of Newcastle-upon-Tyne. Educ.: Royal Grammar School, Newcastle-upon-Tyne. Sheriff of Newcastle-upon-Tyne, 1916–17 ; Lord Mayor of Newcastle-upon-Tyne, 1918–19 ; shipowner and coal exporter ; Chairman of Newcastle Commercial Exchange ; owner of Dunstanburgh Castle, Embleton, Newton, Stamford, Yeavoring and Hethpool Estates in the County of Northumberland ; principal proprietor of "Newcastle Chronicle," "Illustrated Chronicle," "Evening Chronicle," "Weekly Chronicle," "Sporting Man," "North Mail," and "Sunday Sun." War Work: Took an active part in the raising of the Tyneside Commercial Battalions, Northumberland Fusiliers, and was the means of enabling eighty-five British steamers to escape from the Baltic, thus adding about 300,000 tons of carrying capacity to the British Mercantile Marine. Addresses: Thurso House, Newcastle-upon-Tyne ; Hethpool, Northumberland. Clubs: Union (Newcastle-upon-Tyne) ; Junior Constitutional. (K429)

SUTHERLAND, Lieut.-Col. **Bertram Milne,** O.B.E., Aust. A.M.C.

SUTHERLAND, George Alexander, C.B.E. ; s. of the Rev. James Sutherland, D.D., of Aberdeen. Educ.: Universities of Aberdeen and Edinburgh. Physician to the Hampstead General Hospital and the Paddington Green Children's Hospital. War Work: Consulting Physician to the Royal Air Force. Address: 29B, Wimpole Street, W. 1. Club: Scottish Conservative (Edinburgh). (C2983)

SUTHERLAND, Lieut. **Harry Wilson,** M.B.E., M.M.

SUTHERLAND, Lieut.-Col. **James,** D.S.O., O.B.E., R.E. Dep. Director of Railways. (O2340)

SUTHERLAND, Lieut. **James Henry Richardson,** M.B.E., A.F.C., R.A.F.

SUTHERLAND, John, M.B.E.

SUTHERLAND, Lieut. **John,** M.B.E.

SUTHERLAND, 2nd Lieut. **John,** M.B.E., R.A.F.

SUTHERLAND, John Donald, C.B.E., F.S.I., b. 10 Nov. 1865 ; s. of John Sutherland, of Inverness ; m. Kate Belcher, d. of the Rev. Andrew Belcher, M.A., of Fasque. Educ.: Royal Academy, Inverness, and Univ. Edinburgh. Assistant Commissioner for Forestry in Scotland. War Work: Executive Officer Timber Supplies, Scotland ; Director Home-Grown Timber Committee ; Assistant Director of Forestry in France ; Col. in R.E. ; British Representative on Comité Interallie de bois de Guerre, Paris ; Administrative Officer in Les Landes Jura and Vosges, France ; Member of various war committees. Address: 11, Inverleith Row, Edinburgh. Clubs: University (Edinburgh) ; National ; Royal Automobile. (C1333)

SUTHERLAND, Eng.-Lieut. **Joseph,** O.B.E., R.N.

SUTHERLAND, Robert, M.B.E.

SUTHERLAND, Lieut. **William,** M.B.E.

SUTRO, Alfred, O.B.E.

SUTTHERY, Colin Pellatt, O.B.E., b. 13 Aug. 1887 ; s. of Frank Pellatt Sutthery, Solicitor, of Chelmsford, Essex. Electrical Engineer. War Work: On the Staff of The Director of Experiments and Research ; attached to Staff of The Deputy Controller of Armament Production ; Appointed Technical Adviser to the Rear Admiral Controlled Minefields. Address: 83, Cannon Street, London, E.C. 4. (O11412)

SUTTIE, Peter **Edwin,** O.B.E

SUTTON, Albert Edward, M.B.E., b. 26 Oct. 1871 : s. of James Sutton, of Long Eaton, Derby ; m. Ada, d. of Robert Scampton, of Nottingham. Educ.: Long Eaton, Midland Academy. Commandant, British Red Cross Society. Address: 5, Sandringham Avenue, West Bridgford, Nottingham. Club: Constitutional (Nottingham). (M9765)

SUTTON, Rev. **Alfred,** C.B.E., b. 1851 ; s. of James Sutton ; m. Bertha F. E. Walker. Rural Dean, Hon. Canon of

Carlisle ; J.P. and Chairman of County Council for Cumberland. *Address :* Bridekirk Vicarage, Cockermouth. (C2984)

SUTTON, Capt. Arthur Fraser, M.B.E.

SUTTON, Major Bertine Entwistle, D.S.O., O.B.E., M.C., R.A.F. Served in the Great War, 1914–19 (despatches). (O3426)

SUTTON, Cecil Norman Stafford, M.B.E.,

SUTTON, Constance Marion, M.B.E., L.C.A., *b.* 3 June, 1888 ; *d.* of William Robert Sutton, of Thame. *Educ. :* The Grove School, Highgate. *War Work :* Kitchen Sister Royal Surrey County Hospital, Guildford, 1914–16 ; Superintendent, Women's Legion, 1917 ; Assist. Administrator, Q.M.A.A.C., France, 1917 ; Unit Administrator, Q.M.A.A.C., France, 1918–20. *Club :* Forum. (M4610)

SUTTON, Emily Evelyn, M.B.E., *b.* 13 Aug. 1889 ; *d.* of Henry J. Sutton, of Salisbury. *Educ. :* Godolphin School, Salisbury ; Wilts and Bristol Schools of Domestic Economy. Teacher of domestic science ; six years' service under the Wilts County Council. *War Work :* Joined Cookery Section of Women's Legion, Jan. 1917 ; transferred to Q.M.A.A.C., Nov. 1917 ; discharged under termination of engagement, Dec. 1919 ; served as assistant Cook, Head Cook (under W.L.), and as Deputy Administrator, Unit Administrator, and Deputy Controller in Q.M.A.A.C. *Addresses :* 56, Waterloo Gardens, Salisbury ; University Settlement, Bristol. (M6711)

SUTTON, Ernest Phillips Foquett, M.B.E., late Capt. R.A.S.C., *b.* 20 March, 1882 ; *s.* of the late Martin John Sutton, of Reading ; *m.* Hilda Douglas, *d.* of Col. D. F. Douglas-Jones, Wimbledon. *Educ. :* Trinity Coll., Cambridge. Member of Council Bath and West Agricultural Society ; Member of Council of the Kerry and Dexter Cattle Society. *War Work :* 1916–17, Mechanical Transport Officer, attached 163 Siege Battery, B.E.F. ; 1917–18, Officer-in-charge of the Agricultural Scheme, Lines of Communication, B.E.F. *Address :* Sidmouth Grange, nr Reading *Club :* Berkshire. (M3154)

SUTTON, Major Harvey, O.B.E., A.I.F.

SUTTON, John Joseph, M.B.E.

SUTTON, Kathleen Alice, Mrs., M.B.E.

SUTTON, Leonard Goodhart, C.B.E. Rendered public service during Great War. Of the firm of Sutton & Sons, Seed Merchants. (C2985)

SUTTON, Ralph, *b.* 11 May, 1881 ; *s.* of Edmund Sutton, of Manchester. *Educ. :* Shrewsbury, and Oriel Coll., Oxford. Barrister. *War Work :* Legal Adviser, Central Control Board (Liquor Traffic). *Addresses :* 2, Garden Court, Temple, E.C. 4 ; St. Olave's, Chagford, Devon. *Clubs :* Reform ; London Fencing. (O11413)

SUTTON, Richard James, O.B.E., *b.* 17 Feb. 1862 ; *s.* of Joseph Walter Sutton (of Tufnell Park, N. (formerly of Boston, Lincs.) ; *m.* Mary Sophia, *d.* of Francis Hillam, of Shrewsbury. Member of Hornsey Borough Council, Edmonton Board of Guardians, Hornsey Education Committee ; Overseer of the Poor. *War Work :* Chairman, Local Relief Committee ; Hon. Treas. Soldiers' and Sailors' Families Assn. ; Chairman Hornsey War Pensions Committee ; Chairman Defence Committee ; Chairman Voluntary Organisations Committee ; Military Representative Hornsey Local Tribunal, etc. *Address :* 30, Denton Road, Stroud Green, N. 8. (O11414)

SUTTON, Lieut. and Qr.-Mr. Thomas James, M.B.E., R.A.V.C., *b.* 21 Sept. 1877. Enlisted in the Royal Horse Artillery, 1896 ; served in India, 1897–98 ; served in South African War, 1899–1902 ; King's and Queen's Medals, 7 clasps ; served in South Africa, 1910–14. *War Work :* Served in South Africa, 1914 ; France, 1915–16 ; mentioned in despatches ; Mesopotamia, 1918–20 ; mentioned in despatches, 1920 ; in possession of Long Service and Good Conduct Medal, recommended for Meritorious Service Medal ; 1914–15–Star ; B.G.S. Medal ; Allied Medal. *Address :* 27, Genesta Road, Plumstead, Kent. (M4932)

SWABEY, Col. Wilfrid Spedding, C.B., C.M.G., C.B.E., *b.* 25 Feb. 1871 ; *s.* of Thomas Swabey, of Woodcote, Woburn Sands, Co. Beds. ; *m.* Maud, *d.* of S. A. Walker Waters, Assist. Inspector General Royal Irish Constabulary. *Educ. :* Marlborough Coll. Joined King's Own Yorkshire Light Infantry, 1892 ; afterwards transferred to Army Service Corps ; served with Egyptian Army, 1896–99 (2 medals) ; D.A.A.G. South African War, 1899 to 1902 ; (mentioned in despatches, Brevet Majority, 2 medals, 7 clasps). *War Work :* Deputy Director of Transport from Oct. 1914, holding appointments as A.D. of S. and T. Cavalry Corps, DD. of S. and T., Northern L. of C., and DD. of S. and T. Third Army, till proceeding to Italy as D. of S. and T., in Nov. 1917 ; was Brig.-Gen. ; six times mentioned in despatches ; 1914 Star, General Service and Victory Medals, Italian Croce di Guerra, and Order of the Crown of Italy. (C2069)

SWAFFIELD, Ernest, M.B.E.

SWAIN, Col. James, C.B., C.B.E., M.D., F.R.C.S., *b.* 1862 ; *s.* of the late George Swain, of Kingswood, Surrey ; *m.* 1899, Hilda May, *d.* of A. J. Harrison, M.B., J.P. Professor of Surg. and Lecturer in Clinical Surg. Bristol Univ. ; Surg. to Roy. Infirmary, Bristol ; Consulting Surg. Southern Command ; sometime Col. Army Medical Service ; during Great War as Consulting Surg. to British Forces in France, 1916 : Delegate to Inter-Allies Conference, 1917–19 ; Professor of Surg. Univ. Coll. Bristol, 1897–1907 ; Pres. Medico-Chirurgical Soc. 1909–10 ; edited Greig Smith's " Abdominal Surgery " (6th edition). *Address :* 4, Victoria Square, Clifton, Bristol. *Club :* Royal Societies'. (C1989)

SWAIN, Percival Francis, C.B.E., *b.* 14 March, 1887 ; *s.* of

W. A. Swain, of Wynchcroft, Reading ; *m.* Winifred, *d.* of F. W. Balding, of Padworth, Berks. *Educ. :* Reading late University Coll. Principal Clerk, Public Trustee Dept., H.M. Civil Service. *War Work :* Principal Clerk-in-charge, Trading with the Enemy Department of the Public Trustee Dept. *Address :* Dingley, Tilehurst-on-Thames. (C1044)

SWAIN, William Henry, O.B.E.

SWAINE, Ethel, O.B.E.

SWAINSON, Robert Hunter, O.B.E., *b.* 15 Feb. 1882 ; *s.* of William Swainson, of Harrogate ; *m.* Ellen, *d.* of — Holborn, of Darlington. Metropolitan Sec. of the Young Men's Christian Association. *War Work :* 1914–15. Organised Y.M.C.A. military work on Salisbury Plain and with Southern Command, Ireland ; 1915–18, Organising Sec. Y.M.C.A., Munition Workers' Dept. *Address :* Rosslyn Lodge, Hampstead. (O1905)

SWAISH, Sir John, K.B.E., J.P., D.L., *b.* 1 Sept. 1852 ; *s.* of John Swaish, of Bristol ; *m.* Nellie, *d.* of Joshua Mitchell, of Harrogate. *Educ. :* Privately. Alderman of Bristol City Council. *War Work :* Lord Mayor of Bristol, 1913–15 ; organised the local scheme of Bristol's endeavour in Naval, Military, Red Cross, and Munitions ; Chairman of Local Tribunal. (K430)

SWALLOW, Clara, Mrs., M.B.E. ; *d.* of Thomas Hutchinson. of Bamburgh Hall, Northumberland ; *m.* Wardle Asquith, J.P., *s.* of John Swallow, of Percy Gardens, Tynemouth. *War Work :* Commandant of 22nd Durham V.A. Hospital from June, 1915, to Feb. 1919 ; Member of the Easington War Pensions Committee. *Address :* Seaton Hall, New Seaham, Co. Durham. (M9766)

SWALLOW, Lieut. Thomas Asquith, M.B.E., R.G.A. (T.)

SWALLOW, Lieut. William Hugh, O.B.E., R.A.O.C.

SWAN, Capt. John Barry Rankin, M.B.E., R.A.F.

SWAN, Capt. John Henry, M.B.E.

SWAN, Lieut. Kenneth Raydon, O.B.E., R.N.V.R.

SWAN, Mary, Mrs., M.B.E.

SWAN, 2nd Lieut. Robert, M.B.E., R.A.F.

SWAN, Major Robert Arthur, O.B.E.

SWAN, Major Russell Henry Jocelyn, O.B.E., M.S., M.B., F.R.C.S., R.A.M.C. *b.* 20 July, 1876 ; *s.* of R. Jocelyn Swan, of Wallington ; *m.* Una Gladys, *d.* of A. J. Waterlow, of Hurlingham. *Educ. :* Wilson's School, and Guy's Hospital. Surgeon, Cancer Hospital, London, S.W. ; Consulting Surgeon, Walton Cottage Hospital ; Fellow of Royal Society of Medicine, and of Royal Medical Society. *War Work :* Senior Operating Surgeon and Surgical Specialist, Royal Herbert Hospital, Woolwich ; District Consulting Surgeon, Eastern Command ; Surgeon Royal Air Force Hospital, American Red Cross Hospital, Lancaster Gate, and Queen Mary's Royal Naval Hospital, Southend ; served in France ; mentioned in despatches ; author of many articles on military surgery. *Addresses :* 75, Wimpole Street, W. 1. ; Ingram's Copse, Farnham Common, Bucks. (O7758)

SWAN, Capt. Thomas Angus, M.B.E.

SWAN, Charles Robert John ATKIN-, O.B.E., M.B., B.Ch., (Oxon), M.R.C.S. (England), L.R.C.P. (London), F.R.R.P.S., F.R.G.S., *b.* 28 Sept. 1863 ; *s.* of John Thomas Atkin-Swan, Rector, of Fiddington, Somerset ; *m.* Veronica Head, *d.* of Antoine Schlesinger, of Paris and New York. *Educ. :* Newton Abbot Coll. ; Keble Coll., Oxford ; St. George's Hospital. Late Physician and Administrative Officer to R.F.C. Hospitals ; Medical Referee for Anglo-Persian and Burmah Oil Companies. *War Work :* Devised camera for use from an aeroplane, and filters that were fitted in goggles of pilots and observers to prevent dazzle and to assist in seeing through mist ; founded and organised Medical service and Hospitals for the Royal Flying Corps ; selected and appointed staff to Eaton and Bryanston Hospitals ; Lecturer on photography at various aerodromes in England ; devised special hood for pilots and observers, and also apparatus for correcting distortion in the early aerial photographs. *Address :* 3, Chester Place, Hyde Park Square, W. 2. *Club :* Junior Carlton. (O1906)

SWANN, Major Ernest Edward, O.B.E., *b.* 23 Jan. 1879 ; *s.* of Councillor Frederick Swann, of Cambridge ; *m.* Grace, *d.* of Alfred Thompson, of Cambridge. *Educ. :* Perse School, Cambridge. Bank Manager, Barclay's Bank, Ltd., Westcliff-on-Sea ; Hon. Freeman of the Borough of Cambridge ; served with Volunteer Company of the Suffolk Regt. in South African War, 1900–1. *War Work :* Commissioned in the 5th Batt. Essex Regt. (T.F.), afterwards attached to the General Staff, Southern Command, as Chemical Adviser. *Address :* 13, Winton Avenue, Westcliff-on-Sea. (O7759)

SWANN, Grace Elsie, M.B.E.

SWANN, Brig.-Gen. Oliver, C.B., C.B.E., R.N. Col. and a Brig.-Gen. R.A.F. (C1908)

SWANSON, David, M.B.E.

SWANTON, Margaret Eileen Pasley, M.B.E., *b.* 27 March 1890 ; *d.* of Major-General James Hutchinson Swanton (late Royal Marine L.I.), of Woodrow, Yelverton, South Devon. *Educ. :* Western Coll., Plymouth. *War Work :* Emergency work as member of a Voluntary Aid Detachment (Devon 2) from Sept. 1914, to Oct. 1916 ; appointed Divisional Sec., Plymouth Division, British Red Cross Society, Oct. 1916, to present date. *Address :* Woodrow, Yelverton, South Devon. (M9769)

SWANWICK, Laura Beatrix, O.B.E., *b.* 14 Sept. 1874 ; *d.* of H. J. Marshall, late R.N., of Gayton Hall, Ross-on-Wye ; *m.* Bruce, *s.* of Russell Swanwick, of Cirencester. *Educ. :*

Ladies' Coll., Cheltenham ; St. Hilda's Hall, Oxford. *War Work :* Commandant of the Cirencester V. A. Hospital, Dec. 1914, to Dec. 1918, and of V.A.D. Glos. 84, from 1912–20 the Cirencester Hospital had 86 beds, and took cases direct from France. *Address :* The Road House, near Stroud, Glos. *Club :* Ladies' University. (O1907)

SWANZY, Lieut. Francis Hugh, O.B.E., R.A.O.C.

SWAYNE, Lieut.-Col. Edward Hopton, O.B.E.

SWAYNE, Col. Sir Eric John Eagles, K.C.M.G., C.B., C.B.E., *b.* 14 May, 1863 ; *s.* of the late Rev. G. C. Swayne ; *m.* Yda L., *d.* of Sir T. Holdich, and widow of Major Edmund Peach, I.A. Joined Indian Staff Corps ; entered Army, 1883 ; served in Burma, 1886 ; Special duty, Somaliland reconnaissance, 1890 ; Uganda Mutiny and Jubaland, 1898 ; Commanded Somaliland Field Force, 1901 (Brevet Lieut.-Col.) ; O.C. Troops, Somaliland, with local rank of Brig.-Gen. 1904 ; Intelligence Branch, H.Q. India, 1892–98 ; Commissioner and Consul-General for Somali Coast Protectorate, 1902–6 ; Governor, British Honduras, 1906–13 ; Assistant Inspector Recruiting, Northern Command, 1914–17 ; Grand Officer of Order of Crown of Italy. *Address :* 41, Courtfield Road, S.W. (C2053)

SWAYNE, Major Richard Woodward, O.B.E., M.B., B.S. ; R.A.M.C., *s.* of H. E. Swayne, of Monkstown, Co. Dublin. *Educ. :* Durham Univ. Officer-in-Charge Medical Division, 3rd General Hospital, Army of the Rhine. *War Work :* Joined the Northumbrian Casualty Station, Nov. 1914 ; served in France and Belgium in the 2nd, 3rd, 4th, 5th Armies, mostly with the Casualty Clearing Stations ; since July, 1919, Officer-in-Charge Medical Division, 3rd General Hospital, Army of the Rhine. *Address :* Park Lodge, Cambridge Road, Dublin. (O5825)

SWEENIE, Elizabeth, Mrs., M.B.E.

SWEENY, Capt. Sedley Fleming Campbell, O.B.E., R.N.

SWEET, William McMurdo, O.B.E., *b.* 14 Feb. 1860 ; *s.* of the Rev. James Bradby Sweet, of Otterton, Devon ; *m.* May, *d.* of John Frank Hunnard, of London. *Educ. :* Honiton, and Cooper's Hill. Public Works Department, India ; Chief Engineer, Assam, India. *War Work :* Inspection Department, Woolwich Arsenal. *Address :* The Woodlands, Limpley, Stoke, Bath. (O11415)

SWEETING, Henry Carol, O.B.E., *b.* 17 March, 1885 ; *s.* of the late Alfred Charles Sweeting, of Paxton Hall, St. Neots, Hunts. ; *m.* Greta Gladys, *d.* of Alfred Cochrane, of Norton House, Redcar. *Educ. :* Eton and Trinity Hall, Cambridge. Land Agent. *War Work :* Rejoined 5th Batt. King's Royal Rifles on the outbreak of war ; drafted to France, to the 1st Bn. Sept. 1914 ; severely wounded at Ypres, on 26 Oct. 1914 ; passed unfit for further service abroad ; transferred for recruiting duty to Bakewell Sub-Area under H.Q. Staff, Derby, No. 6 District, 1916 ; later transferred to Ministry of National Service ; appointed Assist. Director of National Service, Nov. 1917 ; mentioned in despatches, 1916 ; placed on the Retired List, owing to ill-health caused by wounds, Jan. 1919. *Address :* Cote Heath, Buxton, Derbyshire. (O7760)

SWEETMAN, Capt. Gerald Drysdale, O.B.E., A.M.Inst.C.E., *b.* 24 Jan. 1880 ; *s.* of Henry Sweetman, J.P. of Ryde, Isle of Wight ; *m.* Marie, *d.* of the late John Everard Pollard, of Bristol. *Educ. :* Portsmouth Grammar School. Assistant Surveyor to the Wandsworth Borough Council. *War Service :* Oct. 1914, to April, 1915, engaged by the War Office as Civil Engineer for Works Services ; April, 1915, to Nov. 1919, Inspector of Works, Staff for R.E. Services ; employed in England, on the construction and administration of camps, hospitals, and depots on the Salisbury Plain and Weymouth districts respectively ; served with British Expeditionary Force, North Russia (Murmansk Area) ; mentioned in despatches. *Address :* 15, Dalebury Road, Wandsworth Common, S.W. 17. (O9729)

SWEETMAN, Lieut.-Col. Michael James, O.B.E.

SWENY, Capt. William Halpin Paterson, C.B.E. Capt. R.N.R. (C642)

SWETTENHAM, Lieut.-Col. George Kilner, C.B.E., D.S.O., *b.* 1866 ; *s.* of the late G. F. Swettenham, of South Lodge, Eastbourne ; *m.* Catherine Anne Eleanor, *d.* of the late Very Rev. Augustine FitzGerald, D.D., Dean of Armagh. *Educ. :* Cheltenham Coll. *War Work :* Commanded 5th Batt. Royal Irish Rifles. *Address :* Ravensdale, Mount Pleasant, Co. Louth. (C1782)

SWETTENHAM, Lieut.-Col. William Alexander Wybault, C.B.E., R.G.A., *b.* 16 Dec. 1870 ; *s.* of William Norman, of Belper, Derbyshire. *Educ. :* Shrewsbury School, and Bedford Grammar School. 4 years' Militia Service with the Lancashire Artillery Militia, and 27 years' service in the Royal Regiment of Artillery. *War Work :* Sec. Siege Artillery Committee ; G.S.O. Siege Artillery, War Office ; Brigade Major 2nd Army Heavy Artillery Reserve Group, France, till invalided ; G.S.O. Siege Artillery ; Artillery Bgde. Commander, Commanding R.G.A. Training School, France ; Ministry of Munitions. *Address :* Hurlands, Dunsfold, Surrey. *Club :* Junior Naval and Military. (C2175)

SWIFT, Comm. Clement Charles, O.B.E., R.N.

SWIFT, Dame Sarah Ann, G.B.E., R.R.C., *b.* 22 Nov. 1854 ; *d.* of Robert Swift, of Boston. *Educ. :* Privately. Matron of Guy's Hospital until 1909. *War Work :* Matron-in-chief of the Joint War Committee of the British Red Cross and Order of St. John, from 1914. to 1920. *Address :* 48, Primrose Mansions, S.W. 11. (DG27)

SWINBOURNE, Major Charles Augustus, O.B.E.

SWINBURNE, John Eliot, O.B.E.

SWINDELLS, Major Frank Marshall, O.B.E.

SWINERD, Lieut. and Qr.-Mr. Henry James, M.B.E. R.A.

SWINNERTON, Robert William, M.B.E., J.P. for the County of Warwick, *b.* 7 April, 1848 ; *s.* of Robert Swinnerton, of Weddington Grove, near Nuneaton. *Educ. :* Privately. Chairman Board of Guardians ; Alderman Nuneaton Borough Council ; Co-opted Member Warwickshire Education Committee. *Address :* Linden Lodge, Nuneaton. (M2503)

SWINSON, Ethel, Mrs., M.B.E.,; *d.* of Joseph Sampson Gamgee, Surgeon, of Birmingham ; *m.* Frederick Swinson. *War Work :* Organising Voluntary Helpers in Birmingham District for Munition Workers Auxiliary Committee. *Address :* 12, Augustus Road, Edgbaston. (M9770)

SWINSTEAD, Lieut. Norman Hillyard, M.B.E., R.E.

SWINTON, Elizabeth, Mrs., M.B.E.

SWIRE, William, C.B.E., J.P., *b.* 17 July, 1862 ; *s.* of William Hudson, of Liverpool ; *m.* Jessie Lindsay Edith, *d.* of George Jardine Kidston, J.P., D.L., of Finlaystone, Renfrewshire. *Educ. :* Charterhouse. *War Work :* County Director, Red Cross, Shropshire. *Address :* Longden Manor, Shrewsbury. *Club :* Boodle's ; Conservative. (C643)

SWIRE, William, M.B.E., *b.* 29 Sept. 1872 ; *s.* of Robinson Swire, of Skipton, Yorkshire ; *m.* Ellen, *d.* of Thomas Fish, of Retford, Notts. *Educ. :* Skipton Grammar School. Headmaster of Fleetwood, Lord Street C. School until Feb. 1919, now Headmaster, Leyland, Wes. School. *War Work :* Hon. Sec. Fleetwood War Savings Committee, Food Economy Committee, and of Food Economy and War Bonds Campaigns ; Member of Fleetwood Local Food Committee ; on the panel of Royal Horticultural Society's War-time Garden Advisers. (M4011)

SWITHENBANK, John William, M.B.E.

SWOFFER, Lieut Frank Arthur, M.B.E., R.A.F.

SWORNSBOURNE, Mabel Edith, M.B.E.

SYDENHAM, Eng.-Comm. Frederick William, O.B.E., R.N.

SYDENHAM OF COMBE, George Sydenham Clarke, Lord, G.C.S.I., G.C.M.G., G.C.I.E., G.B.E., F.R.S., *b.* 4 July, 1848 (*see* BURKE'S *Peerage*) ; *s.* of the Rev. W. I. Clarke, late of Knoyle House, Folkestone ; *m.* Phyllis Angelina Rosamund, *d.* of George Morant, late of Grenadier Guards. *Educ. :* Repton Rossall, Haileybury, R.M.A., Woolwich. *War Work :* Chairman Central Appeal Tribunal ; Member Air Board ; President Belgian Field Hospital. *Addresses :* 101, Onslow Square, S.W. ; The Priory, Lumberhurst, Kent. *Club :* Athenæum. (G5)

SYDENHAM, Capt. Lewis George, M.B.E.

SYKES, Lieut.-Col. Arthur, C.B.E., *b.* 22 Oct. 1868 ; *s.* of Alfred Sykes, of Witcham, Cambs ; *m.* Maud Mary, *d.* of John Talyor, of Woodlands, Sutton, Cambs. Joined as a private, 1887 ; promoted to commissioned rank during S. African War ; served on War Office Staff as Inspector of Army Catering, 1912–18. *War Work :* Organisation of the feeding of the fighting forces at home and abroad ; inauguration of system whereby shell propellents were recovered from by-products of troops rations ; appointed Inspector of Administrative Services, Royal Air Force, 1918. *Address :* Henleigh, Kingston Hill. S.W. *Club :* Royal Automobile. (C1909)

SYKES, Capt. Arthur Clifton, D.S.O., O.B.E., *b.* 1891 ; *s.* of the late Adam Sykes, of Wadbury, near Frome ; *m.* 1919, Lorna Evelyn, *d.* of Ernest Stanier, of Elmhurst, Isleworth. Served in the Great War in Mesopotamia, 1914–18 (despatches). *Club :* Army and Navy. (O6711)

SYKES, Sir Charles, K.B.E., M.P., *b.* 1867 ; *s.* of the late Benjamin W. Sykes ; *m.* daughter of the late Benjamin Newsome. Chairman, Sir Charles Sykes and Sons, Ltd., Netherdale, Galashiels. *Address :* Kingsknowes, Galashiels. *Clubs :* National Liberal ; Liberal (Huddersfield). (K110)

SYKES, Charles David, O.B.E., B.Sc. (Lond.), *b.* 21 Jan. 1875 ; *s.* of David Sykes, of West Bromwich ; *m.* Lucy Alice, *d.* of Richard Thorn, of Topsham, S. Devon. *Educ. :* Handsworth Grammar School. General Works Manager, Messrs. Albright and Wilson, Chemical Works. *War Work :* General Works Manager of important H.M. Factory. (O11417)

SYKES, Charles Henry, M.B.E., M.R.C.S., L.R.C.P.

SYKES, Rev. Frank Morris, O.B.E., *b.* 1879 ; *s.* of William Sykes, M.D., of Paignton. *Educ. :* Malvern Coll. ; Selwyn Coll., Cambridge. Vice-Principal, Ordination Test School, Knutsford. *War Work :* B.E.F., Chaplain to the Forces, 1915–19. *Address :* Ordination Test School, Knutsford. (O2745)

SYKES, Major-Gen. Sir Frederick Hugh, G.B.E., K.C.B., *b.* 1877 ; *s.* of Hy. Sykes, of Addiscombe ; *m.* 1920, Isabel Harrington, *e. d.* of Rt. Hon. Andrew Bonar Law, M.P. Appointed 2nd Lieut. 1901 ; Lieut.-Col. 1915 ; Brevet Col. 1918 ; Major-Gen. 1918 ; qualified as Air Pilot, 1911 ; Comm. R.F.C. Military Wing, 1912–14 ; Comm. R.N.A.S. E. Mediterranean, 1915–16 ; Dep. Div. War Office, 1917 ; Chief Air Staff, R.A.F. 1918–19 ; Comm. Gen. Civil Aviation from 1919 ; Comm. Legion of Honour, Order Leopold of Belgium, Vladimir of Russia, American D.S.M. *Clubs :* United Service ; Cavalry. (G46)

SYKES, Capt. George, M.B.E.

SYKES, Major George Arthur, O.B.E., R.A.S.C.

SYKES, Joe Armitage, O.B.E., *b.* 24 Oct. 1864 ; *s.* of William Sykes, of Huddersfield ; *m.* Mary Annie, *d.* of Henry Redfearn, of Huddersfield. *Educ. :* Huddersfield Board School. Merchant. *War Work :* Valuable services rendered to British Prisoners of

War in Turkey. *Address:* Mithad Pacha Han, Sirkedji, Constantinople. *Club:* National Liberal.   (O11418)

SYKES, Joseph Percival, M.B.E.

SYKES, Margaret, Mrs., M.B.E.

SYKES, Mary Louisa, Mrs., M.B.E.; *d.* of George March, of Thorner, near Leeds; *m.* John Thorley (who died), *s.* of John Sykes, of Croes Howell. *War Work:* Organiser, Donor, Commandant, and Matron of own Auxiliary Hospital, Croes Howell, Rossett, Denbighshire. *Address:* Croes Howell, Rossett, Denbighshire.   (M993)

SYKES, Percy Duncan, M.B.E., B.A., *b.* 7 Dec. 1882; *s.* of Thomas Edward Sykes, of Huddersfield; *m.* Alethea Edith, *d.* of George Chandler, of Sutton (Surrey). *Educ.:* Royal Mount School, Colwyn Bay. *War Work:* Contract Department, Admiralty.   (M994)

SYKES, Paymaster-Lieut. Percy Stanley, O.B.E., R.D., R.N.R.

SYKES, Capt. Stanley William, O.B.E., M.C.

SYKES, William Henry, M.B.E., *b.* 5 Jan. 1850; *s.* of James Sykes, of Lindley; *m.* Rhoda, *d.* of Joseph Myers, of Berkenshaw. Late assistant master, Barkerend School; Head Master, Bank Top School, and Wapping Road School; Head-master, 36 years (Slum School). *War Work:* Vice-Chairman, Soldiers' and Sailors' Dependents Relief Committee; with the assistance of the Education Committee formed classes for instructing wounded soldiers. *Address:* 84, Dornsthorpe Street, West Bowling, Bradford Yorks. *Clubs:* Cinderella Club; Liberal Club.   (M2505)

SYKES, Annie, Mrs. KNOWLES-, M.B.E., *b.* 1867; *d.* of John Smith, of Huddersfield, Yorkshire; *m.* Frank, *s.* of Alfred Sykes, of Huddersfield. *Educ.:* Huddersfield and Paris. *War Work:* President of the Ladies' Auxiliary of the Huddersfield Y.M.C.A. during the whole period of war, including canteens in connection with the hospitals; Member of Hudders-field War Savings Committee. *Address:* Fixby, 34, West Heath Drive, Hampstead, N.W. 3.   (M6771)

SYLVESTER, Albert James, C.B.E., *b.* 24 Nov. 1889; *s.* of the late Albert Sylvester, of Harlestone, Staffs. Private Sec. to Sec. of Cabinet and Committee of Imperial Defence. *Address:* 2, Whitehall Gardens, S.W. 1.   (C2986)

SYMES, Capt. John, O.B.E.

SYMES, Major Kenneth, O.B.E.

SYMES, Sandham John, O.B.E., *b.* 25 Feb. 1877; *s.* of Sandham John Symes, of Hill View, Co. Wexford, Ireland; *m.* Grace Annie, *d.* of John Thomas Peacock, of Derby. *Educ.:* Foy's School, Waterford. Engineer; Chief Mechanical Engineers, Dept., Midland Railway. *Address:* 5, Mill Hill Road, Derby.   (O1910)

SYMES, Lieut.-Col. and Qr.-Mr. William, O.B.E., M.B.E., R.M.L.I.

SYMES, William Fitzrow Scudamore Stallard, O.B.E.

SYMINTON, Capt. Ralph, M.B.E., R.F.A. (S.R.)

SYMMONS, Percy James, M.B.E.

SYMON, Lesley Kilmeny, M.B.E.; *s.* of Sir J. H. Symon, of Adelaide, S. Australia. *Educ.:* Privately. *War Work:* Belgian Refugee and Munitions Canteens; Prisoner of War Dept., Camps Library. *Address:* Adelaide, S. Australia.   (M6774)

SYMONDS, Sir Charters James, K.B.E., C.B., M.S., F.R.C.S., *b.* 1852; *s.* of Charles Symonds, of St. John, New Brunswick, Canada; *m.* Fanny Marie, *d.* of Lieut.-Gen. D. Shaw, Indian Army. *Educ.:* Guy's Hospital. and Univ. of London. Consulting Surgeon to Guy's Hospital; Member of Council and Vice-President Royal Coll. of Surgeons. *War Work:* Major, 2nd London General Hospital, 1914; Col. A.M.S.; Consulting Surgeon H.M. Forces, Malta, Salonica, Southern Command, 1915–19. *Address:* 58, Portland Place, W. *Club:* Albemarle.   (K293)

SYMONDS, William North, M.B.E., *b.* 21 Feb. 1872; *s.* of the late Rev. Canon Symonds, of The Rectory, Stockport; *m.* Hilda Brownell, *d.* of the late C. T. Drabble, of Sharston Hall, Northenden. *Educ.:* Eton; Gonville and Caius Coll., Cambridge. Barrister-at-Law. *War Work:* Transport Officer of the East Lancashire Branch of the British Red Cross Society. *Address:* Meadow Brow, Alderley Edge. *Clubs:* Oxford and Cambridge.   (M4014)

SYMONDS, May Josephine, Mrs., LODER-, O.B.E., *d.* of Sir William Vavasour, Bart.; *m.* Major John Fitzgerald Loder-Symonds, S. Staffordshire Regt. (killed in action, 1914), *s.* of Capt. F. Loder-Symonds, R.A., J.P., of Hinton Waldrist, Berks. *War Work:* Free Canteen at Lichfield Station for South Staffordshire Regt. and troops. *Address:* The Close, Saffron Walden, Essex.   (O11419)

SYMONS, Paymaster-Lieut.-Comm. Herebert Edward, O.B.E., R.N.

SYMONS, Major John, O.B.E., R.A.O.C.

SYMONS, Rudolph Victor, O.B.E.

SYMONS, Lieut.-Col. Thomas Henry, O.B.E., M.R.C.S. L.R.C.P.

SYMONS, William Frederick, O.B.E., *b.* 1865. *War Work:* Commandant, 1st City of London Detachment British Red Cross Society; Deputy Director, Ambulance Column, London District, Aug. 1914, to March, 1919. *Address:* 35, Dryburgh Road, Putney.   (O11420)

SYMONS, Sir Robert FOX-, K.B.E., M.R.C.S., L.R.C.P., D.P.H., *b.* 1870; *m.* Maude, R.R.C., 1st Class, *d.* of Joseph Calverley. *Educ.:* Privately. Physician. *War Work:* Head of Auxiliary Hospitals Dept. B.R.C.S. *Address:* 5, Courtfield Gardens, S.W. 7. *Clubs:* Savile; Surrey County Cricket; Royal Cornwall Yacht.   (K172)

SYNNOT, Major Reginald Victor Okes HART-, O.B.E., D.S.O., B.Sc., *b.* 1879; *s.* of the late Major-Gen. Arthur FitzRoy Hart-Synnot, C.B., C.M.G., of Ballymoyer, Co. Armagh; *m.* 1912, Violet Mary Emily Maud, *d.* of the Rev. Lord James Theobald Bagot John Butler, *b.* of the present Marquess of Ormonde (*see* BURKE'S *Peerage*). *Educ.:* King William's Coll.; R.M.C.; S.-E. Agricultural Coll. Wye. Entered E. Surrey Regt. 1899; retired, 1904; served in S. Africa, 1899–1902, on the Staff, present at relief of Ladysmith (despatches twice); Dean of Faculty of Agriculture, Univ. Coll. Reading, since 1909; Capt. Guernsey L.I.; on Head Quarter Staffs of Guernsey Dist. and S. Command, 1915–19. *Club:* Athenæum.   (O7250)

SYNNOTT, Major Percy Joseph Ignatius, O.B.E.

SYRETT, Herbert Sutton, C.B.E., *b.* 20 April, 1877; *s.* of Alfred Syrett, of Sydenham, S.E., J.P.; *m.* Rose, *d.* of — Jenkens, of Fulham. *Educ.:* London Univ. Private Sec. to Mr. Lloyd George, 1915–16; Private Sec. to Mr. Clynes (Food Controller, 1918–19). *War Work:* Sec. to Consumers' Council, Ministry of Food. *Address:* 30, Kensington Mansions, Earls Court, S.W. *Clubs:* National Liberal; Royal Auto-mobile.   (C2987)

SYRETT, Sidney James, M.B.E., *b.* 7 Sept. 1889; *s.* of J. H. Syrett, of 190, West Green Road, London, N. 15; *m.* Elsie Louisa, *d.* of E. Bullen, of 2, Suffolk Road, St. Anns, West Green, N. 15. *Educ.:* City Central Foundation School, London, E.C. Armament Stores Officer, Hong-Kong, China. *War Work:* In connection with the R.N. Cordite Factory, Holton Heath, Dorset. *Address:* Royal Navy Ordnance Depot, Hong-Kong, China.   (M6775)

SYSON, Major Alfred Edward, O.B.E. Croix de Guerre (France).

SYSON, Paymaster-Comm. John Luxmore, O.B.E., R.N.

SZLUMPER, Major Alfred Weeks, C.B.E., M.Inst.C.E., R.E. (T.), *b.* 24 May, 1858; *s.* of the late Albert Szlumper, of Wavertree, Liverpool; *m.* Frances Margaret, *d.* of the late Capt. Williams, of Aberystwyth. *Educ.:* Aberystwyth Grammar School, and Univ. of Wales. Articled, and subse-quently Chief Assistant to Sir James W. Szlumper, M.Inst.C.E.; Resident Engineer on section of G.I.P. Rly., India; for 17 years Divisional Engineer, L. & S. W. Rly., Chief Engineer since April, 1914. *War Work:* As Chief Engineer, L. & S.-W. Rly., carried out important and urgent work including Light Rail-ways, many sidings, etc.; advised as to conveyance of special heavy and out-of-gauge loads, such as Guns, Tanks, etc. *Address:* Glenbuckhouse, Surbiton, Surrey. *Clubs:* St. Stephen's; Roehampton.   (C2988)

TABOR, James, C.B.E., *b.* 25 Jan. 1869; *s.* of James A. C. Tabor, of Gt. Baddow Lodge, Chelmsford; *m.* Margaret Ada Sophia, *d.* of Charles A. Tabor, of Earls Hall, Prittlewell, Essex. *Educ.:* Eton, and Trinity Coll., Cambridge. J.P., D.L., C.A., Essex. *War Work:* Chairman, Essex Local War Pensions Committee; Vice-Chairman, Territorial Force Association, Essex County. *Address:* The Lawn, Rochford, Essex. *Club:* Constitutional.   (C2984)

TABRUM, Ashley, O.B.E., LL.B. (Camb.), *b.* 13 March, 1879; *s.* of Burnett Tabrum, of Bromley, Kent; *m.* Mary Montague, *d.* of Dr. B. E. Fordyce, of Cambridge. *Educ.:* Felsted School. Clerk of the Peace and of the County Council of Cambridgeshire; County Returning Officer, etc. *War Work:* Hon. Sec. Cambridgeshire War Pensions Committee and Cambridgeshire Relief Committee (Prince of Wales' Fund); Sec. Cambridgeshire Appeal Tribunal (Military Service Acts). *Address:* 13, Harvey Road, Cambridge. *Club:* University Pitt (Cambridge).   (O11421)

TABUTEAU, Lieut.-Comm. Reginald Moliere, O.B.E., R.N.

TADEMA, Anna ALMA-, M.B.E.

TADEMA, Laurence ALMA-, C.B.E.; *d.* of the late Sir Lawrence Alma-Tadema, O.M., R.A. Authoress. *War Work:* Founder, with I. J. Paderewski, and Hon. Sec. of the Polish Victims Relief Fund, 1915; founder and Hon. Sec. of the Polish Exiles Protection, 1915; founder and director of Crèche and Schools for the education of Polish Children in England, 1918. *Address:* The Fair Haven, Wittersham, Kent.   (C90)

TADGELL, Capt. Frederick Harold, M.B.E., A.I.F.

TAFFS, Herbert William, M.B.E.

TAGG, Lieut.-Col. George John, M.B.E., R.E.

TAGGART, Sir James, K.B.E., J.P., *b.* 6 Dec. 1849; *m.* Eliza, *d.* of George Reid, of Rothie-Norman. *Educ.:* Port Elphiston; Inverurie Parish School; Aberdeen Mechanics Institution. Entered the Aberdeen Town Council, 1894; Magistrate, 1896; Deputy Lieutenant, 1905; Granite Mer-chant. Lord Provost of Aberdeen and Lord Lieutenant of the County of the City of Aberdeen; and Vice-Admiral of the North Sea since 1914. *Address:* Ashley Lodge, Aberdeen.   (K173)

TAILBY, Lieut. Mark, M.B.E., *b.* Nov. 1888; *s.* of A. Tailby, of Woolwich. *Educ.:* Woolwich Polytechnic. Design-ing Engineer. *War Work:* Three years with Royal Garrison Artillery, and two years as Inspector of Ordnance Machinery (I.O.M.); served in France, Belgium, Russia, and Palestine.   (M7006)

TAINSH, Peter, O.B.E.

TAIT, Major and Qr.-Mr. Andrew Ferdinand, M.B.E., R.A.M.C.

TAIT, Andrew Wilson, C.B.E., *b.* 16 Jan. 1876; *s.* of William Tait, of Edinburgh; *m.* Isabel May, *d.* of George

Allinson, of Ellesmere. *Educ.:* Edinburgh. Chartered Accountant. *War Work:* Chairman of British Aluminium Co., Ltd.; Member of various Government Committees. *Address:* The Oaks, Parkside, Wimbledon Common, S.W. *Clubs:* Junior Carlton; Royal Automobile; Scottish Conservative. (C644)

TAIT, Anne Smith, Mrs., M.B.E.

TAIT, Charles Wilson, M.B.E.

TAIT, Capt. Henry Caldwell, M.B.E.

TAIT, James, M.B.E., *b.* 1853; *s.* of Andrew Tait, of Dumbarton; *m.* Mary Jane, *d.* of Robert Turnbull, of West Hartlepool. *Educ.:* National Schools and Evening Technical Classes. Manager (Engineer) to Messrs. Thurd, Ridley and Sons, Middlesbrough. *War Work:* Organising and Manufacturing of 18-pounder Shrapnel Shells. (M2509)

TAIT, James, M.B.E., *b.* 26 March, 1885; *s.* of Willami Tait, of Edinburgh; *m.* Jane Anne Menzies. *Educ.:* Daniel Stewart's Coll., Edinburgh, and Edinburgh Univ. Chartered Accountant; member of firm of George A. Touche & Co., Chartered Accountants, London. *War Work:* Section Director in Accounts Department of Ministry of Munitions. *Address:* Basildon House, Moorgate Street E.C. 2. (M9778)

TAIT, Lieut.-Col. John Spottiswood, C.B.E. Lieut.-Col. British Columbia Regt.; served in Great War, 1915–19 (mentioned in despatches). (C1838)

TAIT, Capt. William Ironsides, O.B.E., R.E.

TALBOT, Bridget Elizabeth, O.B.E.

TALBOT, Ernest Edward Austin, M.B.E.

TALBOT, Comm. Gerald, C.M.G., O.B.E.

TALBOT, Hugo, O.B.E.

TALBOT DE MALAHIDE, Isabel Charlotte Talbot, Lady, D.B.E., Lady of Grace of the Order of St. John of Jerusalem; *d.* of Robert-Blake Humfrey, of Wroxham House, Norwich, Norfolk; *m.* Richard Wogan, 5th Baron, *s.* of James, Lord Talbot de Malahide, 4th Baron (*see* BURKE'S *Peerage*). *War Work:* President of County Dublin B.R.C.S. *Address:* Malahide Castle, Dublin. *Clubs:* Alexandra; Empress. (D50)

TALBOT, Eng.-Comm. John Charles, O.B.E., R.N.

TALBOT, 2nd Lieut. John Hamilton, M.B.E., R.E.

TALBOT, Julia Elizabeth Mary, Mrs., O.B.E., Lady of Grace of the Order of St. John of Jerusalem; *d.* of Sir Capel Molyneux, 7th Bart. of Castle Dillon, Co. Armagh (*see* BURKE'S *Peerage*); *m.* William John Talbot, of Mount Talbot; Lord Lieutenant of Co. Roscommon, and a J.P. for Cos. Roscommon, Armagh, and Galloway. *Educ.:* At home. County Director for County Armagh of joint Red Cross and St. John Ambulance Association; Chairman, Roscommon Boarding-Out Committee. *War Work:* Acting ;Chairman, Co. Roscommon Local War Pensions Committee; 2 years Chairman, Roscommon Town War Pensions Sub-Committee; President for St. John Ambulance Association, Co. Armagh, Nov. 1194, to Oct. 1919; County Director for Co. Armagh, Oct. 1919, to present date; part organiser, Co. Armagh, "Our Day" Fund, etc. *Addresses:* Mount Talbot, Co. Roscommon; Castle Dillon, Co. Armagh. (O11425)

TALBOT, Matilda Theresa, M.B.E., W.R.A.F.

TALBOT, Dame Meriel Lucy, D.B.E.; *d.* of the late Rt. Hon. John G. Talbot, of Falconhurst, Eden Bridge, Kent. Woman Adviser, Ministry of Agriculture and Fisheries. *War Work:* Member of Home Office Committee for Repatriation of enemy aliens; Director, Women's Branch, Ministry of Agriculture, and responsible for the organisation of the Women's Land Army. *Address:* 14, Moore Street, Chelsea, S.W. 3. *Club:* Ladies' Empire. (D56)

TALBOT, Lieut.-Col. Reginald George, C.B.E., R.A.F., and Comm. R.N., *b.* 25 Jan. 1881; *s.* of Gustavus Arthur Chetwynd-Talbot (*see* BURKE'S *Peerage*, Shrewsbury and Talbot, E.); *m.* Mary Helen Charlotte, *d.* of Hon. H. R. Hepbourne-Scott (*see* BURKE'S *Peerage*, Polwarth, B.). *Address:* R.N.A. Station, Straford, Lincolnshire. (C876)

TALBOT, Hon. Reginald Gilbert Murray, C.B.E., LL.B., *b.* 30 Jan. 1849; *s.* of James, 4th Lord Talbot, of Malahide (*see* BURKE'S *Peerage*); *m.* 1st Edith Lucy Murray; *d.* of the Rev. Jermyn Pratt, of Ryston Hall, Norfolk (who died); 2nd, Richenda, *d.* of the late Charles Buxton, M.P. *Educ.:* Trinity Coll. Cambridge (*see* BURKE'S *Peerage*, Buxton, Bart.). Barrister-at-law. *Address:* 34, St. George's Road, S.W. *Club:* Windham. (C313)

TALLACK, Charles Michael, O.B.E., *b.* 7 June, 1874; *s.* of M. D. Tallack, of Bristol; *m.* Marianne Boultbee, *d.* of J. B. Brooks, J.P., of Finstall, Worcester. *Educ.:* Merchant Venturers' Coll., Bristol. Banker; Chief Accountant and Deputy Sec. Bank of Bengal. *War Work:* Indian War Loans, and Indian War Funds, etc. *Address:* c/o Bank of Bengal, Calcutta. *Clubs:* Bengal (Calcutta); East India United Services (London). (O9856)

TALLACK, Francis Harold Cass, M.B.E.

TALLACK, Thomas, M.B.E.

TALLBOY, George Percy, O.B.E., *b.* 27 June, 1877; *s.* of the late George Frederick Tallboy; *m.* Ina Winifred Bertha, *d.* of the late Capt. W. J. Anderson, R.N., of Chatham. *Educ.:* Midhurst Grammar School, London Univ. (Cobden Club Prize). Sec. "The Times History of the War," in S. Africa; Private Sec. to Mr. L. S. Amery, M.P., 1909–14. *War Work:* Private Sec. to Director of Army Contracts, War Office, 1914–17, Surveyor-General of Supply, War Office, 1917, and to Permanent Sec. Ministry of Food, 1917–18; Head of Correspondence Section, Livestock Branch, Ministry of Food, 1918; Private Sec. to Controller of H.M. Stationery Office, 1918; Licensing Officer, Inter-Allied Rhineland Commission, Coblenz, 1918; in charge of Import and Export Licence Section, Ministry of Food, since 1919. *Address:* 31, Earlsthorpe Road, Sydenham, S.E. (O788)

TALLENT, Edward Killworth, O.B.E.

TALLENTS, Stephen George, C.B., C.B.E., *b.* 20 Oct. 1884; *s.* of G. W. Tallents, of 49, Warwick Square, London, S.W. 1; *m.* Bridget, *d.* of Hugh Hole, of Caunton Manor, Newark. *Educ.:* Harrow, and Balliol Coll., Oxford. Civil Servant. *War Work:* Irish Guards (S.R.), 1914; wounded May, 1915; Ministry of Munitions, 1915–16; a Principal Assist. Sec. Ministry of Food, 1916–19; Chief British Member, Inter-Allied Commission for the Relief and Supply of Poland, 1919; British Commissioner for the Baltic Provinces, 1919–1920. *Address:* 34, Ladbroke Square, W. 11. *Club:* Oxford and Cambridge. (C2360b)

TAMBLYN, Lieut.-Col. David Sobey, D.S.O., O.B.E.; Lieut.-Col. Canadian Army Vet. Corps; served in Great War, 1915–18 (mentioned in despatches). (O6059)

TANDY, Lieut.-Col. Maurice O'Connor, D.S.O., O.B.E., R.E., *b.* 1873. Aden, 1903–4; Great War, 1914–19 (mentioned in despatches). (O6712)

TANCOCK, Charles Crump, M.B.E.

TANCRED, Flying Officer Christopher Humphrey, M.B.E.

TANGYE, Albert William, O.B.E.

TANGYE, Major Richard Trevithick Gilbertstone, O.B.E., J.P., *b.* 26 June. 1875; *s.* of Sir Richard Tangye, of Newquay; *m.* S. E. Frieda, *d.* of J. Kidman, of Liverpool. *Educ.:* Bromsgrove, Trinity Coll., Cambridge. Barrister-at-Law. *War Work:* With British Red Cross Society in France as Voluntary Driver, Nov. 1914, to June, 1916; June, 1916, to Feb. 1919, attached General Staff, G.H.Q., B.E.F.; Feb. 1919, General Staff, G.H.Q., British Army of the Rhine; twice mentioned in despatches, Croix de Guerre avec Palme. *Addresses:* 40, Bramham Gardens, S.W.; Glendorgal ,St. Columb Minor, Cornwall. *Club:* New University. (O8610)

TANNER, Alfred Richard Morley, M.B.E. Staff Accountant in Coal Mines Dept., Board of Trade. (M10260b)

TANNER, Edward, M.B.E.

TANNER, Lieut. Edward Butler, O.B.E., R.N.R., *b.* 10 July, 1865; *s.* of Joseph Thompson Tanner, of Wexford, Ireland; *m.* Annie Esther, *d.* of Henry Johnston, of Tomagaddy, Co. Wexford. *Educ.:* The Tate School, Wexford, and High School, Wexford. In command of cross-Channel passenger steamers owned by L. & N.-W. Rly. Co. *War Work:* Commanding Officer, H.M.S. "Tara" (Owners' Master, Lieut. R.N.R.), Aug. 1914, to Nov. 1915; prisoner of war in Libyan Desert, Nov. 1915, to March, 1916, when rescued by Duke of Westminster; Master of H.M.A.T., "Cambria," Dec. 1918, to present date. *Address:* Ormesby, Walthew Avenue, Holyhead, North Wales. (O11428)

TANNER, Lieut. Guy, M.B.E., R.F.A.

TANNER, John, M.B.E.

TANNER, Mary Elizabeth, M.B.E., *b.* 31 May, 1866, *d.* of Thomas Hawkes Tanner, M.D., of London. *Educ.:* Privately; Bedford; Univ. Coll., London; Federal School of Science, Zurich, Switzerland. *War Work:* One year in Postal Censorship; from 1916–19, directing canteens and recreation huts for Women's Emergency Canteens and British Committee of French Red Cross, with French Army; received from Government of French Republic, Silver Médaille de la Reconnaissance, Française. *Club:* Forum. (M4016)

TANNER, William Allan, O.B.E., *b.* 23 Dec. 1866; *s.* of William Tanner, of Eastville, Bristol; *m.* Eva, *d.* of William Smith, J.P., of Athlone, Ireland. *Educ.:* Merchant Venturers' Schools, Bristol. 1882–89, training and serving as Civil Engineer; 1889–98, attached to Civil Engineering Staff, Royal Engineers on Engineering Works, Dublin District; 1898–1901, Assist. Civil Engineer, Works Department, H.M. Dockyards at Devonport, and later at Portsmouth; 1901–4, Resident Engineer, Rangoon Port Trust, Burmah. *War Work:* Aug. 1914, to Feb. 1915, Police River Patrol, commissioned and ran his own petrol launch on Thames; Feb. 1915, to Nov. 1915, helped in Medical Research Dept.; Nov. 1915, to Nov. 1919, in Ministry of Munitions, Trench Warfare Dept., and Gun Ammunition Dept.; was responsible for supply of (at first) trench guns and ammunition; in 1916 was apponted Director, Aerial Bomb Section, and responsible for whole supply of the Air Board's requirements; in 1918 was appointed controller of Gun Ammunition (C.G.A.), and in 1919 was appointed Deputy Director of Ordnance Supply Department. *Address:* Doonvara, Highbury Road, Wimbledon, S.W1 *Clubs:* Royal Institution; Royal Wimbledon Golf; Roya, Automobile. (O11429)

TANSLEY, Comm. Emily Amelia, M.B.E., *b.* 17 Feb. 1872; *d.* of — Tansley, of London. *Educ.:* Gravesend High School. *War Work:* Qr.-Mr., V.A.D. Kent 16, at Yacht Club, Gravesend, Oct. 1914, to Oct. 1915; Qr.-Mr., All Hallows', Middlestoke, near Rochester, Sept. 1914, to Nov. 1915; also at Great Hermitage, Higham, near Rochester, Nov. 1915, to April, 1918; Commandant, April, 1918, to June, 1919, at The Great Hermitage. *Address:* St. Hilda, Old Road West, Gravesend. (M9802)

TAPERELL, Major Bernard Treleaven, O.B.E., late R.A.S.C.; *m.* 14 Dec. 1920, Henriette Palmyre-Joseph Godin, of Paris. (O1911)

TAPHOUSE, Alfred John, M.B.E.

TAPLIN, Capt. Colin Quintrell, O.B.E., R.A.F.

TAPP, Capt. Arthur Gerard Rhodes Sentance, O.B.E., M.C., *b.* 2 Jan. 1897; *s.* of Arthur Tapp, of The Old Hatchgate, Horley, Surrey. *Educ.:* Winchester Coll. Stock Exchange. *War Work:* Proceeded to France attached as R.A. Officer, Ammunition Park, 37th Div., June, 1915; transferred in same capacity to Indian Corps, Sept. 1915; transferred to XIVth Corps, Nov. 1915; remained with XIVth Corps in France till Nov. 1917, then proceeded with XIVth Corps to Italy; appointed Staff Capt. Heavy Artillery, British Forces in Italy, Dec. 1917, until demobilised, Feb. 1919; Belgian Croix de Guerre, Italian Croce di Guerra, mentioned in Birthday Honours List. *Addresses:* The Old Hatchgate, Horley, Surrey; 3, Tokenhouse Buildings, King's Arms Yard, London, E.C. 2. *Club:* R.A.C. (O6422)

TAPP, Egerton Richard, M.B.E., *b.* 11 Dec. 1868; *s.* of the late William Pearce Tapp, of Bristol; *m.* Bessie Maude Carter, *d.* of William Henry House, of Bristol. *Educ.:* Colston School, Stapleton, Bristol. *War Work:* Special Constable; Hon. Sec. Church Brampton V.A.D. Auxiliary Hospital; also of Weston Favel Primary Hospital. *Address:* Fairlawn, Abington, Northampton. (M9804)

TAPP, Capt. Harold Astley, O.B.E., M.C., R.A.S.C.

TAPP, John Reuban, M.B.E.

TAPPER, Major Kenneth Edwin, O.B.E., M.B.

TARBET, Arthur, M.B.E.

TARGETT, 2nd Lieut. Harry, O.B.E.

TARLTON, Jessie, Mrs., M.B.E.

TARRAN, Major William, O.B.E., T.D., 5th East Surrey Regt. With Unit in India and Mesopotamia. *Address:* 33, Calais Gate, Myatts Park, S.E. 5. (O4255)

TARRANT, Harley, M.B.E. (M10418)

TARRANT, Lieut.-Comm. William Charles, O.B.E., R.N.R.

TARRING, Bateman Brown, O.B.E., *b.* 4 June, 1873; *s.* of F. W. Tarring, of Crouch End; *m.* Elizabeth Blake, *d.* of Alexander Watson, of Dover. *Educ.:* Taunton Coll. Civil Engineer. *War Work:* Construction of the National Shell Filling Factory at Chilwell, Notts, for the Ministry of Munitions, also The Tank Assembling Factory at Chateauroux, France, for the Allies. *Address:* 28, Claremont Road, Surbiton. *Clubs:* Royal Automobile; City Guild of the Worshipful Company of Cooks. (O1912)

TASKER, Arthur, M.B.E.

TASKER, George Edward, M.B.E., *b.* 1868; *s.* of John Tasker, of Oxford. Author of "Ilford Past and Present," "Country Rambles around Ilford," "Country Rambles around Romford," miscellaneous articles in magazines, etc. *War Work:* Confidential Shorthand Writer and Clerk to successive Secretaries of State for War, including F. M. Earl Kitchener, Mr. D. Lloyd George, Earl of Derby, etc. *Address:* 84, Mayfair Avenue, Ilford, Essex. (M9806)

TASKER, Grace Rosina, M.B.E., *b.* 22 Dec. 1884; *d.* of the late John Tasker, late Royal Artillery. *Educ.:* Private Schools. Member of Stirlingshire Education Authority; Member of Stirling Town Council; Hon. Assistant Sec. Stirling Nursing Association; Treas. Ladies' Golf Club; Treas. Stirling Ladies' County Golf Club. *War Work:* Hon. Sec. and Treas. Argyll and Sutherland Highlanders' Prisoners of War Fund; Hon. Sec. and Treas. Stirlingshire Work Depot. *Address:* 22, Clarendon Place, Stirling. (M998)

TASKER, Theodore James, O.B.E., I.C.S.

TATA, Mehrbai, Lady, C.B.E., *d.* of H. J. Bhabha (late Inspector-General of Education, Mysore); *m.* Sir Dorabji Jamseti, J.P., *s.* of the late Jamsetji Nusservanji Tata. *Address:* Esplanade House, Waudby Road, Fort, Bombay. (C2390)

TATAM, Col. Walter John, C.M.G., C.B.E., *b.* 1869. Entered Army Vet. Corps, 1891; Lieut.-Col. 1915; A. Col. 1917; Mohmand and Tirah Expeditionary Forces, 1897–98 (medal with two clasps); S. Africa, 1899–1902, present at defence of Ladysmith (Queen's medal with five clasps, King's medal with two clasps); Great War, 1914–17 (despatches). (C1334)

TATE, Lieut. Frederick Lionel, O.B.E., R.N.V.R.

TATE, Lieut. Henry Percy, M.B.E., R.A.F.

TATE, Col. Robert Ward, C.B.E. Col. and Adj.-Gen. New Zealand Forces. (C373)

TATE, Major Robert William, K.B.E., F.T.C.D., M.A., *b.* 27 Aug. 1872; *s.* of the late Rev. Richard Tate, of Rossinver, Co. Leitrim, Ireland; *m.* Raby Georgina, *d.* of the late William Clarke, of Dublin. *Educ.:* Shrewsbury School (Head boy, 1889–91); St. John's Coll. Cambridge (scholar); Trinity Coll., Dublin. Fellow of Trinity Coll., Dublin, 1908; Tutor, Trinity Coll., Dublin, 1910; Public Orator, Univ. of Dublin since 1914; Major, Commanding Dublin Univ. Contingent, O.T.C., since 1910. *War Work:* Commanded Dublin Univ. Contingent, O.T.C., throughout the war, and was Commandant of Officers' School of Instruction attached thereto from Sept. 1914, to Feb. 1916. *Addresses:* 34, Trinity Coll., Dublin; 9, Brendan Road, Donnybrook, Dublin. *Club:* The Univ. (Dublin). (K431)

TATE, Capt. Simon Marshall, O.B.E.

TATHAM, Col. Charles John Willmer, O.B.E.

TATHAM, Lilian Elizabeth, Mrs., M.B.E.

TATHAM, Capt. Meaburn, O.B.E., M.A., *b.* 14 Aug. 1886; *s.* of Meaburn Talbot Tatham, M.A., J.P., of Northcourt House, Abingdon, Berks; *m.* Bessie Eileen, *d.* of Sir Robert Roden, of Belize, British Honduras (*see* BURKE'S *Peerage*). *Educ.:* Eton, and Balliol Coll., Oxford. Sec. Messrs. Cadbury

Bros., Ltd. *War Work:* Served with Friends' Ambulance Unit, British Red Cross Society, 1915–19 (France and Flanders); Officer Commanding above unit, 1918–19; Chevalier, Ordre de la Couronne, Belgium. *Address:* 111, Middleton Hall Road, King's Norton, Birmingham. (O11430)

TATLOW, Frank, C.B.E. Gen. Manager, Midland Railway since 1918. (C314)

TATTERSALL, Flight-Lieut. James William, M.B.E., R.A.F.

TATTERSALL, Capt. Tom Whitaker, M.B.E., R.A.F.

TATTON, Winifred Eva, Mrs., O.B.E., *d.* of Salisbury Payne, of Blunham, Beds.; *m.* Reginald Arthur, *s.* of Thos. Wm. Tatton, of Wythenshame. *Educ.:* Harrow. *War Work:* Hospital work. (O11431)

TAUNTON, John William Lionel, O.B.E., *b.* 13 July, 1882; *s.* of the late Wm. Whitchurch Taunton. *Educ.:* Victoria Coll., Jersey. *Address:* c/o Sir C. R. McGrigor, Bart, & Co., 39, Panton Street, Haymarket, S.W. 1. (O4256)

TAVENER, Veronica Mary Agnes, M.B.E.

TAYLER, Frank Alfred, M.B.E.

TAYLER, Major Henry Pascoe Blair, D.S.O., O.B.E. Major, Gen. List; S. Africa, 1900 (Queen's medal with four clasps); served in Great War, 1914–18 (mentioned in despatches). (O2746)

TAYLER, Mary Beatrice CHURCHILL-, M.B.E.; *d.* of the late William Moseley Tayler, solicitor, of Gt. James Street, Bedford Row, W.C. *Educ.:* Various schools, and Convent of the Assumption, Kensington, W. 8. *War Work:* Secretarial work in H.M. Procurator-General's Intelligence Department; St. James' Park, and Storey's Gate, S.W. 1 (Prize Court); continuing same work. *Address:* 58, Scarsdale Villas, Kensington, W. 8. (M999)

TAYLEUR, Lieut.-Col. William, O.B.E.

TAYLOR, Alexander Thomson, O.B.E.

TAYLOR, Alfred Ernest, M.B.E., *b.* 7 Oct. 1878; *s.* of William Taylor, of Birmingham. Representative of Messrs. Edgar Allen & Co., Ltd., Imperial Steel Works, Sheffield. *War Work:* Devoted an enormous amount of time in connection with the Sheffield Corps of the St. John Ambulance Brigade, in which held rank of Divisional Superintendent; was also Founder and Commandant of Voluntary Aid Detachment No. 47, West Riding, Yorks (the detachment carried out a considerable part of the wounded convoy detraining at Sheffield, and also rendered other valuable voluntary assistance at the 3rd W.G.H., Sheffield); also undertook other important work on behalf of the Joint Societies of the British Red Cross and the Order of St. John. *Address:* 53, Fossdale Road, Sheffield. *Club:* Reform (Sheffield). (M9810)

TAYLOR, Comm. Alfred Hugh, O.B.E., R.N.

TAYLOR, Capt. and Qr.-Mr. Alfred William, O.B.E.

TAYLOR, Alice Maud Rowson, M.B.E., J.P., *b.* Aug. 1869; *d.* of Joseph Taylor, Cotton-broker, Liverpool. *Educ.:* Private Schools. Justice of the Peace, Co. Lancs.; Commandant, St. John Ambulance Brigade; Chairman, Crosby Division, B.R.C.S.; Governor, Merchant Taylors' School for Girls, Crosby; Member of Executive Committee, Department Household and Social Science, Univ. of London; District Commissioner, Girl Guides. *War Work:* Commandant, Windy Knowe V.A.D. Hospital, Blundellsands, 4 years; Acting-Matron, Seaforth Military Hospital, Liverpool, 3½ years; Hon. Sec. Civic Service League, Blundellsands, 5 years. *Address:* Newstead, Blundelllands, Lancs. *Clubs:* Albemarle; West Lancs Ladies' Golf. (M1000)

TAYLOR, Andrew William, M.B.E.

TAYLOR, Paymaster-Comm. Archibald, O.B.E., R.N.

TAYLOR, Arnold, M.B.E.

TAYLOR, Lieut. Arnold, O.B.E., R.N.R., *b.* 1883; *s.* of Joseph Taylor, of Dukinfield, Cheshire; *m.* Alice, *d.* of Samuel Mallinson, of Ashton-under-Lyne. *Educ.:* Moravian School, Dukinfield. Master Mariner, holding Extra Master's certificate; Capt. of Transport "Rotenfels," under control of India Office; also a Younger Brother of Trinity House, London. *War Work:* Served in Singapore in the R.N.R., and later in Bombay; in Nov. 1914 appointed to command this vessel, and was one of the convoy which brought over the Indian Expeditionary Force to France; subsequently in command continuously running with troops, ammunition, and war stores through the danger zone throughout the submarine menace. *Address:* Oakdene, Smallshaw, Ashton-under-Lyne, Lancs. (O11432)

TAYLOR, Arthur Edwin, O.B.E., *b.* 13 April, 1864; *s.* of the late William Campbell Taylor, of Woolwich; *m.* Annie, *d.* of the late W. A. Peckitt, of Woolwich. *Educ.:* Merchant Taylors' School, London. Assistant Registrar of Joint Stock Companies. *Address:* Rossmoyne, Beckenham Grove, Shortlands, Kent. *Club:* Shortlands Golf. (O11433)

TAYLOR, Arthur Enfield, O.B.E., *b.* 4 Aug. 1875; *s.* of Henry Enfield Taylor, of Chester; *m.* Olive Marjorie, *d.* of Philip Edward Tillard, of Godmanchester. *Educ.:* Rugby. Partner in John Taylor and Sons, Mining Engineers. *War Work:* Ministry of Munitions. *Addresses:* Rothamsted Lodge, Harpenden; 6, Queen Street Place, E.C. (O789)

TAYLOR, 2nd Lieut. Arthur Henry, M.B.E., R.A.F.

TAYLOR, Capt. Arthur Herbert, M.B.E.

TAYLOR, Arthur Thomas, O.B.E.

TAYLOR, Capt. Arthur Trevelyan, C.B.E., R.N. Served in Great War, 1914–19 (mentioned in despatches). (C1945)

TAYLOR, Capt. Basil Wilford, O.B.E., R.A., *b.* 26 Nov. 1883; *s.* of John Wilford Taylor, of Malwa, Seaford. *Educ.:*

Dulwich Coll. Capt. R.A. *War Work :* Officer in the Royal Artillery ; U.K., Dec. 1914, to Sept. 1915 ; France, Sept. 1915, to Dec. 1915 ; Macedonia, Dec. 1915, to May, 1919. *Address :* Malwa, Seaford, Sussex. *Club :* Wellington.
(O6540)

TAYLOR, Capt. Bernard Archie, M.B.E., R.A.F.

TAYLOR, Lieut.-Col. Bertie Harry Waters, C.B.E., *b.* 1874 ; Major and Brevet Lieut.-Col. S. Staffordshire Regt. ; S. Africa, 1889–1902 (Queen's medal with four clasps, King's medal with two clasps) ; S. Nigeria, 1909–10 (medal with clasp) ; Great War, 1914–19 (despatches) ; is Officer of the Legion of Honour.
(C789)

TAYLOR, Bramwell, M.B.E.

TAYLOR, Major Cecil George, O.B.E.

TAYLOR, Capt. Cedric Rowland, O.B.E., M.B.

TAYLOR, Charles, M.B.E.

TAYLOR, Capt. Charles Gerald, O.B.E., R.A.S.C.

TAYLOR, Lieut.-Col. Charles Hillsborough Rimington, O.B.E.

TAYLOR, Major Charles Lancelot Deslandes, O.B.E., R.A.M.C.

TAYLOR, Charles Lewis, M.B.E., V.D.

TAYLOR, Lieut.-Col. ¡Charles Newton, C.B.E. Major, and Hon. Lieut. Col.London Regt. (Reserve). Served in the Great War, 1914–19 (despatches).
(C1783)

TAYLOR, Clara Jane, M.B.E,

TAYLOR, Major Claude Waterhouse Hearne, C.B.E., D.S.O., *b.* 1880 ; *s.* of the late John Henry Taylor ; *m.* Edyth Syra, *d.* of Col. Henry W. Jameson, of Titness Cottage, Sunninghill, Berks. *Educ.:* Eton, and Camb. Univ. Capt. and Brevet Major, Roy. W. Kent Regt. ; served in Great War, 1914–19, as Major (mentioned in despatches). *Address :* 6, Montagu Mansions, Portman Square, W. *Club :* Union.
(C1783)

TAYLOR, Corrie, M.B.E.

TAYLOR, Capt. David, O.B.E.

TAYLOR, David Paton, O.B.E.

TAYLOR, Deborah Phipps, M.B.E.

TAYLOR, Capt. Douglas Compton, O.B.E., R.A.M.C.

TAYLOR, Capt. and Qr.-Mr. Douglas Percy, O.B.E., R.A.M.C. (T.).

TAYLOR, Major Edgar Charles, O.B.E., F.S.I., R.E.

TAYLOR, Capt. Edward Dansy, M.B.E., R.A.S.C.

TAYLOR, Lieut. Edward McKenzie, M.B.E., R'A.S.C.

TAYLOR, Eleanor Bessie Percy, M.B.E. ; *d.* of Percy William Taylor, of Bishop's Stortford. *Educ.:* Privately. Formerly Sec. Victoria League ; subsequently Sec. Colonial Intelligence League. *War Work :* Joint Sec. Professional Classes War Relief Council, for the relief of distress, occasioned by the war, among the professional classes of Great Britain and Ireland. *Address :* 30, Cathcart Road, London, S.W. 10.
(M9813)

TAYLOR, Capt. Sir Eric Stuart, Bart, O.B.E., *b.* 1889 ; *s.* of the late Sir Frederick Taylor, Bart, of Kennington, Co. London. *Educ.:* Clifton Coll. and King's Coll. Camb. M.D., B.A., Camb. ; Capt. R.A.M.C. ; served in the Great War.
(O5836)

TAYLOR, Esther Hilda, M.B.E.

TAYLOR, Lieut. Frank, M.B.E., D.C.M., R.A.S.C., *b.* 14 Nov. 1882 ; *s.* of William and Ellen Taylor, of Manchester. *Educ.:* Technical School, Manchester. Engineer. *War Work :* Enlisted Feb. 1915, in the ranks, joined 3rd Siege Battery, March, 1915, in France ; granted commission for service in the field, May, 1917 ; demobilised Oct. 1919, with rank of Lieut., O.C. 4th Army Siege Park. *Address :* 10, Howe Street Higher Broughton, Manchester.
(M4612)

TAYLOR, Capt. Frank Gillis, M.B.E.

TAYLOR, Fred, M.B.E.

TAYLOR, Frederick, M.B.E.

TAYLOR, Capt. Geoffrey Fell, M.B.E.

TAYLOR, Lieut.-Col. George Bryan Ogilvie, C.B.E. Capt. and Brevet-Major, R.E. Served in the Balkans, Great War, 1914–19 (despatches).
(C1419)

TAYLOR, Lieut. George Reay, O.B.E., R.N.R.

TAYLOR, George Stevenson, O.B.E.

TAYLOR, George Wilson, M.B.E.

TAYLOR, Brig.-Gen. Gerald Kyffin, C.B.E., V.D., *b.* 1863 ; *s.* of the late Ven. W. F. Taylor, D.D., late Archdeacon of Liverpool ; *m.* Bessie, *d.* of the late Thomas Cope, J.P., of Hayton, near Liverpool. *Educ.:* Liverpool Coll. Housing Commissioner for Lancashire and Cheshire (Region C.). *War Work :* Commanding Royal Artillery West Lancashire (Reserve) Division, afterwards the 57th Division, until Jan. 1916 ; subsequently a Military Representative at Liverpool until Oct. 1917 ; then Director of National Service for Lancashire and Cheshire until Jan. 1919. *Club :* Junior Army and Navy.
(C646)

TAYLOR, Lieut.-Col. Gerard Charles, O.B.E., M.A., M.D., R.A.M.C. (T.), *b.* 29 Dec. 1868 ; *s.* of the late Lieut.-Col. Thomas Taylor, of Bengal Staff Corps. *Educ.:* Dulwich Coll. ; Cambridge Univ ; St. Bartholomew's Hospital, London. County Medical Officer of Health, Berkshire. *Addresses :* Shire Hall, Reading ; Sunnyside, Grosvenor Road, Caversham.
(O2941)

TAYLOR, Gwynedd Lefer, M.B.E., J.P., *b.* 23 May, 1895 ; *d.* of the late Capt. H. W. Taylor, of Royal Horse Artillery. *Educ.:* The Beehive, Bexhill-on-Sea. County Sec. Girl Guides for Pembrokeshire. *War Work :* Hon. Assist. Sec. County of Pembroke War Fund ; Member Pembrokeshire War Memorial

Committees ; Member County Distress Committee. *Address :* Dial House, Lamphey, S.O., Pembrokeshire.
(M9816)

TAYLOR, Harold, O.B.E., *b.* 25 Nov. 1866 ; *s.* of the late Ven. W. F. Taylor, D.D., Archdeacon of Liverpool ; *m.* Frances Jane, *d.* of O. H. Williams, J.P., of Liverpool. *Educ.:* Liverpool Coll. *War Work :* National Service Representative, Liverpool ; Deputy Chairman, North Western Regional Shipping Committee ; Member, National Service (Part Time) Committee, Liverpool. *Clubs :* Royal Automobile ; Royal Liverpool Golf (Hoylake).
(O11436)

TAYLOR, Major Harold Blake, C.B.E., R.E. Served in Great War, 1914–19 (mentioned in despatches).
(C1784)

TAYLOR, Rev. Harold Milman Strickland, O.B.E., M.A., *b.* 4 Aug. 1890 ; *s.* of the late Rev. John Charles Taylor, of Harmondsworth ; *m.* Violet Ursula, *d.* of Gerald Hunnybun, of Godmanchester. *Educ.:* Marlborough ; Trinity Coll., Cambridge. Schoolmaster. *War Work :* Chaplain to the Forces in France for 3 years, Jan. 1916, to March, 1919, of which 19 months was spent with R.F.A., 21st Division, and the rest of the time with various units. Headmaster, Cheam School, Surrey.
(O5836)

TAYLOR, Harold Victor, M.B.E., B.Sc., A.R.C.S., *b.* 6 May, 1887 ; *s.* of Albion Taylor, of Thurlbere, Taunton ; *m.* Dorothy Mary, *d.* of Frederick Speedy, of 76, Tulse Hill, *Educ.:* Huish School, Taunton, and The Royal Coll. of Science, South Kensington. Deputy Controller of Horticulture, Ministry of Agriculture and Fisheries, 4, Whitehall Place, London. *War Work :* For the Food Production Department, concerning the increased production of potatoes. *Address :* 4, Whitehall Place, London. *Club :* The Farmers'.
(M2516)

TAYLOR, Lieut. Harry, M.B.E., R.E.

TAYLOR, Lieut.-Comm. Hastings Elwin, O.B.E., R.N.V.R.

TAYLOR, Hon. Col. Herbert Brooke, C.B.E., V.D., D.L., *b.* 6 Oct. 1855 ; *s.* of John Taylor, of Bakewell ; *m.* Mary Taitt, *d.* of the Rev. William Mallalieu, of Ockbrook, Derbyshire. *Educ.:* Privately, and in Switzerland (Lausanne). Solicitor ; Col. commanding 2nd V. Batt. Sherwood Foresters (retired 1904). *War Work :* For some years prior to the war was Hon. Organising Sec. of the Derbyshire Branch of the Red Cross Society, and member of Derbyshire Territorial Force Association ; in Aug. 1914, appointed to Staff of 45th Recruiting Area, Hon. Sec. Derbyshire Recruiting Committee ; 1915, Military Representative Colliery Recruiting Tribunal ; Instructor No. 6 District School of Instruction for Recruiting Officers ; organised Vol. Training Corps in Derbyshire, 8 Batts. Volunteers ; in Nov. 1917, appointed A.D.R. for Derbyshire, and A.D.N.S. ; retired June, 1918. *Address :* The Close, Bakewell. *Club :* County (Derby).
(C833)

TAYLOR, Lieut. Hugh Lamport, O.B.E., R.F.A., *b.* 6 May, 1891 ; *s.* of T. H. Taylor, of Tynemouth ; *m.* Enid Essex, *d.* of R. H. Horrocks, of Manchester. *Educ.:* Tynemouth School. Engineer until 1914. *War Work :* B.E.F, 1915–19. *Address :* c/o Messrs. Cox & Co., 16, Charing Cross.
(O5839)

TAYLOR, Lieut. Hugh Oddin, M.B.E., R.A.S.C.

TAYLOR, Irene, M.B.E.

TAYLOR, Isabella, Mrs., M.B.E.

TAYLOR, Capt. James, O.B.E., R.A.M.C.

TAYLOR, James, C.B.E., M.A., M.D., F.R.C.P., *b.* 1860 ; *s.* of Peter Taylor, of Forres, Scotland ; *m.* Elizabeth Marian, *d.* of Charles Earsham Cooke, of Grimston, Norfolk. *Educ.:* Edinburgh and Germany. Physician National Hospital for Paralysis, etc., Queen Square ; Consulting Physician Moorfield's Eye Hospital, and Queen's Hospital for Children ; Consultant on Staff of Osborne Convalescent Home. *War Work :* Physician to Endsleigh Palace Hospital for Officers ; Committee of Management of Endsleigh Palace Hospital ; Member of War Office Committee on Massage, etc. *Address :* 49, Welbeck Street, W. *Club :* Arts.
(O3123)

TAYLOR, John, O.B.E., M.P., *b.* 25 Dec. 1857 ; *s.* of Robert Taylor, of Cambusbarron, Stirling ; *m.* Agnes Gordon, *d.* of William Wood, of Yoker. *Educ.:* Cambusbarron, Public School, and Stirling Art School. Decorator ; Member of Parliament for Dumbarton Burghs ; previously Provost of Clydebank 15 years. *War Work :* Chairman of Prince of Wales' Fund, Military Tribunal, Food Control, Coal Control, Belgian Relief Fund, Pension Committee, and Labour Exchange Committees ; Member of Glasgow District Advisory Committee on Women's Work, and Dumbartonshire Fund for Disabled Soldiers and Sailors, and all other Local Committees for War Funds. *Address :* Craigforth, Baskerville Road, London, S.W. 18. *Clubs :* National Liberal ; Glasgow Liberal. (O1914)

TAYLOR, John, C.B.E., *b.* 28 Feb. 1861 ; *s.* of Alex. ander Taylor, of Bolton-le-Moors ; *m.* Mary Ann, *d.* of John Roberts, of Bolton. *Educ.:* Privately. Engineer, Director of Mathor and Platt's, Ltd., Manchester. *War Work :* Member of Board of Management of Manchester and District Armaments Output Committee ; Member of Engineering (New Industries) Committee ; Chairman of Electrical Sub-Committee ; Chairman of Lancashire Anti-submarine Committee. *Addresses :* Brywood, Birkdale, Southport ; Helmside, Grasmere, Westmorland. *Club :* Union (Southport).
(C2990)

TAYLOR, John, O.B.E., J.P.

TAYLOR, John, M.B.E.

TAYLOR, John Norman, C.I.E., O.B.E.

TAYLOR, John William, O.B.E., M.D., Ch.B.

TAYLOR, Capt. Julian, O.B.E., F.R.C.S., R.A.M.C. (T.).

TAYLOR, Major Kenyon Davenport, M.B.E.

TAYLOR, Capt. Leicester Edward, M.B.E., R.A.F.

TAYLOR, Lionel Percy Duncuft, O.B.E.

TAYLOR, Capt. Louis Henry, M.B.E., *b.* 20 Dec. 1857; *s.* of Henry Taylor, of Newcastle-on-Tyne; *m.* Emily Miriam, *d.* of William Banks, of Hastings. *Educ.:* Edward VI.'s Grammar School, Morpeth; Univ. School, Hastings. Master Mariner. *War Work:* Carrying on all through the war, without loss of life or ship. *Address:* Woodlands, 92, Elmbourne Road, Tooting Bec Common, London, S.W. 17. *Club:* The National Maritime. (M2517)

TAYLOR, Mabel Frances, M.B.E., *b.* 30 March, 1889. *Educ.:* Belgium and Derby. Appointed Sec. Compass Dept. of the Admiralty, April, 1917. *War Work:* Service in connection with the organisation of the above Dept. *Address:* Admiralty Compass Observatory, Slough, Bucks. (M9820)

TAYLOR, Minnie Elena Scott, Mrs., M.B.E.,

TAYLOR, Major Newman, O.B.E., I.D.F.

TAYLOR, Lieut. Ogden, O.B.E., R.N.V.R.

TAYLOR, Oscar Herbert, M.B.E., *b.* 14 March, 1860; *s.* of the late C. Taylor, of Norwich. *Educ.:* King Edward VI. Middle School, Norwich. Clerk, War Office. *War Work:* Appointed to the War Office in March, 1878, and served there until retirement in March, 1920. *Address:* 53, Buckleigh Road, Streatham Common, S.W. (M9822)

TAYLOR, Percy, O.B.E., *b.* 15 May, 1862; *s.* of Charles Taylor, of Colnbrook, Bucks; *m.* Helen Theresa, *d.* of Frederick Richardson, of Southend. *Educ.:* Privately, and King's Coll., London. Chief Examiner, War Office. *War Work:* Connected with official position. *Address:* Sunnyholme, Amersham Common, Bucks. (O11439)

TAYLOR, Percy Henry, O.B.E.

TAYLOR, Col. Philip Beauchamp, C.B.E. Lieut.-Col. and Brevet Col. R.A.; served in S. Africa, 1899–1901 (despatches, Queen's medal with eight clasps). (C834)

TAYLOR, Lieut. and Qr.-Mr. Richard Allen, M.B.E. M.C.

TAYLOR, Richard Francis, M.B.E.

TAYLOR, Richard Henry, O.B.E.

TAYLOR, Capt. Robert Allan Grant, O.B.E., M.C.

TAYLOR, Capt. Robert Clark, O.B.E.

TAYLOR, Lieut.-Col. Robert James Frederick, C.B.E., *b.* 1873. Lieut.-Col. Notts & Derbyshire Regt. Served in the Great War, 1914–19 (despatches). (C2177)

TAYLOR, Robert Walter, O.B.E.

TAYLOR, Selina Emma, Mrs., M.B.E., *d.* of William Orme, of Hartshorne, widow of Henry Taylor, J.P. *War Work:* War Pensions Committee. *Address:* 250, Edlestow Road, Crewe. (M9823)

TAYLOR, Capt. Sidney Herbert, O.B.E., M.Sc.Tech., *b.* 21 July, 1893; *s.* of George Herbert, of Manchester. *Educ.:* Coll. of Technology, Univ., Manchester. *War Work:* France, 1914; Russia, 1919–20. *Address:* Higher Blackley, Manchester. (O11887)

TAYLOR, Sidney Ormerod, O.B.E.

TAYLOR, Thomas, M.B.E.

TAYLOR, Major Thomas Alexander Hatch, O.B.E., M.C.

TAYLOR, Capt. Thomas McComb, O.B.E., R.N.R.

TAYLOR, Thomas Marris, C.B.E., M.A., *b.* 1871; *s.* of the late George Marris Taylor; *m.* Mary Dorothea, *d.* of the late Walter Wren, of 7, Powis Square, W. *Educ.:* Gonville and Caius Coll. Camb. *War Work:* Appointed Chief of Training Section, Ministry of Munitions, 1915; Assist. Director, Dilution Section, 1916; Dep. Director-Gen. Labour Supply Depart. 1916; Director, 1918; Fellow of Gonville and Caius Coll. Cambridge. *Address:* Whitedale, Hambledon, Hants. *Club:* Oxford and Cambridge. (C69)

TAYLOR, Walter Ross, C.B.E., M.A., LL.B., *b.* 1877; *s.* of the late Rev. Walter Ross Taylor, D.D., of Glasgow; *m.* 1910, Frances, *d.* of the late Robert Orr, of Kinnaird, Stirlingshire. *Educ.:* Glasgow Acad.; Leys School, Camb.; Glasgow and Edinburgh Univs. Advocate, Scotland, 1902; Lecturer on Roman and Criminal Law, School of Law, Cairo, 1905–12; Judge of Court of First Instance, Cairo, 1912–15; Assist. Legal Adviser, Ministries of Public Works, War, and Agriculture, 1915–18; since when he has been Chairman of Supplies Control Board; appointed Counsel to H.H. the Sultan, April, 1919; has 3rd class Order of the Nile. *Address:* Gezira, Cairo, Egypt. (C1096)

TAYLOR, William, O.B.E., J.P., *b.* 1859; *s.* of John R. Taylor, of Leith; *m.* Margaret Henderson, *d.* of W. D. K. Currie, of Leith. *Educ.:* Sheddens Academy, and Free Church Normal School. Member of Leith Education Authority; ex-Chairman Leith Parish Council. *War Work:* Vice-Chairman Leith War Pensions Committee, and Chairman of Executive Committees thereof; Chairman of Executive of Local National Relief (Prince of Wales' Fund) Committee. *Address:* Richmond Lodge, 20, York Road, Leith. (O11431)

TAYLOR, William, O.B.E., *b.* June, 1865; *s.* of Richard Taylor, of Leicester; *m.* Esther Margaret, *d.* of John Coy, of Leicester. *Educ.:* London and City Guilds Coll. Engineer; Governing Director of Taylor, Taylor, and Hobson, Ltd., of Leicester and London. *War Work:* Manufacture of lenses for photography from aircraft, of lenses for rangefinders, telescopes, binoculars, of clinometers, gun sights, inspection-screw gauges, and other instruments of precision; Chairman of Committee on Scientific Apparatus (Ministry of Reconstruction); Chairman of Committees on Optical Instruments and on Standardisation (Department of Scientific and Industrial

Research); Member of Committees on Standardisation of Screw Threads and Limit Gauges, British Engineering Standards Association; Member of Council, Institution of Mechanical Engineers. *Addresses:* Stoughton Street Works, Leicester; Narborough Hall, nr. Leicester. *Club:* Leicestershire. (O3951)

TAYLOR, Col. Sir William, K.B.E., C.B., D.L., *b.* 21 Sept. 1871; *s.* of John Taylor, of Castlefin, Co. Donegal; *m.* Katherine Maria, *d.* of Dr. William Hamilton Walker. *Educ.:* Strabane Academy, Dublin Univ., and R.C.S.I. Surgeon to the Meath Hospital, and Co. Dublin Infirmary; Consulting Surgeon to the Forces in Ireland; Consulting Surgeon to the Combe Lying-in Hospital, and to the Incorporated Dental Hospital; Past President Royal Coll. of Surgeons in Ireland. *War Work:* Consulting Surgeon to the Forces from 1916; organised and maintained the Dublin (83) General Hospital in France, 1917–18; served in France with that Hospital; mentioned in Earl Haig's despatches; created C.B. (Mil.) for work in France and Flanders, June, 1919. *Addresses:* 47, FitzWilliam Square, Dublin; St. Anne's, Killarney, Co. Dublin. *Clubs:* Dublin University; Royal Irish Yacht (Kingston). (K463)

TAYLOR, William Arthur Trevor, M.B.E.

TAYLOR, Sir William Francis Kyffin, K.B.E., J.P., *b.* 3 July, 1854; *s.* of Ven. William Francis Taylor, D.D., Archdeacon of Liverpool; *m.* Mary Fleming, *d.* of Robert Crooks, of Rosemount, Liverpool. *Educ.:* Liverpool Coll.; Exeter Coll., Oxford. Practised as Barrister on Northern Circuit at Liverpool, 1879–94; Q.C. 1895; Recorder of Bolton, 1901–3; Bencher of Inner Temple, 1905; Member of the General Council of the Bar, 1900–11; Judge of Appeal for the Isle of Man, 1918; Presiding Judge, Liverpool Court of Passage since 1903. *Addresses:* 4, Harcourt Buildings, Temple; The Gadlas, Ellesmere, Shropshire. *Club:* Garrick. (K174)

TAYLOR, William Henry, M.B.E., *s.* of William Taylor, of Revesby, Lincolnshire; *m.* Mary Ann Johnstone, *d.* of Thomas Chambers, of Abbey Holme, Cumberland, and Liverpool. *Educ.:* Revesby and Lincoln. Master of the Belmont Institution, Liverpool. *War Work:* During Oct. 1914 over 300 Belgian refugees (ages ranging from a few months to over 70 years) were received in the Belmont Institution; supervised and directed all arrangements for their accommodation and welfare during the following four months; Superintendent conversion of the Institution into Auxiliary Military Hospital (2,000 beds); 20,000 patients passed through the hospital; was Chief Transport Officer under British Red Cross, Liverpool, and had charge of fleet of ambulances and motor cars by means of which nearly 2,000 wounded soldiers were transferred from train to hospital. Provincial Officer in West Lancashire (Freemason). (M9826)

TAYLOR, Major William Henry Forbes, M.B.E., R.A., *b.* 7 May, 1856; *s.* of William Baker Taylor, late Surgeon-General Hon. East India Company's Service, Bombay; *m.* 1st Renira Louisa, 3rd *d.* of late Vice-Admiral Ormsby Johnson, R.N. died 1881, 2nd, Florence Annie, 2nd *d.* of late Rev. E. B. P. Wynne, Rector of Shoeburyness, Essex. *Educ.:* Victoria Coll., Jersey; St. James's Collegiate School, Jersey; R.M. Academy, Woolwich. Commissioned as Lieut. in R.A., Feb. 1876; and served therein in all three branches until retirement in Feb. 1902; then Assist. Private Sec. to Rt. Hon. G. Wyndham, at the Irish Office, and for 17 years in the War Office; Zulu War, 1879, medal and clasp; Kaffir War, 1898, medal; Boer War, medal and 2 clasps. *War Work:* Throughout the Great War at the War Office until Sept. 1919, in the Adjutant-General's Dept.; mentioned in despatches. *Address:* Woodholme, Farnham Royal, Bucks. (M9826)

TAYLOR, William James, O.B.E.

TAYLOR, Major William John, O.B.E. Can. A.P.D.

TAYLOR, Winifred Mary, Mrs., M.B.E. *War Work:* Went from Associated Newspapers, Ltd., London, to join British War Mission, 14 July, 1917, on Lord Northcliffe's Staff. *Addresses:* Carmelite House, London, E.C. 4; 4, Bennett Park, Blackheath, S.E. 3. (M1708)

TAYLOR, Major Gordon, GORDON-, O.B.E., F.R.C.S., *b.* 1878; *s.* of John Taylor; *m.* Florence Mary, *d.* of John Pegnume, of Waltham Abbey. *Educ.:* Aberdeen Univ., and Middlesex Hospital, London. Consulting Surgeon; Surgeon to the Middlesex Hospital, etc. *War Work:* Served in the R.A.M.C. from March, 1915, until Jan. 1919, at Aldershot and in France; sometime Acting Consulting Surgeon to the Fourth Army, B.E.F., etc. *Addresses:* 15, Harley Street; 36, Audley House, Margaret Street, W. *Club:* Caledonian. (O5837)

TAYLOR, Margaret HECTOR, M.B.E., L.L.A.; *d.* of Alexander Hector Taylor, J.P., of Aberdeen. *Educ.:* Aberdeen High School for Girls; Aberdeen Univ. *War Work:* Supervisor of the Women's Records Section, War Office, Whitehall. *Addresses:* Wyldesmead, Morland Close, Hampstead; The Briars, Bieldside, Aberdeenshire. (M9821)

TAYLOR, Major George Philip Du PLAT-, O.B.E., *b.* 28 Feb. 1866; *s.* of the late Colonel J. L. Du Plat-Taylor, C.B., of Combe Revile, Combe; *m.* Sydney Hilda, *d.* of Arthur Hutton Croft, of Aldborough Hall, Yorkshire. *Educ.:* Eton. Major (retired pay) Grenadier Guards. *War Work:* Permanent President District Courts Martial London District. *Address:* 17, Hobart Place, Grosvenor Gardens, London. *Clubs:* Guards'; Bachelor's. (O7107)

TAYLOR, Major Alfred Jesse SUENSON-, O.B.E., M.A.,

Barrister-at-Law, b. 14 Aug. 1893; s. of A. G. Taylor, of Sutton, Surrey; m. Mamie, d. of Albert Suenson, of Copenhagen. Educ.: Epsom Coll., and King's Coll., Cambridge; Middle Temple, London. War Work: Joined the forces in Oct. 1914; commissioned Dec. 1914; served with Supply and Transport Services attached to the Australian and New Zealand Corps, Anzac, Gallipoli, 1915; invalided to England; posted to France, and appointed to Administrative Staff as Deputy Assistant Director of Supplies and Transport, G.H.Q., 1916–19; assisted Ministry of Food, 1919. Addresses: 20, Gloucester Terrace, Hyde Park, W; 1, Essex Court Temple.
(O5832)

TEAGLE, Alice Annie, M.B.E.

TEAGUE, Lieut. George Eric, M.B.E.

TEAR, Richard Frederick Charles, M.B.E., b. 28 Nov. 1858; s. of the late Richard Henry Tear, of Wimbledon, Surrey; m. Louisa, d. of the late Owen Tomlinson, of Wimbledon. Educ.: St. Xaviers, Calcutta, India; South Lambeth Coll., London. Superintendent, Boundary Dept., Ordnance Survey. War Work: Maps.
(M4017)

TEARE, Robert Arminius Beaumont, M.B.E., b. 25 April, 1872; s. of the late Robert Teare, of Liverpool and King's Lynn; m. Alice Margaret, e. d. of Joseph William Johnson, of London. Educ.: King's Lynn (King Edward VII. Grammar School). Entered Civil Service, 1889; Member Hendon Urban District Council since 1913; Overseer since 1916; Chairman Hendon Public Health Committee; Member of Middlesex Districts Joint Smallpox Hospital Board; Member Hendon Education Committee; Governor of Hendon County School; Member West Hendon Nursing Association Committee; Vice-President West Hendon and Colindale Brotherhood. War Work: Member of Hendon Committee of the Soldiers' and Sailors' Families Association from the commencement of the war; Member of Hendon Local War Pensions Committee since its formation in 1916; Hon. Sec. West Hendon War Pensions Committee; Chairman, Pensions Appeals Committee; Chairman, Pensions Grants Committee; Member of the Essex and Middlesex Joint Disablement Committee; Chairman, West Hendon War Relief Committee; Member of the Local Distress Committee (National Relief Fund); Member of the Local Food Control Committee; Member of Fuel Control Committee; Member of Hendon Kitchens Committee; Member of the Housing Executive committee. Address: Wingfield, Station Road, Hendon, N.W. 4.
(M9828)

TEASDALE, Capt. George Arthur James, O.B.E., R.F.A.

TEASDALE, John, M.B.E.

TEBAY, Capt. Frederick Henry, O.B.E., b. 1878. Educ.: City of London School. Engraver. War Work: Siege Artillery. Address: 120, Bedford Hill, London, S.W.
(O2750)

TEBBITT, Mabel, Mrs., M.B.E., b. 7 July, 1875; d. of Edward Carpenter, of Beckenham, Kent; m. Ernest Reginald, s. of Walter Tebbitt of Tunbridge Wells. Educ.: Bromley High School, and Miss Allen Olney, The Hall, Swiss Cottage. War Work: Head Cook from Oct. 1914–16; Quartermaster from Oct. 1916, to March, 1918; Assist. Commandant, March, 1918, to Dec. 1919, of St. Mark's Hospital, Tunbridge Wells, Sussex 92 V.A.D. Addresses: 5A, Grove Hill, Tunbridge Wells, Kent; Barnfield, Hoadley Lane, Crowborough, Sussex.
(M4019)

TEBBS, Capt. Louis George, O.B.E.

TEBBUTT, Arnold, O.B.E., J.P. City of Winchester, b. July, 1858; s. of C. P. Tebbutt, J.P., of Bluntisham, Huntingdonshire; m. E. A. d. of James Marsh, of Stanstead, Essex. Educ.: Bishop Stortford Coll. Chairman of Winchester Liberal Association, etc.; Alderman of County Council of Hampshire. War Work: Acted in advisory capacity to Controller of Mines Department from 1917–20. Address: Claramond, 10, Clifton Road, Winchester.
(O11443)

TEBBUTT, Katherine Rose, M.B.E., b. 10 Feb. 1889; d. of Sidney Tebbutt, of Southampton. Educ.: Pembroke House School, Southampton. Address: Bagenholt, Northlands Road, Southampton.
(M2520)

TEBBUTT, Mary Jessie, M.B.E., b. 23 Aug. 1887; d. of Sidney Tebbutt, of Southampton. Educ.: Pembroke House School, Southampton. Address: Bagenholt, Northlands Road, Southampton.
(M2519)

TEDDER, Alfred Edward, O.B.E.

TEDMAN, Flight-Lieut. Frank, M.B.E., R.A.F.

TEE, Major Charles Clifford, M.B.E., M.C., b. 17 Oct. 1882; s. of William Henry Tee, of Manchester; m. Nina Edith Hoblyn, d. of the late Arthur Malet Hoblyn Oliver. Educ.: Elstree and Harrow. War Work: 1914–15, Royal Irish Rifles in France; Nov. 1915, to April, 1916, Instructor to newly-formed Machine Gun Corps; May, 1916, to Sept. 1918, M.G. Corps in Macedonia; Jan. 1919. to Dec. 1919, Machine Gun Adviser to General Dennikin's Forces in South Russia, also to Generals Wrangel and Schkuro. Address: c/o Messrs. Cox & Co., Army Agents. Clubs: Army and Navy; Queen's; Royal Automobile.
(O9753)

TEE, Major James Henry Stanley, C.B.E. Served in S. Africa, 1900–1 (Queen's medal with seven clasps), and in Great War, 1914–19, as Major R.A.S.C. (T.) (mentioned in despatches).
(C2178)

TEELING, Major Bartholomew Louis Charles, O.B.E., R.A.S.C.

TEESDALE, Kenneth John Marmaduke, M.B.E., Commander of the Order of George I. of Greece, b. 25 Jan. 1871; s. of the Rev. Prebendary Teesdale, of Chichester; m. Louise

Elizabeth Agnes, d. of George G. Thomson, of Edinburgh. Educ.: Winchester Coll.; Magdalen Coll., Oxford. War Work: Service in France with Croix Rouge Française, 1915–16; Ministry of Munitions (Allies and Foreign Supplies Branch), 1916–20. Address: Ulverstone, Peaslake, Guildford, Surrey.
(M2521)

TEGG, Capt. Charles, O.B.E.

TEICHMAN, Major Max, O.B.E., R.A.S.C.

TELFER, Capt. John Edward, O.B.E.

TELFORD, John Charles, O.B.E., A.M.I.C.E., b. 12 April, 1883; s. of John Telford, of Middlesbrough; m. Edith Mary, d. of John Appleton, of Middlesbrough. Educ.: Middlesbrough Grammar School; Hugh Bell School; Middlesbrough High School. Civil Engineer; late Manager of Dorman, Long & Co., Ltd. Constructional Dept., Middlesbrough, now General Manager, Braithwaite & Co., West Bromwich, and Newport, Mon. War Work: Assistant Director of Supplies in the Dept. of the C.G.M.S., Ministry of Shipping. Address: Bloomfield House, Sedgley, nr. Dudley. Club: National Liberal.
(O11445)

TEMPERLEY, Charles, O.B.E.

TEMPERLEY, Capt. Clive Errington, O.B.E., M.C.

TEMPERLEY, Dorothy Mary Gladys, O.B.E.

TEMPERLEY, Major Harold William Vazeille, M.A., O.B.E., b. 20 April, 1879; s. of the late Ernest Temperley, Fellow of Queen's Coll., Cambridge; m. Gladys d. of the late Job Bradford, Barrister-at-law. Educ.: Sherborne School, King's Coll., Cambridge. Tutor in History and Fellow of Peterhouse, Cambridge; Reader in Modern History, Univ. of Cambridge. War Work: Commissioned as Lieut. 2/1st Fife and Forfar Yeomanry, Nov. 1914; Capt. 1915; Major, 1918; General Staff Officer, 1916; Assistant Military Attaché (Serbian G.H.Q. 1918, Belgrade, 1920); has received Roumanian and Serbian decorations. Addresses: Peterhouse, Cambridge; 107, King Henry's Road, Primrose Hill, N.W. 3. Club: Reform.
(O3190)

TEMPERLEY, Major Robert, O.B.E., T.D.

TEMPEST, Henrietta Frances May, Mrs., O.B.E.; d. of Sir Robert T. Tempest. Bart., of Tong Hall, Yorks; m. John Hicks Graves, who assumed the name of Tempest by Royal Licence on his wife's accession to the Tong Estates, of Bradenham, Bucks. War Work: Commandant of Bucks V.A.D. 40, acting Commandant of Perthshire V.A.D. 24; Pres. Red Cross, Perthshire; organised an Auxiliary Hospital of 20 beds at Dalguise, Perthshire, and acted as Commandant of same, from June, 1915, to May, 1919. Addresses: Bradenham House, Bucks.; Tong Hall, Yorks; Dalguise House, Perthshire. Club: Empress.
(O11447)

TEMPEST, Lieut.-Col. Percy Crosland, C.B.E., M.Inst.C.E., Chevalier of the Legion of Honour, Belgian Croix d'officier de l'ordre de Leopold, 1918, b. 24 Feb. 1861; s. of Charles Tempest (Solicitor), of Leeas; m. Evelyn Kate, d. of Alfred Willis, J.P., D.L., of Kemsing, Kent. Educ.: Leeds Grammar School, and Leeds Univ. General Manager and Chief Engineer to the S.E. & C. Rlys. Managing Committee; Engineer to the English Channel Tunnel Co.; Engineer to East London Railway Joint Committee. War Work: Engaged on enlarging the Military Base at Boulogne, 1914–15; assisting the Chemin de Fer du Nord in reconstruction of bridges and other works, throughout the war, as also the Belgian State Railways, and obtaining and shipping supplies to these railways. Address: Crismill, Chislehurst Road, Bromley, Kent.
(C315)

TEMPLE, Comm. John Howard, O.B.E., R.N.V.R.

TEMPLE, Lieut.-Col. Reginald Cecil, O.B.E., R.M.A., b. 13 Aug. 1877; s. of Lieut.-Col. William Temple, V.C., of Co. Monaghan, Ireland; m. Zillah Edith, d. of Vere D. V. Hunt, of Co. Limerick, Ireland. Educ.: Dulwich College. Officer of Royal Marine Artillery; served in Intelligence Department, Admiralty, 1905–10; Intelligence Officer on Staff of C. in C. Mediterranean, 1910–13. War Work: H.M.S. "Ocean" Aug. 1914; to March, 1915; operations in Mesopotamia, Suez Canal, and Dardanelles Military; Governor, Tenedos, March to May; appointed Intelligence Officer (G.S.O.2) on Staff of Vice-Admiral Ægean Squadron, July, 1915, and served in this capacity till July, 1919; Brevet Lieut.-Col. and G.S.O. 1 Feb. 1917. Address: Eastney Barracks, Portsmouth. Club: United Service.
(O4329)

TEMPLE, Robert, M.B.E.

TEMPLE, Major Thomas, O.B.E., R.A., b. 31 Aug. 1883; s. of Col. John Temple, R.F.A.; m. Delia Louisa Kate, d. of A. E. Ryves, Barrister-at-Law. Educ.: Malvern College. R.A. attached to Indian Ordnance Dept. War Work: Mesopotamia, 1917–19; Afghanistan, 1919–20. Address: Heathfield Lodge, Bitterne.
(O6714)

TEMPLE, Walter Middlewood, O.B.E., b. 1872; s. of Michael Temple, of Driffield; m. Alice Temple, d. of Robert Hall Carlton, of Bridlington. Member of the Staff of City of York Education Committee. War Work: Hon. Sec. of the North Riding of Yorkshire County Committee for War Savings Organisation; Hon. Sec. of the City of York War Savings Committee. Addresses: Law Court Buildings, York; Wetherby Road, Acomb, York.
(O11448)

TEMPLER, Col. Henry, O.B.E.

TEMPLER, Lieut.-Col. Walter Francis, C.B.E., b. 28 Aug. 1865; s. of R. B. Templer, of Armagh, Ireland. Educ.: Charterhouse, Pembroke College, Cambridge, and R.M.C. Sandhurst, 87th Royal Irish Fusiliers and Royal Army Pay Department. Address: The Castle, Cape Town.
(C2179)

TEMPLETON, Archibald Angus, M.B.E., b. 22 Aug.

1893 ; *s.* of William Templeton, J.P., C.C., of Torland. *Educ.:* Hamilton Academy, and Glasgow University. Solicitor. *War Work:* Gazetted 15th August 1915 ; France with 1st Black Watch ; attached Staff of 67th Division ; Capt. and Adjutant, 51st Batt. Gordon Highrs. ; returned Civil Employment, Jan. 1919. *Address:* Torland, Dalserf, Lanarkshire.
(M5666)

TEMPLETON, Col. Charles Perry, C.B.E., D.S.O., M.D., C.M., C.A.M.C., *b.* 10 July, 1884 ; *s.* of William Templeton, of Napanee, Ont. ; *m.* Alice (who died 1914), *d.* of Judge T. D. Cumberland, Brandon. *Educ.:* Queen's Coll. Surgeon. *War Work:* 3rd Canadian Field Ambulance, Aug. 1914, to Feb. 1917 ; D.A.D.M.S., 1st Canadian Div. Feb. 1917, to Aug. 1918 ; A.D.M.S., 3rd Canadian Div. Aug. 1918, to May, 1919 ; in France from Feb. 1915, to Feb. 1919 ; C.B.E., D.S.O., despatches three times ; rank of full Colonel. *Address:* Brandon, Manitoba, Canada. *Clubs:* Brandon ; Brandon Golf and County.
(C1356)

TENCH, Lillian Eugenia, O.B.E. ; *d.* of Dr. Edward Beavan Tench, of Ludlow. *Educ.:* London. *War Work:* Second in Command of English Soldiers' and Sailors' Club, Rome. *Address:* c/o Dr. Montague Tench, Dunmow, Essex. (O3952)

TENNANT, Lieut. Ernest William Dalrymple, O.B.E.
TENNANT, Lieut.-Col. Henry Lancelot, O.B.E.
TENNENT, Lieut. Anderson Kirkwood, O.B.E.
TENNENT, Capt. James Moncrieff, O.B.E. R.A.S.C.
TENNENT, John James Colvin, O.B.E., *b.* 26 April, 1861 ; *s.* of James Boursiquot, of Norwood, Surrey ; *m.* Dorothy Elizabeth, *d.* of John Shettle, of Mapperton, Dorset. *Educ.:* Privately. Late Pembroke Artillery Militia. *War Work:* Acting Paymaster, Army Pay Department. *Address:* Redlands, Surbiton Hill, Surrey.
(O11449)

TENNENT, Major Thomas Hastings, O.B.E. (Military Division), retired Pay, late Royal Engineers, *b.* 21 Jan. 1860 ; *s.* of Thomas Tennent, of Glasgow ; *m.* Eliza Jane (who died), *d.* of Thomas Cowley, of London. *Educ.:* Royal Hibernian Military School, Dublin. *War Work:* Equipment of the troops at Aldershot for active service. *Address:* c/o Cox and Co., 16, Charing Cross. S.W.1.
(O3191)

TENNEY, John, C.B.E., I.S.O., *b.* 1856 ; *s.* of John Tenncy, of Treninnow, Cornwall ; *m.* Mary Charlotte Waterlow, *d.* of Philip S. King, of Westminster, formerly wife of R. D. Roberts, D.Sc., of London University. *Educ.:* Privately. Late Principal Clerk, Exchequer and Audit Department (1875-1919). *Address:* The Long House, Hindhead, Surrey. *Club:* National Liberal.
(C2991)

TENNYSON, Ivy Gladys, Mrs., O.B.E., *b.* 29 Jan. 1880 ; *d.* of W. J. Pretious, of Loughton, Essex ; *m.* Charles Bruce, Locker *s.* of the Hon. Lionel Tennyson (*see* BURKE'S *Peerage*). *Educ.:* Canterbury. Sec. of Free Trade Union 1903–09. *War Work:* Head of Women's Establishment Ministry of Munitions, Oct. 1916, to April, 1919. *Address:* 26, Cheyne Row, Chelsea, S.W.
(O797)

TERNAN, Major Henry Augustus Breffney, O.B.E., *b.* 1876 ; *s.* of Col. H. B. Ternan, of Ashley Cottage, Walton-on-Thames. *Educ.:* Lancing and Sandhurst. (Retired) Army. *Club:* Naval and Military.
(O5843)

TERRILL, Lieut. Frank, O.B.E., R.N.
TERRINGTON, Baron, O.B.E.: *see* Woodhouse, H. J. S.
TERRIS, James, O.B.E., *b.* 23 July, 1877 ; *s.* of James Terris, of Kelty ; *m.* Georgina Kennedy, *d.* of George A. Braddon, of Musselburgh. *Educ.:* Kelty Public School. *Address:* 42, West Holmes Gardens, Musselburgh. (O11450)

TERRY, Lieut.-Col. Claude Herbert, O.B.E., A.I.F.
TERRY, Lieut.-Col. Cyril Edward, O.B.E., *b.* 25 April, 1870 ; *s.* of the late Rev. Michael Terry, M.A. ; *m.* Anne Victoria, *d.* of John Latham, F.S.A., of London. *Educ.:* Derby School. Regular Army. *War Work:* France and Flanders. *Address:* Rothesay House, Netley Abbey, Hants.
(O5844)

TERRY, Walter Eyre, M.B.E., M.A., *b.* 1862 ; *s.* of Charles Terry, of Tostock, Suffolk ; *m.* Elsie Augusta (who died), *d.* of Wallace Crothers, of Chew Magna. *Educ.:* Uppingham and Pembroke Coll., Cambridge. *War Work:* Hon. Sec. Red Cross Hospital, Finborough Hall, Suffolk. *Address:* Gt. Finborough, Suffolk.
(M9829)

TETLEY, Herbert Hustler, C.B.E., J.P., *b.* 10 Jan. 1854 ; *s.* of William and Ann Tetley, of Bradford ; *m.* Hannah, *d.* of James Robertshaw, of Great Horton, Bradford. *Educ.:* Commenced working at 7 years of age ; self-educated by home-study and evening classes at Bradford Mechanics' Institute. Printer and Publisher ; City Alderman and Justice of the Peace for City of Bradford ; Chairman of Local Naval and Military War Pensions Committee. *War Work:* Chairman (1915–19), Bradford Lord Mayor's Fund (a voluntary fund for augmenting separation allowances to Soldiers' and Sailors' Dependants) about £200,000 disbursed ; Chairman, Old Age Pensions Committee (1912–19), upon which devolved, during the war, the work of dealing with Soldiers' and Sailors' Dependants, other than wives and children.; Chairman, Naval and Military War Pensions Committee, from its formation in 1915 up to present time ; Lord Mayor of Bradford, 1918. *Addresses:* 16, St. Andrew's Place, Bradford. *Club:* Bradford and County Conservative.
(C2992)

TEVERSHAM, Col. Richard Kinloch, D.S.O., O.B.E., *b.* 1856 ; *s.* of the late Major Mark Teversham ; *m.* 1888, Ethel Mary, *e d.* of W. A. Symonds, sometime Sup. of Central Jail, Coimbatore. Entered Army, 1875 ; Capt. M.S.C. (now Indian Army), 1886 ; Major, 1895 ; Lieut.-Col. 1901 ; Brevet Col.

1904 ; served with Burma Expedition, 1886–87(medal) ; sometime Officiating A.A.G. Madras Command ; appointed a Gen. Staff Officer. 1914.
(O8950)

TEW, Capt. Charles Napier Alexander, O.B.E., R.E.
TEWKSBURY, Searson William, O.B.E.
THACKERAY, Major Joseph Makepeace, O.B.E.
THACKWELL, Major Noel Edmund Osbert, O.B.E., Royal Garrison Artillery, *b.* 16 Dec. 1878 ; *s.* of Lieut.-Col. J. E. L. Thackwell, late 5th Lancers and Cork Artillery, of Aghada Hall, Co. Cork. *Educ.:* Bath College. Instr. Gunnery, Malta, 1908-11, Adjt. Cork Artillery, 1914-15. *War Work:* Adjt. various Siege Training Brigade, 1914 ; B.E.F. (France), 1916 ; operations, July, Aug., 1916 ; Commanded 180 Siege Batty., France, 1916–17 ; Adjt. of Havre Base, 1918–19. *Address:* c/o Mrs. M. R. Bennett, 10, Royal Parade, Cheltenham, Glos.
(O5845)

THADDEUS, Mary, Mrs., M.B.E.
THADDEUS, Mesrop Gabriel, M.B.E.
THADDEUS, Mesrup, M.B.E.
THAIN, Alexander, M.B.E.
THAKE, Frank Edward Seymour, M.B.E.
THANE, Capt. Charles Stuart, M.B.E.
THATCHER, Noel, O.B.E., M.A., LL.B. (Cantab.), Barrister-at-Law, *b.* 17 June, 1871 ; *s.* of R. H. Thatcher, of Wickham, nr. Newbury, Berks. *Educ.:* Newbury Grammar School ; Privately. and St. John's Coll., Cambridge. Mathematical Exhibitioner and Prizeman and Choral Scholar of St. John's Coll., Cambridge, 1891–5 ; Double Honours, Mathematics and Law, 1894–5. Educational work ; Mathematical and Physics Lecturer for 9 years at York Training College, 1904–13 ; Principal of Univ. of London's Goldsmiths' Coll. Hostel for Men, 1913–16 ; work under Ministry of Labour since April, 1919 ; now Assistant to the Sec. of the Industrial Court (formerly Court of Arbitration). *War Work:* Statistician in Mobilisation Directorate of War Office ; Member and Sec. of Committees, and Head of Statistical Section 1917–19 ; Volunteer (East Surrey Regt.), 1916–19 ; Special Constable (Metrop. Police), 1914–19. *Address:* Saverne, Cressingham Grove, Sutton, Surrey.
(O11451)

THATCHER, Capt. Reginald Sparshatt, O.B.E., M.C., B.A., F.R.C.O., (3rd Somerset L.I.), *b.* 11 March, 1888 ; *s.* of the late W. J. Thatcher, of Midsomer Norton, Somerset ; *m.* Ruth, *d.* of the late W. J. Trethowan, of Salisbury. *Educ.:* Royal Coll. of Music, and Worcester Coll., Oxford. Organist and Master of music at Charterhouse. *War Work:* Enlisted 3rd Somerset L.I., Aug. 1914 ; Commission, Oct. 1914 ; served in France, Belgium, Italy, and Germany (Army of Occupation) from May, 1915, to April, 1919 ; served with 2nd Duke of Wellington's, 1st Somerset L.I., H.Q. 4th Division. H.Q. 2nd Army (as D.A.Q.M.G.), and G.H.Q. Italy (as D.A.Q.M.G.) ; mentioned in despatches, Croix de Guerre (French), Corona d'Italia (Chevalier). *Address:* Charterhouse, Godalming.
(O2753)

THEAKSTON, Capt. Francis, O.B.E., R.E.
THEAKSTON, William Pease, M.B.E., J.P.
THELLUSSON, Florence Adeline, M.B.E. Lately head V.A.D. worker at St. Dunstan's, No. 11 House. Now Matron of Ilkley Annexe.
(M10337)

THEOBALD, Charles Henry Gordon Eyre, M.B.E., *b.* 17 March, 1860 ; *s.* of Canon Theobald, of Lasham, Hants. ; *m.* Lucy Anne, *d.* of C. C. Skarratt. *Educ.:* Tonbridge School. *War Work:* Missing Soldiers Department of the Red Cross. *Address:* 11, Egerton Place, London, S.W. 3. *Clubs:* Junior Carlton ; Ranelagh.
(M2524)

THEOBALD, Major Courtney Eleves, O.B.E., R.A.S.C.
THEODOSIUS, Alfred Fletcher, O.B.E., M.A., *b.* 9 Dec. 1866 ; *s.* of the Rev. James Henry Theodosius, M.A., of Stafford. *Educ.:* Bath Coll., and Univ. Coll., Oxford. Tutor in University of Oxford. *War Work:* 1915, worked in France with the French Red Cross ; 1916–17, at Admiralty ; 1917–19, at Ministry of Pensions ; Officer of the Order of Christ (Portugal). *Address:* 13, Merton Street. *Clubs:* Leander ; Gridiron (Oxford) ; Royal Societies' ; Oxford and Cambridge.
(O11452)

THESIGER, Florita Maria-Engracia, Mrs. Arthur, O.B.E., *b.* 31 Jan. 1873 ; *d.* of Edward J. Knight, of Tregroes, Pencoed, Glamorgan ; *m.* Arthur Lionel Bruce (Barrister-at-Law), *s.* of Hon. Sir E. P. Thesiger, K.C.B. (*see* BURKE'S *Peerage*), of 142, Sloane Street. *Educ.:* Privately and Royal Holloway College. *War Work:* Organiser and Hon. Sec. of Princess Louis of Battenberg's (afterwards Lady Milford Haven) Minesweepers' Fund ; Chairman of Finance Committee, Chelsea V.A.D. Hospital. *Address:* Heath Corner, Burgh Heath, Surrey. *Club:* International Women's Franchise.
(O11453)

THESIGER, Hon. Kathleen Mary, Mrs. Wilfred, C.B.E., *b.* 4 Feb. 1880 ; *d.* of Thomas Mercer Cliffe Vigors, of Burgage, Co. Carlow ; *m.* Wilfred Gilbert, *s.* of 2nd Lord Chelmsford (*see* BURKE'S *Peerage*). During the revolution in Abyssinia, Mrs. Thesiger kept the infant and only son of the Heir Apparent at the Legation, and for some months afterwards. *War Work:* Services rendered during the influenza epidemic, Nov. 1918. *Address:* 34, Onslow Square, S.W.
(O11453)

THESIGER, Hon. Percy Mansfield, M.B.E., *b.* 7 Nov. 1869 ; *s.* of Frederick Augustus, 2nd Baron Chelmsford, G.C.B., G.C.V.O. (*see* BURKE'S *Peerage*) ; *m.* Katharine Frances, *d.* of A. F. Wallace, of Candacraig, Strathdon, Aberdeenshire. Served as Lieut. Royal Kent Yeomanry during the Great War. *Address:* 25, Cranley Gdns., S.W. *Club:* Boodle's. (M2525)

THEW, Charlton, M.B.E.

THICKE, Lieut. Claude Stanley, O.B.E., R.N.V.R.

THIRKELL, Lieut. Constantine, M.B.E.

THIRKELL, Capt. Robert Mowbray Winston, M.B.E.

THIRKELL, William, M.B.E.

THIRLWELL, Rev. Thomas William, O.B.E., *b.* 28 Jan. 1876 ; *s.* of John Thirlwell, of Catton, Northumberland ; *m.* Isabella, *d.* of Robert Adams, of Newcastle-on-Tyne. *Educ.:* Newcastle-on-Tyne, and King's College, London. Mission Van Sec., Church Army, 1909–14 ; Chairman of Executive Council, Church Benefit Society. 1913–14 ; Member of Executive Council, Church Benefit Society since 1902 ; Trustee of Church Benefit Society from 1918 ; Parochial Dept. Sec. Church Army since 1918. *War Work :* Sec. of the Church Army War Hospital, 1914–17 ; Personnel Sec., Church Army Hut Dept. 1915–19. *Address :* 12, St. John's Road, Wembley.
(O3953)

THIRSK, Richard, O.B.E., *b.* 3 Oct. 1876. *Educ.:* Edinburgh and the Continent. British Consul at Aarhus, Denmark ; Assistant Sec. to the Commission Internationale Slesvig during the period of the Plebiscite according to the terms of Article 109 of the Treaty of Versailles. *War Work :* Was on various occasions commended by the Lords of the Admiralty and by the Secretary of State for Foreign Affairs for important work in connection with the Blockade. *Clubs :* British Consulate, Aarhus, Denmark. (O3954)

THOM, Frederick Worrall, M.B.E., Can. A.M.C.

THOM, Col. George St. Clair, C.B., C.M.G., C.B.E., M.B., *b.* 1870. *Educ.:* Edinburgh Univ. Entered R.A.M.C. 1894 ; Lieut.-Col. 1915 ; Col. Army Med. Ser. 1917 ; S. African War, 1900–2 (despatches, Queen's medal with three clasps, King's medal with two clasps) ; Great War, 1914–19, on Staff and as Dep. Director of Med. Ser. Russian Expeditionary Force (despatches).
(C2359d)

THOM, Lieut.-Comm. James Maxtone, O.B.E., R.N.

THOM, James Maxtone, O.B.E., M.B., C.M., D.P.H., J.P., *b.* 1863 ; *s.* of the late Alexander Thom, L.R.C.S.E., and M.R.C.S. (Eng.), of Crieff, Perthshire ; *m.* Jessie Ludlam, *d.* of the late George Nesbit Minto, J.P. of Hong Kong and London. *Educ.:* Morrison's Academy, Crieff, and Univ. of Edinburgh. Superintendent, Royal Infirmary, Glasgow. *War Work :* Member of War Executive, Scottish Branch, British Red Cross Society. *Address :* Royal Infirmary, Glasgow. *Clubs :* Scottish Constitutional ; Royal Scottish Automobile. (O11454)

THOM, Robert Absalom, O.B.E., *b.* 1873 ; *s.* of George Thom, of Aberdeen ; *m.* Robina, *d.* of James Wills, of Aberdeen. *Educ.:* Robert Gordon's Coll., Aberdeen. Mechanical Engineer ; Assistant to the Chief Mechanical Engineer, Great Central Railway, Gorton, Manchester. *War Work :* The manufacture, in the Dukinfield and Gorton works of the Great Central Railway Co., of ambulance trains, gun carriages, howitzer carriages, sighting gear, high-explosive shells, cartridge cases, forgings, drop-stampings, etc. *Address :* 11, Loven Terrace, Fairfield, Manchester. (O11455)

THOM, Sir William, K.B.E., Chairman, Blackburn Board of Management, Ministry of Supplies ; Member of the Engineering Trades (New Industries Committee of the Ministry of Reconstruction) ; Director of Messrs. Tates and Thom, Ltd. *Address :* Blackburn (K236)

THOMAS, Flight-Lieut. Alan Miller, M.B.E., R.A.F.

THOMAS, Major Alfred Dominy, O.B.E., T.D., *b.* 26 Sept. 1855 ; *s.* of William Thomas, of Southook, Pembrokeshire ; *m.* Matilda Jane, *d.* of Edwin Pearson, of Bristol. *Educ.:* Clifton Church School, and Trade and Mining School, Bristol. Superintendent of Workshops and Surveyor, Clifton Coll., Bristol. *War Work :* Officer-in-Charge Clothing Store, Range, Buildings, Headquarters, etc., Gloucester County Association (T.F.). Bristol. *Addresses :* Clifton Coll., Bristol ; 9, St. John's Road, Clifton, Bristol. (O11456)

THOMAS, Arnold, M.B.E., *b.* 1882 ; *s.* of James Thomas, of Lewisham ; *m.* May Maud, *d.* of H. M. Stanley, of Dawley, Salop. *Educ.:* City of Westminster School. Draper, etc. *War Work :* Ministry of Food ; War Savings Association ; Herts Special Police. *Address :* Sarnia, Ware Road, Hertford. *Club :* National Liberal. (M4021)

THOMAS, Arthur Augustus, M.B.E., B.A., *b.* 12 Aug. 1862 ; *s.* of David Thomas, of Landore, Swansea ; *m.* Kathleen Lily, *d.* of Marshall Jackman, of Longfield, Kent. *Educ.:* St. Paul's Coll. Cheltenham, Royal Univ. of Ireland, Dublin. Governor of Northern Polytechnic ; Governor of Highbury Hill High School ; sometime Member of L.C.C. for East Islington ; President, Athenian Football League. *War Work :* Hon. Military Representative, Borough of Islington ; Vice-Chairman, S.Northamptonshire Recruiting Committee ; National Service Representative, Islington. *Addresses :* 5, Crown Office Row, Temple ; 5, Elm Grove Road, W. 5. *Club :* National Liberal. (M1009)

THOMAS Capt. Arthur Henry, M.B.E., M.B., R.A.M.C.

THOMAS, Arthur Lloyd, M.B.E., *b.* 5 Nov. 1869 ; *s.* of William Thomas, of Coedpenmaen, Pontypridd ; *m.* Agnes, *d.* of David Jones, of Treforest. *Educ.:* Cardiff Technical Schools ; Cardiff Univ. Schools (National Bronze Medallist, Special Queen's Prizeman, National Science Exhibitioner). Housing Commissioner, Wales and Mon. (Ministry of Health). Consulting Engineer and Architect ; Fellow Surveyors' Institute ; Member Institute Mechanical Engineers ; Member of Council, South Wales' Institute of Architects. *War Work :* Sec. two Red Cross Hospitals ; Sec. Pontypridd and Rhondda

Div. Red Cross ; Asst. County Director Red Cross, Glam *Addresses :* The Grove, Pontypridd ; 23, Gelliwastad Road, Pontypridd. *Club :* National Liberal. (M9831)

THOMAS, Surg.-Comm. Arthur Richard, O.B.E., F.R.C.S., R.N.

THOMAS, Capt. Bernard Henry, O.B.E., R.A.S.C.

THOMAS, Bert, M.B.E.

THOMAS, Capt. Cecil Compton, O.B.E., Can. A.S.C.

THOMAS, Capt. Charles William, C.B.E., R.N. Has Legion of Honour and Mil. Order of Aviz of Portugal.
(C919)

THOMAS, Daniel, C.B.E. Private Secretary to H.M.'s First Commissioner of Works. (C3167)

THOMAS, David, O.B.E., B.A. (London), elected F.L.S. in 1903, *b.* 15 Feb. 1866 ; *s.* of the late David Thomas, of Llanwnen, Cardiganshire ; *m.* Annie, *d.* of the late John Carrington, of Wrexham. *Educ.:* Llanwnen ; Lampeter ; Carmarthen (Graduated in Arts at the Univ. of London in Oct. 1892). Assistant Master at the Penygelli Schools, Wrexham, 1887–90 ; Headmaster of the Borth School, Portmadoc, Carnarvonshire, 1890–93 ; commenced duties as an Inspector of Schools, under the Board of Education, May, 1893. *War Work :* Joint Hon. Sec. to the Cardiganshire County Committee for War Savings. *Addresses :* Eirianfa, Caradoc Road, Aberystwyth ; Board of Education, Whitehall, London, S.W. 1.
(O1916)

THOMAS, Lieut.-Col. David Brodie, O.B.E., *b.* 19 Feb. 1863 ; *s.* of the late Benjamin Thomas, F.R.C.S., Llanelly ; *m.* Gertrude Annie, *d.* of the Rev. Canon Treasurer C. I. Atherton, M.A., of Exeter. *Educ.:* Epsom Coll. ; Oxford Military Coll. ; Naval Military Academy. Chin-Lushai Expedition, 1889–90. *War Work :* 1914–18 ; mentioned in despatches (London Gazette) three times. *Address :* Silvermead, Blackmore Road, Malvern. *Club :* Junior Army and Navy. (O2754)

THOMAS, David John, O.B.E.

THOMAS, Dulcibel Catherine Iltuta, M.B.E., *b.* 20 Jan. 1872 ; *d.* of Iltid Thomas, of Glanmor, Swansea. *War Work :* Member of Swansea Local War Pensions Committee, and Vice-Chairman of a Sub-Committee ; Member of Swansea Rural District War Pensions Committee ; Hon. Sec. Soldiers' and Sailors' Families Association (Swansea and Pontardawe Branch) ; District Representative Women's Branch under Ministry of Agriculture. *Address :* Bryn Neulog, Sketty, Glamorganshire.
(M9832)

THOMAS, Edgar William, C.B.E., *b.* 1879. Member of London Stock Exchange ; Partner in firm of Greenwood and Co. sometime Financial Adviser to Public Trustee. (C1045)

THOMAS, Edward, M.B.E., *b.* 10 March, 1854 ; *s.* of Edward Thomas, of Peurall Farm, near Harlech ; *m.* Cecilia Grant, *d.* of David Lister, of Newcastle, N.B. Canada. *Educ.* Harlech. Ship Master ; twenty-eight years in the service of Messrs. Frederick Leyland & Co., Liverpool. *War Work :* South African Trooping Service in Command of the S.S. "Cestrian" ; also commanded the same ship during the great War, from Aug. 1914 until torpedoed, June, 1917 ; then commanded S.S. "Parisian" and "Bohemian," until Armistice, 1918, in various British and Allied trooping service ; during this time he lost no men except unfortunately three engine-room hands, killed by explosion of enemy torpedo when H.M.S. "Cestrian" was sunk in Ægean Sea, June, 1917, on a voyage from Salonica to Alexandria with part of the 10th Division. *Address :* Overdale, 23, Kelvinside, Gt. Crosby, near Liverpool. (M2529)

THOMAS, Edward George, O.B.E. (January 1920), M.D., C.M., *b.* 2 Oct. 1853 ; eldest *s.* of the Rev G. T. W. Thomas, M.A., formerly Vicar of St. Mark's, Glouc ster ; *m.* Alice Louisa, *d.* of Alfred Moseley, has issue one daughter. *Educ.:* Felsted ; Edinburgh Univ. *War Work :* Civil Surgeon, Guards' Depot, Caterham. 1915 ; raised and First Commandant of Red Cross V.A.D. Surrey 88, 1914 ; mentioned in despatches and brought to the notice of the Secretary of State for War for valuable medical services. *Address :* Haveringwell, Caterham, Surrey. (O11852)

THOMAS, Ethel, O.B.E. Q.M.A.A.C.

THOMAS, Farrar Evelyn, O.B.E.

THOMAS, Capt. Francis Henry Hale, O.B.E., T.D., *b.* 23 June, 1874 ; *s.* of Francis H. Thomas, of Leytonstone. *Educ.:* Wellington Commercial Coll., and Drapers' Co. Secretary's Office, Great Eastern Railway Co. *War Work :* Qr.-Mr. 6th Bn. City of London Rifles, 1914–15 ; Qr.-Mr. and Assist. Adjt. and Qr.-Mr. No. 1 (N.C.) School of Instruction, 1916 ; Adjt. and Qr.-Mr. Senior Officers' School, Aldershot, from Oct. 1916, to Sept. 1919. *Address :* 30, Vernon Road, Leytonstone, Essex, E. 11. (O8951)

THOMAS, Frank Charles, O.B.E., *b.* 26 March, 1865 ; *s.* of the late Philip Edwin Thomas, of Southampton ; *m.* Lucy Mary, *d.* of the late Robert Eveleigh, of Devonshire. *Educ.:* Southampton. Sec. of the Union-Castle Mail Steamships Co. Ltd. Member of Shipping Federation Ltd., London Shipowners' Dock Labour Committee, and London Chamber of Commerce. *War Work :* Local Sec. of the Union-Castle Line at Southampton, 1914–19, dealing there with Company's Steamers engaged in Naval and Military requirements as Hospital Ships, Transports, Armed Cruisers, etc. ; Hon. Sec. Southampton District Munitions (shells, etc.), Committee, 1915–18 ; assisted the Chairman of General Munitions Tribunal (South Western Division), 1915–18 as Employers' Assessor at

Exeter, Basingstoke, Portsmouth, and Southampton. *Addresses:* The Union-Castle Line, 3 and 4, Fenchurch Street, E.C. 3; 44, Crescent Road, Norwood Park, S.E. 25. (O11457)

THOMAS, Capt. George Pollard, O.B.E., R.G.A., *b.* 6 June, 1893; *s.* of H. A. Thomas, of London; *m.* Florence Ruby Beatrice, *d.* of Lieut.-Col. H. K. Gordon (ret.), of Folkestone. *Educ.:* Clifton Coll., and R.M.A., Woolwich. Officer in His Majesty's Land Forces. *War Work:* Gibraltar, 1914; B.E.F., France, 1915–18; attached to American Exped. Force in France as Artillery Instructor, 1918. *Address:* c/o Cox & Co., 16. Charing Cross, S.W. 1. (O2755)

THOMAS, Lieut. Godfrey Herbert, M.B.E., I.A.

THOMAS, Capt. Harold Miles, M.B.E.

THOMAS, Harry Jones, M.B.E.

THOMAS, Henry Franklin, O.B.E.

THOMAS, Lieut. Hugh Hamshaw, M.B.E.

THOMAS, Major Hugh James Protheroe, O.B.E., R.G.A. (T.)

THOMAS, Ivor Cradock, M.V.O., O.B.E., *b.* 4 April, 1861; *s.* of the late Benjamin Thomas, F.R.C.S., of Llanelly, S. Wales; *m.* Laura Mulgrave, *d.* of the late Major-Gen. C. Hardy, R.A., of Dover. *Educ.:* Cowbridge Coll.; Epsom Coll.; R.I.E.C. Coll., Coopers Hill. Chief Engineer, Telegraphs, India, 35 years' service, retired April, 1916. *War Work:* Ministry of Munitions, Priority Department, Nov. 1916, to June, 1919; Section Director. *Address:* Mt. Shali, Sidley, Sussex. *Club:* East India United Service. (O3955)

THOMAS, James Bertram, M.B.E. A.M.Inst.C.E., *b.* 1875; *m.* Elizabeth Annie Wainscott. *Educ.:* Admiralty Schools; Goldsmith's Coll. Seven years on the Naval Designing Staff of Sir W. G. Armstrong, Whitworth & Co.; since 1912, as an Assistant to the Director of Naval Construction, Vickers, Ltd. *War Work:* Superintended the installation of apparatus for protection against mines in over 3000 merchant ships at the chief ports of the British Isles and in the Mediterranean; also all designs of arrangements for submarine attack and protection against mines for the Allied Navies. *Addresses:* 1, Honor Oak Road, Forest Hill, S.E.; Vickers House, Westminster, S.W. (M9833)

THOMAS, Jessie, Mrs., O.B.E., *b.* 1862; eldest *d.* of the late Eli Heyworth, J.P., of Blackburn; widow of Franklin Talbot, eldest *s.* of the late Franklin Thomas, of Blackburn. *Educ.:* Birklands, Hornsey Lane, N. *War Work:* Vice-President Blackburn Branch East Lancs Division; Head of Comforts Section, 1914–19; Chairman of Blackburn Prisoners of War Help Committee. *Address:* Blackburn, Lancs. (O1919)

THOMAS John Frederick Ivor, O.B.E.

THOMAS, Col. Sir John Lynn, K.B.E., C.B., C.M.G., F.R.C.S., *b.* 10 Sept. 1861; *s.* of the late Evan Thomas, of Llandyssol, Cardigan; *m.* daughter of the late Edward Jenkins, of Cardiff. *Educ.:* Privately, London Hospital, and Vienna. Surgeon, King Edward VII.'s Hospital; Consulting Surgeon to many hospitals in the Western Command; Member of the Council of Surgeons, England; served in S. African War with Welsh Hospitals; formerly Senior House Surgeon to the Cardiff Infirmary, and House Surgeon to the London Hospital. etc. *Addresses:* Greenlawn, Pen-y-lan, Cardiff; Stradmore, Cenarth, Carmarthen. *Clubs:* Royal Automobile; Garrick; Cardiff and County (Cardiff). (K197)

THOMAS, Kathleen Kyffin, O.B.E.

THOMAS, Major Lewis, O.B.E.

THOMAS, Lillie, Mrs., O.B.E.

THOMAS, Maude Tuson, O.B.E.

THOMAS, Morgan, O.B.E.

THOMAS, Olive Morton, M.B.E.

THOMAS, Capt. Otho Vincent, O.B.E., R.A.F.

THOMAS, Capt. Percy Edward, O.B.E., A.R.I.B.A., *b.* 1883; *s.* of the late Capt. Christmas Thomas, of Penarth, S. Wales; *m.* Margaret Ethel, *d.* of H. E. Turner. *Educ.:* Hasland House, Penarth, S. Wales. Partner in firm of Ivor Jones and Percy Thomas, Architects, Cardiff; Designer of many well-known buildings in the Principality, including Cardiff Technical College, Merthyr Y.M.C.A., etc.; was one of the ten firms selected in competition for the new Board of Trade Offices, Whitehall; Member of Council, and Hon. Librarian, South Wales Institute of Architects. *War Work:* Joined Artists' Rifles, in 1915; rose through various noncommissioned ranks, and eventually obtained commission in Royal Engineers; was with a Field Company, R.E., on the Somme, 1916–17 Vimy Ridge, etc.; was promoted Capt. and Adjutant, R.E., in Dec. 1917; in June, 1918, was further promoted to Staff Officer to Chief Engineer 13th Corps, and acted in this capacity during the successful advance of the corps over the old 1914 battlefield of Le Cateau, Landrecies, etc.; was demobilised in Feb. 1919; twice mentioned in despatches. *Addresses:* 6 and 7, St. John's Square; 6, Syr David's Avenue, Cardiff. (O5847)

THOMAS, Major Peter David, C.B.E., M.V.O., *b.* 29 Nov. 1873; *s.* of Nicholas Howell Thomas, of Bridge House, Neath, South Wales; *m.* Ada, *d.* of David Isaac, late Under Sheriff of Glamorganshire, of Heathfield, Swansea, Glam. *Educ.:* Neath Proprietary School, and privately. Solicitor; Senior Partner of the firm of Peter Thomas and Clark, 1, Bush Lane, E.C.; Chairman of Hudson, Sykes and Bousfield, of Leeds, Worsted Spinners; Director of Fenton Textile Associations, etc. *War Work:* Lieut. Machine Gun Section, 6th Welsh Regt., from Aug. 1914, to June, 1915; served in France, Oct. 1914 to May, 1915; appointed Organising Sec. to the Ministry of Munitions, Yorkshire Area, July, 1915; resigned, Jan. 1919; gazetted

Capt., July, 1915; gazetted, Feb. 1917, and Feb. 1918, for valuable services rendered in the war; acted on various committees for War Savings, for the Ministry of Reconstruction, the Ministry of Labour, and the Ministry of Munitions; rendered certain services to the Italian Government, and was awarded the Cavaliere of the Crown of Italy in Oct. 1917; was awarded the M.V.O. (4th class) by His Majesty the King, in June, 1918; generally devoted the whole of his time to war work from Aug. 1914, to March, 1919. *Address:* 144, Adelaide Road, N.W. 3. *Clubs:* Junior Carlton; Constitutional; Bath. (C2994)

THOMAS, Lieut.-Col. Reginald Aneurin, C.B.E., R.A.; *b.* 19 July, 1879; *s.* of the late A. H. Thomas, late of Gampola, Ceylon; *m.* Kathleen Mary O'Connel, *d.* of G. C. Bliss, of Glenlyon, Ceylon. *Educ.:* Cheltenham Coll. *Address:* c/o Messrs. Cox & Co. (C1785)

THOMAS, Rev. Richard Albert, O.B.E.

THOMAS, Rev. Richard Everard, M.B.E. Vicar of Bolam, Northumberland. *War Work:* Sec. of the Castle Ward Union War Savings Committee, and Lecturer on Food Economy. *Address:* Bolam Vicarage, Morpeth. (M9835)

THOMAS, Capt. Robert John, O.B.E., R.E.

THOMAS, Capt. Rodall Woodcliffe, O.B.E., R.A.F.

THOMAS, Major Sydney Arnold, O.B.E., R.E.

THOMAS, Capt. Sidney Arthur, M.B.E., R.G.A., *b.* 8 May, 1871; *s.* of William Godfrey Thomas, of Plumstead; *m.* Winifred Kate Mary Whitaker, *d.* of Charles John Williams, of Netley. *Educ.:* Mercer's School. Army. *War Work:* Ordnance Committee. *Address:* 12, Sherard Gardens, Eltham, S.E. 9. (M2552)

THOMAS, Capt. Thomas Charles, O.B.E.

THOMAS, Thomas John, O.B.E. (O12024)

THOMAS, Thomas Shenton Whitelegge, O.B.E., *b.* 10 Oct. 1879; *s.* of the late Rev. T. W. Thomas, of Newton Rectory, Wisbech, Cambs.; *m.* Lucy Marguerite, *d.* of Col. J. A. L. Montgomery, C.S.I., C.B.E., D.L., of Moville, Co. Donegal. *Educ.:* Leatherhead and Queens' Coll., Cambridge. In Colonial Civil Service; appointed Assist. Dist. Commr. East Africa Prot., Aug. 1909; 3rd Assist. Sec., 1 April, 1911; Senior Assist. Sec., 1 April, 1912; Assist. Chief Sec., Uganda, Jan. 1919. *War Work:* Employed throughout the war in the East Africa Prot. Secretariat. *Address:* The Secretariat, Entebbe, Uganda. *Club:* Isthmian. (O8414)

THOMAS, Trevor Meredyth Chitty, O.B.E., M.C., *b.* 28 Nov. 1889; *s.* of Major Harley Thomas, F.S.A., of Escote, Shortlands, Kent. *Educ.:* Cheltenham Coll.; Royal Military Academy, Woolwich. Barrister-at-Law. *War Work:* Served in Belgium and France, May, 1915, to Feb. 1916; mentioned in despatches and awarded Military Cross for services at Battle of Hulloch, 13 Oct. 1915; Courts-Martial Officer and Legal Adviser, Dec. 1916, to Dec. 1917, Harwich Garrison; Dec. 1917, to March, 1919, to Inspector General, Lines of Communication, Italy; twice mentioned in despatches and awarded O.B.E. (Mil. Div.) for services in Italy. *Address:* 3, Elm Court, Temple, E.C. (O6423)

THOMAS, Vyvyan Hood, O.B.E. Hon. Sec., County of Glamorgan Branch of the Soldiers' and Sailors' Families Association. (O11928)

THOMAS, Walter John, O.B.E.

THOMAS, Capt. Walwyn, O.B.E.

THOMAS, William, J.P., O.B.E., *b.* 30 June, 1855; *s.* of William Thomas, of Ucheldrefgoed, Anglesea; *m.* Elizabeth Mary, *d.* of William Scott, J.P., of Gosport. *Educ.:* Privately. Admiralty Surgeon, and Agent; Medical Officer Royal Alexandra Hospital, Rhyl. *War Work:* Medical Officer Red Cross Auxiliary Hospital, Rhyl. *Address:* Clarence House, Rhyl. (O11460)

THOMAS, Sir William Beach, K.B.E. *Educ.:* Shrewsbury and Christ Church, Oxford. War Correspondent on the Staff of the "Daily Mail"; was President of Oxford Univ. Athletic Club. *Address:* Wheathamstead Place, Herts. (K432)

THOMAS, Lieut. William Bryson, M.B.E., Can A.P.C.

THOMAS, William Edmund, O.B.E., J.P., *b.* 8 March, 1859; *s.* of David Thomas, of Llanfabon, Glamorgan; *m.* Katharine, *d.* of David Thomas, of Nelson, Glamorgan. *Educ.:* Edinburgh and London. Physician and Surgeon; Sub-Commissioner, Order of St. John of Jerusalem, Welsh Priory; M.O. Bridgend and Cowbridge Board of Guardians; Surgeon Home Office and Board of Education, Bridgend District; Examiner and Lecturer Order of St. John and British Red Cross Society. *War Work:* Surgeon to Bridgend Section of 3rd Western Military Hospital, and to Auxiliary Voluntary Hospitals. *Address:* Ashfield, Bridgend, Glam. (O11461)

THOMAS, William Gearing, M.B.E.

THOMAS, William Henry, M.B.E., *b.* 23 Aug. 1858; *s.* of Joshua Heneage Thomas, of Pickhill, Yorks. *Educ.:* Cleveland Academy, Middlesbrough. *War Work:* Military Representative; Chairman Advisory Committee; Hon. Area Substitution Officer; Revising Officer and Member of various committees in connection with Recruiting, Tribunals, etc. *Address:* The Ness Linthorpe, Middlesbrough. (M2534)

THOMAS, William Henry, M.B.E.; *s.* of Richard Thomas; *m.* Mary Davidson, *d.* of John Grant Shepherd, J.P. formerly of The Knole, Bournemouth. *Educ.:* Commercial School, Bournemouth. Solicitor; Commissioner for Oaths; Deputy Alderman of City of London; one of H.M. Lieutenants of the City of London; Governor of St. Thomas'

Hospital: Governor of City and Guilds Institute; Hon.-Treas. of the City of London Conservative and Unionist Association; Churchwarden of Wimbledon. *War Work:* Chairman of the Executive Committee. and Founder of the Montenegrin Red Cross and Relief Fund; collected upwards of £80,000, besides tons of clothing and surgical appliances for the smallest and poorest of our Allies; Chevalier de la Legion d'honneur. *Address:* Talbot House, Wimbledon. (M4022)

THOMAS, William Howard, M.B.E., *b.* 5 Jan. 1890; *s.* of the late Frederick George Thomas, of Reading; *m.* Ethel Louise, *d.* of John Mears, of Westcliff-on-Sea. *Educ.:* High School, Harlesden, Middlesex. Member of London and North Western Co.'s Headquarters Staff. since 1905. *War Work:* Private Sec. to late Sir Guy Calthrop, Bart., Controller of Coal Mines. *Address:* 40, Finchley Rd., Westcliff-on-Sea, Essex.
(M9836)

THOMAS, William Thelwall, M.B.E., Ch.M. (Liverpool), F.R.C.S. (Eng.), *b.* 1865; *s.* of John and Elizabeth Thomas, of Liverpool; *m.* Anabel Roxburgh, *d.* of Alexander Spence, of Huntly, N.B. *Educ.:* Liverpool Institute; Glasgow Royal Infirmary School of Medicine; Univ. Coll., Liverpool. Surgeon; Professor of Regional Surgery, Univ. of Liverpool; Surgeon Royal Infirmary, and Lecturer on Clinical Surgery. *War Work:* Surgeon Royal Infirmary Military Beds; Consulting Surgeon to the following:—Wallasey Town Hall Military Hospital, Tropical School Military Hospital, and Crofton Auxiliary Military Hospital, Liverpool. *Addresses:* 84, Rodney Street, Liverpool; Verdala Towers, Allerton, Liverpool. *Club:* Royal Automobile; Reform; University; Athenæum (Liverpool). (M10286)

THOMAS, Beatrice Mary, Mrs. DAWSON-, M.B.E., *b.* 13 Oct. 1870; *d.* of the late Capt. Charles E. Pritchard, of R.F.A., Indian Army; *m.* Edward Morgan, *s.* of the late John B. Dawson-Thomas. *Educ.:* Chateau Roux, Lausanne; Chateau de Montiers, Chateau Thierez, pré Paris, France. *War Work:* Organiser, Commandant, and Hon. Matron of the Military Hospital for W. Somerset Yeomanry, from Nov. 1914, to June, 1915; Organiser of the Red Cross Auxiliary Military Hospital (150 beds) Minehead, Somerset, from Dec. 1915, to May, 1919; both Hospitals at Minehead. *Address:* Harefield, Minehead, Somerset. (M318)

THOMAS, Julia Winifred, Mrs. GRIFFITH-, O.B.E.; *d.* of Walter Lewis, of Llangadock; *m.* Rees Griffith-Thomas, General Manager British Linen Bank. Scotland. *Educ.:* Hillhouse Coll., Haverfordwest; St. Mawr Coll., Chepstow. *War Work:* Five years all round Social Service at Woolwich during war time. *Address:* 42, Moray Place, Edinburgh. (O1145)

THOMAS, S. Lavinia, Mrs. RIDLEY-, M.B.E. *War Work:* Commandant, Ardmillan Auxiliary Military Hospital, Oswestry. (M9834)

THOMAS, Joseph Silvers WILLIAMS-, O.B.E., J.P., *b.* 27 April, 1848; *s.* of Samuel Cox Williams, of Stourbridge; *m.* Lucy Annette, *d.* of Thomas Davies Thomas, of Stourbridge and Denbigh. *Educ.:* Stourbridge and Bromsgrove Grammar Schools. High Sheriff for County of Worcester, 1917–18; assumed by deed poll additional name of Thomas, 1903; Glass Manufacturer by Royal Warrant to H.M. King Edward VI.; Director of several companies; Chairman of Stourbridge Grammar School; also Corbett Hospital; and connected with various other educational institutions. *Address:* Parkfield, Stourbridge, Worcestershire. *Club:* County Worcester.

THOMPSON, Major (T. Lieut.-Col.) Archibald Henry James, O.B.E.

THOMPSON, A. M., O.B.E.

THOMPSON, Comm. Arthur, O.B.E., P. & O. S. N. Co., *b.* 1862. *Educ.:* Privately. *War Work:* Transporting troops throughout the war, also mails and passengers. *Clubs:* R. T. Yacht; R.A.C.; I.A. & N.; Golfers'; Richmond Golf. (O11462)

THOMPSON, Major Cecil Henry Farrer, D.S.O., O.B.E.

THOMPSON, Charles John S., M.B.E., Ph.D.; *s.* of the late John Thompson, formerly of Esholt, Yorkshire; *m.* Ethel May, *d.* of the late Rev. W. H. Tindall, of Weybridge. *Educ.:* Univ. of Liverpool. Curator of the Historical Medical Museum, Wigmore Street, Cavendish Square, W. 1. *War Work:* Commandant British Red Cross; founded and established the Holmleigh Auxiliary Military Hospital at Harrow-on-the-Hill, in Nov. 1914; was Commandant and Officer-in-charge of this institution until it closed, Dec. 1918; the hospital will be perpetuated in the Holmleigh Room, equipped with Zander appliances for the treatment of paralysed soldiers, at the Star and Garter Red Cross Hospital, Richmond. *Address:* Penn Corner, Beaconsfield, Bucks. *Club:* Services. (M9837)

THOMPSON, 2nd Lieut. Charles Stuart, M.B.E., R.F.A.

THOMPSON, Lieut.-Col. Cyril Powney, C.B.E., *b.* Aug. 1864; *s.* of the late Fendall Thompson, B.C.S.; *m.* Mary, *d.* of Lieut.-Gen. R. C. R. Clifford, C.B. *Educ.:* Charterhouse; R.M.C., Sandhurst. Joined Wiltshire Regt. 1885; 3rd Sikhs P.F.F. 1888; Panjab Commission, 1889. *War Work:* Commissioner Multan Division, 1915–19. *Address:* Chamba, Panjab, India. *Club:* East India United Service. (C1981)

THOMPSON, Edgar, O.B.E.

THOMPSON, Edith Marie, C.B.E., *b.* 1879; *d.* of W. F. Thompson, J.P., Barrister-at-Law, of Aldeburgh. *Educ.:* Cheltenham Ladies' Coll.; King's Coll. Univ. of London. Editor of "The Hockey Field," 1901–15; Sec. of Building Fund, Bedford Coll. (Univ. of London); Member of Council All-England Women's Hockey Association, and Ladies' Lacrosse Association. *War Work:* V.A.D., 1914–17; Area Controller,

London District, Q.M.A.A.C., 1917–18; Controller of Inspection, Q.M.A.A.C., 1918; Assistant Chief Controller, Q.M.A.A.C., 1919–20. *Address:* Gables, Aldeburgh, Suffolk. *Club:* Forum. (C2214C)

THOMPSON, Edward, M.B.E.

THOMPSON, Major Edward, O.B.E., R.E.

THOMPSON, Emily, Mrs., O.B.E. (O12025)

THOMPSON, 2nd Lieut. Eric Bertram, M.B.E., R.B.

THOMPSON, Capt. Frank, M.B.E., *b.* 9 Nov. 1848; *s.* of George Thompson, of Blakeney, Norfolk; *m.* Eleanor Marie, *d.* of Joseph Pyman Farmer, of Deopham, Norfolk. *Educ.:* Blakeney School. Master Mariner. *War Work:* Commander of s.s. "Whorlton," as transport for H.M. Grand Fleet during the war, from 1914–18. *Address:* 33, Charlotte Street, South Shields. (O4023)

THOMPSON, Lieut.-Col. Frank Stuart Corbitt, O.B.E.

THOMPSON, Comm. Frederic John, O.B.E., R.D, R.N.R.,

THOMPSON, Surg.-Lieut. Comm. Frederick, O.B.E., L.D.S., R.N.V.R.

THOMPSON, Lieut.-Col. George, O.B.E., T.D.

THOMPSON, George, M.B.E.

THOMPSON, 2nd Lieut. George Albert, M.B.E., R.A.F.

THOMPSON, George Batching, M.B.E.

THOMPSON, Rev. George Herbert, C.B.E., *b.* 1859; *s.* of the late John Thompson, of Bickley, Kent; *m.* Alice Agar, *d.* of Major Francis James Bampfylde, of Bath. *Educ.:* Bickley, and Univ. Coll., Durham. Royal Army Chaplains Department (T.) 3rd class; Major, Commanding Beccles Cadet Corps, R.F.A. *War Work:* County Director of Norfolk B.R.C.S.; raised Norfolk R.A.M.C. (Vol.), and was gazetted Lieut.-Col. Commanding, in 1918. *Address:* Gillingham Rectory, Beccles, Norfolk. (C647)

THOMPSON, George Roger, C.B.E. Chief Engineer in Merchant Service. (C3080)

THOMPSON, George Tyrrell, D.S.O., M.B.E.

THOMPSON, Capt. Harold Willoughby, M.B.E., *b.* 4 April, 1891; *s.* of the late Charles Thompson, of 36, Jermyn Street, S.W. 1. *Educ.:* Tonbridge. Schoolmaster. *War Work:* From 26 Aug. 1914, to 10 Feb. 1920, served as commissioned officer, India, Mesopotamia, and Kurdistan, with the 1/9th Middlesex Regt. *Address:* 3, Finchley Avenue, Hendon Lane, Finchley, N. 3. (M7027)

THOMPSON, Lieut.-Col. Harry Adair, O.B.E.

THOMPSON, Rev. Harry Ernest, M.B.E., *b.* 11 Nov. 1879; *s.* of Ernest Alfred Thompson, of Liverpool, England; *m.* Edith Mary Elizabeth, *d.* of John Bratt, of Birkenhead. *Educ.:* St. Margaret's Liverpool, and Dorchester Coll., Oxon. Clerk in Holy Orders; House Master, St. Andrew's School, Bloemfontein, and Priest-Vicar, Bloemfontein Cathedral. *War Work:* Hon. Sec. Governor-General's Fund, Bloemfontein, July, 1915, to Dec. 1919. *Address:* St. Andrew's School, Bloemfontein, South Africa. *Club:* Bloemfontein. (M6379)

THOMPSON, Helena Agnes Mary, M.B.E., *b.* 1855; *d.* of William Thompson, of Park End, Workington. *War Work:* Soldiers' and Soldiers' Families Association. *Address:* Park End, Workington. (M9838)

THOMPSON Ina Sophia, M.B.E.

THOMPSON, Lieut.-Col. Jacob Jewett, O.B.E., R.E.

THOMPSON, Lieut. James, C.B.E., R.N.R.

THOMPSON, James Benjamin, M.B.E.

THOMPSON, Capt. James Douglas, M.B.E.

THOMPSON, James Osbourne, O.B.E.

THOMPSON, T. Warrant Officer J., M.B.E. Royal Indian Marine.

THOMPSON, Jean Glass, O.B.E., Q.M.A.A.C.

THOMPSON, Jessie Catherine, M.B.E.

THOMPSON, Lieut. John, O.B.E., R.N.R.

THOMPSON, John Barwick, O.B.E.

THOMPSON, Capt. John Foster, O.B.E.

THOMPSON, Hon. Capt. John Hannay, O.B.E., Officier d'Académie, J.P., M.Sc., M.I.C.E., F.R.S.E., M.Soc.C.E. (France), *b.* 17 May, 1869; *s.* of John Thompson, C.E., of Newcastle-on-Tyne; *m.* Mary Isabella, *d.* of Thomas Hodge, of Newcastle-on-Tyne. *Educ.:* Trinity Coll., Harrogate; Durham Coll. of Science, Newcastle-on-Tyne. General Manager and Engineer Dundee Harbour Trust; Lecturer on Dock and Harbour Engineering, St. Andrews Univ.; 2nd V.B. Royal Highlanders, The Black Watch. *War Work:* Member of the Advisory Committee of the Board of Trade on Congestion of Docks; Chairman of the Dundee Port Labour Committee, and Dundee Port and Transit Committee; Member of other committees, and largely engaged in war work in connection with the Port of Dundee. *Address:* Sorbie, Broughty Ferry, Forfarshire. (O11463)

THOMPSON, Alderman John Ockelford, O.B.E., J.P., *b.* 8 Oct. 1872; *s.* of the late Thomas Thompson, Chelmsford; *m.* Emma, *d.* of the late Henry Tanner, of Chelmsford. *Educ.:* King Edward VI. School. Mayor of Chelmsford 1916–17, and 1920–21; Part-Proprietor and Editor of "The Essex Chronicle." *War Work:* Officer in the Volunteers and on Volunteer Special Coastal Service; Commissioner of Boy Scouts; Chairman, Chelmsford District War Pensions Committee; Member of Chelmsford Military Service Tribunal; Chairman, Food Control Committee; Chairman Profiteering Committee; Chairman, Chelmsford District Local Employment Committee; Chairman, Appointments Dept., Ministry of Labour; Chairman, Chelmsford and District Committee for War Savings. *Address:* The Eaves, Chelmsford. (O11464)

THOMPSON, Major John Pickering, O.B.E., I.A.

THOMPSON, Lorna, M.B.E.

THOMPSON, Marion Annie, M.B.E. W.R.A.F.

THOMPSON, Mary, b. 16 Sept. 1855; d. of Francis Thompson. Educ.: Derby. War Work: Commandant of the Red Cross Hospital, Burton-on-Trent, from Aug. 1914 to its close in March, 1919. Address: Ivy Lodge, Stapenhill, Burton-on-Trent. (O804)

THOMPSON, Maurice, M.B.E.

THOMPSON, Major Maurice Scott, O.B.E.

THOMPSON, Nathan, M.B.E.

THOMPSON, Sir Percy, K.B.E.. C.B., b. 18 Dec. 1872; s. of Richard Thompson, J.P., of Whalley Lancashire; m. Daisy Elaine, d. of Leicester Edwards, R.N., Assistant Colonial Secretary, Sierra Leone. Educ.: Rugby, and Brasenose Coll., Oxford. Deputy Chairman of the Board of Inland Revenue. War Work: Financial. Address: 174, Cromwell Road, S.W. 5. Clubs: Union; Royal Automobile. (K433)

THOMPSON, Reginald, O.B.E.

THOMPSON, Lieut. Reginald Ernest, O.B.E,. R.A.S.C.

THOMPSON, Reria, Mrs., M.B.E.

THOMPSON, Major Robert Broadwell, O.B.E., b. 29 Sept. 1874; s. of Amos Thompson, of West Kootenay, B.C.; m. Alma Gertrude, d. of John Henry Lyons, of Manitoba. Educ.: Public and High Schools, Ontario, Canada. Financial Broker; Notary Public; 20 years' service in Active Militia Force of Canada. War Work: At outbreak of war was a Captain in Militia; joined Expeditionary Force in Aug. 1914; in command of "H" Company, 11th (Provisional) Battalion; went to France in Feb. 1915 with the Artillery, 1st Canadian Division; was demobilised in June, 1919; M.B.E. 1918; O.B.E. (Military), 1919; Prince Albert, Sask. (O7939)

THOMPSON, Robert John, O.B.E., b. 27 Sept. 1867. Assistant Sec., Ministry of Agriculture. War Work: Member of the following committees:—Fertilisers, Alcohol, Sulphuric Acid, Sulphate of Ammonia, Phosphates and Potash, and Seeds Advisory Committee, etc. Addresses: 10, Bigwood Road, N.W. 4; Copthorne, Crawley, Sussex. Club: Reform. (O805)

THOMPSON, Samuel Douglas, M.B.E. (M10419)

THOMPSON, Sarah Ann, Mrs., M.B.E.

THOMPSON, Thomas, M.B.E.

THOMPSON, Capt. Thomas, O.B.E.

THOMPSON, Capt. and Qr.-Mr. Walter Wright, O.B.E.

THOMPSON, William, C.B.E., b. 9 Aug. 1858; s. of Benjamin Thompson, of Newcastle-on-Tyne; m. Evelina Frances, d. of William Howey, of Longframlington. Educ.: Public School, Newcastle-on-Tyne. Station Master, N.E.R., Newcastle-on-Tyne, Central Station. War Work: In connection with movement of troops to and from Newcastle-on-Tyne. Address: 32, Simonside Terrace, Heaton, Newcastle-on-Tyne. (C648)

THOMPSON, William Bruce, C.B.E. Managing Director of Caledon Shipbuilding and Engineering Co. (C648)

THOMPSON, William Henry, M.B.E., b. 8 Feb. 1861; s. of John Thompson, of Limerick City, m. Mary, d. of John Kealy, cf Fenagh, Co. Carlow. Educ.: Christian Brothers Schools, Sexton Street, Limerick. District Superintendent, Great Southern and Western Railway, Cork. War Work: Supervision of Railway Transport by special and scheduled trains of British and American Naval (American Fleet stationed at Queenstown) and Military Forces, including general food supplies, arms, equipment, ammunition, etc., between ports and railway stations in the south of Ireland. Address: Tirano, Victoria Road, Cork. (M2538)

THOMPSON, William Nelson, M.B.E.

THOMPSON, Arthur BEEBY-, M.B.E.

THOMPSON, Mary Alice Helen, Mrs. POWNEY-, M.B.E.; d. of Lieut.-General R. C. Clifford, C.B., of Carn Cottage, Belturbet; m. Lieut.-Col. Cyril Powney Thompson. War Work: Managed the Branches of the Red Cross and Comforts for Soldiers in the Multan Division of the Panjab, 1915–19. Address: Chamba, Panjab. (M6259)

THOMPSON, Brig.-Gen. Frederick HACKET-, C.B. C.B.E., b. 1858; s. of the late Charles Henry Thompson, of Bilbrough Hall, Yorks. Entered 79th Regt. 1879; Capt. Queen's Own Cameron Highlanders, 1884; Major, 1894; Lieut.-Col. 1901; Brevet Col. 1904; Col. 1908; Hon. Brig.-Gen. (ret.), 1918; served with Egyptian Expedition, 1882 (medal with clasp, bronze star); Sudan Expedition, 1885–86; Nile Expedition, 1898 (despatches, medal with two clasps, 4th class Osmanieh); S. Africa, 1901–2 (Queen's medal with five clasps); was Comdt. School of Instruction for Mounted Inf. 1906–10; in command of a Dist. 1911–15; Brig. Com. with rank of Brig.-Gen. 1915–18. Club: Naval and Military. (C1506)

THOMPSON, Adam Robert, M.B.E., b. 1865. Civil Servant, 2nd Division Clerk, Board of Trade 1883–1907; Staff Clerk, 1907; First Division Clerk, 1908–19; Staff Officer, Grade 1, Ministry of Transport, 1919. War Work: Railway Department, Board of Trade. Addresses: Ministry of Transport, S.W.1; 6, Dunstan Road, Golders Green, N.W. 11. (M1012)

THOMSON, Capt. Alexander Brackstone, M.B.E.

THOMSON, Capt. Alexander Melen, M.B.E.

THOMSON, Alfred Ebenezer Spence, M.B.E., M.A., LL.B., b. 7 Dec. 1880; s. of William Thomson, of Edinburgh, m. Hilda Margaret Hume, d. of R. D. Ker, W.S., of Edinburgh. Educ.: George Watson's Coll.; Edinburgh Univ.: also studied at Paris (Faculté de Droit); and Heidelberg. Solicitor; partner of Stalker and Thomson, Solicitors, Galashiels. War Work: Red Cross organisation in Selkirkshire. Address: Belmont, Galashiels. Club: Scottish Liberal. (M9845)

THOMSON, Lieut. Alfred Louis, M.B.E., R.A.S.C.

THOMSON, Andrew, O.B.E., b. 17 June, 1856; s. of Andrew Thomson, of Glasgow. Educ.: Glasgow. Cabinet Manufacturer; President Scottish Furniture Manufacturers Assocn.; Expert on Furnishings; Carlton Hotels, London and Johannesburg, Ritz Hotel, London, Royal Automobile Club London, etc. War Work: Expert on furnishing contracts for Navy and Army Canteen in Glasgow and districts; Member of Government Advisory Committee (Furnishing Trades), National Service, also Chairman of Glasgow local committee; Member of Government Advisory Committee (Furnishing Trades) Training of Disabled Sailors and Soldiers, also Chairman of Glasgow and Districts Local Committee; Member of two committees for Belgian relief and furnishing homes in Glasgow. (O11406)

THOMSON, Capt. Anthony Standidge, C.B., C.B.E, b. 1851; s. of the Rev. Anthony Francis Thomson; m. 1888, Alethea Isabella Evans Davis (who died). Com. (ret.) Royal Naval Reserve; Elder Brother of Trinity House; was a Member of Board of Trade Enquiry on Ships' Side Lights, 1895. Addresses: 47, FitzGeorge Avenue, West Kensington, W.; Trinity House, E.C. (C918)

THOMSON, Archibald, M.B.E.

THOMSON, Major Arthur Landsborough, O.B.E.

THOMSON, Brig.-Gen. Christopher Birdwood, C.B.E., D.S.O., b. 1875. Ret. as Hon. Brig.-Gen. 1919 (formerly R.E.); S. Africa, 1899–1902 (despatches, Queen's medal with three clasps, King's medal with two clasps); Balkan Campaign, 1912–13 (medals); Great War, 1914–19, in Palestine (despatches). (C1786)

THOMSON, Constance Emily Temple, Mrs., O.B.E.; d. of R. Temple Frere, of Harley Street; m. Herbert Campbell, s. of David Thomson. War Work: Four years at Central War Supply Depot, Cavendish Square. Address: 34, Queen Anne Street, W. 1. Club: League of Remembrance (1914–1919). (O11467)

THOMSON, Col. Sir Courtauld, K.B.E., Knt. Bach., C.B., M.A., b- 1866; s. of Robert William Thomson. Educ.: Eton, and Magdalen Coll., Oxford. War Work: Chief Commissioner for British Red Cross and Order of St. John for France, Malta, Egypt, Italy, Macedonia, and Near East, 1914–19; attached General Headquarters Staff, B.E.F., Egypt (1916), and Italy (1918); mentioned in despatches four times; Knight of Grace Order of St. John of Jerusalem; Chairman Order of St. John Hospital, Jerusalem; Order of Nile Second Class; Knight Commander of the Order of St. Sava (1917); Italian Military Cross with bar; Grand Officier de l'ordre de Danilo (Montenegro); Cross of Mercy (Serbia); Gold Medal Italian and Serbian Red Cross. Addresses: 59, Pont Street, S.W. 1; Dorney Wood, Burnham, Bucks. Clubs: Reform; Brooks's; Arthur's; New (Edinburgh); Royal St. George's (Sandwich). (K172)

THOMSON, Major Cyril Henry Farrar, D.S.O, C.B.E., Major, London Regt.; Assist. Mil. Sec.; served in Great War (mentioned in despatches). (O2758)

THOMSON, Daniel, M.B.E., b. 28 March, 1875; s. of Charles Thomson, of Cumnock; m. Ellen Mary, d. of David Veitch, of Duns. Educ.: Cumnock, and Glasgow. Headmaster, Duns Public School. War Work: Hon. Sec. and Treas. of the Central War Savings Committee for the County of Berwick. Address: Schoolhouse, Duns. (M9846)

THOMSON, Capt. David, M.B.E.

THOMSON, Capt. David, O.B.E., M.B., R.A.M.C.

THOMSON, David, M.B.E., b. 8 Aug. 1880; s. of David Thomson, of Glasgow; m. Jessie, d. of the late Arch Taylor, of Glasgow. Educ.: Privately. Acting Assistant Architect, H.M. Office of Works. War Work: Concerned in the design and erection of war buildings for H.M.O.W. Address: The Gables, Cheam Common, Worcester Park, Surrey. (M4025)

THOMSON, David George, C.B.E., M.D., b. 1856; s. of Thomas Thomson, of Edinburgh; m. Malina Stromeyer. Sometime Lieut.-Col. R.A.M.C.; commanded Norfolk War Hospital during Great War, 1914–19 (despatches); Med. Sup. County Mental Hospital, Thorpe. Address: Thorpe, Norwich. (C1787)

THOMSON, Elizabeth, M.B.E.

THOMSON, Elizabeth, M.B.E., Q.M.A.A.C.

THOMSON, Frances Beresford, M.B.E.

THOMSON, Frances Ingleton, M.B.E.

THOMSON, Lieut. Frederick Charles, M.B.E., M.P., b. 27 May, 1875; s. of James Wishart Thomson, of Glenpark, Balerno, Midlothian; m. Constance Margaret. d. of Hamilton Andrew Hotson, of 4, Rothesay Terrace, Edinburgh. Educ.: Edinburgh Academy and Univ. Coll., Oxford, also Edinburgh Univ. Advocate of the Scottish Bar; Member of Parliament for South Aberdeen; Parliamentary Private Sec. to Sir R. Horne, President Board of Trade. War Work: Lieut. 1/3rd Scottish Horse, afterwards attached Lovat Scouts; served in Egypt and Salonica; wounded; attached General Staff, War Office. Address: 8, Egerton Place, London, S.W. 3. Clubs: Carlton; Caledonian; Royal Northern (Aberdeen); University (Edinburgh). (M5671)

THOMSON, Major George Henry, O.B.E., R.A.F.

THOMSON, Lieut.-Comm. George Pirie, O.B.E., R.N.

THOMSON, George Rutherford, O.B.E.

THOMSON, Gwyneth Marjory, Mrs., O.B.E., M.A., Oxon., b. 27 Oct 1889; d. of the late Canon Ll. J. M. Bebb, D.D., Principal of St. David's Coll., Lampeter, S. Wales; m. Thomas

Weldon, *s.* of the late Capt. William Thomson, Seaforth Highlanders, of Cloon Eavin, Co. Down, Ireland. *Educ.:* St. Mary's Coll.; Lancaster Gate, and St. Hugh's Coll., Oxford, Honours School of Jurisprudence, Oxford, Class I., June 1911. Sept. 1911 to March, 1917, Investigating Officer, Board of Trade. *War Work:* March, 1917, to Aug. 1917, Commissioner, West Midland Division, National Service for Women ; Aug. 1917, to Aug. 1920, Assistant Commissioner for Enforcement, Ministry of Food, Midland Division. *Address:* Sherford House, Tewkes-Glos. *Club:* University. (O11468)

THOMSON, James, M.B.E.

THOMSON, James Miln, M.B.E., F.I.C., *b.* 15 Feb. 1859 ; *s.* of John Thomson, of Glasgow ; *m.* Barbara Smith, *d.* of Dugald Campbell McLean, of Cam. *Educ.:* Commercial Road Academy and City Analysts Laboratory. Chemist; Manager, Royal Gunpowder Factory, Waltham Abbey. *War Work:* Improvements in explosives greatly used in production ; safety arrangements for factory and workers against aircraft attack. *Address:* Officers' Quarters, Waltham Abbey. (M2541)

THOMSON, Capt. James Oliver, O.B.E.

THOMSON, James Park, C.B.E. (C3204)

THOMSON, Capt. James Robert Karran, O.B.E., M.R.C.S., L.R.C.P., *b.* 13 May, 1890 ; *s.* of Dr. Thomson, of Penrith ; *m.* Laura Frances Mary, *d.* of Lawrence Smith, of Hurstpierpoint. *Educ.:* King William's Coll., Isle of Man, and London Hospital. Medical Practitioner. *War Work:* With R.A.M.C. in Malta, Egypt, Palestine, Syria, etc. *Address:* Bishopyards, Penrith. (O6305)

THOMSON, Lieut.-Col. Sir James Wishart, K.B.E., *b.* 30 July, 1870 ; *s.* of James Wishart Thomson, of Glenpark, Balerm, N.B. ; *m.* Winifred Montgomerie Bell, *d.* of M. Montgomerie Bell. *War Work:* Served in Egypt, 1915–16 ; D.A.Q.M.G., Mesopotamia, 1916–17 ; A.G.M.G., Army H.Q., India, 1917 ; Shipping Controller in India, 1917–18. *Clubs:* Caledonian ; University (Edinburgh). (K249)

THOMSON, John, M.B.E.

THOMSON, John, O.B.E., B.Sc., *b.* 23 Nov. 1881 ; *s.* of David Thomson, of Aberdeen ; *m.* Margaret, *d.* of Alexander Dunlop, of Belfast. *Educ.:* Glasgow Univ. Works Manager to Sir Wm. Arrol & Co., Ltd., Glasgow. *War Work:* Had charge of the manufacture of the steelwork for all the factories and other buildings manufactured by Messrs. Arrol during the war. *Address:* 16, Abbotsford Avenue, Rutherglen, nr. Glasgow. (O1924)

THOMSON, Capt. John James, O.B.E., Can. A.M.C.

THOMSON, Lieut. John Patrick, O.B.E.

THOMSON, Major Kenneth John, M.B.E.

THOMSON, Margaret Edith, Mrs., O.B.E., *b.* 11 Jan. 1868 ; *d.* of Joseph Roseden Stead, of Canterbury ; *m.* Major-Gen. Henry Thomson, C.B. ; *s.* of the late James Thomson, R.A. (ret). *Educ.:* Privately. *War Work:* V.A.D. Commandant, Highland Divisional Clearing Hospital, Bedford, Aug. 1914, to March, 1915 ; V.A.D. Commandant and Acting Matron, Divisional Hospital, Ampthill Road, Bedford, 1915–17 ; Commandant, V.A.D. Hospital, Ampthill Road, Bedford, 1917–19. *Address:* Essilmont, Bedford. *Clubs:* Ladies' Army and Navy ; The V.A.D. Ladies. (O806)

THOMSON, Margaret Eleanor, M.B.E.

THOMSON, Lady Margaret Ellen, M.B.E., M.A., *b.* 19 May, 1867 ; *d.* of C. F. Todhunter, of Christ Church, New Zealand ; *m.* James, *s.* of John Thomson, of Aberdeen. *Educ.:* England and New Zealand. *War Work:* Vice-President, B.R.C.S. ; Assist.-Commandant Bricket House V.A.D. Hospital, St. Albans, 1914–19 ; visitor from New Zealand Red Cross to Napsbury Hospital, 1915–19. *Addresses:* Torrington House, St. Albans. *Club:* New Victorian, Sackville Street. (M4027)

THOMSON, Marion Annie, M.B.E., *b.* 1884 ; *d.* of Laurence Thomson, of Glasgow. *War Work:* 1916–18, Women's Legion motor driver, working for R.F.C. ; 1918–19, Officer in Women's Royal Air Force. (M3458)

THOMSON, Patricia Clay, M.B.E.

THOMSON, Peter Allan, O.B.E., *b.* 22 Jan. 1866 ; *s.* of Peter Thomson. *Educ.:* Alloway School ; Ayr Academy ; Glasgow Univ. Town Clerk of Ayr. *War Work:* Hon. Sec. Ayr Town Savings Committee ; Clerk to the Local Tribunal ; Organised Recruiting Meetings in Ayr ; Hon. Sec. War Memorial Committee. *Address:* 17, Park Circus, Ayr. *Club:* Scottish Conservative (Edinburgh). (O11469)

THOMSON, Robert Cunie, M.B.E.

THOMSON, Brevet-Col. Samuel John, C.I.E., C.B.E., J.P. (Kent), *b.* 17 Jan. 1853 ; *s.* of John Buck Thomson, of Ramsgate, Kent ; *m.* Isabel Gordon, *d.* of Surgeon-Gen. A. Cowie, of Indian Medical Service, London. *Educ.:* St. John's Coll., Hurstpierpoint, and St. Mary's Hospital, London. Indian Medical Service (retired) ; Medical Superintendent, Ministry of Pensions Hospital, Hollymoor, Birmingham. *War Work:* Member Lord Lieutenant of Kent's Emergency Committee for National Purposes, Oct. 1914 ; Administrator, No. 2 Birmingham War Hospital, May, 1915 ; Administrator, Special Military Surgical Hospital, Birmingham, Jan. 1918 up to March, 1920, and also Senior Medical Officer of Birmingham Area. *Address:* South Bank, Tankerton, Whitstable, Kent. *Club:* East Kent (Canterbury). (C2180)

THOMSON, Thomas Craston, O.B.E.

THOMSON, Col. William Gordon, C.B.E., Knight of Grace of the Hospital of St. John of Jerusalem, V.D., D.L., J.P., *b.* 5 March, 1858 ; *s.* of James Thomson, Engineer, of Dundee ; *m.* Isabella Jane, *d.* of Alexander Craik, of Forfar.

Educ.: Dundee Institution, Tay Square, Dundee, and Edinburgh Univ. Retired Engineer, and Jute Spinner and Manufacturer ; Military Member Dundee Territorial Association ; Member of Council Scottish Episcopal Church ; Member Vestry St. Paul's Episcopal Church, Dundee ; on Board of Dundee Industrial Schools and Eye Institution. *War Work:* Red Cross Commissioner for Central Eastern District of Scotland ; Officer in Charge of Auxiliary Hospitals Central Eastern District of Scotland ; Member Territorial Force Association ; County Director Dundee V.A.D. ; Member War Executive Committee, Scottish Branch, British Red Cross Society ; Hon. Sec. City of Dundee Branch Red Cross Society ; Chairman St. Andrew's Ambulance Association ; on Committee of Orthopædic Annexe (local). *Address:* Taychreggan, Broughty Ferry, Dundee. *Club:* Eastern (Dundee). (C1046)

THOMSON, Major William Grant, O.B.E.,

THOMSON, Major William Raymond, O.B.E.., A.P.C.

THOMSON, William Thomas, O.B.E.

THOMSON, Sir William MITCHELL-, K.B.E., M.P., *b.* 1877 ; *s.* of the late Sir Mitchell Mitchell-Thomson, 1st Bart. of Polmood (*see* BURKE'S *Peerage*) ; *m.* Anne Madeline, *d.* of the late Hon. Sir Malcolm D. McEacharn, of Melbourne. *Educ.:* Winchester, and Balliol. Formerly in West Indian business ; M.P. North-West Lanarkshire, 1906 to 1910, for North Down, 1910–18, and for Maryhill Division of Glasgow, since 1918. *War Work:* Lieut., R.N.V.R., 1914 ; Director Restriction of Enemy Supplies Dept., 1916–19 ; British Representative Supreme Economic Council in Paris, 1919 ; Parliamentary Sec. to Ministry of Food, 1920 ; Legion of Honour, and Order of Crown of Italy. *Address:* House of Commons. *Club:* Carlton. (K176)

THOMSON, Sir William ROWAN-, K.B.E., Wh.Sc. (*see* BURKE'S *Peerage*), *b.* 22 April, 1867 ; *s.* of John Thomson, of Glasgow ; *m.* Janet, *d.* of David Rowan, of Glasgow. *Educ.:* Glasgow Academy ; Glasgow Univ. ; Royal Technical Coll., Glasgow. Engineer ; late Senior Partner of David Rowan & Co., Marine Engineers and Boilermakers, Glasgow. *War Work:* Chairman, Glasgow and West of Scotland Munitions Management Committee ; Member of Merchant Shipbuilding Advisory Committee ; Director of Machinery for Auxiliary Ships, Admiralty. *Address:* The Gart, Callander, Perthshire. *Club:* New (Glasgow). (K112)

THOMSON, Brevet-Major Henry Charles Stephens STUART-, O.B.E., A.C.A., *b.* 31 Jan. 1891 ; *s.* of John Thomson, of Edinburgh. *Educ.:* Privately. Associate Chartered Accountant. *War Work:* Aug. 1914 to Sept. 1915, on Active Service, France, with London Scottish ; twice wounded ; transferred R.A.S.C., Sept. 1915 ; received Croix de Guerre avec Palme ; Oct. 1917, Staff Capt. Q.M.G.C. War Office ; June, 1918, Deputy Assistant Director of Supplies ; Q.M.G.C., War Office, in charge Foodstuffs, Shipping and Supply of Forage and Fuel to all Forces ; demobilised 1 Jan. 1920. *Address:* c/o Messrs. Graham, 400, Cathedral Street, Glasgow. *Clubs:* New (Calcutta) ; Royal Automobile. (O7773)

THOMSON, Col. Sir Hugh Davie WHITE-, K.B.E., C.B., C.M.G., D.S.O., *b.* 6 Sept. 1866 ; *s.* of Col. Sir R. T. White-Thomson, K.C.B., of Broomford, Devon ; *m.* Ela Louisa Agatha (who died 1895), *d.* of Rev. J. S. Ruddach. *Educ.:* Eton. Royal Artillery. South Africa, 1899–1900 ; wounded, mentioned in despatches ; D.S.O. *War Work:* France, 1914–16 ; Macedonia, 1916–18 ; wounded, mentioned in despatches. *Address:* 39, Hans Place, S.W. 1. *Club:* Naval and Military.

THORBURN, Dieudonnee Grace, Mrs., M.B.E.

THORBURN, Henrietta Sybil Douglas, Mrs. M.B.E., *b.* 10 July, 1896 ; *d.* of Lieut.-Col. Henry Philip Picot, C.B.E., of 33, Onslow Gardens, London, S.W. 7 ; *m.* Major Stephen Keith, *s.* of Septimus Thorburn, of Old Bracknell House, Bracknell, Berks. *War Work:* In charge of the Packing Department of the British Section of the Berne Bread Bureau aux Prisonniers de Guerre, 1915–16 (affiliated to the Central Prisoners of War Committee, London) ; Hon. Sec. to British Red Cross Organisation in Switzerland, 1916–18 ; Hon. Sec. to the British Interned Branch of the British Red Cross Organisation in Switzerland, 1916–18. (M2287)

THORBURN, Margaret Alison, M.B.E. W.R.N.S.

THORBURN, Major William, O.B.E., T.D., K.O.S.B.

THORBURN, Sir William, K.B.E., C.B., C.M.G., *b.* 7 April, 1861 ; *s.* of John Thorburn, M.D., of Manchester ; *m.* Augusta, *d.* of William Edward Melland, of Middleton, Derbyshire. *Educ.:* Owens Coll., Manchester, etc. Surgeon ; Prof. of Clinical Surgery, Univ. of Manchester ; Senior Hon. Surgeon, Manchester Royal Infirmary. *War Work:* Consulting Surgeon, Malta, Salonica, France. *Address:* Newbury, Victoria Park, Manchester. *Clubs:* Athenæum ; Oriental ; Union (Manchester). (K322a)

THORLEY, William Frederick, M.B.E.

THORMAN, William Henry, M.B.E., M.R.C.S., L.R.C.P.

THORNBERY, Capt. Stanley Russell, M.B.E., R.A.S.C. (T.), *b.* 14 April, 1883 ; *s.* of J. Russell Thornbery, of Glennyolden, Seaford, Sussex. *Educ.:* Forest Hill House School. *War Work:* Served in R.A.S.C. (T.F.) from 30 Oct. 1914, to 24 Feb. 1920 ; Adjutant to 59th N. Mid. Div. Train, 13 May, 1915, to 15 Nov. 1917 ; Adjutant to 67th Home Counties Div. Train, 4 Jan. 1918, to July, 1919. *Address:* Glennyolden, Seaford, Sussex. *Clubs:* Junior Army and Navy ; United R.A.S.C.

THORNE, Anna Elizabeth, Mrs. C.B.E. Has been Mayoress of Cape Town. (C3214)

THORNE, Annie Marion, M.B.E.

THORNE, Berthold Bezly Thorne, O.B.E.. M.D., B.S., *b.* 4 April, 1867 ; *s.* of the late Sir Richard Thorne Thorne, K.C.B., F.R.S. ; *m.* Ruth Golding. *War Work :* Medical Officer of the Military Hospital, Woking, 1916–19. (O4397)

THORNE, Capt. Frederick John, M.B.E., M.B., R.A.M.C.

THORNE, May, O.B.E., F.R.C.S.1., M.D., *b.* 1861 ; *d.* of Joseph and Isabel Thorne, of Shanghai and Southover Grange, Lewes, Sussex. *Educ.:* Miss Phœbe Blyth's School, Edinburgh ; London (Royal Free Hospital) School of Medicine for Women. Surgeon (retired). *War Work :* Attached to R.A.M.C., 1916–19 ; in charge of the following : Hospital for Military Sisters, Floriana, Malta ; Staffs and Departments, Valetta, Malta ; Military Families' Hospital, Valetta, Malta, 1916–18 ; in charge Hospital for Queen Alexandra's Imperial Military Nursing Service, Vincent Square, Westminster, S.W. 1918–19. *Address :* 148, Harley Street, London, W. 1. (O1955)

THORNE, Theophilus, M.B.E.

THORNE, Capt. William Crockett, O.B.E., R.E. (T.)

THORNELY, Daisy, Mrs., O.B.E.

THORNELY, Major John Edmund Burnet, O.B.E., R.A.F.

THORNELY, Margaret Emily, Mrs., O.B.E., *b.* 29 March, 1875 ; *d.* of the late Robert Hill, of Leamington ; *m.* Thomas Heath. *Educ.:* Girl's High School, Leamington. *War Work :* Commandant of Devizes Red Cross Hospital, Jan. 1915. to Oct. 1917 ; the hospital was originally opened for the first contingent of Canadian troops on Salisbury Plain ; afterwards used for British troops ; staffed by Wilts V.A.D.s 1 and 2. (O808)

THORNETON, Arthur Joseph, M.B.E.

THORNHILL, Beatrice Mary Compton, M.B.E.

THORNHILL, Florence A., Mrs., O.B.E., *b.* 1 Nov. 1869 ; *d.* of the Rev. F. Walsham, of Kenill Court, Hereford ; *m.* John Cecil, *s.* of the Rev. W. Thornhill, of Diddington, Hunts. *Educ.:* High School, Newcastle-on-Tyne. Chairman, Drogheda War Pensions Committee ; Vice-President Co. Louth War Pensions Committee ; Member of Advisory Council, Dublin ; Treasurer, Drogheda N.S.P.C.C., etc. *War Work :* Sec. Soldiers' and Sailors' Families Association ; Sec. War Pensions Committee ; Red Cross Work, etc. *Club :* Alexandra. (O11471)

THORNHILL, John Samuel Alphonso McCoan, M.B.E., *b.* 4 May, 1858 ; *s.* of John Thornhill, of Kent ; *m.* Hardy Jane, *d.* of S. Hunt, of Hants. *Educ.:* Duke of York's Military School. Chief Superintendent of Map Printing, Ordnance Survey. *War Work :* Superintended the compilation, printing, etc. (under Col. Sir Charles Close, K.B.E.) of most of the confidential maps and other secret and descriptive documents issued by the Admiralty, War Office, and other Government Departments, to all branches of the public service on all Fronts, and to the Allied Nations and Staffs. (M1015)

THORNLEY, Hubert Gordon, O.B.E., *b.* 16 Jan. 1884 ; *s.* of Robert Thornley, of The Brooklands, Broomsgrove. *Educ.:* Malvern Coll. ; St. Paul's, West Kensington. Clerk of the Peace and of the County Council of the North Riding of Yorkshire ; Registrar of the North Riding Registry of Deeds ; Clerk to the Lieutenancy for the North Riding. *War Work :* Hon. Sec. of the National Service Volunteer Committee and of the Local War Pensions Committee for the North Riding and Clerk of the Appeal Tribunal under the Military Service Acts. *Address :* The Register House, Northallerton. (O11472)

THORNLEY, Reginald Ernest, C.B.E. Senior Establishment Officer, Ministry of Food. (C2996)

THORNLEY, Thomas, O.B.E., *b.* 13 March, 1873 ; *s.* of John Hy. Thornley, of Thornham ; *m.* Anne, *d.* of Gilbert McIntosh, of Falkirk. *Educ.:* England and Scotland. *War Work :* Member of Lord Moulton's Committee, High Explosives (Acid Section) ; Advisory Committee on Food Production, Fertiliser's Section. *Address :* Garthill, Falkirk, Stirlingshire. *Club :* Scottish Constitutional (Glasgow). (O11473)

THORNS, Major Leslie, O.B.E., M.C.

THORNTON, Lieut.-Col. Basil Albert, O.B.E.

THORNTON, Major Charles Edward, O.B.E., *b.* 7 Nov. 1879 ; *s.* of the late Capt. E. B. Thornton ; *m.* Mary Caroline, *d.* of Lt.-Col. H. Thornton, of St. John's, Muggerhanger, Beds. *War Work :* Adjutant, 3rd (Reserve) Batt. Northumberland Fusiliers. *Address :* Sissinghurst, Cranbrook, Kent. *Club :* United Service. (O8955)

THORNTON, Paymaster-Lieut.-Comm. Cyril Joseph, O.B.E., R.N.

THORNTON, Lieut. Doris Cyril, M.B.E., R.E.

THORNTON, Lieut.-Col. Sir Edward Newbury, K.B.E., M.R.C.S.(Eng.),L.R.C.P. (Lond.) D.P.H. (Camb.), J.P.,S.A.M.C. *b.* 10 June, 1878 ; *s.* of Thomas Thornton, of Woolferton, Sporle, Norfolk ; *m.* Maud Annie, *d.* of Lieut.-Col. W. F. Gregory, of Cape Town. *Educ.:* Cheltenham Coll., and London Hospital. Lieut.-Col. S. African Medical Corps and O.C. No. 2 General Hospital for German S.W. African campaign, 1915, and O.C. No. Co., S.A.M.C. ; O.C. S. African Military Hospital and S.A.M.C. Depot, Richmond, Surrey, 1916–20 ; Member of Committee of Management of, and Surgeon to, Queen Mary's Auxiliary Convalescent Hospital for limbless soldiers, Roehampton ; Member of Committee of Management of Queen Mary's Auxiliary Convalescent Hospital for facial injuries, Sidcup ; Member of General Committee, and Chairman of Executive Committee, on Vocational Training of soldiers in the Military Hospitals of the Londo District ; represented S. Africa at the Inter-Allied Conference held in London in 1918 on disablement problems arising out of the war. *Address :* Cartsburn, Waterkloof, Pretoria, S. Africa. *Clubs :* Pretoria and Pretoria Country. (K322c)

THORNTON, Major George James Tharton, O.B.E.

THORNTON, Major-Gen. Sir Henry Worth, K.B.E., *b.* 6 Nov. 1871 ; *s.* of Henry C. Thornton, of Newtown, Penn, U.S.A. ; *m.* Virginia Dike Blair, *d.* of George D. Blair, of New Castle, Pennsylvania, U.S.A. *Educ.:* St. Paul's School, Concord, New Hampshire, U.S.A. ; Univ. of Pennsylvania, Philadelphia, Penn. U.S.A. General Manager, Great Eastern Railway since 1914. *War Work :* July 1916, Commissioned as Lieut.-Col. in Engineer & Rly. Staff Corps ; March 1917, appointed Deputy Director of Inland Waterways and Docks, War Office ; May 1917, Assistant Director-General of Movement and Rlys., War Office, with temp. rank of Col. ; 1918, Deputy Director-General of Movements and Rlys. with temp. rank of Brig.-Gen. ; 1919, Inspector-General of Transportation with temp. rank of Major-Gen. since Jan. 1919 ; March 1919, Awarded Cross of Officer of the Order of Leopold ; May, 1919, American Distinguished Service medal ; 1920, French Legion of Honour. *Address :* Great Eastern Hotel, Liverpool Street, E.C. *Clubs :* Junior Athenæum ; Royal Automobile ; Queen's Mid-Surrey Golf ; Bishop Stortford Golf ; Lotos (New York); Travellers' (Paris).

THORNTON, Major Robert Lawrence, C.B.E., J.P. D.L., M.A., *b.* 17 Sept, 1865 ; *s.* of Robert Thornton, J.P., D.L., of High Cross, Framfield, Sussex, and Thornton-in-Lonsdale, Yorks. ; *m.* Charlotte, *d.* of Rev. Wm. Raynes, of Cambridge. *Educ.:* Eton ; Trinity Coll., Cantab. Chairman, Brighton, Hove, Mid-Sussex Employment Committee, under the Ministry of Labour ; Chairman, East Sussex Standing Joint Committee ; Alderman, East Sussex County Council (Chairman, 1913–16): High Sheriff of Sussex, 1900 ; Deputy Chairman, E. Sussex Quarter Sessions, 1919 ; Chairman, Diocesan Finance Board. *War Work :* Chairman of Appeal Tribunal for East Sussex, Brighton, Hastings, and Eastbourne ; Vice-Chairman, Sussex Emergency Committee ; Chairman, Area Road Transport Committee ; Treas., East Sussex Branch National Relief Fund, also of Belgian Relief Committee ; Member of the County Committee for co-ordinating the war work, etc. *Address :* High Cross, Framfield, Sussex. (C2997)

THORNTON, William, O.B.E.

THORNTON, William Mundell, O.B.E.

THORNTON, Lieut. William Thomas, M.B.E.

THORNYCROFT, Lieut.-Col. Charles Mytton, C.B.E., D.S.O., *b.* 6 Aug. 1879 ; *s.* of Charles Edward Thornycroft, of Highfield, Exmouth (late of Thornycroft Hall, Chelford, Cheshire) ; *m.* Vida Maude, *d.* of G. W. Deakin, of Blowith, Grange-over-Sands. *Educ.:* Eton and Sandhurst. Regular Army, the Manchester Regt.. 1899–1911 ; retired as Captain ; joined Spec. Res. 1911. *War Work :* Rejoined Spec. Res., 3rd Manchester Regt., Aug. 1914 ; France, Dec. 1914, to Sept. 1915 ; Adjutant, 3rd Batt. Manchester Regt., Nov. 1915, to Feb. 1917 ; France, March, 1917, to Aug. 1917 ; Commanding 2/9th Batt. Manchester Regt., Aug. 1917 ; now Commanding 3rd Batt. Manchester Regt. *Address :* Wyecliff House, Breinton, Hereford. (C1788)

THORNYCROFT, Sir John Edward, K.B.E., J.P., *b.* 5 Sept. 1872 ; *s.* of Sir John Isaac Thornycroft, F.R.S., of Bembridge ; *m.* Isabel, *d.* of Albert Bird Ward, of Chiswick. *Educ.:* St. Paul's School. Managing Director of Messrs. John T. Thornycroft & Co. Ltd. *War Work :* Building torpedoboat destroyers, submarines, and coastal motor boats. *Addresses :* 27, Grosvenor Road, Westminster ; Steyne Wood Battery, Bembridge, Isle of Wight. *Clubs :* St. Stephen's ; Ranelagh ; Royal Automobile. (K177)

THORNYCROFT, Lieut. Oliver, O.B.E., R.N.V.R.

THOROGOOD, Capt. Percival Walter, O.B.E., *b.* 10 Sept. 1889 ; *s.* of the late Henry John Thorogood, of Kingston-upon-Thames ; *m.* Dorothy Jeannette. *Educ.:* Tiffins Boys' School, Kingston-on-Thames, and King's Coll., London. Permanent Civil Servant, H.M. Paymaster-General's Dept., Whitehall, S.W. *War Service :* Intelligence Officer, 2/15th Batt., London R. ; Vimy Ridge, France, 1916 ; Company Commander, Salonica and Palestine, 1917 ; appointed to regular commission in the Indian Army ; served (1918) as Company Commander and Adjutant to the 10th Jats on the N.W. Frontier, India, and on the Tigris in Mesopotamia (twice mentioned in despatches). *Address :* Paymaster-General's Office, Whitehall, S.W.1. (O6544)

THOROLD, Rev. Ernest Hayford, O.B.E.

THOROLD, Col. Hayford Douglas, C.B.E., West Riding Regt., *b.* 20 July, 1861 ; *s.* of Maj.-Gen. Reginald Gother Thorold, R.E., of Leamington (*see* BURKE'S *Peerage,* Thorold, Bart.) ; *m.* Mary, *d.* of the late Alexander R. Kirkpatrick, of Donocomper co. Kildare. Served in Great War as Col. Assist. to a Brig.-Gen. in charge of Administration. (C1789)

THORP, Rear-Adm. Charles Frederick, C.B.E., R.N. ; *s.* of the Rev. Frederic Thorp, formerly Rector of Burton Overy ; *m.* 1910, Anne Ethel, *d.* of George Handford. Served in Great War, 1914–19, Comdg. E. Coast Guard Dist. (C2300)

THORP, Capt. Eustace, O.B.E., R.A.M.C.

THORP, Major Gerald, O.B.E., R.E.

THORP, Lieut. Harold John, M.B.E., R.E.

THORP, Lieut.-Col. John Claude, D.S.O., O.B.E., *b.* 1883. Lieut.-Col. Army Ordnance Reserve ; served in Great War, 1914–19 (mentioned in despatches). (O5856)

THORPE, Major and Qr.-Mr. Alfred, M.B.E., *b.* 17 Sept. 1860 ; *s.* of Alfred Thomas Thorpe, of Huntingdon ; *m.* Margaret Sydney, *d.* of Richard Pocock, of Shaldon. *Educ.:* Various Schools. Quartermaster. Bedfordshire Regiment. *War Work :* Quartermaster, 3rd (Special Reserve) B.

Bedfordshire Regiment. *Address:* 85, Goldington Avenue, Bedford.   (M6713)

THORPE, Alfred Charles, O.B.E.

THORPE, Arthur Winton, O.B.E., *b.* 19 Feb. 1865; *s.* of the late Thomas Miller Thorpe, of Winchester: *m.* Alice, *d.* of the late Benjamin Wheeler, of Northampton (*see* BURKE'S *Peerage*, Wheeler, Bart.). Managing Director, the Burke Publishing Co. Ltd. *War Work:* Director of Publicity, Ministry of Food, 1917–18; Headquarters Central Detachment of Metropolitan Special Constabulary, 1915–19. *Addresses:* Swangrove, Chalfont-St. Peter, Bucks; 22, Suffolk Street, S.W. 1. *Clubs:* Junior Carlton; Junior Constitutional; Savage.   (O1926)

THORPE, Hannah Maude Taylor, M.B.E.; *d.* of John Thorpe, of Nottingham. *Educ.:* Nottingham Girls' High School. *War Work:* Commandant of Notts 42 V.A.D.; Hon. Sec. Military Hospital Comforts Committee. *Address:* Brantwood, Barrack Lane, Nottingham. *Club:* V.A.D. (M1017)

THORPE, Helen Mary, M.B.E., *b.* 1884; *d.* of James Thorpe, of Coddington Hall, Notts, an dArdbrecknish, Argyllshire. *Educ.:* Privately. Divisional Sec. City of Westminster Division British Red Cross Society from Jan. 1920. *War Work:* 1914–15, General Red Cross Work; 1915–20, General Service Dept., County of London V.A.D., Headquarters. *Address:* 21, Eccleston Square, S.W. 1. *Club:* V.A.D. Ladies'.   (M9854)

THORPE, Hugh, M.B.E.

THORPE, Professor Jocelyn Field, C.B.E., F.R.S., Ph.D., D.Sc., *b.* 1872; *s.* of the late William George Thorpe, F.S.A.; *m.* Lilian, *d.* of William Briggs, J.P., of Heaton Mersey, Lancashire. *Educ.:* King's Coll., London: Heidelberg Univ. Is an Organic Chemist; a Member of Advisory Council, Depart. of Scientific and Industrial Research; an Associate Member of Ordnance Committee; appointed Professor of Organic Chemistry, Imperial Coll. of Science and Technology, 1914. *Address:* 34, De Vere Gardens, Kensington, W.8. *Club:* Constitutional.   (C70)

THORPE, Capt. John Henry, O.B.E., M.P., *b.* 1887; *s.* of Canon J. H. Thorpe, B.D., R.D., of Stockport. *Educ.:* Leatherhead, and Trinity Coll., Oxford. Barrister-at-Law; Member of Parliament; Member of the Bar Council. *War Work:* 1914, Egyptian Expeditionary Force; 1915, Intelligence Halfa; 1916–17, Appeal Court Reprs. Staffordshire (Military Service Act); 1917–18, Court Martial Officer Canadian Corps, France; 1919, Legal Adviser, Military Gov., Cologne. *Address:* 6, Crown Office Row, Temple, E.C. 4. *Clubs:* Carlton; Constitutional.   (O5857)

THORPE, Stanley William, M.B.E., *b.* 28 Aug. 1884; *s.* of Capt. W. H. Thorpe, of St. Albans; *m.* Beatrice Maud. *Educ.:* Claremont House Coll., St. Albans. Fire Inspector, Chief Officer Kodak Fire Brigade; District Sec. South Midland District, National Fire Brigade Association; Member British Fire Prevention Committee; Member French and Italian Fire Service Federations; Member, Junior Institution of Engineers. *War Work:* Cross Channel messenger, British Red Cross Society, 1914–15; The Brigade under his command saw service with the London Fire Brigade during air raids actually coming into London on 54 occasions, during which period very valuable assistance was rendered in extinguishing large fires caused by bombs dropped from enemy aircraft; this work was done entirely voluntarily and at considerable personal risk to all concerned. *Addresses:* Kodak Fire Station, Wealdstone; Merton, Hide Road, Harrow.   (M9856)

THORPE, Surg.-Capt. Vidal Gunson, C.B.E., L.S.A., M.R.C.S., R.N., *b.* 1864; *s.* of the late Rev. R. O. T. Thorpe, R. of Anstey, Herts; *m.* 1897, Maude, *d.* of the late Fleet-Paymaster C. R. Rodham, R.N. *Educ.:* Merchant Taylors' School; King's Coll. Hospital, London.   (C917)

THORPE, Capt. Walter Benjamin, M.B.E., *b.* 1 Feb. 1877. Regular soldier, Royal Army Service Corps. *Address:* 1, Melbourne Street, Fishergate, York.   (M1018)

THOY, Herbert Dominick, M.B.E.

THRALE, Capt. Peter Ralph Alwen, O.B.E., R.A.V.C. (T.)

THRELFALL, Sir Richard, K.B.E., F.R.S., M.A. (*see* BURKE'S *Peerage*), *b.* 14 Aug. 1861; *s.* of Richard Threlfall, of Hollowforth, Lancs; *m.* Evelyn Agnes, *d.* of John Forster Baird, of Bowmont Hill, Northumberland. *Educ.:* Clifton; Gonville and Caius Coll., Cambs; Univ. of Strassburg. Consulting Engineer. *War Work:* Member of Board of Invention and Research, Munitions Invention Board, Chemical Warfare Committee. *Address:* Oakhurst, Church Road, Edgbaston. *Clubs:* Athenæum; United University; Savile.   (K40)

THRELFORD, Paymaster-Lieut.-Com. William Lacon, M.B.E., R.D., F.C.A.; *s.* of Thomas Threlford, of London. *Educ.:* London, Boulogne, and Strassburg. Fellow of the Institute of Chartered Accountants; Senior partner in W. Lacon Threlford & Co., chartered accountants, 120, London Wall, E.C. 2. *War Work:* Served in Grand Fleet and in Belgian Coast Operations; Sec. to Rear Admiral A. E. A. Grant, Sec. to various Admiralty Committees; Superintending Accountant Admiralty Costing and Investigation Department. *Address:* 120, London Wall, E.C. 2. *Club:* Royal Automobile. (M9857)

THRING, Capt. Frank John, C.B.E., *b.* 1857; *s.* of Gen. J. E. Thring, R.A. Capt. R.N. (ret.).   (C2265)

THRING, Capt. Walter Hugh Charles Samuel, C.B.E. Capt. Royal Australian Navy; as Director Navy War Staff during Great War.   (C3205)

THUBRON, Kate, Mrs., M.B.E.

THUILLIER, Capt. and Qr.-Mr. Ernest, M.B.E., R.E.

THUILLIER, Brig.-Gen. Willoughby, C.B.E. Col. and Hon. Brig.-Gen. (ret.); N.-W. Frontier of India, 1897–98 (medal with clasps); served in Great War, 1914–19 (mentioned in despatches).   (C1790)

THUNDEN, Irene Mary, M.B.E.

THURBURN, Bertha, O.B.E., *b.* 21 June, 1873; *d.* of H. H. Loveday, of Derby; *m.* Robert Augustus, *s.* of Capt. J. P. Thurburn, R.N., of Upper Norwood, S.E. *War Work:* Red Cross work and in charge of the Argentine section of the Anglo-South American Depot, established for the care of volunteers from South America. *Address:* 77, Sussex Gardens, Hyde Park, London. W. 2   (O11475)

THURGOOD, Harry Voce, O.B.E., F.C.A., *b.* 22 Oct. 1861; *s.* of William Henry Thurgood, of Putney; *m.* Helen Zoe, *d.* of William Rueben Rayner, of Putney. *Educ.:* Carshalton House, and King's Coll. School. Deputy Hon. Treas. Princess Mary Village Homes for little girls; Hon. Auditor, Training Ship "Stork;" Joint Hon. Auditor, South Wales Nursing Association; Hon. Auditor, Coll. of Teachers of the Blind. *War Work:* Member of Board of Audit Control; Hon. Auditor of Soldiers' and Sailors' Families Association. *Addresses:* The Oaks, Leatherhead; 11 Queen Victoria Street. E.C.   (O1927)

THURLOW, Edith Marian, M.B.E.

THURSTAN, Lieut. Alan Dorrington, M.B.E., R.E.

THURSTON, Capt. Albert Peter, M.B.E., R.A.F.

THURSTON, Hugh Kingsmill Neville, M.B.E.

THURSTON, Col. Hugh Stanley, C.B., C.M.G., C.B.E., *b.* 1869; *s.* of Hugh Kingsmill Thurston, of Marton, Thornbury, Gloucestershire. Entered Army, 1892; Capt. R.A.M.C. 1895; Major, 1904; Lieut.-Col. 1915; Col. Army Medical Service, 1917; served on the N.W. Frontier of India, 1897–98 (medal with clasp); in the S. African War, 1901–2 (despatches, Queen's medal with three clasps); Great War, 1914–19 (despatches). *Club:* Army & Navy.   (C1325)

THURSTON, Mabel, C.B.E., R.R.C. Matron-in-Chief, New Zealand Army Nursing Staff, during Great War, 1915–19 (mentioned in despatches).   (C1875)

THURSTON, Sir Thomas George Owens, K.B.E., M.I.C.E., M.I.N.A., M.R.S.A., F.N.B.A.; *b.* 1869. Shipbuilding Director and Chief Constructor of Vickers, Ltd.; Managing Director of the Forth Shipbuilding and Engineering Co., Ltd.; and director of many other companies; has been responsible for the design and construction of all classes of war vessels. *Address:* Greenford Hall, Greenford, Middlesex. *Clubs:* Junior Constitutional; Royal Automobile.   (K434)

THWAITES, Joseph Samuel, M.B.E.

THWAITES, Lieut.-Col. Norman Graham, C.B.E., M.V.O., M.C., *b.* 24 June, 1872; *s.* of The Rev. H. Graham Thwaites, of Burnham, Somerset; *m.* Eleanor Lucia, *d.* of Frederick W. Whitridge, of New York, U.S.A. *Educ.:* St. Lawrence Coll. Kent; Germany. Served during South African War, 1899–1901, in South African Light Horse (Queen's Medal, 4 bars); *War Work:* Appointed to 4th Dragoon Guards (Royal Irish), Sept. 1914; mentioned in despatches; wounded at Messines; awarded M.C.; appointed special Mission to U.S.A., 1916; Passport Officer, 1917; appointed A.P.M. New York, 1918; in charge of British Mission, 1919. *Address:* Cambridge Park, Redland, Bristol. *Clubs:* Constitutional, Bath; Fellow Colonial Institute; Racquet and Tennis, New York.   (C1131)

THYNE, John Sinclair, M.B.E.

THYNNE, Katharine Angela, M.B.E., *b.* 20 April, 1893; *d.* of Major General Sir Reginald Thynne, K.C.B., of 24, Park Square, N.W. 1. *Educ.:* Francis Holland Church of England School for Girls, Baker Street, W., and privately. *War Work:* 2½ years at the War Office as Clerk and private Sec., previously at Queen Mary's Needlework Guild (Surgical dressings) 2, Cavendish Square; mentioned in despatches in 1918. *Address:* 24, Park Square, Regent's Park, N.W. 1.   (M9821)

TIARKS, Lieut. Frank Cecil, O.B.E., R.N.V.R.

TIARKS, Sophie Louise, M.B.E., *b.* 10 March, 1880; *d.* of Henry Frederic Tiarks, of Foxbury Chislehurst. *War Work:* A Member of Kent Voluntary Aid Detachment 66 of the British Red Cross Society in 1911; Mobilised in Aug. 1914; worked as a Nursing Member of Kent 66 from Oct. 1914, till Aug. 1918, at Holbrook Lane, and the Gorse Hospitals, Chislehurst; appointed Commandant of Kent 66, Sept. 1918, and worked at the Gorse Hospital till April, 1919. *Address:* Foxbury, Chislehurst, Kent.   (M9862)

TIBBETS, Capt. Charles, C.B.E., M.V.O., *b.* 1872; *s.* of the late Dr. John Tibbets, of Warwick; *m.* 1909, Elsie Bethune, *d.* of Thomas Eastman, of Northwood Park, Winchester. Entered R.N. 1885; Lieut. 1893; Com. 1905; Capt. 1913.

TIBBITS, Lieut.-Comm. Edward, O.B.E., R.D., R.N.R.

TIBBITS, Olive Eleanore, Mrs., M.B.E.

TIBBS, Lieut.-Comm. Ernest Henry, M.B.E., R.A.M.C. (T.)

TICEHURST, Hugh Gorham, M.B.E., M.I.Mech.E., *b.* 12 Nov. 1871; *s.* of Francis William Ticehurst, of Birmingham; *m.* Edith Clara, *d.* of Capt. De Merrall, of Belvedere, S.E. *Educ.:* King Edward VI.'s High School, and Mason Coll., Birmingham Manager and Engineer, The Thames Ammunition Works, Erith, Kent. *War Work:* Manufacture of Fuses, Ammunition, and Bombs, and erection of plant for manufacture of high explosives, and supervising such manufacture. *Addresses:* Telham, Bexley Heath, Kent; Thames Ammunition Works, Ltd., Erith.   (M1020)

TICEHURST, Norman Frederic, O.B.E., M.A., M.B., B.C., F.R.C.S., Eng., *b.* 1 July, 1873 ; *s.* of Augustus Rowland Ticehurst, Huntbourne, High Halden, Kent ; *m.* Ivy, *d.* of Henry Cross, of Greenwich. *Educ.:* Tonbridge School ; Clare Coll., Cambridge ; Guy's Hospital. Assistant Surgeon, East Sussex Hospital, Hastings ; Medical Officer, Beau Site Convalescent Home, Hastings. *War Work :* Medical Officer in Charge Normanhurst Auxiliary Hospital, Battle, Sussex, 1915–19. *Address :* 24, Pevensey Road, St. Leonards-on-sea. *Club :* Fly-Fishers'. (O11476)

TICKELL, Major Richard Eustace, O.B.E.

TIDBURY, Lieut.-Col. (ret.) James, O.B.E., *b.* 4 July, 1852 ; *s.* of Edward Tidbury, of London ; *m.* Agnes, *d.* of Robert Henderson, of Glasgow and Leghorn ; one *s.* and one *d.* *Educ.:* Privately at Dr. Knights' School, and Univ. Coll., London. Commissioned in R.A.M.C., Feb. 1878 ; in Medical Charge, Winchester Depot, 1898–1902 ; Medical Officer to Sandhurst Royal Military Coll., 1902–9 ; in Medical Charge, 1st Battalion Gordon Highlanders at Battle of Tel-el-Kebir, Egypt, 1882 (wounded). *War Work :* Senior Medical Officer, London District, for Recruiting, June, 1915, to March, 1917 ; Commandant, Military Hospital, Woking (Inkerman Barracks), March, 1917, to Jan. 1919. *Address :* North Bend, Maybury, Woking. *Club :* Army and Navy. (O7779)

TIDMARSH, Capt. Charles Baillie, O.B.E.

TIDMARSH, Edwin Russell, O.B.E.

TIDRIDGE, Capt. John Harry, M.B.E.

TIDSWELL, Lieut.-Col. Edmund Samuel Waite, D.S.O., O.B.E., *b.* 1881 ; *s.* of the Rev. S. W. Tidswell, of Harewood Dovercourt ; *m.* 1919, Patricia, *d.* of the late Lieut.-Col. R. C. Pierce, Royal Inniskilling Fusiliers. Entered Leicestershire Regt. 1904 ; Capt. 1912 ; Brevet Major, 1917 ; served in Great War, 1914–19 (despatches) ; appointed a Gen. Staff Officer, 1918, with rank of Lieut.-Col. (C6546)

TIDSWELL, Major Samuel Waite, D.S.O., O.B.E.

TIERNEY, Francis Michael, M.B.E., *b.* 1 April, 1871 ; *s.* of William Tierney, of Nova Scotia ; *m.* Jean, *d.* of John Barron, of Lochee, Scotland. *Educ.:* Public Schools (Halifax and Dartmouth, N.S.). Repairing Atlantic Cables, and looking after the finishing up of the new Cable Ship " Lord Kelvin," finished in 1916 at Newcastle. *War Work :* Chief Engineer of Cable Ships " Minia," and then " Lord Kelvin," owned by the Anglo-American Co. and controlled by The Western Union Cable System. *Address :* Windmill Road, Dartmouth, N.S. Canada. (M9863)

TIFFEN, Doris Ada, Mrs., M.B.E., *b.* 22 Sept. 1893 ; *d.* of Thomas Brandon, of Shooters Hill ; *m.* Laurence, B.Sc. (Lond.), *s.* of Joseph Tiffen, of Brockley. *Educ.:* Woolwich High School. Hon. Sec. Woolwich Children's Care Committees ; Various social works in Woolwich ; Assist. Sec. Juvenile Advisory Committee, Ministry of Labour, Deptford and Lewisham. *War Work :* Superintendent of Women's Staff ; Admiralty Controller's Dept. and Ministry of Shipping, 1916–19. *Address :* 45, Temple Fortune Hill, London, N.W.4. *Club :* 1917. (M2545)

TILBURY, Edith Jane, M.B.E. *War Work :* In charge of Hostels and Huts for the Troops in Rouen, Havre, Dunkirk, and Calais from Jan. 1915 until March, 1920 ; at present engaged in War Graves Visitation Work. *Address :* Hotel L'Avenir, 91, Boulevard Gambetta, Calais. *Clubs :* Rue de Paris, Le Harve, France. (M9864)

TILBY. Henry Albert, O.B.E.

TILL, Lieut.-Col. Percy William WILLIAMS-, O.B.E.

TILL, Violet Beatrice, M.B.E.

TILL, Thomas Marson, O.B.E.

TILLARD, Lieut.-Col. Arthur Basil, C.B.E., D.S.O. *b.* 1870 ; *s.* of Maj.-Gen. John Arthur Tillard, C.B. *Educ.:* Dover Coll. Entered Hampshire Regt. 1890 ; Capt. Indian Army, 1901 ; Major, 1908 ; Lieut.-Col. 1916 ; served in South Lushal, 1892–93 ; operations in Samana, 1897 ; Tirah Expedition, 1897–98 (despatches twice, medal with three clasps) ; Mahsud-Waziri Blockade Expedition, 1901–2 ; Tibet Expedition, 1903–4 (medal). (C3104)

TILLARD, Major Ernest, O.B.E.

TILLARD, Ethel Hilda, Mrs., M.B.E., *b.* 12 Jan. 1886 ; *d.* of W. M. Baker, of Cheltenham ; *m.* Arthur Kenneth Dowell, *s.* of Charles Tillard, of Bathford. *Educ.:* Cheltenham Ladies' Coll. *War Work :* Quartermaster of Race Course Hospital, V.A.D. Glos. 14. *Address :* Bathford, Bath. (M9865)

TILLARD, Capt. John Arthur Stuart, O.B.E., M.C., R.E., *b.* 24 Nov. 1889 ; *s.* of Phillip Edward Tillard, of the Holme, Godmanchester, Huntingdon. *Educ.:* Rugby and Woolwich. *War Work :* Served in R.E. Signals in France and Italy, from Aug. 1914, to July, 1919 ; O.C. 23rd Divisional Signal Company from Sept. 1916, to March, 1919. *Address :* The Holme, Godmanchester, Huntingdon. *Club :* Junior Army and Navy. (O6424)

TILLERAY, Capt. William Arthur James, O.B.E., *b.* 16 Jan. 1879 ; *s.* of William Tilleray, of Dulwich, London ; *m.* Madaline, *d.* of the late Frederick H. Charles, of Westbourne Grove, W. *Educ.:* Mina Road, Secondary School, S.E. Shipping Agent. *War Work :* Commissioned April, 1915 ; served in France, May, 1915, to Oct. 1915 ; Salonica, Nov. 1915, to Sept. 1917 ; Egypt, Oct. 1917, to Nov. 1919 ; mentioned in despatches. *Addresses :* 39, Sydenham Hill, S.E. 26 ; 53, Gracechurch Street, E.C. 3. *Club :* United R.A.S.C. (O6307)

TILLETT, Amy Henrietta, M.B.E., *b.* 4 Jan. 1876. *Educ. :* London School Board. *War Work :* House Matron, The Lord

Derby War Hospital, Warrington, Lancs. *Address :* The Lord Derby War Hospital, Warrington, Lancs. (M9866)

TILLEY, Capt. Harry, M.B.E., R.A.F.

TILLEY, John William, O.B.E.

TILLYARD, Capt. Eustace Mandeville Wetenhall, O.B.E. M.A. (Cantab.), *b.* 19 May, 1889 ; *s.* of A. I. Tillyard, M.A., J.P., of Fordfield, Cambridge ; *m.* Phyllis Beatrice, *d.* of H. M. Cooke, of 3, Porchester Terrace, W. *Educ.:* Perse School, Jesus Coll., Cambridge. Late Fellow of Jesus Coll., Cambridge. *War Work :* Service with 1/4th R. Lanc. Regt. (T.F.) in France, 1915–16 ; with Intelligence Corps, and as British Liaison Officer with Greek Army H.Q. in Salonica, 1916–19 ; Greek Military Cross ; three times mentioned in despatches. *Address :* 31, New Square, Cambridge. (O657)

TILLYARD, Brevet Major Godfrey, O.B.E., R.A.V.C., *b.* 1883 ; *s.* of John Joseph Tillyard, of Norwich. *Educ.:* Bracondale School, Norwich, and privately. Member Royal Col. Veterinary Surgeons ; Commission Royal Army Veterinary Corps, Sept. 1908. *War Work :* Employed in R.A.V.C. in England, Autumn, 1914 ; in Egypt and Salonica in 1915–16 ; Command of Veterinary Hospitals (M.E.F. and Salonica Expeditionary Force) ; Assist. Director Veterinary Services (Egypt and Palestine) from 1917 until termination of war. (O2944)

TILNEY, Mary Elizabeth, M.B.E.

TILNEY, Lieut.-Col. Norman Eccles, C.B.E., D.S.O., R.A., *b.* 1872. China, 1900 (medal) ; served in Great War, 1914–19 (mentioned in despatches). (C1791)

TIMBURY, Henry Thomas, M.B.E., *b.* 10 July, 1865 ; *s.* of Frederick Timbury, of Portsmouth ; *m.* Bessie, *d.* of John Duddleston, of Portsmouth. *Educ.:* Greenwich. *War Work :* Sec. to Senior Naval Officer, and Superintendent of H.M. ships building for H.M. Navy in Clyde District. *Address :* Broomhall, Partick, Glasgow. (M4029)

TIMEWELL, Major Henry A., O.B.E.

TIMEWELL, Herbert William, O.B.E.

TIMINS, Douglas Theodore, M.B.E., M.A. (Cantab,.) F.R.C.I., F.R.B.S., *b.* 9 Nov. 1871 ; *s.* of the Rev. Douglas Cartwright Timins, of Hilfield, Aldenham, Herts ; *m.* Anna Helen Blanche, *d.* of Arthur Barkly, C.M.G., Governor of Heligoland. *Educ.:* Wimbledon ; Jesus Coll., Cambridge ; City and Guilds of London ; Central Technical Coll., South Kensington. Industrial Commissioner to the National Savings Committee, Salisbury Hotel, Fleet Street, E.C. ; Member Birmingham Municipal Council, 1914–19 (retired). *War Work :* Addressed Recruiting Meetings, Birmingham District ; Assistant in Engineering Dept., and Private Sec. to Gen. Manager, Metropolitan Munitions Committee ; Munitions Commissioner to National War Savings Committee (Ministry of Munitions Branch). *Clubs :* Junior Carlton ; Ranelagh ; Queen's ; 1900 ; Union (Birmingham). (O3959)

TIMS, Capt. Edwin George Thomas, M.B.E.

TIMS, Major Henry William Marrett, O.B.E., M.D., R.A.M.C.

TINDALL, Edith Pelham, M.B.E.,;. *d.* of the Rev. Canon Field, and his 1st wife, Eleanor, née Elwes, of Bigby Rectory, Lincs. ; *m.* Charles Miles, *s.* of William Tindall, of Wheatley, nr. Doncaster. *Educ.:* Privately, and at Ladies' Coll., Grantham. *War Work :* Commandant, Wainfleet Red Cross Hospital, Lincs. V.A.D. 50, 1914–19 ; Member of Local War Pensions Committee, and Women's War Agricultural Committee ; District Councillor for Wainfleet, 1902–20. *Address :* Park House, Louth, Lincs. *Club :* V.A.D. (M4030)

TINDALL, Louis Edward, O.B.E., *b.* 17 Oct. 1873 ; *s.* of the late George Tindall, of Newmarket. *Educ.:* Privately. Local Taxation Officer, Norfolk County Council. *War Work :* Hon. Sec. Norfolk County War Savings Committee ; Hon. Sec. Henstead Local War Pensions Committee. *Addresses :* Brunswick Road, Norwich ; The Shirehall, Norwich. (O11482)

TINDALL, Robert, M.B.E., R.A.S.C.

TINDLEY, Francis Oswald, O.B.E., *b.* 26 June, 1883 ; *s.* of Alfred Tindley, of Croydon ; *m.* Lily Marian, *d.* of John Siviour, of Croydon. *Educ.:* The Oval School, Croydon. Export Manager, The Mediterranean Company for General Trade, Ltd. *War Work :* Buyer of Supplies for the Y.M.C.A. with the Forces in all theatres of war. *Address :* The Red Gables, Whitstable, Kent. (O1929)

TINKER, Lieut. Henry William Cossart, O.B.E., R.N.V.R.

TINKLER, Capt. Frederick Usher John, O.B.E., M.C.

TINKLER, Capt. Lionel Maughan, O.B.E., M.C., *b.* 1886 ; *s.* of George Tinkler, of Liverpool. *Educ.:* Privately, and at Liverpool Coll. *War Work :* 1st King Edward's Horse, Aug. 1914 ; transferred to A.P.W.O. Yorkshire Regt., Jan. 1916 ; proceeded overseas to France, June, 1915 ; wounded, July, 1916 ; served again in France, 1917 ; served in France and Italy, 1918 ; on General Staff in South Russia, 1919–20. *Address :* 72, Devonshire Road, Liverpool. *Club :* Junior Army and Navy. (O9755)

TINN, John, M.B.E.

TINNER Lieut.-Col. Sydney Jonathan, O.B.E.

TINNISWOOD, Robert, O.B.E., *b.* 18 Dec. 1879. *Address :* 10, Woodside Lane, N. Finchley, N. 12. (O3960)

TINSLEY, Comm. Richard Bolton, C.B.E., R.N.R.

TINSON, Comm. Charles Wills, O.B.E., R.N.

TIPPING, Arthur Bramble, M.B.E.

TIPPING, Capt. Frank Walter, M.B.E., *b.* 9 March, 1884. Enlisted Oxford and Bucks. Lt. Infy., 1900 ; served South Africa, 1901–2. *War Work :* Corps School of Musketry (Staff

Sergt.), 1914 ; Sgt.-Maj., School of Musketry, Dublin, 1915 ; Commissioned, Dec. 1915 ; Assistant Instructor, School of Musketry, Strensall and Hythe, 1915–19. *Address* : Pytchley, Strensall, York. (M5676)

TIPPING, Capt. Herbert, M.B.E.

TIPPING, Kate Vernon, M.B.E.

TIPPING, Capt. William John, O.B.E.

TIPPINGE, Capt. Leicester Francis Gartside, C.B.E., R.N., *b.* 1855 ; *s.* of the late Rev. Francis Gartside Tippinge, of Sansaw Hall, Shrewsbury. Served in Great War, 1914–19 (mentioned in despatches). (C1946)

TISLEY, Capt. Frederick William, M.B.E., R.E.

TITCHENER, Capt. Harry Stocker, M.B.E., R.A.O.C.

TITLEY, Margaret, Mrs., O.B.E., *m.* John Edward Addison. *War Work* : Organised and superintended the Harrogate Voluntary Ambulance Service from Oct. 1914 to May, 1919, Headquarters, Harrogate. *Address* : Manor Cottage, Cornwall Road, Harrogate, Yorks. *Club* : Lyceum. (O11483)

TITTERINGTON, Edward John Goodall, M.B.E.

TIVY, Evelyn Laura, M.B.E., *b.* 10 Sept. 1879 ; *d.* of William James Tivy, F.R.C.P., F.R.C.S., Victoria Square, Clifton, Bristol. *Educ.* : Privately. Civil Servant. *War Work* : Sec. of the Bristol Advisory Committee, and Manager of the Bristol Juvenile Employment Exchange. *Address* : 42, Royal York Crescent, Clifton, Bristol. (M9867)

TIZARD, Capt. Claude, O.B.E., M.C.

TIZARD, Ethel Annie, M.B.E., *b.* 3 July, 1884 ; *d.* of Capt. T. H. Tizard, C.B., R.N., of 23, Geneva Road, Kingston-on-Thames. *Educ.* : Surbiton Church High School, Kingston-on-Thames. Assist. Sec. to the Rt. Rev. E. S. Talbot, present Bishop of Winchester, 1907–11 ; Sec. to the Rt. Rev. H. M. Burge, D.D., present Bishop of Oxford, 1911, to Aug. 1914 ; Private Sec. to F. C. Abbott, C.B.E., M.C., F.R.C.S., The Hermitage, Bletchingley, 1920. *War Work* : Aug. 1914, to May, 1919, Sec. to Dame Ethel Becher, G.B.E., R.R.C., Matron-in-Chief of Queen Alexandra's Imperial Military Nursing Service, War Office (Royal Army Medical Dept.). (M2547)

TOBIN, Frank, C.B.E., Knight of Grace, Order of St. John of Jerusalem in England, *b.* 1849 ; *s.* of James Aspinall Tobin. Partner in Hornby, Tobin and Ockleston, Stockbrokers, of Liverpool ; Founder of Avenue (Liverpool) Auxiliary Hospital for Officers during the Great War. (C2998)

TOBIN, Capt. Frederick Matthias, M.B.E., R.A.S.C., *b.* 13 Nov. 1879 ; *s.* of Matthias Tobin, of Kingstown, Ireland ; *m.* Catherine, *d.* of James McKay, of Warrington. *Educ.* : Army Schools. Soldier in ranks (Regular), Nov. 1893, to Sept. 1903, 1st Batt. E. Surrey Regt. ; Sept. 1903, to Nov. 1915, R.A.P.C. ; Nov. 1915, to Nov. 1916, R.A.O.C. ; Commissioned, R.A.S.C., Nov. 1916 to date ; Assist. Control Native Labour, Mesop. Exped. Force, Aug.–Sept. 1917 ; Adjutant, 13th Divisional Train ; Officer 18th (Ind.) Division, May, 1920, to date. *War Work* : Aug. 1914, to Nov. 1915, Army Pay Office, Woolwich ; Nov. 1915, to Nov. 1916, East Coast Defences ; Nov. 1916 to date in R.A.S.C. ; Mesop. Exped. Force, Feb. 1917, to date ; Senior Officer 18th (Ind.) Div. ; mentioned in despatches five times. *Address* : 3, Wilton Place, Marmion Road, Southsea, Hants. (M4933)

TOBIN, Major Harry Walter, D.S.O., O.B.E., *b.* 1879 ; *s.* of the late Henry Murray Tobin, I.C.S. ; *m.* Regina, *d.* of the late Archibald Dowdall-Nicolls, J.P., of co. Kildare. *Educ.* : St. Paul's School. Is Major, Indian Army ; served in Great War, 1914–16 (despatches). (O8552)

TOBY, Lieut. William Henry, O.B.E., R.N.R.

TOD, Major Alan Cecil, O.B.E., *b.* 10 Aug. 1887 ; *s.* of A. J. Tod, of Liverpool ; *m.* Helen Marjorie, *d.* of James E. Gordon, of Great Sutton, Cheshire. *Educ.* : Dunchurch, and Wellington. Banker. *Address* : Maryton Grange, Allerton, Liverpool. (O2760)

TOD, Capt. and Qr.-Mr. Alexander Gray, O.B.E., R.A.M.C.

TOD, Arthur White Millar, O.B.E.

TOD, Major David Inman, M.B.E., R.A.S.C.

TOD, Lieut. Frederick Lewis Maitland, M.B.E., R.A.S.C. (T.)

TOD, James Alexander, M.B.E.

TOD, James Niebuhr, C.B.E., *b.* 20 Sept. 1876 ; *s.* of the late John Tod, of St. Albans, Herts. ; *m.* Edith May, *d.* of the late Comm. Keppel Garnier, R.N., of Farnham, Surrey. *Educ.* : Privately. *War Work* : Assisted in securing supplies of textiles ; later appointed Assistant Director of Wool Textile Production. *Address* : Balgownie House, nr. Aberdeen. (C2999)

TOD, Capt. Marcus Niebuhr, O.B.E.

TOD, Robert Paterson, O.B.E., M.I.M.E. Special services during the war in connection with the British Aluminium Company's factory at Kinlochleven. (O11920)

TOD, Major William Norman, O.B.E.

TODD, Lieut. Alexander, M.B.E., R.F.A.

TODD, Col. Arthur George, C.B.E., D.S.O. Lieut.-Col. and Brevet Col. Army Vet. Corps ; Dep. Director of Vet. Services ; served in Great War, 1914–18 (mentioned in despatches). (C790)

TODD, Major Arthur Theodore, O.B.E., M.B., M.R.C.P., R.A.M.C., *b.* 1888 ; *s.* of Rev. M. M. Todd. *Educ.* : Latimer School, Hammersmith ; Edinburgh Univ. Consulting Physician, Rhine Forces. *War Work* : Medical Specialist, 42 C.C.S., France. *Address* : Berry Brow, Huddersfield, Yorks. (O5859)

TODD, Charles, O.B.E., M.D., *b.* 17 Sept. 1869 ; *s.* of J. Todd, of Harraby, Carlisle. *Educ.* : Cambridge, and St. Bartholomew's Hospital, London. Director, Public Health Laboratories, Public Health Department, Cairo, Egypt. *War Work* : Director, Central Military Bacteriological Laboratory, Cairo. *Clubs* : Royal Societies ; Turf (Cairo). (O2133)

TODD, Duncan, O.B.E.

TODD, Edith Mary Elizabeth, M.B.E., *b.* 29 Sept. 1870 ; *d.* of the late George Todd, of Bideford, N. Devon. *Educ.* : At home, and private school. Matron, Q.A.S.M.N. Service. *War Work* : Matron of Men's and Women's Hospitals, Royal Arsenal, Woolwich. (M2548)

TODD, Major Edwin Ernest Enever, O.B.E.

TODD, Lieut.-Col. George Eardley, O.B.E., *b.* 14 Feb. 1881 ; *s.* of George Nicholas Todd ; *m.* Mary, *d.* of David Thomson-Glover. *Educ.* : Blundell's School. Regular (retired) ; served South African Campaign, 1901–1902, with 3rd Welch Regt. Militia ; gazetted Welch Regt., July, 1903 ; served India, South Africa, and Sierra Leone. *War Work* : Seconded to Royal Flying Corps, April, 1913 ; served in France, Egypt, Salonica, and Turkey ; awarded Chevalier Legion of Honour, Croix de Guerre avec Palme, Serbian White Eagle, 1914 Star, Victory Medal, War Medal, and Brevet Lieut.-Col. *Address* : Mundham House, Brooke, Norwich. (O8205)

TODD, Eng.-Comm. George Webster, O.B.E., R.N.R.

TODD, Georgina, Mrs., M.B.E., *b.* 25 June, 1863 ; *d.* of the late George Matthews, of Holly Mount, Maguiresbridge, Co. Fermanagh ; *m.* Armstrong Herbert Swift Todd, M.D. ; *s.* of the late Armstrong Todd, M.D., of Grosvenor Street, Hyde Park, London, W. War Workers Badge ; The Order of St. John War Service Badge ; Egg Collector's Certificate. *War Work* : Commandant V.A.D. 752 Fermanagh, Order of St. John of Jerusalem ; Recruiting Commandant, Co. Fermanagh ; Head of Workroom 5732, Holly Mount, Co. Fermanagh ; Hon. Sec. Co. Fermanagh Red Cross and Order of St. John Ambulance Fund. *Address* : Holly Mount, Maguiresbridge, Co. Fermanagh. (M9869)

TODD, Gerald Frederick, M.B.E., *b.* 3 Aug. 1881 ; *s.* of William Ansell Todd, J.P., late of Bristol ; *m.* Hilda Margaret Bartrum, *d.* of Charles Ackland, of Woking, Surrey. *Educ.* : Clifton ; Malvern Coll. Chartered Accountant ; Partner in Grace Darbyshire and Todd, Chartered Accountants, 24, Clare Street, Bristol. *War Work* : Hon. Sec., Bristol and District War Savings Local Committee. *Address* : Stapleton, Bristol. *Club* : Constitutional (Bristol). (M9870)

TODD, Lieut.-Col. G. M., C.B.E. Lieut.-Col. Canadian Army Pay Corps ; served in Great War, 1915–19 (mentioned in despatches). (C1357)

TODD, John Thomas, M.B.E.

TODD, Reginald, O.B.E., 10 Oct. 1868 ; *s.* of the late James J. Todd, of Aberdeen ; *m.* Lorna, *d.* of Lieut.-Col. Henry John Lawrence, of Parkstone, Dorset. *Educ.* : Fettes Coll., Edinburgh ; Coopers Hill ; Royal Indian Engineering Coll. Civil Engineer ; Deputy to the Agent, Bombay, Baroda, and Central India Rly. *War Work* : Seconded from Bombay, Baroda, and Central India Railway to be Agent of the Madras and Southern Mahratta Railway during the war, 1916–19. *Address* : c/o Henry S. King & Co., Pall Mall. *Club* : East Indian United Service. (O4107)

TODD, Capt. Sam, O.B.E., L.D.S., *b.* 22 June, 1886 ; *s.* of Edward Todd, of Fencehouses, Co. Durham ; *m.* Amy *d.* of the late John George Baty, of Houghton-le-Spring. *Educ.* : Argyle House School, Sunderland, and Durham Univ. Coll. of Medicine. *War Work* : Enlisted Nov. 1914 in R.A.M.C. ; proceeded overseas as Corporal, April, 1915 ; gazetted Lieut. (Dental Surgeon), Aug. 1915, and appointed to No 17 Casualty Clearing Station ; promoted Capt., Aug. 1916, and served continuously overseas in Belgium, France, and Germany until March, 1919 ; mentioned in Sir D. Haig's despatches. *Address* : Church House, Houghton-le-Spring, Co. Durham. (O5860)

TODD, Albert Rudolf LOCHLEIN-, M.B.E.

TODHUNTER, Alice Mrs., O.B.E. ; *d.* of the late Capt. C. W. Losack, late of 93rd Highlanders ; *m.* Hon. Charles George Todhunter, T.C.S., C.S.T., J.P. *War Work* : President, Tinnevelly War Fund (Ladies Branch) ; Ladies' Committee, Madras War Fund ; trained as Superintendent Military Dairy Farm. *Address* : The Hermitage, Mylapore, Madras. (O4108)

TODHUNTER, Benjamin Edward, O.B.E.

TOFFT, Major Walter Henry, M.B.E.

TOGHILL, Edward Sergent, M.B.E.

TOKE, Nicolas Eyare, M.B.E., *b.* 18 March, 1866 ; *s.* of Rev. Nicolas R. Toke, of Pipsden Lodge, Hawkhurst, Kent ; *m.* Ida Julie Françoise, *d.* of Jean Bardy, of Helsingfors, Finland. *Educ.* : London Univ. and Univ. of Lausanne, Switzerland. *War Work* : Representative of the Local Government Board in Folkestone, from Oct. 1916, to April, 1919, with charge of Belgian Refugees and Belgian Soldiers arriving at Folkestone ; Assistant Sec. during the war of the Folkestone War Refugees Committee ; Chevalier de l'Ordre de la Couronne, Belgique. *Address* : Penfillan House, Folkestone. (M9872)

TOLLEMACHE, Capt. Cecil Herbert, M.B.E.

TOLLER, Emma Anne, Mrs., M.B.E. *War Work* : Lady President and Organiser of the Paddington and Ceylon Y.M.C.A. Hut, Stanley Street, W. 2. *Club* : Forum. (M2549)

TOLLER, Capt. George Gordon Taylor, O.B.E., I.A.R.O. (O11769)

TOLMIE, Agnes, O.B.E.

TOM, Henry, M.B.E., H.M's. Consul at Amsterdam. (M1024)

TOMASSON, Capt. William Hugh, Sir, K.B.E., M.V.O., b. 1857; s. of the late William Tomasson, of Grainfoot, Derwent; m. Eliza, d. of the late George Lees, of Ashton, Cheshire. *Educ.:* Clifton. Formerly Capt. Baker's Horse; has been Chief Constable of Nottinghamshire since 1892. *Address:* Woodthorpe, Nottingham. *Clubs:* Boodle's; Pratt's.   (K435)

TOMB, John Walker, O.B.E.

TOMES, Wiliam Jameson, M.B.E.

TOMKINS, Ernest William, O.B.E.

TOMKINS, Stanley Charles, M.B.E.

TOMKINSON, Dora Sloane, O.B.E.

TOMKINSON, Lieut. Geoffrey Stewart, O.B.E., M.C.

TOMKINSON, Major Herbert, O.B.E.

TOMKINSON, Marion, M.B.E.

TOMLEY, John Edward, C.B.E. Chairman of the Joint Disablement Committee (Ministry of Pensions) for North Wales. Chairman of the Hospital and General Purposes Committee (Ministry of Pensions) for North Wales.   (C3168)

TOMLIN, Henry Charles, M.B.E., b. July, 1862. Fruit and Potato Merchant; Member, Leicester Board of Guardians. *War Work:* Member of Potato Control Committee (North Midland Division); Member of Naval and Military War Pensions Committee. *Address:* 21, Junction Road, Leicester. *Club:* Constitutional (Leicester).   (M9873)

TOMLIN, Major Julian Latham, C.B.E., D.S.O., R.E., b. 23 April, 1886; s. of the late Capt. Bankes Tomlin, King's Dragoon Guards, of Dane Court, St. Peters, Isle of Thanet; m. 1 Sept. 1920, Emily Gertrude, d. of Rev. T. G. Falkiner, Vicar of Wythall. *Educ.:* King's School, Canterbury; R.M.A., Woolwich.   (C3000)

TOMLIN, 'Lieut.-Col. Morton James Baring, O.B.E., s. of John Leonard Tomlin, of Thiernswood, by Richmond, Yorkshire; m. May, d. of Thomas Edward Brewitt Hilliard. *Educ.:* Eton, and New Coll., Oxford. Solicitor. *War Work:* Commanded 1/21st Bn. London Regt. at outbreak of war; proceeded to France in March, 1915; invalided home; subsequently commanded 19th (R.) Bn. London Regt. until March, 1919. *Address:* 67, Elm Park Gardens, S.W. 10. *Clubs:* Junior United Service; M.C.C.; Leander.   (O7783)

TOMLING, Flying Officer George Gibson, M.B.E., M.C., R.A.F.

TOMLINSON, Alice May, M.B.E., d. of S. Tomlinson, M.Inst.C.E., of Singapore and Grange. *Educ.:* High School, Saltaire, and Univ. Coll., London. *War Work:* Voluntary Canteen work in Alexandria, 1915–17; in Cairo, from 1917 to March, 1920, in charge of Central Office of the Civilian Employment Bureau for E.E.F., established in Aug. 1917, under the direction of S. H. Wells, C.B.E., for the recruiting of civilians for military work. *Address:* Beechgrove, Grange-over-Sands.   (M9874)

TOMLINSON, Lieut. Davil Holland, M.B.E.

TOMLINSON, Ernest William, O.B.E.

TOMLINSON, Major and Qr.-Mr. Frederick, O.B.E., M.C.

TOMLINSON, Tom Ashton, M.B.E.

TOMPKINS, Engr.-Capt. Albert Edward, C.B.E., R.N., b. 30 May, 1863; s. of the late John Tompkins, of Aveley Hall, Essex; m. Dorothea Frances, d. of Edmund George Reader, of Genoa, Italy. *Educ.:* Private Schools. Royal Navy; Engineer Student, H.M.S. "Marlborough," June, 1878; Engr.-Lieut., April, 1889; Engr.-Comm., Sept. 1901; Engr.-Capt. (ret.), May, 1913; Instructor in Steam and Marine Engineering at R.N. Coll., Greenwich, and Lecturer to R.N. War Colleges, 1902–6; M.I.Mech.E.; author of "Marine Engineering" (a Text-Book), "Turbines," etc. *War Work:* In charge emergency repairs to H.M. ships and mercantile vessels, Clyde district, 1914–17, and at Genoa and N.-W. Italy, from 1917–19. *Address:* Little Brookley, Brockenhurst, Hants.   (C1947)

TOMS, Major Charles Bailey, O.B.E.

TOMS, Lieut. Frederick Bowring, O.B.E., R.N.V.R.

TOMS, Stanley J., M.B.E. Formerly Partner in the firm of Derry and Sons. *War Work:* Joined Red Cross, Sept. 1914; Commandant of London 31 V.A.D., Kensington Div., Feb. 1915; commenced work with London Ambulance Column, March, 1915; became one of the Commandants, bearer section Units V. and VI.; Air Raid work at Kensington Headquarters; demobilised, March, 1919. *Address:* Homestead, Great Missenden, Bucks.   (M9876)

TOMS, Capt. William, M.B.E.

TOMSON, Lieut. Henry Gordon, M.B.E.

TONGE, Edward, M.B.E., M.B., B.S., b. 3 June, 1872; s. of Robert Tonge, of York; m. Kate, d. of William Wilty, of Driffield. *Educ.:* Univ. of Durham, and Pisa. Admiralty Surgeon, Seaton and District; M.O. Beer District; Public Vaccinator, Beer District; Surgeon to Shipping Federation. *War Work:* Admiralty Surgeon; Examining M.O. for East Devon, Lord Kitchener's Army; Commanding Officer and M.O. of the Seaton and District Auxiliary War Hospital (100 beds). *Addresses:* The Grange, Beer, E. Devon; St. Margaret's, Seafield Terrace, Seaton.   (M9877)

TONGE, Lieut. Frederick William John, M.B.E., Officer d'Academie, R.N.V.R., b. 29 July, 1885; s. of John Tonge, of London; m. Evelyn Mary, d. of Frank Drew, of London. *Educ.:* Privately, and Cusack Institute. Clerk, Ministry of Health, and during the war at Admiralty and Ministry of Shipping. *War Work:* Executive work on Staff of Ministry of Shipping; 1917–18, on Staff of British Naval Commander-in-Chief, Mediterranean Station, as Officer-in-Charge of Shipping Intelligence and Statistics, in connection with protection of merchant shipping. *Address:* 243, Norwood Road, Herne Hill.   (M9878)

TONKIN, Harold John, M.B.E., b. 10 March, 1887; s. of James F. Tonkin, of Swindon, Wilts; m. Josepha Kate, d. of John Tippet Angove, of Mutley, Devon. *Educ.:* North Wilts Technical and Secondary School, and London School of Economics (Univ. of London). Works Accountant of the Ashford Locomotive Carriage and Wagon Works of the South-Eastern and Chatham Rly., Co. *Address:* Homeland, Willesborough, Kent.   (M9879)

TONKIN, John, M.B.E.

TONKINSON, Edith, Mrs., M.B.E.

TONKINSON, Capt. and Qr.-Mr. John, M.B.E., R.A.M.C.

TONKS, Major Osmund, O.B.E.

TONNER, James, M.B.E.

TOOGOOD, Lieut.-Col. Arthur Seymour, O.B.E.

TOOGOOD, Lieut.-Col. Frederick Sherman, O.B.E., M.D., R.A.M.C.

TOOGOOD, John James, M.B.E.

TOOHILL, Capt. and Qr.-Mr. Thomas, O.B.E., R.A.S.C.

TOOKEY, Capt. Francis Edwin Friday, M.B.E.

TOOMER, Edith, Mrs., M.B.E.

TOOTH, Helen Katharine, Mrs., O.B.E., b. 5 Sept. 1873; d. of the Rev. C. S. Chilver, of Gate House, Midhurst; m. Howard Henry, M.D., C.B., C.M.G., s. of Frederick Tooth, of Brighton. *Educ.:* Newbury. *War Work:* Sec. Y.M.C.A. Hut at 1st London General Hospital; Vice-Chairman, St. Bartholomew's Hospital Women's Guild. *Address:* 34, Harley Street, W. 1.   (O11485)

TOOTH, Louis Frederick, M.B.E.

TOOTILL, Robert, C.B.E., M.P., b.1850; s. of James Tootill. Town Councillor and a J.P. of Bolton; Member of War Aims Committee, Central Tribunal, and Parliamentary Pensions Bureau; has been Sec. to Bolton Trades Council since 1894; has sat as M.P. for Bolton-le-Moors (Lab.) since Sept. 1914. *Address:* Westward House, Bolton-le-Moors.   (C649)

TOOVEY, Thomas Reginald, M.B.E., b. 21 June, 1878. *Educ.:* Sir W. Borlase, Grammar School, Great Marlow, and the City of London School. Assistant to the Staff Manager, Port of London Authority. *War Work:* Sec. to the Port of London Local Committee of the Port and Transit Executive Committee. *Address:* Ormonde House, High Wycombe.   (M9880)

TOPHAM, Harry, M.B.E.

TOPHAM, Harry, M.B.E., b. 16 Feb. 1873; s. of Christopher and Mary Elizabeth Topham, of Wakefield; m. Jane, d. of William Sidebottom, of Wakefield. *Educ.:* Wakefield Grammar School (Queen Elizabeth's). Clerk to the West Riding of Yorkshire Asylums Board, and to the Scalebor Park Asylum (Private) Visiting Committee. *War Work:* Acted as Clerk to the Wharncliffe War Hospital Committee (2000 beds). *Address:* Asylums Board Office, Wakefield; 1, Rishworth Street, Wakefield. *Club:* Leeds and County.   (M2555)

TOPHAM, Jane Grace Cowan, M.B.E., d. of Lupton T. Topham, of Lutterworth and Middleham. *Educ.:* Privately. *War Work:* Assistant Superintendent and Qr.-Mr. at Lutterworth Auxiliary Hospital. *Address:* Middleham House, Middleham, Yorks.   (M9881)

TOPLIS, James, C.B.E., b. 1876; s. of Frederick Toplis, of Crouch End; m. Ellen Kate, d. of John Jameson, of Southsea, Hants. *Educ.:* St. Paul's School, and Trinity Coll., Cambridge. *War Work:* Financial Adviser in Italy to War Office. *Address:* Army Audit Office, Baghdad, Mesopotamia. (C3001)

TOPLISS, Capt. John, M.B.E., R.A.S.C.

TOPPIN, Lieut.-Col. Henry, O.B.E., b. 15 June, 1868; s. of the Rev. Richard Toppin, late of Tramore; m. Amy Constance, d. of John Greene, of Gaulstown House, Co. Meath. *Educ.:* Trinity Coll., Dublin, and abroad. Resident Magistrate. *War Work:* Attached G.H.Q., Ireland, and to Headquarters of various Special Military Areas in Ireland; Assistant Adjutant-General, G.H.Q., Ireland (Temp.). *Address:* Bally-carney, Tramore. *Club:* Sackville Street, Dublin.   (O8956)

TOPPIN, Paymaster-Sub-Lieut. Maxwell Howard, M.B.E., R.N.R.

TOPPLE, Walter Livingstone, C.B.E. Sup. Electric and Ordnance Accessories Co. (Limited).   (C650)

TORREGGIANI, Antonio Cassar, O.B.E.

TORRIE, Claud Jamieson, O.B.E.

TOSSWILL, Capt. Frank Speare, O.B.E., R.A.O.C., b. 23 June, 1878. Sec. to the Guildford Education Authority, and Director of Technical Instruction. *War Work:* Received H.M. Commission, Jan. 1916; appointed to R.A.O.C., and stationed Dover Ordnance Depot; overseas service, East Africa, May, 1917, until demobilised, May, 1919. *Address:* The Hoo, Wodeland Road, Guildford.   (O4181)

TOSSWILL, Major, Leonard Robert, O.B.E., M.R.C.S., L.R.C.P., D.P.H., b. 12 Jan. 1880; s. of Louis H. Tosswill, M.B., of Exeter; m. Mabel Sylvia, y.d. of G. W. O. Secretan. *Educ.:* Marlborough Coll. Principal Deputy Commissioner of Medical Services, Ministry of Pensions. *War Work:* Served with R.A.M.C. (T.F.) over 12 years, including period of the war; overseas (France), with 1st Division, then as D.A.D.M.S. (Sanitation), H.Q. 4th and 5th Armies; twice mentioned in despatches. *Address:* Southwood, Pinner. *Club:* Authors'. (O5861)

TOTTENHAM, Capt. Francis Loftus, C.B.E., R.N. Served in Great War, 1914–19 (mentioned in despatches). (C1948)

TOTTENHAM, Percy Marmaduke, C.B.E. *b.* 1873; *s.* of Capt. Francis Loftus Tottenham, of Coolmore, Crowborough; *m.* 1909, Angel, *d.* of Edward Mervyn Archdale, M.P., of Riversdale, Fermanagh. Inspector-General of Irrigation, Soudan, 1909–13, and for Lower Egypt, 1914–16; now Under-Secretary of State, Ministry of Public Works, Egypt. (C2361)

TOUGH, George, O.B.E.

TOUGH, James Macgillivray, M.B.E.

TOULMIN, Capt. Francis Justus, O.B.E.

TOURTEL, John Mesny, M.B.E.

TOWER, Comm. Francis Fitzpatrick, O.B.E., R.N.V.R.

TOWER, Comm. Francis Thomas Butler, O.B.E., R.N.

TOWERS, Thomas Peacock, M.B.E., *b.* 1862; *s.* of William Towers, of Paisley; *m.* Margaret, *d.* of John Galbraith, of Paisley. *Educ.:* Paisley and Glasgow Univ. Solicitor. *War Work:* Joint Hon. Sec. Soldiers' and Sailors' Families Association (Paisley Branch), and Sec. Paisley War Pensions Committee till April, 1919. *Address:* 16, Moss Street, Paisley. *Clubs:* Paisley Liberal; Edderslie Golf. (M9883)

TOWILL, Capt. William Frederick, O.B.E., Can. A.V.C.

TOWLE, Arthur Edward, C.B.E., *b.* 1878; *s.* of William Towle, of Rooklands, Torquay; *m.* Mabel Ethel, *d.* of the late Henry Taylor, of St. Peter's, Thanet. *Educ.:* Marlborough. A Railway Officer and Assist. Sec. Ministry of Food during Great War. (C1047)

TOWLE, Arthur Henry, O.B.E.

TOWLE, Lieut.-Col. Sir Francis William, C.B.E., B.A., *b.* 18 April, 1876; *s.* of Wm. Towle, of Rooklands, Torquay; *m.* Emma Annette, widow of Capt. and Adjutant D. A. N. Lomax. 1st Welsh Regt. *Educ.:* Marlborough, and Trinity Coll., Cambridge. Director, Commercial Bank of London; Director, Agricultural Industries, Ltd., and British Glass Industries, Ltd. *War Work:* T. Capt. A.S.C., Nov. 1915; Asst. Inspector Q.M.G.'s Services, Hdqrs., Southern Command, Jan. 1916; Inspector Q.M.G. Services, War Office, and Member of Executive Committee, Army Canteen Committee, on formation, Jan. 1917; appointed Member of Tobacco Control Board on formation, May, 1917; Lieut.-Col., Dec. 1917; Controller at War Office Navy and Army Canteen Board, Dec. 1917; Chairman, Board of Management, N.A.C.B., April, 1918. *Addresses:* 3, Clarence Terrace, Regent's Park, N.W.; Commercial Bank of London, Ltd., 37–41, Gracechurch Street, E.C. *Club:* Bath. (C317)

TOWN, Christopher Edward, M.B.E.

TOWNE, Major Edward Charles Lyndhurst, O.B.E.

TOWNEND, Paymaster-Comm. Alfred Bernard Stairs, O.B.E., R.N, *b.* 5 Oct. 1882; *s.* of the late Rev. Alfred John Townend, B.A., C.F.; *m.* Grace Carina, *d.* of the late Timothy Bevington. *War Work:* Served as Sec. to Hyde Parker and Terrain Committees, 1918–19. (O9196)

TOWNEND, Kathleen M., O.B.E., *b.* 15 May, 1851; *d.* of James Hamilton Townend, of Harefield, Cheam, Surrey. Vice-President for several years of Girls' Friendly Society, and Chairman of its Imperial Committee; Vice-Chairman of the G.F.S. War Emergency Committee from 1916–19. *War Work:* Organising work on behalf of Munition Workers, W.A.A.C.s, and other War workers, by helping to raise funds for the War Emergency Fund to start hostels, clubs, and huts in various places. *Address:* 46, The Ridgways, Golder's Green, N.W. *Club:* Church Imperial Ladies'. (O11490)

TOWNER, Lieut. Henry William, O.B.E., R.G.A.

TOWNLEY, Rev. Charles Francis, C.B.E., *v.* 15 June, 1856; *s.* of Charles Watson Townley, of Fulbourn Manor; *m.* Rosalinde, *d.* of the Rev. Jermyn Pratt, of Ryston Hall, Downham, Norfolk. *Educ.:* Cheam; Eton; Trinity Coll. Cambridge. County Director, Red Cross, Cambs. *War Work:* As County Director. *Address:* Fulbourn Manor, Cambridge. *Club:* Wellington; M.C.C. (C3002)

TOWNLEY, Capt. Herbert Arthur, M.B.E.

TOWNLEY, Rosalinde Cecil, M.B.E.

TOWNSEND, Harry Edward, O.B.E., *b.* April, 1872; *s.* of Richard Montague; *m.* Eleanor, *d.* of James Moulding, of Toxteth, Liverpool. *Educ.:* Privately. Engaged in Commerce. *War Work:* Founded in Sept. 1914, the Bristol Inquiry Bureau, a voluntary organisation for the assistance and entertainment of wounded soldiers; officially acting for the 2nd Southern General, and the Beaufort War Hospitals; acted as Hon. Organising Sec. until March 1918, subsequently leaving Bristol to join the Ministry of Food, London. *Clubs:* Eccentric; Bristol Liberal. (O1149)

TOWNSEND, Capt. Harry Orton, O.B.E.

TOWNSEND, Lucy Mabel, Mrs., M.B.E. *War Work:* Convener of the Central Store for Surgical Dressings, Scottish Branch of the British Red Cross Society. *Address:* 19, Huntly Gardens, Kelvinside, Glasgow. (M1028)

TOWNSEND, Capt. Philip Henry, O.B.E., *b.* 12 Aug. 1881; *s.* of the late Henry Milnes Townsend, of Peterborough; *m.* Gwenyth Gwendoline, *d.* of Robert Roberts, of Chester. *Educ.:* Privately. *War Work:* Mechanical Transport, 1915–20; served in France, Belgium, and Germany from Feb. 1916 to Jan. 1920. *Club:* R.A.S.C. (O5862)

TOWNSHEND, Anna, M.B.E.

TOWNSHEND, Arthur Walter, M.B.E., *b.* 5 Jan. 1859; *s.* of Walter Waters Townshend, of Sussex; *m.* Mary, *d.* of Major Inglesby, of Cape Town. *Educ.:* Uckfield and Eastbourne. Printer; Member of Corporation of Cape Town. *War Work:* President, Y.M.C.A., etc.; Chairman of the Visiting Troops Entertainment Committee, which entertained all troops touching at Cape Town during the war, to the number of 1¼ million men. *Address:* Ridgewood, Tamboer's Kloof, Cape Town. (M1236)

TOWNSHEND, Capt. Francis Horatio Evory, O.B.E., M.C.

TOWNSHEND, Margery, M.B.E.

TOWNSHEND, Lieut. Reginald Brooks, O.B.E., R.N.V.R.

TOWSE, Capt. Ernest Beechcroft Beckwith, V.C., C.B.E., *b.* 1864, *s.* of the late Beckwith Towse; *m.* 1892, Gertrude, *d.* of the late John Christie. Capt. Gordon Highlanders; served with the Chitral Relief Force, 1895 (medal with clasp); N.-W. Frontier of India, 1897–8 (clasps); S. Africa, 1899–1900 (wounded, despatches twice, V.C., Queen's medal, with three clasps); Serj.-at-Arms to H.M. Corps of Gentlemen-at-Arms; Dep. Chm. National Institute for the Blind, and a Knight of Grace of Order of St. John of Jerusalem in England. *Address:* Long Meadow, Goring, Oxon. *Clubs:* Naval and Military; Wellington; Caledonian; United Service. (C3003)

TOWSEY, Brig.-Gen. Francis William, C.M.G., C.B.E., D.S.O., *b.* 1864. Col. W. Yorkshire Regt.; Brig.-Com. with rank of Brig.-Gen.; Ashanti Expedition, 1895–96 (star); Great War, 1914–19 (despatches, Order of St. Maurice and St. Lazarus of Italy). (C1793)

TOYE, Dudley Bulmer, O.B.E., LL.B., *b.* 1888; *s.* of the late Henry Toye. *Educ.:* Privately; London Univ.; Member of the Middle Temple; Campbell Foster Prizeman, 1918. *War Work:* Head of Finance Branch, Restriction of Enemy Supplies Dept., Foreign Office, 1917–19; Sec. 1919–20. *Addresses:* Redhill, Surrey; Ministry of Agriculture and Fisheries, Whitehall Place, S.W. (O11492)

TOYNBEE, Lieut.-Col. Guy Elliston, C.M.G., C.B.E., *b.* 1884. Major and Brevet Lieut.-Col. Army Ser. Corps; served in Great War, 1914–19 (despatches). (C1794)

TOZER, Alfred Robert, O.B.E.

TOZER, Edward John, M.B.E.

TOZER, James Clark, O.B.E., J.P.; *s.* of James S. Tozer, of St. Pennycross, Devon; *m.* Henrietta, *d.* of John Cole Matthews, of Ipplepen, Devon. *Educ.:* Plymouth Grammar School. Wholesale and Retail Drapery Stores. *War Work:* Chairman South Devon Appeal Tribunal. *Address:* Stoke House, Devonport. *Club:* Constitutional. (O11494)

TRACEY, Isabel Audrey, Mrs., M.B.E.

TRACY, Capt. Charles Dunlop, O.B.E.

TRACY, Kate, M.B.E., *b.* 24 Sept. 1870; *d.* of D. J. E. Tracy, of The Elms, Croydon. *War Work:* Quartermaster, Beccles V.A.D. Hospital. *Address:* The Tower House, Beccles. (M9884)

TRACY, Louis, C.B.E., *b.* 18 March, 1863; *s.* of Thomas Tracy, of Whitby, Yorkshire; *m.* Ethel, *d.* of John Morse, of Grosmont, Mon. *Educ.:* Privately, and France. Author. *War Work:* Raised, equipped, and trained half-battalion, 4th North Riding Regiment of Volunteers, 1914–16; joined Headquarter Staff British War Mission in U.S.A., and served under Lord Northcliffe, Lord Reading, and Sir Henry Babington Smith; Liquidator British Bureau of Information, New York. *Club:* Savage; Authors'; New York Yacht; Lotos (New York). (C3004)

TRACY, Lieut.-Col. William Maxwell, O.B.E.

TRACY, Cyprienne Emma Madeleine HANBURY-, O.B.E., *b.* 27 Oct. 1874; *d.* of the Hon. Frederick Hanbury Tracy, of 116, Queen's Gate, London, S.W. (*see* BURKE'S *Peerage*, Sudeley, B.). *War Work:* 1916, fed the wounded Italian soldiers in the trains passing through the railheads on the Carso Front; Nov. 1917 to Feb. 1920, helped at, and afterwards in charge of, British Soldiers' Club at British Base, Italy; mentioned in despatches, 1919. *Address:* The King's Barrow, Wareham, Dorset. (O3961)

TRACY, Major Eric Thomas HANBURY-, O.B.E.

TRAFFORD, Marcus Antonius Johnston de Laves, O.B.E. M.D. Senior Medical Officer, Red Cross Hospital, Turin, Italy. (O11790*h*)

TRAILL, Margaret Isabelle, Mrs., M.B.E.

TRANT, Capt. Alfred William Vincent, O.B.E., *b.* 2 April, 1867; *s.* of William Henry Trant, of Liverpool; *m.* Ann Eliza, *d.* of William Wannop, of Chester. *Educ.:* Merchant Taylors' School, Great Crosby. Extra Master, Merchant Service; Capt. s.s. "Winifredian," Leyland Line; Member Executive Council, Mercantile Marine Service Assoc. *War Work:* Transport Service, and Marine Superintendent, Convoy Section, Admiralty. *Addresses:* 23, Denman Drive, Newsham Park, Liverpool; c/o Messrs. Fredk. Leyland & Co., Ltd., 27, James Street, Liverpool. (O3962)

TRANT, Hope, M.B.E., Hon. Serving Sister Order of St. John of Jerusalem, *b.* 4 Aug. 1888; *d.* of the late Col. Fitzgibbon Trant, D.L., J.P., of Dovea, Co. Tipperary. *Educ.:* Rathgowry, Eastbourne; Trinity Coll., Dublin. *War Work:* V.A.D. Nurse, July, 1915, to Jan. 1917, at No. 6 Stationary and No. 2 General Hospitals, Havre, France; ambulance driver in B.Red Cross Convoy, Le Tréport, July, 1917, to July, 1918; Commandant in charge, General Service V.A.D. Convoy, Abbeville, July, 1918, to Oct. 1919; mentioned in despatches, Nov. 1916. *Address:* Glenart Lodge, Blackrock, Co. Dublin. *Club:* Ladies' V.A.D., Cavendish Square W. (M9886)

TRASK, Capt. Charles Stancomb Lisle, O.B.E.

TRATHAN, Walter, M.B.E.

TRAVERS, Frederick Thomas, O.B.E., M.B., F.R.C.S., *b.* 3 Dec. 1869; *s.* of William Travers, of Kensington; *m.* Doris Henrietta Ellen, *d.* of William Rowlstone, of Gravesend.

Educ.: Blundell's School, and Univ. Coll., Hospital. Senior Surgeon to West Kent General Hospital, Maidstone. *War Work:* Assistant County Director, Kent V.A.D.; Medical officer in charge of The Mote Auxiliary Hospital, Howard de Walden V.A.D. Hospital, Maidstone; consulting Surgeon to Barham Court Auxiliary Hospital, and Hayle Place, V.A.D. Hospital. (O1933)

TRAVERS, Col. Henry Cecil, C.B.E., D.S.O., *b.* 1876. Major and Brevet Lieut.-Col; Acting Col. Army Ordnance Depart.; served in Great War, 1914–19 (mentioned in despatches). (C1391)

TRAVERS, Wing-Comm. James Lindsey, O.B.E., R.A.F.

TRAVERS, Lieut. Sidney Joe, M.B.E., *b.* 9 Dec. 1894; *s.* of Walter Benward Travers, of Kingsdowne-on-Sea. *Educ.:* Dinglewood School, Colwyn Bay. Agriculture. *War Work:* Lieut. in the 5th (Cinque Ports) Batt., The Royal Sussex Regt.; Temp. Instructor Gen. Inf. Section, 14th Corps School, Italy; Act. Adjutant and Act. Quartermaster to the Batt.; commanded British Detachment, Scutari, Albania. *Address:* Hill Top, Kingsdown, Deal, Kent. (M4756)

TRAVERS, Hon. Walter Lancelot, O.B.E.; *s.* of W. Benward Travers, of Mumby, Alford, Lincolnshire. *Educ.:* Alford Grammar School. Member Bengal Legislative Council; Chairman Duars Planters Association; Member Jalpaiguri District Board; Capt. Northern Bengal Mounted Rifles (I.D.F.). *War Work:* Member Rajshahi Selection Committee, and principal non-official member of all war organisations, 1915–19. *Address:* Banadighi Tea Estate, Jalpaiguri (Duars), Bengal. *Club:* Bengal (Calcutta). (O2081)

TRAVERS, Lieut.-Col Wilfrid Irwin, O.B.E., F.R.I.B.A., *b.* 25 April, 1883; *s.* of William Travers, M.D., late of Kensington; *m.* Vera Patty Helsham, *d.* of A. McCausland, M.D., of Swanage. *Educ.:* Uppingham School. Deputy Housing Director to Corporation of Birmingham. *War Work:* Served with Royal Engineers, Jan. 1915, to Jan. 1920, France, Salonica, and Turkey. *Addresses:* 33, Clarendon Road, Edgbaston; Council House, Birmingham. (O6545)

TRAVILL, Lieut. Robert, M.B.E., R.A.O.C.

TRAVIS, Harry, C.B.E., I.S.O., M.I.M.E., *b.* 18 July, 1858; *s.* of John Travis, of Devonport; *m.* Emmeline, *d.* of George Hamlyn, of Roborough, South Devon. *Educ.:* Privately at Devonport. Superintending Engineer, War Office. *War Work:* Engaged under the Director of Transport, War Office, in the provision and general supervision of War Dept. Shipping, and specially of those vessels employed on the Examination Service under Military Control for the pro-' tection of Commercial Ports; assisted as Advising Officer to H.M. Customs and Excise in the provision and working of launches for river patrol purposes in safeguarding the revenue. *Address:* Royal Dockyard, Woolwich. *Club:* Junior Constitutional. (C3005)

TREACY, Alfred Martin, O.B.E.

TREADWELL, Capt. Charles Archibald Lawrance, O.B.E.

TREANOR, Lieut. Francis James, M.B.E., *b.* 23 July, 1873; *s.* of Francis Treanor, of Liverpool; *m.* Jessie Maud, *d.* of Peter Hannay, of Gelston, Kirkcudbrightshire. *Educ.:* St. Francis Xaviers. Foreman, L. & N.W. Rly. Co. *War Work:* S.Q.M.S., Lancashire Hussars Yeomanry, 1914–17; granted Commission in R.A.S.C., 1917; 2 years with 1st Cavalry Division, Reserve Park, in France; 1 year with Highland Divisional train, in France. *Address:* 93, Manningham Road, Liverpool. (M2557)

TREASURE, John William Oran, M.B.E.

TREDEGAR, Courtenay Charles Evan Morgan, the Lord. (*see* BURKE'S *Peerage*), O.B.E., F.S.A., J.P., D.L., R.N.V.R., *b.* 10 April, 1867; *s.* of the late the Hon. F. C. Morgan, J.P., D.L., of Ruperra Castle, Newport, Co. Monmouth; *m.* Lady Katharine Agnes Blanche Carnegie, *d.* of James, 9th Earl of Southesk, K.T. Peer of Realm; County Alderman, Co. Monmouth; Hon. Col. 1st Batt. Monmouthshire Regt.; served in S.A. War, 1900–01, medal and 4 clasps. *War Work:* Lieut. R.N.R. from 7 Aug. to 31 Dec. 1914; Commander, R.N.V.R. Jan. 1915; demobilised, 1919; served with R.N. Division, also Commanded and maintained H.M. Yacht "Liberty IV.,"; has Star, G.S. and Victory medals, and is Knight of Grace of St. John of Jerusalem. *Address:* 37 Bryanston Square. *Clubs:* Turf; White's; Arthur's; Royal Yacht Squadron. (O4449)

TREDENNICK, Major James Paumier, D.S.O., O.B.E., *b.* 1879. Entered Royal Dublin Fusiliers 1900; Capt. 1910; Major, 1915; S. African War, 1900–2 (Queen's medal with three clasps, King's medal with two clasps); Aden, 1903; S. Nigeria, 1905–6; served in Great War, 1914–19, on Staff (despatches). (O5863)

TREDGOLD, Helen, M.B.E.

TREE, Maud, Lady, O.B.E.

TREES, Capt. and Qr.-Mr. Reginald Pearson, M.B.E., *b.* 21 Sept. 1872; *s.* of James Enoch Trees, of Ripon, Yorks.; *m.* Margaret Jane, *d.* of S. Daniels, of St. Johns, Newfoundland. *Educ.:* Ripon National Schools. Enlisted in April, 1889, in the ranks of The King's Liverpool Regt., and served with this Regt. until Oct. 1915. *War Work:* Commissioned as Quartermaster in the 4/5th Loyal North Lancashire Regiment; Sec., Old Comrades Association, the King's Liverpool Regt. *Address:* 29, Palmerston Drive, Litherland, near Liverpool. (M6715)

TREFFRY, Lieut.-Col. Edward, C.M.G., O.B.E., J.P.

TREFUSIS, Dorothy Marguerite Elizabeth, Hon. Mrs.,

O.B.E.; *d.* of Col. Edward William Herbert, C.B., of Orleton, Salop (*see* BURKE'S *Peerage*, Powis, E.); *m.* Robert Henry, *s.* of Charles Rolle, 20th Baron Clinton, by his 2nd wife (*see* BURKE'S *Peerage*). (O8417)

TREGASKIS, Nellie Blanche, Mrs., M.B.E.

TREGONING, Wynn Harold, C.B.E., M.A., *b.* 1876; 4th *s.* of the late John Simmons Tregoning, J.P., D.L., of Landue, Launceston; *m.* Alice Dorothy, *d.* of the late Rev. William Pollexfen Bastard, of Kitley, and Buckland Court, Devon. *Educ.:* Harrow, and Trinity Coll. Cambridge. Civil Engineer; Merchant and Shipowner; on Staff of Ministry of Shipping; Director of Alfred Booth and Co., Ltd., Merchants and Shipowners; and of John S. Tregoning and Co., Ltd., Steel and Tinplate makers; Deputy Chairman of Ship Licensing Committee. *Address:* 57, Campden Hill Road, W. *Clubs:* St. Stephen's; Reform. (C318)

TREHARNE, Frederick Gwilym, O.B.E.

TREHEARN, Sarah Emuss, M.B.E. *War Work:* Hon. Sec. Queen Mary's Needlework Guild, Marlborough Branch; Local Representative, Prisoner of War Fund, Marlborough *Address:* 122, High Street, Marlborough, Wilts. (M4038)

TRELAWNY, James Edward SALUSBURY-, O.B.E.

TRELEAVEN, Charles John, M.B.E.

TRELOAR, Major John Linton, O.B.E.

TREMAINE, Brevet Lieut.-Col. Richard, C.B.E., *b.* 1 May, 1860; *s.* of Richard Tremaine, of Trethurffe, Ladock, Cornwall; *m.* Gertrude, *d.* of Claris Henry Everard Landell, of Landulla, Denmark. *Educ.:* Sherborne; Royal Military Academy, Woolwich. Staff Officer, Lydd Practice Camp; Adjutant Field Artillery Brigade, Aldershot; Commanding Remount Depot, Canterbury. *War Work:* Served on the Remount Department in South African War (Queen's medal, 4 clasps); Great War, 1914–18, Officer-in-charge Royal Garrison Artillery Record Office, Dover, 1916 to 1921; promoted Brevet Lieut.-Col. *Address:* Trethurffe, Griniston Gardens, Folkestone. (C2181)

TREMAYNE, Capt. John Claude Lewis, O.B.E., J.P.

TREMEARNE, Sybil, Mrs., M.B.E.

TREMLETT, Lieut.-Col. Colin Percy, C.B.E., *b.* 5 Aug. 1880; *s.* of Walter William Tremlett, of Exeter. *Educ.:* The Coll., Inverness. *War Work:* Served in India and Mesopotamia. *Address:* Highlands, Exeter. (C1434)

TREMLETT, Capt. Frederic Thomas George, M.B.E.

TRENAM, Lieut. Richard, M.B.E., M.C.

TRENCH, Catherine Anne Swetenham, Mrs., M.B.E.; *d.* of Sir Thos. Lecky, of Greystone Hall, Limavady, Co. Londonderry; *m.* Frederick Charles Bloomfield (who was killed in action 1st July, 1916), *s.* of Henry Bloomfield Trench, of Cangort Park, Shinrone, King's Co., Ireland. Hon. Treas., Limavady District Nursing Association. *War Work:* Member of Co. Londonderry War Pensions Committee, Limavady War Pensions Sub-Committee, and Soldiers' and Sailors' Families Association; collected money for packing and sending bales regularly to the 10th Batt. Royal Inniskilling Fusiliers (Ulster Division); raised money to pay for all parcels sent to local Prisoners of War belonging to all regiments; looked after dependants of soldiers and prisoners of war. *Address:* Greystone Hall, Limavady, Co. Londonderry. (M9887)

TRENCH, Ernest Frederick Crosbie, C.B.E., *b.* 1869; *s.* of George Frederick Trench, J.P., Kerry; *m.* 1895, Netta Wilbraham, *e.* of the late Herbert Wilbraham Taylor, J.P., of Hadley Bourne. M.A. Trin. Coll. Dublin; M.Inst.C.E.; Lieut.-Col. Eng. and Railway Staff Corps, R.E.; Chief Engineer L. & N.W. Ry. *Address:* The Firs, Croxley Green, Herts. *Club:* Union. (C3006)

TRENCH, Col. Frederick Amelius, LE POER-, C.B., C.B.E., A.S.C., *b.* 6 July, 1857; *s.* of Rev. Frederic William Le Poer Trench, rector of Rover and Brun; *m.* Mary Gertrude (*see* BURKE'S *Peerage*, Clancarty, E.) *d.* of late C. W. Roberts, M.R.C.S., of Radstock, Somerset. Served in S. Africa and during Great War. (C1663)

TRENCH, Capt. Ralph Chenevix, O.B.E., M.C.

TRENCH, Major Richard Henry Chenevix, O.B.E.

TRENCH, Gwendoline, Mrs. CHENEVIX, M.B.E., *b.* 31 Oct. 1869; *d.* of Sir John Heron-Maxwell, Bart., of Springkell House, Dumfriesshire (*see* BURKE'S *Peerage*); *m.* Richard Chenevix-Trench, *s.* of Philip Chenevix-Trench, of Botley, Hants. *War Work:* Commandant of the Bangor Women's Voluntary Aid Detachment, who nursed at the Bangor Military Hospital, 1914–15; organised and staffed Penrhyn Cottage V.A.D. Hospital. (M1031)

TRENDELL, Herbert Arthur Previte, M.V.O., C.B.E., *b.* 9 June, 1864; *s.* of the late Sir Arthur Trendell, C.M.G.; *m.* Harriette Constance, *d.* of Randal Thomas Slacke, of Annadale, Co. Leitrim. *Educ.:* Amersham Hall, Caversham, Berks. Chief Clerk, Ceremonial Department, St. James's Palace. *Address:* Ambassador's Court, St. James's Palace, S.W. 1. (O814)

TRESTRAIL, Major Alfred Bond, M.B.E., J.P., V.D., *b.* 5 Feb. 1849; *s.* of the Rev. Frederick Trestrail, D.D., of Clifton, Bristol; *m.* Clara Maud, *d.* of Richard Brodribb Sherring, of Bristol. *Educ.:* Mill Hill School; Amersham Hall; Royal Coll. of Chemistry, and the Royal School of Mines, Jermyn Street. Fellow of Royal Geographical Society; Member of the Geological Association; Vice-President Weston-super-Mare Division Liberal Association. *War Work:* Commandant of the V.A.D. Red Cross Hospital, Clevedon, 1914–19; Commandant of the Clevedon Ladies V.A.D. *Address:* Southdale, Clevedon, Somerset. (M4039)

TREVANION, Stella, O.B.E.: *d.* of Deane Webb, of Portland Place, London, W.; *m.* Charles Graham, *s.* of H. T. Trevanion, of Bournemouth. *Educ.:* Queen's Coll. *War Work:* Hon. Supt. Food, Care, and Clothing Department, Dorset Regt. *Address:* Almondbury, Poole. (O11497)

TREVASKES, Hugh Kennedy, O.B.E., I.C.S.

TREVELYAN, George Macaulay, C.B.E., *b.* 16 Feb. 1876; *s.* of Sir George Trevelyan, of Wallington; *m.* Janet Penrose, *d.* of Humphry Ward, of Stocks. *Educ.:* Harrow, and Trinity, Cambridge. *War Work:* Mission to Serbia for the Serbian Relief Committee, Nov. 1914, to Jan. 1915; Lecturing on Serbia in United States, April to May, 1915; Commandant First British Ambulance Unit (B.R.C.) for Italy, on Isonzo and Piave fronts, Aug. 1915, to Dec. 1918; Italian Silver Medal, and Cavaliere Order of St. Maurice and St. Lazarus, 1919. *Address:* Pen Rose, Berkhamsted. *Clubs:* Athenæum; National Liberal. (C3007)

TREVES, Major Frederick Boileau, O.B.E., R.A.M.C. (T.F.), *b.* 5 Jan. 1880; *s.* of William Knight Treves, of Margate. *Educ.:* Rugby School; Cambridge Univ. Hon. Visiting Surgeon, Royal Sea Bathing Hospital, Margate; Cottage Hospital, Margate, and Victoria Home for Children, Margate. *War Work:* Second in Command, 1/1st South-Eastern Mounted Brigade, Field Ambulance, Aug. 1914; T. Lieut.-Col. Commanding 1/1st South-Eastern Mounted Brigade, Field Ambulance, Oct. 1915, to March, 1917; served in Gallipoli, Western Desert, and Palestine; Major, second in Command, 24th Stationary Hospital, Kantara, E.E.F., Sept. 1917, to May, 1919. *Address:* 32, Dalby Square, Cliftonville, Margate, Kent. *Club:* Union (Margate). (O2945)

TREVETT, Major Charles George, O.B.E., R.A.S.C. (M.T.).

TREVITHICK, Arthur Reginald, C.B.E., *b.* 1858; *s.* of Francis Trevithick, of the Cliff, Penzance; *m.* 1891, Annie, *e. d.* of John Sharp, J.P., of West Cliff, Preston. Locomotive Works Manager, L. & N. W. Ry. and Wagon Sup. 1910–16, since when he has been Carriage Supt. (C3008)

TREVOR, Digby Bruce, O.B.E.

TREVOR, Col. Philip Christian William, C.B.E. Major and T. Col. R.A.O.C.; served in Great War, 1914–19 (mentioned in despatches). (C1795)

TREVOR, Rosamund, Lady, M.B.E.; *d.* of the Hon. Edmund Petre, and widow of William, 4th Earl of Sussex; *m.* 1897, Arthur William Hill-Trevor, Baron, of Brynkinalt Co. Denbigh (*see* BURKE's *Peerage*). (M1032)

TREW, George Harry Male, O.B.E.

TREW, Lieut.-Col. Richard James Fynmore, O.B.E., has Legion of Honour.

TRIBE, Eileen Mary, M.B.E., *b.* 25 Dec. 1893; *d.* of Wilberforce N. Tribe, of Stoke Bishop, Bristol. *Educ.:* Clifton High School; Paris; Berlin. *War Work:* Hon. Sec. Soldiers' and Sailors' Families Assoc., Bristol East, Sept. 1914, to Sept. 1915; Private Sec. to Assistant-Director of Naval Intelligence, Admiralty, May, 1916, to May, 1919. *Address:* Sunnyside, Stoke Bishop, Bristol. (M9888)

TRIBE, T. Capt. Frank Newton, O.B.E.

TRIBE, Major John Charles, O.B.E., R.G.A., *b.* 31 July, 1873; *s.* of W. Tribe, of Portsmouth; *m.* Mary Josephine, *d.* of J. Daly, of Co. Cork. *Educ.:* Royal Naval School, Greenwich. *War Work:* Ordnance Officer, 5th Corps Troops, B.E.F.; O.W. Railhead, B.E.F.; O.K. Railhead, B.E.F.; and Q.R. Depot, I.E.F. *Address:* Claremont, Norfolk Terrace, Brockhurst. (O3008)

TRIBE, Lieut.-Col. Paul Cuningham Edward, O.B.E., R.A.M.C.

TRICK, William Burrows, M.B.E., J.P.

TRICKER, Leonard Charles, M.B.E.

TRICKETT, Major John James, O.B.E., Aust. I.F.

TRICKETT, Wilfrid Richard, O.B.E.

TRIGG, William Ewart Gladstone, M.B.E., *b.* 7 Oct. 1880; *s.* of the late William Trigg, of Walmer, Kent. Deputy Chief Constable of Lincolnshire. *War Work:* Hon. Sec. to Central Organising Committee for Lincolnshire dealing with all emergency matters connected with invasion of county by enemy; rendering of assistance to military. *Address:* County Police Buildings, Lincoln. (M2559)

TRIGGER, Major Alfred Ernest, M.B.E.

TRIGGER, Oliver, M.B.E., F.I.C., F.C.S., *b.* 3 May, 1860; *s.* of the late William Trigger, of the Newbolds Farm, nr. Wolverhampton. *Educ.:* Brewood Grammar School, Staffordshire, and Denstone Coll., Staffs.; Royal Coll. of Chemistry, South Kensington. Analytical Chemist, recently retired from Civil Service after 37 years' work in Departments of War Office Chemist, Woolwich Arsenal. *War Work:* Worked under the Ministry of Munitions in the Directorate of Chemical Inspection, Woolwich Arsenal, first as Deputy Head Chemist, and latterly as Technical Adviser to the Directorate. *Address:* 14, Weech Road, West Hampstead, N.W. 6. (M1034)

TRIM, Sarah Ann, Mrs., O.B.E.

TRIMBLE, Samuel Delmege, O.B.E., *b.* 9 Sept. 1857; *s.* of William Trimble, of Enniskillen, Co. Fermanagh; *m.* 1st Margaret (*d.* 1900), *d.* of Charles Hersée, 2nd Susan, *d.* of William Weir, of 21, Upper Baggot Street, Dublin. *Educ.:* Enniskillen Royal School. Journalist and Newspaper Proprietor; in charge Comforts Fund for the Royal Irish Fusiliers, South African Campaign. *War Work:* 1914–18, inaugurated and in charge Comforts Fund for the Royal Irish Fusiliers, and Prisoners of War Fund, Royal Irish Fusiliers. *Address:* 36, Upper English Street, Armagh. *Club:* Unionist. (O11498)

TRIMEN, Stephen Herbert, O.B.E., *b.* 27 May, 1881; *s.* of Edward Trimen; *m.* Gladys Constance, *d.* of John Grant Morris. *Educ.:* Highgate School, and City and Guilds of London Institutes Technical Coll. Chemist, 1st Class, Egyptian Government Analytical Laboratory, Cairo. *War Work:* Work for Intelligence Dept., E.E.F. *Address:* Government Analytical Laboratory, Cairo, Egypt. *Club:* Gezim Sporting, Cairo. (O11499)

TRINGHAM, Lieut.-Col. Archibald Montgomery, D.S.O., O.B.E., late The Queen's Regt., *b.* 16 Sept. 1869; *s.* of the Rev. W. Tringham, R.D., if Longcross, Surrey; *m.* Mary Eastlake, *d.* of B. W. Leader, R.A., of Burrows Cross, Gomshall. *Educ.:* Charterhouse. *War Work:* Served in France from Sept. 1915, to May, 1918; wounded 28 May, 1918; thrice mentioned in despatches. *Address:* Hurtmore Gap, Godalming. (O8967)

TRINICK, Lieut. Fred, O.B.E., R.N.R.

TRIPE, William Archibald, M.B.E.

TRIPP, Bernard, M.B.E.

TRIPP, Capt. Horace Edgar Howard, O.B.E., R.A.S.C.

TRIPP, Leonard Owen Howard, O.B.E.

TRIPP, William Thomas, M.B.E.

TRIPPAS, Maurice, M.B.E.

TRIST, Lieut. Edward, M.B.E., R.A.F.

TRISTEM, Major Henry, O.B.E., R.A.O.C.

TRITTON, Major Claude Henry, O.B.E.

TRITTON, Sir Seymour Biscoe, K.B.E., M.I.C.E., M.I.N.A., *b.* 1860; *s.* of the late Col. F. B. Tritton, Royal Welsh Fus.; *m.* Alice May, *d.* of Louis Jullion, Ph.D., of Low Fell, Durham. *Educ.:* Haileybury Coll.; Univ. Coll., London. Received technical training at R. & W. Hawthorn's, Engineers, Newcastle-on-Tyne; India, as Assistant Loco. Supt.; Bengal and North-Western Rly. 1885; subsequently entered service of the Government of India, Eastern Bengal Rly; partner in firm of Rendal, Palmer and Tritton, Consulting Engineers to the Government of India; in this capacity acted during the war as adviser to the War Office and Ministry of Munitions for new railway work of all kinds; Chairman of the Standards Committee Conference on Locomotive Design. *Addresses:* 12–14, Dartmouth Street, Westminster, S. W. 1; Hill Manor, Surbiton Hill, Surrey. *Club:* St. Stephen's. (K178)

TROLLOPE, Fabian George, C.B.E., *b.* 1872; *s.* of Col. G. H. Trollope; *m.* 1900, Violet, *d.* of the late William Jebbutt. Chm. Minesweepers Fund. (C3009)

TROTT, Cap. Francis William, O.B.E., M.C., R.A.F.

TROTT, Nelson Hill, M.B.E.; *s.* of Thomas Cleveland Trott, of Yarcombe, Devon; *m.* Edith C., *d.* of Evan Evans, of London. *Educ.:* London. Superintending Engineer. *War Work:* Commenced as Superintending Engineer for the War Office in 1914; joined the Air Ministry Department Works and Buildings, 1917, in charge of the Aerodrome Construction, Lincolnshire; appointed District Engineer for Scotland, in 1919. *Address:* Leafmore, Victoria Avenue, Surbiton. (M9890)

TROTTER, Archibald MacGregor, O.B.E., B.A., J.P. *b.* 7 Sept. 1878; *s.* of John M. Trotter (*see* BURKE's *Landed Gentry*). *Educ.:* Privately, and Trinity Coll., Cambridge. Hon. Sec. Scottish Text Society. *War Work:* County Sec., Midlothian, for Red Cross Society, until 1916; attached at Scottish Branch Red Cross Headquarters, 1915–19; on the staff of the Western District Commissioner (Scottish Branch), as regards Auxiliary Hospital Executive work; Assistant, Organiser of the "France Day" Appeal of the Scottish Branch 1916. *Address:* Colinton House, Colinton, Midlothian, Scotland. *Clubs:* Royal Societies'; New, Edinburgh. (O11500)

TROTTER, Hon. Mrs. Charles William, O.B.E.

TROTTER, Edith Mary, C.B.E.; *d.* of the Rev. Canon H. E. Trotter, of Reading. *War Work:* Hon. work in connection with Care and Comforts Committee, Reading, 1915–16; appointed Assistant Section Controller, Q.M.A.A.C., 1917; later Recruiting Controller for S. Western Division; 1918, Assistant Chief Controller in charge of Personnel, Headquarters, Q.M.A.A.C. *Address:* Horton Lodge, Reading. (C2182)

TROTTER, Brig.-Gen. Gerald Frederick, C.B., C.M.G., C.B.E., D.S.O., M.V.O., *b.* 1871; *s.* of the late Maj.-Gen. Sir Henry Trotter, G.C.V.O. (*see* BURKE's *Peerage*, Gifford, B.). Entered Grenadier Guards, 1892; Capt. 1899; Major, 1907 (retired, 1912); Brevet Lieut.-Col. Reserve of Officers, 1916; Hon. Brig.-Gen. 1918; S. Africa, 1899–1900 (despatches); Great War, 1914–19; A.D.C. to Gov.-Gen. and Com.-in-Chief, Canada, 1909–10; appointed a Brig.-Gen on Gen. Staff, 1917; (C1132)

TROTTER, Harry Woodward, C.B.E. Assist.-Sect. Board of Excise and Customs. (C3010)

TROTTER, Capt. John Frederick Arthur, O.B.E., R.F.A.

TROTTER, Marjorie Ellinor, O.B.E.

TROTTER, Lieut. Philip Coutts, M.B.E., Welsh Guards, *b.* 27 June, 1891; *s.* of Col. Sir Philip Durham Trotter, of Mainhouse, Kelso. *Educ.:* Charterhouse; subsequently Germany and Paris. *War Work:* Intelligence Corps, 1914–16 (mentioned in despatches 1916); Household Battalion, 1916–; 17; severely wounded, Oct. 1917, at Poelcapelle; Welsh Guards, 1918; A.D.C. to Lieut.-Gen. Sir H. Gough, in Finland, 1919. *Address:* Mainhouse, Kelso. *Clubs:* Brooks's; Guards'; Cavendish; Beefsteak; New (Edinburgh). (M7011)

TROUBRIDGE, Lieut. Thomas St. Vincent Wallace, M.B.E., K.R.R.C., *b.* 15 Nov. 1895; *s.* of Capt. Sir T. H.

Troubridge, Bart., of 48, Great Cumberland Place (*see* BURKE'S *Peerage*). *Educ.*: Wellington Coll., and R.M.C., Sandhurst. *War Work*: Served in France and Salonica with K.R.R.C.; wounded, 2nd Battle Ypres; G.S.O., 3, British Mission to Italian H.Q.; awarded Croce di Guerra and Order of the Crown of Italy, by H.M. King of Italy. *Address*: 48, Great Cumberland Place. *Club*: Royal Automobile. (M5687)

TROUNCE, Alice, Mrs., M.B.E., *b.* 5 May, 1869; *d.* of William Skinner, of Woodford, Essex; *m.* Thomas Plomer Trounce, J.P., *s.* of William Trounce, of Helston, Cornwall. *Educ.*: Greenfield House, Waltham Cross. *War Work*: Hon. Sec. to a Y.M.C.A. Hostel for the Royal Gunpowder Factory, Waltham Abbey; Hon. Sec. and finally Vice-President of a Canteen for Munition Workers at Waltham Abbey. *Address*: Bank House, Waltham Abbey, Essex. (M2500)

TROUSSELOT, Major Henry Edward, O.B.E.

TROUT, Major John Charles, O.B.E.

TROUTBECK, Lieut. John Monro, O.B.E.

TROUTON, Edmund Arthur, C.B.E., B.A., *b.* 23 June, 1861; *s.* of Thomas Trouton, of Dublin. *Educ.*: Royal School, Dungannon; Trinity Coll., Dublin. Hon. Sec. County Dublin British Red Cross Society; Hon. Sec. The Adelaide Hospital, Dublin, and Director of Public Companies. *War Work*: Organiser and Chief of the Enquiry Department (British Red Cross) for Wounded and Missing and Prisoners of War (Ireland). *Address*: The Grange, Stillorgan, Co. Dublin. *Clubs*: University (Dublin); Royal Irish Yacht; Bath. (C1048)

TRUBSHAW, Lieut. Arthur Ralph, M.B.E., R.F.A., (T.)

TRUBSHAW, Gwendoline Joyce, C.B.E.; *d.* of the late Ernest Trubshaw, D.L., J.P., of Aelybryn, Llanelly. *Educ.*: Privately. *War Work*: Work in connection with Soldiers' and Sailors' Families Association, and Soldiers' and Sailors' Help Society; Chairman, Llanelly War Pensions Committee, 1917–20; Organiser of Munition Workers' Club; Ministry of Labour Employment Committee (Wales); Llanelly Local War Relief Fund. *Address*: Aelybryn, Llanelly, Carmarthenshire. (C3011)

TRUBSHAW, Wilfred, O.B.E., *b.* 16 June, 1870; *s.* of the late Alfred Trubshaw, M.R.C.S. (Eng.), of Mold, Flintshire; *m.* Bessie André, *d.* of Walter Edward Perkins, J.P., of Astwood Bank, Worcestershire, and Bodegroes, Pwllheli, Carnarvonshire. *Educ.*: Epsom Coll. Admitted Solicitor, Oct. 1893; Assistant Prosecuting Solicitor for Liverpool, 1902–04; Assistant Solicitor to Lancashire County Council, 1904–14; appointed Assistant Chief Constable of Lancashire, 1914. *Address*: Grimsargh House, nr. Preston. *Clubs*: County (Lancaster); Winckley (Preston). (O11502)

TRUEMAN Lady Susan Catherine Harriet, O.B.E., *b.* 19 March, 1854; *d.* of 2nd Earl of Strafford (*see* BURKE'S *Peerage*); *m.* Col. Thomas, *s.* of Thomas Trueman. *Address*: White Hill House, Chesham, Bucks. (O11503)

TRUEMAN, Major Thomas Edwin, O.B.E.

TRUMAN, Col. Egerton Danford, C.B.E.; *m.* 1920, Margery Dalrymple, *d.* of Reginald B. Jacomb, of Ewell, Surrey. Formerly Col. R.E.; served in Mesopotamia, 1914–19. (C1435)

TRUMBLE, Thomas, C.B.E., *b.* 1872; *s.* of the late William Trumble, formerly of Melbourne; *m.* 1899, Katherine Ellen, *d.* of the late Travers Hutchinson. *Educ.*: Wesley Coll. Melbourne. Appointed Acting Sec. Depart. of Defence, Commonwealth of Australia, 1914; Sec. 1918. *Address*: Camberwell, Victoria, Australia. *Clubs*: Athenæum; Naval and Military. (C720)

TRUMPER, John Henry Walwyn, O.B.E., B.A., *b.* 8 Jan. 1885; *s.* of the Rev. J. F. Walwyn Trumper, of Bryngwyn Rectory, Monmouthshire; *m.* Marjorie Cicely, *d.* of Col. Mackay Scobie, C.B., of Armadale, Hereford. *Educ.*: Hereford Cathedral School; St. John's Coll., Cambridge; Wells Theological Coll., Somerset. Educational work in India, 1909–11; Assistant Schoolmaster, Scartcliffe, Englefield Green, Surrey, 1911–13; Educational Work in St. Petersburg, Russia, 1913–14. *War Work*: Gazetted to the 1st Monmouthshire Regt. (T.F.) as 2nd Lieut., 9 Sept. 1914; served on the Ypres front from Feb. to May, 1915; gassed in the 2nd Battle of Ypres, 8 May, and subsequently relinquished commission owing to ill-health, 1916; entered the Foreign Office, May, 1916; resigned, July, 1919; awarded 1914–15 Star, British War Medal, and Allied War Medal. *Club*: National Liberal. (O11504)

TRUSCOTT, Frederick George Walter, M.B.E.

TRUSCOTT, Major Roy Francis, O.B.E.

TRYE, Capt. John Henry, C.B.E., R.N., *b.* 1 June, 1875; *s.* of the late Henry Norwood Trye, J.P., of Hartshill, Co. Warwick; *m.* Elizabeth Martinet, *d.* of Robert Hewitt, of Ardsley-on-Hudson, New York. *Educ.*: H.M.S. "Britannia." *Address*: The Grotto, Leckhampton, Cheltenham. *Club*: Royal Automobile. (C651)

TRYON, Capt. Henry Covey, M.B.E.

TUBB, Capt. Frederick William, O.B.E.

TUBBS, Lucinda Elizabeth Alexandra, Mrs., O.B.E.; *d.* of William McClymont, of Buenos Aires; *m.* Cyril B. Tubbs, *s.* of the late Rev. G. Ibberson-Tubbs, of St. Mary's, Reading. *Educ.*: Privately. *War Work*: Commandant V.A.D. Berks. 44, Albion House Hospital, Newbury, Jan. 1915, to Jan. 1919; kept Annexe open as a club for ex-Service men for a year. *Addresses*: Snelsmore House, Newbury; 15, Chapel Street, Belgrave Square. *Club*: Empress. (O3964)

TUBMANN, Francis de Moag, O.B.E.

TUCK, Alice Mary, M.B.E.

TUCKER, Ada Mary, Mrs., M.B.E.

TUCKER, Lieut.-Col. Albert Napoleon, O.B.E.

TUCKER, Catherine Peterkin, Mrs., M.B.E.

TUCKER, Capt. Charles Edward, O.B.E., R.A.O.C.

TUCKER, Douglas William, M.B.E.

TUCKER, Major Frederic Gordon, O.B.E., T.D., *b.* 18 Nov. 1883; *s.* of Frederick Tucker; *m.* Dorothy Kate, *d.* of Richard Spackman. *Educ.*: Heversham School, Westmorland. Private Sec. to the Parliamentary Sec., Ministry of Transport. *War Work*: Mobilised with 6th London Regt. on 4 Aug. 1914; served 3 years in France and Flanders; D.A.A.G. at General Headquarters, Oct. 1918, to Jan. 1920. *Address*: Bordyke House, Tonbridge. *Club*: Isthmian. (O5866)

TUCKER, Lieut. Frederick James, M.B.E.

TUCKER, George John, M.B.E.

TUCKER, Herbert Carey, O.B.E.

TUCKER, Ina Aveling, M.B.E., *b.* 22 Sept. 1874; *d.* of John Usher Cunningham, of Birkenhead, Cheshire; *m.* Duncan Hayter Froude, *s.* of Lieut.-Gen. Sir C. Tucker, G.C.B., G.C.V.O., of Ashburton, Devon. *Educ.*: Privately. *War Work*: Commandant of 58 Det. V.A.D., Hart House Hospital, Burnham, Som., Jan. 1915, to Aug. 1919. *Address*: Malvernhurst, Burnham, Somerset. *Club*: V.A.D. (M2562)

TUCKER, Capt. Richard Jennings, O.B.E.

TUCKER, Lieut. William Ernest, M.B.E.

TUCKER, Lieut.-Col. William Kington, C.B.E., *b.* 1877; *s.* of W. Lambley Tucker, of Calne, Wilts. Lieut.-Col. R.A.S.C.; Forage Depart. War Office; has Belgian Order of the Crown. (C1796)

TUCKETT, Walter Reginald, O.B.E., M.R.C.S. (Eng.), L.S.A. (Lond.), *b.* 7 Dec. 1859; *s.* of Dr. William Fothergill Tuckett, J.P., late of Clydach, near Abergavenny, and Bath; *m.* Nancie, *d.* of Henry Lewis Soper, of Ilford, Essex. *Educ.*: Privately; King Edward VI. School, Bath; London Hospital; London Univ. Late House Surgeon, House Physician, and Resident Accoucheur to the London Hospital; Resident Medical Officer at the Throat Hospital, Golden Square, and House Surgeon at The West Kent County Hospital, Maidstone; Hon. Consulting Medical Officer to the Charnwood Forest Convalescent Homes, and Hon. Medical Officer to the Children's Home; Medical Officer to Swithland Convalescent Home, and to the Empitts Convalescent Home for Children, Woodhouse Eaves. *War Work*: Hon. Medical Officer in charge of Charnwood Auxiliary Military Hospital; Hon. Medical Officer to Belgian Soldiers at Burton Hall, and Hon. Doctor to Belgian Refugees; mentioned in the list of the Sec. of State for War. *Address*: Woodhouse Eaves, Loughborough. (O11506)

TUCKEY, Rev. James Grove White, C.B.E., M.A., K.H.C., *b.* 5 June, 1864; *s.* of the late Charles Caulfeild Tuckey, of Charleville, Kew; *m.* Emily Louise, *d.* of the late George Mason, of Manchester. *Educ.*: King's School, Canterbury; Trinity Coll., Oxford; Heidelberg Univ. Chaplain to the Forces, 1st Class, ranking as Col.; Assistant Chaplain-General, Southern Command. *War Service*: South African War, 1899–1902, including Defence of Ladysmith and subsequent operations; mentioned in despatches; specially promoted (Queen's Medal, 6 clasps, King's Medal, 2 clasps); Great War: Senior Chaplain 4th Division; Senior Chaplain 3rd Army Corps; Senior Chaplain 2nd Army; then Assistant Chaplain-General, Rouen Area; finally Assistant Chaplain-General, Southern Command; mentioned three times in despatches, and brought to notice of Sec. of State for War for valuable services in connection with the war; 1914 Star, with clasp; British War Medal; Victory Medal, with oakleaf. *Address*: Headquarters, Southern Command, Salisbury. *Club*: Oxford and Cambridge. (C1797)

TUDOR, Major Claude Lechmere St. John, O.B.E., M.C., R.A.S.C., *b.* 27 Dec. 1888; *s.* of the Rev. Owen Lechmere Tudor, of Willingdon; *m.* Kathleen Isabel, *d.* of Hugh Inglis, of Inverness. *Educ.*: Hydneye House, Willingdon; Eastbourne Coll.; R.M.C. Sandhurst. *War Work*: O.C. 2nd Divisional Supply Column, France, Aug. 1914, to Oct. 1914; O.C. 27th (afterwards 55th) Divl. Supply Column, France, Dec. 1914, to Aug. 1916; D.A.D.T., G.H.Q., Salonica, Aug. 1916, to Dec. 1917; O.C. British M.T. Units with Serbian Army, Dec. 1917, to March, 1919. *Addresses*: c/o Sir C. R. McGrigor, Bart., & Co., 39, Panton Street, Haymarket, S.W. 1. (O6549)

TUDOR, Elizabeth, M.B.E.

TUDOR, Capt. Gerald, O.B.E.

TUDOR, Major Lechmere Howell, O.B.E.

TUDSBERY, Francis Cannon, C.B.E., M.A., LL.M., *b.* 9 Jan. 1888; *s.* of J. H. T. Tudsbery, of 100, St. George's Square, S.W. 1; *m.* Isabella Fleming, *d.* of Robert Mackay Sutherland, of Solsgirth. *Educ.*: Dulwich, and King's Coll., Cambridge. Barrister-at-Law, Middle Temple; Yorke Prizeman of Cambridge Univ.; formerly Sec. to the Surplus Government Property Disposal Board. *War Work*: Gazetted 9th Batt. Middlesex Regt., Oct. 1914; Staff Capt., Irish Rebellion, 1916; Major, Deputy Assist. Director, War Office, 1918. *Address*: 1, Mulberry Walk, Chelsea, S.W. 3. *Clubs*: Junior Carlton; Ranelagh. (C3012)

TUFNAIL, Harry Philip, M.B.E.

TUFNELL, Major Wyndham Frederick, M.B.E.

TUFTON, Stella, Hon. Mrs., O.B.E., *b.* 2 Sept. 1879; *d.* of Sir George Faudel-Phillips, 1st Batt., Balls Park, Hertford; *m.* Hon. Charles Henry, C.M.G., *s.* of 1st Baron Hothfield.

War Work: Sec. of Hospital Comforts for four London Hospitals, Territorial Force Nursing Service; Superintendent Alexandra Pavilion for Officers. *Address:* 33, Albert Road, Regent's Park, N.W. 8. (O818)

TUKE, Anna, Mrs., O.B.E.

TUKE, Capt. Godfrey, C.B.E. Com. and Acting Capt. R.N. during Great War, 1914–15, as Senior Naval Officer (mentioned in despatches). (C2301)

TUKE, Major Shirley John Montague, O.B.E., *b.* 10 Sept. 1892; *s.* of George Montague Tuke, of Sutton Valence, Kent; *m.* Mary Grace, *d.* of Thomas Newman, of Pine Hill Ore, Sussex. *Educ.:* Sutton Valence. *Address:* The Limes, Sutton Valence, Kent. (O6716)

TULK, Effie Morris, Mrs., M.B.E.

TULLOCH, Angus Alexander Gregorie, O.B.E.

TULLOCH, Lieut. Hubert Thorold, M.B.E., R.F.A.

TULLOCH, William Forbes, O.B.E., *b.* 1 Aug. 1876; *s.* of William Tulloch, of Glasgow; *m.* Margaret Farquhar, *d.* of John Farquhar. *Educ.:* Leys School, Cambridge, and Abroad. Oil Seed Crusher, and Director of Companies. *War Work:* Special worrk on behalf of the Foreign Office, Ministry of Munitions, and Ministry of Food. *Address:* Heworth Hall, York. *Clubs:* Caledonian; Yorkshire (York); Leeds (Leeds); Western (Glasgow). (O1945)

TULLOCH, Major William John, O.B.E., R.A.M.C.

TULLY, Capt. Claude Lewis Devenish, O.B.E.

TUNBRIDGE, Lieut.-Col. Walter Howard, C.B., C.M.G., C B.E., J.P., *b.* 1850; *s.* of John Nicholas Tunbridge. *Educ.:* Privately. Major and Brevet Lieut.-Col. Australian Artillery; A.D.C. to Gov.-Gen. of Australia: served in S. Africa, 1900–1, as Major Comdg. 3rd Australian Contingent of Mounted Infantry, and in command of 2nd Regt. Rhodesian Field Force (despatches); Great War, as Senior Mechanical Transport Officer. *Address:* Wolverton, Townsville, Queensland. *Club:* N. Queensland (Townsville). (C1364)

TUNKS, Charles James, M.B.E.

TUNKS, Capt. George Patrick D'Arcy Gregory, M.B.E., The Leicestershire Regt., *b.* 26 May, 1888; *s.* of the late George Gregory Tunks, of the Admiralty; *m.* Violet, *d.* of the late Ernest Barker, of Stock Exchange, London. *Educ.:* Privately. *Address:* c/o Cox & Co., 16, Charing Cross. (M5690)

TUNKS, Harold William Gregory, O.B.E., 5 July, 1875; *s.* of the late George Gregory Tunks, of Addlestone, Surrey; *m.* Dorothy, *d.* of the late John Charles Hunter-Pierce, of 51 Devonshire Street, Portland Place, W. *Educ.:* Privately Member of London Stock Exchange. *War Work:* Wing Officer, Army Pay Department. *Address:* 197, Albany Street, Gloucester Gate, London, N.W. *Club:* Thatched House. (O11507)

TUNNARD, Isabel Mary, Mrs., O.B.E., *b.* July 26, 1884; *d.* of W. H. White, of Bloxholm Hall, Lincoln; *m.* Conolly Norman, *s.* of C. T. Tunnard, of Huntingdon. *Educ.:* England and Abroad. Vice-President Boston District, S. Lincs. Branch, British Red Cross Society. *War Work:* V.A.D. work for British Red Cross Society; assisted Central Charities Committee with Repatriation of British civilian prisoners of war. *Address:* West Skirbeck House, Boston, Lincs. (O1946)

TUNNICLIFF, Edward Jones, M.B.E.

TUPMAN, Lieut.-Col. John Arthur, O.B.E.

TURBERVILL, Edith PICTON-, O.B.E.; *d.* of Col. John Picton-Turbervill, of Ewenny Priory, Glamorgan. Vice-President National Y.W.C.A.; Executive Committee National Council of Women; Chairman Criminal Law Amendment Council. *War Work:* Blue Triangle Clubs and Hostels for Service Women and Munition Workers. *Addresses:* Ewenny Priory, Glamorgan; 14, Gayfere Street, Westminster. *Club:* International Franchise. (O653)

TURBETT, Lieut.-Col. Eyre Anthony Weldon, O.B.E.

TURBETT, Lieut.-Comm. Lionel Richard William Tusmell, O.B.E., R.I.M.

TURK, Lieut. Arthur Edward, M.B.E.

TURK, Erich, M.B.E.

TURNBULL, Alice Helen, M.B.E., R.R.C. (1st class); *d.* of the late Andrew Hugh Turnbull, of Edinburgh. 1908–14, Matron Canning Town Women's Settlement Hospital, Plaistow; 1914–20, Lady Supt. Church of Scotland Deaconess Hospital, Edinburgh; at present Supt. of Health Visitors, Edinburgh. *War Work:* Matron's work at the Church of Scot. Deaconess Hospital, with military annexe affiliated to 2nd Scottish General Hospital. *Address:* The Elms, Whitehouse Loan, Edinburgh. (M9897)

TURNBULL, Amy Ruth, M.B.E.; *d.* of the late William Abbott Turnbull, of Vines, Hildenborough, Kent. *Educ.:* Privately, and Brussels. Commandant V.A.D. Kent 44. *War Work:* Joined V.A.D. Kent 44, Oct. 1914, and acted as Commandant's Sec. at Quarry Hill Hospital until July, 1915; was sent to Lyghe Annexe as Acting Lady Supt. until Dec. 1916; promoted Commandant, and had charge of Quarry Hill and Lyghe Hospitals; Hon. Sec. Marchioness Camden's V.A.D. War Fund for Tonbridge and District; passed examination and became entitled to the rank of Assist. Nurse. *Address:* The Mill House, Hildenborough, Kent. (M9898)

TURNBULL, George Drummond, M.B.E., *b.* 10 Sept. 1859; *s.* of Thomas Turnbull; *m.* Sophia, *d.* of Robert Purves, of Howden-on-Tyne. *Educ.:* British Schools, Tyne Dock. Chief Engineer. *War Work:* Traded under Admiralty orders, 1914–16, in S.S. "Wilston," sunk off Pentland Firth; ran S.S. "Iriston" under Admiralty orders, 1916–17, until torpedoed second time in Mediterranean; ran S.S. "Enterprise"

on same work. *Address:* 20, Caird Drive, Partickhill, Glasgow. (M2563)

TURNBULL, Helen Oliver, M.B.E., W.R.N.S.

TURNBULL, Herbert, M.B.E.

TURNBULL, Capt. James, C.B.E., R.D. Com. and A Capt. R.N.R.; served in Great War, 1914–19, as Port Com. of Office, Sydney, Cape Breton (mentioned in despatches). (C1207)

TURNBULL, Jane Holland, C.B.E., M.D., B.S. (Lond.), *b.* 21 May, 1871; *d.* of the late Archibald Turnbull, of 19, Blacket Place, Edinburgh. *Educ.:* St. John's, Lauder Road, Edinburgh; Wilton House School, Reading; London (Royal Free Hospital) School of Medicine for Women. Medical Officer, Ministry of Health; late Obstetrician, New Hospital for Women, Euston Road; late Surgeon, South London Hospital for Women; late Anæsthetist and Lecturer in Anæsthetics, Royal Free Hospital. *War Work:* Physician, Maternity Home Professional Classes War Relief Council; Hon. Anæsthetist, King George Hospital, Stamford Street; Controller of Medical Services, Queen Mary's Army Auxiliary Corps. *Address:* 39, Nottingham Place, London, W. 1. *Club:* Halcyon. (C652)

TURNBULL, John, M.B.E.

TURNBULL, Lucia, Mrs., M.B.E.

TURNBULL, Lieut.-Col. Thomas Eyre, O.B.E.

TURNBULL, Capt. Thomas Montgomerie, M.B.E., R.A.S.C.

TURNBULL, Major William Henry, O.B.E.

TURNER, Ada Mary, Mrs., M.B.E.,

TURNER, Adolphus Frederick Franklyn, M.B.E.,

TURNER, Albert Charles, O.B.E., *b.* 4 Sept. 1888; *s.* of Albert Turner, of Nottingham; *m.* Mabel, *d.* of Thomas Threlfall, of Rochdale and Manchester. *Educ.:* Manchester: Ross Place, Municipal Secondary School, and Coll. of Technology. Secretary and Accountant. *War Work:* Voluntary Aid Detachment, B.R.C.S., London 5 Hammersmith; Head of Finance Department and Chief Accountant, France and Belgium; Commission, H.Q. Boulogne; Joint War Committee, British Red Cross Society, and Order of St. John of Jerusalem in England; Instituted British Red Cross (France) War Savings Association; Hon. Associate Order of St. John; Officier Ordre de la Couronne de Belgique; Cruz Vermelha de Merito da Republica, Portuguesa. *Addresses:* 180, Holland Road, W. 14; 54, Clitheroe Road, Manchester, S.E. (O11509)

TURNER, Lieut. Alfred Charles, M.B.E.

TURNER, Col. Archer Lloyd Marischal, C.B.E., *b.* 1860. China, 1900 (Brevet Lieut.-Col., medal); Great War, 1914–19 (despatches). (C1798)

TURNER, Lieut. Arthur Castle, M.B.E., R.A.S.C. (T.).

TURNER, Ben, O.B.E., J.P., *b.* 25 Aug. 1863; *s.* of Jonathan Turner, of Holmfirth, Yorks; *m.* Elisabeth, *d.* of J. Hopkinson, of Huddersfield. Secretary and Journalist. *War Work:* Mayor for 2½ years during first part of the Great War; Chairman, Batley Pensions Committee; Member, Profiteering Committee, National Wool Control Board, Manpower Board, and Appeal Tribunal. *Address:* 5, Talbot Street, Batley. *Club:* 1917. (O63)

TURNER, Capt. Bernard Wilfred, M.B.E., R.E.

TURNER, Cameron, M.B.E.

TURNER, Caroline, M.B.E.

TURNER, Catherine Mary, M.B.E., *b.* 6 Aug. 1884; *d.* of Sir George Turner, of Newlands Radlett, Herts. *Educ.:* Roedean School, Brighton. *War Work:* Commandant, V.A.D. Herts 42, Wall Hall V.A.D. Hospital, Watford; Assistant County Director for Hertfordshire; V.A.D. Area Commandant, B.R.C.S., Joint Commission, France; Y.W.C.A. Hut Leader with W.A.A.C. in France. *Club:* Forum. (M2566)

TURNER, Mrs. Constance Henry, M.B.E.

TURNER, Elizabeth, Mrs., M.B.E.

TURNER, Emily Eliza, M.B.E., *b.* 13 Feb. 1876; *s.* of James Turner, of City of London. *Educ.:* Central Foundation School, Spital Square, E. Civil Servant; Superintendent of Female Staff, Ministry of Health. *War Work:* Organised and conducted with female labour certain sections of work in the National Health Insurance Commission vacated by mobilisation of men. *Address:* 10, Ranelagh Gardens, Stamford Brook, W. 6. (M9902)

TURNER, Emma Maud, O.B.E., *b.* 30 Nov. 1861; *d.* of John Andrew Turner, of Maitland, New South Wales. *Educ.:* Sydney, New South Wales, and Blackheath, England. Commandant, Dorset 72. *War Work:* Joint Commandant at Crag Head Red Cross Hospital, Bournemouth, from Aug. 1914, till Jan. 1919; Hon. Organiser and Head of Branksome Park Red Cross War Hospital Supply Depot, Feb. 1916, to Feb. 1919. *Club:* Parkstone Golf (Dorset). (O11510)

TURNER, Ernest Edward, O.B.E., J.P., M.A., *s.* of W. B. Turner, of Ponsonby Hall, Cumberland; *m.* Beatrice, *d.* of H. Unwin, of Arle Court, Cheltenham. *Educ.:* Harrow, and Exeter Coll., Oxford. *War Work:* Registrar, Cheltenham Group of Hospitals: Sec. Naunton V.A. Hospital, Cheltenham. *Clubs:* Garrick; Fly Fishers'; Ranelagh. (O11511)

TURNER, Ernest James, C.B.E., *b.* 26 Feb. 1877; *s.* of Arthur James, of Kensington; *m.* Minnie Florence, *d.* of J. Bulgin. *Educ.:* St. Paul's School and Trinity Coll., Cambridge. Assistant Sec. Revenue Department, India Office. *War Work:* Departmental work at the India Office. *Address:* 55, Addison Road, W. 14. *Club:* National Liberal. (C653)

TURNER, Capt. Francis Gordon, O.B.E.

TURNER, Eng.-Lieut.-Comm. Frederick Richard Gordon, O.B.E., R.N.

TURNER, Fredrick William, O.B.E., *b.* 26 Dec. 1858 ; *s.* of John Turner, of Rochdale, Lancs. ; *m.* Elizabeth, *d.* of Edwin Ashworth, of Rochdale, Lancs. *Educ.:* Privately. High Sheriff of the County of Anglesey, 1918–19. *War Work :* Hon. Sec. of the British Red Cross Society for the County of Anglesey. *Address :* The Moorings, Menai Bridge, Anglesey. (O11512)

TURNER, Lieut. Fulham, M.B.E.

TURNER, George, O.B.E., M.A., J.P., *b.* 23 Dec. 1852 ; *s.* of James Hovell Turner, of Cambridge ; *m.* Bertha, *d.* of Wm. Eaden Lilley, of Cambridge. *Educ.:* Perse School, St. Catharine's Coll., Cambridge, and Middle Temple. Alderman (Town Council) and Ex-Mayor ; County Councillor ; Chairman of Profiteering Committee, and of Addenbrooke's Hospital. *War Work :* Chairman of Local Tribunal and of Local War Savings Committee. *Address :* 63, Bateman Street, Cambridge. (O3965)

TURNER, George Argo, O.B.E.

TURNER, Major George Bankart, M.B.E., R.A.F.

TURNER, Capt. George Eli, O.B.E.

TURNER, Sir George Robertson, K.B.E., C.B., *b.* 22 Oct. 1855 ; *s.* of George Turner, of Sussex Gardens, Hyde Park ; *m.* Isabel Beatrice, *d.* of Frederick Augustus Du Croz, J.P., of Courtlands, East Grinstead, Sussex. *Educ.:* Uppingham School. Consulting Surgeon, St. George's Hospital, and Leatherhead School for Blind ; Consulting Surgeon, Railway Passengers Assurance Co. *War Work :* Served from 4 Aug. 1914, to June, 1919, as consultant to the Admiralty ; Surgeon-General, and later Surgeon-Rear-Admiral at the R.N. Hospitals at Chatham and Plymouth ; also Mediterranean, 1915. *Address :* 6, Half Moon Street, Piccadilly, London. *Clubs :* Wellington ; Royal Automobile ; Portland. (K256)

TURNER, Helen, Mrs., O.B.E., *b.* 1872 ; *d.* of Charles Lambert, of Kingswood, Gloucester ; *m.* Philip, *s.* of Arthur James Turner, of Kensington. *War Work :* Matron, Central Red Cross Work Rooms, 1915–19. *Address :* 73, Wimpole Street, London, W. 1. *Club :* New Victorian. (O1948)

TURNER, Helen Gertrude, Mrs., M.B.E., *b.* 1878 ; *d.* of Thomas Francis Burgess, of Lowestoft ; *m.* Sydney, *s.* of the late Walton Turner, J.P., of Ipswich. *Educ.:* Privately. Nurse, trained at the General Hospital, Birmingham ; late Member of the Chartered Nurses Society, London. *War Work :* Founded the first War Hospital Supply Depot in England on 7 Aug. 1914, at Northgate Street, Ipswich ; mentioned in despatches, 1919. *Address :* 12, St. Edmund's Road, Ipswich. (M9903)

TURNER, Major Henry Morton Stanley, M.B.E.

TURNER, Isobel Agnes, M.B.E., B.Sc., *b.* 17 May, 1892 ; *d.* of Edward B. Turner, F.R.C.S., of 21, Westbourne Terrace, W. 2. *Educ.:* St. Mary Coll., Lancaster Gate, and Bedford Coll. for Women, Univ. of London. Assistant Science Mistress, Roedean School, Brighton ; Assistant Inspector Ministry of Health, Insurance Dept. *War Work :* Unit Administrator, Q.M.A.A.C., Eastern Unit, Rouen, and Unit II., Wimereux. *Address :* 21, Westbourne Terrace, London, W. 2. *Club :* Ladies' Athenæum. (M4618)

TURNER, James, M.B.E.

TURNER, James Wilson, O.B.E.

TURNER, Lieut. John George, M.B.E., D.C.M.

TURNER, Sir Joseph, K.B.E., J.P., *b.* 1868 ; *s.* of Joseph Turner, of Sheffield ; *m.* Alice, *d.* of S. Brook, of Huddersfield. *Educ.:* Huddersfield Technical Coll. Chairman, Read, Holliday and Sons, Ltd. ; Director and Manager, British Dyes, Ltd. ; Managing Director of British Dyestuffs Corporation ; Member of Huddersfield Chamber of Commerce ; Governor of Huddersfield Technical Coll. *War Work :* Manufacture of High Explosives and Aniline Dyestuffs. *Address :* Birkby Lodge, Birkby, Huddersfield. *Clubs :* British Empire. (K436)

TURNER, Joseph Harling, C.B.E., J.P.

TURNER, Lucy Aylwin, Mrs. Morten, M.B.E., *b.* 26 May, 1867 ; *d.* of Henry George Matthews, of Portsmouth ; *m.* Henry Morten, *s.* of Henry Turner, of Portsmouth. *Educ.:* Blandford, Dorset. *War Work :* Commandant of private Red Cross Hospital, Lady's Close, Watford ; Vice-President, Red Cross, Girls' Patriotic Club. *Address :* 12, Monmouth Road, Watford. (M784)

TURNER, Col. Martin Newman, C.B., C.M.G., C.B.E., *b.* 1865 ; *s.* of the late Charles Willis Turner, of Blackheath, S.E. ; *m.* Ethel, *d.* of J. S. Hannagan, Dist. and Sessions Judge, Lucknow, and widow of Surg.-Capt. E. Cormack, R.A.M.C. *Educ.:* Blackheath Proprietary School. Entered Duke of Cornwall's L.I. 1890 ; Capt. 1899 ; Major, 1906 ; Lieut.-Col. 1912 ; Col. 1916 ; served with Kachin Hills Expedition, 1889–93 ; Burma Expedition, 1895–96, as Assist. Comdt. Mil. Police (medal with clasp) ; Great War, 1914–15, Comdg. a Batt. of his Regt. (despatches) ; Brig. Com. 1915–19. (C2359g)

TURNER, Capt. Montagu Trevor, O.B.E., M.C., 3rd Royal Sussex Regt., *b.* 30 May, 1881 ; *s.* of the late Montagu Turner, of Cuckfield, Sussex ; *m.* Josephine, *d.* of the late Edmund Watt, Civil Commissioner, Gold Coast. *Educ.:* Harrow. Solicitor. *War Work :* Served with 2nd Batt. The Royal Sussex Regt., Sept. 1914 to Feb. 1915 (present at the first Battle of Ypres) ; 1914 Star with clasp ; Assistant Provost Marshal, 39th Division, 1915–17 ; Assistant Provost Marshal, 6th Army Corps, 1917–19 ; Assistant Provost Marshal

No. 5 (Mersey Defences) Area, 1919–20 ; twice mentioned in despatches. *Address :* Carrick Cottage, St. Mawes, Cornwall. *Clubs :* Junior Carlton ; Marylebone and Free Foresters Cricket. (O2768)

TURNER, Muriel Clara, Mrs., M.B.E.

TURNER, Lieut. Noel Theodor Berwell, M.B.E.

TURNER, Percy F., C.B.E. For voluntary services rendered to the Ministry of Shipping, especially as Private Secretary and Personal Assistant to the Minister. (C3169)

TURNER, Lieut. Percy William, M.B.E., R.E.

TURNER, Philip Dymock, O.B.E., M.D. (Lond.), M.R.C.S. (Eng.), *b.* 7 Oct. 1861 ; *s.* of Benjamin B. Turner, of Tulse Hill, S.W. ; *m.* Jeanne Thérèse, *d.* of Charles Robin, of Paris. *Educ.:* Dulwich Coll. ; Univ. Coll. Hospital ; Paris ; Berlin. Medical Officer of Health, Boro' of Ryde ; Hon. Medical Officer, Royal Isle of Wight County Hospital ; Hon. Surgeon, Royal National Hospital for Consumption, Ventnor, I. of W. ; Fellow of Univ. Coll., London. *War Work :* Medical Officer in sole charge, The Castle Auxiliary Hospital, Ryde. *Addresses :* Sudburg, Ryde, I. of W. ; Ciddy Hall, East Liss, Hants. (O11513)

TURNER, Renard Orlando Sydney, O.B.E., *b.* 12 April, 1885 ; *s.* of Thos. Turner, of Dudley ; *m.* Maud, *d.* of Samuel Woodhead, of Workington. *Educ.*, Privately ; and Technical Coll., West Hartlepool. Director of two Shipping and Trading Companies. *War Work :* 1½ years in the Commercial Section of British Legation, Copenhagen, and 2 years as head of the Shipping and Coal Depts. of the British Legation in Christiania. *Addresses :* 10, Fenchurch Avenue, London, E.C. 3 ; 14, Craven Hill Gardens, W. 2. *Club :* Junior Constitutional. (O11514)

TURNER, Richard, O.B.E., M.B., Ch.M., *b.* 22 Oct. 1856 ; *s.* of the late John Turner, of Ratho. *Educ.:* Edinburgh Univ. Medical practitioner (ret.). *War Work :* Four years' work in V.A.D. Hospital, and in Military Hospital, York, as Medical Officer (civilian). *Temporary Address :* Caledonian Station Hotel, Edinburgh. *Club :* Scottish Conservative (Edinburgh). (O11853)

TURNER, Richard Miles Arundel, O.B.E., *b.* 17 Sept. 1880 ; *s.* of W. R. Eaton Turner, of Bedford ; *m.* Gertrude, *d.* of H. Steensen, of Logismose, Funen. H.M. Commercial Sec., Copenhagen. *War Work :* Commercial Attaché, H.M. Legation, Copenhagen. *Address :* Amaliegade 21, Copenhagen. (O1949)

TURNER, Robert Reginald Johnston, O.B.E.

TURNER, Lieut. Samuel Arthur, M.B.E., R.A.F.

TURNER, Samuel Thomas, O.B.E.

TURNER, Sydney George, O.B.E.

TURNER, William, M.V.O., O.B.E., M.D., M.A., *b.* 1856 ; *s.* of Robert Turner, of Keith, Banffshire. *Educ.:* Univs. of Aberdeen and Edinburgh. Held appointments as House Physician, Royal Infirmary, and Royal Hospital for Sick Children, Edinburgh ; House Surgeon, Glasgow Maternity Hospital ; Colonial Surgeon, Gibraltar, 1882–1914 ; Fellow Royal Society of Medicine. *War Work :* Principal Medical Officer, Milton Hill Military Hospital, Steventon, Berkshire, 1914–19 ; attached to the Staff of Dunblane War Hospital, Scottish Command, 1919. *Addresses :* Strathpeffer, Ross-shire ; Hotel Reina Cristina, Algeciras, Spain. *Club :* Royal Societies'. (O11854)

TURNER, Professor William Ernest Stephen, O.B.E., *b.* 22 Sept. 1881 ; *s.* of William G. Turner, of Smethwick, Staffs. ; *m.* Mary Isobel, *d.* of John Marshall, of Birmingham. *Educ.:* King Edward VI. School, Birmingham, Mason Univ. Coll., and Univ. of Birmingham. Professor of Glass Technology, Univ. of Sheffield ; Hon. Sec. Society of Glass Technology ; Editor (Quarterly) Journal of Society of Glass Technology. *War Work :* General assistance to Optical Munitions, Ministry of Munitions ; to glass manufacturers throughout the country ; in founding new Univ. Department of Glass Technology for research, and to the Society of Glass Technology. *Addresses :* The University, Sheffield ; 30, Whitworth Road, Ranmoor, Sheffield. (O3967)

TURNER, William Glasier, O.B.E.

TURNER, William Leslie, M.B.E.

TURNER, Capt. William Thomas, O.B.E.

TURNER, William Thomas, O.B.E., *b.* 10 Dec. 1888. Civil Servant. *War Work :* In connection with Peace Conference. *Address :* Waimea, Lord Roberts' Avenue, Leigh-on-Sea. (O11518)

TURNER, William Walker, M.B.E., *b.* 25 March, 1871 ; *s.* of Robert Turner, of Oundle, Northants ; *m.* Edith Julia, *d.* of Robert George Noakes, of Peterboro'. *Educ.:* Oundle School. *War Work :* Chief Accountant, Stores Department, British Red Cross Society, Headquarters. *Address :* 95, Ellerton Road, Surbiton, Surrey. (M2508)

TURNER, T. Major Douglas BORDEN-, O.B.E.

TURNER, James LOCKLEY-, O.B.E., Medaille d' Honneur avec Glaivès, late Capt. and Adjutant R.A.S.C., *b.* 25 July. 1889 ; *s.* of George Thomas Turner, of Clifton, Glos. *Educ.:* Clifton Coll. *War Work :* Sub-Inspector, Special Constabulary, Scotland Yard (Transport Section) ; Chief Petty Officer, R.N.V.R. Anti-Aircraft H.Q. Staff, Admiralty ; 4th and 6th Siege Batteries, R.G.A., France ; Adjutant to Senior Mechanical Transport Officer, 18th and 8th Corps, H.Q., France. *Address :* 74, Wigmore Street, W. 1. *Club :* Royal Colonial Institute. (O2767)

TURNER, Blanche SHEARMAN-, Mrs., M.B.E.

TURNER Lieut.-Col. Cuthbert Gambier Ryves

SYDNEY-, D.S.O., O.B.E., *b.* 1883. Major and Brevet Lieut.-Col. R.A.S.C.; Great War, 1914–19, as Lieut.-Col. on Staff (despatches, Legion of Honour, Belgian Order of the Crown, Croix de Guerre). (O3006)

TURNEY, Capt. Fred, O.B.E.

TURNEY, Horace George, O.B.E., M.D., F.R.C.P., *b.* 28 Oct. 1860; *s.* of George Leonard Turney, of Denmark Hill, S.E.; *m.* Margaret, *d.* of William Ferguson, of Edinburgh. *Educ.:* Dulwich and Trinity, Coll., Oxon. Physician to St. Thomas's Hospital. *War Work:* A la suite, 2nd London Gen. Hospital, 1914–19. *Address:* 7, Park Square West, London, N.W.1. (O8958)

TURNOCK, Walter Bertram, O.B.E., *b.* 1876; *s.* of James Turnock, of Ross, Herefordshire; *m.* Margaret Jane, *d.* of John Hughes, of Gowerton, Glam. Works Manager at Port Talbot Steelworks, Port Talbot. *War Work:* Controlling output of Shell Steel, Ship Plates, and other steel manufactures for H.M. Govt. *Address:* Danygraig, Baglan, Briton Ferry, Glam. (O1951)

TURNOR, Lady Mary Katherine C.B.E.; *d.* of Charles, 10th Marquess of Huntly (*see* BURKE'S *Peerage*); *m.* 1866, Edmund Turnor, of Stoke Rochford, Co. Lincoln. (C1049)

TURPIN, Armigill Thomas, O.B.E., *b.* 30 Sept. 1855; *s.* of Thomas Turpin, of Adelaide, South Australia; *m.* Florence Clarissa, *d.* of E. A. R. Williamson, of London. *Educ.:* Privately. Served in H.M. Civil Service, 1875; Assistant Comptroller of Accounts and Stores, Prison Commission, Home Office, 1912; Comptroller, 1920; Hon. Treas. Civil Service Benevolent Fund, 1919. *War Work:* Organised and supervised the manufacture of War Stores in H.M. Prisons, England and Wales, also in various barracks, camps, and schools. *Address:* 76, Underhill Road, Lordship Lane, London, S.E. 22. (O820)

TURPIN, Helena Augusta Mary, Mrs., O.B.E.; *d.* of Hon. A. Y. Bingham (*see* BURKE'S *Peerage*, Clanmorris, B.); *m.* Capt. William Augustus Turpin. *War Work:* Lady Smith-Dorrien's Hospital Bag Depot, from May, 1915, to Feb. 1919. *Address:* 35, Dover Street, W. *Club:* Empress. (O3938)

TURPIN, William, M.B.E.

TURPIN, William Alfred, O.B.E.

TURTILL, Alfred Robert, O.B.E.

TURTON, William Henry, M.B.E.

TURTON, Willie Jack Trevor, O.B.E., M.A., *b.* 21 Nov. 1874; *s.* of the late Lieut.-Gen. Thomas Trevor Turton (Madras Staff Corps), of Lingfield, Surrey; *m.* Mary Christina, *d.* of the late Arthur Godlee, of The Lea, Harborne, Birmingham. *Educ.:* Eton; Trinity Hall, Cambridge. Barrister-at-law; Middle Temple (Western Circuit). General Inspector, Ministry of Health. *Address:* c/o Ministry of Health, Whitehall, S.W. 1. (O1954)

TUTCHER, William Arthur, M.B.E., *b.* 8 April, 1882. *War Work:* Employed in work at War Office, Assist. Dec. War Office Appeals Committee, till Nov. 1915; later Ministry of Pensions. *Address:* The Ferns, Knaphill, Surrey. (M4043)

TWEED, Lieut. John Reginald Howard, M.B.E., I.A.

TWEEDDALE, Candida Louise, Marchioness O.B.E., *b.* 3 May, 1858; *d.* of Count Bartolucci, of Cantiano, Italy; *m.* William George Montague, 10th Marquis of Tweeddale, K.T. (who died). *War Work:* Chairman of Ladies' Emergency Committee, Navy League; hold Special Service Order, Navy League; Y.M.C.A. Order of The Red Triangle. *Address:* 6 Hill Street, Berkeley Square, London. (C3013)

TWEEDALE, James, M.B.E.

TWEEDALE, S., M.B.E.

TWEEDIE, Flight Lieut. Harley Alec, O.B.E., A.F.C.

TWEEDIE, Lieut.-Col. Frank Forbes, O.B.E., R.E.

TWEEDIE, Major Henry Carmichael, D.S.O., O.B.E., *b.* 25 Jan. 1876; *s.* of the late Major-Gen. Michael Tweedie, R.A.; *m.* Catherine Lucy Minnie, *d.* of Col. A. W. Prior, of Lyncroft, Lichfield, Staffs. *Educ.:* R.M.C., Sandhurst. Major, 2nd N. Staffordshire Regt. *War Work:* Kurram Valley Expedition, 1914, and Mohmand Disturbance, 1915, N.W. Frontier, India; 8th South Staffordshire Regt., France; severely wounded, Nov. 1916, on Somme; Commandant, R.A.F. Officers' School, Henley-on-Thames. *Address:* Cairo, Egypt. (O8206)

TWEEDY, Dorothea, M.B.E., *b.* 30 Dec. 1874; *s.* of Henry John Tweedy, of Pendower, Bromley, Kent. *Educ.:* Cheltenham Ladies' Coll. *War Work:* Commandant of V.A.D. Hospital, Springhill, Bromley, Kent. *Address:* Pendower, Bromley, Kent. *Club:* V.A.D. (M4044)

TWEEDY, Edwin, M.B.E.

TWEEDY, George Frederick, O.B.E.

TWEEDY, Hugh James, M.B.E., *b.* 7 Nov. 1858. *War Work:* Hon. Recruiting Officer, Norwood and District, 1914–16; Military Representative and National Service Representative, 1917–18. *Club:* Junior Constitutional. (M9908)

TWEEDY, Capt. William Glenholme, M.B.E.

TWIGG, Albert Percy, O.B.E.

TWIGG, Comm. Francis Walter Despard, O.B.E., R.N.

TWINE, Capt. Frank Percival, M.B.E., M.C., *b.* 11 Dec. 1877; *s.* of Percival Twine, of Worthing; *m.* Mary Jordan, *d.* of George Green, of Fulham. *Educ.:* Worthing. Builder; Member of the firm of Twine & Son, Builders, Worthing. *War Work:* Enlisted, Aug. 1914; served in the 5th Batt. Royal Sussex Regt. (T.F.), France, Feb. 1915; Commissioned, April. 1916; mentioned in despatches; wounded, 1917; rejoined Batt. Dec. 1917, in Italy; A. Capt. Feb. 1917, to Dec. 1918; A. Major, Second-in-Command, Dec. 1918, to March, 1919. *Address:* 12, Crescent Road, Worthing, Sussex. (M3216)

TWINING, Capt. Stephen Herbert, M.B.E., *b.* 28 July, 1895; *s.* of the Rev. W. H. G. Twining, of St. Stephen's Vicarage, Vincent Square, S.W. 1 *Educ.:* Hazelwood, and Lancing Coll. With the firm of Messrs. R. Twining & Co., Ltd., Tea and Coffee Merchants, 216, Strand, W.C. 2 *War Service:* Served in England, France, Belgium, Canada, and Texas; Commissioned, 13th S. B. Batt. Middlesex Regt., Sept. 1914; transferred to General List for duty with Light Trench Mortar Batteries, June, 1916, 73rd L.T.M.B.; attached to R.F.C. as A. Adjutant, April, 1917; No. 80 Canadian Reserve Squadron, June, 1917, Adjutant, School of Aerial Gunnery, R.F.C., Canada. July, 1918; Capt., Wing Adjutant, 60th and 21st Wings R.A.F. March, 1918, H.Q. No. 2 Training Group, attached S.E. Area, R.A.F. *Address:* St. Stephen's Vicarage, Vincent Square, S.W. 1. *Club:* United Sports. (M6074)

TWISS, Col. John Henry, C.B., C.B.E., *b.* 1867; *s.* of Col. Godfrey Twiss, formerly R.A.; of Southsea; *m.* Evelyn, *d.* of Maj.-Gen. A Searle, and widow of John Campbell. *Educ.:* R.M.A. Entered R.E. 1885; Capt. 1895; Brevet Major, 1900; Lieut.-Col. 1911; Col. 1914; S. African War, 1899–1902, on Staff (despatches, Queen's medal with three clasps, King's medal with two clasps); Great War, 1914–19, on Staff, and subsequently as Director of Railways (despatches, Croix de Guerre). (C1799)

TWISS, Mildred Caroline, O.B.E.

TWISS, Lieut.-Col. William Louis Oberkirch, C.B.E., M.C., F.R.G.S., *b.* 1879; *s.* of the Rev. William Christopher Twiss, formerly rector of Worstlingworth and Eyeworth, Beds. Major and Brevet Lieut.-Col. Indian Army; served in China, 1900–1 (despatches, medal with clasp); Tibet, 1903–4 (medal); Great War, 1914–19 (despatches five times, Brevet Lieut.-Col. Legion of Honour, Order of Sacred Treasure of Japan); Knight of Order of St. Olaf (Norway); has bronze medal of Royal Humane Soc. (C2183)

TWIST, Lieut. Thomas, O.B.E.

TWITCHIN, Lieut. Nathaniel Edwards, O.B.E.. R.F.A.

TWYFORD, Dora, O.B.E., *b.* 12 May, 1880; *d.* of Thomas William Twyford, D.L., of Whitmore Hall, Newcastle, Staffordshire. *War Work:* Hon. Sec. Soldiers' and Sailors' Families Association, Hanley Division, from Aug. 1914; Hon. Sec. Hanley Disablement War Pensions Committee; Joint Hon. Sec. Hanley War Pensions Committee; Township Leader of the Whitmore Township, British Red Cross Society, Staffordshire Branch, Newcastle Division. *Address:* Whitmore Hall, Newcastle, Staffordshire. (O11519)

TWYNAM, Nora Cecilia, M.B.E.

TYDEMAN, Ethel, Mrs., M.B.E.

TYLEE, Major Arthur Kellan, O.B.E., R.A.F.

TYLER, Capt. Arthur George, M.B.E.

TYLER, Major Francis Cameron, O.B.E., R.F.A. (ret.), *b.* 29 June, 1874; *s.* of the late Major-Gen. Charles James Tyler, Royal Artillery; *m.* Constance Anne, *d.* of the late John Fair, of Wilderton, Bournemouth. *Educ.:* Charterhouse, and Royal Military Academy, Woolwich. *War Work:* Served as Officer of Reserve; Instructor in Gunnery, School of Instruction, R.H. and R.F.A., Shoeburyness; and on Experimental Staff, at Chapperton Down Artillery School, Salisbury; mentioned in despatches for Home Service. *Address:* Wurlie, West Hill, Ottery St. Mary, Devon. *Club:* Army and Navy. (O1958)

TYLER, Lieut. and Qr.-Mr. Frederick Montague, M.B.E., R.E.

TYLER, Capt. James Herbert, M.B.E., R.A.F.

TYLER, Lieut.-Col Ralph Edward, O.B.E., R.G.A., *b.* 27 July, 1868; *s.* of the late Major-Gen. C. J. Tyler, Royal Artillery, of Eastbourne. *Educ.:* Cheltenham Coll. Commanding Royal Garrison Artillery, Singapore, S.S. *War Work:* Served N.W. Frontier, India, 1897 (medal with clasps); N.W. Frontier Disturbances, 1897; Terah Expedition, 1897–98; South African War, 1899–1902 (Queen's Medal with clasps, King's Medal with clasps, mentioned in despatches, wounded); Major, "B " 94th Bgde., R.F.A., 21st Division, Battle of Loos, 1915; Lieut.-Col., O.C. 57th Heavy Artillery Group, R.G.A., Somme, 1916; Commandant, No. 1 R.G.A., Officer Cadet School, Trowbridge, Jan. to August, 1917; and of Coast Artillery School, Golden Hill, Isle of Wight, Aug. 1917, to June, 1918; C.R.A. Harwich Garrison, March, 1918, to April, 1919; mentioned in despatches. *Address:* c/o Messrs. Cox & Co., 16, Charing Cross. *Club:* Junior Army and Navy. (O7797)

TYLER, George Dacre HARDINGE-, C.B.E., *b.* 17 Feb. 1881; *s.* of William Hardinge-Tyler, Bengal Civil Service; *m.* Alys Merial, *d.* of John Arthur Talbot, of Newtown, Montgomery. *Educ.:* Harrow, and New Coll., Oxford. Barrister-at-law. *War Work:* Assistant in Trade Division, Naval Staff, Admiralty. *Addresses:* Great Missenden, Bucks; 61, Egerton Gardens, S.W. (C3014)

TYLER, Eng.-Comm. Thomas Richard, O.B.E., R.N.R.

TYLER, Walter Edward, M.B.E.

TYLOR, Capt. George Cunningham, O.B.E., R.F.A.

TYMONS, Major Francis Parnell, O.B.E.

TYNDALE, Lieut. Henry Edmund Guise, M.B.E.

TYNDALE, Walter Clifford, O.B.E., M.I.C.E., F.R.S.I., F.G.S., *b.* 26 July, 1853; *s.* of the Rev. Henry Annesley Tyndale, of Holton, Oxon.; *m.* Mary, *d.* of George Tyndale, of Ealing. *Educ.:* Haileybury, and King's Coll., London. Civil Engineer; Sanitary Adviser to the W.D. *War Work:* Advising the W.D. on drainage and water supply in connection with barracks and hut camps in the United Kingdom. *Addresses:* Swallowfield, Ealing; Foresthill, Oxon. (O822)

TYRER, **William Henry**, O.B.E., *b.* 4 Feb. 1876; *s.* of Stephen Tyrer, of Wigan; *m.* Ellen, *d.* of George James Bridge, of Wigan. *Educ.:* Wigan Grammar School. Town Clerk of Wigan; Clerk to Local Education Authority; Borough Prosecuting Solicitor for Wigan; Registration Officer (Representation of the People Act) for Wigan; Hon. Sec. and Solicitor to Maypole Colliery Disaster Fund. *War Work:* Hon. Sec. to Local War Pensions, Local Representative, Belgian Refugees, Munitions, and National Service Committees; Hon. Clerk to Wigan Local Tribunal; Hon. Food Executive Officer. *Address:* Lyndale, Wigan. (O11520)

TYRRELL, **Lieut.-Col. Augustus Charles Lionel**, O.B.E.

TYRRELL, **Col. Charles Robert**, C.B., C.B.E., A.M.S. (ret.), *b.* 2 Dec. 1859; *m.* Agnes Laura Livesey. *War Work:* Employed at War Office, 1914–17; Commissioner of Medical Services, Ministry of National Service, 1917–18; A.D.M.S., London District, 1918–19; Deputy Chief Commissioner, St. John Ambulance Brigade, 1914–19. *Address:* 5, The Green, Wimbledon Common, S.W. 19. *Club:* Junior United Service. (C1800)

TYRRELL, **Pilot Officer John Ernest**, M.B.E., R.A.F.

TYRRELL, **Lieut.-Col. John Frederick**, C.B.E., *b.* 1872. Lieut.-Col. Indian Army; served in the Great War, 1914–18 (despatches thrice); Afghan War, 1919. (C3105)

TYRRELL, **Major Reginald Bramley**, O.B.E., R.A.O.C.

TYRWHITT, **Rev. Canon, the Hon. Leonard Francis**, M.V.O., O.B.E., M.A., *b.* 29 Oct. 1863; *s.* of Sir H. Tyrwhitt, 3rd Bart. (*see* BURKE'S *Peerage*), and Baroness Berners (*see* BURKE'S *Peerage*). *Educ.:* Marlborough, Magdalene Coll., Cambridge; Wells Theological Coll. Curate at Henley-on-Thames, Hendon, Middlesex; Chaplain to H.M.S. "Renown," for tour of T.R.H.'s the Prince and Princess of Wales to India, 1905–6; Vicar of Fenton, 1895–1907; Vice-Provost of Denstone since 1906; Acting Chaplain to the Forces, 1914; mentioned in despatches, Deputy Assist. Chaplain-General, 1918; Rector of Rolleston, since 1907; Canon of St. George's Chapel, Windsor, since 1910; Chaplain in Ordinary to the King. *Addresses:* Rolleston Rectory, Burton-on-Trent; The Cloisters, Windsor. *Club:* Wellington. (O5871)

TYSON, **Lieut. William**, M.B.E.

TYTHERLEIGH, **2nd Lieut. Arthur Henry**, M.B.E.

TYZACK, **Walter**, O.B.E.

UDEN, **Lieut. Walter Jeffery**, M.B.E., R.N., *b.* 9 June, 1886; *s.* of John Uden, of Guston, Kent; *m.* Flora Mary, *d.* of John Moffatt, of Portsmouth. *Educ.:* Privately. Torpedo Depot, Portsmouth, for Inspection of Warheads. *War Work:* In H.M.S. "Canopus" at Falkland, and at Dardanelles; later Ordnance Supply Officer at the Nore. *Address:* H.M.S. "Vernon." (M2572)

UFF, **Capt. Sidney ALBAN-**, O.B.E., R.A.S.C.

UGANDA, **Rt. Rev. John Jamieson Willis, Bishop of**, O.B.E., D.D., *b.* 8 Nov. 1872; *s.* of Sir William Willis, of Lee, Kent. *Educ.:* Haileybury; Pembroke Coll., Camb.; Ridley Hall, Camb. Bishop of Uganda, 1912. *War Work:* Assistance rendered in German East African Campaign, particularly in connection with raising the African Native Medical Corps, and East African Native Transport Corps, from among boys educated in Mission School, Uganda. *Address:* Dunan, Aldeburgh, Suffolk. (O8419)

UMFREVILLE, **Brig.-Gen. Percy**, C.M.G., C.B.E., *b.* 1868. Entered Royal W. Kent Regt. 1887; Capt. 1896; Major, 1905; Brevet Lieut.-Col. 1917; Lieut.-Col. 1919; served in Great War, 1914–19 (mentioned in despatches); appointed Director of Military Prisons in the Field, 1916; Comdt. of a Detention Barracks, 1917; Director of Military Prisons, 1919, with rank of Brig.-Gen. (C1336)

UMNEY, **Percy**, M.B.E.

UNDERHILL, **Francis Olive**, M.B.E.

UNDERHILL, **Hugh Harman**, O.B.E., *b.* 12 June, 1864; *s.* of Paymaster-in-Chief G. W. Underhill, R.N., Lugley House, Newport, I. of W.; *m.* Annie Teresa Mary, *d.* of James Francis Caulfield, late of Manchester. *Educ.:* King's Coll. School, London. Assistant Supt. of Charts, Hydrographic Dept., Admiralty. *War Work:* Employed at Admiralty. *Address:* 50, Nevern Square, S.W. 5. *Clubs:* Royal Thames Yacht; Ranelagh. (O823)

UNDERHILL, **Major Owen**, O.B.E., *b.* 4 Jan. 1887; *s.* of Thomas Underhill, of Tachbrook, near Leamington Spa; *m.* Annie, *d.* of Thomas Corbett, of Wellington. *War Work:* Served in France, 1915–19; wounded; retired. *Addresses:* Prospect Hill Place, Greenock; c/o Cox & Co. (O5872)

UNDERHILL, **Thomas John**, O.B.E., F.I.C., F.C.S., *b.* 16 Sept. 1862. Senior Technical Examining Officer, Food and Clothing for the Royal Navy; for 38 years in H.M. Service; has visited all parts of the world on behalf of Admiralty in connection with Naval Food Supply. *War Work:* Dealing with Naval Stores; holds several silver and bronze medals for Technology from the City of London Guilds Institute and the Society of Arts. *Address:* Stanley, 53, Lanercost Road, Tulse Hill Park, Brixton, S.W. 2. (O11522)

UNDERWOOD, **2nd Lieut. Reginald Edward**, M.B.E.

UNGER, **Lieut. John**, M.B.E., E.A.F.

UNIACKE, **Lieut.-Col. Cecil Dudley Woodgate**, O.B.E., R.A.

UNSWORTH, **Isaac**, O.B.E., *b.* 23 Dec. 1861. Officer,

Salvation Army. *War Work:* Chaplain's duty, mainly among Australian troops, in Egypt, France, and on Salisbury Plain; supervised transport of Red Cross stores from Egypt to Gallipoli and Mudros. *Addresses:* 101, Queen Victoria Street, London, E.C. 4; Royal Colonial Institute, Northumberland Avenue, W.C. 2. (O11523)

UNSWORTH, **Capt. Richard Lewis**, O.B.E., R.A.S.C.

UNTHANK, **Agnes Elizabeth**, M.B.E.

UNWIN, **Lieut. Arthur John**, M.B.E., *b.* 1 July, 1890; *s.* of James Unwin, of Muswell Hill, N. 10. *Educ.:* Newcastle-under-Lyme. Director of Dried Fruits Branch, Ministry of Food. *War Work:* Joined Army, Aug. 1914; active service in Gallipoli and Mesopotamia; wounded. *Address:* 32, Wellington Square, Chelsea, S.W. 3. *Club:* Junior Army and Navy. (M9912)

UNWIN, **Major Frederick Henry**, O.B.E., R.A.F.

UNWIN, **Major Thomas Barton**, O.B.E., M.B., R.A.M.C., *b.* 5 March, 1875; *s.* of John Brooke Unwin, of Dunsmore House, Dunchurch, Rugby; *m.* Amy, *d.* of Thomas Henry Robinson, of Clapham Park, S.W. *Educ.:* Rugby; Univ. of Edinburgh. *Clubs:* Junior United Service; Royal Automobile. (O2769)

UPHAM, **2nd Lieut. John Albert Austin**, M.B.E.

UPHAM, **Paymaster Lieut. John William**, O.B.E., R.N.R.

UPJOHN, **Capt. Dudley Francis**, M.B.E., R.A.F.

UPJOHN, **Lieut.-Col. William George Dismore**, O.B.E., Aust. A.M.C.

UPTON, **Capt. Norman Royce**, M.B.E.

UPTON, **Lieut. Thomas Haynes**, O.B.E., R.E.

UPTON, **William James**, M.B.E.

URE, **Georgiana Jean Elizabeth, Mrs.**, O.B.E.

URE, **Capt. John Holmes**, O.B.E., R.E.

URELL, **Lieut. Valentine**, M.B.E., R.N.

URIE, **John**, O.B.E.

URMSON, **Capt. Gilbert Alexander**, M.B.E., *b.* 4 March, 1884; *s.* of Francis Birley Urmson, of Bampton, Devon; *m.* Dorothea, *d.* of W. N. Hutchings, of Frodsham, Cheshire. *Educ.:* Wellington Coll. Tanner. *War Work:* Served with R.A.S.C. (Supplies) in Mesopotamia from Dec. 1916, to Jan. 1920; two years attached to Director of Supplies and Transport Office, Bagdad. *Address:* Simonsdelf, Frodsham, Cheshire. (M4935)

URQUHART, **Alexander Lewis**, O.B.E., M.B., Ch.B., D.P.H., *b.* April, 1887; *s.* of Alexander Reid Urquhart, M.D., LL.D.; *m.* Annie, *d.* of D. F. Addis, I.C.S. (ret.). *Educ.:* Edinburgh Academy; Edinburgh Univ. Physician; (late) Royal Army Medical Corps; Senior Assistant, Bacteriologist; St. Thomas's Hospital, London. *War Work:* Served in the R.A.M.C. in France, 1914–15; Salonica, 1916–18; O.C. I. Mobile Bacteriological Laboratory, Salonica Army; O.C. Central Laboratory, Salonica Army. *Address:* 31, Sussex Place. Regent's Park, N.W. 1. (O1959)

URQUHART, **Lieut. Charles Ernest**, M.B.E., R.A.O.C.

URQUHART, **Herbert**, M.B.E.

URWICK, **Major Lyndall Fownes**, O.B.E., M.C.

URWICK, **Thirza Beatrice, Mrs.**, O.B.E., *b.* 17 Feb. 1884; *d.* of E. L. Thornton, of Oporto, and Weybridge; *m.* Reginald Henry, *s.* of W. H. Urwick, of London. *War Work:* Hon. Sec. Shropshire Voluntary Aid Organisation, Red Cross Workrooms; Member of Committee, K.S.L.I. Prisoners of War Fund, Hon. Sec. of Clothing Department. *Address:* Council House Court, Shrewsbury. (O1960)

URWIN, **Major John Johnson**, O.B.E., M.B., I.M.S.

USHER, **Archibald Rhys**, M.B.E.

USHER, **Capt. Charles Milne**, O.B.E., *b.* 6 Sept. 1891; *s.* of Robert Usher, of Edinburgh. *Educ.:* Merchiston Castle School. Capt. Gordon Highlanders. *Address:* c/o Messrs. Holt & Co. (O4489B)

USHER, **George Edwin**, M.B.E.

USHER, **Rachel Lilian May**, M.B.E.

USHER, **Tom Caizley**, M.B.E., C.C., *b.* 11 Nov. 1867; *e.s.* of Ralph H. Usher; *m.* Sarah Ann, *d.* of Thomas Jennings, of Darlington. Master Textile Machinery Engineer. *War Work:* Military, National Service Representation; War Pensions Committee; Hospital Committee; and other work. *Address:* Foxhill Bank, Oswaldtwistle. (M9914)

USMAR, **Lieut.-Col. George Henry**, O.B.E.

UTHWATT, **Elsie Mary, Mrs. Andrewes**, O.B.E.; *d.* of the late John C. Small, of Nottingham; *m.* William Andrewes, *s.* of T. Andrewes Uthwatt, of Maids Moreton, Buckingham. *Educ.:* Taunton, Somerset. *War Work:* Commandant from April, 1915, to Feb. 1919, at Burgage Manor Auxiliary Hospital, Southwell, Notts. *Address:* St. Luke's Vicarage, Derby. (O3928)

UTTERTON, **Capt. A.**, M.B.E., R.A.S.C.

UTTON, **Capt. Frederick William**, O.B.E.

VALADIER, **Major Sir Auguste Charles**, K.B.E., C.M.G., *b.* 26 Nov. 1873; *s.* of Charles Jean Baptiste Valadier; *m.* Alice, *d.* of John Maxwell Wright. Dental Surgeon. *War Work:* Joined (volunteered) Red Cross, Aug. 1914; Dental work; organised Maxillo-Facial Hospital, B.E.F.; served as Major until 1919; twice mentioned in despatches; has order of St. John of Jerusalem; Legion of Honour; Mons Medal. *Address:* 47, Ave. Hoche, Paris. *Clubs:* Cercle Voluay, Paris; Cercle Hoche. Racing Club de France. (K446)

VALENTINE, **Catherine, Mrs.**, M.B.E., *b.* 20 Feb. 1859;

d. of Walter Watkins, of Delbury ; *m.* Samuel Herbert, *s.* of John Valentine, of Ludlow. Mayoress of Ludlow from 1913–17. *War Work :* President of Ludlow Branch of Queen Mary's Needlework Guild, from Aug. 1914, to Jan. 1919 ; Medaille de la Reine Elisabeth, for work with Belgian Refugees. *Address :* Hawthornden, Ludlow, Shropshire. (M4046)

VALENTINE, George Herbert, M.B.E.

VALENTINE, Herbert Hughes, M.B.E., *b.* 21 Aug. 1865 ; *s.* of John Valentine, of Ludlow. *Educ. :* Ludlow Grammar School. *War Work :* Chief Clerk, Commanding Royal Engineer's Office, Weymouth. *Address :* 105, Dorchester Road, Weymouth. (M9916)

VALENTINE, Col. Thomas Harcourt Ambrose, C.B.E. Col. New Zealand Forces ; served in Great War, 1915–19 (mentioned in despatches). (C1876)

VALERIE, Capt. John, O.B.E., R.A.F., *b.* 6 March, 1866 ; *m.* Marion Frances, *d.* of the Rev. R. Leslie Morris, late Rector of Brook, Isle of Wight. *Educ. :* Shrewsbury, and Cambridge Univ. Surgeon. *War Work :* Medical Officer to Middlesex Red Cross Hospital, Hanworth Park ; Officer Commanding the Hampton Court Auxiliary Military Hospital ; Capt. in R.A.F. Medical Service. *Address :* The Green, Hampton Court, Middlesex. *Club :* R.A.F. (O11524)

VALLANGE, Capt. Clement, O.B.E., *b.* 1870 ; *s.* of the late William Vallange Condell, of Melbourne, Australia ; *m.* Sylvia Beatrice, *d.* of the late Sir John Madden, G.C.M.G., Lieutenant-Governor of Victoria. *Educ. :* Harrow, and Merton Coll., Oxford. Served in 3rd Batt. The Buffs, South African War ; private Sec. to Governor of Victoria, 1901–3. *War Work :* Intelligence Officer, Sheerness, 1915 ; Ministry of Munitions, 1916–18. *Address :* 5, Basil Mansions, S.W. 3. *Clubs :* Orleans ; R.A.C. (O824)

VALLAT, Lieut.-Col. Frederick William, O.B.E., *b.* 23 Jan. 1875 ; *s.* of G. F. Vallat, of London.; *m.* Marie Irma, *d.* of Jules Maillard, of St. Quentin, France. *Educ. :* St. Paul's. Engineer. *War Work :* Served overseas. *Address :* 26, Stonor Road, West Kensington. *Club :* R.C.Y.C. (O2301)

VALLENTIN, Lieut.-Col. Henry Edward, D.S.O., C.B.E., late R.A., *b.* 5 Jan. 1870 ; *s.* of Sir James Vallentin, of Essex. *m.* Claudine, *d.* of the Rev. R. Orr, Vicar of Thurleigh, Beds. *Educ. :* Haileybury, and Royal Military Academy, Woolwich. *War Work :* Served in France, 1914–16 ; at War Office, 1916–18. *Address :* Eastfield, Weyhill, Andover. *Club :* Army and Navy. (O3197)

VALON, Major Albert Robert, O.B.E., M.C., *b.* 9 June, 1885 ; *s.* of Ernest Julian Daniel Valon, of Charlton, Kent ; *m.* Nellie Hildred, *d.* of Thomas Watson Worke, of Dublin. *Educ. :* Univ. Coll., London. *War Work :* Instructor, Ordnance Coll., Woolwich, 1914–15 ; Aug. 1915, to Jan. 1919, served with B.E.F., France. *Address :* Rathmore, Grosvenor Road, Rathgar, Dublin. (O5876)

VALPY, Bertha, Mrs., O.B.E.

VAN BAERLE, Capt. Edward, O.B.E., *b.* 6 Aug. 1861 ; *s.* of Hislop van Baerle ; *m.* Elizabeth, *d.* of — Kettlewell. *Educ. :* Christ's Hospital. Editorial Staff, Cassels & Co. ; Sub-Editor, " Magazine of Art," 1878–81 ; Editor, " Queenstown Free Press," South Africa, 1882 ; Art Director, Yorkshire Royal Jubilee Exhibition, 1887 ; Commission, Scottish Rifles, (7th Batt.), 1894–1901. *War Work :* Rejoined Scottish Rifles, 1914 ; Staff Capt. 26th Division ; Military Representative, France. *Clubs :* Royal Automobile ; Primrose. (O9915)

VAN BERGEN, Ethel, Mrs., O.B.E. ; *m.* Capt. Harry A. Van Bergen. *Address :* Ferney Hall, Oniburg, Salop. (O3618)

VAN COLLER, Christian Audries Brenk, M.B.E.

VAN COLLER, Major Paul Johannes, O.B.E.

VANDELEUR, Major and Brevet Lieut.-Col. Henry Martley, C.B.E., R.A., *b.* 12 Dec. 1875 ; younger *s.* of the Rev. G. O. Vandeleur, of Ballinamona ; *m.* Theodosia Agnes, *d.* of the late W. H. Sinclair, of Morton Manor, Brading. *Educ. :* Bedford School, and R.M. Academy, Woolwich. *Club :* Army and Navy. (C1801)

VANDELEUR, Mary Evelyn, Mrs., M.B.E.

VAN DEN BERGH, Major Henry Edward, O.B.E., *b.* 1882 ; *s.* of Jacob Van Den Bergh, of London ; *m.* Enid, *d.* of Dr. Macdonald Brown, F.R.C.S., of London. *Educ. :* City of London School, and Abroad. *War Work :* Officer in charge of Supplies, Navy and Army Canteen Board. *Address :* Brook Lodge, Hendon. *Club :* Royal Automobile. (O825)

Van DE POL, Florence Clara, Mrs., M.B.E.

VAN DER BIJL, Kate Amy, Mrs., M.B.E.

VAN DER BYL, Lieut.-Col. Voltelin Albert William, O.B.E.

VANDERFELT, Capt. Sydney Gorton, O.B.E., R.A.S.C.

VAN DER HEUVEL, Frederick William Arthur, Count, O.B.E.

VAN DER MEULEN, Sir Frederick Alan, O.B.E., Knt. Bach., *b.* 1875 ; *s.* of the Rev. G. A. Van der Meulen, of Brook Knoyle, Wilts. ; *m.* Aline, *d.* of Buddle Atkinson, of Woolley Grange, Wilts. *Educ. :* Blundells, Tiverton, and Keble Coll., Oxford. Solicitor-General, Sierra Leone, 1908–1914 ; Judge of Supreme Court, Gambia, 1914–19 ; Puisne Judge, Nigeria, from 1919. *War Work :* Acting Assistant-Principal, War Office, 1917–18. *Address :* Calverley, St. Albans. *Clubs :* Oxford and Cambridge ; Royal Automobile. (O3835)

VANE, Harry Tempest, C.B.E., *b.* 10 Nov. 1874 ; *s.* of James Vane, of Cuxton ; *m.* Florence Emmara Maud, *d.* of Stephen Burley, of Woolwich. Managing Director, D. Napier and Son, Ltd., Acton ; Chairman, Cunard Motor and Carriage Co., Putney. *War Work :* In connection with supplies of Aero Engine and Mechanical Transport. *Address :* Highfield, Beaconsfield, Bucks. *Club :* Royal Automobile. (C71)

VANE, Sybil, M.B.E.

VANES, Edith Mary, Mrs., M.B.E., *b.* 19 Sept. 1863 ; *d.* of Butterworth Broadbent, of Snowlea, Huddersfield ; *m.* the Rev. James Alfred Vanes, Wesleyan Chaplain, Bangalore, *s.* of the Rev. John Vanes, of Ealing. *War Work :* In connection with Wesleyan Soldiers' Home and Club ; Station Hospital, and Red Cross. *Addresses :* 1, Trinity Road, Bangalore ; Longwood Edge, Huddersfield. (M6264)

VAN GRUTTEN, Capt. Winchcombe Norman Carpenter, O.B.E., M.C., late Capt. R.A., *b.* 9 June, 1895 ; *s.* of Lucien S. L. van Grutten, of Rosteague, Portscatho, S.O., Cornwall ; *m.* Enid Winifred, *d.* of the late Lieut.-Col. Robert Barrington-Baker, Naval Ordnance. *Educ. :* Cheltenham Coll. ; King's Coll., Cambridge. *War Work :* Lieut. in C Battery, 103rd Bgde., R.F.A., England, Nov. 1914 ; France, Aug. 1915 ; Adjutant, 103rd Brigade R.F.A., in France, Jan. 1916 to April, 1917 ; Reconnaissance Officer, R.A., H.Q. 18th Corps (Capt.), April, 1917, to July, 1918 ; 8th Corps, July, 1918, to Feb. 1919 ; Croix de Guerre with Gold Star, March 1918. *Addresses :* King's Coll., Cambridge ; Rosteague, Portscatho, S.O., Cornwall. (O2770)

VAN HECKE, Hilda Gertrude, Mrs., M.B.E.

VANKATARAMAYYA, Saguria, Mrs., M.B.E.

VANN, Walter Gerald, M.B.E., A.C.A., *b.* 26 Nov. 1886 ; *s.* of A. M. Vann, M.R.C.S. (Eng.), L.R.C.P., of Durham ; *m.* Ethel Mary, *d.* of W. Rushworth, F.R.I.B.A., of Durham. *Educ. :* Durham School. Chartered Accountant. *War Work :* Organising Sec. to British Farmers' Red Cross Fund, founded by Sir Herbert Brown, K.B.E., which raised over £1,000,000 for British Red Cross Society. *Address :* Dunelm, Chapel Road, Warlingham, Surrey. (M1041)

VANNECK, Arthur Percy, M.B.E., *b.* 4 Oct. 1870 ; *m.* Annie, *d.* of Richard Armstrong. *Educ. :* Balliol Coll., Oxford. Barrister-at-Law. *War Work :* R.N.V.R. (Anti-Aircraft Corps), 1914–16 ; Lieut. R.G.A. (S.R.), 1916–18 ; Staff-Lieut. I. (b), Western Command, 1918–19. *Address :* 43, Westbourne Gardens, London, W. 2. (M2577)

VAN RYNEVELD, Lieut.-Col. Sir Hetperus Andrias, K.B.E., D.S.O., M.C., late R.A.F. Made the pioneer flight with Sir Joseph Quinton Brand, D.S.O., M.C., D.F.C., from London to Cape Town in 1920. Served in Great War ; mentioned in despatches ; has Croix de Guerre, Legion of Honour, and Order of Leopold of Belgium. (K448)

VANSAGNEW, Lieut.-Col., O.B.E.

VANSITTART, Capt. Robert Arnold, M.B.E.

VAN STRAUBENZEE, Brig.-Gen. Casimir Henry Claude, C.B., C.B.E., *b.* 30 Jan. 1864 ; *s.* of Lieut.-Col. Frederick van Straubenzee, late 13th P.A. Somersetshire L.I. ; *m.* Evelyn Thornton, *d.* of Robert Bell, late of Norris Castle, I. of W. *Educ. ;* Sherborne. *War Work :* Commanded Brigade, 1914–16 (twice mentioned in despatches), and subsequently No. 5A District, to June, 1919, when he retired. *Address :* 3, Sussex Mansions, S.W. 7. *Club :* Army and Navy. (C1802)

VAN TYEN, Capt. Martinus Sibillus Jan Casper, M.B.E.

VAN ZIJL, Carel Johannes, O.B.E.

VARDON, Capt. Eric John, M.B.E., *b.* 1 Oct. 1892 ; *s.* of P. J. Vardon, of The Clock House, Bramley, Surrey. *Educ. :* Malvern Coll. Assistant Master, Elstree School. *War Work :* Served with 5th East Surrey Regiment, Sept. 1914, to Dec. 1917 ; with 16th Queens, Dec. 1917, to Nov. 1918 ; and in North Russia, as D.A.A. and Q.M.G. *Addresses :* Elstree School, Elstree, Herts ; The Clock House, Bramley, Surrey. (M5009)

VARDY, George, M.B.E.

VARLEY, Capt. and Qr.-Mr. James, O.B.E., R.A.M.C.

VARLEY, John, M.B.E.

VARNEY, Arthur, M.B.E., *b.* 10 Oct. 1870 ; *s.* of Elizabeth and Alfred Varney, of Belper, Derbyshire ; *m.* Charlotte Ann, *d.* of the late Rev. L. E. Ellis, of Alfreton, Derbyshire. *Educ. :* Public School, Belper, and Saltley Training College, Birmingham. National General Secretary, Y.M.C.A. of New Zealand. *War Work :* In charge of New Zealand Y.M.C.A. War Work during the whole period of the work ; visited England and France in 1916–17. *Address :* Y.M.C.A. Headquarters, Wellington, New Zealand. (M1203)

VARPILLEUX, Capt. Antoine Emilie, M.B.E. (M3445)

VARWELL, Margaret, Mrs., O.B.E. ; *d.* of William Logan, J.P., of Langley Park, Durham ; *m.* Peter, *s.* of Peter Varwell, of Brixham, S. Devon. *War Work :* Assisted in various work at Dartmouth. *Address :* Bank House, Bideford. (O11525)

VARWELL, Millie Gertrude, Mrs., M.B.E., B.A., *b.* 4 Dec. 1891 ; *d.* of the Rev. G. W. Clutterbuck, of Bombay ; *m.* John Browning, *s.* of W. W. Varwell, of Paignton, Devon. *Educ. :* North London Collegiate School, and Birkbeck. *War Work :* Employed in Air Ministry, 1916–19 ; Registry work, and later Private Sec. to Head of Medical Dept. *Address :* 35, Portland Road, N. 4. (M1548)

VASEY, Major Charles James, O.B.E.

VASSE, Kate, M.B.E.

VASSIE, Capt. and Qr.-Mr. Frederick Charles, M.B.E., R.G.A.

VAUGHAN, Arthur Ronald, M.B.E.

VAUGHAN, Major Charles Jerome, O.B.E., R.E.

VAUGHAN, Ethel Irene, M.B.E.

VAUGHAN, Evelyn Goode, Mrs., O.B.E.

VAUGHAN, Major Gomer Miles, O.B.E., R.E.

VAUGHAN, Dame Helen Charlotte Isabella, GWYNNE-, D.B.E., D.Sc., LL.D., b. 21 Jan. 1879 ; d. of Capt. the Hon. A. H. D. Fraser, and granddaughter of 17th Lord Saltoun (see BURKE'S Peerage) ; m. David Thomas, s. of Henry Gwynne-Vaughan, of Cynghordy. Educ.: Cheltenham, and King's Coll., Univ. of London. Head of Dept. of Botany, Birkbeck Coll., London. War Work: Chief Controller, Queen Mary's Army Auxiliary Corps, British Armies in France, from formation, in Feb. 1917, to Sept. 1918 ; Commandant, Women's Royal Air Force, Sept. 1918, to Dec. 1919. Address: 93, Bedford Court Mansions, W. C. 1. Club: Univ. of London. (D37)

VAUGHAN, Col. Herbert Radclyffe, C.B.E. Formerly Col. Warwickshire Regt.; served in Great War, 1914–19 (mentioned in despatches). (C835)

VAUGHAN, Janet Feliza, O.B.E., b. 3 Aug. 1857 ; d. of Hugh Vaughan, of Redland House, Gloucestershire. Educ.: Privately. Hon. Sec. Tone Valley Primrose League. War Work: Raised eight Detachments V.A.D's. and organised Red Cross Hospital for Taunton. Address: Staple Grove, Taunton. (O3930)

VAUGHAN, Lieut. William, M.B.E. R.N.

VAUX, Emily Eve Lellam, Mrs., M.B.E.; d. of Moon Ord, of Sunderland. Educ.: Highfield, and Dresden. War Work: Qr.-Mr. 12th Durham V.A.D., 1911, and 3rd Durham Officers' Hospital, 1914–17 ; Co-President Sunderland Prisoners-of-War Fund ; Hon. Sec. 7th Durham Light Infantry Comforts Fund. Addresses: Grindon, near Sunderland ; Brettanby Manor, Barton, R.S.O., Yorks. (M4047)

VAWDREY, Paymaster-Capt. Charles, C.B.E., b. 1848 ; s. of William Cock ; m. 1st, Mary Louisa Vawdrey, who d., 2nd, Elizabeth, d. of the late Robert Tamblin. Entered R.N. 1864 ; Paymaster Capt.; Abyssinian Expedition, 1867–68 (medal) ; Ashanti War, 1873–74 (medal) ; Egyptian War, 1882 (Egyptian medal, Khedive's Star) ; Great War, 1914–19, at Naval Base, Kingstown ; assumed the surname of Vawdrey in lieu of his patronymic, 1881. Address: Walton Pines, Clevedon, Somerset. (C2302)

VAWDREY, Col. George, C.M.G., C.B.E., b. 6 July, 1872 ; s. of Dr. Vawdrey, late of Farnboro', Hants. Educ.: Privately, and at R.M.C., Sandhurst. A.D. of S. & T., Malta. War Work: S.A. Campaign, 1899–1902 (Queen's Medal, 5 clasps ; King's Medal, 2 clasps. and mentioned in despatches ; Brevet of Major); Great War, 1914–18, O.C. Train 7 Div. ; 4 times mentioned in despatches ; 1914 Star and clasp, General Service and Victory Medals. Club: United Service. (C795)

VEAL, Capt. and Qr.-Mr. Frank, O.B.E.

VEALE, William John, M.B.E.

VEITCH, Robert McLeod, O.B.E., M.D., Ch.B., b. 1881 ; s. of John Veitch, of Edinburgh ; m. Gladys Maud, d. of George Smith, of London. Educ.: Royal High School, Edinburgh ; Edinburgh Univ. Doctor of Medicine ; Commissioner of Medical Services, Ministry of Pensions, London Region. War Work: T. Capt. R.A.M.C., 1914–17 ; France, May, 1915, to Aug. 1916 ; Bacteriologist Isolation Hospital, Etaples ; invalided home, Aug. 1916 ; home service, Aug. 1916, till Dec. 1917 ; transferred Ministry of National Service, Dec. 1917 ; D.C.M.S. Bradford, Nottingham, and London. Address: 31A, High Street, St. John's Wood, N.W. 8. (O11526)

VELLA, Lieut.-Col. Alfred, O.B.E., b. 28 Feb. 1863 ; s. of the late Hon. Francis Vella, C.M.G., Member of the Executive Council and Collector of Customs, Malta ; m. Mary, d. of the late Chev. Francis Pace, K.S.S., President of the Chamber of Commerce, Malta. Educ.: Privately, and Malta Univ. War Work: Lieut.-Col. Commanding Royal Malta Regt. of Artillery ; Officer-in-charge of Records, Permanent Staff ; 1st and 2nd Batts. King's Own Malta Regiment of Militia ; Fire Commander of the Western and North-Western Forts of the island, including Mobile Defence against Submarines ; raised and trained personnel for New Artillery Defences, and to replace Royal Garrison Artillery urgently required elsewhere ; formed a Detachment, Royal Malta Artillery for Coast Defence Work in Alexandria (Egyptian Expeditionary Force). Address: 171, Str. Mercanti, Valetta, Malta. Club: Casino Maltese, Valletta. (O7803)

VELLACOTT, Capt. Philip Northcote, O.B.E., R.A.M.C.

VENABLES, Caroline Emily, O.B.E.

VENABLES, Harry Archbutt, O.B.E.

VENABLES, Margaret, M.B.E.

VENN, Ella Margaret, M.B.E.

VENN, Capt. Hugh Whatley Stevens, O.B.E.

VENN, Capt. Tom Walters, M.B.E., I.A. R. of O., b. 24 Jan. 1882 ; s. of J. Venn, of Crediton, Devon ; m. Margaret Frances, d. of Rev. Robert Greig, of Bedford. Educ.: Crediton Grammar School. The Bombay Steam Navigation Co., Ltd., Bombay ; granted Commission Bombay Volunteer Artillery, Oct. 1914 ; transferred to Indian Army Reserve of Officers, Mar. 1915 ; attached 42nd Deoli Regt. ; officer in charge of War Gifts for the Mesopotamian Forces from Oct. 1916 to Feb. 1919. Address: c/o Bombay Steam Navigation Co., Ltd., Bombay. (M3018)

VENNER, George Edward Sidebottom, M.B.E.

VENNING, Margaret Beatrice, Mrs., O.B.E.,

VENOUR, Capt. Claude Malcolm Hamilton, O.B.E., s. of the late James M. H. Venour, of Wellesbourne, Warwickshire. Officer in Hampshire Regiment ; Chevalier of the Legion of

Honour. Address: Tyne-y-coed, Bettws-y-Coed, N. Wales. Club: United Service. (O7804)

VERBI, Capt. Vladimir Vassil, O.B.E.

VERCOE, Lieut. Edmund, O.B.E.

VERDIER, James William, O.B.E.

VEREKER, Frances Gore, Mrs., M.B.E., b. 1861 ; d. of Robert Manders, of Landscape, Co. Dublin ; m. George Medlicott Vereker, s. of the Hon. John Prendergast Vereker, of 72, Merrion Square, Dublin. Educ.: Privately. War Work: 4½ years Officer-in-charge of Hospital in own house for the Red Cross ; Assist. Commandant of Detachment. Address: Sharpitor, Salcombe, S. Devon. (M4049)

VERGE, Capt. Lionel Arthur Frederick, M.B.E.

VERNEY, Malvina, Mrs., M.B.E.

VERNEY, Lieut.-Col. Reynell Henry, O.B.E.

VERNON, Sir Harry Foley, Bart., C.B.E., V.D., J.P., D.L., M.A., b. 11 April, 1834 ; s. of T. T. Vernon, of Hanbury Hall, Worcestershire ; m. Lady Georgina Sophia Baillie-Hamilton, d. of 10th Earl of Haddington (see BURKE'S Peerage). Educ.: Harrow ; Magdalen Coll., Oxford. M.P. East Worcestershire, 1861–66 ; Master of Worcestershire Foxhounds, 1862–68 ; Col. of 2nd Vol. Br. Worcestershire Regt. 1873–87 ; Hon. Col. (ret.) of Worcestershire Hussars. Address: Hanbury Hall, Droitwich, Worcestershire. (C3015)

VERNON, Percy Venables, O.B.E., M.I.M.E.

VERNON, Lieut. Richard Henry, M.B.E.

VERNON, Lieut. Ronald Clifton, M.B.E., R.E.

VERNON, Capt. Stuart Arthur, O.B.E., M.C.

VERNON, William Hamilton, M.B.E. (M5803)

VERRALL, Marian Elizabeth, M.B.E. ; d. of Henry Verrall, of Brighton. Educ.: Cheltenham Ladies' Coll. War Work: Joint Women's V.A.D. Headquarters. Address: The Lydd, West Hoathly, Sussex. Clubs: Ladies' Univ. ; V.A.D. (M9920)

VERSCHOYLE, Beresford, C.B.E. Chief Engineer, Egyptian State Railways. (C654)

VERSCHOYLE, Capt. Henry Cosby, O.B.E., b. 28 Oct. 1887 ; s. of the late Capt. R. H. Verschoyle, 11th Hussars, Springfield, Ross, Herefordshire ; m. Doris Sophia Lukis, 2nd d. of — Collings, Seigneur of Sark, of La Seigneurie, Sark. Educ.: Rossall. Regular Officer, R.A.S.C. War Work: Promoted Capt. Oct. 1914 ; T. Major, Nov. 1914 ; T. Lieut.-Col. Oct. 1916 ; served in B.E.F. and E.E.F. ; O.C 54th and 60th Divisional Trains ; O.C. Transport Training School, Grantham. Address: 32, Watergate, Grantham. (O6313)

VERYARD, Ernest Thomas, M.B.E., R.N.

VESEY, David, O.B.E., b. 1872 ; s. of the late Ven. Archdeacon F. G. Vesey, of Huntingdon ; m. Caroline Atholl, d. of the late Sir H. Evelyn Oakeley. Educ.: Harrow, and Trinity Coll., Cambridge. Principal, Board of Education. War Work: Legal Draftsman, Ministry of Munitions, 1915–19. Address: 3, Camp View, Wimbledon Common, S.W. 19. Club: United University. (O829)

VESEY, Isabel Constance, O.B.E. War Work: Commandant of the Empress Eugénie's Hospital for Officers, Farnboro' Hill, from 1915–19. Address: Tile Barn, Farnboro', Hants. (O11528)

VESEY, Lieut.-Col. the Hon. Osbert Eustace, C.B.E., R.E., K.M.R., b. 20 Feb. 1884 ; m. Dorothy, d. of William Morisont Stradran of Strood Park, Horsham. Educ.: Eton ; Sandhurst. Late 9th Lancers ; served in Great War. Address: 7, Westbourne Terrace, W. 2. Club: Boodle's. (C1337)

VESEY, Sidney Philip Charles, C.B.E., M.A., J.P., b. 9 March, 1873 ; s. of William Muschamp Vesey, of Upton House, Bagenalstown ; m. Blanche Edith, d. of Edmund N. Power, of Tramore House, Tramore. Educ.: Rugby, and Christchurch, Oxford. War Work: Meetings and Finance Sub-Committee of Parliamentary Recruiting Committee ; Joint Hon. Sec. Meetings Dept. of Parliamentary National Service Committee ; then Member of Meetings Branch of National War Aims Committee ; later served as Capt. in King's Royal Rifle Corps. Address: 14, Heathside, Finchley Road, N.W. 2. Clubs: Junior Carlton ; Constitutional ; Kildare Street. (C655)

VESSEY, Lieut.-Col. Gordon Harry Bowker, O.B.E., R.E.

VIBART, Com. John Fleming, C.B.E. Com. Royal Indian Marine, and Div. Naval Transport Officer, Salonika ; served in Great War, 1914–19 (mentioned in despatches). (C2260)

VICARS, Edward Robert Eckersall, C.B.E., b. 6 March, 1869 ; s. of the late Edward Armstrong Vicars, of Rugby ; m. Evelyn Louisa, d. of the late Edward Ashley Scott, of The Lawn, Rugby. Educ.: Rugby. H.B.M. Consul-General, Marseilles ; previously Clerk in Foreign Office ; Sec. in Diplomatic Service (Athens and Constantinople) ; Sec. to British Delegation to various International Conferences ; Consul at Madeira ; Consul-General at Lyons. War Work: Various, in capacity as Consul-General at Lyons. Addresses: British Consulate General, 8 Rue des Princes, Marseilles ; Villa Belle Vue, Boulevard Bompard, Marseilles. (C656)

VICARS, William, C.B.E.

VICCARS, Major John Ellis, D.S.O., O.B.E., Major Leicester Regt. ; served in Great War, 1915–19 (mentioned in despatches). (O5882)

VICK, Lieut.-Col. Reginald Martin, O.B.E., R.A.M.C. (T.), b. 20 Aug. 1884 ; s. of Richard William Vick, of West Hartlepool ; m. Mary Kate, d. of Reginald J. N. Neville, of 25,

Eccleston Square, W. 1. *Educ.:* The Leys; Jesus Coll., Cambridge; St. Bartholomew's Hospital. Warden of St. Bartholomew's Hospital; Assistant Surgeon St. Bartholomew's Hospital. *War Work:* Section Commander 85th Field Ambulance, 28th Div. (2½ years); Officer-in-charge Surgical Division, Stationary, and General Hospitals, B.S.F., for remainder of war. *Address:* Warden's House, St. Bartholomew's Hospital. *Club:* United University. (O6551)

VICKERMAN, Major Hugh, D.S.O., O.B.E., A.M.I.C.E., M.Sc., *b.* 1880; *s.* of Charles Rankin Vickerman, of Kelburne, Wellington, New Zealand; *m.* 1913, Arabella Colquhoun, *d.* of Henry Allingham Morrow, of Belfast. *Educ.:* Auckland Grammar School and New Zealand University. Civil Engineer; Member of New Zealand Society of Engineers; Major, New Zealand Engineers; during Great War commanded a Tunnelling Co. (despatches). *Address:* Wellington, New Zealand. (O6108)

VICKERMAN, Lieut.-Col. Philip Sefton, O.B.E., M.B., F.R.C.S., *b.* 19 Dec. 1920; *s.* of Charles R. Vickerman, of Wellington, N.Z.; *m.* Betty Stuart, *d.* of John Wallace, of Braidwood, N.S.W. *Educ.:* Auckland Grammar School; Edinburgh University. Medical Practitioner. *War Work:* Royal Victoria Hospital, Netley, Aug. 1914 to April, 1915; No. 19 General Hospital, Alexandria, May 1918 to Aug. 1916; No. 2 Prisoners of War Hospital, Cairo, Aug. 1916. *Address:* 729, Tucuman, Buenos Aires, Argentine. (O2947)

VICKERS, Capt. Charles, M.B.E.

VICKERS, Major Wilmot Gordon Hilton, O.B.E.

VICKERY, Frederick William, O.B.E. *War Work:* Inventor of Munitions of War. *Address:* Flat 44, Whitehall Court, London, S.W. 1. (O11529)

VICKERY, Surg.-Lieut.-Comm. George Gordon, O.B.E., M.B., M.A., R.N.

VICKRESS, Major William Henry, D.S.O., O.B.E., *b.* 18 Feb. 1880; *s.* of the late Thomas Albert Vickress, of Hill, Slinfold, Sussex; *m.* Margaret Jane, *d.* of Robert Thompson, of Sunderland. *Educ.:* Horsham. Solicitor. *War Work:* Special Constable E Division first few months; Commissioned R.A.S.C., Dec. 1914; served in France as Supply Officer, Divisional Troops, 14th Division, May, 1915; Senior Supply Officer, 14th Division, Oct. 1915, to April, 1919; from April to July, 1919, commanded 14th Divisional Train. *Addresses:* The Follies, St. Margaret's Bay, Kent; 24, Royal Crescent, Holland Park Avenue, W. *Club:* Badminton. (O5883)

VIDAL, Major Francis Peter, O.B.E.

VIENER, Rev. Harry Dan Leigh, C.B.E., M.A., R.A.F., *b.* 26 Dec. 1868; *s.* of Mrs. K. V. Viener, of Poulton-le-Fylde, Lancashire. *Educ.:* Malvern Coll.; St. John's Coll., Oxford (Exhibitioner). Late Chaplain Royal Navy, 1901–18; Chaplain-in-Chief, Royal Air Force, from Oct. 1918. *War Work:* Chaplain, H.M.S. "Prince of Wales," Channel and Mediterranean, 1914–15; Chaplain Royal Naval Barracks, Chatham, 1916–18. *Address:* Air Ministry, Kingsway, W.C. 2. *Club:* Royal Air Force. (C2331)

VIGERS, Ruth Sarah, M.B.E.; *d.* of Frederick Vigers of Reigate. *Educ.:* Eastbourne; Ladies Coll., Cheltenham; Paris; Germany. Secretary. *War Work:* From Feb. 1915, has held the post of Assist. Sec. in Lady Dudley's Auxiliary Hospitals Department of the Red Cross. *Address:* The Beeches, Wray Lane, Reigate. (M1045)

VIGERS, Lieut. Thomas Whitehaire, O.B.E., M.C., R.E. (T.).

VIGNE, Lieut.-Comm. Bertram, O.B.E., R.N.

VIGNE, Lieut.-Col. Robert Austen, C.M.G., C.B.E.

VIGO, Capt. Benjamin William, M.B.E., *b.* 17 Feb. 1882; *s.* of David Vigo, of Reading. *Educ.:* King's School, Canterbury, and privately. *War Work:* Served with Red Cross in Mesopotamia, 1916–19. *Addresses:* Kensington High Street, W. 8; Ely Place, E.C. 1. *Club:* Eccentric. (M4051)

VIGOR, Harold Decimus, M.B.E.

VIGORS, Major Cliffe Henry, O.B.E.

VIGRASS, Herbert, O.B.E., *b.* 1869. H.M. Inspector of Schools. *War Work:* Joint Hon. Sec. Hull War Savings Committee; Hon. Organiser East Riding of Yorks. War Savings Committee; Hon. Sec. Beverley War Savings Committee. *Address:* Rudyard, Cottingham, Hull. (O11530)

VILLIERS, Major Arthur, O.B.E., R.A.O.C.

VILLIERS, Lieut.-Col. Charles Walker, C.B.E., D.S.O.

VILLIERS, Comm. Gerald Berkeley, O.B.E.

VILMET, Henry Frederic Vilmet OLDHAM-, M.B.E.

VINCE, John Billinton, M.B.E., *b.* 22 July, 1866; *s.* of Thomas Billinton, of Wakefield, Yorks.; *m.* Jane, *d.* of William Thomas Danahy, of Dublin. *Educ.:* Northampton. Served with the Gloucestershire Regt. for 22 years in Malta, Egypt, India, and St. Helena; holds Queen's South Africa and Long Service Medals. *War Work:* Employed as Supervising Clerk in the Military Secretary's Department, War Office, London, during the whole period of the Great War. *Address:* 41, Richmond Road, Twickenham. (M9921)

VINCENT, Lieut.-Col. Arthur Gustave, C.B.E. Major and T. Lieut.-Col. R.M.L.I.; served in Great War, 1914–19 (mentioned in despatches). (C1949)

VINCENT, Arthur Rose, C.B.E., J.P., D.L., *b.* 9 June, 1876; *s.* of Col. Arthur Vincent, of Summerhill House, Co. Clare; *m.* Maud, *d.* of William B. Brown, of California. *Educ.:* Wellington; Trinity Coll.; College de France. *War Work:* Served with Anglo-American Ambulance, France, 1915–16; Ministry of Information, 1917–18; Representative of Ministry at Chicago, 1918. *Address:* Muckross Abbey, Co. Kerry,

Ireland. *Clubs:* Carleton; White's; Boodle's; Garrick: Kildare Street. (C1050)

VINCENT, Lieut.-Comm. Charles Rogers, O.B.E., R.N.

VINCENT, Cyril Mosson, O.B.E., J.P., *b.* Nov. 1846; *s.* of William Allder Vincent, of Oxford; *m.* Mary Ann, *d.* of Edward Owen, of Moseley, Birmingham. *Educ.:* Wolverhampton. Councillor, Mayor of Oxford, 1915–16. *War Work:* Chairman Oxford Military Tribunal, Food Control, and War Pensions Committees. *Address:* 3, Polstead Road, Oxford. *Club:* Clarendon, Oxford. (O11531)

VINCENT, Lieut.-Col. Frank Lloyd, O.B.E., I.A.

VINCENT, Capt. Frederick Calvert, O.B.E.

VINCENT, Major Sydney, O.B.E., *b.* 27 July, 1875; *s.* of William George Vincent, of Petworth; *m.* Ethel Beatrice, *d.* of Henry Thomas Upton, of Petworth. *Educ.:* Guildford. Builder and Contractor. *War Work:* Commissioned Nov. 1914; detailed for recruiting duties until April, 1916; served in France from April, 1916, to Nov. 1918 with the 8th Royal Sussex, 12th Batt. D.C.L.I., and finally transferred to the Labour Corps; 3 times mentioned in despatches. *Address:* Wilmcote, Angel Street, Petworth, Sussex. (O5885)

VINCENT, Lieut. William, O.B.E., M.C., R.A.S.C. (T.).

VINCENT, Lieut.Col. William James Nathaniel, C.B.E. Lieut.-Col. R.A.M.C.; served in the Great War, 1914–19 (despatches). (C2186)

VINE, Alfred Bertram, M.B.E., M.B. (Lond.), M.R.C.S. (Eng.), L.R.C.P. (Lond.), *b.* 1875; *s.* of the Rev. J. N. Vine, of Bedford; *m.* Ethel, *d.* of the Rev. J. R. Graham. *Educ.:* Bedford. Medical Practitioner; Hon. Medical Officer, Bury Infirmary. *War Work:* Medical· Officer-in-charge, Timberhurst Auxiliary Hospital, Bury; Capt. R.A.M.C. *Address* 179, Manchester Road, Bury. (M9922)

VINES, Capt. Duncan Frederick, R.I.M., O.B.E.

VINEY, Albert William, M.B.E.

VINEY, Lieut.-Col. Horace George, C.M.G., C.B.E., D.S.O. Major Australian Light Horse; A.A. and Q.M.G. with rank of Lieut.-Col.; served in Great War, 1914–19 (mentioned in despatches). (C1365)

VINTCENT, Rose Lilian, Mrs., M.B.E.

VIRGO, John James, C.B.E., J.P. for South Australia, *b.* 22 April, 1865; *s.* of Caleb and Mary Virgo, of South Australia; *m.* Emmeline Dorothy, *d.* of the Rev. F. Aston, of Birmingham. *Educ.:* Glenelg Grammar School, South Australia. Honorary World's representative, Y.M.C.A. *War Work:* Visiting representative of Y.M.C.A. to all war fronts. *Address:* Y.M.C.A., British Empire Union, Tottenham Court Road, W. 1. *Club:* Royal Colonial Institute. (C320)

VISART, Lieut.-Col. Henry Robert (Count de Bury), C.B.E.

VISCHER, Major Hanns, C.B.E. Served in Great War, 1914–19, as Major, Gen. List (mentioned in despatches). (C1149a)

VISGER, Charles, O.B.E., M.R.C.S. (Eng.), L.R.C.P. (Lond.), *b.* 28 Feb. 1875; *s.* of Harman Visger; *m.* Nesta Gwynne (who died), *d.* of Hurst Reay, of London. *Educ.:* Trent Coll.; Univ. Coll.; Hospital, London. Hon. Surgeon; Clevedon Cottage Hospital. *War Work:* M.O. to Oaklands Red Cross Hospital, Clevedon; Capt. R.A.M.C.; Capt. R.A.F.M.S.; mentioned in despatches. *Address:* Beachcroft, Clevedon, Som. (O11532)

VIVIAN, Major Guy Noel, O.B.E.

VIVIAN, Nancy Lycett, M.B.E.

VIVIAN, Valentine Patrick Terrel, C.B.E.

VIZARD, Brig.-Gen. Robert Davenport, C.B.E. Col. and Hon. Brig.-Gen (ret.); Egyptian Expedition, 1882 (medal, bronze star); S. Africa, 1899–1902 (Queen's medal with three clasps); served in the Great War, 1914–19 (despatches). (C2185)

VOICE, Thomas Aubrey, O.B.E., *b.* 4 Aug. 1876; *s.* of Thomas Voice, of East Grinstead; *m.* Gladys Harwood, *d.* of John Arthur Evans Burrup, O.B.E., I.S.O., H.M. Customs (retired). *Educ.:* Cranleigh School, Surrey. Supt., Public Debt Office, Calcutta; at present officiating Chief Accountant and Deputy Sec., Bank of Bengal. *War Work:* Took over charge of the Public Debt Office of India in Nov. 1917, following on the issue of the Indian War Loan; cleared up the arrears, reorganised the office, and successfully dealt with the flotation of the Second Indian War Loan. *Addresses:* c/o Messrs. Coutts & Co., London; c/o Bank of Bengal, Calcutta. (O8313)

VORES, Phillipa, Mrs., M.B.E.

VOSS, Capt. Charles, M.B.E.

VOULES, Francis Minchin, C.B.E.; *s.* of Sir Gordon Blennerhassett Voules, of Bournemouth; *m.* Isabel Janet, *d.* of A. H. Kennedy. *Educ.:* Dulwich Coll., and abroad. Director, Equity and Law Life Assurance Society; Para Electric Rlys. and Lighting Co.; International Light and Power Co.; Kepong Malay Rubber Estates, Ltd. *War Work:* Commissioner for Holland, British Red Cross Society; in charge of instruction, occupation, employment and welfare work of the British Prisoners of War interned in Holland; assisted in the repatriation of our Prisoners after the Armistice; later took charge of the Russian Prisoners of War in the 10th and 7th Army Corps in Germany; Knight of Grace of the Order of St. John of Jerusalem. *Addresses:* Orchard House, Kensington, W. 14; 65, Bishopsgate, E.C. *Clubs:* Reform; City of London; Royal Automobile; Royal Wimbledon, and Stoke Poges Golf. (C3070)

VOYSEY, Violet Mary Annesley, C.B.E., *b.* 1880; *d.* of Annesley Wesley Voysey, of Queensland. *Educ.:* Sydney,

Australia. *War Work:* During three years at Admiralty House, Queenstown, with her uncle, Admiral Sir Lewis Rayly, Commander-in-Chief; President and Treas. of Queenstown War Work Fund; Commandant of Queenstown V.A.D.'s.; Vice-President of Local War Pensions Committee; established and worked canteen, and personal assistance for survivors from torpedoed ships, who numbered over 4500 during the three years; Member of Cork Red Cross, and Munster's Prisoners of War Fund. (C3016)

VULLIAMY, Grace, C.B.E. Rendered assistance to British Civilians and Prisoners of War in Holland during Great War. (C1051)

VYSE, Ethel Mary, Mrs., M.B.E.

VYVYAN, Philip Henry Norris Nugent, O.B.E.

WACE, Brig.-Gen. Edward Gurth, C.B.E., D.S.O., R.E.

WACHE, Ethel Evelyna, M.B.E.

WACKRILL, Major Walter Frederick, O B.E., late R.E., *b.* 26 Feb. 1893; *s.* of George Wackrill, of Harborne, Birmingham. *Educ.:* Birmingham. Civil Servant; Ministry of Health; Sec. National Health Joint Committee. *War Work:* Enlisted Sept. 1914; commissioned, July, 1915, in Royal Fusiliers; transferred Royal Engineers, May, 1917; B.E.F., France, May, 1916, to Nov. 1917; Italy, Nov. 1917, to Jan. 1919; G.H.Q., 9B., Feb. 1919, to Oct. 1919. *Address:* 26, Melrose Gardens, New Malden, Surrey. *Club:* Junior Army and Navy. (O6425)

WADDILOVE, Capt. George Edward DARLEY-, O.B.E.

WADDINGHAM, Lieut. George, M.B.E.

WADDINGHAM, William Hart, M.B.E., *b.* 14 June, 1878; *s.* of William K. Waddingham, of Elsham, Lincolnshire; *m.* Norah, *d.* of C. H. Murray, of Newcastle-on-Tyne. *Educ.:* Sedbergh. Engineer with Messrs. Armstrong, Whitworth & Co., Ltd., Elswick Works, Newcastle-on-Tyne. *War Work:* Associated with the design, manufacture, and testing of Torpedo Tubes for Submarines, Destroyers, and Cruisers for British Navy. *Address:* 22, Haldane Terrace, Newcastle-on-Tyne. (M4052)

WADDINGTON, Eubule John, O.B.E.

WADDINGTON, Lieut. Henry, M.B.E.

WADDINGTON, Capt. William James, O.B.E.

WADDY, Capt. Arthur Cyril, O.B.E., *b.* 14 Sept. 1892; *s.* of Henry Turner Waddy, of The Priory, Worcester Park, Surrey. *Educ.:* The Leys School, and Caius Coll., Cambridge. *War Work:* Oct. 1914, to July, 1915, Despatch Rider, R.E., France; served in R.F.A., Oct. 1915, to Nov. 1919, in France, Belgium, and Germany. *Address:* The Priory, Worcester Park, Surrey. (O5886)

WADE, Elmira Margaret Louisa, M.B.E.; *d.* of George Edward Wade, of 1, Wilton Place, S.W., and Stubbings, Berks. *Educ.:* London and Abroad. *War Work:* V.A.D. Berks 20; Temp. Clerk, War Office; Personal assistant, Ministry of Munitions; Administrative Assistant, Aircraft Production Dept. *Address:* 1, Wilton Place, Knightsbridge, S.W. 1. *Clubs:* Victoria; United Societies'. (M9925)

WADE, Francis Richard, O.B.E.

WADE, Capt. George Bridges, M.B.E., R.E.

WADE, James Owen David, O.B.E., F.R.C.S.

WADE, Sidney, M.B.E. Chief Clerk in a Section of Directorate of Surplus Stores and Salvage in connection with the clearing up of Salvage and disposal both at home and abroad. (M10338)

WADE, Thomas Callander, M.B.E., M.A., LL.B., *b.* 30 April, 1867; *s.* of the Rev George Wade, of Falkirk. *Educ.:* Royal High School, Edinburgh, and Edinburgh Univ. *War Work:* County Director for Stirlingshire for Red Cross Society. *Address:* Woodcroft, Larbert, Stirlingshire. (M2587)

WADE, Capt. Thomas Kingsmill, O.B.E., Can. A.S.C.

WADE, Sir William, Knt. Bach., C.B.E. Alderman, J.P., Lord Mayor of Bradford. Has shown great energy in many activities connected with the War. (C3171)

WADE, Capt. William, O.B.E.

WADE, Capt. William John, M.B.E.

WADLEY, Lieut.-Col. Edgar John, C.B.E., D.S.O., M.R.C.V.S. (Lond.), *b.* 1880; *s.* of Thomas Wadley, of Penarth; *m.* 1906, Nancy, *d.* of Pierce Ryan. *Educ.:* Bath. Entered Army Vet. Corps, 1903; Capt. 1908; Major, 1915; Brevet Lieut.-Col. 1918; S. African War, 1901–2 (medal with five clasps) Great War, 1914–19 (despatches). (C1339)

WAGER, Euclid Brookes, M.B.E., R.G.A.

WAGER, May Frances, Mrs., M.B.E.

WAGG, Lieut. Henry John, O.B.E., R.N.V.R.

WAGGETT, Constance, Mrs., O.B.E., *b.* 10 June, 1863; *d.* of Quintin Twiss, of 9, Chester Street; *m.* Ernest Blechynden, D.S.O., M.B., B.Ch., *s.* of John Waggett, M.D., of Notting Hill. *Educ.:* Privately, and in France. *War Work:* Organised and superintended a dinner room (Soldiers' and Sailors' Families Association) for women, and children under school age; Chairman of Ladies' Committee for equipment of War Wards, Charing Cross Hospital; Y.M.C.A., and Church Army Recreation Huts in France from Feb. 1915, to Dec. 1919; Hon. Head Lady of Church Army Hut Workers in France. *Address:* 39, Wimpole Street. *Club:* Sesame. (O3972)

WAGGOTT, Edward, M.B.E.

WAGHORN, Capt. Hugh Colin, M.B.E.

WAGHORNE, John, M.B.E.

WAGSTAFF, George Leonard, O.B.E.

WAGSTAFF, Harry Finnis, M.B.E.

WAGSTAFF, Lewis Cecil, O.B.E.

WAGSTAFFE, Ellen Charlotte, Mrs., M.B.E., *b.* 17 Oct) 1871; *d.* of John Lester, of Somersetshire. *Educ.:* Cardiff Univ. Head Mistress under the Barry Education Authority; President, Local Branch, N.U.T.; President, South Wales and Monmouthshire Association of Welfare Workers. *War Work:* Chief Welfare Supervisor, National Shell Factory, Newport, Mon.; Superintendent, Juvenile Unemployment Welfare Centre; instituted a very successful War Savings Association; Member Local Advisory Committee, and practically all other local war committees. *Address:* Ivydene, Dewsland Park, Newport, Mon. (M2590)

WAGSTAFFE, Capt. William Warwick, O.B.E., M.B., F.R.C.S., R.A.M.C. (S.R.).

WAIGHT, Daisy Olive, Mrs., M.B.E., *b.* 7 July, 1887; *d.* of George Giles Vining, of Motcombe, Dorset; *m.* Thomas Henry, *s.* of Thomas James Waight, of Clapham Park, S.W. *Educ.:* Privately. Supervisor in charge of Telephone Exchange at War Office, which post she held during the war. *Address:* Gipstead, 175, Crowborough Road, Streatham, S.W. 17. (M9926)

WAIN, Capt. Douglas, O.B.E.

WAIN, Thomas, M.B.E., *b.* 27 May, 1868; *s.* of the late J. R. Wain, of Tunstall, Staffs; *m.* Alice Mary, *d.* of Joseph Grocott, of Chapel Chorlton, Staffs. *Educ.:* Osmonds, Shelton, Staffs. Managing Director, National Timber Co., Ltd., etc. *War Work:* Organiser and Commandant of Chester Detachment British Red Cross Transport, Cheshire 7 (T.), which carried about 76,000 wounded soldiers during the war; dealt with transport for all ambulance trains coming to Chester, and transport of sick and wounded for over 40 Red Cross and Military Hospitals in Western Command. *Address:* Roseville, Dee Banks, Chester. (M4053)

WAINWRIGHT, Amy Grace, Mrs., M.B.E., *b.* 20 Aug. 1869; *d.* of W. A. B. Williams, of London; *m.* Charles Henry, J.P., *s.* of C. J. Wainwright, of Finchley. *Educ.:* Dover. *War Work:* Y.M.C.A. Canteen at the Aircraft Manufacturing Co., Hendon. N.W., 2¼ years; for 7 months Vice-President. *Address:* Hill House, Edgware, Middlesex. (M9927)

WAINWRIGHT, Col. Charles Richard, M.B.E., T.D., J P., D.L., *b.* 22 Feb. 1866; *s.* of Joel Wainwright, of Ludworth, Derbyshire; *m.* Ada Lavinia, *d.* of James Hulme, of Marple, Cheshire. *Educ.:* Cheetham Collegiate School. Mayor of the Borough of Ashton-under-Lyne, 1914–16; Hon. Col. 9th Batt. Manchester Regt.; Hon. Col. 181st Brigade, R.F.A. *War Work:* Raised 181st Brigade, R.F.A., and 143rd Battery, R.G.A.; Chairman of Ashton-under-Lyne Tribunal. *Address:* Brabyns House, Marple, Cheshire. *Clubs:* Junior Army and Navy; Constitutional (Manchester). (M1051)

WAINWRIGHT, Lieut. Edwin Moira, O.B.E.

WAINWRIGHT, George Bertram, O.B.E., M.B., *b.* 23 Feb. 1880; *s.* of Sir James Wainwright, of Norney Grange, Godalming; *m.* Florence Maud, *d.* of Robert Bagot Everard, of Hillbrow, Bournemouth. *Educ.:* Haileybury; Trinity Coll., Cambridge; St. Thomas's Hospital. M.O. Twyford School Working Dispensary. *War Work:* M.O. Red Cross Hospital, Winchester; M.O. in charge of officers and men quartered in Winchester, and their wives and families. *Address:* Freelands, Winchester. (O11534)

WAINWRIGHT, Mabel Francis Hewitt, M.B.E.

WAIT, Col. Hugh Godfrey Killigrew, C.B.E., D.S.O., *b.* 1871; *m.* 1905, Helen Mary Lothian, *d.* of the late Gen. Sir Lothian Nicholson, K.C.B., R.E. (*see* BURKE'S *Peerage,* Romilly, B.). Lieut.-Col. R.E.; served in Great War, 1914–19 (despatches); Chief Instructor, School of Electric Lighting, 1910–12; School of Mil. Engineering, 1912–15; appointed A.Q.M.G. 1916; Dep. Director at War Office, 1919, with rank of Col. (C1406)

WAITE, Alice May, M.B.E.

WAITE, Eva, M.B.E.

WAITE, James, M.B.E., *b.* 1867; *s.* of Peter Waite, of Adelaide, S. Australia; *m.* Louise, *d.* of John R. Nicholson, of Carlisle. *Educ.:* Australia, and Leeds Univ. Inspecting and Metallurgical Engineer, with Messrs. C. P. Sandberg, Consulting Engineers, 40, Grosvenor Gardens, S.W. *War Work:* Under Director of Inspection of Munitions Areas, Sheffield, for investigation of defects, etc., in shell steel. *Address:* 45, Queen's Road, St. John's Wood, N.W. (M2592)

WAITE, Capt. Robert Bruce, M.B.E., R.F.A.

WAITE, William Vincent, O.B.E., M.I.Mech.E., A.M.I.E.E., *b.* 2 Feb. 1877; *s.* of William Waite, of Bristol. *Educ.:* Shepton Mallet Grammar School. Works Manager, Marshall, Sons & Co., Ltd., Gainsborough. *War Work:* Production of naval gun mountings, tanks, aeroplanes, shells, and war vehicles at above works. *Address:* Middlefield House, Gainsborough. (O1962)

WAKE, Richard, O.B.E., C.E.. *b.* 1870; *s.* of G. F. Wake, of Clifton Hampden, Oxon; *m.* Marion Letitia, *d.* of Henry Cowley, of Clapton. *Educ.:* Privately. Civil Engineer; Director of Technical Education, County of Wicklow, Ireland; Managing Director. *War Work:* Section Chief (Birmingham), Dept. of Small Arms and Machine Gun Supply, Ministry of Munitions; Consulting Engineer, Belgian Government Arms Factory; Vice-Chairman, Engineering Board, Midland Area, Ministry of Munitions; Chevalier of Belgian Order of the Crown. *Address:* 86, Yardley Road, Birmingham. (O3973)

WAKEFIELD, Col. Sir Charles Cheers, Bart., C.B.E., *s.* of John Wakefield, of H.M. Customs; *m.* Sarah Frances

Graham, Dame of Grace of St. John of Jerusalem. *Educ.*: Liverpool Institute. Governing Director of C. C. Wakefield & Co., Ltd., Oil Manufacturers ; Director, North British and Mercantile Insurance Co. ; Lord Mayor of London, 1915–16 ; Alderman of the City of London ; has Order of Legion of Honour, Order of the Crown of Belgium, Order of Leopold of Belgium, Knight of Grace of St. John of Jerusalem ; County Commandant of the City of London Regt. ; Hon. Col. of the Royal Garrison Artillery ; a Lieut. for the City ; President of the Bridewell and Bethlem Hospitals ; P.G.W. in English Freemasonry. *Address*: Hythe, Kent. *Club*: United Service. (C1803)

WAKEFIELD, Frank Howard, M.B.E., *b.* 1 July, 1897 ; *s.* of William Howard Wakefield, of Reading, Berks. *Educ.*: Newtown, Reading, and Whitehill Higher Grade, Glasgow. Civil Servant, Assistant Clerk, War Office. *War Work*: Employed in Casualty Department, War Office ; employed as Supervisor of Section of Regiments, Prisoners of War Section, and Correspondence Section. *Addresses*: 2, Courtenay Square, Kennington, S.E. 11 ; 149, Onslow Drive, Dennistoun, Glasgow. (M9928)

WAKEFIELD, George Edward Campbell, O.B.E., *b.* 16 April, 1873 ; *s.* of G. E. Wakefield, of Punjab Commission. Sec. to the Government of H.E.H. the Nizam ; has Kaisar-i-Hind Gold Medal. *Address*: Hyderabad, Deccan, India. (O2098)

WAKEFIELD, Capt. Hubert Steven, O.B.E.

WAKEFIELD, Squadron-Leader Hugh Claude, O.B.E., R.A.F.

WAKEFIELD, William Birkbeck, M.B.E. ; *s.* of W. Wakefield, of Kendal ; *m.* Elizabeth, *d* of — Davison. (M2593)

WAKEHAM, Capt. Frederick, O.B.E.

WAKELIN, Lieut.-Col. Arthur Brittan, O.B.E.

WAKELIN, Capt. James Glencorse, O.B.E., *b.* 1888 ; *s.* of Henry Wakelin, of Edinburgh ; *m.* Adelaide, *d.* of W. F. McHardy, of Drumblair, and Auchernach, Aberdeenshire. *Educ.*: Edinburgh Academy. Advocate ; M.A., LL.B. *War Work*: Served with Royal Scots Fusiliers, Gallipoli, spring, 1915 ; wounded later, 1915 ; appointed officer in charge of Recruiting at Ayr for Ayrshire and Wigtownshire, 1917–19. *Address*: Drumblair, Aberdeenshire ; 14, Drummond Place, Edinburgh. *Club*: Caledonian United Service (Edinburgh). (O3199)

WAKELING, Elizabeth, Mrs., O.B.E., A.R.R.C., *b.* 1862 ; *d.* of Hugh Hunter, of Barassie, Troon, Ayrshire ; *m.* Thomas George, *s.* of George Lionel Wakeling, of Essex. *Educ.*: Ayr Academy. *War Work*: Assistant Matron to Dame Swift, Matron-in-Chief ; Trained Nursing Service of the Joint War Committee of British Red Cross and the Order of St. John of Jerusalem in England. *Address*: 46, Palace Gardens Terrace, Kensington, London. (O11535)

WAKELING, George Henry, O.B.E., M.A. Fellow of Brasenose Coll., Oxford. *War Work*: Sec. War Trade Intelligence Department. *Address*: 5, Northmoor Road, Oxford. (O11536)

WAKELING, Capt. Thomas George, O.B.E., R.A.M.C., *b.* 1864 ; *s.* of George Lionel Wakeling, of Essex ; *m.* Elizabeth Aitken, *d.* of Hugh Hunter, of Barassie, Troon. *Educ.*: London Univ. and St. Bartholomew's Hospital. Senior Medical Officer, East London, 1915–17 ; President of Officers' Standing Medical Board ; Prince of Wales' Hospital, London. *Address*: 46, Palace Gardens Terrace, Kensington, W. 8. *Clubs*: Royal Automobile ; Alexandra Yacht. (O1964)

WALCOTT, Capt. Colpoys Cleland, C.B.E., R.N. For services in connection with the Imperial War Museum. (C3172)

WALDEGRAVE, Alfred John, M.B.E., *b.* 18 Nov. 1872. Civil Servant. *War Work*: Post Office Investments. *Address*: Oxhey, Watford. (M2594)

WALDEGRAVE, Alice, Mrs., M.B.E., *b.* 1863 ; *d.* of C. O. Millett, of Marazion, Cornwall ; *m.* Samuel Edmund, *s.* of Samuel Waldegrave, Bishop Carlisle. *War Work*: Quartermaster of the Castle Hospital, Sherborne, and pre-war Sec. of the Sherborne Division of the British Red Cross Society. *Address*: Poyntington, Sherborne, Dorset. (M2595)

WALDEGRAVE, Mary Dorothea, Countess of, D.B.E., *b.* 25 March, 1850 ; *d.* of 1st Earl of Selborne, of Blackmoor Liss, Hampshire (*see* BURKE'S *Peerage*) ; *m.* William Frederick, Earl Waldegrave, *s.* of William Frederick, Viscount Chewton (*see* BURKE'S *Peerage*). *Educ.*: Privately. Deputy President, Somerset Branch of the British Red Cross Society ; Member of Somerset County Education Committee. *War Work*: Red Cross work in Somerset. *Address*: Chewton Priory, Bath. *Clubs*: Forum ; Ladies' Bath and County. (D31)

WALDEN, Robert Woolley, C.B.E., J.P. Late Mayor of Westminster ; Knight Officer, Vasa Sweden and Crown of Belgium. *War Work*: Chairman of the Metropolitan Asylums Board ; Chairman, Earl's Court, Alexandra Palace and Edmonton Belgium Refugees Committees ; Deputy Chairman for "F" Section, Tribunal of Appeal for County of London (Military) ; Chairman of Food Control Committee, Westminster City Council, Member Standing Joint Committee, National Reserve. *Address*: Bella Vista, Warlingham, Surrey. *Club*: St. Stephen's. (C3017)

WALDEN, Thomas, M.B.E.

WALDEN, William Herbert, O.B.E.

WALDOCK, Lieut. Charles William, M.B.E., *b.* 20 Aug. 1885 ; *s.* of A. Waldock, of St. Ives, Hunts ; *m.* Ruby Dorothy,

d. of S. W. Scott, of London and niece of Sir Leicester Harmsworth, Bart. (*see* BURKE'S *Peerage*). *Educ.*: St. Ives, Hunts, Grammar School. *War Work*: Corporal, 19th Royal Fusiliers, Public Schools Brigade, Oct. 1914, to June 1916 ; served in France during winter 1915–16 ; gazetted 2nd Lieut. Bedford and Herts Regt., July, 1916 ; seconded to King's African Rifles, Oct. 1916 ; served with 3rd Regt. in East Africa ; invalided to S. Africa, Jan. 1918, attached to Simonstown Depot 1918, during 1919 on the Staff of South African Military Command as Garrison Adjutant ; while at Simonstown wrote and produced a revue which was the means of raising nearly £1000 for charities. (M6718)

WALDRON, Major and Qr.-Mr. Charles, M.B.E.

WALDRON, Capt. Edward Joseph, O.B.E.

WALDRON, 2nd Lieut. Frank, M.B.E.

WALDRON, Capt. and Qr.-Mr. William, O.B.E.

WALE, Henry William, C.B.E., J.P., *b.* 1874. Member of City Council for Coventry, and Chairman of its Appeal Tribunal (Coventry and Dist.). *Address*: 15, Terry Road, Coventry. (C658)

WALE, Capt. William Alfred, M.B.E.

WALEY, Capt. Eric George Simon, O.B.E.

WALEY, Capt. Frederick George, C.B.E. Rendered service in connection with Coal Supplies, Commonwealth of Australia, during the Great War. (C3207)

WALFORD, 2nd Lieut. Harry Norman, M.B.E., R.A.S.C.

WALKER, Sir Alexander, K.B.E., ; *b.* 1869 *s.* of Alexander Walker, of Kilmarnock ; *m.* 1895. Director of John Walker & Sons (Lim.) Distillers. Rendered service to Ministry of Munitions and other Depts., during the Great War ; was connected with Disposal Board, Ministry of Munitions. (K464)

WALKER, Alexander, C.B.E., F.S.I., J.P., *b.* 28 March, 1866 ; *s.* of Andrew Walker, of Glasgow ; *m.* Jessie, *d.* of John Winchester, J.P., of Loanhead, Buckie. *Educ.*: Wilson School, Glasgow, and Glasgow Univ. Solicitor ; for many years Deputy Town Clerk, Glasgow, now holding the offices of City Assessor under the Lands Valuation Acts ; Registration Officer under the Representation of the People Act, and Surveyor of Municipal Rates, Glasgow. *War Work*: Hon. Sec. of the Glasgow Corporation Belgian Refugee Committee, who gave hospitality to about 20,000 Belgian Refugees, and raised the necessary funds to maintain them ; also did work for the Admiralty in connection with the housing of Shipyard workers, etc. *Addresses*: 18, Queen's Gate, Downhill, Glasgow ; City Chambers, Glasgow. *Clubs*: Royal Automobile ; Liberal ; Royal Scottish Automobile (Glasgow). (C659)

WALKER, Alexander Mann, M.B.E.

WALKER, Major and Qr.-Mr. Archibald, O.B.E., R.E.

WALKER, Comm. Arthur Horace, O.B.E., R.E.

WALKER, Lieut. Austine Harington, O.B.E., R.A.F.

WALKER, Charles, M.B.E., *b.* 3 Oct. 1874 ; *s.* of James Walker, of Forfar ; *m.* Elizabeth Robbie, *d.* of Alexander Gair, of Tannadice. *Educ.*: Forfar. Superintendent of Police, Wishaw Division of Lanarkshire. *War Work*: Assistant Chief of Police at Gretna. *Address*: Ivy Cottage, Wishaw. (M9930)

WALKER, Charles Alfred Le Maistre, C.B.E.

WALKER, Major Charles Bishop, O.B.E., R.A.S.C.

WALKER, Charles Craven Howell, M.B.E.

WALKER, Charles Edmund, M.B.E.

WALKER, Eadith Campbell, C.B.E., *b.* 1874 ; *d.* of the late Thomas Walker. Rendered services in connection with Red Cross movement, N.S. Wales, during Great War. *Address*: Yaralla, Concord, Sydney, N.S. Wales. *Clubs*: Ladies' Empire ; Queen's (Sydney). (C721)

WALKER, Edward, M.D., M.R.C.S., *b.* 25 Feb. 1863 ; *s.* of Samuel Walker, of Golcar, nr. Huddersfield ; *m.* Ethel, *d.* of Samuel Learoyd, of Huddersfield. *Educ.*: Edinburgh Univ. Hon. Physician, Royal Infirmary, Huddersfield ; ex-President, Huddersfield Medical Society, and Chairman, Huddersfield Division British Medical Association ; Governor, Technical Coll., Huddersfield ; Member Free Library Committee ; formerly Member of Education Committee, and of the Huddersfield School Board. *War Work*: Hon. Sec. Local Medical War Committee ; Member National Service Medical Board ; Recruiting Medical Officer, Huddersfield District. *Address*: Spring Bank, Huddersfield. (M9931)

WALKER, Capt. Edward McAllen, O.B.E., R.A.F.

WALKER, Major Eric Bolingbroke, M.B.E., M.C.

WALKER, Col. Francis John, C.B.E., V.D., J.P., *b.* 29 Oct. 1859 ; *s.* of John West Walker, of Hundleby House, Spilsby ; *m.* Maria Edith, M.B.E., *d.* of Pereira Brown, of Glentworth Hall, Lincoln. *Educ.*: St. Bartholomew's Hospital, and Univ. of Durham. H.M. Coroner for parts of Lindsey. *War Work*: County Director, B.R.C.S., North Lincolnshire Branch ; Medical Officer in charge Spilsby Auxiliary Hospital. *Address*: St. Damian, Spilsby, Lincolnshire. (C3018)

WALKER, Lieut.-Col. Francis Spring, C.B.E., R.A.M.C., *b.* 6 Jan. 1876 ; *s.* of Anster Fitzgeral Walker, M.D., Glenbergh, Co. Kerry ; *m.* Rosamond Margaret, *d.* of Capt. Richard Chute, of Leabrook, Tralee. *Educ.*: Royal Coll. of Surgeons, Dublin, and Trinity Coll., Dublin. Regular Officer, joined Army, in 1900. *War Work*: Served in France with 16th Field Ambulance, 6th Division ; in command Hospital-carrier "Vladivian" at Suvla Bay ; O.C. No. 3 Convalescent Camp, Ghain Tuffeyh, Malta ; O.C. Military Hospital, Taunton, and Military Hospital, Cork ; retired May, 1920. *Address*: Woodquest, Crosshaven, Co. Cork. (C1804)

WALKER, Lieut. Frederick Rutley, M.B.E. I.A.,

WALKER, Capt. Frederic William, O.B.E., b. 21 Feb. 1870; s. of Edward Walker, of Newcastle-upon-Tyne; m. Rose, d. of Major H. J. King, of the Royal Scots Greys. Staff Capt., War Office, Under Sec. of States' Dept.; Lieut.-Col. 2/4th Hampshire Regt. Cadet Batt.; Assistant Hon. Sec. the Royal Tournament. *War Work:* With Headquarters Staff, 1st Army, Central Force, under Gen. Sir Horace Smith-Dorrien; Army H.Q. Staff, War Office, under Major-Gen. the Earl of Scarborough; identified with the reorganisation of the Cadet Force. *Addresses:* 73, St. James' Street, S.W.; The White Cottage, Horsell Woking. *Clubs:* Junior Carlton; Junior Constitutional; Royal Automobile. (O11538)

WALKER, Capt. George, M.B.E.

WALKER, George, M.B.E.

WALKER, Lieut. George, O.B.E., M.C., R.E.

WALKER, Capt. and Qr.-Mr. George Beresford, M.B.E., M.C., R.A.M.C., b. 18 Oct. 1871; s. of James Beresford Walker. *Educ.:* Battersea. *War Work:* Served from 1914–19 in France and Mesopotamia. *Address:* R.A.M.C. Officers' Mess, London, S.W. 1. (M4936)

WALKER, Major George Croxton, O.B.E.,M.C., R.E. (T.).

WALKER, Lieut. George David, M.B.E., I.A.R.O. (M6780g)

WALKER, Lieut.-Col. George Kemp, C.I.E., O.B.E., b. 20 March, 1872; s. of William Alfred Walker, of Warwick, England; m. Ethel Maria, d. of William Herbert Wall, of Stoke Prior, Worcs. *Educ.:* Warwick School; Royal Veterinary Coll., London. Principal, Punjab Veterinary Coll., Lahore, India. *War Work:* Officer Commanding, 35th Poona Batt., I.V.F.; Conducting Officer, Mesopotamia Expeditionary Force. *Address:* Lahore, India. *Clubs:* United Service (Simla); Western India (Poona). (O2369)

WALKER, Lieut. Harold Frederick, M.B.E., R.A.F.

WALKER, Harry, O.B.E.

WALKER, Henry, C.B.E. Deputy Chief Inspector for Mines. (C3019)

WALKER, Herbert Arthur, M.B.E.

WALKER, Lieut.-Col. Herbert Sutherland, C.B.E., b. 29 Sept. 1864; s. of Gen. W. Walker, Indian Medical Service; m. Josephine Helen, d. of W. R. Freeman, of Murtle, N.B. *Educ.:* Rugby; Sandhurst; Staff Coll. The Cameronians (Scottish Rifles), Brevet Major, 1897; Brevet Lieut.-Col., 1899; Chief Constable of Worcestershire from 1903. *War Work:* Chief Permit Officer, Intelligence Division, War Office, 1914–19. *Address:* The Cross House, Powyke, Worcester. *Club:* County (Worcester). (C660)

WALKER, T. Capt. James Blake, O.B.E., R.A.V.C.

WALKER, Jessie Winchester, Mrs., M.B.E., b. 1871; d. of John Winchester, J.P., of Loanhead, Portessie; m. Alexander, C.B.E., J.P., F.S.I., s. of Andrew Walker, of Glasgow. *Educ.:* Buckie, Banffshire. *War Work:* Member of the Glasgow Corporation Belgian Refugee Ladies Committee, who gave hospitality to over 18,000 refugees in Scotland, and by voluntary subscriptions defrayed the expenses thereof; also worked in connection with war hospitals; holder of Belgian Queen Elizabeth Medal. *Address:* 8, Queen's Gate, Downanhill, Glasgow. (M9933)

WALKER, Major John, O.B.E., D.C.M.

WALKER, John, M.B.E.

WALKER, John, O.B.E.

WALKER, Flight-Lieut. John Briton, O.B.E., R.A.F.

WALKER, Lieut.-Col. John Douglas Glen, D.S.O., O.B.E.

WALKER, John Drummond, M.B.E.

WALKER, John Frederick, M.B.E.

WALKER, John Hamilton, M.B.E.

WALKER, John Jeffrey, M.B.E. Senior Assistant Inspector of Munitions Areas, Ministry of Munitions. (M10260c)

WALKER, Capt. John Philip, M.B.E., R.A.F.

WALKER, Capt. John William, O.B.E., F.S.A., J.P., R.A.M.C. (T.), b. 15 Oct. 1859; s. of Thomas Walker, J.P., of Chapelthorpe Hall, Wakefield; m. Constance Elizabeth, d. of Samuel Holdsworth, J.P., of Burneytops House, Wakefield. *Educ.:* Rossall; Univ. Coll., Hospital, London. Vice-President, Trustee, and Consulting Surgeon, Clayton Hospital, Wakefield; Visiting Justice, H.M. Prison, Wakefield; Hon. Life Member, St. John Ambulance Association; Governor of the Wakefield Charities; represents Diocese of Wakefield in House of Laymen; late President, Wakefield Institute of Literature and Science. *War Work:* Gazetted Capt., R.A.M.C. (T.), and appointed on the Staff of 2nd Northern General Hospital, Beckett Park, Leeds; started an auxiliary hospital; representative of the County Branch of the St. John Ambulance Association. *Address:* The Grange, East Hagbourne, Berks. (O11540)

WALKER, John William Thomson, O.B.E., M.B., C.M., F.R.C.S.; s. of John H. Walker, of Westwood, Newport, Fife; m. Isabella, d. of Sir Michael Nairn, Bart., Dysart House, and Rankeilour, Fife (see BURKE'S *Peerage*). *Educ.:* Edinburgh Univ.; Vienna. Surgeon; Senior Urologist and Lecturer on Urology, King's Coll. Hospital; Surgeon to St. Peter's Hospital for Stone. *War Work:* Surgeon to the King George Military Hospital, King Edward VII.'s Hospital for Officers, Lady Carnarvon's Hospital, Lady Ridley's Hospital, Star and Garter; Member of Advisory Committee to Director-General. *Addresses:* 30, Queen Anne Street, London, W. 1.; Burntwood, Goring-on-Thames, Oxon. *Club:* Caledonian. (O4398)

WALKER, Capt. Joseph, M.B.E., b. 1877; s. of the late

Charles Hy. Walker, of Lindley. Solicitor; Commissioner for Oaths. *War Work:* Commissioned in 2/5th Duke of Wellington's (West Riding Regt.) in 1914; served until 1919; wounded with B.E.F., France, 62nd (West Riding) Division, in 1917; mentioned in despatches. *Address:* Marsh House, Lindley, Huddersfield. *Club:* Huddersfield. (M4310)

WALKER, Rev. Joseph Robert, M.B.E.

WALKER, Lieut. Keith Jerome, M.B.E.

WALKER, Lucy, Mrs., M.B.E., b. 14 Dec. 1862; m. James Clough Walker. *War Work:* 1914–15, assisted Woman's Club for Wives and Mothers of men serving; also at Y.M.C.A. Hut and Soldiers' Recreation Room; 1915–19, worked at York War Hospital Supply Depot from start to finish; also assisted at Artificial Limb Depot. (M9935)

WALKER, Mabel Caroline, O.B.E.; d. of Col. Sir George Gustavus Walker, K.C.B., Crawfordton, Dumfriesshire. *Educ.:* Crawfordton, Dumfriesshire, and London. From 1897 to 1908 Hon. Supt. of Institutes for Soldiers in South Africa; from 1908 to the present time founder and Hon. Supt. of the Soldiers' Institute, York, of which Field Marshal Earl Roberts was President. *War Work:* From Dec. 1914, to June, 1917, was a hospital visitor and writer for the wounded in Wimereux near Boulogne; upon returning to York, enlarged the Institute for Soldiers, and opened a hostel-annexe for the relatives of wounded and sick soldiers in the Military Hospital. *Address:* The Soldiers' Institute, Wenlock Terrace, York. *Club:* New Alliance. (O11541)

WALKER, Margaret, O.B.E.

WALKER, Margaret Dewar, Mrs., M.B.E.

WALKER, Maria Edith, Mrs., M.B.E., b. Nov. 1864; d. of Pereira Brown, Glenworth Hall; m. Francis John, C.B.E., s. of John West Walker of Spilsby. *Educ.:* Brighton. *War Work:* Commandant of V.A.D. 24 Lincs; Officer-in-Charge of Spilsby Auxiliary Hospital. *Address:* St. Damian, Spilsby, Lincolnshire. *Club:* Ladies' V.A.D. (M1057)

WALKER, Major(A. Lieut.-Col.) Norman Dunbar, O.B.E., M.B., Ch.B. (Edin.), D.P.H., R.A.M.C., b. 21 Aug. 1876; s. of A. Dunbar Walker, of Hampstead, London; m. Norah Dorothy, d. of F. K. Cunliffe, of P.W.D. (India) (see BURKE'S *Peerage*). *Educ.:* Haileybury and Merchiston. Assistant Director of Hygiene, Western Command; Regular Officer; Civil Surgeon, South Africa, 1900–1 *War Work:* Baluchistan, 1914–15; Siestan, 1916; Mesopotamian Expeditionary Force, 1916–18; Afghan War, 1919. *Address:* c/o Holt & Co., 3, Whitehall Place, S.W. (O6718)

WALKER, Captain Percy, M.B.E.

WALKER, Rev. Raymond Elliston, O.B.E.

WALKER, Reginald Field, M.B.E., M.R.C.S., L.R.C.P., b. 2 June, 1864; s. of E. W. Walker, of Esher. *Educ.:* Charterhouse. Hon. Surgeon, Esher and Thames Ditton Cottage Hospital. *War Work:* Hon. Surgeon, H.R.H. the Duchess of Albany's Hospital for Officers; Hon. Surgeon, Mrs. Moreing's Hospital at Moore Place, Esher; Hon. Surgeon, Esher Red Cross Hospital. *Address:* The New House, Esher, Surrey. (M9936)

WALKER, Lieut. Reginald Henry, M.B.E., R.E.

WALKER, Robert, M.B.E.

WALKER, Robert John, C.B.E., b. 23 Dec. 1870. Honours Medallist, Naval Architecture; Joint Managing Director of the Parsons Marine Steam Turbine Co., Ltd., Wallsend-on-Tyne. *War Work:* Associated with the Hon. Sir Charles A. Parsons, K.C.B., F.R.S., in his development of the Steam Turbine for the propulsion of War and Merchant ships. *Address:* Kingmead, Riding-Mill, Northumberland. *Clubs:* British Empire; Royal Automobile. (C3020)

WALKER, Capt. Samuel, M.B.E.

WALKER, Captain Thomas Herbert, M.bB.E.

WALKER, Major Thomas Molineaux, O.B.E.

WALKER, Capt. and Hon. Major William, C.B.E., T.D., M.I.M.E., M.I.M.M., b. 26 Dec. 1863; s. of William Walker, of Hinderwell, Yorkshire; m. Margaret, d. of the late Thomas Dickinson, of Saltburn-by-the-Sea. *Educ.:* Coatham Grammar School, Redcar, Yorkshire. Mining Engineer; H.M. Chief Inspector of Mines. *War Work:* Member of Coal Export Committee; Chairman, Mines Rescue Apparatus Research Committee; Central Colliery Recruiting Court; Distribution of Coal and Coke Committee. *Address:* Mapledene, Ashtead, Surrey. (C662)

WALKER, Lieut. William, M.B.E.

WALKER, William, C.B.E., b. 1863; formerly H.M. Inspector of Mines. Director of Health and Safety, Mines Department Board of Trade. (C662)

WALKER, Winifred Jane, O.B.E.; d. of Frederick J. Walker, of Myton Lodge, Warwick. *War Work:* Worked at Hill House Hospital, Warwick as Quartermaster, 1915–16, and as Commandant, 1916–19. *Address:* Myton Lodge, Warwick. *Club:* Albemarle. (O11544)

WALKER, Eliza BAGSHAWE-, M.B.E.

WALKER, Sophie, Mrs., GAMBLE-, M.B.E., b. 21 Nov. 1872; d. of Joseph Henry Nixon, of Chester; m. Sam, s. of Benjamin Walker, of Bradford. *Educ.:* Wilton House School, Chester. Incorporated Society Trained Masseuses. *War Work:* At the request of the B.R.C.S. opened and filled the position of Commandant-in-charge of Lancaster House Red Cross Hospital, later for Limbless Sailors and Soldiers, Whalley Range, Manchester. *Address:* Ladies' Club, Deansgate, Manchester. (M9937)

WALKER, Lieut.-Col. Joseph Walker HIGGS-, O.B.E.

WALKER, Thomas Charles Bruce MACKINTOSH, O.B.E.

WALKER, Major Archibald STODART-, M.B.E., M.A., M.B., C.M., F.R.C.P., R.A.M.C., *b.* 16 April, 1869; *s.* of David S. Walker, of Luthrie, Fife. *Educ.:* Edinburgh; Paris; Balogna. Assistant Director, Ministry of Pensions; late Assistant Professor of Institutes of Medicine, and of Clinical Medicine, Univ. of Edin.; President, Student's Representative Council; President of Union, Univ. of Edin.; Chairman, Scottish Modern Arts Association; author of many works on Literary Criticism, Biography, Philosophy, Sport, Fiction, Verse, and contributor to reviews and magazines. *War Work:* Sec. Queen Alexandra Hospital for Officers, 1914; joined R.A.M.C. 1915; Capt. 1916; Major, 1918; Chief Registrar and Acting Commandant, the King's Lancashire Military Convalescent Hospital; mentioned in Sec. of State for War's List. *Club:* Caledonian. (M5657)

WALKER, Lieut.-Comm. William Frederic WAKE-, O.B.E.

WALKEY, Lieut.-Col. Rev. Frank John, O.B.E, M.C., *b.* 10 Nov. 1874; *s.* of Thomas Durston Walkey, of Sidmouth, Devonshire; *m.* Phillis, *d.* of the Rev. C. Trim Johnson, of Southbourne, Hants. *Educ.:* Osborne House School, Romsay, and Metropolitan Coll., Newington Butts, S.E. Baptist Minister; now Assistant Principal Chaplain, United Army Board, Egyptian Expeditionary Force. *War Work:* Member of Gateshead Volunteer Training Corps, Jan. to July, 1915; Officiating Clergyman, 63rd Div., Aug. to Oct. 1915; Commissioned C.F., Oct. 1915; served with 63rd Northumbrian Division in England Oct. 1915 to April, 1916; appointed United Board Chaplain, 162nd Brigade, 54th Division, E.E.F., May, 1916; in action with 1/4th Northampton Regiment at Gaza, March, April, and Nov. 1917; Palestine, Nov. to Dec. 1917; Senior U.B. Chaplain, Mesopotamia, May, 1918; Assistant Principal Chaplain United Board, Egypt, Nov. 1918; twice mentioned in despatches. *Addresses:* Baptist Church House, Southampton Row, W.C.; c/o Sir C. R. McGrigor, Bart., & Co., Army Agents., London. (O6720)

WALKLEY, Major Daniel, O.B.E.

WALL, Lieut.-Col. Allan Copinger, O.B.E.

WALL, Capt. Anthony Herbert William, O.B.E. M.C., R.A.F.

WALL, Arthur, O.B.E. Director of Dairy Produce in America for the Ministry of Food. (O11791a)

WALL, Arthur Joseph, O.B.E., *b.* 27 Aug. 1861; *s.* of Capt. Michael Wall, of London; *m.* Jessie Elizabeth (who died, Feb. 1907), *d.* of William Pratt, of London. *Educ.:* Battersea Grammar School. Joined the Prison Commission, Sept. 1880; appointed Assistant Sec. 1910, and Sec. 1919. *War Work:* Much work in connection with interned aliens. *Addresses:* Prison Commission, Home Office, S.W.; Grange Cottage, 34, Amerland Road, Wandsworth, S.W. 18. (O1967)

WALL, Arthur Thomas, O.B.E.

WALL, Lieut.-Col. Charles Percivale Bligh, O.B.E., M.D.

WALL, Lieut.-Col. George, C.M.G., C.B.E.. Gen. List, Australian Inf.; served in Great War, 1915–19. (C1846)

WALL, Maud Amy Margaret, M.B.E., W.R.N.S.

WALL, William Joseph, M.B.E.

WALLACE, Agnes Kendall, Mrs., M.B.E.; *d.* of John Fair, of Wilderton, Bournemouth; *m.* John Agnew Wallace, D.L., J.P. *War Work:* County Sec. Red Cross Society. *Address:* Lochryan, Stranraer, Wigtownshire. (M4056)

WALLACE, Augusta Maud, Lady, M.B.E.; *d.* of Sir Thomas Clouston, of Holodyke, Orkney; *m.* Sir David, K.B.E. (*q.v.*), *s.* of David Wallace, of Balgrummo, Fife. *Educ.:* St. Leonards School, St. Andrews, and Paris. *War Work:* Organised and acted as Hon Sec. from 1915–19 of the Edinburgh Victoria League Clubs for Overseas Soldiers; appointed by military authorities one of the organisers of the reception and feeding of 40,000 repatriated prisoners of war arriving at Leith. *Addresses:* 29, Charlotte Square, Edinburgh; Holodyke, Orkney. *Clubs:* Forum; Caledonian (Edinburgh). (M1060)

WALLACE, Eng.-Comm. Charles James Mitchell, O.B.E., R.N.

WALLACE, Major Charles John, D.S.O., O.B.E., M.C., *b.* 1890; *s.* of Lieut.-Col. Hugh Robert Wallace, D.S.O.. Capt. and Brevet Major, Highland L.I.; served in Great War (mentioned in despatches). (O2777)

WALLACE, Brevet-Lieut.-Col. Sir David, K.B.E., C.M.G., F.R.C.S., R.A.M.C. (T.), *b.* July, 1862; *s.* of David Wallace, of Balgrummo, Fife; *m.* Augusta Maud, M.B.E. (*q.v.*) *d.* of the late Sir Thomas Clouston, of Edinburgh. *Educ.:* Dollar Academy, and Edinburgh Univ. Surgeon, Edinburgh Royal Infirmary; Senior Lecturer and Examiner in Clinical Surgery, Univ. of Edinburgh. *War Work:* Brevet Lieut.-Col. No. 2 Scottish General Hospital; Red Cross Commissioner, Eastern District of Scotland; Military Inspector of Auxiliary Hospitals, Eastern District of Scotland. *Address:* 29, Charlotte Square, Edinburgh. *Club:* University (Edinburgh). (K437)

WALLACE, Falconer Lewis, O.B.E., *b.* 1870; *s.* of Alexander F. Wallace, of Candacraig, Strathdon, and 20, Hyde Park Gardens, W.; *m.* Kathleen Anne, *d.* of Admiral Arthur Paget. *Educ.:* Privately, and Cambridge Univ. Director of Wallace Brothers & Co., Ltd., 4, Crosby Square, London, E.C. 3. *War Work:* Employed at War Office; Commission Internationale de Ravitaillement; Investigations into Wages and Conditions of Agricultural Labour, also Farming Costs and Profit and Loss Accounts. *Addresses:* Tillypronie, Tarland, Aberdeenshire; Balcairn, Oldmeldrum, Aberdeenshire; Candacraig, Strathdon, Aberdeenshire; 40, Brook Street, London, W. 1. *Clubs:* Brooks's; Windham; Boodle's. (O832)

WALLACE, Major Forbes Thomson, O.B.E., J.P., *b* 13 Dec. 1874; *s.* of Michael Thomson Wallace, of Leven, Fife; *m.* Mary Rollo, *d.* of James Clark, of Largo. *Educ.:* Leven; Waid Academy, Anstruther; Edinburgh Univ. S.S.C. and Notary Public; Agent of British Linen Bank. *War Work:* Served with 1/7th Black Watch, 1914–15, in Scotland and France; thereafter employed on staff duties in France till 1919. *Addresses:* many Ernsyde, Links Road, Leven; British Linen Bank, Leven. *Clubs:* Innerleven; Conservative (Edin.). (O5892)

WALLACE, James Alfred, M.B.E.

WALLACE, Major James Hill, O.B.E.

WALLACE, John, O.B.E., M.B., C.M.

WALLACE, Capt. John, O.B.E., M.A., M.B., R.A.M.C. (T. *b.* 18 March, 1878; *s.* of Thomas Wallace, M.D., J.P., of Cardiff; *m.* Lilian Beatrice, *d.* of John Lenton, J.P., of Newport, Mon. *Educ.:* Rugby; Oxford Univ.; St. Thomas's Hospital. Director of Medical Services, Ministry of Pensions. *War Work:* Served with 2nd Welsh Field Ambulance. R.A.M.C. (T.) at Suvla Bay; attached H.Q. Western Command; attached War Office; Commissioner of Medical Services, Ministry of National Service. *Address:* 45, Pembroke Square, Earl's Court, W. 8. (O1969)

WALLACE, Col. Sir Johnstone, K.B.E., J.P., *b.* 20 Oct. 1861; *s.* of Thomas Wallace, of Castledawson; *m.* Norah, *d.* of John B. Bowes, of Newcastle-upon-Tyne. *Educ.:* Westgate Academy, and Rutherford Technical Coll. Iron and Steel Exporter and Merchant; Director of the English Insurance Co., Ltd.; Alderman; Sheriff (1906–7); Lord Mayor (1913–14) of Newcastle-upon-Tyne; Chairman of Finance Committee; Chairman of Laing Art Gallery; Vice-Chairman of Education Committee. *War Work:* 1914, was responsible for raising Tyneside Brigades of Northumberland Fusiliers (two brigades and reserves); instituted Lord Mayor's War Relief Fund; Hon. Col. of Northumberland Fusiliers; was Deputy Director of Trades Section in National Service Ministry. *Address:* Parkholme, Newcastle-upon-Tyne. *Clubs:* Junior Constitutional; Northern Conservative (Newcastle-upon-Tyne). (K41)

WALLACE, John Thompson, M.B.E.

WALLACE, Sir Lawrence Aubrey, K.B.E., C.M.G., *b.* 1857; *s.* of John Henry Wallace, *m.* Marguerite Marie, C.B.E., *d.* of Henry Duboc, of Le Havre. Administrator of Northern Rhodesia (ret.). *War Work:* As Administrator of Northern Rhodesia, where von Lettow surrendered. *Address:* Lynton, Bromley Grove, Shortlands, Kent. *Club:* Royal Societies'. (K125)

WALLACE, Margaret Janet, M.B.E.

WALLACE, Marguerite Marie, Lady, C.B.E.; *d.* of Prof. Henry Duboc, of Le Havre, France; *m.* Sir Lawrence Aubrey, K.B.E. (*see* BURKE'S *Peerage*), *s.* of the late John Henry Wallace. *Address:* Nynton, Bromley Grove, Shortlands, Kent. (C2027)

WALLACE, Ottiline, Mrs., O.B.E., W.R.N.S.

WALLACE, Col. Robert Hugh, C.B., C.B.E., M.A., D.L., *b.* 14 Dec. 1860; *s.* of the late William Nevin Wallace, D.L., of Downpatrick, Co. Down; *m.* Caroline Wilhelmina, *d.* of John Benjamin Twigg, of Cootstown, Co. Tyrone. *Educ.:* Harrow, and B.N.C., Oxford. Solicitor, and Land Agent. *War Work:* Organised and commanded successively 17th (Reserve) Batt. Royal Irish Rifles, and 19th Batt. Royal Irish Rifles. *Address:* Myra Castle, Downpatrick; Waterfoot, Newcastle, Co. Down. *Clubs:* Carlton; Ulster (Belfast). (C2188)

WALLACE, Lieut. Robert Stuart, M.B.E.

WALLACE, William, C.B.E., J.P.; *s.* of William Wallace, of Glasgow; *m.* Barbara, *d.* of Alexander Munro. *Educ.:* Glasgow Academy and Univ. Sheriff-Substitute of Argyllshire; Advocate of Scottish Bar; author of numerous legal works. *War Work:* President of West Highland Sailors' and Soldiers' Home; Sub-commandant of Argyllshire National Guards; Hon. Sec. and Treas. of Lorne Division of Red Cross Society from 1912–16; Chairman of West Highland Reconstruction and of Oban and District Local Employment Committees. *Address:* Glenlee, Oban, Argyllshire. *Clubs:* Scottish Conservative (Edinburgh); Royal Highland Yacht (Oban). (C3021)

WALLACE, William Reeve, O.B.E., *b.* 1 July, 1873; *s.* of William Wallace, of the Bank of England. *Educ.:* St. Paul's. Admitted a Solicitor, 1896; Official Solicitor's Dept., Royal Courts of Justice, 1896–1902; entered Privy Council Office, 1902; Chief Clerk, Judicial Dept., Privy Council Office, since 1909. *War Work:* Acting Superintending Aliens Officer, 1916–19. *Addresses:* Judicial Dept., Privy Council Office, S.W. 1; 4, Waverton Street, Mayfair, W. 1. *Clubs:* Athenæum; Savile. (O833)

WALLACE, Charles Nugent HOPE-, M.B.E.

WALLER, Rev. Alfred George, O.B.E.

WALLER, Major Edgar Hardress, O.B.E., R.A.S.C.

WALLER, Lieut.-Col. Edmund, O.B.E., I.A.

WALLERS, Sir Evelyn A., M.B.E.

WALLER, Capt. James Hardress de Warrenne, D.S.O., O.B.E., M.Sc., M.I.E.E., *b.* 31 July, 1884; *s.* of George Arthur Waller, of Prior Park and Luska, Nenagh; *m.* Beatrice Francis, *d.* of Richard John Kinkead, M.D., of Forster House, Galway. *Educ.:* Queen's Coll., Cork. Chief Engineer, Waller Housing Corporation, 16, Albemarle Street, W. 1. *War Work:* Served in Royal Engineers (Field Company) at Gallipoli and Salonica;

late Acting Major ; Chief Technical Adviser in Reinforced Concrete Construction to Controller-General, Merchant Shipbuilding. *Address :* Luska, Nenagh. (O11547)

WALLER, John, M.B.E., *b.* 13 June, 1862. Deputy Chief Constable, Durham. (M9940)

WALLER, Col. Stanier, C.V.O., O.B.E.

WALLERS, Sir Evelyn Ashley, K.B.E., *b.* 28 May 1876 ; *m.* Mary Elsie Dumbelton, of Elstree. *Educ. :* Enfield. Went to Transvaal, 1897. President of the Transvaal Chamber of Mines. *Address :* Elstree, West Parktown, Johannesburg. *Clubs :* Rand . Country ; Johannesburg. (K187)

WALLINGER, Capt. William Arnold, O.B.E.

WALLINGTON, Augusta Frances, O.B.E. ; *d.* of the late Sir John W. Wallington, K.C.B., of Keevil Manor, Trowbridge, Wiltshire. *War Work :* Commandant of Trowbridge Red Cross Hospital from Jan. 1915, to April, 1919. *Address :* Hilperton, Trowbridge, Wiltshire. (O11548)

WALLINGTON, Major Christopher Thomas, O.B.E., R.A.O.C.

WALLIS, Claude Dudley, M.B.E., *b* 31 Dec. 1885 ; *s.* of Henry Clobery Wallis, of Dieppe, France. *Educ. :* Bedford, and Europe. Colonial Civil Service ; Sec. to the Government of the Zanzibar Protectorate. *War Work :* Military Commandant and Officer-in-Charge of the occupied Enemy Territory in Central East Africa, comprised by the Island of Mafia and its adjacent islands. *Address :* Zanzibar, East Africa. (M6489)

WALLIS, Lieut.-Col. Henry Clifford, O.B.E., R.A.S.C.

WALLIS, Henry Richard, C.M.G., C.B.E.

WALLIS, Robert, M.B.E.

WALLIS, Lieut. Tacy Millett Winstanley, O.B.E., R.N.V.R.

WALMSLEY, Ben, C.B.E., *b.* 24 March, 1871 ; *s.* of Thomas M. Walmsley, of Bolton-le-Moors ; *m.* Laura Waldyve Champernowne, *d.* of the Rev. J. Willington, of Fen End. *Educ. :* Giggleswick. *War Work :* Ministry of Munitions, May, 1916, to June, 1919 ; Director of Pig Iron Section, Iron and Steel Department ; later Director of Iron and Steel Contracts, finally Controller, Ferrous Metals Department. *Address :* Baddesley Grange, Northam, N. Devon. *Clubs :* Bath ; Royal North Devon Golf (Westward Ho !) (C3022)

WALMSLEY, Capt. George, O.B.E., K.R.R.C.

WALMSLEY, Capt. Harry Hendon, O.B.E., R.A.F.

WALPOLE, Charles Archibald, O.B.E., *b.* 25 March, 1881 ; *s.* of Sir Charles Walpole, of Broadford Chobham (*see* BURKE'S *Peerage*). *Educ. :* Eton, and Trinity Coll. Cambridge. General Manager, Anglo-Persian Oil Co., Ltd., Mohammerah, Persian Gulf. *War Work :* Held the above position throughout the war, during which the Anglo-Persian Oil Co supplied the entire requirements of the Mesopotamia Expeditionary Force of oil, petrol, etc. *Address :* Mohammerah, Persian Gulf. *Clubs .* New University ; East India United Services. (O4144)

WALPOLE, Hugh Seymour, C.B.E., *b.* 13 March, 1884 ; *s.* of the Rt. Rev. George Henry Somerset Walpole (*see* BURKE'S *Peerage* Orford, E.). (C322)

WALSH, Ann Pollexfen, Mrs., M.B.E.,

WALSH, Capt. Arthur, M.B.E.

WALSH, Arthur Edward, M.B.E.

WALSH, Capt. George Gould, O.B.E., I.A.R.O.

WALSH, Flying Officer George Victor, M.B.E., R.A.F.

WALSH, Ivy, Mrs., O.B.E.

WALSH, Lieut.-Col. John Gustavus Russell, O.B.E., *b.* 1865 ; *s.* of Col. C. G. Walsh, of 15th Sikhs ; *m.* Frances May, *d.* of Arthur Norcott, of Park, Doneraile, Co. Cork. *Educ. :* Privately ; Royal Military Coll., Sandhurst. Gazetted Royal Berks. Regt. in 1887 ; served in Burma, 1888, medal and clasp, and throughout S. African War, Queen and King's Medals, 2 clasps each. *War Work :* Served in India with 2nd Batt. Royal Berks. Regt. Oct. 1914 ; France, Nov. 1914 ; dangerously wounded ; Commandant of Command Depot since June, 1916 ; transferred to Command Regimental Depot, Nov. 1917 ; retired, Nov. 1919 ; Mons Star (1914 and clasp). G.S. Medal, and Victory Medal. *Club :* Junior Army and Navy. (O7808)

WALSH, Marguerite Mary, M.B.E.

WALSH, William Thomas, M.B.E.

WALSH, William Trevor Hayne, M.B.E., M.A. (Oxon.). *b.* 26 June, 1866 ; *s.* of the late William Walsh, Bishop, Archdeacon, and Canon of Canterbury. *Educ. :* Berkhamsted ; Merchant Taylors' ; St. John's Coll., Oxford. Assistant Master, Mercers' School ; Assistant Sec. Kent Education Committee ; Sub-Section Director, Training Section, Ministry of Munitions ; Section Director, Training Department, Ministry of Labour. *War Work :* Ministry of Munitions (Training Section) from Jan. 1916. *Address :* Chillenden, 38, Temple Fortune Lane, Hendon, N.W. 4. *Club :* Athenæum. (M9944)

WALSHE, Major Francis Martin Rose, O.B.E., M.D., R.A.M.C.

WALSHE, Paymaster-Comm. Francis Weldon, O.B.E., R.N.

WALTER, Major Albert Elijah, O.B.E., I.M.S.

WALTER, Capt. Archibald Stephen, O.B.E.

WALTER, Edna, M.B.E.

WALTER, Margaret Jean, Mrs. Albert Elijah, M.B.E.

WALTER, Capt. Weever Kenneth, M.B.E.

WALTERS, Lieut.-Col. Alfred, O.B.E., T.D., *b.* 1867 ; *s.* of Richard Walters, of Falmouth ; *m.* Florence Elizabeth, *d.* of James Thomas, of Portscatho. *Educ. :* The Coll., Truro. Solicitor. *War Work :* Commanding T.F. Depot, Duke of

Cornwall's Light Infantry ; served in Command, Labour Corps Record Office, Nottingham. *Address :* Camborne, Cornwall. (O4280)

WALTERS, Evelyn Mayura, Mrs., C.B.E., *b.* 1881 ; *d.* of Conrad William Engleheart, of 6, Shaftesbury Villas, W. 8 ; *m.* Comm. Richard Huth Walters, D.S.O., R.N. *Educ. :* Privately, and Hyde Park New Coll. London. Hon. Sec. and Director, Kensington Div. B.R.C.S. during Great War. (C323)

WALTERS, Henry Beauchamp, O.B.E., M.A., F.S.A., *b.* 6 April, 1867 ; *s.* of the Rev. William Walters, Vicar of Oldham, Lancs, afterwards Archdeacon of Worcester ; *m.* Margaret, *d.* of Francis Edward Thompson, of Marlborough, and 16, Primrose Hill Road, N.W. *Educ. :* Eton, and King's Coll., Cambridge. Dept. of Greek and Roman Antiquities, British Museum, Assistant Keeper from 1911. *War Work :* Head of Naval Supplies Section, Commission Internationale de Ravitaillement, 1916–19. *Addresses :* 36, Oppidans Road, N.W. 3 ; British Museum, W.C. 1. (O11549)

WALTERS, Henry Blanchard, O.B.E., M.R.C.S., L.R.C.P (Lond.), *b.* 20 Nov. 1879 ; *s.* of John Walters, M.B., of Reigate ; *m.* Grace, *d.* of Robert Heppenstall, of Ealing. *Educ. :* Clifton Coll. *War Work :* M.O. V.A. Hospital, Chudleigh, Sir Ernest Cable's Hospital for Officers, Teignmouth, Canadian Forestry Corps, Mamhead and Kenton Camps, and P.O.W. Camp, Starcross. *Address :* Fairlea, Chudleigh, S. Devon. (O11550)

WALTERS, Capt. and Qr.-Mr. John Douglas, M.B.E., R.E.

WALTERS, Lieut.-Col. Robert Francis, O.B.E.

WALTERS, Samuel, M.B.E.

WALTERS, Winifred Edith, M.B.E. ; *d.* of R. E. Walters, of Wales. Trained Nurse, Lady Superintendent, Civil Hospital, Karachi. *War Work :* Worked in Officers' Overseas Sick and Wounded War Section of the Civil Hospital, Karachi, Sind, India. *Address :* Civil Hospital, Karachi, Sind, India. (M6268)

WALTHALL, Capt. Henry Douglas Delves, O.B.E.

WALTHAM, Amy, O.B.E. ; *d.* of the late Thomas Perrett Waltham, of Spaxton Court, Somerset. *War Work :* Assist. County Director of the Berkshire Branch of the British Red Cross Society. *Address :* 53, Russell Street, Reading. (O11551)

WALTON, Cecil, O.B.E., J.P.

WALTON, Lieut. Cyril Glanmore, M.B.E., R.E. (T.).

WALTON, Frank Neville, O.B.E., *s.* of Thomas Walton, of Cold Brayfield, Bucks. Banker. *War Work :* Bankers to Armies of Occupation, E.E.F., M.E.F. and I.E.F., and Australian and N. Zealand Forces. *Address :* Koubbeh Bridge, Cairo. *Clubs :* Constitutional ; Automobile ; Turf (Cairo). (O1152)

WALTON, Major George Laird, O.B.E., R.E.

WALTON, Lieut.-Col. Granville, O.B.E., R.E.

WALTON, Harold Conrad, M.B.E.

WALTON, Major Harry, M.B.E., I.A.R.O.

WALTON, Comm. Henry Lavington, O.B.E., R.D., R.N.R. ; *s.* of John Walton, of York ; *m.* Georgina Helen Burns, *d.* of Capt. W. B. Lawrence, of Hull. *Educ. :* St. Olave's School, York. Marine Superintendent, Ellerman's Wilson Line, Wilson and N.E. Rly. Shipping Co. ; Hon. Commander, Hull Boys' Naval Brigade ; Member of Navy League Sea Training, and of National War Savings Committees. *War Work :* Marine Supt. Ellerman Wilson Line. *Address :* Westmont, Newland Park, Hull. (O11553)

WALTON, John Thomas, M.B.E.

WALTON, Nellie, Mrs., M.B.E., *b.* 6 Jan. 1876 ; *d.* of John de Horne, of London ; *m.* Alexander Frederic Walton (killed in action). *War Work :* Head of Registry, and Women's Welfare Supervisor in War Priorities Committee (Branch of War Cabinet), and in co-ordination of Demobilisation Section, War Cabinet Offices. (M9947)

WALTON, Lieut.-Col. Robert Henry, O.B.E., M.D., F.R.C.S.

WALTON, Stanley, M.B.E.

WALTON, Sydney, C.B.E., *b.* 25 Oct. 1882 ; *s.* of Robert Thomas Walton, of Weardale ; *m.* Emma, *d.* of Ralph White, of Gosforth. *Educ. :* Univ. Coll., Durham. Journalist, *War Work :* Ministry of Munitions : Ministry of Food, personal staff of Lord Rhondda and later the Principal ; Private Sec. to the Food Controller. *Address :* 5, St. James's Place, London, S.W. 1. *Clubs :* Devonshire ; Aldwych. (C663)

WALTON, Thomas Frederick, O.B.E.

WALTON, Sir William, K.B.E., J.P. for Berkshire, *b.* 1844 ; *s.* of Charles Walton, of Croydon. Vice-President, Admiralty Transport Arbitration Board ; formerly Head of Walton's & Co., Solicitors. *Address :* Donington Holt, Newbury, Bucks. *Club :* Reform. (K42)

WALWYN, Major Charles Lawrence Tyndale, D.S.O., O.B.E., M.C., R.H.A., *b.* 20 April, 1920 ; *s.* of Col. James Walwyn, of Croft-y-Bwla, Monmouth. *Educ. :* Stubbington House, Fareham, and Wellington Coll. *War Work :* Lieut. E Battery, R.H.A., 3rd Cav. Bgde. ; served in France from Aug. 1914, and throughout the war. *Address :* R.A. Mess, Weedon, Northants. *Club :* Junior United Service. (O8963)

WALWYN, Flying Officer Roderick Aylward SHEPHEARD-, M.B.E., R.A.F.

WANLISS, Lieut.-Col. Cecil, O.B.E., (ret. pay), *b.* 19 Oct. 1866 ; 3rd *s.* of T. D. Wanliss, late Member of Legislative Council of Victoria, Australia ; *m.* Honora Louise, *d.* of Major J. Vaughan-Arbuckle, Royal Marine Light Infantry. *Educ. :* Royal Military Coll., Sandhurst. *War Work :* Served in France with the B.E.F. in command of the 2nd Bn. South Lancashire

Regt., and subsequently in command of the 10th Batt. South Lancashire Regt., and 52nd B.l. Manchester Regt. ; proceeded with the latter battalion to Germany in Feb. 1919, where it formed part of the Rhine Army ; appointed to the Inter-Allied Rhineland High Commission in Jan. 1920. *Address :* Rhineland High Commission, Cologne. (O7813)

WANSBROUGH, Lieut.-Col. Thomas Percival, C.B.E., A.I.A., F.C.I.I., *b.* 4 June, 1875 ; *s.* of the late Rev. Chas. E. Wansbrough ; *m.* Fuchsia Gertrude, *d.* of the late J. Lyddon Roberts. *Educ. :* Kingswood School, Bath. Assistant Sec., Eagle, Star, and British Dominions Insurance Co., Ltd., Royal Exchange Avenue, London, E.C. *War Work :* Assistant to Deputy Director of Supplies Investigation Department Supply Directorate, British Expeditionary Force, France, Nov. 1914, to March, 1919. *Addresses :* 22, Regents Court, Hanover Gate, London, N.W. ; 3, London Wall Buildings, E.C. *Club :* Gresham. (C1342)

WARBURG, Capt. Oscar Emanuel, O.B.E., *b.* 6 Feb 1876 : *s.* of Fredric Elias Warburg, of London ; *m.* Catherine Widdrington, *d.* of Mr. Justice Byrne. *Educ. :* Trinity Coll., Cambridge. Member of the London County Council from 1910. *War Work :* Served in R.G.A. (S.R.) and Intelligence Corps. *Addresses :* 2, Craven Hill, London, W. 2 ; Boidier, Headley, Epsom. *Clubs :* Reform ; Gresham. (O7814)

WARBURTON, Alfred, M.B.E., *b.* 19 May, 1873 ; *s.* of Alfred Warburton, of Altrincham ; *m.* Maria, *d.* of John Windle, of Moss Side, Manchester. Departmental Director at Chas. Macintosh Co., Ltd., India Rubber Manufacturers, Manchester ; served through the South African campaign with the R.A.M.C. *War Work :* Did duty for B.R.C.S. at Moorlands Hospital, Kersal ; later was appointed Officer-in-charge of Station Party for the unloading of ambulance trains at Mayfield Station, Manchester, and was given the rank of Commandant. *Address :* Cathcart, Richmond Avenue, Prestwich. (M9950)

WARBURTON, Surg.-Lieut.-Comdr. Llewellyn Rhys, O.B.E., R.N.

WARBURTON, Mabel Clarisse, M.B.E., *b.* 22 June, 1879 ; *d.* of Thomas Frederick Warburton, of King's Langley, Herts. *Educ. :* Cheltenham Coll. Late Principal of British Syrian Training Coll., Beyrout, Syria ; now Principal of British High School for Girls, Jerusalem. *War Work :* Canteen work in Cairo ; Service in Minieh Hospital, Upper Egypt, during the Senussi campaign, May, 1916, to Sept. 1916 ; Relief work in Palestine under the Syria and Palestine Relief Fund. *Addresses :* British High School, Jerusalem, Palestine ; Bradwell House, near Wolverton, Bucks. (M9951)

WARBURTON, Lieut. Peter, M.B.E., R.G.A., and R.F.A.

WARBURTON, Thomas, O.B.E., *b.* 6 June, 1852 ; *s.* of Thomas Warburton, of Heaton Mersey ; *m.* Clara, *d.* of Enos Barrowclough, of Heaton Mersey. *Educ. :* Heaton Mersey. Managing Director, Bleachers Association, Ltd., 4, Norfolk Street, Manchester. *War Work :* Assisting Government in labour matters, the supply of munitions, and surgical requisites. *Address :* The Hollies, Woodbrook Road, Alderley Edge, Cheshire. (O835)

WARBURTON, Walter Granville, M.B.E., J.P., *b.* 11 April, 1877 ; *s.* of Thomas Warburton, of Manchester ; *m.* Edith, *d.* of Frank Reddaway, J.P., of Winmarleigh Hall, Garstang. *Educ. :* Manchester. Civil Engineer. *War Work :* Deputy Coal Controller, India. *Address :* Bombay. *Clubs :* R.A.C., London ; Yacht (Bombay) ; Sind (Karachi). (O8134)

WARD, Ada Grace, Mrs., M.B.E., *b.* 18 March, 1868 ; *d.* of William Hall, of Treelands, Leckhampton ; *m.* Charles Albert John, *s.* of George Ward, of Fairfield House, Leckhampton. *Educ. :* Chellnham. *War Work :* Commandant of Leckhampton Court V.A. Hospital, and Glos. 42 detachment. *Address :* Treelands, Leckhampton. (M2601)

WARD, Capt. Alexander Ivan, M.B.E., D.A.I.

WARD, Lieut.-Col. Arthur Blackwood, C.B.E., D.S.O., B.A., M.B., B.C. (Cantab), M.R.C.S. (Eng.), L.R.C.P. (Lond.), *b.* 2 July, 1870 ; *s.* of the late John Hext Ward, of New Wandsworth, and H.M. Inland Revenue ; *m.* Angela Susan Dorothea, *d.* of the late Henry Finch, J.P., of Redheath, Herts. *Educ. :* Christ's Hospital, Selwyn Coll. Cambridge, and St. Bartholomew's Hospital, London. Commissioner of Medical Services, Ministry of Pensions. *War Work :* Officer Commanding No. 1 General Hospital, Cape Town (German S.-W. African Campaign); Officer Commanding 1st South African General Hospital, B.E.F. France ; D.D.M.S. South African Contingent (T. Col.). *Addresses :* Headquarters, Ministry of Pensions, Stoney Street, Nottingham ; Western House, East Leake, Notts. (C2203)

WARD, Col. Arthur John Hanslip, M.B.E., V.D., *b.* 20 July, 1859 ; *s.* of Robert Arthur Ward, of Ray Park, Maidenhead ; *m.* Eleanor Katherine Mignot Ward, *d.* of John Brown, of Altwood, Maidenhead. *Educ. :* Cranford Coll., Maidenhead. Solicitor ; Town Clerk of Harwich ; Registrar of County Court ; Deputy Lieut. of Essex. *War Work :* late Chairman of Harwich Garrison Emergency Committee and Chief Special Constable ; Member of Advisory Committee for County. *Address :* The Gables, Dovercourt. (M4059)

WARD, Lieut.-Col. Basil Seth, O.B.E.

WARD, Beatrice Gascoigne, O.B.E.

WARD, Comm. Bernard John Hamilton, O.B.E.

WARD, Caroline Theodora, Mrs., M.B.E., *b.* 7 June, 1868 ; *d.* of Frank Pooley, of Liverpool ; *m.* Frank, *s.* of Thomas Ward, of Oxford. *Educ. :* Privately. Sister, Guy's Hospital. *War Work :* Commandant of V.A.D. Surrey 88 ; also of Burntwood Red Cross Hospital of Caterham, Surrey. *Club :* Ladies' Army and Navy. (M1064)

WARD, Paymaster-Capt. Charles Allen, C.B.E., R.N. Served in Great War, 1914–19 (mentioned in despatches). (C1950)

WARD, Charlotte Sarah, Mrs., M.B.E.

WARD, Lieut.-Col. Edward, M.B.E., *b.* 10 Oct. 1852 ; *s.* of William Robert Ward, of Co. Down, Ireland ; *m.* Harriette Caroline, *d.* of J. S. Maconchy, of Kilvare, Templeogue, Co. Dublin. *Educ. :* Winchester Coll. Royal Artillery. *War Work :* Assistant Inspector, Army Inspection Staff, at Royal Arsenal, Woolwich. *Address :* c/o Messrs. Cox & Co., 16, Charing Cross. *Club :* Naval and Military. (M2602)

WARD, Sir Edward Willis Duncan, Bart., G.B.E., K.C.B., K.C.V.O., *b.* 17 Oct. 1853 ; *s.* of Capt. John Ward, R.N. ; *m.* Florence Caroline, *d.* of H. M. Simons. *Educ. :* Privately. Chairman and Director of several companies ; Officer of Legion of Honour, and Knight of Grace Order of St. John of Jerusalem. *War Work :* Commanding and Chief Staff Officer Metropolitan Special Constabulary ; Director-General of Voluntary Organisations ; Chairman of Camps Library ; in administrative charge of Colonial Contingents, 1914 ; Member of Overseas Forces Committee ; Chairman of Council Union Jack Club for Sailors and Soldiers ; Chairman of Union Jack Hostel for married Sailors and Soldiers and their families ; Chairman of Royal Society for Prevention of Cruelty to Animals. *Address :* 5, Welbraham Place, Sloane Street, London, S.W. *Clubs :* Carlton ; Travellers' ; United Service ; Ranelagh ; Junior Naval and Military. (G44)

WARD, Lieut.-Col. Ellacott Leamon, C.B.E., I.M.S., *b.* 28 April, 1873 ; *s.* of William Philip Ward, of Plymouth ; *m.* Charlotte Lyne, *d.* of William Edward Lyne Veale, of Plymouth. *Educ. :* King's School, Chester. Inspector-General of Prisons, Punjab, India. *War Work :* Raised two Labour Battalions from prisoners in Punjab jails ; re-organised Punjab Jail Department for war work. *Clubs :* East India United Service (London) ; United Service (Simla) ; Punjab (Lahore, India). (C1093)

WARD, Elsmie, M.B.E.

WARD, Ernest, M B.E., M.R.C.S., L.R.C.P.

WARD, Frederick Josiah, C.B.E., *b.* 1861 ; *m.* Rose, *d.* of George Greaves Brooks. Entered Admiralty Service, 1887 ; appointed Superintendent of Torpedo Stores, May, 1917, and Deputy Director of Armament Supply. Jan. 1919. *Address :* Fairlight, Elm Bank Gardens, Barnes, Surrey. *Club :* Royal Automobile. (C3023)

WARD, Col. Gerard Arnold, C.B.E. Col. New Zeala..d Forces ; served in Great War, 1915–19 (mentioned in despatches). (C1877)

WARD, Henry, M.B.E., J.P. for Somerset, *b.* 29 Feb. 1848 ; *s.* of Henry Ward, of Hayle, Cornwall ; *m.* Isabella Margaret, *d.* of William May, of Lanceston, Cornwall. *Educ. :* Crowern, Cornwall. Chairman of Council Weston-super-Mare ; Magistrate. *War Work :* Chairman of Tribunal, War Savings Committee, Food Control, Coal Control, and Belgian Refugee Committees. *Address :* Beeulieu, Clarence Park, Weston-super-Mare. *Club :* Weston County. (M9953)

WARD, Lieut.-Col. Henry Charles Swinburne, O.B.E.

WARD, Capt. Horace Edward, O.B.E.

WARD, Howard Percy, M.B.E., M.B., M.R.C.S.

WARD, Hon. James Templeton, Hon. Lady, C.B.E., Lady of Grace of St. John of Jerusalem, *d.* of the late Hon. Whitelaw Reid, U.S.A. Ambassador in London ; *m.* Major the Hon. Sir John Hubert, K.C.V.O., C.V.O., M.V.O. ; Equerry in Ordinary to King Edward VII., 2nd *s.* of 1st Earl of Dudley (*see* BURKE'S *Peerage*). *Addresses :* Dudley House, Park Lane ; Chilton, Hungerford, Berks. (C664)

WARD, Jeannie Wright, M.B.E., *d.* John Lipson Ward, J.P., of Belgrave House, Leicester. *Educ. :* Wyggest n High School, Leicester. *War Work :* Welfare Supervision at National Projectile Factory, Nottingham ; Organised Recreation Huts for the Q.M.A.A.C. and W.R.A.F. in the Southern Command for the Y.W.C.A. *Address :* Belgrave House, Leicester. (M4060)

WARD, Major John, O.B.E., *b.* June, 1858 ; *s.* of the late George Ward, of Co. Galway ; *m.* Esther, *d.* of the late Joseph Jordan, of Co. Down. *Educ. :* Privately. Chief Recruiting Officer, Dublin. *War Work :* Served in the South African War, 1899–1902 ; mentioned in despatches ; Queen's Medal, six clasps ; King's Medal, two clasps ; promoted Major for Distinguished Service 1910 ; 1914–20, Chief Recruiting Officer Dublin Area. *Address :* 4, Elm Grove, Ranelagh, Dublin. (O3200)

WARD, Lieut.-Comm. John Chappell, M.B.E.

WARD, Major John Dudley, O.B.E. A.P.D.

WARD, John Henry, M.B.E.

WARD, Comm. John Richard Le Hunte, C.B.E., R.N., *b.* 18 March, 1870 ; *s.* of Thomas Le Hunte Ward, C.B. (*see* BURKE'S *Peerage*, Bangor, V.) ; *m.* Violet Ella Mary, *d.* of the late Col. B. E. Ward (*see* BURKE'S *Peerage*, Bangor, V.). *Address :* Heath Cottage, Yelverton, S. Devon. *Club :* Army and Navy. (C2228)

WARD, Capt. and Qr.-Mr. John Stanley, O.B.E., Can. A.M.C.

WARD, Engineer-Capt. John Tom Hickman, C.B.E., M.V.O., R.N., *b.* 1862. Engineer, 1889 ; Chief Engineer, 1898 ; Engineer-Comm. 1902 ; Engineer-Capt. (ret.), 1912 ; served in Roy. Yacht "Victoria and Albert," 1908–12 ; on Staff of Senior Naval Officer, Liverpool, 1914–19. (C2326)

WARD, Major Joseph Corbett, O.B.E.

WARD, Leonard, O.B.E.

WARD, Capt. and Qr.-Mr. Lionel Antony Parry, O.B.E., A.I.F.

WARD, Mary Alexandria, M.B.E., R.R.C., *b.* 13 July, 1866; *s.* of John Mosebury Ward, of Brentwood, Essex. Nursing Sister in Nigeria from 1899–1917 under the Colonial Government; now Matron Princess Christian Mission Hospital, Sierra Leone: nursing at Cape Coast Castle during Ashanti rising, 1900 (Ashanti Medal); at Tower Hill Military Hospital Sierra Leone during influenza epidemic 1918. *Address:* Princess Christian Mission Hospital, Sierra Leone, W. African. (M9956)

WARD, Lieut.-Col. Montague Charles Pearson, C.B.E., R.A., *b.* 1869. Served in Great War, 1914–19 (mentioned in despatches). (C1805)

WARD, Capt. the Hon. Robert Arthur, O.B.E., *b.* 23 Feb. 1871; *s.* of William, 1st Earl of Dudley, of Witley Court, Worcester (*see* BURKE'S *Peerage*); *m.* Lady Mary, *d.* of 4th Earl of Gosford, of Gosford Castle, Co. Armagh, Ireland (*see* BURKE'S *Peerage*). *Educ.:* Eton, and Trinity Hall, Cambridge. *War Work:* Served on General Staff in France, Flanders, Gallipoli, Egypt, Russia, and Italy, 1914–19. *Address:* Turf Club, London. (O8964)

WARD, Theresa Dorothea, Lady, C.B.E.; *d.* of — de Smith; *m.* Rt. Hon. Sir Joseph Ward, P.C., K.C.M.G., 1st Bart., *s.* of William Thomas Ward. *Address:* 122, Twakori Road, Wellington, New Zealand. (C374)

WARD, Major and Qr.-Mr. Thomas, O.B.E.

WARD, Lieut. Tom, M.B.E.

WARD, Thomas Henry, M.B.E., *b.* 28 April, 1886. Civil Service Clerk. *War Work:* Sec. and Assistant Director, Central Register of Belgian Refugees; appointed Chevalier de l'Ordre de la Couronne by H.M. the King of Belgium. (M9957)

WARD, Col. Walter Reginald, C.B.E. Col. Canadian Gen. List. (C84)

WARD, Lieut.-Col. William, O.B.E., L.R.I.B.A., *b.* 31 May, 1879; *s.* of William Henry Ward, of Bangor, Co. Down, Ireland, and Handsworth, Staffordshire; *m.* Eleanor Hirst, only *d.* of W. Rylands Mellor, of Lapworth, Warwickshire. *Educ.:* Rugby. *War Work:* Served with B.E.F. France and Belgium, 242nd Brigade, R.F.A., seconded in Dec. 1917, to Ministry of Munitions; transferred in March, 1918, to Ministry of Labour; District Director appointments Dept. for counties of Stafford, Warwick, Salop, Worcester, Hereford, Gloucester, Oxford, Bucks. and Berks. Member of Executive Committee of the Officers Association, Birmingham Branch. *Address:* Darley Mill, Knowle, Warwickshire. *Club:* Union, Birmingham. (O11555)

WARD, William Pettit, O.B.E.

WARD, Capt. William Robert, O.B.E.

WARD, Isabel Mary, Mrs. DESBOROUGH-, M.B.E., *b.* 7 July, 1877; *d.* of William Burnyeat, J.P., D.L., of Millgrove, Whitehaven; *m.* George, *s.* of William C. Ward, of Victoria, B.C. *Educ.:* Cheltenham. *War Work:* Commandant of V.A.D., 12 Cumberland, and Whitehaven Auxiliary Military Hospital. *Address:* Rosehill, Whitehaven. (M9955)

WARDE, Ambrose Huntington, O.B.E., M.R.C.S., L.R.C.P.

WARDE, Lieut.-Col. Charles Edward, O.B.E.

WARDE, Sir Charles Edward, Bart., O.B.E., J.P., D.L., *b.* 25 Dec. 1845; *s.* of General Sir Edward Warde; *m.* Helen Caroline, *d.* of the late Viscount de Stern. Late 4th Hussars; Commanded West Kent Yeomanry, 1898–1905; M.P. for Mid Kent, 1892–1918. *War Work:* Commanded the 4th Royal West Kent Volunteer Battalions through the War; converted House into a Private Hospital. *Address:* Barham Court, Maidstone. *Clubs:* Carlton; Naval and Military; Automobile. (O7818)

WARDE, Capt. Frank, O.B.E.

WARDE, Lieut.-Col. Henry Murray Ashley, C.B.E., *b.* 3 Sept. 1850; *s.* of Sir Edward Warde, K.B.C., R.H.A.; *m.* Louisa Annie (who died 24 Dec. 1916), *d.* of Wilmot Lane, Indian Civil Service. *Educ.:* Privately. Served in the XIX Hussars, from 1872–95; Chief Constable of the County of Kent from 1895. *War Work:* Supervision of the Police, most strenuous work owing to the frequent raids over and enormous War Traffic through Kent. *Address:* Gallants, East Farleigh, Maidstone. *Clubs:* Junior United Service; Cavalry. (C3024)

WARDELL, Lieut. John Stewart Michael, M.B.E.

WARDEN, Henry George, M.B.E.

WARDEN, Lieut.-Col. John Weightman, D.S.O., O.B.E., *b.* 1871; *s.* of George Albert Warden; *m.* Jessie Evelyn Whittaker, of Pittsfield, Mass, U.S.A. Lieut.-Col. Canadian Inf., serving at War Office; Coronation medal (1911); S. African Constabulary, 1901–6; S. African War, 1901–2 (Queen's medal with five clasps); Great War, 1914–19 (wounded, despatches twice). *Clubs:* Junior Naval and Military; United Service (Vancouver). (O4267)

WARDEN, Capt. Robert Campbell, C.B.E..

WARDEN, Comm. Robert Cunningham, O.B.E., R.D., R.N.R.

WARDER, Gerald Edwin, M.B.E.,

WARDLE, Charles, M.B.E.

WARDLE, Flora, Mrs., M.B.E.

WARDLE, Percy Thomas, M.B.E.

WARDLE, Capt. William George James, M.B.E., R.A.F.

WARDROP, Major David Rish, O.B.E., A.P.D.

WARDROPER, Capt. Arthur Kingsley, M.B.E.

WARDROPER, Lieut. Percy Redesdale, M.B.E.

WARE, Major-Gen. Sir Fabian Arthur Goulstone, K.B.E., C.B., C.M.G., *b.* 17 June, 1869; *s.* of Charles Carew Ware, of Clifton: *m.* Anna Margaret, *d.* of W. E. Phibbs, of Clifton. *Educ.:* Privately; Universities of London and Paris (B. ès Science). Permanent Vice-Chairman, Imperial War Graves Commission. *War Work:* 1914, Commanded Red Cross Unit at Front; 1915, Director of Graves Registration and Enquiries, B.E.F., France; 1917, Director-General of G.R. and E., War Office; mentioned in despatches (twice); Commander Order of Leopold (Belgium); Chevalier Légion d'honneur; Croix de Guerre with palms (France). *Address:* 41, Gloucester Terrace, London, W. 2. (K445)

WARE, Louisa, M.B.E., *b.* Jan. 1873; *d.* of James Ware, of Wanstead. Head Mistress of the Wanstead Church of England Infants' School. *War Work:* Red Cross Nurse, attached to Essex 56 Detachment; Hon. Sec. of the Wanstead War Savings Committee at its formation in Oct. 1916, and held this Office until the end of the year, 1919. *Address:* 13, Gordon Road, Wanstead, E. 11. (M9959)

WARE, Ralph Ernest, M.B.E., F.C.A., *b.* 14 May, 1883; *s.* of Charles Stancomb Ware, of Bristol; *m.* Hilda Marguerite, *d.* of O. Croom Johnson, of Clifton. *Educ.:* Clevedon. Chartered Accountant Partner in Ware, Ward & Co., Bristol, Exeter, and Torquay. *War Work:* 2nd Lieut. Army Cyclist Corps; attached from 1918–19 to Ministry of Munitions, as Assistant Director of Finance to Central Stores Department, owing to ill health contracted on service. *Addresses:* Rodney House, Union Road, Exeter; 50, High Street, Exeter; 7, Unity Street, College Green, Bristol; 4, Fleet Street, Torquay. *Clubs:* Devon and County (Exeter). (M9960)

WARE, Capt. Sampson Weston Percy, O.B.E., R.E. (T.)

WAREHAM, Paymaster-Lieut. Stuart Waldron, O.B.E., R.N.

WARING, Lieut.-Col. Edmund Henry, O.B.E.

WARING, Eleanor Gladys, O.B.E., *b.* 1894; *d.* of Sir Samuel Waring, Bart., of Foots-Cray Place, Kent. *Educ.:* Folkestone. Divisional Commissioner, Girl Guides. *War Work:* Worked in connection with Hosp. Entertainments for wounded, and raising funds for War Charities, Local Girl Guide organization for Princes of Wales' Fund and Y.M.C.A. Hut Fund, also flowers and vegetables grown for R.C. Hospital. *Address:* Foots-Cray Place, Kent; 13, Portland Place, W. 1; Gopsall, Atherstone. *Club:* Phyllis Court (Henley). (O11557)

WARING, Harold, C.B.E., *b.* 2 Feb. 1881; *s.* of the late S. J. Waring, of Liverpool; *m.* Iris Amie Kelso, *d.* of George Eccles Kelso King, of Sydney, Australia. *Educ.:* Privately. Director and Manager of the Alliance Aeroplane Co. Ltd. *War Work:* Aeroplane Manufacture. *Address:* 37, Hyde Park Gate, S.W. 7. *Club:* Royal Automobile. (C3026)

WARING, Col. Holburt Jacob, C.B.E., M.D. F R.C.S., R.A.M.C. (T.).

WARING, Margaret Elizabeth, M.B.E.

WARING, Lady Susan Elizabeth Clementine, C.B.E., *b.* 9 Aug. 1879; *d.* of 10th Marquess, of Tweeddale (*see* BURKE'S *Peerage*); *m.* Walter, *s.* of Charles Waring, M.P., and has issue two daughters. *Educ.:* Privately. *War Work:* Administrator of Lennel Auxiliary Hospital for Officers, specialising in neurasthenic cases, Oct. 1914, to Dec. 1918; has Belgian medal of Queen Elizabeth. *Addresses:* Lennel, Coldstream, Scotland; The Moult, Salcombe, S. Devon; 1, Prince's Row, S.W. 1. *Club:* Bath. (C324)

WARK, Hector, M.B.E., R.F.A.

WARK, Lieut. John Lean, M.B.E.

WARLEIGH, Capt. Percival Henry, C.B.E., R.N., *b.* 1873; *s.* of Henry Smith Warleigh, of Southampton; *m.* Marion Ina, *d.* of William Alder, of Lymington, Hants. Great War, 1914–16; Flag Capt., Port Depot Ship, Rosyth, 1916–19. *Address:* 2, Bruce Road, Southsea. (C2240)

WARLOW, Camilla Allan, Mrs. PICTON-, M.B.E.; *d.* of the late J. R. Aitcnison, of India Office; *m.* Alick John, *s.* of Colonel J. Picton Turbervill, of Ewenny Priory, Bridgend, Glamorgan. *Educ.:* Privately. Admiralty, Woman Inspector. *War Work:* Originator and Hon. Sec. Bread, Blanket and Invalid Comforts Funds for Prisoners of War; 1916, went to Copenhagen at request of British Red Cross; 1917, in charge of a Y.M.C.A. Canteen in Holland for interned British Prisoners from Germany. *Address:* 1, St. Minver Road, Bedford. (M9961)

WARMSLEY, Jennie, Mrs., M.B.E.

WARNEFORD, Major, Walter Wyndham Hanbury, O.B.E., *b.* July, 1866; *s.* of Canon J. H. Warneford, late of Warneford Place, Wilts.; *m.* Mary Elizabeth, *d.* of A. Goodall, of Halifax. *Educ.:* Newark and Windsor. Superintendent of the Wagon Dept. of the L. and N.W. Rly. Co.; late 2nd C.R.E. (R.V.) *War Work:* 1914, as Manager of Crewe Works arranged the special plant for the production of fuses, shells, drop forge and other munition work; as Superintendent of Wagon Dept. in 1916 supplied stock for Transport work. *Address:* Lansdowne House, Huyton, Liverpool. *Club:* Services, Stratford Place. (O11558)

WARNER, Lieut.-Col. Charles Edward, V.D., *b.* 2 Jan. 1865; *s.* of George Daniel Warner, of Tonbridge, Kent; *m.* Ethel Constantia Catharine, *d.* of the late David Cornfoot, of Lancaster Gate, London. *Educ.:* Tonbridge. Solicitor; Registrar County Court; Clerk to County Justices; Clerk to Commissioners of Taxes; Clerk to Visiting Justices under Lunacy Acts and Mental Deficiency Acts. *War Work:* Commanded 2/1 Kent Cyclist Batt., Nov. 1914, to disbandment,

May, 1919; demobilised, Oct. 1919. *Address:* Coldharbour Park, Hildenborough, Kent. *Club:* Tonbridge. (O7820)

WARNER, Major and Qr.-Mr. Cuthbert Philip, O.B.E.

WARNER, Major Rev. David Victor, O.B.E.

WARNER, Sir Frank, K.B.E., C.C., *b.* 13 Sept. 1862; *s.* of Benjamin Warner, of Wanstead, Essex; *m.* Kate Dennis, *d.* of Edmund Strange Parsons, of King's Lynn. *Educ.:* Privately and at Lyons. Adviser to the Board of Trade on Textiles, 1917–20; Chairman of the Advisory Committees on silk Production, Imperial Institute, British Silk Research Association, and of Board of Trade Committee on British Industries Fairs; Vice-Chairman of the British Empire Flax-growing Commitee, Board of Trade; Member of various Councils connected with Board of Trade, Textiles and Industries; Delegate at various Board of Trade and Foreign Office congresses, 1910–19; read papers before many learned societies. *Addresses:* Woodcroft, Nottingham, Kent; Newgate Street, London, E.C. 1. *Club:* Royal Automobile. (K113)

WARNER, Henry Brooks, O.B.E., *b.* 28 Sept. 1880; *s.* of Joseph Henry Warner, Kt., of 62, Eaton Square, S.W. *Educ.:* Eton, and Trinity Coll., Cambridge. Barrister-at-Law. *War Work:* Temp. Clerk in Foreign Office from June, 1915, to Aug. 1919. *Address:* 1, Sumner Place, S.W. 7. *Club:* Union. (O837)

WARNER, Lionel Ashton Piers, C.B.E., *b.* 30 April, 1875; *s.* of the late Major Ashton C. Warner, of 20th Hussars, and Chief Constable of Bedfordshire; *m.* Nina Mary, *d.* of the late Capt. Matthew Liddon, of Iron Acton, Glos. *Educ.:* Marlborough. General Manager Mersey, Docks and Harbour Board, Liverpool. *War Work:* Director of Ports Branch, Ministry of Shipping; Member of Port and Transit Executive Committee, East and West Coast Diversion Committee, etc. *Address:* 46, Wellington Road, New Brighton, Cheshire. *Club:* Royal Societies'. (C1053)

WARNER, Capt. Pelham Francis, M.B.E.

WARNER, Surrey, O.B.E., *b.* 27 Aug. 1861. *Educ.:* Cranleigh. Carriage and Waggon Superintendent, London and South Western Railway. *War Work:* Railway work; a member of the Ambulance Train Committee. *Address:* 85, Westridge Road, Southampton. *Club:* Royal Southampton Yacht. (O11559)

WARNER, Sydney Jeannetta, O.B.E., W.R.N.S.

WARNOCK, David, O.B.E.

WARNOCK, Capt. James, O.B.E., R.A.M.C.

WARNOCK, William Findlay, M.B.E., *b.* 31 March, 1871; *s.* of George Warnock, late of Lesmahagow, Upper Ward of Lanarkshire; *m.* Isabella Smith, *d.* of M. Smith, of Worcester. *Educ.:* Glasgow. Chief Ship Draughtsman of Messrs. John Brown & Co., Clydebank; Member of the Institute of Engineers and Shipbuilders in Scotland. *War Work:* Drawing Office work in connection with Battleships and Battle Cruisers, and other war vessels, built by J. Brown & Co., 1914–18. *Address:* Belhaven, Dalmuir, Dumbartonshire. (M2606)

WARR, Howard Grove, M.B.E.

WARRACK, Frances Jane, M.B.E., *b.* 29 Sept. 1864; *d.* of James Warrack, of Montrose, Forfarshire. Town Councillor, St. Andrews, Fife. *War Work:* Convener, Soldiers' Club, St. Andrews (Nat. Union Women Workers), 1914–16; Commandant, Scottish Soldiers' Club, Boulogne, Jan. 1917, to Nov. 1919; St. Andrews Caravan, Devastated Areas, 1919. *Address:* 3, Playfair Terrace, St. Andrews, Fife. *Club:* Forum. (M4061)

WARRACK, Sir James Howard, K.B.E., *b.* 11 Dec. 1855; *s.* of the late James Warrack, of Montrose; *m.* Dorothy Cooper, *d.* of the late George Todd, C.A., of Edinburgh. *Educ.:* Montrose Academy. Late President of the Chamber of Shipping of the United Kingdom; Member of Council of Shipping Federation, of the British Imperial Council of Commerce, and of Committee of Lloyd's Register of Shipping; Deputy Chairman Edinburgh Chamber of Commerce; Director of the Bank of Scotland, Caledonian Insurance Co., and North British Rubber Co., Ltd. *War Work:* Member of the Admiralty Transport Arbitration Board, and of the Board of Trade War Risks Advisory Committee. *Address:* 38, Palmerston Place, Edinburgh. *Club:* Junior Constitutional. (K237)

WARRAND, Major Duncan Grant, O.B.E., M.A., F.S.A., *b.* 16 March, 1877; *s.* of the late Col. A. J. C. Warrand, of Bught, Inverness-shire, and Ryefield, Ross-shire; *m.* Daisy Helen, *d.* of the late Col. H. Burnley-Campbell, of Ormidale, Argyll. *Educ.:* Wellington Coll., Berks.; Univ. Coll., Oxford. *War Work:* Capt. 3rd Batt. Seaforth Highlanders, Aug. to Nov. 1914; served in France with 2nd Batt Seaforth Highlanders, Nov. 1914, to March, 1915; Staff Capt. G.H.Q. 3rd Echelon, B.E.F., June, 1915, to Jan. 1917; D.A.A.G. Jan. 1917, to Nov. 1918; despatches 3 times; Major, Aug. 1918. *Address:* Ormidale, Glendaruel, Argyll. *Club:* United University. (O1978)

WARRE, Major Felix Walter, O.B.E., M.C.

WARRE, George Francis, C.B.E., Formerly Head of Motor Boat Depart. British Red Cross Society; Donor of Rest House for Nurses, Rocquebrune, Riviera, during Great War. (C1054)

WARRE, Comm. Philip Asheson, O.B.E., R.N.

WARREN, Sir Alfred Haman, O.B.E., J.P., M.P., *b.* 1856; *s.* of Richard Sambull, of Callington, Cornwall; *m.* Jane Macey, *d.* of George Castle, of Deal. *Educ.:* City of London Coll. M.P. for Edmonton. *War Work:* Five years Mayor of Poplar, 1913–18; raised Poplar Volunteers (Lieut.-Col.); Chairman of Tribunal; recruited large number for Army; raised large sums for War Charities. *Address:* Mountain Ash, Wanstead. (O1979)

WARREN, Capt. Claude Alfred Reuben, M.B.E.

WARREN, Rev. Claude Bertram, O.B.E.

WARREN, Capt. David Bruce, O.B.E.

WARREN, Lieut. Desmond Cecil Robert, M.B.E., R.A.S.C.

WARREN, Edith Ella, Mrs., O.B.E.; *d.* of the late John Grant Jackson; *m.* Lieut.-Col. Dawson, late The Queen's Regt., R.W.S. (killed in action, Sept. 1914), *s.* of the late Maj.-Gen., Dawson Stockley Warren, C.B. *War Work:* Hon. Sec. The Queen's (Royal West Surrey) Regt. Prisoners of War Fund, the work being carried on at Stoughton Barracks, Guildford. *Address:* Stoughton, Guildford. (O11560)

WARREN, Edith Mary, M.B.E.

WARREN, Ellen Winifred Anne, Mrs., M.B.E., *b.* 13 Oct. 1875. *War Work:* Secretary, then President of Bristol South Branch of the Soldiers' and Sailors' Families Association, and of the War Pensions Committee, Aug. 1914, to May, 1919. *Address:* Llanfoist, Clifton Down, Bristol. (M9963)

WARREN, Frederick John, M.B.E., F.S.A.A., J.P., *b.* 14 April, 1865; *s.* of Charles Warren, of Haverfordwest; *m.* Annie Elizabeth, *d.* of P. Griffiths, of Haverfordwest. *Educ.:* Haverfordwest. Borough Accountant of Haverfordwest; Public Auditor of Co-operative Societies appointed by H.M. Treasury; Professional Auditor to County Compensation Authorities of Carmarthen and Pembroke, and to Joint Standing Committee for Pembrokeshire. *War Work:* Hon. Sec. Local War Savings and War Loans Committees; Author of the War Savings Song, "Sing a Song of Sixpence"; Member of Governing Body of Church in Wales, of St. David's Diocesan Conference and Finance Board, and of the Council of the Historical Society of West Wales; An ovate of the Welsh Gorsedd. (M9964)

WARREN, Lieut. Henry William, M.B.E.

WARREN, Surg.-Comm. Leonard, C.B.E., M.B., R.N.

WARREN, Margaret Maxwell, O.B.E.

WARREN, Marmont, M.B.E.

WARREN, Matthew, M.B.E., *b.* 9 Feb. 1868; *s.* of Peter Warren, of Macclesfield; *m.* Beatrice, *d.* of Edward Clark, of Tettenhall, nr. Wolverhampton. *Educ.:* Macclesfield Public School. Clerk to Llandaff and Dinas-Powis Rural District Council, Glamorgan. *War Work:* Sec. and Executive Officer to Food Control Committee; Clerk to Local Military Tribunal; Sec. and Treas. to District War Pensions Committee; Clerk to Local Registration Authority. *Addresses:* St. Elmo, Radyr, Glamorgan; Park House, Park Place, Cardiff. (M9965)

WARREN, Col. Peter, C.M.G., C.B.E., *b.* 1866; *s.* of the late William Ellis Warren, of Paignton, Devon; *m.* Helen, Marian, *d.* of James Squire Steele. Col. R.E.; S. African War, 1901–2 (Queen's medal with five clasps); served in Great War, 1914–19, as Dep. Director Army Postal Services, British Expeditionary Force, and subsequently as Director, Army Postal Service, Mediterranean, Egyptian, and Salonica Expeditionary Forces (despatches six times, Order of the Nile, 1914 star with clasp). *Address:* 9, Plympton Road, Brondesbury, N.W. (C1392)

WARREN, Lieut.-Col. Philip Ridsdale, O.B.E., R.E., *b.* 7 Sept. 1874; *s.* of Rev. William Warren, of Kinsale, Co. Cork, Ireland; *m.* Evelyn Agneta; *d.* of F. A. Bevan, J.P., of 1, Tilney Street, Park Lane, London. *Educ.:* Malvern. Civil Engineer. *War Work:* Port Construction Engineer, under Director-General of Transport, France, and afterwards Assistant Director-General of Transport, G.H.Q., France. *Address:* Sports Club, St' James' Square, London. (O5897)

WARREN, Major Thomas Richard Pennefather, C.B.E., R.A.S.C., *b.* 12 Sept. 1883; *s.* of Thomas Robert Warren J.P. R.N., (see BURKE'S *Peerage*, Warren, Bart.); *m.* Ada Bene Costello (Stella), *d.* of the late Col. Charles Hely, of Woodstock, Co. Waterford. Res. Mag. for N.R. Tipperary, 1919–20; served in Great War. (C1806)

WARREN, William, O.B.E.

WARREN, Major William Robert Vaughton, O.B.E., M.C., R.A.S.C.

WARREN, Col. William Robinson, C.B.E., D.S.O., 1882. Entered R.A. 1900; Major, Brevet Lieut.-Col. and T. Col.; Great War, 1914–18 (mentioned in despatches). (C2360c)

WARRENER, Major and Qr.-Mr. John, O.B.E.

WARRINER, Fred, M.B.E.

WARRIOR, Edith Mary, M.B.E., *b.* 17 May, 1887; *d.* of Henry Warrior, of Northallerton, Yorks. *Educ.:* Ripon and Harrogate. *War Work:* Enrolled in Q.M.A.A.C., Dec. 1917, as Asst. Administrator; attached Area Controller, London District; promoted to rank of Unit Administrator, Aug. 1918; promoted and transferred to H.Q., Northern Command as Deputy Controller-in-charge Areas 1 and 2, Feb. 1919; demobilised March, 1920. *Address:* 6, North Avenue, Ealing, W. 13. (M5709)

WARRY, Lieut.-Col. Bertram Arthur, O.B.E., *b.* 22 Sept. 1865; *s.* of George Deedes Warry, of Shapwick, Somerset; *m.* Mary Shafto, *d.* of David Shafto Hawks. *Educ.:* Winchester. *Address:* Shapwick House, Bridgwater, Somerset. *Club:* United Service. (O7822)

WARSELL, Edith, M.B.E.

WARTON, Major Charles Percival Fenwick, O.B.E.

WARTON, Florence Ethel, O.B.E., W.R.N.S.

WARTON, Capt. John Fenwick, C.M.G., C.B.E., *b.* 1879. Capt. R.N. and Senior Naval Officer, Danube; served in Great War 1914–19; present at battle of Jutland; with Mission to N. Russia. and in White Sea. (C2368)

WARWICK, Capt. Norman Richard Coombe, O.B.E.

WASEY, Evelyn Mary, M.B.E., b. 6 April, 1895; d. of Edward J. S. Wasey, J.P., of Bradley Court, Newbury, Berks. Educ.: Highgate. War Work: Employed at Ministry of Pensions and at War Office, first as Clerk and later as Lady supervisor. Address: Bradley Court, Chieveley, Newbury, Berks. (M9967)

WASHBOURN, William, C.B.E., b. 1862; s. of William Washbourn, of Blackfriars, Gloucester; m. Mabel Woods. Senior Surgeon, Gloucestershire Royal Infirmary and Eye Institution. War Work: Medical Officer-in-charge, Gloucester Red Cross Hospital; Civil Surgeon-in-charge Recruiting, Gloucester. Address: Blackfriars, Gloucester. (C3027)

WATCHLIN, Lieut. Alexander, O.B.E., R.N.R.

WATERFIELD, May Constance Flora, M.B.E., b. 1872; d. of Ottiwell, of Nackington House, Canterbury. War Work: Commandant of Dame John A.P., Canterbury; served in France at Etaples from June, 1915, till April, 1916; invalided home; General Service Supt., June, 1917; Unit Commandant, July, 1919. Address: The Awmby, Eastry. (M4063)

WATERHOUSE, Agnes May, C.B.E., R.R.C. Chief Sup. Queen Alexandra's Mil. Nursing Service, India. (C2045)

WATERHOUSE, Sir Nicholas Edwin, K.B.E., b. 24 Aug. 1877; s. of Edwin Waterhouse, of Holmbury St. Mary, Surrey; m. Audrey Hale, d. of Lieut.-Col. T. H. Lewin, of Abinger, Surrey. Educ.: Winchester, and New Coll., Oxford. Chartered Accountant. War Work: Employed at War Office. Address: 71, Victoria Road, Kensington, London, W. (K438)

WATERHOUSE, Paymaster-Comm. Thomas Ryder, O.B.E., R.N.

WATERLOW, Sydney Philip Perigal, C.B.E., M.A., b. 22 Oct. 1878; s. of George Sydney Waterlow (see BURKE'S Peerage); m. 1st, 10 Nov. 1902, Alice Isabella, o.d. of the Rt. Hon. Sir Frederick Pollock, 3rd Bart.; 2ndly, Helen Margery, d. of Gustav Eckhard. Educ.: Eton, and Trinity Coll., Cambridge. Senior Clerk in the Foreign Office. War Work: Engaged in the Contraband Department of the Foreign Office, April, 1916, to Jan. 1919; British Representative on the Inter-Allied Commission at Paris for the occupied territory of Germany during 1919. Address: Parsonage House, Oare, Marlborough, Wilts. (C3028)

WATERLOW, Sir William Alfred, K.B.E., b. 1871; s. of late James Jameson Waterlow, of 25, Park Crescent, W.; m. Adelaide Hay, d. of Thomas Gordon, of Edinburgh. Educ.: Marlborough. Admitted a solicitor, 1896; Joint Managing Director of Waterlow & Sons, Ltd. Address: Harrow Weald, Middlesex. (K238)

WATERMAN, Elizabeth Margaret, Mrs., M.B.E., b. 11 Aug. 1875; d. of George Moore, of Maidenhead; m. Alfred Edward Stanton Waterman, s. of Alfred Waterman, of London. Educ.: Baker Street C. of E. High School. Commandant Kent V.A.D. 42; late Commandant Rosherville and Ingress Abbey V.A.D. Hospitals. War Work: Aug. 1914, Recruited and trained fresh members for the Gravesend Voluntary Aid Detachments; Sept. 1914, took over duties of School Nurse to release Territorial Nurse; Oct. 1914, helped prepare and open Yacht Club V.A.D. Hospital, Gravesend; Nov. 1914, helped prepare and open Rosherville V.A.D. Hospital, Kent, and there worked as Matron, being appointed Commandant of Rosherville and Ingress Abbey V.A.D. Hospitals in June, 1917. Address: The Parade, St. Mawes, Cornwall. (M9968)

WATERS, Alfred John, M.B.E.

WATERS, Charles Joseph, M.B.E. Assistant Town Clerk, Wandsworth. War Work: District Supervisor National Registration Act, 1915; Clerk to Borough of Wandsworth Cultivation Society and the Committee of the Borough Council, which secured over 5000 allotments in the Borough, 1917; Deputy Executive Officer, Borough of Wandsworth Food Control Committee, 1917-19. Address: 26, Killarney Road, Wandsworth, S.W. 18. (M9969)

WATERS, Donald, M.B.E., b. 26 April, 1851; s. of John Waters, of Watten, Caithness; m. Ellen, d. of Alfred Widley, of Blackheath, London. Educ.: Watten. Late Superintendent, Metropolitan Police; Associate of Royal Colonial Institute. War Work: Strictly confidential. Address: 28, Wilbury Avenue, Hove, Sussex. (M2608)

WATERS, Major George Frederick, M.B.E., R.E.

WATERS, Lieut.-Col. John Dallas, C.B.E., D.S.O., b. 1889; m. 1919, the Hon. Lettice, d. of 2nd Baron Newton (see BURKE'S Peerage), and widow of Capt. John Egerton-Warburton (see BURKE'S Peerage, Grey-Egerton, Bart.). T. Major and Acting Lieut.-Col. Roy. Fusiliers; served in Great War, 1914-18 (despatches four times). Addresses: Arley Hall, Northwich, Cheshire; 9, Berkeley Square. (C134)

WATERS, Owen, O.B.E.

WATERS, Robert Abraham Samuel, O.B.E.

WATERS, Major Robert Sydney, O.B.E.. I.A.

WATERS, Roger Donald, O.B.E.

WATERS, Major Walter James, O.B.E., R.A.M.C., b. 19 May, 1876; s. of Alfred Waters, R.N.; m. Annette Violet, d. of Surgeon-General James Fairweather, Indian Army. Educ.: St. Thomas's Hospital, London. War Work: O.C. 16th General Hospital and 21st C.C.S., France. Address: c/o Messrs. Holt & Co., 3, Whitehall Place, S.W. 1. (O5899)

WATERSON, Frances, Mrs., M.B.E.

WATHEN, Lieut.-Col. Edward Owen, O.B.E.

WATHEN, Frederick Blunt, M.B.E., b. 12 June, 1877; s. of the late William Hulbert Wathen, of Westerham, Kent; m. Louisa, d. of the late Charles Walker, J.P., D.L., of Brettargh

Holt, Westmorland. Educ.: St. Paul's. General Traffic Manager, Madras and Southern Mahratta Railway. Address: Plaxtole, Nungumbaukum, Madras. Clubs: Madras; Marylebone Cricket. (M4226)

WATKINS, Arthur Glyn, M.B.E., A.M.I.M.E., b. 18 Nov. 1882; s. of the late Archdeacon of Perth, Western Australia; m. Marion Eileen, d. of C. G. Bannister-Hall, of London. Educ.: Perth High School, Western Australia. Western Australian Government Railways; Crown Agents for the Colonies, London; Messrs. John Lysaght, Ltd., Newport, Mon. War Work: General Manager and afterwards Director, Gloucester National Filling Factory for Ministry of Munitions. Address: York Lodge, Cheltenham. (M1067)

WATKINS, Arthur Muriel, M.B.E., M.R.C.S. (Eng.), L.R.C.P. (Lond.), b. 11 March, 1862; s. of John Webb Watkins, M.D., of Stonelegh, Newton-le-Willows, Lancashire; m. Laura Anne Burdett; d. of John Frederick Young, of Bulmershe Lodge, Reading. Educ.: Privately; Univ. Coll. Liverpool, and London. Hon. Surgeon, Whitchurch Cottage Hospital; Medical Officer, Whitchurch Union Workhouse. War Work: Surgeon, Bronghall and Cloverley V.A.D. Hospitals, Whitchurch, Salop; Assistant Medical Officer, Prees Heath Military Hospital. Address: Dodington, Whitchurch, Salop. (M9970)

WATKINS, Dorothy Emily, M.B.E.

WATKINS, Lieut. Frank, M.B.F., E.A.F.

WATKINS, Col. Frederic Mostyn, C.B.E.; b. 1873. Lieut. Col. and T. Col. Army Pay Depart.; N.-W. Frontier of India,1897-98 (medal with two clasps); Great War, 1914-19 (despatches). (C1807)

WATKINS, Major Henry George, C.B.E.

WATKINS, Jane Gertrude, C.B.E., b. 30 Sept. 1864; d. of James Gwyllam Watkins, of Hereford. Educ.: Privately. Trained at St. Bartholomew's Hospital, London, 1895; Sister, Kasr-el-Aini Hospital, Cairo, 1895-98; Matron, Victoria Nursing Home, Cairo, 1898-1916; Matron Anglo-American Hospital from 1916. War Work: Training V.A.D.s, Cairo, 1914-15; Red Cross work, Officers' Hospital, 1916-17; Matron, only English Civilian Hospital in Cairo, 1916, to end of War. Address: Anglo-American Hospital, Gezireh, Cairo. (O11564)

WATKINS, John Stewart, O.B.E., b. 2 Dec. 1862; s. of William Watkins, of 75, Mark Lane, London; m. Florence Maud, d. of Walter Thomas Kirton, of Bournemouth. Educ.: Eastbourne. Tug owner. War Work: Commercial Advisor on Tugs to Ministry of Shipping. Address: Loddenden Manor, Staplehurst. Club: Royal Automobile. (O11565)

WATKINS, Major Joseph Harold, M.B.E.

WATKINS, Maria Heloise, Mrs., O.B.E.

WATKINS, Lieut.-Col. Oscar Ferris, C.B.E., D.S.O., M.A., b. 23 Dec. 1877; s. of Ven. O. D. Watkins, of Holywell Vicarage, Oxford; m. Olga Florence, d. of Baillie Grohman, of Matzen, Tyrol. Educ.: Marlborough and Oxford. Native Affairs Department, Kenya Colony. Fellow of Royal Colonial Institute and Royal Anthropological Institute. War Work: Director of Military Labour; mentioned in despatches. Address: Nairobi, Kenya Colony. Club: Royal Societies'. (C744)

WATKINS, Rev. Owen Spencer, C.M.G., C.B.E., b. 28 Feb. 1873; s. of Rev. Owen Watkins, Wesleyan Minister; m. 1st, Sadie Soul, only d. of W. Mathias, of H.M. Dockyard, Malta (who died 1910), 2nd, Ethel Elizabeth, e.d. of G. George, of Llandilo. Educ.: Bath and Richmond. C.F., 1st Class, (Wesleyan), Assistant Chaplain-General. Eastern Command; Assistant Sec. Wesleyan Navy, Army, and Air Force Board; Hon. Sec. Duke of Connaught's Soldiers' and Sailors' Home.; International Force in Crete, 1897-99; Nile Expedition, 1898, Battle of Khartoum (despatches, Queen's Medal, Egyptian Medal and clasp); one of four chaplains who conducted Memorial Service for Gordon at Khartoum; S. African War, 1899-1900 (three times mentioned in despatches; Queen's Medal, with five clasps). War Work: 1914-19, France, 5th Division, 1914-17; H.Q. Third Army as Assistant Principal Chaplain, 1917-18; Italy, 1918-19; Principal Chaplain (Brig.-Gen.); (mentioned in despatches four times, 1914 Star with clasp, Victory and War Medals); author of several books. Address: 20, Mortimer Road, West Ealing, W. 13. (C1407)

WATKINS, Lieut. Purcell John, M.B.E., R.E.

WATKINS, 2nd Lieut. Thomas Percival Holmes, M.B.E., b. 30 July, 1877; s. of Thomas Watkins, of The Wern, Pontypool; m. Margaret, d. of James Jenkins, of Pontypool. Educ.: King's School, Canterbury. Solicitor; Commissioner for Oaths; Supt. Registrar and Clerk to the Guardians of the Pontypool Union; Clerk to the Pontypool Rural and Panteg Urban District Councils and Old Age Pensions Committees. War Work: 2nd Lieut. 1st Vol. Batt., Monmouthshire Regt.; Sec. Griffithstown Aux. Mil. Hospital (Poor Law Institution, 370 beds); Clerk to Panteg Local Tribunal, Hon. Sec. local War Pensions, Recruiting, War Loan, Committees. Address: Shirley, Griffithstown. (M1068)

WATKINS, William, M.B.E., b. 23 May, 1860; s. of John Watkins, of Aberystwyth; m. Augusta Braham, d. of the late Rev. George Horrocks, of Preston. Educ.: Llandovery. Solicitor; Registrar of Newtown County Court and District Registrar of the High Court. War Work: Chairman of Newtown War Pensions Committee; Vice-Chairman of Local Committee and Disablement Committee of County of Montgomery; Sec. for County, of Soldiers' and Sailors' Families Association. Address: Delguan, Newtown, N. Wales. (M9971)

WATKINS, William Edward, O.B.E., b. 19 Jan. 1864; s. of William Watkins, of Monmouth. Educ.: Culham Coll., and Leipzig Univ. Director of Education to East Suffolk Education Authority. *War Work :* Lectured on Food Economy and War Savings ; organised Economy exhibitions ; at Ministry of Food organised Cookery demonstrations throughout Great Britain ; developed a scheme for feeding children in School Canteens. *Address :* St. Malo, South Hill, Felixstowe. (O3975)

WATKINS, Capt. and Qr.-Mr. William John, M.B.E.

WATLING, Lieut.-Col. Francis Wyatt, C.B.E., D.S.O., *b.* 1869 ; Lieut.-Col. R.E. ; N.-W. Frontier of India, 1897 (despatches, medal with two clasps) ; served in Great War, 1914–19 (mentioned in despatches) (C1344)

WATLING, Lieut. John Basil, M.B.E., R.E. (T.)

WATLING, Capt. John William, O.B.E., R.N.R., *b.* 30 Oct. 1862 ; *s.* of William Watling of Littlehampton ; *m.* Maude Ellen, *d.* of Frederick A. Power, of Birmingham. *War Work :* Commanded s.s. "Intaba" as commissioned ship from Aug. 1914 as a flotilla supply ship. squadron supply ship, mystery ship, and lastly transport carrying troops and repatriating German prisoners to July, 1919. *Address :* c/o London County and Westminster Bank, Blackheath, S.E. 3. *Club :* Durban (Natal). (O11566)

WATLINGTON, Victor, M.B.E.

WATNEY, Constance, M.B.E.

WATNEY, Capt. Ernest Alfred William, O.B.E.

WATNEY, Col. Frank Dormay, C.B.E., *b.* 1870 ; *s.* of John Watney, of Shermanbury House, Reigate ; *m.* Margaret Graham (has Order of Mercy), *d.* of the Rev. George Richardson, of Winchester Coll. Hants. Lieut.-Col. and Hon. Col. Roy. W. Surrey Regt. (T.F.) ; D.L. for Surrey ; Great War, 1914–19 (despatches, 3rd class Order of the Nile) (C1393)

WATNEY, Major Gilbert John, O.B.E.

WATNEY, Major Ronald Denby, O.B.E., R.W.Kent Rgt.

WATSON, Agnes Mary, Mrs., M.B.E., *b.* 4 Aug. 1889 ; *d.* of William Bird, of Sheffield (Eng.), and Vancouver (B.C.) ; *m.* Arthur Ernest, *s.* of John Thomas Watson, of York. *Educ. :* Privately, and at Leeds. *War Work :* Junior Administrative Assistant 4½ years in the Naval Store Department, Admiralty. *Address :* 77 Castellain Mansions, W. 9. (M9973)

WATSON, Albert Harold Joseph, M.B.E.

WATSON, Lieut. Alexander Milne, M.B.E., R.A.F.

WATSON, Capt. Alexander Pirie, O.B.E., M.B., F.R.C.S., R.A.M.C. (T.).

WATSON, Lieut.-Col. Alexander Thomas. O.B.E.

WATSON, Capt Andrew McCrae, O.B.E., E.A.F.

WATSON, Arthur, C.B.E.

WATSON, Lieut.-Col. Arthur, C.B.E., *b.* 1873 ; *s.* of Daniel Watson, of Manchester. Gen. Manager, Lancashire and Yorkshire Railway ; Member of Railway Executive Committee, Board of Trade ; Lieut.-Col. R.E. (T.F.), Railway Engineer and Staff Corps ; M.I.C.E. ; was Chairman of Sups. Conference, Railway Clearing House, 1915–18. (C72)

WATSON, Arthur Egerton, C.B.E., Controller of Finance Ministry of Munitions. (C3029)

WATSON, Arthur William, M.B.E.

WATSON, Arthur William, C.B.E., I.C.S., *b.* 16 Nov. 1874 ; *s.* of James Watson, M.D., of Dormans House, Dormans Park, Surrey ; *m.* Marion, *d.* of W. H. Ashwin, J.P., D.L., of Bretforton Manor, Evesham. *Educ. :* Cheltenham, Uppingham, and Magdalene Coll., Cambridge. Appointed to Indian Civil Service, 1898 ; served in Bihar, Chota Nagpur, and Bengal, in various capacities ; Sec. to the Bengal Government Legislative Department, 1913. *War Work :* Various Committees in Calcutta ; Ministry of Munitions (Deputy Assist.-Sec.), 1915 ; Ministry of Labour (Assist.-Sec.), 1918 ; Principal Asst. Sec. 1919. *Addresses :* Dormans House, Dormans Park, Surrey ; 22, Douglas Mansions, Cromwell Road, S.W. *Club :* Travellers'. (C3030)

WATSON Lieut. Basil Barnar M.B.E.

WATSON, Lieut.-Col. Charles Scott Moncrieff Chalmers, D.S.O., O.B.E., *b.* 1881. Major and Acting Lieut.-Col. R.E. (O6770)

WATSON, Dorothy Bannerman, Mrs., O.B.E., *b.* 5 Feb. 1878 ; *d.* of the late James Ramsay, of York ; *m.* Henry Angus, *s.* of Rev. Wm. Watson, M.A., of Forres. *War Work :* Commandant Clifford Street V.A.D. Hospital, York, 2 years ; Asst. County Director, W. Riding, Yorks. *Address :* 6, St. George's Place, York. *Club :* Ladies' Automobile. (O3976)

WATSON, Major Douglas Home, O.B.E., *b.* 23 March, 1878 ; *s.* of A. C. Watson, of Edinburgh ; *m.* Jean Armour, *d.* of S. D. Black, of Edinburgh. *Educ. :* Edinburgh. Principal Clerk, Ministry of Pensions. *War Work :* Adjutant 2/5th Royal Scots ; D.A.A.G. War Office ; Regional Recorder, Ministry of National Service, London and South-Eastern Region. *Address :* 3. Gloucester Place, Edinburgh. *Club :* Scottish Arts (Edinburgh). (O3977)

WATSON, Capt. Earl Basil Kenmure, M.B.E., *b.* 22 Aug 1882 ; *s.* of James Watson, of 35, Duke Street, Hamilton Canada ; *m.* Marie Laure, *d.* of Emile Hauzer, of Verviers, Belgium. *Educ. :* Trinity Coll., Port Hope, Ontario. P.P.C. L.I. Regiment. *War Work :* Served with P.P.C.L.I. Aug. 1914, to Sept. 1915 ; transferred to 8th London Regt. ; appointed A.P.M. Jan. 1917, and served at areas in above appointment, Etaples, 9th Scottish Division. St. Germain, Mont d'Or, Paris, Avancourt, Trouville, Ostend ; wounded May, 1915. *Address :* P.P.C. L.I., Wolseley Barracks, London. *Club :* London Hunt, Country. (M4620)

WATSON, Edith Deverell, Mrs., O.B.E.

WATSON, Edith Hay, Mrs., M.B.E., *b.* 9 July, 1865 ; *d.* of Henry Burrows, of Doe Park, Woolton, Liverpool ; *m.* John Henry Douglas, *s.* of John Watson, of Edinburgh. *War Work :* Commandant of V.A.D. Kent 18 ; Pembury V.A.D. Hospital. *Address :* Broad Oak, Brenchley, Kent. (M9975)

WATSON, Edith Margaret, C.B.E. Private Sec. to Chancellor of Exchequer. (C1055)

WATSON, Ernest Ansley, O.B.E., M.Sc., *b.* 4 April, 1887 ; *s.* of Charles J. Watson, of Birmingham ; *m.* Elizabeth, *d.* of James Cotterill, of Coventry. *Educ. :* Birmingham and Liverpool Univ. Electrical Engineer. *War Work :* Technical Director of M.L. Magneto Synd., Ltd., Coventry, manufacturers of magnetos, particularly for aeroplane engines ; developed magnetos for rotary and other aeroplane engines. *Address :* 2, St. Andrew's Road, Coventry ; Victoria Works, Coventry. (O11567)

WATSON, Eva Gordon, Mrs., M.B.E., *d.* of H. M. Chase, of Bengal Civil Service. *War Work :* Organiser of Queen Mary's Needlework Guild at St. Andrews, Fife. *Clubs :* New Victorian ; The End House, S. Andrews, Fife. *Clubs :* New Victorian ; St. Rules. (M4064)

WATSON, Major Evelyn Cyril, O.B.E., *b.* 28 April, 1883 ; *s.* of Farnel Watson, of Isleworth : *m.* Dulce Lilian Watson, *d.* of W. J. Bush-Salmon, of Stanwell. *Educ. :* Uppingham. Gazetted in the 4th Essex Regt. as a 2nd Lieut. 1899, and in 7th Dragoon Guards, 1902, and served in South African War, 1900–1. *War Work :* 1914–18, with the 5th Cav. Division in France. *Address :* 7th Dragoon Guards (attached Machine Gun Corps Cav.), Somerset Barracks, Shorncliffe. *Club :* Cavalry. (O7825)

WATSON, Evelyn Elenor, Mrs., O.B.E.

WATSON, Frank, O.B.E.

WATSON, Frank Pears, O.B.E.

WATSON, Major Forrester Colvin, O.B.E., M.C., *b.* 26 July, 1878 ; *s.* of William Farnell Watson, late of Henfold, Dorking, Surrey ; *m.* Cecilia, *d.* of — Grimston, of Earls Colne, Essex. *Educ. :* Rugby. Major 3rd (K.O.) Hussars, retired and on the Reserve of Officers (3rd R.O.) Hussars. *War Work :* Served in South African War, Feb. 1900–01, Queen's and King's medals ; Adjutant, 3rd (K.O.) Hussars, went abroad with Regt. Aug. 1914 ; Staff Capt., 1st Divisional Artillery, Jan. 1916 ; D.A.Q.M.G., 3rd Corps., Oct. 1916. *Address :* The Chantry, Harlow, Essex. *Club :* Cavalry. (O5901)

WATSON, Capt. Frederick Whittaker, M.B.E.

WATSON, Capt. George Leybourne, O.B.E.

WATSON, George Trustram, O.B.E.

WATSON, Paymaster-Lieut.-Comm. George William, O.B.E., R.N.

WATSON, Gilbert, M.B.E.

WATSON, Gwendoline Isabel, Mrs., M.B.E.

WATSON, Harris, M.B.S.

WATSON, Major-Gen. Sir Harris Davis, K.B.E., C.M.G., C.I.E., M.V.O., 9th Ghurka Rifles ; *b.* 18 July, 1866 ; *s.* of late Gen. Sir John Watson, G.C.B., V.C. Entered Dorset Regt., 1885 ; Captain Indian Army, 1896 ; Major, 1903, Lieut.-Col. 1904 ; Col. 1914 ; served Sikkur Expedition, 1888 ; Chin Nushai Expedition, 1899–1902 ; China, 1900–1 ; Great War, 1914–18 ; has Order of the Nile, 3rd Class ; extra Equerry to H.M. the King. *Address :* Dehra Dun, India. (K272)

WATSON, Henry, O.B.E.

WATSON, Henry, O.B.E.

WATSON, Major Henry Angus, C.B.E., R.E. (T.), *b.* 18 Aug. 1863 , *s.* of Rev. Wm. Watson, M.A., of Forres, Scotland ; *m.* Dorothy Bannerman ; *d.* of James Ramsay, M.D., of York. *Educ. :* Privately, Aberdeen, and Edinburgh Univ. General Superintendent, N.E.R. *War Work :* Railway Transport work for Northern Command. *Address :* 6, St. George's Place, York. *Clubs :* Constitutional ; Royal and Ancient Golf. (C325)

WATSON, Henry Talbot, O.B.E., *b.* 1 July, 1866 ; *s.* of Charles Watson, of Valparaiso, Chile. *Educ. :* Columbia Coll., New York, U.S.A. *War Work :* Second in command of British Military Control Bureau, Paris. *Address :* 25, Avenue des Champs, Elysées, Paris. *Clubs :* White's ; St. James'. (O11570)

WATSON, Capt. Horace Cyril, C.B.E., R.N., *b.* 1876 ; *s.* of the Rev. Arthur Watson, of The Grange, West Cowes, Isle of Wight. Great War, 1914–19, as Navigating Officer and with Patrol and Ocean Escort (despatches) ; appointed Capt.-Attendant and King's Harbour Master at Malta, 1910. *Address :* H.M.'s Dockyard, Malta. *Clubs :* Junior Army and Navy ; Royal London Yacht. (C1208)

WATSON, Rear-Admiral Hugh Dudley Richards, C.B. C.B.E., M.V.O., *b.* 20 April, 1872 ; *s.* of the Rev. William Watson, of Saltfleetby, Lincolnshire ; *m.* Janie Amina, sister of 1st Viscount Cowdray (*see* BURKE's *Peerage*), *d.* of George Pearson, of Brickendonbury, Herts. *Educ. :* Llandaff Cathedral School, and Naval Educational Establishments. Served in the Royal Navy between 1885 and 1914 ; amongst other appointments commanded the first expedition of men-of-war over the Yangtse river rapids in 1898–1901 ; Naval attaché to British Embassy, Berlin, 1910–13. *War Work :* As Captain Royal Navy, commanded the following ships during the war : H.M ships "Essex," "Bellerophon," and "Canada." *Address :* 40, Cadogan Square, London. *Clubs :* Marlborough ; Naval and Military. (C2275)

WATSON, Isaac Adolphus Herbert, O.B.E., *b.* 1 Sept. 1869 ; *s.* of Isaac Watson, of Portsmouth ; *m.* Clara, *d.* of J. Johnson, of Linthorpe, Yorks. *Educ. :* Privately, and

Bensberg, Germany. Superintendent of Stores and Transport, H.M. Stationery Office. *Address :* Dinsdale, South Norwood, Surrey. (O841)

WATSON, Isabella Clark, M.B.E., V.A.D.

WATSON, Isobel, Mrs., O.B.E.

WATSON, James, M.B.E.

WATSON, James, O.B.E., J.P., D.L., *b.* 1848; *s.* of Thomas Watson, of Dalry, Millmark, Kirkcudbrightshire; *m. d.* of Thomas Deacon, of Southsea. *Educ. :* Sanguhar Academy. Retired; Member of Edinburgh Town Council; Chairman, Commission of Public Health Committee. *War Work :* Recruiting; Military Tribunal; Controller and Sec. of Municipal War Comforts Committee; Chairman of War Pensions Local Tribunal (all voluntary). *Address :* Abington, McLaren Road, Edinburgh. *Club :* Scottish Liberal (Edinburgh). (O11572)

WATSON, Lieut.-Col. James Kiero, C.M.G., C.V.O., C.B.E., D.S.O., *s.* of the late Major-Gen. J. K. Watson, late 60th Rifles; *m.* Katharine Emelia; *d.* of H. C. Nisbet, of The Old House, Wimbledon. *Educ. :* Clifton Coll., and R.A.M.C., Sandhurst. Joined King's Royal Rifles, 1885; served in Chin Hills, Burma (medal and clasp); attached Egyptian Army, 1894–99; Dongola and Khartoum Expeditions, 1896–99 (despatches, D.S.O., Brevet-Majority, 4th Class Medjidieh and 3rd Class Osmanieh); S. African War, 1899–1901 (despatches, C.M.G.); A.D.C. to Lord Kitchener, 1895–1901; returned to Egyptian Army as A.A.G., 1901; retired, 1905; 1st A.D.C. to H.H. The Khedive, 1905–14. *War Work :* D.A.A.G. in France, 1914–15; Commandant, Advanced Base, Cape Helles, 1915 till evacuation, Gallipoli; military attaché, Egypt, 1915–19; Order of the Sword of Sweden and Legion of Honour. *Address :* Gorse Cottage, Fleet, Hants. *Club :* Naval and Military. (C1394)

WATSON, Major James Robert, O.B.E., A.P.D.

WATSON, Major James Taylor, C.B.E.,

WATSON, Comm. John, M.B.E., J.P.

WATSON, Major John, O.B.E., R.A.O.C.

WATSON, John, M.B.E., *b.* 2 May, 1864; *s.* of John Watson, of Shirburn, Oxfordshire. *Educ. :* Univ. Coll. School. District Valuer, Inland Revenue Department. *War Work :* Aug. 1914, to March, 1917, organised for the southern part of the Northern Command a Corps of Army Guides as part of the Territorial Forces, primarily intended to guide the Army in case of invasion, but employed in anti-aircraft defence and general intelligence work; March, 1917, to June, 1919, with permission of Inland Revenue Department acted in an honorary capacity as Chief Executive Officer to the Yorks, West Riding Agricultural Executive Committee. (M2614)

WATSON, John Alfred, O.B.E., J.P.; *s.* of William Watson, late of Balsall, Warwickshire; *m.* Mary Ann, *d.* of John Lea, of Birmingham. *Educ. :* Privately. County Councillor for Warwickshire, and Chairman for Warwickshire War Pension Local Committee. *War Work :* Chairman of Warwickshire Local War Pension Committee. *Address :* Chadwick Manor, Knowle, Warwickshire. (O11573)

WATSON, Capt. John Charles, M.B.E., R.A.F.

WATSON, John Henderson, O.B.E.

WATSON, Joseph Thomas, M.B.E., *b.* 30 May, 1863; *s.* of Joseph Watson, of London; *m.* Louise Mary, *d.* of Linscott. *Educ. :* Ealing. Councillor, St. Marylebone Borough Council; Hon. Sec. London Playing Fields Society. *War Work :* National Service Representative for St. Marylebone; organised the feeding of 150 pigs at Zoological Gardens from house refuse; organised the collection and salvage of waste products from house refuse. *Clubs :* Royal Automobile; M.C.C.; Edgware Golf; Huckwell Heath Golf. (M9978)

WATSON, Lieut.-Col. Julien, O.B.E., M.C., R.E.

WATSON, Major Lewis James Fort, M.B.E.

WATSON, Eng.-Comm. Lewis Jones, O.B.E., R.N.

WATSON, Margaret Jane, Mrs., M.B.E.

WATSON, Marguerite Audrey, Mrs., M.B.E.

WATSON, Maud Edith Eleanor, M.B.E.

WATSON, Mildred Jane Musgrave, M.B.E.

WATSON, Capt. Noel Sutcliffe Ogilvy, M.B.E., R.E.

WATSON, Pamela Ethel, Mrs., M.B.E.

WATSON, Lieut. Robert Campbell, O.B.E., R.N.R.

WATSON, Thomas, M.B.E.

WATSON, 2nd Lieut. Victor Fsevlod, M.B.E., R.G.A.

WATSON, Victor James Carter, M.B.E.

WATSON, Wallace, M.B.E., R.N.R.

WATSON, Lieut. William, M.B.E.

WATSON, Capt. William, M.B.E.

WATSON, Capt. William Charles, M.B.E.

WATSON, Capt. William Douglas, O.B.E., M.C., R.A.

WATSON, William Elder, O.B.E., J.P., *b.* 2 Feb. 1866; *s.* of A. R. Watson, of Springlands, Elgin; *m.* Mary Evaline, *d.* of Lachlan Mackintosh, of Old Lodge, Elgin. *Educ. :* Elgin Academy. *War Work :* Appeal Tribunal for Inverness, Moray, and Nairn Shires. *Address :* Moray Bank, Elgin. (O843)

WATSON, Capt. William F., O.B.E., *b.* 6 Sept. 1888; *s.* of F. Hazell Watson, of Hurst House, Woodford Green, Essex; *m.* Emily Delano, *d.* of Robert Halfhead, of Beech Hall, Woodford Green, Essex. *War Work :* Active Service at the Dardanelles, in Egypt, Palestine, and France. (O5902)

WATSON, William George, M.B.E.

WATSON, William Joseph Gabriel, M.B.E.

WATSON, William Law, M.B.E.

WATSON, Capt. William Linton, O.B.E., I.M.S.

WATSON, William Milne, O.B.E.

WATSON, Lieut. William Robert, O.B.E., R.N.V.R.

WATSON, William Wallace, M.B.E.

WATSON, Alexandra Mary, Mrs. CHALMERS-, C.B.E., M.D., *b.* 1872; *d.* of Auckland Campbell Geddes; *m.* Douglas Chalmers, *d.* of Walter Watson, M.D. of Midcalder. *Educ. :* South Hampstead High School, and Edinburgh Univ. Chairman, Time and Tide Publishing Co.; Vice-President, Medical Women's Federation; Chairman, Edinburgh Women Citizens Association; Member of Committee and Hon. Sec. Edinburgh Hospital for Women and Children, Queen Victoria's Jubilee Nurses, Central Committee Scotland, Queen Mary's Nursing Home, Edinburgh. *War Work :* Hon. Sec. Women's Emergency Corps, Edinburgh; Organiser and first Chief Controller, W.A.A.C. *Address :* 11, Walker Street, Edinburgh. *Club :* Caledonian Ladies' (Edinburgh). (C73)

WATSON, Sir Charles Gordon GORDON-, K.B.E., C.M.G., F.R.C.S., *b.* 1874; *s.* of the Rev. H. G. Watson, M.A., of The Wilderness, Woburn Sands, Beds; *m.* 1917, Alice Geraldine Mary, *d.* of the late C. J. Teevan, of Woodside Court, Croydon. *Educ :* St. Mark's, Windsor, and St. Bartholomew's Hospital. Surgeon, St. Bartholomew's Hospital, St. Mark's Hospital, and St. Andrew's Hospital; Consulting Surgeon, Metropolitan Hospital. Civil Surgeon in South African War, 1899–1901; Hon. previously Temp. Col. A.M.S. *War Work :* Consulting Surgeon, B.E.F., France and Italy, 1914–19. *Addresses :* 82, Harley Street, W. 1; Highwood Cottage, Harpsden, Henley-on-Thames. *Clubs :* Royal Automobile; Bath. (K275)

WATSON, Charles HERON-, O.B.E., M.A., *b.* 1871; *s.* of the late Sir Patrick Heron-Watson, of Edinburgh. *Educ. :* Edinburgh Academy, and Univ., and Paris. Commissioner to the Sutherlandshire Boy Scouts. *War Work :* Scout Commissioner on Admiralty Coastwatching Services, 1914–18. *Address :* Achinduic Lodge, Invershi, Sutherlandshire. *Clubs :* Caledonian; University (Edinburgh). (O419)

WATSON, Mildred Jane MUSGRAVE-, M.B.E.; *d.* of the late Capt. Musgrave-Watson, Royal Fusiliers. *Educ. :* Notting Hill High School. Sec. of the Publicity Committee of the Children's Country Holidays Fund; Hon. Sec. of Women's Advisory Committee of National Savings Committee. *War Work :* 1915–16, Sec. Serbian Relief Fund, received the Serbian Croix de Misére; 1916, Sec. to British Women's Star and Garter Hospital Building Fund; 1916–20, Head of Women's Section of National War Savings Committee. *Address :* 4, Upper Gloucester Place, N.W. *Club :* Ladies' Army and Navy. (M2616)

WATT, Alexander Strahan, C.B.E. *Address :* 82, Boundary Road, St. John's Wood, N.W. (C326)

WATT, Charles Frederick, O.B.E., *b.* 9 Aug. 1882; *s.* of Charles Watt, late of 6, Grosvenor Terrace, Glasgow; *m.* Marion Gillies, *d.* of James C. Gillies, of New York. *Educ. :* Edinburgh Academy. *War Work :* Director and Vice-President of the Wheat Export Co., Inc., New York, U.S.A., 1916–20, which was the Official Representative and Agent of the Royal Commission on Wheat Supplies, London, for the purchase of Cereals and Cereal products in the United States and Canada; Buyer of all Rye and Barley in U.S.A. and Canada. *Addresses :* 361, Produce Exchange, New York, U.S.A.; c/o Samuel Sanday & Co., Holland House, London. *Clubs :* Flushing Country (Long Island, U.S.A.); Canadian (New York); and British Schools and Universities (New York). (O11575)

WATT, Capt. George, M.B.E., *b.* 4 Feb. 1851; *s.* of the late George Watt, of Aberdeenshire; *m.* Jane, *d.* of Alexander McLeod, of Stornoway. *Educ. :* Stornoway. Late Mercantile Marine, and Member of Stornoway School Board; now Harbour Master at Stornoway. *War Work :* Employed as Senior Pilot to the Admiralty on the Stornoway Base. (M9985)

WATT, Lieut. James, M.B.E.

WATT, Capt. John William, M.B.E.

WATT, Madge Robertson, Mrs., M.B.E.

WATT, Margaret Rose, Mrs., M.B.E., *b.* 4 June, 1870; *d.* of Henry Robertson, K.C., of Collingwood, Canada; *m.* Alfred Tennyson, *s.* of Hugh Watt, M.P., of British Columbia. *Educ. :* Privately, and at Univ. of Toronto, Victoria, Canada. President, Univ. Women's Club, 1912; Member Senate Univ. of British Columbia, 1913–18. *War Work :* Founded and 1st Chairman, British Columbia War Service Committee, 1914, for visiting hospitals in England; Founded Women's Institute Movement in the British Isles, 1915–17; Chief Organiser, Women's Institutes Board of Agriculture, 1917–19; Chairman, Advisory Board Women's Institutes, Department of Agriculture, British Columbia, 1910; delivered over 1000 addresses on increasing food supply. *Addresses :* Selsey, Melchkin, Victoria, British Columbia; c/o Bank of Montreal, London; 9, Waterloo Place, London. *Clubs :* Lyceum; University Women's (Victoria, Canada). (M2617)

WATT, Lieut.-Col. Walter Oswald, O.B.E.

WATT, Capt. William McIver, M.B.E.

WATTERS, John, M.B.E.

WATTERSON, Percy Gill, M.B.E., A.C.A., *b.* 23 Aug. 1887; *s.* of Robert Watterson, of Leeds. *Educ. :* Leeds. Chief Accountant, League of Nations. *War Work :* Finance and Accounts Manager, Berne (Switzerland), Office of the Ministry of Munitions. (M9986)

WATTLEWORTH, Capt. James Percy, O.B.E., R.F.A.(T.).

WATTON, Capt. George, M.B.E., R.G.A.

WATTS, Arthur Francis, M.B.E., B.A., *b,* 31 Oct. 1872; *s.* of the Rev. Arthur Watts, L.Th., F.G.S., F.R.G.S., Rector

of Witton Gilbert, Durham. *Educ.:* Durham Grammar School, and Durham Univ. Assistant Master at Crypt Grammar School, Gloucester. *War Work:* Qr.-Mr. of Glos. 60 V.A.D. 1910–15; Commandant, Glos. 25 from 1915; Transport Officer, Gloucester City Area, 1914–19; Qr.-Mr. and Hon. Sec. Great Western Hospital, 1914–17; County Commissariat Officer, 1917–19. *Addresses:* Crypt Grammar School, Gloucester; Yew Tree Villa, Tuffley, Gloucester.
(M9987)

WATTS, Charles Haynes, M.B.E.

WATTS, Charles Manly, O.B.E.

WATTS, Charlotte Helen, Mrs., M.B.E.

WATTS, Edgar Charles, O.B.E., *b.* 3 Oct. 1871; *s.* of Charles Watts, of Smarden, Kent; *m.* Edith Mary, *d.* of John Palmer, of Sergeants' Inn. *Educ.:* Clapham Collegiate School, and King's Coll. Naval Store Officer under the Admiralty. *War Work:* Naval Store Officer, H.M. Dockyard, Sheerness, 1914–15; Chatham, 1915–17; Coal Controller, Gibraltar, 1917–19. *Address:* H.M. Dockyard, Devonport.   (O844)

WATTS, Emily, Mrs., M.B.E.

WATTS, Capt. Francis Mapleton Iremonger, M.B.E. *b.* 1 July, 1895; *s.* of Francis Watts, of Laureston Lodge, Newton Abbot, S. Devon. *Educ.:* Newton Coll., Newton Abbot, and R.M.C., Sandhurst. Solicitor. *War Work:* Served abroad with Worcestershire Regt., 1915; wounded; seconded to R.F.C., and served overseas with 24th Squadron, 1916; Mesopotamia, 1918–19. *Address:* Laureston Lodge, Newton Abbot, S. Devon.   (M6084)

WATTS, Henry Charles, M.B.E., D.Sc., *b.* 5 Feb. 1892; *s.* of C. F. Watts, of Bristol. *Educ.:* Bristol Univ. Director, Ogilvie and Partners, Consulting Aeronautical Engineers. *War Work:* Head of Propeller Designs Branch, Air Ministry. *Address:* Gwdyr Chambers, 104, High Holborn, W.C. 1.
(M1071)

WATTS, Hugh Edmund, M.B.E., Ph.D., B.Sc., F.I.C., F.C.S., *b.* 5 Dec. 1888; *s.* of Thomas William Watts, of Gordon House, Hutton, Essex. *Educ.:* Mercers' School; King's Coll., London; Univ. of Zürich. Sec. to the Factories Branch of the Department of Explosives Supplies, and to the Gretna-Waltham Abbey Committee; Technical Adviser to Major-Gen. Sir F. R. Bingham, K.C.M.G., C.B., of the Military Inter-Allied Commission of Control, Berlin, with rank of Lieut.-Col. *War Work:* Sec. to the Factories Branch of the Department of Explosives Supplies. *Address:* Gordon House, Hutton, Essex. *Clubs:* Royal Societies'; Chemical Industry; Univ. of London.   (M9990)

WATTS, Lieut.-Col. Humphrey, O.B.E., T.D., B.A., *b.* 15 Sept. 1880; *s.* of James Watts, of Abney Hall, Cheadle, Cheshire; *m.* Gladys Mary, *d.* of Sir Edward Parkes, M.P., of Edgbaston, Birmingham. *Educ.:* Brasenose Coll., Oxford. Merchant. *War Work:* Went to France Feb. 1915, with 5th (Earl of Chester's) Batt., the Cheshire Regt.; invalided home and held various appointments connected with Musketry and Lewis Gun instruction. *Address:* Haslington Hall, N. Crewe. *Club:* Isthmian.   (O7828)

WATTS, Major John Hunter, O.B.E., R.A.S.C.

WATTS, Lieut.-Col. Luther, O.B.E., V.D., *b.* 6 Oct. 1861; *s.* of Alderman W. H. Watts, J.P., C.C., late Lord Mayor of Liverpool; *m.* Bertha, *d.* of T. E. Priest, of Liverpool. *Educ.:* Liverpool Institute. *War Work:* O.C. 1/9th Batt. King's Liverpool Regt.; served with 1st and 2nd Army in France; Town Major and District Commandant, St. Pol, from June, 1917, to June, 1919; has British and Allied War Medals, Edward VII. and George V. Coronation Medals, Volunteer Officers' Decoration and Long Service Medal, Territorial Force Medal. *Address:* Sinhala, Aughton, Ormskirk, Lancashire. *Club:* Junior Army and Navy.   (O5904)

WATTS, Mary Manning, M.B.E.; *d.* of the late William Manning Watts, of Belsize Park, Hampstead, London. *Educ.:* Privately. *War Work:* Joint organiser of Belgian Hostel and Club, from Sept. 1914, to July, 1915, and of Hampstead War Hospital Supply Depot, July, 1915, to March, 1919. *Address:* 1, Compayne Gardens, Hampstead, N.W. (M9991)

WATTS, Patterson, O.B.E.

WATTS, Philip James, O.B.E., M.I.E.E., *b.* 4 April, 1873; *s.* of James Watts, of Orlingbury Rectory, Northants; *m.* Isabella Fox, *d.* of Archibald Kitchin, of Whitehaven. *Educ.:* King's School, Canterbury, and Faraday House, London. Electrical Engineer under the Admiralty. *War Work:* In charge of the Electrical Department of H.M. Dockyard, Sheerness. *Address:* 4, Naval Terrace, Sheerness.
(O1576)

WATTS, Major Roger John, O.B.E.

WAUCHOPE, Lieut. David, M.B.E.

WAUCHOPE, Jean Mary, Mrs., C.B.E.; *m.* Gen. Wauchope, of Niddrie, C.B., C.M.G. (who died). *War Work:* President for Midlothian Soldiers' and Sailors' Families Association; Lady President, Midlothian Y.M.C.A.; Edinburgh Executive Red Cross; Chairman, Siberton Local Pensions; Council Y.W.C.A. *Addresses:* Niddrie, Marischal, Craigmillar, Midlothian; The Hall, Yetham, Kelso. (C3031)

WAUCHOPE, Robert Stuart, O.B.E.

WAUGH, Alfred Charles, M.B.E., R.N.

WAUGH, Walter Charles, M.B.E., *b.* 6 March, 1884; *s.* of Walter Waugh, of Chigwell Hall, Chigwell, Essex. *Educ.:* Forest School and abroad. Partner of Walter Waugh & Co., Chemical Merchants and Manufacturers. *War Work:* Section Director, Mineral Oil Production Dept. of the Ministry of Munitions; Chiefly responsible for allocating supplies of home

produced oils for the Admiralty. *Addresses:* Chigwell Hall, Essex; 4, Lloyds Avenue, London, E.C. 3. *Club:* Royal Automobile.   (M9992)

WAV, Effie, Mrs., M.B.E.

WAVERTREE, Sophie Florence Nothrop, Lady, C.B.E., *d.* of Algernon Thomas Brinsley Sheridan, D.L., of Frampton Court, Dorset; *m.* William Hall Walker, 1st Baron Wavertree (*see* BURKE'S *Peerage*); *s.* of Sir Andrew Barclay Walker, 1st Bart. of Gateacre. *Addresses:* Horlsey Hall, Gresford, Denbighshire; Sandy Brow, Tarporley, Cheshire; Sussex Lodge, Regent's Park, N.W.   (C661)

WAVISH, Samuel John, O.B.E.

WAWN, Dominique, O.B.E., *b.* 29 July, 1871; *s.* of Middlemost Wawn, of Sunderland; *m.* Eileen, *d.* of Capt. F. Crohan, of Indian Army. *Educ.:* Neuwied, Germany. *War Work:* On Staff of Controller-General of Merchant Shipping as Chief Inspector for all North East Coast shipbuilding yards and engine and boiler works. *Address:* Cleadon Tower, near Sunderland. *Club:* Sunderland.   (O11577)

WAY, Albert Edward, M.B.E., R.N.

WAY, Capt. Arthur, M.B.E., *b.* 1848; *s.* of W. B. Jennings Way; *m.* Ellen, *d.* of — Bee, of Lancaster. *Educ.:* Beamshaw Academy, New Forest. Extra Master in the Mercantile Marine. *War Work:* Master of Transport " Gregynog 673 "; served throughout the war. *Address:* 8, Sandbourne Road, Poole, Dorset. *Club:* Liberal, Sunderland.   (M4066)

WAY, Lieut.-Col. Bromley G. V., C.B.E., M.V.O., *b.* 30 Nov. 1873; *e.s.* of the late Rev. Bromley Way. *Educ.:* Wellington Coll., and New Coll., Oxford. Gazetted, 2nd Batt. the Sherwood Foresters, 1896; promoted Capt. 1900; Major, 1915; Brevet Lieut.-Col., 1918; Adjutant, 2nd Batt., 1904–7; A.D.C. to G.O.C. in Command Aldershot Command, 1907–10; A.M.S., Aldershot Command, 1910–12; Assistant Director of Movements, War Office, 1918–20; served with 2nd Batt. Tirah Expedition, 1897 (Indian Frontier Medal); S. Africa, with Mounted Infantry, 1900–1 (Queen's S. African Medal); France, 1914 (1914 Star, British and Victory Medals), Legion of Honour (Croix d'Officier), 1918, Crown of Belgium (Croix d'Officier), 1919. *Address:* c/o Messrs. Cox & Co. *Clubs:* Naval and Military; Boodle's.   (C1808)

WAY, Edith, Caroline, Mrs., M.B.E., *b.* 8 Oct. 1871; *d.* of Surgeon-Major John Mennie, of Bombay Medical Service; *m.* Theodore Alban Henry, I.C.S., *s.* of Dr. F. W. Way, of Southsea. *Educ.:* Southsea. *War Work:* Sec. St. John Ambulance Association, Red Cross work, Naini Tal. United Provinces, India; twice mentioned in gazette of India. *Address:* c/o T. A. H. Way, Indian Civil Service, United Provinces, India. *Agents:* Messrs. H. S. King & Co., 9, Pall Mall, London, S.W.   (M6269)

WAY, Lieut. Francis Robert, O.B.E., R.A.S.C., (T.).

WAY, Lieut. John Dover, M.B.E.

WAY, Philip Greville Hugh, M.B.E., *b.* 15 April, 1865; *s.* of the Rev. John Hugh Way, of Henbury; *m.* Dorothy Constance, *d.* of C. C. Cave, of 13, Cranley Gardens. *War Work:* Organising Sec. War Savings Association for Lincs, and Vice-Chairman for Horticultural Sub-Committee, Kesteven, Lincs. *Address:* Merriott House, Merriott, Crewkerne, Som.
(M4067)

WAY, Comm. Robert Lewis, O.B.E.,R.N.

WAYLEN, Capt. Donald Campbell, M.B.E. R.A.F.

WAYMAN, Lieut.-Col. Henry Holdsworth, O.B.E., D.L., *b.* 1876; 2nd *s.* of William Henry Wayman, of Halifax. *Educ.:* Edinburgh and Bonn. *War Work:* Served in ·S. Africa, 1899–1902 (Mounted Infantry; despatches), and in Great War in France, 1915–17 (despatches); Commanded 3rd Batt. West Riding Regt., 1910–17. *Address:* South Field, Halifax, Yorks. *Clubs:* Bucks; Junior United Service.   (O8967)

WAYMAN, Lieut.-Col. Myers, O.B.E., F.S.S., F.I.S.A.; *s.* of Myers Wayman, of Valebrooke, Sunderland, and Egglestone, Yorks; *m.* Margaret Winifred, *d.* of William Bland, of Shildon, Durham. *Educ.:* Sunderland, and Christ's Coll., Cambridge. Director of Appointments Department, Ministry of Labour; Member of a large number of Councils, Boards, and Committees in connection with education and resettlement. *War Work:* Lieut.-Col. H.M. Forces; War Service, 1914–19, Durham Light Infantry; seriously wounded, Armentières, 1916. *Address:* Wetherby, Yorks. *Clubs:* Rotary (Leeds); Services (Sheffield).   (O3979)

WAYNE, Francis Herman Milford, O.B.E., M.A., *b.* 14 July, 1863; *s.* of the late Col. Herman Wayne, J.P., of Tickwood Hall, Much Wenlock; *m.* Charlotte Isabella Blanche, *d.* of the late Sir George Kinloch, Bart., of Kinloch, Meigle, N.B. *Educ.:* Rugby and Cambridge. Assistant County Director British Red Cross Society, East Sussex. *War Work:* Hon. Agent for Food Supplies, British Red Cross Society, Sussex. *Address:* Campfield, Battle, Sussex. *Club:* Windham.   (O11578)

WAYNE, Capt. Frederick William, O.B.E.

WEAKFORD, Charles Frederick, M,B.E.

WEAKNER, John Johnson, M.B.E.

WEALE, Eng.-Lieut. Henry Searle, O.B.E., R.N.

WEATHERALL, Capt. Nigel Edward, O.B.E.

WEATHERHEAD, Adam, M.B.E. Shipbuilder; Managing Director, W. Harkess and Son, Ltd. *War Work:* Superintendent of Special Constabulary; carried out important work for the Admiralty. *Address:* The Moorings, Cornfield Road, Middlesbrough. *Club:* Cleveland.   (M1072)

WEATHERHEAD, Robert, O.B.E., B.A., R.N.

WEATHERILL, Henry, O.B.E.

WEAVER, Alexander Charles, M.B.E.

WEAVER, Arthur John, M.B.E., J.P., *b.* 13 Feb. 1863 ; *s.* of Arthur Weaver, of Walsall ; *m.* Mary Jane, *d.* of Samuel White, of Walsall. *Educ.:* Queen Mary's Grammar School, Walsall. Magistrate ; Member of Advisory Committee to Wolverhampton Borough Justices ; Vice-Chairman, Labour Employment Committee, Vice-Chairman, Food Committee ; President, Wolverhampton Trades and Labour Council ; active worker in Sunday Morning Adult School Movement. *War Work:* Served on Advisory Committee to Military Tribunal ; Member of Soldiers' and Sailors' Disablement Committee. *Address:* 12, Raby Street, Wolverhampton.
(M9994)

WEAVER, Capt. Charles Henry, M.B.E., *b.* 1 Jan. 1888. *War Work:* Served with Red Cross, Alexandria, 1915, and Mesopotamia, 1916–19, as Assistant Commissioner. *Address:* Boxmoor, Herts. (M2620)

WEAVER, Frederick William Herron, O.B.E.

WEAVER, Gertrude Cleave, Mrs., M.B.E., *b.* 20 Oct. 1881 ; *d.* of Harry Westbrook, of Binfield, Berkshire ; *m.* William Henry Weaver, of the International Labour Office, Geneva. *Educ.:* North Dulwich. Civil Servant, Administrative Officer of the International Labour Office, League of Nations, Geneva, formerly Assistant Inspector in National Health Insurance Commission. *War Work:* Woman Chief of Staff in (Enemy) Prisoners of War Information Bureau ; Staff of 400 women speaking practically every European and many Oriental languages. *Address:* International Labour Office (Bureau International du Travail), Geneva. *Club:* 1917.
(M2627)

WEAVER, Henry, M.B.E.

WEAVER, Capt. John, M.B.E., *b.* 18 Sept. 1867 ; *s.* of William Weaver, of Lewes, Sussex ; *m.* Margaret, *d.* of Cornelius Conning, of Isle of Whithorn. *Educ.:* Privately. Master, both Sailing and Steam ; Master of Cruising Yacht. *War Work:* Deputy Head Coast Watcher, Headquarters, Whitefield Road, Govan ; Official District, Wigtownshire Coast from Glasserton to Dinnans Head. *Address:* Harbour House, Isle of Whithorn, Wigtownshire, N.B. (M9996)

WEAVER, John Henry, C.B.E. ; *s.* of John Weaver, of Doncaster. Ch. Censor for Union of S. Africa and Imperial Dep. Ch. Censor for S. Africa during Great War. *Address:* Pretoria, Transvaal. (C762)

WEAVER, Sir Lawrence, K.B.E., F.S.A., Hon. A.R.I.B.A., *b.* 2 July, 1876 ; *s.* of W. F. Weaver ; *m.* Kathleen, *d.* of the late Major-Gen. E. T. W. Purcell, R.A. *Educ.:* Clifton Coll. Director-General, Land and Supplies Dept., and Second Secretary, Ministry of Agriculture and Fisheries ; Chairman, National Institute of Agricultural Botany ; Hon. Treas. Housing Association for Officers' Families. *War Work:* Anti-Aircraft Corps, R.N.V.R., 1915–17 ; Controller of Supplies, Food Production Dept., 1917–18. *Address:* 38, Hamilton Terrace, N.W. 8. *Clubs:* Reform ; Farmers'. (K439)

WEAVER, Percy Willian, M.B.E., *b.* 6 Nov. 1882 ; *s.* of Henry Weaver, M.B.E., of Stourport, Worcs. (late Station Supt., G. W. Rly., Paddington). *Educ.:* Newbury and Reading. Railway Traffic Officer ; Assistant Goods Manager, Egyptian State Railways, Cairo. *War Work:* Supervision of Military Railway Traffic on the Egyptian State Railways at various points, particularly at Kantara West station. *Address:* Helmieh, near Cairo, Egypt. *Clubs:* Constitutional ; Turf (Cairo) ; Union (Alexandria). (M1148)

WEBB, Arthur George, M.B.E.

WEBB, Col. Sir Arthur Lisle Ambrose, K.B.E., C.B. C.M.G., *b.* 19 July, 1871 Lieut. R.A.M.C., 1899 ; Capt., 1902 ; Major, 1911 ; Lieut.-Col. 1014 ; served S. Africa, 1899–1902 (Queen's Medal, 5 clasps ; King's Medal, 2 clasps) ; Great War, 1914–18 ; mentioned in despatches ; Director-General A.M.S. (K470)

WEBB, Benjamin, M.B.E., R.E.

WEBB, Cecil Dunstan, O.B.E.

WEBB, Lieut. Cyril Charles William, M.B.E., R.A.S.C.

WEBB, Major Edward Clive, O.B.E., F.R.C.V.S., *b.* 8 March, 1881 ; *s.* of Edward Samuel Webb, of Brighton ; *m.* Edith, *d.* of — Lewis. *Educ.:* Privately, and Royal Veterinary Coll. R.A.V.C. *War Work:* 1914, Sudan (Egyptian Army) ; 1915, M.E.F., Cairo ; 1915–16, D.A.D.V.S., 36th (Ulster) Div., France ; 1916–18, No. 1 Convalescent Horse Depot ; No. 24 Veterinary Hospital, France. *Club:* Junior Naval and Military. (O1987)

WEBB, Ella Gertrude Amy, Mrs., M.B.E., M.D., *b.* 16 Oct. 1877 ; *d.* of Charles T. Ovenden, Dean of St. Patrick's Cathedral, Dublin ; *m.* George, F.T.C.D., *s.* of Randolph Webb, Surgeon-General, R.A.M.C. *Educ.:* Queen's Coll., Harley Street ; Royal Univ., Dublin ; Berlin ; Vienna. Anæsthetist and Physician in charge of out-patient department for children, Adelaide Hospital, Dublin ; Physician to St. Ultan's Infant Hospital. *War Work:* Organisation of St. John Ambulance Brigade in Ireland, as Lady District Supt., No. 12 (Irish) District ; Member of Joint War Committee Hospitals. *Address:* 20, Hatch Street, Dublin. (M1073)

WEBB, Frank Hart, M.B.E.

WEBB, Lieut.-Col. Frederick Edward Apthorpe, O.B.E., R.A.M.C. (T.).

WEBB, Frederick James, O.B.E., J.P., *b.* 20 Aug. 1871 ; *s.* of Joseph Webb, of Wells, Somerset ; *m.* Gertrude Marie Louise, *d.* of Edward Garrett, of Sherborne, Dorset. *Educ.:* Blue Schools, Wells, Somerset. Accountant and Valuer ; Director of several companies ; Councillor for Borough of

Bournemouth ; Past High Chief Ranger, Ancient Order of Foresters Friendly Society. *War Work:* Chairman of Bournemouth War Savings Control Committee, First Victory War Loan Committee, Food Control Propaganda and Statutory Committees (resigned), War Pensions Statutory Committee, and Member of various committees doing voluntary war work. *Addresses:* 1, Yelverton Road, Bournemouth ; Glencoe, Branksome Park, Bournemouth. (O11579)

WEBB, Capt. and Qr.-Mr. Frederick John, M.B.E.

WEBB, Lieut.-Col. George Richard, M.B.E., V.D.

WEBB, Major. G. R. H., O.B.E., R.E.

WEBB, George William Cutler, O.B.E.

WEBB, Gladys Vivien, M.B.E., Q.M.A.A.C.

WEBB, Harry James C.B.E. A Member of Roy. Corps of Naval Constructors ; Ch. Constructor and Sup., Dockyard Branch, Controllers' Depart., Admiralty. *Address:* Admiralty, Whitehall. S.W. (C328)

WEBB, Major Henry Smith, M.B.E., *b.* 25 Nov. 1845 ; *s.* of James Webb, of Deptford, Kent ; *m.* Jane, *d.* of W. Sharman, of Maidstone, Kent. *Educ.:* Morden House, Greenwich, Kent. Quartermaster (ret.), R.A.M.C. *War Work:* Did duty at Base Depot Medical Stores, Bristol, Sept. 1914 ; transferred to Military Hospital, Bethnal Green, London, April, 1915. *Address:* 15, Lansdowne Road, Seven Kings, Ilford. (M5716)

WEBB, Herbert Stephen, M.B.E.

WEBB, Capt. Hugh Edwin, M.B.E., R.E.

WEBB, Comm. John Henry, O.B.E., R.N.R., *b.* 26 May, 1871 ; *s.* of Richard Webb, of Dunderrow, Kingsale, Co. Cork ; *m.* Kathleen Henrietta, *d.* of John McClean Thompson of Dublin. *Educ.:* Banden, Co. Cork. Harbour Master and Pilot Superintendent, Dublin ; Commissioner of Irish Lights. *War Work:* Assisted in embarkation of troops to and from Dublin ; salvage of torpedoed vessels, also services rendered during Irish Rebellion ; mentioned in despatches. *Address:* St. Melloco, Castle Avenue, Contarf, Dublin. (O11571)

WEBB, Capt. John Montague, O.B.E.

WEBB, Major John Robert Douglas, O.B.E., I.M.S.

WEBB, Paymaster-Lieut. Lancelot Vere, O.B.E., R.N.

WEBB, Sir Montagu de Pomeroy, Knt. Bach., C.I.E., C.B.E., *b.* 1869 ; *s.* of W. W. Webb, solicitor of Bristol and London ; *m.* 1908, Catharine Frances, *d.* of Col. Frederick Charles Wood Rideout, Indian Army. Sometime Chairman of Karachi Chamber of Commerce ; Additional Member of Bombay Legislative Council ; is Founder of the War League of India. *Address:* Karachi, India. (C352)

WEBB, Percy Henry, M.B.E., F.R.N.S., *b.* 22 Dec. 1856 ; *s.* of William Webb, of The Welches, Bentley, Hants ; *m.* Sarah Jane, *d.* of Frederic Andrews, of Cox Bridge, Farnham, Surrey. *Educ.:* Marlborough. Clerk of the Walton-upon-Thames Urban District Council ; Vestry Clerk of Walton-upon-Thames ; Clerk of Walton and Weybridge Old Age Pension Committee ; Hon. Treas. of the Royal Numi matic Society. *War Work:* Member (acting as clerk) of Walton-upon-Thames Military Tribunal ; Hon. Sec. and Hon. Treas. Walton War Pensions Committee ; Joint Hon. Sec. Walton, Hersham, and Oatlands National Emergency Committee ; Member of numerous other committees. *Addresses:* The Garden, Walton-on-Thames ; 4 & 5, West Smithfield, London, E.C. 1. (M9999)

WEBB, Major Philip, O.B.E., R.A.O.C.

WEBB, Philip George Lancelot, C.B., C.B.E., M.A., *b.* 4 Aug. 1856 ; *s.* of the Rev. Benjamin Webb, of St. Andrew's, Well Street, Prebendary of St. Paul's. *Educ.:* Westminster, and Christ Church, Oxford. Assistant Comptroller of Patents ; Hon. Sec. of the Handel Society. *War Work:* Establishment Officer in Ministry of Munitions, 1915–16 ; Deputy Controller of Petrol, Board of Trade, 1916–19. *Address:* 12, Lancaster Gate Terrace, London, W. 2. *Clubs:* New University ; Oxford and Cambridge Musical. (C329)

WEBB, Major Robert Edward, O.B.E., *b.* 29 Jan. 1875 ; *s.* of Major W. Webb, late Black Watch, of Hove ; *m.* Dulcie, *d.* of — Mabert, of Allahabad, India. *Educ.:* Mercer's Coll., Limerick. *War Work:* Served in S. African War, 1900, as Sergt. in Burma Mounted Infantry ; Great War, 1914–18 (mentioned in despatches). *Address:* 2nd Battn. York and Lancs. Regt., Persia. (O2780)

WEBB, Lieut. Sidney George, M.B.E.

WEBB, Stephen Rev. Llewellyn, O.B.E., L.Th. Durh., *b.* 7 Aug. 1885 ; *s.* of the late George Fortescue Webb, M.R.C.S., L.S.A. Chaplain to the Forces. *Address:* c/o. The Chaplain-General, War Office. (O2312)

WEBB, Capt. and Qr.-Mr. Thomas, M.B.E., R.A.S.C.

WEBB, Major William Francis, Richmond, D.S.O., O.B.E.

WEBBE, William Harold, C.B.E., B.A. (Cantab.), *b.* 30 Sept. 1885 ; *s.* of John. H. Webbe, of Birmingham ; *m.* Constance Laura Jane, *d.* of W. A. Harrison, of Birmingham. *Educ.:* King Edward's School, Birmingham, and Queen's Coll., Cambridge. 28th Wrangler, 1907 ; H.M. Inspector of Schools, 1910–20 ; Ministry of Munitions, 1915–20 ; Merchant from 1920. *War Work:* Ministry of Munitions ; Private Sec. to General Sec., and later to Parliamentary and Financial Sec. (Rt. Hon. Sir L. Worthington Evans, Bart., M.P.), Controller, Ferrous Metals and Warlike Stores Section, Disposal Board. *Address:* Queen's Park, Caterham, Surrey. *Club:* Junior Army and Navy. (C3032)

WEBBER, Amherst, O.B.E.

WEBBER, Major Horace Armine William, C.B.E., *b.* 28 March, 1880 ; *s.* of the late Felix Hussey Webber, of

Swansea; *m.* Grace Vernon, *d.* of William Pinder, of British Columbia. *Educ.*: Eton. Regular Officer, Royal Artillery. *War Work*: Served in France. *Address*: Nether House, Gaddesby, Leicestershire. *Club*: Cavalry. (C1137)

WEBBER, Capt. Hubert Arthur Cornwall, O.B.E., R.M.L.I.

WEBBER, Katharine Stanton, M.B.E.

WEBBER, Mowbray Frederick Vivian James Arthur, M.B.E., J.P. Cambs, *b.* 25 Nov. 1866; *s.* of Vivian Arthur Webber, of Ryde, Isle of Wight; *m.* Amy Affleck, *d.* of Joseph Grimond, of Carbet Castle, Broughty Ferry, Kinnettles, Forfarshire. *Educ.*: Appledencombe, Isle of Wight. Alderman, Cambs County Council; Chairman of Finance Committee, and of Visiting Committee, Fulbourn Mental Hospital; Income and Land Tax Commissioner; Treas. Cambs and Isle of Ely Nursing Association. *War Work*: Commandant, Shepreth Auxiliary Hospital, Cambs, 21 beds; Member of Advisory Committee, Melbourn Local Tribunal; 1st Treas. Cambs War Refugee Committee; Chairman and Sec. Thepreth Belgian Refugee Committee. *Clubs*: Royal Automobile; Cambridge County. (M10001)

WEBBER, Lieut.-Col. Ralph Gowland, O.B.E.

WEBER, Barbara, Mrs., M.B.E., *b.* 1871; *d.* of John Fyfe, of Aberdeen; *m.* Edward, *s.* of Frederic Weber, of London. District Chairman, War Pensions Committee. *War Work*: Hon. Organiser, Barnet War Hospital Supply Depot; Member of Red Cross, Food Control, and Food Economy Committees; Hon. Sec. War Savings Association. *Address*: Hadley Bourne, Barnet. (M10002)

WEBLEY, Flora Mary, Mrs., O.B.E.

WEBLEY, Capt. William Thomas, M.B.E., R.A.F.

WEBSTER, Capt Alexander, M.B.E.

WEBSTER, Arthur Douglas, O.B.E., V.D., M.D., D.Sc., F.R.C.P.

WEBSTER, Sir Augustus Frederick Walpole Edward, Bart., O.B.E., J.P., *b.* 6 Feb. 1864; *s.* of Sir Augustus Frederick Webster, Bart., of Battle Abbey (*see* BURKE'S *Peerage*); *m.* Mabel (who died), *d.* of Henry Corsley. *Educ.*: Eton. *War Work*: Served Reserve Batt. Grenadier Guards, 1914–19. *Address*: Battle Abbey, Sussex. *Clubs*: Guards'; Bachelors'; Authors'. (O7833)

WEBSTER, Avice, M.B.E., *b.* 30 Oct. 1863; *d.* of the late Thomas Webster, Q.C., of 2, Pump Court Temple. *Educ.*: Notting Hill High School. *War Work*: Hon. Organising Sec. of voluntary workers in scheme for quick meals at Coffee Stalls in Royal Arsenal, Woolwich, under Welfare Supervision Dept. of the Arsenal, June, 1915, to Jan. 1919. *Address*: 46, Brunswick Gardens, Kensington. (M4069)

WEBSTER, Major Charles Robert, O.B.E.

WEBSTER, Lieut. Frank Coutts, O.B.E., R.A.O.C.

WEBSTER, George, O.B.E., *b.* 22 June, 1870; *s.* of George Webster, of Rochdale; *m.* Mary, *d.* of Joseph Butterworth, of Rochdale. *Educ.*: Privately. General Manager of Tramways. *War Work*: Hon. Sec. 1915–16, afterwards Member of Board of Management, Rochdale Area, Munitions Board, and Rochdale National Shell Factory; organised War Savings in Munition Factories in Rochdale Area, representing the Ministry of Munitions. *Address*: 342, Edenfield Road, Rochdale. (O3980)

WEBSTER, Capt. George Frederick Anderson, O.B.E., R.A.O.C.

WEBSTER, Georgina, M.B.E.

WEBSTER, Capt. Godfrey George, O.B.E., R.N.

WEBSTER, Gustavus William, M.B.E.

WEBSTER, Major Harold Weatherald, O.B.E., Can. A.S.C. (M.T.)

WEBSTER, James Alexander, M.B.E.

WEBSTER, Capt. John Alexander, C.B.E., M.V.O., *b.* 1874; *s.* of John Webster, Bar.-at-Law, of Southband, Newton Abbot; *m.* Lalia, *d.* of the Hon. Mr. Justice Wallace Graham, of Halifax, Nova Scotia. Entered R.N. 1887; Lieut. 1895; Com. 1907; Capt. 1914; was Navigating Com. of "Indomitable" during Prince of Wales's visit to Canada, 1908; subsequently Naval Assist. Navigation Depart., Admiralty. (C1957)

WEBSTER, Lieut. and Qr.-Mr. Joseph Henry, M.B.E., M.C.

WEBSTER, Dame May, D.B.E., *d.* of Alfred Whitty, Journalist and Writer; *m.* Ben Webster, *s.* of William Shakespeare Webster. *Educ.*: Privately. Actress. *War Work*: Chairman, British Women's Hospitals Committee, Three Arts Women's Employment Fund, Era War Distress Fund, United Suffragists Women's War Club, Theatrical Ladies' Guild, and Actresses' Franchise League; worked on Women's Emergency Corps, and helped to organise many charity entertainments. *Address*: 31, Bedford Street, Strand. *Clubs*: Three Arts; International Women's Franchise. (D21)

WEBSTER, Lieut. Noel Edwin, O.B.E., M.C.

WEBSTER, Violet Helen, M.B.E.

WEBSTER, William, C.B.E., J.P., *b.* 21 Sept. 1866; *s.* of Wm. Webster, of Springburn, Glasgow, and Fraserburgh, Aberdeenshire; *m.* Mary Russell, *d.* of Wm. Hughes, of Springburn, Glasgow. *Educ.*: Glasgow. General Sec. Scottish Liberal Federation; Hon. Sec. Scottish Home Rule Council. *War Work*: Joint Chief Organiser of Joint Political Voluntary Recruiting Committee; Deputy Commissioner for Scotland of National Service Department (Agricultural Section); Member of first Scottish War Savings Committee; Scottish War Aims Committee; and other National work. *Clubs*: Scottish Liberal (Edinburgh); Glasgow Liberal (Glasgow); National Liberal. (C665)

WEDD, Major Aubrey Pattisson Wallman, O.B.E., R.E.

WEDDERBURN, Alexander Dundas Ogilvy, C.B.E., K.C., J.P., *b.* 7 Aug. 1854; *s.* of James Alexander Wedderburn, of Auchterhouse, Forfarshire; *m.* Mathilde (who died, 1898), *d.* of Henry William Segelcke. *Educ.*: Haileybury; Balliol Coll., Oxford. Recorder of Gravesend, 1897; a Bencher of the Inner Temple, 1908; one of the leaders of the Parliamentary Bar; Joint Editor (with the late Sir Edward T. Cook, K.B.E.) of the Library Edition of Ruskin, 1903–12. *War Work*: Worked in the Enquiry for the Wounded and Missing Department of the Red Cross Society, and was Director of the London Area of that Department from Jan. 1916, till April, 1919. *Address*: 8, Ormonde Gate, Chelsea, S.W. 3; The Hoo, Willingdon, Sussex. *Clubs*: Travellers'; St. Stephen's; Society of Dilettanti. (C3033)

WEDDERBURN, Charles David St. Clair, O.B.E.

WEDDERBURN, Henry Kellerman Hamilton, O.B.E.

WEDDERBURN, Robert Rowell, O.B.E.

WEDDERBURN, Ernest MACLAGAN-, O.B.E., W.S., D.Sc., *b.* 3 Feb. 1884; *s.* of A. S. Maclagan-Wedderburn, of Pearsie; *m.* Mary, *d.* of the Rev. T. S. Goldie, of Granton. *Educ.*: Edinburgh Univ. Member of firm of Carment, Wedderburn, and Watson, W.S., Edinburgh; Hon. Sec. Scottish Meteorological Society. *War Work*: Meteorologist attached to Headquarters at Gallipoli and Salonica; thereafter Assistant Supt. of Experiments, Shoeburyness. *Address*: 6, Succoth Gardens, Edinburgh. *Clubs*: Caledonian; Caledonian U.S. (Edinburgh). (O3981)

WEDDERSPOON, Lieut. Arthur Alexander, M.B.E., R.E.

WEDGWOOD, Mary Euphrazia, M.B.E.; *d.* of Godfrey Wedgwood, of Idlerocks, Stone, Staffs. *Educ.*: St. Leonards School, St. Andrews. *War Work*: V.A.D., Mrs. Watkin's Canteens for the Italian wounded on the Isonzo Front; British soldiers' clubs in the forward area of the Italian Expeditionary Force; awarded Italian Military Cross. *Addresses*: 120, St. James' Court, London, S.W. 1; Idlerocks, Stone, Staffs. *Club*: Albemarle. (M10004)

WEDLAKE, John, M.B.E.

WEEDALL, John, M.B.E.

WEEKES, Capt. Henry Holman, O.B.E., M.D., M.R.C.S. (Eng.), L.R.C.P. (Lond.), *b.* 1868; *s.* of Henry Weekes, J.P., C.A., M.R.C.S. (Eng.), L.R.C.P. (Edin.), of Mansion House, Old Brompton, Kent; *m.* Constance, *d.* of Sir Francis Hicks, J.P., D.L., of Oakfield, Streatham Hill, London. *Educ.*: Eastbourne Coll.; Epsom Coll.; Univ. Coll. Hospital, London. Late Physician to St. Bartholomew's Hospital, Rochester. *War Work*: Commanding Officer to Military Ambulance Trains in England and France, for 4 years; Examining Recruits during the first 5 months of war. *Address*: West Hill, Ottery St. Mary, Devon. (O7835)

WEEKES, Lieut.-Col. Henry Wilson, D.S.O., O.B.E., *b.* 1870; *s.* of the late Rev. W. J. Weekes. Entered R.E. 1888; Major, 1907; Lieut.-Col. 1915; served in Chitral Relief Force, 1895 (medal with clasp); Great War, 1915–19 (despatches twice). (O3202)

WEEKS, Major Harold Ernest, O.B.E.

WEEKS, Percy Frank, M.B.E., *b.* 9 Oct. 1871; *s.* of Frank Weeks, of Newport, Isle of Wight; *m.* 1st, Eveline Ada Chapman, 2nd, Ethel Adelaide Farmer. *Educ.*: Newport Grammar School. *War Work*: Inspector, Ramsgate Special Constabulary. *Address*: 1, Queen Street, Ramsgate. (M10007)

WEGENER, Capt. John Frederick William, M.B.E., A.I.F.

WEGUELIN, Ethel Mary Josephine, Mrs., C.B.E., *b.* 1862; *d.* of Thomas Fuller, of 13, Chesterfield Street, Mayfair; *m.* Arthur Gerald, *s.* of Thomas M. Weguelin, of 44, Grosvenor Gardens, S.W. *Educ.*: Privately. Lady of Grace of the Order of St. John of Jerusalem. *War Work*: Organiser and Hon. Sec. of War Hospital Supply Depots, Isle of Wight, 1915–17; Hon. Organising Sec. Officers' Record Department Central Prisoners of War Committee April, 1917 to March, 1919. *Address*: 23, Pelham Crescent, S.W. 7. *Club*: Ladies' Automobile. (C3034)

WEHNER, Major Arthur Francis Percival, O.B.E., R.G.A., *b.* 15 March, 1883; *s.* of Percival A. H. Wehner, of Eastbourne; *m.* Phyllis, *d.* of the late Lieut.-Col. R. Holyoake, R.A.M.C. *Educ.*: Wellington Coll., and Royal Military Academy. *War Work*: Served with B.E.F., France; Instructor in Gunnery, Central Siege School, Lydd; 1914 Star; G.S. Medal; Victory Medal. *Address*: c/o Messrs. Cox & Co., 16, Charing Cross, S.W. 1. *Club*: Junior Army and Navy. (O7836)

WEIGALL, Lieut. Graham Selwyn, O.B.E., R.N.R.

WEIGALL, Rachel Priscilla, M.B.E., *b.* 21 Aug. 1879; *d.* of Henry Weigall, of Southwood House, Ramsgate. *War Work*: 4 years' service as Sec. (Aug. 1914, to April, 1916), Quartermaster (April, 1916, to Aug. 1917), and Commandant (Aug. 1917) to Kent 2 V.A.D. Hospital, Ramsgate; in charge of Canteen and Medical Huts for Women Workers at Richboro' Camp, March, 1918, to Nov. 1918. (M4070)

WEIGALL, Reginald Edward, O.B.E., M.B.

WEIGHELL, Walter, M.B.E., *b.* 25 Sept. 1880; *s.* of James J. Weighell, of Stocksfield, Northumberland. *Educ.*: Newcastle-on-Tyne. Second Division Clerk in Foreign Office, from April, 1899; Assistant Registrar, Foreign Office, Feb. 1920. *War Work:* In Registry of Foreign Office. *Address:* Glenleigh, 285, Abbey Road, Belvedere, Kent. (M1076)

WEIGHILL, Allice, Mrs., M.B.E.

WEIGHTNMA, Fleet-Surg. Alfred Ernest, O.B.E., R.N.

WEIGHTMAN, Lieut. Reginald, M.B.E., Can. A.S.C.

WEINTHAL, Leo, O.B.E.; Chevalier of the Order of the Crown of Belgium.

WEIR, Lieut. David Alexander, M.B.E.

WEIR, Edith Margaret Mary, M.B.E. *War Work:* Ministry of Munitions; Foreign Office; Ministry of Pensions. (M10009)

WEIR, George Jackson, M.B.E., *b.* 6 July, 1882; *s.* of Walter Weir, Merchant, of Glasgow; *m.* Marguerita Isabella (who died), *d.* of Henry Moncrieffe Guthrie, of Perth, Scotland. *Educ.:* Glasgow. Chief Accountant, British Cellulose and Chemical Manufacturing Co., Ltd., London and Spondon, Derbyshire. *War Work:* Joined special costing staff of Ministry of Munitions of War in Sept. 1915, from Nobel's Explosives Co., Ltd., Glasgow; Director of National Factories' Cost Statistics till Jan. 1920. *Address:* Hermiston, Stepps, Lanarkshire. (M1077)

WEIR, Brig.-Gen. James George, C.M.G., C.B.E., *b.* 1862. Is Lieut.-Col. R.F.A.; T. Brig.-Gen.; served in Great War, 1914–19 (Order of Crown of Italy, Legion of Honour). (C1910)

WEIR, Lieut. John, O.B.E., R.N.V.R.

WEIR, Lieut. Col. Peter, O.B.E., *b.* 4 Oct 1892; *s.* of the late J. W. A. Weir, I.C.S., of Sulby, Isle of Man; *m.* Margaret Isobel, *d.* of the late Francis Robinson Watson, of the Bank of Madras. *Educ.:* Cheltenham Coll.; Wadham Coll., Oxford. Settler, Kenya Colony. *War Work:* R.A.S.C., France, 1914–16, with Indian and British Cavalry; 1917–19, Mesopotamia and Persia; subsequently commanding No. 5 M.T. Column (mentioned in despatches). *Addresses:* Inversburg, Nakuru, Kenya Colony; Sulby, Isle of Man. (O4262)

WEIR, Lieut. Robert J., O.B.E., R.N.R.

WEIR, Capt. Robert Yaxley, O.B.E.

WEIR, Major Thomas Duncan, M.B.E., R.E.

WEIR, William Goold, O.B.E., M.I.N.A., *b.* March, 1862; *s.* of James Weir, of Glasgow; *m.* Mary Goold, *d.* of John Kerr, of Glasgow. *Educ.:* Glasgow Univ. Engineer and Boilermaker; partner in the firm of David Rowan & Co., who were engaged in work for the Admiralty almost exclusively during the whole period of the war. *Addresses:* 190, Nithsdale Road, Glasgow; 231, Elliot Street, Glasgow. *Club:* Liberal (Glasgow). (O849)

WELBORN, George Coulson, O.B.E.

WELBY, Lieut.-Col. Sir Alfred Cholmeley Earle, K.B.E., J.P., *b.* 22 Aug. 1849; *s.* of Sir Glynne Earle Welby, Bart., of Denton Hall, Grantham (*see* BURKE'S *Peerage*); *m.* Alice Désirée, *d.* of A. E. Copland Griffiths, of Meadow Bank, Melksham. *Educ.:* Eton Coll. Lieut.-Col. Commanding Royal Scots Greys, 1892–96; has Order of St. Anne of Russia, 2nd Class and jewelled; M.P. for Taunton, 1895–1906. *War Work:* Sec. Royal Patriotic Fund Corporation; Acting Sec. War Pensions Statutory Committee, 1915–16. *Addresses:* 18, Chester Street, Belgrave Square, S.W. 1; The Mill House, Stowford, Bradford-on-Avon. *Clubs:* Carlton; 1900. (K114)

WELCH, George, M.B.E.

WELCH, Joseph Hubbard, M.B.E., *b.* 18 Nov. 1873; *s.* of Joseph Welch, of Laglands, Reigate; *m.* Violet Lee, *d.* of James Dickson, D.L., of Miltown House, Dungannon. *Educ.:* Winchester. *War Work:* Hon. Sec. British Red Cross Society and Order of St. John of Jerusalem for City of Derry and County of Donegal. *Address:* Dunruadh, Londonderry. *Clubs:* Northern Counties (Londonderry); Junior Constitutional. (M10011)

WELCH, Lilian Emily, M.B.E.

WELCH, Leiut, Maurice Cleary, M.B.E., Aust. A.O.C.

WELCH, Jessie Muriel KEMP-, M.B.E.; *d.* of Charles Durant Kemp-Welch, J.P., D.L., of 2, Porchester Gate, W. 2. *War Work:* Commandant of Paddington V.A.D. Orthopædic Hospital, April, 1916, to July, 1919. *Address:* 30, St. Mary's Mansions, W. 2. *Club:* Ladies' V.A.D. (M4071)

WELCH, John Howard KEMP-, M.B.E., *b.* 1881; *s.* of C. D. Kemp-Welch, J.P., D.L., of Sunningdale. *Educ.:* Eton, and Univ. Coll., London. Engineer. *War Work:* Superintending production of Mines and Depth Charges. *Address:* 20, The Avenue, Beckenham, Kent. (M629)

WELCHMAN, Capt. Godfrey de Vere, O.B.E., R.F.A., *b.* 20 Aug. 1894; *s.* of Rev. H. de Vere Welchman, M.A., of Exeter. *Educ.:* Cathedral School, Exeter; Royal Military Academy. *War Work:* 1914–19, served in France, Egypt, Gallipoli, and Mesopotamia; 3 times mentioned in despatches. *Addresses:* R.A. Mess, Bordon, Hants.; Alphington, Exeter. (O6724)

WELCHMAN, Major Sidney Chaytor, O.B.E., Chevalier of the Order of Leopold of Belgium.

WELDON, Winifred, Lady, O.B.E.; *d.* of the late Col. Varty Rogers, of Broxmore Park, Hants.; *m.* Col. Sir Anthony Arthur Weldon, 6th Bart. (who died) (*see* BURKE'S *Peerage*). Organised war work and war collections in Co. Kildare, in the absence on service of her husband, who was Lord Lieutenant of the County; collected considerable sums of money for Queen Mary's Fund for Women, Red Cross, and for Kildare soldiers in France and Germany; organised classes for instruction in Red Cross duties, and weekly egg collections in Town Hall,

Athy; organised a committee to assist women regarding their pensions, separation allowances, and started in Co. Kildare the system of adopting Prisoners of War in Germany. *Address:* Kilmorony, Athy, Co. Kildare, Ireland. (O11583)

WELFORD, Robert Anthony Ettrick, O.B.E., *b.* 15 Sept. 1883; *s.* of Robert Welford, of North Hylton, Co. Durham; *m.* Dorothy Elaine, *d.* of Joseph Firminger, of Aldwick, Bognor. *Educ.:* Denstone Coll. Chief Investigation Officer, Ministry of Munitions, N.W. Area; Chief Conciliation Officer, N.W. Area, Wages and Arbitration Dept., Ministry of Labour. *War Work:* Settling strikes and labour disputes of all kinds. *Addresses:* Littlewood, Warlsey, Lancs.; 77, Shudehill, Manchester. (O1989)

WELLBORNE, Major Cyril de Montfort, O.B.E., I.A.

WELLER, Pilot Officer Herbert Humphries, M.B.E.

WELLESLEY, Major Cecil George, O.B.E.

WELLET, Florence Maud, Mrs., M.B.E.

WELLINGS, Major Evelyn Valentine, O.B.E., R.A.S.C.

WELLINGTON, Lieut. Robert, M.B.E., M.C.

WELLMAN, Francis Alfred, O.B.E.

WELLS, Capt. and Qr.-Mr. Arthur George, O.B.E., D.C.M. R.A.S.C.

WELLS, Major Charles Alexander, O.B.E.

WELLS, Capt. Charles Edward, M.B.E.

WELLS, Flight-Lieut. Frederick Kynaston, M.B.E., R.A.F.

WELLS, Lieut.-Col. Hardy Vesey, C.B.E. Lieut.Col. R.A.F.; served in Great War, 1914–19 (mentioned in despatches). (C1911)

WELLS, Harold Arthur Thompson, M.B.E.

WELLS, Lieut. Henry Bensley, M.B.E., *b.* 12 Jan. 1891; *s.* of Thomas Edward Wells, of 9, Petersham Terrace, S.W. 7. *Educ.:* Winchester, and Magdalen Coll., Oxford. Barrister-at-Law. *War Work:* Served in France with 6th London Bgde., R.F.A., from March, 1915, to July, 1915; Gunnery Instructor in England from Nov. 1915, to July, 1916; Eastern Command Headquarters, from July, 1916, to Oct. 1917; War Office from Oct. 1917, to Jan. 1919. *Address:* 9, Petersham Terrace, London, S.W. 7. *Clubs:* Junior Carlton; Vincents (Oxford); Leander; M.C.C. (M5720)

WELLS, James Laurence, O.B.E., *b.* 11 Sept. 1877; *s.* of Jonathan Wells, of Glasgow; *m.* Isabella Graham, *d.* of Gordon Young, of Glasgow. *Educ.:* Glasgow. *War Work:* Deputy Food Commissioner for Glasgow and West of Scotland Division of Ministry of Food; Hon. Sec. Glasgow War Savings Committee; Hon. Organiser of all Glasgow's War Loan Campaigns. *Address:* 90, Marlborough Avenue, Broomhill, Glasgow. *Club:* Constitutional (Glasgow). (O3983)

WELLS, Major John Stuart Kerr, C.B.E., *b.* 1873; *s.* of the late Capt. John Wells, of Monaghan, Ireland; *m.* Mary Florence, 3rd *d.* of the late Major C. Brenan, of Lifford, co. Donegal. Hon. Major and Dist. Resident, Nyasaland Protectorate; German E. Africa during Great War as Political Officer. *Address:* Zomba, Nyasaland. (C742)

WELLS, John Wardle, M.B.E., *b.* 18 Aug. 1881; *s.* of Richard Wells, of Ringshall, Berkhamsted; *m.* Fanny, *d.* of Francis Rogers, of Lt. Gaddesden, Berkhamsted. *Educ.:* St. John's Coll., York. Head Master, Boys' School, Abbots Langley. *War Work:* Hon. Sec. Abbots Langley War Savings Association, and Food Control Sub-Committee; Special Constable, Herts Constabulary. *Address:* School House, Abbotts Langley, Herts. (M10013)

WELLS, Capt. Joseph Douglas, O.B.E., M.B., R.A.S.C. (T.).

WELLS, Joseph Francis, M.B.E.

WELLS, Capt. Sir Lionel De Lautour, Knt. Bach., C.B., C.M.G., C.B.E., *b.* 1859; *s.* of the late W. S. Wells, of Bitterne Court, Hants; *m.* Ida Caroline, *d.* of the late Joseph Busk, of Codicote Lodge, Welwyn, Herts. *Educ.:* Cheltenham. Entered R.N. 1871; Lieut. 1881; Com. 1892; Capt. (ret.), 1901; was Ch. Officer Metropolitan Fire Brig. 1896–1903; Ch. Agent of Conservative Party, 1903–5; served during Egyptian War, 1882; Dardanelles, 1915 (despatches, D.S.M. of U.S.A.). *Address:* Houghton Lodge, Stockbridge, Hants. *Clubs:* United Service; Royal Naval (Portsmouth). (C920)

WELLS, Mildmay Francis, M.B.E., *b.* 31 Dec. 1888; *s.* of the Rev. H. M. Wells, of 17, Queen's Gate Gardens, London, S.W. *Educ.:* Eton. Banker. *War Work:* Several appointments in Ministry of Munitions, including that of Sec. Mineral Resources Development Branch; Private Sec. to Rt. Hon. Sir Lancing Worthington Evans, when Parliamentary Sec., Ministry of Munitions, and subsequently when Minister of Blockade, and Minister of Pensions. *Address:* Travellers' Club, Pall Mall. *Clubs:* Travellers'; Bachelors'; Savile. (M2624)

WELLS, Muriel Grace, Mrs., M.B.E., *b.* 25 Aug. 1892; *d.* of Josiah Beddow, of Thorverton, Devonshire; *m.* Alfred Waters, *s.* of Alfred George Wells, of Osterley Park. *Educ.:* Chateau de Blanc Pignon, Boulogne. Junior Assistant Administrator, Mobilisation Directorate, War Office. *War Work:* V.A.D., 1914–15; War Office, 1916–20. *Address:* 39, Pembroke Square, Kensington, W. 8. (M3524)

WELLS, Selkirk, M.B.E., *b.* 1878; *s.* of Frede ick Wells, of Chelmsford; *m.* Isabel Frances Barbara, *d.* of Christopher Wilson, of Rigmaden Park, Westmorland. Late Captain. *Clubs:* Bachelors'; Travellers'. (M2625)

WELLS, Capt. Stanley Walter, M.B.E., R.A.S.C.

WELLS, Sydney Herbert, C.B.E., *b.* 1865. Director-General of Department of Technical Education, Egyptian Government. *War Work:* Director of Civilian Employment for E.E.F., 1918–20 (Egypt and Palestine); mentioned in despatches. *Address :* Cairo, Egypt. *Clubs :* Royal Societies'; Turf (Cairo). (C1056)

WELLS, Thomas George Raymond, O.B.E., A.C.A., *b.* 11 Sept. 1880; *s.* of Wallace Wells, of Norwich; *m.* Ethel Blanche, *d.* of James Robinson, of London. *Educ. :* Privately. Chartered Accountant. *War Work :* Organised Inspection, Storage, and Distribution of Meat Supplies to H.M. Forces at home and abroad. *Addresses :* Lamb Building, Temple; Brampton, Huntingdon. *Clubs :* National Sporting; Huntingdon County. (O850)

WELLS, Victor Ernest, M.B.E.

WELLS, William George, M.B.E.

WELLS, Major Russell Primrose COLLINGS-, D.S.O., O.B.E., *b.* 1882; *s.* of Arthur Collings Wells, J.P., of Caddington Hall, near Dunstable. *Educ. :* Elstree, and Harrow. Major (ret.), 15th Hussars; served in Great War, 1914–19 (mentioned in despatches); assumed by deed-poll, 1919, the additional surname of Collings. *Address :* Caddington Hall, near Dunstable. *Club .* Cavalry. (O2949)

WELLS, Capt. Robert Charles OWEN-, M.B.E., M.A., *b.* 20 Dec. 1865; *s.* of Chas. Wells, M.D., of Maidenhead; *m.* Lucy Violet, *d.* of A. Dulahe, of Maidenhead. *Educ. :* Epsom Coll., and Oxford. Barrister-at-Law. *War Work :* Three years in Mesopotamia, and Adjutant of Basra and Bagdad Depot. *Address :* Castle Hill Lodge, Maidenhead. (M4939)

WELLS, Capt. Thomas Henry SANDERSON-, M.B.E., M.D., J.P., *b.* 12 March, 1871; *s.* of John Septimus Wells, of Banbury; *m.* Agnes Macpherson, *d.* of J. Macpherson Laurie, D.L., J.P., of Weymouth. *Educ. :* All Saints' School, Bloxham. Surgeon, Princess Christian Hospital, Weymouth. *War Work :* Capt., R.A.M.C., Egypt, British Red Cross Hospital, Eizeh; Capt. Dorset Volunteer Medical Corps; Surgeon, Princess Christian Hospital, and V.A.D. Dorset 38. *Address :* 14, Victoria Terrace, Weymouth. *Clubs :* County (Weymouth); Royal Automobile. (M10287)

WELMAN, Lieut.-Col. Harvey, O.B.E.

WELMAN, Helen Owen, Mrs., M.B.E.

WELSFORD, Evelyn J., M.B.E., F.L.S., F.R.M.S.; *d.* of Richard Sherring Welsford, of Ceylon. *Educ. :* Blackheath High School. Research Assistant in Plant Pathology, Imperial Coll. of Science. *War Work :* Queen Mary's Army Auxiliary Corps, as Senior Unit Administrator, Abbeville Area; served overseas from April, 1917, to Oct. 1919. *Club :* Forum. (M4624)

WELSFORD, Lieut. Herbert Gray, M.B.E., R.A.F.

WELSH, Cecile Campbell, Mrs., M.B.E.

WELSH, Major David Thomson, O.B.E.

WELSH, James Frederick, M.B.E,. R.N.

WELSH, John George, M.B.E.. R.M.

WEMYSS, Lieut.-Col. John Maurice COLCHESTER-, O.B.E.

WEMYSS, Sir (Maynard) Francis COLCHESTER-, K.B.E., D.L., J.P., *b.* 12 March, 1872; *s.* of Maynard Willoughby Colchester-Wemyss, of Westbury Court, Glos; *m.* Maria Alice, *d.* of the late General Disney Leith, C.B., of Glenkindie, Aberdeenshire. *Educ. :* Eton, and Sandhurst. Served in Scottish Rifles, 1890–1903, India, South Africa, and at home; Director Gloucester Railway Carriage and Wagon Works. *War Work :* Sec. Glos. Territorial Association. Hon. County Director, British Red Cross Society, Gloucestershire; Hon. Director of Food Economy in Auxiliary Military Hospitals, England and Wales. *Address :* Ravensworth, Cheltenham. *Clubs :* Caledonian; Fly Fishers'; New (Cheltenham). (K441)

WEMYSS, Maynard Willoughby COLCHESTER-, C.B.E., J.P., D.L., *b.* 14 Aug. 1846; *s.* of Capt. Francis Wemyss, Bombay Engineers; *m.* Mary Clere, *d.* of the Rev. E. Newton Dickenson, Chaplain, India. *Educ. :* Eton, and Woolwich Academy. Served in Royal Artillery; Chairman, Gloucestershire County Council. *War Work :* Work connected with the Gloucestershire County Council; for three years Honorary Chief Constable for the County. *Address :* Westbury Court, Westbury-on-Severn, N. Newnham, Glos. (C132)

WEMYSS, Major Robert Dunbar SINCLAIR-, O.B.E.

WENCH, Una Margaret Kerry, M.B.E., B.Sc.; *d.* of Henry Sellick Wench, of Leamington Spa. *Educ. :* Leamington High School; Birmingham Univ.; Bedford Coll., London Univ.; Cambridge Training Coll. Technical Assistant to the Engineer of the Underground Railways, 1919–20; Science Mistress, Gosport and Alverstoke Secondary School from 1920. *War Work :* Administrative Assistant in the Priority Department, Ministry of Munitions, Dec. 1916–18; Director of Food Machinery Sub-section, 1918–19. *Addresses :* Bedford House, York Place, Portman Square, W.1; 60, Warwick St. West, Leamington Spa. (M10014)

WENHAM, Basil Eliot, O.B.E.

WENLEY, George Seton Veitch, M.B.E.

WENN, Lieut. Frederick William, O.B.E., R.N.

WENSLEY, Frederick Porter, M.B.E., *b.* 28 March, 1865; *s.* of George Wensley, Stogumber, Somerset; *m.* Laura Elizabeth, *d.* of William Martin, of Hadlow, Kent. Detective Supt. Metropolitan Police, New Scotland Yard, S.W.; awarded the King's Police Medal. *War Work :* Assisted in the investigation of the causes of many of the explosions on land and sea; effecting the arrest of numerous persons for conspiring to defeat the Military Service Act; assisted in the enforcing of the Alien Enemies Act, and other similar services. *Address :* Lucholm, 22, Powys Lane, Palmers Green, London, N. (M18015)

WENTWORTH, Joseph, M.B.E., A.M.I.C.E., *b.* 23 Nov. 1862; *s.* of Edward Wentworth, of East Leaze, Aldbourne, Wiltshire. Civil Engineer and connected for many years with the British Gas Light Co. at Hull, Portsea Island Gas Works, Portsmouth, and Aldershot Gas and Water Co., Aldershot. *War Work :* Assistant Inspector of Gun Ammunition in the Inspection Department of Woolwich Arsenal and in charge of the Birmingham Area of that Department in the Empty Fuse Section. *Address :* East Leaze, Baydon, R.S.O., Wilts. (M10016)

WENYON, Col. Charles Morley, C.M.G., C.B.E., M.B., B.Sc.; *s.* of the Rev. C. Weynon, M.D. *Educ. :* Univ. Coll., London. Lieut.-Col. and T. Col. R.A.M.C. *Address :* 7, Vallance Road, Alexandra Park, Wood Green, N 22. (C1421)

WERNER, Edmund Arthur Robert, O.B.E., B.A., *b.* 19 April, 1872; *s.* of Robert Werner, of Lee, Kent; *m.* Annie Christian MacRitchie, *d.* of Robert Kilgour, of Glasgow. *Educ. :* Blackheath, and St. John's Coll., Cambridge. H.M. Inspector of Factories. *War Work :* Chairman of Standing Joint Committee of Employers and Operatives (for Recruiting), Pottery Industry, and of Leek Textile Trades; Hon. Member, Pottery National Council, and Chairman of Demobilisation Committee. *Addresses :* Basford, Stoke-on-Trent; Town Hall Chambers, Stoke-on-Trent. (O852)

WESLEY, Major Frank William, O.B.E., M.D., B.S. (Lond.), *b.* 6 Nov. 1869; *s.* of Wm. Hy. Wesley, of R.A.S., Burlington House, Piccadilly, London, W. *Educ. :* University Coll., London; Univ. Coll. Hospital. *War Work :* T. Capt. in the R.A.M.C. 4½ years; 4 years' overseas service in Malta, on Western Front, and with the Rhine Army. *Address :* 4, Oxford Street, Nottingham. *Clubs :* Nottingham and Nott United Services. (O5911)

WEST, Major Arthur John, O.B.E., T.D., *b.* 12 April, 1873; *s.* of George West, of Beechwood, Dunstable; *m.* Daisy Margaret, *d.* of Arthur William Larkman, of Kensington. *Educ. :* Emanuel School. Managing Director, Cubitt Estates, Ltd.; Military Member of Surrey Territorial Force Association from 1919; Member of Wandsworth Borough Council from 1912; Hon. Clerk to Lord Lieutenant of Surrey's Magisterial Advisory Committee from 1911; Member 2nd Vol. Batt. Royal Fusiliers from 1896 to 1901, Surrey (Q.M.R.) Yeomanry, 1901–20. *War Work :* Surrey (Q.M.R.) Yeomanry in England Aug. 1914, to May, 1915; Staff Appointment, May. 1915, to July, 1916 (England and France); Special Investigation Officer, Ministry of Munitions, July, 1916, to Jan. 1917; Director in Ministry of Food, Jan. 1917, to Dec. 1919. *Address :* 175, King's Avenue, Clapham Park, S.W. 12. *Club :* Junior Constitutional. (O11585,

WEST, Hon. Mrs. Augustus William, O.B.E.

WEST, Charles, M.B.E.

WEST, Lieut.-Col. Charles James, O.B.E., M.D., R.A.M.C., *b.* 10 Aug. 1863; *s.* of James West, of Shepton Mallet, Somerset; *m.* Mary Morrison, *d.* of J. Milling, of Harrogate. *Educ. :* King's Coll., London. Doctor of Medicine. *War Work :* Four years in Southern Command. *Address :* Hermitage, Newbury, Berkshire. (O7840)

WEST, David Cockburn, M.B.E., *b.* 5 Oct. 1879; *s.* of Charles West, of Wallsend; *m.* Sarah Ann, *d.* of William Robinson, of Barrow-in-Furness. Assistant District Sec., Rechabites Friendly Society and Approved Society; Hon. worker in Church and Sunday School and Social Centre work. *War Work :* Hon. Sec. from inception of Wallsend Savings Committee, responsible for organising the various War Loan Campaigns, and War Food Economy Campaign; Member of Food Control and Fuel Committees; actively connected with local appeals for War Relief Fund, Queen Mary's Guild, etc. *Address :* 16, Rochdale Street, Wallsend-on-Tyne. (M10017)

WEST, Dora, O.B.E.; *d.* of Alderman W. H. West, J.P., of Holbeach, Lincs. From 1919, Sec. to the Food Controller, the Right Hon. C. A. McCurdy, K.C., M.P. *War Work :* 1916–18, Sec. to Military Representative, County Appeal Tribunal, Monmouthshire; Hon. Sec., Monmouthshire Women's Recruiting Committee. *Address :* 21, Lexham Gardens, W. 8. *Club :* Forum. (O11586)

WEST, Edward, M.B.E., *b.* 5 Oct. 1859; *s.* of Edward West, late of New Brompton, Kent; *m.* Emma Charlotte, *d.* of John Nunn, of Stowmarket, Suffolk. *Educ. :* Royal Engineers School, Brompton. Superintendent of " W " Division, Metropolitan Police, Brixton. *War Work :* In connection with Aliens, and Air Raids, during the whole period of war. *Address :* 90, Helix Road, Brixton, London, S.W. 2. (M10018)

WEST, Ellen, M.B.E.,

WEST, Frederick Joseph, C.B.E. Director and General Manager, West's Gas Improvement Co., Ltd.; Manager of Munitions Board of Management during the Great War. (C3035)

WEST, Frederick William, O.B.E., *b.* 21 April, 1860; *s.* of Thomas West, of Calverton, Bucks. *Educ. :* Privately. Lecturer on Railway Economics, London and Manchester; Chairman of Inter-departmental Government and Railway Advisory Committee, Fruit and Vegetables. *War Work :* Re-organisation of Military and Naval Transport at Boulogne, 1915; expert adviser to Port and Transit Committee on manipulation of Shipping Traffic at Ports, 1916; directing handling of war material in the London area during the course of the war. *Addresses :* Hayes Lea, Bromley, Kent; S.E. & C. Railway, Superintendent's Office, Victoria Station. (O11587)

WEST, Major George Frederick Parrett, C.B.E., R.E.

WEST, George Philip, O.B.E., *b.* 14 April, 1867; *s.* of

the late George West, of Gillingham, Kent ; *m.* Rose, *d.* of the late Frederick Boorman, of New Brompton. *Educ.*: Commercial School, New Brompton, and Royal Dockyard School, Chatham. Director of Archibald Russell, Ltd., Coalmasters, Director of other Limited Companies. General Manager, Messrs. David Colville & Sons, Ltd., Glengarnock Works, Scotland. *War Work :* Chief Steel Superintendent, for all Steel producing districts in Great Britain, and served under directions of Admiralty and Ministry of Munitions. *Address :* Barrington House, Beith, Ayrshire, Scotland.   (O1991)

WEST, James Grey, M.B.E.

WEST, James Hales, M.B.E. *b.* 10 Aug. 1862. Superintendent, Metropolitan Police (retired). *War Work :* Many additional phases of police work brought about by the War. *Address :* 24, Albion Road, Clapham, S.W. 8.   (M1079)

WEST, John Edward, O.B.E., *b.* 17 June, 1855 ; *s.* of Hugh Brookshaw West, of Congleton, Cheshire, and Stoke-on-Trent ; *m.* Corinda Dight, *d.* of Richard Pengelly Almond, of Newark-on-Trent. *Educ.:* Stoke-on-Trent. Land Agent. *War Work :* Commandant Scopwick House Auxiliary Hospital, Lincolnshire, 1914–19. *Address :* Blankney, Lincoln. (O11588)

WEST, Leonard Henry, O.B.E., LL.D., C.A., J.P., *b.* 1864 ; *s.* of Edward Henry West, of Glenrock, Brough, East Yorks. *Educ.:* Privately, and London Univ. Vice-Chairman, Bucks County Council ; Chairman, Bucks County Insurance Committee ; President, Mid-Bucks Unionist Association ; Member of the Central Midwives Board. *War Work :* Chairman Bucks War Pensions Committee, and of Agricultural Executive Committee ; Deputy Chairman Bucks Agricultural Wages Committee. *Address :* Quinton Cottage, Bucks. *Club :* Junior Constitutional.   (O11589)

WEST, Lieut.-Col. Richard Melbourne, O.B.E., D.S.O., M.D., M.R.C.S., L.R.C.P. Served in Great War (mentioned in despatches).   (O7841)

WEST, Stanley George Norman, M.B.E., *b.* 12 June, 1878 ; *s.* of the late George Norman West, of Rochester, Kent. Supervising Clerk, War Office. Served with Imperial Yeomanry (Rough Riders) in South African War, 1900–1902 ; employed at War Office during the Great War. *Address :* Normanhurst, 50, Homefield Road, Chiswick, W. 4.   (M10020)

WEST, Capt. Stewart Ellis Lawrence, C.M.G., O.B.E.

WEST, Capt. Thomas Samuel, M.B.E.

WEST, Capt. William George, M.B.E.

WEST, Lieut. William Tom, O.B.E., R.N.R.

WEST, Major-Gen. the Hon. Sir Charles John, SACK-VILLE-, K.B.E., C.M.G. ; *b.* 10 Aug. 1870 ; *s.* of Lieut.-Col. William Edward Sackville-West ; *m.* Maude Cecilia, *d.* of late Capt. Matthew John Bell, of Bourne Park, Kent (*see* BURKE'S *Landed Gentry*). *Educ. :* Winchester, and R.M.C. Formerly Col. K.R.R.C. ; British Military Representative on late Allied War Council, and a Member of the Army Council ; served in Manipur Expedition 1891 (mentioned in despatches) ; S. Africa, 1899 as A.D.C. to Gen. the Right Hon. Sir R. H. Buller, G.C.B., K.C.M.G. (mentioned in despatches). European War, 1914–17 (mentioned in despatches).   (K283)

WESTACOTT, William John Henry, M.B.E., R.N.

WESTAWAY, Richard Ernest, O.B.E., J.P.

WESTBROOK, G. L. : *see* Weaver G. L., Mrs.

WESTBURY, Lieut. Frederick Newell, O.B.E., R.E.

WESTCAR, Major Charles Henry Beeston PRESCOTT-, O.B.E., *b.* 16 May, 1881 ; *s.* of Charles William Prescott-Westcar, of Strode Park, Herne, Kent ; *m.* Sara Judith, *d.* of Major-General W. E. Warrand, R.E., of Westhorpe Hall, Notts. *Educ. :* Wellington Coll. ; Sandhurst Coll. J.P. for Kent, 1903 ; late Lieut. 14th Hussars ; Farming and Engineering. *War Work :* Mobilised with Royal East Kent Yeomanry, 1914 ; Staff, 1915–17 ; Tank Corps, 1917 ; Inspector of Guns, 1918. *Address :* Strode Park, Herne, Kent. *Club :* Orleans.   (O7594)

WESTCOTT, Lieut.-Col. George, O.B.E

WESTCOTT, Lieut. George Henry, M.B.E., *b.* 21 Dec. 1888 ; *s.* of G. C. Westcott, of Bristol ; *m.* Marion, *d.* of M. L. Fry, of Oldlands, near Bristol. *Educ. :* Bristol. Railway Carriage Engineer. *War Work :* Workshops of R.A.S.C. (M.T.) *Address :* Montacute Villa, 25, Ashley Hill, Bristol. (M5722)

WESTCOTT, John Richard, M.B.E.

WESTELL, Benjamin, M.B.E.

WESTELL, Edgar Lawton, M.B.E.

WESTERN, Lieut. James George, M.B.E., R.A.F.

WESTERN, Col. John Sutton Edward, C.B.E. Col. Indian Army (ret.) ; Waziri Expedition, 1881 ; Hazara Expedition, 1888 (despatches, medal with clasp) ; Waziristan Expedition, 1894–95 (clasp) ; N.-W. Frontier of India, 1902 ; Great War, 1914–19 (despatches).   (C1809)

WESTHEAD, Marian Lucy, M.B.E.

WESTLAKE, Frederick Arthur, O.B.E., *b.* 10 Feb. 1883 ; *s.* of the late Alfred Westlake, of Gloucester ; *m.* Annie, *d.* of the late Adam Handyside, of Edinburgh. Civil Servant. *War Work :* Employment Department, Ministry of Labour. *Address :* 36, Blenheim Gardens, Wallington, Surrey. (O1992)

WESTLAKE, John Harold, M.B.E., R.N.

WESTLAND, John Lowe, M.B.E.

WESTMACOTT, Charles Babington, O.B.E.

WESTMACOTT, Brig.-Gen. Claude Berners, C.B.E. T. Brig.-Gen., and an A.D.C. ; served in Great War, 1914–19 (mentioned in despatches).   (C1810)

WESTMACOTT, Col. Frederick Hibbart, C.B.E. Lieut.-Col. and Brevet Col. R.A.M.C. (T.) ; served in Great War, 1914–19 (mentioned in despatches).   (C1346)

WESTMACOTT, Major Herbert Horatio Spencer, O.B.E.

WESTMACOTT, James Richard, M.B.E., *b.* 11 Aug. 1856 ; *s.* of Richard Penton Westmacott, of Newbury ; *m.* Marie Teresa, *d.* of Thomas Spurway. *Educ.:* Privately. *War Work :* Special work in a department of the War Office. *Address :* 19, Deauville Road, Clapham Park, S.W. 4. (M10024)

WESTMACOTT, Major Reginald Granville, O.B.E.

WESTMACOTT, Major Thomas Horatio, O.B.E.

WESTMINSTER, the Right Reverend Adam Urias de Pencier, Bishop of, O.B.E., M.A., D.D., *b.* 9 Feb. 1866 ; *s.* of Peter Theodore de Pencier, of Marlboro', Ontario, Canada ; *m.* Nina Fredericka, *d.* of Fred Wells, Col. 1st Royals, *Educ.:* Trinity Coll., Toronto. *War Work :* Chaplain, 1915–19. *Address :* 1346, Pendrell Street, Vancouver, B.C. *Club :* Vancouver.   (O1744)

WESTMINSTER, Constance Edwina (Mrs. Lewis), Duchess of, C.B.E., *d.* of late Col. William Cornwallis-West, of Ruthin Castle, Co. Denbigh (*see* BURKE'S *Peerage*, de la West, E.) ; *m.* 1st, Sir Hugh Richard Arthur Grosvenor, G.C.V.O., D.S.O., Duke of Westminster (*see* BURKE'S *Peerage*), from whom she obtained a divorce ; 2nd, Capt. James Fitzpatrick Lewis, late R.A.F. *Address :* Annesley Bank, Lyndhurst, Hants.   (C667)

WESTMORE, Lieut.-Com. Henry George Gardiner, D.S.O., O.B.E., R.N.R. (ret.). Served in Great War, 1914–19 (mentioned in despatches).   (C9412)

WESTMORLAND, Anthony Mildmay Julian Jane, Earl of, C.B.E., *b.* 16 Aug. 1859 ; *s.* of Francis William Henry, 12th Earl of Westmorland (*see* BURKE'S *Peerage*) ; *m.* 1st, Lady Sybil Mary St. Clair-Erskine (who died 1910), *d.* of 4th Earl of Rosslyn (*see* BURKE'S *Peerage*) ; 2nd, Catharine Louise, *d.* of late Rev. John Samuel Seale. Also holds title of Baron Burghash ; J.P. Northants ; Col. and A.D.C. to the King ; Temp. Lieut.-Col. Special Reserve Lancashire Fusiliers ; late commanding 3rd Batt. Northamptonshire Regt. ; and hon. Major in the Army. *Address :* Woodstock Park, Sittingbourne, Kent. *Club.:* Marlborough.   (C836)

WESTMORLAND, Josephine, Mrs., M.B.E.

WESTON, Edith Ivy, M.B.E. ; *d.* of Sidney Cooper Weston, of Folkestone. *Educ.:* Mount School, York. Town Councillor, Folkestone. *War Work :* Superintending supply of food to Belgian refugees and soldiers on Folkestone Harbour. *Address :* 32, Sandgate Road, Folkestone. *Club :* St. Andrew's House.   (M1082)

WESTON, Right Reverend Frank, Bishop of Zanzibar, O.B.E. : *see* Zanzibar, Bishop of.

WESTON, Henry Gould, M.B.E.

WESTON, Lieut.-Col. Reginald Salter, C.M.G., O.B.E., *b.* 10 Aug. 1867 ; *s.* of William Weston, late of Abbey Wood, Kent. *Educ.:* Marlborough Coll. Joined 2nd Batt. Manchester Regt. in 1888 ; served in India, on the Punjab Frontier with the Malakand Field Force (medal and clasp, and thanks of Government of India) ; Aden, in Central Africa, with K.A.R., 1899–1900 ; Adjutant 3rd Batt. Manchester Regt., with which he served in South Africa till disbanded ; rejoined 2nd Batt. at home ; to Ireland 1909 till Aug. 1914, when he proceeded as 2nd in command with B.E.F. to France. *War Work :* Present at Mons and retreat, and many other battles ; in command of regiment at Wulverghem and Ypres, and on Somme ; mentioned in despatches ; wounded twice ; raised and commanded 12th Batt. East Lancs Regt., commanded 70th Training Reserve Battalion, 3rd Batt. Welsh Regt., attached Northern Command H.Q. York ; Commandant No. 1 Area P. of War, Eastern Command, till Nov. 1919 ; retired. *Address :* Elmsgate, Steeple Ashton, Trowbridge, Wilts. *Club :* Naval and Military.   (O7844)

WESTON, Robert Ogilvy, M.B.E.

WESTROPP, Lieut. John Francis Ralph MASSY-, M.B.E., *b.* 6 April, 1891 ; *s.* of Col. John Massy-Westropp, C.M.G., of Doonass, Clonlara, Limerick, Ireland ; *m.* Gabrielle Evelyn, *d.* of Col. C. A. S. Montgomery, of Fort Royal, Rathmullen, Co. Donegal, Ireland. *Educ.:* Cheltenham Coll. Princess Victoria's Royal Irish Fusiliers. *War Work :* France, Aug. 1914, with 1st R. Irish Fusiliers ; retreat from Mons ; 1st and 2nd Battle of Ypres ; wounded Ypres, 1915 ; left for Salonica, May, 1916 ; remained there with 2nd Batt. R. Irish Fusiliers, and as A.P.M. Salonica until Armistice ; proceeded Batum, Black Sea, Nov. 1918, as A.P.M. ; left Constantinople, June, 1919, for home, and posted 2nd Batt. R. Irish Fusiliers at Dover. *Addresses :* Doonass Clonlara, Limerick, Ireland ; Grand Shaft Barracks, Dover. *Club :* Royal Automobile.   (M4810)

WESTROPP, Capt. Richard Gibbings, O.B.E.

WESTWOOD, William, O.B.E.

WESTWOOD, Andrew, O.B.E., M.B.

WETHERALL, Major John Andrew Chilton, O.B.E., *b.* 22 March, 1862 ; *s.* of Capt. John William Wetherall, of Geddington Priory, Northamptonshire ; *m.* Annie Frances, *d.* of Major Bannister, of The Warrens, Kelvedon. *Educ.:* Privately. Northampton and Rutland Militia, 1879 ; Northamptonshire Regt. (Regular Army), 1884 ; retired 1903 ; Sec. to Northamptonshire Territorial Force Association, 1908 ; South Africa (Queen's Medal, 2 clasps). *War Work :* Preparation in readiness for war, all works connected with the duties of a Sec. of Territorial Force, such as mobilisation, recruiting, clothing, equipping, etc. ; recruiting volunteer units to take places of Territorial units serving abroad. *Address :* Billing Arborns, Moulton, Northampton.   (O853)

WETHERALL, Col. William Alexander, C.B.E., J.P.,

D.L., U.S.L. Indian Army, *b.* 8 April, 1847 ; *s.* of the Rev. J. E. Wetherall, of Brereton, Staffs ; *m.* Alice Jane, *d.* of the Rev. T. Bonney, of Rugeley. *Educ. :* The Royal Academy, Gosport ; Royal Mil. Coll., Sandhurst. Member of Territorial Force Association, Staffs ; Urban District Council, Rugeley. *War Work :* County Director, Auxiliary Hospitals, and V.A.D., Staffordshire. *Address :* 30, Church Street, Rugeley. *Club :* Junior United Service. (C3037)

WETHERED, Ernest Handel Cossham, O.B.E., M.A., LL.B., *b.* 18 July, 1878 ; *s.* of Edward Bestbridge Wethered, J.P., of Cheltenham, and Totland Bay, I. of W. ; *m.* Jessie Marian, *d.* of the late Rev. Richard Ward, Rural Dean, Vicar of St. George's, Newcastle, Staffs. *Educ. :* Cheltenham Coll. ; Pembroke Coll., Cambridge. Barrister-at-Law ; Member of Western Circuit, and of Somerset, Bristol, and Bath Sessions ; an appointed Member of Trade Boards ; Chairman of Court of Referees for Bristol Kingswood, Bath, and Trowbridge District. *War Work :* Chairman of Bristol Local Munitions Tribunal ; Chairman of Swindon Local Munitions Tribunal ; Chairman of Court of Referees for Bristol and Swindon District : Assistant Commissioner (Enforcement of Orders) S.W. Div. Ministry of Food ; assisted in forming the National Council of the Pottery Industry, the first National Joint Industrial Council under the Whitley Scheme to be recognised by the Government ; Chairman of Advisory Wages Board for Disabled Sailors and Soldiers, for the County Borough of Bristol ; Treas. of the Bristol Association for Voluntary Organisations ; Associated with the National Adult School Union, the Workers' Educational Association, and other Social and Educational work. *Addresses :* Albion Chambers, Bristol ; 2, Pump Court, Temple, E.C. ; The Avenue, Clifton, Bristol. *Clubs :* Bristol Constitutional ; Bristol Cavendish. (O11592)

WETHERED, Mina Ricketts Sarah Elizabeth, O.B.E., *b.* 1881 ; *d.* of Edward Bestbridge Wethered, J.P., of Heathercroft, Totland Bay, I. of W. *Educ. :* Cheltenham Ladies' Coll. *War Work :* Hon. Organising Sec. Voluntary Organisations, Gloucestershire and Bristol. *Address :* Heathercroft, Totland Bay, I. of W. *Club :* New Century. (O1994)

WETHERELL, Major William Edward May, O.B.E., *b.* 1 July, 1872 ; *s.* of Col. R. M. Wetherell, of St. Leonards-on-Sea ; *m.* Norah Emma Mary, *d.* of Robert Fitzgerald, of Lisheen, Co. Tipperary. *Educ. :* Cheltenham College. Regular Army, Bedfordshire Regt. (retired). *War Work :* Served with 7th Division, B.E.F. ; Instructor R.M. College ; Army Gymnastic Staff. *Address :* St. Leonard's-on-Sea. (O7845)

WETHEY, Paymaster-Lieut. Edwin Howard, O.B.E.

WEYMAN, Major Edward Colpitts, O.B.E.

WHALEY, Francis Henry, M.B.E.

WHALLEY, Frank Douglas, C.B.E. Ministry of Munitions. (C3173)

WHARHIRST, Alfred John, M.B.E., B.A., *b.* 1881 ; *s.* of John Wharhirst, of Highgate, London ; *m.* Hannah, *d.* of Peter Deuchar, of Thirsk, Yorks. *Educ. :* Stationers', Hornsey, N., and Univ. Coll. of Wales, Aberystwyth. Senior History and Geography Master, Municipal Secondary School, Lincoln. *War Work :* Hon. Sec. to Lincoln War Savings Committee. *Address :* Granville House, Carline Road, Lincoln. (M101027)

WHARTON, Charles Joseph, O.B.E., M.I.E.E., *b.* 1857 ; *s.* of Rev. C. C. Wharton, of Allesley, nr. Coventry *t m.* Mary Sybil, *d.* of James Sandys, M.D., of The Slade, Stroud, Glos., *Educ. :* Coventry, Worthing, and privately. Consulting Engineer. *War Work :* Deputy Director of Inspection under War Office and Ministry of Munitions ; Technical Inspection of shell and gun ammunition generally. *Addresses :* Bursledon, Hants ; 44, Bedford Row, London, W.C. 1. *Clubs :* St. Stephen's ; Royal Corinthian Yacht. (O854)

WHARTON, Edith Hilda, M.B.E., *b.* June, 1890 ; *d.* of Admiral Sir W. J. L. Wharton. *Educ. :* Levana School. *War Work :* Commandant of V.A.D. Hospital, Withyham, Sussex, 1914–19. *Address :* Fisher's Gate, Withyham, Sussex. *Club :* New Century (M4075)

WHARTON, Frederick Malcolm, M.B.E., F.I.C., *b.* 22 April, 1875 ; *s.* of Frederick Wharton, late of Kings Heath, Birmingham ; *m.* Juliana Hampton, *d.* of William B. Stokes, of Newent, Glos. *Educ. :* King Edward VI. School, Camp Hill, Birmingham ; Univ., Birmingham. Metallurgical and Technical Chemist ; Director and Works Manager to the Hall Street Metal Rolling Co., Western Road, Birmingham. *War Work :* Works Manager to the New Explosives Co., Ltd., Stowmarket, Suffolk ; Manufacturing Cordite, Guncotton, Aeroplane Dope, etc. *Address :* 74, Stanmore Road, Edgbaston, Birmingham. *Club :* Camp Hill Old Edwardians. (M2631)

WHARTON, Frederick Percival, O.B.E.

WHARTON, Major Richard George, O.B.E., R.M.L.I.

WHARTON, Capt. Stanley, O.B.E.

WHARTON, Col. William Henry Anthoney, O.B.E., V.D., T.D., J.P., D.L., A.D.C. to the King. *b.* Nov. 1859, *s.* of J. T. Wharton, of Skelton Castle ; *m.* Elizabeth Sophia Mytton, *d.* of the late Rev. Robert John Harrison, of Caerhowel, Montgomeryshire. *Educ. :* Eton and Cambridge. *War Work :* Commanded 4th (Reserve) Yorkshire Regt., and 24th Provisional Bn. ; Group Commandant, N.R.Y. Volunteers. *Address :* Skelton Castle, Skelton - in - Cleveland. *Clubs :* Bachelors' ; Boodle's ; Carlton. (O855)

WHATLEY, Capt. Norman, M.B.E.

WHATMAN, Florence Emma Jemima, O.B.E. ; *d.* of James Whatman, of Vinters, Maidstone. *War Work :* Hon. Treasurer and Sec. Soldiers' and Sailors' Families Association, Bearsted and Maidstone Division ; Hon. Treas. War Pensions, Maidstone Sub-Committee. (O11594)

WHAYMAN, Engineer-Capt. William Matthias, C.B.E., R.N. Engineer Manager, Rosyth Dockyard ; sometime Chief Engineer, Pembroke Dockyard. *Address :* H.M. Dockyard, Rosyth. (C2327)

WHEAT, Thomas Milnes, M.B.E., B.A., Lond., *b.* 22 Sept. 1876 ; *s.* of Rev. J. M. Wheat, of 84, Lee Road, Blackheath ; *m.* Constance Mary, *d.* of the late Rev. C. G. Wheat. *Educ. :* Montpellier School, Paignton. *War Work :* Hon. Treas. and Chief Clerk, City of Lincoln War Pensions Committee ; Hon. Sec. Incorporated Soldiers' and Sailors' Help Society, Lincoln. *Address :* Tarleton House, Woodhall Spa. (M10028)

WHEATLEY, Capt. Christopher William, M.B.E.

WHEATLEY, Major Henry Harold, O.B.E., M.C., R.E.

WHEATLEY, Major Mervyn James, O.B.E. ; Sudan Civil Service, late Dorset Regt. *Address :* Windholme, Parkstone, Dorset. (O4122)

WHEATLEY, Thomas Angas, M.B.E., *b.* 5 April, 1855 ; *s.* of Thomas Hodgson Wheatley, of Rotherham, Yorks. ; *m.* Edith, *d.* of Charles B. James, of Redditch. *Educ. :* Privately. *War Work :* Engineering in special reference to appliances for destroying U boats. *Address :* Neswick, Wimbledon Common. *Club :* St. Stephen's. (M1083)

WHEBLE, Ursula Mary, M.B.E., *b.* 1862 ; *d.* of James Wheble, of Bulmershe Court, Reading, and Lady Catherine Wheble (*see* BURKE'S *Peerage*, Howth E.). *Educ. :* Privately. *War Work :* Superintendent, War Hospital Supplies Depot, Reading. *Address :* Hungerford Lodge, Reading. (M2632)

WHEELER, Annie Margaret, Mrs., O.B.E.

WHEELER, Arthur George, M.B.E.

WHEELER, Major Charles, O.B.E. M.I.A.E., F.R.S.A.: *b.* 2 Aug. 1875 ; *s.* of William Wheeler, of Westminster ; *m.* Jane, *d.* of Joseph Hadley, of Northampton. *Educ. :* City of Westminster School. Chief Automobile Engineer, General Post Office. *War Work :* Officer-in-Charge, Inspection Branch R.A.S.C.(M.T.), Aldershot, 1914 ; laid out and appointed Officer in charge of American Spare Parts Depot, London, 1916 ; and Sub-Depots, Home M.T.D. London ; devised store Accounting System for Mechanical Transport Stores ; subsequently adopted in all Depots. *Address :* Casula, Bushey Grove Road, Bushey, Herts. (O7846)

WHEELER, Lieut.-Col. Charles Alexander, O.B.E., R.E.

WHEELER, Capt. Douglas Bingham, M.B.E., A.I.F.

WHEELER, Edith Mary, C.B.E., *b.* 3 Oct. 1867 ; *d.* of Seaton Forrest Milligan, M.R.I.A., of Bangor, Co. Down ; *m.* George Herbert, *s.* of the late Thos. Kennedy Wheeler, M.D., of Belfast. *Educ. :* Belfast and Hanover. *War Work :* Aug. 4 1914, to Jan. 1919, Hon. Sec. to War Hospital Supply Committee, Belfast, which distributed help to local and foreign hospitals, ambulances, hospital ships, and to Belgian, French, and Servian Reliefs ; also gave honorary services in the translation of foreign documents and papers. *Address :* Thornhill Gardens, Marlborough Park, Belfast. (C3038)

WHEELER, Edward Thomas, M.B.E.

WHEELER, Col. Edward Vincent Vashon, O.B.E., J.P., D.L., *b.* 3 June, 1858 ; *s.* of Edward Vincent Wheeler, of Kyrewood, Tenbury ; *m.* Elizabeth Ellen Winwood, *d.* of Sir Wm. Smith, Bart., late of Eardiston, Worcestershire. *Educ. :* Eton and Trinity Coll., Tenbury. Farmer and Landowner ; Vice-Chairman, Worcestershire County Council. *War Work :* Commanding 2/7th Battalion Worcestershire Regt. ; Chairman, Worcestershire War Agricultural Committee. *Address :* Newnham Court, Tenbury. (O1995)

WHEELER, George Herbert, M.B.E., A.M.Inst.Y., *b.* 4 June, 1881 ; *s.* of George Wheeler, of Old Charlton, Kent ; *m.* Alice, *d.* of Philip Keates, of Wimbledon, Surrey. *Educ. :* Roan Grammar School, Greenwich, and London School of Economics. Assist.-Sec. Railway Executive Committee (Board of Trade), from July, 1917 ; Sec. to that Committee from June, 1919 ; Sec. to Committee of Railway General Managers from Jan. 1920. *Addresses :* 35, Parliament Street, Westminster, S.W. 1 ; 10, Stanley Road, Wimbledon, S.W. (M10030)

WHEELER, Rev. Harold William, O.B.E.

WHEELER, Henry Charles, M.B.E., *b.* 7 March, 1877 ; *s.* of Francis Wheeler, of Hounslow ; *m.* Adelaide, *d.* of John David Darling, of Twickenham. *Educ. :* Board School, Hounslow, Middlesex. Chief of the Rolling Stock Department, L. & S.W. Rly. *War Work :* Organising the formation of Military, Naval and Ambulance trains ; controlling the movements of rolling stock throughout the system of the L. & S.W. Rly. *Address :* 96, Clifton Road, Kingston Hill, Kingston-on-Thames, Surrey. (M10031)

WHEELER, Herbert Edward Ogle, O.B.E., *b.* 13 May, 1878 ; *s.* of His Honour T. W. Wheeler, of Kensington ; *m.* Edith Catherine, *d.* of William Gandy, M.R.C.S., of Upper Norwood. *Educ. :* Windlesham House, Brighton, and Uppingham. Assistant Superintendent of the Line, South Eastern and Chatham Railway. *War Work :* S.E. & C. Rly., as London District Traffic Superintendent and Assistant Superintendent of the Line. *Address :* The Lee, Plaistow Lane, Bromley, Kent. (O1996)

WHEELER, Capt. Roland Chamberlain, M.B.E.

WHEELER, Capt. Roy Lambert, O.B.E., *b.* 28 Aug. 1886 ; *s.* of Franklin Wheeler, of North Vancouver, Canada. *Educ. :* Belgrave and Wingham, Ontario, Canada. Railway

Employee, C.P.R. *War Work:* Enlisted Nov. 1914; overseas to England, Jan. 1915; to France, Feb. 1915 (reinforcement to P.P.C.L.I.); wounded, May, 1915 (2nd Battle of Ypres); commissioned to B.C. Regt., Nov. 1916; seconded under War Office for Railway Operating Div., R.E., May, 1917; continuous service as Traffic Officer, 58th B.G.O.C., R.O.D., T., March, 1919; transferred to Royal Engineers, and embarked for South Russian Mission, April, 1919; employed on travelling supervision; Major, D.A.D.R.T., Crimea, Feb. 1920, until withdrawal of Mission end of June, 1920. *Addresses:* 157, Second St. E., North Vancouver, Canada; c/o Bank of Montreal. Waterloo Place, London, S.W. 1. (O9757)

WHEELER, Samuel Gerald De Courcey, O.B.E.

WHEELER, William, C.M.G., O.B.E.

WHEELER, Florence, Mrs. BOURNE-, M.B.E., *b.* 27 Sept. 1870; *d.* of Francis N. Smith, of Wingfield Park, Ambergate, Derbyshire; *m.* Joseph Bourne-Wheeler, 2nd *s.* of Rev. Wm. C. Wheeler, of Southborough, Kent. *War Work:* War Hospital Supply Depot, 1915; Hon. Sec. of the Sherwood Foresters Prisoners of War Regimental Care Committee, June, 1915, to March, 1919. *Address:* Netherlea, Holbrook, Derby. *Club:* The Forum. (M4077)

WHEELWRIGHT, Capt. Edward Lycett, O.B.E.

WHEELWRIGHT, Major Talbot Hodwen, O.B.E.

WHELAN, Lieut.-Col. Joseph Francis, D.S.O., O.B.E., M.B., B.Sc., R.A.M.C., *b.* 1873. *Educ.:* Dublin Univ. S. Africa, 1900–2 (Queen's medal with three clasps, King's medal with two clasps); Great War, 1914–19 (despatches). (O6727)

WHELER, Florence Ffaith Hastings, Mrs., O.B.E.

WHELER, Major Granville Charles Hastings, C.B.E., M.P.

WHELON, Emily Mildred, O.B.E., *b.* 27 Dec. 1887; *d.* of William Whelon, of Lancaster. Hon. Sec. of the Prisoners of War Care Committee of the King's Own Royal Lancaster Regiment from 1916–18. *Address:* Croftlands, Lancaster. (O11595)

WHERRY, Albert Edward Kerkham, O.B.E., *b.* 24 Aug. 1874; *s.* of the late Alderman W. R. Wherry, J.P., of The Cedars, Bourne; *m.* Evelyn. *d.* of Alderman E. J. Grummitt, of Stainfield, Bourne. *Educ.:* Privately. Treas. and Hon. Sec. National Association of Corn and Agricultural Merchants; Member of the Council of the Agricultural Seed Trade Association. *War Work:* Member of the Control of Crops Committee (Ministry of Food), Home Cereals Committee (Royal Commission on Wheat Supplies), Cereal Seeds Advisory Committee, and Fertilisers Distribution Committee (Board of Agriculture and Fisheries). *Address:* Qu'Appelle, Bourne, Lincs. *Clubs:* Junior Constitutional, W.; Hunstanton Golf; Luffenham Heath Golf. (O11596)

WHIDBORNE, Lieut. Charles Stanley Lucas, M.B.E.

WHIDBORNE, Winifred Biehl, Mrs., M.B.E.

WHIFFEN, Major Stanley White, O.B.E., R.A.S.C.

WHIFFIN, Major George Greenhough, O.B.E.

WHIGHAM, Walter Kennedy, O.B.E., *b.* 6 June, 1878; *s.* of the late D. D. Whigham, of Dunearn, Prestwick, N.B.; *m.* Jacqueline, *d.* of Baron Henri de Salignac Fénélon, of Hermaville, Pas de Calais, France. Merchant. Director, Bank of England, North Eastern Railway, British Investment Trust, Ltd., and the Mercantile Investment and General Trust Company, Ltd. *War Work:* Re-joined Territorial Force, 6th North Staffordshire Regt., 7 Aug. 1914; proceeded to France, March, 1915, with Battalion; joined headquarters 51st (Highland) Division, Sept. 1915, and 4th Corps, March, 1918; returned from France, Jan. 1919. *Addresses:* 2, Chesham Street, London, S.W. 1; Dunearn, Sandwich, Kent. *Clubs:* Union; Prestwick Golf; Royal St. George's Golf. (O5916)

WHILES, George Frederick, M.B.E.

WHILLER, Annie, Mrs., O.B.E.

WHINNEY, Sir Arthur Francis, K.B.E., *b.* 16 Dec. 1865; *s.* of Frederick Whinney, of Avenue Road, Regent's Park, N.W.; *m.* Amy Elizabeth, *d.* of William Golden, of Chalcot Crescent, Regent's Park, N.W. *Educ.:* Privately and France. Chartered Accountant. *War Work:* Adviser upon Costs of Production to the Admiralty; Assistant Accountant-General of the Navy; Member of Sub-Committee upon Admiralty Contracts; Hon. Consulting Accountant to the Admiralty. *Clubs:* Reform; Bath; British Empire; Gresham. (K239)

WHINNEY, Gladys, M.B.E.

WHINNEY, Major Harold Fife, D.S.O., O.B.E., *b.* 1878. Major Roy. Fusiliers (City of London Regt.); Gen. Staff Officer; served during Great War, 1914–18 (despatches, Legion of Honour). (O8969)

WHISH, Comm. Eric Vipam, O.B.E., R.I.M.

WHISTLER, Lieut. Godfrey Fuller, M.B.E., R.F.A.

WHITAKER, Col. Albert Edward, C.B.E., T.D., J.P., D.L., *b.* 9 May, 1860; *s.* of J. Whitaker, of Hesley Hall, Yorks.; *m.* Eileen, M.B.E., *d.* of Col. J. Croker, of Ballinagarde, Co. Limerick. *Educ.:* Harrow. High Sheriff for Notts., 1921. *War Work:* Served in Afghanistan 1879–80. and Egypt, 1914–16. *Address:* Babworth Hall, Retford, Notts. *Clubs:* Naval and Military; Arthur's. (C2191)

WHITAKER, Bt.-Major Arthur Marmaduke, O.B.E.

WHITAKER, Major Benjamin, M.B.E.

WHITAKER, Eileen, Mrs., M.B.E.; *d.* of Col. J. Croker, of Ballinagarde, Co. Limerick; *m.* Col. A. E. Whitaker. *War Work:* Managed and maintained an Auxiliary Hospital for 4 years, at Babworth Hall, Notts. *Address:* Babworth Hall, Retford, Notts. (M2635)

WHITAKER, Frances Henrietta, M.B.E.

WHITAKER, Capt. George Backhouse, O.B.E., R.E.

WHITAKER, Capt. Harold Braithwait, M.B.E., R.E.

WHITAKER, Capt. Raymond, M.B.E., R.A.F.

WHITAKER, Thorp, O.B.E.

WHITAMORE, Major Vernon Northwood, O.B.E. I.M.S.

WHITBOURN, Ernest, M.B.E., R.A.S.C.

WHITBREAD, Beatrice, O.B.E.

WHITBREAD, Edward, M.B.E., *b.* 19 Jan. 1852; *s.* of Henry Whitbread, of Cheltenham; *m.* Louisa Amelia, *d.* of Henry Beard, of Cheltenham. *Educ.:* Privately. Hon. Treas. to the Chamber of Commerce and Traders' Assoc., and for Town Development Fund. *War Work:* Hon. Treas. to the Local Prisoners of War Fund, and for Soldiers' Welcome Home Funds. (M10033)

WHITBY, Alfred James, M.B.E.

WHITBY, Beatrice Mary Elizabeth, M.B.E.

WHITBY, Stafford Beeston, M.B.E., *b.* 27 Dec. 1860; *s.* of Rev. W. Whitby, of Manningtree, Essex; *m.* Hettie, *d.* of G. Smith, of Audlem, Cheshire. *Educ.:* Retford Grammar School. *War Work:* Lecturer to the troops; Voluntary Recruiting; Hon. Sec. Soldiers' Club, Hull; Representative of the National War Aims Committee; V.A.D. Hospital Hon. Staff. *Addresses:* 23, Prince's Avenue, Hull; 8, Victoria Avenue, Hull. (M10035)

WHITCOMBE, Adeline Elizabeth, M.B.E.; *d.* of J. C. Whitcombe. Hon. Assist.-Sec. P.W.M.F. *War Work:* 1914–19, Women's Branch War and Relief Fund, Poona. *Address:* 10, Phayre Road, Poona, India. (M2796)

WHITCOMBE, Julia May, M.B.E.; *d.* of J. C. Whitcombe. Supt. Clothing Department. *War Work:* 1914–19, Women's Branch Bombay Presidency War Relief Fund, Poona. *Address:* 10, Phayre Road, Poona, India. (M4229)

WHITE, Arthur, C.B.E.

WHITE, Arthur, O.B.E., *b.* 19 April, 1875. Assistant to Supt. of the Line, L.B. & S.C.R. *War Work:* Principally in connection with transport of troops and war material. *Address:* Hobart Villa, Heathview Road, Thornton Heath. (O11660)

WHITE, Arthur, M.B.E., *b.* 16 Sept. 1865. *Educ.:* Chaloner's School, Braunton, North Devon. Superintendent Metropolitan Police. (ret.) *War Work:* In charge of the Executive Department at New Scotland Yard; special onerous duties in connection with air raids and war work generally. *Address:* 2, Grenville Terrace, Northam, N. Devon. (M1085)

WHITE, Eng.-Comm. Arthur Frederick, O.B.E., R.N.

WHITE, Arthur Rabbitts, O.B.E., J.P., D.L., *b.* 19 June, 1859; *s.* of John White, of Zeals, Wilts; *m.* Minnie Beauchamp; *d.* of William B. Beauchamp, of Norton Hall, Somerset. *Educ.:* Queenwood Coll., Hants. Member of the Wilts County Council; Chairman of the Mere Rural District Council; Chairman of the Mere Board of Guardians; Governor of the Dauntry Agricultural School; Member of the Council of the Bath and West of England Agricultural Society. *War Work:* Chairman of the Wilts War Agricultural Committee; Chairman of the Wilts County War Executive Committee; Chairman of the Mere Local Tribunal. *Address:* Charnage, Mere, Wiltshire. (O856)

WHITE, Lieut.-Col. Basil Cherrington, O.B.E.

WHITE, Major Bruce Gordon, M.B.E., R.E.

WHITE, Charles, M.B.E.

WHITE, Charles Arthur, M.B.E., B.Sc. (Lond.), M.Sc. (Birm.), *b.* 21 Oct. 1862. *Educ.:* Imperial Coll. of Science and Technology, and Univ. of Birmingham. Principal, Aston Technical School. *War Work:* Director, Munitions Training Centre, Aston Technical School, Aug. 1915, to Nov. 1918; this centre trained over 2000 men and women successfully for various forms of Munitions work. *Address:* 14, Grosvenor Road, Handsworth, Birmingham. (M2636)

WHITE, Lieut. Charles Clement Stuart, M.B.E., R.E.

WHITE, Major Charles Francis, O.B.E., M.B., B.Ch., B.A.O., R.A.M.C., *b.* 27 Jan. 1879; *s.* of the late Dr. William Dudley White, of Dublin; *m.* Ellen, *d.* of David Hamilton, of Ballina, Co. Mayo. *Educ.:* Belvedere Coll.; University Coll., Dublin. Officer Commanding, Military Hospital, Rochester Row, London. *War Work:* Medical Officer to 8th Howitzer Brigade, R.F.A.; attached 13th Field Ambulance (5th Division); afterwards in charge of Surgical Division of 39th General Hospital. *Address:* 33, Emperor's Gate, South Kensington. (O5917)

WHITE, Capt. Charles Henry, O.B.E., R.A.S.C.

WHITE, Clare, O.B.E., *b.* 22 May, 1853; *s.* of William White, of Cirencester; *m.* Maude Janvrin, *d.* of Frederick Augustus Vincent, B.D., late Rector of Elsted, Sussex. *Educ.:* Grammar School and St. Thomas', Cirencester. Diocesan Sec. C.E.T.S. Winchester Diocese; General Sec. Royal Army Temperance Association; Honorary Financial Representative, Royal Army Temperance Association. *War Work:* Visiting Prisoners of war camps; organising erection of hutments; delivering lectures to troops at the Front and organising branches of R.A.T.A. in the New Army. *Address:* 11, Ramillies Road, Chiswick, W. 4. (O1997)

WHITE, Major Edwin E., O.B.E., R.A.S.C.

WHITE, Lieut.-Col. Ernest William, C.B.E., M.B. (Lond.), M.R.C.P. (Lond.), A.K.C., R.A.M.C., *b.* 22 Jan. 1851; *s.* of Richard White, of Heathfield House, Norwich; *m.* Harriett, *d.* of Samson Bowyer, of Maesbury, Salop. *Educ.:* King Edward VI. School, Bury St. Edmund's; King's Coll., London;

Norfolk and Norwich Hospital; and King's Coll. Hospital, London. Emeritus Professor, King's Coll., London; Professor of Psychological Medicine, King's Coll., London (1890–1910); Physician Superintendent City of London Asylum (1887–1905); Mental Consultant to Western Command, 1916 to date; President Medico-Psychological Association of Gt. Britain and Ireland, 1903–4. *War Work :* Appointed Mental Consultant to Western Command, Dec. 1916, as Hon. Major R.A.M.C.; promoted Hon. Lieut.-Col., R.A.M.C., Oct. 1917; Lieut.-Col. R.A.M.C., July, 1918; since July, 1919, has had the supervision and disposal of all the Army Mental Hospital patients in England, Wales, Scotland, Ireland, and from overseas *via* Netley Hospital. *Addresses :* Fenstanton, Christchurch Road, London, S.W. 2; Betley House, near Shrewsbury. *Clubs :* Constitutional and Shropshire. (C3082)

WHITE, Brevet-Major FitzGibbon Grove, D.S.O., O.B.E.

WHITE, the Hon. Francis William, O.B.E., *b.* 23 May, 1873; *s.* of 2nd Lord Annaly, of Luttrelstown, Co. Dublin (*see* BURKE'S *Peerage*); *m.* Anna Elizabeth, *d.* of — Jaeger, of New Zealand. *Educ :* Harrow. *War Work :* Army Remount Service. *Address :* 77, New Cavendish Street, London, W. (O7850)

WHITE, Frank George, M.B.E.

WHITE, Frederick, O.B.E.

WHITE, Frederick Wallis, M.B.E., A.M.I.M.E., *b.* 16 Aug. 1886; *s.* of Charles White, of Charlton, Kent. Assistant Manager, Inspection Dept., Ministry of Munitions. *War Work :* In charge Small Arms Ammunition Shop, Royal Arsenal, 1914–15; in charge of staff of nearly 6000 hands employed at the Small Arms Ammunition Inspection Buildings, Park Royal, N.W., 1915–19. *Addresses :* 2, Brookhill Road, Woolwich, S.E. 18; 7, Apsley Terrace, Acton, W. 3. *Clubs :* Mill Hill Park Cricket; Woolwich Polytechnic Athletic. (M10037)

WHITE, Lieut.-Comm. George Colvin, O.B.E., R.N.V.R.

WHITE, Capt. George Gilmour, O.B.E.

WHITE, George Thomas, O.B.E., J.P., for Exeter, *b.* 8 June, 1857; *s.* of the late Richard Dunning White, Vice-Admiral, C.B., of Exeter; *m.* Mary Katharine Sidney, *d.* of Lieut.-Col. Charles Sidney Hawkins, D.L., J.P., of Malvern Hill House, Cheltenham. *Educ :* Royal Naval School, New Cross. Assist.-Supt. H.M. Penal Settlement, British Guiana, 1879–89; J.P. for British Guiana, 1881; Governor Glendairy Prison, Barbados, 1889–94; Superintendent of Prisons, Trinidad, 1894–1901; Chairman Heavitree Urban District Council, 1913. *War Work :* Hon. Treas. Exeter Local War Pensions Committee; Chairman, Heavitree District, Exeter War Relief Fund for Dependants of Sailors and Soldiers, 1914–18; Hon. Sec. Exeter Belgian Refugees' Committee and Member of Devon and Cornwall War Refugees' Committee on Amalgamation with Exeter (Medal du Roi Albert); Chairman, Exeter and District Local Advisory Committee, 1917–20. *Address :* 11, Baring Crescent, Exeter. *Clubs :* Devon and Exeter. (O11601)

WHITE, Col. Gerald Verner, C.B.E., *b.* 1897, *s.* of the late Hon. Peter White, P.C.; *m.* Mary Elizabeth Tretes. *Educ :* Pembroke Public and High School, Ontario; McGill Univ. Col. Canadian Forces; Director of Timber Operations, Canadian Forestry Corps; elected to Canadian Parliament, 1906. *Address :* Pembroke, Ontario. *Club :* Rideau (Ottawa). (C330)

WHITE, Major Henry Herbert Ronald, D.S.O., O.B.E., J.P., D.L., *b.* 1870; *s.* of the late Maj.-Gen. Henry George White, J.P., D.L., of Lough Eske Castle, co. Donegal; *m.* Florence Geraldine, *d.* of Sir John Arnott, 1st Bt. (*see* BURKE'S *Peerage*). *Educ :* Rugby, and R.M.C. Formerly Capt. King's Roy. Rifle Corps; Major. Roy. Fusiliers; High Sheriff, co. Donegal, 1912; S. Africa, 1901–2 (Queen's medal with four clasps); Somaliland, 1903–4 (medal with two clasps); Great War, 1914–19 (despatches); Nyasaland Field Force, 1918, as Lieut.-Col. *Address :* Lough Eske Castle, co. Donegal. *Clubs :* Army and Navy; Royal Automobile (O8970)

WHITE, Hilda Ann, M.B.E.

WHITE, Major and Qr.-Mr. James, M.B.E., R.E.

WHITE, Jesse Obediah, M.B.E.

WHITE, Jessie McHardie, M.B.E.

WHITE, Major John, O.B.E., R.E.

WHITE, John Arthur Temple, O.B.E., M.R.C.S., L.R.C.P., *b.* 17 June, 1866; *s.* of John Branford White, of Norfolk, and Colonial Civil Service; *m.* Alice Edith, *d.* of Col. Henry John Brownrigg, C.B. *Educ :* Abroad and St. Bartholomew's Hospital. *War Work :* Medical Officer, Hillsborough Military Hospital, Harlow; Civilian M.O. various London Regiments and Anti-Aircraft Gun Stations. *Address :* Hatfield Broad Oak, Essex. (O11602)

WHITE, John Bell, C.B.E., J.P., *b.* 1857; *s.* of the late W. Bell White, of Dublin; *m.* Jane, *d.* of the late David Davis, of Maes-y-ffynon, Aberdare, and Tan-y-coed, Arthog, and widow of Thomas Babington Jones, of Glynpedr, Crickhowell. Barrister, Inner Temple, 1893; Hon. Capt. R.N.R. : an Assoc. of Institute of Naval Architects ; a Member of Conjoint Board of Scientific Soc., and a Younger Brother of the Trinity House ; was Assist. Director of Naval Recruiting, 1917–19 ; editor of the "Law Magazine and Review." *Addresses :* 3, Paper Buildings, Temple, E.C.; Alderbourne Manor, Gerrard's Cross, Bucks. *Clubs :* Athenæum; Savage; Farmers'; Caledonian. (C1169)

WHITE, 2nd Lieut. John Charles, M.B.E., R.A.F.

WHITE, Capt. John Christian, O.B.E., M.C.

WHITE, Capt. John Sinclair, O.B.E., M.B., R.A.M.C.

WHITE, Kathleen Cameron, M.B.E.

WHITE, Mabel, Mrs., M.B.E.; *d.* of Matthew Ben Shaw, R.M., Cape Civil Service, Transkeian Territories; *m.* Arthur Edward, *s.* of Thomas White, of County Wexford, Ireland. Trained Nurse; served through Boer War at Ladysmith and Howick, with No. 3 General Hospital (South African Medal); joined British South African Co.'s Nursing Service, 1902. *War Work :* Founder and Organising Sec. of the Gwelo Red Cross Working Party, for sending comforts to 1st R.R. in S.W. Africa. Hospital ship "Ebani," S. Rhodesian Column on N. Border; 2nd R.R. in East Africa, Nairobe Hospital, 2nd R.R. overseas, and donations to St. Dunstan's Home, Richmond Hospital, Maitland Institute. *Address :* Erin-go-bragh Estate, P.O. Box 100, Gwelo, S. Rhodesia. (M6494)

WHITE, Madge Macarthur, O.B.E., *b.* 28 March, 1891, *d.* of John White, of Glasgow. *Educ :* Privately. Private Sec. to Rt. Hon. Christopher Addison, M.D., M.P., Board of Education, 1914–15; Ministry of Munitions, 1915–17; Ministry of Reconstruction, 1917–19; Local Government Board, 1919; Ministry of Health. (O1998)

WHITE, Major Maurice Forbes, O.B.E., M.B., I.M.S.

WHITE, Minnie Beauchamp, Mrs., O.B.E. ; *d.* of Wm. Beauchamp, of Norton Hall, near Bath; *m.* Arthur R. White, O.B.E., D.L., J.P. *War Work :* Commandant of Mere V.A.D. Hospital, 1914–19. *Address :* Charnage, Mere, Wilts. *Club :* V.A.D. Ladies'. (O11603)

WHITE, Percival, M.B.E., F.S.A.A., *b.* 2 July, 1881; *s.* of William John White, of Plymouth. *Educ :* Corporation Grammar School, Plymouth. Incorporated Accountant. *War Work :* Hon. Sec. Plymouth War Savings Committee, 1916–20; Organised Food Economy Campaign; Hon. Auditor, V.A.D. Hospital, Plymouth. *Address :* The Knowle, Mannamead, Plymouth. *Club :* Yelverton Golf. (M2638)

WHITE, Percy Ernest, M.B.E.

WHITE, Comm. Richard Forster, O.B.E., R.N.

WHITE, Robert, C.B.E. Assist. Director, Wool Textile Production, War Office. (C3039)

WHITE, Lieut.-Col. Robert Fortescue Moresby, O.B.E., V.D., *b.* 8 May, 1862; *s.* of Robert Azlack White, of Grantham; *m.* Editha Lamorna, *d.* of the Rev. George Cardew, of St. Minver, East Lyss, Hants. *Educ :* Magnus School, Newark. Solicitor; Clerk to Lieutenancy, County of Lincoln; Clerk to Magistrates, Spittlegate Petty Sessional Division of County; Clerk of the Peace, Borough of Grantham; Clerk to Commissioners of Taxes. *War Work :* Served on Army Headquarters, H.D., as Headquarters Commandant, July, 1915, to June, 1918; and D.A.A.G. Headquarters Northern Command, York, June, 1918, to Jan. 1919. *Address :* Grantham. (O7852)

WHITE, Professor Robert George, M.B.E. M.S.C.

WHITE, Robert George, M.B.E.

WHITE, Robert William, M.B.E., R.A.S.C.

WHITE, Samuel James, O.B.E., M.C.

WHITE, Major William Blomfield, O.B.E. (O9058)

WHITE, Amber, Mrs. BLANCO-, O.B.E., *b.* 1 July, 1887; *d.* of the Hon. W. Pember Reeves, of New Zealand; *m.* George Rivers, *s.* of Thomas Blanco White, of Putney. *Educ :* Kensington High School, and Newnham Coll., Cambridge. Novelist; now in Ministry of Labour; Member of the National Whitley Council for the Civil Service. *War Work :* Director of Women's Wages, Ministry of Munitions. *Address :* 44, Downshire Hill, Hampstead. (O11598)

WHITE, Lieut. Arthur BLAIR-, M.B.E., R.F.A.

WHITE, Major Charles James BROOMAN-, C.B.E., *b.* 1883; *s.* of Richard Charles Brooman-White, of Arddarroch, Dumbarton; *m.* 1907, Idalea Hastings, *d.* of the late William Hearne, of Hearne, Texas, U.S.A. Major Gen. List; served in Great War, 1914–19 (mentioned in despatches). (C1123)

WHITE, Col. Percy CARR-, C.B.E., M.B.

WHITE, Capt. Ernest COSTLEY-, O.B.E.

WHITE, Capt. Cyril Francis DOUGLAS-, M.B.E., R.A.S.C.

WHITE, Brevet Major Maurice Fitzgibbon GROVE-, D.S.O., O.B.E., R.E., *b.* 7 Dec. 1887; *s.* of Col. James Grove-White, C.M.G., J.P., D.L., of Kilbyrne, Doneraile, Co. Cork, and Rockfield, Cappagh, Co. Waterford; *m.* Bernice Agnes, *d.* of D. F. W. Parlane. *Educ :* St. Andrew's Coll., Grahamstown, Cape Colony; Wellington Coll.; R.M.A., Woolwich. *War Work :* 54th Field Co. R.E., France; General Staff of 13th Corps. and G.H.Q., France. *Address :* c/o Cox & Co., 16, Charing Cross. *Club :* Army and Navy. (O5921)

WHITE, Sir William HALE-, K.B.E., M.D., F.R.C.P., *b.* 7 Nov. 1857; *s.* of William Hale-White, of Groombridge, Kent (known as Mark Rutherford, Author); *m.* Edith Jane Spencer, *d.* of Alfred Downing Fripp, R.W.S., of Hampstead, N.W. *Educ :* Framlingham, and Guy's Hospital. Consulting Physician to Guy's Hospital. *War Work :* Brevet Col. R.A.M.C.(T.), 2nd London General Hospital; Chairman, H.M. Queen Mary's Royal Naval Hospital, Southend; Physician to King Edward VII. Hospital for Officers, and to the American Women's Hospital for Officers; served on numerous War Committees and Boards. *Address :* 38, Wimpole Street, London. W. 1. *Club :* Athenæum. (K240)

WHITE, Arethusa Flora Gartside, Mrs. LEIGH-, O.B.E., *b.* 3 June, 1885; *d.* of Peter Hawker, of Longparish, Hants.; *m.* Edward Egerton (who died), *s.* of Egerton Leigh, of Jodrell Hall, Cheshire. *War Work :* Chairman, Bantry War Pensions Sub-Committee; Vice- and Acting Chairman, County Cork Local War Pensions Committee, 1917–18; Hon. Sec., Cork County Soldiers' and Sailors' Families Association, and Bantry

Voluntary Recruiting Committee; President, Bantry District Association, and Bantry Voluntary Aid Committee (controlling Station Buffet, Prisoners' Parcels, Comforts, National Egg Collection); Superintendent, Y.M.C.A. Club, Bantry; also worked for British and Foreign Sailors' Society and B.R.C.S., Cork. *Address:* Bantry House, Bantry, Co. Cork. *Clubs:* Ladies' Athenæum; Empress. (O11599)

WHITE, Major Robert STANDISH-, O.B.E., R.A.M.C.

WHITEHEAD, Alfred Kershaw, M.B.E., *b.* 14 April, 1873; *s.* of Samuel Whitehead, of Oldham; *m.* Nellie Murray, *d.* of Charles Edwin Dyer, of London. *Educ.:* Wesleyan School, Glodwick, Oldham, and Wesleyan Training Coll., Westminster, S.W. Headmaster, Whickham Council School, Durham Education Committee. *War Work:* Member of Executive Durham County War Savings Committee, and Sec. of the Whickham Urban District War Savings Committee. *Address:* Ash Villa, Whickham. (M4079)

WHITEHEAD, Arthur John, M.B.E.

WHITEHEAD, Lieut.-Col. Herbert Mansfield, O.B.E.

WHITEHEAD, Irene, Mrs., M.B.E.

WHITEHEAD, Isobel, Mrs., C.B.E., *b.* 1872; *d.* of the late Rev. John Duncan, Vicar of Calne, Rural Dean of Avebury, and Canon of Salisbury; *m.* 1903, the Rt. Rev. Henry Whitehead, Lord Bishop of Madras. *Educ.:* Head of Women's Services in connection with Furlough and Convalescent camps in India during the Great War. Has Kaisir-i-Hind medal. (C1982)

WHITEHEAD, Major John, O.B.E.

WHITEHEAD, Mary Catherine, Mrs., M.B.E., *b.* 1 June, 1862; *d.* of the late Henry Haes, of Caterham Valley, Surrey; *m.* the late Charles Whitehead, *s.* of the late Charles Whitehead, of London, N. *Educ.:* North London Collegiate School, and Wiesbaden. *War Work:* Belgian Refugee work; Canteen work, Woolwich Arsenal, and King's Cross Y.M.C.A. Hut, for 4 years, originally as a worker and afterwards as Lady Superintendent. *Address:* Westways, Burke's Road, Beaconsfield, Bucks. (M2639)

WHITEHEAD, Maude Lillian, M.B.E., *d.* of the late George Whitehead, of Deighton Grove, York. *War Work:* Commandant of Escrick Red Cross Hospital, Escrick, York, from 1914–19. *Address:* Deighton Grove, York. (M4080)

WHITEHEAD, Lieut.-Comm. Norman, O.B.E., R.N.

WHITEHEAD, Lieut. William, M.B.E.

WHITEHORN, Lieut. Roy Drummond, M.B.E., M.A., *b.* 4 Aug. 1891; *s.* of Joseph H. Whitehorn, of 74, Canfield Gardens, London, N.W. 6. *Educ.:* St. Paul's School, London; Trinity and Westminster Colls., Cambridge. *War Work:* Lieut., 37th Calcutta Presidency Batt., Indian Defence Force; National Sec. for Army Work, Y.M.C.A. of India, Burma, and Ceylon, 1915–19; mentioned in despatches, July, 1919. *Addresses:* 74, Canfield Gardens, London, N.W. 6; Trinity Coll., Cambridge. *Club:* Hawks, Cambridge. (M2640)

WHITEHORNE, Major Arthur Cecil, O.B.E.

WHITEHOUSE, Edwin St. John, M.B.E., M.R.C.S., L.R.C.P., *b.* 1867; *s.* of H. B. Whitehouse, of Sedgley, Staffs. *Educ.:* Wolverhampton School, Cambridge, and Birmingham. Medical Practitioner, Medical Officer, Solihull and Meriden Joint Isolation Hospital. *War Work:* Medical Officer-in-charge Hermitage, V.A.D. Hospital, Solihull (Auxiliary to 1st Southern General Hospital). *Address:* Solihull, Warwickshire. (M19042)

WHITEHOUSE, John, M.B.E., *b.* 29 May, 1875. Clerk to the Barrow Insurance Committee; Fellow of the Faculty of Insurance. *War Work:* Vice-Chairman of the Local War Pensions Committee; Member of the Finance Committee; Member of the Local Training Committee for Discharged Sailors and Soldiers; Member of Lord Roberts' Workshop Memorial Committee; Member of the Executive Committee Barrow War Memorial; Member of the Prince of Wales' Committee, War Savings Committee, Old Age Pensions Committee, and Council for Combating Venereal Disease. *Addresses:* 92, Duke Street; 20 Windsor Street, Barrow-in-Furness. (M10043)

WHITEHOUSE, Capt. John Hubert, O.B.E.

WHITELAW, Robert Pender, C.B.E., *b.* 22 April, 1865; *s.* of Robert Whitelaw, of Stirling, Scotland; *m.* Helen, *d.* of Robert Watson, of Coatbridge. *Educ.:* West of Scotland Technical Coll., Coatbridge. Superintendent, H.M. Factory, Avonmouth. *War Work:* A contractor in S. Africa, came to England in 1915 to assist the Ministry of Munitions; supervised the construction of H.M. Factory, Queensferry, of which he became works manager; transferred to Gretna, and afterwards to Avonmouth, where he filled the dual posts of construction manager and superintendent. *Address:* H.M. Factory, Avonmouth. *Club:* The Rand, Johannesburg, South Africa. (C3040)

WHITELEY, Capt. Cyprian Charles Oswald, O.B.E., T.D.

WHITELEY, Feather Ogden, O.B.E., F.S.S., F.S.A.A., *b.* 4 Oct. 1877; *s.* of the late Simeon Whiteley, Professor of Music, of Bradford; *m.* Annie, *d.* of the late Abel Kershaw, Worsted Spinner, of Oxenhope. *Educ.:* Horton Coll., and privately. City Treas. of Bradford; admitted Incorporated Accountant in 1912; elected a Fellow of the Society in 1914; elected a Member of the Council of the Society of Incorporated Accountants and Auditors, 1920; Fellow, Member of the Executive Council, and Past President of the Institute of Municipal Treasurers and Accountants. *War Work:* Commanded 4th (Vol.) Batt. Prince of Wales' Own West Yorkshire Regt.; Hon. Treas. of European War, Bradford Lord Mayor's

Fund, Belgian National Relief (Bradford) Fund, Belgian Refugees' Fund, Serbian Relief Fund, Polish Relief Fund, " Lusitania " Relief Fund, Y.M.C.A. War Memorial and National Fund, Bradford Flag Days Organisation; Hon. Sec. and Treas. of Bradford War Pensions Committee. *Address:* Highfield View, Idle, Bradford. *Clubs:* Union (Bradford); Northern Counties'. (O11604)

WHITELEY, Martha Annie, O.B.E., D.Sc., F.I.C., *b.* 11 Nov. 1866; *d.* of William Sedgwick Whiteley, of London. *Educ.:* Kensington High School; Royal Holloway Coll.; Royal Coll. of Science, South Kensington. *War Work:* Superintendent of Organic Chemistry Laboratories, Imperial Coll. of Science and Technology, South Kensington, under Ministry of Munitions; Research work for Chemical Warfare Department, Ministry of Munitions; Superintendent of research work carried out in Organic Chemistry Laboratories, South Kensington, for Royal Society's War Committee. *Address:* 111, Castlenau, Barnes, London, S.W. 13. *Club:* Lyceum. (O2001)

WHITELEY, Major Percival, O.B.E.

WHITELEY, Lieut. the Hon Ronald George, O.B.E., B.A., *b.* 1890; *s.* of George Whiteley, Baron Marchamley. *Educ.:* Magdalen Coll., Oxford. Late Major R.G.A. *Address:* Charnley Manor, nr. Wantage, Bucks. (O7853)

WHITEMAN, Major Francis Edward, O.B.E.

WHITEMAN, George Hewitt, O.B.E.

WHITFIELD, Avery Alfred, M.B.E.

WHITFIELD, Capt. Frederick Ernest Banister, M.B.E., R.A.F

WHITFIELD, Lieut. George Arthur, O.B.E., R.N.R.

WHITFIELD, Muriel Frances, Mrs., M.B.E.

WHITFIELD, Com. Paul, D.S.O., O.B.E., R.N. Served in Great War, 1914–19 (mentioned in despatches). (O9662)

WHITFIELD, Major Robert Langton Digby, O.B.E., R.A.O.C.

WHITING, Ernest James, M.B.E., R.N.

WHITING, Capt. Maurice Henry, O.B.E., F.R.C.S., *b.* 12 Oct. 1885; *s.* of Henry Whiting, of Long Acre, West Ealing; *m.* Blanche Beatrice, *d.* of Edward Aggas, of Torquay. *Educ.:* Mill Hill School; Downing Coll., Cambridge; Middlesex Hospital. Pathologist to the Royal London Ophthalmic Hospital; Ophthalmic Surgeon to Paddington Green Children's Hospital, and St. Saviour's Hospital. *War Work:* Lieut. and Capt. R.A.M.C.; Ophthalmic Specialist, Shorncliffe Military Hospital; 13th Stationary Hospital, Boulogne (afterwards the 83rd (Dublin) General Hospital), Dec. 1914, to March, 1919. *Address:* 9, Welbeck Street, W. 1. (O5922)

WHITING, William Robert Gerald, M.B.E., M.A., M.I.N.A., *b.* 15 May, 1884; *s.* of W. H. Whiting, C.B., of West Ealing; *m.* Irene Helena, *d.* of Professor Henry Stroud, of Armstrong Coll. *Educ.:* Mill Hill School, and Cambridge Univ. Personal Assistant to General Manager, Sir W. G. Armstrong, Whitworth & Co.'s Shipyard Department. *War Work:* Had charge of the construction of submarines built by the above firm. *Address:* Armstrong Naval Yard, Newcastle-on-Tyne. (M1089)

WHITLA, Major Valentine George, O.B.E.

WHITLEY, Leonard Vincent, M.B.E.

WHITLOCK, Col. George Frederic Ashford, C.B.E., R.E., *b.* 16 April, 1868; *s.* of Capt. George F. T. Whitlock, of H.M. 84th (York and Lancaster) Regt.; *m.* 1st, Rebecca Margaret, *d.* of Horatio J. Sprague, H.M. Consul, Gibraltar, d. 1903; 2nd, Annie Florence, *d.* of W. L. T. Foy, D.L., J.P., of Henley-on-Thames, and 22, Down Street, W. *Educ.:* Royal Naval School, New Cross. Ordnance Survey, 1897–1903; Assistant British Commissioner, Yola-Chad Boundary Commission, 1903–4; British Commissioner, Yola-Cross River Boundary Commission, 1907–9; Chief Instructor in Surveying, School of Military Engineering, Chatham, 1909–13; Ordnance Survey, 1913–19; British Commissioner, Inter-Allied Boundary Commission, Germany—Belgium Boundary, 1919–20. *War Work:* Assisting in the preparation of the maps for the armies at the Front, and work of a similar nature for the Admiralty and Air Force. *Address:* 30, Winn Road, Southampton. *Clubs:* Army and Navy; Junior Naval and Military; Geographical. (C1133)

WHITLOCK, Roland Whitelocke, O.B.E.

WHITMEE, Andrew Conder, M.B.E.

WHITMORE, Violet Francis Elizabeth, Mrs., O.B.E., *b.* 1 Nov. 1877; *d.* of the late Sir Wm. H. Houldsworth, Bart. *m.* Lieut.-Col. Francis Henry Douglas Charlton, C.M.G., D.S.O., T.D., *s.* of the late Capt. Douglas Whitmore. *Educ.:* Privately. *War Work:* Commandant, Essex 12, and worked from 1917–19 at Military Auxiliary Hospital, Orsett; served on Local War Pensions Committee; Member of the Essex Executive Committee, B.R.C.S.; Commandant of the Essex Reserve V.A.D. *Address:* Orsett Hall, Grays, Essex. (O11605)

WHITT, Edith, M.B.E., *b.* 8 July, 1871; *d.* of Thomas Pickels, of Manchester. Teacher of Domestic Science, Leeds Education Committee. *War Work:* Demonstrator under Ministry of Food; Supervisor, National Kitchen, Leeds. (M4081)

WHITTAKER, George, O.B.E., C.C., *b.* 18 April, 1856; *s.* of Edmund Whittaker, of Hall Green, near Birmingham; *m.* Marion Ellen, *d.* of Henry Whittaker, of Churchill. *Educ.:* Hall Green School. *War Work:* Recruiting; Registering; Organising Labour for Land Work; organising Farmer's

Sales in Aid of Red Cross Funds, several of the sales realising from £1000 to over £3000 each. *Address:* Veldifer House, near Hereford. (O3987)

WHITTAKER, Joseph Henry, M.B.E.

WHITTAKER, Capt. and Qr.-Mr. Laurence, M.B.E., R.A.M.C.

WHITTAKER, Mary Fanny, M.B.E.

WHITTAKER, Capt. William Edward de Bagnlegh, M.B.E.

WHITTALL, Frederick Edwin, C.B.E., *b.* 20 April, 1864; *s.* of Sir William Whittall, Kt., of Constantinople. *War Work:* At the request of the Admiralty, organised a regular intelligence service with Constantinople during the Dardanelles Campaign; collaborated with A. J. Waugh, C.M.G., at H.B.M.'s Legation, Athens, in the control of Greek Export and Import Trade. *Address:* Constantinople. (C3041)

WHITTALL, Herbert Octavius, O.B.E., *b.* 1 Sept. 1858; *s.* of James Whittall, of Smyrna; *m.* Louisa Jane, *d.* of Edward Maltass, of Smyrna. *Educ.:* Christ's Coll., Finchley. Merchant and Director of various British Limited Liability Companies connected with Asia Minor; Member of the Committee of Management of the British Seamen's Hospital, Smyrna. *War Work:* Chairman of the British Relief Committee; Chairman of the Committee appointed by the Dutch Minister at Constantinople for the care of British prisoners of war in Turkey, repatriated through Smyrna; Confidential Adviser to the first British Military and Naval authorities in Smyrna after the Armistice. *Address:* Smyrna. (O11606)

WHITTALL, Lieut.-Comm. Hugh C., O.B.E., .R.N.V.R.

WHITTEN, George Jackson, M.B.E.

WHITTERIDGE, Lieut. Percy Claydon, M.B.E.

WHITTINGDALE, John Flasby Laurance, O.B.E., B.A., M.B (Cantab), M.R.C.S. (Eng.), *b.* 6 Oct. 1858; *s.* of William Lucas Whittingdale, of Ellerbeck, Thornton-in-Linedale; *m.* Maria Irene, *d.* of William Jennings, of Fritwell. *Educ.:* Cambridge and Edinburgh Univs. Surgeon to the Yeatman Hospital; Medical Officer, Sherborne School and Ladies' Coll. *War Work:* M.O. Yeatman Hospital, and Castle Red Cross Hospital. *Address:* Grosvenor Lodge, Sherborne, Dorset. (O11607)

WHITTINGHAM, Hilda Kate, O.B.E., M.B., B.S.

WHITTINGHAM, Comm. Wallace Edgar, O.B.E., R.D., R.N.R.

WHITTINGTON, Brig.-Gen. Cecil Henry, C.M.G., C.B.E., *b.* 1 Feb. 1878; *s.* of the late Rev. R. E. Whittington, of Bath; *m.* Mary Cecil, *d.* of Mulville Thomson, of Bath. *Educ.:* Bath Coll. Director of Mather & Platt, Ltd., Engineers. *War Work:* Commission in the Royal Flying Corps; rose to Brig.-Gen. in the Royal Air Force. *Address:* Queen Anne's Mansions, Westminster, S.W. 1. *Clubs:* Royal Air Force; Roehampton. (C877)

WHITTINGTON, Major Richard Auguste William, M.B.E. Officer commanding Western Group Middlesex, R.A-S.C. Motor Transport (Volunteers). (M10340)

WHITTINGTON, Capt. William, M.B.E.

WHITTLE, Fortescue Glynn, M.B.E., *b.* 29 Jan. 1886; *s.* of E. M. Glynn Whittle, M.D. (Cantab), M.R.C.P., of Liverpool. *Educ.:* The Liverpool Coll. Audit Office, Mersey Docks and Harbour Board. *War Work:* Commissioned in A.S.C. (T.F.) Sept. 1914, and served with 57th (West Lancs.) Div. 1914–16; served in Mesopotamia, 1917–19 (promoted Acting Capt. 1918); mentioned in despatches, Nov. 1918. *Address:* Garth Drive, Allerton. *Club:* Junior Conservative (Liverpool). (M4290)

WHITTLE, Lieut.-Col. Herbert John, M.B.E.

WHITTLE, William Henry, M.B.E., R.N.R.

WHITTON, Lieut.-Col. David Alexander, O.B.E.

WHITTY, Capt. Gerald Joseph, O.B.E., M.C., *b.* 4 Aug. 1895; *s.* of John J. Whitty, of St. Johns, Newfoundland. *Educ.:* Holy Cross Schools, St. Johns, Newfoundland. Sec. Great War Veteran's Association. Newfoundland. *War Work:* 3½ years overseas active service. *Address:* 346, Water Street West, St. Johns, Newfoundland. *Club:* B.I.S. (O8031)

WHITTY, William, M.B.E., *b.* 22 Aug. 1866; *s.* of Edward and Rose Whitty, Barton-in-Humber; *m.* Mary, *d.* of Cutsforth Knapton, of Brigg, Lincs. *Educ.:* St. Augustine's School, Barton-on-Humber. Superintendent and Deputy Chief Constable; Grimsby Borough Police. *War Work:* Service during the war in organising and supervising a large body of Special Constables, billetting, and various work in connection with the military, alien regulations, and air raids. *Address:* 17, Town Hall Street, Grimsby. (M10049)

WHITWORTH, Capt. Charles Warwick, M.B.E., T.D., *b.* 18 Jan. 1878; *s.* of Joseph Whitworth, of Harrogate; *m.* Alice Marion, *d.* of William C. Lupton, of Bradford. *Educ.:* Uppingham. Barrister-at-Law. *War Work:* General service. *Address:* Park Place. Harrogate. *Clubs:* Carlton; Junior Carlton; Bath. (M5727)

WHITWORTH, Edith, Mrs., M.B.E., *b.* 18 Oct. 1866; *d.* of Frank Dawson, of Bury; *m.* Albert Gladstone, *s.* of John Whitworth, of Rochdale. Police Court Missionary and Probation Officer; appointed by Swindon Borough Bench. *War Work:* Member of Swindon Local Tribunal; Chairman of Ladies' Committee which undertook the care of all Motherless or Orphan children of soldiers and sailors; organiser and Member of Committee of Weekly Meetings, including tea and concert, for Widows and Dependants of soldiers and sailors; Member of Local Branch of Soldiers' and Sailors' Families Association; Member of Prisoners of War and Belgian Relief

Committee; Member of War Savings Committee; Y.M.C.A. worker; Member of Local War Pensions Committee. *Address:* The Ferns, Dixon Street, Swindon. (M10056)

WHITWORTH, Lieut. Geoffrey Budibent, M.B.E.

WHITWORTH, Walter Stanley, M.B.E.

WHYATT, Charles Sidney, M.B.E., *b.* 30 Jan. 1855. *Educ.:* Privately. Late Assistant Marine Superintendent, Great Eastern Rly. Co., Parkeston Quay. *War Work:* Under Railway Control, supervising and arranging transit, and working of Naval Stores at a Naval Base during the war. *Address:* 16, Fairlawn Park, Chiswick, London, W. 4. (M10051)

WHYTE, Lieut. Colin Campbell, M.B.E.

WHYTE, Capt. James Cunningham, M.B.E.

WHYTE, John, O.B.E.

WHYTE, Robert, M.B.E., *b.* 29 Jan. 1874; *s.* of John Whyte, of Lanark, N.B.; *m.* Isabella, *d.* of Wm. Stout, of Kirkwall, Orkney. *Educ.:* Lanark Grammar School, and Edinburgh Univ. Solicitor, Supreme Courts of Scotland, and Notary Public S.S.C., N.P. *War Work:* Sec. of War Savings Committee, and organiser of Leith War Loan Campaigns and the local organisations. *Address:* Belverley Trinity, Edinburgh. (M10052)

WHYTE, William de Burgh, O.B.E.

WHYTE, William Edward, O.B.E.

WICKERSHAM, Capt. John, O.B.E., R.A.M.C., *b.* 13 Oct. 1871; *s.* of Thomas Wickersham, of Horsham; *m.* Emily, *d.* of James Morris, of Eastbourne. *Educ.:* Horsham Grammar School. *War Work:* Expeditionary Force, France and Belgium, Oct. 1914, to Oct. 1919. *Address:* No. 3, British General Hospital, Basrah, Mesopotamia. (O5924)

WICKES, Charles HAMILTON-, C.B.E., *b.* 8 Aug. 1866; *s.* of Thomas H. Wickes, late of Indian Service D.P.W., Chief Engineer, North-West Provinces; *m.* Florence Edith Bisset, *d.* of Richard Crossley, J.P., of Accrington. *Educ.:* All Hallows Grammar School, Honiton, Devon. Solicitor, 1885–92; Commerce, 1892–1908; first to hold appointment H.M. Trade Commissioner to Commonwealth of Australia, 1908–12; first to hold double appointment of H.M Trade Commissioner to Dominion of Canada and Newfoundland, 1912–18; H.M. Senior Trade Commissioner in the Service, 1917–20. *War Work:* H.M. Trade Commissioner to Dominion of Canada in charge of Commission to investigate timber resources of Newfoundland and maritime provinces of Canada; Director at Whitehall of Post-War market enquiry to ascertain the oversea demand for British Manufactures after the conclusion of hostilities. *Address:* Broad Oak, Northwood, Middlesex. *Clubs:* Constitutional; City Carlton. (C3042)

WICKHAM, Lieut.-Comm. Evelyn Twysden, O.B.E., R.N.

WICKHAM, Frederick, O.B.E.

WICKHAM, Surg.-Lieut.-Comm. Frederick St. Barbe, O.B.E., R.N.,

WICKHAM, Brig.-Gen. John Avenal, C.B.E. Served in the Great War 1914–19 (mentioned in despatches). (C2054)

WICKS, Ernest Arthur, M.B.E.

WICKS, Major Gerald Hamilton, O.B.E., R.E.

WICKS, Lieut.-Col. Henry William Cairns, O.B.E., D.S.O., *b.* 1881; *s.* of Henry Wicks. Entered Seaforth Highlanders (Ross-shire Buffs, the Duke of Albany's), 1900; Capt. 1906; Major, 1915; Zakka Khel and Mohmand Expedition, 1908; Great War, 1914–19, as a Gen. Staff Officer (despatches); appointed Lieut.-Col. comdg. a Physical Training School, 1918. (O5925)

WIDDERSON, Capt. Andrew James, O.B.E.

WIDDOWSON, Dorothy, M.B.E.

WIDDOWSON, Howell Young, O.B.E.

WIGAN, Aubrey John GRAHAM-, M.B.E., *b.* 3 Sept. 1897; *s.* of John Alfred Graham-Wigan, of Oakwood Park, Maidstone. *Educ.:* Eton Coll. *Address:* Oakwood Park, Maidstone. (M2645)

WIGGETT, John Howitson, M.B.E.

WIGGINS, Major Carl, O.B.E., R.A.O.C.

WIGHT, Mabel, M.B.E., *b.* 1876; *d.* of Wm. Dundas Wight. *Educ.:* Caldicot Towers, Bushey Heath. Herts. *War Work:* Hon. Sec. of St. John Auxiliary Hospital, Penarth, March, 1915, to June, 1919. *Address:* Falconhyrst, Bradford Place, Penarth, Glam. (M10055)

WIGHTMAN, Florence Oldfield, M.B.E.; *d.* of the Rev. W. A. Wightman, of Stillingfleet, York. *War Work:* Head of Bandage Room Department, York War Hospital Supply Depot, 1915–19. (M10056)

WIGHTMAN, Lieut. Henry Christopher, O.B.E., R.E.(T.).

WIGHTMAN, Owen William, C.B.E., J.P., *b.* 29 Dec. 1869; *s.* of the Rev. William Arnett Wightman, of Stillingfleet, York; *m.* Ethel Maria, *d.* of Henry Hall, of Alton, Hants. *Educ.:* Radley, and Exeter Coll., Oxford. Maltster; Director Brewing Branch, Ministry of Food. *War Work:* Hon. Lieut. Herts. Volunteer Regiment. *Address:* Bengeo, Herts. *Club:* Royal Automobile. (C3043)

WIGLEY, Lieut.-Col. George Alfred, O.B.E., *b.* 1872; *s.* of George Wigley, of Nottingham; *m.* Annie Louise, *d.* of William Pidcock, of Nottingham. *Educ.:* Merchant Taylors' School. *War Work:* Commanded 2/7th Sherwood Foresters, Sept. 1914, to July, 1915; Commanded 7th T.F. Reserve Batt. Sherwood Foresters, July, 1915, to March, 1919. *Address:* Wingfield, Lucknow Avenue, Nottingham. *Club:* County (Nottingham). (O7856)

WIGLEY, Kathleen Sinclair, Mrs., M.B.E.

WIGLEY, Thomas, M.B.E.

WIGNALL, Edith Marguerite, M.B.E., *d.* of Edwin Sate, of 14, Park Street; *m.* Frederick William, *s.* of Walter Barton Wignall, of Spital, Cheshire. *War Work:* Commandant of Tattenhall and The Rookery Hospitals, Oct. 1914, to April, 1919. *Addresses:* The Rookery, Tattenhall, Cheshire; Cambusmore, The Mound, Sutherland. (M2646)

WIGRAM, Agnes Vernon, Mrs. Henry Francis, O.B.E.

WIGRAM, Col. Kenneth, C.B., C.B.E., D.S.O., *b.* Dec. 5 1875; *s.* of late Herbert Wigram, late I.C.S. *Educ.:* Winchester chester and Sandhurst. General Staff (Director of Staff Duties), Army Headquarters, India. *War Work:* General Staff, Army Headquarters, India, Aug. 1914, to May, 1915; General Staff, G.H.Q. France, June, 1915, to Sept. 1918; R.A.F. H.Q., France, Oct. 1918, till Armistice. *Club:* United Service. (C1912)

WILBERFORCE, Major Arthur Roland George, O.B.E. *b.* 21 Dec. 1877; *s.* of the Rt. Rev. Ernest Wilberforce, late Bishop of Chichester. *Educ.:* Winchester, and Christ Church, Oxford. Deputy Assistant Director, Q.M.G. Canteens, War Office. *War Work:* Served with 2nd Batt. Royal Sussex Regt. in France, 1914; severely wounded; attached Gen. Staff, War Office, 1915, to Sept. 1916; Staff Capt., 5A District, Sept. 1916, to Sept. 1918; Private Sec. to Q.M.G., War Office, Sept. 1918, to March, 1919. *Address:* 17, Eccleston Square, S.W. 1. *Clubs:* Naval and Military; Royal Automobile. (O7857)

WILBERFORCE, Brig.-Gen. Sir Herbert William K.B.E., C.B., C.M.G., *b.* 4 July, 1866; *s.* of the late Venerable Wilberforce, of Westminster Abbey; *m.* Eleanor Catherine, *d.* of Major-Gen. E. Micklem, of Rosehill, Henley-on-Thames. *Educ.:* Eton and Sandhurst. *War Work:* Served in France continuously from Aug. 1914, until Jan. 1920, first as Lieut.-Col. Commanding Queen's Bays, latterly as Base Commandant, Boulogne; Knight of Grace, St. John of Jerusalem, Croix de Commander Legion of Honour (France); Grand Officer Military Order of Avis (Portugal). *Address:* Kingswood, Medmenham, Marlow. *Clubs:* Cavalry; Royal Automobile. (K321b)

WILBRAHAM, Capt. Henry Dudley, O.B.E.

WILBRAHAM, Major Hugh Edward, M.B.E.

WILBRAHAM, Lady Alice Maud BOOTLE-, O.B.E., *b.* 22 June, 1861; *d.* of 1st Earl of Lathom, of Lathom House, Ormskirk (see BURKE'S *Peerage*). *Educ.:* Privately. Lady District Superintendent London District, St. John Ambulance Brigade. *War Work:* Started and organised Queen Mary's Royal Naval Hospital, Southend-on-Sea; President, Silver Thimble Fund, which collected over £70,000; worked in Canteens; King Edward's Coronation Medal; King George's Coronation Medal; Long Service Medal; Sister St. John of Jerusalem; Order of Queen Elizabeth of Belgium. *Address:* 26, Lower Sloane Street, S.W. 1. (O11609)

WILBRAHAM, Evelyn Caryl Bootle, O.B.E., Ph.D., F.I.C., F.C.S., *b.* 8 June, 1877; *s.* of Col. Arthur B. Wilbraham. *Educ.:* Clifton Coll., and Leipzig Univ. *War Work:* Superintendent of H.M. High Explosives Factory, Rainham, Essex; afterwards technical adviser to Explosives Dept. of the Ministry of Munitions; Liaison Officer to Gun and Ammunition Filling Dept. of Ministry of Munitions. *Address:* 28, Ovington Square, S.W. 3. *Clubs:* Royal Institution; Royal Aero.; Chemical Industry. (O2007)

WILBY, Col. Arthur William Roger, O.B.E., C.E., *b.* 27 March, 1875; *s.* of the late Lieut. A. E. Wilby, 61st Regt.; *m.* Eva Mary, *d.* of Arthur P. Blathwayt, of Northwood Grange, Middlesex. *Educ.:* Upper Canada Coll., Toronto, Canada; R.M.C., Kingston, Canada. Agent for British Columbia, of the Marine Dept., Federal Government of Canada. *War Work:* Gazetted as Captain to the 62nd Batt. C.E.F., June, 1915; promoted Major, Dec. 1915; transferred to the 48th Batt. C.E.F. on proceeding to France, Aug. 1916; appointed D.A.D. of Labour for Canadian Corps, April, 1917; appointed Labour Commandant Canadian Corps with rank of Colonel, April, 1918; returned to Canada and demobilised, Aug. 1919; *Address:* Victoria, British Columbia. *Club:* Union; Victoria. (C1358)

WILCOCK, Lieut. Albert Edward, O.B.E., R.N.V.R.

WILCOCK, Joseph, M.B.E., *b.* 23 March, 1858; *s.* of Joseph Wilcock, of Preston Lancashire; *m.* Annie, *d.* of Jacob Hindle, of Nelson, Lanc. *Educ.:* Marton School, Blackpool. Superintendent, Lancashire County Constabulary. *War Work:* General War work in Connection with local munition works. *Address:* 87, Seaforth Road, Seaforth, Liverpool. (M10060)

WILD, Lieut. John Robert Francis, C.B.E., R.N.V.R. Accompanied the Shackleton Antartic Expeditions. (C3044)

WILD, Norman Ward, M.B.E.

WILD, Robert Vaughan, O.B.E.

WILD, Brig.-Gen. Ralph Kirby BAGNALL-, C.M.G., C.B.E., *b.* 1873; *s.* of Ralph Bagnall Bagnall-Wild, J.P., of The Manor House, Costock, Loughborough; *m.* Maida, *d.* of the late John Devereux, of Hereford. Brevet Major, R.E. Reserve, and Lieut.-Col. and T. Brig.-Gen., R.A.F. (C1885)

WILDBORE, Albert Milton, M.B.E., R.N.

WILDER, Edward Hunter, M.B.E., Commissioned Boatswain, R.N., *b.* 1 May, 1870; *s.* of David Hunter Wilder, of Dalkeith, Scotland; *m.* Evelyn Blanche, *d.* of William Fryer, of Portsmouth. *Educ.:* Greenwich R.H. School. Assistant to King's Harbour Master, Gibraltar Dockyard; in charge of Boom Defence and Moorings, Berthing and Sailing of Ships in convoys, Salvage work, etc. *Addresses:* Richmond,

London Road, nr. Horndean, Hants.; H.M. Dockyard, Gibraltar. (M2648)

WILDING, Edward, C.B.E., *b.* 25 Nov. 1875; *s.* of Henry Wilding, of Liverpool; *m.* Marion Emily, *d.* of William Shilton, of Burton-on-Trent. *Educ.:* Liverpool Institute; R.N.E. Coll., Devonport; R.N. Coll., Greenwich. Managing Director of Harland & Wolff, Ltd.; Deputy Director of Designs under Controller General of Merchant Shipbuilding, 1918–19. *Address:* 6, Royal Terrace, Lisburn Road, Belfast. *Club:* Ulster Reform. (C3045)

WILDING, 2nd Lieut. Henry, M.B.E.

WILDING, Capt. Michael Henley, C.B.E., R.N. Served in Great War, 1914–19 (mentioned in despatches). (C2284)

WILDMAN, Major Sam Beck, O.B.E., R.A.S.C., *b.* 21 Aug. 1868. Superintendent No 1 Remount Depot, Dublin. *War Work:* In addition to superintending Remount Depot was assistant to the Inspector of Remounts, Irish Command, from 1914–17; Supervised the Embarkation and disembarkation of horses at the Port of Dublin. (O3205)

WILDY, Comm. Edmund, O B.E., V.D., R.N.V.R.

WILDY, Capt. Harold Adams, O.B.E., M.G.C.

WILES, Capt. Harold Herbert, M.B.E.,

WILEY, Capt. Thomas Paul, O.B.E., *b.* 2 Dec. 1883; *s.* of late Arthur John, of Oulton Broad, Suffolk; *m.* Eileen Mary, *d.* of Doctor Joseph Alexander Tooner, late of Broad Street, Pendleton. *Educ.:* Rossall School, Fleetwood, Lancs. Engineer and Local Manager of Waygood-Otis Ltd., Lift Makers, London. *War Work:* In charge of 610th Fortress Company, R.E.; responsible for Defence Electric Lighting, Milford Haven Garrison. *Address:* 90, Princess Street, Manchester. (O7858)

WILFORD, Major Edmund Ernest, D.S.O., O.B.E., *b.* 1876; *s.* of the late Col. Edmund Percival Wilford, Gloucestershire Regt.; *m.* Rachel Lancaster Sharpe. *Educ.:* Clifton Coll. Major Indian Army; Great War, 1914–19 as Lieut.-Col. York and Lancaster Regt., and subsequently Major Roy. Defence Corps (despatches). *Club:* Royal Automobile. (O7860)

WILFORD, Edward Charles, M.B.E.

WIKLE, Bessie Dayrell, M.B.E., *b.* 18 Oct. 1890; *d.* of the late Augustus Wilké, of Epsom, Surrey. *Educ.:* Lee High School for Girls. *War Work:* Club Leader and organiser of The Daughters of the Empire Club, Upper Norwood, since Jan. 1915, under the auspices of the Y.W.C.A. *Address:* Thimbleby, South Vale, Upper Norwood, S.E. 19. (M10061)

WILKIE, Surg.-Lieut.-Comm. David Percival Dalbrick, O.B.E., M.B., R.N.V.R.

WILKIE, Helen Gertrude, Mrs., C.B.E.; *d.* of late Reginald Reynolds, of 28, Clarendon Square, Leamington; *m.* E. O. Hales Wilkie (Major, Worcestershire Regt. ret.), *s.* of the late General Hales Wilkie, of Ellington, Kent. *War Work:* Founder, Organiser, and Hon. Sec. The Womens Emergency Canteens for soldiers, founded Jan. 1915, closed June, 1919; Canteens on the French Front and at the Gare du Nord and Gare de Lyon, Paris, for Allied troops; transport of Wounded and much relief work. *Address:* 9, Grove Court, Drayton Gdns., S.W. 10. (C3046)

WILKIE, Capt. James Bowman, M.B.E., M.B., R.A.M.C.

WILKIE, Major Robert, O.B.E., R.A.S.C.

WILKIN, Rear-Adm. Henry Douglas, C.B.E., D.S.O., J.P. (West Riding of Yorkshire (1920) R.N., *b.* 27 March, 1862; *s.* of Major H. J. Wilkin, of 11th and 7th Hussars; *m.* Elfrida Bertha, *d.* of Egbert Iveson, of Charters, Ascot. *Educ.:* Eastman's Preparatory School and H.M.S. "Britannia." *War Work:* Senior Naval Officer at Belfast. *Address:* Wetherby Grange, Wetherby, Yorks. *Clubs:* United Service; Royal Naval (Portsmouth); Yorkshire. (C2328)

WILKINS, Capt. Dennison Alfred, M.B.E., *b.* 28 July, 1892; *s.* of late A. D. Wilkins, of 21, Pemberley Avenue, Bedford. *Educ.:* Bedford School, and Sandhurst. *War Work:* Severely wounded at Second battle of Ypres, April, 1915; Adjutant, Anti-Aircraft Command, 1916; on Staff from 1917–20; mentioned "London Gazette," March, 1920. *Address:* 21, Pemberley Avenue, Bedford. *Club:* United Service. (M5729)

WILKINS, Elizabeth Bastable, O.B.E., *b.* 24 Feb. 1883; *d.* of Stephen Wilkins, of Shaftesbury. Nursing Sister. *War Work:* Assistant to Miss Edith Cavell, Brussels, Belgium, 1914–15; Sister in Charge B. Red Cross Hospital St. Fagan's Castle, Glam., S. Wales, March, 1916, to March, 1919. *Addresses:* Yeatman Hospital, Sherborne, Dorset; Stour, Shaftesbury, Dorset. (O11610)

WILKINS, Frederick Charles Sydney, O.B.E.

WILKINS, Harold, M.B.E.

WILKINS, Capt. John, O.B.E.

WILKINS, Louisa, Mrs. Roland Field, O.B.E.

WILKINS, Margaret Mabel, M.B.E.

WILKINS, Lieut. Raymond, O.B.E., R.A.O.C.

WILKINS, Col. Thomas James Hackett, O.B.E.,M.R.C.P.E., L.R.C.S.E., I.M.S., *b.* 6 Oct. 1850; *s.* of Thomas Wilkins, Deputy Registrar, High Court, Madras; *m.* Alicia Caroline Evelyn, *d.* of Lieut.-Col. Felix Richard Vincent Jervis, of the Bengal Army. *Educ.:* Ootacamund Grammar School; Madras; Edinburgh; and special Hospitals in London. Took part in the Burma expedition in 1884–85; S.M.O. of the Tongoo-Nyngan Column under Col. Dicken, received medal and clasp; retired from I.M.S. as Divisional P.M.O., the 9th Secunderabad Division, late Madras Command; President of the Recruiting Medical Board at Great Scotland Yard, under Military authorities;

Senior Chairman and Deputy Commissioner of the Medical Boards at Whitehall under the Ministry of National Services, and Deputy Commissioner of Medical Services in the Ministry of Pensions ; in charge of the Discharge Board of the Royal Air Force, at Blandford, Halton Camp, and Uxbridge. *Address :* c/o Messrs. Coutts & Co., 440, Strand, London, W.C. 2. (O11612)

WILKINSON, Clennell Anstruther, M.B.E.

WILKINSON, Christopher Henry George, M.B.E.

WILKINSON, Surg.-Lieut.-Comm. Edward Aubrey Guy, O.B.E., B.A., R.N.

WILKINSON, Capt. Edward John, O.B.E.

WILKINSON, T. Warrant Officer Ernest, M.B.E., Royal Indian Marine. (M6780h)

WILKINSON, Frederick, C.B.E.

WILKINSON, Col. George Alexander Eason, C.B.E., D.S.O., *b.* 1860 ; *s.* of the late Matthew Wilkinson of Middle-thorpe Hall, Yorkshire ; *m.* 1886· the Hon. Caroline Catherine Horsley-Beresford, *d.* of 3rd Baron Decies (*see* BURKE'S *Peerage*) J.P. for W. and E. Ridings of Yorkshire ; Hon.-Major in the Army ; Lieut.-Col. Royal Defence Corps, 1914–19 ; formerly Lieut.-Col. Comdg. and Hon. Col. 4th Bn. Sherwood Foresters (Notts. and Derbyshire Regt.). Served in S. Africa, 1900–1 (severely wounded, despatches). *Address :* Dring-houses Manor, York. (C837)

WILKINSON, Capt. Gerrard Napier, O.B.E., I.A.

WILKINSON, Harry Cuthbert William, M.B.E.

WILKINSON, Harry William John, M.B.E.

WILKINSON, Major, Brevet Lieut.-Col., Henry Benfield Des Voeux, C.B.E., D.S.O., Durham Light Infantry, *b.* 18 Oct. 1870 ; *s.* of Major H. C. Wilkinson, of Oswald House, nr. Durham ; *m.* Bridget, *d.* of Col. T. B. Cookson, C.B., of Meldon Park, Morpeth. *Educ.:* Cheam School ; Wellington Coll. ; Sandhurst ; Staff Coll. *War Work :* D.A.A. and Q.M.G., South African War ; G.S.O.2, 1st Peshawar Div. Expedition against Bunurwals, 1914 ; Provost Marshal, Indian Corps, D.A.A., and Q.M.G. Lahore Division ; A.A. and Q.M.G. 33rd Division ; A.A. and Q.M.G., 23rd Division ; A.A. and Q.M.G. 68th Division. *Address :* 20, Cliveden Place, S.W. *Club :* Army and Navy. (C1814)

WILKINSON, Rev. Horace Ricardo, O.B.E., R.N.

WILKINSON, Howitt Key, M.B.E.

WILKINSON, John, O.B.E.

WILKINSON, Kenneth Douglas, O.B.E., *b.* 17 April, 1886 ; *s.* of Rev. H. C. Wilkinson, of High Leigh, Cheshire ; *m.* Phebe Helena, *d.* of Capt. C. H. Homewood, of Wallasey, Cheshire. *Educ.:* Berkhamsted, and Birmingham Univ. Assistant Physician General Hospital Birmingham ; Physician to Out-patients, Children's Hospital, Birmingham. *War Work :* Served successively as Lieut., Capt., and Major in R.A.M.C. (T.) (Medical Specialist). *Address :* 91, Cornwall Street, Birmingham. (O5928)

WILKINSON, Martin, M.B.E.

WILKINSON, Capt. Noel Read Ellershaw, O.B.E., R.A.S.C.

WILKINSON, Lieut.-Comm. Norman, O.B.E., R.I., R.N.V.R., *b.* 24 Nov. 1878 ; *s.* of T. C. Wilkinson ; *m.* Evelyn Harriet, *d.* of Rev. Murdo Mackenzie, Swatow, China. *Educ.:* Berkhamsted. Artist. *War Work :* Lieut.-Comm. R.N.V.R., served in various theatres of war ; 1917, originated and carried out the system of " Dazzle " Painting as applied to Merchant Vessels for protection against Torpedo attack ; this system was officially adopted by all the Allied maritime nations. *Address :* 40, Marlborough Hill, St. John's Wood, N.W. 8. *Clubs :* Royal Thames Yacht ; St. John's Wood Arts. (O861)

WILKINSON, Lieut. Ralph Thomas, O.B.E., R.N.V.R.

WILKINSON, Rev. Richard Brindle, O.B.E., *b.* 5 May, 1886 ; *s.* of R. Wilkinson, of Hoghton, nr. Preston ; *m.* Mary, *d.* of Thos. Bretherton, of Hoghton nr. Preston. *Educ.:* Didsbury Coll., Manchester. Wesleyan Minister. *War Work :* Fourth Class Chaplain from April, 1915, to June, 1919 ; attached to 6th and 29th Divisions ; served with these Divisions in France, Flanders, and Germany, during that period. *Address :* Daisy Bank, Rhodes, Manchester. (O2783)

WILKINSON, Lieut. Robert Joseph, M.B.E.

WILKS, Capt. Frank Stanley, O.B.E., *b.* 1 July, 1882 ; *s.* of E. T. Wilks, F.R.G.S., C.C., of Watford ; *m.* Winifred, *d.* of F. H. Freeth, of Putney. *Educ.:* Mill Hill School. Chartered Accountant. *War Work :* Gazetted Lieut. in the R.A.S.C., Aug. 1915 ; appointed Supply Officer 156th Inf. Bde., 52nd Division, Dec. 1915 ; served with the division on Gallipoli, Egypt, Sinai, Palestine, and France ; promoted Capt. Sept. 1916 ; thrice mentioned in despatches. *Addresses :* 26, Kingsfield Road, Watford, Herts, ; 31, Lombard Street, E.C. (O5930)

WILKS, T. Major John Eason, O.B.E., R.A.S.C.

WILLAN, Surg.-Comm. Robert Joseph, M.V.O. O.B.E., V.D., M.B., R.N.V.R., *b.* 1878 ; *s.* of John Willan, J.P., of Durham ; *m.* Dorothy Eleanor, *d.* of J. B. Shawyer, of Carlisle. *Educ.:* Durham. T. Hon. Surgeon, Royal Victoria Infirmary, Newcastle-on-Tyne. *War Work :* Served in R.N. Hospital Ships, " Drina," " Plassy," and " Karapara," Aug. 1914, to Sept. 1918, at R.N. Hospital, Haslar, Sept. 1918, to July, 1919. *Address :* 6, Kensington Terrace, Newcastle-on-Tyne. *Club :* Union. (O9509)

WILLANS, Gordon Jenne, M.B.E.

WILLCOCK, Rev. John, O.B.E., D.D., D.Litt., *b.* 18 April, 1853 ; *s.* of John Willcock, of Northwich, Cheshire ; *m.* Annie Bannatyne, *d.* of William Malcolmson, of Lerwick.

Educ.: Liverpool High School, and Edinburgh Univ. Minister of United Free Church of Scotland. *War Work :* Sec. of War Savings Associations for County of Zetland, Sec. of Soldiers' and Sailors' Families Association. *Address :* St. Ringan's Manse, Lerwick, Shetland. (O11613)

WILLCOCKS, Major George Charles, O.B.E., M.C., Aust. A.M.C.

WILLCOX, Capt. Howard James Lionel Walter Kox, C.B.E., R.N. Served in Great War, 1914–19, with Ocean Escort (mentioned in despatches). (C1209)

WILLCOX, Capt. William Garratt, M.B.E., *b.* 23 April, 1879 ; *s.* of James Willcox, of Putney. *Educ.:* Privately. *War Work :* Sec. to British Farmers' Red Cross Fund ; assisting Sir Herbert Brown in the raising of a Fund of £1,053,000 in this connection ; executive organiser to the Frances Day branch of the French Red Cross ; now Sec. to the Appeal Department of Earl Haig's Officers' Association. (M10064)

WILLCOX, William Henry, O.B.E., *b.* 5 Dec. 1871 ; *s.* of Henry Willcox, of Spalding ; *m.* Lucy Mabel, *d.* of Andrew Aitken, of Spalding. *Educ.:* Spalding Grammar School. H.M. Civil Service ; Administrative Officer of the First Division ; Assistant Sec. to the Commissioners of the Royal Hospital, Chelsea. *War Work :* Chief Civil Officer in charge of work connected with the award of disability pensions to Warrant Officers, N.C.O.s and men invalided from the Army from the beginning of the war until the creation of the Ministry of Pensions ; continued in charge of work connected with the award of Long Service Pensions, awards for Distinguished Conduct Medals in addition to pension, as well as other duties relating to the permanent appointment of Assistant Sec. to the Commissioners of the Royal Hospital, Chelsea ; for the first year of its existence assisted the Ministry of Pensions in an advisory capacity. *Address :* The Royal Hospital, Chelsea, S.W. 3. (O11614)

WILLER, Herbert Humphries, M.B.E.

WILLERT, Sir Arthur, K.B.E., *b.* 19 May, 1882 ; *s.* of late P. F. Willert, of Headington Hill, Oxford ; *m.* Florence, *d.* of late Sir Walter Simpson, Bart., of Balabraes, Ayton, Scotland (*see* BURKE'S *Peerage*). *Educ.:* Eton, Balliol Coll., Oxford. Correspondent of the " Times " at Washington, U.S.A. ; joined staff of " Times," 1905 ; correspondent of the " Times " at Washington, 1910–17 ; Sec. British War Mission in Washington, and representative there of Ministry of Information, 1917–18. *Address :* Headington Hill, Oxford. *Club :* Metropolitan (Washington). (K241)

WILLES, Lieut. Harry, M.B.E., R.G.A. (S.R.).

WILLETT, Henry Goodrich, C.B.E. Secretary to the Trinity House for 48 years. (C1055)

WILLETT, Lieut. Hugh, M.B.E., R.E.

WILLETT, John Eddowes, C.B.E., J.P., Knight of Grace of Order of St. John of Jerusalem, *b.* 23 April, 1853 ; *s.* of John Spencer Willett, of Liverpool. *Educ.:* Privately. Alder-man of County Borough of Southport ; Chairman of Finance Committee ; Mayor of Southport, 1907–8, 1914–5 ; Vice-Chairman Southport Unionist Association ; Member of West Lancashire Territorial Association ; Member of York House of Laymen and of National Church Assembly ; Churchwarden, All Saints, Southport, 1897–1919 ; Merchant and Shipowner, Liverpool, and Director International Navigation Co., Ltd. ; Hon. Freeman of the Borough of Southport. *War Work :* As Mayor of Southport during the first year of the War carried out numerous duties as Chairman of Committees for raising funds and providing for comforts of troops, and continued in all such committees till end of war ; President of the Southport St. John V.A.D. Hospital, 1915–19 ; Military Representative and National Service Representative at Local Tribunal, 1915–19 ; Hon. Battalion Commandant in the Lancashire Volunteer Brigade, 1915 ; has Medaille du Roi Albert, 1920. *Address :* 3, Park Road, Southport. *Clubs :* Conservative (Liverpool) ; Conservative (Southport) ; Hesketh Golf (Southport). (C3048)

WILLETT, Major Lewis Howard, O.B.E.

WILLETT, Thomas Charles, M.B.E., *b.* 1884 ; *s.* of Thomas Willett, of Wandsworth ; *m.* Marie Lavinia, *d.* of William Henry Windmill, L.D.S., R.C.S.I., of Wandsworth. *Educ.:* Honey-well Higher Grade School. Sec. to the Mayor of Wandsworth. *War Work :* Hon. Secretary Borough of Wandsworth War Savings Committee (organised Tank, Gun, War Weapons, and Victory Loan Campaigns) ; Hon. Sec. Borough of Wandsworth Assn. of Vol. Workers (mentioned in despatches by War Office) ; Sec. Prince of Wales' National Relief Fund ; Hon. Sec Surrey Prisoners of War Fund, Wandsworth ; Hon. Sec. 13th East Surrey Regt. Comforts Fund, and also Hon. Sec. to various other organisations connected with the war. (M10065)

WILLEY, Lieut.-Col. Francis Vernon, C.M.G., C.B.E., M.V.O., M.A., M.P., *b.* 1884 ; *s.* of Francis Willey, J.P., of Blyth Hall, Notts. *Educ.:* Eton and Magdalen Coll., Oxford. A partner in the firm of Francis Willey & Co., wool merchant's, of Bradford, Yorkshire, and Boston, U.S.A. ; Major, Notts (Sherwood Rangers) Yeo. (T.D.), attached T. Lieut.-Col., R.A.O.C. ; Controller of Wool Supplies, Min. of Munitions Supply ; has sat as M.P. for S. Div. of Bradford since Dec. 1918. *Address :* Blyth Hall, via Rotherham, Notts. *Clubs :* Carlton ; St Stephen's ; Bath ; Cavalry ; Hurlingham. (C1812)

WILLIAMS, Major Albert, O.B.E.

WILLIAMS, Albert George, M.B.E., *b.* 9 Sept. 1881 ; *s.* of Albert Kurtch Williams, of Kew ; *m.* Elsie, *d.* of John Hammett, of Richmond. *Educ.:* Tiffin's School, Kingston-on-Thames. Principal Observer at the National Physical

Laboratory. *War Work:* Inspection of Optical Munitions for H.M. Navy, etc. *Address:* 242, Sandycombe Road, Kew Gardens. (M4084)

WILLIAMS, Lieut. Albert Henry, O.B.E., R.A.O.C. (T.).

WILLIAMS, Capt. Albert Howard, O.B.E.

WILLIAMS, Capt. Alfred Dalby Ross, O.B.E., R.G.A. (T.).

WILLIAMS, Capt. and Qr.-Mr. Alfred Edwin, O.B.E.

WILLIAMS, Surg.-Lieut. Alfred Gregson, O.B.E., R.N.

WILLIAMS, Lieut. Alfred Harry, O.B.E., R.A.S.C.

WILLIAMS, Amy Katharine, O.B.E. *Educ.:* Privately. Headmistress L.C.C. School; Executive National Union of Teachers; Past President London Teachers' Association; Treasurer L.C.C. Women Teachers' Union. *War Work:* Committee L.C.C. Women Teachers' effort for supplying comforts for wounded soldiers; National War Savings Committee (Women's Advisory Committee); Committee (National Union of Teachers) War Aid Fund; Committee National Union of Teachers' Belgian Relief Fund; and Prince of Wales' War Aid Fund; assisted in organising collections for Ambulances, Red Cross Funds, Blue Cross Funds, Blinded Soldiers' Fund, Blinded Soldiers' Children Fund, Army Huts Fund, Jack Cornwell Fund. *Address:* L.C.C. School, Broadwater Road, Tooting. (O11615)

WILLIAMS, Annie Margery, Mrs., O.B.E.

WILLIAMS, Major Archard Trevor, O.B.E., R.A.S.C. (T.), *b.* 10 May, 1885; *s.* of the late W. Maurice Williams, of Leicester; *m.* Violet Ysobel, *d.* of J. Bruce-Payne, M.A., of Bishop Stortford, Herts. *Educ.:* Stoneygate School, Leicester, and King's School, Canterbury. Qualified as a Solicitor in 1908; joined A.S.C. (T.) as 2/Lieut. on 7 July, 1908; promoted Capt. 18 May, 1910; Member of the Leicestershire Territorial Association; Member of the National Service League. *War Work:* Mobilised, Lincoln and Leicester Bde. Co. A.S.C. (T.), on outbreak of War in Aug. 1914, and served during the War in the 46th, 59th, 58th, and 34th (Eastern) Divisions; twice mentioned in despatches; promoted T. Major, Oct. 1915; Major, June, 1916; at present O.C. R.A.S.C., Ripon. *Addresses:* c/o Sir Chas. R. McGrigor, Bart., and Co., 39, Panton Street, Haymarket; c/o J. Bruce-Payne, M.A., Bishop Stortford, Herts. (O5933)

WILLIAMS, Lieut.-Col. Arthur Cecil, C.B.E., Royal Artillery, *b.* 24 Feb. 1871; *s.* of J. B. Williams. *Educ.:* Portsmouth Grammar School, and Royal Military Academy; Fellow of the Optical Society; Director of Inspection of Optical Supplies during the war; Chief Instructor in Range Finding, Great Britain, 1919–20. *Club:* Junior United Service. (C1813)

WILLIAMS, Major Arthur Donald John Bedwood, O.B.E.

WILLIAMS, Major Arthur Frederick Basil, O.B.E.

WILLIAMS, Lieut. Arthur James, M.B.E.

WILLIAMS, Arthur Moray, O.B.E., M.A., *b.* 6 March, 1878; *s.* of Rev. J. A. Williams. late Vicar of Alderminster, Stratford-on-Avon; *m.* Mabel Lizzie, *d.* of Edward Unwin, of Shortlands, Kent. *Educ.:* Felsted and Cambridge. Chief Assistant County Director Hampshire Territorial Force Association; Sec. to the Trustees of the Home of Recovery for Surgical Convalescents in Hampshire. *Address:* Cherrycroft, Petersfield, Hants. *Club:* Public Schools. (O2010)

WILLIAMS, Arthur Owen, M.B.E.

WILLIAMS, Charles, O.B.E.

WILLIAMS, Lieut. Charles, M.B.E., R.E.

WILLIAMS, Major Charles Edward, O.B.E., M.I.Mech.E., *b.* 11 Jan. 1873; *s.* of D. E. Williams, of Brecon. *Educ.:* Llandovery Coll., Carmarthenshire. Mechanical Engineer; Deputy Chief Inspecting Engineer to the Crown Agents for the Colonies. *War Work:* War Office, as Staff Captain, 1915–17; Ministry of Munitions as Director; 1918 until termination of war, as Major and D.A.D. at War Office. *Address:* 4, Millbank, Westminster. *Club:* St. Stephen's. (O863)

WILLIAMS, Charles George, M.B.E.

WILLIAMS, Charles Robert Thomas, O.B.E.

WILLIAMS, Lieut. Charles Sydney, M.B.E., R.A.S.C.

WILLIAMS, Capt. Cyril Theodore, O.B.E., E. Surrey Regt. (O11788)

WILLIAMS, Daisy, Mrs., M.B.E. Area Inspector of Women's Forage Corps, R.A.S.C. (M10340)

WILLIAMS, David, O.B.E.

WILLIAMS, 2nd Lieut. David Eric, M.B.E., R.A.F.

WILLIAMS, Sir Dawson, Knt. Bach., C.B.E., M.D., F.R.C.P., *b.* 1854; *s.* of the Rev. John Mack Williams, formerly Rector of Burnby, Yorkshire; *m.* 1882, Catherine (who died 1917), *d.* of Robert Kirkpatrick-Howart, of Mabie, Kircudbrightshire. Editor, *British Medical Journal;* Consulting Physician, E. London Hospital for Children. Rendered service to R.A.M.C. during Great War. *Addresses:* Wall End, Bourne End; 2F, Portman Mansions, Marylebone Road, W. 1. *Clubs:* Garrick; Bath. (C304a)

WILLIAMS, Edith, Mrs., M.B.E., B.A. (Lond.). Commandant, V.A.D. Carnarvon 22, British Red Cross Society, since 1912. *War Work:* Organiser and acted as Hon. Sec. Pwllheli Women's War Relief Association, 1914–19; as Commandant, supplied nurses for temporary hospital for troops in training in Pwllheli, and occasional nurses for Wern Hospital, Portmadoc. *Address:* Haulfryn, Pwllheli, N. Wales. (M10067)

WILLIAMS, Capt. Edward Richard, M.B.E., L.R.C.P. (Lond.), M.R.C.S. (Eng.), R.A.M.C. (T.) (ret.). Hon. Medical

Officer, Carmarthenshire Infirmary; Medical Officer, H.M. Prison, Carmarthen. *War Work:* Medical Officer in Charge of Troops, Carmarthen; Medical Officer, Carmarthen Auxiliary Hospital. *Address:* 36, Spilman Street, Carmarthen. (M10068)

WILLIAMS, Emma Christine, Mrs., M.B.E., M.B., B.S.

WILLIAMS, Ernest Graham, M.B.E., *b.* 29 April, 1875; *s.* of Henry Williams, of Clapham Common; *m.* Dorothy Grace, *d.* of — Nerney, of Wandsworth. *Educ.:* Privately. Civil Servant in Board of Trade. *War Work:* Admiralty and Ministry of Shipping. (M1095)

WILLIAMS, Ernest Thomas, O.B.E., M.I.E.E., *b.* 9 Oct. 1877; *s.* of W. H. Williams, of Manchester and Blackpool; *m.* Maggie Clarke, *d.* of Richard Catleugh, of Hunstanton. *Educ.:* Manchester Technical Coll. Electrical Engineer; Assistant Director of Electrical Engineering, Admiralty. *War Work:* Electrical Engineer, Hong Kong Naval Base; Electrical Engineer, Admiralty, later Assistant Director of Electrical Engineering, responsible amongst other items for the electrical equipment of Shore and Air Stations, Aircraft and Auxiliary Naval Vessels. *Address:* 11, The Drive, Golder's Green. (O11617)

WILLIAMS, Capt. Ernest Ulysses, O.B.E., M.R.C.S., L.R.C.P., late R.A.M.C., *b.* 1880; *s.* of Alfred Dawson, of London; *m.* Emma Christine, *d.* of Charles Pillman. *Educ.:* Kings Coll. School and Hospital. Radiographer, Royal Free Hospital and Queen's Hospital, London. *War Work:* Served under French, Servian, and Russian Red Cross, 1914–16; attached numerous Hospitals as Consultant 1916–17; attached War Office, 1917–19; received Mons Medal, Order of St. Sava, Balkan Red Cross Medal, O.B.E. *Address:* 128, Harley Street, W. 1. *Clubs:* National Sporting; Royal Automobile; Royal Botanical Society; Royal Society of Medicine. (O7864)

WILLIAMS, Major Francis Cartwright, O.B.E.

WILLIAMS, Frank Eliot, O.B.E., *b.* 2 Sept. 1881; *s.* of William Williams, of London; *m.* Marian Jane, *d.* of Harry Frost, of Wimbledon. *Educ.:* University Coll. School. General Manager of the European Gas Co., Ltd. *War Work:* Chairman of an Export Licensing Committee of the War Trade Department. *Address:* Ocklynge Manor House, Mill Road, Eastbourne; Finsbury House, Blomfield Street, London, E.C. *Club:* Reform. (O864)

WILLIAMS, Major Frank Harry, O.B.E., M.C., R.E.

WILLIAMS, Capt. Frederick Thomas, M.B.E.

WILLIAMS, Friend Isaacs, M.B.E., I.A.D.

WILLIAMS, Rev. Garfield, O.B.E.

WILLIAMS, George Owen, M.B.E., *b.* 2 April, 1873; *s.* of William Williams, of Ruthin; *m.* Elizabeth Ann, *d.* of Jonathan Rawling, of Llandudno. *Educ.:* Ruthin Board School. Railway Official; Councillor and Ex-Chairman, Prestatyn Urban District Council. *War Work:* Chairman, Prestatyn Food Control Committee and Allotment Holders' Association; Hon. Sec. Prestatyn and District, Tontine Approved Society, War Savings Association; Chairman of Prestatyn Urban District Council; Hon. Sec. Prestatyn Prisoners of War Fund. *Address:* Gwynlys, Prestatyn. (M19069)

WILLIAMS, Lieut. Gerald Atherton, M.B.E., R.A.F.

WILLIAMS, Capt. Harold, M.B.E., *b.* 17 July, 1883; *s.* of the Rev. Henry Hugh Williams, late of Brilley Vicarage, Herefordshire; *m.* Evelyn Diana Stonhouse, *d.* of Major Vansittart Pochin, of Market Harborough. *Educ.:* Cheltenham Coll. *War Work:* Enlisted in Motor Machine Gun Service; Commissioned in France 1916; transferred to Royal Army Service Corps; invalided to England, 1917; Adjutant, R.A.S.C., Bulford, 1917–19; Adjutant, Embarkation Depot, R.A.S.C., Portsmouth, 1919–20. *Address:* Minehead and West Somerset Club, Minehead. (M5732)

WILLIAMS, Lieut. Harold, O.B.E., R.E.

WILLIAMS, Capt. Harold Baskerville, O.B.E., R.A.V.C. (S.R.)

WILLIAMS, Harris Gregory, O.B.E., *b.* 4 April, 1870; *s.* of Samuel Gregory Williams, of Plymouth; *m.* Blanche Ford, *d.* of W. J. Harris, of Dulwich. *Educ.:* Reading School; R.N. Engineering Coll., Keyham; and Royal Naval Coll., Greenwich. Naval Architect; General Manager and Chief Naval Architect of Sir W. G. Armstrong, Whitworth & Co., Ltd., Shipyard Department. *War Work:* Construction of submarines, airships, and other war vessels. *Address:* 6, Windsor Crescent, Newcastle-on-Tyne. *Club:* Royal Automobile. (O3992)

WILLIAMS, Helen Lucy, M.B.E.,

WILLIAMS, Capt. Henry Claude, O.B.E., R.A.S.C. (T.F. Res.), *b.* 15 Jan. 1891; *s.* of Henry Williams, Surgeon, of Nottingham. *Educ.:* Gresham's School, Norfolk. *War Work:* Served in France and Belgium for 4½ years in 46th, 21st, and 3rd Cavalry Divisions; twice mentioned in despatches. *Clubs:* Services; Eccentric. (O5935)

WILLIAMS, Rev. Henry Morrison, O.B.E.

WILLIAMS, Henry Owen, O.B.E., I.S.O.

WILLIAMS, Hilda, O.B.E.

WILLIAMS, Isabel Rose, M.B.E.; *d.* of the Rev. A. H. Williams, M.A., late Rural Dean and Rector of Alcester, Chaplain to Queen Victoria and King Edward V. *War Work:* Lady President of the Waterloo Y.M.C.A. Hut, 1916–20. *Address:* Heatherlea, Worcester Park, Surrey. (M1096)

WILLIAMS, Lieut. James Leslie, C.M.G., M.B.E.

WILLIAMS, Jessie Wilhelmine, Mrs., M.B.E.

WILLIAMS, Major John, M.B.E., M.C.

WILLIAMS, Lieut.-Col. John, C.B.E. Lieut.-Col. comdg. Anzac Provost Corps.   (C331)

WILLIAMS, Capt. John Clive, O.B.E.

WILLIAMS, John Edgar, M.B.E., M.I.E.E., A.M.I.M.E., *b.* 4 April, 1880. Electrical and Mechanical Engineer. *War Work:* Sudan Government and Egyptian Army for the Darfour Expedition, in civilian capacity as Consulting Engineer for Mechanical Transport. *Address:* Sudan Public Works, Khartoum. *Club:* Sudan.   (M2827)

WILLIAMS, John Fischir, C.B.E., *b.* 26 Feb. 1870; *s.* of John Williams, of 5, Elvaston Place, London; *m.* Eleanor Marjorie Hay, *d.* of Robert Evelyn Murray, of Hascombe, Godalming. *Educ.:* Harrow, and New Coll., Oxford. Barrister-at-Law, Lincoln's Inn; Assistant Legal Adviser, Home Office; British Legal Adviser on the Reparation Commission, Paris. *Address:* Lamledra, Gorran Haven, Cornwall. *Club:* Athenæum.   (C75)

WILLIAMS, Major John Montague, M.B.E., R.E.

WILLIAMS, John Seth, M.B.E.

WILLIAMS, Lawrence Frederic Rushbrook, O.B.E.

WILLIAMS, Leonard Henry, M.B.E.

WILLIAMS, Capt. Leonard Lowther, M.B.E., M.B., R.E.

WILLIAMS, Capt. Leslie, M.B.E.

WILLIAMS, Mabel Catherine St. John, Mrs., O.B.E.

WILLIAMS, Mary Christian, Mrs., C.B.E.; *d.* of Sir Frederick Martyn Williams, Bart., of Goonvrea, Perranworthal, Cornwall (*see* BURKE'S *Peerage*); *m.* John Charles, *s.* of John Michael Williams, of Caerhays Castle, Gorran, Cornwall. *War Work:* Organising Sec. and for 4¼ years O.C. of Auxiliary Home Hospital, Launceston. *Addresses:* Caerhays Castle, Gorran, R.S.O., Cornwall; Werrington Park, Launceston, Cornwall.   (C3050)

WILLIAMS, Morgan, M.B.E., M.A., *b.* 1860; *s.* of Morgan B. Williams, of Killay House, Glamorgan. *Educ.:* London Univ. Coll. School, and Caius Coll., Cambridge. Consulting Engineer (retired). *War Work:* Commander of Headquarters Detachment Metropolitan Special Constabulary; served on Priority Committee, Ministry of Munitions (High Explosives Dept.) *Address:* 13, King's Bench Walk, Temple, E.C. 4. *Club:* Reform; New University; Eighty.   (M10071)

WILLIAMS, Lieut.-Col. Norman Rees, M.B.E., A.I.F.

WILLIAMS, Oliver Morrice, O.B.E.

WILLIAMS, Capt. Owen, M.B.E., R.A.F.

WILLIAMS, Lieut. Percy Alec, M.B.E.

WILLIAMS, Philip, O.B.E., *b.* 7 Dec. 1862; *s.* of Philip Williams, of Llanfihangel, Nant Bran, Breconshire. Silk Mercers. *War Work:* Acted as expert adviser to 15th and 18th Batts. R.W.F., Kit and Clothing Committees; also expert adviser to National Fund for Welsh Troops. *Addresses:* 312, Earls Court Road, S.W. 5; Rockdean, Camden Hill, Cranbrook, Kent. *Clubs:* National Liberal; Eccentric.   (O11620)

WILLIAMS, Lieut. Ralph, M.B.E., *b.* 13 April, 1892; *s.* of Charles Frederick Williams. *Educ.:* Cambridge House School. *War Work:* Prince of Wales' Own Civil Service Rifles, Aug. 1914, to Dec. 1915; active service, March, 1915; Gazetted, 2nd Lieut.,.8th The King's Own (R.L.) Regt., Dec. 1915; wounded, Ypres, March, 1916; Lieut., July, 1917; specially employed Board of Trade and Foreign Office, Jan. 1917, to April, 1919; discharged through wounds. *Club:* Badminton.   (M4326)

WILLIAMS, Richard, M.B.E.,. M.R.C.S., L.R.C.P.

WILLIAMS, Lieut.-Col. Richard, D.S.O., O.B.E., Major and T. Lieut.-Col. Australian Flying Corps. Served in Great War (mentioned in despatches).   (O3435)

WILLIAMS, Lieut. Richard Barclay, M.B.E., R.E. (T.).

WILLIAMS, Major Richard Charles Whittaker, O.B.E. R.F.A.

WILLIAMS, Capt. Richard John, O.B.E.; *s.* of Lieut.-Col. M. Scott Williams, of Woolland House, Blandford, Dorset; *m.* Eileen, *d.* of Edward Smith, of London. *Educ.:* Harrow and Exeter Coll., Oxford. Engineer. *War Work:* Instructor on Caterpillar Tractors; in command of Tractors laying the 12-inch pipe line from Kantara to Gaza and Beersheba; O.C. M.T., 103rd Bgde. R.G.A., during last advance from Jerusalem through Nablus. *Addresses:* Base, Heavy Repair Workshops, M.T., Alexandria; Woolland House, Blandford, Dorset.
(O8656)

WILLIAMS, Richard John, O.B.E., J.P. for the County of Carnarvon; *s.* of John Williams, of Blaenan Festiniog; *m.* Mary Emily, *d.* of Hugh Pritchard, of Liverpool. *Educ.:* Blaenan Festiniog; Towyn Academy; Liverpool Institute. Director in Messrs. Morris and Jones (1919), Ltd., Liverpool; Mayor of Bangor 1913-20. *War Work:* Chairman, Tribunal; Chairman, Sub-Committee, Pensions and War Savings Committee; Vice-Chairman, Carnarvonshire Pensions; Member and Vice-Chairman, Appeals Committee; Alderman, City Council; Member, County Council; Chairman, Industrial Council, North Wales; Chairman, War Distress Committee, and of Belgian Refugees Committee; Chairman, Food Committee; Member, Profiteering and Coal Committees. *Address:* Cynfal, Bangor. *Club:* Bangor Liberal.   (O11621)

WILLIAMS, Richard Trefor, M.B.E.

WILLIAMS, Major Robert Drake, M.B.E., R.E.

WILLIAMS, Roderick, M.B.E.

WILLIAMS, Capt. Roger Francis, M.B.E., R.E.

WILLIAMS, Major Ronald Frederick, O.B.E.,

WILLIAMS, Major Stanley Walter, O.B.E., R.A.M.C.

WILLIAMS, Thomas, M.B.E.

WILLIAMS, Thomas, O.B.E., *b.* 31 Jan. 1861; *s.* of James Joseph Williams, of Yeovil, Somerset; *m.* Rebecca J. Williams, *d.* of Benjamin Wright, of Cork, Ireland. *Educ.:* Privately. Superintendent, Metropolitan Police. *War Work:* General Police work including duties connected with air raids, and alien enemies. *Address:* 59, Sherriff Road, West Hampstead, N.W.   (O11622)

WILLIAMS, Capt. Thomas Acland, C.B.E., Com. and A. Capt., R.N. Served in Great War, 1914–19 with Ocean Escort (mentioned in despatches).   (C1210)

WILLIAMS, Thomas Richard, O.B.E., *b.* 3 Dec. 1864; *s.* of Richard Williams, of Cwmtwrch, Breconshire; *m.* Rachel, *d.* of Evan Evans, of Ystalyfera, Glam. *Educ.:* Bangor Coll. Inspector of Schools, Board of Education, Whitehall. *War Work:* Hon. Sec. of the Northumberland War Savings Committee; Member of the National Savings Assembly. *Address:* 17, Granville Gardens, Jesmond, Newcastle-on-Tyne. (O11623)

WILLIAMS, Major Vivian Dunbar Stanley, O.B.E., 5th D. Gds. (Ret.), *b.* 20 Sept. 1885; *s.* of the late Capt. G. S. Williams, of Brooksby Hall; *m.* Violet Mary Thellusson, *d.* of the Rev. Canon H. T. Wood, of Aldbury. *Educ.:* Harrow. Hertfordshire Militia, 5th Dragoon Guards. *War Work:* Went out with Expeditionary Force to France in Aug. 1914; retreat from Mons; severely wounded 1st Battle of Ypres; rejoined Regt. in France, 1917; invalided home with appendicitis, 1918; Headquarters Staff, Aldershot, 1918–19. *Address:* Greens Norton Court, Towcester. *Club:* Cavalry.   (O7867)

WILLIAMS, Brevet-Major Walton d'Eichtal, O.B.E.

WILLIAMS, Wilfred Howard, C.B.E., *b.* 1878; *s.* of Sir (Isaac) Thomas Williams, of Oakdene, St. Margaret's, Middlesex. *War Work:* Director of Inland Transport, Ministry of Munitions.   (C332)

WILLIAMS, Capt. William Edward Rees, O.B.E., M.B., I.M.S.

WILLIAMS, William Frederick, M.B.E., M.A. (Cantab.), *b.* 24th Nov. 1885; *s.* of the late William Lymington Williams, of Coolhurst, Bournemouth; *m.* Enid, *d.* of Howard Frederick Norton, of Glenroy, Croydon. *Educ.:* Haileybury Coll., and Clare Coll., Cambridge. Underwriting Member of Lloyd's. *War Work:* Gazetted to a Commission in the Royal Engineers, in Jan. 1916; served in France from Sept. 1916, to the Armistice; mentioned in Earl Haig's despatch of Nov. 8, 1918. *Address:* Brook House, East Grinstead, Sussex.   (M4627)

WILLIAMS, W. George, M.B.E. *War Work:* Joined Carmarthen 5 Red Cross Detachment, Sept. 1913; appointed Commandant of the detachment at the outbreak of war; responsible for the transport of the sick and wounded soldiers to the four Red Cross Hospitals in the county, namely, Carmarthen, Llandovery, Dolgarreg, and Llanelly; May, 1918, elected a Member of the British Red Cross Society; Oct. 1918, name inscribed upon the Roll of Honourable Service of the British Red Cross Society for services rendered in connection with the war, and received certificate of congratulations and thanks signed by Queen Alexandra.   (M10075)

WILLIAMS, William Henry, M.B.E., 18 Sept. 1871; *s.* of William Williams, of West Bromwich; *m.* Louisa, *d.* of Henry Bond, of Norfolk. *Educ.:* West Bromwich. Managing Director of Aston Chain and Hook Co., Ltd., Bromford, Erdington, Birmingham. *War Work:* Assisted in recruiting; collected funds for food for the Belgians; persuaded employees to invest in War Loan; invented special machinery for making shell bands at the rate of 1200 per hour. *Address:* Bromford House, Bromford Lane, Erdington. *Clubs:* Cosmopolitan; Royal Automobile; Calumet.   (M4085)

WILLIAMS, 2nd Lieut. William Herbert, M.B.E.

WILLIAMS, Capt. William Lewis, M.B.E.

WILLIAMS, Hon. William Micah, O.B.E.

WILLIAMS, William Nance, O.B.E.

WILLIAMS, William Thomas, O.B.E.

WILLIAMS, Winifred Mary, Hon. Mrs. M.B.E.; *d.* of 2nd Baron Addington, of Addington, Winslow, Bucks.; *m.* Berkeley Cole Wilmot; *s.* of Edward Wilmot Williams, of Herringston, Dorchester. *War Work:* Hon. Sec. Yorkshire Regiment Prisoners of War Committee. *Address:* Herringston, Dorchester; 36, Ennismore Gardens, London, S.W.
(M10077)

WILLIAMS, Sir Arthur John ALLEN-, K.B.E., C.M.G., M.I.C.E., *b.* 30 Nov. 1869; *s.* of the late William Williams, of Tower Hill, Fishguard; *m.* Ursula Mary, *d.* of Francis Allen, J.P., of Cockley Cley Hall, Swaffham, Norfolk. *Educ.:* Haverfordwest Grammar School, and Royal Indian Engineering Coll., Cooper's Hill. Member of firm of Westley, Williams, and Henderson, Ltd., Public Works Contractors, 3, Copthall Buildings, E.C. 2. *War Work:* T. Lieut. R.E., June, 1915, to Dec. 1916; promoted Major, Dec. 1916; Lieut.-Col., Col. and finally Brig.-Gen. (temp.), 27 Dec. 1917; from Dec. 1916, to Dec. 1919, in command at Richborough as Commandant, is Officer of the Legion of Honour. *Address:* Beach Lodge, Littlehampton. *Club:* Reform.   (K465)

WILLIAMS, Paymaster-Lieut.-Comm. Maurice Marcel Frederic CONDE-, O.B.E., R.N.

WILLIAMS, Sub-Lieut. Nevill Glennie GARNONS-, M.B.E., R.N.

WILLIAMS, Lieut. Reuben Henry GWYN-, O.B.E.

WILLIAMS, Lieut.-Col. Reginald Guy HUE-, O.B.E., *b.* 22 April, 1873; *s.* of F. Hue-Williams, of Uplands, Leatherhead; *m.* Amy Gladys, *d.* of Charles W. Elsden, of Beckenham. *Educ.:* Charterhouse. Stock Exchange, London. *War Work:*

Joined 2/5th East Surrey Regt., Oct. 1914 ; raised and commanded 3/5th East Surrey Regt., Aug. 1915 ; commanded 5th Res. Batt. East Surrey Regt., Sept. 1916, to April, 1919. *Address* : 15, Malbrook Road, Putney, S.W. 15. *Club* : Junior Army and Navy. (O7301)

WILLIAMS, Sir William Ellis HUME-, K.B.E., K.C., M.P., B.A., LL.D. ; *s.* of J. W. Hume-Williams, Barrister-at-law. *Educ.* : Trinity Hall, Cambridge. Called to the Bar, 1881 ; contested North Monmouthshire, 1895 ; Frome Division of Somerset, 1900 ; North Kensington, 1906 ; Recorder of Bury St. Edmunds, 1901–8, and of Norwich, 1905 ; Member of Central Prisoners of War Committee ; Liaison Officer between War Trade Dept. and Commission Internationale de Ravitaillement ; Knight of Grace of the Order of St. John of Jeruslaem. *Address* : 59, Pall Mall, S.W. *Clubs* : Carlton ; Junior Carlton ; New Oxford and Cambridge ; Constitutional. (K179)

WILLIAMS, Alice Gwynllyan, Mrs., LEE-, O.B.E., *b.* 1859 ; *d.* of William Phillip Price, of Tibberton Court, Gloucester ; *m.* Charles Lee, *s.* of the Rev. David Williams, Rector of Pewsey, Wilts. *Educ.* : Privately. *War Work* : Commandant of Red Cross Hospital, Great Western Road, Gloucester. *Address* : Tuffley Knoll, Gloucester. (O499)

WILLIAMS, Major Gordon W. MONIER-, O.B.E., M.A., *b.* 17 April, 1881 ; *s.* of M.F. Monier-Williams, of Old Parks, Stoke D'Abernon ; *m.* Dorothy Winifred, *d.* of Charles Sumner Hoare. Capt. 12th London Regt., Sept. 1914 ; seconded to R.E., May 1915, A. Major, Feb. 1916 ; served in France, May, 1915, to Nov. 1918 ; attached Staff 5th Army, April 1917, to March, 1918 ; and Fourth Army, March, 1918, to Nov. 1918, as Chemical Adviser ; twice mentioned in despatches. *Address* : Lower Farm, Stoke D'Abernon, Surrey. (O5590)

WILLIAMS, Major Roy Thornton MONIER-, O.B.E.

WILLIAMS, Janet, Mrs. PRICE-, M.B.E.

WILLIAMS, Lieut. Douglas PRICE-, O.B.E., R.N.V.R.

WILLIAMSON, Hon. Agnes Freda, Lady, O.B.E., sister of 2nd Baron Herschell ; *m.* as his 2nd wife, Right Hon. Sir Architect, 1st Bart., P.C., M.P., *s.* of late Stephen Williamson, M.P., of Edinburgh. *Addresses* : 36, Belgrave Square ; Glenogil, Kirriemuir, Forfarshire. (O11625)

WILLIAMSON, Capt. Alexander, O.B.E.

WILLIAMSON, Andrew, O.B.E.

WILLIAMSON, Colin Martin, C.B.E., *b.* 29 Oct. 1887 ; *s.* of James Williamson, of Boreham Wood, Herts. ; *m.* Gertrude Alice, *d.* of Frederick Parsons, of Hove. *Educ.* : Brighton Grammar School. Managing Director of the Williamson Kinematograph Co., Ltd. *War Work* : Invented the automatic camera for use in the air, and other photographic appliances for the Royal Air Force. *Addresses* : 36, Ambrose Avenue, N.W. 11 ; Litchfield Gardens, N.W. 10. (C3051)

WILLIAMSON, Florence, Mrs., M.B.E.

WILLIAMSON, Francis, M.B.E., *b.* 22 July, 1882 ; *s.* of Frank, of London ; *m.* Anice Louisa, *d.* of Charles Goodspeed, of Observatory Road, S.A. *Educ.* : Uckfield and Brighton Colleges. Secretary to various public committees. ; served through Boer War, Queen's Medal, 5 clasps ; dangerously wounded Noodgedacht, 13 Dec. 1900 ; Life Pensioner. *Address* : Francistown, Bechuanaland Protectorate. (M6495)

WILLIAMSON, Brig.-Gen. Frederic Herbert, C.B.E., *b.* 1876 ; *s.* of George Williamson, of Ringley, Manchester ; *m.* 1901, Florence May, *d.* of the late William Dawson, of Huddersfield. *Educ.* : Grammar School, Manchester ; Balliol Coll., Oxford. Brig.-Gen. R.E. (Reserve) ; Director of Army Postal Service, and Assist. Sec., G.P.O. *Address* : Wolverton, Egmont Road, Sutton. (C333)

WILLIAMSON, Major George William, O.B.E.

WILLIAMSON, Harry Captain, O.B.E.

WILLIAMSON, Henry, M.B.E.

WILLIAMSON, Horace, M.B.E.

WILLIAMSON, James, O.B.E.

WILLIAMSON, James, M.B.E., *b.* 1854. Member Local War Pensions Committee, Old Age Pensions Committee, Joint Committee Discharged Soldiers' and Sailors' Employment, and King's Lynn and District National Health Committee. *War Work* : Assist. Hon. Sec. Sailors' and Soldiers' Families Association, from Oct. 1914 ; Hon. Sec. Statutory Pension Committee until taken over by the War Pension Committee ; Hon. Sec. to War Pensions Committee until 1918–19 ; Hon Sec. King's Lynn and District War Savings Committee. *Address* : Checker Street, King's Lynn, Norfolk. (M10078),

WILLIAMSON, James, M.B.E.

WILLIAMSON, Lieut.-Col. Michael, O.B.E., J.P., I.A. (ret.), *b.* 4 April, 1865 ; *s.* of John Williamson, of Bruff, Co. Limerick ; *m.* Rhoda Mary, *d.* of John Christopher White, of Cork. *Educ.* : Trinity Coll., Dublin. Resident Magistrate for Limerick ; served 26 years in Indian Army ; retired, 1913. *War Work* : Raised, and commanded in the field, the 8th Batt. Royal Munster Fusiliers, until the battalion was wiped out ; afterwards commanded 5th Royal Munster Fusiliers, and two other Battalions. *Clubs* : Junior Naval and Military ; Hibernian United Service ; County Limerick ; Calcutta Turf. (O3994)

WILLIAMSON, Rhoda Mary Westropp, M.B.E., *b.* 1 Aug. 1890 ; *d.* of Lieut.-Col. Michael Williamson, O.B.E., late Indian Army, Resident Magistrate, Limerick. *Educ.* : Duncan House, Clevedon, Somerset. *War Work* : Worked in R.S.A.A. Inspection Factory, Park Royal, Acton. W., in 1915, and afterwards in the Finance Dept., War Office, until Dec. 1919. *Address* : Roorkee, North Circular Road, Limerick, Ireland. (M2654)

WILLIAMSON, Richard, C.B.E., *b.* 1 July, 1863 ; *s.* of James Williamson, of Montrose. *Educ.* : Privately. Managing Director Scottish Cinematograph Company. *War Work* : Worked in connection with Government allowances and pensions for a period of 4½ years, dealing with over 400,000 cases ; maintained a staff at own expense at a cost of over £2,000. *Addresses* : 94, West Regent Street, Glasgow ; Westerton, Callander, Perthshire. (C669)

WILLIAMSON, Major Richard Charles, M.B.E.

WILLIAMSON, Robert, C.B.E., J.P., Managing Director of Mount Stuart Dry Docks Co. (Limited), John Shearman and Co. (Limited), and Mordey, Carney and Co. (Limited), of Cardiff, Barry and Newport. (C670)

WILLIAMSON, Capt. William James, M.B.E. Master Fleet Mail Steamer, " St. Ninian."

WILLICOT, Capt. George Frederick William, M.B.E., M.C., R.E.,

WILLINGDON, Sir Freeman Freeman-Thomas, Lord, G.C.I.E., G.B.E., *b.* 12 Sept. 1866 ; *s.* of late Frederick Freeman-Thomas, of Ratton and Yapton, Sussex ; *m.* Lady Marie Adelaide, D.B.E., C.I., *d.* of 1st Earl Brassey (*see* BURKE'S *Peerage*). *Educ.* : Eton, and Trinity Coll., Cambridge. Is a Knight of Grace of Order of St. John of Jerusalem ; J.P. for Sussex and a member of the East India Assoc. ; was an A.D.C. to Governor of Victoria, 1895–98 ; and a Junior Lord of the Treasury, Dec. 1905– to Jan. 1906 ; appointed a Lord-in-Waiting to H.M. 1911 ; Governor of Bombay, 1913, and of Fort St. George, Madras, from 1919 ; Major, Sussex Yeomanry ; assumed the additional name of Freeman, 1892 ; M.P. for Hastings, 1900–6 ; and for S.E. Division of Cornwall, 1906–10. *Addresses* : Government House, Madras ; 5, Lygon Place, Grosvenor Gardens. *Clubs* : Brooks's ; Bachelor's (*see* BURKE'S *Peerage*). (G15)

WILLINGDON, Marie Adelaide, Lady, D.B.E., C.I. ; *d.* of 1st Earl Brassey (*see* BURKE'S *Peerage*) ; *m.* Freeman Freeman-Thomas, Lord Willingdon, G.C.S.I., G.C.I.E., G.B.E., *s.* of late Frederick Freeman-Thomas, of Ratton and Yapton, Sussex. Is a Lady of Grace of the Order of St. John of Jerusalem. *Addresses* : Government House, Madras ; 5, Lygon Place, Grosvenor Gardens, S.W. (D7)

WILLINGTON, William Thomas, O.B.E., J.P.

WILLIS, Arthur, M.B.E., J.P. for Middlesex, *b.* 19 June, 1858 ; *s.* of William Willis, of Sheffield ; *m.* Catharine, *d.* of Henry Wormall, of Ilfracombe. *Educ.* : Ecclesall Coll., Sheffield. Hon. Lieut.-Col. (Vols.) ; Chairman, Southgate Urban District Council, 1914–15, and 1915–16 ; Member of Council since 1907 ; Chairman of the Fire Brigade Committee for 14 years. *War Work* : Chairman, Southgate Citizens' Committee (Prince of Wales' Fund), Enfield Division Parliamentary Recruiting Committee, Southgate Local Recruiting Committee, Southgate Voluntary Aid Organisation, and House Committee Grovelands Auxiliary War Hospital, 170 beds ; Hon. Lieut.-Col. and Hon. Commandant 1st Vol. Batt. Middlesex Regt. ; raised Southgate Special Constabulary ; Chairman, Southgate Local Tribunal, and of Southgate Oneman Business Committee ; Director of Sub-Section, Special Dept. Ministry of Munitions, and served in H.M.O.W. Division Special Constabulary ; served on Middlesex and on Southgate War Pensions Committees, and on Southgate Prisoners of War Fund Committee. *Address* : 20, Elm Park Road, Winchmore Hill, London, N. 21. (M10080)

WILLIS, Lieut. Cecil Herbert Stanley, M.B.E.

WILLIS, Charles, M.B.E.

WILLIS, Capt. Charles Armine, O.B.E.

WILLIS, Ernest Horatio, O.B.E.

WILLIS, Frederick Bainbridge, M.B.E.

WILLIS, Sir Frederick James, K.B.E., C.B., J.P., Commander of the Order of Leopold, *b.* 16 March, 1865 ; *s.* of Joseph Willis, of Bristol ; *m.* Agnes Maude, *d.* of H. J. Infield, J.P., of Brighton. Barrister-at-Law ; Principal Assistant Sec. in Ministry of Health. *War Work* : Had charge of Government work on behalf of Belgian Refugees. *Address* : Ministry of Health, Whitehall, S.W. *Club* : Reform. (K442)

WILLIS, Major Harry Richard James, M.B.E.

WILLIS, Rt. Rev. John Jameseon, O.B.E., D.D. : *see* Uganda. Bishop of.

WILLIS, Maud Mary, Mrs., M.B.E., Medaille de la Reine Elizabeth, Belgium, *b.* 7 Jan. 1878 ; *d.* of John Hall, J.P., C.C., of Scarborough ; *m.* William Brooke, Solicitor, *s.* of Gervase Butterill Willis, of Rotherham. *Educ.* : Privately. *War Work* : Sec. Belgian Refugees, Rotherham, 1914, to their return ; Member of Prisoner of War Committee, and Pensions Committee from commencement to date. *Address* : Abbeville, Rotherham. (M2656)

WILLIS, Rev. Michael Hamilton Gibson, M.B.E., M.A., T.C.D., *b.* 29 Sept. 1864 ; *s.* of Hamilton Willis, of Dublin ; *m.* Elizabeth Shortt, *d.* of William Stewart Mollan, of Belfast. *Educ.* : High School, Dublin ; Trinity Coll., Dublin. Rector of Donaghadee. *War Work* : Hon. Sec. and County Director for Down for British Red Cross Society. *Address* : Rectory, Donaghadee. *Club* : Donaghadee Golf. (M2657)

WILLIS, Capt. Richard Dunn, O.B.E.

WILLIS, 2nd Lieut. Thomas, M.B.E., R.A.F.

WILLIS, Zwinglius Frank, O.B.E.

WILLMER, Lieut. Edward Albert Brittain, O.B.E., A.M.I.C.E., *b.* 4 Jan. 1881 ; *s.* of Edward Willmer, of Hove ; *m.* Anne Fleming, *d.* of Cornelius B. Fish, of New York, U.S.A. *Educ.* : Mercer's School, Holborn, London. Civil and Mechanical Engineer. *War Work* : Commissioned 2nd Lieut. in R.E.,

1915; trained 4 months in Chatham Military Engineering Coll.; on Western Front, Belgium, winter, 1915–16; invalided, April, 1916, and seconded to British Ministry of Munitions in U.S.A., on Staff of Sir E. Muir; promoted Lieut., Oct. 1916; promoted Assistant Director of Production, under Sir H. Japp, Sept. 1917; had charge of production of fuses, explosives, machinery, metals, and miscellaneous products and drawing up reports on new labour-saving devices for production of munitions, later drawing up reports for Glassware Dept. of British Ministry of Munitions on labour-saving devices; recommended for Captaincy. *Addresses:* 7, Seafield Road, Hove; Parliament Mansions, Victoria St., Westminister, S.W. 1.
(O11629)

WILLMORE, Ida, Mrs., M.B.E.

WILLMOT, Capt. Arthur Charles, O.B.E.

WILLMOT, Nellie Pratchett, Mrs., M.B.E., *b.* 17 July, 1869; *d.* of John Heatley, of Eaton-upon-Tern, Shropshire; *m.* George Dyott Willmot, J.P., *s.* of Francis Willmot, of Moseley, Birmingham. *War Work:* Commandant of the Vicarage Auxiliary Hospital, Coleshill, Warwickshire, June, 1915, to Feb. 1919, during which time over one thousand patients passed through the hospital. *Address:* Coleshill, Warwickshire. *Club:* Three Counties'. (M4087)

WILLMOTT, Capt. Frederick William, M.B.E.

WILLOCK, Air-Commodore Frederick George, C.B.E., D.S.O., R.A.F. Served in the Great War, 1914–18 (despatches).
(C2330)

WILLOUGHBY, Bertha Jane, O.B.E., Can. A.M.C.

WILLOUGHBY, Esther Ann, Hon. Mrs., O.B.E., *b.* 7 Jan. 1872; *d.* of Sir Charles William Strickland, Bart., of Boynton, Bridlington; *m.* Lieut.-Col. the Hon. Tatton Lane-Fox Willoughby, 6th *s.* of 8th Baron Middleton, of Birdsall Malton (*see* BURKE'S *Peerage*). *War Work:* Sec. Buckrose Division Soldiers' and Sailors' Families Association, Sec. and Treas. Buckrose War Pensions for Families; Vice-Chairman East Riding of Yorkshire Local War Pensions Committee. *Address:* Howsham Hall, York. (O11630)

WILLOUGHBY, James Frederick Digby, O.B.E., M.R.C.S., L.R.C.P., J.P.

WILLOUGHBY, John William, M.B.E.

WILLOUGHBY, Paymaster-Lieut. Reginald Stephen, O.B.E., R.N.R.

WILLOUGHBY DE BROKE, Marie Frances Lisette Lady, O.B.E., *b.* 20 Oct. 1868; *d.* of the late Charles A. Hanbury, of Belmont and Strathgarve; *m.* Lord Richard Greville Verney, *s.* of Henry, 18th Baron Willoughby de Broke (d. 1902), of Compton Verney, Warwick (*see* BURKE'S *Peerage*). *War Work:* Co. Commandant of Kineton Auxiliary Hospital of 110 beds; care of Belgian refugees; County Collector for Pearl Necklace; collected £7500 for Richmond Star and Garter Home for disabled soldiers and sailors. *Address:* Compton Verney, Warwick. *Clubs:* Ladies' Empire; Ladies' Imperial; V.A.D. (O1145)

WILLOX, 2nd Lieut. George Martin, M.B.E.

WILLS, Charles, O.B.E.

WILLS, Major Edgar Vernon, O.B.E.

WILLS, Sir Gilbert Alan Hamilton, O.B.E., M.A., J.P., M.P., *b.* 28 March, 1880; *s.* of Sir Frederick Wills (*see* BURKE'S *Peerage*); *m.* Victoria May, *d.* of Rear-Admiral Sir Edward Chichester, C.B., C.M.G., of Youlston, Devon. *Educ.:* Privately, and Magdalen Coll., Oxford. M.P. (Unionist), Taunton, 1912–18; M.P. Weston-super-Mare, 1918. *War Work:* Major Royal North Devon Yeomanry (Gallipoli, 1915); T. Lieut.-Col., Machine Gun Corps (France, 1917–18); despatches. *Address:* Batsford Park, Moreton-in-Marsh, Glos. *Clubs:* Carlton; Junior Carlton; Cavalry; Arthur's. (O2787)

WILLS, Marian Margaret, M.B.E.; *d.* of the late Rev. Edmund Wills, of Barkston, Lincs. *War Work:* Organising Sec., American Women's War Relief Fund, 1914–18, comprising American Women's War Hospital, Paignton; American Women's Hospital for Officers, Lancaster Gate, London; worked with American Red Cross. *Addresses:* 184, Buckingham Palace Road, S.W. 1; Pearcey's Cottage, Bosham, Sussex. (M2658)

WILLS, Surg.-Lieut.-Comm. Walter Kenneth, O.B.E., M.B., R.N.V.R.

WILLS, Dame Janet Stancomb Graham, STANCOMB-, D.B.E., F.S.A.; *d.* of the late George Perkins Stancomb, of Trowbridge, and niece and adopted daughter of 1st Baron Winterstoke (extinct), whose surname of Wills she has assumed in addition to that of Stancomb. President Royal West of England Academy, Bristol; Town Councillor for Ramsgate; Member Education Committee, Higher Education Committee, Ramsgate; Chairman, Library Committee. *War Work:* Served on various Ramsgate Committees connected with the war (Local Tribunal, Prince of Wales' Fund, Canadian Fund, Food Control, etc.). *Addresses:* 25, Hyde Park Gardens, W. 2; East Court, Ramsgate. (D20)

WILLSHER, John Edward, M.B.E., R.E.

WILLSHER, Capt. and Qr.-Mr. John Wingfield, M.B.E., R.A.M.C.

WILLSON, Major Christopher, O.B.E., J.P.; *s.* of George Willson, late of Ramsgate. *Educ.:* Privately. Assistant Superintendent Victoria Gaol, Hong Kong. *War Work:* Served in China with R.G.A., in France with R.F.A., and in Archangel (mentioned in despatches). *Club:* Hong Kong.
(O9710)

WILLSON, Emily Mary, M.B.E.; *d.* of John Willson

Bexhill-on-Sea. *War Work:* Commandant of Red Cross Hospital, Cantelupe Road, Bexhill-on-Sea, Dec. 1914, to April, 1919. *Address:* Ryecotes, Wilton Road, Bexhill-on-Sea. (M10082)

WILLSON, Harold Leonard James, M.B.E., Assoc.M.Inst. N.A., *b.* 30 July, 1891; *s.* of H. A. Willson, of Portsmouth; *m.* Ellen, *d.* of Frederick Richard Groves, of Portsmouth. *Educ.:* Secondary Day School, H.M. Dockyard, and Technical Institute. Inspector of Shipping, Transport Dept., Admiralty, S.W. *War Work:* Engaged in supervision of work in fitting and refitting Transports (Naval and Military) for carrying troops, horses, etc., also in planning and fitting of Naval and Military Hospital Ships and Ambulance Transports, etc.; later in the reconditioning of such vessels for their return to the various owners. *Address:* 36A, Louisville Road, Upper Tooting, S.W. 17. (M10083)

WILLSON, Major Herbert Stuart, O.B.E., R.A.O.C.

WILLSON, Major John Hughes, M.B.E., *b.* 28 Feb. 1857; *s.* of William L. Willson, Master Mariner, of Folkestons, who was drowned from a lifeboat off Calais, 17 Jan. 1867; *m.* Jane Eugenie, *d.* of Capt. M. E. Matthews, Master Mariner, of Akyab, who was drowned. *Educ.:* Greenwich Coll. Joined Messrs. A. Woodward & Co., Ship Chandlers, Akyab, 1877; joined Preventive Customs Dept. as Inspector, 1880; appointed Head Assistant, Deputy Commissioner's Office, Kyaukpyu, 1889; Superintendent, Arakan Commissioner's Office, 1893; Extra Assistant Commissioner, 1907; retired, 1916, after 36 years' service. Joined as Private, Akyab Det. of Rangoon Vol. Rifle Corps, 1893; appointed 2nd Lieut. Reserve Coy. Vol. Rifle Corps, Kyaukpyu, 1894; promoted Lieut. 1896; Capt. 1909; took command of Akyab Det. 1909; retired as Major, 1916; awarded Long Service Medal, 1902; Volunteer Decoration, 1904; appointed Municipal Commissioner, 1904; Vice.-President, 1919; Hon. Secretary, King Edward VII. Memorial Industrial School, 1914–20; St. Mark's Church Committee, 1891–1920; and Red Cross Fund Committee, 1919. *Address:* Akyab, Burmah, India. (M6271)

WILLSON, Laura, Mrs., M.B.E.

WILLSON, Nellie Marie, M.B.E.

WILLSON, Percy Arden, M.B.E., *b.* 27 May, 1862; *s.* of the late Thomas Willson, of Knaptoft Hall, Leicestershire; *m.* Annie Wilson, *d.* of the late James Robertson, of Glasgow. *Educ.:* Oundle School. *War Work:* Chairman, Lambeth War Savings Committee; Hon. Treas., Lambeth C War Pensions Sub-Committee. *Address:* 19, St. John's Road, S.W. 9. (M10084)

WILLSON, Rose, Mrs., M.B.E., *b.* 30 Aug. 1862; *d.* of Rev. H. C. de St. Croix, late of Figheldean, Wilts.; *m.* Rev. Vere Francis Willson (d. 1917). *War Work:* Hospital at own house, Rauceby Hall, Grantham, until 1917. *Address:* The Grey House, Little Hampden, Great Missenden, Bucks. (M1101)

WILLSON, Thomas Olaf, C.B.E., M.A. (Chevalier de l'Ordre de la Couronne), *b.* 29 July, 1880; *s.* of Rev. T. B. Willson, M.A., D.Litt., of West Woodhay, Rectory, Newbury; *m.* Constance Horsburgh, *d.* of Walter Basil Cowan, of St. Kilda, Sidmouth. *Educ.:* Westminster and Keble Coll., Oxford. Assistant Sec. for Higher Education, Berkshire Education Committee, 1905–19; Assistant Sec. for Education, Oxfordshire Education Committee, 1919; Sec. for Education, Oxfordshire Education Committee from Sept. 1920. *War Work:* H.A.C. 1914–15; T.F. Reserve, General List. May, 1915, to Jan. 1919; Special duty with Foreign Office, Department of Information, and Ministry of Information, at home and abroad. *Address:* 13, Bevington Road, Oxford. (C671)

WILMAN, 2nd Lieut. Edgar Arthur, M.B.E., R.E.

WILMER, Lieut. Edward Albert Brittain, O.B.E.

WILMOT, Edith, Mrs., O.B.E., *b.* 18 June, 1877; *d.* of the late Joseph Cadman; *m.* Philip McKinnell Corbould, *s.* of George Wilmot, of Rio. *War Work:* Assistant County Director of the Plymouth Branch of the British Red Cross Society; equipped and organised V.A. Hospital. *Address:* 2, Crescent Villas, Plymouth. *Clubs:* Ladies' Victoria. (O3995)

WILMOT, Major Hugh EARDLEY-, O.B.E.

WILMOT, Jane Millicent, Mrs. EARDLEY-, O.B.E.; *d.* of the late Sir James Scott, Bart., of Yews Windermere; *m.* Edward Gwynne, *s.* of Robert Eardley-Wilmot, J.P., of Petworth. *War Work:* Commandant Training Coll. V.A.D. Hospital, York. *Address:* Corner House, Gerrards Cross, Bucks. (O11632)

WILMOT, Capt. Percy EARDLEY-, O.B.E.

WILMSHURST, Thomas Percival, M.B.E., *b.* 1869; *s.* of Edwin Wilmshurst, Retford, Notts; *m.* Henrietta Louise, *d.* of Thos. Reynolds, of Wells. *Educ.:* King Edward VI. School, Retford. Borough Electrical Engineer, Derby. *War Work:* Supply of electric power to munition factories; Commander, Derby Borough Special Constabulary. *Address:* Lime Leigh, Burton Road, Derby. (M10085)

WILSOM, Major Charles Percival, O.B.E., Aust. A.P.C.

WILSON, Alexander, O.B.E., *b.* 1864; *s.* of James Wilson, of Edinburgh; *m.* Barbara, *d.* of J. Buchanan, of Edinburgh. *Educ.:* Privately, and Heriot-Watt Coll., Edinburgh. Assistant General Manager, North Eastern Railway; Sec. Hull Joint Dock Co. *War Work:* Railway administration. *Addresses:* c/o Beckett & Co., Bankers, Harrogate; N.E. Rly., York. (O2018)

WILSON, Alexander, O.B.E., *b.* 20 April, 1855; *s* of

John Wilson, of Kirkmay, Leven ; *m.* Margaret, *d.* of John Philip Denhead, Kennoway. *Educ.:* Leven School ; Birbeck Coll. ; Royal Technical Coll., Glasgow. Civil Engineer ; late Chief Engineer and General Manager of Glasgow Corporation Gas Department. *War Work:* Assisted the Explosives Dept. of the Government in organising the Gas Works in Scotland for the production of Benzol and Toluol to be used in the manufacture of explosives. *Address:* Baronald, Promenade, Leven, Fifeshire. *Clubs:* Royal Scottish Automobile ; Innerleven Golf. (O11633)

WILSON, Capt. Alexander Morice, M.B.E.

WILSON, Alexander Poole, M.B.E.

WILSON, Capt. Andrew, O.B.E., I.O.D.

WILSON, T. Major Andrew, M.B.E., R.E.

WILSON, Lieut. Andrew McCrae, M.B.E., H.L.I. and R.A.F.

WILSON, Annie Wilhelmina Elizabeth, Lady. M.B.E. ; *d.* of the late Rev. Henry Smythe ; *m.* Surg.-Gen. Sir William Deane, K.C.M.G., M.B., L.R.C.S.I., *s.* of J. Deane Wilson, of Rathdownay, Queen's County. *Address:* Moorside, Westfield, Sussex. (M10088)

WILSON, Aphra Phyllis, M.B.E., *b.* 18 Jan. 1895 ; *d.* of George Morton Wilson, C.M., M.B. (Edin.), of Pendyffryn Hall, Penmaenmawr. *Educ.:* Queen Anne's School, Caversham. *War Work:* Women's Volunteer Reserve, Canteen Work, and Motor Transport, 1915–Sept. 1917 ; Q.M.A.A.C., Sept. 1917, to Dec. 1919. *Address:* 116, Fellows Road, N.W. 3. *Club:* International Women's Franchise. (M5738)

WILSON, Capt. Archibald, O.B.E., M.C., R.A.M.C. (S.R.).

WILSON, Archie John Landles, M.B.E.

WILSON, Capt. Arnot Milne, O.B.E., R.A.S.C.

WILSON, Capt. Arthur Cecil James, O.B.E.

WILSON, Major Arthur Ernest, O.B.E.

WILSON, Arthur Maitland, O.B.E., J.P., D.L.

WILSON, Lieut.-Col. Arthur Maclean, O.B.E.

WILSON, Benedict John, O.B.E.

WILSON, Beryl Charlotte Mary, Mrs., C.B.E. Manager Free Buffet, Waterloo Station during Great War. (C3052)

WILSON, Cecil Mary, Lady, C.B.E. ; *d.* of the late George Cecil Gore Wray, J.P., of Ardnawana, Donegal ; *m.* Field Marshal Sir Henry Hughes Wilson, Bt., K.C.B., C.B., D.S.O., Rifle Brigade, *s.* of James Wilson, D.L., J.P., of Currygrane Edgeworthstown, Ireland. *Addresses:* Currygrane, Edgeworthstown, Ireland ; Grove End, Bagshot, Surrey ; 36, Eaton Place, S.W. 1. (C1059)

WILSON, Lieut. Charles Ernest, M.B.E.

WILSON, Col. Charles Henry Luttrell Fahie, C.B.E., late R.A., *b.* 24 Aug. 1858 ; *s.* of the late Gen. C. W. Wilson, of Royal Artillery ; *m.* Mabel Margaret, *d.* of Claude James Erskine, I.C.S. *Educ.:* Privately, and R.M. Academy, Woolwich. *War Work:* A.D.O.S., Aldershot Command, from Dec. 1914, to Aug. 1919. *Address:* Harlington, Fleet, Hampshire. (C838)

WILSON, Charles James, O.B.E. Voluntary research worker, Ministry of Munitions. (O11791*b*)

WILSON, Capt. Charles Spencer, O.B.E.

WILSON, Charlotte Mary, Mrs., O.B.E., *b.* 1854 ; *d.* of R. Spencer Martin, M.D., of Whitley Grange, Reading ; *m.* Arthur, *s.* of Rev. Daniel Wilson, Vicar and Rural Dean of Islington, Prebendary of St. Paul's. *Educ.:* Newnham Coll., Cambridge. *War Work:* Organiser and General Hon. Sec. of War Prisoners Fund for Oxfordshire and Buckingham Regiments, Spring, 1915, to end of war. *Addresses:* Queen Anne's Mansions, London, S.W. 1 ; The Nook, Pepgraed Common, Oxon. (O3996)

WILSON, Capt. Cyril, M.B.E. Censor, Alexandria. (M10260*e*)

WILSON, Col. Cyril Edward, C.M.G., C.B.E., D.S.O., R. of O., *b.* 9 March, 1873 ; *s.* of the late Major-General Sir Charles Wilson, K.C.B., K.C.M.G., D.C.L., etc., of Royal Engineers ; *m.* Beryl Marie, *d.* of Col. W. Hunter Little, of Harestock Lodge, Winchester. *Educ.:* Clifton Coll., and R.M.C. Sandhurst. Entered Army October, 1893 ; served in Nile Expeditions, 1898 and 1899 (attached to Egyptian Army) ; South African War, 1900–2 ; Egyptian Army and Sudan Government, 1902 to date. *War Work:* Commanded Red Sea District, Aug. 1914, to July, 1916 ; appointed British Military and Political Representative in the Hejaz ,July, 1916, to Dec. 1919. Order of the Blue Nile (2nd class) ; El Nakda (Grand Cordon) Medjidieh (3rd class) ; officer of the Legion of Honour. *Address:* Port Sudan, Sudan. *Club:* Army and Navy. (C2065)

WILSON, Daniel Ellis, O.B.E., A.M.I.C.E., A.M.I.M.E., *b.* 15 Sept. 1866 ; *s.* of the late James Wilson, Pasha, of Cairo, Egypt. *Educ.:* Liverpool Coll. Engineer. *War Work:* Inspector of Munitions Areas, Ministry of Munitions, 1915–19. *Address:* 54, Mortlake Road, Kew Gardens, Surrey. (O11636)

WILSON, David, O.B.E., A.M.I.E.E., *b.* 1874 ; *s.* of David Wilson, of Dundee, N.B. ; *m.* Florence Audrey, *d.* of Frederic Jones, L.D.S., R.C.S., of Carlisle. *Educ.:* Harris Academy, Dundee. *War Work:* Technical Adviser to Coal Controller. *Address:* Dunholme, Park Road, Radlett, Herts. *Club:* Royal Automobile. (O3997)

WILSON, Dorothy Holmes, M.B.E.

WILSON, Edith Annie, Mrs., M.B.E, *b.* 24 Oct. 1881 ; *d.* of John Thomas Parrish, of Newcastle-on-Tyne ; *m.* Capt. Frederick Gordon, M.C., *s.* of William Arthur Wilson, of Newcastle-on-Tyne. *War Work:* Member of the Tyneside Scottish

(N.F.) Dependants Committee ; worked in Armstrong's Munitions Factory ; Hon. Superintendent Y.W.C.A. Munitions Canteen, Scotswood. *Address:* The Lodge, The Drive, Gosforth, Northumberland. (M2659)

WILSON, Edith Frances, Mrs., M.B.E.

WILSON, Edith Marguerite, M.B.E.

WILSON, Edith Matilda Clementine, Mrs., M.B.E.

WILSON, Lieut.-Col. Edward Arthur, O.B.E., M.C.

WILLSON, Emily Mary, M.B.E.

WILSON, Ernest George, C.B.E., *b.* 3 Sept. 1875 ; *s.* of George Wilson, of Northumberland. *Educ.:* Privately. Traffic Manager, Uganda Railway. *War Work:* In charge of the transport by rail of troops and supplies landing in B.E. Africa for G.E. African campaign. *Address:* Nairobi, B.E. Africa. *Club:* Sports. (C3053)

WILSON, Florence Aline, Mrs., M.B.E.

WILSON, Lieut.-Col. Francis Bertram, O.B.E.

WILSON, Lieut.-Col. Francis Walter Ernest, C.B.E., Can. A.M.C.

WILSON, Frank, O.B.E.

WILSON, Capt. Frank Gordon, O.B.E., R.A.F.

WILSON, Frederick Wallace, M.B.E., M.R.C.S. (Eng.), L.R.C.P. (Lond.), *b.* 7 Sept. 1866. *Educ.:* Guy's Hospital. *War Work:* Hon. Anæsthetist and Ophthalmic Surgeon Princess Club Hospital for Wounded Soldiers, Bermondsey ; Acting Surgeon-in-charge Outpatients, and acting Anæsthetist to Outpatients, Guy's Hospital ; Medical Officer-in-charge Messrs. Peek, Frean & Co., Ltd., Air Raid Shelters ; Divisional Inspector of Bermondsey Branch, British Red Cross Society. *Address:* c/o Peek, Frean & Co., Ltd., S.E. 16. (M10289)

WILSON, George, O.B.E., *b.* 30 Oct. 1850 ; *s.* of John Wilson, of York ; *m.* Florence, *d.* of Frederick Hall, M.R.C.S., of Southampton. *War Work:* For five years, Hon. Assistant to the Col. in charge of No. 2 Infantry Records Office, York ; in charge of the Department for the Distribution of Medals for the Yorkshire Regiments affiliated with that Office. *Address:* Linton Lodge, York. *Club:* St. Leonards (York). (O11637)

WILSON, George Alexander, M.B.E.

WILSON, George Alexander, O.B.E., *b.* 7 Dec. 1869 ; *s.* of James Wilson, of Arnhall, Huntly ; *m.* Jane Ann, *d.* of Thomas Clapperton, of Potterton House, Aberdeenshire. *Educ.:* Huntly (Gordon Schools), and Aberdeen Univ. Advocate ; Sec. and Treas. of Central Aberdeenshire Liberal Association, and Sec. and Treas. of the Aberdeenshire and Kincardineshire Licence Holders' Association. *War Work:* Commandant of the City of Aberdeen Special Constabulary ; Military Representative and National Service Representative for the City of Aberdeen ; Clerk to the Advisory Committee of the Aberdeen District of Parishes (Northern) Division ; Joint Sec. of West Aberdeenshire Derby Recruiting Scheme. *Addresses:* 77, Crown Street, Aberdeen ; St. Leonards, King's Gate, Aberdeen. *Clubs:* University ; Royal Golf (Aberdeen). (O11638)

WILSON, Capt. George Gatherer, O.B.E.

WILSON, George Gordon, O.B.E., *b* 1 March, 1854 ; *s.* of Capt. Bracey Robson Wilson, of Sunderland, Durham ; *m.* Corina, *d.* of Emanuel Laurence Grillo, of Lima, Peru *Educ.:* Privately. His Britannic Majesty's Consul for Peru with the exception of the Department of Loreto ; President of the British Benevolent Society at Callao, and of the Mission to Seamen, Callao ; Captain of the International Fire Brigade, " Salvadora Callao " ; 1st Lieut. of No. 1 Ambulance Corps during the war between Peru and Chile, 1879–81. *War Work:* During the European War devoted whole time to Consular and War duties at Callao and Lima. *Address:* c/o British Consulate, Callao, Peru. *Clubs:* The Club (Callao) ; The Phœnix (Lima). (O868)

WILSON, George Heron, C.B.E., J.P., *b.* Jan. 1868 ; *s.* of Charles John Wilson, of Deanfield, Hawick ; *m.* Julia, *d.* of Andrew Tod, of Edinburgh. *Educ.:* George Watson's Coll. Provost of Hawick ; Vice-Chairman Roxburghshire Education, and Chairman Roxburghshire National Insurance Committees. *War Work:* Deputy Controller Priority Dept., Ministry of Munitions ; Member of Interim Court of Arbitration, Ministry of Labour. *Club:* Caledonian. (C3054)

WILSON, Geraldine, O.B.E., *b.* Sept. 1888 ; *d.* of the late Col. J. G. Wilson, C.B., of Cliffe Hall, Darlington. *Educ.:* Privately. Vice-President British Red Cross Society for North Riding of Yorkshire ; Commandant V.A.D. Yorks 36 ; Representative of National Assoc. of Landworkers on North Riding Executive Agricultural Committee under Board of Agriculture. *War Work:* Commandant of Yorks 36 Red Cross Auxiliary Hospital ; Organising Sec., 1917–18, for Women Landworkers in the N. Riding of Yorkshire under the Board of Agriculture. *Address:* Mansfield House, Darlington. *Club:* Forum. (O867)

WILSON, Brevet-Lieut.-Col. Godfrey Harold Alfred, O.B.E.

WILSON, Miss Grace Margaret, C.B.E., R.R.C. *War Work:* Principal Matron, Australian Army Nursing Service. (C778)

WILSON, Major Gregg, O.B.E.

WILSON, Haigh Robson, O.B.E., *b.* 12 Oct. 1880 ; *s.* of John Bowron Wilson, of Darlington, England ; *m.* Elsie, *d.* of Benjamin Jacques Swales, of Fleetwood, Lancs. *Educ.:* Higher Grade School, Crouch End, London ; City of London Technical Coll. Engineer. *War Work:* Served in Royal Naval Air Service ; transferred 1915 to Technical Staff, Ministry of Munitions ; later transferred to Resettlement Department,

Ministry of Labour. *Addresses*: 9, Brian Avenue, Monkseaton, Northumberland; 41, Chandos Road, Finchley, London, N. (O11639)

WILSON, Harold Inchbald, C.B.E.

WILSON, Harry Gouldie, M.B.E., F.C.A.

WILSON, Harry James, O.B.E., *b.* 9 July, 1870; *s.* of James Wilson, of Baldavie, Banffshire; *m.* Margaret Wilhelmina, *d.* of the Rev. James Leith Ironside, M.A., of Aberdour, Aberdeenshire. *Educ.*: Banff, and Aberdeen. H.M. Superintending Inspector of Factories for Scotland, and North of Ireland. *War Work*: Member of West of Scotland Armaments Committee; Commissioner for National Service for Scotland. *Address*: Strathview Gardens, Bearsden, Dumbartonshire. (O870)

WILSON, Helen, M.B.E., *b.* 1862; *d.* of John Wilson, of Bantaskine. *War Work*: Y.M.C.A. Canteen Work in France for four and a half years. *Address*: Bantaskine, Falkirk, Stirlingshire. (M4091)

WILSON, Helena Jane, Mrs., O.B.E., *b.* 2 June, 1858; *d.* of the late Rev. Samuel Charlton, Rector of Tydd St. Giles, near Wisbech, Cambs; *m.* Mervyn Seppings Wilson, B.A. (Cantab.), M.R.C.S.; *s.* of the late Francis Read. Commandant Wilts 6; Representative on Wilts County Committee for care of the Blind in Chippenham Union; Hon. Sec. and Treas. of Finance Sub-Committee, Wilts. *War Work*: Commandant of Red Cross Hospital Chippenham (100 beds). *Address*: 19, St. Mary Street, Chippenham, Wilts. *Club*: V.A.D. (O3998)

WILSON, Henry, M.B.E. *Educ.*: Grammar School, Market Rasen. Acting Accountant, Army Audit Staff, War Office. *War Work*: In Finance Dept. of the War Office. (M10091)

WILSON, Lieut.-Col. Henry, O.B.E., *b.* 27 March, 1880; *s.* of Henry Wilson, of Carnach Polmont, Stirlingshire; *m.* Janet, *d.* of Thomas Ritchie, of Grangemouth. *Educ.*: Falkirk High School. Architect. *War Work*: Served with 51st Divisional Train, B.E.F., and 22nd Divisional Train, R.A.S.C., Salonica, E.F. *Addresses*: Boness Road, Grangemouth; Carnach, Polmont. (O6557)

WILSON, Capt. Henry Adrian Fitzroy, O.B.E.

WILSON, Capt. Henry Alexander James, O.B.E., R.A.F.

WILSON, Lieut.-Col. Henry Christopher Bruce, O.B.E., B.A., J.P., *b.* 12 Jan. 1875; *s.* of Henry S. L. Wilson, of Crofton Hall, near Wakefield, J.P., late 13th Light Dragoons and East Yorkshire Regt. (*see* BURKE'S *Landed Gentry*); *m.* Alma Marie, *d.* of Rev. Louis Le Bouvier, Chev. Order Orange and Nassau. *Educ.*: Winchester, New Coll., Oxon. *War Work*: Rejoined 3rd K.O.Y.L.I., 8 Aug. 1914; France, Nov. 1914, 21st Brigade, 7th Division; severely wounded, Neuve Chapelle, Mar. 1915; commanding drafting battalion from Aug. 1915, to Aug. 1919. *Address*: Crofton Hall, Crofton, Wakefield. *Club*: Junior United Service. (O7871)

WILSON, Capt. Henry Joseph Fullock, M.B.E.

WILSON, Sir Henry Francis (Harry), K.C.M.G., K.B.E., *b.* 8 Aug. 1859; *s.* of Rev. William Grieve Wilson, J.P., Rector of Forncett St. Peter, Norfolk; *m.* Isabella Dora, *d.* of Admiral Sir Robert Smart, K.C.B., K.H., of Rothbury House, Chiswick Mall. *Educ.*: Rugby, and Trinity Coll., Cambridge. Barrister-at-law; Sec. of the Royal Colonial Institute; Chairman of the North Charterland Exploration Company, 1910, Ltd., and Director of the Eagle, Star and British Dominions Insurance Company, Ltd. (English and Scottish Board); formerly Colonial Sec. and Acting Lieut.-Governor of the Orange River Colony; Legal Assistant at the Colonial Office, and Private Sec. to the late Right Hon. J. Chamberlain, Sec. of State for the Colonies; Foundation Scholar and Fellow of Trinity Coll., Camb. *War Work*: Member of the Empire Land Settlement Committee and Sec. of the War Services Committee of the Royal Colonial Institute; Commander of the Order of Leopold II. for services rendered to the Belgian Colonial Office. *Addresses*: Lennox House, 43, Ovington Square, London, S.W.; Pencraig Court, Ross-on-Wye, Herefordshire. *Clubs*: Albemarle; Authors'. (K320)

WILSON, Capt. Herbert Ward, O.B.E.. M.C.

WILSON, Capt. Horace Bagster, O.B.E., R.A.M.C.

WILSON, Horace John, C.B., C.B.E., *b.* 23 Aug. 1882; *s.* of Harry Wilson, of Bournemouth; *m.* Emily, *d.* of John Sheather, of Beckley. *Educ.*: Kurnella School, Bournemouth; London School of Economics. Principal Assistant Sec., Ministry of Labour. *War Work*: Sec., Committee on Production and Special Arbitration Tribunal, Munitions of War Acts, 1915–18. *Addresses*: Montagu House, Whitehall, S.W. 1; 14, Whitehall Road, Harrow-on-the-Hill. (C335)

WILSON, Col. Hubert Malcolm, O.B.E.

WILSON, Hubert Wilberforce, O.B.E., *b.* 10 Jan. 1867; *s.* of Wilberforce Wilson, of Hong Kong. *Educ.*: Univ. School, Hastings, and Privately. Consul-General for the Rep. of Ecuador and Chargé d'Affaires in the absence of the Minister. *War Work*: Consular and Diplomatic Services in connection with the war. *Address*: British Legation, Quito. *Club*: Junior Constitutional; Royal Automobile. (O871)

WILSON, Pay-Sub-Lieut. Hugh Brown, M.B.E., R.N.V.R.

WILSON, Humphrey Bowstead, O.B.E., M.B., *b.* 1 Nov. 1883; *s.* of Joseph Bowstead Wilson, of Oakfield, Worcester. *Educ.*: Charterhouse and Pembroke Coll., Cambridge. Anæsthetist to St. Thomas' Hospital, Hospital for Sick Children, Gt. Ormond Street. *War Work*: Aug. 1914, to April, 1919,

Surgical Specialist to 5th Casualty Clearing Station. *Address*: 27, Gloucester Terrace, Hyde Park, London. *Club*: Bath. (O2789)

WILSON, Ivy Madge, Mrs., M.B.E., *b.* 19 Jan. 1893; *d.* of H. A. Cunis, of Kèramos, Woldingham, Surrey; *m.* Major A. Wilson, M.C. *Educ.*: Blackheath High School. *War Work*: Personal Assistant to Chief Establishment Officer Dept. of Aircraft Production; Assistant Sec., Ministry of Munitions. *Addresses*: 26, Cantonments, Cawnpore, India; Kèramos, Woldingham, Surrey. (M10093)

WILSON, James, M.B.E.

WILSON, James, O.B.E., *b.* 29 Nov. 1858; *s.* of James Wilson, of Faversham, Kent; *m.* Clara, *d.* of Henry Butt, of Tewkesbury. *Educ.*: Privately. Town Clerk of St. Marylebone; Registration Officer and Returning Officer; Food Officer and Fuel Overseer; formerly Clerk to Croydon Rural District Council, and previously assistant clerk to Guardians at Croydon and Paddington. *War Work*: Recruiting; National and Local Relief Funds; Hon. Clerk, Military Service Tribunal, National Registration, National Service, National Kitchen, Food Control. *Addresses*: 99, Marylebone Road, N.W.; 48, Holland Road, Westcliffe-on-Sea. (O11640)

WILSON, James Alexander, M.B.E., M.D.

WILSON, James Alexander, O.B.E., M.D.; *m.* Sara, *d.* of William Corner. *Educ.*: Glasgow Univ. Surgeon. *War Work*: Resident Surgeon at the Lord Derby War Hospital, Warrington, for four years. *Address*: 4, Central Avenue, Cambuslang, nr. Glasgow. (O11857)

WILSON, James Arthur, M.B.E.

WILSON, James Naismith, M.B.E.

WILSON, Capt. James Robert Menzies, O.B.E., R.E.

WILSON, Jeanie Stewart Ramsay, O.B.E., R.R.C.

WILSON, Jessie Millar, M.B.E., *b.* 27 April, 1871; *d.* of James Stephen Wilson. July 1915, to Nov. 1918, worked for the Y.M.C.A. at Hut 15, Harfleur, provided every comfort for men proceeding to the front from base at Le Havre. *War Work*: Nov. 1918, to Aug. 1919, Australian, British and New Zealand Y.M.C.A. Hotel Windsor, Paris, for men on leave; British representative-in-charge with Captain Wright (Australia). *Address*: Belmont, Otley, Yorkshire. (M10096)

WILSON, Rev. John, M.B.E.

WILSON, Major John, O.B.E.

WILSON, Comm. John, O.B.E., R.N.R.

WILSON, John, M.B.E.

WILSON, Capt. John, O.B.E.

WILSON, Capt. John, M.B.E.

WILSON, Capt. John Alexander, O.B.E., R.A.M.C.

WILSON, John Bowie, M.B.E.

WILSON, Lieut.-Col. John George Yule, C.B.E., R.A.S.C. (ret.), *b.* 1853. Served in the Zulu Campaign, 1879 (medal with clasp); Egyptian Expedition, 1884 (medal, bronze star); Great War, 1914–19 (despatches). (C1815)

WILSON, John Henry, C.B.E., *b.* 6 Aug. 1862; *s.* of John Wilson. *Educ.*: Lancing Coll.; France; Switzerland. Seven years member of the Legislative Council of the British East Africa Protectorate. *War Work*: Special Constable and on a Government commission to the Persian Gulf and Mesopotamia. *Address*: Claridge's Hotel, London. *Clubs*: Bachelors'; Oriental; City of London. (C672)

WILSON, John Hughes, M.B.E., V.D.

WILSON, Rev. John Plumpton, O.B.E., *b.* 1 Jan. 1868; *s.* of Rev. Plumpton Wilson, of Horbling, Lincs.; *m.* Mary Elinor; *d.* of Canon John Mason Mason, of Whitfield, Northumberland. *Educ.*: Rossall and Queen's Coll., Oxford. Clerk in Holy Orders. Rector of Hedenham, Norfolk; Clerical Sec. to the Bishop of Gibraltar. *War Work*: Chaplain, C. of E., 21st Corps, H.Q., E.E.F.; mentioned in despatches. *Addresses*: Hedenham Rectory, Bungay; Gibraltar Diocesan Office, Church House, Westminster. (O2951)

WILSON, Lieut.-Col. John Stewart, O.B.E., R.E., *b.* 8 June, 1872; *s.* of Robert Wilson, of Glasgow. *War Work*: Served with British Army in France from June, 1915, to Nov. 1919; thrice mentioned in despatches. (O5941)

WILSON, Joseph Havelock, C.B.E., M.P., *b. s.* of John, of Sunderland; *m.* Jane Ann, *d.* of William Watham, of South Shields. *Educ.*: Boys' British School, Sunderland. President National Sailors' and Firemen's Union of Great Britain and Ireland; Chairman Seafarers' Joint Council; President International Seafarers' Federation. *War Work*: Recruiting for the Army, Navy, Merchant Service; assisted with War Savings. *Addresses*: 76, Victoria Street, London; 56, The Ridgeway, Golders Green, N.W. *Club*: National Liberal. (C77)

WILSON, Lieut.-Col. Joseph Maitland, C.B.E., J.P., *b.* 1868; *s.* of the late Lieut.-Col. Fuller Maitland Wilson, of Stowlangtoft Hall, Bury St. Edmunds. *Educ.*: Eton and Christ Church, Oxford. Capt. and Hon. Major, Reserve of Officers (Special Reserve), Co.; Director V.A.D. for Suffolk; Hon. Lieut.-Col. Suffolk Med. Vol. Corps; a J.P. for Suffolk; served with S. Africa with Imperial Yeo. *Club*: Arthur's. (C673)

WILSON, Maggie Scot, Mrs., M.B.E.

WILSON, Marguerite Rowley, Mrs., M.B.E., *b.* 7 July, 1864; *d.* of Myles Kennedy, J.P., of Stone Cross, Ulverston; *m.* Harry Constantine Wilson, *s.* of Henry Charles Wilson, of Prestwich, Manchester. *Educ.*: Privately. *War Work*: V.A.D. work at Ash, Canterbury, 1914–15, as Quartermaster to Kent 128; 1916–19, as Quartermaster and Commandant. *Club*: V.A.D., London. (M2662)

WILSON, Capt. Neville Frederick Jarvis, C.M.G., C.B.E., *b.* 1865 ; *s.* of the late Maj.-Gen. Charles Watson Wilson, R.A. ; *m.* Helena Dorothy, who died, 1917, *d.* of the late Brig.-Gen. Hunter Alexander Goghlan, Army Med. Depart. *Educ.:* St. John's Coll., and Royal Academy, Gosport. Royal Indian Marine ; served in Burma War, in Suakin, and in E. Africa ; Assist. Port Officer, Bombay, 1904–7 ; Port Officer, Karachi, 1909–14. *War Work :* Marine Transport Officer (despatches) 1914–17 ; appointed Dep. Director of Royal Indian Marine, 1916. Principal Naval Transport Officer for the East Indies from 1920. (C695)

WILSON, Oreana Fanny, Mrs., C.B.E.

WILSON, Rev. Piers Holt, O.B.E., *b.* 3 Jan. 1883 ; *s.* of George Holt Wilson, of Redgrave Hall, Suffolk. *Educ.:* Sherborne ; Oriel Coll., Oxford ; Wells Theological Coll. *War Work :* Chaplain to Scottish Horse Brigade in Gallipoli and Egypt, 1915–16 ; Royal Air Force in France, and Belgium, 1916–19. *Address :* 120, North Street, St. Andrews, N.B. (O5942)

WILSON, Lieut. Ralph Justly Chatterton, M.B.E., *b.* 1880 ; *s.* of T. B. Wilson, late County Inspector R.I.C. *Educ.:* Portora Royal School, Enniskillen and Trinity Coll., Dublin. *War Work :* 1915, German S.W. Africa ; France, R.A.S.C. (M.T.), 39th Division. *Club :* Tipperary County (Clonmel). (M4630)

WILSON, Capt. Reginald Maitland, O.B.E.

WILSON, Reginald Page Campbell, C.B.E., M.I.C.E., M.I.E.E., M.Cons.E., *b.* 1866 ; *s.* of Charles Herbert Ball Wilson, of Calcutta, and Hay (Brecon) ; *m.* Ada Sarah, *d.* of S. H. Behrend, of Liverpool. *Educ.:* Privately. Consulting Engineer. *War Work :* Enlisted as A.B. in R.N.V.R., May 1915 ; Woolwich Inspection Dept., Jan. 1916 ; Ministry of Munitions, Oct. 1917 ; Assistant Controller Seaplanes, Jan. 1918 ; Director Aeronautical Supplies, Jan. 1919. *Address :* 58, Wynnstay Gardens, Kensington, W. 8. *Clubs :* Junior Carlton : Ranelagh : Royal Air Force. (C3055)

WILSON, Richard William, O.B.E.

WILSON, Lieut. Ritchie, M.B.E., R.F.A. (T.)

WILSON, Robert, M.B.E., *b.* 7 June, 1865 ; *s.* of Robert Wilson, of Helmsley, Yorks ; *m.* Annie Margaret, *d.* of James T. Robinson, of Thormanby Hill, Easingwold, Yorks. *Educ.:* C. of E. School, Helmsley, Yorks. Clerk to the Chipping Sodbury Board of Guardians ; Rural District Council, etc., Chipping Sodbury, Glos. *War Work :* Hon. Sec. National Registration, National Service, War Charities, War Relief Committee, War Savings Organisation and Campaign, Recruiting, Belgian Refugees, Food Economy Campaign, War Agricultural Organisation, and Prisoners of War Fund ; Clerk to Local Tribunal War Pensions Committee, Food Control Committee, and Coal Control Committee. *Address :* The Cliff, Old Sodbury, Glos. (M10098)

WILSON, Robert Alexander, M.B.E., *b.* 3 June, 1850 ; *s.* of Thomas Wilson, of Sligo, Ireland ; *m.* Mary, *d.* of John Lawson, of Newcastle-on-Tyne. *Educ.:* Ballysodare Collooney and Sligo. Wholesale Clothier. *War Work :* Special Constable, Newcastle-on-Tyne, Group Leader. *Address :* 2, Lambton Road, Newcastle-on-Tyne. *Clubs :* Liberal (Newcastle) Portland Park Bowling. (M10099)

WILSON, Robert James, M.B.E., *b.* 21 Feb. 1876 ; *s.* of Thomas Wilson, of Shinrone, King's County, Ireland ; *m.* Susannah Anne, *d.* of William Henry Baker, of Culmstock, Devon. *Educ.:* Duke of York's Royal Military School. Managing Clerk in Treasury Solicitor's Department. *War Work :* Legal work for Admiralty in connection with H.M. ships. *Address :* 334, Merton Road, Wandsworth, S.W. 18. (M2663)

WILSON, Lieut. Roy Vincent, M.B.E., A.I.F.

WILSON, Stewart, M.B.E.

WILSON, 2nd Lieut. Sholto Douglas Major, M.B.E.

WILSON, Major and Qr.-Mr. Thomas, O.B.E., R.A.S.C.

WILSON, Thomas, O.B.E., J.P., *b.* 2 Feb. 1846 ; *s.* of James Wilson, of Glasgow ; *m.* Elizabeth (who died), *d.* of John Johnston, of Glasgow. *Educ.:* Parish School, and Glasgow Univ. Drapery Warehouseman. *War Work :* Military Tribunal, Lanarkshire. *Address :* 17, Fotheringay Road, Glasgow. *Clubs :* Liberal (Glasgow). (O872)

WILSON, Thomas, O.B.E.

WILSON, Rev. Thomas Augustine, O.B.E.

WILSON, Sir Thomas Fleming, K.B.E., J.P., *b.* 1862 ; *s.* of John Wilson, of Glasgow ; *m.* Helen, *d.* of the late William Barr, J.P., of Noantead, Uddingston. *Educ.:* Glasgow High School ; Glasgow Univ. A member of Lanarkshire County Council for fifteen years ; Chairman Committee on Public Health ; M.P. for North-East Lancashire, 1910–11 ; Partner in the firm of Wilson, Chalmers and Hendry, Solicitors, Glasgow. *Addresses :* Flemington House, Uddingston ; 40, Vincent Place, Glasgow. *Clubs :* National Liberal ; Glasgow Liberal. (K180)

WILSON, Walter Caradine, O.B.E.

WILSON, Lieut. Wilfred Wellington, M.B.E.,

WILSON, William, O.B.E.,

WILSON, William, M.B.E.

WILSON, William, M.B.E.

WILSON, William, O.B.E., J.P., *b.* 24 April, 1871 ; *s.* of William Wilson, of Stratford House, Atherstone ; *m.* Evelyn Muriel, *d.* of Frederick H. Farquharson, Jamaica, B.W.I. Merchant ; Member of Executive Committee of Jamaica Imperial Association ; Member of British Empire Producers Association ; Member of Royal Colonial Institute. *War Work :*

Originator of Jamaica War Contingent ; Chairman of Jamaica War Contingent Committee ; Member of Central Recruiting Committee ; Trustee of Jamaica War Trust Fund ; Member of Pensions and Allowances Committee ; nominated Member of Committee of Baden Powell Boy Scouts, Jamaica. *Address :* The White House, Kingston, Jamaica. *Clubs :* West India, and Overseas, (London) ; The Jamaica, St. Andrews, The Liguanea, Jamaica). (O1016)

WILSON, William John Denman, M.B.E.

WILSON, William Major, M.B.E.; *b.* 1867 ; *s.* of John Wilson, of Kilmarnock, N.B. Staff Clerk, Local Government Board (now Ministry of Health). *War Work :* Care, etc., of the Belgian Refugees. *Address :* 30, Morton Gardens, Wallington, Surrey. (M2664)

WILSON, Major William Perceval, O.B.E.

WILSON, Capt. and Qr.-Mr. William Robert, M.B.E.

WILSON, Caroline Adini, Mrs. CARUS-, M.B.E.,*b.* 25 June, 1897 ; *d.* of the Rev. Henry Gardner Hills, Vicar of St. Thomas', Portman Square ; *m.* Frederick Maynard, *s.* of Rev. Frederick Neville Carus-Wilson, of St. Petersburg Place, London. *Educ.:* Clapham High School. *War Work :* Orderly at Kent 50 V.A.D. Hospital, Oakley, Bromley Common, Kent, May, 1915 to Dec. 1915 ; Clerk in the Secretary's Department of the War Office, Dec. 1915 to March, 1919 ; Junior Administrative Assistant in charge of sub-section dealing with the encoding of telegrams, Aug. 1918 to March, 1919. *Address :* Millfield, Keston, Kent. (M10089)

WILSON, Sir William GREY-, K.C.M.G., K.B.E., *b.* 1852 ; *s.* of late Andrew Wilson, Inspector-Gen. of Hospitals, H.E.I.C.S. ; *m.* Margaret, *d.* of Robert Glasgow Brown, of Broadstairs, Ayrshire. *Educ.:* Cheltenham Coll., and France. Clerk of the Executive and Legislative Councils of British Honduras, 1878 ; A. Magistrate, Orange Walk, 1879–80, and 1880–1 ; Assistant Colonial Sec. and Treas., Sierra Leone, 1883–4 ; Assistant Colonial Sec., Gold Coast, 1884–86 ; Colonial Sec., St. Helena, 1886–87, Administrator there, 1887–90 ; Governor, Commander-in-Chief, and A. Chief Justice, 1890–97 ; Governor, and Chief Justice of the Falkland Islands 1897–1904, and Governor and Commander-in-Chief of the Bahama Islands, 1904–12. *War Work :* Sec. and Chairman of the Central Committee for National Patriotic Organisations, which was founded in Nov. 1914, as the result of an appeal in the papers signed by all the notable men of the day. *Clubs :* Isthmian ; Junior Carlton. (K75)

WILSON, Capt. Albert Edgar SIDDONS-, M.B.E., R.A.F.

WILSON, Minnie Elisabeth, Lady, MARYON-, O.B.E.,*b.* 22 May, 1863 : *d.* of Gen. Thornhill, of Lavender Farm, Ascot ; *m.* Sir Spencer J. *s.* of Sir Spencer Maryon-Wilson, of Charlton House, Kent (*see* BURKE'S *Peerage*). *Educ.:* Abroad. *War Work :* Vice-President of County of London ; Chairman of Greenwich and Woolwich District Committee ; Hon. Commandant Charlton House Hospital ; worked at Canteens, War Supply Depot. *Address :* Bury Hill, Dorking ; 9, Victoria Square. (O11642)

WILSONE, Lieut. Comm. Thomas Clarence, O.B.E., R.N.

WILTON, Jemima, Mrs., M.B.E.

WILTS, Captain and Brevet Major, Frederick Vavasour Broome, D.S.O., O.B.E., M.C., R.E.

WILTSHIRE, Major Harold Waterlow, D.S.O., O.B.E., M.D. Served in the Great War, 1914–18 (despatches). (O6558)

WILYMAN, Capt. Charles, M.B.E.

WIMBLE, Sir John Bowring, K.B.E., *b.* 1868 ; *s.* of John Wimble ; *m.* Anne Mason, *d.* of William Fothergill Batho. *Educ.:* Clifton Coll. Shipowner ; Director of C. T. Bowring & Co., Ltd., of Liverpool, London, Cardiff, New York, and St. John's, Newfoundland ; Chairman Metropolitan Life Assurance Society ; Member of the Port of London Authority. *War Work :* Chairman London Shipowners and Transport Workers ; Military Service Committee ; Member of the Port and Transit Executive Committee. *Addresses :* 23, Cambridge Square, Hyde Park, W. 2 ; Huntercombe, near Henley-on-Thames. *Clubs :* Union ; Bath ; City of London ; Ranelagh. (K242)

WIMBORNE, Lady Cornelia Henrietta Maria, O.B.E.

WIMPERIS, Major Harry Egerton, O.B.E., M.A., late R.A.F., *b.* 27 Aug. 1876 ; *s.* of Joseph Price Wimperis, of London ; *m.* Grace d'Avray, *d.* of Sir George Parkin K.C.M.G., LL.D., D.C.L., of London (*see* BURKE'S *Peerage*). *Educ.:* Imperial Coll. of Science, and Caius Coll., Cambridge. Head of Air Ministry Laboratory ; Head of Navigation Research at Air Ministry. *War Work :* Lieut. and Lieut.-Comdr. R.N.V.R.; Major R.A.F.in charge of Bomb Sighting Research at Admiralty, Air Board, and Air Ministry ; Inventor of various Service instruments for this purpose, and for Air Navigation. *Address :* Grahamsfield, Goring-on-Thames. *Club :* Athenæum. (O893)

WINBY, Thomas, M.B.E., *b.* 16 Nov. 1871 ; *s.* of Henry Freeman Winby, of Crewe ; *m.* Kate, *d.* of John Pearce, of Market Drayton, Salop. *Educ.:* Crewe. Fuel Superintendent L. & N.W. Rly. *War Work :* Assistant to Chief Coal Controller (late Sir Guy Calthrop). *Address :* Euston Station, London. (M10102)

WINCH, Capt. Arthur Bluett, M.B.E.

WINCH, Major Aubrey Brooke, M.B.E.

WINCH, Capt. Stanley Brooke, O.B.E., R.A.O.C.

WINCHESTER, Charlotte Josephine, Marchioness of, G.B.E. ; *d.* of late Col. J. S. Howard, of Ballina Park, Co. Wicklow, and widow of Samuel Garnett, of Arch Hall, County Neath ; *m.* Henry William Montagu Paulet, 16th Marquess of Winchester (*see* BURKE'S *Peerage*). *War Work :* President

Hampshire Branch British Red Cross Society, 1909–20; Member Voluntary Aid Advisory Sub-Committee; Joint Women's V.A.D. Committee; Netley Red Cross Auxiliary Hospital Committee; V.A.D. Uniform Committee; South African and Rhodesian Officers' Residential Club Committee; Rhodesian Soldiers' Comfort Fund Committee. *Club :* Ladies' Empire.

WINDEATT, Major George Edward, O.B.E.

WINDER, Ada Mary, M.B.E., *b.* 24 July, 1877; *d.* of the late Col. Edward Noblett, of The Wallands, Lewes; *m.* Arthur Wellesley, *s.* of Thomas Winder, of Cork. *Educ. :* Cheltenham Ladies Coll. *War Work :* Work in connection with the B.R.C.S. *Address :* Mount Verdon, Cork. *Club :* New Century. (M2665)

WINDER, Arthur Wellesley, O.B.E., B.A., LL.D., *b.* 7 Dec. 1868; *s.* of Thomas Winder, of Mount Verdon, Cork; *m.* Ada Mary, *d.* of Col. Edward Noblett, late Royal Irish Regt. Solicitor. *War Work :* Work in connection with the B.R.C.S., St. John's Ambulance and other Societies. *Address :* Mount Verdon, Cork. *Club :* Cork. (O11643)

WINDER, Charles Bertram, M.B.E., *b.* 1 Oct. 1876; *s.* of Charles James Winder, of The Holt, Barnacre, Garstang. *Educ. :* Privately; The Royal Agricultural Coll., Cirencester. *War Work :* Voluntary Ambulance driver in France and Italy; later acting O.C. for the B.R.C.S. Abbeville Store; finally Adjutant of the Boulogne Base Convoys. *Addresses :* c/o C. J. Winder, The Holt, Barnacre, Garstang; Wellesley Farm, Salisbury, Rhodesia. (M10103)

WINDER, Capt. Francis Arthur, O.B.E., B.A., M.B., B.Ch., B.A.O., R.A.M.C., *b.* 16 March, 1872; *s.* of Edward William Winder, of Stillorgan, Co. Dublin. *Educ. :* Rathmines School, and Trinity Coll., Dublin. General Practitioner of Medicine. *War Work :* Founder of Glasnevin Company of "G.R." Volunteer Training Corps; served 1915–19 in R.A.M.C. with service in Mediterranean, India, Mesopotamia, German East Africa, France, and Egypt. *Address :* 170, Botanic Road, Glasnevin, Dublin. (O5945)

WINDER, Penelope, Mrs., M.B.E.

WINDEYER, William Archibald, M.B.E.

WINDHAM, William, C.B.E., *b.* 1864; *s.* of Ashe Windham, of Wawne Hall, co. York (*see* BURKE'S *Peerage*), Bowyer-Smith); *m.* 1894, Blanche Marie, *d.* of the late Achille Erneste Titren, of Durban. Gov. Sec., Zululand, 1882–7; Reg.-Gen. Natal, 1901; Sec. for Native Affairs, Transvaal, 1901–10; Board of Trade, England, 1912–17; Ministry of Labour from 1917. (C76)

WINDIATE, Albert, M.B.E.

WINDLE, Alfred Rawlinson, O.B.E., *b.* 5 July, 1862; *s.* of late Rev. William Windle, M.A., Rector of St. Stephen's, Walbrook, E.C. *Educ. :* Blackheath, and King's Coll., London. Chairman, Birmingham Railway Carriage and Wagon Co., Ltd., Smethwick, Staffs. *War Work :* Chairman, War Pensions Committee, Wolverhampton; Sec. and Treas. Soldiers' and Sailors' Families Association, Wolverhampton. *Address :* Redhill, Farnham, Surrey. *Club :* British Empire; Royal N. Devon Golf, Westward Ho ! (O11644)

WINDLE, Lieut. Charles Howard, O.B.E., R.N.V.R.

WINDRUM, Capt. and Qr.-Mr. James Moffet, M.B.E.

WINDSOR, Arthur Whalesby, M.B.E.

WINDSOR, Capt. Maurice, M.B.E.

WINDUS, Capt. George Ryley, M.B.E.

WINEARLS, Henry Martin, O.B.E., *b.* 1859; *s.* of late Henry Winearls, of Westacre, Norfolk. *Educ. :* Shrewsbury School. Assist. Official Receiver in Companies Winding-up, 1893–1913; Chief Clerk, Companies Dept., Board of Trade, 1913; Comptroller Companies Dept., Board of Trade, 1919. *Address :* 65, George Street, Portman Square, W. 1. *Club :* Union. (O2024)

WINFIELD, Capt. Frederick Butwell, O.B.E., R.A.M.C.

WINFIELD, Richard, M.B.E., *b.* 29 March, 1867; *s.* of Richard Winfield, of Manchester; *m.* Elizabeth, *d.* of William Bennett, of Salford, Manchester. *Educ. :* Derby. Chief Outdoor Representative, Great Northern Rly. Co., Manchester. *War Work :* Board of Trade, Coal Mines Dept.; Divisional Officer Manchester, Lancashire, and Lancaster North-Western Division, 1917–20. (M10107)

WING, Fred Augustus, M.B.E., *b.* 16 Feb. 1881; *s.* of Fred Wing, of Cambridge; *m.* Florence May, *d.* of George Stevens, of Loughborough. *Educ. :* Pelly Memorial School, and King's Coll. Staff Clerk in His Majesty's Civil Service, Secretary's Department, Admiralty. *Address :* 93, Holland Road, S.W. 9. (M4095)

WINGATE, Catherine Leslie, Lady, O.B.E.

WINGATE, Gen. Sir Francis Reginald, Bart., G.C.B., G.C.V.O., G.B.E., K.C.M.G., D.S.O., D.C.L. (Oxon.), LL.D. (Edin.), *b.* 25 June, 1861; *s.* of late Andrew Wingate, of Broadfield, Renfrewshire N.B.; *m.* Catherine Leslie, D.B.E., *d.* of late Capt. Joseph Sparkhall Rundle, R.N. *Educ. :* St. Heliers, Jersey, and R.M.A., Woolwich. Col. Commandant, Royal Artillery; Hon. Col. 7th Manchesters (T.); formerly Sirdar of the Egyptian Army, Governor-General of the Sudan, and High Commissioner for Egypt. *War Work :* Organised numerous expeditions in the Sudan, including the reconquest of the Darfur Province in 1916; General Officer commanding the Hedjaz Operations, 1916–19; several times mentioned in despatches for services in connection with Military Operations in the Near East, whilst High Commissioner for Egypt; President Red Cross Society (Egyptian Branch), 1916–19; Knight of Grace of St. John of Jerusalem. *Address :* Knockenhair,

Dunbar, Scotland. *Clubs :* Army and Navy; Beefsteak; British Empire. (G30)

WINGATE, Major George Frederick Richard, O.B.E., R.A.

WINGATE, Gerald Henry, M.B.E.

WINGFIELD, Lieut.-Col. John Maurice, D.S.O., O.B.E., F.R.G.S., F.Z.S., J.P., *b.* 1 Feb. 1863; *s.* of J. H. L. Wingfield, of Tickencote Hall, Stamford. *Educ. :* Harrow, and Trinity Coll., Cambridge. High Sheriff of Rutland, 1911. *War Work :* Served in S. Africa, 1899–1900; Great War, 1914–18. *Addresses :* Tickencote Hall, Stamford; Market Overton, Oakham; D, 5, The Albany, Piccadilly. *Clubs :* Guards'; Turf; Carlton; Arthur's; Wellington. (O3206)

WINN, Rowland, M.B.E.

WINNETT, Major Albert William, O.B.E.

WINNIFRITH, Rev. Douglas Percy, O.B.E., M.A., *b.* 17 Aug. 1875; *s.* of Rev. A. Winnifrith, M.A., of Hythe, Kent; *m.* Margaret Louise, *d.* of Dr. T. L. Macartney, of Sefton Park, Liverpool. *Educ. :* Pembroke Coll., Oxford. Curate from 1899–1904; Chaplain to the Forces from 1904; Hon. Chaplain to Lord Lieut. of Ireland, 1919. *War Work :* Chaplain in charge of 14th Infantry Brigade, Aug. 1914; twice mentioned in despatches. *Address :* c/o Sir C. R. McGrigor, Bart. & Co., 39, Panton Street, Haymarket. (O7876)

WINNY, William Humphris, O.B.E., A.M.I.E.E., *b.* Aug. 1867; *s.* of William Winny, of London. *Educ. :* Brewer's Grammar School; Finsbury Technical Coll. Assistant Staff Engineer, G.P.O. *War Work :* In command of the London District of the St. John Ambulance Brigade during and since the war; organised in conjunction with the Police Authorities schemes for relief of air raid victims and help for those in air raid shelters. *Address :* 61, Chancery Lane, W.C. 2. (O874)

WINRAM, Agnes Rankine, Mrs., O.B.E.; *d.* of John Williamson, of Powfoulis, Airth, Stirlingshire; *m.* James, *s.* of George Winram, of Coldingham, Berwickshire. Hon. Convener of Cradle Committee, Child Welfare Scheme, City Chambers, Edinburgh; also Voluntary Health Visitor, Child Welfare Scheme. *War Work :* Originator and Hon. Organising Sec. of the Fund for British Soldiers interned in Germany; this Fund, instituted in 1914, was the first to be formed in the British Isles for the purpose of sending parcels of foodstuffs, clothing, etc., to the British Prisoners of War in Germany; all the work was voluntary. *Addresses :* 2, Warrender Park Crescent, Edinburgh; Rosebank Cottage, Belhaven, Dunbar. (O4001)

WINSER, Charles, O.B.E.

WINSTANLEY, Denys Arthur, M.B.E., *b.* 5 Dec. 1877; Fellow of Trinity Coll., Cambridge. (M10109)

WINSTANLEY, Capt. Henry Parr M.B.E., R.A.S.C.

WINSTANLEY, Herbert, M.B.E., *b.* 7 Aug. 1885; *s.* of John Winstanley, of Liverpool; *m.* Esther Marian *d.* of William Henry McCarter, of Birkenhead. *Educ. :* Liverpool Institute. Chief Inspector, Liverpool City Police. *War Work :* In charge of Aliens Registration Department, Liverpool. *Address :* Easby, Mersey Road, Liverpool. (M10110)

WINSTANLEY, John, M.B.E., R.N.

WINTER, Squadron-Leader Alexander Charles, O.B.E., R.A.F., *b.* 26 April, 1887; *s.* of the Rev. Canon E. G. A. Winter, D.D., of East Bradenham, Norfolk; *m.* Rachel Charlotte, *d.* of Col. G. F A. Cresswell, C.V.O., V.D., of King's Lynn. *Educ. :* Trinity Coll., Glenalmond. Entered Royal Navy, 1904; served in Accountant Branch of R.N., 1904–18, mostly on Staff; Sec. to British Naval Mission to Greece, 1913–16. *War Work :* Sec. to Admiral Commanding British Adriatic Squadron, H.M.S. "Queen"; Staff Officer, 1st Class (Lieut.-Col.) in R.A.F., April, 1918, to end of war; has Order of Redeemer of Greece (1913), and Order of Crown of Italy (1916). *Clubs :* R.A.F.; United Sports; Princes Tennis and Racquets. (O2025)

WINTER, George Mitchell, O.B.E., M.R.C.S., L.R.C.P., J.P.

WINTER, Henry Elsbury, M.B.E., *b.* 1867; *s.* of James Winter, of Carlisle; *m.* Katharine Evelyn, *d.* of William Jameson, of Salisbury. *Educ. :* Waterloo Coll., Northampton, and Grammar School, Salisbury. Auctioneer and Estate Agent. *War Work :* Organiser of Carlisle Special Constabulary, and took prominent work therewith throughout war; organiser and Manager of the Carlisle Soldiers' and Sailors' Rest Rooms; Treas. Local Central War Savings Committee; Treas. of Cumberland and Westmorland Care Committee for Prisoners of War; Treas. Carlisle Citizens League. *Address :* Shaftesbury House, Howard Place, Carlisle. (M1106)

WINTER, Lieut. Herbert Marmaduke, M.B.E., *b.* 10 Oct. 1889; *s.* of the Hon. M. G. Winter, C.B.E., M.L.C., of St. John's, Newfoundland; *m.* Edythe, *d.* of Geo. J. Hayward, of St. John's, Newfoundland. *Educ. :* Bishop Field Coll., St. John's, and Rossall School, Lancashire. Accountant with firm of T. and M. Winter, St. John's; Member, Board of Trade. *War Work :* Attached Musketry Staff, Royal Newfoundland Regt. Depot, at Ayr, Scotland, and Musketry Staff Headquarters, St. John's, Newfoundland. *Address :* Omrac, King's Bridge Road, St. John's, Newfoundland. *Clubs :* Bally Haly; Golf and Country. (M5903)

WINTER, Hon. Marmaduke George, C.B.E., M.L.C.

WINTER, Mildred Marion, Mrs., M.B.E.

WINTER, Col. William Robert, O.B.E.

WINTERBOTHAM, Clara Frances, M.B.E., *b.* 2 Aug. 1880; *d.* of the late James Batten Winterbotham, of Cranley Lodge, Cheltenham. *Educ. :* Cheltenham Ladies' Coll.

Councillor on the Cheltenham Town Council; Member of the Cheltenham Education Committee. *War Work :* The London Hospital, Whitechapel, Oct. 1914, to May, 1915 ; V.A.D. Staff Nurse at St. John Hospital, Cheltenham, June, 1915, to June, 1918 ; Quartermaster at same, June, 1918, to March, 1919 ; Member of Local Food Control, and Fuel and Lighting Committees. *Address :* Cranley Lodge, Cheltenham. (M10111)

WINTERBOTTOM, Albert, O.B.E. Chief Constable, Hartlepool. *Address :* Marine Parade, Hartlepool. (O4646)

WINTERBOTTOM, George William, O.B.E.

WINTERBOTTOM, Paymaster-Capt. Thomas, C.B.E., R.N. *War Work :* 1914–19, at Naval Base, Portland. (C2303)

WINTON, Rev. Walter Sim, M.B.E.

WINTOUR, Major-Gen. FitzGerald, C.B., C.B.E., *b.* 1860 ; *s.* of the late Rev. FitzGerald Wintour, of High Hayland, Barnsley ; *m.* 1st 1899, Cicily Winifred who died 1904, *d.* of the late Col. Sir Walter Thomas William Spencer Stanhope, K.C.B., of Cannon Hall, Barnsley (*see* BURKE'S *Peerage*), 2nd in 1912, Alice Jane Blanche, *d.* of the late Major John Frederick Foster (*see* BURKE'S *Peerage*, Foster of Glyde Court). Entered Army, 1880 ; Capt. and Brevet Major, 1887 ; Brevet Lieut.-Col., 1900 ; Lieut.-Col. 1904 ; Col., 1908, Hon. Major-Gen., 1918 (ret.), served with the Egyptian Expedition, 1882 (medal, bronze star) ; Soudan Expedition, 1884–5 (despatches, clasp) ; Soudan 1885–6 ; N. W. Frontier of India, 1897 on Staff (despatches, medal with clasp) ; S. Africa, 1899–1901 (despatches, medal with two bars) ; served in the Great War, 1914–15. (C839a)

WINTOUR, Francis, O.B.E.

WINTZ, Sophia Gertrude Wintz, D.B.E. ; *d.* of Augustus Wintz, of Schaffhausen, Switzerland. *Educ. :* Girls' Coll., Fareham, Hants. *War Work :* Associated with Miss Weston in her work for the Sailors of the Royal Navy, since 1876. *Address :* Royal Sailors Rest, Devonport and Portsmouth. (D57)

WINWOOD, Lieut.-Col. William Quintyne, C.M.G., D.S.O., O.B.E., *b.* 1873 ; *s.* of the Rev. Henry Hoyte Winwood, M.A., of 11, Cavendish Crescent, Bath ; *m.* 1909, Gertrude Dolben, *d.* of the late Rev. Dolben Paul, Rector of Bearwood, and widow of T. Bryon Hope, of Harwood, Newbury. Entered 5th Dragoon Guards, 1893 ; became Capt. 1901 ; Major, 1904 ; Lieut.-Col. 1914 ; served in S. Africa, 1899–1902, taking part in the defence of Ladysmith (despatches) ; in the Great War, 1914–18 ; Commanded 5th Dragoon Guards in the field from Sept. 1914, to May, 1918 ; Commandant, Cavalry Corps School in France until the conclusion of hostilities (wounded, despatches, Order of Leopold of Belgium, Croix de Guerre) ; was Assist. Mil. Sec. to Com.-in-Chief, S. Africa, 1907–8. *Clubs :* Cavalry ; Army and Navy. (O2790)

WINZAR, Sidney Herbert, M.B.E., R.N.

WISE, Alexander, O.B.E.

WISE, Capt. Cuthbert Walter, O.B.E., M.C., R.A.S.C.

WISE, Lieut.-Col. Henry Edward Disbrowe, C.B.E., Col. 3rd Notts. and Derbyshire Regt. Served in the Great War, 1914–19 (despatches). (C1826)

WISE, Percy Furlong, M.B.E.

WISE, Thomas, O.B.E., *b.* 1850 ; *s.* of Thomas Wise, of Boston, Banker. *Educ. :* Cheltenham Coll. *War Work :* Chairman, Chartered Accountants Advisory Committee, Ministry of National Service. *Address :* 27, Eldon Road, Kensington, W. 8. *Clubs :* Travellers ; City Carlton. (O11649)

WISEMAN, Francis Augustus John Bartholomew, O.B.E., R.A.F.

WISHART, Frederick, O.B.E., M.A., LL.B., *b.* 25 July, 1888 ; *s.* of F. W. F. Wishart, of Westerfolds, Morayshire. *Educ. :* Aberdeen Grammar School ; Aberdeen Univ. ; Balliol Coll., Oxford. Barrister. *War Work :* Ministry of Munitions of War, 1916–19 ; Personal Assistant to Controller, 1917, and Assistant Controller, 1918, Munitions Timber Supplies Department. *Addresses :* Westerfolds, Elgin, Morayshire ; 1, Temple Gardens, Temple, E.C. 4. (O11650)

WITHALL, Major Latham August, O.B.E.,

WITHER, Major Harold Stephen BIGG-, O.B.E.

WITHERBY, Lieut. Harry Forbes, M.B.E., R.N.V.R.

WITHERDEN, Charlotte Mary, Mrs., O.B.E.

WITHERS, Gerald Mould, M.B.E.

WITHERS, John James, C.B.E., *b.* 21 Dec. 1863 ; *s.* of James Tuck Withers, of Arundel Street, Strand ; *m.* Caroline Gifford, *d.* of — Ransford, of 22, Sussex Square, Hyde Park. *Educ. :* Eton, and King's Coll., Cambridge. Solicitor ; Senior Partner in firm of Withers, Bensons, Currie, Williams & Co ; Fellow of St. Catharine's Coll., Cambridge. *War Work :* Assisted Propaganda Dept. and Ministry of Information during the war, both as legal adviser and otherwise. *Addresses :* 4, Arundel Street, Strand, London ; 54, Gloucester Terrace, Hyde Park. *Clubs :* Oxford and Cambridge ; Garrick ; Alpine ; Leander. (C336)

WITHYCOMBE, Robert, M.B.E.

WITNEY, Lieut. John Humphrey, M.B.E., R.A.O.C.

WITT, Lieut. Albert Thomas Edgar, M.B.E. R.A.F.

WITT, Robert Clermont, C.B.E., M.A., *b.* 16 Jan. 1872 ; *s.* of G. A. Witt ; *m.* Mary Helene, *d.* of Charles Henry Marten, Blackheath. *Educ. :* Clifton Coll. ; New Coll., Oxford. Trustee of the National Gallery ; Trustee of the National Gallery of British Art (Tate) ; Vice-Chairman, National Art Collections Fund ; Chairman, National Loan Collection Trust. *War Work :* Assisted in Treasury Solicitor's Department.

Address : 32, Portman Square, W. 1. *Clubs :* Royal Automobile ; Burlington Fine Arts ; Leander Rowing. (C674)

WITTHAUS, Gabriel Thorold, M.B.E., A.C.I.S., *b.* 6 Sept. 1888 ; *s.* of the late F. E. Witthaus, of High Barnet ; *m.* Florence, *d.* of the late James Kerry, of Highbury, London. *Educ. :* Queen Elizabeth's Grammar School, Barnet, and Caterham. *War Work :* Enlisted in The Queen's (R.W. Surrey) Regt., and later commissioned in The Norfolk Regt. ; Overseas service, India, 1917–18 ; Mesopotamia, 1918–19. (M7030)

WITTS, Gulielma Ewart, Mrs., M.B.E.

WITTS, Capt. John Travell, M.B.E.

WITTY, Lieut. Charles Harry, M.B.E., R.A.F.

WOAKES, Capt. William James Primet, O.B.E., R.A.S.C.

WODEHOUSE, Amy Violet, Mrs. O.B.E., *b.* 16 Oct. 1876 ; *d.* of John Swinton Isaac, of Boughton Park, Worcester ; *m.* Lieut.-Col. Ernest Charles Forbes, D.S.O. (killed in action), *s.* of Lieut.-Col. Charles Wodehouse, C.I.E. *War Work :* Hon. Sec. and Organiser of Worcestershire Regimental Comforts Fund, which despatched Comforts to the various Batts. of the Worcestershire Regt. at the front, and looked after all the Prisoners of War of the Worcestershire Regiment, Worcestershire Yeomanry. *Address :* 11, Prince of Wales Terrace, W. 8. (O2027)

WODEHOUSE, Lieut.-Col. Robert Elmer, O.B.E.

WOLFE, Ernest Montague, M.B.E.

WOLFE, George Charles, C.B.E. Assist. Audit Officer, Military Supply Accounts, India. *Address :* Simla, India. (C1983)

WOLFE, Eng.-Comm. Henry Eccles, O.B.E., R.N.

WOLFE, Humbert, C.B.E. *War Work :* Controller, Labour Regulation Depart. Ministry of Munitions ; appointed an Assist. Sec. Ministry of Labour, 1919. (C337)

WOLFENDEN, Ralph, M.B.E., M.Sc., A.M.I.Mech.E., *b.* 18 Feb. 1884 ; *s.* of J. W. Wolfenden, J.P., of Heyside, Lancs. *Educ. :* Victoria Univ. of Manchester, and Middle Temple. Barrister-at-Law ; Lecturer in Engineering in King's Coll., London, W.C. ; Examiner for the B.Sc. (Eng.) of the Univ. of London. *War Work :* Assistant-in-Charge, Gauge Testing Department, National Physical Laboratory, Teddington, Middlesex. *Address :* King's College, London, W.C. (M1109)

WOLFERSTAN, Evelyn, M.B.E.

WOLFF, Major Henry Philip, O.B.E.

WOLFF, Lieut. James Daniel, M.B.E., R.A.

WOLFF, Joseph, O.B.E.

WOLFF, Lieut. Mark Arthur, O.B.E.

WOLLEN, Emily Hilda, M.B.E.

WOLMARANS, Capt. Martinus Johannes, O.B.E.

WOLSTENHOLME, Capt. Thomas Blakeway, O.B.E., R.A.M.C. (T.).

WOLVERTON, Edith Amelia, Lady, C.B.E. ; *d.* of 1st Earl of Dudley ; *m.* Frederic Glyn, D.L., 4th Baron Wolverton, *s.* of Vice-Admiral Hon. Harry Carr, C.B., C.S. *Address :* 26, St. James' Place, S.W. 1. (C338)

WOMBWELL, Lieut. and Qr.-Mr. Fred, M.B.E.

WONHAM, Paymaster-Capt. Charles Scrivener, C.B.E., R.N. Served in the Great War, 1914–19 (despatches). (C1952)

WOOD, Alexander, M.B.E. M.M.R.

WOOD, Capt. Alexander, M.B.E.

WOOD, Rev. Alexander, O.B.E.

WOOD, Major Alexander Lewis Sandison, O.B.E.

WOOD, Eng.-Comm. Alfred Oswald, O.B.E., R.N.

WOOD, Col. Attewell Henry, C.B.E., *b.* 1854. Formerly Lieut.-Col. and Brevet Col. Connaught Rangers (ret. 1906) ; served on the N.-W. Frontier of India, 1897–98 (medal with two clasps) ; Nile Expedition, 1898 (medal) ; S. Africa, 1899–1900 (despatches twice, Queen's medal with three clasps) ; Great War, 1914–19. (C751a)

WOOD, Augustus Ottewell, C.B.E. Chief Manager, Imperial Bank of Persia, Teheran. *Address :* Teheran, Persia. (C675)

WOOD, Benjamin, M.B.E., late Staff Quartermaster-Sergeant Army, Pay Corps, *b.* 28 Aug. 1855 ; *s.* of John Wood, of Bushby, Leicestershire ; *m.* Mary, *d.* of Robert Barron Braik, of Aberdeen. Army Scripture Reader. *War Work :* Went to France in Nov. 1914, and as Senior Army Scripture Reader superintended the whole of the work of the Army Scripture Readers' Society with the B.E.F. in France from that date to the end of June, 1919. *Address :* 36, Claremont Road, Alexandra Park, Manchester. (M10116)

WOOD, Benjamin George, O.B.E., J.P.

WOOD, Brooks Crompton, C.B.E. Acted as Chairman of Egyptian Cotton Official Values Committee. (C3174)

WOOD, Charles, O.B.E., F.C.S., *b.* 6 Jan. 1864 ; *s.* of William Wood, of Bradford ; *m.* Gertrude, *d.* of John Dawson, of Skipton. *Educ. :* Cambridge Grammar School and Birkenhead School. Gas Engineer and General Manager, Bradford Corporation. *War Work :* Coal Control, Ministry of Munitions, Explosives Dept. and Fuel Oil Production Dept. *Address :* Rosse Mount, Heaton, Bradford. (O11652)

WOOD, Col. Charles Knight, O.B.E., R.E. (ret.), *b.* 1 July, 1851 ; *s.* of Miles Astman Wood, of Orchardleigh, Ledbury, Herefordshire ; *m.* Lilian Arden, *d.* of Rev. George Arden, M.A., of Dunsford, Devonshire. *Educ. :* Cheltenham. Nile Expedition, 1886 ; Boer War : Chief Engineer to General Sir Redvers Buller ; twice mentioned in despatches ; Brevet Colonel ; Secretary to Herefordshire Territorial Force Association since 1908. *Address :* The Lower Venn, Marden, Hereford. *Club :* Primrose. (O3208)

WOOD, Cyril George Russ, O.B.E., F.R.C.S. (Eng.), *b.* 3 Aug. 1869 ; *s.* of Cyril Wood, of Bath, *m.* Fanny Mein, *d.* of Chas. Steele, of Clifton, Bristol. *Educ. :* Bristol. Surgeon to the Shropshire Eye, Ear, and Throat Hospital ; Ophthalmic Surgeon to Salop Royal Infirmary, Montgomeryshire Infirmary. *War Work :* Special work in Western Command in Eye, Ear, and Throat departments, throughout the whole period of the war. *Address :* 12, St. John's Hill, Shrewsbury.   (O4400)

WOOD, David William, M.B.E.

WOOD, Dennis, M.B.E.

WOOD, Dorothy Wood, Lady, M.B.E. ; *d.* of James Harwood, of Manchester ; *m.* as his second wife, Sir Edward Graham, *s.* of the Rev. Thomas Smith Wood. *Address :* West Heath House, West Heath Road, Hampstead.   (M10118)

WOOD, Major Douglas, O.B.E.

WOOD, Lieut.-Col. Ernest, D.S.O., O.B.E., *b.* 28 Sept. 1871 ; *s.* of Lieut.-Col. J. Wood, of Military Train ; *m.* Ellen Caroline, *d.* of Peter Wessels, of Kroonstad, O.F.S. *Educ. :* Trinity Coll., Dublin. Joined the King's Own Scottish Borderers as 2nd Lieut. June, 1894 ; transferred to the R.A.S.C. April, 1896 ; Capt. Jan. 1901 ; Major, June, 1911 ; Lieut.-Col. Jan. 1916. *War Work :* Served with the 7th Division and 5th Division in France, Belgium, and Italy ; twice mentioned in despatches. *Address :* c/o Sir Charles McGrigor, Bart., & Co., London.   (O2793)

WOOD, Ethel Mary, Mrs., C.B.E. ; *d.* of Quintin Hogg, Founder of Regent Street Polytechnic ; *m.* Herbert Frederic Wood, Major, 9th Lancers and R.A.F. (who died 1918), *s.* of Lieut.-Col. Wood, C.B., of Kibworth, Leicester. Sec. London War Pensions Committee. *War Work :* Hon. Sec. County of London Soldiers' and Sailors' Families Association, Aug. 1914–17 ; Member and Hon. Organiser of London War Pensions Committee, June, 1916, to Aug. 1917, when appointed paid secretary ; week-end munition worker and evening Woman Patrol. *Address :* 4, Park Village East, N.W. 1. *Club :* New County.   (C3081)

WOOD, Col. Evelyn FitzGerald Mitchell, D.S.O., O.B.E., R.G.A., R. of O., *b.* 16 Nov. 1869 ; *s.* of the late Field-Marshall Sir (Henry) Evelyn Wood, V.C., G.C.B., G.C.M.G., D.C.L. (*see* BURKE'S *Peerage*) ; *m.* 1st, 20 March, 1893, Lilian, *d.* of the late Charles Edward Hutton, of 63, Porchester Terrace, W. ; 2nd, Kathleen (Alla), *d.* of R. R. Morton, and widow of Hatherley Page Wood (*see* BURKE'S *Peerage*, Wood of Hatherley House). Lieut.-Col. London Brigade, R.G.A. ; Major, Reserve of Officers, Royal Dragoons ; Hon. Col. in the Army ; Sec. City of London Territorial Force Association ; one of the Lieuts. for the City of London ; served in Ashanti and in S. Africa. *Address :* Warden Hall, Willingdale Doe, Ongar, Essex. *Club :* Army and Navy.   (O3209)

WOOD, Frances Mary, M.B.E. ; *d.* of Herbert Wood, of Wolverhampton. *War Work :* Personal assistant to Chief of Engineering Section and Controller of Mild Steel Wire, Manufacture Contracts Branch, War Office. *Address :* 13, Owen Mansions, London, W. 14.   (M1110)

WOOD, Capt. Frank Thomas Herbert, O.B.E., M.D., B.Sc., R.A.M.C. (T.), *b.* 17 Nov. 1882. *Educ. :* Guy's Hospital. Medical Officer of Health, County Borough of Bootle. *War Work :* O.C. 1/1st Home Counties Divisional Sanitary Section ; engaged in sanitary work with 67th Division in England until Sept. 1916 ; then proceeded with unit to join Mesop. Exped. Force ; appointed Health Officer (Civil) for Basra, Dec. 1916, to Jan. 1919. *Address :* Health Dept., Town Hall, Bootle. (O4264)

WOOD, Frederick, O.B.E.

WOOD, Frederick Benjamin, O.B.E. ; lately British Consul at Patras, has Order of the Redeemer of Greece.   (O11654)

WOOD, Gamble Ekin Vickers, M.B.E., *b.* 24 June, 1876 ; *s.* of Lewis Wood ; *m.* Kate, *d.* of — Weston, of Folkestone. *War Work :* Folkestone War Refugees Committee ; Sub-Section Director, Ministry of Munitions, for direct purchase of shell components and gauges. *Addresses :* 39, Brompton Square ; Vale Vottage, Downley, nr. High Wycombe. *Club :* Constitutional.   (M2668)

WOOD, Capt. Geoffrey, O.B.E., M.C,

WOOD, George Albert Thomas, O.B.E., R.N.R.

WOOD, Surg.-Lieut.-Comdr. George E., R.E.

WOOD, George Ellis, M.B.E.

WOOD, Capt. George Jervis, O.B.E.

WOOD, Lieut. George Neville, O.B.E., Cross of St. Anne's " of Russia, *b.* 4 May, 1898 ; *s.* of Frederick Wood, of Cheltenham Road, Bristol. *Educ. :* Colston's School and Sandhurst Military Coll. *War Work :* Commissioned, 1916 ; France, Sept. 1916 ; wounded, March, 1917 ; Instructor No 17 O.C.B., Kinmell Park, Sept. 1917 ; Russia, B.M.M.,, April, 1919 ; now with the Greek Army in Turkey as one of the Allied Representatives.   (O11889)

WOOD, Gertrude, M.B.E.

WOOD, Gladys, M.B.E.

WOOD, Grace Anna Mary, Mrs., O.B.E.

WOOD, Grace Eliza, Mrs., M.B.E.

WOOD, 2nd Lieut. Harold John, M.B.E.

WOOD, Harold John, O.B.E., *b.* 21 Nov. 1885 ; *s.* of John Wood, of Cheam, Surrey ; *m.* Marianne Suzanne Sophie, *d.* of Leopold Henri Lavaivre, of Paris. *Educ. :* Privately. *War Work :* 10th Batt. (Res.) Border Regiment, attached General Staff, Special Missions, New York and South America. *Address :* Rua da Quitanda, 143, Rio de Janeiro.   (O11655)

WOOD, Harry Brounton, M.B.E.

WOOD, Col. Hastings St. Leger, C.B.E., D.S.O., *b.* 1856 ; *s.* of the late Lieut.-Gen. Sir (Henry) Hastings Afleck Wood,

K.C.B. ; *m.* 1891, Mary Judith Vaughton, *d.* of the Rev. J. Parker, formerly Rector of Willoughby and Wysall, Notts. Entered 15th Regt. 1877 ; Capt. E. Yorkshire Regt. 1886 ; Major, Dorsetshire Regt. 1895 ; Lieut.-Col. 1900 ; Brevet Col. 1906 ; Col. 1908 (h.-p. 1908) ; retired, 1910 ; served during Afghan War, 1879–80, as A.D.C. (severely wounded, horse killed, medal) ; Nile Expedition, 1884–85 (despatches specially, medal with clasp, bronze star) ; Burmah Campaign, 1887–88 ; D.A.A. and Q.M.G. (despatches, medal with two clasps) ; Tirah Expedition, 1897–98, as D.A.A.G. (despatches, medal with two clasps) ; D.A.A.G. Madras, 1897–99 ; A.A.G. 1899–1902 ; D.A.A.G. Jersey, 1904–8 ; appointed A.A.G. Roy. Guernsey Mil. 1911 ; A.A. and Q.M.G. 1914. *Club :* Naval and Military.   (C1817)

WOOD, Henrietta, Mrs., M.B.E.

WOOD, James, O.B.E.

WOOD, Lieut. James Henry, O.B.E., R.A.O.C.

WOOD, Capt. John Edward, O.B.E., T.F.R.

WOOD, Major John Hardy, O.B.E., *b.* 12 April, 1877 ; *s.* of Arthur Hardy Wood, of Duddleswell, Sussex ; *m.* Catherine Hazebruck, *d.* of Henry Staker, of Newbrough, Northumberland. *Educ. :* Stubbington House, Fareham. Durham Light Infantry ; served with W. African Frontier Forces. *Address :* 14, Warrington Place, Dublin. *Clubs :* Naval and Military ; Union (Brighton).   (O8976)

WOOD, Capt. John Lawrence, O.B.E., R.A.M.C.

WOOD, Lieut.-Col. John Livingstone, O.B.E., V.D.

WOOD, Capt. John William, O.B.E.

WOOD, Capt. Leonard Stanley, M.B.E.

WOOD, Louisa Jane, M.B.E.

WOOD, Maud, Mrs., M.B.E.

WOOD, May, M.B.E. ; *d.* of the late Robert Brindley Wood, of Uttoxeter. Was Deputy Clerk and Treas. of the Town of Kentville, Nova Scotia, Canada ; from 1906 Private Sec. to the Managing Director of the Underground Electric Railways Company of London, Ltd. ; from 1910 Clerk in Charge of Accounts, Road Board. *War Work :* Accounting in connection with the road works carried out by the Road Board for the War Department, Admiralty, Air Ministry. and other Government Departments during the war.   (M10125)

WOOD, Sister Minnie, O.B.E., *b.* Oct. 1882 ; *d.* of Charles W. Wood, of Sandal, Yorkshire. *Educ. :* Miss Sandbach's Private School, Hull, Yorks. Nursing Sister in Queen Alexandra's Imperial Military Nursing Service. *War Work :* Ward Sister in General Hospitals in Versailles and Boulogne, from Aug. 1914, to Nov. 1916 ; afterwards Sister-in-Charge, 44th Casualty Clearing Station from Nov. 1916, to Aug. 1919, in France, Belgium, and Germany. *Address :* Military Hospital Devonport. *Club :* Imperial Nurses'.   (O5953)

WOOD, Capt. Murdick McKenzie, O.B.E., R.A.F.

WOOD, Robert Henry, C.B.E., *b.* 1860 ; *s.* of John George Wood, W.S., of Edinburgh ; *m.* 1904, Elaine, *d.* of Col. F. Bell, of Stand House, Fermoy, co. Cork. Hon. Sec., Cork County War Pensions Local Committee. *Address :* Castle Hyde, Fermoy. *Clubs :* Thatched House ; Royal Automobile ; County (Cork).   (C3056)

WOOD, Capt. Roy Wilds Fry, M.B.E.

WOOD, Russell Howard, C.B.E., Acting Food Commr., S. Midland Div. Ministry of Food.   (C3057)

WOOD, Lieut. Thomas, M.B.E.

WOOD, Thomas Alfred, M.B.E.

WOOD, Prof. Thomas Barlow, C.B.E., M.A., F.R.S., *b.* 1869 ; *s.* of the late Brittain Dawes Wood, of Field Dalling, Norfolk ; *m.* 1914, Margaret Isabel, *d.* of Edwin Sloper Beaven, of Warminster. *Educ. :* High School, Newcastle-under-Lyme and Gonville and Caius Coll. Camb. Draper's Professor of Agriculture, Camb. Univ. ; sometime Member of Development Comm. *Address :* Springfield,; Cambridge. *Clubs :* Saville ; Farmers'.   (C339)

WOOD, William, M.B.E., *b.* 12 July, 1884 ; *s.* of George Henry Wood, of Woodlands, Oakenshaw, nr. Bradford ; *m.* Jane Ellen, *d.* of Gaythorne Hodgson, of Oakenshaw, nr. Bradford, *Educ. :* Elementary, and at Cleckheaton Technical School. Assistant Overseer and Collector of Rates for Cleckheaton and Gomersal Parishes, Spenborough, Yorks. *War Work :* Vice-Chairman Spenborough War Pensions Committee, Cleckheaton European War Fund, Prisoners of War Fund, Soldiers' and Sailors' Help Society ; Sec. to Trustees Spenborough War Memorial Fund.   (M10126)

WOOD, William, O.B.E.

WOOD, Lieut.-Col. William Albert, C.B.E., Major, Brevet Lieut.-Col. and temporary Col. R.A.V.C. during Great War.   (C1436)

WOOD, Capt. William Cranna, O.B.E., J.P.

WOOD, William Francis John, C.B.E., B.Sc., *b.* 1876 ; *s.* of the late Alphonse Wood, of Osborne House, Barnsley ; *m.* 1902, Eliza Beatrice, *d.* of Dr. John Haslam, of New College, Harrogate. *Educ. :* Sheffield and Leeds Univs. Chairman and Managing Director of Derby Crown Glass Co.. Ltd. Ryland's, Glass and Engineering Co., Ltd., and Wood Bros. Glass Co. Ltd. ; Fellow of Institute of Chemistry ; Pres. of Society of Glass Technology ; Chairman, British Chemical Ware Manufacturers' Assocn. ; J.P. for Barnsley. *Address :* Ardsley House, nr. Barnsley.   (C1060)

WOOD, Eng.-Comm. William Henry, C.B.E., R.N.

WOOD, William Henry, M.B.E.

WOOD, William John, O.B.E., *b.* 15 March, 1871. *Educ. :* Christ Church, New North Road, London, N. Member of the Willesden Board of Guardians ; Master Printer ; Founder,

Chairman, and Managing Director of Wood and Rozelaar, Ltd., London, E.C. *War Work :* Special and honorary of an Advisory nature to the Board of Trade, Coal Mines Dept., during the great coal shortage and crisis of 1918. *Address :* Brondesbury House, Willesden Lane, N.W. 6. *Club :* Eccentric.
(O11659)

WOOD, Capt. William Lyon, O.B.E., R.E.

WOOD, William, KING-, C.I.E., C.B.E., *b.* 1867 ; *s.* of the late Capt. W. Wood, Public Works Depart. Bombay ; *m.* Daisy Grace, *d.* of Sir Hugh Adcock, C.M.G. (*see* BURKE'S *Peerage*). *Educ. :* Dollar Acad. N.B. Served in S. Africa, 1900-1, with Middlesex Imperial Yeo. (despatches, medal with three clasps) ; Director, Persian Section, Indo-European Telegraph Depart. ; assumed by deed poll, 1909, the additional surname of King. *Address :* Teheran, Persia. *Club :* Junior Naval and Military.
(C1973)

WOOD, Lieut.-Col. Sir James LEIGH-, K.B.E., C.B., C.M.G. ; *b.* 1870 ; *s.* of the late James William Wood ; *m.* 1900, Joanna Elizabeth, *d.* of the late Walter Turnbull. A Gov. and Almoner of Christ's Hospital ; Com. of Order of Leopold of Belgium ; Knight of Grace of Order of St. John of Jerusalem in England. Served in the S. African war 1899-1900 (despatches twice, Queen's medal) ; Q.M.G. Staff and A.A.G. at War Office during Great War. *Address :* 24, Great Cumberland Place, W. *Clubs :* Brooks's ; Oriental.
(K290)

WOODALL, Capt. John Dane, M.B.E., M.C., R.A.

WOODALL, Norah, Mrs., M.B.E.

WOODBURN, Lieut.-Col. Thomas Stanley, C.B.E., Australian Forces, Ch. Commr. Australian Comforts Fund during Great War.
(C677)

WOODCOCK, Major George Cyril, O.B.E., R.M.A., *b.* 26 May, 1879 ; *s.* of the late Col. H. F. Woodcock, of Bengal Army. *Educ. :* Dulwich Coll. *War Work :* Grand Fleet ; R.M.A., Howitzer Brigade, B.E.F. France ; R.M. Garrison, Ægean Army of Black Sea. *Club :* United Service.
(O9676)

WOODCOCK, Harold Brookfield, M.B.E., M.B., *b.* 2 March, 1874 ; *s.* of Samuel Woodcock, of Manchester ; *m.* Florence Walteling, *d.* of W. W. Lecomber, of Manchester and Llandudno. *Educ. :* Manchester Grammar School, and Owens Coll. *War Work :* Medical Officer in charge of Seymour Park Military Hospital (2nd Western General Hospital). *Address :* The Sycamores, Old Trafford, Manchester.
(M10288)

WOODCOCK, Wing-Com. Harold Larpent, C.B.E., R.A.F. Served in Great War, 1914-19 (mentioned in despatches).
(C2343)

WOODCOCK, Henry Chadwick, M.B.E., M.R.C.S., L.R.C.P.

WOODCOCK, Walter Shellake, M.B.E.

WOODCOCK, William Stanley, M.B.E., *b.* 14 June, 1873 ; *s.* of William Plant Woodcock, of Bury, Lancs ; *m.* Ethel, *d.* of Col. T. R. Jolly, M.B.E., of Preston. *Educ. :* Rossall. Solicitor ; Clerk to Walton-le-Dale Urban District Council. *War Work :* Acting Deputy Commissioner, St. John Ambulance Brigade *Address :* 178, Station Road, Bamber Bridge.
(M2669)

WOODELL, Florence Ernestine, M.B.E.

WOODESON, Edward Seymour, M.B.E., *b.* 27 July, 1884 ; *s.* of Edwin Thomas Woodeson, of Tilehurst, Reading, Berks ; *m.* Alice Rose, *d.* of Nelson Geal, of St. Leonards-on-Sea. *Educ. :* Elementary and Secondary Schools, Reading. Dep. Ch. Constable and Chief Clerk, Norfolk Constabulary. *Address :* County Police Headquarters, Norwich. (M10130)

WOODFIELD, Col. Anthony Hudson, C.M.G., O.B.E., R.A.O.C., *b.* 26 June, 1867 ; *s.* of the late Matthew Woodifield ; *m.* Nellie, *d.* of the late Rev. Albert Willan. *Educ. :* Cheltenham ; R.M.A., Woolwich. Royal Artillery from Feb. 1886, to March, 1900 ; Army Ordnance Department from April, 1900, to present date. *War Work :* Served in Egypt from beginning of Great War to April, 1916. *Club :* United Service.
(O878)

WOODFORD, Charles Merllynn, M.B.E.

WOODFORD, Isabel Charlotte, M.B.E.

WOODGATE, Alfred, C.B.E., *b.* 1860 ; *s.* of the late Thomas Woodgate, of Hampton Wick. *Educ. :* Privately. Entered Education Dept. 1879 ; Assist. Sec. Ministry of Shipping ; Senior Clerk, National Health Insurance Comm. 1912-16.
(C340)

WOODGATE, 2nd Lieut. F. C. I., M.B.E.

WOODGER, Lieut. John Surry, O.B.E., *b.* 10 April, 1896 ; *s.* of John Woodger, of Lowestoft. *Educ. :* Charterhouse ; R.M.C., Sandhurst. *War Work :* A.S.C., first commissioned, 1915. *Address :* Woodside, Lowestoft. (O5955)

WOODHAMS, Walter Lee, M.B.E.

WOODHEAD, Esther, M.B.E.

WOODHEAD, Col. Sir German Sims, K.B.E., M.D., F.R.C.P., F.R.S.E., *b.* 29 April, 1855 ; *s.* of the late Joseph Woodhead, of Holmfirth ; *m.* Harriett Elizabeth St. Clair Eskine, *d.* of James Yates, of Edinburgh. *Educ. :* Huddersfield Coll., Edinburgh Univ., and abroad. President Royal Med. Soc. 1878 ; Assist. Com. to the Royal Commission on Tuberculosis, 1892-95 ; Lieut.-Col. R.A.M.C ; Brevet Col. A.M.S., 1917 ; Inspector of Laboratories in Military Hospitals in U.K. ; formerly Adviser in Pathology to the War Office ; Member Imperial Cancer Research Fund ; Member Scottish Universities Committee, etc., etc. *Address :* Dysart House, Luard Road, Cambridge. *Clubs :* Athenæun ; Savage ; National Liberal ; Carnarvonshire ; Royston ; Gog-Magog.
(K287)

WOODHEAD, Henry George Wandesford, C.B.E. Rendered service in connection with British interests in China during Great War.
(C3058)

WOODHEAD, Herbert Miall, M.B.E., M.B., C.M.

WOODHOUSE, Arthur William Webster, C.B.E., H.M.B. Consul-General for Moscow, *b.* 31 May, 1867 ; *s.* of the late Arthur Woodhouse, H.B.M. Consul for Riga ; *m.* Marie Petrovna, *d.* of Peter Klimov, of Petrograd. *Educ. :* Oxenford House, Jersey ; Paris ; Odessa. Entered British Consulate-General at Odessa as Clerk, Oct. 1886 ; employed on the Afghan Boundary Commission Sept., 1887, to Feb. 1888 ; appointed Vice-Consul at Batoum, June, 1891, Odessa, April, 1893, Nicolaiev, April, 1895, Boston, Feb. 1905 ; Consul, St. Pierre-Miquelon, March, 1906, Thorshavn, Feb. 1907, Petrograd, Oct. 1907 ; Consul-General, New Orleans, April, 1919, Moscow, Feb. 1920. *War Work :* Petrograd during whole war and the Revolution ; voluntarily remained behind at Petrograd when the British Embassy left, Feb. 1918 ; carried on, with whole Consular Staff, till Aug. 1918 ; imprisoned in dungeons of Peter and Paul Fortress with other British officials and civilians arrested during Bolshevic armed raid on Embassy. *Address :* c/o Foreign Office, London, S.W. 1. *Club :* British Russia.
(C3059)

WOODHOUSE, Major Brierly, O.B.E., R.A.S.C.

WOODHOUSE, Lieut. Harold James Selborne, Baron Terrington, O.B.E., *b.* 8 May, 1877 ; *e. s.* of the Right Hon. James Thomas, 1st Baron Terrington of Huddersfield, Yorks (*see* BURKE'S *Peerage*) ; *m.* Vera Florence Annie, widow of Guy Ivo Sebright. *Educ. :* Marlborough. *War Work :* Recruiting Officer, Westminster and St. Pancras, 1916 ; Substitution Officer, West London Area, 1917 ; Military Representative and National Service Representative, Hammersmith and Paddington, 1917-18. *Addresses :* 11, Clarges Street, W. ; Spinfield, Marlow Bucks. *Clubs :* Bath ; Royal Thames Yacht ; Royal Automobile.
(O4003)

WOODHOUSE, Paymaster-Lieut.-Comm. Hector Roy MacKenzie, O.B.E., R.N.

WOODHOUSE, Herbert, C.B.E., M.A., LL.D., J.P., *b.* 1 Dec. 1859 ; *s.* of James Woodhouse, of Manchester ; *m.* Frances Harriette, *d.* of William J. Halliday, of Manchester. *Educ. :* Manchester Grammar School, and Trinity Hall Cambridge. Clerk of the Peace for City and County of Kingston-upon-Hull ; Commissioner for Oaths. President, North-West Hull Unionist Association ; Member of Law Committee, Leeds Univ. *War Work :* Chairman, Hull and East Riding Appeal Tribunal and of National Service (Hull) Tribunals Committee. *Addresses :* Eastfield House, Roos, E. Yorks ; Carlton House, The Park, Hull. *Club :* Hull and East Riding.
(C3060)

WOODHOUSE, Hon. Horace Marton, C.B.E., B.A., *b.* 27 Oct. 1887 ; 2nd *s.* of the late Rt. Hon. Lord Terrington, of Huddersfield (*see* BURKE'S *Peerage*) ; *m.* Valérie, *d.* of George Allen Phillips, of Eden Bridge, Kent. *Educ. :* Winchester ; New Coll., Oxford. Barrister-at-law (1911) ; Assistant Sec. Ministry of Food (1919) ; Member of Central Committee ; Chairman of Wool Sub-Committee (Profiteering Act, 1919). *Address :* 14, Abingdon Court, Kensington, W. 8 ; *Clubs :* Reform ; Bath.
(C1061)

WOODHOUSE, Lieut.-Col. Percy St. John Rance, O.B.E.

WOODIWISS, Major and Qr.-Mr. Edwin Sydney, M.B.E., Can. A.M.C.

WOODLEY, Lieut.-Col. Ernest James, O.B.E., *b.* 26 April, 1867 ; *s.* of Matthew Fuller Woodley, of Folkestone ; *m.* Selma Isabella, *d.* of Anders Ohlsson, of Cape Town, South Africa. *Educ. :* Tonbridge School. Lieut.-Col. (ret.). Reserve of Officers. *War Work :* Rejoined from the Reserve of Officers, Aug. 1914, served till June, 1919 ; Officer-in-Charge of a Section of Infantry Records, General Headquarters, 3rd Echelon, B.E.F. *Address :* Seckford Hall, Woodbridge, Suffolk. *Club :* Junior United Service.
(O2784)

WOODLOCK, 2nd Lieut. David William Fair, M.B.E.

WOODMAN, Norah Blanche, M.B.E., *b.* 12 April, 1885. *Educ. :* St. Helen's, Northwood, Middlesex. Trained Nurse ; Now Matron, Lambeth Infirmary. *War Work :* Matron of War Refugees Camp, Earl's Court, S.W. *Address :* Lambeth Infirmary, Brook Street, Kennington, S.E. 11. (M2671)

WOODMORE, William James, M.B.E.

WOODROFFE, Alban James, M.B.E.

WOODROFFE, Brig.-Gen. Charles Richard, C.M.G., C.B.E., *b.* 4 July, 1878 ; *s.* of the late G. W. P. Woodroffe, Royal Horse Guards ; *m.* Eleanor Mary, *d.* of the late Henry Barlow-Webb, of Holmdale, Holmbury St. Mary. *Educ. :* Radley. Joined R. Sussex Artillery Militia, 1896-98 ; Royal Artillery, 1898 ; Capt. 1906 ; Major, 1914 ; attached Japanese Army, 1907-8 ; Japanese Interpreter, 1907 ; Adjutant, R.H.A., 1909-13 ; Staff Capt. 1913-14 ; D.A.Q.M.G. 1914-15 ; A.Q.M.G. 1915-16 ; D.A. and Q.M.G. 1917-18 ; served S. Africa, 1899-1902 (despatches, 2 medals, 5 clasps) ; European War, 1914-18 (C.M.G., C.B.E., Brevet Lieut.-Col., despatches 6 times) ; Officer Legion of Honour ; Order of Crown of Belgium ; Croix de Guerre (Belgian) ; Croix de Guerre (French) ; Order of Sacred Treasure, 2nd class. *Clubs :* Army and Navy ; Ranelagh ; Royal Automobile.
(C1134)

WOODROFFE, Henry, O.B.E.

WOODROFFE, Capt. Norman Frederic, O.B.E.

WOODROFFE, William Henry Plukenett, C.B.E. Director of Road Transport, Labour and Material, Ministry of Food, during Great War.
(C1062)

WOODROOFE, Henry, M.B.E.

WOODRUFF, Capt. Charles Reynolds, M.B.E., R.A.M.C. (T.).

WOODRUFFE, Major John Sheldon, D.S.O., O.B.E.. *b.* 1879. Roy. Sussex Regt.; S. Africa, 1898–1902 (Queen's medal with two clasps, King's medal with two clasps): Great War, 1914–18 (despatches). (O9711)

WOODS, Alfred, O.B.E.

WOODS, (Charlie) Roland, M.B.E., F.C.S., *b.* 11 April, 1885; *s.* of Charlie Woods, A.C.P., of Sandown I.O.W.; *m.* Sarah Hedley, *d.* of Thomas Anthony Widdrington, of Catford, S.E. *Educ.:* Strand School; King's Coll.; Birkbeck Coll., London, and Gray's Inn. Assistant Sec. of the National Federation of Iron and Steel Manufacturers; Hon. Lector of the United Girls' School Mission, North Camberwell. *War Work:* Aug. 1914, joined Emergency Staff of the Commercial Intelligence Branch of the Board of Trade; 1915, Assistant to H.M. Trade Commissioners in Canada; 1916, Sec. of Departmental Committee on the Iron and Steel Trades; 1917, Sec. of Committee on the Utilisation and Feeding of Horses; 1918, Sec. of the Committee for the Administration of the Non-Ferrous Metals Act (Board of Trade). *Addresses:* Temple Bar House, Fleet Street; Canvey, Marine Parade, Leigh-on-Sea, Essex. *Club:* Essex Yacht. (M1114)

WOODS, Constance Ada, Mrs., O.B.E.

WOODS, Edith Louisa Sophia, Mrs., M.B.E., *b.* 15 April, 1893; *d.* of Thomas John Humphreys, of Greenwich; *m.* William Henry, *s.* of Capt. Henry William Woods, of Folkestone. *Educ.:* Royal Merchant Seamen's Orphanage at Snaresbrook. Joined the staff of Messrs. Andrew Weir & Co. at the age of 16, as telephone operator, gradually working upwards as Shorthand Typist to the Private Department. *War Work:* Accompanied Mr. Andrew Weir (now the Rt. Hon. Lord Inverforth, J.P.), to the War Office, when he became the Surveyor General of Supply, serving in the capacity of lady Secretary. *Address:* 46, Lucerne Road, Thornton Heath, Surrey. (M573)

WOODS, Surg.-Lieut. George Edmund, OB.E., L.D.S., R.N.V.R.

WOODS, Major Harold, O.B.E., M.D.

WOODS, Major James Cowan, O.B.E.

WOODS, Sir James Williams, K.B.E. (1919). Director of Purchases, British War Mission in U.S.A. (K243)

WOODS, John Alexander Inglis, M.B.E.

WOODS, Dr. Lionel Dudley, O.B.E., *b.* 24 Nov. 1885; *s.* of Thomas Arthur, of Rose Lodge, Douglas, Isle of Man. *Educ.:* King Williams Coll., Isle of Man. Hon. Surgeon, Nobles Hospital, Isle of Man; has Order of St. Sava, 4th class, and Legion of Honour. *War Work:* Gazetted Lieut. R.A.M.C. Aug. 1914; Capt. Aug. 1915; Major, Sept. 1917; Surgical Specialist, Royal Victoria Hospital, Netley, Aug. 1914, to June, 1916; from then till May, 1919, 37th General Hospital, Salonica Army, attached Royal Serbian Army; Surgical Specialist and Officer-in-Charge of Surgical Division of that hospital. *Address:* 6, Albert Terrace, Douglas, Isle of Man. (O6559)

WOODS, Margery Adah, M.B.E.; *d.* of late Captain Arthur C. Woods, R.N. *War Work:* Finance Dept., Ministry of Munitions, Aug. 1916, to Sept. 1920. (M10135)

WOODS, Raymond Wybrow, C.B.E., *b.* 28 Aug. 1882; *s.* of James Chapman Woods, of Hillside, Swansea; *m.* Maud Emily Fenn, *d.* of Walter Reginald Collins, of Langland Bay, Glam. *Educ.:* Cathedral School, Hereford. *War Work:* Hon. Procurator-General, Prize Department; Chief Clerk, Treasury Solicitor's Department. *War Work:* In charge of Naval Prize work in the Department of H.M. Procurator-General. *Address:* 13, Upper Phillimore Gardens, W. 8. *Clubs:* Garrick; Roehampton. (C341)

WOODS, Sqdn.-Leader Reginald Herbert, O.B.E., M.C., R.A.F.

WOODS, Major Rickard John, O.B.E.

WOODS, Fleet-Surg. Samuel Henry, O.B.E., B.Ch., B.A., R.N.

WOODS, Walter William, M.B.E., M.C., R.A.S.C.

WOODS, Rev. William Maitland, O.B.E., V.D.

WOODWARD, Charles William, M.B.E., *b.* 21 June, 1886, *s.* of Henry Woodward, of Plumstead. *Educ.:* City of London School. Civil Servant; Assistant Principal, Board of Education. *War Work:* Principal of Division, and Sec. to the War Office Commodities Committee in the War Trade Department, Westminster. *Address:* Park View, Parkview Road, Welling, Kent. (M2678)

WOODWARD, Lieut. Frederick Hugh, M.B.E., *b.* 24 March, 1878; *s.* of Thomas Hopkins Woodward, of Blackheath. *Educ.:* Cheltenham Grammar School, and Abroad. Produce Broker, Rootham Woodward & Co., Colonial House, 17, Tooley Street, S.E. 1. *War Work:* Arranged Prize Sales for Marshal of Admiralty, 1915; joined R.A.S.C., 1915; Officer-in-charge Accounts Forage Committee, Midland Area, 1916; Assistant Buyer in U.S.A. for British Ministry of Food, and Allied Provision Export Commission, Oct. 1916, to June, 1917; Deputy Director (in charge) British Ministry of Food (Canada); Member Dairy Produce Commission; Liasson Officer between French, Belgian, and Italian Govts., and Canadian Govts., for Food supplies, June, 1917, to June, 1918. *Address:* 43, Lee Road, Blackheath, London, S.E. 3. *Clubs:* Royal Automobile; United R.A.S.C. (M10136)

WOODWARD, Capt. Frederick William, O.B.E.

WOODWARD, George Ernest, C.B.E., *b.* 26 April, 1865; *s.* of John Woodward of Dorking; *m.* Mildred, *d.* of William Aste, of Streatham. *Educ.:* Privately. Admiralty Service since 1883; now Senior Armament Supply Officer, Chatham District. *War Work:* 1912–17, in charge of Ammunition Supply Section, Naval Ordnance Dept., Admiralty; 1917–19, Director of Ammunition Production, Admiralty. *Address:* Upnor Castle, nr. Rochester. (C678)

WOODWARD, Sydney John, M.B.E., *b.* 19 March, 1882; *s.* of Henry Woodward, of Paddington; *m.* Emily, *d.* of Michael McKigney, of Ballicallin, Co. Londonderry. Steward, Queen Mary's Hospital for children, Carshalton, Surrey. *War Work:* First Superintendent of Poland Street Refugee Home under Jewish Authorities; Works Manager, Belgian War Refugees Camp, Earl's Court Exhibition, 1914–19. *Address:* Queen Mary's Hospital for Children, Carshalton, Surrey. (M4099)

WOODWARD, Capt. Vivian John, O.B.E.

WOODWARD, Capt. William Henry, M.B.E.

WOODWARK, Col. Arthur Stanley, C.M.G., C.B.E., M.D. *b.* 1875; *s.* of G. S. Woodwark, J.P., *m.* 1912, Hilda Mary, *d.* of Sir Richard Atkinson Robinson. Col. Army Med. Ser. *Address:* 4, Harley Street, W.1. (C1818)

WOODWARK, Major George Graham, C.B.E., *b.* 1 July, 1876; *s.* of George Smith Woodwark, of King's Lynn. *Educ.:* King Edward VII. Grammar School. Vice-Consul for France; Member of King's Lynn Borough Council, and of Norfolk Territorial Force Association. *War Work:* Commanded Battalions in England and France; mentioned in despatches; awarded the Legion of Honour, 1918; served in the British War Mission to the U.S.A. *Addresses:* 4. Harley Street, W. 1; Croylands, King's Lynn. *Club:* National Sporting. (C3061)

WOODWRIGHT, Surg.-Rear Adm., Charles Sharman, C.B.E., R.N. Served in Great War, 1914–19, as Principal Med. Officer, Sudan (mentioned in despatches). (C2304)

WOODYEAR, Irene M., M.B.E.; *d.* of John A. S. Woodyear. *War Work:* Intelligence Branch, War Office. (M1115)

WOOLCOCK, William James Uglow, C.B.E., M.P., *b.* 6 Sept 1878; *s.* of the Rev. James Woolcock, of Penzance; *m.* Katherine Maud, *d.* of J. T. Homer, J P., of Witchampton. *Educ.:* Privately. Barrister-at-Law; Parliamentary Private Sec. to Ministry of Munitions; General Manager of the Association of British Chemical Manufacturers. *War Work:* Chairman, Committee 5 (Medical Supplies), Surveyor-General's Department, War Office. *Address:* 166, Piccadilly, W. 1. *Clubs:* Royal Automobile; National Liberal; Chemical Industry. (C3062)

WOOLCOMBE, Lilian Mary, M.B.E.

WOOLCOTT, Francis Mary, Mrs., C.B.E. Hon. Organiser of Button Fund during the Great War. (C368)

WOOLDRIDGE, Capt. Gilbert de Lacy, O.B.E., R.A.F.

WOOLDRIDGE, Jane Anne, M.B.E.; *d.* of Thomas Wooldridge, of Hungerford. *Educ.:* Privately in England, Paris, and Germany. Joined the British Red Cross Society, 1910; Commandant of Berks. 42, 1911; *War Work:* Opened Hospital, Feb. 1915, in Hungerford Technical Institute with twelve beds; at request of War Office, increased to forty beds; auxiliary to Tedworth Military Hospital. *Address:* The Bridge House, Hungerford. (M10138)

WOOLDRIDGE, Walter, M.B.E., R.N.R.

WOOLER, Lieut. Lionel Sykes, M.B.E., R.A.

WOOLF, Albert Morris, O.B.E., *b.* 3 Nov. 1856; *s.* of Edward Woolf, of 1, Marlborough Place, N.W.; *m.* Martha, *d.* of Henry Isaacs, of Auckland, N.Z. *Educ.:* Neumageus School, Kew. Vice-President of the United Synagogue. *War Work:* Jewish War Service Committee; Vice-President of the Jewish Belgian Refugee Committee, under the Local Government Board. *Address:* 52, Priory Road, London, N.W. *Club:* British Empire. (O11662)

WOOLF, Capt. Edward Savile, O.B.E., *b.* 12 Oct. 1896; *s.* of Major H. G. Woolf, of Semley, Woking; *m.* Mildred Lucy, *d.* of F. E. Scully. *Educ.:* Malvern Coll.; R.M.C., Sandhurst. *War Work:* With R.A.S.C. in France, July, 1915, to May, 1920; D.A.D.T. (G.H.Q.), May, 1918. *Address:* Buller Barracks, Aldershot. *Club:* R.A.S.C. (O5957)

WOOLF, Mortimer, O.B.E.. *b.* 23 April, 1857; *s.* of Edward Woolf, of London; *m.* Miriam, *d.* of John Jonas, of London. *Educ.:* Privately. Manufacturer. *War Work:* Interested in, and assisted Belgian Refugees. *Address:* Mayfield, Mortimer Crescent, London, N.W. *Clubs:* British Empire; Royal Automobile. (O11662)

WOOLF, Paymaster-Comm. Thomas Alfred, O.B.E., R.N.

WOOLFE, Capt. Francis Alexander, M.B.E., R.A.F.

WOOLL, Capt. Edward, O.B.E.

WOOLLAM, Henry, O.B.E., J.P., *b.* 7 Aug. 1862; *s.* of John Woollam, of Wem. Shropshire; *m.* Clementine, *d.* of Christopher G. Polwin, of Falmouth. *Educ.:* British School, Wem, Shropshire. *War Work:* Assistant Commissioner and Chief Distribution Officer for Midland Division, Ministry of Food. *Address:* Greenfield Villa, Wem, Shropshire. (O11664)

WOOLLARD, Frank George, M.B.E., *b.* 22 Sept. 1883; *s.* of George Woollard, of London; *m.* Katherine Elizabeth, *d.* of Henry Richards, of London. *Educ.:* City of London School. Assistant Managing Director, E. G. Wrigley & Co., Ltd.; Member of Council of Institution of Automobile Engineers. *War Work:* Design and Construction of Motor Transport and Tank Components. *Address:* 8, Hall Road, Handsworth, Birmingham. (M1116)

WOOLLCOMBE, Rev. Edward Percival, O.B.E.

WOOLLCOMBE, Lilian Mary, M.B.E.; *d.* of Richard Woollcombe, of 31, Cleveland Square. *War Work:* Red Cross

V.A.D., Oct. 1914, to May, 1919, in various parts of France; mentioned in despatches. *Address:* 31, Cleveland Square, London, W. 2. *Club:* Portsmouth. (M10137)

WOOLLCOMBE, Capt. Malcolm Louis, O.B.E.

WOOLLETT, Major Sydney Winslow, O.B.E., R.A.M.C.

WOOLLEY, Alfred, O.B.E.

WOOLLEY, Constance Maria, M.B.E.

WOOLLEY, Frederick George, M.B.E.

WOOLLEY, Lieut. Ivor William, O.B.E., R.A.S.C.

WOOLLEY, Capt. Reginald George, M.B.E.

WOOLLEY, Walter James, C.B.E.

WOOLLEY, Comm. William, O.B.E., R.N.

WOOLLISCROFT, George Williams, O.B.E., J.P.

WOOLMER, Andrew Charles, O.B.E.

WOOLMER, Charles Edward, O.B.E., *b.* 23 April, 1875; *s.* of E. S. Woolmer, of London; *m.* Ada Louise, *d.* of William Avens, of Portsmouth. *Educ.:* Privately. Sec. to Commodore, Hong-Kong Naval Yard, 1902–5; Sec. to Admiral Superintendent, Malta Naval Yard, 1911–19; Cashier, Rosyth Naval Yard, 1919. *War Work:* Sec. to the Admiral Supt. and Senior Naval Officer of Malta Yard; also Cashier of Malta Yard, and responsible for distributing money to the Mediterranean and Adriatic Fleets throughout the War. (O1167)

WOOLRYCH, Capt. Stanley Herbert Cunliffe, O.B.E.

WOOLSTON, Thomas Henry, C.B.E., J.P., D.L., *b.* 10 March, 1855; *s.* of Samuel Hames Woolston, of Wellingborough; *m.* Florence Katherine, *d.* of William Moxon, M.R.C.S., J.P., of Northampton. *Educ.:* Wellingborough Grammar School, and St. Paul's, Stony Stratford. County Director, Northamptonshire Auxiliary Military Hospitals and V.A.D.s, Northamptonshire T.F.A.; Knight of Grace of Order of St. John of Jerusalem in England; Member of Board of Management of Northampton General Hospital, and Vice-Chairman of Finance Committee; Chairman of Northampton Crippled Children's Fund; Hon. Commissioner St. John Ambulance Brigade. *War Work:* County Director Auxiliary Military Hospitals, 1600 beds, V.A.D.s, and transport of Sick and Wounded Soldiers during whole period of war. *Addresses:* 53, East Park Parade, Northampton; The White Cottage, Caister-on-Sea, Norfolk. (C679)

WOOLWAY, Capt. Charles Gordon, M.B.E., R.E.

WOOMBELL, Capt. Thomas, M.B.E., K.R.R.C.

WOOSLEY, Capt. Ernest Harry, M.B.E., R.A.O.C.

WOOSNAM, Capt. Charles Earnshaw, O.B.E., *b.* 2 Dec. 1886; *s.* of George Woosnam, of Newtown, Mont. Solicitor; Member of Birmingham Citizens' Committee. *War Work:* Staff Capt., Q.M.G., War Office. *Address:* 19, Waterloo Street, Birmingham. *Club:* Royal Automobile. (O7883)

WOOTTON, Capt. Herbert, M.B.E.

WOOTTON, Capt. Herbert Arthur, M.B.E.

WORDIE, Major William, O.B.E., R.A.S.C. (T.).

WORDINGHAM, Charles Henry, C.B.E., M.I.C.E. M.I.E.E., M.I.M.E., A.I.N.A., F.S.A., *b.* 14 April, 1866; *s.* of William Hales Wordingham, of Twickenham; *m.* Emily Anne, *d.* of Charles John West, of Maryboro', Queensland. *Educ.:* King's Coll. School, London, and King's Coll., London. Past President, Institution of Electrical Engineers; Past President, Incorporated Municipal Electrical Association; City Electrical Engineer, Manchester, 1893–1901; Director of Electrical Engineering, Admiralty, 1903–18; Consulting Engineer, advising numerous Local Authorities and others, including large electric supply schemes, *e.g.* Greater London, promoted by the Conference of London Boroughs, East Midland, etc. *War Work:* Responsible both during and before the war for the design and superintendence, during construction and erection, of the electrical equipment of the whole of H.M. ships of all classes; also for the electrical equipment of Rosyth Dockyard, and of all the Naval Air Stations, and for advising on all important questions of electric light and power in connection with the Royal Dockyards and other shore establishments. *Addresses:* 7, Victoria Street, Westminster, London, S.W. 1; 11, Mosley Street, Manchester; Beechgrove, Ridgeway Road, Redhill, Surrey. *Clubs:* St. Stephen's; Engineers'. (C680)

WORDSWORTH, Annie Elizabeth, M.B.E., *d.* of John Wordsworth. *Educ.:* Dolgelley, and Univ., Bangor. Head Mistress, Victoria Girls' School, Wrexham. *War Work:* Organised voluntary labour to deal with filing, etc., of registration cards; Organising Sec. under Women's Branch, Board of Agriculture, Denbighshire; Divisional Organiser, Board of Agriculture, for S. Wales. *Address:* Victoria School, Wrexham. (M2674)

WORGAN, Lieut.-Col. Sydney Drummond, C.B.E. Lieut.-Col. and Staff-Paymaster, Army Pay Depart.; served in Great War, 1914–19 (mentioned in despatches). (C1135)

WORK, Thomas Budge, O.B.E.

WORKMAN, Alice Hill, O.B.E.

WORKMAN, Margaret Elliot, O.B.E.

WORKMAN, Leiut.-Col. Wolston Thomas, C.B.E. Lieut.-Col. Canadian Chap. Sers. (C1141)

WORLEY, Sir Arthur, Knt. Bach., C.B.E., F.C.I.I., *b.* 10 May, 1871; *s.* of Philip Worley, of Manchester; *m.* Edith, *d.* of Thomas Kay, of Pendleton. *Educ.:* Manchester. General Manager, North British and Mercantile Insur. Co.; Manager, Railway Passengers Assurance Company; Manager, Ocean Marine Insurance Co., Ltd.; Chairman, Fine Art and General Insurance Co., Ltd. *War Work:* Member of the Advisory Committee to the Ministry of Munitions under the Explosives Liability Act. *Address:* 61, Threadneedle Street, E.C. 2; The Gables, Oxshott, Surrey. *Clubs:* Constitutional; British Empire. (C681)

WORLIDGE, Capt. Edward, C.B.E.

WORLLEDGE, Edward William, O.B.E., M.A., J.P.. *b.* 27 Jan. 1850; *s.* of His Honour the late Judge Worlledge, of Ipswich; *m.* Edith Georgiana, *d.* of the late Rev. William Wigston, of Rushmere Vicarage, Ipswich. *Educ.:* Ipswich School, and Jesus College, Cambridge. District Registrar of the High Court of Justice; Registrar and High Bailiff of County Court; 4 times Mayor of the County Borough of Great Yarmouth, and for 30 years Chairman of the Local Education Authority. *War Work:* Mayor during two years of the War (1915–17); also Chairman of the Local Tribunal, and of the Local War Pensions, Food Control, War Savings, and Employment Committees. *Address:* 10, Albert Square, Great Yarmouth. (O11668)

WORLLEDGE, Capt. John Penry Garnons, O.B.E., R.E.

WORMALD, Arthur, O.B.E.

WORMALD, Sir John, K.B.E., M.I.C.E., J.P., *b.* 1 July, 1859; *m.* Eleanor Mabel, *d.* of the late Henry Simms, of Oriel Lodge, Bath. *Educ.:* Royal High School, and Univ. Edinburgh. Director of Mather & Platt, Ltd., Engineers, of Manchester and Westminster; J.P. (Oxford); High Sheriff, 1916–17; Lord of the Manor of North Stoke; was a Member of the Munitions Finance Board, and Chairman of the Industrial and General Services Committee of the War Cabinet Committee, 1916–19. *Addresses:* 37, Sloane Street, S.W. 1; Springs, North Stoke, Oxfordshire. *Clubs:* Brooks's; Cavendish. (K244)

WORMALD, Rev. Robert Leonard, M.B.E.

WORMALD, Walter, M.B.E.

WORMALD, William, O.B.E., *b.* 23 Sept. 1871; *s.* of William Wormald, of Wakefield; *m.* Bessie, *d.* of John Cranke, of Cumberland. *Educ.:* Leeds Higher Grade School. Railway District Agent. *War Work:* Chairman of War Pensions Committee; War Savings Committee; Food Control Committee; Recruiting Officers' Advisory Committee. *Club:* Rotherham Unionist. (O11669)

WORRALL, Gladstone Walter, M.B.E., M.Sc., D.Eng., *b.* 1 March, 1881; *s.* of Robert John Worrall, of Liverpool; *m.* Winifred Emily, *g.d.* of Alderman Thomas Cook, J.P., of Birkenhead. *Educ.:* Liverpool Univ.; Technische Hochschule, Karlsruhe. Consulting Electrical Engineer, Vulcan Boiler and General Insurance Co., Ltd. *War Work:* Chief Engineer, H.M. Factory, Penrhyndeudraeth; Electrical Engineer, H.M. Factory, Henbury; Superintendent Engineer, Ammonium Nitrate Section, Explosives Dept., Ministry of Munitions; Chief Inspector of Factory Construction, Chemical Gas Section, Factories Branch, Ministry of Munitions; Works Manager, Electro Bleach and By-Products, Ltd., Middlewich (manufacturers of Poison Gas and other war chemicals). *Address:* The Priory, Middlewich. (M10143)

WORSDELL, Brevet-Major Geoffrey Bradford, O.B.E., Alexandra, Princess of Wales' Own Yorkshire Regt (Signal Service), *b.* 16 Feb. 1883; *s.* of Wilson Worsdell, J.P., of Ascot; *m.* Winifred Mary, *d.* of John Livesey Lea, J.P., of Wakefield. *Educ.:* Charterhouse, and Trinity Coll., Cambridge. First gazetted, Sept. 1906; Capt., Jan. 1915. *Addresses:* c/o Messrs. Holt & Co., 3, Whitehall Place, London, S.W.; The Glebe, South Ascot, Berks. (O6734)

WORSLEY, Comm. Frank Arthur, D.S.O., O.B.E., R.D., R.N.R., *b.* 1872; *s.* of Henry Theophilus Worsley, of Akaroa, N.Z. *Educ.:* Christchurch, New Zealand. Master Mariner and Explorer (commanded Sir E. Shackleton's ship, S.Y. "Endurance," and navigated boat 800 m. from Elephant I. to S. Georgia). *War Work:* Commanded H.M.S. "P.61," H.M. mystery ship "Paugloss," H.M.S. "Cricket," and H.M.S. "M.24"; rammed and sank German submarine; captured the captain and towed oiler "San Ziferino" while pursued by German submarines; served 1 year with army under Gen. Ironsides, as Director of Arctic Equipment for Archangel Front; won bar to D.S.O., and 2nd Class St. Stanislaus, in actions against Bolsheviks. *Address:* Ringloes, Fendalton, Christchurch, New Zealand. *Club:* Road. (O11670)

WORSLEY, Geoffrey, O.B.E.

WORSSAM, Lieut. Charles Archie, O.B.E., R.A.O.C.

WORSWICK, Major Thomas, O.B.E., R.A.F.

WORSWICK, Gertrude, Mrs. Worsley, O.B.E., *b.* 28 Jan. 1884; *d.* of F. E. Harding, of Old Springs, Market Drayton; *m.* Richard, *s.* of Major William Worsley Worswick, of Normanton Hall, Hinckley. *Educ.:* Privately. *War Work:* Joint Management of Catholic Clubs in France; worked at those at Harve, Etaples, and Dunkirk, and at Cologne. *Address:* Normanton Hall, Hinckley. (O2035)

WORT, Capt. Walter Edward, O.B.E., M.I.M.E., M.I.N.A. I.O.M., R.A.O.C.; *s.* of Walter Wort, of Teddington; *m.* Frances Edith, *d.* of John Dennis, of Newport. *Educ.:* Waverley Coll., Eastbourne; Anerly Coll., Anerly. Consulting Engineer and Naval Architect. *War Work:* Had charge of Army Ordnance Workshops on the Doiran front, also took workshops through Turkey and Bulgaria on the advancing of our forces; was inspector of Ordnance Machinery with the B.E.F., March, 1916, to April, 1919. (O6560)

WORTH, Major Reginald, O.B.E., M.B., R.A.M.C.

WORTH, Capt. William Percy, M.B.E.

WORTHAM, Lieut.-Col. Harold Charles Webster Hale, C.B.E., D.S.O.

WORTHINGTON, Frank Vigers, C.B.E., F.R.G.S., F.Z.S., *b.* 21 April, 1874; *s.* of late James Worthington, of Belcombe Brook, Bradford-on-Avon; *m.* Gladys Elma, *d.* of Major K. F. Maclachlan, late R.H.A. *Educ.:* Repton. Sec. for Native

Affairs and Judge of the Administrator's Court, Northern Rhodesia ; retired, Jan. 1914. *War Work :* 1915–19, Deputy Chief Postal Censor ; O.B.E., 1917 ; Deputy Director-General of Awards, Ministry of Pensions, 1919 ; C.B.E., 1920. *Address :* 20, Montpelier Square, Knightsbridge. *Club :* St. James'   (C3063)

WORTHINGTON, Major Frank, D.S.O., O.B.E., R.A.M.C.

WORTHINGTON, Gwenyth, M.B.E., *b.* 2 June, 1888 ; *d.* of late Ernest Andrew, of Hillesdon, Leek, Staffs. *Educ. :* St. Mandé, Paris. At present training at St. Thomas's Hospital, S.E. 1. *War Work :* Commandant of Red Cross Hospital, Foxlowe, Leek, Dec. 1914, to March, 1919. *Address :* Hillesdon, Leek, Staffs. *Club :* Lady Golfers'   (M2677)

WORTHINGTON, Lieut. John Ramsay, M.B.E.

WORTHINGTON, Nora Mary Bayley, M.B.E., *b.* 24 Aug. 1883 ; *d.* of Arthur Bayley Worthington, of Charlton, Singleton, Chichester. *Educ. :* Worcester Park School, Surrey, and Brussels. *War Work :* 1916–17 Commandant in charge of the Post Office at the B.R.C.S. Hdqrs., Boulogne ; 1917–20, Commandant in charge of G.S. V.A.D. Units at St. Omer, Trouville, Havre, and Wimereux. *Address :* Charlton, Singleton, Chichester. *Clubs :* Portsmouth ; V.A.D. Ladies'.   (M2676)

WORTHINGTON, Robert Alfred, O.B.E., M.B., B.C., F.R.C.S.

WORTHINGTON, Thomas, C.B.E. Sometime Head of Commercial Intelligence Depart. Board of Trade.   (C342)

WORTHINGTON, Capt. William Wilfred, O.B.E.

WORTLEY, Edward Jocelyn, M.B.E.

WORTLEY, Capt. Ernest Dixon, O.B.E., R.A.M.C.

WORTLEY, Violet, Hon. Mrs. E. STUART-, C.B.E., *b.* 1866 ; *d.* of James Alexander Guthrie, of Craigie ; *m.* Edward, *s.* of Hon. Francis Stuart-Wortley (*see* BURKE'S *Peerage,* Wharncliffe, E.) *War Work :* Worked in connection with the Y.M.C.A. *Address :* Highcliffe Castle, Christchurch.   (C312)

WOTHERSPOON, Ellen, O.B.E. Hon. Organiser, Tunbridge Wells Association of Voluntary Workers.   (O11791c)

WOTHERSPOON, Capt. John Armour, M.B.E., R.E.

WOTTON, Walter John, M.B.E.,

WOTZEL, Anthony Andrew Augustine, O.B.E., F.S.S., *b.* 22 Aug. 1864 ; *s.* of late C. A. Wotzel, of Mountain View, Laurel Hill, Limerick, Ireland ; *m.* Mary Elizabeth ; *d.* of Patrick Dillon Irwin, of Fern Hall, Co. Roscommon. *Educ. :* Privately, and King's Coll., London. Appointed to Board of Trade, Nov. 1883, after open competitive examination ; appointed Registrar of Conciliation Boards in 1897 ; translator to the Board of Trade in 1905 ; Chief Staff Officer, Board of Trade in 1913 ; Principal Clerk, Ministry of Labour, 1916. *War Work :* Editor of " Economic Notes " (from Enemy Press), showing changes in enemy's fighting capacity from the economic point of view. *Address :* Bohemia, Belmont, Surrey. (O882)

WRAITH, Col. Ernest Arnold, C.B.E., D.S.O., *b.* 1876 ; *s.* of A. Wraith, of Wakefield ; *m.* Gwendolen, *d.* of O'Connell Jones, of Saltburn-by-Sea. *Educ. :* Wakefield School and Victoria University. Late Hon. Surgeon, Derbyshire Children's Hospital ; Civil Surgeon, S. African War, 1900–1. *War Work :* O.C. 1st N. Midland Field Ambulance, 1914–18 ; A.D.M.S., 58th Division, 1918–19 ;' thrice mentioned in despatches. *Address :* Little Stretton, Salop. *Clubs :* Derby ; Shrewsbury.   (C1348)

WRANGHAM, Lieut.-Col. William, O.B.E., M.D., R.A.M.C.

WRATE, Paymaster-Lieut. James Frederick, M.B.E., R.N.

WRATISLAW, Albert Charles, C.B., C.M.G., C.B.E., *b.* 17 Oct. 1862 ; *s.* of Rev. A. H. Wratislaw, of Bury St. Edmund's. *Educ. :* Rossall. Consul-General at Tabriz, Canea, Salonica, and Beyrout. *Address :* 13, York House, Kensington, W. 8.   (C682)

WRAY, Cecil James, M.B.E.

WRAY, Ellen, M.B.E.

WRAY, Rev. Frederick William, C.M.G., C.B.E., *b.* 1864 ; *s.* of Robert Mackie Wray. Curate of Dookie, Victoria, 1894–96 ; Minister of Euroa, Victoria, 1896–1902 ; Rector of St. Cuthbert, Yarrawonga, 1902–13 ; since when he has been Rector of Rushworth, Victoria ; S. African War, 1900–2. as Chap. Australian troops (medal with six clasps) ; Great War, 1914–19, as Chap. Australian Imperial Forces (despatches twice). *Address :* Rushworth, Victoria, Australia. (C1847)

WRAY, John James, M.B.E., R.G.A.

WRAY, Lieut.-Col. John Willoughby, C.B.E. Indian Army (ret.) ; served in Great War, 1914–19 (mentioned in despatches).   (C1136)

WRAY, Comm. Thomas Henry ROBERTS-, O.B.E., R.D., R.N.V.R.

WREN Albert Charles, M.B.E.

WREN, Evelyn Emma Amelia, Mrs., O.B.E., *b.* 12 July, 1854 ; *d.* of Beale Blackwell Colvin, of Pishobury, Herts., and Monkhams, Waltham Abbey, Essex ; *m.* Joseph, *s.* of George Wren, of King Street, Edinburgh. *War Work :* Vice-President of the Lexden and Winstree Division of Essex V.A.D. ; Commandant of Gostwycke Hospital Colchester, Oct. 1914, to March, 1917 ; Member of the Red Cross Executive Committee for Essex. *Address :* Colneford House, White Colne, Essex.   (O4004)

WRENCH, Capt. Charles Croydon, M.B.E., R.A.S.C.

WREY, Lieut.-Comm. Edward Charles, O.B.E.

WREY, Capt. William Sherard, BOURCHIER-, C.M.G., C.B.E., R.N., *b.* 1865 ; *s.* of Sir Henry Bourchier-Wrey, 10th

Baronet of Tawstock Court, Barnstaple, Devon (*see* BURKE'S *Peerage*) ; *m.* Flora Bathurst, *d.* of Vice-Admiral Greive, of Ord House, Berwick-on-Tweed. Midshipman H.M.S. " Superb " at Bombardment of Alexandria, 1882, and at Suakim, 1884 (medal, 2 clasps, bronze star) ; promoted Commander for services as 2nd in command Naval Brigade, Relief of Pekin, 1900 ; mentioned in despatches (medal and clasp). *War Work :* Served as Principal Naval Transport Officer, Southampton, with rank of Commodore ; Officer of Order Crown of Belgium, 1917 ; Japanese Order of the Sacred Treasure, 1918 ; Distinguished Service Medal of U.S. America, 1919 ; British War and Victory Medals. Elected Hon. Member of Royal Yacht Squadron, 1901. *Address :* Taw Green, Westbourne, Sussex. *Club :* Naval and Military.   (C1593)

WRIGHT, Comm. Alexander Galloway, O.B.E., R.N.

WRIGHT, Brevet Lieut.-Col. Alfred, C.B.E., R.A.M.C., *b.* 1863 ; *s.* of John Wright, M.D., J.P., of Wynberg, S. Africa. *m.* Mabel K., *d.* of William Fleming, of M.L.A., S. Africa. *Educ. :* St. Bartholomew's Hospital. Entered R.A.M.C., 1887, served in S. African War. *War Work :* Imperial Medical Administrative Officer, S. Africa Military Command at Cape, Base of Operations for German S.W. and E. African Campaigns, 1914–19. *Address :* c/o Messrs. Holt & Co., Bankers, London.   (C2192)

WRIGHT, Sir Almroth Edward, K.B.E., C.B., M.D., F.R.S., *b.* 1861 ; *s.* of the late Rev. Charles H. H. Wright, D.D. ; *m.* Jane Georgina, *d.* of R. M. Wilson, J.P., of Carlcarrigan, Co. Kildare. *Educ. :* Dublin Univ. and abroad. Demonstrator of Pathology, Cambridge, 1887 ; Army Medical School,' Netley, 1892–1902 ; of Physiology, Sydney, 1889 ; Member of the Indian Plague Commission, 1898–1900 ; Originator of the System of Anti-Typhoid Inoculation and Therapeutic Inoculation for Bacterial Infections ; served as Consultant Physician in France during Great War, 1914–19 ; Hon. F.R.C.S.I. ; Hon. Sc.D. (Dublin and Leeds), Fothergillian Gold Medal, Med. Soc. of London, 1908 ; Hungarian Prize, International Med. Congress, Lond. 1910 ; Le Conte Prize, Academy des Sciénces, 1915 ; Hon. Burgess of the City of Belfast ; Director of the Dept. for Therapeutic Inoculation St. Mary's Hospital, Paddington, W. ; attached to the Med. Research Service under the Nat. Ins. Act ; Professor of Experimental Pathology, Univ. of London. Gold Medallist Roy. Soc. Med. and Institute of France ; Foreign Member of the Academie de Medécine, Paris. *Address :* 6, Pembroke Square, W. 8.   (K192)

WRIGHT, Arthur, O.B.E.

WRIGHT, Arthur James, M.B.E., J.P.

WRIGHT, Capt. Arthur John, O.B.E., R.A.O.C.

WRIGHT, Rev. Arthur Yeomans, M.B.E., *b.* 6 Feb. 1889 ; *s.* of Rev. John Wright, of Shrewsbury. *Educ. :* Woodhouse Grove School, Yorks., and Headingley Coll., Leeds. Wesleyan Chaplain to the Forces. *War Work :* First Nonconformist Chaplain appointed to I.E.F. " D " (Mesopotamia) ; Basra, Sept. 1915, with the 6th (Indian) Division at Battle of Ctesiphon, the retirement, and through the siege of Kut-el-Amara ; prisoner of war in Turkey, April, 1916, to Nov. 1918. *Addresses :* Ipsley, Underdale Road, Shrewsbury, England ; Wesleyan Manse, Kirkee, Poona, India.   (M6520)

WRIGHT, Calvin, M.B.E.

WRIGHT, Cecily Gertrude, Mrs., C.B.E. ; *d.* of Henry Cartwright, of London ; *m.* William Frederick, *s.* of William Thomas Wright, of Middlesex. *Educ. :* Privately. *War Work :* Hon. Organiser and Director of the Sutton War Hospital Supply Depot and Surgical Requisities Association in connection with Queen Mary's Needlework Guild. *Address :* Lismore, Langley Park, Sutton, Surrey.   (C3064)

WRIGHT, Capt. Charles, M.B.E., R.A.O.C.

WRIGHT, Charles Francis, O.B.E., *b.* 1865 ; *s.* of Charles Francis Wright, of Birmingham ; *m.* Bertha, *d.* of Samuel Pettit, of Stanwick, Northants. *Educ. :* King Edward's School, Birmingham. Appointed H.M. Inspector of Factories, 1892, and H.M. Supt. Inspector, 1913. *War Work :* Commissioner, Ministry of National Service, 1917 ; Technical Adviser to Reserved Occupations Committee, 1915–18 ; Chairman of Committee for the replacement of men by women in the Woollen and Worsted Industry, and in the Cutlery Industry. *Address :* West Park, Leeds.   (O882)

WRIGHT, Capt. Charles Seymour, O.B.E., M.C., R.E. (T.).

WRIGHT, Clare Elise Ellington, M.B.E., *b.* 20 Sept. 1888 ; *d.* of Arthur Wright, of London. *Educ. :* Privately. and Oxford and London Universities. Sec. to Professor W. G. S. Adams, All Souls Coll., Oxford, 1912. *War Work :* Editor of " Daily Notes from the Foreign Press on Economic Subjects," in War Trade Intelligence Department, 1915–19. *Address :* The Hanburies, Eastbourne. *Club :* Forum.   (M2680)

WRIGHT, Lieut. Douglas William, M.B.E,

WRIGHT, Edmund, M.B.E.

WRIGHT, Lieut.-Col. Edward Constable, O.B.E.

WRIGHT, Col. Ernest Granville, C.B.E., *b.* 1865 ; served with the Burma Expedition 1886–9 (medal with two clasps) ; China Lushai Expedition 1889–90 (clasp) ; Tibet, 1903–4 (medal) ; Great War, 1914–19 (mentioned in despatches).   (C1819)

WRIGHT, Ernest John, O.B.E.

WRIGHT, Major Ernest Trevor Langebear, D.S.O., O.B.E., R.A.S.C. Formerly Capt. Hussars ; S. Africa, 1901–2 (Queen's medal with five clasps, King's medal with two clasps) ; Great War, 1914–19 (despatches twice).   (O5966)

WRIGHT, Florence Helena, M.B.E., b. 1868; d. of George Thomas Wright, J.P., of Longstone Hall, Derbyshire. *Educ.*: Lausanne, Switzerland. Commandant, Llandudno Branch of B.R.C.S. since 1912. *War Work*: Organised hospital in 1914 with 25 beds, nursing first the sick of the Welsh Brigade training in the town, later taking overseas cases, and increasing the beds to 120. *Address*: Preswylfa, Abbey Road, Llandudno. (M2682)

WRIGHT, Col. Francis Granville, C.B.E., b. 1865. Burma Expedition, 1886–89 (medal with two clasps); Chin Lushai Expedition, 1889–90 (clasp); Tibet, 1903–4 (medal); Great War, 1914–19 (despatches). (C1819)

WRIGHT, Lieut. Frank Thomas, M.B.E.

WRIGHT, Frank Wilson, O.B.E.

WRIGHT, Col. George, C.B.E., D.S.O., b. 1860; s. of the late Robert John Wright, of Norwich. Entered R.A. 1879; Capt., 1887; Major, 1897; Lieut.-Col., 1904; Col. 1909 (ret.); served in S. Africa, 1900–1 (despatches, D.S.O.); Command of troops in Rhodesia, 1902; Commanding R.A. in Straits Settlements, 1904–7; Shoeburyness, 1907–9; Appointed Gen. Staff Officer, 1914. (C1820)

WRIGHT, George Hudson, O.B.E.

WRIGHT, Lieut. and Qr.-Mr. Harry, M.B.E.

WRIGHT, Henry, O.B.E.,

WRIGHT, Major Horace Leaf, O.B.E.

WRIGHT, Hugh, M.B.E.

WRIGHT, Lieut.-Col. James, O.B.E., R.E.

WRIGHT, James Brown, C.B.E., LL.D., B.A., b. 1861; s. of Samuel Wright, J.P., of Newbliss, Co. Monaghan; m. Zara, d. of late Trevor Corry, of Belmont, Newry. *Educ.*: Trinity Coll., Dublin. Joined R.I. Constabulary as Cadet, 1887; appointed District Inspector, 1888, and served in the counties of Cork and Limerick and City of Belfast; appointed Chief Constable of Newcastle-upon-Tyne, 1899, and still serving as such. *War Work*: Assisted Naval and Military authorities and was responsible for the carrying out of all police arrangements in an important centre, and as mobilising officer of Fire Brigade, for fire protection in the N.E. of England; Member of Commission on Irish Police Pay, 1919; Member of Police Council, 1920. *Address*: 84, Osborne Road, Newcastle-upon-Tyne. (C683)

WRIGHT, James Brown, M.B.E., b. 25 April, 1851; s. of Elias Wright, of Salisbury; m. Marian, d. of William Charles Newman, of Pimlico. *Educ.*: St. Martin's National School, Salisbury. Liberal Political Agent for Evesham Division. *War Work*: Hon. Sec. Evesham Division Parliamentary Recruiting Committee, and for National Service; Sub-Advisory National War Aims; National War Savings Local Committee; Sec. to the Worcestershire War Agricultural Sub-Committee dealing with 4 camps of German prisoners employed in Agriculture. *Address*: 20, Northwick Road, Evesham. (M10146)

WRIGHT, John, M.B.E., b. 18 Feb. 1857; s. of Thomas Wright, of Bishopbriggs, Lanarkshire; m. Bessie, d. of Robert Haddow, of Dumbarton. *Educ.*: Cadder Public School, Bishopbriggs. Superintendent in the Dumbartonshire Constabulary at Helensburgh. *War Work*: Rendered valuable service to the officer in charge of the Intelligence Department of the War Office, in connection with the military policy in dealing with aliens and persons suspected of acting against the interests of the country. *Address*: Iridholm, Helensburgh. (M10148)

WRIGHT, John Brown, O.B.E., b. 23 Dec. 1872; s. of William Wright, of Glasgow; m. Cecilia Thom, d. of Alexander Mason, of Glasgow. *Educ.*: Hutcheson's Grammar School, Glasgow. Late Deputy Director of Cheese for Ministry of Food; now one of the Managing Directors of the Harris (Calne) and the General Produce Co., Ltd., Bristol and London, S.W. *War Work*: Organised and managed the department for controlled Imported Cheese for the Board of Trade from June, 1917; formulated and launched the first complete Food Control Scheme in Great Britain, which was for Imported Cheese; managed this department for the Board of Trade until end of year 1917, when the whole department was taken over by the Ministry of Food; took charge of the commercial section of the Cheese Division of the Ministry of Food from 1918 until 1920; formulated and launched complete schemes for control of Home Cheese right through from producer to consumer; co-ordinated the control of both Imported and Home Cheese so as to allow of consumers all over the country obtaining cheese at one flat rate irrespective of source of supply or original cost; supplied all cheese requirements of the Army and Navy. *Address*: Meldreth, Bridle Road, Purley, Surrey. *Club*: Royal Automobile. (O4005)

WRIGHT, John Graham, C.B.E., b. 1873; s. of late William G. Wright, of Irvine, Ayrshire; m. Elizabeth Macfarlan, d. of the late John Young, of Cross Lynne, New Kilpatrick. *Educ.*: Blair Lodge, Stirlingshire. Partner in the firm of Wright, Graham & Co., Glasgow and London. *War Work*: Deputy Director of Overseas Ship Purchase, Ministry of Shipping. *Address*: Invereil, Dirleton, Haddingtonshire. *Clubs*: Caledonian; Royal Societies; New (Glasgow). (C3065)

WRIGHT, Capt John Henry, O.B.E., R.A.V.C. (T.), b. 1 May, 1873; s. of late John Wright, of Whitchurch, Salop; m. Florence Gertrude, d. of late Andrew George Hunter, Rockcliffe Hall, nr. Flint, N. Wales. *Educ.*: Chester and Whitchurch Grammar School, and New Vety. Coll., Edinburgh. Veterinary Surgeon, private practice; firm, Lawson & Wright, Great Bridgewater Street, Manchester. *War Work*: Veterinary

Officer, Duke of Lancs. Own Yeomanry, Aug. 1915, to May, 1916; Veterinary Officer, Beds Yeomanry, 1st Cav. Div., June to Sept. 1915; Veterinary Officer, 50th Northumbrian Div., Sept. to July, 1917; D.A.D.V.S., 9th Scottish Div., July 1917, to April 1919. *Address*: Clayton House, Fallowfield, Manchester. *Club*: Arts (Manchester). (O5964)

WRIGHT, J. M., M.B.E.,

WRIGHT, Paymaster-Comm. John Turnbull, M.B.E., R.N.

WRIGHT, Prof. Mark Robinson, M.B.E. M.A., b. 3 July, 1854; s. of late John Wright, of Willington, Northumberland; m. Ellen Phoebe, d. of late James Franklyn Cooper, of Birmingham. *Educ.*: Borough Road College. Professor of Education, Armstrong Coll., Newcastle-upon-Tyne, in the University of Durham. Member of Senate of Durham Univ.; Chairman of Higher Education Sub-Committee, Gateshead; Chairman of Governors of Whitley and Monkseaton High School; Governor of Samuel King's School, Alston; Chairman of Managers of Whitley Bay Schools; Chairman of Gateshead and District Local Employment Committee. *War Work*: Chairman of Local Tribunal for Whitley and District. *Address*: Lonsdale, St. George's Crescent, Monkseaton, Northumberland. *Club*: Liberal (Newcastle-on-Tyne). (M1120)

WRIGHT, Mary Veronica, M.B.E.

WRIGHT, Maurice Beresford, O.B.E., M.D., b. 30 Jan. 1872; s. of Philip Wright, of Mellington Hall, Churchstoke, Montgomeryshire; m. Elisabeth Eleanor, d. of Bridges Plumptre, of Goodnestone Park, near Canterbury, Kent. *Educ.*: Cambridge, and Edinburgh Univs. *War Work*: Hon. Medical Sec. to Lord Knutsford's Special Hospitals for Officers; Major, R.A.M.C.; Mental Specialist to Eastern Command. *Addresses*: 4, Devonshire Place, W. 1; Wood End, Beaconsfield, Bucks. *Club*: Arts. (O7887)

WRIGHT, Paymaster-Lieut. Noel, O.B.E., R.N.

WRIGHT, Stephen, M.B.E.

WRIGHT, Capt. Sydney Arthur, M.B.E., R.A.S.C.

WRIGHT, Thomas, M.B.E.

WRIGHT, Thomas Henry, M.B.E.

WRIGHT, Major Thomas Kendall, M.B.E.

WRIGHT, William, M.B.E.

WRIGHT, William, M.B.E., b. 14 Dec. 1853; s. of William Wright, of Norwood; m. Elizabeth, d. of — Crussel, of Bishop Stortford. *Educ.*: Norwood and Royal School of Science, South Kensington. Resident Engineer at the Crystal Palace. *War Work*: Temporary Admiralty Works Officer, during the War period when the Crystal Palace was used as a Training Depot for the Navy. *Address*: 20, Becondale Road, Upper Norwood, London, S.E. (M1122)

WRIGHT, Col. William Burgess, C.I.E., C.B.E., V.D., Indian Auxiliary Forces (ret.). Late General Traffic Manager, Madras and Southern Mahratta Railway. *War Work*: Was appointed Railway Staff Officer in the Regular Army, Nov. 1914, and served for five years; mentioned in despatches. *Address*: Belassi Lee, Southwick, Sussex. *Club*: Junior Army and Navy. (C1821)

WRIGHT, Col. Sir William Charles, K.B.E., C.B., J.P. Glamorganshire, Knight Commander of the Crown of Italy, and Officier Legion d'Honneur, b. 1876; s. of Sir John Roper Wright, Bart., of Wydcombe Manor, Bath (see BURKE'S *Peerage*); m. Maud, d. of late Isaac Butler, J.P., of Panteg, Monmouthshire. *Educ.*: Privately. *War Work*: Served from 1st day of the War as Officer of Supply Transport, Milford Haven Defences, and afterwards at the Ministry of Munitions, as Controller of Iron and Steel Production; many times in France and Italy on this work. *Address*: 31, Prince's Gate, London. (K443)

WRIGHT, Lieut. William James Turnbull, M.B.E., R.A.F.

WRIGHT, Major William Owen, O.B.E.

WRIGHT, Helen, Muriel BARTON-, Mrs., M.B.E.

WRIGHT, May, Mrs. HALL-, M.B.E.

WRIGHTON Amelia, Mrs., M.B.E.

WRIGHTSON, Capt. Charles Archibald Wise, C.B.E., R.N., b. 11 July, 1874; s. of Sir Thomas Wrightson, 1st Bart., of Neastan Hall, Co. Durban (see BURKE'S *Peerage*). (C2329)

WRIGLEY, Constance, M.B.E.

WRIGLEY, Lilian, Mrs., O.B.E.; d. of John Dodd, J.P., of Oldham; m. Alan, s. of Roscoe Wrigley, of Oldham. *Educ.*: Privately. *War Work*: Commandant, 62 EL, Oldham B.R.C.S., 1911; equipped and worked an Orthopædic Dept. at Rock Bank Auxiliary Hospital, 1915; equipped and ran an Orthopædic Clinic under the auspices of the Cheshire Red Cross at Macclesfield. *Address*: Upton Priory, nr. Macclesfield, Cheshire. (O11673)

WRIGLEY, Vincent Shiers, M.B.E.

WUIDART, Jules Reuleaux, M.B.E., b. 29 Dec. 1879; s. of Jules Wuidart, Officier de l'ordre de la Couronne, of St. Hubert, Belgium; m. Madeleine Millicent, d. of Edward Strange. *Educ.*: Eastbourne, Liege, and Stockholm. *War Work*: Assisted in organising Shell Fuze Factory; later with Ministry of Munitions, Gun Ammunition Dept. *Address*: Pillars, Northwood. *Club*: Cavendish. (M16152)

WURTZBURG, Margaret Caroline, M.B.E.

WYATT, Lieut.-Col. Archibald, O.B.E., T.D., D.L., b. 29 April, 1872; s. of Francis William Wyatt, of Nutbourne, Sussex; m. Constance Kate, d. of Henry Thomas Upton, of Petworth, Sussex. *Educ.*: Portsmouth Grammar School. Surveyor. *War Work*: Served in Territorial Force, Aug. 1914 to June, 1919, India and Mesopotamia. *Address :* East Lodge, Fareham, Hants. (O6735)

WYATT, Ethel, M.B.E.

WYATT, Major Francis Joseph Caldwell, O.B.E., M.C., R.E.

WYATT, Comm. John Oliver, O.B.E., R.N.

WYATT, Lieut.-Col. John Railton, O.B.E.

WYATT, Katharine Montagu, M.B.E. ; *s.* of Thomas Henry Wyatt, M.V.O., I.S.O., T.D., of Weston Patrick, Basingstoke, Hants. *War Work :* Divisional Sec. Chelsea Red Cross, and Commandant V.A.D. London 52 ; Commandant of Chelsea Red Cross Officers' Hospital, 40, Upper Grosvenor Street ; Commandant of all the V.A.D.s of London 52 at the Ridley Hospital, 1914–19 ; and of Russian and Swedish Hospitals for English Officers. *Addresses :* St. Andrew's Rectory, Holborn, E.C. ; Weston Patrick, Basingstoke, Hants. (M2687)

WYATT, Major Philip Humphrey, O.B.E., R.A.S.C.

WYATT, Major Travers Carey, O.B.E., M.A., *b.* 24 Feb. 1887 ; *s.* of A. J. Wyatt, of Christ's Coll., Cambridge. *Educ. :* Leys School, and Christ's Coll., Cambridge. Staff of Engineering Department, Cambridge Univ. *War Work :* France and Belgium, 1915–18 ; British Army of the Rhine, 1919. *Addresses :* 6, Queen Anne Terrace, Cambridge ; Christ's College, Cambridge. (O5967)

WYBROW, Albert William, M.B.E. *War Work :* On outbreak of war was Commandant of No. 5 Detachment, City of London Red Cross ; later organised and commanded Air Raid Relief Unit, a mobile body of men who were on duty (in all air raids) in various parts of London ; also organised Hospital Service which supplied men for various hospitals to assist in ward duties, operations, and X-ray cases, etc. *Address :* 2, Lonsdale Avenue, Wembley, Middlesex. (M10154)

WYCHE, Katharine, O.B.E. ; *d.* late William Dalla Husband, F.R.C.S., D.L. West Riding, Yorkshire, of York and Clifton ; *m.* William (who died Nov. 1919), *s.* of the late William Wyche, of Postlance. *Educ. :* Clifton and Dover. *War Work :* Served and worked on Mayoress of Bournemouth's War Work Committee from Aug. 1914 ; organiser of the War Hospital Supply Depot, Q.M.N.G. Surgical Branch, from 1915. *Address :* Holcombe, Cavendish Place, Bournemouth. (O11674)

WYKE, Clement James, M.B.E., A.M.I.Mech.E., A.M.I.A.E., F.R.M.S., *b.* 19 Oct. 1884 ; *s.* of John Wyke, of Overley, Wellington, Salop ; *m.* Elizabeth, *d.* of James Phillips, of Whitefields, Wellington, Salop. *Educ. :* School of Technology, Salford. Partner in Greaves and Wyke, Electrical and Mechanical Engineers, Manchester. *War Work :* Engineering Organiser to Ministry of Munitions ; Deputy Chief Dilution Officer, North-Western Area, Ministry of Munitions, Head Office, Manchester. *Address :* Harefield, Gt, Clowes Street, Manchester. (M10256e)

WYKES, Leonard Graveney, M.B.E.

WYKES, William Henry, M.B.E., *b.* 11 Sept. 1848 ; *s.* of William Henry Wykes, of Derby. *War Work :* Superintending Clerk, Registration Head Quarters, Central Force and Eastern Command. (M10155)

WYLD, Florence Maria, M.B.E.

WYLD, Frances Mary, M.B.E.

WYLDE, Major Lennard Francis George Stoven, O.B.E., I.A.

WYLES, John Edward, O.B.E.

WYLEY, Capt. Donald Henry FitzThomas, O.B.E., M.C., R.F.A. (T.).

WYLEY, Major John Deane Newbank, O.B.E., R.M.A.

WYLIE, Lieut.-Col. David Storer, C.M.G., C.B.E., M.B., F.R.C.S. Served with New Zealand Forces during Great War. (C1578)

WYLIE, Sqdn.-Leader Hamilton Neil, M.B.E., R.A.F.

WYLIE, James, C.B.E., *b.* 15 June, 1875 ; *s.* of late James Hamilton Wylie, of 4, Lawn Road, Hampstead, N.W. *Educ. :* Manchester Grammar School and Wadham Coll., Oxford. Barrister-at-law ; was Assist. Sec. to Royal Commission on Shipping Rings in 1909 ; was till April, 1920, Dramatic Critic of "Illustrated Sporting and Dramatic News," and Assistant Dramatic Critic of "Westminster Gazette." *War Work :* Temp. Legal Assistant in Department of H.M. Solicitor to the Treasury, Oct. 1914, to March, 1919. *Addresses :* 1, South Square, Gray's Inn, W.C. 1 ; 1, Temple Gardens, Temple, E.C. 4. (C1063)

WYLIE, Maria Elizabeth, Mrs., M.B.E.

WYLIE, Lilian O'Meira, Mrs. DOUGHTIE-, O.B.E., R.R.C.

WYLLIE, Lieut.-Col. Harold, O.B.E., 1st Wilts Regt. and R.A.F., *b.* 29 June, 1880 ; *s.* of W. L. Wyllie, R.A., R.E., of Point ; *m.* Margaret, *d.* of Edmund Boyle, of Castle Comer. *Educ. :* Littlejohns, Greenwich ; Smyths, Southsea. Marine Artist ; soldier ; aeroplane pilot. *War Work :* South Africa. 1902 ; R.F.C. and R.A.F., France and Home Defence, 1914–19. *Address :* Tower House, Point, Portsmouth. *Clubs :* Royal Corinthian Yacht ; Royal Portsmouth Corinthian Yacht. (O3440)

WYLSON, Oswald Cane, M.B.E., F.R.I.B.A., *b.* 6 April, 1858 ; *s.* of James Wylson, of London ; *m.* Katharine, *d.* of B. Murgatroyd, of Yorkshire. *Educ. :* King's Coll. School, London. Architect. *War Work :* Services as Hon. Deputy Chief Surveyor of the British Fire Prevention Committee in relation to the protection from fire of hospitals, camps, etc., for the B.R.C.S. *Addresses :* 1 and 2 Henrietta Street, Strand, London ; Beaconsdene, Tankerton, Kent. *Clubs :* Royal Corinthian Yacht ; Royal Automobile. (M10156

WYNCH, Lionel Maling, C.I.E., C.B.E., *b.* 21 July, 1864 ; *s.* of William Maling Wynch, of Rose Hill, Lyme Regis ; *m.* Violet Harriet, *d.* of Sir A. T. Arundel, of Glebefields, Guildford (*see* BURKE'S *Peerage*). *Educ. :* Bedford Grammar School ; Balliol Coll., Oxon. Indian Civil Service ; Private Sec. to Governor of Madras, 1901–1906 ; Sec. to Government of Madras Revenue Dept. ; Member of the Viceroy's Legislative Council, 1914. *War Work :* Administrator, British Farmers' Typhus Hospital, Belgrade, 1915 ; Deputy Commissioner British Red Cross, France, 1916–19 ; mentioned in despatches. *Address :* Pine Hill, Camberley. *Clubs :* Junior Carlton ; East India United Service. (C343)

WYNCOLL, Capt. Hugh Edmund Fowler, O.B.E., M.C., R.A.F.

WYNDHAM, Lieut.-Col. Charles John, C.B.E., J.P., *b.* 17 June, 1844 ; *s.* of Col. Charles Wyndham, M.P., of Rogate Lodge, Sussex ; *m* Laura Sophia (who died), *d.* of the late Rev. the Hon. Alfred Wodehouse (*see* BURKE'S *Peerage*). *Educ. :* Eton, and R.M.C., Sandhurst. Alderman of Sussex. *War Work :* Boer War, 1881 ; with Nile Expedition, 1889 ; County Director British Red Cross and Order of St. John of Jerusalem for Sussex, 1909–16. *Address :* Heathfield Lodge, Midhurst, Sussex. *Club :* Junior United Service. (C344)

WYNDHAM, Percy, C.I.E., C.B.E., *b.* 13 Dec. 1867 ; *s.* of Horace Robert Wyndham, of Cockermouth. *Educ. :* Giggleswick School, Yorkshire ; Queen's Coll., Oxford. Indian Civil Service ; Commissioner Kumaon Division, United Provinces, India. *War Work :* Trooper in the Indian Defence Force ; Supervised the recruiting for combatants and labour corps in the hill districts of the Kumaon Division. *Address :* Hatton Hall, Naini Tal. *Club :* East India United Service. (C389)

WYNESS, Ada, Mrs., O.B.E.

WYNN, Wing-Comm Alfred Hearst Wynn Elias, O.B.E., R.A.F.

WYNN, Elizabeth Ida, Mrs. WILLIAMS-, M.B.E. ; *d.* of George William Lowther, of Swillington, Yorks ; *m.* Robert William Herbert Watkin, *s.* of Col. Herbert Watkin Williams-Wynn, of Cefn, St. Asaph. *War Work :* County Sec. of the B.R.C.S., Denbighshire. (M1098)

WYNNE, Frederick Grant, M.B.E.

WYNNE, Jessie, Mrs., O.B.E.

WYNNE, Mary Carleton, Mrs., C.B.E. ; *d.* of Edward A. Parke, of Mount Temple, Sligo ; *m.* Albert Edward, M.D., F.R.C.S.I., *s.* of William Wynne. *War Work :* Head of North Wall Soldiers' and Sailors' Free Buffet ; head of Packing Room, War Hospitals Supply Depot, Merrion Square ; Assistant at Royal Dublin Fusiliers Parcels Depot. *Address :* 27, Westland Row, Dublin. (C3066)

WYNNE, Nora, M.B.E.

WYNNE, Major Owen Evelyn, O.B.E., R.E. *b.* 14 June, 1887 ; *e.s.* of General Sir Arthur S. Wynne, G.C.B., of Haybergill, Warcop, Westmorland. *Educ. :* Wellington Coll. ; R.M.A. Woolwich. Commissioner Anglo-Belgian (Rhodesian-Congo) Boundary Commission, 1911–13 ; G.S.O. 3 Geographical Section G. S. War Office, March, 1914 ; Geographical Representative, British Delegation, Peace Conference, Paris, 1919. *War Work :* Officer-in-charge Maps, L. of C., B.E.F., France, Aug. 1914 ; Comm. D Airline Section, R.E., Nov. 1914 ; Comm. 4th Divisional Signal Co. R.E. March, 1915 ; G.S.O. 3, 49th Division, July, 1915 ; Brigade-Major 147th Infantry Brigade, June, 1916 ; G.S.O. 2 in charge German Sub-Section War Office, Feb. 1917 ; G.S.O. 2 Intelligence, G.H.Q., France, Feb. 1918 ; despatches 3 times ; Brevet Major, June, 1916 ; O.B.E., Jan. 1919 ; Chevalier of the Order of the Crown (Belgium). *Club :* Army and Navy. (O2798)

WYNNE, Thomas Joseph, O.B.E.

WYNNES, James Cumming, M.B.E.

WYNTER, Comm. Gerald Charles, D.S.O., O.B.E., R.N.

WYNYARD, Major Edward George D.S.O., O.B.E., *b.* 1861 ; *s.* of the late William Wynyard, J.P., of Hursley, Winchester ; *m.* Sarah Louise, *d.* of James G. Worts, of Toronto. *Educ. :* Charterhouse. Entered King's (Liverpool Regt.), 1883 ; specially selected for promotion to Capt. Welsh Regt. 1890 ; retired, 1903 ; Burma Campaign, 1885–7 (despatches twice) ; Instructor in Fortification at Roy. Mil. Coll. Sandhurst, 1890–97 ; rejoined, 1914 ; appointed Major, Liverpool Regt. 1914 ; Army Ordnance Depart. 1915 ; again retired, 1919 ; received Roy. Humane Society's bronze medal, 1894. *Clubs :* Wellington ; Sports. (O7891)

WYNYARD, Lieut.-Col. Richard Damer, O.B.E.

WYON, Sir Albert William, K.B.E., *b.* 1869 ; *s.* of Leonard Charles Wyon, Head of firm of Price, Waterhouse & Co., and Govt. Auditor of Railways, and Govt. Accountant, Controlled Canals, etc. (K245)

WYSE, Richard, M.B.E., M.D., M.A.

WYTHES, Aline, Mrs. Ernest James, O.B.E., *d.* of Sir John Henry Thorold, Bt. (*see* BURKE'S *Peerage*) ; *m.* Ernest James, C.B.E., *s.* of the late George Edward Wythes, F.R.G.S. (O885)

WYTHES, Ernest James, C.B.E., *b.* 1858 ; *s.* of the late George Edward Wythes, F.R.G.S. ; *m.* Aline, B.E., (*q.v.*) *d.* of Sir John Henry Thorold 12th Bt. (*see* BURKE'S *Peerage*). J.P. for Essex ; Co. Director, Auxiliary Hospitals and V.A.D.'s Essex during the Great War. (C3067)

YAPP, Sir Arthur Keysall, K.B.E., *b.* 12 March, 1869 : *s.* of the late Richard Keysall Yapp, of Orleton, Herefordshire ; *m.* Alice Maude, *d.* of the late T. Hesketh Higson, of Southport.

Educ.: Hereford County Coll. National Sec. Y.M.C.A. *Addresses:* Highfield House, Enfield; 13, Russell Square, W.C. 1. *Club:* National. (K43)

YARBOROUGH, Marcia Amelia Mary, BaronessFauconberg and Conyers, Countess of, O.B.E., Lady of Justice of St. John of Jerusalem, *b.* 18 Oct. 1863; *d.* of 12th Baron Conyers (*see* BURKE'S *Peerage*), and 15th Baron D'Arcy de Knayth; *m.* Charles Alfred Pelham, 4th Earl of Yarborough, *s.* of 3rd Earl of Yarborough (*see* BURKE'S *Peerage*). *War Work:* Matron of Brocklesby Park Hospital, 1914–19. *Address:* Brocklesby Park, Lincolnshire. (O11676)

YARROW, Lieut. George Ernest, M.B.E.

YARROW, Harold Edgar, C.B.E., *b.* 11 Aug. 1884; *s.* of Sir Alfred Yarrow, Bart., Hindhead, Surrey; *m.* Eleanor Etheldreda, *d.* of the Rev. Canon W. H. M. H. Aitken, of Norwich. *Educ.:* Bedford Grammar School. *War Work:* Managing Director of Messrs. Yarrow & Co., Ltd., who were engaged in building Torpedo Boat Destroyers, Submarines and Gunboats for the British Navy; Chairman of Limbs and Appliances Committee of the Princess Scottish Hospital for Limbless Sailors and Soldiers. *Address:* Fairlawn, Bearsden, Dumbartonshire. *Clubs:* Royal Automobile; Western (Glasgow). (C345)

YATES, Albert James, M.B.E., R.A.S.C.

YATES, Lieut.-Col. Arthur St. John, O.B.E., M.C., R.E., *b.* 23 July, 1882; *s.* of Col. H. T. S. Yates, late R.A.; *m.* Ethel, *d.* of Col. J. Barry, late R.A.M.C. *Address:* c/o Messrs Cox & Co. *Club:* Junior Army and Navy. (O5968)

YATES, Col. Clarence Montague, C.B.E., M.V.O., M.C., *b.* 1881. Entered Royal Warwickshire Regt. 1901; became Capt. The King's (Liverpool Regt.) 1910; Major and Col. (ret.) 1920; S. African War, 1900–1 (Queen's medal with three clasps); served in the Great War, 1914–16 (despatches). Legion of Honour. (C2055)

YATES, Lieut. Donald Russell Martin, O.B.E., I.A.R.O.

YATES, Florence, M.B.E.

YATES, Major Henry Irving Frederick, O.B.E. M.C., R.A.F.

YATES, James, M.B.E.,' *b.* 11 Sept. 1871; *s.* of Peter Yates, of Rhodes, Manchester; *m.* Mary, *d.* of Richard Pendleton, of Harefield, Middlesex. Superintendent of Police in charge of the North Lonsdale Division of Lancashire. *War Work:* Specially appointed Chief Superintendent and Deputy Chief Officer of the Gretna Police Force (Ministry of Munitions); lent by the Lancashire County Police Authority on 1 June, 1917, to assist in the organisation of the Gretna Force; served there until 31 Oct. 1918. *Address:* Neville House, Ulverston. *Clubs:* Lonsdale North Police Athletic; County Bowling (Ulverston); Ulverston Cricket. (M10159)

YATES, Capt. John Henry, O.B.E., R.A.V.C.

YEARSLEY, Clare Elizabeth, Mrs., M.B.E.

YEATES, Capt. Percy Thomas Arthur, M.B.E.

YEATES, Capt. Robert Montford Michaelson, M.B.E., I.A.R.O.

YEATMAN, Lieut.-Col. Charleton, O.B.E., Aust. A.M.C.

YEAXLEE, Basil Alfred, Rev., O.B.E., B.A., *b.* 2 Dec. 1883; *s.* of Alfred George Yeaxlee, of Southsea, Hants; *m.* Annie Julie Mary, *d.* of the late Thomas Leadbeater, M.R.C.S., F.R.C.P., of Southsea. *Educ.:* Privately; King's Coll., London; New Coll., London; Mansfield Coll., Oxford. Minister Emmanuel Congregational Church, Bootle, 1909–11; Educational Sec. London Missionary Society, 1911–13, and Editor, United Council for Missionary Education, 1911–15; Editor, National Council of Y.M.C.A.'s, 1915–16; Sec. Y.M.C.A. Universities Committee, 1916 to present time; Joint Hon. Sec. Educational Settlements Association; Member of Ministry of Reconstruction Committee on Adult Education (Master of Balliol's Committee), 1917–19; Author of "An Educated Nation" and "Working Out the Fisher Act." *War Work:* Responsible for all the educational work of the Y.M.C.A. carried on through the Universities Committee in co-operation with the War Office and respective G.H.Q. in France, Italy, Salonica, Egypt, Palestine, and Home Command, as also among munition workers, this including work of Red Triangle library and Music Section. *Addresses:* 24, Hayne Road, Beckenham, Kent; Y.M.C.A. Headquarters, 13, Russell Square, W.C. 1. *Club:* University of London. (O4006)

YELD, Ellen, M.B.E.

YELD, Major Richard Kingsley, O.B.E., I.A.R.O.

YELLOLY, Robert, M.B.E., *b.* 17 Sept. 1882; *s.* of the late Robert Yelloly, of Berwick-upon-Tweed; *m.* Sarah, *d.* of the late Patrick Davis, of Berwick-upon-Tweed. *Educ.:* Corporation School and Academy, Berwick-upon-Tweed. Chief Constable of Wakefield; formerly Superintendent and Chief Clerk, Newcastle-upon-Tyne Police. *War Work:* As a Police Officer holding a very responsible position in a large and important Police Force (Newcastle-upon-Tyne), was specially commended by Home Office for work in connection with aliens and suspected persons. *Address:* Wakefield. (M10162)

YELLOWLEES, Capt. Henry, O.B.E., R.A.M.C.

YELLOWLEES, Henry, O.B.E., M.D., F.R.C.P.S. (Glas.), R.A.M.C., *b.* 11 June, 1888; *s.* of David Yellowlees, M.D., of Glasgow; *m.* Dorothy, *d.* of Major A. J. Davis, of London. *Educ.:* Kelvinside Academy, and Glasgow Univ. Senior Assistant Physician, Edinburgh Royal Asylum. *War Work:* Mental Specialist, Etaples Area, 1915–18; designed and arranged accommodation for nervous and mental cases in the district, and personally treated 2200 cases of mental disorder

in soldiers, and many more cases of nerve shock in addition. *Address:* Craig House, Edinburgh. (O5970)

YELVERTON, Rev. Erik Esskildsen, O.B.E.

YEO, Capt. Moritz Rodwell, O.B.E., R.M.L.I., *b.* 1 Sept. 1884; *s.* of John Yeo, of 106, Penylan Road, Cardiff; *m.* Flora Irma, *d.* of the late Andrew Macfarlane, of Bournemouth. *Educ.:* Wellingborough Grammar School, and Dulwich Coll. Joined Royal Marine Light Infantry as 2nd Lieut. Sept. 1903; continuous service since; promoted Lieut. July, 1904; Capt. Sept. 1914. *War Work:* Ordinary duties as Capt. R.M.L.I. afloat and ashore; seconded for duty on Naval Staff, Gibraltar, April, 1917, and employed as such till end of war. *Address:* Royal Marine Barracks, Plymouth. *Club:* Union, Malta. (O9378)

YEO, Richard Forster, M.B.E.

YEOMAN, John Pattison, M.B.E.

YEOMAN, Sophia Bruce, O.B.E.; *d.* of the late Rev. Constantine Bernard Yeoman. *War Work:* Commandant, Sleights Red Cross Hospital. *Address:* Woodlands, Sleights, Yorkshire. *Club:* Sesame. (O886)

YEOMANS, Capt. Charles Fredsall, O.B.E., R.A.F.

YERBURGH, Capt. Richard Guy Cecil, O.B.E.

YETTS, Major Walter Perceval, O.B.E., M.R.C.S., L.R.C.P., Staff Surgeon, R.N. (ret.), *b.* 25 April, 1878; *s.* of the late A. M. Yetts; *m.* Gwendoline Mary, *d.* of the late Dr. D. Hughes. *Educ.:* Bradfield Coll., Berks; St. Bartholomew's Hospital; Edinburgh and Lausanne Univs. R.N. Medical Service, 1903–12; Acting Physician, H.B.M. Legation, Peking, 1913. *War Work:* Temporary Commission in R.A.M.C. from Aug. 1914, to Aug. 1919, holding appointment as Deputy Assistant Director of Medical Services, and latterly specially employed at War Office; Deputy Commissioner of Medical Services, Ministry of Pensions, 1919–20; Medical Officer, Ministry of Health, May, 1920. *Address:* 29, Redcliffe Gardens, S.W. 10. *Club:* Junior United Service. (O7893)

YOCKNEY, Alfred, M.B.E., *b.* 13 Feb. 1878; *s.* of John S. Yockney; *m.* Mabel Blanche, *d.* of Capt. J. T. Partridge, R.N. *Educ.:* The Woodlands, Hitchin, and Alleyn's School, Dulwich. Assistant Librarian, Royal Institute of British Architects; Editor, "The Art Journal." *War Work:* Government Publications; Sec. Pictorial Propaganda Committee, Ministry of Information. *Address:* 32, South Side, Clapham Common, S.W. *Club:* London Rowing. (M4103)

YOLLAND, Hon. Lieut.-Col. John Horatio, C.B.E., M.R.C.S. (Eng.), L.S.A. (Lond), R.A.M.C. (V.), Esquire, Order of St. John of Jerusalem, *b.* 18 Dec. 1863; *s.* of the late John Yolland, of Hoylake, Birkenhead; *m.* Emily Constance, *d.* of the late Henry Railton, of Snittlegarter, Carlisle. *Educ.:* King William's Coll., Isle of Man, and Univ. Coll. Hospital, London. Hon. Surgeon, Bromley Cottage Hospital. *War Work:* Hon. Sec. and Treas. Kent County War Fund; Chief Staff Officer, Kent V.A.D.; Officer-in-Charge, Kent R.A.M.C. (V.) *Address:* 53, Bromley Common, Bromley, Kent. (C346)

YORK, Capt. William Douglas COLIN-, O.B.E.

YORKE, Col. Frederick Augustus, O.B.E., late R.A. (Staff); *s.* of Major-Gen. F. A. Yorke, R.E., of Tunbridge Wells; *m.* Lucy Elizabeth, *d.* of the late Dr. C. E. Hayes Newington, of Ticehurst, Sussex. *Educ.:* R.M.A., Woolwich. Assist. Commandant, R.M.A., Woolwich, 1895–1900; commanded Royal Horse and Field Artillery in Ireland, 1900–2; appointed Assist. Military Sec. War Office, which post was held until retirement, May, 1903. *War Work:* Called up, April, 1915; raised a R.F.A. Brigade (168th) at Huddersfield, Yorks; commanded 189th R.F.A. Brigade, Aldershot; 1916, appointed Commandant, Royal Horse Artillery Training School (T.F.), Larkhill and Bulford; now Commanding Hants R.A.S.C., M.T. (V.). *Address:* Southfield, Twyford, Winchester. *Club:* Army and Navy. (O3210)

YORKE, Gladys Dunlop, Hon. Mrs. Alfred, O.B.E.; *d.* of the late A. V. Dunlop Best; *m.* Alfred Ernest Frederick Yorke, *s.* of the late Earl of Hardwicke (*see* BURKE'S *Peerage*). *War Work:* Co.-Supt. with the Hon. Mrs. Charles Tufton, O.B.E., of the Alexandra Pavilion for Officers, Victoria Station, 1915–19. *Address:* 1, Manchester Square, London, W. 1. *Club:* Bath. (O11677)

YORKE, Lieut. John, O.B.E., R.F.A.

YORKE, Lieut. Maurice Francis, O.B.E., R.N.V.R.

YORKE, T. Capt. Noel Leigh, O.B.E., R.A.S.C.

YORSTOUN, Lieut. Morden Archibald CARTHEW-, M.B.E.

YORWERTH, Capt. Thomas Jenkin, M.B.E., *b.* 26 Nov. 1870; *s.* of William Yorwerth, of Cowbridge; *m.* Gwendoline, *d.* of Thomas John, of Aburthin. *Educ.:* Cowbridge Grammar School. Auctioneer; Sec. Glamorgan Agricultural Society. *War Work:* District Purchasing Officer Supplies (D.P.O.S.) for South Wales and Monmouthshire. *Address:* 65, High Street, Cowbridge, Glam. *Club:* Farmers'. (M5759)

YOUDEN, Lieut.-Col. William Alfred, O.B.E., T.D.

YOULE, Paymaster-Lieut. George Arthur, O.B.E., R.N.

YOUNG, Allan Carruth, O.B.E., J.P., *b.* 1859; *s.* of John Young, of Fulwood, Renfrewshire; *m.* Annie, *d.* of Henry Franklin, of Broadwater, Herts. Owning occupier of land in Wilts. *War Work:* Chairman of Wilts County Committee; served on many Committees; Hon. Purchasing Officer for Wilts, 1914–15, reorganising this work with marked success and showing a large saving on the turnover. *Address:* Drumreagh, Bournemouth. *Club:* Bournemouth. (O11678)

YOUNG, Capt. Andrew, O.B.E., R.A.F.

YOUNG, Col. Archibald, C.B.E., V.D. Served in Great War, 1914–19 (mentioned in despatches). (C1822)

YOUNG, Sir Arthur Henderson, G.C.M.G., K.B.E., *b.* 31 Oct. 1854; *s.* of the late Col. Keith Young, C.B., Judge Advocate-General for India; *m.* Evelyn Ann, *d.* of 2nd Marquess of Ailsa (*see* BURKE'S *Peerage*). *Educ.:* Edinburgh Academy; Rugby; R.M.C., Sandhurst. Late Capt. 27th Inniskillings; Local Commandant, Military Police, Kyrenia, Cyprus, 1878; appointed Commissioner, Pagho, 1878; Chief Sec. to Government, Cyprus, 1894; Colonial Sec. Straits Settlements, 1906–11; Chief Sec. Federated Malay States, Feb. 1911; Governor and Commander-in-Chief of the Straits Settlements, and High Commissioner Malay States, Sept. 1911, to Dec. 1919. *War Work:* Governor and Commander-in-Chief, Straits Settlements; and High Commissioner, Malay States, throughout the war. *Address:* Spring Grove, Sunningdale, Berks. *Clubs:* Army and Navy; Royal Automobile; New (Edinburgh). (K126)

YOUNG, Arthur Primrose, O.B.E., M.I.E.E., M.I.A.E., *b.* 2 July, 1885; *s.* of William Young, of Prestwick, Ayrshire, Scotland; *m.* Lillie Louisa, *d.* of Abel Porter, of Rugby. *Educ.:* Finsbury Technical Coll., London. Chief Engineer, Coventry Magneto Works, B.T.H. Co., Ltd.; Hon. Sec. Coventry Lecture Society; author of numerous papers delivered to learned societies. *War Work:* Took a leading part in the creation of the British Magneto Industry; designed the B.T.H. Co.'s type A.V. Polar Inductor Magneto, which was used almost exclusively on 8-cylinder Aero Engines during the war; lectured to the R.A.F. in France, on Magnetos, in Jan. 1919. *Addresses:* B.T.H. Co., Coventry; Dovedale, Kenilworth. (O11679)

YOUNG, Capt. Bertram John, M.B.E.

YOUNG, Charles Robert, O.B.E.

YOUNG, Lieut. Charlie, M.B.E., R.A.V.C.

YOUNG, Lieut. Christopher Harding, M.B.E., R.A.F.

YOUNG, Clarence Ross, M.B.E., *b.* 25 Aug. 1877; *s.* of Jesse Young; *m.* Marian Laird, *d.* of John Gilbert Rendall. Civil Servant, Local Government Board (now merged in Ministry of Health). *War Work:* Special service in a variety of war work. *Address:* St. Margarets, Langley Drive, Wanstead. (M2690)

YOUNG, Colin, M.B.E., J.P.

YOUNG, Constance E., M.B.E., *b.* 20 May, 1886; *d.* of Frederick Wright, of Wembley; *m.* Sydney Mountford Young (28th Co. of London (Artist's), killed in action; *s.* of Alfred W. Young, of Ealing. *Educ.:* Haberdashers' Aske's Girls' School, Acton, W. *War Work:* Women's Legion, Aug. 1916 (Cookery Section); Q.M.A.A.C., 1917; Assist. Administrator, Dec. 1917; Unit Administrator, 1918–19. *Address:* 94, Swinderby Road, Wembley. *Club:* Women's United Services. (M6728)

YOUNG, Daniel Henderson Luck, C.B.E., J.P., D.L. Director of Recruiting and of National Service, Northern Region. (C684)

YOUNG, Lieut.-Col. David Douglas, C.B.E. T. Lieut.-Col. Special List; served in Great War, 1914–19 (mentioned in despatches). (C1823)

YOUNG, David Wilberforce, M.B.E.

YOUNG, Edward Willie, O.B.E., *b.* 11 June, 1867; *s.* of Edward Young, of Islington; *m.* Beatrice Mary, *d.* of Daniel Sharman, of Huddersfield. *Educ.:* City of London Coll., and Durham Univ. Chartered Sec. (A.C.I.S.); Sec. Comptroller to His Grace, the Duke of Northumberland. *War Work:* Hon. Sec. to the British Red Cross Society (County of Middlesex); the Middlesex Joint V.A.D. Committee; Demobilisation and Reconstruction Committee. *Address:* Syon Park Cottage, Brentford, Middlesex. *Club:* Cavendish. (O11680)

YOUNG, Eng.-Lieut.-Comm. Edwin Walton, O.B.E., R.N.

YOUNG, Elizabeth Diana, M.B.E.

YOUNG, Capt. Ernest William Gilmour, O.B.E., M.C., M.B., R.A.M.C.

YOUNG, F. R., Mrs., M.B.E.

YOUNG, Lieut.-Col. Sir Frank Popham, K.B.E., C.I.E., *b.* 24 Dec. 1863; *m.* 1st, Winifred Ethel (d. 1902), *d.* of Col. J. A. L. Montgomery, C.S.I.; 2nd, Elizabeth Anne Marens, née Beckett, of San Francisco, U.S.A. Entered Indian Army, 1884; Capt. 1885; Major, 1902; Lieut.-Col. 1910; Dep. Commissioner, Punjab; Colonisation Officer, Chenab Canar Settlement; Commissioner Pakada State; Commissioner Rawal Pindi Dis., Punjab. Commissioner of the Rawal Pindi Division of the Punjab during the war. The Rawal Pindi Division led the Indian Empire in providing soldiers for the Army. *Addresses:* Punjab, India; c/o Grindlay & Co., 54, Parliament Street, S.W. 1. *Clubs:* East India; United Service; Royal Automobile. (K182)

YOUNG, Lieut.-Col. Fred Armstrong, O.B.E., Can. A.M.C.

YOUNG, Capt. Frederick Hugh, O.B.E., R.A.M.C.

YOUNG, Paymaster-Lieut. Frederick Richard, M.B.E., R.N.R.

YOUNG, Frederick William, C.B.E., O.B.E., R.N.

YOUNG, Commodore Sir Frederick William, K.B.E., R.N.R., *b.* 23 Dec. 1858. Naval Salvage Adviser; late Chief Surveyor, Liverpool Salvage Association; Member of the Institute of Mechanical Engineers; Officer of the Crown of Belgium, United States Navy Cross. *War Work:* Director of salvage operations to H.M. Fleet and merchant ships damaged in action; clearance of Belgian ports after Armistice; raising of "Vindictive," "Intrepid," and "Iphigenia," etc.; served from 1914 and still employed on Belgian coast. *Address:* 14, Cheyne Row, Chelsea. (K467)

YOUNG, George, M.B.E.

YOUNG, George, M.B.E.

YOUNG, George Macdonald, M.B.E.

YOUNG, Comm. Harold Francis John, O.B.E., R.N.

YOUNG, Harry Maurice, M.B.E.

YOUNG, Capt. Harry Robert, M.B.E.

YOUNG, Brig.-Gen. Henry Alfred C.I.E., C.B.E., R.A., *b.* 1867. Director of Ordnance Factories, India, with rank of Col. (C2046)

YOUNG, Lieut.-Col. Hugh Corbett TAYLOR-, O.B.E., Aust. A.M.C.

YOUNG, 2nd Lieut. Hugh Joseph, M.B.E., R.A.F.

YOUNG, Major James, M.B.E., I.A.R.O.

YOUNG, Eng.-Lieut.-Comm. James, O.B.E., R.D., R.N.R.

YOUNG, James, O.B.E., A.R.C.Sc., *b.* 14 Dec. 1861; *s.* of James Young, of Co. Down, Ireland. *Educ.:* Privately, and Royal Coll. of Science. Professor in Science, R.M.A., Woolwich. *War Work:* Training of cadets and officers of the New Armies and scientific research. *Addresses:* R.M.A., Woolwich; 12, Edge Hill, Plumstead, S.E. 18. (O888)

YOUNG, James Robert Spencer, M.B.E., *b.* 5 Jan. 1882; *s.* of Edward Robert Young, of Llanelly; *m.* Constance Frances Morton, *d.* of Theodore Morton-Jones, Admiral R.N., of Brixton. *Educ.:* County School, Llanelly. Solicitor. *War Work:* Engaged in Legal Department, Air Ministry. *Addresses:* Thomas Ditton, Surrey; 31, Wardour Street, W. 1. (M10169)

YOUNG, Flying-Officer James William, M.B.E., R.A.F.

YOUNG, James Wolstan, O.B.E.

YOUNG, John, O.B.E., *b.* 1858; *s.* of John Young, of Falkirk, Scotland; *m.* Jennie, *d.* of C. F. Finch, of London. *Educ.:* Privately. Engineer and Manager of the British Gas Light Company's Hull Station; now retired. *War Work:* A Member of Lord Moulton's Committee; Supervisor of the counties of Northumberland, Durham, and Yorkshire for that committee; Commander of Special Constables. (O11681)

YOUNG, Capt. John Ross, O.B.E.

YOUNG, Joseph Samuel, O.B.E.

YOUNG, Nathaniel James, M.B.E., *b.* Oct. 1877; *s.* of Nathaniel Young, of Clutton, Somerset. *Educ.:* Cameley Schools, Somerset; Private Academy, Bristol. General Manager, Electricity and Tramways Department, Newport Corporation, Newport, Mon.; Joint Sec. of the District Joint Industrial Council for the Tramways Industry, South Wales Area. *War Work:* Considerable assistance given in transport problems in South Wales; Hon. Sec. of the Board of Trade Advisory Committee in the South Wales Area. *Addresses:* Town Hall, Newport, Mon.; Bellevue, Belmont Hill, Caerleon, Mon. *Club:* Monmouthshire (Newport). (M10170)

YOUNG, Patricia Annie, M.B.E., *b.* Jan. 1866; *d.* of Major Thomas Young, of Lincluden House, Stewartry of Kirkcudbright. *War Work:* Hon. Sec. and Treas. Dumfries and Maxwelltown Women's War Relief Executive, 1914–19; Hon. Sec. and Treas. and Joint Superintendent of Hospital Supplies Depot, 1915–19; Hon. Sec. Sailors' and Soldiers' Buffet, Dumfries Station, 1916–19; worked for three years in Maxwelltown Red Cross Hospital. *Address:* Lincluden House, Stewartry of Kirkcudbright. *Clubs:* Ladies' Army and Navy; Border Counties Ladies' (Dumfries). (M1128)

YOUNG, Patrick, O.B.E.

YOUNG, T. Col. Patrick Charles, C.B.E., late T. Col. R.E., *b.* 22 Jan. 1880; *s.* of Peter Alexander Young, M.D., J.P., of Edinburgh; *m.* Elizabeth Harvey, *d.* of Patrick Turnbull, C.A., of Edinburgh. *Educ.:* Edinburgh Academy, and Christ's Coll. Cambridge. 1903–16, P.W.D. India; Assistant General Manager, N.W.R.; Assist. Sec. and official Sec. to the Railway Board; now Acting General Manager, the Pailan Mining Administration. *War Work:* Engineer-in-Chief, Nushki Extension Railway, Baluchistan; Deputy Chief Railway Construction Engineer, France; Assist. Inspector-General of Transportation, France, has Legion of Honour. *Addresses:* Tientsin, N. China; 1, Royal Circus, Edinburgh. (C1824)

YOUNG, Sister Pauline, C.B.E.

YOUNG, Major Richard Ashmur Blair, O.B.E., A.P.D.

YOUNG, Capt. Richard Horton, M.B.E., *b.* 21 Dec. 1879; *s.* of the late Capt. R. N. Young, R.H.A., of Orlingbury, Northants. *Educ.:* Oxford Military Coll. *War Work:* 3rd Royal Warwickshire Regt.; served with 1st and 2nd Batts. in France, Mons Medal, 1914; Adjutant to No. 6 and No. 13 Officer Cadet Batt. *Address:* Bloxham, Banbury. *Club:* Badminton. (M5763)

YOUNG, Lieut. Richard Linsley, M.B.E.

YOUNG, Robert, O.B.E., M.P., *b.* 26 Jan. 1872; *s.* of Robert Young, of Glasgow; *m.* Bessie Laurina, *d.* of C. J. Choldcroft, of Oxford. *Educ.:* Elementary Schools and Ruskin Coll. Oxford. Late Gen. Sec. Amalgamated Society of Engineers, now Member of Parliament, Newton Division of Lancashire. *War Work:* Appointed by Minister of Munitions to visit the Front to select soldier engineers for war work at home; Member of Army Demobilisation Committee, Demobilisation of Civil War Workers' Committee, and of National Maritime Board. *Address:* 213, Barry Road, Dulwich, S.E. 22. (O70)

YOUNG, Robert Arthur, C.B.E., M.D., B.Sc., F.R.C.P., *b.* 6 Nov. 1871; *s.* of the late William Young, of London; *m.* Fanny Caroline Phœbe, *d.* of the late Robert Muirhead Kennedy, I.C.S. *Educ.:* United Westminster Schools; King's Coll.; Middlesex Hospital. Physician to the Middlesex and Brompton Hospitals. *War Work:* Physician in charge of Medical Military Wards, Middlesex Hospital; Senior Physician, City of London Red Cross Hospital, Finsbury Square. *Address:* 57, Harley Street, London, W.1.; Heath View, Tiptree, Essex. *Club:* Savage. (C4124)

YOUNG, Robert Hellyer, O.B.E.

YOUNG, Sidney, O.B.E., *b.* 1869; *s.* of John Young; *m.* Ellen Mary *d.* of J. B. Penistan. Chairman of British and Argentine Meat Co., Ltd., Las Palmas Produce Co., Ltd., "K" Steamship Co., Ltd., and Director of Planet Assurance Co., Ltd. *War Work:* The first Director of Meat Supplies under Lord Rhondda, and after on the Meat and Livestock Advisory Committee at the Ministry of Food; also an *ex officio* Member of the River Plate Refrigerated Tonnage Committee at the Board of Trade, the Meat and Allied Trades Red Cross Fund Committee, and of the Officers' Association Committee. *Address:* Redmile, Sevenoaks, Kent. *Clubs:* Argentine; Alpine. (O890)

YOUNG, Rev. Stanislaus Dominic, D.S.O., O.B.E., *b.* 7 May, 1884; *s.* of O. W. Young, F.S.I., of Liverpool. *Educ.:* Downside School; Liverpool Univ. (Law School); Christ's Coll., Cambridge (M.A.). Priest in Roman Catholic Church; Member of Benedictine Community, Downside Abbey; Headmaster, Ealing Priory School. *War Work:* Chaplain to Forces, Feb. 1915, to Aug. 1919; France, April, 1915, to Aug. 1919; thrice mentioned in despatches. *Address:* Ealing Priory School, Ealing, W.5. (O5973)

YOUNG, Pilot-Officer Stanley Gordon, M.B.E., R.A.F.

YOUNG, Lieut. Stanley Harris, O.B.E., R.N.V.R., *b.* 5 March, 1888; *s.* of the late Harry Woodward Young, of Hampstead; *m.* Jessie, *d.* of William Francis Drewe, of Upper Norwood. *Educ.:* Schorne Coll., Bucks., and H.M.S. "Worcester." Partner in firm of Trafford and Young, Surveyors, 100, Jermyn Street, S.W.1. *War Work:* Joined Anti-Aircraft Corps, R.N.V.R. in Oct. 1914; Commissioned as Sub-Lieut. R.N.V.R., and went to sea in various craft, bases, Lerwick and Dover, Oct. 1915; promoted to Lieut., command of M.L. 306, base, Swansea, Oct. 1916; qualified as Gunnery Lieut., bases, Larne and Granton. *Addresses:* 15, Dunmore Road, Wimbledon; 100, Jermyn Street, S.W.1. (O3596)

YOUNG, Sydney Roles, O.B.E., *b.* 25 March, 1866; *s.* of Thomas Young, of Clapham; *m.* Florence Priscilla, *d.* of Henry Lawry, of St. Minver, Cornwall. *Educ.:* St. Walter St. John's School, Battersea. Superintending Clerk, Department of the Accountant-General of the Navy, Admiralty. *War Work:* Head of the Salary Branch, Admiralty. *Address:* 76, Bromfelde Road, Clapham, S.W.4. (O11683)

YOUNG, Thomas, M.B.E., N.D.A., F.S.I., *b.* 25 Oct. 1879; *s.* of Thomas Young, J.P., of Newbigging, Methven, Perthshire. *Educ.:* Sharps, Perth; West of Scotland Coll. of Agriculture, Glasgow. Lecturer in Estate Management in Agricultural Coll., Aspatria, Cumberland, Oct. 1901, to July, 1908; on staff of Edinburgh and East of Scotland Coll. of Agriculture as Organiser and Lecturer in Agriculture in County of Fife, Oct. 1908, to date. *War Work:* Sec. and Executive Officer to Fife Agricultural Executive Committees for Increased Food Production; Sec. to Fife Women's County Agricultural Committee for Organisation of Women Labour; Agricultural Superintendent under the Ministry of Agriculture and Fisheries for the reintroduction of Flax Production in Scotland as a war measure for the manufacture of Aeroplane Wings; Sec. to the Fife Flax Advisory Committee; author of a first prize scheme for the settlement of discharged and disabled soldiers and sailors on the land. (M1129)

YOUNG, Major Thomas Dunlop, O.B.E.

YOUNG, Thomas Pettigrew, M.B.E.

YOUNG, Lieut.-Comm. Thomas Wallace, O.B.E., R.N.R.

YOUNG, Lieut. Wallace Melville, M.B.E.

YOUNG, Capt. Walter Gerald Paul, O.B.E.

YOUNG, Major William, O.B.E., V.D., M.B., C.M.

YOUNG, Capt. William Alexander, O.B.E., *b.* July, 1884; *s.* of John Young, of The Manor, Fisherton de la Mere, Wilts; *m.* Marion Edith, *d.* of David G. Mitchell, of Wynyards, Wimbledon. *Educ.:* Glasgow Academy, and Fettes Coll., Edinburgh. Shipowner and Shipbroker; Partner in firms of W. A. Young & Co., and Hansen Bros., Young and Gillett, 7, Union Court, E.C.2. *War Work:* Mobilised Aug. 1914, with the London Scottish, in which he was 2nd Lieut.; immediately after outbreak of war was promoted Capt. and detailed to the raising and training of new battalions; eventually went to France, and after serving in the trenches was severely wounded at the first Battle of Arras; sent home and found unfit for further active service; on discharge from hospital was posted to the Ministry of Shipping, where he was chiefly associated with the Requisition of the Dutch steamers in British Ports in 1918; superintended the management of the fleet thus acquired by the British Government along with a large number of time-chartered neutral vessels; after the Armistice redelivered all the neutral steamers acquired by the British Government to their nationals. *Addresses:* 9, Woodhayes Road, Wimbledon Common; c/o W. A. Young & Co., 7, Union Court, Old Broad Street, E.C.2. *Club:* Caledonian. (O11685)

YOUNG, Sir William Douglas, K.B.E., C.M.G.; *s.* of the late W. Alexander George Young, C.M.G., Governor of Gold Coast Colony. *Educ.:* Charterhouse, Entered Colonial Service, 1877; Chief Clerk, Government Secretary Office, British Guiana, 1889; Assistant Colonial Secretary, Mauritius 1895; Acting Colonial Secretary, 2½ years; Commissioner, Turks and Caicos Islands, 1901; Administrator Dominica, 1906–13; Acting Governor and Commander-in-Chief, Leeward Islands, 1909; Administrator-Colonial Secretary, Santa Lucia, 1913–14; Acting Governor and Commander-in-Chief, Windward Islands, 1914; Governor and Commander-in-Chief, Falkland Islands, since 1914. *Address:* Government House, Stanley, Falkland Islands. *Club:* Isthmian. (K321a)

YOUNG, Capt. William Edward, M.B.E., M.S.C.R.; *s.* of the late Rev. William Frederick Young, M.A., B.D., of Co. Tipperary, Ireland; *m.* Lilian Mary, *d.* of the late Reuben Ross, of Ross, Gloucestershire. *Educ.:* St. Peter's School, York; Canada. Commandant, Metropolitan Police Reserve, and Hon. General Sec. of the Free Church of England (Episcopal); late Royal Dragoons, Royal Irish Constabulary, Legion of Frontiersmen, National Reserve, etc. *War Work:* Commander, Metropolitan Special Constabulary, Metropolitan Observation Service; served on numerous committees, including the Veterans' Association, Land Settlement, War Orphans, Seamen's, etc. *Addresses:* Nenagh, Thames Ditton, Surrey; Royal Colonial Institute, Northumberland Avenue, London. *Club:* Tamesis Sailing. (M4104)

YOUNG, William James, C.B.E. Rendered services to Shipping during Great War. (C369)

YOUNG, William Ronald, O.B.E.

YOUNG, Winifred, Mrs., M.B.E., M.A., B.Sc. (St. Andrews), *b.* 10 June, 1890; *d.* of James Ross, J.P., of Canisbay Lodge, Newport, Fife; *m.* Charles Robert, *s.* of Robert Young, of Nottingham. *Educ.:* Univ. of St. Andrews. Formerly Carnegie Research Scholar and Fellow, Univ. of St. Andrews. *War Work:* Preparation of rare drugs for National Health Insurance Commission at Univ. of St. Andrews; investigation of problems connected with chemical warfare; Technical Assistant, H.Q. Offices, Chemical Warfare Department, Ministry of Munitions. *Address:* 14B, Belsize Lane, Hampstead, N.W. (M10172)

YOUNGE, Joseph Samuel, O.B.E., J.P.; *s.* of William Younge, of Ballinamana, Galway; *m.* Edith Mary, *d.* of John O'Connor, of Dublin. *Educ.:* Model School, Galway. *War Work:* Worked for 4½ years in the cause of recruiting in Ireland, and received letters of thanks from prominent members of the Army and Navy. (O11682)

YOUNGER, Jessie Alice, O.B.E., *b.* 23 Sept. 1871; *d.* of George Younger, of 10, Lynedoch Crescent, Glasgow. *Educ.:* The Park School, Glasgow; Cambridge Univ. (Girton Coll., Cambridge). Civil Servant; Chief Woman Officer, Ministry of Labour, Employment Department. *War Work:* Recruiting women labour for Munition Factories; for substitution; and for Women's Auxiliary War Services. *Addresses:* Divisional Office, Ministry of Labour, 44, Drumsheugh Gardens, Edinburgh; 6, Osborne Terrace, Edinburgh. *Clubs:* Lyceum; Ladies' Caledonian (Edinburgh); Kelvin (Glasgow); Literary (Glasgow). (O2042)

YOUNGER, Lieut.-Col. John Henderson, O.B.E.

YOUNGER, Rt. Hon. Sir Robert, G.B.E., *b.* 12 Sept. 1861; *s.* of James Younger, of Alloa. *Educ.:* Edinburgh Academy, and Balliol Coll., Oxford. Lord Justice of Appeal. *War Work:* Joint Chairman of Aliens' Internment and Repatriation Committee, 1915–17; Chairman of Government Committee on Treatment by the Enemy of British Prisoners of War; a British Delegate at the Hague Conference with German Delegates on the Treatment of Prisoners of War in 1917; Chairman of Home Office Committee on Interned Enemy Aliens, 1919. *Address:* 73, South Audley Street, W.C. *Clubs:* Athenæum; Oxford and Cambridge; New University; Garrick; Bachelors'; New (Edinburgh). (G12)

YOUNGHUSBAND, Arthur Delavel, C.S.I., C.B.E., *b.* 1854; *s.* of the late Gen. Robert Romer Younghusband, C.B., of 106, Pembroke Road, Clifton, Bristol; *m.* Maud Helen, *d.* of Lewis Gordon. *Educ.:* Rugby; Clifton Coll.; Balliol Coll. Oxford. Entered I.C.S. 1875; Assist. Commr. Central Provinces, 1891; Dep. Commr. 1892; Commr. 1897; M.L.C. Bombay, 1903; Member of Council of Viceroy of India, 1904; Commr. in Sind, 1905; retired, 1912; has Kaisir-i-Hind medal. *Address:* Priory House, Long Bennington, near Grantham. (C3069)

YOUNGHUSBAND, Herbert William, M.B.E.

YOUNGHUSBAND, Jonathan, M.B.E. Censor, Durban. (M10260)

YOUNGMAN, Annie, M.B.E., *b.* 21 April, 1894. *Educ.:* Watford. Junior Administrative Assist., Ministry of Shipping. *War Work:* Canteen work at the Eagle Hut. *Address:* 84, Shaftesbury Road, Crouch Hill, London, N. (M2691)

YOUNGMAN, Walter, M.B.E.

YOUNGSON, Alexander, M.B.E., R.N.R.

YOURDI, Lieut.-Col. John Robert, O.B.E., B.A., M.B., B.Ch., R.A.M.C., *b.* 6 Feb. 1855; *s.* of Nicholas George Yourdi, of Queenstown, Co. Cork; *m.* Hilda Margaret, *d.* of J. H. Rive, of Southview, St. Saviour's, Jersey, C.I. *Educ.:* Trinity Coll., Dublin. Served in the Egyptian Campaign, 1882, Medal and Khedive Star; officiating Principal Medical Officer, 9th (Secunderabad) Division, India, 1906; Senior Medical

Officer, Jersey District, 1907–10. *War Work :* Re-employed at outbreak of the war ; served as S.M.O. Jersey District, Nov. 1914, to April, 1919 ; President of Recruiting Medical Board under the Jersey Military Service Act ; mentioned for valuable service rendered in connection with the war, 1917. *Address :* Spring Bank, St. Heliers, Jersey. *Club :* Victoria (Jersey).   (O7897)

YOXALL, George, O.B.E.

YUILL, Lieut. Alexander Claude Roy, O.B.E., R.N.V.R.

YULE, Capt. Charles Bernard Besly, O.B.E., R.A.

YULE, George Udny, C.B.E., *b.* 1871 ; *s.* of the late Sir George Udny Yule, K.C.S.I., C.B. *Educ.:* Winchester, and Univ. Coll. London. Hon. M.A. Camb. 1913 ; appointed Univ. Lecturer in Statistics, Cambridge, 1912 ; Head of Statistics and Information Branch (later Director of Requirements), Ministry of Food, 1917 ; employed in Army Contracts Depart. 1915–16. *Address :* St. John's College, Cambridge. *Club :* Savile.   (C349)

YULE, Capt. Jack Seymour, O.B.E., *b.* 29 Sept. 1889 ; *s.* of George Udny Yule, of Calcutta. *Educ.:* Repton, R.M.A., Woolwich. Royal Engineers, employed as Staff Officer ; Chief Signal Officer (British Forces on the Rhine). *Club :* Junior United Service.   (O8611)

YULE, Capt. John Stirling, M.B.E., R.F.A. (T.).

ZAHAROFF, Sir Basil, G.C.B., G.B.E., *b.* 1850. *Educ.:* London and Paris. Doctor of Laws, Paris ; Banker. *War Work :* Founded Professorships of Aviation at Universities of Paris, Petrograd, and London ; also Marshal Foch Professorship of French Literature at Oxford University ; Field Marshal Haig Professorship of English Literature at Paris University ; has Grand Cross of Legion of Honour. *Addresses :* 53, Avenue Hoche, Paris ; Chateau de Balincourt, Seine-et-Oise, France. *Club :* Marlborough.

ZANZIBAR, Rt. Rev. Frank Weston, Bishop of, O.B.E., M.A., D.D., *b.* 1871 ; 4th *s.* of R. W. G. Weston. Chaplain of St. Andrew's Coll. Zanzibar, 1898–99 ; Warden, St. Mark's Theological Coll. Zanzibar, 1899—1901 ; Principal, St. Andrew's Training Coll. Kiungani, Zanzibar, 1901–8 ; Chancellor of Zanzibar Cathedral, 1904–8 ; Hon. Maj. Zanz. Carrier Corps, 1916 (mentioned in despatches, 1917).   (O2235)

ZOBEL, Elizabeth, Mrs., M.B.E.

THE MOST EXCELLENT ORDER OF THE BRITISH EMPIRE.

SOVEREIGN OF THE ORDER,

H.M. THE KING.

GRAND MASTER AND FIRST OR PRINCIPAL KNIGHT GRAND CROSS,
H.R.H. THE PRINCE OF WALES, K.G., 4 JUNE 1917.

KNIGHTS GRAND CROSS.

(G.B.E.)

(M.) signifies Military Division.

1 Connaught, Field-Marshal H.R.H. The Duke of, 4 June, 1917.
2 Gladstone, Viscount, 4 June, 1917.
3 Emmott, Lord, 4 June, 1917.
4 Moulton, Lord, 4 June, 1917.
5 Sydenham, Lord, 4 June, 1917.
6 Strathclyde, Lord, 4 June, 1917.
8 Stanley, Hon. Sir Arthur, 4 June, 1917.
9 Geddes, Rt. Hon. Sir Eric Campbell, 4 June, 1917.
10 Pearson, Sir (Cyril) Arthur, Bart., 4 June, 1917.
11 Sankey, Sir John, 4 June, 1917.
12 Younger, Sir Robert, 4 June, 1917.
14 Chelmsford, Lord, 4 Dec. 1917.
15 Willington, Lord, 4 Dec. 1917.
16 Hyderabad, H.H. Nizam-ul-Daula Nawab Mir Sir Usman Ali Khan Bahadur, Fatch Yang of, 4 Dec. 1917.
17 Mysore, H.H. Maharaja Sri Sir Krishnaraja Wadiyar Bahadur of, 4 Dec. 1917.
18 Scindhia of Gwalior, H.H. Maharaja Sir MadhoRao Bahadur, 4 Dec. 1917.
19 Jammu and Kashmir, H.H. Maharaja Sir Pratap Singh Bahadur of, G.C.S.I., G.C.I.E., 1 Jan. 1918.;
20 Jaipur, H.H. Maharajadhiraja Sir Sawai Madho Singh Bahadur of, G.C.S.I., G.C.I.E., G.C.V.O., 1 Jan. 1918.
21 Kotah, H.H. Maharao Sir Umed Singh Bahadur of, G.C.S.I., G.C.I.E., 1 Jan. 1918.
22 Patiala, H.H. Maharajadhiraja Sri Sir Bhupindar Singh Mahindar Bahadur, of, G.C.I.E., 1 Jan. 1918.
23 Dunlop, Sir Thomas, Bart., 1 Jan. 1918.
24 Ellis, Sir William Henry, 1 Jan., 1918.
25 Garton, Sir Richard Charles, 1 Jan. 1918.
26 Harrel, Rt. Hon. Sir David, 1 Jan. 1918.
27 Hudson, Sir Robert Arundell, 1 Jan. 1918.
28 Lee of Fareham, Lord, 1 Jan. 1918.
29 Plender, Sir William, 1 Jan. 1918.
30 Wingate, Sir Francis Reginald, 1 Jan. 1918.

31 Brooks, Sir Arthur David, 3 June, 1918.
32 Garstin, Sir William Edmund, 3 June, 1918.
33 Gordon, Sir Charles Blair, 3 June, 1918.
34 Plymouth, Earl of, 3 June, 1918.
35 Strong, Rt. Reverend Sir Thomas Banks, 3 June, 1918.
37 Liverpool, Earl of, 3 June, 1918.
38 Miles, Sir Herbert Scott Gould, 3 June, 1918.
39 Sclater, Sir Henry Crichton, 1 Jan. 1919. (M.)
40 Durnford, Sir Walter, 1 Jan. 1919.
41 Ellis, Sir Charles Edward, 1 Jan. 1919.
42 Peel, Viscount, 1 Jan. 1919.
43 Raglan, Lord, 1 Jan. 1919.
44 Ward, Sir Edward Willis Duncan, Bart. 1 Jan. 1919.
45 Nawanagar, H.H. Jam of, 3 June, 1919. (M.)
46 Sykes, Sir Frederick Hugh, 26 Aug. 1919.
48 Chilston, Viscount, 1 Jan. 1920.
49 Gibb, Sir Alexander, 1 Jan. 1920.
51 Harris, Sir Charles, 1 Jan. 1920.
52 Highmore, Sir Nathaniel Joseph, 1 Jan. 1920.
53 Horne, Rt. Hon. Sir Robert Stevenson, 1 Jan., 1920.
54 Kindersley, Sir Robert Molesworth, 1 Jan. 1920.
55 Livesey, Sir Harry, 1 Jan. 1920.
56 Meath, Earl of. 1 Jan. 1920.
57 Munro, Sir Thomas, 1 Jan. 1920.
58 Denison-Pender, Sir John, 1 Jan. 1920.
59 Ridsdale Sir Edward Aurelian, 1 Jan. 1920.
60 Shipley, Sir Arthur Everett, 1 Jan. 1920.
61 Smith, Sir Henry Babington, 1 Jan. 1920.
62 Bates, Sir Percy Elly, Bart., 5 June, 1920.
63 MacLeod, Sir John Larne, 5 June, 1920.
64 Robinson, Sir Thomas Bilbe, 5 June, 1920.
65 Samuel, Rt. Hon. Sir Herbert Louis, 11 June 1920.
66 Cox, Sir Edward Owen, 15 Oct. 1920.
67 Haking, Sir Richard Cyril Byrne, 1 Jan. 1921 (M.)
68 Bikaner, H.H. The Maharaja of, 1 Jan. 1921. (M.)
69 Scarborough, Earl of, 12 Feb. 1921. (M.)

DAMES GRAND CROSS.

(G.B.E.)

H.M. THE QUEEN, 24 Aug. 1917.
H.M. QUEEN ALEXANDRA, 1 Jan. 1918.

1 Lawley, Annie Allen, Hon. Lady, 4 June, 1917.
2 Paget, Louisa Margaret Leila Weymss, Lady, 4 June, 1917.
3 Reid, Flora, Lady, 4 June, 1917.
4 Furse, Dame Katharine, 4 June, 1917.
5 Chelmsford, Francis Charlotte, Lady, 4 Dec. 1917.
6 Bhopal, H.H. Nawab Sultan Jahan Begum of, 1 Jan. 1918.
7 Ampthill, Margaret, Lady, C.I., 1 Jan. 1918.
9 Dawson, Aimée Evelyn, Lady, 1 Jan. 1918.
10 Montrose, Violet Hermione, Duchess of, 1 Jan. 1918.
11 Northcliffe, Mary Elizabeth, Viscountess, 1 Jan. 1918.
12 Liverpool, Annette Louise, Countess of, 1 Jan. 1918.
13 Christian, H.R.H. Princess, 3 June, 1918.
14 Argyll, H.R.H. Princess Louise, Duchess of, 3 June, 1918.
15 Helena Victoria, H.H. Princess. C.I., 3 June, 1918.
16 Becher, Dame Ethel Hope, 3 June, 1918. (M.)
17 Harcourt, Mary Ethel, Viscountess, 3 June, 1918.

19 Winchester, Charlotte Josephine, Marchioness of, 3 June, 1918.
20 McCarthy, Dame Emma Maud, 3 June, 1918. (M.)
21 Novar, Helen Hermione, Viscountess, 3 June, 1918.
22 Browne, Dame Sidney Jane, 1 Jan. 1919. (M.)
23 Beatrice, H.R.H. Princess, 1 Jan. 1919.
24 Marie Louise, H.H. Princess, 1 Jan. 1919.
26 Buxton, Mildred, Viscountess, 1 Jan. 1919.
27 Swift, Dame Sarah Ann, 1 Jan. 1919.
28 Waterford, Beatrix Frances, Marchioness of, 1 Jan. 1919.
29 Airlie, Mabell Frances Elizabeth, Countess of, 1 Jan. 1920.
30 Lansdowne, Maud Evelyn, Marchioness of, 1 Jan. 1920.
31 Reading, Alice Edith, Countess of, 1 Jan. 1920.
32 de Saumarez, Annie, Lady, 1 Jan. 1920.
33 George, Dame Margaret Lloyd, 16 Aug. 1920.

KNIGHTS COMMANDERS.
(K.B.E.)

1 Fellowes, Rt. Hon. Sir Ailwyn Edward, 4 June, 1917.
2 Maclean, Rt. Hon. Sir Donald, 4 June, 1917.
3 Goschen, Hon. Sir William Henry, 4 June, 1917.
9 Raven, Sir Vincent Litchfield, 4 June, 1917.
10 Anderson, Sir Alan Garrett, 4 June, 1917.
11 Austin, Sir Herbert, 4 June, 1917.
12 Bledisloe, Lord, 4 June, 1917.
13 Bell, Sir Thomas, 4 June, 1917.
14 Carter, Sir George John, 4 June. 1917,
15 Clerk, Sir Dugald, 4 June, 1917.
16 Cleland, Sir Charles John. 4 June, 1917.
17 Cullen of Ashbourne, Brien Ibrican, Lord, 4 June, 1917.
18 Collingwood, Sir William, 4 June, 1917.
19 Fielding, Sir Charles William, 4 June, 1917.
20 Findlay, Sir John Ritchie, 4 June, 1917.
22 Harris, Sir Henry Percy, 4 June, 1917.
23 Herbert, Sir Alfred Edward, 4 June, 1917.
24 Hunter, Sir John, 4 June, 1917.
25 Irvin, Sir John Hannell, 4 June, 1917.
26 Jackson, Sir Cyril, 4 June, 1917.
27 Jackson, Sir Herbert Samuel, 4 June, 1917.
29 Llewelyn, Sir Leonard Wilkinson, 4 June, 1917.
30 Macassey, Sir Lynden, 4 June, 1917.
31 Morgan, Sir Herbert Edward, 4 June, 1917.
32 Partridge, Sir Cecil, 4 June, 1917.
33 Pollock Sir Ernest Murray, 4 June 1917
34 Robinson, Sir Thomas, 4 June, 1919.
35 Roberts, Sir Arthur Cornelius, 4 June, 1917.
36 Robbins, Sir Edmund, 4 June, 1917.
37 Samuel, Sir John Smith, 4 June, 1917.
38 Stewart, Sir Edward, 4 June, 1917.
39 Stokes, Sir Frederick Wilfred Scott, 4 June, 1917.
40 Threlfall, Sir Richard, 4 June, 1917.
41 Wallace, Sir Johnstone, 4 June, 1917.
42 Walton, Sir William, 4 June, 1917. (M.)
43 Yapp, Sir Arthur Keysall, 4 June, 1917.
44 Dhar, H.H. Raja Sir Udaji Rao Puar of, 4 Dec. 1917.
45 Hewett, Sir John Prescott, 4 Dec. 1917.
46 Cleveland, Sir Charles Raitt, 4 Dec. 1917.
48 Aglen, Sir Francis Arthur, 1 Jan. 1918.
49 Baillie, Sir Frank, 1 Jan. 1918.
50 Barlow, Sir Clement Anderson Montague, 1 Jan. 1918.
51 Beale, Sir John Field, 1 Jan, 1918.
52 Beatson, Sir George Thomas, 1 Jan. 1918.
53 Becker, Sir Walter, 1 Jan. 1918.
54 Caird, Sir Andrew, 1 Jan. 1918.
55 Cantlie, Sir James, 1 Jan. 1918.
56 Close, Sir Charles Frederick, 1 Jan. 1918.
57 Davies, Sir Alfred Thomas, 1 Jan. 1918.
58 Davies, Sir Joseph, 1 Jan. 1918.
59 Davison, Sir William Henry, 1 Jan. 1918.
60 Dennis, Sir Alfred Hull, 1 Jan. 1918.
61 Dickinson, Rt. Hon. Sir Willoughby Hyett, 1 Jan. 1918.
62 Don, Sir William, 1 Jan. 1918.
63 Dorman, Sir Arthur John, 1 Jan. 1918.
64 Elliott, Sir Bignell George, 1 Jan. 1918.
65 Eve, Sir Herbert Trustram, 1 Jan. 1918.
66 Fletcher, Sir Walter Morley, 1 Jan. 1918.
67 Forwood, Sir William Bower, 1 Jan. 1918.
68 Fowler, Sir Henry, 1 Jan. 1918. (M.)
69 Galloway, Sir James, 1 Jan. 1918. (M.)
71 Goadby, Sir Kenneth Weldon, 1 Jan. 1918.
72 Goldfinch, Sir Arthur Horne, 1 Jan. 1918.
73 Goode, Sir William Athelstane Meredith, 1 Jan. 1918.
74 Gracie, Sir Alexander, 1 Jan. 1918.
75 Grey-Wilson, Sir William, 1 Jan. 1918.
76 Guthrie, Sir Connop, 1 Jan. 1918.
77 Hall, Sir Frederick, 1 Jan. 1918.
78 Harris, Sir Arthur Ambrose Hall, 1 Jan. 1918.
79 Henderson, Sir Frederick Ness, 1 Jan. 1918.
80 Henriques, Sir Philip Gutterez, 1 Jan. 1918.
81 Hiley, Sir Ernest Varvill, 1 Jan. 1918.
82 Holbrook, Sir Arthur Richard, 1 Jan. 1918.
84 Hunter, Sir George Burton, 1 Jan. 1918.
85 Jackson, Sir Louis Charles, 1 Jan. 1918. (M.)
86 Jarmay, Sir John Gustave, 1 Jan. 1918.
87 Jones, Sir Edgar Rees, 1 Jan. 1918.
88 Jones, Sir Robert, 1 Jan. 1918.
89 Kenderdine, Sir Charles Halestaff, 1 Jan. 1918.
91 Lloyd, Sir John Hall Seymour, 1 Jan. 1918. (M.)
92 Mann, Sir John, 1 Jan. 1918.

93 Marshall, Sir Arthur Harold, 1 Jan. 1918.
94 May, Sir George Ernest, 1 Jan. 1918.
95 McClelland, Sir Peter Hannay, 1 Jan. 1918.
96 McKechnie, Sir James, 1 Jan. 1918.
97 Ogilvie, Sir Andrew Muter John, 1 Jan. 1918.
98 Penson, Sir Thomas Henry, 1 Jan. 1918.
99 Penton, Sir Edward, 1 Jan. 1918.
100 Preston, Sir Frederick George Panizzi, 1 Jan. 1918.
102 Robertson, Sir Robert, 1 Jan. 1918.
103 Rowell, Sir Herbert Babington, 1 Jan. 1918.
104 Smith, Sir Harry, 1 Jan. 1918.
105 Stewart, Sir Charles John, 1 Jan. 1918.
106 Storey, Sir Thomas James, 1 Jan. 1918.
107 Stothert, Sir Percy Kendall, 1 Jan. 1918.
109 Stuart, Sir Campbell, 1 Jan. 1918.
110 Sykes, Sir Charles, 1 Jan. 1918.
112 Thomson, Sir William Rowan, 1 Jan. 1918.
113 Warner, Sir Frank, 1 Jan. 1918.
114 Welby, Sir Alfred Cholmeley Earle, 1 Jan. 1918.
115 Stack, Sir Lee Oliver FitzMaurice, 1 Jan. 1918.
116 Barrett, Sir James William, 1 Jan. 1918.
117 Clarkson, Sir William, 1 Jan. 1918.
119 Steward, Sir George, 1 Jan. 1918.
121 McGrath, Sir Patrick Thomas, 1 Jan. 1918.
122 Caruana, Most Rev. Maurice, Bishop of Malta, 1 Jan. 1918.
123 im Thurn, Sir Everard Ferdinand, 1 Jan. 1918.
124 Manning, Sir William Henry, 1 Jan. 1918.
125 Wallace, Sir Laurence Aubrey, 1 Jan. 1918.
126 Young, Sir Arthur Henderson, 1 Jan. 1918.
127 Bourne, Sir Henry Roland Murray, 24 May, 1918.
128 Goold-Adams, Sir Henry Edward Fane, 3 June, 1918. (M.)
129 Archer, Sir John, 3 June, 1918.
130 Readett-Bayley, Sir Henry Dennis, 3 June, 1918.
131 Benn, Sir Arthur Shirley, 3 June, 1918.
132 Brittain, Sir Harry, 3 June, 1918.
133 Byrne, Sir Joseph Aloysius, 3 June, 1918.
134 Caine, Sir Hall, 3 June. 1918.
135 Chambers, Sir Theodore Gervase, 3 June, 1918.
136 Cobb, Sir Cyril Stephen, 3 June, 1918.
137 Connell, Sir Robert Lowden, 3 June, 1918.
138 Cooke, Sir Edward Marriott, 3 June, 1918.
139 Darwin, Sir Horace, June 3, 1918.
140 Duthie, Sir John, 3 June, 1918.
141 Esplen, Sir John, 3 June, 1918.
142 Ferguson, Sir John, 3 June, 1918.
143 Garnsey, Sir Gilbert Francis, 3 June, 1918.
144 Hadcock, Sir Albert George, 3 June, 1918.
145 Harrison, Sir Cecil Reeves, 3 June, 1918.
146 Henn, Sir Sydney Herbert Holcroft, 3 June, 1918.
147 Holmden, Sir Osborn George, 3 June, 1918.
148 Houston, Sir Alexander Cruikshank, 3 June, 1918.
149 Japp, Sir Henry, 3 June, 1918.
150 Kinnear, Sir Walter Samuel, 3 June, 1918.
151 Levick, Sir Hugh Gwynne, 3 June, 1918.
153 Lowrey, Sir Joseph, 3 June, 1918.
154 Lumsden, Sir John, 3 June, 1918.
155 McGowan, Sir Harry Duncan, 3 June, 1918.
156 Mackenzie, Sir William Warrender, 3 June, 1918.
157 Mendl, Sir Sigismund Ferdinand, 3 June, 1918.
158 Middleton, Sir Thomas Hudson, 3 June, 1918.
159 Nathan, Sir Frederic Lewis, 3 June, 1918.
160 Nimmo, Sir Adam, 3 June, 1918.
161 Orpen, Sir William Newenham Montague, 3 June, 1918.
162 Peirse, Sir Richard Henry, 3 June, 1918. (M.)
163 Perry, Sir Percival Lea Dewhurst, 3 June, 1918.
164 Peters, Sir Lindley Byron, 3 June, 1918.
166 Sinclair, Sir Walrond Arthur Frank, 3 June, 1918. (M.)
167 Smith, Sir Allan MacGregor, 3 June, 1918.
168 Spencer, Sir Thomas Harris, 3 June, 1918.
169 Spicer, Sir Howard Handsly, 3 June, 1918.
170 Stern, Sir Albert, 3 June, 1918.
171 Stewart, Sir Robert King, 3 June, 1918.
172 Fox-Symons, Sir Robert, 3 June, 1918.
173 Taggart, Sir James, 3 June, 1918.
174 Taylor, Sir William Francis Kyffin, 3 June, 1918.
175 Thomson, Sir Courtauld, 3 June, 1918.
176 Mitchell-Thomson, Sir William, Bart., 3 June, 1918.
177 Thornycroft, Sir John Edward, 3 June, 1918.
178 Tritton, Sir Seymour Biscoe, 3 June, 1918.
179 Hume-Williams, Sir William Ellis, 3 June, 1918.
180 Wilson, Sir Thomas Fleming, 3 June, 1918.

181 Bhagwati Prasad Singh, Maharaja Bahadur Sir, 3 June, 1918.
182 Young, Sir Frank Popham, 3 June, 1918.
183 Darbhanga, Maharaja Sir Rameshwar Singh Bahadur of, 3 June, 1918.
184 Pirajirao, Sir Bapu Sahib Ghatge, 3 June, 1918.
185 Harvey, Sir George Samuel Abercrombie, 3 June, 1918.
186 French, Sir John Russell, 3 June, 1918.
187 Wallers, Sir Evelyn Ashley, 3 June, 1918.
188 Cashin, Hon. Sir Michael Patrick, 3 June, 1918.
189 Adams, Sir Arthur Robert, 3 June, 1918.
190 Duff, Sir Hector Livingstone, 3 June, 1919.
191 Price, Sir Rhys Howell, 19 Dec, 1918. (M.)
192 Wright, Sir Almroth Edward, 1 Jan. 1919. (M.)
193 Friend, Rt. Hon. Sir Lovick Barnsby, 1 Jan. 1919. (M.)
194 Hickson, Sir Samuel, 1 Jan. 1919. (M.)
195 Thornton, Sir Henry Worth, 1 Jan. 1919. (M.)
196 Brown, Sir George McLaren, 1 Jan. 1919. (M.)
197 Thomas, Sir John Lynn, 1 Jan. 1919. (M.)
198 Bruce-Porter, Sir Harry Edwin Bruce, 1 Jan. 1919. (M.)
199 Ommanney, Sir Robert Nelson, 1 Jan. 1919. (M.)
200 Inglefield, Sir Edward Fitzmaurice, 1 Jan. 1919. (M.)
201 Pears, Sir Edmund Radcliffe, 1 Jan. 1919. (M.)
202 Boys, Sir Francis Theodore, 1 Jan. 1919.
203 Budd, Sir Cecil Lindsay, 1 Jan. 1919.
204 Burnett, Sir Edward Napier, 1 Jan. 1919.
205 Butler, Sir Geoffrey, 1 Jan. 1919.
206 Carmichael, Sir James, 1 Jan. 1919.
207 Clement, Sir Thomas, 1 Jan. 1919.
208 Kinloch-Cooke, Sir Clement, 1 Jan. 1919.
209 Tudor-Craig, Sir Algernon, 1 Jan. 1919.
210 Curtis, Sir Richard James, 1 Jan. 1919.
211 Daniels, Sir Percy, 1 Jan. 1919.
212 Eyles, Sir Alfred, 1 Jan. 1919.
213 Gibson, Sir Herbert, 1 Jan. 1919.
214 Green, Sir Frederick, 1 Jan. 1919.
215 Haggard, Sir Henry Rider, 1 Jan. 1919.
216 Halsey, Sir Laurence Edward, 1 Jan. 1919.
217 Jones, Sir William John, 1 Jan. 1919.
218 Lees, Sir John McKie, 1 Jan. 1919.
219 Leslie, Sir Norman Alexander, 1 Jan. 1919.
220 Mackenzie, Sir Alexander, 1 Jan. 1919.
221 McLaughlin, Sir Henry, 1 Jan. 1919.
222 Mansell, Sir John Herbert, 1 Jan. 1919.
223 Mansell, Sir John Herbert, 1 Jan. 1919.
224 Maxwell, Sir William, 1 Jan. 1919.
225 Newton, Sir George Douglas Cochrane, 1 Jan. 1919.
226 Pares, Sir Bernard, 1 Jan. 1919.
227 Pedder, Sir John, 1 Jan. 1919.
228 Piggott, Sir George Bettesworth, 1 Jan. 1919.
229 Polson, Sir Thomas Andrew, 1 Jan. 1919.
230 Pope, Sir William Jackson, 1 Jan. 1919.
231 Reid, Sir George Archdall O'Brien, 1 Jan. 1919.
232 Rhind, Sir Thomas Duncan, 1 Jan. 1919. (M.)
233 Sparks, Sir Ashley, 1 Jan. 1919.
234 Standing, Sir Guy, 1 Jan. 1919.
235 Strahan, Sir Aubrey, 1 Jan. 1919.
236 Thom, Sir William, 1 Jan. 1919.
237 Warrack, Sir James Howard, 1 Jan. 1919.
238 Waterlow, Sir William Alfred, 1 Jan. 1919.
239 Whinney, Sir Arthur Francis, 1 Jan. 1919.
240 White, Sir William Hale, 1 Jan. 1919.
241 Willert, Sir Arthur, 1 Jan. 1919.
242 Wimble, Sir John Bowring, 1 Jan. 1919.
243 Woods, Sir James Williams, 1 Jan. 1919.
244 Wormald, Sir John, 1 Jan. 1919.
245 Wyon, Sir Albert William, 1 Jan. 1919.
246 Dennys, Sir Hector Travers, 1 Jan. 1919.
247 Reed, Sir Stanley, 1 Jan. 1919.
248 Richards, Sir Henry George, 1 Jan. 1919.
249 Thomson, Sir James Wishart, 1 Jan. 1919.
250 Bernard, Sir Edgar Edwin, 1 Jan. 1919.
251 Stavert, Sir William Ewen, 1 Jan. 1919.
252 Hambro, Sir Eric, 1 Jan. 1919.
253 Collins, Sir Godfrey Pattison, 1 Jan. 1919. (M.)
254 Headlam, Sir John Emerson Wharton, 1 Jan. 1919. (M.)
255 Creswell, Sir William Rooke, 1 April, 1919. (M.)
256 Turner, Sir George Robertson, 1 April, 1919. (M.)
257 Vaughan-Lee, Sir Charles Lionel, 3 June, 1919. (M.)
258 Pryn, Sir William Wenmoth, 3 June, 1919. (M.)
259 Handyside, Sir Patrick Brodie, 3 June, 1919. (M.)
260 Cust, Sir Herbert Edward Purey-, 3 June, 1919. (M.)
261 McNabb, Sir Daniel Joseph Patrick, 3 June, 1919. (M.)
262 Nance, Sir Arthur Stanley, 3 June, 1919. (M.)
263 Alton, Sir Francis Cooke, 3 June, 1919. (M.)
264 Khan, Nawab Sir Bahram, 3 June, 1919.
265 Singh, Raja Sir Daljit, 3 June, 1919.
266 Sitole, Sardar Sir Appaji Rao, 3 June, 1919.
267 Murray, Sir Valentine, 3 June, 1919. (M.)
268 Ballance, Sir Hamilton Ashley, 3 June, 1919. (M.)
269 Firth, Sir Robert Hammill, 3 June, 1919. (M.)
270 Money, Sir Arthur Wigram, 3 June, 1919. (M.)
271 Jackson, Sir Robert Whyte Melville, 3 June, 1919. (M.)
272 Watson, Sir Harry Davis, 3 June, 1919. (M.)
273 Bowman-Manifold, Sir Michael Graham Egerton, 3 June, 1919. (M.)
274 Clayton, Sir Gilbert Falkingham, 3 June, 1919. (M.)
275 Gordon-Watson, Sir Charles Gordon, 3 June, 1919. (M.)
276 Long, Sir Arthur, 3 June, 1919. (M.)
277 White-Thomson, Sir Hugh Davie, 3 June, 1919. (M.)

278 Forbes, Sir Arthur William, 3 June, 1919. (M.)
280 Seymour, Sir Edward Hamilton, 3 June, 1919. (M.)
281 Dick, Sir Arthur Robert, 3 June, 1919. (M.)
282 Ridout, Sir Dudley Howard, 3 June, 1919. (M.)
283 Sackville-West, Hon. Sir Charles John, 3 June, 1919. (M.)
284 Poole, Sir Frederick Cuthbert, 3 June, 1919. (M.)
285 Stanistreet, Sir George Bradshaw, 3 June, 1919. (M.)
286 Davy, Sir Henry, 3 June, 1919. (M.)
287 Woodhead, Sir German Sims, 3 June, 1919. (M.)
288 Murphy, Sir Shirley Forster, 3 June, 1919. (M.)
289 Power, Sir D'Arcy, 3 June, 1919. (M.)
290 Wood, Sir James Leigh, 3 June, 1919. (M.)
291 Gray, Sir Henry McIlree Williamson, 3 June, 1919. (M.)
292 Mayo-Robson, Sir Arthur William, 3 June, 1919. (M.)
293 Symonds, Sir Charters James, 3 June, 1919. (M.)
294 Mott, Sir Frederick Walker, 3 June, 1919. (M.)
295 Jones, Sir Robert, 3 June, 1919. (M.)
296 Reid, Sir Archibald Douglas, 3 June, 1919. (M.)
297 Belfield, Sir Herbert Eversley, 3 June, 1919. (M.)
298 Bond, Sir Francis George, 3 June, 1919. (M.)
299 Bewicke-Copley, Sir Robert Calverley Alington, 3 June, 1919. (M.)
301 Pain, Sir George William Hacket, 3 June, 1919. (M.)
302 Raban, Sir Edward, 3 June, 1919. (M.)
303 Balfour, Sir Alfred Granville, 3 June, 1919. (M.)
304 Morgan, Sir Hill Godfrey, 3 June, 1919. (M.)
305 Browne, Lord Arthur Howe, 3 June, 1919. (M.)
306 Kell, Sir Vernon George Waldegrave, 3 June, 1919. (M.)
307 Edis, Sir Robert William, 3 June, 1919. (M.)
308 MacKenzie, Sir Robert Campbell, 3 June, 1919. (M.)
309 Bedford, Herbrand Arthur, Duke of, 3 June, 1919. (M.)
310 Ryan, Sir Charles Snodgrass, 3 June, 1919. (M.)
311 McCay, Hon. Sir James Whiteside, 3 June, 1919. (M.)
312 Crosbie, Sir John Chalker, 3 June, 1919.
313 Cotts, Sir William Dingwall Mitchell, 3 June, 1919.
314 Fowle, Sir Henry Walter Hamilton, 3 June, 1919.
315 Hands, Sir Harry, 3 June, 1919.
316 Stanford, Hon. Sir Walter Ernest Mortimer, 3 June, 1919.
317 Bowring, Sir Charles Calvert, 3 June, 1919.
318 Fuller, Sir Francis Charles Bernard Dudley, 3 June, 1919.
319 Grey, Sir Raleigh, 3 June, 1919.
320 Wilson, Sir Henry Francis, 3 June, 1919.
321a Young, Sir William Douglas, 3 June, 1919.
321b Wilberforce, Sir Herbert William, 3 June, 1919. (M.)
321c Macauley, Sir George Bohun, 3 June, 1919. (M.)
321d Mackenzie-Kennedy, Sir Edward Charles William, 3 June, 1919. (M.)
321e Ross, Sir Walter Charteris, 3 June, 1919. (M.)
321f Hedley, Sir Walter Coote, 3 June, 1919. (M.)
321g Heron, Sir Thomas, 3 June, 1919. (M.)
321h Stiles, Sir Harold Jalland, 3 June, 1919. (M.)
322a Thorburn, Sir William, 3 June, 1919. (M.)
322b Yarde-Buller, Hon. Sir Henry, 3 June, 1919. (M.)
322c Thornton, Sir Edward Newbury, 3 June, 1919. (M.)
323 Brown, Sir Arthur Whitten, 27 June, 1919.
324 Rowlatt, Sir Frederick Terry, 5 Dec. 1919.
325 Jackson, Sir Herbert William, 5 Dec. 1919.
326 Smith, Sir Ross Macpherson, 26 Dec. 1919.
327 Smith, Sir Keith Macpherson, 26 Dec. 1919.
328 Couchman, Sir Francis Dundas, 30 Dec. 1919.
329 Hart, Sir George Sanky, 30 Dec. 1919.
330 Kaul, Sir Diwan Bahadur Dayer Kishan, 30 Dec. 1919.]
331 McRobert, Sir Alexander, 30 Dec. 1919.
332 Stileman, Sir Harry Hampson, 1 Jan. 1920. (M.)
333 Ellis, Sir Edward Henry Fitzhardinge Heaton-, 1 Jan. 1920. (M.)
334 Hatch, Sir Ernest Frederick George, Bart., 1 Jan. 1920.
335 Rhodes, Sir Robert Heaton, 1 Jan. 1920.
336 Brooke, Sir Harry Vesey, 1 Jan. 1920.
337 Abell, Sir Westcott Stile, 1 Jan. 1920.
338 Abrahamson, Sir Martin Arnold, 1 Jan. 1920.
339 Agnew, Sir Patrick Dalreagle, 1 Jan. 1920.
340 Alexander, Sir William, 1 Jan. 1920.
341 Ashdown, Sir George Henry, 1 Jan. 1920.
342 Badock, Sir Henry Walter, 1 Jan. 1920.
343 Baker, Sir Thomas, 1 Jan. 1920.
344 Balfour, Sir Isaac Bayley, 1 Jan. 1920.
345 Baynham, Sir Walter de Mouchet, 1 Jan. 1920.
346 Barraclough, Sir Samuel Henry Egerton, 1 Jan. 1920.
347 Beattie, Sir James, 1 Jan. 1920.
348 Beeton, Sir Mayson Moss, 1 Jan. 1920.
349 Berridge, Sir Thomas Henry Devereux, 1 Jan. 1920.
350 Berry, Sir Walter Wheeler, 1 Jan. 1920.
351 Blake, Sir Arthur Ernest, 1 Jan. 1920.
352 Bragg, Sir William Henry, 1 Jan. 1920.
354 Brown, Sir Herbert, 1 Jan. 1920.
355 Burn, Sir Joseph, 1 Jan. 1920.
356 Butler, Sir Cyril Kendall, 1 Jan. 1920.
357 Campbell, Sir Gordon Huntly, 1 Jan. 1920.
358 Chance, Sir Frederick William, 1 Jan. 1920.
359 Charles, Sir James Thomas Walter, 1 Jan. 1920.
360 Chave, Sir Benjamin, 1 Jan. 1920.
361 Cohen, Sir Robert Waley, 1 Jan. 1920.
362 Colefax, Sir Henry Arthur, 1 Jan. 1920.
363 Currie, Sir James, 1 Jan. 1920.
364 Demetriadi, Sir Stephen, 1 Jan. 1920.
365 Dennis, Sir Raymond Herbert, 1 Jan. 1920.
366 Devonshire, Sir James Lyne, 1 Jan. 1920.
367 Dewrance, Sir John, 1 Jan. 1920.

368 Diamond, Sir William Henry, 1 Jan. 1920.
369 Down, Sir Charles Edward, 1 Jan. 1920.
370 Elphinstone, Sir George Keith Buller, 1 Jan. 1920.
371 Fisher, Sir Thomas, 1 Jan. 1920.
372 Fitch, Sir Cecil Edwin, 1 Jan. 1920.
373 Freeman, Sir Philip Horace, 1 Jan. 1920.
374 German, Sir James, 1 Jan. 1920.
375 Gibbons, Sir Walter, 1 Jan. 1920.
376 Gibbs, Sir Philip Hamilton, 1 Jan. 1920.
377 Goschen, Sir William Henry Neville, 1 Jan. 1920.
378 Lloyd-Greame, Sir Philip, 1 Jan. 1920.
379 Gridley, Sir Arnold Babb, 1 Jan. 1920.
380 Harmer, Sir Sidney Frederic, 1 Jan. 1920.
381 Harris, Sir Austin Edward, 1 Jan. 1920.
382 Harvey, Sir Ernest Maes, 1 Jan. 1920.
383 Hearn, Sir Walter Risley, 1 Jan. 1920.
384 Hertslet, Sir Cecil, 1 Jan. 1920.
385 Hodsdon, Sir James William Beeman, 1 Jan. 1920.
386 Hutchings, Sir Alan, 1 Jan. 1920.
387 Johnston, Sir George Lawson, 1 Jan. 1920
388 Jones, Sir Bertram Hyde, 1 Jan. 1920.
389 Knudsen, Sir Karl Fredrik, 1 Jan. 1920.
390 Legg, Sir George Edward Wickham, 1 Jan. 1920.
391 Lobnitz, Sir Frederick, 1 Jan. 1920.
392 Lucan, Earl of, 1 Jan. 1920.
393 Macardle, Sir Thomas Callan, 1 Jan. 1920.
394 Macleod, Sir Frederick Larkins, 1 Jan. 1920.
395 Macnaghten, Hon. Sir Malcolm Martin, 1 Jan. 1920.
396 Macneal, Sir Hector Murray, 1 Jan. 1920.
397 Mansfield, Sir Alfred, 1 Jan. 1920.
398 Mayhew, Sir Basil Edgar, 1 Jan. 1920.
399 Metcalfe, Sir George, 1 Jan. 1920.
400 Mooney, Sir John Joseph, 1 Jan. 1920.
401 Murray, Sir George, 1 Jan. 1920.
402 Nicol, Sir Thomas Drysdale, 1 Jan. 1920.
403 Notley, Sir Franke Bartlett Stuart, 1 Jan. 1920.
404 Oman, Sir Charles William Chadwick, 1 Jan. 1920.
405 O'Neill, Sir Arthur Eugene, 1 Jan. 1920.
406 Packe, Sir Edward Hussey, 1 Jan. 1920.
407 Paton, Sir Alfred Vaughan, 1 Jan. 1920.
408 Petavel, Sir Joseph Ernest, 1 Jan. 1920.
409 Petersen, Sir William, 1 Jan. 1920.
410 Phillips, Sir Percival, 1 Jan. 1920.
411 Prothero, Sir George Walter, 1 Jan. 1920.
412 Rae, Sir James Robert, 1 Jan. 1920.
413 Raeburn, Sir Ernest Manifold, 1 Jan. 1920.
414 Renwick, Sir Harry Benedetto, 1 Jan. 1920.
415 Robinson, Sir Harry Perry, 1 Jan. 1920.
416 Robson, Sir Herbert Thomas, 1 Jan. 1920.
417 Ruck, Sir Richard Matthews, 1 Jan. 1920.
418 Russell, Sir Herbert William Henry, 1 Jan. 1920.
419 Salvidge, Sir Archibald Tutton James, 1 Jan. 1920.
420 Samson, Sir Edward Marlay, 1 Jan. 1920.
421 Sanders, Sir Charles John Ough, 1 Jan. 1920.
422 Schooling, Sir William, 1 Jan. 1920.
423 Simmons, Sir William Anker, 1 Jan. 1920.
424 Singer, Sir Mortimer, 1 Jan. 1920.
425 Sladen, Sir Sampson, 1 Jan. 1920.
426 Smethurst, Sir Thomas, 1 Jan. 1920
427 Smith, Sir Malcolm, 1 Jan. 1920.
428 Snagge, Sir Harold Edward, 1 Jan. 1920.

429 Sutherland, Sir Arthur Munro, 1 Jan. 1920.
430 Swaish, Sir John, 1 Jan. 1920.
431 Tate, Sir Robert William, 1 Jan. 1920.
432 Thomas, Sir William Beach, 1 Jan. 1920.
433 Thompson, Sir Percy, 1 Jan. 1920.
434 Thurston, Sir Thomas George Owens, 1 Jan. 1920.
435 Tomasson, Sir William Hugh, 1 Jan. 1920.
436 Turner, Sir Joseph, 1 Jan. 1920.
437 Wallace, Sir David, 1 Jan. 1920.
438 Waterhouse, Sir Nicholas Edwin, 1 Jan. 1920.
439 Weaver, Sir Lawrence, 1 Jan. 1920.
440 Webb, Sir Arthur Lisle Ambrose, 1 Jan. 1920.
441 Colchester-Wemyss, Sir Maynard Francis, 1 Jan. 1920.
442 Willis, Sir Frederick James, 1 Jan. 1920.
443 Wright, Sir William Charles, 1 Jan. 1920.
443a Densham, Sir Harry Percival, 1 Jan. 1920.
443b Fraser, Sir Drummond, 1 Jan. 1920.
443c O'Conor, Sir John, 1 Jan. 1920.
443d Dukes, Sir Paul, 1 Jan. 1920.
444 Colyer, Sir James Frank, 30 Jan. 1920.
445 Ware, Sir Fabian Arthur Goulstone, 23 Feb. 1920. (M.)
446 Valadier, Sir Auguste Charles, 3 March, 1920.
446a Percy, Sir John Samuel Jocelyn, 15 March, 1920.
447 Share, Sir Hamnet Holditch, 16 April, 1920.
448 Van Ryneveld, Sir Helperus Andrias, 14 May, 1920.
449 Brand, Sir Christopher Joseph Quintin, 14 May, 1920.
450 Apsey, Sir John, 5 June, 1920.
451 Bowater, Sir Frederick William, 5 June, 1920.
452 D'Egville, Sir Howard, 5 June, 1920.
453 Elliot, Sir James Duncan, 5 June, 1920.
454 Finlay, Sir William, 5 June, 1920.
455 Grant, Sir James Dundas-, 5 June, 1920.
456 Grayson, Sir Henry Mulleneux, 5 June, 1920.
457 Harvey, Sir Ernest Musgrave, 5 June, 1920.
458 Holt, Sir Vesey George Mackenzie, 5 June, 1920.
459 Lawson, Sir Arnold, 5 June, 1920.
460 Peat, Sir William Henry, 5 June, 1920.
461 Proctor, Sir Philip Bridger, 5 June, 1920.
462 Stamp, Sir Josiah Charles, 5 June, 1920.
463 Taylor, Sir William, 5 June, 1920.
464 Walker, Sir Alexander, 5 June, 1920.
465 Williams, Sir Archer John Allen-, 5 June, 1920.
466 Hayter, Sir William Goodenough, 24 Aug. 1920.
467 Young, Sir Frederick William, 5 Oct. 1920.
468 Braddon, Hon. Sir Henry Yule, 15 Oct. 1920.
469 Brookman, Sir George, 15 Oct. 1920.
470 David, Sir Tannatt William Edgeworth, 15 Oct. 1920.
471 Gibson, Sir Robert, 15 Oct. 1920.
472 Henley, Sir Thomas, 15 Oct. 1920.
473 McBeath, Sir William George, 15 Oct. 1920.
474 Meeks, Hon. Sir Alfred William, 15 Oct. 1920.
475 Rickard, Sir Arthur, 15 Oct. 1920.
476 Smith, Sir James Joynton, 15 Oct. 1920.
477 Blankenberg, Sir Reginald Andrew, 15 Oct. 1920.
478 Browne, Hon. Sir Albert, 15 Oct. 1920.
479 Dalrymple, Sir William, 15 Oct. 1920.
480 Edwards, Sir Alfred Hamilton Mackenzie, 15 Oct. 1920.
481 Clarke, Sir Arthur Wellesley, 22 Oct. 1920.
482 Smith, Sir Thomas James, 1 Nov. 1920.
483 Cunningham, Sir George, Jan. 1921.
484 Leveson-Gower, Sir George Granville, 1 Jan. 1921.

DAMES COMMANDERS.
(D.B.E.)

1 Londonderry, Edith, Marchioness of, 4 June, 1917. (M.)
2 Dufferin and Ava, Hariot Georgina, Marchioness of, 4 June, 1917.
3 Byron, Fanny Lucy, Lady, 4 June, 1917.
4 Lyttelton, Hon. Dame Edith Sophy, 4 June, 1917.
5 Lees, Dame Sarah Anne, 4 June, 1917.
6 Pentland, Marjorie Adeline, Lady, 4 Dec. 1917.
7 Willingdon, Marie Adelaide, Lady, 4 Dec. 1917.
8 Anstruther, Hon. Dame Eva Isabella Henriette, 1 Jan. 1918.
9 Arnott, Caroline Sydney, Lady, 1 Jan. 1918.
10 Burnett, Dame Maud, 1 Jan. 1918.
11 Godman, Dame Alice Mary, 1 Jan. 1918.
12 Jekyll, Agnes Lowndes, Lady, 1 Jan. 1918.
13 Livingstone, Dame Adelaide, 1 Jan. 1918.
14 Locke-King, Dame Ethel, 1 Jan. 1918.
15 Lugard, Flora, Lady, 1 Jan. 1918.
16 Vaughan-Pryse-Rice, Dame Margaret Ker, 1 Jan. 1918.
17 Ridley, Rosamond Cornelia Gwladys, Viscountess, 1 Jan. 1918.
18 Sclater, Edith Harriet, Lady, 1 Jan. 1918.
19 Smith-Dorrien, Olive Crofton, Lady, 1 Jan. 1918.
20 Wills, Dame Janet Stancomb, 1 Jan. 1918.
21 Webster, Dame May, 1 Jan. 1918.
22 Armstrong, Dame Helen Proctor (Madame Melba), 1 Jan. 1918.
23 Davidson, Margaret Agnes, Lady, 1 Jan. 1918.
24 Atholl, Katharine Marjory, Duchess of, 3 June, 1918.
25 Bell, Florence Eveleen Eleanore, Lady, 3 June, 1918.
26 Bevan, Hon. Dame Maud Elizabeth, 3 June, 1918.
27 Bute, Augusta Mary Monica, Marchioness of, 3 June, 1918.
28 Donner, Anna Maria, Lady, 3 June, 1918.
29 Reid, Dame Clarissa, 3 June, 1918.
30 Roberts, Aileen Mary, Countess, 3 June, 1918.

31 Waldegrave, Mary Dorothea, Countess, 3 June, 1918.
32 Leach, Dame Florence Edith Victoria, 1 Jan. 1919. (M.)
33 Crowdy, Dame Rachel Eleanor, 1 Jan. 1919.
34 Henderson, Henrietta Caroline, Lady, 1 Jan. 1919.
35 Lennox, Lady Blanche Gordon, 1 Jan. 1919.
36 Mount Stephen, Gian, Lady, 1 Jan. 1919.
37 Gwynne-Vaughan, Dame Helen Charlotte Isabella, 3 June, 1919. (M.)
38 Monro, Mary Caroline, Hon. Lady, 3 June, 1919.
39 O'Dwyer, Una, Lady, 3 June, 1919.
40 Oram, Dame Sarah Elizabeth, 3 June, 1919. (M.)
41 Northcote, Alice, Lady, 3 June, 1919.
42 Darnley, Florence Rose, Countess of, 3 June, 1919.
43 Harrowby, Mabel Danvers, Countess of, 3 June, 1919.
44 Chisholm, Dame Alice, 1 Jan. 1920.
45 Eglinton and Winton, Janet Lucretia, Countess of, 1 Jan. 1920.
46 Gosford, Louisa Augusta Beatrice, Countess of, 1 Jan. 1920.
47 Pope-Hennessy, Dame Una Constance, 1 Jan. 1920.
48 Hunt, Dame Catherine Reeve, 1 Jan. 1920.
49 Leicester, Alice Emily, Countess of, 1 Jan. 1920.
50 Talbot de Malahide, Isabel Charlotte, Lady, 1 Jan. 1920.
51 Oliver, Beryl Carnegy, Lady, 1 Jan. 1920.
52 Rhondda, Sybil Margaret, Viscountess, 1 Jan. 1920.
53 Butt-Rumford, Dame Clara, 1 Jan. 1920.
54 Samuel, Dame Louise Victoria, 1 Jan. 1920.
55 Shakespear, Dame Ethel Mary Reader, 1 Jan. 1920.
56 Talbot, Dame Meriel Lucy, 1 Jan. 1920.
57 Wintz, Dame Sophia Gertrude, 1 Jan. 1920.
58 Wingate, Catherine Leslie, Lady, 1 Jan. 1920.
59 Mond, Violet Florence Mabel, Lady, 5 June, 1920.
60 Pearson, Ethel Maud, Lady, 5 June, 1920.
61 Buller, Dame Audrey Charlotte Georgina, 5 June, 1920.

COMMANDERS.

(C.B.E.)

1 Appleton, William Archibald, 4 June, 1917.
2 Amory, Sir Ian Murray, Bart., 4 June, 1917.
3 Garrett-Anderson, Louisa, 4 June, 1917.
4 Baker, Professor Herbert Brereton, 4 June, 1917.
5 Baker, Gwendoline, Mrs. Cecil, 4 June, 1917.
6 Barker, Lilian Charlotte, 4 June, 1917.
7 Barclay, Colville Adrian de Rune, 4 June, 1917.
8 Barrett, Florence Elizabeth, Lady, 4 June, 1917.
9 Bairstow, Leonard, 4 June, 1917.
10 Barnett, Henrietta Octavia, Mrs. Samuel Augustus, 4 June, 1917.
11 Bell, Gertrude Margaret Lowthian, 4 June, 1917.
12 Bryant, Charles William, 4 June, 1917.
13 Blane, William, 4 June, 1917.
14 Brownlie, James Thomas, 4 June, 1917.
15 Moss-Blundell, Henry Seymour, 4 June, 1917.
16 Bellamy, Albert, 4 June, 1917.
18 Carter, Albert Thomas, 4 June, 1917.
19 Chapman, Sir Sydney John, 4 June, 1917.
20 Chorlton, Alan Ernest Leofric, 4 June, 1917.
21 Collinson, Alfred Howe, 4 June, 1917.
25 Gaskell, Helen Mary, Mrs. Henry Brooks, 4 June, 1917.
26 Geldart, William Martin, 4 June, 1917.
27 Gordon, Archibald Alexander, 4 June, 1917.
29 Harbord, Frank William, 4 June, 1917.
30 Hart, Thomas Wheeler, 4 June, 1917.
31 Harvey, Ernest Musgrave, 4 June, 1917.
32 Hogg, Margaret, 4 June, 1917.
33 Hope, George Irving, 4 June, 1917.
34 Irving, Herbert Cavan, 4 June, 1917.
35 Jacobson, Ernest Nathaniel Joseph, 4 June, 1917.
36 Keeble, Professor Frederick William, 4 June, 1917.
37 Lambert, Arthur Bradley, 4 June, 1917.
38 Laing, Andrew, 4 June, 1917.
39 Layton, Walter Thomas, 4 June, 1917.
40 Lindley, Hon. Francis Oswald, 4 June, 1917.
43 Macmillan, Margaret, 4 June, 1917.
44 McIntosh, Annie, 4 June, 1917.
45 Marks, Sir George Croydon, 4 June, 1917.
46 Mathew, Charles James, 4 June, 1917.
47 Maudslay, Algernon, 4 June, 1917.
49 Montefiore, Edmund Sebag-, 4 June, 1917.
50 Murray, Flora, 4 June, 1917.
51 Norman, Florence Priscilla, Hon. Lady, 4 June, 1917.
52 Norman, Herman Cameron 4 June, 1917.
53 Parker, Charles Sandbach, 4 June, 1917.
54 Padwick, Francis Herbert, 4 June, 1917.
55 Young, Sister Pauline, 4 June, 1917.
56 Perry, Robert Grosvenor, 4 June, 1917.
58 Pavy, Dorothea, Mrs. Gordon Augustus, 4 June, 1917.
59 Pybus, Percy John, 4 June, 1917.
60 Roxburgh, Eleanor Mary Ann, Lady, 4 June, 1917.
61 Scharlieb, Mary Ann Dacomb, Mrs. William Mason, 4 June, 1917.
62 Sclater, Charlotte Seymour, Mrs. William Lutley, 4 June, 1917.
63 Scott, Sophie Beatrix Mary, Lady, 4 June, 1917.
64 Sexton, James, 4 June, 1917.
65 Smith, Lancelot Grey Hugh, 4 June, 1917.
66 Stevens, Clement Henry, 4 June, 1917.
67 Still, Alicia Lloyd, 4 June, 1917.
68 Stokes, Edith Nellie, Mrs. Leonard Aloysuis Scott, 4 June, 1917.
69 Taylor, Thomas Marris, 4 June, 1917.
70 Thorpe, Professor Jocelyn Field, 4 June, 1917.
71 Vane, Harry Tempest, 4 June, 1917.
72 Watson, Arthur, 4 June, 1917.
73 Watson, Alexandra Mary, Mrs. Douglas Chalmers, 4 June, 1917.
75 Williams, John Fischer, 4 June, 1917.
76 Windham, William, 4 June, 1917.
77 Wilson, Joseph Havelock, 4 June, 1917.
79 Manipur, H.H. Raja Chura Chand Singh, Raja of, 4 Dec. 1917.
80 Crooke-Lawless, Sir Warren Roland, 4 Dec. 1917.
81 Bobbili, Maharaja Sri Rao Sir Venkatasveta Chalapati Ranga Rao Bahadur of, 4 Dec. 1917.
82 Anderson, Sir Arthur Robert, 4 Dec. 1917.
83 Abdulla Ibn Yusuf Ali, 4 Dec. 1917.
85 Alton, John Arthur, 1 Jan. 1918.

86 Aldington, Charles, 1 Jan. 1918.
87 Allen, Ernest Joshua, 1 Jan. 1918.
88 Allen, Ernest King, 1 Jan. 1918.
89 Allen, Richard William, 1 Jan. 1918.
90 Alma-Tadema, Lawrence, 1 Jan. 1918.
91 Anderson, Adelaide Mary, 1 Jan. 1918.
92 Anderson, John Hubback, 1 Jan. 1918. (M.)
93 Anderson, William James, 1 Jan. 1918.
94 Angell, Frederick John, 1 Jan. 1918. (M.)
95 Anstruther, Mildred Harriet, Lady, 1 Jan. 1918.
97 Armitage, Cecil Henry, 1 Jan. 1918.
99 Ashley, Frank, 1 Jan. 1918.
100 Askwith, Ellen, Lady, 1 Jan. 1918.
101 Bacon, Frederick Joseph, 1 Jan. 1918.
102 Bagshawe, Bernal, 1 Jan. 1918.
103 Bain, David, 1 Jan. 1918.
104 Baines, Sir Frank, 1 Jan. 1918.
105 Barlow, James Alan Noel, 1 Jan. 1918.
106 Barrios, Benjamin, 1 Jan. 1918.
107 Barrow, Oscar Theodore, 1 Jan. 1918.
108 Bate, Thomas Elwood Lindesay, 1 Jan. 1918.
109 Bean, John Harper, 1 Jan. 1918.
110 Bellhouse, Gerald, 1 Jan. 1918.
112 Blyth, Alfred Carleton, 1 Jan. 1918.
113 Brackenbury, Hereward Irenius, 1 Jan. 1918.
114 Bradley, Thomas John, 1 Jan. 1918.
115 Broadbent, Benjamin, 1 Jan. 1918.
116 Bromhead, Alfred Claude, 1 Jan. 1918.
118 Brown, James, 1 Jan. 1918.
119 Bryant, Sir Francis Morgan, 1 Jan. 1918.
120 Brydon, James Herbert, 1 Jan. 1918.
122 Peabody, Kathleen, 1 Jan. 1918.
123 Burney, Sydney Bernard, 1 Jan. 1918.
125 Carmichael, James Forrest Halkett, 1 Jan. 1918.
126 Catto, Thomas Sivewright, 1 Jan. 1918.
127 Chamberlain, Fernley John, 1 Jan. 1918.
128 Chandos-Pole-Gell, Harry Anthony, 1 Jan. 1918.
129 Cheshire, Professor Frederic John, 1 Jan. 1918.
130 Churchill, Clementine Ogilvy, Mrs. Winston Leonard, 1 Jan. 1918.
131 Clerke, Augustus Basil Holt, 1 Jan. 1918. (M.)
132 Colchester-Wemyss, Maynard Willoughby, 1 Jan. 1918.
133 Cooke, Charles John Bowen, 1 Jan. 1918.
134 Cox, Edwin Charles, 1 Jan. 1918.
135 Cripps, Hon. Leonard Harrison, 1 Jan. 1918. (M.)
136 Daniel, Edward Yorke, 1 Jan. 1918.
137 Davidson, Albert, 1 Jan. 1918.
138 Davidson, Stuart, 1 Jan. 1918. (M.)
139 Davies, Charles Llewelyn, 1 Jan. 1918.
140 Davies, Ernest, 1 Jan. 1918.
141 Davis, Henry William Carless, 1 Jan. 1918.
142 Davis, John Samuel Champion, 1 Jan. 1918.
144 Dendy, Edward Evershed, 1 Jan. 1918.
145 Dennistoun, Robert Maxwell, 1 Jan. 1918. (M.)
146 Dixon, Arthur Lewis, 1 Jan. 1918.
147 Dormer, Lord, 1 Jan. 1918. (M.)
148 Duncombe, Charles William Ernest, 1 Jan. 1918.
149 Durham, Frances Hermia, 1 Jan. 1918.
150 Dyke, Arthur James, 1 Jan. 1918.
151 Ebden, Agnes Murray, Mrs., 1 Jan. 1918.
152 Edgar, Ethel, Lady, 1 Jan. 1918.
153 Edwards, George, 1 Jan. 1918.
154 Evans, William James, 1 Jan. 1918.
155 Ewing, Peter Dewar, 1 Jan. 1918.
156 Ferard, John Edward, 1 Jan. 1918.
157 Ffinch, Matthew Benjamin Dipnall, 1 Jan. 1918.
158 Fieldhouse, William John, 1 Jan. 1918.
159 FitzGerald, Edward, 1 Jan. 1918.
160 Fitzherbert-Brockholes, William Joseph, 1 Jan. 1918.
161 Fitzpatrick, Herbert Lindsay, 1 Jan. 1918.
162 Folker, Horace Shepherd, 1 Jan. 1918.
163 Follows, John Henry, 1 Jan. 1918.
164 Forber, Edward Rodolph, 1 Jan. 1918.
165 Foster, Sir William Yorke, Bart., 1 Jan. 1918. (M.)
166 Fowler, George Herbert, 1 Jan. 1918.
167 Frederick, George Charles, 1 Jan. 1918. (M.)
168 Fry, George Samuel, 1 Jan. 1918.
169 Fyfe, Thomas Alexander, 1 Jan. 1918.
170 Garnett, Frank Walls, 1 Jan. 1918.
171 Garrett, Frank, 1 Jan. 1918.
172 Garrod, Heathcote William, 1 Jan. 1918.

2 P

173 Gascoigne, Laura Gwendolen, Mrs., 1 Jan. 1918.
174 Gaselee, Stephen, 1 Jan. 1918.
175 Gaskell, Joseph, 1 Jan. 1918. (M.)
176 Gauntlett, Mager Frederic, 1 Jan. 1918.
177 Gibbon, Ioan Gwilym, 1 Jan. 1918.
178 Gibbs, Victoria Florence de Burgh, Mrs., 1 Jan. 1918.
179 Gilmour, David, 1 Jan. 1918.
180 Glendinning, Henry, 1 Jan. 1918.
181 Gordon, Lewis, 1 Jan. 1918.
182 Gore, St. John Corbet, 1 Jan. 1918.
183 Goschen, George Joachim, Viscount, 1 Jan. 1918.
184 Graves, Robert Ernest, 1 Jan. 1918.
185 Grierson, William Wylie, 1 Jan. 1918.
186 Grosvenor. Rosamund, Lady Henry, 1 Jan. 1918.
187 Guise, Anselm Verner Lee, 1 Jan. 1918.
188 Hadfield, Frances Bett, Lady, 1 Jan. 1918.
189 Hadley, Arthur Edward, 1 Jan. 1918.
190 Haigh, Ernest Varley, 1 Jan. 1918.
191 Hall, Arthur Henry, 1 Jan. 1918.
192 Harrison, John, 1 Jan. 1918.
193 Harwood, Ralph Endersby, 1 Jan. 1918.
194 Hawk, William, 1 Jan. 1918.
195 Hazel, Alfred Ernest William, 1 Jan. 1918.
196 Helbert, Geoffrey Gladstone, 1 Jan. 1918. (M.)
197 Hetherington, Thomas Gerard, 1 Jan. 1918.
198 Higgins, Alexander Pearce, 1 Jan. 1918.
199 Hodgkinson, Professor William Richard, 1 Jan. 1918.
200 Holmes, Arthur William, 1 Jan. 1918.
201 Hope, Collingwood, 1 Jan. 1918.
202 Hope, John Wilson, 1 Jan. 1918.
203 Horne, Leonard Thomas, 1 Jan. 1918.
204 Horne, Lancelot Worthy, 1 Jan. 1918.
205 Hunt, George Henry, 1 Jan. 1918.
206 Hunter, Summers, 1 Jan. 1918.
207 Hurcomb, Cyril William, 1 Jan. 1918.
209 Jackson, Daniel, 1 Jan. 1918.
211 Jenkins, Walter St. David, 1 Jan. 1918.
212 Jonas, Harry Marshall, 1 Jan. 1918.
213 Jones, Charles Henry, 1 Jan. 1918.
214 Jowitt, Frederick McCulloch, 1 Jan. 1918.
215 Judd, Harold Godfrey, 1 Jan. 1918.
216 Kent, Walter George, 1 Jan. 1918.
217 Killin, Robert, 1 Jan. 1918.
218 Lawrence, Alfred Clive. 1 Jan. 1918.
220 Lempfert, Rudolph Gustav Karl, 1 Jan. 1918.
222 Lewtas, John Tweedy, 1 Jan. 1918. (M.)
223 London, Edgar Stanford, 1 Jan. 1918.
224 Lucas, Arthur, 1 Jan. 1918.
225 Luke, William Joseph, 1 Jan. 1918.
226 Lysaght, William Royse, 1 Jan. 1918.
227 Mackie, Horacio George Arthur, 1 Jan. 1918.
228 MacLean, James Borrowman, 1 Jan. 1918.
229 MacLellan, William Turner, 1 Jan. 1918.
231 Macnaghten, Terence Charles, 1 Jan. 1918.
232 Maconochie, Charles Cornelius, 1 Jan. 1918.
233 Maginness, Edmund John, 1 Jan. 1918.
234 Maguire, James Rochfort, 1 Jan. 1918.
235 Malcolm, George, 1 Jan. 1918.
237 Marr, Sir James, Bart., 1 Jan. 1918
238 Marsden, Sir Thomas Rodgerson, 1 Jan. 1918.
239 Masterman, Edward Alexander Dimsdale, 1 Jan. 1918. (M.)
240 Mather, Arthur Stanley, 1 Jan. 1918.
241 Matthews, Valentine, 1 Jan. 1918. (M.)
242 Maunsell, Richard Edward Lloyd, 1 Jan. 1918.
243 McCowen, Oliver Hill, 1 Jan. 1918.
244 McLaren, Hon. Henry Duncan, 1 Jan. 1918.
245 McLean, James Reynolds, 1 Jan. 1918. (M.)
246 McMillan, William Bentley, 1 Jan. 1918.
247 Measures, Harry Bell, 1 Jan. 1918.
248 Mellor, Francis Hamilton, 1 Jan. 1918.
249 Mitchell, Frank Herbert, 1 Jan. 1918.
250 Mitchell, Robert, 1 Jan. 1918.
252 Montgomery, James Alexander Lawrence, 1 Jan. 1918.
253 Morgan, Charles Langbridge, 1 Jan. 1918.
254 Morgan, Hopkin, 1 Jan. 1918.
255 Mottram, Thomas Harry, 1 Jan. 1918.
256 Mount, William Arthur, 1 Jan. 1918.
257 Naef, Conrad James, 1 Jan. 1918.
258 Neylan, Daniel, 1 Jan. 1918.
259 Norton, Thomas, 1 Jan. 1918.
261 Palmer, Claud Bowes, 1 Jan. 1918.
262 Parsons, Edward Howard Thornbrough, 1 Jan. 1918.
263 Peech, James, 1 Jan. 1918.
265 Piggott, Henry Howard, 1 Jan. 1918.
266 Pinder, Charles Ralph, 1 Jan. 1918.
267 Pledge, Henry, 1 Jan. 1918.
269 Procter, Helen Matilda, Lady, 1 Jan. 1918.
270 Railton, James, 1 Jan. 1918.
271 Rawson, Harry, 1 Jan. 1918.
272 Rea, George Grey, 1 Jan. 1918.
273 Reid, Hugh, 1 Jan. 1918.
274 Relton, Arthur John, 1 Jan. 1918.
276 Richmond, John Richie, 1 Jan. 1918.
277 Roberts, Gervase Henry, 1 Jan. 1918.
278 Robertson, John, 1 Jan. 1918.
279 Robinson, William, 1 Jan. 1918.
280 Robinson, Sir William Arthur, 1 Jan. 1918.
281 Rodney, Corisande, Lady, 1 Jan. 1918.
282 Ross, Archibald John Campbell, 1 Jan. 1918.

283 Rowland, John, 1 Jan. 1918.
284 Rudolf, Robert Dawson, 1 Jan. 1918. (M.)
285 Rundell, Matthew Adkins, 1 Jan. 1918.
287 Sandberg, Nils Percy Patrick, 1 Jan. 1918.
289 Sanders, William Stephen, 1 Jan. 1918.
290 Sarel, William Samuel, 1 Jan. 1918.
291 Scott, Finlay Forbes, 1 Jan. 1918.
292 Scott-Riddell, John, 1 Jan. 1918.
293 Senior, Albert, 1 Jan. 1918.
294 Siddeley, John Davenport, 1 Jan. 1918.
296 Smallwood, Arthur William, 1 Jan. 1918.
297 Smith, Fredcrick, 1 Jan. 1918.
298 Smith, Hon. George John, 1 Jan. 1918. (M.)
299 Smith, Launcelot Eustace, 1 Jan. 1918.
300 Sopwith, Thomas Octave Murdoch, 1 Jan. 1918.
301 Spens, William, 1 Jan. 1918.
302 Squires, Ernest Edward William, 1 Jan. 1918.
303 Stamp, Josiah Charles, 1 Jan. 1918.
304 Stephens, Lockhart, 1 Jan. 1918.
305 Stevenson, Frances Louise, 1 Jan. 1918.
306 Stevenson, Thomas Henry Craig, 1 Jan. 1918.
307 Stewart-Mackenzie, Mary Margaret, Mrs. 1 Jan. 1918.
308 Still, William Chester, 1 Jan. 1918.
309 Stone, John William, 1 Jan. 1918.
310 Streatfield, Lucy Granville, Mrs., 1 Jan. 1918.
311 Stuart, John, 1 Jan. 1918.
312 Stuart Wortley Violet, Hon. Mrs. Edward James, 1 Jan. 1918.
313 Talbot, Hon. Reginald Gilbert Murray, 1 Jan. 1918.
314 Tatlow, Frank, 1 Jan. 1918.
315 Tempest, Percy Crosland, 1 Jan. 1918.
317 Towle, Sir Francis William, 1 Jan. 1918. (M.)
318 Tregoning, Wynn Harold, 1 Jan. 1918.
319 Turner, Joseph Harling, 1 Jan. 1918.
320 Virgo, John James, 1 Jan. 1918.
322 Walpole, Hugh, 1 Jan. 1918.
323 Walters, Evelyn Mayura, Mrs. Richard Huth, 1 Jan. 1918.
324 Waring, Lady Susan Elizabeth Clémentine, 1 Jan. 1918.
325 Watson, Henry Angus, 1 Jan. 1918.
326 Watt, Alexander Strahan, 1 Jan. 1918.
328 Webb, Harry James, 1 Jan. 1918.
329 Webb, Philip George Lancelot, 1 Jan. 1918.
330 White, Gerald Verner, 1 Jan. 1918. (M.)
331 Williams, John, 1 Jan. 1918. (M.)
332 Williams, Wilfred Howard, 1 Jan. 1918.
333 Williamson, Frederic Herbert, 1 Jan. 1918.
334 Bund, John William Willis, 1 Jan. 1918.
335 Wilson, Horace John, 1 Jan. 1918.
336 Withers, John James, 1 Jan. 1918.
337 Wolfe, Humbert, 1 Jan. 1918.
338 Wolverton, Edith Amelia, Lady, 1 Jan. 1918.
339 Wood, Professor Thomas Barlow, 1 Jan. 1918.
340 Woodgate, Alfred, 1 Jan. 1918.
341 Woods, Raymond Wybrow, 1 Jan. 1918.
342 Worthington, Thomas, 1 Jan. 1918.
343 Wynch, Lionel Maling, 1 Jan. 1918
344 Wyndham, Charles John, 1 Jan. 1918.
345 Yarrow, Harold Edgar. 1 Jan. 1918.
346 Yolland, John Horatio, 1 Jan. 1918.
347 Yule, George Udny. 1 Jan. 1918.
348 Meston, Jeanie, Lady, 1 Jan. 1918.
350 Highet, Sir Robert Swan, 1 Jan. 1918.
351 Faridoon Daula Bahadur, Nawab Sir, 1 Jan. 1918.
352 Webb, Sir Montague de Pomeroy, 1 Jan. 1918
353 Dowson, Ernest Macleod. 1 Jan. 1918.
354 Crawley, Cecil Gordon, 1 Jan. 1918.
355 Sterry, Wasey, 1 Jan. 1918.
356 Burnett-Stuart, George Eustace, 1 Jan. 1918.
357 Antill, Mary, Mrs., 1 Jan. 1918.
358 Budden, Henry Ebenezer, 1 Jan. 1918.
359 Delprat, Guillaume Daniel, 1 Jan. 1918.
360 Hennessy, Mary, Lady, 1 Jan. 1918.
361 Henty, Beatrice, 1 Jan. 1918.
362 Lamb, Frank de Villiers, 1 Jan. 1918.
363 Lyle, Clare Frances Isabel, Mrs., 1 Jan. 1918.
364 McKay, Hugh Victor, 1 Jan. 1918.
365 Masson, Mary, Mrs. Orme, 1 Jan. 1918.
366 Mitchell, Eliza Fraser, Mrs., 1 Jan. 1918.
367 Oldershaw, William James Norman, 1 Jan. 1918.
368 Woolcott, Frances Mary, Mrs., 1 Jan. 1918.
369 Young, William James, 1 Jan. 1918.
370 Luke, Jacobina, Mrs. John Pearce, 1 Jan. 1918.
371 Massey, Christina Allen, Mrs., 1 Jan. 1918.
372 Nolan, Robert Howard, 1 Jan. 1918.
373 Tate, Robert Ward, 1 Jan. 1918. (M.)
374 Ward, Theresa Dorothea, Lady, 1 Jan. 1918.
375 Wilson, Oriana Fanny, Mrs., 1 Jan. 1918.
376 Carter, Hester Marion, Mrs. 1 Jan. 1918.
377 Chappell, Ernest, 1 Jan. 1918.
378 Christopherson, Douglas, 1 Jan. 1918.
379 Wilson-Fox, Hon. Eleanor Birch, 1 Jan. 1918.
380 Rose-Innes, Jessie Dodd, Lady, 1 Jan. 1918.
383 Clift, Hon. James Augustus, 1 Jan. 1918.
384 Agnew, Andrew, 1 Jan. 1918.
385 Best, Thomas Alexander Vans, 1 Jan. 1918.
386 Bowring, Ethel Dorothy, Lady Charles Calvert, 1 Jan. 1918.
387 Bury, Francis George, 1 Jan. 1918.
388 Burrowes, Thomas Fraser, 1 Jan. 1918.

COMMANDERS.

389 Carter, Hon. Sir William Morris, 1 Jan. 1918.
390 Clifford, Elizabeth Lydia Rosabelle, Lady, 1 Jan. 1918.
391 De Mel, Henry Lawson, 1 Jan. 1918.
392 Evans, Sir Frederick, 1 Jan. 1918.
393 Gollan, Sir Henry Cowper, 1 Jan. 1918.
394 Goode, Richard Allmond Jeffrey, 1 Jan. 1918.
395 Jenkin, Francis Charles, 1 Jan. 1918.
396 Johnston, Reginald Fleming, 1 Jan. 1918.
397 Kemp, Joseph Horsford, 1 Jan. 1918.
398 Kitson, Albert Ernest, 1 Jan. 1918.
399 Marks, Henry, 1 Jan. 1918.
400 Methuen, Mary Ethel, Lady, 1 Jan. 1918.
401 Miles, Alice, Lady, 1 Jan. 1918.
402 Nana Ofori Atta, Paramount Chief of Akin Abuakwa, 1 Jan. 1918.
403 Slater, Alexander Ransford, 1 Jan. 1918.
404 Souchon, Hippolyte Louis Wiehe de Coudray, 1 Jan. 1918.
405 Beavis, Arthur Beagley, 1 Jan. 1918.
407 Egerton, Lady Mabelle Annie, 1 Jan. 1918.
408 Goligher, Hugh Garvin, 1 Jan. 1918. (M.)
410 Horne, Edward William, 1 Jan. 1918. (M.)
411 Partridge, Sydney George, 1 Jan. 1918. (M.)
412 Peckitt, Robert Godfrey, 1 Jan. 1918.
413 Barrett, Edith Helen, 24 May, 1918.
414 Edginton, Clyde, 24 May, 1918.
415 Fairfax, James Oswald, 24 May, 1918.
416 Hayward, Edwyn Walton, 24 May, 1918.
417 Hordern, Anthony, 24 May, 1918.
418 Abdy, Anthony John, 3 June, 1918. (M.)
419 Aberconway, Laura Elizabeth, Lady, 3 June, 1918.
420 Adam, James, 3 June, 1918.
421 Adams, Thomas, 3 June, 1918.
422 Allin, Samuel John Henry Wallis, 3 June, 1918.
423 Andrews, Francis Arthur Lavington, 3 June, 1918. (M.)
424 Asher, Augustus Gordon Grant, 3 June, 1918.
425 Bailey, Gertrude Mary, Mrs., 3 June, 1918.
426 Bairnsfather, George Edward Beckwith, 3 June, 1918. (M.)
427 Baly, Edward Charles Cyril, 3 June, 1918.
428 Barcroft, Joseph, 3 June, 1918.
429 Barrie, Charles Coupar, 3 June, 1918.
430 Beatty, Rose Mabel, Mrs., 3 June, 1918.
431 Beck, Conrad, 3 June, 1918.
432 Beckett, Muriel Helen Florence, Hon. Mrs. Rupert Evelyn, 3 June, 1918.
433 Beith, John Hay, 3 June, 1918.
434 Belcher, Ernest Albert, 3 June, 1918.
435 Bell, Robert, 3 June, 1918.
436 Benet, Henry Vere Fane, 3 June, 1918. (M.)
437 Benn, Ernest John Pickstone, 3 June, 1918.
438 Benson, Frank, 3 June, 1918. (M.)
439 Bidwell, Rt. Rev. Monsignor Manuel John, Bishop, 3 June, 1918.
440 Blaylock, Harry Woodburn, 3 June, 1918.
442 Boulton, Sir Harold Edwin, Bart., 3 June, 1918.
443 Bradfield, William Walter, 3 June, 1918.
444 Brooks, Florence, Hon. Mrs. Marshall Jones, 3 June, 1918.
445 Brown, W., 3 June, 1918.
446 Browning, Jeffrey, 3 June, 1918.
447 Buckler, Georgina Grenfell, Mrs., 3 June, 1918.
448 Buckley, William, 3 June, 1918.
450 Burt, Sir Henry Parsall, 3 June, 1918.
451 Cameron, Sir Hector Clare, 3 June, 1918.
452 Carter, George Wallace, 3 June, 1918.
453 Caunter, James Eales, 3 June, 1918. (M.)
454 Cave, Sir Thomas Sturmy, 3 June, 1918.
455 Chandler, Alfred, 3 June, 1918.
456 Cheetham, Anastasie, Lady, 3 June, 1918.
457 Chisholm, Robert, 3 June, 1918.
458 Churchill, Arthur Gillespie, 3 June, 1918. (M.)
459 Churchward, George Jackson, 3 June, 1918.
460 Clapham, John Harold, 3 June, 1918.
461 Clark, Ernest, 3 June, 1918.
462 Clarke, Joseph Percival, 3 June, 1918.
463 Clegg, Sir William Edwin, 3 June, 1918.
464 Coates, David Wilson, 3 June, 1918.
465 Cobb, Herbert Mansfield, 3 June, 1918.
466 Cocks, William, 3 June, 1918.
467 Codling, William Richard, 3 June, 1918.
468 Cole, Herbert Covington, 3 June, 1918. (M.)
469 Collard, Alfred Stephen, 3 June, 1918.
470 Compton, Lord Douglas James Cecil, 3 June, 1918. (M.)
471 Cooper, James Alexander, 3 June, 1918.
472 Cornwallis, Fiennes Stanley Wykeham, 3 June, 1918.
473 Courtney, Edmund Arthur Waldegrave, 3 June, 1918. (M.)
474 Cox, Thomas, 3 June, 1918.
476 Craig, John, 3 June, 1918.
477 Cranston, Sir Robert, 3 June, 1918. (M.)
478 Crowdy, Mary, 3 June, 1918.
479 Cummings, David Charles, 3 June, 1918.
480 Curzon, Edith Bassett, Mrs. Ernest Charles Penn, 3 June, 1918.
481 Dally, Thomas, 3 June, 1918.
482 Davenport, Muriel, Mrs. Bromley, 3 June, 1918.
483 Denny, Henry Samuel, 3 June, 1918.
484 Denny, Maurice Edward, 3 June, 1918.
485 Dickson, Henry Newton, 3 June, 1918.
486 Dixon, Harold Baily, 3 June, 1918.
487 Dobrée, Alfred, 3 June, 1918.
488 Dodds, Helen, Lady, 3 June, 1918.

489 Dodgson, Campbell, 3 June, 1918.
490 Donohue, William Edward, 3 June, 1918. (M.)
491 Drake, Henry Dowrish, 3 June, 1918. (M.)
492 Grant-Duff, Edith Florence, Lady, 3 June, 1918.
493 Dulanty, John Whelan, 3 June, 1918.
494 Eddison, Albert, 3 June, 1918.
495 Evans, John Owain, 3 June, 1918.
496 Eve, Arthur Stewart, 3 June, 1918.
497 Fitzroy, Muriel, Hon. Mrs. Edward Algernon, 3 June, 1918.
498 Fleet, Henry Louis, 3 June, 1918.
499 Fletcher, Albert, 3 June, 1918. (M.)
500 Fraser, William, 3 June, 1918.
502 Gibson, Myra MacIndoe, Mrs., 3 June, 1918.
503 Goddard, Alexander, 3 June, 1918.
504 Golightly, Robert Edmund, 3 June, 1918. (M.)
505 Gonner, Edward Carter Kersey, 3 June, 1918.
506 Goode, Henry Abel, 3 June, 1918.
507 Hamilton-Grace, Gladys, Mrs. Raymond Sheffield, 3 June, 1918.
508 Grant, Samuel Charles Norton, 3 June, 1918. (M.)
509 Greaves, John Ernest, 3 June, 1918.
510 Green, John Alfred Henderson, 3 June, 1918.
511 Greenwell, Francis John, 3 June, 1918.
512 Greenwood, Robert Morrell, 3 June, 1918.
513 Greg, John Ronald, 3 June, 1918.
514 Guggisberg, Lilian Decima Moore, Mrs., 3 June, 1918.
515 Hallé, Elinor Marie Jessie, 3 June, 1918.
516 Hankey, Basil Howard Alers, 3 June, 1918.
517 Hercy, Francis Hugh George, 3 June, 1918. (M.)
518 Higgins, Sir Sydney George, 3 June, 1918.
519 Hill, Alfred John, 3 June, 1918.
520 Hoare, Geoffrey Lennard, 3 June, 1918. (M.)
521 Hocking, William John, 3 June, 1918.
522 Holford, Mary Eleanor Gwynne, Mrs., 3 June, 1918.
523 Hollingsworth, Howard, 3 June, 1918.
525 Howard, Stephen Goodwin, 3 June, 1918.
526 Hudson, Harry Kynoch, 3 June, 1918.
527 Huggett, James, 3 June, 1918.
528 Hughes, Evan, 3 June, 1918.
529 Hughes, John Arthur, 3 June, 1918.
530 Hughes, Sydney Herbert George, 3 June, 1918.
531 Hunt, Albert, 3 June, 1918.
532 Iliffe, Edward Mauger, 3 June, 1918.
533 Jackson, Sir Henry Mather, Bart., 3 June, 1918.
534 James, Alfred Henry, 3 June, 1918.
535 James, William Henry, 3 June, 1918. (M.)
536 Jenkins, Francis Conway, 3 June, 1918. (M.)
537 Jenkinson, Mark Webster, 3 June, 1918.
538 Jervoise, Edmund Purefoy Ellis, 3 June, 1918.
539 Johnson, Henry Langhorne, 3 June, 1918.
541 Joseph, Francis L'Estrange, 3 June, 1918. (M.)
543 Knowles, Frank, 3 June, 1918. (M.)
544 Lane, Harry Philip Parnell, 3 June, 1918.
545 Lang, Charles Russell, 3 June, 1918.
547 Legge, Thomas Morison, 3 June, 1918.
548 Lenn, Frank, 3 June, 1918. (M.)
549 Lethbridge, Marion Eva, 3 June, 1918.
550 Letts, William Malmesbury, 3 June, 1918.
551 Lister, Charles Ashton, 3 June, 1918.
553 Lucas, Edward William, 3 June, 1918.
555 MacDonald, Rev. John Howard, 3 June, 1918. (M.)
556 MacGuckin, Charles John Graham, 3 June, 1918.
557 MacKay, Robert John, 3 June, 1918.
558 Mackworth, John Dolben, 3 June, 1918. (M.)
559 McLean, William Richard James, 3 June, 1918. (M.)
560 McLellan, William, 3 June, 1918. (M.)
561 McNair, Arnold Duncan, 3 June, 1918.
562 Mager, Sydney, 3 June, 1918.
563 Margerison, Lawrence, 3 June, 1918.
564 Marriott, Herbert, 3 June, 1918.
565 Marsh, William, 3 June, 1918.
566 Martin, George Walter Howard, 3 June, 1918. (M.)
567 Melland, Norman, 3 June, 1918.
568 Mensforth, Holberry, 3 June, 1918.
569 Milne, John Alexander, 3 June, 1918.
570 Moens, Seaburne Godfrey Arthur May, 3 June, 1918.
571 Moncrieff, John Mitchell, 3 June, 1918.
572 Monfries, Charles Babington Smith, 3 June, 1918.
573 Monsell, Caroline Mary Sybil, Mrs. Bolton Meredith Eyres, 3 June, 1918.
574 Morris, Thomas Henry, 3 June, 1918.
575 Moylan, John Fitzgerald, 3 June, 1918.
576 Murray, Hugh, 3 June, 1918.
577 Nash, George Howard, 3 June, 1918.
578 Newlands, John, 3 June, 1918.
579 Nicholson, John Sanctuary, 3 June, 1918. (M.)
580 Norris, Henry, 3 June, 1918.
581 Norton, Robert Frederick, 3 June, 1918.
582 Noyes, Alfred, 3 June, 1918.
583 Nuttall, Thomas Downham, 3 June, 1918.
584 Orr, Charles Roger, 3 June, 1918.
585 Oxley, John Stewart, 3 June, 1918.
586 Page, Frederick Handley, 3 June, 1918.
587 Page, William Morton, 3 June, 1918.
588 Paget, Eden Wilberforce, 3 June, 1918.
589 Parkes, William Henry, 3 June, 1918. (M.)
590 Parsons, William Roskilly, 3 June, 1918. (M.)
591 Paul, Denis, 3 June, 1918. (M.)

592 Payne, Sylvia May, Mrs., 3 June, 1918.
593 Penoyre, John, 3 June, 1918.
594 Peters, Arthur, 3 June, 1918.
595 Phillips, Thomas William, 3 June, 1918.
596 Picot, Henry Philip, 3 June, 1918. (M.)
597 Potter, Edmund, 3 June, 1918.
598 Powell, James Leslie Grove, 3 June, 1918. (M.)
599 Price, William, 3 June, 1918. (M.)
600 Procter, Sir Henry Edward Edleston, 3 June, 1918.
601 Radstock, Lord, 3 June, 1918.
602 Rait, Robert Sangster, 3 June, 1918.
603 Richardson, Sir Albion Henry Herbert, 3 June, 1918.
604 Ridley, Cecil Guy, 3 June, 1918.
605 Robertson, Struan Gordon, 3 June, 1918. (M.)
606 Robinson, Andrew, 3 June, 1918.
607 Rogers, Edith Louise Julie, Lady, 3 June, 1918.
608 Ruddock, Thomas Emerson, 3 June, 1918.
609 Ryall, Sir Charles, 3 June, 1918.
610 Ryan, Charles Montgomerie, 3 June, 1918. (M.)
611 Ryan, Mervyn Frederick, 3 June, 1918.
612 Salisbury, Francis, 3 June, 1918.
613 Sampson, John, 3 June, 1918.
615 Sayer, Maxwell Barcham, 3 June, 1918. (M.)
617 Scott, Charles, 3 June, 1918.
618 Seager, John Renwick, 3 June, 1918.
619 Selway, Cornelius James, 3 June, 1918.
620 Sewell, John Thomas Beadsworth, 3 June, 1918.
621 Sharman, Charles Henry Ludovic, 3 June, 1918. (M.)
622 Smith, Albert William, 3 June, 1918. (M.)
623 Roach-Smith, Charles, 3 June, 1918. (M.)
624 Shrapnell-Smith, Edward Shrapnell, 3 June, 1918.
625 Smith, George Scoby, 3 June, 1918.
626 Smith, Henry White, 3 June, 1918.
627 Smith, James Cruickshank, 3 June, 1918.
628 Darvil-Smith, Percy George, 3 June, 1918.
629 Smith, Robert John, 3 June, 1918.
631 Smithe, Ida Elizabeth, Mrs., 3 June, 1918.
632 Somerleyton, Phyllis, Lady, 3 June, 1918.
634 Stanley, Joseph Henry, 3 June, 1918.
635 Steele, W. H., 3 June, 1918.
636 Stevens, Frank Augustus Douglas, 3 June, 1918. (M.)
637 Stevenson, James Verdier, 3 June, 1918.
638 Stevenson, William March, 3 June, 1918.
640 Strange, Edward Fairbrother, 3 June, 1918.
641 Strong, John, 3 June, 1918.
642 Sweny, William Halpin Paterson, 3 June, 1918. (M.)
643 Swire, William, 3 June, 1918.
644 Tait, Andrew Wilson, 3 June, 1918.
646 Kyffin-Taylor, Gerald, 3 June, 1918. (M.)
647 Thompson, Rev. George Herbert, 3 June, 1918.
648 Thompson, William Bruce, 3 June, 1918.
649 Tootill, Robert, 3 June, 1918.
650 Topple, Walter Livingstone, 3 June, 1918.
651 Trye, John Henry, 3 June, 1918. (M.)
652 Turnbull, Jane Holland, 3 June, 1918. (M.)
653 Turner, Ernest James, 3 June, 1918.
654 Verschoyle, Beresford St. George, 3 June, 1918.
655 Vesey, Sidney Philip Charles, 3 June, 1918.
656 Vicars, Edward Robert Eckersall, 3 June, 1918.
657 Des Vœux, Hylda Henrietta, Lady, 3 June, 1918.
658 Wale, Henry William, 3 June, 1918.
659 Walker, Alexander, 3 June, 1918.
660 Walker, Herbert Sutherland, 3 June, 1918.
661 Wavertree, Sophie Florence Lothrop, Lady, 3 June, 1918.
662 Walker, William, 3 June, 1918.
663 Walton, Sydney, 3 June, 1918.
664 Ward, Jean Templeton, Hon. Lady, 3 June, 1918.
665 Webster, William, 3 June, 1918.
666 West, George Frederick Parrett, 3 June, 1918.
667 Westminster, Constance Edwina, Duchess of, 3 June, 1918.
669 Williamson, Richard, 3 June, 1918.
670 Williamson, Robert, 3 June, 1918.
671 Willson, Thomas Olaf, 3 June, 1918.
672 Wilson, John Henry, 3 June, 1918.
673 Wilson, Joseph Maitland, 3 June, 1918.
674 Witt, Robert Clermont, 3 June, 1918.
675 Wood, Augustus Ottiwell, 3 June, 1918.
676 Wood, William Henry, 3 June, 1918.
677 Woodburn, Thomas Stanley, 3 June, 1918. (M.)
678 Woodward, George Ernest, 3 June, 1918.
679 Woolston, Thomas Henry, 3 June, 1918.
680 Wordingham, Charles Henry, 3 June, 1918.
681 Worley, Sir Arthur, 3 June, 1918.
682 Wratislaw, Albert Charles, 3 June, 1918.
683 Wright, James Brown, 3 June, 1918.
684 Young, Daniel Henderson Lusk, 3 June, 1918.
685 Robertson, Charlotte, Lady, 3 June, 1918.
686 Ebrahim, Sir Fazalbhoy Currimbhoy, 3 June, 1918.
687 Carter, Sir Frank Willington, 3 June, 1918.
688 Hallifax, Charles Joseph, 3 June, 1918.
689 Wyndham, Percy, 3 June, 1918.
690 Mountford, Lewis James, 3 June, 1918.
691 Elliott, Alfred Charles, 3 June, 1918.
692 Ali, Shaikh Ashgar, 3 June, 1918.
693 Wilson-Johnston, Joseph, 3 June, 1918.
694 Brander, William Browne, 3 June, 1918.
695 Wilson, Neville Frederick Jarvis, 3 June, 1918.
696 Fawcett, Edward Pinder, 3 June, 1918.

697 Pithapuranes, Sri Raja, Rao Venkata Kumara Mahipati Surya Rao Bahadur of, 3 June, 1918.
698 Birkmyre, Sir Archibald, Bart., 3 June, 1918.
699 Buck, Edward John, 3 June, 1918.
700 Mullick, Sarat Kumar, 3 June, 1918.
701 Hayter, William Goodenough, 3 June, 1918.
702 Dudgeon, Gerald Cecil, 3 June, 1918.
703 Goodman, Cyril, 3 June, 1918.
704 Feilden, Randle Montagu, 3 June, 1918.
705 Bolton, Senator William Kinsey, 3 June, 1918.
706 Bright, Alfred, 3 June, 1918.
707 Draper, Thomas Percy, 3 June, 1918.
708 Gibson, Robert, 3 June, 1918.
709 Hunter, David, 3 June, 1918.
710 Kerr, William Warren, 3 June, 1918.
711 Leitch, Walter, 3 June, 1918.
712 Lockyer, Nicholas Colston, 3 June, 1918.
713 McBeath, William George, 3 June, 1918.
714 McColl, George Guthrie, 3 June, 1918.
715 McKay, Benjamin Thomas, 3 June, 1918.
716 Masson, Professor David Orme, 3 June, 1918.
717 Owen, Langer, 3 June, 1918.
718 Raws, William Lennen, 3 June, 1918.
719 Smith, Mary Isobel Barr, Mrs., 3 June, 1918.
720 Trumble, Thomas, 3 June, 1918.
721 Walker, Eadith, 3 June, 1918.
722 Chaffey, Ralph Anderson, 3 June, 1918. (M.)
723 Fowlds, Hon. George, 3 June, 1918.
724 Hardwicke, Countess of, 3 June, 1918.
725 Hunter, Thomas Anderson, 3 June, 1918. (M.!
726 Mackenzie, Helen, 3 June, 1918.
727 Nichols, Joseph Cowie, 3 June, 1918. (M.)
728 Fort, George Seymour, 3 June, 1918.
729 Pargiter, David Scott, 3 June, 1918.
730 Browning, Adeline Elizabeth, Mrs., 3 June, 1918.
731 Grieve, Walter Baine, 3 June, 1918.
732 Chaplin, Margaret Seton, Lady, 3 June, 1918.
733 Chesnaye, Christian Purefoy, 3 June, 1918.
734 Crompton, Robert, 3 June, 1918.
735 Derrick, George Alexander, 3 June, 1918. (M.)
736 Masterman, Thomas Spry, 3 June, 1918. (M.)
737 Marshall, Elizabeth Middleton Ord, Mrs., 3 June, 1918.
738 Refalo, Sir Michel Angelo, 3 June, 1918.
739 Silburn, Percy Arthur Baxter, 3 June, 1918.
740 Smith, Lucie MacDuff, Lady, 3 June, 1918.
741 Wallis, Henry Richard, 3 June, 1918.
742 Wells, John Stuart Kerr, 3 June, 1918.
743 Morison, Sir Theodore, 3 June, 1918. (M.)
744 Watkins, Oscar Ferris, 3 June, 1918. (M.)
745 Barnes, Harold C. E., 3 June, 1918. (M.)
746 Soane, Ely Banister, 3 June, 1918.
747 Molesworth, William, 3 June, 1918. (M.)
748 Sheen, Alfred William, 3 June, 1918. (M.)
750 Smith, Walter William Marriott, 3 June, 1918. (M.)
751a Wood, Attiwell Henry, 3 June, 1918. (M.)
751b Belfield, Florence, Lady, 3 June, 1918.
752 Greenwood, Jonathan William, 22 Aug. 1918. (M.)
753 Gutsche, Clemens, 22 Aug. 1918. (M.)
754 Harvey, Francis George, 22 Aug. 1918. (M.)
756 Smith, James Irvine, 22 Aug. 1918. (M.)
757a Sturman, Albert Edward, 22 Aug. 1918. (M.)
757c Moncrieff, George Hay, 14 Oct. 1918.
758 Giles, Godfrey Hill, 19 Dec. 1918. (M.)
760 Hodgson, Greenwood, 19 Dec. 1918. (M.)
761 Hughes, Alfred Mahony, 19 Dec. 1918. (M.)
762 Weaver, John Henry, 19 Dec. 1918.
763 Woolley, Walter James, 19 Dec. 1918.
764 Brooke, Hugh Fenwick, 1 Jan. 1919. (M.)
765 Caulfield, Francis William John, 1 Jan. 1919. (M.)
766 Crosse, Rev. Arthur John William, 1 Jan. 1919. (M.)
767 Dunsterville, Arthur Bruce, 1 Jan. 1919. (M.)
768 Laughton, Joseph Vinters, 1 Jan. 1919. (M.)
769 Magniac, Charles Lane, 1 Jan. 1919. (M.)
770 Philips, Lewis Francis, 1 Jan. 1919. (M.)
771 Poett, Joseph Howard, 1 Jan. 1919. (M.)
772 de Bury and de Bocarme, Henry Robert Visart, Count, 1 Jan. 1919.
773 Fetherstonhaugh, William Samuel, 1 Jan. 1919. (M.)
774 Jarvis, Arthur Murray, 1 Jan. 1919. (M.)
775 Johnson, George Hamilton, 1 Jan. 1919. (M.)
776 Miller, John Lawrence, 1 Jan. 1919. (M.)
777 Ridley, Ethel Blanche, 1 Jan. 1919. (M.)
778 Wilson, Grace Margaret, 1 Jan. 1919. (M.)
779 Ainsworth, William John, 1 Jan. 1919. (M.)
780 Choyce, Charles Coley, 1 Jan. 1919. (M.)
781 Cooper, Lyall Newcombe, 1 Jan. 1919. (M.)
782 Cunningham, Aylmer Basil, 1 Jan. 1919. (M.)
783 Garner, Cathcart, 1 Jan. 1919. (M.)
784 Hay, George Lennox, 1 Jan. 1919. (M.)
785 Mainwaring, Watkin Randle Kynaston, 1 Jan. 1919. (M.)
786 Pollock, Evelyn, 1 Jan. 1919. (M.)
787 Rawlins, Arthur Kennedy, 1 Jan. 1919. (M.)
788 Storrs, Ronald Henry Amherst, 1 Jan. 1919. (M.)
789 Taylor, Bertie Harry Waters, 1 Jan. 1919. (M.)
790 Todd, Arthur George, 1 Jan. 1919. (M.)
791 Dixon, Graham Patrick, 1 Jan. 1919. (M.)
792 Fulton, David, 1 Jan. 1919. (M.)
793 McLeish, Duncan, 1 Jan. 1919. (M.)
794 Newton, Frank Graham, 1 Jan. 1919. (M.)

COMMANDERS.

795 Vawdrey, George, 1 Jan. 1919. (M.)
796 Abbott, Herbert Edward Stacy, 1 Jan. 1919. (M.)
797 Alexander, Charles Henry, 1 Jan. 1919. (M.)
798 Arnold, Alfred James, 1 Jan. 1919. (M.)
799 Baird, Edward William David, 1 Jan. 1919. (M.)
800 Bicket, William Neilson, 1 Jan. 1919. (M.)
801 Bond, Chetwynd Rokeby Alfred, 1 Jan. 1919. (M.)
802 Browning, Frederick Henry, 1 Jan. 1919. (M.)
803 Rattray, Paul Robert Burn Clerk, 1 Jan. 1919. (M.)
804 Cathcart, Charles Walker, 1 Jan. 1919. (M.)
805 Clarke, Thomas Henry Matthews, 1 Jan. 1919. (M.)
806 Clay, Henry, 1 Jan. 1919. (M.)
807 Cloete, Evelyn Rivers Henry Josias, 1 Jan. 1919. (M.)
808 Combe, Lionel, 1 Jan, 1919. (M.)
809 Dansey-Browning, George, 1 Jan. 1919. (M.)
810 Daubeney, Edward Kaye, 1 Jan. 1919. (M.)
811 Dawson, Algernon Cecil, 1 Jan. 1919. (M.)
812 Exham, Simeon Hardy, 1 Jan. 1919. (M.)
813 Fayrer, Sir Joseph, Bart., 1 Jan. 1919. (M.)
814 Finnis, Henry, 1 Jan. 1919. (M.)
815 Fowle, Thomas Ernle, 1 Jan. 1919. (M.)
816 Gibson, Robert John Harvey, 1 Jan. 1919. (M.)
817 Grogan, Edward George, 1 Jan. 1919. (M.)
818 Home, Robert Elton, 1 Jan. 1919. (M.)
819 Humphrys, Charles Vesey, 1 Jan. 1919. (M.)
820 Jack, Herbert Rowett Henry, 1 Jan. 1919. (M.)
821 Jennings, Richard, 1 Jan. 1919. (M.)
822 Kemp, Sir Kenneth Hagar, Bart., 1 Jan. 1919. (M.)
823 Learoyd, Charles Douglas, 1 Jan. 1919. (M.)
824 Loscombe, Arthur Russell, 1 Jan. 1919. (M.)
825 Lumley, Francis Douglas, 1 Jan. 1919. (M.)
826 Macgeagh, Henry Davies Foster, 1 Jan. 1919. (M.)
827 Madoc, Henry William, 1 Jan. 1919. (M.)
828 Markwick, Ernest Elliott, 1 Jan. 1919. (M.)
829 Miller, Alfred Douglas, 1 Jan. 1919. (M.)
830 Neilson, Henry John, 1 Jan. 1919. (M.)
831 Scovell, George Julian Selwyn, 1 Jan. 1919. (M.)
832 Souttar, Henry Session, 1 Jan. 1919. (M.)
833 Taylor, Herbert Brooke, 1 Jan. 1919. (M.)
834 Taylor, Philip Beauchamp, 1 Jan. 1919.
835 Vaughan, Herbert Radclyffe, 1 Jan. 1919. (M.)
836 Westmorland, Anthony Mildmay Julian, Earl of, 1 Jan. 1919. (M.)
837 Wilkinson, George Alexander Eason, 1 Jan. 1919. (M.)
838 Wilson, Charles Henry Luttrell Fahie, 1 Jan. 1919. (M.)
839a Wintour, Fitzgerald, 1 Jan. 1919. (M.)
839b Helyar, Arthur Beaumont, 1 Jan. 1919.
840 Farmer, George Devey, 1 Jan. 1919. (M.)
841 Smythe, William Ross, 1 Jan. 1919. (M.)
842 Stewart, John, 1 Jan. 1919. (M.)
843 Ward, Walter Reginald, 1 Jan. 1919. (M.)
844 Griffiths, Thomas, 1 Jan. 1919. (M.)
845 McGlinn, John Patrick, 1 Jan. 1919. (M.)
846 McWhae, Douglas Murray, 1 Jan. 1919. (M.)
847 Maudsley, Sir Henry Carr, 1 Jan. 1919. (M.)
848 Macdonald, William Marshall, 1 Jan. 1919. (M.)
849 McLean, Henry John, 1 Jan. 1919. (M.)
850 Richardson, George Spafford, 1 Jan. 1919. (M.)
852 Barry, Thomas David Collis, 1 Jan. 1919. (M.)
853 Cave-Browne-Cave, Thomas Reginald, 1 Jan. 1919. (M.)
854 Cleaver, Frederick Holden, 1 Jan. 1919. (M.)
855 Courtney, Christopher Lloyd, 1 Jan. 1919.
856 Drake, Francis Richard, 1 Jan. 1919. (M.)
857 Drury, Richard Frederick, 1 Jan. 1919. (M.)
858 Ellis, Herbert Charles, 1 Jan. 1919. (M.)
859 Flack, Martin William, 1 Jan. 1919. (M.)
860 Gill, Napier John, 1 Jan. 1919.
861 Halahan, John Crosby, 1 Jan. 1919. (M.)
862 Heald, Charles Brehmer, 1 Jan. 1919. (M.)
863 Hoare, Francis Richard Gurney, 1 Jan. 1919. (M.)
864 Holt, Harold Edward Sherwin, 1 Jan. 1919. (M.)
865 Home, James Murray, 1 Jan. 1919. (M.)
866 Houison-Craufurd, John Archibald, 1 Jan. 1919. (M.)
867 Leslie, Sir Norman Roderick Alexander David, Bart. 1 Jan. 1919. (M.)
868 Maclean, Archibald Campbell Holms, 1 Jan. 1919. (M.)
869 Moore, Harold Arthur, 1 Jan. 1919. (M.)
870 Muecke, Francis Frederick, 1 Jan. 1919. (M.)
871 Ogilvie, Alec, 1 Jan. 1919. (M.)
872 Powell, Douglas, 1 Jan. 1919. (M.)
873 Randall, Charles Russel Jekyl, 1 Jan. 1919. (M.)
874 Steel, John Miles, 1 Jan. 1919. (M.)
875 Stoney, Ralph Durrant Sadleir, 1 Jan. 1919. (M.)
876 Talbot, Reginald George, 1 Jan. 1919. (M.)
877 Whittington, Cecil Henry, 1 Jan. 1919. (M.)
878 Bather, Rowland Henry, 1 Jan. 1919. (M.)
879 Boyer, George Christopher Aubin, 1 Jan. 1919. (M.)
880 Broatch, George Thomas, 1 Jan. 1919. (M.)
881 Bruce, Wilfred Montague, 1 Jan. 1919. (M.)
882 Bell, Adolphus Edmund, 1 Jan. 1919. (M.)
883 Crease, Thomas Evans, 1 Jan. 1919. (M.)
884 Coke, John Gilbert de Odingsells, 1 Jan. 1919. (M.)
885 Chetwode, George Knightley, 1 Jan. 1919. (M.)
886 Cummins, Henry Ashley Travers, 1 Jan. 1919. (M.)
888 Clarke, Arthur Wellesley, 1 Jan. 1919. (M.)
889 Dunbar, Charles Augustus Royer Flood, 1 Jan. 1919. (M.)
890 Dreyer, Frederic Charles, 1 Jan. 1919. (M.)
891 Duncan, George, 1 Jan. 1919. (M.)
892 Daintree, John Dodson, 1 Jan. 1919. (M.)

893 Garforth, Francis Edmund Musgrave, 1 Jan. 1919. (M.)
894 Golding, Thomas, 1 Jan. 1919. (M.)
895 Hall, Hugh Seymour, 1 Jan. 1919. (M.)
896 Halsey, Arthur, 1 Jan. 1919. (M.)
897 Hibbert, Hugh Thomas, 1 Jan. 1919. (M.)
898 Jones, Owen, 1 Jan. 1919. (M.)
899 Lafone, Albert Sumner, 1 Jan. 1919. (M.)
900 Langdon, Charles Henry Clarke, 1 Jan. 1919. (M.
901 Lees, Edgar, 1 Jan. 1919. (M.)
902 Learmonth, Frederick Charles, 1 Jan. 1919. (M.)
903 Lewis, Frank Oswald, 1 Jan. 1919. (M.)
904 Lucas, Armytage Anthony, 1 Jan. 1919. (M.)
905 Le Brun, William Henry, 1 Jan. 1919. (M.)
906 Mansell, George Robert, 1 Jan. 1919. (M.)
907 Marshall, Oswald Percival, 1 Jan. 1919. (M.)
908 Metcalfe, Henry Wray, 1 Jan. 1919. (M.)
909 Murray, George William, 1 Jan. 1919. (M.)
910 Osborne, John Warde, 1 Jan. 1919. (M.)
911 Pollen, Francis Hungerford, 1 Jan. 1919. (M.)
912 Rostron, Arthur Henry, 1 Jan. 1919. (M.)
913 Roome, George William, 1 Jan. 1919. (M.)
914 Robinson, Harry, 1 Jan. 1919.
916 Smith, Charles Valentine, 1 Jan. 1919.
917 Thorpe, Vidal Gunson, 1 Jan. 1919.
918 Thomson, Anthony Standidge, 1 Jan. 1919. (M.)
919 Thomas, Charles William, 1 Jan. 1919. (M.)
920 Wells, Sir Lionel de Lautour, 1 Jan. 1919. (M.)
921 Crowdy, Edith Frances, 1 Jan. 1919. (M.)
922 Abrahall, Bennet Hoskyns-, 1 Jan. 1919. (M.)
923 Acheson, Annie Crawford, 1 Jan. 1919. (M.)
924 Aspden, Newton Hartley, 1 Jan. 1919.
925 Bacon, Constance Alice, Mrs., 1 Jan. 1919.
926 Baker, Arthur, 1 Jan. 1919.
927 Banister, George Henry, 1 Jan. 1919.
928 Barry, Arthur John, 1 Jan. 1919.
929 Bayne, Charles Walter, 1 Jan. 1919.
930 Benson, William John, 1 Jan. 1919.
931 Benthall, John Lawrence, 1 Jan. 1919.
932 Black, William George, 1 Jan. 1919.
933 Booth, Mary Booth, 1 Jan. 1919.
934 Bourne, Thomas Johnstone, 1 Jan. 1919.
935 Boyd, William, 1 Jan. 1919.
936 Brunskill, Catherine Lavinia, Mrs., 1 Jan. 1919.
937 Burbidge, Sir Richard Woodman, Bart., 1 Jan. 1919.
938 Campbell, John Macmaster, 1 Jan. 1919.
940 Charles, Ernest Bruce, 1 Jan. 1919.
941 Clayton, George Christopher, 1 Jan. 1919.
942 Cobb, John William, 1 Jan. 1919.
943 Coles, Richard James, 1 Jan. 1919.
944 Colvin, Lady Gwendoline Audrey Adeline Brudenell, 1 Jan. 1919.
945 Connolly, William Patrick Joseph, 1 Jan. 1919.
946 Crawford, Andrew, 1 Jan. 1919.
947 Crisford, George Northcote, 1 Jan. 1919.
948 Crookston, John Gray, 1 Jan. 1919.
949 Dale, Henry Hallett, 1 Jan. 1919.
950 Darling, John Ford, 1 Jan. 1919.
951 Dawkins, Charles William, 1 Jan. 1919.
953 Drogheda, Kathleen, Countess of, 1 Jan. 1919.
954 Drower, John Edmund, 1 Jan. 1919.
955 Williams-Drummond, Francis Dudley, 1 Jan. 1919.
956 Eichholz, Alfred, 1 Jan. 1919.
957 Robertson-Eustace, Marjory Edith, Mrs., 1 Jan. 1919.
958 Fedden, Katharine Waldo Douglas, Mrs., 1 Jan. 1919
959 Fish, Walter George, 1 Jan. 1919.
960 Fisher, Charles Browning, 1 Jan. 1919.
961 FitzGerald, Francis John, 1 Jan. 1919.
962 Forman, Rev. Adam, 1 Jan. 1919.
963 Foster, Wilfrid Lionel, 1 Jan. 1919.
964 Fountain, Annie Christine, 1 Jan. 1919.
965 Fryer, Walter John, 1 Jan. 1919.
966 Garnett, James Clerk Maxwell, 1 Jan. 1919.
967 Gibson, Hope, 1 Jan. 1919.
968 Davies-Gilbert, Grace Catherine Rose, Mrs., 1 Jan. 1919.
969 Gladstone, Maud Ernestine, Hon. Mrs. Henry Neville, 1 Jan. 1919.
970 Goddard, Ernest Hope, 1 Jan. 1919.
971 Grant, Neil Forbes, 1 Jan. 1919.
972 Greene, John Arch, 1 Jan. 1919.
973 Grey, Mabel Laura, Countess, 1 Jan. 1919.
974 Groves, Herbert Austen, 1 Jan. 1919.
975 Haines, William Joseph, 1 Jan. 1919.
977 Hammond, Dayrell Talbot, 1 Jan. 1919. (M.)
978 Hannen, Lancelot, 1 Jan. 1919.
979 Hartshorn, Stuart, 1 Jan. 1919. (M.)
980 Hastings, Frank, 1 Jan. 1919.
981 Chadwyck-Healey, Sir Gerald Edward, Bart., 1 Jan. 1919.
982 Herbert, Lady Victoria Alexandrina Mary Cecil, 1 Jan. 1918.
983 Hood, David Wilson, 1 Jan. 1919.
984 Jamieson, Stanley Wyndham, 1 Jan. 1919.
985 Jones, David Thomas, 1 Jan. 1919.
986 Heath-Jones, Edgar, 1 Jan. 1918.
987 Keary, James Donald, 1 Jan. 1919.
988 Kent, Chris Shotter, 1 Jan. 1919.
989 Lackie, William Walker, 1 Jan. 1919
990 Leng, Hilary Howard, 1 Jan. 1919.
991 Lewis, John, 1 Jan. 1919.
992 Lister, Sir Robert Ashton, 1 Jan. 1919.

993 Lloyd, Albert Henry, 1 Jan. 1919.
994 Lloyd, Samuel Cook, 1 Jan. 1919.
995 Lowe, Arthur Labron, 1 Jan. 1919.
996 Lyle, Samuel, 1 Jan. 1919.
997 McCall, Charles William Home, 1 Jan. 1919.
998 McCullagh, Margaret Craig, Lady, 1 Jan. 1919.
999 McDougall, Alexander Patrick, 1 Jan. 1919.
1000 Maclagan, Eric Robert Dalrymple, 1 Jan. 1919.
1002 McMordie, Julia, Mrs., 1 Jan. 1919.
1003 March, Hilda Madeleine, Countess of, 1 Jan. 1919.
1004 Marjoribanks, Dudley Sinclair, 1 Jan. 1919.
1005 Mellersh, Arthur, 1 Jan. 1919.
1006 Menzies, Thomas Graham, 1 Jan. 1919.
1007 Mitchell, Peter Chalmers, 1 Jan. 1919. (M.)
1008 Moffat, John, 1 Jan. 1919.
1009 Morgan, George, 1 Jan. 1919.
1010 Murray, Helen Mary, Hon. Lady, 1 Jan. 1919.
1011 Nichols, Charles Lee, 1 Jan. 1919.
1012 Obré, Henry, 1 Jan. 1919.
1013 O'Keeffe, James George, 1 Jan. 1919.
1015 Oliver, Charles Augustus, 1 Jan. 1919.
1016 Hughes-Onslow, Henry, 1 Jan. 1919.
1017 Orchard, Jonathan, 1 Jan. 1919.
1018 Paget, Henry Edward Clarence, 1 Jan. 1919.
1019 Pakeman, John Robert, 1 Jan. 1919.
1020 Pearce, Standen Leonard, 1 Jan. 1919.
1021 Pearson, Louis Frederick, 1 Jan. 1919.
1022 Pelham, Frederick Sidney, 1 Jan. 1919.
1023 Pembroke and Montgomery, Beatrice Eleanor, Countess of, 1 Jan. 1919.
1024 Peto, Geoffrey Kelsall, 1 Jan. 1919. (M.)
1025 Piercy, William, 1 Jan. 1919.
1026 Pigott, Richard, 1 Jan. 1919.
1028 Reiss, Charles Julius, 1 Jan. 1919.
1029 Roberts, George Quinlan, 1 Jan. 1919.
1030 Robey, George, 1 Jan. 1919.
1031 Rolleston, Lady Charlotte Emma Maud, 1 Jan. 1919.
1032 Ross, James Stirling, 1 Jan. 1919.
1033 Haynes-Rudge, Florence, Mrs., 1 Jan. 1919.
1034 Sampson, Alexander Whitehead, 1 Jan. 1919.
1035 Seddon, Harry Sterratt, 1 Jan. 1919.
1036 Selbie, Robert Hope, 1 Jan. 1919.
1037 Shaw, Thomas, 1 Jan. 1919.
1038 Shaw, William Barbour, 1 Jan. 1919.
1039 Simmonds, Herbert John, 1 Jan. 1919.
1040 Sloan, Robert Patrick, 1 Jan. 1919.
1041 Stobart, Hugh Morton, 1 Jan. 1919.
1042 Stonestreet, George William, 1 Jan. 1919.
1043 Strain, James Bruce, 1 Jan. 1919.
1044 Swain, Percival Francis, 1 Jan. 1919.
1045 Thomas, Edgar William, 1 Jan. 1919.
1046 Thomson, William Gordon, 1 Jan. 1919.
1047 Towle, Arthur Edward, 1 Jan. 1919.
1048 Trouton, Edmund Arthur, 1 Jan. 1919.
1049 Turnor, Lady Mary Katherine, 1 Jan. 1919.
1050 Vincent, Arthur Rose, 1 Jan. 1919.
1051 Vulliamy, Grace, 1 Jan. 1919.
1053 Warner, Lionel Ashton Piers, 1 Jan. 1919.
1054 Warre, George Francis, 1 Jan. 1919.
1055 Watson, Edith Margaret, 1 Jan. 1919.
1056 Wells, Sidney Henry, 1 Jan. 1919.
1057 Willett, Henry Goodrich, 1 Jan. 1919.
1058 Willett, Henry Goodrich, 1 Jan. 1919.
1059 Wilson, Cecil Mary, Lady, 1 Jan. 1919.
1060 Wood, William Francis John, 1 Jan. 1919.
1061 Woodhouse, Hon. Horace Marton, 1 Jan. 1919.
1062 Woodroffe, William Henry Plukenett, 1 Jan. 1919.
1063 Wylie, James, 1 Jan. 1919.
1064 Allum, Frederick Warner, 1 Jan. 1919.
1065 Beyts, William George, 1 Jan. 1919.
1066 Boalth, Victor Hope, 1 Jan. 1919.
1067 Campbell, Charles Stewart, 1 Jan. 1919.
1068 Cardew, Evelyn Roberta, Lady, 1 Jan. 1919.
1069 Carmichael, Gertrude, Mrs., 1 Jan. 1919.
1070 Close, Harold Arden, 1 Jan. 1919.
1071 Coubrough, Anthony Cathcart, 1 Jan. 1919.
1072 Sudhal Deo, Raja, 1 Jan. 1919.
1073 Denham, Godfrey Charles, 1 Jan. 1919.
1074 Ferrier, Thomas Archibald, 1 Jan. 1919.
1075 Fitzpatrick, James Alexander Ossory, 1 Jan. 1919.
1076 Harcourt, Henry, 1 Jan. 1919.
1077 Hardiman, John Percy, 1 Jan. 1919.
1078 Harnett, William Falkiner, 1 Jan. 1919.
1079 Holberton, Edgar Joseph, 1 Jan. 1919.
1080 Holmes, Henry Burvill, 1 Jan. 1919.
1081 Fa yaz Ali Khan, Nawab Mumtaz-ud-Daula Sir Muhammad, 1 Jan. 1919.
1082 Mubariz Khan Tiwana, Nawab Malik Muhammad, 1 Jan. 1919.
1083 Lindsay, Darcy, 1 Jan. 1919.
1084 Lyons, Miriam Isabel, Mrs., 1 Jan. 1919.
1085 Mitra, Bhupendra Nath, 1 Jan. 1919.
1086 Molony, Edmund Alexander, 1 Jan. 1919.
1087 Murray, Sir Alexander Robertson, 1 Jan. 1919.
1088 O'Brien, Aubrey John, 1 Jan. 1919.
1089 Orr, James Peter, 1 Jan. 1919.
1090 Pearce, Charles Marshall, 1 Jan. 1919.
1091 Petrie, David, 1 Jan. 1919.
1092 Stanley, Sir John, 1 Jan. 1919.
1093 Ward, Ellacott Leamon, 1 Jan. 1919.

1094 Langley, John, 1 Jan. 1919.
1095 Boys, Henry Ward, 1 Jan. 1919.
1096 Ross-Taylor, Walter, 1 Jan. 1919.
1097 Midwinter, Edward Colpoys, 1 Jan. 1919.
1098 King, Henry Douglas, 1 Jan. 1919. (M.)
1099 Phillips, Geoffrey Francis, 1 Jan. 1919.
1100 Boase, William Norman, 1 Jan. 1919.
1101 Campbell, Robert Garrett, 1 Jan. 1919.
1103 Bond, James Henry Robinson, 1 Jan. 1919. (M.)
1104 Day, Ven. Archdeacon Charles Victor Parkerson, 1 Jan. 1919. (M.)
1105 Dickson, Ernest, 1 Jan. 1919. (M.)
1106 Green, Sebert Francis St. Davids, 1 Jan. 1919. (M.)
1107 Hawker, Claude Julian, 1 Jan. 1919. (M.)
1108 Jones, Beatrice Isabel, 1 Jan. 1919. (M.)
1109 Knott, Rev. Alfred Ernest, 1 Jan. 1919. (M.)
1110 Lane, William Byam, 1 Jan. 1919. (M.)
1111 Oakes, Richard, 1 Jan. 1919. (M.)
1112 Pitkeathly, James Scott, 1 Jan. 1919. (M.)
1113 Stone, Rev. Henry Cecil Brough, 1 Jan. 1919. (M.)
1114 Flick, Charles Leonard, 1 Jan. 1919. (M.)
1115 McCarthy, James Joseph, 1 Jan. 1919. (M.)
1116 Anderson, Edmund Buller, 1 Jan. 1919. (M.)
1117 Daniel, Charles James, 1 Jan. 1919. (M.)
1118 McNish, George, 1 Jan. 1919. (M.)
1119 Stewart, Louisa Mary, 1 Jan. 1919. (M.)
1120 Messer, Arthur Albert, 1 Jan. 1919. (M.)
1121 Soltau, Alfred Bertram, 1 Jan. 1919. (M.)
1122 Osborne, Rosabelle, 1 Jan. 1919. (M.)
1123 Brooman-White, Charles James, 1 Jan. 1919. (M.)
1124 Buller, Walter Thomas More, 1 Jan. 1919. (M.)
1125 Cormack, John Dewar, 1 Jan. 1919. (M.)
1126 Daubeny, Reginald Ernest, 1 Jan. 1919. (M.)
1127 Hutchinson, Robert Schlesinger, 1 Jan. 1919. (M.)
1128 Johnston, William James, 1 Jan. 1919. (M.)
1129 Mitchell-Innes, Edward Alfred, 1 Jan. 1919. (M.)
1130 Peel, Herbert Haworth, 1 Jan. 1919. (M.)
1131 Thwaites, Norman Graham, 1 Jan. 1919. (M.)
1132 Trotter, Gerald Frederic, 1 Jan. 1919. (M.)
1133 Whitlock, George Frederic Ashford, 1 Jan. 1919. (M.)
1134 Woodroffe, Charles Richard, 1 Jan. 1919. (M.)
1135 Worgan, Sydney Drummond, 1 Jan. 1919. (M.)
1136 Wray, John Willoughby, 1 Jan. 1919. (M.)
1137 Webber, Horace Armine William, 1 Jan. 1919. (M.)
1138 Dowie, Lawrence Adam, 1 Jan. 1919. (M.)
1139 Hyde, James Reid, 1 Jan. 1919. (M.)
1140 Macpherson, Duncan Gordon, 1 Jan. 1919. (M.)
1141 Workman, Wolston Thomas, 1 Jan. 1919. (M.)
1142 Conyers, Evelyn Augusta, 1 Jan. 1919. (M.)
1143 Durrant, Rt. Rev. Henry Bickersteth, 1 Jan. 1919.
1144 Barth, Hon. Jacob William, 1 Jan. 1919.
1145 Macdonald, Archibald Campbell, 1 Jan. 1919.
1146 Brandon, Vivian Ronald, 12 Feb. 1919. (M.)
1147 Rayment, Guy Varley, 12 Feb. 1919. (M.)
1148 Tinsley, Richard Bolton, 12 Feb. 1919. (M.)
1149a Vischer, Hanns, 12 Feb. 1919. (M.)
1149b Paterson, Andrew Melville, 12 Feb. 1919. (M.)
1150 Alcock, Reginald, 18 Feb. 1919.
1151 Anderson, Alexander Richard, 18 Feb. 1919.
1152 Frankling, Herbert George, 18 Feb. 1919.
1153 Greene, William Henry Clayton, 18 Feb. 1919.
1154 Hogarth, Robert George, 18 Feb. 1919.
1155 Howard, Russell John, 18 Feb. 1919.
1156 Howarth, William James, 18 Feb. 1919.
1157 May, Bennett, 18 Feb. 1919.
1158 Morton, William Cuthbert, 18 Feb. 1919.
1159 Nicholson, Frank, 18 Feb. 1919.
1160 Rice-Oxley, Alfred James, 18 Feb. 1919.
1161a Simpson, Thomas Young, 18 Feb. 1919.
1161b Cornock-Taylor, Gerald Oldroyd, 25 Feb. 1919. (M.)
1161c Hazel, Albert William, 31 March, 1919.
1162 Carey, Walter, 1 April, 1919. (M.)
1163 Fraser, Gordon Colquhoun, 1 April, 1919.
1164 Harrel, William Vesey, 1 April, 1919. (M.)
1165 Innes, James William Guy, 1 April, 1919. (M.)
1166 Miller, Grenville Acton, 1 April, 1919. (M.)
1167 Rowley, Howard Fiennes Julius, 1 April, 1919. (M.)
1168 Slee, John Ambrose, 1 April, 1919. (M.)
1169 White, John Bell, 1 April, 1919. (M.)
1170 Payne, Christopher Russell, 22 April, 1919. (M.)
1171 Pitts, Percy, 11 April, 1919. (M.)
1172 Cane, Mary Lucy, Mrs., 9 May, 1919. (M.)
1173 Dakyns, Winifred, Mrs., 9 May, 1919. (M.)
1174a Hare, Dorothy Christian, 9 May, 1919. (M.)
1174b Brown, William George Charteris, 24 May, 1919. (M.)
1175 Adam, Herbert Algernon, 27 May, 1919. (M.)
1176 Anderson, Maxwell Hendry, 27 May, 1919. (M.)
1177 Beck, Oliver Lawrence, 27 May, 1919. (M.)
1178 Blackett, Henry, 27 May, 1919. (M.)
1179 Bowden-Smith, William, 27 May, 1919. (M.)
1180 Bush, James Tobin, 27 May, 1919. (M.)
1181 Church, William Drummond, 27 May, 1919. (M.)
1182 Clark, Henry William Alfred, 27 May, 1919. (M.)
1183 Clarke, Henry James Langford, 27 May, 1919. (M.)
1184 Coppinger, Robert Henry, 27 May, 1919. (M.)
1185 Corbett, Godfrey Edwin, 27 May, 1919. (M.)
1186 Foot, Cunningham Robert de Clare, 27 May, 1919. (M.)
1188 Hewett, Paul, 27 May, 1919. (M.)
1189 Howard, William Gilbert, 27 May, 1919. (M.)

COMMANDERS.

1190 Howson, John, 27 May, 1919. (M.)
1191 Hughes, Edward Llewellyn, 27 May, 1919. (M.)
1192 Hyde, Richard, 27 May, 1919. (M.)
1193 Irvin, William Dion, 27 May, 1919. (M.)
1194 Leith, George Piercy, 27 May, 1919. (M.)
1195 McKinstry, Edward Robert, 27 May, 1919. (M.)
1196 Moore, Nithsdale Carleton Atkinson, 27 May, 1919. (M.)
1198 Mulleneux, Hugh Bowring, 27 May, 1919. (M.)
1199 Parish, Arthur John, 27 May, 1919. (M.)
1200 Parker, Walter Henry, 27 May, 1919. (M.)
1201 Plenderleath, Claude William Manners, 27 May, 1919. (M.)
1202 Purefoy, Richard Purefoy Fitz-Gerald, 27 May, 1919. (M.)
1203 Rashleigh, Vernon Stanhope, 27 May, 1919. (M.)
1204 Roberts, John, 27 May, 1919. (M.)
1205 Simpson, Cortland Herbert, 27 May, 1919. (M.)
1206 Staunton, Hugh Geoffrey, 27 May, 1919. (M.)
1207 Turnbull, James, 27 May, 1919. (M.)
1208 Watson, Horace Cyril, 27 May, 1919. (M.)
1209 Willcox, Howard James Lionel Walter Kox, 27 May, 1919. (M.)
1210 Williams, Thomas Acland, 27 May, 1919. (M.)
1211 Wright, Alexander Galloway, 27 May, 1919. (M.)
1212 Abercrombie, Charles Murray, 3 June, 1919. (M.)
1213 Addie, John Heathcote, 3 June, 1919,. (M.)
1214 Alexander, John Donald, 3 June, 1919. (M.)
1215 Anderson, James Dalgleish. 3 June, 1919. (M.)
1216 Ardee, Reginald Le Normand, Lord, 3 June, 1919. (M.)
1217 Arnold, Herbert Tollemache, 3 June, 1919. (M.)
1218 Baker, Jasper, 3 June, 1919. (M.)
1219 Barnett, Alfred George, 3 June, 1919. (M.)
1220 Begbie, Frank Warburton, 3 June, 1919. (M.)
1221 Beveridge, Wilfred William Ogilvy, 3 June, 1919. (M.)
1222 Blount, Edward Augustine, 3 June, 1919. (M.)
1224 Bowen, Arthur Winniett Nunn, 3 June, 1919. (M.)
1225 Bradford, Sir John Rose, 3 June, 1919. (M.)
1226 Braithwaite, Francis Powell, 3 June, 1919. (M.)
1227 Branson, William Philip Sutcliffe, 3 June, 1919.
1228 Bromley-Davenport, William, 3 June, 1919. (M.)
1229 Browne, Sherwood Dighton, 3 June, 1919. (M.)
1230 Burke, Bernard Bruce, 3 June, 1919. (M.)
1231 Burrows, Harold, 3 June, 1919. (M.)
1232 Bush, James Paul, 3 June, 1919. (M.)
1233 Callender, Eustace Maude, 3 June, 1919.
1234 Campbell, John Hay, 3 June, 1919. (M.)
1235 Carden, Rev. John, 3 June, 1919. (M.)
1236 Church, George Ross Marryat, 3 June, 1919. (M.)
1237 Clay, John, 3 June, 1919. (M.)
1238 Cooper, Robert Higham, 3 June, 1919. (M.)
1239 Cordeaux, Edward Kyme, 3 June, 1919.
1240 Couper, John Duncan Campbell, 3 June, 1919.
1241 Cowie, Henry Edward Colvin, 3 June, 1919. (M.)
1242 Cranford, Robert Langely, 3 June, 1919. (M.)
1243 Davy, Lila, 3 June, 1919. (M.)
1244 Eames, William L'Estrange, 3 June, 1919. (M.)
1245 Elliott, Thomas Renton, 3 June, 1919. (M.)
1246 Elsner, Otto William Alexander, 3 June, 1919. (M.)
1247 Erskine, Henry Adeane, 3 June, 1919. (M.)
1248 Fegen, Magrath Fogarty, 3 June, 1919. (M.)
1249 Fleming, John Gibson, 3 June, 1919. (M.)
1250 Frankau, Claude Howard Stanley, 3 June, 1919. (M.)
1251 Fraser, Thomas, 3 June, 1919. (M.)
1252 Fraser, Forbes, 3 June, 1919. (M.)
1253 Gibb, Evan, 3 June. 1919. (M.)
1254 Gibbard, Thomas Wykes, 3 June, 1919. (M.)
1255 Goldsmith, George Mills, 3 June, 1919. (M.)
1256 Graham, Charles Percy, 3 June, 1919. (M.)
1257 Grattan, Henry William, 3 June, 1919. (M.)
1258 Gray, Archibald Montague Henry, 3 June, 1919. (M.)
1259 Guest, Rt. Hon. Frederick Edward, 3 June, 1919. (M.)
1260 Gwynne, Rt. Rev. Llewellyn Henry, Bishop, 3 June, 1919. (M.)
1261 Harper, John Robinson, 3 June, 1919. (M.)
1262 Harrison, Cholmely Edward Carl Branfill, 3 June, 1919. (M.)
1263 Hartley, Harold, 3 June, 1919. (M.)
1264 Hayes, Edwin Charles, 3 June, 1919. (M.)
1265 Henniker, Alan Major, 3 June, 1919. (M.)
1266 Hicks, Sir Maxwell, 3 June, 1919. (M.)
1267 Higgs, Frederick William, 3 June, 1919. (M.)
1268 Holmes, Gordon Morgan, 3 June, 1919. (M.)
1269 Howkins, Cyril Henry, 3 June, 1919. (M.)
1270 Hudleston, Wilfrid Edward, 3 June, 1919. (M.)
1271 Hunt, Frederick Welsley, 3 June, 1919. (M.)
1272 Hyde, Dermot Owen, 3 June, 1919. (M.)
1273 Jackson, George Scott, 3 June, 1919. (M.)
1274 Jenney, Archibald Offley, 3 June, 1919. (M.)
1275 Keddie, Herbert William Graham, 3 June, 1919. (M.)
1276 Kelly, Francis, 3 June, 1919. (M.)
1277 Ker, Charles Arthur, 3 June, 1919. (M.)
1278 Larken, Edmund, 3 June, 1919. (M.)
1279 Lecky, John Gage, 3 June, 1919.
1280 Legge, Reginald Francis, 3 June, 1919. (M.)
1281 Lindsay, Alexander Dunlop, 3 June, 1919. (M.)
1282 Lindsay, Ernest Charles, 3 June, 1919. (M.)
1283 Longmore, John Constantine Gordon, 3 June, 1919. (M.)
1284 Lyell, David, 3 June, 1919. (M.)
1285 MacCormac, Henry, 3 June, 1919. (M.)
1286 MacLaughlin, Arthur Maunsell, 3 June, 1919.

1287 Macleod, Robert Lockhart Ross, 3 June, 1919. (M.)
1288 McNalty, Arthur George Preston, 3 June, 1919. (M.)
1289 Man, Hubert William, 3 June, 1919. (M.)
1290 Masters, Rev. Thomas Heywood, 3 June, 1919. (M.)
1291 Maud, Harry, 3 June, 1919. (M.)
1292 Miller, Charles Hewitt, 1 June, 1919. (M.)
1293 Miller, Edward Darley, 3 June, 1919. (M.)
1294 Money, Robert Cotton, 3 June, 1919. (M.)
1296 Morgan, Frederick James, 3 June, 1919. (M.)
1297 Mount, Alan Henry Lawrence, 3 June, 1919. (M.)
1298 Nelson, Percy Reginald, 3 June, 1919. (M.)
1299 Newsom, Augustus Charles, 3 June, 1919. (M.)
1300 Pallin, William Alfred, 3 June, 1919. (M.)
1301 Pearson, Walter Bagot, 3 June, 1919. (M.)
1302 Perry, Ernest Middleton, 3 June, 1919. (M.)
1303 Peterkin, Charles Duncan, 3 June, 1919. (M.)
1304 Pilcher, Edgar Montagu, 3 June, 1919. (M.)
1305 Pollock, Charles Edward, 3 June, 1919. (M.)
1306 Pollok, Robert Valentine, 3 June, 1919. (M.)
1307 Prynne, Harold Vernon, 3 June, 1919. (M.)
1308 Radcliffe Frederick Walter, 3 June, 1919. (M.)
1309 Radnor, Jacob, Pleydell-Bouverie, Earl of, 3 June, 1919. (M.)
1310 Ramsbottom-Isherwood, Charles Edward, 3 June, 1919. (M.)
1311 Ramsden, Herbert Frechville Smythe, 3 June, 1919. (M.)
1312 Rawnsley, Claude, 3 June, 1919. (M.)
1313 Reid, Frederick James, 3 June, 1919. (M.)
1314 Reynolds, Reginald Philip Neri, 3 June, 1919. (M.)
1315 Ricardo, Ambrose St. Quintin, 3 June, 1919. (M.)
1316 Robertson, John, 3 June, 1919. (M.)
1318 Rudd, Thomas William, 3 June, 1919. (M.)
1319 Saint, Charles Frederick Morris, 3 June, 1919. (M.)
1320 Sargent, Harry Neptune, 3 June, 1919. (M.)
1321 Savile, George Walter Wrey, 3 June, 1919. (M.)
1322 Searle, Frank, 3 June, 1919. (M.)
1323 Shaw, Francis Stewart Kennedy, 3 June, 1919. (M.)
1324 Silver, John Payzant, 3 June, 1919. (M.)
1325 Simpson, Lightly Stapleton, 3 June, 1919. (M.)
1326 Smith, Rev. Charles William, 3 June, 1919. (M.)
1327 Spencer, Charles Louis, 3 June, 1919. (M.)
1328 Starr, Frederick Newton Gisboine, 3 June, 1919. (M.)
1329 Statham, John Charles Baron, 3 June, 1919. (M.)
1330 Steward, Godfrey Robert Viveash, 3 June, 1919. (M.)
1331 Stewart, Rev. Frank White, 3 June, 1919. (M.)
1332 Stirling, Sir George Murray Home, Bart., 3 June, 1919. (M.)
1333 Sutherland, John Donald, 3 June, 1919. (M.)
1334 Tatam, Walter John, 3 June, 1919. (M.)
1335 Thurston, Hugh Stanley, 3 June, 1919. (M.)
1336 Umfreville, Percy, 3 June, 1919. (M.)
1337 Vesey, Hon. Osbert Eustace, 3 June, 1919. (M.)
1339 Wadley, Edward John, 3 June, 1919. (M.)
1342 Wansbrough, Thomas Percival, 3 June, 1919. (M.)
1343 Watkins, Henry George, 3 June, 1919. (M.)
1344 Watling, Francis Wyatt, 3 June, 1919. (M.)
1345 Webb-Johnson, Alfred Edward, 3 June, 1919. (M.)
1346 Westmacott, Frederick Hibbart, 3 June, 1919. (M.)
1348 Wraith, Ernest Arnold, 3 June, 1919. (M.)
1349 Drum, Lorne, 3 June, 1919. (M.)
1350 Fallis, Rev. George Oliver, 3 June, 1919. (M.)
1351 Griffin, Atholl Edwin, 3 June, 1919. (M.)
1352 Hogan, Edward Vincent, 3 June, 1919. (M.)
1354 Ripley, Blair, 3 June, 1919. (M.)
1355 Simpson, Robert Mills, 3 June, 1919. (M.)
1356 Templeton, Charles Perry, 3 June, 1919. (M.)
1357 Todd, Guy Mansfield, 3 June, 1919. (M.)
1358 Wilby, Arthur William Roger, 3 June, 1919. (M.)
1359 Wilson, Francis Walter Ernest, 3 June, 1919. (M.)
1360 Davis, Charles Herbert, 3 June, 1919. (M.)
1361 Leane, Edwin Thomas, 3 June, 1919. (M.)
1362 Marks, Alexander Hammett, 3 June, 1919. (M.)
1363 Shepherd, Arthur Edmund, 3 June, 1919. (M.)
1364 Tunbridge, Walter Howard, 3 June, 1919. (M.)
1365 Viney, Horace George, 3 June, 1919. (M.)
1366 Duff, Charles de Vertus, 3 June, 1919. (M.)
1367 Abraham, James Johnstone, 3 June, 1919. (M.)
1368 Badcock, Gerald Eliot, 3 June, 1919. (M.)
1369 Bagshawe, Herbert Vale, 3 June, 1919. (M.)
1370 Beach, Thomas Boswell, 3 June, 1919. (M.)
1371 Blunt, Conrad Edward Grant, 3 June, 1919. (M.)
1372 Bury, Lindsay Edward, 3 June, 1919. (M.)
1373 Cornwallis, Kinahan, 3 June, 1919. (M.)
1374 Cowan, John Marshall, 3 June, 1919. (M.)
1375 Davies, George Freshfield, 3 June, 1919. (M.)
1376 Dawnay, Alan Geoffrey Charles, 3 June, 1919. (M.)
1377 Day, Rev. Edward Rouverie, 3 June, 1919. (M.)
1378 Dobbin, William James Knowles, 3 June, 1919. (M.)
1379 Elliott, William, 3 June, 1919. (M.)
1380 Gabriel, Edmund Vivian, 3 June, 1919. (M.)
1381 Hopkinson, Henry Charles Barwick, 3 June, 1919. (M.)
1382 Huskisson, William Gordon, 3 June, 1919. (M.)
1383 Jellicoe, Richard Carey, 3 June, 1919. (M.)
1385 McCandlish, Patrick Dalmahoy, 3 June, 1919. (M.)
1386 Nicoll, Peter Strachan, 3 June, 1919. (M.)
1387 Paul, Ernest Moncrieff, 3 June, 1919. (M.)
1388 Rice, Cecil Edward, 3 June, 1919. (M.)
1389 Savile, Robert Vesey, 3 June, 1919. (M.)
1390 Shute, Cyril Aveling, 3 June, 1919. (M.)

1391 Travers, Henry Cecil, 3 June, 1919. (M.)
1392 Warren, Peter, 3 June, 1919. (M.)
1393 Watney, Frank Dormay, 3 June, 1919. (M.)
1394 Watson, James Keiro, 3 June, 1919. (M.)
1395 Croll, David Gifford, 3 June, 1919. (M.)
1396 Chaytor, D'Arcy, 3 June, 1919. (M.)
1397 Mackesy, Charles Ernest Randolph, 3 June, 1919. (M.)
1398 Campbell, Robert Morris, 3 June, 1919. (M.)
1399 Hale, Thomas Wyatt, 3 June, 1919. (M.)
1400 Hobbins, Thomas Phillips, 3 June, 1919. (M.)
1401 Robertson, James Currie, 3 June, 1919. (M.)
1402 Rose, Ernest Albert, 3 June, 1919. (M.)
1403 Rowe, Williams Hugh Cecil, 3 June, 1919. (M.)
1404 Stephenson, Robert, 3 June, 1919. (M.)
1405 Stewart-Dick-Cunyngham, Sir William, Bart., 3 June, 1919. (M.)
1406 Wait, Hugh Godfrey Killigrew, 3 June, 1919. (M.)
1407 Watkins, Rev. Owen Spencer, 3 June, 1919. (M.)
1408 Dowell, George William, 3 June, 1919. (M.)
1409 Dudgeon, Leonard Stanley, 3 June, 1919. (M.)
1410 Falconer, Arthur Wellesley, 3 June, 1919. (M.)
1411 Gauntlett, Eric Gerald, 3 June, 1919. (M.)
1412 Hooper, Harry Upington, 3 June, 1919. (M.)
1413 Jaffray, Rev. William Stevenson, 3 June, 1919. (M.)
1414 Morcom, Reginald Keble, 3 June, 1919. (M.)
1415 Payne, Herbert Chidgey Brine, 3 June, 1919. (M.)
1416 Rhodes, Godfrey Dean, 3 June, 1919. (M.)
1417 Shuttleworth, Digby Inglis, 3 June, 1919. (M.)
1418 Smith, William Hugh Usher, 3 June, 1919. (M.)
1419 Taylor, George Brian Ogilvie, 3 June, 1919. (M.)
1420 Villiers, Charles Walter, 3 June, 1919. (M.)
1421 Wenyon, Charles Morley, 3 June, 1919. (M.)
1422 Browne, Philip Henry, 3 June, 1919. (M.)
1423 Canny, James Clare Macnamara, 3 June, 1919. (M.)
1424 Frost, Frank Dutton, 3 June, 1919. (M.)
1425 Garrow, Robert George, 3 June, 1919. (M.)
1426 Lang, Elliot Brownlow, 3 June, 1919. (M.)
1427 Leland, Francis William George, 3 June, 1919. (M.)
1428 Macrae, Robert Scarth Farquhar, 3 June, 1919. (M.)
1429 McVittie, Robert Henry, 3 June, 1919. (M.)
1430 Morris, Arthur Hugh, 3 June, 1919. (M.)
1431 Morton. Hugh Murray, 3 June, 1919. (M.)
1432 Ratsey, Harold Edward, 3 June, 1919. (M.)
1433 Starr, William Henderson, 3 June, 1919. (M.)
1434 Tremlett, Colin Percy, 3 June, 1919. (M.)
1435 Truman, Egerton Danford, 3 June, 1919. (M.)
1436 Wood, William Albert, 3 June, 1919. (M.)
1437 Dwyer, Ernest, 3 June, 1919. (M.)
1438 Graham, Robert Blackall, 3 June, 1919. (M.)
1439 Nussey, Albert Henry Mortimer, 3 June, 1919. (M.)
1440 Elliot, Gilbert Sutherland McDowell, 3 June, 1919. (M.)
1441 Adair, Hugh Robert, 3 June, 1919. (M.)
1442 Adams, Gofton Gee, 3 June, 1919. (M.)
1443 Adams, Lewis Charles, 3 June, 1919. (M.)
1444 Adamson, Robert Hay, 3 June, 1919. (M.)
1445 Alford, Rev. Josiah George, 3 June, 1919. (M.)
1446 Armstrong. Thomas Graves Lowry Herbert, 3 June, 1919. (M.)
1447 Armstrong-Jones, Sir Robert, 3 June, 1919. (M.)
1448 Aytoun. Andrew, 3 June, 1919. (M.)
1449 Bailey, Alfred John, 3 June, 1919. (M.)
1450 Barclay, Robert Leatham, 3 June, 1919. (M.)
1451 Baring, Hon. Everard, 3 June, 1919. (M.)
1452 Barker, Frederick George, 3 June, 1919. (M.)
1453 Barrett-Lennard, John, 3 June. 1919. (M.)
1454 Barry, Stanley Leonard, 3 June, 1919. (M.)
1455 Barton, Alfred Yarker, 3 June, 1919. (M.)
1456 Batt, Reginald Cossley, 3 June, 1919. (M.)
1457 Baylay, Frederick, 3 June, 1919. (M.)
1458 Bayley, Arthur George, 3 June, 1919. (M.)
1459 Beadon, Roger Hammet, 3 June, 1919. (M.)
1460 Beauchamp, Sir Frank, Bart., 3 June, 1919. (M.)
1461 Becher, Andrew Cracroft, 3 June, 1919. (M.)
1462 Glasier, Frank Bedford-, 3 June, 1919. (M.)
1463 Belfield, Sydney, 3 June, 1919. (M.)
1464 Bernard, William Kingsmill, 3 June, 1919. (M.)
1465 Bickerstaffe-Drew, Rt. Rev. Monsignor, Count Francis Browning Drew, 3 June, 1919. (M.)
1466 Bigham, Hon. Charles Clive, 3 June, 1919. (M.)
1467 Billington, Lawson, 3 June, 1919. (M.)
1468 Birdwood, George Christopher McDowall, 3 June, 1919. (M.)
1469 Blackett, William Cuthbert, 3 June, 1919. (M.)
1470 Blandford, Laurence James, 3 June, 1919. (M.)
1471 Bliss, Thomas Gordon Cumming, 3 June, 1919. (M.)
1472 Blunt, Charles Jasper, 3 June, 1919. (M.)
1473 Blyth, James, 3 June, 1919. (M.)
1474 Boase, George Orlebar, 3 June, 1919. (M.)
1475 Boles, Dennis Fortescue, 3 June, 1919. (M.)
1476 Rooker, George Edward Nussey, 3 June, 1919. (M.)
1477 Bonomi, Joseph Ignatius, 3 June, 1919. (M.)
1478 Bowly, William Arthur Travell, 3 June, 1919. (M.)
1479 Boyd, Mossom Archibald, 3 June, 1919. (M.)
1480 Brereton, Frederick Sadlier, 3 June, 1919. (M.)
1481 Bromilow, Walter, 3 June, 1919. (M.)
1482 Brooke, Ronald George, 3 June, 1919. (M.)
1483 Browne, Abraham Walker, 3 June, 1919. (M.)
1484 Brownlow, Charles William, 3 June, 1919. (M.)
1485 Bruce. Clarence Dalrymple, 3 June, 1919. (M.)
1486 Bryant, Frederick Carkeet, 3 June, 1919. (M.)

1487 Buchan. Charles Forbes, 3 June, 1919. (M.)
1488 Buckle, Cuthbert, 3 June, 1919. (M.)
1489 Buckley. George Alexander MacLean, 3 June, 1919. (M.)
1490 Burdon, Rowland. 3 June, 1919. (M.)
1491 Burn-Murdoch, John Francis, 3 June, 1919. (M.)
1492 Burne, Rainald Owen, 3 June, 1919. (M.)
1493 Burney, Herbert Henry, 3 June, 1919. (M.)
1494 Burrell, Sir Merrik Raymond, Bart., 3 June, 1919. (M.)
1495 Burrows, Edmund Augustine. 3 June, 1919. (M.)
1496 Butler, Henry Hugh, 3 June, 1919. (M.)
1497 Bythell, William John, 3 June, 1919. (M.)
1498 Cadell, Harry Ernest, 3 June, 1919. (M.)
1499 Caithness, Norman Macleod Buchan, Earl of, 3 June, 1919. (M.)
1500 Calley, Thomas Charles Pleydell, 3 June, 1919. (M.)
1501 Calvert, James, 3 June, 1919. (M.)
1502 Campbell, Hon Ralph Alexander, 3 June, 1919. (M.)
1503 Campbell. William MacLaren, 3 June, 1919. (M.)
1504 Cardew, George Hereward, 3 June, 1919. (M.)
1505 Carless, Albert, 3 June, 1919. (M.)
1506 Carleton, Montgomery Launcelot, 3 June, 1919. (M.)
1507 Carr, Edward Elliott, 3 June, 1919. (M.)
1508 Carter, Charles Herbert Philip, 3 June, 1919. (M.)
1509 Carter, Ernest Augustus Frederick, 3 June, 1919. (M.)
1510 Champion-De-Crespigny, George Harrison, 3 June, 1919.
1511 Chance, Sir Arthur, 3 June, 1919. (M.)
1512 Chatterton, Frank Beauchamp Macaulay, 3 June, 1919. (M.)
1513 Cholmondeley, Hugh Cecil. 3 June, 1919. (M.)
1514 Clarke, Herman, 3 June, 1919. (M.)
1515 Clay, Ernest Charles, 3 June, 1919. (M.)
1516 Clifford, Ernest Thomas, 3 June, 1919. (M.)
1517 Clifford, Walter Rees, 3 June, 1919. (M.)
1518 Cleeve, Herbert, 3 June, 1919. (M.)
1519 Cockburn, George, 3 June, 1919. (M.)
1520 Coleridge, Hugh Fortescue, 3 June, 1919. (M.)
1521 Collard, Alexander Arthur, Lysons 3 June, 1919. (M.)
1522 Collard, Arthur William, 3 June, 1919. (M.)
1523 Colvin, Forrester Farnell, 3 June, 1919. (M.)
1524 Conway-Gordon, Gwynnedd, 3 June, 1919. (M.)
1525 Cooper, Harry, 3 June, 1919. (M.)
1526 Cottell, Reginald James Cope, 3 June, 1919. (M.)
1527 Cousins, Arthur George, 3 June, 1919. (M.)
1528 Cox, Edward Geoffrey Hippisley, 3 June, 1919. (M.)
1529 Craig, Sir Maurice, 3 June, 1919. (M.)
1530 Craig, Robert Annesley, 3 June, 1919. (M.)
1531 Crampton, Philip John Ribton, 3 June, 1919. (M.)
1532 Craster, Edmund Henry Bertram, 3 June, 1919. (M.)
1533 Crofton-Atkins, Cyril Randell, 3 June, 1919. (M.)
1534 Crookham, Rev. William Thomas Rupert, 3 June, 1919. (M.)
1535 Curry, Montagu Creighton, 3 June, 1919. (M.)
1536 Cunningham, George Glencairn, 3 June, 1919. (M.)
1537 Daniell, Frederick Francis Williamson, 3 June, 1919. (M.)
1538 Dashwood, Edmund William, 3 June, 1919. (M.)
1539 Deane, Richard Woodforde, 3 June, 1919. (M.)
1540 Etheridge, De Courcy Cecil, 3 June, 1919. (M.)
1541 De Hoghton, Sir James, Bart., 3 June, 1919. (M.)
1542 De Jersey, William Grant, 3 June, 1919. (M.)
1543 De Watteville, Herman Gaston, 3 June, 1919. (M.)
1544 Denison. Henry, 3 June, 1919. (M.)
1545 Doran, John Crampton Morton, 3 June, 1919.
1546 Dunfee, Vickers, 3 June, 1919. (M.)
1547 Dunne, William, 3 June, 1919. (M.)
1548 Easton, Philip George, 3 June, 1919. (M.)
1549 Edmondson, James Heslam, 3 June, 1919. (M.)
1550 Edwards, Henry John, 3 June, 1919. (M.)
1551 Edwards, William Bickerton, 3 June, 1919. (M.)
1552 Egan, Michael Henry, 3 June, 1919. (M.)
1553 Ellis, Charles Conyngham, 3 June, 1919. (M.)
1554 Ellis, Henrietta Christobel, 3 June, 1919. (M.)
1555 Elmslie, Christiana Deanes, 3 June, 1919. (M.)
1556 Eteson, Harold Carleton Wetherall, 3 June, 1919. (M.)
1557 Farquharson, Arthur Spenser Loat, 3 June, 1919. (M.)
1558 Fell, Robert Black, 3 June, 1919. (M.)
1559 Fenwick, Edward Hurry, 3 June, 1919. (M.)
1560 Ferrar, Henry Minchin, 3 June, 1919. (M.)
1561 Finch, Hamilton Walter Edward, 3 June, 1919. (M.)
1562 Findlay, Harold. 3 June, 1919. (M.)
1563 Fisher-Rowe, Herbert Mayow 3 June, 1919. (M.)
1564 Fitzpatrick, Ernest Richard, 3 June, 1919. (M.)
1565 Fitzwilliam. Sir William Charles De Meuron, Earl, 3 June, 1919. (M.)
1566 Foley, Frank Wigram, 3 June, 1919. (M.)
1567 Follett, Henry Spencer 3 June 1919. (M.)
1568 Foster, Alfred James, 3 June, 1919. (M.)
1569 Foster, Arthur Bruce, 3 June, 1919. (M.)
1570 Foster Henry Needham, 3 June, 1919. (M.)
1571 Francis, Charles John, 3 June, 1919. (M.)
1573 French, Herbert, 3 June, 1919. (M.)
1574 Frith, Cyril Halsted. 3 June, 1919. (M.)
1575 Gardner, Charles James Hookham, 3 June, 1919. (M.)
1576 Garrett, Arthur Newson Bruff, 3 June, 1919. (M.)
1578 Geddes, George Hessing, 3 June, 1919. (M.)
1579 Gemmel, Archibald Burns, 3 June, 1919. (M.)
1580 Gilbert, Arthur Robert, 3 June, 1919. (M.)
1581 Gilpin, Frederick Charles Almon, 3 June, 1919. (M.)
1582 Glanusk, Joseph Henry Russell, Lord, 3 June, 1919. (M.)

1584 Gordon, Mervyn Henry, 3 June, 1919. (M.)
1585 Gordon-Steward, Charles Steward, 3 June, 1919. (M.)
1586 Gorell, Ronald Gorell Barnes, Lord, 3 June, 1919. (M.)
1587 Gorges, Edmund Howard, 3 June, 1919. (M.)
1588 Gough, Alan Percy George, 3 June, 1919. (M.)
1589 Gould, Sir Alfred Pearce, 3 June, 1919. (M.)
1590 Graham, Gilbert Maxwell Adair, 3 June, 1919. (M.)
1591 Greenly, John Henry Maitland, 3 June, 1919. (M.)
1592 Greg, Robert Alexander, 3 June, 1919. (M.)
1593 Gretton, John, 3 June, 1919. (M.)
1594 Gribbon, Walter Harold, 3 June, 1919. (M.)
1595 Grove, Edward Aickin William Stewart, 3 June, 1919. (M.)
1596 Hacket-Thompson, Frederick, 3 June, 1919. (M.)
1597 Hackett, Robert Isaac Dalby, 3 June, 1919. (M.)
1598 Hall, Ven. Archdeacon Henry Armstrong, 3 June, 1919. (M.)
1599 Hall, Sir John Richard, Bart., 3 June, 1919. (M.)
1600 Hambro, Harold Everard, 3 June, 1919. (M.)
1601 Hamilton-Cox, Arthur Francis, 3 June, 1919. (M.)
1602 Hammond, Frederick Dawson, 3 June, 1919. (M.)
1603 Hankey, John Cyril Giffard Alers, 3 June, 1919. (M.)
1604 Hare, Charles Tristram Melville, 3 June, 1919. (M.)
1605 Harrison, Louis Kenneth, 3 June, 1919. (M.)
1606 Hart, Charles Joseph, 3 June, 1919. (M.)
1607 Harvey, David, 3 June, 1919. (M.)
1608 Hawkins, Herbert Pennell, 3 June, 1919. (M.)
1609 Haynes, Kenneth Edward, 3 June, 1919. (M.)
1610 Heaton-Ellis, Charles Henry Brabazon, 3 June, 1919. (M.)
1611 Helliwell, John Percival, 3 June, 1919. (M.)
1612 Hepburne-Scott, Hon. Walter George, Master of Polwarth, 3 June, 1919. (M.)
1614 Hesketh, Rawdon John Isherwood, 3 June, 1919. (M.)
1615 Hezlet, Robert Knox, 3 June, 1919. (M.)
1616 Hill, Charles Henry, 3 June, 1919. (M.)
1617 Hill, Francis Robert, 3 June, 1919. (M.)
1618 Hill, Robert Montague, 3 June, 1919. (M.)
1619 Hill, Walter de Marchet, 3 June, 1919. (M .
1620 Grove-Hills, Edmond Herbert, 3 June, 1919. (M.)
1621 Hoadley, Jane, 3 June, 1919. (M.)
1622 Holford, Sir George Lindsay, 3 June, 1919. (M.)
1623 Holmes, Hardress Gilbert, 3 June, 1919. (M.)
1624 Hordern, Rev. Arthur Venables Calvely, 3 June, 1919. (M.)
1625 Horniblow, Emilie Hilda, 3 June, 1919. (M.)
1626 Hoskyn, John Cunningham Moore, 3 June, 1919. (M.)
1627 Howard, Francis James Leigh, 3 June, 1919. (M.)
1628 Howe, Randall Charles Annesley, 3 June, 1919. (M.)
1629 Hume, John James Francis, 3 June, 1919. (M.)
1630 Hunt, Godfrey Massy Vere, 3 June, 1919. (M.)
1631 Iremonger, Edgar Assheton, 3 June, 1919. (M.)
1632 Jack, Archibald, 3 June, 1919. (M.)
1633 James, Frederick, 3 June, 1919. (M.)
1634 James, Rev. Canon Sidney Rhodes, 3 June, 1919. (M.)
1635 Jenkins, Noble Fleming, 3 June, 1919. (M.)
1636 Jennings, Edward Charles, 3 June, 1919. (M.)
1637 Jerrard, Augustus George Almes, 3 June, 1919. (M.)
1638 Johnston, Henry Halcro, 3 June, 1919. (M.)
1639 Johnston, Osmond Moncrieff, 3 June, 1919. (M.)
1640 Johnstone, Hope, 3 June, 1919. (M.)
1641 Jones, Cyril Vivian, 3 June, 1919. (M.)
1642 Julian, Oliver Richard Archer, 3 June, 1919. (M.)
1643 Keane, Richard Henry, 3 June, 1919. (M.)
1644 Kempton, Charles Leslie, 3 June, 1919. (M.)
1645 Kennard, Henry Gerard Hegan, 3 June, 1919. (M.)
1646 Kimber, Edmund Gibbs, 3 June, 1919. (M.)
1647 King, Charles Dickson, 3 June, 1919. (M.)
1648 Kirk, John Charles, 3 June, 1919. (M.)
1649 Kirkpatrick, Ivone, 3 June, 1919. (M.)
1650 Koe, Lancelot Charles, 3 June, 1919. (M.)
1651 Land, William Henry, 3 June, 1919. (M.)
1652 Lane, Samuel Wellington, 3 June, 1919. (M.)
1653 Langley, John Penrice, 3 June, 1919. (M.)
1654 Larking, Reginald Nesbitt Wingfield, 3 June, 1919. (M.)
1655 Leach, Harold Pemberton, 3 June, 1919. (M.)
1656 Leather, Kenneth John Walters, 3 June, 1919. (M.)
1657 Lee, Francis, 3 June, 1919. (M.)
1658 Lees, Charles Archibald, 3 June, 1919. (M.)
1659 Legard, Alfred Digby, 3 June, 1919. (M.)
1660 Leith, Henry Gordon, 3 June, 1919. (M.)
1661 Le Marchant, Edward Thomas, 3 June, 1919. (M.)
1662 Lemonius, Gerald MacLean, 3 June, 1919. (M.)
1663 Le-Poer-Trench, Frederick Amelius, 3 June, 1919. (M.)
1664 Leslie, Sir John, Bart., 3 June, 1919. (M.)
1665 Levita, Cecil Bingham, 3 June, 1919. (M.)
1666 Liddell, Clive Gerard, 3 June, 1919. (M.)
1667 Little, Malcolm Orme, 3 June, 1919. (M.)
1668 Lloyd, Samuel Eyre Massy, 3 June, 1919. (M.)
1669 Lloyd-Carson, Charles John, 3 June, 1919. (M.)
1670 Lord, John Robert, 3 June, 1919.
1671 Lowry, James, 3 June, 1919. (M.)
1672 Ludlow, Edmund Ranald Owen, 3 June, 1919. (M.)
1673 Luff, Arthur Pearson, 3 June, 1919. (M.)
1674 Lyle, Hugh Thomas, 3 June, 1919. (M.)
1675 Lynch, David, 3 June, 1919. (M.)
1676 McCalmont, Barklie Cairns, 3 June, 1919. (M.)
1677 McClymont, Robert Arthur, 3 June, 1919. (M.)
1678 McFerran, Edwin Millar Gilliland, 3 June, 1919. (M.)
1680 McKie, John, 3 June, 1919. (M.)
1681 Mackintosh of Mackintosh, Alfred Donald, The, 3 June, 1919. (M.)

1682 Mackintosh, George, 3 June, 1919. (M.)
1683 Macpherson, Rev. Ewen George Fitzroy, 3 June, 1919. (M.)
1684 Markham, Charles John, 3 June, 1919. (M.)
1685 Marriott, John, 3 June, 1919. (M.)
1686 Marsh, Frank, 3 June, 1919. (M.)
1687 Martin, Ernest Edmund, 3 June, 1919. (M.)
1688 Martin, James Fitzgerald, 3 June, 1919. (M.)
1689 Marwood, Henry, 3 June, 1919. (M.)
1690 Mason-MacFarlane, David James, 3 June, 1919. (M.)
1691 Massy, Percy Hugh Hamon, 3 June, 1919. (M.)
1692 Maunsell, Francis Richard, 3 June, 1919. (M.)
1693 Meeres, Charles Stuart, 3 June, 1919. (M.)
1694 Meldon, James Austen, 3 June, 1919. (M.)
1695 Mellor, Robert Ramsden, 3 June, 1919. (M.)
1696 Metcalfe-Smith, Bertram, 3 June, 1919. (M.)
1698 Middleton, William Crawford, 3 June, 1919. (M.)
1699 Miles, George Edward, 3 June, 1919. (M.)
1700 Miller, Hugh de Burgh, 3 June, 1919. (M.)
1701 Montagu, Edward, 3 June, 1919. (M.)
1702 Moore, Arthur Trevelyan, 3 June, 1919. (M.)
1703 Moore, Robert Reginald Heber, 3 June, 1919. (M.)
1704 Moore-Lane, William, 3 June, 1919. (M.)
1705 Morgan, Alexander Braithwaite, 3 June, 1919. (M.)
1706 Morton, Edward, 3 June, 1919. (M.)
1707 Moullin, Charles William Mansell, 3 June, 1919. (M.)
1708 Muller, George Herbert, 3 June, 1919. (M.)
1709 Murphy, Rev. William, 3 June, 1919. (M.)
1710 Murray, Eric Madden, 3 June, 1919. (M.)
1711 Murray-Smith, Arthur, 3 June, 1919. (M.)
1712a Nelson, Edgar Forbes, 3 June, 1919. (M.)
1712b Neve, Edward John, 3 June, 1919. (M.)
1713 Newland, Edmund Walcott, 3 June, 1919. (M.)
1714 Niblett, Herbert, 3 June, 1919. (M.)
1715 Noblett, Louis Hemington, 3 June, 1919. (M.)
1716 Northumberland, Alan Ian, Duke of, 3 June, 1919. (M.)
1717 Nugent, Walter Vyvian, 3 June, 1919. (M.)
1718 O'Brien, Edmund Donough John, 3 June, 1919. (M.)
1719 O'Carroll, Joseph Francis, 3 June, 1919. (M.)
1720 O'Donoghue, Montague Ernest, 3 June, 1919. (M.)
1721 O'Leary, Tom Evelyn, 3 June, 1919. (M.)
1722 Oliver, Rev. Richard John Deane, 3 June, 1919 (M.)
1723 O'Meagher, John Kevin, 3 June, 1919. (M.)
1724 Onslow, Cranley Charlton, 3 June, 1919. (M.)
1725 Ostrehan, Francis George Rodney, 3 June, 1919. (M.)
1726 O'Sullivan, Daniel, 3 June, 1919. (M.)
1727 Owen, William Hugh, 3 June, 1919. (M.)
1728 Owens, Robert Leonce, 3 June, 1919. (M.)
1729 Parr, Clements, 3 June, 1919. (M.)
1730 Parry, Henry Jules, 3 June, 1919. (M.)
1731 Parry, Llewelyn England Sidney, 3 June, 1919. (M.)
1732 Parsons, John Herbert, 3 June, 1919. (M.)
1733 Paterson, Stanley, 3 June, 1919. (M.)
1734 Peacock, Rev. Charles Alfred, 3 June, 1919. (M.)
1735 Pearce, Cyril Harvey, 3 June, 1919. (M.)
1736 Pearson, George Thomson, 3 June, 1919. (M.)
1737 Perceval, Charles Cecil, 3 June, 1919. (M.)
1738 Perkins, Edwin King, 3 June, 1919. (M.)
1739 Perkins, Hugh Wharton, 3 June, 1919. (M.)
1740 Phillips, George Ingleton, 3 June, 1919. (M.)
1741 Pike, Cuthbert Joseph, 3 June, 1919. (M.)
1742 Pinhorn, Henry Quinten, 3 June, 1919. (M.)
1743 Plunkett, Edward Abadie, 3 June, 1919. (M.)
1744 Poulton, Arthur Faulconer, 3 June, 1919. (M.)
1745 Powell, Philip Lionel William, 3 June, 1919. (M.)
1746 Prendergast, Theodore John Warrender, 3 June, 1919. (M.)
1747 Pulling, Rev. Edward Herbert, 3 June, 1919. (M.)
1748 Purvis, John Spottiswoode, 3 June, 1919. (M.)
1749 Raper, Henry Stanley, 3 June, 1919. (M.)
1750 Remnant, Sir James Farquharson, Bart., 3 June, 1919. (M.)
1751 Richards, Gertrude Mary, 3 June, 1919. (M.)
1752 Roberts, Arthur Noel, 3 June, 1919. (M.)
1753 Roberts, Henry Robert, 3 June, 1919. (M.)
1754 Rolleston, Lancelot William, 3 June, 1919. (M.)
1755 Roper, Alexander William, 3 June, 1919. (M.)
1756 Rows, Richard Gundry, 3 June, 1919. (M.)
1757 Savage, Morris Boscawen, 3 June, 1919. (M.)
1758 Sawyer, Charles Edward, 3 June, 1919. (M.)
1759 Scholfield, George Peabody, 3 June, 1919. (M.)
1760 Selby, Rev. William John, 3 June, 1919. (M.)
1761 Shaftesbury, Sir Anthony Ashley-Cooper, Earl of, 3 June, 1919. (M.)
1762 Shakerley, Sir Walter Geoffrey, Bart., 3 June, 1919. (M.)
1763 Shawe, Charles, 3 June, 1919. (M.)
1764 Sherren, James, 3 June, 1919. (M.)
1765 Smith, Anne Beadsmore, 3 June, 1919. (M.)
1766 Smith, Peter Caldwell, 3 June, 1919. (M.)
1767 Smith-Neill, James William, 3 June, 1919. (M.)
1768 Smithson, Walter Charles, 3 June, 1919. (M.)
1769 Smyth, Robert Napier, 3 June, 1919. (M.)
1770 Sparshott, Margaret Elwin, 3 June, 1919. (M.)
1771 Spears, Edward Louis, 3 June, 1919. (M.)
1772 Stansfeld, James Rawdon, 3 June, 1919. (M.)
1773 Stansfield, Thomas Edward Knowles, 3 June, 1919. (M.)
1774 Stenning, John Frederick, 3 June, 1919. (M.)
1775 Stewart, Patrick Alexander Vansitart 3 June, 1919. (M.)
1776 Stewart, William Robert, 3 June, 1919. (M.)

1777 Stobart, George Herbert, 3 June, 1919. (M.)
1778 Stordy, Robert John, 3 June, 1919. (M.)
1779 Stradbroke, George Edward John Mowbray, Earl of, 3 June, 1919. (M.)
1780 Strutt, Edward Lisle, 3 June, 1919. (M.)
1781 Sulivan, Ernest Frederic, 3 June, 1919. (M.)
1782 Swettenham, George Kilner, 3 June, 1919. (M.)
1783 Taylor, Charles Newton, 3 June, 1919. (M.)
1784 Taylor, Harold Blake, 3 June, 1919. (M.)
1785 Thomas, Reginald Aneurin, 3 June, 1919. (M.)
1786 Thomson, Christopher Birdwood, 3 June, 1919. (M.)
1787 Thomson, David George, 3 June, 1919. (M.)
1788 Thornycroft, Charles Mytton, 3 June, 1919. (M.)
1789 Thorold, Hayford Douglas, 3 June, 1919. (M.)
1790 Thuillier, Willoughby, 3 June, 1919. (M.)
1791 Tilney, Norman Eccles, 3 June, 1919. (M.)
1792 Todd, Octavius, 3 June, 1919. (M.)
1793 Towsey, Francis William, 3 June, 1919. (M.)
1794 Toynbee, Guy Elliston, 3 June, 1919. (M.)
1795 Trevor, Philip Christian William, 3 June, 1919. (M.)
1796 Tucker, William Kington, 3 June, 1919. (M.)
1797 Tuckey, Rev. James Grove White, 3 June, 1919. (M.)
1798 Turner, Archer Lloyd Marischal, 3 June, 1919. (M.)
1799 Twiss, John Henry, 3 June, 1919. (M.)
1800 Tyrrell, Charles Robert, 3 June, 1919. (M.)
1801 Vandeleur, Henry Martley, 3 June, 1919. (M.)
1802 Van Straubenzee, Casimir Henry Claude, 3 June, 1919. (M.)
1803 Wakefield, Sir Charles Cheers, Bart., 3 June, 1919. (M.)
1804 Walker, Francis Spring, 3 June, 1919. (M.)
1805 Ward, Montague Charles Pearson, 3 June, 1919. (M.)
1806 Warren, Thomas Richard Pennefather, 3 June, 1919. (M.)
1807 Watkins, Fredric Mostyn, 3 June, 1919. (M.)
1808 Way, Bromley George Vere, 3 June, 1919. (M.)
1809 Western, John Sutton Edward, 3 June, 1919. (M.)
1810 Westmacott, Claude Berners, 3 June, 1919. (M.)
1812 Willey, Francis Vernon, 3 June, 1919. (M.)
1813 Williams, Arthur Cecil, 3 June, 1919. (M.)
1814 Wilkinson, Henry Benfield Des Voeux, 3 June, 1919. (M.)
1815 Wilson, John George Yule, 3 June, 1919. (M.)
1816 Wise, Henry Edward Disbrowe, 3 June, 1919. (M.)
1817 Wood, Hastings St. Leger, 3 June, 1919. (M.)
1818 Woodwark, Arthur Stanley, 3 June, 1919. (M.)
1819 Wright, Ernest Granville, 3 June, 1919. (M.)
1820 Wright, George, 3 June, 1919. (M.)
1821 Wright, William Burgess, 3 June, 1919. (M.)
1822 Young, Archibald, 3 June, 1919. (M.)
1823 Young, David Douglas, 3 June, 1919. (M.)
1824 Young, Patrick Charles, 3 June, 1919. (M.)
1825 Adami, John George, 3 June, 1919. (M.)
1826 Almond, Rev. Canon John McPherson, 3 June, 1919. (M.)
1827 Armstrong, John Alexander, 3 June, 1919. (M.)
1828 Bosworth, Samuel Medbury, 3 June, 1919. (M.)
1829 Bridges, James Whiteside, 3 June, 1919. (M.)
1830 Brown, Ernest Rudolf, 3 June, 1919. (M.)
1831 Buell, William Senkler, 3 June, 1919. (M.)
1832 Goldsmith, Perry Gladstone, 3 June, 1919. (M.)
1833 Hutchison, James Alexander, 3 June, 1919. (M.)
1834 McKeown, Walter, 3 June, 1919. (M.)
1835 Robertson, Herman Melchior, 3 June, 1919. (M.)
1836 Ruttan, Charles Millidge, 3 June, 1919. (M.)
1837 Skinner, Frederick St. Duthus, 3 June, 1919. (M.)
1838 Tait, John Spottiswood, 3 June, 1919. (M.)
1840 Davidson, Ethel Sarah, 3 June, 1919. (M.)
1841 Gray, Ethel, 3 June, 1919. (M.)
1842 Holden, Rev. Albert Thomas, 3 June, 1919. (M.)
1843 Kellett, Adelaide Maud, 3 June, 1919. (M.)
1844 Long, George Merrick, 3 June, 1919. (M.)
1845 Millard, Reginald Jefferey, 3 June, 1919. (M.)
1846 Wall, George, 3 June, 1919. (M.)
1847 Wray, Rev. Frederick William, 3 June, 1919. (M.)
1848 Acland, Hugh Thomas Dyke, 3 June, 1919. (M.)
1849 Carberry, Anderson Robert Dillon, 3 June, 1919. (M.)
1850 Christie, Joseph McNaughton, 3 June, 1919. (M.)
1851 Cooke, Percival Robert, 3 June, 1919. (M.)
1852 Cooper, Charles James, 3 June, 1919. (M.)
1853 Dawson, Thomas Henry, 3 June, 1919. (M.)
1854 Falconer, Alexander Robertson, 3 June, 1919. (M.)
1855 Gabites, George Edward, 3 June, 1919. (M.)
1856 Hall, George Thompson, 3 June, 1919. (M.)
1857 Hiley, Ernest Haviland, 3 June, 1919. (M.)
1858 Hume, John Edward, 3 June, 1919. (M.)
1859 Hutchen, James William, 3 June, 1919. (M.)
1860 Leahy, John Patrick Daunt, 3 June, 1919. (M.)
1861 Major, Charles Thomas, 3 June, 1919. (M.)
1862 Makgill, Robert Haldane, 3 June, 1919. (M.)
1863 Mill, Thomas, 3 June, 1919. (M.)
1864 Pilkington, Herbert Edward, 3 June, 1919. (M.)
1865 Pringle, David, 3 June, 1919. (M.)
1866 Purdy, James Robert, 3 June, 1919. (M.)
1867 Reakes, Charles John, 3 June, 1919. (M.)
1868 Reed, John Ranken, 3 June, 1919. (M.)
1869 Roberts, Alexander Fowler, 3 June, 1919. (M.)
1870 Robertson, James Herbert Graham, 3 June, 1919. (M.)
1871 Sleeman, James Lewis, 3 June, 1919. (M.)
1872 Smith, Edmund Robinson, 3 June, 1919. (M.)
1873 Strong, William James, 3 June, 1919. (M.)

1874 Studholme, John, 3 June, 1919. (M.)
1875 Thurston, Mabel, 3 June, 1919. (M.)
1876 Valentine, Thomas Harcourt Ambrose, 3 June, 1919. (M.)
1877 Ward, Gerard Arnold, 3 June, 1919. (M.)
1878 Wylie, David Storer, 3 June, 1919. (M.)
1879 Baker, James Mitchell, 3 June, 1919. (M.)
1880 Burgess, Charles Roscoe, 3 June, 1919. (M.)
1881 Edwards, Robert Richard, 3 June, 1919. (M.)
1882 Hodson, Frederick Arthur, 3 June, 1919. (M.)
1883 Stock, Philip Graham, 3 June, 1919. (M.)
1884 Montgomerie, Alexander, 3 June, 1919. (M.)
1885 Bagnall-Wild, Ralph Kirkby, 3 June, 1919. (M.)
1886 Bartley, Bryan Cole, 3 June, 1919. (M.)
1887 Bent, Arthur Milton, 3 June, 1919. (M.)
1888 Boyle, Hon. John David, 3 June, 1919. (M.)
1889 Burnett, Charles Stuart, 3 June, 1919. (M.)
1890 Cooke, Bertram Hewett Hunter, 3 June, 1919. (M.)
1891 Davidson, Edward Humphrey, 3 June, 1919. (M.)
1892 Drew, Bertie Clephane Hawley, 3 June, 1919. (M.)
1893 Dunville, John, 3 June, 1919. (M.)
1894 Ellington, Sir, Edward Leonard, 3 June, 1919. (M.)
1895 Herbert, Philip Lee William, 3 June, 1919. (M.)
1896 Hoare, Cuthbert Gurney, 3 June, 1919. (M.)
1897 Jenkin, Charles Frewen, 3 June, 1919. (M.)
1898 Marindin, Cecil Colvile, 3 June, 1919. (M.)
1899 Melville, Edward Patrick Alexander, 3 June, 1919. (M.)
1900 More, Robert Henry, 3 June, 1919. (M.)
1901 Mulock, Redford Henry, 3 June, 1919. (M.)
1902 Newall, Cyril Louis Norton, 3 June, 1919. (M.)
1903 Osmond, Edward, 3 June, 1919. (M.)
1904 Pitcher, Duncan Le Geyt, 3 June, 1919. (M.)
1905 Russell, Reginald Edmund Maghlin, 3 June, 1919. (M.)
1906 Ryan, William John, 3 June, 1919. (M.)
1907 Smith, Sidney Ernest, 3 June, 1919. (M.)
1908 Swann, Oliver, 3 June, 1919. (M.)
1909 Sykes, Arthur, 3 June, 1919. (M.)
1910 Weir, James George, 3 June, 1919. (M.)
1911 Wells, Hardy Vesey, 3 June, 1919. (M.)
1912 Wigram, Kenneth, 3 June, 1919. (M.)
1913 Andrews, Octavius William, 3 June, 1919. (M.)
1914 Barnes, George Edward, 3 June, 1919. (M.)
1915 Barrett, Dacre Lennard, 3 June, 1919. (M.)
1916 Chilcott, Ronald Evered, 3 June, 1919. (M.)
1917 Clarke, Arthur Calvert, 3 June, 1919. (M.)
1918 Clinton-Baker, Lewis, 3 June, 1919. (M.)
1919 Colclough, Beauchamp Urquhart, 3 June, 1919. (M.)
1920 Crisp, Arthur Samuel, 3 June, 1919. (M.)
1921 Drury, William Price, 3 June, 1919. (M.)
1922 Eldred, Edward Henry, 3 June, 1919. (M.)
1923 Ferguson, Samuel Pringle, 3 June, 1919. (M.)
1924 Fleet, Ernest James, 3 June, 1919. (M.)
1925 Harris, Gerald Noel Anstice, 3 June, 1919. (M.)
1927 Heming, Thomas Henry, 3 June, 1919. (M.)
1928 Hinchcliffe, William Fryer, 3 June, 1919. (M.)
1929 Holmes, John Dickenson, 3 June, 1919. (M.)
1930 James, Hon. Cuthbert, 3 June, 1919. (M.)
1931 Jones, Rev. Percy Herbert, 3 June, 1919. (M.)
1932 McKew, Rev. Robert, 3 June, 1919. (M.)
1933 Meredyth, Charles Edward Hughes, 3 June, 1919. (M.)
1934 Moorshead, Herbert Brooks, 3 June, 1919. (M.)
1935 Penfold, William George Edward, 3 June, 1919. (M.)
1936 Rees, John David, 3 June, 1919. (M.)
1937 Rodet, Ernest William, 3 June, 1919. (M.)
1938 Ryan, Frank Edward Cavendish, 3 June, 1919. (M.)
1939 Silk, Ernest Edwin, 3 June, 1919. (M.)
1940 Simmons, George Thomas, 3 June, 1919. (M.)
1941 Smyth, Morris Henry, 3 June, 1919. (M.)
1942 Stephens, Lindsay James, 3 June, 1919. (M.)
1943 Stevens, Charles, 3 June, 1919. (M.)
1944 Stevens, John Greet, 3 June, 1919. (M.)
1945 Taylor, Arthur Trevelyan, 3 June, 1919. (M.)
1946 Tippinge, Leicester Francis Gartside, 3 June, 1919. (M.)
1947 Tompkins, Albert Edward, 3 June, 1919. (M.)
1948 Tottenham, Francis Loftus, 3 June, 1919. (M.)
1949 Vincent, Arthur Gustave, 3 June, 1919. (M.)
1950 Ward, Charles Henry Allen, 3 June, 1919. (M.)
1951 Webster, John Alexander, 3 June, 1919. (M.)
1952 Wonham, Charles Scrivener, 3 June, 1919. (M.)
1953 Wrey, William Bourchier Sherard, 3 June, 1919. (M.)
1956 Anderson, Eric Oswald, 3 June, 1919.
1957 Bray, Denys de Saumarez, 3 June, 1919.
1958 Calnan, Denis, 3 June, 1919.
1959 Cobb, Henry Venn, 3 June, 1919.
1960 Cochran, Alexander, 3 June, 1919.
1961 Cottle, Adela, Mrs., 3 June, 1919.
1962 Craddock, Frances Henrietta, Lady, 3 June, 1919.
1963 Davies, Arthur, 3 June, 1919.
1964 Deo, Maharaja Ramanuj Saran Singh, 3 June, 1919.
1965 Fraser, Constance, Lady, 3 June, 1919.
1966 French, Lewis, 3 June, 1919.
1967 Gracey, Hugh Kirkwood, 3 June, 1919.
1968 Hammond, Egbert Laurie Lucas, 3 June, 1919.
1969 Henderson, John Wright, 3 June, 1919.
1970 John, Edwin, 3 June, 1919.
1971 Khan, Jalal-ud-Daula Nawab Muhammad Khurshed Ali, 3 June, 1919.
1972 Khan Tiwana, Malik Sir Umar Hayat, 3 June, 1919.
1973 King-Wood, William, 3 June, 1919.

COMMANDERS.

1974 Knapp, Arthur Rowland, 3 June, 1919.
1975 Leftwich, Charles Gerrans, 3 June, 1919.
1976 Legge, Francis Cecil, 3 June, 1919.
1977 Lindsay, Harry Alexander Fanshawe, 3 June, 1919.
1978 Miller, Sir Leslie Creery, 3 June, 1919.
1979 Singh, Maharaja Bahadur Keshav Prashad, 3 June, 1919.
1980 Preston, Arthur, 3 June, 1919.
1981 Thompson, Cyril Powney, 3 June, 1919.
1982 Whitehead, Isabel, Mrs., 3 June, 1919.
1983 Wolfe, George Charles, 3 June, 1919.
1984 Chapman, Archibald John, 3 June, 1919. (M.)
1985 Sinclair, Hugh Montgomerie, 3 June, 1919. (M.)
1986 Barling, Sir Harry Gilbert, Bart., 3 June, 1919. (M.)
1987 Forster, David, 3 June, 1919. (M.)
1988 Parish, Woodbine, 3 June, 1919. (M.)
1989 Swain, James, 3 June, 1919. (M.)
1990 Adamson, John, 3 June, 1919.
1991 Burnett, Ethel Mary, 3 June, 1919.
1992 Clark, James John, 3 June, 1919.
1993 Day, Albert Cecil, 3 June, 1919.
1994 Gunson, James Henry, 3 June, 1919.
1995 Holland, Henry, 3 June, 1919.
1996 MacDonald Ronald Macintosh, 3 June 1919.
1997 Montgomery, William Hugh, 3 June, 1919.
1998 Rolleston, Iris Brenda, Mrs., 3 June, 1919.
1999 Browne, Albert, 3 June, 1919.
2000 Chappe, Penelope Louise, Mrs., 3 June, 1919.
2001 Dunn, James Stormont, 3 June, 1919.
2002 Godley, Godfrey Archibald, 3 June, 1919.
2003 Herbst, John Frederick, 3 June, 1919.
2004 Long, Arthur Tilney, 3 June, 1919.
2005 Manning, William, 3 June, 1919.
2006 Pim, James Howard, 3 June, 1919.
2007 Richardson, Lewis, 3 June, 1919.
2008 Hall, Thomas Andrew, 3 June, 1919.
2009 Morris, Edward Robert, 3 June, 1919.
2010 Pitts, Mary, Mrs., 3 June, 1919.
2011 Rendell, Robert George, 3 June, 1919.
2012 Winter, Hon. Marmaduke George, 3 June, 1919.
2013 Ainsworth, John, 3 June, 1919.
2014 Baker, Alma, 3 June, 1919.
2015 Bertram, Edith Marion, Lady, 3 June, 1919.
2016 Boyes, Charles Edward, 3 June, 1919.
2017 Boyle, Sir Alexander George, 3 June, 1919.
2018 Church, Arthur Frederick, 3 June, 1919.
2019 Fletcher, Arthur George Murchison, 3 June, 1919.
2020 Hollis, Alfred Claud, 3 June, 1919.
2021 Noel, Martial Louis Auguste, 3 June, 1919.
2022 Pountney, Arthur Meek, 3 June, 1919.
2023 Ryder, Lady Frances, 3 June, 1919.
2024 Sinclair, John Houston, 3 June, 1919.
2025 Slyne, Denis, 3 June, 1919.
2026 Stubbs, Winifred Marjory, Lady, 3 June, 1919.
2027 Wallace, Marguerite Marie, Lady, 3 June, 1919.
2028 Barnardo, Frederick Adolphus Fleming, 3 June, 1919. (M.)
2029 Barstow, Henry, 3 June, 1919. (M.)
2030 Blakeney, William Edward Albemarle, 3 June, 1919. (M.)
2031 Campbell, George Polding, 3 June, 1919. (M.)
2032 Dunwoodie, Lallah Bessie, 3 June, 1919. (M.)
2033 Eustace, Alexander Henry, 3 June, 1919. (M.)
2034 Evans, George Henry, 3 June, 1919. (M.)
2035 Jones, Benjamin Henry, 3 June, 1919. (M.)
2036 Kaye, Cecil, 3 June, 1919. (M.)
2037 Lindsay, Henry Arthur Peyton, 3 June, 1919. (M.
2038 Luke, Thomas Mawe, 3 June, 1919. (M.)
2039 Lush, John, 3 June, 1919. (M.)
2040 Ogilvie, Edward Collingwood, 3 June, 1919. (M.)
2041 Picton, Reginald Ernest, 3 June, 1919. (M.)
2042 Rait, Helen Anna Macdonald, 3 June, 1919. (M.)
2043 Spence, Alexander Hierom Ogilvy, 3 June, 1919. (M.)
2044 Stuart, William Desmond Villiers-, 3 June, 1919. (M.)
2045 Waterhouse, Agnes May, 3 June, 1919. (M.)
2046 Young, Henry Alfred, 3 June, 1919. (M.)
2047 Brockbank, John Grahame, 3 June, 1919. (M.)
2048 Clark, D'Arcy Melville, 3 June, 1919. (M.)
2049 McDouall, Robert, 3 June, 1919. (M.)
2050 Miller, John Harry, 3 June, 1919. (M.)
2051 Myers, Charles Samuel, 3 June, 1919. (M.)
2052 Purdon, Richard Ireland, 3 June, 1919. (M.)
2053 Swayne, Sir Eric John Eagles, 3 June, 1919. (M.)
2054 Wickham, John Avenel, 3 June, 1919. (M.)
2055 Yates, Clarence Montague, 3 June, 1919. (M.)
2056 McAvity, Thomas Malcolm, 3 June, 1919. (M.)
2057 Bolton, Charles Arthur, 3 June, 1919. (M)
2058 Hall, George Clifford Miller, 3 June, 1919. (M.)
2059 Cooper, William Weldon Herring-, 3 June, 1919. (M.)
2060 Howell, Wilfrid Russell, 3 June, 1919. (M.)
2061 Kinahan, George Frederick Hudson-, 3 June, 1919. (M.)
2062 Joyce, Pierce Charles, 3 June, 1919. (M.)
2063 McCheane, Montagu William Hiley, 3 June, 1919. (M.)
2064 Sudds, William Benjamin, 3 June, 1919. (M.)
2065 Wilson, Cyril Edward, 3 June, 1919. (M.)
2066 Walton, Robert Henry, 3 June, 1919. (M.)
2067 Bartholomew, Arthur Wollaston, 3 June, 1919. (M.)
2068 Riddell, Edward Vausittart Dick, 3 June, 1919. (M.)
2069 Swabey, Wilfred Spedding, 3 June, 1919. (M.)
2070 Brough, Alan, 3 June, 1919. (M.)
2071 Learmouth, Agnes Moore, Mrs.Livingstone-, 3 June, 1919. (M.)

2072 Rawlinson, Alfred, 3 June, 1919. (M.)
2073 Striedinger, Oscar, 3 June, 1919. (M.)
2074 Harris, Herbert Sextus, 3 June, 1919. (M.)
2075 Acworth, Louis Raymond, 3 June, 1919. (M.)
2076 Allen, Edward Watts, 3 June, 1919. (M.)
2077 Bailey, John Henry, 3 June, 1919. (M.)
2078 Bateson, Rev. Joseph Harter, 3 June, 1919. (M.)
2079 Bentinck, Walter Guy, Baron, 3 June, 1919. (M.)
2080 Blachford, James Vincent, 3 June, 1919. (M.)
2081 Blagrove, Henry John, 3 June, 1919. (M.)
2082 Blewitt, William Edward, 3 June, 1919. (M.)
2083 Blore, Herbert Richard, 3 June, 1919. (M.)
2085 Cadogan, Earl, 3 June, 1919. (M.)
2086 Carey, Carteret Walter, 3 June, 1919. (M.)
2087 Churchward, Rev. Marcus Wellesley, 3 June, 1919. (M.)
2088 Clarke, William Gay, 3 June, 1919. (M.)
2089 Cobb, Henry Frederick, 3 June, 1919. (M.)
2090 Cochrane, Robert Cecil, 3 June, 1919. (M.)
2091 Cook, Herbert George, 3 June, 1919. (M.)
2092 Cooke, Claude Edward Arthur, 3 June, 1919. (M.)
2093 Corbett, Robert Lorimer, 3 June, 1919. (M.)
2094 Cornwall, James Handyside Marshall, 3 June, 1919. (M).
2095 Coulson, Basil John Blenkinsopp, 3 June, 1919. (M.)
2096 Coulson, Frank Morris, 3 June, 1919. (M.)
2097 Crossley, Arthur William, 3 June, 1919. (M.)
2098 Dauntesey, William Bathurst, 3 June, 1919. (M.)
2099 Douglas, Robert Vaughan, 3 June, 1919. (M.)
2100 Drummond, Laurence George, 3 June, 1919. (M.)
2101 Dumble, Wilfrid Chatterton, 3 June, 1919. (M.)
2102 Earl, Austin, 3 June, 1919. (M.)
2103 Eliot, Nevill, 3 June, 1919. (M.)
2104 Engleheart, Evelyn Linzee, 3 June, 1919. (M.)
2105 Falls, Horace Edward, 3 June, 1919. (M.)
2106 Fitzmaurice, Robert, 3 June, 1919. (M.)
2107 Gattie, Vernon Rodney Montagu, 3 June, 1919. (M.)
2108 Gibb, Ronald Charles, 3 June, 1919. (M.)
2109 Gill, James Herbert Wainwright, 3 June, 1919. (M.)
2110 Gillies, Harold Delf, 3 June, 1919. (M.)
2111 Goodall, Edwin, 3 June, 1919. (M.)
2112 Gordon, William Eagleson, 3 June, 1919. (M.)
2113 Grant, Sir Arthur, Bart., 3 June, 1919. (M.)
2114 Grattan, O'Donnell Colley, 3 June, 1919. (M.)
2115 Harding, William, 3 June, 1919. (M.)
2117 Hart, Henry Travers, 3 June, 1919. (M.)
2118 Healey, Coryndon William Rutherford, 3 June, 1919. (M.)
2119 Scott, Archibald Malcolm Henderson-, 3 June, 1919. (M.)
2121 Hooley, Vernon Vavasour, 3 June, 1919. (M.)
2122 Ingram, John O'Donnell, 3 June, 1919. (M.)
2123 Isham, Ralph Heyward, 3 June, 1919. (M.)
2124 Jebb, Gladwyn Dundas, 3 June, 1919. (M.)
2125 Johnson, Frederick Francis, 3 June, 1919. (M.)
2126 Johnson, Philip Henry, 3 June, 1919. (M.)
2127 Johnson, Richard Francis, 3 June, 1919. (M.)
2128 Jolly, Joan Vera Douglas, Mrs., 3 June, 1919. (M.)
2129 Mitton, George Jones, 3 June, 1919. (M.)
2130 Keay, John, 3 June, 1919. (M.)
2131 Slaney, Francis Gerald Kenyon-, 3 June, 1919. (M.)
2132 Kidd, Harold Andrew, 3 June, 1919. (M.)
2133 Kisch, Frederick Hermann, 3 June, 1919. (M.)
2134 Clarke, John de Winton Lardner-, 3 June, 1919. (M.)
2135 Lithgow, James, 3 June, 1919. (M.)
2136 Lloyd, Frederick Lindsay, 3 June, 1919. (M.)
2137 Filgate, Arthur Robert Patten Macartney-, 3 June, 1919. (M.)
2138 McCullah, Albert, 3 June, 1919. (M.)
2139 MacGwire, John Edward, 3 June, 1919. (M.)
2140 MacKay, Rev. Patrick Robson, 3 June, 1919. (M.)
2141 Maud, Philip, 3 June, 1919. (M.)
2142 Maurice, David Blake, 3 June, 1919. (M.)
2143 Midwood, Harrison 3 June, 1919. (M.)
2144 Moody, Arthur Hatfield, 3 June, 1919. (M.)
2145 Moore, Francis Hamilton, 3 June, 1919. (M.)
2146 Mornement, Edward, 3 June, 1919. (M.)
2147 Northen, Arthur, 3 June, 1919. (M.)
2148 Oldfield, Christopher George, 3 June, 1919. (M.)
2149 Oliver, William James, 3 June, 1919. (M.)
2150 Oram, Harry Kendall, 3 June, 1919. (M.)
2151 Ormond, Arthur William, 3 June, 1919. (M.)
2152 Orr, Frank George, 3 June, 1919. (M.)
2153 Paul, Walter Reginald, 3 June, 1919. (M.)
2154 Pearce, Rt. Rev. Ernest Harold, 3 June, 1919. (M.)
2155 Percival, Harold Franz Passawer, 3 June, 1919. (M.)
2156 Percy, Lord William Richard, 3 June, 1919. (M.)
2157 Potter, James Archer, 3 June, 1919. (M.)
2158 Prichard, Hubert Cecil, 3 June, 1919. (M.)
2159 Rainey, John Wakefield, 3 June, 1919. (M.)
2160 Rolland, Charles Edward Tulloch, 3 June, 1919. (M.)
2161 Samson, Louis Lort Rhys, 3 June, 1919. (M.)
2162 Satow, Hugh Ralph, 3 June, 1919. (M.)
2163 Crawford, Robert Gordon Sharman-, 3 June, 1919. (M.)
2164 Sheldrake, Edward Nodin, 3 June, 1919. (M.)
2165 Short, Ernest William George, 3 June, 1919. (M.)
2166 Simon, Maximilian St. Leger, 3 June, 1919. (M.)
2167 Simpson, Alexander, 3 June, 1919. (M.)
2168 Smallman, Arthur Briton, 3 June, 1919. (M.)
2169 Smith, Richard Talbot Snowden-, 3 June, 1919. (M.)
2170 Somerville, John Arthur Coghill, 3 June, 1919. (M.)
2171 Spiller, Lionel Wallace, 3 June, 1919. (M.)
2172 Stomm, Paul William John Augustus, 3 June, 1919. (M.)

2173 Clitherow, John Bouchier Stracey-, 3 June, 1919. (M.)
2174 Stuart, Donald Mackenzie, 3 June, 1919. (M.)
2175 Swettenham, William Alexander Whybault, 3 June, 1919. (M.)
2177 Taylor, Robert James Frederick, 3 June, 1919. (M.)
2178 Tee, James Henry Stanley, 3 June, 1919. (M.)
2179 Templer, Walter Francis, 3 June, 1919. (M.)
2180 Thomson, Samuel John, 3 June, 1919. (M.)
2181 Tremaine, Richard, 3 June, 1919. (M.)
2182 Trotter, Edith Mary, 3 June, 1919. (M.)
2183 Twiss, William Louis Oberkirch, 3 June, 1919. (M.)
2184 Vigne, Robert Austen, 3 June, 1919. (M.)
2185 Vizard, Robert Davenport, 3 June, 1919. (M.)
2186 Vincent, William James Nathaniel, 3 June, 1919. (M.)
2187 Wakefield, Rt. Rev. Henry Russell, 3 June, 1919. (M.)
2188 Wallace, Robert Hugh, 3 June, 1919. (M.)
2189 Waring, Holburt Jacob, 3 June, 1919. (M.)
2190 Wheler, Granville Charles Hastings, 3 June, 1919. (M.)
2191 Whitaker, Albert Edward, 3 June, 1919. (M.)
2192 Wright, Alfred, 3 June, 1919. (M.)
2193 Burston, Samuel Roy, 3 June, 1919. (M.)
2194 Newland, Henry Simpson, 3 June, 1919. (M.)
2195 Newmarch, Bernard James, 3 June, 1919. (M.)
2196 Stewart, John Mitchell Young, 3 June, 1919. (M.)
2197 Fitz-Herbert, Norman, 3 June, 1919. (M.)
2198 Home, George, 3 June, 1919. (M.)
2199 McKibbin, Thomas, 3 June, 1919. (M.)
2201 Inglis, Russell Tracy-, 3 June, 1919 (M.)
2202 Watson, James Taylor, 3 June, 1919. (M.)
2203 Ward, Arthur Blackwood, 3 June, 1919. (M.)
2204 Franklin, William Hodson, 3 June, 1919. (M.)
2205 Rendell, Walter Frederick, 3 June, 1919. (M.)
2206 Bayley, Stuart Farquharson, 3 June, 1919. (M.)
2207 Chamier, William, 3 June, 1919. (M.)
2208 Dorai, Bhairava Ramachandra, 3 June, 1919. (M.)
2209 Jang, Ganpat Rao Raghunath Rajwade Shaukat, 3 June, 1919. (M.)
2210 Singh, Kanwar Jeoray, 3 June, 1919. (M.)
2211 Singh, Thahur Pratab, 3 June, 1919. (M.)
2212a Storey, Robert Douglas, 3 June, 1919. (M.)
2212b Beckett, William Thomas Clifford, 3 June, 1919. (M.)
2212c Cameron, Cecil Aylmer, 3 June, 1919. (M.)
2212d Hulton, John Meredith, 3 June, 1919. (M.)
2212e Johnson, Robert Arthur, 3 June, 1919. (M.)
2212f Johnston, Eric Archibald, 3 June, 1919. (M.)
2212g Morley, Lyddon Charteris, 3 June, 1919. (M.)
2212h Neilson, John Fraser, 3 June, 1919. (M.)
2213a Brook, Reginald James, 3 June, 1919. (M.)
2213b Cartwright, Francis Lennox, 3 June, 1919. (M.)
2213c Clarke, John Thomas, 3 June, 1919. (M.)
2213d Stayner, Richard Winslow, 3 June, 1919 (M.)
2213e Lewis, Henry Augustus, 3 June, 1919. (M.)
2213f Evans, Charles Harford Bowle-, 3 June, 1919. (M.)
2213g Blackden, Leonard Shadwell, 3 June, 1919. (M.)
2213h McClymont, Rev. James Alexander, 3 June, 1919. (M.)
2214a Morris, Richard John, 3 June, 1919. (M.)
2214b Reed, John Arthur Wemyss, 3 June, 1919. (M.)
2214c Thompson, Edith Marie, 3 June, 1919. (M.)
2214d Banning, Stephen Thomas, 3 May, 1919. (M.)
2214e Ellissen, Herbert, 3 June, 1919. (M.)
2214f Mowat, Magnus, 3 June, 1919. (M.)
2214g Newton, Henry, 3 June, 1919. (M.)
2214h Stronach, Robert Summers, 3 June, 1919. (M.)
2215a Abbey, Walter Bulmer Tait, 3 June, 1919. (M.)
2215b Burne, Lindsay Elliott Lumley, 3 June, 1919. (M.)
2215c Keatinge, Rt. Rev. William, Bishop, 3 June, 1919. (M.)
2215d Hanson, Rev. David Hamilton, 3 June, 1919. (M.)
2215e Acklom, Cecil Ryther, 11 June, 1919. (M.)
2215f Blake, Albert Valentine, 11 June, 1919. (M.)
2215g Brown, Percy George, 11 June, 1919. (M.)
2216 Candy, Algernon Henry Chester, 11 June, 1919. (M.)
2217 Carruthers, David John, 11 June, 1919. (M.)
2218 Cuming, Robert Stevenson Dalton, 11 June, 1919. (M.)
2219 Dixon, Kennett, 11 June, 1919. (M.)
2220 Finlay, George, 11 June, 1919. (M.)
2221 Garde, Robert Boles, 11 June, 1919. (M.)
2222 Kent, Walter James, 11 June, 1919. (M.)
2223 Keyes, Adrian St. Vincent, 11 June, 1919. (M.)
2224 Kiddle, Kerrison, 11 June, 1919. (M.)
2225 Meadus, Harry Howard, 11 June, 1919. (M.)
2226 Parker, Willam Ramsey, 11 June, 1919. (M.)
2227 Rashbrook, Henry Samuel, 11 June, 1919. (M.)
2228 Ward, John Richard Le Hunte, 11 June, 1919. (M.)
2230 Hardy, Charles Talbot, 21 June, 1919. (M.)
2231 Moir, William Mitchell, 21 June, 1919. (M.)
2232 Bamber, Wyndham Lerrier, 27 June, 1919. (M.)
2234 Colvin, Ragnar Musgrave, 27 June, 1919. (M.)
2235 Dicks, Henry Leage, 27 June, 1919. (M.)
2236 May, Arthur de Kewer Livius, 27 June, 1919. (M.)
2237 Penfold, Marchant Hubert, 27 June, 1919. (M.)
2238 Powlett, Frederick Armand, 27 June, 1919. (M.)
2239 Silver, Mortimer L'Estrange, 27 June, 1919. (M.)
2240 Warleigh, Percival Henry, 27 June, 1919. (M.)
2241 Ballard, George Norman, 30 June, 1919. (M.)
2242 Acheson, Albert Edward, 4 July, 1919. (M.)
2243 Allenby, Frederick Claud Hynman, 4 July, 1919. (M.)
2244 Blake, James Thompson, 4 July, 1919. (M.)
2245 Cave, George Ellis, 4 July, 1919. (M.)
2246 Crawford, Charles Wispington Glover, 4 July, 1919. (M.)

2247 de Wet, Thomas Olaff, 4 July, 1919. (M.,
2248 Douglas, Sholto Grant, 4 July, 1919. (M.)
2249 Evans, Frederick James, 4 July, 1919. (M.)
2250 Garrett, Peter Bruff, 4 July, 1919. (M.)
2251 Gregory, George, 4 July, 1919. (M.)
2252 Gush, Alfred William, 4 July, 1919. (M.)
2253 Hewett, George Stuart, 4 July, 1919. (M.)
2254 Sumner, Berkeley Holme-, 4 July, 1919. (M.)
2255 Huddleston, Ernest Whiteside, 4 July, 1919. (M.)
2256 Jefferson, Henry, 4 July, 1919. (M.)
2257 Leggatt, Charles William Stares, 4 July, 1919. (M.)
2258 Leighton, John Albert, 4 July, 1919. (M.)
2259 Macdonald, David James, 4 July, 1919. (M.)
2260 Newman, Edward John Kendall, 4 July, 1919. (M.)
2261 Perfect, Herbert Mosley, 4 July, 1919. (M.)
2262 Pritchard, Francis Burnett, 4 July, 1919. (M.)
2263 Rowsell, Clarence Ralph, 4 July, 1919. (M.)
2264 Satow, Lawrence de Wahl, 4 July, 1919. (M.)
2265 Thring, Frank John, 4 July, 1919. (M.)
2266 Vibart, John Fleming, 4 July, 1919. (M.)
2267 Caulfield, James Montgomery, 10 July, 1919. (M.)
2268 Egerton, Philip, 10 July, 1919. (M.)
2269 Eliot, Ralph, 10 July, 1919. (M.)
2270 Hill, Marcus Rowley, 10 July, 1919. (M.)
2271 Hopwood, Geoffrey, 10 July, 1919. (M.)
2272 Paul, Oliver Richard, 10 July, 1919. (M.)
2273 Richards, John Arthur, 10 July, 1919. (M.)
2274 Stewart, Arthur Courtenay, 10 July, 1919. (M.)
2275 Watson, Hugh Dudley Richards, 10 July, 1919. (M.)
2276 Bethune, Henry Leonard, 12 July, 1919. (M.)
2277 Brocklebank, Henry Cyril Royds, 12 July, 1919. (M.)
2278 Fanshawe, Basil Hew, 12 July, 1919. (M.)
2279 Hargraves, Herbert James, 12 July, 1919. (M.)
2280 Martin, Harry Cutfield, 12 July, 1919. (M.)
2281 Osmaston, Cecil Alvend Fitzherbert, 12 July, 1919. (M.)
2282 Cotton, Richard Greville Arthur Wellington Stapleton-, 12 July, 1919. (M.)
2283 Tibbits, Charles, 12 July, 1919. (M.)
2284 Wilding, Michael Henley, 12 July, 1919. (M.)
2285 Adams, Henry George Homer, 17 July, 1919. (M.)
2286 Crampton, Denis Burke, 17 July, 1919. (M.)
2287 Gregory, Ernest Foster, 17 July, 1919. (M.)
2288 Hickson, Gerald Robert Stedall, 17 July, 1919. (M.)
2289 Homfray, John Robert Henry, 17 July, 1919. (M.)
2290 Betts, Ernest Edward Alexander, 31 July, 1919. (M.)
2291 Dunn, Arthur Edward, 31 July, 1919. (M.)
2292 Grant, Arthur Robert, 31 July, 1919. (M.)
2293 im Thurn, John Knowles, 31 July, 1919. (M.)
2294 O'Sullivan, Hugh Dermod Evan, 31 July, 1919. (M.)
2295 Cameron, Cyril St. Clair, 11 Aug. 1919. (M.)
2296 Dawson, Henry, 11 Aug. 1919. (M.)
2298 Meredyth, Arthur Gwyn Moreton. 11 Aug. 1919. (M.)
2299 Robertson, John Hercules, 11 Aug. 1919. (M.)
2300 Thorp, Charles Frederick, 11 Aug. 1919. (M.)
2301 Tuke, Godfrey, 11 Aug. 1919. (M.)
2302 Vawdrey, Charles, 11 Aug. 1919. (M.)
2303 Winterbottom, Thomas, 11 Aug. 1919. (M.)
2304 Woodwright, Charles Sharman, 22 Aug. 1919. (M.)
2305 Scott, George Herbert, 23 Aug. 1919.
2306 Blunt, William Frederick, 16 Sept. 1919. (M.)
2307 Boyle, Harry Lumsden, 16 Sept. 1919. (M.)
2308 Crichton, Peter Thomson, 16 Sept. 1919. (M.)
2309 Ford, Richard Vernon Tredinnick, 16 Sept. 1919. (M.)
2310 Brown, Frederick Dundas Gilpin-, 16 Sept. 1919. (M.)
2311 Hallett, Theodore John, 16 Sept. 1919. (M.)
2312 Genn, Otto Herman Hawke-, 16 Sept. 1919. (M.)
2313 Hughes, Arthur Beckett, 16 Sept. 1919. (M.)
2314 Huntingford, Walter Legh, 16 Sept. 1919. (M.)
2315 Kelly, William Henry, 16 Sept. 1919. (M.)
2316 Layton, Percival Norman, 16 Sept. 1919. (M.)
2317 Meadus, William Henry, 16 Sept. 1919. (M.)
2318 Mountifield, James, 16 Sept. 1919. (M.)
2319 Murray, John Adam, 16 Sept. 1919. (M.)
2320 Nelson, Maurice Henry Horatio, 16 Sept. 1919. (M.)
2321 Risk, Richard Henry Little, 16 Sept. 1919. (M.)
2322 Scott, Albert Charles, 16 Sept. 1919. (M.)
2323 Smith, Bertram Hornsby, 16 Sept. 1919. (M.)
2324 Smith, Charles Appleton, 16 Sept. 1919. (M.)
2325 Wace, Stephen Charles, 16 Sept. 1919. (M.)
2326 Ward, John Tom Hickman, 16 Sept. 1919. (M.)
2327 Whayman, William Matthias, 16 Sept. 1919. (M.)
2328 Wilkin, Henry Douglas, 16 Sept. 1919. (M.)
2329 Wrightson, Charles Archibald Wise, 16 Sept. 1919. (M.)
2330 Willock, Frederick George, 10 Oct. 1919. (M.)
2331 Viener, Rev. Harry Dan Leigh, 10 Oct. 1919. (M.)
2332 Cunningham, Alexander Duncan, 10 Oct. 1919. (M.)
2333 Munro, Lewis, 10 Oct. 1919. (M.)
2334 Beatty, William Dawson, 10 Oct. 1919. (M.)
2335 Birley, James Leatham, 10 Oct. 1919. (M.)
2336 Boothby, Frederick Lewis Maitland, 10 Oct. 1919. (M.)
2337 Courtney, Ivon Terence, 10 Oct. 1919. (M.)
2338 Griffith, Edward Hugh, 10 Oct. 1919. (M.)
2339 Mead, John, 10 Oct. 1919. (M.)
2340 Outram, Harold William Sydney, 10 Oct. 1919. (M.)
2341 Pink, Richard Charles Montague, 10 Oct. 1919. (M.)
2342 Playfair, Frederick Hope Grant 10 Oct. 1919. (M.)
2343 Woodcock, Harold Larpent, 10 Oct. 1919. (M.)
2344 Burch, William Edward Scarth, 10 Oct. 1919. (M.)
2345 Cheatle, Arthur Henry, 10 Oct. 1919. (M.)

COMMANDERS.

2346 Dreyer, Georges, 10 Oct. 1919. (M.)
2347 Peal, Edward Raymond, 10 Oct. 1919. (M.)
2348 Reiss, Alexander Emil Jacques, 10 Oct. 1919. (M.)
2349 Fairfield, Josephine Letitia Denny, 10 Oct. 1919. (M.)
2350 Hogarth, Archibald Henry, 10 Oct. 1919. (M.)
2351 Airey, Harold Morris, 17 Oct. 1919. (M.)
2352 Dewar, Kenneth Gilbert Balmain, 17 Oct. 1919. (M.)
2353 Finnis, George Home, 17 Oct. 1919. (M.)
2354 James, Ralph Ernest Haweis, 17 Oct. 1919. (M.)
2355 Knox, Henry Owen, 17 Oct. 1919. (M.)
2356 Lane, Henry Gerald Elliot, 17 Oct. 1919. (M.)
2357 Skelton, Reginald William, 17 Oct. 1919. (M.)
2358 Edwards, Graham Richard Leicester, 11 Nov. 1919. (M.)
2359a Pearse, Claude Alwin Rombulow-, 11 Nov. 1919. (M.)
2359b Johnson, Walter Russell, 11 Nov. 1919. (M.)
2359c Marshall, Eric Stewart, 11 Nov. 1919. (M.)
2359d Thom, George St. Clair, 11 Nov. 1919. (M.)
2359e Moore, Thomas Cecil Russell, 11 Nov. 1919.
2359f Schuster, George Ernest, 11 Nov. 1919. (M.)
2359g Turner, Martin Newman, 11 Nov. 1919. (M.)
2359h Leckie, John Edwards, 11 Nov. 1919. (M.)
2360a Herapath, Lionel, 11 Nov. 1919. (M.)
2360b Tallents, Stephen George, 11 Nov. 1919. (M.)
2360c Warren, William Robinson, 11 Nov. 1919. (M.)
2360d De Wolff, Charles Esmond, 11 Nov. 1919. (M.)
2360e Sidney, Edward, 28 Nov. 1919. (M.)
2361 Tottenham, Percy Marmaduke, 5 Dec. 1919.
2362 Hornsby, Bertram, 5 Dec. 1919.
2363 Carver, Sydney Ralph Pitts, 5 Dec. 1919.
2364 Garsia, Herbert George Anderson, 5 Dec. 1919.
2365 Christopherson, John Brian, 5 Dec. 1919.
2366 Crowfoot, John Winter, 5 Dec. 1919.
2367 Kerr, William Munro, 12 Dec. 1919. (M.)
2368 Warton, John Fenwick, 12 Dec. 1919. (M.)
2369 Bone, Reginald John, 22 Dec. 1919. (M.)
2369a Jackson, Henry Leigh, 22 Dec. 1919.
2370 Agabeg, Frank Joseph, 30 Dec. 1919.
2371 Bhore, Joseph William, 30 Dec. 1919.
2372 Bowman, Humphrey Ernest, 30 Dec. 1919.
2373 Butler, Montagu Sherard Dawes, 30 Dec. 1919.
2374 Clarke, Charles Agacy, 30 Dec. 1919.
2375 Clutterbuck, Peter Henry, 30 Dec. 1919.
2376 Cox, John Hugh, 30 Dec. 1919.
2377 Crosthwaite, Henry Robert, 30 Dec. 1919.
2378 de Montmorency, Geoffrey Fitz Hervey, 30 Dec. 1919.
2379 Elmes, Cecil Henry, 30 Dec. 1919.
2380 Forbes, Alexander, 30 Dec. 1919.
2381 Gait, Christian Maud, Lady, 30 Dec. 1919.
2382 Gall, Robert Laing Bruce, 30 Dec. 1919.
2383 Hailey, Hammett Reginald Clode, 30 Dec. 1919.
2384 Heaton, Mary Meredyth, Lady, 30 Dec. 1919.
2385 Khan, Sardar Bahadur Nawab Mehrab, 30 Dec. 1919.
2386 Jones, Frederick Archibald Leslie, 30 Dec. 1919.
2387 Macphail, Rev. Earle Monteith, 30 Dec. 1919.
2388 McCarthy, Frank, 30 Dec. 1919.
2389 McWilliam, Andrew, 30 Dec. 1919.
2390 Mistri, Kaikhushroo Manekshah, 30 Dec. 1919.
2391 Noyce, Frank, 30 Dec. 1919.
2392 Rhodes, Campbell Ward, 30 Dec. 1919.
2393 Rogers, Arthur Burden Campbell, 30 Dec. 1919.
2394 Simpson, George Clarke, 30 Dec. 1919.
2395 Singh, Raja Sadeshri Pashad Narayan, 30 Dec. 1919.
2396 Tata Mehrbai, Lady, 30 Dec. 1919.
2397 Beattie, Alexander Elder, 1 Jan. 1920.
2398 Cecil, Alicia Margaret, Hon. Mrs. Evelyn, 1 Jan. 1920.
2399 Grosvenor, Caroline Susan Theodora, Hon. Mrs. Norman, 1 Jan. 1920.
2400 Joyce, Ellen, Hon. Mrs. James Gerald, 1 Jan. 1920.
2401 Lefroy, Grace, 1 Jan. 1920.
2402 McClellan, Frank Campbell, 1 Jan. 1920.
2403 Markham, Lucy Bertram, Lady, 1 Jan. 1920.
2404 Abbott, Francis Charles, 1 Jan. 1920.
2405 Abrahams, Arthur Cecil, 1 Jan. 1920.
2406 Ackland, Robert Craig, 1 Jan. 1920.
2407 Acland, Alfred Dyke, 1 Jan. 1920.
2408 Acton, Ellen Marion, 1 Jan. 1920.
2409 Acton, Frederick, 1 Jan. 1920.
2410 Albright, George Stacey, 1 Jan. 1920.
2411 Allen, Herbert Warner, 1 Jan. 1920.
2412 Allen, Oswald Coleman, 1 Jan. 1920.
2413 Allen, Walter Macarthur, 1 Jan. 1920.
2414 Allison, James, 1 Jan. 1920.
2415 Allison, Richard John, 1 Jan. 1920.
2416 Alston, Hilda, Mrs., 1 Jan. 1920.
2417 Amery, William Bankes, 1 Jan. 1920.
2418 Anderson, David Martin, 1 Jan. 1920.
2419 Anderson, James, 1 Jan. 1920.
2420 Anderson, James Edward, 1 Jan. 1920.
2421 Anderson, Lydia Elizabeth, Lady, 1 Jan. 1920.
2422 Anderson, William Thomas, 1 Jan. 1920.
2423 Ansell, George Frederic, 1 Jan. 1920.
2424 Armstrong, John Warneford Scobell, 1 Jan. 1920.
2425 Ashhurst, William Henry, 1 Jan. 1920.
2426 Atkinson, Edward Hale Tindal, 1 Jan. 1920.
2427 Aveling, Arthur Francis, 1 Jan. 1920.
2428 Badeley, Henry John Fanshawe, 1 Jan. 1920.
2429 Baines, Hubert, 1 Jan. 1920.
2430 Baird, Douglas Heriot, 1 Jan. 1920.
2431 Ballinger, John, 1 Jan. 1920.

2432 Bandon, Georgina Dorothea Harriet, Countess of, 1 Jan. 1920.
2433 Barber, James William, 1 Jan. 1920.
2434 Barnes, Edwin Clay, 1 Jan. 1920.
2435 Barr, Sir James, 1 Jan. 1920.
2436 Barr, John, 1 Jan. 1920.
2437 Barr, Venie Ainsworth, Mrs., 1 Jan. 1920.
2438 Barratt, Frances, Lady Layland-, 1 Jan. 1920.
2439 Barrows, Elliot Thomas, 1 Jan. 1920.
2440 Bartlett, Charles Alfred, 1 Jan. 1920.
2441 Batchelor, Emily, 1 Jan. 1920.
2442 Beard, Joseph James, 1 Jan. 1920.
2443 Beausire, Clara Constance, 1 Jan. 1920.
2444 Bell, Charles Francis, 1 Jan. 1920.
2445 Bell, Henry McGrady, 1 Jan. 1920.
2446 Benson, Philip de Gylpyn, 1 Jan. 1920.
2447 Bertram, Francis George Lawder, 1 Jan. 1920.
2448 Betterton, Henry Bucknall, 1 Jan. 1920.
2449 Bewick, Ralph Martin, 1 Jan. 1920.
2450 Beynon, John Wyndham, 1 Jan. 1920.
2451 Bibby, Frank, 1 Jan. 1920
2452 Binns, Arthur, 1 Jan. 1920.
2453 Blackburn, William Ernest, 1 Jan. 1920.
2454 Blackwell, Francis Victor, 1 Jan. 1920.
2456 Blain, Herbert Edwin, 1 Jan. 1920.
2457 Blake, Edwin Holmes, 1 Jan. 1920.
2458 Bohane, Albert Edward, 1 Jan. 1920.
2459 Botterell, Percy Dunville, 1 Jan. 1920.
2460 Bower, Robert Lister, 1 Jan. 1920.
2461 Boyd, Alexander William Keown-, 1 Jan. 1920.
2462 Boyd, Harry Robert, 1 Jan. 1920.
2463 Boyne, Margaret Selina, Viscountess, 1 Jan. 1920.
2464 Bradly, Henry George, 1 Jan. 1920.
2465 Bradshaw William Graham, 1 Jan. 1920.
2466 Bramah, David, 1 Jan. 1920.
2467 Brickwell, Alfred James, 1 Jan. 1920.
2468 Bridge, Joseph James Rabnett, 1 Jan. 1920.
2469 Briggs, James, 1 Jan. 1920.
2470 Brims, Charles William, 1 Jan. 1920,
2471 Briscoe, William Richard Brunskill, 1 Jan. 1920.
2472 Brooke, Edward Geoffrey de Capell, 1 Jan. 1920.
2473 Brooks, Florence Ethel, Lady, 1 Jan. 1920.
2474 Browett, Leonard, 1 Jan. 1920.
2475 Brown, Charles John, 1 Jan. 1920.
2476 Brown, Frank James, 1 Jan. 1920.
2477 Brown, John Edwin Ambrose, 1 Jan. 1920.
2478 Brown, Joseph Pearce, 1 Jan. 1920.
2479 Brown, Nicol Paton, 1 Jan. 1920.
2480 Brown, Robert Cunyngham, 1 Jan. 1920.
2481 Bryce, James McKie, 1 Jan. 1920.
2482 Buchanan, James Courtney, 1 Jan. 1920.
2483 Buchanan, Joseph Andrew William, 1 Jan. 1920.
2484 Buckingham, Sir Henry Cecil, 1 Jan. 1920.
2485 Buckley, Wilfred, 1 Jan. 1920.
2486 Bull, Edward Bagnall-, 1 Jan. 1920.
2487 Buller, Ralph Buller Hughes-, 1 Jan. 1920.
2488 Bullock, Ralph, 1 Jan. 1920.
2489 Burditt, George Frederick, 1 Jan. 1920.
2490 Burnham, John Charles, 1 Jan. 1920.
2491 Button, Howard, 1 Jan. 1920.
2492 Byrom, Thomas Emmett, 1 Jan. 1920.
2493 Cairns, William Murray, 1 Jan. 1920.
2494 Calder, James Charles, 1 Jan. 1920.
2495 Caldwell, Francis, 1 Jan. 1920.
2496 Callendar, Hugh Longbourne, 1 Jan. 1920.
2497 Carr-Calthrop, Christopher William, 1 Jan. 1920.
2498 Camden, Joan Marion, Marchioness, 1 Jan. 1920.
2499 Campbell, Alexander, 1 Jan. 1920.
2500 Campbell, Gerald FitzGerald, 1 Jan. 1920.
2501 Campbell, Harry, 1 Jan. 1920.
2502 Candler, Edmund, 1 Jan. 1920.
2503 Cane, Arthur Beresford, 1 Jan. 1920.
2504 Carbutt, Francis, 1 Jan. 1920.
2505 Carlile, Sir (Edward) Hildred, Bart. 1 Jan. 1920.
2506 Carlton, Arthur, 1 Jan. 1920.
2507 Carnegie, David, 1 Jan. 1920.
2508 Carpenter, Charles Claude, 1 Jan. 1920.
2509 Carr, Edward Hallett, 1 Jan. 1920.
2510 Carr, Francis Howard, 1 Jan. 1920.
2511 Carr, William Theodore, 1 Jan. 1920.
2512 Cathery, Edmund, 1 Jan. 1920.
2513 Caton, Richard, 1 Jan. 1920.
2514 Chambers, George Lawson, 1 Jan. 1920.
2515 Chambers, James Thomas, 1 Jan. 1920.
2516 Charley, Harold Richard, 1 Jan. 1920.
2517 Clarke, John Courtenay, 1 Jan. 1920.
2518 Clarke, William John, 1 Jan. 1920.
2519 Clauson, Albert Charles, 1 Jan. 1920.
2520 Clough, Frederic Horton, 1 Jan. 1920.
2521 Clow, William, 1 Jan. 1920.
2522 Coates, William, 1 Jan. 1920.
2523 Cobbold, Herbert St. George, 1 Jan. 1920.
2524 Cockeram, William Henry, 1 Jan. 1920.
2525 Codrington, Adela Harriet, Lady, 1 Jan. 1920.
2526 Cole, Harold William, 1 Jan. 1920.
2527 Comben, Robert Stone, 1 Jan. 1920.
2528 Constable, Andrew Henderson Briggs, 1 Jan. 1920.
2529 Cooper, Mary Emma, Lady, 1 Jan. 1920.
2530 Corkhill, Percy Fullerton, 1 Jan. 1920.

2531 Corkran, Florence Caroline, Mrs. Seymour, 1 Jan 1920.
2532 Cotter, Joseph, 1 Jan. 1920.
2533 Coulcher, Mary Caroline, 1 Jan. 1920.
2534 Craig, Alexander, 1 Jan. 1920.
2535 Craig, Emily Mary. Lady Tudor-, 1 Jan. 1920.
2536 Cresswell, John Edwards, 1 Jan. 1920.
2537 Crewdson, Bernard Francis, 1 Jan. 1920.
2538 Crichton. Lady Jane Emma, 1 Jan. 1920.
2539 Croysdill, Clifford William, 1 Jan. 1920.
2540 Cubitt, Hon. Helen Laura, 1 Jan. 1920.
2541 Culling, James William Henry, 1 Jan. 1920.
2542 Cunliffe, Hon. Cecilie Victoria, Lady, 1 Jan. 1920.
2543 Cunningham, Lallie, 1 Jan. 1920.
2544 Cunningham, Mary Elizabeth, 1 Jan. 1920.
2545 Curre, William Edward Carne, 1 Jan. 1920.
2546 Dale, Charles Ernest, 1 Jan. 1920.
2547 Dalrymple, James, 1 Jan. 1920.
2548 Dalwood, John Hall-, 1 Jan. 1920.
2549 Dalzell, Reginald, Alexander, 1 Jan. 1920.
2550 Dartmouth, Mary, Countess of, 1 Jan. 1920.
2551 Davidson, James, 1 Jan. 1920.
2552 Davies, Alfred Thomas, 1 Jan. 1920.
2553 Davies, John Cecil, 1 Jan. 1920.
2554 Davies, John Robert, 1 Jan. 1920.
2555 Davies, Richard, 1 Jan. 1920.
2556 Deacon, Henry Wade, 1 Jan. 1920.
2557 Denman, Gertrude Mary, Lady, 1 Jan. 1920.
2558 Denniss, George Hamson, 1 Jan. 1920.
2559 Denny, Barbara Mary, Mrs., 1 Jan. 1920.
2560 Desborough, Arthur Peregrine Henry, 1 Jan. 1920.
2561 Despard, Herbert John, 1 Jan. 1920.
2562 Diack, Sir Alexander Henderson, 1 Jan. 1920.
2563 Dillon, Richards Henry, 1 Jan. 1920.
2564 Dixon, Gertrude Caroline, 1 Jan. 1920.
2565 Dobson, Bernard Henry, 1 Jan. 1920.
2566 Dominy, Reginald Hugh, 1 Jan. 1920.
2567 Donaldson, Norman Patrick, 1 Jan. 1920.
2568 Donnan, Frederick George, 1 Jan. 1920.
2569 Dottridge, Edwin Thomas, 1 Jan. 1920.
2570 Dougan, James Lockhart, 1 Jan. 1920.
2571 Downie, Fairbairn, 1 Jan. 1920.
2572 Drake, Bernard Harpur, 1 Jan. 1920.
2573 Drury, Amy Gertrude, Lady, 1 Jan. 1920.
2574 Duff, Thomas Duff Gordon, 1 Jan. 1920.
2575 Dunn, Patrick Smith, 1 Jan. 1920.
2576 Durell, Arthur James Vavasor, 1 Jan. 1920.
2577 Durell, Rev. John Carlyon Vavasor, 1 Jan. 1920.
2578 Durrant, Sir Arthur Isaac, 1 Jan. 1920.
2579 Earle, Gerald Frederick, 1 Jan. 1920.
2580 Easton, George, 1 Jan. 1920.
2581 Edgcumbe, John Aubrey Pearce-, 1 Jan. 1920.
2582 Edmeades, Alfred, 1 Jan. 1920.
2583 Edwards, Charles Lewis, 1 Jan. 1920.
2584 Edwards, John, 1 Jan. 1920.
2585 Eggar, James, 1 Jan. 1920.
2586 Elderton, William Palin, 1 Jan. 1920.
2587 Elliot, Frederick Barnard, 1 Jan. 1920.
2588 Elveden, Gwendolen Florence Mary, Viscountess, 1 Jan. 1920.
2589 Evans, Evan Laming, 1 Jan. 1920.
2590 Evans, Frederick George, 1 Jan. 1920.
2591 Evans, Henry, 1 Jan. 1920.
2592 Evans, Herbert, 1 Jan. 1920.
2593 Evans, Thomas, 1 Jan. 1920.
2594 Ewart, William Herbert Lee, 1 Jan. 1920.
2595 Fagan, Charles Edward, 1 Jan. 1920.
2596 Faire, Arthur William, 1 Jan. 1920.
2597 Falk, Oswald Toynbee, 1 Jan. 1920.
2598 Farr, William Edward, 1 Jan. 1920.
2599 Fathers, Henry, 1 Jan. 1920.
2600 Faulkner, Alfred Edward, 1 Jan. 1920.
2601 Fehr, Frank Emil, 1 Jan. 1920.
2602 Fell, Aubrey Llewellyn Coventry, 1 Jan. 1920.
2603 Fells, John Manger, 1 Jan. 1920.
2604 Ferard, Arthur George, 1 Jan. 1920.
2605 Ferguson, Arthur George, 1 Jan. 1920.
2606 Ferguson, Fergus James, 1 Jan. 1920.
2607 Fiennes, Gerard Yorke Twisleton-Wykeham-, 1 Jan. 1920.
2608 Findlay, Jean Elmslie Henderson, 1 Jan. 1920.
2609 FitzGerald, Marion, Mrs., 1 Jan. 1920.
2610 Fleming, Arthur Percy Morris, 1 Jan. 1920.
2611 Fletcher, Clarence George Eugene, 1 Jan. 1920.
2612 Fletcher, Nora Kathleen, 1 Jan. 1920.
2613 Floersheim, Cecil, 1 Jan. 1920.
2614 Fortescue, Emily, Countess, 1 Jan. 1920.
2615 Foster, Sir Norris Tildesley, 1 Jan. 1920.
2616 Frankland, Percy Faraday, 1 Jan. 1920.
2617 Freeman, John Joseph, 1 Jan. 1920.
2618 Freeman, Sterry Baines, 1 Jan. 1920.
2619 Freir, Walter Leo, 1 Jan. 1920.
2620 Fremantle, Barberina Rogers, Hon. Lady, 1 Jan. 1920.
2621 Fullerton, James, 1 Jan. 1920.
2622 Gairns, James Mather, 1 Jan. 1920.
2623 Gallier, William Henry, 1 Jan. 1920.
2624 Gambell, Thomas Francis, 1 Jan. 1920.
2625 Gandy, Henry Garnett, 1 Jan. 1920.
2626 Gates, Thomas Frank, 1 Jan. 1920.

2627 Gaunt, Percy Reginald, 1 Jan. 1920.
2628 Gavin, William, 1 Jan. 1920.
2629 Gibb, Maurice Sylvester, 1 Jan. 1920.
2630 Gick, William John, 1 Jan. 1920.
2631 Gillies, James, 1 Jan. 1920.
2632 Glanusk, Editha Elma, Lady, 1 Jan. 1920.
2633 Glover, Thomas, 1 Jan. 1920.
2634 Gollin, Alfred, 1 Jan. 1920.
2635 Goodfellow, Thomas Ashton, 1 Jan. 1920.
2636 Goodwin, Frederick Rice, 1 Jan. 1920.
2637 Gordon, James, 1 Jan. 1920.
2638 Gorvin, John Henry, 1 Jan. 1920.
2639 Gossage, Alfred Milne, 1 Jan. 1920.
2640 Graham, Allan James, 1 Jan. 1920.
2641 Graham, James, 1 Jan. 1920.
2642 Graham, John Irvine, 1 Jan. 1920.
2643 Graham, Sydney, 1 Jan. 1920.
2644 Granville, Alexander, 1 Jan. 1920.
2645 Grayson, Henry Mulleneux, 1 Jan. 1920.
2646 Green, Frederick William Edridge-, 1 Jan. 1920.
2647 Greenwood, Margery, Lady, 1 Jan. 1920.
2648 Greig, John, 1 Jan. 1920.
2649 Gresley, Herbert Nigel, 1 Jan. 1920.
2650 Griffith, Walter Spencer Anderson, 1 Jan. 1920.
2651 Griffith, Sir William Brandford, 1 Jan. 1920.
2652 Grinling, William James, 1 Jan. 1920.
2653 Gronow, Albert George, 1 Jan. 1920.
2654 Groves, Charles Nixon, 1 Jan. 1920.
2655 Grylls, Charles John Tench Bedford, 1 Jan. 1920.
2656 Gwynne, Nevile Gwyn, 1 Jan. 1920.
2657 Hadow, Sir William Henry, 1 Jan. 1920.
2658 Haig, Thomas Wolseley, 1 Jan. 1920.
2659 Hambelton, Alexander Elvin Sherwin, 1 Jan. 1920.
2660 Hamilton, Andrew, 1 Jan. 1920.
2661 Hamilton, John Baillie, 1 Jan. 1920.
2662 Hanbury, Noel, 1 Jan. 1920.
2663 Hands, William Joseph, 1 Jan. 1920.
2664 Hanman, William Thomas, 1 Jan. 1920.
2665 Hargreaves, John Henry, 1 Jan. 1920.
2666 Harris, Ernest Alfred, 1 Jan. 1920.
2667 Harry, William, 1 Jan. 1920.
2668 Hatton, George, 1 Jan. 1920.
2669 Heming, George Booth, 1 Jan. 1920.
2670 Hemingway, Charles Robert, 1 Jan. 1920.
2671 Henderson, Duncan, 1 Jan. 1920.
2672 Henley, Thomas, 1 Jan. 1920.
2673 Henson, John James, 1 Jan. 1920.
2674 Herdman, William Abbott, 1 Jan. 1920.
2675 Heriot, William Maitland-, 1 Jan. 1920.
2676 Higgins, Edward John, 1 Jan. 1919.
2677 Higginson, Charles James, 1 Jan. 1920.
2678 Hignett, Dorothy Eleanor Augusta, Mrs., 1 Jan. 1920.
2679 Hilliar, Harry William, 1 Jan. 1920.
2680 Hinks, Arthur Robert, 1 Jan. 1920.
2681 Hitchcock, Eldred Frederick, 1 Jan. 1920.
2682 Hoare, William Douro, 1 Jan. 1920.
2683 Hockaday, William Thomas, 1 Jan. 1920.
2684 Holbrook, Claude Vivian, 1 Jan. 1920.
2685 Holland, Leonard Duncan, 1 Jan. 1920.
2686 Hollingworth, Edward, 1 Jan. 1920.
2687 Holt, Sir Edward, Bart., 1 Jan. 1920.
2688 Homer, John Twigg, 1 Jan. 1920.
2689 Hooper, Barrington, 1 Jan. 1920.
2690 Hopkins, Rev. Charles Plomer, 1 Jan. 1920.
2691 Hornsby, Frederick Middleton, 1 Jan. 1920.
2692 Horsley, Albert Beresford, 1 Jan. 1920.
2693 Hough, Edwin Leadam, 1 Jan. 1920.
2694 Howard, Mabel, Lady, 1 Jan. 1920.
2695 Howell, John, 1 Jan. 1920.
2696 Howlett, Charles Edgar, 1 Jan. 1920.
2697 Howlett, Edmund Henry, 1 Jan. 1920.
2698 Howley, Richard Joseph, 1 Jan. 1920.
2699 Hudleston, Francis Josiah, 1 Jan. 1920.
2700 Hughes, George, 1 Jan. 1920.
2701 Human, Arnold Henry, 1 Jan. 1920.
2702 Humphreys, George William, 1 Jan. 1920.
2703 Hunt, Stanley Herbert, 1 Jan. 1920.
2704 Hunter, Phillip Vassar, 1 Jan. 1920.
2705 Hutchins, George D'Oyly, 1 Jan. 1920.
2706 Impey, Lawrence, 1 Jan. 1920.
2707 Innes, Cecil Mitchell-, 1 Jan. 1920.
2708 Inskip, Thomas Walker Hobart, 1 Jan. 1920.
2709 Irvine, James Colquhoun, 1 Jan. 1920.
2710 Isaac, Joseph Charles, 1 Jan. 1920.
2711 Jack, Alexander Mackenzie, 1 Jan. 1920.
2712 Jackson, Arnold Nugent Strode Strode-, 1 Jan. 1920.
2713 James, Arthur Godfrey, 1 Jan. 1920.
2714 James, Thomas David, 1 Jan. 1920.
2715 Jeeves, William John, 1 Jan. 1920.
2716 Jersey, Margaret Elizabeth, Dowager Countess of, 1 Jan. 1920.
2717 Johns, Arthur William, 1 Jan. 1920.
2718 Johnson, Dennis Ross-, 1 Jan. 1920.
2719 Johnson, Hugh Spencer, 1 Jan. 1920.
2720 Johnston, Sir Duncan Alexander, 1 Jan. 1920.
2721 Johnstone, Robert William, 1 Jan. 1920.
2723 Jones, Cadwaladr Bryner, 1 Jan. 1920.
2724 Jones, David Rocyn, 1 Jan. 1920.
2725 Jones, Llewelyn Hugh-, 1 Jan. 1920.

COMMANDERS.

2726 Jones, Morey Quayle, 1 Jan. 1920.
2727 Jones. Thomas Rees, 1 Jan. 1920.
2728 Jordan, John, 1 Jan. 1920.
2729 Judd, Thomas Langley, 1 Jan. 1920.
2730 Kelly, Elizabeth Harlott, Miss 1 Jan. 1920.
2731 Kerr, James Rutherford, 1 Jan. 1920.
2732 Kettlewell, Arthur Bradley, 1 Jan. 1920.
2733 Killick, John Spencer, 1 Jan. 1920.
2735 King, James Edward, 1 Jan. 1920.
2736 King, James Foster, 1 Jan. 1920.
2737 Kinnaird, Hon. Emily Cecilia, 1 Jan. 1920.
2738 Kitching, Theodore Hopkins, 1 Jan. 1920.
2739 Konstam, Edwin Max, 1 Jan. 1920.
2740 Koppel, Percy Alexander, 1 Jan. 1920.
2741 Krohn, Herman Alexander, 1 Jan. 1920.
2742 Laird, Roy Macgregor, 1 Jan. 1920.
2743 Laird, William, 1 Jan. 1920.
2744 Lampson, Curtis Walter, 1 Jan. 1920.
2745 Lang, Patrick Keith, 1 Jan. 1920.
2746 Larke, William James, 1 Jan. 1920.
2747 Larkin, Herbert Benjamin George, 1 Jan. 1920.
2748 Lawn, James Gunson, 1 Jan. 1920.
2749 Lawrence, Dorothy Helen, Lady, 1 Jan. 1920.
2750 Lawrence, Lester James Harvey, 1 Jan. 1920.
2751 Lazenby, Frederick George, 1 Jan. 1920.
2752 Leavis, Henry, 1 Jan. 1920.
2753 Lee, Mary Ess, Mrs. Welsh-, 1 Jan. 1920.
2754 Lee, William Alexander, 1 Jan. 1920.
2755 Leeper, Alexander Wigram Allen, 1 Jan. 1920.
2756 Leeper, Reginald Wildig Allen, 1 Jan. 1920.
2757 Leggett, Henry Aufrère, 1 Jan. 1920.
2758 Leigh, Norah Marjorie, Lady, 1 Jan. 1920.
2759 Lewis, Lucas Reginald, 1 Jan. 1920.
2760 Lillico, William Lionel James, 1 Jan. 1920
2761 Lindsay, Eugénie Josephine, Mrs., 1 Jan. 1920.
2763 Locke, Arthur, 1 Jan. 1920.
2764 Longbotham, Hugh Ashley, 1 Jan. 1920.
2765 Longridge, Michael, 1 Jan. 1920.
2766 Lonsdale, Grace Cicelie, Countess of, 1 Jan. 1920.
2767 Love, Richard Archibald, 1 Jan. 1920.
2768 Lovell, William George, 1 Jan. 1920.
2769 Lovett, Rev. Canon Ernest Neville, 1 Jan. 1920.
2770 Lowry, Thomas Martin, 1 Jan. 1920.
2771 Lucas, William Henry, 1 Jan. 1920.
2772 McArthur, William Lyon, 1 Jan. 1920.
2773 McCormack, Arthur John, 1 Jan. 1920.
2774 McDonnell, Aeneas Ronald, 1 Jan. 1920.
2775 Macgregor. John Julius, 1 Jan. 1920.
2776 Mackay, James Francis, 1 Jan. 1920.
2777 Mackenzie, Lady Marjory Louisa, 1 Jan. 1920.
2778 MacKinnon, Madeleine Frances, Lady, 1 Jan. 1920.
2779 Mackintosh of Mackintosh, Harriet Diana Arabella Mary, Mrs., 1 Jan. 1920.
2780 MacMurray, James Hamish, 1 Jan. 1920.
2781 Macnab, William, 1 Jan. 1920.
2782 McPherson, Henry Alexander, 1 Jan. 1920.
2783 Maddick, Edmund Distin, 1 Jan. 1920.
2784 Maistre, Charles le, 1 Jan. 1920.
2785 Mallet, Matilde. Lady, 1 Jan. 1920.
2786 Malmesbury, Dorothy, Countess of, 1 Jan. 1920.
2787 Manners, Mildred Mary, Lady Robert, 1 Jan. 1920.
2788 Manuel, Stephen, 1 Jan. 1920.
2789 Marchant, Rev. James, 1 Jan. 1920.
2790 Marillier, Frank William, 1 Jan. 1920.
2791 Markbreiter, Charles Gustavus, 1 Jan. 1920.
2792 Markham, Theodora Chevallier, Lady, 1 Jan. 1920.
2793 Marks, Geoffrey, 1 Jan. 1920.
2794 Marling, Lucia, Lady, 1 Jan. 1920.
2795 Marshall, Kenneth McLean, 1 Jan. 1920.
2796 Marsham, George,1 Jan. 1920.
2797 Martin, Hubert Stanley, 1 Jan. 1920.
2798 Martyr, Richard Edward, 1 Jan. 1920.
2799 Massey, William Thomas, 1 Jan. 1920.
2800 le Masurier, James, 1 Jan. 1920.
2801 Mathias, Lewis James, 1 Jan. 1920.
2802 May, Barry, 1 Jan. 1920.
2803 Meade, Francis Henry, 1 Jan. 1920.
2804 Melrose, John. 1 Jan. 1920.
2805 Melville, William, 1 Jan. 1920.
2806 Merricks, Frank, 1 Jan. 1920.
2807 Michie, Charles, 1 Jan. 1920.
2808 Michie, James, 1 Jan. 1920.
2809 Michie, Mary Agnes, Mrs. Coutts, 1 Jan. 1920.
2810 Mills, Arthur John, 1 Jan. 1920.
2811 Milne, Kenneth John, 1 Jan. 1920.
2812 Minter, Percy, 1 Jan. 1920.
2813 Mole, Lancelot Eldin de, 1 Jan. 1920.
2814 Moneypenny, Sir Frederick William, 1 Jan. 1920.
2815 Montgomery, William Alexander, 1 Jan. 1920.
2816 Moore, Rev. David Keys, 1 Jan. 1920.
2817 Moore, Thomas Warren, 1 Jan. 1920.
2818 Moresby, Walter Halliday, 1 Jan. 1920.
2819 Morgan, David Watts, 1 Jan. 1920.
2820 Morley, George, 1 Jan. 1920.
2821 Morley. James Wycliffe Headlem-, 1 Jan. 1920.
2822 Morrell, Alfred, 1 Jan. 1920.
2823 Morris, Ernest William, 1 Jan. 1920.
2824 Morrison, Agnes Brysson, Mrs., 1 Jan. 1920.
2825 Morrison, Julia Minnie, Mrs. 1 Jan. 1920.

2826 Mullins, Arthur, 1 Jan. 1920.
2827 Mummery, John Howard, 1 Jan. 1920.
2828 Myers, Arthur Wallis, 1 Jan. 1920.
2829 Napier, Cecilia Jane, Mrs., 1 Jan. 1920.
2830 Narbeth, John Harper, 1 Jan. 1920.
2831 Needham, James Ernest, 1 Jan. 1920.
2832 Nevill, Florence Mary, Lady George, 1 Jan. 1920.
2833 Newbolt, George Palmerston, 1 Jan. 1920.
2834 Newlands, Alexander, 1 Jan. 1920.
2835 Newton, Ernest, 1 Jan. 1920.
2836 Newton, Robert Henry, 1 Jan. 1920.
2837 Nicholl, Allan Hume, 1 Jan. 1920.
2838 Nicholls, Richard Howell, 1 Jan. 1920.
2839 Nicholson, Ivor Percy, 1 Jan. 1920.
2840 Norrie, Beatrice, Mrs., 1 Jan. 1920.
2841 Norris, Francis Edward Boshear, 1 Jan. 1920.
2842 North, Rev. Frank, 1 Jan. 1920.
2843 Northbrook, Florence Anita Eyre, Countess of, 1 Jan. 1920.
2844 Northumberland, Helen Magdalen, Duchess of, 1 Jan. 1920.
2845 Oakes, James, 1 Jan. 1920.
2846 O'Brien, Richard Alfred, 1 Jan. 1920.
2847 Olive, James William, 1 Jan. 1920.
2848 Oliver, John William Lambton, 1 Jan. 1920.
2849 Oliver, Philip Milner, 1 Jan. 1920.
2850 O'Mahony, Pierce de Lacy (The O'Mahony), 1 Jan. 1920.
2851 Onslow, Marion, Mrs. Denzil Hughes-, 1 Jan. 1920.
2852 Onslow, Violet Marcia Catherine Warwick, Countess of, 1 Jan. 1920.
2853 Orange, George James, 1 Jan. 1920.
2854 Orchard, Alfred John, 1 Jan. 1920.
2855 Orr, William James, 1 Jan. 1920.
2856 Overman, Henry Jacob, 1 Jan. 1920.
2857 Owen, Frederick Cunliffe-, 1 Jan. 1920.
2858 Page, Robert Palgrave, 1 Jan. 1920.
2859 Parker, Charles Thomas, 1 Jan. 1920.
2860 Parker, Owen, 1 Jan. 1920.
2861 Parlett. Harry Edgar, 1 Jan. 1920.
2862 Parry, Charles de Courcy, 1 Jan. 1920
2863 Parry, William John, 1 Jan. 1920.
2864 Paterson, Mary Muirhead, 1 Jan. 1920.
2865 Paus, Christopher Lintrup, 1 Jan. 1920.
2866 Payne, Charles, 1 Jan. 1920.
2867 Pearson, Charles Child, 1 Jan. 1920.
2868 Pease, Joseph Gerald, 1 Jan. 1920.
2869 Peile, Henry, 1 Jan. 1920.
2870 Pender, James, 1 Jan. 1920.
2871 Perkins, Frederick William, 1 Jan. 1920.
2873 Peyton, Guy Wynne Alfred, 1 Jan. 1920.
2874 Philipps, Mai Alice Magdalene, Lady, 1 Jan. 1920.
2875 Pickersgill, William, 1 Jan. 1920.
2876 Pinckney, John Robert Hugh, 1 Jan. 1920.
2877 Portal, Florence Elizabeth Mary, Lady, 1 Jan. 1920.
2878 Porter, John Fletcher, 1 Jan. 1920.
2879 Potter, John Alexander, 1 Jan. 1920.
2880 Potts, William Thomas, 1 Jan. 1920.
2881 Powell, George Allan, 1 Jan. 1920.
2882 Powell, Harry James, 1 Jan. 1920.
2883 Prescott, William Henry, 1 Jan. 1920.
2884 Preston, Alistair Houstoun-Boswell-, 1 Jan. 1920.
2885 Preston, George Frederic, 1 Jan. 1920.
2886 Preston, Sidney, 1 Jan. 1920.
2887 Prosser, Ernest Albert, 1 Jan. 1920.
2888 Pullinger, Thomas Charles Willis, 1 Jan. 1920.
2889 Quick, Eliza Ellen, Mrs., 1 Jan. 1920.
2890 Raeburn, William Norman, 1 Jan. 1920.
2891 Rafter, Charles Haughton, 1 Jan. 1920.
2892 Raikes, Henry St. John Digby, 1 Jan. 1920.
2893 Ramsay, William, 1 Jan. 1920.
2894 Ramsden, Dorothy, Mrs., 1 Jan. 1920.
2895 Reay, William Thomas, 1 Jan. 1920.
2896 Redpath, Robert, 1 Jan. 1920.
2897 Rees, Howell, 1 Jan. 1920.
2898 Reid, May, 1 Jan. 1920.
2899 Reid, Robert Whyte, 1 Jan. 1920.
2900 Reid, William Paton, 1 Jan. 1920.
2901 Rennie, Horace Watt, 1 Jan. 1920.
2902 Ricardo, Francis Cecil, 1 Jan. 1920.
2903 Richards, Albert Edwin George, 1 Jan. 1920.
2904 Richards, Rupert Peel, 1 Jan. 1920.
2905 Richards, William, 1 Jan. 1920.
2906 Robbins, Rowland Richard, 1 Jan. 1920.
2907 Roberts, Charles Abraham, 1 Jan. 1920.
2908 Roberts, George Augustus, 1 Jan. 1920.
2909 Roberts, Sir Walworth Howland, 1 Jan. 1920.
2910 Robinson, James, 1 Jan. 1920.
2911 Robinson, John, 1 Jan. 1920.
2912 Robinson, John George, 1 Jan. 1920.
2913 Robinson, Leonard Nicholas, 1 Jan. 1920.
2914 Robinson, William Henry, 1 Jan. 1920.
2915 Rogers, Muriel Augusta Gillian, Mrs. Coltman-, 1 Jan. 1920.
2916 Rogerson, Albert Chorley, 1 Jan. 1920.
2917 Ross, Roderick, 1 Jan. 1920.
2918 Rostern, Joseph, 1 Jan. 1920.
2919 Rothchild, Marie. Mrs. de, 1 Jan. 1920.
2920 Rothwell, James Herbert, 1 Jan. 1920
2921 Roundell, Christopher Foulis, 1 Jan. 1920.
2922 Rowland, Frank Mortimer, 1 Jan. 1920.

2923 Rucker, Reginald Wynn, 1 Jan. 1920.
2924 Rumbold, Etheldred Constantia, Lady, 1 Jan. 1920.
2925 Runtz, Sidney Westwood, 1 Jan. 1920.
2926 Russell, Frederick Vernon, 1 Jan, 1920.
2927 St. Helier, Susan Mary Elizabeth, Lady, 1 Jan. 1920.
2928 Salmon, Isidore, 1 Jan. 1920.
2929 Sandberg, Christer Peter, 1 Jan. 1920.
2930 Sandes, Elizabeth, 1 Jan. 1920.
2931 Sankey, Matthew Henry Phineas Riall, 1 Jan. 1920.
2932 Sarjeant, Frederick Arthur, 1 Jan. 1920.
2933 Sassoon, Eugenie Louise Judith, Mrs., 1 Jan. 1920.
2934 Sawyer, George Alexander, 1 Jan. 1920.
2935 Scholey, Harry, 1 Jan. 1920.
2936 Scott, Andrew, 1 Jan. 1920.
2937 Scott, Sidney, 1 Jan. 1920.
2938 Sears, John Edward, 1 Jan, 1920.
2939 Segrave, Thomas George, 1 Jan. 1920.
2940 Selby, Francis James, 1 Jan. 1920.
2941 Sexton, Walter, 1 Jan. 1920.
2942 Shakerley, Hilda Mary, Lady, 1 Jan. 1920.
2943 Sharp, Alphonse, 1 Jan. 1920.
2944 Shaw, Richard James Herbert, 1 Jan. 1920.
2045 Shearme, Edward Haweis, 1 Jan. 1920.
2946 Shedden, Lewis, 1 Jan. 1920.
2947 Sheffield, Mary Katharine, Lady, 1 Jan. 1920.
2948 Shepherd, Joseph Wilfrid, 1 Jan. 1920.
2949 Shorto, William Alfred Thomas, 1 Jan. 1920.
2950 Simond, Charles François, 1 Jan. 1920.
2951 Simonis, Henry, 1 Jan. 1920.
2952 Simpkin, Oswald Richard Arthur, 1 Jan. 1920.
2953 Simpson, Joseph, 1 Jan. 1920.
2954 Simpson, William Hirst, 1 Jan. 1920.
2955 Simson, Richard Arbuthnot, 1 Jan. 1920.
2956 Sire, Henry Alphonse, 1 Jan. 1920.
2957 Slater, George, 1 Jan. 1920.
2958 Smallwood, Richard Coningsby, 1 Jan. 1920
2959 Smeal, Joseph, 1 Jan. 1920.
2960 Smith, Alic Halford, 1 Jan. 1920.
2961 Smith, David Baird-, 1 Jan. 1920.
2962 Smith, Herbert Melville, 1 Jan. 1920.
2963 Smith, Thomas William, 1 Jan. 1920.
2964 Snowden, Arthur de Winton, 1 Jan. 1920.
2965 Snowden, Cyril Ralph, 1 Jan. 1920.
2966 Sparks, Charles Pratt, 1 Jan. 1920.
2967 Spreckley, Herbert William, 1 Jan. 1920.
2968 Stamer, Arthur Cowie, 1 Jan. 1920.
2969 Stanton, Thomas Ernest, 1 Jan. 1920.
2970 Stemp, Charles Hubert, 1 Jan. 1920.
2971 Stewart, Lady Alice Emma Shaw-, 1 Jan. 1920.
2972 Stewart, Ellen Frances, Mrs., 1 Jan. 1920.
2973 Stewart, James King, 1 Jan. 1920.
2974 Stewart, Valentine Peter Beardmore, 1 Jan,. 1920.
2975 Stockings, Arthur Perry, 1 Jan. 1920.
2976 Stoddart, Kenneth Bowring, 1 Jan. 1920.
2977 Strang, Alexander Ronald, 1 Jan. 1920.
2978 Strode, Edward David Chetham, 1 Jan. 1920.
2979 Strutt, Geoffrey St. John, 1 Jan. 1920.
2980 Stuart, Charles Kennedy-Craufurd-, 1 Jan. 1920.
2981 Stubbs, George, 1 Jan. 1920.
2982 Suart, Montagu Wemyss, 1 Jan. 1920.
2983 Sutherland, George Alexander, 1 Jan. 1920.
2984 Sutton, Rev. Canon Alfred, 1 Jan. 1920.
2985 Sutton, Leonard Goodhart, 1 Jan. 1920.
2986 Sylvester, Albert James, 1 Jan. 1920.
2987 Syrett, Herbert Sutton, 1 Jan. 1920.
2988 Szlumper, Alfred Weeks, 1 Jan. 1920.
2989 Tabor, James, 1 Jan. 1920.
2990 Taylor, John, 1 Jan. 1920.
2991 Tenney, John, 1 Jan. 1920.
2992 Tetley, Herbert Hustler, 1 Jan. 1920.
2993 Thesiger, Kathleen Mary, Hon. Mrs. Wilfred, 1 Jan. 1920.
2994 Thomas, Peter David, 1 Jan. 1920.
2995 Thompson, James, 1 Jan. 1920.
2996 Thornley, Reginald Ernest, 1 Jan. 1920.
2997 Thornton, Robert Lawrence, 1 Jan. 1920.
2998 Tobin, Frank, 1 Jan. 1920.
2999 Tod, James Niebuhr, 1 Jan. 1920.
3000 Tomlin, Julian Latham, 1 Jan. 1920.
3001 Toplis, James, 1 Jan. 1920.
3002 Townley, Rev. Charles Francis, 1 Jan. 1920.
3003 Towse, Ernest Beachcroft Beckwith, 1 Jan. 1920.
3004 Tracy, Louis, 1 Jan. 1920.
3005 Travis, Harry, 1 Jan. 1920.
3006 Trench, Ernest Frederic Crosbie, 1 Jan. 1920.
3007 Trevelyan, George Macaulay, 1 Jan. 1920.
3008 Trevithick, Arthur Reginald, 1 Jan. 1920.
3009 Trollope, Fabian George, 1 Jan. 1920.
3010 Trotter, Harry Woodward, 1 Jan. 1920.
3011 Trubshaw, Gwendoline Joyce, 1 Jan. 1920.
3012 Tudsbery, Francis Cannon, 1 Jan. 1920.
3013 Tweeddale, Candida Louise, Marchioness of, 1 Jan. 1920.
3014 Tyler, George Dacre Hardinge-, 1 Jan. 1920.
3015 Vernon, Sir Harry Foley, Bart., 1 Jan. 1920.
3016 Voysey, Violet Mary Annesley, 1 Jan. 1920.
3017 Walden, Robert Wooley, 1 Jan. 1920.
3018 Walker, Francis John, 1 Jan. 1920.
3019 Walker, Henry, 1 Jan. 1920.
3020 Walker, Robert John, 1 Jan. 1920

3021 Wallace, William, 1 Jan. 1920.
3022 Walmsley, Ben, 1 Jan. 1920.
3023 Ward, Frederick Josiah, 1 Jan. 1920.
3024 Warde, Henry Murray Ashley, 1 Jan 1920.
3025 Warden, Robert Campbell, 1 Jan. 1920.
3026 Waring, Harold, 1 Jan. 1920.
3027 Washbourn, William, 1 Jan. 1920
3028 Waterlow, Sydney Philip Perigal, 1 Jan. 1920.
3029 Watson, Arthur Egerton, 1 Jan. 1920.
3030 Watson, Arthur William, 1 Jan. 1920.
3031 Wauchope, Jean Mary, Mrs., 1 Jan. 1920.
3032 Webbe, William Harold, 1 Jan. 1920.
3033 Wedderburn, Alexander Dundas Ogilvy, 1 Jan. 1920.
3034 Weguelin, Ethel, Mrs., 1 Jan. 1920.
3035 West, Frederick Joseph, 1 Jan. 1920.
3036 Westminster, Katharine Caroline, Dowager Duchess of, 1 Jan. 1920
3037 Wetherall, William Alexander, 1 Jan. 1920.
3038 Wheeler, Edith Mary, Mrs., 1 Jan. 1920.
3039 White, Robert, 1 Jan. 1920.
3040 Whitelaw, Robert Pender, 1 Jan. 1920.
3041 Whittall, Frederick Edwin, 1 Jan. 1920.
3042 Wickes, Charles Hamilton-, 1 Jan. 1920.
3043 Wightman, Owen William, 1 Jan. 1920.
3044 Wild, John Robert Francis, 1 Jan. 1920.
3045 Wilding, Edward, 1 Jan. 1920.
3046 Wilkie, Helen Gertrude, Mrs., 1 Jan. 1920.
3047 Wilkinson, Frederick, 1 Jan. 1920.
3048 Willett, John Eddowes, 1 Jan. 1920.
3049 Williams, Sir Dawson, 1 Jan. 1920.
3050 Williams, Mary Christian, Mrs., 1 Jan. 1920.
3051 Williamson, Colin Martin, 1 Jan. 1920.
3052 Wilson, Beryl Charlotte Mary, Mrs., 1 Jan. 1920.
3053 Wilson, Ernest George, 1 Jan 1920.
3054 Wilson, George Heron, 1 Jan. 1920.
3055 Wilson, Reginald Page Campbell, 1 Jan. 1920.
3056 Wood, Robert Henry, 1 Jan. 1920.
3057 Wood, Russell Howard, 1 Jan. 1920.
3058 Woodhead, Henry George Wandesford, 1 Jan. 1920.
3059 Woodhouse, Arthur William Webster, 1 Jan. 1920.
3060 Woodhouse, Herbert, 1 Jan. 1920.
3061 Woodwark, George Graham, 1 Jan. 1920.
3062 Woolcock, William James Uglow, 1 Jan. 1920.
3063 Worthington, Frank Vigers, 1 Jan. 1920.
3064 Wright, Cecily Gertrude, Mrs., 1 Jan. 1920.
3065 Wright, John Graham, 1 Jan. 1920.
3066 Wynne, Mary Carleton, Mrs., 1 Jan. 1920.
3067 Wythes, Ernest James, 1 Jan. 1920.
3068 Young, Patrick, 1 Jan. 1920.
3069 Younghusband, Arthur Delaval, 1 Jan. 1920.
3070 Voules, Francis Minchin, 1 Jan. 1920.
3071 Barker, Tom Battersby, 1 Jan. 1920.
3072 Bennett, John Wheeler Wheeler-, 1 Jan. 1920.
3073 Bull, George Lucien, 1 Jan. 1920.
3074 Butler, Lily Isabella, 1 Jan. 1920.
3075 Buttersworth, Reginald, 1 Jan. 1920.
3076 Chrimes, Frank. 1 Jan. 1920.
3077 Faunthorpe, John Champion, 1 Jan. 1920.
3078 Gittens, Henry, 1 Jan. 1920.
3079 Morkhill, William Lucius, 1 Jan. 1920.
3080 Thompson, George Roger, 1 Jan. 1920.
3081 Wood, Ethel Mary, Mrs. Herbert Frederick, 1 Jan. 1920.
3082 White, Ernest William, 1 Jan. 1920. (M.)
3083 Bainbridge, William Frank, 1 Jan. 1920. (M.)
3084 Boileau, Etienne Partridge, 1 Jan. 1920. (M.)
3085 Boulton, Harold, 1 Jan. 1920.
3086 Bright, Reginald Arthur, 1 Jan. 1920. (M.)
3087 Brooke, Harry Morris Mitchelson, 1 Jan. 1920. (M.)
3088 White, Percy, Carr-, 1 Jan. 1920. (M.)
3089 Dobbs, Charles Fairlie. 1 Jan. 1920. (M.)
3090 Hepenstal, Maxwell Edward, 1 Jan. 1920. (M.)
3091 Douglas, Archibald Philip, 1 Jan. 1920. (M.)
3092 Edwardes, Alexander Coburn, 1 Jan. 1920. (M.)
3093 Fetherstonhaugh, William Albany, 1 Jan. 1920. (M.)
3094 Gill, James Geoffrey, 1 Jan. 1920. (M.)
3095 Hyslop, Francis, 1 Jan. 1920 (M.)
3096 Keen, William John, 1 Jan. 1920. (M.)
3097 Larnder, Eugene William, 1 Jan. 1920. (M.)
3098 Maurice, George Thelwall Kindersley, 1 Jan. 1920. (M.)
3099 Ommanney, Charles Vernon, 1 Jan. 1920. (M.)
3100 Evans, Granville Pennefather-, 1 Jan. 1920. (M.)
3101 Rice, Sidney Mervyn, 1 Jan. 1920. (M.)
3102 Palmer, Frederick Carey Stukeley Samborne-, 1 Jan. 1920.
3103 St. John, Henry Beauchamp, 1 Jan. 1920. (M.)
3104 Tillard, Arthur Basil, 1 Jan. 1920. (M.)
3105 Tyrrell, John Frederick, 1 Jan. 1920. (M.)
3106a Bartlett, Ellis Ashmead-, 1 Jan. 1920.
3106b Davies, Madalen Augusta Lavinia, 1 Jan. 1920.
3106c Duke, Reginald Franklyn Hare, 1 Jan 1920.
3106d Given, Ernest Cranston, 1 Jan. 1920.
3106e Lawson, Lady Wilma, 1 Jan. 1920.
3106f Lebus, Herman Andrew Harris, 1 Jan. 1920.
3106g McDonald, Allan Macdonald, 1 Jan. 1920.
3106h Pitts, Joseph, 1 Jan. 1920.
3107a Campbell, Archibald Young Gibbs, 1 Jan. 1920.
3107b Clarke, Orme Bigland, 1 Jan. 1920.
3107c Fordyce, John Gordon, 1 Jan. 1920.
3107d Spry, Henry Ernest, 1 Jan. 1920.

COMMANDERS.

3107e Allen, Atwell Hayes. 9 Jan. 1920. (M.)
3108 Blacker, George, 30 Jan. 1920.
3109 Bolton, Charles, 30 Jan. 1920.
3110 Bond, Charles Hubert, 30 Jan. 1920.
3111 Carr, John Walter, 30 Jan. 1920.
3112 Chambers, Helen, 30 Jan. 1920.
3113 Drummond, David, 30 Jan. 1920.
3114 Furber, Edward Price, 30 Jan. 1920.
3115 Lambert, Florence Barrie, 30 Jan. 1920.
3116 Lett, Hugh, 30 Jan. 1920.
3117 Lewis, Thomas, 30 Jan. 1920.
3118 Lister, Thomas David, 30 Jan. 1920.
3119 McGavin, Lawrie Hugh, 30 Jan. 1920.
3220 Paterson, Herbert John, 30 Jan. 1920.
3221 Sinclair, John, 30 Jan. 1920.
3122 Smith, Sir Thomas Rudolph Hampden, Bart., 30 Jan. 1920.
3123 Taylor, James, 30 Jan. 1920.
3124 Young, Robert Arthur, 30 Jan. 1920.
3125 Archdale, Nicholas Edward, 8 March, 1920. (M.)
3126 Cotton, Arthur Stedman, 15 March, 1920. (M.)
3127 Harrison, Walter Lewis, 15 March, 1920. (M.)
3128 Radclyffe, Charles Raymond, 15 March, 1920. (M.)
3129 Rowlandson, Herbert Wynward, 15 March, 1920. (M.)
3130 Ling, Robert Walton, 15 March, 1920. (M.)
3130a Eldridge, George Bernard, 23 Apr. 1920. (M.)
3130b Frowd, William Smeeton, 23 Apr. 1920. (M.)
3130c Harvey, John, 23 Apr. 1920. (M.)
3130d Hose, Walter, 23 Apr. 1920. (M.)
3130e Story, William Oswald, 23 Apr. 1920. (M.)
3131 Barker, Charles William Panton, 5 June, 1920.
3132 Beeman, C., May, 5 June, 1920.
3133 Bull, George, 5 June, 1920.
3134 Caine, Gordon Ralph Hall, 5 June, 1920.
3135 Carlisle, Rev. John Charles, 5 June, 1920.
3136 Coplestone, Frederick, 5 June, 1920.
3137 Danger, Frank Charles, 5 June, 1920.
3138 Howard de Walden and Seaford, Margherita, Baroness, 3 June, 1920.
3139 Donald, Colin George, 5 June, 1920.
3140 Dyer, Edward Jerome, 5 June, 1920.
3141 Fraser, Mrs. Irene Gladys, 5 June, 1920.
3142 Gibson, John Constant, 5 June, 1920.
3143 Gibson, William, 5 June, 1920.
3144 Glaneley, Ada Mary, Baroness, 5 June, 1920.
3145 Goudge, J. A., 5 June, 1920.
3146 Graeme, Patrick Neal Sutherland, 5 June, 1920.
3147 Graham, Maurice, 5 June, 1920.
3148 Hancock, George Charles, 5 June, 1920.
3149 Hynard, William George, 5 June, 1920.
3150 Jordan, Alfred Charles, 5 June, 1920.
3151 Lascelles, Edward ffrancis Ward, 5 June, 1920.
3152 Limerick, May Josephine, Countess of, 5 June, 1920.
3153 Low, John Spencer, 5 June, 1920.
3154 Lyall, Beatrix Margaret, Mrs., 5 June, 1920.
3155 Madge, Henry Ashley, 5 June, 1920.
3156 Maude, Edith Caroline, Mrs., 5 June, 1920.
3157 Mollison, William Mayhew, 5 June, 1920.

3158 Moody, Charles Henry, 5 June, 1920.
3159 Noal, Richard John, 5 June, 1920.
3160 North, Margaret Caird, Mrs., 5 June, 1920.
3161 Ovans, Hugh Lambert, 5 June, 1920.
3162 Pearse, James, 5 June, 1920.
3163 Perkin, Frederick Mollwo, 5 June, 1920.
3164 Stanton, Charles Butt, 5 June, 1920.
3165 Soundy, Sir John Thomas, 5 June, 1920.
3166 Stanley, Lady Beatrix Taylour, 5 June, 1920.
3167 Thomas, Daniel, 5 June, 1920.
3168 Tomley, John Edward, 5 June, 1920.
3169 Turner, Percy F., 5 June, 1920.
3170 Venables, Harry Archbutt, 5 June, 1920.
3171 Wade, Sir William, 5 June, 1920.
3172 Walcott, Colpoys Cleland, 5 June, 1920.
3173 Whalley, Frank Douglas, 5 June, 1920.
3174 Wood, Brooks Crompton, 5 June, 1920.
3175 Barne, William Bradley Gosset, 9 July, 1920. (M.)
3176 Reid, Hector Gowans, 9 July, 1920. (M.)
3177 Roch, Horace Samson, 9 July, 1920. (M.)
3178 Archer, John Oliver, 12 July, 1920. (M.)
3179 Martin, Norman Macdonald, 12 July, 1920. (M.)
3180 Maund, Arthur Clinton, 12 July, 1920. (M.)
3181 Minchin, Frederick Frank, 12 July, 1920. (M.)
3182 Crispin, Edward Smyth, 24 Aug. 1920.
3183 Macallan, Arthur Ferguson, 24 Aug. 1920.
3184 Morice, George Farquhar, 24 Aug. 1920.
3185 Phillimore, Valentine Egerton Bagot, 7 Sept. 1920. (M.)
3185a. Nalder, Leonard Fielding, 20 Sept. 1920. (M.)
3186 Brewis, Charles Richard Wynn, 15 Oct. 1920.
3187 Cridland, Frank, 15 Oct. 1920.
3188 Dunn, Alfred Cuthbert, 15 Oct. 1920.
3189 Earp, Charles Anthony, 15 Oct. 1920.
3190 Earp, Hon. George Frederick, 15 Oct. 1920.
3191 Garner, Walter Wesley, 15 Oct. 1920.
3192 Grant, Duncan Walter, 15 Oct. 1920.
3193 Green, Thomas Ernest, 15 Oct. 1920.
3194 Greenwood, William Frederick, 15 Oct. 1920.
3195 Gunn, Frank Lindsay, 15 Oct. 1920.
3196 Jess, Carl Herman, 15 Oct. 1920.
3197 Johnston, George Jamieson, 15 Oct. 1920.
3198 Johnstone, William Downs, 15 Oct. 1920.
3199 Macandie, George Lionel, 15 Oct. 1920.
3200 Newland, John, 15 Oct. 1920.
3201 Nicholson, George Gibb, 15 Oct. 1920.
3202 Orchard, Hon. Richard Beaumont, 15 Oct. 1920.
3203 Robertson, William Nathaniel, 15 Oct. 1920.
3204 Thomson, James Park, 15 Oct. 1920.
3205 Thring, Walter Hugh Charles Samuel, 15 Oct. 1920.
3206 Vicars, William, 15 Oct. 1920.
3207 Waley, Frederick George, 15 Oct. 1920.
3208 Walker, Charles Alfred Le Messurier, 15 Oct. 1920.
3209 Frostick, James Arthur, 15 Oct. 1920.
3210 Giovanetti, Constantine William, 15 Oct. 1920.
3211 Jeppe, Julius, 15 Oct. 1920.
3212 Lewis, Ernest Harry, 15 Oct. 1920.
3213 Rees, David, 15 Oct. 1920.
3214 Thorne, Anna Elizabeth, Mrs., 15 Oct. 1920.
3215 Myles, Thomas William, 24 Dec. 1920.

OFFICERS.

(O.B.E.).

1 Balgarnie, Wilfred, 4 June, 1917.
2 Beresford, Denis Robert Pack, 4 June, 1917.
3 Birkin, Ethel Lilian, 4 June, 1917.
4 Blackwell, Thomas Geoffrey, 4 June, 1917.
5 Brockington, William Allport, 4 June, 1917.
6 Brodrick, William John Henry, 4 June, 1917.
7 Brown, James, 4 June, 1917.
8 Broughton, Gladys Mary, 4 June, 1917.
9 Chandler, Francis, 4 June, 1917.
10 Coller, Frederick Ernest Watts, 4 June, 1917.
11 Courtney, Janet Elizabeth, Mrs. William Leonard, 4 June, 1917.
12 Cumming, George, 4 June, 1917.
13 Davies, Edward Futcher, 4 June, 1917.
14 Dease, Mabel Mary Frances, Mrs. Edmund James, 4 June, 1917.
15 de Rothschild, Lionel Nathan, 4 June, 1917. (M.)
17 Fox, Tom, 4 June, 1917.
18 Burgoyne, Sydney Thomas, 4 June, 1920. (M.)
19 Field, Michael Birt, 4 June, 1917.
20 Galbraith, Samuel, 4 June, 1917.
21 Gordon, William, 4 June, 1917.
22 Gee, Alan, 4 June, 1917.
23 Gilmour David, 4 June, 1917.
24 Harben, Guy Philip, 4 June, 1917.
25 Hart, William Edward, 4 June, 1917.
26 Hodgson, Henry Michael, 4 June, 1917.
27 Hudson, Walter, 4 June, 1917.
28 Jayne, Ethel Basil, 4 June, 1917.
30 Langridge, Francis Barton, 4 June, 1917.
31 Larke, William James, 4 June, 1917.
32 McLennan, John Cunningham, 4 June, 1917
33 McNeill, Charles FitzRoy Ponsonby, 4 June, 1917.
35 Matthews, Florence, Mrs. Arthur Kennard, 4 June, 1917.
36 Millar, Duncan McFayden, 4 June, 1917.
38 Mosses, William, 4 June, 1917.
39 Mounsey, George Augustus, 4 June, 1917.
40 Musgrave, Henry, 4 June, 1917.
41 Nelson, William Ernest, 4 June, 1917.
42 Nicholl, David Arthur, 4 June, 1917.
43 Paget, Lady Muriel Evelyn Vernon, 4 June, 1917.
44 Parkinson, Albert Ernest, 4 June, 1917.
45 Parr, Robert John, 4 June, 1917.
46 Poulton, Edward Lawrence, 4 June, 1917.
47 Postlethwaite, William Taylor, 4 June, 1917.
48 Pratt, Edith Helen, 4 June, 1917.
49 Raffety, Harold Vesey, 4 June, 1917.
51 Rolfe, Sybil Katherine, Mrs. Clive Neville-, 4 June, 1917.
52 Robinson, William Cornforth, 4 June, 1917.
53 Rose, Felix, 4 June, 1917.
54 Saunders, Elsie, 4 June, 1917.
55 Silley, John Henry, 4 June, 1917.
57 Simson, Lena, Mrs. Henry John Forbes, 4 June, 1917.
58 Smith, Frank, 4 June, 1917.
59 Smith, William Brownhill, 4 June, 1917.
60 Bunning, George Harold Stuart, 4 June, 1917.
61 Stewart, James, 4 June, 1917.
63 Turner, Ben, 4 June, 1917.
64 Wilkins, Louisa, Mrs. Roland Field, 4 June, 1917.
65 Watts, Patterson, 4 June, 1917.
66 Wilson, Harold Inchbald, 4 June, 1917.
69 Farrer, Hon. Cecil Claude, 4 June, 1917.
70 Young, Robert, 4 June, 1917.
71 Ramsay, Margaret, Lady, 4 Dec. 1917.
72 Singh, Rai Bahadur Buta of Rawalpindi, 4 Dec. 1917.
74 Symons, Thomas Henry, 4 Dec. 1917.
75 Mitra Rai, Sahib Rajeshwar, 4 Dec. 1917.
76 Heale, Robert John Wingfield, 4 Dec. 1917.
77 Sethna, Phiroye Kharsedji, 4 Dec. 1917.
78 Carter, Edward Clark, 4 Dec. 1917.
79 Adam, Robert, 1 Jan. 1918.
80 Ainscough, Thomas Martland, 1 Jan. 1918.
81 Alcorn, Alexander, 1 Jan. 1918.
82 Allan, Evelyn Julia, Mrs., 1 Jan. 1918.
83 Allan, James, 1 Jan. 1918.
84 Allden, Harry, 1 Jan. 1918.
85 Allen, John, 1 Jan. 1918.
86 Allen, Mary Sophia, 1 Jan. 1918.
88 Allen, William George, 1 Jan. 1918.
89 Allen, William Henry, 1 Jan. 1918.
90 Alsop, James Willcox, 1 Jan. 1918.

91 Anderson, Amy Douglas Knyveton, Mrs., 1 Jan. 1918.
92 Anderson, Lois Dessurne, 1 Jan. 1918.
94 Anderson, Thomas George, 1 Jan. 1918.
95 Anwyl-Passingham, Augustus Mervyn Owen Anwyl, 1 Jan. 1918. (M.)
96 Archer, Henry William, 1 Jan. 1918.
97 Armstrong, Francis Logie, 1 Jan. 1918. (M.)
98 Armstrong, Henry, 1 Jan. 1918.
99 Glenarthur, Lady, 1 Jan. 1918.
100 Foakes, Edward Lindsay Ashley, 1 Jan. 1918. (M.)
101 Atkin, Peter Wilson, 1 Jan. 1918.
102 Ayre, Amos Lowrey, 1 Jan. 1918.
103 Bagenal, Philip Henry, 1 Jan. 1918.
104 Bagnall, Francis Edward, 1 Jan. 1918.
105 Bailey, Arthur Stowey, 1 Jan. 1918.
106 Baines, Edward George Graham Talbot, 1 Jan. 1918. (M.)
108 Baker, Alfred Gabriel, 1 Jan. 1918.
109 Baker, George Stephen, 1 Jan. 1918.
110 Baker, John William, 1 Jan. 1918.
111 Balfour, Robert John, 1 Jan. 1918.
112 Banbury, Charlotte Marie-Louise, Mrs., 1 Jan. 1918.
113 Barber, William, 1 Jan. 1918.
115 Barnard, Ernest Augustus William, 1 Jan. 1918.
116 Barnes, Annie Ethel, Mrs., 1 Jan. 1918.
117 Barnes, Henry, 1 Jan. 1918.
118 Barnes, James Sidney, 1 Jan. 1918.
119 Barnett, James Rennie, 1 Jan. 1918.
120 Barrow, Alfred, 1 Jan. 1918.
121 Bartlett, Edmund Burton, 1 Jan. 1918.
122 Bartlett, Frederick William, 1 Jan. 1918.
123 Barwick, Frederick Mortimer, 1 Jan. 1918.
124 Basset, William Fortescue, 1 Jan. 1918.
125 Bastard, Ernest William, 1 Jan. 1918.
126 Bather, Muriel, Mrs., 1 Jan. 1918.
127 Battersby, James Allan, 1 Jan. 1918
128 Baxter, Edith, Lady, 1 Jan. 1918.
129 Baxter, Peter McLeod, 1 Jan. 1918.
130 Baylay, Willoughby Lake, 1 Jan. 1918.
131 Beamer, Ernest Edward Boyce, 1 Jan. 1918.
133 Beaton, George Howard, 1 Jan. 1918.
135 Bednall, Alfred, 1 Jan. 1918.
136 Beevor, Susan Heard, Mrs. John Hare, 1 Jan. 1918.
137 Bell, Hubert Dowson, 1 Jan. 1918.
138 Bell, William Thomas, 1 Jan. 1918.
139 Bell-Irving, Richard, 1 Jan. 1918. (M.)
140 Bennett, Geoffrey Thomas, 1 Jan. 1918.
141 Berriman, Algernon Edward, 1 Jan. 1918.
142 Berrow, William Lewis, 1 Jan. 1918.
143 Bertie-Perkins, Alys Mary, Mrs., 1 Jan. 1918.
145 Corbet, Rosamond, Mrs. Bertram D'Avenant, 1 Jan. 1918.
147 Betts, Lionel Oxborrow, 1 Jan. 1918. (M.)
148 Bing, Herbert, 1 Jan. 1918.
149 Binns, Oswell Barritt, 1 Jan. 1918.
150 Birks, Gerald Walker, 1 Jan. 1918. (M.)
151 Bissett, John, 1 Jan. 1918.
152 Black, Archibald Campbell, 1 Jan. 1918. (M.)
153 Blair, David, 1 Jan. 1918. (M.)
154 Blake, Frank, 1 Jan. 1918.
155 Blakemore, Frederick, 1 Jan. 1918. (M.)
156 Bloomfield, Constance Caldwell, 1 Jan. 1918.
157 Blount, Clara, Mrs. Edward Aston Charles Marie, 1 Jan. 1918.
158 Bogle, James Cairns, 1 Jan. 1918.
159 Boland, Henry Patrick, 1 Jan. 1918.
160 Bonny, William, 1 Jan. 1918.
161 Booth, Harry, 1 Jan. 1918.
162 Booth, William Henry, 1 Jan. 1918. (M.)
163 Boothby, Francis Stewart Evelyn, 1 Jan. 1918. (M.)
164 Borley, John Oliver, 1 Jan. 1918.
166 Bottomley, William Cecil, 1 Jan. 1918.
167 Bourdeaux, John, 1 Jan. 1918.
168 Bowater, Sarah Fanny, Lady, 1 Jan. 1918.
169 Bowden, John, 1 Jan. 1918. (M.)
170 Bowers, Frederick Gatus, 1 Jan. 1918.
171 Bowman, Thomas Anderson, 1 Jan. 1918.
172 Bowman, William Turnbull, 1 Jan. 1918.
173 Boyd, Arthur, 1 Jan. 1918. (M.)
175 Boyland, Sydney Edward, 1 Jan. 1918.
176 Bramwell, Hugh, 1 Jan. 1918.
177 Bremner, David Alexander, 1 Jan. 1918.
178 Brierley, Edgar, 1 Jan. 1918.

181 Brown, Archibald, 1 Jan. 1918.
182 Brown, Jonathan Boswell, 1 Jan. 1918.
183 Brown, Wilfred Gordon, 1 Jan. 1918.
185 Bruce, Charles Matthewes, 1 Jan. 1918.
186 Bruce, Ellen Maud, Lady, 1 Jan. 1918.
187 Bryant, Frederick, 1 Jan. 1918.
188 Buchanan, Jane, 1 Jan. 1918.
190 Buckland, Alfred Virgoe, 1 Jan. 1918.
191 Bulpitt, Walter Henry, 1 Jan. 1918.
192 Burch, Frederick, 1 Jan. 1918. (M.)
193 Burgess Kenneth Paul, 1 Jan. 1919.
194 Burke, Hubert Francis Daubeny, 1 Jan. 1918.
195 Burke, May, Mrs., 1 Jan. 1918.
196 Burn, Ethel Louise, Hon. Mrs. Charles Rosdew, 1 Jan. 1918.
197 Burnett, Ethel, 1 Jan. 1918.
198 Burnside, Ethel Margaret, 1 Jan. 1918.
199 Burton, William, 1 Jan. 1918. (M.)
200 Burton, William Parker, 1 Jan. 1918.
201 Bush, Margery, Mrs., 1 Jan. 1918.
202 Busteed, Henry Richard, 1 Jan. 1918. (M.)
203 Butler, Arthur Francis, 1 Jan. 1918.
204 Cable, William John, 1 Jan. 1918.
205 Cadbury, Elizabeth Mary, Mrs., 1 Jan. 1918.
206 Caillard, Lily Eliza Frances, Lady, 1 Jan. 1918
207 Caldecott-Smith, Percy Pyne, 1 Jan. 1918.
208 Caldwell, Mary Louisa, 1 Jan. 1918.
209 Cambray, Philip, 1 Jan. 1918.
211 Campbell, Alexander, 1 Jan. 1918.
212 Campbell, Florence Ishbell, 1 Jan. 1918.
213 Campbell, Gordon Charles Henry, 1 Jan. 1918.
214 Capron, Athol John, 1 Jan. 1918.
215 Carden, Mary Gertrude, Mrs., 1 Jan. 1918.
216 Carl, Frederick, 1 Jan. 1918.
217 Carlile, Walter, 1 Jan. 1918.
218 Carrick, Earl of, 1 Jan. 1918. (M.)
219 Carter, William Allan, 1 Jan. 1918.
220 Carter, Edward Henry, 1 Jan. 1918.
221 Cator, Maud, Mrs., 1 Jan. 1918.
222 Cauvin, William Stephen, 1 Jan. 1918. (M.)
223 Chalmers, Robert Arthur, 1 Jan. 1918. (M.)
224 Champion, John Alfred Cuthbert, 1 Jan. 1918.
225 Champion, Samuel Stewart, 1 Jan. 1918.
228 Chichester, Dehra, Mrs. Robert Peel Dawson Spencer, 1 Jan. 1918.
229 Chichester, Earl of, 1 Jan. 1918. (M.)
230 Churchill, Henry, 1 Jan. 1918.
231 Clark, George, 1 Jan. 1918. (M.)
232 Clark, William Henry Dennis, 1 Jan. 1918. (M.)
233 Clarke, Geoffrey Rothe, 1 Jan. 1918.
234 Clarke, James Alexander, 1 Jan. 1918.
237 Clay, Robert, 1 Jan. 1918.
238 Cleaver, Harris Peugeot, 1 Jan. 1918
239 Cochrane, Andrew, 1 Jan. 1918.
240 Cockburn, George Bertram, 1 Jan. 1918.
241 Cocke, Thomas Dudley, 1 Jan. 1918. (M.)
242 Coggan, William, 1 Jan. 1918.
243 Cole, William George, 1 Jan. 1918.
245 Collett, John Alsager, 1 Jan. 1918. (M.)
246 Colmore, Reginald Blayney Bulteel, 1 Jan. 1918.
247 Conacher, Charles Leonard, 1 Jan. 1918. (M.)
248 Constable, Arthur Douglas, 1 Jan. 1918.
249 Cooper, Elizabeth, 1 Jan. 1918.
250 Cooper, Ernest Napier, 1 Jan. 1918.
251 Coppock, Harry Stowe, 1 Jan. 1918.
253 Coventry, Fulwar Cecil Ashton, 1 Jan. 1918.
254 Cowen, Jane, 1 Jan. 1918.
255 Cox, Bernard Henry, 1 Jan. 1918.
256 Cox, Oswald, 1 Jan. 1918.
257 Craig, William Brownfield, 1 Jan. 1918.
258 Cramond, John McGregor, 1 Jan. 1918.
259 Crane, Charles Paston, 1 Jan. 1918. (M.)
261 Cree, Laura Alexander Bell, Mrs., 1 Jan. 1918.
262 Creswell, Francis Samuel, 1 Jan. 1918. (M.)
263 Croft, Ernest Samuel, 1 Jan. 1918.
264 Crompton, Claud, 1 Jan. 1918.
265 Cropper, Edward, 1 Jan. 1918.
266 Crosbie-Hill, Marjorie, 1 Jan. 1918.
267 Crosby, Josiah, 1 Jan. 1918.
268 Cross, Richard Basil, 1 Jan. 1918.
270 Cuff, Herbert Edmond, 1 Jan. 1918.
272 Cummins, Herbert Ashley Cunard, 1 Jan. 1918.
274 Cunliffe, William, 1 Jan. 1918.
275 Cunnington, Frederick Joseph, 1 Jan. 1918.
276 Cuthbert, Kathleen Alice, Mrs. James Harold, 1 Jan. 1918.
277 Cuthbertson, Clive, 1 Jan. 1918.
279 Dagnall, William John, 1 Jan. 1918.
280 Dallinger, Percy Gough, 1 Jan. 1918.
281 Dana, Robert Washington, 1 Jan. 1918.
282 Davidson, James Stewart, 1 Jan. 1918.
283 Davies, Andrew William, 1 Jan. 1918. (M.
284 Davis, William Northcote, 1 Jan. 1918.
285 Dawson, Albert Edward, 1 Jan. 1918. (M.)
287 de Montmorency, Hervey Angus, 1 Jan. 1918.
288 Dendy Frederick Walter, 1 Jan. 1918.
289 Denne, Mark Thomas, 1 Jan. 1918.
290 Denniston, Alexander Guthrie, 1 Jan. 1918. (M.)
291 de Rougemont, Muriel Evelyn, Mrs. Cecil Henry, 1 Jan. 1918.

292 Dickens, Henry Charles, 1 Jan. 1918.
293 Dillon, Thomas Cantrel, 1 Jan. 1918.
296 Dixon, William Vibart, 1 Jan. 1918.
297 Downs, James, 1 Jan. 1918.
299 Dudgeon, Margaret, Mrs. Robert Francis, 1 Jan. 1918.
300 Duff, Mildred Mabel Gordon, Mrs., 1 Jan. 1918.
301 Duffin, Earle Calder, 1 Jan. 1918. (M.)
302 Duggan, George Chester, 1 Jan. 1918.
303 Duncan, Leland Lewis, 1 Jan. 1918.
304 Dunstan, Malcolm James Rowley, 1 Jan. 1918.
305 Durant, Percy, 1 Jan. 1918.
307 Dyball, William Moore, 1 Jan. 1918.
309 Easten, Stephen, 1 Jan. 1918.
310 Ebben, Henry Stuart, 1 Jan. 1918. (M.)
311 Edmond, John, 1 Jan. 1918.
312 Edmunds, Leslie Wynn, 1 Jan. 1918. (M.)
313 Edwardes, David John William, 1 Jan. 1918.
314 Edwards, Charles James, 1 Jan. 1918.
315 Edwards, George Henry, 1 Jan. 1918.
318 Eldred, Edwin Charles, 1 Jan. 1918.
321 Ellis, John Henry, 1 Jan. 1918.
322 Elvy, Thomas Elvy, 1 Jan. 1918.
323 Emberton, John, 1 Jan. 1918.
324 Evans, Corris William, 1 Jan. 1918.
326 Evans, Thomas Henry Royston, 1 Jan. 1918.
327 Everett, Basil Preston, 1 Jan. 1918.
329 Fairholme, Edward George Robert, 1 Jan. 1918. (M.)
330 Farmer, Robert Crosbie, 1 Jan. 1918.
331 Fass, Herbert Ernest, 1 Jan. 1918.
332 Fedarb, Frederick James, 1 Jan. 1918.
333 Fielden, Dora, Mrs., 1 Jan. 1918.
334 Fisher, Charles Stanley, 1 Jan. 1918. (M.)
335 Fletcher, Walter Blunt, 1 Jan. 1918. (M)
336 Foreman, Sir Henry, 1 Jan. 1918.
337 Hamilton, Dowager Duchess of, 1 Jan. 1918.
338 Fortescue, Cecil Lewis, 1 Jan. 1918.
339 Fortington, Harold Augustus, 1 Jan. 1918
340 Foster, James, 1 Jan. 1918.
341 Francis, Joseph, 1 Jan. 1918.
342 Franklin, Leonard Benjamin, 1 Jan. 1918.
343 Franklin, Robert Francis, 1 Jan. 1918.
344 Frazer, Thomas, 1 Jan. 1918.
345 Freeman, Robert, 1 Jan. 1918.
346 Freiligrath, Otto Tennent Eastman, 1 Jan. 1918. (M.)
347 French, Hon. Essex Eleonora, 1 Jan. 1918.
348 French, Henry Leon, 1 Jan. 1918.
349 French, Reginald Thomas George, 1 Jan. 1918.
350 Frost, Edward John Allan, 1 Jan. 1918.
351 Frost, Mark Edwin Pescott, 1 Jan. 1918.
352 Fulcher, George Arthur, 1 Jan. 1918. (M.)
353 Fulton, David Bowie, 1 Jan. 1918.
354 Game, Henry, 1 Jan. 1918. (M.)
355 Gandell, William Raleigh Kerr, 1 Jan. 1918.
356 Gandy, Eric Worsley, 1 Jan. 1918. (M.)
357 Gardner, Annie Elizabeth, 1 Jan. 1918.
358 Gardom, Edward Theodore, 1 Jan. 1918.
359 Garvey, John William Frederick, 1 Jan. 1918. (M.)
360 Gentry, George, 1 Jan. 1918.
362 Gibb, William Doig, 1 Jan. 1918.
363 Gibson, Joseph Hamilton, 1 Jan. 1918.
364 Gibson, John Watson, 1 Jan. 1918.
366 Giffard, Jack, 1 Jan. 1918. (M.)
367 Gilchrist, Archibald, 1 Jan. 1918.
368 Gill, Walter Brudenell, 1 Jan. 1918. (M.)
369 Gledhill, John, 1 Jan. 1918.
370 Glenny, William James, 1 Jan. 1918.
371 Goalen, James Thomas, 1 Jan. 1918.
372 Godman, Edward Shirley, 1 Jan. 1918.
373 Goldsmid, Lionel Frederic, 1 Jan. 1918.
374 Gomersall, Edward, 1 Jan. 1918.
375 Goodsir, Gertrude Esperance, Mrs., 1 Jan. 1918.
376 Goodwin, Ernest, 1 Jan. 1918. (M.)
377 Goolden, Walter Herbert Lewis, 1 Jan. 1918. (M.)
378 Gordon, Henry Erskine, 1 Jan. 1918.
379 Gordon, William James, 1 Jan. 1918.
380 Gowans, Thomas, 1 Jan. 1918.
381 Gowing, Warden, 1 Jan. 1918.
382 Graham, Mary Louise, Marchioness of, 1 Jan. 1918
384 Graham, Arthur John Wood, 1 Jan. 1918.
387 Grant, Selwyn Seafield, 1 Jan. 1918.
388 Grant, William, 1 Jan. 1918. (M.)
390 Grapes, John, 1 Jan. 1918.
391 Gray, Robert, 1 Jan. 1918.
392 Green, Edward William, 1 Jan. 1918.
393 Green, James Alexander, 1 Jan. 1918. (M.)
394 Green, Mary Anne, Mrs., 1 Jan. 1918.
395 Grehan, Francis, 1 Jan. 1918. (M.)
396 Greig, Donald McNeill, 1 Jan. 1918. (M.)
397 Greville, Hon. Mrs. Alwyn Henry Fulke, 1 Jan. 1918.
398 Griffiths, Sarah Gilbert, Mrs., 1 Jan. 1918.
399 Grimbly, Richard Henry, 1 Jan. 1918.
400 Grimshaw, Wilfrid, 1 Jan. 1918.
401 Grinsted, Harold, 1 Jan. 1918. (M.)
402 Gundill, William Edward, 1 Jan. 1918.
403 Haggard, Godfrey Digby Napier, 1 Jan. 1918.
405 Hannay, Jane Ewing, Mrs., 1 Jan. 1918.
406 Harding, Alfred John, 1 Jan. 1918.
407 Hare, Samuel, 1 Jan. 1918.
408 Harker, John Allen, 1 Jan. 1918.

410 Harrison, Emily Margaret, Mrs. Frederick James, 1 Jan. 1918.
411 Hartley, Richard Frederick, 1 Jan. 1918.
412 Hartshorn, Vernon, 1 Jan. 1918.
413 Hart-Smith, Theodore Edward, 1 Jan. 1918.
414 Hatfield, Ada Sophia Lucy, Mrs., 1 Jan. 1918.
415 Hatherley, Cyril George, 1 Jan. 1918.
417 Hebert, Charles, 1 Jan. 1918.
418 Herbert, Philip, 1 Jan. 1918. (M.)
419 Heron-Watson, Charles, 1 Jan. 1918.
421 Hiley, Wilfrid Edward, 1 Jan. 1918.
422 Hill, Archibald Vivian, 1 Jan. 1918. (M.)
423 Hilleary, George Edward, 1 Jan. 1918.
424 Hinks, Percy John, 1 Jan. 1918.
425 Hoare, Albert Ernest, 1 Jan. 1918.
426 Hodgens, John, 1 Jan. 1918. (M.)
427 Hodgson, Charles Courtenay, 1 Jan. 1918.
428 Hodgson, John Alexander, 1 Jan. 1918.
429 Hodgson, Elizabeth Odeyne, Hon. Mrs. Francis Henry, 1 Jan. 1918.
430 Holden, Norman Edward, 1 Jan. 1918. (M.)
431 Holland, Julia, 1 Jan. 1918.
432 Holley, Alfred Ewart, 1 Jan. 1918.
433 Holmes, Constance, 1 Jan. 1918.
434 Holmes, Lt.Col. Gerard Robert Addison, 1 Jan. 1918. (M.)
435 Holmes, William, 1 Jan. 1918.
436 Honey, William John, 1 Jan. 1918. (M.)
437 Horne, Frederic, 1 Jan. 1918.
439 Howard, Cecil Harry St. Leger, 1 Jan. 1918. M.)
440 Howard, Frederick James, 1 Jan. 1918.
441 Howell, Godfrey Valentine, 1 Jan. 1918.
442 Hughes, Arthur, 1 Jan. 1918.
443 Hughes-Gibb, Aubrey Patrick, 1 Jan. 1918.
444 Humphreys, Gilbert, 1 Jan. 1918.
445 Hunt, John, 1 Jan. 1918.
446 Hunt, Joseph, 1 Jan. 1918.
447 Hunter, Thomas Charles, 1 Jan. 1918.
449 Hutchinson, Arthur, 1 Jan. 1918.
452 Infeld, Louis, 1 Jan. 1918.
453 Ingram, Edward Maurice Berkeley, 1 Jan. 1918.
454 Ireland, William Edward, 1 Jan. 1918.
455 Irwin, Thomas Cuthbert, 1 Jan. 1918. (M.)
456 Jacks, Harold Benjamin, 1 Jan. 1918.
457 Jackson, John, 1 Jan. 1918.
458 Jackson, Laura, Mrs., 1 Jan. 1918.
460 James, George Charles, 1 Jan. 1918.
461 Jarrott, Charles, 1 Jan. 1918. (M.)
462 Jefferies, Henry Charles, 1 Jan. 1918.
463 Johnston, William Douglas, 1 Jan. 1918.
464 Jonas, Harold Driver, 1 Jan. 1918. (M.)
465 Jones, Arthur, 1 Jan. 1918.
466 Jones, Arthur Dansey, 1 Jan. 1918.
467 Jones, Patrick Nicholas Hill, 1 Jan. 1918.
469 Jones, Theodore Warren, 1 Jan. 1918. (M.)
470 Jones, John Francis, 1 Jan. 1918.
471 Joyce, Thomas Athol, 1 Jan. 1918. (M.)
472 Kay, Andrew Cassels, 1 Jan. 1918.
473 Kaye, Sydney Herbert, 1 Jan. 1918.
474 Keenlyside, Rupert Hales Headlam, 1 Jan. 1918.
475 Kelly, Alfred Evans, 1 Jan. 1918.
477 Kelman, Rev. John, 1 Jan. 1918.
478 Kenrick, Hubert Wynn, 1 Jan. 1918. (M.)
479 Kerr, Lady Anne, 1 Jan. 1918.
480 Kidner, Samuel, 1 Jan. 1918.
481 Kimpton, Arthur Ernest, 1 Jan. 1918.
482 King, Mary Liddon, 1 Jan. 1918.
483 Kingston, William, 1 Jan. 1918. (M.)
485 Kirkus, Arthur Ernest, 1 Jan. 1918.
486 Kirkwood, William Dennett, 1 Jan. 1920.
487 Kissane, Matthew, 1 Jan. 1918.
488 Knight, Christopher Newman, 1 Jan. 1918.
489 Knowles, Constance Mary, Lady, 1 Jan. 1918.
491 Landau, Herman, 1 Jan. 1918.
492 Lascelles, Evelyn Louisa, 1 Jan. 1918.
493 Langton, George Philip, 1 Jan. 1918.
494 Learmont, John, 1 Jan. 1918. (M.)
495 le Breton, Clement Martin, 1 Jan. 1918.
496 Ledlie, James Crawford, 1 Jan. 1918.
497 Lee, John William, 1 Jan. 1918.
499 Lee-Williams, Alice Gwynllyan, Mrs., 1 Jan. 1918.
501 Lewers, Hugh Bunnett, 1 Jan. 1918. (M.)
502 Lewin, Lady Ada Edwina Stewart, 1 Jan. 1918.
503 Lewis, Herbert David William, 1 Jan. 1918.
504 Lewis, Ruth, Mrs. John Herbert, 1 Jan. 1918.
505 Lidderdale, Alan Wadsworth, 1 Jan. 1918.
506 Lindley, Tinsley, 1 Jan. 1918.
507 Lindsay, James Brown, 1 Jan. 1918.
508 Lister, Francis Vivian, 1 Jan. 1918. (M.)
510 Lloyd, Arthur Athelwold, 1 Jan. 1918. (M.)
511 Loch, George Richard Boycott, 1 Jan. 1918.
512 Lomax, John, 1 Jan. 1918.
514 Low, William, 1 Jan. 1918.
516 Lowther, Mildred, 1 Jan. 1918.
517 Lugard, Edward James, 1 Jan. 1918. (M.)
518 Lupton, Charles, 1 Jan. 1918.
519 MacAlpine, Cyril Douglas Hughes, 1 Jan. 1918. (M.)
520 MacAlpine, Reginald John, 1 Jan. 1918. (M.)
521 Macaulay, Thomas Symington, 1 Jan. 1918.
522 MacDonald, Rev. Angus, 1 Jan. 1918. (M.)
523 MacDonald, George William, 1 Jan. 1918.
524 Macdonald, James, 1 Jan. 1918.
525 Macdonald, Sheena, Mrs., 1 Jan. 1918.
526 Macfarlane, Hugh, 1 Jan. 1918.
527 Macfarlane, Peter, 1 Jan. 1918.
528 Mackenzie, Finlay Matheson, 1 Jan. 1918
529 Mackintosh, John, 1 Jan. 1918.
530 MacLennan, William, 1 Jan. 1918.
531 MacLintock, Charles Henry, 1 Jan. 1918.
532 Macmillan, Alexander, 1 Jan. 1918. (M.)
533 Macrosty, Henry William, 1 Jan. 1918.
535 Mainwaring, Mary Sybil, Mrs., 1 Jan. 1918.
536 Mair, Jessy, Mrs. 1 Jan. 1918.
537 Major, Albany Featherstonehaugh, 1 Jan. 1918.
538 Man, Frederick Henry Dumas, 1 Jan. 1918.
539 Mansbridge, Henry, 1 Jan. 1918. (M.)
540 Manton, Arthur Woodroffe, 1 Jan. 1918.
541 Maplesden, Charles William, 1 Jan. 1918.
542 Marsden, Winifred, 1 Jan. 1918.
543 Marsh, Ernest William, 1 Jan. 1918.
544 Marsham, Joan, Hon. Mrs. Sydney Edward, 1 Jan. 1918.
545 Martin, Charles Selwyn, 1 Jan. 1918.
547 Mason, Alexander Neil, 1 Jan. 1918.
548 Matson, James, 1 Jan. 1918.
549 Matthews. Arthur, 1 Jan. 1918.
550 Matthews, Thomas Leigh, 1 Jan. 1918.
551 Matthey, Percy, 1 Jan. 1918.
552 Maxwell, Alexander Gordon, 1 Jan. 1918. (M)
553 Maxwell, Leslie Blythe, 1 Jan. 1918.
554 Maxwell, Richard Cowdy, 1 Jan. 1918.
555 May, Katharine Edith, Mrs., 1 Jan. 1918.
556 McAdam, Frances, Mrs., 1 Jan. 1918.
557 McAughey, John, 1 Jan. 1918. (M.)
558 McAuliffe, Rev. Edmond, 1 Jan. 1918. (M.)
559 McCaffery, James, 1 Jan. 1918.
561 McCann, John, 1 Jan. 1918.
562 McCann, Robert, 1 Jan. 1918.
563 McClelland, William, 1 Jan. 1918.
564 McConnel, William Holdsworth, 1 Jan. 1918. (M.)
565 McEwen, Thomas, 1 Jan. 1918.
566 McFarlane, Andrew, 1 Jan. 1918.
567 McFarlane, Joseph, 1 Jan. 1918.
568 McFerran, Howard Addison, 1 Jan. 1918.
569 McGowan, James, 1 Jan. 1918.
570 McKeown. John James, 1 Jan. 1918.
572 McLaren, Richard, 1 Jan. 1918.
573 McLean, Peter, 1 Jan. 1918.
574 McNeil, Neil, 1 Jan. 1918.
575 McPherson, Gilbert, 1 Jan. 1918.
576 McPherson. John, 1 Jan. 1918. (M.)
577 Medd, Wilfrid, 1 Jan. 1918.
579 Menzies, Alexander James Pople, 1 Jan. 1918.
580 Metson, George, 1 Jan. 1918. (M.)
581 Michell, George Babbington, 1 Jan. 1918.
582 Millar, William, 1 Jan. 1918.
583 Miller, Arnold Henry, 1 Jan. 1918.
584 Miller, Frank Lawrence, 1 Jan. 1918.
585 Mobbs, Arthur Noel, 1 Jan. 1918.
586 Moffat, James, 1 Jan. 1918.
587 Moir, Alexander, 1 Jan. 1918.
588 Molyneux, Thomas Fell, 1 Jan. 1918.
591 Monteith, David Taylor, 1 Jan. 1918.
592 Moore, Evelyn, 1 Jan. 1918.
593 Moore, Harold. 1 Jan. 1918.
594 More, Jasper Frederick, 1 Jan. 1918.
595 Moreland, Harold, 1 Jan. 1918. (M.)
597 Morris, Henry, 1 Jan. 1918.
598 Morrison, John, 1 Jan. 1918.
599 Morrow, George Andrew, 1 Jan. 1918.
600 Mott, Owen Edward, 1 Jan. 1918.
601 Mulherion, George Frederick, 1 Jan. 1918.
602 Murison, William, 1 Jan. 1918.
603 Murray, Howard, 1 Jan. 1918.
604 Murray, James, 1 Jan. 1918.
605 Murray, Thomas Roberts, 1 Jan. 1918.
606 Napier, Arthur Lenox, 1 Jan. 1918. (M.)
607 Nash. William, 1 Jan. 1918.
608 Nevill, Walter Elphinstone, 1 Jan. 1918. (M.)
609 Newall, Ethel Nest, Mrs. Geoffrey Stirling, 1 Jan. 1918.
610 Newitt, Leonard, 1 Jan. 1918.
611 Newlands, Archibald, 1 Jan. 1918.
612 Nunburnholme, Dowager Lady, 1 Jan. 1918.
613 Nutt, Francis George, 1 Jan. 1918.
616 Oldham, Reta, 1 Jan. 1918.
619 Onslow, Earl of, 1 Jan. 1918. (M.)
621 Osgood, Frederic Stanley, 1 Jan. 1918.
622 Ovans, Charles Phipps John, 1 Jan. 1918. (M.)
625 Palmer, Marian, Mrs. Claude Bowes, 1 Jan. 1918.
626 Palmer, Philip, 1 Jan. 1918.
627 Pardoe, Elizabeth Wentworth, Mrs., 1 Jan. 1918.
628 Park Thomas 1 Jan. 1918.
629 Parker, Sir George Phillips, 1 Jan. 1918.
631 Parker-Jervis, Ethel Mary, 1 Jan. 1918.
633 Paterson, Clifford Copland, 1 Jan. 1918.
634 Paterson, Thomas, 1 Jan. 1918.
636 Patterson, Robert George, 1 Jan. 1918.
638 Payne, Walter, 1 Jan. 1918.
639 Pearce, Ernest Alfred John, 1 Jan. 1918.
640 Pearce-Serocold, Claud, 1 Jan. 1918. (M.)

641 Pease, Evelyn. 1 Jan. 1918.
642 Pease, Lucy Victoria, Mrs., 1 Jan. 1918.
643 Peel, Constance Dorothy Evelyn, Mrs., 1 Jan. 1918.
644 Pendarves, Alice Louisa, Mrs., 1 Jan. 1918.
645 Penhorwood, Sydney Lewis, 1 Jan. 1918. (M.)
646 Penrose, Emily, 1 Jan. 1918.
648 Perrin, William Gordon, 1 Jan. 1918. (M.)
649 Pettifor, William, 1 Jan. 1918.
650 Philip, Arthur Edward, 1 Jan. 1918.
651 Phillips, Herbert, 1 Jan. 1918.
652 Phillpotts, Owen Surtees, 1 Jan. 1918.
653 Picton-Turbervill, Edith, 1 Jan. 1918.
654 Piercy, Mary Louisa, Mrs., 1 Jan. 1918.
655 Pitcher, Albert John, 1 Jan. 1918.
656 Platt, William Charles, 1 Jan. 1918.
657 Plumer, Lady, 1 Jan. 1918.
659 Pool, Augustus Frank, 1 Jan. 1918.
660 Porter, Herbert, 1 Jan. 1918.
661 Porter, Mansel Loudon, 1 Jan. 1918. (M.)
662 Prismall, Edwin, 1 Jan. 1918. (M.)
663 Procter, Charles James, 1 Jan. 1918.
664 Prosser, Walter Byron, 1 Jan. 1918.
665 Pulford, William John, 1 Jan. 1918.
666 Rabbit, Edward Joseph, 1 Jan. 1918.
667 Smith, Alan Rae, 1 Jan. 1918. (M.)
668 Raikes, Francis Edward, 1 Jan. 1918.
670 Ralston, Andrew Agnew, 1 Jan. 1918.
671 Randall, James, 1 Jan. 1918. (M.)
672 Rankin, Hugh Fraser, 1 Jan. 1918.
673 Ranson, Joseph Barlow, 1 Jan. 1918.
674 Ratcliff, Constance Lilian, 1 Jan. 1918.
675 Ratcliffe, Henry Stephenson, 1 Jan. 1918.
676 Reckitt, Philip Bealby, 1 Jan. 1918.
677 Reed, Frank William, 1 Jan. 1918.
678 Reed, William, 1 Jan. 1918.
679 Reekie, William Maxwell, 1 Jan. 1918.
680 Reeks, James Albert, 1 Jan. 1918. (M.)
681 Rees, James Daniel, 1 Jan. 1918.
682 Regan, Maurice Ambrose, 1 Jan. 1918. (M.)
683 Reid, George, 1 Jan. 1918.
684 Riddell, William George, 1 Jan. 1918.
685 Ridley, Mary Stephanie, Mrs. Henry Matthew, 1 Jan. 1918.
686 Riley, Edmond John, 1 Jan. 1918.
687 Rind, Walter Lockhart, 1 Jan. 1918.
688 Ritchie, Hugh, 1 Jan. 1918.
689 Roberts, Richard Gilbert, 1 Jan. 1918. (M.)
690 Roberts-Wray, Thomas Henry, 1 Jan. 1918. (M.)
691 Robertson, John, 1 Jan. 1918.
692 Robertson, William, 1 Jan. 1918. (M.)
693 Robinson, Edwin, 1 Jan. 1918.
694 Robinson, Roy Lister, 1 Jan. 1918.
696 Roddam, Roddam John, 1 Jan. 1918. (M.)
697 Roe, Alliott Verdon, 1 Jan. 1918.
698 Rogers, Tanner Montague, 1 Jan. 1918. (M.)
700 Rosher, Noel Burn, 1 Jan. 1918.
701 Ross, Hugh Henderson, 1 Jan. 1918.
702 Rotter, Godfrey, 1 Jan. 1918.
704 Rowley, Amy Isabel, Lady, 1 Jan. 1918.
705 Royce, Frederick Henry, 1 Jan. 1918.
706 Ruck-Keene, Robert Francis, 1 Jan. 1918. (M.)
707 Ruddle, Frank William, 1 Jan. 1918.
708 Runge, Norah Cecil, Mrs., 1 Jan. 1918.
709 Russell, Edward John, 1 Jan. 1918.
711 Russell, John, 1 Jan. 1918.
712 Rutherford, Annie, 1 Jan. 1918.
713 Thomson, George Rutherford, 1 Jan. 1918.
714 Ryan, John, 1 Jan. 1918.
716 Sandison, David, 1 Jan. 1918.
717 Sargeaunt, Bertram Edward, 1 Jan. 1918.
718 Saunders, Frederick James, 1 Jan. 1918.
719 Savill, Edwin, 1 Jan. 1918.
720 Saville, Francis Ernest, 1 Jan. 1918.
721 Sawday, Albert Edwin, 1 Jan. 1918.
724 Serjeantson, Cecil Myles, 1 Jan. 1918. (M.)
725 Sexton, Eric James, 1 Jan. 1918. (M.)
726 Sharp, Frederic Joseph, 1 Jan. 1918. (M.)
727 Sharples, George Bertrand, 1 Jan. 1918.
728 Sharpley, Edward Burgess, 1 Jan. 1918.
730 Shepherd, William Constable, 1 Jan. 1918. (M.)
731 Sheppard, Frank, 1 Jan. 1918.
734 Simonds, Robert Henville, 1 Jan. 1918. (M.)
735 Skene, Philip George Moncrieff, 1 Jan. 1918. (M.)
736 Skipwith, Sophia Flora, Mrs. Grey Townsend, 1 Jan. 1918.
737 Skipworth, George Philip, 1 Jan. 1918.
738 Smith, Alfred, 1 Jan. 1918.
739 Smith, Charles, 1 Jan. 1918.
740 Smith, Ernest Wentworth, 1 Jan. 1918.
741 Smith, Frank Edward, 1 Jan. 1918.
742 Smith, George Henry Cheverton, 1 Jan. 1918.
744 Smith, John Arthur, 1 Jan. 1918.
746 Smith, Thomas Blampey, 1 Jan. 1918.
747 Smith, William Sydney, 1 Jan. 1918.
748 Snowden, Florence Mary, Mrs., 1 Jan. 1918.
749 Southam, Frederick Neil, 1 Jan. 1918.
750 Southgate, Charles Joseph, 1 Jan. 1918.
751 Spencer, Mary Gertrude Catherine Hitchcock, 1 Jan. 1918.
752 Squire, Rose Elizabeth. 1 Jan. 1918.
753 Stainforth, Rowland Hill, 1 Jan. 1918. (M.)

754 Staniland, Alfred Edward, 1 Jan. 1918.
755 Stapley, Frank Robert, 1 Jan. 1918.
756 Steel, Thomas Heron, 1 Jan. 1918. (M.)
757 Stein, Charles, 1 Jan. 1918.
759 Stenson, George Routledge, 1 Jan. 1918.
760 Stephenson, Richard Henry, 1 Jan. 1918.
761 Stevens, Frederick, 1 Jan. 1918.
762 Stevens, Ida Kathleen, 1 Jan. 1918. (M.)
763 Stevens, Patrick William Joseph, 1 Jan. 1918.
764 Stevenson, May Margaret, 1 Jan. 1918.
766 Stewart, Alice Margaret, Mrs., 1 Jan. 1918.
767 Stewart, Athole, 1 Jan. 1918.
768 Stewart, James, 1 Jan. 1918.
770 Stewart, William Allison, 1 Jan. 1918.
771 Stirk, Rufus, 1 Jan. 1918.
772 Stirling, Thomas Willing, 1 Jan. 1918. (M.)
773 Stobart, Frederick William, 1 Jan. 1918.
775 Stow, Harry Vane, 1 Jan. 1918.
776 Strachey, Henrietta Mary Amy, Mrs. John St. Loe, 1 Jan. 1918.
777 Streatfeild, Evelyn Olive, Mrs., 1 Jan. 1918.
778 Clark, Mary Corisande, Mrs. John Bayfield, 1 Jan. 1918
779 Strutt, Emily Mary Charlotte, Mrs., 1 Jan. 1918.
780 Stuart, John, 1 Jan. 1918. (M.)
782 Sunderland, Brian Gresley Elton, 1 Jan. 1918. (M.)
783 Suter, George Edward, 1 Jan. 1918.
785 Swain, William Henry, 1 Jan. 1918.
787 Symes, Kenneth, 1 Jan. 1918. (M.)
788 Tallboy, George Percy, 1 Jan. 1918.
789 Taylor, Arthur Enfield, 1 Jan. 1918.
790 Taylor, David, 1 Jan. 1918.
791 Taylor, George Stevenson, 1 Jan. 1918.
793 Taylor, Richard Henry, 1 Jan. 1918.
794 Taylor, Thomas McComb, 1 Jan. 1918.
795 Tebbs, Louis George, 1 Jan. 1918.
796 Tedder, Alfred Edward, 1 Jan. 1918.
797 Tennyson, Ivy Gladys, Mrs. Charles Bruce, 1 Jan. 1918.
798 Thomas, David John, 1 Jan. 1918.
800 Thomas, John, 1 Jan. 1918.
801 Thomas, Lillie, Mrs., 1 Jan. 1918.
802 Thomas, Walter John, 1 Jan. 1918.
803 Thompson, John Barwick, 1 Jan. 1918. (M.)
804 Thompson, Mary, 1 Jan. 1918.
805 Thompson, Robert John, 1 Jan. 1918.
806 Thomson, Margaret Edith, Mrs., 1 Jan. 1918.
807 Thomson, William Thomas, 1 Jan. 1918.
808 Thornely, Daisy, Mrs., 1 Jan. 1918.
810 Thornton, William, 1 Jan. 1918.
811 Todd, Duncan, 1 Jan. 1918.
812 Todd, Edwin Ernest Enever, 1 Jan. 1918. (M.)
813 Towsey, Joseph Henry, 1 Jan. 1918.
814 Trendell, Herbert Arthur Previté, 1 Jan. 1918.
815 Trew, George Harry Male, 1 Jan. 1918.
818 Tufton, Stella, Hon. Mrs. Charles Henry, 1 Jan. 1918.
810 Turner, William Thomas, 1 Jan. 1918.
820 Turpin, Armigill Thomas, 1 Jan. 1918.
821 Tweedy, George Frederick, 1 Jan. 1918.
822 Tyndale, Walter Clifford, 1 Jan. 1918.
823 Underhill, Hugh Harman, 1 Jan. 1918.
824 Vallange, Clement, 1 Jan. 1918. (M.)
825 Van den Bergh, Henry Edward, 1 Jan. 1918. (M.)
827 Verdier, James William, 1 Jan. 1918.
828 Vernon, Percy Venables, 1 Jan. 1918.
829 Vesey, David Arthur Fitzgerald, 1 Jan. 1918.
830 Vidal, Francis Peter, 1 Jan. 1918. (M.)
831 Walker, Harry, 1 Jan. 1918.
832 Wallace, Falconer Lewis, 1 Jan. 1918.
833 Wallace, William Reeve, 1 Jan. 1918.
834 Walton, Cecil, 1 Jan. 1918.
835 Warburton, Thomas, 1 Jan. 1918.
836 Ward, Leonard, 1 Jan. 1918.
837 Warner, Henry Brooks, 1 Jan. 1918.
838 Waters, Robert Abraham Samuel, 1 Jan. 1918.
840 Watson, Henry, 1 Jan. 1918.
841 Watson, Isaac Adolphus Herbert, 1 Jan. 1918.
843 Watson, William Elder, 1 Jan. 1918.
844 Watts, Edgar Charles, 1 Jan. 1918.
845 Weatherill, Henry, 1 Jan. 1918.
846 Weaver, Frederick William Herron, 1 Jan. 1918.
847 Webb, Cecil Dunstan, 1 Jan. 1918.
848 Webber, Amherst, 1 Jan. 1918.
849 Weir, William Goold, 1 Jan. 1918.
850 Wells, Thomas George Raymond, 1 Jan. 1918.
851 Wenham, Basil Eliot, 1 Jan. 1918.
852 Werner, Edmund Arthur Robert, 1 Jan. 1918.
853 Wetherall, John Andrew Chilton, 1 Jan. 1918. (M.)
854 Wharton, Charles Joseph, 1 Jan. 1918.
855 Wharton, William Henry Anthony, 1 Jan. 1918. (M.)
856 White, Arthur Rabbitts, 1 Jan. 1918.
857 White, Frederick, 1 Jan. 1918.
858 Wickham, Frederick, 1 Jan. 1918.
859 Wicks, Gerald Hamilton, 1 Jan. 1918. (M.)
860 Wildy, Edmund, 1 Jan. 1918. (M.)
861 Wilkinson, Norman, 1 Jan. 1918. (M.)
863 Williams, Charles Edward, 1 Jan. 1918. (M.)
864 Williams, Frank Eliot, 1 Jan. 1918.
865 Williams, Ronald Frederick, 1 Jan. 1918. (M.)
866 Wilson, Arthur Maitland, 1 Jan. 1918.
867 Wilson, Geraldine, Mrs., 1 Jan. 1918.

868 Wilson, George Gordon, 1 Jan. 1918.
870 Wilson, Harry James, 1 Jan. 1918.
871 Wilson, Hubert Wilberforce, 1 Jan. 1918.
872 Wilson, Thomas, 1 Jan. 1918.
873 Wimperis, Harry Egerton, 1 Jan. 1918. (M.)
874 Winny, William Humphris, 1 Jan. 1918.
875 Wood, James, 1 Jan. 1918.
878 Woodifield, Anthony Hudson, 1 Jan. 1918. (M.)
882 Wotzel, Anthony Andrew Augustine, 1 Jan. 1918.
883 Wright, Charles Francis, 1 Jan. 1918.
884 Wynne-Edwards, Hugh Copner, 1 Jan. 1918.
885 Wythes, Aline, Mrs. Ernest James, 1 Jan. 1918.
886 Yeoman, Sophia Bruce, 1 Jan. 1918.
888 Young, James, 1 Jan. 1918.
889 Young, Robert Hellyer, 1 Jan. 1918.
890 Young, Sidney, 1 Jan. 1918.
891 Yule, Charles Bernard Besly, 1 Jan. 1918. (M.)
893 Jacob, Arthur Leslie, 1 Jan. 1918.
894 Ramsay, Arthur Dennys Gilbert, 1 Jan. 1918.
895 Huddleston, Henry Batten, 1 Jan. 1918.
898 Jehangir, Cowasji, 1 Jan. 1918.
900 Downie, Thomas Steel, 1 Jan. 1918.
901 Carnegie, Arthur Alexander, 1 Jan. 1918.
903 Lloyd, Arthur Thomas, 1 Jan. 1918.
904 Hopkins, James Francis Gordon, 1 Jan. 1918.
905 MacCallan, Arthur Ferguson, 1 Jan. 1918.
907 Grogan, Edward Harry, 1 Jan. 1918.
909 Watson, Frank Pears, 1 Jan. 1918.
910 Hewins, Harold Preece, 1 Jan. 1918.
911 Iles, George Ehret, 1 Jan. 1918.
912 Hodgson, Clement Gaukroger, 1 Jan. 1918.
913 Hornblower, William Crothers, 1 Jan. 1918.
914 Macnaghten, Norman Donnelly, 1 Jan. 1918.
915 Anderson, Elizabeth, Mrs., 1 Jan. 1918.
916 Arnold, Percy, 1 Jan. 1918.
918 Campion, Charles Austin Bunworth, 1 Jan. 1918.
919 Chomley, Mary Elizabeth Maud, 1 Jan. 1918.
920 Creswell, Adelaide, Lady, 1 Jan. 1918.
921 Deakin, Vera, 1 Jan. 1918.
923 Gilruth, Jeannie, Mrs., 1 Jan. 1918.
924 James, Gwyneforde, Lady, 1 Jan. 1918.
925 Miller, Annie Emily, 1 Jan. 1918.
926 Miller, Mary Elizabeth, Lady, 1 Jan. 1918.
927 Owen, Gladys, 1 Jan. 1918.
928 Parker, Florence Mary, Mrs., 1 Jan. 1918.
929 Robertson, Philadelphia Una, 1 Jan. 1918.
930 Thomas, Kathleen Kyffin, 1 Jan. 1918.
931 Tucker, Herbert Carey, 1 Jan. 1918.
932 Weigall, Reginald Edward, 1 Jan. 1918.
933 Boyle, Fanny. Mrs. Alexander, 1 Jan. 1918
934 Carroll, Heni Materoa, Lady, 1 Jan. 1918.
936 Coates, Lavinia, 1 Jan. 1918.
937 Duthie, David Whamond, 1 Jan. 1918.
939 Gunson, Jessie, Mrs., 1 Jan. 1918.
941 Holland, Jane, Mrs., 1 Jan. 1918.
942 Lowry, Helen, 1 Jan. 1918.
943 Pomare, Miria Woodbine, Mrs., 1 Jan. 1918.
944 Rhodes, Arthur Edgar Gravenor, 1 Jan. 1918.
946 Rutherford, Eva Lydia, Mrs., 1 Jan. 1918.
947 Stewart, Mary Downie, 1 Jan. 1918.
948 Wigram, Agnes Vernon, Mrs. Henry Francis, 1 Jan. 1918.
949 Williams, Hilda, 1 Jan. 1918.
950 Amphlett, Theodora Mildred, Mrs., 1 Jan. 1918.
951 Anstey, Norman, 1 Jan. 1918.
952 Blankenberg, Reginald Andrew, 1 Jan. 1918.
954 Ponsonby, Hon. Mrs. Maurice George Jesser, 1 Jan. 1918.
956 Clark, Gowan Cresswell Strange, 1 Jan. 1918.
957 Davis, Mary Elizabeth, Mrs., 1 Jan. 1918.
958 Greenacre, Walter, 1 Jan. 1918.
959 Juta, Helen Lena, Lady, 1 Jan. 1918.
960 Lewis, Elizabeth Tryphena, Mrs., 1 Jan. 1918.
961 Mackeurtan, Ellen Maria Louisa, Mrs., 1 Jan. 1918.
962 Marx, Susannah Brandt, Mrs., 1 Jan. 1918.
963 Nicolson, Joseph Henry, 1 Jan. 1918.
964 O'Hara, John Wesley, 1 Jan. 1918.
965 Parker, John, 1 Jan. 1918.
966 Sampson, Henry William, 1 Jan. 1918.
967 Smartt, Sybil Annie, Lady, 1 Jan. 1918.
968 Solomon, Maud Elizabeth, Lady, 1 Jan. 1918.
970 Sturman, Edward Albert, 1 Jan. 1918.
971 Taylor, John, 1 Jan. 1918.
972 van Zijl, Carel Johannes, 1 Jan. 1918. (M.)
974 Conroy, Charles O'Neill, 1 Jan. 1918.
975 Emerson, Katherine, Mrs., 1 Jan. 1918.
977 MacPherson, Eleonora Thompson, Mrs., 1 Jan. 1918.
979 Paterson, Florence Lavinia, Mrs., 1 Jan. 1918.
981 Alabaster, Chaloner Grenville, 1 Jan. 1918.
982 Allwood, John Humber, 1 Jan. 1918.
983 Berne, James Leo, 1 Jan. 1918.
984 Bullock, Amy Isabel, Lady, 1 Jan. 1918.
985 Cook, Albert Ruskin, 1 Jan. 1918.
986 Cran, James, 1 Jan. 1918.
987 de Freitas, Anthony, 1 Jan. 1918.
988 Drayton, Gertrude, 1 Jan. 1918.
989 Egerton, Ada Maud, Lady, 1 Jan. 1918.
990 Felton, Muriel Harriet, Mrs., 1 Jan. 1918.
991 Fisher, John Campbell, 1 Jan. 1918.
992 Fletcher, Stanley Hewitt, 1 Jan. 1918.
993 Furley, John Talfourd, 1 Jan. 1918.

994 Murray, Hon. Mrs. Ronald Thomas Graham, 1 Jan. 1918.
995 Huggins, George Frederick, 1 Jan. 1918.
996 Jackson, Edward St. John, 1 Jan. 1918.
997 James, Williard Frank, 1 Jan. 1918.
998 Jebb, Robert Russell Horsley, 1 Jan. 1918.
999 Johnston, Margaret Emmeline, Mrs. James Thomason, 1 Jan. 1918.
1000 Keng, Lim Boon, 1 Jan. 1918.
1001 Malcolm, Harcourt Gladstone, 1 Jan. 1918.
1002 McDonald, James Gordon, 1 Jan. 1918.
1003 Nicholson, Sybil Helen, Lady, 1 Jan. 1918.
1004 Nicolls, Edward Hugh Dyneley, 1 Jan. 1918.
1005 Patron, Joseph Armand, 1 Jan. 1918.
1006 Probyn, Emily, Lady, 1 Jan. 1918.
1007 Radcliffe, Cecily, Mrs., 1 Jan. 1918.
1008 Radford, Beatrice Letitia May, Mrs., 1 Jan. 1918.
1009 Rippon, Joseph, 1 Jan. 1918.
1010 Scicluna, Corinna, Marchesa, 1 Jan. 1918.
1011 Sharp, Ernest Hamilton, 1 Jan. 1918.
1012 Simpson, Hubert Ashton Laselve, 1 Jan. 1918.
1013 Spurling, Stanley Salisbury, 1 Jan. 1918.
1014 Stabb, Sir Newton John, 1 Jan. 1918.
1015 Swinbourne, Charles Augustus, 1 Jan. 1918. (M.)
1016 Wilson, William, 1 Jan. 1918.
1017 Austin, William, 1 Jan. 1918.
1018 Boraston, John Herbert, 1 Jan. 1920. (M.)
1019 Bragg, William Lawrence, 1 Jan. 1918. (M.)
1021 Clifford, William Henry, 1 Jan. 1918. (M.)
1022 Currie, Isabel, Mrs., 1 Jan. 1918.
1023 Duke, Richard Hare, 1 Jan. 1918.
1024 Fitch, Rev. Edward Arnold, 1 Jan. 1918. (M.)
1025 Fowler, Charles Edward Percy, 1 Jan. 1918. (M.)
1026 Green, Francis Arthur, 1 Jan. 1918. (M.)
1027 Griffith, George Herbert, 1 Jan. 1918.
1028 Higgin-Birket, Myles, 1 Jan. 1918. (M.)
1029 Jessop, William, 1 Jan. 1918.
1030 Magrath, Charles John, 1 Jan. 1918.
1032 Tod, Marcus Niebuhr, 1 Jan. 1918. (M.)
1034 Wright, Edward Constable, 1 Jan. 1918. (M.)
1037 Absale, John Hilling, 3 June, 1918.
1040 Adcock, Frank Ezra, 3 June, 1918. (M.)
1041 Adey, John Kellerman, 1 Jan. 1918. (M.)
1042 Agnew, Charles Morland, 3 June, 1918.
1043 Agnew, Samuel Montagu, 3 June, 1918. (M.)
1044 Aitken, James Herbert, 3 June, 1918.
1045 Akerman, John Camille, 3 June, 1918.
1046 Alexander, Frederick, 3 June, 1918.
1047 Allan, James, 3 June, 1918.
1048 Allardice, William McDiarmid, 3 June, 1918. (M.)
1049 Allen, Clementina Dorothy, 3 June, 1918.
1052 Alvarez, Justin Charles William, 3 June, 1918.
1053 Anderson, Arthur, 3 June, 1918.
1054 Anderson, Charles Harrison Murray, 3 June, 1918. (M.)
1055 Anderson, Dora, Mrs., 3 June, 1918.
1056 Anderson, Eric Harper, 3 June, 1918.
1057 Anderson, William, 3 June, 1918.
1058 Apthorp, Beatrice Mary, 3 June, 1918.
1059 Armstrong, Francis Philip, 3 June, 1918. (M.)
1060 Arscott, William Herbert, 3 June, 1918. (M.)
1061 Aston, Reginald Godfrey, 3 June, 1918. (M.)
1062 Atha, Charles Gurney, 3 June, 1918.
1063 Atkinson, Georgina Jane, 3 June, 1918.
1064 Attwood, Edward Lewis, 3 June, 1918.
1065 Audus, Henry Joseph Francis, 3 June, 1918. (M.)
1066 Avern, James Waters Earnscliffe, 3 June, 1918. (M.)
1067 Badger, James Carol, 3 June, 1918.
1068 Badshah, Kavas Jamas, 3 June, 1918.
1069 Bailey, Duncan, 3 June, 1918.
1071 Baillie, Granville Hugh, 3 June, 1918.
1072 Baillieu, Clive Latham, 3 June, 1918. (M.)
1073 Baker, George, 3 June, 1918.
1074 Baker, Richard Lawrence, 3 June, 1918. (M.)
1075 Balaam, Charles John, 3 June, 1918. (M.)
1076 Burton-Baldry, Walter Burton, 3 June, 1918. (M.)
1077 Baldwin, Edmund Chaplin, 3 June, 1918.
1078 Baldwin, Lucy, Mrs., 3 June, 1918.
1079 Ball, William Valentine, 3 June, 1918.
1080 Balme, Archibald Hamilton, 3 June, 1918.
1081 Bamford, Harry William Morrey, 3 June, 1918. (M.)
1082 Banfield, Richard, 3 June, 1918.
1083 Barbour, Anna Edwards, Mrs., 3 June, 1918.
1085 Baring, Hon. Maurice, 3 June, 1918. (M.)
1086 Barkas, Thomas Cooke, 3 June, 1918.
1087 Barnard, Arthur John Chichester, 3 June, 1918. (M.)
1088 Barnardiston, Katherine Weston, Mrs. Ernald, 3 June, 1918.
1089 Barnes, Frank Purcell, 3 June, 1918. (M.)
1090 Barnes, James Burden, 3 June, 1918.
1091 Barnsley, George, 3 June, 1918. (M.)
1092 Barnwell, Frank Sowter, 3 June, 1918. (M.)
1093 Barrett, Geoffrey Foster, 3 June, 1918.
1094 Barry, Bernard John Wolfe Wolfe-, 3 June, 1918.
1095 Barry, David, 3 June, 1918.
1096 Bartholomew, John, 3 June, 1918.
1097 Barton, Emma Alice, Mrs., 3 June, 1918.
1099 Bates, Herbert, 3 June, 1918.
1100 Bates, William, 3 June, 1918.
1101 Bayley, Roland, 3 June, 1918.

1102 Beaumont, Violet Marie Louise, Baroness, 3 June, 1918.
1103 Beckett, Ivy Nina, Mrs., 3 June, 1918.
1104 Bellamy, Charles Glynn Hughes, 3 June, 1918. (M.)
1106 Bennett, Reginald Allbon, 3 June, 1918.
1108 Berners, John Anstruther, 3 June, 1918.
1109 Bettington, Egerton Mitford, 3 June, 1918. (M.)
1110 Bilsland, Robert, 3 June, 1918.
1111 Binyon, Basil, 3 June, 1918. (M.)
1112 Bird, James, 3 June, 1918. (M.)
1113 Bispham, James Webb, 3 June, 1918. (M.)
1114 Blackburne-Farrer, Edward Richard, 3 June, 1918. (M.)
1115 Blackler, Leonard, 3 June, 1918. (M.)
1116 Blacklock, Thomas, 3 June, 1918.
1117 Blackshaw, John Frank, 3 June, 1918.
1118 Blake, Harry, 3 June, 1918.
1119 Blaker, Sir John George, Bart., 3 June, 1918.
1120 Blandford, Herbert John George, 3 June, 1918.
1121 de Blaquiere, Marie Lucienne Henriette Adine, Lady, 3 June, 1918.
1122 Bloomfield, James, 3 June, 1918. (M.)
1124 Blundell, Bryan Seymour Moss-, 3 June, 1918. (M.)
1125 Boar, William Henry, 3 June, 1918.
1126 Board, William John, 3 June, 1918.
1127 Bond, John, 3 June, 1918.
1128 Bond, John Robert, 3 June, 1918.
1129 Booth, Erskine, 3 June, 1918.
1131 Borrie, Walter, 3 June, 1918.
1132 Boswell, Percy George Hamnal, 3 June, 1918.
1133 Bower, Thomas Stanley, 3 June, 1918.
1134 Boyce, Godfrey Hale, 3 June, 1918.
1135 Boyton, Robert Alexander Stewart, 3 June, 1918.
1136 Bradbury, William Percy, 3 June, 1918. (M.)
1137 Bradford, William, 3 June, 1918.
1138 Bradshaw, Frank, 3 June, 1918.
1139 Bradshaw, Granville Eastwood, 3 June, 1918.
1140 Bramall, Ernest Edward Peel, 3 June, 1918. (M.)
1141 Brand, Robert Harvey, 3 June, 1918. (M.)
1142 Brett, Hon. Maurice Vymer Baliol, 3 June, 1918. (M.)
1143 Broad, Gordon Leslie, 3 June, 1918. (M.)
1144 Broadwood, Francis, 3 June, 1918. (M.)
1145 Willoughby de Broke, Marie Frances Lisette, Lady, 3 June, 1918.
1147 Brothers, Orlando Frank, 3 June, 1918. (M.)
1148 Brown, Alice, 3 June, 1918.
1149 Brown, Archibald Hall, 3 June, 1918.
1150 Browne, Lady Mary Isabel Peyronnet, 3 June, 1918.
1152 Bruce, Alexander, 3 June, 1918. (M).
1153 Bruce, Edward Walrond de Wells, 3 June, 1918.
1154 Bruce, William Joseph Willett, 3 June, 1918.
1155 Brunton, John Norman, 3 June, 1918.
1156 Bryant, George Herbert, 3 June, 1918. (M.)
1157 Buckley, Edward John, 3 June 1918. (M.)
1158 Budgett, Georgiana Essie, Mrs., 3 June, 1918.
1159 Buist, William Huntley, 3 June, 1918.
1160 Bulleid, Charles Henry, 3 June, 1918.
1161 Bullen, William Henry Chambers, 3 June, 1918. (M.)
1162 Bulloch, Marion Maria, 3 June, 1918.
1163 Burgess, William Edward, 3 June, 1918. (M.)
1164 Burne, Newdigate Addington Knightley, 3 June, 1918. (M.)
1165 Burnet, Sarah Elizabeth, 3 June, 1918.
1166 Burnie, William Beckit, 3 June, 1918.
1167 Burton, Rev. Canon Harry Darwin, 3 June, 1918. (M.)
1168 Bushrod, Frank, 3 June, 1918.
1169 Butcher, Samuel Foster, 3 June, 1918.
1170 Butler, Albert, 3 June, 1918.
1171 Butler, Harold George, 3 June, 1918.
1172 Butterworth, Jabez, 3 June, 1918. (M.)
1173 Buxton, Lucy Ethel, Mrs. Gerald, 3 June, 1918.
1174 Buxton, Mary Emma, Hon. Mrs. Francis William, 3 June, 1918.
1175 Byne, Roland Martin, 3 June, 1918. (M.)
1176 Byrom, Charles Reginald, 3 June, 1918.
1177 Cabuche, Henry Leon, 3 June, 1918. (M.)
1178 Cairns, Rev. David Smith, 3 June, 1918.
1180 Caldwell, Michael Alexander, 3 June, 1918. (M.)
1181 Callan, Joseph, 3 June, 1918.
1182 Calverley, Louisa Mary, Mrs., 3 June, 1918.
1183 Campbell, Donald, 3 June, 1918.
1184 Campbell, Mary Vereker Hamilton-, 3 June, 1918.
1185 Campos, Victor Ribeiro d'Almeida, 3 June, 1918. (M.)
1186 Du Cane, Charles George, 3 June, 1918. (M.)
1187 Cannons, Edwin Galton, 3 June, 1918.
1188 Cargill, Alexander, 3 June, 1918.
1189 Carpenter, Charles Howard, 3 June, 1918.
1190 Carr, Alexander, 3 June, 1918.
1191 Carr, Reginald Childers Culling, 3 June, 1918.
1192 Carter, Flora Mactavish, Mrs., 3 June, 1918.
1193 Carter, Herbert Parkinson, 3 June, 1918.
1194 Cary, Reginald Ormsby, 3 June, 1918.
1195 Cathles, Albert, 3 June, 1918.
1196 Cave, Beatrice Julia, Mrs. Charles Henry, 3 June, 1918.
1197 Cavendish, Elizabeth Janet, Hon. Mrs. William Edwin, 3 June, 1918.
1198 Chaldecott, Harold Richards, 3 June, 1918.
1199 Chamberlain, Helen, Mrs., 3 June, 1918.
1200 Chambers, Frank William, 3 June, 1918.
1201 Chamier, John Adrian, 3 June, 1918. (M.)

1202 Chaplin, Reginald Spencer, 3 June, 1918. (M.)
1203 Chapman, Edward Henry, 3 June, 1918. (M.)
1204 Charlton, Rowland Hugh, 3 June, 1918.
1205 Charrington, Elinor Mary, Mrs., 3 June, 1918.
1206 Chassar, William Charles, 3 June, 1918. (M.)
1207 Cheetham, Eva Christine, Mrs., 3 June, 1918.
1208 Chettle, Henry Francis, 3 June, 1918. (M.)
1209 Chill, Edwin Albert, 3 June, 1918.
1210 Cholmeley, Robert Francis, 3 June, 1918.
1211 Chute, Mervyn Lyde, 3 June, 1918. (M.)
1212 Clapham, Douglas, 3 June, 1918. (M.)
1213 Claret, Frank Henry, 3 June, 1918.
1214 Clark, Frederick Ourry, 3 June, 1918.
1217 Clay, William Henry Christy, 3 June, 1918. (M.)
1218 Clipperton, Ella Elizabeth, Mrs. Charles Bell Child, 3 June, 1918.
1219 Clowes, Mary Knight, 3 June, 1918.
1220 Coates, Thomas Seymour, 3 June, 1918. (M.)
1222 Cockburn, David, 3 June, 1918. (M.)
1223 Cockburn, Ernest Radcliffe, 3 June, 1918. (M.)
1224 Cockburn, George Ernest, 3 June, 1918.
1225 Cockell, Anthony Stuart Buckland-, 3 June, 1918.
1226 Coke, Basil Elmsley, 3 June, 1918. (M.)
1227 Coleman, George Henry, 3 June, 1918.
1228 Coleman, Patrick Eugene, 3 June, 1918. (M.)
1229 Collett, Charles Benjamin, 3 June, 1918.
1230 Concannon, Henry, 3 June, 1918.
1231 Coope, Raymond Henry, 3 June, 1918.
1232 Cooper, Vivian Bolton Douglas, 3 June, 1918. (M.)
1234 Corbett, Sybel, 3 June, 1918.
1235 Cornish, William Delhi, 3 June, 1918.
1236 Cosgrove, James, 3 June, 1918.
1237 Cotterell, Mabel, 3 June, 1918.
1238 Coulon, Frederick, 3 June, 1918. (M.)
1239 Couper, John Charles, 3 June, 1918.
1240 Cox, Alfred, 3 June, 1918.
1241 Cox, Irene Winifred, 3 June, 1918.
1242 Crafter, Richard Andrew, 3 June, 1918.
1243 Craig, Eustace Neville, 3 June, 1918.
1244 Craig, William, 3 June, 1918.
1245 Crisp, John, 3 June, 1918.
1246 Croal, George Crammond, 3 June, 1918.
1247 Croker, Crofton, 3 June, 1918. (M.)
1248 Crook, William Montgomery, 3 June, 1918.
1249 Crow, Alwyn Douglas, 3 June, 1918. (M.)
1251 Crowdy, Isabel, 3 June, 1918.
1252 Cruddas, William John, 3 June, 1918.
1253 Cruickshank, Alexander Thomas, 3 June, 1918.
1254 Culver, Edith Bruce, Mrs., 3 June, 1918.
1255 Cumming, Alexander Charles, 3 June, 1918.
1256 Cunningham, Barbara Martin, 3 June, 1918.
1257 Curry, James William, 3 June, 1918.
1258 Dainton, Sydney Herbert George, 3 June, 1918. (M.)
1259 Dale, Alywn Percy, 3 June, 1918. (M.)
1260 Dalgleish, James William Ogilvy-, 3 June, 1918. (M.)
1261 Dalrymple, Joseph, 3 June, 1918. (M.)
1262 Dalziel, Norman Pearson, 3 June, 1918.
1263 Daniell, Thomas Edward St. Clare, 3 June, 1918. (M.)
1266 Davies, Charles Robert, 3 June, 1918. (M.)
1267 Davies, Ethel, Mrs. Price-, 3 June, 1918.
1269 Davies, Thomas Evan, 3 June, 1918.
1270 Davies, William Henry Saxon, 3 June, 1918.
1271 Davis, Sidney George, 3 June, 1918. (M.)
1273 Dawnay, Sybil Mary, 3 June, 1918.
1274 Dawson, Arthur James, 3 June, 1918.
1275 Dawson, Minnie Ethel, Lady, 3 June, 1918.
1276 Day, Edmund, 3 June, 1918. (M.)
1278 Deane, Augusta, 3 June, 1918.
1279 Delany, William, 3 June, 1918. (M.)
1280 Denham, Arthur Christopher, 3 June, 1918.
1281 Dennis, Bertram Ramsey, 3 June, 1918. (M.)
1282 Despard, Beatrice Lorne, Mrs., 3 June, 1918.
1283 Dexter, Edward, 3 June, 1918.
1284 Dexter, Thomas Edward, 3 June, 1918.
1285 Dickson, Isabel Anne, 3 June, 1918.
1286 Dickson, Norman, 3 June, 1918.
1287 Diggins, Arthur, 3 June, 1918.
1288 Dignam, Edmund Grattan, 3 June, 1918.
1289 Dimmer, John Francis, 3 June, 1918. (M.)
1290 Dimsdale, Beatrice, Dowager Lady, 3 June, 1918.
1291 Dixon, Edward, 3 June, 1918.
1292 Dixon, Leonard Alexander, 3 June, 1918.
1293 Dodds, Thomas Liddell, 3 June, 1918.
1294 Dodsworth, Sir Matthew Blayney Smith-, Bart., 3 June 1918.
1295 Dodsworth, Robinson Irving, 3 June, 1918.
1296 Dolton, Herbert Edward, 3 June, 1918.
1297 Dorman, Bedford Lockwood, 3 June, 1918.
1298 Douglas, Alfred, 3 June, 1918.
1299 Doyle, James Bernard Harvey, 3 June, 1918. (M.)
1300 Drinkwater, Katharine Rosebery, Mrs., 3 June, 1918.
1301 Druitt, Reginald Ernest, 3 June, 1918.
1302 Drummond, Robert, 3 June, 1918.
1303 Drury, Geoffrey Herbert, 3 June, 1918.
1304 Drysdale, John Douglas, 3 June, 1918. (M.)
1305 Dugdale, Maud Violet, Mrs., 3 June, 1918.
1306 Duncan, James, 3 June, 1918.
1307 Dunlop, Charles, 3 June, 1918. (M.)
1808 Dunnett, Rev. George Victor, 3 June, 1918. (M.)

1309 Dunsheath, Percy, 3 June, 1918. (M.)
1310 Durnford, Philip Barton, 3 June, 1918.
1311 Edmed, Frank George, 3 June, 1918.
1314 Edwards, William Rea, 3 June, 1918.
1315 Egan, George, 3 June, 1918.
1316 Elgood, Frank Minshull, 3 June, 1918.
1317 Elles, Arthur Warre, 3 June. 1918. (M.)
1318 Ellicock, Samuel, 3 June, 1918.
1319 Ellis, James Valentine, 3 June, 1918.
1320 Elwood, Elisha, 3 June, 1918.
1321 Emett, Frederick William, 3 June, 1918.
1322 Ennis, Lawrence, 3 June, 1918.
1323 Evans, Henry Morton Glyn, 3 June, 1918. (M.)
1324 Evans, Herbert Walter Lloyd, 3 June, 1918.
1325 Evans, Richard, 3 June, 1918.
1326 Evelyn, Gwendolen Evelyn Maud, 3 June, 1918.
1327 Ewart, Ernest Andrew, 3 June, 1918. (M.)
1328 Eyre, John, 3 June, 1918.
1329 Faber, Oscar, 3 June, 1918.
1330 Fairbank, William, 3 June, 1918.
1331 Farmer, Samuel William, 3 June, 1918.
1332 Farnsworth, Alfred William, 3 June, 1918.
1333 Fender, Thomas, 3 June, 1918.
1334 Ffiske, William Henry, 3 June, 1918.
1335 Field, Herbert Stanley, 3 June, 1918.
1336 Field, Joseph Henry, 3 June, 1918.
1337 Fiennes, Florence Agnes, Hon. Lady Twistleton-Wykeham-, 3 June, 1918.
1338 Finch, William, 3 June, 1918.
1339 Finlay, Frank Dalzell, 3 June, 1918. (M.)
1340 Finlayson, Duncan, 3 June, 1918.
1342 Fleming, John Grant, 3 June, 1918. (M.)
1343 Fletcher, Frank Purser, 3 June, 1918.
1344 Flett, John Smith, 3 June, 1918.
1345 Flower, Leila Beatrice, Mrs., 3 June, 1918.
1346 Ford, Allen Edward, 3 June, 1918.
1347 Forsdick, Edward Thomas, 3 June, 1918. (M.)
1348 Forsdike, George Frederick, 3 June, 1918.
1349 Forster, John Vernon, 3 June, 1918.
1350 Foster, John Vere, 3 June, 1918. (M.)
1351 Fowler, Ralph Howard, 3 June, 1918.
1352 Fowler, Robert Copp, 3 June, 1918.
1353 Francis, Herbert William Sidney, 3 June, 1918.
1354 Franey, George Ernest, 3 June, 1918.
1355 Freeth, Francis Arthur, 3 June, 1918.
1356 Fricker, Guy Carey, 3 June, 1918.
1357 Fry, Beatrice, Mrs., 3 June, 1918.
1358 Fry, Theodore Wilfrid, 3 June, 1918.
1359 Fuller, Mabel, Mrs. Robert Fleetwood, 3 June, 1918.
1360 Gandy, Gerard Knipe, 3 June, 1918.
1361 Gandy, Henry George, 3 June, 1918. (M.)
1362 Ganson, Robert Dowell, 3 June, 1918.
1364 Gaskell, Holbrook, 3 June, 1918.
1367 Gatty, Lina Mary, Mrs. Alexander John Scott-, 3 June, 1918.
1368 Gaunt, Walter Henry, 3 June, 1918.
1369 George, John, 3 June, 1918.
1370 Gibson, Herbert Mends, 3 June, 1918.
1371 Gibson, Richard Edward, 3 June, 1918. (M.)
1372 Gilchrist, John MacAuslan, 3 June, 1918.
1374 Glaser, Herbert, 3 June, 1918.
1375 Glynn, Thomas George Powell, 3 June, 1918. (M.)
1376 Gobey, Francis Edward, 3 June, 1918.
1377 Goddard, Charles Ernest, 3 June, 1918.
1378 Godfray, John Charles Lerrier, 3 June, 1918. (M.)
1379 Gold, Harcourt Gilbey, 3 June, 1918. (M.)
1380 Gordon, James Scott, 3 June, 1918.
1381 Gordon, James Tennant, 3 June, 1918.
1384 Gott, Violet Alice, Mrs., 3 June, 1918.
1385 Graham, Thomas Harkness, 3 June, 1918.
1386 Granville, Dennis, 3 June, 1918.
1387 Grasett, Edward Douglas, 3 June, 1918.
1388 Grassick, Frederick, 3 June, 1918.
1389 Graves, Cecil Alexander Hope, 3 June, 1918. (M.)
1390 Gray, James Carter, 3 June, 1918.
1391 Green, Ethel Mary, Mrs., 3 June, 1918.
1392 Green, John, 3 June, 1918. (M.)
1393 Green, Sir John Little, 3 June, 1918.
1394 Greenwell, Charles Okey, 3 June, 1918. (M.)
1395 Greer, Alured Ussher, 1 June, 1918. (M.)
1396 Gregory, Alfred, 3 June, 1918. (M.)
1397 de Grey, Nigel, 3 June, 1918. (M.)
1398 Grey, Lady Sybil, 3 June, 1918.
1399 Grieve, Richard Albany, 3 June, 1918. (M.)
1400 Grigor, William Ernest, 3 June, 1918. (M.)
1401 Gripper, Basil Jasper, 3 June, 1918. (M.)
1402 Grove, Frank, 3 June, 1918.
1403 Grundy, Samuel Percy, 3 June, 1918.
1405 Gull, Sir William Cameron, Bart., 3 June, 1918.
1406 Gunn, John Alexander, 3 June, 1918.
1407 Gush, Arthur Sydney, 3 June, 1918. (M.)
1408 Gwyn, Edith, Mrs. Moore-, 3 June, 1918.
1409 Haines, John Thomas Augustus, 3 June, 1918.
1411 Hall, Annie, Mrs., 3 June, 1918.
1412 Hall, Charles John Ernest, 3 June, 1918.
1413 Hall, Frederick Walter, 3 June, 1918.
1414 Hall, Herbert Gordon Lewis, 3 June, 1918. (M.)
1415 Hall, Martin Julian, 3 June, 1918.
1416 Hallett, Frederic Greville, 3 June, 1918.

1417 Hamil., John Molyneux, 3 June, 1918. (M.)
1418 Hamilton, Charles Gipps, 3 June, 1918.
1419 Hanbury, Effield Dorothy Cecil, Mrs. Cecil, 3 June, 1918.
1420 Hancock, Charles Frederick, 3 June, 1918.
1421 Handover, Harry George, 3 June, 1918.
1423 Hannah, John Miller, 3 June, 1918.
1424 Hanson, John Richard, 3 June, 1918. (M.)
1425 Hanson, Paul Rennard, 3 June, 1918. (M.)
1426 Hanson, Reginald John Edward, 3 June, 1918. (M.)
1427 Harding, Egerton Stephen Somers, 3 June, 1918.
1428 Hardisty, William Frederick James, 3 June, 1918. (M.)
1429 Hardman, Frances May Holford, Mrs., 3 June, 1918.
1430 Harker, Edward, 3 June, 1918.
1431 Harley, David, 3 June, 1918.
1432 Harper, Arthur David, 3 June, 1918. (M.)
1433 Harper, John Bradford, 3 June, 1918.
1434 Harries, Herbert Frederick, 3 June, 1918.
1435 Harris, George Henry, 3 June, 1918.
1436 Harris, George Montagu, 3 June, 1918.
1438 Harrison, William, 3 June, 1918.
1439 Harrison, William Edward, 3 June, 1918. (M.)
1440 Harston, John Edwin, 3 June, 1918.
1441 Harstone, John Brunton, 3 June, 1918. (M.)
1443 Hartley, Harry, 3 June, 1918.
1444 Hartree, William, 3 June, 1918.
1446 de Havilland, Geoffrey, 3 June, 1918. (M.)
1447 Hay, Algernon Richard Francis, 3 June, 1918.
1448 Hay, James Lawrence, 3 June, 1918.
1449 Haycraft, George Tolman, 3 June, 1918.
1450 Hayes, George Patrick, 3 June, 1918.
1451 Hayward, Ernest Addison Stanley, 3 June, 1918.
1452 Head, Geoffrey, 3 June, 1918. (M.)
1453 Heakes, Samuel Rigbye, 3 June, 1918. (M.)
1454 Heasman, Albert Edward, 3 June, 1918. (M.)
1455 Heath, Meyrick William, 3 June, 1918.
1456 Heatley, William Robertson, 3 June, 1918.
1457 Heaton, Margaret Elizabeth, Mrs., 3 June, 1918.
1458 Hedderwick, Ethel Marian, Mrs., 3 June, 1918.
1459 Helmore, George Reginald, 3 June, 1918.
1460 Henderson, Kenneth George, 3 June, 1918. (M.)
1461 Herbert, Rosalie Margaret, 3 June, 1918.
1462 Hetherington, Roger Gaskell, 3 June, 1918.
1463 Hewlett, Francis Esmé Theodore, 3 June, 1918. (M.)
1464 Hickes, Edward Weston, 3 June, 1918. (M.)
1465 Hicks, William Thomas, 3 June, 1918. (M.)
1468 Hill, George Bernard, 3 June, 1918. (M.)
1469 Hill, Henry Leonard Gauntlett, 3 June, 1918. (M.)
1470 Hill, Thomas Eustace, 3 June, 1918.
1471 Hilleary, Edward Langdale, 3 June, 1918. (M.)
1472 Hind, Arthur Mayger, 3 June, 1918. (M.)
1473 Hinks, Frederick George, 3 June, 1918.
1474 Hippisley, Richard John Bayntun, 3 June, 1918. (M.)
1475 Hird, Frank, 3 June, 1918.
1476 Hodgson, Arthur John, 3 June, 1918.
1477 Hodgson, Joseph Willoughby, 3 June, 1918.
1478 Hodgson, Patrick Kirkman, 3 June, 1918. (M.)
1479 Hogarth, William, 3 June, 1918.
1480 Hogg, Robert Henry, 3 June, 1918. (M.)
1481 Holden, John Edward, 3 June, 1918.
1482 Holliday, Lionel Brook, 3 June, 1918.
1483 Hollins, Dora Emily Susan, Lady, 3 June, 1918.
1484 Holmes, Henry Nicholls, 3 June, 1918.
1485 Holmes, Horace Gordon, 3 June, 1918.
1486 Holmes, Robert Blake Worsley, 3 June, 1918. (M.)
1487 Holt, Thomas Herbert, 3 June, 1918.
1489 Honey, Annie Violet, 3 June, 1918.
1490 Hooper, Alexander Francis Anderson, 3 June, 1918. (M.)
1491 Hooper, Wallis Dawson, 3 June, 1918. (M.)
1492 Hope, Edward William, 3 June, 1918.
1494 Horne, John William, 3 June, 1918.
1495 Hoskyns, Mabella Harriette Georgina, Mrs., 3 June, 1918.
1496 Howard, Henry Ralph Mowbray, 3 June, 1918. (M.)
1497 Hudlass, Felix William, 3 June, 1918.
1499 Hudson, Fanny Marian, 3 June, 1918.
1500 Hudson, Hilda Phœbe, 3 June, 1918.
1501 Hughes, Phyllis May, Lady, 23 June, 1918.
1502 Hulton, William Arthur Hyde, 3 June, 1918.
1503 Humphrys, John Goundrill, 3 June, 1918.
1504 Hunloke, Sylvia, Mrs. Philip, 3 June, 1918.
1505 Hunt, Jesse Brookes, 3 June, 1918.
1506 Hunter, Alexander, 3 June, 1918.
1507 Hutchinson, Henry Norton, 3 June, 1918.
1508 Hutchinson, Walter Ernest, 3 June, 1918.
1509 Ilbert, Joyce Violet, 3 June, 1918.
1510 Inglis, Hugh, 3 June, 1918.
1511 Iron, John, 3 June, 1918.
1512 Irving, Lewis Allen, 3 June, 1918.
1513 James, Fullarton, 3 June, 1918.
1514 James, Robert Percival, 3 June, 1918.
1515 James, Wilhelmina Martha, 3 June, 1918.
1516 James, William John, 3 June, 1918.
1517 Jeffes, George Ernest, 3 June, 1918.
1518 Jenkin, Henry Archibald, 3 June, 1918.
1519 Jessiman, George Gaston, 3 June, 1918. (M.)
1520 Johnson, Arthur Henry, 3 June, 1918.
1521 Johnson, Robert Stewart, 3 June, 1918.
1522 Johnston, Arthur Hammersley, 3 June, 1918.
1523 Johnstone, Joseph, 3 June, 1918.
1524 Johnstone, Josephine, Mrs. John Heywood, 3 June, 1918.

1525 Jones, Aneurin, 3 June, 1918.
1526 Jones, Charles Hugh le Palleur, 3 June, 1918. (M.)
1527 Jones, David Gwilym, 3 June, 1918. (M.)
1528 Jones, Ethel Mary, 3 June, 1918.
1529 Jones, Glyn Howard Howard-, 3 June, 1918. (M.)
1530 Jones, Richard Evan. 3 June, 1918.
1531 Jones, Tom Bruce, 3 June, 1918.
1532 Jones, William, 3 June, 1918. (M.)
1533 Joseph, Ernest Martin, 3 June, 1918. (M.)
1534 Josselyn, John, 3 June, 1918. (M.)
1535 Joy, Sydney Cooper, 3 June, 1918.
1537 Kah., Frederick, 3 June, 1918.
1539 Keary, George, 3 June, 1918.
1540 Keene, John Limrick, 3 June, 1918.
1541 Keene, Thomas Mann, 3 June, 1918. (M.)
1542 Keith, Angus, 3 June, 1918.
1543 Kelly, Hilda Margaret Catherine, 3 June, 1918.
1544 Kendall, William Henry, 3 June, 1918.
1545 Kennedy, James Montagu Bowle, 3 June 1918. (M.)
1547 Kerr, Allen Coulter, 3 June, 1918.
1548 Kershaw, Abraham, 3 June, 1918.
1549 Kershaw, Edward Bertram Hilton, 3 June, 1918.
1550 Kershaw, Frederick William. 3 June, 1918.
1551 Kinahan, John, 3 June, 1918.
1552 Kincaid, James Scott, 3 June, 1918.
1553 Kindersley, Guy, 3 June, 1918. (M.)
1554 King, Rev. Thomas Joseph, 3 June, 1918. (M.)
1555 Kingston, George Henry, 3 June, 1918.
1556 Kinloch, Sir George, Bart., 3 June, 1918.
1558 Kirk, Norah, Mrs. 3 June, 1918.
1559 Kirwin, Joseph John, 3 June, 1918. (M.)
1560 Knox, Robert Graeme, 3 June, 1918. (M.)
1561 Knyfton, Edith Mary, Mrs. Graves-, 3 June, 1918.
1562 Lacey, Solomon James, 3 June, 1918. (M.)
1563 Laing, Hugh, 3 June, 1918.
1564 Lamb, Andrew, 3 June, 1918.
1565 Lamb, Malcolm Henry Mortimer, 3 June, 1918. (M.)
1566 Lane, Francis Lawrence, 3 June, 1918.
1567 Langridge, William, 3 June, 1918.
1568 Lapsley, Claude Charles, 3 June, 1918.
1570 Lawless, Emily Anne, Lady Crooke-, 3 June, 1918.
1571 Lawrence, John Henry, 3 June, 1918. (M.)
1572 Lawson, Francis Bernard, 3 June, 1918. (M.)
1573 Lawton, Frank Warburton, 8 June, 1918.
1574 Layland, Henry, 3 June, 1918. (M.)
1575 Lea, George Edward, 3 June, 1918.
1576 Leach, Richard, 3 June, 1918.
1577 Leake, Frederick Osborne Simeon, 3 June, 1918.
1579 Ledgard, Reginald Armitage, 3 June. 1918.
1580 Lee, William Lauriston Melville, 3 June 1918.
1581 Lees, Ebenezer Antony, 3 June, 1918.
1582 Leese, Vernon Francis, 3 June, 1918.
1583 Leete, William Chambers, 3 June, 1918.
1584 Lefevre, Frederick Charles, 3 June, 1918.
1585 Lemon, Ernest John Hutchings, 3 June, 1918.
1586 Lench, Harry, 3 June, 1918.
1587 Lenthall, Charles Bertram, 3 June, 1918. (M.)
1588 Leon, Joseph, 3 June, 1918. (M.)
1589 Leslie, Robert, 3 June, 1918.
1590 Lester, John Bingley Garland, 3 June, 1918.
1591 Lethaby, Tom, 3 June, 1918. (M.)
1592 Levick, Thomas Henry Cariton, 3 June, 1918.
1593 Lewer, Arthur John, 3 June, 1918 (M.)
1594 Lewis, Arthur Francis Owen, 3 June, 1918. (M.)
1595 Lincoln, John Bebrouth, 3 June, 1918.
1596 Lindley, William Burns, 3 June, 1918.
1597 Lindsay, Henry Edith Arthur, 3 June, 1918. (M.)
1598 Lindsay, Lady Kathleen, 3 June, 1918.
1599 Littlewood, Alfred William. 3 June, 1918. (M.)
1600 Llewellyn, Joseph Millro, 3 June, 1918.
1601 Lloyd, Charles, 3 June, 1918. (M.)
1602 Lloyd, Ernest Herbert, 3 June, 1918. (M.)
1603 Lloyd, George William, 3 June, 1918.
1604 Lloyd, Nathaniel, 3 June, 1918.
1605 Lobban, Alexander Harper, 3 June, 1918.
1606 Loch, Ruth, 3 June, 1918.
1607 Long, Michael John, 3 June, 1918. (M.)
1608 Lothian, James, 3 June, 1918.
1609 Loveday, William Dunmore, 3 June, 1918.
1611 Luce, Emily Gertrude, 3 June. 1918.
1612 Lumley, Constance Ellinor, Hon. Mrs. Osbert Victor George Atheling, 3 June, 1918.
1613 Lyne, Harry, 3 June, 1918.
1614 Lytton, Hon. Neville Stephen, 3 June, 1918. (M.)
1615 Mabee, Oliver Hugel, 3 June, 1918. (M.)
1616 Macartney, James, 3 June, 1918.
1617 McBain, Alexander Richardson, 3 June, 1918.
1618 McClintock, Antonia, Mrs., 3 June, 1918.
1620 McCracken, David Edenfield, 3 June, 1918.
1622 MacDonald, Hector Munro, 3 June, 1918.
1623 MacDonald, Rev. Robert Gordon, 3 June, 1918.
1624 Mackay, Nora, 3 June, 1918.
1625 Mackenzie, John Hugh Munro, 3 June, 1918.
1626 Mackie, Tom Darke, 3 June, 1918. (M.)
1627 McLaren, Alexander Ernest. 3 June, 1918.
1628 McMath, John, 3 June, 1918.
1629 McMullen, William Halliburton, 3 June, 1918.
1630 Macrae, Donald MacNaughton, 3 June, 1918. (M.)
1631 Madden, William Thomas, 3 June 1918.

1633 Main, William Smith, 3 June. 1918.
1634 Maitland, Edward Bellasis Wightman, 3 June, 1918.
1635 Maitland, William Whitaker, 3 June. 1918.
1636 Maloney, Edward, 3 June, 1918.
1637 Man, Joseph, 3 June, 1918. (M.)
1638 Mann, Francis Oscar, 3 June, 1918.
1639 Mansfield, Henry Lattin, 3 June, 1918. (M.)
1640 Mansfield, Ralph Sheldon, 3 June, 1918. (M.)
1641 Mansfield, Thomas Edward, 3 June, 1918.
1642 Mansford, Henry, 3 June, 1918. (M.)
1643 Maples, Edward William, 3 June, 1918.
1645 Marr, John Lynn, 3 June, 1918.
1646 Marsden, John, 3 June, 1918. (M.)
1647 Marshall, Arthur James, 3 June, 1918. (M.)
1648 Marsham, Hon. Reginald Hastings, 3 June, 1918. (M.)
1649 Martin, Alfred James, 3 June, 1918.
1650 Martin, David, 3 June, 1918.
1651 Martin, William Lewis, 3 June, 1918. (M.)
1652 Martindale, Hilda, 3 June, 1918.
1653 Maskall, George Stephen, 3 June, 1918.
1654 Maslin, Charles James, 3 June, 1918.
1655 Mathias, James Herbert, 3 June, 1918. (M.)
1656 Maton, Reginald Foster Pitt, 3 June, 1918. (M.)
1657 Maxwell, Charles Henderson, 3 June, 1918. (M.)
1658 May, Henry John, 3 June, 1918.
1659 Mayne, Otway, 3 June, 1918.
1660 Melville, Arthur Henry Leslie-, 3 June, 1918.
1661 Menzies, Major Robert. 3 June, 1918. (M.)
1662 Merrells, Thomas Arthur, 3 June, 1918.
1663 Merriman, Frank Boyd, 3 June, 1918. (M.)
1664 Mewburn, Frank Hamilton, 3 June, 1918. (M.)
1665 Michell, Marie Louise, Mrs., 3 June, 1918.
1666 Milford, Sydney William, 3 June, 1918.
1667 Miller, Thomas Lodwick, 3 June, 1918.
1668 Milliken, Gertrude Andrews, Mrs., 3 June, 1918.
1669 Millington, Herbert Ashlin, 3 June, 1918.
1670 Milne, John Archibald Douglas, 3 June, 1918.
1671 Milner, Sarah Elizabeth, Mrs., 3 June, 1918.
1672 Mitchell, Frank Carlyle, 3 June, 1918.
1674 Moffatt, James, 3 June, 1918.
1676 Monckton, Thomas Anthony, 3 June, 1918. **(M.)**
1677 Moreton, Loftus Balfour, 3 June, 1918.
1678 Morisons, Jules Louis, 3 June, 1918.
1680 Morris, Alfred Drummond Warrington-, 3 June, 1918. (M.)
1681 Morris, Thomas Robertson, 3 June. 1918.
1682 Morris, William Richard, 3 June, 1918.
1683 Morrison, Sidney William, 3 June, 1918.
1685 Moscrop Andrew, 3 June, 1918.
1686 Moth, Rev. John Charles, 3 June, 1918. (M.)
1688 Mountjoy, John Percy, 3 June, 1918.
1689 Moxon, John, 3 June, 1918.
1690 Moyses, Harry John Swenson, 3 June, 1918.
1691 Muir, James Ernest, 3 June, 1918.
1692 Muirhead, John, 3 June, 1918.
1693 Mulligan, William Percival, 3 June, 1918. (M.)
1694 Munro, Donald, 3 June, 1918.
1695 Muntzer, George Frederick, 3 June, 1918.
1696 Murray, Alexander, 3 June, 1918.
1697 Murray, William, 3 June, 1918. (M.)
1698 Muspratt, Horace, 3 June, 1918.
1699 Myers, Dudley Borron, 3 June, 1918.
1700 Myles, Charles Duncan, 3 June, 1918. (M.)
1701 Nash, William John Charles, 3 June, 1918.
1702 Neish, Colin Graham, 3 June, 1918. (M.)
1703 Nelson, Henry, 3 June, 1918. (M.)
1704 Nelson, William, 3 June, 1918.
1705 Nelthorpe, Robert Nassau Sutton-, 3 June, 1918.
1706 Newell, Frederick William Monk, 3 June, 1918. (M.)
1707 Newnham, John Montague, 3 June, 1918.
1708 Nicholson, Robert Beattie, 3 June, 1918.
1710 Norman, Frank Arthur, 3 June, 1918.
1712 Oakley, Harry Ekermans, 3 June, 1918.
1713 O'Conor, Maude, Mrs. Edmond, 3 June, 1918.
1714 Okeden, Violet Parry-, 3 June, 1918.
1715 Oliver, Percy Lane, 3 June, 1918.
1716 Orme, Frederick George, 3 June. 1918. (M.)
1717 Osman, Alfred Henry, 3 June, 1918. (M.)
1718 Owen, Alfred Lloyd, 3 June, 1918. (M.)
1719 Owen, Edward Tudor, 3 June, 1918.
1720 Owen, John, 3 June, 1918.
1721 Owen, Reginald Charles Lloyd, 3 June, 1918. (M.)
1722 Paffard, Reginald Douglas, 3 June, 1918. (M.)
1723 Palmer, Eric Barton, 3 June, 1918.
1724 Palmer, Vivian Trestrail Dampier, 3 June, 1918. (M.)
1725 Palmer, William Harold, 3 June, 1918.
1726 Pam, Maude Le Clerc, Mrs., 3 June, 1918.
1727 Parker, Charles Percival ,3 June 1918. (M.)
1728 Parkes, Edward, 3 June, 1918.
1730 Parry, Ernest Gambier, 3 June, 1918.
1731 Passingham, Robert Townshend Anwyl-, 3 June, 1918 (M.)
1732 Paterson, Louise, Mrs., 3 June, 1918.
1733 Payne, Joseph, 3 June, 1918.
1734 Payne, Richard Alfred Ernest, 3 June, 1918.
1735 Peace, Edwin, 3 June, 1918.
1736 Peak, William Herbert, 3 June, 1918.
1738 Pearson, Robert John Addison, 3 June, 1918.
1740 Peel, Robert, 3 June, 1918. (M.)
1741 Peirse, Henrietta, Lady Beresford-, 3 June, 1918.
1742 Pelham, Maude Katherine, 3 June, 1918.

1744 de Pencier, Rt. Rev. Adam Urias, Bishop, 3 June, 1918. (M.)
1745 Penney, Peter John, 3 June, 1918.
1746 Perrett, Thomas Edwin, 3 June 1918. (M.)
1747 Perrier, John William, 3 June, 1918. (M.)
1748 Peskett, Leonard, 3 June, 1918.
1749 Petrie, James, 3 June, 1918.
1750 Petter, Edith Mary, Mrs., 3 June, 1918.
1751 Pharazyn, Godfrey Norris, 3 June, 1918.
1752 Phayre, Richard, 3 June, 1918.
1753 Philip, James Charles, 3 June, 1918.
1754 Phillips, Ernest Harold, 3 June, 1918.
1755 Phillips, Ernest William, 3 June, 1918.
1756 Phillips, Frederick Solomon, 3 June, 1918.
1757 Phillips, George Percy Achilles, 3 June, 1918. (M.)
1758 Phillips, Henry Percy, 3 June, 1918.
1759 Phillips, Lilian Marion Estelle, Mrs., 3 June, 1918.
1760 Phillipson, John, 3 June, 1918. (M.)
1761 Phillpotts, Bertha, 3 June, 1918.
1762 Pigott, Henry Lionel, 3 June, 1918. (M.)
1763 Pigott, John Glyn, 3 June, 1918. (M.)
1764 Pim, John, 3 June, 1918. (M.)
1765 Pim, Violet May, Mrs., 3 June, 1918.
1766 Pirie, Duncan Vernon, 3 June, 1918. (M.)
1767 Pitt, Fanny Sarah Marion, Mrs., 3 June, 1918.
1768 Platt, Isaiah, 3 June, 1918.
1769 Playfair, Charles Murray, 3 June, 1918. (M.)
1770 Pollock, Arthur Jocelyn Coleman, 3 June, 1918. (M.)
1771 Pollok, Robert, 3 June, 1918.
1772 Pott, Walter, 3 June, 1918.
1773 Potts, Reginald, 3 June, 1918.
1774 Potts, Thomas Worthington, 3 June, 1918.
1775 Powell, Kate Haidée, Mrs., 3 June, 1918.
1776 Powell, Herbert James Bingham, 3 June, 1918.
1777 Prescott, Charles William Beeston, 3 June, 1918.
1778 Preston, William Edward, 3 June, 1918.
1779 Price, Henry Gilbert, 3 June, 1918.
1780 Prust, Robert Bateman, 3 June, 1918. (M.)
1783 Purdy, William Frank, 3 June, 1918.
1784 Quelch, Arthur Temple, 3 June, 1918.
1785 Quest, Arthur Charles, 3 June, 1918.
1787 Ramsay, James, 3 June, 1918.
1788 Randolph, Thomas Henry, 3 June, 1918.
1789 Ravenshaw, Rose Constance, Mrs. Hurdis Secundus Lalande, 3 June, 1918.
1790 Rawlinson, Rev. Bernard Stephen, 3 June, 1918. (M.)
1791 Rayner, Alfred, 3 June, 1918.
1792 Ready, Basil Tobin, 3 June, 1918. (M.)
1793 Reed, Thomas Morley, 3 June, 1918. (M.)
1794 Reeves, William Harvey, 3 June, 1918.
1795 Reid, Percy Lester, 3 June, 1918. (M.)
1796 Reid, Robert, 3 June, 1918.
1798 Restall, Walter Tapley, 3 June, 1918.
1799 Retallack, John Ley, 3 June, 1918. (M.)
1800 Reynolds, Edgar Hercules, 3 June, 1918. (M.)
1801 Reynolds, Harold Bulkeley, 3 June, 1918.
1803 Richards, George Cobley Smyth-, 3 June, 1918.
1804 Richards, Harold, 3 June, 1918. (M.)
1805 Richardson, Charles William, 3 June, 1918. (M.)
1806 Richardson, Sidney Sherlock, 3 June, 1918. (M.)
1807 Riches, Henry, 3 June, 1918.
1808 Rigg, Richard, 3 June, 1918.
1809 Rintoul, William, 3 June, 1918.
1810 Roberts, Alfred Henry, 3 June, 1918.
1811 Roberts, Richard Cowan, 3 June, 1918. (M.)
1812 Roberts, William, 3 June, 1918.
1813 Robertson, Duncan John, 3 June, 1918.
1814 Robertson, James Alexander, 3 June, 1918.
1815 Robinson, Dorothy Eyre, 3 June, 1918.
1816 Robinson, Maurice Alexander, 3 June, 1918.
1817 Robinson, Samuel, 3 June, 1918.
1818 Rogers, Charles Herman, 3 June, 1918. (M.)
1819 Rogers, Herbert Edwin Wright, 3 June, 1918.
1820 Rogers, John, 3 June, 1918.
1821 Rogers, John, 3 June, 1918.
1822 Rooke, Alfred Shipton, 3 June, 1918. (M.)
1823 Ross, William David, 3 June, 1918. (M.)
1824 Ross, William Henry, 3 June, 1918.
1825 De Rougemont, Frank, 3 June, 1918.
1826 Rowe, George John, 3 June, 1918.
1827 Rowland, Margaret Lilian, Mrs., 3 June, 1918.
1828 Roxby, Francis Maude, 3 June, 1918. (M.)
1829 Rudkin, Hugh Ernest, 3 June, 1918. (M.)
1830 Rundle, Henry John Montague, 3 June, 1918. (M.)
1831 Russell, George Dearle, 3 June, 1918.
1832 Ruthen, Sir Charles Tamlin, 3 June, 1918.
1833 Ryder, George Thomas, 3 June, 1918.
1834 Salcombe, Ernest Walter, 3 June 1918.
1835 Salmond, Mary Augusta Compton, Mrs., 3 June, 1918.
1836 Sample, Charles Herbert, 3 June, 1918.
1837 Sandbach, Ina Douglas Pennant, Hon. Mrs. Arthur Edmund, 3 June, 1918.
1838 Sandeman, Isabella Emma, Mrs., 3 June, 1918.
1839 Sandeman, Ronald Leighton, 3 June, 1918.
1840 Sanders, Percy Alan, 3 June, 1918.
1841 Sandes, Thomas Lewis Lindsay, 3 June, 1918. (M.)
1842 Satow, Harold Eustace, 3 June, 1918.
1843 Satterly, Charles Skinner, 3 June, 1918.
1844 de Saumarez, Jane Anne, Lady, 3 June, 1918.
1845 Saunders, Samuel Edgar, 3 June, 1918.

1846 Say, Richard, 3 June, 1918. (M.)
1847 Scholes, Joseph, 3 June, 1918.
1848 Scott, Louisa Leslie Florence, Mrs., 3 June, 1918.
1849 Scully, Vincent Marcus Barron, 3 June, 1918. (M.)
1850 Senior, George Gaunt, 3 June, 1918.
1851 Shannon, Rev. William Floyd, 3 June, 1918. (M.)
1852 Sharples, Richard William, 3 June, 1918.
1853 Shaughnessy, Edward Herbert, 3 June, 1918.
1854 Shaw, Robert, 3 June, 1918. (M.)
1855 Shearman, Montague, 3 June, 1918.
1857 Shephard, Walter Rider, 3 June, 1918.
1858 Sherman, Carlton Collingwood, 3 June, 1918. (M.)
1859 Short, Hugh, 3 June, 1918. (M.)
1860 Shove, Cyril Ambrose, 3 June, 1918. (M.)
1861 Shute, Charles William, 3 June, 1918.
1862 Shuter, James Percy, 3 June, 1918.
1863 Sieber, John Frederick, 3 June, 1918.
1864 Silverthorne, James William Bradford, 3 June, 1918. (M.)
1865 Skentelbery, George Arthur, 3 June, 1918.
1866 Skinner, Donald Chipman, 3 June, 1918. (M.)
1867 Sleight, Ernest, 3 June, 1918. (M.)
1868 Smallwood, George Clarence, 3 June, 1918.
1869 Smiles, Samuel, 3 June, 1918.
1870 Smith, David Joseph, 3 June, 1918. (M.)
1871 Smith, Frances Louise Mrs. Kyrle-, 3 June, 1918.
1872 Smith, Robert James, 3 June, 1918.
1873 Smith, Sydney Edwin, 3 June, 1918.
1874 Smith, William James, 3 June, 1918.
1875 Smythe, Altamont, 3 June, 1918.
1876 Smyth, Frederick Wilkinson, 3 June, 1918. (M.)
1877 Snider, Irvine Robinson, 3 June, 1918. (M.)
1879 Somers, Frank, 3 June, 1918.
1880 Southey, John Henry Willes, 3 June, 1918. (M.)
1881 Spaight, James Moloney, 3 June, 1918.
1883 Speranza, Victor Ernest, 3 June, 1918. (M.)
1884 Spoor, Benjamin Charles, 3 June, 1918.
1885 Stallybrass, William Teulon Swan, 3 June, 1918.
1886 Stanger, Ernest William, 3 June, 1918.
1887 Stanhope, Adèle, Hon. Mrs. Charles Hay Scudamore, 3 June, 1918.
1888 Steel, Alfred Ernest, 3 June, 1918.
1889 Stevens, Edith, Mrs., 3 June, 1918.
1890 Stewart, Archibald Thomas, 3 June, 1918. (M.)
1891 Stewart, Percy Malcolm, 3 June, 1918.
1892 Stobart, Henry John Scott, 3 June, 1918.
1893 Stobart, Jessica Octavia, Mrs., 3 June, 1918.
1894 Stoker, George Herbert, 3 June, 1918.
1895 Stoker, Gilbert, 3 June, 1918.
1896 Stoneham, Edgar Cooper, 3 June, 1918.
1897 Stovold, Herbert William, 3 June, 1918.
1898 Stradbroke, Helena Violet Alice, Countess of, 3 June, 1918.
1899 Stuart, Edward John, 3 June, 1918. (M.)
1900 Stuart, Laura Elizabeth, Mrs., 3 June, 1918.
1901 Stunt, Edith Melba, Mrs., 3 June, 1918.
1902 Sturdy, Edward Vyse, 3 June, 1918.
1903 Sumner, Leonard, 3 June, 1918.
1904 Sutro, Alfred, 3 June, 1918.
1905 Swainson, Robert Hunter, 3 June, 1918.
1906 Swan, Charles Robert John Atkin, 3 June, 1918.
1907 Swanwick, Laura Beatrix, Mrs., 3 June, 1918.
1908 Swayne, Edward Hopton, 3 June, 1918. (M.)
1909 Sykes, George Arthur, 3 June, 1918. (M.)
1910 Symes, Sandham John, 3 June, 1918.
1911 Taperell, Bernard Treleaven, 3 June, 1918. (M.)
1912 Tarring, Bateman Brown, 3 June, 1918.
1913 Taylor, John, 3 June, 1918.
1914 Taylor, John, 3 June, 1918.
1915 Taylor, Thomas Alexander Hatch, 3 June, 1918. (M.)
1916 Thomas, David, 3 June, 1918.
1917 Thomas, Ethel, 3 June, 1918. (M.)
1918 Thomas, Farrar Wolferston, 3 June, 1918.
1919 Thomas, Jessie, Mrs., 3 June, 1918.
1920 Thomas, John Frederick Ivor, 3 June, 1918.
1921 Thomas, Joseph Silvers Williams-, 3 June, 1918.
1922 Thompson, Archibald Henry James, 3 June, 1918. (M.)
1923 Thompson, William Peter, 3 June, 1918.
1924 Thomson, John, 3 June, 1918.
1925 Thorne, May, 3 June, 1918.
1926 Thorpe, Arthur Winton, 3 June, 1918.
1927 Thurgood, Harry Voce, 3 June, 1918.
1929 Tindley, Francis Oswald, 3 June, 1918.
1930 Todhunter, Benjamin Edward, 3 June, 1918.
1931 Townshend, Francis Horatio Evory, 3 June, 1918. (M.)
1933 Travers, Frederick Thomas, 3 June, 1918.
1934 Tremayne, John Claude Lewis, 3 June, 1918. (M.)
1936 Trew, Richard James Fynmore, 3 June, 1918. (M.)
1937 Trickett, Wilfrid Richard, 3 June, 1918.
1938 Tritton, Claude Henry, 3 June, 1918. (M.)
1940 Trotter, John Frederick Arthur, 3 June, 1918. (M.)
1942 Tubb, Frederick William, 3 June, 1918.
1944 Tulloch, Angus Alexander Gregorie, 3 June, 1918.
1945 Tulloch, William Forbes, 3 June, 1918.
1946 Tunnard, Isabel Mary, Mrs., 3 June, 1918.
1947 Turbett, Eyre Anthony Weldon 3 June, 1918. (M.)
1948 Turner, Helen Burgess, Mrs., 3 June, 1918.
1949 Turner, Richard Miles Arundel Eaton, 3 June, 1918.
1950 Turney, Fred, 3 June, 1918.
1951 Turnock, Walter Bertram, 3 June, 1918.
1952 Turpin, William Alfred, 3 June, 1918.

1953 Turtill, Alfred Robert, 3 June, 1918.
1954 Turton, Willie Jack Trevor. 3 June, 1918.
1955 Twigg, Albert Percy, 3 June, 1918.
1956 Twiss, Mildred Caroline, 3 June, 1918.
1957 Twist, Thomas, 3 June, 1918. (M.)
1958 Tyler, Francis Cameron, 3 June, 1918. (M.)
1959 Urquhart, Alexander Lewis, 3 June, 1918. (M.)
1960 Urwick, Thirza Beatrice, Mrs., 3 June, 1918.
1962 Waite, William Vincent, 3 June, 1918.
1963 Wakelin, Arthur Brittan, 3 June, 1918. (M.)
1964 Wakeling, Thomas George, 3 June, 1918.
1966 Walker, Nigel Ouchterlony, 3 June, 1918. (M.)
1967 Wall, Arthur Joseph, 3 June, 1918.
1968 Wallace, James Hill, 3 June, 1918.
1969 Wallace, John, 3 June, 1918. (M.)
1970 Waller, Stanier, 3 June, 1918.
1972 Walmsley, Harry Henden, 3 June, 1918. (M.)
1974 Warde, Frank, 3 June, 1918. (M.)
1975 de Wardt, John Isaac, 3 June, 1918.
1977 Warnock, David, 3 June, 1918.
1978 Warrand, Duncan Grant, 3 June, 1918. (M.)
1979 Warren, Sir Alfred Haman, 3 June, 1918.
1981 Watson, Henry, 3 June, 1918.
1982 Watson, John Henderson, 3 June, 1918.
1983 Watts, Charles Manley, 3 June, 1918.
1984 Watts, John Hunter, 3 June, 1918. (M.)
1985 Wavish, Samuel John, 3 June, 1918.
1986 Wayne, Frederick William, 3 June, 1918. (M.)
1987 Webb, Edward Clive, 3 June, 1918. (M.)
1988 Weightman, Alfred Ernest, 3 June, 1918. (M.)
1989 Welford, Robert Anthony Ettrick, 3 June, 1918.
1990 West, Edith Maria, Hon. Mrs. Augustus William, 3 June, 1918.
1991 West, George Philp, 3 June, 1918.
1992 Westlake, Frederick Arthur, 3 June, 1918.
1994 Wethered, Mina Ricketts Sarah Elizabeth, 3 June, 1918.
1995 Wheeler, Edward Vincent Vashon, 3 June, 1918.
1996 Wheeler, Herbert Edward Ogle, 3 June, 1918.
1997 White, Clare, 3 June, 1918.
1998 White, Madge Macarthur, 3 June, 1918.
1999 Whitehouse, John Hubert, 3 June, 1918. (M.)
2000 Whiteley, Cyprian Charles Oswald, 3 June, 1918. (M.)
2001 Whiteley, Martha Annie, 3 June, 1918.
2002 Whiteman, George Hewitt, 3 June, 1918.
2003 Whitlock, Roland Whitelocke, 3 June, 1918.
2004 Whyte, John, 3 June, 1918.
2007 Wilbraham, Evelyn Caryl Bootle-, 3 June, 1918.
2008 Wilcock, Albert Edward, 3 June, 1918. (M.)
2009 Wilkinson, John, 3 June, 1918.
2010 Williams, Arthur Moray, 3 June, 1918.
2011 Williams, David, 3 June, 1918.
2012 Williams, Henry Owen, 3 June, 1918.
2013 Williams, Annie Margery, Mrs., 3 June, 1918.
2014 Williams, Mabel Catherine St. John, Mrs., 3 June, 1918.
2015 Williams, Walton d'Eichtal, 3 June, 1918. (M.)
2016 Williamson, Alexander, 3 June, 1918.
2017 Willis, Zwinglius Frank, 3 June, 1918.
2018 Wilson, Alexander, 3 June, 1918.
2019 Wilson, Edward Arthur, 3 June, 1918. (M.)
2020 Wilson, Francis Bertram, 3 June, 1918. (M.)
2021 Wilson, Frank, 3 June, 1918.
2022 Wilson, John, 3 June, 1918. (M.)
2023 Wimborne, Cornelia Henrietta Maria, Dowager Baroness, 3 June, 1918.
2024 Winearls, Henry Martin, 3 June, 1918.
2025 Winter, Alexander Charles, 3 June, 1918. (M.)
2026 Wither, Harold Stephen Bigg-, 3 June, 1918. (M.)
2027 Wodehouse, Amy Violet, Mrs. Ernest Charles Forbes, 3 June, 1918.
2028 Wood, Benjamin George, 3 June, 1918.
2030 Woods, Samuel Henry, 3 June, 1918. (M.)
2031 Work, Thomas Budge, 3 June, 1918.
2032 Workman, Alice Hill, Mrs. Charles McNeil, 3 June, 1918.
2033 Workman, Margaret Elliot, 3 June, 1918.
2034 Wormald, Arthur, 3 June, 1918.
2035 Worswick, Frances Gertrude Somers Worsley, Mrs., 3 June, 1918.
2036 Wright, Frank Wilson, 3 June, 1918.
2037 Wright, George Hudson, 3 June, 1918.
2038 Wyatt, Francis Joseph Caldwell, 3 June, 1918. (M.)
2039 Young, Charles Robert, 3 June, 1918.
2041 Young, Thomas Dunlop, 3 June, 1918. (M.)
2042 Younger, Jessie Alice, 3 June, 1918.
2043 Kanika, Raja Rajendra Narayan Bhanja Deo, of, 3 June, 1918.
2044 Singh Amawan, Raja Harihar Prasad Narayan, 3 June, 1918.
2045 Mackenzie, James, 3 June, 1918.
2046 Lovett, Clara Crofton, Lady, 3 June, 1918.
2048 Walsh, Ivy, Mrs., 3 June, 1918.
2049 Gurdon, Ada, Mrs., 3 June, 1918.
2050 Standen, Oona, Mrs., 3 June, 1918.
2051 Reid, Beatrice, Mrs., 3 June, 1918.
2052 Stowell, Vere Arthur, 3 June, 1918.
2053 Conyngham, Elsie Margaret, Lady Lenox-, 3 June, 1918.
2054 Pugh, Archibald John, 3 June, 1918.
2056 Blakeway, Evelyn, Mrs. Denys Brooke, 3 June, 1918.
2057 Howard, William Henry Ker, 3 June, 1918.
2058 Murtrie, David James, 3 June, 1918.

2059 Cumming, Marjorie Stevenson, Mrs., 3 June, 1918.
2060 Roy, Jotindra Nath, 3 June, 1918.
2061 Goudge, Joseph Ernest, 3 June, 1918.
2062 Campbell, John, 3 June, 1918.
2063 Khan, Ghazanfar Ali, 3 June, 1918.
2064 Clay, Joseph Miles, 3 June, 1918.
2065 Crawford, James Muir, 3 June, 1918.
2066 McDonald, Archibald Anthony, 3 June, 1918.
2067 Vines, Duncan Frederick, 3 June, 1918.
2068 Hutchinson, William Gordon, 3 June, 1918.
2069 Gunter, Eustace Edward, 3 June, 1918.
2070 Vivian, Valentine Patrick Terrel, 3 June, 1918.
2071 Prideaux, Frank Winckworth Austice, 3 June, 1918.
2072 Lal, Isa Charan Chandu, 3 June, 1918.
2073 Ross, Henry, 3 June, 1918.
2074 Hotson, John Ernest Buttery, 3 June, 1918.
2075 Bradfield, Ernest William Charles, 3 June, 1918.
2076 Tuke, Anna, Mrs., 3 June, 1918.
2077 Crum, Sir Walter Erskine, 3 June, 1918.
2078 Stott, Hugh, 3 June, 1918.
2079 Copeland, David Patrick, 3 June, 1918.
2080 Peuch, Albert Gottlieb, 3 June, 1918.
2081 Travers, Walter Lancelot, 3 June, 1918.
2082 Burkitt, Francis Holy, 3 June, 1918.
2083 Adam, John Hunter, 3 June, 1918.
2084 Ashford, John, 3 June, 1918.
2085 Dunbar-Brander, Archibald Alexander, 3 June, 1918.
2086 Deo, Raja Brij Mohan, 3 June, 1918.
2087 Tiwana, Nawab Malik Khuda Bakhsh Khan, 3 June, 1918.
2089 Adams, Richard Percival, 3 June, 1918.
2090 Rumboll, Arthur Charles, 3 June, 1918.
2091 Gray, William David, 3 June, 1918.
2092 Browne, John Coggin, 3 June, 1918.
2093 Purssell, Richard Stanley, 3 June, 1918.
2094 Bonner, Thomas William, 3 June, 1918.
2095 Fraser, William Stuart, 3 June, 1918.
2096 Nicholson, Catherine, Lady, 3 June, 1918.
2097 Miller, Margaret Julia, Lady, 3 June, 1918.
2098 Wakefield, George Edward Campbell, 3 June, 1918.
2099 Sattasar, Rao Bahadur Thakur Hari Singh, of, 3 June, 1918.
2100 Rani Surat Kunwar, 3 June, 1918.
2101 Khan Bahadur Sardar Abdul Hamid, 3 June, 1918.
2102 Raja Sansi, Sardar Raghbir Singh, of, 3 June, 1918.
2103 Wedderburn, Charles David St. Clair, 3 June, 1918.
2104 de Glanville, Oscar, 3 June, 1918.
2105 Rai Bahadur Lala Sheo Parshad, 3 June, 1918.
2107 Bennett, Frank Douglas, 3 June, 1918.
2109 Hormusji Cowasjee Dinshaw, 3 June, 1918.
2110 Jehangir Hormasji Kothari, 3 June, 1918.
2111 Jamsetji Framjee Madan, 3 June, 1918.
2112 Kanakarayan Tirufelvam Paul, 3 June, 1918.
2113 Rai Bahadur Sir Kailash Chandra Bose, 3 June, 1918.
2114 Risaldar Chaudhri Amar Singh, 3 June, 1918.
2115 Rai Chhote Lal Bahadur, 3 June, 1918.
2116 Bellairs, Robert George, 3 June, 1918.
2117 Armstrong, John William, 3 June, 1918.
2118 Kumar Sheonandan Prasad Singh, 3 June, 1918.
2119 Diwan Tek Chand, 3 June, 1918.
2120 Carstairs, William Ramage, 3 June, 1918.
2122 Mansell, Richard Vivian, 3 June, 1918.
2123 Dadabhoy, Jarbanoo, Mrs., 3 June, 1918.
2124 Dewan Shujat Ali Khan, 3 June, 1918.
2125 Rani Abhayeswari Debi, 3 June, 1918.
2126 Coggan, Robert Denby, 3 June, 1918.
2127 Ezra, Alfred, 3 June, 1918.
2128 Nirmul Chunder Sen, 3 June, 1918.
2129 Briggs, William Albert, 3 June, 1918.
2130 Alban, Arthur David, 3 June, 1918.
2131 Ball, John, 3 June, 1918.
2132 Pearson, Burton, 3 June, 1918.
2133 Todd, Charles, 3 June, 1918.
2134 Preston, Arthur Sansome, 3 June, 1918.
2135 Hastings, William, 3 June, 1918.
2136 Monteith-Smith, Robert Earle, 3 June, 1918.
2137 Branch, Albert Ernest, 3 June, 1918.
2139 Page, Charles Herbert, 3 June, 1918.
2140 McKey, Charles, 3 June, 1918.
2141 Dent, Lancelot Wilkinson, 3 June, 1918.
2142 Ashton, Helen, Mrs., 3 June, 1918.
2144 Brownlow, Frederick Hugh Cust, 3 June, 1918.
2145 Campbell, Joseph Alexander, 3 June, 1918.
2146 Doery, George Henry, 3 June, 1918.
2147 Downes, Doris Mary, Mrs., 3 June, 1918.
2148 Fairbairn, Frederick William, 3 June, 1918.
2149 Farr, Muriel, 3 June, 1918.
2150 Gillespie, James Macgregor, 3 June, 1918.
2151 Greenwood, William Frederick, 3 June, 1918.
2152 Hall, Jane, Mrs., 3 June, 1918.
2153 Hill, Edith, 3 June, 1918.
2154 Hood, Georgina, Mrs., 3 June, 1918.
2155 Hughes, Agnes Eva, Mrs., 3 June, 1918.
2156 Johnson, Winifred Farnell, 3 June, 1918.
2157 Kiddle, John Beacham, 3 June, 1918.
2158 Lazarus, Emanuel Samuel, 3 June, 1918.
2159 McInerney, Marguerratta, Mrs., 3 June, 1918.
2160 McIntyre, Ronald George, 3 June, 1918.
2161 Mackinnon Eleanor Vokes Irby, Mrs., 3 June, 1918.

2162 Mailer, Ramsay, 3 June, 1918.
2163 Mitchell, James, 3 June, 1918.
2164 Moore, Henry Byron, 3 June, 1918.
2165 Nettlefold, Robert, 3 June, 1918.
2166 Nicholls, Helen, Lady, 3 June, 1918.
2167 Pitt, Harry Arthur, 3 June, 1918.
2168 Rankin, Alexander Donald, 3 June, 1918.
2169 Riley, Joseph Albert, 3 June, 1918.
2170 Roberts, Alfred Jabez, 3 June, 1918.
2171 Scobie, Grace Locke, 3 June, 1918.
2172 Stirling, Hon. Sir John Lancelot, 3 June, 1918.
2173 Tolmie, Agnes, 3 June, 1918.
2174 Treacy, Alfred Martin, 3 June, 1918.
2175 Westmacott, Charles Babington, 3 June, 1918.
2176 Willington, William Thomas, 3 June, 1918.
2177 Bean, Jane Ann, Mrs., 3 June, 1918.
2178 Bidwill, William Edward, 3 June, 1918.
2179 Buckleton, Alice Australia Gertrude, Mrs., 3 June 1918.
2180 Close, Etta, 3 June, 1918.
2181 Elliot, George, 3 June, 1918.
2182 Empson, Agnes Dyke, Mrs., 3 June, 1918.
2183 Flesher, James Arthur, 3 June, 1918.
2184 Harper, George, 3 June, 1918.
2185 Herbert, Arthur Stanley, 3 June, 1918. (M.)
2186 Hill, Elizabeth Ann, Mrs., 3 June, 1918.
2187 Hodder, Henry Charles, 3 June, 1918.
2188 King, Rev. Vincent George Bryan, 3 June, 1918.
2189 Love, Ripeka Wharawhara, Mrs., 3 June, 1918.
2190 Macfarlane, Edith Mary, Mrs., 3 June, 1918.
2191 Miles, Alfred Henry, 3 June, 1918.
2192 Moorhouse, Jessie Matilda, Mrs., 3 June, 1918.
2193 Mutu, Rahera Muriwai, Mrs., 3 June, 1918.
2194 Rhodes, Ellen Laura Amy, Mrs., 3 June, 1918
2195 Rattray, Francis Cochrane, 3 June, 1918.
2196 Tripp, Leonard Owen Howard, 3 June, 1918.
2197 Wood, Grace Anna Mary, Mrs., 3 June, 1918.
2198 Allen, Thomas Frederick, 3 June, 1918.
2199 Cornell, Frederick Carruthers, 3 June, 1918.
2200 Crewe, Helen Agnes Josephine, Lady, 3 June, 1918.
2201 Dichmont, Katherine, Mrs., 3 June, 1918.
2202 Hands, Aletta Catherine, Mrs., 3 June, 1918.
2203 Maggs, Agnes Mary, Mrs., 3 June, 1918.
2204 Mardall, George Stratford, 3 June, 1918.
2205 Mackenzie, Thomas William, 3 June, 1918.
2206 O'Brien, William John, 3 June, 1918.
2207 Panchaud, Harry George Louis, 3 June, 1918.
2208 Rees, David, 3 June, 1918.
2209 Smith, Lillie Edith, Lady, 3 June, 1918.
2210 Smith, Arthur Herbert, 3 June, 1918.
2211 Steel, Barbara Joanna, Lady, 3 June, 1918.
2212 Brehm, Mary Chisholm, Mrs., 3 June, 1918.
2213 Oke, Sophy, Mrs., 3 June, 1918.
2214 Power, Margaret Mary, Mrs., 3 June, 1918.
2215 Barnes, John Albert, 3 June, 1918.
2216 Berkeley, John Henry Astley, 3 June, 1918.
2217 Bolton, Wilfrid Nash, 3 June, 1918.
2218 Costley-White, Ernest, 3 June, 1918.
2219 Croad, Hector, 3 June, 1918.
2220 Edwards, Kate, Lady, 3 June, 1918.
2221 Elliot, Frederick Mitchell, 3 June, 1918.
2222 Francis, Percy James, 3 June, 1918.
2223 Greenwood, Alfred Craven, 3 June, 1918.
2224 Hallifax, Edwin Richard, 3 June, 1918.
2225 Hearsey, Herbert Hyde Young, 3 June, 1918.
2226 Jardine, Douglas James, 3 June, 1918.
2227 Johnson, Edward Odlum, 3 June, 1918.
2228 Keyte, Vincent John, 3 June, 1918.
2229 May, John Ivo Cecil, 3 June, 1918.
2230 Messer, Charles McIlvaine, 3 June, 1918.
2231 Nutt, Walter Frederick, 3 June, 1918.
2232 Park, James Harvey Williamson, 3 June, 1918.
2233 Phillips, William Lambert Collyer, 3 June, 1918.
2234 Sauzier, Emile, 3 June, 1918.
2235 Weston, Rt. Rev. Frank, 3 June, 1918.
2236 Wheeler, William, 3 June, 1918.
2237 de Wolf, Francis George, 3 June, 1918. (M.)
2238 Fraser, David Hammand, 3 June, 1918. (M.)
2239 Gagnon, Joseph Thomas Emile, 3 June, 1918. (M.)
2240 Hopkins, Gilbert Rivers, 3 June, 1918. (M.)
2241 Lash, John Francis, 3 June, 1918. (M.)
2242 McMahon, Sir Horace Westropp, Bart., 3 June, 1918. (M.)
2243 Mills, Walter Henry, 3 June, 1918. (M.)
2244 Atherton, Stanley, 3 June, 1918. (M.)
2245 Betts, Hyla Hume, 2 June, 1918. (M.)
2246 Clarence, Arthur Arderne, 3 June, 1918. (M.)
2247 Greenstreet, Reginald Hawkins, 3 June, 1918. (M.)
2248 Greenwell, Percy 3 June 1918. (M.)
2249 Hughes, Edmond Locock, 3 June, 1918. (M.)
2250 Knowles, James, 3 June, 1918. (M.)
2251 McTurk, Alexander Gladstone, 3 June, 1918. (M.)
2252 Parks, John Hegan, 3 June, 1918. (M.)
2253 Rees, Herbert, 3 June, 1918. (M.)
2255 Scott-Harden, Henry Spencer, 3 June, 1918. (M.)
2256 Spranger, Francis Jeffries, 3 June, 1918. (M.)
2257 Angus, Robert, 3 June, 1918. (M.)
2258 Baker, Alfred Henry, 3 June, 1918. (M.)
2259 Bamford, Reginald Mayall, 3 June, 1918. (M.)
2260 Blackshaw, George Neville, 3 June, 1918. (M.)
2261 Borrie, David Forbes, 3 June, 1918. (M.)

2262 Boyd, John Henry, 3 June, 1918. (M)
2263 Campbell. Arthur Colin Clyde, 3 June, 1918. (M.)
2264 Carter, Frederick George, 3 June, 1918. (M.)
2265 Carter, Gerald Vernon, 3 June, 1918. (M.)
2266 Christophers, Samuel Richard, 3 June, 1918. (M.)
2267 Clerici, Charles John Emile, 3 June, 1918.
2268 Duffy, Thomas Augustine, 3 June, 1918. (M.)
2269 Dunlop, William, 3 June, 1918. (M.)
2270 Fleming, William Ernest, 3 June, 1918. (M.)
2272 Garstin, Richard Hart, 3 June, 1918. (M.)
2273 Glover, Edward Norman, 3 June, 1918. (M.)
2274 Goldie, Kenneth Oswald, 3 June, 1918. (M.)
2275 Gordon, John de la Hay, 3 June, 1918. (M.)
2276 Gunter, Clarence Preston, 3 June, 1918. (M.)
2277 Harvey, Ralph Oswald, 3 June, 1918. (M.)
2278 Hope, Percy Morehouse, 3 June, 1918. (M.)
2279 Innes, Robert McGregor, 3 June, 1918. (M.)
2280 Jones, Rev. Albert, 3 June, 1918. (M.)
2281 Jones, Herbert Cavendish, 3 June, 1918. (M.)
2282 Kent, Leslie Martin, 3 June, 1918. (M.)
2283 Kidby, Edward William Brand, 3 June, 1918. (M.)
2284 Kirkwood, Andrew Samuel, 3 June, 1918.
2286 Lewis, Rev. Percy, 3 June, 1918. (M.)
2287 Livesay, Waterworth Bligh, 3 June, 1918. (M.)
2288 Low, Peter Dunstan. 3 June, 1918. (M.)
2289 Macdonald, Alexander, 3 June, 1918.
2290 Mackie, Frederick Percival, 3 June, 1918. (M.)
2292 Mann, Algernon Edward, 3 June, 1918. (M.)
2293 Mullins, Rev. William, 3 June, 1918. (M.)
2294 Pennefather, John Broderick, 3 June, 1918. (M.)
2295 Reynolds, Herbert James Blakemore, 3 June, 1918. (M.)
2296 Rowlings, Alfred Lefevre, 3 June, 1918. (M.)
2297 Smith, Bertram Gilbert, 3 June, 1918. (M.)
2298 Swindells, Frank Marshall, 3 June, 1918. (M.)
2299 Thompson, Thomas, 3 June, 1918. (M.)
2301 Vallat, Frederick William, 3 June, 1918. (M.)
2312 Webb, Rev. Stephen Llewellyn, 3 June, 1918. (M.)
2303 Akers, Wilfred Stuart, 3 June, 1918. (M.)
2304 Barbour, Archibald Robertson, 3 June, 1918. (M.)
2305 Browne, Edward Denis, 3 June, 1918. (M.)
2306 Cadiz, Charles James Roche Galway, 3 June, 1918. (M.)
2307 Christie. William Edward Tolfrey, 3 June, 1918. (M.)
2308 Cole, Aubrey de Plat Thorold, 3 June, 1918. (M.)
2309 Coote, John Methuen, 3 June, 1918. (M.)
2310 Craven, Albert, 3 June, 1918. (M.)
2311 Dickens, Willie Hyde, 3 June, 1918. (M.)
2312 Elkington, James Llewellyn Meredith, 3 June, 1918. (M.)
2313 Fisher, Charles Taylor, 3 June, 1918. (M.)
2314 Garnier, Charles Newdigate, 3 June, 1918. (M.)
2315 Gordon, Robert, 3 June, 1918. (M.)
2316 Grant, Robert Charles, 3 June, 1918. (M.)
2317 Gray, Hubert Wilfred, 3 June, 1918. (M.)
2318 Hopkins, Raymond Beechey, 3 June, 1918. (M.)
2319 Horne, Henry Hastings, 3 June, 1918. (M.)
2320 Laverton, Henry Sanderson, 3 June, 1918. (M.)
2321 Logan, Robert Hector, 3 June, 1918. (M.)
2322 Macaulay, Donald, 3 June, 1918. (M.)
2323 McMaster, Patrick Garnet Walsh, 3 June, 1918. (M.)
2324 McNeice, Arthur Charles Davenport, 3 June, 1918. (M.)
2325 Malan, Leslie Noel, 3 June, 1918. (M.)
2326 Manning, Arthur Pitcher, 3 June, 1918. (M.)
2327 Maynard, George Darell, 3 June, 1918. (M.)
2328 Miller, William Duncan, 3 June, 1918. (M.)
2329 Murray, Lennox Biggar, 3 June, 1918. (M.)
2330 Newland, Victor Marra, 3 June, 1918. (M.)
2331 Pike, Montague Headland, 3 June, 1918. (M.)
2332 Pitt, Bernard, 3 June, 1918. (M.)
2333 Read, Hector, 3 June, 1918. (M.)
2334 Richardson, Henry William Arbuckle, 3 June, 1918. (M.)
2335 Rost, Ernest Reinhold, 3 June, 1918. (M.)
2336 Scholtz, Edmund John, 3 June, 1918. (M.)
2337 Scott, Eustace Lindsay, 3 June, 1918. (M.)
2338 Smellie, John Hugh, 3 June, 1918. (M.)
2339 Southon, Charles Edward, 3 June, 1918. (M.)
2340 Sutherland, James, 3 June, 1918. (M.)
2341 Ward, Joseph Corbett, 3 June, 1918. (M.)
2342 Warwick, Norman Richard Coombe, 3 June, 1918. (M.)
2343 Webster, Charles Robert, 3 June, 1918. (M.)
2344 Whiteley, Percival, 3 June, 1918. (M.)
2345 Wilkinson, Edward John, 3 June, 1918. (M.)
2346 Gibbon, Edward, 3 June, 1918. (M.)
2349 Reilly, Bernard Rawdon, 3 June, 1918. (M.)
2350 Ogg, Arthur Charles, 3 June, 1918. (M.)
2351 Angell, Charles Henry Cooper, 3 June, 1918.
2353 Cox, Belle, Lady, 3 June, 1918.
2354 Dewar-Durie, Robert, 3 June, 1918.
2355 Faulkner, Sydney Neal, 3 June, 1918.
2356 Jackson, Aline Louise, Lady, 3 June, 1918.
2357 Kittermaster, Harold Baxter, 3 June, 1918.
2358 Knox, Ethel Laura, Mrs. Stuart George, 3 June, 1918.
2359 Lee, Herbert Newton, 3 June, 1918. (M.)
2360 Lorimer, Hilda, Mrs., 3 June, 1918.
2361 Medland, James William, 3 June, 1918.
2362 Spurrier, Alfred Henry, 3 June, 1918.
2363 Thorpe, Alfred Charles, 3 June, 1918.
2364 Watkins, Maria Heloise, Mrs., 3 June, 1918.
2365 Watson, Evelyn Elenor, Mrs., 3 June, 1918.
2366 Clifton, Arthur John, 3 June, 1918. (M.)
2367 Drayson, Alfred Percy, 3 June, 1918. (M.)

2368 Halland, Gordon Herbert Ramsay, 3 June, 1918. (M.)
2369 Walker, George Kemp, 3 June, 1918. (M.)
2370 Walter, Albert Elijah, 3 June, 1918. (M.)
2370a Batten, Edward Fetherstonhaugh, 3 June, 1918. (M.)
2371 Brown, Harry Egerton, 22 Aug. 1918. (M.)
2372 Cope, Thomas Francis, 22 Aug. 1918. (M.)
2373 Meiners, Leo Udo Hugo, 22 Aug. 1918. (M.)
2374 Morton, Robert, 22 Aug. 1918. (M.)
2375 Creagh, Elizabeth Rymer, Mrs., 22 Aug. 1918. (M.)
2376 Van Coller, Paul Johannes, 19 Dec. 1918. (M.)
2377 Cumming, Adam Bennett, 19 Dec. 1918. (M.)
2378 Curran, Theophilus John, 19 Dec. 1918. (M.)
2379 Grant, Ronald Charles, 19 Dec. 1918. (M.)
2380 Hartling, Edward Hadley, 19 Dec. 1918. (M.)
2381 Harvey, Arthur Kenneth Le Rai, 19 Dec. 1918. (M.)
2382 Hurst, Godfrey Thomas, 19 Dec. 1918. (M.)
2383 Judd, Bertram Christopher, 19 Dec. 1918. (M.)
2384 De Kock, Gervase Meyer, 19 Dec. 1918. (M.)
2385 McGregor, John Robertson, 19 Dec. 1918. (M.)
2386 McLoughlin, Mark Wilson, 19 Dec. 1918. (M.)
2387 Mursell, Henry Temple, 19 Dec. 1918. (M.)
2388 Nutt, Mary Ann Margaret, 19 Dec. 1918. (M.)
2389 Salmon, Hedley, 19 Dec. 1918.
2390 Adams, Josiah Logan, 1 Jan. 1919. (M.)
2391 Adams, Harold Cotterell, 1 Jan. 1919. (M.)
2392 Adams, William Henry, 1 Jan. 1919. (M.)
2393 Addison-Smith, Chilton Lind, 1 Jan. 1919. (M.)
2394 Adye-Curran, William John Patrick, 1 Jan. 1919. (M.)
2395 Allan, Norman, 1 Jan. 1919. (M.)
2396 Allard, William, 1 Jan. 1919. (M.)
2397 Allcard, Rupert, 1 Jan. 1919. (M.)
2398 Allen, Abraham, 1 Jan. 1919. (M.)
2399 Allin, Henry Chester, 1 Jan. 1919. (M.)
2400 Ambrose, John Goldwell, 1 Jan. 1919. (M.)
2401 Anderson, Nevill, 1 Jan. 1919. (M.)
2402 Anderson-Pelham, Alfred, 1 Jan. 1919. (M.)
2403 Arkle, John Stanley, 1 Jan. 1919. (M.)
2404 Ascott, William, 1 Jan. 1919. (M.)
2405 Atkin, Edward, 1 Jan. 1919. (M.)
2406 Atkinson, Arthur, 1 Jan. 1919. (M.)
2407 Atkinson, John, 1 Jan. 1919. (M.)
2408 Atter, Harold Frederick, 1 Jan. 1919. (M.)
2409 Baker, Frank, 1 Jan. 1919. (M.)
2410 Balfour, Nigel Harington, 1 Jan. 1919. (M.)
2411 Balston, Thomas, 1 Jan. 1919. (M.)
2412 Bangor, Maxwell Richard Crosbie Ward, Viscount, 1 Jan. 1919. (M.)
2413 Barber, Thomas, 1 Jan. 1919. (M.)
2414 Barker, Norman Leslie, 1 Jan. 1919. (M.)
2415 Barnes, Rev. Sydney Reeves, 1 Jan. 1919. (M.)
2416 Barron, Sydney Norman, 1 Jan. 1919. (M.)
2418 Barrow, Harold Percy Waller, 1 Jan. 1919. (M.)
2419 Bartlett, Edward George, 1 Jan. 1919. (M.)
2420 Baxter, Charles Botterill, 1 Jan. 1919. (M.)
2421 Beacham, Robert William, 1 Jan. 1919. (M.)
2422 Beale, Basil Perry, 1 Jan. 1919. (M.)
2423 Beasley, Horace Owen Compton, 1 Jan. 1919. (M.)
2424 Bell, Richard Carmichael, 1 Jan. 1919. (M.)
2426 Beney, Arthur, 1 Jan. 1919. (M.)
2427 Bennett, Thomas Edwin, 1 Jan. 1919. (M.)
2428 Berkeley, Christopher Robert, 1 Jan. 1919. (M.)
2429 Besant, Reginald Edgar, 1 Jan. 1919. (M.)
2430 Birks, Falconer Mofrat, 1 Jan. 1919. (M.)
2432 Blades, John, 1 Jan. 1919. (M.)
2433 Blake, Charles Frederick, 1 Jan. 1919. (M.)
2434 Blumberg, Henry d'Arnim, 1 Jan. 1919. (M.)
2435 Bonner, Stanley Abbott, 1 Jan. 1919. (M.)
2436 Borden-Turner, Douglas, 1 Jan. 1919. (M.)
2437 Bowden, Jonathan Scott, 1 Jan. 1919. (M.)
2438 Bowyer, Arthur William, 1 Jan. 1919. (M.)
2439 Boyd, Rev. Arthur Hamilton, 1 Jan. 1919. (M.)
2440 Brander, James Maudsley, 1 Jan. 1919. (M.)
2441 Braybrooke, Henry George, 1 Jan. 1919. (M.)
2442 Brenan, Frederick Rudolf Esmonde Dowes, 1 Jan. 1919. (M.)
2443 Bressey, Charles Herbert, 1 Jan. 1919. (M.)
2444 Briggs, Arthur Edwin, 1 Jan. 1919. (M.)
2445 Brinson, Harold Neilson, 1 Jan. 1919. (M.)
2446 Brown, George S., 1 Jan. 1919. (M.)
2447 Brown, Thomas, 1 Jan. 1919. (M.)
2448 Bull, Frederick Julius, 1 Jan. 1919. (M.)
2449 Bulman, John James, 1 Jan. 1919. (M.)
2450 Burlton, Launcelot Henry Beaumont, 1 Jan. 1919. (M.)
2451 Burn, Eric Francis, 1 Jan. 1919. (M.)
2453 Burt, Reginald Stevens, 1 Jan. 1919. (M.)
2454 Burtenshaw, Arthur, 1 Jan. 1919. (M.)
2455 Burton, Percy Collingwood, 1 Jan. 1919. (M.)
2456 Butler, Arnold Charles Paul, 1 Jan. 1919. (M.)
2457 Butler, Frank Norman, 1 Jan. 1919. (M.)
2458 Butler, Henry Basil Bacon, 1 Jan. 1919. (M.)
2459 Cadge, Christopher Rawlinson, 1 Jan. 1919. (M.)
2460 Calverley, Edmond Leveson, 1 Jan. 1919. (M.)
2461 Camp, Ernest Walter, 1 Jan. 1919. (M.)
2462 Campbell, Archibald Sydney, 1 Jan. 1919. (M.)
2463 Cansdale, Cyril, 1 Jan. 1919. (M.)
2464 Cantrell-Hubbersty, William Philip Cantrell, 1 Jan. 1919. (M.)
2465 Carr, Francis Tullius Fay, 1 Jan. 1919. (M.)
2466 Carr, Lawrence, 1 Jan. 1919. (M.)

2467 Cartwright, Edward Rogers, 1 Jan. 1919. (M.)
2468 Chaplin, Henry Slater, 1 Jan. 1919. (M.)
2469 Chapman, Guy Patterson, 1 Jan. 1919. (M.)
2470 Chapman, John Damian, 1 Jan. 1919. (M.)
2471 Charles, Richard, 1 Jan. 1919. (M.)
2472 Chignell, Robert, 1 Jan. 1919. (M.)
2473 Child, Armando Dumas, 1 Jan. 1919. (M.)
2474 Clegg, Sydney James, 1 Jan. 1919. (M.)
2475 Cockburn, Clarence Beaufort, 1 Jan. 1919. (M.)
2476 Collins, Arthur Francis St. Clair, 1 Jan. 1919. (M.)
2477 Cooper, Robert William, 1 Jan. 1919. (M.)
2478 Cooper, William Linford Edward, 1 Jan. 1919. (M.)
2479 Cordner, Edward James O'Cinidi, 1 Jan. 1919. (M.)
2480 Cotton, William Ernest Leslie, 1 Jan. 1919. (M.)
2481 Coutts, Malcolm, 1 Jan. 1919. (M.)
2482 Cowan, Eric Tennant, 1 Jan. 1919. (M.)
2483 Coward, Noel Anthony, 1 Jan. 1919. (M.)
2484 Craster, John Evelyn Edmund, 1 Jan. 1919. (M.)
2485 Crowe, Henry Aubrey, 1 Jan. 1919. (M.)
2486 Davidson, John, 1 Jan. 1919. (M.)
2487 Davis, Alexander Horace, 1 Jan. 1919. (M.)
2488 Davison, William Henderson, 1 Jan. 1919. (M.)
2489 Day, Christian Richard John, 1 Jan. 1919. (M.)
2490 Dayer-Smith, Percy William, 1 Jan. 1919. (M.)
2491 De Carrara-Rivers, Arthur Joseph, 1 Jan. 1919. (M.)
2492 De Salis, Herbert Joseph Norman, 1 Jan. 1919. (M.)
2493 De Trafford, Rudolf Edgar Francis, 1 Jan. 1919. (M.)
2494 Devlin, Joseph, 1 Jan. 1919. (M.)
2495 Dickerson, Frederick Thomas, 1 Jan. 1919. (M.)
2496 Dickie, William Stewart, 1 Jan. 1919. (M.)
2497 Dimmock, Harry Lionel Ffortington, 1 Jan. 1919. (M.)
2498 Douglass, Rev. Frederick Wingfield, 1 Jan. 1919. (M.)
2499 Dowling, Thomas, 1 Jan. 1919. (M.)
2500 Drake, John Hughes, 1 Jan. 1919. (M.)
2501 Duncan, Rev. George Simpson, 1 Jan. 1919. (M.)
2502 Dunsterville, Arthur Geoffrey, 1 Jan. 1919. (M.)
2503 Durham, Frank Rogers, 1 Jan. 1919. (M.)
2504 Duthie, Arthur Murray, 1 Jan. 1919. (M.)
2505 Edden, Reginald Percival Sidney, 1 Jan. 1919. (M.)
2506 Edmonds, Courtenay Harold Wish, 1 Jan. 1919. (M.)
2507 Egginton, John, 1 Jan. 1919. (M.)
2508 Ellis, George William, 1 Jan. 1919. (M.)
2509 Etherington-Smith, Harry Launcelot, 1 Jan. 1919. (M.)
2510 Euan-Smith, Cyril McLaurin, 1 Jan. 1919. (M.)
2511 Evans, Arthur Kelly, 1 Jan. 1919. (M.)
2512 Fane, Frederick Navaire, 1 Jan. 1919. (M.)
2513 Field, Edward Elgar, 1 Jan. 1919. (M.)
2514 Fitzgerald, Maurice Edward William, 1 Jan. 1919. (M.)
2515 Foster, Dennis, 1 Jan. 1919. (M.)
2516 Fox, Frank, 1 Jan. 1919. (M.)
2517 Fox, Walter, 1 Jan. 1919. (M.)
2518 Frood, Thomas Martin, 1 Jan. 1919. (M.)
2519 Gabb, Samuel Alwyne, 1 Jan. 1919. (M.)
2520 Gammon, John Charles, 1 Jan. 1919. (M.)
2521 Gamon, Humphrey Percival, 1 Jan. 1919. (M.)
2522 Gardner, John Cyril, 1 Jan. 1919. (M.)
2523 Gaye, Rev. Herbert Charles, 1 Jan. 1919. (M.)
2524 Geddes, Alexander Ebenezer McLean, 1 Jan. 1919. (M.)
2525 George, Charles Dennis Victor, 1 Jan. 1919. (M.)
2526 Giffin, William Herbert Dore, 1 Jan. 1919. (M.)
2527 Goddard, Francis Ambrose D'Oyley, 1 Jan. 1919. (M.)
2528 Goffin, Sydney Frederick Herbert, 1 Jan. 1919. (M.)
2529 Gold, Ernest, 1 Jan. 1919. (M.)
2530 Gonsalves, George, 1 Jan. 1919. (M.)
2531 Gooderidge, Robert Aubrey, 1 Jan. 1919. (M.)
2532 Gould, Willis, 1 Jan. 1919. (M.)
2533 Goulding, Edward Sainsbury, 1 Jan. 1919. (M.)
2534 Graham, Charles Ronald, 1 Jan. 1919. (M.)
2535 Graham, Harold John, 1 Jan. 1919. (M.)
2536 Grant, Stuart Colquhoun, 1 Jan. 1919. (M.)
2537 Grasett, Geoffrey William, 1 Jan. 1919. (M.)
2538 Gray, Alexander Mungo, 1 Jan. 1919. (M.)
2539 Gray, George Douglas, 1 Jan. 1919. (M.)
2540 Greaves, Francis Ley Augustus, 1 Jan. 1919. (M.)
2541 Green, Thomas, 1 Jan. 1919. (M.)
2542 Greenall, James Macintosh, 1 Jan. 1919. (M.)
2543 Greg, Arthur Hyde, 1 Jan. 1919. (M.)
2544 Griffith, Llewelyn Wyn, 1 Jan. 1919. (M.)
2545 Groom, Edmond Arthur Hudson, 1 Jan. 1919. (M.)
2546 Hacking, Douglas Hewitt, 1 Jan. 1919. (M.)
2547 Hall, Norman McLeod, 1 Jan. 1919. (M.)
2548 Halligan, Joseph Thomas, 1 Jan. 1919. (M.)
2549 Hamilton, Albert, 1 Jan. 1919. (M.)
2550 Hammersley-Smith, Ralph Henry, 1 Jan. 1919. (M.)
2551 Hancock, Thomas Watson, 1 Jan. 1919. (M.)
2552 Harbinson, William Dawson, 1 Jan. 1919. (M.)
2553 Hardy, Walter, 1 Jan. 1919. (M.)
2554 Hare, R. George Powel, 1 Jan. 1919. (M.)
2555 Harrison, Frank, 1 Jan. 1919. (M.)
2556 Hart, Gilbert, 1 Jan. 1919. (M.)
2557 Harvey, Percy Edgar, 1 Jan. 1919. (M.)
2558 Hay, James George, 1 Jan. 1919. (M.)
2559 Hebb, John Harry, 1 Jan. 1919. (M.)
2560 Henderson, Alan Keith, 1 Jan. 1919. (M.)
2561 Henderson, Alexander Mitchell, 1 Jan. 1919. (M.)
2562 Henderson, Herbert Purse, 1 Jan. 1919. (M.)
2563 Henderson, John Steill, 1 Jan. 1919. (M.)
2564 Henderson, Matthew Bolan, 1 Jan. 1919. (M.)
2565 Heppel, Hugh Middleton, 1 Jan. 1919. (M.)

2566 Herbertson, James John William, 1 Jan. 1919. (M.)
2567 Higgins, Cecil Matthew, 1 Jan. 1919. (M.)
2568 Higgins, William George, 1 Jan. 1919. (M.)
2569 Hill, John, 1 Jan. 1919. (M.)
2570 Hill, John Arthur, 1 Jan. 1919. (M.)
2571 Hill, Reginald Day Finch, 1 Jan. 1919. (M.)
2572 Hitchings, Oswald Thomas, 1 Jan. 1919. (M.)
2573 Hobbs, Reginald Arthur, 1 Jan. 1919. (M.)
2574 Hogarth, Lionel Brewer, 1 Jan. 1919. (M.)
2575 Holland, Henry William, 1 Jan. 1919. (M.)
2576 Holman, Bernard Whelpton, 1 Jan. 1919. (M.)
2577 Holmes, Samuel Edward, 1 Jan. 1919. (M.)
2578 Hornidge, Edward Stewart, 1 Jan. 1919. (M.)
2579 Horsfield, George William, 1 Jan. 1919. (M.)
2580 Houston, Thomas, 1 Jan. 1919. (M.)
2581 Hughes, William Rawson, 1 Jan. 1919. (M.)
2582 Hull, Charles Robert Ingham, 1 Jan. 1919. (M.)
2583 Huskinson, Charles John, 1 Jan. 1919. (M.)
2584 Impson, Herbert John, 1 Jan. 1919. (M.)
2585 Ingpen, Arthur Lockyer, 1 Jan. 1919. (M.)
2586 Isaacs, Isaac Benjamin, 1 Jan. 1919. (M.)
2587 Jagger, Hugh Cleivion, 1 Jan. 1919. (M.)
2588 Johnson, Arthur Ainslie, 1 Jan. 1919. (M.)
2589 Jones, Henry James, 1 Jan. 1919. (M.)
2590 Judd, Henry Alexander, 1 Jan. 1919. (M.)
2591 Jury, Arthur Ernest, 1 Jan. 1919. (M.)
2593 Kennington, Arthur James, 1 Jan. 1919. (M.)
2594 Kerr, William Lord Coke, 1 Jan. 1919. (M.)
2595 Keymer, Rev. Bernard William, 1 Jan. 1919. (M.)
2596 King, William Bernard Robinson, 1 Jan. 1919. (M.)
2597 King, William Henry Daniel, 1 Jan. 1919. (M.)
2598 Kinnersley, William Harold, 1 Jan. 1919. (M.)
2599 Kitson, Hubert Vernon, 1 Jan. 1919. (M.)
2600 Lane, Harold Arthur, 1 Jan. 1919. (M.)
2601 Langman, Thomas Witheridge, 1 Jan. 1919. (M.)
2602 Larter, Percy John, 1 Jan. 1919. (M.)
2604 Laurie, Robert Douglas, 1 Jan. 1919. (M.)
2605 Lawson, Eric St. John, 1 Jan. 1919. (M.)
2606 Lawson, John Hanson, 1 Jan. 1919. (M.)
2607 Lawson, Wentworth Dillon, 1 Jan. 1919. (M.)
2608 Leake, Claude Lancelot, 1 Jan. 1919. (M.)
2609 Lee, Arthur Neale, 1 Jan. 1919. (M.)
2610 Lempriere, Lancelot Raoul, 1 Jan. 1919. (M.)
2611 Leresche, Percy Vere, 1 Jan. 1919. (M.)
2612 Leslie, Bradford, 1 Jan. 1919. (M.)
2613 Lewis, Wilfred Hubert Poyer, 1 Jan. 1919. (M.)
2614 Lindsell, Wilfred Gordon, 1 Jan. 1919. (M.)
2615 Lodge, Thomas Arthur, 1 Jan. 1919. (M.)
2616 Long, Sydney Herbert, 1 Jan. 1919. (M.)
2617 Lough, Reginald Dawson Hopcraft, 1 Jan. 1919. (M.)
2618 Lovatt, Harry Leslie Bache, 1 Jan. 1919. (M.)
2619 Lowry, Frederick James Sharples, 1 Jan. 1919. (M.)
2620 Loyd, Robert Lindsay, 1 Jan. 1919. (M.)
2621 Lynde, Gilbert Somerville, 1 Jan. 1919. (M.)
2622 McArthur, James, 1 Jan. 1919. (M.)
2623 McCammon, Frank Alexander, 1 Jan. 1919. (M.)
2624 McCullough, Robert Stuart, 1 Jan. 1919. (M.)
2625 McDonald, Duncan, 1 Jan. 1919. (M.)
2626 McGuire, Bernard Aloysius, 1 Jan. 1919. (M.)
2627 McGuire, George Patrick, 1 Jan. 1919. (M.)
2628 McLachlan, James William Francis, 1 Jan. 1919. (M.)
2629 McLellan, Charles Alexander, 1 Jan. 1919. (M.)
2630 McLeod, James Walter, 1 Jan. 1919. (M.)
2631 Mahoney, Daniel, 1 Jan. 1919. (M.)
2632 Marchant, William Francis, 1 Jan. 1919. (M.)
2633 Marten, Leslie Howard, 1 Jan. 1919. (M.)
2634 Mason, Albert Wilberforce, 1 Jan. 1919. (M.)
2635 Mason, Henry George, 1 Jan. 1919. (M.)
2636 Mason, Lawrence, 1 Jan. 1919. (M.)
2637 Massey, Charles Montague Hamilton, 1 Jan. 1919. (M.)
2638 Maurice, Lawrence Colley, 1 Jan. 1919. (M.)
2639 Mawby, Arthur Willders Montague, 1 Jan. 1919. (M.)
2640 Melville, George David, 1 Jan. 1919. (M.)
2641 Miles-Cadman, Rev. Cecil Frank, 1 Jan. 1919. (M.)
2642 Mills, Ernest James, 1 Jan. 1919. (M.)
2643 Mills, Geoffrey Horner, 1 Jan. 1919. (M.)
2644 Mills, James Jesse, 1 Jan. 1919. (M.)
2645 Moggridge, Harry Weston, 1 Jan. 1919. (M.)
2646 Molony, Brian Charles, 1 Jan. 1919. (M.)
2647 Monier-Williams, Roy Thornton, 1 Jan. 1919. (M.)
2648 Morgan, Bernard Donald Crawford, 1 Jan. 1919. (M.)
2649 Morgan, George Urquhart, 1 Jan. 1919. (M.)
2650 Morgan-Grenville, Hon. Harry Nugent, 1 Jan. 1919. (M.)
2651 Morrison, John Fraser, 1 Jan. 1919. (M.)
2652 Mullings, James Finbarr, 1 Jan. 1919. (M.)
2653 Mumford, Wilfred George, 1 Jan. 1919. (M.)
2654 Naylor, Rev. Alfred Thomas Arthur, 1 Jan. 1919. (M.)
2655 Neale, William Walter Raymond, 1 Jan. 1919. (M.)
2656 Nelson, James Owen, 1 Jan. 1919. (M.)
2657 Neville, Maurice Michael, 1 Jan. 1919. (M.)
2658 Newbold, William, 1 Jan. 1919. (M.)
2659 Newman, John Campin, 1 Jan. 1919. (M.)
2660 Nicholas, Samuel William, 1 Jan. 1919. (M.)
2661 Nicholas, Tressilian Charles, 1 Jan. 1919. (M.)
2662 Oakley, John Gretton, 1 Jan. 1919. (M.)
2663 Odlum, Benjamin Alexander, 1 Jan. 1919. (M.)
2664 Oldfield, John William, 1 Jan. 1919. (M.)
2665 Oswald, Christopher Percy, 1 Jan. 1917. (M.)
2666 Packard, Joseph Thomas, 1 Jan. 1919. (M.)

2667 Parker, Edward Augustus, 1 Jan. 1919. (M.)
2668 Parks, Ernest William, 1 Jan. 1919. (M.)
2669 Patchett, Arthur Nesbit, 1 Jan. 1919. (M.)
2670 Patridge, Edward Henry William 1 Jan. 1919. (M.)
2671 Peach, Leonard Thomas, 1 Jan. 1919. (M.)
2672 Pearson, Richard William, 1 Jan. 1919. (M.)
2673 Pellew, Edward Irving Pownel, 1 Jan. 1919. (M.)
2674 Pepper, Thomas Oswald, 1 Jan. 1919. (M.)
2675 Pitt, George John, 1 Jan. 1919. (M.)
2676 Potter, Cyril Charlie Hamilton, 1 Jan. 1919. (M.)
2677 Potter, Thomas, 1 Jan. 1919. (M.)
2678 Power, Richard Pascal, 1 Jan. 1919. (M.)
2679 Prance, Basil C., 1 Jan. 1919. (M.)
2680 Price, Frank, 1 Jan. 1919. (M.)
2681 Price, William Edward, 1 Jan. 1919. (M.)
2682 Prunell, Rev. William Alfred, 1 Jan. 1919. (M.)
2683 Pugh, William John, 1 Jan. 1919. (M.)
2684 Quilter, Eustace Cuthbert, 1 Jan. 1919. (M.)
2685 Radcliff, Arthur Samuel, 1 Jan. 1919. (M.)
2686 Raikes, Kenneth Cochrane, 1 Jan. 1919. (M.)
2687 Ramsay, Jeffrey, 1 Jan. 1919. (M.)
2688 Ramsbotham, Herwald, 1 Jan. 1919. (M.)
2689 Rathbone, Charles Arthur, 1 Jan. 1919. (M.)
2690 Renouf, Cyril Percival, 1 Jan. 1919. (M.)
2691 Reynolds, Walter Philip Kearns, 1 Jan. 1919. (M.)
2692 Riach, Alexander Robertson, 1 Jan. 1919. (M.)
2693 Rice, Arthur Henry, 1 Jan. 1919. (M.)
2694 Richardson, Thomas William, 1 Jan. 1919. (M.)
2695 Rickman, Arthur Patrick William, 1 Jan. 1919. (M.)
2696 Ritchie, Thomas Clark, 1 Jan. 1919. (M.)
2697 Roberts, Geoffray Dorling, 1 Jan. 1919. (M.)
2698 Robertson, Andrew Clark, 1 Jan. 1919. (M.)
2699 Rolling, Bernard Ismay, 1 Jan. 1919. (M.)
2700 Roth, Albert Alexander, 1 Jan. 1919. (M.)
2701 Rothwell, William Edward, 1 Jan. 1919. (M.)
2702 Rountree, Arthur Noel, 1 Jan. 1919. (M.)
2703 Rouse, Alfred Corrie, 1 Jan. 1919. (M.)
2704 Rowden, Ernest George, 1 Jan. 1919. (M.)
2705 Royds, Albert Henry, 1 Jan. 1919. (M.)
2706 Saunders, Alan Arthur, 1 Jan. 1919. (M.)
2707 Scotland, Alexander Patterson, 1 Jan. 1919. (M.)
2708 Scott, Hon. Michael, 1 Jan. 1919. (M.)
2709 Selby-Lowndes, William, 1 Jan. 1919. (M.)
2710 Serjeant, Theophilus Hengist, 1 Jan. 1919. (M.)
2711 Sharp, Aubrey Temple, 1 Jan. 1919. (M.)
2712 Shaw, Frederick Arthur, 1 Jan. 1919. (M.)
2713 Shaw, Peter, 1 Jan. 1919. (M.)
2714 Sigrist, Edward, 1 Jan. 1919. (M.)
2715 Simpson, Alexander Petrie, 1 Jan. 1919. (M.)
2716 Smellie, William Thomas, 1 Jan. 1919. (M.)
2717 Smith, Albert George, 1 Jan. 1919. (M.)
2718 Smith, John William, 1 Jan. 1919. (M.)
2719 Smith, Leslie Harcourt, 1 Jan. 1919. (M.)
2721 Somervell, Arnold Colin, 1 Jan. 1919. (M.)
2722 Spedding, Edward Wilfred, 1 Jan. 1919. (M.)
2723 Speed, Ralph Henley, 1 Jan. 1919. (M.)
2724 Spencer, Harold Ernest, 1 Jan. 1919. (M.)
2726 Springhall, John Winchester, 1 Jan. 1919. (M.)
2727 Stackpoole, George William Robert, 1 Jan. 1919. (M.)
2728 Stafford, Waddington, 1 Jan. 1919. (M.)
2729 Stanford, William, 1 Jan. 1919. (M.)
2730 Stanley, James, 1 Jan. 1919. (M.)
2731 Stanton, Reginald William Starkey, 1 Jan. 1919. (M.
2732 Starr, Frank Joseph, 1 Jan. 1919. (M.)
2733 Stephens, Hubert Stanley, 1 Jan. 1919. (M.)
2734 Stevenson, James, 1 Jan. 1919. (M.)
2735 Stewart, Herbert Arthur, 1 Jan. 1919. (M.)
2736 Stewart, William Hendry Burgess, 1 Jan. 1919. (M.)
2737 Stokes, George Edward, 1 Jan. 1919. (M.)
2738 Stone, Philip Arthur, 1 Jan. 1919. (M.)
2739 Storey, Alan Thomas Trevor, 1 Jan. 1919. (M.)
2740 Sumner, Orlando, 1 Jan. 1919. (M.)
2741 Sutcliffe, William Greenwood, 1 Jan. 1919. (M.)
2742 Sutherland, Arthur Henry Carr, 1 Jan. 1919. (M.)
2743 Swallow, William Hugh, 1 Jan. 1919. (M.)
2744 Swanzy, Francis Hugh, 1 Jan. 1919. (M.)
2745 Sykes, Rev. Frank Morris, 1 Jan. 1919. (M.)
2746 Tayler, Henry Pascoe Blair, 1 Jan. 1919. (M.)
2747 Taylor, Alfred William, 1 Jan. 1919. (M.)
2748 Taylor, Charles Gerald, 1 Jan. 1919. (M.)
2749 Taylor, Charles Hillsborough Rimington, 1 Jan. 1919. (M.)
2750 Tebay, Frederick Henry, 1 Jan. 1919. (M.)
2751 Tennant. Henry Lancelot, 1 Jan. 1919. (M.)
2752 Thackeray, Joseph Makepeace, 1 Jan. 1919. (M.)
2753 Thatcher, Reginald Sparshatt, 1 Jan. 1919. (M.)
2754 Thomas, David Brodie, 1 Jan. 1919. (M.)
2755 Thomas, George Pollard, 1 Jan. 1919. (M.)
2756 Thomas, Sydney Arnold, 1 Jan. 1919. (M.)
2757 Thomas, Thomas Charles, 1 Jan. 1919. (M.)
2758 Thompson, Cecil Henry Farrer, 1 Jan. 1919. (M.)
2759 Thompson, Reginald Ernest, 1 Jan. 1919. (M.)
2760 Tod, Alan Charles, 1 Jan. 1919. (M.)
2761 Tomkinson, Geoffrey Stewart, 1 Jan. 1919. (M.)
2762 Toohill, Thomas. 1 Jan. 1919. (M.)
2763 Towne, Edward Charles Lyndhurst, 1 Jan. 1919. (M.)
2764 Trask, Charles Stancomb Lisle, 1 Jan. 1919. (M.)
2765 Tribe, Frank Newton, 1 Jan. 1919. (M.)
2766 Tudor, Lechmere Howell, 1 Jan. 1919. (M.)

OFFICERS.

2767 Turner, James Lockley, 1 Jan. 1919. (M.)
2768 Turner, Montagu Trevor, 1 Jan. 1919. (M.)
2769 Unwin, Thomas Barton, 1 Jan. 1919. (M.)
2770 Van Grutten, Winchcombe Norman Carpenter, 1 Jan. 1919. (M.)
2771 Van der Byl, Voltelin Albert William, 1 Jan. 1919. (M.)
2772 Varley, James, 1 Jan. 1919. (M.)
2773 Vivian, Guy Noel, 1 Jan. 1919. (M.)
2774 Wagstaffe, William Warwick, 1 Jan. 1919. (M.)
2775 Walker, James Blake, 1 Jan. 1919. (M.)
2776 Walker, Kenneth Macfarlane, 1 Jan. 1919. (M.)
2777 Wallace, Charles John, 1 Jan. 1919. (M.)
2778 Walthall, Henry Douglas Delves, 1 Jan. 1919. (M.)
2779 Warre, Felix Walter, 1 Jan. 1919. (M.)
2780 Webb, Robert Edward, 1 Jan. 1919. (M.)
2781 Webster, George Frederick Anderson, 1 Jan. 1919. (M.)
2782 Whitehead, Herbert Mansfield, 1 Jan. 1919. (M.)
2783 Wilkinson, Rev. Richard B., 1 Jan. 1919. (M.)
2784 Wilks, John Eason, 1 Jan. 1919. (M.)
2785 Williams, Alfred Dalby Ross, 1 Jan. 1919. (M.)
2786 Williams, Roger Francis, 1 Jan. 1919. (M.)
2787 Wills, Sir Gilbert Alan Hamilton, Bart., 1 Jan. 1919. (M.)
2788 Wilson, Andrew, 1 Jan. 1919. (M.)
2789 Wilson, Humphrey Bowstead, 1 Jan. 1919. (M.)
2790 Winwood, William Quintyne, 1 Jan. 1919. (M.)
2791 Wolstenholme, Thomas Blakeway, 1 Jan. 1919. (M.)
2792 Wood, Alexander Lewis Sandison, 1 Jan. 1919. (M.)
2793 Wood, Ernest, 1 Jan. 1919. (M.)
2794 Woodley, Ernest James, 1 Jan. 1919. (M.)
2795 Worsam, Charles Archie, 1 Jan. 1919. (M.)
2796 Worthington, Frank, 1 Jan. 1919. (M.)
2797 Wyley, Donald Henry FitzThomas, 1 Jan. 1919. (M.)
2798 Wynne, Owen Evelyn, 1 Jan. 1919. (M.)
2799 Yorke, Noel Leigh, 1 Jan. 1919. (M.)
2800 Alderson, William Frederick, 1 Jan. 1919. (M.)
2801 Archibald, George Grassie, 1 Jan. 1919. (M.)
2802 Armstrong, Nevill Alexander Drummond, 1 Jan. 1919. (M.)
2803 Birch, George Russell, 1 Jan. 1919. (M.)
2804 Brown, Percy Gordon, 1 Jan. 1919. (M.)
2805 Burgess, John Frederick, 1 Jan. 1919. (M.)
2806 Carew, Frank John, 1 Jan. 1919. (M.)
2807 Cowan, Harry James, 1 Jan. 1919. (M.)
2808 Dulmage, Anson, 1 Jan. 1919. (M.)
2809 Fisher, George Wilfred, 1 Jan. 1919. (M.)
2810 Grimsdick, John Dennin, 1 Jan. 1919. (M.)
2811 Herchmer, William Sinclair, 1 Jan. 1919. (M.)
2812 Hill, Hedley, 1 Jan. 1919. (M.)
2813 Hurd, William Burton, 1 Jan. 1919. (M.)
2814 Lettice, William Henry, 1 Jan. 1919. (M.)
2815 Lindsay, Norman James, 1 Jan. 1919. (M.)
2816 McEwen, Robert James, 1 Jan. 1919. (M.)
2817 McLeod, James William, 1 Jan. 1919. (M.)
2818 Mackintosh, William Cameron, 1 Jan. 1919. (M.)
2819 Maxwell, Charles Barker, 1 Jan. 1919. (M.)
2820 Montgomery-Campbell, Henry, 1 Jan. 1919. (M.)
2821 Munroe, Hugh Edwin, 1 Jan. 1919. (M.)
2822 Murray, Kenneth A., 1 Jan. 1919. (M.)
2823 Orr, Harold, 1 Jan. 1919. (M.)
2824 Palmer, Creighton Ross, 1 Jan. 1919. (M.)
2825 Richards, Samuel Charles, 1 Jan. 1919. (M.)
2826 Richardson, Albert Angus, 1 Jan. 1919. (M.)
2827 Robertson, William Adam, 1 Jan. 1919. (M.)
2828 Robinson, Charles Wilson, 1 Jan. 1919. (M.)
2829 Robinson, William Henry, 1 Jan. 1919. (M.)
2830 Scott, Charles McAdam, 1 Jan. 1919. (M.)
2831 Thomas, Cecil Compton, 1 Jan. 1919. (M.)
2832 Thomson, William Raymond, 1 Jan. 1919. (M.)
2833 Utton, Frederick William, 1 Jan. 1919. (M.)
2834 Webster, Harold Weatherald, 1 Jan. 1919. (M.)
2835 Willoughby, Bertha Jane, 1 Jan. 1919. (M.)
2836 Anderson, Robert Cairns Amis, 1 Jan. 1919. (M.)
2837 Chirnside, Robert Gordon, 1 Jan. 1919. (M.)
2838 Donnelly, John William, 1 Jan. 1919. (M.)
2839 David Moore, 1 Jan. 1919. (M.)
2840 Finn, Charles Napier, 1 Jan. 1919. (M.)
2841 Hamilton, William Lockhart, 1 Jan. 1919. (M.)
2842 Hargreaves, Gordon John Cooper, 1 Jan. 1919. (M.)
2843 Helsham, Charles Howard, 1 Jan. 1919. (M.)
2844 Henley, Frank Le Leu, 1 Jan. 1919. (M.)
2845 Hore, Reginald Mitchell, 1 Jan. 1919. (M.)
2846 Hunn, Sydney Arthur, 1 Jan. 1919. (M.)
2847 Hyman, Arthur Wellesley, 1 Jan. 1919. (M.)
2848 Lacey, Samuel Barningham, 1 Jan. 1919. (M.)
2849 Lane, Harry James, 1 Jan. 1919. (M.)
2850 McColl, John Thomas, 1 Jan. 1919. (M.)
2851 Maclure, Alfred Fay, 1 Jan. 1918. (M.)
2852 Officer, Keith, 1 Jan. 1919. (M.)
2853 Parker, Leslie Clive, 1 Jan. 1919. (M.)
2854 Robinson, Charles Walter, 1 Jan. 1919. (M.)
2855 Sanderson, William Lauchlan, 1 Jan. 1919. (M.)
2856 Saunders, Frank Veall, 1 Jan. 1919. (M.)
2857 Sturdee, Vernon Asleton Hobart, 1 Jan. 1919. (M.)
2858 Upjohn, William George Dismore, 1 Jan. 1919. (M.)
2859 Ward, Lionel Antony Parry, 1 Jan. 1919. (M.)
2860 Hindley, Frank Lawton, 1 Jan. 1919. (M.)
2861 Parker, Frank Woolmer, 1 Jan. 1919. (M.)
2863 Shera, Louis Murray, 1 Jan. 1919. (M.)
2864 Alderson, James Richard, 1 Jan. 1919. (M.)

2865 Bartrum, Vere Ayscott, 1 Jan. 1919. (M.)
2866 Beveridge, Thomas Blackwood, 1 Jan. 1919. (M.)
2867 Binney, Arthur Thomson, 1 Jan. 1919. (M.)
2868 Boyle, Walter, 1 Jan. 1919. (M.)
2869 Briercliffe, Rupert, 1 Jan. 1919. (M.)
2870 Bustard, Frank, 1 Jan. 1919. (M.)
2871 Butter, Francis Sam, 1 Jan. 1919. (M.)
2872 Campbell, Roy Neil Boyd, 1 Jan. 1919. (M.)
2873 Carson, David Simpson, 1 Jan. 1919. (M.)
2874 Clark, Lionel Melville, 1 Jan. 1919. (M.)
2875 Clark, Robert Leaver, 1 Jan. 1919. (M.)
2876 Clauson, Gerald Leslie Makins, 1 Jan. 1919. (M.)
2877 Corder, Arthur Annerley, 1 Jan. 1919. (M.)
2878 Couturier, Rev. Felix, 1 Jan. 1919. (M.)
2879 Crichton, George Keeble, 1 Jan. 1919. (M.)
2880 Crosthwaite, William Henry, 1 Jan. 1919. (M.)
2881 Cunningham, Percy Henry, 1 Jan. 1919. (M.)
2882 Dale, Wilfred John, 1 Jan. 1919. (M.)
2883 de Paravicini, Percy Chandos Farquhar, 1 Jan. 1919. (M.)
2884 Des Clayes, Camille, 1 Jan. 1919. (M.)
2885 Diggle, Frank Holt, 1 Jan. 1919. (M.)
2886 Draper, Charles Frederick, 1 Jan. 1919. (M.)
2887 Duberly, Montagu Richard William, 1 Jan. 1919. (M.)
2888 Dunstan, Albert Edward, 1 Jan. 1919. (M.)
2889 Dyson, William, 1 Jan. 1919. (M.)
2890 Ellis, William Francis, 1 Jan. 1919. (M.)
2891 Fitzgerald. Rev. James Charles, 1 Jan. 1919. (M.)
2892 Fletcher, Alexander Kempson, 1 Jan. 1919. (M.)
2893 Forbes, William Wood, 1 Jan. 1919. (M.)
2894 Fox, Harold Arthur, 1 Jan. 1919. (M.)
2895 Gilchrist, Norman Stephen, 1 Jan. 1919. (M.)
2896 Godding, James, 1 Jan. 1919. (M.)
2897 Gracie, Farquhar, 1 Jan. 1919. (M.)
2898 Graham, David Livingstone, 1 Jan. 1919. (M.)
2899 Granville, Court, 1 Jan. 1919. (M.)
2900 Graves, Robert Windham, 1 Jan. 1919. (M.)
2901 Gray-Donald, George, 1 Jan. 1919. (M.)
2902 Gregory, Hugh Manley, 1 Jan. 1919. (M.)
2903 Haddad, Gabriel, 1 Jan. 1919. (M.)
2904 Haddon, Reginald Cutler, 1 Jan. 1919. (M.)
2905 Halsey, Walter Johnston, 1 Jan. 1919. (M.)
2906 Hill, John Edgar, 1 Jan. 1919. (M.)
2907 Houghton, Richardson Johnson, 1 Jan. 1919. (M.)
2908 How, Eustace Arnold, 1 Jan. 1919. (M.)
2909 Hubbard, John Francis, 1 Jan. 1919. (M.)
2910 Inglis, John, 1 Jan. 1919. (M.)
2911 Jolliffe, Arthur Henry, 1 Jan. 1919. (M.)
2912 Justice, Philip Welman, 1 Jan. 1919. (M.)
2913 Kennedy, Thomas Fuller, 1 Jan. 1919. (M.)
2914 Lake, Ernest, 1 Jan. 1919. (M.)
2915 McDonald, George Frederick Handel, 1 Jan. 1919. (M.)
2916 MacDonnell, Mervyn Sorly, 1 Jan. 1919. (M.)
2917 Mackenzie, John William, 1 Jan. 1919. (M.)
2918 Macowan, Norman James, 1 Jan. 1919. (M.)
2919 Mitchell, Lachlan Martin Victor, 1 Jan. 1919. (M.)
2920 Moore, Harry Francis Beauchamp Seymour, 1 Jan. 1919. (M.)
2921 Odell, Oswald Facer, 1 Jan. 1919. (M.)
2922 Pearson, Hugh Frederick Archie, 1 Jan. 1919. (M.)
2923 Pigott, St. John Renwick, 1 Jan. 1919. (M.)
2924 Protheroe-Smith, Hugh Bateman, 1 Jan. 1919. (M.)
2925 Ratcliff, Charles John, 1 Jan. 1919. (M.)
2926 Ritchie, William, 1 Jan. 1919. (M.)
2927 Rodliffe, Thomas, 1 Jan. 1919. (M.)
2928 Ryder, Charles Frederick, 1 Jan. 1919. (M.)
2929 Scott, Robert Hamilton, 1 Jan. 1919. (M.)
2930 Simpson, Arthur William Woodman, 1 Jan. 1919. (M.)
2931 Smith, Charles William, 1 Jan. 1919. (M.)
2932 Smith, Vincent, 1 Jan. 1919. (M.)
2933 Smithers, Hubert, 1 Jan. 1919. (M.)
2934 Stammers, George Elliot Frank, 1 Jan. 1919. (M.)
2935 Stern, Frederic Claude, 1 Jan. 1919. (M.)
2936 Stirling, Rev. John Featherstone, 1 Jan. 1919. (M.)
2937 Stout, Percy Wyfold, 1 Jan. 1919. (M.)
2939 Synnott, Percy Joseph Ignatius, 1 Jan. 1919. (M.)
2940 Tait, William Ironsides, 1 Jan. 1919. (M.)
2941 Taylor, Gerard Charles, 1 Jan. 1919. (M.)
2942 Templer, Henry, 1 Jan. 1919. (M.)
2943 Tillard, Ernest, 1 Jan. 1919. (M.)
2944 Tillyard, Godfrey Ebenezer, 1 Jan. 1919. (M.)
2945 Treves, Frederick Beaumont, 1 Jan. 1919. (M.)
2946 Ure, John Holmes, 1 Jan. 1919. (M.)
2947 Vickerman, Phillip Sefton, 1 Jan. 1919. (M.)
2948 Watson, Alexander Paul, 1 Jan. 1919. (M.)
2949 Wells, Russell Primrose Collings-, 1 Jan. 1919. (M.)
2950 Williams, Albert, 1 Jan. 1919. (M.)
2951 Wilson, Rev. John Plumpton, 1 Jan. 1919. (M.)
2952 Woods, Harold, 1 Jan. 1919. (M.)
2953 Wright, Horace Leaf, 1 Jan. 1919. (M.)
2954 Madan, Kaikobad Rustonyf, 1 Jan. 1919. (M.)
2955 Blackburn, Charles Bickerton, 1 Jan. 1919. (M.)
2956 Fairley, Niel Hamilton, 1 Jan. 1919. (M.)
2957 Fowler, Robert, 1 Jan. 1919. (M.)
2958 Hammond, John Henry, 1 Jan. 1919. (M.)
2959 Kendall, John, 1 Jan. 1919. (M.)
2960 Storey, John Colvin, 1 Jan. 1919. (M.)
2961 Trickett, John James, 1 Jan. 1919. (M.)
2962 Woods, Rev. William Maitland, 1 Jan. 1919. (M.)
2963 Shauki, El Miralai Ali Bay, 1 Jan. 1919. (M.)

2964 Shalabi, El Bimbashi Mohammed Effendi Kamel, 1 Jan. 1919. (M.)
2965 Beckett, Rev. Maurice Thomas, 1 Jan. 1919. (M.)
2966 Bone, Thomas, 1 Jan. 1919. (M.)
2967 Brown, Frank Leader, 1 Jan. 1919. (M.)
2968 Brown, Vernon, 1 Jan. 1919. (M.)
2969 Browne, George Willis, 1 Jan. 1919. (M.)
2970 Butler, Sir Richard Pierce, Bart., 1 Jan. 1919. (M.)
2971 Clements, Thomas, 1 Jan. 1919. (M.)
2972 Coates, Christopher George, 1 Jan. 1919. (M.)
2973 Coltman, Edward Sinnott, 1 Jan. 1919. (M.)
2974 Cotton, Vere Egerton, 1 Jan. 1919. (M.)
2975 Cunynghame, Sir Percy Francis, Bart., 1 Jan. 1919. (M.)
2976 Dewhurst, Norman, 1 Jan. 1919. (M.)
2977 Eales, William John, 1 Jan. 1919. (M.)
2978 Eatherley, William, 1 Jan. 1919. (M.)
2979 Evans, David Howard, 1 Jan. 1919. (M.)
2980 Hay, Arthur Kennet, 1 Jan. 1919. (M.)
2981 Hill, John Sturgess Burow, 1 Jan. 1919. (M.)
2982 Hippisley, Arthur, 1 Jan. 1919. (M.)
2983 Hoare, Henry Noel, 1 Jan. 1919. (M.)
2984 Hodgkinson, Harry Drake, 1 Jan. 1919. (M.)
2985 Holmes, Reginald Valentine, 1 Jan. 1919. (M.)
2986 Inch, Thomas Douglas, 1 Jan. 1919. (M.)
2987 Inskipp, Percy Sidney, 1 Jan. 1919. (M.)
2988 Jones, Bernard Frederick, 1 Jan. 1919. (M.)
2989 Jones, Gerald Francis, 1 Jan. 1919. (M.)
2990 Limb, Frank, 1 Jan. 1919. (M.)
2991 Longdin, Herbert William, 1 Jan. 1919. (M.)
2992 Mitchell, Frank Brigham, 1 Jan. 1919. (M.)
2993 Murray, Patrick Moncreiff, 1 Jan. 1919. (M.)
2994 Myddleton, Cornelius William, 1 Jan. 1919. (M.)
2995 Norbury, Frank Herbert, 1 Jan. 1919. (M.)
2996 Owen, Herbert Charles, 1 Jan. 1919. (M.)
2997 Picken, Andrew, 1 Jan. 1919. (M.)
2998 Pryce, Wilfred Harry, 1 Jan. 1919. (M.)
2999 Ratcliffe, Herbert James, 1 Jan. 1919. (M.)
3000 Ridley, Richard Cooke, 1 Jan. 1919. (M.)
3001 Roberts, Arthur Henry, 1 Jan. 1919. (M.)
3003 Spurling, Dennis, 1 Jan. 1919. (M.)
3004 Starkey, Dickinson, 1 Jan. 1919. (M.)
3005 Stothert, William, 1 Jan. 1919. (M.)
3006 Sydney-Turner, Cuthbert Gambier Ryves, 1 Jan. 1919. (M.)
3007 Tipping, William John, 1 Jan. 1919. (M.)
3008 Tribe, John Charles, 1 Jan. 1919. (M.)
3009 Vaughan, Charles Jerome, 1 Jan. 1919. (M.)
3010 Vyvyan, Philip Henry Norris Nugent, 1 Jan. 1919. (M.)
3011 Wells, Joseph Douglas, 1 Jan. 1919. (M.)
3012 Wood, Douglas, 1 Jan. 1919. (M.)
3013 Allan, William Murray, 1 Jan. 1919. (M.)
3014 Anderson, David Irving, 1 Jan. 1919. (M.)
3016 Bakewell, George Victor, 1 Jan. 1919. (M.)
3017 Barker, Francis Brock, 1 Jan. 1919. (M.)
3018 Barkley, Thomas Yuille, 1 Jan. 1919. (M.)
3020 Birch, Alfred Granville, 1 Jan. 1919. (M.)
3021 Boulter, Edgar Charles, 1 Jan. 1919. (M)
3022 Boyle, Michael, 1 Jan. 1919. (M.)
3023 Briggs, Warwick Wellington, 1 Jan. 1919. (M.)
3024 Bryant, Robert Francis, 1 Jan. 1919. (M.)
3025 Chambers, Harold Tullis, 1 Jan. 1919. (M.)
3026 Coleman, Amos Hubert, 1 Jan. 1919. (M.)
3027 Cremetti, Paul Eugene, 1 Jan. 1919. (M.)
3028 Davies, Joseph Edward, 1 Jan. 1919. (M.)
3029 Delmege, James Anthony, 1 Jan. 1919. (M.)
3031 Douglas-Campbell, Archibald, 1 Jan. 1919. (M.)
3032 Downie, Frederick Habler, 1 Jan. 1919. (M.)
3033 Elwes, William Burton, 1 Jan. 1919. (M.)
3034 Elworthy, Robert Richard, 1 Jan. 1919. (M.)
3035 Ffooks, William Archdall, 1 Jan. 1919. (M.)
3036 FitzJohn, Geoffrey Nigel, 1 Jan. 1919. (M.)
3037 Foley, Walter Barham, 1 Jan. 1919. (M.)
3038 Fox, Charles Horace, 1 Jan. 1919. (M.)
3039 Galwey, William Rickards, 1 Jan. 1919. (M.)
3040 Garnier, Rev. Thomas Vernon, 1 Jan. 1919. (M.)
3041 Goad, Harold Elsdale, 1 Jan. 1919. (M.)
3042 Gray, John, 1 Jan. 1919. (M.)
3043 Harrison, Walter Lewis, 1 Jan. 1919. (M.)
3045 Hornabrook, Rev. John Oliver, 1 Jan. 1919. (M.)
3046 Jackson, Oswald Egerton Orme, 1 Jan. 1919. (M.)
3047 Judson, Daniel, 1 Jan. 1919. (M.)
3048 Kidson, Edward, 1 Jan. 1919. (M.)
3049 Knight-Bruce, James Comyn Lewis, 1 Jan. 1919. (M.)
3050 Lefroy, Langlois Massey, 1 Jan. 1919. (M.)
3051 McColl, Hugh Ernest, 1 Jan. 1919. (M.)
3052 Mitchell, Peter, 1 Jan. 1919. (M.)
3053 Moir, George, 1 Jan. 1919. (M.)
3054 Orange-Bromehead, Francis Edward, 1 Jan. 1919. (M.)
3055 Paddey, John Elliott, 1 Jan. 1919. (M.)
3056 Parkhouse, John Bardsley, 1 Jan. 1919. (M.)
3057 Parkhouse, Stanley Ernest, 1 Jan. 1919. (M.)
3058 Perkins, William Jackson, 1 Jan. 1919. (M.)
3059 Purdie, Rev. Albert Bertrand, 1 Jan. 1919. (M.)
3060 Scholes, Walter Nevelle, 1 Jan. 1919. (M.)
3061 Shingleton, Leslie, 1 Jan. 1919. (M.)
3062 Smith, Arthur William, 1 Jan. 1919. (M.)
3064 Taylor, Julian, 1 Jan. 1919. (M.)
3065 Verschoyle-Campbell, William Henry McNeile, 1 Jan. 1919. (M.)

3067 Walker, Charles Bishop, 1 Jan. 1919. (M.)
3068 Webb, Frederick Edward Apthorpe, 1 Jan. 1919. (M.)
3069 Webb-Peploe, Rev. Howard Melville, 1 Jan. 1919. (M.)
3070 Wellings, Evelyn Valentine, 1 Jan. 1919. (M.)
3071 Wheelwright, Edward Lycett, 1 Jan. 1919. (M.)
3072 Wilson, Reginald Maitland, 1 Jan. 1919. (M.)
3073a Wyatt, Philip Humphrey, 1 Jan. 1919. (M.)
3073b Neobard, Harold John Cooke, 1 Jan. 1919. (M.)
3074 Chambers, F., 1 Jan. 1919. (M.)
3075 Chenevix-Trench, Ralph, 1 Jan. 1919. (M.)
3076 Kearn, A .W., 1 Jan. 1919. (M.)
3077 Steele, G., 1 Jan. 1919. (M.)
3078 Stokes, Ralph Shenton Griffin, 1 Jan. 1919. (M.)
3079 Burton, R. B. S., 1 Jan. 1919. (M.)
3080 Adair, Alexander Cecil, 1 Jan. 1919. (M.)
3081 Allan, William David, 1 Jan. 1919. (M.)
3082 Anderson, Roy Dunlop, 1 Jan. 1919. (M.)
3083 Arnold, Francis Havard, 1 Jan. 1919. (M.)
3084 Atkinson, Alice Lilian, 1 Jan. 1919. (M.)
3085 Atkinson, Thomas John Day, 1 Jan. 1919. (M.)
3086 Bagnall, Ralph, 1 Jan. 1919. (M.)
3087 Ball, George Joseph, 1 Jan. 1919. (M.)
3088 Barnes, Harold Douglas, 1 Jan. 1919. (M.)
3089 Beale, Walter William, 1 Jan. 1919. (M.)
3090 Beatson, Leonard Frank, 1 Jan. 1919. (M.)
3091 Bell, Morris James, 1 Jan. 1919. (M.)
3092 Bennett, Alexander John Munro, 1 Jan. 1919. (M.)
3093 Bevis, Cecil Bevis, 1 Jan. 1919. (M.)
3094 Block, Maurice William Palmer, 1 Jan. 1919. (M.)
3095 Braid, Arthur Reade, 1 Jan. 1919. (M.)
3096 Breakey, Arthur John, 1 Jan. 1919. (M.)
3097 Broadley, Phillip John, 1 Jan. 1919. (M.)
3098 Bryant, Arthur Rolfe, 1 Jan. 1919. (M.)
3099 Bucknill, Thomas Alfred Townsend, 1 Jan. 1919. (M.)
3100 Bull, William Henry, 1 Jan. 1919. (M.)
3101 Burton, Sydney Collard, 1 Jan. 1919. (M.)
3102 Caldwell, Arthur Lewis, 1 Jan. 1919. (M.)
3103 Clapshaw, Aquila, 1 Jan. 1919. (M.)
3104 Cooke, Robert Joseph, 1 Jan. 1919. (M.)
3105 Corbet, Francis Wellington, 1 Jan. 1919. (M.)
3106 Cowan, Peter Hood. 1 Jan. 1919. (M.)
3107 Cowley, James William, 1 Jan. 1919. (M.)
3108 Cox, Joshua John, 1 Jan. 1919. (M.)
3109 Dewing, Robert Henry, 1 Jan. 1919. (M.)
3110 Dibben, Cecil Reginald, 1 Jan. 1919. (M.)
3111 Dittman, William Ewart, 1 Jan. 1919. (M.)
3112 Dixon, Charles Joseph, 1 Jan. 1919. (M.)
3114 Eaton, William Arnold. 1 Jan. 1919. (M.)
3115 Ellis, James Logan, 1 Jan. 1919. (M.)
3116 Ellis, Philip, 1 Jan. 1919. (M.)
3117 Emley, Maurice Woodman, 1 Jan. 1919. (M.)
3118 English, Charles Ernest, 1 Jan. 1919. (M.)
3119 Etches, Charles Edward, 1 Jan. 1919. (M.)
3120 Feilden, Edward Leyland Cooke, 1 Jan. 1919. (M.)
3121 Forrest, David, 1 Jan. 1919. (M.)
3122 Gair, Sinclair, 1 Jan. 1919. (M.)
3123 Gavin, Frederick James, 1 Jan. 1919. (M.)
3124 Griffin, Edward Christian, 1 Jan. 1919. (M.)
3125 Haddon, Andrew, 1 Jan. 1919. (M.)
3127 Hartcup, William Richard Monyns, 1 Jan. 1919. (M.)
3128 Haythorne, Winifred S., 1 Jan. 1919. (M.)
3130 Higgins, Joseph Thomas, 1 Jan. 1919. (M.)
3131 Hincks, Henry, 1 Jan. 1919. (M.)
3132 Horniblow, Edith Marjory, 1 Jan. 1919. (M.)
3134 Irvine, Matthew, 1 Jan. 1919. (M.)
3135 Jackson, Maximilian, 1 Jan. 1919. (M.)
3136 Jickling, Charles Maurice, 1 Jan. 1919. (M.)
3137 Johnson, Raymond, 1 Jan. 1919. (M.)
3138 Kelley, Frederick Arthur, 1 Jan. 1919. (M.)
3139 Kendall, John, 1 Jan. 1919. (M.)
3140 Lambert, Francis John, 1 Jan. 1919. (M.)
3141 Lang-Hyde, John Irvine, 1 Jan. 1919. (M.)
3142 Lascelles, Ernest, 1 Jan. 1919. (M.)
3143 Leathes, Carteret de Mussenden, 1 Jan. 1919. (M.)
3144 Lee-Evans, George, 1 Jan. 1919. (M.)
3145 Ludlow, Fred Ball, 1 Jan. 1919. (M.)
3146 McGuire, Michael, 1 Jan. 1919. (M.)
3147 Mailins, John Robert, 1 Jan. 1919. (M.)
3148 Manners-Howe, Thomas Harris, 1 Jan. 1919. (M.)
3149 Marsack, Edward Lethbridge, 1 Jan. 1919. (M.)
3150 Mathews, Henry Edmunds, 1 Jan. 1919. (M.)
3151 Mathias, Oswald Llewellyn, 1 Jan. 1919. (M.)
3152 Maxted, Charles Stenteford, 1 Jan. 1919. (M.)
3153 Mayer, Gaston, 1 Jan. 1919. (M.)
3154 Michod, Percy Douglas, 1 Jan. 1919. (M.)
3156 Munro, James McVicar, 1 Jan. 1919. (M.)
3157 Napier, John Steward, 1 Jan. 1919. (M.)
3158 New, Claud E., 1 Jan. 1919. (M.)
3159 Newbold, Ambrose William, 1 Jan. 1919. (M.)
3160 Newton, Harry Kottingham, 1 Jan. 1919. (M.)
3161 North, Edward, 1 Jan. 1919. (M.)
3162 Payne, Charles, 1 Jan. 1919. (M.)
3163 Pedley, Oswald Henry, 1 Jan. 1919. (M.)
3164 Pickin, William David, 1 Jan. 1919. (M.)
3165 Pollock, Evelyn Hay, 1 Jan. 1919. (M.)
3166 Pomeroy, Hon. Ralph Legge, 1 Jan. 1919. (M.)
3167 Reynolds, Frank Romilly, 1 Jan. 1919. (M.)
3168 Richardson. Philip Wigham, 1 Jan. 1919. (M.)
3169 Rickman Graham Egerton, 1 Jan. 1919. (M.)

3170 Roberts, Adeline, 1 Jan. 1919. (M.)
3171 Rodick, William, 1 Jan. 1919. (M.)
3172 Rodwell, Francis John, 1 Jan. 1919. (M.)
3173 Rogerson, John Edwin, 1 Jan. 1919. (M.)
3174 Rowe, Henry Gordon, 1 Jan. 1919. (M.)
3176 Scratchley, Victor Henry Sylvester, 1 Jan. 1919. (M.)
3177 Shannon, John, 1 Jan. 1919. (M.)
3178 Short, Oswald Murton, 1 Jan. 1919. (M.)
3179 Simson, Rupert, 1 Jan. 1919. (M.)
3180 Skeats, Thomas George, 1 Jan. 1919. (M.)
3181 Smyly, Richard Josiah, 1 Jan. 1919. (M.)
3182 Smyth, Benjamin, 1 Jan. 1919. (M.)
3183 Soames, Walter Field, 1 Jan. 1919. (M.)
3184 Somers, John Percy, 1 Jan. 1919. (M.)
3185 Spread, Eustace John William, 1 Jan. 1919. (M.)
3186 Stacke, Hedley Herbert, 1 Jan. 1919. (M.)
3187 Stewart-Bam, Sir Pieter Canzius van Blommestein, 1 Jan. 1919. (M.)
3189 Tatham, Charles John Willmer, 1 Jan. 1919. (M.)
3190 Temperley, Harold William Vazeille, 1 Jan. 1919. (M.)
3191 Tennent, Thomas Hastings, 1 Jan. 1919. (M.)
3193 Thompson, Harry Adair, 1 Jan. 1919. (M.)
3194 Thompson, Jean Glass, 1 Jan. 1919. (M.)
3195 Treffry, Edward, 1 Jan. 1919. (M.)
3196 Tristem, Henry, 1 Jan. 1919. (M.)
3197 Vallentin, Henry Edward, 1 Jan. 1919. (M.)
3198 Vigors, Henry, 1 Jan. 1919. (M.)
3199 Wakelin, James Glencorse, 1 Jan. 1919. (M.)
3200 Ward, John, 1 Jan. 1919. (M.)
3201 Warner, Cuthbert Philip, 1 Jan. 1919. (M.)
3202 Weekes, Henry Wilson, 1 Jan. 1919. (M.)
3203 Wheeler, Charles Alexander, 1 Jan. 1919. (M.)
3205 Wildman, Sam Beck, 1 Jan. 1919. (M.)
3206 Wingfield, John Maurice, 1 Jan. 1919. (M.)
3207 Wiseman-Clarke, Charles Camden, 1 Jan. 1919. (M.)
3208 Wood, Charles Knight, 1 Jan. 1919. (M.)
3209 Wood, Evelyn Fitzgerald Michell, 1 Jan. 1919. (M.)
3210 Yorke, Frederick Augustus, 1 Jan. 1919. (M.)
3211 Anderson, Frederick Walter Gale, 1 Jan. 1919. (M.)
3212 Caldwell, Thomas Richey, 1 Jan. 1919. (M.)
3213 Campbell, Charles Vincent, 1 Jan. 1919. (M.)
3214 Cassels, George Hamilton, 1 Jan. 1919. (M.)
3215 Cornett, Alexander Don, 1 Jan. 1919. (M.)
3217 Fordham, John Guerney, 1 Jan. 1919. (M.)
3218 Gillies, Austin Bain, 1 Jan. 1919. (M.)
3219 Goodall, James Roberts, 1 Jan. 1919. (M.)
3220 Jeffery, John, 1 Jan. 1919. (M.)
3221 Lindsay, James Hawkins, 1 Jan. 1919. (M.)
3222 McGillivray, Percy Crannell, 1 Jan. 1919. (M.)
3223 Morrison, William Geekie, 1 Jan. 1919. (M.)
3224 Mowbray, John Arthur Clark, 1 Jan. 1919. (M.)
3225 Raikes, Richard, 1 Jan. 1919. (M.)
3226 Routh, Jason Rudolph, 1 Jan. 1919. (M.)
3227 Smith, Albert Alexander, 1 Jan. 1919. (M.)
3228 Swinburne, John Eliot, 1 Jan. 1919. (M.)
3229 Winnett, Albert William, 1 Jan. 1919. (M.)
3231 Beamish, Francis Teulon, 1 Jan. 1919. (M.)
3232 Bruggey, Stephen, 1 Jan. 1919. (M.)
3233 Down, John Egbert, 1 Jan. 1919. (M.)
3234 Sherington, Guy, 1 Jan. 1919. (M.)
3235 Sutherland, Bertram Milne, 1 Jan. 1919. (M.)
3236 Watt, Walter Oswald, 1 Jan. 1919. (M.)
3237 Willcocks, George Charles, 1 Jan. 1919. (M.)
3238 Yeatman, Charleton, 1 Jan. 1919. (M.)
3239 Brandon, Percy de Bathe, 1 Jan. 1919. (M.)
3240 Brewis, Andrew Seymour, 1 Jan. 1919. (M.)
3241 Bruce, William, 1 Jan. 1919. (M.)
3242 Lawry, Raymond Alexander Reid, 1 Jan. 1919.
3243 Mills, Henry Percival, 1 Jan. 1919. (M.)
3244 Pearson, Maurice Grey, 1 Jan. 1919. (M.)
3245 Abell, Charles Francis, 1 Jan. 1919. (M.)
3246 Abell, George Henry, 1 Jan. 1919. (M.)
3247 Addenbrooke-Prout, Reginald, 1 Jan. 1919. (M.)
3248 Anne, George Chartlon, 1 Jan. 1919. (M.)
3249 Atkinson, Felton Clayson, 1 Jan. 1919. (M.)
3250 Atkinson, Harold Gordon, 1 Jan. 1919. (M.)
3251 Atkinson-Clark, Henry Fox, 1 Jan. 1919. (M.)
3252 Aubrey, Herbert Arthur Reginald, 1 Jan. 1919. (M.)
3253 Auker, Lawrence, 1 Jan. 1919. (M.)
3254 Axford, Sidney Robert, 1 Jan. 1919. (M.)
3255 Aylwin, William Edgar, 1 Jan. 1919. (M.)
3256 Ball, Lionel Percy, 1 Jan. 1919. (M.)
3257 Barmby, Aiden James Wharton, 1 Jan. 1919. (M)
3258 Barnfield, Allen Stewart, 1 Jan. 1919. (M.)
3259 Barton, Robert John Ferguson, 1 Jan. 1919. (M.)
3260 Baxenden, Thomas George, 1 Jan. 1919. (M.)
3261 Bayes, John George, 1 Jan. 1919. (M.)
3262 Bell, Victor Douglas, 1 Jan. 1919. (M.)
3263 Beor, Bertram Richard White, 1 Jan. 1919. (M.)
3264 Beuttler, Edward Gerald Oakley, 1 Jan. 1919. (M.)
3265 Blowey, Henry Francis Tozer, 1 Jan. 1919. (M.)
3266 Bonham-Carter, Ian Malcolm, 1 Jan. 1919. (M.)
3267 Bonnett, Claude Herbert Dick, 1 Jan. 1919. (M.)
3268 Bowen, James Bevan, 1 Jan. 1919. (M.)
3269 Bromet, Geoffrey Rhodes, 1 Jan. 1919. (M.)
3270 Brown, Francis Giles, 1 Jan. 1919. (M.)
3271 Bullen, Thomas, 1 Jan. 1919. (M.)
3272 Budgen, William Douglas, 1 Jan. 1919. (M.)
3273 Bullock, Christopher Llewellyn, 1 Jan. 1919. (M.)

3274 Burge, Cyril Gordon, 1 Jan. 1919. (M.)
3275 Burt, John Wotherspoon, 1 Jan. 1919. (M.)
3276 Buss, Horace Austin, 1 Jan. 1919. (M.)
3277 Butter, Charles Adrian James, 1 Jan. 1919. (M.)
3278 Cameron, Donald Hay, 1 Jan. 1919. (M.)
3279 Carbery, Edward Oliver Bamford, 1 Jan. 1919. (M.)
3280 Carey, Rowland Dobree, 1 Jan. 1919. (M.)
3281 Carter, Silas Bernard Foley, 1 Jan. 1919. (M.)
3282 Chambers, Frederick Foster, 1 Jan. 1919. (M.)
3283 Cockburn, Ronald, 1 Jan. 1919. (M.)
3285 Conner, Daniel Goodwin, 1 Jan. 1919. (M.)
3286 Cook, Robert Ewing, 1 Jan. 1919. (M.)
3287 Cooke, Ion Alexander Scott, 1 Jan. 1919. (M.)
3288 Cooper, James Percy Carre, 1 Jan. 1919. (M.)
3289 Corin, Herbert John, 1 Jan. 1919. (M.)
3290 Cruickshank, Jasper Wallace, 1 Jan. 1919. (M.)
3291 Cumming, Howard, 1 Jan. 1919. (M.)
3292 Davies, Walford, 1 Jan. 1919. (M.)
3293 Curtis, Walter John Brice, 1 Jan. 1919. (M.)
3294 Davis, Francis Robert Edward, 1 Jan. 1919. (M.)
3295 Denton, Harold Bentley, 1 Jan. 1919. (M.)
3296 de Sarigny, Rene, 1 Jan. 1919. (M.)
3298 Duffus, Chester Stairs, 1 Jan. 1919. (M.)
3300 Edge, Percy Granville, 1 Jan. 1919. (M.)
3301 Edmonds, Charles Humphrey Kingsman, 1 Jan. 1919. (M.)
3302 Eggar, Thomas Macdonald, 1 Jan. 1919. (M.)
3303 Elliott, James Boyne, 1 Jan. 1919. (M.)
3304 Everitt, Stuart Oswald, 1 Jan. 1919. (M.)
3305 Farthing, William Walter, 1 Jan. 1919. (M.)
3306 Fell, Louis Frederick Rudston, 1 Jan. 1919. (M.)
3307 Fernie, William James, 1 Jan. 1919. (M.)
3308 Fraser, Cecil, 1 Jan. 1919. (M.)
3309 Fraser, Francis William Ian Victor, 1 Jan. 1919. (M.)
3310 Fraser, George William Frederick, 1 Jan. 1919. (M.)
3311 Freeman, Max, 1 Jan. 1919. (M.)
3312 Gamble, Charles William, 1 Jan. 1919. (M.)
3313 Garrett, Thomas Richard Henty, 1 Jan. 1919. (M.)
3314 Gibson, William Walker, 1 Jan. 1919. (M.)
3315 Gilmore, Thomas Edward, 1 Jan. 1919. (M.)
3316 Goble, Stanley James, 1 Jan. 1919. (M.)
3317 Goldsmith, Norman, 1 Jan. 1919. (M.)
3318 Gordon, Cedric Foskett, 1 Jan. 1919. (M.)
3319 Gray, Frank James, 1 Jan. 1919. (M.)
3320 Guest, Hon. Lionel George William, 1 Jan. 1919. (M.)
3321 Hall, Alfred Kingsley, 1 Jan. 1919. (M.)
3322 Halford, Ernest Samuel, 1 Jan. 1919. (M.)
3323 Hammond, William Stanley, 1 Jan. 1919. (M.)
3324 Hannay, George Daniel, 1 Jan. 1919. (M.)
3325 Hawkins, John Frederick, 1 Jan. 1919. (M.)
3326 Hayes, Robert Cholerton, 1 Jan. 1919. (M.)
3327 Hazelton, George, 1 Jan. 1919. (M.)
3328 Hellawell, Alfred Stanley, 1 Jan. 1919. (M.)
3329 Heyn, Richard Gustavus, 1 Jan. 1919. (M.)
3330 Hills, John Harris, 1 Jan. 1919. (M.)
3331 Hilton-Jones, Robert, 1 Jan. 1919. (M.)
3332 Hodgson, William, 1 Jan. 1919. (M.)
3333 Holloway, Ernest, 1 Jan. 1919. (M.)
3334 Howard, Ernest James, 1 Jan. 1919. (M.)
3335 Johnston, Ernest Henry, 1 Jan. 1919. (M.)
3336 Jolly, Frank, 1 Jan. 1919. (M.)
3337 Kennedy, Stuart Samuel, 1 Jan. 1919. (M.)
3338 Krabbé, Charles Frederick, 1 Jan. 1919. (M.)
3339 Krabbé, Clarence Brehmer, 1 Jan. 1919. (M.)
3340 Laing, George, 1 Jan. 1919. (M.)
3341 Lang, James Arthur Maule, 1 Jan. 1919. (M.)
3342 Lang, William Henry, 1 Jan. 1919. (M.)
3343 Langdon, Henry Charles Theodore, 1 Jan. 1919. (M.)
3344 Laws, Frederick Charles Victor, 1 Jan. 1919. (M.)
3345 Lecomber, Harold Roger, 1 Jan. 1919. (M.)
3346 L'Estrange-Malone, Cecil John, 1 Jan. 1919. (M.)
3347 Lilley, Leonard Moore, 1 Jan. 1919. (M.)
3348 Lindsell, Reginald Stuart, 1 Jan. 1919. (M.)
3349 Lintott, John William, 1 Jan. 1919. (M.)
3350 Logan, Philip Norman, 1 Jan. 1919. (M.)
3351 Long, William Dickson, 1 Jan. 1919. (M.)
3352 Longridge, Theodore Ernle, 1 Jan. 1919. (M.)
3353 Lucas, Frederick William, 1 Jan. 1919. (M.)
3354 Lyons, Thomas, 1 Jan. 1919. (M.)
3355 McClure, George Buchanan, 1 Jan. 1919. (M.)
3356 McClure, Samuel, 1 Jan. 1919. (M.)
3357 McCrindle, James Ronald, 1 Jan. 1919. (M.)
3358 McLaren, Colin Temple, 1 Jan. 1919. (M.)
3359 Marsh, William Lockwood, 1 Jan. 1919. (M.)
3360 Maitland, Reginald Ferdinando, 1 Jan. 1919. (M.)
3361 Martin, Alfred Ridley, 1 Jan. 1919. (M.)
3362 Martin, Thomas, 1 Jan. 1919. (M.)
3363 Maycock, Richard Beauchamp, 1 Jan. 1919. (M.)
3364 Measures, Arthur Harold, 1 Jan. 1919. (M.)
3365 Medhurst, Charles Edward Hastings, 1 Jan. 1919. (M.)
3367 Methven, Malcolm David, 1 Jan. 1919. (M.)
3368 Michie, William Charles, 1 Jan. 1919. (M.)
3369 Miley, Arnold John, 1 Jan. 1919. (M.)
3370 Mornement, Robert Harry, 1 Jan. 1919. (M.)
3371 Morris, Alfred Samuel, 1 Jan. 1919. (M.)
3372 Mounsey, Roland James, 1 Jan. 1919. (M.)
3373 Murfitt, Charles Joseph, 1 Jan. 1919. (M.)
3374 Murrell, Percy Murray John, 1 Jan. 1919. (M.)
3375 Nairn, Douglas Gordon, 1 Jan. 1919. (M.)

2 R

THE ORDER OF THE BRITISH EMPIRE.

3376 Nevill, Stanley Sharp, 1 Jan. 1919. (M.)
3377 Newall, Norman Dakeyne, 1 Jan. 1919. (M.)
3378 Newman, Leslie, 1 Jan. 1919. (M.)
3379 Newton-Clare, Herbert John. 1 Jan. 1919. (M.)
3380 Noel, Francis Arthur Gerard, 1 Jan. 1919. (M.)
3381 North, John Tom, 1 Jan. 1919. (M.)
3382 Northover, Harry Robert, 1 Jan. 1919. (M.)
3383 Ogden, Charles Percy, 1 Jan. 1919. (M.)
3384 O'Reilly, Brefney Rolph, 1 Jan. 1919. (M.)
3385 Paul, Henry William Moncrieff, 1 Jan. 1919. (M.)
3386 Peacock, Gerald Selwyn, 1 Jan. 1919. (M.)
3387 Pearce, Joseph, 1 Jan. 1919. (M.)
3388 Perrin, Eugene Courtney, 1 Jan. 1919. (M.)
3389 Phillips, Thomas Brocklehurst, 1 Jan. 1919. (M.)
3390 Pidgeon, Geoffrey Denzie, 1 Jan. 1919. (M.)
3391 Pillers, Robert Kingsley, 1 Jan. 1919. (M.)
3392 Polyblank, William Joseph, 1 Jan. 1919. (M.)
3393 Powell, Enoch, 1 Jan. 1919. (M.)
3394 Pretyman, George Frederick, 1 Jan. 1919. (M.)
3395 Prince, Charles Edmond, 1 Jan. 1919. (M.)
3396 Pulford, Conway Walker Heath, 1 Jan. 1919. (M.)
3397 Pulham, Frederick Bygrave, 1 Jan. 1919. (M.)
3398 Raffles, Stamford Cecil, 1 Jan. 1919. (M.)
3399 Raikes, William Oswell, 1 Jan. 1919. (M.)
3400 Rainsford-Hannay, Donald, 1 Jan. 1919. (M.)
3401 Rees, George Martin Treherne, 1 Jan. 1919. (M.)
3402 Reid, Robert Alburne, 1 Jan. 1919. (M.)
3403 Richmond, Vincent Crane, 1 Jan. 1919. (M.)
3404 Robertson, Thomas Edward, 1 Jan. 1919. (M.)
3405 Robinson, Alexander Augustus Edmund, 1 Jan. 1919. (M.)
3406 Robinson, Alick Christopher, 1 Jan. 1919. (M.)
3407 Rubie, John, 1 Jan. 1919. (M.)
3408 Sadler, Leslie, 1 Jan. 1919. (M.)
3410 Scholte, Frederick Lewellen, 1 Jan. 1919. (M.)
3411 Shelmerdine, Francis Claude, 1 Jan. 1919. (M.)
3412 Simon, Rt. Hon. Sir John Allsebrook, 1 Jan. 1919. (M.)
3413 Sinclair-Hill, Gerald Arthur, 1 Jan. 1919. (M.)
3414 Sippe, Sidney Vincent, 1 Jan. 1919. (M.)
3415 Smith, Charles Gainer, 1 Jan. 1919. (M.)
3417 Spittle, John Trevor, 1 Jan. 1919. (M.)
3418 Stammers, Frederick Gunning, 1 Jan. 1919. (M.)
3419 Stapleton, Edward Parker, 1 Jan. 1919. (M.)
3420 Starling, John, 1 Jan. 1919. (M.)
3421 Stedman, Ernest Walker, 1 Jan. 1919. (M.)
3422 Steele-Perkins, Alfred Horace Steele, 1 Jan. 1919. (M.)
3423 Stephens, Frank Harold, 1 Jan. 1919. (M.)
3424 Stokes, Edward, 1 Jan. 1919. (M.)
3425 Struben, Arthur, 1 Jan. 1919. (M.)
3426 Sutton, Bertine Entwistle, 1 Jan. 1919. (M.)
3427 Thomas, Otho Vincent, 1 Jan. 1919. (M.)
3428 Thomas, Rudall Woodliffe, 1 Jan. 1919. (M.)
3429 Thornely, John Edmund Burnet, 1 Jan. 1919. (M.)
3430 Trott, Francis William, 1 Jan. 1919. (M.)
3431 Tylee, Arthur Kellan, 1 Jan. 1919. (M.)
3432 Wall, Anthony Herbert William, 1 Jan. 1919. (M.)
3433 Ward-Brown, Vere, 1 Jan. 1919. (M.)
3434 Williams, Francis Cartwright, 1 Jan. 1919. (M.)
3435 Williams, Richard, 1 Jan. 1919. (M.)
3436 Wilson, Frank Gordon, 1 Jan. 1919. (M.)
3437 Wiseman, Francis Augustus John Bartholomew, 1 Jan. 1919. (M.)
3438 Wood, Murdick McKenzie, 1 Jan. 1919. (M.)
3439 Wooldridge, Gilbert de Lacy, 1 Jan. 1919. (M.)
3440 Wyllie, Harold, 1 Jan. 1919. (M.)
3441 Wynn, Alfred Hearst Wynn Elias, 1 Jan. 1919. (M.)
3442 Young, Walter Gerald Paul, 1 Jan. 1919. (M.)
3443 Powell, Winifred, Mrs., 1 Jan. 1919. (M.)
3444 Edwards, Mary, Mrs., 1 Jan. 1919. (M.)
3445 Moss, Margaret, Mrs., 1 Jan. 1919. (M.)
3446 Anstey, Henry Charles, 1 Jan. 1919. (M.)
3448 Atkinson, William, 1 Jan. 1919. (M.)
3449 Barff, Arthur Douglas, 1 Jan. 1919. (M.)
3450 Bartlett, John Holderness, 1 Jan. 1919. (M.)
3451 Bate, Richard Francis, 1 Jan. 1919. (M.)
3452 Baynham, Henry, 1 Jan. 1919. (M.)
3453 Beal, Norman Hugh, 1 Jan. 1919. (M.)
3454 Bean, Arthur, 1 Jan. 1919. (M.)
3455 Bennett, Edward Morden, 1 Jan. 1919. (M.)
3456 Bennett, Martin Gilbert, 1 Jan. 1919. (M.)
3457 Bernacchi, Louis Charles, 1 Jan. 1919. (M.)
3458 Birch, Fred, 1 Jan. 1919. (M.)
3459 Bond, Arthur George Hayes, 1 Jan. 1919. (M.)
3460 Borrissow, Charles Kirby, 1 Jan. 1919. (M.)
3461 Bowen, Gerald Percival, 1 Jan. 1919. (M.)
3462 Brown, Duncan Tatton, 1 Jan. 1919. (M.)
3464 Browne, Harold Ernest, 1 Jan. 1919. (M.)
3465 Buchan, John Robertson, 1 Jan. 1919. (M.)
3466 Bull, Wilfrid James, 1 Jan. 1919. (M.)
3467 Bunbury, Charles Thomas Alexander, 1 Jan. 1919. (M.)
3468 Burt, Arthur Stanley, 1 Jan. 1919. (M.)
3469 Cable, James Frederick, 1 Jan. 1919. (M.)
3470 Carr, Christopher George, 1 Jan. 1919. (M.)
3472 Constable, James Sandford, 1 Jan. 1919. (M.)
3473 Cook, Alexander James, 1 Jan. 1919. (M.)
3474 Cooper, Archibald Frederick, 1 Jan. 1919. (M.)
3475 Corbyn, Frederick Jams Harold, 1 Jan. 1919. (M.)
3476 Cottrell, William Henry, 1 Jan. 1919. (M.)
3477 Cox, Herbert Spencer, 1 Jan. 1919. (M.)

3478 Davey, Charles Henry, 1 Jan. 1919. (M.)
3479 Day, Roderick Wilson, 1 Jan. 1919. (M.)
3480 Dibben, Arthur Douglas Harry, 1 Jan. 1919. (M.)
3481 Dowling, Horace Edward, 1 Jan. 1919. (M.)
3482 Drury, Edward Dumerque, 1 Jan. 1919. (M.)
3483 Dunn, Robert Ewart, 1 Jan. 1919. (M.)
3484 Dunning, Thomas William John, 1 Jan. 1919. (M.)
3485 Eachus, Thomas, 1 Jan. 1919. (M.)
3486 Edmond, Robert, 1 Jan. 1919. (M.)
3487 Emery, Herbert Denham, 1 Jan. 1919. (M.)
3488 Enright, William George Ewart, 1 Jan. 1919. (M.)
3489 Farish, James Risk, 1 Jan. 1919. (M.)
3490 Farquharson, John Philips, 1 Jan. 1919. (M.)
3491 Fforde, Thomas Roderick, 1 Jan. 1919. (M.)
3492 Ford, Reginald Bertram, 1 Jan. 1919. (M.)
3493 Freeman, Benson Fletcher, 1 Jan. 1919. (M.)
3495 Gilhespy, John William Edward, 1 Jan. 1919. (M.)
3496 Gillespie, Andrew, 1 Jan. 1919. (M.)
3497 Gillies, John, 1 Jan. 1919. (M.)
3498 Glegg-Smith, William, 1 Jan. 1919. (M.)
3499 Goddard, Norris, 1 Jan. 1919. (M.)
3500 Graham, Rev. Christopher, 1 Jan. 1919. (M.)
3501 Graham, William Air 1 Jan. 1919. (M.)
3505 Hanson, Herbert James, 1 Jan. 1919. (M.)
3506 Hardie, Robert, 1 Jan. 1919. (M.)
3507 Hastings, Edward George Godolphin, 1 Jan. 1919. (M.)
3508 Haszard, Gerald Fenwick, 1 Jan. 1919. (M.)
3509 Hayes, Robert, 1 Jan. 1919. (M.)
3510 Haynes, Frederick Gambier, 1 Jan. 1919. (M.)
3511 Heaton, Charles Howard, 1 Jan. 1919. (M.)
3512 Heddles, Thomas Mann, 1 Jan. 1919. (M.)
3513 Hefford, Edward Owen, 1 Jan. 1919. (M.)
3514 Hill, Gerald Dudley, 1 Jan. 1919. (M.)
3515 Hoare, Stephen Leonard, 1 Jan. 1919. (M.)
3517 Horne, Charles Frederick, 1 Jan. 1919. (M.)
3518 Howard, Henry Mowbray, 1 Jan. 1919. (M.)
3519 Hutchings, Samuel Louis, 1 Jan. 1919. (M.)
3520 Iles, Arthur Ernest, 1 Jan. 1919. (M.)
3521 Isherwood, Harold, 1 Jan. 1919. (M.)
3522 Jackson, Harold Gordon, 1 Jan. 1919. (M.)
3523 Jenkinson, Thomas Norman, 1 Jan. 1919. (M.)
3525 Jones, Hubert Louis, 1 Jan. 1919. (M.)
3526 Kelly, John, 1 Jan. 1919. (M.)
3527 King, C. W., 1 Jan. 1919. (M.)
3528 Lee, Herbert Victor, 1 Jan. 1919. (M.)
3529 Lester, Arthur Ellis, 1 Jan. 1919. (M.)
3530 Liston, Andrew Graham, 1 Jan. 1919. (M.)
3531 Lyttleton, Stephen Clive, 1 Jan. 1919. (M.)
3532 McCormick-Goodhart, Leander, 1 Jan. 1919. (M.)
3533 McGrath, Redmond Walter, 1 Jan. 1919. (M.)
3534 McRitchie, William MacPherson, 1 Jan. 1919. (M.)
3535 MacKay, Robert Henry Ramsay, 1 Jan. 1919. (M.)
3536 Macmillan, James Charles Newsome, 1 Jan. 1919. (M.)
3537 Mace, Frederick William, 1 Jan. 1919. (M.)
3538 Martyn, John, 1 Jan. 1919. (M.)
3539 May, James Rees, 1 Jan. 1919. (M.)
3541 Minter, Joseph Alfred, 1 Jan. 1919. (M.)
3542 Moore, Albert John Campbell, 1 Jan. 1919. (M.)
3543 Moore, Hartley Russell Gwennap, 1 Jan. 1919. (M.)
3544 Morris, Leslie Miles, 1 Jan. 1919. (M.)
3545 Mountstephens, Richard, 1 Jan. 1919. (M.)
3546 Palmer, Edwin Mansergh, 1 Jan. 1919. (M.)
3547 Parry, Gladwyn, 1 Jan. 1919. (M.)
3548 Penny, Herbert Lloyd, 1 Jan. 1919. (M.)
3550 Pilditch, Cyril Harold Lee, 1 Jan. 1919. (M.)
3551 Pougnet, John Maurice Barbes, 1 Jan. 1919. (M.)
3552 Pover, Thomas Pierce, 1 Jan. 1919. (M.)
3553 Price, William Alfred, 1 Jan. 1919. (M.)
3554 Prior, Cunningham, 1 Jan. 1919. (M.)
3555 Richards, John Osment, 1 Jan. 1919. (M.)
3556 Riley, Gerard Brook, 1 Jan. 1919. (M.)
3557 Roskruge, Francis John, 1 Jan. 1919. (M.)
3558 Ruxton, William Mill, 1 Jan. 1919. (M.)
3559 Ryan, Walter Thomas, 1 Jan. 1919. (M.)
3560 Sandieson, John, 1 Jan. 1919. (M.)
3561 Seabrook, James Alfred, 1 Jan. 1919. (M.)
3562 Shaw, Ernest Albert, 1 Jan. 1919. (M.)
3563 Siddals, John, 1 Jan. 1919. (M.)
3564 Simpson, James, 1 Jan. 1919. (M.)
3565 Slaney, Charles Wynne, 1 Jan. 1919. (M.)
3566 Smart, Harold Nevil, 1 Jan. 1919. (M.)
3568 Smith, Frederick H., 1 Jan. 1919. (M.)
3569 Snelling, Norman George Fowler, 1 Jan. 1919. (M.)
3570 Sparrow, William George, 1 Jan. 1919. (M.)
3571 Stapylton, Martyn Frederic, 1 Jan. 1919. (M.)
3572 Swann-Mason, Rev. Richard Swann, 1 Jan. 1919. (M.)
3573 Symes, William, 1 Jan. 1919. (M.)
3574 Tabuteau, Reginald Molière, 1 Jan. 1919. (M.)
3575 Talbot, John Charles, 1 Jan. 1919. (M.)
3576 Tarrant, William Charles, 1 Jan. 1919. (M.)
3577 Temple, John Howard, 1 Jan. 1919. (M.)
3578 Thom, James Henry, 1 Jan. 1919. (M.)
3580 Tinker, Henry William Cossart, 1 Jan. 1919. (M.)
3581 Townshend, Reginald Brooks, 1 Jan. 1919. (M.)
3582 Upham, John William, 1 Jan. 1919. (M.)
3583 Vigne, Bertram, 1 Jan. 1919. (M.)
3584 Vincent, Charles Rogers, 1 Jan. 1919. (M.)
3585 Wallace, Charles James Mitchell, 1 Jan. 1919. (M.)
3586 Wallis, Tacy Millett Winstanley, 1 Jan. 1919. (M.)

610

3588 Watchlin, Alexander, 1 Jan. 1919. (M.)
3589 Watson, William Robert, 1 Jan. 1919. (M.)
3590 Way, Robert Lewis, 1 Jan. 1919. (M.)
3591 Webster, Godfrey George, 1 Jan. 1919. (M.)
3592 White, Hans Thomas Fell, 1 Jan. 1919. (M.)
3593 Whittingham, Wallace Edgar, 1 Jan. 1919. (M.)
3594 Windle, Charles Howard, 1 Jan. 1919. (M.)
3595 Wrey, Edward Charles, 1 Jan. 1919. (M.)
3596 Young, Stanley Harris, 1 Jan. 1919. (M.)
3597 Young, Thomas Wallace, 1 Jan. 1919. (M.)
3598 Gillon, Nina, Mrs. Stair Andrew, 1 Jan. 1919. (M.)
3599 Wallace, Ottilie, Mrs., 1 Jan. 1919. (M.)
3601 Anderson, Alexander Colin, 1 Jan. 1919.
3602 Anderson, Maurice Fitzgerald, 1 Jan. 1919.
3603 Angel, Sydney James Hounsell, 1 Jan. 1919.
3604 Armstrong, Francis Joseph, 1 Jan. 1919.
3605 Atkin, Percy Harland, 1 Jan. 1919.
3606 Austen, Harold Cholmley Mansfield, 1 Jan. 1919.
3607 Aveline, William Rebotier, 1 Jan. 1919.
3608 Baillie, James Black, 1 Jan. 1919.
3609 Barber, William David, 1 Jan. 1919.
3610 Barber, Mabel Emily, 1 Jan. 1919.
3611 Barnes, Thomas James, 1 Jan. 1919.
3612 Baron, Barclay, 1 Jan. 1919.
3613 Bates, Sir Richard Dawson, 1 Jan. 1919.
3614 Batty, Rev. Basil Staunton, 1 Jan. 1919.
3615 Beauchamp, Agneta Frances, 1 Jan. 1919.
3616 Bell, Charles Thornhill, 1 Jan. 1919. (M.)
3617 Bennett, Arthur Henry, 1 Jan. 1919.
3618 Van Bergen, Ethel, Mrs., 1 Jan. 1919.
3619 Bevan, Jean, Mrs., 1 Jan. 1919.
3620 Bigge, Edith Lindsay, Lady Selby-, 1 Jan. 1919.
3621 Binney, Harold William Meares, 1 Jan.1919.
3622 Birkett, Matthew Stevenson, 1 Jan. 1919.
3623 Bishop, Pearl Hall, Mrs., 1 Jan. 1919.
3624 Blake, Owen Vincent, 1 Jan. 1919.
3625 Blythen, Stanley, 1 Jan. 1919.
3626 Booth, Alfred Watson, 1 Jan. 1919.
3627 Borthwick, Albert William, 1 Jan. 1919.
3628 Boughey, George Menteth, 1 Jan. 1919.
3629 Bourdeaux, Henry Frank, 1 Jan. 1919.
3630 Bowen, William Korff, 1 Jan. 1919.
3631 Bradford, Mary, Lady, 1 Jan. 1919.
3632 Brand, Edward Murray, 1 Jan. 1919.
3633 Brassey, Maude Helena, Hon. Mrs., 1 Jan. 1919.
3634 Brechin, Rev. Edwin James, 1 Jan. 1919.
3635 Brighten, Edgcumbe Rendle, 1 Jan. 1919.
3636 Broadmead, Edith, Mrs., 1 Jan. 1919.
3637 Brougham, Diana Isabel, Hon. Mrs., 1 Jan. 1919
3638 Bruce, Marion, Mrs., 1 Jan. 1919.
3639 Du Buisson, Henry, 1 Jan. 1919.
3641 Bulman, George Purvis, 1 Jan. 1919. (M.)
3642 Burchardt, Christiana Mary, 1 Jan. 1919.
3643 Burns, Hon. Emily Dunbar, 1 Jan. 1919.
3644 Bussell, Albert Cecil, 1 Jan. 1919. (M.)
3645 Bussell, Percy Dale, 1 Jan. 1919.
3646 Buxton, Frances Mary, 1 Jan. 1919.
3647 Byron, Margaret Dorothy, 1 Jan. 1919.
3648 Cadbury, Laurence John, 1 Jan. 1919.
3649 Calder, Reginald Colin, 1 Jan. 1919.
3650 Campbell, Archibald Charles, 1 Jan. 1919.
3651 Campion, Mary Gertrude, 1 Jan. 1919.
3652 Cannon, Percival Charles, 1 Jan. 1919. (M.)
3653 Cantlie, Mabel Barclay, Lady, 1 Jan. 1919.
3654 Case, Thomas Henry Towler, 1 Jan. 1919.
3655 Chalmers, Kenneth Edlmann, 1 Jan. 1919.
3656 Chivers, George Tanner, 1 Jan. 1919.
3657 Clarke, Harold Thomas, 1 Jan. 1919.
3658 Cliff, Edith Maud, 1 Jan. 1919.
3659 Clutterbuck, Lewis St. John Rawlinson, 1 Jan. 1919.
3660 Cochrane, Blair Onslow, 1 Jan. 1919.
3662 Cocks, Albert Edward, 1 Jan. 1919.
3663 Codd, Arthur William, 1 Jan. 1919.
3665 Colson, Charles Henry, 1 Jan. 1919.
3666 Combridge, Cornelius, 1 Jan. 1919.
3667 Cookson, Kenneth, 1 Jan. 1919.
3668 Cooper, Charlotte Leonora, Lady, 1 Jan. 1919.
3669 Corless, Richard, 1 Jan. 1919.
3671 Costello, Frederick, 1 Jan. 1919.
3672 Courtney, Reginald Sydney, 1 Jan. 1919.
3673 Cox, Aedan, 1 Jan. 1919. (M.)
3674 Cribbes, George, 1 Jan. 1919.
3675 Crosbie, Maxwell Arthur, 1 Jan. 1919.
3676 Crowley, Cuthbert, 1 Jan. 1919.
3677 Crowther, William, 1 Jan. 1919.
3678 Culley, Zella Evelyn, Mrs. Leather, 1 Jan. 1919.
3679 Cumming, John Fleetwood, 1 Jan. 1919. (M.)
3680 Curr, Thomas, 1 Jan. 1919.
3681 Curry, Phillip Arthur, 1 Jan. 1919.
3682 Cutbush, Mabel Jane, 1 Jan. 1919.
3683 David, Maud Anne, 1 Jan. 1919.
3684 Davidson, George, 1 Jan. 1919.
3685 Davies, Edwin Harold, 1 Jan. 1919.
3686 Davies, Thomas, 1 Jan. 1919.
3687 Davis, Florence Mary, Mrs., 1 Jan. 1919.
3688 Davis, Kenneth Randall, 1 Jan. 1919.
3689 Davy, Francis Herbert Mountjoy Nelson Humphrey-, 1 Jan. 1919.
3690 Disraeli, Marion Grace, Mrs., 1 Jan. 1919.

3691 Dobbs, George Cadell, 1 Jan. 1919.
3692 Doncaster, Robert, 1 Jan. 1919.
3694 Drake, William Henry Milverton, 1 Jan. 1919.
3695 Dunn, James Dunn, 1 Jan. 1919.
3696 Durler, Nora Kathleen, Mrs., 1 Jan. 1919.
3697 Eastham, William Pelham, 1 Jan. 1919.
3698 Edmonds, William Stanley, 1 Jan. 1919.
3699 Edwards, George, 1 Jan. 1919.
3700 Elford, Archibald Selton, 1 Jan. 1919.
3701 Elliott, Alexander Macbeth, 1 Jan. 1919.
3703 Enness, Minnie, Mrs., 1 Jan. 1919.
3704 Esplen, James Jonhstone, 1 Jan. 1919.
3705 Etherton, George Hammond, 1 Jan. 1919.
3706 Ewen, John Taylor, 1 Jan. 1919.
3707 Fardell, Flora Emily, 1 Jan. 1919.
3708 Farren, Hugh Richard, 1 Jan. 1919.
3709 Ferguson, Alfred Cornwall, 1 Jan. 1919.
3710 Ferguson, Anthony, 1 Jan. 1919.
3711 Ferguson, Louis, 1 Jan. 1919.
3712 Fife, William, 1 Jan. 1919.
3713 Finlayson, David John, 1 Jan. 1919.
3714 Foot, George Edgar, 1 Jan. 1919.
3715 Forbes, Arthur Charles, 1 Jan. 1919.
3716 Ford, Everard Allen, 1 Jan. 1919.
3717 Forster, John James, 1 Jan. 1919.
3718 Foster, Robert John, 1 Jan. 1919.
3719 Fowler, Margaret Mary Maitland, Mrs., 1 Jan. 1919.
3720 Fraser, Florence, Mrs., 1 Jan. 1919.
3721 Fulton, Hamilton, 1 Jan. 1919.
3722 Garcia, Henry John Edward, 1 Jan. 1919.
3723 Gardner, John Campbell, 1 Jan. 1919. (M.)
3724 George, William, 1 Jan. 1919.
3725 Gibbs, Henry, 1 Jan. 1919.
3726 Gibson, Charles Stanley, 1 Jan. 1919.
3727 Gillett, Edwin, 1 Jan. 1919.
3728 Gleghorn, Thomas Richard, 1 Jan. 1919.
3729 Goldsmith, Edward, 1 Jan. 1919.
3731 Good, John, 1 Jan. 1919.
3732 Goodall, Clarence Noel, 1 Jan. 1919.
3733 Goodenough, Henrietta Margaret, Hon. Mrs., 1 Jan. 1919.
3734 Gower, Robert Vaughan, 1 Jan. 1919.
3735 Graham, Mary Bremner, 1 Jan. 1919.
3736 Greer, Olivia Mary, Mrs., 1 Jan. 1919.
3737 Grey, John Temperley, 1 Jan. 1919.
3738 Grimwood, James, 1 Jan. 1919.
3739 Gurney, Catherine, 1 Jan. 1919.
3740 Hambly, George Francis, 1 Jan. 1919.
3741 Handford, John James William, 1 Jan. 1919.
3742 Harding, John Rudge, 1 Jan. 1919.
3743 Hardisty, Arthur Hobson, 1 Jan. 1919.
3744 Harrison, Henry, 1 Jan. 1919. (M.)
3745 Hay, David Allan, 1 Jan. 1919.
3746 Hayne, Frederick William, 1 Jan. 1919.
3747 Hedley, Mary Elizabeth, Mrs., 1 Jan. 1919.
3748 Henderson, Eveleen Mary, Mrs., 1 Jan. 1919.
3749 Hendriks, Henry Leslie, 1 Jan. 1919.
3750 Henry, Alice Helen, Mrs., 1 Jan. 1919.
3751 Hewan, Elliot Dunville, 1 Jan. 1919.
3753 Hiley, Mary, Mrs., 1 Jan. 1919.
3754 Hindley, Edith Cairns, 1 Jan. 1919.
3755 Hoad, Lewis, 1 Jan. 1919.
3756 Hobbs, Walter Edward, 1 Jan. 1919.
3757 Hobden, Gideon, 1 Jan. 1919.
3758 Hodgson, Edward Highton, 1 Jan. 1919.
3759 Hogg, John Ewer Jefferson, 1 Jan. 1919.
3760 Holland, Robert Wolstenholme, 1 Jan. 1919.
3761 Holt, Frederick, 1 Jan. 1919.
3762 Horner, Frances Jane, Lady, 1 Jan. 1919.
3763 Horton, Ernest Charles, 1 Jan. 1919.
3764 Houston, Charles Marshall, 1 Jan. 1919.
3765 Hulme, Agnes Maud, 1 Jan. 1919.
3766 Hunt, John Herbert, 1 Jan. 1919.
3767 Huth, Bertha, Mrs., 1 Jan. 1919.
3768 Hyde, Katharine Anne, Mrs., 1 Jan. 1919.
3769 Isaacs, Mariette, Mrs., 1 Jan. 1919.
3770 Jacob, John Hier, 1 Jan. 1919.
3771 James, Frederick Ernest, 1 Jan. 1919.
3772 Johnson, Mary, Mrs., 1 Jan. 1919.
3774 Jones, Ernest Stephens, 1 Jan. 1919.
3775 Jones, Reginald John Wallis-, 1 Jan. 1919. (M.)
3776 Jones, Samuel Glynne, 1 Jan. 1919.
3777 Joy, Henry, 1 Jan. 1919.
3778 Kay, Mary Lees, Mrs., 1 Jan. 1919.
3779 Keatinge, Reginald Heber, 1 Jan. 1919.
3780 Kelcey, William Foord-, 1 Jan. 1919.
3781 Kendall, William Thomas, 1 Jan. 1919.
3782 Kennedy, John Macfarlane, 1 Jan. 1919.
3783 Kerr, Martha, Mrs., 1 Jan. 1919.
3784 Kerr, Muriel Constance, Mrs., 1 Jan. 1919.
3785 Kimber, Augustus Charles Edmund, 1 Jan. 1919.
3786 King, Alice Cicell, 1 Jan. 1919.
3787 King, Henry Smails, 1 Jan. 1919.
3788 King, William Frederick, 1 Jan. 1919.
3789 Kittoe, Montague Francis Markham Sloane-, 1 Jan. 1919. (M.)
3790 Knight, Ethel Corbet, 1 Jan. 1919.
3791 Knowles, Christine, 1 Jan. 1919.
3792 Kouyoumdjian, Manouk, 1 Jan. 1919.
3793 Laurie, Annie Macpherson, Mrs., 1 Jan. 1919.

3794 Leech, Samuel Chetwynd, 1 Jan. 1919.
3795 Legros, Lucien Alphonse, 1 Jan. 1919.
3796 Lewis, Henry, 1 Jan. 1919.
3797 Lewis, John, 1 Jan. 1919.
3798 Lewis, Margaret Blanche, 1 Jan. 1919.
3799 Linton, Charles, 1 Jan. 1919.
3800 Lloyd, Thomas Henry, 1 Jan. 1919. (M.)
3801 Locke, William, 1 Jan. 1919.
3802 Lohden, Frederick Charles, 1 Jan. 1919.
3803 Long, Edward Ernest, 1 Jan. 1919.
3804 Loudon, Mary Sophia, Mrs., 1 Jan. 1919.
3805 Lunn, John Reuben, 1 Jan. 1919.
3806 Luttrell, Mary Fownes, 1 Jan. 1919.
3807 Macewen, Hugh Allan, 1 Jan. 1919.
3808 Macfarlane, James Colquhoun, 1 Jan. 1919.
3809 McFarlane, Lauchlan Grant, 1 Jan. 1919.
3810 Macfarlane, Malcolm, 1 Jan. 1919.
3811 McGrigor, Margaret Annie Kay, Mrs., 1 Jan. 1919.
3812 McKenzie, Hon. Robert Donald, 1 Jan. 1919.
3813 McLean, John Reid, 1 Jan. 1919.
3814 MacLeod Murray, 1 Jan. 1919. (M.)
3816 McNab, Wallace John, 1 Jan. 1919.
3817 Maconochie, Robert Henry, 1 Jan. 1919.
3818 Macoun, James, 1 Jan. 1919.
3819 Macphail, Douglas Ross, 1 Jan. 1919.
3820 MacPherson, Thomas, 1 Jan. 1919.
3821 Macqueen, Frances Helen, Mrs., 1 Jan. 1919.
3822 MacSwinney, Elsie Trant, 1 Jan. 1919.
3823 Manley, Kate, 1 Jan. 1919.
3824 Manning, Edith Lindsay, 1 Jan. 1919.
3825 Marlow, Edmund George, 1 Jan. 1919.
3826 Marquand, Alan Herbert, 1 Jan. 1919.
3827 Marrack, Philip Edward, 1 Jan. 1919.
3828 Marshall, Arthur Timothy, 1 Jan. 1919.
3829 Marshall, William Lee, 1 Jan. 1919.
3830 Maynard, Dudley Christopher, 1 Jan. 1919.
3831 Mayne, Olga Moseley, 1 Jan. 1919.
3832 Mayo, Robert Hobart, 1 Jan. 1919. (M.)
3833 Measor, Henry Arthur, 1 Jan. 1919.
3834 Measures, Benjamin, 1 Jan. 1919.
3835 Meulen, Frederick Alan Van der, 1 Jan. 1919.
3836 Middleton, William Aberdein, 1 Jan. 1919.
3837 Miles, William, 1 Jan. 1919.
3838 Miller, Ellen Cameron, Mrs., 1 Jan. 1919.
3839 Miller, Irene Helen, Mrs., 1 Jan. 1919.
3840 Milne, George Torrance, 1 Jan. 1919.
3841 Mitchell, Albert Ernest, 1 Jan. 1919.
3842 Morgan, William Henry, 1 Jan. 1919.
3843 Morison, William Roger, 1 Jan. 1919.
3844 Morris, Cynthia Gertrude, Mrs., 1 Jan. 1919.
3845 Moseley, Miriam Louise, Mrs., 1 Jan. 1919.
3846 Mostyn, Mary Florence Edith, Lady, 1 Jan. 1919.
3847 Mudie, Annie Bertha, Mrs., 1 Jan. 1919.
3848 Mundy, Catherine, Mrs. Miller, 1 Jan. 1919.
3849 Murchie, Archibald, 1 Jan. 1919.
3851 Nisbet, Henry Kingscote, 1 Jan. 1919.
3852 Norbury, Lionel Edward Close, 1 Jan. 1919.
3853 Norman, Percy George, 1 Jan. 1919.
3854 Northam, Walter Arthur, 1 Jan. 1919.
3855 Nuttall, May, Mrs., 1 Jan. 1919.
3856 O'Brien, Beatrice Jane, 1 Jan. 1919.
3857 O'Donnell, James Rodney, 1 Jan. 1919.
3858 Oliver, Arthur Maule, 1 Jan. 1919.
3859 O'Neill, Herbert Charles, 1 Jan. 1919.
3860 Onslow, Harriet Katharine, 1 Jan. 1919.
3862 Palmer, Walter Benjamin, 1 Jan. 1919.
3863 Pate, George, 1 Jan. 1919.
3864 Patterson, George, 1 Jan. 1919.
3865 Paul, William Francis, 1 Jan. 1919.
3867 Peck, Margaret Catharine, 1 Jan. 1919.
3868 Perrin, Rev. Howard Nasmith, 1 Jan. 1919.
3869 Phillip, William Littlejohn, 1 Jan. 1919.
3870 Phillips, John Robert, 1 Jan. 1919.
3871 Pinkney, Samuel Renny, 1 Jan. 1919.
3872 De La Poer, Mary Olivia, Hon. Mrs., 1 Jan. 1919.
3873 Powell, Margaret Joyce, 1 Jan. 1919.
3874 Pretyman, Lady Beatrice Adine, 1 Jan. 1919.
3875 Quayle, John, 1 Jan. 1919.
3876 Raikes, Ernest Barkley, 1 Jan. 1919.
3877 Ramsay, John Maclean, 1 Jan. 1919.
3878 Rankine, Alexander Oliver, 1 Jan. 1919.
3879 Rawlinson, Ralph George Joynson, 1 Jan. 1919.
3880 Reading, Harry Thomas, 1 Jan. 1919.
3881 Rees, David Valentine, 1 Jan. 1919.
3882 Rees, Joseph Cook, 1 Jan. 1919.
3883 Reid, Charles, 1 Jan. 1919.
3884 Ricardo, Katherine Alice, 1 Jan. 1919.
3885 Rice, Fabian Arthur Besant, 1 Jan. 1919.
3886 Richardson, Harry, 1 Jan. 1919.
3887 Riseley, Arthur Henry, 1 Jan. 1919.
3888 Roads, Edith Mary, 1 Jan. 1919.
3889 Robb, John McLorinan, 1 Jan. 1919.
3890 Roberts, Edward Coleridge, 1 Jan. 1919.
3891 Robinson, Katharine Haigh, 1 Jan. 1919.
3892 Robinson, Sir Thomas, 1 Jan. 1919.
3893 Rogers, John Henry, 1 Jan. 1919.
3894 Rollin, Ambrose, 1 Jan. 1919.
3895 Ross, Frederick Alexander, 1 Jan. 1919.
3896 Row, Bessie Rose, 1 Jan. 1919.

3897 Rowcliffe, Clementina Elizabeth Hope, Mrs., 1 Jan. 1919.
3898 Rowell, Henry Snowden, 1 Jan. 1919.
3899 Roxburghe, Anne Emily, Dowager Duchess of, 1 Jan. 1919.
3900 Russell, Hon. Eustace Scott Hamilton-, 1 Jan. 1919.
3901 Russell, Henry Hartley Aloysius, 1 Jan. 1919. (M.)
3902 Ryle, Herbert, 1 Jan. 1919.
3903 Safford, Stella Fanny, 1 Jan. 1919.
3904 St. Clair, Hon. Lockhart Matthew, 1 Jan. 1919.
3905 Sandeman, David Alexander Stewart, 1 Jan. 1919
3906 Sandhurst, Eleanor Mary Caroline, Viscountess, 1 Jan. 1919.
3907 Saunders, George William, 1 Jan. 1919.
3908 Sayers, Joseph, 1 Jan. 1919.
3909 Scholfield, William Farrar, 1 Jan. 1919.
3910 Scott, Adam, 1 Jan. 1919.
3911 Seatle, John Bridson, 1 Jan. 1919.
3912 de Segundo, Charles Sempill, 1 Jan. 1919. (M.)
3913 Selby, Prideaux George, 1 Jan. 1919.
3914 Sells, Julia Perronet, Mrs., 1 Jan. 1919.
3916 Shaw, George Ernest, 1 Jan. 1919.
3917 Shaw, Gwendoline Mary, 1 Jan. 1919.
3918 Shepperd, Walter Henry, 1 Jan. 1919.
3919 Siltzer, Violet Mary, Mrs., 1 Jan. 1919.
3920 Sim, James, 1 Jan. 1919.
3921 Simmons, Stanley Hall, 1 Jan. 1919.
3923 Sinclair, Donald Boase, 1 Jan. 1919. (M.)
3924 Singleton, James Edward, 1 Jan. 1919.
3925 Sitters, Percy Henry Smart, 1 Jan. 1919.
3926 Skeggs, James Buteux, 1 Jan. 1919.
3927 Smail, James Cameron, 1 Jan. 1919.
3928 Small, Elsie Mary, 1 Jan. 1919.
3929 Smith, Edward Rawdon, 1 Jan. 1919. (M.)
3930 Smith, Frances Mary, 1 Jan. 1919.
3931 Smith, Frederick Crawford, 1 Jan. 1919.
3932 Smith, Marshall King, 1 Jan. 1919.
3933 Smith, Sarah Helen, 1 Jan. 1919.
3935 Spear, Wilfrid Guy, 1 Jan. 1919.
3937 Stark, James, 1 Jan. 1919.
3938 Stedman, Isabel Margaret, 1 Jan. 1919.
3939 Stephenson, Philippa Anna Frederica, Mrs., 1 Jan. 1919.
3940 Steward, Alexandrina Ryrie, Mrs., 1 Jan. 1919.
3941 Stewart, John, 1 Jan. 1919.
3942 Stickland, John Northover, 1 Jan. 1919
3943 Stilwell, George Robert Fabris, 1 Jan. 1919.
3945 Stocks, Andrew Denys, 1 Jan. 1919.
3946 Stokes, Irene Mary, 1 Jan. 1919.
3947 Studd, John Edward Kynaston, 1 Jan. 1919.
3950 Taylor, Alexander Thomson, 1 Jan. 1919.
3951 Taylor, William, 1 Jan. 1919.
3952 Tench, Lillian Eugenia, 1 Jan. 1919.
3953 Thirlwell, Thomas William, 1 Jan. 1919.
3954 Thirsk, Richard, 1 Jan. 1919.
3955 Thomas, Ivor Cradock, 1 Jan. 1919.
3956 Thomas, Maude Tuson, 1 Jan. 1919.
3957 Thompson, George Roger, 1 Jan. 1919.
3958 Till, Thomas Marson, 1 Jan. 1919.
3959 Timins, Douglas Theodore, 1 Jan. 1919.
3960 Tinniswood, Robert, 1 Jan. 1919.
3961 Tracy, Cyprienne Emma Madeleine Hanbury-, 1 Jan. 1919.
3962 Trant, Alfred William Vincent, 1 Jan. 1919.
3963 Trotter, Ellinor, Hon. Mrs., 1 Jan. 1919.
3964 Tubbs, Lucinda Elizabeth Alexandra, Mrs., 1 Jan. 1919.
3965 Turner, George, 1 Jan. 1919.
3966 Turner, Samuel Thomas, 1 Jan. 1919.
3967 Turner, William Ernest Stephen, 1 Jan. 1919.
3968 Turpin, Helena Augusta Mary, Mrs., 1 Jan. 1919.
3969 Urie, John, 1 Jan. 1919.
3970 Vaughan, Janet Feliza, 1 Jan. 1919.
3971 Venables, Caroline Emily, 1 Jan. 1919.
3972 Waggett, Constance, Mrs., 1 Jan. 1919.
3973 Wake, Richard, 1 Jan. 1919.
3974 Waters, Roger Donald, 1 Jan. 1919.
3975 Watkins, William Edward, 1 Jan. 1919.
3976 Watson, Dorothy Bannerman, Mrs., 1 Jan. 1919.
3977 Watson, Douglas Home, 1 Jan. 1919. (M.)
3978 Watson, Edith Deverell, Mrs., 1 Jan. 1919.
3979 Wayman, Myers, 1 Jan. 1919.
3980 Webster, George, 1 Jan. 1919.
3981 Wedderburn, Ernest Maclagan-, 1 Jan. 1919. (M.)
3982 Welborn, George Coulson, 1 Jan. 1919.
3983 Wells, James Laurence, 1 Jan. 1919.
3984 Wheler, Florence Ffaith, Mrs. Hastings, 1 Jan. 1919.
3985 Whiller, Annie, Mrs., 1 Jan. 1919.
3986 Whitbread, Beatrice, 1 Jan. 1919.
3987 Whittaker, George, 1 Jan. 1919.
3988 Whyte, William de Burgh, 1 Jan. 1919.
3989 Whyte, William Edward, 1 Jan. 1919.
3990 Wilkins, John, 1 Jan. 1919.
3991 Williams, Charles, 1 Jan. 1919.
3992 Williams, Harris Gregory, 1 Jan. 1919.
3993 Williams, William Nance, 1 Jan. 1919.
3994 Williamson, Michael, 1 Jan. 1919. (M.)
3995 Wilmot, Edith, Mrs., 1 Jan. 1919.
3996 Wilson, Charlotte Mary, Mrs., 1 Jan. 1919.
3997 Wilson, David, 1 Jan. 1919.
3998 Wilson, Helena Jane, Mrs., 1 Jan. 1919.
3999 Wilson, Henry Adrian Fitzroy, 1 Jan. 1919.
4000 Wilson, Richard William, 1 Jan. 1919.

4001 Winram, Agnes Rankine, Mrs., 1 Jan. 1919.
4002 Winter, George Mitchell, 1 Jan. 1919.
4003 Terrington, Lord, 1 Jan. 1919. (M.)
4004 Wren, Evelyn Emma Amelia, Mrs., 1 Jan. 1919.
4005 Wright, John Brown, 1 Jan. 1919.
4006 Yeaxlee, Rev. Basil Alfred, 1 Jan. 1919.
4007 Abbott, John Harold, 1 Jan. 1919.
4008 Addis, Frederick Henry, 1 Jan. 1919.
4009 Balfour, Alfred Stevenson, 1 Jan. 1919.
4010 Bali, Rai Rajeshwar, 1 Jan. 1919.
4011 Barne, Rev. George Dunsford, 1 Jan. 1919.
4012 Bell, Arthur Morton, 1 Jan. 1919.
4013 Best, Hon. James William, 1 Jan. 1919.
4014 Beyts, Clement Ayerst, 1 Jan. 1919.
4015 Bingley, Mabel Katherine, Lady, 1 Jan. 1919.
4016 Black, Rev. James, 1 Jan. 1919.
4017 Blackstock, George, 1 Jan. 1919.
4018 Branford, Harold, 1 Jan. 1919.
4019 Broke-Smith, Philip William Lilian, 1 Jan. 1919.
4020 Brown, Arthur Cecil, 1 Jan. 1919.
4021 Bruce, Charles Edward, 1 Jan. 1919.
4022 Burrup, John Arthur Evans, 1 Jan. 1919.
4023 Chand, Rao Bahadur Choudhri Lal, 1 Jan. 1919.
4024 Chand, Rai Bahadur Lala Karam, 1 Jan. 1919.
4025 Chase, Alfred James, 1 Jan. 1919.
4026 Chenevix-Trench, Richard Henry, 1 Jan. 1919.
4027 Coburn, Marmaduke Robert, 1 Jan. 1919.
4028 Collins, Godfrey Ferdinando Stratford, 1 Jan. 1919.
4029 Cooke, Thomas Fothergill, 1 Jan. 1919.
4030 Cowley, Robert Mansfield, 1 Jan. 1919.
4031 Davys, Maud Lilian, Mrs., 1 Jan. 1919.
4032 Deo, Rani Chandelin Ju, 1 Jan. 1919.
4033 Digby-Beste, Henry Aloysius Bruno, 1 Jan. 1919.
4034 Drake, John Collard Bernard, 1 Jan. 1919.
4035 Ellis, Kate Hannah, Mrs., 1 Jan. 1919.
4036 Elwes, Aline, Mrs., 1 Jan. 1919.
4037 Feiling, Keith Grahame, 1 Jan. 1919.
4038 Ferguson, John Alexander, 1 Jan. 1919.
4039 Ferrar, Michael Lloyd, 1 Jan. 1919.
4040 Gamlen, Robert Loraine, 1 Jan. 1919.
4041 Gilbert, James Ainsworth, 1 Jan. 1919.
4042 Girard, Marie, Mrs., 1 Jan. 1919.
4043 Godden, James William Mineard, 1 Jan. 1919.
4044 Hannyngton, Mary, Mrs. John Arthur, 1 Jan. 1919.
4045 Harris, Thomas Guy Marriott, 1 Jan. 1919.
4046 Hopkins, Robert Hemiss Handasyd, 1 Jan. 1919.
4047 Hopkyns, William Stenning, 1 Jan. 1919.
4048 Hunt, Francis Dillon, 1 Jan. 1919.
4049 Husain, Khan Bahadur Muhammad Aziz-ud-Din, 1 Jan. 1919.
4050 Husain, Shaikh Shahid, 1 Jan. 1919.
4051 Kendrick, Sidney John, 1 Jan. 1919.
4052 Khan, Khan Bahadar Nawao Muhammad Muzammi-lullah, 1 Jan. 1919.
4053 Khan, Khan Bahadur Arbab Dost Muhammad, 1 Jan. 1919.
4054 Khan, Kahn Bahadur Malik Muhammad Amin, 1 Jan. 1919.
4055 Latouche, George Henry Stransham, 1 Jan. 1919.
4056 Leigh, Maxwell Studdy, 1 Jan. 1919.
4057 LeMesurier, Thomas Henry, 1 Jan. 1919.
4058 Litster, William James, 1 Jan. 1919.
4059 Loch, Edward Campbell, 1 Jan. 1919.
4060 Lomas, Hugh Arthur, 1 Jan. 1919.
4061 Luxmore, Ethel, Mrs., 1 Jan. 1919.
4062 MacCaw, Vivian Hardy, 1 Jan. 1919.
4063 Maffey, Dorothy, Mrs., 1 Jan. 1919.
4064 Majid, Abdul, 1 Jan. 1919.
4065 Marker, Kahn Bahadur Ardeshir Dossabhoy. 1 Jan. 1919.
4066 Martin, Frederick Barclay, 1 Jan. 1919.
4067 Mason, Adeline, Mrs., 1 Jan. 1919.
4068 Mathers, Rev. James, 1 Jan. 1919.
4069 McMichael, John Fisher, 1 Jan. 1919.
4070 McNair, Arthur Wyndham, 1 Jan. 1919.
4071 Meikle, John James, 1 Jan. 1919.
4072 Mitchell, Hugh Henry Gordon, 1 Jan. 1919.
4073 Money, Wigram Seymour Elliot, 1 Jan. 1919.
4074 Montefiore, Claude Emanuel, 1 Jan. 1919.
4075 Mort, Arthur, 1 Jan. 1919.
4076 Mules, Sir Horace Charles, 1 Jan. 1919.
4077 Mumford, Charles Allan, 1 Jan. 1919.
4078 Nelson, Arthur Edward, 1 Jan. 1919.
4079 Oakden, Ralph, 1 Jan. 1919.
4080 Page, Frederick James, 1 Jan. 1919.
4081 Paterson, Herbert John, 1 Jan. 1919.
4082 Powell, Hon. John, 1 Jan. 1919.
4084 Robinson, Horace Astell Lynn, 1 Jan. 1919.
4085 Rodger, Alexander, 1 Jan. 1919.
4087 Rudkin, George Drury, 1 Jan. 1919.
4088 Sah, Raja Lokendra, 1 Jan. 1919.
4089 Sands, Charles Edward Walker, 1 Jan. 1919.
4090 Scott, Ernest Alexander, 1 Jan. 1919.
4091 Shah, Khan Bahadur Sayyid Mahdi, 1 Jan. 1919.
4092 Shelton, Robert Melvin, 1 Jan. 1919.
4093 Silvester, Colin Joseph, 1 Jan. 1919.
4094 Simkins, Helen, Mrs., 1 Jan. 1919.
4095 Singh, Rai Bahadur Bhaiya Ganga Baksh, 1 Jan. 1919.
4096 Singh, Sardar Bahadur Gajjan, 1 Jan. 1919.

4097 Singh, Raja Parbal Partab, 1 Jan. 1919.
4098 Stevens, James Algernon, 1 Jan. 1919.
4099 Stewart, Helen Osmer, Mrs., 1 Jan. 1919.
4100 Stow, Alexander Montagu, 1 Jan. 1919.
4101 Street, Clare, Mrs., 1 Jan. 1919.
4102 Swaine, Ethel, 1 Jan. 1919.
4103 Symons. Rudolph Victor, 1 Jan. 1919.
4104 Tha, Maung Po, 1 Jan. 1919.
4105 Thompson Edgar, 1 Jan. 1919.
4106 Thompson, Frank Stuart Corbitt 1 Jan. 1919.
4107 Todd, Reginald, 1 Jan. 1919.
4108 Todhunter, Alice, Mrs., 1 Jan. 1919.
4109 Tomb, John Walker, 1 Jan. 1919.
4110 Trevor, Digby Bruce, 1 Jan. 1919.
4111 Tsong, Lim Chin, 1 Jan. 1919.
4112 Turner, James Wilson, 1 Jan. 1919.
4113 Ure, Georgina Jean Elizabeth, Mrs., 1 Jan. 1919.
4114 Walpole, Charles Archibald, 1 Jan. 1919.
4115 Williams, Rev. Garfield, 1 Jan. 1919.
4116 Worsley, Geoffrey, 1 Jan. 1919.
4117 Hornblower, George Davis, 1 Jan. 1919.
4118 Garvice, Chudleigh, 1 Jan. 1919.
4119 Madden, Frank Cole, 1 Jan. 1919.
4120 Scott, John Archibald, 1 Jan. 1919.
4121 Rolo, Robert, 1 Jan. 1919.
4122 Wheatley, Mervyn James, 1 Jan. 1919.
4123 Hewison, Robert, 1 Jan. 1919.
4124 Huddleston, Arthur James Croft, 1 Jan. 1919.
4125 Willis, Charles Armine, 1 Jan. 1919.
4126 Ker, Hugh T., 1 Jan. 1919. (M.)
4127 Adams, John Basil Franklin, 1 Jan. 1919. (M.)
4128 Appleby, Kinloch Arthur, 1 Jan. 1919. (M.)
4129 Avery, John Edgar, 1 Jan. 1919. (M.)
4130 Wall, Charles Percivale Bligh, 1 Jan. 1919. (M.)
4131 Block, Isidore Jack, 1 Jan. 1919. (M.)
4132 Britten, Wallace Ernest, 1 Jan. 1919. (M.)
4133 Brown, Arthur Edmund, 1 Jan. 1919. (M.)
4134 Carolin, George Ievers, 1 Jan. 1919. (M.)
4135 Carpenter, Henry, 1 Jan. 1919. (M.)
4136 Connan, John Cranmer, 1 Jan. 1919. (M.)
4137 Cossey, Harry John Moore, 1 Jan. 1919. (M.)
4138 Cotton, Maurice John, 1Jan. 1919. (M.)
4139 Dudgeon, Arthur Frederick, 1 Jan. 1919. (M.)
4140 Du Frayer, Alfred Henry, 1 Jan. 1919. (M.)
4141 Eldred, Arthur George, 1 Jan. 1919. (M.)
4142 Gardner, Frederick William, 1 Jan. 1919. (M.)
4143 Geipel, Kenneth Shute, 1 Jan. 1919. (M.)
4144 Graham, Charles Townley, 1 Jan. 1919. (M.)
4145 Harvey, Robert Bald, 1 Jan. 1919. (M.)
4146 Henderson, Christopher Woodall, 1 Jan. 1919. (M.)
4147 Hoare, Charles E., 1 Jan. 1919. (M.)
4148 Home, George Archibald Swinton, 1 Jan. 1919. (M.)
4151 Howie, Adrian Morrison, 1 Jan. 1919. (M.)
4152 Hudson, Charles, 1 Jan. 1919. (M.)
4153 Jackson, Thomas Eldridge, 1 Jan. 1919. (M.)
4154 Jeffery, George Russell, 1 Jan. 1919. (M.)
4155 Jones, Basil Dennis, 1 Jan. 1919. (M.)
4156 Kettle, Harry Philip, 1 Jan. 1919. (M.)
4157 Lynn, William Davies Eliott, 1 Jan. 1919. (M.)
4158 Madge, Quintus, 1 Jan. 1919. (M.)
4159 Margach, Lewis Grant, 1 Jan. 1919. (M.)
4160 Marshall, Legh Richmond Herbert Peter, 1 Jan. 1919. (M.)
4161 Mason, Samuel, 1 Jan. 1919. (M.)
4162 Millar, George McGregor, 1 Jan. 1919. (M.)
4163 Moore, George James, 1 Jan. 1919. (M.)
4164 Morris, James Hulbert, 1 Jan. 1919. (M.)
4165 Murton, Ivo Murray, 1 Jan. 1919. (M.)
4166 Orde-Browne, Granville St. John, 1 Jan. 1919. (M.)
4167 Overell, Percy William, 1 Jan. 1919. (M.)
4168 Page, Francis James, 1 Jan. 1919. (M.)
4169 Phillips, Percival, 1 Jan. 1919. (M.)
4170 Puntis, Walter Ernest, 1 Jan. 1919. (M.)
4171 Roberts, Cecil Henry Woolcott, 1 Jan. 1919. (M.)
4172 Saville-Farr, Arthur James Melancthon, 1 Jan. 1919. (M.)
4173 Semple, Robert, 1 Jan. 1919. (M.)
4174 Simpson, William Slessor, 1 Jan. 1919. (M.)
4175 Smith, Albert Augustus, 1 Jan. 1919. (M.)
4176 Smith, Allison Eugene, 1 Jan. 1919. (M.)
4177 Smith, Ronald Maskelyen, 1 Jan. 1919. (M.)
4178 Standish-White, Robert, 1 Jan. 1919. (M.)
4179 Stokes, Francis Maurice Collins, 1 Jan. 1919. (M)
4180 Thomson, John Patrick, 1 Jan. 1919. (M.)
4181 Tosswill, Frank Speare, 1 Jan. 1919. (M.)
4182 Trelawny, James Edward Salusbury, 1 Jan. 1919. (M.)
4183 Turner, George Ell, 1 Jan. 1919. (M.)
4184 Verbi, Vladimir Vassil, 1 Jan. 1919. (M.)
4185 West, Stewart Ellis Lawrence, 1 Jan. 1919. (M.)
4186 Aitken, Allan Beacon, 1 Jan. 1919. (M.)
4187 Aldham, Michael Seymour, 1 Jan. 1919. (M.)
4188 Alexander, Robert Donald Thain, 1 Jan. 1919. (M.)
4189 Blaker, William Frederick, 1 Jan. 1919. (M.)
4190 Boyce, Clement James, 1 Jan. 1919. (M.)
4191 Brock, Charles Henry, 1 Jan. 1919. (M.)
4192 Brunskill, John Handfield, 1 Jan. 1919. (M.)
4193 Burn, Robert Nathaniel, 1 Jan. 1919. (M.)
4194 Cardwell, William Arthur, 1 Jan. 1919. (M.)
4195 Carty, Samuel Wilfrid, 1 Jan. 1919. (M.)
4196 Cathcart, George Elliot, 1 Jan. 1919. (M.)
4197 Chambers, Robert Alexander 1 Jan. 1919. (M.)

4198 Clifton, Rev. Edward James, 1 Jan. 1919. (M.)
4199 Cockerell, Frederick Peyps, 1 Jan. 1919. (M.)
4200 Cooper, Raymond Willoughby, 1 Jan. 1919. (M.)
4201 Crawford, Stanley Charles Russell, 1 Jan. 1919. (M.)
4202 Davidson, Colin Keppel, 1 Jan. 1919. (M.)
4203 Davies, Llewellyn Wynne, 1 Jan. 1919. (M.)
4204 Davy, Gerald Henry, 1 Jan. 1919. (M.)
4205 Eve, George Thomas, 1 Jan. 1919. (M.)
4206 Farrell, Rev. Bernard, 1 Jan. 1919. (M.)
4207 Frost, George Hewitt, 1 Jan. 1919. (M.)
4208 Furlong, Rev. Hubert, 1 Jan. 1919. (M.)
4209 Griffin, Arthur Cecil, 1 Jan. 1919. (M.)
4210 Guays, Frank Lewis, 1 Jan. 1919. (M.)
4211 Gumbley, Douglas William Mew, 1 Jan. 1919. (M.)
4212 Harris, John Richard, 1 Jan. 1919. (M.)
4213 Harvey, Bertram Lionel, 1 Jan. 1919. (M.)
4214 Hawkes, Frank Roxburgh, 1 Jan. 1919. (M.)
4215 Hendry, Frank Coutts, 1 Jan. 1919. (M.)
4216 Hewer, John Radborn, 1 Jan. 1919. (M.)
4217 Hill, Alfred Lyon, 1 Jan. 1919. (M.)
4218 Howe, William Tuxford, 1 Jan. 1919. (M.)
4219 Howell, Hector Lionel, 1 Jan. 1919. (M.)
4220 Hunter, Reginald Gordon Pulteney, 1 Jan. 1919. (M.)
4221 Hyatt, Percival Taylor, 1 Jan. 1919. (M.)
4222 John, Nichol Shaw, 1 Jan. 1919. (M.)
4223 Johnson, Harold Cecil John, 1 Jan. 1919.
4224 Jones, Percival Walter Edwin, 1 Jan. 1919. (M)
4225 Kauntze, Bertram Charles, 1 Jan. 1919. (M.)
4226 Kemble, Paul Berthon, 1 Jan. 1919. (M.)
4227 Lakin, Colin Arthur, 1 Jan. 1919. (M.)
4228 Lamb, David Ogilvy Wright, 1 Jan. 1919. (M.)
4229 Lander, Arthur, 1 Jan. 1919. (M.)
4230 Leslie, Seymour Granger, 1 Jan. 1919. (M.)
4231 Little, Cuthbert Joseph Harwood, 1 Jan. 1919. (M.)
4232 Loverock, Robert Charles, 1 Jan. 1919. (M.)
4233 Marshall, Gerald Struan, 1 Jan. 1919. (M.)
4234 Mellsop, John Arthur, 1 Jan. 1919. (M.)
4235 Metcalfe, Joseph Noel, 1 Jan. 1919. (M.)
4236 Mitchell, John Phimister, 1 Jan. 1919. (M.)
4237 Moillet, Hubert Mainwaring Keir, 1 Jan. 1919. (M.)
4238 Neilson, Ronald Braco Stenhouse, 1 Jan. 1919. (M.)
4239 Nelson, John Joseph Harper, 1 Jan. 1919. (M.)
4240 Newell, Stanley Monk, 1 Jan. 1919. (M.)
4241 O'Connor, James Lynch, 1 Jan. 1919. (M.)
4242 Penny, Cyril John, 1 Jan. 1919. (M.)
4243 Pope, Seymour Fell, 1 Jan. 1919. (M.)
4244 Preedy, Clement, 1 Jan. 1919. (M.)
4245 Rawson, Geoffrey, 1 Jan. 1919. (M.)
4246 Revnell, Rev. Arthur Jesse, 1 Jan. 1919. (M.)
4247 Riccard, John Stanley, 1 Jan. 1919. (M.)
4248 Robertson, Hugh Given, 1 Jan. 1919.
4249 Scott, Maitland Bodley, 1 Jan. 1919. (M.)
4250 Sheath, William Archibald Sidney, 1 Jan. 1919. (M.) .
4251 Spence, Richard Bennett, 1 Jan. 1919. (M.)
4252 Starkey, Herbert James, 1 Jan. 1919. (M.)
4253 Stevens, Thomas Harry Gouldsworthy, 1 Jan. 1919. (M.)
4254 Storey, Robert, 1 Jan. 1919. (M.)
4255 Tarran, William, 1 Jan. 1919. (M.)
4256 Taunton, John William Lionel, 1 Jan. 1919. (M.)
4257 Turner, Percy William, 1 Jan. 1919. (M.)
4258 Wagstaff, Lewis Cecil, 1 Jan. 1919. (M.)
4259 Waring, Edmund Henry, 1 Jan. 1919. (M.)
4260 Watson, William Douglas, 1 Jan. 1919. (M.)
4261 Weatherall, Nigel Edward 1 Jan. 1919. (M.)
4262 Weir, Peter, 1 Jan. 1919. (M.)
4263 Willis, Richard Dunn, 1 Jan. 1919. (M.)
4264 Wood, Frank Thomas Herbert, 1 Jan. 1919.
4265 Woodhouse, Percy St. John Rance, 1 Jan. 1919. (M.)
4266 Yeld, Richard Kingsley, 1 Jan. 1919. (M.)
4267 Warden, John Weightman, 1 Jan. 1919. (M.)
4268 Starnes, Fred, 1 Jan. 1919. (M.)
4269 Aylward, William, 1 Jan. 1919. (M.)
4270 Churchill, Herbert Forbes, 1 Jan. 1919. (M.)
4271 Collier, Edwin Arthur, 1 Jan. 1919. (M.)
4272 Cox, Humphrey John Hamilton, 1 Jan. 1919. (M.)
4273 Fleming, Baldwyn Henry Francis, 1 Jan. 1919. (M.)
4274 Goodwyn, Julius Henry, 1 Jan. 1919. (M.)
4275 Horner, John FitzLloyd, 1 Jan. 1919. (M.)
4276 Ingilby, John Ughtred McDowall, 1 Jan. 1919. (M.)
4277 Maunsell, Charles Henry Wray, 1 Jan. 1919. (M.)
4278 Read, Philip Austin Ottley, 1 Jan. 1919. (M.)
4279 Richardson, Frederick, 1 Jan. 1919. (M.)
4280 Waiters, Alfred, 1 Jan. 1919. (M.)
4281 Williams, Richard Charles Whittaker, 1 Jan. 1919. (M.)
4282 Duke, Basil Lawrence, 1 Jan. 1919. (M.)
4283 Castellan, Victor Edward, 1 Jan. 1919. (M.)
4284 Davies, Charles Frederick Fellows, 1 Jan. 1919. (M.)
4285 Packford, Charles William, 1 Jan. 1919. (M.)
4286 Shadforth, Harold Anthony, 1 Jan. 1919. (M.)
4287 Cameron, Annie Buchanan, 1 Jan. 1919. (M.)
4288 Humphreys, Elizabeth Clement, 1 Jan. 1919. (M.)
4289 Boulton, James Arthur, 1 Jan. 1919. (M.)
4290 Browne, Francis John, 1 Jan. 1919. (M.)
4291 Eastman, Edward George, 1 Jan. 1919. (M.)
4292 Lessing, Edward Albert, 1 Jan. 1919. (M.)
4293 Pinder, Francis William Stanley, 1 Jan. 1919. (M.)
4294 Robertson, Thomas Alexander, 1 Jan. 1919. (M.)
4295 Schwabe, Charles Parker, 1 Jan. 1919. (M.)
4296 Steveni, Leo, 1 Jan. 1919. (M.)

4297 Bell, James MacKintosh, 1 Jan. 1919. (M.)
4298 Bruce, Charles Edward, 1 Jan. 1919. (M.)
4299 Ruck, Richard Conyers, 1 Jan. 1919. (M.)
4300 Stubbs, Shirley Graham, 1 Jan. 1919. (M.)
4301 Airey, Rowland Montagu, 1 Jan. 1919. (M.)
4302 Anscombe, Richard Stanley, 1 Jan. 1919. (M.)
4303 Ball, Edward, 1 Jan. 1919. (M.)
4304 Bell, Matthew Gerald Edward, 1 Jan. 1919. (M.)
4305 Bruce, Arthur Carlyon, 1 Jan. 1919. (M.)
4306 Currie, Philip John Reginald, 1 Jan. 1919. (M.)
4307 Field, Raymond Ernest, 1 Jan. 1919. (M.)
4308 Greene, Wilfred Arthur, 1 Jan. 1919. (M.)
4309 Griffith-Jones, Morgan Phillips, 1 Jan. 1919. (M.)
4310 Jayne, Arthur Alfred, 1 Jan. 1919. (M.)
4311 Jephson, P. H. R., 1 Jan. 1919. (M.)
4312 Parry, Arthur Haydon, 1 Jan. 1919. (M.)
4313 Ravenscroft, John Arthur, 1 Jan. 1919. (M.)
4314 Richardson, James, 1 Jan. 1919. (M.)
4315 Robertson-Durham, James Alexander, 1 Jan. 1919. (M.)
4316 Rose, Ivor Sainte Croix, 1 Jan. 1919. (M.)
4317 Walkley, Daniel, 1 Jan. 1919. (M.)
4318 Wilson, Walter Carandini, 1 Jan. 1919. (M.)
4319 Alley, Herbert Rutton, 1 Jan. 1919. (M.)
4320 Kingman, Abner, 1 Jan. 1919. (M.)
4321 Miller, Walter, 1 Jan. 1919. (M.)
4322 Angelo, Alfred, 1 Jan. 1919.
4323 Fairhurst, Archibald, 1 Jan. 1919.
4325 Moir, Ian, 1 Jan. 1919.
4326 Hemsted, Rupert William, 1 Jan. 1919.
4327 Beatty, Francis Montague Algernon, 1 Jan. 1919.
4328a Pierce, Helen, 1 Jan. 1919.
4328b Smith, Arthur Henderson, 1 Jan. 1919. (M.)
4328c Stokes, William Noel, 1 Jan. 1919. (M.)
4328d Ball, George Joseph, 1 Jan. 1919. (M.)
4329 Temple, Reginald Cecil, 12 Feb. 1919. (M.)
4330 Sinclair, Walter, 12 Feb. 1919. (M.)
4331 Eady, George Griffin, 12 Feb. 1919. (M.)
4332 Binns, Cuthbert Evelyn, 12 Feb. 1919. (M.)
4333 Myres, John Linton, 12 Feb. 1919. (M.)
4334 Hudson, Charles Edward, 12 Feb. 1919. (M.)
4335 Sykes, Percy Stanley, 12 Feb. 1919. (M.)
4336 Tiarkes, Frank Cecil, 12 Feb. 1919. (M.)
4337 Clarke, William Francis, 12 Feb. 1919. (M.)
4338 Johnson, Thomas Frank, 12 Feb. 1919. (M.)
4339 Hall, Archibald Holte, 12 Feb. 1919. (M.)
4340 Reid, Lionel, 12 Feb. 1919. (M.)
4341 Boyce, Ernest Thomas, 12 Feb. 1919. (M.)
4342 Hooker, Charles William Ross, 12 Feb. 1919. (M.)
4343 Van der Heuvel, Frederick William Arthur, Count, 12 Feb. 1919. (M.)
4344 Dickinson, James, 12 Feb. 1919. (M.)
4345 Landau, Henry, 12 Feb. 1919. (M.)
4346 Aitken, Robert Young, 18 Feb. 1919.
4347 Andrews, George Edward Genge-, 18 Feb. 1919.
4348 Atkinson, George James Mouncey, 18 Feb. 1919.
4349 Banks, Isaac, 18 Feb. 1919.
4350 Barter, Richard Henry, 18 Feb. 1919.
4351 Bentall, William Charles, 18 Feb. 1919.
4352 Blackett, Edward Joseph, 18 Feb. 1919.
4353 Blomfield, Joseph, 18 Feb. 1919.
4354 Brown, Frederick Lenox Harman, 18 Feb. 1919.
4355 Cadge, William Hotson, 18 Feb. 1919.
4356 Cashen, John, 18 Feb. 1919.
4357 Day, James John, 18 Feb. 1919.
4358 Elliott, John, 18 Feb. 1919.
4359 Elton, Henry Brown, 18 Feb. 1919.
4360 Ewart, David, 18 Feb. 1919.
4361 Fairweather, Francis Harold, 18 Feb. 1919.
4362 Farnell, Henry Dawson, 18 Feb. 1919.
4363 Fison, Edmund Towers, 18 Feb. 1919.
4364 Fleming, James Finlayson, 18 Feb. 1919.
4365 Fox, Joseph Vincent, 18 Feb. 1919.
4366 Giles, John Dudgeon, 18 Feb. 1919.
4367 Godwin, Herbert James, 18 Feb. 1919.
4368 Gordon, James Edward, 18 Feb. 1919.
4369 Guillemard, Bernard James, 18 Feb. 1919.
4370 Harrison, John Atkinson, 18 Feb. 1919.
4371 Harvey, Joshua Harold, 18 Feb. 1919.
4372 Hawke, Edward Drummond Hay, 18 Feb. 1919.
4373 Hunton, Alfred William, 18 Feb. 1919.
4374 Jeremy, Mary Ethel, 18 Feb. 1919.
4376 Kempe, Charles Gilbert Burrington, 18 Feb. 1919.
4377 Key, Martin Aston, 18 Feb. 1919.
4378 Liston, Mary Forbes, 18 Feb. 1919.
4379 MacFadden, Cecil John Read, 18 Feb. 1919.
4380 Mackintosh, John, 18 Feb. 1919.
4381 Mitchell, Arthur Martin, 18 Feb. 1919.
4382 Orrin, Herbert Charles, 18 Feb. 1919.
4383 Peacocke, Reginald Christopher, 18 Feb. 1919.
4384 Percival, George Henry, 18 Feb. 1919.
4385 Pinching, Charles James, 18 Feb. 1919.
4386 Pringle, Arthur Young, 18 Feb. 1919.
4387 Radcliffe, Frank, 18 Feb. 1919.
4388 Rice, Bernard, 18 Feb. 1919.
4389 Rogers, Kenneth, 18 Feb. 1919.
4390 Ross, Winifred Margaret, 18 Feb. 1919.
4391 Shore, Lewis Erle, 18 Feb. 1919.
4393 Simmons, Edward Walpole, 18 Feb. 1919.
4394 Somers, Charles Dudley, 18 Feb. 1919.

4395 Stoney, Florence Ada, 18 Feb. 1919.
4396 Taylor, John William, 18 Feb. 1919.
4397 Thorne, Berthold Bezly Thorne, 18 Feb. 1919.
4398 Walker, John William Thomson, 18 Feb. 1919.
4399 Webster, Arthur Douglas, 18 Feb. 1919.
4400 Wood, Cyril George Russ, 18 Feb. 1919.
4401 Worthington, Robert Alfred, 18 Feb. 1919.
4402 Humphrey, John Cave, 17 March, 1919. (M.)
4403 Walker, Arthur Horace, 17 March, 1919. (M.)
4404 Davis, John Cecil, 17 March, 1919.
4405 Clegg, John Harry Kay, 17 March, 1919. (M.)
4406 Woodhouse, Hector Roy MacKenzie, 17 March, 1919. (M.)
4407 Daniels, Ernest Stuart, 17 March, 1919. (M.)
4408 Richards, Edward, 17 March, 1919. (M.)
4409 Youle, George Arthur, 17 March, 1919. (M.)
4410 Fox, William Henry, 24 March, 1919. (M.)
4411 Harvey, James Robertson, 24 March, 1919. (M.)
4412 Hulme-Goodier, Robert Simes, 24 March, 1919. (M.)
4413 Seropian, Charles Dickran Oliver Déodat, 24 March, 1919. (M.)
4414 Bolton, Richard Edmund Cornforth, 1 April, 1919. (M.)
4415 Breton, Colin Guy, 1 April, 1919. (M.)
4416 Broderick, Richard, 1 April, 1919. (M.)
4417 Burgess, Herbert Smith, 1 April, 1919. (M.)
4418 Bushe, Charles Kendal, 1 April, 1919. (M.)
4419 Capper, Henry Douglas, 1 April, 1919. (M.)
4420 Chamberlin, Trevor Ronald, 1 April, 1919. (M.)
4421 Coates, Joseph Edward, 1 April, 1919. (M.)
4422 Crawford, James Robert, 1 April, 1919. (M.)
4423 Donaldson, Ernest, 1 April, 1919. (M.)
4424 Duffett, Edward, 1 April, 1919. (M.)
4425 Dunraven, Earl of, 1 April, 1919.
4426 Eady, Frederick William Edward, 1 April, 1919. (M.)
4427 Feilding, Hon. Francis Everard Henry Joseph, 1 April, 1919. (M.)
4429 Freeman, Sidney Charles, 1 April, 1919. (M.)
4430 Frith, William Willoughby Cole, 1 April, 1919. (M.)
4431 Gill, Henry Dale, 1 April, 1919. (M.)
4432 Hailes, David Augustus, 1 April, 1919. (M.)
4433 Haslam, William Heywood, 1 April, 1919. (M.)
4434 Hemsley, Arthur Cyril, 1 April, 1919. (M.)
4435 Houghton, Sydney Charles, 1 April, 1919. (M.)
4436 Hunn, John Alfred, 1 April, 1919. (M.)
4437 Kilroy, Willie Dickson, 1 April, 1919. (M.)
4438 MacDermott, Anthony Francis Joseph, 1 April, 1910. (M.)
4439 Murray, Charles Geoffrey, 1 April, 1919. (M.)
4440 Pinchin, John Fitzmaurice, 1 April, 1919. (M.)
4441 Pollock, J. Donald, 1 April, 1919. (M.)
4442 Price, Thomas Slater, 1 April, 1919. (M.)
4443 Reeve, Arthur William Simms, 1 April, 1919. (M.)
4444 Robinson, Leonard, 1 April, 1919. (M.)
4445 Scott, Evelyn Dennis, 1 April, 1919. (M.)
4446 Sims, William, 1 April, 1919. (M.)
4447 Simpson, William, 1 April, 1919. (M.)
4448 Syson, Alfred Edward, 1 April, 1919. (M.)
4449 Tredegar, Lord, 1 April, 1919. (M.)
4450 Wharton, Richard George, 1 April, 1919. (M.)
4451 Wilkinson, Ralph Thomas, 1 April, 1919. (M.)
4452 Wolfe, Henry Eccles, 1 April, 1919. (M.)
4453 Searle, Sydney, 5 April, 1919. (M.)
4454 Sampson, Leslie Norman, 5 April, 1919. (M.)
4455 Davies, William John Abbott, 5 April, 1919. (M.)
4456 Carter, Thomas Gilbert, 11 April, 1919. (M.)
4457 Toms, Frederick Bowering, 11 April, 1919. (M.)
4458 Groome, Frederick Thompson, 11 April, 1919. (M.)
4459 Osburn, Harold, 11 April, 1919. (M.)
4460 Clark, Gordon Lilico, 11 April, 1919. (M.)
4461 Pipon, James Murray, 22 April, 1919. (M.)
4462 Porter, Robert Milne, 22 April, 1919. (M.)
4463 Bremner, Archibald Gordon, 22 April, 1919. (M.)
4464 Tyler, Thomas Richard, 22 April, 1919. (M.)
4465 Bowden, Harry James, 22 April, 1919. (M.)
4466 Lee, Vaughan Alexander Edward Hanning-, 22 April, 1919. (M.)
4467 Cooper, Charles Purcell, 22 April, 1919. (M.)
4468 Hudson, Henry Victor, 22 April, 1919. (M.)
4469 Besant, Henry Francis, 22 April, 1919. (M.)
4470 Forrester, William Thomson, 22 April, 1919. (M.)
4471 Malpas, James Herbert, 22 April, 1919. (M.)
4472 Nicholls, Arthur Sydney Moir, 22 April, 1919. (M.)
4473 Wethey, Edwin Howard, 22 April, 1919. (M.)
4474 Woolf, Thomas Alfred, 22 April, 1919. (M.)
4475 Bourchier, John Arthur Fitz-warine, 22 April, 1919. (M.)
4476 Collins, Arthur Rutherford Dundas, 22 April, 1919. (M.)
4477 Trinick, Fred, 22 April, 1919. (M.)
4478 Ridyard, Arnold, 22 April, 1919. (M.)
4479 Learmonth, Archibald Thomas, 22 April, 1919. (M.)
4480 Lawlor, Leslie, 22 April, 1919. (M.)
4481 Colbourne, Walter Sydney, 22 April, 1919. (M.)
4482 Lloyd, Rowland Owen, 22 April, 1919. (M.)
4483 Capon, Selwyn Norman, 22 April, 1919. (M.)
4484 Ranson, Percy, 22 April, 1919. (M.)
4485 McKichan, John James, 22 April, 1919. (M.)
4486 Hoar, Henry Samuel, 22 April, 1919. (M.)
4487 Ewart, Francis, 22 April, 1919. (M.)
4488a Selwin, Percy, 22 April, 1919. (M.)
4488b Rivers, Walter Samuel, 5 May, 1919. (M.)
4488c Armstrong, Francis Harold Courtenay, 5 May, 1919. (M.)

4488d Cowan, David John, 5 May, 1919. (M.)
4488e Finch, Lionel Hugh Knightley, 5 May, 1919. (M.)
4488f Juriss, Maximilian, 5 May, 1919. (M.)
4488g Leighton, Thomas William, 5 May, 1919. (M.)
4488h Mitchell, Wright, 5 May, 1919. (M.)
4489a Roberts, Arthur Edward Stokes-, 5 May, 1919. (M.)
4489b Usher, Charles Milne, 5 May, 1919. (M.)
4489c Park, Frank Stewart, 5 May, 1919. (M.)
4489d Mills, Charles, 5 May, 1919. (M.)
4489e Anderson, William, 5 May, 1919. (M.)
4889 Beale, Helen Mary, 9 May, 1919. (M.)
4890 Bennet, Mary Barbara, 9 May, 1919. (M.)
4891 Bennett, Catherine Elizabeth, 9 May, 1919. (M.)
4892 Currey, Muriel Innes, 9 May, 1919. (M.)
4893 Jermyn, Ida Mary, 9 May, 1919. (M.)
4894 de L'Hôpital, Winifride Mary, Mrs., 9 May, 1919. (M.)
4895 Maclennan, Anna Buchanan, 9 May, 1919. (M.)
4896 Matheson, Ethel Ivy Flora, 9 May, 1919. (M.)
4897 Merston, Ethel Gladys, 9 May, 1919. (M.)
4898 Monkhouse, Marjorie Mary, 9 May, 1919. (M.)
4899 Northcote, Evelyn Maud, Hon. Mrs., 9 May, 1919. (M.)
4900 Penrose, Katherine St. Aubyn, 9 May, 1919. (M.)
4901 Royden, Ethel Martha, 9 May, 1919. (M.)
4902 Valpy, Mrs. Bertha, 9 May, 1919. (M.)
4903 Warner, Sydney Jeannetta, 9 May, 1919. (M.)
4904 Warton, Florence Ethel, 9 May, 1919. (M.)
4905 Campbell, Victor Lindsey Arbuthnot, 24 May, 1919. (M.)
4906 Rennie, Alexander, 24 May, 1919. (M.)
4907 Graham, Thomas Alexander, 24 May, 1919. (M.)
4908 Todd, George Webster, 24 May, 1919. (M.)
4909 Young, James, 24 May, 1919. (M.)
4910 Warden, Robert Cunningham, 24 May, 1919. (M.)
4911 Paterson, Robert Ormiston, 24 May, 1919. (M.)
4912 Clare, Harold Ernest, 24 May, 1919. (M.)
4913 Masters, Albert Frederick, 24 May, 1919. (M.)
4914 Ryan, Thomas Philip, 24 May, 1919. (M.)
4915 Driscoll, Robert, 24 May, 1919. (M.)
4916 Polehampton, John, 24 May, 1919. (M.)
4917 Eglen, Arthur Harold, 24 May, 1919. (M.)
4918 Anning, William James, 27 May, 1919. (M.)
4919 Beautement, Harold, 27 May, 1919. (M.)
4920 Beare, Stanley Samuel, 27 May, 1919. (M.)
4921 Bevan, George Hope, 27 May, 1919. (M.)
4922 Blomfield, Myles Aldington, 27 May, 1919. (M.)
4923 Callwell, Eberhard William Ernest, 27 May 1919. (M.)
4924 Clark, Roland Arbuthnot, 27 May, 1919. (M.)
4925 Close, Rev. Richard Bevill Middleton, 27 May, 1919.
4926 Congdon, William Sydney Philip, 27 May, 1919. (M.)
4927 Davies, Bertram Harold, 27 May, 1919. (M.)
4928 Edwards, Macleod Gamul Arthur, 27 May, 1919. (M.)
4929 Harrison, William Rhodes, 27 May, 1919. (M.)
4930 Hodge, John Macky, 27 May, 1919. (M.)
4931 Lawder, Keith Macleod, 27 May, 1919. (M.)
4932 Lyon, Alexander, 27 May, 1919. (M.)
4933 McConkey, Henry, 27 May, 1919. (M.)
4934 Macleod, William Simon Fraser, 27 May, 1919. (M.)
4935 Purdon, Henry Maurice Chidley, 27 May, 1919. (M.)
4936 Spriggs, Harold James Duthoit, 27 May, 1919. (M.)
4937 Symons, Herebert Edward, 27 May, 1919. (M.)
4938 Talbot, Gerald, 27 May, 1919. (M.)
4939 Wyatt, John Oliver, 27 May, 1919. (M.)
4940 Adams, Edwin Plimpton, 3 June, 1919. (M.)
4941 Adams, Thomas Henry, 3 June, 1919. (M.)
4942 Alban-Uff, Sidney, 3 June, 1919. (M.)
4943 Aldridge, Evelyn, 3 June, 1919. (M.)
4944 Alexandre, Philip George, 3 June, 1919. (M.)
4945 Alford, Sidney Ernest, 3 June, 1919. (M.)
4946 Alkin, Richard Ley, 3 June, 1919. (M.)
4947 Allard, Philip, 3 June, 1919. (M.)
4948 Allan, Bryce, 3 June, 1919. (M.)
4949 Allen, Francis John, 3 June, 1919. (M.)
4950 Allen, Frederick John, 3 June, 1919. (M.)
4951 Anderson, Francis Henry Middleton, 3 June, 1919. (M.)
4952 Anderson, James Douglas, 3 June, 1919. (M.)
4953 Anderson, Neil Gordon, 3 June, 1919. (M.)
4954 Anderson, Robert Gray, 3 June, 1919. (M.)
4955 Anderson, Thomas Andrew Irving, 3 June, 1919. (M.)
4956 Anderson, William, 3 June, 1919. (M.)
4957 Anderson, Wilfred Arthur Duncombe, 3 June, 1919. (M.)
4958 Andrew, George Lionel, 3 June, 1919. (M.)
4959 Angus, William Brodie Gurney, 3 June, 1919. (M.)
4960 Aris, Alexander Frederick, 3 June, 1919. (M.)
4961 Armstrong, Samuel Richard, 3 June, 1919. (M.)
4962 Armstrong, Godfrey George, 3 June, 1919. (M.)
4963 Armstrong, Sereld John, 3 June, 1919. (M.)
4964 Ash, Ernest, 3 June, 1919. (M.)
4965 Ashford, Frederick Henry, 3 June, 1919. (M.)
4966 Attwood, Reginald Guy, 3 June, 1919. (M.)
4967 Bacon, Cyril William, 3 June, 1919. (M.)
4968 Baird, William Merrilees, 3 June, 1919. (M.)
4969 Baker, Arthur Frederick, 3 June, 1919. (M.)
4970 Baker, Herbert, 3 June, 1919. (M.)
4971 Baker, Joseph Samuel, 3 June, 1919. (M.)
4972 Balders, Dudley Vere Morley, 3 June, 1919. (M.)
4973 Ball, Harry Standish, 3 June, 1919. (M.)
4974 Ballard, Gilbert Alfred, 3 June, 1919. (M.)
4975 Balleine, Rev. Austin Humphrey, 3 June, 1919. (M.)
4976 Barrett, Hugh Scott, 3 June, 1919. (M.)
4977 Barron, Cyril Alexander, 3 June, 1919. (M.)

4978 Barry, John Hewitt, 3 June, 1919. (M.)
4979 Barton, Charles Percival, 3 June, 1919. (M.)
4980 Bashford, Ernest Francis, 3 June, 1919. (M.)
4981 Batchelor, Arthur, 3 June, 1919. (M.)
4982 Bates, Hubert Tunstall, 3 June, 1919. (M.)
4983 Batson, Herbert Mackenzie, 3 June, 1919. (M.)
4984 Batty, Edgar Douglas, 3 June, 1919. (M.)
4985 Bawden, Frederick Henry, 3 June, 1919. (M.)
4986 Baxter, Arthur, 3 June, 1919. (M.)
4987 Baxter, David Charles, 3 June, 1919. (M.)
4988 Bazett, Henry Cuthbert, 3 June, 1919. (M.)
4989 Beard, Samuel Trevor, 3 June, 1919. (M.)
4990 Beatty, William John, 3 June, 1919. (M.)
4991 Beaumont, Henry George, 3 June, 1919. (M.)
4992 Beavis, Philip Ernest. 3 June, 1919. (M.)
4993 Bebb. Roland Harry, 3 June, 1919. (M.)
4994 Beckett, Charles Stephenson, 3 June, 1919. (M.)
4995 Bell, Thomas Carmichael, 3 June, 1919. (M.)
4996 Bemrose, William Lloyd, 3 June, 1919. (M.)
4997 Bennette, Bernard John Taylor, 3 June, 1919. (M.)
4998 Bennett, Norman Carmichael, 3 June, 1919. (M.)
4999 Bennett, Thomas William, 3 June, 1919. (M.)
5000 Bennett, William, 3 June, 1919. (M.)
5001 Benson, Hugh, 3 June, 1919. (M.)
5002 Benson, George Augustus, 3 June, 1919. (M.)
5003 Beresford. Gerald Waddington, 3 June, 1919. (M.)
5004 Bernard, Oliver Percy, 3 June, 1919. (M.)
5005 Berry, Winslow Seymour Sterling, 3 June, 1919. (M.)
5006 Best, Sigismund Payne, 3 June, 1919. (M.)
5007 Bewicke, Calverly, 3 June, 1919. (M.)
5008 Biddulph, Alfred James, 3 June, 1919. (M.)
5009 Bigg, William Charles, 3 June, 1919. (M.)
5010 Birch, Montague, 3 June, 1919. (M.)
5011 Birch, William Kenning, 3 June, 1919. (M.)
5012 Bird, Ronald Trevor Wilberforce, 3 June, 1919. (M.)
5013 Blackburn, Lionel Oddy Gaskell, 3 June, 1919. (M.)
5014 Blake, Harold Henry, 3 June, 1919. (M.)
5015 Blake, William Lascelles Fitzgerald, 3 June, 1919. (M.)
5016 Bliss, William Edward, 3 June, 1919. (M.)
5017 Blunt, Gerald Charles Gordon, 3 June, 1919. (M.)
5018 Boag, Henry, 3 June, 1919. (M.)
5019 Boggs, Arthur Beaumont, 3 June, 1919 (M.)
5020 Bond, Mildred Mary, 3 June, 1919. (M·.)
5021 Bond, William Cotesworth, 3 June, 1919. (M.)
5022 Bostock, John Edward, 3 June, 1919 (M.)
5023 Bostock, Thomas Herbert Geoffrey, 3 June, 1919. (M.)
5024 Bosworth, Laurence Owen, 3 June, 1919. (M.)
5025 Bourne, Thomas Richard Arter, 3 June, 1919. (M.)
5026 Bowater, Norman James, 3 June, 1919. (M.)
5027 Bower, Lancelot Tregonwell Syndercombe, 3 June, 1919. (M.)
5028 Bowhay, Alfred Benjamin, 3 June, 1919. (M.)
5029 Bowman, George Edward, 3 June, 1919. (M.)
5030 Bownass, William Everett, 3 June, 1919. (M.)
5031 Bowra, Edward Valentine, 3 June, 1919. (M.)
5032 Bowron, Henry, 3 June, 1919. (M.)
5033 Boys, Herbert Augustus, 3 June, 1919. (M.)
5035 Bray, Eustace Arthur, 3 June, 1919. (M.)
5036 Brennan, William, 3 June, 1919. (M.)
5037 Brewin, Harry, 3 June, 1919. (M.(
5038 Brice, Albert Victor, 3 June, 1919. (M.)
5039 Brierley, Eustace Carlile, 3 June, 1919. (M.)
5040 Briggs, Henry Stackpoole, 3 June, 1919. (M.)
5041 Briggs, Waldo Raven, 3 June, 1919. (M.)
5042 Brightman, Eustace Webster, 3 June, 1919. (M.)
5043 Bristed, Richard Bower, 3 June, 1919. (M.)
5044 Brister, Joseph Fane, 3 June, 1919. (M.)
5045 Bromley-Davenport, Hugh Richard, 3 June, 1919. (M.)
5046 Broster, Lennox Ross, 3 June, 1919. (M.)
5047 Brown, Alwin, 3 June, 1919. (M.)
5048 Brown, Geoffrey Mainwaring, 3 June, 1919. (M.)
5049 Brown, Henry, 3 June, 1919. (M.)
5050 Brown, Rev. William Joseph, 3 June, 1919. (M.)
5051 Brown, Rev. Hugh, 3 June, 1919. (M.)
5052 Browne, Cyril Edward, 3 June, 1919. (M.)
5053 Bruce, John, 3 June, 1919. (M.)
5054 Brunton, Guy, 3 June, 1919. (M.)
5055 Bryce, Francis, 3 June, 1919. (M.)
5056 Bryans, Maurice, 3 June, 1919. (M.)
5057 Buchanan, Arthur Louis Hamilton, 3 June, 1919. (M.)
5058 Burlace, Leslie Binmore, 3 June, 1919. (M)
5059 Burchell, James Melvill, 3 June, 1919. (M.)
5060 Burland, Leonard, 3 June, 1919. (M.)
5061 Burn-Callender, Cuthbert, 3 June, 1919. (M.)
5062 Burstall, Edgar Bryan, 3 June, 1919. (M.)
5063 Burton, Henry Walter, 3 June, 1919. (M.)
5064 Butler, Frederick William, 3 June, 1919. (M.)
5065 Butler, James Ramsay Montagu, 3 June, 1919. (M.)
5066 Byrne, Gerald Bertram, 3 June, 1919. (M.)
5067 Cameron, John, 3 June, 1919. (M.)
5068 Campbell, Duncan, 3 June, 1919. (M.)
5069 Campbell, Francis Ernest Archer, 3 June, 1919. (M.)
5070 Campbell, Lewis Gordon, 3 June, 1919. (M.)
5071 Campbell, Thomas, 3 June, 1919. (M.)
5072 Campbell, William Little, 3 June, 1919. (M.)
5073 Canham, Ernest Reginald, 3 June, 1919. (M.)
5074 Cannon, William Butler, 3 June, 1919. (M.)
5075 Carkeet-James, Edward Hamilton, 3 June, 1919. (M.)
5076 Carmichael, James Charles Gordon, 3 June, 1919. (M.)

5077 Carmichael, James Duncan, 3 June, 1919. (M.)
5078 Carrington, Noel Lewis, 3 June, 1919. (M.)
5079 Carrington, William, 3 June, 1919. (M.)
5080 Carruthers, Francis E., 3 June, 1919. (M.)
5081 Carstairs, Albert Joseph Henry, 3 June, 1919. (M.).
5082 Carter, Ernest Walker Augustus, 3 June, 1919. (M)
5083 Carter, Gerald Francis, 3 June, 1919. (M.)
5084 Carter, Thomas Moravian, 3 June, 1919. (M.)
5085 Case, Arthur, 3 June, 1919. (M.)
5086 Cassera, Anthony Aloysius, 3 June, 1919. (M.)
5087 Cavanagh, Henry James, 3 June, 1919. (M.)
5088 Cazenove, Percy, 3 June, 1919. (M.)
5089 Chadwick, Alan Wentworth, 3 June, 1919. (M.)
5090 Chambers, Sydney Arthur, 3 June, 1919. (M.)
5091 Chapman, Leonard, 3 June, 1919. (M.)
5092 Charley, Leslie William, 3 June, 1919. (M.)
5093 Charnock, Richard. 3 June, 1919. (M.)
5094 Charteris, Rev. William Cramb, 3 June, 1919. (M.)
5095 Cheales, Ralph Darley, 3 June, 1919. (M.)
5096 Cheriton, William George Lloyd, 3 June, 1919. (M.)
5098 Christie, Lionel Ronald, 3 June, 1919. (M.)
5099 Clark, Herbert James, 3 June, 1919. (M.)
5100 Clark, Hugh Bryan, 3 June, 1919. (M.)
5101 Clarke, Charles Hugh, 3 June, 1919. (M.)
5102 Clarke, Gerald, 3 June, 1919. (M.)
5103 Clarke, Joseph Edward, 3 June, 1919. (M.)
5104 Clarke, Richard Cristopher, 3 June, 1919. (M.)
5105 Clay, Frank Septimus, 3 June, 1919. (M.)
5106 Clayton-East, George Frederick Lancelot, 3 June, 1919. (M.)
5107 Cleeve, Charles Edward, 3 June, 1919. (M.)
5108 Cliff, Arthur, 3 June, 1919. (M.)
5109 Clogstoun, Herbert Cunningham, 3 June, 1919. (M.)
5110 Close, Francis Morton, 3 June, 1919. (M.)
5111 Clouston, Noel Stewart, 3 June, 1919. (M.)
5112 Clowes, Ethel Robin, 3 June, 1919. (M.)
5113 Coales, Herbert Wallis, 3 June, 1919. (M.)
5114 Coates, Edward Clive, 3 June, 1919. (M.)
5115 Coates, Joseph Michael Smith, 3 June, 1919. (M.)
5116 Codrington. Geoffrey Ronald, 3 June, 1919. (M.)
5117 Coghlan, Daniel, 3 June, 1919. (M.)
5118 Colchester-Wemyss, John Maurice, 3 June, 1919. (M.)
5119 Cole, Harold Linter, 3 June, 1919. (M.)
5120 Cole, Henry Walter George, 3 June, 1919. (M.)
5121 Colin-York, William Douglas, 3 June, 1919. (M.)
5122 Colley, William Harold, 3 June, 1919. (M.)
5123 Colquhoun, Victor Alexander, 3 June, 1919. (M.)
5124 Colvile, Charles Rowe, 3 June, 1919. (M.)
5125 Colyer, Claude Gray, 3 June, 1919. (M.)
5126 Constable, Clifford Edward, 3 June, 1919. (M.)
5127 Cook, Victor Chandler, 3 June, 1919. (M.)
5128 Cook, William Ernest, 3 June, 1919. (M.)
5129 Cook, James, 3 June, 1919. (M.)
5130 Cooke, Philip Andrew, 3 June, 1919. (M.)
5131 Coombs, Frederick Middleton, 3 June, 1919. (M.)
5132 Cooper, Harold Octavius, 3 June, 1919. (M.)
5133 Corbett, Daniel Maurice, 3 June, 1919. (M.)
5134 Corbishley, Mary Cecilia, 3 June, 1919. (M.)
5135 Corfield, Frederick Alleyne, 3 June, 1919. (M.)
5136 Cork, Reginald Philip, 3 June, 1919. (M.)
5137 Cornish-Bowden, Robert Kenrick, 3 June, 1919. (M.)
5138 Corrall, George Edward, 3 June, 1919. (M.)
5139 Cottle, Peter James, 3 June, 1919. (M.)
5140 Cousins, Robert William, 3 June, 1919. (M.)
5141 Coulson, Thomas, 3 June, 1919. (M.)
5142 Cox, Percy Alexander, 3 June, 1919. (M.)
5143 Cox, Reginald Woodruff, 3 June, 1919. (M.)
5144 Coy, Frederick, 3 June, 1919. (M.)
5145 Crabtree, Ernest Granville, 3 June, 1919. (M.)
5146 Craig, John Gibson, 3 June, 1919. (M.)
5147 Craig, Newman Lombard, 3 June, 1919. (M.)
5148 Craig, Thomas, 3 June, 1919. (M.)
5149 Crawford, John Martin Maynard, 3 June, 1919. (M.)
5150 Crewe, Frank, 3 June, 1919. (M.)
5151 Crockett, Leonard Marshall, 3 June. 1919. (M.)
5152 Crosby, Reginald Douglas, 3 June, 1919. (M.)
5153 Crosthwaite, Arthur Tonley, 3 June, 1919. (M.)
5154 Crowe, Joseph John, 3 June, 1919. (M.)
5155 Cruickshank, Robert Scott, 3 June, 1919. (M.)
5156 Cruickshank, Rev. William Walker, 3 June, 1919. (M.)
5157 Crump, Edward Harold, 3 June 1919. (M.)
5158 Cuckow, Philip Edwin, 3 June, 1919. (M.)
5159 Cumberlege, Barry Stephenson 3 June, 1919. (M.)
5160 Cunningham, Rev. Canon Bertram Keir, 3 June, 1919. (M.).
5161 Cunningham, John Francis, 3 June, 1919. (M.)
5162 Cursiter, Stanley, 3 June, 1919. (M.)
5163 Curtis, Cecil Montagu Drury 3 June, 1919. (M.)
5164 Cutting, Frank, 3 June, 1919. (M.)
5165 Dadson, Reginald Thornton. 3 June, 1919. (M.)
5166 Dale, John, 3 June, 1919. (M.)
5167 Dalgleish, William Brown, 3 June, 1919. (M.)
5168 Daniels, Lindsay Sydney, 3 June, 1919. (M.)
5169 Davenport, Charles Malcolm, 3 June, 1919. (M.)
5170 Davidson, Hugh Stevenson, 3 June, 1919. (M.)
5171 Davidson, James MacFarlane, 3 June, 1919. (M.)
5172 Davies, Ernest James, 3 June, 1919. (M.)
5173 Davies, Harry Cornwall, 3 June, 1919. (M.)
5174 Davies, John, 3 June, 1919. (M.)
5175 Davis, Frank Gordon, 3 June, 1919. (M.)

5176 Davis, Leslie Stalman, 3 June, 1919. (M.)
5177 Dawson, John Kenneth Bonsfield, 3 June, 1919. (M.)
5178 Deakin, Ralph, 3 June, 1919. (M.)
5179 De Bathe, Maximilian John, 3 June, 1919. (M.)
5180 De Bavay, Auguste John Charles, 3 June, 1919. (M.)
5181 Dechair, George Herbert Blackett, 3 June, 1919. (M.)
5182 De La Cour, George, 3 June, 1919. (M.)
5183 De Montmorency, Hervey Guy Francis Edward, 3 June, 1919. (M.)
5184 Dent, Arthur, 3 June, 1919. (M.)
5185 De Paula, Frederic Rudolf Mackley, 3 June, 1919. (M.)
5186 De Putron, Adele, 3 June, 1919. (M.)
5187 De Soissons, Pierre Amedee de Savoie Carignan, 3 June, 1919. (M.)
5188 Devas, Rev. Francis Charles, 3 June, 1919. (M.)
5189 Devas, Rev. Philip Dominic, 3 June, 1919. (M.)
5190 Dickinson, George Joseph, 3 June, 1919. (M.)
5191 Dickinson, Richard Frederick O'Toole, 3 June, 1919. (M.)
5192 Dickinson, William Michael Kington, 3 June, 1919. (M.)
5193 Dimock, John Francis Douglas, 3 June, 1919. (M.)
5194 Dinwiddie, Melville, 3 June, 1919. (M.)
5195 Dix, Henry Philip, 3 June, 1919. (M.)
5196 Dixon, Arthur Tollemache, 3 June, 1919. (M.)
5197 Dixon, George Seymour, 3 June, 1919. (M.)
5198 Dixon, Robert Garside, 3 June, 1919. (M.)
5199 Dixon, William Chester, 3 June, 1919. (M.)
5200 Dobbins, Roy Samuel, 3 June, 1919. (M.)
5201 Dobbs, Conway Richard, 3 June, 1919. (M.)
5202 Dodds, Archibald Forbes, 3 June, 1919. (M.)
5203 Dodds, Jackson, 3 June, 1919. (M.)
5204 Dodsworth, Benjamin, 3 June, 1919. (M.)
5205 Donald, William Hamish, 3 June, 1919. (M.)
5206 Donaldson, Arthur William Hunter, 3 June, 1919. (M.)
5207 Douglass, James Henry, 3 June, 1919. (M.)
5208 Douthwaite, William Bernard, 3 June, 1919. (M.)
5209 Dowson, Oscar Follett, 3 June, 1919. (M.)
5210 Driberg, James Douglas, 3 June, 1919. (M.)
5211 Drury, Thomas, 3 June, 1919. (M.)
5212 Dukes, Cuthbert, 3 June, 1919. (M.)
5214 Du Breul, Frederick Alexander, 3 June, 1919. (M.)
5215 Duncan, Rev. James, 3 June, 1919. (M.)
5216 Duncan, David Blaikie, 3 June, 1919. (M.)
5217 Duncan, James Matthews, 3 June, 1919. (M.)
5218 Duncan, William, 3 June, 1919. (M.)
5219 Dundas, Allan Charlesworth, 3 June, 1919. (M.)
5220 Dymock, Arthur, 3 June, 1919. (M.)
5221 Dyson, Harry Hugo Bernard, 3 June, 1919. (M.)
5222 Earle, Augustus Thornhill, 3 June, 1919. (M.)
5223 Earwaker, Ralph Parsons, 3 June, 1919. (M.)
5224 Eaton, Henry Rayner, 3 June, 1919. (M.)
5225 Esgington, Herbert, 3 June, 1919. (M.)
5226 Edgington, Walter, 3 June, 1919. (M.)
5227 Edser, Edmund, 3 June, 1919. (M.)
5228 Edwards, John Augustus, 3 June, 1919. (M.)
5229 Edwards, Rev. Nathaniel Walter Allan, 3 June, 1919. (M.)
5230 Edwards, Walter Bernard, 3 June, 1919. (M.)
5231 Edwards-Ker, Douglas Rous, 3 June, 1919. (M.)
5232 Elgood, Leonard Alsager, 3 June, 1919. (M.)
5233 Elkan, Clarence John, 3 June, 1919. (M.)
5234 Ellwood, Arthur Addison, 3 June, 1919. (M.)
5235 Erskine-Murray, Robert, 3 June, 1919. (M.)
5236 Erwin, Harry, 3 June, 1919. (M.)
5237 Espley, Arthur James, 3 June, 1919. (M.)
5238 Evans, John, 3 June, 1919. (M.)
5239 Evans, William Richard, 3 June, 1919. (M.)
5240 Evans, William Stanley, 3 June, 1919. (M.)
5241 Everidge, John, 3 June, 1919. (M.)
5242 Ewart, Gerald Valentine, 3 June, 1919. (M.)
5243 Fargus, Nigel Harry Skinner, 3 June, 1919. (M.)
5244 Fasson, Thomas William, 3 June, 1919. (M.)
5245 Fawcus, James Scott, 3 June, 1919. (M.)
5246 Feiling, Gladys Maud, Mrs., 3 June, 1919. (M.)
5247 Fenn, Ernest Edward, 3 June, 1919. (M.)
5248 Fenner, Ralph Lennox, 3 June, 1919. (M.)
5249 Fenton, Samuel Greame, 3 June, 1919. (M.)
5250 Ferguson, James, 3 June, 1919. (M.)
5251 Ferguson, Montgomery du Bois, 3 June, 1919. (M.)
5252 Fernie, Ralph, 3 June, 1919. (M.)
5253 Ferrier, Charles Gordon, 3 June, 1919. (M.)
5254 Field, Rev. William, 3 June, 1919. (M.)
5255 Figg, Charles Arthur, 3 June, 1919. (M.)
5256 Finch, William Robert Edward Heneage, 3 June, 1919. (M.)
5257 Fisher, Otto Sarony, 3 June, 1919. (M.)
5258 Flook, Walter Bryan, 3 June, 1919. (M.)
5259 Flowers, Stephen, 3 June, 1919. (M.)
5260 Foley, Gerald Robert Edward, 3 June, 1919. (M.)
5261 Foley, Mary Gladys Corinne, 3 June, 1919. (M.)
5262 Foley, Peter Trant, 3 June, 1919. (M.)
5263 Foot, Robert William, 3 June, 1919. (M.)
5264 Forbes, Ronald Foster, 3 June, 1919. (M.)
5265 Forbes, Charles, 3 June, 1919. (M.)
5266 Ford, Stanley William, 3 June, 1919. (M.)
5267 Foster, Arthur Norman, 3 June, 1919. (M.)
5268 Foster, Edward, 3 June, 1919. (M.)
5269 Foster, Frank Broome, 3 June, 1919. (M.)
5270 Foster, Kennedy, 3 June, 1919. (M.)
5271 Foster, Michael George, 3 June, 1919. (M.)
5272 Fox, William, 3 June, 1919. (M.)

5273 Frampton, Henry Frank, 3 June, 1919. (M.)
5274 Franklin, Edward, 3 June, 1919. (M.)
5275 Fraser, James Wilson, 3 June, 1919. (M.)
5276 Fraser, Thomas Lockhead, 3 June, 1919. (M.)
5277 Frederick, Sir Charles Edward St. John, Bart., 3 June, 1919. (M.)
5278 Fulton, John Sidney, 3 June, 1919. (M.)
5279 Furber, Montague, 3 June, 1919. (M.)
5280 Furlong, Dennis Walter, 3 June, 1919. (M.)
5281 Gabe, Howell Woodwell, 3 June, 1919. (M.)
5282 Gadban, Victor John, 3 June, 1919. (M.)
5283 Gamble, Henry, 3 June, 1919. (M.)
5284 Garraway, Frank Harold, 3 June, 1919. (M.)
5285 Gaunt, Arthur, 3 June, 1919. (M.)
5286 Gaye, Arthur Stretton, 3 June, 1919. (M.)
5287 Geddes, William John, 3 June, 1919. (M.)
5288 George, Wilfred Harold, 3 June, 1919. (M.)
5289 Gibb, William Morrison, 3 June, 1919. (M.)
5290 Gibbons, Gerald Francis Petvin, 3 June, 1919. (M.)
5291 Gibbons, Oliver Thomas Brice, 3 June, 1919. (M.)
5292 Giblet, Robert Harold, 3 June, 1919. (M.)
5293 Gibson, Arthur Clare Vernon, 3 June, 1919. (M.)
5294 Gilchrist, Archibald John, 3 June, 1919. (M.)
5295 Giles, Hylton Lloyd, 3 June, 1919. (M.)
5296 Gillett, Bernard George, 3 June, 1919. (M.)
5297 Gilligan, Geoffrey Goyer, 3 June, 1919. (M.)
5298 Gimbert, William Bertie, 3 June, 1919. (M.)
5299 Godley, Francis William Crewe, 3 June, 1919. (M.)
5300 Goff, Hugh Stuart Trevor, 3 June, 1919. (M.)
5301 Goldingham, Robert Elphinstone Dalrymple, 3 June, 1919. (M.)
5302 Goldney, Henry Wetherall, 3 June, 1919. (M.)
5303 Gordon-Forbes, Bertram Francis Alex., 3 June, 1919. (M.)
5304 Gore-Langton, Francis Wilfred, 3 June, 1919. (M.)
5305 Gorrie, Henry James, 3 June, 1919. (M.)
5306 Goulden, Charles Bernard, 3 June, 1919. (M.)
5307 Graham, David James, 3 June, 1919. (M.)
5308 Graham, John St. John, 3 June, 1919. (M.)
5309 Graham, James Wells, 3 June, 1919. (M.)
5310 Grant-Peterkin, Montagu James, 3 June, 1919. (M.)
5311 Gray, Arthur Claypon Horner, 3 June, 1919. (M.)
5312 Gray, Joseph Alexander, 3 June, 1919. (M.)
5313 Gray, Reginald Wentworth, 3 June, 1919. (M.)
5314 Green, Douglas Harold, 3 June, 1919. (M.)
5315 Green, William Robert, 3 June, 1919. (M.)
5316 Greenhill, Frederick William, 3 June, 1919. (M.)
5317 Greig, Albert David, 3 June, 1919. (M.)
5318 Greig, Kenneth Clunie, 3 June, 1919. (M.)
5319 Greville, Charles Beresford Fulke Greville, Lord, 3 June, 1919. (M.)
5320 Grierson, Ernest Moore, 3 June, 1919. (M.)
5321 Guinness, Owen Charles, 3 June, 1919. (M.)
5322 Gurney, John Cedric, 3 June, 1919. (M.)
5323 Guy, Edward Martin, 3 June, 1919. (M.)
5324 Hagan, Rev. Edward James, 3 June, 1919. (M.)
5325 Haig, John Alicius, 3 June, 1919. (M.)
5326 Hake, Henry Engelbert, 3 June, 1919. (M.)
5327 Hall, Bertram Arthur Montagu, 3 June, 1919. (M.)
5328 Hall, Rev. James Thomas, 3 June, 1919. (M.)
5329 Hall, Vincent Claud, 3 June, 1919. (M.)
5330 Hall, William Henry, 3 June, 1919. (M.)
5331 Hamilton, Alexander George, 3 June, 1919. (M.)
5332 Hamilton, Norman Chivas, 3 June, 1919. (M.)
5333 Hamlyn, Ralph Ashton, 3 June, 1919. (M.)
5334 Hanbury, Geoffrey Hyde Barday, 3 June, 1919. (M.)
5335 Hanbury, Rev. Guy Somerset, 3 June, 1919. (M.)
5336 Hancock, William Venning Glanville, 3 June, 1919. (M.)
5337 Hanna, William Gemmill Chalmers, 3 June, 1919. (M.)
5338 Hannen, Nicholas James, 3 June, 1919. (M.)
5339 Harding, Arthur George, 3 June, 1919. (M.)
5340 Harding, Philip Edward, 3 June, 1919. (M.)
5341 Harding, Richard Spalding, 3 June, 1919. (M.)
5342 Hardwick, Noel de Courcy, 3 June, 1919. (M.)
5343 Hardy, Frank Buckland, 3 June, 1919. (M.)
5344 Harewood, Rev. Ernest James, 3 June, 1919. (M.)
5345 Hargreaves, Laurence Appleyard, 3 June, 1919. (M.)
5346 Harker, Rev. Thomas Alphonsus, 3 June, 1919. (M.)
5347 Harper, Reginald Tristram, 3 June, 1919. (M.)
5348 Harpham, Harold D., 3 June, 1919. (M.)
5349 Harpur, William Lewis, 3 June, 1919. (M.)
5350 Harris, Guy Summerell, 3 June, 1919. (M.)
5351 Harris, Leopold Jonas, 3 June, 1919. (M.)
5352 Harrison, Frank, 3 June, 1919. (M.)
5353 Harrison, Francis Edward, 3 June, 1919. (M.)
5354 Hartley, James Norman Jackson, 3 June, 1919. (M.)
5355 Hartshorn, Arthur Hastings, 3 June, 1919. (M.)
5356 Hastie, Stuart Henderson, 3 June, 1919. (M.)
5357 Hastings, John Henry, 3 June, 1919. (M.)
5358 Hawkins, George, 3 June, 1919. (M.)
5359 Hawkins, Harold John Charlton, 3 June, 1919. (M.)
5360 Headlam, Cuthbert Morley, 3 June, 1919. (M.)
5361 Hearne, Edward, 3 June, 1919. (M.)
5362 Heathcote, Gilbert Stanley, 3 June, 1919. (M.)
5363 Henderson, Hon. Arnold, 3 June, 1919. (M.)
5364 Hennessy, George Richard, 3 June, 1919. (M.)
5365 Herbert Edward Dave Asher, 3 June, 1919. (M.)
5366 Herbert, Henry Carden, 3 June, 1919. (M.)
5367 Herdman, Arthur Cochran, 3 June, 1919. (M.)
5368 Herrick, William, 3 June, 1919. (M.)

5369 Herron, Robert Charles, 3 June, 1919. (M.)
5370 Heslop, Alfred Herbert, 3 June, 1919. (M.)
5371 Heyde, Douglas, 3 June, 1919. (M.)
5372 Heymann, Francis Albert, 3 June, 1919. (M.)
5373 Heyworth-Savage, Cecil Francis, 3 June, 1919. (M.)
5374 Hibbard, Thomas, 3 June, 1919. (M.)
5375 Hibbert, George, 3 June, 1919. (M.)
5376 Hickes, Lancelot Daryl, 3 June, 1919. (M.)
5377 Higgins, Thomas Twistington, 3 June, 1919. (M.)
5378 Hill, Herbert John, 3 June, 1919. (M.)
5379 Hill, Lionel Edward, 3 June, 1919. (M.)
5380 Hills, Charles Edward, 3 June, 1919. (M.)
5381 Hills, Reginald Playfair, 3 June, 1919. (M.)
5382 Hinde, Harold Montague, 3 June, 1919. (M.)
5383 Hindmarsh, Harold Hammond, 3 June, 1919. (M.)
5384 Hobart, Claud Vere Cavendish, 3 June, 1919. (M.)
5385 Holden, Rev. Philip Giffard, 3 June, 1919. (M.)
5386 Holdich, William Jeffkins, 3 June, 1919. (M.)
5387 Holdsworth, John Evelyn, 3 June, 1919. (M.)
5388 Holland, Ronald Morris, 3 June, 1919. (M.)
5389 Holland, Theodore Samuel, 3 June, 1919. (M.)
5390 Holland, Vyvyan Beresford, 3 June, 1919. (M.)
5391 Holley, George, 3 June, 1919. (M.)
5392 Hollond, Henry Arthur, 3 June, 1919. (M.)
5393 Holloway, Arthur Joseph, 3 June, 1919. (M.)
5394 Holmes, Dan Campbell, 3 June, 1919. (M.)
5395 Holmes-Brown, Alfred Ernest, 3 June, 1919. (M.)
5396 Hone, Thomas Nathaniel, 3 June, 1919. (M.)
5397 Hope, Charles William Menelaus, 3 June, 1919. (M.)
5398 Hope-Johnstone, Charles Spread, 3 June, 1919. (M.)
5399 Hopkins, Thomas Hollis, 3 June, 1919. (M.)
5400 Hossack, James Davidson, 3 June, 1919. (M.)
5401 Howard, Hugh Roberts, 3 June, 1919. (M.)
5402 Howell, Norman, 3 June, 1919. (M.)
5403 Hubbard, Reginald Kirshaw, 3 June, 1919. (M.)
5404 Huck, John, 3 June, 1919. (M.)
5405 Hudson, Ernest John, 3 June, 1919. (M.)
5406 Hudson, Robert Challis, 3 June, 1919. (M.)
5407 Hughes, Frederick St. John, 3 June, 1919. (M.)
5408 Hughes-Jones, John Trevor, 3 June, 1919. (M.)
5410 Humphreys, Henry Herbert, 3 June, 1919. (M.)
5411 Hunkin, Rev. Joseph Wellington, 3 June, 1919. (M.)
5412 Hunter, Cecil Stuart, 3 June, 1919. (M.)
5413 Huntington, Herbert Francis Searancks, 3 June, 1919. (M.)
5414 Hurst, Arthur Reginald, 3 June, 1919. (M.)
5415 Hussey, Arthur Vivian, 3 June, 1919. (M.)
5416 Hutchinson, Tnomas Massie, 3 June, 1919. (M.)
5417 Ince, Eric Henry Philip Blundell, 3 June, 1919. (M.)
5418 Inglis, Alexander Reid, 3 June, 1919. (M.)
5419 Ingram, Bruce Stirling, 3 June, 1919. (M.)
5420 Inskip, Arthur Cecil, 3 June, 1919. (M.)
5421 Jackson, Swinscho James, 3 June, 1919. (M.)
5422 Jacob, Rev. John Thomas, 3 June, 1919. (M.)
5423 Jacobs, Jonathan, 3 June, 1919. (M.)
5424 Jameson, David Napier, 3 June, 1919. (M.)
5425 Jarvis, Charles Francis Cracroft, 3 June, 1919. (M.)
5426 Jefferson, Herbert, 3 June, 1919. (M.)
5427 Jenner, Lawrence Wynyard, 3 June, 1919. (M.)
5428 Jennings, Leonard, 3 June, 1919. (M.)
5429 Jessop, Bernard, 3 June, 1919. (M.)
5430 Johnson, Frederick William, 3 June, 1919. (M.)
5431 Johnston, Harry Bertram, 3 June, 1919. (M.)
5432 Johnston, John, 3 June, 1919. (M.)
5433 Johnston, Robert George, 3 June, 1919. (M.)
5434 Jones, Charles, 3 June, 1919. (M.)
5435 Jones, Gladys Alicia, Mrs., 3 June, 1919. (M.)
5436 Jones, John, 3 June, 1919. (M.)
5437 Jones, John Lloyd Charles, 3 June, 1919. (M.)
5438 Jones, John Howard, 3 June, 1919. (M.)
5439 Jordan, Harold George, 3 June, 1919. (M.)
5440 Joscelyne, Frederic Percy, 3 June, 1919. (M.)
5441 Keep, Thomas Bettsworth, 3 June, 1919. (M.)
5442 Keith, George Theodore Elphinstone, 3 June, 1919. (M.)
5443 Keller, Rudolph Henry, 3 June, 1919. (M.)
5444 Kellner, Philip Travice Rubie, 3 June, 1919. (M.)
5445 Kelly, Arthur Lindsay, 3 June, 1919. (M.)
5446 Kendall, Rev. George, 3 June, 1919. (M.)
5447 Kemp, Edgar Stephen, 3 June, 1919. (M.)
5448 Kennedy, Archibald Arrol, 3 June, 1919. (M.)
5449 Kensington, Guy Belfield, 3 June, 1919. (M.)
5450 Keppel, John Joseph Guiney, 3 June, 1919. (M.)
5451 King, Colin, 3 June, 1919. (M.)
5452 King, Frank, 3 June, 1919. (M.)
5453 King, Lancelot Noel Friedrick Irving, 3 June, 1919. (M.)
5454 King, Leonard Algernon Bertram, 3 June, 1919. (M.)
5455 Kirby, William, 3 June, 1919. (M.)
5456 Kitson Alan Kennedy, 3 June, 1919. (M.)
5457 Kitson, Walter Frederick Clifford, 3 June, 1919. (M.)
5458 Knight, Cecil Davenport, 3 June, 1919. (M.)
5459 Knight, Ernest, 3 June, 1919. (M.)
5460 Knight, William Collins, 3 June, 1919. (M.)
5461 Knott, George Patrick, 3 June, 1919. (M.)
5462 Knowling, Arthur Ernest George, 3 June, 1919. (M.)
5463 Knuthsen, Louis Francis, 3 June, 1919. (M.)
5464 Knyvett, Rev. Carey Frederick, 3 June, 1919. (M.)
5465 Kohan, Charles Mendel, 3 June, 1919. (M.)
5466 Kuhne, Carl Hans, 3 June, 1919. (M.)
5467 Lang, James, 3 June, 1919. (M.)

5468 Lawrence, Alfred, 3 June, 1919. (M.)
5469 Lawson, Ernest Evelyn Lister, 3 June, 1919. (M.)
5470 Leche, John Hurleston, 3 June, 1919. (M.)
5471 Lee, Herbert Benjamin, 3 June, 1919. (M.)
5472 Lee, Lennie Henry, 3 June, 1919. (M.)
5473 Lees, George, 3 June, 1919. (M.)
5474 Legg, Cecil Henry, 3 June, 1919. (M.)
5475 Legh, Frank Bertram, 3 June, 1919. (M.)
5476 Leslie, Robert Walter Dickson, 3 June, 1919. (M.)
5477 Levey, Joseph Henry, 3 June, 1919. (M.)
5478 Lewis, James Charles, 3 June, 1919. (M.)
5479 Lewis, Thomas Percy, 3 June, 1919. (M.)
5480 Liddle, Dudley Mark Percy, 3 June, 1919. (M.)
5481 Lindsay, Walker Stewart, 3 June, 1919. (M.)
5482 Lindsey, Rev. Charles Edward Chaloner, 3 June, 1919. (M.)
5483 Little, D'Arcy Hunter, 3 June, 1919. (M.)
5484 Livesey, Everard Frederick Ernest, 3 June, 1919. (M.)
5485 Livingstone, John Stewart, 3 June, 1919. (M.)
5486 Livingstone, Robert Heaton, 3 June, 1919. (M.)
5487 Llewellin, Charles Herbert, 3 June, 1919. (M.)
5489 Lloyd, John Daniel Stuart, 3 June, 1919. (M.)
5490 Lloyd, Llewellyn Hubert, 3 June, 1919. (M.)
5491 Lock, Arthur, 3 June, 1919. (M.)
5492 Lockhart, Norman Charles, 3 June, 1919. (M.)
5493 Lockie, John, 3 June, 1919. (M.)
5494 Logan, Frederick Robert, 3 June, 1919. (M.)
5495 Long, Walter, 3 June, 1919. (M.)
5496 Lord, Henry Hardman, 3 June, 1919. (M.)
5497 Lorimer, James Vass, 3 June, 1919. (M.)
5498 Loveridge, Cecil Hubert, 3 June, 1919. (M.)
5499 Lowe, Alice Mary, 3 June, 1919. (M.)
5500 Low, James Lawson, 3 June, 1919. (M.)
5501 Lowther-Clarke, Mervyn Hanbury, 3 June, 1919. (M.)
5502 Ludlow-Hewitt, Alfred, 3 June, 1919. (M.)
5503 Lumb, Norman Peace Lacy, 3 June, 1919. (M.)
5505 Lyle, John Clifford Vacy, 3 June, 1919. (M.)
5506 Lyon, Kenneth, 3 June, 1919. (M.)
5507 McArthur, William James, 3 June, 1919. (M.)
5508 Macauley, Elizabeth Lusk, 3 June, 1919. (M.)
5509 MacColl, Henry Hector, 3 June, 1919. (M.)
5510 Maconachie, Charles Ogle, 3 June, 1919. (M.)
5511 McCracken, Frederic de Cree, 3 June, 1919. (M.)
5512 MacDona, Cuthbert Laud, 3 June, 1919. (M.)
5513 McDonald, Charles James Lewis, 3 June, 1919. (M.)
5514 MacDonald, Francis Caven, 3 June, 1919. (M.)
5515 McDonald, James Ratcliff, 3 June, 1919. (M.)
5516 MacDonald, Duncan, 3 June, 1919. (M.)
5517 MacDougall, Frederick George, 3 June, 1919. (M.)
5518 McDougall, William Allen, 3 June, 1919. (M.)
5519 McDowell, Alexander, 3 June, 1919. (M.)
5520 MacEwen, William, 3 June, 1919. (M.)
5521 MacFie, Ronald Bute, 3 June, 1919. (M.)
5522 McGrigor, Alexander Muir, 3 June, 1919. (M.)
5523 McHugh, Rev. Daniel John, 3 June, 1919. (M.)
5524 MacKay, Robert Whyte, 3 June, 1919. (M.)
5525 MacKenzie, Colin, 3 June, 1919. (M.)
5526 MacKenzie, Alexander, 3 June, 1919. (M.)
5527 McLachlan, James, 3 June, 1919. (M.)
5528 MacLeod, Adam Gordon, 3 June, 1919. (M.)
5529 MacMahon, Gerald Patrick Ruadh, 3 June, 1919. (M.)
5530 MacMillan, Rev. John Victor, 3 June, 1919. (M.)
5531 MacPherson, Ernest Ronald, 3 June, 1919. (M.)
5532 MacPherson, Malcolm Munro, 3 June, 1919. (M.)
5533 MacSwiney, John Charles, 3 June, 1919. (M.)
5534 MacVey, Thomas, 3 June, 1919. (M.)
5535 Major, William Reginald, 3 June, 1919. (M.)
5536 Malyon, Frank Haistone, 3 June, 1919. (M.)
5537 Mann, Percival Ramsey, 3 June, 1919. (M.)
5538 Marr, David Murdock, 3 June, 1919. (M.)
5539 Marriott, Herbert, 3 June, 1919. (M.)
5540 Marriott, Samuel Warburton, 3 June, 1919. (M.)
5541 Marriott-Dodington, Roger, 3 June, 1919. (M.)
5542 Marsden, John Henry Frederick, 3 June, 1919. (M.)
5543 Marsh, Octavius-de-Burgh, 3 June, 1919. (M.)
5544 Marshall, Geoffrey, 3 June, 1919. (M.)
5545 Marshall, Hugh John Cole, 3 June, 1919. (M.)
5546 Marshall, Isa Carswell, 3 June, 1919. (M.)
5547 Martin, Charles James, 3 June, 1919. (M.)
5548 Martin, Gerald Hamilton, 3 June, 1919. (M.)
5549 Martyn, Anthony Wood, 3 June, 1919. (M.)
5550 Martyn, Samuel, 3 June, 1919. (M.)
5551 Mascall, Maurice Edward, 3 June, 1919. (M.)
5553 Mason, Robert Wyllie, 3 June, 1919. (M.)
5554 Massie, Robert, 3 June, 1919. (M.)
5555 Masterson, William, 3 June, 1919. (M.)
5556 Matcham, William Eyre, 3 June, 1919. (M.)
5557 Matchett, Harry Gerald Keith, 3 June, 1919. (M.)
5558 Matthews, David, 3 June, 1919. (M.)
5559 Matheson, Edmond George, 3 June, 1919. (M.)
5560 Mathew, Felton Arthur Hamilton, 3 June, 1919. (M.)
5561 Matthews, Herbert, 3 June, 1919. (M.)
5562 Mattocks, Richard Mawson, 3 June, 1919. (M.)
5563 Maude, Charles Raymond, 3 June, 1919. (M.)
5564 Maude, Christian George, 3 June, 1919. (M.)
5565 Maude, Ronald Edmund, 3 June, 1919. (M.)
5566 Maund, Ernest Ricardo, 3 June, 1919. (M.)
5567 Maunsell, Octavius Studdert, 3 June, 1919. (M.)
5568 Mawson, William Willmott, 3 June, 1919. (M.)

5569 May, Noel Bankart, 3 June, 1919. (M.)
5570 Maycock, Arthur Hubert, 3 June, 1919. (M.)
5571 Meagher, Denis John, 3 June, 1919. (M.)
5572 Meagher, Henry Louis, 3 June, 1919. (M.)
5573 Measham, Richard John Rupert, 3 June, 1919. (M.)
5574 Medcalfe, John Clarence, 3 June, 1919. (M.)
5575 Mellor, John Seymour, 3 June, 1919. (M.)
5576 Meredith, Henry Chase, 3 June, 1919. (M.)
5577 Metford, Francis Killigrew Seymour, 3 June, 1919. (M.)
5578 Metivier, Harry Vincent Mercer, 3 June, 1919. (M.)
5579 Meynell, Everard Charles, 3 June, 1919. (M.)
5580 Meynell, Robert Alexander Lindley, 3 June, 1919. (M.)
5581 Mildred, Spencer, 3 June, 1919. (M.)
5582 Miller, James Cousins, 3 June, 1919. (M.)
5583 Milligan, Edward Thomas Campbell, 3 June, 1919. (M.)
5584 Millward, Harry Dacres, 3 June, 1919. (M.)
5585 Mitchell, John Malcolm, 3 June, 1919. (M.)
5586 Mold, Leonard Ernest, 3 June, 1919. (M.)
5587 Moncrieff, Roger Murray, 3 June, 1919. (M.)
5588 Monckton-Arundell, Hon. George Vere, 3 June, 1919. (M.)
5589 Money, Kenneth Robertson, 3 June, 1919. (M.)
5590 Monier-Williams, Gordon Wickham, 3 June, 1919. (M.)
5591 Montagu, Frederick James Osbaldeston, 3 June, 1919. (M.)
5592 Montagu, St. John Edward, 3 June, 1919. (M.)
5593 Montagu, Vivian Charles, 3 June, 1919. (M.)
5594 Montague, Charles Edward, 3 June, 1919. (M.)
5595 Monteith, Hugh Glencairn, 3 June, 1919. (M.)
5596 Mood, John Muspratt, 3 June, 1919. (M.)
5597 Moon, Jasper, 3 June, 1919. (M.)
5598 Moore, James, 3 June, 1919. (M.)
5599 Moore, James York, 3 June, 1919. (M.)
5600 Moore, Robert Foster, 3 June, 1919. (M.)
5601 Moran, John William, 3 June, 1919. (M.)
5602 Morgan, Stanley Herbert, 3 June, 1919. (M.)
5603 Morgan, Thomas Henry, 3 June, 1919. (M.)
5604 Morison, Ernest, 3 June, 1919. (M.)
5605 Morrell, Arthur Claude, 3 June, 1919. (M.)
5606 Morris, Frederick, 3 June, 1919. (M.)
5607 Morrison, John Tertius, 3 June, 1919. (M.)
5608 Morton, Edwin Ralph Maddison, 3 Jan. 1919. (M.)
5609 Morwood, Arthur, 3 June, 1919. (M.)
5610 Moss, Kenneth Neville, 3 June, 1919. (M.)
5611 Moxon, Francis Henry, 3 June, 1919. (M.)
5612 Mudge, Albert Edward Phayre, 3 June, 1919. (M.)
5613 Muir, George, 3 June, 1919. (M.)
5614 Mundy, Robert Godfrey, 3 June, 1919. (M.)
5615 Munn, Leonard, 3 June, 1919. (M.)
5616 Murdoch, Robert, 3 June, 1919. (M.)
5617 Murphy, John, 3 June, 1919. (M.)
5618 Murray, Walter, 3 June, 1919. (M.)
5619 Myles, Walter Andrew, 3 June, 1919. (M.)
5620 Napier, Charles James, 3 June, 1919. (M.)
5621 Neate, Alfred, 3 June, 1919. (M.)
5622 Neate, Frederick Harry, 3 June, 1919. (M.)
5623 Needham, Alfred Owen, 3 June, 1919. (M.)
5624 Needham, James Easthope, 3 June, 1919. (M.)
5625 Neil, George London, 3 June, 1919. (M.)
5626 Newell, Leopold Monk, 3 June, 1919. (M.)
5627 Newman, Frederick Herbert, 3 June, 1919. (M.)
5628 Newman, Richard Ernest Upton, 3 June, 1919. (M.)
5629 Newman, Vincent Chester, 3 June, 1919. (M.)
5630 Newsome, Charles Todd, 3 June, 1919. (M.)
5631 Nicholas, Edward Hall, 3 June, 1919. (M.)
5632 Nicholls, James Edward, 3 June, 1919. (M.)
5633 Nicholson, Henry Scoble, 3 June, 1919. (M.)
5634 Nicol, Rev. George Erskine, 3 June, 1919. (M.)
5635 Nicol, Randall James, 3 June, 1919. (M.)
5636 Nicoll, Frederick Alan Benson, 3 June, 1919. (M.)
5637 Noble, Bertram Wilfred, 3 June, 1919. (M.)
5638 Noel, Hon. Charles Hubert Francis, 3 June, 1919. (M.)
5639 Norman, Edward Hubert, 3 June, 1919. (M.)
5640 Northcott, Harold James, 3 June, 1919. (M.)
5641 Norwood, Charles John, 3 June, 1919. (M.)
5642 Oates, William, 3 June, 1919. (M.)
5643 O'Donnell, John, 3 June, 1919. (M.)
5644 O'Grady, Robert Louis, 3 June, 1919. (M.)
5646 O'Hara, Ernest, 3 June, 1919. (M.)
5646 O'Kelly, John William, 3 June, 1919. (M.)
5647 Oldham, Rev. Gordon Miles Staveley, 3 June, 1919. (M.)
5648 Oliver, Edward Victor, 3 June, 1919. (M.)
5649 Oliver, Matthew William Baillie, 3 June, 1919. (M.)
5650 Olley, Arthur Edward, 3 June, 1919. (M.)
5651 Ollivant, Rupert Charles, 3 June, 1919. (M.)
5652 O'Riordan, Henry Michael, 3 June, 1919. (M.)
5653 Ormiston, Thomas Maclay, 3 June, 1919. (M.)
5654 Osborne, John Williams, 3 June, 1919. (M.)
5655 Osler, James Bell, 4 June, 1919. (M.)
5656 Owen, Bertram Maurice, 3 June, 1919. (M.)
5657 Palin, Randle Harry, 3 June, 1919. (M.)
5658 Palmer, Alexander Croyden, 3 June, 1919. (M.)
5659 Palmer, Herbert James Leslie, 3 June, 1919. (M.)
5660 Pam, Albert, 3 June, 1919. (M.)
5661 Pam, Edgar, 3 June, 1919. (M.)
5662 Parker, Beltran William, 3 June, 1919. (M.)
5663 Parker, Frances Mary, 3 June, 1919. (M.)
5664 Parker, Rev. Joseph, 3 June, 1919. (M.)
5665 Parker, Sidney James, 3 June, 1919. (M.)
5666 Parkin, Herbert Denis, 3 June, 1919. (M.)

5667 Paterson, Matthew Wallace, 3 June, 1919. (M.)
5668 Pawle, Hanbury, 3 June, 1919. (M.)
5669 Peachey, William Ellis, 3 June, 1919. (M.)
5670 Peake, Edward Gordon, 3 June, 1919. (M.)
5671 Pearce, Edward Oscar, 3 June, 1919. (M.)
5672 Pearson, Basil Lancelot, 3 June, 1919. (M.)
5673 Peattie, Donald Munroe, 3 June, 1919. (M.)
5674 Pearsall, Sidney James, 3 June, 1919. (M.)
5675 Pellereau, John Cyril Etienne, 3 June, 1919. (M.)
5676 Penrose, Edward Samuel, 3 June, 1919. (M.)
5677 Perkins, William Hughes, 3 June, 1919. (M.)
5678 Perry, Henry Marrian Joseph, 3 June, 1919. (M.)
5679 Peterson, Guy Lansbury, 3 June, 1919. (M.)
5680 Peyton, William de Malet, 3 June, 1919. (M.)
5681 Philpot, Albert John, 3 June, 1919. (M.)
5682 Pierce, William Robertus, 3 June, 1919. (M.)
5683 Pillow, Frederick William, 3 June, 1919. (M.)
5684 Pinniger, Albert Edward, 3 June, 1919. (M.)
5685 Platts, Matthew George, 3 June, 1919. (M.)
5686 Plucknett, Frederick, 3 June, 1919. (M.)
5687 Plunkett, James Joseph, 3 June, 1919. (M.)
5688 Poole, Francis Garden, 3 June, 1919. (M.)
5689 Pooles, Mark, 3 June, 1919. (M.)
5690 Pope, Andrew Noble, 3 June, 1919. (M.)
5691 Poyser, John, 3 June, 1919. (M.)
5692 Prescott-Roberts, Prescott Anson, 3 June, 1919. (M.)
5693 Price, Charles Weaver, 3 June, 1919. (M.)
5694 Pridden, Edith Mary, 3 June, 1919. (M.)
5695 Procter, Edward, 3 June, 1919. (M.)
5696 Pryce-Jones, Albert Westlake, 3 June, 1919. (M.)
5697 Pullar, George Douglas, 3 June, 1919. (M.)
5698 Pullar, John Lindsay, 3 June, 1919. (M.)
5699 Pym, Charles Evelyn, 3 June, 1919. (M.)
5700 Rainsford, George, 3 June, 1919. (M.)
5701 Ramage, William, 3 June, 1919. (M.)
5702 Ramsay, Ronald Arthur, 3 June, 1919. (M.)
5703 Raper, Ernest Charles, 3 June, 1919. (M.)
5704 Raymond, Harold, 3 June, 1919. (M.)
5705 Raymond, Hugh Phillips, 3 June, 1919. (M.)
5706 Reckitt, Charles Edward Hay, 3 June, 1919. (M.)
5707 Redfern, Arthur Edward, 3 June, 1919. (M.)
5708 Rees, Blethyn Treherne, 3 June, 1919. (M.)
5709 Rees, William Arthur, 3 June, 1919. (M.)
5710 Rees-Mogg, Graham Beauchamp Coxeter, 3 June, 1919. (M.)
5711 Renton, William Clifford, 3 June, 1919. (M.)
5712 Rich, Theodore, 3 June, 1919. (M.)
5713 Richards, Malcolm John, 3 June, 1919. (M.)
5714 Richardson, Harry, 3 June, 1919. (M.)
5715 Richmond, John Duncan, 3 June, 1919. (M.)
5716 Ridley, Hon. Jasper Nicholas, 3 June, 1919. (M.)
5717 Rigden, William Percy, 3 June, 1919. (M.)
5718 Ritchie, Michael Balfour Hutchison, 3 June, 1919. (M.)
5719 Ritchie, Robert Linton, 3 June, 1919. (M.)
5720 Roberts, James Ernest Helme, 3 June, 1919. (M.)
5721 Robertson, Alfred Leopold, 3 June, 1919. (M.)
5723 Robertson, Frederick William, 3 June, 1919. (M)
5724 Robertson, Robert Charles, 3 June, 1919. (M.)
5725 Robinson, Augustus Francis, 3 June, 1919. (M.)
5726 Robson, John, 3 June, 1919. (M.)
5727 Rockett, Herbert Charles, 3 June, 1919. (M.)
5728 Roderick, Henry Buckley, 3 June, 1919. (M.)
5729 Rogers, Henry Waters Lyttleton, 3 June, 1919. (M.)
5730 Rollinson, Harry Duggan, 3 June, 1919. (M.)
5731 Romer, Charles Robert Ritchie, 3 June, 1919. (M.)
5732 Romer, Robert Wolfgang, 3 June, 1919. (M.)
5733 Ronan, Walter Joseph, 3 June, 1919. (M.)
5734 Rook, William Robert, 3 June, 1919. (M.)
5735 Roseveare, Leslie, 3 June, 1919. (M.)
5736 Ross, Angus, 3 June, 1919. (M.)
5737 Ross, Charles Thomas, 3 June, 1919. (M.)
5738 Rowell, William Henry, 3 June, 1919. (M.)
5739 Ruck-Keene, Harry Lancelot, 3 June, 1919. (M.)
5740 Russell, Ernest Gordon, 3 June, 1919. (M.)
5741 Russell, William Sydney Kemp, 3 June, 1919. (M.)
5742 Rutherford, Percival Thomas, 3 June, 1919. (M.)
5743 Ruttledge, Thomas Geoffrey, 3 June, 1919. (M.)
5744 Ruxton, Robert Minturn Clarges, 3 June, 1919. (M.)
5745 Ryan, Pierce Neimeyer, 3 June, 1919. (M.)
5746 Ryan, Rev. William, 3 June, 1919. (M.)
5747 Sampson, Herbert Henry, 3 June, 1919. (M.)
5748 Sandars, Edmund Thomas, 3 June, 1919. (M.)
5749 Sandon, James Francis, 3 June, 1919. (M.)
5750 Sanguinetti, William Roger, 3 June, 1919. (M.)
5751 Sarchet, Rev. William Henry, 3 June, 1919. (M.)
5752 Satchwell, Ernest, 3 June, 1919. (M.)
5753 Satow, Graham Francis Henry, 3 June, 1919. (M.)
5755 Scawin, Harold Willis, 3 June, 1919. (M.)
5756 Scholtz, Ellis Keith, 3 June, 1919. (M.)
5757 Schonland, Basil Ferdinand Jamieson, 3 June, 1919. (M.)
5758 Scorgie, Norman Gibb, 3 June, 1919. (M.)
5759 Scott, David Jobson, 3 June, 1919. (M.)
5760 Scott, Frank, 3 June, 1919. (M.)
5761 Scott, James Edward, 3 June, 1919. (M.)
5762 Scott, John Creagh, 3 June, 1919. (M.)
5763 Scruby, Frank Sutherland, 3 June, 1919. (M.)
5764 Seale, Edward Wilmot, 3 June, 1919. (M.)
5765 Sealy, Philip Temple, 3 June, 1919. (M.)

5766 Selby, Edward James, 3 June, 1919. (M.)
5767 Sells, Martin Perronet, 3 June, 1919. (M.)
5768 Selous, William Boyd, 3 June, 1919. (M.)
5769 Shackleton, Alfred George, 3 June, 1919. (M.)
5770 Shackleton, Herbert Park, 3 June, 1919. (M.)
5771 Sharpe, Gerald Whittaker, 3 June, 1919. (M.)
5772 Sharples, Frank Deeks, 3 June, 1919. (M.)
5773 Shaw, Arthur Godfrey, 3 June, 1919. (M.)
5774 Shaw, Thomas Alfred, 3 June, 1919. (M.)
5775 Sheppard, Helen Mildred, 3 June, 1919. (M.)
5776 Shilton, Frederick Walton, 3 June, 1919. (M.)
5777 Shipp, Frederick Edgar, 3 June, 1919. (M.)
5778 Sidebottom, John Kercheval, 3 June, 1919. (M.)
5779 Simpson, Edward Herbert, 3 June, 1919. (M.)
5780 Simpson, George Charles Edward, 3 June, 1919. (M.)
5781 Simpson, Selwyn George, 3 June, 1919. (M.)
5782 Simson, Harold, 3 June, 1919. (M.)
5783 Sissons, Henry Arnott, 3 June, 1919. (M.)
5784 Smith, Augustus William, 3 June, 1919. (M.)
5785 Smith, Daniel Rowland, 3 June, 1919. (M.)
5786 Smith, Felix Patrick, 3 June, 1919. (M.)
5787 Smith, George William, 3 June, 1919. (M.)
5788 Smith, Isaac Claude Victor, 3 June, 1919. (M.
5789 Smith, Samuel Boylan, 3 June, 1919. (M.)
5790 Smith, Stanley, 3 June, 1919. (M.)
5791 Smythe, Patrick Cecil, 3 June, 1919. (M.)
5792 Sorley, Gerald Merson. 3 June, 1919. (M.)
5793 Spafford, Percy Lionel, 3 June, 1919. (M.)
5794 Speke, Herbert Benjamin, 3 June, 1919. (M.)
5795 Spoor, Sidney George, 3 June, 1919. (M.)
5796 Spyer, George, 3 June, 1919. (M.)
5798 Stack, Rev. James, 3 June, 1919. (M.)
5799 Stallard, Robert Humphry, 3 June, 1919. (M.)
5800 Stallard, Sydney, 3 June. 1919. (M.)
5801 Stanhope, Colin Lundin, 3 June, 1919. (M.)
5802 Stanley. Ernest Raymond, 3 June, 1919. (M.)
5803 Stannard, Frank Charles, 3 June, 1919. (M.)
5804 Statham, Reginald Samuel Sherrard, 3 June, 1919. (M.)
5805 Steel, Gabriel, 3 June, 1919. (M.)
5806 Stephen, Guy Neville, 3 June. 1919. (M.)
5807 Stevens, Edward James, 3 June, 1919. (M.)
5808 Stevenson, Bertrand James, 3 June, 1919. (M.)
5809 Stevenson, George Henderson, 3 June, 1919. (M.)
5810 Stewart. Aubrey George Battersby, 3 June, 1919. (M.)
5811 Stewart, Donald MacIver, 3 June, 1919. (M.)
5812 Stewart, William Henry, 3 June, 1919. (M.)
5813 Stickings, Ralph William Ewart, 3 June, 1919. (M.)
5814 Stirling, Patrick Douglas, 3 June, 1919. (M.)
5815 Stirling, William, 3 June, 1919. (M.)
5816 Stobie, William, 3 June, 1919. (M.)
5817 Stockwell, Hugh Charles, 3 June, 1919. (M.)
5818 Stokes, Adrian, 3 June, 1919. (M.)
5819 Stokes, Henry, 3 June, 1919. (M.)
5820 Storr, Francis Holland, 3 June, 1919. (M.)
5821 Stow, George, 3 June, 1919. (M.)
5822 Streatfield, Granville Edward Stewart, 3 June, 1919. (M.)
5823 Stuckey, Edward Joseph, 3 June, 1919. (M.)
5824 Surtees, Robert Lambton, 3 June, 1919. (M.)
5825 Swayne, Richard Woodward, 3 June, 1919. (M.)
5826 Sweetman, Michael James, 3 June, 1919. (M.)
5827 Sykes, Stanley William, 3 June, 1919. (M.)
5828 Symes, John, 3 June, 1919. (M.)
5829 Tagg, George John, 3 June, 1919. (M.)
5830 Targett, Harry, 3 June, 1919. (M.)
5831 Tayleur, William, 3 June, 1919. (M.)
5832 Taylor, Alfred Jessie, 3 June, 1919. (M.)
5833 Taylor, Douglas Compton, 3 June, 1919. (M.)
5834 Taylor, Douglas Percy, 3 June, 1919. (M.)
5835 Taylor, Edgar Charles, 3 June, 1919. (M.)
5836 Taylor, Eric Stewart, 3 June, 1919. (M.)
5837 Taylor, Gordon, 3 June, 1919. (M.)
5838 Taylor, Rev. Harold Milman Strickland, 3 June, 1919. (M.)
5839 Taylor, Hugh Lamport, 3 June, 1919. (M.)
5840 Teasdale. George Arthur James, 3 June, 1919. (M.)
5841 Teeling, Bartholomew Louis Charles, 3 June, 1919. (M.)
5842 Tennant, Ernest William Dalrymple, 3 June, 1919. (M.)
5843 Ternan, Henry Augustus Breffney, 3 June, 1919. (M.)
5844 Terry, Cyril Edward, 3 June, 1919. (M.)
5845 Thackwell, Noel Edmund Osbert, 3 June, 1919. (M.)
5846 Thomas, Bernard Henry, 3 June, 1919. (M.)
5847 Thomas, Percy Edward, 3 June, 1919. (M.)
5848 Thomas, Rev. Richard Albert, 3 June, 1919. (M.)
5849 Thomas, Robert John, 3 June, 1919. (M.)
5850 Thomson Arthur Landsborough, 3 June, 1919. (M.)
5851 Thompson, Edward, 3 June, 1919. (M.)
5852 Thompson, James Osbourne, 3 June, 1919. (M.)
5853 Thompson, Walter Wright, 3 June, 1919. (M.)
5854 Thorns, Leslie, 3 June, 1919. (M.)
5855 Thornton, Basil Albert, 3 June, 1919. (M.)
5856 Thorp, John Claud, 3 June, 1919. (M.)
5857 Thorpe, John Henry, 3 June, 1919. (M.)
5858 Tizard, Claude, 3 June, 1919. (M.)
5859 Todd, Arthur Theodore, 3 June, 1919. (M.)
5860 Todd, Sam, 3 June, 1919. (M.)
5861 Tosswill, Leonard Robert, 3 June, 1919. (M.)
5862 Townsend, Philip Henry, 3 June, 1919. (M.)
5863 Tredennick, James Paumier, 3 June, 1919. (M.)

5864 Tripp, Horace Edgar Howard, 3 June, 1919. (M.)
5865 Truscott, Roy Francis, 3 June, 1919. (M.)
5866 Tucker, Frederick Gordon, 3 June, 1919. (M.)
5867 Tudor, Gerald, 3 June, 1919. (M.)
5868 Tully, Claude Lewis Devenish, 3 June, 1919. (M.)
5869 Turner, Francis Gordon, 3 June, 1919. (M.)
5870 Tylor, George Cunningham, 3 June, 1919. (M.)
5871 Tyrwhitt, Rev. Canon Hon. Leonard Francis, 3 June, 1919. (M.)
5872 Underhill, Owen, 3 June, 1919. (M.)
5873 Unsworth, Richard Lewis, 3 June, 1919. (M.)
5874 Upton, Thomas Haynes, 3 June, 1919. (M.)
5875 Urwick, Lyndall Fownes, 3 June, 1919. (M.)
5876 Valon, Albert Robert, 3 June, 1919. (M.)
5877 Vaughan, Arthur Owen, 3 June, 1919. (M.)
5878 Veal, Frank, 3 June, 1919. (M.)
5879 Vellacott, Philip Northcote, 3 June, 1919. (M.)
5880 Venn, Hugh Whatley Stevens, 3 June, 1919. (M.)
5881 Vercoe, Edmund, 3 June, 1919. (M.)
5882 Viccars, John Ellis, 3 June, 1919. (M.)
5883 Vickress, William Henry, 3 June, 1919. (M.)
5884 Vigers, Thomas Whitehaire, 3 June, 1919. (M.)
5885 Vincent, Sydney, 3 June, 1919. (M.)
5886 Waddy, Arthur Cyril, 3 June, 1919. (M.)
5887 Wain, Douglas, 3 June, 1919. (M.)
5888 Wainwright, Edwin Moira, 3 June, 1919. (M.)
5889 Walker, Edward McAllen, 3 June, 1919. (M.)
5890 Walker, George, 3 June, 1919. (M.)
5891 Walker, John Douglas Glen, 3 June, 1919. (M.)
5892 Wallace, Forbes Thompson, 3 June, 1919. (M.)
5893 Waller, Edgar Hardress, 3 June, 1919. (M.)
5894 Wallinger, William Arnold, 3 June, 1919. (M.)
5895 Wanklyn-James, Charles Wilmot, 3 June, 1919. (M.)
5896 Warren, David Bruce, 3 June, 1919. (M.)
5897 Warren, Philip Ridsdale, 3 June, 1919. (M.)
5898 Warren, William Robert Vaughton, 3 June, 1919. (M.)
5899 Waters, Walter James, 3 June, 1919. (M.)
5900 Watney, Ernest Alfred William, 3 June, 1919. (M.)
5901 Watson, Forrester Colvin, 3 June, 1919. (M.)
5902 Watson, William Frank, 3 June, 1919. (M.)
5903 Wattleworth, James Percy, 3 June, 1919. (M.)
5904 Watts, Lowther, 3 June, 1919. (M.)
5905 Webster, Frank Coutts, 3 June, 1919. (M.)
5906 Webster, Noel Edwin, 3 June, 1919. (M.)
5907 Wedd, Aubrey Pattisson Wallman, 3 June, 1919. (M.)
5908 Weir, Robert Yaxley, 3 June, 1919. (M.)
5909 Wells, Arthur George, 3 June, 1919. (M.)
5910 Wells, Charles Alexander, 3 June, 1919. (M.)
5911 Wesley, Frank William, 3 June, 1919. (M.)
5912 Westmacott, Reginald Granville, 3 June, 1919. (M.)
5913 Westmacott, Thomas Horatio, 3 June, 1919. (M.)
5914 Wheatley, Henry Harold, 3 June, 1919. (M.)
5915 Whiffen, Stanley White, 3 June, 1919. (M.)
5916 Whigham, Walter Kennedy, 3 June, 1919. (M.)
5917 White, Charles Francis, 3 June, 1919. (M.)
5918 White, Edwin E., 3 June, 1919. (M.)
5919 White, George Gilmour, 3 June, 1919. (M.)
5920 White, John, 3 June, 1919. (M.)
5921 White, Maurice FitzGibbon Grove, 3 June, 1919. (M.)
5922 Whiting, Maurice Henry, 3 June, 1919. (M.)
5923 Whitla, Valentine George, 3 June, 1919. (M.)
5924 Wickersham, John, 3 June, 1919. (M.)
5925 Wicks, Henry William Cairns, 3 June, 1919. (M.)
5926 Widderson, Andrew James, 3 June, 1919. (M.)
5927 Wilkins, Raymond, 3 June, 1919. (M.)
5928 Wilkinson, Kenneth Douglas, 3 June, 1919. (M.)
5929 Wilkinson, Noel Read Ellershaw, 3 June, 1919. (M.)
5930 Wilks, Frank Stanley, 3 June, 1919. (M.)
5931 Williams, Albert Henry, 3 June, 1919. (M.)
5932 Williams, Alfred Edwin, 3 June, 1919. (M.)
5933 Williams, Archard Trevor, 3 June, 1919. (M.)
5934 Williams, Frank Harry, 3 June, 1919. (M.)
5935 Williams, Henry Claude, 3 June, 1919. (M.)
5936 Williams-Freeman, Arthur Peere, 3 June, 1919. (M.)
5937 Wilson, Archibald, 3 June, 1919. (M.)
5938 Wilson, Arthur Ernest, 3 June, 1919. (M.)
5939 Wilson, George Gatherer, 3 June, 1919. (M.)
5940 Wilson, John Alexander, 3 June, 1919. (M.)
5941 Wilson, John Stewart, 3 June, 1919. (M.)
5942 Wilson, Rev. Piers Holt, 3 June, 1919. (M.)
5943 Winch, Stanley Brooke, 3 June, 1919. (M.)
5944 Windeatt, George Edward, 3 June, 1919. (M.)
5945 Winder, Francis Arthur, 3 June, 1919. (M.)
5946 Winfield, Frederick Butwell, 3 June, 1919. (M.)
5947 Wolff, Henry Philip, 3 June, 1919. (M.)
5948 Wolridge-Gordon, Walter Gordon. 3 June, 1919. (M.)
5949 Wood, George Jervis, 3 June, 1919. (M.)
5950 Wood, James Henry, 3 June, 1919. (M.)
5951 Wood, John Edward, 3 June, 1919. (M.)
5952 Wood, John Lawrence, 3 June, 1919. (M.)
5953 Wood, Minnie, 3 June, 1919. (M.)
5954 Wood, William Lyon, 3 June, 1919. (M.)
5955 Woodger, John Surry, 3 June, 1919. (M.)
5956 Woodward, Vivian John, 3 June, 1919. (M.)
5957 Woolf, Edward Saville, 3 June, 1919. (M.)
5958 Wooll, Edward, 3 June, 1919. (M.)
5959 Woollcombe, Rev. Edward Percival, 3 June, 1919. (M.)
5960 Woolley, Ivor William, 3 June, 1919. (M.)
5961 Woolrych, Stanley Herbert Cunliffe, 3 June, 1919. (M.)

5962 Worlledge, John Penry Garnons, 3 June, 1919. (M.)
5963 Wright, Arthur John, 3 June, 1919. (M.)
5964 Wright, John Henry, 3 June, 1919. (M.)
5965 Wright, Charles Seymour, 3 June, 1919. (M.)
5966 Wright, Ernest Trevor Langebear, 3 June, 1919. (M.)
5967 Wyatt, Travers Carey, 3 June, 1919. (M.)
5968 Yates, Arthur St. John, 3 June, 1919. (M.)
5969 Yates, John Henry, 3 June, 1919. (M.)
5970 Yellowlees, Henry, 3 June, 1919. (M.)
5971 Yelverton, Rev. Erik Esskildsen, 3 June, 1919. (M.)
5972 Yorke, John, 3 June, 1919. (M.)
5973 Young, Rev. Stanislaus Dominic, 3 June, 1919. (M.)
5974 Acheson, Thomas Stuart, 3 June, 1919. (M.)
5975 Alexander, Kay, 3 June, 1919. (M.)
5976 Allen, Jesse, 3 June, 1919. (M.)
5977 Armour, John Douglas, 3 June. 1919. (M.)
5978 Ball, John Clements, 3 June, 1919. (M.)
5979 Bennett, Allan Edward Kingston, 3 June, 1919. (M.)
5980 Bissett, James, 3 June, 1919. (M.)
5981 Bovey, Wilfred, 3 June, 1919. (M.)
5982 Burke, Edmund Albert, 3 June, 1919. (M.)
5983 Carey, Leslie Clement, 3 June, 1919. (M.)
5984 Carroll, William, 3 June, 1919. (M.)
5985 Church, Eric James, 3 June, 1919. (M.)
5986 Cline, John George, 3 June, 1919. (M.)
5987 Colville, Cyril Prichard, 3 June, 1919. (M.)
5988 Cooper, Henry Sloane, 3 June, 1919. (M.)
5989 Delaute, Frederic Joseph, 3 June, 1919. (M.)
5990 Duhault, Joseph Rene Jacques, 3 June, 1919. (M.)
5991 Earchman, Archibald, 3 June, 1919. (M.)
5992 Ellis, Arthur William Mickle. 3 June, 1919. (M.)
5993 Erlebach, Cyril Woodland, 3 June, 1919. (M.)
5994 Findlay, William Henri de la Tour d'Auvergne, 3 June, 1919. (M.)
5995 Findley, Harold Bruce, 3 June, 1919. (M.)
5996 Finney, Wilfred Josiah, 3 June, 1919. (M.)
5997 Foster, Albert Percy. 3 June, 1919. (M.)
5998 Gault, Andrew Hamilton, 3 June, 1919. (M.)
5999 Geary, George Reginald, 3 June, 1919. (M.)
6000 George, FitzRoy, 3 June, 1919. (M.)
6001 Gibsone, William Waring Primrose, 3 June, 1919. (M.)
6002 Gordon, Edward Montgomery, 3 June, 1919. (M.)
6003 Graham, Vivien Horace, 3 June, 1919. (M.)
6004 Hale. Thomas, 3 June, 1919. (M.)
6005 Hardy, Hermann Alfred, 3 June, 1919. (M.)
6006 Harty, William, 3 June, 1919. (M.)
6007 Herbert, Harold, 3 June, 1919. (M.)
6008 Herd, Walter, 3 June, 1919. (M.)
6009 Irwin, Basil Herbert John, 3 June, 1919. (M.)
6010 Jack, John Gordon, 3 June, 1919. (M.)
6011 Jennings, George Leslie, 3 June, 1919. (M.)
6012 Johnston, Benjamin James, 3 June, 1919. (M.)
6013 Jones, Arthur Llewelyn, 3 June, 1919. (M.)
6014 Jones, Lorne Fauntleroy, 3 June, 1919. (M.)
6015 Kemmis Betty, Hubert, 3 June, 1919. (M.)
6016 Lacroix, Lucien, 3 June, 1919. (M.)
6017 Landon, Arthur Henry Whittington, 3 June, 1919. (M.)
6018 Larkin, Gerald Ross, 3 June, 1919. (M.)
6019 Macaulay, Archibald Francis, 3 June, 1919. (M.)
6020 McGreer, Rev. Arthur Huffman, 3 June, 1919. (M.)
6021 McGugan, Donald, 3 June, 1919. (M.)
6022 MacKay, Donald Morrison, 3 June, 1919. (M.)
6023 McKinery, John William Herbert, 3 June, 1919. (M.)
6024 Mackinnon, Cecil Gordon, 3 June, 1919. (M.)
6025 McMurray, William Hamilton, 3 June, 1919. (M.)
6026 McNeil, James Howard, 3 June, 1919. (M.)
6027 Main, William Wright, 3 June, 1919. (M.)
6028 Marshall, Harry A., 3 June, 1919. (M.)
6029 Marshall, James Frederick Stewart, 3 June, 1919. (M.)
6030 Martin, Herbert Walter, 3 June, 1919. (M.)
6031 Mason, Douglas Herbert Campbell, 3 June, 1919. (M.)
6032 Mathews, Robert Gordon, 3 June, 1919. (M.)
6033 Mermagen, Ernest Wallace, 3 June, 1919. (M.)
6034 Morton, Arthur William, 3 June, 1919. (M.)
6035 O'Gorman, Rev. John Joseph, 3 June, 1919. (M.)
6036 O'Sullivan, Richard Benjamin, 3 June, 1919. (M.)
6037 Parmelee, James Grannis, 3 June, 1919. (M.)
6038 Pattullo, James Burleigh, 3 June, 1919. (M.)
6039 Pearson, Gilbert Livermore, 3 June, 1919. (M.)
6040 Philpot, David, 3 June, 1919. (M.)
6041 Preston, Marvin James, 3 June, 1919. (M.)
6042 Ramsay, Kenneth Allan, 3 June, 1919. (M.)
6043 Reason, Clifford Hamilton, 3 June, 1919. (M.)
6044 Reed-Lewis, William John Duane, 3 June, 1919. (M.)
6045 Richardson, Frederick, 3 June, 1919. (M.)
6046 Richardson, William Augustus, 3 June, 1919. (M.)
6047 Roaf, James Richardson, 3 June, 1919. (M.)
6048 Robertson, Russell Butler, 3 June, 1919. (M.)
6049 Shatford, Rev. Allan, 3 June, 1919. (M.)
6050 Smith, Richard Stephenson, 3 June, 1919. (M.)
6051 Sowden, Felix Musgrave, 3 June, 1919. (M.)
6052 Spink, Bertram John William, 3 June, 1919. (M.)
6053 Spry, Daniel William Bigelows, 3 June, 1919. (M.)
6054 Stewart, John Douglas Reginald, 3 June, 1919. (M.)
6055 Stewart, Peter Donald, 3 June, 1919. (M.)
6056 Still, James, 3 June, 1919. (M.)
6057 Streight, Samuel James, 3 June, 1919. (M.)
6058 Sugden, John Leslie, 3 June, 1919. (M.)
6059 Tamblyn, David Soley, 3 June, 1919. (M.)

6060 Taylor, William John, 3 June, 1919. (M.)
6061 Towill, William Frederick, 3 June, 1919. (M.)
6062 Wade, Thomas Kingsmill, 3 June, 1919. (M.)
6063 Waldron, William, 3 June, 1919. (M.)
6064 Ward, John Stanley, 3 June, 1919. (M.)
6065 Worthington, William Wilfred, 3 June, 1919. (M.
6066 Young, Fred Armstrong, 3 June. 1919. (M.)
6067 Bath, Charles Hubert, 3 June, 1919. (M.)
6068 Bell, George, 3 June, 1919. (M.)
6069 Blanshard, Ernest Gladstone, 3 June, 1919. (M.)
6070 Bushell, Edward Harry, 3 June, 1919. (M.)
6071 Chapman, James Austin, 3 June, 1919. (M.)
6072 Dike, Edward Henry, 3 June, 1919. (M.)
6073 Farrar, John William, 3 June, 1919. (M.)
6074 Fiaschi, Piers, 3 June, 1919. (M.)
6075 Fry, Walter Arnold Le Roy, 3 June, 1919. (M.)
6076 Greenlees, Alexander McPhee, 3 June, 1919. (M.)
6077 Hardie, John Leslie, 3 June, 1919. (M.)
6078 Harrison, Charles Henry, 3 June, 1919. (M.)
6079 Harrison, Henry Coromandel Watsford, 3 June, 1919. (M.)
6080 Jack, Walter, 3 June, 1919. (M.)
6081 James, Edward Stewart, 3 June, 1919. (M.)
6082 Kerr, Robert, 3 June, 1919. (M.)
6083 Lawton, Frederick Donald Herbert Blois, 3 June, 1919. (M.)
6084 Macindoe, Robert Hall Forman, 3 June, 1919. (M.)
6085 Manning, Charles Henry Ernest, 3 June, 1919. (M.)
6086 Mellor, Thomas Reginald, 3 June, 1919. (M.)
6087 Morrell, Roy, 3 June, 1919. (M.)
6088 Moulden, Arnold Meredith, 3 June, 1919. (M.)
6089 Nugent. Hector Alexander, 3 June, 1919. (M.)
6090 Peters, Gordon, 3 June, 1919. (M.)
6091 Playfair, Thomas Alfred Jack, 3 June, 1919. (M.)
6092 Plant, Eric Clive Pegus, 3 June, 1919. (M.)
6093 Simonson, Paul William, 3 June, 1919. (M.)
6094 Stacy, Valentine Osborne, 3 June, 1919. (M.)
6095 Stevenson, Walter Ormond, 3 June, 1919. (M.)
6096 Taplin, Colin Quintrell, 3 June, 1919. (M.)
6097 Tinkler, Frederick Usher John, 3 June, 1919. (M.)
6098 Townsend, Harry Orton, 3 June, 1919. (M.)
6099 Trousselot, Henry Edward, 3 June, 1919. (M.)
6100 Wilson, Herbert Ward, 3 June, 1919. (M.)
6101 Wynyard-Joss, Alexander, 3 June, 1919. (M.)
6102 Edgar, Peter Maxwell, 3 June, 1919. (M.)
6103 Gossage, Charles Ingram, 3 June, 1919. (M.)
6104 Hutchinson, George Rowland, 3 June, 1919. (M.)
6105 McCurdy, David, 3 June, 1919. (M.)
6106 Muir, Allan Stanley, 3 June, 1919. (M.)
6107 Reid, Harold Avery, 3 June, 1919. (M.)
6108 Vickerman, Hugh, 3 June, 1919. (M.)
6109 Bowles, Ernest, 3 June, 1919. (M.)
6110 Cameron, Cecil Stevenson, 3 June, 1919. (M.)
6111 Collins, Frederick, 3 June, 1919. (M.)
6112 Emmett, Joseph James Cheere, 3 June, 1919. (M.)
6113 Fawous, Alfred, 3 June, 1919. (M.)
6114 Geddes, William Louis, 3 June, 1919. (M.)
6116 Jacobsz, Jan, 3 June, 1919. (M.)
6117 Lennox, Rev. John C. F., 3 June, 1919. (M.)
6118 Marshall, Henry Edmund, 3 June, 1919. (M.)
6119 Ross, Findlay McKay, 3 June, 1919. (M.)
6120 Sproule, Harper, 3 June, 1919. (M.)
6121 Usmar, George Henry, 3 June, 1919. (M.)
6122 McNeill, Hector, 3 June, 1919. (M.)
6123 Thomson, William Grant, 3 June, 1919. (M.)
6124 Adams, Alexander, 3 June, 1919. (M.)
6125 Aitkin, James Alexander Hamilton, 3 June, 1919. (M.)
6126 Alexander, James Ulick Francis Canning, 3 June, 1919. (M.)
6127 Allen, Charles Henry, 3 June, 1919. (M.)
6128 Andrew, Richard Hynman, 3 June, 1919. (M.)
6129 Armbruster, Charles Hubert, 3 June, 1919. (M.)
6130 Armitage, Philip Melland, 3 June, 1919. (M.)
6131 Ash, Harold Garton, 3 June, 1919. (M.)
6132 Bacon, Charles Raymond Kenrick, 3 June, 1919. (M.)
6133 Bally, Edward Downes, 3 June, 1919. (M.)
6134 Barker, Frederic Allan, 3 June, 1919. (M.)
6135 Barker, Charles Ainslie, 3 June, 1919. (M.)
6136 Bartlett, Horace John, 3 June, 1919. (M.)
6137 Bashford, Radcliffe James Lindsay, 3 June, 1919. (M.)
6138 Bates, Mark, 3 June, 1919. (M.)
6139 Beaumont, Henry, 3 June, 1919. (M.)
6140 Bentwich, Norman de Mattos, 3 June, 1919. (M.)
6141 Biggs, John James Egerton, 3 June, 1919. (M.)
6142 Blenkarne, Harold Morgan, 3 June, 1919. (M.)
6143 Bradley, James Lennox, 3 June, 1919. (M.)
6144 Bramall, Harold, 3 June, 1919. (M.)
6145 Bremner, James Morrison Gardiner, 3 June, 1919. (M.)
6146 Bridgwater, Havard Noel, 3 June, 1919. (M.)
6147 Brougham, James Henry Chamberlain, 3 June, 1919. (M.)
6148 Brown, Adam, 3 June, 1919. (M.)
6149 Brown, William, 3 June, 1919. (M.)
6150 Buckland, Lionel, 3 June, 1919. (M.)
6151 Campbell, John Cameron, 3 June, 1919. (M.)
6152 Carter, George James, 3 June, 1919. (M.)
6153 Cash, Rev. William Wilson, 3 June, 1919. (M.)
6154 Chesterman, Clement Clapton, 3 June, 1919. (M.)
6155 Chetwynd, Arthur Henry Talbot, 3 June, 1919. (M.)
6156 Cholmondeley, Lord George Hugo, 3 June, 1919. (M.)
6157 Clarke, James Bryce, 3 June, 1919. (M.)

6158 Cobden, George Gough, 3 June, 1919. (M.)
6159 Coles, Lawrence Walter, 3 June, 1919. (M.)
6160 Craig, Colin McKean, 3 June, 1919. (M.)
6161 Crerar, Robert, 3 June, 1919. (M.)
6162 Cumberbatch, Hugh Carlton, 3 June, 1919. (M.)
6163 Davidson, Norman Granville Walshe, 3 June, 1919. (M.)
6164 Day, Rev. Arthur, 3 June, 1919. (M.)
6165 Deas, Percy Boscombe, 3 June, 1919. (M.)
6166 Delme-Radcliffe, Seymour Arthur, 3 June, 1919. (M.)
6167 Dickinson, William Henry, 3 June, 1919. (M.)
6168 Dix, Robert Malam, 3 June, 1919. (M.)
6169 Dodgson, Arthur Douglas, 3 June, 1919. (M.)
6170 Duffield, Edgar Willoughby, 3 June, 1919. (M.)
6171 Dun, George, 3 June, 1919. (M.)
6172 Dunbar, Henry John, 3 June, 1919. (M.)
6173 Dunlop, William George, 3 June, 1919. (M.)
6174 Eastwood, Frederick Norman, 3 June, 1919. (M.)
6175 Echlin, Joseph Edward O'Brien, 3 June, 1919. (M.)
6177 Ellery, Cecil Langdon, 3 June, 1919. (M.)
6178 Evans, Arthur, 3 June, 1919. (M.)
6179 Fail, Frederick, 3 June, 1919. (M.)
6180 Ferguson, Alexander Robert, 3 June, 1919. (M.)
6181 Fisher, Walter Harington, 3 June, 1919. (M.)
6182 Flood, Charles Bertram, 3 June, 1919. (M.)
6183 Forbes, Hon. Bertram Aloysius, 3 June, 1919. (M.)
6184 Foster, Charles La Trobe, 3 June, 1919. (M.)
6185 Fox, John, 3 June, 1919. (M.)
6186 Gill, Ernest William, 3 June, 1919. (M.)
6187 Goodeve, Thomas Edward, 3 June, 1919. (M.)
6188 Gordon, Annesley De Rinzy, 3 June, 1919. (M.)
6189 Gotto, Robert Porter Corry, 3 June, 1919. (M.)
6190 Graham, William Thomson, 3 June, 1919. (M.)
6191 Grant, Andrew, 3 June, 1919. (M.)
6192 Gubbins, Stamer, 3 June, 1919. (M.)
6193 Gunnell, Dudley, 3 June, 1919. (M.)
6194 Halliwell, William Arthur, 3 June, 1919. (M.)
6195 Handley, Arthur, 3 June, 1919. (M.)
6196 Hassall, Owen, 3 June, 1919. (M.)
6197 Haultain, William Francis Theodore, 3 June, 1919. (M.)
6198 Hayley, Sidney Thomas, 3 June, 1919. (M.)
6199 Heron, George Wykeham, 3 June, 1919. (M.)
6201 Higgs, Henry Joseph, 3 June, 1919. (M.)
6202 Hinde, Alfred Buckley, 3 June, 1919. (M.)
6203 Hobart, Percy Cleghorn Stanley, 3 June, 1919. (M.)
6204 Hodgson, William Ewart, 3 June, 1919. (M.)
6205 Holgate, Maurice James, 3 June, 1919. (M.)
6206 Holmes, Maurice Gerald, 3 June, 1919. (M.)
6207 Horn, D'Arcy, 3 June, 1919. (M.)
6208 Horne, Rev. Edwin de Jersey, 3 June, 1919. (M.)
6209 Horn, Percy Sutherland, 3 June, 1919. (M.)
6210 Howell, Herbert Gwynne, 3 June, 1919. (M.)
6211 Hutchinson, James Lawrie McKie, 3 June, 1919. (M.)
6212 Inglis, Alexander Francis, 3 June, 1919. (M.)
6213 Isaac, Thomas Austin, 3 June, 1919. (M.)
6214 Jackson, George Erskine, 3 June, 1919. (M.)
6215 Jaggard, George, 3 June, 1919. (M.)
6216 Jardine, William Christopher, 3 June, 1919. (M.
6217 Jones, Seymour Whitworth, 3 June, 1919. (M.)
6218 Kerr, Charles, 3 June, 1919. (M.)
6219 Kerr, Norman Munroe, 3 June, 1919. (M.)
6220 Lash, Ivor Richard de Warraine, 3 June, 1919. (M.)
6221 Leach, Richard Ernest Howell, 3 June, 1919. (M.)
6222 Leask, James Bruce, 3 June, 1919. (M.)
6223 Leggat, George Leggat, 3 June, 1919. (M.)
6224 Leman, Harry Charles, 3 June, 1919. (M.)
6225 L'Estrange, Henry Roland, 3 June, 1919. (M.)
6226 Linklater, George James, 3 June, 1919. (M.)
6227 Long, William Edward, 3 June, 1919. (M.)
6228 Lord, Percy Calvert, 3 June, 1919. (M.)
6229 Lornie, Peter, 3 June, 1919. (M.)
6230 Lowe, Stanley Philip, 3 June, 1919. (M.)
6231 McCosh, Robert, 3 June, 1919. (M.)
6232 MacDonald, Ronald, 3 June, 1919. (M.)
6233 McGowan, James Alexander, 3 June, 1919. (M.)
6234 MacGregor, Alexander Stewart Murray, 3 June, 1919. (M.)
6235 McIntyre, Peter, 3 June, 1919. (M.)
6236 MacQueen, Robert Haldane, 3 June, 1919. (M.)
6237 McRitchie, Charles Bell, 3 June, 1919. (M.)
6238 Malhotra, Rom Charndr, 3 June, 1919. (M.)
6239 Mann, Harry Ainsley, 3 June, 1919. (M.)
6240 Marshall, Colin Andrew, 3 June, 1919. (M.)
6241 Mason, Frederic Eugene, 3 June, 1919. (M.)
6243 Mathieson, William, 3 June, 1919. (M.)
6244 Medley, Edward Arnold, 3 June, 1919. (M.)
6245 Middleton, Edward Meredyth, 3 June, 1919. (M.)
6246 Middleton, Walter, 3 June, 1919. (M.)
6247 Millar, Rev. Peter Carmichael, 3 June, 1919. M.)
6248 Mills, Eric, 3 June, 1919. (M.)
6249 Milne, Charles, 3 June, 1919. (M.)
6250 Milward, Robert Spencer, 3 June, 1919. (M.)
6251 Mirlees, Arthur John, 3 June, 1919. (M.)
6252 Moore, Alfred William, 3 June, 1919. (M.)
6253 Morland, Algernon, 3 June, 1919. (M.)
6254 Morrell, Henry, 3 June, 1919. (M.)
6255 Morten, Raymond Laroche Alexander Burdett, 3 June, 1919. (M.)
6256 Musker, Herbert, 3 June, 1919. (M.)
6257 Nathan, Arthur Frederic, 3 June, 1919. (M.)

6258 Needham, Joseph George, 3 June, 1919. (M.)
6259 Neilson, George Clement, 3 June, 1919. (M.)
6260 Nicholls, Gregory Basil Treglisson, 3 June, 1919. (M.)
6262 Oppenheim, Robert William, 3 June, 1919. (M.)
6263 Owen, Roger Carmichael Robert, 3 June, 1919. (M.)
6264 Packer, Rev. George Francis, 3 June, 1919. (M.)
6265 Parisotti, Rev. Albert, 3 June, 1919. (M.)
6266 Parker, Arthur Stanley, 3 June, 1919. (M.)
6267 Pemberton, Edward Gerald, 3 June, 1919. (M.)
6268 Percy-Smith, Douglas Cyril, 3 June, 1919. (M.)
6269 Phillips, Rees, 3 June, 1919. (M.)
6270 Pole, Wellesley Tudor, 3 June, 1919. (M.)
6271 Pooler, John Read, 3 June, 1919. (M.)
6272 Porter, James Douglas, 3 June, 1919. (M.)
6273 Postlethwaite, Francis John Marshall, 3 June, 1919. (M.)
6274 Rabaghati, Dancan Silvestro, 3 June, 1919. (M.)
6275 Rae, James Gordon, 3 June, 1919. (M.)
6276 Rankin, Frederick Powlett, 3 June, 1919. (M.)
6277 Raven-Hart, James Milleville, 3 June, 1919. (M.)
6278 Raymond, Eben Lindsay, 3 June, 1919. (M.)
6279 Rayner, Arthur Ernest, 3 June, 1919. (M.)
6280 Rickett, Gerald Russell, 3 June, 1919. (M.)
6281 Ridley, Geoffrey William, 3 June, 1919. (M.)
6282 Ritchie, William Thomas, 3 June, 1919. (M.)
6283 Robertson, Andrew, 3 June, 1919. (M.)
6284 Robertson, John William, 3 June, 1919. (M.)
6285 Ross, William John, 3 June, 1919. (M.)
6286 Rothschild, Sydney Henry, 3 June, 1919. (M.)
6287 Sanderson, Francis Robert, 3 June, 1919. (M.)
6288 Sandes, Charles William Wallace, 3 June, 1919. (M.)
6289 Scott, Percy Alexander, 3 June, 1919. (M.)
6290 Scrimgeour, Frederic John, 3 June, 1919. (M.)
6291 Seccombe, John William Smyth, 3 June, 1919. (M.)
6292 Sewell, John, 3 June, 1919. (M.)
6293 Sharp, Wilfred, 3 June, 1919. (M.)
6294 Simson, Robert, 3 June, 1919. (M.)
6295 Spinks, Charlton Watson, 3 June, 1919. (M.)
6296 Stafford, Percy Beaumont, 3 June, 1919. (M.)
6297 Starkey, Henry Samuel Crichton, 3 June, 1919. (M.)
6298 Stephenson, Basil, 3 June, 1919. (M.)
6299 Stewart, George Herbert, 3 June, 1919. (M.)
6301 Smith, Walter William, 3 June, 1919. (M.)
6302 Strathearn, John, 3 June, 1919. (M.)
6303 Strong, Robert Henry, 3 June, 1919. (M.)
6304 Tegg, Charles, 3 June, 1919. (M.)
6305 Thomson, James Robert Karrow, 3 June, 1919. (M.)
6306 Thorp, Eustace, 3 June, 1919. (M.)
6307 Tilleray, William Arthur James, 3 June, 1919. (M.)
6308 Tomkinson, Herbert, 3 June, 1919. (M.)
6310 Urwin, John Johnson, 3 June, 1919. (M.)
6311 Vacy-Ash, William Maxwell, 3 June, 1919. (M.)
6313 Verschoyle, Henry Prittie Cosby, 3 June, 1919. (M.)
6314 Vessey, Gordon Harry Bowker, 3 June, 1919. (M.)
6315 Vincent, William, 3 June, 1919. (M.)
6316 Wakeham, Frederick, 3 June, 1919. (M.)
6317 Walshe, Francis Martin Rouse, 3 June, 1919. (M.)
6318 Ware, Sampson Weston Percy, 3 June, 1919. (M.)
6319 Way, Francis Robert, 3 June, 1919. (M.)
6321 Westropp, Richard Gibbings, 3 June, 1919. (M.)
6322 White, Maurice Forbes, 3 June, 1919. (M.)
6323 Wightman, Henry Christopher, 3 June, 1919. (M.)
6324 Williams, Harold Baskerville, 3 June, 1919. (M.)
6325 Willson, Herbert Stuart, 3 June, 1919. (M.)
6326 Wood, Rev. Alexander, 3 June, 1919. (M.)
6327 Wood, John William, 3 June, 1919. (M.)
6328 Woodward, Frederick William, 3 June, 1919. (M.)
6329 Young, Ernest William Gilmore, 3 June, 1919. (M.)
6330 Linton, Adam Pearce, 3 June, 1919. (M.)
6331 White, Basil Cherrington, 3 June, 1919. (M.)
6332 Bisdee, John Hutton, 3 June, 1919. (M.)
6333 Davidson, Arthur Madgwick, 3 June, 1919. (M.)
6334 Dickinson, Francis Sidney, 3 June, 1919. (M.)
6335 Henry, James Douglas, 3 June, 1919. (M.)
6336 Kirkwood, William Love, 3 June, 1919. (M.)
6337 Saw, Athelstan John Henton, 3 June, 1919. (M.)
6338 Summons, Walter Ernest, 3 June, 1919. (M.)
6339 Hercus, Charles Ernest, 3 June, 1919. (M.)
6340 Abdel Khalik Eff Talaat (Bimbashi), 3 June, 1919. (M.)
6341 Adam, Ronald Forbes, 3 June, 1919. (M.)
6342 Argles, Guy Arthur Eustace, 3 June, 1919. (M.)
6343 Baily, Clifford Allan, 3 June, 1919. (M.)
6344 Belchem, Owen King, 3 June, 1919. (M.)
6345 Berlandina, Herbert Hillel, 3 June, 1919. (M.)
6346 Bowen, John Francis, 3 June, 1919. (M.)
6347 Boyd, Clive Kingsley, 3 June, 1919. (M.)
6348 Bramhall, Charles, 3 June, 1919. (M.)
6349 Brown, Montagu Wilhelm, 3 June, 1919. (M.)
6350 Browning, Langley, 3 June, 1919. (M.)
6351 Buckley, Peter Burton, 3 June, 1919. (M.)
6352 Butler, Rev. Richard Urban, 3 June, 1919. (M.)
6353 Carroll, Patrick Alphonsus, 3 June, 1919. (M.)
6354 Chichester, Hon. Arthur Claud Spencer, 3 June, 1919. (M.)
6355 Chute, Rev. Anthony William, 3 June, 1919. (M.)
6356 Coplans, Myer, 3 June, 1919. (M.)
6357 Curling, Joseph, 3 June, 1919. (M.)
6358 Davids, Maurice, 3 June, 1919. (M.)
6359 Day, Robert William, 3 June, 1919. (M.)
6360 de Soissons, Louis Emmanuel Jean Guy de Savoie Carignan, 3 June, 1919. (M.)

OFFICERS.

6361 Dixon, Frederick Frank, 3 June, 1919. (M.)
6362 Dyas, Richard Seymour Vivian, 3 June, 1919. (M.)
6363 Evans, William Martin, 3 June, 1919. (M.)
6364 Farquhar, FitzRoy, 3 June, 1919. (M.)
6365 Ferguson, Wallace, 3 June, 1919. (M.)
6366 Forrest, James, 3 June, 1919. (M.)
6367 Foster, Francis Kenelm, 3 June, 1919. (M.)
6368 Fulford, Henry Edward, 3 June, 1919. (M.)
6369 Gardner, George Herbert, 3 June, 1919. (M.)
6370 Gates, Edward Alfred, 3 June, 1919. (M.)
6371 Gibbon, Thomas Holroyd, 3 June, 1919. (M.)
6372 Gibson, Alan Keith, 3 June, 1919. (M.)
6373 Gill, John Galbraith, 3 June, 1919. (M.)
6374 Goldsmid, Cyril Julian, 3 June, 1919. (M.)
6375 Grindley, Hugh Henry, 3 June, 1919. (M.)
6376 Grinsell, George Herbert, 3 June, 1919. (M.)
6377 Gwatkin, Archibald James, 3 June, 1919. (M.)
6378 Hayter, Gordon Willis, 3 June, 1919. (M.)
6379 Hewitt, Alfred Scott, 3 June, 1919. (M.)
6380 Hilliard, James Joseph, 3 June, 1919. (M.)
6381 Hopkinson, Miles Staveley, 3 June, 1919. (M.)
6382 Horton, Sydney Charles, 3 June, 1919. (M.)
6383 Hughes, Rev. Randolph, 3 June, 1919. (M.)
6384 Hunter, George Noel, 3 June, 1919. (M.)
6385 Irving, John Duckworth, 3 June, 1919. (M.)
6386 Ivory, Harold Frank, 3 June, 1919. (M.)
6387 Jardine, John, 3 June, 1919. (M.)
6388 Jeff, Robert Hunter, 3 June, 1919. (M.)
6389 Keenan, Augustine Henry, 3 June, 1919. (M.)
6390 Kenworthy, Harold, 3 June, 1919. (M.)
6391 Leese, Neville, 3 June, 1919. (M.)
6392 Legh, Hon. Piers Walter, 3 June, 1919. (M.)
6393 Le Mesurier, Algernon George, 3 June, 1919. (M.)
6394 Lipsett, Lewis Richard, 3 June, 1919. (M.)
6395 Lowe, Sydney Joseph, 3 June, 1919. (M.)
6396 Lucas, Reginald Hutchinson, 3 June, 1919. (M.)
6397 McCliment, Rev. Robert James, 3 June, 1919. (M.)
6398 McMurtrie, Basil Flexman, 3 June, 1919. (M.)
6399 Matthews, William John Richardson, 3 June, 1919. (M.)
6400 Mitchell, Charles, 3 June, 1919. (M.)
6401 Morris, Edwin Logie, 3 June, 1919. (M.)
6402 Murphy, Rev. Thomas Carlyle, 3 June, 1919. (M.)
6404 Nicholl, Charles Carlyon, 3 June, 1919. (M.)
6405 Parker, Reginald Frank, 3 June, 1919. (M.)
6406 Parkes, William Ashley, 3 June, 1919. (M.)
6407 Phillips, Charles Kendall, 3 June, 1919. (M.)
6408 Plews, Harry, 3 June, 1919. (M.)
6409 Potter, Benjamin Henry, 3 June, 1919. (M.)
6410 Ramsden, Eugene, 3 June, 1919. (M.)
6411 Rean, William Henry, 3 June, 1919. (M.)
6412 Rolleston, Arthur George, 3 June, 1919. (M.)
6413 Sarjeant, Leonard James, 3 June, 1919. (M.)
6414 Sclater, Frank Arthur, 3 June, 1919. (M.)
6415 Shaddick, Rev. Harvey George Hastings, 3 June, 1919. (M.)
6416 Sharp, George Edward, 3 June, 1919. (M.)
6417 Shoetensack, Edgar Leonard, 3 June, 1919. (M.)
6418 Smyth, Humphrey Etwall, 3 June, 1919. (M.)
6419 Southee, Ethelbert Ambrook, 3 June, 1919. (M.)
6420 Spurrier, George Stretton, 3 June, 1919. (M.)
6421 Stearns, Cyril Ernest, 3 June, 1019. (M.)
6422 Tapp, Arthur Gerard Rhodes Sentance, 3 June, 1919. (M.)
6423 Thomas, Trevor Meredyth Chitty, 3 June, 1919. (M.)
6424 Tillard, John Arthur Stuart, 3 June, 1919. (M.)
6425 Wackrill, Walter Frederick, 3 June, 1919. (M.)
6426 Williams, John Clive, 3 June, 1919. (M.)
6427 Wilson, Arnot Milne, 3 June, 1919. (M.)
6428 Wilson, Hubert Malcolm, 3 June, 1919. (M.)
6429 Yerburgh, Richard Guy, 3 June, 1919. (M.)
6430 Anderson, Albert Roland, 3 June, 1919. (M.)
6431 Armour, George Denholm, 3 June, 1919. (M.)
6432 Arnot, William, 3 June, 1919. (M.)
6433 Ashton, Cecil Charles Gough, 3 June, 1919. (M.)
6434 Barritt, Wesley, 3 June, 1919. (M.)
6435 Barstow, Thomas Clement Erskine, 3 June, 1919. (M.)
6436 Barton, Bertram Claude, 3 June, 1919. (M.)
6437 Beall, Frank William, 3 June, 1919. (M.)
6438 Bingham, William Henry, 3 June, 1919. (M.)
6439 Breadmore, Reginald George, 3 June, 1919. (M.)
6440 Brereton, Rev. Eric Hugh, 3 June, 1919. (M.)
6441 Brierley, Norman Howarth, 3 June, 1919. (M.)
6442 Brock, William, 3 June, 1919. (M.)
6443 Brown, Albert James Studd, 3 June, 1919. (M.)
6444 Burn, Reginald William, 3 June, 1919. (M.)
6445 Butterworth, Arthur Bernard, 3 June, 1919. (M.)
6446 Burt-Marshall, David Bannerman, 3 June, 1919. (M.)
6447 Cameron, Donald Cunninghame, 3 June, 1919. (M.)
6448 Campbell, Malcolm Hay Alexander, 3 June, 1919. (M.)
6449 Campbell, John MacKnight, 3 June, 1919. (M.)
6450 Cane, Arthur Skedling, 3 June, 1919. (M.)
6451 Cardwell, Charles Alexander, 3 June, 1919. (M.)
6452 Carleton, Hon. Dudley Massey Piggott, 3 June, 1919. (M.)
6453 Castle, Leonard James, 3 June, 1919. (M.)
6454 Chambers, Rev. Frank Hanson, 3 June, 1919. (M.)
6455 Collas, Francis Jervoise, 3 June, 1919. (M.)
6456 Crailsham, Harry Rollo, 3 June, 1919. (M.)
6457 Cumberland, Thomas Daily, 3 June, 1919. (M.)
6458 Cuthbertson, John Ernest Moncrieff, 3 June, 1919. (M.)
6459 Dalyell, Elsie Jean, 3 June, 1919. (M.)
6460 Darby, Alexander White, 3 June, 1919. (M.)

6461 Davies, Rev. David, 3 June, 1919. (M.)
6462 Douglas, Archibald Sholto George, 3 June, 1919. (M.)
6463 Edwards, Harry Melville, 3 June, 1919. (M.)
6464 Ellis, Hector Charles, 3 June, 1919. (M.)
6465 England, Philip Remington, 3 June, 1919. (M.)
6466 Fairbank, Harold Arthur Thomas, 3 June, 1919. (M.)
6467 Ferguson, Rev. Fergus, 3 June, 1919. (M.)
6468 Ferry, Cuthbert Edmund Caulfield, 3 June, 1919. (M.)
6469 Fish, Phillip Henry, 3 June, 1919. (M.)
6470 Fox, James Joseph, 3 June, 1919. (M.)
6471 Giffard, Walter Longueville, 3 June, 1919. (M.)
6472 Godwin, George, 3 June, 1919. (M.)
6473 Goodwin, George, 3 June, 1919. (M.)
6474 Gosling, William Richard, 3 June, 1919. (M.)
6475 Gough, Arthur Trevor, 3 June, 1919. (M.)
6476 Hearne, Francis George, 3 June, 1919. (M.)
6477 Hele, Thomas Shirley, 3 June, 1919. (M.)
6478 Henderson, John Gilbert, 3 June, 1919. (M.)
6479 Heurtley, Walter, 3 June, 1919. (M.)
6480 Holme, Alfred Siegfried, 3 June, 1919. (M.)
6481 Holland, Thomas George, 3 June, 1919. (M.)
6482 Hopkin, Frank, 3 June, 1919. (M.)
6483 Horn, William Herbert Gascoine, 3 June, 1919. (M.)
6484 Horlick, James Nockells, 3 June, 1919. (M.)
6485 Jackson, Robert Hugh Holmes, 3 June, 1919. (M.)
6486 James, Herbert Ellison Rhodes, 3 June, 1919. (M.)
6487 Jameson, Aaron, 3 June, 1919. (M.)
6488 Jamieson, Alexander Harvey Morro, 3 June, 1919. (M.)
6489 Jarvis, Thomas Stanley Wiles, 3 June, 1919. (M.)
6490 Jones, John Arnold, 3 June, 1919. (M.)
6491 Kidd, Alexander Edward, 3 June, 1919. (M.)
6492 Kirkness, Lewis Hawker, 3 June, 1919. (M.)
6493 Knight, Alfred John Hammond, 3 June, 1919. (M.)
6494 Langley, Albert Ernest, 3 June, 1919. (M.)
6495 Leatham, Nigel Clere, 3 June, 1919. (M.)
6496 Lepper, Elizabeth Herdman, 3 June, 1919. (M.)
6497 Lightfoot, Leslie Jabez, 3 June, 1919. (M.)
6498 Lucas, Charles Alfred, 3 June, 1919. (M.)
6499 Lucie-Smith, John Alfred, 3 June, 1919. (M.)
6500 Luck, Sidney Ivor, 3 June, 1919. (M.)
6501 Lyle, Arthur Nevin, 3 June, 1919. (M.)
6502 Lyndon, Rev. Charles Henry Preston, 3 June, 1919. (M.)
6503 MacDonnell, Alister Maxwell, 3 June, 1919. (M.)
6504 MacGregor, James St. Cuthbert, 3 June, 1919. (M.)
6505 MacNab, Ronald Charles, 3 June, 1919. (M.)
6506 MacQueen, Loudon Hope, 3 June, 1919. (M.)
6507 Marlow, Arthur Lambert, 3 June, 1919. (M.)
6508 Matheson, Ian McLeod Angus, 3 June, 1919. (M.)
6509 Michie, Henry Maurice, 3 June, 1919. (M.)
6510 Milne, Rev. John Lloyd, 3 June, 1919. (M.)
6511 Morris, George Philip, 3 June, 1919. (M.)
6512 Morrison, John Norman, 3 June, 1919. (M.)
6513 Murley, Rev. James Reginald de Courcy O'Grady, 3 June, 1919. (M.)
6514 Nash, Ryder Percival, 3 June, 1919. (M.)
6515 Nasmith, George William, 3 June, 1919. (M.)
6516 Neill, Joseph, 3 June, 1919. (M.)
6517 Newey, Frank, 3 June, 1919. (M.)
6518 O'Brien, Rev. Thomas Francis, 3 June, 1919. (M.)
6519 Pauncefort-Munday, Henry Clement, 3 June, 1919. (M.)
6520 Peatt, Ernest Snowden Wallace, 3 June, 1919. (M.)
6521 Penhale, Richard Hugh, 3 June, 1919. (M.)
6522 Pritchard, Richard Graham, 3 June, 1919. (M.)
6523 Ramsbottom, John, 3 June, 1919. (M.)
6524 Richardson, Frederick, 3 June, 1919. (M.)
6525 Robinson, Cyril Ellett, 3 June, 1919. (M.)
6526 Ronald, Reginald Stanley, 3 June, 1919. (M.)
6527 Rooke, John Wentworth, 3 June, 1919. (M.)
6528 Roscoe, Harry, 3 June, 1919. (M.)
6529 Rule, John Allan, 3 June, 1919. (M.)
6530 Saunders, John Augustus, 3 June, 1919. (M.)
6531 Sellers, Rev. Harold Gordon, 3 June, 1919. (M.)
6532 Smythe, Harry Alexander, 3 June, 1919. (M.)
6533 South, Thomas, 3 June, 1919. (M.)
6534 Spurway, John Edward, 3 June, 1919. (M.)
6535 Stericker, Stanley, 3 June, 1919. (M.)
6536 Stokes, Claude Bayfield, 3 June, 1919. (M.)
6537 Stokes, Leslie Eric Sheldon, 3 June, 1919. (M.)
6538 Stott, James Robert, 3 June, 1919. (M.)
6539 Stourton, Herbert Marmaduke Joseph, 3 June, 1919. (M.)
6540 Taylor, Basil Wilford, 3 June, 1919. (M.)
6541 Temperley, Clive Errington, 3 June, 1919. (M.)
6542 Thompson, John Pickering, 3 June, 1919. (M.)
6543 Thompson, Maurice Scott, 3 June, 1919. (M.)
6544 Thorogood, Percival Walter, 3 June, 1919. (M.)
6545 Thrale, Peter Ralph Alwen, 3 June, 1919. (M.)
6546 Tidswell, Edmund Samuel Walte, 3 June, 1919. (M.)
6547 Tillyard, Eustace Mandeville Witenhall, 3 June, 1919. (M.)
6548 Travers, Wilfred Irwin, 3 June, 1919. (M.)
6549 Tudor, Claude Lechmere St. John, 3 June, 1919. (M.)
6550 Tweedie, Frank Forbes, 3 June, 1919. (M.)
6551 Vick, Reginald Martin, 3 June, 1919. (M.)
6552 Wallis, Henry Clifford, 3 June, 1919. (M.)
6553 Warnock, James, 3 June, 1919. (M.)
6554 Warren-Lambert, Arthur, 3 June, 1919. (M.)
6555 Watts, Roger John, 3 June, 1919. (M.)
6556 White, Charles Henry, 3 June, 1919. (M.)
6557 Wilson, Henry, 3 June, 1919. (M.)

6558 Wiltshire, Harold Waterlow, 3 June, 1919. (M.
6559 Woods, Lionel Dudley, 3 June, 1919. (M.)
6560 Wort, Walter Edward, 3 June, 1919. (M.)
6561 Wright, James, 3 June, 1919. (M.)
6562 Young, Frederick Hugh, 3 June, 1919. (M.)
6563 Young, William Alexander, 3 June, 1919. (M.)]
6564 Newcombe, Harold Kenzie, 3 June, 1919. (M.)
6565 Chevens, Herbert Glyn, 3 June, 1919. (M.)
6566 Alderman, Robert Edward, 3 June, 1919. (M.)
6567 Ames, William Rex, 3 June, 1919. (M.)
6568 Auchinleck, Claud John Eyre, 3 June, 1919. (M.)
6569 Bagshawe, Edward Leonard, 3 June, 1919. (M.)
6570 Bampfield, George Charles, 3 June, 1919. (M.)
6571 Bartholomew, Allen Gilbert, 3 June, 1919. (M.)
6572 Bell, Alec Jeffrey, 3 June, 1919. (M.)
6573 Bell, Herbert, 3 June, 1919. (M.)
6574 Bispham, George, 3 June, 1919. (M.)
6575 Blackwell, Henry, 3 June, 1919. (M.)
6576 Blake, Arthur Locke, 3 June, 1919. (M.)
6577 Blew, Nellie, 3 June, 1919. (M.)
6578 Body, John, 3 June, 1919. (M.)
6579 Bourne, Walter Fitzgerald, 3 June, 1919. (M.)
6580 Bramley, Percy Brooke, 3 June, 1919. (M.)
6581 Bridcut, Sydney Haynes, 3 June, 1919. (M.)
6582 Broad, Robert Norman Dymoke, 3 June, 1919. (M.)
6583 Brook, Thomas Fleetwood, 3 June, 1919. (M.)
6584 Brown, James Hardy, 3 June, 1919. (M.)
6585 Brown, John Bayley Fairfax, 3 June, 1919. (M.)
6586 Browne, Denis Robert Howe, 3 June, 1919. (M.)
6587 Brownrigg, Rev. Ernest Graham, 3 June, 1919. (M.)
6588 Burn, Alexander Henderson, 3 June, 1919. (M.)
6589 Burn, William George, 3 June, 1919. (M.)
6590 Bushell, Christopher Wyndowe, 3 June, 1919. (M.)
6591 Callaghan, Joseph Aloysius, 3 June, 1919. (M.)
6592 Campbell, John Maurice Hardman, 3 June, 1919. (M.)
6593 Chandler, Arthur Frederick Neale, 3 June, 1919. (M.)
6594 Christie, Joseph James, 3 June, 1919. (M.)
6595 Clarke, Arthur John, 3 June, 1919. (M.)
6596 Clarke, Aubrey Martin, 3 June, 1919. (M.)
6597 Clarke, Richard Charles, 3 June, 1919. (M.)
6598 Coleman, Reginald Ernest, 3 June, 1919. (M.)
6599 Coleridge, Percy Lovel, 3 June, 1919. (M.)
6600 Corner, Williams, 3 June, 1919. (M.)
6601 Cruddas, Hamilton Maxwell, 3 June, 1919. (M.)
6602 Cuming, Robert John, 3 June, 1919. (M.)
6603 Daniels, Arthur Marston, 3 June, 1919. (M.)
6604 Davidson, John, 3 June, 1919. (M.)
6605 Davis, William, 3 June, 1919. (M.)
6606 Dawson, Frank Donald 3 June, 1919. (M.)
6607 Dennys. Guy Tullock. 3 June, 1919. (M.
6608 De Woolfson, Albert Henry Frederick, 3 June, 1919. (M.)
6609 Drake, William Barnard, 3 June, 1919. (M.)
6610 Drew, Francis Grenville, 3 June, 1919. (M.)
6611 Dunbar, Leslie, 3 June, 1919. (M.)
6612 Dundas, Patrick Henry, 3 June, 1919. (M.)
6613 Dunn, Wilfred James, 3 June, 1919. (M.)
6614 Dunnett, Rev. William Alexander, 3 June, 1919. (M.)
6615 Exham, Harold, 3 June, 1919. (M.)
6616 Fanshawe, Lionel Arthur, 3 June, 1919. (M.)
6617 Ferry, Edward Stanton Henry, 3 June, 1919. (M.)
6618 Fisher, Cecil James, 3 June, 1919. (M.)
6619 Fitzgerald, Arthur, 3 June, 1919. (M.)
6620 Flack, Hugh Lidwell, 3 June, 1919. (M.)
6621 Flowers, Cyril, 3 June, 1919. (M.)
6622 Foster, John George, 3 June, 1919. (M.)
6623 Fremantle, Francis Edward, 3 June, 1919. (M.)
6624 Garson, Herbert Leslie, 3 June, 1919. (M.)
6625 Goddard, Eric Norman, 3 June, 1919. (M.)
6626 Godwin-Austen, Alfred Reade, 3 June, 1919. (M.)
6627 Gore, Frederic Lawrence, 3 June, 1919. (M.)
6628 Grylls, Glynn, 3 June, 1919. (M.)
6629 Gwyn-Williams, Reuben Henry, 3 June, 1919. (M.)
6630 Hadrill, Henry Clement, 3 June, 1919. (M.)
6631 Hall, Leonard Joseph, 3 June, 1919. (M.)
6632 Hall, Sidney Lewis, 3 June, 1919. (M.)
6633 Harding, Kenneth O'Brien, 3 June, 1919. (M.)
6634 Harris, Archibald John, 3 June, 1919. (M.)
6635 Heaslop, Adair Colpoys, 3 June, 1919. (M.)
6636 Henderson, Rev. Hamilton Dunstan, 3 June, 1919. (M.)
6637 Higson, Frank, 3 June, 1919. (M.)
6638 Hiles, Morton, 3 June, 1919. (M.)
6639 Hipwell, Rev. Richard Senior, 3 June, 1919. (M.)
6640 Hobson, Rev. Edmund Joseph, 3 June, 1919. (M.)
6641 Hodge, Reginald Thomas Keble, 3 June, 1919. (M.)
6642 Hutson, Henry Porter Wolseley, 3 June, 1919. (M.)
6643 Ingram, Charles Robert, 3 June, 1919. (M.)
6644 Inwood, Charles Herbert, 3 June, 1919. (M.)
6645 James, Rev. Percival Walter, 3 June, 1919. (M.)
6646 Jarvis, Oswald Duke, 3 June, 1919. (M.)
6647 John, Jordan Constantine, 3 June, 1919. (M.)
6648 Jones, Charles Grey Peyton, 3 June, 1919. (M.)
6649 Jones, Sydney Herbert, 3 June, 1919. (M.)
6650 Kirkpatrick, Charles, 3 June, 1919. (M.)
6651 Knowland, George Henry, 3 June, 1919. (M.)
6652 Lawrence, Cecil John Rhodes, 3 June, 1919. (M.)
6653 Lightfoot, Kenneth, 3 June, 1919. (M.)
6654 MacArthur, Donald Hector Colin, 3 June, 1919. (M.)
6655 MacDermott, William, 3 June, 1919. (M.)
6656 MacDonald, Ian Thomas Aliston, 3 June, 1919. (M.)

6657 MacGurk, Nioll Austin, 3 June, 1919. (M.)
6658 MacHutchon, Edwin Gray, 3 June, 1919. (M.)
6659 MacMillan, Archibald, 3 June, 1919. (M.)
6660 McNaughtan, William, 3 June, 1919. (M.)
6661 MacPherson, Duncan Gordon, 3 June, 1919. (M.)
6662 Mainwaring, Rev. John, 3 June, 1919. (M.)
6663 Manderson, Robert Wardlaw, 3 June, 1919. (M.)
6664 Marr, Hugh, 3 June, 1919. (M.)
6665 Marriott, Donald James, 3 June, 1919. (M.)
6666 Maxwell, Percy Alexander, 3 June, 1919. (M.)
6667 Miller, Archibald Thomas, 3 June, 1919. (M.)
6668 Miller, John Alfred Tennant, 3 June, 1919. (M.)
6669 Milne-Henderson, Thomas Maxwell, 3 June, 1919. (M.)
6670 Mocatta, Valentine Elkin, 3 June, 1919. (M.)
6671 Molony, John Barre de Winton, 3 June, 1919. (M.)
6672 Molony, Rev. John Patrick, 3 June, 1919. (M.)
6673 Mullings, Joseph Randolf, 3 June, 1919. (M.)
6674 Munro, Edward Brodie, 3 June, 1919. (M.)
6675 Murray, Stuart, 3 June, 1919. (M.)
6676 Niblett, Harry Edwin Newton, 3 June, 1919. (M.)
6677 Nicholl, Earle McKillop, 3 June, 1919. (M.)
6678 Nicholls, Reginald Latham, 3 June, 1919. (M.)
6679 Neild, Ralph, 3 June, 1919. (M.)
6680 O'Brien, Joseph, 3 June, 1919. (M.)
6681 O'Bryen, Charles William, 3 June, 1919. (M.)
6682 Palmer, Charles William Gustavis, 3 June, 1919. (M.)
6683 Park, Rev. William Robert, 3 June, 1919. (M.)
6684 Parker, Edwin Charles Lewis, 3 June, 1919. (M.)
6685 Pepper, Henry, 3 June, 1919. (M.)
6686 Porteous, Percy Guynedd, 3 June, 1919. (M.)
6687 Pritchard, Jack Mervyn, 3 June, 1919. (M.)
6688 Protheroe, Arthur Havard, 3 June, 1919. (M.)
6689 Reader, Ernest John Ward, 3 June, 1919. (M.)
6690 Redman, Henry Gordon, 3 June, 1919. (M.)
6691 Reed, George Stanley, 3 June, 1919. (M.)
6692 Reid, Walter Clarke, 3 June, 1919. (M.)
6693 Reynolds, Ernest Brayley, 3 June, 1919. (M.)
6694 Rothera, Percy, 3 June, 1919. (M.)
6695 Rountree, Arthur Fitzgerald, 3 June, 1919. (M.)
6696 Rowlandson, Herbert Wynyard, 3 June, 1919. (M.)
6697 Russell, Harry William, 3 June, 1919. (M.)
6698 Sassoon, Arthur Meyer, 3 June, 1919. (M.)
6699 Sellwood, Frank Greaves, 3 June, 1919. (M.)
6700 Skinner, Ernest William, 3 June, 1919. (M.)
6701 Sloper, John Smith, 3 June, 1919. (M.)
6702 Smith, Edward Percival Allman, 3 June, 1919. (M.)
6703 Somerville, Donald Bradley, 3 June, 1919. (M.)
6704 Spens, William Patrick, 3 June, 1919. (M.)
6705 Stevenson, Harry Daniel Muhldoroff, 3 June, 1919. (M.)
6706 Stewart, William Archibald, 3 June, 1919. (M.)
6707 Stoddart, Guy, 3 June, 1919. (M.)
6708 Stokes, Hugh Gabriel, 3 June, 1919. (M.)
6709 Stone, Alan Gething, 3 June, 1919. (M.)
6710 Stoneham, Hugh Frederic, 3 June, 1919. (M.)
6711 Sykes, Arthur Clifton, 3 June, 1919. (M.)
6712 Tandy, Maurice O'Connor, 3 June, 1919. (M.)
6713 Taylor, Cedric Rowland, 3 June, 1919. (M.)
6714 Temple, Thomas, 3 June, 1919. (M.)
6715 Theobald, Courtney Eleves, 3 June, 1919. (M.)
6716 Tuke, Shirley John Montague, 3 June, 1919. (M.)
6717 Turbett, Lionel Richard William Tusmell, 3 June, 1919. (M.)
6718 Walker, Norman Dunbar, 3 June, 1919. (M.)
6719 Walker, Rev. Raymond Elliston, 3 June, 1919. (M.)
6720 Walkey, Rev. Frank John, 3 June, 1919. (M.)
6721 Warren, Rev. Claude Bertram, 3 June, 1919. (M.)
6722 Warton, Charles Percival Fenwick, 3 June, 1919. (M.)
6723 Watson, William Linton, 3 June, 1919. (M.)
6724 Welchman, Godfrey De Vere, 3 June, 1919. (M.)
6725 Wellborne, Cyril de Montfort, 3 June, 1919. (M.)
6726 Wheeler, Rev. Harold William, 3 June, 1919. (M.)
6727 Whelan, Joseph Francis, 3 June, 1919. (M.)
6728 Whitamore, Vernon Northwood, 3 June, 1919. (M.)
6729 Wheelwright, Talbot Hodwen, 3 June, 1919. (M.)
6730 Williams, William Edward Rees, 3 June, 1919. (M.)
6731 Wilson, Jeanie Stewart Ramsay, 3 June, 1919. (M.)
6732 Wilkinson, Gerrard Napier, 3 June, 1919. (M.)
6733 Wood, Geoffrey, 3 June, 1919. (M.)
6734 Worsdell, Geoffrey Bradford, 3 June, 1919. (M.)
6735 Wyatt, Archibald, 3 June, 1919. (M.)
6736 Yates, Donald Russell Martin, 3 June, 1919. (M.)
6737 Hillary, Michael James, 3 June, 1919. (M.)
6738 White, Samuel James, 3 June, 1919. (M.)
6739 Knight, Robert Charles, 3 June, 1919. (M.)
6740 Wakefield, Hubert Steven, 3 June, 1919. (M.)
6741 Andrews, Neale, 3 June, 1919. (M.)
6742 Atkinson, Herbert Benjamin, 3 June, 1919. (M.)
6743 Chalmers, William, 3 June, 1919. (M.)
6744 Collisson, Percival Lorimer, 3 June, 1919. (M.)
6745 Dashwood, Arthur Paul, 3 June, 1919. (M.)
6746 Duke, Herbert Lyndhurst, 3 June, 1919. (M.)
6747 Furlong, Sydney Joseph Verner, 3 June, 1919. (M.)
6748 Hardy, John Lawton, 3 June, 1919. (M.)
6749 Harvey, Robert Bleeck Leech, 3 June, 1919. (M.)
6750 Jeffreys, Henry Albert Gravious, 3 June, 1919. (M.)
6751 Jennings, Percy John, 3 June, 1919. (M.)
6753 Kidd, James Dunlop, 3 June, 1919. (M.)
6754 Lawrence, Ernest Harry Thorn, 3 June, 1919. (M.)
6755 Leonard, John Douglas, 3 June, 1919. (M.)

OFFICERS.

6756 Marshall, Frederick Herbert James, 3 June, 1919. (M.)
6757 Montgomery, James Thomas, 3 June, 1919. (M.)
6758 Mortimer, Leslie, 3 June, 1919. (M.)
6759 Muggeridge, Charles Ernest, 3 June, 1919. (M.)
6760 Page, Rev. Walter Sutton, 3 June, 1919. (M.)
6761 Palmer, Edward Henry Banks, 3 June, 1919. (M.)
6762 Parkinson, Arthur Charles Cosmo, 3 June, 1919. (M.)
6763 Paterson, John, 3 June, 1919. (M.)
6764 Rogan, Rev. Peter, 3 June, 1919. (M.)
6765 Russell, Alexander, 3 June, 1919. (M.)
6766 Shilson, Bernard William, 3 June, 1919. (M.)
6767 Smith, Geoffrey Lionel, 3 June, 1919. (M.)
6768 Solomon, Harold Josiah, 3 June, 1919. (M.)
6769 Watson, Andrew McCrae, 3 June, 1919. (M.)
6770 Watson, Charles Scott Moncreiff Chalmers, 3 June, 1919. (M.)
6771 Whitehorne, Arthur Cecil, 3 June, 1919. (M.)
6772 Williams, Arthur Donald John Bedwood, 3 June, 1919. (M.)
6773 Willmot, Arthur Charles, 3 June, 1919. (M.)
6774 Woakes, William James Primet, 3 June, 1919. (M.)
6775 Bateman, James Cecil, 3 June, 1919. (M.)
6776 Bell, Rudolph John, 3 June, 1919. (M.)
6777 Bromilow, Bernard Heatherington, 3 June, 1919. (M.)
6778 Dunbar, Robert Murray, 3 June, 1919. (M.)
6779 Field, William Vincent, 3 June, 1919. (M.)
6780 Grinsell, Jack, 3 June, 1919. (M.)
6781 Guinness, Earnest Whitmore Newton, 3 June, 1919. (M.)
6782 Hornby, Henry Epton, 3 June, 1919. (M.)
6783 Hosken, Courteney Charles, 3 June, 1919. (M.)
6784 Ronald, George, 3 June, 1919. (M.)
6785 Thornton, George James Tharton, 3 June, 1919. (M.)
6786 Cumming, Arthur Willie, 3 June, 1919. (M.)
6787 Klerck, Willem Jan, 3 June, 1919. (M.)
6788 Langebrink, Andries, 3 June, 1919. (M.)
6789 Nicholson, Richard Granville, 3 June, 1919. (M.)
6790 Boutflower, Geoffrey, 3 June, 1919. (M.)
6791 Carter, Edward Philip, 3 June, 1919. (M.)
6792 Cautley, Harry Llewellyn, 3 June, 1919. (M.)
6793 Coker, Lewis Aubrey, 3 June, 1919. (M.)
6794 Coxon, Alfred Walter, 3 June, 1919. (M.)
6795 Crawley, Richard Parry, 3 June, 1919. (M.)
6796 Criswell, Walter, 3 June, 1919. (M.)
6797 Croydon, George, 3 June, 1919. (M.)
6798 De Falbe, Christian Frederick George William, 3 June, 1919. (M.)
6799 Dykes, Kingsley, 3 June, 1919. (M.)
6800 Jay, William Cunliffe Pickersgill, 3 June, 1919. (M.)
6801 Kennedy, William Nicol Watson, 3 June, 1919. (M.)
6802 McDermott, Thomas, 3 June, 1919. (M.)
6803 Mohr, Stanley Melborne, 3 June, 1919. (M.)
6804 Moore, Francis, 3 June, 1919. (M.)
6805 Mould, John Alfred, 3 June, 1919. (M.)
6806 Pitts, Joseph, 3 June, 1919. (M.)
6807 Poole, John Sanderson, 3 June, 1919. (M.)
6808 Roeber, William Carl Trorey, 3 June, 1919. (M.)
6809 Smith, Robert Hunter, 3 June, 1919. (M.)
6810 Whitaker, George Backhouse, 3 June, 1919. (M.)
6811 Mills, Paul Hubert, 3 June, 1919. (M.)
6812 Bellwood, Cecil Power, 3 June, 1919. (M.)
6813 Holmes, Barnard, 3 June, 1919. (M.)
6814 Kilby, James Wheatley, 3 June, 1919. (M.)
6815 MacKilligin, Robert Springett, 3 June, 1919. (M.
6816 Moores, Frank Gerald Guise, 3 June, 1919. (M.)
6817 Nye, Arthur Field, 3 June, 1919. (M.)
6818 Penn, Henry Albert, 3 June, 1919. (M.)
6819 Renwick, John, 3 June, 1919. (M.)
6820 Shackleton, Sir Ernest Henry, 3 June, 1919. (M.)
6821 Sweeny, Sedley Fleming Campbell, 3 June, 1919. (M.)
6822 Macrae, Ian Macpherson, 3 June, 1919. (M.)
6823 Pullman, Gerald Cozens, 3 June, 1919. (M.)
6824 Stroughill, Mabel Anna, 3 June, 1919. (M.)
6825 Ablett, Charles Anthony, 3 June, 1919. (M.)
6826 Abrahams, Adolphe, 3 June, 1919. (M.)
6827 Acres, Thomas George, 3 June, 1919. (M.)
6828 Adams, John Cadwallader, 3 June, 1919. (M.)
6829 Addenbrooke, Joseph Saunders, 3 June, 1919. (M.)
6830 Ahern, Michael David, 3 June, 1919. (M.)
6831 Aherne, Denis, 3 June, 1919. (M.)
6832 Alexander, Arthur Charles Bridgeman, 3 June, 1919. (M.)
6835 Alston, John Stirling, 3 June, 1919. (M.)
6836 Alwood, William Albert, 3 June, 1919. (M.)
6837 Anderson-Pelham, Cecil Henry, 3 June, 1919. (M.)
6838 Anderson, John Samuel, 3 June, 1919. (M.)
6839 Andrewes, Frederick William, 3 June, 1919. (M.)
6840 Appleyard, George Crossley, 3 June, 1919. (M.)
6841 Arbuthnot, Malcolm Alexander, 3 June, 1919. (M.)
6842 Archdale, Rev. Mervyn, 3 June, 1919. (M.)
6843 Archer, Samuel Frank Alderson, 3 June, 1919. (M.)
6844 Armitage, Charles Leathley, 3 June, 1919. (M.)
6845 Armstrong, James Alexander, 3 June, 1919. (M.)
6846 Arnott, Edward Whinstone, 3 June, 1919. (M.)
6847 Ashwell, Herbert George, 3 June, 1919. (M.)
6848 Aspinall, Hugh Harry Haworth, 3 June, 1919. (M.)
6849 Atchley, Charles Atherton, 3 June, 1919. (M.)
6850 Atherton, George Bramall, 3 June, 1919. (M.)
6852 Atthill, Anthony William Maunsell, 3 June, 1919. (M.)
6853 Auld, Samuel James Manson, 3 June, 1919. (M.)
6854 Auld, William, 3 June, 1919. (M.)

6855 Badcock, George Henry, 3 June, 1919. (M.)
6856 Bagnall, Arthur Henry, 3 June, 1919. (M.)
6857 Bagnall, Richard Dayrell, 3 June, 1919. (M.)
6858 Bailey, Arthur Charles, 3 June, 1910. (M.)
6859 Bailey, Percy James, 3 June, 1919. (M.)
6860 Baker, Frederick Guy Stirling, 3 June, 1919. (M.)
6861 Baker-Baker, William Henry, 3 June, 1919. (M.)
6862 Baker-Carr, Henry Barchard Fenwick, 3 June, 1919. (M.)
6863 Balfour, Edward William Sturgis, 3 June, 1919. (M.)
6864 Balfour, Hon. James Moncrieff, 3 June, 1919. (M.)
6865 Ball, Alexander Douglas, 3 June, 1919. (M.)
6866 Ball, Walter Craven, 3 June, 1919. (M.)
6867 Ballantyne, David, 3 June, 1919. (M.)
6868 Bamford, Percy, 3 June, 1919. (M.)
6869 Bannatyne, Gilbert Alex., 3 June, 1919. (M.)
6870 Barham, Thomas Foster, 3 June, 1919. (M.)
6871 Baring, Hon. Hugo, 3 June, 1919. (M.)
6872 Barkshire, Charles Robert, 3 June, 1919. (M.)
6873 Barron, Neil MacKechnie, 3 June, 1919. (M.)
6874 Bartholomew, William Barker, 3 June, 1919. (M.)
6875 Bartlett, Rev. Reginald, 3 June, 1919. (M.)
6876 Bass, William, 3 June, 1919. (M.)
6877 Bassett, Francis Marshall, 3 June, 1919. (M.)
6878 Bassett, John Retallack, 3 June, 1919. (M.)
6879 Bastard, William Edmund Pollexfen, 3 June, 1919. (M.),
6880 Batho, George William Hyde, 3 June, 1919. (M.)
6881 Batten, Herbert Cary George, 3 June, 1919. (M.)
6882 Bayley, Abingdon Robert, 3 June, 1919. (M.)
6883 Baynes, Douglas Dyneley, 3 June, 1919. (M.)
6884 Beales, William Lear, 3 June, 1919. (M.)
6885 Beamish, William Robert de la Cour, 3 June, 1919. (M.)
6886 Beasley, Myddelton, 3 June, 1919. (M.)
6887 Beaumont, Eugene Guy Euston, 3 June, 1919. (M.)
6888 Beddoes, Claude Eagles Willoughby, 3 June, 1919. (M.)
6889 Bedingfield, Henry Howard, 3 June, 1919. (M.)
6890 Begbey, Henry, 3 June, 1919. (M.)
6891 Behrens, Edgar Charles, 3 June, 1919. (M.)
6893 Bell, Clive Vincent Moberley, 3 June, 1919. (M.)
6894 Bell, George Gerald, 3 June, 1919. (M.)
6895 Bell-Irving, Andrew, 3 June , 1919. (M.)
6896 Bennett, James, 3 June, 1919. (M.)
6897 Benskin, Joseph, 3 June, 1919. (M.)
6898 Benson, Ralph Hawtrey, 3 June, 1919. (M.)
6899 Benzie, Robert Marr, 3 June, 1919. (M.)
6900 Beresford, John de la Poer, 3 June, 1919. (M.)
6901 Lindsay, Peter, 3 June, 1919. (M.)
6902 Berkeley, Rupert Edric Gifford, 3 June, 1919. (M.)
6903 Bernard, John, 3 June, 1919. (M.)
6904 Bernays, Rev. Stewart Frederick Lewis, 3 June, 1919 (M.)
6905 Berrow, John, 3 June, 1919. (M.)
6906 Berryman, Henry Arthur, 3 June, 1919. (M.)
6907 Berthon, Charles Peter, 3 June, 1919. (M.)
6908 Best, Alfred, 3 June, 1919. (M.)
6909 Beverley, Samuel, 3 June, 1910. (M.)
6910 Biggs, Charles William, 3 June, 1919. (M.)
6911 Bilderbeck, William John How, 3 June, 1919. (M.)
6912 Bingham, Sir Albert Edward, Bart., 3 June, 1919. (M.)
6913 Binny, Steuart Murrey, 3 June, 1919. (M.)
6914 Bird, Lawrence Wilfred, 3 June, 1919. (M.)
6915 Birkin, Philip Austen, 3 June, 1919. (M.)
6916 Birt, Arthur Watson, 3 June, 1919. (M.)
6917 Bishop, Charles Alder, 3 June, 1919. (M.)
6918 Bishop, Joseph George, 3 June, 1919. (M.)
6919 Bishop, Nathaniel, 3 June, 1919. (M.)
6920 Black, N., 3 June, 1919. (M.)
6921 Blackburn, Thomas, 3 June, 1919. (M.)
6922 Blair-Imrie, Hew Francis, 3 June, 1919. (M.)
6923 Blois, Eustace William, 3 June, 1919. (M.)
6924 Blomefield, Wilmot, 3 June, 1919. (M.)
6925 Blundell-Hollinshead-Blundell, Cuthbert Leigh, 3 June, 1919. (M.)
6926 Body, Kenneth Martin, 3 June, 1919. (M.)
6927 Bolam, Robert Alfred, 3 June, 1919. (M.)
6928 Bourne, Frank, 3 June, 1919. (M.)
6929 Bowers, Mansell, 3 June, 1919. (M.)
6930 Bower Ismay, Charles, 3 June, 1919. (M.)
6931 Bowles, Ludlow Tonson, 3 June, 1919. (M.)
6932 Bowring, Edward Langley, 3 June, 1919. (M.)
6933 Boyd, Arthur Octavian, 3 June, 1919. (M.)
6934 Branson, Frederick Henry Ewart, 3 June, 1919. (M.)
6935 Bray, Rev. Albert Edward, 3 June, 1919. (M.)
6936 Bremridge, Richard Harding, 3 June, 1919. (M.)
6937 Bridges, Arthur Brodie Hamilton, 3 June, 1919. (M.)
6938 Bridges, Edward James, 3 June, 1919. (M.)
6939 Brierly, James Leslie, 3 June, 1919. (M.)
6940 Briggs, George Ewbank, 3 June, 1919. (M.)
6941 Brightman, Charles John, 3 June, 1919. (M.)
6942 Brightman, John Henry, 3 June, 1919. (M.)
6943 Brinckman, Rowland, 3 June, 1919. (M.)
6944 Brittan, Reginald, 3 June, 1919. (M.)
6945 Britten, William Albert, 3 June, 1919. (M.)
6946 Brosnan, Rev. John Brodie, 3 June, 1919. (M.)
6947 Brown, Arthur Rudston, 3 June, 1919. (M.)
6949 Browne, Tom Bousquet, 3 June, 1919. (M.)
6950 Bruce, George Robert, 3 June, 1919. (M.)
6951 Buchanan, George Herbert, 3 June, 1919. (M.)
6952 Buchanan, Michael Rowland Gray, 3 June, 1919. (M.)
6953 Buckinghamshire, Sidney Carr, Earl of, 3 June, 1919. (M.)

2 s

6954 Buckley, Edward Duncombe Henry, 3 June, 1919. (M.)
6955 Buckmaster, Henry Stephen Guy, 3 June, 1919. (M.)
6956 Buffham, Lewis William, 3 June, 1919. (M.)
6957 Burdon, Edward Griffiths George, 3 June, 1919. (M.)
6958 Burke, Denis Joseph Gerard, 3 June, 1919. (M.)
6959 Burnand, Montague Berthon, 3 June, 1919. (M.)
6960 Burnand, Richard Frank, 3 June, 1919. (M.)
6961 Burnell-Nugent, Frank Henry, 3 June, 1919. (M.)
6962 Burnett, Alexander Edwin, 3 June, 1919. (M.)
6963 Burnett, John Chaplyn, 3 June, 1919. (M.)
6964 Burnett, Leslie Trew, 3 June, 1919. (M.)
6965 Burnett-Hitchcock, Harry William Geddes, 3 June, 1919. (M.)
6966 Burrell, Charles William Wilberforce, 3 June, 1919. (M.)
6967 Burton, Edmund Gerald, 3 June, 1919. (M.)
6968 Burton, Henrietta, 3 June, 1919. (M.)
6969 Burton, Herbert Edgar, 3 June, 1919. (M.)
6970 Bury-Barry, James Robert, 3 June, 1919. (M.)
6971 Byam, William, 3 June, 1919. (M.)
6972 Byrne, Richard, 3 June, 1919. (M.)
6973 Cairns, Rev. John, 3 June, 1919. (M.)
6974 Campbell, Arthur, 3 June, 1919. (M.)
6975 Campbell, Charles, 3 June, 1919. (M.)
6976 Campden, Arthur Edward Joseph Noel, Viscount, 3 June, 1919. (M.)
6977 Carden, Edward David, 3 June, 1919. (M.)
6978 Cardew, Francis Gordon, 3 June, 1919. (M.)
6979 Carlyle, Thomas, 3 June, 1919. (M.)
6980 Carr, Charles Cattley, 3 June, 1919. (M.)
6981 Carter, William Tom, 3 June, 1919. (M.)
6982 Carruthers, Robert Jardine, 3 June, 1919. (M.)
6983 Cartwright, Richard Bernard, 3 June, 1919. (M.)
6984 Cassel, Louis, 3 June, 1919. (M.)
6985 Causton, Edward Postle Gwyn, 3 June, 1919. (M.)
6986 Challis, Oswald, 3 June, 1919. (M.)
6987 Chance, Ernest Washington, 3 June, 1919. (M.)
6988 Chance, Maurice, 3 June, 1919. (M.)
6989 Chandler, Cecil John Golding, 3 June, 1919. (M.)
6990 Chapman, George James, 3 June, 1919. (M.)
6991 Chapman, Joseph Thomas, 3 June, 1919. (M.)
6992 Chapman, T. H., 3 June, 1919. (M.)
6993 Chatterley, Frank Martin, 3 June, 1919. (M.)
6994 Chellew, Thomas John, 3 June, 1919. (M.)
6995 Chesney, Dennis, 3 June, 1919. (M.)
6996 Chichester, Walter Raleigh, 3 June, 1919. (M.)
6997 Chirnside, John Percy, 3 June, 1919. (M.)
6998 Christie, James, 3 June, 1919. (M.)
6999 Chubb, Harry Emory, 3 June, 1919. (M.)
7000 Churston, John Reginald Lopes, Lord, 3 June, 1919. (M.)
7001 Clark, Robert, 3 June, 1919. (M.)
7002 Clayton, Emilius, 3 June, 1919. (M.)
7003 Clemens, Lionel Alfred, 3 June, 1919. (M.)
7004 Clive, Harry, 3 June, 1919. (M.)
7005 Clifton, Ernest Hamilton, 3 June, 1919. (M.)
7006 Clough, Henry Kenny, 3 June, 1919. (M.)
7007 Coates, Thomas, 3 June, 1919. (M.)
7008 Cockburn, Walter George, 3 June, 1919. (M.)
7009 Cochrane, Thomas Henry, 3 June, 1919. (M.)
7010 Cochrane. William Percy, 3 June, 1919. (M.)
7011 Coddington, Herbert Adolphe, 3 June, 1919. (M.)
7012 Coleman, Thomas Everit, 3 June, 1919. (M.)
7013 Cohen, Sir Herbert Benjamin, 3 June, 1919. (M.)
7014 Coldwell, Reginald Charles, 3 June, 1919. (M.)
7015 Cole, John Albert, 3 June, 1919. (M.)
7016 Collier, Mortimer Calmady, 3 June, 1919. (M.)
7017 Collingwood, Bertram James, 3 June, 1919. (M.)
7018 Collins, Charles Howell Groset, 3 June, 1919. (M.)
7019 Collins, Rev. Edward Hycynth, 3 June, 1919. (M.)
7020 Colquhoun, Arthur Hugh, 3 June, 1919. (M.)
7021 Colville, Charles Eliezer, 3 June, 1919. (M.)
7022 Combe, James Scarth, 3 June. 1919. (M.)
7025 Coningham, Alfred Evelyn, 3 June, 1919. (M.)
7026 Cook, Sidney George, 3 June, 1919. (M.)
7027 Cooke, Martin Alfred, 3 June, 1919. (M.)
7028 Cookson, Philip Blencowe, 3 June, 1919. (M.)
7029 Cooper, Eustace Nugent Fitzgeorge de Radcliffe, 3 June, 1919. (M.)
7030 Cooper, George Alexander Conacher, 3 June, 1919. (M.)
7031 Cooper, Harry, 3 June, 1919. (M.)
7032 Corkery, Martin Percy, 3 June, 1919. (M.)
7033 Cory, Evan James Trevor, 3 June, 1919. (M.)
7034 Court, Sidney Herbert, 3 June, 1919. (M.)
7035 Cowan, John, 3 June, 1919. (M.)
7036 Cowling, John, 3 June, 1919. (M.)
7037 Cowper, Lionel Ilfred, 3 June, 1919. (M.)
7038 Cox, Horace Beresford, 3 June, 1919. (M.)
7039 Coxhead, Thomas Langhorne, 3 June, 1919. (M.)
7040 Crabbie, John Edward, 3 June, 1919. (M.)
7041 Cran, Peter McLellan, 3 June, 1919. (M.)
7042 Crane, Lucius Fairchild, 3 June, 1919. (M.)
7043 Crane, Robert Eugene, 3 June, 1919. (M.)
7044 Craster, Albert Kenneth Graves, 3 June, 1919. (M.)
7045 Craven, John, 3 June, 1919. (M.)
7046 Crawley, Charles, 3 June, 1919. (M.)
7047 Creagh, Edward Cottingham, 3 June, 1919. (M.)
7048 Critchlow, John, 3 June, 1919. (M.)
7049 Crocker, Arthur Albert, 3 June, 1919. (M.)
7050 Croft, Tom, 3 June, 1919. (M.)
7051 Crosskey, Cecil, 3 June, 1919. (M.)

7052 Crossley, Eric, 3 June, 1919. (M.)
7053 Cruickshank, Percy Hamilton, 3 June, 1919. (M.)
7054 Crump, Eldon Annesley, 3 June, 1919. (M.)
7055 Cumberlege, Cleland Bulstrode, 3 June, 1919. (M.)
7057 Cunningham, Frederick George, 3 June, 1919. (M.)
7059 Dailley, Wilfred Gordon Beale, 3 June, 1919. (M.)
7060 Dale, Claude Henry, 3 June, 1919 (M.)
7061 Daniel, Walter, 3 June, 1919. (M.)
7062 Daniell, Humphrey Averell, 3 June, 1919. (M.)
7063 Dansey, Edward Mashiter, 3 June, 1919. (M.)
7064 Darley, Henry Read, 3 June, 1919. (M.)
7065 Dartnell, George Bruce, 3 June, 1919. (M.)
7066 Daubuz, Claude, 3 June, 1919. (M.)
7067 Davies, Edward Owen, 3 June, 1919. (M.)
7068 Davis, Bryant Fitzwilliam Richard, 3 June, 1919. (M.)
7069 Davis, Cecil, 3 June, 1919. (M.)
7070 Davis, Sidney Alfred, 3 June, 1919. (M.)
7071 Dawson, William Richard, 3 June, 1919. (M.)
7072 Daynes, William Herbert, 3 June, 1919. (M.)
7073 Dean, Arthur Cecil Hamilton, 3 June, 1919. (M.)
7074 Dearnley, Walter Nathan, 3 June, 1919. (M.)
7075 Debenham, Frank, 3 June, 1919. (M.)
7076 Denham, Harold Alfred, 3 June, 1919. (M.)
7077 Denniston, John Dewar, 3 June, 1919. (M.)
7078 Denny, William Alfred Charles, 3 June, 1919. (M.)
7079 De Vic Carey, Lewis Adolphus, 3 June, 1919. (M.)
7080 Devine, James, 3 June, 1919. (M.)
7081 Devine, James Arthur, 3 June, 1919. (M.)
7082 Des Voeux, Henry, 3 June, 1919. (M.)
7083 Dewar, Michael Bruce Urquhart, 3 June, 1919. (M.)
7084 De Witt, Ferdinand, 3 June, 1919. (M.)
7085 Dewing, Sidney Herbert, 3 June, 1919. (M.)
7086 Dickinson, Joseph Espin, 3 June, 1919. (M.)
7087 Dickson, Robert Milne, 3 June, 1919. (M.)
7088 Dickson, William, 3 June, 1919. (M.)
7089 Dill, Thomas Melville, 3 June, 1919. (M.)
7090 Dimmock, Henry Peers, 3 June, 1919. (M.)
7091 Dixon, Edward Travers, 3 June, 1919. (M.)
7092 Dobson, Andrew Edward Augustus, 3 June, 1919. (M.)
7093 Dockrell, George Shannon, 3 June, 1919. (M.)
7094 Dod, Francis Sandford, 3 June, 1919. (M.)
7095 Doidge, Herbert Frederick, 3 June, 1919. (M.)
7096 Doig, Claude Prendergast, 3 June, 1919. (M.)
7097 Doland, George Frederick, 3 June, 1919. (M.)
7098 Dooner, William Dundas, 3 June, 1919. (M.)
7099 Dove, Percy William, 3 June, 1919. (M.)
7100 Down, Halkett Walton Money, 3 June, 1919. (M.)
7101 Downing, Henry John, 3 June, 1919. (M.)
7102 Drew, John Summers, 3 June, 1919. (M.)
7103 Drew, Tom Maxwell, 3 June, 1919. (M.)
7104 Dudfield, Reginald Samuel Orme, 3 June, 1919. (M.)
7105 Dudley, Harold Ward, 3 June, 1919. (M.)
7106 Duffy, Michael Louis, 3 June, 1919. (M.)
7107 Du Plat, Taylor, George Philip, 3 June, 1919. (M.)
7108 Dunn, Robert Charles, 3 June, 1919. (M.)
7109 Dyke, John Samuel, 3 June, 1919. (M.)
7110 Eardley-Wilmot, Hugh, 3 June, 1919. (M.)
7111 Eardley-Wilmot, Percy, 3 June, 1919. (M.)
7112 Earp, Lewis Thomas Jerome, 3 June, 1919. (M.)
7113 Eaton, B. J., 3 June, 1919. (M.)
7114 Edwards, Lionel Charles, 3 June, 1919. (M.)
7115 Ehrmann, Albert, 3 June, 1919. (M.)
7116 Elgee, Ernest Alfred, 3 June, 1919. (M.)
7117 Elliott, Stanley, 3 June, 1919. (M.)
7118 Ellis, Richard Stanley, 3 June, 1919. (M.)
7119 Elmslie, Reginald Cheyne, 3 June, 1919. (M.)
7120 Elton, Herbert Averill, 3 June, 1919. (M.)
7121 Elworthy, William Rowe, 3 June, 1919. (M.)
7122 Emmet, Ernest Arnold, 3 June, 1919. (M.)
7124 England, Richard Travell, 3 June, 1919. (M.)
7125 English, William, 3 June, 1919. (M.)
7126 Ennis, Rev. Alexander Dallas Lecky, 3 June, 1919. (M.)
7127 Esslemont, Mrs. Dora Longair, 3 June, 1919. (M.)
7128 Evans, Arthur Henry, 3 June, 1919. (M.)
7129 Evans, Cecil Hugh Silvester, 3 June, 1919. (M.)
7130 Ewing, Isabella Mercer, 3 June, 1919. (M.)
7131 Ezechiel, James, 3 June, 1919. (M.)
7132 Fagan, Charles Horace John, 3 June, 1919. (M.)
7133 Fairbairn, David Alexander, 3 June, 1919. (M.)
7134 Fairbairn, James Ross, 3 June, 1919. (M.)
7135 Falkner, Henry George, 3 June, 1919. (M.)
7136 Farrell, Gilbert Valentine, 3 June, 1919. (M.)
7137 Fawcett, Edward George Duncan, 3 June 1919. (M.)
7138 Fearenside, Edmund, 3 June, 1919. (M.)
7139 Fellowes, Charles Grincill, 3 June, 1919. (M.)
7140 Ferguson, Donald, 3 June, 1919. (M.)
7141 Ferguson, Spencer Charles, 3 June, 1919. (M.)
7142 Field, Christopher Senior, 3 June, 1919. (M.)
7143 Fincken, Vernon Shaw Taylor, 3 June, 1919. (M.)
7144 Findlay, Richard John, 3 June, 1919. (M.)
7145 Finlayson, William Thomas, 3 June, 1919. (M.)
7146 Fish, Colin, 3 June, 1919. (M.)
7147 Fitch, Vernon Frederick, 3 June, 1919. (M.)
7148 Fitzgerald, Gordon William, 3 June, 1919. (M.)
7149 Fitzgerald, William Coulson, 3 June, 1919. (M.)
7150 Fitzwarrenne-Despencer-Robertson, James Archibald St. George, 3 June, 1919. (M.)
7151 Fleming, Henry Slane, 3 June, 1919. (M.)
7152 Fletcher, Henry Rivers, 3 June, 1919. (M.)

7153 Flew, Edwin Howard, 3 June, 1919. (M.)
7154 Flinn, William Henry, 3 June, 1919. (M.)
7155 Fogg, Herbert George Henry, 3 June, 1919. (M.)
7157 Foran, Robert, 3 June, 1919. (M.)
7158 Ford, George Newton, 3 June, 1919. (M.)
7159 Ford, John Theodore, 3 June, 1919. (M.)
7160 Foreman, Cornelius William, 3 June, 1919. (M.)
7161 Formby, Hugh Carlton, 3 June, 1919. (M.)
7162 Formby, John, 3 June, 1919. (M.)
7163 Forster, Charles Matthew, 3 June, 1919. (M.)
7164 Fosbery, Widenham Francis Widenham, 3 June, 1919. (M.)
7165 Foulerton, Alexander Grant Russell, 3 June, 1919. (M.)
7166 Fowler, George Curran, 3 June, 1919. (M.)
7167 Fox, Robert Michael Douglas, 3 June, 1919. (M.)
7168 Frazer, George Warren, 3 June, 1919. (M.)
7169 Freer, Harry Branston, 3 June, 1919. (M.)
7170 Frye, Colin Charlwood, 3 June, 1919. (M.)
7171 Fryer, Cecil Robert, 3 June, 1919. (M.)
7172 Reynardson, Arthur Acland-Hood, 3 June 1919. (M.)
7173 Gair, Charles John Dickenson, 3 June, 1919. (M.)
7174 Galtrey, Sidney, 3 June, 1919. (M.)
7175 Galloway, James Muir, 3 June, 1919. (M.)
7176 Gardner, FitzRoy, 3 June, 1919. (M.)
7177 Garrett, Frederick Charles, 3 June, 1919. (M.)
7178 Garratt, Lawrence Challoner, 3 June, 1919. (M.)
7179 Gemmell, William Alexander Stuart, 3 June, 1919. (M.)
7180 Gervers, Dorothy, Mrs. Charles T., 3 June, 1919. (M.)
7181 Gilbert-Cooper, William Naunton Roger, 3 June, 1919. (M.)
7182 Giles, Godfrey Douglas, 3 June, 1919. (M.)
7183 Giles, Arthur Herbert Wainwright, 3 June, 1919. (M.)
7185 Gillam, Vincent Andrew, 3 June, 1919. (M.)
7186 Gillies, James Adam Kirkwood, 3 June, 1919. (M.)
7187 Gilling, Henry Thomas, 3 June, 1919. (M.)
7188 Gimingham, Conrad Theodore, 3 June, 1919. (M.)
7189 Gleeson, Andrew Fitzwilliam, 3 June, 1919. (M)
7190 Glover, James Alison, 3 June, 1919. (M.)
7191 Gluckstein, Montague, 3 June, 1919. (M.)
7192 Godley, Alfred Davis, 3 June, 1919. (M.)
7193 Goldsmith, Frank, 3 June, 1919. (M.)
7194 Golla, Frederick Lucien, 3 June, 1919. (M.)
7195 Goodall, Edward Wilberforce, 3 June, 1919. (M.)
7196 Goodden, Robert Blunde, 3 June, 1919. (M.)
7197 Goodwin, Aubrey, 3 June, 1919. (M.)
7198 Gordon, Edward Ian Drumearn, 3 June, 1919. (M.)
7199 Gordon, George, 3 June, 1919. (M.)
7200 Gover, William Cyril, 3 June, 1919. (M.)
7201 Grant, William Francis Newby, 3 June, 1919. (M.)
7202 Grant, William Griffith, 3 June, 1919. (M.)
7203 Gray, Alexander Charles Edward, 3 June, 1919. (M.)
7204 Green, Rev. Earnest William, 3 June, 1919. (M.)
7205 Gregg, James, 3 June, 1919. (M.)
7206 Gregson, Lancelot Mare, 2 June, 1919. (M.)
7207 Gresson, Robert Holmes Arbuthnot, 3 June, 1919. (M.)
7208 Griffith, Gronwy Robert, 3 June, 1919. (M.)
7209 Griffiths, Charles, 3 June, 1919. (M.)
7210 Griffiths, Noel Marshall, 3 June, 1919. (M.)
7211 Griffiths, Rev. Trevor, 3 June, 1919. (M.)
7212 Grigson, Thomas Reginald, 3 June, 1919. (M.)
7213 Grimshaw, William Edwin, 3 June, 1919. (M.)
7214 Griss, John Ellis, 3 June, 1919. (M.)
7215 Grubb, John James, 3 June, 1919. (M.)
7216 Gubbins, Martin Nepean Traill, 3 June, 1919. (M.)
7217 Guthrie, Robert Lindsay, 3 June, 1919. (M.)
7218 Guthrie, Robert Lyall, 3 June, 1919. (M.)
7219 Gyngell, George, 3 June, 1919. (M.)
7220 Hackett, Patrick, 3 June, 1919. (M.)
7221 Hacking, Arthur, 3 June, 1919. (M.)
7222 Haggitt, Edward Dashwood, 3 June, 1919. (M.)
7223 Hale, Walter Churchill, 3 June, 1919. (M.)
7224 Hales, Rev. James Tooke, 3 June, 1919. (M.)
7225 Halford, Michael Francis, 3 June, 1919. (M.)
7226 Hall, Alexander Nelson, 3 June, 1919. (M.)
7227 Hall, Douglas, 3 June, 1919. (M.)
7228 Hall, George Leslie, 3 June, 1919. (M.)
7229 Hall, Rev. Richard, 3 June, 1919. (M.)
7230 Hallsworth, Harry Mainwaring, 3 June, 1919. (M.)
7231 Hambleton, Herbert Adolph, 3 June, 1919. (M.)
7232 Hamilton, Ronald James, 3 June, 1919. (M.)
7233 Hamlin, Richard James, 3 June, 1919. (M.)
7234 Hamlett, Harry Williams, 3 June, 1919. (M.)
7235 Hanbury, Everard Ernest, 3 June, 1919. (M.)
7236 Tracy, Eric Thomas Henry Hanbury, 3 June, 1919. (M.)
7237 Hankey, William Hubert Alers, 3 June, 1919. (M.)
7238 Hannay, Charles Graham, 3 June, 1919. (M.)
7239 Hanson, Rev. Robert Edward Vernon, 3 June, 1919. (M.)
7240 Harding, Cecil Redfern, 3 June, 1919. (M.)
7241 Hardy, Confred Napier Mitchell, 3 June, 1919. (M.)
7242 Harlow, George Henry, 3 June, 1919. (M.)
7243 Harris, Charles Sydney, 3 June, 1919. (M.)
7244 Harris, Emanuel Vincent, 3 June, 1919. (M.)
7245 Harris, George Arthur, 3 June, 1919. (M.)
7246 Harris, Walter Reginald, 3 June, 1919. (M.)
7247 Harrison, John Stubbs, 3 June, 1919. (M.)
7248 Hart, Ernest James, 3 June, 1919. (M.)
7249 Hart, Kenneth Eugene, 3 June, 1919. (M.)
7250 Hart-Cox, Ernest William, 3 June, 1919. (M.)
7251 Hart-Synnot, Ronald Victor Okes, 3 June, 1919. (M.)

7252 Harvey, Frank Barrington, 3 June, 1919. (M.)
7253 Haughton, Henry Wilfred, 3 June, 1919. (M.)
7254 Hawkes, John Alfred, 3 June. 1919. (M.)
7255 Hawkins, Henry, 3 June, 1919. (M.)
7256 Haworth, Frederick, 3 June, 1919. (M.)
7257 Hayden, Frederick Arthur, 3 June, 1919. (M.)
7258 Hayes, George Sullivan Clifford, 3 June, 1919. (M.)
7259 Headley, Arthur William Ainley, 3 June, 1919. (M.)
7960 Heard, Samuel Ferguson, 3 June, 1919. (M.)
7261 Hearn, Michael Leo, 3 June, 1919. (M.)
7262 Heatley, Thomas George, 3 June, 1919. (M.)
7263 Helps, Rowland Philip Arthur, 3 June, 1919. (M.)
7264 Hely-Hutchinson, Coote Robert, 3 June, 1919. (M.)
7265 Henderson, John Acheson, 3 June, 1919. (M.)
7266 Heneage, Hon. George Edward, 3 June, 1919. (M.)
7267 Hennell, Sir Reginald, 3 June, 1919. (M.)
7268 Henry, Alfred Stanley, 3 June, 1919. (M.)
7269 Herbert, Ernest Roland, 3 June, 1919. (M.)
7270 Herne, Arthur Cecil, 3 June, 1919. (M.)
7271 Herridge, George James, 3 June, 1919. (M.)
7272 Hervey, Gerald Charles Iwin, 3 June, 1919. (M.)
7273 Hewett, Edward Vincent Osborne, 3 June, 1919. (M.)
7274 Hewitt, John Theodore, 3 June, 1919. (M.)
7275 Heywood, Noel, 3 June, 1919. (M.)
7276 Higgins, John Esmond Longuet, 3 June, 1919. (M.)
7277 Higgs-Walker, Joseph Walker, 3 June, 1919. (M.)
7278 Hill, Frederick George, 3 June, 1919. (M.)
7279 Hill, Frank William Rowland, 3 June, 1919. (M.)
7280 Hill, Trevor Montague, 3 June, 1919. (M.)
7281 Hillyard, John William, 3 June, 1919. (M.)
7282 Hilton, R. S., 3 June, 1919. (M.)
7283 Hine, Thomas Guy Macaulay, 3 June, 1919. (M.)
7284 Hingston, Alfred Joseph, 3 June, 1919. (M.)
7285 Hoare, Herbert, 3 June, 1919. (M.)
7286 Hodgkinson, Robert Frank Byron, 3 June, 1919. (M.)
7287 Holdich, Thomas White, 3 June, 1919. (M.)
7288 Holdsworth, John Joseph, 3 June, 1919. (M.)
7289 Holford, Charles Frederick, 3 June, 1919. (M.)
7290 Holland, Wilfred, 3 June, 1919. (M.)
7291 Home, William Edward, 3 June, 1919. (M.)
7292 Hood, Grosvenor Arthur Alexander, Viscount, 3 June, 1919. (M.)
7294 Hooper, Herbert Ross, 3 June, 1919. (M.)
7295 Hope, Sir John Augustus, Bart., 3 June, 1919. (M.)
7296 Hopkins, Percy Alfred, 3 June, 1919. (M.)
7297 Horn, Robert Victor Galbraith, 3 June, 1919. (M.)
7298 Howells, Wilfred Allen, 3 June, 1919. (M.)
7299 Hoyle, Edward Jonas, 3 June, 1919. (M.)
7300 Hoyle, Emanuel, 3 June, 1919. (M.)
7301 Hue-Williams, Reginald Guy, 3 June, 1919. (M.)
7302 Hughes, Claud Gillan Erskine, 3 June, 1919. (M.)
7303 Hughes, Ernest Cranmer, 3 June, 1919. (M.)
7304 Hughman, Gordon Stewart, 3 June, 1919. (M.)
7305 Humphrey, Bernard, 3 June, 1919 (M.)
7306 Humphreys, Percy Harry Illingworth, 3 June, 1919. (M.)
7307 Humphreys, William, 3 June, 1919. (M.)
7308 Hunt, Thomas Edward Carew, 3 June, 1919. (M.)
7309 Hunter, Evan Austin, 3 June, 1919. (M.)
7310 Hunter, Herbert Patrick, 3 June, 1919. (M.)
7311 Hunter, Maurice, 3 June, 1919. (M.)
7312 Hurst, Arthur Frederick, 3 June, 1919. (M.)
7313 Inglis, Charles Edward, 3 June, 1919. (M.)
7314 Inns, Jeremiah, 3 June, 1919. (M.)
7315 Irby, Leonard Paul, 3 June, 1919. (M.)
7316 Iremonger, Ernest Lascelles, 3 June, 1919. (M.)
7317 Jackson, Jessie Millicent, 3 June, 1919. (M.)
7318 Jackson, Samuel, 3 June, 1919. (M.)
7319 Jameson, George Lionel, 3 June, 1919. (M.)
7320 Janes, Ernest, 3 June, 1919. (M.)
7321 Jardine, William, 3 June, 1919. (M.)
7322 Jarvis, William Bertie, 3 June, 1919. (M.)
7323 Jeffreys, Patrick Douglas, 3 June, 1919. (M.)
7324 Jelley, Reginald Frank, 3 June, 1919. (M.)
7325 Jellicorse, Harold, 3 June, 1919. (M.)
7326 Jeffery, Reginald, 3 June, 1919. (M.)
7327 Jenkins, George John, 3 June, 1919. (M.)
7328 Jenkins, John Alexander, 3 June, 1919. (M.)
7329 Joel, Herbert Cecil, 3 June, 1919. (M.)
7330 Johns, Frederick Nelson, 3 June, 1919. (M.)
7331 Johnson, Albert, 3 June, 1919. (M.)
7332 Johnson, Henry Campbell, 3 June, 1919. (M.)
7333 Johnston, Bruce Campbell, 3 June, 1919. (M.)
7334 Jones, Edgar Williams, 3 June, 1919. (M.)
7335 Jones, Russell, 3 June, 1919. (M.)
7336 Jopp, Stephen James Melville, 3 June, 1919. (M.)
7337 Jupp, William Alfred, 3 June, 1919. (M.)
7338 Joy, Herbert Alfred, 3 June, 1919. (M.)
7339 Kaulbach, Henry Albert, 3 June, 1919. (M.)
7340 Kay, Herbert Davenport, 3 June, 1919. (M.)
7341 Keays, Cyril Arthur, 3 June, 1919. (M.)
7342 Keene, John James, 3 June, 1919. (M.)
7343 Keith, Gerald, 3 June, 1919. (M.)
7344 Kellett, James Albert, 3 June, 1919. (M.)
7345 Kelly, Richard Cecil, 3 June, 1919. (M.)
7346 Kemmis-Betty, William Redmond Prendergast, 3 June, 1919. (M.)
7347 Kerrison, Edmund Roger Allday, 3 June, 1919. (M.)
7348 Key, Robert Ellis, 3 June, 1919. (M.)
7349 Kimmitt, Robert Robertson, 3 June, 1919. (M.)

7350 King, William Henry, 3 June, 1919. (M.)
7351 Kingston, John Rudolph, 3 June, 1919. (M.)
7352 Kinloch, Rev. Michael Ward, 3 June, 1919. (M.)
7353 Kirby, Edmund Bertram, 3 June, 1919. (M.)
7354 Kirk, Albert Edward, 3 June 1919. (M.)
7355 Kirkland, James, 3 June, 1919. (M.)
7356 Kirsop, Alexander Kennedy, 3 June, 1919. (M.)
7357 Kitson, Alexander Wentworth, 3 June, 1919. (M.)
7358 Kitson, Paul Hengrave, 3 June, 1919. (M.)
7359 Knight, Charles Louis William Morley, 3 June, 1919. (M.)
7360 Knox, James Stuart, 3 June, 1919. (M.)
7361 Laidlaw, John Brown, 3 June, 1919. (M.)
7362 Lambert, Bertram, 3 June, 1919. (M.)
7363 Lambert, George Herbert, 3 June, 1919. (M.)
7364 Lambert, Thomas Erskine, 3 June, 1919. (M.)
7365 Lambton, George Charles, 3 June, 1919. (M.)
7366 Laming, Henry Thornton, 3 June, 1919. (M.)
7367 Langdale, Philip, 3 June, 1919. (M.)
7368 Langworthy-Parry, Percy Edward, 3 June, 1919. (M.)
7369 Lascelles, George Reginald, 3 June, 1919. (M.)
7370 Laskey, Walter William, 3 June, 1919. (M.)
7371 Latham, John Ion, 3 June, 1919. (M.)
7372 Lathbury, Ernest Browning, 3 June, 1919. (M.)
7373 Laverton, Herbert Curling, 3 June, 1919. (M.)
7374 Law, Robert William Rowland, 3 June, 1919. (M.)
7375 Lawrence, Hervey Major, 3 June, 1919. (M.)
7376 Leahy, Henry Gordon, 3 June, 1919. (M.)
7377 Leamy, Alfred, 3 June, 1919. (M.)
7378 Ledward, Harold, 3 June, 1919. (M.)
7379 Lee, John Robert, 3 June, 1919. (M.)
7380 Lees, Roderick Livingstone, 3 June, 1919. (M.)
7381 Lefebure, Victor, 3 June, 1919. (M.)
7382 Leggett, Edward James, 3 June, 1919. (M.)
7383 Leggett, Robert Anthony Cleghorn Linington, 3 June, 1919. (M.)
7384 Leigh, Geoffrey Hamilton, 3 June, 1919. (M.)
7385 Le Rossignol, H. S., 3 June, 1919. (M.)
7386 Lethbridge, Robert Thomas Morland, 3 June, 1919. (M.)
7387 Leveson-Gower, Charles Cameron, 3 June, 1919. (M.)
7388 Lewis, George Ernest, 3 June, 1919 (M.)
7389 Ley, Cuthbert Hillyer, 3 June, 1919. (M.)
7390 Lickman, Harry Sylvanus, 3 June, 1919. (M.)
7391 Link, Willie Cresswell, 3 June, 1919. (M.)
7392 Linlithgow, Victor Alexander John, Marquis of, 3 June, 1919. (M.)
7393 Lister-Kaye, Sir John, Bart., 3 June, 1919. (M.)
7394 Little, John, 3 June, 1919. (M.)
7395 Litton, Marchall William, 3 June, 1919. (M.)
7396 Lloyd, George William David Bowen, 3 June, 1919. (M.)
7397 Lodge, Thomas, 3 June, 1919. (M.)
7398 Logan, Francis Carleton Logan, 3 June, 1919. (M.)
7399 Logan, William, 3 June, 1919. (M.)
7400 Lomer, Sydney Francis McIlree, 3 June, 1919. (M.)
7401 Long, Gerard Hanslip, 3 June, 1919. (M.)
7402 Longden, Henry John Leicester, 3 June, 1919. (M.)
7403 Low, Charles Frederick Gemley, 3 June, 1919. (M.)
7404 Low, James Lindsay, 3 June, 1919. (M.)
7405 Lowe, Andrew Alfred, 3 June, 1919. (M.)
7406 Lowe, Thomas Enoch, 3 June, 1919. (M.)
7407 Lucas, Reginald Hugh, 3 June, 1919. (M.)
7408 Lucas, Thomas Lucas Woodwright, 3 June, 1919. (M.)
7409 Lumley, Dudley Owen, 3 June, 1919. (M.)
7410 Lyde, Edith Mary, 3 June, 1919. (M.)
7411 Lyle, Arthur Abram, 3 June, 1919. (M.)
7412 Lyle, Oliver, 3 June, 1919. (M.)
7413 McArthur, Charles Joseph Edward Addis, 3 June, 1919. (M.)
7414 McCance, Henry Montray Jones, 3 June, 1919. (M.)
7415 McClellan, Frederick Ewing, 3 June, 1919. (M.)
7416 McCormack, Michael, 3 June, 1919. (M.)
7417 McDermott, John, 3 June, 1919. (M.)
7418 Macdiarmid, Peter, 3 June, 1919. (M.)
7419 Macdonald, Andrew Edward, 3 June, 1919. (M.)
7420 Macdonald, Angus G., 3 June, 1919. (M.)
7421 McDonald, James, 3 June, 1919. (M.)
7422 McDougall, John McI., 3 June, 1919. (M.)
7423 McDowell, Donald Keith, 3 June, 1919. (M.)
7424 McDowell, Samuel Johnson, 3 June, 1919. (M.)
7425 McEwen, James, 3 June, 1919. (M.)
7426 McFall, Albert William Crawford, 3 June, 1919. (M.)
7427 McGuinness, Charles Hamilton, 3 June, 1919. (M.)
7428 MacIndoe, James Douglas, 3 June, 1919. (M.)
7429 MacKenzie, Alexander Donald, 3 June, 1919. (M.)
7430 Mackenzie, Colin Mansfield, 3 June, 1919. (M.)
7431 Mackenzie, Eric Francis Wallace, 3 June, 1919. (M.)
7432 McKergow, Robert Wilson, 3 June, 1919. (M.)
7433 McKerrell, Reginald L'Estrange, 3 June, 1919. (M.)
7434 MacKinnon, Archibald Donald, 3 June, 1919. (M.)
7435 MacLeod, Rev. John, 3 June, 1919. (M.)
7436 McMahon, Kellerman Eyre, 3 June, 1919. (M.)
7437 McMunn, Andrew, 3 June, 1919. (M.)
7438 MacPherson, Rev. Ranald, 3 June, 1919. (M.)
7439 Macready, Gordon Nevil, 3 June, 1919. (M.)
7440 Magill, Henry Patrick, 3 June, 1919. (M.)
7441 Mahe de Chenal de la Bourdonnais, Charles, H.H. Prince, 3 June, 1919. (M.)
7442 Maitland, Frederick Colin, Viscount, 3 June, 1919. (M.)
7443 Maitland-Jones, Arthur Griffiths, 3 June, 1919. (M.)
7444 Makalua, Matthew James Manuia, 3 June, 1919. (M.)

7445 Malim, Edward John, 3 June, 1919. (M.)
7446 Manley, John Charles Medland, 3 June, 1919. (M.)
7447 Manley, William Edward, 3 June, 1919. (M.)
7448 Marians, Reginald Ingram, 3 June, 1919. (M.)
7449 Marks, Edward Seaborn, 3 June, 1919. (M.)
7450 Marples, Morris Edgar, 3 June, 1919. (M.)
7451 Marsden, Charles Howard, 3 June, 1919. (M.)
7452 Marshall, Herbert Westmorland, 3 June, 1919. (M.)
7453 Marshall, Mark Henry, 3 June, 1919. (M.)
7454 Martin, Charles Jasper, 3 June, 1919. (M.)
7455 Martin, Horace, 3 June, 1919. (M.)
7456 Maskell, William Edward, 3 June, 1919. (M.)
7457 Mason, James Ernest, 3 June, 1919. (M.)
7458 Master, Frederick Hill, 3 June, 1919. (M.)
7459 Mather, William Harold, 3 June, 1919. (M.)
7460 Matthews, Edward, 3 June, 1919. (M.)
7461 Matthews, Ernest James, 3 June, 1919. (M.)
7462 Matthews, Llewellin Washington, 3 June, 1919. (M.
7463 Maunsell, Richard John Caswell. 3 June, 1919. (M.)
7464 May, Arthur Henry, 3 June, 1919. (M.)
7465 May, Arthur John, 3 June, 1919. (M.)
7466 Mayhew, Mark James, 3 June, 1919. (M.)
7467 Mayor, Edgar William, 3 June, 1919. (M.)
7468 Mead, Charles, 3 June, 1919. (M.)
7469 Meade, Harry Edward, 3 June, 1919. (M.)
7470 Mellis, William, 3 June, 1919. (M.)
7471 Mepham, Charles Edward, 3 June, 1919. (M.)
7472 Messel, Leonard Charles Rudolph, 3 June, 1919. (M.)
7473 Messiter, Charles Bayard, 3 June, 1919. (M.)
7474 Methuen, Lionel Harry, 3 June, 1919. (M.)
7475 Milburn, Charles Henry, 3 June, 1919. (M.)
7476 Milburn, Thomas Alan, 3 June, 1919. (M.)
7477 Millican, Harry Cyril, 3 June, 1919. (M.)
7478 Millman, Francis Henry, 3 June, 1919. (M.)
7479 Millman, William Henry Ennor, 3 June, 1919. (M.)
7480 Milne, George Wardlaw, 3 June, 1919. (M.)
7481 Mitchell, Arthur Brownlow, 3 June, 1919. (M.)
7482 Mitchell, Spencer, 3 June, 1919. (M.)
7483 Molony, Francis Arthur, 3 June, 1919. (M.)
7484 Monro, John Duncan, 3 June, 1919. (M.)
7485 Montague-Douglas-Scott, Lord George William, 3 June, 1919. (M.)
7486 Montague, Stewart Francis, 3 June, 1919. (M.)
7487 Montgomerie, Victor Robert, 3 June, 1919. (M.)
7488 Moore, James Stuart Hamilton, 3 June, 1919. (M.)
7489 Moore, William, 3 June, 1919. (M.)
7490 Morgan, Kenyon Pascoe Vaughan, 3 June, 1919. (M.)
7491 Morgans, Godfrey Ewart, 3 June, 1919. (M.)
7492 Morrison-Bell, Ernest FitzRoy, 3 June, 1919. (M.)
7493 Morrow, John Smythe, 3 June, 1919. (M.)
7494 Morton-Clarke, James Thomas, 3 June, 1919. (M.)
7495 Motherwell, Gavin Black Loudon, 3 June, 1919. (M.)
7496 Moulton, John Coney, 3 June, 1919. (M.)
7497 Moxon, Herbert William, 3 June, 1919. (M.)
7498 Muir, John, 3 June, 1919. (M.)
7499 Muir, Robert Bunten, 3 June, 1919. (M.)
7500 Mulholland, Hon. Charles Henry George, 3 June, 1919. (M.)
7501 Murphy, James, 3 June, 1919. (M.)
7502 Murray, Alan Sim, 3 June, 1919. (M.)
7503 Murray, Everitt, George Dunne, 3 June, 1919. (M.)
7504 Murray, William Alfred, 3 June, 1919. (M.)
7505 Musgrave, William Newcome, 3 June, 1919. (M.)
7506 Nathan, Edward Jonah, 3 June, 1919. (M.)
7507 Nelson, Arthur, 3 June, 1919. (M.)
7508 Nelson, William, 3 June, 1919. (M.)
7509 Nesbit, George, 3 June, 1919. (M.)
7510 Nesbitt-Dufort, Cyril John, 3 June, 1919. (M.)
7511 Newham, William Henry, 3 June, 1919. (M.)
7512 Newton, Stephen Guy, 3 June, 1919. (M.)
7513 Newton, Thomas Cochrane, 3 June, 1919. (M.)
7514 Nevill, Cosmos Charles Richard, 3 June, 1919. (M.)
7515 Nicol, John, 3 June, 1919. (M.)
7516 Nicholls, Edward Alfred, 3 June, 1919. (M.)
7517 Nicholson, Thomas Brinsley, 3 June, 1919. (M.)
7518 Nicholson, Stephen William, 3 June, 1919. (M.)
7519 Nind, Henry James, 3 June, 1919. (M.)
7520 Nix, Charles George Ashburton, 3 June, 1919. (M.)
7521 Noble, Richard, 3 June, 1919. (M.)
7522 Nornabell, Henry Marshall, 3 June, 1919. (M.)
7523 Nugent, George Roubiliac Hodges, 3 June, 1919. (M.)
7524 O'Brien, John, 3 June, 1919. (M.)
7525 O'Donel, Manus Basil Hugh, 3 June, 1919. (M.)
7526 Ogier, L. L'H. R., 3 June, 1919. (M.)
7527 Ogilvie, Alan Grant, 3 June, 1919. (M.
7528 Ogilvie, Alexander, 3 June, 1919. (M.)
7529 Ogle, Arthur Bertram, 3 June, 1919. (M.)
7531 Oppenheim, Arthur Edwin, 3 June, 1919. (M.)
7532 Orford, William Oswald, 3 June, 1919. (M.)
7533 Ormsby-Johnson, Guy Allen Colpoys, 3 June, 1919. (M).
7535 O'Sullivan, Patrick, 3 June, 1919. (M.)
7536 Oswald, Robert James William, 3 June, 1919. (M.)
7537 Outram, Francis Davidson, 3 June, 1919. (M.)
7538 Owtram, Herbert Hawkesworth, 3 June, 1919. (M.)
7539 Packe, Edmund Christopher, 3 June, 1919. (M.)
7540 Packe, Frederick Edward, 3 June, 1919. (M.)
7541 Padfield, Frederick Henry, 3 June, 1919. (M.)
7542 Palmer, Archibald James, 3 June, 1919. (M.)
7543 Palmer, Ernest Henry, 3 June, 1919. (M.)

7544 Pardoe, Edward Percy Hamilton, 3 June, 1919. (M.)
7545 Parkin, Francis Hearle, 3 June, 1919. (M.)
7546 Parkinson, Percival George, 3 June, 1919. (M.)
7547 Parkyn, Harry Gordon, 3 June, 1919. (M.)
7548 Parmiter, Charles Lister, 3 June, 1919. (M.)
7549 Parr, Cecil William Chase, 3 June, 1919. (M.)
7550 Part, Dealtrey Charles, 3 June, 1919. (M.)
7551 Parry, Cecil Morgan, 3 June, 1919. (M.)
7552 Parsons, Christopher Thackray, 3 June, 1919. (M.)
7553 Paske, Edward Lake, 3 June, 1919. (M.)
7554 Patch, James, 3 June, 1919. (M.)
7555 Patterson, Daniel Wells, 3 June, 1919. (M.)
7556 Pattinson, George Hedworth, 3 June, 1919. (M.)
7557 Paxman, William, 3 June, 1919. (M.)
7558 Peake, Walter King, 3 June, 1919. (M.)
7559 Pearce, John Wesley, 3 June, 1919. (M.)
7560 Pearce, William, 3 June, 1919. (M.)
7561 Pearson, Charles Edmund, 3 June, 1919. (M.)
7562 Pearson, John Barrington, 3 June, 1919. (M.)
7563 Pearson, Robert Stanley, 3 June, 1919. (M.)
7564 Pease, Ernest Hubert, 3 June, 1919. (M.)
7565 Peebles, Arthur Charlesworth, 3 June, 1919. (M.)
7566 Penketh, James, 3 June, 1919. (M.)
7567 Perceval, Francis Westby, 3 June, 1919. (M.)
7568 Perkins, Albert Augustus, 3 June, 1919. (M.)
7569 Pery-Knox-Gore, Aubrey Edmond, 3 June, 1919. (M.)
7570 Petre, Henry Cecil, 3 June, 1919. (M.)
7571 Phillips, Cyril Charles, 3 June, 1919. (M.)
7572 Phillips, Charles Edmund Stanley, 3 June, 1919. (M.)
7573 Phillips, Ernest William, 3 June, 1919. (M.)
7574 Phillips, William John, 3 June, 1919. (M.)
7575 Pickett, Alfred Cleveland, 3 June, 1919. (M.)
7576 Pigott, Wellesley George, 3 June, 1919. (M.)
7577 Pirie, William Rattray, 3 June, 1919. (M.)
7578 Pitt, George Newton, 3 June, 1919. (M.)
7579 Pixley, Stewart Aitken, 3 June, 1919. (M.)
7580 Pocock, James Charles, 3 June, 1919. (M.)
7581 Pocock, Sydney Elsdon, 3 June, 1919. (M.)
7582 Pollard, Arthur Erskine St. Vincent, 3 June, 1919. (M.)
7583 Pollok, Allan Bingham, 3 June, 1919. (M.)
7584 Pollok-Morris, Thomas Anselan, 3 June, 1919. (M.)
7585 Poole, Henry Reynold, 3 June, 1919. (M.)
7586 Porges, Edmund Daniel, 3 June, 1919. (M.)
7588 Potter, Thomas James, 3 June, 1919. (M.)
7589 Potts, Charles, 3 June, 1919. (M.)
7590 Poulton, Faville Clement, 3 June, 1919. (M.)
7591 Powell, George Robert, 3 June, 1919. (M.)
7592 Pownall, Assheton, 3 June, 1919. (M.)
7593 Pratt, James Davidson, 3 June, 1919. (M.)
7594 Prescott-Westcar, Charles Henry Beeston, 3 June, 1919. (M.)
7595 Pretty, William Tertius, 3 June, 1919. (M.)
7596 Prewer, William Henry Russell, 3 June, 1919. (M.)
7597 Pridham, Geoffrey Robert, 3 June, 1919. (M.)
7598 Priestley, Beatrice Ada, 3 June, 1919. (M.)
7599 Priestly, William, 3 June, 1919. (M.)
7600 Primrose, Alexander Ferguson, 3 June, 1919. (M.)
7601 Pringle, Seton Sidney, 3 June, 1919. (M.)
7602 Prior, Harold Astley Somerset, 3 June, 1919. (M.)
7603 Probert, William Godfrey, 3 June, 1919. (M.)
7604 Prout, William Thomas, 3 June, 1919. (M.)
7605 Purser, Arthur William, 3 June, 1919. (M.)
7606 Purser, Francis Carmichael, 3 June, 1919. (M.)
7607 Purves, Thomas Fortune, 3 June, 1919. (M.)
7608 Pyle, George Elliot Aubone, 3 June, 1919. (M.)
7609 Pyne, Frederick Dennis, 3 June, 1919. (M.)
7610 Quirke, Raymond Fitzwilliam, 3 June, 1919. (M.)
7611 Raley, William Ensley, 2 June, 1919. (M.)
7612 Rankin, Thomas, 3 June, 1919. (M.)
7613 Raw, Rev. Albert Edward, 3 June, 1919. (M.)
7614 Rawson, Geoffrey Grahame, 3 June, 1919. (M.)
7615 Read, Archibald Hugh, 3 June, 1919. (M.)
7616 Reavell, George, 3 June, 1919. (M.)
7617 Reeves, Patrick John, 3 June, 1919. (M.)
7618 Redman, Sidney George, 3 June, 1919. (M.)
7619 Rendel, Richard Meadows, 3 June, 1919. (M.)
7620 Rendall, Thomas Shuttleworth, 3 June, 1919. (M.)
7621 Reynolds, Louis George Stanley, 3 June, 1919. (M.)
7622 Reynolds, Sidney Latimer, 3 June, 1919. (M.)
7623 Reynolds, William Charles Noel, 3 June, 1919. (M.)
7624 Rhodes, Hubert Victor, 3 June, 1919. (M.)
7625 Rhodes, Stanislas Matthew Hastings, 3 June, 1919. (M.)
7626 Riall, Malcolm Brown Bookey, 3 June, 1919. (M.)
7627 Richards, Henry Meredyth, 3 June, 1919. (M.)
7628 Richards, John Charles Field, 3 June, 1919. (M.)
7629 Richardson, Thomas, 3 June, 1919. (M.)
7630 Richardson, Edwin Hautonville, 3 June, 1919. (M.)
7631 Richardson-Griffiths, Charles du Plat, 3 June, 1919. (M.)
7632 Riddell, Brownlow, 3 June, 1919. (M.)
7633 Ridgway, Robert Edward, 3 June, 1919. (M.)
7634 Ritchie, Blyth, 3 June, 1919. (M.)
7635 Ripley, Edward Guy, 3 June, 1919. (M.)
7636 Roberts, Arthur Neil Stewart, 3 June, 1919. (M.)
7638 Roberts, George Fossett, 3 June, 1919. (M.)
7639 Roberts, Hugh Bradley, 3 June, 1919. (M.)
7640 Robertson, David Stephen, 3 June, 1919. (M.)
7641 Robertson, Frederick William, 3 June, 1919. (M.)
7642 Robertson, John Kerr, 3 June, 1919. (M.)

7643 Robertson, Malcolm, 3 June, 1919. (M.)
7645 Roche, Benjamin Robert, 3 June, 1919. (M.)
7647 Rogers, Lincoln Coslett, 3 June, 1919. (M.)
7647 Rogers, Thomas Leslie, 3 June, 1919. (M.)
7648 Rose, Ambrose George, 3 June, 1919. (M.)
7649 Ross, Conrad, 3 June, 1919. (M.)
7650 Ross, William, 3 June, 1919. (M.)
7651 Rostron, Philip Simpson, 3 June, 1919. (M.)
7652 Rowan, Robert Houston, 3 June, 1919. (M.)
7653 Rowbotham, Farnel, 3 June, 1919. (M.)
7654 Rowell, Charles, 3 June, 1919. (M.)
7655 Rowlands, Robert Pugh, 3 June, 1919. (M.)
7656 Royds, Edmund, 3 June, 1919. (M.)
7657 Royle, Ernest Rupert, 3 June, 1919. (M.)
7658 Rummins, Henry, 3 June, 1919. (M.)
7659 Rundle, Charles, 3 June, 1919. (M.)
7660 Rundall, Frank Montagu, 3 June, 1919. (M.)
7661 Russell, Edmond Cecil, 3 June, 1919. (M.)
7662 Russell, Thomas, 3 June, 1919. (M.)
7663 Ryan, Hugh Septimus Kroenig, 3 June, 1919. (M.)
7664 Sallis, Daniel, 3 June, 1919. (M.)
7665 Sanders, Samuel George, 3 June, 1919. (M.)
7666 Sands, Robert William Philip, 3 June, 1919. (M.)
7667 Sarson, John Edward, 3 June, 1919. (M.)
7668 Satterthwaite, Clement Richard, 3 June, 1919. (M.)
7669 Saunders-Knox-Gore, William Arthur Gore, 3 June, 1919. (M.)
7670 Saunders-O'Mahoney, Charles Carleton, 3 June, 1919. (M.)
7671 Savile, Clare Ruxton Uvedale, 3 June, 1919. (M.)
7672 Sayer, George William, 3 June, 1919. (M.)
7673 Sayers, Raymond Cecil, 3 June, 1919. (M.)
7675 Schofield, William Ernest, 3 June, 1919. (M.)
7676 Scott, Ivor Buchanan Wyndham, 3 June, 1919. (M.)
7677 Scott, James, 3 June, 1919. (M.)
7678 Scratton, Edward William Howet Blackburn, 3 June, 1919. (M.)
7679 Searight, James Gerald Lamb, 3 June, 1919. (M.)
7680 Seth-Smith, Keith John, 3 June, 1919. (M.)
7681 Seymour, Edward, 3 June, 1919. (M.)
7682 Seymour, Evelyn Francis Edward, 3 June, 1919. (M.)
7683 Seymour, Lionel, 3 June, 1919. (M.)
7684 Seys, Roger Cecil, 3 June, 1919. (M.)
7685 Shadwell, Leonard Julius, 3 June, 1919. (M.)
7686 Sharp, Rowland, 3 June, 1919. (M.)
7687 Shaw, James Henry Montague, 3 June, 1919. (M.)
7688 Sheedy, Thomas, 3 June, 1919. (M.)
7689 Sheppard, Eric William, 3 June, 1919. (M.)
7690 Shore, George William, 3 June, 1919. (M.)
7691 Shorto, Henry George, 3 June, 1919. (M.)
7692 Sime, W. Malacca, 3 June, 1919. (M.)
7693 Sims, John Henry Lang, 3 June, 1919. (M.)
7694 Sinclair-Wemyss, Robert Dunbar, 3 June, 1919. (M.)
7695 Skaife, Eric Ommanney, 3 June, 1919. (M.)
7697 Smart, Thomas Fraser Mackenzie, 3 June, 1919. (M.)
7698 Smethurst, William Wintringham, 3 June, 1919. (M.)
7699 Smith, Arthur William, 3 June, 1919. (M.)
7700 Smith, Charles Edward, 3 June, 1919. (M.)
7701 Smith, George Frederick, 3 June, 1919. (M.)
7702 Smith, Clarence Gorton Ross, 3 June, 1919. (M.)
7703 Smith, Frederick Hargreaves, 3 June, 1919. (M.)
7704 Smith, George Rainier De Herriez, 3 June, 1919. (M.)
7705 Smith, George Wilson, 3 June, 1919. (M.)
7706 Smith, Julian Carter Carrington, 3 June, 1919. (M.)
7707 Smith, S., 3 June, 1919. (M.)
7708 Smith, William Stanley, 3 June, 1919. (M.)
7709 Smithett, Henry Cecil East, 3 June, 1919. (M.)
7710 Smithwick, Standish George, 3 June, 1919. (M.)
7711 Smyly, Frederick Philip, 3 June, 1919. (M.)
7712 Snelling, Leonard Fowler, 3 June, 1919. (M.)
7714 Soames, Arthur Granville, 3 June, 1919. (M.)
7715 Southampton, Charles Henry Fitzroy, 3 June, 1919. (M.)
7716 Sowerby, Edward Chayton, 3 June, 1919. (M.)
7717 Spafford, Arthur Owen, 3 June, 1919. (M.)
7718 Sparrow, Walter Augustus, 3 June, 1919. (M.)
7719 Spencer, Harrison, 3 June, 1919. (M.)
7720 Spencer, Herbert Eames, 3 June, 1919. (M.)
7721 Spencer, Walter George, 3 June, 1919. (M.)
7722 Spens, Archibald Borthwick, 3 June, 1919. (M.)
7723 Spens, John Ivan, 3 June, 1919. (M.)
7724 Squires, Thomas L., 3 June, 1919. (M.)
7725 Stamberg, Arthur Clement, 3 June, 1919. (M.)
7726 Standage, Henry Edmund, 3 June, 1919. (M.)
7727 Standish, William Percy, 3 June, 1919. (M.)
7728 Stanley, Robert Vinin Stanley, 3 June, 1919. (M.)
7729 Stanley-Jones, William Henry, 3 June, 1919. (M.)
7730 Stannus, Gerald Walter James Fitzgerald, 3 June, 1919. (M.)
7731 St. Aubyn, Guy Stewart, 3 June, 1919. (M.)
7732 Stanford, Frederick Owen, 3 June, 1919. (M.)
7733 Stapylton, Miles John, 3 June, 1919. (M.)
7734 Stavers, John, 3 June, 1919. (M.)
7735 Steele, Henry Squire, 3 June, 1919. (M.)
7736 Stenning, Henry Alexander, 3 June, 1919. (M.)
7737 Stephen, George Andrew, 3 June, 1919. (M.)
7738 Stephens, Francis Trant, 3 June, 1919. (M.)
7739 Stephens, Leslie Nalder, 3 June, 1919. (M.)
7740 Stephenson, John, 3 June, 1919. (M.)
7741 Stevens, Frederick John, 3 June, 1919. (M.)

7742 Stevenson, Robert, 3 June, 1919. (M.)
7743 Steward, Reginald Holden, 3 June, 1919. (M.)
7744 Stewart, Albert Fortescue, 3 June, 1919. (M.)
7745 Stewart, Charles, 3 June, 1919. (M.)
7746 Stewart, James Allan, 3 June, 1919. (M.)
7747 Stewart, Alexander Brodie Seton, 3 June, 1919. (M.)
7748 Stewart, James, 3 June, 1919. (M.)
7749 Stobie, Harold Ramsay, 3 June, 1919. (M.)
7750 Stokes, Hubert Francis, 3 June, 1919. (M.)
7751 Stopford, James Richard Neville, Vicount, 3 June, 1919. (M.)
7752 Stott, Herbert, 3 June, 1919. (M.)
7753 Stott, William Harle, 3 June, 1919. (M.)
7754 Stoyle, William, 3 June, 1919. (M.)
7755 Street, Cecil John Charles, 3 June, 1919. (M.)
7756 Struben, Robert Henry, 3 June, 1919. (M.)
7757 Sullivan, George Kingston, 3 June, 1919. (M.)
7758 Swan, Russell Henry Jocelyn, 3 June, 1919. (M.)
7759 Swann, Ernest Edward, 3 June, 1919. (M.)
7760 Sweeting, Henry Carol, 3 June, 1919. (M.)
7762 Taylor, Cecil George, 3 June, 1919. (M.)
7763 Taylor, Charles Lancelot Deslandes, 3 June, 1919. (M.)
7764 Taylor, James, 3 June, 1919. (M.)
7765 Taylor, Robert Clark, 3 June, 1919. (M.)
7766 Teichman, Max, 3 June, 1919. (M.)
7767 Temperley, Robert, 3 June, 1919. (M.)
7768 Tennent, Henry Moncrieff, 3 June, 1919. (M.)
7769 Theakston, Francis, 3 June, 1919. (M.)
7770 Thomas, Lewis, 3 June, 1919. (M.)
7771 Thompson, A. M., 3 June, 1919. (M.)
7772 Thompson, George, 3 June, 1919. (M.)
7773 Thomson, Henry Charles Stephens, 3 June, 1919. (M.)
7774 Thomson, David, 3 June, 1919. (M.)
7775 Thorburn, William, 3 June, 1919. (M.)
7776 Thorne, William Crockett, 3 June, 1919. (M.)
7777 Thorp, Gerald, 3 June, 1919. (M.)
7778 Tickell, Richard Eustace, 3 June, 1919. (M.)
7779 Tidbury, James, 3 June, 1919. (M.)
7780 Tims, Henry William Marrett, 3 June, 1919. (M.)
7781 Tod, Alexander Gray, 3 June, 1919. (M.)
7782 Tod, William Norman, 3 June, 1919. (M.)
7783 Tomlin, Morton James Baring, 3 June, 1919. (M.)
7784 Tomlin-Money-Shewan, Robert Ernest, 3 June, 1919. (M.)
7785 Toms, Charles Bailey, 3 June, 1919. (M.)
7786 Toogood, Arthur Seymour, 3 June, 1919. (M.)
7787 Toogood, Frederick Sherman, 3 June, 1919. (M.)
7788 Towner, Henry William, 3 June, 1919. (M.)
7789 Tracy, William Maxwell, 3 June, 1919. (M.)
7790 Tribe, Paul Cuningham Edward, 3 June, 1919. (M.)
7791 Trout, John Charles, 3 June, 1919. (M.)
7792 Troutbeck, John Munro, 3 June, 1919. (M.)
7793 Tucker, Albert Napoleon, 3 June, 1919. (M.)
7794 Tucker, Richard Jennings, 3 June, 1919. (M.)
7795 Tulloch, William John, 3 June, 1919. (M.)
7796 Tupman, John Arthur, 3 June, 1919. (M.)
7797 Tyler, Ralph Edward, 3 June, 1919. (M.)
7798 Tyrrell, Reginald Bramley, 3 June, 1919. (M.)
7799 Vanderfelt, Sydney Gorton, 3 June, 1919. (M.)
7800 Vansagnew, John, 3 June, 1919. (M.)
7801 Vasey, Charles James, 3 June, 1919. (M.)
7802 Vaughan, Gomer Miles, 3 June, 1919. (M.)
7803 Vella, Alfred, 3 June, 1919. (M.)
7804 Venour, Claude Malcolm Hamilton, 3 June, 1919. (M.)
7806 Walker, Archibald, 3 June, 1919. (M.)
7807 Walker, John, 3 June, 1919. (M.)
7808 Walsh, John Gustavus Russell, 3 June, 1919. (M.)
7809 Walter, Archibald Stephen, 3 June, 1919. (M.)
7810 Walters, Robert Francis, 3 June, 1919. (M.)
7811 Walton, George Laird, 3 June, 1919. (M.)
7812 Walton, Granville, 3 June, 1919. (M.)
7813 Wanliss, Cecil, 3 June, 1919. (M.)
7814 Warburg, Oscar Emanuel, 3 June, 1919. (M.)
7815 Ward, Beatrice Gascoigne, 3 June, 1919. (M.)
7816 Ward, John Dudley, 3 June, 1919. (M.)
7817 Ward, Thomas, 3 June, 1919. (M.)
7818 Warde, Sir Charles Edward, Bart., 3 June, 1919. (M.)
7819 Wardrop, David Risk, 3 June, 1919. (M.)
7820 Warner, Charles Edward, 3 June, 1919. (M.)
7821 Warrener, John, 3 June, 1919. (M.)
7822 Warry, Bertram Arthur, 3 June, 1919. (M.)
7823 Waters, Robert Sydney, 3 June, 1919. (M.)
7824 Wathen, Edward Owen, 3 June, 1919. (M.)
7825 Watson, Evelyn Cyril, 3 June, 1919. (M.)
7826 Watson, George Leybourne, 3 June, 1919. (M.)
7827 Watson, James Robert, 3 June, 1919. (M.)
7828 Watts, Humphrey, 3 June, 1919 (M.)
7829 Webb, G. R. H., 3 June, 1919. (M.)
7830 Webb, John Montague, 3 June, 1919. (M.)
7831 Webb, Philip, 3 June, 1919. (M.)
7832 Webber, Ralph Gowland, 3 June, 1919. (M.)
7833 Webster, Sir Augustus Frederick Walpole Edward, Bart., 3 June, 1919. (M.)
7834 Webster, Charles Kingsley, 3 June, 1919. (M.)
7835 Weekes, Henry Holman, 3 June, 1919. (M.)
7836 Wehner, Arthur Francis Percival, 3 June, 1919. (M.)
7837 Wellesley, Cecil George, 3 June, 1919. (M.)
7838 Welman, Harvey, 3 June, 1919. (M.)
7839 Welsh, David Thomson, 3 June, 1919. (M.)

7840 West, Charles James, 3 June, 1919. (M.)
7841 West, Richard Melbourne, 3 June, 1919. (M.)
7842 Westbury, Frederick Newell, 3 June, 1919. (M.)
7843 Westcott, George, 3 June, 1919. (M.)
7844 Weston, Reginald Salter, 3 June, 1919. (M.)
7845 Wetherell, William Edward May, 3 June, 1919. (M.)
7846 Wheeler, Charles, 3 June, 1919. (M.)
7847 Whiffin, George Greenhough, 3 June, 1919. (M.)
7848 Whitaker, Arthur Marmaduke, 3 June, 1919. (M.)
7849 White, Hon. Ernest William, 3 June, 1919. (M.)
7850 White, Hon. Francis William, 3 June, 1919. (M.
7851 White, John Christian, 3 June, 1919. (M.)
7852 White, Robert Fortescue Moresby, 3 June, 1919. (M.)
7853 Whiteley, Hon. Ronald George, 3 June, 1919. (M.)
7854 Whitfield, Robert Langton Digby, 3 June, 1919. (M.)
7855 Wiggins, Carl, 3 June, 1919. (M.)
7856 Wigley, George Alfred, 3 June, 1919. (M.)
7857 Wilberforce, Arthur Roland George, 3 June, 1919. (M.)
7858 Wiley, Thomas Paul, 3 June, 1919. (M.)
7860 Wilford, Edmund Ernest, 3 June, 1919. (M.)
7861 Williams, Arthur Frederick Basil, 3 June, 1919. (M.)
7862 Williams, Alfred Harry, 3 June, 1919. (M.)
7863 Williams, Albert Howard, 3 June, 1919. (M.)
7864 Williams, Ernest Ulysses, 3 June, 1919. (M.)
7865 Williams, Harold, 3 June, 1919. (M.)
7866 Williams, Stanley Walter, 3 June, 1919. (M.)
7867 Williams, Vivian Dunbar Stanley, 3 June, 1919. (M.)
7869 Wilson, Charles Spencer, 3 June, 1919. (M.)
7870 Wilson, Godfrey Harold Alfred, 3 June, 1919. (M.)
7871 Wilson, Henry Christopher Bruce, 3 June, 1919. (M.)
7872 Wilson, James Robert Menzies, 3 June. 1919. (M.)
7873 Wilson. William Perceval, 3 June, 1919. (M.)
7874 Wimberley, Douglas George Nugent, Irving 3 June, 1919. (M.)
7876 Winnifrith Rev. Douglas Percy, 3 June, 1919. (M.)
7877 Winter, William Robert, 3 June, 1919. (M.)
7878 Wolfe-Barry, Kenneth, 3 June, 1919. (M.)
7879 Woodroffe, Norman Frederic, 3 June, 1919. (M.)
7880 Woods, James Cowan, 3 June, 1919. (M.)
7881 Woods, Rickard John, 3 June, 1919. (M.)
7882 Woollett, Sydney Winslow, 3 June, 1919. (M.)
7883 Woosnam, Charles Earnshaw, 3 June, 1919. (M.)
7884 Worth, Reginald, 3 June, 1919. (M.)
7885 Wortley, Ernest Dixon, 3 June, 1919. (M.)
7886 Wrangham, William, 3 June, 1919. (M.)
7887 Wright, Maurice Beresford, 3 June, 1919. (M.)
7888 Wright, Stephen, 3 June, 1919. (M.)
7889 Wyatt, John Railton, 3 June, 1919. (M.)
7890 Wyndham Quin, Charles Frederick, 3 June, 1919. (M.)
7891 Wynyard, Edward George, 3 June, 1919. (M.)
7892 Wynyard, Richard Damer, 3 June, 1919. (M.)
7893 Yetts, Walter Perceval, 3 June, 1919. (M.)
7894 Youden, William Alfred, 3 June, 1919. (M.)
7895 Young, Richard Ashmur Blair, 3 June, 1919. (M.)
7896 Younger, John Henderson, 3 June, 1919. (M.)
7897 Yourdi, John Robert, 3 June, 1919. (M.)
7898 Baxter, David Lionel MacKenzie, 3 June, 1919. (M.)
7899 Bentley, William Joseph, 3 June, 1919. (M.)
7900 Brown, Claude, 3 June, 1919. (M.)
7901 Chown, Stanley Gordon, 3 June, 1919. (M.)
7902 Clifford, Ernest Stanley, 3 June, 1919. (M.)
7903 Cole, Cole Edward Cooper, 3 June, 1919. (M.)
7904 Complin, Edward Charles, 3 June, 1919. (M.)
7905 Cowan, Robert Cecil, 3 June, 1919. (M.)
7906 Davy, Frederick, 3 June, 1919. (M.)
7907 Elliot, Henry Charles Schomberg, 3 June, 1919. (M.)
7908 Fell, James Pemberton, 3 June, 1919. (M.)
7909 Gibson, Orland Kingsley, 3 June, 1919. (M.)
7910 Hewgill, William Herbert, 3 June, 1919. (M.)
7911 Huggins, Samuel John, 3 June, 1919. (M.)
7912 Inglis, William Clarence. 3 June, 1919. (M.)
7913 Kappele, John Logan, 3 June, 1919. (M.)
7914 Ker, Thomas Reginald, 3 June, 1919. (M.)
7915 Knox, Rev. John, 3 June, 1919. (M.)
7916 Lobley, Owen Rickell, 3 June, 1919. (M.)
7917 McCormack, Carson Alexander Vivian, 3 June, 1919. (M.)
7918 MacGillivray, Gordon Leslie, 3 June, 1919. (M.)
7919 MacInnis, Carlyle William. 3 June, 1919. (M.)
7920 MacKay, Daniel Sayre, 3 June, 1919. (M.)
7921 MacKenzie, Thomas Roderick, 3 June, 1919. (M.)
7922 MacPhail, Sir Andrew, 3 June, 1919. (M.)
7923 McPherson, Charles Duncan, 3 June, 1919. (M.)
7924 Mason, Edward George, 3 June, 1919. (M.)
7925 Milne, William Harcourt, 3 June, 1919. (M.)
7926 Monks, Kelson Charles Harley, 3 June, 1919. (M.)
7927 Moorhead, Charles Andrews, 3 June, 1919. (M.)
7928 Muirhead, William Harry, 3 June, 1919. (M.)
7929 Myatt, Arthur Egbert, 3 June, 1919. (M.)
7930 Neiley, Bayard Lamont, 3 June, 1919. (M.)
7931 Nicholson, William James, 3 June, 1919. (M.)
7932 Robson, John Wintour, 3 June, 1919. (M.)
7933 Rush, Frederick Charles, 3 June, 1919. (M.)
7935 Spencer, Fred, 3 June, 1919. (M.)
7936 Sprague, Daniel Emes, 3 June, 1919. (M.)
7937 Stirrett, Albert Newton, 3 June, 1919. (M.)
7938 Tate, Simon Marshall, 3 June, 1919. (M.)
7939 Thompson, Robert Broadwell, 3 June, 1919. (M.)
7940 Thomson, John James, 3 June, 1919. (M.)

7941 Tinner, Sydney Jonathan, 3 June, 1919. (M.)
7942 Walker, Thomas Molineaux, 3 June, 1919. (M.)
7943 Warner, Rev. David Victor, 3 June, 1919. (M.)
7944 Weyman, Edward Colpitts, 3 June, 1919. (M.)
7945 Wharton, Stanley, 3 June, 1919. (M.)
7946 Whitton, David Alexander, 3 June, 1919. (M.)
7947 Wilson, Rev. Thomas Augustine, 3 June, 1919. (M.)
7948 Wodehouse, Robert Elmer, 3 June, 1919. (M.)
7949 Wolff, Mark Arthur, 3 June, 1919. (M.)
7950 Brain, Hugh Gerner, 3 June, 1919. (M.)
7951 Cook, Alexander, 3 June, 1919. (M.)
7952 Crane, Francis Leopold, 3 June, 1919. (M.)
7953 Dennis, Charles Edgar, 3 June, 1919. (M.)
7954 Gibson, Norman Maxwell, 3 June, 1919. (M.)
7955 Gowing, Reginald Mack, 3 June, 1919. (M.)
7956 Griffiths, Cyril Tracy, 3 June, 1919. (M.)
7957 Hogben, George Justice, 3 June, 1919. (M.)
7958 Holder, Stanley Borwood, 3 June, 1919. (M.)
7959 Howard, Charles Holmes, 3 June, 1919. (M.)
7960 Jackson, Alfred, 3 June, 1919. (M.)
7961 Jeffries, Lewis Wilmer, 3 June, 1919. (M.)
7962 Knight, Glen Alburn William James, 3 June, 1919. (M.)
7963 Macdonald, John, 3 June, 1919. (M.)
7964 Marshall, William Henry, 3 June, 1919. (M.)
7965 Miles, Rev. Frederick James, 3 June, 1919. (M.)
7966 Moon, Alfred, 3 June, 1919. (M.)
7967 Page, Frederick William, 3 June, 1919. (M.)
7968 Playford, Elliott Frank, 3 June, 1919. (M.)
7969 Taylor-Young, Hugh Corbett, 3 June, 1919. (M.)
7970 Treloar, John Linton, 3 June, 1919. (M.)
7971 Wilsom, Charles Percival, 3 June, 1919. (M.)
7972 Withall, Latham August, 3 June, 1919. (M.)
7973 Acland, Leopold George Dyke, 3 June, 1919. (M.)
7974 Andrew, Phillip Oywalk, 3 June, 1919. (M.)
7975 Andrews, Charles Eric, 3 June, 1919. (M.)
7976 Baigent, Cyril Victor, 3 June, 1919. (M.)
7977 Banks, George Bertram, 3 June, 1919. (M.)
7978 Barclay, George, 3 June, 1919. (M.)
7979 Bernau, Henry Ferdinand, 3 June, 1919. (M.)
7980 Bowerbank, Frederick Thompson, 3 June, 1919. (M.)
7981 Colbeck, Edumand Harry, 3 June, 1919. (M.)
7982 Fenwick, David Eardley, 3 June, 1919. (M.)
7983 Fenwick, George Ernest Oswald, 3 June, 1919. (M.)
7984 Gow, Reginald Ronald, 3 June, 1919. (M.)
7985 Hogg, Alexander Wilson, 3 June, 1919. (M.)
7986 Hovey, Gordon, 3 June, 1919. (M.)
7987 Izard, Arnold Woodford, 3 June, 1919. (M.)
7988 Jacob, Archdeacon John Attwood, 3 June, 1919. (M.)
7989 Kay, William, 3 June, 1919. (M.)
7990 Lawless, Thomas, 3 June, 1919. (M.)
7991 Levien, Norman James, 3 June, 1919. (M.)
7992 Little, William, 3 June, 1919. (M.)
7993 McChristell, Thomas, 3 June, 1919. (M.)
7994 Marchant, Eric Lachlan, 3 June, 1919. (M.)
7995 Mounsey, John, 3 June, 1919. (M.)
7996 Newcomb, Neville, 3 June, 1919. (M.)
7997 Ostler, Francis Edward, 3 June, 1919. (M.)
7998 Peacock, Henry, 3 June, 1919. (M.)
7999 Pickerill, Henry Percy, 3 June, 1919. (M.)
8000 Turnbull, William Henry, 3 June, 1919. (M.)
8001 Tymons, Francis Parnell, 3 June, 1919. (M.)
8002 Westmacott, Herbert Horatio Spencer, 3 June, 1919. (M.)
8003 Averre, William James, 3 June, 1919. (M.)
8004 Baker, Harry Cecil, 3 June, 1919. (M.)
8005 Balfour, Harry Hyndman, 3 June, 1919. (M.)
8006 Dacomb, Leonard Sydney, 3 June, 1919. (M.)
8007 Daniels, Henry Douglas, 3 June, 1919. (M.)
8008 Deane, Robert, 3 June, 1919. (M.)
8009 Fincham, John William George, 3 June, 1919. (M.)
8010 Fox, Edward Thornton, 3 June, 1919. (M.)
8011 Horwich, David, 3 June, 1919. (M.)
8012 Lange, Richard Charles, 3 June, 1919. (M.)
8013 Maxwell, Raymond, 3 June, 1919. (M.)
8014 Menzies, Donald, 3 June, 1919. (M.)
8015 Napier, Francis, 3 June, 1919. (M.)
8016 Orford, Herbert John, 3 June, 1919. (M.)
8017 Parker, Robert Derwent, 3 June, 1919. (M.)
8018 Pepper, Arthur Llewellyn, 3 June, 1919. (M.)
8019 Phillips, William James, 3 June, 1919. (M.)
8020 Porter, Charles, 3 June, 1919. (M.)
8021 Rann, Alfred Edward, 3 June, 1919. (M.)
8022 Rigby, James Charles Alexander 3 June, 1919. (M.)
8023 Sellick, Alfred James, 3 June, 1919. (M.)
8024 Trevett, Charles George, 3 June, 1919. (M.)
8025 Wolmarans, Martinus Johannes, 3 June, 1919. (M.)
8026 Emerson, George Michael, 3 June, 1919. (M.)
8027 Greene, William Howe, 3 June, 1919. (M.)
8028 Knight, James St. Pierre, 3 June, 1919. (M.)
8029 Patterson, Lamont, 3 June, 1919. (M.)
8030 Timewell, Henry A., 3 June, 1919. (M.)
8031 Whitty, Gerald Joseph, 3 June, 1919. (M.)
8032 Adams, Paul, 3 June, 1919. (M.)
8033 Addison, Sydney Wentworth, 3 June, 1919. (M.)
8034 Albrecht, Vaudrey Adolph, 3 June, 1919. (M.)
8035 Anderson, Ruper Darnley, 3 June, 1919. (M.)
8036 Archer, John Oliver, 3 June, 1919. (M.)
8037 Armitage, William Bryan, 3 June, 1919. (M.)
8038 Arrol-Hunter, John Eric, 3 June, 1919. (M.)

8039 Atkins, William Ringrose Gelston, 3 June, 1919. (M.)
8040 Awcock, Charles Henry, 3 June, 1919. (M.)
8041 Baldwin, John Eustace Arthur, 3 June, 1919. (M.)
8042 Banks, James Harvey, 3 June, 1919. (M.)
8043 Bateman, George Deane, 3 June, 1919. (M.)
8044 Beachcroft, Philip Maurice, 3 June, 1919. (M.)
8046 Beaufort, Victor Alexander, 3 June, 1919. (M.)
8047 Bell, Charles Hugh, 3 June, 1919. (M.)
8048 Belton, Andrew, 3 June, 1919. (M.)
8049 Bently, Harold Rothwell, 3 June, 1919. (M.)
8050 Berry, Rev. Robert Seymour Brendon Stirling, 3 June, 1919. (M.)
8051 Bishop, Percy, 3 June, 1919. (M.)
8052 Blyth, John Dunbar, 3 June, 1919. (M.)
8053 Bovill, Carlos, 3 June, 1919. (M.)
8054 Brabazon, Hon. Claude Maitland Patrick, 3 June, 1919. (M.)
8055 Bradley, Charles Raymond Strathearn, 3 June, 1919. (M.)
8056 Bradley, John Stanley Travers, 3 June, 1919. (M.)
8057 Briggs, Edward Featherstone, 3 June, 1919. (M.)
8058 Brinsmead, Horace Clowes, 3 June, 1919. (M.)
8059 Briscoe, Edward James, 3 June, 1919. (M.)
8060 Brook, Reginald Vernon Charlesworth, 3 June, 1919. (M.)
8061 Burchall, Percival Russell, 3 June, 1919. (M.)
8062 Burrowes, Louis Arundell, 3 June, 1919. (M.)
8063 Buxton, Vincent, 3 June, 1919. (M.)
8064 Campbell, Charles Ferguson, 3 June, 1910. (M.)
8065 Campbell, Hugh, 3 June, 1919. (M.)
8066 Chainey, George Barrett, 3 June, 1919. (M.)
8068 Child, Arthur James, 3 June, 1919. (M.)
8069 Clark, Adrian John, 3 June, 1919. (M.)
8070 Cockerell, Henry, 3 June, 1919. (M.)
8071 Collier, Richard Hamilton, 3 June, 1919. (M.)
8072 Cook, Leonard Barnaby, 3 June, 1919. (M.)
8073 Cooper, Frederick Ernest, 3 June, 1919. (M.)
8074 Cordingley, John Walter, 3 June, 1919. (M.)
8075 Cosway, Leopold Harold Baskerville, 3 June, 1919. (M.)
8078 Darby, Maurice Ormonde, 3 June, 1919. (M.)
8079 Davies, John Hallmark, 3 June, 1919. (M.)
8080 Deacon, Martin, 3 June, 1919. (M.)
8081 de Dombasle, Guy Cyril St. Pourgin, 3 June, 1919. (M.)
8082 Delacombe, Harry, 3 June, 1919. (M.)
8083 de Poix, Ralph Busick Claude Marie Tyrel, 3 June, 1919. (M.)
8084 Dickson, James, 3 June, 1919. (M.)
8085 Dixon-Spain, John Edward, 3 June, 1919. (M.)
8086 Dixon-Spain, Gerald, 3 June, 1919. (M.)
8087 Dobson, Geoffrey William, 3 June, 1919. (M.)
8088 Dobson, Maurice Rowland, 3 June, 1919. (M.)
8089 Dyer, James Frederick, 3 June, 1919. (M.)
8090 Ellerton, Alban Spenser, 3 June, 1919. (M.)
8091 Evans, Audrey Thomas, 3 June, 1919. (M.)
8092 Evans, William Sandford, 3 June, 1919. (M.)
8093 Everett, Reginald Marsh, 3 June, 1919. (M.)
8094 Faithful, George Ferdinand Hay, 3 June, 1919. (M.)
8095 Farley, Reuben Llewelyn, 3 June, 1919. (M.)
8096 Fill, Samuel John Vincent, 3 June, 1919. (M.)
8097 Fisher, Hubert Frank, 3 June, 1919. (M.)
8098 Ford, Harry Gilbert, 3 June, 1919. (M.)
8099 Gadsby, Philip, 3 June, 1919. (M.)
8100 Gendle, Albert Edgar, 3 June, 1919. (M.)
8101 Goad, David, 3 June, 1919. (M.)
8102 Godden, Guy Langham, 3 June, 1919. (M.)
8103 Goddard, Richard Ernest, 3 June, 1919. (M.)
8104 Gordon, Harry Francis Adam, 3 June, 1919. (M.)
8105 Gordon, James William, 3 June, 1919. (M.)
8107 Gude, Gerald, 3 June, 1919. (M.)
8108 Hall, Robert, 3 June, 1919. (M.)
8109 Hall, William Wellington, 3 June, 1919. (M.)
8111 Hargrave, William Bowen, 3 June, 1919. (M.)
8112 Harnett, Edward St. Clair, 3 June, 1919. (M.)
8113 Harrison, Cuthbert Alfred Lakin, 3 June, 1919. (M.)
8114 Hartley, Alan Pickup, 3 June, 1919. (M.)
8115 Hawksford, Francis Henry, 3 June, 1919. (M.)
8116 Hearn, Edward Michael William, 3 June, 1919. (M.)
8117 Hebden, Sacheverell Arthur, 3 June, 1919. (M.)
8118 Hellyer, Francis Edgcombe, 3 June, 1919. (M.)
8119 Hirtzel, Clement Henry Armitage, 3 June, 1919. (M.)
8121 Humphery, George Edward Woods, 3 June, 1919. (M.)
8122 Hunter, Albert, 3 June, 1919. (M.)
8123 Iron, Douglas, 3 June, 1919. (M.)
8124 James, Dennis Cory, 3 June, 1919. (M.)
8125 Jenkins, Frederick Howard, 3 June, 1919. (M.)
8126 Jones, John Fleming, 3 June, 1919. (M.)
8127 Jupp, William Dallas Loney, 3 June, 1919. (M.)
8128 Keegan, Michael, 3 June, 1919. (M.)
8129 Kirby, Frank Howard, 3 June, 1919. (M.)
8130 Lambert, William Clement, 3 June, 1919. (M.)
8131 Landon, Joseph Herbert Arthur, 3 June, 1919. (M.)
8132 Landry, Pierre Alfred, 3 June, 1919. (M.)
8133 Lawder, Cecil Edward, 3 June, 1919. (M.)
8134 Layard, Arthur Raymond, 3 June, 1919. (M.)
8135 Lerwill, Francis William Henry, 3 June, 1919. (M.)
8136 Levick, Albert, 3 June, 1919. (M.)
8137 Lindquist, Oskar, 3 June, 1919. (M.)
8138 Lyall, Peter Douglas Lorne, 3 June, 1919. (M.)
8139 Lywood, Oswyn George William Clifford, 3 June, 1919. (M.)

8140 MacCullum, Alfred Erasmus Geoffrey, 3 June, 1919. (M.)
8141 McLean, Kenneth Hugh, 3 June, 1919. (M.)
8142 MacLeod, Thomas, 3 June, 1919. (M.)
8143 Maidstone, Guy Montagu George, Viscount, 3 June, 1919. (M.)
8144 Mansell, Reginald Baynes, 3 June, 1919. (M.)
8145 Maybury, Harry Percy, 3 June, 1919. (M.)
8146 Michell, Herbert Arthur, 3 June, 1919. (M.)
8147 Miller, Allister Mackintosh, 3 June, 1919. (M.)
8148 Milman, Hugh, 3 June, 1919. (M.)
8149 Mitchell, Richard Galbraith, 3 June 1919. (M.)
8150 Money, Rowland, 3 June, 1919. (M.)
8151 Monk, Errol Francis, 3 June, 1919. (M.)
8152 Moore, Arthur Thomas, 3 June, 1919. (M.)
8153 Morle, Denzil Adair Bartlett, 3 June, 1919. (M.)
8155 Neame, Arthur Lawrence Cecil, 3 June, 1919. (M.)
8156 Nevatt, Christopher George, 3 June, 1919. (M.)
8157 Nicholl, Hazleton Robson, 3 June, 1919. (M.)
8158 Nicolle, John MacArthur, 3 June, 1919. (M.)
8159 Nixon, Sydney, 3 June, 1919. (M.)
8160 Oliver, Douglas Austin, 3 June, 1919. (M.)
8161 Palmer, Leonard Edgcombe, 3 June, 1919. (M.)
8162 Parkes, Charles Herbert, 3 June, 1919. (M.)
8163 Parr, Sydney Charles, 3 June, 1919. (M.)
8164 Peck, Richard Hallam, 3 June, 1919. (M.)
8165 Penberthy, Phillip Pearce Clay, 3 June, 1919. (M.)
8166 Pope, William Henry, 3 June, 1919. (M.)
8167 Powell, Eric Walter, 3 June, 1919. (M.)
8168 Pratt-Barlow, Lucy Marjorie Kathleen, Mrs., 3 June, 1919. (M.)
8169 Pritchard, John Edward Maddock, 3 June, 1919. (M.)
8170 Pryce, Walter John Dakyns, 3 June, 1919. (M.)
8171 Rasmusen, Charles Francis, 3 June, 1919. (M.)
8172 Read, Geoffrey Jervis, 3 June, 1919. (M.)
8173 Rees, Lionel Wilmot Brabazon, 3 June, 1919. (M.)
8174 Rippon, Thomas Stanley, 3 June, 1919. (M.)
8175 Robertson, Charles MacIver, 3 June, 1919. (M.)
8176 Robertson, Hector Murdoch Maxwell 3 June. 1919. (M.)
8177 Robinson, Richard Stirling, 3 June, 1919. (M.)
8178 Roche, Nelson Joseph, 3 June, 1919. (M.)
8179 Rodwell, James Theodore, 3 June, 1919. (M.)
8180 Rome, Samuel Greenless, 3 June, 1919. (M.)
8181 Ross, Andrew Alexander, 3 June, 1919. (M.)
8182 Ross-Hume, Alexander, 3 June, 1919. (M.)
8183 Russell, Hon. Victor Alexander Frederick Villiers, 3 June, 1919. (M.)
8184 Samson, Felix Rumney, 3 June, 1919. (M.)
8185 Selby, Ernest, 3 June, 1919. (M.)
8186 Sewell, John Percy Claude, 3 June, 1919. (M.)
8187 Shaw, Harry Turner, 3 June, 1919. (M.)
8188 Sidgreaves, Arthur Frederick, 3 June, 1919. (M.)
8189 Smith, George Edward, 3 June, 1919. (M.)
8190 Smith, James Drummond, 3 June, 1919. (M.)
8191 Smith, Sydney William, 3 June, 1919. (M.)
8192 Smith, William Edwin, 3 June, 1919. (M.)
8193 Somers-Clarke, Geoffrey, 3 June, 1919. (M.)
8194 Speed, Douglas Charles Leyland, 3 June, 1919. (M.)
8195 Steel, Frank, 3 June, 1919. (M.)
8196 Steel, John Valentine, 3 June, 1919. (M.)
8197 Stevens, Frank Douglas, 3 June, 1919. (M.)
8198 Stevens, George, 3 June, 1919. (M.)
8199 Stewart, Jack, 3 June, 1919. (M.)
8200 Stradling, Alfred Hugh, 3 June, 1919. (M.)
8201 Strain, Lawrence Hugh, 3 June, 1919. (M.)
8202 Stratton, Howard Wallace, 3 June, 1919. (M.)
8203 Sulivan, Lionel Michael Patrick, 3 June, 1919. (M.,)
8204 Thomson, George Henry, 3 June, 1919. (M.)
8205 Todd, George Eardley, 3 June, 1919. (M.)
8206 Tweedie, Henry Carmichael, 3 June, 1919. (M.)
8207 Unwin, Frederick Henry 3 June, 1919. (M.)
8208 Verney, Reynell Henry, 3 June, 1919. (M.)
8209 Waddington, William James, 3 June, 1919. (M.)
8210 Wade, William, 3 June, 1919. (M.)
8212 Watson, Alexander Thomas, 3 June, 1919. (M.)
8213 Williamson, George William, 3 June, 1919. (M.)
8214 Wilson, Henry Alexander James, 3 June, 1919. (M.)
8215 Winch, Aubrey Brooke, 3 June, 1919. (M.)
8216 Wise, Cuthbert Walter, 3 June, 1919. (M.)
8217 Worswick, Thomas, 3 June, 1919. (M.)
8218 Wyncoll, Hugh Edmund Fowler, 3 June, 1919. (M.)
8219 Yates, Henry Irving Frederick, 3 June, 1919. (M.)
8220 Yeomans, Charles Fredsall, 3 June, 1919. (M.)
8221 Young, Andrew, 3 June, 1919. (M.)
8222 Failes, Rev. Bernard James, 3 June, 1919. (M.)
8223 Jones, Rev. Francis Horace, 3 June, 1919. (M.)
8224 Kendall, Rev. Henry Ewing, 3 June, 1919. (M.)
8225 Kent, Rev. Norman Braund, 3 June, 1919. (M.)
8226 Knight-Adkin, Rev. Walter Kenrick, 3 June, 1919. (M.)
8227 Wilkinson, Rev. Horace Ricardo, 3 June, 1919.
8228 Ahmad, Kahn Bahadur Kazi Aziz-ud-Din, 3 June, 1919.
8229 Ahmad, Maulvi Nizam-ud-Din, 3 June, 1919.
8230 Alder, Wilfrid, 3 June, 1919.
8231 Armstrong, Arthur Campbell, 3 June, 1919.
8232 Banerji, Satish Chandra, 3 June, 1919.
8233 Barnard, Albert Alfred, 3 June, 1919.
8234 Barton, Sybil, Mrs., 3 June, 1919.
8235 Bayley, Edward Charles, 3 June, 1919.
8236 Bell, Evelyn Mary, Mrs., 3 June, 1919.
8237 Berthoud, Edward Henry, 3 June, 1919.

8238 Bhonsle, Sambhaji Rao, 3 June, 1919.
8239 Blunt, Edward Arthur Henry, 3 June, 1919.
8240 Carson, Charles William Charteris, 3 June, 1919.
8241 Channer, Frederick Francis Ralph, 3 June, 1919.
8242 Coldstream, John Clayton, 3 June, 1919.
8243 Cooke, Henry Moore Annesley, 3 June, 1919.
8244 Cross-Barratt, May, Mrs., 3 June, 1919.
8245 Crosthwaite, Charles Gilbert, 3 June, 1919.
8246 Dixon, Edgar George, 3 June, 1919.
8247 Donald, Duncan, 3 June, 1919.
8248 Duncan, Houston, 3 June, 1919.
8249 Duval, Ethel, Mrs., 3 June, 1919.
8250 Ellis, Thomas Peter, 3 June, 1919.
8252 Fermor, Lewis Leigh, 3 June, 1919.
8253 Fowler, May, Mrs. Francis John, 3 June, 1919.
8254 Fraser, John Hugh Ronald, 3 June, 1919.
8255 Greig, William Best, 3 June, 1919.
8256 Griffith, Francis Charles, 3 June, 1919.
8257 Guilford, Rev. Canon Edward, 3 June, 1919.
8258 Gupta, Ashoke Chandra, 3 June, 1919.
8259 Hajibhoy, Seth Bandeali, 3 June, 1919.
8260 Hingston, Clayton Alexander Francis, 3 June, 1919.
8261 Hudson, Kate Evans, Lady, 3 June, 1919.
8262 Innes, Charles, 3 June, 1919.
8263 Jackson, Samuel, 3 June, 1919.
8264 Jatia, Rai Bahadur Onkar Mull, 3 June, 1919
8265 Johnson, Mary Eliot, Mrs., 3 June, 1919.
8266 Johnstone, Dr. James Glansey, 3 June, 1919.
8267 Khan, Nawab Abdul Rahim, 3 June, 1919.
8268 Talpur, Khan Bahadur Mir Ghulam Mahomed Khan of, 3 June, 1919.
8269 Khan, Sahibzada Muhammad Jafar Ali, 3 June, 1919.
8270 Lal, Rai Bahadur Seth Sukh, 3 June, 1919.
8271 Lemon, Guy Talbot, 3 June, 1919.
8272 Lupton, Samuel, 3 June, 1919.
8273 Lyons, Charles Michael, 3 June, 1919.
8274 Macfarlane, James Wallace, 3 June, 1919.
8275 Macpherson, Duncan Iver, 3 June, 1919.
8276 Madden, Samuel Fitzgerald, 3 June, 1919.
8277 Madhavial, Lady Chinubhai, 3 June, 1919.
8278 Maude, Maude, Mrs., 3 June, 1919.
8279 Miller, William Charles Walmer, 3 June, 1919.
8280 Mohatta, Rao Bahadur Seth Goverdhandas Motilal, 3 June, 1919.
8281 Moncrieff-Smith, Hilda Mary, Mrs., 3 June, 1919.
8282 Moodie, Adam Wilson, 3 June, 1919.
8283 Murray, Miss Violet, 3 June, 1919.
8284 Mylrea, Charles Stanley Garland, 3 June, 1919.
8285 O'Brian, Herbert Edgar Whitehead, 3 June, 1919.
8286 O'Meara, Eugene John, 3 June, 1919.
8287 Oughton, Ernest, 3 June, 1919.
8288 Pershad, Rai Sahib Mathura, 3 June, 1919
8289 Powell, William Wallace, 3 June, 1919.
8290 Prasad, Kunwar Jagdish, 3 June, 1919.
8291 Qayum, Abdul, 3 June, 1919.
8292 Reith, Alexander Murray, 3 June, 1919.
8293 Richards, Frances Maud Lyster, Lady, 3 June, 1919.
8294 Richardson, George Alexander, 3 June, 1919.
8295 Richmond, Alice, Mrs., 3 June, 1919.
8296 Roberts, Montgomery Browne, 3 June, 1919.
8297 Robertson, Stuart Duncan, 3 June, 1919.
8298 Sarup, Rai Bahadur Ram, 3 June, 1919.
8299 Singh, Sardar Bahadur Bhai Arjan, 3 June, 1919.
8300 Singh, Diwan Chet, 3 June, 1919.
8301 Singh, Rai Bahadur Thakur Dhonkal, 3 June, 1919.
8302 Singh, Sardar Gopal, 3 June, 1919.
8303 Singh, Kanwar Raghbir, 3 June, 1919.
8304 Singh, Raja Raghuraj, 3 June, 1919.
8305 Singh, Ram, 3 June, 1919.
8306 Spence, Hon. Christina Philippa Agnes, Mrs., 3 June, 1919.
8307 Stevens, Leonard Cordinge, 3 June, 1919.
8308 Stiffe, Norman Cecil, 3 June, 1919.
8309 Stoddard, George Frederick, 3 June, 1919.
8310 Symes, William Fitzroy Scudamore Stallard, 3 June, 1919.
8311 Tomkins, Ernest William, 3 June, 1919.
8312 Trevaskis, Hugh Kennedy, 3 June, 1919.
8313 Voice, Thomas Aubrey, 3 June, 1919.
8314 Warburton, Walter Granville, 3 June, 1919.
8315 Ward, William Robert, 3 June, 1919.
8316 Williamson, Andrew, 3 June, 1919.
8317 Wylde, Lennard Francis George Stovin, 3 June, 1919.
8318 Brodick, Thomas Noel, 3 June, 1919.
8319 Burgess, Frederick James, 3 June. 1919.
8320 Burnett, James, 3 June, 1919.
8321 Clark, Donald George, 3 June, 1919.
8322 Cleary, Rt. Rev. Henry William, 3 June, 1919.
8323 Cooper, Daniel George Arthur, 3 June, 1919.
8324 Day, Victor Grace, 3 June, 1919.
8325 Earl, Frederick, 3 June, 1919.
8326 Evans, James Sim, 3 June, 1919.
8327 Fache, George Cox, 3 June, 1919.
8328 Fell, Frederick Chandos Courtenay, 3 June, 1919.
8329 Findlay, James, 3 June, 1919.
8330 Fraser, Malcolm, 3 June, 1919.
8331 Hislop, James, 3 June, 1919.
8332 Montgomery, William Barr, 3 June, 1919.
8333 Moss, Thomas, 3 June, 1919.

OFFICERS.

8334 Myers, Vera Anita, Mrs., 3 June, 1919.
8335 Poynton, John William, 3 June, 1919.
8336 Rhodes, George Edward, 3 June, 1919.
8337 Ronaldson, Thomas Sheriff, 3 June, 1919.
8338 Shirer, Rev. William, 3 June, 1919.
8339 Scholefield, Guy Hardy, 3 June, 1919.
8340 Shirtcliffe, George, 3 June, 1919.
8341 Sprott, Rt. Rev. Thomas Henry, 3 June, 1919.
8342 Topia, Kingi, 3 June, 1919.
8343 Wilson, Thomas, 3 June, 1919.
8344 Beer, George Stephen, 3 June, 1919.
8345 Birch, George Ernest, 3 June, 1919.
8346 Bray, Paul Dudley, 3 June, 11919.
8347 Cluver, Paul Dietrich, 3 June, 1919.
8348 Cooke, Herbert Sutton, 3 June, 1919.
8349 Crichton, Jean, Mrs. Cullen, 3 June, 1919.
8350 Dent, Richard Court, 3 June, 1919.
8351 Duquemin, Eveline Mary, Mrs., 3 June, 1919.
8352 Earle, William Francis, 3 June, 1919.
8353 Fairbairn, John, 3 June, 1919.
8354 Frood, Bertha Helen, Mrs., 3 June, 1919.
8355 Godley, Richard Shearman, 3 June, 1919.
8356 Gray, George Douglas, 3 June, 1919.
8357 Mathers, Mary Augusta, Mrs., 3 June, 1919.
8358 Miller, Charles Cecil, 3 June, 1919.
8359 Murray, Charles Frederick Kennan, 3 June, 1919.
8360 O'Reilly, Thomas Leslie, 3 June, 1919.
8361 Orr, John, 3 June, 1919.
8362 Rockey, Willie, 3 June, 1919.
8363 Rowland, Frederick, 3 June, 1919.
8364 Searle, Emma Jane, Mrs., 3 June, 1919.
8365 Skeels, Lewis Serecold, 3 June, 1919.
8366 Sommerville, James, 3 June, 1919.
8367 Taylor, Percy Henry, 3 June, 1919.
8368 Weinthal, Leo, 3 June, 1919.
8369 Winser, Charles, 3 June, 1919.
8370 Wynne, Thomas Joseph, 3 June, 1919.
8371 Hutchings, Charles Henry, 3 June, 1919.
8372 Morris, Francis Joseph, 3 June, 1919.
8373 Parsons, Rachael Fannie, Mrs., 3 June, 1919
8374 Roper, Ann, Mrs., 3 June, 1919.
8375 Squarey, Robert Thomas, 3 June, 1919.
8376 Summers, Patrick Joseph, 3 June, 1919.
8378 Azzopardi, Francesco, 3 June, 1919.
8379 Bagenal, Charles James, 3 June, 1919.
8380 Baines, Denis Lynch, 3 June, 1919.
8381 Chamberlain, William, 3 June, 1919.
8382 Cooper, Philip Ward, 3 June, 1919.
8383 Crook, John Rowland, 3 June, 1919.
8384 Sen, Eu Tong, 3 June, 1919.
8385 Gosling, Francis Goodwin, 3 June, 1919.
8386 Haddon-Smith, Izy Constance, Lady, 3 June, 1919.
8387 Harper, Charles Henry, 3 June, 1919.
8388 Harrisson, Sydney Thirlwall, 3 June, 1919.
8390 Hillyer, Herbert Keys, 3 June, 1919.
8391 Howard, Joseph, 3 June, 1919.
8392 Jones, Malcolm Ludlow, 3 June, 1919.
8393 Kay, William Gemmell, 3 June, 1919.
8394 King, Godfrey James, 3 June, 1919.
8395 Lochhead, James, 3 June, 1919.
8396 Lynch, James Challenor, 3 June, 1919.
8397 Macdonald of the Isles, Celia Violet, 3 June, 1919.
8398 MacDonald, Ranald, 3 June, 1919.
8399 Macintyre, Duncan Charles, 3 June, 1919.
8400 MacLelland, Hugh, 3 June, 1919.
8402 Morris, Edward Gilbert, 3 June, 1919.
8403 Parnis, Alfredo, 3 June, 1919.
8404 Phillips, Elizabeth Miller, Mrs., 3 June, 1919.
8405 Rabici, Ratu Joni Antonio, 3 June, 1919.
8406 Rew, Charles Edward Daliel Oldham, 3 June, 1919.
8407 Smith, Stanley Rivers-, 3 June, 1919.
8408 Robertson, John Argyll, 3 June, 1919.
8409 Roy, Thomas, 3 June, 1919.
8410 Sackett, Rev. Alfred Barrett, 3 June, 1919.
8411 Scott, Frederick Emelius, 3 June, 1919
8412 Stack, Alan Edward, 3 June, 1919.
8413 Taylor, Robert Walter, 3 June, 1919.
8414 Thomas, Thomas Shenton Whitelegge, 3 June, 1919.
8415 Tonks, Osmund, 3 June, 1919.
8416 Torreggiani, Antonio Cassar, 3 June, 1919.
8417 Trefusis, Dorothy Marguerite Elizabeth, Hon. Mrs., 3 June, 1919.
8418 Waddington, Eubule John, 3 June, 1919.
8419 Willis, Rt. Rev. John Jameson, 3 June, 1919.
8420 Buller, Francis Elliot, 3 June, 1919. (M.)
8421 Butters, Adams, 3 June, 1919. (M.)
8422 Hamilton, Frederick Arthur, 3 June, 1919. (M.)
8423 Kane, John Leonard Kirkpatrick, 3 June, 1919. (M.)
8424 Robinson, Charles, 3 June, 1919. (M.)
8425 Adams, John Hughes, 3 June, 1919. (M.)
8426 Adams, Kenneth Lemesle, 3 June, 1919. (M.)
8427 Alexander, Heber Maitland, 3 June, 1919. (M.)
8428 Andrews, Frank Leon, 3 June, 1919. (M.)
8429 Arneil, London, 3 June, 1919. (M.)
8430 Babonau, Alexander Frederick, 3 June, 1919. (M.)
8431 Baird, Alexander Edwin, 3 June, 1919. (M.)
8432 Baird, Randolph Eustace Wemyss, 3 June, 1919. (M.)
8433 Baker, Wilfred Bertram, 3 June, 1919. (M.)
8434 Ball, Eric Percy, 3 June, 1919. (M.)

8435 Barnes, Lawrance Edward, 3 June, 1919. (M.)
8436 Bell, Arthur Hugh, 3 June, 1919. (M.)
8437 Benson, William John Phillip, 3 June, 1919. (M.)
8438 Bonnyman, Francis James Cosmos, 3 June, 1919. (M.)
8439 Bourne, Walter Kemp, 3 June, 1919. (M.)
8440 Bradbury, Arthur Lyle, 3 June, 1919. (M.)
8441 Brewin, Thomas James, 3 June, 1919. (M.)
8442 Brewis, Roddison Douglas, 3 June, 1919. (M.)
8443 Bruce, John, 3 June, 1919. (M.)
8444 Bucknall, William Beverley, 3 June, 1919. (M.)
8445 Burdon, Walter Boyd Chandlers, 3 June, 1919. (M.)
8446 Cairns, James, 3 June, 1919. (M.)
8447 Carr, Charles, 3 June, 1919. (M.)
8448 Carruthers, John Harvey de Wiederhold, 3 June, 1919 (M.)
8449 Carter, Ernest Pasley, 3 June, 1919.
8450 Chamier, William St. George, 3 June, 1919. (M.)
8451 Cobb, Charles, 3 June, 1919. (M.)
8452 Compton, Clifton William McGrath, 3 June, 1919. (M.)
8453 Constable, William Charles, 3 June, 1919. (M.)
8454 Coppinger, Francis Romney, 3 June, 1919. (M.)
8455 Cotton, Percy Vernon, 3 June, 1919. (M.)
8456 Cumberlege, Archibald Farrington, 3 June, 1919. (M.)
8457 Dallas, Alexander Egerton, 3 June, 1919. (M.)
8458 Daniell, John Acheson Staines, 3 June, 1919. (M.)
8459 Davies, John Francis, 3 June, 1919. (M.)
8460 Davis, Charles Thomas, 3 June, 1919. (M.)
8461 Dease, Conley Edward, 3 June, 1919. (M.)
8462 De la Bere, Hugh Pleydell, 3 June, 1919. (M.)
8463 Dwane, Herbert Milton, 3 June, 1919. (M.)
8464 Errington, John Perrin, 3 June, 1919. (M.)
8465 Farquharson, Christopher William, 3 June, 1919. (M)
8466 Fleming, John Kenneth Sprot, 3 June, 1919. (M.)
8467 Forbes, Alister Esme Buchan, 3 June, 1919. (M.)
8468 Franklin, George Denne, 3 June, 1919. (M.)
8469 Freel, Joseph, 3 June, 1919. (M.)
8470 Frost, Augustine Thomas, 3 June, 1919. (M.)
8471 Frost, William Arthur, 3 June, 1919. (M.)
8473 Gaunt, Cecil Robert, 3 June, 1919. (M.)
8474 Gilpin, George, 3 June, 1919. (M.)
8475 Gittings, Thomas Albert, 3 June, 1919. (M.
8476 Gosling, Graham, 3 June, 1919. (M.)
8477 Graveson, Henry, 3 June, 1919. (M.)
8478 Grimston Lionel Augustus, 3 June, 1919. (M.)
8479 Haig, David Price, 3 June, 1919. (M.)
8480 Harward, Robert Blake, 3 June, 1919. (M.)
8481 Hawks, George Augustus, 3 June, 1919. (M.)
8482 Hayes, Francis Bernard, 3 June, 1919. (M.)
8483 Heaton, Trevor Braby, 3 June, 1919. (M.)
8484 Hewlett, Kenelm, 3 June, 1919. (M.)
8485 Heycock, Charles Hensman, 3 June, 1919. (M.)
8486 Hinde, Henry Thomas Langford, 3 June, 1919. (M.)
8487 Hopkins, Lewis Egerton, 3 June, 1919. (M.)
8488 Hulbert, Thomas Ernest, 3 June, 1919. (M.)
8489 Humphrey, John, 3 June, 1919. (M.)
8490 Hunt, Frederick Eckstein, 3 June, 1919. (M.)
8491 Hynes, Brian Mansfield, 3 June, 1919. (M.)
8492 Irving, Miles, 3 June, 1919. (M.)
8493 Johnstone, Beresford Assheton, 3 June, 1919. (M.)
8494 Johnstone, David Patrick, 3 June, 1919. (M.)
8495 Kirkwood, Andrew Torton, 3 June, 1919. (M.)
8496 Leathes, Herbert de Mussenden, 3 June, 1919. (M.)
8497 Jones, Leycester Hudson Leslie-, 3 June, 1919. (M.)
8498 Lethbridge, Sydney, 3 June, 1919. (M.)
8499 Ley, Arthur Edwin Hale, 3 June, 1919. (M.)
8500 Lindesay, Frederick Sinclair, 3 June, 1919. (M.)
8501 McElwaine, Erick James Dalby, 3 June, 1919. (M.)
8502 Macpherson, George Cook, 3 June, 1919. (M.)
8503 Malet, Robert James, 3 June, 1919. (M.)
8504 Manners, Charles Manners, 3 June, 1919. (M.)
8505 Marsh, Cunliffe Herbert, 3 June, 1919. (M.)
8506 Mason, Alfred Sidell, 3 June, 1919. (M.)
8507 Matthews, Frank Melvin, 3 June, 1919. (M.)
8508 Meadows, George Stephen, 3 June, 1919. (M.)
8509 Miles, Sir Charles William, 3 June, 1919. (M.)
8510 Miller, Frank Edwin, 3 June, 1919. (M.)
8511 Minty, Thomas William, 3 June, 1919. (M.)
8512 Molloy, Gerald Macleay, 3 June, 1919. (M.)
8513 Moore, Herbert William, 3 June, 1919. (M.)
8514 Moore, William Gale, 3 June, 1919. (M.)
8515 More, Paxton St. Clair, 3 June, 1919. (M.)
8516 Mudie, Robert Francis, 3 June, 1919. (M.)
8517 Muir, Archibald Huleath Huntley, 3 June, 1919. (M.)
8518 Muir, Wingate Wemyss, 3 June, 1919. (M.)
8519 Nevill, Henry Rivers, 3 June, 1919. (M.)
8520 Nicholson, Roger Brighouse, 3 June, 1919. (M.)
8521 Noel, Kenneth Hugh, 3 June, 1919. (M.)
8522 Osborne, George Henry, 3 June, 1919. (M.)
8523 Ouseley, Joseph William Glynn, 3 June, 1919. (M.)
8524 Parsons, Frederick George, 3 June, 1919. (M.)
8525 Paull, James Rabley, 3 June, 1919. (M.)
8526 Pierpoint, Harry William, 3 June, 1919. (M.)
8527 Prescott, John Joseph Whitworth, 3 June, 1919. (M.)
8528 Preston, Eyre Evans, 3 June, 1919. (M.)
8529 Preston, William John Phaelim, 3 June, 1919. (M.)
8530 Reed, William Louis Lindsay, 3 June, 1919. (M.)
8531 Richardson, Rosslyn James Dilyell, 3 June, 1919. (M.)
8533 Robinson, William Pasley, 3 June, 1919. (M.)
8534 Sandeman, Alfred Patrick, 3 June, 1919. (M.)

8535 Sanford, George Batthyany, 3 June, 1919. (M.)
8536 Saunders, Ernest Howle, 3 June, 1919. (M.)
8537 Shepherd, Walter Isaac, 3 June, 1919. (M.)
8538 Sherer, John Corrie, 3 June, 1919. (M.)
8539 Skinner, Alexandra Baird, 3 June, 1919. (M.)
8540 Smith, Charles Harold, 3 June, 1919. (M.)
8541 Smith, G. Graham, 3 June, 1919. (M.)
8542 Smith, Maurice Castle, 3 June, 1919. (M.)
8543 Smith, William Frank, 3 June, 1919. (M.)
8544 Spalding, William Burrington, 3 June, 1919. (M.)
8545 Spring, George Conrad, 3 June, 1919. (M.)
8546 Stansfield, Cyril Grey, 3 June, 1919. (M.)
8547 Steele, Charles Edward Beevor, 3 June, 1919. (M.)
8548 Bennett, John Sterndale, 3 June, 1919. (M.)
8549 Stiffe, Archibald Francis Everett, 3 June, 1919. (M.)
8551 Taylor, Newman, 3 June, 1919. (M.)
8552 Tobin, Harry Walter, 3 June, 1919. (M.)
8553 Torrie, Claud Jameson, 3 June, 1919. (M.)
8554 Turnbull, Thomas Eyre, 3 June, 1919. (M.)
8555 Tyrrell, Augustus Charles Lionel, 3 June, 1919. (M.)
8556 Villiers, Arthur, 3 June, 1919. (M.)
8557 Vincent, Frank Lloyd, 3 June, 1919. (M.)
8558 Wall, Allan Copinger, 3 June, 1919. (M.)
8559 Waller, Edmund, 3 June, 1919. (M.)
8560 Walsh, George Gould, 3 June, 1919. (M.)
8561 Ward, Basil Seth, 3 June, 1919. (M.)
8562 Ward, Henry Charles Swinburne, 3 June, 1919. (M.)
8563 Webb, John Robert Douglas, 3 June, 1919. (M.)
8564 Weekes, Harold Ernest, 3 June, 1919. (M.)
8565 Whish, Eric Vipam, 3 June, 1919. (M.)
8566 Wildy, Harold Adams, 3 June, 1919. (M.)
8567 Wills, Edgar Vernon, 3 June, 1919. (M.)
8568 Wilson, Andrew, 3 June, 1919. (M.)
8569 Wright, William Owen, 3 June, 1919. (M.)
8570 Kalkhushru, Sorat, 3 June, 1919. (M.)
8571 Rimington, Percy William, 3 June, 1919. (M.)
8572 Appleton, Edith Elizabeth, 3 June, 1919. (M.)
8573 Bennett, Douglas Raymond, 3 June, 1919. (M.)
8574 Bristow, Frank Anstie, 3 June, 1919. (M.)
8575 Broughton, Geoffrey Delves, 3 June, 1919. (M.)
8576 Calder, George, 3 June, 1919. (M.)
8577 Cragg, William Joseph, 3 June, 1919. (M.)
8578 De Hochepied-Larpent, Lionel William Peppe, 3 June, 1919. (M.)
8579 Duggan, Martin Joseph, 3 June, 1919. (M.)
8580 Easby, Nora, 3 June, 1919. (M.)
8581 Elwes, Francis Guy Robert, 3 June, 1919. (M.)
8582 Farrow, Frederick Denny, 3 June, 1919. (M.)
8583 Flint, George William, 3 June, 1919. (M.)
8584 Fraser, Pierce Butler, 3 June, 1919. (M.)
8585 Gammon, Frank, Leonard, 3 June, 1919. (M.)
8586 Gatehouse, Hugh, 3 June, 1919. (M.)
8587 Gibbon, Rev. Henry Hensman, 3 June, 1919. (M.)
8588 Gurley, John Herbert, 3 June, 1919. (M.)
8589 Haldane, Henry Chicheley, 3 June, 1919. (M.)
8590 Holden, Alexander Henry Shuttleworth, 3 June, 1919. (M.)
8591 Howard, Arthur Henry, 3 June, 1919. (M.)
8592 Knudsen, Orric Joures, 3 June, 1919. (M.)
8593 Bell, James Logan-, 3 June, 1919. (M.)
8594 MacFarlane, Fane Andrew James, 3 June, 1919. (M.)
8595 Maclear, Ronald, 3 June, 1919. (M.)
8596 McSheehy, Oswald William, 3 June, 1919. (M.)
8597 Malet, Sir Harry Charles, 3 June, 1919. (M.)
8598 O'Neill, Charles Sefton, 3 June, 1919. (M.)
8599 Phipps, Frederick Reginald, 3 June, 1919. (M.)
8600 Potter, Frank Thomas, 3 June, 1919. (M.)
8601a Ramsay, James Gordon, 3 June, 1919. (M.)
8601b Rankin, Henry Charles Deans, 3 June, 1919. (M.)
8602 Salmond, Robert Williamson Asher, 3 June, 1919. (M.)
8603 Scott, Donald Charles, 3 June, 1919. (M.)
8604 Sewell, Douglas Arden Dalrymple, 3 June, 1919. (M.)
8605 Sidgwick, Harry Christopher, 3 June, 1919. (M.)
8606 Sikes, Charles William Booth, 3 June, 1919. (M.)
8607 Simmonds, Roy, 3 June, 1919. (M.)
8608 Sinkinson, Alfred Le Mesurier, 3 June, 1919. (M.)
8609 Sproule, James Chambers, 3 June, 1919. (M.)
8610 Tangye, Richard Trevithick Gilbertstone, 3 June, 1919. (M.)
8611 Yule, Jack Seymour, 3 June, 1919. (M.)
8612 Sadashive, Krishna Bapat Risaldar, 3 June, 1919. (M.)
8613 Blackstock, George Gooderham, 3 June, 1919. (M.)
8614 Donaldson, Robert Inglis, 3 June, 1919. (M.)
8615 Vernon, Stuart Arthur, 3 June, 1919. (M.)
8616 Francis, Frederick Howard, 3 June, 1919. (M.)
8617 Gullett, Sydney Wolton, 3 June, 1919. (M.)
8618 Abramson, Albert, 3 June, 1919. (M.)
8619 Archer, Basil Henry, 3 June, 1919. (M.)
8620 Gould, Edward Sabine Baring-, 3 June, 1919. (M.)
8621 Barron, John Bernard, 3 June, 1919. (M.)
8622 Black, Hutcheson Campbell, 3 June, 1919. (M.)
8623 Ensor, Frederick Charles Curme, 3 June, 1919. (M.)
8624 Goodchild, Thomas Phillip, 3 June, 1919. (M.)
8625 Harris, Edward Ross, 3 June, 1919. (M.)
8626 Hewitt, Albert Claud, 3 June, 1919. (M.)
8627 Hines, John Tatham, 3 June, 1919. (M.)
8628 Holland, Kenneth George, 3 June, 1919. (M.)
8629 Howard, William, 3 June, 1919. (M.)
8630 Linton, George Purdie, 3 June, 1919. (M.)

8631 MacDonald, John Robert, 3 June, 1919. (M.)
8632 MacIlvenna, John, 3 June, 1919. (M.)
8633 MacKenzie, William, 3 June, 1919. (M.)
8634 MacLaren, Geoffrey, 3 June, 1919. (M.)
8635 Moody, Edward Thomas, 3 June, 1919. (M.)
8636 Mortimer, Frederick George Crofton, 3 June, 1919. (M.)
8637 Nicholas, John, 3 June, 1919. (M.)
8638 Nicol, George, 3 June, 1919. (M.)
8639 Olden, George William, 3 June, 1919. (M.)
8640 Ommanney, Walter Montagu, 3 June, 1919. (M.)
8642 Ramsey, Graham Colville, 3 June, 1919. (M.)
8643 Randell, Alan Summers, 3 June, 1919. (M.)
8644 Richmond, Arthur Eaton, 3 June, 1919. (M.)
8645 Roberts, Rev. Henry George, 3 June, 1919. (M.)
8646 Roberts, Charles Cecil Gwynedd, 3 June, 1919. (M.)
8647 Roose, Gerald Unna Bond, 3 June, 1919. (M.)
8648 Ross, Duncan, 3 June, 1919. (M.)
8649 Saunders, Percy Tunstable, 3 June, 1919. (M.)
8650 Scott, James Harry, 3 June, 1919. (M.)
8651 Stewart, Percy Peter James, 3 June, 1919. (M.)
8652 Tucker, Charles Edward, 3 June, 1919. (M.)
8653 Waley, Eric George Simon, 3 June, 1919.
8654 Whitehead, John, 3 June, 1919. (M.)
8655 Whiteman, Francis Edward, 3 June, 1919. (M.)
8656 Williams, Richard John 3 June, 1919. (M.)
8657 Wordie, William, 3 June, 1919. (M.)
8658 El Sagh-Kolaghasi-Mahmound-Effendi-Hilmi-el-Samaa 3 June, 1919. (M.)
8660 Mehr, Mohammad Khan, 3 June, 1919. (M.)
8661 Chauvel, James Allan, 3 June, 1919. (M.)
8662 Comins, Francis Aloysius, 3 June, 1919. (M.)
8663 Darley, Thomas Henry, 3 June, 1919. (M.)
8664 Jarman, Cecil Trevelyan, 3 June, 1919. (M.)
8665 Johnston, Percy Leo, 3 June, 1919. (M.)
8666 Phillips, Francis Hardwick, 3 June, 1919.
8667 Price, Columbus Leigh, 3 June, 1919. (M.)
8668 Sutton, Harvey, 3 June, 1919. (M.)
8669 Croft, Geraldine May, 3 June, 1919. (M.)
8670 Saunders, Ernest Victor, 3 June, 1919. (M.)
8671 Wilkie, Robert, 3 June, 1919. (M.)
8672 Ainley, Richard, 3 June, 1919. (M.)
8673 Anderson, Francis Edward, 3 June, 1919. (M.)
8674 Andrews, George Henry, 3 June, 1919. (M.)
8675 Browne, Arthur Ernest Bankhead-, 3 June, 1919. (M.)
8676 Barrell, William Henry, 3 June, 1919. (M.)
8677 Block, Bernard Alfred Leopold, 3 June, 1919. (M.)
8678 Brammall, Leslie Hinchcliffe, 3 June, 1919. (M.)
8679 Brown, Francis Robert, 3 June, 1919. (M.)
8680 Brown, James Carleton, 3 June, 1919. (M.)
8681 Bullock, Herbert Poe Story, 3 June, 1919. (M.)
8682 Corking, James William, 3 June, 1919. (M.)
8683 Crompton, James, 3 June, 1919. (M.)
8684 Davis, Bernard, Langridge, 3 June, 1919. (M.)
8685 De Freitas, Julian Migron, 3 June, 1919. (M.)
8686 Elkins, Walter Henry, 3 June, 1919. (M.)
8687 Everett, Raymond Charles, 3 June, 1919. (M.)
8688 Farmer, Horace Edwin, 3 June, 1919. (M.)
8689 Frogley, Walter James, 3 June, 1919. (M.)
8690 Galbraith, James Ponsonby, 3 June, 1919. (M.)
8691 Geddes, Rex Wilshire, 3 June, 1919. (M.)
8692 Glasby, Walter George, 3 June, 1919. (M.)
8693 Herschell, Allan, 3 June, 1919. (M.)
8694 Hitchcock, Percy Albion, 3 June, 1919. (M.)
8695 Hine, Walter, 3 June, 1919. (M.)
8696 Hollway, Edith Blake, 3 June, 1919. (M.)
8697 Hosken, William Leslie, 3 June, 1919. (M.)
8698 Jones, William, Edward 3 June, 1919. (M.)
8699 King, Albert Lewin, 3 June, 1919. (M.)
8700 Leman, George Edward, 3 June, 1919. (M.)
8701 Marks, John Barkly, 3 June, 1919. (M.)
8702 Mason, John Henry, 3 June, 1919. (M.)
8703 Maxwell, Ernest Cassel, 3 June, 1919. (M.)
8704 Mason, Godfrey Noel Grey Monck-, 3 June, 1919. (M.)
8705 Peach, Benjamin Neave, 3 June, 1919. (M.)
8706 Raikes, Robert Cecil Montague, 3 June, 1919. (M.)
8707 Rawlings, Geoffrey Nares, 3 June, 1919. (M.)
8708 Rawlins, Howard St. George, 3 June, 1919. (M.)
8709 Revillon, Joseph Whistler, 3 June, 1919. (M.)
8710 Sale, Arthur Bromwich, 3 June, 1919. (M.)
8711 Saunders, George Muskett, 3 June, 1919. (M.)
8712 Scott, John Philips, 3 June, 1919. (M.)
8713 Scruby, William Sidney James, 3 June, 1919. (M.)
8714 Sidney, Ernest Hemming, 3 June, 1919. (M.)
8715 Silley, Edward Charles, 3 June, 1919. (M.)
8716 Stalker, John, 3 June, 1919. (M.)
8717 Stewart, Robert Neil, 3 June, 1919. (M.)
8718 Strahan, Geoffrey Cartaret, 3 June, 1919. (M.)
8719 Stow, David Fenwick, 3 June, 1919. (M.)
8720 Tew, Charles Napier Alexander, 3 June, 1919. (M.)
8721 Till, Percy William Williams-, 3 June, 1919. (M.)
8722 Young, John Ross, 3 June, 1919. (M.)
8723 Barron, Frederick Wilmot, 3 June, 1919. (M.)
8725 Lane, Frank Bernard, 3 June, 1919. (M.)
8726 Abbott, William George, 3 June, 1919. (M.)
8727 Fleischl, Walter, 3 June, 1919. (M.)
8728 Flynn, Rev. William Joseph, 3 June, 1919. (M.)
8729 Smyth, Robert Milner-, 3 June, 1919. (M.)
8730 Alleyne, Charles Foster, 3 June, 1919. (M.)
8731 Anson, Ernest St. George, 3 June, 1919. (M.)

OFFICERS.

8732 Applin, Reginald Vincent Kemperfeldt, 3 June, 1919. (M.)
8733 Armstrong, George Medlicott, 3 June, 1919. (M.)
8734 Arthur, Harry Robert, 3 June, 1919. (M.)
8735 Arthur, John Starling, 3 June, 1919. (M.)
8736 Austin, Aldfred Edward, 3 June, 1919. (M.)
8737 Austin, Frederick William, 3 June, 1919. (M.)
8738 Badger, Thomas Reginald, 3 June, 1919. (M.)
8739 Baird, Andrew Henry, 3 June, 1919. (M.)
8740 Bartels, Olive, 3 June, 1919. (M.)
8741 Bale, Francis Herbert, 3 June, 1919. (M.)
8742 Beaver, Robert Atwood, 3 June, 1919. (M.)
8743 Bigge, George Orde, 3 June, 1919. (M.)
8744 Birch, Lewis Henry Peregrive, 3 June, 1919. (M.)
8745 Bird, Richard Martin, 3 June, 1919. (M.)
8746 Bland, Maurice George, 3 June, 1919. (M.)
8747 Bloomburgh, Joseph Hugh, 3 June, 1919. (M.)
8748 Blundell, Charles Wilson, 3 June, 1919. (M.)
8749 Booty, Lester Browning, 3 June, 1919. (M.)
8750 Bowen, Albert Stephen, 3 June, 1919. (M.)
8751 Boyle, Henry Edmund Gaskin, 3 June, 1919. (M.)
8752 Brown, Alexander, 3 June, 1919. (M.)
8753 Brown, Algernon Gordon, 3 June, 1919. (M.)
8754 Brown, Frederick Alexander William, 3 June, 1919. (M.)
8755 Brown, Gilbert Alexander Murray, 3 June, 1919. (M.)
8756 Brown, Harold Blumfield, 3 June, 1919. (M.)
8757 Bruen, William, 3 June, 1919. (M.)
8758 Bucknall, Roger, 3 June, 1919. (M.)
8759 Burn, Charles Rosdew, 3 June, 1919. (M.)
8760 Caddington, Thomas George Augustus, 3 June, 1919. (M.)
8761 Carter, John Leslie Graydon, 3 June, 1919. (M.)
8762 Carey, William Havilland, 3 June, 1919. (M.)
8763 Carey, Hon. Lucius Plantagenet, 3 June, 1919. (M.)
8764 Child, Gerald Alfred, 3 June, 1919. (M.)
8765 Clark, James Jeffery, 3 June, 1919. (M.)
8766 Clements, Mrs. Dora, 3 June, 1919. (M.)
8767 Cleveland, Arthur John, 3 June, 1919. (M.)
8768 Clover, Edgar, 3 June, 1919. (M.)
8769 Collins, Michael Abdy, 3 June, 1919. (M.)
8770 Cook, Mrs. Grace Muriel, 3 June, 1919. (M.)
8771 Cook, William Littlejohn, 3 June, 1919. (M.)
8772 Cooke, Cedric Franklin, 3 June, 1919. (M.)
8773 Cooke, William Edward Hinchley, 3 June, 1919. (M.)
8774 Cooney, Ralph Carson, 3 June, 1919. (M.)
8775 Cordeaux, William Wilfred, 3 June, 1919. (M.)
8776 Couper, Peter, 3 June, 1919. (M.)
8777 Craik, George Thomas, 3 June, 1919. (M.)
8778 Craven, Hon. Rupert Cecil, 3 June, 1919. (M.)
8779 Craven, Earl of, 3 June, 1919. (M.)
8780 Crook, Arthur, 3 June, 1919. (M.)
8781 Crutchley, Ernest Tristram, 3 June, 1919. (M.)
8782 Daly, Charles Calthorpe de Burgh, 3 June, 1919. (M.)
8783 Daniell, John Clarmont, 3 June, 1919. (M.)
8784 Waddilove, George Edward Darley-, 3 June, 1919. (M.)
8785 Daukes, Sidney Herbert, 3 June, 1919. (M.)
8786 Daucey, Thursby Henry Ernest, 3 June, 1919. (M.)
8787 Davies, Reginald Laidlow, 3 June, 1919. (M.)
8788 Davison, Duncan Athol, 3 June, 1919. (M.)
8789 Day, Benjamin, 3 June, 1919. (M.)
8790 Day, William Leigh Maule, 3 June, 1919. (M.)
8791 Deakin, Charles, 3 June, 1919. (M.)
8792 Wheeler, Samuel Gerald De Courcey, 3 June, 1919. (M.)
8793 Derry, Arthur, 3 June, 1919. (M.)
8794 Devine, Henry, 3 June, 1919. (M.)
8795 Dixon, Herbert, 3 June, 1919. (M.)
8796 Dixon, Sydney Wentworth, 3 June, 1919. (M.)
8797 Hepenstal, Lambert John Dopping-, 3 June, 1919. (M.)
8798 Drummond, Cyril Alexander Fraser, 3 June, 1919. (M.)
8799 Duke, Edward, 3 June, 1919. (M.)
8800 Dunscombe, Nicholas Blake, 3 June, 1919. (M.)
8801 Eager, Richard, 3 June, 1919. (M.)
8802 Eldridge, Ernest James Morritt, 3 June, 1919. (M.)
8803 Elgee, Samuel Charles, 3 June, 1919. (M.)
8804 Eliot, Christian Edward Cornwallis, 3 June, 1919. (M.)
8805 Everest, William Charles Robert, 3 June, 1919. (M.)
8806 Fitzgerald, Thomas Patrick, 3 June, 1919. (M.)
8807 Forsdick, William Henry, 3 June, 1919. (M.)
8808 Frost, Geoffrey Meadows, 3 June, 1919. (M.)
8809 Gaitskell, Henry Walter, 3 June, 1919. (M.)
8810 Garton, William George Alfred, 3 June, 1919. (M.)
8811 Gibson, Jane, 3 June, 1919. (M.)
8812 Gibson, Thornley Carbutt, 3 June, 1919. (M.)
8813 Gifford, Herbert Llewellyn, 3 June, 1919. (M.)
8814 Gillman, Herbert, 3 June, 1919. (M.)
8815 Godfery, Masters Van Somere, 3 June, 1919. (M.)
8816 Good, Thomas Saxty, 3 June, 1919. (M.)
8817 Gordon, Philip James, 3 June, 1919. (M.)
8818 Grange, Charles D'Oyly, 3 June, 1919. (M.)
8819 Greet, Cecil Anstey, 3 June, 1919. (M.)
8820 Guerin, Charles Joseph, 3 June, 1919. (M.)
8821 Gwynne, Frederick William Davies, 3 June, 1919. (M.)
8822 Hadkinson, Percival, 3 June, 1919. (M.)
8823 Hall, John, 3 June, 1919. (M.)
8824 Hamilton, Claude Melville Bruce, 3 June, 1919. (M.)
8825 Hankey, George Frederick Barnard, 3 June, 1919. (M.)
8826 Hawksworth, John Ledlie Inglis, 3 June, 1919. (M.)
8827 Hay, Malcolm Vivian, 3 June, 1919. (M.)
8828 Hay, Peter Stewart, 3 June, 1919. (M.)

8829 Hazard, Cecil James, 3 June, 1919. (M.)
8830 Henderson, Garnet Montgomery Hume, 3 June, 1919. (M.)
8831 Hendry, Alexander William, 3 June, 1919. (M.)
8832 Henry, Hugh, 3 June, 1919. (M.)
8833 Hepworth, Frank Arthur, 3 June, 1919. (M.)
8834 Hervey, Gerald Augustus Frederic, 3 June, 1919. (M.)
8835 Heseltine, Christopher, 3 June, 1919. (M.)
8836 Heywood, Thomas George Gordon, 3 June, 1919. (M.)
8837 Hill, Leslie Rowley, 3 June, 1919. (M.)
8838 Hindlip, Charles Allsopp, Lord, 3 June, 1919. (M.)
8839 Hughes, Robert, 3 June, 1919. (M.)
8840 Hunter, James, 3 June, 1919. (M.)
8841 Ilchester, Earl of, 3 June, 1919. (M.)
8842 Ingram, Francis Manning, 3 June, 1919. (M.)
8843 Irvine, Charles Alexander Lindsay, 3 June, 1919. (M.)
8844 James, Eustace Lindsay Haweis, 3 June, 1919. (M.)
8845 Jefferys, Arthur Harold, 3 June, 1919. (M.)
8846 Johnson, Edgar David, 3 June, 1919. (M.)
8847 Jones, William Henry, 3 June, 1919. (M.)
8848 Kemple, John Howard, 3 June, 1919. (M.)
8849 Kendall, John Kaye, 3 June, 1919. (M.)
8850 Kidley, Alexander John, 3 June, 1919. (M.)
8851 King, David Barty, 3 June, 1919. (M.)
8852 Kinsman, William Augustus Cecil, 3 June 1919. (M.)
8853 Kirby, William Lewis Clark, 3 June. 1919. (M.)
8854 Lamb, Claude Carnegie, 3 June, 1919. (M.)
8855 Langton, Theobald Michael, 3 June, 1919. (M.)
8856 Lawrence, Frederick George, 3 June, 1919. (M.)
8857 Leith, Alexander Robert, 3 June, 1919. (M.)
8858 Conyngham, William Arbuthnot Lenox, 3 June, 1919. (M.)
8861 Liddell, Eric Manfre, 3 June. 1919. (M.)
8862 Lindsay, William George, 3 June, 1919. (M.)
8863 Loughborough, Arthur Harold, 3 June, 1919. (M.)
8864 Lowther, Hon. Lancelot Edward, 3 June, 1919. (M.)
8865 Luscombe, George Augustus, 3 June, 1919. (M.)
8866 Lyons, Henry Edward, 3 June, 1919. (M.)
8867 MacArthur, William Porter, 3 June, 1919. (M.)
8868 MacDonald, John Alexander, 3 June, 1919. (M.)
8869 McGrigor, Dalziel Buchanan, 3 June, 1919. (M.)
8870 MacKay, William Murray, 3 June, 1919. (M.)
8871 MacKenzie, William Scobie, 3 June, 1919. (M.)
8872 MacKinnon, Alexander Dugald, 3 June, 1919. (M.)
8873 MacMahon. Neil Cullum Mildred, 3 June, 1919. (M.)
8874 MacPhail, Hector Duncan, 3 June, 1919. (M.)
8875 MacPhie, John James, 3 June, 1919. (M.)
8876 Malcolm, William Alister, 3 June, 1919. (M.)
8877 Marriott, William Mason, 3 June, 1919. (M.)
8878 Marsden, William Murray, 3 June, 1919. (M.)
8879 Matthews, Durham Simpson, 3 June, 1919. (M.)
8880 Mattinson, Arthur Bowman, 3 June, 1919. (M.)
8881 Maxwell, Edward Boyd, 3 June, 1919. (M.)
8882 Meadows, Alice Margaret, 3 June, 1919. (M.)
8883 Miller, Alfred, 3 June, 1919. (M.)
8884 Mitchell, Rev. Percy Robert, 3 June, 1919. (M.)
8885 Scott, David John Montagu-Douglas-, 3 June, 1919. (M.)
8886 Monteith, Joseph Basil Lawrence, 3 June, 1919. (M.)
8887 Morse, Thomas Ricketts, 3 June, 1919. (M.)
8888 Morsley, John William, 3 June, 1919. (M.)
8889 Morton, Charles Alexander, 3 June, 1919. (M.)
8890 Murray, Robert William, 3 June, 1919. (M.)
8891 Murray, William Cochrane, 3 June, 1919. (M.)
8892 Nason, Henry Hyde Williamson, 3 June, 1919. (M.)
8893 Neave, Charles Alexander, 3 June, 1919. (M.)
8894 King, Francis John Newton-, 3 June, 1919. (M.)
8895 Noon, Charles, 3 June, 1919. (M.)
8896 Northen, Frank, 3 June, 1919. (M.)
8897 O'Callaghan, Rev. James, 3 June, 1919. (M.)
8898 O'Farrell, Rev. Francis, 3 June, 1919. (M.)
8899 O'Neill, Arthur, 3 June, 1919. (M.)
8900 O'Reilly, Rev. James, 3 June, 1919. (M.)
8901 Orpen, Anthony Schroeder, 3 June, 1919. (M.)
8902 Oxley, Frederick John, 3 June, 1919. (M.)
8903 Patterson, Harold Dorman, 3 June, 1919. (M.)
8904 Peacocke, Goodrick Thomas, 3 June, 1919. (M.)
8905 Pearce, Wallace George James. 3 June, 1919. (M.)
8906 Pemberton, Francis Seaton, 3 June, 1919. (M.)
8907 Peters, John Weston Parsons, 3 June, 1919. (M.)
8908 Phillips, John Robert Parry, 3 June, 1919. (M.)
8909 Phillips, William Albert, 3 June, 1919. (M.)
8910 Pine, Charles, 3 June, 1919. (M.)
8911 Powell, Harold Haines, 3 June 1919. (M.)
8912 Prater, George, 3 June, 1919. (M.)
8913 Pugh, George Wilfred, 3 June, 1919. (M.)
8914 Pym, Frederick Harry Norris, 3 June, 1919. (M.)
8915 Ramsey, Arthur Douglas, 3 June, 1919. (M.)
8916 Reilly, James Miles Townsend, 3 June, 1919. (M.)
8917 Richards, Arthur Carew, 3 June, 1919. (M.)
8918 Richards, Rev. Sydney William Letcher, 3 June, 1919. (M.)
8919 Ridings, Cecil, 3 June, 1919. (M.)
8920 Roberts, Hugh Dennison, 3 June. 1919. (M.)
8912 Roberts, Hamilton Walker, 3 June, 1919. (M.)
8922 Roberts, Norcliffe, 3 June, 1919. (M.)
8923 Robertson, Kenneth Struan, 3 June, 1919. (M.)
8924 Robinson, Ernest, 3 June, 1919. (M.)
8925 Robinson, Henry, 3 June, 1919. (M.)
8926 Rodgers, Frederick Millar, 3 June. 1919. (M.)
8927 Romer, Malcolm, 3 June, 1919. (M.)

8928 Ross, Edward Henry, 3 June, 1919. (M.)
8929 Ross, Hew Dalrymyple, 3 June, 1919. (M.)
8930 Rowden. Arthur Roger, 3 June, 1919. (M.)
8931 Rudd, Hubert, 3 June. 1919. (M.)
8932 Sanders, Grace Louise, 3 June, 1919. (M.)
8933 Scale, John Dymoke. 3 June, 1919. (M.)
8934 Sharpe, Alfred Gerald Meredith, 3 June, 1919. (M.)
8935 Shearburn, Alan Darvil, 3 June, 1919. (M.)
8936 Singleton, Henry, 3 June, 1919. (M.)
8937 Slowan, William John More, 3 June, 1919. (M.)
8938 Smith, Albert, 3 June, 1919. (M.)
8939 Smith, Starley Alwyn, 3 June, 1919. (M.)
8940 Smith, Sidney James, 3 June, 1919. (M.)
8941 Soames, Gerald, 3 June, 1919. (M.)
8942 Somerset, Somers, 3 June, 1919. (M.)
8943 Spratley, Thomas James, 3 June, 1919. (M.)
8944 Stephenson, Stanley George, 3 June, 1919. (M.)
8945 Stewart Charles Ravenscroft, 3 June, 1919. (M.)
8946 Stewart, Gertrude, 3 June, 1919. (M.)
8947 Strickland, Guy Tyrone, 3 June, 1919. (M.)
8948 Stuart, Frederick Joshua, 3 June, 1919. (M.)
8949 Suffern, Alexander Canning, 3 June, 1919. (M.)
8950 Teversham, Richard Kinlock, 3 June, 1919. (M.)
8951 Thomas, Francis Henry Hale, 3 June, 1919. (M.)
8952 Thomas, Hugh James Protheroe, 3 June, 1919. (M.)
8953 Thornton, Charles Edward, 3 June, 1919. (M.)
8954 Thorold, Rev. Ernest Hayford, 3 June, 1919. (M.)
8955 Tomlinson, Frederick, 3 June, 1919. (M.)
8956 Toppin, Henry, 3 June, 1919. (M.)
8957 Tringham, Archibald Montgomery, 3 June, 1919. (M.)
8958 Turney, Horace George, 3 June, 1919. (M.)
8959 Vincent, Frederick Calvert, 3 June, 1919. (M.)
8960 Waldron, Edward Joseph, 3 June, 1919. (M.)
8961 Wallington, Christopher Thomas, 3 June, 1919. (M.)
8962 Walmsley, George, 3 June, 1919. (M.)
8963 Walwyn, Charles Lawrence Tyndall, 3 June, 1919. (M.)
8964 Ward, Hon. Robert Arthur, 3 June, 1919. (M.)
8965 Watson, Julien, 3 June, 1919. (M.)
8966 Watson, John, 3 June, 1919. (M.)
8967 Wayman, Henry Holdsworth, 3 June, 1919. (M.)
8968 Welchman, Sidney Chaytor, 3 June, 1919. (M.)
8969 Whinney, Harold Fife, 3 June, 1919. (M.)
8970 White, Henry Herbert Ronald, 3 June, 1919. (M.
8971 Wilbraham, Henry Dudley, 3 June, 1919. (M.)
8972 Willett, Lewis Howard, 3 June, 1919. (M.)
8973 Wilson, Horace Bagster, 3 June, 1919. (M.)
8974 Wilson, Thomas, 3 June, 1919. (M.)
8975 Wingate, George Frederic Richard, 3 June, 1919. (M.
8976 Wood, John Hardy, 3 June, 1919. (M.)
8977 Woodhouse, Brierly, 3 June, 1919. (M.)
8978 Woollcombe, Malcolm Louis, 3 June, 1919. (M.)
8979 Wright, Kenneth Crause, 3 June, 1919. (M.)
8980 Anderson, Thomas Lynewolde, 3 June, 1919. (M.)
8981 Bladen, Rev. Albert Percy, 3 June, 1919. (M.)
8982 Blight, George Elmo, 3 June, 1919. (M.)
8983 Brown, John Herald Balfour, 3 June, 1919. (M.)
8984 Brumwell, Rev. Donald Stanley, 3 June, 1919. (M.
8985 Finlay, George, 3 June, 1919. (M.)
8986 Fletcher, Cecil John, 3 June, 1919. (M.)
8987 Fogarty, Joseph Patrick, 3 June, 1919. (M.)
8988 Fuhrman, Osmond Charles William, 3 June, 1919. (M.)
8989 Gault, Rev. James Archibald, 3 June, 1919. (M.)
8990 Gunn, James Robert, 3 June, 1919. (M.)
8991 Haslam, Thomas Wilfred, 3 June, 1919. (M.)
8992 Makeham, Rev Edward, 3 June, 1919. (M.)
8993 Mayman, Rupert Livingstone, 3 June, 1919. (M.)
8994 Middleton, Sydney Albert, 3 June, 1919. (M.)
8995 Neale, John Arnold, 3 June, 1919. (M.)
8996 Ross, Clara Louisa, 3 June, 1919. (M.)
8997 Sabeston, Robert, 3 June, 1919. (M.)
8998 Sawers, John Boothman, 3 June, 1919. (M.)
8999 Terry, Claude Herbert, 3 June 1919. (M.)
9000 Williams, Norman Reep, 3 June, 1919. (M.)
9001 Archey, Gilbert Edward, 3 June, 1919. (M.)
9002 Beamish, Eric Hamilton, 3 June, 1919. (M.)
9003 Bolton, Samuel James, 3 June, 1919. (M).
9004 Brown, John Falconer, 3 June, 1919. (M.)
9005 Buchanan, Henry Meredith, 3 June, 1919. (M.)
9006 Davies, Leofric Pearson, 3 June, 1919. (M.)
9007 McCurdy, Donald Archibald, 3 June, 1919. (M.)
9008 May, Charles Edward, 3 June, 1919. (M.)
9009 Mewett, James Edward Hedley 3 June. 1919. (M.)
9010 Oram, Harry, 3 June, 1919. (M.)
9011 Stout, Thomas Duncan McGregor, 3 June, 1919. (M.)
9012 Tapper, Kenneth Edwin, 3 June, 1919. (M.)
9013 Treadwell, Charles Archibald Lawrance, 3 June, 1919. (M.)
9014 Davison, Charles Gray, 3 June, 1919. (M.)
9015 Gordon, William Lennox, 3 June, 1919. (M.)
9016 MacDougall, Ian, 3 June, 1919. (M.)
9017 Medlicott, Richard Frederick Cavendish, 3 June, 1919 (M.)
9018 Mullins, Henry Rubert, 3 June, 1919. (M.)
9019 Robertson, George Watson, 3 June, 1919. (M.)
9020 Thomas, Walwyn, 3 June, 1919. (M.)
9021 Baxter, Robert Hugh Neville, 3 June, 1919. (M.)
9022 Berridge, Harold, 3 June, 1919. (M.)
9023 Daldy, Alexander William, 3 June, 1919. (M.)
9024 Finnis, Herbert Cobb, 3 June, 1919. (M.)

9025 Gwynne, Clement Wansbrough, 3 June, 1919 (M.)
9026 Jadav, Pandurung Rao, 3 June, 1919. (M.)
9027 Khan, Iqbal Mahomed, 3 June, 1919. (M.)
9028 MacEwan, Andrew Kenneth, 3 June, 1919. (M.)
9029 Nottidge, George. 3 June. 1919. (M.)
9030 Row, Raghabendra, 3 June, 1919. (M.)
9031 Rush, John Shipman, 3 June, 1919. (M.)
9032 Samund, Abdul, 3 June, 1919. (M.)
9033 Shairp, Henry Frank, 3 June, 1919. (M.)
9034 Shine, Eugene Percy Forrest, 3 June, 1919. (M.)
9035 Singh, Rao Bahadur Rao Balbir, 3 June, 1919. (M.)
9036 Singh, Sardar Bahardur Chanda, 3 June, 1919. (M.)
9037 Singh, Dais Raj Ranjit, 3 June, 1919. (M.)
9038 Singh, Rajhumar Ranjit, 3 June, 1919. (M.)
9039 Wilson, John Arthur Maclean, 3 June, 1919. (M.)
9040 Baring, Thomas Esme, 3 June, 1919. (M.)
9041 Brooke, John Chadwick, 3 June, 1919. (M.)
9042 Campbell, Ian Percy Fitzgerald, 3 June, 1919. (M.)
9043 Edwards, T. H., 3 June, 1919. (M.)
9044 Graham, Hamilton Maurice Howgrave-, 3 June, 1919. (M.)
9045 Kirkwood, Thomas William, 3 June, 1919. (M.)
9046 Montefiore. Leonard Nathaniel, 3 June, 1919. (M.)
9047 Newbery, James Wilfred Trevor, 3 June, 1919. (M.)
9048 Parker, Sir William Lorenzo, Bart., 3 June, 1919. (M.)
9049 Price, Walter Dennis, 3 June, 1919. (M.)
9050 Robson, Archibald, 3 June, 1919. (M.)
9051 Doidge, R. C., 3 June, 1919. (M.)
9052 McHaffie, George Addison, 3 June, 1919. (M.)
9053a Renaud, Ernest James. 3 June, 1919. (M.)
9053b Anderson, Alexander, 3 June, 1919. (M.)
9053c Huffam, William Tyers Christopher, 3 June, 1919 (M.)
9053d Black, George Cumine Strahan, 3 June, 1919. (M.)
9053e Bonar, Hew Hunter, 3 June, 1919. (M.)
9053f Bown, Herbert, 3 June, 1919. (M.)
9053g Cooper, Geoffrey Beauchamp Astley, 3 June, 1919. (M.)
9053h Dudding, Thomas Scarborough, 3 June, 1919. (M.)
9054a Dutton, Ralph Matthew Legge, 3 June, 1919. (M.)
9054b Jones, Richard Reginald Glynne-, 3 June, 1919. (M.)
9054c Jacomb, Frederick Basil Wood, 3 June, 1919. (M.)
9054d Lapsley, William, 3 June, 1919. (M.)
9054e Lyall, William James, 3 June, 1919. (M.)
9054f Palmer, John Harald Gore, 3 June, 1919. (M.)
9054g Porter, Herbert Charles Vivian, 3 June, 1919. (M.)
9054h Singer, Charles Archibald, 3 June, 1919. (M.)
9055a Taylor, John Norman, 3 June, 1919. (M.)
9055b Tennent, Anderson Kirkwood, 3 June, 1919. (M.)
9055c Bostock, James, 3 June, 1919. (M.)
9055d Brighten, Claude William, 3 June, 1919. (M.)
9055e Ellison, Craufurd Tait, 3 June, 1919. (M.)
9055f Lewis, Ernest William, 3 June, 1919. (M.)
9055g Meares.HughPoynder, 3 June, 1919. (M.)
9055h Rendle,William Edgcumbe, 3 June, 1919. (M.)
9056a Ritson, Cuthbert Ward, 3 June, 1919. (M.)
9056b Tracy, Charles Dunlop, 3 June, 1919. (M.)
9056c Wilson, Gregg, 3 June, 1919. (M.)
9056d Gowans, James Dakers, 3 June, 1919. (M.)
9056e Khan, Ajab, 3 June, 1919. (M.)
9056f Vickers, Wilmot Gordon Hilton, 3 June, 1919. (M.)
9056g Collings, F. J., 3 June, 1919. (M.)
9056h Wedderburn, Henry Kellerman Hamilton-, 3 June, 1919. (M.)
9057a McCallum, Robert Towson, 3 June, 1919. (M.)
9057b Trueman, Thomas Edwin, 3 June, 1919. (M.)
9057c Watson, Basil Barnard, 3 June, 1919. (M.)
9057d Farran, George Lambert, 3 June, 1919. (M.)
9057e Greer, William Niven, 3 June, 1919. (M.)
9057f Mouat, Charles George Kay-, 3 June, 1919. (M.)
9057g Marshall, Hannath Douglas, 3 June, 1919. (M.)
9057h O'Malley, David Vincent, 3 June, 1919. (M.)
9058a Scott, George Edward, 3 June, 1919. (M.)
9058b White, White Bolmfield, 3 June, 1919. (M.)
9058c Anderson, Arthur Robert, 11 June, 1919. (M.)
9058d Ayre, Leslie Charles Edward, 11 June, 1919. (M.)
9058e Bates, Reginald Barrington, 11 June, 1919. (M.)
9058f Bath, Alan George, 11 June, 1919. (M.)
9058g Bills, Walter William, 11 June, 1919. (M.)
9059 Borrett, Jack Tuthill, 11 June, 1919. (M.)
9060 Bott, Leslie Charles, 11 June, 1919. (M.)
9061 Bowing, John, 11 June, 1919. (M.)
9062 Boyle, James Charles, 11 June, 1919. (M.)
9063 Bray, John Evelyn, 11 June, 1919. (M.)
9064 Brewer, Charles Samuel, 11 June, 1919. (M.)
9065 Brown, William, John Archer, 11 June, 1919. (M.)
9066 Buchanan, Frederic Gray, 11 June, 1919. (M.)
9067 Candy, Geoffrey Charles, 11 June, 1919. (M.)
9068 Candy, John, 11 June, 1919. (M.)
9069 Catto, Andrew Yule, 11 June, 1919. (M.)
9070 Cavill, Herbert John, 11 June, 1919. (M.)
9071 Cole, Archiblad Charles, 11 June, 1919. (M.)
9072 Coleman, Patrick Peter, 11 June, 1919. (M.)
9073 Colles, Ernest Dudley Gordon, 11 June, 1919. (M.
9074 Collins, Charles Edward, 11 June, 1919. (M.)
9075 Colwill, George Henry, 11 June, 1919. (M.)
9076 Connors, Ernest John, 11 June, 1919. (M.)
9077 Coote, Bernard Trotter, 11 June, 1919. (M.)
9078 Craven, Charles Worthington, 11 June, 1919. (M.)
9079 Crowther, William Reginald Denys, 11 June, 1919. (M.)
9080 Cudlip, Edwin William, 11 June, 1919. (M.)

9081 Cumberlege. Marcus Victor, 11 June, 1919. (M.)
9082 Damant, Guybon Chesney Castell, 11 June, 1919. (M.)
9083 Davis, William Thomas, 11 June, 1919. (M.)
9084 Eason, Victor Cecil Gould, 11 June, 1919. (M.)
9085 Ellis, Thomas, 11 June, 1919. (M.)
9086 Fildes, Paul G., 11 June, 1919. (M.)
9087 Garwood, Hugh Sydney, 11 June, 1919. (M.)
9088 Gilbert, Archibald, 11 June, 1919. (M.)
9089 Good, Henry John Graham, 11 June, 1919. (M.)
9090 Gocld, Hubert, 11 June, 1919.
9091 Hamilton-Gordon, Hugh, 11 June, 1919. (M.)
9092 Harris, Percy George, 11 June, 1919. (M.)
9093 Harrison, Geoffrey Brancker, 11 June, 1919. (M.)
9094 Hart, William, 11 June, 1919. (M.)
9095 Hastings, James Frederick Arthur, 11 June, 1919. (M.)
9096 Heather, Paul, 11 June, 1919. (M.)
9097 Horsey, Frank Lankester, 11 June, 1919. (M.)
9098 Jackson, Stanley, 11 June, 1919. (M.)
9099 Janion, Arthur Cyril Austin, 11 June, 1919. (M.)
9100 Jeans, George, 11 June, 1919. (M.)
9101 Kay, Ivo James, 11 June, 1919. (M.)
9102 Kerr, Fairfax Moresby, 11 June, 1919. (M.)
9103 Lane-Poole, Richard Hayden, Owen, 11 June, 1919. (M.)
9104 Llewellyn, Llewellyn Evan Hugh, 11 June, 1919. (M.)
9105 McKinlay, Alfred White, 11 June, 1919. (M.)
9106 MacLean, Harper, 11 June, 1919. (M.)
9107 Mann, William Selwyn, 11 June, 1919. (M.)
9108 Martin, Edward George, 11 June, 1919. (M.)
9109 Moore, Gerald, 11 June, 1919. (M.)
9110 Morley, Cornelius Cecil, 11 June, 1919. (M.)
9111 Moseley, Edward James, 11 June, 1919. (M.)
9112 Murray, Arthur John Layard, 11 June, 1919. (M.)
9113 O'Connor, Thomas Reginald Gill, 11 June, 1919. (M.)
9114 Orchard, Edwin Harold, 11 June, 1919. (M.)
9115 Orton, John Henry, 11 June, 1919. (M.)
9116 Palfreman, Edwin, 11 June, 1919. (M.)
9117 Parsons, Stanley Seymour Conway, 11 June, 1919. (M.)
9118 Pratt, Edwin, 11 June, 1919. (M.)
9119 Prendergast, John Arnoux, 11 June, 1919. (M.)
9120 Robins, Leslie, 11 June, 1919. (M.)
9121 Romer, Frederick, 11 June, 1919. (M.)
9122 Rudland, Henry Alfred, 11 June, 1919. (M.)
9123 Shee, Richard John, 11 June, 1919. (M.)
9124 Simon, Arnold, 11 June, 1919. (M.)
9125 Stocker, Percy, 11 June, 1919. (M.)
9126 Swan, Kenneth Raydon, 11 June, 1919. (M.)
9127 Thomson, George Pirie, 11 June, 1919. (M.)
9128 Thornton, Cyril Joseph, 11 June, 1919. (M.)
9129 Tower, Francis Fitzpatrick, 11 June, 1919. (M.)
9130 Turner, Frederick Richard Gordon, 11 June, 1919. (M.)
9131 Twigg, Francis Walter Despard, 11 June, 1919. (M.)
9132 Wood, Alfred Oswald, 11 June, 1919. (M.)
9133 Wynter, Gerald Charles, 11 June, 1919. (M.)
9134 Yorke, Maurice Francis, 11 June, 1919. (M.)
9135 Barnes, George Edwin Olaf, 21 June, 1919. (M.)
9136 Blackburn, Albert Edward, 21 June, 1919. (M.)
9137 Blumberg, Frederick Thomas, 21 June, 1919.
9138 Brady, John Joseph Hugh, 21 June, 1919. (M.)
9139 Browne, Robley Henry John, 21 June, 1919. (M.)
9140 Compton, Edward Bathurst, 21 June, 1919. (M.)
9141 Elstob, Eric Bramley, 21 June, 1919. (M.)
9142 Hamnett, Bernard, 21 June, 1919. (M.)
9143 Hooper, Geoffroy William Winsmore, 21 June, 1919. (M.)
9144 Large, Edwin Ryder, 21 June, 1919.
9145 Mann, William Burridge, 21 June, 1919. (M.)
9146 Miles, Francis Nigel, 21 June, 1919. (M.)
9147 Moorsom, Winstanley Robert Coverdale, 21 June, 1919.
9148 Morgan, John Hamilton, 21 June, 1919. (M.)
9149 Pelham-Kent, Arthur Clifton, 21 June, 1919. (M.)
9150 Sarel, Colin Alfred Molyneux, 21 June, 1919. (M.)
9151 Waterhouse, Thomas Ryder, 21 June, 1919. (M.)
9152 Watson, George William, 21 June, 1919. (M.)
9153 Whitehead, Norman, 21 June, 1919. (M.)
9154 Ahern, Michael John, 27 June, 1919. (M.)
9155 Allenby, John Norfolk, 27 June, 1919. (M.)
9156 Bate, Francis William, 27 June, 1919. (M.)
9157 Bennetts, Sydney, 27 June, 1919. (M.)
9158 Chichester, Ivor Francis, 27 June, 1919. (M.)
9159 Colbeck, Charles Edward Beeby, 27 June, 1919. (M.)
9160 Williams, Maurice Marcel Frederic Condé-, 27 June, 1919. (M.)
9161 Cornwallis, Oswald Wykeham, 27 June, 1919. (M.)
9162 Dingli, Adrian, 27 June, 1919. (M.)
9163 Dunkley, George William, 27 June, 1919. (M.)
9164 Edgell, John Augustine, 27 June, 1919. (M.)
9165 Salmond, Kenneth Gofton-, 27 June, 1919. (M.)
9166 Goolden, Archibald Campbell, 27 June, 1919. (M.)
9168 Henslowe, Ernest, 27 June, 1919. (M.)
9169 Hodgson, Oswald Tylston, 27 June, 1919. (M.)
9170 Humphrey, Percy Edward May, 27 June, 1919. (M.)
9171 Johnston, William, 27 June, 1919. (M.)
9172 Kennedy, James, 27 June, 1919. (M.)
9173 Markham, Ernest Lacey, 27 June, 1919. (M.)
9174 Martin, Thomas, 27 June, 1919. (M.)
9175 Medd. Walter Hall, 27 June, 1919. (M.)
9176 Merry, Colin Campbell, 27 June, 1919. (M.)
9177 Mills, Gerald Edgell, 27 June, 1919. (M.)
9178 Muir, Allan Thompson, 27 June, 1919. (M.)

9180 Nathan, George Emanuel, 27 June. 1919. (M.)
9181 Nicholas, Ernest, 27 June, 1919. (M.)
9182 Parker, Frederick William, 27 June, 1919. (M.)
9183 Parsons, Oswy Lonsdale, 27 June, 1919. (M.)
9184 Phillips, Richard Hood Grant, 27 June, 1919. (M.)
9185 Pocock, Herbert Cheyney, 27 June, 1919. (M.)
9186 Rising, Francis Simon, 27 June, 1919. (M.)
9187 Roberts, Arthur Cecil, 27 June, 1919. (M.)
9188 Robertson, James Anderson Brown, 27 June, 1919. (M.)
9189 Rosevere, Edward James, 27 June, 1919. (M.)
9190 Sandford, Cecil Stanley, 27 June, 1919.
9191 Shaw, Francis Blewitt, 27 June, 1919. (M.)
9192 Smithson, Alfred Edward, 27 June, 1919. (M.)
9193 Stevenson, Ian Teacher, 27 June, 1919. (M.)
9194 Taylor, George Reay, 27 June, 1919. (M.)
9195 Thornycroft, Oliver, 27 June, 1919. (M.)
9196 Townend, Alfred Bernard Stairs, 27 June, 1919. (M.)
9197 Wagg, Henry John, 27 June, 1919. (M.)
9198 Ward, Bernard John Hamilton, 27 June, 1919. (M.)
9199 Webber, Hubert Arthur Cornwall, 27 June, 1919. (M.)
9200 Woolley, William, 27 June, 1919. (M.)
9201 Young, Harold Francis John, 27 June, 1919. (M.)
9202 Blanchflower. Edward Charles, 30 June, 1919. (M.)
9203 Delius, Daniel Edwin St. Martin, 30 June, 1919. (M.)
9204 Dixon, Alan, 30 June, 1919. (M.)
9205 Glennie, Hugh Gardiner, 30 June, 1919. (M.)
9206 Hamilton, James Jack, 30 June, 1919. (M.)
9207 Innes, Arthur, 30 June, 1919. (M.)
9208 Leportier, Theodore, 30 June, 1919. (M.)
9209 McMickam, Walter Campbell, 30 June, 1919. (M.)
9210 Money, Norman Angel Kyrle, 30 June, 1919. (M.)
9211 Newman, James Benjamin, 30 June, 1919. (M.)
9212 Norcock, Charles Vernon Lowcay, 30 June, 1919. (M.)
9213 Pickering, William Alfred, 30 June, 1919. (M.)
9214 Potts, Thomas Moffett, 30 June, 1919. (M.)
9215 Reid, Joseph Alfred, 30 June, 1919. (M.)
9216 Smith, Philip Albert, 30 June, 1919. (M.)
9217 Strickland, Henry, 30 June, 1919. (M.)
9219 Thompson, John, 30 June, 1919. (M.)
9220 Baxendale, Basil Francis, 4 July, 1919. (M.)
9221 Bickley, Reginald Courteney, 4 July, 1919. (M.)
9222 Broome, Thomas Charles, 4 July, 1919. (M.)
9223 Cartwright, Charles Chesters, 4 July, 1919. (M.)
9224 Clarke, Maurice Harvey, 4 July, 1919. (M.)
9225 Crouch, Charles Henry Anson, 4 July, 1919. (M.)
9226 Dawes, Hugh Campbell Frederick. 4 July. 1919. (M.)
9227 Fenwick, Henry Clennell, 4 July, 1919. (M.)
9228 Fenwick, Maurice George Fenwick Bissett, 4 July, 1919. (M.)
9229 Froggatt, Charles Edward, 4 July, 1919. (M.)
9230 Gibbs, Stanley, 4 July, 1919. (M.)
9231 Gilroy, Henry Errington, 4 July, 1919. (M.)
9232 Grant, Arthur Syme, 4 July, 1919. (M.)
9233 Greig, Donald, 4 July, 1919. (M.)
9234 Griffith, Charles Harry, 4 July, 1919. (M.)
9235 Harrison, Thomas, 4 July, 1919. (M.)
9236 Hemsley, Alexander Guy, 4 July, 1919. (M.)
9237 Holloway, Graham Charles, 4 July, 1919. (M.)
9238 Horsburgh, Gordon Staveley, 4 July, 1919. (M.)
9239 Jackson, Thomas Edwin, 4 July, 1919. (M.)
9240 Jones, John Herbert, 4 July, 1919. (M.)
9241 King, Joseph, 4 July, 1919. (M.)
9242 Kitcat, Henry Jeffreys de Winton, 4 July, 1919. (M.)
9243 Landon, Edward Cyril Turton, 4 July, 1919. (M.)
9244 Lay, John Richard, 4 July, 1919. (M.)
9245 Lee, Emsley Mark, 4 July, 1919. (M.)
9246 Lockhart, Murray MacGregor, 4 July, 1919. (M.)
9247 Lockyer, Sydney de Bohun, 4 July, 1919. (M.)
9248 McBroom, Samuel, 4 July, 1919 (M.)
9249 McKay, William Kirby, 4 July, 1919. (M.)
9250 Partridge, Reginald Montague, 4 July, 1919. (M.)
9251 Phillips, Frederick Brown, 4 July 1919. (M.)
9252 Rice, James, 4 July, 1919. (M.)
9253 Richardson, Francis Joseph, 4 July, 1919. (M.)
9254 Ridgway, Bertram Henry Akroyd, 4 July, 1919. (M.)
9255 Smith, Henry Edward Goves Scott-, 4 July, 1919. (M.)
9256 Shipton, Francis Henry Eldred, 4 July, 1919. (M.)
9257 Stonehouse, Andrew Woodhouse, 4 July, 1919. (M.)
9258 Stubbs, Sydenham Ernest, 4 July, 1919. (M.)
9259 Taylor, Ogden, 4 July, 1919. (M.)
9260 Tibbits, Edward, 4 July, 1919. (M.)
9261 Toby. William Henry, 4 July, 1919. (M.)
9262 Walshe, Francis Weldon, 4 July, 1919. M.)
9263 Whittle, William Henry, 4 July, 1919. (M.)
9264 Appleyard, Rollo, 10 July, 1919. (M.)
9265 Bannatyne, Archibald Brown, 10 July, 1919. (M.)
9266 Barker, Albert, 10 July, 1919. (M.)
9267 Barrett, Richard William, 10 July, 1919. (M.)
9268 Brett, George Henry, 10 July, 1919. (M.)
9269 Brewer, Frederick Henry, 10 July, 1919. (M.)
9270 Brock, Donald Carey, 10 July, 1919. (M.)
9271 Carey, Basil Ernest, 10 July, 1919. (M.)
9272 Courage, Archibald Vesey, 10 July, 1919. (M.)
9273 Cross, Cecil Woodrow, 10 July, 1919. (M.)
9274 Eliot, Montague Charles, 10 July, 1919. (M.)
9275 Forbes, William Stonach Foster, 10 July, 1919. (M.)
9276 Froude, Anthony Ashley, 10 July, 1919. (M.)
9277 Graves, Cornelius Blackwell, 10 July, 1919. (M.)
9278 Gray, William, 10 July, 1919. (M.)

9279 Hall, Hamilton John Burnett, 10 July, 1919. (M.)
9280 Hamilton, James, 10 July, 1919. (M.)
9281 Hammond, Bert Ernest, 10 July, 1919. (M.)
9282 Hargrave, John Eustace, 10 July, 1919. (M.)
9283 Hervey, Richard George, 10 July, 1919. (M.)
9284 Hordern, Lionel Herbert, 10 July, 1919. (M.)
9285 Hughes, William Henry, 10 July, 1919. (M.)
9286 King, James Henry, 10 July, 1919. (M.)
9287 Knox, John Frederick, 10 July, 1919. (M.)
9288 Lapage, Walter Neville, 10 July, 1919. (M.)
9289 MacBrayne, Laurence, 10 July, 1919. (M.)
9290 Mackie, George William, 10 July, 1919. (M.)
9291 Matthews, Thomas Samuel, 10 July, 1919. (M.)
9292 Morgon, James Kendle, 10 July, 1919. (M.)
9293 Murray, Neil Smith, 10 July, 1919. (M.)
9294 Peattie, Alexander Bonnie, 10 July, 1919. (M.)
9295 Robinson, Leonard Mould, 10 July, 1919. (M.)
9296 Rodham, Cuthbert Halliburton, 10 July, 1919. (M.
9297 Russell, Edward Holden, 10 July, 1919. (M.)
9298 Smiles, Stephen Hudson, 10 July, 1919. (M.)
9299 Tate, Frederick Lionel, 10 July, 1919. (M.)
9300 Thicke, Claude Stanley, 10 July, 1919. (M.)
9301 Villiers, Gerald Berkeley, 10 July, 1919. (M.)
9302 Watney, Gilbert John, 10 July, 1919. (M.)
9303 Russell, Harold David Watts-, 10 July, 1919. (M.)
9304 Baker, Gordon St. George Wildman, 12 July, 1919. (M.)
9305 Bell, John Fawcett, 12 July, 1919. (M.)
9306 Davis, Reginald Unwin, 12 July, 1919. (M.)
9307 Figgins, John William, 12 July, 1919. (M.)
9308 Gibson, Frederick John Butler, 12 July, 1919. (M.)
9309 Herivel, Sidney Peck, 12 July, 1919. (M.)
9310 Maconochie, Charles Ernest, 12 July, 1919. (M.)
9311 Martin, Alfred, 12 July, 1919. (M.)
9313 Painter, Arthur Collett, 12 July, 1919. (M.)
9314 Saunders, Arthur Patrick, 12 July, 1919. (M.)
9315 Simson, Arthur Fraser, 12 July, 1919. (M.)
9316 Sutherland, Joseph, 12 July, 1919. (M.)
9317 White, Richard Forster, 12 July, 1919. (M.)
9318 Willoughby, Reginald Stephen, 12 July, 1919. (M.)
9319 Wright, Noel, 12 July, 1919. (M.)
9320 Young, Edwin Walton, 12 July, 1919. (M.)
9321 Abbott. Bernard Edwin, 17 July, 1919. (M.)
9322 Allan, John Hunter, 17 July, 1919. (M.)
9323 Allen, James, 17 July, 1919. (M.)
9324 Ashton, Reginald William Alexander, 17 July, 1919. (M.)
9325 Barter, Frederick, 17 July, 1919. (M.)
9326 Cannan, George William, 17 July, 1919. (M.)
9327 Cassy, Alexander William, 17 July, 1919. (M.)
9328 Clausen, Hugh, 17 July, 1919. (M.)
9329 Crabb, William Charles Pascoe, 17 July, 1919. (M.)
9330 Cross, Charles Henry Dennis, 17 July, 1919. (M.)
9331 Dove, John Scott, 17 July, 1919. (M.)
9332 Drew, Thomas Bernard, 17 July, 1919. (M.)
9333 Elliott, Frank, 17 July, 1919. (M.)
9334 Falle, H. de C., 17 July, 1919. (M.)
9335 Fisher, Douglas Blake, 17 July, 1919. (M.)
9336 Fisher, William Newton, 17 July, 1919. (M.)
9337 Fraser, Bruce Austin, 17 July, 1919. (M.)
9338 Gillespie, Harold Evelyn, 17 July, 1919. (M.)
9339 Gregory, Leslie, 17 July, 1919. (M.)
9340 Haines, Henry Ronald, 17 July, 1919. (M.)
9341 Hall, Samuel Howard, 17 July, 1919. (M.)
9342 Harwood, Henry Harwood, 17 July, 1919. (M.)
9343 Haves, Thomas, 17 July, 1919. (M.)
9344 Hewitt, Brian Lifford, 17 July, 1919. (M.)
9345 Hughes, Evan Jukes, 17 July, 1919. (M.)
9346 Hawkesworth, Richard Arthur, 17 July, 1919. (M.)
9347 Jermain, Harry Bingham, 17 July, 1919. (M.)
9348 Keily, Charles Joseph, 17 July, 1919. (M.)
9349 Lawson, John Cuthbert, 17 July, 1919. (M.)
9350 Leahy, James Palmer, 17 July, 1919. (M.)
9351 Kaye, Russell Lister-, 17 July, 1919. (M.)
9352 Lucas, Charles Anthony Cecil, 17 July, 1919. (M.)
9353 McGrath, Harry Nisbet, 17 July, 1919. (M.)
9354 MacKeown, Robert John, 17 July, 1919. (M.)
9355 Marriott, Horace Bruce, 17 July, 1919. (M.)
9356 Metcalfe, Bruce, 17 July, 1919. (M.)
9357 More, George Irwin Sanctuary, 17 July, 1919. (M.)
9358 Nash, Walter Macdonald, 17 July, 1919. (M.)
9359 Neligan, Eric Claude, 17 July, 1919. (M.)
9360 Nelson, Robert Douglas, 17 July, 1919. (M.)
9361 Pape, Percy John, 17 July, 1919. (M.)
9362 Rattey, William, 17 July, 1919. (M.)
9364 Rogers, Henry, 17 July, 1919. (M.)
9365 Skinner, William Shelford, 17 July, 1919. (M.)
9366 Startin, Robert Arthur. 17 July, 1919. (M.)
9367 Stevenson, Ernest, 17 July, 1919. (M.)
9368 Sydenham, Frederick William, 17 July, 1919. (M.)
9369 Terrill, Frank, 17 July, 1919. (M.)
9370 Tinson, Charles Wills, 17 July, 1919. (M.)
9371 Tower, Francis Thomas Butler, 17 July, 1919. (M.)
9372 Walker, William Frederic Wake-, 17 July, 1919. (M.)
9373 Watson, Lewis Jones, 17 July, 1919. (M.)
9374 Webb, Lancelot Vere, 17 July, 1919. (M.)
9375 White, Arthur Frederick, 17 July, 1919. (M.)
9376 Wilkinson, Edward Aubrey Guy, 17 July, 1919. (M.)
9377 Wright, John Turnbull, 17 July, 1919. (M.)
9378 Yeo, Moritz Rodwell, 17 July, 1919. (M.)
9379 Bisset, William David, 31 July, 1919. (M.)

9380 Briggs, Charles, 31 July, 1919. (M.)
9381 Butcher, Victor George, 31 July, 1919. (M.)
9382 Chater, Francis Arthur, 31 July, 1919. (M.)
9383 Cornabé, William Eckford, 31 July, 1919. (M.)
9384 Draper, Philip Nelson, 31 July, 1919. (M.)
9385 Edmonds, Archibald Charles Mackay, 31 July, 1919. (M.)
9386 Evans, Alfred Englefield, 31 July, 1919. (M.)
9387 Fairbairn, Bernard William Murray, 31 July, 1919. (M.)
9388 Findlay, George William Marshall, 31 July, 1919. (M.)
9389 Flood, Otto Barnes Patrick, 31 July, 1919. (M.)
9390 Freyberg, Geoffrey Herbert, 31 July, 1919. (M.)
9391 Grant, Malcolm Kenneth, 31 July, 1919. (M.)
9392 Hunter, Harry, 31 July, 1919. (M.)
9393 Irving, Robert Beaufin, 31 July, 1919. (M.)
9394 Jollye, Godfrey Herbert, 31 July, 1919. (M.)
9395 Jones, Isaac, 31 July, 1919. (M.)
9396 Jones, Rupert Oswald, 31 July, 1919. (M.)
9397 May, Archibald Seaburne, 31 July, 1919. (M.)
9398 Meeson, Charles Mortimore, 31 July, 1919. (M.)
9399 Mills, Tom Lakin, 31 July, 1919. (M.)
9400 Mittell, Richard William, 31 July, 1919. (M.)
9401 Patterson, Julian Francis Chichester, 31 July, 1919. (M.)
9402 Peterkin, William, 31 July, 1919. (M.)
9403 Powell, Malcolm Cecil, 31 July, 1919. (M.)
9404 Putt, William Pearce, 31 July, 1919. (M.)
9405 Rankine, Roger Aiken, 31 July, 1919. (M.)
9406 Smith, Clifford Edward Heathcote, 31 July, 1919. (M.)
9407 Smithers, William Henry Grant, 31 July, 1919. (M.)
9408 Swift, Clement Charles, 31 July, 1919. (M.)
9409 Warre, Philip Acheson, 31 July, 1919. (M.)
9410 Weatherhead, Robert, 31 July, 1919. (M.)
9411 Weigall, Graham Selwyn, 31 July, 1919. (M.)
9412 Westmore, Henry George Gardiner, 31 July, 1919. (M.)
9413 Whitfield, George Arthur, 31 July, 1919. (M.)
9414 Bell, Aidan Isaac, 11 Aug. 1919. (M.)
9415 Blake-Reed, John Seymour, 11 Aug. 1919. (M.)
9416 Boyd, John Mossom, 11 Aug. 1919. (M.)
9417 Brown, Richard Charles, 11 Aug. 1919. (M.)
9418 Clarke, George Edgar, 11 Aug. 1919. (M.)
9419 Clarke, James Richard Plomer, 11 Aug. 1919. (M.)
9420 Cunningham, Charlie Allen Chichester, 11 Aug. 1919. (M.)
9421 Dewar, Alfred Charles, 11 Aug. 1919. (M.)
9422 Duggan, Eyre Sturdy, 11 Aug. 1919. (M.)
9423 Eliott, Gerald Otho Rooskie, 11 Aug. 1919. (M.)
9424 Evans, Harold Ernest, 11 Aug. 1919. (M.)
9425 Fielder, Stanley, 11 Aug. 1919. (M.)
9426 Firth, Bernard, 11 Aug. 1919. (M.)
9427 Fraser, James Gordon, 11 Aug. 1919. (M.)
9428 Grenville-Grey, Grenville, 11 Aug. 1919. (M.)
9429 Heayberd, William Valentine, 11 Aug. 1919. (M.)
9430 Holborn, Arthur Savory, 11 Aug. 1919. (M.)
9431 Howden, Ian D. C., 11 Aug. 1919. (M.)
9432 Hugill, Réne Charles, 11 Aug. 1919. (M.)
9433 Jones, Frank Murcheson, 11 Aug. 1919. (M.)
9434 Lewis, Guy Perdell, 11 Aug. 1919. (M.)
9435 Martin, Andrew, 11 Aug. 1919. (M.)
9436 Mayo, Herbert Coates, 11 Aug. 1919. (M.)
9437 Parkes, Alfred John, 11 Aug. 1919. (M.)
9438 Parry, Herbert Lyell, 11 Aug. 1919. (M.)
9439 Shipman, Frederick L., 11 Aug. 1919. (M.)
9440 Syson, John Luxmore, 11 Aug. 1919. (M.)
9441 Taylor, Hastings Elwin, 11 Aug. 1919. (M.)
9442 White, George Colvin, 11 Aug. 1919. (M.)
9443 Wickham, Evelyn Twysden, 11 Aug. 1919. (M.)
9444 Alton, Francis Cooke, 22 Aug. 1919. (M.)
9446 Barton, Samuel Saxton, 22 Aug. 1919. (M.)
9447 Beaton, Thomas, 22 Aug. 1919. (M.)
9448 Bellwood, Kenneth Bonson, 22 Aug. 1919. (M.)
9449 Blackman, William Stephen, 11 Aug. 1919. (M.)
9450 Bringan, James Campbell, 22 Aug. 1919. (M.)
9451 Brownfield, Owen Deane, 22 Aug. 1919. (M.)
9452 Buddle, Roger, 22 Aug. 1919. (M.)
9453 Burns, Henry, 22 Aug. 1919. (M.)
9454 Button, Philip Norman, 22 Aug. 1919. (M.)
9455 Campbell, John Alexander Langford, 22 Aug. 1919. (M.)
9456 Carey, Richard Stocker, 22 Aug. 1919. (M.)
9457 Clift, Hugh, 22 Aug. 1919. (M.)
9458 Dixon, Walter Ernest, 22 Aug. 1919. (M.)
9459 Duck, William Agar Scholefield, 22 Aug. 1919. (M.)
9460 Dudley, Sheldon Francis, 22 Aug. 1919. (M.)
9461 Ellis, Gordon Ernest Dormer, 22 Aug. 1919. (M.)
9462 Eykyn, Frederick Bentley, 22 Aug. 1919. (M.)
9463 Fairbank, John Gerald Atkinson, 22 Aug. 1919. (M.)
9464 Fawkes, Marmaduke, 22 Aug. 1919. (M.)
9465 Fletcher, Edward Ernest, 22 Aug. 1919. (M.)
9466 Francis, Thomas Evan, 22 Aug. 1919. (M.)
9467 Goldie, Walton Leigh Mackinnon, 22 Aug. 1919. (M.)
9468 Goss, Leslie Stewart, 22 Aug. 1919. (M.)
9469 Grimwade, Sidney Wilfred, 22 Aug. 1919. (M.)
9470 Halahan, Thomas Dufour, 22 Aug. 1919. (M.)
9471 Harker, William Edmund, 22 Aug. 1919. (M.)
9472 Herman, Ashley Ernest, 22 Aug. 1919. (M.)
9473 Holton, Ernest Charles, 22 Aug. 1919. (M.)
9474 Hughes, Cecil Hugh Myddleton, 22 Aug. 1919. (M.)
9475 Jeffery, Thomas Walter, 22 Aug. 1919. (M.)
9476 Lambert, John, 22 Aug. 1919. (M.)
9477 Lorimer, Duncan, 22 Aug. 1919. (M.)
9478 Lynch, Gerald Roche, 22 Aug. 1919. (M.)

9479 Lyster, Ronald Guy, 22 Aug. 1919. (M.)
9480 McCowen, Gerald Roche, 22 Aug. 1919. (M.)
9481 Mann, Harold Cory, 22 Aug. 1919. (M.)
9482 Margetts, Horace Palmer, 22 Aug. 1919. (M.)
9483 Martin, William Ludgate, 22 Aug. 1919. (M.)
9484 Mayne, Cyril Frederick, 22 Aug. 1919. (M.)
9485 Morris, Claude Woodham, 22 Aug. 1919. (M.)
9486 Morson, Albert Clifford, 22 Aug. 1919. (M.)
9487 Nunn, Gerald, 22 Aug. 1919. (M.)
9488 Ormsby, William Edwin, 22 Aug. 1919. (M.)
9489 Palmer, John Ramsey, 22 Aug. 1919. (M.)
9490 Parkes, Oscar, 22 Aug. 1919. (M.)
9491 Percival, Harold Fey, 22 Aug. 1919. (M.)
9492 Richardson, Alan Harvey, 22 Aug. 1919. (M.)
9493 Rodd, Montague Louis Bouchier, 22 Aug. 1919. (M.)
9494 Schlesinger, Edward Gustave, 22 Aug. 1919. (M.)
9495 Shewell, Herbert Wells Bayly, 22 Aug. 1919. (M.)
9496 Smith, Reginald Eccles, 22 Aug. 1919. (M.)
9497 Stat, Paul Hohling Mills, 22 Aug. 1919. (M.)
9498 Steegmann, Edward John, 22 Aug. 1919. (M.)
9499 Stephens, Horace Elliot Rose, 22 Aug. 1919. (M.)
9500 Stewart, Robert William Glennan, 22 Aug. 1919. (M.)
9501 Sturdee, Edwin Lawrence, 22 Aug. 1919. (M.)
9502 Sutcliffe, Percy Temple, 22 Aug. 1919. (M.)
9503 Thomas, Arthur Richard, 22 Aug. 1919. (M.)
9504 Thompson, Frederick, 22 Aug. 1919. (M.)
9505 Vickery, George Gordon, 22 Aug. 1919. (M.)
9506 Warburton, Llewellyn Rhys, 22 Aug. 1919. (M.)
9507 Warren, Leonard, 22 Aug. 1919. (M.)
9508 Wilkie, David Percival Dalbrick, 22 Aug. 1919. (M.)
9509 Willan, Robert Joseph, 22 Aug. 1919. (M.)
9510 Williams, Alfred Gregson, 22 Aug. 1919. (M.)
9511 Wills, Walter Kenneth, 22 Aug. 1919. (M.)
9512 Woods, George Edmund, 22 Aug. 1919. (M.)
9513 Allen, George Roland Gordon, 16 Sept. 1919. (M.)
9514 Andrews, Henry Osmond, 16 Sept. 1919. (M.)
9515 Baker, Frederick John, 16 Sept. 1919. (M.)
9516 Beaumont, Godfrey Lancaster, 16 Sept. 1919. (M.)
9517 Boswell, Albert Edouard, 16 Sept. 1919. (M.)
9518 Boucher, Henry Charles Russel, 16 Sept. 1919. (M.)
9519 Bullock, Charles Arthur, 16 Sept. 1919. (M.)
9520 Campbell, James Douglas, 16 Sept. 1919. (M.)
9521 Carlton, George Frederick, 16 Sept. 1919. (M.)
9522 Cator, Robert, 16 Sept. 1919. (M.)
9523 Clarke, Charles Childs, 16 Sept. 1919. (M.)
9524 Colegrave, William Henry, 16 Sept. 1919. (M.)
9525 Comber, Thomas Geoffrey, 16 Sept. 1919. (M.)
9526 Copleston, Reginald Gay, 16 Sept. 1919. (M.)
9527 Cripps, Arthur Edward William, 16 Sept. 1919. (M.)
9528 Cull, Malcolm Giffard Stebbing, 16 Sept. 1919. (M.)
9529 Demuth, Richard Harold, 16 Sept. 1919. (M.)
9530 Donohue, William James, 16 Sept. 1919. (M.)
9531 Douglas, Hon. Ronald John Walton Sholto, 16 Sept. 1919. (M.)
9532 Drake, James Woodard 16 Sept. 1010. (M.)
9533 Duncan, George Ernest, 16 Sept. 1919. (M.)
9534 Eagleton, Henry Arthur, 16 Sept. 1919. (M.)
9535 Elliott, Stephen Percy, 16 Sept. 1919. (M.)
9536 Embling, Rev. Hugh John, 16 Sept. 1919. (M.)
9537 Evans, Richard Samuel, 16 Sept. 1919. (M.)
9538 Faviell, Douglas, 16 Sept. 1919. (M.)
9540 Garrett, John Raymond, 16 Sept. 1919. (M.)
9541 Gaskell, Arthur, 16 Sept. 1919. (M.)
9542 Gibbons, Robert Reginald, 16 Sept. 1919. (M.)
9543 Gibson, Charles Mends, 16 Sept. 1919. (M.)
9544 Gibson, Isham Worsley, 16 Sept. 1919. (M.)
9545 Gordon, Walter Hamilton, 16 Sept. 1919. (M.)
9546 Green, Henry William Gordon-, 16 Sept. 1919. (M.)
9547 Graham, Charles Frederick Oliver, 16 Sept. 1919. (M.)
9548 Hail, Frederick William, 16 Sept. 1919. (M.)
9549 Harrington, Arthur George, 16 Sept. 1919. (M.)
9550 Harris, Herbert William, 16 Sept. 1919. (M.)
9551 Haszard, Henry Vivian Moore, 16 Sept. 1919. (M.)
9552 Highfield, William, 16 Sept. 1919. (M.)
9553 Homer, John Leonard, 16 Sept. 1919. (M.)
9554 Hunton, Thomas Lionel, 16 Sept. 1919. (M.)
9555 Jeffery, George Hoare, 16 Sept. 1919. (M.)
9556 Kiddle, John, 16 Sept. 1919. (M.)
9557 Lake, Atwell Henry, 16 Sept. 1919. (M.)
9558 Lambert, John Hamilton, 16 Sept. 1919. (M.)
9559 Learoyd, Leonard, 16 Sept. 1919. (M.)
9560 Logan, James Henry, 16 Sept. 1919. (M.)
9561 Mackenzie, Edward Montagu Compton, 16 Sept. 1919. (M.)
9562 New, Arthur Henry, 16 Sept. 1919. (M.)
9563 Oldham, Ronald Wolseley, 16 Sept. 1919. (M.)
9564 Owens, John Daniel, 16 Sept. 1919. (M.)
9565 Palmer, Bennet, 16 Sept. 1919. (M.)
9566 Palmer, Reginald Howard, 16 Sept. 1919. (M.)
9567 Parker, Ernest Edward, 16 Sept. 1919. (M.)
9568 Pemberton, William, 16 Sept. 1919. (M.)
9569 Philpott, Henry Goschen, 16 Sept. 1919. (M.)
9570 Pickering, Frederick, 16 Sept. 1919. (M.)
9571 Williams, Douglas Price-, 16 Sept. 1919. (M.)
9572 Pullibank, John Blackler, 16 Sept. 1919. (M.)
9573 Reade, Arthur George Lawrence, 16 Sept. 1919. (M.)
9574 Richards, Augustus Gluckstein, 16 Sept. 1919. (M.)
9575 Richardson, Charles Dene, 16 Sept. 1919. (M.)
9576 Richardson, Hugh Maclean, 16 Sept. 1919. (M.)

9577 Rogers, Hugh Hext, 16 Sept. 1919. (M.)
9578 Seccombe, Edward Arthur John, 16 Sept. 1919. (M.)
9579 Slessor, Herbert, 16 Sept. 1919. (M.)
9580 Smith, Edgar Charles, 16 Sept. 1919. (M.)
9581 Snepp, John Wansey, 16 Sept. 1919. (M.)
9582 Strange, Jack Ronald Stewart, 16 Sept. 1919. (M.)
9583 Stringer, Reginald Heber, 16 Sept. 1919. (M.)
9584 Thompson, Frederic John, 16 Sept. 1919. (M.)
9585 Weir, John, 16 Sept. 1919. (M.)
9586 Weir, Robert J., 16 Sept. 1919. (M.)
9587 Wenn, Frederick William, 16 Sept. 1919. (M.)
9588 West, William Tom, 16 Sept. 1919. (M.)
9589 Whittall, Hugh C., 16 Sept. 1919. (M.)
9590 Wood, George Albert Thomas, 16 Sept. 1919. (M.)
9591 Wyley, John Deane Newbank, 16 Sept. 1919. (M.)
9592 Yuill, Alexander Claude Roy, 16 Sept. 1919. (M.)
9593 Baker, Allan Hugh Sancroft, 10 Oct. 1919. (M.)
9594 Boyd, Owen Tudor, 10 Oct. 1919. (M.)
9595 Forbes, James Louis, 10 Oct. 1919. (M.)
9596 Kearsey, Alexander Horace Cyril, 10 Oct. 1919. (M.)
9597 Kirby, Claude, 10 Oct. 1919. (M.)
9598 Nye, Alfred Thomas Larcom, 10 Oct. 1919. (M.)
9599 Ranken, Francis, 10 Oct. 1919. (M.)
9600 Richardson, Albert Victor John, 10 Oct. 1919. (M.)
9601 Restler, James Douglas Kendall, 10 Oct. 1919. (M.)
9602 Travers, James Lindsey, 10 Oct. 1919. (M.)
9603 Davson, Ivan Buchanan, 10 Oct. 1919. (M.)
9604 Bourke, John Patrick, 10 Oct. 1919. (M.)
9605 Bowdler, Archibald Penhryn, 10 Oct. 1919. (M.)
9606 Boyle, Archibald Robert, 10 Oct. 1919. (M.)
9607 Carr, Alfred George Horsley, 10 Oct. 1919. (M.)
9608 Cherry, Ernest William Fraser, 10 Oct. 1919. (M.)
9609 Cox, Henry Ashley, 10 Oct. 1919. (M.)
9610 Guilfoyle, William James Yule, 10 Oct. 1919. (M.)
9611 Kennedy, David Henry, 10 Oct. 1919. (M.)
9612 Leith, Thomas Geoffrey, 10 Oct. 1919. (M.)
9613 Lewis, Charles Henry, 10 Oct. 1919. (M.)
9614 Lidderdale, John Henry, 10 Oct. 1919. (M.)
9615 Saunders, Edgar Stopford, 10 Oct. 1919. (M.)
9616 Stewart, Charles John, 10 Oct. 1919. (M.)
9617 Wakefield, Hugh Claude, 10 Oct. 1919. (M.)
9618 Woods, Reginald Herbert, 10 Oct. 1919. (M.)
9619 Bridgeman, Percival Cunningham Allen, 10 Oct. 1919. (M.)
9620 Clements, Edward Cecil, 10 Oct. 1919. (M.)
9621 de Francia, Jean, 10 Oct. 1919. (M.)
9622 Hartley, Arthur Clifford, 10 Oct. 1919. (M.)
9623 Hull, Tom Grove, 10 Oct. 1919. (M.)
9624 Lees, Thomas Orde Hans, 10 Oct. 1919. (M.)
9625 Macpherson, Osborne Cluny, 10 Oct. 1919. (M.)
9626 Mitchell, John Mitchell, 10 Oct. 1919. (M.)
9627 Park, William, 10 Oct. 1919. (M.)
9628 Sanders, Douglas Brooking, 10 Oct. 1919. (M.)
9629 Snape, Albert Edward, 10 Oct. 1919. (M.)
9630 Baker, Cyril Bennett, 10 Oct. 1919. (M.)
9631 Crosie, Dudley Stuart Kay, 10 Oct. 1919. (M.)
9632 Evans, Geoffrey Fanington, 10 Oct. 1919. (M.)
9633 Gordon, David, 10 Oct. 1919. (M.)
9634 Humfress, Harold Tunmer, 10 Oct. 1919. (M.)
9635 Kaye, George William Clarkson, 10 Oct. 1919. (M.)
9636 Munro, David, 10 Oct. 1919. (M.)
9637 Shepherd, George Granville, 10 Oct. 1919. (M.)
9638 Smith, William Percy, 10 Oct. 1919. (M.)
9639 Walker, John Briton, 10 Oct. 1919. (M.)
9640 Curlett, Kathleen Lottie, 10 Oct. 1919. (M.)
9641 Doughty-Wylie, Mrs. Lilian Oimara, 10 Oct. 1919. (M.)
9642 Bingham, Hon. Edward Barry Stewart, 17 Oct. 1919. (M.)
9643 Bishop, Walter George, 17 Oct. 1919. (M.)
9644 Causton, Joseph, 17 Oct. 1919. (M.)
9645 Clavell, Richard Charles, 17 Oct. 1919. (M.)
9646 Cope, Lidbrooke Frank, 17 Oct. 1919. (M.)
9647 Craig, Archibald Maxwell, 17 Oct. 1919. (M.)
9648 Cross, James, 17 Oct. 1919. (M.)
9649 Fitch, Henry Maldon, 17 Oct. 1919. (M.)
9650 Gedye, Nicholas George, 17 Oct. 1919. (M.)
9651 Hewitt, Heathcote George, 17 Oct. 1919. (M.)
9652 Hind, Norman Sinclair, 17 Oct. 1919. (M.)
9653 Key, George, 17 Oct. 1919. (M.)
9654 Macdonald, Malcolm Henry Somerled, 17 Oct. 1919. (M.)
9655 Palmer, William, 17 Oct. 1919. (M.)
9656 Phillips, Algernon Wynn Pendennis, 17 Oct. 1919. (M.)
9657 Prendergast, Edmund James, 17 Oct. 1919. (M.)
9658 Rankin, Francis James, 17 Oct. 1919. (M.)
9659 Scaife, John Andrew Hanson, 17 Oct. 1919. (M.)
9660 Struben, Charles Frederick William, 17 Oct. 1919. (M.)
9661 Taylor, Alfred Hugh, 17 Oct. 1919. (M.)
9662 Whitfield, Paul, 17 Oct. 1919. (M.)
9663 Banks, Francis Rodwell, 11 Nov. 1919. (M.)
9664 Coombs, Thomas Edward, 11 Nov. 1919. (M.)
9665 Douglas, James, 11 Nov. 1919. (M.)
9666 Franks, Maurice Cardinall, 11 Nov. 1919. (M.)
9667 Greig, Alexander Collie, 11 Nov. 1919. (M.)
9668 Hay, Hon. Sereld Mordaunt, Alan Joscelyn, 11 Nov. 1919. (M.)
9369 Lawrance, Kenneth Edward, 11 Nov. 1919. (M.)
9670 Malcolm, Pulteney William, 11 Nov. 1919. (M.)
9671 Millar, Frank Ernest, 11 Nov. 1919. (M.)
9672 Parnell, Gerald Langston, 11 Nov. 1919. (M.)
9673 Privett, George John, 11 Nov. 1919. (M.)

9674 Robinson, Eric Gascoigne, 11 Nov. 1919. (M.)
9675 Shadwell, Lancelot Horace Augustus, 11 Nov. 1919. (M.)
9676 Woodcock, George Cyril, 11 Nov. 1919. (M.)
9677 Acton, William Cawley, 11 Nov. 1919. (M.)
9678 Arnold, Allan Cholmondeley, 11 Nov. 1919. (M.)
9679 Baxter, George, 11 Nov. 1919. (M.)
9680 Borland, James Henry George, 11 Nov. 1919. (M.)
9681 Brown, James Parry, 11 Nov. 1919. (M.)
9682 Bunce, William Leslie, 11 Nov. 1919. (M.)
9683 Candy, Cairns, 11 Nov. 1919. (M.)
9684 Clarke, William James, 11 Nov. 1919. (M.)
9685 Brown, George Conway-, 11 Nov. 1919. (M.)
9686 Crossman, Robert Francis, 11 Nov. 1919. (M.)
9687 Curwen, John Spedding, 11 Nov. 1919. (M.)
9688 Dawes. Henry Halford, 11 Nov. 1919. (M.)
9689 Garratt, Clarence Herbert, 11 Nov. 1919. (M.)
9690 Gordon, Grahame Masey, 11 Nov. 1919. (M.)
9691 Graham, Joseph William, 11 Nov. 1919. (M.)
9692 Hull, Gordon Burnett Gifford, 11 Nov. 1919. (M.)
9693 Irwin, Alfred William Adamson, 11 Nov. 1919. (M.)
9694 Lake, Bruce Launcelot, 11 Nov. 1919. (M.)
9695 Lund, George Percy, 11 Nov. 1919. (M.)
9696 Macadam, Ivison Stevonson, 11 Nov. 1919. (M.)
9697 McBride, Stuart George, 11 Nov. 1919. (M.)
9698 Mackenzie, Kenneth Davidson, 11 Nov. 1919. (M.)
9699 McLeod, Leonard Frederick, 11 Nov. 1919. (M.)
9700 Murray, William Alexander Kininmouth, 11 Nov. 1919. (M.)
9701 Musgrave, Bernard, 11 Nov. 1919. (M.)
9702 Neighbour, Sidney William, 11 Nov. 1919. (M.)
9703 Poignant, Axel Jonas Alfred, 11 Nov. 1919. (M.)
9704 Rahilly, John Maurice Bisdee, 11 Nov. 1919. (M.)
9705 Richmond, Thomas Heyliger, 11 Nov. 1919. (M.)
9706 Smith, James, 11 Nov. 1919. (M.)
9707 Strachan, Ernest Frederick, 11 Nov. 1919. (M.)
9708 Swan, Robert Arthur, 11 Nov. 1919. (M.)
9709 Uniacke, Cecil Dudley Woodgate, 11 Nov. 1919. (M.)
9710 Willson, Christopher, 11 Nov. 1919. (M.)
9711 Woodruffe, John Sheldon, 11 Nov. 1919. (M.)
9712 Addington, Lord, 11 Nov. 1919. (M.)
9713 Andrews, Albion Ernest, 11 Nov. 1919. (M.)
9714 Bellamy, Hugh Maurice, 11 Nov. 1919. (M.)
9715 Dale, William Henry, 11 Nov. 1919. (M.)
9716 Dobb, Harry Raymond, 11 Nov. 1919. (M.)
9717 Franklin, Herbert Joseph, 11 Nov. 1919. (M.)
9718 Hewson, Frank Lloyd, 11 Nov. 1919. (M.)
9719 Keane, Charles George Gordon, 11 Nov. 1919. (M.)
9720 Lewis, Edward Trevor, 11 Nov. 1919. (M.)
9721 Macklin, Alexander Hepburn, 11 Nov. 1919. (M.)
9722 Palmer, Charles Ernest, 11 Nov. 1919. (M.)
9723 Pringle, Charles Herford, 11 Nov. 1919. (M.)
9724 Robertson, Colin John Trevelyan, 11 Nov. 1919. (M.)
9725 Samuelson, Cecil Llewellyn, 11 Nov. 1919. (M.)
9726 Sandison, John Forbes William, 11 Nov. 1919. (M.)
9727 Smyth, Bernard Owen, 11 Nov. 1919. (M.)
9728 Somerville, Thomas Victor, 11 Nov. 1919. (M.)
9729 Sweetman, Gerald Drysdale, 11 Nov. 1919. (M.)
9730 Thompson, Jacob Jewett, 11 Nov. 1919. (M.)
9731 Walker. George Croxton, 11 Nov. 1919. (M.)
9732 Ward, Horace Edward, 11 Nov. 1919. (M.)
9733 Allen, Edmund Drury, 11 Nov. 1919. (M.)
9734 Bavin. Arthur Julian Walter, 11 Nov. 1919. (M.)
9735 Greenslade, Cyrus, 11 Nov. 1919. (M.)
9736 Beal, Richard Edward Bruce, 11 Nov. 1919. (M.)
9737 Butcher, Trevor Aveling, 11 Nov. 1919. (M.)
9738 Carter, John Reginald, 11 Nov. 1919. (M.)
9739 Craig, Hugh Morton, 11 Nov. 1919. (M.)
9740 Donovan, Thomas, 11 Nov. 1919. (M.)
9741 Douglas, George Robert Poynter, 11 Nov. 1919. (M.)
9742 Edwards, Reginald Owen, 11 Nov. 1919. (M.)
9743 Forwood, Harry, 11 Nov. 1919. (M.)
9744 Fox, Thomas Laurence, 11 Nov. 1919. (M.)
9745 Kent, Wilfred Francis, 11 Nov. 1919. (M.)
9746 Lumsden, Reginald Lewis, 11 Nov. 1919. (M.)
9747 Owen, Richard, 11 Nov. 1919. (M.)
9748 Prickett, Frederick Cecil, 11 Nov. 1919. (M.)
9749 Smith, Harry Cyril, 11 Nov. 1919. (M.)
9750 Stamp, Arthur Frederick, 11 Nov. 1919. (M.)
9751 Tapp, Harold Astley, 11 Nov. 1919. (M.)
9752 Taylor, Robert Allan Grant, 11 Nov. 1919. (M.)
9753 Tee, Charles Clifford, 11 Nov. 1919. (M.)
9754 Thompson. John Foster, 11 Nov. 1919. (M.)
9755 Tinkler, Lionel Maughan, 11 Nov. 1919. (M.)
9756 Twitchin, Nathaniel Edwards, 11 Nov. 1919. (M.)
9757 Wheeler, Roy Lambert, 11 Nov. 1919. (M.)
9758 Aldworth, Thomas Preston, 15 Nov. 1919. (M.)
9759 Collins, Hugh Michael, 15 Nov. 1919. (M.)
9760 Duncan, Henry Clare, 15 Nov. 1919. (M.)
9761 Faris, John George, 15 Nov. 1919. (M.)
9762 Grant, James Forgan, 15 Nov. 1919. (M.)
9763 Holliday, John Cecil Hamilton, 15 Nov. 1919. (M.)
9764 Maturin, Hugh Geoffrey, 15 Nov. 1919. (M.)
9765 Spitteler, Alfred, 15 Nov. 1919. (M.)
9767 Ring, James Sinclair, Henry 28 Nov. 1919. (M.)
9768 Rutherford, Zerube Baillie, 28 Nov. 1919. (M.)
9769 Mohammed Bey Wifki, El Kaimakam, 26 Nov. 1919. (M.)
9770 Mohammed Effendi Shahin, Bimbashi, 26 Nov. 1919. (M.)
9771 Wild, Robert Vaughan, 5 Dec. 1919.
9772 Russell, Thomas Wentworth, 5 Dec. 1919.

9773 Marshall, John MacMillan, 5 Dec. 1919.
9774 Ingram, Alexander Gordon, 5 Dec. 1919.
9775 Wise, Alexander, 5 Dec. 1919.
9776 Dowson, Kenneth, 5 Dec. 1919.
9777 Job, Herbert Shipley, 5 Dec. 1919.
9778 Struve, Kenneth Chetwood Price, 5 Dec. 1919.
9779 Lyall, Charles Elliott, 5 Dec. 1919.
9780 More, Richard Edwardes, 5 Dec. 1919.
9781 Browne, Cecil Pownall, 5 Dec. 1919.
9782 Craig, James Douglas, 5 Dec. 1919.
9783 Burges, Frank, 5 Dec. 1919.
9784 Flint, Samuel Kirk, 5 Dec. 1919.
9785 Brown, Cecil Thomas, 12 Dec. 1919. (M.)
9786 Carson, John Findlay, 12 Dec. 1919. (M.)
9787 Dunkley, Stanley Fitzroy, 12 Dec. 1919. (M.)
9788 Hammond, William Charles Thomas, 12 Dec. 1919. (M.
9789 Hudson, John Augustine, 12 Dec. 1919. (M.)
9790 Langley, Gerald Maxwell Bradshaw, 12 Dec. 1919. (M.)
9791 Lockett, Herbert Anthony, 12 Dec. 1919. (M.)
9792 McGiffin, Robert Hunter, 12 Dec. 1919. (M.)
9793 Roch, Sydney George, 12 Dec. 1919. (M.)
9794 Sanders, Arthur Addison, 12 Dec. 1919. (M.)
9795 Wickham, Frederick St. Barbe, 12 Dec. 1919. (M.)
9796 Pritchard, Isabel Lace, Mrs., 12 Dec. 1919. (M.)
9797 Merritt, George, 12 Dec. 1919. (M.)
9798 Balmer, Ruth, 22 Dec. 1919. (M.)
9799 Carey, Alfred David, 22 Dec. 1919. (M.)
9800 Christmas, Jessie, Mrs.. 22 Dec. 1919. (M.)
9801 de Ville, Edward Alexander de Lossy, 22 Dec. 1919. (M.)
9802 MacLaren, Archibald Stuart Charles Stuart-, 22 Dec. 1919. (M.)
9803 Roe, Robert Lloyd, 22 Dec. 1919. (M.)
9804 Armitage, Louisa Mary, 30 Dec. 1919.
9805 Baker, Conyers, 30 Dec. 1919.
9806 Blanford, Harry Richard, 30 Dec. 1919.
9807 Cassels, Walter Seton, 30 Dec. 1919.
9808 Chand, Lala Ratan, 30 Dec. 1919.
9809 Chettle, Lisbeth, Mrs., 30 Dec. 1919.
9810 Clayton, Rev. Albert Charles, 30 Dec. 1919.
9811 Colvin, Clement Preston, 30 Dec. 1919.
9812 Crawford, Frederick Leslie, 30 Dec. 1919.
9813 Curtis, Agnes Eleanor. Lady, 30 Dec. 1919.
9814 Deo, Raja Chandrashekar Prasad Singh, 30 Dec. 1919.
9815 Dobholkar, Visantrao Annandrao, 30 Dec. 1919.
9816 Douglas, Helen Mary Isabel, Mrs., 30 Dec. 1919.
9817 Du Bern, Jules Emile, 30 Dec. 1919.
9818 Gayer, Mary Hazell, Mrs.. 30 Dec. 1919.
9819 Gleeson, Edward John, 30 Dec. 1919.
9820 Gray, John, 30 Dec. 1919.
9821 Ullah, Muhammed Habib-, 30 Dec. 1919.
9822 Hale, William Stather, 30 Dec. 1919.
9823 Hall, John Frederick, 30 Dec. 1919.
9824 Hezlett, Mary Kathleen, Mrs., 30 Dec. 1919.
9825 Hibberd, Julia Florence, 30 Dec. 1919.
9826 Holder, Charles Howard, 30 Dec. 1919.
9827 Kemball, Hattie, Lady, 30 Dec. 1919.
9828 Khan, Nawab Shaikh Ahmad Husain, 30 Dec. 1919.
9829 Khan, Khan Sahib Shah Nawaz, 30 Dec. 1919.
9830 Lapraik, John, 30 Dec. 1919.
9831 Latifii, Alma, 30 Dec. 1919.
9832 Lea, Measham, 30 Dec. 1919.
9833 Lincoln, Cecil Henning, 30 Dec. 1919.
9834 Lupton, Walter James Edwin, 30 Dec. 1919.
9835 Malan, Charles Huntingford, 30 Dec. 1919.
9836 Messa, Banin Menahem, 30 Dec. 1919.
9837 Neilson, William Hardcastle, 30 Dec. 1919.
9838 Newby, Styan, 30 Dec. 1919.
9839 Grace, Mrs. Norie. 30 Dec. 1919.
9840 Parlby, Joshua, 30 Dec. 1919.
9841 Prasad, Rai Ashtbhuja, 30 Dec. 1919.
9842 Prasad, Raja Lalta, 30 Dec. 1919.
9843 Smith, Montague Bentley Talbot Paske-, 30 Dec. 1919.
9844 Patel, Khan Bahadur Burjorji Dorabji, 30 Dec. 1919.
9845 Philipe, George William Vitalli de Rhe, 30 Dec. 1919.
9846 Powell, Samuel Arthur, 30 Dec. 1919.
9847 Price, Edwin Lessware, 30 Dec. 1919.
9848 Prideaux, Constance Mary, Mrs., 30 Dec. 1919.
9849 Sahib, Khan Bahadur Muhammad Bazlullah, 30 Dec. 1919.
9850 Singh, Raja Partab Bahadur, 30 Dec. 1919.
9851 Singh, Rai Bahadur Kunwar Bharat, 30 Dec. 1919.
9852 Singh, Rai Bahadur Suraj Baksh, 30 Dec. 1919.
9853 Singh, Sardar Bahadur Sardar Dal, 30 Dec. 1919.
9854 Stones, Frederick, 30 Dec. 1919.
9855 Suttie, Peter Edwin, 30 Dec. 1919.
9856 Tallack, Charles Michael, 30 Dec. 1919.
9857 Tasker, Theodore James, 30 Dec. 1919.
9858 Thaper, Rai Bahadur Kunj Behari, 30 Dec. 1919.
9859 Williams, Lawrence Frederic Rushbrook, 30 Dec. 1919.
9860 Wright, Arthur, 30 Dec. 1919.
9861 Wyness, Ada, Mrs., 30 Dec. 1919.
9862 Young, James Wolstan, 30 Dec. 1919.
9863 Barber, Richard Alexander, 1 Jan. 1920.
9864 Kelham, Bimbashi Robert Arthur Langdale, 1 Jan. 1920.
9865 Abbott, George Edward, 1 Jan. 1920.
9866 Abbott, Joseph Edward, 1 Jan. 1920.
9867 Abell, Thomas Bertrand, 1 Jan. 1920.
9868 Abraham, John William, 1 Jan. 1920.
9869 Acfield, Wilfred Cosens, 1 Jan. 1920.

OFFICERS.

9870 Adams, Arthur Botwell, 1 Jan. 1920.
9871 Adams, Edward William, 1 Jan. 1920.
9872 Adams, William, 1 Jan. 1920.
9873 Adams, William John, 1 Jan. 1920.
9874 Addington, Maud Florence, 1 Jan. 1920.
9875 Adeane, Jean Henrietta, 1 Jan. 1920.
9876 Aitken, David Jeffrey, 1 Jan. 1920.
9877 Aldridge, Allen Garnies, 1 Jan. 1920.
9878 Aldridge, Samuel Kendrick, 1 Jan. 1920.
9879 Alexander, George Edward, 1 Jan. 1920.
9880 Alexander, James Young, 1 Jan. 1920.
9881 Rose, Mrs. Alexander, 1 Jan. 1920.
9882 Allan, Edith Mary, Lady Havelock-, 1 Jan. 1920.
9883 Allan, Herbert William, 1 Jan. 1920.
9884 Allan, Jessie Whyte, 1 Jan. 1920.
9885 Allcock, William Barnes, 1 Jan. 1920.
9886 Allen, Arthur Denby, 1 Jan. 1920.
9887 Allen, Percy Ruskin, 1 Jan. 1920.
9888 Allen, Stella Ada May, 1 Jan. 1920.
9889 Allibone, Abraham Cory, 1 Jan. 1920.
9890 Allison John Neve, 1 Jan. 1920.
9891 Amory, Alexandra, Lady Heathcoat-, 1 Jan. 1920.
9892 Amos, Mary Beatrice, 1 Jan. 1920.
9893 Ancaster, Eloise Lawrence, Countess of, 1 Jan. 1920.
9894 Anderson, Charles John, 1 Jan. 1920.
9895 Andrew, Rev G. Findlay, 1 Jan. 1920.
9896 Angier, Frederick Leigh, 1 Jan. 1920.
9897 Annand. John Fowler, 1 Jan. 1920.
9898 Antrobus, George Pollock, 1 Jan. 1920.
9899 Arbuthnot, Evelyn Mary, 1 Jan. 1920.
9900 Archer, William David, 1 Jan. 1920.
9901 Argles, Agnes, Mrs., 1 Jan. 1920.
9902 Arkle, Arthur Henry, 1 Jan. 1920.
9903 Arman, Edward William James, 1 Jan. 1920.
9904 Armitage Stanley Holt, 1 Jan. 1920.
9905 Armstrong, John Henry Nicholas, 1 Jan. 1920.
9906 Arnold, Alfred Henry, 1 Jan. 1920.
9907 Arthur, Rev. John William, 1 Jan. 1920.
9908 Ash, Alfred James, 1 Jan. 1920.
9909 Ashford, William, 1 Jan. 1920.
9910 Ashton, Antonio, 1 Jan. 1920.
9911 Astle, William, 1 Jan. 1920.
9912 Atcheson, William, 1 Jan. 1920.
9913 Aylmer, Arthur Lintott, 1 Jan. 1920
9914 Bacon, Rupert Alfred, 1 Jan. 1920.
9915 Van Baerle, Edward Thomas William, 1 Jan. 1920.
9916 Bagshaw, William, 1 Jan. 1920.
9917 Bailey, Edwin Benjamin, 1 Jan. 1920.
9918 Bailey, Harold James, 1 Jan. 1920.
9919 Baillie, Ronald Hugh, 1 Jan. 1920.
9920 Baily, Joseph Macdonald, 1 Jan. 1920.
9921 Bain, Mary Jane, Mrs., 1 Jan. 1920.
9922 Baird, Malcolm, 1 Jan. 1920.
9923 Baiss, Llewelyn Arnold, 1 Jan. 1920.
9924 Baker, Edward Charles Stuart, 1 Jan. 1920.
9925 Baker, John Edgar, 1 Jan. 1920.
9926 Balfour, David, 1 Jan. 1920.
9927 Ball, William Theodore 1 Jan. 1920.
9928 Ballantyne, John, 1 Jan. 1920.
9929 Bamber, Herbert, 1 Jan. 1920.
9930 Banister, John, 1 Jan. 1920.
9931 Banner, Allan William, 1 Jan. 1920.
9932 Bantoft, William, 1 Jan. 1920.
9933 Barclay, Alfred Ernest, 1 Jan. 1920.
9934 Barclay, Jeanie, Mrs. Coats, 1 Jan. 1920.
9935 Barclay, William Robb, 1 Jan. 1920.
9936 Barnacle, Arthur Henry, 1 Jan. 1920.
9937 Barnard, Edmund Broughton, 1 Jan. 1920.
9938 Barnes, Edgar George, 1 Jan. 1920.
9939 Barnes, Leonard Stewart, 1 Jan. 1920.
9940 Barnes, Mary Elizabeth, Mrs. 1 Jan. 1920.
9941 Barrie, David Watson, 1 Jan. 1920.
9942 Barron, Rev. Douglas Gordon, 1 Jan. 1920.
9943 Bartholomew, Clarence Edward, 1 Jan. 1920.
9944 Barton, Ernest Mortlock, 1 Jan. 1920.
9945 Bartram, Euphemia Walker, Mrs., 1 Jan. 1920.
9946 Bass, Edith, 1 Jan. 1920.
9947 Bassett, Arthur Tilney, 1 Jan. 1920.
9948 Bassom, Arthur Ernest, 1 Jan. 1920.
9949 Batchelor, John William, 1 Jan. 1920.
9950 Batchelor, Mary Anne Northway, Mrs., 1 Jan. 1920.
9951 Bate, Henry Francis, 1 Jan. 1920.
9952 Bates, Lilian Douglas, Mrs., 1 Jan. 1920.
9953 Bates, Thomas Edward Bowen, 1 Jan. 1920.
9954 Bates, William Richard, 1 Jan. 1920.
9955 Bathurst, Frederick Marlay, 1 Jan. 1920.
9956 Bathurst, Katharine Mary Delicia, Lady Hervey-, 1 Jan. 1920.
9957 Batty, Edmund, 1 Jan. 1920.
9958 Baxter, Fane Fleming, 1 Jan. 1920.
9959 Bayford, Robert Frederic, 1 Jan. 1920.
9960 Baynes, Edward William, 1 Jan. 1920.
9961 Beard, Marian Gertrude, 1 Jan. 1920.
9962 Beardmore, Joseph George, 1 Jan. 1920.
9963 Beath, David Leslie, 1 Jan. 1920.
9964 Beatty, Andrew Henry, 1 Jan. 1920.
9965 Beavan, Francis John, 1 Jan. 1920.
9966 Audsley-Beaver, Ida Scott, 1 Jan. 1920.
9967 Bebb, Herbert Llewellyn Mountfort, 1 Jan. 1920.

9968 Beckwith, Arthur, 1 Jan. 1920.
9969 Beddington, Reginald, 1 Jan. 1920.
9970 Beer, Lina, Mrs., 1 Jan. 1920.
9971 Begg, Alexander Clarke, 1 Jan. 1920.
9972 Belben, Frank, 1 Jan. 1920.
9973 Belchamber, Frederick Augustus, 1 Jan. 1920.
9974 Bell, Andrew Riddell, 1 Jan. 1920.
9975 Bell, Harold Idris, 1 Jan. 1920.
9976 Bell, Robert Arthur, 1 Jan. 1920.
9977 Bell, Thomas Norman Jarvis, 1 Jan. 1920.
9978 Bendall, James Lucas, 1 Jan. 1920.
9979 Bennett, James William, 1 Jan. 1920.
9980 Bennett, Peter Frederick Blaker, 1 Jan. 1920.
9981 Berisford, Harold, 1 Jan. 1920.
9982 Berry, Arthur, 1 Jan. 1920.
9983 Berry, Harry Poole, 1 Jan. 1920.
9984 Berry, William, 1 Jan. 1920.
9985 Bersey, Stanley Howard, 1 Jan. 1920.
9986 Bethell, Phyllis Mary Hermoine, 1 Jan. 1920.
9987 Bevan, Edwyn Robert, 1 Jan. 1920.
9988 Bevan, Ernest Alltree, 1 Jan. 1920.
9989 Bickersteth John Joseph, 1 Jan. 1920.
9990 Biddulph, Eleanor, Lady, 1 Jan. 1920.
9991 Bingham, Constance Gwendoline, 1 Jan. 1920.
9992 Bingley, Robert Noel Glanville, 1 Jan. 1920.
9993 Bird, William John Butterworth, 1 Jan. 1920.
9994 Birkett, Annie, 1 Jan. 1920.
9995 Bisacre, Frederick Francis Percival, 1 Jan. 1920.
9996 Bishop, Charles Arthur, 1 Jan. 1920.
9997 Bishop, Rosa Ethel, Mrs., 1 Jan. 1920.
9998 Blackburn, Robert, 1 Jan. 1920.
9999 Blackley, Lucy Ida, Mrs., 1 Jan. 1920.
10,000 Blakey, George, 1 Jan. 1920.
10,001 Blaxland, George Thomas, 1 Jan. 1920.
10,002 Blennerhasset, Nesta Georgie, 1 Jan. 1920.
10,003 Bliss, Gertrude Alice, 1 Jan. 1920.
10,004 Blount, Edward Charles Aston Marle, 1 Jan. 1920.
10,005 Bloye, George Herbert, 1 Jan. 1920.
10,006 Blunt, Rev. Arthur Stanley Vaughan, 1 Jan. 1920.
10,007 Boden, Oliver, 1 Jan. 1920.
10,008 Boggon, Richard Octavius, 1 Jan. 1920.
10,009 Bolt, George, 1 Jan. 1920.
10,010 Bolter, Henry James, 1 Jan. 1920.
10,011 Bond, John, 1 Jan. 1920.
10,012 Bond, Nigel de Mandeville, 1 Jan. 1920.
10,013 Bond, Reginald Francis George, 1 Jan. 1920.
10,014 Bonsey, Harold Robert Yerburgh-, 1 Jan. 1920.
10,015 Bonus, Florence, Mrs., 1 Jan. 1920.
10,016 Boobyer, John Edwards, 1 Jan. 1920.
10,017 Booth, Frederic Lancelot, 1 Jan. 1920.
10,018 Booth, John, 1 Jan. 1920.
10,019 Borthwick, Jemina, 1 Jan. 1920.
10,020 Bott, Henry, 1 Jan. 1920.
10,021 Bottomley, Francis Carr, 1 Jan. 1920.
10,022 Boulding, Richard Sidney Henry, 1 Jan. 1920.
10,023 Bourke, Hon. Terence Theobald, 1 Jan. 1920.
10,024 Bousfield, Edith Margaret, Mrs., 1 Jan. 1920.
10,025 Bower, Beatrice Lilian Chivars, 1 Jan. 1920.
10,026 Bowes, Elizabeth, Mrs., 1 Jan. 1920.
10,027 Bowis, William John, 1 Jan. 1920.
10,028 Bownas, Francis Osborne, 1 Jan. 1920.
10,029 Bowyer, John Charles, 1 Jan. 1920.
10,030 Boys, Walter Guy Robert, 1 Jan. 1920.
10,031 Bradwell, William Howard, 1 Jan. 1920.
10,032 Brady, Rev. Canon Henry Westby, 1 Jan. 1920.
10,033 Branch, Charles Churchill, 1 Jan. 1920.
10,034 Brass, Thomas Francis, 1 Jan. 1920.
10,035 Brayden, William John Henry, 1 Jan. 1920.
10,036 Breach, William Hall, 1 Jan. 1920.
10,037 Brett, Rev. William, 1 Jan. 1920.
10,038 Brewer, Frederic William, 1 Jan. 1920.
10,039 Brewer, Griffith, 1 Jan. 1920.
10,040 Briggs, Albert, 1 Jan. 1920.
10,041 Briggs, Henry, 1 Jan. 1920.
10,042 Briggs, William, 1 Jan. 1920.
10,043 Brightman, Frank, 1 Jan. 1920.
10,044 Brocklebank, Thomas Harlehurst, 1 Jan. 1920.
10,045 Brodie, Caroline Violet Mary, Mrs. Brodie of, 1 Jan. 1920.
10,046 Brooke, John Walter, 1 Jan. 1920.
10,047 Brookes, Albert Edward, 1 Jan. 1920.
10,048 Brooks, Ernest, 1 Jan. 1920.
10,049 Brooy, Amelia Fanny, Mrs. La, 1 Jan. 1920.
10,050 Brousson, Robert Parey, 1 Jan. 1920.
10,051 Brown, Alice Elizabeth, Mrs., 1 Jan. 1920.
10,052 Brown, Edward Walter, 1 Jan. 1920.
10,053 Brown, Frederick Benjamin, 1 Jan. 1920.
10,054 Brown, Herbert Henry, 1 Jan. 1920.
10,055 Brown, Janet Gilmour, 1 Jan. 1920.
10,056 Brown, Robert Campbell, 1 Jan. 1920.
10,057 Brown, Simon Stubbs, 1 Jan. 1920.
10,058 Brown, Tom, 1 Jan. 1920.
10,059 Browne, Gerald Macleay, 1 Jan. 1920.
10,060 Browne, Henry William Langley, 1 Jan. 1920.
10,061 Brownfield, Harry Munyard, 1 Jan. 1920.
10,062 Browning, Harry, 1 Jan. 1920.
10,063 Bruce, John Charles, 1 Jan. 1920.
10,064 Bruce, Mary Elizabeth, Lady, 1 Jan. 1920.
10,065 Bruce, Robert Arthur, 1 Jan. 1920.

2 T

10,066 Bruce, William Joseph, 1 Jan. 1920.
10,067 Brunton, John Dixon, 1 Jan. 1920.
10,068 Brydone, James Marr, 1 Jan. 1920.
10,069 Bryett, Henry, 1 Jan. 1920.
10,070 Buchanan, Robert John, 1 Jan. 1920.
10,071 Buckingham, James Frank, 1 Jan. 1920.
10,072 Buckley, Arthur Burton, 1 Jan. 1920.
10,073 Buckley, James William, 1 Jan. 1920.
10,074 Buckmaster, Harry Cuthbert. 1 Jan. 1920.
10,075 Buckmaster, William, 1 Jan. 1920.
10,076 Bull, George Frederick, 1 Jan. 1920.
10,077 Bull, Thomas Tollemache Jackson, 1 Jan. 1920.
10,078 Buller, Hon. Lilah Constance, Lady Manningham-, 1 Jan. 1920.
10,079 Bullwinkle, Leonard Albert. 1 Jan. 1920.
10,080 Bundock, Charles Slade, 1 Jan. 1920.
10,081 Burden, Albert Edmund Charles, 1 Jan. 1920.
10,082 Burke, Fred, 1 Jan. 1920.
10,083 Burleigh, Cecil Charles, 1 Jan. 1920.
10,084 Burrage, Cyril Charles Webb, 1 Jan. 1920.
10,085 Burrell, Frederic William White, 1 Jan. 1920.
10,086 Burridge, Arthur, 1 Jan. 1920.
10,087 Burton, William John, 1 Jan. 1920.
10,088 Bury, Ernest, 1 Jan. 1920.
10,089 Butler, Mildred Mary, Mrs., 1 Jan. 1920.
10,090 Butler, Samuel Flowers, 1 Jan. 1920.
10,091 Buxton Alfred Mellor, 1 Jan. 1920.
10,092 Buxton, Violet, Mrs., 1 Jan. 1920.
10,093 Bygrave, William Thomas, 1 Jan. 1920.
10,094 Byrne, Violet Julia, 1 Jan. 1920.
10,095 Bythell, William James Storey, 1 Jan. 1920.
10,096 Cabrol, Dom Fernand, Lord Abbot of the Order of Benedictines, 1 Jan. 1920.
10,097 Call, Hamilton, 1 Jan. 1920.
10,098 Calladine, Ernest Thompson, 1 Jan. 1920.
10,099 Callard, Cuthbert Richard, 1 Jan. 1920.
10,100 Callender, Edward Henry William, 1 Jan. 1920.
10,101 Calwell, William, 1 Jan 1920.
10,102 Campbell, Archibald, 1 Jan. 1920.
10,103 Campbell, Charles Ivor Rae, 1 Jan. 1920.
10,104 Campbell, Colin. 1 Jan. 1920.
10,105 Campbell, Duncan, of Inverneill, 1 Jan. 1920.
10,106 Campbell, Emily, Mrs. Muirhead, 1 Jan. 1920.
10,107 Campbell, James Alexander West, 1 Jan. 1920.
10,108 Campbell, John Arthur, 1 Jan. 1920.
10,109 Campbell, John St. Clair, 1 Jan. 1920.
10,110 Campion, Edwin William, 1 Jan. 1920.
10,111 Cannell, Harry Hardman, 1 Jan. 1920.
10,112 Canning, Joseph Herbert, 1 Jan. 1920.
10,113 Capstick, John Walton, 1 Jan. 1920.
10,114 Cardew George Arthur, 1 Jan. 1920.
10,115 Carlton, Thomas, 1 Jan. 1920.
10,116 Carmichael, Evelyn George Massey, 1 Jan. 1920.
10,117 Carmichael. Montgomery, 1 Jan. 1920.
10,118 Carnegie, Edward Hugo Wakefield Fullerton-, 1 Jan. 1920.
10,119 Carnegie, Francis, 1 Jan. 1920.
10,120 Carpenter, Alexander Scott Jarvis, 1 Jan. 1920.
10,121 Carr, Mary, 1 Jan. 1920.
10,122 Carter, Eustace George, 1 Jan. 1920.
10,123 Carter, Rei Alfred Deakin, 1 Jan. 1920.
10,124 Carter. Stanley Bronislaw, 1 Jan. 1920.
10,125 Cary, Arthur Deering Lucius, 1 Jan. 1920.
10,126 Cass, Gertrude Margaret Carew, 1 Jan. 1920.
10,127 Catmur, Benjamin, 1 Jan. 1920.
10,128 Cave, Wilhelmina Mary Henrietta, Mrs., 1 Jan. 1920.
10 129 Caw, William Strathie, 1 Jan. 1920.
10,130 Chalmers, Jessie Elder, Mrs., 1 Jan. 1920.
10,131 Chalmers, Robert, 1 Jan. 1920.
10,132 Chapman, Edward Stuart, 1 Jan. 1920.
10,133 Chapman, Harry Ernest, 1 Jan. 1920.
10,134 Chapman, John Barnett, 1 Jan. 1920.
10,135 Chapman, Oswald Cotton, 1 Jan. 1920.
10 136 Chapman, Richard Herbert, 1 Jan. 1920.
10,137 Chapman, Walter, 1 Jan. 1920.
10,138 Charleson, Bruno Arthur, 1 Jan. 1920.
10,139 Charrington, John Douglas, 1 Jan. 1920.
10,140 Chave, Benjamin, 1 Jan. 1920.
10,141 Chaytor, Herbert Stanley, 1 Jan. 1920.
10,142 Cheetham, Rev. Robert Darbyshire, 1 Jan. 1920.
10,143 Chichester, Shane Randolph, 1 Jan. 1920.
10,144 Chilver, James Thomas, 1 Jan. 1920.
10,145 Chipman. Leontine, 1 Jan. 1920.
10,146 Cholmondeley, Winifred Ida, Marchioness of, 1 Jan. 1920.
10,147 Christian, Edward Hompesch, 1 Jan. 1920.
10,148 Christian, Louis de Bylandt, 1 Jan. 1920.
10,149 Christie, James Robertson, 1 Jan, 1920.
10,150 Christie, John Cubie. 1 Jan. 1920.
10,151 Churchill, Augusta, Lady Edward Spencer-, 1 Jan. 1920.
10,152 Churton, Ethel Blanche, Mrs., 1 Jan. 1920.
10,153 Clapcott, Charles Blackstone, 1 Jan. 1920.
10,154 Clark, Edward Mellish, 1 Jan. 1920.
10,155 Clayton, William Ellis, 1 Jan. 1920.
10,156 Clonbrock, Augusta Caroline, Lady, 1 Jan. 1920.
10,157 Clouston, Thomas Harold, 1 Jan. 1920.
10,158 Clower, William, 1 Jan. 1920.
10,159 Clowes, Mina Maud Dacre, Mrs., 1 Jan. 1920.

10,160 Clubb, Leonard, 1 Jan. 1920.
10,161 Coats, Marie Jeanne, Lady, 1 Jan. 1920.
10,162 Cobbold, Alfred Townshend, 1 Jan. 1920.
10,163 Cults, Gertrude Julia Georgina, Baroness Cochrane of, 1 Jan. 1920.
10,164 Cockburn, Charles, 1 Jan. 1920.
10,165 Cockburn, John Henry, 1 Jan. 1920.
10,166 Cockell, Norman Alexander Lindsey, 1 Jan. 1920.
10,167 Cockerell, John Pepys, 1 Jan. 1920.
10,168 Cockerell, Leslie Maurice, 1 Jan. 1920.
10,169 Cockington, Arthur John, 1 Jan. 1920.
10,170 Cockshott, John James, 1 Jan. 1920.
10,171 Cohen, Hannah Floretta, 1 Jan. 1920.
10,172 Cohen, Philip, 1 Jan. 1920.
10,173 Cole, Laura Edith, 1 Jan. 1920.
10,174 Cole, Lilian Seymour, Mrs., 1 Jan. 1920.
10,175 Cole, Stanton Wilding, 1 Jan. 1920.
10,176 Coleing, Charles Thomas, 1 Jan. 1920.
10,177 Coleridge, Ellen Gertrude, Mrs., 1 Jan. 1920.
10,178 Coles, Walter George. 1 Jan. 1920.
10,179 Coley, Phillip, 1 Jan. 1920.
10,180 Collingwood, Alfred Henry, 1 Jan. 1920.
10,181 Collins, Lady Evelyn Anne, 1 Jan. 1920.
10,182 Collins, Frank Moore, 1 Jan. 1920.
10,183 Collins, Harold Edmund, 1 Jan. 1920.
10,184 Collins, Percy John, 1 Jan. 1919.
10,185 Collinson, Arthur, 1 Jan. 1920.
10,186 Colman. Edith Margaret, Mrs., 1 Jan. 1920.
10,187 Colt, Thomas Archer, 1 Jan. 1920.
10,188 Comyns, Algernon Charles. 1 Jan. 1920.
10,189 Connal, Kenneth Hugh Munro, 1 Jan. 1920.
10,190 Conyngham, Eva. Mrs. Lennox-, 1 Jan. 1920.
10,191 Coode, Montgomery Penrose, 1 Jan. 1920.
10,192 Cook, Thomas, 1 Jan. 1920.
10,193 Cook, William Wallace, 1 Jan. 1920.
10,194 Cooke, John Galwey, 1 Jan. 1920.
10,195 Cooke, Joseph, 1 Jan. 1920.
10,196 Cooke, Margery Randal, Mrs., 1 Jan. 1920.
10,197 Cooke, Philip Tatton Davies-, 1 Jan. 1920.
10,198 Cooper, Alice, 1 Jan. 1920.
10,199 Cooper, Ethel Beatrice, 1 Jan. 1920.
10,200 Cooper, Harold Merriman, 1 Jan. 1920.
10,201 Cooper, Hon. Rose Ellen, Mrs., 1 Jan. 1920.
10,202 Cooper, Thomas Mackay, 1 Jan. 1920.
10,203 Cooper, Wilbraham Villiers, 1 Jan. 1920.
10,204 Corfield, Hon. Mary Hay. Mrs., 1 Jan. 1920.
10,205 Corlett, Arthur Ready, 1 Jan. 1920.
10,206 Corlette, Hubert Christian, 1 Jan. 1920.
10,207 Corrie, William Malcolm, 1 Jan. 1920.
10 208 Cotton. Charles, 1 Jan. 1920.
10,209 Cotton, Olive Harriet, Mrs. Stapleton, 1 Jan. 1920.
10,210 Court, Charles Edward, 1 Jan. 1920.
10,211 Coward, Randulph Lewis, 1 Jan. 1920.
10,212 Cowcher, William Brainsford, 1 Jan. 1920.
10,213 Cowell, Edward Hudson, 1 Jan. 1920.
10,214 Cowtan, Arthur Barnard, 1 Jan. 1920.
10,215 Cox, Frederick Nutter, 1 Jan. 1920.
10,216 Cox, Gerald, 1 Jan. 1920.
10 217 Cox. Sybil Mary, Mrs., 1 Jan. 1920.
10,218 Coxwell, Charles Blake, 1 Jan. 1920.
10,219 Crabb, Maud Mary, Mrs., 1 Jan. 1920.
10,220 Cranfield, Mary, 1 Jan. 1920.
10,221 Craufurd. Emily Maud, Mrs. Houison-, 1 Jan. 1920.
10,222 Craven, Henry, 1 Jan. 1920.
10,223 Crawshay, de Barri, 1 Jan. 1920.
10,224 Cree, Thomas Deacon, 1 Jan. 1920.
10,225 Creswick, James Paul, 1 Jan. 1920.
10,226 Crighton, John, 1 Jan. 1920.
10,227 Crisp, Charles Doland, 1 Jan. 1920.
10,228 Critchley, Herbert Lawson, 1 Jan. 1920.
10,229 Croker, Alice Georgiana, 1 Jan. 1920.
10,230 Crompton, Charles, 1 Jan. 1920.
10,231 Crosskill, Reginald Charles Osborne, 1 Jan. 1920.
10,232 Crossman, Francis Ward, 1 Jan. 1920.
10,233 Crowther, Lawrence, 1 Jan. 1920.
10,234 Croxford, Charles Henry, 1 Jan. 1920.
10,235 Du Croz, Grace Jessie, Mrs., 1 Jan. 1920.
10,236 Crozier, William, 1 Jan. 1920.
10,237 Cruickshank, Alexander Jaffray, 1 Jan. 1920.
10,238 Crump, Charles, 1 Jan. 1920.
10,239 Crump, Percy Charles, 1 Jan. 1920.
10,240 Crutchfield, Henry, 1 Jan. 1920.
10,241 Cuff, Anne Holland, Mrs., 1 Jan. 1920.
10,242 Cuffey, Edward, 1 Jan. 1920.
10,243 Cullis, Winifred Clara, 1 Jan. 1920.
10,244 Culpin, George Francis. 1 Jan. 1920.
10,246 Cumming, Alexander, 1 Jan. 1920.
10,247 Cumming, Beatrice, Mrs., 1 Jan. 1920.
10,248 Cunliffe, Walter, 1 Jan. 1920.
10,249 Cunningham, John, 1 Jan. 1920.
10,250 Curry, William Fortescue, 1 Jan. 1920.
10,251 Curtis, Frederick, 1 Jan. 1920.
10,252 Dadson, Sophie Portlock, 1 Jan. 1920.
10,253 Daffern, Thomas Wells, 1 Jan. 1920.
10,254 Dain, John Henry, 1 Jan. 1920.
10,255 Dale, Rev. Percy John, 1 Jan. 1920.
10,256 Dalrymple, Lady Marjorie Louise, 1 Jan. 1920.
10,257 Dalton, Michael, 1 Jan. 1920.
10,258 Daltry, Henry James, 1 Jan. 1920.

10,259 Dance, Charles William, 1 Jan. 1920.
10,260 Dannatt, Frank Cedric, 1 Jan. 1920.
10,261 Darnell, Edward, 1 Jan. 1920.
10,262 Darnell, George, 1 Jan. 1920.
10,263 Darroch, Rev. John, 1 Jan. 1920.
10,264 Dashper, Alice Hester, Mrs., 1 Jan. 1920.
10,265 Dashwood, Cyril Russell, 1 Jan. 1920.
10,266 Davey, Annie, Mrs. 1 Jan. 1920.
10,267 Davey, Grace Emilie, 1 Jan. 1920.
10,268 Davey, Harold William, 1 Jan. 1920.
10,269 Davey, William Hamilton, 1 Jan. 1920.
10,270 Davidson, Frances Joan, Mrs., 1 Jan. 1920.
10,271 Davidson, George Frederick, 1 Jan. 1920.
10,272 Davidson, Williamina Saida, 1 Jan. 1920.
10,273 Davies, Arthur Vernon, 1 Jan. 1920.
10,274 Davies, David Thomas, 1 Jan. 1920.
10,275 Davies, Edward Owen Watkin-, 1 Jan. 1920.
10,276 Davies, Ernest Herbert, 1 Jan. 1920.
10,277 Davies, Evan Edward, 1 Jan. 1920.
10,278 Davies, Frederick Charles, 1 Jan. 1920.
10,279 Davies, Henry, 1 Jan. 1920.
10,280 Davies, James David, 1 Jan. 1920.
10,281 Davies, Rev. William Wynn, 1 Jan. 1920.
10,282 Davis, Edward Henry Meggs, 1 Jan. 1920.
10,283 Davis, Evelyn Mary, Mrs. Bramwell, 1 Jan. 1920.
10,284 Davis, Harry Lewer. 1 Jan. 1920.
10,285 Davis, Thomas Ruddock, 1 Jan. 1920.
10,286 Davison, Daniel, 1 Jan. 1920.
10,287 Davison, Minnie Gibson, Mrs., 1 Jan. 1920.
10,288 Dawes, Jesse Cooper, 1 Jan. 1920.
10,289 Dawson, Errington, 1 Jan. 1920.
10,290 Dawson, Sidney Stanley, 1 Jan. 1920.
10,291 Dawson, William, 1 Jan. 1920.
10,292 Deacon, Edgar Reginald, 1 Jan. 1920.
10,293 Deane, Charles Chatterton, 1 Jan. 1920.
10,294 Dearden, Clarence Reginald, 1 Jan. 1920.
10,295 Debenham, Amy, 1 Jan. 1920.
10,296 Delany, Thomas William, 1 Jan. 1920.
10,297 D'Elboux, Louis, 1 Jan. 1920.
10,298 Denby, Clara Sophia, Lady, 1 Jan. 1920.
10,299 Dendy, John, 1 Jan. 1920.
10,300 Denning, Arthur du Pré, 1 Jan. 1920.
10,301 Dent, Edith Vere, Mrs., 1 Jan. 1920.
10,302 Devenish, Bertha, Mrs., 1 Jan. 1920.
10,303 Devine, John, 1 Jan. 1920.
10,304 Dewhurst, Counsell, 1 Jan. 1920.
10,305 Dick, Helen Maybel Kathleen, Mrs., 1 Jan. 1920.
10,306 Dick, Margaret Mary Douglas, 1 Jan. 1920.
10,307 Dickie, Robert Charles, 1 Jan. 1920.
10,308 Dickson, Robinson Simpson, 1 Jan. 1920.
10,309 Dill, John Frederick Gordon, 1 Jan. 1920.
10,310 Dix, Arthur Harold, 1 Jan. 1920.
10,311 Dixon, Charles Egerton, 1 Jan. 1920.
10,312 Dodd, John William, 1 Jan. 1920.
10,313 Dodds, Lionel Graham, 1 Jan. 1920.
10,314 Dodds, Mary Janet, 1 Jan. 1919.
10,315 Dolphin, John Byron, 1 Jan. 1920.
10,316 Domville, Edward James, 1 Jan. 1920.
10,317 Doubleday, Charles Edward, 1 Jan. 1920.
10,318 Douglas, Robert James, 1 Jan. 1920.
10,319 Douglas, Samuel Henry, 1 Jan. 1920.
10,320 Dowding, Dorothy Carwithen, 1 Jan. 1920.
10,321 Dower, Mary, Mrs. Gough-, 1 Jan. 1920.
10,322 Downes, Thomas, 1 Jan. 1920.
10,323 Downey, Thomas, 1 Jan. 1920.
10,324 Drake, James Ernest, 1 Jan. 1920.
10,325 Dreaper, William Porter, 1 Jan. 1920.
10,326 Drysdale, Charles Vickery, 1 Jan. 1920.
10,327 Duberly, Ida Mary Villiers, Mrs., 1 Jan. 1920.
10,328 Dudley, George James, 1 Jan. 1920.
10,329 Dudley, William Edward, 1 Jan. 1920.
10,330 Duffield, Walter Dowsett, 1 Jan. 1920.
10,331 Dugdale, Ethel Innes, Mrs., 1 Jan. 1920.
10,332 Dumbell, James Burns, 1 Jan. 1920.
10,333 Duncalfe, Lucy Harding, Mrs.. 1 Jan. 1920.
10,334 Dunleath, Norah Louisa Fanny, Baroness, 1 Jan. 1920.
10,335 Dunlop, Frederick George, 1 Jan. 1920.
10,336 Dunlop, William Louis Martial, 1 Jan. 1920.
10,337 Dunn, Frederick William, 1 Jan. 1920.
10,338 Dunn, George Owen William, 1 Jan. 1920.
10,339 Dunwoody, Robert Browne, 1 Jan. 1920.
10,340 Duthie, David Hutcheon, 1 Jan. 1920.
10,341 Duval, Rev. Stephen Peachey, 1 Jan. 1920.
10,342 Dyke, David Nicholas, 1 Jan. 1920.
10,343 Dykes, Ellen, Mrs., 1 Jan. 1920.
10,344 Dymond, Charles Joseph, 1 Jan. 1920.
10,345 Dymond, Edmund Robert, 1 Jan. 1920.
10,346 Dymond, Mary Evelyn, 1 Jan. 1920.
10,347 Eason, John Charles Malcolm, 1 Jan. 1920.
10,348 Eastwood, William Hastings, 1 Jan. 1920.
10,349 Eberle, James Fuller, 1 Jan. 1920.
10,350 Eckersley, Frank, 1 Jan. 1920.
10,351 Eden, Charles Hamilton, 1 Jan. 1920.
10,352 Eden, Sybil Frances, Lady, 1 Jan. 1920.
10,353 Edge, George, 1 Jan. 1920.
10,354 Edmunds, Wilfred Hawksley, 1 Jan. 1920.
10,355 Edwards, Jean, Mrs., 1 Jan. 1920.
10,356 Edwards, James Herbert, 1 Jan. 1920.
10,357 Edwards, John Vaughan, 1 Jan. 1920.

10,358 Edwards, Percy, 1 Jan. 1920.
10,359 Edwards, William Robert, 1 Jan. 1920.
10,360 Egerton, Dorothy Charlotte, 1 Jan. 1920.
10,361 Elder, David, 1 Jan. 1920.
10,362 Elgood, Cornelia Bonté Sheldon, Mrs., 1 Jan. 1920.
10,363 Elles, Edmund Hardie, 1 Jan. 1920.
10,364 Elliott, Claude Aurelius, 1 Jan. 1920.
10,365 Ellis, Edward George, 1 Jan. 1920.
10,366 Ellis, Gertrude, Lady Heaton-, 1 Jan. 1920.
10,367 Ellis, Inez Blanche, Lady, 1 Jan. 1920.
10,368 Ellson, George, 1 Jan. 1920.
10,369 Elsmere, Maude Alice, 1 Jan. 1920.
10,370 Emra, Frederic Harcourt, 1 Jan. 1920.
10,371 Engelbach, Charles Richard Fox, 1 Jan. 1920.
10,372 England, Alfred Colborne, 1 Jan. 1920.
10,373 Estill, John Henry, 1 Jan. 1920.
10,374 Evans, Annie Lloyd, Mrs., 1 Jan. 1920.
10,375 Evans, Christopher Douglas, 1 Jan. 1920.
10,376 Evans, Edward Victor, 1 Jan. 1920.
10,377 Evans, Ethel Frances, Mrs., 1 Jan. 1920.
10,378 Evans, Fisher Henry Freke, 1 Jan. 1920.
10,379 Evans, William Augustus Bulkeley-, 1 Jan. 1920
10,380 Everett, Lionel Decimus Longcroft, 1 Jan. 1920.
10,381 Everitt, Robert Gordon, 1 Jan. 1920.
10,382 Eyre, Gervas Malcolm, 1 Jan. 1920.
10,383 Fagge, Mabel Muriel Hilton, 1 Jan. 1920.
10,384 Fair, Blanche Alicia, 1 Jan. 1920.
10,385 Falconer, Lieut.-Col. John, Bey, 1 Jan. 1920.
10,386 Farndale, Joseph, 1 Jan. 1920.
10,387 Faulkner, Roger, 1 Jan. 1920.
10,388 Fawcett, Frederick, 1 Jan. 1920.
10,389 Fawcett, Percy William, 1 Jan. 1920.
10,390 Fawcus, Arthur Francis, 1 Jan. 1920.
10,391 Fell, William, 1 Jan. 1920.
10,392 Fellows, Evelyn Emma, 1 Jan. 1920.
10,393 Fellows, George, 1 Jan. 1920.
10,394 Felton, John Robinson, 1 Jan. 1920.
10,395 Fenner, Sidney, 1 Jan. 1920.
10,396 Fenton, William Walter, 1 Jan. 1920.
10,397 Fernley, James, 1 Jan. 1920.
10,398 Fetherstonhaugh, Margaret, Mrs., 1 Jan. 1920.
10,399 Filer, Samuel, 1 Jan. 1920.
10,400 Finch, Sidney, 1 Jan. 1920.
10,401 Firmin, Norman Haynes, 1 Jan. 1920.
10,402 Firmstone, Emily Florence, 1 Jan. 1920.
10,403 Fisher, Frederick Furryan, 1 Jan. 1920.
10,404 Fittall, Robert John, 1 Jan. 1920.
10,405 FitzGerald, Edward Henry, 1 Jan. 1920.
10,406 Fitzwilliam, Maud Frederica Elizabeth, Countess, 1 Jan. 1920.
10,407 Fleming, John Arnold, 1 Jan. 1920.
10,408 Fleming, John Lancelot, 1 Jan. 1920.
10,409 Fleming, Rev. James William, 1 Jan. 1920.
10,410 Fleming, Sarah Kate, Mrs., 1 Jan. 1920.
10,411 Fletcher, Henry Francis, 1 Jan. 1920.
10,412 Fletcher, William Frederick Ashby, 1 Jan. 1920.
10,413 Flint, Samuel, 1 Jan. 1920.
10,414 Foà Ferdinand Eugene, 1 Jan. 1920.
10,415 Folker, Herbert Henry, 1 Jan. 1920.
10,416 Ford, Norman Thomas, 1 Jan. 1920.
10,417 Fordham, Edward Wilfrid, 1 Jan. 1920.
10,418 Forrest, John William, 1 Jan. 1920.
10,419 Forrester, James, 1 Jan. 1920.
10,420 Forster, John, 1 Jan. 1920.
10,421 Foster, Evelyn Mary, Mrs., 1 Jan. 1920.
10,422 Foster, Phipps Bentley, 1 Jan. 1920.
10,423 Foster, Reginald, 1 Jan. 1920.
10,424 Foucar, Alexander Ferdinand Emile, 1 Jan. 1920.
10,425 Fowler, Lionel John Porter, 1 Jan. 1920.
10,426 Fox, David Henry, 1 Jan. 1920.
10,427 Fox, John Jacob, 1 Jan. 1920.
10,428 Fox, Walter St. John, 1 Jan. 1920.
10,429 Francis, Alfred George, 1 Jan. 1920.
10,430 Francis, Harvey, 1 Jan. 1920.
10,431 Francis, John Horace, 1 Jan. 1920.
10,432 Frank, Peter, 1 Jan. 1920.
10,433 Franklin, Richard, 1 Jan. 1920.
10,434 Frazer, Wilson Ray, 1 Jan. 1920.
10,435 Freeman, Alice, Mrs., 1 Jan. 1920.
10,436 Freeth, Dorothy Ierne, 1 Jan. 1920.
10,437 Frere, Frank Horace, 1 Jan. 1920.
10,438 Fry, Ellen Margaret, Mrs., 1 Jan. 1920.
10,439 Fryer, George Ernest, 1 Jan. 1920.
10,440 Fullerton, Alexander Moffitt, 1 Jan. 1920.
10,442 Furse, Jean Adelaide, Lady, 1 Jan. 1920.
10,443 Gale, Arthur John, 1 Jan. 1920.
10,444 Gale, Rev. James Randolph Courtenay, 1 Jan. 1920.
10,445 Gallagher, John, 1 Jan. 1920.
10,446 Galland, Alfred Jules Louis, 1 Jan. 1920.
10,447 Galloway, Alexander Rudolf, 1 Jan. 1920.
10,449 Gange, Ambrose Day, 1 Jan. 1920.
10,450 Gann, Edmond Thomas, 1 Jan. 1920.
10,451 Gardner, George Frederick, 1 Jan. 1920.
10,452 Gardner, John, 1 Jan. 1920.
10,453 Gardner, Joseph William, 1 Jan. 1920.
10,454 Gardner, Thomas Edward, 1 Jan. 1920.
10,455 Garland, Charles Tuller, 1 Jan. 1920.
10,456 Garland, John William, 1 Jan. 1920.
10,457 Garner, Joseph Richardson, 1 Jan. 1920.

10,458 Garry, Francis Nicholas Arbuthnot, 1 Jan. 1920.
10,459 Gaskill, Jackson, 1 Jan. 1920.
10,460 Gatacre, Hon. Beatrix Wickens, Lady, 1 Jan. 1920.
10,461 Gay, Charlotte Evelyn, 1 Jan. 1920.
10,462 Gibb, William Thomas, 1 Jan. 1920.
10,463 Gibbons, William Michael, 1 Jan. 1920.
10,464 Gibbs, Brandreth, 1 Jan. 1920.
10,465 Gibbs, Hon. Mildred Dorothea, 1 Jan. 1920.
10,466 Gibson, Alfred Edgar, 1 Jan. 1920.
10,467 Gibson, Finlay Albert, 1 Jan. 1920.
10,468 Gibson, George McLean, 1 Jan. 1920.
10,469 Gibson, William Howieson, 1 Jan. 1920.
10,470 Gibson, William John, 1 Jan. 1920.
10,471 Giffard, Mary Constance, Mrs., 1 Jan. 1920
10,472 Gilfillan, Samuel James, 1 Jan. 1920.
10,473 Gill, Frank, 1 Jan. 1920.
10,474 Gill, Joseph Withers-, 1 Jan. 1920.
10,475 Gill, William Briggs, 1 Jan. 1920.
10,476 Gillman, Arthur William, 1 Jan. 1920.
10,477 Gilmour, Robert, 1 Jan. 1920.
10,478 Gilroy, John 1 Jan. 1920.
10,479 Gjers, Annie Gatenby, Mrs., 1 Jan. 1920.
10,480 Glanville, William Henry, 1 Jan. 1920.
10,481 Glass, Alexander, 1 Jan. 1920.
10,482 Glass, Henry Matier, 1 Jan. 1920.
10,483 Glaze, Charles William Livock, 1 Jan. 1920.
10,484 Gleichen, Lady Helena Emily, 1 Jan. 1920.
10,485 Glen, Elizabeth Hope, 1 Jan. 1920.
10,486 Glover, Kathleen, Mrs., 1 Jan. 1920.
10,487 Gluckstein, Joseph, 1 Jan. 1920.
10,488 Glyn, Augusta Carr, 1 Jan. 1920.
10,489 Gold, Gerald Gilbey, 1 Jan. 1920.
10,490 Goldie, Valentine Francis Taubman, 1 Jan. 1920.
10,491 Goldney, Alice Frances Holbrow, Lady, 1 Jan. 1920.
10,492 Gollin, George, 1 Jan. 1920.
10,493 Good, Thomas, 1 Jan. 1920.
10,494 Goodman, Coleman, 1 Jan. 1920.
10,495 Goodyear, Charles Ernest, 1 Jan. 1920.
10,496 Goodyer, Thomas Boyce, 1 Jan. 1920.
10,497 Gordon, Alexander Stewart, 1 Jan. 1920.
10,498 Gordon, Dora Helen, Mrs., 1 Jan. 1920.
10,499 Gordon, Douglas George Hamilton, 1 Jan. 1920.
10,500 Gordon, George Robert, 1 Jan. 1920.
10,501 Gordon, Henry Sharpe, 1 Jan. 1920.
10,502 Gordon, Robert, 1 Jan. 1920.
10,503 Gott, Walter, 1 Jan. 1920.
10,504 Gotts, John Benjamin, 1 Jan. 1920.
10,505 Goudie, Peter Augustus, 1 Jan. 1920.
10,506 Gough, Arthur Edward, 1 Jan. 1920.
10,507 Gough, Joseph Salmon, 1 Jan. 1920.
10,508 Goulding, Harry Wilson, 1 Jan. 1920.
10,509 Gowan, Francis Edward, 1 Jan. 1920.
10,510 Grace, George William, 1 Jan. 1920.
10,511 Graddon, Ernest Edgar, 1 Jan. 1920.
10,512 Graff, Francis Stephen, 1 Jan. 1920.
10,513 Grafton, Alexander, 1 Jan. 1920.
10,514 Graham, Duncan, 1 Jan. 1920.
10,515 Graham, Joseph, 1 Jan. 1920.
10,516 Granard, Beatrice, Countess of, 1 Jan. 1920.
10,517 Grant, Alexander, 1 Jan. 1920.
10,518 Graves, Rev. Robert Vernon Ottley, 1 Jan. 1920.
10,519 Gray, Edith Mary Spencer, Mrs., 1 Jan. 1920.
10,520 Gray, Robert Whytlaw Whytlaw-, 1 Jan. 1920.
10,521 Gray, Ronald Birdseye, 1 Jan. 1920.
10,522 Green, Edwin Collier, 1 Jan. 1920.
10,523 Green, Frederick Michael, 1 Jan. 1920.
10,524 Green, Helen Mowbray, Mrs. Vincent-, 1 Jan. 1920
10,525 Green, Margaret Bennett, Mrs., 1 Jan. 1920.
10,526 Greenall, Cyril Edward, 1 Jan. 1920.
10,527 Greene, Kathleen, 1 Jan. 1920.
10,528 Greenwood, George David, 1 Jan. 1920.
10,529 Gregory, Alfred John, 1 Jan. 1920.
10,530 Gregory, John, 1 Jan. 1920.
10,531 Grenside, Thomas Reed, 1 Jan. 1920.
10,532 Grey, Thomas, 1 Jan. 1920.
10,533 Grierson, George Arthur, 1 Jan. 1920.
10,534 Grieve, George Butler, 1 Jan. 1920.
10,535 Griffin, John, 1 Jan. 1920.
10,536 Griffin, William Lashford, 1 Jan. 1920.
10,537 Griffiths, Arthur, 1 Jan. 1920.
10,538 Griffiths Arthur, 1 Jan. 1920.
10,539 Griffiths, Charles Bedlington, 1 Jan. 1920.
10,540 Griffiths, David Llewellyn, 1 Jan. 1920.
10,541 Griffiths, Herbert Richard, 1 Jan. 1920.
10,542 Griffiths, Thomas Henry, 1 Jan. 1920.
10,543 Gruchy, Frederick de Quetteville De, 1 Jan. 1920.
10,544 Gruchy, William Geary De, 1 Jan. 1920.
10,545 Grundy, Robert Taylor, 1 Jan. 1920.
10,546 Haddo, George Gordon, Earl of, 1 Jan. 1920.
10,547 Hadfield, Ernest, 1 Jan. 1920.
10,548 Haggart, James Dewar, 1 Jan. 1920.
10,549 Hall, Charles Stuart, 1 Jan. 1920.
10,550 Hall, Rev. John, 1 Jan. 1920.
10,551 Hall, John Herbert, 1 Jan. 1920.
10,552 Hall, Oscar Standring, 1 Jan. 1920.
10,553 Hall, Percival Stanhope, 1 Jan. 1920.
10,554 Hall, Robert Mills, 1 Jan. 1920.
10,555 Hall, Walter, 1 Jan. 1920.
10,556 Hall, William Carby, 1 Jan. 1920.

10,557 Hallett, Norton Joseph Hughes-, 1 Jan. 1920.
10,558 Hamersley, John Henry, 1 Jan. 1920.
10,559 Hamilton, Kate Gibson, Mrs., 1 Jan. 1920.
10,560 Hammond, William Cecil, 1 Jan. 1920.
10,561 Hanbury, Arthur Marcus, 1 Jan. 1920.
10,562 Hanbury, John James, 1 Jan. 1920.
10,563 Handasyde, George Harris, 1 Jan. 1920.
10,564 Harbord, Richard Arthur, 1 Jan. 1920.
10,565 Harding, William Percy, 1 Jan. 1920.
10,566 Hardy, Gladys Rivers, 1 Jan. 1920.
10,567 Hargood, Harry, 1 Jan. 1920.
10,568 Hargrave, Mary Montague, Mrs., 1 Jan. 1920.
10,569 Harrington, Ernest John, 1 Jan. 1920.
10,570 Harrison, Florence Ada, Mrs., 1 Jan. 1920.
10,571 Harrison, George Alfred, 1 Jan. 1920.
10,572 Harrison, Rosamond Mary, 1 Jan. 1920.
10,573 Harrop, William, 1 Jan. 1920.
10,574 Hart, James MacGregor, 1 Jan. 1920.
10,575 Hart, Philip Theodore, 1 Jan. 1920.
10,576 Harvey, Rev. Edward Douglas Lennox, 1 Jan. 1920.
10,577 Harvey, Emma Jessie, Mrs., 1 Jan. 1920.
10,578 Harvey, Joseph Massey, 1 Jan. 1920.
10,579 Harvie, Charles Frederick, 1 Jan. 1920.
10,580 Harwood, John Edward, 1 Jan. 1920.
10,581 Haseler, William Rabone, 1 Jan. 1920.
10,582 Hassell, Charles Joseph, 1 Jan. 1920.
10,583 Hatch, Frederick Henry, 1 Jan. 1920.
10,584 Hattersley, John, 1 Jan. 1920.
10,585 Haughton, Marjorie Wilhelmina, 1 Jan. 1920.
10,586 Hauxwell, Samuel, 1 Jan. 1920.
10,587 Hawes, George William Spencer, 1 Jan. 1920.
10,588 Hawtrey, Wilfred Robert John, 1 Jan. 1920.
10,589 Hay, Mary Elizabeth Dalrymple, 1 Jan. 1920.
10,590 Haycock, Herbert Clement, 1 Jan. 1920.
10,591 Haylock, Ernest Edwin, 1 Jan. 1920.
10,592 Hazlehurst, George, 1 Jan. 1920.
10,593 Hazlerigg, Grey, 1 Jan. 1920.
10,594 Headland, Robert Vincent, 1 Jan. 1920
10,595 Heald, Charles Ernest, 1 Jan. 1920.
10,596 Healey, Basil, 1 Jan. 1920.
10,597 Heasman, Arthur William, 1 Jan. 1920.
10,598 Heath, Cuthbert Eden, 1 Jan. 1920.
10,599 Heathcote, Charles Francis, 1 Jan. 1920
10,600 Heaton, John, 1 Jan. 1920.
10,601 Hedge, George Tullidge, 1 Jan. 1920.
10,602 Hedley, Oswald William Edward, 1 Jan. 1920.
10,603 Heeps, James, 1 Jan. 1920.
10,604 Hellier, Maurice, 1 Jan. 1920.
10,605 Henderson, George, 1 Jan. 1920.
10,606 Henderson, John Hossell, 1 Jan. 1920.
10,607 Henderson, Kate, Mrs., 1 Jan. 1920.
10,608 Henderson, Robert Cron, 1 Jan. 1920.
10,609 Henderson, William Alexander Cruickshank, 1 Jan. 1920.
10,610 Hendriks, Cecil Morgan, 1 Jan. 1920.
10,611 Hendry, John, 1 Jan. 1920.
10,612 Henry, Florence Vaughan Mitchell-, 1 Jan. 1920.
10,613 Henson, George Herbert, 1 Jan. 1920.
10,614 Herbert, Adelaide Jane, Mrs., 1 Jan. 1920.
10,615 Heron, Harold Hastings, 1 Jan. 1920.
10,616 Hett, Janie, Mrs., 1 Jan. 1920.
10,617 Hett, Reginald, 1 Jan. 1920.
10,618 Hewelcke, Theodore William, 1 Jan. 1920.
10,619 Hewer, Basil, 1 Jan. 1920.
10,620 Hewer, Cecil Mackenzie, 1 Jan. 1920.
10,621 Hewer, Edward Septimus Earnshaw, 1 Jan. 1920.
10,622 Hewett, Charles Ernest, 1 Jan. 1920.
10,623 Hewson, James Archibald, 1 Jan. 1920.
10,624 Heylin, Henry Brougham, 1 Jan. 1920.
10,625 Hick, Benjamin, 1 Jan. 1920.
10,626 Hickman, John Blair Smith, 1 Jan. 1920.
10,627 Hickson, William Henry, 1 Jan. 1920.
10,628 Higgins, William, 1 Jan. 1920.
10,629 Hill, Alex, 1 Jan. 1920.
10,630 Hill, Christopher John, 1 Jan. 1920.
10,631 Hill, Robert, 1 Jan. 1920.
10,633 Hillingdon, Alice Marian, Lady, 1 Jan. 1920.
10,634 Hincks, William Edwin, 1 Jan. 1920.
10,635 Hind, Wilhelmina Maria, Mrs., 1 Jan. 1920.
10,636 Hinnell, Joseph Squier, 1 Jan. 1920.
10,637 Hitchcock Thomas Gilbert, 1 Jan. 1920.
10,638 Hobbs, Herbert, 1 Jan. 1920.
10,639 Hobday, Kingsford George, 1 Jan. 1920.
10,640 Hobson, Arthur John, 1 Jan. 1920.
10,641 Hocking, R. C., 1 Jan. 1920.
10,642 Hodgson, Benjamin, 1 Jan. 1920.
10,643 Hodgson, Edgar Stanley, 1 Jan. 1920.
10,644 Hodgson, Malcolm Elliott, 1 Jan. 1920.
10,645 Hodkinson, John Alfred, 1 Jan. 1920.
10,646 Holdforth, Harold, 1 Jan. 1920.
10,647 Hollings, Nina Augusta Stracey, Mrs., 1 Jan. 1920.
10,648 Hollins, Edith Blanche, Mrs., 1 Jan. 1920.
10,649 Hollway, Geoffrey Fynes, 1 Jan. 1920.
10,650 Holloway, William Henry, 1 Jan. 1920.
10,651 Holman, Phyllis, 1 Jan. 1920.
10,652 Holmes, Herbert Thomas, 1 Jan. 1920.
10,653 Holmes, Joseph Edward Leo, 1 Jan. 1920.
10,654 Holt, Florence Annie, Mrs. Lyster-, 1 Jan. 1920.
10,655 Holt, Frederick Appleby, 1 Jan. 1920.

OFFICERS.

10,656 Holt, Thomas, 1 Jan. 1920.
10,657 Homfray, Ernest Randolph Popkin, 1 Jan. 1920.
10,658 Hooper, Alfred, 1 Jan. 1920.
10,659 Hooper, George Henry James, 1 Jan. 1920.
10,660 Hope, Mabel Ellen, Mrs., 1 Jan. 1920.
10,661 Hope, Hon. Mary, Lady, 1 Jan. 1920.
10,662 Hopkins, Thomas Edmund, 1 Jan. 1920.
10,663 Hopping, Sydney, 1 Jan. 1920.
10,664 Hopwood, Eleanor Mary, 1 Jan. 1920.
10,665 Horne, Alexander Robert, 1 Jan. 1920.
10,666 Horne, Henry Spence, 1 Jan. 1920.
10,667 Horobin, Oliver Wil iam, 1 Jan. 1920.
10,668 Horton, Percy Thomas, 1 Jan. 1920.
10,669 Houldsworth, Joseph, 1 Jan. 1920.
10,670 Hourston, Margaret Anne, Mrs., 1 Jan. 1920.
10,671 Housden, James Anderson, 1 Jan. 1920.
10,672 Houston, Henry James, 1 Jan. 1920.
10,673 Howard, Carter William, 1 Jan. 1920.
10,674 Howard, William James, 1 Jan. 1920.
10,675 Howarth, Osbert John Radcliffe, 1 Jan. 1920.
10,676 Howe, John Allen, 1 Jan. 1920.
10,677 Hughes, Ethel Blanche, Mrs. Price-, 1 Jan. 1920.
10,678 Hughes, Rev. Hugh Michael, 1 Jan. 1920.
10,679 Hughes, Thomas, 1 Jan. 1920.
10,680 Huie, Richard William, 1 Jan. 1920.
10,682 Hume, Blanche, Mrs., 1 Jan. 1920.
10,683 Humfrey, John Charles Willis, 1 Jan. 1920.
10,684 Hunt, Thomas, 1 Jan. 1920.
10,685 Hunter, David, 1 Jan. 1920.
10,686 Hunter, James, 1 Jan. 1920.
10,688 Hunter, Margaret Bruce, 1 Jan. 1920.
10,689 Hunter, Thomas Briggs, 1 Jan. 1920.
10,690 Hunton, Edgar Barton, 1 Jan. 1920.
10,691 Hurst, Christopher Salkeld, 1 Jan. 1920.
10,692 Hurst, John, 1 Jan. 1920.
10,693 Hussey, John Walton, 1 Jan. 1920.
10,694 Hutchinson, Lucy, Mrs., 1 Jan. 1920.
10,695 Hutchinson, Wilfred Leavold, 1 Jan. 1920.
10,696 Hutsel, Robert, 1 Jan. 1920.
10,697 Hutton, William, 1 Jan. 1920.
10,698 Hyde, Charles, 1 Jan. 1920.
10,699 Ibbetson, Alexander, 1 Jan. 1920.
10,700 Ingham, William Henry, 1 Jan. 1920.
10,701 Inglefield, Julia Katharine Margaret, Lady, 1 Jan. 1920.
10,702 Ingram, Joseph, 1 Jan. 1920.
10,703 Inman, Arnold, 1 Jan. 1920.
10,704 Innes, James, 1 Jan. 1920.
10,705 Inskip, Grace Hampden, 1 Jan. 1920.
10,706 Irwin, George Robert, 1 Jan. 1920.
10,707 Irwin, Thomas James, 1 Jan. 1920.
10,708 Isaacs, Harry Michael, 1 Jan. 1920.
10,709 Ives, William Henry Martin, 1 Jan. 1920.
10,710 Jack, John William, 1 Jan. 1920.
10,711 Jackling, Percival, 1 Jan. 1920.
10,712 Jackson, Ada Frances, Lady Mather, 1 Jan. 1920.
10,713 Jackson, Andrew Eric, 1 Jan. 1920.
10,714 Jackson, Gwendoline Doris, Mrs., 1 Jan. 1920.
10,715 Jackson, John William, 1 Jan. 1920.
10,716 Jacob, Edmund Henry, 1 Jan. 1920.
10,717 Jacobs, Julius, 1 Jan. 1920.
10,718 James, Eric Ibbetson, 1 Jan. 1920.
10,719 James, Gwilym Cristor, 1 Jan. 1920.
10,720 James, Gwilym Prosser, 1 Jan. 1920.
10,721 James, Jenkin, 1 Jan. 1920.
10,722 James, Rebecca Green, Mrs., 1 Jan. 1920.
10,723 James, Sidney Frederick, 1 Jan. 1920.
10,724 James, William Henry, 1 Jan. 1920.
10,725 James, William Isaac, 1 Jan. 1920.
10,726 Jarmay, Charlotte E., Lady, 1 Jan. 1920.
10,727 Jay, Edward Aubrey Hastings, 1 Jan. 1920
10,728 Jayne, Ronald Garland, 1 Jan. 1920.
10,729 Jeffery, Florence Augusta, 1 Jan. 1920.
10,730 Jeffery, Margaret Ann, 1 Jan. 1920.
10,731 Jeffries, Martha, Mrs., 1 Jan. 1920.
10,732 Jenkins, Ann Nora, Mrs., 1 Jan. 1920.
10,733 Jenkins, Herbert George, 1 Jan. 1920.
10,734 Jenkins, Thomas Lewis, 1 Jan. 1920.
10,735 Jenkinson, Alfred James, 1 Jan. 1920.
10,736 Jewell, Bertie, 1 Jan. 1920.
10 737 Jewell, Henry James, 1 Jan. 1920.
10,738 Jodrell, Mary Rennell, Lady Cotton, 1 Jan. 1920.
10,739 Johnson, Alfred Joseph, 1 Jan. 1920.
10,740 Johnson, Ernest James, 1 Jan. 1920.
10,741 Johnson, Henry, 1 Jan. 1920.
10,742 Johnson, James, 1 Jan. 1920.
10,743 Johnson, Sydney Frederick, 1 Jan. 1920.
10,744 Johnson, Walter, 1 Jan. 1920.
10,745 Johnston, Hon. Winifred Mary, Lady, 1 Jan. 1920.
10,746 Jones, Abel John, 1 Jan. 1920.
10,747 Jones, Alice Gray, Mrs., 1 Jan. 1920.
10,748 Jones, Alice Pownall, Mrs. Caton-, 1 Jan. 1920.
10,749 Jones, Frederick William, 1 Jan. 1920.
10,750 Jones, Glynne, 1 Jan. 1920.
10,751 Jones, Herbert Charles, 1 Jan. 1920.
10,752 Jones, John Phillips, 1 Jan. 1920.
10,753 Jones, Margaret, 1 Jan. 1920.
10,754 Jones, Richard Edward, 1 Jan. 1920.
10,755 Jones, Ronald Herbert, 1 Jan. 1920.

10,756 Jones, William Henry, 1 Jan. 1920.
10,757 Jones, Walter Lindley-, 1 Jan. 1920.
10,758 Joy, Henry Holmes, 1 Jan. 1920.
10,759 Joyner, Cerdric Batson, 1 Jan. 1920.
10,760 Joynt, Richard Lane, 1 Jan. 1920.
10,761 Kalker, Emanuel, 1 Jan. 1920.
10,762 Kaufman, Louis, 1 Jan. 1920.
10,763 Kaye, Evan, 1 Jan. 1920.
10,764 Keel, William Henry, 1 Jan. 1920.
10,765 Keen, Katherine Elizabeth, Mrs., 1 Jan. 1920
10,766 Keene, Henry Furse, 1 Jan. 1920.
10,767 Kemm, Stephanie Lilian Septima, Mrs., 1 Jan. 1920.
10,768 Kennedy, Alexander, 1 Jan. 1920.
10,769 Keogh, Joseph Wiseman, 1 Jan. 1920.
10,770 Kerr, Errol, 1 Jan. 1920.
10,771 Kerr, Harold, 1 Jan. 1920.
10,772 Kerr, Kenelm, 1 Jan. 1920.
10,773 Kershaw, John Felix, 1 Jan. 1920.
10,774 Kerslake, Arthur Thomas, 1 Jan. 1920.
10,775 Kett, George Robert, 1 Jan. 1920.
10,776 Kettles, William, 1 Jan. 1920.
10,777 Keymer, Daniel Thomas, 1 Jan. 1920.
10,778 Keyser, Maurice Max, 1 Jan. 1920.
10,779 Kimberley, Paul, 1 Jan. 1920.
10,780 King, John Alexander, 1 Jan. 1920.
10,781 King, John Charles, 1 Jan. 1920.
10,782 Kingham, Robert Dixon, 1 Jan. 1920.
10,783 Kinnear, Thomas John, 1 Jan. 1920.
10,784 Kirby, George, 1 Jan. 1920.
10,785 Kitcat, Rev. Henry James, 1 Jan. 1920.
10,786 Kitchen, Preston, 1 Jan. 1920.
10,787 Kitchin, John William, 1 Jan. 1920.
10,788 Knill, Charles Henry, 1 Jan. 1920.
10,789 Knott, Harry Ernest ,1 Jan. 1920.
10,790 Knowles, Sir Lees, Bart., 1 Jan. 1920.
10,791 Knowles, Thornton, 1 Jan. 1920.
10,792 Krohn, Alice, Mrs., 1 Jan. 1920.
10,793 Kyle, Phillip Kyle, 1 Jan. 1920.
10,794 Lafontaine, Henry Philip Leopold Cart de, 1 Jan. 1920.
10,795 Lake, Ada Louise, 1 Jan. 1920.
10,796 Lambert, Stanley Harrison, 1 Jan. 1920.
10,797 Lambie, Robert, 1 Jan. 1920.
10,798 Laming, Richard Valentine, 1 Jan. 1920.
10,800 Lane, Daniel de Moura, 1 Jan. 1920.
10,801 Lane, Frederick, 1 Jan. 1920.
10,802 Langmaid, Ernest Richard, 1 Jan. 1920.
10,803 Lanham, Laurence, 1 Jan. 1920.
10,804 Lansdown, Charles Ewbank, 1 Jan. 1920.
10,805 Larnder, Harold Frederick, 1 Jan. 1920.
10,806 Lascelles, Edward Charles Ponsonby, 1 Jan. 1920.
10,807 Lascot, Frank Leslie, 1 Jan. 1920.
10,808 Latham, Percy James, 1 Jan. 1920.
10,809 Lauder, William Belth, 1 Jan. 1920.
10,810 Law, David, 1 Jan. 1920.
10,811 Lawrenson, Thomas Alfred, 1 Jan. 1920.
10,812 Lawson, Catherine Adah, Mrs. Kerr-, 1 Jan. 1920
10,813 Lea, Frederick Charles, 1 Jan. 1920.
10,814 Leach, Marian, Mrs., 1 Jan. 1920.
10,815 Leak, Daniel Arthur, 1 Jan. 1920.
10,816 Leake, Sidney Henry, 1 Jan. 1920
10,817 Lee, George, 1 Jan. 1920.
10,818 Lee, Hugh Warren, 1 Jan. 1920.
10,819 Lee, Sarah Josephine, Mrs., 1 Jan. 1920.
10,820 Leeman, Walter Joseph, 1 Jan. 1920.
10,821 Lees, William Clare, 1 Jan. 1920.
10,822 Leigh, Reginald Gerard, 1 Jan. 1920.
10,823 Leighton, Gerald Rowley, 1 Jan. 1920.
10,824 Lendrum, John Black, 1 Jan. 1920.
10,825 Lescher, Thomas Edward, 1 Jan. 1920.
10,826 Leslie, Lewis Francis, 1 Jan. 1920.
10,827 Lewis, Annie Caton, Mrs., 1 Jan. 1920.
10,828 Lewis, George Frederick, 1 Jan. 1920.
10,829 Lewis, John, 1 Jan. 1920.
10,830 Lewis, Kate, Mrs., 1 Jan. 1920.
10,831 Lewis, Llewelyn, 1 Jan. 1920.
10,832 Lewis, William John, 1 Jan. 1920.
10,833 Liddell, Hilda Kathleen, 1 Jan. 1920.
10,834 Liddington, Ezra William Edmund, 1 Jan. 1920.
10,835 Lindon, John Benjamin, 1 Jan. 1920.
10,836 Lindsay, Lionel Arthur, 1 Jan. 1920.
10,837 Lineham, Samuel, 1 Jan. 1920.
10,838 Linthorne, Richard Roope, 1 Jan. 1920
10,839 Livesley, Edwin, 1 Jan. 1920.
10,840 Llewellyn, Frederick Allen, 1 Jan. 1920.
10,841 Llewellyn, William Ewart, 1 Jan. 1920.
10,842 Lloyd, Cyril Edward, 1 Jan. 1920.
10,843 Lloyd, Francis Seymour, 1 Jan. 1920.
10,844 Lobjoit, William George, 1 Jan. 1920.
10,845 Lockett, Emma, Mrs., 1 Jan. 1920.
10,846 Lockyer, Frank Joshua, 1 Jan. 1920.
10,847 Lodge, Samuel Durham, 1 Jan. 1920.
10,848 Lomax, Edith Annie, 1 Jan. 1920.
10,849 Lombard, Rev. Bousfield Swan, 1 Jan. 1920.
10,850 London, Francis Henry, 1 Jan. 1920.
10,851 London, William Shakespeare, 1 Jan. 1920.
10,852 Loney, Henry Frith, 1 Jan. 1920.
10,853 Long, Archibald Percy, 1 Jan. 1920.
10,854 Long, Sibell, Hon. Mrs. Walter, 1 Jan. 1920.
10,855 Longcroft, Gwendoline Mary, 1 Jan. 1920

10,856 Longdon, Arthur Frederick, 1 Jan, 1920.
10,857 Longmore, Philip Raynsford, 1 Jan. 1920.
10,858 Loraine, William George, 1 Jan. 1920.
10,859 Lord, Charles Lupton, 1 Jan. 1920.
10,860 Lowe, Percy Roycroft, 1 Jan. 1920.
10,861 Lowis, Horace Lake, 1 Jan. 1920.
10,862 Lowson, Kenneth John, 1 Jan. 1920.
10,863 Lowthian, Harold Douglas, 1 Jan. 1920.
10,864 Lucan, Violet, Countess of, 1 Jan. 1920.
10,865 Luke, Alfred James, 1 Jan. 1920.
10,866 Lumsden, Thomas, 1 Jan. 1920.
10,867 Luttrell, Eva Fownes, 1 Jan. 1920.
10,868 Lyddon, Alfred Jonathan, 1 Jan. 1920.
10,869 Lyndon, Arnold, 1 Jan. 1920.
10,870 MacAlister, Sir John Young Walker, 1 Jan. 1920.
10,871 McAlpine, George, 1 Jan. 1920.
10,872 McBarnet, Alexander Cockburn, 1 Jan. 1920.
10,873 MacCallum, James Dalgleish Kellie-, 1 Jan. 1920.
10,874 McConnell, William Alexander, 1 Jan. 1920.
10,875 McCorquodale, Norman, 1 Jan. 1920.
10,876 McDermaid, Neil John, 1 Jan. 1920.
10,877 McDonald, Charles, 1 Jan. 1920.
10,878 Macdonald, Duncan Finlayson, 1 Jan. 1920.
10,879 Macdonald, James, 1 Jan. 1920.
10,880 Macdonald, Kenneth, 1 Jan. 1920.
10,881 MacDougall, Alice Mary, Lady Patten-, 1 Jan. 1920.
10,882 McDougall, Edith, 1 Jan. 1920.
10,883 McDowall, Charles, 1 Jan. 1920.
10,884 McEwan, John Robert, 1 Jan. 1920.
10,885 McEwen, Frederick Charles, 1 Jan. 1920.
10,886 Macfarlane, Alexander, 1 Jan. 1920.
10,887 Macfarlane, John Miller, 1 Jan. 1920.
10,888 McGeogh, Alexander, 1 Jan. 1920.
10,889 McGowan, James, 1 Jan. 1920.
10,890 MacGregor, John, 1 Jan. 1920.
10,891 McIlroy, Anne Louise, 1 Jan. 1920.
10,892 McIntyre, James Lewis, 1 Jan. 1920.
10,893 Macintyre, John Andrew, 1 Jan. 1920.
10,894 Mackay, Neil, 1 Jan. 1920.
10,895 Mackenzie, Beatrice Anna, Mrs. Fraser-, 1 Jan. 1920.
10,896 Mackenzie, Henrietta Mary, Lady, 1 Jan. 1920.
10,897 Mackenzie, Millicent, Mrs., 1 Jan. 1920.
10,898 McKenzie, William, 1 Jan. 1920.
10,899 MacKillop, Edward Laurence, 1 Jan. 1920.
10,900 McKinna, Alexander, 1 Jan. 1920.
10,901 Mackintosh, James, 1 Jan. 1920.
10,902 Mackintosh, Norna Susan, Mrs., 1 Jan. 1920.
10,903 Macklin, Edward Lionel, 1 Jan. 1920.
10,904 McLachlan, Arthur Cecil, 1 Jan. 1920.
10,905 McLachlan, Isabella Brodie, 1 Jan. 1920.
10,906 McLaughlin, William Reginald, 1 Jan. 1920.
10,907 McLean, Alexander Colin, 1 Jan. 1920.
10,908 Maclean, Agnes, 1 Jan. 1920.
10,909 MacMillan, Archibald Macpherson, 1 Jan. 1920
10,910 Macmillan, Agnes Olive, 1 Jan. 1920.
10,911 McNab, James, 1 Jan. 1920.
10,912 Macneill, William, 1 Jan. 1920.
10,913 McQuibban, Lewis, 1 Jan. 1920.
10,914 MacRae, Lady Margaret, 1 Jan. 1920.
10,915 Madin, Charles Gilbert, 1 Jan. 1920.
10,916 Maggs, Percy Harold, 1 Jan. 1920.
10,917 Mahon, Lilian Frances, Mrs., 1 Jan. 1920.
10,918 Mair, John Bagrie, 1 Jan. 1920.
10,919 Malby, Henry Arthur, 1 Jan. 1920.
10,920 Malcolmson, Norman, 1 Jan. 1920.
10,921 Malins, Mary Selina Beatrice, 1 Jan. 1920.
10,922 Mallinson, Frederick, 1 Jan. 1920.
10,923 Mander, John Harold, 1 Jan. 1920.
10,924 Manning, Lionel John, 1 Jan. 1920.
10,925 Manning, Nathaniel Samuel, 1 Jan. 1920.
10,926 Marcy, Janie, 1 Jan. 1920.
10,927 Marks, Richard Harris, 1 Jan. 1920.
10,928 Marsden, James Whittaker, 1 Jan. 1920.
10,929 Marsden, William Allen, 1 Jan. 1920.
10,930 Marshall, Howard, 1 Jan. 1920.
10,931 Marter, Alice Eleanor, 1 Jan. 1920.
10,932 Martin, Arthur, 1 Jan. 1920.
10,933 Martin, Gerald, 1 Jan. 1920.
10,934 Martin, James Cecil, 1 Jan. 1920.
10,935 Mason, Alfred, 1 Jan. 1920.
10,936 Mason, Cecil Charles, 1 Jan. 1920.
10,937 Mason, David, 1 Jan. 1920.
10,938 Mason, Evelyn Margaret, Lady, 1 Jan. 1920.
10,939 Mason, Mary Margaret, Mrs., 1 Jan. 1920.
10,940 Mather, Joseph Louis, 1 Jan. 1920.
10,941 Matheson, Wilhelmina Jean, Mrs., 1 Jan. 1920.
10,942 Mathewson, Alfred Eugene, 1 Jan. 1920.
10,943 Maxwell, William Jardine Herries, 1 Jan. 1920.
10,944 May, Eric Maurice, 1 Jan. 1920.
10,945 May, Lily Julia, Lady, 1 Jan. 1920.
10,946 Maycock, Thomas Langley, 1 Jan. 1920.
10,947 Maynard, Harry Payne, 1 Jan. 1920.
10,948 Mayne, Jasper Graham, 1 Jan. 1920.
10,949 Mayne, William, 1 Jan. 1920.
10,950 Mayo, Henry Herbert Worsfold, 1 Jan. 1920.
10,951 Meade, Richard John Edward, 1 Jan. 1920.
10,952 Meighan, John McNair, 1 Jan. 1920.
10,953 Melly, George Henry, 1 Jan. 1920.
10,054 Melville, Beresford Valentine, 1 Jan. 1920.

10,955 Menary, Thomas George, 1 Jan. 1920.
10,956 Mercer, John Swan, 1 Jan. 1920.
10,957 Meredith, Hugh Owen, 1 Jan. 1920.
10,958 Merivale, Bernard, 1 Jan. 1920.
10,959 Merry, William John Collings, 1 Jan. 1920.
10,960 Metcalfe, Thomas Edward, 1 Jan. 1920.
10,961 Middlemas, Robert, 1 Jan. 1920.
10,962 Middleton, Mary Katharine, Mrs., 1 Jan. 1920.
10,963 Midmer, Thomas William, 1 Jan. 1920.
10,964 Mildmay, Cecil Francis, Mrs. W. H. St. John, 1 Jan. 1920.
10,965 Miles, Alfred, 1 Jan. 1920.
10,966 Miles, Harry Powell, 1 Jan. 1920.
10,967 Miles, Sybil Marguerite Gonne, Mrs., 1 Jan. 1920.
10,968 Millar, James, 1 Jan. 1920.
10,969 Miller, Anne, 1 Jan. 1920.
10,970 Milligan, Robert Arthur, 1 Jan. 1920.
10,971 Millington, David, 1 Jan. 1920.
10,972 Millson, George, 1 Jan. 1920.
10,973 Minton, Richard Caldwell, 1 Jan. 1920.
10,974 Mitchell, John Edwin, 1 Jan. 1920.
10,975 Mitchell, Peter, 1 Jan. 1920.
10,976 Mitchison, Mary Emeline, Mrs., 1 Jan. 1920.
10,976a Moat. William, 1 Jan. 1920.
10,977 Mock, William John, 1 Jan. 1920.
10,978 Modlin, Isaac Gibson, 1 Jan. 1920.
10,979 Moger, Walter Henry, 1 Jan. 1920.
10,980 Moir, Charles Robert, 1 Jan. 1920.
10,981 Moir, Margaret Bruce, Lady, 1 Jan. 1920.
10,982 Monckton, William Leopold, 1 Jan. 1920.
10,983 Moncrieff, Jane Mary Scott-, 1 Jan. 1920.
10,984 Moncrieff, John, 1 Jan. 1920.
10,985 Money, Mildred Catherine, Mrs., 1 Jan. 1920.
10,986 Monkhouse, John Parry, 1 Jan. 1920.
10,987 Monro, Alexander James Falconer, 1 Jan. 1920.
10,988 Montgomery, Walter Basil Graham, 1 Jan. 1920
10,989 Moon, Rosa, 1 Jan. 1920.
10,990 Moore, Charles Henry, 1 Jan. 1920.
10,991 Morant, William George, 1 Jan. 1920.
10,992 More, Thomas Jasper Mytton, 1 Jan. 1920.
10,993 Morgan, Edward Lleurwg, 1 Jan. 1920.
10,994 Morgan, Effie Blanche, Mrs., 1 Jan. 1920.
10,995 Morgan, Gilbert Thomas, 1 Jan. 1920.
10,996 Morley, Arthur, 1 Jan. 1920.
10,997 Morley, Ida Rose, Mrs., 1 Jan. 1920.
10,998 Morphy, Arthur, 1 Jan. 1920.
10,999 Morris, Florence Muriel, 1 Jan. 1920.
11,000 Morris, Henry, 1 Jan. 1920.
11,001 Morrison, Archibald Cameron, 1 Jan. 1920.
11,002 Morrison, John, 1 Jan. 1920.
11,003 Morrison, John, 1 Jan. 1920.
11,004 Morrison, John Dow, 1 Jan. 1920.
11,005 Mortimer. Joseph, 1 Jan. 1920.
11,006 Mortimer, Ralph George Elphinstone, 1 Jan. 1920.
11,007 Mortimer, William Alfred, 1 Jan. 1920.
11,008 Morton, Hugh, 1 Jan. 1920.
11,009 Mosey, James Yeoman, 1 Jan. 1920.
11,010 Mount, Hilda Lucy Adelaide, Mrs., 1 Jan. 1920.
11,011 Mountgarret, Robina Marion, The Viscountess, 1 Jan. 1920.
11,012 Mozley, William, 1 Jan. 1920.
11,013 Mugliston, Francis Hugh, 1 Jan. 1920.
11,014 Muir, John, 1 Jan. 1920.
11,015 Muirhead, Frank Stirling, 1 Jan. 1920.
11,016 Munby, Mary Forth, 1 Jan. 1920.
11,017 Munday, John Augustus, 1 Jan. 1920.
11,018 Munkhouse, Alfred Frederick O'Gorman-, 1 Jan. 1920.
11,019 Munro, Hugh George, 1 Jan. 1920.
11,020 Munro, Rev. James Lorimer, 1 Jan. 1920.
11,021 Munro, John Edward, 1 Jan. 1920.
11,022 Murison, Annie Alice, Mrs., 1 Jan. 1920.
11,023 Murray, Clarisse Maria Guthrie, Mrs., 1 Jan. 1920.
11,024 Murray, Emma Cecilia, Lady Wyndham, 1 Jan. 1920.
11,025 Murray, Gertrude Margaret, Mrs., 1 Jan. 1920.
11,026 Murray, John, 1 Jan. 1920.
11,027 Murray, John, 1 Jan. 1920.
11,028 Murray, Mary Stewart, 1 Jan. 1920.
11,029 Murray, Richard, 1 Jan. 1920.
11,030 Murray, William, 1 Jan. 1920.
11,031 Murry, John Middleton, 1 Jan. 1920.
11,032 Muttlebury, Stanley Duff, 1 Jan. 1920.
11,033 Myers, James Eckersley, 1 Jan. 1920.
11,034 Myers, Leopold, 1 Jan. 1920.
11,035 Mylne, Katharine Isabel, 1 Jan. 1920.
11,036 Nadin, Joseph, 1 Jan. 1920.
11,037 Nash, Agnes Kathleen Mary, Lady, 1 Jan. 1920.
11,038 Naylor, Henry William Letts. 1 Jan. 1920.
11,039 Needham, John Hewson, 1 Jan. 1920.
11,040 Nesbitt, Edward John Beaumont-, 1 Jan. 1920.
11,041 Newberry, Percy Edward, 1 Jan. 1920.
11,042 Newcastle, Kathleen Florence May, Duchess of, 1 Jan. 1920.
11,043 Newell, Frank, 1 Jan. 1920.
11,044 Newman, William, 1 Jan. 1920.
11,045 Newton, Elizabeth Louisa, 1 Jan. 1920.
11,046 Nicholls, Frederick Lucius, 1 Jan. 1920.
11,047 Nicholls, George, 1 Jan. 1920.
11,048 Nicholson, David Walter, 1 Jan. 1920.
11,049 Nicholson, William Henry, 1 Jan. 1920.
11,050 Nicol, Robert Gordon, 1 Jan. 1920.

11,051 Normanby, Gertrude Stansfield, Marchioness of, 1 Jan. 1920.
11,052 Norton, Ethel Ada, Mrs., 1 Jan. 1920.
11,053 Norton, Grace Madeleine, Mrs., 1 Jan. 1920.
11,054 Norton, Herbert John, 1 Jan. 1920.
11,055 Norton, Robert Henry, 1 Jan. 1920.
11,056 Nunneley, Frederick Pitcairn, 1 Jan. 1920.
11,057 Nutter, Alfred Barrett, 1 Jan. 1920.
11,058 Oakshott, Ronald Stanley, 1 Jan. 1920.
11,059 Oates, William Henry, 1 Jan. 1920.
11,060 O'Donovan, William James, 1 Jan. 1920.
11,061 Ogston, Walter Henry, 1 Jan. 1920.
11,062 O'Hara, Charles Kean, 1 Jan. 1920.
11,063 Oldham, Alfred, 1 Jan. 1920.
11,064 Oliphant, William Elwin, 1 Jan. 1920.
11,065 Olive, Eustace John Parke, 1 Jan. 1920.
11,066 Openshaw, James, 1 Jan. 1920.
11,067 Ord, Evelyne Mary, 1 Jan. 1920.
11,068 Ord, William Wallis, 1 Jan. 1920.
11,069 Orme, Thomas Charles Rushmer, 1 Jan. 1920.
11,070 Ormerod, Marion Grace, Mrs., 1 Jan. 1920.
11,071 Orpen, Hon. Sybil Margaret, Mrs., 1 Jan. 1920.
11,072 Orr, John, 1 Jan. 1920.
11,073 Osborne, Frederick William, 1 Jan. 1920.
11,074 Oswald, Maude, Mrs., 1 Jan. 1920.
11,075 Oswald, Percy Cunningham, 1 Jan. 1920.
11,076 Owen, Robert David, 1 Jan. 1920.
11,078 Oyler, Alexander Wilfrid, 1 Jan. 1920.
11,079 Paget, Rosalind Margaret, Mrs., 1 Jan. 1920.
11,080 Paish, Leonard Alfred, 1 Jan. 1920.
11,081 Palmer, Louise Madeleine, Mrs., 1 Jan. 1920.
11,082 Palmer, Robert Edward, 1 Jan. 1920.
11,083 Panckridge, William Panckridge, 1 Jan. 1920.
11,084 Pape, William George, 1 Jan. 1920.
11,085 Papworth, Frederic William, 1 Jan. 1920.
11,086 Parker, Edwin Thorley, 1 Jan. 1920.
11,087 Parker, Haydon, 1 Jan. 1920.
11,088 Parker, Reginald Barcroft, 1 Jan. 1920.
11,089 Parry, Hugh Lloyd, 1 Jan. 1920.
11,090 Parry, John, 1 Jan. 1920.
11,091 Partington, Charles Frederick, 1 Jan. 1920.
11,092 Passingham, Edith Laura, Mrs., 1 Jan. 1920.
11,093 Paterson, James Graham, 1 Jan. 1920.
11,094 Patman, Frederick, 1 Jan. 1920.
11,095 Paton, Benjamin Lewis, 1 Jan. 1920.
11,096 Paton, Mary Emma, 1 Jan. 1920.
11,097 Pattinson, Henry, 1 Jan. 1920.
11,098 Paul, Walter Wyatt, 1 Jan. 1920.
11,099 Paul, Eveline Alice Wanda, Lady, 1 Jan. 1920.
11,100 Paull, James George, 1 Jan. 1920.
11,101 Payn, Thomas, 1 Jan. 1920.
11,102 Payne, Clifford, 1 Jan. 1920.
11,103 Payne, Rev. Francis Reginald Chassereau, 1 Jan. 1920.
11,104 Peachey, George Wyatt, 1 Jan. 1920.
11,105 Peaker, Alfred, 1 Jan. 1920.
11,106 Pearce, Thomas, 1 Jan. 1920.
11,107 Pearson, Geoffrey Hope, 1 Jan. 1920.
11,108 Pease, Ella, 1 Jan. 1920.
11,109 Peel, Walter, 1 Jan. 1920.
11,110 Pelham, Hon. Georgina, Mrs. Anderson-, 1 Jan. 1920.
11,111 Pelham, Louisa Keith, Hon. Mrs. Thomas, 1 Jan. 1920.
11,112 Pemberton, Eleanora Blanshard, 1 Jan. 1920.
11,113 Penrose, Nevill Coghill, 1 Jan. 1920.
11,114 Peploe, Alfred, 1 Jan. 1920.
11,115 Perkin, Herbert, 1 Jan. 1920.
11,116 Perry, Edward Verdon, 1 Jan. 1920.
11,117 Perry, George Henry, 1 Jan. 1920.
11,118 Perry, Muriel, 1 Jan. 1920.
11,119 Peto, Dorothy Olivia Georgiana, 1 Jan. 1920.
11,120 Petre, Francis Loraine, 1 Jan. 1920.
11,121 Petrie, Thomas Alexander, 1 Jan. 1920.
11,122 Phelps, Joseph Bryan William, 1 Jan. 1920.
11,123 Phelps, Joseph Harold, 1 Jan. 1920.
11,124 Philips, Edward Mark, 1 Jan. 1920.
11,125 Philipps, Marian Isobel, Lady, 1 Jan. 1920.
11,126 Phillips, Acton, 1 Jan. 1920.
11,127 Phillips, Edith Helen, Mrs., 1 Jan. 1920.
11,128 Phillips, Henry Archibald Allen, 1 Jan. 1920.
11,129 Phizackerley, George Thompson, 1 Jan. 1920.
11,130 Picton, Lionel James, 1 Jan. 1920.
11,131 Pike John 1 Jan. 1920.
11,132 Pike, Robert 1 Jan. 1920.
11,133 Pilcher, Richard Bertram, 1 Jan. 1920.
11,134 Pilgrim, Ida Helen, Mrs., 1 Jan. 1920.
11,135 Pilter, Sir John George, 1 Jan. 1920.
11,136 Pinckney, Leonard Durnford, 1 Jan. 1920.
11,137 Pinkham, Charles, 1 Jan. 1920.
11,138 Pinnington, Francis Stanislaus, 1 Jan. 1920.
11,139 Piper, George, 1 Jan. 1920.
11,140 Piper, Oliver James Southwell, 1 Jan. 1920.
11,141 Pitman, Arthur Joseph, 1 Jan. 1920.
11,142 Pitts, Robert Henry, 1 Jan. 1920.
11,143 Plackett, James William, 1 Jan. 1920.
11,144 Plage, John Philip, 1 Jan. 1920.
11,145 Pledge, Cecil Fenwick de, 1 Jan. 1920.
11,146 Plummer, Wilfrid Henry Coates, 1 Jan. 1920.
11,147 Pollock, Samuel Alexander, 1 Jan. 1920.
11,148 Polwhele, Arthur Carne, 1 Jan. 1920.

11,149 Ponsonby, Hon. Cyril Walter, 1 Jan. 1920.
11,150 Pooley, Robert, 1 Jan. 1920.
11,151 Pooley, Warner Lake, 1 Jan. 1920.
11,152 Porter, Frank, 1 Jan. 1920.
11,153 Porter, Ludovic Charles, 1 Jan. 1920.
11,154 Potter, Edith, Mrs., 1 Jan. 1920.
11,155 Powell, James Ablitt Pasiful, 1 Jan. 1920.
11,156 Powell, Joseph, 1 Jan. 1920.
11,157 Prance, Geoffrey Hammett, 1 Jan. 1920.
11,158 Preece, George, 1 Jan. 1920.
11,159 Price, Percy Howard, 1 Jan. 1920.
11,160 Priestley, Robert Chambers, 1 Jan. 1920.
11,161 Pringle, James Scott, 1 Jan. 1920.
11,162 Pritchard, Henry Ambrose, 1 Jan. 1920.
11,163 Pritchard, Henry Gibbon, 1 Jan. 1920.
11,164 Pritchett, Theodore, 1 Jan. 1920.
11,165 Probst, John Charles, 1 Jan. 1920.
11,166 Procter, George Henderson, 1 Jan. 1920.
11,167 Pryse, Nina Katherine Angharad, Lady Webley-Parry-, 1 Jan. 1920.
11,168 Punchard, John Alfred, 1 Jan. 1920.
11,169 Purcell, Matthew Henry, 1 Jan. 1920.
11,170 Purdom, John Ritchie, 1 Jan. 1920.
11,171 Purnell, William Ralph, 1 Jan. 1920.
11,172 Pyke, Cyril Cameron, 1 Jan. 1920.
11,173 Pyke, Harold Reason, 1 Jan. 1920.
11,174 Quarmby, Herbert Henry, 1 Jan. 1920.
11,175 Quass, Phineas, 1 Jan. 1920.
11,176 Quennell, Robert William, 1 Jan. 1920.
11,177 Rabino, Hyacinth Louis, 1 Jan. 1920.
11,178 Rainbow, William Thomas, 1 Jan. 1920.
11,179 Ramsay, Alexander, 1 Jan. 1920.
11,180 Ramsay, Ermyntrude Sidwell, Mrs., 1 Jan. 1920.
11,181 Randall, Alec Walter George, 1 Jan. 1920.
11,182 Randolph, George Boscawen, 1 Jan. 1920.
11,183 Ransome, Edward Coleby, 1 Jan. 1920.
11,184 Rawes, Stanley, 1 Jan. 1920.
11,185 Rawlins, Louisa Geraldine, Mrs., 1 Jan. 1920.
11,186 Rawnsley, Helen Maud, Mrs., 1 Jan. 1920.
11,187 Rayner, Eva Alexina Snoad, Mrs., 1 Jan. 1920.
11,188 Read, Francis Edward, 1 Jan. 1920.
11,189 Reddie, Constance Katharine Mary, Mrs., 1 Jan. 1920.
11,190 Reddoch, John Simpson, 1 Jan. 1920.
11,191 Redman, George Herbert, 1 Jan. 1920.
11,192 Reed, Thomas Danby, 1 Jan. 1920.
11,193 Reep, William, 1 Jan. 1920.
11,194 Reeves, John James, 1 Jan. 1920.
11,195 Reilly, Charles Herbert, 1 Jan. 1920.
11,196 Remington, Alfred Arnold, 1 Jan. 1920.
11,197 Renshaw, Samuel Henry, 1 Jan. 1920.
11,198 Reynolds, Reginald Carey, 1 Jan. 1920.
11,199 Rhodes, Edward Hugh, 1 Jan. 1920.
11,200 Rice, Hon. Helen Sarah, Mrs., 1 Jan. 1920.
11,201 Richards, John, 1 Jan. 1920.
11,202 Richards, John Thomas, 1 Jan. 1920.
11,203 Richardson, Bernhard Hermann, 1 Jan. 1920.
11,204 Richardson, Dunsford, 1 Jan. 1920.
11,205 Richardson, Florence Ellen, Lady, 1 Jan. 1920.
11,206 Richardson, Herbert Lindsley, 1 Jan. 1920.
11,207 Richardson, Jerusha Davidson, Mrs., 1 Jan. 1920
11,208 Richardson, Kathleen Rayner, 1 Jan. 1920.
11,209 Richardson, Percy, 1 Jan. 1920.
11,210 Richmond, Daniel, 1 Jan. 1920.
11,211 Richordson, James Birrell, 1 Jan. 1920.
11,212 Rickard, Charles Ernest, 1 Jan. 1920.
11,213 Rickett, Hubert Cecil, 1 Jan. 1920.
11,214 Rider, Douglas, 1 Jan. 1920.
11,215 Rider, Lewis Herbert, 1 Jan. 1920.
11,216 Ridley, Clarence Oliver, 1 Jan. 1920.
11,217 Ridley, John Henry Llewellyn, 1 Jan. 1920.
11,218 Rigg, Rowland William, 1 Jan. 1920.
11,219 Riordan, John McMahon, 1 Jan. 1920.
11,220 Rishworth, Albert Henry, 1 Jan. 1920.
11,221 Rivers, Arthur Thomas, 1 Jan. 1920.
11,222 Riviere, Evelyn, 1 Jan. 1920.
11,223 Rob, Joseph William, 1 Jan. 1920.
11,224 Robb, James Jenkins, 1 Jan. 1920.
11,225 Roberts, Ernest, 1 Jan. 1920.
11,226 Roberts, Hon. Marie Theresa, Mrs. Phillips-, 1 Jan. 1920.
11,227 Roberts, Reginald, 1 Jan. 1920.
11,228 Robertson, Charles, 1 Jan. 1920.
11,229 Robertson, Charles Bruce, 1 Jan. 1920.
11,230 Robertson, James Stewart, 1 Jan. 1920.
11,231 Robertson, Kate Ann, Lady, 1 Jan. 1920.
11,232 Robertson, Robert, 1 Jan. 1920.
11,233 Robertson, William, 1 Jan. 1920.
11,234 Robertson, Charles George, 1 Jan. 1920.
11,235 Robin, Alexander Gibson, 1 Jan. 1920.
11,236 Robin, Matthew, 1 Jan. 1920.
11,237 Robinson, Frederick Field, 1 Jan. 1920.
11,238 Robinson, Leonard Bambridge, 1 Jan. 1920.
11,239 Robinson, Rev. Samuel Fairbrother, 1 Jan. 1920.
11,240 Robson, Philip Warwick, 1 Jan. 1920.
11,241 Rodgers, Charles, 1 Jan. 1920.
11,242 Rogers, Rev. Edgar, 1 Jan. 1920.
11,243 Rogers, Hugh Innes, 1 Jan. 1920.
11,244 Rollason, Walter Herbert, 1 Jan. 1920.
11,245 Romer, Robert Leslie, 1 Jan. 1920.

11,246 Roper, John Gregson, 1 Jan. 1920.
11,247 Rose, Edith, 1 Jan. 1920.
11,248 Rose, Edward Armstrong, 1 Jan. 1920.
11,249 Ross, Alice Constance, Mrs., 1 Jan. 1920.
11,250 Rossmore, Mittie, Baroness, 1 Jan. 1920.
11,251 Round, Arthur, 1 Jan. 1920.
11,252 Royle, George, 1 Jan. 1920.
11,253 Rudder, Charles Joseph, 1 Jan. 1920.
11,254 Rudgard, Henry John, 1 Jan. 1920.
11,255 Ruffell, Frederick, 1 Jan. 1920.
11,256 Russell, William David, 1 Jan. 1920.
11,257 Rutherford, Ernest Victor Buckley, 1 Jan. 1920.
11,258 Ruthven, Hon. Charles Edward Stuart Hore-, 1 Jan. 1920.
11,259 Ryder, Lady Mary Maud, 1 Jan. 1920.
11,260 Sadler, Annie, 1 Jan. 1920.
11,261 Sadler, James, 1 Jan. 1920.
11,262 Sainsbury, Edgar John, 1 Jan. 1920.
11,263 St. Aubyn, Ingeborg Alfhild, Lady Molesworth-, 1 Jan. 1920.
11,264 St. Clair, Frank Verity, 1 Jan. 1920.
11,265 St. Quintin, Arthur Newton, 1 Jan. 1920.
11,266 Salmond, Elaine Marguerite, Mrs., 1 Jan. 1920.
11,267 Samble, Read, 1 Jan. 1920.
11,268 Sampson, George Frederick, 1 Jan. 1920.
11,269 Samuelson, Sybil Charlotte Eleanor, Mrs., 1 Jan. 1920.
11,270 Sandars, Gertrude Marian, Mrs., 1 Jan. 1920.
11,271 Sandberg, Oscar Fridolf Alexander, 1 Jan. 1920.
11,272 Sandlands, Paul Ernest, 1 Jan. 1920.
11,273 Sargant, Francis William, 1 Jan. 1920.
11,274 Sargent, Frederick Albert, 1 Jan. 1920.
11,275 Saunders, George, 1 Jan. 1920.
11,276 Sayers, Josiah, 1 Jan. 1920.
11,277 Scarr, George, 1 Jan. 1920.
11,278 Scholefield, Cotterill, 1 Jan. 1920.
11,279 Schreiber, Arthur Thomas, 1 Jan. 1920.
11,280 Scott, Alice Mary, 1 Jan. 1920.
11,281 Scott, Charles Robert, 1 Jan. 1920.
11,282 Scott, William, 1 Jan. 1920.
11,283 Scott, William Harding, 1 Jan. 1920.
11,284 Screech, Alfred Leonard, 1 Jan. 1920.
11,285 Screech, Alfred Leonard, 1 Jan. 1920.
11,286 Scriven, Charles, 1 Jan. 1920.
11,287 Scrivener, William Charles, 1 Jan. 1920.
11,288 Secretan, Hubert Arthur, 1 Jan. 1920.
11,289 Segar, John, 1 Jan. 1920.
11,290 Selby, Edmond Wallace, 1 Jan. 1920.
11,291 Sellers, Frederick Custance, 1 Jan. 1920.
11,292 Sells, Charles de Grave, 1 Jan. 1920.
11,293 Shacklock, Henry Stephen, 1 Jan. 1920.
11,294 Shafto, Helena Rosa. Mrs. Duncombe-, 1 Jan. 1920.
11,295 Shann, Lilian Alice, Mrs., 1 Jan. 1920.
11,296 Shapley, William Gilbert, 1 Jan. 1920.
11,297 Shaw, Adela Constance Alexandrina, Mrs., 1 Jan. 1920.
11,298 Shaw, Lisa Rebecca, Mrs. Gresham, 1 Jan. 1920.
11,299 Shaw, William Vernon, 1 Jan. 1920.
11,300 Shearer, James, 1 Jan. 1920.
11,301 Sheat, William James Oliver, 1 Jan. 1920.
11,302 Sheffield, Joseph, 1 Jan. 1920.
11,303 Sheffield, Julia Mary, Lady, 1 Jan. 1920.
11,304 Sheilds, Francis Wentworth-, 1 Jan. 1920.
11,305 Shepherd, Percy Edward, 1 Jan. 1920.
11,306 Sherbrooke, Margaret Macdonald, Mrs., 1 Jan. 1920.
11,308 Shiffner, Elsie, Lady, 1 Jan. 1920.
11,309 Shore, Thomas William, 1 Jan. 1920.
11,310 Shorto, Henry Ralph Trenchard, 1 Jan. 1920.
11,311 Showers, Edward Maclean, 1 Jan. 1920.
11,312 Shuckburgh, Honor Zoe, Lady, 1 Jan. 1920.
11,313 Sibley, Edith Waters, Mrs., 1 Jan. 1920.
11,314 Sim, John, 1 Jan. 1920.
11,315 Simmonds, Charles, 1 Jan. 1920.
11,316 Simmons, John Barnett, 1 Jan. 1920.
11,317 Simon, Emily Anne, Mrs., 1 Jan. 1920.
11,318 Simonds, Cecilia Elizabeth Beatrice, Mrs., 1 Jan. 1920.
11,319 Simpson, Annie Louise, 1 Jan. 1920.
11,320 Simpson, Clement Pearson, 1 Jan. 1920.
11,321 Simpson, James Bertie, 1 Jan. 1920.
11,322 Sims, Alfred James, 1 Jan. 1920.
11,323 Sinclair, Andrew Macgregor, 1 Jan. 1920.
11,324 Sinclair, Barbara Margaret Anne, 1 Jan. 1920.
11,325 Sinclair, James Donald, 1 Jan. 1920.
11,326 Singer, Aline Madeleine Charlotte, Lady, 1 Jan. 1920.
11,327 Sinnott, John, 1 Jan. 1920.
11,328 Skeet, Arthur Robert, 1 Jan. 1920.
11,329 Sketch, Samuel Bolt, 1 Jan. 1920.
11,330 Slocombe, Frank Edwin, 1 Jan. 1920.
11,331 Smeddle, John Henry, 1 Jan. 1920.
11,332 Smeeton, Charles William, 1 Jan. 1920.
11,333 Smith, Alwyn Dudley, 1 Jan. 1920.
11,334 Smith, Arthur Croxton, 1 Jan. 1920.
11,335 Smith, Cicely, Mrs., 1 Jan. 1920.
11,336 Smith, Clarence Dalrymple, 1 Jan. 1920.
11,337 Smith, Constance Isabella Stuart, 1 Jan. 1920.
11,338 Smith, Edith Flora, Mrs., 1 Jan. 1920.
11,339 Smith, Harold Lea-, 1 Jan. 1920.
11,340 Smith, Henry John, 1 Jan. 1920.
11,341 Smith, Henry Watson, 1 Jan. 1920.
11,342 Smith, Herbert Francis, 1 Jan. 1920.
11,843 Smith, John William, 1 Jan. 1920.
11,344 Smith, Joseph Kent, 1 Jan. 1920.

11,345 Smith, Percy Campbell, 1 Jan. 1920.
11,346 Smith, Robert Adam, 1 Jan. 1920.
11,347 Smith, St. Osyth Mahala Eustace, 1 Jan. 1920.
11,348 Smith, Victor Vyvian Cuthbertson, 1 Jan. 1920.
11,349 Smith, William Charles Clifford, 1 Jan. 1920.
11,350 Smith, William George, 1 Jan. 1920.
11,351 Smithson, John George, 1 Jan. 1920.
11,352 Smyth, Barbara, Mrs. Ross, 1 Jan. 1920.
11,353 Smyth, George Edward, 1 Jan. 1920.
11,354 Smyth, John George, 1 Jan. 1920.
11,355 Snape, Henry Lloyd, 1 Jan. 1920.
11,356 Snell, John Beddome, 1 Jan. 1920.
11,357 Soundy, William Henry, 1 Jan. 1920.
11,358 Sparkes, Henry, 1 Jan. 1920.
11,359 Sparkes, James Noel, 1 Jan. 1920.
11,360 Spence, Alexander, 1 Jan. 1920.
11,361 Spence, James Beveridge, 1 Jan. 1920.
11,362 Spencer, Christopher John, 1 Jan. 1920.
11,363 Spencer, Rev. Henry Thomas, 1 Jan. 1920.
11,364 Spender, Arthur Francis, 1 Jan. 1920
11,365 Spensley, James Calvert, 1 Jan. 1920.
11,366 Spratt, Laura Gertrude, 1 Jan. 1920.
11,367 Sprott, James, 1 Jan. 1920.
11,368 Stafford, Salvatore Guattari-, 1 Jan. 1920.
11,369 Stainthorpe, William Waters, 1 Jan. 1920.
11,370 Stamford, Emma Pauline, Mrs., 1 Jan. 1920.
11,371 Stamford, Elizabeth Louisa Penelope, Countess of, 1 Jan. 1920.
11,372 Stanier, William Henry, 1 Jan. 1920.
11,373 Stanion, Oliver Bown, 1 Jan. 1920.
11,374 Stanley, Olivia Elizabeth, Mrs. Sloane- (Dowager Countess Cairns), 1 Jan. 1920.
11,375 Stanton, Harold Westwood, 1 Jan. 1920.
11,376 Stark, John, 1 Jan. 1920.
11,377 Stark, John, 1 Jan. 1920.
11,378 Steel, Alexander, 1 Jan. 1920.
11,379 Stenhouse, Joseph Russell, 1 Jan. 1920.
11,380 Stephen, Henry, 1 Jan. 1920
11,381 Stephens, Charles Hoak, 1 Jan. 1920.
11,382 Stephens, William Edgar, 1 Jan. 1920.
11,383 Stephenson, Joseph, 1 Jan. 1920.
11,384 Sterry, John, 1 Jan. 1920.
11,385 Steuart, James, 1 Jan. 1920.
11,386 Stevens, Harold Blythen, 1 Jan. 1920.
11,387 Stevenson, James Maxton, 1 Jan. 1920.
11,388 Stevenson, William King, 1 Jan. 1920.
11,389 Stewart, Angus, 1 Jan. 1920.
11,390 Stewart, Charles, 1 Jan. 1920.
11,391 Stewart, Mary Beatrice Sydney, Mrs. Shaw, 1 Jan. 1920.
11,392 Stirling, George Harry Miller-, 1 Jan. 1920.
11,393 Stirling, John, 1 Jan. 1920.
11,394 Stirling, Hon. Margaret Mary, Mrs. A., 1 Jan. 1920.
11,395 Stobart, Bessie, Mrs., 1 Jan. 1920.
11,396 Stocker, Edward Barlow, 1 Jan. 1920.
11,397 Stockley, Henry Hudson Fraser, 1 Jan. 1920.
11,398 Stoneham, Allen Henry Philip, 1 Jan. 1920.
11,399 Stonham, Edwin Earle, 1 Jan. 1920.
11,400 Stopher, Arthur James, 1 Jan. 1920.
11,401 Storey, Ethel Mary Hutton, 1 Jan. 1920.
11,402 Storey, Joseph Kearon, 1 Jan. 1920.
11,403 Storey, Mary Gladys, 1 Jan. 1920.
11,404 Strickland, William Henry, 1 Jan. 1920.
11,405 Strode, George Sydney Strode, 1 Jan. 1920.
11,406 Stromeyer, Charles Edmond, 1 Jan. 1920.
11,407 Stubbs, Arthur, 1 Jan. 1920.
11,408 Studdert. Frederick Naunton, 1 Jan. 1920.
11,409 Sumner, Harold, 1 Jan. 1920.
11,410 Sutcliffe, Frances Edith, 1 Jan. 1920.
11,411 Sutcliffe, John Hamer, 1 Jan. 1920.
11,412 Sutthery, Colin Pellatt, 1 Jan. 1920.
11,413 Sutton, Ralph, 1 Jan. 1920.
11,414 Sutton, Richard James, 1 Jan. 1920.
11,415 Sweet, William McMurdo, 1 Jan. 1920.
11,416 Swinton, Elizabeth, Mrs., 1 Jan. 1920.
11,417 Sykes, Charles David 1 Jan. 1920.
11,418 Sykes, Joe Armitage, 1 Jan. 1920.
11,419 Symonds, Mary Josephine, Mrs. Loder-, 1 Jan. 1920.
11,420 Symons, William Frederick, 1 Jan. 1920.
11,421 Tabrum, Ashley, 1 Jan. 1920.
11,422 Tainsh, Peter, 1 Jan. 1920.
11,423 Talbot, Bridget Elizabeth, 1 Jan. 1920.
11,424 Talbot, Hugo, 1 Jan. 1920.
11,425 Talbot, Julia Elizabeth Mary, Mrs., 1 Jan. 1920.
11,426 Tallent, Edward Killworth, 1 Jan. 1920.
11,427 Tangye, Albert William, 1 Jan. 1920.
11,428 Tanner, Edward Butler, 1 Jan. 1920.
11,429 Tanner, William Allan, 1 Jan. 1920.
11,430 Tatham, Meaburn, 1 Jan. 1920.
11,431 Tatton, Winifred Eva, Mrs., 1 Jan. 1920.
11,432 Taylor, Arnold, 1 Jan. 1920.
11,433 Taylor, Arthur Edwin, 1 Jan. 1920.
11,434 Taylor, Arthur Thomas, 1 Jan. 1920.
11,435 Taylor, David Paton, 1 Jan. 1920.
11,436 Taylor, Harold, 1 Jan. 1920.
11,437 Taylor, John, 1 Jan. 1920.
11,438 Taylor, Lionel Percy Duncuft, 1 Jan. 1920.
11,439 Taylor, Percy, 1 Jan. 1920.
11,440 Taylor, Sidney Ormerod, 1 Jan. 1920.
11,441 Taylor, William, 1 Jan. 1920.

11,442 Taylor, William James, 1 Jan. 1920.
11,443 Tebbutt, Arnold, 1 Jan. 1920.
11,444 Telfer, John Edward. 1 Jan. 1920.
11,445 Telford, John Charles, 1 Jan. 1920.
11,446 Temperley, Charles, 1 Jan. 1920.
11,447 Tempest, Henrietta Frances May, Mrs., 1 Jan. 1920.
11,448 Temple, Walter Middlewood, 1 Jan. 1920.
11,449 Tennent, John James Colvin, 1 Jan. 1920.
11,450 Terris, James, 1 Jan. 1920
11,451 Thatcher, Noel, 1 Jan. 1920.
11,452 Theodosius, Alfred Fletcher, 1 Jan. 1920.
11,453 Thesiger, Florita Maria-Engracia, Mrs., 1 Jan. 1920.
11,454 Thom, James Maxtone, 1 Jan. 1920.
11,455 Thom, Robert Absalom, 1 Jan. 1920.
11,456 Thomas, Alfred Dominy, 1 Jan. 1920.
11,457 Thomas, Frank Charles, 1 Jan. 1920.
11,458 Thomas, Julia Winifred, Mrs. Griffith-, 1 Jan. 1920.
11,459 Thomas, Morgan, 1 Jan. 1920.
11,460 Thomas, William, 1 Jan. 1920.
11,461 Thomas, William Edmund, 1 Jan. 1920.
11,462 Thompson, Arthur, 1 Jan. 1920.
11,463 Thompson, John Hannay, 1 Jan. 1920.
11,464 Thompson, John Ockelford, 1 Jan. 1920.
11,465 Thompson, Reginald, 1 Jan. 1920.
11,466 Thomson, Andrew, 1 Jan. 1920.
11,467 Thomson, Constance Emily Temple, Mrs., 1 Jan. 1920.
11,468 Thomson, Gwyneth Marjory, Mrs., 1 Jan. 1920.
11,469 Thomson, Peter Allan, 1 Jan. 1920.
11,470 Thomson, Thomas Craston, 1 Jan. 1920.
11,471 Thornhill, Florence Augusta, Mrs., 1 Jan. 1920.
11,472 Thornley, Hubert Gordon, 1 Jan. 1920.
11,473 Thornley, Thomas, 1 Jan. 1920.
11,474 Thornton, William Mundell, 1 Jan. 1920.
11,475 Thurburn, Bertha, Mrs., 1 Jan. 1920.
11,476 Ticehurst, Norman Frederic, 1 Jan. 1920.
11,477 Tidmarsh, Charles Baillie, 1 Jan. 1920.
11,478 Tidmarsh, Edwin Russell, 1 Jan. 1920.
11,479 Tilby, Henry Albert, 1 Jan. 1920.
11,480 Tilley, John William, 1 Jan. 1920.
11,481 Timewell, Herbert William, 1 Jan. 1920.
11,482 Tindall, Louis Edward, 1 Jan. 1920.
11,483 Titley, Margaret, Mrs., 1 Jan. 1920.
11,484 Tomkinson, Dora Sloane, 1 Jan. 1920.
11,485 Tooth, Helen Katherine, Mrs., 1 Jan. 1920.
11,486 Topham, Harry, 1 Jan. 1920.
11,487 Tough, George, 1 Jan. 1920.
11,488 Toulmin, Francis Justus, 1 Jan. 1920.
11,489 Towle, Arthur Henry, 1 Jan. 1920.
11,490 Townend, Kathleen Mary, 1 Jan. 1920.
11,491 Townsend, Harry Edward, 1 Jan. 1920.
11,492 Toye, Dudley Bulmer, 1 Jan. 1920.
11,493 Tozer, Alfred Robert, 1 Jan. 1920.
11,494 Tozer, James Clark, 1 Jan. 1920.
11,495 Tree, Maud Helen Louise, Lady, 1 Jan. 1920
11,496 Treharne, Frederick Gwilym, 1 Jan. 1920.
11,497 Trevanion, Stella, Mrs., 1 Jan. 1920.
11,498 Trimble, Samuel Delmege, 1 Jan. 1920.
11,499 Trimen, Stephen Herbert, 1 Jan. 1920.
11,500 Trotter, Archibald McGregor, 1 Jan. 1920.
11,501 Trotter, Marjorie Ellinor, 1 Jan. 1920.
11,502 Trubshaw, Wilfred, 1 Jan. 1920.
11,503 Trueman, Lady Susan Catherine Harriet, 1 Jan. 1920.
11,504 Trumper, John Henry Walwyn , 1 Jan. 1920.
11,505 Tubmann, Francis de Moag, 1 Jan. 1920.
11,506 Tuckett, Walter Reginald, 1 Jan. 1920.
11,507 Tunks, Harold William Gregory, 1 Jan. 1920.
11,508 Turckheim, Alfred De, 1 Jan. 1920.
11,509 Turner, Albert Charles, 1 Jan. 1920.
11,510 Turner, Emma Maud, 1 Jan. 1920.
11,511 Turner, Ernest Edward, 1 Jan. 1920.
11,512 Turner, Frederick William, 1 Jan. 1920.
11,513 Turner, Philip Dymoch, 1 Jan. 1920.
11,514 Turner, Renard Orlando Sydney, 1 Jan. 1920.
11,515 Turner, Robert Reginald Johnston, 1 Jan. 1920.
11,516 Turner, Sydney George, 1 Jan. 1920.
11,517 Turner, William Glasier, 1 Jan. 1920.
11,518 Turner, William Thomas, 1 Jan. 1920.
11,519 Twyford, Dora, 1 Jan. 1920.
11,520 Tyrer, William Henry, 1 Jan. 1920.
11,521 Tyzack, Walter, 1 Jan. 1920.
11,522 Underhill, Thomas John, 1 Jan. 1920.
11,523 Unsworth, Isaac, 1 Jan. 1920.
11,524 Valerie, John, 1 Jan. 1920.
11,525 Varwell, Margaret, Mrs., 1 Jan. 1920.
11,526 Veitch, Robert McLeod, 1 Jan. 1920.
11,527 Venning, Margaret Beatrice, Mrs., 1 Jan. 1920.
11,528 Vesey, Isabel Constance, 1 Jan. 1920.
11,529 Vickery, Frederick William, 1 Jan. 1920.
11,530 Vigrass, Herbert, 1 Jan. 1920.
11,531 Vincent, Cyril Mosson, 1 Jan. 1920.
11,532 Visger, Charles, 1 Jan. 1920.
11,533 Wagstaff, George Leonard, 1 Jan. 1920.
11,534 Wainwright, George Bartram, 1 Jan. 1920.
11,535 Wakeling, Elizabeth, Mrs., 1 Jan. 1920.
11,536 Wakeling, George Henry, 1 Jan. 1920.
11,537 Walden, William Herbert, 1 Jan. 1920.
11,538 Walker, Frederic William, 1 Jan. 1920.
11,539 Walker, John, 1 Jan. 1920.
11,540 Walker, John William, 1 Jan. 1920.

11,541 Walker, Mabel Caroline, 1 Jan. 1920.
11,542 Walker, Margaret, 1 Jan. 1920.
11,543 Walker, Thomas Charles Bruce Mackintosh-, 1 Jan. 1920.
11,544 Walker, Winifred Jane, 1 Jan. 1920.
11,545 Wall, Arthur Thomas, 1 Jan. 1920.
11,546 Wallace, John, 1 Jan. 1920.
11,547 Waller, James Hardress de Warrenne, 1 Jan. 1920.
11,548 Wallington, Augusta Frances, 1 Jan. 1920.
11,549 Walters, Henry Beauchamp, 1 Jan. 1920.
11,550 Walters, Henry Blanchard, 1 Jan. 1920.
11,551 Waltham, Amy, 1 Jan. 1920.
11,552 Walton, Frank Neville, 1 Jan. 1920.
11,553 Walton, Henry Lavington, 1 Jan. 1920.
11,554 Walton, Thomas Frederick, 1 Jan. 1920.
11,555 Ward, William, 1 Jan. 1920.
11,556 Ward, William Pettit, 1 Jan. 1920.
11,557 Waring, Eleanor Gladys, 1 Jan. 1920.
11,558 Warneford, Walter Wyndham Hanbury, **1 Jan. 1920.**
11,559 Warner, Surrey, 1 Jan. 1920.
11,560 Warren, Edith Ella, Mrs., 1 Jan. 1920.
11,561 Warren, Margaret Maxwell, Mrs., 1 Jan. 1920.
11,562 Warren, William, 1 Jan. 1920.
11,563 Waters, Owen, 1 Jan. 1920.
11,564 Watkins, Jane Gertrude, 1 Jan. 1920.
11,565 Watkins, John Stewart, 1 Jan. 1920.
11,566 Watling, John William, 1 Jan. 1920.
11,567 Watson, Ernest Ansley, 1 Jan. 1920.
11,568 Watson, Frank, 1 Jan. 1920.
11,569 Watson, George Trustram, 1 Jan. 1920.
11,570 Watson, Henry Talbot, 1 Jan. 1920.
11,571 Watson, Isobel, Mrs., 1 Jan. 1920.
11,572 Watson, James, 1 Jan. 1920.
11,573 Watson, John Alfred, 1 Jan. 1920.
11,574 Watson, William Milne, 1 Jan. 1920.
11,575 Watt, Charles Frederick, 1 Jan. 1920.
11,576 Watts, Philip James, 1 Jan. 1920.
11,577 Wawn, Dominique, 1 Jan. 1920.
11,578 Wayne, Francis Herman Milford, 1 Jan. 1920.
11,579 Webb, Frederick James, 1 Jan. 1920.
11,580 Webb, George William Cutler, 1 Jan. 1920.
11,581 Webb, John Henry, 1 Jan. 1920.
11,582 Wedderburn, Robert Rowell, 1 Jan. 1920.
11,583 Weldon, Winifred, Lady, 1 Jan. 1920.
11,584 Wellman, Francis Alfred, 1 Jan. 1920.
11,585 West, Arthur John, 1 Jan. 1920.
11,586 West, Dora, 1 Jan. 1920.
11,587 West, Frederick William, 1 Jan. 1920.
11,588 West, John Edward, 1 Jan. 1920
11,589 West, Leonard Henry, 1 Jan. 1920.
11,590 Westaway, Richard Ernest, 1 Jan. 1920.
11,591 Westwood, Andrew, 1 Jan. 1920.
11,592 Wethered, Ernest Handel Cossham, 1 Jan. 1920.
11,593 Wharton, Frederick Percival, 1 Jan. 1920.
11,594 Whatman, Florence Emma Jemima, 1 Jan. 1920.
11,595 Whelon, Emily Mildred, 1 Jan. 1920.
11,596 Wherry, Albert Edward Kerkham, 1 Jan. 1920
11,597 Whitaker, Thorp, 1 Jan. 1920.
11,598 White, Amber, Mrs. Blanco, 1 Jan. 1920.
11,599 White, Arethusa Flora Gartside, Mrs. Leigh-, 1 Jan. 1920.
11,600 White, Arthur, 1 Jan. 1920.
11,601 White, George Thomas, 1 Jan. 1920.
11,602 White, John Arthur Temple, 1 Jan. 1920.
11,603 White, Minnie Beauchamp, Mrs., 1 Jan. 1920.
11,604 Whiteley, Feather Ogden, 1 Jan. 1920.
11,605 Whitmore, Violet Frances Elizabeth, Mrs., 1 Jan. 1920
11,606 Whittall, Frederick Octavius, 1 Jan. 1920.
11,607 Whittingdale, John Flasby Lawrance, 1 Jan. 1920.
11,608 Whittingham, Hilda Kate, 1 Jan. 1920.
11,609 Wilbraham, Lady Alice Maud Bootle-, 1 Jan. 1920.
11,610 Wilkins, Elizabeth Bastable, 1 Jan. 1920.
11,611 Wilkins, Frederick Charles Sydney, 1 Jan. 1920.
11,612 Wilkins, Thomas James Hackett, 1 Jan. 1920.
11,613 Willcock, Rev. John, 1 Jan. 1920.
11,614 Willcox, William Henry, 1 Jan. 1920.
11,615 Williams, Amy Katharine, 1 Jan. 1920.
11,616 Williams, Charles Robert Thomas, 1 Jan. 1920.
11,617 Williams, Ernest Thomas, 1 Jan. 1920.
11,618 Williams, Rev. Henry Morrison, 1 Jan. 1920.
11,619 Williams, John Seth, 1 Jan. 1920.
11,620 Williams, Philip, 1 Jan. 1920.
11,621 Williams, Richard John, 1 Jan. 1920.
11,622 Williams, Thomas, 1 Jan. 1920.
11,623 Williams, Thomas Richard, 1 Jan. 1920.
11,624 Williams, William Thomas, 1 Jan. 1920.
11,625 Williamson, Hon. Agnes Freda, Lady, 1 Jan. 1920.
11,626 Williamson, Harry, 1 Jan. 1920.
11,627 Williamson, James, 1 Jan. 1920.
11,628 Willis, Charles, 1 Jan. 1920.
11,629 Willmer, Edward Albert Brittain, 1 Jan. 1920.
11,630 Willoughby, Esther Ann, Mrs. T., 1 Jan. 1920.
11,631 Willoughby, James Frederick Digby, 1 Jan. 1920.
11,632 Wilmot, Jane Millicent, Mrs. Eardley-, 1 Jan. 1920
11,633 Wilson, Alexander, 1 Jan. 1920.
11,634 Wilson, Arthur Cecil James, 1 Jan. 1920.
11,635 Wilson, Benedict John, 1 Jan. 1920.
11,636 Wilson, Daniel Ellis, 1 Jan. 1920.
11,637 Wilson, George, 1 Jan. 1920.

11,638 Wilson, George Alexander, 1 Jan. 1920.
11,639 Wilson, Haigh Robson, 1 Jan. 1920.
11,640 Wilson, James, 1 Jan. 1920.
11,641 Wilson, John, 1 Jan. 1920.
11,642 Wilson, Minnie Elizabeth, Lady Maryon-, 1 Jan. 1920.
11,643 Winder, Arthur Wellesley, 1 Jan. 1920.
11,644 Windle, Alfred Rawlinson, 1 Jan. 1920.
11,645 Windus, George Ryley, 1 Jan. 1920.
11,646 Winterbottom, Albert, 1 Jan. 1920.
11,647 Winterbottom, George William, 1 Jan. 1920.
11,648 Wintour, Francis, 1 Jan. 1920.
11,649 Wise, Thomas, 1 Jan. 1920.
11,650 Wishart, Frederick, 1 Jan. 1920.
11,651 Wolff, Joseph, 1 Jan. 1920.
11,652 Wood, Charles, 1 Jan. 1920.
11,653 Wood, Frederick, 1 Jan. 1920.
11,654 Wood, Frederick Benjamin, 1 Jan. 1920.
11,655 Wood, Harold John, 1 Jan. 1920.
11,656 Wood, John Livingstone, 1 Jan. 1920.
11,657 Wood, William, 1 Jan. 1920.
11,658 Wood, William Cranna, 1 Jan. 1920.
11,659 Wood, William John, 1 Jan. 1920.
11,660 Woodroffe, Henry, 1 Jan. 1920.
11,661 Woods, Alfred, 1 Jan. 1920.
11,662 Woolf, Albert Morris, 1 Jan. 1920.
11,663 Woolf, Mortimer, 1 Jan. 1920.
11,664 Woollam, Henry, 1 Jan. 1920.
11,665 Woolliscroft, George William, 1 Jan. 1920.
11,666 Woolmer, Andrew Charles, 1 Jan. 1920.
11,667 Woolmer, Charles Edward, 1 Jan. 1920.
11,668 Worlledge, Edward William, 1 Jan. 1920.
11,669 Wormald, William, 1 Jan. 1920.
11,670 Worsley, Frank Arthur, 1 Jan. 1920.
11,671 Wright, Ernest John, 1 Jan. 1920.
11,672 Wright, Henry, 1 Jan. 1920.
11,673 Wrigley, Lilian, Mrs., 1 Jan. 1920.
11,674 Wyche, Katharine, Mrs., 1 Jan. 1920.
11,675 Wyles, John Edward, 1 Jan. 1920.
11,676 Yarborough, Marcia Amelia Mary, Countess of, 1 Jan. 1920.
11,677 Yorke, Gladys. Hon. Mrs. Alfred, 1 Jan. 1920.
11,678 Young, Allen Carruth, 1 Jan. 1920.
11,679 Young, Arthur Primrose, 1 Jan. 1920.
11,680 Young, Edward Willie, 1 Jan. 1920.
11,681 Young, John, 1 Jan. 1920.
11,682 Young, Joseph Samuel, 1 Jan. 1920.
11,683 Young, Sydney Roles, 1 Jan. 1920.
11,684 Young, William, 1 Jan. 1920.
11,685 Young, William Alexander, 1 Jan. 1920.
11,686 Yoxall, George, 1 Jan. 1920.
11,687 Andel, Harry Rudolph, 1 Jan. 1920.
11,688 Arthur, George Stanley, 1 Jan. 1920.
11,689 Blair, Frank Younger, 1 Jan. 1920.
11,690 Bonhote, Mary Baxter, Mrs., 1 Jan. 1920.
11,691 Booth, Henry Bennion-, 1 Jan. 1920.
11,692 Canning, Lionel Edgar, 1 Jan. 1920.
11,693 Capito, Charles Erik, 1 Jan. 1920.
11,694 Cattell, Arthur Shelton Goodricke, 1 Jan. 1920.
11,695 Collier, Hon. John, 1 Jan. 1920.
11,696 Cowper, Muriel, 1 Jan. 1920.
11,697 England, Walter William, 1 Jan. 1920.
11,698 Evans, Griffith Charles, 1 Jan. 1920.
11,699 Eyre, Edmond, 1 Jan. 1920.
11,700 Foster, Frank, 1 Jan. 1920.
11,701 Gardner, Harry Geary, 1 Jan. 1920.
11,702 Hunter, Campbell, Murray, 1 Jan. 1920.
11,703 Leslie, Theodore, 1 Jan. 1920.
11,704 Loveday, Arthur Frederic, 1 Jan. 1920.
11,705 McHardy, William, 1 Jan. 1920.
11,706 MacPhillamy, Verania, 1 Jan. 1920.
11,707 Maer, Constance Muriel, Mrs. Astley, 1 Jan. 1920.
11,708 Mason, Joseph Warren Teets, 1 Jan. 1920.
11,709 Melsom, George Washington, 1 Jan. 1920.
11,710 Pratt, Henry Francis, 1 Jan. 1920.
11,711 Small, Frederick Trouton, 1 Jan. 1920.
11,712 Smythe, Theodore William, 1 Jan. 1920.
11,713 Temperley, Dorothy Mary Gladys, 1 Jan. 1920.
11,714 Thompson, Arthur Beeby, 1 Jan. 1920.
11,715 Timewell, Herbert William, 1 Jan. 1920.
11,716 Tod, Arthur White Millar, 1 Jan. 1920.
11,717 Wills, Charles, 1 Jan. 1920.
11,718 Wilson, John, 1 Jan. 1920.
11,719 Wooley, Alfred, 1 Jan. 1920.
11,720 Abdul Samad Shah, 1 Jan. 1920. (M.)
11,721 Abdul Majid Khan, 1 Jan. 1920. (M.)
11,722 Anson, George Frank Wemyss, 1 Jan. 1920. (M.)
11,723 Arthur, Lionel Francis, 1 Jan. 1920. (M.)
11,724 Bethell, Leonard Arthur, 1 Jan. 1920. (M.)
11,725 Bharucha, Phirozshah Byramji, 1 Jan. 1920. (M.)
11,726 Bird, William Arthur Henry, 1 Jan. 1920. (M.)
11,727 Blackmore, Herbert Stuart, 1 Jan. 1920. (M.)
11,728 Boutflower, Edward Cyril, 1 Jan. 1920. (M.)
11,729 Bulteel, Cecil Edward, 1 Jan. 1920. (M.)
11,730 Burmester, Zante Gower, 1 Jan. 1920. (M.)
11,731 Butler, Charles Walter, 1 Jan. 1920. (M.)
11,732 Cameron, Alexander, 1 Jan. 1920. (M.)
11,733 Collins, Lionel Peter, 1 Jan. 1920. (M.)
11,734 Craster, George, 1 Jan. 1920. (M.)
11,735 Davenport, Colin, 1 Jan. 1920. (M.)

11,736 De Sousa, Pascal John, 1 Jan. 1920. (M.)
11,737 Dunlop, William Bruce, 1 Jan. 1920. (M.)
11,738 Roberts, Kenneth Farquharson Farquharson-, 1 Jan. 1920. (M.)
11,739 Farrell, Robert, 1 Jan. 1920. (M.)
11,740 Forbes, Gordon Harold Norman, 1 Jan. 1920. (M.)
11,741 Gilmore, Alice Maud, 1 Jan. 1920. (M.)
11,742 Gupta, Bhola Nath, 1 Jan. 1920. (M.)
11,743 Hall, Charles Frank, 1 Jan. 1920. (M.)
11,744 Haws, Albert Henry, 1 Jan. 1920. (M.)
11,745 Huban, John Patrick, 1 Jan. 1920. (M.)
11,746 Lillingston, Frederick Francis Innes-, 1 Jan. 1920. (M.)
11,747 Jones, Vincent Strickland, 1 Jan. 1920. (M.)
11,748 Kendall, Sydney Robert Gordon, 1 Jan. 1920. (M.)
11,749 King, Charles John Stuart, 1 Jan. 1920. (M.)
11,750 Landon, Cyril, 1 Jan. 1920. (M.)
11,751 Macdonald, Reginald Henry, 1 Jan. 1920. (M.)
11,752 McRae, Henry St. George Murray, 1 Jan. 1920. (M.)
11,753 Martin, Hugh Gray, 1 Jan. 1920. (M.)
11,754 Matson, John, 1 Jan. 1920. (M.)
11,755 Murphy, Robert Walpole, 1 Jan. 1920. (M.)
11,756 Myles, Robert Boulton, 1 Jan. 1920. (M.)
11,757 Nawab Talib Mehdi Khan, 1 Jan. 1920. (M.)
11,758 Nicol, William Hutton, 1 Jan. 1920. (M.)
11,759 Norrie, Forster Heddle Brown, 1 Jan. 1920. (M.)
11,760 Parsons, Arthur Edward Broadbent, 1 Jan. 1920. (M.)
11,761 Pengelly, George Hastings, 1 Jan. 1920. (M.)
11,762 Pillay, Aiyappin Padmanabbha, 1 Jan. 1920. (M.)
11,763 Pritchard, Hugh Robert Norman, 1 Jan. 1920. (M.)
11,764 Quinan, Edward Pellew, 1 Jan. 1920. (M.)
11,765 Ryles, Charlie. 1 Jan. 1920. (M.)
11,766 Skinner, Robert Bruce, 1 Jan. 1920. (M.)
11,767 Steward, Edward Merivale, 1 Jan. 1920. (M.)
11,768 Strong, Cecil Alfred, 1 Jan. 1920. (M.)
11,769 Toller, George Gordon Taylor, 1 Jan. 1920. (M.)
11,770 Pattenson, Edwin Cooke Tylden-, 1 Jan. 1920. (M.)
11,771 Stuart, John Patrick Villiers, 1 Jan. 1920. (M.)
11,772 Watney, Ronald Denby, 1 Jan. 1920. (M.)
11,773 Wauchope, Robert Stuart, 1 Jan. 1920. (M.)
11,774 Webb, William Francis Richmond, 1 Jan. 1920. (M.)
11,775 Browne, William Walker, 1 Jan. 1920. (M.)
11,776 Deedes, Ralph Bouverie, 1 Jan. 1920. (M.)
11,777 Gardiner, Herbert William, 1 Jan. 1920. (M.)
11,778 Gillespie, Rollo St. John, 1 Jan. 1920. (M.)
11,779 Harrison, Christopher Heathfield, 1 Jan. 1920. (M.)
11,780 Kearns, William Irving, 1 Jan. 1920. (M.)
11,781 Kelly, Patrick Anselm, 1 Jan. 1920. (M.)
11,782 Murphy, Alfred, 1 Jan. 1920. (M.)
11,783 Petrie, John Campbell Eggar, 1 Jan. 1920. (M.)
11,784 Stagg, Montague, 1 Jan. 1920. (M.)
11,784a Allaway, Henry, 1 Jan. 1920.
11,784b Baynes, Charlotte Augusta, Mrs., 1 Jan. 1920.
11,784c de Beaufort, Arnoud Jan, 1 Jan. 1920.
11,784d Benn, Charles Anthony, 1 Jan. 1920.
11,784e Blane, Amy Henrietta, Lady, 1 Jan. 1920.
11,784f Blennerhassett, William Lewis, 1 Jan. 1920.
11,784g Brooke, John Warwick, 1 Jan. 1920.
11,784h Bullen, Frederick John, 1 Jan. 1920.
11,785a Claughton, Harold, 1 Jan. 1920.
11,785b Cooper, Willie, 1 Jan. 1920.
11,785c Davidson, Ellen Beatrice, Mrs., 1 Jan. 1920.
11,785d Davis, Alfred Maurice, 1 Jan. 1920.
11,785e Deeks, Stephen John, 1 Jan. 1920.
11,785f Fitzgerald, William, 1 Jan. 1920.
11,785g Footman, Harold, 1 Jan. 1920.
11,785h Glenton, Arthur Hastings Septimus, 1 Jan. 1923.
11,786a Gracie, Robert Spencer, 1 Jan. 1920.
11,786b Harrison, Stanley, 1 Jan. 1920.
11,786c Harvey, Edward Murray, 1 Jan. 1920.
11,786d Henderson, Mrs. Beatrice Elizabeth, 1 Jan. 1920.
11,786e Hopkins, Harry Sinclair, 1 Jan. 1920.
11,786f Hopkinson, Gwendolen Blanche, 1 Jan. 1920.
11,786g Hughes, Harry, 1 Jan. 1920.
11,786h Inman, Cecil Daubeny, 1 Jan. 1920.
11,787a Buchanan-Jardine, Lady Ethel Mary, 1 Jan. 1920.
11,787b Keane, John, 1 Jan. 1920.
11,787c Ley, Henry James, 1 Jan. 1920.
11,787d Mackinnon, Lucy Vere, Mrs., 1 Jan. 1920.
11,787e Medcalf, William Harold, 1 Jan. 1920.
11,787f Milne, James William, 1 Jan. 1920.
11,787g Morgan, Eleanor Elizabeth Bamlet, Mrs., 1 Jan. 1920
11,787h Neville, Ralph, 1 Jan. 1920.
11,788a O'Gorman, Mrs. Flora, 1 Jan. 1920.
11,788b Palaeologus, Harriott Oatman, Mrs., 1 Jan. 1920.
11,788c Parker, William Edwin, 1 Jan. 1920.
11,788d Pritchard, Hugh John Mostyn, 1 Jan. 1920.
11,788e Revell, Alfred Edgar, 1 Jan. 1920.
11,788f Roche, A. W., 1 Jan. 1920.
11,788g Schultze, Alfred Cecil Dunbar-, 1 Jan. 1920.
11,788h Thomas, Henry Franklin, 1 Jan. 1920.
11,789a Wade, Francis Richard, 1 Jan. 1920.
11,789b Webley, Flora Mary, Mrs., 1 Jan. 1920.
11,789c Westwood, William, 1 Jan. 1920.
11,789d Young, William Ronald, 1 Jan. 1920.
11,789e Binns, Douglas Thomson, 1 Jan. 1920.
11,789f Byrde, Edwin Augustus, 1 Jan. 1920.
11,789g Dives, Evelyn Scott, Mrs., 1 Jan. 1920.
11,789h Hayman, Albert Melville, 1 Jan. 1920.
11,790a Henderson, Henry Ludwig, 1 Jan. 1920.

OFFICERS.

11,790b Lacey, William Henry Westwood, 1 Jan. 1920.
11,790c Lewis, Helen, 1 Jan. 1920.
11,790d McConaghy, Minnie Bevernand, 1 Jan. 1920.
11,790e Mawson, Sir Douglas, 1 Jan. 1920.
11,790f Osborne, Margaret, 1 Jan. 1920.
11,790g Ross, Stewart Buckle Carne, 1 Jan. 1920.
11,790h Trafford, Marcus Antonius Johnston de Lavis-, 1 Jan. 1920.
11,791a Wall, Arthur, 1 Jan. 1920.
11,791b Wilson, Charles James, 1 Jan. 1920.
11,791c Wotherspoon, Ellen, 1 Jan. 1920.
11,791d Lewis, Leonard Carey, 9 Jan. 1920. (M.)
11,791e Wilsone, Thomas Clarence, 22 Jan. 1920. (M.)
11,791f Alpin, William George Patrick, 30 Jan. 1920.
11,791g Anderson, William Dunlop, 30 Jan. 1920
11,791h Baker, Thomas, 30 Jan. 1920.
11,792a Barlow, Thomas William Naylor, 30 Jan. 1920.
11,792b Barnard, John Henry, 30 Jan. 1920.
11,792c Boden, John Smedley, 30 Jan. 1920.
11,793 Boon, John Goodisson, 30 Jan. 1920.
11,794 Bubb, Charles Henry, 30 Jan. 1920.
11,795 Buckley, Winifred Finnimore, 30 Jan. 1920.
11,796 Burgess, William Frederick Richardson, 30 Jan. 1920.
11,797 Burrows, Adam Clarke, 30 Jan. 1920.
11,798 Comber, Charles Thomas Thornton, 30 Jan. 1920.
11,799 Dagger, Richard, 30 Jan. 1920.
11,800 Davidson, Robert Gibson, 30 Jan. 1920.
11,801 Dickinson, William Henry, 30 Jan. 1920.
11,802 Dillon, Luke Gerald, 30 Jan. 1920.
11,803 Garratt, George Campbell, 30 Jan. 1920.
11,804 Gell, Henry Willingham, 30 Jan. 1920.
11,805 Gostling, Thomas Preston, 30 Jan. 1920.
11,806 Greenwood, Edwin Climson, 30 Jan. 1920.
11,807 Hanafy. John Zaky, 30 Jan. 1920.
11,808 Hawley, Arthur, 30 Jan. 1920.
11,809 Hay, Kenneth Robert, 30 Jan. 1920.
11,810 Hern, William, 30 Jan. 1920.
11,811 Herring, Herbert Thomas, 30 Jan. 1920.
11,813 Humphreys, Richard, 30 Jan. 1920.
11,814 James, William Warwick, 30 Jan. 1920.
11,815 Jewell, William Henry, 30 Jan. 1920.
11,816 Johnson, Harold Jossé, 30 Jan. 1920.
11,817 Jones, Richard Nelson, 30 Jan. 1920.
11,818 Kilvert, John Ellis, 30 Jan. 1920.
11,819 Laws, Percy Charles Willoughby, 30 Jan. 1920.
11,820 Lees, Kenneth Arthur, 30 Jan. 1920.
11,821 Low, Richard Marsden Hutchinson-, 30 Jan. 1920.
11,821a McCrea, Hugh Moreland, 30 Jan. 1920.
11,822 McDonald, Niel, 30 Jan. 1920.
11,823 McEwen, William Fullerton, 30 Jan. 1920.
11,824 Magill, Ethel Mary, 30 Jan. 1920.
11,825 Mansel, Charles John Linskill, 30 Jan. 1920.
11,826 Morison, Albert Edward, 30 Jan. 1920.
11,827 Moss, Enoch, 30 Jan. 1920.
11,828 Murray, Robert Alexander, 30 Jan. 1920.
11,829 Newby, Gervase Edward, 30 Jan. 1920.
11,830 Northcroft, George, 30 Jan. 1920.
11,831 Nourse, William John Chichele, 30 Jan. 1920.
11,832 Palmer, John Irwin, 30 Jan. 1920.
11,833 Parrott, Arthur Hughes, 30 Jan. 1920.
11,834 Payne, Joseph Lewin, 30 Jan. 1920.
11,835 Peacocke, George John, 30 Jan. 1920.
11,836 Philip, James Porter, 30 Jan. 1920.
11,837 Pinhey, Eustace Townley, 30 Jan. 1920.
11,838 Porter, Joseph Francis, 30 Jan. 1920.
11,839 Prosser, Thomas Gilbert, 30 Jan. 1920.
11,840 Reed, John Arthur, 30 Jan. 1920.
11,841 Rendall, Percy John, 30 Jan. 1920.
11,842 Rodway, Barron John, 30 Jan. 1920.
11,843 Rowlands, Richard Alun, 30 Jan. 1920.
11,844 Sainsbury, Harrington, 30 Jan. 1920.
11,845 Shelswell, Oscar Berridge, 30 Jan. 1920.
11,846 Sheppard, Amy, 30 Jan. 1920.
11,847 Smiley, George Kennedy, 30 Jan. 1920.
11,848 Southern, John Acton, 30 Jan. 1920.
11,849 Stansfield, George Sutcliffe, 30 Jan. 1920.
11,850 Stawell, Roldolph de Salis, 30 Jan. 1920.
11,851 Strover, Henry William Martyn, 30 Jan. 1920.
11,852 Thomas, Edward George, 30 Jan. 1920.
11,853 Turner, Richard, 30 Jan. 1920.
11,854 Turner, William, 30 Jan. 1920.
11,855 Wade, James Owen David, 30 Jan. 1920.
11,856 Warde, Ambrose Huntington, 30 Jan. 1920.
11,857 Wilson, James Alexander, 30 Jan. 1920.
11,858 Briggs, Henry Smalley, 8 March, 1920. (M.)
11,859 Fendick, Walter Robert, 8 March, 1920. (M.)
11,860 Goldsworthy, John Arthur, 8 March, 1920. (M.)
11,861 Greene, John Wilmer, 8 March, 1920. (M.)
11,862 Hall, Arthur Colin, 8 March, 1920. (M.)
11,863 Harvey, Cecil Russell Hains, 8 March, 1920. (M.)
11,864 Hely, Hamilton McMath, 8 March, 1920. (M.)
11,865 Langford, Horace Trevor St. Ledger, 8 March, 1920. (M.)
11,866 Lockington, Arthur Esme, 8 March, 1920. (M.)
11,867 Mills, Charles James, 8 March, 1920. (M.)
11,868 Murdoch, Hugh Campbell, 8 March, 1920. (M.)
11,869 Rapkin, Geoffrey Jennings, 8 March, 1920. (M.)
11,870 Shelton, Frederick Soltau, 8 March, 1920. (M.)
11,871 Stone, Charles Edward, 8 March, 1920. (M.)
11,872 Styles, Edward Goggin, 8 March, 1920. (M.)

11,873 Taylor, Archibald, 8 March, 1920. (M.)
11,874 Wareham, Stuart, Waldron, 8 March, 1920. (M.)
11,875 Watson, Robert Campbell, 8 March, 1920. (M.)
11,876 Weale, Henry Searle, 8 March, 1920. (M.)
11,877 Browne, Claude Melville, 15 March, 1920. (M.)
11,878 Cragg, Robert Herbert, 15 March, 1920. (M.)
11,879 Darby, George, 15 March, 1920. (M.)
11,880 Hickie, George William, 15 March, 1920. (M.)
11,881 Mitchell, John Marsters, 15 March, 1920. (M.)
11,882 O'Brien, Lennox Brett, 15 March, 1920. (M.)
11,883 Pascoe, Cluad Alfred Leonard, 15 March, 1920. (M.)
11,884 Simpson, Gilbert, 15 March, 1920. (M.)
11,885 Stanton, Reginald, 15 March, 1920. (M.)
11,886 Symons, John, 15 March, 1920. (M.)
11,887 Taylor, Sidney Herbert, 15 March, 1920. (M.)
11,888 Williams, Cyril Theodore, 15 March, 1920. (M.)
11,889 Wood, George Neville, 15 March, 1920. (M.)
11,889a Atwood, Arthur Francis Lysons, 23 Apr. 1920. (M.)
11,889b Edwards, Charles Peter, 23 Apr. 1920. (M.)
11,889c Purdon, Alick, 23 Apr. 1920. (M.)
11,889d Ross, John Kenneth Leveson, 23 Apr. 1920. (M.)
11,889e Stuart, Charles Joseph, 23 Apr. 1920. (M.)
11,890 Bakewell, Robert Turle, 5 June, 1920.
11,891 Bates, Ellen Marie, Mrs., 5 June, 1920.
11,892 Black, Archibald, 5 June, 1920.
11,893 Bott, Carl Lotherington, Glen-, 5 June, 1920.
11,894 Bradley, Rose Marian, 5 June, 1920.
11,895 Brocklebank, Agnes Sylvia, 5 June, 1920.
11,896 Buck, Philip, 5 June, 1920.
11,897 Carey, Florence Margaret, Mrs. Carteret-, 5 June 1920.
11,898 Clarke, Hope Elizabeth, Hope-, 5 June, 1920.
11,899 Clerk, Robert Mildmay, 5 June, 1920.
11,900 Cowell, Marie, 5 June, 1920.
11,901 Dove, Edward James, 5 June, 1920.
11,902 Fava, Albert Bernard, 5 June, 1920.
11,903 Fitton, John Herbert, 5 June, 1920.
11,904 Gilmour, John, 5 June, 1920.
11,905 Glyn, Margot Elinor, 5 June, 1920.
11,906 Harvey, Tom Horace, 5 June, 1920.
11,907 Jackson, Robert, 5 June, 1920.
11,908 Jury, Horatius Arthur, 5 June, 1920.
11,909 King, Nelly Maria, 5 June, 1920.
11,910 Lees, William, 5 June, 1920.
11,911 Lewis, John Thomas, 5 June, 1920.
11,912 Light, Edgar William, 5 June, 1920.
11,913 Keeble, Lillah, Mrs., 5 June, 1920.
11,914 McClean, Rev. Canon Richard Arthur, 5 June, 1920.
11,915 McMillan, James, 5 June, 1920.
11,916 Mactaggart, John Norman, 5 June, 1920.
11,917 Maude, Jenny Maria Catherine, Mrs., 5 June 1920.
11,918 Morant Lydia Louisa, 5 June, 1920.
11,919 Munro, William John, 5 June, 1920.
11,920 Pain, Dorothy Alice, 5 June, 1920.
11,921 Peake, Wilfred Stevenson, 5 June, 1920.
11,922 Anderson, Mrs. Powell-, 5 June, 1920.
11,923 Power, Margaret, 5 June, 1920.
11,924 Scott, Florence Oswald, Mrs., 5 June, 1920.
11,925 Speers, Frederick Solomon, 5 June, 1920.
11,926 Strang, Duncan, 5 June, 1920.
11,927 Street, Charles Edmund, 5 June, 1920.
11,928 Thomas, Vyvyan Hood, 5 June, 1920.
11,929 Tod, Robert Paterson, 5 June, 1920.
11,930 Geard, Reginald Cheniston, 30 June, 1920. (M.)
11,931 Bruce, William Robert, 12 July, 1920. (M.)
11,892 Clemson, Alfred William, 12 July, 1920. (M.)
11,933 Collinshaw, Raymond, 12 July, 1920. (M.)
11,934 Slatter, Leonard Horatio, 12 July, 1920. (M.)
11,935 Tweedie, Harley Alec, 12 July, 1920. (M.)
11,936 Archer, Henry George Fuller, 24 Aug. 1920.
11,937 Flower, Stanley Smyth, 24 Aug. 1920.
11,938 Fraser, Hugh, 24 Aug. 1920.
11,939 Garland, Herbert, 24 Aug. 1920.
11,940 Grundy, Robert Taylor, 24 Aug. 1920.
11,941 Lucas, Alfred, 24 Aug. 1920.
11,942 Matthew, John Godfrey, 24 Aug. 1920.
11,943 Pender, William Edmonstone, 24 Aug. 1920.
11,944 Shepherd, John Dawson, 24 Aug. 1920.
11,945 Mockett, Hugh Brooke, 25 Aug. 1920. (M.)
11,945a Murdoch, Ian Burn, 20 Sept. 1920. (M.)
11,945b Johnson, William Frederick, 20 Sept. 1920. (M.)
11,945c Macintyre, Francis Peter, 20 Sept. 1920. (M.)
11,945d Witts, Frederick Vavasour Broome, 20 Sept. 1920. (M.)
11,946 Hobson, Hugh George, 24 Sept. 1920. (M.)
11,946a Rawlings, Henry Barnard, 15 Oct. 1920. (M.)
11,947 Baillieu, Arthur Sydney, 15 Oct. 1920.
11,948 Barter, John Reginald, 15 Oct. 1920.
11,949 Bell, Marcus, 15 Oct. 1920.
11,950 Bennett, Edward George, 15 Oct. 1920.
11,951 Bennett, Violet, Mrs., 15 Oct. 1920.
11,952 Blythe, Archibald Lewis, 15 Oct. 1920.
11,953 Bolton, Arthur Leon, 15 Oct. 1920.
11,954 Brereton, Victor le Gay, 15 Oct. 1920.
11,955 Brodribb, Noel Kenrice Stevens, 15 Oct. 1920.
11,956 Bromwich, George Herbert, 15 Oct. 1920.
11,957 Buck, Henry, 15 Oct. 1920.
11,958 Bucknell, Norman Charles, 15 Oct. 1920.
11,959 Busby, William Dalrymple, 15 Oct. 1920.
11,960 Castle, Gordon Harwood, 15 Oct. 1920.
11,961 Cochrane, William John, 15 Oct. 1920.

THE ORDER OF THE BRITISH EMPIRE.

11,962 Collins, Elizabeth Ann, Mrs., 15 Oct. 1920
11,963 Cowan, Edith Dircksey, Mrs., 15 Oct. 1920.
11,964 Cowdell-Barrett, Mary Beatrice, Mrs., 15 Oct. 1920.
11,965 Cowley, Lady Marie, 15 Oct. 1920.
11,966 Crowther, Ethel Annie, Mrs., 15 Oct. 1920.
11,967 Currie, Lorna May, Mrs., 15 Oct. 1920.
11,968 Daglish, Edith, Mrs., 15 Oct. 1920.
11,969 Davies, James, 15 Oct. 1920.
11,970 de Bavay, August Joseph François, 15 Oct. 1920.
11,971 Downes, Sarah Elizabeth, Mrs., 15 Oct. 1920.
11,972 Fraser, Jessie, Mrs., 15 Oct. 1920.
11,973 Freeman, Arthur David, 15 Oct. 1920.
11,974 Garvan, Claire Frances, 15 Oct. 1920.
11,975 Gibson, William Alfred, 15 Oct. 1920.
11,976 Good, Minnie Agnes, Mrs., 15 Oct. 1920.
11,977 Grant, Lilian, Mrs., 15 Oct. 1920.
11,978 Grayndler, Edward, 15 Oct. 1920.
11,979 Hancock, Annie Maria, Mrs., 15 Oct. 1920.
11,980 Hay, James, 15 Oct. 1920.
11,981 Henderson, John Brownlie, 15 Oct. 1920.
11,982 Hitchcock, Howard, 15 Oct. 1920.
11,983 Hixson, Francis William, 15 Oct. 1920.
11,984 Hoare, Robert Richard, 15 Oct. 1920.
11,985 Holden, Edge Anthony, 15 Oct. 1920.
11,986 Holme, Ernest Rudolph, 15 Oct. 1920.
11,987 Horden, Eva, Mrs., 15 Oct. 1920.
11,988 Jones, Harold Edward, 15 Oct. 1920.
11,989 Knowles, George Shaw, 15 Oct. 1920.
11,990 Leitch, John, 15 Oct. 1920.
11,991 Lendon, Lucy Isabel, Mrs., 15 Oct. 1920.
11,992 Lewis, Reginald Jamieson, 15 Oct. 1920.
11,993 Little, Robert, 15 Oct. 1920.
11,994 Lysaght, Herbert Royse, 15 Oct. 1920.
11,995 Mackay, Hon. James Alexander Kenneth, 15 Oct. 1920.
11,996 McRobert, William Graham, 15 Oct. 1920.
11,997 Maguire, Matthew Michael, 15 Oct. 1920.
11,998 Marsh, Malcolm Ready, 15 Oct. 1920.
11,999 Martin, Albert, 15 Oct. 1920.
12,000 Merry, George Pitlow, 15 Oct. 1920.
12,001 Moorehead, Harold Percival, 15 Oct. 1920.
12,002 Mort, Mary Laidley Marjorie, 15 Oct. 1920.
12,003 Nangle, James, 15 Oct. 1920.
12,004 Owen, Percy Thomas, 15 Oct. 1920.
12,005 Parnell, John William, 15 Oct. 1920.
12,006 Paterson, Daniel Gavin, 15 Oct. 1920.
11,007 Poynton, Hon. Alexander, 15 Oct. 1920.
12,008 Preston, Herbert James, 15 Oct. 1920.
12,009 Reid, Pauline, Mrs., 15 Oct. 1920.
12,010 Rentoul, Rt. Rev. John Laurence. 15 Oct. 1920.
12,011 Richardson, Helen Morewood, Mrs., 15 Oct. 1920.
11,012 Ridley, Rev. Charles Lawrence, 15 Oct. 1920.
12,013 Riley, Most Rev. Charles Owen Leaver, Archbishop, 15 Oct. 1920.
12,014 Robertson, William St. Leonards, 15 Oct. 1920.

12,015 Rothwell, Thomas James, 15 Oct. 1920.
12,016 Russell, Delia Constance Mrs., 15 Oct. 1920.
12,017 Russell, Herbert Ernest Henry, 15 Oct. 1920.
12,018 Ryan, Victor Herbert, 15 Oct. 1920.
12,019 Sanders, Lewis Samuel, 15 Oct. 1920.
12,020 Semmens, James Michael, 15 Oct. 1920.
12,021 Serle, Edwin Hamilton, 15 Oct. 1920.
12,022 Sinclair, Russell, 15 Oct. 1920.
12,023 Smith, George Wishart, 15 Oct. 1920.
12,024 Spurgeon, Charles Herbert, 15 Oct. 1920.
12,025 Starling, John Henry, 15 Oct. 1920.
12,026 Tewksbury, Pearson William, 15 Oct. 1920.
12,027 Thomas, Thomas John, 15 Oct. 1920.
12,028 Thompson, Emily, Mrs., 15 Oct. 1920.
12,029 Tomlinson, Ernest William, 15 Oct. 1920.
12,030 Trim, Sarah Ann, Mrs., 15 Oct. 1920.
12,031 Turner, George Argo, 15 Oct. 1920.
12,032 Vaughan, Evelyn Goode, Mrs., 15 Oct. 1920.
12,033 Weller, Rev. Alfred George, 15 Oct. 1920.
12,034 Wheeler, Annie Margaret, Mrs., 15 Oct. 1920.
12,035 Williams, Oliver Morrice, 15 Oct. 1920.
12,036 Williams, Hon. William Micah, 15 Oct. 1920.
12,037 Willis, Ernest Horatio, 15 Oct. 1920.
12,038 Witherden, Charlotte Mary, Mrs., 15 Oct. 1920.
12,039 Wynne, Jessie, Mrs., 15 Oct. 1920.
12,040 Ewen, Greta, 15 Oct. 1920.
12,041 Widdowson, Howell Young, 15 Oct. 1920.
12,042 Anderson, Charles Thompson, 15 Oct. 1920.
12,043 Anderson, Charles Llewellyn, 15 Oct. 1920.
12,044 Bateman, Walter Slade, 15 Oct. 1920.
12,045 Brown, Daniel MacLaren, 15 Oct. 1920.
12,046 Carter, John Gordon, 15 Oct. 1920.
12,047 Collie, James, 15 Oct. 1920.
12,048 Duncan, Peter Milne, 15 Oct. 1920.
12,049 Faure, Pieter Jacobus van Breda, 15 Oct. 1920.
12,050 Fitzpatrick, Gerald Coleman, 15 Oct. 1920.
12,051 Finch, Josiah Robert, 15 Oct. 1920.
12,052 Holmes, William, 15 Oct. 1920.
12,053 Kirkness, John Johnston, 15 Oct. 1920.
12,054 Langley, Cecil Ernest Herrick, 15 Oct. 1920.
12,055 Lewes, John Guy Robert, 15 Oct. 1920.
12,056 Murray, Phœbe Henrietta, Mrs., 15 Oct. 1920.
12,057 Manning, Charles Nicolson, 15 Oct. 1920.
12,058 Pienaar, Filippus Fourie, 15 Oct. 1920.
12,059 Price, Bernard, 15 Oct. 1920.
12,060 Rawbone, Annie Christine, Mrs., 15 Oct. 1920.
12,061 Faber, George Valdemar, 16 Oct. 1920. (M.)
12,062 Gerhardi, William Alexander, 16 Oct. 1920. (M.)
12,063 Hughes, Bernard, 16 Oct. 1920. (M.)
12,064 Lycett, Cyril Vernon Lechmere, 31 Oct. 1920. (M.)
12,065 Jones, Everard John Hardman, 12 Nov. 1920. (M.)
12,066 Jordan, William Thomas Arthur, 12 Nov. 1920. (M.)
12,067 Smyth, Geoffrey Thomas, 12 Nov. 1920. (M.)
12,068 Bangay, James Barrington, 24 Dec. 1920.

MEMBERS.

(M.B.E.)

1 Ard, Rachel Maud, 4 June, 1917
4 Bassett, Rosa, 4 June, 1917.
7 Beard, Ernest Somerville, 4 June, 1917. (M.)
8 Cape, Thomas, 4 June, 1917
9 Chesterton, Sidney James, 4 June, 1917.
10 Carr, William, 4 June, 1917.
12 Coates, R. H., 4 June, 1917.
13 Cocking, Albert, 4 June, 1917.
14 Collingwood, Edith Florence, 4 June, 1917.
15 Dawtry, W. F., 4 June, 1917.
16 Dickens, Sidney John Oldacres, 4 June, 1917.
18 Edwards, Joseph, 4 June, 1917.
19 Fisher, Josephine Hilda, Mrs. Herbert, 4 June, 1917.
21 Grant. William Charles, 4 June, 1917.
22 Hudson, J. H., 4 June, 1917.
23 Hughes, Elizabeth Phillips, 4 June, 1917.
24 Hunt. William, 4 June, 1917.
25 Hunter, Catherine Augusta, Mrs. Harry Osborn, 4 June, 1917.
26 Jackson, Mary, 4 June, 1917.
27 Jones, W. H., 4 June, 1917.
28 Jemminson, H., 4 June, 1917.
30 Kean, Charles, 4 June, 1917.
31 Landon, Katherine Ann Brenda, 4 June, 1917.
33 MacNalty, Mary, Mrs., 4 June, 1917.
34 Milligan, George, 4 June, 1917.
35 Mills, Robert Clarkson, 4 June, 1917.
36 Moore, Ernest Reginald, 4 June, 1917.
38 Moss, Henry, 4 June, 1917.
39 Oldershaw, Albert William, 4 June, 1917.
42 Price, George, 4 June, 1917.
43 Pringle, George Cossar, 4 June, 1917.
44 Pritchard, Herbert Alfred, 3 June, 1917.
45 Sainsbury, Charles, 4 June, 1917.
46 Schofield, Herbert, 4 June, 1917.
47 Simcox, William, 4 June, 1917.
49 Taylor, Corrie, 4 June, 1917.
50 Tricker, Leonard Charles, 4 June, 1917.
51 Wilkins, Harold, 4 June, 1917.
52 Willson, Laura, Mrs., 4 June, 1917.
53 Waterson, Frances, Mrs., 4 June, 1917.
54 Dennys, Lucy Maud Massy, Lady, 4 Dec. 1917.
56 MacFadyen, Jessie, Mrs., 4 Dec. 1917.
57 Purshotamdas Thakurdas, 4 Dec. 1917.
58 Sardar Bahadur Hanwant Singh, 4 Dec. 1917.
59 Tharle-Hughes, Reginald, 4 Dec. 1917.
60 Rowland, Frederick, 4 Dec. 1917.
61 Lahore, Rai Bahadur Lala Kunj Behari Thapur of, 4 Dec. 1917.
63 Khan Bahadur Arab Dost Mahomed Khan of Tahkal Bala, Peshawar, 4 Dec. 1917.
64 Kothavala, Hector Ratanji, 4 Dec. 1917.
65 Wilson, John, 4 Dec. 1917.
66 Abram, Ethel May, Mrs., 1 Jan. 1918.
67 Hood, Margaret Acland, 1 Jan. 1918.
69 Addiscott, William James, 1 Jan. 1918.
70 Affleck, Florence Bessie, 1 Jan. 1918.
71 Aikman, Andrew, 1 Jan. 1918.
72 Aitkenhead, William, 1 Jan. 1918.
73 Aldridge, Ernest Charles, 1 Jan. 1918.
75 Sinclair, Stroma Alexander-, 1 Jan. 1918.
76 Alison, Charles Hugh, 1 Jan. 1918.
77 Allan, George Macdonald, 1 Jan. 1918.
78 Allan, Ida, Mrs., 1 Jan. 1918.
79 Allan, Thomas Easton, 1 Jan. 1918.
80 Allchin, Thomas Cuthbert, 1 Jan. 1918.
82 Allen, Alan Bruce, 1 Jan. 1918.
83 Allen, Frank, 1 Jan. 1918.
84 Amos, Alfred, 1 Jan. 1918.
85 Andrews, Henry Leonard Herbert, 1 Jan. 1918.
86 Applebey, Malcolm Percival, 1 Jan. 1918.
88 Arnott, Florence Evelyn, Mrs., 1 Jan. 1918.
89 Arthur, Olive Juana, Mrs., James, 1 Jan. 1918.
90 Ascroft, Robert William, 1 Jan. 1918.
91 Ashbridge, Harry Hales, 1 Jan. 1918.
92 Ashley, Ernest Gilman, 1 Jan. 1918.
93 Ashton, John Herbert, 1 Jan. 1918. (M.)
94 Ashworth, Wilfred Adam, 1 Jan. 1918.
95 Atkinson, Carleton Richard Bucky, 1 Jan. 1918.
96 Atkinson, Margaret Winifred, 1 Jan. 1918. (M.)
97 Attwell, Sydney Watson, 1 Jan. 1918.
98 Auger, Albert Raymond, 1 Jan. 1918. (M.)

99 Auret, Frances Victoria, 1 Jan. 1918.
101 Back, Stanley, 1 Jan. 1918.
102 Bacon, Eustace Vivian, 1 Jan. 1918.
103 Baker, Francis, 1 Jan. 1918.
104 Baker, John, 1 Jan. 1918. (M.)
105 Baker, Percy Montagu, 1 Jan. 1918.
106 Baker, Thomas Edgar, 1 Jan. 1918.
107 Baker, William Ernest, 1 Jan. 1918.
109 Ballard, Joseph Alfred William, 1 Jan. 1918.
110 Bannatyne, Victoria Vera, Mrs., 1 Jan. 1918.
111 Bannerman, Alexander, 1 Jan. 1918.
112 Barber, Frances Amy, 1 Jan. 1918.
113 Barber, Samuel Henry, 1 Jan. 1918.
114 Barber, William Clarence, 1 Jan. 1918.
115 Barker, Thomas, 1 Jan. 1918.
116 Barnes, Douglas, 1 Jan. 1918. (M.)
118 Baron, Herbert Harry, 1 Jan. 1918.
119 Barras, Harold Wilmot, 1 Jan. 1918. (M.)
120 Barrett, Kenneth Delmar, 1 Jan. 1918.
121 Barrett, William James, 1 Jan. 1918.
122 Barrington, Thomas Barwell, 1 Jan. 1918. (M.)
123 Barron, Alexander, 1 Jan. 1918. (M.)
124 Barron, Jonathan, 1 Jan. 1918.
126 Barton, Harriet, Mrs. Maurice Charles, 1 Jan. 1918.
127 Bate, William, 1 Jan. 1918.
128 Ironside, Helen Maud Bax-, 1 Jan. 1918.
130 Bayne, Bertha Marguerite, Mrs. John, 1 Jan. 1918.
131 Bearder, John William, 1 Jan. 1918.
132 Beaver, Edith Maude, 1 Jan. 1918.
133 Beddall, Herbert Bowman, 1 Jan. 1918.
135 Beddoe, James Stuart, 1 Jan. 1918.
136 Bedford, Richard William, 1 Jan. 1918.
137 Belcher, Evelyn, 1 Jan. 1918.
138 Bell, Violet Caroline, 1 Jan. 1918.
139 Bellaney, David Ernest, 1 Jan. 1918. (M.)
140 Bellasis, Gwendolen Edith, 1 Jan. 1918.
141 Bennett, Ernest Lampeer, 1 Jan. 1918.
143 Beresford, John Baldwin, 1 Jan. 1918.
144 Bernard, Alice Eleanor, 1 Jan. 1918.
146 Bevan, F. H., 1 Jan. 1918.
147 Biddle, Lois, 1 Jan. 1918.
148 Bignold, William Henry, 1 Jan. 1918.
149 Birbeck, Thomas Edson, 1 Jan. 1918.
150 Birch, Bertha, Mrs., 1 Jan. 1918.
151 Birkett, Tom, 1 Jan. 1918.
153 Black, Dora Winifred, 1 Jan. 1918.
154 Blackett, Frances Charlotte Isabella, 1 Jan. 1918.
155 Blair, Malcolm, 1 Jan. 1918.
156 Blake, Jack Percy, 1 Jan. 1918.
157 Blamey, Thomas, 1 Jan. 1918.
158 Blay, John Augustus, 1 Jan. 1918. (M.)
159 Blennerhassett, Arthur, 1 Jan. 1918. (M.)
160 Blennerhassett, Nesta, Mrs., 1 Jan. 1918.
161 Bonner, John William Arundel, 1 Jan. 1918.
164 Box, Harold Arthur, 1 Jan. 1918.
165 Boycott, Lota, Mrs., 1 Jan. 1918.
166 Boyd, Elizabeth Frances, 1 Jan. 1918.
167 Boyer, Albert Edward, 1 Jan. 1918.
168 Boys, Henry Cecil, 1 Jan. 1918. (M.)
169 Bradbury, William Embrey, 1 Jan. 1918.
170 Bradley, Henry Edward Manning, 1 Jan. 1918.
172 Brett, Hon. Oliver Sylvian, 1 Jan. 1918. (M.)
173 Brightman, Edith Marian, Mrs., 1 Jan. 1918.
175 Brown, Charles Frederick, 1 Jan. 1918.
176 Brown, Edwin, 1 Jan. 1918. (M.)
177 Brown, Fannie Florence, Mrs., 1 Jan. 1918.
178 Brown, George Drake, 1 Jan. 1918.
179 Brown, Helen Grace Rae, 1 Jan. 1918. (M.)
180 Browne, Tomyns Reginald, 1 Jan. 1918.
181 Bruce, Bertha Marguerita, 1 Jan. 1918.
182 Bruce, Maye, 1 Jan. 1918.
183 Bryan, John Lockton, 1 Jan. 1918.
184 Bryant, Herbert William, 1 Jan. 1918.
185 Bryson, Frederick Francis Smith, 1 Jan. 1918.
186 Buckman, James, 1 Jan. 1918.
187 Bullock, Herbert Charles Stuart, 1 Jan. 1918. (M.)
188 Bumpus, Alfred Adolphus, 1 Jan. 1918.
189 Bumstead, Richard Edward, 1 Jan. 1918.
190 Bunton, Samuel, 1 Jan. 1918.
192 Burgess, Arthur William, 1 Jan. 1918.
193 Burgess, Elspeth, Mrs., 1 Jan. 1918.
194 Burleigh, John Laurence, 1 Jan. 1918.

195 Burling, George Alfred, 1 Jan. 1918.
196 Murdoch, Regiaulde de Maule, Mrs. Burn-, 1 Jan. 1918.
197 Burns, Helen Jaqueline, Mrs., 1 Jan. 1918.
198 Burrough, Hedley Gravett, 1 Jan. 1918.
199 Burrow, Leopold Arthur, 1 Jan. 1918.
200 Burrows, Kate Ellen, 1 Jan. 1918.
201 Burt, John, 1 Jan. 1918.
202 Ballantine, Ethel Codogan Burton, 1 Jan. 1918.
203 Burton-Mackenzie, Isabel, 1 Jan. 1918.
204 Bury, John Edwin, 1 Jan. 1918.
205 Caines, Clement Guy, 1 Jan. 1918.
206 Cairns, John, 1 Jan. 1918.
207 Cameron, Norman Restell, 1 Jan. 1918.
209 Campbell, Clementina Henrietta, Mrs., 1 Jan. 1918.
210 Campbell, Colin Clyde, 1 Jan. 1918. (M.)
211 Campbell, David Bishop, 1 Jan. 1918. (M.)
212 Campbell, Gilbert, 1 Jan. 1918.
215 Campey, Thomas Epton, 1 Jan. 1918. (M.)
216 Candler, Henry, 1 Jan. 1918.
217 Carnegie, William, 1 Jan. 1918.
218 Carroll, Thomas William, 1 Jan. 1918.
219 Carter, Francis Tavor, 1 Jan. 1918.
220 Carter, William, 1 Jan. 1918.
221 Carver, Albert Wing, 1 Jan. 1918.
222 Cassidi, Francis Richard, 1 Jan. 1918.
224 Chadwick, Thomas, 1 Jan. 1918.
225 Chalkley, Alfred Philip, 1 Jan. 1918.
226 Chalkley, Francis Henry, 1 Jan. 1918. (M.)
228 Challinor, William Robert, 1 Jan. 1918.
229 Chalmers, Margaret, 1 Jan. 1918.
230 Chambers, Harry, 1 Jan. 1918.
231 Chantrey, Guy Mortimer, 1 Jan. 1918.
232 Charlton, Charles Joseph, 1 Jan. 1918. (M.)
233 Chiesman, Harry, 1 Jan. 1918.
234 Childers, Mary Alden, Mrs. Erskine, 1 Jan. 1918.
235 Chinery, Elizabeth, Mrs., 1 Jan. 1918.
236 Clark, Sir John Maurice, Bart., 1 Jan. 1919. (M.)
237 Clark, Owen Aly, 1 Jan. 1918.
238 Clarke, Walter Leonard, 1 Jan. 1918.
239 Clarke, Edith, Mrs., 1 Jan. 1918.
240 Clarke, Thomas Henry, 1 Jan. 1918.
242 Clayton, Charles Henry James, 1 Jan. 1918.
243 Clegg, Margaret Penelope, 1 Jan. 1918.
244 Clowes, Edith Emily, Mrs. Peter Legh, 1 Jan. 1918.
245 Cluett, Alfred William Ayers, 1 Jan. 1918.
246 Coast, Ernest Frederick, 1 Jan. 1918.
248 Cobb, Robert Bennett, 1 Jan. 1918.
250 Cock, Edward, 1 Jan. 1918.
251 Cockerell, Douglas Bennett, 1 Jan. 1918.
252 Coffey, Frank William, 1 Jan. 1918.
253 Cole, Edward George, 1 Jan. 1918.
255 Coley, William, 1 Jan. 1918. (M.)
256 Colledge, Francis William, 1 Jan. 1918.
257 Collins, Lionel Dennis, 1 Jan. 1918.
258 Collinson, Beatrice Annie, 1 Jan. 1918.
259 Coltman, Walter William, 1 Jan. 1918.
260 Compton, Charles Leonard, 1 Jan. 1918.
261 Coningham, Geraldine Emily, Mrs., 1 Jan. 1918.
262 Connell, Jessie Murdoch, Mrs., 1 Jan. 1918.
263 Conner, James, 1 Jan. 1918.
264 Cook, Fred Compigné, 1 Jan. 1918.
265 Cook, Richard Frederic, 1 Jan. 1918.
266 Cooke, Cuthbert Cresswell, 1 Jan. 1918.
267 Cooksey, Henry James, 1 Jan. 1918.
268 Coombe, Arthur Henry, 1 Jan. 1918.
269 Coombs, William Walter, 1 Jan. 1918.
270 Cooper, Bertram George, 1 Jan. 1918.
271 Cooper, Henry, 1 Jan. 1918. (M.)
272 Cooper, H. M., 1 Jan. 1918. (M.)
273 Cooper, James, 1 Jan. 1918.
274 Cooper, John, 1 Jan. 1918.
275 Copus, Clarence George, 1 Jan. 1918.
276 Corbett, Edward Richard Trevor, 1 Jan. 1918.
277 Cordeaux, Hilda Eliza Agar, Mrs., 1 Jan. 1918.
278 Corner, Sylvia, 1 Jan. 1918. (M.)
279 Corrigan, John, 1 Jan. 1918.
280 Cowan, Howard Denys Russell, 1 Jan. 1918.
281 Cowan, William, 1 Jan. 1918.
283 Craig, Juliet Sisley, Mrs., 1 Jan. 1918.
284 Crawley, James, 1 Jan. 1918.
285 Creegan, Edward Patrick, 1 Jan. 1918.
286 Cripps, Gerald Faulkner, 1 Jan. 1918.
287 Crisp, Helena Jane, 1 Jan. 1918.
289 Crocker, Gordon George, 1 Jan. 1918. (M.)
290 Crockett, William Gordon, 1 Jan. 1918.
291 Cromar, George Scott, 1 Jan. 1918.
292 Crompton-Roberts, Winifred Eyre, Mrs., 1 Jan. 1918.
293 Cropper, Ann Ellen, Mrs., 1 Jan. 1918.
294 Cross, Ernest, 1 Jan. 1918.
295 Cross, Robert, 1 Jan. 1918.
296 Cruickshank, William, 1 Jan. 1918.
297 Cumming, Janet Baron, 1 Jan. 1918.
298 Cuninghame, Margaret Georgiana, 1 Jan. 1918.
299 Currie, Marghuerita Copeland, 1 Jan. 1918.
300 Cusens, George Charles, 1 Jan. 1918.
301 Cuthbertson, John, 1 Jan. 1918.
302 Cutler, Ernest Edward, 1 Jan. 1918.
303 Cutler, Roy Victor, 1 Jan. 1918. (M.)
304 Daglish, James, 1 Jan. 1918.
305 Darlow, Ellen Frances, Mrs., 1 Jan. 1918.

306 Darrach, William Elliott, 1 Jan. 1918.
309 Davies, Sophia Katherine, Mrs., 1 Jan. 1918.
312 Davies, Gwilym Meirion, 1 Jan. 1918.
313 Davies, Hugh Christopher, 1 Jan. 1918.
314 Davies, Walter, 1 Jan. 1918.
315 Daw, Thomas, 1 Jan. 1918. (M.)
316 Dawkins, Horace Christian, 1 Jan. 1918.
317 Dawson, George William, 1 Jan. 1918.
318 Dawson-Thomas, Beatrice Mary, 1 Jan. 1918.
319 Day, George, 1 Jan. 1918.
321 Dean, Frederic William Charles, 1 Jan. 1918.
322 Dean, Seth Ellis, 1 Jan. 1918.
323 Deane, Phyllis Lucy, Mrs. James, 1 Jan. 1918.
324 Deighton, Albert, 1 Jan. 1918.
325 Denniston, Adam Fairrie, 1 Jan. 1918.
326 Dent, Hubert Augustus, 1 Jan. 1918.
327 Digby, Lady Lilian Mary Harriet Diana, 1 Jan. 1918.
328 Dixon, Charles William, 1 Jan. 1918.
329 Doig, Annie Emilia Scott Elliott, Mrs., 1 Jan. 1918.
330 Donald, William, 1 Jan. 1918.
331 Dorrell, William John, 1 Jan. 1918.
332 Dougherty, Aileen Margaret, 1 Jan. 1918.
333 Douglas, Allie Vibert, 1 Jan. 1918.
334 Down, Percy Bissett, 1 Jan. 1918.
335 Drake, John, 1 Jan. 1918.
336 Drinkwater, Sidney William, 1 Jan. 1918.
337 Smith, Edith Marion Drummond, Mrs., 1 Jan. 1918.
338 Drysdale, Duncan, 1 Jan. 1918.
339 Dudding, Bernard Phineas, 1 Jan. 1918.
340 Duke, Reginald Franklin Hare, 1 Jan. 1918.
341 Dunbar, Frank Hay, 1 Jan. 1918.
342 Dunley, James, 1 Jan. 1918.
345 Dupe, Mabel Alethea, Mrs., 1 Jan. 1918.
346 Dupré, Frederick Harold, 1 Jan. 1918.
347 Durley, R. J., 1 Jan. 1918. (M.)
348 Durran, William, 1 Jan. 1918.
349 Dutton, Beatrice Aimée, Mrs., 1 Jan. 1918.
350 Eadie, Harold George, 1 Jan. 1918.
351 Eagar, Edward Herbert, 1 Jan. 1918.
352 Eborall, Herbert, 1 Jan. 1918.
353 Ede, Stuart Strickland Moore, 1 Jan. 1918.
354 Edmonds, John Francis, 1 Jan. 1918.
355 Edwards, Edith Constance, Mrs., 1 Jan. 1918.
356 Edwards, Hester Mary, Mrs. (M.)
357 Elbourne, Edward Tregaskiss, 1 Jan. 1918.
359 Elliott, Mabel Beatrice, 1 Jan. 1918.
360 Elliott, William, 1 Jan. 1918.
361 Ellis, Amy Amelia, Mrs., 1 Jan. 1918.
362 Ellison, Frank, 1 Jan. 1918.
363 Emery, Horace Milton, 1 Jan. 1918.
364 Emmett, George Ernest, 1 Jan. 1918.
365 Eshelby, Frederick George, 1 Jan. 1918.
366 Esslemont, George Gall, 1 Jan. 1918.
367 Estill, Harriet, 1 Jan. 1918.
369 Everest, Edward Percy, 1 Jan. 1918.
370 Fage, James Alfred, 1 Jan. 1918.
371 Faikney, Robert, 1 Jan. 1918.
372 Fairholme, Marie-Antoinette, Mrs., 1 Jan. 1918.
373 Falconer, James, 1 Jan. 1918.
374 Fane, Samuel Maddams, 1 Jan. 1918.
375 Farley, Edwin Wood Thorp, 1 Jan. 1918.
376 Farquharson, Alexander, 1 Jan. 1918.
377 Farraday, William, 1 Jan. 1918. (M.)
378 Farren, William Scott, 1 Jan. 1918. (M.)
379 Feast, Edith M., Mrs.. 1 Jan. 1918.
381 Fellowes, Alfred Ernest, 1 Jan. 1918.
382 Fenton, Alexander, 1 Jan. 1918. (M.)
383 Fenton, Charles Ernest, 1 Jan. 1918.
384 Fenwick, Harriet Frances 1 Jan. 1918.
385 Ferguson, Alpin, 1 Jan. 1918. (M.)
387 Findlay, Elizabeth Susan, 1 Jan. 1918.
388 Findlay-Hamilton, Georgina Julia, Mrs., 1 Jan. 1918.
389 Finlay, May, 1 Jan. 1918. (M.)
391 Finnimore, Benjamin Kingston, 1 Jan. 1918.
392 Firth, Clare Jane, Mrs., 1 Jan. 1918.
393 Fisher, Honoria Mary, 1 Jan. 1918.
394 FitzMaurice, Henry, 1 Jan. 1918.
395 Flannery, Harold Fortescue, 1 Jan. 1918. (M.)
396 Fletcher, Basil, 1 Jan. 1918.
397 Foggo, Watson, 1 Jan. 1918.
398 Follett, Robert Charles, 1 Jan. 1918.
399 Forbes, Mary Constance, 1 Jan. 1918.
400 Ford, John, 1 Jan. 1918.
401 Forrest, William Robinson Lidderdale, 1 Jan. 1918.
402 Forster, Andrew, 1 Jan. 1918.
404 Fossey, Frederick Walter, 1 Jan. 1918.
405 Foster, Henry Knollys, 1 Jan. 1918.
406 Foster, William Melville, 1 Jan. 1918.
407 Fowell, Edward Turner, 1 Jan. 1918.
408 Fowle, Helene, Mrs. John, 1 Jan. 1918.
409 Fowler, Eveline Georgina, 1 Jan. 1918.
411 Fraser, Evelyn Margaret, 1 Jan. 1918.
412 Fraser, Thomas Houston, 1 Jan. 1918.
413 Frewen, Edward James, 1 Jan. 1918.
414 Frisby, Elizabeth Rowley, 1 Jan. 1918.
415 Froud, William Percy, 1 Jan. 1918.
416 Fry, Dorothy Margaret, 1 Jan. 1918.
417 Fry, John James, 1 Jan. 1918. (M.)
418 Fuller, Walter Everard, 1 Jan. 1918.
419 Galilee, Mary Edith, 1 Jan. 1918.

420 Gall, Christian McDowall, 1 Jan. 1918.
421 Gamble, John Dunn. 1 Jan. 1918.
423 Gard, Albert, 1 Jan. 1918.
424 Gardner, Nora Hilton, 1 Jan. 1918.
425 Garnett, Caroline Sugden, Mrs., 1 Jan. 1918.
426 Garnett, Helen Maude Dorothy, 1 Jan. 1918.
427 Garside, Constance Elizabeth, 1 Jan. 1918.
428 Geake, William Henry Gregory, 1 Jan. 1918. (M.)
429 Genower, Reginald, 1 Jan. 1918.
430 Geoghegan, William, 1 Jan. 1918.
431 Gibb, Allan, 1 Jan. 1918.
433 Gibson, Jane Margaret Francis, 1 Jan. 1918. (M.)
435 Gibson, William Charles Ernest, 1 Jan. 1918.
436 Giffard, Thomas Arthur Walter, 1 Jan. 1918.
437 Gilbert, George Julian, 1 Jan. 1918.
438 Gilbert, Violet Adeline, 1 Jan. 1918.
439 Giles, Robert, 1 Jan. 1918.
440 Gillingham, James Searle. 1 Jan. 1918.
441 Glennie, Maud, 1 Jan. 1918.
442 Glennie, Patrick Gordon, 1 Jan. 1918.
443 Godding, James William Sleigh, 1 Jan. 1918.
444 Godfrey, Albert Hamilton, 1 Jan. 1918.
445 Going, Fanny Augusta, Mrs., 1 Jan. 1918.
448 Gooch, Herbert, 1 Jan. 1918.
449 Goodall, Stanley Vernon, 1 Jan. 1918.
450 Goodchild, Alwyn Valerie, Mrs., 1 Jan. 1918.
451 Goodland, Joshua, 1 Jan. 1918.
452 Goodwin, Walter, 1 Jan. 1918.
453 Goodyear, Clarie Helen, 1 Jan. 1918.
454 Goodyear, Percy, 1 Jan. 1918.
455 Gordon, George, 1 Jan. 1918.
457 Gordon-Steward, Lily, Mrs., 1 Jan. 1918.
458 Gorman, Gorman, 1 Jan. 1918. (M.)
459 Gorton, Sandford George. 1 Jan. 1918.
462 Gould, Claude William Shepard, 1 Jan. 1918.
464 Graham, Christopher Colborne, 1 Jan. 1918.
465 Graham, Cuthbert, 1 Jan. 1918. (M.)
466 Graham, David Morgan, 1 Jan. 1918.
468 Graves, Reginald Coupland, 1 Jan. 1918.
469 Gray, Charles Harold, 1 Jan. 1918.
470 Gray, William, 1 Jan. 1918.
471 Greaves, Constance Mary, Mrs., 1 Jan. 1918.
472 Green, Alexander John, 1 Jan. 1918.
473 Green, Hettie Mary, Mrs., 1 Jan. 1918.
474 Greenfield, Edith Mary, 1 Jan. 1918.
476 Gregson, Alvero Church. 1 Jan. 1918.
478 Grey, Charles William, 1 Jan. 1918.
479 Grieve, James Dyce, 1 Jan. 1918.
480 Griffith, Rev. Ellis Hughes, 1 Jan. 1918.
481 Griffiths, Helen Maud, Mrs., 1 Jan. 1918.
482 Grimbly, James Thomas, 1 Jan. 1918.
483 Grimsdall, Henry, 1 Jan. 1918.
484 Grimsley, Ellen Maud, 1 Jan. 1918.
485 Gritton, John, 1 Jan. 1918.
486 Groom, Susannah, 1 Jan. 1918.
487 Groom, Professor Percy, 1 Jan. 1918.
489 Grundy, Allan Wilson, 1 Jan. 1918.
491 Gubbins, Matilda Ida, Mrs., 1 Jan. 1918.
492 Gummer, Philip Edward, 1 Jan. 1918. (M.)
493 Guthrie-Smith, Olive Francis, Mrs., 1 Jan. 1918.
494 Hadden, Frederick Weston, 1 Jan. 1918.
495 Hadnutt, William, 1 Jan. 1918.
496 Haigh, Bernard Parker, 1 Jan. 1918.
497 Hall, Harry Francis, 1 Jan. 1918.
498 Hall, John, 1 Jan. 1918.
499 Halloran, John William, 1 Jan. 1918.
500 Hamilton, Emily Moore, 1 Jan. 1918.
502 Hankinson, George, 1 Jan. 1918.
503 Hanna, Arthur Leonard, 1 Jan. 1918. (M.)
504 Hanson, Clarence Oldham, 1 Jan. 1918.
505 Hanton, Peter Kydd, 1 Jan. 1918.
506 Hardman, James, 1 Jan. 1918.
507 Hardy, Frank Philip, 1 Jan. 1918.
508 Harries, George Samuel, 1 Jan. 1918. (M.)
509 Harris, Ethel, 1 Jan. 1918.
510 Harris, Samuel Wallace, 1 Jan. 1918. (M.)
511 Harris, William Thomas Hooper, 1 Jan. 1918.
512 Hart-Cox, George, 1 Jan. 1918.
513 Harvey, Edward John Morewood, 1 Jan. 1918. (M.)
514 Harvey, Edwin William, 1 Jan. 1918.
515 Harvey, Nicholas Charles, 1 Jan. 1918. (M.)
516 Harvey, William, 1 Jan. 1918.
518 Harwood, James Henry, 1 Jan. 1918.
519 Haskins, Arthur, 1 Jan. 1918.
521 Hastie, Peter, 1 Jan. 1918.
522 Haswell, Robert, 1 Jan. 1918.
523 Hawkins, Albert Victor, 1 Jan. 1918.
524 Hawkins, Thomas Shirley, 1 Jan. 1918.
525 Hay, Henrietta Louisa, 1 Jan. 1918.
526 Hayes, Arthur W., 1 Jan. 1918.
527 Hayes, Fredric James, 1 Jan. 1918.
528 Headley, Robert Hollowell, 1 Jan. 1918.
530 Heath, Herbert Charles Selwyn, 1 Jan. 1918. (M.)
531 Hebb, Florence Agnes, 1 Jan. 1918.
532 Henderson, Alice Craig, 1 Jan. 1918.
533 Henderson. George Blake, 1 Jan. 1918.
534 Henry, Jane Selina, Mrs., 1 Jan. 1918.
535 Henry, John, 1 Jan. 1918,
536 Herbert, Agnes Mary, 1 Jan. 1918.
537 Hewetson, John Tordiffe, 1 Jan. 1918.

538 Heynes, James Baylis, 1 Jan. 1918.
539 Hibberd, Henry George. 1 Jan. 1918.
540 Higman, Frank Sidney, 1 Jan. 1918.
541 Higson, Elizabeth Annie, Mrs., 1 Jan. 1918.
542 Hill, Arthur James, 1 Jan. 1918.
545 Hines, Arthur Sidney, 1 Jan. 1918.
546 Hobart, Violet Verve, Mrs. Claud Vere Cavendish, 1 Jan. 1918.
547 Hocking, William Stanley, 1 Jan. 1918.
548 Hogan, Arthur, 1 Jan. 1918.
550 Hoile, George Vincent, 1 Jan. 1918. (M.)
551 Holgate-Smith, Frank, 1 Jan. 1918.
552 Holland, Edith Clara, 1 Jan. 1918.
553 Holloway, Frank Herbert, 1 Jan. 1918.
554 Holmes, Annie Gertrude, Mrs., 1 Jan. 1918.
555 Hooper, Charles Stuart, 1 Jan. 1918.
556 Hope-Wallace, Charles Nugent, 1 Jan. 1918.
557 Hopkins, Harry Sinclair, 1 Jan. 1918.
559 Hopps, Walter, 1 Jan. 1918.
560 Horden, Florence Julia, Mrs., 1 Jan. 1918.
561 Horne, Andrew Coutts, 1 Jan. 1918.
563 Hornibrook, John Laurence, 1 Jan. 1918.
564 Houghton, E. F., 1 Jan. 1918.
565 Houston, Alexander McLean, 1 Jan. 1918.
566 Howard, Arthur Henry, 1 Jan. 1918.
568 Howard, Holly, Mrs., 1 Jan. 1918.
569 Huddart, Alfred Harry, 1 Jan. 1918. (M.)
571 Hughes, Edward, 1 Jan. 1918.
572 Huleatt, Helen Cornelia, 1 Jan. 1918.
573 Humphreys, Edith Louisa Sophia, 1 Jan. 1918.
574 Humphreys, Harold Goundrill, 1 Jan. 1918.
575 Hunt, Charles Henry, 1 Jan. 1918.
576 Hunt, Joseph Henry, 1 Jan. 1918.
577 Hunt, William Wright, 1 Jan. 1918.
578 Hunter, John Leslie, 1 Jan. 1918.
579 Hunter, Marion Janet, 1 Jan. 1918.
582 Hutt, Alfred, 1 Jan. 1918. (M.)
583 Hutt, John, 1 Jan. 1918. (M.)
584 Hutton, William Ross, 1 Jan. 1918.
585 Ilsley, Arthur Frederick, 1 Jan. 1918.
586 Impey, Frank, 1 Jan. 1918.
587 Inglis, Kate, 1 Jan. 1918.
588 Ireland, Blanche, 1 Jan. 1918. (M.)
590 Jack, James Robertson, 1 Jan. 1918.
591 Jackson, Alice Mabel Erskine, 1 Jan. 1918.
592 Jackson, Arthur, 1 Jan. 1918.
593 Jackson, Hugh Willan, 1 Jan. 1918.
594 Jackson, Joseph Clough, 1 Jan. 1918.
595 James, James Picton, 1 Jan. 1918.
596 James, Thomas Gwynfab, 1 Jan. 1918.
597 James, William Arthur, 1 Jan. 1918.
598 Jamieson, Alexander, 1 Jan. 1918.
599 Jamieson, Charles Fleming, 1 Jan. 1918.
601 Jeffreys, Charles Nicholas Theodore, 1 Jan. 1918.
603 Jenkins, Albert David, 1 Jan. 1918.
604 Jerrard, Garnett Longsdon, 1 Jan. 1918.
605 Jewell, Frank Ashton, 1 Jan. 1918.
607 Johnson, Frederick William, 1 Jan. 1918.
608 Johnson, Samuel, 1 Jan. 1918.
609 Johnson, William, 1 Jan. 1918.
610 Jolly, John, 1 Jan. 1918.
611 Jones, Edmund Vaughan, 1 Jan. 1918.
612 Jones, George, 1 Jan. 1918.
613 Jones, Harold Spencer, 1 Jan. 1918.
614 Jones, James Stuart, 1 Jan. 1918.
615 Jones, Richard, 1 Jan. 1918. (M.)
616 Jones, Walter Owen, 1 Jan. 1918.
619 Judge, Wybrants, 1 Jan. 1918. (M.)
620 Justice, Charles Ernest William, 1 Jan. 1918.
621 Kay, Sydney Entwisle, 1 Jan. 1918.
622 Kearney, Arthur Richard, 1 Jan. 1918.
623 Keary, Margaret Alice, 1 Jan. 1918.
624 Smith, Annie Margaret Keeble, Mrs., 1 Jan. 1918.
626 Kelly, Frank Arthur, 1 Jan. 1918.
627 Kelly, James, 1 Jan. 1918.
628 Kelly, Robert, 1 Jan. 1918.
629 Welch, John Howard Kemp-, 1 Jan. 1918.
630 Kenny, William James, 1 Jan. 1918.
631 Keough, Frederick, 1 Jan. 1918. (M.)
632 Ker, Helen Bethea, Mrs., 1 Jan. 1918.
633 Kidd, Gladys Louise, 1 Jan. 1918.
634 Kidson, Arthur Frederic, 1 Jan. 1918.
635 Killmayer, Leon Joseph, 1 Jan. 1918. (M.)
636 King, Norah, Mrs., 1 Jan. 1918.
638 Kirk, Mabel Cecil, Mrs., 1 Jan. 1918.
639 Kirkwood, Richard Cameron, 1 Jan. 1918.
640 Klitz, Wilfrid Robert, 1 Jan. 1918.
641 Knight, Frank, 1 Jan. 1918.
642 Knight, George, 1 Jan. 1918.
643 Knocker, George Stodart, 1 Jan. 1918.
644 Lack, Edwin, 1 Jan. 1918.
646 Lamb, Brydon, 1 Jan. 1918.
647 Lamb, Dorothy, 1 Jan. 1918.
648 Landells, Helena Jane, 1 Jan. 1918.
649 Lane, Harry Joseph, 1 Jan. 1918.
650 Langlands, George, 1 Jan. 1918.
651 Lapham, Robert John, 1 Jan. 1918. (M.)
652 Larter, Alfred Tabois, 1 Jan. 1918.
653 Laurie, Herbert, 1 Jan. 1918. (M.)
654 Lawes, Ernest Lingwood, 1 Jan. 1918.

655 Lawrence, Aubrey Trevor, 1 Jan. 1918.
656 Lawrence, James, 1 Jan. 1918. (M.)
657 Laws, Ernest, 1 Jan. 1918.
658 Layton, Maud Matilda, 1 Jan. 1918.
659 Leck, William, 1 Jan. 1918.
660 Leese, Clive, 1 Jan. 1918. (M.)
661 Leggett, Arthur, 1 Jan. 1918.
662 Legh-Jones, George, 1 Jan. 1918.
663 Lemesurier, Edwin Philip, 1 Jan. 1918. (M.)
664 Levi, Louis, 1 Jan. 1918.
665 Lewis, Janet Marion Terry, 1 Jan. 1918.
666 Liddiard, Jessie, 1 Jan. 1918.
668 Lightbody, Henry, 1 Jan. 1918.
669 Lillicrap, Charles Swift, 1 Jan. 1918.
670 Linfield, Frederic Cæsar, 1 Jan. 1918.
671 Linnell, Agnes Evelyn, Mrs., 1 Jan. 1918.
672 Litchfield, John Walter, 1 Jan. 1918. (M.)
673 Little, William, 1 Jan. 1918.
674 Livesey, Geraldine, 1 Jan. 1918.
677 Lloyd, Daniel Charles, 1 Jan. 1918.
678 Jones, Alice Lloyd, Mrs., 1 Jan. 1918.
680 Bunce, Thomas Lockwood, 1 Jan. 1918.
682 Longbotham, Arthur Thompson, 1 Jan. 1918.
686 Lovett, Frederic Reynolds, 1 Jan. 1918.
687 Lowe, Arthur Henry, 1 Jan. 1918. (M.)
689 Lowe, Dorothy Ann Shelmerdine, 1 Jan. 1918.
690 Luck, Robert, 1 Jan. 1918.
692 Lyne, Horace Sampson, 1 Jan. 1918.
694 Macdonald, Eva Flora Caroline, 1 Jan. 1918.
695 Macdonald, Florence, 1 Jan. 1918.
696 Macdonald, John Angus, 1 Jan. 1918.
698 Macfarlane, Walter Mace, 1 Jan. 1918.
699 Macgregor, Archibald Bow, 1 Jan. 1918.
701 Machtig, Eric, 1 Jan. 1918.
703 MacKay, Colin, 1 Jan. 1918.
704 Mackay, John George, 1 Jan. 1918.
705 Mackrow, George Frank, 1 Jan. 1918.
706 MacLellan, William Archibald, 1 Jan. 1918.
707 MacQueen, John, 1 Jan. 1918.
708 Macqueen, Margaret Marsden, 1 Jan. 1918.
709 Maeers, Frank, 1 Jan. 1918.
710 Main, Melville Pownall, 1 Jan. 1918.
711 Maitland, Adam, 1 Jan. 1918.
712 Makins, Agatha Caroline, 1 Jan. 1918.
713 Malcolm, Jeanne Marie, Mrs., 1 Jan. 1918.
714 Malcolm, William, 1 Jan. 1918.
715 Mallett, John Moore, 1 Jan. 1918.
717 Mann, Gerard Noel Cornwallis, 1 Jan. 1918.
718 Mann, William Henry, 1 Jan. 1918.
719 Manning, Albert John, 1 Jan. 1918.
720 Marchbank, Helen Millicent, 1 Jan. 1918.
721 Marriott, Ethel Gertrude, Mrs., 1 Jan. 1918.
722 Martin, Beatrix Maria, 1 Jan. 1918.
723 Martin, Ernest Charles, 1 Jan. 1918.
724 Martin, John Bentick, 1 Jan. 1918.
725 Mason, William Thomas, 1 Jan. 1918.
727 Maton, William Henry George, 1 Jan. 1918. (M.)
728 Matthews, Thomas, 1 Jan. 1918. (M.)
729 Matthews, William Thomas, 1 Jan. 1918.
730 Mavrogordato, Paul John, 1 Jan. 1918.
731 Mayberry, Lucy Powys, Mrs., 1 Jan. 1918.
732 Mayes, Henry George, 1 Jan. 1918. (M.)
734 McCall, David, 1 Jan. 1918.
735 McCammon, George William Richardson, 1 Jan. 1918.
736 McCormick Gerald Bernard, 1 Jan. 1918.
737 McCutchan, William Charles, 1 Jan. 1918. (M.)
738 McDonald, Alexander, 1 Jan. 1918. (M.)
739 McGavin, Maude, 1 Jan. 1918.
741 McLachlan, Donald McBrayne, 1 Jan. 1918.
742 McLaren, Maurice Paterson, 1 Jan. 1918.
743 McLean, Esther Fanny, Mrs., 1 Jan. 1918.
745 McLean, Matthew Adam, 1 Jan. 1918.
749 Medrow, Walter Alfred, 1 Jan. 1918.
752 Menzies, Charles Duncan, 1 Jan. 1918.
753 Merriman, Henry John, 1 Jan. 1918.
754 Metcalfe, Edith Minna, 1 Jan. 1918.
755 Methven, John, 1 Jan. 1918.
756 Michell, John Deeble, 1 Jan. 1918.
758 Middleton, Frederick George, 1 Jan. 1918. (M.)
759 Millar, Ella Morison, Mrs., 1 Jan. 1918.
760 Miller, Annie, 1 Jan. 1918.
761 Mills, John Edwin, 1 Jan. 1918.
762 Millward, Richard Tudor, 1 Jan. 1918.
763 Milne, George, 1 Jan. 1918.
764 Milne, John Ferguson, 1 Jan. 1918.
765 Milne, John Robertson, 1 Jan. 1918.
766 Mingard, Herbert Samuel, 1 Jan. 1918.
767 Mitchell, George Bennett, 1 Jan. 1918.
768 Mitchell, John Adamson, 1 Jan. 1918.
769 Mitchell, Walter, 1 Jan. 1918.
770 Moberly, James Edward, 1 Jan. 1918. (M.)
771 Moffatt, Alexander George, 1 Jan. 1918.
772 Moir, Annie Maitland, 1 Jan. 1918.
773 Moll, Frederick William, 1 Jan. 1918.
774 Monk, Owen, 1 Jan. 1918.
775 Monk, William Dusar, 1 Jan. 1918.
776 Monkhouse, Olive Eleanor, 1 Jan. 1918.
777 Montford, Eleanora, 1 Jan. 1918.
778 Montgomerie, Isabella Macalister, 1 Jan. 1918.
779 Morgan, John, 1 Jan. 1918.

780 Morgan, William, 1 Jan. 1918. (M.)
781 Morris, Frederick Montague Augustus, 1 Jan. 1918. (M.)
782 Morson, Arthur, 1 Jan. 1918.
783 Mort, John William, 1 Jan. 1918. (M.)
784 Morten-Turner, Lucy Aylwin, Mrs., 1 Jan. 1918.
786 Moseley, Arthur Herbert, 1 Jan. 1918.
787 Moss, George Sinclair, 1 Jan. 1918.
788 Munford, Frank Jago, 1 Jan. 1918.
789 Murphy, Henry Palmer, 1 Jan. 1918.
790 Murphy, Jerome Bernard, 1 Jan. 1918.
791 Murray, James Robertson, 1 Jan. 1918.
792 Mylrea, Mrs. Maynard, 1 Jan. 1918.
793 Nairn, George Alexander Stokes, 1 Jan. 1918. (M.)
794 Naish, Harold Walter, 1 Jan. 1918.
796 Neame, Ada Grace, Mrs., 1 Jan. 1918.
797 Neame, Thomas, 1 Jan. 1918. (M.)
798 Needham, James Henry, 1 Jan. 1918.
799 Nelson, William, 1 Jan. 1918.
800 Nicholas, Alice Jane Winifred, 1 Jan. 1918.
801 Nicholson, Evelyn Joanna, Mrs., 1 Jan. 1918.
802 Nicholson, John Steel, 1 Jan. 1918. (M.)
803 Nicol, John Strathdel, 1 Jan. 1918.
805 Northam, James, 1 Jan. 1918.
806 Northcott, George H. A., 1 Jan. 1918.
807 Notley, Leslie Richard, 1 Jan. 1918.
808 Nott, Harry Augustus, 1 Jan. 1918.
809 Oakeshott, Reuben, 1 Jan. 1918.
810 Ogilvie, Helen Leslie, 1 Jan. 1918.
812 O'Reilly, Arthur, 1 Jan. 1918.
813 Ormston, John Maurice, 1 Jan. 1918.
815 Orton, C. J., 1 Jan. 1918.
816 Oswald, Ethel Margaret Oswald, 1 Jan. 1918.
817 Ottewill, James Thomas, 1 Jan. 1918.
819 Owen, John Albert, 1 Jan. 1918.
820 Owen, Richard Trevor Tudor, 1 Jan. 1918. (M.)
821 Page, Edward, 1 Jan. 1918.
822 Pallin, Sydney David, 1 Jan. 1918.
823 Palmer, Horace Frank, 1 Jan. 1918.
824 Palmer, May Blanche, Mrs., 1 Jan. 1918.
826 Parker, Percy Frank, 1 Jan. 1918. (M.)
827 Parker, Sidney Ernest, 1 Jan. 1918. (M.)
828 Parr, George Herbert Edmeston, 1 Jan. 1918.
829 Paul, Janie Ramsbottom, Mrs., 1 Jan. 1918.
830 Paull, Catherine Swan, Mrs., 1 Jan. 1918.
831 Payne, Janet, Mrs., 1 Jan. 1918.
832 Pead, Winifred, 1 Jan. 1918.
833 Pearce, Agnes Isobel, 1 Jan. 1918.
835 Peet, Howard, 1 Jan. 1918.
836 Peirce, Richard Gall, 1 Jan. 1918.
837 Pell, Henry William, 1 Jan. 1918.
838 Pelling, Charlie, 1 Jan. 1918.
840 Peters, Bernard Richard, 1 Jan. 1918.
841 Peters, Cecil James Razzell, 1 Jan. 1918.
842 Pettet, Walter Bell, 1 Jan. 1918.
843 Phillips, David, 1 Jan. 1918.
844 Phillips, Henry Dixon, 1 Jan. 1918.
845 Phillips, Henry Thomas, 1 Jan. 1918.
846 Phillips, James Falkner, 1 Jan. 1918
847 Phillips, John Henry, 1 Jan. 1918.
848 Phillips, Walter John, 1 Jan. 1918.
849 Pickering, Alice Mabel, Mrs., 1 Jan. 1918.
850 Pilling, Henry, 1 Jan. 1918.
851 Pinchard, Rev. Arnold Theophilus Biddulph, 1 Jan. 1918.
853 Piper, Arthur, 1 Jan. 1918.
854 Pippard, Alfred John Sutton, 1 Jan. 1918.
855 Pledger, Charles Russell, 1 Jan. 1918.
856 Pomeroy, Amy, Mrs., 1 Jan. 1918.
857 Porter, Amy, Mrs., 1 Jan. 1918.
858 Porters, Robert Halstead, 1 Jan. 1918. (M.)
859 Potter, Francis Martin, 1 Jan. 1918.
860 Poultney, Edward Cecil, 1 Jan. 1918.
861 Power, George, 1 Jan. 1918.
862 Poynter, Vernon Hamilton, 1 Jan. 1918.
863 Smith, Maye Alice Pressley, 1 Jan. 1918.
864 Price, Ernest, 1 Jan. 1918.
865 Price-Williams, Janet, Mrs., 1 Jan. 1918.
866 Prime, Frederick Charles, 1 Jan. 1918. (M.)
867 Prower, Ernest Edward, 1 Jan. 1918.
868 Prytherch, Henry James, 1 Jan. 1918.
869 Purchas, Frederick Hayden, 1 Jan. 1918.
870 Quick, Henry James, 1 Jan. 1918.
871 Quilter, Joseph Rogers, 1 Jan. 1918.
872 Radcliffe, John, 1 Jan. 1918.
873 Rankin, George William, 1 Jan. 1918.
874 Rankin, John Arthur, 1 Jan. 1918.
875 Read, George Daniel, 1 Jan. 1918.
876 Reading, Joseph William, 1 Jan. 1918.
877 Readman, Annie Bradley, Mrs., 1 Jan. 1918.
878 Reid, Charles Clements, 1 Jan. 1918.
879 Reid, Isabella Elizabeth, 1 Jan. 1918.
880 Remington, Percy Thorndon, 1 Jan. 1918. (M.)
881 Reynolds, Clement Unsworth, 1 Jan. 1918.
882 Reynolds, William Howe, 1 Jan. 1918.
883 Riach, David Mackinlay Potter, 1 Jan. 1918. (M
884 Rice, Percy Christopher, 1 Jan. 1918.
885 Richardson, George Herbert, 1 Jan. 1918.
886 Richardson, Peter, 1 Jan. 1918.
887 Rickett, Alfred Charles James, 1 Jan. 1918.
888 Rider, Graham Stanley, 1 Jan. 1918.
890 Riordan, Patrick, 1 Jan. 1918.

MEMBERS.

892 Ritchie, Sir James William, Bart., 1 Jan. 1918.
894 Roberts, Herbert Wallace, 1 Jan. 1918.
895 Robertshaw, Robert Henry, 1 Jan. 1918.
896 Robertson, John, 1 Jan. 1918.
897 Robertson, James Constable, 1 Jan. 1918.
898 Robertson, Winifred Agnes Florence, 1 Jan. 1918.
899 Robinson, George Lovely, 1 Jan. 1918.
900 Robinson, William Charles, 1 Jan. 1918.
901 Robson, James, 1 Jan. 1918.
902 Rogers, George James Nicholas, 1 Jan. 1918.
903 Rogers, Richard Hawke, 1 Jan. 1918.
904 Rogers, Thomas Edward, 1 Jan. 1918.
905 Romney, William, 1 Jan. 1918.
906 Ronca, James Francis, 1 Jan. 1918.
908 Rossall, Jane, 1 Jan. 1918.
909 Rowbotham, James MacKean, 1 Jan. 1918.
910 Rowland, Arthur Maynard, 1 Jan. 1918.
911 Rowley, Mildred, 1 Jan. 1918
912 Rowlinson, Henry George, 1 Jan. 1918.
913 Roworth, Harry James, 1 Jan. 1918.
914 Rowse, Arthur Albert, 1 Jan. 1918.
915 Royle, Thomas Wright, 1 Jan. 1918.
916 Rush, William, 1 Jan. 1918. (M.)
917 Rust, Percy, 1 Jan. 1918. (M.)
918 Rutter, Herbert Llewellyn, 1 Jan. 1918.
920 Sadler, Henry, 1 Jan. 1918. (M.)
922 Sandeman, Ella Victoire, 1 Jan. 1918.
924 Sargent, Walter Anthony, 1 Jan. 1918.
926 Saunders, Edward, 1 Jan. 1918.
928 Saunders, Thomas Arthur, 1 Jan. 1918.
929 Schiff, Ernst, 1 Jan. 1918.
931 Seddon, James, 1 Jan. 1918.
933 Seymour, Lettice, 1 Jan. 1918.
934 Shacklady, Thomas George, 1 Jan. 1918.
937 Shilstone, Walter Richard, 1 Jan. 1918. (M.)
938 Shorey, Percy Thomas, 1 Jan. 1918.
939 Siddle, Robert, 1 Jan. 1918.
940 Sidebottom, Herbert, 1 Jan. 1918.
941 Sillar, Arthur Molyneux, 1 Jan. 1918.
942 Simmonds, Percy, 1 Jan. 1918.
943 Simpson, John Leonard, 1 Jan. 1918.
944 Sinclair, George Greig, 1 Jan. 1918.
945 Sitwell, William Sacheverel, 1 Jan. 1918.
946 Skinner, Edward John, 1 Jan. 1918.
948 Smith, Alexander, 1 Jan. 1918.
949 Smith, Albert, 1 Jan. 1918.
951 Smith, Frank William, 1 Jan. 1918.
952 Smith, Gladys Augusta, 1 Jan. 1918.
953 Smith, Harold, 1 Jan. 1918.
954 Smith, Harold Robert, 1 Jan. 1918.
955 Smith, James Alfred, 1 Jan. 1918.
956 Smith, Rodney, 1 Jan. 1918.
957 Smith, Sydney, 1 Jan. 1918.
959 Smith, Stanley George Drew, 1 Jan. 1918. (M.)
960 Smyth, Francis Watson, 1 Jan. 1918.
962 Snowden, Frederick Cousins, 1 Jan. 1918.
963 Sommerville, John, 1 Jan. 1918.
965 Spiller, Edward Francis, 1 Jan. 1918.
966 Spivey, Charles Henry Hughes, 1 Jan. 1918. (M.)
967 Springate, Edward Tom, 1 Jan. 1918.
968 Spragge, Samuel, 1 Jan. 1918.
969 Squirrell, Joseph Cooper, 1 Jan. 1918.
970 Stacey, Fanny, 1 Jan. 1918.
971 Stafford, John, 1 Jan. 1918.
972 Stafford, James William, 1 Jan. 1918.
973 Stansfield, Louis Donald, 1 Jan. 1918.
974 Staple, Rev. Richard, 1 Jan. 1918.
976 Stevenson, Herbert Given, 1 Jan. 1918.
977 Stewart, Elizabeth Woodhead, Mrs., 1 Jan. 1918.
978 Stewart, Jean Carruthers, 1 Jan. 1918.
979 Stewart, John, 1 Jan. 1918.
980 Stewart, Robert, 1 Jan. 1918.
981 Still, Ernest Henry, 1 Jan. 1918.
982 Stokes, Richard Albert, 1 Jan. 1918.
983 Stone, Leslie Norman Waldegrave, 1 Jan. 1918. (M.)
985 Storey, John, 1 Jan. 1918.
986 Strevens, Irene, 1 Jan. 1918.
987 Stringer, Ernest Edward, 1 Jan. 1918.
989 Stuckey, Ellen Elizabeth, 1 Jan. 1918.
991 Sutton, Arthur Fraser, 1 Jan. 1918. (M.)
992 Sydenham, Lewis George, 1 Jan. 1918.
993 Sykes, Mary Louisa, Mrs., 1 Jan. 1918.
994 Sykes, Percy Duncan, 1 Jan. 1918.
996 Tancock, Charles Crump, 1 Jan. 1918.
997 Tapp, John Reuben, 1 Jan. 1918.
998 Tasker, Grace Rosina, 1 Jan. 1918.
999 Tayler, Mary Beatrice Churchill, 1 Jan. 1918.
1000 Taylor, Alice Maud Rowson, 1 Jan. 1918.
1002 Taylor, Charles, 1 Jan. 1918.
1003 Taylor, Esther Hilda, 1 Jan. 1918
1004 Taylor, George Wilson, 1 Jan. 1918.
1008 Thew, Charlton, 1 Jan. 1918.
1009 Thomas, Arthur Augustus, 1 Jan. 1918.
1010 Thomas, Olive Morton, 1 Jan. 1918.
1011 Thompson, George, 1 Jan. 1918.
1012 Thomson, Adam Robert, 1 Jan. 1918.
1013 Thomson, Archibald, 1 Jan. 1918.
1014 Thomson, Margaret Eleanor, 1 Jan. 1918.
1015 Thornhill, John Samuel Alphonso McCoan, 1 Jan. 1918.

1017 Thorpe, Hannah Maud Taylor, 1 Jan. 1918.
1018 Thorpe, Walter Benjamin, 1 Jan. 1918. (M.)
1019 Thurston, Hugh Kingsmill Neville, 1 Jan. 1918.
1020 Ticehurst, Hugh Gorham, 1 Jan. 1918.
1021 Till, Violet Beatrice, 1 Jan. 1918.
1022 Tims, Edwin George Thomas, 1 Jan. 1918. (M.)
1023 Toft, Walter Henry, 1 Jan. 1918. (M.)
1024 Tom, Henry, 1 Jan. 1918.
1025 Tomkinson, Marion, 1 Jan. 1918.
1026 Tourtel, John Mesny, 1 Jan. 1918.
1028 Townsend, Lucy Mabel, Mrs., 1 Jan. 1918.
1029 Townshend, Anna, 1 Jan. 1918.
1030 Tozer, Edward John, 1 Jan. 1918.
1031 Trench, Gwendoline Heron, Mrs. Richard Bayley Chenevix, 1 Jan. 1918.
1032 Trevor, Rosamond, Lady, 1 Jan. 1918.
1033 Trick, William Burrows, 1 Jan. 1918.
1034 Trigger, Oliver, 1 Jan. 1918.
1036 Turner, Ada Mary, Mrs., 1 Jan. 1918.
1037 Turner, George Bankart, 1 Jan. 1918. (M.)
1039 Turton, William Henry, 1 Jan. 1918.
1040 Tweedale, James, 1 Jan. 1918.
1041 Vann, Walter Gerald, 1 Jan. 1918.
1042 Vardy, George, 1 Jan. 1918.
1043 Varley, John, 1 Jan. 1918.
1044 Vaughan, Arthur Ronald, 1 Jan. 1918.
1045 Vigers, Ruth Sarah, 1 Jan. 1918.
1046 Vigor, Harold Decimus, 1 Jan. 1918.
1047 Viney, Albert William, 1 Jan. 1918.
1048 Vivian, Nancy Lycett, Lady, 1 Jan. 1918.
1049 Wade, Francis Richard, 1 Jan. 1918.
1050 Waggott, Edward, 1 Jan. 1918.
1051 Wainwright, Charles Richard, 1 Jan. 1918.
1052 Waite, Alice May, 1 Jan. 1918.
1053 Walker, Alexander Mann, 1 Jan. 1918.
1054 Walker, Charles Edmund, 1 Jan. 1918.
1055 Walker, John Drummond, 1 Jan. 1918.
1056 Walker, John Frederick, 1 Jan. 1918.
1057 Walker, Maria Edith, Mrs., 1 Jan. 1918.
1058 Walker, Robert, 1 Jan. 1918.
1059 Walker, William, 1 Jan. 1918. (M.)
1060 Wallace, Augusta Maud, Lady, 1 Jan. 1918.
1061 Wallis, Robert, 1 Jan. 1918.
1062 Walton, John Thomas, 1 Jan. 1918.
1064 Ward, Caroline Theodora, Mrs., 1 Jan. 1918.
1065 Wardle, Charles, 1 Jan. 1918.
1066 Wardle, Percy Thomas, 1 Jan. 1918.
1067 Watkins, Arthur Glyn, 1 Jan. 1918.
1068 Watkins, Thomas Percival Holmes, 1 Jan. 1918.
1069 Watson, Isabella Clark, 1 Jan. 1918
1070 Watson, William George, 1 Jan. 1918.
1071 Watts, Henry Charles, 1 Jan. 1918.
1072 Weatherhead, Adam, 1 Jan. 1918.
1073 Webb, Ella Gertrude Amy, Mrs., 1 Jan. 1918.
1075 Webb, Herbert Stephen, 1 Jan. 1918.
1076 Weighell, Walter, 1 Jan. 1918.
1077 Weir, George Jackson, 1 Jan. 1918.
1078 Welsh, Cécile Campbell, Mrs., 1 Jan. 1918.
1079 West, James Hales, 1 Jan. 1918.
1080 West, William George, 1 Jan. 1918. (M.)
1081 Westland, John Lowe, 1 Jan. 1918.
1082 Weston, Edith Ivy, 1 Jan. 1918.
1083 Wheatley, Thomas Angas, 1 Jan. 1918.
1084 Whitby, Alfred James, 1 Jan. 1918.
1085 White, Arthur, 1 Jan. 1918.
1086 White, Jesse Obadiah, 1 Jan. 1918.
1087 White, Percy Ernest, 1 Jan. 1918.
1088 White, Professor Robert George, 1 Jan. 1918.
1089 Whiting, Gerald, 1 Jan. 1918.
1090 Whitten, George Jackson, 1 Jan. 1918.
1091 Whitteridge, Percy Claydon, 1 Jan. 1918. (M.)
1092 Whittle, Herbert John, 1 Jan. 1918.
1093 Wilkinson, Christopher Henry George, 1 Jan. 1918.
1095 Williams, Ernest Graham, 1 Jan. 1918.
1096 Williams, Isabel Rose, 1 Jan. 1918.
1097 Williamson, Richard Charles, 1 Jan. 1918. (M.)
1098 Williams-Wynn, Elizabeth Ida, Mrs. Robert William Herbert Watkin, 1 Jan. 1918.
1099 Willicot, George Frederick William, 1 Jan. 1918. (M.)
1100 Willis, Cecil Herbert Stanley, 1 Jan. 1918. (M.)
1101 Willson, Rose, Mrs., 1 Jan. 1918.
1103 Wilson, Harry Gouldie, 1 Jan. 1918.
1104 Wilson, William, 1 Jan. 1918.
1105 Winn, Rowland, 1 Jan. 1918.
1106 Winter, Henry Elsbury, 1 Jan. 1918.
1107 Smith, Constance Evelyn Winwood-, 1 Jan. 1918.
1108 Wise, Percy Furlong, 1 Jan. 1918.
1109 Wolfenden, Ralph, 1 Jan. 1918.
1110 Wood, Frances Mary, 1 Jan. 1918.
1111 Wood, Thomas, 1 Jan. 1918.
1112 Woodford, Charles Merllynn, 1 Jan. 1918.
1113 Wood-Hill, Amy, Mrs., 1 Jan. 1918.
1114 Woods, Charlie Roland, 1 Jan. 1918.
1115 Woodyear, Irene, 1 Jan. 1918.
1116 Woollard, Frank George, 1 Jan. 1918.
1118 Wotton, Walter John, 1 Jan. 1918.
1120 Wright, Professor Mark Robinson, 1 Jan. 1918.
1121 Wright, William, 1 Jan. 1918.
1122 Wright, William, 1 Jan. 1918.
1123 Wykes, Leonard Graveney, 1 Jan. 1918.

1124 Wynne, Nora, 1 Jan. 1918.
1125 Young, David Wilberforce, 1 Jan. 1918.
1127 Young, George, 1 Jan. 1918.
1128 Young, Patricia, 1 Jan. 1918.
1129 Young, Thomas, 1 Jan. 1918.
1130 Youngman, Walter, 1 Jan. 1918.
1131 Barton, Lilian, Mrs., 1 Jan. 1918.
1132 Durell, Deaconess Margaret, 1 Jan. 1918.
1133 Thubron, Kate, Mrs., 1 Jan. 1918.
1134 McCarthy, May, Mrs., 1 Jan. 1918.
1135 Spencer, Edith, 1 Jan. 1918.
1136 Wyld, Florence Maria, 1 Jan. 1918.
1137 Bird, Herbert Ruben, 1 Jan. 1918.
1138 Naik, Rao Bahadur Rango Govind, 1 Jan. 1918.
1139 Judge, Charles Edward Miller, 1 Jan. 1918.
1140 Jones, Frank Henry, 1 Jan. 1918.
1141 Fulford, Edward Oliver Heywood, 1 Jan. 1918
1143 McIntosh, John, 1 Jan. 1918.
1144 Douglas, George, 1 Jan. 1918.
1146 Middleton, George Burnett, 1 Jan. 1918.
1147 Skelly, Henry Wilfrid, 1 Jan. 1918.
1148 Weaver, Percy, 1 Jan. 1918.
1149 Mason, Herbert, 1 Jan. 1918.
1150 Moore, Pye, 1 Jan. 1918.
1151 Boxall, George, 1 Jan. 1918.
1152 Potts, Allen Calder, 1 Jan. 1918.
1153 Dennett, Sydney, 1 Jan. 1918.
1154 Austin, Albert Sydney, 1 Jan. 1918.
1155 Calthrop, Hugh V. E., 1 Jan. 1918.
1156 Cave, H. C., 1 Jan. 1918.
1157 Dean, Ida Florence, Mrs., 1 Jan. 1918.
1158 de Boise, Frank, 1 Jan. 1918.
1159 Draper, Thomas Percy, 1 Jan. 1918.
1160 Egan, Kate, 1 Jan. 1918.
1161 Elworthy, E. G., 1 Jan. 1918.
1162 Isbister, W. J., 1 Jan. 1918
1163 Laidley, Ethel, Mrs., 1 Jan. 1918.
1164 Robertson, W. T., 1 Jan. 1918.
1165 Sinclair, Robert Albert Dunbar, 1 Jan. 1918.
1166 Skene, Lillias Margaret, Mrs., 1 Jan. 1918.
1167 Stephen, Nancy Consett, 1 Jan. 1918.
1169 Bissland Emma, Mrs., 1 Jan. 1918.
1170 Burgess, Ann, Mrs., 1 Jan. 1918.
1171 Burt, Jean, 1 Jan. 1918.
1172 Coradine, Sarah Ann, Mrs., 1 Jan. 1918.
1173 Crawford, Harriette Sophia, Mrs., 1 Jan. 1918.
1174 Donaldson, George Lester, 1 Jan. 1918.
1176 Fenton, Edith, 1 Jan. 1918.
1177 Forrester, Elizabeth, Mrs., 1 Jan. 1918.
1178 Gibbons, Hope, 1 Jan. 1918.
1179 Guinness, Florence, Mrs., 1 Jan. 1918.
1180 Harding, Margaret, Mrs., 1 Jan. 1918.
1181 Hawke, Leah Lucy, Mrs., 1 Jan. 1918.
1182 Jack, Douglas William, 1 Jan. 1918.
1183 Kirkpatrick, Mary Hawkins, Mrs., 1 Jan. 1918
1184 Larner, Victor John, 1 Jan. 1918.
1185 Leaver, Kate Rose, Mrs., 1 Jan. 1918.
1186 Levinge, Edward George, 1 Jan. 1918.
1187 McLean, Isabel, 1 Jan. 1918.
1188 Manning, Arthur Edward, 1 Jan. 1918.
1189 Moorhouse, William Henry Sefton, 1 Jan. 1918.
1190 Nash, Elizabeth Lily, Mrs., 1 Jan. 1918.
1191 Ngata, Arihia Kane, Mrs., 1 Jan. 1918.
1192 Perry, George Albert, 1 Jan. 1918.
1193 Robertson, Herbert James Duncan, 1 Jan. 1918.
1195 Sherratt, Alice Georgina, Mrs., 1 Jan. 1918.
1196 Simpson, Jean, Mrs., 1 Jan. 1918.
1197 Snodgrass, William Wallace, 1 Jan. 1918.
1198 Spedding, Belle, 1 Jan. 1918.
1199 Stead, William, 1 Jan. 1918.
1200 Thompson, Maurice, 1 Jan. 1918.
1201 Thomson, Patricia Clay, 1 Jan. 1918.
1202 Treleaven, Charles John, 1 Jan. 1918.
1203 Varney, Arthur, 1 Jan. 1918.
1204 Webster, Georgina, 1 Jan. 1918.
1205 Barnett, Ezra John, 1 Jan. 1918.
1206 Bourne, Lucy Dorothea, Lady, 1 Jan. 1918.
1207 Calder, William Beale, 1 Jan. 1918.
1208 Clark, Herbert Ernest, 1 Jan. 1918.
1209 Clarkson, Francis George, 1 Jan. 1918.
1211 Dougall, John, 1 Jan. 1918.
1212 Dunlop, Robert, 1 Jan. 1918.
1215 Faure, Pieter Jacobus van Breda, 1 Jan. 1918.
1216 Fraser, Laura Vivienne, Mrs., 1 Jan. 1918.
1217 Friedlander, Grace Christian, Mrs., 1 Jan. 1918.
1218 Giovanetti, Constantine William, 1 Jan. 1918.
1219 Girdwood, Alexander Forsyth, 1 Jan. 1918.
1220 How, Willoughby, 1 Jan. 1918.
1221 Izod, Edwin Gilbert, 1 Jan. 1918.
1222 Kemsey, John Chambers, 1 Jan. 1918.
1223 Martin, Elizabeth Evelyn, Mrs., 1 Jan. 1918.
1224 Moller, Justina Wilhelmina Nancy, Mrs., 1 Jan. 1918.
1225 Murray, Susan Ann, Mrs., 1 Jan. 1918.
1226 Nuttall, Maria, Mrs., 1 Jan. 1918.
1227 Orr, John, 1 Jan. 1918.
1228 Parker, Mary Jeannette, 1 Jan. 1918.
1229 Parkyns, Thomas Samuel, 1 Jan. 1918.
1230 Rees, Catherine Mary, Mrs., 1 Jan. 1918.
1233 Sleith, Thomas, 1 Jan. 1918.
1234 Stowe, Richard Walter, 1 Jan. 1918.

1236 Townshend, Arthur Walter, 1 Jan. 1918.
1237 Van der Bijl, Kate Amy, Mrs., 1 Jan. 1918.
1238 Vintcent, Rose Lilian, Mrs., 1 Jan. 1918.
1241 Blackall, William Walker, 1 Jan. 1918.
1242 Burke, Vincent Patrick, 1 Jan. 1918.
1243 Curtis, Rev. Levi, 1 Jan. 1918.
1244 Green, Elizabeth Selina, Mrs., 1 Jan. 1918.
1245 Hayward, Annie, 1 Jan. 1918.
1246 McKay, Mary, 1 Jan. 1918.
1247 Morris, Eliza Mary Jane, Mrs., 1 Jan. 1918.
1248 Rennie, William Hoyles, 1 Jan. 1918.
1249 Steer, Frank, 1 Jan. 1918.
1250 Bell, Edward, 1 Jan. 1918. (M.)
1251 Bonavia, Marie, Mrs. Edgar, 1 Jan. 1918.
1252 Bowen, Ellen, Mrs., 1 Jan. 1918.
1253 Briscoe, Ada Ellen, Mrs., 1 Jan. 1918.
1254 Bruce, Robert Randal, 1 Jan. 1918.
1255 Cassels, John Borlase, 1 Jan. 1918.
1257 Clumeck, Marie, Mrs., 1 Jan. 1918.
1258 Collymore, Frederick Appleton, 1 Jan. 1918.
1259 Cook, Katharine, Mrs., 1 Jan. 1918.
1260 Cummings, Emanuel Henry, 1 Jan. 1918.
1261 de Cordova, Judith, Mrs., 1 Jan. 1918.
1262 Douglas, Annie Jane, 1 Jan. 1918.
1263 Draper, Christopher Robert Burroughs, 1 Jan. 1918.
1264 Fitzpatrick, Matthew McKean, 1 Jan. 1918.
1266 Fraser, Percy Louis Alexander, 1 Jan. 1918.
1267 Fremantle, John Morton, 1 Jan. 1918.
1268 Goodall, Edward Basil Herbert, 1 Jan. 1918.
1269 Griffin, Eugene Patrick, 1 Jan. 1918.
1270 Hand, John Pierce, 1 Jan. 1918.
1271 Hutchinson, Robert Oliphant, 1 Jan. 1918.
1272 Johnson, Agnes Norah, Mrs., 1 Jan. 1918.
1273 Jones, Edgar Anderson Averaye, 1 Jan. 1918.
1274 Kearney, Tereza Mary, 1 Jan. 1918.
1275 Lanitis, Vrasidas Demitriou, 1 Jan. 1918.
1276 Guan, Lee Choon, 1 Jan. 1918.
1277 Lofthouse, Elizabeth Ann, Mrs., 1 Jan. 1918.
1278 Lyons, George Graham Percy, 1 Jan. 1918.
1279 Mifsud, Anne Gill, Mrs., 1 Jan. 1918.
1280 Moseley, Mary, 1 Jan. 1918.
1282 Popham, Henry Bradshaw, 1 Jan. 1918.
1283 Rattray, Robert Sutherland, 1 Jan. 1918.
1284 Reid, Maria Jean, Mrs., 1 Jan. 1918.
1286 Sheppard, Herbert St. John, 1 Jan. 1918.
1287 Stanley, William Blakeney, 1 Jan. 1918.
1288 Toogood, John James, 1 Jan. 1918.
1289 Tremlett, Frederic Thomas George, 1 Jan. 1918.
1290 Tucker, Ada Mary, Mrs., 1 Jan. 1918.
1291 Usher, Archibald Rhys, 1 Jan. 1918.
1292 Webster, Gustavus William, 1 Jan. 1918.
1293 Wells, Charles Edward, 1 Jan. 1918.
1294 Wood, Thomas Alfred, 1 Jan. 1918.
1296 Beasley, Madeleine, 1 Jan. 1918.
1297 Beeby-Thompson, Arthur, 1 Jan. 1918.
1298 Buchan, Andrew, 1 Jan. 1918. (M.)
1299 Coke, Hon. Mrs. Arthur George, 1 Jan. 1918.
1300 Collins, Gladys Mary, 1 Jan. 1918. (M.)
1301 Duckworth, Francis Robinson Gladstone, 1 Jan 1918. (M.)
1302 Finch, George Ingle, 1 Jan. 1918. (M.)
1303 Frood, Mary Sophia, 1 Jan. 1918. (M.)
1304 Gill, Lilias Ida, Mrs., 1 Jan. 1918. (M.)
1307 Kenyon, Margaret Kilroy, Mrs., 1 Jan. 1918. (M.)
1308 Lench, William F., 1 Jan. 1918. (M.)
1311 Owens, William, 1 Jan. 1918.
1314 Swithenbank, John William, 1 Jan. 1918.
1314a Johnston, Francis, 15 Feb. 1918. (M.)
1315 Fisken. Alice Maude. 24 May, 1918.
1316 Fisken, Lily Edith, 24 May, 1918.
1317 Kiddle, John Lindsay, 24 May, 1918.
1318 Smith, Percy, 24 May, 1918.
1319 Pomfret, Edith Mary, Mrs., 24 May, 1918.
1320 Abbott, Charles Reginald, 3 June, 1918. (M.)
1321 Abbott, John Dixon, 3 June, 1918.
1322 Acraman, Ivor Yorath, 3 June, 1918.
1323 Adamson, John S†ockton, 3 June, 1918.
1324 Adcock, Fred, 3 June, 1918.
1325 Addy, Ernest, 3 June, 1918. (M.)
1326 Ainslie, Eustace Montagu Lafone, 3 June, 1918. (M.)
1327 Aitchison, Agnes Mary, 3 June, 1918.
1328 Aitken, Andrew, 3 June, 1918.
1329 Alcock, Violet May, 3 June, 1918.
1330 Aldam, Sarah Julia, Mrs. William Wright Warde, 3 June, 1918
1331 Alder, George, 3 June, 1918.
1333 Aldridge, William Frederick, 3 June, 1918.
1334 Alexander, Samuel Grant, 3 June, 1918.
1335 Allan, James Craig, 3 June, 1918. (M.)
1336 Allen, Michael Henry Percival, 3 June, 1918. (M.)
1337 Allinson, Ephraim, 3 June, 1918.
1338 Allison, Thomas, 3 June, 1918.
1339 Allum, Horace Benjamin, 3 June, 1918.
1340 Ambrose, Philip Fermor, 3 June, 1918.
1341 Amey, Fulcher, 3 June, 1918. (M.)
1342 Amy, Lillian Eva, Mrs., 3 June, 1918.
1343 Anderson, Charles, 3 June, 1918.
1344 Anderson, Charles James, 3 June, 1918.
1345 Anderson, Daisy Kate, 3 June, 1918.
1346 Anderson, George, 3 June, 1918.

MEMBERS.

1347 Anderson, Percy, 3 June, 1918. (M.)
1348 Andrews, Cyril Rogers, 3 June, 1918. (M.)
1350 Andrews, Horace George, 3 June, 1918.
1351 Appleby, Geoffrey Edmund, 3 June, 1918. (M.)
1352 Archer, Thomas William, 3 June, 1918.
1353 Armitstead, Thomas, 3 June, 1918. (M.)
1354 Armstrong, Robert Bayles, 3 June, 1918.
1355 Armstrong, Thomas Edward Steele, 3 June, 1918. (M.)
1356 Arnold, Henry George, 3 June, 1918.
1357 Ashford, Mary Adelaide, Mrs., 3 June, 1918.
1358 Ashton, George Kerfoot, 3 June, 1918.
1359 Atherton, William Thomas Finley, 3 June, 1918. (M.)
1360 Atkinson, Dorothea, Mrs.. 3 June, 1918.
1361 Atkinson, Lucy Mary Montagu, 3 June, 1918.
1362 Audland, William Edward, 3 June, 1918.
1364 Ayres, Henry John, 3 June, 1918.
1365 Backhouse, Edith Frances, 3 June, 1918.
1366 Bailey, Cyril, 3 June, 1918.
1367 Bailey, Sidney Alfred, 3 June, 1918.
1368 Bailey, William Edward, 3 June, 1918. (M.)
1369 Baillie, Elizabeth Margaret, Mrs., 3 June, 1918.
1370 Baines, John William Owen, 3 June, 1918.
1371 Baird, Constance Kennedy, 3 June, 1918.
1372 Baker, Atheling Herbert, 3 June, 1918.
1373 Ball, Frank Clement, 3 June, 1919. (M.)
1374 Bamford, Louisa Orme, Mrs., 3 June, 1918.
1375 Bancroft, James, 3 June, 1918.
1376 Bannerman, David Armitage, 3 June, 1918.
1377 Barber, Louis Walter, 3 June, 1918. (M.)
1378 Barker, Evelyn, Mrs., 3 June, 1918.
1379 Barker, Harold Hastings, 3 June, 1918.
1381 Barnett, Geoffrey Arthur, 3 June, 1918. (M.)
1382 Barnett, Samuel Henry Gilmore, 3 June, 1918.
1383 Barns, Stephen Allen, 3 June, 1918.
1384 Baron, Hilda Madeleine, Mrs., 3 June, 1918.
1385 Barton, Ernest Wilfred Edwards, 3 June, 1918.
1386 Bassett, John William Abell, 3 June, 1918.
1387 Batch, Edward, 3 June, 1918.
1388 Bate, Mary, Mrs., 3 June, 1918.
1389 Bates, Charles William, 3 June, 1918.
1390 Batger, Janet Mary, Mrs., 3 June, 1918.
1391 Batten, Beatrix Marguerite, 3 June, 1918.
1392 Batten, John Thomas, 3 June, 1918. (M.)
1393 Batten, Winifred Eleanor Sarah, 3 June, 1918.
1394 Batty, George Henry, 3 June, 1918. (M.)
1395 Bayliss, Edward Swayn, 3 June, 1918.
1396 Bayliss, Gilbert Thomas, 3 June, 1918.
1397 Baynes, Charlotte Augusta, 3 June, 1918.
1398 Beanes, Warwick Henry, 3 June, 1918.
1399 Beard, Richard Frith, 3 June, 1918.
1400 Beattle, John Millar, 3 June, 1918.
1401 Brecroft, Arthur Edward, 3 June, 1918. (M.)
1402 Begg, Donald Glassford, 3 June, 1918.
1403 Bell, Charles David Jarrett, 3 June, 1918.
1404 Bainbridge-Bell, Kathleen Audrey Danvers, 3 June, 1918.
1405 Bell, Lee, 3 June, 1918. (M.)
1406 Benjamin, Florence Sarah, Mrs., 3 June, 1918.
1407 Bennett, William Roger, 3 June, 1918.
1408 Benson, Bessie, Mrs., 3 June, 1918.
1409 Beresford, Charles Frederick Delaval, 3 June, 1918.
1410 Berry, Mary Ann, 3 June, 1918. (M.)
1411 Bethell, William Edmund, 3 June, 1918.
1412 Bickley, Nora Magdalen, Mrs., 3 June, 1918.
1414 Bilton, Christina Turnbull, 3 June, 1918.
1415 Binnie, Annie Janet, Mrs., 3 June, 1918.
1416 Binns, Aubrey Brian, 3 June, 1918.
1417 Birch, Wyndham Lindsay, 3 June, 1918. (M.)
1418 Bird, Douglas Joseph, 3 June, 1918. (M.)
1419 Birrell, Hugh, 3 June, 1918.
1420 Birtwistle, Philip, 3 June, 1918.
1421 Bishop, Richard Winsor, 3 June, 1918.
1422 Black, Gordon Boyes, 3 June, 1918. (M.)
1423 Blackett, Mortimer Charles, 3 June, 1918. (M.)
1424 Blackman, Ida Louisa, 3 June, 1918.
1425 Blackwell, Harry Cooper, 3 June, 1918.
1426 Blackwell, Hilda, 3 June, 1918.
1427 Blair, Atholl, 3 June, 1918.
1428 Blair, Robert, 3 June, 1918.
1429 Blamires, Mary, Mrs., 3 June, 1918.
1430 Blaylock, Robert, 3 June, 1918.
1432 Bloor, Frank Robert, 3 June, 1918. (M.)
1433 Blount, Mary, 3 June, 1918.
1434 Blyth, Hon. Mrs. James Audley, 3 June, 1918.
1435 Bolt, Daniel Roberts, 3 June, 1918.
1436 Bolton, Edwin, 3 June, 1918.
1437 Bond, James Ryding, 3 June, 1918.
1439 Bonser, William Frederic, 3 June, 1918.
1441 Boosey, Madge, 3 June, 1918.
1442 Booth, Maud, 3 June, 1918.
1443 Borland, Robert Gordon, 3 June, 1918.
1444 Bosanquet, Thomas Albert Edward James, 3 June 1918. (M.)
1445 Boulnois, Emma Mrs., 3 June, 1918.
1446 Bourn, Thomas William, 3 June, 1918.
1447 Bowles, Elizabeth, 3 June, 1918.
1448 Bowman, Alfred Thomas, 3 June, 1918.
1450 Boyd, Anne Jamieson, 3 June, 1918.
1451 Brackenbury, Florence Adelia, Mrs.. 3 June, 1918.
1452 Bradshaw, Stanley Goodwin, 3 June, 1918. (M.)
1453 Brain, Edwin Lewton-, 3 June, 1918.

1455 Brake, Ethel Primrose, Mrs., 3 June, 1918.
1456 Bramwell, Percy, 3 June, 1918.
1457 Shairp, Gertrude Ethel, Mrs. Algernon, 3 June, 1918.
1458 Bremner, David, 3 June, 1918.
1459 Brennan, Vincent Talbot, 3 June, 1918.
1460 Brewis, Thomas Stamp, 3 June, 1918. (M.)
1461 Brice, Mary Helen Thorpe, 3 June, 1918.
1462 Brickenden, Charles, 3 June, 1918.
1463 Bridger, Stanley Alexander, 3 June, 1918.
1464 Brien, Owen, 3 June, 1918.
1465 Briggs, Elsie Baron, 3 June, 1918.
1466 Brill, Gwendoline Mary, 3 June, 1918.
1467 Brodie, Arthur William, 3 June, 1918.
1468 Brodie, Rhoda, 3 June, 1918.
1469 Brooks, Alice, Mrs., 3 June, 1918.
1470 Broome, Louis Egerton, 3 June, 1918. (M.)
1471 Broomfield, Frederick Harry, 3 June, 1918.
1472 Brown, Albert Thomas, 3 June, 1918.
1473 Brown, Cecil Norman, 3 June, 1918. (M.)
1474 Brown, Cicely Leadley-, 3 June, 1918.
1475 Brown, Cuthbert, 3 June, 1918.
1476 Brown, David, 3 June, 1918.
1477 Brown, Everard Kenneth, 3 June, 1918. (M
1478 Brown, Geoffrey William, 3 June, 1918. (M.)
1479 Brown, George Thomas, 3 June, 1918. (M.)
1480 Brown, Harry Percy, 3 June, 1918.
1481 Brown, Margaret Bennett, 3 June, 1918.
1482 Brown, Mary Louisa Hester, Mrs. Clerke-, 3 June, 1918.
1483 Brown, Reginald, 3 June, 1918.
1484 Bruce, Charles Brudenell, 3 June, 1918
1485 Bruce, Elizabeth, Mrs., 3 June, 1918.
1486 Bryning, Emma Jane, 3 June, 1918.
1487 Buchanan, Rhoda Agnes, Mrs., 3 June, 1918.
1488 Buck, Frank Steele, 3 June, 1918.
1489 Buck, Margaret, Mrs., 3 June, 1918.
1490 Buckle, Ethel Agnes, Mrs., 3 June, 1918.
1491 Bulkley, Mildred Emily, 3 June, 1918.
1492 Bullen, Gertrude, 3 June, 1918.
1494 Bunch, William Henry, 3 June, 1918.
1495 Bunney, Michael, 3 June, 1918.
1496 Burden, Walter Patrick, 3 June, 1918. (M.)
1497 Burder, Walter Chapman, 3 June, 1918.
1499 Burne, Louisa Joan, Mrs., 3 June, 1918.
1500 Burnet, William Hodgson, 3 June, 1918.
1501 Burrage, David Alexander, 3 June, 1918. (M.)
1502 Burridge, John Harold, 3 June, 1918.
1503 Burt, Frank Playfair, 3 June, 1918.
1504 Butcher, George Henry, 3 June, 1918.
1505 Butcher, Sidney Herbert, 3 June, 1918
1506 Butler, Harold, 3 June, 1918.
1507 Caird, Francis Pratt, 3 June, 1918.
1508 Caldwell, Bruce McGregor, 3 June, 1918. (M.)
1509 Caldwell, David, 3 June, 1918.
1510 Calvert, Rupert Harry, 3 June, 1918.
1511 Cameron, William Scott, 3 June, 1918.
1512 Campbell, Annie Campbell, 3 June, 1918.
1513 Campbell, Frederick Harold, 3 June, 1918. (M.)
1514 Campbell, Henry Kenyon, 3 June, 1918.
1515 Campbell, William Robert, 3 June, 1918.
1516 Carbonell, Edith Frances, 3 June, 1918.
1517 Carr, John, 3 June, 1918. (M.)
1518 Carter, Charles Maurice, 3 June, 1918.
1519 Carter, George, 3 June, 1918.
1520 Cartmail, Daisy Olive, 3 June. 1918.
1521 Carver, Mary Glendinning, 3 June, 1918.
1522 Catley, Clare, 3 June, 1918.
1523 Causton, Ida Jessie, Mrs., 3 June, 1918.
1524 Cavan, Samuel Edward, 3 June, 1918.
1525 Cawood, Charles John, 3 June, 1918.
1526 Cayley, Dora, 3 June, 1918.
1527 Chaplin, Frank, 3 June, 1918.
1528 Chapman, Florence, 3 June, 1918.
1529 Chapman, George Russell, 3 June, 1918.
1530 Cherry, Edward Hazlehurst, 3 June, 1918.
1531 Childs, James, 3 June, 1918.
1532 Chippendale, Martha, 3 June, 1918.
1533 Chune, Helen Gertrude, 3 June, 1918.
1534 Churchward, George Charles, 3 June, 1918.
1535 Chuter, Arthur George, 3 June, 1918.
1536 Claremont, Adel Dorothy, Mrs., 3 June, 1918.
1538 Clark, John Martin, 3 June, 1918. (M.)
1539 Clark, William Morrison, 3 June, 1918. (M.)
1540 Clarke, Francis William, 3 June, 1918.
1541 Claughton, Harold, 3 June, 1918.
1542 Clegg, Alfred, 3 June, 1918.
1543 Clegg, Bella, Mrs., 3 June, 1918.
1544 Clegg, Ethel Theodora, 3 June, 1918. (M.)
1545 Clements, Fred, 3 June, 1918.
1546 Clough, William, 3 June, 1918.
1547 Clucas, Alfred Henry, 3 June, 1918. (M.)
1548 Clutterbuck, Millie Gertrude, 3 June, 1918.
1549 Cochran, Dora Alexandrina, 3 June, 1918.
1550 Cockburn, John Alexander, 3 June, 1918.
1551 Coe, Charles George, 3 June, 1918. (M.)
1552 Cole, Charles Henry, 3 June, 1918.
1553 Coleman, Arthur Charles, 3 June, 1918.
1555 Colley, Thomas Bellasyse, 3 June, 1918. (M.)
1556 Collier, Willoughby, 3 June, 1918.
1557 Collins, Abraham Bennett, 3 June, 1918. (M.)
1558 Collins, George Alfred, 3 June, 1918.

1559 Collins. John Howarth, 3 June, 1918.
1560 Collis, Frederick, 3 June, 1918.
1561 Colman, Joseph Leonard, 3 June, 1918. (M.)
1562 Colville, Hon. George Charles, 3 June, 1918.
1563 Combe, Harvey Alexander Brabazon, 3 June, 1918. (M.)
1564 Connett, William, 3 June, 1918.
1565 Consterdine, Rudolph, 3 June, 1918.
1566 Conway, Agnes Ethel, 3 June, 1918.
1567 Cooke, William John, 3 June, 1918.
1568 Coombs, Edward Alfred, 3 June, 1918.
1569 Cooper, Allan Ernest, 3 June, 1918.
1570 Cooper, Eleanor Valentine, 3 June, 1918.
1571 Cooper, Harry Gordon, 3 June, 1918.
1572 Cope, Geoffrey Silverwood, 3 June, 1918.
1573 Corah, John Reginald, 3 June, 1918.
1574 Corbet, Hon. Mrs. Reginald, 3 June, 1918.
1575 Corner, Kate Agnes, 3 June, 1918.
1576 Corrie, Donald Welldon, 3 June, 1918.
1577 Cory, Mabel Emily Hartridge, Mrs., 3 June, 1918.
1578 Cottell, Amy Joan, 3 June, 1918.
1579 Cotterell, Thomas Sturge, 3 June, 1918.
1580 Cotton, George Frederick, 3 June, 1918.
1581 Cotton, James Temple, 3 June, 1918.
1582 Couper, John, 3 June, 1918. (M.)
1583 Couratin, Paul Evelyn, 3 June, 1918.
1584 Course, Sarah Denton, Mrs., 3 June, 1918.
1585 Court, Eleanor Rosina, 3 June, 1918.
1587 Cowley, Norah Louisa, 3 June, 1918.
1588 Cowling, Eleanor, Mrs., 3 June, 1918.
1589 Cox, Charles Edwin, 3 June, 1918.
1590 Cox, Stephen, 3 June, 1918.
1591 Coyne, Russell, 3 June, 1918. (M.)
1592 Cracknell, Nora Frances Elizabeth, 3 June, 1918.
1593 Cranfield, Guy William, 3 June, 1918. (M.)
1594 Crang, James, 3 June, 1918.
1595 Crawford, Alexander, 3 June, 1918.
1596 Crawford, Barbara Grace Rutherford, Mrs., 3 June, 1918.
1597 Crawford, James, 3 June, 1918. (M.)
1598 Crawley, Cecil, Mrs., 3 June, 1918.
1599 Cree, Isabella Warden, 3 June, 1918.
1601 Cripps, Lucy Davis, 3 June, 1918.
1602 Critchinson, William Thomas, 3 June, 1918.
1603 Crook, George Henry Holland, 3 June, 1918. (M.)
1604 Crosby, Ada, 3 June, 1918.
1605 Cross, Charles Garsed, 3 June, 1918. (M.)
1606 Cross, Minnie Eleanor Elizabeth, 3 June, 1918.
1607 Crowe, George Gorden, 3 June, 1918.
1608 Croxton, Edith Miriam, Mrs., 3 June, 1918.
1609 Cudlip, Ethel Annie Lina Pender-, 3 June, 1918.
1610 Culbard, Amelia Jane Chisholm, 3 June, 1918.
1612 Cunningham, Edith Usher, 3 June, 1918.
1613 Cuthbertson, William Darling, 3 June, 1918.
1616 Dalmahoy, Emily Marion, 3 June, 1918.
1617 Dalston, Norman Howard Maxwell, 3 June, 1918. (M.)
1618 Daly, Amy, Mrs., 3 June, 1918.
1619 Daly, Hon. Florence Maria, 3 June, 1918.
1620 Darby, Margaret, 3 June, 1918.
1621 Darker, Charlotte Tarry, 3 June, 1918.
1622 Darnell, Thomas Noah, 3 June, 1918.
1623 Dashwood, Sidney Lewes, 3 June, 1918. (M.)
1624 Datta, Surendra Kumar, 3 June, 1918.
1625 Daubeny, Mabel Agnes, 3 June, 1918.
1626 David, Morgan Edwin, 3 June, 1918.
1627 Davidson, Elizabeth, Mrs., 3 June, 1918.
1628 Davidson, John Hay, 3 June, 1918.
1629 Davies, Ashton, 3 June, 1918.
1630 Davies, David Gordon, 3 June, 1918.
1631 Davies, Dorothy Kevill-, Mrs., 13 June, 1918.
1632 Davies, Ivor, 3 June, 1918.
1633 Davies, Owen, 3 June, 1918.
1634 Davies, Thomas, 3 June, 1918.
1635 Davies, William, 3 June, 1918.
1636 Davis, Charles, 3 June, 1918.
1638 Davis, Owen, 3 June, 1918.
1639 Dawson, Arthur Robert, 3 June, 1918.
1640 Dawson, Frederick William, 3 June, 1918.
1641 Day, Gertrude Margaret, 3 June, 1918.
1642 Deacon, Mary Ariel Stewart, Mrs., 3 June, 1918.
1643 Dean, Basil, 3 June, 1918.
1645 Dempsey, Cornelius Thomas, 3 June, 1918. (M.)
1646 Dennis, H. A., 3 June, 1918.
1647 Denny, Norah, 3 June, 1918.
1648 Devereux, Ethel Mary, Mrs., 3 June, 1918.
1649 Dick, Octavius Pelly, 3 June, 1918.
1650 Dickey, Archibald Alexander George, 3 June, 1918.
1651 Dickie, James, 3 June, 1918.
1652 Dickinson, Emily Frances, Mrs., 3 June, 1918.
1653 Dickinson, William, 3 June, 1918.
1654 Disney, Rev. Anthony Edward Denny, 3 June, 1918.
1655 Dive, Horace, 3 June, 1918.
1656 Dix, Selina, 3 June, 1918.
1657 Dixey, Evelyn Hilda, 3 June, 1918.
1658 Dodd, Peter, 3 June, 1918.
1659 Dodwell, Charles Money, 3 June, 1918.
1660 Doig, David, 3 June, 1918.
1661 Donald, Cecile, Mrs., 3 June, 1918.
1662 Donald, Ethel Maud, 3 June, 1918.
1663 Dooley, John, 3 June, 1918. (M.)
1664 Dooley, Raymond, 3 June, 1918. (M.)
1665 Doughty, Frederick George, 3 June, 1918. (M.)

1666 Dow, James William, 3 June, 1918.
1667 Dower, Edward Maxwell, 3 June, 1918.
1668 Downs, John Henry, 3 June, 1918.
1669 Drake, Frank, 3 June, 1918.
1670 Drake, Tom, 3 June, 1918. (M.)
1672 Drower, Gertrude Louise, 3 June, 1918.
1673 Drummond, Charles James, 3 June, 1918.
1674 Duckworth, Robert, 3 June, 1918.
1675 Dudley, Edward Joseph Scott, 3 June, 1918. (M.)
1676 Duff, Victoria Adelaide Alexandrina Grant-, 3 June, 1918.
1677 Dufton, Dorothy, 3 June, 1918.
1678 Duncan, George Leopold, 3 June, 1918.
1679 Duncan, George Wilson, 3 June, 1918. (M.)
1680 Dunk, Harry William, 3 June, 1918.
1681 Durrant, Walter Charles, 3 June, 1918.
1682 Eastcott, Henry John, 3 June, 1918.
1683 Eastick, Charles Esau, 3 June, 1918.
1685 Eddy, Edward George, 3 June, 1918.
1687 Edgecombe, Ethel, Mrs., 3 June, 1918.
1688 Edkins, Beresford Harry Huey, 3 June, 1918. (M.)
1690 Edwards, Annie Doulton-, 3 June, 1918.
1691 Edwards, Ivor, 3 June, 1918.
1692 Egerton, Christian Mary, 3 June, 1918.
1693 Elborne, Sydney Lipscomb, 3 June, 1918.
1694 Elliott, Blanche Beatrice, 3 June, 1918.
1695 Ellis, Minnie, 3 June, 1918.
1696 Ellison, William Reynolds, 3 June, 1918. (M.)
1697 Elsdon, Francis William, 3 June, 1918.
1698 Esplin, Annie, 3 June, 1918.
1699 Ethelston, Ruth Frances, Mrs., 3 June, 1918.
1700 Evans, Arthur Ernest, 3 June, 1918.
1701 Evans, Edwin, 3 June, 1918.
1703 Evans, Gweneth Kate Moy-, 3 June, 1918.
1704 Evans, S., 3 June, 1918.
1705 Evens, Elizabeth Mary, Mrs., 3 June, 1918.
1706 Fanner, Henry Robert, 3 June, 1918.
1707 Fathers, Alice Mary, 3 June, 1918.
1708 Taylor, Winifred Mary, Mrs., 3 June, 1918.
1709 Fenwick, Ernest Guy, 3 June, 1919. (M.)
1710 Ferguson, Amy, Mrs., 3 June, 1918.
1711 Fergusson, Robert Loftus, 3 June, 1918.
1712 Ferns, Walter, 3 June, 1918.
1713 Ferris, Pierce, 3 June, 1918. (M.)
1714 Fielden, Mysie, Mrs., 3 June, 1918.
1715 Figgis, Howard Bradley, 3 June, 1918.
1716 Finch, Marie Isabel, 3 June, 1918.
1717 Firth, John William, 3 June, 1918.
1718 Flavell, Thomas, 3 June, 1918.
1719 Fleming, Frederic John, 3 June, 1918.
1720 Fletcher, John William, 3 June, 1918. (M.)
1721 Flower, John Walter, 3 June, 1918.
1722 Fludyer, Augusta Frances, Lady, 3 June, 1918.
1724 Fooks, Philip Edward Broadley, 3 June, 1918. (M)
1725 Foot, Phyllis Margaret, Mrs., 3 June, 1918.
1726 Forbes, Duncan, 3 June, 1918.
1727 Forges, Charles Lee des, 3 June, 1918.
1728 Foster, James Evelyn, 3 June, 1918. (M.)
1729 Foster, Thomas Burdall, 3 June, 1918.
1730 Foster, William, 3 June, 1918. (M.)
1732 Fowler, Charles Henry, 3 June, 1918. (M.)
1733 Fox, William Harris. 3 June, 1918. (M.)
1734 Foxall, Arthur, 3 June, 1918.
1735 Foyster, Arthur Henry, 3 June, 1918.
1736 Francis, Elizabeth Lydia, Mrs. Bult-, 3 June, 1918.
1737 Francis, Guy, 3 June, 1918.
1739 Franklin, Lilian Annie Margueretta, 3 June, 1918.
1740 Fraser, K. R., Mrs., 3 June, 1918.
1741 Fraser, Catherine, 3 June, 1918.
1742 Freegard, Charles Gordon, 3 June, 1918. (M.)
1743 Frew, Harry, 3 June, 1918. (M.)
1744 Frost, Robert Henry, 3 June, 1918. (M.)
1745 Frost, Sydney George, 3 June, 1918. (M.)
1746 Fullager, Leo Alfred, 3 June, 1918.
1747 Fullerton, James Glen, 3 June, 1918.
1748 Fyson, Alfred, 3 June, 1918.
1749 Gadd, Helen, Mrs., 3 June, 1918.
1750 Gales, John Russell, 3 June, 1918. (M.)
1751 Galton, Mary Louisa, Mrs. Wheler-, 3 June, 1918.
1753 Game, Winifred, 3 June, 1918.
1756 Garland, Herbert, 3 June, 1918.
1757 Garlick, Edith, 3 June, 1918.
1758 Garlick, Richard, 3 June, 1918.
1759 Garner, Arthur, 3 June, 1918.
1760 Garrett, Charles Scott, 3 June, 1918.
1761 Garvagh, Alice Florence, Baroness, 3 June, 1918.
1762 Geddes, George, 3 June, 1918.
1763 Gemmill, Jane, Mrs., 3 June, 1918.
1764 Geoghegan, Ethel Constance, 3 June, 1918.
1766 Gibson, Grace, Mrs., 3 June, 1918.
1769 Gilby, Frank, 3 June, 1918. (M.)
1770 Giles, Robert Edgar, 3 June, 1918.
1772 Gillespie, James, 3 June, 1918.
1773 Gillett, Thomas, 3 June, 1918.
1774 Gillon, Dorothy Gladys, 3 June, 1918.
1775 Gilmour, James, 3 June, 1918.
1776 Gilpin, William John, 3 June, 1918.
1777 Gimson, Margaret, 3 June, 1918.
1778 Gladwell, Athelstan Louis, 3 June, 1918. (M.)
1779 Glazebrook, Monica, 3 June, 1918.
1780 Glen, James Morrison, 3 June 1918.

1781 Glendenning, William Purvis, 3 June, 1918.
1782 Glew, Frederick Harrison, 3 June, 1918.
1783 Goddard, Ernest, 3 June, 1918. (M.)
1784 Godsell, Cornelius, 3 June, 1918.
1785 Gold, Maud Mary, Mrs., 3 June, 1918.
1786 Goldingham, Isobel Frances, 3 June, 1918.
1787 Goodall, Amy Sophia, 3 June, 1918.
1788 Goodwin, John Thomas, 3 June, 1918.
1789 Goodwin, Minnie, Mrs., 3 June, 1918.
1790 Goodyear, Mabel, 3 June, 1918.
1791 Gordon, Isidore Heyam, 3 June, 1918.
1792 Gordon, Lisa Mary, 3 June, 1918. (M.)
1793 Gorman, James Thomas, 3 June, 1918.
1794 Gorringe, Emmeline Mary Vallance, Mrs., 3 June, 1918.
1795 Gouk, William, 3 June, 1918.
1796 Gould, Harold Miller, 3 June, 1918.
1798 Grandin, Ernest, 3 June, 1918.
1799 Grantham, Jane Marian, Mrs. 3 June, 1918.
1800 Graves, Frances Marjorie, 3 June, 1918.
1802 Gray, Percy, 3 June, 1918.
1803 Gray, Robert, 3 June, 1918.
1804 Gray, Valentine Edgar, 3 June, 1918. (M.)
1806 Greaves, Richard Henry, 3 June, 1918.
1807 Green, Alice, 3 June, 1918.
1808 Green, Arthur Stanley, 3 June, 1918.
1810 Green, William Isaac, 3 June, 1918.
1811 Greenall, Fred, 3 June 1918.
1812 Greener, Charles Edward, 3 June, 1918.
1813 Greenwood, William, 3 June, 1918.
1814 Gregory, Basil Francis, 3 June, 1918.
1815 Gregory, Frances Violet, 3 June, 1918.
1816 Gregory, John, 3 June, 1918.
1817 Grey, Mary Lizette, 3 June, 1918.
1818 Grice, Geoffrey, 3 June, 1918. (M.)
1819 Griffin, James Henry, 3 June, 1918.
1820 Griffith, George Devonald, 3 June, 1918. (M.)
1821 Griffith, Louisa, 3 June, 1918.
1822 Griffiths, George Edward, 3 June, 1918.
1823 Grimsey, J. R., 3 June, 1918.
1824 Grose, Frederick, 3 June, 1918.
1825 Grounds, Thomas Collier, 3 June, 1918.
1826 Grumbar, Julian Charles, 3 June, 1918.
1827 Guild, James Bennett, 3 June, 1918.
1828 Guilford, Hannah, 3 June, 1918.
1829 Gunn, Alexander, 3 June, 1918.
1830 Gunton, George, 3 June, 1918.
1831 Gurling, James, 3 June, 1918.
1832 Gurney, Mabel Annie, Mrs., 3 June, 1918.
1833 Hackett, William Jennens, 3 June, 1918.
1834 Hale, Thomas Edward Sherwood, 3 June, 1918.
1835 Hales, Willes, 3 June, 1918. (M.)
1836 Hall, Anthony, 3 June, 1918.
1837 Hall, Alice Mary, 3 June, 1918.
1839 Hall, George Frederick 3 June, 1918. (M.)
1840 Hall, Henry, 3 June, 1918.
1841 Hall, John Job, 3 June, 1918.
1843 Hall, Thomas, 3 June, 1918.
1844 Halse, Edyth Mary, Mrs., 3 June, 1918.
1845 Hamilton, Jane Ethel, 3 June, 1918.
1847 Hancock, Frederick, 3 June, 1918.
1848 Hankins, Albert Edward, 3 June, 1918.
1849 Hannaford, Sarah Ann Pike, 3 June, 1918.
1850 Harburn, Ellen Frances, 3 June, 1918.
1851 Hardie, John, 3 June, 1918.
1852 Harding, John Stafford Goldie, 3 June, 1918. (M.)
1853 Hardy, Henry Harrison, 3 June, 1918. (M.)
1854 Harman, Rowland George, 3 June, 1918.
1855 Harris, William Blandford 3 June, 1918.
1856 Harrison, William John, 3 June, 1918. (M.)
1857 Harrold, John Blake, 3 June, 1918.
1858 Harry, Herbert Edward, 3 June, 1918. (M.)
1859 Hart, Ernest Sidney Walter, 3 June, 1918.
1860 Hart, Jane Elizabeth, Mrs., 3 June, 1918.
1861 Hartland, Lilian Mary, Mrs., 3 June, 1918.
1862 Harwood, Alfred, 3 June, 1918. (M.)
1863 Harwood, Gertrude, Mrs., 3 June, 1918.
1865 Hasthorpe, Alice, 3 June, 1918.
1866 Hawker, Frank, 3 June, 1918.
1867 Hawker, Frank Feodor Wynne, 3 June, 1918.
1868 Hawker, Harry George, 3 June, 1918.
1869 Hawkins, John Alfred, 3 June, 1918.
1870 Hawson, Millar Wright, 3 June, 1918.
1871 Hay, Althea Maud, 3 June, 1918.
1872 Hayes, Agnes, 3 June, 1918.
1874 Haynes, George William, 3 June, 1918. (M.)
1875 Hayse, Thomas William James, 3 June, 1918.
1876 Hazlehurst, George, 3 June, 1918.
1877 Heap, Iris Evelina Margaret Campbell, 3 June, 1918.
1878 Heap, Stephen, 3 June, 1918.
1879 Heath, Thomas Arthur, 3 June, 1918. (M.)
1880 Hebron, Arthur Edward, 3 June, 1918.
1881 Helcké, Wilfred Fulleylove, 3 June, 1918.
1882 Henderson, Freda Marguerite Dorothy, Mrs., 3 June, 1918.
1883 Henderson, John, 3 June, 1918.
1884 Henderson, Mabel, Mrs., 3 June, 1918.
1885 Hendin, Alexander James, 3 June, 1918.
1886 Hetherington, William Carruthers, 3 June, 1918.
1887 Hewitt, Eileen Mabel, 3 June, 1918.
1888 Hewitt, Thomas, 3 June, 1918.

1889 Hicks, Nicholas John, 3 June, 1918. (M.)
1890 Hicks, Thomas William, 3 June, 1918.
1891 Higgins, John, 3 June. 1918. (M.)
1892 Higgon, Catherine Octavia, Mrs., 3 June, 1918.
1893 Hill, Ledger Story, 3 June, 1918. (M.)
1894 Hilliar, Robert James, 3 June, 1918.
1895 Hilliard, Gladys Elizabeth Clark, 3 June, 1918.
1897 Hills, Henry, 3 June, 1918. (M.)
1898 Hills, Isabel Sinton, Mrs., 3 June, 1918.
1900 Hinchliffe, Arthur 3 June, 1918. (M.)
1901 Hinchliffe, Robert, 3 June, 1918.
1902 Hines, Ernest Edward, 3 June, 1918.
1903 Hird, Thomas Cullen, 3 June, 1918.
1904 Hitchcock, Lawrence Hiron, 3 June, 1918. (M.)
1905 Hobday, John William, 3 June, 1918.
1907 Hodge, Richard Henry, 3 June, 1918. (M.)
1908 Hogarth, William Anthony, 3 June, 1918.
1909 Hollins, Mary Clare, 3 June, 1918.
1910 Holloway, Reginald, 3 June, 1918. (M.)
1912 Hope, Herbert George, 3 June, 1918.
1913 Hope, John, 3 June, 1918.
1914 Hopgood, Francis George, 3 June, 1918.
1915 Hopkins, Muriel Margaret, 3 June, 1918.
1917 Hopkinson, Allen Haigh, 3 June, 1918. (M.)
1918 Hopper, Percy Clarence, 3 June, 1918.
1920 Horstmann, Gustav Otto Henry, 3 June, 1918.
1921 Houston, Thomas, 3 June, 1918.
1922 Howard, Annie, 3 June, 1918.
1923 Howard, Catherine Meriel, Lady, 3 June, 1918.
1924 Howes, William Trotman, 3 June, 1918.
1925 Howie, Christina Lamond, Mrs., 3 June, 1918.
1926 Howlett, Frank, 3 June, 1918.
1927 Hughes, George Wall Wall Bagot, 3 June, 1918.
1929 Hugill, Herbert, 3 June, 1918.
1930 Hume, William, 3 June, 1918.
1931 Humphrey, Thomas Clements, 3 June, 1918.
1932 Humphries. Albert. 3 June. 1918.
1933 Hunt, George, 3 June, 1918. (M.)
1934 Hunter, Edith Lena, 3 June, 1918.
1935 Hunter, George Albert, 3 June, 1918.
1937 Hutchins, Arthur Edmund, 3 June, 1918.
1938 Hutton, Stamorfd, 3 June, 1918.
1939 Huxford, Ernest Henry, 3 June, 1918.
1940 Huxter, Muriel Kathleen, 3 June, 1918.
1941 Inglis, Henry Maxwell Burton, 3 June, 1918. (M.)
1944 Innes, James Oliver, 3 June, 1918. (M.)
1945 Irby, Gerald Howard Boteler, 3 June, 1918. (M.)
1946 Irvine, Lionel Herbert, 3 June, 1918. (M.)
1947 Irving, Isabella, Mrs. Bell-, 3 June, 1918.
1948 Jackson, Margaret Lilian Cowper, Mrs., 3 June, 1918.
1949 Jackson, Roland, 3 June, 1918.
1950 Jackson, Violette Mary, Mrs., 3 June, 1918.
1951 James, Diana Lily, Mrs., 3 June, 1918.
1952 James, Henry Maunsell, 3 June, 1918.
1953 James, Iris Silburn, Mrs., 3 June, 1918.
1954 James, Ivor Lough, 3 June, 1918.
1955 James, Josephine Selina, Mrs., 3 June, 1918.
1956 Jazdouska, Mary Margaret, 3 June, 1918.
1957 Jefferys, Edward Compton, 3 June, 1918.
1958 Jenkins, Rees, 3 June, 1918. (M.)
1959 Jenkinson, Stanley Noel, 3 June, 1918.
1960 Joanes, Walter, 3 June, 1918. (M.)
1961 Jobling, Thomas, 3 June, 1918.
1962 Johnson, Cuthbert, 3 June, 1918. (M.)
1963 Johnson, Walter, 3 June, 1918.
1965 Johnston, Winifred Blanche, Mrs., 3 June, 1918.
1966 Jolly, Thomas Riley, 3 June, 1918. (M.)
1968 Jones, Brainard Arthur Robinson, 3 June, 1918. (M.)
1969 Jones, David Marteine, 3 June, 1918.
1970 Jones, Dorothea Adelaide Lowry Pughe, 3 June, 1918.
1972 Jones, Frederick Tobias, 3 June. 1918.
1974 Jones, Lillie, Mrs. Highfield-, 3 June, 1918.
1975 Joughin, John Clague, 3 June, 1918.
1976 Joynson, Margaret Beatrice Ethel, 3 June, 1918.
1977 Keevil, Ambrose, 3 June, 1918. (M.)
1978 Keightley, Mary, 3 June, 1918.
1979 Keir, William, 3 June, 1918.
1980 Kelly, Eleanor Sarah, 3 June, 1918. (M.)
1981 Kelly, Henry Titus, 3 June, 1918.
1982 Kemble, Henry, 3 June, 1918.
1983 Kemper, Joseph, 3 June, 1918. (M.)
1984 Kendall, Charlotte Emma Mabel, 3 June, 1918.
1985 Kenrick, Sylvia, 3 June, 1918.
1986 Kent, Arthur Thomas, 3 June, 1918.
1987 Kenyon, Thomas, 3 June, 1918.
1988 Kenyon, Thomas Allan, 3 June, 1918.
1990 Kew, John Charles, 3 June, 1918.
1991 Kimber, Thomas, 3 June, 1918.
1992 Kimmins, James Charles Clegg, 3 June, 1918.
1993 Kindersley, Katherine Emma, 3 June, 1918.
1994 King, Rev. Thomas, 3 June, 1918.
1995 King, William Samuel, 3 June, 1918.
1997 Kingsland, John Edward, 3 June, 1918.
1998 Kinloch, Charles, 3 June, 1918.
1999 Kinsman, Harry Jeoffrey, 3 June, 1918.
2000 Kirby, George Clarvis, 3 June, 1918.
2001 Kirby, Marion Ellen, 3 June, 1918.
2002 Kirkpatrick, Robert, 3 June, 1918. (M.)
2003 Kirwan, Florence Sydney Brudenell, 3 June, 1918.
2004 Kitching, Fanny Rushall, 3 June, 1918.

2005 Knight, Christina Graham, 3 June, 1918.
2006 Knights, Henry Newton, 3 June, 1918.
2007 Knocker, Reginald Edward, 3 June, 1918.
2008 Knox, Alice, Lady, 3 June, 1918.
2009 Korn, George Ernest, 3 June, 1918.
2011 Kynoch, Minnie, 3 June, 1918.
2012 Lambert, Blanche Sarah, 3 June, 1918.
2013 Lance, O., 3 June, 1918.
2014 Lane, Charlotte Jane, Lady Arbuthnot, 3 June, 1918.
2015 Lang, Stuart Jackson, 3 June, 1918.
2016 Langley, Percy James, 3 June, 1918.
2017 Langridge, Herbert, 3 June, 1918.
2018 Latey, William, 3 June, 1918.
2019 Lawrence, Angel Lawrence, 3 June, 1918.
2020 Lawrence, Elizabeth Mary Hilda, Mrs., 3 June, 1918.
2023 Lawson, Mildred Zacyntha, Mrs., 3 June, 1918.
2024 Lawther, James Alfred, 3 June, 1918.
2025 Leach, William, 3 June, 1918.
2026 Lee, Loraine, 3 June, 1918.
2027 Leeson, Gladys Mary, 3 June, 1918.
2028 Leinster, Elsie Maude, 3 June, 1918.
2031 Lerry, George Geoffrey, 3 June, 1918.
2032 Lethbridge, Harold Octavius, 3 June, 1918. (M.)
2033 Letty, William, 3 June, 1918.
2034 Lewis, John, 3 June, 1918.
2035 Lewis, William Reed-, 3 June, 1918.
2036 Lewis, Wyndham, 3 June, 1918.
2037 Liddell, Dorothy Mary, 3 June 1918.
2038 Liddle, Thomas, 3 June, 1918.
2040 Lindley, Walter, 3 June, 1918.
2042 Lindsay, Harold Robert, 3 June, 1918. (M.)
2043 Ling, Herbert Westwood, 3 June, 1918. (M.)
2044 Lipman, Samuel Niman, 3 June, 1918.
2045 Lister, William, 3 June, 1918. (M.)
2046 Lloyd, Harry Duncaff, 3 June, 1918. (M.)
2047 Lloyd, Herbert Alan, 3 June, 1918. (M.)
2048 Lobb, William Stephen, 3 June, 1918.
2049 Loch, Emily Elizabeth, 3 June, 1918.
2051 Loftin, Florence, Mrs., 3 June, 1918.
2052 Logan, William Malcolm, 3 June, 1918.
2053 Lomax, Mabel Sarah, 3 June, 1918.
2054 Long, Katherine Ellis, Mrs., 3 June, 1918.
2055 Long, William, 3 June, 1918.
2056 Longmuir, Percy, 3 June, 1918.
2057 Lord, Charles Ernest, 3 June, 1918.
2059 Lowe, William Herbert, 3 June, 1918. (M.)
2060 Lucas, Terence, 3 June, 1918.
2062 Luker, Herbert William, 3 June, 1918.
2063 Lumsden, Thomas William, 3 June, 1918.
2064 Lund, Edmund, 3 June, 1918.
2065 Lund, Janet, Mrs., 3 June, 1918.
2066 Lush, Hubert, 3 June, 1918. (M.)
2067 Luxon, George William, 3 June, 1918. (M.)
2068 Lyall, Mellicent, 3 June, 1918.
2069 Lyell, Hon. Mrs. Charles Henry, 3 June, 1918
2070 Lyle, Alexander McIntosh, 3 June, 1918.
2071 Lynch, Patrick, 3 June, 1918.
2072 Lynne, Audrey, 3 June, 1918.
2073 Lyon, Richard Charles, 3 June, 1918.
2074 McAlister, John, 3 June, 1918.
2075 McAnally, Sibyl La Fontaine, 3 June, 1918.
2076 McCarthy, Ignatius James John, 3 June, 1918.
2077 McClelland, Andrew, 3 June, 1918.
2078 McClure, Mary, Lady, 3 June, 1918.
2079 McCorkell, Dudley Evelyn Bruce, 3 June, 1918.
2080 McCrae, James, 3 June, 1918. (M.)
2082 Macdonald of the Isles, Godfrey Middleton Bosville, 3 June, 1918.
2083 McDonnell, Walter James, 3 June, 1918.
2085 Macfarlane, James Arthur Henderson, 3 June, 1918.
2086 McFerran, Emily, 3 June, 1918.
2087 McGevor, John, 3 June, 1918. (M.)
2088 McGilchrist, Thomas Brown, 3 June, 1918.
2089 MacGregor, Joseph, 3 June, 1918.
2090 MacGregor, Robert William, 3 June, 1918.
2091 McGuinness, Ethel Theresa, 3 June, 1918.
2092 McGuiness, Mary Jane, 3 June, 1918.
2093 McIlvenna, James Graham, 3 June, 1918.
2094 Macintyre, Duncan Mackinnon, 3 June, 1918.
2096 McIntyre, William, 3 June, 1918.
2097 Mackenzie, Donald, 3 June, 1918.
2098 McKenzie, John, 3 June, 1918.
2099 McKersie, Marion, Mrs., 3 June, 1918.
2100 Mackie, Thomas Callender Campbell, 3 June, 1918.
2102 Mackinnon, Alister, 3 June, 1918.
2103 MacLachlan, James, 3 June, 1918.
2104 Maclagan, Douglas Philip, 3 June, 1918.
2105 McLaren, John, 3 June, 1918.
2106 MacLean, Charles Allan, 3 June, 1918. (M.)
2107 McLean, John Hair Kirk, 3 June, 1918.
2108 Maclure, Margaret Eleanor, 3 June, 1918.
2109 McMahon, Albert James, 3 June, 1918. (M.)
2110 McMaster, Hugh, 3 June, 1918.
2111 MacNab, Margaret Grahame Bryce 3 June, 1918.
2112 McPherson, Dougal Campbell, 3 June, 1918. (M.)
2113 McPherson, Thomas, 3 June, 1918.
2114 McQuillen, William, 3 June, 1918.
2115 McRae, Alexander, 3 June, 1918.
2116 Macrae, Herbert Alexander, 3 June, 1918.
2117 McReddie, Margaret, Mrs. 3 June 1918.

2118 McRobbie, David, 3 June, 1918.
2119 Mactavish, Herbert James, 3 June, 1918. (M.)
2120 McVicar, Neil, 3 June, 1918.
2121 McWilliam, Dorothy, 3 June, 1918.
2122 Magnus, William Robert, 3 June, 1918.
2123 Maguire, Richard Kenneth Calton, 3 June, 1918. (M.)
2124 Malim, John Charles, 3 June, 1918.
2126 Mann, James Henderson, 3 June, 1918. (M.)
2127 Manners, James Benjamin, 3 June, 1918. (M.)
2129 Mansell, Arthur, 3 June, 1918.
2130 Manwell, Gertrude Thompson, 3 June, 1918.
2131 Maples, Euretta Mary, 3 June, 1918.
2132 Markham, Anna Elizabeth Daisy, Mrs., 3 June, 1918.
2133 Marshall, David Gregory, 3 June, 1918.
2134 Marshall, Ethel Margaret, 3 June, 1918.
2135 Martin, James Wright, 3 June, 1918. (M.)
2136 Martineau, Edith, Mrs., 3 June, 1918.
2137 Martinelli, Alfred, 3 June, 1918.
2138 Masson, James Irvine Orme, 3 June, 1918.
2139 Masters, Wilfrid John, 3 June, 1918.
2140 Masterton, John, 3 June, 1918.
2141 Matcham, Sydney Harold, 3 June, 1918. (M.)
2142 Mathers, John Jephson, 3 June. 1918.
2143 Matheson, Percy Ewing, 3 June, 1918.
2144 Matthews, Basil Garland-, 3 June. 1918. (M.)
2145 Mattinson, Thomas Herbert, 3 June, 1918.
2146 Mauger, Jean Adolphe, 3 June, 1918.
2147 Mawle, Sidney Joseph, 3 June, 1918.
2148 Maxse, Marjorie, 3 June, 1918.
2149 Maxwell, Frances Jane, Mrs. Patrick Heron-, 3 June 1918.
2150 Maxwell, Stephen John, 3 June, 1918.
2151 May, William Henry, 3 June, 1918. (M.)
2153 Meaby, Walter Alfred, 3 June, 1918.
2154 Medd, Jesse Simpson, 3 June, 1918.
2155 Meglaughlin, Barry, 3 June, 1918.
2156 Mellonie, Thomas Cyril, 3 June, 1918. (M.)
2157 Mellor, John, 3 June, 1918.
2158 Melville, John Mitchell, 3 June, 1918.
2159 Merchant, John Lewis, 3 June, 1918.
2160 Merry, Henry Edward, 3 June, 1918. (M.)
2161 Metcalfe, Harold William, 3 June, 1918. (M.)
2162 Micklethwait, Frances Mary Gore, 3 June, 1918.
2163 Middlemas, Percy, 3 June, 1918. (M.)
2164 Middleton, George Francis, 3 June, 1918.
2165 Milburn, William, 3 June, 1918.
2166 Mildren, William, 3 June, 1918. (M.)
2168 Millar, Exley Livingston, 3 June, 1918. (M.)
2169 Milledge, Minnie, 3 June, 1918.
2170 Miller, Alexander, 3 June, 1918.
2171 Miller, Edith Mary, Mrs., 3 June, 1918.
2172 Mills, Charles Augustus, 3 June. 1918.
2173 Mills, Florence Leyland, 3 June, 1918.
2174 Milne, Margaret Smith, 3 June, 1918. (M.)
2175 Minett, Francis Colin, 3 June, 1918. (M.)
2176 Mirehouse, Henry William, 3 June, 1918. (M.)
2177 Mitchell, James Knight, 3 June, 1918.
2178 Mitchell, William Boyd, 3 June, 1918. (M.)
2179 Moir, Alexander Penrose David, 3 June, 1918.
2180 Moir, Thomas, 3 June, 1918.
2181 Molyneaux, Thomas, 3 June, 1918.
2182 Montefiore, Geoffrey Edmund Sebag-, 3 June, 1918. (M.)
2183 Moore, Annie, Mrs., 3 June, 1918.
2184 Moore, Cecil Arbuthnot St. George, 3 June, 1918. (M.)
2185 Moore, Harry Formby, 3 June, 1918. (M.)
2188 Mordey, Thomas, 3 June, 1918.
2189 Morgan, Bessie, 3 June, 1918.
2190 Morgan, Edward Barcham, 3 June, 1918.
2191 Morgan, Margaret Alice Agnes, Mrs., 3 June, 1918.
2192 Morle, Helena Frances, 3 June, 1918.
2193 Morrey, Percy, 3 June, 1918. (M.)
2194 Morris, Arthur, 3 June, 1918.
2195 Morris, Charles Edward, 3 June, 1918.
2196 Morris, Etheldreda, 3 June 1918.
2198 Morris, Hardwick Grant, 3 June, 1918.
2199 Morris, Jean Anderson, 3 June, 1918.
2200 Morris, William Anthony, 3 June, 1918.
2201 Morrison, James Augustus, 3 June, 1918.
2202 Morrison, John, 3 June, 1918.
2204 Morse, Leopold George Esmond, 3 June, 1918.
2205 Mortimore, Clifford Charles, 3 June, 1918.
2206 Morton, Elsie Eleanor, 3 June, 1918.
2207 Morton, John Darnley Mitford, 3 June, 1918. (M.)
2208 Mousley, Arthur, 3 June, 1918.
2209 Mowat, Annie Angus, 3 June, 1918.
2210 Mudd, Edith Emily, 3 June, 1918.
2211 Muller, Percy Maxwell-, 3 June, 1918.
2212 Mulligan, Clifford Victor, 3 June, 1918. (M.)
2213 Mullins, George William, 3 June, 1918.
2214 Murrant, Ernest Henry, 3 June, 1918.
2215 Musgrave, Arthur Stanley Gordon, 3 June, 1918. (M.)
2216 Myatt, Agnes Rose, 3 June, 1918.
2219 Napier, James Ross, 3 June, 1918. (M.)
2220 Nash, Blanche Thompson, 3 June, 1918.
2221 Nash, Frank Horace Elliott, 3 June, 1918. (M.)
2222 Nash, Henry, 3 June, 1918.
2223 Naylor, William James, 3 June, 1918.
2224 Neill, Eric Vansittart Ernest, 3 June, 1918. (M.)
2225 Nevile, Maria Elizabeth, 3 June, 1918.
2226 Newall, John Walker, 3 June, 1918.

2227 Newton, Charles Wemyss, 3 June, 1918.
2228 Newton, John Charles, 3 June, 1918.
2229 Nicholls, George Thomas, 3 June, 1918.
2230 Nichols, Dorothea Marian, 3 June, 1918.
2231 Nicholson, Florence Isabel, Mrs., 3 June, 1918.
2232 Nicholson, Malcolm, 3 June, 1918. (M.)
2233 Nicholson, Reginald, 3 June, 1918.
2234 Nicholson, Samuel Thomas, 3 June, 1918.
2235 Nicol, Quintin Anderson, 3 June, 1918.
2236 Niven, Charles Bain, 3 June, 1918.
2237 Noal, Frederick Worth, 3 June, 1918.
2238 Novis, William Herbert, 3 June, 1918.
2239 Offord, Alfred James, 3 June, 1918.
2241 Ogilvy, Diana Elizabeth Maria, 3 June, 1918.
2242 Oldfield, Norman, 3 June, 1918.
2243 Oldmeadow, George Edward, 3 June, 1918.
2244 Olive, Annie Gordon, Mrs., 3 June, 1918.
2245 Oliver, John David, 3 June, 1918.
2246 O'Meara, Daniel John, 3 June, 1918. (M.)
2247 Ormerod, Annie, 3 June, 1918.
2248 Osborne, Albert Alfred, 3 June, 1918.
2250 Ost, William Lewis, 3 June, 1918. (M.)
2251 O'Sullivan, Gerald Hendon, 3 June, 1918.
2252 Outram, Haidée Maria, Mrs. William, 3 June, 1918.
2253 Oxburgh, George Stanley, 3 June. 1918.
2254 Oxland, Thomas Benjamin, 3 June, 1918.
2255 Packer, Henry Walter Percy, 3 June, 1918.
2256 Page, Agnes Margaret, Mrs., 3 June, 1918.
2257 Painting, Helen, 3 June, 1918.
2258 Palin, Helen Grace, 3 June, 1918. (M.)
2259 Paling, Vincent, 3 June, 1918.
2260 Palmer, Clara, 3 June, 1918.
2261 Palmer, Hubert Leslie, 3 June, 1918. (M.)
2262 Palmer, William, 3 June, 1918. (M.)
2263 Parker, Charles, 3 June, 1918.
2264 Parkin, James Edward, 3 June, 1918. (M.)
2265 Parkinson, James, 3 June, 1918.
2266 Parry, Mary Evelyn, 3 June, 1918.
2267 Partington, James Riddick, 3 June, 1918. (M.)
2268 Patenall, Clara Poynton, Mrs., 3 June, 1918.
2269 Patrick, Neil James Kennedy-Cochran-, 3 June, 1918. (M.)
2270 Payne, George, 3 June, 1918. (M.)
2271 Payne, Herbert, 3 June, 1918.
2272 Payne, Lily, 3 June, 1918.
2273 Peacock, Alice Evelyn, 3 June, 1918.
2274 Peacock, May Beauchamp, 3 June. 1918.
2275 Pearce, John, 3 June, 1918.
2276 Pearson, John Howard, 3 June, 1918.
2277 Pennell, Charles Waldegrave, 3 June, 1918.
2278 Pennell, Frederick, 3 June, 1918.
2279 Peppercorn, Geoffrey Arthur, 3 June, 1918. (M.)
2280 Perry, Ada Stair, 3 June, 1918.
2281 Pescod, Joseph Hind, 3 June, 1918.
2282 Phelps, Fanny Elizabeth, 3 June, 1918.
2283 Phillips, Cecilia Lucas, 3 June 1918.
2284 Phillips, George Lort, 3 June, 1918. (M.)
2285 Picken, Richard Nelson, 3 June, 1918 (M.)
2286 Pickering Edward Fitzgerald Samuel, 3 June, 1918. (M.)
2287 Thorburn, Henrietta Sybil Douglas, Mrs. Stephen Keith 3 June, 1918.
2288 Pilkington, Leonard Garnier, 3 June, 1918.
2289 Pine, John Henry, 3 June, 1918. (M.)
2291 Pitt, Nellie Flora, 3 June, 1918.
2292 Plaister, William Edward, 3 June, 1918. (M.)
2293 Platt, Oswald Gordon, 3 June, 1918. (M.)
2294 Poate, Herbert, 3 June, 1918.
2295 Pocock, Dorothy Martha, 3 June, 1918.
2296 Poole, Arthur Reginald, 3 June, 1918.
2297 Pooley, Arthur Milnes, 3 June, 1918.
2299 Powne, Leslie, 3 June, 1918.
2300 Prentice, William Francis, 3 June, 1918. (M.)
2301 Preston, Mark Rushworth, 3 June, 1918.
2302 Preston, William Edward, 3 June, 1918.
2303 Price, James Beer, 3 June, 1918.
2304 Price, Violet Amelia, Mrs., 3 June, 1918.
2305 Prichard, Alice Maud, Mrs., 3 June, 1918.
2307 Prince, Edwin James, 3 June, 1918.
2308 Proger, Harriet Gertrude, Mrs., 3 June. 1918.
2309 Prowse, Albert Edward, 3 June, 1918.
2310 Pryor, Ethne Philippa, Mrs., 3 June, 1918.
2311 Purvis, William Frederick, 3 June, 1918.
2312 Pyke, William Thomas, 3 June, 1918. (M.)
2313 Quann, John James, 3 June, 1918.
2316 Quick, Sidney Curtis, 3 June, 1918.
2317 Radford, Dorothy, Mrs., 3 June, 1918.
2318 Radford, Joseph Charles, 3 June, 1918.
2320 Rainford, Thomas, 3 June, 1918.
2321 Ramsbottom, Edmund Cecil, 3 June, 1918.
2322 Ramsay, Francis Graham, 3 June, 1918.
2323 Rankine, William, 3 June, 1918.
2325 Ratcliff, Sydney, 3 June, 1918. (M.)
2326 Raven, Norman Vincent, 3 June, 1918. (M.)
2327 Rawlinson, Leonard, 3 June, 1918.
2329 Raynor, Robert Osmond, 3 June, 1918. (M.)
2330 Reader, Thomas, 3 June, 1918.
2331 Reavill, Ernest Alfred, 3 June, 1918.
2332 Reed, Edwin, 3 June, 1918.
2333 Rees, Ernest Wilmot, 3 June, 1918.

2334 Rees, Henry, 3 June, 1918.
2335 Rees, T. E., 3 June, 1918.
2336 Reeve, William Booth, 3 June, 1918.
2337 Reeves, George, 3 June, 1918. (M.)
2338 Reynolds, Ethel Maude, 3 June, 1918.
2339 Richards, Percival Stanley, 3 June, 1918. (M.)
2340 Richardson, Rev. Albert Thomas, 3 June, 1918.
2341 Richardson, Annie Bertha, Mrs., 3 June, 1918.
2342 Richardson, Harry, 3 June, 1918.
2343 Richardson, Mary Anita, Mrs., 3 June, 1918.
2344 Rideal, Eric Keightley, 3 June, 1918. (M.)
2345 Riordan, Thomas Mortimer, 3 June, 1918.
2346 Ritchie, John, 3 June, 1918. (M.)
2347 Ritchings, Mary Thompson, 3 June, 1918.
2348 Roberts, David Richard, 3 June, 1918.
2349 Roberts, Gomer, 3 June, 1918.
2350 Roberts, Henry David, 3 June, 1918.
2351 Roberts, Herbert Charles, 3 June, 1918.
2352 Roberts, John, 3 June, 1918. (M.)
2353 Robertson, Archibald Campbell, 3 June, 1918.
2354 Robertson, Richard Frederick, 3 June, 1918.
2355 Robinson, Thomas Ingle, 3 June, 1918.
2356 Rodger, James Allison, 3 June, 1918.
2357 Rodham, Robert, 3 June, 1918.
2358 Roebuck, Samuel, 3 June, 1918.
2360 Rogers, Henry, 3 June, 1918.
2362 Rogers, James George, 3 June, 1918. (M.)
2363 Rogers, Joan, 3 June, 1918.
2364 Romer, Leila Harriette, Mrs., 3 June, 1918.
2365 Rose, James, 3 June, 1918.
2366 Ross, James Maxwell, 3 June, 1918.
2367 Ross, John David McBeath, 3 June, 1918.
2368 Ross, Stella Maude Dalrymple, 3 June, 1918.
2369 Rowe, John William, 3 June, 1918.
2370 Rowe, Mabel Ruth, Mrs., 3 June, 1918.
2371 Rowe, William George, 3 June, 1918.
2372 Rowland, Joseph Samuel, 3 June, 1918.
2373 Rowley, Charles Donovan, 3 June, 1918. (M.)
2374 Royce, Elizabeth Lilian, 3 June, 1918.
2375 Rudge, Louise Alice, 3 June, 1918.
2376 Runciman, Henry Weir, 3 June, 1918.
2377 Rush, Thomas Arthur Edwin, 3 June, 1918. (M.)
2378 Russell, Diana, 3 June, 1918.
2379 Russell, Rachel Augusta, 3 June, 1918.
2380 Russell, William Sidney, 3 June, 1918.
2381 Ruston, Henry Thomas, 3 June, 1918.
2382 Rutland, George Henry, 3 June, 1918.
2383 Sage, Allen Molyneux Baxter, 3 June, 1918.
2384 Salter, William Henry, 3 June, 1918.
2385 Sambridge, William, 3 June, 1918.
2386 Sample, Leslie, 3 June. 1918. (M.)
2387 Sampson, Howard, 3 June, 1918. (M.)
2388 Sandford, Elizabeth, 3 June, 1918.
2389 Sankey, Henry John, 3 June, 1918.
2390 Sargint, Olga Joyce Forbes, Mrs., 3 June, 1918.
2391 Saunders, Ina, Mrs., 3 June, 1918.
2392 Savage, John Clifford, 3 June, 1918. (M.)
2393 Sayer, Harold Edward, 3 June, 1918.
2394 Scarfe, Fred, 3 June, 1918.
2395 Scarlett, Albert Edward, 3 June, 1918.
2396 Scatterty, Agnes, Mrs., 3 June, 1918.
2397 Schofield, James Rimmer, 3 June, 1918.
2398 Scott, Eloise Irene, 3 June, 1918.
2399 Scott, Gladys Mary, 3 June, 1918.
2400 Scott, James, 3 June, 1918.
2401 Scott, John, 3 June, 1918.
2402 Scott, Muriel Elena, 3 June, 1918. (M.)
2404 Segrue, George Edward, 3 June, 1918. (M.)
2405 Semmons, Foster James, 3 June, 1918. (M.)
2406 Settle, Agnes Hannah, Mrs., 3 June, 1918.
2407 Seward, Alfred Charles, 3 June, 1918.
2408 Seymour, Frank, 3 June, 1918.
2409 Shackleton, Kathleen, 3 June, 1918.
2410 Sharp, Gerald Whittaker, 3 June, 1918.
2411 Sharp, William, 3 June, 1918. (M.)
2412 Sharpe, James Edward, 3 June, 1918.
2413 Shaw, Gertrude, 3 June, 1918.
2414 Shaw, Herbert, 3 June, 1918.
2415 Shaw, Katherine, Mrs., 3 June, 1918.
2416 Shawcross, George Nuttall, 3 June, 1918.
2417 Sheffield, Mary Edith, 3 June, 1918.
2418 Short, John, 3 June, 1918. (M.)
2419 Siddon, Emily Frances, 3 June, 1918.
2421 Simpson, Geoffrey Hugh, 3 June, 1918. (M.)
2422 Simpson, Herbert, 3 June, 1918. (M.)
2424 Sinclair, Edward, 3 June, 1918. (M.)
2425 Sinclair, Samuel Christian, 3 June, 1918. (M.)
2426 Skelton, William Simmonds, 3 June, 1918.
2427 Skiffington, Donald McLean, 3 June, 1918.
2428 Skinner, Herbert Fenton, 3 June, 1918. (M.)
2429 Skurray, Ernest Clement, 3 June, 1918.
2430 Slade, George Frederick, 3 June, 1918.
2431 Smale, Bertram Haylock, 3 June, 1918.
2432 Smallbones, Robert Townsend, 3 June, 1918.
2433 Smallwood, Henry Sankey, 3 June, 1918.
2434 Smedley, Charles Frederick, 3 June, 1918. (M.)
2435 Smedley, Olive Truda Marsden-, 3 June, 1918.
2436 Smedley, William Henry, 3 June, 1918.
2488 Smith, Annie Hansley, 3 June, 1918.
2439 Smith, Aubrey Golding, 3 June, 1918.

2440 Smith, Constance Maitland Wilson, Mrs., 3 June, 1918.
2441 Smith, Dempster, 3 June, 1918.
2442 Smith, Fred John, 3 June, 1918.
2443 Smith George Geoffrey, 3 June, 1918. (M.)
2444 Smith, Herbert Edwin, 3 June, 1918.
2445 Smith, Anne Huntingdon Melville, Mrs., 3 June, 1918.
2446 Smith, James Albert, 3 June, 1918. (M.)
2448 Smithers, Walter, 3 June, 1918. (M.)
2449 Smy, Alfred, 3 June, 1918.
2450 Smythe, Albert Charles Butler-, 3 June, 1918.
2451 Snaith, Adam Currie, 3 June, 1918.
2452 Songhurst, Fred Hibbard, 3 June, 1918. (M.)
2453 Sorby, Gertrude Vera, 3 June, 1918.
2455 Sparkes, Stanley, 3 June, 1918.
2456 Spence, Caroline Mary, Mrs., 3 June, 1918.
2457 Spencer, Henry Bath, 3 June, 1918.
2458 Spencer, John Haywood. 3 June, 1918.
2459 Spicer, Alfred, 3 June, 1918.
2460 Spiers, Gavin, 3 June, 1918.
2461 Spikins, Armande, Mrs., 3 June, 1918.
2462 Spite, Eva Harvey, 3 June, 1918.
2463 Stafford, Reginald Vernon, 3 June, 1918. (M.)
2464 Stagg, George Ernest. 3 June, 1918. (M.)
2465 Stainforth, Gladys Margaret, 3 June, 1918.
2467 Stampe, Bernard Coatsworth, 3 June, 1918.
2468 Stanley, Leonard, 3 June, 1918.
2469 Stanton, Frederick William, 3 June, 1918. (M.)
2470 Stapledon, Reginald George, 3 June, 1918.
2471 Stark, Frank Tapscott, 3 June, 1918.
2473 Staunton, George Sydney, 3 June, 1918.
2474 Steeds, Ethel Mary, 3 June, 1918.
2475 Steel, Charles Walter, 3 June, 1918.
2476 Stephen, Henry Brown Torrie, 3 June, 1918. (M.)
2477 Stephens, Amy Frances Caroline, 3 June, 1918.
2478 Stephenson, Marjory, 3 June, 1918.
2479 Stevenson, John Horne, 3 June, 1918.
2480 Stevenson, Samuel, 3 June, 1918.
2481 Stewart, Mary Jane, 3 June, 1918.
2482 Still, Marjorie Ellen, 3 June, 1918.
2483 Stirling, Charles Frederick, 3 June, 1918. (M.)
2484 Stoddard, John Wilkie, 3 June, 1918. (M.)
2485 Stone, Isaac, 3 June, 1918.
2486 Storey, Henry, 3 June, 1918.
2487 Stoughton, Maud Eleanor, 3 June, 1918.
2488 Stovell, Frederick, 3 June, 1918. (M.)
2489 Strachan, James, 3 June, 1918.
2490 Strang, Matthew Smellie, 3 June, 1918.
2491 Strother, Cyril John, 3 June, 1918. (M.)
2492 Stuart, Florence Louise, Lady, 3 June, 1918.
2493 Stuart, George Barclay, 3 June, 1918.
2494 Sturdee, Arthur Hope, 3 June, 1918.
2495 Sturt, Ethel Hariette, Mrs., 3 June, 1918.
2496 Sullivan, Joseph, 3 June, 1918.
2497 Summers, Ada Jane, Mrs., 3 June, 1918.
2499 Sutherland, John, 3 June, 1918.
2500 Sutton, Cecil Norman Stafford, 3 June, 1918.
2501 Sutton, John Joseph, 3 June, 1918.
2502 Swanson, David, 3 June, 1918.
2503 Swinnerton, Robert William, 3 June, 1918.
2504 Sykes, Joseph Percival, 3 June, 1918.
2505 Sykes, William Henry, 3 June, 1918.
2508 Tadema, Anna Alma, 3 June, 1918.
2509 Tait, James, 3 June, 1918.
2511 Tanner, Edward, 3 June, 1918.
2512 Taylor, Bramwell, 3 June, 1918.
2514 Taylor, Frank Gellie, 3 June, 1918. (M.)
2515 Taylor, Geoffrey Fell, 3 June, 1918. (M.)
2516 Taylor, Harold Victor, 3 June, 1918.
2517 Taylor, Louis Henry, 3 June, 1918.
2518 Taylor, Richard Francis, 3 June, 1918.
2519 Tebbutt, Mary Jessie. 1918.
2520 Tebbutt, Katherine Rose, 3 June, 1918.
2521 Teesdale, Kenneth John Marmaduke, 3 June, 1918.
2522 Temple, Robert. 3 June, 1918.
2523 Thake, Frank Edward Seymour, 3 June, 1918.
2524 Theobald, Charles Henry Gordon Eyre, 3 June, 1918.
2525 Thesiger, Hon. Percy Mansfield, 3 June, 1918. (M.)
2526 Thirkell, Constantine, 3 June, 1918.
2527 Thirkell, William, 3 June, 1918.
2528 Thomas, Bert, 3 June, 1918.
2529 Thomas, Edward, 3 June, 1918.
2531 Thomas, Harry Jones, 3 June, 1918.
2532 Thomas, Sidney Arthur, 3 June, 1918. (M.)
2533 Thomas, William Gearing, 3 June, 1918.
2534 Thomas, William Henry, 3 June, 1918.
2535 Thompson, Edward, 3 June, 1918.
2536 Thompson, Jessie Catherine, 3 June, 1918.
2538 Thompson, William Henry, 3 June, 1918.
2539 Thompson, William Nelson, 3 June, 1918.
2540 Thomson, James, 3 June, 1918.
2541 Thomson, James Miln, 3 June, 1918.
2542 Thornhill, Beatrice Mary Compton, 3 June, 1918.
2543 Thyne, John Sinclair, 3 June, 1918.
2545 Tiffen, Doris Ada, Mrs., 3 June, 1918.
2546 Tinn, John, 3 June, 1918.
2547 Tizard, Ethel Annie, 3 June, 1918. (M.)
2548 Todd, Edith Mary Elizabeth, 3 June, 1918. (M.)
2549 Toller, Emma Anne, Mrs., 3 June, 1918.
2551 Tonner, James, 3 June, 1918.
2552 Tooth, Louis Frederick, 3 June, 1918.

2553 Topham, Harry, 3 June, 1918.
2554 Town, Christopher Edward, 3 June, 1918.
2555 Townshend, Margery, 3 June, 1918.
2556 Trathan, Walter, 3 June, 1918.
2557 Treanor, Francis James, 3 June, 1918. (M.)
2559 Trigg, William Ewart Gladstone, 3 June, 1918.
2560 Trounce, Alice, Mrs., 3 June, 1918.
2561 Tucker, George John, 3 June, 1918.
2562 Tucker, Ina Aveling, Mrs., 3 June, 1918.
2563 Turnbull, George Drummond, 3 June, 1918.
2564 Turner, Adolphus Frederick Franklyn, 3 June, 1918.
2565 Turner, Cameron, 3 June, 1918.
2566 Turner, Catherine Mary, 3 June 1918.
2568 Turner, William Walker 3 June, 1918.
2569 Tweedale, S., 3 June, 1918.
2570 Tweedy, William Glenholme, 3 June, 1918. (M.)
2571 Tytherleigh, Arthur Henry, 3 June, 1918. (M.)
2572 Uden, Walter Jeffery, 3 June, 1918. (M.)
2573 Umney, Percy, 3 June, 1918.
2574 Usher, Rachel Lilian May, 3 June 1918.
2575 Le Vack, William, 3 June, 1918.
2576 Vane, Sybil, 3 June, 1918.
2577 Vanneck, Arthur Percy, 3 June, 1918. (M.)
2578 Vansittart, Robert Arnold, 3 June, 1918. (M.)
2579 Vaughan, William, 3 June, 1918. (M.)
2580 Veale, William John, 3 June, 1918.
2582 Venables, Margaret, 3 June, 1918.
2583 Venn, Ella Margaret, 3 June, 1918.
2584 Vickers, Charles, 3 June, 1918.
2585 Vilmet, Henry Frederic Vilmet Oldham-, 3 June, 1918.
2586 Waddingham, George, 3 June, 1918. (M.)
2587 Wade, Thomas Callander, 3 June, 1918.
2588 Wade, William John, 3 June, 1918.
2589 Waghorne, John, 3 June, 1918.
2590 Wagstaffe, Ellen Charlotte, Mrs., 3 June, 1918.
2591 Wainwright, Mabel Frances Hewitt, 3 June, 1918
2592 Waite, James, 3 June, 1918.
2593 Wakefield, William Birkbeck, 3 June, 1918.
2594 Waldegrave, Alfred John, 3 June, 1918.
2595 Waldegrave, Alice, Mrs., 3 June, 1918.
2597 Walker, Keith Jerome, 3 June, 1918. (M.)
2598 Wall, William Joseph, 3 June, 1918.
2600 Walter, Edna, 3 June, 1918.
2601 Ward, Ada Grace, Mrs., 3 June, 1918.
2602 Ward, Edward, 3 June, 1918. (M.)
2603 Ward, John Henry, 3 June, 1918.
2604 Ward, Tom, 3 June, 1918. (M.)
2605 Wardroper, Arthur Kingsley, 3 June, 1918. (M.)
2606 Warnock, William Findlay, 3 June, 1918.
2607 Warren, Marmont, 3 June, 1918.
2608 Waters, Donald, 3 June, 1918.
2609 Watkins, Dorothy Emily, 3 June, 1918.
2612 Watson, Albert Harold Joseph, 3 June, 1918.
2613 Watson, James, 3 June, 1918.
2614 Watson, John, 3 June, 1918.
2615 Watson, Marguerite Audrey, Mrs., 3 June, 1918.
2616 Watson, Mildred Jane Musgrave, 3 June, 1918.
2617 Watt, Madge Robertson, Mrs., 3 June, 1918.
2618 Watt, John William, 3 June, 1918.
2619 Watters. John, 3 June, 1918.
2620 Weaver, Charles Henry, 3 June, 1918.
2621 Webster, Alexander, 3 June, 1918.
2622 Welch, Lilian Emily, 3 June, 1918.
2623 Wellington, Robert, 3 June, 1918.
2624 Wells, Mildmay Francis, 3 June, 1918
2625 Wells, Selkirk, 3 June, 1918.
2626 West, Charles. 3 June, 1918. (M.)
2627 Westbrook, Gertrude Cleave. 3 June, 1918
2628 Westcott, John Richard, 3 June, 1918.
2630 Weston, Henry Gould, 3 June, 1918.
2631 Wharton, Frederick Malcolm, 3 June, 1918.
2632 Wheble, Ursula Mary, 3 June, 1918.
2633 Wheeler, Edward Thomas, 3 June, 1918.
2634 Whiles, George Frederick, 3 June, 1918.
2635 Whitaker, Eileen, Mrs. 3 June, 1918.
2636 White, Charles Arthur, 3 June, 1918.
2637 White, Jessie McHardie, 3 June, 1918. (M.)
2638 White, Percival, 3 June, 1918.
2639 Whitehead, Mary Catharine, Mrs., 3 June, 1918.
2640 Whitehorn, Roy Drummond, 3 June, 1918.
2641 Whitfield, Frederick Ernest Banister. 3 June, 1918. (M.)
2642 Whiting, Ernest James, 3 June, 1918. (M.)
2643 Whittaker, Mary Fanny, 3 June, 1918.
2644 Whitworth, Geoffrey Budibent, 3 June, 1918.
2645 Wigan, Aubrey John Graham-, 3 June, 1918. (M.)
2646 Wignall, Edith Marguerite, Mrs., 3 June, 1918.
2647 Wild, Norman Ward, 3 June, 1918.
2648 Wilder, Edward H., 3 June, 1918. (M.)
2649 Wilkins, Margaret Mabel. 3 June, 1918.
2650 Wilkinson, Martin, 3 June, 1918.
2651 Williams, Emma Christine, Mrs., 3 June, 1918.
2652 Williams, Leonard Henry, 3 June, 1918.
2653 Williams, Percy Alec, 3 June, 1918. (M.)
2654 Williamson, Rhoda Mary Westropp, 3 June, 1918.
2656 Willis, Maud Mary, Mrs., 3 June, 1918.
2657 Willis, Rev. Michael Hamilton Gibson, 3 June, 1918.
2658 Wills, Marian Margaret, 3 June, 1918.
2659 Wilson, Edith Annie, Mrs., 3 June, 1918.
2660 Wilson, George Alexander, 3 June, 1918.

2661 Wilson, James, 3 June, 1918.
2662 Wilson, Margaret Rowley, Mrs., 3 June, 1918.
2663 Wilson, Robert James, 3 June, 1918.
2664 Wilson, William Major, 3 June, 1918.
2665 Winder, Ada Mary, Mrs., 3 June, 1918.
2666 Witts, John Travell, 3 June, 1918. (M.)
2667 Wolferstan, Evelyn, 3 June, 1918.
2668 Wood, Gamble Ekin Vickers, 3 June, 1918.
2669 Woodcock, William Stanley, 3 June. 1918.
2670 Woodhams, Walter Lee, 3 June, 1918.
2671 Woodman, Norah Blanche, 3 June, 1918.
2672 Woods, Constance Ada. Mrs., 3 June. 1918.
2673 Woodward, Charles William, 3 June, 1918.
2674 Wordsworth, Annie Elizabeth. 3 June, 1918.
2675 Worth, William Percy, 3 June, 1918.
2676 Worthington, Nora Mary Bayley, 3 June, 1918
2677 Worthington, Gwenyth, 3 June, 1918.
2678 Wren, Albert Charles, 3 June, 1918.
2679 Wright, Calvin, 3 June, 1918.
2680 Wright, Clare Elise Ellington, 3 June, 1918.
2681 Wright, Douglas William, 3 June, 1918. (M.)
2682 Wright, Florence Helena, 3 June, 1918.
2683 Wright, Mary Veronica, 3 June. 1918.
2685 Wright, Thomas, 3 June, 1918.
2686 Wrigley, Constance. 3 June, 1918.
2687 Wyatt, Katharina Montagu. 3 June, 1918.
2689 Yeld, Ellen, 3 June, 1918.
2690 Young, Clarence Ross, 3 June, 1918.
2691 Youngman, Annie, 3 June, 1918.
2693 Hardy, Ismay Gertrude, Mrs., 3 June, 1918.
2694 Gracey, Mabel Alice, Mrs., 3 June, 1918.
2695 Kealy, Tempe, Mrs., 3 June, 1918.
2696 Jackson, Dorothy Starr, Mrs., 3 June, 1918.
2697 Browning, Mary Louisa, Mrs.. 3 June, 1918.
2698 Fremantle, Vera Evelyn Selina, Mrs. Selwyn Howe, 3 June, 1918.
2699 Gupta, Jnanendra Nath, 3 June, 1918.
2700 Clarke, Antoinette, Mrs., 3 June, 1918.
2701 Mumford, Hilda, Mrs., 3 June. 1918.
2702 Hemingway, Stennet. Mrs., 3 June, 1918.
2703 Dutt, Mrs., 3 June, 1918.
2704 Nevill, Euphan, Mrs., 3 June, 1918.
2705 Peirse, Florence Ida, Mrs., 3 June. 1918.
2706 Playfair, Caro, Mrs., 3 June, 1918.
2707 Laslett, Charles Frederick, 2 June, 1918.
2708 Milne, Alice Stuart, Mrs., 3 June, 1918.
2709 Sullivan, Robina Olive, Mrs., 3 June, 1918.
2710 Broomfield, Dorothy, Mrs., 3 June. 1918.
2711 Ayyar, Visalakshi Narayana, Mrs., 3 June, 1918.
2712 Arbery, James, 3 June, 1918.
2713 Ward, John Chappell, 3 June, 1918.
2715 Ray, Prasanna Kumar, Mrs., 3 June, 1918.
2716 Chazal, Dora Stewert, Mrs. de, 3 June, 1918.
2717 Shaw, Herbert Hunley, 3 June, 1918.
2718 Badu Budh Sen, 3 June, 1018
2719 Gurtu, Pandit Mannohan Nath, 3 June, 1918.
2720 Singh, Babu Sardar, 3 June, 1918.
2721 Tahsildar, Pandit Ganga Dutt Joshi, 3 June, 1918.
2722 Havock, Donald St. John, 3 June, 1918.
2723 Robertson, Richard, 3 June, 1918.
2724 Gittings, Gwendoline. Mrs., 3 June, 1918.
2725 Green, Thomas George, 3 June, 1918.
2726 Nawab of Dera. Nawab Ahmed Nawaz Khan, Saddozai, 3 June, 1918.
2727 Powell, Ernest Robert, 3 June. 1918.
2728 Naidu, Rao Bahadur Shrinivasulu, 3 June, 1918.
2729 Rao, M. Narsing, 3 June, 1918.
2730 Hayward, William, 3 June, 1918.
2731 Gregson, Thomas, 3 June. 1918.
2732 Knowles, Charles James, 3 June, 1918.
2733 Devasahayam, Sardar Bahadur, 3 June, 1918.
2734 Kathait, Bishan Singh, Sardar Bahadur, 3 June. 1918.
2735 Gupta, Babu Srimanta Kumar Das, 3 June, 1918.
2736 Sen, Nirmal Sankar, 3 June, 1918.
2737 Anderson, Percival James, 3 June, 1918.
2738 Khan, Munshi Muhammad Zaman, 3 June, 1918.
2739 Khan, Sardar Bahadur, 3 June, 1918.
2740 Nath, Lala Amar, 3 June, 1918.
2741 Khan, Abdul Majid, 3 June, 1918.
2742 Singh, Babu Shyam Naryan, 3 June, 1918.
2743 Bose, Babu Arun Kumar, 3 June, 1918.
2744 Patnaik, Babu Lakshminarayan, 3 June, 1918.
2745 Pardhi, Ramchandra Moreshwar, 3 June, 1918.
2746 Ali, Khan Sahib Ishtiak, 3 June, 1918.
2747 Nath, Rai Bahadur Bhola, 3 June, 1918.
2748 Manik, U. Kmuin, Siem of Mylliem, Assam, 3 June, 1918.
2749 Harison, U., Siem of Rambray, Assam, 3 June, 1918.
2750 Alston, Frances Carr Ross, Mrs., 3 June, 1918.
2751 Ghatak, Narendra Nath, 3 June, 1918.
2752 Ram, Pandit Daulat, 3 June, 1918.
2753 Cowasji, Serene, Mrs., 3 June, 1918.
2754 Bhandari, Rai Bahadur Gopal Das, 3 June, 1918.
2755 Chand, Rai Bahadur Pandit Davi, 3 June, 1918.
2756 Dass, Babu Pyari Lal, 3 June, 1918.
2757 Das, Babu Kamini Kumar, 3 June, 1918.
2758 Jaywant, Ram Krishna Raoji, 3 June, 1918.
2759 Hayes, Lillian May McCaully, Mrs., 3 June, 1918.
2760 Bhajekar, Vinayak Narayan, 3 June, 1918.
2761 Chaudhuri, Surat Kunwar, 3 June, 1918.
2762 Hindmarsh, Edwin Andrew Cuthbert, 3 June, 1918.

2763 Wright, May, Mrs. Hall-, 3 June, 1918.
2764 Brierly, Clement Hall, 3 June, 1918.
2765 Khan, Subedar Wali Muhammad, 3 June, 1918.
2766 Robson, Helene, Mrs.. 3 June, 1918.
2767 Tydeman, Ethel, Mrs., 3 June, 1918.
2768 Reaks, Sidney Hugh, 3 June, 1918.
2769 Ilahi, Khan Bahadur Chaudhuri Karam, 3 June, 1918.
2770 Gopal, Rai Sahib Lala Ram, 3 June, 1918.
2771 Ali, Khan Sahib Chaudhri Fazal, 3 June, 1918.
2772 Khan of Kotla, Khan Bahadur Arbab Muhammad Azam, 3 June, 1918.
2773 Sethi, of Peshawar, Khan Bahadur Haji Karim Bakhsh, 3 June, 1918.
2774 Khiomal, Lekhraj, 3 June, 1918.
2775 Vakil, Pestan Shah Nussedwanji, 3 June, 1918.
2776 Wiggett, John Howitson, 3 June, 1918.
2777 Gillespie, Margaret, 3 June, 1918.
2778 Chaudhuri, Raja Mahendra Ranjan Ray, 3 June, 1918.
2779 Singh, Babu Manindra Chandra, 3 June, 1918.
2781 Grant, Norman, 3 June, 1918.
2782 Singh, Babu Shiba Prasad, of Jharia, 3 June, 1918.
2783 Gupta, Rai Sahib Chandra Narayan, 3 June, 1918.
2784 Hart, Maurice Roberts Wilson, 3 June, 1918.
2785 Avargal, M. R. Ry. Tiruvadi Chidambara Ramaswami Sarma, 3 June, 1918.
2786 Hussain, Khan Sahib Sayad Nazir, 3 June, 1918.
2787 Sen, Babu Upendra Nath. 3 June, 1918.
2788 Ghose, Babu Atal Chandra, 3 June, 1918.
2789 Antia, Jamsetji Dinshaw, 3 June, 1918.
2790 Davis, Georgina Jessie Chisholm, Mrs., 3 June, 1918.
2791 Spence, Mary Denham, Mrs., 3 June, 1918.
2792 M. R. Ry. Diwan Bahadur Mandayam Ananda Pillay Parthasarathi Ayyangar Avargal, B.L., 3 June, 1918.
2793 Jessop, Gertrude, 3 June, 1918.
2794 Carrick, Margaret, 3 June, 1918.
2795 Deaken, Margaret, Mrs., 3 June, 1918.
2796 Whitcombe, Adeline Elizabeth, 3 June, 1918.
2797 Palit, Lokendra Nath. Mrs., 3 June, 1918.
2798 Ewing, Annie, 3 June, 1918.
2799 Husain, Khan Bahadur Mir Tawaqqul, 3 June, 1918.
2800 Khan, Nawab Ahmad Saiyed, 3 June, 1918.
2801 Ram, Chaudhri Data, 3 June, 1918.
2802 Joshi, Rai Bahadur Dharma Nand, 3 June, 1918.
2803 Kishan, Pandit Maharaj, 3 June, 1918.
2804 Ali, Subedar-Major Ashaq, 3 June, 1918.
2805 Khan, Mian Yar Muhammad, 3 June, 1918.
2806 Ram, Resaldar Bahadur Sahaj, 3 June, 1918.
2807 Singh, Sardar Fateh, 3 June, 1918.
2808 Singh, Raja Fateh, 3 June, 1918.
2809 Wardle, Flora, Mrs., 3 June, 1918.
2811 Sangma, Babu Jagin, 3 June, 1918.
2812 Latif, Khan Sahib Maulvi Mohammad Abdul, 3 June, 1918.
2813 Shah, Rai Sahib Lala Tirath Ram, 3 June, 1918.
2814 Muhammad. Khan Bahadur Wadera Nur, 3 June, 1918.
2815 Hart, Henry, 3 June, 1918.
2816 Vores, Philippa, Mrs., 3 June, 1918.
2817 East, Percy Harry, 3 June, 1918.
2818 Hall, Charles Leavers, 3 June, 1918.
2819 Johnstone, Arthur Henry, 3 June, 1918.
2820 Craig, Alexander Robertson, 3 June, 1918.
2821 Williams, Arthur Owen, 3 June, 1918.
2822 Bury, George Wyman, 3 June, 1918.
2823 Kennedy, Rev. Samuel Hanna, 3 June, 1918.
2824 Merton, Arthur Sidney, 3 June, 1918.
2825 Storrar, George Ronald, 3 June, 1918.
2826 Walker, Charles Craven Howell, 3 June, 1918.
2827 Williams, John Edgar, 3 June, 1918.
2828 Bolland, Arthur Philip, 3 June, 1918.
2829 Abraham, Constance Palgrave, Mrs.. 3 June, 1918.
2830 Bankart, Alfred Seymour, 3 June, 1918.
2831 Bethell, Thyra Talvase, Mrs., 3 June, 1918.
2832 Boden, Annie Sanetta, Mrs., 3 June, 1918.
2833 Bollard, Louisa, Mrs.. 3 June, 1918.
2834 Chilton, Elizabeth, Mrs., 3 June, 1918.
2835 Conn, Robert, 3 June, 1918.
2836 Corry, Alice Maude, Mrs., 3 June, 1918.
2837 Crooke, Jane Duthie, Mrs., 3 June, 1918.
2838 Donaldson, Ada Maud, Mrs., 3 June, 1918.
2839 Findlay, Ellen Kent, Mrs., 3 June, 1918.
2840 Galbraith, Marion, Mrs., 3 June, 1918.
2841 George, William Henry Harrison, 3 June, 1918.
2842 Graham, Helen, 3 June, 1918.
2843 Grimmond, Margaret Isabella, Mrs., 3 June, 1918.
2844 Hill, Jessie, Mrs., 3 June, 1918.
2845 Lee, Jane Winfield, Mrs., 3 June, 1918.
2846 Lock, Esther Georgina, Mrs., 3 June. 1918.
2847 MacGibbon, Mabel Jane, 3 June, 1918.
2848 MacKay, Isobelle Mary Agnes, Mrs., 3 June, 1918.
2849 Mackenzie, Jessie, 3 June, 1918.
2850 Maguire, Emily Herbert, Mrs., 3 June, 1918.
2851 Mete, Erina, Mrs., 3 June, 1918.
2852 Morris, Cecilia Margaret, 3 June, 1918.
2853 Murphy, Hannah, Mrs., 3 June, 1918.
2854 Nathan, Sybil Caroline. 3 June, 1918.
2855 Petrie, Helen Young, Mrs., 3 June, 1918.
2856 Raymond, Mary, Mrs., 3 June, 1918.
2857 Reeve, Joan Leslie, Mrs., 3 June, 1918.
2858 Robin, Maggie, 3 June, 1918.
2859 Shallcrass, Robert William 3 June, 1918.

2860 Smith, Charles Bowtell, 3 June, 1918.
2861 Smith, Mary Euphemia Roseborough, Mrs., 3 June, 1918
2863 Thompson, Riria, Mrs., 3 June, 1918.
2864 Tripe, William Archibald, 3 June, 1918.
2865 Ward, Charlotte Sarah, Mrs., 3 June, 1918.
2866 Webster, Violet Helen, 3 June, 1918.
2867 Wilkinson, Howitt Key, 3 June, 1918.
2868 Williams, Helen Lucy, 3 June, 1918.
2869 Akerman, Conrad, 3 June, 1918.
2870 Andrews, Annie Burt, Mrs., 3 June, 1918.
2871 Burman, Thomas, 3 June, 1918.
2872 Burnside, Robert Henery, 3 June, 1918.
2873 Campbell, Ethel Margaret, 3 June, 1918.
2874 Clapp, Rev. Charles Herbert, 3 June, 1918.
2875 Colborne, Christina Johanna Petronella, Mrs., 3 June, 1918.
2876 Currie, Richard, 3 June, 1918.
2877 Davis, Anna Gronow, Mrs., 3 June, 1918.
2878 Dudley, Sophie, Mrs., 3 June, 1918.
2879 Freer, Maude Alice, 3 June, 1918.
2880 French, John Williar, 3 June, 1918.
2881 Gaisford, Harriet Helen, Mrs., 3 June, 1918.
2882 Ganteaume, Patrick Padron Joseph, 3 June, 1918.
2883 Gibaud, Agnes Mary, Mrs., 3 June, 1918.
2884 Gill, Daisy Lee Heywood, Mrs., 3 June, 1918.
2885 Gillespie, Sara, Mrs., 3 June, 1918.
2886 Goble, Annie Harriet, Mrs., 3 June, 1918.
2887 Green, Arthur James, 3 June, 1918.
2888 Griffith, Alison Lockhart, 3 June, 1918.
2889 Hollander, Ethel Mary, Mrs., 3 June, 1918.
2890 Hosking, William Samuel Victor, 3 June, 1918.
2891 Hutchinson, Bertha Charlotte, Mrs., 3 June, 1918.
2892 Jacques, Rev. George Henry Paul, 3 June, 1918.
2893 Kleinenberg, Maude Ellen, Mrs., 3 June, 1918.
2894 Lamont, James, 3 June, 1918.
2895 Lennox, Jessie Orr, Mrs., 3 June, 1918.
2896 Long, John Percy, 3 June, 1918.
2897 Miles, Blanch Kate, Mrs. Beere-, 3 June, 1918.
2898 Neave, John Sims, 3 June, 1918.
2899 Parkes, Lily Beatrice, Mrs., 3 June, 1918
2900 Poynter, William Dyke, 3 June, 1918.
2901 Reynolds, Harriet Sarah, Mrs., 3 June, 1918.
2902 Robinson, Beatrice Evelyn Eugenie, Mrs., 3 June, 1918
2903 Shearer, David, 3 June, 1918.
2904 Strachan, Robert, 3 June, 1918.
2905 Style, Sydney Richard, 3 June, 1918.
2906 Urquhart, Herbert, 3 June, 1918.
2907 Willson, Nellie Marie, 3 June, 1918.
2908 Wylie, Maria Elizabeth, Mrs., 3 June, 1918.
2909 Angel, Frederick William, 3 June, 1918.
2910 Facey, Edith Mary, Mrs., 3 June, 1918.
2911 Goodison, Mary, Mrs., 3 June, 1918.
2912 Harvey, Christina, Mrs., 3 June, 1918.
2913 Knox, Sara, 3 June, 1918.
2914 Macpherson, Violette, 3 June, 1918.
2915 Morris, John William, 3 June, 1918.
2916 O'Reilly, Isabella, Mrs., 3 June, 1918.
2917 Ryan, Isabel, Mrs., 3 June, 1918.
2918 Sclater, Eliza, Mrs., 3 June, 1918.
2919 Scott, Katherine, Mrs., 3 June, 1918.
2920 Wilton, Jemima, Mrs., 3 June, 1918.
2921 Abraham, John Conrad, 3 June, 1918.
2922 Addison, Joseph Bartlett, 3 June, 1918.
2923 Armitage, Ethel, Mrs., 3 June, 1918.
2924 Atterbury, William Joseph, 3 June, 1918.
2925 Baldock, Henry Augustus, 3 June, 1918.
2926 Bartolo, Antonio, 3 June, 1918.
2927 Basch, Bertha, Mrs., 3 June, 1918.
2928 Blackden, Mary Helen Bennett, Mrs., 3 June, 1918.
2929 Blanshard Isabella Miller, Mrs., 3 June, 1918.
2930 Borg, George, 3 June, 1918.
2931 Branch, Irene, Mrs., 3 June, 1918.
2932 Cargill, John Henry, 3 June, 1918.
2933 Clinckett, Robert James, 3 June, 1918.
2934 Cocks, Edward Charles, 3 June, 1918.
2935 Connal, Sophia Lucy Mackworth, Mrs., 3 June, 1918.
2936 Corsi, Anthony Joseph, 3 June, 1918.
2938 Da Costa, Altamont, 3 June, 1918.
2939 Drury, Edward Herbert Merivale, 3 June, 1918.
2940 Ebden, Elizabeth, Mrs., 3 June, 1918.
2941 Elcombe, Minnie Eliza, Mrs., 3 June, 1918.
2942 Fowlie, Mary, Mrs., 3 June, 1918.
2943 Gardner, Arthur Edward, 3 June, 1918.
2944 Goddard, Thomas Neilson, 3 June, 1918.
2945 Harnett, Leslie Bennett, Mrs., 3 June, 1918.
2946 Harris, Henry Lewis, 3 June, 1918.
2947 Howard, Robert, 3 June, 1918.
2948 Hutson, John, 3 June, 1918.
2949 Kerr, Walter Coke, 3 June, 1918.
2950 Kerr, Maud Coke, Mrs., 3 June, 1918.
2953 Matthews, Philip Edwin, 3 June, 1918.
2954 Moggridge, Norah, Mrs., 3 June, 1918.
2955 Philip, Fullerton Bell, 3 June, 1918.
2956 Saunders, Maude Irene, 3 June, 1918.
2957 Sinclair, Muriel Eveleen Kathleen, Mrs., 3 June, 1918.
2958 Smith, George Milner, 3 June, 1918.
2959 Tarlton, Jessie, Mrs., 3 June, 1918.
2961 Turner, Henry Morton Stanley, 3 June, 1918.
2962 Verney, Malvina, Mrs., 3 June, 1918.
2963 Baxendale, Gertrude Mary, Mrs. Vincent-, 3 June, 1918.

2964 Watney, Constance, 3 June, 1918.
2965 Withycombe, Robert, 3 June, 1918.
2966 Coombs, Percy, 3 June, 1918.
2967 Craft, Samuel Louis, 3 June, 1918. (M.)
2968 Gray, Herbert Chester, 3 June, 1918. (M.)
2969 Lock, James Steele, 3 June, 1918. (M.)
2970 McMullen, William Albert, 3 June, 1918. (M.)
2971 Murray, Reginald Myrie, 3 June, 1918. (M.)
2972 Rudden, Bernard, 3 June, 1918. (M.)
2973 Circuitt, George Francis Langdald, 3 June, 1918. (M.)
2974 Hemper, John Richard, 3 June, 1918. (M.)
2975 Steen, Royston Dunbar, 3 June, 1918. (M.)
2976 Barnett, Alfred Henry, 3 June, 1918. (M.)
2978 Blackburn, Rev. Burdus Redford, 3 June, 1918. (M.)
2979 Bowen, Charles Henry Croasdaile, 3 June, 1918. (M.)
2980 Bratby, Samuel Henry, 3 June, 1918. (M.)
2982 Buckner, Johnstone Stanley, 3 June, 1918. (M.)
2983 Childs, Edmund, 3 June, 1918. (M.)
2984 Cowan, Percy John, 3 June, 1918. (M.)
2985 Duncan, Godfrey Alexander, 3 June, 1918. (M.)
2986 Elliott, George Frederick, 3 June, 1918. (M.)
2987 Ferguson, John, 3 June, 1918. (M.)
2988 Fleming, Rev. Michael Joseph, 3 June, 1918. (M.)
2989 Flint, Alfred William, 3 June, 1918. (M.)
2990 Glanville, Ernest Alfred, 3 June, 1918. (M.)
2991 Hedges, Harold Edward, 3 June, 1918. (M.)
2992 Hony, Henry Charles, 3 June, 1918. (M.)
2993 Hurst, Ian, 3 June, 1918. (M.)
2994 Hyde-Smith, Valentine Gardner, 3 June, 1918. (M.)
2995 Johnson, Alfred William, 3 June, 1918. (M.)
2996 Kunal, Chandra Sen, 3 June, 1918. (M.)
2997 Lakeland, William John, 3 June, 1918. (M.)
2998 Littlejohns, Alfred Edwin, 3 June, 1918. (M.)
2999 Mackay, Frank Forbes, 3 June, 1918. (M.)
3000 MacNeill, Rev. John Henry Horton, 3 June, 1918. (M.)
3001 Martin, Robert, 3 June, 1918. (M.)
3002 Molyneux, Rev. Frederick Merivale, 3 June, 1918. (M.)
3003 Morgan, Percival Robert, 3 June, 1918. (M.)
3004 Nichols, Frederick William, 3 June, 1918. (M.)
3005 O'Leary, Michael George, 3 June, 1918. (M.)
3006 O'Rooke, George Mackenzie, 3 June, 1918. (M.)
3007 Orr, George, 3 June, 1918. (M.)
3008 Pollard, Armell Richard, 3 June, 1918. (M.)
3009 Reed, George Washington, 3 June, 1918. (M.)
3011 Scholefield, Maurice Theodore, 3 June, 1918. (M.)
3012 Scott, James, 3 June, 1918. (M.)
3013 Shand, George, 3 June, 1918. (M.)
3014 Smith, Charles Probyn, 3 June, 1918. (M.)
3015 Smithson, Edward, 3 June, 1918. (M.)
3016 Stowell, George Christopher, 3 June, 1918. (M.)
3017 Thompson, Eric Bertram, 3 June, 1918. (M.)
3018 Venn, Tom Walters, 3 June, 1918. (M.)
3019 Way, John Dover, 3 June, 1918. (M.)
3020 Wilkinson, Robert Joseph, 3 June, 1918 (M.)
3021 Wood, Leonard Stanley, 3 June, 1918. (M.)
3022 Wormald, Rev. Robert Leonard, 3 June, 1918. (M.)
3023 Wright, Frank Thomas, 3 June, 1918. (M.)
3027 Boazman, Henry, 3 June, 1918. (M.)
3028 Botha, Gerhardus Maritz, 3 June, 1918. (M.)
3029 Bottomley, Clarence Fereday, 3 June, 1918. (M.)
3030 Broome, Lewis John, 3 June, 1918. (M.)
3031 Bunting, Sheldon Arthur Stewart, 3 June, 1918. (M.)
3032 Bury, Raymond, 3 June, 1918. (M.)
3033 Caldwell, William James, 3 June, 1918. (M.)
3034 Carpenter, Geoffrey Douglas Hale, 3 June, 1918. (M.)
3035 Carswell, James Ernest Ingham, 3 June, 1918. (M.)
3036 Christison, Fred Hamilton, 3 June, 1918. (M.)
3037 Cresswell, Herbert Pinkney, 3 June, 1918. (M.)
3038 Davies, George Frederick, 3 June, 1918. (M.)
3039 Davis, Valfred Emanuel, 3 June, 1918. (M.)
3040 de Barcaye, Hugo Seeman, 3 June, 1918. (M.)
3041 de Maine, Lionel Thomas, 3 June, 1918. (M.)
3043 Fleming, Geoffrey Balmano, 3 June, 1918. (M.)
3044 Fludder, George, 3 June, 1918. (M.)
3046 Fuge, William Valentine Greatraks, 3 June, 1918. (M.)
3047 Grant, Charles Cameron, 3 June, 1918. (M.)
3048 Greenwood, T., 3 June, 1918. (M.)
3049 Harris, Edgar David, 3 June, 1918. (M.)
3050 Healey, Harry, 3 June, 1918. (M.)
3051 Hollis, Wilfrid Norman, 3 June, 1918. (M.)
3052 Hughes, Robert Edwarde Armour, 3 June, 1918. (M.)
3053 Humphreys, Robert Arthur, 3 June, 1918. (M.)
3054 Innes, Cameron Starr, 3 June, 1918. (M.)
3055 Jones, William, 3 June, 1918. (M.)
3056 Kauntz, William Henry, 3 June, 1918. (M.)
3057 Leapingwell, Louis Albert, 3 June, 1918. (M.)
3058 McIntyre, Donald, 3 June, 1918. (M.)
3059 McLaren, Douglas, 3 June, 1918. (M.)
3060 Murrell, Henry Francis, 3 June, 1918. (M.)
3061 Pearse, Robert Bernard, 3 June, 1918. (M.)
3062 Potter, Frederick Effingham, 3 June, 1918. (M.)
3063 Reid, Eric, 3 June, 1918. (M.)
3064 Rennie, Andy Gerald, 3 June, 1918. (M.)
3065 Rossiter, Frederick Norman Chambers, 3 June, 1918. (M.)
3066 Ruffle, William Harry, 3 June, 1918. (M.)
3067 Saunders, Henry Hume, 3 June, 1918. (M.)
3068 Sheedy, Frederick John, 3 June, 1918. (M.)
3069 Slingsby, Charles Richard, 3 June, 1918. (M.)
3070 Southey, Maurice Edward, 3 June, 1918. (M.)
3071 Stead, Norman, 3 June, 1918. (M.)

MEMBERS.

3072 Stradling, Charles Anstice, 3 June, 1918. (M.)
3073 Stuart, Donald Richard, 3 June, 1918. (M.)
3075 Stuart, Thane Charles, 3 June, 1918. (M.)
3076 Van Tyen, Martinus Sibillus Jan Casper, 3 June, 1918. (M.)
3077 Walker, Rev. Joseph Robert, 3 June, 1918. (M.)
3078 Watkins, Purcell John, 3 June, 1918. (M.)
3079 Watt, James, 3 June, 1918. (M.)
3080 Wheeler, Roland Chamberlain, 3 June, 1918. (M.)
3084 de Felice, Rodolfo, 3 June, 1918. (M.)
3085 Crotty, Trevor, 3 June, 1918. (M.)
3086 Blaney, George, 3 June, 1918.
3087 Buhagiar, Peter, 3 June, 1918.
3088 Cameron, Clarence St. Clair, 3 June, 1918.
3089 Caterall, John, 3 June, 1918.
3090 Cunningham, Gordon, 3 June, 1918.
3091 Ferguson, May Glendening, Mrs., 3 June, 1918.
3092 Gabain, Adele, Mrs., 3 June, 1918.
3093 Harris, Leonard David John, 3 June, 1918.
3094 Hartley, Albert, 3 June, 1918.
3095 Harwood, George, 3 June, 1918.
3096 Hilliard, Robert 3 June, 1918.
3097 McCraken, John, 3 June, 1918.
3098 Moir, William Robertson, 3 June, 1918.
3099 Strong, William Henry, 3 June, 1918.
3100a Thoy, Herbert Dominick, 3 June, 1918.
3100b Guthrie, William Alexander, 3 June, 1918.
3100c Sullivan, John Andrew, 3 June, 1918.
3100d Facey, Lilian Maud, Mrs., 3 June, 1918.
3101 Fenton, Henry Walter, 22 Aug. 1918. (M.)
3102 Lovelace, Peter Leo, 22 Aug. 1918. (M.)
3103 McPhail, Lachlan Rose, 22 Aug. 1918. (M.)
3104 Wauchope, David, 22 Aug. 1918. (M.)
3105 Jones, Arthur Melville, 22 Aug. 1918. (M.)
3106 Ings, George Benjamin, 19 Dec. 1918. (M.)
3107 Basden, Albert Edward, 19 Dec. 1918.
3108 Brocklebank, Stanley Hartree, 19 Dec. 1918.
3109 Jordan, Herbert James, 19 Dec. 1918.
3110 Lewis, Ernest Harry, 19 Dec. 1918.
3111 Macandrew, Evan, 19 Dec. 1918.
3112 Sheldon, Thomas Alfred, 19 Dec. 1918.
3112a Garraway, Leonard, 28 Dec. 1918.
3113 Barbier, Isabella Eugenie Marie, 1 Jan. 1919. (M.)
3114 Beresford, Henry Edward, 1 Jan. 1919. (M.)
3115 Binnie, James Ballentyne, 1 Jan. 1919. (M.)
3116 Brand, Erle Bergo, 1 Jan. 1919. (M.)
3117 Butters, James Waugh, 1 Jan. 1919. (M.)
3118 Chase, Louisa Maud, 1 Jan. 1919. (M.)
3120 Dilworth, Charles, 1 Jan. 1919. (M.)
3121 Dobson, William Frederick, 1 Jan. 1919. (M.)
3122 Dunell, Alan Gordon, 1 Jan. 1919. (M.)
3123 Faviell, Mrs. Mary Sanderson, 1 Jan. 1919. (M.)
3124 Gale, Frederick Richard, 1 Jan. 1919. (M.)
3125 Goodyear, Geoffrey, 1 Jan. 1919. (M.)
3126 Gough, Herbert John, 1 Jan. 1919. (M.)
3127 Green, Lionel Havercroft, 1 Jan. 1919. (M.)
3128 Halliday, Charles William, 1 Jan. 1919. (M.)
3129 Hampton, Charles Sweet, 1 Jan. 1919. (M.)
3130 Harrison, Joseph Lawrence, 1 Jan. 1919. (M.)
3131 Heath, Roland John, 1 Jan. 1919. (M.)
3132 Hill, Arthur, 1 Jan. 1919. (M.)
3133 Hingston, Cicely Lamorna, 1 Jan. 1919. (M.)
3134 Hogg, William, 1 Jan. 1919. (M.)
3135 Hopkinson, Harold, 1 Jan. 1919. (M.)
3136 Houghton, Elizabeth, Mrs., 1 Jan. 1919. (M.)
3137 Hughes, John Archibald, 1 Jan. 1919. (M.)
3138 Hyde, Ethel Vivian, Mrs., 1 Jan. 1919. (M.)
3139 Johnston, Annie Emily Blanche, Mrs., 1 Jan. 1919. (M.)
3140 Joyce, Francis Matthew, 1 Jan. 1919. (M.)
3141 Keery, William James, 1 Jan. 1919. (M.)
3142 Lambert, Miriam Constance, 1 Jan. 1919. (M.)
3143 Lutwyche, Margaret Ruby, Mrs., 1 Jan. 1919. (M.)
3144 Mackenzie, Murdo, 1 Jan. 1919. (M.)
3145 Mallet, Frank Charles, 1 Jan. 1919. (M.)
3146 Neale, Clara, 1 Jan. 1919. (M.)
3147 Plowman, William Albert, 1 Jan. 1919. (M.)
3148 Proud, William, 1 Jan. 1919. (M.)
3149 Rowlatt, John Henry, 1 Jan. 1919. (M.)
3150 Saunders, Molly, 1 Jan. 1919. (M.)
3151 Scott, Flora Murray, 1 Jan. 1919. (M.)
3152 Shepherd, Cornelius, 1 Jan. 1919. (M.)
3153 Spring, George Robert, 1 Jan. 1919. (M.)
3154 Sutton, Ernest Phillips Foquet, 1 Jan. 1919. (M.)
3155 Thomson, Elizabeth, 1 Jan. 1920. (M.)
3156 Wilkinson, Harry Cuthbert William, 1 Jan, 1919. (M.)
3157 Willett, Hugh, 1 Jan. 1919. (M.)
3158 Wilman, Edgar Arthur, 1 Jan. 1919. (M.)
3159 Narain, Subadar Lachmi, 1 Jan. 1919. (M.)
3160 Hutchinson, Thomas Herbert, 1 Jan. 1919. (M.)
3161 McLachlan, Allan, 1 Jan. 1919. (M.)
3162 McCallum, Alexander, 1 Jan. 1919. (M.)
3163 Smith, George, 1 Jan. 1919. (M.)
3164 Aitchison, George, 1 Jan. 1919. (M.)
3165 Baldwin, Walter James, 1 Jan. 1919. (M.)
3166 Barber, James, 1 Jan. 1919. (M.)
3167 Barnes, James Cecil Lawson, 1 Jan. 1919. (M.)
3168 Blake, William Betts, 1 Jan. 1919. (M.)
3169 Bullock, Frank Henry William, 1 Jan. 1919. (M.)
3170 Cudmore, Frederick William, 1 Jan. 1919. (M.)
3171 Douglas-White, Cyril Francis, 1 Jan. 1919. (M.)

3172 Evans, Richard Endell, 1 Jan. 1919. (M.)
3173 Eyres, Charles Lionel, 1 Jan. 1919. (M.)
3174 Frampton, Napier Paul, 1 Jan. 1919. (M.)
3175 Gardner, Reginald Lowood, 1 Jan. 1919. (M.)
3176 Green, Gerald Gilbert, 1 Jan. 1919. (M.)
3177 Green, Joseph, 1 Jan. 1919. (M.)
3178 Green, William, 1 Jan. 1919. (M.)
3179 Hahn, Adolph, 1 Jan. 1919. (M.)
3180 Hamilton-Grierson, Philip Francis, 1 Jan. 1919. (M.)
3181 Hay, William Ross, 1 Jan. 1919. (M.)
3182 Holden, Fred, 1 Jan. 1919. (M.)
3183 Hope, Arthur Clement, 1 Jan. 1919. (M.)
3184 Irons, Thomas William, 1 Jan. 1919. (M.)
3185 Kerry, Arthur Henry Gould, 1 Jan. 1919. (M.)
3186 Lewis, Frederick, 1 Jan. 1919. (M.)
3188 Malyn, Donald Paton, 1 Jan. 1919. (M.)
3189 Merry, Edgar James, 1 Jan. 1919. (M.)
3190 Powell, Thomas Percy Prosser, 1 Jan. 1919. (M.)
3191 Sergeant, Herbert Lee, 1 Jan. 1919. (M.)
3192 Shreeve, Arthur William, 1 Jan. 1919. (M.)
3193 Slaughter, Ernest William, 1 Jan. 1919. (M.)
3194 Smith, James Hampstead, 1 Jan. 1919. (M.)
3195 Sowman, Ulric Doncaster, 1 Jan. 1919. (M.)
3196 Stoddard, Ernest Algernon, 1 Jan. 1919. (M.)
3197 Stratton, James Phillips, 1 Jan. 1919. (M.)
3198 Wilson, Sholto Douglas Major, 1 Jan. 1919. (M.)
3199 Buckland, Philip Percival, 1 Jan. 1919. (M.)
3200 Frost, Wilfreu John Thomas, 1 Jan. 1919. (M.)
3201 Kadi, El Saghkolaghasi Abdel Azim Effendi Abd El, 1 Jan. 1919. (M.)
3202 Amer, El Mulazim-Awal Anwar Effendi, 1 Jan. 1919. (M.)
3203 Shoucair, El Yuzbashi Halim Effendi Sulman, 1 Jan. 1919. (M.)
3204 Akle, El Yuzbashi (T. Saghkolaghasi) Mohammed Effendi, 1 Jan. 1919. (M.)
3205 Lufti, El Bimbashi Saleh Effendi, 1 Jan. 1919. (M.)
3206 Bampfield, Lewis Adolphus, 1 Jan. 1919. (M.)
3207 Benson, Trevor Gaulter, 1 Jan. 1919. (M.)
3208 Brown, Lawrence, 1 Jan. 1919. (M.)
3209 Carlisle, William, 1 Jan. 1919. (M.)
3210 Daly, Oscar Bedford, 1 Jan. 1919. (M.)
3211 Gibson, Francis Edmund, 1 Jan. 1919. (M.)
3212 McClintock-Bunbury, Hon. Thomas Leopold, 1 Jan 1919. (M.)
3213 Moss, Frederic William, 1 Jan. 1919. (M.)
3214 Rose, Thomas Whately, 1 Jan. 1919. (M.)
3215 Smith, John, 1 Jan. 1919. (M.)
3216 Twine, Frank Percival, 1 Jan. 1919. (M.)
3217 Williams, William Herbert, 1 Jan. 1919. (M.)
3218 Young, Richard Linsley, 1 Jan. 1919. (M.)
3219 Bernays, Geoffrey Charles Arrowsmith, 1 Jan. 1919. (M.)
3220 Blaikie, Thomas Hugh Conolly, 1 Jan. 1919. (M.)
3221 Bliss, Theodore Stephen, 1 Jan. 1919. (M.)
3222 Breton, Norton, 1 Jan. 1919. (M.)
3223 Clarke, Hugh Franklin, 1 Jan. 1919. (M.)
3224 Court, Henry Darlington Harold, 1 Jan. 1919. (M.)
3225 Duckett, William Knight, 1 Jan. 1919. (M.)
3226 Fontaine, Frederick Charles, 1 Jan. 1919. (M.)
3227 Leslie-Melville, Hon. David William, 1 Jan. 1919. (M.)
3228 Mansell, Reginald Anson, 1 Jan. 1919. (M.)
3231 Pallis, Andreas, 1 Jan. 1919. (M.)
3233 Reynolds, Walter Deveson, 1 Jan. 1919. (M.)
3234 Robson, Thomas Buston, 1 Jan. 1919. (M.)
3235 Stevens, Gordon, 1 Jan. 1919. (M.)
3236 Johnstone, John Hamilton Lane, 1 Jan. 1919. (M.)
3237 Sturdy, A. E., 1 Jan. 1919. (M.)
3238 Utterton, A., 1 Jan. 1919. (M.)
3239 Adams, Robert Frank, 1 Jan. 1919. (M.)
3240 Allen, Doreen, 1 Jan. 1919. (M.)
3241 Alston, Rowland Allison, 1 Jan. 1919. (M.)
3242 Balls William Daniel Chamberlain, 1 Jan. 1919. (M.)
3243 Banger, John Henry Adolphus, 1 Jan. 1919. (M.)
3244 Bayley, Benjamin Croft, 1 Jan. 1919. (M.)
3245 Bishop, John Evitt, 1 Jan. 1919. (M.)
3246 Britton, Walter Peaston, 1 Jan. 1919. (M.)
3247 Brooks, Henry Arthur, 1 Jan. 1919. (M.)
3248 Brooks, John Rowe, 1 Jan. 1919. (M.)
3249 Brown, Arthur Walter, 1 Jan. 1919. (M.)
3250 Budd, Charles, 1 Jan. 1919. (M.)
3251 Budge, James William, 1 Jan. 1919. (M.)
3252 Cemlyn-Jones, Elias Wynne, 1 Jan. 1919. (M.)
3253 Chapman, Marie Langslow, 1 Jan. 1919. (M.)
3254 Clay, Beatrice L., 1 Jan. 1919. (M.)
3255 Cooper, Thomas, 1 Jan. 1919. (M.)
3256 Cope, Noel Harwood, 1 Jan. 1919. (M.)
3257 Cowan, Alexander Henry, 1 Jan. 1919. (M.)
3258 Craigie, Muriel, 1 Jan. 1919. (M.)
3259 Curry, Edward, 1 Jan. 1919. (M.)
3260 Cursley, Samuel, 1 Jan. 1919. (M.)
3261 Desmond, Arthur Edward, 1 Jan. 1919. (M.)
3262 Edwards, William, 1 Jan. 1919. (M.)
3263 Ellis, Arthur Evelyn Paul, 1 Jan. 1919. (M.)
3264 Emerson, Thomas William, 1 Jan. 1919. (M.)
3265 Forrest, Robert, 1 Jan. 1919. (M.)
3266 Freeman, Percy Tom, 1 Jan. 1919. (M.)
3267 Gamage, Cecil Murdoch, 1 Jan. 1919.
3268 Garnier, Alan Parry, 1 Jan. 1919. (M.)
3269 Gethin, Randolph G., 1 Jan. 1919. (M.)
3270 Gough, Robert Thomas, 1 Jan. 1919. (M.)
3271 Heath, Sidney John, 1 Jan. 1919. (M.)

3272 Hetherington, Graham, 1 Jan. 1919. (M.)
3273 Holland, Francis, 1 Jan. 1919. (M.)
3274 Holme, Charles Geoffrey, 1 Jan. 1919. (M.)
3275 Holmes, Hubert Jack, 1 Jan. 1919. (M.)
3276 Horton, Vernon Grove, 1 Jan. 1919. (M.)
3277 Hutchings, W. F., 1 Jan. 1919. (M.)
3278 Johnson, Horace Swales, 1 Jan. 1919. (M.)
3279 Jones, Harry Beresford, 1 Jan. 1919 (M.)
3280 Kirkby, Edward William, 1 Jan. 1919. (M.)
3281 Klein, Adrian Bernard L., 1 Jan. 1919. (M.)
3282 Knapp, E. C., 1 Jan. 1919. (M.)
3283 Landon, Joseph Whittington, 1 Jan. 1919. (M.)
3284 Lawrence, Francis Henry, 1 Jan. 1919. (M.)
3285 Lawson, John Boyd, 1 Jan. 1919. (M.)
3286 Leneghan, Mary, 1 Jan. 1919. (M.)
3287 Lister, George, 1 Jan. 1919. (M.)
3288 Lloyd, Ethel Vernon, Mrs., 1 Jan. 1919. (M.)
3289 Macleod, James Keith, 1 Jan. 1919. (M.)
3290 Martin, John Newton, 1 Jan. 1919. (M.)
3291 Meredith, H. A., 1 Jan. 1919. (M.)
3292 Mitchell, James, 1 Jan. 1919. (M.)
3293 Morris, Rhys Hopkin, 1 Jan. 1919. (M.)
3294 Read, Hugh A. Moutray-, 1 Jan. 1919. (M.)
3295 Muirhead, James Calder, 1 Jan. 1919. (M.)
3297 Naish, Francis Clement Prideaux, 1 Jan. 1919. (M.)
3298 Nightingale, Thomas George Hull, 1 Jan. 1919. (M.)
3299 O'Kelly, Edward Joseph, 1 Jan. 1919. (M.)
3300 Oliver, Richard, 1 Jan. 1919. (M.)
3302 Patrick, John McDonald, 1 Jan. 1919. (M.)
3303 Pegrum, Abraham William, 1 Jan. 1919 (M.)
3304 Popplestone, William Gilbert, 1 Jan. 1919. (M.)
3305 Post, Donnell Shepard, 1 Jan. 1919. (M.)
3306 Rayner, George Henry, 1 Jan. 1919. (M.)
3307 Rayner, Walter John, 1 Jan. 1919. (M.)
3308 Reeder, Robert John, 1 Jan. 1919. (M.)
3309 Rennie, George, 1 Jan. 1919. (M.)
3310 Rix, Dudley Gerald, 1 Jan. 1919. (M.)
3311 Saul, Joseph, 1 Jan. 1919. (M.)
3312 Scrimgeour, James, 1 Jan. 1919. (M.)
3313 Shield, John Gilson, 1 Jan. 1919. (M.)
3314 Solly, William, 1 Jan. 1919. (M.)
3315 Springate, Albert Edward, 1 Jan. 1919. (M.)
3316 Stallan, Herbert Alfred, 1 Jan. 1919. (M.)
3317 Stirling, Hugh William, 1 Jan. 1919. (M.)
3318 Stirling, John, 1 Jan. 1919. (M.)
3319 Storey, John William, 1 Jan. 1919. (M.)
3320 Streeter, Gertrude M. H., Mrs., 1 Jan. 1919. (M.)
3321 Stringer, Herbert Alfred, 1 Jan. 1919. (M.)
3322 Taylor, Arthur Herbert, 1 Jan. 1919. (M.)
3324 Whittaker, Laurence, 1 Jan. 1919. (M.)
3325 Richardson, William Wigham-, 1 Jan. 1919. (M.
3326 Willsher, John Wingfield, 1 Jan. 1919. (M.)
3327 Woombell, Thomas, 1 Jan. 1919. (M.)
3328 Watkins, Joseph Harold, 1 Jan. 1919. (M.)
3329 Webb, Sidney George, 1 Jan. 1919. (M.)
3330 Barry, Arthur Cressy, 1 Jan. 1919. (M.)
3331 King, George, 1 Jan. 1919. (M.)
3332 Lee, Eric Alfred, 1 Jan. 1919. (M.)
3334 Murphy, Clarence Robert, 1 Jan. 1919. (M.)
3335 Perrin, William Andrew, 1 Jan. 1919. (M.)
3336 Price, William, 1 Jan. 1919. (M.)
3337 Prior, William Henry, 1 Jan. 1919. (M.)
3338 Savage, James Edmund, 1 Jan. 1919. (M.)
3339 Eastgate, Henry, 1 Jan. 1919. (M.)
3340 Forsythe, Gordon Harris, 1 Jan. 1919. (M.)
3343 McGowan, Henry Edward, 1 Jan. 1919. (M.)
3344 Magnay, Christopher Robert Alexander, 1 Jan. 1919. (M.)
3345 Staples-Brown, Richard Charles, 1 Jan. 1919. (M.)
3346 Jamieson, Edmund Charles Kean, 1 Jan. 1919. (M.)
3347 Walker, Eric Bolingbroke, 1 Jan. 1919. (M.)
3348 Whyte, James Cunningham, 1 Jan. 1919. (M.)
3349 Achurch, George Philip, 1 Jan. 1919. (M.)
3350 Adams, John Leonard, 1 Jan. 1919. (M.)
3351 Allen, Arthur Dunscombe, 1 Jan. 1919. (M.)
3352 Anderson, Henry Graeme, 1 Jan. 1919. (M.)
3353 Attrill, Charles, 1 Jan. 1919. (M.)
3354 Bagge, Harry James, 1 Jan. 1919. (M.)
3355 Bellew, Edward Henry, 1 Jan. 1919. (M.)
3356 Bentley, Walter Owen, 1 Jan. 1919. (M.)
3357 Brittain, Arthur William, 1 Jan. 1919. (M.)
3358 Bruce-Clarke, William Robert, 1 Jan. 1919. (M.)
3359 Butler, Fernand Charles, 1 Jan. 1919. (M.)
3360 Carr, Leslie Wilden, 1 Jan. 1919. (M.)
3361 Catherall, John Eric, 1 Jan. 1919. (M.)
3362 Catleugh, John Harwood, 1 Jan. 1919. (M.)
3363 Cheshire, Archibald Sidney, 1 Jan. 1919. (M.)
3364 Christie, Fred, 1 Jan. 1919. (M.)
3365 Clift, John George Neilson, 1 Jan. 1919. (M.)
3366 Clogstoun, Herbert Prinsep Somers, 1 Jan. 1919. (M.)
3367 Cole, William, 1 Jan. 1919. (M.)
3368 Colquhoun, Edgar Edmund, 1 Jan. 1919. (M.)
3369 Cooke, James Henry, 1 Jan. 1919. (M.)
3370 Corby, Hugh George, 1 Jan. 1919. (M.)
3371 Cort, William Percy, 1 Jan. 1919. (M.)
3372 Courtney, Reginald Aloysius, 1 Jan. 1919. (M.)
3373 Creswell, Keppel Archibald Cameron, 1 Jan. 1919. (M.)
3374 Denison, Amos Allan, 1 Jan. 1919. (M.)
3375 Dew, William James, 1 Jan. 1919. (M.)
3376 Drudge, Ernest O., 1 Jan. 1919. (M.)
3377 Ellis, Samuel Howard, 1 Jan. 1919. (M.)

3378 Felkin, Samuel Denys, 1 Jan. 1919. (M.)
3379 Ferguson, John Herbert, 1 Jan. 1919. (M.)
3380 Fielding, Walter Harrison, 1 Jan. 1919. (M.)
3381 Fortescue, Albert Edward Muspratt, 1 Jan. 1919. (M.)
3382 Fraser, George Gerald Rae, 1 Jan. 1919. (M.)
3383 Freemantle, Robert McGorman, 1 Jan. 1919. (M.)
3384 Furniss, John Hunt, 1 Jan. 1919. (M.)
3385 Hill, Harold Gardiner-, 1 Jan. 1919. (M.)
3386 Greenhough, Arthur Basil Wickham, 1 Jan. 1919. (M)
3387 Gregory, Arthur Leslie, 1 Jan. 1919. (M.)
3388 Handman, Adolph Herbert, 1 Jan. 1919. (M.)
3389 Hansford, Albert Urbane, 1 Jan. 1919. (M.)
3390 Hart, William Whiddon, 1 Jan. 1919. (M.)
3391 Heanly, Wilfred Edward Graham, 1 Jan. 1919. (M.)
3392 Hemsley, Noel, 1 Jan. 1919. (M.)
3393 Hetherington, Charles Goldby, 1 Jan. 1919. (M.)
3394 Hingston, Alfred, 1 Jan. 1919. (M.)
3395 Hostings, James Walter, 1 Jan. 1919. (M.)
3396 Hoyland, Philip Charles, 1 Jan. 1919. (M.)
3397 Humphries, Eric Beresford, 1 Jan. 1919. (M.)
3398 Humphreys, Robert Henry, 1 Jan. 1919. (M.)
3399 Hunter, John, 1 Jan. 1919. (M.)
3400 Iredale, Frederick Mitchell, 1 Jan. 1919. (M.)
3401 James, Maurice Jewison, 1 Jan. 1919. (M.)
3402 Jones, Thomas Pargeter, 1 Jan. 1919. (M.)
3403 Knight, Alfred, 1 Jan. 1919. (M.)
3404 Lander, Leonard Edward, 1 Jan. 1919. (M.)
3405 Lee, Alistair, 1 Jan. 1919. (M.)
3406 Levey, Bernard Alexander, 1 Jan. 1919. (M.)
3407 Lienard, Walter, 1 Jan. 1919. (M.)
3408 Lingard, William, 1 Jan. 1919. (M.)
3409 Lyall, George Henry Hudson, 1 Jan. 1919. (M.)
3410 Lyall, William Hooker, 1 Jan. 1919. (M.)
3411 Lyne, Edgar, 1 Jan. 1919. (M.)
3412 MacKilligan, Alister Pelham, 1 Jan. 1919. (M.)
3413 McLean, Robert Knox, 1 Jan. 1919. (M.)
3414 McMullen, John Alexander, 1 Jan. 1919. (M.)
3416 Molyneux, Edward Arthur, 1 Jan. 1919. (M.)
3417 Mullard, Stanley Robert, 1 Jan. 1919. (M.)
3418 Newman, Herbert John Greatrex, 1 Jan. 1919. (M.)
3419 Osborn, Tom Douglas Hamilton, 1 Jan. 1919. (M.)
3420 Ovens, Alexander Rutherford, 1 Jan. 1919. (M.)
3421 Peddell, Thomas Arthur, 1 Jan. 1919. (M.)
3422 Ramage, George, 1 Jan. 1919. (M.)
3423 Read, John Victor, 1 Jan. 1919. (M.)
3424 Richardson, Colin Spencer, 1 Jan. 1919. (M.)
3425 Ruttle, Jacob Sutcliffe, 1 Jan. 1919. (M.)
3426 Scarff, Frederick William, 1 Jan. 1919. (M.)
3427 Scoble, Walter Alfred, 1 Jan. 1919. (M.)
3428 Sharples, John Butterfield, 1 Jan. 1919. (M.)
3429 Slater, James Henry, 1 Jan. 1919. (M.)
3430 Smith, Alexander Glegg, 1 Jan. 1919. (M.)
3431 Smith, Charles Hodgkinson, 1 Jan. 1919. (M.)
3432 Smith, Henry Joseph Cecil, 1 Jan. 1919. (M.)
3433 Peach, Robert Stephenson-, 1 Jan. 1919. (M.)
3434 Stevenson, Robert Little, 1 Jan. 1919. (M.)
3435 Stroud, George John, 1 Jan. 1919. (M.)
3436 Sutherland, James Henry Richardson, 1 Jan. 1919. (M.)
3437 Tate, Henry Percy, 1 Jan. 1919. (M.)
3438 Tattersall, Tom Whitaker, 1 Jan. 1919. (M.)
3439 Thompson, Charles Stuart, 1 Jan. 1919. (M.)
3440 Thompson, George Albert, 1 Jan. 1919. (M.)
3441 Tilley, Harry, 1 Jan. 1919. (M.)
3442 Turner, Samuel Arthur, 1 Jan. 1919. (M.)
3443 Tyler, James Herbert, 1 Jan. 1919. (M.)
3444 Upjohn, Dudley Francis, 1 Jan. 1919. (M.)
3445 Verpilleux, Antoine Emile, 1 Jan. 1919. (M.)
3446 Waite, Robert Bruce, 1 Jan. 1919. (M.)
3447 Walker, John Philip, 1 Jan. 1919. (M.)
3448 Watson, John Charles, 1 Jan. 1919. (M.)
3449 Webley, William Thomas, 1 Jan. 1919. (M.)
3450 Welsford, Herbert Gray, 1 Jan. 1919. (M.)
3451 Whitaker, Raymond, 1 Jan. 1919. (M.)
3452 White, John Charles, 1 Jan. 1919. (M.)
3453 Willis, Thomas, 1 Jan. 1919. (M.)
3454 Witt, Albert Thomas Edgar, 1 Jan. 1919. (M.)
3455 Witty, Charles Harry, 1 Jan. 1919. (M.)
3456 Young, Christopher Harding, 1 Jan. 1919. (M.)
3457 Talbot, Matilda Theresa, 1 Jan. 1919. (M.)
3458 Thompson, Marion Annie, 1 Jan. 1919. (M.)
3459 Tibbits, Olive Eleanore, Mrs., 1 Jan. 1919. (M.)
3460 Gething, Charlotte Bathasar, Mrs., 1 Jan. 1919. (M.)
3461 Ablett, Frank, 1 Jan. 1919. (M.)
3462 Alexander, George Hamilton, 1 Jan. 1919. (M.)
3464 Black, Alfred Stephen, 1 Jan. 1919. (M.)
3465 Budge, Henry, 1 Jan. 1919. (M.)
3466 Cary, Henry John, 1 Jan. 1919. (M.)
3467 Diver, James Michael, 1 Jan. 1919. (M.)
3468 Gracie, Duncan McAuley, 1 Jan. 1919. (M.)
3469 Harrington, George, 1 Jan. 1919. (M.)
3470 Hovells, Ernest William, 1 Jan. 1919. (M.)
3471 Long, William Edward, 1 Jan. 1919. (M.)
3472 Macbeth, Allan, 1 Jan. 1919. (M.)
3473 Miller, Ernest Charles, 1 Jan. 1919. (M.)
3474 Morgan, James Walwyn Gynlais, 1 Jan. 1919. (M.)
3475 Shepherd, John Ernest, 1 Jan. 1919. (M.)
3476 Waugh, Alfred Charles, 1 Jan. 1919. (M.)
3477 Wilson, Hugh Brown, 1 Jan. 1919. (M.)
3478 Wooldridge, Walter, 1 Jan. 1919. (M.)
3479 Dannatt, Elsie Mary, 1 Jan. 1919. (M.)

MEMBERS.

3480 Acland, Katharine, 1 Jan. 1919.
3481 Adams, Frank, 1 Jan. 1919.
3482 Adams, John, 1 Jan. 1919.
3483 Adams, Robert Ernest Kennedy, 1 Jan. 1919.
3484 Aitken, Jean Reid, 1 Jan. 1919.
3485 Alcock, Edgar, 1 Jan. 1919.
3486 Alexander, Stanley Walter. 1 Jan. 1919.
3487 Allnutt, Arthur Joseph, 1 Jan. 1919.
3488 Amor, Emma, Mrs., 1 Jan. 1919
3489 Anderson, Annie Maria, Mrs., 1 Jan. 1919.
3490 Andrews, Charles Henry, 1 Jan. 1919.
3491 Andrews, Leonard, 1 Jan. 1919.
3492 Armitage, Elsie Barbara, 1 Jan. 1919.
3493 Arnold, George, 1 Jan. 1919.
3494 Ascough, Matthew Mather, 1 Jan. 1919.
3495 Ashton, Arthur, 1 Jan. 1919.
3496 Aslett, William Stacey, 1 Jan. 1919.
3497 Astin, Arthur, 1 Jan. 1919.
3498 Atkins, May Clara, Lady Crofton, 1 Jan. 1919.
3499 Atkinson, Harold Waring, 1 Jan. 1919.
3500 Ayrton, George, 1 Jan. 1919.
3501 Backhouse, Indiana Richenda, 1 Jan. 1919.
3502 Baigent, William, 1 Jan. 1919.
3503 Baker, Ada Mary, 1 Jan. 1919.
3504 Ball, Francis Livingstone, 1 Jan. 1919.
3505 Ballantine, Alice Liardet, 1 Jan. 1919.
3506 Baring, Eva Hermoine, Lady, 1 Jan. 1919.
3507 Barling, Edith Madge. 1 Jan. 1919.
3508 Barlow, Henry Arthur, 1 Jan. 1919.
3509 Barlow, William Tait, 1 Jan. 1919.
3510 Barnes, Edith Helen, Lady, 1 Jan. 1919.
3511 Barnett, Ada, 1 Jan. 1919.
3512 Barrington, Sir Charles Burton, 1 Jan. 1919.
3513 Barry, Lady Grace, 1 Jan. 1919.
3514 Barry, John Armstrong, 1 Jan. 1919.
3515 Barton, Gilbert William, 1 Jan. 1919.
3516 Bates, Henry Baker, 1 Jan. 1919.
3517 Batten, Frederick William, 1 Jan. 1919.
3518 Battle, George Richard, 1 Jan. 1919.
3519 Baxter, Harry Percy, 1 Jan. 1919.
3520 Bazeley, Marjorie Letitia, Mrs., 1 Jan. 1919.
3521 Beard, John James, 1 Jan. 1919.
3522 Beazley, Arthur Tetley, 1 Jan. 1919. (M.)
3523 Beazley, Herbert George, 1 Jan. 1919.
3524 Beddow, Muriel Grace, 1 Jan. 1919.
3525 Bennett, George Edward, 1 Jan 1919.
3526 Bennett, Isaac Vaughan, 1 Jan. 1919.
3527 Best, Charles William, 1 Jan. 1919.
3528 Binns, Joseph, 1 Jan. 1919.
3529 Birch, Janet Elizabeth, Mrs., 1 Jan. 1919.
3530 Bird, Jessie, Mrs., 1 Jan. 1919.
3531 Bobart, Henry Hodgkinson, 1 Jan. 1919.
3532 Bosanquet, Theodora, 1 Jan. 1919.
3533 Bourn, George, 1 Jan. 1919.
3534 Bowen, Thomas, 1 Jan. 1919.
3535 Bowman, James Robert, 1 Jan. 1919.
3536 Boyce, Adam, 1 Jan. 1919.
3537 Bradden, Elliot, 1 Jan. 1919.
3539 Broad, Frederick Laurence, 1 Jan. 1919. (M.)
3540 Brock, George Sandison, 1 Jan. 1919.
3541 Brocklehurst, Herbert Cecil, 1 Jan. 1919.
3542 Brodie, Marial, 1 Jan. 1919.
3543 Brown, Annie Kathleen, 1 Jan. 1919.
3544 Brown, James, 1 Jan. 1919.
3545 Brown, Minnie, 1 Jan. 1919.
3546 Brumell, Mary, Mrs., 1 Jan. 1919.
3547 Bullock, John William, 1 Jan. 1919.
3548 Bullock, Margaret Annie, 1 Jan. 1919.
3549 Bunker, Nellie, 1 Jan. 1919.
3550 Burley, Alison, 1 Jan. 1919.
3551 Burns, Norah Dalrymple, 1 Jan. 1919.
3552 Burstall, Henry Robert John, 1 Jan. 1919.
3553 Burton, Frances Westbrook, 1 Jan. 1919.
3554 Bush, Helen Ethel, Mrs. Harry Stebbing, 1 Jan. 1919.
3555 Bushby, Maud Alice, 1 Jan. 1919.
3556 Butcher, Marjorie Alma, 1 Jan. 1919.
3557 Butler, John Lawrence, 1 Jan. 1919.
3558 Butler, Nina, 1 Jan. 1919.
3559 Buttenshaw, George Eskholme, 1 Jan. 1919.
3560 Buxton, Edward, 1 Jan. 1919.
3561 Buxton, Laura, Mrs. Edward Gurney, 1 Jan. 1919
3562 Byatt, Ernest Henry, 1 Jan. 1919.
3563 Byles, Emma Mary, 1 Jan. 1919.
3564 Campbell, Lady Angela Mary Alice, 1 Jan. 1919.
3565 Campbell, Vera Harriett Antill, 1 Jan. 1919.
3566 Carey, Robert Edward, 1 Jan. 1919.
3567 Castell, Rose Catharine Clanmorris, Mrs., 1 Jan. 1919.
3568 Chaplin, Constance Helena, 1 Jan. 1919.
3569 Chatterton, Julia, Mrs., 1 Jan. 1919.
3570 Cheshire, Frederic Brandon, 1 Jan. 1919.
3571 Chidgey, Hugh Thomas Arthur, 1 Jan. 1919.
3572 Church, Thomas Henry, 1 Jan. 1919.
3573 Churchill, Laura, Mrs., 1 Jan. 1919.
3574 Clay, Frederick Septimus, 1 Jan. 1919.
3575 Clayton, Harry, 1 Jan. 1919.
3576 Clegg, Elizabeth, Mrs., 1 Jan. 1919.
3577 Elgin, Katherine Elizabeth, Countess, 1 Jan. 1919.
3578 Cock, James Wearne, 1 Jan. 1919.
3579 Colegrave, Elizabeth Violet, Mrs., 1 Jan. 1919.
3580 Coleridge, Frances May, 1 Jan. 1919.

3581 May, Ellen Evelyn, Mrs., J.J.I.C. 1 Jan. 1919.
3582 Collins, Lesbia, 1 Jan. 1919.
3583 Colona, Gilbert Edmond Chalmers, 1 Jan. 1919.
3584 Compton, John, 1 Jan. 1919.
3585 Connolly, Matthew, 1 Jan. 1919.
3586 Connolly, William Frederick, 1 Jan. 1919.
3587 Connor, William James, 1 Jan. 1919.
3588 Cooper, Robert Llewellyn Wilson, 1 Jan. 1919.
3589 Corkran, Sybil Florence, 1 Jan. 1919.
3590 Cottle, Clifford John, 1 Jan. 1919.
3591 Cotton, Alonzo, 1 Jan. 1919.
3592 Cox, Constance Louise, Mrs., 1 Jan. 1919.
3593 Cox, Sydney, 1 Jan. 1919.
3595 Crombie, Henry, 1 Jan. 1919.
3596 Crooke, Victor, 1 Jan. 1919.
3597 Cross, Bertram Charles, 1 Jan. 1919.
3598 Crossley, Audrey, Mrs., 1 Jan. 1919.
3599 Culross, James, 1 Jan. 1919.
3600 Cunninghame, James Fraser, 1 Jan. 1919.
3601 Curnow, Benjamin Henry, 1 Jan. 1919.
3602 Currie, Gertrude Barclay, Mrs., 1 Jan. 1919.
3603 Dale, William John, 1 Jan. 1919.
3604 Davies, Alphonso William James, 1 Jan. 1919.
3605 Davies, John Howell, 1 Jan. 1919.
3606 Davies, Milfred Lucy, Mrs., 1 Jan. 1919.
3607 Dawes, Helen Frances, 1 Jan. 1919.
3608 Dean, Edward George, 1 Jan. 1919.
3609 Deedes, Rose Elinor, Mrs., 1 Jan. 1919.
3610 Denny, Rosalind Mary, 1 Jan. 1919.
3611 Devonshire, Marie, 1 Jan. 1919.
3612 Dick, Gladys Helen, 1 Jan. 1919.
3614 Dixon, Elizabeth Amy, Mrs., 1 Jan. 1919.
3616 Dowbiggin, Annie, 1 Jan. 1919.
3617 Duggan, Eva, 1 Jan. 1919.
3618 Duncan, Elsie Eppielow, 1 Jan. 1919.
3619 Dunlop, Elizabeth Dorothea, 1 Jan. 1919.
3620 Dunne, James, 1 Jan. 1919.
3621 Stewart-Dyer, Terence Armiston, 1 Jan. 1919.
3622 East, Alfred Ernest, 1 Jan. 1919.
3623 Eden, Morton Frederick, 1 Jan. 1919.
3624 Edgar, Alice, 1 Jan. 1919.
3625 Edmunds, Elizabeth, Mrs., 1 Jan. 1919.
3626 Edmunds, John Parry, 1 Jan. 1919.
3627 Edwards, Gladys Maude, 1 Jan. 1919.
3628 Edwards, Richards, 1 Jan. 1919.
3629 Eldridge, William John, 1 Jan. 1919.
3630 Ellery, Kathleen Frances Elizabeth, Mrs., 1 Jan. 1919.
3631 Ellis, George Stanley, 1 Jan. 1919.
3632 Evans, Agnes Louisa, Mrs., 1 Jan. 1919.
3633 Ewen, Elias, 1 Jan. 1919.
3634 Fairbank, Amy Helena Margaret, 1 Jan. 1919.
3635 Farmer, Henry Edward, 1 Jan. 1919.
3636 Farren, Rev. George Erle, 1 Jan. 1919.
3637 Feiling, Ethel Bessie, Mrs., 1 Jan. 1919.
3638 Fell, Marion Isobel, Mrs., 1 Jan. 1919.
3639 Fetherstonhaugh, Victoria Shaw, Mrs., 1 Jan. 1919.
3640 Fidler, George Thomas, 1 Jan. 1919.
3641 Field, Mabel Clara Hawkes, 1 Jan. 1919.
3642 Figgis, Ruby Norah, 1 Jan. 1919.
3643 Filder, Charles Lavington, 1 Jan. 1919.
3644 Findlay, James Arthur, 1 Jan. 1919.
3645 Forbes, Eliza Mary, 1 Jan. 1919.
3646 Foreshew, Ernest, 1 Jan. 1919.
3648 Fozard, Harry Edwin, 1 Jan. 1919. (M.)
3649 France, Reginald, 1 Jan. 1919.
3650 Francis, Percy Alexander 1 Jan. 1919.
3651 Fraser, James, 1 Jan. 1919.
3652 Friend, Dorothy, 1 Jan. 1919.
3654 Gallaway, Agnes Lottie, Mrs., 1 Jan. 1919.
3655 Gander, Bernard Vincent, 1 Jan. 1919.
3656 Gardiner, Alice Marie, Mrs., 1 Jan. 1919.
3657 Gardner, Dorothy, 1 Jan. 1919.
3658 Garforth, Hylda Maria Madeline, Hon. Mrs., 1 Jan. 1919.
3659 Garner, Lizzie, Mrs., 1 Jan. 1919.
3660 Garrett, James Charles, 1 Jan. 1919.
3661 Gask, Eleanor, 1 Jan. 1919.
3662 Gaskell, Catharine Julia, 1 Jan. 1919.
3663 Gaussen, Marguerite, Mrs., 1 Jan. 1919.
3664 Gentle, Robert, 1 Jan. 1919.
3665 George, Arthur Hereford Wykeham-, 1 Jan. 1919.
3666 Gilchrist, George Prowse, 1 Jan. 1919.
3667 Gillespie, William James, 1 Jan. 1919.
3668 Girdlestone, Emily, 1 Jan. 1919.
3669 Girling, Marjorie, 1 Jan. 1919.
3670 Gladwell, Ethel Dorothy, Mrs., 1 Jan. 1919.
3671 Glanfield, Olive, 1 Jan. 1919.
3672 Glegg, Robert, 1 Jan. 1919.
3673 Glen, James Hutchison, 1 Jan. 1919.
3674 Gluckstein, Francesca, Mrs., 1 Jan. 1919.
3675 Gordon, George Henry, 1 Jan. 1919.
3676 Graham, Sophia Augusta, 1 Jan. 1919.
3677 Grant, Alexander Philip Foulerton, 1 Jan. 1919.
3678 Grant, Donald Ernest, 1 Jan. 1919. (M.)
3679 Gray, Alice, 1 Jan. 1919.
3680 Gray, Andrew, 1 Jan. 1919.
3681 Greaves, Stanley Haldane Linford, 1 Jan. 1919.
3683 Greenham George Frederick, 1 Jan. 1919.
3685 Grimes, John, 1 Jan. 1919.
3686 Gros, Edith Katharine, Mrs. Le, 1 Jan. 1919.
3687 Grose, Woodman Cole, 1 Jan. 1919.

3688 Grosvenor, Lady Mabel Florence Mary, 1 Jan. 1919.
3689 Gubbins, Helen Frances Hartopp, Mrs., 1 Jan. 1919.
3690 Gulston, Agneta Annie Justina Stepney, 1 Jan. 1919.
3691 Gurney, Sarah Gamzee, Mrs., 1 Jan. 1919.
3692 Hains, Charles Brazier, 1 Jan. 1919.
3693 Hall, Evelyn Alice, Mrs., 1 Jan. 1919.
3694 Hall, Ernest Frederick, 1 Jan. 1919
3695 Hamilton, Margaret Gordon Hans. Mrs., 1 Jan. 1919.
3696 Hankins, Ivy Winifred, 1 Jan. 1919.
3697 Hare, William Henry, 1 Jan. 1919.
3698 Harris, Charles Hubert, 1 Jan. 1919.
3699 Harris, Helen, Mrs., 1 Jan. 1919.
3700 Harris, Marjorie Maxwell, 1 Jan. 1919.
3701 Hawes, Charles Henry, 1 Jan. 1919.
3702 Hayes, James Waldegrave, 1 Jan. 1919.
3703 Hayward, Percy Christopher Gallimore, 1 Jan. 1919.　(M.)
3704 Head, Herbert Harry Thomas, 1 Jan. 1919.
3705 Heath, John Henry, 1 Jan. 1919.
3706 Heelis, Marion, 1 Jan. 1919.
3707 Henderson, Charles Allen, 1 Jan. 1919.
3708 Henderson, Hubert Douglas, 1 Jan. 1919.
3709 Henderson, Laura Catharine, 1 Jan. 1919.
3710 Henderson, Violet, 1 Jan. 1919.
3711 Henley, Hon. Mrs. Sylvia Laura, 1 Jan. 1919.
3712 Henshilwood, George, 1 Jan. 1919.
3713 Hepburn, Thomas, 1 Jan. 1919.
3714 Herford, Caroline, 1 Jan. 1919.
3715 Hewett, Reginald, 1 Jan. 1919.
3716 Hewkin, Edwin Percy, 1 Jan. 1919.
3717 Heywood, Ivy Lenore, 1 Jan. 1919.
3718 Hicks, Corona, 1 Jan. 1919.
3719 Highton, William Thomas, 1 Jan. 1919.
3720 Hildyard, Gertrude Mary, Mrs. d'Arcy-, 1 Jan. 1919.
3721 Hilton, George Grimmer, 1 Jan. 1919
3722 Hobson, Charles Kenneth, 1 Jan. 1919.
3723 Hobson, William Edward, 1 Jan. 1919.
3724 Hodgson, Lillie, Mrs., 1 Jan. 1919.
3725 Hoffmann, Anne Avery, Mrs., 1 Jan. 1919.
3727 Holden, Ethel Mary, Mrs., 1 Jan. 1919.
3728 Holloway, Arthur William, 1 Jan. 1919.
3729 Holt, Constance, 1 Jan. 1919.
3730 Holt, Frederick William, 1 Jan. 1919.
3731 Hooper, Francis William, 1 Jan. 1919.
3732 Hore, Alexie, 1 Jan. 1919.
3733 Horstmann, Sidney Adolph, 1 Jan. 1919.
3735 How, Ethel Mary Beatrice, Mrs., 1 Jan. 1919.
3736 Howard, John Palmer, 1 Jan. 1919.
3737 Hoyle, George, 1 Jan. 1919.
3738 Hughes, Frances, 1 Jan. 1919.
3739 Hughes, Gibbard Richard, 1 Jan. 1919.
3740 Huish, Lizzie, Mrs., 1 Jan. 1919.
3741 Hullett, Gertrude Cecilia, 1 Jan. 1919.
3742 Hulse, Hilda Gertrude Overs, Mrs., 1 Jan. 1919.
3743 Humphreys, George Oscar, 1 Jan. 1919.
3744 Hunter, John Henry, 1 Jan. 1919.
3745 Hutchinson, Frances Catherine Maude Haynes, 1 Jan. 1919.
3746 Hutchison, Helen Duguid, 1 Jan. 1919.
3747 Huxley, Henry Scott, 1 Jan. 1919.
3748 Iles, Annie Christease, 1 Jan. 1919.
3749 Impey, Isabella Edith, 1 Jan. 1919.
3750 Inglis, Walter George, 1 Jan. 1919.
3751 Ireland, Herbert James, 1 Jan. 1919.
3752 Irvine, Margaret Elizabeth, Mrs. Charles Irvine Douglas- 1 Jan. 1919.
3753 Jackman, Douglas Arthur John, 1 Jan. 1919.
3754 Jackson, William Henry Congreve, 1 Jan. 1919.
3755 James, Dudley William Henry, 1 Jan. 1919.
3756 James, Herbert William, 1 Jan. 1919.
3758 Jebb, Georgina Martha, Mrs., 1 Jan. 1919.
3759 Jeeves, Isabel Blanche, 1 Jan. 1919.
3760 Jefferies, Marguerite, 1 Jan. 1919.
3761 Jeffrey, Edward James, 1 Jan. 1919.
3762 Jenkins, Frances Edith, 1 Jan. 1919.
3763 Jenkins, Jenkin, 1 Jan. 1919.
3764 Jennings, Ida, Mrs., 1 Jan. 1919.
3765 Jerram, Frederick Horace Oldershaw, 1 Jan. 1919.
3766 Johnson, Dorothy, 1 Jan. 1919.
3767 Johnson, Edith Clara, 1 Jan. 1919.
3768 Johnson, John Ben, 1 Jan. 1919.
3769 Johnson, Violet Charlotte, Mrs., 1 Jan. 1919.
3770 Johnson, Violet Seymour, Mrs., 1 Jan. 1919.
3771 Johnston, John Ewing, 1 Jan. 1919.
3772 Johnston, Mary Ingham, Mrs., 1 Jan. 1919.
3773 Johnstone, Ethel Rose, Mrs., 1 Jan. 1919.
3774 Johnstone, Frances Lucy, 1 Jan. 1919.
3775 Jones, Margaret Ellen, 1 Jan. 1919.
3776 Jones, Ann Laugharne Phillips Griffith, 1 Jan. 1919.
3778 Jones, Thomas Lionel, 1 Jan. 1919.
3779 Jones, William Tudor, 1 Jan. 1919.
3780 Jordan, William Ezra, 1 Jan. 1919.
3781 Joy, George William, 1 Jan. 1919.
3782 Kay, Edward, 1 Jan. 1919.
3783 Keeling, Dorothy Clarissa, 1 Jan. 1919.
3784 Kemble, Virginia Margaret, 1 Jan. 1919.
3785 Kennedy, James Hutchinson, 1 Jan. 1919.
3786 Kentish, Hilda Mary, Mrs., 1 Jan. 1919.
3787 Kentish, Ida Clementina, 1 Jan. 1919.
3788 Knibb, Frederick Charles, 1 Jan. 1919.
3789 Lacey, Ada, 1 Jan. 1919.

3790 Lambourn, Frank Harper, 1 Jan. 1919.
3791 Laming, Evelyn Hamar, Mrs., 1 Jan. 1919
3792 Lander, Richard Gilbert, 1 Jan. 1919.
3793 Lander, Sidney Montem, 1 Jan. 1919
3794 Langston, Jessie Eleanor, 1 Jan. 1919.
3795 Large, Robert James, 1 Jan. 1919.
3796 Latham, George, 1 Jan. 1919.
3797 Lattey, Maud, 1 Jan. 1919.
3798 Law, Laura Jessie, 1 Jan. 1919.
3799 Lawrence, Thomas David, 1 Jan. 1919.
3800 Leaver, Frederick John, 1 Jan. 1919.
3801 Leighton, Jane Creagh, 1 Jan. 1919.
3802 Leslie, Arthur Trevor O'Bryen, 1 Jan. 1919.
3803 Lester, Léontine Isabelle Emmeline, Mrs., 1 Jan. 1919.
3804 Lewin, Isabella Marion, Mrs., 1 Jan. 1919.
3805 Ligat, John Mackinlay, 1 Jan. 1919.
3806 Lightfoot, C. H., Mrs., 1 Jan. 1919.
3807 Lile, Henry John, 1 Jan. 1919.
3808 Limming, William Thomas, 1 Jan. 1919.
3809 Lindsell, Iris le Strange, 1 Jan. 1919.
3810 Lister, Rev. Irvine, 1 Jan. 1919.
3811 Little, James Mason, 1 Jan. 1919.
3812 Lloyd, Fred, 1 Jan. 1919.
3813 Long, Arthur William, 1 Jan. 1919.
3814 Lowman, Rose Frances, 1 Jan. 1919.
3815 Lumsden, William Watt, 1 Jan. 1919.
3816 Lyon, Isabella Romanes, Mrs., 1 Jan. 1919.
3817 McBride, John Corbet, 1 Jan. 1919.
3818 McCarthy, John William Henry, 1 Jan. 1919.
3819 McClellan, Sarah Georgina Corbetta, Mrs., 1 Jan. 1919.
3820 Mace, William Ethrington, 1 Jan. 1919.
3821 Macklin, Barbara, Mrs., 1 Jan. 1919.
3822 Maclean, Thomas Finlay, 1 Jan. 1919.
3823 McLean, 1 Jan. 1919.
3824 McNaughton, John Love, 1 Jan. 1919.
3825 McNeile, Mary Bridget, 1 Jan. 1919.
3826 McPherson, Thomas, 1 Jan. 1919.
3827 McRae, Bessie, Mrs., 1 Jan. 1919.
3828 Magruder, Maryel Alpina, Mrs., 1 Jan. 1919.
3829 Maleham, George Edgar, 1 Jan. 1919.
3830 Mann, Walter George, 1 Jan. 1919.
3831 Massie, Anne, 1 Jan. 1919.
3832 Mauvan, Agnes Jessie, 1 Jan. 1919.
3833 Mawby, Lilian Edith, 1 Jan. 1919.
3834 Maxwell, Marion Winefrid, 1 Jan. 1919.
3835 May, Irene Harriet Bourne Seaburne Bourne-, 1 Jan. 1919.
3836 May, Walter Baillie, 1 Jan. 1919.
3837 Meakin, George Healey, 1 Jan. 1919.
3838 Meakin, Mary Ridgway, 1 Jan. 1919.
3839 Medcalf, Herbert, 1 Jan. 1919.　(M.)
3840 Meek, Elizabeth Muriel Grant-, 1 Jan. 1919.
3841 Merriles, Alexander Horsburgh, 1 Jan. 1919.
3842 Merry, Henry Edward Dilke, 1 Jan. 1919.
3843 Mervyn, Muriel Hermione Marion, 1 Jan. 1919.
3844 Michaelis, Marie, 1 Jan. 1919.
3845 Middlemiss, John, 1 Jan. 1919.
3846 Middleton, John, 1 Jan. 1919.
3847 Midgley, John William, 1 Jan. 1919.
3849 Millar, Henry Horatio, 1 Jan. 1919.
3850 Milligan, Helena Mary, Mrs., 1 Jan. 1919.
3851 Mills, Janet Mélanie Ailsa, 1 Jan. 1919.
3852 Monck, Louise Emilia, 1 Jan. 1919.
3853 Moore, Herbert Joseph, 1 Jan. 1919.
3854 Morgan, Harold Roland, 1 Jan. 1919.
3855 Morgan, Robert Upton, 1 Jan. 1919.
3856 Morrison, Florence Mildred, Mrs., 1 Jan. 1919.
3857 Mortimer, Robert Richardson, 1 Jan. 1919.
3858 Muirhead, Hon. Mrs. Katharine Charlotte Elizabeth Stewart, 1 Jan. 1919.
3859 Mundy, William Charles, 1 Jan. 1919.
3860 Murch, John, 1 Jan. 1919.
3861 Murphy, Ellen Theodora, Lady, 1 Jan. 1919.
3862 Neame, Maud Kathleen Frances, Mrs., 1 Jan. 1919.
3863 Neilson, Katherine Helen, 1 Jan. 1919.
3864 New, Evelyn Helen Johnston, 1 Jan. 1919
3865 Newton, Susan, Mrs., 1 Jan. 1919.
3866 Nicholson, Thomas, 1 Jan. 1919.
3867 Nicoll, Thomas Alexander, 1 Jan. 1919.
3868 Nightingale, Thomas Herbert, 1 Jan. 1919.
3869 Norton, Eleanor Millicent, 1 Jan. 1919.
3870 Norton, Jessie Jane Jardine, Mrs., 1 Jan. 1919.
3871 Oakshett, Owen James, 1 Jan. 1919.
3872 O'Byrne, John, 1 Jan. 1919.
3873 O'Callaghan, Richard Grainger Dennis, 1 Jan. 1919.
3874 Ogden, Alice, 1 Jan. 1919.
3875 Oliver, Charlotte, 1 Jan. 1919.
3876 Orman, Frederick Brook, 1 Jan. 1919.
3877 Orpen, Ida Grace Victoria, 1 Jan. 1919.
3878 Osborne, David, 1 Jan. 1919.
3879 Ouzman, William Charles, 1 Jan. 1919.
3880 Owen, Frederick William, 1 Jan. 1919.
3881 Owen, Thomas, 1 Jan. 1919.
3882 Page, James, 1 Jan. 1919.
3883 Page, William Charles, 1 Jan. 1919.
3884 Painter, Thomas Abbott, 1 Jan. 1919.
3885 Palmer, Nellie Hurcomb, 1 Jan. 1919.
3886 Pascoe, Frederick Richard, 1 Jan. 1919.
3887 Paterson, Thomas, 1 Jan. 1919.
3888 Pawson, Herbert Alfred James, 1 Jan. 1919.

3890 Pearce, William Sidney, 1 Jan. 1919.
3891 Peek, William Heath, 1 Jan. 1919.
3892 Penny, Richard, 1 Jan. 1919.
3893 Perkins, Sydney, 1 Jan. 1919.
3894 Pérot, Louise Pauline, 1 Jan. 1919.
3895 Phillimore, Ethel Maud, 1 Jan. 1919.
3896 Philip, Alexander John, 1 Jan. 1919.
3897 Phillips, Eric Taylor, 1 Jan. 1919.
3898 Phillips, Margaret, Mrs., 1 Jan. 1919.
3899 Philpot, Harold Percy, 1 Jan. 1919.
3900 Philpot, Thomas, 1 Jan. 1919.
3901 Philps, Evelyn Chapman, Mrs., 1 Jan. 1919.
3902 Pickles, Edward Llewellyn, 1 Jan. 1919.
3903 Player, William John Percy, 1 Jan. 1919.
3904 Pochin, Edmund Arthur Norman, 1 Jan. 1919.
3905 Pochin, Harold Nichols, 1 Jan. 1919.
3906 Pollard, Frederick Ernest, 1 Jan. 1919. (M.)
3907 Portal, Louise Rosemary Kathleen Virgina, Lady, 1 Jan. 1919.
3908 Pott, Katharine Frances Wilson, 1 Jan. 1919.
3909 Powell, Hugh Falkenberg, 1 Jan. 1919.
3910 Powney, Cecil Du Pre Penton, 1 Jan. 1919.
3911 Prendergast, Maud Dora Josephine, 1 Jan. 1919.
3912 Price, Gertrude Rangeley Stanley, Mrs., 1 Jan. 1919.
3913 Price, Richard, 1 Jan. 1919.
3914 Prichard, Richard John, 1 Jan. 1919.
3915 Pride, Herbert Charles, 1 Jan. 1919.
3916 Proctor, Vernon, 1 Jan. 1919.
3917 Putnam, William Clarke, 1 Jan. 1919.
3918 Ramsay, James, 1 Jan. 1919.
3920 Redstone, Lilian Jane, 1 Jan. 1919.
3921 Reed, Alice Clay, Mrs., 1 Jan. 1919.
3922 Reed, Harbottle, 1 Jan. 1919.
3923 Rees, Frederick William, 1 Jan. 1919.
3924 Reeve, Georgina Ruth, 1 Jan. 1919.
3925 Reid, David Alexander, 1 Jan. 1919.
3926 Reiss, Phyllis Emily, Mrs., 1 Jan. 1919.
3927 Rendle, Evangeline Annette Harriett, Mrs., 1 Jan. 1919.
3929 Reynolds, Arthur Charles, 1 Jan. 1919.
3930 Reynolds, Henry George, 1 Jan. 1919.
3931 Rhodes, Caroline Maud, Mrs., 1 Jan. 1919.
3932 Richards, Francis Bartlett, 1 Jan. 1919.
3933 Richmond, Annie Catherine Mary, 1 Jan. 1919.
3934 Ridsdale, Herbert Wheatley, 1 Jan. 1919.
3935 Ritchie, Mary, Mrs., 1 Jan. 1919.
3936 Roberts, Ronald Cleave, 1 Jan. 1919.
3937 Robertson, Annie, 1 Jan. 1919.
3938 Robertson, Mary Elizabette, 1 Jan. 1919.
3940 Robinson, Elizabeth Street, Mrs., 1 Jan. 1919.
3941 Robinson, Robert Hervey St. Clair, 1 Jan. 1919.
3942 Robson, Constance Evelyn, Mrs., 1 Jan. 1919.
3943 Roche, Elizabeth Jane, 1 Jan. 1919.
3944 Rogers, Henry Montague, 1 Jan. 1919.
3945 Rogers, Rose Sophia, 1 Jan. 1919.
3946 Rolfe, Ethel Blanche, 1 Jan. 1919.
3947 Ross, Gladys Ethel, 1 Jan. 1919.
3948 Rotton, Letitia, 1 Jan. 1919.
3949 Rule, Alexander, 1 Jan. 1919.
3950 Russell, Alexandra Alberta, 1 Jan. 1919.
3951 Russell, Rev. Cecil Edward, 1 Jan. 1919.
3952 Russell, Mildred, 1 Jan. 1919.
3953 Rusten, John Albert Edgar, 1 Jan. 1919.
3954 Ryland, Edith Smith, Mrs., 1 Jan. 1919.
3955 Salmond, Elaine Marguerite, Mrs., 1 Jan. 1919.
3956 Samson, Howard Lewis, 1 Jan. 1919.
3957 Sandwell, Percy William, 1 Jan. 1919.
3958 Savage, Joseph, 1 Jan. 1919.
3959 Saville, Daniel Benjamin Sheriff, 1 Jan. 1919.
3960 Scott, Ina Lochhead, 1 Jan. 1919.
3961 Scott, John, 1 Jan. 1919.
3962 Shaw, Donald Stuart, 1 Jan. 1919.
3963 Shaw, Elsie Marie, 1 Jan. 1919.
3964 Sheppard, John Tresidder, 1 Jan. 1919.
3965 Shipley, Walter Henry Foster, 1 Jan. 1919.
3966 Shorter, Albert Edward, 1 Jan. 1919.
3967 Sidebottom, Samuel, 1 Jan. 1919.
3968 Simcock, James, 1 Jan. 1919.
3969 Simmons, Frederick, 1 Jan. 1919.
3970 Simpson, David, 1 Jan. 1919.
3971 Skipwith, Richard Edward, 1 Jan. 1920.
3972 Slater, Quintin Fleming, 1 Jan. 1919.
3973 Slator, Edward, 1 Jan. 1919.
3974 Slaughter, Leonard Lansdell, 1 Jan. 1919.
3975 Smart, John Manson, 1 Jan. 1919.
3976 Smith, Arthur Ives, 1 Jan. 1919.
3977 Smith, Ernest Arthur, 1 Jan. 1919.
3978 Smith, Lewis William, 1 Jan. 1919.
3979 Smith, Noel William Kelland Isbister, 1 Jan. 1919.
3980 Smyth, Ethel Downing, Mrs., 1 Jan. 1919.
3981 Smyth, John Cecil, 1 Jan. 1919.
3982 Soames, Mabel Janet, Mrs., 1 Jan. 1919.
3983 Solly, Henry William, 1 Jan. 1919.
3984 Sparrow, Guy, 1 Jan. 1919.
3985 Spearman, Jessie Aubrey, Mrs., 1 Jan. 1919.
3986 Spellar, William David, 1 Jan. 1919.
3987 Spence, Alfred, 1 Jan. 1919.
3988 Spencer, Gladys Marion, 1 Jan. 1919.
3989 Spencer, William Arthur, 1 Jan. 1919.
3990 Stack, Susan, Mrs., 1 Jan. 1919.
3991 Stanworth, James, 1 Jan. 1919.

3992 Starbuck, Thomas William, 1 Jan. 1919.
3993 Steele, Alfred Lilburn, 1 Jan. 1919.
3994 Steele, Reginald Johns, 1 Jan. 1919.
3995 Stenning, William Lees, 1 Jan. 1919.
3996 Stevens, George Douglas, 1 Jan. 1919.
3997 Stevenson, Arnold, 1 Jan. 1919.
3998 Stevenson, Stansmore Leslie Dean Macaulay, Mrs., 1 Jan. 1919.
3999 Stewart, Edward Pakenham, 1 Jan. 1919.
4000 Stewart. Isabella Forbes, 1 Jan. 1919.
4001 Stewart, James, 1 Jan. 1919.
4002 Stewart, William Alexander, 1 Jan. 1919.
4004 Stoddart, Swinton, 1 Jan. 1919.
4005 Stokes, Madel Louise, 1 Jan. 1919.
4006 Storey, Wilfred Robinson, 1 Jan. 1919.
4007 Stubbington, Ruby, 1 Jan. 1919.
4008 Sturgeon, Robert Wallace, 1 Jan. 1919.
4009 Sutherland, Alexander, 1 Jan. 1919.
4010 Sutton, Kathleen Alice, Mrs., 1 Jan. 1919.
4011 Swire, William, 1 Jan. 1919.
4012 Swornsbourne, Mabel Edith, 1 Jan. 1919.
4013 Sykes, George, 1 Jan. 1919. (M.)
4014 Symonds, William North, 1 Jan. 1919.
4015 Tallack, Francis Harold Cass, 1 Jan. 1919.
4016 Tanner, Mary Elizabeth, 1 Jan. 1919.
4017 Tear, Richard Frederick Charles, 1 Jan. 1919
4018 Teasdale, John, 1 Jan. 1919.
4019 Tebbitt, Mabel, Mrs., 1 Jan. 1919.
4021 Thomas, Arnold, 1 Jan. 1919.
4022 Thomas, William Henry, 1 Jan. 1919.
4023 Thompson, Frank, 1 Jan. 1919.
4024 Thompson, George Tyrrell, 1 Jan. 1919.
4025 Thomson, David, 1 Jan. 1919. (M.)
4026 Thomson, John, 1 Jan. 1919.
4027 Thomson, Margaret Ellen, Lady, 1 Jan. 1919.
4028 Thorne, Annie Marion, 1 Jan. 1919.
4029 Timbury, Henry Thomas, 1 Jan. 1919.
4030 Tindall, Edith Pelham, Mrs., 1 Jan. 1919.
4031 Tipping, Arthur Bramble, Mrs., 1 Jan. 1919.
4032 Tod, David Inman, 1 Jan. 1919. (M.)
4033 Todd, John Thomas, 1 Jan. 1919.
4034 Toghill, Edward Sergent, 1 Jan. 1919.
4035 Tonkin, John, 1 Jan. 1919.
4036 Toomer, Edith, Mrs., 1 Jan. 1919.
4037 Townley, Rosalinde Cecil, 1 Jan. 1919.
4038 Trehearne, Sarah Emuss, 1 Jan. 1919.
4039 Trestrail, Alfred Bond, 1 Jan. 1919.
4040 Tufnail, Harry Philip, 1 Jan. 1919.
4041 Tufnell, Wyndham Frederick, 1 Jan. 1919. (M.)
4042 Turnbull, John, 1 Jan. 1919.
4043 Tutcher, William Arthur, 1 Jan. 1919.
4044 Tweedy, Dorothea, 1 Jan. 1919.
4045 Upton, William James, 1 Jan. 1919.
4046 Valentine, Catherine, Mrs., 1 Jan. 1919.
4047 Vaux, Emily Eve Lellam, Mrs., 1 Jan. 1919.
4048 Venner, George Edward Sidebottom, 1 Jan. 1919.
4049 Vereker, Frances Gore, Mrs. George Medlicott, 1 Jan. 1919.
4050 Verge, Lionel Arthur Frederick, 1 Jan. 1919. (M.)
4051 Vigo, Benjamin William, 1 Jan. 1919.
4052 Waddingham, William Hart, 1 Jan. 1919.
4053 Wain, Thomas, 1 Jan. 1919.
4054 Walker, Eliza Bagshawe-, 1 Jan. 1919.
4055 Walker, Percy, 1 Jan. 1919.
4056 Wallace, Agnes Kendall, Mrs., 1 Jan. 1919.
4059 Ward, Arthur John Hanslip, 1 Jan. 1919.
4060 Ward, Jeannie Wright, 1 Jan. 1919.
4061 Warrack, Frances Jane, 1 Jan. 1919.
4062 Warren, Edith Mary, 1 Jan. 1919.
4063 Waterfield, May Constance Flora, 1 Jan. 1919.
4064 Watson, Eva Gordon, Mrs., 1 Jan. 1919.
4065 Watts, Charles Haynes, 1 Jan. 1919.
4066 Way, Arthur, 1 Jan. 1919.
4067 Way, Philip Greville Hugh, 1 Jan. 1919.
4068 Weakner, John Johnson, 1 Jan. 1919.
4069 Webster, Avice, 1 Jan. 1919.
4070 Weigall, Caroline Rachel Selina Priscilla, 1 Jan. 1919.
4071 Welch, Jessie Muriel Kemp-, 1 Jan. 1919.
4072 Wells, Victor Ernest, 1 Jan. 1919.
4073 Wenley, George Seton Veitch, 1 Jan. 1919.
4074 West, James Grey, 1 Jan. 1919.
4075 Wharton, Edith Hilda, 1 Jan. 1919.
4076 Wheatley, Christopher William, 1 Jan. 1919.
4077 Wheeler, Florence Louisa Felicia, Mrs. Bourne-, 1 Jan. 1919.
4078 Whitaker, Frances Henrietta, 1 Jan. 1919.
4079 Whitehead, Alfred Kershaw, 1 Jan. 1919.
4080 Whitehead, Maude Lilian, 1 Jan. 1919.
4081 Whitt, Edith, Mrs., 1 Jan. 1919.
4082 Wilford, Edward Charles, 1 Jan. 1919.
4083 Wilkinson, Harry William John, 1 Jan. 1919.
4084 Williams, Albert George, 1 Jan. 1919.
4085 Williams, William Henry, 1 Jan. 1919.
4086 Williams, William Henry, 1 Jan. 1919.
4087 Willmot, Nellie Pratchett, Mrs., 1 Jan. 1919.
4088 Willoughby, John William, 1 Jan. 1919.
4089 Wilson, Dorothy Holmes, 1 Jan. 1919.
4090 Wilson, Edith Marguerite, 1 Jan. 1919.
4091 Wilson, Helen, 1 Jan. 1919.
4092 Wilyman, Charles, 1 Jan. 1919.

4094 Windsor, Arthur Whalesby, 1 Jan. 1919.
4095 Wing, Fred Augustus, 1 Jan. 1919.
4096 Winter, Mildred Marion, Mrs., 1 Jan. 1919.
4097 Wood, William Henry, 1 Jan. 1919.
4098 Woodhead, Esther, 1 Jan. 1919.
4099 Woodward, Sidney John, 1 Jan. 1919.
4100 Wright, Hugh, 1 Jan. 1919.
4101 Wyld, Frances Mary, 1 Jan. 1919.
4102 Wynne, Frederick Grant, 1 Jan. 1919.
4103 Yockney, Alfred, 1 Jan. 1919.
4104 Young, William Edward, 1 Jan. 1919.
4105 Younghusband, Herbert William, 1 Jan. 1919.
4106 Mya, Ebrahim Ahmed, alias Be Shwe, 1 Jan. 1919.
4107 Alexander, Juliet, Mrs., 1 Jan. 1919.
4108 Armitstead, Henry, 1 Jan. 1919.
4109 Bakhsh, Shaikh Mahbub, 1 Jan. 1919.
4110 Barker, Raymond Thomas, 1 Jan. 1919.
4111 Beachcroft, Betty, Mrs., 1 Jan. 1919.
4112 Beard, William, 1 Jan. 1919.
4113 Bennett, Arthur Russell, 1 Jan. 1919.
4114 Bhore, Margaret Wilke, Mrs., 1 Jan. 1919.
4115 Billimoria, Shapurji Bomanji, 1 Jan. 1919.
4116 Birch, George, 1 Jan. 1919.
4117 Black, Muriel, Mrs., 1 Jan. 1919.
4118 Brent, Margaret, Mrs., 1 Jan. 1919.
4119 Brereton, Charles Cecil Trelawny, 1 Jan. 1919.
4120 Buckner, Frederick Percival, 1 Jan. 1919.
4121 Burt, Bryce Chudleigh, 1 Jan. 1919.
4122 Bya, Maung Maung, 1 Jan. 1919.
4123 Chand, Lala Fateh, 1 Jan. 1919.
4124 Chand, Pandit Narayan, 1 Jan. 1919.
4125 Chandar, Lala Ram, 1 Jan. 1919.
4126 Cole, Claude Willoughby, 1 Jan. 1919.
4127 Collier, Joseph Veasy, 1 Jan. 1919.
4128 Cowan, John, 1 Jan. 1919.
4130 Cuttriss, Charles Arthur, 1 Jan. 1919.
4131 Dastur, Sunbai Kaikobad, Mrs., 1 Jan. 1919.
4132 Davidson, Marion, Mrs., 1 Jan. 1919.
4133 De, Sarojini, Mrs., 1 Jan. 1919.
4134 Dennis, Rendall Hamilton, 1 Jan. 1919.
4135 Dunne, Walter Clement Goddard, 1 Jan. 1919.
4136 Edye, Ernest Henry Huish, 1 Jan. 1919.
4137 Eggar, Mildred Fanny, 1 Jan. 1919.
4138 Franklin, Mabel, 1 Jan. 1919.
4139 Glackan, Sydney Hugh, 1 Jan. 1919.
4140 Gomes, Bernard Francis, 1 Jan. 1919.
4141 Greaves, Isabel, 1 Jan. 1919.
4142 Guan, Quah Cheng, 1 Jan. 1919.
4143 Habib, Maulvi Muhammad Savan, 1 Jan. 1919.
4144 Hai, Mian Abdul, 1 Jan. 1919.
4145 Hall, Frederick Joseph, 1 Jan. 1919.
4146 Hammond, Ernest Walter, 1 Jan. 1919.
4147 Harvey, Anita, Mrs., 1 Jan. 1919.
4148 Hind, Robert William, 1 Jan. 1919.
4149 Hitchcock, Richard Howard, 1 Jan. 1919.
4150 Jan, Chaudhri Nabi, 1 Jan. 1919.
4151 Jarry, Rev. Frederick William, 1 Jan. 1919.
4152 Johnstone, Thomas White, 1 Jan. 1919.
4153 Khan, Sardar Bahadur Sardar Abdul Rashid, 1 Jan. 1919.
4154 Khan, Khan Sahib Ahmed Mir, 1 Jan. 1919.
4155 Khan, Khan Bahadur Ain-ud-Din, 1 Jan. 1919.
4156 Khan, Chaudhri Ali Akbar, 1 Jan. 1919.
4157 Khan, Malik Allah Bakhsh, 1 Jan. 1919.
4158 Khan, Malik Ghulam Muhammad, 1 Jan. 1919.
4159 Khan, Subedar-Major Khan Bahadur Kurban Ali, 1 Jan. 1919.
4160 Khan, Khan Bahadur Mohammed Ashraff, 1 Jan. 1919.
4161 Khan, Khan Bahadur Munshi Muhammad Ali, 1 Jan. 1919.
4162 Khan, Khan Bahadur Musa, 1 Jan. 1919.
4163 Khan, Khan Bahadur Sohbat, 1 Jan. 1919.
4164 Khan, Khan Bahadur Sardar Wahab, 1 Jan. 1919.
4165 Kirkpatrick, Cecil William, 1 Jan. 1919.
4166 Kirwan, Lionel Edward, 1 Jan. 1919.
4167 Kothawala, Malcolm Rataji, 1 Jan. 1919.
4168 Lajoie, Louis Patrick, 1 Jan. 1919.
4169 Lal, Chaudhri Kishori, 1 Jan. 1919.
4170 Lalkalka, Ilinabai, 1 Jan. 1919.
4171 Lane, Ernest, 1 Jan. 1919.
4172 Langer, Charles Frederick, 1 Jan. 1919.
4173 Langley, Frank, 1 Jan. 1919.
4175 Lawrence, Alexander Samuel, 1 Jan. 1919.
4176 Leach, Arthur John, 1 Jan. 1919.
4177 Leach, Milton, 1 Jan. 1919.
4178 Lee, Frederick Reginald, 1 Jan. 1919.
4179 Letton, Charles Thomas, 1 Jan 1919.
4181 Manibhai, Bai Champabahen, 1 Jan. 1919.
4182 Mann, David Barry, 1 Jan. 1919.
4183 May, Charlotte Dorothea, Mrs., 1 Jan. 1919.
4184 McPherson, Duncan Louis, 1 Jan. 1919.
4185 Mehta, Homia, Mrs., 1 Jan. 1919.
4186 Muhammad, Shaikh Yakub Vazir, 1 Jan. 1919.
4187 Mule, Bhalchandra Vaman, 1 Jan. 1919.
4188 Nag, Khagendra Chandra, 1 Jan. 1919.
4189 Narayan, Pandit Anand, 1 Jan. 1919.
4190 Nath, Rai Bahadur Amar, 1 Jan. 1919.
4191 Nath, Lala Baij, 1 Jan. 1919.
4192 Newton, Zoe Ellesmere Davidson, Mrs., 1 Jan. 1919.
4193 Nun, Malik Sahib Khan, 1 Jan. 1919.
4194 Nyun, Maung, 1 Jan. 1919.

4195 Ostrehan, Malcolm, 1 Jan. 1919.
4196 Padam, Rajaram Tukaram, 1 Jan. 1919.
4197 Pant, Pandit Bhola Dat, 1 Jan. 1919.
4198 Pattadar, Babu Rajani Kanta, 1 Jan. 1919.
4199 Pennell, Dorothy, Mrs., 1 Jan. 1919.
4200 Perkins, Winifred Ward, Mrs., 1 Jan. 1919.
4201 Phillips, John Ruskin, 1 Jan. 1919.
4202 Pillay, Hari Krishna, 1 Jan. 1919.
4203 Price, Julian Hugh, 1 Jan. 1919.
4204 Pudumji, Hirabai, Mrs., 1 Jan. 1919.
4205 Rai, Rai Bahadur Biswambhar, 1 Jan. 1919.
4206 Ramanbhai, Vidhyagouri, Mrs., 1 Jan. 1919.
4207 Roberts, Charles Herbert, 1 Jan. 1919.
4208 Rozario, Michael Anthony, 1 Jan. 1919.
4209 Ruegg, Alfred James, 1 Jan. 1919.
4210 Saheb, Kunvari Rupalbai, 1 Jan. 1919.
4211 Saligram, Rai Bahadur, 1 Jan. 1919.
4212 Sarkar, Babu Panchanan, 1 Jan. 1919.
4213 Singh, Bawa Bhag, 1 Jan. 1919.
4214 Singh, Lieutenant Ishar, 1 Jan. 1919.
4215 Singh, Munshi Sundar, 1 Jan. 1919.
4216 Stewart, Maude, Mrs., 1 Jan. 1919.
4217 Swan, Mary, Mrs., 1 Jan. 1919.
4218 Taylor, Charles Lewis, 1 Jan. 1919.
4219 Taylor, Thomas, 1 Jan. 1919.
4220 Thaddeus, Mesrup, 1 Jan. 1919.
4221 Thorne, Theophilis, 1 Jan. 1919.
4222 Turner, Muriel Clara, Mrs., 1 Jan. 1919
4223 Tomes, William Jameson, 1 Jan. 1919.
4224 Wagstaff, Harry Finnis, 1 Jan. 1919.
4225 Walker, Margaret Dewar, Mrs., 1 Jan. 1919
4226 Wathen, Frederick Blunt, 1 Jan. 1919.
4227 Webb, George Richard, 1 Jan. 1919.
4228 Welman, Helen Owen, Mrs., 1 Jan. 1919.
4229 Whitcombe, May Julia, 1 Jan. 1919.
4230 Williamson, Florence, Mrs., 1 Jan. 1919.
4231 Williamson, Horace, 1 Jan. 1919.
4232 Shapley, George William Thomas, 1 Jan. 1919.
4233 Patterson, William Baker, 1 Jan. 1919.
4234 Bennett, George Wilfred, 1 Jan. 1919.
4235 Bardsley, Robert Vickers, 1 Jan. 1919.
4236 Warder, Gerald Edwin, 1 Jan. 1919.
4237 Forster, Arnold John, 1 Jan. 1919.
4238 Butcher, Alfred William, 1 Jan. 1919. (M.)
4239 Collier, Frank Norton Proctor, 1 Jan. 1919. (M.)
4240 Corrie, William Edward, 1 Jan. 1919. (M.)
4241 Davies, Fred, 1 Jan. 1919. (M.)
4242 Davis, Spencer, 1 Jan. 1919. (M.)
4243 De Wet, Nicholas Johannes, 1 Jan. 1919. (M.)
4244 Ellis, Reuben, 1 Jan. 1919. (M.)
4245 Hopkins, Francis Arthur, 1 Jan. 1919. (M.)
4246 Humberseth, John Johansen, 1 Jan. 1919. (M.)
4247 Huxtable, Geoffrey, 1 Jan. 1919. (M.)
4248 Mills, Charles Egerton, 1 Jan. 1919. (M.)
4249 Pomeroy, Arthur William Joblins, 1 Jan. 1919. (M.)
4250 Powell, William Clive, 1 Jan. 1919. (M.)
4251 Ross, Alexander Joseph, 1 Jan. 1919. (M.)
4252 Saies, Lorenso, 1 Jan. 1919. (M.)
4253 Small, William, 1 Jan. 1919. (M.)
4254 Sutherland, John, 1 Jan. 1919. (M.)
4255 Tryon, Henry Covey, 1 Jan. 1919. (M.)
4256 Wardroper, Percy Redesdale, 1 Jan. 1919. (M.)
4257 Willox, George Martin, 1 Jan. 1919. (M.)
4258 Woodlock, David William Fair, 1 Jan. 1919. (M.)
4259 Ash, Frederick Cecil, 1 Jan. 1919. (M.)
4260 Bampton, John Augustus Hamilton, 1 Jan. 1919. (M.)
4261 Banks, Thomas Rivers, 1 Jan. 1919. (M.)
4262 Belchamber, Douglas Foster, 1 Jan. 1919. (M.)
4263 Blackwood, Noel Pinkstan O'Reilly, 1 Jan. 1919. (M.)
4264 Broadbent, John Stuart, 1 Jan. 1919. (M.)
4265 Butler, Richard Jefferson, 1 Jan. 1919. (M.)
4266 Campbell, Malcolm, 1 Jan. 1919. (M.)
4267 Coutts, Colin, 1 Jan. 1919. (M.)
4268 Davies, Sellick, 1 Jan. 1919. (M.)
4269 Denny, William Bernard Valentine, 1 Jan. 1919. (M.)
4270 Everett, Roland Tylor, 1 Jan. 1919. (M.)
4271 Ezra, Ellice, 1 Jan. 1919. (M.)
4272 Gerard, Charles Edward, 1 Jan 1919. (M.)
4273 Gibbs, Gerard Yardley, 1 Jan. 1919. (M.)
4274 Gladstone, Albert Charles, 1 Jan. 1919. (M.)
4275 Grey, Percy, 1 Jan. 1919. (M.)
4276 Gwatkin, Reginald Dugleby Stapleton, 1 Jan. 1919. (M.)
4277 Harding, Robert Arthur Cotton, 1 Jan. 1919. (M.)
4278 Lee, John Dalby, 1 Jan. 1919. (M.)
4279 Monks, Thomas Vernon, 1 Jan. 1919. (M.)
4280 Montgomerie, William Dunn, 1 Jan. 1919. (M.)
4281 Morgan, Hugh, 1 Jan. 1919. (M.)
4282 Ord, Benjamin, 1 Jan. 1919. (M.)
4283 Pattinson, Edward Harold, 1 Jan. 1919. (M.)
4284 Salmon, Ronald Martin, 1 Jan. 1919. (M.)
4285 Shedden, William St. John, 1 Jan. 1919. (M.)
4286 Tysoe-Smith, George, 1 Jan. 1919. (M.)
4287 Vernon, Ronald Clifton, 1 Jan. 1919. (M.)
4288 Waris-ud-Din, Rev., 1 Jan. 1919. (M.)
4289 Whidborne, Charles Stanley Lucas, 1 Jan. 1919. (M.)
4290 Whittle, Fortescue Glynne, 1 Jan. 1919. (M.)
4291 Baker, Francis Barrington, 1 Jan. 1919. (M.)
4292 Barrow, Claude, 1 Jan. 1919. (M.)
4293 Barry, Louis Charles, 1 Jan. 1919. (M.)
4294 Bogle, Robert, 1 Jan. 1919. (M.)

4295 Chandler, John Marsden, 1 Jan. 1919. (M.)
4296 Dingle, Henry James, 1 Jan. 1919. (M.)
4297 Dinsdale, Thomas Errington Coutts, 1 Jan. 1919. (M.)
4298 Fawcett, Walter, 1 Jan. 1919. (M.)
4299 George, Willy Oswald, 1 Jan. 1919. (M.)
4300 Gibson, John George, 1 Jan. 1919. (M.)
4301 Holman, Joseph Guest, 1 Jan. 1919. (M.)
4302 Hudson, William, 1 Jan. 1919. (M.)
4303 Hunt, Henry Charles, 1 Jan. 1919. (M.)
4305 Smith, Charles William Gates, 1 Jan. 1919. (M.)
4306 Spurling, Charles George, 1 Jan. 1919. (M.)
4307 Stillwell, Gloria Ethel Ada, 1 Jan. 1919. (M.)
4308 Townley, Herbert Arthur, 1 Jan. 1919. (M.)
4310 Walker, Joseph, 1 Jan. 1919. (M.)
4311 Walsh, Arthur, 1 Jan. 1919. (M.)
4312 Whitehead, William, 1 Jan. 1919. (M.)
4313 Wrench, Charles Croyden, 1 Jan. 1919. (M.)
4314 Tod, Frederick Lewis Maitland, 1 Jan. 1919. (M.)
4315 Cripps, George Wilfitt, 1 Jan. 1919. (M.)
4316 Walton, Cyril Glanmore, 1 Jan. 1919. (M.)
4317 Effendi, Mulazim Tani Zaki Selim, 1 Jan. 1919. (M.)
4318 Beattie, Edward Allsop, 1 Jan. 1919. (M.)
4319 Allan, James Lambertini, 1 Jan. 1919. (M.)
4320 Barraclough, Jackson Gurth, 1 Jan. 1919. (M.)
4321 Browne, Charles James, 1 Jan. 1919. (M.)
4322 Hill, Garrington Lewis Watson, 1 Jan. 1919. (M.)
4323 Mallett, Thomas Robert, 1 Jan. 1919. (M.)
4324 Ward, Alexander Ivan, 1 Jan. 1919. (M.)
4325 Wardell, John Stewart Michael, 1 Jan. 1919. (M.)
4326 Williams, Ralph, 1 Jan. 1919. (M.)
4327 Arklie, Edgar Vincent, 1 Jan. 1919.
4328 Barker, Nellie, 1 Jan. 1919.
4329 Booth, Albert Joseph, 1 Jan. 1919.
4330 Cosgriff, Eugene, 1 Jan. 1919.
4331 Lorraine, Ellen Mary, 1 Jan. 1919.
4332 Shujath, Ali, 1 Jan. 1919. (M.)
4333 Thaddeus, Mesrop Gabriel, 1 Jan. 1919.
4334 Barton-Wright, Helen Muriel, Mrs., 1 Jan. 1919.
4335 Legat, Kathleen, Mrs., 1 Jan. 1919.
4336 Llewellyn, Clara Maud, 1 Jan. 1919.
4337 Philips, Enid, Mrs., 1 Jan. 1919.
4338 Baillie, Amelia Martha, Mrs., 1 Jan. 1919.
4339 Blewitt, Ethel Louisa Herries, 1 Jan. 1919.
4340 Fletcher, Fanny, 1 Jan. 1919.
4341 Hall, Rosina Marion, 1 Jan. 1919.
4342 Leary, Dennis Donald, 1 Jan. 1919.
4343 Millward, Thomas, 1 Jan. 1919.
4344 Nettleship, William Sharp, 1 Jan. 1919.
4345 Richardson, Mabel, 1 Jan. 1919.
4346 Roark, John, 1 Jan. 1919.
4347 Roberts, Florence Alice, 1 Jan. 1919.
4348 Gordon, Grace, 1 Jan. 1919.
4349 Joyce, Francis Raoul, 1 Jan. 1919.
4350 Gillespie, Gerald James, 12 Feb. 1919. (M.)
4351 Cunningham, Andrew, 12 Feb. 1919. (M.)
4352 Dalton, Ernest Albert Llewellyn, 12 Feb. 1919. (M.)
4353 Northey, Henry John, 15 Feb. 1919. (M.)
4354 Veryard, Ernest Thomas, 20 Feb. 1919. (M.)
4355 Johnson, James 24 March, 1919. (M.)
4356 O'Brien, Eugene Herbert, 24 March, 1919. (M.)
4357 Meachem, Frank, 24 March, 1919. (M.)
4358 Austin, Walter, 1 April, 1919. (M.)
4359 Gearing, Ernest Handley, 1 April, 1919. (M.)
4360 Samways, William Henry, 1 April, 1919. (M.)
4361 Stone, Ernest Stracey, 1 April, 1919. (M.)
4362 Ling, Robert, 11 April, 1919. (M.)
4363 Lloyd, Leonard Wynne, 22 April, 1919. (M.)
4364 Saville, Cyril Arthur, 22 April, 1919. (M.)
4365 Gale, Ernest John Albert, 22 April, 1919. (M.)
4366a Gasparro, Francis Christopher, 22 April, 1919. (M.)
4366b Cowan, Herbert Gladstone, 5 May, 1919. (M.)
4366c Praeger, Isonard Paul, 5 May, 1919. (M.)
4366d Davies, Alewyn Thomas, 5 May, 1919. (M.)
4366e Chidson, Montagu Reaney, 5 May, 1919. (M.)
4366f Cole, Robert Frank, 5 May, 1919. (M.)
4366g Goble, William Richard, 5 May, 1919. (M.)
4366h Holt, Edwin Brook, 5 May, 1919. (M.)
4367a Wells, Harold Arthur Thompson, 5 May, 1919. (M.)
4367b Austin, Bertram Herbert, 5 May, 1919. (M.)
4367c Short, John, 5 May, 1919.
4367d Corridon, Richard, 5 May, 1919. (M.)
4367e Kerr, Charles William Ernest, 5 May, 1919. (M.)
4367f Best, Eleanor, 9 May, 1919. (M.)
4368 Bradshaw, Frances Evelyn, 9 May, 1919. (M.)
4369 Craster, Barbara Marion, 9 May, 1919. (M.)
4370 Crisp, Annette Ina, 9 May, 1919. (M.)
4371 Eastwood, Mrs. Dorothy Sybil Montague, 9 May, 1919. (M.)
4372 Farrell, Margaret Georgina Mary, 9 May, 1919. (M.)
4373 Franklin, Olga Heather, 9 May, 1919. (M.)
4374 Eagar, Margery, Mrs., 9 May, 1919. (M.)
4375 Gye, Irene Alice, 9 May, 1919. (M.)
4376 Hardie, Muriel, 9 May, 1919. (M.)
4377 Horsey, Mrs. Ada Noel, 9 May, 1919. (M.)
4378 James, Eleanor Marian, 9 May, 1919. (M.)
4379 James, Katharine Margaret, 9 May, 1919. (M.)
4380 Johnston, Elizabeth Gairdner, 9 May, 1919. (M.)
4381 Johnston, Mrs. Florence, 9 May, 1919. (M.)
4382 Kersey, Winifred Esdaile, 9 May, 1919. (M.)
4383 Laughton, Elvira Sibyl Marie, 9 May, 1919. (M.)

4384 MacDonald, Marian Louie, 9 May, 1919. (M.)
4385 Macleod, Olive Moultrie, 9 May, 1919. (M.)
4386 MacEwan, Jean Margaret, 9 May, 1919. (M.)
4387 Mouat, Basilina Ninian, 9 May, 1919. (M.)
4388 Maunsell, Mary Helen Maxwell, 9 May, 1919. (M.)
4389 Pettit, Mrs. Isobel Helena Courtney, 9 May, 1919. (M.)
4390 Robinson, Norah Gertrude, 9 May, 1919. (M.)
4391 Rope, Irene Mary, 9 May, 1919. (M.)
4392 Rubenstein, Vera Rachel, Mrs., 9 May, 1919. (M.)
4393 Strickland, Mary Constance Elizabeth Christine, 9 May, 1919. (M.)
4394 Thorburn, Margaret Alison, 9 May, 1919. (M.)
4395 Turnbull, Helen Oliver, 9 May, 1919. (M.)
4396 Wall, Maud Amy Margaret, 9 May, 1919. (M.)
4397 Rainier, Gladys Mary, Mrs., 9 May, 1919. (M.)
4398 Robbins, William Henry, 24 May, 1919. (M.)
4399 Youngson, Alexander, 24 May, 1919. (M.)
4400 Lewis, William, 24 May, 1919. (M.)
4401 Brown, Donald Eadie, 27 May, 1919. (M.)
4402 Charlier, Leonard Clayton, 27 May, 1919. (M.)
4403 Farnley, Arthur Hambleton, 27 May, 1919. (M.)
4404 McCusker, Ralph Henry John, 27 May, 1919. (M.)
4405 Mitchelmore, Augustus John, 27 May, 1919. (M.)
4406 Rea, Basil Soame, 27 May, 1919. (M.)
4407 Witherby, Harry Forbes, 27 May, 1919. (M.)
4408 Adcock, Frank, 3 June, 1919. (M.)
4409 Allan, William, 3 June, 1919. (M.)
4410 Allingham, Gerald Carlyle, 3 June, 1919. (M.)
4411 Arundell, John Henry, 3 June, 1919. (M.)
4412 Armitage, Walter Cleveland, 3 June, 1919. (M.)
4413 Atkins, Charles Henry, 3 June, 1919. (M.)
4414 Attenborough, Ernest, 3 June, 1919. (M.)
4415 Bannon, John Joseph, 3 June, 1919. (M.)
4416 Barnett, Edwin Ernest, 3 June, 1919. (M.)
4417 Battle, William Scoley, 3 June, 1919. (M.)
4418 Beer, Arthur James, 3 June, 1919. (M.)
4419 Bennett, Alice Mary, 3 June, 1919. (M.)
4420 Bevan, Marmaduke, 3 June, 1919. (M.)
4421 Bishop, Arthur Grimwade, 3 June, 1919. (M.)
4422 Blackwood, Edgar Derwent, 3 June, 1919. (M.)
4423 Blair-White, Arthur, 3 June, 1919. (M.)
4424 Bleck, George Sebastian, 3 June, 1919. (M.)
4425 Bond, Cyril Henry Charles, 3 June, 1919. (M.)
4426 Brand, Stanley Hunt, 3 June, 1919. (M.)
4427 Brewster, William Thomas, 3 June, 1919. (M.)
4428 Brice, Ernest Gottlieb Isdeal, 3 June, 1919. (M.)
4429 Brown, George Wauchop Stewart, 3 June, 1919. (M.)
4430 Brown, Phillis Warden, 3 June, 1919. (M.)
4431 Bryan, Godfrey Middleton Eric, 3 June, 1919. (M
4432 Bryan, Thomas Edward, 3 June, 1919. (M.)
4433 Bulteel, Walter Beresford, 3 June, 1919. (M.)
4434 Bulteel, Walter Beresford, 3 June, 1919. (M.)
4435 Busby, Thomas Frederick, 3 June, 1919. (M.)
4436 Cable, Norah Evelyn, 3 June, 1919. (M.)
4137 Campbell, Donald George, 3 June, 1919. (M.)
4438 Campbell, John, 3 June, 1919. (M.)
4439 Carey, Albert John, 3 June, 1919. (M.)
4440 Carey, Hattie Maud, 3 June, 1919. (M.)
4441 Cary, Rupert Tristram Oliver, 3 June, 1919. (M.)
4442 Carr, John William, 3 June, 1919. (M.)
4443 Carthew-Yorstoun, Morden Archibald, 3 June, 1919. (M.)
4444 Challice, Sydney, 3 June, 1919. (M.)
4445 Clark, Martin Harry, 3 June, 1919. (M.)
4446 Clarke, Ernest Herbert, 3 June, 1919. (M.)
4447 Claye, Fred Wainwright, 3 June, 1919. (M.)
4448 Clegg, Herbert Edmund, 3 June, 1919. (M.)
4449 Clements, William Joseph, 3 June, 1919. (M.)
4450 Clemishaw, John, 3 June, 1919. (M.)
4451 Coates, Ernest, 3 June, 1919. (M.)
4452 Combes, Percy Matthew, 3 June, 1919. (M.)
4453 Connell, John, 3 June, 1919. (M.)
4454 Cooper, Francis John, 3 June, 1919. (M.)
4455 Corney, Albert, 3 June, 1919. (M.)
1556 Costello, George Arthur, 3 June, 1919. (M.)
4457 Cotton, Harry, 3 June, 1919. (M.)
4458 Craig, William James Robert, 3 June, 1919. (M.)
4459 Cranston, Thomas, 3 June, 1919. (M.)
4460 Crombie, Colin Ross, 3 June, 1919. (M.)
4461 Cumming, Percy, 3 June, 1919. (M.)
4462 Daglish, Gladys, 3 June, 1919. (M.)
4463 Davis, John, 3 June, 1919. (M.)
4464 Anderson, Gladys, Mrs., 3 June, 1919. (M.
4465 Doolan, Edmond, 3 June, 1919. (M.)
4466 Dugon, Arnold Louis, 3 June, 1919. (M.)
4467 Dundas, Betty, Mrs., 3 June, 1919. (M.)
4468 Dunham, Walter, 3 June, 1919. (M.)
4469 Egan, William, 3 June, 1919. (M.)
4470 Eldred, Elizabeth Francis, Mrs., 3 June, 1919. (M.)
4471 Elkin, Charlotte Emily, 3 June, 1919. (M.)
4472 Elliott, James Henry, 3 June, 1919. (M.)
4473 Elmore, Percy, 3 June, 1919. (M.)
4474 Eustace, Albert Victor, 3 June, 1919. (M.)
4475 Everett, Charles Falconer Guy, 3 June, 1919. (M.)
4476 Farmer, Frank Morley, 3 June, 1919. (M.)
4477 Field, Eric Athelstane, 3 June, 1919. (M.)
4478 Field, Edward Hubert, 3 June, 1919. (M.)
4479 Field, William Samuel, 3 June, 1919. (M.)
4480 Fitzgerald, Frank, 3 June, 1919. (M.)
4481 Fitzsimon, Samuel Ernest Sydney, 3 June, 1919. (M.)
4482 Ford, Harry Spry, 3 June, 1919. (M.)

4483 Foster, Cecily Penrose, 3 June, 1919. (M.)
4484 Fox, James Bartholomew, 3 June, 1919. (M.)
4485 Francis, Ada Emily, 3 June, 1919. (M.)
4486 Francis, Arnold Eardley, 3 June, 1919. (M.)
4487 Fry, Walter 3 June, 1919. (M.)
4488 Gardiner, Edward Cecil, 3 June, 1919. (M.)
4489 Gee, George Augustine, 3 June, 1919. (M.)
4490 Glason, John Appollonius, 3 June, 1919. (M.)
4491 Glencross, Julia. 3 June, 1919. (M.)
4492 Godfrey, Alfred Philip, 3 June, 1919. (M.)
4493 Gower, John Forbes, 3 June, 1919. (M.)
4494 Green, William Holmes, 3 June, 1919. (M.)
4495 Griffiths, William Crynant 3 June, 1919. (M.)
4496 Gunn, James, 3 June, 1919. (M.)
4497 Hampton, Thomas, 3 June, 1919. (M.)
4498 Hanbury Nigel, 3 June, 1919. (M.)
4499 Hancock, Frank, 3 June, 1919. (M.)
4500 Handy, William 3 June, 1919. (M.)
4501 Hanscombe, Stanley William, 3 June, 1919. (M.)
4502 Harcher, Ernest Edwin, 3 June, 1919. (M.)
4503 Harcourt-Brown, Monica, 3 June, 1919. (M.)
4504 Harding, Wyndham John Dorney, 3 June, 1919. (M.)
4505 Harford, Winifred Maud B., 3 June, 1919. (M.)
4506 Harman, Edmund, 3 June, 1919. (M.)
4507 Harold, Joseph, 3 June, 1919. (M.)
4508 Harrison, George, 3 June, 1919. (M.)
4509 Hartley, Richard Warburton, 3 June, 1919. (M.)
4510 Harvey, Austin Mozart, 3 June, 1919. (M.)
4511 Hatch, Ethel Francis, 3 June, 1919. (M.)
4512 Hatch, William Ashton, 3 June, 1919. (M.)
4513 Hartnell, Walter George, 3 June, 1919. (M.)
4514 Hawkes, Comley, 3 June, 1919. (M.)
4515 Hawkins, A'bert Gordon Jones, 3 June, 1919. (M.)
4516 Hayes, Ernest George, 3 June, 1919. (M.)
4517 Haywood, Harry, 3 June, 1919. (M.)
4518 Henderson, Charles Hender, 3 June, 1919. (M.)
4519 Heyworth, Beatrice Hestietha Gundreda, 3 June, 1919. (M.)
4520 Hicks, Arthur Samuel, 3 June, 1919. (M.)
4521 Hill, Frank, 3 June, 1919. (M.)
4522 Hill, Thomas Edgar, 3 June, 1919. (M.)
4523 Hobbs, Irene Decima, 3 June, 1919. (M.)
4524 Hollidge, Alec, 3 June, 1919. (M.)
4525 Holywood, Matthew, 3 June, 1919. (M.)
4526 Hunt, Thomas, 3 June, 1919. (M.)
4527 Ingle, Harry Cyril, 3 June, 1919. (M.)
4528 Isaac, William Rudolph Vernon, 3 June, 1919. (M.)
4529 Jackman. Cornelius John Gershom, 3 June, 1919. (M.)
4530 Jackson, Leonard Edward Selmas, 3 June, 1919. (M.)
4531 Jones, Francis Henry, 3 June, 1919. (M.)
4532 Johnson, Diana Mabel, 3 June, 1919. (M.)
4533 King, George William, 3 June, 1919. (M.)
4534 Kingston. Alfred Thomas, 3 June, 1919. (M.)
4535 Kinross, Ann Mary, 3 June, 1919. (M.)
4536 Kippen, James William, 3 June, 1919. (M.)
4537 Leatherbarrow, Edward John, 3 June, 1919. (M.)
4538 Leverett, Frederick William, 3 June. 1919. (M.)
4539 Lewarn, Herbert Stanley, 3 June, 1919. (M.)
4540 Lightfoot, Harriet, 3 June, 1919. (M.)
4541 Lisle, Arthur, 3 June, 1919. (M.)
4542 Lorimer, Christian Gray, 3 June, 1919. (M.)
4543 Lyon, Francis Hamilton, 3 June. 1919. (M.)
4544 Lyon, Violet Dorothy Agnes, 3 June, 1919. (M.)
4545 McLaren, John William, 3 June, 1919. (M.)
4546 Mander, Albert, 3 June, 1919. (M.)
4547 Manton, John, 3 June, 1919. (M.)
4548 Maile, Alfred Charles William, 3 June, 1919. (M.)
4549 Marsden, Ethel, 3 June, 1919. (M.)
4550 Martin, Alfred Walter, 3 June, 1919. (M.)
4551 Mashiter, Thomas, 3 June, 1919. (M.)
4552 Mathews, Charles Bernard, 3 June, 1919. (M.)
4553 Merrick, Frederick Thomas. 3 June, 1919. (M.)
4554 Middlemass, Agnes Lizzie, Mrs., 3 June, 1919. (M.)
4555 Mills, Esther Mary, 3 June, 1919. (M.)
4556 Morgan, Cecil May, 3 June, 1919. (M.)
4557 Milne, Isabella Steele, 3 June, 1919. (M.)
4558 Morris, William Henry, 3 June, 1919. (M.)
4559 Narracot, Isabella Frances, 3 June, 1919. (M.)
4560 Nathan, Stanley John. 3 June, 1919. (M.)
4561 Newman, James Colin, 3 June, 1919. (M.)
4562 Nicolls, Heloise Scott, 3 June, 1919. (M.)
4563 Oakley, Harry Lawrence, 3 June, 1919. (M.)
4564 O'Gorman, Count Robert Jean Marie Gaspard, 3 June, 1919. (M.)
4565 Ost, Henry John, 3 June, 1919. (M.)
4566 Ottman, Amelia Gertrude, Mrs., 3 June, 1919. (M.)
4567 Page, George Albert, 3 June, 1919. (M.)
4568 Parker, John, 3 June, 1919. (M.)
4569 Parker, John Joslin, 3 June, 1919. (M.)
4570 Parr, William Henry, 3 June, 1919. (M.)
4571 Patten, Alan Stewart, 3 June, 1919. (M.)
4572 Pearce. Herbert Cecil, 3 June, 1919. (M.)
4573 Pearsall, Richard Montague Stack, 3 June, 1919. (M.)
4574 Perch, William John, 3 June, 1919. (M.)
4575 Perryer, Harold William, 3 June, 1919. (M.)
4576 Phillips, Ernest Thomas Adams, 3 June, 1919. (M.)
4577 Phillips, Harold Lionel, 3 June, 1919. (M.)
4578 Phillpotts, Lillian Lestella Elizabeth Georgina, 3 June, 1919. (M.)
4579 Pilkington, Dennis Fielden, 3 June, 1919. (M.)

4580 Potier, George, 3 June, 1919. (M.)
4581 Powell, Wilfred Monsell, 3 June, 1919. (M.)
4582 Rayner, Harry, 3 June, 1919. (M.)
4583 Regan, Percy Raphael, 3 June, 1919. (M.)
4584 Reynolds, Margaret Maude, Mrs., 3 June, 1919. (M.)
4585 Roberts, George James, 3 June, 1919. (M.)
4586 Robinson, Harold, 3 June, 1919. (M.)
4587 Rushworth, Mary, 3 June, 1919. (M.)
4588 Schaverine, Samuel, 3 June, 1919. (M.)
4589 Scott, William, 3 June, 1919. (M.)
4590 Sellers, Harry, 3 June, 1919. (M.)
4591 Shorney, Frederick William, 3 June, 1919. (M.)
4592 Simpson, Malcolm Macrae, 3 June, 1919. (M.)
4593 Small, George James, 3 June, 1919. (M.)
4594 Smith, Dennis William, 3 June, 1919. (M.)
4595 Smith, Sydney George, 3 June, 1919. (M.)
4596 Smith, Frank Robinson, 3 June, 1919. (M.)
4597 Smith, Cecil Edward Bartholomew, 3 June, 1919. (M.)
4598 Smith, Ernest Alfred, 3 June, 1919. (M.)
4599 Sorrell, Herbert Alfred George, 3 June, 1919. (M.)
4600 Spall, Leslie Alan, 3 June, 1919. (M.)
4601 Spencer, Harry, 3 June, 1919. (M.)
4602 Stanhope, Cicely, 3 June, 1919. (M.)
4603 Stapleton, Frederick, 3 June, 1919. (M.)
4604 Starkey, Margaret, Mrs., 3 June, 1919. (M.)
4605 Steer, George Patrick, 3 June, 1919. (M.)
4606 Stephens, Sidney Francis Hood, 3 June, 1919. (M.)
4607 Stevens, Reginald, 3 June. 1919. (M.)
4608 Strang, William, 3 June, 1919. (M.)
4609 Strange, John, 3 June, 1919. (M.)
4610 Sutton, Constance Marion. 3 June, 1919. (M.)
4611 Tarbet, Arthur, 3 June, 1919. (M.)
4612 Taylor, Frank, 3 June, 1919. (M.)
4613 Thornton, William Thomas, 3 June, 1919. (M.)
4614 Tibbs, Ernest Henry, 3 June, 1919. (M.)
4615 Tindall, Robert, 3 June, 1919. (M.)
4616 Trippas, Maurice, 3 June, 1919. (M.)
4617 Trubshaw, Arthur Ralph, 3 June, 1919. (M.)
4618 Turner, Isobel Agnes, 3 June, 1919. (M.)
4619 Wager, Euclid Brookes, 3 June, 1919. (M.)
4620 Watson, Earl Basil Kenmure, 3 June, 1919. M.)
4621 Webb, Cyril Charles William, 3 June, 1919. (M.)
4622 Webb, Gladys Vivien, 3 June, 1919. (M.)
4623 Webster, Joseph Henry, 3 June, 1919. (M.)
4624 Welsford, Evelyn Janie, 3 June, 1919. (M.)
4625 Whitbourn, Ernest, 3 June, 1919. (M.)
4626 White, Robert William, 3 June, 1919. (M.)
4627 Williams, William Frederick, 3 June, 1919. (M.)
4628 Williams, Roderick, 3 June, 1919. (M.)
4629 Wilson, Ritchie, 3 June, 1919. (M.)
4630 Wilson, Ralph Justly Chatterton, 3 June, 1919. (M.)
4631 Woodford, Isabel Charlotte, 3 June, 1919. (M.)
4632 Woods, John Alexander Inglis, 3 June, 1919. (M.)
4633 Woods, Walter William, 3 June, 1919. (M.)
4634 Wooler, Lionel Sykes, 3 June, 1919. (M.)
4635 Wray, John James, 3 June, 1919. (M.)
4636 Wright, Harry, 3 June, 1919. (M.)
4637 Yates, Albert James, 3 June, 1919. (M.)
4638 Young, Frederick William, 3 June, 1919. (M.)
4639 Carless, William Edward, 3 June, 1919. (M.)
4640 Coles, Harry Victor, 3 June, 1919. (M.)
4641 Craig, Alexander Meldrum, 3 June, 1919. (M.)
4642 Driver, George Osborne Hitchin, 3 June, 1919. (M.)
4643 Harding, Alfred Burcham, 3 June. 1919. (M.)
4644 Hewett, Cecil Allan, 3 June, 1919. (M.)
4645 Humphries, Henry Hurl, 3 June, 1919. (M.)
4646 MacDonell, Ian McLean, 3 June, 1919. (M.)
4647 Palmer, Edward George, 3 June, 1919. (M.)
4648 Rider, William Rider, 3 June, 1919. (M.)
4649 Stanley, Arthur, 3 June, 1919. (M.)
4650 Thom, Frederick Worrall, 3 June, 1919. (M.)
4651 Weightman, Reginald, 3 June, 1919. (M.)
4652 Andrews, Leslie Frank, 3 June, 1919. (M.)
4653 Brissenden, Edwin Mayhow, 3 June, 1919. (M.)
4654 Cruise, Albert John, 3 June, 1919. (M.)
4655 Dening, Maberley Ester, 3 June, 1919. (M.)
4656 Harrington, John, 3 June, 1919. (M.)
4657 Hills, Loftus, 3 June, 1919. (M.)
4658 Irwin, Stanley, 3 June, 1919. (M.)
4659 Murray, James Edward, 3 June, 1919. (M.)
4660 Stanbury, Ernest Borland, 3 June, 1919. (M.)
4661 Teague, George Eric. 3 June, 1919. (M.)
4662 Welch, Maurice Cleary, 3 June, 1919. (M.)
4663 Carter, Henry Lower, 3 June, 1919. (M.)
4664 Lucas, Gordon Tate, 3 June, 1919. (M.)
4665 Kimberley, Henry, 3 June, 1919. (M.)
4666 Alden, Arthur Rhodes, 3 June, 1919. (M.)
4667 Anastasie, Joseph Anastasi, 3 June, 1919. (M.)
4668 Angel, Walter Douglas, 3 June. 1919. (M.)
4669 Bawden, Cornelius Roberts, 3 June, 1919. (M.)
4670 Blomfield, Sydney Thomas, 3 June, 1919. (M.)
4671 Brown, Alfred Thomas, 3 June, 1919. (M.)
4672 Cassels, James Houston, 3 June, 1919. (M.)
4673 Christie, Harold, 3 June, 1919. (M.)
4674 Davies, William Thomas, 3 June, 1919. (M.)
4675 Ewen, David, 3 June, 1919. (M.)
4676 Ford, Thomas, 3 June, 1919. (M.)
4677 Gann, Ernest Henry, 3 June, 1919. (M.)
4679 Greaves, Walter, 3 June, 1919. (M.)
4680 Griffiths, David John, 3 June, 1919. (M.)

4681 Headwards, Horace, 3 June, 1919. (M.)
4682 Henley, Francis Antony Haste, 3 June, 1919. (M.)
4683 Higgins, Arthur Hall, 3 June, 1919. (M.)
4684 Ingram, Alexander Gordon, 3 June, 1919. (M.)
4685 Jamison, Robert Edward, 3 June, 1919. (M.)
4686 Jenkins, Stanley Evan, 3 June, 1919. (M.)
4687 Jones, Joseph, 3 June, 1919. (M.)
4688 Jones, Thomas Cecil, 3 June, 1919. (M.)
4689 Kennedy, Duncan, 3 June, 1919. (M.)
4690 Kenny-Levick, Vivian Mortimer, 3 June, 1919. (M.)
4691 Kinghorn, Douglas Charles, 3 June, 1919. (M.)
4692 Lucas, Reginald William Owen, 3 June, 1919. (M.)
4693 Lucas, William, 3 June, 1919. (M.)
4694 Miles, Cecil James, 3 June, 1919. (M.)
4695 Millard, Claud John, 3 June, 1919. (M.)
4696 Morgan, David, 3 June, 1919. (M.)
4697 Newport, George Charles, 3 June, 1919. (M.)
4698 Oliphant, Andrew John, 3 June, 1919. (M.)
4699 Pegg, Thomas Edgar, 3 June, 1919. (M.)
4700 Robinson, Bernal, 3 June, 1919. (M.)
4701 Roddis, Ernest, 3 June, 1919. (M.)
4702 Rowe, George Richard, 3 June, 1919. (M.)
4703 Shepherd, Philip William, 3 June, 1919. (M.)
4704 Sherlock, David Thomas Joseph, 3 June, 1919. (M.)
4705 Smith, George Clarke, 3 June, 1919. (M.)
4706 Smith, Thomas, 3 June, 1919. (M.)
4707 Smith, Thomas Harold, 3 June, 1919. (M.)
4708 Spinney, Thomas George, 3 June, 1918. (M.)
4709 Stoodley, Fred, 3 June, 1919. (M.)
4710 Taylor, Edward McKenzie, 3 June, 1919. (M.)
4711 Thomas, Godfrey Herbert, 3 June, 1919. (M.)
4712 Thuillier, Ernest, 3 June, 1919. (M.)
4713 Turk, Arthur Edward, 3 June, 1919. (M.)
4714 Voss, Charles, 3 June, 1919. (M.)
4715 Wedderspoon, Arthur Alexander, 3 June, 1919. (M.)
4716 Brown, Robert William, 3 June, 1919. (M.)
4717 Stewart, Keith Lindsay, 3 June, 1919. (M.)
4718 Abdel Azim Effendi (Saghkolaghasi), 3 June, 1919. (M.)
4719 Mohammed Abdel Aziz Sharaf (Yuzbashi), 3 June, 1919. (M.)
4720 Mohammed Effendi Miazi (Saghkolaghasi), 3 June, 1919. (M.)
4721 Sadek Eff Ibrahim El Mula (Yuzbashi), 3 June, 1919. (M.)
4722 Anderson, William John Skeat, 3 June, 1919. (M.)
4723 Armstrong, George William, 3 June, 1919. (M.)
4724 Bundock, Charles, 3 June, 1919. (M.)
4725 Burrows, Amos, 3 June, 1919. (M.)
4726 Cottle, Joseph, 3 June, 1919. (M.)
4727 Dodds, Theodore Edwin, 3 June, 1919. (M.)
4728 Edwards, William Manning, 3 June, 1919. (M.)
4729 Everson, Thurston Hicks, 3 June, 1919. (M.)
4730 Eyre, John Benedict, 3 June, 1919. (M.)
4731 Fenn, Sydney Albert, 3 June, 1919. (M.)
4732 Fieldhouse, Arthur, 3 June, 1919. (M.)
4733 Fry, Douglas Gaskoin, 3 June, 1919. (M.)
4734 Furler, Herbert John, 3 June, 1919. (M.)
4735 Gilchrist, Henry Thomas, 3 June, 1919. (M.)
4736 Hacker, Douglas Walter Stewart, 3 June, 1919. (M.)
4737 Hamilton Smith, Norman, 3 June, 1919. (M.)
4738 Hopcraft, Harry Douglas, 3 June, 1919. (M.)
4739 Hudson, Alfred, 3 June, 1919. (M.)
4740 Jones, Harry Carder, 3 June, 1919. (M.)
4741 Kilvert, Charles Robert, 3 June, 1919. (M.)
4742 Langston, William, 3 June, 1919. (M.)
4743 Levy, Joseph, 3 June, 1919. (M.)
4744 Lovett, William Edward, 3 June, 1919. (M.)
4745 Mackay, James Eugene, 3 June, 1919. (M.)
4746 Madden, Guy Ross, 3 June, 1919. (M.)
4747 Matthews, Noel Lane, 3 June, 1919. (M.)
4748 Nelson, Joe, 3 June, 1919. (M.)
4749 Ratcliffe, Charles Plummer, 3 June, 1919. (M.)
4750 Sainsbury, Eric John, 3 June, 1919. (M.)
4751 Slater, John Alan, 3 June, 1919. (M.)
4752 Smith, Denton, 3 June, 1919. (M.)
4753 Strina, Gerald Lionel, 3 June, 1919. (M.)
4754 Syminton, Ralph, 3 June, 1919. (M.)
4755 Taylor, Richard Allen, 3 June, 1919. (M.)
4756 Travers, Sydney Stanley Joe, 3 June, 1919. (M.)
4757 Turner, Arthur Castle, 3 June, 1919. (M.)
4758 Walford, Harry Norman, 3 June, 1919. (M.)
4759 Walker, William, 3 June, 1919. (M.)
4760 Watling, John Basil, 3 June, 1919. (M.)
4761 Williams, Charles Sydney, 3 June, 1919. (M.)
4762 Willsher, John Edward, 3 June, 1919. (M.)
4763 Andrewes, Cyril John, 3 June, 1919. (M.)
4764 Barker, Eric Clement, 3 June, 1919. (M.)
4765 Barker, John Percival, 3 June, 1919. (M.)
4766 Black, Graeme Morrison, 3 June, 1919. (M.)
4767 Blake, George Shearsley, 3 June, 1919. (M.)
4768 Brooke, Joshua Rupert Ingham, 3 June, 1919. (M.)
4769 Brough, Frederick Arthur, 3 June, 1919.
4770 Browning, Herbert, 3 June, 1919. (M.)
4771 Bruce, Ian Robert Cranford George Mary, 3 June, 1919. (M.)
4772 Bruno, Hugh Alan Bruno, 3 June, 1919. (M.)
4773 Cadoux, Bernard Temple, 3 June, 1919. (M.)
4774 Charnand, Frederick Christian, 3 June, 1919. (M.)
4775 Chidson, Lowthian Hume, 3 June, 1919. (M.)
4776 Cree, Harold Frederick, 3 June, 1919. (M.)
4777 Dew, Reginald Francis, 3 June, 1919. (M.)

4778 East, Arthur William, 3 June, 1919. (M.)
4779 Erby, Henry William, 3 June, 1919. (M.)
4780 Eyre, Richard Philip Hastings, 3 June, 1919. (M.)
4781 Faulkner, Henry Robert, 3 June, 1919. (M.)
4782 Fetherston, Henry Barry, 3 June, 1919. (M.)
4783 Forster, Edward Seymour, 3 June, 1919. (M.)
4785 Freeman, George Herbert, 3 June, 1919. (M.)
4786 Gattie, Brian Berkeley, 3 June, 1919. (M.)
4787 Goate, Ernest Edward, 3 June, 1919. (M.)
4788 Godsell, James Stanley Peel, 3 June, 1919. (M.)
4789 Gout, Evelyn Rudolf Albert John, 3 June, 1919. (M.
4790 Gower, John Richard, 3 June, 1919. (M.)
4791 Greenlees, Robert Wallace, 3 June, 1919. (M.)
4792 Hext, Arthur Charles, 3 June, 1919. (M.)
4793 Horan, Preston, 3 June, 1919. (M.)
4794 Hoyland, Harold Allan Dilke, 3 June, 1919. (M.)
4795 Hudson, Roland Cecil, 3 June, 1919. (M.)
4796 Humphries, Hubert John, 3 June, 1919. (M.)
4797 Ibbotson, Archie William, 3 June, 1910. (M.)
4798 Jardine, John, 3 June, 1919. (M.)
4799 Kenny, Vincent Raymond, 3 June, 1919. (M.)
4800 King, Malcolm, 3 June, 1919. (M.)
4801 Knight, Alfred James, 3 June, 1919. (M.)
4802 Kitching, Harold Edward, 3 June, 1919. (M.)
4803 La Fontaine, Edward Leonard, 3 June, 1919. (M.)
4804 Lambert, Roger Uredale, 3 June, 1919. (M.)
4805 Luxton, William John, 3 June, 1919. (M.)
4806 McCormick, Henry Charles Gordon, 3 June, 1919. (M.)
4807 McEacharn, Niel Boyd Watson, 3 June, 1919. (M.)
4808 MacGuire, Edward Robert Mileson, 3 June, 1919. (M.)
4809 Martin, Harrison, 3 June, 1919. (M.)
4810 Massy-Westropp, John Francis Ralph, 3 June, 1919. (M.)
4811 Matthews, Ernest Francis K., 3 June, 1919. (M.)
4813 Miller, Joseph Charles, 3 June, 1919. (M.)
4814 Minter, George Ash, 3 June, 1919. (M.)
4815 Morris, Archibald, 3 June, 1919. (M.)
4816 Nares, Ramsay Llewellyn Ives, 3 June, 1919. (M.)
4817 Noble, Crawford, 3 June, 1919. (M.)
4818 Parry, William Francis Vaughan, 3 June, 1919. (M.)
4819 Partington, Thomas, 3 June, 1919. (M.)
4820 Perkins, James, 3 June, 1919. (M.)
4821 Rose, Harold Oldham, 3 June, 1919. (M.)
4822 Saunders, Harry Francis, 3 June, 1919. (M.)
4823 Smith, George Henry Gould, 3 June, 1919. (M.)
4824 Steele, Matthew Garvan, 3 June, 1919. (M.)
4825 Stirling, John, 3 June, 1919. (M.)
4826 Strachan, Charles John, 3 June, 1919. (M.)
4827 Swan, Thomas Angus, 3 June, 1919. (M.)
4828 Taylor, Hugh Oddin, 3 June, 1919. (M.)
4829 Thomson, Kenneth John, 3 June, 1919. (M.)
4830 Tomson, Henry Gordon, 3 June, 1919. (M.)
4831 Weir, David Alexander, 3 June, 1919. (M.)
4832 White, Charles Clement Stuart, 3 June, 1919. (M.)
4833 Woodall, John Dane, 3 June, 1919. (M.)
4834 Aitchison, Robert Smith, 3 June, 1919. (M.)
4835 Anderson, Alexander, 3 June, 1919. (M.)
4836 Andrews, Ernest Courtney Harold Norman, 3 June, 1919. (M.)
4837 Ashcroft, William, 3 June, 1919. (M.)
4838 Azevedo, Alec Eustace, 3 June, 1919. (M.)
4839 Banister, Fred, 3 June, 1919. (M.)
4840 Barber, Charles Gordon, 3 June, 1919. (M.)
4841 Batterbury, George Henry, 3 June, 1919. (M.)
4842 Bell, John Aiton, 3 June, 1919. (M.)
4843 Bender, William Edward Gustave, 3 June, 1919. (M.)
4844 Bevan, Gilbert John Beckford, 3 June, 1919. (M.)
4845 Beynon, John, 3 June, 1919. (M.)
4846 Blair, John Milligan, 3 June, 1919. (M.)
4847 Booth, Arthur Newton, 3 June, 1919. (M.)
4848 Brewin, George Grahame, 3 June, 1919. (M.)
4849 Brown, Douglas Archibald Guillan, 3 June, 1919. (M.)
4850 Burgess, Robert Ashfield, 3 June, 1919. (M.)
4851 Butcher, Charlie Robert, 3 June, 1919. (M.)
4852 Master, Archie George Chester-, 3 June, 1919. (M.)
4853 Coghlan, Edward Maurice Ernest, 3 June, 1919. (M.)
4854 Cooper, Charles Herbert, 3 June, 1919. (M.)
4855 Cox, Edward Orme, 3 June, 1919. (M.)
4856 Crowther, Harold Oakes, 3 June, 1919. (M.)
4857 Daly, Agnes, 3 June, 1919. (M.)
4858 Danson, Thomas, 3 June, 1919. (M.)
4859 Davison, James Edwin, 3 June, 1919. (M.)
4860 Dearing, Sidney Arthur, 3 June, 1919. (M.)
4861 de Robeck, John Henry Edward, 3 June, 1919. (M.)
4862 Dickens, William Samuel, 3 June, 1919. (M.)
4863 Donkin, Herbert Julyan, 3 June, 1919. (M.)
4864 Dredge, Austin Edward Makinson, 3 June, 1919. (M.)
4865 Duthie, Barbara Elder, 3 June, 1919. (M.)
4866 Eccleston, Henry Charles, 3 June, 1919. (M.)
4867 Elliott, Myles Layman Farr, 3 June, 1919. (M.)
4868 Falgar, Richard Joseph, 3 June, 1919. (M.)
4869 Filmer, Walter George Harry, 3 June, 1919. (M.)
4870 Finlay, John, 3 June, 1919. (M.)
4871 Forster, George Henry, 3 June, 1919. (M.)
4872 Fulcher, Ernest William Popplewell, 3 June, 1919. (M.)
4873 Galvin, Alfred, 3 June, 1919. (M.)
4874 Grant, Leslie Iam, 3 June, 1919. (M.)
4875 Gravett, George William, 3 June, 1919. (M.)
4876 Gutteridge, Leonard, 3 June, 1919. (M.)
4877 Harbottle, Denis Leslie, 3 June, 1919. (M.)

4878 Hardy, Victor, 3 June, 1919. (M.)
4879 Harris, Claude Pickering, 3 June, 1919. (M.)
4880 Hill, Robert Charles, 3 June, 1919. (M.)
4881 Hinks, Edward, 3 June, 1919. (M.)
4882 Holmes, Alfred Henry Robert, 3 June, 1919.
4883 Holt, Alec Horace Edward Litton, 3 June, 1919. (M.)
4884 Hopkins, John Boyd, 3 June, 1919. (M.)
4885 Hulbert, Leonard, 3 June, 1919. (M.)
4886 Jackson, Herbert, 3 June, 1919. (M.)
4887 Kingsberry, William Henry, 3 June, 1919. (M.)
4889 Kitching, Douglas Woolley, 3 June, 1919. (M.)
4890 Lines, Reginald Edward, 3 June, 1919. (M.)
4891 Long, Walter, 3 June, 1919. (M.)
4892 McGrath, William Henry, 3 June, 1919. (M.)
4893 McNair, George Douglas, 3 June, 1919. (M.)
4894 Malcolm, Frederick Arthur, 3 June, 1919. (M.)
4895 Martin, Gilbert Charles, 3 June, 1919. (M.)
4896 Massey, Everard Ernest, 3 June, 1919. (M.)
4897 Matthews, Harry, 3 June, 1919. (M.)
4898 May, Ernest, 3 June, 1919. (M.)
4899 Mercer, George Joseph, 3 June, 1919. (M.)
4900 Minns, Alfred, 3 June, 1919. (M.)
4901 Morgan, William Harold, 3 June, 1919. (M.)
4902 Mockett, Vere, 3 June, 1919. (M.)
4903 Moore, John Sarel, 3 June, 1919. (M.)
4904 Musgrave, Francis Peete, 3 June, 1919. (M.)
4905 Myers, Nathan Coleman, 3 June. 1919. (M.)
4906 Nicholl, Edwin McKillop, 3 June, 1919. (M.)
4907 Openshaw, George Arthur, 3 June, 1919. (M.)
4908 Owens, Joseph Hubert, 3 June, 1919.
4909 Parsley, Walter, 3 June, 1919. (M.)
4910 Pragnell, Donovan William Alan, 3 June, 1919. (M.)
4911 Penman, Victor Robert, 3 June, 1919. (M.)
4912 Power, Gerald Hugh, 3 June, 1919. (M.)
4913 Pring, John Nathaniel, 3 June, 1919. (M.)
4914 Ramsbotham, Richard Bury, 3 June, 1919. (M.)
4915 Rana-Jodha Jung, Bahadur, 3 June, 1919. (M.)
4916 Reilly, Charles Oliver Calcott, 3 June, 1919. (M.)
4917 Renfrew, Robert, 3 June, 1919. (M.)
4918 Rennick, Denis Kingston, 3 June, 1919. (M.)
4919 Ridley, Ernest Rupert, 3 June, 1919. (M.)
4920 Rose, Clifford, 3 June, 1919. (M.)
4921 Ross, Alexander Lewis, 3 June, 1919. (M.)
4922 Rowlands, Archibald, 3 June, 1919. (M.)
4923 Salberg, Frank James, 3 June, 1919. (M.)
4924 Shurmur, Stanley Emberick, 3 June, 1919. (M.)
4925 Sievwright, Andrew George Hume, 3 June, 1919. (M.)
4926 Smith, Ralph William, 3 June, 1919. (M.)
4927 Smith, Thomas, 3 June, 1919. (M.)
4928 Snelgar, John Thomas, 3 June, 1919. (M.)
4929 Spear, Richard William, 3 June, 1919. (M.)
4930 Stribling, William James Leonard, 3 June, 1919. (M.)
4931 Steward, Charles Arthur Cholmley, 3 June, 1919. (M.)
4932 Sutton, Thomas James, 3 June, 1919. (M.)
4933 Tobin, Frederick Matthias, 3 June, 1919. (M.)
4934 Tweed, John Reginald Howard, 3 June, 1919. (M.)
4935 Urmson, Gilbert Alexander, 3 June, 1919. (M.)
4936 Walker, George Benisford, 3 June, 1919. (M.)
4937 Walker, Reginald Henry, 3 June, 1919. (M.)
4938 Walton, Harry, 3 June, 1919. (M.)
4939 Wells, Robert Charles Owen, 3 June, 1919. (M.)
4940 Wilson, Charles Ernest, 3 June, 1919. (M.)
4941 Williams, Robert Drake, 3 June, 1919. (M.)
4942 Williams, Leslie, 3 June, 1919. (M.)
4943 Worthington, John Ramsay, 3 June, 1919. (M.)
4944 Whyte, Colin Campbell, 3 June, 1919. (M.)
4945 Martin, Robert Fiennes Wykeham-, 3 June, 1919. (M.)
4946 Yeates, Robert Montford Michaelson, 3 June, 1919. (M.)
4947 Moore, Frederick Ernest, 3 June, 1919. (M.)
4048 Anderson, Alfred Thomas Duncan, 3 June, 1919. (M.)
4949 Armstrong, Howard Wolfenden, 3 June, 1919. (M.)
4950 Baker, Charles Matthew, 3 June, 1919. (M.)
4951 Black, Alexander, 3 June, 1919. (M.)
4952 Butler, George Guy, 3 June, 1919. (M.)
4953 Collins, Edward Redvers Kerington, 3 June, 1919. (M.)
4954 Crawford, Andrew, 3 June, 1919. (M.)
4955 Doble, William Alfred, 3 June, 1919. (M.)
4956 Evans, George Windham Wright, 3 June, 1919. (M.)
4957 Fillion, Rev. Joseph, 3 June, 1919. (M.)
4958 Graham, Walter, 3 June, 1919. (M.)
4959 Greig, John Isdale, 3 June, 1919. (M.)
4960 Hack, Rev. Robert, 3 June, 1919.
4961 Innes, Robert, 3 June, 1919. (M.)
4962 King-Magee, Arthur Fitzherbert, 3 June, 1919.
4963 Loveridge, Frederick, 3 June, 1919. (M.)
4964 McCormack, Rev. John Bernard, 3 June, 1919. (M.)
4965 Maddams, William Samuel, 3 June, 1919.
4966 Martin, George William, 3 June, 1919. (M.)
4967 Michie, Andrew, 3 June, 1919. (M.)
4968 Mullan, Henry Felix, 3 June. 1919. (M.)
4969 Mussanji Walugembe, Joseph (Prince), 3 June, 1919. (M.)
4970 Nightingale, William Maxwell, 3 June, 1919. (M.)
4971 Pheysey, Frederick Cecil, 3 June, 1919. (M.)
4972 Quirk, Edward John Joseph, 3 June, 1919. (M.)
4973 Rapley, William Sydney, 3 June, 1919. (M.)
4974 Robertson, James Sin, 3 June, 1919. (M.)
4975 Robins, Veral Glen, 3 June, 1919. (M.)
4976 Saunders, Frederick, 3 June, 1919. (M.)
4977 Stanley, Robert, 3 June, 1919. (M.)
4978 Stock, Ernest Elliot, 3 June, 1919. (M.)

4979 Suffield, William Joseph, 3 June, 1919. (M.)
4980 Unger, John, 3 June, 1919. (M.)
4981 Urquhart, Charles Ernest, 3 June, 1919. (M.)
4982 Watkins, Frank, 3 June, 1919. (M.)
4983 Whitaker, Harold Braithwait, 3 June, 1919. (M.)
4984 Wilkie, James Bowman, 3 June, 1919. (M.)
4985 Beatty, Herbert James, 3 June, 1919. (M.)
4986 Bowen, Frank Hart. 3 June, 1919. (M.)
4987 Brown, John, 3 June, 1919. (M.)
4988 Clegg, Robert Edward, 3 June, 1919. (M.)
4989 De Lisle, Rev. Hugh Frederick, 3 June, 1919. (M.)
4990 Douglas, Robert Douglas Argyll, 3 June, 1919. (M.)
4991 Fraser, David, 3 June, 1919. (M.)
4992 Hamilton, William Vickery, 3 June, 1919. (M.)
4993 Henrey, James Osler, 3 June, 1919. (M.)
4994 Houghton, Walter John, 3 June, 1919. (M.)
4995 Lane, Wilhelm Heinreich Christian Ahrens, 3 June, 1919 (M.)
4996 McPherson, Stuart Mackintosh, 3 June, 1919. (M.)
4997 Manseth, William Alfred, 3 June, 1919. (M.)
4998 Pattle, Rupert James Hartwell, 3 June, 1919. (M.)
4999 Turner, Fulham, 3 June, 1919. (M.)
5000 Watson, William, 3 June, 1919. (M.)
5001 Collet, Arthur William, 3 June, 1919. (M.)
5002 Smith, Charles Newbald, 3 June, 1919. (M.)
5003 Clarke, Leslie Ebenezer, 3 June, 1919. (M.)
5004 Cooper, Cecil Aubrey, 3 June. 1919. (M.)
5005 Evans, Frederic, 3 June, 1919. (M.)
5006 Hodson, Leopold Percival, 3 June, 1919. (M.)
5007 McNair, Matthew Barr. 3 June. 1919. (M.)
5008 Rendel, William Vincent, 3 June, 1919. (M.)
5009 Vardon, Eric John, 3 June, 1919. (M.)
5010 Watson, Victor Fsevlod, 3 June, 1919. (M.)
5011 Whistler, Godfrey Fuller, 3 June, 1919.
5012 Burke, Allan Frederick, 3 June 1919. (M.)
5013 Fenning, Robert William, 3 June, 1919. (M.)
5014 Johnson, Ernest Alfred, 3 June, 1919. (M.)
5015 Littlehales, Joseph Thomas, 3 June, 1919. (M.)
5016 McKerchar, 3 June. 1919. (M.)
5017 Clayton, Norman Willis. 3 June, 1919. (M.)
5018 Eden, Geoffrey Morten, 3 June, 1919. (M.)
5019 Abbot-Anderson, Louis Goodrich, 3 June, 1919. (M.)
5020 Acheson, James, 3 June, 1919. (M.)
5021 Adair, Francis Robert, 3 June. 1919. (M.)
5022 Adams, Herbert Windham, 3 June, 1919. (M.)
5023 Adcock, Frederick Harold, 3 June, 1919. (M.)
5024 Adkins, George, 3 June, 1919. (M.)
5025 Adler, Herbert Marcus, 3 June, 1919. (M.)
5026 Aitkin, John Christie, 3 June, 1919. (M.)
5027 Akhurst, William Harry, 3 June, 1919. (M.)
5028 Albany, Sidney Charles, 3 June, 1919. (M.)
5029 Alcock, Charles William, 3 June, 1919. (M.)
5030 Allen, Charles Edward, 3 June, 1919. (M.)
5031 Allnatt, Alfred Ernest, 3 June, 1919. (M.)
5032 Andersor, Henry, 3 June, 1919. (M.)
5033 Anderson, Robert William, 3 June, 1919. (M.)
5034 Anderson, Thomas Percival, 3 June, 1919. (M.)
5036 Anson, George Wilfred, 3 June, 1919. (M.)
5037 Arbuthnot, Lionel Gough, 3 June, 1919. (M.)
5038 Armstrong, Cyril, 3 June, 1919. (M.)
5039 Aston, Thomas, 3 June. 1919. (M.)
5040 Atkins, Henry Albert, 3 June, 1919. (M.)
5041 Atkinson, Arthur George, 3 June, 1919. (M.)
5042 Atkinson, Arthur Joseph, 3 June, 1919. (M.)
5043 Axten, Ernest Henry, 3 June, 1919. (M.)
5044 Ayden, Arthur John, 3 June, 1919. (M.)
5045 Backhaus, Frederick, 3 June, 1919. (M.)
5046 Bacon, James, 3 June, 1919. (M.)
5047 Bailey, Herbert John, 3 June. 1919. (M.)
5048 Baillie, George Bertram, 3 June. 1919. (M.)
5049 Baillie, Roderick, 3 June, 1919. (M.)
5050 Baines, George Norman. 3 June, 1919. (M.)
5051 Munton, Horace Munton Baker-, 3 June, 1919. (M.)
5052 Ball, Sydney Arthur, 3 June, 1919. (M.)
5053 Bannatyne, Arthur Gordon, 3 June, 1919. (M.)
5054 Barbary, John Ewart Trounce, 3 June, 1919. (M.)
5055 Barber, George Henry, 3 June, 1919. (M.)
5056 Barclay, Henry Gladstone, 3 June, 1919. (M.)
5057 Barnett, Albert Edward, 3 June, 1919. (M.)
5059 Barnfield, William George, 3 June, 1919. (M.)
5060 Barr, Charles Nicholson, 3 June, 1919. (M.)
5061 Barratt, Arthur Walker, 3 June, 1919. (M.)
5062 Barrington, Herbert Cecil, 3 June, 1919. (M.)
5063 Bartie, Edward William, 3 June, 1919. (M.)
5064 Barton, George, 3 June, 1919. (M.)
5065 Batchelor, Ronald George, 3 June, 1919. (M.)
5066 Baxter, Henry George, 3 June, 1919. (M.)
5067 Bean, Robert Charles, June, 1919. (M.)
5068 Beattie, Arthur Joseph, 3 June, 1919. (M.)
5069 Beesley, Lewis Henry, 3 June, 1919. (M.)
5070 Beeton, Thomas Guy, 3 June, 1919. (M.)
5071 Benn, Edward Hugh, 3 June, 1919. (M.)
5072 Benn, Walter, 3 June, 1919. (M.)
5073 Bennett, Archie, 3 June, 1919. (M.)
5074 Bentliff, Philip Barnett, 3 June, 1919. (M.)
5075 Beresford-Peirse, Arthur Cecil Procter de la Poer, 3 June, 1919. (M.)
5076 Bertram, Robert, 3 June, 1919. (M.)
5077 Beszant, William George, 3 June, 1919. (M.)
5078 Binns, Frederick, 3 June, 1919. (M.)

MEMBERS.

5080 Bird, Mary Cecilia, 3 June, 1919. (M.)
5081 Bishop, Robert Odell, 3 June, 1919. (M.)
5082 Bishop, Stanley, 3 June, 1919. (M.)
5083 Bisset, Rev. Mordaunt Elrington, 3 June, 1919. (M.)
5084 Blackburn, Walter James, 3 June, 1919. (M.)
5085 Blackmore, Charles Nelson Lindsley, 3 June, 1919. (M.)
5086 Blackwell, Cecil Patrick, 3 June, 1919. (M.)
5087 Blair, Alexander, 3 June, 1919. (M.)
5088 Blunt, Hubert Porter, 3 June, 1919. (M.)
5089 Boland, Samuel, 3 June, 1919. (M.)
5090 Bolton, Frederick, 3 June, 1919. (M.)
5091 Bosustow, John Coulson, 3 June, 1919. (M.
5092 Bott, Olive, 3 June, 1919. (M.)
5093 Bowers, John, 3 June, 1919. (M.)
5094 Bowes-Robinson, Cecil, 3 June, 1919. (M.)
5095 Bowhill, Thomas, 3 June, 1919. (M.)
5096 Boyle, Cecil Hefferon, 3 June, 1919. (M.)
5097 Bradbury, George Richardson, 3 June, 1919. (M.)
5098 Bradford, James 3 June, 1919. (M.)
5099 Brady, Sydney Edward Joseph, 3 June, 1919. (M.)
5100 Brash, Ernest Livett, 3 June, 1919. (M.)
5101 Bratby, George Henry, 3 June, 1919. (M.)
5102 Brett, John Vaughan, 3 June, 1919. (M.)
5103 Bridges, Frederick Thomas, 3 June, 1919. (M.)
5104 Bright, Harold Norman, 3 June, 1919. (M.)
5105 Broadway, Eric Evans, 3 June, 1919. (M.)
5106 Brock, William Stewart Ranulf, 3 June, 1919. (M.)
5107 Brodie, Henry Campbell, 3 June, 1919. (M.)
5108 Brodie, Richard, 3 June, 1919. (M.)
5109 Brook, Leonard Thornicraft, 3 June, 1919. (M.)
5110 Brooks, George Thomas Adams, 3 June, 1919. (M.)
5111 Broughton, Cecil Howard, 3 June, 1919. (M.)
5112 Brown, Arthur Richard Dupuis, 3 June, 1919. (M.)
5113 Brown, Frederick, 3 June, 1919. (M.)
5115 Brown, Stanley, 3 June, 1919. (M.)
5116 Brown-Constable, Alice Amelia, 3 June, 1919. (M.)
5117 Bruty, William Glynes, 3 June, 1919. (M.)
5118 Bryant, Thomas Hedley, 3 June, 1919. (M.)
5119 Buchanan, James Frederick, 3 June, 1919. (M.)
5120 Bugler, William Thomas Hansford, 3 June, 1919. (M.)
5121 Bull, William, 3 June, 1919. (M.)
5122 Bullock, Harold Malcolm, 3 June, 1919. (M.)
5123 Bullock, John Walter, 3 June, 1919. (M.)
5124 Burgoyne, Clarence, 3 June, 1919. (M.)
5125 Burke, Hugh St. George, 3 June, 1919. (M.)
5126 Burns, Edward James, 3 June, 1919. (M.)
5127 Burrows, James Douglas, 3 June, 1919. (M.)
5128 Burt, Reginald Edward, 3 June, 1919. (M.)
5129 Burton, Rev. Harold John Chandos. 3 June, 1919. (M.)
5130 Butler, Eustace Norman, 3 June, 1919. (M.)
5131 Butler, James Bayley, 3 June, 1919. (M.)
5132 Butler, James Dickson, 3 June, 1919. (M.)
5133 Buxton, Claude Henry, 3 June, 1919. (M.)
5134 Cahill, Albert, 3 June, 1919. (M.)
5135 Caldicott, Charles Holt, 3 June, 1919. (M.)
5136 Calvey, Charles 3 June, 1919. (M.)
5137 Cameron, Alexander Duncan, 3 June, 1919. (M.)
5138 Cameron, Thomas Duncan, 3 June, 1919. (M.)
5139 Campbell, Harold James, 3 June, 1919. (M.)
5140 Campion-Coles, John Monck, 3 June, 1919. (M.)
5141 Carden, John Valentine, 3 June, 1919. (M.)
5142 Carrington, Sidney John Ness, 3 June, 1919. (M.)
5143 Carse, John R., 3 June, 1919. (M.)
5144 Carter, Charles Frederick Beall, 3 June, 1919. (M.)
5145 Carter, Thomas Benjamin, 3 June, 1919. (M.)
5146 Cavaye, Ronald James, 3 June, 1919. (M.)
5147 Chambers, George Kirby, 3 June, 1919. (M.)
5148 Chandler, Frederick Joseph, 3 June, 1919. (M.)
5149 Chandler, Hugh Elphinstone, 3 June, 1919. (M.)
5150 Cheeswright, Frederick Grahame, 3 June, 1919. (M.)
5151 Chenery, George, 3 June, 1919. (M.)
5152 Chesterton, Hugh, 3 June, 1919. (M.)
5153 Child, Cyril Holland, 3 June, 1919. (M.)
5154 Christian, Charles, 3 June, 1919.
5155 Christison, McCulloch, 3 June, 1919. (M.)
5156 Christopherson, Kenneth, 3 June, 1919. (M.)
5157 Clapham, Athol England, 3 June, 1919. (M.)
5158 Clark, Hubert Charles, 3 June, 1919. (M.)
5159 Clarke, Derrick Ansell, 3 June, 1919. (M.)
5160 Clarke, Frederick, 3 June, 1919. (M.)
5161 Clay, Ernest, 3 June, 1919. (M)
5162 Clegg, Thomas Harry, 3 June, 1919. (M.)
5163 Clements, Frederick James, 3 June, 1919. (M.)
5164 Clout, Charles William, 3 June, 1919. (M.)
5165 Clover, Frederick William, 3 June, 1919. (M.)
5166 Cobb, Henry Percy, 3 June, 1919. (M.)
5167 Cokayne, Thomas, 3 June, 1919. (M.)
5168 Cole, David Henry, 3 June, 1919. (M.)
5169 Cole, Fritz William, 3 June, 1919. (M.)
5170 Cole, Lowry Arthur Casamajor, 3 June, 1919. (M.)
5171 Collins, William Henry, 3 June, 1919. (M.)
5172 Connolly, Hugh Francis, 3 June, 1919. (M.)
5173 Cooksey, Frank Reginald, 3 June, 1919. (M.)
5174 Coombes, William James, 3 June, 1919. (M.)
5175 Cooper, Ansell Edgar, 3 June, 1919. (M.)
5176 Cooper, Bryan Ricco, 3 June, 1919. (M.)
5177 Cooper, Richard Tennant, 3 June, 1919. (M.)
5178 Cooper, Samuel Edward, 3 June, 1919. (M.)
5179 Cordeaux, Melville Charles Dymock, 3 June, 1919. (M.)
5180 Cosgrave, Frederick John, 3 June, 1919. (M.)

5181 Cosgrove, Thomas Patrick, 3 June, 1919. (M.)
5182 Coulson, Horace Wilkinson, 3 June, 1919. (M.)
5183 Coulter, Percival Arthur, 3 June, 1919. (M.)
5184 Cousens, Arthur Bertie, 3 June, 1919. (M.)
5185 Cowley, Ernest, 3 June, 1919. (M.)
5186 Cox, George, 3 June, 1919. (M.)
5187 Cox, Keith Trenchard, 3 June, 1919. (M.)
5188 Coyle, James, 3 June, 1919. (M.)
5189 Coyne, Denis, 3 June, 1919. (M.)
5190 Craig, Graham, 3 June, 1919. (M.)
5191 Crane, James Henry, 3 June, 1919. (M.)
5192 Crankshaw, Eric Norman Spencer, 3 June, 1919. (M.)
5193 Crapper, Harold Sugden, 3 June, 1919. (M.)
5194 Cripps, Henry Rivers, 3 June, 1919. (M.)
5195 Crosbie, William Maxwell, 3 June, 1919. (M.)
5196 Cross, Arthur Gordon, 3 June, 1919. (M.)
5197 Crosse, James Frederick, 3 June, 1919. (M.)
5198 Crossley, George Henry, 3 June, 1919. (M.)
5199 Cullen, William John, 3 June, 1919 (M.)
5200 Cunliffe, Norman, 3 June, 1919. (M.)
5201 Curtis, Annie, Mrs., 3 June, 1919. (M.)
5202 Curtis, William Arthur, 3 June, 1919. (M.)
5204 Dann, William Squire, 3 June, 1919. (M.)
5205 Darby, John Edward, 3 June, 1919. (M.)
5206 D'Arcy, George Graham, 3 June, 1919. (M.)
5207 Davidson, Alec Stuart, 3 June, 1919. (M.)
5208 Davies, David Owen, 3 June, 1919. (M.)
5209 Davies, Charles Beverley, 3 June, 1919. (M.)
5210 Davies, Richard Llewellyn, 3 June, 1919. (M.)
5211 Davis, Robert, 3 June, 1919. (M.)
5212 Davoren, Carmen, 3 June, 1919 (M.)
5213 Dawson, Herbert Milner, 3 June, 1919. (M.)
5214 Dawson, William Bell, 3 June, 1919. (M.)
5215 Day, George Albert John, 3 June, 1919. (M.)
5216 Day, William, 3 June, 1919. (M.)
5217 Dean, Walter Thomas, 3 June, 1919. (M.)
5218 Deedes, John Gordon, 3 June, 1919. (M.)
5219 Jones, Edward Denby-, 3 June, 1919. (M.)
5220 De St. Croix, Leslie Lawson, 3 June, 1919. (M.)
5221 De Tuyll, Frank, 3 June, 1919. (M.)
5222 Dicker, Arthur Seymour Hamilton, 3 June, 1919. (M.)
5223 Dicker, Gilbert Charles Hamilton, 3 June, 1919. (M.)
5224 Dillon, Robert, 3 June, 1919. (M.)
5225 Doggrell, Enos, 3 June, 1919. (M.)
5226 Doherty, Francis Cecil, 3 June, 1919. (M.)
5227 Dolmage, Francis Alfred Emilio, 3 June, 1919. (M.)
5228 Donald, George Reid, 3 June, 1919. (M.)
5229 Douglas, John Turner, 3 June, 1919. (M.)
5230 Dowdell, George James, 3 June, 1919. (M.)
5231 Duarte, Edgar Thurston, 3 June, 1919. (M.)
5232 Dudley, Cyril Raymond, 3 June, 1919. (M.)
5233 Duncan, Charles, 3 June, 1919. (M.)
5234 Duncan, Thomas, 3 June, 1919. (M.)
5235 Durbridge, William, 3 June, 1919. (M.)
5236 Eastwood, Samuel Cosby, 3 June, 1919. (M.)
5237 Ecroyd, Frederick Thomas, 3 June, 1919. (M.)
5238 Edge, Arthur Broughton, 3 June, 1919. (M.)
5239 Edwards, Charles Joseph. 3 June, 1919. (M.)
5240 Edwards, John Henry, 3 June, 1919. (M.)
5241 Eley, Henry Gerard, 3 June, 1919. (M.)
5242 Eliot, John Alfred Roy, 3 June, 1919. (M.)
5243 Ellis, Harry Charles, 3 June, 1919. (M.)
5244 Ellison, William Richard, 3 June, 1919. (M.)
5245 Elsworthy, Alexander Lockhart, 3 June, 1919. (M.)
5246 Englefield, William, 3 June, 1919. (M.)
5247 Evans, Bernard Scott, 3 June, 1919. (M.)
5248 Evans, Evan Reginald, 3 June, 1919. (M.)
5249 Evans, Henry John Archibald, 3 June, 1919. (M.)
5250 Evans, Samuel Earnest, 3 June, 1919. (M.)
5251 Evatt, James Wrigley, 3 June, 1919. (M.)
5252 Fairbairns, Mary Elizabeth, 3 June, 1919. (M.)
5253 Farquhar, Rev. Henry, 3 June, 1919. (M.)
5254 Farmer, Frank, 3 June, 1919. (M.)
5255 Farrance, Harry, 3 June, 1919. (M.)
5256 Fenton, Cecil, 3 June, 1919. (M.)
5257 Fenton, John, 3 June, 1919. (M.)
5258 Fenton-Jones, William Fenton, 3 June, 1919. (M.)
5259 Fergusson, John Caldwell, 3 June, 1919. (M.)
5260 Field, David, 3 June, 1919. (M.)
5261 Finlay, Harry William, 3 June, 1919. (M.)
5262 Fish, George Drummond, 3 June, 1919. (M.)
5263 Fisher, Claude Frederick Urquhart, 3 June, 1919. (M.)
5264 Fitchett, William Graham Lawson, 3 June, 1919. (M.)
5265 Fitzwater, Wilfred George, 3 June, 1919. (M.)
5266 Footner, Bertram Maughan, 3 June, 1919. (M.)
5267 Forsdyke, Albert Victor Wells, 3 June, 1919. (M.)
5268 Forster, Frederick Norman, 3 June, 1919. (M.)
5269 Foster-Melliar, John Kenelm, 3 June, 1919. (M.)
5270 Franks, Rudolph Keane, 3 June, 1919. (M.)
5271 Fraser, Angus George, 3 June, 1919. (M.)
5272 Fraser, George Alexander, 3 June, 1919. (M.)
5273 Fraser, John James, 3 June, 1919. (M.)
5274 Froude, Charles William, 3 June, 1919. (M.)
5275 Fryer, Sydney Ernest, 3 June, 1919. (M.)
5276 Fuller, Charles, 3 June, 1919. (M.)
5277 Gale, Henry Arthur, 3 June, 1919. (M.)
5278 Gallie, Sydney, 3 June, 1919. (M.)
5279 Garton, Willoughby Lewis, 3 June, 1919. (M.)
5280 Gatliff, Geoffrey Gatliff, 3 June, 1919. (M.)
5281 Gedge, Denny Victor, 3 June, 1919. (M.)

5282 George, Richard Westropp, 3 June, 1919. (M.)
5283 Gibb, Andrew Dewar, 3 June, 1919. (M.)
5284 Gibson, James Baily, 3 June, 1919. (M.)
5285 Gibson, John Montgomery, 3 June, 1919. (M.)
5286 Gielgud, Lewis Evelyn, 3 June, 1919. (M.)
5287 Gilchrist, Elizabeth MacFarlane, 3 June, 1919. (M.)
5288 Gillam, Vernon, 3 June, 1919. (M.)
5289 Gillespie, William Ernest, 3 June, 1919. (M.)
5290 Godfray, Mowatt, 3 June, 1919. (M.)
5291 Goggin, John, 3 June, 1919. (M.)
5292 Goldman, Charles Sidney, 3 June, 1919. (M.)
5293 Goldman, Julius Israel, 3 June, 1919. (M.)
5294 Goldsmith, Frank, 3 June, 1919. (M.)
5295 Goodall, Francis Harrison, 3 June, 1919. (M.)
5296 Goodwin, Arthur, 3 June, 1919. (M.)
5297 Gow, Peter Graham, 3 June, 1919. (M.)
5298 Graham-Barrow, Jess, Mrs., 3 June, 1919. (M.)
5299 Grant, Andrew, 3 June, 1919. (M.)
5300 Gray, Elliott Cecil George, 3 June, 1919. (M.)
5301 Gray, George, 3 June, 1919. (M.)
5302 Green, Robert, 3 June, 1919. (M.)
5303 Greenlees, Janet Campbell, 3 June, 1919. (M.)
5304 Greenwell, Bernard Eyre, 3 June, 1919. (M.)
5305 Greenwood, Charles Stainforth, 3 June, 1919. (M.)
5306 Gretton, Richard Henry, 3 June, 1919. (M.)
5307 Griffin, Arthur James, 3 June, 1919. (M.)
5308 Grist, William Alfred, 3 June, 1919. (M.)
5309 Groome, Walter, 3 June, 1919. (M.)
5310 Gull, Alfred Henry, 3 June, 1919. (M.)
5311 Gunn, John, 3 June, 1919. (M.)
5312 Gunton, Herbert Charles, 3 June, 1919. (M.)
5313 Guy, Percy Claude, 3 June, 1919. (M.)
5314 Hacker, William Henry, 3 June, 1919. (M.)
5315 Hall, Edgar, 3 June, 1919. (M.)
5316 Hall, Harry Reginald Holland, 3 June, 1919. (M.)
5318 Halloran, William James, 3 June, 1919. (M.)
5319 Handley-Read, Edward Harry, 3 June, 1919. (M.)
5320 Hanney, Michael John, 3 June, 1919. (M.)
5321 Hardy, Henry Stewart, 3 June, 1919. (M.)
5322 Hargroves, William Robert, 3 June, 1919. (M.)
5323 Harley, Ernest William James, 3 June, 1919. (M.)
5324 Harmer, Ronald Frederick, 3 June, 1919. (M.)
5325 Harper, John Stanley, 3 June, 1919. (M.)
5326 Harpur, John Latimer, 3 June, 1919. (M.)
5327 Harris, Francis George, 3 June, 1919. (M.)
5329 Harrison, Leonard Charles, 3 June, 1919. (M.)
5330 Hartington, Edward William Spencer Cavendish, Marquis of, 3 June, 1919. (M.)
5331 Harvey, William. 3 June, 1919. (M.)
5332 Haviland, Reginald Henry 3 June, 1919. (M.)
5333 Haviland, Wilfred Pullan, 3 June, 1919. (M.)
5334 Hearn, George Henry Seymour, 3 June, 1919. (M.)
5335 Hedley, Thomas, 3 June, 1919. (M.)
5336 Hedley, Theodore Fenwick, 3 June, 1919. (M.)
5337 Helden, Frederick, 3 June, 1919. (M.)
5338 Hellyer, Ernest Palmer, 3 June, 1919. (M.)
5339 Henderson, Ian Macdonald, 3 June, 1919. (M.)
5340 Henshaw, John Thomas, 3 June, 1919. (M.)
5341 Henshaw, Thomas, 3 June, 1919. (M.)
5342 Herbert, George, 3 June, 1919. (M.)
5343 Heseltine, Conrad Pelham, 3 June, 1919. (M.)
5344 Hesketh, William Henry, 3 June, 1919. (M.)
5345 Hicks, Joseph Marmaduke, 3 June, 1919. (M.)
5346 Hide, Lewis, 3 June, 1919. (M)
5347 Higson, Percy John, 3 June, 1919. (M.)
5348 Higson, William, 3 June, 1919. (M.)
5349 Hill, Robert, 3 June, 1919. (M.)
5350 Hinton, William Henry, 3 June, 1919. (M.)
5351 Hitchcock, Roland George, 3 June, 1919. (M.)
5352 Hogan, Thomas, 3 June, 1919. (M.)
5353 Holden, Ernest Frank, 3 June, 1919. (M.)
5354 Holland, Edgar Stopford, 3 June, 1919. (M.)
5355 Holmes, Arthur Ernest, 3 June, 1919. (M.)
5356 Hopperton, Henry Edward, 3 June, 1919. (M.)
5357 Hoskins, Wallace Edward, 3 June, 1919. (M.)
5358 Howard, Septimus Carolus, 3 June, 1919. (M.)
5359 Howell, Owen A., 3 June, 1919. (M.)
5360 Hudson, Charles, 3 June, 1919. (M.)
5361 Huggard, Rev. Richard, 3 June, 1919. (M.)
5362 Hume, Hugh Bliss Torriano, 3 June, 1919. (M.)
5363 Humphreys, Thomas, 3 June, 1919. (M.)
5364 Hunt, Reginald Noel, 3 June, 1919. (M.)
5365 Hunter, John Francis Stuart, 3 June, 1919. (M.)
5366 Hunter-Blair, Reginald Stanley, 3 June, 1919. (M.)
5367 Hurle, Alfred Edward, 3 June, 1919. (M.)
5368 Hussey, Henry, 3 June, 1919. (M.)
5369 Huyshe, Rowland Radcliffe, 3 June, 1919. (M.)
5370 Ibbitson, George, 3 June, 1919. (M.)
5371 Imrie, George Blair, 3 June, 1919. (M.)
5372 Ince, Bernard Sidney, 3 June, 1919. (M.)
5373 Innes, George Alexander, 3 June, 1919. (M.)
5374 Ionides, Helen Euphrosyne, 3 June, 1919. (M.)
5375 Ireland, James Augustus, 3 June, 1919. (M.)
5377 Jackson, Francis Munton, 3 June, 1919. (M.)
5378 James, Edward Lionel Luscombe, 3 June, 1919. (M.)
5379 Janson, Frederick Ernest, 3 June, 1919. (M.)
5380 Jay, Stanley, 3 June, 1919. (M.)
5381 Jenks, Herbert William, 3 June, 1919. (M.)
5382 Jessap, Charles Townsley, 3 June, 1919. (M.)
5383 Johns, Frederick, 3 June, 1919. (M.)

5384 Johns, William Alexander, 3 June, 1919. (M.)
5385 Johnson, Reginald, 3 June, 1919. (M.)
5386 Jones, Oswell, 3 June, 1919. (M.)
5387 Jones, Robert, 3 June, 1919. (M.)
5388 Jones, William Everard Tyldesley, 3 June, 1919. (M.)
5389 Joslin, Evelyn Whyaid, 3 June, 1919. (M.)
5391 Keefe, Ernest, 3 June, 1919. (M.)
5392 Keeping, Harold Balfour, 3 June, 1919. (M.)
5393 Keer, Raymond Wilfred Cordy, 3 June, 1919. (M.)
5394 Keitley, Cyril Humby, 3 June, 1919. (M.)
5395 Kekewich, Sydney, 3 June, 1919. (M.)
5396 Kelly, Thomas, 3 June, 1919. (M.)
5397 Kennedy, Charles Matheson, 3 June, 1919. (M.)
5398 Kennedy, Douglas Neil, 3 June, 1919. (M.)
5399 Kennedy, Walter Stewart, 3 June, 1919. (M.)
5400 Kenny, Louis, 3 June, 1919. (M.)
5401 Kerr, Robert, 3 June, 1919. (M.)
5403 Kimberley, Harold William, 3 June, 1919. (M.)
5404 Kingdon, Albert Arthur, 3 June, 1919. (M.)
5405 Kingston, Charles, 3 June, 1919. (M.)
5407 Lambie, George, 3 June, 1919. (M.)
5408 Lanigan-O'Keefe, Francis Stephen, 3 June, 1919. (M.)
5409 Laurie, Rawdon Hastings St. Barbe, 3 June, 1919. (M.)
5410 Laurie, William, 3 June, 1919. (M.)
5411 Lavery, Andrew, 3 June, 1919. (M.)
5412 Lawler, Robert Edward, 3 June, 1919. (M.)
5413 Leaver, Gray, 3 June, 1919. (M.)
5414 Lee, Albert Victor, 3 June, 1919. (M.)
5415 Lee, George, 3 June, 1919. (M.)
5416 Leonard, Thomas Goulton, 3 June, 1919. (M.)
5417 Leslie, Charles William, 3 June, 1919. (M.)
5418 Leveson-Gower, Cecil Oliver Gresham, 3 June, 1910. (M.)
5419 Levy, Jeanne Athol, 3 June, 1919. (M.)
5420 Lewis, Orpheus William Henry, 3 June, 1919. (M.)
5421 Lindop, Patrick, 3 June, 1919. (M.)
5422 Lippold, Albert Arthur, 3 June, 1919. (M.)
5423 Lithiby, Beatrice Ethel, 3 June, 1919. (M.)
5424 Loudon, Thomas, 3 June, 1919. (M.)
5425 Longbotham, Charles Rawson, 3 June, 1919. (M.)
5426 Longworth, Ernest Victor, 3 June, 1919. (M.)
5427 Lucy, John Charles Hampden, 3 June, 1919. (M.)
5429 Lumley, Charles Hope, 3 June, 1919. (M.)
5430 Lumsden, Charles Ernest, 3 June, 1919. (M.)
5432 McAlister, Daniel Archibald, 3 June, 1919. (M.)
5433 McAvoy, John, 3 June, 1919. (M.)
5434 McColl, Henrietta Sunderland, 3 June, 1919. (M.)
5435 McCulloch, John Smith, 3 June, 1919. (M.)
5436 MacDonald, Allen Fraser, 3 June, 1919. (M.)
5437 MacDonald, Ewen William Charles, 3 June, 1919. (M.)
5438 McDonald, James, 3 June, 1919. (M.)
5439 McDonald, James, 3 June, 1919. (M.)
5440 MacDonald, Robert Parker, 3 June, 1919. (M.)
5441 McDougall, Alfred, 3 June, 1919. (M.)
5442 McIver, Walter, 3 June, 1919. (M.)
5443 McKay, Robert James, 3 June, 1919. (M.)
5444 McKechnie, George, 3 June, 1919. (M.)
5445 McLaren, Robert, 3 June, 1919. (M.)
5446 McLean, Alan, 3 June, 1919. (M.)
5447 McLeish, James, 3 June, 1919. (M.)
5448 McClellan, Creighton William, 3 June, 1919. (M.)
5449 McMullen, Kenrick James, 3 June, 1919. (M.)
5450 MacPhail, Agnew Main, 3 June, 1919. (M.)
5451 Manico, Arthur, 3 June, 1919. (M.)
5452 Mann, Grace, 3 June, 1919. (M.)
5453 Mann, Thomas Clifford, 3 June, 1919. (M.)
5454 Mansfield, James Walter, 3 June, 1919. (M.)
5455 Marchant, Frederick James, 3 June, 1919. (M.)
5456 Mason, Horace George, 3 June, 1919. (M.)
5457 Masters, Denis MacPherson, 3 June, 1919. (M.)
5458 Matheson, Frederick William, 3 June, 1919. (M.)
5459 Mathews, George Alfred, 3 June, 1919. (M.)
5460 Matthews, Clement Norman, 3 June, 1919. (M.)
5461 Meadows, Henry George, 3 June, 1919. (M.)
5462 Merrett, Francis George, 3 June, 1919. (M.)
5463 Metcalfe, Harry Francis, 3 June, 1919. (M.)
5464 Metcalfe, Percy Kynaston, 3 June, 1919. (M.)
5465 Middleton, George, 3 June, 1919. (M.)
5466 Midgeley, Sam, 3 June, 1919. (M.)
5467 Miles, Alfred George, 3 June, 1919. (M.)
5468 Mill, John Smith Tindal, 3 June, 1919. (M.)
5469 Milliken, Ernest Norman, 3 June, 1919. (M.)
5470 Mills, Harry Sturgess, 3 June, 1919. (M.)
5471 Milton, James Clymo, 3 June, 1919. (M.)
5472 Mitchell, Margaret Florence, 3 June, 1919. (M.)
5473 Mitchell, William Alfred James, 3 June, 1919. (M.)
5474 Moir, Archibald Patrick, 3 June, 1919. (M.)
5475 Molineux, George, 3 June, 1919. (M.)
5476 Moncrieff, Malcolm Matthew, 3 June, 1919. (M.)
5477 Monk, John Bird, 3 June, 1919. (M.)
5478 Moor, Marjorie, 3 June, 1919. (M.)
5479 Moore, Harold Mead, 3 June, 1919. (M.)
5480 Moore, Richard William, 3 June, 1919. (M.)
5481 Moore, William Arthur, 3 June, 1919. (M.)
5482 Moreton, Arthur Ernest, 3 June, 1919. (M.)
5483 Morgan, Arthur Richard, 3 June, 1919. (M.)
5484 Morgan, John Scammell, 3 June, 1919. (M.)
5485 Morgan, Phillip Sydney, 3 June, 1919. (M.)
5486 Morgan, Sydney Cope, 3 June, 1919. (M.)
5487 Morris, Edward, 3 June, 1919. (M.)
5488 Morris, Frederick Herbert, 3 June, 1919. (M.)

5489 Morris, Rev. Patrick Joseph, 3 June, 1919. (M.)
5490 Morris, William Henry, 3 June, 1919. (M.)
5491 Morton, George Bowen, 3 June, 1919. (M.)
5492 Morton, Robert Connell, 3 June, 1919. (M.)
5493 Mumford, Harry George, 3 June, 1919. (M.)
5494 Munday, Alfred, 3 June, 1919. (M.)
5495 Murgatroyd, Dorothy Sarah, Mrs., 3 June, 1919. (M.)
5496 Murphy, Francis Philip Sydney, 3 June, 1919. (M.)
5497 Nash, Francis Joseph, 3 June, 1919. (M.)
5498 Nelson, David, 3 June, 1919. (M.)
5499 Newton, Giles Fendall, 3 June, 1919. (M.)
5500 Nias, Herbert John, 3 June, 1919. (M.)
5501 Nicholson, Christabel, 3 June, 1919. (M.)
5502 Nicholson, Norwood, 3 June, 1919. (M.)
5503 Noyes, Edwin Brownrigg, 3 June, 1919. (M.)
5504 Oates, Frank, 3 June, 1919. (M.)
5505 Oborn, Joseph, 3 June, 1919. (M.)
5506 O'Brien, James Matthew, 3 June, 1919. (M.)
5507 Orchard, Edward Henslow, 3 June, 1919. (M.)
5508 Ottley, Robert Bruce Hamilton, 3 June, 1919. (M.)
5509 Ovens, Jean Broomfield Wier, 3 June, 1919. (M.)
5510 Page, Harold James, 3 June, 1919. (M.)
5511 Palmer, Basil Owen, 3 June, 1919. (M.)
5512 Palmer, Ellen Amelia, Mrs., 3 June, 1919. (M.)
5513 Paramor, Frank Richard, 3 June, 1919. (M.)
5514 Parker, Hugh Love, 3 June, 1919. (M.)
5515 Parker, Thomas Mayor, 3 June, 1919. (M.)
5516 Parker, Wilfred Watson, 3 June, 1919. (M.)
5517 Parkes, Dorothy Phœbe, Mrs., 3 June, 1919. (M.)
5518 Passmore, Herbert, 3 June, 1919. (M.)
5519 Payne, Tom, 3 June, 1919. (M.)
5520 Pearson, Henry John, 3 June, 1919. (M.)
5521 Peart, Charles, 3 June, 1919. (M.)
5522 Peck, Victor Newton, 3 June, 1919. (M.)
5523 Peddie, John Ronald, 3 June, 1919. (M.)
5524 Peel, Albert William, 3 June, 1919. (M.)
5525 Pellatt, Hamilton Francis Moore, 3 June, 1919. (M.)
5526 Pelly, Evelyn, 3 June, 1919. (M.)
5527 Percival, Alexander Philip, 3 June, 1919. (M.)
5528 Perkins, Lewis Arthur, 3 June, 1919. (M.)
5529 Perry, Violet, 3 June, 1919. (M.)
5530 Peters, Cecil Wyburn, 3 June, 1919. (M.)
5531 Philips, Harry Vaughan, 3 June, 1919. (M.)
5532 Phillips, Horace Stock, 3 June, 1919. (M.)
5533 Phillips, James Charles Joseph, 3 June, 1919. (M.)
5534 Phillips, William Austin, 3 June, 1919. (M.)
5535 Phipps, Henry Croly, 3 June, 1919. (M.)
5536 Pickering, John Russell, 3 June, 1919. (M.)
5537 Pigé-Leschallas, Henry, 3 June, 1919. (M.)
5538 Pinder, Arthur William, 3 June, 1919. (M.)
5539 Pinsent, Arthur, 3 June, 1919. (M.)
5540 Platt, Claude Bernard Meister, 3 June, 1919. (M.)
5541 Platt, Sydney Frank, 3 June, 1919. (M.)
5542 Pleydell-Bouverie, Humphrey, 3 June, 1919. (M.)
5543 Pocock, Elisha John, 3 June, 1919. (M.)
5545 Porter, Samuel Lowry, 3 June, 1919. (M.)
5546 Post, George Henry Draper, 3 June, 1919. (M.)
5547 Power, George Teevan, 3 June, 1919. (M.)
5548 Power, Frank Trevor, 3 June, 1919. (M.)
5549 Prioleau, Lynch Hamilton, 3 June, 1919. (M.)
5550 Procter, Roger Cecil, 3 June, 1919. (M.)
5551 Quayle, Edwin, 3 June, 1919. (M.)
5552 Quick, Abraham, 3 June, 1919. (M.)
5553 Quinn, John James, 3 June, 1919. (M.)
5554 Rackham, George John, 3 June, 1919. (M.)
5555 Rait, Alexander Macpherson, 3 June, 1919. (M.)
5556 Ramsdale, James Ellwood, 3 June, 1919. (M.)
5557 Randall, Richard Walter Kimbal, 3 June, 1919. (M.)
5558 Rawlinson, Arthur Richard, 3 June, 1919. (M.)
5559 Rayner, Oswald Theodore, 3 June, 1919. (M.)
5560 Read, Alfred, 3 June, 1919. (M.)
5561 Redlich, Stefan, 3 June, 1919. (M.)
5562 Reed, Baron Noel, 3 June, 1919. (M.)
5563 Rees, Harry, 3 June, 1919. (M.)
5564 Reeves, Edward Charles, 3 June, 1919. (M.)
5565 Reid, Isaac William, 3 June, 1919. (M.)
5566 Reid, James, 3 June, 1919. (M.)
5567 Reilly, Thomas, 3 June, 1919. (M.)
5568 Rennet, David, 3 June, 1919. (M.)
5569 Reynish, James Bruce, 3 June, 1919. (M.)
5570 Reynolds, Philip George, 3 June, 1919. (M.)
5571 Richards, Province Wellesley, 3 June, 1919. (M.)
5572 Ricketts, Joseph, 3 June, 1919. (M.)
5573 Riddell, Douglas Errington, 3 June, 1919. (M.)
5574 Rigby, Robert Stacey Marks, 3 June, 1919. (M.)
5576 Robertson, Adam McCall, 3 June, 1919. (M.)
5577 Roberts, George William Pearson, 3 June, 1919. (M.)
5578 Roberts, Talbot Vivian Waymen, 3 June, 1919. (M.)
5579 Robertson, Frederick William, 3 June, 1919. (M.)
5580 Robertson, Margaret Agnes Josepha, 3 June, 1919. (M.)
5581 Robinson, William Henry, 3 June, 1919. (M.)
5582 Roche, Alfred Lyttleton, 3 June, 1919. (M.)
5583 Rogers, Gilbert, 3 June, 1919. (M.)
5584 Rogers, Lilian May, 3 June, 1919. (M.)
5585 Rogers, William Aldrich, 3 June, 1919. (M.)
5586 Rolfe, Charles Bertram, 3 June, 1919. (M.)
5587 Rose, Norman Frank, 3 June, 1919. (M.)
5588 Rosling, Cecil, 3 June, 1919. (M.)
5589 Rouse, William Sydney, 3 June, 1919. (M.)
5590 Rowe, James Stewart, 3 June, 1919. (M.)

5591 Rowe, Wilfred Aubrey, 3 June, 1919. (M.)
5592 Rowlatt, Charles James, 3 June, 1919. (M.)
5593 Rowlatt, Frederick George, 3 June, 1919. (M.)
5594 Rycroft, Albert, 3 June, 1919. (M.)
5595 Rycroft, Frederick, 3 June, 1919. (M.)
5596 Sandberg, Judith Mary, 3 June, 1919. (M.)
5597 Sandeman, William Wellington, 3 June, 1919. (M.)
5598 Sandercock, Archie, 3 June, 1919. (M.)
5600 Sangster, Thomas Alexander Gardner, 3 June, 1919. (M.)
5601 Saward, Frank Robert, 3 June, 1919. (M.)
5602 Scholes, George Ernest, 3 June, 1919. (M.)
5603 Scott, Arthur Frank, 3 June, 1919. (M.)
5604 Scott, Eustace Edward, 3 June, 1919. (M.)
5605 Scott, George Alfred, 3 June, 1919. (M.)
5606 Scott, Keith Stanley Malcolm, 3 June, 1919. (M.)
5607 Scott, Walter Nedham, 3 June, 1919. (M.)
5608 Scrivener, Harry Stanley, 3 June, 1919. (M.)
5609 Scudamore, William George, 3 June, 1919. (M.)
5610 Searle, Arthur Mackenzie, 3 June, 1919. (M.)
5611 Seeley, Rev. John, 3 June, 1919. (M.)
5612 Sergeant, Archibald Joseph, 3 June, 1919. (M.)
5613 Shallis, Boydell, 3 June, 1919. (M.)
5614 Shannon, Richard, 3 June, 1919. (M.)
5615 Sharland, Ernest John, 3 June, 1919. (M.)
5616 Sharles, Frederick Francis, 3 June, 1919. (M.)
5617 Shaw, James William, 3 June, 1919. (M.)
5618 Shean, Walter, 3 June, 1919. (M.)
5619 Shefford, Alan Douglas Edward, 3 June, 1919. (M.)
5620 Shelmerdine, Harry Neal, 3 June, 1919. (M.)
5621 Shelton, Harry Gordon, 3 June, 1919. (M.)
5622 Shields, Oswald Clive Graeme, 3 June, 1919. (M.)
5623 Shillington, Elizabeth Mildred, 3 June, 1919. (M.)
5624 Shore, Alfred George, 3 June, 1919. (M.)
5625 Showell, Charles Frederick, 3 June, 1919. (M.)
5626 Silverwood-Cope, Alan Lachlan, 3 June, 1919. (M.)
5627 Simmett, William Edward, 3 June, 1919. (M.)
5628 Sinclair, Robert John, 3 June, 1919. (M.)
5629 Sinfield, Thomas, 3 June, 1919. (M.)
5630 Sinnatt, Frank Sturdy, 3 June, 1919. (M.)
5631 Skelton, Allan, 3 June, 1919. (M.)
5632 Smith, Donald Woodford, 3 June, 1919. (M.)
5633 Smith, Harold James, 3 June, 1919. (M.)
5634 Smith, James William, 3 June, 1919. (M.)
5635 Smith, Mary Amelia, 3 June, 1919. (M.)
5637 Smith, Soloman Charles Kaines, 3 June, 1919. (M.)
5638 Smith, Thomas Joseph, 3 June, 1919. (M.)
5639 Spence, Andrew, 3 June, 1919. (M.)
5640 Spence, John Charles, 3 June, 1919. (M.)
5641 Spence, Lockhart James, 3 June, 1919. (M.)
5642 Spencer, Gerald Theodosius Leigh, 3 June, 1919. (M.)
5643 Spillane, Richard, 3 June, 1919. (M.)
5644 Spinks, Edwin Gardiner, 3 June, 1919. (M.)
5645 Spittal, John Kerr, 3 June, 1919. (M.)
5646 Squire, Walter Ernest, 3 June, 1919. (M.)
5647 St. Clair-Ford, Leicester, 3 June, 1919. (M.)
5648 Stack, Norah Blake, 3 June, 1919. (M.)
5649 Stafford, Edward, 3 June, 1919. (M.)
5650 Stanley, Herbert Vernon, 3 June, 1919. (M.)
5651 Steggall, Robert Ernest, 3 June, 1919. (M.)
5652 Stelling, Carl David, 3 June, 1919. (M.)
5653 Stericker, John, 3 June, 1919. (M.)
5654 Stewart, Angus Matheson, 3 June, 1919. (M.)
5655 Stewart, John Henry George, 3 June, 1919. (M.)
5656 Stitt, Iza, 3 June, 1919. (M.)
5657 Stodart-Walker, Archibald, 3 June, 1919. (M.)
5658 Stringer, Hubert Leslie, 3 June, 1919. (M.)
5659 Stubbs, Harry, 3 June, 1919. (M.)
5660 Sturgess, Charles, 3 June, 1919. (M.)
5661 Swallow, Thomas Asquith, 3 June, 1919. (M.)
5662 Swinerd, Henry James, 3 June, 1919. (M.)
5663 Swinstead, Norman Hillyard, 3 June, 1919. (M.)
5664 Taylor, Edward Dansy, 3 June, 1919. (M.)
5665 Taylor, Harry, 3 June, 1919. (M.)
5666 Templeton, Archibald Angus, 3 June, 1919. (M.)
5667 Thomas, Arthur Henry, 3 June, 1919. (M.)
5668 Thomas, Harold Miles, 3 June, 1919. (M.)
5669 Thomson, Alexander Brackstone, 3 June, 1919. (M.)
5670 Thomson, Alfred Louis, 3 June, 1919. (M.)
5671 Thomson, Frederick Charles, 3 June, 1919. (M.)
5672 Thornbery, Stanley Russell, 3 June, 1919. (M.)
5673 Thorne, Frederick John, 3 June, 1919. (M.)
5674 Thorp, Harold John, 3 June, 1919. (M.)
5675 Thurstan, Alan Dorrington, 3 June, 1919. (M.)
5676 Tipping, Frank Walter, 3 June, 1919. (M.)
5677 Tisley, Frederick William, 3 June, 1919. (M.)
5678 Titchener, Harry Stocker, 3 June, 1919. (M.)
5679 Todd, Alexander, 3 June, 1919. (M.)
5680 Tomkins, Stanley Charles, 3 June, 1919. (M.)
5681 Toms, William, 3 June, 1919. (M.)
5682 Tonkinson John, 3 June, 1919. (M.)
5683 Tookey, Francis Edwin Friday, 3 June, 1919. (M.)
5684 Topliss, John, 3 June, 1919. (M.)
5685 Travill, Robert, 3 June, 1919. (M.)
5686 Trenam, Richard, 3 June, 1919. (M.)
5687 Troubridge, Thomas St. Vincent Wallace, 3 June, 1919. (M.)
5688 Tucker, Frederick James, 3 June, 1919. (M.)
5689 Tulloch, Hubert Thorold, 3 June, 1919. (M.)
5690 Tunks, George Patrick D'Arcy Gregory, 3 June, 1919. (M.)

5691 Turnbull, Thomas Montgomerie, 3 June, 1919. (M.)
5692 Turner, Alfred Charles, 3 June, 1919. (M.)
5693 Turner, Bernard Wilfred, 3 June, 1919. (M.)
5694 Tyndale, Henry Edmund Guise, 3 June, 1919. (M.)
5695 Tyson, William, 3 June, 1919. (M.)
5696 Underwood, Reginald Edward, 3 June, 1919. (M.)
5697 Upham, John Albert Austin, 3 June, 1919. (M.)
5698 Vassie, Frederick Charles, 3 June, 1919. (M.)
5699 Vernon, Richard Henry, 3 June, 1919. (M.)
5700 Wade, George Bridges, 3 June, 1919. (M.)
5701 Wale, William Alfred, 3 June, 1919. (M.)
5702 Walker, Austine Harington, 3 June, 1919. (M.)
5703 Walker, Samuel, 3 June, 1919. (M.)
5704 Walter, Weever Kenneth, 3 June, 1919. (M.)
5705 Wark, Hector, 3 June, 1919. (M.)
5706 Wark, John Lean, 3 June, 1919. (M.)
5707 Warren, Claude Alfred Reuben, 3 June, 1919. (M.)
5708 Warren, Henry William, 3 June, 1919. (M.)
5709 Warrior, Edith Mary, 3 June, 1919. (M.)
5710 Waters, George Frederick Mary, 3 June, 1919. (M.)
5711 Watkins, William John, 3 June, 1919. (M.)
5712 Watson, Frederick Whittaker, 3 June, 1919. (M.)
5713 Watson, Noel Sutcliffe Ogilvy, 3 June, 1919. (M.)
5714 Watson, William Charles, 3 June, 1919. (M.)
5715 Webb, Frederick John, 3 June, 1919. (M.)
5716 Webb, Henry Smith, 3 June, 1919. (M.)
5717 Webb, Thomas, 3 June, 1919. (M.)
5718 Weir, Thomas Duncan, 3 June, 1919. (M.)
5720 Wells, Henry Bensley, 3 June, 1919. (M.)
5721 Wells, Stanley Walter, 3 June, 1919. (M.)
5722 Westcott, George Henry, 3 June, 1919. (M.)
5723 Whatley, Norman, 3 June, 1919. (M.)
5724 White, Bruce Gordon, 3 June, 1919. (M.)
5725 Whittaker, William Edward de Bagnlegh, 3 June, 1919. (M.)
5726 Whittington, William, 3 June, 1919. (M.)
5727 Whitworth, Charles Warwick, 3 June, 1919. (M.)
5728 Wiles, Harold Herbert, 3 June, 1919. (M.)
5729 Wilkins, Dennison Alfred, 3 June, 1919. (M.)
5730 Willes, Harry, 3 June, 1919. (M.)
5731 Williams, Charles, 3 June, 1919. (M.)
5732 Williams, Harold, 3 June, 1919. (M.)
5733 Williams, John Montague, 3 June, 1919. (M.)
5734 Williams, Leonard Lowther, 3 June, 1919. (M.)
5735 Williams, Richard Barclay, 3 June, 1919. (M.)
5736 Willis, Harry Richard James, 3 June, 1919. (M.)
5737 Willmott, Frederick William, 3 June, 1919. (M.)
5738 Wilson, Aphra Phyllis, 3 June, 1919. (M.)
5739 Wilson, John, 3 June, 1919. (M.)
5740 Wilson, William Robert, 3 June, 1919. (M.)
5741 Winch, Arthur Bluett, 3 June, 1919. (M.)
5742 Windrum, James Moffet, 3 June, 1919. (M.)
5743 Winstanley, Henry Parr, 3 June, 1919. (M.)
5744 Wolff, James Daniel, 3 June, 1919. (M.)
5745 Wombwell, Fred, 3 June, 1919. (M.)
5746 Wood, Alexander, 3 June, 1919. (M.)
5747 Wood, Edith Francis, 3 June, 1919. (M.)
5748 Woodruff, Charles Reynolds, 3 June, 1919. (M.)
5749 Woolley, Reginald George, 3 June, 1919. (M.)
5750 Woolway, Charles Gordon, 3 June, 1919. (M.)
5751 Woosley, Ernest Harry, 3 June, 1919. (M.)
5752 Wootton, Herbert, 3 June, 1919. (M.)
5753 Wootton, Herbert Arthur, 3 June, 1919. (M.)
5754 Wotherspoon, John Armour, 3 June, 1919. (M.)
5755 Wright, Charles, 3 June, 1919. (M.)
5756 Wright, Sydney Arthur, 3 June, 1919. (M.)
5757 Wright, Thomas Kendall, 3 June, 1919. (M.)
5758 Yarrow, George Ernest, 3 June, 1919. (M.)
5759 Yorwerth, Thomas Jenkin, 3 June, 1919. (M.)
5760 Young, Bertram John, 3 June, 1919. (M.)
5761 Young, Charlie, 3 June, 1919. (M.)
5762 Young, Harry Robert, 3 June, 1919. (M.)
5763 Young, Richard Horton, 3 June, 1919. (M.)
5764 Yule, John Stirling, 3 June, 1919. (M.)
5765 Bagot, Christopher George Seymour, 3 June, 1919. (M.)
5766 Caine, Martin Surney, 3 June, 1919. (M.)
5767 Castle, Ivor, 3 June, 1919. (M.)
5768 Clarke, Thomas Walter, 3 June, 1919. (M.)
5769 Cox, Alexander, 3 June, 1919. (M.)
5770 Currie, Thomas Dickson, 3 June, 1919. (M.)
5771 Curry, Charles Townley, 3 June, 1919. (M.)
5772 Duggan, Harry Van Norman, 3 June, 1919. (M.)
5773 Evans, John Edward, 3 June, 1919. (M.)
5774 Gallon, Thomas Heaton, 3 June, 1919. (M.)
5775 Gault, William James, 3 June, 1919. (M.)
5776 Gibson, George E., 3 June, 1919. (M.)
5777 Gordon, Arthur Douglas, 3 June, 1919. (M.)
5778 Gordon, Stewart, 3 June, 1919. (M.)
5779 Hardman, Walter, 3 June, 1919. (M.)
5780 Harrison, Harry, 3 June, 1919. (M.)
5781 Holden, Frederick Morgan, 3 June, 1919. (M.)
5782 Hora, Hansord, 3 June, 1919. (M.)
5783 Hutcheson, John, 3 June, 1919. (M.)
5784 Jaminson, Samuel Jones, 3 June, 1919. (M.)
5785 Johnson, Edwin William, 3 June, 1919. (M.)
5786 Jones, William Henry, 3 June, 1919. (M.)
5787 McDerment, William, 3 June, 1919. (M.)
5788 McLean, James, 3 June, 1919. (M.)
5789 Perry, Joseph Charles, 3 June, 1919. (M.)
5790 Rice, William Henry, 3 June, 1919. (M.)

5791 Robinson, George William, 3 June, 1919. (M.)
5792 Seybold, John Clifford, 3 June, 1919. (M.)
5793 Sheff, John, 3 June, 1919. (M.)
5794 Simpson, George Wilmot Rae, 3 June, 1919. (M.)
5795 Sinclair, Andrew Gibson, 3 June, 1919. (M.)
5796 Slayter, John Howard, 3 June, 1919. (M.)
5797 Smith, Stanley Oscar, 3 June, 1919. (M.)
5798 Smythe, Frank Aldham, 3 June, 1919. (M.)
5799 Starratt, Harry Joseph, 3 June, 1919. (M.)
5800 Sutherland, Harry Wilson, 3 June, 1919. (M.)
5801 Thomas, William Bryson, 3 June, 1919. (M.)
5802 Tomlinson, Davil Holland, 3 June, 1919. (M.)
5803 Vernon, William Hamilton, 3 June, 1919. (M.)
5804 Wilson, Wilfred Wellington, 3 June, 1919. (M.)
5805 Woodiwiss, Edwin Sydney, 3 June, 1919. (M.)
5806 Andrewes, Robert Lancelot, 3 June, 1919. (M.)
5807 Berryman, Mark, 3 June, 1919. (M.)
5808 Bingle, William Reginald, 3 June, 1919. (M.)
5809 Broad, Archibald du Bourg, 3 June, 1919. (M.)
5810 Brown, Joseph Hector, 3 June, 1919. (M.)
5811 Caro, Phillip, 3 June, 1919. (M.)
5812 Carr, Gerald Mossman, 3 June, 1919. (M.)
5813 Charlesworth, Arthur, 3 June, 1919. (M.)
5814 Crome, Harry, 3 June, 1919. (M.)
5815 Crooks, David Robert, 3 June, 1919. (M.)
5816 Davy, Cyril, 3 June, 1919. (M.)
5817 Docker, Cyril Talbot, 3 June, 1919. (M.)
5818 Drummond, John Raymond, 3 June, 1919. (M.)
5819 Grace, Theodore Phillip, 3 June, 1919. (M.)
5820 Hall, Ernest Virtue, 3 June, 1919. (M.)
5821 Hall, Harold Stanley George, 3 June, 1919. (M.)
5822 Healy, Reginald Stafford, 3 June, 1919. (M.)
5823 Henry, John Herbert Wallace, 3 June, 1919. (M.)
5824 Herriott, William Malcolm, 3 June, 1919. (M.)
5825 Ikin, Harry Claude, 3 June, 1919. (M.)
5826 Jessep, Alfred James, 3 June, 1919. (M.)
5827 Laird, Frederick Nicholas, 3 June, 1919. (M.)
5828 Lampe, Frederick Ernest, 3 June, 1919. (M.)
5829 Langslow, Melville Cecil, 3 June, 1919. (M.)
5830 Lawrence, Eric Nathan Samuel, 3 June, 1919. (M.)
5831 Levy, Theodore Harold, 3 June, 1919. (M.)
5832 Long, Edmund James, 3 June, 1919. (M.)
5833 McLennan, Kenneth, 3 June, 1919. (M.)
5834 Mohr, Reginald Harry, 3 June, 1919. (M.)
5835 Murphy, Reginald William, 3 June, 1919. (M.)
5836 Murray, John Francis Stuart 3 June, 1919. (M.)
5837 Newlands, Alexander, 3 June, 1919. (M.)
5838 Norris, Harold, 3 June, 1919. (M.)
5839 Price, Cecil Stanley, 3 June, 1919. (M.)
5840 Robley, Vernon Edward, 3 June, 1919. (M.)
5841 Rossiter, Thomas Frederick, 3 June, 1919. (M.)
5842 Smith, Miles Staniforth Cator, 3 June, 1919. (M.)
5843 Sorensen, Michael, 3 June, 1919. (M.)
5844 Spittal, Charles Edward, 3 June, 1919. (M.)
5845 Thirkell, Robert Mowbray Winston, 3 June, 1919. (M.)
5846 Tyler, Arthur George, 3 June, 1919. (M.)
5847 Wheeler, Douglas Bingham, 3 June, 1919. (M.)
5848 Wilson, Roy Vincent, 3 June, 1919. (M.)
5849 Atwell, William, 3 June, 1919. (M.)
5850 Bell, Norman, 3 June, 1919. (M.)
5851 Booth, Charles Henry, 3 June, 1919. (M.)
5852 Bosworth, John Thomas, 3 June, 1919. (M.)
5853 Brocks, Arthur William, 3 June, 1919. (M.)
5854 Brown, Henry Harwood, 3 June, 1919. (M.)
5855 Colclough, William Cæsar Sarsfield, 3 June, 1919. (M.)
5856 Corrigan, Albert Arthur, 3 June, 1919. (M.)
5857 Cossgrove, David Cecil Wallace, 3 June, 1919. (M.)
5858 Crowther, Walter, 3 June, 1919. (M.)
5859 Dobson, William, 3 June, 1919. (M.)
5860 Ewen, David Alexander, 3 June, 1919. (M.)
5861 Gentry, Frederick Charles, 3 June, 1919. (M.)
5862 Hursthouse, William Richmond, 3 June, 1919. (M.
5863 Isaacs, David Nathan, 3 June, 1919. (M.)
5864 Jack, William, 3 June, 1919. (M.)
5865 Jolly, Henry, 3 June, 1919. (M.)
5866 Kirk, James Robert, 3 June, 1919. (M.)
5867 Lowe, Edward Cronin, 3 June, 1919. (M.)
5868 Malden, Rev. Edward Elliott, 3 June, 1919. (M.)
5869 Martin, James Seaton, 3 June, 1919. (M.)
5870 Matthews, Robert Saxon, 3 June, 1919. (M.)
5871 Mellows, Samuel, 3 June, 1919. (M.)
5872 Moller, Oden, 3 June, 1919. (M.)
5873 Northcote, James Alfred, 3 June, 1919. (M.)
5874 Nutsford, Henry Charles, 3 June, 1919. (M.)
5875 Oram, Matthew Henry, 3 June, 1919. (M.)
5876 Osborne, Henry William, 3 June, 1919. (M.)
5877 Pettit, William Haddon, 3 June, 1919. (M.)
5878 Porteous, Lawrence Victor, 3 June, 1919. (M.)
5879 Pryor, William, 3 June, 1919. (M.)
5880 Quartley, Arthur Gilbert, 3 June, 1919. (M.)
5881 Redmond, Henry Joseph, 3 June, 1919. (M.)
5882 Ridler, Arthur James, 3 June, 1919. (M.)
5883 Ringland, Thomas Hazlett, 3 June, 1919. (M.)
5884 Rishworth, Norman John, 3 June, 1919. (M.)
5885 Shand, David Brett, 3 June, 1919. (M.)
5886 Walker, George, 3 June, 1919. (M.)
5887 Winton, Rev. Walter Sim, 3 June, 1919. (M.)
5888 Wood, Roy Wilds Fry, 3 June, 1919. (M.)
5889 Coghlan, Gerald Spencer, 3 June, 1919. (M.)
5890 Ellis, Norman Nuttall, 3 June, 1919. (M.)

5891 Knibbs, Arthur Reginald, 3 June, 1919. (M.)
5892 Legge, Edward Alder, 3 June, 1919. (M.)
5894 Tucker, William Ernest, 3 June, 1919. (M.)
5895 Walker, John Hamilton, 3 June, 1919. (M.)
5896 Anderson, Hugh A., 3 June, 1919. (M.)
5897 Duley, Cryil C., 3 June, 1919. (M.)
5898 Howley, James, 3 June, 1919. (M.)
5899 Marshall, Frederick W., 3 June, 1919. (M.)
5900 O'Grady, J. J., 3 June, 1919. (M.
5901 Outerbridge, Herbert A., 3 June, 1919. (M.)
5902 Reeves, William, 3 June, 1919. (M.)
5903 Winter, Herbert M., 3 June, 1919. (M.)
5904 Adkins, William John, 3 June, 1919. (M.)
5905 Amor, Stanley Long, 3 June, 1919. (M.)
5906 Andrews, Joseph Claude, 3 June, 1919. (M.)
5907 Angell, Bruce Othniel, 3 June, 1919. (M.)
5908 Arnot, William Mills, 3 June, 1919. (M.)
5909 Axten, Henry James, 3 June, 1919. (M.)
5911 Barber, Percy Charles, 3 June, 1919. (M.)
5912 Barnaby, Hazen Ottis, 3 June, 1919. (M.)
5913 Barr, Philip Henry, 3 June, 1919. (M.)
5914 Bayley, Constance Theodora, 3 June, 1919. (M.)
5915 Beeton, Bernard James, 3 June, 1919. (M.)
5916 Belli-Bivar, Roderick, 3 June, 1919. (M.)
5917 Belt, Charles Burnley, 3 June, 1919. (M.)
5918 Betteridge, Harold Leonard, 3 June, 1919. (M.)
5919 Biggs, Jack Pelham Percival Leslie, 3 June, 1919. (M.)
5920 Bird, Edmund Ivan Montford, 3 June, 1919. (M.)
5921 Booker, Harry, 3 June, 1919. (M.)
5922 Bonnyman, John Alexander, 3 June, 1919. (M.)
5923 Bowring, William, 3 June, 1919. (M.)
5924 Brackenboro, Henry Edwin, 3 June, 1919. (M.)
5925 Brockbank, Charles Joseph, 3 June, 1919. (M.)
5926 Brown, John, 3 June, 1919. (M.)
5927 Bryant, Walter Edward George, 3 June, 1919. (M.)
5928 Burnett, Thomas Leslie Forbes, 3 June, 1919. (M.)
5929 Burns, Patrick John, 3 June, 1919. (M.)
5930 Burt, Walter Leslie, 3 June, 1919. (M.)
5931 Bygrave, Leonard Charles, 3 June, 1919. (M.)
5932 Cairns, David, 3 June, 1919. (M.)
5933 Cambridge, Arthur Edward, 3 June, 1919. (M.)
5934 Campbell, Malcolm, 3 June, 1919. (M.)
5935 Carmody, Ernest Partick, 3 June, 1919. (M.)
5936 Carnley, Mary, Mrs., 3 June, 1919. (M.)
5937 Carter, Alfred William, 3 June, 1919. (M.)
5938 Cassels, Hamilton, 3 June, 1919. (M.)
5939 Castings, Walter Rumley, 3 June, 1919. (M.)
5940 Chambré, John, 3 June, 1919. (M.)
5941 Chandler, Charles Kingsley, 3 June, 1919. (M.)
5942 Cheeseman, Bernard, 3 June, 1919. (M.)
5943 Clare, Samuel, 3 June, 1919. (M.)
5944 Colbeck, Paul, 3 June, 1919. (M.)
5945 Collet, Richard Awdrey White, 3 June, 1919. (M.)
5946 Cooper, Walter Jackson, 3 June, 1919. (M.)
5947 Crane, Bertie Frederick, 3 June, 1919. (M.)
5948 Cranmer, Alexander Thomas, 3 June, 1919. (M.)
5949 Cranmer, William Ernest, 3 June, 1919. (M.)
5950 Crichton, Henry Lumsden, 3 June, 1919. (M.)
5951 Crofton, Richard Llewellyn, 3 June, 1919. (M.)
5952 Crothers, Wallace Guy Murdock, 3 June, 1919. (M.)
5953 Currington, Stanley, 3 June, 1919. (M.)
5954 Curtis, John Dorrien Constable, 3 June, 1919. (M.)
5955 Dance, Frank, 3 June, 1919. (M.)
5956 Dand, James Huddart, 3 June, 1919. (M.)
5957 Dawes, Henry, 3 June, 1919. (M.)
5958 Dawson, William, 3 June, 1919. (M.)
5959 Day, Florence, Mrs., 3 June, 1919. (M.)
5960 Dean, George Edward Morgan, 3 June, 1919. (M.)
5961 Donald, Robert, 3 June, 1919. (M.)
5962 Eckford, Francis George, 3 June, 1919. (M.)
5963 Everett, Raymond Walter, 3 June, 1919. (M.)
5964 Fairbrother, Hugh Kingsley, 3 June, 1919. (M.)
5965 Fawdry, Thomas, 3 June, 1919. (M.)
5966 Firmin, Cyril Alfred, 3 June, 1919. (M.)
5967 Fitzgerald, Maurice Bolton, 3 June, 1919. (M.)
5968 Frankish, John Raven, 3 June, 1919. (M.)
5969 Freeborn, Leonard, 3 June, 1919. (M.)
5970 Freeman, Sidney Thomas, 3 June, 1919. (M.)
5971 Frost, Oliver Harry, 3 June, 1919. (M.)
5972 Fry, Alfred Andrew, 3 June, 1919. (M.)
5973 Fuller, Norman Berwick, 3 June, 1919. (M.)
5974 Fulton, Angus Robertson, 3 June, 1919. (M.)
5975 Fyfe, Robert George, 3 June, 1919. (M.)
5976 Geer, Ernest Walter, 3 June, 1919. (M.)
5977 Gerrard, Thomas Maitland, 3 June, 1919. (M.)
5978 Giles, Harry Herbert, 3 June, 1919. (M.)
5979 Godfrey, Stanley Charles, 3 June, 1919. (M.)
5980 Golding, George Francis, 3 June, 1919. (M.)
5981 Graham, Robert Clark, 3 June, 1919. (M.)
5982 Grave, Frederick, 3 June, 1919. (M.)
5983 Griggs, Alfred George, 3 June, 1919. (M.)
5984 Groome, Auckland William Wollaston, 3 June, 1919. (M.)
5985 Gwyer, Percy Edward, 3 June, 1919. (M.)
5986 Gordon, Thomas Grove, 3 June, 1919. (M.)
5987 Halcrow, Marjorie, Mrs., 3 June, 1919. (M.)
5988 Hayward, William, 3 June, 1919. (M.)
5989 Henshall, Leonard, 3 June, 1919. (M.)
5990 Hill, George Alexander, 3 June, 1919. (M.)
5991 Hodgson, Charles Edward, 3 June, 1919. (M.)
5992 Hulbert, Harry, 3 June, 1919. (M.)

5994 Jones, Henry, 3 June, 1919. (M.)
5995 Kavanagh, Henry Richard, 3 June, 1919. (M.)
5996 Kewley, William Graham, 3 June, 1919. (M.)
5998 Knight, John Morgan, 3 June, 1919. (M.)
5999 Knollys, Edward George William Tyrwhitt, 3 June, 1919. (M.)
6000 Knox, Errol Galbraith, 3 June, 1919. (M.)
6001 Langmuir, John William, 3 June, 1919. (M.)
6002 Langridge, Edwin Joseph, 3 June, 1919. (M.)
6003 Leigh-Bennett, Ernest Pendarves, 3 June, 1919. (M.)
6004 Livingstone, Alexander Frederick, 3 June, 1919. (M.)
6005 Lott, Robert Elgin Lloyd, 3 June, 1919. (M.)
6006 McBain, Percival Alexander, 3 June, 1919. (M.)
6007 Macrostie, Reginald David Gorrie, 3 June, 1919. (M.)
6008 Macdonald, Ronald, 3 June, 1919. (M.)
6009 Maley, William John, 3 June, 1919. (M.)
6010 Mallett, Henry Clifford, 3 June, 1919. (M.)
6011 Manwell, David Thomas William, 3 June, 1919. (M.)
6012 Marchant, Alfred Palmer, 3 June, 1919. (M.)
6013 Mars, Lionel Jackson, 3 June, 1919. (M.)
6014 Marson, Thomas Bertrand, 3 June, 1919. (M.)
6015 Mawdsley, James Buckland, 3 June, 1919. (M.)
6016 Meek, Kenneth Alexander, 3 June, 1919. (M.)
6017 Mitchell, Donald Robert, 3 June, 1919. (M.)
6018 Morris, Harold Spencer, 3 June, 1919. (M.)
6019 Morrissey, Patrick Henry, 3 June, 1919. (M.)
6020 Muir, Dorothy Coward, 3 June, 1919. (M.)
6021 Murphy, Frank, 3 June, 1919. (M.)
6022 Nesbitt, Thomas Hunter, 3 June, 1919. (M.)
6023 Newton, Florence Mai Shedlock, Mrs., 3 June, 1919. (M.)
6024 Newton-Clare, Walter Shackfield, 3 June, 1919. (M.)
6025 Nicholson, Bernard John, 3 June, 1919. (M.)
6026 Noel, Charlotte, 3 June, 1919. (M.)
6027 Northcote, Harry Peter, 3 June, 1919. (M.)
6028 Nuttall, William Ewart, 3 June, 1919. (M.)
6029 Palmer, Gilbert, 3 June, 1919. (M.)
6030 Panter, George William, 3 June, 1919. (M.)
6031 Pearce, Kathleen, 3 June, 1919. (M.)
6033 Pertwee, Gwenlliam, Mrs., 3 June, 1919. (M.)
6034 Petch, Frederick, 3 June, 1919. (M.)
6035 Phipps, William, 3 June, 1919. (M.)
6036 Pinckney, David Ward, 3 June, 1919. (M.
6037 Pinkerton, James Morton, 3 June, 1919. (M.)
6038 Porter, Edward Ernest, 3 June, 1919. (M.)
6039 Postlethwaite, Frederick Hartley, 3 June, 1919. (M.)
6040 Powell, Frank James Bickley, 3 June, 1919. (M.)
6041 Pugh, William Peter Boulton, 3 June, 1919. (M.)
6042 Raine, John Charles, 3 June, 1919. (M.)
6043 Rathburn, Aileen, Mrs., 3 June, 1919. (M.)
6044 Rees, David Morris, 3 June, 1919. (M.)
6045 Ricketts, Walter, 3 June, 1919. (M.)
6046 Ridley, Albert, 3 June, 1919. (M.)
6047 Rivers-Smith, Eric, 3 June, 1919. (M.)
6048 Robinson, James, 3 June, 1919. (M.)
6049 Rogers, George Wase, 3 June, 1919. (M.)
6050 Roper, George Orchard, 3 June, 1919. (M.)
6051 Ross, Alexander Jacob Meyer, 3 June, 1919. (M.)
6052 Rowe, Arthur Alfred, 3 June, 1919. (M.)
6053 Rowe, Charles William, 3 June, 1919. (M.)
6054 Scandrett, James Herbert, 3 June, 1919. (M.)
6055 Siddons-Wilson, Albert Edgar, 3 June, 1919. (M.)
6056 Sladden, Robert John, 3 June, 1919. (M.)
6057 Smart, Archibald Guelph Holdsworth, 3 June, 1919. (M.)
6058 Stansfield, Harold, 3 June, 1919. (M.)
6059 Stevenson, Douglas Stuart, 3 June, 1919. (M.)
6060 Stronach, John Grant McKenzie Martin, 3 June, 1919. (M.)
6061 Susans, Frank, 3 June, 1919. (M.)
6062 Sutherland, John, 3 June, 1919. (M.)
6063 Sutherland, William, 3 June, 1919. (M.)
6064 Swan, John Barry Rankin, 3 June, 1919. (M.)
6065 Swan, Robert, 3 June, 1919. (M.)
6066 Swoffer, Frank Arthur, 3 June, 1919. (M.)
6067 Taylor, Arthur Henry, 3 June, 1919. (M.)
6068 Taylor, Bernard Archie, 3 June, 1919. (M.)
6069 Taylor, Leicester Edward, 3 June, 1919. (M.)
6070 Thomas, Hugh Hamshaw, 3 June, 1919. (M.)
6071 Thomson, Elizabeth, 3 June, 1919. (M.)
6072 Thurston, Albert Peter, 3 June, 1919. (M.)
6073 Trist, Edward, 3 June, 1919. (M.)
6074 Twining, Stephen Herbert, 3 June, 1919. (M.)
6075 Waddington, Henry, 3 June, 1919. (M.)
6076 Waghorn, Hugh Colin, 3 June, 1919. (M.)
6077 Waldron, Frank, 3 June, 1919. (M.)
6078 Walker, Harold Frederick, 3 June, 1919. (M.)
6079 Warburton, Peter, 3 June, 1919. (M.)
6080 Wardle, William George James, 3 June, 1919. (M.)
6081 Watson, Alexander Milne, 3 June, 1919. (M.)
6082 Watson, William, 3 June, 1919. (M.)
6083 Watt, William McIver, 3 June, 1919. (M.)
6084 Watts, Francis Mapleton Iremonger, 3 June, 1919. (M.)
6085 Waylen, Donald Campbell, 3 June, 1919. (M.)
6086 Western, James George, 3 June, 1919. (M.)
6087 Williams, Frederick Thomas, 3 June, 1919. (M.)
6088 Williams, Gerald Atherton, 3 June, 1919. (M.)
6089 Williams, Owen, 3 June, 1919. (M.)
6090 Wilson, Andrew McCrae, 3 June, 1919. (M.)
6091 Wilson, Alexander Morice, 3 June, 1919. (M.)
6092 Woolfe, Francis Alexander, 3 June, 1919. (M.)
6093* Wright, William James Turnbull, 3 June, 1919. (M.)

6094 Young, Hugh Joseph, 3 June, 1919. (M.)
6095 Abel, Walter Charles, 3 June, 1919.
6096 Aiyar, Chidambara Rajagopala, 3 June, 1919.
6097 Alexander, Alfred, 3 June, 1919.
6098 Alexander, Margaret, Mrs., 3 June, 1919.
6099 Anderson, Eleanor Florence, 3 June, 1919.
6100 Anson, Maud, Mrs., 3 June, 1919.
6101 Armour, William Staveley, 3 June, 1919.
6102 Avargal, M. R. Ry. Rao Bahadur Tiruvalyangudi Vija-
      yaraghava Achariyar, 3 June, 1919.
6103 Bahadur, Rai Sahib Raj, 3 June, 1919.
6104 Baker, Augustus, 3 June, 1919.
6105 Baldwin, Christine, Mrs. Guy Melfort, 3 June, 1919.
6106 Balthazar, Helen, Mrs., 3 June, 1919. (M.)
6107 Bamford, Walter Cecil, 3 June, 1919. (M.)
6108 Bewley, Constance, Mrs., 3 June, 1919.
6109 Booker, Cissie, Mrs., 3 June, 1919.
6110 Borlase, Rev. John Jennings Dingle, 3 June, 1919.
6111 Bose, Sharnalata, Mrs., 3 June, 1919.
6112 Bowles, Charles William, 3 June, 1919.
6113 Bruce, Hon. Finetta Madeline Julia, Mrs. Charles Gran-
      ville, 3 June, 1919.
6114 Buist, Florence, Mrs., 3 June, 1919.
6115 Byrne, Kathleen, Mrs., 3 June, 1919.
6116 Cain, Sarah, Mrs., 3 June, 1919.
6117 Captain, Manijeh Sorabjee, 3 June, 1919.
6118 Cartwright, Mary, 3 June, 1919.
6119 Casson, Gertrude, Mrs., 3 June, 1919.
6120 Chand, Babu Bishan, 3 June, 1919.
6121 Chandra, Lala Ram, 3 June, 1919.
6122 Chapman, George Alfred, 3 June, 1919.
6123 Chatterjee, Babu Sukumar, 3 June, 1919.
6124 Chatterton, Alice, Mrs., 3 June, 1919.
6125 de Chaudhuri, Babu Guru Charan, 3 June, 1919.
6126 Clark, Hugh Cook, 3 June, 1919.
6127 Clarke, Reuben Arthur, 3 June, 1919.
6128 Compton, Edna Katharine, Mrs., 3 June, 1919.
6129 Cox, Ethel Sophie, Mrs., 3 June, 1919.
6130 Cox, Evelin Florence Conran, Mrs., 3 June, 1919.
6131 Das, Babu Birendra Kishor, 3 June, 1919.
6132 Dean, George Edward, 3 June, 1919.
6133 Dhatrak, Rao Sahib Rukhmaji Mankoji, 3 June 1919.
6134 Dutt, Babu Jogesh Chandra, 3 June, 1919.
6135 Dwane, Ernest Henry, 3 June, 1919.
6136 Ebrahimji, Sind, Kahn Sahib Shaik, 3 June, 1919.
6137 Engineer, Bhicaijee Ardeshir, 3 June, 1919.
6138 Ewart, Evelyn, Mrs., 3 June, 1919.
6139 Eyres, Edmund, 3 June, 1919.
6140 Fagan, Rhoda, Mrs., 3 June, 1919.
6141 Fink, Kenneth De Quincey, 3 June, 1919.
6142 Firminger, Eveline, Mrs., 3 June, 1919.
6143 Fisk, Elsie Beatrice, 3 June, 1919.
6144 Freitas, Hubert St. Clair, 3 June, 1919.
6145 Frizelle, Frances Emily, Mrs., 3 June, 1919.
6146 Fry, Alfred Joseph, 3 June, 1919.
6147 Gaiger, Grace Elizabeth, 3 June, 1919.
6148 Gopal, Lala Ram, 3 June, 1919.
6149 Govindarajulu, Rose, 3 June, 1919.
6150 Gracias, Hyginus Dominie, 3 June, 1919.
6151 Gupta, Sarat Kumar Datta, 3 June, 1919.
6152 Guthrie, Alan, 3 June, 1919.
6153 Gwyther, Louise Banks, Mrs., 3 June, 1919.
6154 Gyaw, Maung Myat Tha, 3 June, 1919.
6155 Gyi, Ma Le, 3 June, 1919.
6156 Hall, George Thomas, 3 June, 1919.
6157 Hanrahan, William George Augustin, 3 June, 1919
6158 Haslehurst, Harold Maitland, 3 June, 1919.
6159 Hearn, Phyllis, Mrs., 3 June, 1919.
6160 Herbert, Margaret, Mrs., 3 June, 1919.
6161 Hickley, Alice, Mrs. Victor North, 3 June, 1919.
6162 Highton, Arthur Denys Salusbury, 3 June, 1919.
6163 Hmyin, Ma E., 3 June, 1919.
6164 Hogan, Eva, Mrs., 3 June, 1919.
6165 Hunt, Gladys Muriel, Mrs., 3 June, 1919.
6166 Imrie, May, Mrs., 3 June, 1919.
6167 Ingram, George Skinner, 3 June, 1919.
6168 Isaac, John Rajaratnam, 3 June, 1919.
6169 Jackson, Violet, Mrs., 3 June, 1919.
6170 Johnston, Edith Alma, Mrs., 3 June, 1919.
6171 Johnston, Rosalie, Mrs., 3 June, 1919.
6172 Joshi, Pandit Satyanand, 3 June, 1919.
6173 Kanoo, Khan Sahib Yusuf, 3 June, 1919.
6174 Kempster, Ruby, Mrs., 3 June, 1919.
6175 Kendall, Joseph Abner, 3 June, 1919.
6176 Kenyon, Rose Alice, 3 June, 1919.
6177 Khan, Khan Bahadur Muhammad Abdul Karim, 3 June,
      1919.
6178 Khan, Ali Sher, 3 June, 1919.
6179 Khan, Nawab Allahdad, 3 June, 1919.
6180 Khan Arbab, Khan Bahadur Mir Ahmad, 3 June, 1919.
6181 Khan, Khan Bahadur Ghulam Qadir, 3 June, 1919.
6182 Khan, Khan Sahib Jangul, 3 June, 1919.
6183 Khan, Khan Bahadur Sardar Mian, 3 June, 1919.
6184 Khan, Khwaja Muhammad Abdul Majid, 3 June, 1919.
6185 Khan, Khan Bahadur Shakar, 3 June, 1919.
6186 Khan, Kunwar Muhammad Ubaidullah, 3 June, 1919.
6187 Khan, Zaka-ud-din, 3 June, 1919.
6188 Knollys, Ethelred Mary, Mrs., 3 June, 1919.
6189 Laver, Samuel, 3 June, 1919.
6190 Laville, Ellen, 3 June, 1919.

6191 Lee, Harriet Louise, Mrs., 3 June, 1919.
6192 Lister, Charles, 3 June, 1919.
6193 Lobo, Diogo Xavier, 3 June, 1919.
6194 Loughlin, Francis James, 3 June, 1919.
6195 Lowsley, Ethel, Mrs., 3 June, 1919.
6196 Lucas, Rev. Bernard, 3 June, 1919.
6197 MacIver, Agnes Edith Stewart, 3 June, 1919.
6198 Mackay, William George, 3 June, 1919.
6199 Mackenzie, Malcolm Ayers, 3 June, 1919.
6200 Madeley, Edith Mary, Mrs., 3 June, 1919.
6201 Mahawa, Dinshaw Eduljee, 3 June, 1919.
6202 Maheshri, Babu Kishen Lal, 3 June, 1919.
6203 Mal, Rai Bahadur Lala Harji, 3 June, 1919.
6204 Marak, Babu Gangsin, 3 June, 1919.
6205 Marker, Doraha Nusserwanji, 3 June, 1919.
6206 McHugh, Harry Ralph, 3 June, 1919.
6207 Michael, Rao Sahib Antony Simon Gabriel, 3 June, 1919.
6208 Michael, Lewis William, 3 June, 1919.
6209 Mignon, Edith Agnes Ida, Mrs., 3 June, 1919.
6210 Minson, Herbert, 3 June, 1919.
6211 Morrison, Henry St. John, 3 June, 1919.
6212 Muhammad, Abul Lais Saad-ud-Din, 3 June, 1919.
6213 Narain, Lala Raj, 3 June, 1919.
6214 Narayan, Lala Suraj, 3 June, 1919.
6215 Nath, Pandit Kashi, 3 June, 1919.
6216 Newton, Alice Elizabeth Maud, Mrs., 3 June, 1919.
6218 Oliphant, John Ninian, 3 June, 1919.
6219 Palekar, Rao Sahib Balkrishna Anant, 3 June, 1919.
6220 Parsons, Ronald, 3 June, 1919.
6221 Patel, Babu Anirudha, 3 June, 1919.
6222 Phelps, Maude Marion, Mrs., 3 June, 1919.
6223 Philipe, Mary Catherine, Mrs. De Rhe, 3 June, 1919.
6224 Pocklington, Amy, Mrs., 3 June, 1919.
6225 Powell, Edith, Mrs., 3 June, 1919.
6226 Prasad, Lala Sheo, 3 June, 1919.
6227 Pratt, May, Mrs., 3 June, 1919.
6228 Ram, Rai Bahadur Lala Barkat, 3 June, 1919.
6229 Rankin, Mary Ellen, Mrs., 3 June, 1919.
6230 Riley, Richard, 3 June, 1919.
6231 Rivett-Carnac, Lilian Muriel, Mrs., 3 June, 1919.
6232 Robertson, Janet, 3 June, 1919
6233 Rodericks, John Joseph Fisher, 3 June, 1919.
6234 Rodgers, Rivers Thomas, 3 June, 1919.
6235 Roy, Babu Niranjan, 3 June, 1919.
6236 Sailor, Rao Bahadur Keshavji Nathu, 3 June, 1919.
6238 Sells, Arthur Freakish, 3 June, 1919.
6239 Shah, Khan Bahadur Mian Musharraf, 3 June, 1919.
6240 Shah, Khan Bahadur Syed Mehr, 3 June, 1919.
6241 Shaw, Cyril Hay, 3 June, 1919.
6242 Shin, Maung Ba, 3 June, 1919.
6243 Simpson, Winifred, Mrs., 3 June, 1919.
6244 Singh, Rai Amarpal, 3 June, 1919.
6245 Singh, Chaudhri Brij Raj Saran, 3 June, 1919.
6246 Singh, Chaudhri Dhiri, 3 June, 1919.
6247 Singh, Chaudhri Nihal, 3 June, 1919.
6248 Singh, Bhai Gurbakhsh, 3 June, 1919.
6249 Singh, Hira, 3 June, 1919.
6250 Singh, Rai Bahadur Bhai Lehna, 3 June, 1919.
6251 Sladen, Mary, Mrs., 3 June, 1919.
6252 Slater, Alexander Frederick, 3 June, 1919.
6253 Soames, Una, Mrs., 3 June, 1919.
6254 Stephenson, Gertrude, Mrs., 3 June, 1919.
6255 Sterling, Thomas Smith, 3 June, 1919.
6256 Stratford, Lenna Mary, 3 June, 1919.
6257 Tait, Anne Smith, Mrs., 3 June, 1919.
6258 Thaddeus, Mary, Mrs., 3 June, 1919.
6259 Thompson, Mary Powney, Mrs., 3 June, 1919.
6260 Tonkinson, Edith, Mrs., 3 June, 1919.
6261 Turnbull, Lucia, Mrs., 3 June, 1919.
6262 Turner, Constance, Mrs. Henry, 3 June, 1919.
6263 Vaidya, Rao Sahib Govind Mahadeo, 3 June, 1919.
6264 Vanes, Edith Mary, Mrs., 3 June, 1919.
6265 Wadia, Ardeshir Dosabhai, 3 June, 1919.
6266 Waller-Senior, Hellen Stuart, Mrs., 3 June, 1919.
6267 Walter, Margaret Jean, Mrs., Albert Eliza, 3 June, 1919.
6268 Walter, Winifred Edith, 3 June, 1919.
6269 Way, Edith, Mrs., 3 June, 1919.
6270 Willmore, Ida, Mrs., 3 June, 1919.
6271 Wilson, John Hughes, 3 June, 1919.
6272 Woodall, Norah, Mrs., 3 June, 1919.
6273 Adams, Alfred Montague, 3 June, 1919.
6274 Barton, Rachel Mary, Mrs., 3 June, 1919.
6275 Blackwell, Margaret Brown, Mrs., 3 June, 1919.
6276 Bloomfield, Hilda, Mrs., 3 June, 1919.
6277 Blundell, Annie Elizabeth, Mrs., 3 June, 1919.
6278 Bowie, Janet, Mrs., 3 June, 1919.
6279 Brown, Violet McConochie, Mrs., 3 June, 1919.
6280 Burgess, Charles Hayward, 3 June, 1919.
6281 Burt, Alexander, 3 June, 1919.
6282 Castro, Edith, Mrs. de, 3 June, 1919.
6283 Charles, Esther, 3 June, 1919.
6284 Clark, Lydia, 3 June, 1919.
6285 Cooper, Ethel Mary, 3 June, 1919.
6286 Courage, Frances Zoe, Mrs., 3 June, 1919.
6287 Crawford, Gertrude Alice, Mrs., 3 June, 1919.
6288 Cuff, Ethel, Mrs., 3 June, 1919.
6289 Dawson, Hannah, 3 June, 1919.
6290 Dixon, George Finley, 3 June, 1919.
6291 Ellison, Mabel, Mrs., 3 June, 1919.
6292 Gerard, Harold, 3 June, 1919.

6293 Greenslade, Louisa Grace Charlotte, Mrs., 3 June, 1919.
6294 Gunnion, Thomas, 3 June, 1919.
6295 Guthrie, Brenda, 3 June, 1919.
6296 Harcourt, Eveline Alice Marian, 3 June, 1919.
6297 Harrison, Kate, 3 June, 1919.
6298 H rrington, Henry William, 3 June, 1919.
6299 Helmore, Heathcote George, 3 June, 1919.
6300 Hill, Emma Carey, Mrs., 3 June, 1919.
6301 Hislop, Margaret Mary Annie, Mrs., 3 June, 1919.
6082 Hitchen, Ann Margaret, Mrs., 3 June, 1919.
6303 Holdsworth, Elizabeth Annie, Mrs., 3 June, 1919.
6304 Holdsworth, William Godfrey, 3 June, 1919.
6305 Kelsey, Lavinia Jano, 3 June, 1919.
6306 King, Emma Ethel Maud Ford, 3 June, 1919.
6307 King, Sarah Hannah, Mrs., 3 June, 1919.
6308 Lovell, James, 3 June, 1919.
6309 Macassey, Ethel Constance Chapman, 3 June, 1919.
6310 MacDonald, Mina, 3 June, 1919.
6311 McDonnell, Mysie, 3 June, 1919.
6312 McDougall, Agnes, Mrs, 3 June, 1919.
6313 McGregor, Pura, Mrs., 3 June, 1919.
6314 Maling, Nesta Gertrude, Mrs., 3 June, 1919.
6315 Marris, Basil Arthur, 3 June, 1919.
6316 Martin, Alfred Andrew, 3 June, 1919.
6317 Matthews, Frederick Gwillian, 3 June, 1919.
6318 Millton, James Dothie, 3 June, 1919.
6319 Moeller, Winnifred, Mrs., 3 June, 1919.
6320 Murray, Janet, 3 June, 1919.
6321 O'Neill, Leo Francis, 3 June, 1919.
6322 Page, Jessie Ellen, Mrs., 3 June, 1919.
6323 Philson, Lucy, Mrs., 3 June, 1919.
6324 Potter, Mary Ann, Mrs., 3 June, 1919.
6325 Rodda, George Charles, 3 June, 1919.
6326 Russell, William Archibald, 3 June, 1919.
6327 Scales, George Herbert, 3 June, 1919.
6328 Smart, Annie Wilhelmina, Mrs., 3 June, 1919.
6329 Smith, Lilly Mary, Mrs., 3 June, 1919.
6330 Spencer, Martha, Mrs., 3 June, 1919.
6381 Stevenson, Florence Johanna, Mrs., 3 June 1919.
6332 Tripp, Bernard, 3 June, 1919.
6333 Tunks, Charles James, 3 June, 1919.
6334 Wallace, James Alfred, 3 June, 1919.
6335 Ward, Elsmie, 3 June, 1919.
6336 White, Charles, 3 June, 1919.
6337 Wray, Cecil James, 3 June, 1919.
6338 Wray, Ellen, 3 June, 1919.
6339 Young, Mrs. F. R., 3 June, 1919.
6340 Anderson, Julia Ada, Mrs., 3 June, 1919.
6341 Appleyard, Agnes McWhirter, Mrs., 3 June, 1919.
6342 Addie, Julia Constance, Mrs., 3 June, 1919.
6343 Black, Charles William, 3 June, 1919.
6344 Champion, Mary Ann, Mrs., 3 June, 1919.
6345 Cowin, Norris Tynwald, 3 June, 1919.
6346 Conchie, Jean, Mrs., 3 June, 1919.
6347 Catchpole, Alfred Edward, 3 June, 1919.
6348 Downing, Robert Edward, 3 June, 1919.
6349 Grattan, Caroline Elizabeth, Mrs. Edgar, 3 June, 1919.
6350 Eales, Sydney York, 3 June, 1919.
6351 Fisher, Amy Anderson, Mrs., 3 June, 1919.
6352 Fair, Robert Wilson, 3 June, 1919.
6353 Field, Mathilde, Mrs., 3 June, 1919.
6354 Garlake, Dorothy Eleanor, Mrs., 3 June, 1919.
6355 Giddy, Lilian Napier, Mrs., 3 June, 1919.
6356 Grieve, Catherine Ramsay Laburn, Mrs., 3 June, 1919.
6357 Herman, Lena, Mrs., 3 June, 1919.
6358 Howard, Helen Edith, Mrs., 3 June, 1919.
6359 Hale, Lancelot Hugh Dowman, 3 June, 1919.
6360 Herbert-Smith, Christine Louise, Mrs., 3 June, 1919.
6361 Lydall, Edward Wykeman, 3 June, 1919.
6362 Laing, John George, 3 June, 1919.
6363 McIntyre, Donald Arderne, 3 June, 1919.
6364 Naggs, Leonard Bertram, 3 June, 1919.
6365 MacDonogh, George Frederick, 3 June, 1919.
6366 Miller, Thomas Maskew, 3 June, 1919.
6367 Nethersole, Harrison Ralph, 3 June, 1919.
6368 Nivison, William, 3 June, 1919.
6369 Nel, Charles Paul Leonard, 3 June, 1919.
6370 Prince, Constance Perrott, 3 June, 1919.
6371 Poritt, Hannah Mary, Mrs., 3 June, 1919.
6372 Redhill, Samuel, 3 June, 1919.
6373 Rogers, Dorothy Heyward, 3 June, 1919.
6374 Rogers, Fergus Carstairs, 3 June, 1919.
6375 Trigger, Alfred Ernest, 3 June, 1919.
6376 Tatham, Lilian Elizabeth, Mrs., 3 June, 1919.
6377 Taylor, Minnie Elena Scott, Mrs., 3 June, 1919.
6378 Thompson, George Batching, 3 June, 1919.
6379 Thompson, Rev. Harry Ernest, 3 June, 1919.
6380 Watson, Gilbert, 3 June, 1919.
6381 Wallace, Margaret Janet, 3 June, 1919.
6382 Way, Effie, Mrs., 3 June, 1919.
6383 Ayre, Charles Pascoe, 3 June, 1919.
6384 Blackburn, Alfred Charles, 3 June, 1919.
6385 Clift, Agnes, Mrs., 3 June, 1919.
6386 Clift, Mildred, 3 June, 1919.
6388 Fisher, Janet Aitken, Mrs., 3 June, 1919.
6389 Fitzgerald, Henry Frederick, 3 June, 1919.
6390 Harvey, Ethel, Mrs., 3 June, 1919.
6391 Hollands, Emily Hannah, Mrs., 3 June, 1919.
6392 Holloway, Henrietta Palfrey, Mrs., 3 June, 1919.
6393 Horwood, Reuben, 3 June, 1919.

6394 Kennedy, Helen, Mrs., 3 June, 1919.
6395 Lauder, Elizabeth Shaw, 3 June, 1919.
6396 MacDonald, Flora Emma, Mrs., 3 June, 1919.
6397 MacDonnell, Richard, 3 June, 1919.
6398 MacPherson, Margaret, Mrs., 3 June, 1919.
6399 Moore, George Frederick, 3 June, 1919.
6400 Petten, Eliza, Mrs., 3 June, 1919.
6401 Robinson, John Alexander, 3 June, 1919.
6402 Somerton, Caroline Augusta, Mrs., 3 June, 1919.
6403 Steer, Charles Robert, 3 June, 1919.
6404 Swaffield, Ernest, 3 June, 1919.
6405 Thompson, Sarah Ann, Mrs., 3 June, 1919.
6406 Tulk, Effie Morris, Mrs., 3 June, 1919.
6407 Ainsworth, Ina Cameron, Mrs. John, 3 June, 1919.
6408 Aldworth, Dorothea Anne Harvey, Mrs., 3 June, 1919.
6409 Armbruster, Hubert, 3 June, 1919.
6410 Arrigo, Edgar, 3 June, 1919.
6411 Bagshawe, Francis John, 3 June, 1919.
6412 Bancroft, Blanche, Mrs., 3 June, 1919.
6413 Bartley, William, 3 June, 1919.
6414 Belcher, Charles Frederick, 3 June, 1919.
6415 Bennett, Agnes, Mrs., 3 June, 1919.
6416 Bernard, Albert Victor, 3 June, 1919.
6417 Bettington, Maud, Mrs., 3 June, 1919.
6418 Bryant, Robert William, 3 June, 1919.
6420 Bullock, James Arthur Edward, 3 June, 1919.
6421 Bushell, John James, 3 June, 1919.
6422 Cardona, Lewis Borg, 3 June, 1919.
6423 Casolani, Henry, 3 June, 1919.
6424 Chataway, Louise, Mrs., 3 June, 1919.
6425 Cipriani, Albert Henry, 3 June, 1919.
6426 Clarke, Percival Herbert, 3 June, 1919.
6427 Clementi, Marie Penelope Rose, Mrs. Cecil, 3 June, 1919.
6428 Conyers, Ada Blanche Pierce, Mrs., 3 June, 1919.
6429 Cookson, Percy Charles, 3 June, 1919.
6430 Copeman, Edward Arden, 3 June, 1919.
6431 Corsi, Manuel Gregory, 3 June, 1919.
6432 Cowley, Alexander Percy, 3 June, 1919.
6433 Critien, Attilio, 3 June, 1919.
6434 de Fonseka, Edmund Clarke, 3 June, 1919.
6435 de Freitas, Dora Florence, Mrs. 3 June, 1919.
6436 de Soyce, Mary Margaret, Mrs., 3 June, 1919.
6437 Drew, Florence Grace, Mrs.. 3 June, 1919.
6438 Evans, Maude Elletred, 3 June, 1919.
6439 Dilke, Beaumont Albany Fetherstone-, 3 June, 1919.
6440 Ffrench, Alfred E., 3 June, 1919.
6441 Flint, Violet Amy, Mrs., 3 June, 1919.
6442 Fuller, Elfrida Mary, Lady, 3 June, 1919.
6443 Rutter, Joseph Gatt, 3 June, 1919.
6444 Gordon, Gladys, Mrs., 3 June, 1919.
6445 Gregory, Charles William, 3 June, 1919.
6446 Greig, Alexander, 3 June, 1919.
6447 Hayford, Joseph Ephraim Casely, 3 June, 1919.
6448 Henocksburg, Josephine Norie, Mrs., 3 June, 1919.
6449 Hewett, James Henry, 3 June, 1919.
6450 Heyman, Frances Patton, Mrs., 3 June, 1919.
6451 Hickling, Alice, Mrs., 3 June, 1919.
6452 Hinkson, Ernest Augustus, 3 June, 1919.
6453 Hobley, Alice Mary, Mrs. Charles William, 3 June, 1919.
6454 Hobson, Dorothy, Mrs., 3 June, 1919.
6455 Hodgson, Anthony, 3 June, 1919.
6456 Huyshe-Eliot, Ann, Mrs., 3 June, 1919.
6457 Ingham, Sybil, Mrs., 3 June, 1919.
6458 Johnson, Hubert Lawrence, 3 June, 1919.
6459 Lezard. Herbert Lewis, 3 June, 1919.
6460 Long, Hilda Charlotte, Mrs., 3 June, 1919.
6461 Lyall, George, 3 June, 1919.
6462 McCutchin, Sydney Cameron, 3 June, 1919.
6463 Macintyre, James Colin, 3 June, 1919.
6464 McKeartan, Mary, Mrs., 3 June, 1919.
6465 Mackie, Annie, 3 June, 1919.
6466 McLaughlan, Henry Peter Marius, 3 June, 1919.
6467 Merriefield, Albert, 3 June, 1919.
6468 Myers, Horace, 3 June, 1919.
6469 Paul, Ruth Ethel, Mrs., 3 June, 1919.
6470 Percival, Mary, Mrs., 3 June, 1919.
6471 Perez, Mary, Mrs., 3 June, 1919.
6472 Perryman, Percy Wilbraham, 3 June, 1919.
6473 Phillips, Emily, Mrs., 3 June, 1919.
6474 Pitt, Charles Peniston, 3 June, 1919.
6475 Poole, George Arthur Evered, 3 June, 1919.
6476 Pordage, Anna, Mrs., 3 June, 1919.
6477 Postlethwaite, John Rutherford Parkin, 3 June, 1919.
6478 Sandford, Thomas Frederick, 3 June, 1919.
6479 Scanlen, Emilie, Mrs., 3 June, 1919.
6480 Shearman-Turner, Blanche, Mrs., 3 June, 1919.
6481 Sherwood, Montague Earle, 3 June, 1919.
6482 Stabb, Ethel, Mrs. 3 June, 1919.
6483 Sutherland, Robert, 3 June, 1919.
6484 Sweenie, Elizabeth, 3 June, 1919.
6485 Thorburn, Dieudonnée Grace, Mrs., 3 June, 1919.
6486 Tredgold, Helen, 3 June, 1919.
6487 Twynam, Nora Cecilia, 3 June, 1919.
6488 Visram, Abdulrasul Allidina, 3 June, 1919.
6489 Wallis, Claud Dudley, 3 June, 1919.
6490 Warr, Howard Grove, 3 June, 1919.
6491 Watson, Gwendoline Isabel, Mrs., 3 June, 1919.
6492 Watson, Margaret Jane, Mrs., 3 June, 1919.
6493 Westmorland, Josephine, Mrs., 3 June, 1919.
6494 White, Mabel, Mrs., 3 June, 1919.

6495 Williamson, Francis, 3 June, 1919.
6496 Wortley, Edward Jocelyn, 3 June, 1919.
6497 Young, George Macdonald, 3 June, 1919.
6498 Hales, Walter Percy, 3 June, 1919. (M.)
6499 Nash, William, 3 June, 1919. (M.)
6500 Jones, Reginald Teague-, 3 June, 1919. (M.)
6501 Shah, Abdul Samad, 3 June, 1919. (M.)
6502 Baddeley, Henry, 3 June, 1919. (M.)
6503 Berry, William James, 3 June, 1919. (M.)
6504 Betteridge, George William, 3 June, 1919. (M.)
6505 Cheers, Joseph McGregor, 3 June, 1919. (M.)
6506 Claridge, John Watson Lawson, 3 June, 1919. (M.)
6507 Cubbon, Richard, 3 June, 1919. (M.)
6508 Godinho, Paul Xavier, 3 June, 1919. (M.)
6509 Goode, Thomas Charles, 3 June, 1919. (M.)
6510 Hodgen, Gordon West, 3 June, 1919. (M.)
6511 Norris, William Albert, 3 June, 1919. (M.)
6512 Rogers, Alfred George, 3 June, 1919. (M.)
6513 Shoulder, Henry, 3 June, 1919. (M.)
6514 Somerville, George Aytoun, 3 June, 1919. (M.)
6515 Tanner, Guy, 3 June, 1919. (M.)
6516 Nun, Malik Sardar Khan, 3 June, 1919. (M.)
6517 Khan, Muhammad Feroz, 3 June, 1919. (M.)
6518 Mullan, Rev. Father John, 3 June, 1919. (M.)
6519 Spooner, Rev. Harold, 3 June, 1919. (M.)
6520 Wright, Rev. Arthur Yeomans, 3 June, 1919. (M.)
6521 Barker, Herbert, 3 June, 1919. (M.)
6522 Bayes, Sidney Henry, 3 June, 1919. (M.)
6523 Cash, Samuel, 3 June, 1919. (M.)
6524 Crabbe, Sidney Charles, 3 June, 1919. (M.)
6525 Dabell, William Bates, 3 June, 1919. (M.)
6526 Freestone, Sidney, 3 June, 1919. (M.)
6527 Gooderham, George Frederick Robert, 3 June, 1910. (M.)
6528 Heard, Charles Campbell, 3 June, 1919. (M.)
6529 Hickie, Henry, 3 June, 1919. (M.)
6530 Hind, Leslie Glossop, 3 June, 1919. (M.)
6531 Hofman, Augustus, 3 June, 1919. (M.)
6532 Jones, Reginald Vickers, 3 June, 1919. (M.)
6533 Jones, Thomas, 3 June, 1919. (M.)
6534 Kennedy, Horas Graham, 3 June, 1919. (M.)
6535 Mason, Algernon Montague Wilson, 3 June, 1919. (M.)
6536 Moses, Joseph Henry Gronow, 3 June, 1919. (M.)
6537 Munday, William Thomas, 3 June, 1919. (M.)
6538 Munford, Alfred James, 3 June, 1919. (M.)
6539 Rea, Donald, 3 June, 1919. (M.)
6540 Solomon, Joseph, 3 June, 1919. (M.)
6541 Tait, Andrew Ferdinand, 3 June, 1919. (M.)
6542 Watton, George, 3 June, 1919. (M.)
6543 Webb, Benjamin, 3 June, 1919. (M.)
6544 White, James, 3 June, 1919. (M.)
6545 Bailey, Thomas Henry, 3 June, 1919. (M.)
6546 Bennett, Thomas Parks, 3 June, 1919. (M.)
6547 Gingold, Frederick Maurice, 3 June, 1919. (M.)
6548 Haywood, Norman Alphonso, 3 June, 1919. (M.)
6549 Henderson, Walter Salkeld, 3 June, 1919. (M.)
6550 Leach, Frank, 3 June, 1919. (M.)
6551 Lindsay, Alfred Stewart, 3 June, 1919. (M.)
6552 O'Meara, Michael Aloysius, 3 June, 1919. (M.)
6553 Paddle, Albert, 3 June, 1919. (M.)
6554 Pennefather, Edward Cyril, 3 June, 1919. (M.)
6555 Smith, Henry Surridge, 3 June, 1919. (M.)
6556 Steele, Thomas, 3 June, 1919. (M.)
6557 Mulazim, Awal Salama Yusef Effendi, 3 June, 1919. (M.)
6558 Boyle, John Valentine, 3 June, 1919. (M.)
6559 Hosking, Cyril William, 3 June, 1919. (M.)
6560 Robertson, Walter Allan, 3 June, 1919. (M.)
6561 Sturman, Charles, 3 June, 1919. (M.)
6562 Lockington, Harry Aloysius, 3 June, 1919. (M.)
6563 Allardyce, Kenneth James, 3 June, 1919. (M.)
6564 Horner, Harry, 3 June, 1919. (M.)
6565 Ashton, Robert, 3 June, 1919. (M.)
6566 Baker, Francis Pearson, 3 June, 1919. (M.)
6567 Bingham, Charles Frederick, 3 June, 1919. (M.)
6568 Brewitt, Charles Patrick, 3 June, 1919. (M.)
6569 Cameron, William Macpherson, 3 June, 1919. (M.)
6570 Clarke, Henry, 3 June, 1919. (M.)
6571 Cooper, Harry, 3 June, 1919. (M.)
6572 Hall, Bertram James Leslie, 3 June, 1919. (M.)
6573 Hardwick, Frank, 3 June, 1919. (M.)
6574 Higham, Frank David, 3 June, 1919. (M.)
6575 Hunter, Alfred Philip, 3 June, 1919. (M.)
6576 Hurry, Sydney Charles, 3 June, 1919. (M.)
6577 McGillivray, Clifford, 3 June, 1919. (M.)
6578 Marshall, George Sims, 3 June, 1919. (M.)
6579 Mottram, Francis Henry, 3 June, 1919. (M.)
6580 Photiades, Nicolas John, 3 June, 1919. (M.)
6581 Pollock, Douglas Warren, 3 June, 1919. (M.)
6582 Roberts, Norman Stanley, 3 June, 1919. (M.)
6583 Robinson, Percy Gilbert, 3 June, 1919. (M.)
6584 Thornton, Doris Cyril, 3 June, 1919. (M.)
6585 Young, Wallace Melville, 3 June, 1919. (M.)
6586 Woodward, William Henry, 3 June, 1919. (M.)
6587 Mbaruk Bukheit, 3 June, 1919. (M.)
6588 Patterson, D. H., 3 June, 1919. (M.)
6589 Ackers, Irene Mary, 3 June, 1919. (M.)
6590 Adamson, George Robert, 3 June, 1919. (M.)
6591 Aldom, Herbert Raymond Salisbury, 3 June, 1919. (M.)
6592 Allen, Charles William Edward, 3 June, 1919. (M.)
6593 Anderson, Mary Addison, 3 June, 1919. (M.)
6594 Anderson, Mary Gardiner, 3 June, 1919. (M.)

6595 Arland, John Alfred, 3 June, 1919. (M.)
6596 Aspinall, Gladys Hester, 3 June, 1919. (M.)
6597 Baker, Ernest Frederick, 3 June, 1919. (M.)
6598 Balbi, Henry Alexander, 3 June, 1919. (M.)
6599 Bannerman, Glenny Franklin, 3 June, 1919. (M.)
6600 Bateman, Frank Graham, 3 June, 1919. (M.)
6601 Bennett, Gilbert Hedley, 3 June, 1919. (M.)
6602 Benson, John James Charles, 3 June, 1919. (M.)
6603 Birrell, Edward, 3 June, 1919. (M.)
6604 Broomhall, Harold George, 3 June, 1919. (M.)
6605 Brown, Sheila Macpherson, 3 June, 1919. (M.)
6606 Brown, William, 3 June, 1919. (M.)
6607 Bulmer, Newlove, 3 June, 1919. (M.)
6608 Cale, William Frederick, 3 June, 1919. (M.)
6609 Camfield, Charles Nathaniel, 3 June, 1919. (M.)
6610 Cannan, Astley Cuthbert, 3 June, 1919. (M.)
6611 Capon, Herbert William Thomas, 3 June, 1919. (M.)
6612 Charlesworth, William, 3 June, 1919. (M.)
6613 Clark, Horace Gordon, 3 June, 1919. (M.)
6614 Clark, Louis Spencer, 3 June, 1919. (M.)
6615 Clarke, Ethel May, 3 June, 1919. (M.)
6616 Clarke, Joseph, 3 June, 1919. (M.)
6617 Colby, Henry James, 3 June, 1919. (M.)
6618 Colquhoun, James Clifton, 3 June, 1919. (M.)
6619 Collins, Timothy, 3 June, 1919. (M.)
6620 Connery, William Laurence, 3 June, 1919. (M.)
6621 Cook, Percy Frederick, 3 June, 1919. (M.)
6622 Crowden, Henry Clarence, 3 June, 1919. (M.)
6623 Curtis, Amy, 3 June, 1919. (M.)
6624 Davis, Eugene Charles Henry, 3 June, 1919. (M.)
6625 Dawkins, Ernest Walton, 3 June, 1919. (M.)
6626 Dorrington, Frederick James, 3 June, 1919. (M.)
6627 Drayson, Thomas, 3 June, 1919. (M.)
6628 Druitt, Hilda, 3 June, 1919. (M.)
6629 Eastick, Alfred, 3 June, 1919. (M.)
6630 Edwards, Ina Leonora, 3 June, 1919. (M.)
6631 Evans, William John, 3 June, 1919. (M.)
6632 Everett, Ralph Marven, 3 June, 1919. (M.)
6633 Fairbairn, Elizabeth Brown, 3 June, 1919. (M.)
6634 Fairbrother, William George, 3 June, 1919. (M.)
6635 Farnham, Samuel, 3 June, 1919. (M.)
6636 Farrell, James Robert, 3 June, 1919. (M.)
6637 Fawsitt, Hubert Harcourt Morland, 3 June, 1919. (M.)
6638 Gilliard, William Thomas, 3 June, 1919. (M.)
6639 Graham, James, 3 June, 1919. (M.)
6640 Grayson, Rev. Joseph Watson, 3 June, 1919. (M.)
6641 Gunther, Frederick Albert, 3 June, 1919. (M.)
6642 Hamilton, Frank Tracey, 3 June, 1919. (M.)
6643 Haskins, Edith Mabel, 3 June, 1919. (M.)
6645 Hay, Charlotte Maud, 3 June, 1919. (M.)
6646 Hayes, Denis, 3 June, 1919. (M.)
6647 Hayes, George Frederick Lacey, 3 June, 1910. (M.)
6648 Hayter, John, 3 June, 1919. (M.)
6649 Heath, Walter Henry, 3 June, 1919. (M.)
6650 Hendry, James, 3 June, 1919. (M.)
6651 Heyer, George, 3 June, 1919. (M.)
6652 Hickey, Jeremiah, 3 June, 1919. (M.)
6653 Higgins, Charles Henry Prangnell, 3 June, 1910. (M.)
6654 Hill, Ernest Edward, 3 June, 1919. (M.)
6655 Howlett, John Flemyng, 3 June, 1919. (M.)
6656 Hughes, Rev. Levi Gethin, 3 June, 1919. (M.)
6657 Hutchinson, Annie Irene, 3 June, 1919. (M.)
6658 Jabotinsky, Vladimir, 3 June, 1919. (M.)
6659 Johnson, Sidney, 3 June, 1919. (M.)
6660 Jones, Hugh Calvert Francis, 3 June, 1919. (M.)
6661 Jones, Mary, 3 June, 1919. (M.)
6662 Joyce, Sterndale, 3 June, 1919. (M.)
6663 King, James Edward, 3 June, 1919. (M.)
6664 Kinnersly, George Edward, 3 June, 1919. (M.)
6665 Laman, Ernest Kirkland, 3 June, 1919. (M.)
6666 Lane, Margaret, Mrs., 3 June, 1919. (M.)
6667 Laracy, Patrick Joseph, 3 June, 1919. (M.)
6668 Lindsay-Smith, Lindsay, 3 June, 1919. (M.)
6669 Lloyd, Amy Margaret Helen, 3 June, 1919. (M.)
6670 Long, Robert Claude, 3 June, 1919. (M.)
6671 McCarthy, Henry, 3 June, 1919. (M.)
6672 MacKay, Christian Frances Nora, 3 June, 1919. (M.)
6673 MacRory, Adam John Charles, 3 June, 1919. (M.)
6674 Marks, Herbert Elton, 3 June, 1919. (M.)
6675 Marshall, Reginald Ross, 3 June, 1919. (M.)
6676 Matthews, William Reginald, 3 June, 1919. (M.)
6677 Meltruish, John Barradale, 3 June, 1919. (M.)
6678 Melles, Robert Ernest, 3 June, 1919. (M.)
6679 Mitchell, Alfred Henry, 3 June, 1919. (M.)
6680 Mooney, Cecil Douglas, 3 June, 1919. (M.)
6681 More, Thomas, 3 June, 1919. (M.)
6682 Morton, Alfred, 3 June, 1919. (M.)
6685 Nye, Violet Mary, 3 June, 1919. (M.)
6686 Jones, Herbert Oakes-, 3 June, 1919. (M.)
6687 Parker, Charles Anson, 3 June, 1919. (M.)
6688 Parker, Henry Charles, 3 June, 1919. (M.)
6689 Parsons, William Henry, 3 June, 1919. (M.)
6691 Percival, Philip Mason, 3 June, 1919. (M.)
6692 Pollard, Pedr, 3 June, 1919. (M.)
6693 Pontin, William James Henry, 3 June, 1919. (M.)
6694 Reeves, John Horace, 3 June, 1919. (M.)
6695 Reynaud, Edward Henry, 3 June, 1919. (M.)
6696 Ridding, Reginald, 3 June, 1919. (M.)
6697 Ripley, Horace Stephens, 3 June, 1919. (M.)
6698 Robertson, Alexander Smith, 3 June, 1919. (M.)

6699 Robinson, William Edward, 3 June, 1919. (M.)
6700 Rogers, Harry George, 3 June, 1919. (M.)
6701 Rushton, Leveson, 3 June, 1919. (M.)
6702 Sainsbury, Flora Gregory, 3 June, 1919. (M.)
6703 Savona, William, 3 June, 1919. (M.)
6704 Shearwood, Thomas, 3 June, 1919. (M.)
6705 Sinfield, Alfred, 3 June, 1919. (M.)
6706 Singer, David Charles, 3 June, 1919. (M.)
6707 Smith, Frank, 3 June, 1919. (M.)
6708 Smith, Robert Melville, 3 June, 1919. (M.)
6709 Stephens, John Kyle, 3 June, 1919. (M.)
6710 Sterndale, Hilda Alice, 3 June, 1919. (M.)
6711 Sutton, Emily Evelyn, 3 June, 1919. (M.)
6712 Taylor, Kenyon Davenport, 3 June, 1919. (M.)
6713 Thorpe, Alfred, 3 June, 1919. (M.)
6714 Tidridge, John Harry, 3 June, 1919. (M.)
6715 Trees, Reginald Pearson, 3 June, 1919. (M.)
6716 Turner, Laurence Beddome, 3 June, 1919. (M.)
6717 Tyler, Frederick Montague, 3 June, 1919. (M.)
6718 Waldock, Charles William, 3 June, 1919. (M.)
6719 Waldron, Charles, 3 June, 1919. (M.)
6720 Wallace, Robert Stuart, 3 June, 1919. (M.)
6721 Walters, John Douglas, 3 June, 1919. (M.)
6722 Warner, Pelham Francis, 3 June, 1919. (M.)
6723 Watson, Lewis James Fort, 3 June, 1919. (M.)
6724 Webb, Hugh Edwin, 3 June, 1919. (M.)
6725 Whitaker, Benjamin, 3 June, 1919. (M.)
6726 Wood, Harold John, 3 June, 1919. (M.)
6727 Woodgate, F. C. I., 3 June, 1919. (M.)
6728 Young, Constance Emily, Mrs., 3 June, 1919. (M.)
6729 Addison, Lancelot Mark, 3 June, 1919. (M.)
6730 Balfour, John, 3 June, 1919. (M.)
6731 Bland, Frederick Edward, 3 June, 1919. (M.)
6732 Cocks, Robert, 3 June, 1919. (M.)
6733 Day George, 3 June, 1919. (M.)
6734 Fennelly, Philip, 3 June, 1919. (M.)
6735 Hughes, Cyril Emerson, 3 June, 1919. (M.)
6736 Murphy, Rev. Charles, 3 June, 1919. (M.)
6737 Murphy, Peter Kevin, 3 June, 1919. (M.)
6738 Phillips, Herbert Thomas, 3 June, 1919. (M.)
6739 Scott, Walter, 3 June, 1919. (M.)
6740 Tadgell, Frederick Harold, 3 June, 1919. (M.)
6741 Wegener, John Frederick William, 3 June, 1919. (M.)
6742 Williams, James Leslie, 3 June, 1919. (M.)
6743 Burdekin, Cyril Blake, 3 June, 1919. (M.)
6744 Cahill, John Walter Frederick, 3 June, 1919. (M.)
6745 Chisholm, Percy, 3 June, 1919. (M.)
6746 Fordham, Percy John Richmond, 3 June, 1919. (M.)
6747 Hale, Sylvester Gresham, 3 June, 1919. (M.)
6748 Hay, Sydney Hartley, 3 June, 1919. (M.)
6749 Hosking, Arthur, 3 June, 1919. (M.)
6750 Mothes, Frederick William, 3 June, 1919. (M.)
6751 Noseda, Paul Rodolfe, 3 June, 1919. (M.)
6752 Sheridan, Norman Charles, 3 June, 1919. (M.)
6753 Tait, Henry Caldwell, 3 June, 1919. (M.)
6754 Tipping, Herbert, 3 June, 1919. (M.)
6755 West, Thomas Samuel, 3 June, 1919. (M.)
6756 Brebner, Innes Wares, 3 June, 1919. (M.)
6757 Coney, Cecil Frederick, 3 June, 1919. (M.)
6758 Croft, George Henry Belton, 3 June, 1919. (M.)
6759 Harris, Harry Bertram, 3 June, 1919. (M.)
6760 Heeley, Henry Norman, 3 June, 1919. (M.)
6761 Johnson, William Josiah, 3 June, 1919. (M.)
6762 Lagerwall, Frank Alfred, 3 June, 1919. (M.)
6763 Newell, Will, 3 June, 1919. (M)
6764 Oakeley, Henry Echley Herbert, 3 June, 1919. (M.)
6765 Thomson, Alexander Melen, 3 June, 1919. (M.)
6766 Brown, Arthur George, 3 June, 1919. (M.)
6767 Love, George William, 3 June, 1919. (M.)
6768 Seng, Sardar, Kamal, 3 June, 1919. (M.)
6769 Kendall, Ramsay George, 3 June, 1919. (M.)
6770 McCullagh, Francis, 3 June, 1919. (M.)
6771 Middleton, Herbert Edgar, 3 June, 1919. (M.)
6772 Orloff, Eugene, 3 June, 1919. (M.)
6773 Padfield, James Carpenter, 3 June, 1919. (M.)
6774 Peacock, Henry Kartchkal, 3 June, 1919. (M.)
6775 Sandelson, David Isambard, 3 June, 1919. (M.)
6776 Talbot, John Hamilton, 3 June, 1919. (M.)
6777 Williams, Arthur James, 3 June, 1919. (M.)
6778 McGill, Thomas Carlisle, 3 June, 1919. (M.)
6779a El Yusbashi Mohamed Effendi Murad el Shahel, 3 June, 1919. (M.)
6779b Brears, Tom, 3 June, 1919. (M.)
6779c Colam, Rosslyn Leigh, 3 June, 1919. (M.)
6779d Dunbar, William Robert, 3 June, 1919. (M.)
6779e Jarrett, Herbert Ernest, 3 June, 1919. (M.)
6779f Abdel Aziz Eff Mansour, Mulazim Awal, 3 June, 1919. (M.)
6779g Mahammed Eff Shefik Amin, Yousbashi, 3 June, 1919. (M.)
6779h Mohammed Eff Yusri, Yousbashi, 3 June, 1919. (M.)
6780a Gruner, Harold Eric, 3 June, 1919. (M.)
6780b Riviere, Eugene Gonzague, 3 June, 1919. (M.)
6780c Ross, Charles Arthur, 3 June, 1919. (M.)
6780d Beaman, Val Arden Hulme, 3 June, 1919. (M.)
6780e Copeland, John Hugh, 3 June, 1919. (M.)
6780f Hallett, Henry Philip Hughes, 3 June, 1919. (M.
6780g Walker, George David, 3 June, 1919. (M.)
6780h Wilkinson, Eric John, 3 June, 1919. (M.)
6781a Douglass, James Douglas Thesiger, 3 June, 1919. (M.)

6781b Eltham, James Frederick, 3 June, 1919. (M.)
6781c Allwright, Samuel Robert, 3 June, 1919. (M.)
6781d Bailey, George William Bryant, 3 June, 1919. (M.)
6781e Blackwood, Albert, 3 June, 1919. (M.)
6781f Boor Singh, Jemdr., 3 June, 1919. (M.)
6781g Bridge, John Henry, 3 June, 1919. (M.)
6781h Collinson, John Carson, 3 June, 1919. (M.)
6782a Coxe, Charles Robert, 3 June, 1919. (M.)
6782b Davis, Enoch, 3 June, 1919. (M.)
6782c Durham, William Robert, 3 June, 1919. (M.)
6782d Ewaz Khan, Risaldar, 3 June, 1919. (M.)
6782e Farmer, Christopher Alfred, 3 June, 1919. (M.)
6782f Garnett, William, 3 June, 1919. (M.)
6782g Hayhurst, John Henry Joseph, 3 June, 1919. (M.)
6782h Hem Raj, Jemdr., 3 June, 1919. (M.)
6783a Hobbs, William Christian, 3 June, 1919. (M.)
6783b Kent, William, 3 June, 1919. (M.)
6783c Macdonald, Hector Ian, 3 June, 1919. (M.)
6783d Mir Jafar Khan, Sardar Bahadur, 3 June, 1919. (M.)
6783e Mohammed Fazil, Jemdr., 3 June, 1919. (M.)
6783f Morris, Wilfred, 3 June, 1919. (M.)
6783g Parke, Robert, 3 June, 1919. (M.)
6783h Phillips, George Henry, 3 June, 1919. (M.)
6784a Prem Singh, Jemdr., 3 June, 1919. (M.)
6784b Rice, Thomas, 3 June, 1919. (M.)
6784c Shahbaz Khan, Subdr., 3 June, 1919. (M.)
6784d Smyth, Richard, 3 June, 1919. (M.)
6784e Snowdon, John Henry, 3 June, 1919. (M)
6784f Walsh, James Edward, 3 June, 1919. (M.)
6784g Wazir Muhammad, Jemdr., 3 June, 1919. (M.)
6784h Barnsley, John G., 3 June, 1919. (M.)
6785a Bryson, John, 3 June, 1919. (M.)
6785b Burrows, Alexander, 3 June, 1919. (M.)
6785c Chandler, S., 3 June, 1919. (M.)
6785d Elliott, George P., 3 June, 1919. (M.)
6785e Green, Albert Victor, 3 June, 1919. (M.)
6785f Lovett, Arthur Harrison, 3 June, 1919. (M.)
6785g McNeil, A., 3 June, 1919. (M.)
6785h Metcalfe, Robert, 3 June, 1919. (M.)
6786a Pereira, Vincent Manoel Francis, 3 June, 1919. (M.)
6786b Pointing, Albert E., 3 June, 1919. (M.)
6786c Thompson, J., 3 June, 1919. (M.)
6786d Wilkinson, Ernest, 3 June, 1919. (M.)
6786e Abbey, Douglas Wilson, 11 June, 1919. (M.)
6786f Adkin, Guy Tempest, 11 June, 1919. (M.)
6786g Bennett, Ernest Reginald, 11 June, 1919. .(M.)
6786h Harness, Robert John, 11 June, 1919. (M.)
3787a Hopkins, Thomas, 11 June, 1919. (M.)
6787b May, Andrew, 11 June, 1919. (M.)
6787c Noble, Alexander, 11 June, 1919. (M.)
6787d Shields, William Cecil, 11 June, 1919. (M.)
6788 Stevens, Walter William Spencer, 11 June, 1919. (M.)
6789 Way, Albert Edward, 11 June, 1919. (M.)
6790 Wrate, James Frederick, 11 June, 1919. (M.)
6791 Elder, Andrew, 21 June, 1919. (M.)
6792 Finch, Charles Edwin, 21 June, 1919. (M.)
6793 Gordon, Frank Sinclair, 21 June, 1919. (M.)
6794 Rice, Arthur John, 21 June, 1919. (M.)
6795 Rodway, George Frederick, 21 June, 1919. (M.)
6796 Austin, Walter Alexander, 27 June, 1919. (M.)
6797 Bendell, Albert, 27 June, 1919. (M.)
6798 Blake, Alfred, 27 June, 1919.
6799 Blow, Henry Charles, 27 June, 1919. (M.)
6800 Harris, William, 27 June, 1919. (M.)
6801 Herbert, Guy Frederick, 27 June, 1919. (M.)
6802 Hopkins, Harry, 27 June, 1919. (M.)
6803 Jones, Sydney Herbert, 27 June, 1919. (M.)
6804 Kelleway, Percy Dixon, 27 June, 1919. (M.)
6805 Marchant, Frank, 27 June, 1919. (M.)
6806 Milne, Edward Arthur, 27 June, 1919. (M.)
6807 Overhead, William Henry, 27 June, 1919. (M.)
6808 Rawlings, Herbert Henry, 27 June, 1919. (M.)
6809 Shannon, Frank Ernest, 27 June, 1919. (M.)
6810 Singleton, Albert Henry, 27 June, 1919. (M.)
6811 Smith, Alfred Charles, 27 June, 1919. (M.)
6812 Bates, Walter, 30 June, 1919. (M.)
6813 Gammon, John Thomas, 30 June, 1919. (M.)
6814 Holmes, Robert, 30 June, 1919. (M.)
6815 Carpenter, George, 4 July, 1919. (M.)
6816 Duncan, Alec James, 4 July, 1919. (M.)
6817 Evans, Joseph Owen, 4 July, 1919. (M.)
6818 Gobbitt, Reginald Harry Sutton, 4 July, 1919. (M.)
6819 Harris, George William, 4 July, 1919. (M.)
6820 Joy, Charles Edward, 4 July, 1919. (M.)
6821 Neasham, John Robert, 4 July, 1919. (M.)
6822 Pike, Evan Cuthbert, 4 July, 1919. (M.)
6823 Sheldrake, John William, 4 July, 1919. (M.)
6824 Young, Frederick Richard, 4 July, 1919. (M.)
6825 Cant, John, 10 July, 1919. (M.)
6826 Fletcher, Evelyn Norman Robert, 10 July, 1919. (M.)
6827 Paris, William Richard 10 July, 1919. (M.)
6828 Pearse, Hender Trevenen, 10 July, 1919. (M.)
6829 Barnes, John, 12 July, 1919. (M.)
6830 Burrage, Henry James, 12 July, 1919. (M.)
6831 Felton, Charles, 12 July, 1919. (M.)
6832 Howell, Cecil Ingledew, 12 July, 1919. (M.)
6833 McGill, Edmund Allan, 12 July, 1919. (M.)
6834 Thain, Alexander, 12 July, 1919. (M.)
6835 Wood, Alexander, 12 July, 1919. (M.)
6836 Austin, Arthur, 17 July, 1919. (M.)

6837 Ayling, William, 17 July, 1919. (M.)
6838 Bailey, Arthur Hubert, 17 July, 1919.
6839 Bloodworth, William Snow, 17 July, 1919. (M.)
6840 Bown, Joseph, 17 July, 1919. (M.)
6841 Bradby, Matthew Samuel, 17 July, 1919. (M.)
6842 Brown, John Steven, 17 July, 1919. (M.)
6843 Bunt, Richard Charles, 17 July, 1919. (M.)
6844 Cameron, John, 17 July, 1919. (M.)
6845 Carter, Frederick James, 17 July, 1919. (M.)
6846 Clark, Ewbank, 17 July, 1919. (M.)
6847 Dunn, Harold Stuart, 17 July, 1919. (M.)
6848 Elliott, Maurice Herbert, 17 July, 1919. (M.)
6849 Everett, Douglas Henry, 17 July, 1919. (M.)
6850 Gray, Donald Nixon, 17 July, 1919. (M.)
6851 Hanning. Charles Horatio, 17 July, 1919. (M.)
6852 Heraud, Stanley Francis, 17 July, 1919. (M.)
6853 Jackson, Norman, 17 July, 1919. (M.)
6854 Kimber, Ernest, 17 July, 1919. (M.)
6855 Lendy, Thomas, 17 July, 1919. (M.)
6856 Lynch, Herbert Arthur, 17 July, 1919. (M.)
6857 Maitland, Arthur Albert, 17 July, 1919. (M.)
6858 Montgomery, Walter Ernest, 17 July, 1919. (M.)
6859 Morrissey, William, 17 July, 1919. (M.)
6860 Newman, Henry Charles, 17 July, 1919. (M.)
6861 Pantling, Frederick, 17 July, 1919. (M.)
6862 Prideaux, George Edward, 17 July, 1919. (M.
6863 Prince, George, 17 July, 1919. (M.)
6864 Shaw, Robert, John 17 July, 1919. (M.)
6865 Spittle, Edward Alfred, 17 July, 1919. (M.)
6866 Toppin, Maxwell Howard, 17 July, 1919. (M.)
6867 Westacott, William John Henry, 17 July, 1919. (M.)
6868 Westlake, John Harold, 17 July, 1919. (M.)
6869 Bagnall, Reginald Douglas, 31 July, 1919. (M.)
6870 Botterill, Frank Owen, 31 July, 1919. (M.)
6871 Bower, David, 31 July, 1919. (M.)
6872 Burrows. John Thomas Ladbrooke, 31 July, 1919. (M.)
6873 Evans, Evan, 31 July, 1919. (M.)
6874 Fulton, Robert Arthur, 31 July, 1919. (M.)
6875 Green, George James, 31 July, 1919. (M.)
6876 Hammond, Stephen Thomas, 31 July, 1919. (M.)
6877 John, Henry Brynmor, 31 July, 1919. (M.)
6878 Knight, Samuel Henry, 3 July, 1919. (M.)
6879 Lillicrap, Herbert Richard, 31 July, 1919. (M.)
6880 Martin, Frank Lewis, 31 July, 1919. (M.)
6881 Nightingale, William Joseph Edward, 31 July, 1919. (M.).
6882 Ogle, John, 31 July, 1919. (M.)
6883 Regan, Robert Henry, 31 July, 1919. (M.)
6884 Welsh, John George, 31 July, 1919. (M.)
6885 Welsh, James Frederick, 31 July, 1919. (M.)
6886 Draisey, John William James, 11 Aug. 1919. (M.)
6887 Eddy, Charles, 11 Aug. 1919. (M.)
6888 Lamb, Edwin Daniel, 11 Aug. 1919. (M.)
6889 Newmarch, Henry Clarence, 11 Aug. 1919. (M.)
6890 Rhind, William Alexander, 11 Aug. 1919. (M.)
6891 Roberts, Charles John, 11 Aug. 1919. (M.)
6892 Snell, Philip William, 11 Aug. 1919 (M.)
6893 Beever, Claude Henry, 16 Sept. 1919. (M.)
6894 Buchan, Robert, 16 Sept. 1919. (M.)
6895 Butler, Francis John, 16 Sept. 1919. (M.)
6896 Cahill, John, 16 Sept. 1919. (M.)
6897 Coleman, William Francis, 16 Sept. 1919. (M.)
6898 Croucher, Edward William, 16 Sept. 1919. (M.)
6899 Davies, John Wilfred, 16 Sept. 1919. (M.)
6900 Forbes, Robert, 16 Sept. 1919. (M.)
6901 Fuller, James, 16 Sept. 1919. (M.)
6902 Williams, Nevill Glennie Garnons-, 16 Sept. 1919. (M.)
6903 Hole, Edwin, 16 Sept. 1919. (M.)
6904 Hughes, William, 16 Sept. 1919. (M.)
6905 Invermee, Robert, 16 Sept. 1919. (M.)
6906 Larter, Charles Seymour, 16 Sept. 1919. (M.)
6907 Quincey, George, 16 Sept. 1919 (M.)
6908 Ralph, Alexander, 16 Sept. 1919. (M.)
6909 Renshaw, John William, 16 Sept. 1919. (M.)
6910 Sullivan, Richard, 16 Sept. 1919. (M.)
6911 Urell, Valentine, 16 Sept. 1919. (M.)
6912 Winstanley, John, 16 Sept. 1919. (M.)
6913 Barker, Ernest Bernard, 10 Oct. 1919. (M.)
6914 Wylie, Hamilton Neil, 10 Oct. 1919. (M.)
6915 Armstrong, Tom, 10 Oct. 1919. (M.)
6916 Berwick, William Edwin, 10 Oct. 1919. (M.)
6917 Dakin, Humphrey Burns, 10 Oct. 1919. (M.)
6918 Gunn, Donald Benjamin, 10 Oct. 1919. (M.)
6919 Hutchinson, Hubery Gerald, 10 Oct. 1919. (M.)
6920 Ledeboer, John Raymond, 10 Oct. 1919. (M.)
6921 Sumner, James Arthur Chester, 10 Oct. 1919. (M.)
6922 Tedman, Frank, 10 Oct. 1919. (M.)
6923 Wells, Frederick Kynaston, 10 Oct. 1919. (M.)
6924 Crooks, Lindsay, 10 Oct. 1919. (M.)
6925 Dawson, Alexander John, 10 Oct. 1919. (M.)
6926 Dracopoli, Ignatius Nicholas, 10 Oct. 1919. (M.)
6927 Furnival, John Megarry, 10 Oct. 1919. (M.)
6928 Greening, Thomas, 10 Oct. 1919. (M.)
6929 Ralston, Gavin, 10 Oct. 1919. (M.)
6930 Burdett, Henry Stanton, 10 Oct. 1919. (M.)
6931 Cameron, Donald Phillips, 10 Oct. 1919. (M.)
6932 Hughes, Alfred Thomas, 10 Oct. 1919. (M.)
6933 Lehmann, Henry David, 10 Oct. 1919. (M.)
6934 Shaw, Walter Langston, 10 Oct. 1919. (M.)
6935 Shepheard-Walwyn, Roderick Aylward, 10 Oct. 1919. (M.)

6936 Stroud, George Thomas, 10 Oct. 1919. (M.)
6937 Tancred, Christopher Humphrey, 10 Oct. 1919. (M.)
6938 Walsh, George Victor, 10 Oct. 1919. (M.)
6939 Blackmore, Alfred Charles, 10 Oct. 1919. (M.)
6940 Critchley, William Edwin, 10 Oct. 1919. (M.)
6941 Humphreys, Walter Ebenezer, 10 Oct. 1919. (M.)
6942 Ross, Tascar Alan, 10 Oct. 1919. (M.)
6943 Shortridge, Guy Chester, 10 Oct. 1919. (M.)
6944 Tyrrell, John Ernest, 10 Oct. 1919.
6945 Young, Stanley Gordon, 10 Oct. 1919. (M.)
6946 Chauncey, Alice Louise, 10 Oct. 1919. (M.)
6947 Appleton, William Arnold, 17 Oct. 1919. (M.)
6948 Grant, G. B. Macpherson, 17 Oct. 1919. (M.)
6949 Lovatt, John Vincent Stratford, 17 Oct. 1919. (M.)
6950 Osborn, William Albert, 17 Oct. 1919. (M.)
6951 Oswald, David James Tosh, 17 Oct. 1919. (M.)
6952 Pitt, George Philip, 17 Oct. 1919. (M.)
6953 Plant, David Thomas, 17 Oct. 1919. (M.)
6954 Sawyers, William Henry, 17 Oct. 1919. (M.)
6955 Benoy, William John, 11 Nov. 1919. (M.)
6956 Harries, Ernest Bertram, 11 Nov. 1919. (M.)
6957 McCarthy, Sidney James, 11 Nov. 1919. (M.)
6958 Winzar, Sidney Herbert, 11 Nov. 1919. (M.)
6959 Bland, Albert, 11 Nov. 1919. (M.)
6960 Broad, Arthur Nowell, 11 Nov. 1919. (M.)
6961 Bryson, Charles, 11 Nov. 1919. (M.)
6962 Drysdale, John Syme, 11 Nov. 1919. (M.)
6963 Garside, Cecil, 11 Nov. 1919. (M.)
6964 Higgins, Robert Henry Constable, 11 Nov. 1919. (M.)
6965 Hindell, Harold Goodall, 11 Nov. 1919. (M.)
6966 Holder, Alfred Edward, 11 Nov. 1919. (M.)
6967 Howard, Alfred Thomas Stewart, 11 Nov. 1919. (M.)
6968 Jeal, Joseph, 11 Nov. 1919. (M.)
6969 Joyce, Ernest Percy, 11 Nov. 1919. (M.)
6970 Kininmonth, Alec Marshall, 11 Nov. 1919. (M.)
6971 Langmead, Harold Francis, 11 Nov. 1919. (M.)
6972 Leonard, Guiseppe Stanley, 11 Nov. 1919. (M.)
6973 Lord, Godfrey James, 11 Nov. 1919. (M.)
6974 Martine, William Robert, 11 Nov. 1919. (M.)
6975 Paddon, John Locke, 11 Nov. 1919. (M.)
6976 Perkins, Harry Dunbar, 11 Nov. 1919. (M.)
6977 Phelphs, Seth Arthur Rose, 11 Nov. 1919. (M.)
6978 Phipps, Paul Campbell, 11 Nov. 1919. (M.)
6979 Rankin, William Robert Theodore, 11 Nov. 1919. (M.)
6980 Smith, Charles Frederick Tate, 11 Nov. 1919. (M.)
6981 Smith, Eric Payton, 11 Nov. 1919. (M.)
6982 Stokes, William Henry, 11 Nov. 1919. (M.)
6983 Tollemache, Cecil Herbert, 11 Nov. 1919. (M.)
6984 Upton, Norman Royce, 11 Nov. 1919. (M.)
6985 Warren, Desmond Cecil Robert, 11 Nov. 1919. (M.)
6986 Wilding, Henry, 11 Nov. 1919. (M.)
6987 Williams, John, 11 Nov. 1919. (M.)
6988 Nowitsky, Vladimir, 11 Nov. 1919. (M.)
6989 Pepler, Seth Bernard, 11 Nov. 1919. (M.)
6990 Dainton, William Charles Annable-, 11 Nov. 1919. (M.)
6991 Beale, Allan Oswald Rufus, 11 Nov. 1919. (M.)
6992 Beale, Geoffrey Scott, 11 Nov. 1919. (M.)
6993 Birse, Arthur Herbert, 11 Nov. 1919. (M.)
6994 Coghlan, George Edmond, 11 Nov. 1919. (M.)
6995 Fagan, Charles Walter, 11 Nov. 1919. (M.)
6996 Forbes, James George Annand, 11 Nov. 1919. (M.)
6997 Grainger, Charles, 11 Nov. 1919. (M.)
6998 Jagger, William, 11 Nov. 1919. (M.)
6999 Le Roy, Donovan, 11 Nov. 1919. (M.)
7000 Lynott, Michael Joseph, 11 Nov. 1919. (M.)
7001 Mende, Nickolas Edwin, 11 Nov. 1919. (M.)
7002 Neame, George Austin, 11 Nov. 1919. (M.)
7003 Read, Sidney, 11 Nov. 1919. (M.)
7004 Reed, Thomas, 11 Nov. 1919. (M.)
7005 Small, Victor, 11 Nov. 1919. (M.)
7006 Tailby, Mark, 11 Nov. 1919. (M.)
7007 Witney, John Humphrey, 11 Nov. 1919. (M.)
7008 Bentley, R., 11 Nov. 1919. (M.)
7009 Cole, Harold Ralph C., 11 Nov. 1919. (M.)
7010 FitzGerald, John Sidney North, 11 Nov. 1919. (M.)
7011 Trotter, Philip Coutts, 11 Nov. 1919. (M.)
7012 Capstick, Hugh Patrick, 11 Nov. 1919. (M.)
7013 Hobson, Bruce, 11 Nov. 1919. (M.)
7014 Leycester, Philip Wrey, 11 Nov. 1919. (M.)
7015 O'Dell, Edward Seymour, 11 Nov. 1919. (M.)
7016 Rowbottom, Wilmos William Boxall, 11 Nov. 1919. (M.)
7017 Sharpe, Frederick William, 11 Nov. 1919. (M.)
7018 Shaw, Reginald Frank, 11 Nov. 1919. (M.)
7019 Smith, Harold Howard, 11 Nov. 1919. (M.)
7020 Thompson, James Douglas, 11 Nov. 1919. (M.)
7021 Sandels, Cecil Arthur Anglesea,- 11 Nov. 1919. (M.)
7022 Hewett, Arthur, 11 Nov. 1919. (M.)
7023 Brown, Alfred Claude, 15 Nov. 1919. (M.)
7024 Longstaffe, John Walter, 15 Nov. 1919. (M.)
7025 Pender, William Stanhope, 15 Nov. 1919. (M.)
7026 Romilly, Herbrand Alan, 15 Nov. 1919. (M.)
7027 Thompson, Hugh Willoughby, 15 Nov. 1919. (M.)
7028 Turner, Noel Theodor Berwell, 15 Nov. 1919. (M.)
7029 Walker, Frederick Rutley, 15 Nov. 1919. (M.)
7030 Witthaus, Gabriel Thorald, 15 Nov. 1919. (M.)
7030a Beveridge, Edmund Walter St. Clair, 23 Nov. 1919. (M.)
7031 Barry, Jack Leslie, 28 Nov. 1919. (M.)
7032 Davies, John Trevor, 28 Nov. 1919. (M.)
7033 Ellis, Frederick Rowland, 28 Nov. 1919. (M.)

7034 Brunton, Robert Godfree, 5 Dec. 1919.
7035 Rowntree, John Harvey Woodville, 5 Dec. 1919.
7036 Philip, John, 5 Dec. 1919.
7037 Blyth, Charles Edward, 5 Dec. 1919.
7038 Newton, George Burns, 5 Dec. 1919.
7039 Hennings, William, 5 Dec. 1919.
7040 Louch, Arthur Charles Innes, 5 Dec. 1919.
7041 Beard, Norah, Mrs., 5 Dec. 1919.
7042 Dunn, Ellen S., Mrs., 5 Dec. 1919.
7043 White, Robert George, 5 Dec. 1919.
7044 Hayward Curling, 5 Dec., 1919.
7045 Baily, Robert Edward Hartwell, 5 Dec. 1919.
7046 Howell, Alban Berkley Butts, 5 Dec. 1919.
7047 Parker, Arthur Claude, 5 Dec. 1919.
7048 Beddison, Francis William, 5 Dec. 1919.
7049 Egford, George Henry, 12 Dec. 1919. (M.)
7050 Wildbore, Albert Milton, 12 Dec. 1919. (M.)
7051 Batcheldor, William, 22 Dec. 1919. (M.)
7052 Borland, William, 22 Dec. 1919. (M.)
7053 Fraser, Norman Graham, 22 Dec. 1919. (M.)
7054 Gardiner, Stanley James, 22 Dec. 1919. (M.)
7055 Hoile, William Henry, 22 Dec. 1919. (M.)
7056 Jukes, Alfred, 22 Dec. 1919. (M.)
7057 Lang, Albert Frank, 22 Dec. 1919. (M.)
7058 Moore, Gordon, 22 Dec. 1919. (M.)
7059 Tattersall, James William, 22 Dec. 1919. (M.)
7060 Thomas, Alan Miller, 22 Dec. 1919. (M.)
7061 Tomling, George Gibson, 22 Dec. 1919. (M.)
7062 Williams, David Eric, 22 Dec. 1919. (M.)
7063 Young, James William ,22 Dec. 1919. (M.)
7064 Aiyar, Rao Bahadur Pinnavasal Ramaswama Vengu, 30 Dec. 1919.
7065 Ali, Khan Bahadur Mir Diwan, 30 Dec. 1919.
7066 Ali, Maulvi Saiyid Ijaz, 30 Dec. 1919.
7067 Amir-ud-Din, Shaikh, 30 Dec. 1919.
7068 Avargal, Rao Sahib Pettachi Karuppan, 30 Dec. 1919.
7069 Barne, Dorothy Kate, Mrs., 30 Dec. 1919.
7071 Britto, Valentine, 30 Dec. 1919.
7072 Brookes, Arthur Stuart, 30 Dec. 1919.
7073 Buchanan, Margaret, Mrs., 30 Dec. 1919.
7074 Cameron, Cyril Claude, 30 Dec. 1919.
7075 Campagnac, Charles Haswell, 30 Dec. 1919.
7076 Chandra, Lala Ram, 30 Dec. 1919.
7077 Clarke, Douglas Allen, 30 Dec. 1919.
7078 Cole, Sybil, Mrs., 30 Dec. 1919.
7079 Coombes, George Noble, 30 Dec. 1919.
7080 Cooverji, Khan Sahib Sorabji, 30 Dec. 1919.
7081 Cuthbert, Alexander, 30 Dec. 1919.
7082 Davies, Agnes, 30 Dec. 1919.
7083 Day, Andrew Sinclair, 30 Dec. 1919.
7084 Dayal, Seth Prabh, 30 Dec. 1919.
7085 Debenham, Walter Charles, 30 Dec. 1919.
7086 Dickson, Lorna, Mrs., 30 Dec. 1919.
7087 Din, Khan Bahadur Maulvi Ahmed, 30 Dec. 1919.
7088 Din, Khan Bahadur Munshi Ahmad, 30 Dec. 1919.
7089 Evans, Rev. Edward, 30 Dec. 1919.
7090 Fowle, Edward, 30 Dec. 1919.
7091 Gahan, Patrick John, 30 Dec. 1919.
7092 Gajendragadkar, Gopal Lakshman, 30 Dec. 1919
7093 Ganguly, Rai Akhoy Bhusan, 30 Dec. 1919.
7094 Gonet, Adolphe Joseph Louis, 30 Dec. 1919.
7095 Gopal, Lala Ram, 30 Dec. 1919.
7096 Green, Leslie Benton, 30 Dec. 1919.
7097 Hakim, Wadero Abdul, 30 Dec. 1919.
7098 Hamlyn, Henrietta, Mrs., 30 Dec. 1919.
7099 Harold, May, Mrs., 30 Dec. 1919.
7100 Heycock, Florence, Mrs., 30 Dec. 1919.
7101 Higgs, Ernest Bertram, 30 Dec. 1919.
7102 Hodges, George Ernest, 30 Dec. 1919.
7103 Holme, Nellie, Mrs., 30 Dec. 1919.
7104 Hunt, Geraldine, 30 Dec. 1919.
7105 Husain, Chaudri Mujtaba, 30 Dec. 1919.
7106 Husain, Khan Sahib Tasaddug, 30 Dec. 1919.
7107 Hyland, Charles John, 30 Dec. 1919.
7108 Jehangir, Hilla Cowasji, Mrs., 30 Dec. 1919.
7109 Jones, Antoinette Manget, Mrs., 30 Dec. 1919.
7110 Joseph, Charles Henry, 30 Dec. 1919.
7111 Kempster, James Charles, 30 Dec. 1919.
7112 Khair-ud-din, 30 Dec. 1919.
7113 Khan, Saiyid Ahmad Ali, 30 Dec. 1919.
7114 Khan, Begum Mustapha, 30 Dec. 1919.
7115 King-Church, Mabel, Mrs., 30 Dec. 1919.
7116 Kirkpatrick, John, 30 Dec. 1919.
7117 Kunning, Arthur Blandford, 30 Dec. 1919.
7118 Laird, Nellie, Mrs., 30 Dec. 1919.
7119 Lal, Munshi Chiman, 30 Dec. 1919.
7120 Lal, Lala Faranga, 30 Dec. 1919.
7121 Lambourn, Norah, Mrs., 30 Dec. 1919.
7122 Lennox, Agnes Margaret, Mrs.. 30 Dec. 1919.
7123 Liddiard, Edgar Stratton, 30 Dec. 1919.
7124 Lidierth, James Eugene, 30 Dec. 1919.
7125 Lilley, Arthur Winfield, 30 Dec. 1919.
7126 Low, Frederick Edward, 30 Dec. 1919.
7127 McCausland, Gertrude, Mrs., 30 Dec., 1919
7128 Mackenzie, Dorothy Helen, Mrs., 30 Dec. 1919.
7129 MacLeod, Herwald Byrne, 30 Dec. 1919.
7130 Mahamad, Shaikh, 30 Dec. 1919.
7131 Maynard, Mildred, Mrs., 30 Dec. 1919.
7132 Mulcahy, James Hamilton, 30 Dec. 1919.
7133 Nanavati, Collie Erach, Mrs., 30 Dec. 1919.

7134 Narayan, Pandit Bishan, 30 Dec. 1919.
7135 Oakley, Winifred, Mrs., 30 Dec. 1919.
7136 O'Donnel, Edith, Mrs., 30 Dec. 1919.
7137 O'Donnell, John David, 30 Dec. 1919.
7138 Oldfield, Geraldine, Mrs., 30 Dec. 1919.
7139 Osborn, Howard Harry, 30 Dec. 1919.
7140 Osgerby, Isabel, Mrs., 30 Dec. 1919.
7141 Oung, May Hla, Mrs., 30 Dec. 1919.
7142 Panthaki, Dosabhai Framji, 30 Dec. 1919.
7143 Parsons, Bertha, Mrs., 30 Dec. 1919.
7144 Patwardhan, Rao Bahadur Damodar Bapu Rao 30 Dec. 1919.
7145 Peachey, Rev. Robert William, 30 Dec. 1919.
7146 Peppe, Marion, Mrs., 30 Dec. 1919.
7147 Peters, Alice, Mrs., 30 Dec. 1919.
7148 Petit, Jaijee Jehangir, Mrs., 30 Dec. 1919.
7149 Phadke, Vasudev Vishnu, 30 Dec. 1919.
7150 Pillai, Hannah Sargon Ponnuswami, Mrs., 30 Dec. 1919.
7151 Pinches, Nora, Mrs., 30 Dec. 1919.
7152 Potter, Edith Madelene, 30 Dec. 1919.
7153 Prasad, Munshi Ambe, 30 Dec. 1919.
7154 Quinn, George Edwin Walter, 30 Dec. 1919.
7155 Ramsay, Ermyntrude Sidwell, Mrs., 30 Dec. 1919.
7156 Redl, Mary Beatrice, Mrs., 30 Dec. 1919.
7157 Reeks, Reginald Rupert, 30 Dec. 1919.
7158 Scott, James Reid, 30 Dec. 1919.
7159 Shaikh, Muhammad Kadir, 30 Dec. 1919.
7160 Singh, Randhir, 30 Dec. 1919.
7161 Sinha, Madan Mohan, 30 Dec. 1919.
7162 Sleigh, Constance, Mrs., 30 Dec. 1919.
7163 Steen, Minnie, Mrs., 30 Dec. 1919.
7164 Stephen, Henry Buckingham, 30 Dec. 1919.
7165 Sullivan, Michael Allen Patrick, 30 Dec. 1919.
7166 Tremearne, Sybil, Mrs., 30 Dec. 1919.
7167 Tudor Owen, Muriel, Mrs.. 30 Dec. 1919.
7168 Venkataramayya, Saguna, Mrs., 30 Dec. 1919.
7169 Weakford, Charles Frederick, 30 Dec. 1919.
7170 Wells, William George, 30 Dec. 1919.
7171 Wilson, Maggie Scott, Mrs., 30 Dec. 1919.
7172 Wilson, Stewart, 30 Dec. 1919.
7173 Wood, Henrietta, Mrs., 30 Dec. 1919.
7174 Zobel, Elizabeth, Mrs., 30 Dec. 1919.
7175 Abbiss, William Frederick, 1 Jan. 1920.
7176 Abbott, Mary Joyce, 1 Jan. 1920.
7177 Abbott, Tom Bland, 1 Jan. 1920.
7178 Aberdein, Florence Margaret, 1 Jan. 1920.
7179 Abrahams, Joseph Godchaux, 1 Jan. 1920.
7180 Ackland, Vera, Mrs., 1 Jan. 1920.
7181 Adam, Mary, 1 Jan. 1920.
7182 Adams, Edgar, 1 Jan. 1920.
7183 Adams, Thomas Herbert, 1 Jan. 1920.
7184 Adams, Matthew Henry, 1 Jan. 1920.
7185 Addison, Guy Frederick, 1 Jan. 1920.
7186 Aglionby, Rosa Frances, 1 Jan. 1920.
7187 Agnew, Andrew, 1 Jan. 1920.
7188 Aitken, Adeline, Mrs., 1 Jan. 1920.
7189 Aitken, Constance Margaret, 1 Jan. 1920.
7190 Aitken, John Malcolm, 1 Jan. 1920.
7191 Akers, Charles Wrightson, 1 Jan. 1920.
7192 Alcide, Edward Augustus, 1 Jan. 1920.
7193 Aldis, Arthur Cyril Webb, 1 Jan. 1920.
7194 Alexander, Alfred, 1 Jan. 1920.
7195 Alexander, Donald Clark, 1 Jan. 1920.
7196 Alexander, Edith Margaret, Mrs., 1 Jan. 1920.
7197 Alexander, Eleanor Jane, 1 Jan. 1920.
7198 Alexander, John William, 1 Jan. 1920.
7199 Allen, Elsie Clara, 1 Jan. 1920.
7200 Allen, Francis, 1 Jan. 1920.
7201 Allen, George James, 1 Jan. 1920
7202 Allen, John, 1 Jan. 1920.
7203 Allen, Margaret Louise, Mrs., 1 Jan. 1920.
7204 Alleyne, Stella Margaret, 1 Jan. 1920.
7205 Allison, George Henry, 1 Jan. 1920.
7206 Allum, Herbert George, 1 Jan. 1920.
7207 Alston, Charles Henry, 1 Jan. 1920.
7208 Ambler, Joseph Edward, 1 Jan. 1920.
7209 Anderson, Agnes Hilda, Mrs., 1 Jan. 1920.
7210 Anderson, Frances Lightbourne Trimingham, 1 Jan. 1920.
7211 Anderson, Francis, 1 Jan. 1920.
7212 Anderson, George Reinhardt, 1 Jan. 1920.
7213 Anderson, Joan Anderson, Mrs. Scott-, 1 Jan. 1920.
7214 Anderton, James Edwin, 1 Jan. 1920.
7215 Andrew, Bennett Harvey, 1 Jan. 1920.
7216 Andrews, Arthur William, 1 Jan. 1920.
7217 Andrews, Elizabeth, 1 Jan. 1920.
7218 Andrews, George, 1 Jan. 1920.
7219 Andrews, Helen, 1 Jan. 1920.
7220 Andrews, Walter Gower, 1 Jan. 1920.
7221 Angus, John, 1 Jan. 1920.
7222 Annan, Margaret, 1 Jan. 1920.
7223 Annett, Henry Edward, 1 Jan. 1920.
7224 Anstruther, Hon. Eleonora, Mrs., 1 Jan. 1920.
7225 Anthony, Isaac John, 1 Jan. 1920.
7226 Apperly, David Cooper, 1 Jan. 1920.
7227 Appleton, Janet, Mrs., 1 Jan. 1920.
7228 Appleton, Mary, Mrs., 1 Jan. 1920.
7229 Arbuthnot, Constance, Lady, 1 Jan. 1920.
7230 Arbuthnot, Elizabeth Fountaine, Mrs., 1 Jan. 1920.
7231 Archibald, David, 1 Jan. 1920.
7232 Ardern, Frederick, 1 Jan. 1920.

7233 Argo, Archibald, 1 Jan. 1920.
7234 Armitstead, Thomas, 1 Jan. 1920.
7235 Armytage, Frederic Fairburn, 1 Jan. 1920.
7236 Arnison, Christine Mary, Mrs., 1 Jan. 1920.
7237 Arnott, Francis William, 1 Jan. 1920.
7238 Arundel, Grace, 1 Jan. 1920.
7239 Ashley, Anne, 1 Jan. 1920.
7240 Ashley, Martha Nixon Greenwood, Mrs., 1 Jan. 1920.
7241 Ashmole, William Hadley, 1 Jan. 1920.
7242 Ashton, Harold, 1 Jan. 1920.
7243 Ashworth, Tom, 1 Jan. 1920.
7244 Askew, Percy, 1 Jan. 1920.
7245 Astbury, Sarah, Mrs., 1 Jan. 1920.
7246 Atcherley, Ethel Mary, 1 Jan. 1920.
7247 Atkins, Gertrude, 1 Jan. 1920.
7248 Atkinson, George Arthur, 1 Jan. 1920.
7249 Atkinson, John Parkinson, 1 Jan. 1920.
7250 Austin, Gertrude Hannah, 1 Jan. 1920.
7251 Austin, Henry Edmund, 1 Jan. 1920.
7252 Austin, Thomas George, 1 Jan. 1920.
7253 Austin, William Walter, 1 Jan. 1920.
7254 Awburn, Harriet, Mrs. (Madame Hallé), 1 Jan. 1920.
7255 Awdry, Olive Muriel, Mrs., 1 Jan. 1920.
7256 Aylmer, George Mason, 1 Jan. 1920.
7257 Ayres, Robert Alfred, 1 Jan. 1920.
7258 Backhouse, Edwin, 1 Jan. 1920.
7259 Baggallay, Patience Gertrude, 1 Jan. 1920.
7260 Bagwell, William Henry, 1 Jan. 1920.
7261 Baikie, William Baikie, 1 Jan. 1920.
7262 Bailey, Clement William, 1 Jan. 1920.
7263 Bailey, Florence Emily, Mrs., 1 Jan. 1920.
7264 Bailey, George William, 1 Jan. 1920.
7265 Bailey, James Rhodes, 1 Jan. 1920.
7266 Bailey, Margaret Fanny, Mrs., 1 Jan. 1920.
7267 Bailey, Robert William Harvey, 1 Jan. 1920.
7268 Baily, Edwin, 1 Jan. 1920.
7269 Baily, Harold, 1 Jan. 1920.
7270 Bain, Herbert Barr, 1 Jan. 1920.
7271 Bainton, Edward Cecil, 1 Jan. 1920.
7272 Baird, Alexander McDonald, 1 Jan. 1920.
7273 Baird, Blanche Mary, Mrs., 1 Jan. 1920.
7274 Baker, Edwin Emmanuel, 1 Jan. 1920.
7275 Baker, Gerald Percival, 1 Jan. 1920.
7276 Baker, Horace William, 1 Jan. 1920.
7277 Baker, Isabel Noeline, 1 Jan. 1920.
7278 Baker, John, 1 Jan. 1920.
7279 Baker, John Frederick William, 1 Jan. 1920.
7280 Baker, Maggie Ethel, 1 Jan. 1920.
7281 Baker, Isabella Winifred, Mrs., 1 Jan. 1920.
7282 Baker, Muriel Carew, 1 Jan. 1920.
7283 Baldwin, Arthur George, 1 Jan. 1920.
7284 Baldwin, Rev. Charles Henry Robert, 1 Jan. 1920.
7285 Baldwin, Sam, 1 Jan. 1920.
7286 Balfour, Jessie Edith, 1 Jan. 1920.
7287 Ball, Frederick Ernest, 1 Jan. 1920.
7288 Ball, James, 1 Jan. 1920.
7289 Ball, Walter Mills, 1 Jan. 1920.
7290 Ballantyne, Allan Opie, 1 Jan. 1920.
7291 Ballantyne, Andrew, 1 Jan. 1920.
7292 Balmford, Joseph William, 1 Jan. 1920.
7293 Bamford, Herbert Richard, 1 Jan. 1920.
7294 Banner, Wilfred, 1 Jan. 1920.
7295 Barber, Arthur Powell, 1 Jan. 1920.
7296 Barber, Maude Helen, 1 Jan. 1920.
7297 Barclay, Hannah Maud, Mrs., 1 Jan. 1920.
7298 Baring, Harold Herman John, 1 Jan. 1920.
7299 Barker, Christabel Buchanan, 1 Jan. 1920.
7300 Barker, Frederick Rowland, 1 Jan. 1920.
7301 Barker, William, 1 Jan. 1920.
7302 Barker, William, 1 Jan. 1920.
7303 Barkworth, Minnie Mabel, Mrs., 1 Jan. 1920.
7304 Barlow, James, 1 Jan. 1920.
7305 Barlow, Sydney, 1 Jan. 1920.
7306 Barnaby, Stanley Skoulding, 1 Jan. 1920.
7307 Barnard, Cyril Wyndham, 1 Jan. 1920.
7308 Barnard, John Henry Owen, 1 Jan. 1920.
7309 Barnes, Helen Elizabeth, 1 Jan. 1920.
7310 Barnes, Minne Craig, Mrs., 1 Jan. 1920.
7311 Barnett, Margaret Elizabeth, Mrs., 1 Jan. 1920
7312 Barns, George Delbridge, 1 Jan. 1920.
7313 Barrett, Hannah Madge, 1 Jan. 1920.
7314 Barrett, Kate Eveline, 1 Jan. 1920.
7315 Barratt, Milan, Mrs., 1 Jan. 1920.
7316 Barrow, Ellen Janet Innes, 1 Jan. 1920.
7317 Barrowcliff, Marmaduke, 1 Jan. 1920.
7318 Barrows, Lucy Adeline, 1 Jan. 1920.
7319 Barry, Thomas Ernest, 1 Jan. 1920.
7320 Barsdorf, Ralph, 1 Jan. 1920.
7321 Bartholomew, William, 1 Jan. 1920.
7322 Bartlett, Thom, 1 Jan. 1920.
7323 Barton, Harry, 1 Jan. 1920.
7324 Barton, Isabel Eleanor, 1 Jan. 1920.
7325 Bartrum, Marian, Mrs., 1 Jan. 1920.
7326 Barwell, Henry Edward, 1 Jan. 1920.
7327 Bassett, Ernest Thomas Walter, 1 Jan. 1920.
7328 Basset, Helen, Mrs., 1 Jan. 1920.
7329 Bateman, Edward Colston, 1 Jan. 1920.
7330 Bateman, John, 1 Jan. 1920.
7331 Bates, Mary Beatrice, 1 Jan. 1920.
7332 Bates, William Edward, 1 Jan. 1920.

7333 Bathgate, Adam, 1 Jan. 1920.
7334 Battle, Richard, 1 Jan. 1920
7335 Batty, James, 1 Jan. 1920.
7336 Baynes, Lucy Draffen, 1 Jan. 1920.
7337 Baxter, Stewart, 1 Jan. 1920.
7338 Bazley, Walter Stanley, 1 Jan. 1920.
7339 Beale, Frances Helen, Mrs. FitzGerald, 1 Jan. 1920.
7340 Beale, Richard Henry, 1 Jan. 1920.
7341 Beard, Charles Albert, 1 Jan. 1920.
7342 Beardsley, Eleanor Jemina, 1 Jan. 1920.
7343 Beattie, Rachel, Lady, 1 Jan. 1920.
7344 Beavan, Ernest Charles Edward, 1 Jan. 1920.
7345 Beavon, John, 1 Jan. 1920.
7346 Becher, Cecil Leycester, 1 Jan. 1920.
7347 Beck, Albert George, 1 Jan. 1920.
7348 Beck, Frank Harold, 1 Jan. 1920.
7349 Beckenham, Harry Anstead, 1 Jan. 1920.
7350 Beckett, William Marrow, 1 Jan. 1920.
7351 Beecroft, Alfred, 1 Jan. 1920.
7352 Beeden, Harry, 1 Jan. 1920.
7353 Beedie, Robert Mitchell, 1 Jan. 1920.
7354 Belcher, Edmund Charles, 1 Jan. 1920.
7355 Bell, Andrew, 1 Jan. 1920.
7356 Bell, Enoch, 1 Jan. 1920.
7357 Bell, Francis James, 1 Jan. 1920.
7358 Bellman, Charles Harold, 1 Jan. 1920.
7359 Bennett, Ada Mary, 1 Jan. 1920.
7360 Bennett, Edward, 1 Jan. 1920.
7361 Bennett, Joseph, 1 Jan. 1920.
7362 Bennett, Josephine Katherine, 1 Jan. 1920.
7363 Bennett, Leonora, Mrs., 1 Jan. 1920.
7364 Bennett, Nina Bessie, 1 Jan. 1920.
7365 Bennett, William Henry, 1 Jan. 1920.
7366 Benson, Edward Frederic, 1 Jan. 1920.
7367 Benson, John, 1 Jan. 1920.
7368 Benyon, Edith Marion, 1 Jan. 1920.
7369 Berisford, Margaret, Mrs., 1 Jan. 1920.
7370 Berkeley, Eva Mary FitzHardinge, Baroness, 1 Jan. 1920.
7371 Berkley, Ernest James Gibson, 1 Jan. 1920.
7372 Berry, John Joseph, 1 Jan. 1920.
7373 Bertenshaw, Benjamin James, 1 Jan. 1920.
7374 Besant, Frederick William, 1 Jan. 1920.
7375 Bestwick, William, 1 Jan. 1920.
7376 Bevan, Edward Morris, 1 Jan. 1920.
7377 Beveridge, Rev. John, 1 Jan. 1920.
7378 Beverly, Elizabeth Amelia, 1 Jan. 1920.
7379 Beynon, Ruth, 1 Jan. 1920.
7380 Beynon, Vernon Bryan Crowther-, 1 Jan. 1920.
7381 Biddiscombe, George, 1 Jan. 1920.
7382 Bidwell, Elvir Linda, Mrs., 1 Jan. 1920.
7383 Bigby, Dorothy Anne, 1 Jan. 1920.
7384 Biggs, Ambrose Joseph, 1 Jan. 1920.
7385 Biggs, Arthur Holland, 1 Jan. 1920.
7386 Birch, Charles, 1 Jan. 1920.
7387 Birch, John, 1 Jan. 1920.
7388 Birchby, Henry William Briton, 1 Jan. 1920.
7389 Bird, Henry Linsell, 1 Jan. 1920.
7390 Birtles, John Edward, 1 Jan. 1920.
7391 Bishop, Alice Margaret, 1 Jan. 1920.
7392 Bishop, Louisa Emma, Mrs., 1 Jan. 1920.
7393 Bishop, William George, 1 Jan. 1920.
7394 Bishop, William Henry, 1 Jan. 1920.
7395 Bisset, Ormond Douglas, 1 Jan. 1920.
7396 Black, Rena Denholm Menzies, 1 Jan. 1920.
7397 Blackadder, David, 1 Jan. 1920.
7398 Blackburne, Editha Marjorie, Mrs. Ireland-, 1 Jan. 1920.
7399 Blackhurst, Arthur, 1 Jan. 1920.
7400 Blackmore, Constance Marie, 1 Jan. 1920.
7401 Blackshaw, James William, 1 Jan. 1920.
7402 Blake, Charles Thomas, 1 Jan. 1920.
7403 Blake, Ellen Una, Mrs., 1 Jan. 1920.
7404 Blake, Percival, 1 Jan. 1920.
7405 Blake, Percy Francis Ward, 1 Jan. 1920.
7406 Blamey, Helen Dale. 1 Jan. 1920.
7407 Blanchard, Edward Cooper, 1 Jan. 1920.
7408 Blanck, Sydney Frank, 1 Jan. 1920.
7409 Blandford, Edward Cornelius, 1 Jan. 1920.
7410 Blatch, William Bernard, 1 Jan. 1920.
7411 Blewett, Joseph, 1 Jan. 1920.
7412 Blewett, Martin, 1 Jan. 1920.
7413 Bliss, John William, 1 Jan. 1920.
7414 Blossom, James, 1 Jan. 1920.
7415 Blount, Angela Mary, 1 Jan. 1920.
7416 Blount, Edith Margaret, 1 Jan. 1920.
7417 Bloxam, Frank Abel, 1 Jan. 1920.
7418 Bloxam, Henrietta, 1 Jan. 1920.
7419 Blundell, Agnes Mary Frances, 1 Jan. 1920.
7420 Blundell, Harry James, 1 Jan. 1920.
7421 Blyth, Alice Maud, 1 Jan. 1920.
7422 Blyth, Dora Elizabeth, 1 Jan. 1920.
7423 Boadella, Alfred Herbert, 1 Jan. 1920.
7424 Bodin, Samuel, 1 Jan. 1920.
7425 Bolas, Harold, 1 Jan. 1920.
7426 Bolckow, Henry William Ferdinand, 1 Jan. 1920.
7427 Boldero, Margery Florence, Mrs., 1 Jan. 1920.
7428 Bolton, Henry Hargreaves, 1 Jan. 1920.
7429 Bonallo, Nina Helen, Mrs., 1 Jan. 1920.
7430 Bond, George Leslie, 1 Jan. 1920.
7431 Bonner, Eveleen Caroline, Mrs., 1 Jan. 1920.

7432 Bonsall, Gertrude Elizabeth, Mrs., 1 Jan. 1920.
7433 Booker, Joseph, 1 Jan. 1920.
7434 Boorn, George Stanley, 1 Jan. 1920.
7435 Booth, Ernest Witton, 1 Jan. 1920.
7436 Booth, Frederick Knight, 1 Jan. 1920.
7437 Borrajo, Edward Joseph William, 1 Jan. 1920.
7438 Bostock, Adelaide Hannah Eliza Annie, Mrs., 1 Jan. 1920.
7439 Bottomley, James Henry, 1 Jan. 1920.
7440 Boucher, Elizabeth Staniforth, Mrs., 1 Jan. 1920.
7441 Bouffler, Marjorie Minnie, 1 Jan. 1920.
7442 Boundy, Elsie Maria, 1 Jan. 1920.
7443 Bourn, George Frederick, 1 Jan. 1920.
7444 Bourne, Lily Anne, Mrs., 1 Jan. 1920.
7445 Bowden, Edgar Alfred, 1 Jan. 1920.
7446 Bowden, Joseph. 1 Jan. 1920.
7447 Bower, Elias, 1 Jan. 1920.
7448 Bower, Percival, 1 Jan. 1920.
7449 Bowley, Alfred, 1 Jan. 1920.
7450 Bowman, James Henry, 1 Jan. 1920.
7451 Bowman, Richard Oxley, 1 Jan. 1920.
7452 Boyanton Ernest, 1 Jan. 1920.
7453 Boyce, James Stuart, 1 Jan. 1920.
7454 Boycott, Ethel Aline, 1 Jan. 1920.
7455 Boyd, Gladys Margaret, 1 Jan. 1920.
7456 Boyd, Hugh, 1 Jan. 1920.
7457 Boyd, Katharine Faraday, 1 Jan. 1920.
7458 Boydell, Thomas, 1 Jan. 1920.
7459 Boyle, Irene Florinda Maud, 1 Jan. 1920.
7460 Boyle, Louise Judith, Lady, 1 Jan. 1920.
7461 Boyle, Percy, 1 Jan. 1920.
7462 Braby, Wallace, 1 Jan. 1920.
7463 Bradburn, Albert Edward, 1 Jan. 1920.
7464 Bradford, Beryl Angelica Selby, Mrs., 1 Jan. 1920.
7465 Bradshaw, Laura Katherine, 1 Jan. 1920.
7466 Brady, Ralph Hollinshed, 1 Jan. 1920.
7467 Braggins, Edith Annie, 1 Jan. 1920.
7468 Braithwaite, Stanley Nesham, 1 Jan. 1920.
7469 Brakes, Harry, 1 Jan. 1920.
7470 Brand, Ethert, 1 Jan. 1920.
7471 Brand, Henry, 1 Jan. 1920.
7472 Braybrooke, Henry Mellor, 1 Jan. 1920.
7473 Braybrooks, Gladys Marian, Mrs., 1 Jan. 1920.
7474 Brereton, Katherine Blanche, 1 Jan. 1920.
7475 Brewis, Arthur William, 1 Jan. 1920.
7476 Bridge, Josiah, 1 Jan. 1920.
7477 Bridger, Donald Keith, 1 Jan. 1920.
7478 Bridgland, Richard John, 1 Jan. 1920.
7479 Briggs, Helen, Mrs. Currer-, 1 Jan. 1920.
7480 Briggs, Margaret Ellen, Mrs., 1 Jan. 1920.
7481 Briggs, Mary Alice, Mrs., 1 Jan. 1920.
7482 Brightman, Thomas, 1 Jan. 1920.
7483 Brindley, Louis Kirwan, 1 Jan. 1920.
7484 Brindley, William, 1 Jan. 1920.
7485 Brinnand, John Thomas, 1 Jan. 1920.
7486 Brisley, Maud Isabel, Mrs., 1 Jan. 1920.
7487 Brittain, Ernest George, 1 Jan. 1920.
7488 Britten, Charles Douglas, 1 Jan. 1920.
7489 Britten, Regina.d Wellesley, 1 Jan. 1920.
7490 Britton, Ellen Alice, 1 Jan. 1920.
7491 Broadbent, Margaret Emily, 1 Jan. 1920.
7492 Broadwood, Anna Maria Hennen, 1 Jan. 1920.
7493 Brock, Edith Balfour, 1 Jan. 1920.
7494 Brocklesby, Isabel, Mrs., 1 Jan. 1920.
7495 Brodihgan, Mary Christina, 1 Jan. 1920
7496 Bromhead, Ethel, 1 Jan. 1920.
7497 Bromwich, Frederick Dudman, 1 Jan. 1920.
7498 Brook, Arthur, 1 Jan. 1920.
7499 Brook, Mabel Frances, Mrs., 1 Jan. 1920.
7500 Brooke, Grace Milicent, 1 Jan. 1920.
7501 Brooke, Margery Jean, Mrs., 1 Jan. 1920.
7502 Brooks, Charles John Wood, 1 Jan. 1920.
7503 Brooks, Gladys Muriel, 1 Jan. 1920.
7504 Brooks, Charlotte Elizabeth, Lady, 1 Jan. 1920.
7505 Brooks, George Harold, 1 Jan. 1920.
7506 Brown, Agnes Elizabeth, 1 Jan. 1919.
7507 Brown, Bertram John, 1 Jan. 1920.
7508 Brown, Dorothy Ann, Mrs., 1 Jan. 1920.
7509 Brown, Edward John, 1 Jan. 1920.
7510 Brown, Emily May, 1 Jan. 1920.
7511 Brown, Ernest Addison, 1 Jan. 1920.
7512 Brown, George, 1 Jan. 1920.
7513 Brown, James, 1 Jan. 1920.
7514 Brown, Marian, Lady, 1 Jan. 1920.
7515 Brown, Robert Burns, 1 Jan. 1920.
7516 Brown, Robert Cyril, 1 Jan. 1920.
7517 Brown, Theophilus Edward, 1 Jan. 1920.
7518 Brown, Walter Ritchie, 1 Jan. 1920.
7519 Brown, William Henry George, 1 Jan. 1920.
7520 Brown, William Robert, 1 Jan. 1920.
7521 Browne, Dorothy Mary, 1 Jan. 1920.
7522 Browne, Douglas, 1 Jan. 1920.
7523 Browne, George Herbert, 1 Jan. 1920.
7524 Browne, Mildred Frances, 1 Jan. 1920.
7525 Browning, Albert Charles, 1 Jan. 1920.
7526 Brownsword, Walter, 1 Jan. 1920.
7527 Bruce, Alexander, 1 Jan. 1920.
7528 Bruce, Lady Constance Veronica, 1 Jan. 1920.
7529 Bruce, Evelyn Susan, 1 Jan. 1920.
7530 Bruce, George, 1 Jan. 1920.
7531 Bruce, Violet Dorothy Evelyn, Hon. Mrs. George, 1 Jan 1920.

7532 Brune, Cecely Alice, Mrs. Prideaux-, 1 Jan. 1920.
7533 Brunyate, Bertha Maud Vipond, Lady, 1 Jan. 1920.
7534 Bryant, Mary Louisa, 1 Jan. 1920.
7535 Buchan, William, 1 Jan. 1920.
7536 Bucnanan, Andrew, 1 Jan. 1920.
7537 Buchanan, Archibald Samuel, 1 Jan. 1920.
7538 Buck, Edward Horace, 1 Jan. 1920.
7539 Buckland, Isabel Maud, Mrs., 1 Jan. 1920.
7540 Buckland, Rawlin George Samuel, 1 Jan. 1920.
7541 Buckley, Joan Brunner, 1 Jan. 1920.
7542 Buckmaster, Dorothy Mary, Mrs., 1 Jan. 1920.
7543 Bucknall, Nathalie, Mrs., 1 Jan. 1920.
7544 Buckner, Albert Walter, 1 Jan. 1920.
7545 Budd, Henry George, 1 Jan. 1920.
7546 Budge, John, 1 Jan. 1920.
7547 Bugden, Sarah Amy, 1 Jan. 1920.
7548 Bull, Maude Ellen, 1 Jan. 1920.
7549 Bullen, Daisy May, 1 Jan. 1920.
7550 Bullough, Frank, 1 Jan. 1920.
7551 Bulman, Mary Helen, Mrs., 1 Jan. 1920.
7552 Bulmer, Francis Bertram, 1 Jan. 1920.
7553 Burall, Henry Charles, 1 Jan. 1920.
7554 Burchatt, Ernest Edward, 1 Jan. 1920.
7555 Burcher, Frederick Edward. 1 Jan. 1920.
7556 Burdekin, Lizzie, Mrs., 1 Jan. 1920.
7557 Burges, Frederick Augustus L'Estrange, 1 Jan. 1920.
7558 Burgess, Arthur Edward, 1 Jan. 1920.
7559 Burls, Herbert Thomas, 1 Jan. 1920.
7560 Burn, Muriel Lyell, 1 Jan. 1920.
7561 Burnett, Alexander, 1 Jan. 1920.
7562 Burnett, Ernest Joseph, 1 Jan. 1920.
7563 Burnett, James Taylor, 1 Jan. 1920.
7564 Burnett, Mary, 1 Jan. 1920.
7565 Burns, Donald George, 1 Jan. 1920.
7566 Burnyeat, John, 1 Jan. 1920.
7567 Burrowes, Henry Ambrose, 1 Jan. 1920.
7568 Burrows, Anna Louisa, Mrs., 1 Jan. 1920.
7569 Burrows, Thomas Enos, 1 Jan. 1920.
7570 Burt, James, 1 Jan. 1920.
7571 Burton, David Fowler, 1 Jan. 1920.
7572 Burton, Donald, 1 Jan. 1920.
7573 Burton, Kenneth, 1 Jan. 1920.
7574 Burton, Walter William John, 1 Jan. 1920.
7575 Bush, Albert Edward, 1 Jan. 1920.
7576 Bushell, Sybil Dorothy, 1 Jan. 1920.
7577 Butcher, Doris Ruth, 1 Jan. 1920.
7578 Butcher, Henry James, 1 Jan. 1920.
7579 Butler, Daphne Kendall, 1 Jan. 1920.
7580 Butler, Harold Branson, 1 Jan. 1920.
7581 Butler, Henry John, 1 Jan. 1920.
7582 Butler, Herbert George, 1 Jan. 1920.
7583 Butler, John Ingham, 1 Jan. 1920.
7584 Butler, Leonard Frederick George, 1 Jan. 1920.
7585 Button, Thomas Frederick, 1 Jan. 1920.
7586 Buxton, Mary Aline, Mrs., 1 Jan. 1920.
7587 Byrne, Louisa Mary, Mrs., 1 Jan. 1920.
7588 Cadell, Fairley Charlotte, Mrs., 1 Jan. 1920.
7589 Caffyn, Margaret Louise, 1 Jan. 1920.
7590 Caine, Elizabeth, Mrs., 1 Jan. 1920.
7591 Callaghan, John Martin, 1 Jan. 1920.
7592 Calvert, Harry, 1 Jan. 1920.
7593 Calvert, Harry Thornton, 1 Jan. 1920.
7494 Calvert, Tom, 1 Jan. 1920.
7595 Cambridge, Hilda Margaret, Mrs. Pickard-, 1 Jan. 1920.
7596 Camburn, Caleb, 1 Jan. 1920.
7597 Cameron, Allan, 1 Jan. 1920.
7598 Cameron, Charlotte, Mrs., 1 Jan. 1920.
7599 Cameron, James, 1 Jan. 1920.
7600 Camp, Edwin James, 1 Jan. 1920.
7601 Camp, Henry John, 1 Jan. 1920.
7602 Campbell, Donald, 1 Jan. 1920.
7603 Campbell, Douglas Robert, 1 Jan. 1920.
7604 Campbell, Georgina Jane, Mrs., 1 Jan. 1920.
7605 Campbell, Geraldine Georgina, 1 Jan. 1920.
7606 Campbell, Henry Samuel, 1 Jan. 1920.
7607 Campbell, Ina, Mrs., 1 Jan. 1920.
7608 Campbell, John, 1 Jan. 1920.
7609 Campbell, John Archibald, 1 Jan. 1920.
7610 Campbell, Nicol, 1 Jan. 1920.
7611 Cannell, Daniel George, 1 Jan. 1920.
7612 Cant, William Edmund, 1 Jan. 1920.
7613 Cantley, John Cargill, 1 Jan. 1920.
7614 Capleton, Ernest Carlile, 1 Jan. 1920.
7615 Card, Ernest, 1 Jan. 1920.
7616 Cardy, William Edward Jesse, 1 Jan. 1920.
7617 Careless, Beatrice Anne, 1 Jan. 1920.
7618 Carey, Arthur William Joseph Greenwood Macleod, 1 Jan. 1920.
7619 Carey, Geoffrey Newman, 1 Jan 1920.
7620 Carey, Joseph James Seymour, 1 Jan. 1920.
7621 Carle, James, 1 Jan. 1920.
7622 Carlile, Charles, 1 Jan. 1920.
7623 Carmichael, Andrew, 1 Jan. 1920.
7624 Carmichael, Winifred Mary, Mrs., 1 Jan. 1920.
7625 Carnegie, Agnes, Mrs. Lindsay-, 1 Jan. 1920.
7626 Carpenter, Ethel, Mrs. Boyd-, 1 Jan. 1920.
7627 Carr, David Leslie, 1 Jan. 1920.
7628 Carr, David Whiston, 1 Jan. 1920.
7629 Carr, George Alexander, 1 Jan. 1920.
7630 Carrington, John William Richard, 1 Jan. 1920.

2 Y

7631 Carter, Frederick James, 1 Jan. 1920.
7632 Carter, Maud Eleanor, Mrs., 1 Jan. 1920.
7633 Carter, Wilfrid George, 1 Jan. 1920.
7634 Cartmell, Annie, Lady, 1 Jan. 1920.
7635 Carvell, John Maclean, 1 Jan. 1920.
7636 Carver, Helena Philae Olive Virginia Maxwell, Mrs., 1 Jan. 1920.
7637 Carver, Olive McLaren, 1 Jan. 1920.
7638 Cash, Ernest William, 1 Jan. 1920.
7639 Casson, Emily Marjorie, 1 Jan. 1920.
7640 Castle, Hubert William, 1 Jan. 1920.
7641 Castle, Montague Wilson, 1 Jan. 1920.
7642 Cattanach, Jean Lorimer, 1 Jan. 1920.
7643 Cave-Browne-Cave, Beatrice Mabel, 1 Jan. 1920.
7644 Cay, Albert, 1 Jan. 1920.
7645 Chadwick, Harry Bernard Clarke, 1 Jan. 1920.
7646 Chadwick, Edith Caroline, 1 Jan. 1920.
7647 Chalker, Alfred Caulke, 1 Jan. 1920.
7648 Chamberlain, Alfred John, 1 Jan. 1920.
7649 Chambers, Evelyn Marion, 1 Jan. 1920.
7650 Chambers, Francis George, 1 Jan. 1920.
7651 Chambers, Henry, 1 Jan. 1920.
7652 Champness, Edward Leslie, 1 Jan. 1920.
7653 Champneys, Edith, Mrs., 1 Jan. 1920.
7654 Chandler, William Goerge, 1 Jan. 1920.
7655 Chanter, Francis William, 1 Jan. 1920.
7656 Chanter, Frederick, 1 Jan. 1920.
7657 Chantler, John Dale, 1 Jan. 1920.
7658 Chapman, Edmund Alumsby, 1 Jan. 1920.
7659 Chapman, Edward Henry, 1 Jan. 1920.
7660 Chapman, James Gardiner, 1 Jan. 1920.
7661 Chapman, James Henry, 1 Jan. 1920.
7662 Chapman, Maud Jewell, Mrs., 1 Jan. 1920.
7663 Charles, Gertrude Mary, Mrs., 1 Jan. 1920.
7664 Charlesworth, William Herbert Rudolph, 1 Jan. 1920.
7665 Chase, Alice Eleanor, 1 Jan. 1920.
7666 Chatfield, Frederick, 1 Jan. 1920.
7667 Chatterton, Elizabeth Eva, Mrs., 1 Jan. 1920.
7668 Chavasse, Frances Hannah, Lady, 1 Jan. 1920.
7669 Cheshire, Herbert Henry, 1 Jan. 1920.
7670 Chester, Jack Granado, 1 Jan. 1920.
7671 Cheyne, Charles, 1 Jan. 1920.
7672 Chilcott, Gregory Hall, 1 Jan. 1920.
7673 Childs, Emma Catherine, Mrs., 1 Jan. 1920.
7674 Ching, Horace Edwin, 1 Jan. 1920.
7675 Chittenden, Doris Mary, 1 Jan. 1920.
7676 Christie, Annie, 1 Jan. 1920.
7677 Christopherson, Alice Catherine, Mrs., 1 Jan. 1920.
7678 Church, Charlotte Mary Viola, 1 Jan. 1920.
7679 Clanwilliam, Muriel Mary Temple, Countess of, 1 Jan. 1920.
7680 Clapperton, Gladys Laura, Mrs., 1 Jan. 1920.
7681 Clark, Alice Fanny, Mrs., 1 Jan. 1920.
7682 Clark, Arthur Percy Stanley, 1 Jan. 1920.
7683 Clark, Elizabeth Mary, Mrs., 1 Jan. 1920.
7684 Clark, George Henry, 1 Jan. 1920.
7685 Clark, Harry, 1 Jan. 1920.
7686 Clark, Joseph Sains, 1 Jan. 1920.
7687 Clarke, Arthur Ernest, 1 Jan. 1920.
7688 Clarke, Dora Gunning Elwin, 1 Jan. 1920.
7689 Clarke, George Whitlock, 1 Jan. 1920.
7690 Clarke, Helen Blanche, Mrs., 1 Jan. 1920.
7691 Clarke, Leslie Chatfield-, 1 Jan. 1920.
7692 Clarke, Percy Daniel, 1 Jan. 1920.
7693 Clarkson, Elkanah, 1 Jan. 1920.
7694 Clay, Mignon Elvira, Mrs., 1 Jan. 1920.
7695 Clayton, James, 1 Jan. 1920.
7696 Clayton, Thomas, 1 Jan. 1920.
7697 Clegg, Fanny, 1 Jan. 1920.
7698 Clinch, Sidney Herbert, 1 Jan. 1920
7699 Clinkard, Charles Ernest, 1 Jan. 1920.
7700 Clothier, Frederick Nelson, 1 Jan. 1920.
7701 Cloux, Frank Louis Whitmarsh, 1 Jan. 1920.
7702 Clover, Dorothy Margaret, Mrs., 1 Jan. 1920.
7703 Clutterbuck, Sydney Ernest, 1 Jan. 1920.
7704 Cobb, Monica Mary Geikie, 1 Jan. 1920.
7705 Cobden, Alfred Sydney, 1 Jan. 1920.
7706 Cochrane, Edith Rose, 1 Jan. 1920.
7707 Cochrane, Ethel, 1 Jan. 1920.
7708 Cochrane, Ethel Isabel Virginia, Mrs., 1 Jan. 1920.
7709 Cockburn, Dorothy, 1 Jan. 1920.
7710 Cockerell, Florence Elizabeth, Mrs., 1 Jan. 1920.
7711 Cohen, Marjorie Emmeline, 1 Jan. 1920.
7712 Cohen, Philip, 1 Jan. 1920.
7713 Coke, Lady Mabel, 1 Jan. 1920.
7714 Colbourne, Robert Bertram, 1 Jan. 1920.
7715 Colchester, Annie Frances Julia, Mrs., 1 Jan. 1920.
7716 Cole, Annie Violet, Mrs., 1 Jan. 1920.
7717 Cole, Francis Joseph, 1 Jan. 1920.
7718 Cole, James Edward, 1 Jan. 1920.
7719 Cole, Robert Clifford, 1 Jan. 1920.
7720 Cole, Seymour, 1 Jan. 1920.
7721 Collard, Cecil Wharton, 1 Jan. 1920.
7722 Collins, Alice Godiva Thorold, 1 Jan. 1920.
7723 Collins, Christabel, 1 Jan. 1920.
7724 Collins, George William, 1 Jan. 1920.
7725 Collins, Katharine Wilson, Mrs., 1 Jan. 1920.
7726 Collins, Sibyl Ida, Mrs. Abdy, 1 Jan. 1920.
7727 Collins, William Joseph, 1 Jan. 1920.
7728 Colls, Herbert Ailby, 1 Jan. 1920.

7729 Colquhoun, Emily Margaret, 1 Jan. 1920.
7730 Coltman, Grace, Mrs., 1 Jan. 1920.
7731 Combe, Nigel Victor, 1 Jan. 1920.
7732 Comer, George Richard, 1 Jan. 1920.
7733 Comerford, Matthew, 1 Jan. 1920.
7734 Compton, Henry, 1 Jan. 1920.
7735 Conibear, James Handford, 1 Jan. 1920.
7736 Connochie, Henry Joseph Bexfield, 1 Jan. 1920.
7737 Connolly, Thomas Francis, 1 Jan. 1920.
7738 Connor, Anthony John, 1 Jan. 1920.
7739 Constantine, Arthur Heaton, 1 Jan. 1920.
7740 Constantine, William Windley, 1 Jan. 1920.
7741 Cook, Albert Sydney, 1 Jan. 1920.
7742 Cook, Charles Lever, 1 Jan. 1920.
7743 Cook, James, 1 Jan. 1920.
7744 Cook, William Frederick, 1 Jan. 1920.
7745 Cooke, Clara Mabel, Mrs., 1 Jan. 1920.
7746 Cooke, Edward Henry William, 1 Jan. 1920.
7747 Cooke, Frank Alexander, 1 Jan. 1920.
7748 Cooke, Frank James, 1 Jan. 1920.
7749 Cooke, Howard Francis Vernon, 1 Jan. 1920.
7750 Cooke, William Herrick, 1 Jan. 1920.
7751 Cookson, Thomas Hatton, 1 Jan. 1920.
7752 Coombes, Sydney Cooper, 1 Jan. 1920.
7753 Coope, Amy Monica, 1 Jan. 1920.
7754 Cooper, Edward Stroud, 1 Jan. 1920.
7755 Cooper, Henry Harold, 1 Jan. 1920.
7756 Cooper, Howard Samuel, 1 Jan. 1920.
7757 Cooper, Juanita Carlota, Mrs., 1 Jan. 1920.
7758 Cooper Marion Helen, 1 Jan. 1920.
7759 Cooper, Rev. William Henry Hewlett, 1 Jan. 1920.
7760 Cordeaux, Edith, Mrs., 1 Jan. 1920.
7761 Corkran, Helena Muriel Seymour, 1 Jan. 1920.
7762 Cormack, George, 1 Jan. 1920.
7763 Corns, Frederick Samson, 1 Jan. 1920.
7764 Corscaden, Fannie Evelyn, Mrs., 1 Jan. 1920.
7765 Cosens, Peter Hunter, 1 Jan. 1920.
7766 Coster, Gaius William, 1 Jan. 1920.
7767 Costigan, Charles Samuel, 1 Jan. 1920.
7768 Cotton, Annie, Mrs., 1 Jan. 1920.
7769 Cotton, Archibald James, 1 Jan. 1920
7770 Coulson, Edith Mabel, 1 Jan. 1920.
7771 Coulson, William Ernest, 1 Jan. 1920.
7772 Counahan, Michael Tyrell, 1 Jan. 1920.
7773 Court, Lilian, 1 Jan. 1920.
7774 Court, Lilian Ethel, 1 Jan. 1920.
7775 Court, William Albert, 1 Jan. 1920.
7776 Coutts, Frederick, 1 Jan. 1920.
7777 Couzens, Arthur Wilson, 1 Jan. 1920.
7778 Coventry, Mary Jane, 1 Jan. 1920.
7779 Cowdroy, Charlotte Jane Howarth, 1 Jan. 1920.
7780 Cowley, James Arthur, 1 Jan. 1920.
7781 Cowper, Mary Bourne, Mrs., 1 Jan. 1920.
7782 Cox, Arthur William Franklin, 1 Jan. 1920.
7783 Cox, James Henry, 1 Jan. 1920
7784 Cox, Percy Walter, 1 Jan. 1920.
7785 Cox, Ralph Bouverie, 1 Jan. 1920.
7786 Cox, Joseph Peter, 1 Jan. 1920.
7787 Cox, Veronica Mary Machell, 1 Jan. 1920.
7788 Craig, Walter Elder, 1 Jan. 1920.
7789 Cramp, Annie Elizabeth, Mrs., 1 Jan. 1920.
7790 Cran, George, 1 Jan. 1920.
7791 Crapnell, Stanley Richard, 1 Jan. 1920.
7792 Craske, Mary, 1 Jan. 1920.
7793 Craven, Edward Joseph Eclipsis, 1 Jan. 1920.
7794 Crawford, Daniel, 1 Jan. 1920.
7795 Crawford, Thomas, 1 Jan. 1920.
7796 Crawley, Gertrude, 1 Jan. 1920.
7797 Cresswell, Catherine Gwladys, 1 Jan. 1920.
7798 Croft, Charles Rowland, 1 Jan. 1920.
7799 Crofton Augusta Maude, Mrs., 1 Jan. 1920.
7800 Cromwell, Oliver Underwood, 1 Jan. 1920.
7801 Cropper, Marjorie Constance, Mrs., 1 Jan. 1920.
7802 Crosher, William Samuel, 1 Jan. 1920.
7803 Crosland, Clarence Field, 1 Jan. 1920.
7804 Cross, Arthur, 1 Jan. 1920.
7805 Cross, Edward Alfred, 1 Jan. 1920.
7806 Cross, Grenville Burgess, 1 Jan. 1920.
7807 Cross, Robert William Ryder, 1 Jan. 1920.
7808 Crossingham, Agatha Gwendoline Rees, 1 Jan. 1920.
7809 Croucher, Wilfrid Gladstone, 1 Jan. 1920.
7810 Crow, Ada Maud, 1 Jan. 1920.
7811 Crow, John, 1 Jan. 1920.
7812 Cruickshank, George, 1 Jan. 1920.
7813 Cruickshank, James, 1 Jan. 1920.
7814 Cuddeford, Arthur Charles, 1 Jan. 1920.
7815 Cuff, Stanley Geikie, 1 Jan. 1920.
7816 Culley, James, 1 Jan. 1920.
7817 Cullis, Mary Aeldrin, 1 Jan. 1920.
7818 Cullum, Henry John, 1 Jan. 1920.
7819 Culshaw, Frank, 1 Jan. 1920.
7820 Culver, Albert Leopold, 1 Jan. 1920.
7821 Cumming, Andrew Lawrance, 1 Jan. 1920.
7822 Cumming, Ethel Maud, Mrs., 1 Jan. 1920.
7823 Cummings, John Thomas, 1 Jan. 1920.
7824 Cuninghame, Helen Ethel, Mrs., 1 Jan. 1920.
7825 Cunnington, Lily Maria, Mrs., 1 Jan. 1920.
7826 Currall, Henrietta Frances, Mrs., 1 Jan. 1920.
7827 Cursons, George Robert Alfred, 1 Jan. 1920.
7828 Curtis, John William, 1 Jan. 1920.

MEMBERS.

7829 Curwen, Elizabeth Caroline Colebrook Gordon, Mrs., 1 Jan. 1920.
7830 Dadson, Mary Alice Portlock. 1 Jan. 1920.
7831 Dakin, Francis George, 1 Jan. 1920.
7832 Dakin, Margaret Evelyn Harrison, 1 Jan. 1920.
7833 Dale, Mary Frances, 1 Jan. 1920.
7834 Dale, Albert Ernest, 1 Jan. 1920.
7835 Dale, Cicely Susan, 1 Jan. 1920.
7836 Dale, Henry Angley Lewis-, 1 Jan. 1920.
7837 Dalmahoy, Lilias Edith Jean, 1 Jan. 1920.
7838 Dalrymple, Thomas, 1 Jan. 1920.
7839 Dalrymple, William, 1 Jan. 1920.
7840 Dalton, James Henry Chesshyre, 1 Jan. 1920.
7841 Dalton, William, 1 Jan. 1920.
7842 Dance, Samuel Richard, 1 Jan. 1920.
7843 Dane, Frederick Hopper, 1 Jan. 1920.
7844 Dane, James Whiteside, 1 Jan. 1920.
7845 Dane, John Stephenson, 1 Jan. 1920.
7846 Daniels, Margaret Frances, 1 Jan. 1920.
7847 Dann, John Charles, 1 Jan. 1920.
7848 D'Arcy, William James Buchanan, 1 Jan. 1920.
7849 Dargie, Albert, 1 Jan. 1920.
7850 Dashwood, Geva Vereker, Mrs., 1 Jan. 1920.
7851 Davenport, Daniel, 1 Jan. 1920.
7852 Davenport, Flora Gladys, 1 Jan. 1920.
7853 Davey, Benjamin Alfred, 1 Jan. 1920.
7854 Davey, Herbert John, 1 Jan. 1920.
7855 Davie, James Gordon. 1 Jan. 1920.
7857 Davies, Clara Maud, Mrs., 1 Jan. 1920.
7858 Davies, Emily Geraldine, Mrs., 1 Jan. 1920.
7859 Davies, Ernest James, 1 Jan. 1920.
7860 Davies, George, 1 Jan. 1920.
7861 Davies, Henry Ivor, 1 Jan. 1920.
7862 Davies, Isabel Warwick, Mrs., 1 Jan. 1920.
7863 Davies, Julia, 1 Jan. 1920.
7864 Davies, Morgan, 1 Jan. 1920.
7865 Davies, Robert Yarnell, 1 Jan. 1920.
7866 Davies, Louisa, Mrs. Russell, 1 Jan. 1920.
7867 Davies, Thomas Edward, 1 Jan. 1920.
7868 Davies, William Lloyd, 1 Jan. 1920.
7869 Davis, Albert Alfred, 1 Jan. 1920.
7870 Davis, Gershom Willoughby Cecil, 1 Jan. 1920
7871 Davis, Lilian Bertha, 1 Jan. 1920.
7872 Davis, Sydney Carlile, 1 Jan. 1920.
7873 Davison, Edward Anderson, 1 Jan. 1920.
7874 Davison, John William, 1 Jan. 1920.
7875 Dawes, Elizabeth Lilian, Mrs., 1 Jan. 1920.
7876 Dawkins, William Paxton, 1 Jan. 1920.
7877 Dawson, Agnes, 1 Jan. 1920.
7878 Dawson, Agnes Elizabeth, Mrs., 1 Jan. 1920.
7879 Dawson, Anne, 1 Jan. 1920.
7880 Dawson, Cecily, 1 Jan. 1920.
7881 Day, Edward Philip, 1 Jan. 1920.
7882 Day, Ernest Cockburn, 1 Jan. 1920.
7883 Day, George, 1 Jan. 1920.
7884 Day, Maud FitzGerald, 1 Jan. 1920.
7885 Day, Thomas Frederick, 1 Jan. 1920.
7886 Day, William Thomas, 1 Jan. 1290.
7887 Deacon, Clara, 1 Jan. 1920.
7888 Dempster, William Thomas, 1 Jan. 1920.
7889 Denholm, John Maxwell, 1 Jan. 1920.
7890 Denholm, Walter Windebank, 1 Jan. 1920.
7891 Dennis, Anna Emily, 1 Jan. 1920.
7892 Denniston, Mary Grace, Mrs., 1 Jan. 1920.
7893 Dent, Herbert Crowley, 1 Jan. 1920.
7894 Desborough, Walter, 1 Jan. 1920.
7895 Devereux, Augustine, 1 Jan. 1920.
7896 Dewhurst, John Henry, 1 Jan. 1920.
7897 Dey, Alexander, 1 Jan. 1920.
7898 Dezest, Frank, 1 Jan. 1920.
7899 D'Harty, William Cornelius, 1 Jan. 1920.
7900 Dick, Henry Charles, 1 Jan. 1920.
7901 Dick, James Scott, 1 Jan. 1920.
7902 Dick, Marion Edith, Mrs., 1 Jan. 1920.
7903 Dicks, Eustace James Carey, 1 Jan. 1920.
7904 Digby, Emily, 1 Jan. 1920.
7905 Diggins, William Samuel, 1 Jan. 1920.
7906 Dilby, Arthur George. 1 Jan. 1920.
7907 Dilks, Alice Irene, 1 Jan. 1920.
7908 Dillon, Malcolm, 1 Jan. 1920.
7909 Dillon, Stella Margaret, 1 Jan. 1920.
7910 Ditchfield, Richard Thomas, 1 Jan. 1920.
7911 Dix, Edith Amy, Mrs., 1 Jan. 1920.
7912 Dixon, Jennie, Mrs., 1 Jan. 1920.
7913 Dixon, Kate Alice, Mrs., 1 Jan. 1920.
7914 Dixon, Walter Reginald, 1 Jan. 1920.
7915 Dobbin, William Wood, 1 Jan. 1920.
7916 Dobbings, William, 1 Jan. 1920.
7917 Dobie, Herbert, 1 Jan. 1920.
7918 Dockery, Owen, 1 Jan. 1920.
7919 Doherty, Arthur Edward, 1 Jan. 1920.
7920 Dollond, Alfred Walter, 1 Jan. 1920.
7921 Donald, Robert, 1 Jan. 1920.
7922 Door, Reginald Edmund, 1 Jan. 1920.
7923 Doran, David John, 1 Jan. 1920.
7924 Dormer, Alfred James, 1 Jan. 1920.
7925 Dott, George. 1 Jan. 1920.
7926 Doughty, Beatrice Mary Constance, 1 Jan. 1920.
7927 Douglass, James Robertson, 1 Jan. 1920.
7928 Doulton, Alice Duneau, 1 Jan. 1920.

7929 Dove, Margaret Anne, Mrs., 1 Jan. 1920.
7930 Dover, Alice Eliza, Mrs., 1 Jan. 1920.
7931 Dow, Mary, Mrs., 1 Jan. 1920.
7932 Dowler, Edwin Harold, 1 Jan. 1920.
7933 Down, Thomas Beadle, 1 Jan. 1920.
7934 Downing, Pansy, 1 Jan. 1920.
7935 Dowsing, Herbert Leopold, 1 Jan. 192
7936 Drage, Elinor Katharine, 1 Jan. 1920.
7937 Drake, Annie, Mrs., 1 Jan. 1920.
7938 Drake, Ellen Mary, Mrs., 1 Jan. 1920.
7939 Drake, Kathleen Tyrwhitt, 1 Jan. 1920.
7940 Drakeford, William Dusantoy, 1 Jan. 1920.
7941 Drapes, Thomas Lambert, 1 Jan. 1920.
7942 Dray, Evelyn Muriel, 1 Jan. 1920.
7943 Drew, James William, 1 Jan. 1920.
7944 Drew, Lorna Auchterlonie, 1 Jan. 1920.
7945 Drummond, Mary Jane, 1 Jan. 1920.
7946 Dubois. Frederick, 1 Jan. 1920.
7947 Duddy, Philip Menross, 1 Jan. 1920.
7948 Dudgeon, Florence Margaret, 1 Jan. 1920.
7949 Duffes, Hilda Ethel Paterson, 1 Jan. 1920.
7950 Dugdale, Hilda, 1 Jan. 1920.
7951 Duggan Rev. Mother Mary, 1 Jan. 1920.
7952 Duggan, Motherwell, 1 Jan. 1920.
7953 Duggleby, Constance Mary, Mrs., 1 Jan. 1920.
7954 Dunalley, Frances Mary, Baroness, 1 Jan. 1920.
7955 Duncan, George, 1 Jan. 1920.
7956 Duncan, George Douglass, 1 Jan. 1920.
7957 Duncan, George Forest, 1 Jan. 1920.
7958 Duncan, Robert, 1 Jan. 1920.
7959 Duncan, William Lindsay, 1 Jan. 1920.
7960 Dunderdale, Robert Harold Webster, 1 Jan. 1920.
7961 Dunell, Marion, Mrs., 1 Jan. 1920.
7962 Dunkin, William Henry, 1 Jan. 1920.
7963 Dunlop, Mary Janet Murray-, 1 Jan. 1920.
7964 Dunn, Marion Prudence, 1 Jan. 1920.
7965 Dupré, Percy Vivian, 1 Jan. 1920.
7966 Durant, William James, 1 Jan. 1920.
7967 Durham, John Hope, 1 Jan. 1920.
7968 Dutton, Mildred, 1 Jan. 1920.
7969 Dutton, Peter Irving, 1 Jan. 1920.
7970 Dyas, William George, 1 Jan. 1920.
7971 Dyer, Alfred Thomas, 1 Jan. 1920.
7972 Dyer, John Luther, 1 Jan. 1920.
7973 Dyer, Robert Broomfield, 1 Jan. 1920.
7974 Dykes, Kathleen Ellison, Mrs., 1 Jan. 1920.
7975 Dyson, John Richard Haigh, 1 Jan. 1920.
7976 Eager, Joseph Henry, 1 Jan. 1920.
7977 Eagles, Joseph William, 1 Jan. 1920.
7978 Eames, Florence Mabel, 1 Jan. 1920.
7979 Earle, Betty, Mrs., 1 Jan. 1920.
7980 Eastwood, Mabel, 1 Jan. 1920.
7981 Eborall, Edith, 1 Jan. 1920.
7982 Ede, Henry William, 1 Jan. 1920.
7983 Eden, Mary Frances Dove, Mrs., 1 Jan. 1920.
7984 Edgar, James Winterbottom, 1 Jan. 1920.
7985 Edmiston, Iris Dorothy, 1 Jan. 1920.
7986 Edmunds, Flavell, 1 Jan. 1920.
7987 Edwardes, Charles Whitfield, 1 Jan. 1920.
7988 Edwards, Arthur Joseph, 1 Jan. 1920.
7989 Edwards, Bogdan Edward Jastrzabski, 1 Jan. 1920.
7990 Edwards, Elizabeth Alice, 1 Jan. 1920.
7991 Edwards, Emma Dorothy, Mrs., 1 Jan. 1920.
7992 Edwards, Ernest Arthur, 1 Jan. 1920.
7993 Edwards, Mabel Constance, Mrs., 1 Jan. 1920.
7994 Edwards, Roger Bellis, 1 Jan. 1920.
7995 Edwards, Thomas Ramsay King-, 1 Jan. 1920.
7996 Edwards, William Buckland, 1 Jan. 1920.
7997 Edwards, William Ernest, 1 Jan. 1920.
7998 Eggleshaw, Frank Herbert, 1 Jan. 1920.
7999 Ehrenfest, Muriel Alice Adela, 1 Jan. 1920.
8000 Eland, Ruth Adelaide, 1 Jan. 1920.
8001 Eliot, Kate Marianne, 1 Jan. 1920.
8002 Elles, Gertrude Lilian, 1 Jan. 1920.
8003 Elliot, Bessie Clarke, Mrs., 1 Jan. 1920.
8004 Elliott, Arthur Campbell, 1 Jan. 1920.
8005 Elliott, Charles Edward, 1 Jan. 1920.
8006 Elliott, Charles John, 1 Jan. 1920.
8007 Ellis, Albert Edward, 1 Jan. 1920.
8008 Ellis, Charles Leonard, 1 Jan. 1920.
8009 Ellison, Anne, Mrs., 1 Jan. 1920.
8010 Elmsall, William de Cardonnel, 1 Jan. 1920.
8011 Elmslie, Edward Cooch Stewart, 1 Jan. 1920.
8012 Elton, Mable Thérèse, 1 Jan. 1920.
8013 Elwes, Henry Geoffrey, 1 Jan. 1920.
8014 Emler, Frederick William, 1 Jan. 1920.
8015 England, Harry, 1 Jan. 1920.
8016 Engleheart Matilda Mary, Mrs., 1 Jan. 1920.
8017 Enthoven, Augusta Gabriele Eden, Mrs., 1 Jan. 1920.
8018 Entwistle, Joseph, 1 Jan. 1920.
8019 Erskine, Walter Hugh, 1 Jan. 1920.
8020 Etheridge, Arthur Thomas, 1 Jan. 1920.
8021 Etheridge, Herbert, 1 Jan. 1920.
8022 Eunson, Milicent, Mrs., 1 Jan. 1920.
8023 Evans, Abel Joseph, 1 Jan. 1920.
8024 Evans, Claude Victor, 1 Jan. 1920.
8025 Evans, Edith Mary, 1 Jan. 1920.
8026 Evans, Frank Hedley, 1 Jan. 1920.
8027 Evans, Gladys Richardson, 1 Jan. 1920.
8028 Evans, Harry Loft, 1 Jan. 1920.

8029 Evans, Herbert, 1 Jan. 1920.
8030 Evans, John Thomas, 1 Jan. 1920.
8031 Evans, Walter David, 1 Jan. 1920.
8032 Evans, William James, 1 Jan. 1920.
8033 Evans, William Owen, 1 Jan. 1920.
8034 Eve, William Charles Pittuck, 1 Jan. 1920.
8035 Eyles, Herbert Charles, 1 Jan. 1920.
8036 Eyre, Julia Philadelphia, Mrs., 1 Jan. 1920.
8037 Facer, Hedley Humphrey, 1 Jan. 1920.
8038 Fairbairn, Ethel Fulton, 1 Jan. 1920.
8039 Fairbrother, Thomas, 1 Jan. 1920.
8040 Fairey, Charles Richard, 1 Jan. 1920.
8041 Fairley, Lucy Rosalind, Mrs., 1 Jan. 1920.
8042 Fairley, William, 1 Jan. 1920.
8043 Fairlie, Jessie Mary, Mrs., 1 Jan. 1920.
8044 Bull, Annie, Mrs., 1 Jan. 1920.
8045 Falkus, Richard Uriah, 1 Jan. 1920.
8046 Fallon, Thomas Joseph Aloysius Fallon, 1 Jan. 1920.
8047 Farmer, William Henry, 1 Jan. 1920.
8048 Farmery, John, 1 Jan. 1920.
8049 Farnell, Beatrice Isabel, 1 Jan. 1920.
8050 Farnsworth, Frank Smedley, 1 Jan. 1920.
8051 Farran, Helen Isabel. 1 Jan. 1920.
8052 Farrant, Mary Josephine, Mrs., 1 Jan. 1920.
8053 Farrell, Henry William, 1 Jan. 1920.
8054 Farrer, Julia Frances, 1 Jan. 1920.
8055 Farrow, Arthur Edward, 1 Jan. 1920.
8056 Farrow, William, 1 Jan. 1920.
8057 Farwell, George Douglas, 1 Jan. 1920.
8058 Favell, Millicent Elizabeth, 1 Jan. 1920.
8059 Fawsett, Frank, 1 Jan. 1920.
8060 Fear, Thomas Richard, 1 Jan. 1920.
8061 Fearfield, Marjorie Pollard, Mrs., 1 Jan. 1920.
8062 Featherstone, John Thomas, 1 Jan. 1920.
8063 Fedden, Alfred Hubert Roy, 1 Jan. 1920.
8064 Fellows, Gertrude Elizabeth, 1 Jan. 1920.
8065 Felton, Edgar Hall, 1 Jan. 1920.
8066 Fenelon, Martin Joseph, 1 Jan. 1920.
8067 Ferguson, Anna Wise, Mrs., 1 Jan. 1920.
8068 Ferguson, Frances Madeleine, Mrs., 1 Jan. 1920.
8069 Ferguson, Gilbert, 1 Jan. 1920.
8071 Ferguson, James Strathearn, 1 Jan. 1920.
8072 Fergusson, Margaret Heriot, 1 Jan. 1920.
8073 Feuerheerd, Marietta Robertine, 1 Jan. 1920.
8074 Ffoulkes, Katharine Mary, Mrs., 1 Jan. 1920.
8075 Fidoe, Alfred Joseph, 1 Jan. 1920.
8076 Field, John William, 1 Jan. 1920.
8077 Fielder, Charles James, 1 Jan. 1920.
8078 Fielding, Frederick, 1 Jan. 1920.
8079 Fielding, Henry, 1 Jan. 1920.
8080 Finch, Daisy Amelia, 1 Jan. 1920.
8081 Finlay. William George, 1 Jan. 1920.
8082 Finlinson, Ethel Mary, Mrs., 1 Jan. 1920.
8083 Finnis, Herbert, 1 Jan. 1920.
8084 Fisher, Edward Lamley, 1 Jan. 1920.
8085 Fisher, Ellinor Jane, Mrs., 1 Jan. 1920.
8086 Fisher, Ethel Sophia, Mrs., 1 Jan. 1920.
8087 Fisher, Frederick Ludolph, 1 Jan. 1920.
8088 Fisher, Hubert William Warwick, 1 Jan. 1920.
8089 Fisher, Katharine, 1 Jan. 1920.
8090 Fisher, Samuel Joseph, 1 Jan. 1920.
8091 Fitt, Adelaide, Mrs., 1 Jan. 1920.
8092 FitzGerald, Rev. Henry Purefoy, 1 Jan. 1920.
8093 Fitzpatrick, Alice Harriet, 1 Jan. 1920.
8094 Fleming, Edith May, 1 Jan. 1920.
8095 Fleming, Frederick Alexander, 1 Jan. 1920.
8096 Fletcher, Frederick John, 1 Jan. 1920.
8097 Fletcher, Violet Eastwood, 1 Jan. 1920.
8098 Flint, Frederick Theodore, 1 Jan. 1920.
8099 Folland, Henry Phillip, 1 Jan. 1920.
8100 Fooks, Amy Harriet, 1 Jan. 1920.
8101 Foord, Walter James, 1 Jan. 1920.
8102 Forbes, Barbara Donald, Mrs., 1 Jan. 1920.
8103 Forbes, James, 1 Jan. 1920.
8104 Forbes, William, 1 Jan. 1920.
8105 Ford, Arthur Clow, 1 Jan. 1920.
8106 Ford, Thomas Benjamin, 1 Jan. 1920.
8107 Ford, William George, 1 Jan. 1920.
8108 Forman, Bernard Gilpin, 1 Jan. 1920.
8109 Forrest, Alfred Wightman, 1 Jan. 1920.
8110 Forrest, Thomas Walker Amsworth, 1 Jan. 1920.
8111 Forrester, Miriam, 1 Jan. 1920.
8112 Forster, Aquila, 1 Jan. 1920.
8113 Forster, Douglas Wakefield, 1 Jan. 1920.
8114 Forster, Matthew, 1 Jan. 1920.
8115 Forster, William, 1 Jan. 1920.
8116 Fortington, Edna Winifred, Mrs., 1 Jan. 1920.
8117 Fortye, Grace, 1 Jan. 1920.
8118 Fossati, Mary Mussely, 1 Jan. 1920.
8119 Foster, Marion Ferguson, 1 Jan. 1920.
8120 Fowle, William, 1 Jan. 1920.
8121 Fowler, Charles Roy, 1 Jan. 1920.
8122 Fowler, Ethel Ada, Mrs., 1 Jan. 1920.
8123 Fowler, Gertrude Irene, 1 Jan. 1920.
8124 Fox, Marshall Nathaniel, 1 Jan. 1920.
8125 Fox, Violet Beatrice, 1 Jan. 1920.
8126 Foyster, Constance Helena, 1 Jan. 1920.
8127 France, William Ernest, 1 Jan. 1920.
8128 Franceys, Amy Constance, Mrs., 1 Jan. 1920.
8129 Francis, George Chaplin, 1 Jan. 1920.

8130 Francis, Katherine Lilian, Mrs., 1 Jan. 1920.
8131 Franklin, Arthur Sumpter, 1 Jan. 1920.
8132 Frankling, Albert Edward, 1 Jan. 1920.
8133 Fraser, Gordon Lushington, 1 Jan. 1920.
8134 Fraser, Hugh, 1 Jan. 1920.
8135 Fraser, Sarah Louise, 1 Jan. 1920.
8136 Fraser, Robert, 1 Jan. 1920.
8137 Freeman, Phillip Anthony Mallows, 1 Jan. 1920.
8138 Freke, Ambrose Eyre Hussey-, 1 Jan. 1920.
8139 French, Herbert Edward, 1 Jan. 1920.
8140 French, James Frederick, 1 Jan. 1920.
8141 French, Louis Emanuel, 1 Jan. 1920.
8142 French, William Henry, 1 Jan. 1920.
8143 Frere, Laetitia Helen, 1 Jan. 1920.
8144 Frewen, Violet Helen, 1 Jan. 1920.
8145 Frost, Ann Lucy, Mrs., 1 Jan. 1920
8146 Frost, Percy, 1 Jan. 1920.
8147 Fry, Frederick William, 1 Jan. 1920.
8148 Fryer, Frances Mary, Mrs., 1 Jan. 1920.
8149 Fulford, Catherine, 1 Jan. 1920.
8150 Fuller, Mabel Frances, 1 Jan. 1920.
8151 Fuller, Mary Frances, Mrs., 1 Jan. 1920.
8152 Fulljames, Edith Marianne, Mrs., 1 Jan. 1920.
8153 Furner, Duncan Campbell, 1 Jan. 1920.
8154 Gaddum, Arthur Graham, 1 Jan. 1920.
8155 Gahan, Rev. Horace Stirling Townsend, 1 Jan. 1920.
8156 Gair, Christina Ellen, Mrs., 1 Jan. 1920.
8157 Gaisford, Gertrude Emma Frances, 1 Jan. 1920
8158 Gallaway, James Henry, 1 Jan. 1920.
8159 Galloway, Kathleen Frances Elaine, 1 Jan. 1920.
8160 Galloway, Mary Hellene, Mrs., 1 Jan. 1920.
8161 Gamble, William Michael Hudson Julius, 1 Jan. 1920.
8162 Gane, Percy James, 1 Jan. 1920.
8163 Gant, Wilfred Robert Pinfold, 1 Jan. 1920.
8164 Gard, William Garrard Snowdon, 1 Jan. 1920.
8165 Gardiner, Frederick Henry, 1 Jan. 1920.
8166 Gardiner, Henry Willoughby, 1 Jan. 1920.
8167 Gardiner, Robert Fulton, 1 Jan. 1920.
8168 Gardiner, William Rattray, 1 Jan. 1920.
8169 Gardner, Jessie, Mrs., 1 Jan. 1920.
8170 Gardner, William Reid, 1 Jan. 1920.
8171 Garford, Marian, 1 Jan. 1920.
8172 Garland, Arthur Edward, 1 Jan. 1920.
8173 Garland, Hilda Margaret, 1 Jan. 1920.
8174 Garner, Harry, 1 Jan. 1920.
8175 Garratt, Herbert, 1 Jan. 1920.
8176 Garrett, Edith, Mrs., 1 Jan. 1920.
8177 Garrow, Alexander, 1 Jan. 1920.
8178 Garry, Thomas Gerald, 1 Jan. 1920.
8179 Garton, Albert, 1 Jan. 1920.
8180 Garvey, Harrie, Mrs., 1 Jan. 1920.
8181 Garwood, Edmund John, 1 Jan. 1920.
8182 Gaskin, John, 1 Jan. 1920.
8183 Gates, William Henry, 1 Jan. 1920.
8184 Gayton, Joseph, 1 Jan. 1920.
8185 Gear, Elizabeth Anne, Mrs., 1 Jan. 1920.
8186 Geary, Henry Valentine, 1 Jan. 1920.
8187 Gedge, John Henry Barnes, 1 Jan. 1920.
8188 Gee, Frederick Whitfield, 1 Jan. 1920.
8189 Gemmell Alice Caroline Anne, 1 Jan. 1920.
8190 Genders, Reginald, 1 Jan. 1920.
8191 Gent, William Henry, 1 Jan. 1920.
8192 George, Samuel, 1 Jan. 1920.
8193 George, William Frank, 1 Jan. 1920.
8194 Georges, Edith Alexa, Mrs., 1 Jan. 1920.
8195 Gibb, Elizabeth, 1 Jan. 1920.
8196 Gibson, Edward, 1 Jan. 1920.
8197 Gibson, James Albert, 1 Jan. 1920.
8198 Gibson, Lawrence, 1 Jan. 1920.
8199 Gibson, Thomas George, 1 Jan. 1920.
8200 Gifford, Emma, Mrs., 1 Jan. 1920.
8201 Gilbertson, Mary Campbell Bisset, Mrs., 1 Jan. 1920.
8202 Gilburd, William Robert, 1 Jan. 1920.
8203 Giles, Arthur, 1 Jan. 1920.
8204 Gillanders, Frances Geraldine, Mrs. Mackenzie-, 1 Jan. 1920.
8205 Giller, George Samuel, 1 Jan. 1920.
8206 Gillett, Henry William, 1 Jan. 1920.
8207 Gillett, John Cornelius, 1 Jan. 1920.
8208 Gillott, Mary Aloysia, 1 Jan. 1920.
8209 Gilmore, Fred Peden, 1 Jan. 1920.
8210 Gilmour, Robert, 1 Jan. 1920.
8211 Gilmour, Robert Scott, 1 Jan. 1920.
8212 Gilroy, James Boyd, 1 Jan. 1920.
8213 Given, John Cecil Mackmurdo, 1 Jan. 1920.
8214 Gladwyn, Sidney Charles, 1 Jan. 1920.
8215 Glaysher, Henry Charles, 1 Jan. 1920.
8216 Glayzer, Edward John, 1 Jan. 1920.
8217 Glossop, Charles Henry, 1 Jan. 1920.
8218 Goad, Edwin Henry, 1 Jan. 1920.
8219 Goad, Frederick Lockhart, 1 Jan. 1920.
8220 Godfrey, Norah, Mrs., 1 Jan. 1920.
8221 Godwin, George Batley, 1 Jan. 1920.
8222 Goff, Emily Gertrude, 1 Jan. 1920.
8223 Goldsworthy Frederick James, 1 Jan. 1920.
8224 Gollance, Ernest Marcus, 1 Jan. 1920.
8225 Gollin, Walter Josephson, 1 Jan 1920.
8226 Gooch, Eva Conway Everard, Mrs., 1 Jan. 1920.
8227 Gooch Ivy, 1 Jan. 1920.
8228 Goodbody, Lydia Maria, Mrs., 1 Jan. 1920.

MEMBERS.

8229 Gooch, Henry Martyn, 1 Jan. 1920.
8230 Goodden, Caroline, Mrs., 1 Jan. 1920.
8231 Goodrich, Walter Francis, 1 Jan. 1920.
8232 Goodwin, Charles Arthur, 1 Jan. 1920.
8233 Goodwin, John Henry, 1 Jan. 1920.
8234 Gordon, Edward Pirie-, 1 Jan. 1920.
8235 Gordon, Ellinor Maud, Mrs. More-, 1 Jan. 1920
8236 Gorman, William, 1 Jan. 1920.
8237 Gosling, William, 1 Jan. 1920.
8238 Goss, Lilian May, 1 Jan. 1920.
8239 Gosse, Hope Wilkes, 1 Jan. 1920.
8240 Gough, Kathleen Mona, 1 Jan. 1920.
8241 Gould, William Edward Thomas, 1 Jan. 1920.
8242 Gracey, Edmund, 1 Jan. 1920.
8243 Gracie, William McAuley, 1 Jan. 1920.
8244 Graham, James, 1 Jan. 1920.
8245 Graham, Jannet, 1 Jan. 1920.
8246 Graham, Robert Balfour, 1 Jan. 1920.
8248 Graham, Thomas H., 1 Jan. 1920.
8249 Graham, William, 1 Jan. 1920.
8250 Grant, Agnes Jane, Mrs., 1 Jan. 1920.
8251 Grant, Emma Egerton, Mrs., 1 Jan. 1920.
8252 Grant, Ethel Ogilvie, 1 Jan. 1920.
8253 Granville, Agatha, 1 Jan. 1920.
8254 Graves, Margrett Massy, Mrs., 1 Jan. 1920.
8255 Gray, Ada Leila, Mrs., 1 Jan. 1920.
8256 Gray, Julie Hunter, Mrs., 1 Jan. 1920.
8257 Gray, Robert, 1 Jan. 1920.
8258 Greathead, Alice Charlotte, Mrs., 1 Jan. 1920.
8259 Grech, Elizabeth Constance Vittoria, 1 Jan. 1920.
8260 Green, Alfred John, 1 Jan. 1920.
8261 Green, Henry Martyn, 1 Jan. 1920.
8262 Green, Henry William, 1 Jan. 1920.
8263 Greenaway, Thomas Joseph, 1 Jan. 1920.
8264 Greenhalgh, Frederick William, 1 Jan. 1920.
8265 Greenland, Dora, Mrs., 1 Jan. 1920.
8266 Greenland, William John Steward, 1 Jan. 1920.
8267 Greenup, William, 1 Jan. 1920.
8268 Greenway, Bessie, 1 Jan. 1920.
8269 Greenwood, Fred, 1 Jan. 1920.
8270 Greenwood, Josémée Marguerite, 1 Jan. 1920.
8271 Gregory, Alfred Thomas, 1 Jan. 1920.
8272 Gregory, Arthur Lamden, 1 Jan. 1920.
8273 Gregory, Ethel Amy, 1 Jan. 1920.
8274 Gregory, Harry William George, 1 Jan. 1920.
8275 Gregson, George Woolley, 1 Jan. 1920.
8276 Greig, Margaret Eunice, Mrs., 1 Jan. 1920.
8277 Greig, Phyllis Evelyn, Mrs., 1 Jan. 1920.
8278 Grier, Francis, 1 Jan. 1920.
8279 Griffiths, Griffith Nathan, 1 Jan. 1920.
8280 Griffiths, Ida Mildred Mary, 1 Jan. 1920.
8281 Griffiths, Marion, Mrs., 1 Jan. 1920.
8282 Griffiths, Sarah Ann, Mrs., 1 Jan. 1920.
8283 Griffiths, Walter James, 1 Jan. 1920.
8284 Grime, Joseph Crookes, 1 Jan. 1920.
8285 Grimsdale, Blanche Emma, Mrs., 1 Jan. 1920.
8286 Grimsdale, William, 1 Jan. 1920.
8287 Grimwade, Isabella Emily, Mrs., 1 Jan. 1920.
8288 Groves, Mary, Mrs., 1 Jan. 1920.
8289 Grubb, Charles John Edward, 1 Jan. 1920.
8290 Gruchy, Amy Douglas de, 1 Jan. 1920.
8291 Grundy, Emily Susan, Mrs., 1 Jan. 1920.
8292 Grundy, Lily, 1 Jan. 1920.
8293 Guinness, Kenelm Edward Lee Guinness, 1 Jan. 1920.
8294 Gunn, Edith Milner, 1 Jan. 1920.
8295 Gunn, George, 1 Jan. 1920.
8296 Gunson, Alice Maud, 1 Jan. 1920.
8297 Gunton, Ernest, 1 Jan. 1920.
8298 Gurney, Cecily Jane, 1 Jan. 1920.
8299 Gurteen, Horace, 1 Jan. 1920.
8300 Gyles, John William, 1 Jan. 1920.
8301 Hackett, John, 1 Jan. 1920.
8302 Hadfield, John White, 1 Jan. 1920.
8303 Hadley, Joanna Margaret, Mrs., 1 Jan. 1920.
8304 Haffield, Walter Milford Paget, 1 Jan. 1920.
8305 Haggard, Lilias Margitson Rider, 1 Jan. 1920.
8306 Haig, Mary Lilian, 1 Jan. 1920.
8307 Haigh, George William, 1 Jan. 1920.
8308 Hains, John James, 1 Jan. 1920.
8309 Hainworth, Edward Marrack, 1 Jan. 1920.
8310 Hair, John Hugh, 1 Jan. 1920.
8311 Hale, Felix, 1 Jan. 1920.
8312 Hale, Muriel Alice Mary, 1 Jan. 1920.
8313 Hale, Reginald, 1 Jan. 1920.
8314 Haler, Percy James, 1 Jan. 1920.
8315 Hall, Elizabeth Ellen, Mrs., 1 Jan. 1920.
8316 Hall, Frederick Holland, 1 Jan. 1920.
8317 Hall, Henry Leonard, 1 Jan. 1920.
8318 Hall, James, 1 Jan. 1920.
8319 Hall, Mary Eleanor, Mrs., 1 Jan. 1920.
8320 Hall, Matthew, 1 Jan. 1920.
8321 Hallam, Ernest Robert Francis, 1 Jan. 1920.
8322 Halliday, William Jamieson, 1 Jan. 1920.
8323 Hallifax, Percy, 1 Jan. 1920.
8324 Halliwell, David, 1 Jan. 1920.
8325 Halliwell, John, 1 Jan. 1920.
8326 Halsey, George, 1 Jan. 1920.
8327 Haly, Herbert John, 1 Jan. 1920.
8328 Hamer, Dorothy, 1 Jan. 1920.
8329 Hamilton, Ethel Mary, 1 Jan. 1920.

8330 Hamlyn, Mary Sylvia Calmady-, 1 Jan. 1920.
8331 Hammick, Lucy Mabel, 1 Jan. 1920.
8332 Hammond, Emmeline Mary, Mrs., 1 Jan. 1920.
8333 Hampshire, Frederick, 1 Jan. 1920.
8334 Hampton, Clement Edward, 1 Jan. 1920.
8335 Hancock, Alice Maud Nancy, Lady Burford, 1 Jan. 1920.
8336 Hancock, Aline Marie, Mrs., 1 Jan. 1920.
8337 Hancock, William Hern, 1 Jan. 1920.
8338 Hancox, Cecil John, 1 Jan. 1920.
8339 Handford, Margaret Emma, Mrs., 1 Jan. 1920.
8340 Handley, Kirk, 1 Jan. 1920.
8341 Hankinson, Charles James, 1 Jan. 1920.
8342 Hanna, Ellen Victoria, Mrs., 1 Jan. 1920.
8343 Hannaford, Claude, 1 Jan. 1920.
8344 Hannan, George James Bryce 1 Jan. 1920.
8345 Hanscomb, Henry Charles, 1 Jan. 1920.
8346 Hansen, Alma, 1 Jan. 1920.
8347 Hansen, Sven Wohlford, 1 Jan. 1920.
8348 Hansford, Ernest William Harry, 1 Jan. 1920.
8249 Happell, David, 1 Jan. 1920.
8350 Hardie, Annie, 1 Jan. 1920.
8351 Harding, Ethel Emma, Mrs., 1 Jan. 1920.
8352 Hardy, Dorothy Clara, 1 Jan. 1920.
8353 Hardy, Margaret Jane, 1 Jan. 1920.
8354 Hardy, Margaret Joy Cozens-, 1 Jan. 1920.
8356 Hardy, William Eversley, 1 Jan. 1920.
8357 Hare, Francis Edward, 1 Jan. 1920.
8358 Hare, George Frederick, 1 Jan. 1920.
8359 Harington, Wanda Grace, 1 Jan. 1920.
8360 Harlock, Emily, Mrs., 1 Jan. 1920.
8361 Harlock, Wilfred, 1 Jan. 1920.
8362 Harlow, Frederick James, 1 Jan. 1920.
8363 Harnden, Alfred Charles, 1 Jan. 1920.
8364 Harnett, William Augustus, 1 Jan. 1920.
8365 Harper, Edward Thomas, 1 Jan. 1920.
8366 Harper, Francis Henry, 1 Jan. 1920.
8367 Harper, Sydney, 1 Jan. 1920.
8368 Harries, Owen, 1 Jan. 1920.
8369 Harris, Thomas Henry, 1 Jan. 1920.
8370 Harrington, Henry Augustus, 1 Jan. 1920.
8371 Harris, Andrew, 1 Jan. 1920.
8372 Harris, Charles, 1 Jan. 1920.
8373 Harris, Faith Frances, Mrs., 1 Jan. 1920.
8374 Harris, Francis William Robert, 1 Jan. 1920.
8375 Harris, George Hardy, 1 Jan. 1920.
8376 Harris, Henry Arthur, 1 Jan. 1920.
8377 Harris, Rev. John Charles, 1 Jan. 1920.
8378 Harris, Lillie Crawford, Mrs., 1 Jan. 1920.
8379 Harris, Mary Gertrude, 1 Jan. 1920.
8380 Harris, William Rowland, 1 Jan. 1920.
8381 Harrison, Elsie Lydia, 1 Jan. 1920.
8382 Harrison, Evelyn, 1 Jan. 1920.
8383 Harrison, Freda, 1 Jan. 1920.
8384 Harrison, Gwynedd Helen Lightfoot, 1 Jan. 1920.
8385 Harrison, Hilda Mary, 1 Jan. 1920.
8386 Harrison, Muriel Evelyn, 1 Jan. 1920.
8387 Harrison, Sydney Thomas Walker, 1 Jan. 1920.
8388 Harrison, William Walter, 1 Jan. 1920.
8389 Harrisson, James, 1 Jan. 1920.
8390 Harry, Richard John, 1 Jan. 1920.
8391 Harsley, Martha, Mrs., 1 Jan. 1920.
8392 Hart, Charles James, 1 Jan. 1920.
8393 Hart, Cyril Herbert, 1 Jan. 1920.
8394 Hart, James, 1 Jan. 1920.
8395 Hart, Surrey Rutherford, 1 Jan. 1920.
8396 Harvey, Winifred Beatrice, 1 Jan. 1920.
8397 Harward, Mabel, Mrs., 1 Jan. 1920.
8398 Harward, Rev. Reginald Cuthbert, 1 Jan. 1920.
8399 Harwood, Margaret, 1 Jan. 1920.
8400 Haslam, Francis Meadows, 1 Jan. 1920
8401 Hastings, Albert, 1 Jan. 1920.
8402 Haswell, John Watson, 1 Jan. 1920.
8403 Hatton, James Thomas 1 Jan. 1920.
8404 Haughton, Francis George, 1 Jan. 1920.
8405 Hawke, Dora Annie, Mrs., 1 Jan. 1920.
8406 Hawkes, Violet, 1 Jan. 1920.
8407 Hawkins, Beatrice Hen, 1 Jan. 1920.
8408 Hawkins, Florence Beatrice, Mrs., 1 Jan. 1920.
8409 Hawkins, Sarah Annie Moss, 1 Jan. 1920.
8410 Hawksworth, William, 1 Jan. 1920.
8411 Hay, Eveline Anstey, Mrs. Drummond, 1 Jan. 1920.
8412 Hayes, Annie Rosina, Mrs., 1 Jan. 1920.
8413 Hayes, John Joseph, 1 Jan. 1920.
8414 Hayne, Louis Brightwell, 1 Jan. 1920.
8415 Haynes, George, 1 Jan. 1920.
8416 Hayward, John Robert Baxter, 1 Jan. 1920.
8417 Hayward, Margaret Frances Curtis-, 1 Jan. 1920
8418 Heads, John George, 1 Jan. 1920.
8419 Healey, John Edridge, 1 Jan. 1920.
8420 Hean, Walter John, 1 Jan. 1920.
8421 Heap, Edward Barlow, 1 Jan. 1920.
8422 Heaps, James, 1 Jan. 1920.
8423 Hearnden, Horace Richard 1 Jan. 1920.
8424 Hearsey, Dorothy Maud, Mrs., 1 Jan. 1920.
8425 Heath, George Augustine, 1 Jan. 1920.
8426 Heath, Samuel, 1 Jan. 1920.
8427 Heathcote, Lucy Lyttelton, Mrs., 1 Jan. 1920.
8428 Heatley, Thomas Common, 1 Jan. 1920.
8429 Heatly, Richard Fade Goff, 1 Jan. 1920.

8430 Heaton, Mary, 1 Jan. 1920.
8431 Hebblethwaite, Reginald Sidney, 1 Jan. 1920.
8432 Hedderwick, Mary, Mrs., 1 Jan. 1920.
8433 Hedge, Henry Walter, 1 Jan. 1920.
8434 Hedges, Alfred James, 1 Jan. 1920.
8435 Heggie, Amelia Young, Mrs., 1 Jan. 1920
8436 Helm, William, 1 Jan. 1920.
8437 Hemphrey, Bernard, 1 Jan. 1920.
8438 Henderson, George, 1 Jan. 1920.
8439 Henderson, Harry Frederick, 1 Jan. 1920
8440 Henderson, John Percy, 1 Jan. 1920.
8441 Henderson, Marjorie Grace Seton, 1 Jan. 1920.
8442 Henderson, Rosa Agnes, 1 Jan. 1920.
8443 Henrotin Jessie, Mrs., 1 Jan. 1920.
8444 Henry, Margaret Jane, Mrs., 1 Jan. 1920.
8445 Henry, Reginald George, 1 Jan. 1920.
8446 Henshaw, Thomas Arthur, 1 Jan. 1920.
8447 Herapath, Margaret Edith, Mrs., 1 Jan. 1920.
8448 Heraud, Victor Carpenter, 1 Jan. 1920.
8449 Herdman, Maud Harriet, Mrs., 1 Jan. 1920.
8450 Heron, Cyril Renton, 1 Jan. 1920.
8451 Herr, Helena, 1 Jan. 1920.
8452 Hewitt, Sarah, Mrs., 1 Jan. 1920.
8453 Hewlett, Beatrice, 1 Jan. 1920.
8454 Hibbs, Frank Edward, 1 Jan. 1920.
8455 Hickley, Sybil Louise, Mrs. North-, 1 Jan. 1920.
8456 Hicklin, Samuel, 1 Jan. 1920.
8457 Hickman, Kenneth Claude Devereux, 1 Jan. 1920.
8458 Hicks, Amy Maud, 1 Jan. 1920.
8459 Hicks, John William, 1 Jan. 1920.
8460 Hickson, Elizabeth, Mrs., 1 Jan. 1920.
8461 Hide, Annie May Constance, Mrs., 1 Jan. 1920.
8462 Higgin, Elizabeth Philadelphia Lockhart, Mrs., 1 Jan. 1920.
8463 Higgins, Arthur Gordon, 1 Jan. 1920.
8464 Higgon, Victor James, 1 Jan. 1920.
8465 Higgs, Charles James, 1 Jan. 1920.
8466 Higman, Joseph Cresswell, 1 Jan. 1920.
8467 Hignett, Alice, Mrs., 1 Jan. 1920.
8468 Hildyard, Cicely Frances 1 Jan. 1920.
8469 Hill, Alfred Roland, 1 Jan. 1920.
8470 Hill, George Grayson, 1 Jan. 1920.
8471 Hill, George James, 1 Jan. 1920.
8472 Hill, Harry, 1 Jan. 1920.
8473 Hill, Helen Agatha, 1 Jan. 1920.
8474 Hillkirk, Evelyn Margaret. 1 Jan. 1920.
8475 Hillman. George Brown, 1 Jan. 1920.
8476 Hills, Lucy, 1 Jan. 1920.
8477 Hills, Reginald Thomas, 1 Jan. 1920.
8478 Hilton, Evelyn, 1 Jan. 1920.
8479 Hilton, Mary, 1 Jan. 1920.
8480 Hinton, Margaret Searle, 1 Jan. 1920.
8481 Hitch, Lilian, 1 Jan. 1920.
8482 Hitchcock, Katherine Elizabeth, Mrs., 1 Jan. 1920.
8483 Hitchon, Witham, 1 Jan. 1920.
8484 Hives, Ernest Walter, 1 Jan. 1920.
8485 Hoare, Daisy, Mrs., 1 Jan. 1920.
8486 Hoare, Juliana Margaret, 1 Jan. 1920.
8487 Hoare, Frances Louisa Gurney, 1 Jan. 1920.
8488 Hobbs, May Elliot, Mrs., 1 Jan. 1920.
8489 Hocking, Francis Almond, 1 Jan. 1920.
8490 Hockridge, Alfred George, 1 Jan. 1920.
8491 Hodes, Francis Percy, 1 Jan. 1920.
8492 Hodge, Alfred, 1 Jan. 1920.
8493 Hodge, Rebecca Prince, 1 Jan. 1920.
8494 Hodges, James Robert, 1 Jan. 1920.
8495 Hodgkinson Thomas Thorpe, 1 Jan. 1920.
8496 Hodgson, Jonathan Wright, 1 Jan. 1920.
8497 Hodsman, Henry James, 1 Jan. 1920.
8498 Hodson, Violet, 1 Jan. 1920.
8499 Hoffman, Emilie, 1 Jan. 1920.
8500 Holderness, Barry Layton, 1 Jan. 1920.
8501 Holland, Mary Blanche 1 Jan. 1920.
8502 Holland, Thomas, 1 Jan. 1920.
8503 Hollander. John William, 1 Jan. 1920.
8504 Hollick, Frank 1 Jan. 1920.
8505 Hollingdale, Harold John, 1 Jan. 1920.
8506 Hollins, Rotha Mary, 1 Jan. 1920.
8507 Hollis, John Walter, 1 Jan. 1920.
8508 Holloway, Arthur Brissenden, 1 Jan. 1920.
8509 Holloway, Herbert Benjamin, 1 Jan. 1920.
8510 Holmes, Margaret Ann Mrs., 1 Jan. 1920.
8511 Holt, Gertrude Mary, 1 Jan. 1920.
8512 Holt, James Marston, 1 Jan. 1920.
8513 Hood, Joseph, 1 Jan. 1920.
8514 Hookers, Edith, Mrs., 1 Jan. 1920.
8515 Hooper, Florence Mary Alice, Mrs., 1 Jan. 1920.
8516 Hooper, Helen Elizabeth, 1 Jan. 1920.
8517 Hooper, John, 1 Jan. 1920.
8518 Hopkins, Charles James William, 1 Jan. 1920.
8519 Hopkins, Frederick Friend, 1 Jan. 1920.
8520 Hopper, James, 1 Jan. 1920.
8521 Hopps, William George, 1 Jan. 1920.
8522 Horn, Edith Mabel Freeman-, 1 Jan. 1920.
8523 Horn Gerald, 1 Jan. 1920.
8524 Hornbuckle, Thomas, 1 Jan. 1920.
8525 Hornby, Anna, Mrs. Phipps, 1 Jan. 1920.
8526 Horne, Marjorie, Mrs., 1 Jan. 1920.
8527 Horridge, Herbert William, 1 Jan. 1920.
8528 Horsburgh, Florence Gertrude, 1 Jan. 1920.

8529 Horsburgh, Lambert Gordon, 1 Jan. 1920.
8530 Horsfield, James, 1 Jan. 1920.
8531 Horsfield, Robert Lund, 1 Jan. 1920.
8532 Horsman, Ernest George, 1 Jan. 1920.
8533 Hothersall, William Christian, 1 Jan. 1920.
8534 House, Charles Edward George, 1 Jan. 1920.
8535 Howard, Hon. Bernard Edward Fitzalan. 1 Jan. 1920.
8536 Howard, Francis, 1 Jan. 1920.
8537 Howard, Mary, Mrs., 1 Jan. 1920.
8538 Howe, Albert Edward, 1 Jan. 1920.
8539 Howe, Clarence Samuel, 1 Jan. 1920.
8540 Howe, Francis Cecil, 1 Jan. 1920.
8541 Howell, Charles Frederick, 1 Jan. 1920.
8542 Howell, Ivor Morris, 1 Jan. 1920.
8543 Howell. Joseph, 1 Jan. 1920.
8544 Howells, William Wallace, 1 Jan. 1920.
8545 Howes, Arthur James, 1 Jan. 1920.
8546 Howse, Gilbert, 1 Jan. 1920.
8547 Hoyle, George Herbert, 1 Jan. 1920.
8548 Hoyle, Philip John, 1 Jan. 1920.
8549 Hubbert, Oliver John, 1 Jan. 1920.
8550 Huddlestone, Frieda, Mrs., 1 Jan. 1920.
8551 Hudson, Albert Edward, 1 Jan. 1920.
8552 Hudson, Alfred, 1 Jan. 1920.
8553 Hudson, George, 1 Jan. 1920.
8554 Hudson, Joe, 1 Jan. 1920.
8555 Hudson, Russell, 1 Jan. 1920.
8556 Hudson, Samuel, 1 Jan. 1920.
8557 Huggins, Amy Christine Adela, 1 Jan. 1920.
8558 Huggins, Elizabeth Annie, Mrs., 1 Jan. 1920.
8559 Hughes, Albert, 1 Jan. 1920.
8560 Hughes, Charles, 1 Jan. 1920.
8561 Hughes, Dulcie, 1 Jan. 1920.
8562 Hughes, Frederick Richard, 1 Jan. 1920.
8563 Hughes, John Gwilym, 1 Jan. 1920.
8564 Hughes, Richard Lloyd, 1 Jan. 1920.
8565 Hughes, Thomas John, 1 Jan. 1920.
8566 Hughes, William Henry, 1 Jan. 1920.
8567 Hull, Charles, 1 Jan. 1920.
8568 Hulme, Gilbert Ratcliffe, 1 Jan. 1920.
8569 Hume, Alexander Walter, 1 Jan. 1920.
8570 Hunt, Arthur Henry William, 1 Jan. 1920.
8571 Hunt, Francis Cecil, 1 Jan. 1920.
8572 Hunt, Lilian Hart, 1 Jan. 1920.
8573 Hunt, Stanley Percival, 1 Jan. 1920.
8574 Hunter, William Robert, 1 Jan. 1920.
8575 Huntley Alfred Henry, 1 Jan. 1920.
8576 Hurley, Charles Richard, 1 Jan. 1920.
8577 Hurlston, William, 1 Jan. 1920.
8578 Hurson, James, 1 Jan. 1920.
8579 Hussey, Annie, 1 Jan. 1920.
8580 Hutcheon, Ada Mary, Mrs., 1 Jan. 1920.
8581 Hutcheon, Alexander Byres, 1 Jan. 1920.
8582 Hutcheson, Grace, 1 Jan. 1920.
8583 Hutchison, Agnes Hood, Mrs., 1 Jan. 1920.
8584 Hutchison, Alexander, 1 Jan. 1920.
8585 Hutchison, Sarah Hannah, Mrs., 1 Jan. 1920.
8586 Hutton, Arnold William, 1 Jan. 1920.
8587 Hyslop, Irene Murray, 1 Jan. 1920.
8588 Hyslop, James, 1 Jan. 1920.
8589 Hyson, Herbert Augustine Henry, 1 Jan. 1920
8590 Idle, Percy, 1 Jan. 1920.
8591 Ifould, Edwin, 1 Jan. 1920.
8592 Imison, Herbert, 1 Jan. 1920.
8593 Ingilby, Marjorie Cecily, Mrs., 1 Jan. 1920.
8594 Ingram, Alfred Sydenham, 1 Jan. 1920.
8595 Inman, Ernest Stobart, 1 Jan. 1920.
8596 Iredale, Joe, 1 Jan. 1920.
8597 Ireland, Henry Ralph, 1 Jan. 1920.
8598 Ireland, Myrtle, Mrs. De Courcy, 1 Jan. 1920.
8599 Irish, Elsie Celia, 1 Jan. 1920.
8600 Irvine, John Maitland, 1 Jan. 1920.
8601 Irving, John, 1 Jan. 1920.
8602 Irwin, Jean Percival, Mrs., 1 Jan. 1920.
8603 Irwin Sarah, Mrs., 1 Jan. 1920.
8604 Isaac, Charles, 1 Jan. 1920.
8605 Isaac, John Edward, 1 Jan. 1920.
8606 Isaacs, Ellis, 1 Jan. 1920.
8607 Ivell, Grace Mary, 1 Jan. 1920.
8608 Jacka, Hilda Tyacke, 1 Jan. 1920.
8609 Jackson, Daniel Noel, 1 Jan. 1920.
8610 Jackson, Edward Siddall, 1 Jan. 1920.
8611 Jackson, Freda Christelle, 1 Jan. 1920.
8612 Jackson, Maud Mary, Mrs., 1 Jan. 1920.
8613 Jacobs, Dorothy Isabel, 1 Jan. 1920.
8614 Jacobs, Louis, 1 Jan. 1920.
8615 Jakeway, George, 1 Jan. 1920.
8616 James, Frank Treharne, 1 Jan. 1920.
8617 James, Frederick John, 1 Jan. 1920.
8618 James, Helen Mary (Penel), Mrs. Fullarton-, 1 Jan. 1920.
8619 Jameson Erskine Dawson, 1 Jan. 1920.
8620 Jameson William Storm, 1 Jan. 1920.
8621 Jamieson, Adam James, 1 Jan. 1920.
8622 Japp, George Allison, 1 Jan. 1920.
8623 Jardim, Antonietta Marcial, 1 Jan. 1920.
8624 Jarratt, Elizabeth Lankester, Mrs., 1 Jan. 1920.
8625 Jarrold, Alice Isobella, Mrs., 1 Jan. 1920.
8626 Jarvis, Alfred William, 1 Jan. 1920.
8627 Jarvis, Enid Sybil, 1 Jan. 1920.
8628 Jeal George, 1 Jan. 1920.

MEMBERS.

8629 Jeffery, Benjamin James Thomas, 1 Jan. 1920.
8630 Jeffery, Herbert Athelstan 1 Jan. 1920.
8631 Jekyll, Annie, 1 Jan. 1920.
8632 Jenkins, Mary Ann, Mrs., 1 Jan. 1920.
8633 Jenkins, Percy Fitzgerald, 1 Jan. 1920.
8634 Jenkinson, Mary Adeline, 1 Jan. 1920.
8635 Jennens, Lenore Sybil, Mrs., 1 Jan. 1920.
8636 Jennings, Arthur Oldham, 1 Jan. 1920.
8637 Jennings, Harry John, 1 Jan. 1920.
8638 Jennings, Leonard William, 1 Jan. 1920.
8639 Jensen, Winifred, Mrs., 1 Jan. 1920.
8640 Jephcott, Susan, Mrs., 1 Jan. 1920.
8641 Jervoise, Edwyn, 1 Jan. 1920.
8642 Jesson, George Arthur Touchet 1 Jan. 1920.
8643 Jesty, Ernest, 1 Jan. 1920.
8644 Jeune, Charles Henry, 1 Jan. 1920.
8645 Jimenez, Vivian Eustace, 1 Jan. 1920.
8646 Johns, Richard John, 1 Jan. 1920.
8647 Johnson, Adela, Mrs., 1 Jan. 1920.
8648 Johnson, Edwin Thomas, 1 Jan. 1920.
8649 Johnson, Rev. Gifford Henry, 1 Jan. 1920.
8650 Johnson, James William, 1 Jan. 1920.
8651 Johnson, Margaret Lilian, 1 Jan. 1920.
8652 Johnson, Percy Richard, 1 Jan. 1920.
8653 Johnson, Richard Spencer, 1 Jan. 1920.
8654 Johnson, Rosa Webb-, 1 Jan. 1920.
8655 Johnson, William Henry, 1 Jan. 1920.
8656 Johnston, Charles Saint 1 Jan. 1920.
8657 Johnstone, Alexander, 1 Jan. 1920.
8658 Johnstone, James Drummond, 1 Jan. 1920.
8659 Jones, Arthur Palm, 1 Jan. 1920.
8660 Jones, Bessie Lyon, Mrs., 1 Jan. 1920.
8661 Jones, Cecil Barclay, 1 Jan. 1920.
8662 Jones, Charles Leupolt, 1 Jan. 1920.
8663 Jones, Edith Muriel, Mrs., 1 Jan. 1920.
8664 Jones, George Henry Walter, 1 Jan. 1920.
8665 Jones, Hannah, 1 Jan. 1920.
8666 Jones, Henry John Alfred, 1 Jan. 1920.
8667 Jones, Herbert Arthur, 1 Jan. 1920.
8668 Jones, John, 1 Jan. 1920.
8669 Jones, John, 1 Jan. 1920.
8670 Jones, John Colenso, 1 Jan. 1920.
8671 Jones, John Hugh, 1 Jan. 1920.
8672 Jones, John William, 1 Jan. 1920.
8673 Jones, Joseph, 1 Jan. 1920.
8674 Jones, Llewellyn Thomas, 1 Jan. 1920.
8675 Jones, Owen Thomas, 1 Jan. 1920.
8676 Jones, Robert Arthur, 1 Jan. 1920.
8677 Jones, William, 1 Jan. 1920.
8678 Jones, William James Wallis-, 1 Jan. 1920.
8679 Jordan, Charles William, 1 Jan. 1920.
8680 Jordan, William Henry, 1 Jan. 1920.
8681 Joseph, David, 1 Jan. 1920.
8682 Joseph, Janie, 1 Jan. 1920.
8683 Joslin, William Joseph, 1 Jan. 1920.
8684 Joy, Jane Madeleine, Mrs., 1 Jan. 1920.
8685 Judd, Leonard William, 1 Jan. 1920.
8686 Kastor, Ella Marguerite, 1 Jan. 1920.
8687 Kay, David, 1 Jan. 1920.
8688 Kay, William Norrie, 1 Jan. 1920.
8689 Kearns, Haidée Ida, Mrs., 1 Jan. 1920.
8690 Keeson, Peridot Cuthbert, 1 Jan. 1920.
8691 Kelham, Margaret Ethel Mrs., 1 Jan. 1920.
8692 Kelly, Edmund Walsh, 1 Jan. 1920.
8693 Kemble, Katherine Charlotte, 1 Jan. 1920.
8694 Kemp, Amelia Susanna, Mrs., 1 Jan. 1920.
8695 Kemp, Charles Richard William, 1 Jan. 1920.
8696 Kemp, Herbert Edward, 1 Jan. 1920.
8697 Kemp, William, 1 Jan. 1920.
8698 Kemp, William Henry, 1 Jan. 1920.
8699 Kendall, Beatrice, 1 Jan. 1920.
8700 Kendall, Kathleen Addison, Mrs., 1 Jan. 1920.
8701 Kennedy, Walter, 1 Jan. 1.920.
8702 Kennell, Joseph, 1 Jan. 1920.
8703 Kenyon, Milly Esther Innes, Mrs., 1 Jan. 1920.
8704 Kerr, Sybil Mary, 1 Jan. 1920.
8705 Kesteven, Clement Percy, 1 Jan. 1920.
8706 Kettell, James Henry, 1 Jan. 1920.
8707 Kidson, Edith Marian, 1 Jan. 1920.
8708 Kidson, Jessie Cecilia Brownlie, Mrs., 1 Jan. 1920.
8709 Kilgour, Martin Hamilton, 1 Jan. 1920.
8710 Kilner, Charles Scott, 1 Jan. 1920.
8711 Kimber, Florence Edith, 1 Jan. 1920.
8712 Kindersley, Ada Molesworth, 1 Jan. 1920.
8713 King, John, 1 Jan. 1920.
8714 Kingsbury, Kathleen, 1 Jan. 1920.
8715 Kingzett, Norman Froggatt, 1 Jan. 1920.
8716 Kinnear, James Francis, 1 Jan. 1920.
8717 Kiralfy, Gerald Archibald, 1 Jan. 1920.
8718 Kirke, Sarah Elizabeth, Mrs, 1 Jan. 1920.
8719 Kirkwood, Ethel Kate, Mrs., 1 Jan. 1920.
8720 Kissock, William Henry, 1 Jan. 1920.
8721 Knight, Enid Mary, 1 Jan. 1920.
8722 Knight, Florence Mary, Mrs., 1 Jan. 1920.
8723 Knight, John, 1 Jan. 1920.
8724 Knight, Violet Hannah, Mrs., 1 Jan. 1920.
8725 Knighton, Thomas Spencer, 1 Jan. 1920.
8726 Knoop, Evelyn Elizabeth, Mrs. De, 1 Jan. 1920.
8727 Knox, David Alexander, 1 Jan. 1920.
8728 Lacey, Ellen, 1 Jan. 1920.

8729 Lacey, Henry Cubitt, 1 Jan. 1920.
8730 Laidlay, Jane Eileen, Mrs., 1 Jan. 1920.
8731 Laing George Smith, 1 Jan. 1920.
8732 Lake, Alfred Samuel, 1 Jan. 1920.
8733 Laker, Alfred, 1 Jan. 1920.
8734 Lamb, Emily Frances Edith, 1 Jan. 1920.
8735 Lambert, Henrietta Isabella, Mrs., 1 Jan. 1920.
8736 Lambert, Octavius Edward, 1 Jan. 1920.
8737 Lambert, Olive Mary, 1 Jan. 1920.
8738 Lambton, Dorothy, 1 Jan. 1920.
8739 Lamont, John Macnab, 1 Jan. 1920.
8740 Lane, Helena, Mrs., 1 Jan. 1920.
8741 Lang, John Henry, 1 Jan. 1920.
8742 Langford, Frederic Charles, 1 Jan. 1920.
8743 Langley, George Johnson, 1 Jan. 1920.
8744 Langridge, Harry Dickinson, 1 Jan. 1920.
8745 Langstaff, William Henry, 1 Jan. 1920.
8746 Langton, Albert Smith, 1 Jan. 1920.
8747 Large, Frederick George, 1 Jan. 1920.
8748 Larkman, Raymond, 1 Jan. 1920.
8749 Larsson, Carl Alfred, 1 Jan. 1920.
8750 Latter, Eva, 1 Jan. 1920.
8751 Latter, Flora, 1 Jan. 1920.
8752 Lattimore, Ralph, 1 Jan. 1920.
8753 Laurenson, George, 1 Jan. 1920.
8755 Law, Bertha, Mrs., 1 Jan. 1920.
8756 Lawford, Emma Ada, 1 Jan. 1920.
8757 Lawrance, Dora Muriel, 1 Jan. 1920.
8758 Lawrence, Isaac, 1 Jan. 1920.
8759 Lawrence, Margaret Alice, Lady, 1 Jan. 1920.
8760 Lawry, William, 1 Jan. 1920.
8761 Lawson, Emma Louisa, 1 Jan. 1920.
8762 Lawson, Noel John Cecil, 1 Jan. 1920.
8763 Lawson, William, 1 Jan. 1920.
8764 Leach, Charles Henry, 1 Jan. 1920.
8765 Leach, Claude Pemberton, 1 Jan. 1920.
8766 Leach, Mary Sumner, 1 Jan. 1920.
8767 Lean, Jannette Winifred, 1 Jan. 1920.
8768 Leaning, William, 1 Jan. 1920.
8769 Lecourt, Rev. Gustave Alexander, 1 Jan. 1920.
8770 Ledbury, Rowland Egbert, 1 Jan. 1920.
8771 Ledger, Sidney Seaward, 1 Jan. 1920.
8772 Ledingham, Alexander, 1 Jan. 1920.
8773 Lee, George, 1 Jan. 1920.
8774 Lee, Henry Blott 1 Jan. 1920.
8775 Lee, John Thomas, 1 Jan. 1920.
8776 Lee, Mabel Meryck, Mrs., 1 Jan. 1920.
8777 Lee, Rev. Canon William, 1 Jan. 1920.
8778 Lee, William John, 1 Jan. 1920.
8779 Leech, Beatrice Ellen, Mrs., 1 Jan. 1920.
8780 Leedom, Beatrice Lucy, Mrs., 1 Jan. 1920.
8781 Leeper, Elizabeth Anne, Mrs., 1 Jan. 1920.
8782 Leetham, Ethel Mary, 1 Jan. 1920.
8783 Leigh, Alan de Verd, 1 Jan. 1920.
8784 Leigh, Charles Edward, 1 Jan. 1920.
8785 Lemon, Margaretta Louisa, Mrs., 1 Jan. 1920.
8786 Leslie, Emily Florence, Mrs., 1 Jan. 1920.
8787 Leslie, George, 1 Jan. 1920.
8788 Lesser, Catherine Maud, Mrs., 1 Jan. 1920.
8789 Lester, Horace Lenton, 1 Jan. 1920.
8790 Levitt, Robert Thorp, 1 Jan. 1920.
8791 Lewellen, Florence Beatrice, Mrs., 1 Jan. 1920.
8792 Lewes, Mary Louisa 1 Jan. 1920.
8793 Lewin, Percy Evans, 1 Jan. 1920.
8794 Lewis, Alice Pansy Mary, 1 Jan. 1920.
8795 Lewis, Benjamin Joseph, 1 Jan. 1920.
8796 Lewis, Edwin, 1 Jan. 1920.
8797 Lewis, Sarah Agnes Jane, Mrs., 1 Jan. 1920.
8798 Lewis, Thomas Henry, 1 Jan. 1920.
8799 Lewis, William John, 1 Jan. 1920.
8800 Lewty, Mary, Mrs., 1 Jan. 1920.
8801 Liddell, Rhoda Caroline Anna, 1 Jan. 1920.
8802 Liddell, Violet Constance, 1 Jan. 1920.
8803 Lightfoot, Theresa, Mrs., 1 Jan. 1920.
8804 Lightwood, Francis Harry, 1 Jan. 1920.
8805 Liburn, Bethea, Mrs., 1 Jan. 1920.
8806 Lilley, Kate, 1 Jan. 1920.
8807 Lindsay, Alexander Harvey, 1 Jan. 1920.
8808 Lindsay, Eliza Hunter, 1 Jan. 1920.
8809 Linfoot, William Ernest, 1 Jan. 1920.
8810 Link, Emily Ethel, 1 Jan. 1920.
8811 Linton, Charles Astell George, 1 Jan. 1920.
8812 Lintott, Walter, 1 Jan. 1920.
8814 Livingstone, Marion Isabella Rose, Mrs. Fenton- 1 Jan. 1920.
8815 Lloyd, Arthur Harold, 1 Jan. 1920.
8816 Lloyd, Christopher, 1 Jan. 1920.
8817 Lloyd, Frances, Mrs. Merrick, 1 Jan. 1920.
8818 Lloyd, Frederick Propert Jones-, 1 Jan. 1920.
8819 Lloyd, George Maybrey, 1 Jan. 1920.
8820 Lloyd, John, 1 Jan. 1920.
8821 Lloyd, John Daniel, 1 Jan. 1920.
8822 Lloyd, John William, 1 Jan. 1920.
8823 Lloyd, Thomas Joseph, 1 Jan. 1920.
8824 Lloyd, Reginald William, 1 Jan. 1920.
8825 Llywarch, Gerard, 1 Jan. 1920.
8826 Locock, Katharine Beatrice, 1 Jan. 1920.
8827 Loder, Henrietta Mabel, Mrs. 1 Jan. 1920.
8828 Lomax, Frederick, 1 Jan. 1920.
8829 Longcroft, Cecil James, 1 Jan. 1920.

8830 Lord, Arthur Ernest, 1 Jan. 1920.
8831 Lord, William John, 1 Jan. 1920.
8832 Lovelock, Charles Prior, 1 Jan. 1920.
8833 Lowe, Henry, 1 Jan. 1920.
8834 Lowndes, William Frederick Lowdnes Frith-, 1 Jan. 1920.
8835 Luard Louise Henrietta, Mrs., 1 Jan. 1920.
8836 Lucas, Mia, Mrs., 1 Jan. 1920.
8837 Luck, Ernest Bertram, 1 Jan. 1920.
8838 Luckhurst, Allen Edward James, 1 Jan. 1920.
8839 Luddington, Leila Arthur, Mrs., 1 Jan. 1920.
8840 Ludford, George Frederick, 1 Jan. 1920.
8841 Luffman, Brooke Laud, 1 Jan. 1920.
8842 Luffman, John George Innes, 1 Jan. 1920.
8843 Lumley, Eva, 1 Jan. 1920
8844 Lumsden, John Brown, 1 Jan. 1920.
8845 Lumsden, William Henry, 1 Jan. 1920.
8846 Lungley, George William, 1 Jan. 1920.
8847 Lunn, William Henry, 1 Jan. 1920.
8848 Lupton, Anne Muriel, 1 Jan. 1920.
8849 Lyddon, Katherine, Mrs., 1 Jan. 1920.
8850 Lyel, Percival Charles, 1 Jan. 1920.
8851 Lyell, Maud Mary, 1 Jan. 1920.
8852 Lymburn, Mary Jane Dickie, 1 Jan. 1920.
8853 Lynn, Tryner 1 Jan. 1920.
8854 Lyons, Harry, 1 Jan. 1920.
8855 Macafee, Annie Harner, Mrs., 1 Jan. 1920.
8856 Macan, Dorothy Vernon, 1 Jan. 1920.
8857 McArthur, Gladys Forbes, 1 Jan. 1920.
8858 McBright, David Samuel, 1 Jan. 1920.
8859 McBryde, Tom Murray, 1 Jan. 1920.
8860 McCall, Amy Kerr, 1 Jan. 1920.
8861 Macall, William Neil, 1 Jan. 1920.
8862 McCallum, Dugald, 1 Jan. 1920.
8863 MacCartie, Flora Theodosia, 1 Jan. 1920.
8864 McClure, Janet Mary, 1 Jan. 1920.
8865 McClymont, Lillie Atkinson, 1 Jan. 1920.
8866 McCreery, Emilia, Mrs., 1 Jan. 1920.
8867 Macdonald, Amy Beatrice, Mrs., 1 Jan. 1920.
8868 Macdonald, Charles, 1 Jan. 1920.
8869 Macdonald, Elsie Hay, 1 Jan. 1920.
8870 Macdonald, Johanna Margaret, Mrs., 1 Jan. 1920.
8871 Macdonald, John, 1 Jan. 1920.
8872 McDonald, John, 1 Jan. 1920.
8873 Macdonald, John, 1 Jan. 1920.
8874 Macdonald, Margaret Clare, 1 Jan. 1920.
8875 McDonald, Reginald Henry, 1 Jan. 1920.
8876 Macdonald, Wilfrid Frank, 1 Jan. 1920.
8877 McDougall, Donald, 1 Jan. 1920.
8878 McDougall, Harold James, 1 Jan. 1920.
8879 Macey, Josiah, 1 Jan. 1920.
8880 McFadyen, Duncan, 1 Jan. 1920.
8881 McFerran, Sarah Helen, 1 Jan. 1920.
8882 Macfie, Mary Jane, Mrs., 1 Jan. 1920.
8883 McGeorge, Mary, Mrs., 1 Jan. 1920.
8884 McGilvray, James Anderson, 1 Jan. 1920.
8885 McGill, Alice Mary, Mrs., 1 Jan. 1920.
8886 McGonigal, Margaret Dorothy, 1 Jan. 1920.
8887 McGowan, Margaret Jane, Mrs., 1 Jan. 1920.
8888 M'Grath, Wellington Albert, 1 Jan. 1920.
8889 Macgregor, John Alister, 1 Jan. 1920.
8890 McGuinness, Norah Mary Ursula, 1 Jan. 1920.
8891 McIntosh, Alexander, 1 Jan. 1920.
8892 McIntosh, Alexander Hugh, 1 Jan. 1920.
8893 Mack, Peter, 1 Jan. 1920.
8894 Mackarness, Mildred Blankley, Mrs., 1 Jan. 1920.
8895 Mackay, Murdoch, 1 Jan. 1920.
8896 Mackenzie, Dorothy Rose, 1 Jan. 1920.
8897 Mackenzie, Frances Louisa, 1 Jan. 1920.
8898 Mackenzie, Kenneth Child, 1 Jan. 1920.
8899 Mackenzie, May, Lady, 1 Jan. 1920.
8900 Mackenzie, Mina, 1 Jan. 1920.
8901 MacKenzie, Peter, 1 Jan. 1920.
8902 McKerrow, Alexandrina, 1 Jan. 1920.
8903 Mackidd, Barbara Winifred Logan, 1 Jan. 1920.
8904 Mackle, George, 1 Jan. 1920.
8905 McKillop, Margaret, Mrs., 1 Jan. 1920.
8906 Mackinder, Charles Henry, 1 Jan. 1920.
8907 Mackintosh, Alexander, 1 Jan. 1920.
8908 Mackintosh, Donald Grant, 1 Jan. 1920.
8909 Mackintosh, Herbert Bannerman, 1 Jan. 1920.
8910 McLachlan, Guendolen Mab, Mrs., 1 Jan. 1920.
8911 MacLachan, Morrison, 1 Jan. 1920.
8912 McLagan, Douglas Craig, 1 Jan. 1920.
8913 McLaren, Nellie Hessel, Mrs., 1 Jan. 1920.
8914 McLaughlin, Hubert William Charles, 1 Jan. 1920.
8915 McLaughlin, Patrick Joseph, 1 Jan. 1920.
8916 Maclean, Marion Louise, Mrs., 1 Jan. 1920.
8917 MacLeod, Harold Hay Brodie, 1 Jan. 1920.
8918 Maclure, Harry Julius, 1 Jan. 1920.
8919 McMahon, Michael, 1 Jan. 1920.
8920 McMenamin, Peter Paul, 1 Jan. 1920.
8921 McMenemy, Frank, 1 Jan. 1920.
8922 MacMillan, William, 1 Jan. 1920.
8923 McMillan, Sara Jane, Mrs., 1 Jan. 1920.
8924 McMurdo, Archibald Hugh, 1 Jan. 1920.
8925 McNeill, Eileen Maud Mary, 1 Jan. 1920.
8926 MacNeill, Malcolm, 1 Jan. 1920.
8927 McNicoll, David, 1 Jan. 1920.
8928 Macphail, Dugald, 1 Jan. 1920.
8929 Macrae, Elizabeth Nina, 1 Jan. 1920.

8930 McRaith, John Warden, 1 Jan. 1920.
8931 MacSwinney, Nora Kathleen, 1 Jan. 1920.
8932 Mactier, Henry Carter, 1 Jan. 1920.
8933 McTurk, Isabel, Mrs., 1 Jan. 1920.
8934 Maddison, Charles Henry, 1 Jan. 1920.
8935 Madge, Gwendolen Mary Gladys, 1 Jan. 1920.
8936 Magee, Thomas, 1 Jan. 1920.
8937 Magor, Edward Manuel, 1 Jan. 1920.
8938 Main, Ernest William, 1 Jan. 1920.
8939 Mair, Robert, 1 Jan. 1920.
8940 Mainz, Ernest, 1 Jan. 1920.
8941 Maitland, Jean Hamilton, Mrs., 1 Jan. 1920.
8942 Malcolm, George William, 1 Jan. 1920.
8943 Malerbi, James Michael, 1 Jan. 1920.
8944 Malim, Julia, Mrs., 1 Jan. 1920.
8945 Mallen, James, 1 Jan. 1920.
8946 Malloch, Ethel Josephine Victoria, Mrs., 1 Jan. 1920.
8947 Maloney, William Donnellan, 1 Jan. 1920.
8948 Maltby, William Graham, 1 Jan. 1920.
8949 Mamos, Monsignore Giovanni, 1 Jan. 1920.
8950 Maniece, William Christopher Henry, 1 Jan. 1920.
8951 Mann, Frederick William, 1 Jan. 1920.
8952 Mann, Sydney Frederick, 1 Jan. 1920.
8953 Mansell, Rosalie, 1 Jan. 1920.
8954 Mansfield, Norman Polety, 1 Jan. 1920.
8955 Manson, Albert James, 1 Jan. 1920.
8956 March, Joseph Ogdin, 1 Jan. 1920.
8957 Marchand, Isidore Henri Alphonse, 1 Jan. 1920.
8958 Marchant, Herbert George, 1 Jan. 1920.
8959 Margetson, Florence Nys, Mrs., 1 Jan. 1920.
8960 Marindin, Gertrude Florence Evelyn, Mrs., 1 Jan. 1920.
8961 Marlow, George William Augustus, 1 Jan. 1920.
8962 Marsden, Frank, 1 Jan. 1920.
8963 Marsden, Herbert Harrison, 1 Jan. 1920.
8964 Marsh, Constance Mabel Worsey, 1 Jan. 1920.
8965 Marsh, Edith Eleanor Mary, Mrs. Chisenhale, 1 Jan. 1920.
8966 Marshall, Albert Edward, 1 Jan. 1920.
8967 Marshall, James Currie, 1 Jan. 1920.
8968 Marshall, Janet Sophia, Mrs., 1 Jan. 1920.
8969 Marshall, William, 1 Jan. 1920.
8970 Martin, Francis Edward, 1 Jan. 1920.
8971 Martin, Sir James, 1 Jan. 1920.
8972 Martin, May Angela, Mrs., 1 Jan. 1920.
8973 Martin, William, 1 Jan. 1920.
8974 Maskens, Harry Frederick, 1 Jan. 1920.
8975 Mason, Florence Irene, 1 Jan. 1920.
8976 Mason, Frank John, 1 Jan. 1920.
8977 Mason, John Wright, 1 Jan. 1920.
8978 Mason, Walter, 1 Jan. 1920.
8979 Masterton, Rev. John, 1 Jan. 1920.
8980 Mather, Alice, Mrs., 1 Jan. 1920.
8981 Mather, Alice Lilian, 1 Jan. 1920.
8982 Maton, William Clifford, 1 Jan. 1920.
8983 Matthew, Ruth Mary, Mrs., 1 Jan. 1920.
8984 Matthews, Alice May, 1 Jan. 1920.
8985 Matthews, Edward Henry, 1 Jan. 1920.
8986 Matthews, Olive Harrington, 1 Jan. 1920.
8987 Matthews, Robert Lee, 1 Jan. 1920.
8988 Matthews, Sarah Emily, 1 Jan 1920.
8989 Matthewson, Thomas, 1 Jan. 1920.
8990 Maurice, Thomas Cooper, 1 Jan. 1920.
8991 Maurice, Walter Byron, 1 Jan. 1920.
8992 Maxtone, Robert Young, 1 Jan. 1920.
8993 Maxwell, Adeline Helen, Mrs. Heron-, 1 Jan. 1920.
8994 Maxwell, Mary Alexandra, 1 Jan. 1920.
8995 Maxwell, William Blackley, 1 Jan. 1920.
8996 May, Edith, Mrs., 1 Jan. 1920.
8997 May, William George, 1 Jan. 1920.
8998 Mayer, John, 1 Jan. 1920.
8999 Mayes, Howard, 1 Jan. 1920.
9000 Maynard, Annie Evelyn, Mrs., 1 Jan. 1920.
9001 Mears, Grace Edith, 1 Jan. 1920.
9002 Medwin, Gladys Leslie, 1 Jan. 1920.
9003 Mee, Oliver, 1 Jan. 1920.
9004 Meehan, Francis Edward, 1 Jan. 1920.
9005 Meiggs, Mary Effie, 1 Jan. 1920.
9006 Meigh, Edward, 1 Jan. 1920.
9007 Melandre, Joseph, 1 Jan. 1920.
9008 Melling, Thomas William, 1 Jan. 1920.
9009 Mellor, Juliet Vivien, 1 Jan. 1920.
9010 Mellor, William Charles, 1 Jan. 1920.
9011 Mellows, William Thomas, 1 Jan. 1920.
9012 Mellstrom, Charles Gustav, 1 Jan. 1920.
9013 Melville, James, 1 Jan. 1920.
9014 Mercer, William Ayerst, 1 Jan. 1920.
9015 Merchant, John Victor Jabez, 1 Jan. 1920.
9016 Meredith, Ann Maude, 1 Jan. 1920.
9017 Merrick, Frederick William, 1 Jan. 1920.
9018 Messel, Maud Frances, Mrs., 1 Jan. 1920.
9019 Metcalfe, Claude, 1 Jan. 1920.
9020 Metcalfe, George Arthur, 1 Jan. 1920.
9021 Miall, Frank Berger, 1 Jan. 1920.
9022 Micklem, Eva, Mrs., 1 Jan. 1920.
9023 Middleton, John, 1 Jan. 1920.
9024 Miles, Leopold, 1 Jan. 1920.
9025 Millar, Peter, 1 Jan. 1920.
9026 Millard, Ernest Alfred, 1 Jan. 1920,
9027 Miller, Amy Bessie, Mrs., 1 Jan. 1920.
9028 Miller, Charles Edward Augustus, 1 Jan. 1920.
9029 Miller, Charles Thomas Narramore, 1 Jan. 1920.

9031 Miller, David Simpson, 1 Jan. 1920.
9032 Miller, Edmund Josiah, 1 Jan. 1920.
9033 Miller, Harold Tibbatts, 1 Jan. 1920.
9034 Miller, James, 1 Jan. 1920.
9035 Miller, Joseph Edward, 1 Jan. 1920.
9036 Miller, Sidney James, 1 Jan. 1920.
9037 Milligan, John Arthur, 1 Jan. 1920.
9038 Millinger, Thomas, 1 Jan. 1920.
9039 Millington, John Price, 1 Jan. 1920.
9040 Mills, Arthur, 1 Jan. 1920.
9041 Mills, Samuel, 1 Jan. 1920.
9042 Mills, Hon. Violet Louisa, 1 Jan. 1920.
9043 Mills, William Henry, 1 Jan. 1920.
9044 Mills, Zae, 1 Jan. 1920.
9045 Milne, Claire Marjoribanks, Lady, 1 Jan. 1920.
9046 Milne, Florence, Mrs., 1 Jan. 1920.
9047 Milward, Eliza Margaret, 1 Jan. 1920.
9048 Minchin, Arthur, 1 Jan. 1920.
9049 Mitchell, Alexander, 1 Jan. 1920.
9050 Mitchell, Elisabeth Duff, 1 Jan. 1920.
9051 Mitchell, Hélène Penelope Doris, 1 Jan. 1920.
9052 Mitchell, John Methven, 1 Jan. 1920.
9053 Mitchell, Lawrence Yuill, 1 Jan. 1920.
9054 Mitchell, Mary Birch, 1 Jan. 1920.
9055 Mitchell, Robert, 1 Jan. 1920.
9056 Mitchell, Thomas John, 1 Jan. 1920.
9057 Mitford, Dorothy Frances, 1 Jan. 1920.
9058 Mizen, Frederick George, 1 Jan. 1920.
9059 Moffat, George, 1 Jan. 1920.
9060 Moffat, Rennie John, 1 Jan. 1920.
9061 Moir, John Watson, 1 Jan. 1920.
9062 Mole, Charles Johns, 1 Jan. 1920.
9063 Mole, Ernest, 1 Jan. 1920.
9064 Molloy, Gwendolen Beatrice Sanchia May, Mrs., 1 Jan. 1920.
9065 Molyneux, Caroline Elizabeth, Hon. Mrs. Caryl, 1 Jan. 1920.
9066 Monk, Geoffrey, 1 Jan. 1920.
9067 Monk, William Alfred, 1 Jan. 1920.
9068 Montgomerie, Mary, Molineux-, 1 Jan. 1920.
9069 Montgomery, John, 1 Jan. 1920.
9070 Montgomery, Mary Maud, Mrs. Purvis-Russell- 1 Jan. 1920.
9071 Montgomery, Samuel, 1 Jan. 1920.
9072 Moon, Malinda Ann, 1 Jan. 1920.
9073 Mooney, Alexander Patrick, 1 Jan. 1920.
9074 Mooney, Rev. George Elderkin, 1 Jan. 1920.
9075 Moore, Arthur Frederick, 1 Jan. 1920.
9076 Moore, John, 1 Jan. 1920.
9077 Moore, John George, 1 Jan. 1920.
9078 Moore, John Thomas, 1 Jan. 1920.
9079 Moore, Margaret, 1 Jan. 1920.
9080 Moore, Margaret Stuart, Mrs., 1 Jan. 1920.
9081 Moore, Muriel, Mrs., 1 Jan. 1920.
9082 Moore, Thomas Edwin, 1 Jan. 1920.
9083 Moore, William Gunn, 1 Jan. 1920.
9084 Moran, Selina, Mrs., 1 Jan. 1920.
9085 Morgan, Edith Lilian, 1 Jan. 1920.
9086 Morgan, Eileen Cynthia Marjorie, 1 Jan. 1920
9087 Morgan, Ethel Marion, 1 Jan. 1920.
9088 Morgan, Robert Henry, 1 Jan. 1920.
9089 Morgan, Thomas, 1 Jan. 1920.
9090 Morgan, William Richard, 1 Jan. 1920.
9091 Morris, Frank, 1 Jan. 1920.
9092 Morris, Harry, 1 Jan. 1920.
9093 Morris, Iorwerth, 1 Jan. 1920.
9094 Morris, John, 1 Jan. 1920.
9095 Morris, Max Cyril, 1 Jan. 1920.
9096 Morrison, John, 1 Jan. 1920.
9097 Mortimer, Muriel Ida Mary, Mrs., 1 Jan. 1920.
9098 Mortimer, Reginald Mortimer Higgs, 1 Jan. 1920.
9099 Mortished, John, 1 Jan. 1920.
9100 Moscrip, Holbourn Jackson, 1 Jan. 1920.
9101 Moseley, Louise, 1 Jan 1920.
9102 Mostyn, Hon. Pamela Georgine, Mrs. Lloyd-, 1 Jan. 1920.
9103 Mowbray, George, 1 Jan. 1920.
9104 Mudge, Jenny, 1 Jan. 1920.
9105 Muirhead, Essa Gemmell, Mrs., 1 Jan. 1920.
9106 Mulhallen, Vivian Brew-, 1 Jan. 1920.
9107 Müller, Lilian, Mrs., 1 Jan. 1920.
9108 Mullineux, John, 1 Jan. 1920.
9109 Mumford, Agnes, Mrs., 1 Jan. 1920.
9110 Mungall, Walter Heggie, 1 Jan. 1920.
9111 Mungavin, George Walter, 1 Jan. 1920.
9112 Mure, Emily May, Mrs., 1 Jan. 1920.
9113 Murgatroyd, William John, 1 Jan. 1920.
9114 Murphy, James, 1 Jan. 1920.
9115 Murray, Amelia Henrietta, Mrs., 1 Jan. 1920.
9116 Murray, Edith, Mrs., 1 Jan. 1920.
9117 Murray, Frederick, 1 Jan. 1920.
9118 Murray, Josephine, 1 Jan. 1920.
9119 Murray, Robert Alexander, 1 Jan. 1920.
9120 Murray, William, 1 Jan. 1920.
9121 Murton, Alice Hope, Mrs., 1 Jan. 1920.
9122 Musgrave, Catherine Wares Rittle, 1 Jan. 1920.
9123 Musgrave, William Noel Sagar-, 1 Jan. 1920.
9124 Musguin, William Charles, 1 Jan. 1920.
9125 Musson, Arthur, 1 Jan. 1920.
9126 Mustarde, John Clark, 1 Jan. 1920.
9127 Myers, Harry Cecil, 1 Jan. 1920.

9128 Myers, Lancelot Brainard, 1 Jan. 1920.
9129 Mylchreest, Thomas, 1 Jan. 1920.
9130 Mylius, Wilhelmina Leonie, 1 Jan. 1920.
9131 Nancarrow, Charlotte Alice, Mrs., 1 Jan. 1920.
9132 Napier, Norman Wilson, 1 Jan. 1920.
9133 Nash, Alice Emma, 1 Jan. 1920.
9134 Nash, Dorothea, 1 Jan. 1920.
9135 Nash, Elsie Kathleen, 1 Jan. 1920.
9136 Nash, Lilian Mary Hamel, 1 Jan. 1920.
9137 Nawton, Daisy, Mrs., 1 Jan. 1920.
9138 Nayler, Joseph, 1 Jan. 1920.
9139 Neave, William, 1 Jan. 1920.
9140 Neill, William Reid, 1 Jan. 1920.
9141 Neish, Elizabeth Oliver, 1 Jan. 1920.
9142 Nelson, Charlotte Mabel, 1 Jan. 1920.
9143 Ness, Helen Dorothy Parker, 1 Jan. 1920.
9144 Newall, Helen Frances, Mrs. Stirling-, 1 Jan. 1920.
9145 Newby, Albert Ernest, 1 Jan. 1920.
9146 Newel, Rose Alice, Mrs., 1 Jan. 1920.
9147 Newman, William, 1 Jan. 1920.
9148 Newmarch, Edward, 1 Jan. 1920.
9149 Newnham, Charles, 1 Jan. 1920.
9150 Newton, Frederick, 1 Jan. 1920.
9151 Nicholls, Ada Casterton, Mrs., 1 Jan. 1920.
9152 Nicholls, Arthur Burleigh, 1 Jan. 1920.
9153 Nicholls, Evelyn, 1 Jan. 1920.
9154 Nicholls, Thomas, 1 Jan. 1920.
9155 Nicholls, William, 1 Jan. 1920.
9156 Nichols, John Alexander, 1 Jan. 1920.
9157 Nichols, Thomas George, 1 Jan. 1920.
9158 Nicol, Charlotte, 1 Jan. 1920.
9159 Nicoll, William Harry, 1 Jan. 1920.
9160 Nield, Faërie Edith Lilian, Mrs., 1 Jan. 1920.
9161 Nisbet, Robert, 1 Jan. 1920.
9162 Nixon, Margaret Eva, 1 Jan. 1920.
9163 Noble, George Anderson, 1 Jan. 1920.
9164 Nolan, Elizabeth Florence Mary, 1 Jan. 1920.
9165 Norie, Thomas, 1 Jan. 1920.
9166 Norman, Jennie Gilkinson, Mrs., 1 Jan. 1920.
9167 Normington, Arthur Edward, 1 Jan. 1920.
9168 Norrish, Edith Gladys Barrett, 1 Jan. 1920.
9169 North, Frank, 1 Jan. 1920.
9170 Northcote, Jabez Charles, 1 Jan. 1920.
9171 Nott, Marjorie, 1 Jan. 1920.
9172 Nuttall, Edmund, 1 Jan. 1920.
9173 Nuttall, William, 1 Jan. 1920.
9174 Oakley, Alice Annette, Mrs., 1 Jan. 1920.
9175 Oakeshott, Claude Albert, 1 Jan. 1920.
9176 Oakeshott, Frances Maude, Mrs., 1 Jan. 1920.
9177 Oakshott, Julia Maud, 1 Jan. 1920.
9178 O'Brien, Charles Henry William, 1 Jan. 1920.
9179 O'Brien, Herbert Charles, 1 Jan. 1920.
9180 O'Brien, Florence Mary, Mrs. Vere, 1 Jan. 1920.
9181 O'Connell, Cormac John, 1 Jan. 1920.
9182 O'Connor, Henry, 1 Jan. 1920.
9183 O'Donel, John, 1 Jan. 1920.
9184 O'Donoghue, Mary, 1 Jan. 1920.
9185 Offord, Frederick George, 1 Jan. 1920.
9186 O'Hara, Ethel, Mrs., 1 Jan. 1920.
9187 Oldham, Hugh Falconer, 1 Jan. 1920.
9188 Olive, May Winifred, 1 Jan. 1920.
9189 Oliver, Charles Thomas, 1 Jan. 1920.
9190 Oliver, John Pervey, 1 Jan. 1920.
9191 Olivier, Edith Maud, 1 Jan. 1920.
9192 Olver, Bertie Cecil, 1 Jan. 1920.
9193 Openshaw, Edith Newbold, 1 Jan. 1920.
9194 Openshaw, Florence, Mrs., 1 Jan. 1920.
9195 Orange, Lionel, 1 Jan. 1920.
9196 Ord, Mark Curry, 1 Jan. 1920.
9197 Orford, John, 1 Jan. 1920.
9198 Orme, Marie, Mrs., 1 Jan. 1920.
9199 O'Rorke, Gertrude Isabel, Mrs., 1 Jan. 1920.
9200 Orton, William, 1 Jan. 1920.
9201 Ostle, Helen Muriel, 1 Jan. 1920.
9202 Ottaway, John, 1 Jan. 1920.
9203 Ouseley, William, 1 Jan. 1920.
9204 Ouvry, Ernest Carrington, 1 Jan. 1920.
9205 Owen, Griffith Ellis, 1 Jan. 1920.
9206 Owen, Harry Collinson, 1 Jan. 1920.
9207 Oyston, William Fletcher, 1 Jan. 1920.
9208 Paddison, William Perceval, 1 Jan. 1920.
9209 Page, Ethel Augusta, 1 Jan. 1920.
9210 Page, Howard John, 1 Jan. 1920.
9211 Page, John Foulger, 1 Jan. 1920.
9212 Page, Reginald, 1 Jan. 1920.
9213 Pakington, Hon. Mary Augusta, 1 Jan. 1920.
9214 Palmer Florence Mary, 1 Jan. 1920.
9215 Palmer, Rosa Jane, 1 Jan. 1920.
9216 Palmer, William Henry, 1 Jan. 1920.
9217 Pannell, Charles Thomas, 1 Jan. 1920.
9218 Panther, Helen Annie, Mrs., 1 Jan. 1920.
9219 Parish, Henry, 1 Jan. 1920.
9220 Park, Ernest William, 1 Jan. 1920.
9221 Parker, Ethel Elizabeth, 1 Jan. 1920.
9222 Parker, James George, 1 Jan. 1920.
9223 Parker, Ronald Francis, 1 Jan. 1920.
9224 Parker, Bertha Theodora England, 1 Jan. 1920.
9225 Parkes, Colin Egbert, 1 Jan. 1920.
9226 Parkes, Edwin, 1 Jan. 1920.
9227 Parkin, Fanny Ida, Mrs., 1 Jan. 1920.

9228 Parkin, Joseph Henry, 1 Jan. 1920.
9229 Parkinson, Frederick Henry, 1 Jan. 1920.
9230 Parkinson, Janet, 1 Jan. 1920.
9231 Parkinson, John Frederick Main, 1 Jan. 1920.
9232 Parkinson, Walter, 1 Jan. 1920.
9233 Parnaby, John Murray, 1 Jan. 1920.
9234 Parsons, Arthur Ambrose, 1 Jan. 1920.
9235 Parsons, Charles O'Connor, 1 Jan. 1920.
9236 Parsons, Joan Dorothea Langton, 1 Jan. 1920.
9237 Parsons, John Edward Hocking, 1 Jan. 1920.
9238 Partington, Mary Alice, Mrs., 1 Jan. 1920.
9239 Partington, Willie Percival Hindley, 1 Jan. 1920.
9240 Partridge, Sydney John, 1 Jan. 1920.
9241 Pass, Ralph, 1 Jan. 1920.
9242 Paterson, Doris Hirst, 1 Jan. 1920.
9243 Paterson, John Wilson, 1 Jan. 1920.
9244 Paterson, Mary Agnes, Mrs., 1 Jan. 1920.
9245 Paton, Daniel Shaw, 1 Jan. 1920.
9246 Patterson, Robert Hogarth, 1 Jan. 1920.
9247 Patterson, Walter, 1 Jan. 1920.
9248 Pattle, Cecil Frederic, 1 Jan. 1920.
9249 Pattrick, Emma, Mrs., 1 Jan. 1920.
9250 Paul, Minnie, Mrs., 1 Jan. 1920.
9251 Pauli, Emily Anne, Mrs., 1 Jan. 1920.
9252 Pawley, Katherine Alice, 1 Jan. 1920.
9253 Payne, Arthur, 1 Jan. 1920.
9254 Payne, Ellen, 1 Jan. 1920.
9255 Payne, Hazel Vivienne, 1 Jan. 1920.
9256 Payne, Percy John, 1 Jan. 1920.
9257 Payne, Stephen, 1 Jan. 1920.
9258 Peace, John William, 1 Jan. 1920.
9259 Peacocke, Aungier, 1 Jan. 1920.
9260 Peacocke, Ethel Helen, Mrs., 1 Jan. 1920.
9261 Peake, Emily Marion, Mrs., 1 Jan. 1920.
9262 Pearce, James, 1 Jan. 1920.
9263 Pearce, John William, 1 Jan. 1920.
9264 Pearman, Ernest Albert, 1 Jan. 1920.
9265 Pearse, Eleanor, 1 Jan. 1920.
9266 Pearson, Arthur Frederick, 1 Jan. 1920.
9267 Pearson, Robert James, 1 Jan. 1920.
9268 Pearson, William Henry, 1 Jan. 1920.
9269 Peck, Elfrida Mary, 1 Jan. 1920.
9270 Peck, Frederick George, 1 Jan. 1920.
9271 Peddie, Francis Grove, 1 Jan. 1920.
9272 Peddle, Cyril James, 1 Jan. 1920.
9273 Peel, Cicely, 1 Jan. 1920.
9274 Peel, Dorothy Mary Grace, Mrs., 1 Jan. 1920.
9275 Penney, Mary Bentley, 1 Jan. 1920.
9276 Penning, Walter, 1 Jan. 1920.
9277 Pepper, Charles, 1 Jan. 1920.
9278 Pepper, William James, 1 Jan. 1920.
9279 Percy, Gladys May, Mrs. Heber-, 1 Jan. 1920.
9280 Perdue, Florence Louise Sophia, 1 Jan. 1920.
9281 Perkins, Charles Clifforde, 1 Jan. 1920.
9282 Perrin, Alfred William, 1 Jan. 1920.
9283 Perrin, John Edward, 1 Jan. 1920.
9284 Perry, William, 1 Jan. 1920.
9285 Peters, Herbert John, 1 Jan. 1920.
9286 Peters, Henry Robert, 1 Jan. 1920.
9287 Petherick, Wallace, 1 Jan. 1920.
9288 Pettyfer, Percy William, 1 Jan. 1920.
9289 Philip, Elsie Green, Mrs., 1 Jan. 1920.
9290 Philip, Katherine Laura, Mrs., 1 Jan. 1920.
9291 Philips, Helena Adelaide Sara, Mrs., 1 Jan. 1920.
9292 Phillibrown, George Ernest, 1 Jan. 1920.
9293 Phillips, Helena Creed, 1 Jan. 1920.
9294 Phillips, Harry Joseph, 1 Jan. 1920.
9295 Phillips, Wallace Henry, 1 Jan. 1920.
9296 Phillips, William James, 1 Jan. 1920.,
9297 Philpot, Joseph Henry, 1 Jan. 1920.
9298 Phœnix, Herbert Ray, 1 Jan. 1920.
9299 Phythian, Thomas Ewart, 1 Jan. 1920.
9300 Pickard, Henry, 1 Jan. 1920.
9301 Picken, Anna Craig, Mrs., 1 Jan. 1920.
9302 Pickering, Fred, 1 Jan. 1920.
9303 Pickering, Percy, 1 Jan. 1920.
9304 Pickford, Hurd, 1 Jan. 1920.
9305 Pierce, Elsie Louisa, Mrs., 1 Jan. 1920.
9306 Pierce, Thomas John, 1 Jan. 1920.
9307 Pierpoint, Marie Eugénie, Mrs., 1 Jan. 1920.
9308 Pierson, Reginald Kershaw, 1 Jan. 1920.
9309 Pightling, Garnet, 1 Jan. 1920.
9310 Pike, Emma, 1 Jan. 1920.
9311 Pilcher, Cecil Westland, 1 Jan. 1920.
9312 Pin, Violet Constance Letitia Mary, 1 Jan. 1920.
9313 Pincombe Arthur, 1 Jan. 1920.
9314 Pipe, Nellie, Mrs., 1 Jan. 1920.
9315 Pitman, Arthur James, 1 Jan. 1920.
9316 Pitt, Arthur George, 1 Jan. 1920.
9317 Pitt, Inez Mary, Mrs., 1 Jan. 1920.
9318 Platt, William Alexander, 1 Jan. 1920.
9319 Platt, William Alexander, 1 Jan. 1920.
9320 Platten, Samuel Henry, 1 Jan. 1920.
9321 Plevin, Mary Jean, 1 Jan. 1920.
9322 Plummer, Arthur Bertram, 1 Jan. 1920.
9323 Poë, Muriel Gladys, 1 Jan. 1920.
9324 Pollard, Charles, 1 Jan. 1920.
9325 Pollock, Catherine Heutig, 1 Jan. 1920.
9326 Pollock, John Wilson, 1 Jan. 1920.
9327 Pond, Ethel Augusta, Mrs., 1 Jan. 1920.
9328 Ponsonby, Diamond Louise Constance, 1 Jan. 1920.

9329 Poole, George Francis, 1 Jan. 1920.
9330 Poole, Herbert Richard, 1 Jan. 1920.
9331 Pope, Frances Madge, 1 Jan. 1920.
9332 Popplewell, Violet May, 1 Jan. 1920.
9333 Porter, Elizabeth Allison, Mrs., 1 Jan. 1920.
9334 Pott, Evelyn Mabel, 1 Jan. 1920.
9335 Pott, Gladys Sydney, 1 Jan. 1920.
9336 Potts, Dorothy Feilden, Mrs., 1 Jan. 1920.
9337 Potts, George Louis, 1 Jan. 1920.
9338 Poultney, Samuel Levi, 1 Jan. 1920.
9339 Poupart, William John, 1 Jan. 1920.
9340 Powell, Benjamin Henry, 1 Jan. 1920.
9341 Powell, Clare Carew, Mrs., 1 Jan. 1920.
9342 Powell, David, 1 Jan. 1920.
9343 Powell, Bimbashi Felix Edmund, Bey, 1 Jan. 1920.
9344 Powell, Frank Grove, 1 Jan. 1920.
9345 Powell, George Henry, 1 Jan. 1920.
9346 Power, James Augustine, 1 Jan. 1920.
9347 Power, Leila, 1 Jan. 1920.
9348 Pratt, Charlotte Amyand Powys, Mrs., 1 Jan. 1920.
9349 Pratt, Elizabeth Worth, 1 Jan. 1920.
9350 Pratt, Frances Margaret Ethel, Mrs., 1 Jan. 1920.
9351 Pratt, Frank, 1 Jan. 1920.
9352 Pratt, Frank Herbert, 1 Jan. 1920.
9353 Pratt, Hilda Gertrude, 1 Jan. 1920.
9354 Prentice, Joseph, 1 Jan. 1920.
9355 Prescott, Charles Clark, 1 Jan. 1920.
9356 Prescott, Constance Alice, 1 Jan. 1920.
9357 Presland, Claud William, 1 Jan. 1920.
9358 Preston, Mary Augusta Margaret Nicol, Mrs. Campbell 1 Jan. 1920.
9359 Pretty, Marguerite Emily, Mrs., 1 Jan. 1920.
9360 Price, Annie Vincent, 1 Jan. 1920.
9361 Price, Cyril Oliver Rose, 1 Jan. 1920.
9362 Price, Edward French, 1 Jan. 1920.
9363 Price, John Glanville, 1 Jan. 1920.
9364 Price, Joseph Thomas, 1 Jan. 1920.
9365 Prichard, Mabel Henrietta Mrs., 1 Jan. 1920.
9366 Prichard, Samuel David, 1 Jan. 1920.
9367 Priest, James Damer-, 1 Jan. 1920.
9368 Priest, Joseph, 1 Jan. 1920.
9369 Pringle, Ethel Louisa, Mrs., 1 Jan. 1920.
9370 Pritchard, Charles William, 1 Jan. 1920.
9371 Pritchard, Mary Ellen, Mrs., 1 Jan. 1920.
9372 Proctor, Doris Brownsword, 1 Jan. 1920.
9373 Prowse, John Skardon, 1 Jan. 1920.
9374 Puckle, Emily Alice, 1 Jan. 1920.
9375 Puddey, Henry, 1 Jan. 1920.
9376 Puddicombe, John, 1 Jan. 1920.
9377 Pullinger, Dorothée Aurélie, 1 Jan. 1920.
9378 Purcell, Thomas Edwin, 1 Jan. 1920.
9379 Purdue, Harry Roy, 1 Jan. 1920.
9380 Purnell, Edward Kelly, 1 Jan. 1920.
9381 Purslow, Samuel, 1 Jan. 1920.
9382 Purssell, Francis William, 1 Jan. 1920.
9383 Purvis, Bertha Maud Isabella, 1 Jan. 1920.
9384 Purvis, Isabelle Marie, Mrs., 1 Jan. 1920.
9385 Puttock, Muriel, Mrs., 1 Jan. 1920.
9386 Pygall, Frank Thomas, 1 Jan. 1920
9387 Pyman, Elizabeth, 1 Jan. 1920.
9388 Ractliffe, Dorothy Mary, 1 Jan. 1920.
9389 Radcliffe, Robert, 1 Jan. 1920.
9390 Radford, Lily Annie, Mrs., 1 Jan. 1920.
9391 Rae, Alexander Frederick, 1 Jan. 1920.
9392 Raikes, Hilda, Mrs., 1 Jan. 1920.
9393 Raikes, Hilda Taunton, 1 Jan. 1920.
9394 Raine, William Stephenson, 1 Jan. 1920.
9395 Raitt, Charles Palmer, 1 Jan. 1920.
9396 Ralston, Helen Ripley, Mrs., 1 Jan. 1920.
9397 Ramsay, Eleanor, Mrs., 1 Jan. 1920.
9398 Ramsay, Helen Margaret, 1 Jan. 1920.
9399 Ramsay, Margaret Evelyn. 1 Jan. 1920.
9400 Ramsay, Arthur George, 1 Jan. 1920.
9401 Randell, Reginald Maurice Henry, 1 Jan. 1920.
9402 Ranken, Charles Ernest, 1 Jan. 1920.
9403 Ransom, Herbert Charles, 1 Jan. 1920.
9404 Raphael, Effie, Mrs., 1 Jan. 1920.
9405 Ratcliffe, Herbert Coakley, 1 Jan. 1920.
9406 Rawles, Kate Eleanor, Mrs., 1 Jan. 1920.
9407 Rawlins, Frank William, 1 Jan. 1920.
9408 Rawstorne, Maria Harriet, 1 Jan. 1920.
9409 Ray, Helen MacLaine, 1 Jan. 1920.
9410 Read, George William, 1 Jan. 1920.
9411 Read, Lilian, Mrs. Rudston-, 1 Jan. 1920.
9412 Read Mary Ada Alice, Mrs. 1 Jan. 1920.
9413 Reddish, George Joseph, 1 Jan. 1920.
9414 Reed, Leah Lewis, Mrs., 1 Jan. 1920.
9415 Reed, Margaret Haythorne, 1 Jan. 1920.
9416 Rees, David John, 1 Jan. 1920.
9417 Rees, Henry Bernard, 1 Jan. 1920.
9418 Rees, John, 1 Jan. 1920.
9419 Reeves, Mary Sybil, 1 Jan. 1920.
9420 Rehm, Eveline Lucy, 1 Jan. 1920.
9421 Reid, Andrew, 1 Jan. 1920.
9422 Reid, Frederick William, 1 Jan. 1920.
9423 Reid, James, 1 Jan. 1920.
9424 Reid, Thomas, 1 Jan. 1920.
9425 Reid, William, 1 Jan. 1920.
9426 Reid, William, 1 Jan. 1920.
9427 Reid, Sir William, 1 Jan. 1920.

9428 Reid, William Macdonald, 1 Jan. 1920.
9429 Reith, Jean Stuart, 1 Jan. 1920.
9430 Relph, John William, 1 Jan. 1920.
9431 Repton, Guy George, 1 Jan. 1920.
9432 Reside, David Alexander, 1 Jan. 1920.
9433 Reynolds, Arthur, 1 Jan. 1920.
9434 Reynolds, William, 1 Jan. 1920.
9435 Riach, George, 1 Jan. 1920.
9436 Richards, Eleanora Kathleen, Mrs., 1 Jan. 1920.
9437 Richards, Jane Wilson Dixon, Mrs., 1 Jan. 1920.
9438 Richards, John Samuel, 1 Jan. 1920.
9439 Richardson, David, 1 Jan. 1920.
9441 Richardson, John William, 1 Jan. 1920.
9442 Richardson, Maria Isabel, Mrs., 1 Jan. 1920.
9443 Richardson, Peter, 1 Jan. 1920.
9444 Richardson, William, 1 Jan. 1920.
9445 Rickard, Barbara, 1 Jan. 1920.
9446 Rickenbach, Frieda, 1 Jan. 1920.
9447 Ridehalgh, Gertrude Mary, 1 Jan. 1920.
9448 Ridland, Charles Forbes, 1 Jan. 1920.
9449 Ridley, Eustace, 1 Jan. 1920.
9450 Ridley, Mary Constance, 1 Jan. 1920.
9451 Rigg, Hubert MacMullen, 1 Jan. 1920.
9452 Riley, George Willis, 1 Jan. 1920.
9453 Rimer, Alfred Henry, 1 Jan. 1920.
9454 Rimington, Frederick James, 1 Jan. 1920.
9455 Ritchie, Alice Maude, 1 Jan. 1920.
9456 Ritchie, Charles John, 1 Jan. 1920.
9457 Rivet, Albert Robert, 1 Jan. 1920.
9458 Rix, Lucy Mrs., 1 Jan. 1920.
9459 Road, Alfred, 1 Jan. 1920.
9460 Robbins, Gertrude Florence Eveline, Mrs., 1 Jan. 1920.
9461 Robertson, Margaret Hill, Mrs., 1 Jan. 1920.
9462 Roberts, Arthur Harry, 1 Jan. 1920.
9463 Roberts, Evan, 1 Jan. 1920.
9464 Roberts, Irene Helen, Mrs., 1 Jan. 1920.
9465 Roberts, William Ivor, 1 Jan. 1920.
9466 Robertson, Ann Margaret, 1 Jan. 1920.
9467 Robertson, Arthur Hurles, 1 Jan. 1920.
9468 Robertson, George, 1 Jan. 1920.
9469 Robertson, Jean Dewar, 1 Jan. 1920.
9470 Robertson, William, 1 Jan. 1920.
9471 Robertson, William Eugene, 1 Jan. 1920.
9472 Robinow, William, 1 Jan. 1920.
9473 Robins, Harry George, 1 Jan. 1920.
9474 Robinson, Charles, 1 Jan. 1920.
9475 Robinson, Doris Firth, 1 Jan. 1920.
9476 Robinson, Edward, 1 Jan. 1920.
9477 Robinson, Frederick Anthony, 1 Jan. 1920.
9478 Robinson, George Fox, 1 Jan. 1920.
9479 Robinson, Henry William Bradley, 1 Jan. 1920.
9480 Robinson, James Thomas, 1 Jan. 1920.
9481 Robinson, Percy Holland, 1 Jan. 1920.
9482 Robinson, William Walker, 1 Jan. 1920.
9483 Robson, James, 1 Jan. 1920.
9484 Robson, William Tuke, 1 Jan. 1920.
9485 Rochdale, Beatrice Mary, Baroness, 1 Jan. 1920.
9486 Roche, Francis Patrick, 1 Jan. 1920.
9487 Rodhouse, Alfred Edward, 1 Jan. 1920.
9488 Roffe, John, 1 Jan. 1920.
9489 Roger, Herbert Campbell, 1 Jan. 1920.
9490 Rogers, Florence Crichton, Mrs., 1 Jan. 1920.
9491 Rogers, Frederick Henry, 1 Jan. 1920.
9492 Rogers, Gilbert, 1 Jan. 1920.
9493 Rogers, Mary Georgina Helen, Mrs., 1 Jan. 1920.
9494 Rogers, Timothy, 1 Jan. 1920.
9495 Rogerson, William Henry, 1 Jan. 1920.
9496 Rolfe, Richard Alfred, 1 Jan. 1920.
9497 Rollings, William George Benjamin, 1 Jan. 1920.
9498 Rollo, William John, 1 Jan. 1920.
9499 Rolt, Frederick Henry, 1 Jan. 1920.
9500 Ronald, James, 1 Jan. 1920.
9501 Ronaldson, Thomas Percy, 1 Jan. 1920.
9502 Rorison, George Henry, 1 Jan. 1920.
9503 Rose, Hannah Catherine, 1 Jan. 1920.
9504 Rose, Harold Greenwell, 1 Jan. 1920.
9505 Roskrow, Albert Cyril, 1 Jan. 1920.
9506 Ross, Millicent Ellen, 1 Jan. 1920.
9507 Rosser, Thomas Newland, 1 Jan. 1920.
9508 Rouquette, Gladys Howard, Mrs., 1 Jan. 1920.
9509 Rouse, Alfred Robert, 1 Jan. 1920.
9510 Routledge, Thomas, 1 Jan. 1920.
9511 Rowe, Alfred Edward, 1 Jan. 1920.
9512 Rowe, Arthur William, 1 Jan. 1920.
9513 Rowledge, Arthur John, 1 Jan. 1920.
9514 Royds, Annie Bourne, 1 Jan. 1920.
9515 Royds, Margaret Ada, Mrs., 1 Jan. 1920.
9516 Roylance, Ethel Manford, Mrs., 1 Jan. 1920.
9517 Royle, Leonard, 1 Jan. 1920.
9518 Roythorne, Herbert, 1 Jan. 1920.
9519 Ruby, Anna Colburn, 1 Jan. 1920.
9520 Ruddick, John, 1 Jan. 1920.
9521 Ruddin, John Henry, 1 Jan. 1920.
9522 Ruddle, George, 1 Jan. 1920.
9523 Ruffer, Ferdinand Robert, 1 Jan. 1920.
9524 Rushall, Richard Boswell, 1 Jan. 1920.
9525 Russell, Arthur Edward Ian Montague, 1 Jan. 1920.
9526 Russell, Ethel, Mrs., 1 Jan. 1920.
9527 Russell, George Shipton, 1 Jan. 1920.
9528 Russell, Henry Alexander, 1 Jan. 1920.

9529 Russell, Janie, 1 Jan. 1920.
9530 Russell, John, 1 Jan. 1920.
9531 Russell, Mary Ruth, Lady, 1 Jan. 1920.
9532 Rutter, Richard Golden, 1 Jan. 1920.
9533 Rvcroft, Percy Edward, 1 Jan. 1920.
9534 Sabine, Dorothy Gladys, 1 Jan. 1920.
9535 Saer, John, 1 Jan. 1920.
9536 Sage, Arthur Reginald, 1 Jan. 1920.
9537 Saint, Rosa Charlotte, 1 Jan. 1920.
9538 St. Barbe, Henry, 1 Jan. 1920.
9539 St. Lawrence, Bertha Mary, Mrs. Gaisford-, 1 Jan. 1920.
9540 Salmon, Joseph Harold, 1 Jan. 1920.
9541 Salmon, William John Cecil Redford, 1 Jan. 1920.
9542 Salsbury, Albert Edward, 1 Jan. 1920.
9543 Samuel, Argia Alicia Casmira, Mrs., 1 Jan. 1920.
9544 Samuel, Thomas John, 1 Jan. 1920.
9545 Sammut, Florence, Mrs., 1 Jan. 1920.
9546 Sanders, Hilda, Mrs., 1 Jan. 1920.
9547 Sansom, William Campbell, 1 Jan. 1920.
9548 Saunders, Lilian Beatrice Anna, 1 Jan. 1920.
9549 Saunders, Thomas Edward, 1 Jan. 1920.
9550 Sawdon, Frank Reginald, 1 Jan. 1920.
9551 Sawyer, Hedley, 1 Jan. 1920.
9552 Saxon, Amy, Mrs., 1 Jan. 1920.
9553 Saxton, Amy Harriette, 1 Jan. 1920.
9554 Say, Geoffrey Baldwin, 1 Jan. 1920.
9555 Sayer, Thomas Lewes, 1 Jan. 1920.
9556 Scanlon, Leonard Edmund, 1 Jan. 1920.
9557 Scannell, James Berchmans, 1 Jan. 1920.
9558 Schierwater, Charles Adolf, 1 Jan. 1920.
9559 Schiff, Otto, 1 Jan. 1920.
9560 Schlesinger, Richard Alphonse, 1 Jan. 1920.
9561 Schofield, Joseph, 1 Jan. 1920.
9562 Scholefield, George Edward, 1 Jan. 1920.
9563 Scorer, Frank, 1 Jan. 1920.
9564 Scott, Alexander Thomas, 1 Jan. 1920.
9565 Scott, Archibald, 1 Jan. 1920.
9566 Scott, Elizabeth Mabel, 1 Jan. 1920.
9567 Scott, Frank Stanley, 1 Jan. 1920.
9568 Scott, Isabel Mary Gordon, 1 Jan. 1920.
9569 Scott, Isabella, 1 Jan. 1920.
9570 Scott, Nora Carlyle, 1 Jan. 1920.
9571 Scott, Robert, 1 Jan. 1920.
9572 Scott, Robert, 1 Jan. 1920.
9573 Scott, Thomas John, 1 Jan. 1920.
9574 Screech, George Ernest, 1 Jan. 1920.
9575 Scrimshaw, Ellen Mary, Mrs., 1 Jan. 1920.
9576 Scudamore. Sybil Frances, Mrs. Lucas-, 1 Jan. 1920.
9577 Scully, James Donald, 1 Jan. 1920.
9578 Scurlock, Daniel, 1 Jan. 1920.
9579 Searle, Susan Margaret, 1 Jan. 1920.
9580 Searles, Sydney William, 1 Jan. 1920.
9581 Seaton; Peter, 1 Jan. 1920.
9582 Seddon, Thomas, 1 Jan. 1920.
9583 Sedgwick, Susie, 1 Jan. 1920.
9584 Selby, Elizabeth Mary Alice, Mrs., 1 Jan. 1920.
9585 Selby, Thomas James, 1 Jan. 1920.
9586 Sell, Edith Lilian, Mrs., 1 Jan. 1920.
9587 Selous, Gerald Holgate, 1 Jan. 1920.
9588 Senn, Charles Herman, 1 Jan. 1920.
9589 Sergeant, Wilfred Oswald Faithfull, 1 Jan. 1920.
9590 Seyfang, Eveline Mary, 1 Jan. 1920.
9591 Seymour, Arthur George, 1 Jan. 1920.
9592 Seymour, Cynthia Charlotte, 1 Jan. 1920.
9593 Seymour, Frederick Powell, 1 Jan. 1920.
9594 Shand, Eliza Eveline Kynoch-, 1 Jan. 1920.
9595 Shannons, Frederick Alfred, 1 Jan. 1920.
9596 Sharp, James, 1 Jan. 1920.
9597 Sharpe, Daniel Crawford, 1 Jan. 1920.
9598 Sharrock, Alice Edith, 1 Jan. 1920.
9599 Shaw, David Nairn, 1 Jan. 1920.
9600 Shaw, Edward Harry, 1 Jan. 1920.
9601 Shaw, Helen Brown, Mrs., 1 Jan. 1920.
9602 Shaw, Josephine, Mrs. Rawson-, 1 Jan. 1920.
9603 Shaw, Mary Margaret, 1 Jan. 1920.
9604 Shaw, Richard Holgate, 1 Jan. 1920.
9605 Sheldon, Harold, 1 Jan. 1920.
9606 Shepherd, Charles Edward, 1 Jan. 1920.
9607 Shepherd, Charles Herbert, 1 Jan. 1920.
9608 Shepherd, Frederick Hawkesworth Sinclair, 1 Jan. 1920.
9609 Sheppard, Alfred Edwin, 1 Jan. 1920.
9610 Sheppard, Mary Constance, 1 Jan. 1920.
9611 Sheppard, Walter, 1 Jan. 1920.
9612 Shillaker, James Frederick, 1 Jan. 1920.
9613 Shirres, Christian, 1 Jan. 1920.
9614 Shorland, Elizabeth Freeman, Mrs., 1 Jan. 1920.
9615 Short, Henry, 1 Jan. 1920.
9616 Shotton, Charles, 1 Jan. 1920.
9617 Shubrick, Eleanor Mary, 1 Jan. 1920.
9618 Sibbald Arthur Trevitt, 1 Jan. 1920.
9619 Sidney, Leicester Philip, 1 Jan. 1920.
9620 Sigrist, Frederick, 1 Jan. 1920.
9621 Sim, James, 1 Jan. 1920.
9622 Simey, Alma Margaret, Mrs., 1 Jan. 1920.
9623 Simmonds, Frederick Victor, 1 Jan. 1920.
9624 Simmons, Frederic Vital, 1 Jan. 1920.
9625 Simpkins, Ernest Charles, 1 Jan. 1920.
9626 Simpson, Alfred, 1 Jan. 1920.
9627 Simpson, Jeanie Nelson Taylor, Mrs., 1 Jan. 1920.
9628 Simpson, John William, 1 Jan. 1920.

9629 Simpson, Mary Helen, 1 Jan. 1920.
9630 Simpson, William Arthur John, 1 Jan. 1920.
9631 Sims, John William, 1 Jan. 1920.
9632 Sinclair, George Fraser, 1 Jan. 1920.
9633 Sinclair, Ellen Lowry, 1 Jan. 1920.
9634 Skeens, Frederick, 1 Jan. 1920.
9635 Skelsey, Richard Robert, 1 Jan. 1920.
9636 Skerman, Oscar, 1 Jan. 1920.
9637 Skevington, Frank, 1 Jan. 1920.
9638 Skilbeck, Mary Alethea, Mrs., 1 Jan. 1920.
9639 Skinner, Christian Laing, 1 Jan. 1920.
9640 Skipper, Henry Hubert, 1 Jan. 1920.
9641 Skirrow, Florence, 1 Jan. 1920.
9642 Slade, Edward Charles, 1 Jan. 1920.
9643 Slade, Mary Elizabeth, 1 Jan. 1920.
9644 Slater, Alexander, 1 Jan. 1920.
9645 Slater, George Frederick, 1 Jan. 1920.
9646 Slater, John Gladstone, 1 Jan. 1920.
9647 Smale, Samuel, 1 Jan. 1920.
9648 Small, John, 1 Jan. 1920.
9649 Small, William Keane, 1 Jan. 1920.
9650 Smart, Herbert Samuel, 1 Jan. 1920.
9651 Smellie, James, 1 Jan. 1920.
9652 Smith, Constance Brightman, Mrs. Bassett-, 1 Jan. 1920.
9653 Smith, Edith Mabel, Mrs., 1 Jan. 1920.
9654 Smith, Edwin Thomas, 1 Jan. 1920.
9655 Smith, Elizabeth Frances Jane Oke, 1 Jan. 1920.
9656 Smith, Ella Gertrude Castleman-, 1 Jan. 1920.
9657 Smith, Ernest William, 1 Jan. 1920.
9658 Smith, Eva Agnes, 1 Jan. 1920.
9659 Smith, Frederick Robertson, 1 Jan. 1920.
9660 Smith, George Frederick, 1 Jan. 1920.
9661 Smith, Helen, Mrs. Willoughby-, 1 Jan. 1920.
9662 Smith, James, 1 Jan. 1920.
9663 Smith, James, 1 Jan. 1920.
9664 Smith, John, 1 Jan. 1920.
9665 Smith, John Llewellin, 1 Jan. 1920.
9666 Smith, Joseph Alfred Punton, 1 Jan. 1920.
9667 Smith, Mabel Rouse-, 1 Jan. 1920.
9668 Smith, Margaret Newbigging, 1 Jan. 1920.
9669 Smith, Percival, 1 Jan. 1920.
9670 Smith, Sarah Louisa, Mrs., 1 Jan. 1920.
9671 Smith, Stanley William, 1 Jan. 1920.
9672 Smith, Thomas Armstrong, 1 Jan. 1920.
9673 Smith, Thomas Sinclair, 1 Jan. 1920.
9674 Smith, Wyke Catterson-, 1 Jan. 1920
9675 Smith, William Haynes, 1 Jan. 1920.
9676 Smith, William Joseph, 1 Jan. 1920.
9677 Smyth, Jane Robinson, Mrs., 1 Jan. 1920.
9678 Snodgrass, Burns, 1 Jan. 1920.
9679 Snow, Daisy, Mrs., 1 Jan. 1920.
9680 Snow, Hilda Gertrude, 1 Jan. 1920.
9681 Snowdon, John Henry Reed, 1 Jan. 1920.
9682 Snowie, James, 1 Jan. 1920.
9683 Soman, Mariette Eileen, 1 Jan. 1920.
9684 Sotham, Louise Victoria Gisela, Mrs., 1 Jan. 1920.
9685 Soutar, Charles, 1 Jan. 1920.
9686 Southam, Arthur Henry Ridgway, 1 Jan. 1920.
9687 Southam, Thomas Frank, 1 Jan. 1920.
9688 Spadaccini, Henry, 1 Jan. 1920.
9689 Spencer, Blanche Mary, Mrs., 1 Jan. 1920.
9690 Spencer, Henry, 1 Jan. 1920.
9691 Spencer, Thomas, 1 Jan. 1920.
9692 Spiller, John Wyatt, 1 Jan. 1920.
9693 Spottiswoode, Robert Collinson D'Esterre, 1 Jan. 1920.
9694 Squance, Muriel Mary, 1 Jan. 1920.
9695 Staddon, Kate Elizabeth, Mrs., 1 Jan. 1920.
9696 Stagg, Arthur George, 1 Jan. 1920.
9697 Stainthorp, Amy, 1 Jan. 1920.
9698 Stalker, John, 1 Jan. 1920.
9699 Stalley, Ernest Alfred, 1 Jan. 1920.
9700 Stanbury, George Crocker, 1 Jan. 1920.
9701 Stanley, Rowland John, 1 Jan. 1920.
9702 Stanton, Ernest William, 1 Jan. 1920.
9703 Stanton, Helen Emma, 1 Jan. 1902.
9704 Stebbing, Henry Mark, 1 Jan. 1920.
9705 Stedman, Albert Douglas, 1 Jan. 1920.
9708 Stenning, Jessie, 1 Jan. 1920.
9709 Stephens, Adelaide Charlotte Edith, Mrs., 1 Jan. 1920.
9710 Stephens, Edwin, 1 Jan. 1920.
9711 Stephens, Einna Gwendolen, 1 Jan. 1920.
9712 Stephens, William John, 1 Jan. 1920.
9713 Stert, Mabel, 1 Jan. 1920.
9714 Steuart, Maud Anne Sophia, Mrs., 1 Jan. 1920.
9715 Stevens, Arthur Michael Bygholm, 1 Jan. 1920.
9716 Stevens, Frederick Charles, 1 Jan. 1920.
9717 Stevenson, Eileen, Mrs., 1 Jan. 1920.
9718 Stevenson, Hilda, 1 Jan. 1920.
9719 Stevenson, Rev. Hugh, 1 Jan. 1920.
9720 Stevenson, John Proctor, 1 Jan. 1920.
9721 Steward, William Arthur Briault, 1 Jan. 1920.
9722 Stewart, Agnes Paterson, Mrs., 1 Jan. 1920.
9723 Stewart, Charles, 1 Jan. 1920.
9724 Stewart, Donald Alexander, 1 Jan. 1920.
9725 Stewart, Duncan, 1 Jan. 1920.
9726 Stewart, Ethel, 1 Jan. 1920.
9727 Stewart, Hugh Henry Boyd, 1 Jan. 1920.
9728 Stewart, Walter Grahame, 1 Jan. 1920.
9729 Stewart, Walter Richard Shaw, 1 Jan. 1920.
9730 Stewart, William, 1 Jan. 1920.

9731 Stickney, Evelyn Mary, 1 Jan. 1920.
9732 Stigger, Horace Charles, 1 Jan. 1920.
9733 Stobart, Harriet Katie, Mrs., 1 Jan. 1920.
9734 Stocks, George, 1 Jan. 1920.
9735 Stoddard, Reginald Thomas, 1 Jan. 1920.
9736 Stokes, Robert Day, 1 Jan. 1920.
9737 Stokes, Sarah Shelton, Mrs., 1 Jan. 1920.
9738 Stone, Benjamin Garne, 1 Jan. 1920.
9739 Stone, Henry, 1 Jan. 1920.
9740 Stoneham, Florence Marie Louisa, Mrs., 1 Jan. 1920
9741 Stoneman, John Oliver Veysey, 1 Jan. 1920.
9742 Stones, John, 1 Jan. 1920.
9743 Stopford, Annette Hilda, 1 Jan. 1920.
9744 Storey, Florence Lizzie, 1 Jan. 1920.
9745 Storey, George Alexander, 1 Jan. 1920.
9746 Storrie, John Hay Atwall, 1 Jan. 1920.
9747 Stowell, Harold Joseph, 1 Jan. 1920.
9748 Strachan, John, 1 Jan. 1920.
9749 Stratford, Rosalin Mabel, Mrs. Wingfield-, 1 Jan. 1920.
9750 Stratton, Percy Montague, 1 Jan. 1920.
9751 Stratton, Robert, 1 Jan. 1920.
9752 Straus, Blanche, Mrs., 1 Jan. 1920.
9753 Straw, Arthur Roger, 1 Jan. 1920.
9754 Street, Joseph Mansfield, 1 Jan. 1920.
9755 Stringer, Frederick, 1 Jan. 1920.
9756 Stroud, Arthur, 1 Jan. 1920.
9757 Stroud, Arthur May, 1 Jan. 1920.
9758 Stuart, Winefriede Fairless, Mrs. Fairless, 1 Jan. 1920.
9759 Studdart, Isabel, Mrs. Naunton-, 1 Jan. 1290.
9760 Sudbury, Evelyn Mary, 1 Jan. 1920.
9761 Sullivan, Dorothy Evelyn, 1 Jan. 1920.
9762 Sullivan, Daniel, 1 Jan. 1920.
9763 Sulman, Helena Catharine, 1 Jan. 1920.
9764 Summers, Edward Joseph, 1 Jan. 1920.
9765 Sutton, Albert Edward, 1 Jan. 1920.
9766 Swallow, Clara, Mrs., 1 Jan. 1920.
9767 Swan, John Henry, 1 Jan. 1920.
9768 Swann, Grace Elsie, 1 Jan. 1920.
9769 Swanton, Margaret Eileen Pasley, 1 Jan. 1920.
9770 Swinson, Ethel, Mrs., 1 Jan. 1920.
9771 Sykes, Annie, Mrs. Knowles, 1 Jan. 1920.
9772 Sykes, Charles Henry, 1 Jan. 1920.
9773 Sykes, Margaret, Mrs., 1 Jan. 1920.
9774 Symon, Lesley Kilmeny, 1 Jan. 1920.
9775 Syrett, Sidney James, 1 Jan. 1920.
9776 Taffs, Herbert William, 1 Jan. 1920.
9777 Tait, Charles Wilson, 1 Jan. 1920.
9778 Tait, James, 1 Jan. 1920.
9779 Talbot, Ernest Edward Austin, 1 Jan. 1920.
9800 Tallack, Thomas, 1 Jan. 1920.
9801 Tanner, John, 1 Jan. 1920.
9802 Tansley, Emily Amelia, 1 Jan. 1920.
9803 Taphouse, Alfred John, 1 Jan. 1920.
9804 Tapp, Egerton Richard, 1 Jan. 1920.
9805 Tasker, Arthur, 1 Jan. 1920.
9806 Tasker, George Edward, 1 Jan. 1920.
9807 Tavener, Veronica Mary Agnes, 1 Jan. 1920.
9808 Tayler, Frank Alfred, 1 Jan. 1920.
9809 Taylor, Arnold, 1 Jan. 1920.
9810 Taylor, Alfred Ernest, 1 Jan. 1920.
9811 Taylor, Andrew William, 1 Jan. 1920.
9812 Taylor, Clara Jane, 1 Jan. 1920.
9813 Taylor, Eleanor Bessie Percy, 1 Jan. 1920.
9814 Taylor, Fred, 1 Jan. 1920.
9815 Taylor, Frederick, 1 Jan. 1920.
9816 Taylor, Gwynnedd Lefer, 1 Jan. 1920.
9817 Taylor, Irene, 1 Jan. 1920.
9818 Taylor, Isabella, Mrs., 1 Jan. 1920.
9819 Taylor, John, 1 Jan. 1920.
9820 Taylor, Mabel Frances, 1 Jan. 1920.
9821 Taylor, Margaret Hector, 1 Jan. 1920.
9822 Taylor, Oscar Herbert, 1 Jan. 1920.
9823 Taylor, Selina Emma, Mrs., 1 Jan. 1920.
9824 Taylor, William Arthur Trevor, 1 Jan. 1920.
9825 Taylor, William Henry, 1 Jan. 1920.
9826 Taylor, William Henry Forbes, 1 Jan. 1920.
9827 Teagle, Alice Annie, Mrs., 1 Jan. 1920.
9828 Teare, Robert Arminius Beaumont, 1 Jan. 1920.
9829 Terry, Walter Eyre, 1 Jan. 1920.
9830 Theakston, William Pease, 1 Jan. 1920.
9831 Thomas, Arthur Lloyd, 1 Jan. 1920.
9832 Thomas, Dulcibel Catherine Ktuta, 1 Jan. 1920.
9833 Thomas, James Bertram, 1 Jan. 1920.
9834 Thomas, Lavinia, Mrs. Ridley-, 1 Jan. 1920.
9835 Thomas, Rev. Richard Everard, 1 Jan. 1920.
9836 Thomas, William Howard, 1 Jan. 1920.
9837 Thompson, Charles John Samuel, 1 Jan. 1920.
9838 Thompson, Helena Agnes Mary, 1 Jan. 1920.
9839 Thompson, Ina Sophia, 1 Jan. 1920.
9840 Thompson, James Benjamin, 1 Jan. 1920.
9841 Thompson, Lorna, 1 Jan. 1920.
9842 Thompson, Nathan, 1 Jan. 1920.
9843 Thompson, Thomas, 1 Jan. 1920.
9844 Thompson, William, 1 Jan. 1920.
9845 Thomson, Alfred Ebenzer Spence, 1 Jan. 1920.
9846 Thomson, Daniel, 1 Jan. 1920.
9847 Thomson, David, 1 Jan. 1920.
9848 Thomson, Frances Beresford, 1 Jan. 1920.
9849 Thomson, Frances Ingleton, 1 Jan. 1920.
9850 Thomson, Robert Currie, 1 Jan. 1920.

9851 Thorley, William Frederick, 1 Jan. 1920.
9852 Thorman, William Henry, 1 Jan. 1920.
9854 Thorpe, Helen Mary, 1 Jan. 1920.
9855 Thorpe, Hugh, 1 Jan. 1920.
9856 Thorpe, Stanley William, 1 Jan. 1920.
9857 Threlford, William Lacon, 1 Jan. 1920.
9858 Thunder, Irene Mary, 1 Jan. 1920.
9859 Thurlow, Edith Marian, 1 Jan. 1920.
9860 Thwaites, Joseph Samuel, 1 Jan. 1920.
9861 Thynne, Katharine Angela, 1 Jan. 1920.
9862 Tiarks, Sophie Louise, 1 Jan. 1920.
9863 Tierney, Francis Michael, 1 Jan. 1920.
9864 Tilbury, Edith Jane, 1 Jan. 1920.
9865 Tillard, Ethel Hilda, Mrs., 1 Jan. 1920.
9866 Tillett, Amy Henrietta, 1 Jan. 1920.
9867 Tivy, Evelyn Laura, 1 Jan. 1920.
9868 Tod, James Alexander, 1 Jan. 1920.
9869 Todd, Georgina, Mrs., 1 Jan. 1920.
9870 Todd, Gerald Frederick, 1 Jan. 1920.
9871 Todd, Albert Rudolf Lochlein-, 1 Jan. 1920.
9872 Toke, Nicolas Eyare, 1 Jan. 1920.
9873 Tomlin, Henry Charles, 1 Jan. 1920.
9874 Tomlinson, Alice May, 1 Jan. 1920.
9875 Tomlinson, Tom Ashton, 1 Jan. 1920.
9876 Toms, Stanley Joseph, 1 Jan. 1920.
9877 Tonge, Edward, 1 Jan. 1920.
9878 Tonge, Frederick William John, 1 Jan. 1920.
9879 Tonkin, Harold John, 1 Jan. 1920.
9880 Toovey, Thomas Reginald, 1 Jan. 1920.
9881 Topham, Jane Grace Cowan, 1 Jan. 1920.
9882 Tough, James Macgillivray, 1 Jan. 1920.
9883 Towers, Thomas Peacock, 1 Jan. 1920.
9884 Tracy, Kate Adelaide, 1 Jan. 1920.
9885 Traill, Margaret Isabelle, Mrs., 1 Jan. 1920.
9886 Trant, Hope, 1 Jan. 1920.
9887 Trench, Catherine Ann e Swetenham, Mrs., 1 Jan. 1920.
9888 Tribe, Eileen Mary, 1 Jan. 1920.
9889 Tripp, William Thomas, 1 Jan. 1920.
9890 Trott, Nelson Hill, 1 Jan. 1920.
9891 Truscott, Frederick George Walter, 1 Jan. 1920.
9892 Tucker, Catherine Peterkin, Mrs., 1 Jan. 1920.
9893 Tucker, Douglas William, 1 Jan. 1920.
9894 Tudor, Elizabeth, 1 Jan. 1920.
9895 Tunnicliff, Edward Jones, 1 Jan. 1920.
9896 Turk, Erich, 1 Jan. 1920.
9897 Turnbull, Alice Helen, 1 Jan. 1920.
9898 Turnbull, Amy Ruth, 1 Jan. 1920.
9899 Turnbull, Herbert, 1 Jan. 1920.
9900 Turner, Caroline, Mrs., 1 Jan. 1920.
9901 Turner, Elizabeth, Mrs., 1 Jan. 1920.
9902 Turner, Emily Eliza, 1 Jan. 1920.
9903 Turner, Helen Gertrude, Mrs., 1 Jan. 1920.
9904 Turner, James, 1 Jan. 1920.
9905 Turner, William Leslie, 1 Jan. 1920.
9906 Turpin, William, 1 Jan. 1920.
9907 Tweedy, Edwin, 1 Jan. 1920.
9908 Tweedy, Hugh James, 1 Jan. 1920.
9909 Tyler, Walter Edward, 1 Jan. 1920.
9910 Underwood, Eric Gordon, 1 Jan. 1920.
9911 Unthank, Agnes Elizabeth, 1 Jan. 1920.
9912 Unwin, Arthur John, 1 Jan. 1920.
9913 Usher, George Edwin, 1 Jan. 1920.
9914 Usher, Tom Caizley, 1 Jan. 1920.
9915 Valentine, George Herbert, 1 Jan. 1920.
9916 Valentine, Herbert Hughes, 1 Jan. 1920.
9917 Vandeleur, Mary Evelyn, Mrs., 1 Jan. 1920.
9918 Vasse, Kate, Mrs., 1 Jan. 1920.
9919 Vaughan, Ethel Irene, 1 Jan. 1920.
9920 Verrall, Marian Elizabeth, 1 Jan. 1920.
9921 Vince, John Billinton, 1 Jan. 1920.
9922 Vine, Alfred Bertram, 1 Jan. 1920.
9923 des Voeux, Violet Samana, 1 Jan. 1920.
9924 Vyse, Ethel May, Mrs., 1 Jan. 1920.
9925 Wade, Elmira Margaret Louisa, 1 Jan. 1920.
9926 Waight, Daisy Olive, Mrs., 1 Jan. 1920.
9927 Wainwright, Amy Grace, Mrs., 1 Jan. 1920.
9928 Wakefield, Frank Howard, 1 Jan. 1920.
9929 Walden, Thomas, 1 Jan. 1920.
9930 Walker, Charles, 1 Jan. 1920.
9931 Walker, Edward, 1 Jan. 1920.
9932 Walker, George, 1 Jan. 1920.
9933 Walker, Jessie Winchester, Mrs., 1 Jan. 1920.
9934 Walker, John, 1 Jan. 1920.
9935 Walker, Lucy, Mrs., 1 Jan. 1920.
9936 Walker, Reginald Field, 1 Jan. 1920.
9937 Walker, Sophie, Mrs. Gamble-, 1 Jan. 1920.
9938 Walker, Thomas Herbert, 1 Jan. 1920.
9939 Wallace, John Thompson, 1 Jan. 1920.
9940 Waller, John, 1 Jan. 1920.
9941 Walsh, Ann Pollexfen, Mrs., 1 Jan. 1920.
9942 Walsh, Arthur Edward, 1 Jan. 1920.
9943 Walsh, Marguerite Mary, 1 Jan. 1920.
9944 Walsh, William Trevor Hayne, 1 Jan. 1920.
9945 Walsh, William Thomas, 1 Jan. 1920.
9946 Walters, Samuel, 1 Jan. 1920.
9947 Walton, Nellie, Mrs., 1 Jan. 1920.
9948 Walton, Harold Conrad, 1 Jan. 1920.
9949 Walton, Stanley, 1 Jan. 1920.
9950 Warburton, Alfred, 1 Jan. 1920.
9951 Warburton, Mabel Clarisse, 1 Jan. 1920.

9952 Ward, Ernest, 1 Jan. 1920.
9953 Ward, Henry, 1 Jan. 1920.
9954 Ward, Howard Percy, 1 Jan. 1920
9955 Ward, Isabel Mary Desborough, Mrs., 1 Jan. 1920.
9956 Ward, Mary Alexandria, 1 Jan. 1920.
9957 Ward, Thomas Henry, 1 Jan. 1920.
9958 Warden, Henry George, 1 Jan. 1920.
9959 Ware, Louisa, 1 Jan. 1920.
9960 Ware, Ralph Ernest, 1 Jan. 1920.
9961 Warlow, Camilla Allan, Mrs. Picton-, 1 Jan. 1920.
9962 Warmsley, Jennie, Mrs., 1 Jan. 1920.
9963 Warren, Ellen Winifred Anne, Mrs., 1 Jan. 1920.
9964 Warren, Frederick John, 1 Jan. 1920.
9965 Warren, Matthew, 1 Jan. 1920.
9966 Warriner, Fred, 1 Jan. 1920.
9967 Wasey, Evelyn Mary, 1 Jan. 1920.
9968 Waterman, Elizabeth Margaret, Mrs., 1 Jan. 1920.
9969 Waters, Charles Joseph, 1 Jan. 1920.
9970 Watkins, Arthur Muriel, 1 Jan. 1920.
9971 Watkins, William, 1 Jan. 1920.
9972 Watlington, Victor, 1 Jan. 1920.
9973 Watson, Agnes Mary, Mrs., 1 Jan. 1920.
9974 Watson, Arthur William, 1 Jan. 1920.
9975 Watson, Edith Hay, Mrs., 1 Jan. 1920.
9976 Watson, Harris, 1 Jan. 1920.
9977 Watson, John, 1 Jan. 1920.
9978 Watson, Joseph Thomas, 1 Jan. 1920.
9979 Watson, Maud Edith Eleanor, 1 Jan. 1920.
9980 Watson, Pamela Ethel, Mrs., 1 Jan. 1920.
9981 Watson, Thomas, 1 Jan. 1920.
9982 Watson, Victor James Carter, 1 Jan. 1920.
9983 Watson, William Law, 1 Jan. 1920.
9984 Watson, William Wallace, 1 Jan. 1920.
9985 Watt, George, 1 Jan. 1920.
9986 Watterson, Percy Gill, 1 Jan. 1920.
9987 Watts, Arthur Francis, 1 Jan. 1920.
9988 Watts, Charlotte Helen, Mrs., 1 Jan. 1920.
9989 Watts, Emily, Mrs., 1 Jan. 1920.
9990 Watts, Hugh Edmund, 1 Jan. 1920.
9991 Watts, Mary Manning, 1 Jan. 1920.
9992 Waugh, Walter Charles, 1 Jan. 1920.
9993 Weaver, Alexander Charles, 1 Jan. 1920.
9994 Weaver, Arthur John, 1 Jan. 1920.
9995 Weaver, Henry, 1 Jan. 1920.
9996 Weaver, John, 1 Jan. 1920.
9997 Webb, Arthur George, 1 Jan. 1920.
9998 Webb, Frank Hart, 1 Jan. 1920.
9999 Webb, Percy Henry, 1 Jan. 1920.
10,000 Webber, Katharine Stanton, 1 Jan. 1920.
10,001 Webber, Mowbray Frederick Vivian James Arthur, 1 Jan. 1920.
10,002 Weber, Barbara, Mrs., 1 Jan. 1920.
10,003 Webster, James Alexander, 1 Jan. 1920.
10,004 Wedgwood, Mary Euphrazia, 1 Jan. 1920.
10,005 Wedlake, John, 1 Jan. 1920.
10,006 Weedall, John, 1 Jan. 1920.
10,007 Weeks, Percy Frank, 1 Jan. 1920.
10,008 Weighill, Allice, Mrs., 1 Jan. 1920.
10,009 Weir, Edith Margaret Mary, 1 Jan. 1920.
10,010 Welch, George, 1 Jan. 1920.
10,011 Welch, Joseph Hubbard, 1 Jan. 1920.
10,012 Wells, Joseph Francis, 1 Jan. 1920.
10,013 Wells, John Wardle, 1 Jan. 1920.
10,014 Wench, Una Margaret Kerry, 1 Jan. 1920.
10,015 Wensley, Frederick Porter, 1 Jan. 1920.
10,016 Wentworth, Joseph, 1 Jan. 1920.
10,017 West, David Cockburn, 1 Jan. 1920.
10,018 West, Edward, 1 Jan. 1920.
10,019 West, Ellen, 1 Jan. 1920.
10,020 West, Stanley George Norman, 1 Jan. 1920.
10,021 Westell, Benjamin, 1 Jan. 1920.
10,022 Westell, Edgar Lawton, 1 Jan. 1920.
10,023 Westhead, Marian Lucy, 1 Jan. 1920.
10,024 Westmacott, James Richard, 1 Jan. 1920.
10,025 Weston, Robert Ogilvy, 1 Jan. 1920.
10,026 Whaley, Francis Henry, 1 Jan. 1920.
10,027 Wharhirst, Alfred John, 1 Jan. 1920.
10,028 Wheat, Thomas Milnes, 1 Jan. 1920.
10,029 Wheeler, Arthur George, 1 Jan. 1920.
10,030 Wheeler, George Herbert, 1 Jan. 1920.
10,031 Wheeler, Henry Charles, 1 Jan. 1920.
10,032 Whinney, Gladys, 1 Jan. 1920.
10,033 Whitbread, Edward, 1 Jan. 1920.
10,034 Whitby, Beatrice Mary Elizabeth, 1 Jan. 1920.
10,035 Whitby, Stafford Beeston, 1 Jan. 1920.
10,036 White, Frank George, 1 Jan. 1920.
10,037 White, Frederick Wallis, 1 Jan. 1920.
10,038 White, Hilda Annie, 1 Jan. 1920.
10,039 White, Kathleen Cameron, 1 Jan. 1920.
10,040 Whitehead, Arthur John, 1 Jan. 1920
10,041 Whitehead, Irene Mrs., 1 Jan. 1920.
10,042 Whitehouse, Edwin St. John, 1 Jan. 1920.
10,043 Whitehouse, John, 1 Jan. 1920.
10,044 Whitfield, Muriel Frances, Mrs., 1 Jan. 1920.
10,045 Whitfield, Avery Alfred, 1 Jan. 1920.
10,046 Whitley, Leonard Vincent, 1 Jan. 1920.
10,047 Whitmee, Andrew Conder, 1 Jan. 1920.
10,048 Whittaker, Joseph Henry, 1 Jan. 1920.
10,049 Whitty, William, 1 Jan. 1920.
10,050 Whitworth, Edith, Mrs., 1 Jan. 1920.

10,051 Whyatt, Charles Sidney, 1 Jan. 1920.
10,052 Whyte, Robert, 1 Jan. 1920.
10,053 Wicks, Ernest Arthur, 1 Jan. 1920.
10,054 Widdowson, Dorothy, 1 Jan. 1920.
10,055 Wight, Mabel, 1 Jan. 1920.
10,056 Wightman, Florence Oldfield, 1 Jan. 1920.
10,057 Wigley, Kathleen Sinclair, Mrs., 1 Jan. 1920.
10,058 Wigley, Thomas, 1 Jan. 1920.
10,059 Wilbraham, Hugh Edward, 1 Jan. 1920.
10,060 Wilcock, Joseph, 1 Jan. 1920.
10,061 Wilké, Bessie Dayrell, 1 Jan. 1920.
10,062 Wilkinson, Clenell Anstruther, 1 Jan. 1920.
10,063 Willans, Gordon Jeune, 1 Jan. 1920.
10,064 Willcox, William Garratt, 1 Jan. 1920.
10,065 Willett, Thomas Charles, 1 Jan. 1920.
10,066 Williams, Charles George, 1 Jan. 1920,
10,067 Williams, Edith, Mrs., 1 Jan. 1920.
10,068 Williams, Edward Richard, 1 Jan. 1920.
10,069 Williams, George Owen, 1 Jan. 1920.
10,070 Williams, Jessie Wilhelmina, Mrs. Herbert, 1 Jan. 1920.
10,071 Williams, Morgan, 1 Jan. 1920.
10,072 Williams, Richard, 1 Jan. 1920.
10,073 Williams, Richard Trefor, 1 Jan. 1920.
10,074 Williams, Thomas, 1 Jan. 1920.
10,075 Williams, William George, 1 Jan. 1920.
10,076 Williams, William Lewis, 1 Jan. 1920.
10,077 Williams, Winifred Mary, Mrs. Berkeley, 1 Jan. 1920.
10,078 Williamson, James, 1 Jan. 1920.
10,079 Williamson, James, 1 Jan. 1920.
10,080 Willis, Arthur, 1 Jan. 1920.
10,081 Willis, Frederick Bainbridge, 1 Jan. 1920.
10,082 Willson, Emily Mary, 1 Jan. 1920.
10,083 Willson, Harold Leonard James, 1 Jan. 1920.
10,084 Willson, Percy Arden, 1 Jan. 1920.
10,085 Wilmshurst, Thomas Percival, 1 Jan. 1920.
10,087 Wilson, Alexander Poole, 1 Jan. 1920.
10,088 Wilson, Annie Wilhelmina, Lady, 1 Jan. 1920.
10,089 Wilson, Caroline Adini, Mrs. Carus-, 1 Jan. 1920.
10,090 Wilson, Edith Matilda Clementine, Mrs., 1 Jan. 1920.
10,091 Wilson, Henry, 1 Jan. 1920.
10,092 Wilson, Henry Joseph Fullock, 1 Jan. 1920.
10,093 Wilson, Ivy Madge, Mrs., 1 Jan. 1920.
10,094 Wilson, James Arthur, 1 Jan. 1920.
10,095 Wilson, James Naismith, 1 Jan. 1920.
10,096 Wilson, Jessie Millar. 1 Jan. 1920.
10,097 Wilson, Rev. John, 1 Jan. 1920.
10,098 Wilson, Robert, 1 Jan. 1920.
10,099 Wilson, Robert Alexander, 1 Jan. 1920.
10,100 Wilson, William, 1 Jan. 1920.
10,101 Wilson, William John Denman, 1 Jan. 1920.
10,102 Winby, Thomas, 1 Jan. 1920.
10,103 Winder, Charles Bertram, 1 Jan. 1920.
10,104 Winder, Penelope, Mrs., 1 Jan. 1920.
10,105 Windiate, Albert, 1 Jan. 1920.
10,106 Windsor, Maurice, 1 Jan. 1920.
10,107 Winfield, Richard, 1 Jan. 1920.
10,108 Wingate, Gerald Henry, 1 Jan. 1920.
10,109 Winstanley. Denys Arthur, 1 Jan. 1920.
10,110 Winstanley, Herbert, 1 Jan. 1920.
10,111 Winterbotham, Clara Frances, 1 Jan. 1920.
10,112 Withers. George Mould, 1 Jan. 1920.
10,113 Witts, Gulielma Ewart, Mrs., 1 Jan. 1920.
10,114 Wolfe, Ernest Montague, 1 Jan. 1920.
10,115 Wollen, Emily Hilda, 1 Jan. 1920.
10,116 Wood, Benjamin, 1 Jan. 1920.
10,117 Wood, David William, 1 Jan. 1920.
10,118 Wood, Dorothy, Lady, 1 Jan. 1920.
10,119 Wood, George Ellis, 1 Jan. 1920.
10,120 Wood, Gertrude, 1 Jan. 1920.
10,121 Wood, Gladys, 1 Jan. 1920.
10,122 Wood, Grace Eliza, Mrs., 1 Jan. 1920.
10,123 Wood, Harry Brounton, 1 Jan. 1920.
10,124 Wood, Louisa Jane, 1 Jan. 1920.
10,125 Wood, May, 1 Jan. 1920.
10,126 Wood, William, 1 Jan. 1920.
10,127 Woodcock, Henry Chadwick, 1 Jan. 1920.
10,128 Woodcock, Walter Shellaker, 1 Jan. 1920.
10,129 Woodell, Florence Ernestine, 1 Jan. 1920.
10,130 Woodeson, Edward Seymour, 1 Jan. 1920.
10,131 Woodhead, Herbert Miall, 1 Jan. 1920.
10,132 Woodmore, William James, 1 Jan. 1920.
10,133 Woodroffe, Alban James, 1 Jan. 1920.
10,134 Woodroofe, Henry, 1 Jan. 1920.
10,135 Woods, Margery Adah, 1 Jan. 1920.
10,136 Woodward, Frederick Hugh, 1 Jan. 1920.
10,137 Woolcombe, Lilian Mary, 1 Jan. 1920.
10,138 Wooldridge, Jane Anne, 1 Jan. 1920.
10,139 Woolley, Constance Maria, 1 Jan. 1920.
10,140 Woolley, Frederick George, 1 Jan. 1920.
10,141 Worlidge, Edward, 1 Jan. 1920.
10,142 Wormald, Walter, 1 Jan. 1920.
10,143 Worrall, Gladstone Walter, 1 Jan. 1920.
10,144 Wright, Arthur James, 1 Jan. 1920.
10,145 Wright, Edmund, 1 Jan. 1920.
10,146 Wright, James Brown, 1 Jan. 1920.
10,147 Wright, J. M., 1 Jan. 1920.
10,148 Wright, John, 1 Jan. 1920.
10,149 Wright, Thomas Henry, 1 Jan. 1920.
10,150 Wrighton, Amelia, Mrs., 1 Jan. 1920.
10,151 Wrigley, Vincent Shiers, 1 Jan. 1920.

10,152 Wuidart, Jules Reuleaux ,1 Jan. 1920.
10,153 Wurtzburg, Margaret Caroline, 1 Jan. 1920.
10,154 Wybrow, Albert William, 1 Jan. 1920.
10,155 Wykes, William Henry, 1 Jan. 1920.
10,156 Wylson, Oswald Cane, 1 Jan. 1920.
10,157 Wynnes, James Cumming, 1 Jan. 1920.
10,158 Yates, Florence, 1 Jan. 1920.
10,159 Yates, James, 1 Jan. 1920.
10,160 Yearsley, Clare Elizabeth, Mrs., 1 Jan. 1920.
10,161 Yeates, Percy Thomas Arthur, 1 Jan. 1920.
10,162 Yelloly, Robert, 1 Jan. 1920.
10,163 Yeo, Richard Forster, 1 Jan. 1920.
10,164 Yeoman, John Pattison, 1 Jan. 1920.
10,165 Young, Colin, 1 Jan. 1920.
10,166 Young, Elizabeth Diana, 1 Jan. 1920.
10,167 Young, George, 1 Jan. 1920.
10,168 Young, Harry Maurice, 1 Jan. 1920.
10,169 Young, James Robert Spencer, 1 Jan. 1920.
10,170 Young, Nathaniel James, 1 Jan. 1920.
10,171 Young, Thomas Pettigrew, 1 Jan. 1920.
10,172 Young, Winifred, Mrs., 1 Jan. 1920.
10,173 Bennett, George Richard, 1 Jan. 1920.
10,174 Bustard, George, 1 Jan. 1920.
10,175 Byas, Hugh Fulton, 1 Jan. 1920.
10,176 Carter, Thomas, 1 Jan. 1920.
10,177 Cockburn, James Lowrie, 1 Jan. 1920.
10,178 Craig, Robert James, 1 Jan. 1920.
10,179 Cumming, Ida Georgina, 1 Jan. 1920.
10,180 Cuthbert, Helena Eliza, Mrs., 1 Jan. 1920.
10,181 Dexter, Thomas, 1 Jan. 1920.
10,182 Dickson, Beatrice Beaupré, Mrs., 1 Jan. 1920.
10,183 Eckford, Reginald Henderson, 1 Jan. 1920.
10,184 Evans, Edward Pritchard, 1 Jan. 1920.
10,185 Fairweather, Amelia, Mrs., 1 Jan. 1920.
10,186 Farra, Robert Edward, 1 Jan. 1920.
10,187 Gibson, Agnes, Mrs., 1 Jan. 1920.
10,188 Gibson, William, 1 Jan. 1920.
10,189 Gowan, George D'Olier, 1 Jan. 1920.
10,190 Goward, Raymond Spencer, 1 Jan. 1920.
10,191 Griffith, Griffith, 1 Jan. 1920.
10,192 Hadkinson, Frederick, 1 Jan. 1920.
10,193 Harrison, Frederick, 1 Jan. 1920.
10,194 Hide, Arthur, 1 Jan. 1920.
10,195 Hogarth, Frederick William, 1 Jan. 1920.
10,196 Hogg, John Drummond, 1 Jan. 1920.
10,197 Howie, Leila Adeline, Mrs., 1 Jan. 1920.
10,198 Inglis, Dorothy Winifred, Mrs., 1 Jan. 1920.
10,199 Irwin, Eric Barnby, 1 Jan. 1920.
10,200 Johnson, Percy Faraday, 1 Jan. 1920.
10,201 Jones, Herbert Thomas Averay-, 1 Jan. 1920.
10,202 Lawson, Nellie Elizabeth, Mrs., 1 Jan. 1920.
10,203 Macdonald, Herman Arthur, 1 Jan. 1920.
10,204 Maclean, Henrietta Laura, Mrs., 1 Jan. 1920.
10,205 McMurray, Elizabeth Eleanor, Mrs., 1 Jan. 1920.
10,206 Marsh, Jane, Mrs., Earle, 1 Jan. 1920.
10,207 Pardon, Eva, Mrs., 1 Jan. 1920.
10,208 St. Maur, Nina Mabel Mary, Mrs., 1 Jan. 1920.
10,209 Simpson, Jane, Mrs., 1 Jan. 1920.
10,210 Underhill, Frances Olive, 1 Jan. 1920.
10,211 Wilson, Florence Aline, Mrs., 1 Jan. 1920.
10,212 Abdullah Khan, Jemadar, 1 Jan. 1920. (M.)
10,213 Alexander, Arnold, 1 Jan. 1920. (M.)
10,214 Attar Sing, Jemadar, 1 Jan. 1920. (M.)
10,215 Chester, Stephen Charles Robert, 1 Jan. 1920. (M.)
10,216 Dawson, Keith Cyril Darlington, 1 Jan. 1920. (M.)
10,217 Dickson, Eric James, 1 Jan. 1920. (M.)
10,218 Dobson, George Herbert, 1 Jan. 1920. (M.)
10,219 Dyer, Albert John, 1 Jan. 1920. (M.)
10,220 Glazebrook, Edward John, 1 Jan. 1920. (M.)
10,221 Hakim Khan, Risaldar, 1 Jan. 1920. (M.)
10,222 Hamilton, Patrick Swinglehurst, 1 Jan. 1920. (M.)
10,223 Harridence, Robert Treslove, 1 Jan. 1920. (M.)
10,224 Howes, William Thomas, 1 Jan. 1920.
10,225 Khan Sahib Boi Khan, Bahudur, 1 Jan. 1920. (M.)
10,226 Khan Sikandar Hayat Khan, Khadar, 1 Jan. 1920. (M.)
10,227 Looney, Daniel, 1 Jan. 1920. (M.)
10,228 Lovell. William Day. 1 Jan. 1920. (M.)
10,229 Lowther, Thomas Edwin, 1 Jan. 1920. (M.)
10,230 McKim, Frederick George, 1 Jan. 1920. (M.)
10,231 Muhammad Skarif Khan, Jemadar, 1 Jan. 1920. (M.)
10,232 Naughton, Thomas Henry, 1 Jan. 1920. (M.)
10,233 Platt, William Percival, 1 Jan. 1920. (M.)
10,234 Johnson, Joseph Pratt, 1 Jan. 1920. (M.)
10,235 Ranade, Yashwan Bhicajee, 1 Jan. 1920. (M.)
10,236 Rayner, Ralph Herbert, 1 Jan. 1920. (M.)
10,237 Ryder, Edward Northern, 1 Jan. 1920. (M.)
10,238 Shah Bumber, Subadar, 1 Jan. 1920. (M.)
10,239 Stirling, Charles McKldd, 1 Jan. 1920. (M.)
10,240 Williams, Friend Isaac, 1 Jan. 1920. (M.)
10,241 Yasin Khan, 1 Jan. 1920. (M.)
10,242 Young, James, 1 Jan. 1920. (M.)
10,243 Graham, Ronald, 1 Jan. 1920. (M.)
10,244 Morrow, Charles Thomas, 1 Jan. 1920. (M.)
10,244a Addiscott, Elizabeth Mary, 1 Jan. 1920.
10,244b Alexander, Margaret Katharine, Hon. Mrs. Walter, 1 Jan. 1920.
10,244c Anderson, James Alexander, 1 Jan. 1920.
10,244d Banner, Myra, Mrs., 1 Jan. 1920.
10,244e Beresford, Dorothy, Mrs., 1 Jan. 1920.
10,244f Blake, William Henry, 1 Jan. 1920.

MEMBERS.

10,244g Blenkinsop, John Matthewson, 1 Jan. 1920.
10,244h Blood, Hon. Geraldine Mary, Mrs., 1 Jan. 1920.
10,245a Bowman, Hugh, 1 Jan. 1920.
10,245b Bridge, Arthur George, 1 Jan. 1920.
10,245c Bryant, William Henry, 1 Jan. 1920.
10,245d Burtt, William Edmund, 1 Jan. 1920.
10,245e Du Cane, Arthur George, 1 Jan. 1920.
10,245f Chilton, Ruth Helen Jane, Mrs., 1 Jan. 1920.
10,245g Cole, Albert Percy, 1 Jan. 1920.
10,245h Congreve, Eirene, Mrs., 1 Jan. 1920.
10,246a Cornwell, Lily Elizabeth Frances, 1 Jan. 1920.
10,246b Craske, Mabel Annetta, 1 Jan. 1920.
10,246c Crone, William, 1 Jan. 1920.
10,246d Crowe, William, 1 Jan. 1920.
10,246e Cumming, Phœbe Eleanor, Mrs., 1 Jan. 1920.
10,246f Cutforth, John Ashlin, 1 Jan. 1920.
10,246g Dease, Mary O'Kelly, 1 Jan. 1920.
10,246h Defries, Wolf, 1 Jan. 1920.
10,247a Donald, David Angus, 1 Jan. 1920.
10,247b Douglas, Gwendoline Ethel, Mrs., Sholto-, 1 Jan. 1920
10,247c Duncan, Margaret Elmslie, 1 Jan. 1920.
10,247d Elkington, William, 1 Jan. 1920.
10,247e Evans, Harold Butler Wyn, 1 Jan. 1920.
10,247f Fasey, William, 1 Jan. 1920.
10,247g Fielding, Thomas Henry, 1 Jan. 1920.
10,248a Flanagan, Mary, 1 Jan. 1920.
10,248b Fox, Arthur Wingate, 1 Jan. 1920.
10,248c French, Hilda Dillwyn, 1 Jan. 1920.
10,248d Gammon, Edith Olive, 1 Jan. 1920.
10,248e Gartside, Vincent, 1 Jan. 1920.
10,248f Gordon, Frank Lindsay, 1 Jan. 1920.
10,248g Gratwick, Doris Hilda, Mrs., 1 Jan. 1920.
10,248h Gurling, Albert Edwin, 1 Jan. 1920.
10,249a Hall, Audrey Elizabeth Kathleen, 1 Jan. 1920.
10,249b Hammond, Edith, 1 Jan. 1920.
10,249c Hannon, Marion Coulson, 1 Jan. 1920.
10,249d Hauxwell, Francis, 1 Jan. 1920.
10,249e Henning, Gladys, Mrs., 1 Jan. 1920.
10,249f Hook, Reginald Myles, 1 Jan. 1920.
10,249g Howard, Violet Angel, Mrs., 1 Jan. 1920.
10,249h Howell, George, 1 Jan. 1920.
10,250a Hubble, William Collister, 1 Jan. 1920.
10,250b Hutchinson, Beryl Butterworth, 1 Jan. 1920.
10,250c Jenkinson, William Russell, 1 Jan. 1920.
10,250d Jones, John, 1 Jan. 1920.
10,250e King, Basil, 1 Jan. 1920.
10,250f Knowles, George Potter, 1 Jan. 1920.
10,250g Kydd, Oswald Jensen, 1 Jan. 1920.
10,250h Lambourne, Christopher, 1 Jan. 1920.
10,251a Lavy, Rev. Ernest Edward, 1 Jan. 1920.
10,251b Leal, Winifred Marie Louise, 1 Jan. 1920.
10,251c Lilly, Walter Elsworthy, 1 Jan. 1920.
10,251d Little, James Raymond, 1 Jan. 1920.
10,251e Lund, Wilfred George, 1 Jan. 1920.
10,251f McQuade, William, 1 Jan. 1920.
10,251g Macredie, Hastings George Cunningham, 1 Jan. 1920.
10,251h Mahony, Mary Ellen, 1 Jan. 1920.
10,252a Mallinson, Clarice Elsie, 1 Jan. 1920.
10,252b Miller, Joseph, 1 Jan. 1920.
10,252c Moffat, Elijah James, 1 Jan. 1920.
10,252d Ogilvy, Walter, 1 Jan. 1920.
10,252e Perrey, Albert Victor George, 1 Jan. 1920.
10,252f Van de Pol, Florence Clara, Mrs., 1 Jan. 1920.
10,252g Prest, Ellen Gertrude, 1 Jan. 1920.
10,252h Reid, Thomas Ebenezer, 1 Jan. 1920.
10,253a Rickman, Mary Charlotte Murray, 1 Jan. 1920.
10,253b Riley, Henry, 1 Jan. 1920.
10,253c Robertson, James, 1 Jan. 1920.
10,253d Robertson, Margaret Ida, 1 Jan. 1920.
10,253e Robinson, Dorothy Faith, 1 Jan. 1920.
10,253f Sedgwick, Richard Romney, 1 Jan. 1920.
10,253g Shackleton, William, 1 Jan. 1920.
10,253h Shaw, Isabella Mackintosh, 1 Jan. 1920.
10,254a Smith, Frederick Herbert, 1 Jan. 1920.
10,254b Smith, Mathew, 1 Jan. 1920.
10,254d Stansfield, John Firth, 1 Jan. 1920.
10,254e Steele, Arnold Francis, 1 Jan. 1920.
10,254f Stephens, Albert, 1 Jan. 1920.
10,254g Stock, Enid Amy, Mrs., 1 Jan. 1920.
10,254h Strawn, Frances May, Mrs., 1 Jan. 1920.
10,255a Stuart, Charles Edward, 1 Jan. 1920.
10,255b Taylor, Deborah Phipps, 1 Jan. 1920.
10,255c Thorneloe, Arthur Joseph, 1 Jan. 1920.
10,255d Titterington, Edward John Goodall, 1 Jan. 1920.
10,255e Tracey, Isabel Audrey, Mrs., 1 Jan. 1920.
10,255f Tuck, Alice Mary, 1 Jan. 1920.
10,255g Wager, May Frances, Mrs., 1 Jan. 1920.
10,255h Walker, Herbert Arthur, 1 Jan. 1920.
10,256a Waring, Margaret Elizabeth, 1 Jan. 1920.
10,256b Williamson, Henry, 1 Jan. 1920.
10,256c Wood, Dennis, 1 Jan. 1920.
10,256d Wood, Maud, Mrs., 1 Jan. 1920.
10,256e Wyke, Clement James, 1 Jan. 1920.
10,256f Aling, Gerrit, 1 Jan. 1920.
10,256g Allen, David Hugonin Satow, 1 Jan. 1920.
10,256h Anderson, George William Strachan, 1 Jan. 1920.
10,257a Balfe, Kathleen, 1 Jan. 1920.
10,257b Barry, Arthur J., 1 Jan. 1920.
10,257c Brown, Patrick Campbell Cowley-, 1 Jan. 1920.
10,257d Bruffa, John, 1 Jan. 1920.

10,257e Campbell, Arthur Lang, 1 Jan. 1920.
10,257f Campbell, Olga Margaret, 1 Jan. 1920.
10,257g Chubb, William Lindsay, 1 Jan. 1920.
10,257h Davies, Horace Victor, 1 Jan. 1920.
10,258a Frances, Edith, Mrs., 1 Jan. 1920.
10,258b Fraser, Clive Stewart, 1 Jan. 1920.
10,258c Gordon, John Cornewall Duff, 1 Jan. 1920.
10,258d Greatorex, Ronald Henry, 1 Jan. 1920.
10,258e Hodson, Thomas Stuart, 1 Jan. 1920.
10,258f Holmes, Gertrude Eirene, 1 Jan. 1920.
10,258g Irving, Henry Edward, 1 Jan. 1920.
10,258h Johnson, William Thomas, 1 Jan. 1920.
10,259a Lloyd, Edmund, 1 Jan. 1920.
10,259b Mallalieu, Vernon, 1 Jan. 1920.
10,259c Marshall, Gertrude Mary, Mrs., 1 Jan. 1920.
10,259d Martin, Gaston Pacroe de, 1 Jan. 1920.
10,259e Mathews, Leslie, 1 Jan. 1920.
10,259f Mullins, Alfred James, 1 Jan. 1920.
10,259g Ness, Bertha, Mrs., 1 Jan. 1920.
10,259h Price, Sydney Reginald, 1 Jan. 1920.
10,260a Rome, Francis John de, 1 Jan. 1920.
10,260b Tanner, Alfred Richard, Morley, 1 Jan. 1920.
10,260c Walker, John Jeffrey, 1 Jan. 1920.
10,260d Williamson, William James, 1 Jan. 1920.
10,260e Wilson, Cyril, 1 Jan. 1920.
10,260f Younghusband, Jonathan, 1 Jan. 1920.
10,260g Miller, Frederick William, 9 Jan. 1920. (M.)
10,260h Watson, Wallace, 22 Jan. 1920. (M.)
10,261a Askin, Thomas Cuming, 30 Jan. 1920.
10,261b Bailey, Reginald Threlfall, 30 Jan. 1920.
10,261c Bigley, Francis William Hudson, 30 Jan. 1920.
10,261d Blackledge, William Thomas, 30 Jan. 1920.
10,261e Blood, Joseph FitzGerald, 30 Jan. 1920.
10,261f Brockbank, Edward Mansfield, 30 Jan. 1920.
10,261g Chaff, Thomas Waycott, 30 Jan. 1920.
10,261h Chapman, Paul Morgan, 30 Jan. 1920.
10,262a Clarke, Andrew Campbell, 30 Jan. 1920.
10,262b Craig, John, 30 Jan. 1920.
10,262c Cruickshank, James Bell, 30 Jan. 1920.
10,262d Darwin, George Henry, 30 Jan. 1920.
10,262e Fardon, John Henry, 30 Jan. 1920.
10,262f Ferguson, Charles Henry, 30 Jan. 1920.
10,262g Gamble, Mercier, 30 Jan. 1920.
10,262h Hadfield, Charles Frederick, 30 Jan. 1920.
10,263 Hamilton, John Stirling-, 30 Jan. 1920.
10,264 Hedley, Edward Williams, 30 Jan. 1920.
10,265 Helme, George Edgar, 30 Jan. 1920.
10,266 Hughes, John Brierley, 30 Jan. 1920.
10,267 Hutchinson, George Arnold, 30 Jan. 1920.
10,268 Ironside, Catherine Mary, 30 Jan. 1920.
10,269 Jamieson, Thomas Hill, 30 Jan. 1920.
10,270 Lindsay, William Joseph, 30 Jan. 1920.
10,271 McClelland, William, 30 Jan. 1920.
10,272 MacGill, George, 30 Jan. 1920.
10,273 Mackie, Mary Campbell, Mrs., 30 Jan. 1920
10,274 McWatters, John Courtenay, 30 Jan. 1920.
10,275 Melvin, Frank Widowfield, 30 Jan. 1920.
10,276 Moore, Williams Struthers, 30 Jan. 1920.
10,277 Moyles, John George, 30 Jan. 1920.
10,278 Murphy, Maurice Michael, 30 Jan. 1920.
10,279 Nixon, Herbert Thomlinson, 30 Jan. 1920.
10,280 Noble, John, 30 Jan. 1920.
10,281 Palmer, Sydney Joseph, 30 Jan. 1920.
10,282 Prentice, William Hogg, 30 Jan. 1920.
10,283 Rust, John, 30 Jan. 1920.
10,284 Stenhouse, James Wilson, 30 Jan. 1920.
10,285 Stopford, John Sebastian Bach, 30 Jan. 1920.
10,286 Thomas, William Thelwall, 30 Jan. 1920.
10,287 Wells, Thomas Henry Sanderson-, 30 Jan. 1920.
10,288 Woodcock, Harold Brookfield, 30 Jan. 1920.
10,289 Wilson, Frederick Wallace, 30 Jan. 1920.
10,290 Wyse, Richard, 30 Jan. 1920.
10,291 Chbbon, Percy Gordon, 8 March, 1902. (M.)
10,292 Cox, George Henry, 8 March, 1920. (M.)
10,293 Haines, Samuel James, 8 March, 1920. (M.)
10,294 Myott, John, 8 March, 1920. (M.)
10,295 Plummer, John Robert, 8 March, 1920. (M.)
10,296 Power, Charles Louis, 8 March, 1920. (M.)
10,297 Royall, William, 8 March, 1920. (M.)
10,298 Alsop, Anthony, 15 March, 1920. (M.)
10,299 Andrews, Sidney Byron, 15 March, 1920. (M.)
10,300 Duguid, David Robertson, 15 March, 1920. (M.)
10,301 Pilkington, Percy, 15 March, 1920. (M.)
10,302 Turner, John George, 15 March, 1920. (M.)
10,302a Davey, John Henry, 23 April, 1920. (M.)
10,302b Haines, Ernest, 23 Apr. 1920. (M.)
10,302c McGuirk, Henry Francis, 23 Apr. 1920. (M.)
10,302d Ridges, Robert Vigurs, 23 Apr. 1920. (M.)
10,303 Allen, Ernest Thomas William, 5 June, 1920.
10,304 Arnot, John Wilkie, 5 June, 1920.
10,305 Bell, Constance Mildred, 5 June, 1920.
10,306 Black, Herbert Duncan, 5 June, 1920.
10,307 Bradley, Lesley Ripley, 5 June, 1920.
10,308 Brewer, Ella Nora Dorothy, 5 June, 1920.
10,309 Clarke, Harry Charles, 5 June, 1920.
10,310 De la Cour, Miss, 5 June, 1920.
10,311 Dinwiddie, Agnes Letitia, Blount-, 5 June, 1920.
10,312 Dooner, William Toke, 5 June, 1920.
10,313 Duncombe, Emily Katharine Louisa, 5 June, 1920.
10,314 Earl, Edward Franklyn, 5 June, 1920.

THE ORDER OF THE BRITISH EMPIRE.

10,315 Edgar, Jonathan Cyril, 5 June, 1920.
10,316 Etheredge, Charles Douglas, 5 June, 1920.
10,317 Finch, Madeline Constance, 5 June, 1920.
10,318 Garratt, Dorothy Agnes, 5 June, 1920.
10,319 Glover, Inez Marguerite, 5 June, 1920.
10,320 Groser, Phyliss, 5 June, 1920.
10,321 Hall, Aline Margaret, 5 June, 1920.
10,322 Harkness, Edith Geraldine, 5 June, 1920.
10,323 Hughes, J. H., 5 June, 1920.
10,324 Kendall, John Murray, 5 June, 1920.
10,325 Knutford, Lilian May, Mrs., 5 June, 1920.
10,326 Kopetzky, Adolf, 5 June, 1920.
10,327 Kuhner, Charles Henry, 5 June, 1920.
10,329 Lovell, Laura Mary, Mrs., 5 June, 1920.
10,330 Moffatt, Elijah James, 5 June, 1920.
10,331 Morgan, Anne Lalande, Lady, 5 June, 1920.
10,332 Moss, Wilfred, 5 June, 1920.
10,333 Price, Emily Annie, 5 June, 1920.
10,334 Read, Mary Amy, 5 June, 1920.
10,335 Stapleton, May Cotton, 5 June, 1920.
10,336 Struthers, John, 5 June, 1920.
10,337 Thellusson, Florence Adeline, 5 June, 1920.
10,338 Wade, Sidney, 5 June, 1920.
10,339 Walker, H. A., 5 June, 1920.
10,340 Whittington, Richard Auguste William, 5 June, 1920.
10,341 Williams, Daisy, Mrs., 5 June, 1920.
10,342 Cottle, Jack, 12 July, 1920. (M.)
10,343 Cox, Albert John, 12 July, 1920. (M.)
10,344 Jezzard, Frank, 12 July, 1920. (M.)
10,345 Carnac, Wildred John Rivett-, 12 July, 1920. (M.)
10,346 Willer, Herbert Humphries, 12 July, 1920. (M.)
10,347 Allen, Henry Charles, 24 Aug. 1920.
10,348 Clark, J. A., 24 Aug. 1920.
10,349 Cookson, Christopher, 24 Aug. 1920.
10,350 Curtis, William, 24 Aug. 1920.
10,351 Hague, S., 24 Aug. 1920.
10,352 Hamilton, Claud Aubrey Douglas, 24 Aug. 1920.
10,353 Harle, Charles, 24 Aug. 20.
10,354 Henderson, Alexander, 24 Aug. 1920.
10,355 Henderson, Helen, 24 Aug. 1920.
10,356 Hewgill, Edward Burnip, 24 Aug. 1920.
10,357 Logan, William, 24 Aug. 1920.
10,358 Morrison, Kate, 24 Aug. 1920.
10,359 Philippedes, Nessib Cleanthes, 24 Aug. 1920.
10,360 Smith, George Foster, 24 Aug. 1920.
10,361 Treasure, John William Oran, 24 Aug. 1920.
10,362 Watson, William Joseph Gabriel, 24 Aug. 1920.
10,363 Maule, William Harry Fowke, 25 Aug. 1920. (M.)
10,364 Dundersale, Wilfred Albert, 7 Sept. 1920.
10,365 Addison, Stanley, 15 Oct. 1920.
10,366 Allan, Rev. Tom, 15 Oct. 1920.
10,367 Anderson, Helen Agnes, Mrs., 15 Oct. 1920.
10,368 Angelo, Mary Colquhoun, Mrs. Fox-, 15 Oct. 1920.
10,369 Ogilvy, Harry Lort Stephen Balfour-, 15 Oct. 1920.
10,370 Barnes, Katherine Florence, Mrs., 15 Oct. 1920.
10,371 Barton, Albert Edward, 15 Oct. 1920.
10,372 Beebe, William, 15 Oct. 1920.
10,373 Borrow, John Richard Travers Eales, 15 Oct. 1920.
10,374 Botten, Joseph, 15 Oct. 1920.
10,375 Browning, Elizabeth Anne, Mrs., 15 Oct. 1920.
10,376 Butters, John Henry, 15 Oct. 1920.
10,377 Clydesdale, Alexander McAlister, 15 Oct. 1920.
10,378 Campbell, John Honeyford, 15 Oct. 1920.
10,379 Collins, Emily Ila, 15 Oct. 1920.
10,380 Conder, Walter Tasman, 15 Oct. 1920.
10,381 Evans, Annie Elethea, 15 Oct. 1920.
10,382 Evans, Victor Hallen, 15 Oct. 1920.
10,383 Farmer, George Albert, 15 Oct. 1920.
10,384 Ferguson, William Francis, 15 Oct. 1920.
10,385 Fitzgerald, John Thomas, 15 Oct. 1920.
10,386 Hadley, Frederick Augustus, 15 Oct. 1920.
10,387 Ham. Edwin George, 15 Oct. 1920.
10,388 Hamilton, Albert Edwin, 15 Oct. 1920.
10,389 Hardie, James March, 15 Oct. 1920.
10,390 Harrap, George Edward, 15 Oct. 1920.
10,391 Harrison, Tom Curtis, 15 Oct. 1920.
10,392 Hicks, Thomas, 15 Oct. 1920.
10,393 Hill, Charles, 15 Oct. 1920.
10,394 Hiscox, George, 15 Oct. 1920.
10,395 Holmes, Elsie May, 15 Oct. 1920.
10,396 Holyman, Honora, Mrs , 15 Oct. 1920.
10,397 Hordern, Herbert Vivian, 15 Oct. 1920.

10,398 Lean, James Malcolm, 15 Oct. 1920.
10,399 Lunn, Samuel, 15 Oct. 1920.
10,400 MacCallum, Archibald Donald. 15 Oct. 1920.
10,401 McDonald, Rebecca Anne, 15 Oct. 1920.
10,402 McElhone, William Percy, 15 Oct. 1920.
10 403 MacFarlane, Stuart Gordon, 15 Oct. 1920.
10,404 Mathison, Mary Martin, Mrs., 15 Oct. 1920.
10,405 Montgomery, William, 15 Oct. 1920.
10,406 Moors. Florence Donald, 15 Oct. 1920.
10,407 Nance, Thomas Pierce Hains, 15 Oct. 1920.
10,408 Newman, William Augustin, 15 Oct. 1920.
10,409 Osborne, William Henry, 15 Oct. 1920.
10,410 Parker, Arthur Charles, 15 Oct. 1920.
10,411 Parker, Ethel Wyborn, 15 Oct. 1920.
10,412 Pearson, Wesley Marshall, 15 Oct. 1920.
10,413 Sands, Robert Sydney, 15 Oct. 1920.
10,414 Saunders, Florence Margaret, 15 Oct. 1920.
10,415 Solomon Edward, 15 Oct. 1920.
10,416 Smith, Helen Nora, Mrs., 15 Oct. 1920.
10.417 Tarrant, Harley, 15 Oct. 1920.
10,418 Thompson, Samuel Douglas, 15 Oct. 1920.
10,419 Wache, Ethel Evelyna, 15 Oct. 1920.
10,420 Waite, Eva, 15 Oct. 1920.
10,421 Wassell, Edith, 15 Oct. 1920.
10,422 Weller, Florence Maud, Mrs., 15 Oct. 1920.
10,423 Wilson, Archie John Landles, 15 Oct. 1920.
10,424 Wilson, John Bowie, 15 Oct. 1920.
10,425 Windeyer, William Archibald, 15 Oct. 1920.
10,426 Wyatt, Ethel, 15 Oct. 1920.
10,427 Bickford, Charles Frederick, 15 Oct. 1920.
10,428 Bull, Esther, Mrs., 15 Oct. 1920.
10,429 Lovell, Elizabeth Isabel, Mrs., 15 Oct. 1920.
10,430 Baines, Florence, Mrs., 15 Oct. 1920.
10,431 Balfour, Bertha Elsie, Mrs., 15 Oct. 1920.
10,432 Bate, John Osborn Shepperton, 15 Oct. 1920.
10,433 Batho, Charles Philip Arthur, 15 Oct. 1920.
10,434 Campbell, Isabel Edwards, Mrs., 15 Oct. 1920
10,435 Campbell, William, 15 Oct. 1920.
10,436 Cleland, John Stockwin, 15 Oct. 1920.
10,437 Corke, Edward Stanton, 15 Oct. 1920.
10,438 Dyason, Ernest Clement, 15 Oct. 1920.
10,439 Eadie, Robert, 15 Oct. 1920.
10,440 Egan. Hulda, Mrs., 15 Oct. 1920.
10,441 Fernie, James, 15 Oct. 1920.
10,442 Fourie, Louis, 15 Oct. 1920.
10,443 Fynn, Ethel Mary, Mrs., 15 Oct. 1920.
10,444 Fraser, Henry Paterson, 15 Oct. 1920.
10,445 Garrard. Alice Mary, Mrs., 15 Oct. 1920.
10,446 Hahn, Carl Hugo Linsingen, 15 Oct. 1920.
10,447 Head, Arthur, 15 Oct. 1920.
10,448 Hill, Henry Grenville, 15 Oct. 1920.
10,449 Kemsley, Kate Annie, Mrs., 15 Oct. 1920.
10,450 Kennedy, John Morgan, 15 Oct. 1920.
10,451 Lamont, Hellen, 15 Oct. 1920.
10,452 Lea, Doris, 15 Oct. 1920.
10,453 McAlister, William Douglas, 15 Oct. 1920.
10,454 Morgan, Walter Llewellyn, 15 Oct. 1920.
10,455 Morgan, Tom Henry, 15 Oct. 1920.
10,456 Murray, Edward, 15 Oct. 1920.
10,457 Morkel Paul Andrew, 15 Oct. 1920.
10,458 Nottingham, William, 15 Oct. 1920.
10,459 Penfold, William Cowan, 15 Oct. 1920.
10,460 Ramsey, Florence Edith, Mrs., 15 Oct. 1920.
10,461 Riseley, John William, 15 Oct. 1920.
10,462 Salmon, Mary Eburn, Mrs., 15 Oct. 1920.
10,463 Shaw, Mary Charlotte, Mrs., 15 Oct. 1920.
10,464 Sloan, David, 15 Oct. 1920.
10,465 Smith, Herbert Parker Hastings, 15 Oct. 1920.
10,466 Tilney, Mary Elizabeth, 15 Oct. 1920.
10,467 Tregaskis, Nellie Blanch, Mrs., 15 Oct. 1920.
10,468 van Coller, Christian Andries Brenk, 15 Oct. 1920.
10,469 Waters, Alfred John, 15 Oct. 1920.
10,470 Whidborne, Winifred Biehl, Mrs., 15 Oct. 1920.
10,471 Whitworth, Walter Stanley, 15 Oct. 1920.
10,472 Wilson, Edith Frances, Mrs., 15 Oct. 1920.
10,473 Furlong, Margaret Helen, 15 Oct. 1920.
10,474 Salter, Albert Hugh, 15 Oct. 1920.
10,475 Small, Hannah, Mrs., 15 Oct. 1920.
10,476 Snow, William, 31 Oct. 1920. (M.)
10,477 Ellick, James Elliott, 12 Nov. 1920. (M.)
10,478 Reynolds, Andrew Bishop, 23 Nov. 1920.
10 479 Norman, Gunner Richard, R.N., 4 Feb. 1921.

OFFICIALS OF THE ORDER.

Prelate.—Rt. Hon. and Right Rev. The Bishop of London, K.C.V.O.
King of Arms.—Gen. the Rt. Hon. Sir Arthur Henry Fitzroy Paget, G.C.B., K.C.V.O.
Registrar.—Registrar and Secretary of the Central Chancery of the Order of Knighthood.
Secretary.—Permanent Under-Secretary of State for the Home Department.
Gentleman Usher of the Purple Rod.—Sir Frederic George Kenyon, K.C.B.

www.ingramcontent.com/pod-product-compliance
Lightning Source LLC
Chambersburg PA
CBHW081424270326
41932CB00019B/3095